ISBN 978-0-428-68944-5
PIBN 11300611

1 MONTH OF FREE READING

at

www.ForgottenBooks.com

By purchasing this book you are eligible for one month membership to ForgottenBooks.com, giving you unlimited access to our entire collection of over 1,000,000 titles via our web site and mobile apps.

To claim your free month visit:

www.forgottenbooks.com/free1300611

* Offer is valid for 45 days from date of purchase. Terms and conditions apply.

English
Français
Deutsche
Italiano
Español
Português

www.forgottenbooks.com

Mythology Photography **Fiction** Fishing Christianity **Art** Cooking Essays Buddhism Freemasonry Medicine **Biology** Music **Ancient Egypt** Evolution Carpentry Physics Dance Geology **Mathematics** Fitness Shakespeare **Folklore** Yoga Marketing **Confidence** Immortality Biographies Poetry **Psychology** Witchcraft Electronics Chemistry History **Law** Accounting **Philosophy** Anthropology Alchemy Drama Quantum Mechanics Atheism Sexual Health **Ancient History** **Entrepreneurship** Languages Sport Paleontology Needlework Islam **Metaphysics** Investment Archaeology Parenting Statistics Criminology **Motivational**

Supplement to
The Investors' Review, July 15, 1898.]

THE

Investors' Review.

FOUNDED FEBRUARY 1892.

EDITED BY

A. J. WILSON.

Weekly Issue, Vol. I., January 8 to July 1, 1898

(*Being Vol. XI. in consecutive Series*).

LONDON:

CLEMENT WILSON,

NORFOLK HOUSE, NORFOLK STREET, W.C.

PRINTED BY
MESSRS. LOVE & WYMAN, LIMITED,
74-76, GREAT QUEEN STREET, LINCOLN'S INN FIELDS,
LONDON, W.C.

Supplement to The Investors' Review, July 15, 1898.

INDEX TO VOL. I.

A

B

C

D

E

F

M

N

O

P

R

S

T

U

V

W

Y

Z

The Investors' Review

Vol. I.—No. 1. New Series. FRIDAY, JANUARY 7, 1898. Price 6d.

CONTENTS

PAGE

The Investors' Review.

To our Readers.

SOME few words seem in place as to the aims embodied in this new weekly financial paper. For a long time back the Editor's friends have told him that there was room for such a paper, and he now puts their opinions to the test of experience. All along the publication of a magazine only once a month has been hampering and unsatisfactory. No possible effort could prevent some portion of the criticisms thus tardily produced from being behind the times. Many things had to be allowed to pass unnoticed, and readers appeared, in consequence, so distant at times to the writers that the effect was similar to speaking in an empty chamber. In the weekly INVESTORS' REVIEW writers and readers will at least be nearer to each other, and blows aimed at living impostures will fall less frequently on carcases already dead.

THE chief purpose of the REVIEW is not warfare with any class or political creed, but to be a storehouse of facts; facts about trade, about industry, about man's conquests over Nature; facts first and everywhere—inferences from facts afterwards. To the test of reality we shall always desire to bring the opinions expressed. Nothing shall be wilfully misrepresented in these columns, nothing set down from sinister motive; and if we err, as must now and then happen with the best intentions, the error shall always be frankly acknowledged.

ONE thing we beg readers not to do—they should not judge by the first number, nor look in it for all the things we hope in time to accomplish. A first number is always the hardest of all to put before the world. Everything is new; the machinery, as it were, has no yet been worked smooth at the joints. Some things bulk too largely, others are treated with insufficient breadth; there will be omissions and perhaps redundencies, but with time defects will be overcome if diligence and the desire to work always towards perfection count for anything in this world.

ONE object has always been before us, and that is, to supply people who do not live in London with information which should be useful to them in dealing with their money. The REVIEW has never been produced merely for the benefit of the crowd in Throgmorton-street, and to a considerable extent experience has justified the efforts made to give it a wider scope. There is no part of the civilised world into which the monthly INVESTORS' REVIEW did not go. To tell the truth about financial operations and schemes is often neither pleasant nor profitable, but we determined, when we began, to do this as far as in us lay, and readers may depend upon it that we shall not slacken in the endeavour now. Criticism is not always pleasant, and frequently those it is meant to benefit are the first to resent it. Holders of shares bought at fictitious prices do not relish being told that their possessions are not worth the money given for them. Sometimes the criticisms may come too late to save the public from serious loss, and that we cannot help, for if a security is bad to begin with no amount of analysis or denunciation can set it right. A good deal, however, of the criticism hitherto given in this REVIEW—in fact, we may say the bulk of it—has been directed to make things better, not to destroy. Few securities are so good as to have no point at which they can be improved; even Consols, perfect as they are, the most substantial security in the world, may be bought too dear. And if we see a Government pursuing a policy, through its Sinking Fund and Savings Bank investments, which tends to force the price up artificially, surely it is in the interests of the investing public to attack that policy, especially if it not only involves loss to individual investors, but likewise large ultimate deficits in the public accounts, which the nation will have to make good.

LOOKED at in this humbler, matter-of-fact aspect the attitude of this REVIEW is that of the doubtist who stands in the market. No bent is more constant on the Stock Exchange than the tendency to send prices up and up always, to unattainable heights. The man in the market is nearly always over-sanguine. When he sees a stock rising in price, his imagination catches fire and discovers heights to be reached which no ordinary mortal can behold. We stand against this tendency—between the man who means to buy and the market which wants to sell. To call us mere pessimists for taking up this attitude is not to exhibit gratitude, but that cannot be helped in these days. We know very well from a long experience that people who may at first denounce will, by-and-bye, be ready to commend. When this REVIEW was originally started and began to prick the bubbles of finance brought into being before the crisis of November, 1890, many correspondents, in writing to express their gratitude for the light it then began to throw into the dark places of company-mongering, declared that if they had only been privileged to read our exposures before the crisis broke out they would have been saved from serious losses. Our attitude is precisely the same now as it was six years ago, but the gratitude has not of late been so abundantly expressed. People have forgotten the severe lessons of the Baring crisis and its sequels. Many glamours of finance have again come over them and fired their imaginations with hopes of easy gain. But it will not be for long. The elements which go to produce a crisis have been accumulating fast during the last two or three years, and it would not surprise us if before the century closes the country should stand face to face with a far more destructive credit storm than that which was so threatening seven years back. Onlookers, it should not be forgotten, see most of every game, and the INVESTORS' REVIEW is merely an onlooker. Its conductors join not in the play.

IT will be obvious that the REVIEW differs very considerably in its new shape from the monthly one, and that it is now largely occupied with tables of figures and price lists of securities. In this, however, it in some measure but reverts to its original form as a quarterly to which was appended the entire stock exchange list, and the intention has always been to make this publication a medium of information about prices. The list which had to be dropped in the REVIEW was resuscitated in the quarterly index, which is still good. In laying down the lines of the weekly paper the choice lay between again making the attempt to present its subscribers with a complete weekly list of Stock Exchange prices and the easier, much more profitable, and far less troublesome business of filling so many pages a week with reports of company meetings. We had little hesitation in choosing.

REPORTS of meetings have mostly ceased to be independent so far as the weekly Press is concerned, and have sunk to the position of advertisements paid for on a more or less high scale. Editors of financial papers who admit such reports, placing them amongst the editorial matter without the slightest indication that they are mere advertisements, appear to us to surrender their independence in more ways than one. To begin with, the board of the most trumpery company in existence which chooses to spend the money of its shareholders in paying five, ten, or twenty guineas to each one of so many papers in order to have an official report of a shareholders' meeting published as editorial matter can dictate what shall be inserted, thus depriving an editor of the power to say what and what shall not be laid before his readers. Then undoubtedly such official reports act as a gag upon criticism, and payment for their publication as editorial matter is often a mere bribe. They also frequently prevent any ventilation of shareholders' grievances by omitting everything unpleasant to directors.

No reports of this description will ever be published in the INVESTORS' REVIEW. If a board of directors deems it expedient to advertise in its columns an official version of a shareholders' meeting such version must appear in its proper place, among our advertisements. But although shut to official matter of this kind, published as though under our responsibility, the editorial columns will always be open to the ventilation of genuine grievances, impartially, and without any attempt to favour one side more than another.

IT will be obvious that the attempt to conduct a weekly paper on these lines is a somewhat arduous one, and perfection in the arrangements of details, or in the order and mass of information presented, is not to be attained in one month or in six. We may lay down the lines upon which it is the intention to work, but the design has to be filled slowly in bit by bit. Perfection can only be attained, if it is ever attained, after long and patient labour. But readers may be assured that there will be no slackening in the effort to attain something approaching perfection, and if they will not only bear with shortcomings only too visible at the outset, but at the same time help us with suggestions, criticisms, new information, hints of any practical kind, they will earn our gratitude.

Economic and Financial Notes and Correspondence.

HOME AFFAIRS.

THE Revenue for the last quarter of the year was good, and Sir Michael Hicks-Beach will again have a surplus to deal with. It may be one million and might be two. Looking at the Imperial portion of the Revenue alone, it might seem that the nation had tired a little of drinking, for the Customs dropped a little compared with the previous year, but that may be tea or coffee. There is no need to fear the future in this respect while the Excise returns continue to flourish, and they have flourished amazingly in the past year. On the gross Revenue, which includes the doles given to local spending bodies, the increase was £630,000. Taking the gross income from all sources the entire gain for the nine months has been £2,378,000, of which about one million goes to swell the local authorities' portion and £1,400,000 is retained by the Treasury. What will the Government do with the probable surplus? Remit taxation? We may be sure it will not do that. All the money will be spent and much more, and in all probability the next great change in the burden of the taxes will be another penny added to the income tax.

OR shall we have a brand new Customs tariff on the "reciprocity" or *Zollverein* system, so beautifully exemplified by Canada, which, out of her love of the "flag" and of us, generously permits British goods to bear import duties on an average 4 per cent. higher than those of the United States—40 per cent. against 36? Some day we might rise to the height of such generosity.

THE *Star*, which has distinguished itself by exposing the evil deeds of the American monopolists who have acquired the control of the petroleum oil trade, announced a week ago that the Rothschilds had entered into competition with the Rockefellers with Russian oil whose flash point is 103 deg. This is good news, which should be made a note of and acted upon by every householder. It has been a scandal that the law of the land has allowed people, especially the poor, to be murdered throughout the country, or maimed and disfigured for life, every day in the week by explosions of the "low flash" oil supplied by the American monopolist. This new Russian oil which Messrs. Rothschild and their partners are introducing in England is to be known as the "Anchor" Oil, and will be sold at the same price as the abominable trash foisted upon us from the United States. In all probability the Americans will not allow this new oil to get upon the market without a more or less prolonged fight, which will involve very heavy losses to their competitors. It would be a great shame if the British public sat passive in this contest. They ought to help those who are seeking to supply them with an article as safe as water, so far as any risk of explosion is concerned. And the way to help is to imitate the tactics of the American town of Columbus, Miss. Its people boycotted the Rockefeller gang. We should refuse, absolutely, to take anything from the oilman except this "Anchor" oil. If the British consumer does this, there will be an end of the pernicious monopoly which is responsible for such a multitude of deaths here every year.

ON Monday last the re-organisation plan of the Trustees, Executors, &c., Corporation, Limited, was duly carried. It excited much discontent among shareholders, and is strikingly unjust, but as a matter of course it was carried. Opposition by shareholders never seems able to organise itself. Many a time have we tried to work up something like unity and strength among the discontented, but never remember a case in which we really succeeded. On the face of it this scheme is bad, were it for no other reason than that it perpetuates the founders' share abomination, giving to five new founders' shares of £10 each one-eighth of the net profits after 10 per cent. has been paid on the ordinary shares, from which £4. 10s. has been written off as completely lost. Half the reserve formed under sub-section "A" of clause 7 of the memorandum of association also goes to these five founders' shares. In the matter of dividends, we do not suppose the founders' shares will ever be worth anything, but in the event of winding-up, which is as likely as not to be the ultimate fate of this wretched concern, their holders might come in for a substantial amount. However it is no use bewailing; the thing is done, and the fruits of it will remain with those who did it.

IT was stated the other day by some semi-official authority or other that the despatch of British troops to "stiffen" the Egyptian force in the Soudan "meant nothing." It was surely not complimentary to Sir H. Kitchener to assert that he had asked for the help of three or four British battalions when he "meant nothing." Of course he had a meaning, and the events of the week have shown that it is probably a much more important meaning than was, at first suspected. The first explanation was that the Sirdar anticipated a Dervish attack on his position at Berber. The Dervishes have not yet made a movement towards it; but, of course, they may do so at any moment; and if they do go, and are defeated, as they must be, then for some reason, not explained, we may "make a rush" for Khartoum. Perhaps, however, the latter place is the real aim of the "stiffened" expedition. Letters from members of the French Marchand expedition have this week been published, much to the chagrin of the *Temps*, who thinks the publication only serviceable to the enemies of France, and go to show that the primary object of that mysterious expedition was to checkmate England on the Nile. It may even have had instructions to go on to Khartoum; but, whether so instructed or not, it is not impossible that Sir H. Kitchener wishes to get there as soon as possible to wait and to watch for that mysterious French expedition, which is now believed to be nearing the sources of the Nile. What France desires by going there, and whether England is anxious to forestall her aims, are matters on which we must wait for further enlightenment. These are times of secrecy and mystery.

OUR Consul-General in Norway, in his report on the trade of 1896 in that small but steadily progressive community, preaches another little sermon on the stiff-necked character of the British merchant in his dealings with his foreign customers. He likes their custom, but does nothing to attract it, and a good deal to repel it. The consequence is that even Norwegians, who in general rather prefer Englishmen, are being driven to deal with Germans, Frenchmen, Belgians, and Dutchmen. In grain, for example, groceries, textiles, hair, skins, manufactured wooden goods, various vegetable products, paper, and manufactured mineral goods, England is already behind Germany to the extent of about a million and a half sterling. France, Belgium, and Holland are also ahead of us in many things. It is the old and now too familiar story. Our foreign rivals study the wants of their customers; we do not. They have their commercial travellers scouring the country for orders. English merchants seem content with inundating the British Consulate with catalogues and price lists, and probably are surprised that Norwegian dealers never see them. Why should they go to the British Consulate for English catalogues or price lists, when they find foreign commercial travellers bringing their catalogues and price lists to the Norwegian traders' doors—all made up, too, in decimal and metric figures, while John Bull scorns to diverge from his pound sterling and his pound avoirdupois?

INDICATIONS are daily accumulating of the evil influence the engineering dispute is having upon trade. A twelvemonth ago shipbuilders rejoiced in the fact that they had sufficient orders booked to keep them going for a year. Orders are still numerous, but they cannot be executed. Vessels which should have been delivered months ago are still unfinished, and will remain so until the wilful engineers return to work. The copper statistics for December indicate dulness, while there would assuredly have been considerable briskness but for the incubus of the lock-out. Worse than all, perhaps, is the report that a Glasgow iron foundry, which employs about 2,500 hands in the making of locomotive and other engines, is about to transfer its works to Belgium. There can be little doubt that other firms will follow this example if this deplorable dispute is prolonged much further. If they would take the agitators with them we should be glad.

THE following letter on the subject deserves to be carefully read:—

SIR,—Can you find space for a few lines in your REVIEW on the engineering dispute, from one who has carefully read and materially profited by every number of the INVESTORS' REVIEW which has been issued since it started as a quarterly, and who now hails it as a weekly, and wishes it a prosperous career? During the past six months I have had many conversations with members of the Masters' Federation, and of the Amalgamated Society of Engineers, and I am astonished that, with the reciprocal feelings of goodwill expressed by each towards the other, this war has continued so long. Some of the men in London who are now working eight hours have told me that they would rather work the nine hours and not rouse up their homes so early in the morning to make a breakfast, which has to last them until dinner-time, six hours later, when they feel faint and worn out. If this sentiment is general, why has it not made itself felt at the recent ballot of the men? Simply because a large proportion of the men are confused as to what they are fighting for, and many others have not the courage to vote against the policy of their union, which forms the staple conversation in train, tram, public-house, and club-room, led by their younger and more militant members. A quiet chat at home by their own firesides proves that they do not believe that the masters wish to "smash" their union, and as for the eight hours, as one man expressed it, "he was a poor specimen who could not work nine." As we all know, a week consists of seven days of twenty-four hours each. Surely no man in average health could be injured by working fifty-six hours out of 168, leaving a balance of 112 for rest and recreation, one hour's work for two hours' rest. When Mr. Barnes speaks of fifty-six hours a week being too long, owing to the "intensity of the work," he may not be aware that not half of the members of his society, taking all the year round, work more than forty-eight hours a week. How few men in an engineering establishment make a full week's wages, and how many are marked in the wages-book as bad time-keepers? A London employer, who, much against his will, had to concede the eight hours, informed me a few days ago that for the first fortnight after the change his workmen almost to a man were in their places when the engine started in the morning; now they had reverted back to the old state of affairs, and instead of making forty-eight hours, they were making forty-four and forty-six hours a week. The masters cannot allow sentiment to guide them in a matter which is purely one of pounds, shillings, and pence, and have frankly told the men's leaders that fifty-six hours' pay cannot, owing to foreign competition, be given for forty-eight hours' work. If the men are really in earnest they will vote for forty-eight hours, with forty-eight hours' pay, a test of sincerity which their leaders have never had the courage to apply. Mr. Barnes and Mr. Sellicks now find themselves in a very illogical and embarrassing position. At the recent conference the amended terms of management were accepted by them, provided the masters conceded fifty-one hours. They cannot, therefore, now maintain that the employers are attempting to destroy "trades unionism generally," or if they do, why did they barter away their birthright for so miserable a mess of pottage as a paltry concession of three hours a week? The barometer points to prolonged resistance, but what will be the certain upshot? Many masters will never again open their shops to union men, as they are now full up with non-unionists, and the handy lads and men now being daily taken on, are gaining skill every hour the trained men are idly walking the streets, losing their deftness.—Yours, &c.,

ONE WHO HAS BEEN BOTH A MAN AND MASTER.

January 6, 1898.

COLONIAL NOTES.

ACCORDING to the Government accounts just received, the total revenue of the Cape of Good Hope for 1896 was £7,241,311. The estimated revenue for 1897-98 is £6,715,000, while the estimated expenditure for the same period is £6,741,151, showing a deficit of £26,151. The Jubilee celebrations cost the Colonial Government £26,000—£1,000 for the representation of the Colony in London during the celebrations here, and £25,000 in contributions in aid of hospitals and kindred institutions to be erected in commemoration of her Majesty's record reign. The decreases in expenditure are not very formidable, as a rule, but there is a diminution in the estimated expenditure on posts and telegraphs amounting to £37,455. Towards the revenue it is calculated that the railways will contribute £3,360,000, the Customs £1,900,000, the Post Office £308,000, and the telegraphs £130,000. Stamped licences may yield £135,000, blank stamps £175,000, and the bank notes duty £7,000. The land revenue is estimated at £148,000, while £75,000 is set down for the sale of Government property. The existing debt of the Colony amounts to £27,388,405. But where does our "ironclad" come in?

THE prevailing tone of the official report on the Colony of British Honduras for 1896 is cheerful. The increased export duty of 50 cents a ton on logwood fell 3,230 dols. short of paying off the charges on this special tax; but it was promptly resolved to issue an Ordinance re-imposing a duty of 1 dol. a barrel on beef and pork, which, it was expected, would add approximately 14,000 dols. a year to the ordinary revenue of the colony. The total general revenue for 1896 was 302,686 dols., while the expenditure was 269,877 dols.; so that the outgoings were well within the incomings. The revenue for 1896 was more by 48,074 dols. than that of 1895, while the expenditure for the same year was 15,084 dols. less than that of 1895. If the saving is modest, it is at least satisfactory. On the whole, the colony gives a good account of itself, but there seems plenty of room for agriculturists; for, of its estimated acreage of 4,839,408, only 52,600 acres are returned as being under cultivation. The post-office is a costly institution. Its total revenue for 1896 was 6,492 dols., and the expenditure 17,117 dols. But postal business is steadily increasing.

APPENDED to this note is a letter from Renmark South Australia, which ought to have the attention of our Colonial Office. It is shameful to see the Government of that Colony coolly ignoring its moral responsibilities in the way this letter sets forth. All that appears to be wanted is £15,000 to put the irrigation works, on which the existence of Renmark depends, into efficient working order. We need not give over again the miserable story of Chaffey Bros., and their Irrigation Colonies. It was told on several occasions at great length in the monthly issue of this REVIEW, which was threatened with a libel action for daring to speak the truth. Chaffey Bros. have gone, but during their existence they flooded this country with circulars so enticingly worded that numbers of people were induced to invest their money in the fruit-growing ventures, and many to emigrate to Mildura and Renmark. Unquestionably, the Governments both of Victoria and South Australia made themselves responsible for the promises of those American gentlemen Victoria has recognised its responsibility by coming to the help of the Mildura settlers. South Australia refuses. This ought to be energetically protested against in the interests of public morals, as well as in those of the unfortunate people now struggling despairingly to avert absolute ruin on the lands of Renmark. Without the pumped-up water of the Murray River the place is a desert.

Renmark, South Australia, November 8, 1897.

SIR,—I have been desired by my committee to address you on the subject of the present position of the Chaffey Irrigation Settlement of Renmark.

From the nature of your previous references to Messrs. Chaffey's enterprises, you will probably be aware that the liquidation of these contractors discovered the irrigation system to be in a very incomplete and inefficient state. The papers I have the honour to enclose will generally show you the causes of this condition of affairs, as well as the grounds upon which appeals have been made to the South Australian Parliament for redress.

At the sister settlement of Mildura, an accommodation of similar disputes has been arranged. The influence of a large mortgagee interest upon the Victorian Government was successfully exerted, and although the compromise involves the Mildura settlers in a liability for repayment of a loan of over £40,000, and the land owners have pledged themselves to buy-over again the irrigation system included in their purchase-moneys, they are freed at once from heavily-increased water rates, and will avoid the discredit which an agitation involves. Unhappily for this settlement, this influence in sufficient volume is not at command; and in its absence the South Australian Government has specifically refused to do anything. Parliament, we are assured on high authority, will follow suit. Under these circumstances the settlers, an overwhelming proportion of whom were drawn from England, look for the influence and assistance of the Home Press, in the hope that an ultimate appeal to the Imperial Parliament may be avoided.

It has been suggested by my committee that a demand for redress of Renmark grievances in your REVIEW would procure that attention which has been denied to reasonable and respectful representations on the spot. It is submitted that the repudiation of any and all liability to our settlers, in respect of the non-fulfilment of conditions accepted from Government agents, contains the essence of that wider repudiation to which a State turns only in the last resort And that the credit of South Australia is as much involved in the present issue as in the flotation of any of the South Australian public loans on the London market. The Chaffey enterprise was an appeal to English capital, organised between the Government of this province and its agents. The conditions of that appeal have never been satisfied, and are now repudiated by the principals. I, therefore, respectfully suggest that the case is one for your attention as a recognised guardian of English investors.

Hoping for your invaluable aid, I have the honour to be, Sir, your obedient servant, CHAS. MORANT, Lieut.-Col.,

Chairman of the Renmark Defence Committee.

THE revenue of New South Wales only fell off about £190,000 in the second half of 1897, and still amounted to £4,423,200, which is a mighty sum for the Colony to raise in a drought-afflicted year. It is that, even admitting that the gross receipts of the railways, which are national property, account for, say, a million and a half of it. How long this scale of income can be kept up by a population of less than a million and a half is always the serious question. But New South Wales has her liberal trade policy in her favour, and the more thoroughly she carries this out the better is her chance. The worst blow to her would come from India were that misruled dependency to fall into financial difficulties. And she is going to refresh herself with a million and a half from our pockets. So everything is all right.

WE cannot say that the annual report of the New Zealand Government Insurance Commissioner for the year 1896, published six months ago, and which we have just come across, pleases us much. For one thing, ratio of expenses to premium income is still very high, nearly 20½ per cent. taken on the assumption that all the premiums are for the whole life. It would really be considerably higher if the cost of the endowment business was calculated on the basis of the duration of the premiums it brings in. Again, it does not seem to us that the valuation by which a gross surplus of assets over liabilities amounting to £225,000 is brought out is a good one. A 4 per cent. Hm. "nominal basis" is employed, but a special reserve is said to be created, which brings the net valuation virtually down to 3⅝ per cent. This is clumsy at best, and even the lower rate is much too high for prudence in these days. Least of all do we admire the way the funds are invested. These funds aggregate £2,646,158 and of this amount £465,999 is lent out on the Government Office's own policies. Another £872,000 is in Government securities, and not less than £812,565 is in "mortgages on property." Perhaps the first two items ought to pass without criticism, although we do not envy policyholders the quality of the security offered by New Zealand Government stock. But what of these mortgages? We in this country know by the most painful experience the quality New Zealand real estate possesses of shrinking in value until it becomes an unknown quantity. Where are these mortgages located, and on what sort of property? We notice that the department has been obliged to foreclose on £30,000 worth of property thus mortgaged; and besides the huge aggregate under this head, it seems to own "landed and house property" to the value of more than £116,000. Explanations are wanted here, but we fear they are not likely to be forthcoming from the present Government of the Colony.

We shall be as pleased as Punch if the anticipations in the following letter come true :—

DIMBULA VALLEY (CEYLON) TEA COMPANY, LIMITED.
16, Philpot-lane, London, E.C.,
December 1, 1897.

SIR,—My attention has been drawn to your article in the INVESTORS' REVIEW for October headed "A Weak Tea Company." With reference to the writer's comments on the Dimbula valley (Ceylon) Tea Company, Limited, I can only say they are unfair in the comparison drawn between this company and the other two named.

In the first place, the writer of the article adds to the company's capital £6,250, the amount of the mortgages which were taken over when the estates were purchased. These mortgages could only be paid off at certain dates, but the company hold the amount ready to pay them at due date.

In estimating whether our capital is high or low the amount of mortgages should, therefore, not have been added. Then our profit of £14,595. 1s. 8d. was practically derived from 1,440 acres of bearing tea, or at the rate of £10 per acre net profit, whilst I assert without any fear of contradiction that the average profit for the whole of Ceylon is not over £5 per acre.

This shows that the dictum is all wrong of the writer of the article, to the effect that "any tea company's capital which stands over £50 an acre is over capitalised," because it is manifest that a company's gardens which turn out a net profit of over £10 an acre must be worth more than those giving only half that, or even less. The only estate belonging to the company absolutely in full bearing last year gave over £16 per acre profit, and I am aware that it has done something like this for several years. Therefore, no rule such as the writer lays down is applicable to Ceylon, or any other gardens.

I would, in conclusion, point out that in judging the stability or otherwise of a tea company as a safe dividend-paying concern, the net profit per pound of tea realised is the most important guide. A company whose net profit per pound is but a penny, is surely in a very different position from one whose profit is 4d., as was, and, I hope, always will be, the position of this company.

Should tea drop 1d. a pound, a capital of £50 would be a bit high, would it not?—Yours faithfully,

JAMES SINCLAIR.

FOREIGN NOTES.

The papers have lately been giving us scraps of news about a new "wheat corner" which has been engineered in Chicago by a man named Joseph Leiter. We did not care much about it, knowing that such things will be done now and then in spite of the warnings from the past. The American mind cannot be happy until it enjoys a monopoly of something, and brave gamblers have again and again attempted to establish a temporary one in wheat. But wheat is not like oil wells, nor even as bounty nourished beet sugar, and Mr. McKinley has not yet fenced round its production in the States with a prohibition tariff on imported grain.

So Mr. Joseph Leiter appears to have failed, like all who have gone before him, if we may believe a highly-coloured account of the "deal" supplied by Messrs. Armour & Co., the corned beef people, and printed in Wednesday's *Financial Times*. Mr. P. D. Armour, it seems, entered the lists against the champion of the "bulls," and sold him all the wheat he could take. Six million bushels Mr. Leiter bought, all to be delivered by the end of December, and Mr. Armour has delivered it. In the battle of the giants the unrivalled organisation of his house of business, and such ingenuity and resource as was implied in keeping the ice in Duluth harbour and in the "Soo" Canal free by tugs until the wheat boats got out and through, carried the day, and the question now is, what will Mr. Joseph Leiter do with his six million bushels? Go bankrupt over them, perhaps, and help us to cheaper bread. Nobody will pity him should the worst befall, and yet he must be a man of pluck.

Mr. Dingley is exceedingly happy with the condition of the United States Revenue. He thinks his tariff is all right and sure to make surpluses blossom as a rose might on the roof of the Capitol. And if not he still has the remedy of more taxes to fall back upon, happy man that he is. Facts, however, hardly appear to bear him out. Take the New England Cotton Industry as an example. In the Fall River Mills wages were reduced 10 per cent. on Monday last, and the sad confession has to be made that home consumption is not able to take the product of American Cotton mills running full time. Their owners must either get foreign markets for their goods or shut down. How they are to get foreign markets under the Dingley tariff is a problem we are much interested in watching them try to solve. What makes the position all the funnier is that mills in the Southern States are successfully competing with those in New England. So that we shall soon have the cut-throat method of business in this industry just as fully developed as among railroads through raw territories. But plants in hot-houses do have a tendency to crowd each other to death.

President Miller, of the Milwaukee Railway, says that the Western Railroads are not making much profit in spite of their larger business because of the prevalence of rate cutting. It is very candid and honest of him to tell us this. If he would go a step further and let us know who profits by the cutting we should be deeply grateful. The singular fact which we begin to note on this side is, that railroad managers never by any chance become poorer by the policy which ruins their shareholders and nominal masters. On the contrary, from a stockholder's point of view, the worse the profit to him the more rapid is usually the progress of managers towards the blessed state of the millionaire. At present, unless for objects of private profit, there seems no reason why the Grainger roads of the North-West should engage in apparently tearing business out of each others grasp. To undertake to carry goods for unprofitable freights is perhaps excusable when the amount of business doing is not enough to go round, but when the lines are all well laden with traffic eagerly pressed forward, we cannot see why the carriers should be so anxious to conduct business at a loss. Probably there are rings of traders receiving favoured treatment and sharing with the conductors of the roads the gains thus dishonestly obtained. We wait for more light, sceptical on many points.

If it be the case that Marshal Blanco, the new Governor-General of Cuba, has made a demand on the

Spanish Government for sixty million pesetas a month, two-thirds of which are for the expenses of the war, not only are the troubles of that unhappy land not yet at an end, but the difficulties of the Spanish Treasury must surely soon reach a climax. Sixty millions of pesetas amount to about two millions sterling in the present depreciated state of Spanish currency—say £25,000,000 a year, and Spain lumbers along with heavy deficits irrespective of this. Under ordinary circumstances she could no more find this money out of normal resources than her neighbour, Portugal, could. So the Marshal's demand immediately implies a fresh loan on the security of the Customs, amounting to two hundred million pesetas, part of which is to be used to enable the Bank of Spain to still further swell out its excessive note circulation. That is what we infer from the statement that, forty million pesetas of the loan will be retained by the Bank of Spain as a guarantee for the money it is to advance to the Government to meet Marshal Blanco's requirements; and another hundred million besides on Cuban bonds now pledged to the Bank of Spain, is, if possible, to be sold to the public. Spain is not really a poor country in some senses—it is only poverty-stricken. The people also are indifferent taxpayers, so that although the foreign trade is increasing, both import and export, the Customs revenue is declining. What the end will be it seems hardly necessary to say. The wonder to us is that Spain has kept up an appearance of solvency for so long under the strain. Blessed, for its present Government, are the financiers of Paris.

IN his report to the Foreign Office—a veritable trade romance in its way—on the enormous development of the trade and commerce of Japan—a veritable romance in its way—Mr. Brenan certainly speaks very plainly as to the want of commercial morality among the Japanese. They are declared to be worse than the Chinese in this respect. You may accept Chinese goods "on the faith of a Chinaman's honesty," but it is not so with Japanese goods. These have all to be very carefully inspected before delivery is accepted. According to Mr. Brenan, gradual deterioration seems the inevitable fate of all articles of Japanese manufacture. Their match trade, which was rapidly driving all competitors out of Eastern markets, is said to be greatly depressed, if not on the road to ruin, because of fraudulent practices. The Japanese merchant has no credit; it is scarcely possible to keep the ordinary Japanese to the terms of a contract. This is very sad, no doubt; but is it not possible that the traders of Japan may yet learn by experience the value of commercial honesty? Even in England that was a knowledge of slow growth. It is not so very long since there were grievous complaints of the comparative absence of commercial morality among English traders and manufacturers.

BUT, in spite of these drawbacks, Japanese trade progresses at a most extraordinary pace. In twenty-six years the value of the foreign trade of Japan has grown from 48,000,000 dols. to 288,000,000 dols. In the course of the last seven years, the imports into Japan have increased by 90,000,000 yen, and the exports by 74,500,000 yen. In this, Great Britain and the British possessions have participated to the extent of 50,500,000 yen while all other countries put together improved their position to the extent of only 29,000,000 yen. That is all very satisfactory in itself, and there should be no difficulty in the British merchant and manufacturer keeping the lead if they will only submit to push and to display a little more "sweet reasonableness" and patience in dealing with the natives. But the complaint comes from Japan as from so many other quarters, that the British dealer is not so careful in cultivating customers as are the dealers of other countries—more especially America and Germany. Of course, these are at present far behind us in the race, and, to make any headway at all, they must exert their utmost energies in increasing their business. But, as Mr. Brenan wisely says, "if other nations push, and we remain inactive, we shall drop behind."

RUSSIA has now got a good, honest, thumping national debt of 6,101,339,902 roubles, say 600 millions sterling, and a bit. Its total rose in 1897 by about 116 million roubles gross, owing to the issue of 490 rentes, &c., to buy the Vistula, the Moscow-Brest, and the Moscow-Smolensk Railways, and its net increase was about 51 million roubles after allowing for amortisation, &c. This noble debt is represented to some extent by revenue-yielding iron roads; but it took 296 millions odd roubles for its service last year, and will require 272 millions this, or over 20 per cent. of the whole revenue of the State.

THE situation in the Far East has cleared up a very little. It is officially announced that Germany has "leased" Kiao-Chau from China. However bad things may look for her, Germany can now at least say, with documentary proof to back her, that she has not "annexed" that famous bay. The "mailed fist" may have been put forth, but by the moderation of China it was not necessary to use it. Things have, therefore, been made comfortable for the Kaiser. The lease runs for fifty years; will it be necessary to have a formal renewal of it? We doubt it; but much may happen between now and then. But how much is Germany to pay for her lease in rent or tribute? The official record saith not; and the probabilities are that the "rent," if anything is to be paid, will be a peppercorn one. Now will come the question as to whether Kiao-Chau is to be regarded as a free port. Will the other Powers demand the free use of it under the "most favoured nation clause?"

WE shall know that by and by. Meantime, it is said that this "most favoured nation clause" briefly embodies the policy followed by England in China. She demands—as yet—no new port for herself, but tells China that whatever ports she gives to other powers must be as free to all as are the Treaty ports. American journalists applaud this statement of policy; and undoubtedly it is the right course to pursue. England's greatest interest in China is freedom of trade, and this would be in grave danger if there were to be any exclusive dealing in Chinese ports. It would be idle to attempt overtaking all the rumours of the week concerning China. Those of the one day were generally contradicted by others of the next, and most of them are forgotten.

BELGIAN industry must have been in a specially vigorous condition during 1896, for we find from our Vice-Consul's report on the coal industry of the province of Liège for 1896 that the output was 5,241,220 tons, or

192,936 tons greater than in 1895, and 184,789 tons more than in 1890, a year of extraordinary prosperity. This increase in the output of coal was almost entirely due to the greater demand for the coals used for industrial purposes. The profit made by thirty mines at work in 1895 was 2,513,600 frs.; of thirty-three mines in 1896, 3,607,850 frs., or an increase of 1,094,250 frs. About thirty years ago, the quantity of coal produced in the province of Liège was 2,564,550 tons, or less than half of the present day. The owners seem to be totally unaffected by the sinister prophecies of the failure of the supply. That is for the far future.

There is much that is interesting in the British Consular report on the trade and commerce of Hungary for 1896-7. Ever since the close of its memorable struggle with Austria, Hungary has devoted itself with no little energy and perseverance to the development of trade and manufactures. But in this respect it is still, to use a familiar colloquialism, "On the make." It is in the transition stage between agriculture and commerce; and the former is still, by a long way, the leading industry, three-fourths of the population depending upon it for their subsistence. Of its agriculture, however, the British Consul-General can only say that "it is far from being in a hopeless condition." High-farming is practised, and the importation and manufacture of the best agricultural machinery are very large. Indeed, several English manufacturers of modern agricultural machines have found it to their advantage to establish branches in Hungary.

Hungary's principal exports are corn, flour, cattle, and wines. From Great Britain she imports chiefly cotton and woollen goods, raw iron, steel, machinery, platinum articles, and steamships. Seven-tenths of the exports to England consist of meal, the remainder being made up of raw sugar, oak-gall extract, barley, mineral waters, and sawing materials. Recently British manufacturers and merchants have shown increasing interest in Hungarian industries. They have inundated the British Consulate, not with comparatively useless catalogues and price lists, but with applications for information as to the best way of initiating or of developing various branches ofcommerce and industry. Our Consul has supplied these with the best information available, and in time we may see English capital going more freely to the help of Hungarian trade.

Although the Russian bureaucrats, with their stupid system of secrecy in all things, refuse to allow the agricultural statistics gathered yearly a wider circulation than that of their own inner circle, the British Consul at Batoum has contrived in various ways to collect a considerable amount of useful information, which is fairly accurate so far as it goes. It is not a very cheerful picture that he draws. The cereal crops have been a complete failure in the Trans-Caucasian province, so much so that the peasants must be dependent on Government, or other outside sources, for the seeds for next year's crops. They are an ignorant, superstitious, and prejudiced people, these peasants; but farmers of some substance and intelligence do rise up among them; and these, we are told, are showing an inclination to use modern agricultural implements in place of the primitive "scratchers of the ground" to which the common peasantry cling. As a consequence, there is a movement, so far favoured by the Government, for the reduction of the Customs duties on foreign-made agricultural implements, and, if this is successful, the Consul thinks there would be a good opening for English enterprise in this line.

It is difficult to say what success has attended the experiments in tea-growing, begun some years ago on the Russian Imperial domains near Batoum. The yield from the trees planted has been too insignificant to be remunerative, but the domain officials do not seem to have lost hope, as they are trying to induce the neighbouring peasants to plant tea shrubs by the offer of seed for nothing. A still more remarkable fact, however, is the decision of a Moscow firm greatly to extend the area they at present have under tea cultivation. They seem to have found their previous experiments sufficiently successful at least to promise profit in the future. The cultivation of the American cotton plant would appear to have been a decided success. The red rust, a disease which has not yet attacked the local cotton plant, has to some extent damaged the yield for the present year in the Trans-Caucasus; but the crop will still be abundant, and in the Trans-Caspian territory they have 100,000 acres under American cotton—a fact, perhaps, worth noting in Manchester.

We have received the following in reply to an article in the November number of the monthly issue of the Investors' Review:—

The Imperial Continental Waterworks, Limited,
35, New Broad-street,
London, December 30, 1897.

Sir,—Under the heading of "The Proposed New Waterworks for Genoa" there appeared in your issue of last month, a letter, dated 16th October, 1897, which you stated was written by Mr. Frederick A. Y. Brown, of Granet, Brown & Co., English Bankers, Genoa. That letter endeavours to criticise the Debenture Issue of this company made on 9th October last, and seeks to impugn the statements in this company's prospectus of that issue. No one should be denied the right of *fair* criticism, but the intention of Mr. Brown's letter is self-evident, and my directors can only conclude that his fears concerning the ultimate consequences to the company of which he is a director, when the works of this company (excavations and preliminary works for which are now being proceeded with, and steel mains being shipped) are completed, have so far misled him as to cause him to make statements which are proved to be incorrect, even by the engineer-in-chief of his own company in his report printed in 1893, as also by the Royal Decree of November 17, 1887, but these are too lengthy to quote in this letter; the originals, however, and notarial translations thereof can be seen at any time. My directors can only assume that Mr. Brown when writing his letter of October 16 last, forgot the existence of these and other important documents. Mr. Brown's misleading statements are of a very serious and important nature, and while apologising to you for the great, but necessary, length of this reply, embodying as it must do, Mr. Deacon's refutal of Mr. Brown's statements from the engineering point, and a letter addressed to this company from fifty-two leading citizens of Genoa, including members of the Legislature, the Municipal Council of Genoa, and other Municipal Councils, and of land owners, merchants, manufacturers, and professional men, which my directors hope amply refutes Mr. Brown's statement that the residents in the Bisagno valley are "well supplied with water." I am instructed to request that you will, in fairness to this company, give the same publicity to this communication and annexed letters as you gave to Mr. Brown's letter. I am also instructed to say that this company has no need, nor does it intend, to compete at first with existing supplies. The population without any adequate public supply and to whose houses my company at first proposes to lay on its water, will yield a revenue quite equal to that named in the prospectus of this company, without, my directors think, encroaching on the parts now supplied by Mr. Brown's Company, but when this company increases its service beyond that sphere into the parts of Genoa at present very meagrely supplied by pipes with impure water, my directors think it may be safely left with the inhabitants of Genoa to say whether they prefer paying for a constant and unrestricted supply, under high pressure, of pure water such as this company will supply, or for the meagre supply of impure water which they are now receiving.—I am, sir, your obedient servant,

Ernest J. R. Dodd, *Secretary.*

To the Directors of the Imperial Continental Waterworks, Limited.

Victoria Mansions, 32, Victoria-street,
Westminster, S.W.
December 28, 1897.

GENTLEMEN,—In compliance with a request contained in the secretary's letter of the 10th inst., drawing my attention to a communication from Mr. Frederick A. Y. Brown, of Genoa, which appeared in the INVESTOR'S REVIEW for November, I have the honour to report as follows:—In that communication Mr. Brown impugns certain statements made in your prospectus, and others made in my report dated July 20, 1897. It is due to you that I should reply to Mr. Brown's statements, so far as they concern the information I have afforded you.

1. Mr. Brown's letter contains ten paragraphs. The first two do not touch my statements, and the third introduces my name incorrectly in connection with a statement in the prospectus issued by the company, but not contained in my report. Apart from this, I am of opinion concerning that statement that no adequate public supply has been afforded to the "population lying next to the company's proposed reservoir."

2. In the fourth paragraph Mr. Brown says that he is in a position to contradict flatly my statement that the company of which he is a director "has somewhat more than reached the limits of its resources in respect of water-supply." I believe my statement to be accurate even under the restricted mode of distribution adopted, and it would still be true in the driest seasons even if Mr. Brown's company were empowered to take water from the Gorzente without limit. Their concession, however, only permits the withdrawal of 250 litres per second, a quantity many times more than the flow of the stream in dry weather, and which Signor Niccolo Bruno, the engineer-in-chief of the company, says at page 30 of his Report of 1893, had been shown in 1885 to be insufficient to cope with the demand. ("La convenienza di aumentare la potenzialità della derivazione, essendosi dimostrata impari alle richieste quella dei 250 litri d'acqua al l'domandati dagli Ing Grillo e fratelli Bruno.") How much more insufficient must it now be having regard to the great increase of the population of Genoa since that date, and to the fact that the company's statutory powers of withdrawal have not in the interval been increased.

3. But it must be borne in mind that quite apart from insufficiency at the sources, the present Genoa supplies are restricted to a very serious extent by the mode in which they are distributed to the tenement. It is an undoubted fact that the people of Genoa have no experience of that constant and unrestricted supply of water under high pressure, paid for (so far as domestic consumption is concerned) without reference to the quality used, which in this country is regarded as a sanitary necessity.

4. Towards the end of the fourth paragraph Mr. Brown quotes, incorrectly, the statement following, which is contained in my report:—"I have been informed that even after the repair of the lower reservoir the authorities have not permitted it to be filled," and states that he is able to contradict it flatly. By the word "filled" I mean "filled." I do not mean, and no one would suppose I meant, that I had been informed that the reservoir in question had not been used at all. The reservoir is used, but owing to the defective construction of its retaining dam, a Commission was in 1885-6 appointed by the Government upon the report of which Commission an injunction was issued in 1886 by the Ministry of Public Works limiting the height to which water might be stored in the reservoir. Further, that Commission made certain recommendations for the strengthening of the dam, which I understand from the report of the engineer-in-chief of its owners have not been carried out. It is reasonable, therefore, to suppose that the injunction is still in force, and I am informed that it has not been withdrawn. I do not, of course, doubt Mr. Brown's statement that the reservoir was filled on an occasion in October, 1892, but if the upper part of it is used, and the injunction has not been withdrawn, it is improperly used, and having personally examined the dam in 1892 I can imagine nothing but dire need of additional water which would justify so dangerous an expedient as the filling of the upper part of this reservoir, even if there were no human dwellings in the valleys between it and the sea.

5. The fifth and sixth paragraphs of Mr. Brown's letter contain further statements about the Gorzente works, and do not relate to your company's proposed works.

6. In the seventh paragraph Mr. Brown incorrectly quotes the purport of my report, and, having done so, proceeds to draw inferences from the incorrect quotation. The paragraph in question deals with my assertion as to the sufficiency of the gathering ground included in your company's concession. I have thoroughly satisfied myself by prolonged gauging and investigation that every word of my report upon this subject is justified. In the same paragraph, when comparing the resources of your company with those of the Gorzente Company, of which he is a director, Mr. Brown has entirely omitted to mention the Bisagno area, which, in addition to the adjacent Concasca area, is covered by your Concession. The two areas together contain 9,750 acres, and will supply enormously more water than I have yet spoken of.

7. The eighth paragraph of Mr. Brown's letter contains further remarks concerning his company. As an engineer, I am enabled to state that the inference which would be drawn from his conclusion as to the additional supply to be obtained from an additional reservoir on the Gorzente would be incorrect, even if the company had power to abstract more water.

8. The ninth and last paragraphs are expressions of opinion to which it is not necessary that I should reply.

9. From a physical point of view there cannot be any doubt that the sources included in the Bisagno and Concasca areas present immense advantages over those utilised by the Gorzente Company which are drawn from less than half the area, and are situated at a distance from Genoa more than three times as great. I regard it as a misfortune to the city of Genoa that waters of such remarkable purity, and at so short a distance, have not yet been properly utilised.—I am, gentlemen, your obedient servant,

(Signed) GEORGE F. DEACON.

The following letter has been addressed to the company by fifty two residents in Genoa, whose signatures are attached:—"We are extremely pleased to learn from the communication made to us that your company have decided to carry out shortly the conveyance (or derivation) of the water from the torrents of Concasca and Bisagno, for the purpose of supplying with the purest water the valley of Bisagno, Genoa and neighbouring towns. A want is by this means satisfied and a long-felt need will be supplied, and thus benefiting not only the city and townships where the water is delivered, but also the company undertaking the works. And while we thank you for the information afforded us and applaud the initiative taken by your company, we earnestly hope and wish that the aqueduct so sorely needed may as soon as possible become an accomplished fact." (Here follow the signatures.)

The Queensland National Bank.

DEFRAUDED Australian Bank depositors and students interested in the moral development of our Australasian settlements will find much to interest them in the report of the Committee appointed to investigate the affairs of this Bank, the text of which has now reached this country. Some may remember that the London Board of the Bank was so tremendously sensitive, so conscious of surpassing virtue, that it resented the slightest whisper about the solvency of the institution in the crisis of 1893, and even went so far as to commence an action against the *Standard*, claiming £100,000 damages because that newspaper had published a slender fragment of the truth. Of this Board we shall have more to say presently. In the meantime, let us look at what the Committee has disclosed. First, it tells us that the total losses of the Bank from its formation down to June 30, 1896, have amounted to £3,497,803. This is a fairly tidy sum, but the details cause surprise that it was not larger, and we are not at all sure that it is not considerably larger. But as it stands, it is a proof of marvellous, if peculiar, enterprise; for how was this money lost? According to the report before us, barely 7 per cent. of it disappeared in agricultural advances, and less than 14 per cent. in pastoral; but fully 35½ per cent. vanished in what is euphemistically described as commercial undertakings, 22 per cent. in mining adventures, and 21 per cent. in what might be called miscellaneous leaks. The details entered into are of the most romantic description, and, as usual, the directors knew nothing. They trusted to the manager, the manager acted by blind routine, the auditors did what the manager told them, and they were all a happy family until the crash came. Even after the crash, the directors went on comfortably as before. They constructed illusory balance-sheets and paid dividends, which were not earned, on the share capital of the re-constructed bank to the tune of £40,300. In fact, the bank made no profits after its re-construction any more than before, but continued its unbroken record of losses; and we do not believe it is making any profit now; in fact, like Mr. *Punch's* costermonger, in regard to this affair "We don't think much of nuffin'."

But let us get to the heart of the story. Who were the most valiant appropriators of the bank's money? Quite a crowd of small money-sucking accounts are mentioned by the Committee, some of them so graphically that we may quote the text just to lighten the narrative, and to illustrate how banking business can be done in an enterprising and progressive settlement run on bushranger or ticket-of-leave principles. Just read this :—

For each advance with which we dealt we asked by whom it was sanctioned, and in the great majority of cases the answer was "no record." We asked what limit was fixed for each account, and to this query, with very few exceptions, we obtained the same reply. As an extreme instance, we cite a laconic report in the case of an account on which we estimated a deficiency of £7,500, and off which various sums, amounting in all to £14,800, had been previously written :—

"By whom sanctioned?—No record.

"Authorised limit?—No record.

"Value of securities at the time?—No record.

"Commenced with a charge for a cheque-book, and steadily ran up until the bank took over the property."

And this :—

The half-yearly reports on advances of some of the branch managers were absurdly optimistic and misleading.

Here is a case in point in connection with an account on which the bank has lost £30,500. In June, 1889, the manager reported as follows :—"Of the highest character and standing. This is our largest and most profitable account. Their business is extensive both in town and country, and for the most part very sound." In the following half-year the same manager's report resolved itself into the brief obituary notice—"Estate assigned; see security number so-and-so."

In the majority of cases, however, we are happy to say that we believe the branch managers to-day to be competent, careful men.

We can do things pretty freely in the old country and must not hold our heads too high, but this rather beats our "form." It is nothing though to what that renowned statesman and pioneer of all sorts of things, Sir Thomas M'Ilwraith, ex-Prime Minister of Queensland, ex-Finance Minister, and so forth, and so forth, K.C.M.G. in addition, and now of obscure address, was able to accomplish with the assistance of his friend and partner, Mr. E. R. Drury, C.M.G., the remarkable man who condescended to act as general manager of the bank. What Sir Thomas precisely owes the creditors of the old bank we are not sure that the Committee makes quite clear to us, but then, as its members say, "it was most unfortunate" that they should have been without the benefit of Sir Thomas's "oral testimony." He produced his evidence through an attorney who was evidently ignorant of many things, although we do not in the least doubt "a thoroughly intelligent witness." Putting one thing and another together the Committee has come to the conclusion that on June 30, 1896, Sir Thomas M'Ilwraith's indebtedness to the bank at head office, and in respect of accounts in his own name was £251,461. Against this security amounting to £60,700 was held, leaving the deficiency of £190,761, but this is only the beginning of the tale. Sir Thomas is also held responsible by the Committee to the defunct original Queensland National Bank for £39,674, representing advances to the Mount Perry Copper Company, and the whole of this has been written off as irrecoverable, for £16,608 advanced to the Palmer River Gold Mining Company, also all written off, and for £15,928 the amount lost on what is described as the Ida Accounts.*

These items added together come to £247,043, quite a respectable total, but scarcely large enough, we imagine, to indicate the true greatness of Sir Thomas's mind. Its towering grandeur may be dimly perceived from the story of the Ravenswood account, described thus in the report :—

The "Ravenswood" account is referred to as follows by Mr. Stuart : —"Date opened—March, 1887 ; by whom sanctioned—no record ; authorised limit—no record ; security taken—nil. The account commences with a cheque for £3,631 drawn to No. 1, and with accumulated interest represents the debt as written off in December.

A mere bagatelle this, but luminous of its sort. Less light yielding, but suggestive also, are the dealings with the ex-Prime Minister of the Colony, and the ex-General Manager, Mr. Drury. It is popularly supposed, by the way, that Mr. Drury suddenly died a natural death at a convenient moment, but private gossip at once ascribed his death as being due to his own hand ; and it is now alleged that he is no more dead than Sir Thomas, but only "beavering" till the storm blows by. What he and Sir Thomas did together had best be given in the words of the report. They do not require to be moralised over to any great extent :—

Exclusive of the "Ravenswood Account." Sir Thomas had, on June 30, 1896, at the head office, eight separate overdrawn accounts, totalling, as we have said, a quarter of a million sterling, but he asserts that in six out of the eight accounts (amounting in the aggregate to £160,000 in round figures) the late Mr. E. R. Drury was his full partner. The following are the accounts for which it is alleged that the late Mr. Drury is jointly liable :—No. 2 account, representing Mount Morgan shares ; No. 4 account, representing the purchase of shares in the Hydraulic Company, and in the Colonial Land Company; "Dotswood Account" ; "Newcastle Brewery Account" ; "Adelaide-street Land Account" ; "Land Account." There is nothing on record in the books of the bank which would serve to establish the alleged partnership. But there is a letter from Sir Thomas to the late Mr. Drury, dated at Westminster Palace Hotel, London, January 29, 1896, and in this letter Sir Thomas specifically reminds the late Mr. Drury of his liability in connection with the several accounts already mentioned. That letter, of course, arrived here after Mr. Drury's death. In a subsequent letter addressed to the present general manager, Sir Thomas refers to the various transactions as follows :—"No. 2 account. This was an account opened by Mr. Drury for him and myself, founded on the purchase by him of various Mount Morgan shares from time to time. . . . . No. 4 account was opened by Mr. Drury for the purchase between us of certain shares in the United Colonial Land Company and the Sydney Hydraulic Company. Newcastle Brewery Account the late Mr. Drury and I were responsible for. The Adelaide-street Land Account (Dr. £38,493) was for land purchased by Mr. Drury and —— and myself. ——'s portion was divided from ours, and the balance remaining is the foundation of the account." We think it right to say here that the Bank has no security whatever for the last-mentioned advance. "Land Account I am unable to explain, but take it to be for two pieces of land," &c. And he concludes as follows :—"At all events, in the whole account, Mr. E. R. Drury was an equal sharer with myself. This advance, also is entirely unsecured.

Sir Thomas McIlwraith and his friend Mr. Drury, thus by Sir Thomas's own admissions, did what they liked with the money furnished by British depositors and others, and, at the time of the closing of the Bank the pair had open no less than eight separate overdrawn accounts at the head office of the Bank, exclusive of the Ravenswood account, and the two men obviously played with the funds as pickpockets of a gambling disposition might play at Monte Carlo. Securities, where there are any, held by the Bank against advances to Sir Thomas, have depreciated enormously, and it is all very sad of course ; and the late Mr. Drury "stood

* The following reveals a little of the darkness surrounding this account :—Thomas M'Ilwraith "Ida Account."—On the 9th February, 1882, Sir Thomas M'Ilwraith wrote to the late Mr. Drury as follows :—"I enclose cheques (2) for £3,600 each, signed T. M'I., Ida Account. Will you kindly open the account in that form?" This account was closed at the head office on 30th December, 1884, by a transfer of the balance—then Dr. £10,369 18s. 8d. —to the account of the Palmer River Gold Mining Company at Maytown branch, from which £10,000 was written off as irrecoverable in December, 1885.

indebted," £67,744 to the Bank at the time of his decease, £30,242 of it being written off as lost, with another £16,480 to follow. But Mr. Drury is dead—or held to be—and his defalcations are useful mainly as affording directors a chance of excusing themselves. This is how one of them does that. Bold as a warrior in triple brass was this Mr. Webster until the truth begun to be dug out :—

In the early days of the Bank, the directors sanctioned an advance to the deceased gentleman of £600, and subsequently this was extended to £2,000. So far as the minutes go, no application for further advances came before the board, and we were assured by two directors—Messrs. Hart and Morehead—that they were ignorant of the existence of this large advance until after the late Mr. Drury's death. Mr. A. B. Webster, on being questioned on this subject, replied as follows :—"When I was auditor I knew Mr. Drury had an overdraft at the Bank, which I thought was irregular. I was told that this was a land speculation in South Brisbane bridge lands, and that it was amply secured. Mr. Pritchard informed me of this. When I became a director a certain time elapsed between the date of my resignation as auditor and election (Mr. Webster signed the balance-sheet June 30, 1889, as auditor, and took his seat on the board on May 7, 1890), and the account was never brought before the board. I also thought that the account was authorised. I made no enquiry when I went on the board, as I was under the impression that the advance was in order, and that it was not increasing." It would thus appear that the late Mr. Drury, as general manager of the Bank, made large advances to himself, without the sanction of the board, on security that might or might not have been considered full cover at the time. There can be no doubt that there has been a large shrinkage in the value of that security, and that the consequent loss is considerable. We refer to this matter with the utmost reluctance, and we wish to remind you that had the deceased gentleman been able to speak for himself he might have put a different complexion upon a transaction which, we are bound to admit, bears an ugly aspect in its present form. We are much indebted to Mr. Victor Drury, attorney for Mrs. Drury, who courteously gave us the fullest information as to the great decline in the values of properties purchased by his late uncle and held as security by the Bank. We are of opinion that the late Mr. Drury was wrong in incurring large monetary obligations to the Bank—of which he was general manager—without the formal sanction of his board. We desire to record our appreciation of the action of the widow of the deceased in voluntarily surrendering certain securities to the Bank which have since realised over £4,000.

This is sweetly consoling, to be sure; and Mr. Drury was a most honourable man; we are all honourable men. Yea, even Sir Thomas M'Ilwraith, of whose adventures and financial gambols at the Bank's charges the Committee speaks with becoming sorrow. He owes this and that; but what would you, flayed depositor? Was he not a mighty power in the land? Nevertheless, the accumulated interest due on his private account alone amounts to £27,000, and it is not yet paid it up, although, of course, he will pay when "luck" improves with him and times mend. He seems to have been a man of great gullibility in regard to mines, and to have been always dabbling in something, caring not a straw so long as the Bank was loser, and not he. But, through his attorney, he declares that a large part of the debt is due as much to Mr. Drury as himself, Mr. Drury being his "full partner." So let us vow vengeance on Drury, and salute Sir Thomas as a great "Imperial" patriot badly guided.

One point has been hotly debated in the Colony; it has only an academic interest here. The Committee reports that the Bank was in such a precarious position at the end of 1892 as to render it necessary for the Government of the Colony to come to its relief by borrowing £600,000 from the Bank of England to enable it to pay the dividends on the Colony's debt. This transaction was faintly known in London at the time, and must have been perfectly known to the London Board. As soon as possible in 1893 a public loan was issued for Queensland by the Bank of England, so that the said Bank might get its money back again from the pockets of the British investors, and thus escape what would otherwise have been an absolute dead loss to-day. Of course, statements of this kind cast the gravest reflection, not only upon the Government of Queensland, but upon the London Board of its Bank, and Sir Samuel Griffiths, another ex-Premier, who carried out the transaction on behalf of the Colony, wrote to the Brisbane papers to deny that this money had been borrowed for any such purpose. The Queensland Premier also made a statement by way of an explanation, which explained nothing. The money was lent to the Government, they say, not to the Bank; but it really does not matter a straw what the ostensible reason for the borrowing was—the actual fact being that this £600,000 providentially prevented both the Colony and the Bank from stopping payment.

The committee gently informs us that the loss caused to the Bank by the "boom" in Mount Morgan Mine shares "may be moderately computed at £350,000." Did not some of the servants of the Bank emerge more than millionaires from this boom? Are not some of them now swaggering around in London Society, rubbing shoulders with Princes, and intriguing for "titles"? "It is fortunate for the Bank," adds the Committee, "that one of the largest shareholders in the mine headed the financial revel, and took upon his own shoulders liabilities of great magnitude." Perhaps; but the £350,000 "moderately" vanished.

In conclusion, may we be allowed to ask a question about the position of the London Directors in regard to this miserable story of criminal finance. Are they perfectly innocent of any knowledge of what was going on in the Colony? They were supposed to be all men of business, and some of them were reputed to be men of sense also. As directors, they held a position of great responsibility towards the thousands of British depositors who lent money to the Bank on the faith of their names. In their own interest, we imagine, they ought now to demand an investigation into the affairs of the Bank on this side, and if they are innocent of all knowledge of Sir Thomas M'Ilwraith and Mr. Drury's "enterprise," of the thievish proceedings in Brisbane, they would rejoice were investigation made even in a Criminal Court. Whether these gentlemen take steps to have themselves cleared or not, they must expect to be judged by their conduct in relation to this unclean business. The mealy-mouthed language of the Brisbane Committee sometimes excites amazement as one reads it, sometimes contemptuous disgust. They slur over vile betrayals of trust, shameless robberies, the most basely-concocted frauds, as if they were mere errors of judgment, the trivial peccadilloes of men too eager to get on and become rich to pause and give a thought about the morality of their proceedings. But such language is not likely to be employed in this country. Both the Queensland Government and the National Bank appear to us to have been in the hands of a set of unscrupulous knaves, and the London board of the Bank, unconsciously no doubt, but still in actual fact, was the associate of this set of thieves, through whose operations the British public has lost incalculable sums of money. Will those four men try to do anything now to rehabilitate their character, to dissociate themselves fully and convincingly from all participation in the deeds of those Colonial rogues? They may be quite sure that if they adopt the policy of remaining silent under it all, a brand will be put upon their names which will blacken them for ever in the memory of their fellow countrymen.

Our Position in China.

It is well that we should keep calm about the movements of Germany and Russia in China, although commercially we have a greater stake there than all the rest of the world put together. And should it be the case that Sir Robert Hart is to be succeeded in the control of the Imperial Customs by a German or a Russian, we may certainly look for it that our commerce will be seriously interfered with. So far as England herself is concerned, there might be compensations, but the matter is much more serious when we take India into account. The revenue of our Indian dependency from opium, sold principally to China, has been falling off somewhat rapidly of late years, but it still amounts to nearly sixty million rupees a year and were the decay of this source of income to be hastened by influences hostile to the finances of India, so gravely compromised by domestic mismanagement, the consequences might be serious indeed. From this point of view Russia may be able to deal a far more deadly blow at our Indian Empire than by anything she has done in Central Asia. While we have been wasting the bravest of our troops in the foolish endeavour to subdue mountain tribes, always an untameable species of human being; while we have been making roads to facilitate the entrance of an enemy into the plains of India, Russia has reached forth her hand in the far east and grasped the control of Northern China. Both Russia and Germany bear us no good will commercially, and will be at one in all probability in injuring our commerce. All this is true, and still there is nothing much to be afraid of if we do not make the mistake of folding our hands and waiting on events. There has been far too much of the "let slide" in our foreign policy since the present Government came into power. Bold words have been spoken, but the deeds have been futile. When the news first became public that Russia had agreed to guarantee a loan for China in exchange for certain concessions, including the right to carry her Trans-Siberian Railway across Manchuria, we urged in the monthly issue of this Review for July, 1895, that our true policy, as a counter-move, was to ally ourselves with Japan. The wisdom of this course must be still more apparent to-day, and if we neglect to make friends of the Japanese, to work with them, and to back them up in the conflict which is impending between them and the Powers that stepped in and robbed them of the fruits of their victory, the day may not be distant when we shall find ourselves driven out of the commerce of China altogether. Enterprising and clever as the Japanese are, the trade they could give us is not sufficient to compensate us for the much larger business which we do now with the immense population of the Chinese Empire. It is quite conceivable, moreover, that if we neglect Japan she too might be overwhelmed by the combined attack of Russia and Germany, and herself become a dependency of one or other of these powers. This is a contingency too dreadful to be contemplated with equanimity; and, if there be anything in our boast that we are the friends of the free, we certainly ought to make haste to let the Japanese know whether we mean to help them in every just quarrel. Not only so, but, in proof of our capacity to do this, we ought to establish at one or more points of the Chinese coast. A naval post, for our fleet is absolutely necessary there—one at least, but there will be no harm in our having more—one, and that the most important in the South, and another a point of observation somewhere in the neighbourhood of the Gulf of Pi-chi-li. It would hardly be possible to illustrate more strikingly the sham nature of the Imperialist boasting now in fashion, than to contrast our apathy in this matter of the further Eas and our immense interest there, with the zeal and impetuosity with which we rush into costly wars in regions of the earth where there is no trade for us to do, except it may be the insignificant trade surrounding gold digging, and where we cannot settle any of our surplus population. It may be said we cannot settle any of it in China, a country already teeming with people, and that is so; but there is almost unlimited scope for the extension of profitable channels of employment in the civilising and guiding of this great mass of people, and of trade. And the question we have to settle with ourselves is, Shall this be done with our help, or without it? Are we to lead the way, as hitherto, or fall back into the third or fourth place?

When we speak of establishing posts on the Chinese coast, it is by no means our purpose to advocate any imitation of the piratical example set by Germany and Russia. Whatever ports we may require as a refuge for our fleet in the Chinese seas, or as fortified posts of observation, ought to be acquired by purchase, either as freehold outright or on a long lease. There can be no doubt at all that Pekin would be only too pleased at the present time to listen to any offer of money, and it, therefore, is a splendid moment for striking a bargain. We might obtain a harbour or arsenal in the Canton River, a position near the mouth of the Yang-Tsze-Kiang, that great river of Central China, the commerce of which we are bound by the instinct of self-preservation to keep under our own control; and if it were necessary and not too alarming, we might even possess ourselves of the port of Wei-Hai-Wei, failing that, some place on the Gulf of Pi-chi-li, near the mouth of the Hoang-Ho, might be available. In short, our naval commanders out in that region should be instructed to promptly examine the most likely points on the coast of the Chinese Empire for the establishment of naval arsenals and depots, and negotiations ought to be at once entered into with the Tsung-Li-Yamen for the acquisition of the points selected, with a suitable amount of land in their neighbourhood. If it cost us two or three millions to acquire the necessary territory and harbours, the money might easily be raised on a short annuity, and would be money well spent. It would also give most seasonable help to the Chinese Government, which is in a more impecunious condition than it was even at the close of the Tai-ping Rebellion. And better this, surely, than another loan "guaranteed" by Russia, under conditions sure to hasten the collapse of the Tartar Empire in her favour.

As we write the rumour circulates that the British Government is about to stand sponsor with the London Market for a loan to China. The *Times* of Wednesday, quoting the *Cologne Gazette*, put the amount at £16,000,000, and made some very sensible remarks about the supposed policy of England in the matter. On principle, the guarantee of the credit of one State by another cannot well be defended; but expediency sometimes overrides principle in this world, and the habit is spreading which substitutes the *main mort* for the "mailed fist" as leading agent in the subjugation of the weak by the strong. A mortgage on China might not be a bad investment for us; and, provided our Government takes care to obtain substantial concessions from that of Pekin, we might do worse than help the Chinese out of their great impecuniosity. The *rendezvous* port, or ports, for our fleet might be bought or leased as the Germans have leased KiaoChau, and, in addition, ten or more millions might be raised on England's acceptances, so that, say, provided that all Chinese ports, not only on the sea but on the great water-ways, were thrown open to trade, that the Customs service was put definitely under British control, and that order is introduced into the provincial dues—squeezes, *Likin*, or whatever they may be in matters of finance—now too arbitrarily levied by the semi-independent governors. It would be hopeless, we imagine, to attempt to assume the direct management of any portion of the internal revenue, but British Consular Agents ought to be distributed over the whole Empire, and ample guarantees taken for their safety. Under some such conditions a loan might be endorsed by us and China delivered from her present embarrassments without offence to the Japanese, whose trade would benefit by the reforms as well as ours. With the Japanese for our allies and the Chinese under permanent and enforcible obligation to us we need not care much whether Russia and Germany are offended or not. Nor need we interfere with Russian designs on Northern China.

Critical Index to New Investments.

As far as possible the contents of this REVIEW will deal week by week with the affairs of the week. In a first number, however, some slight latitude may be admitted. We do not propose to go back for a month and to examine the prospectuses issued during the month which has elapsed since our final monthly issue appeared in the usual way readers have been accustomed to under this heading, but a little general discourse upon the more prominent features of recent company promotion may not be out of place.

Towards the end of the year the pace at which companies were manufactured for public consumption became fast and furious, and the quality of the wares offered did not improve with the quantity. On the contrary, the faster the pace grew, the wilder became the projects in which imaginative promoters sought to interest the public. What could be more fantastic, for example, than Youde's Bill-Posting, Limited, a new venture whose flaring advertisements dazzled the eye of the newspaper reader for a week or more before Christmas. That a thing of this kind, organised by a man of no strong position in the world of finance or business, possessing no monopoly in the bill-posting trade, or anything else, should have the effrontery to ask for two and a quarter millions of money is something to marvel at. Happily this thing failed, and the subscriptions were returned. The Trinidad Lake Asphalte Company, with its modest £900,000 in shares and debentures, appears to be another example of cupidity gone mad. We believe this pitch lake, for it is more pitch than asphalte, was originally worked by a company with a few thousand pounds capital, and now it comes forward with the demand for this enormous sum at the instance of a vendor from America. If the Clerk of the Fulham Vestry is to be credited, the substance in which this company proposes to deal is not suitable for paving streets; but that does not matter if only shares are subscribed.

We might go on instancing company after company, brought out with the most extravagant pretensions, and making the most unheard-of demands on the purse of the public, and on its credulity. It is hardly worth while, and yet there is one company about which we should like to say a word, because of the man nominally at the head of it. Considerable surprise was expressed in the City when the Marquis of Dufferin and Ava, who has been Governor-General both of Canada and of India, and who but recently retired from the post of British Ambassador to France, allowed himself to be nominated chairman of the London and Globe Finance Corporation, Limited, a concern on all fours with the lamented and badly reduced Trustees, Executors, and Securities Insurance Corporation, Limited, founded by Mr. Leopold Salomons. That is to say, this London and Globe Corporation is a company-promoting agency whose principal purpose is to make as much money as possible out of the things it creates or buys cheap to sell dear. This may be all very well for the ordinary financist, whose only object in life is to get speedily rich, but it is not a business in which a nobleman and gentleman can take part without injury to his position and discredit to his order.

The worst of it is, that having once entered into partnership with financial gentlemen in operations of this sort a man has to go on obeying their orders, and, accordingly, we find the Marquis of Dufferin and Ava going before the public as chairman of an affair called the British America Corporation, Limited, with a nominal share capital of a million and a half in £1 shares. Alongside the Marquis we also find Lord Loch, a brother director of his on the London and Globe concern, and also an ex-member of the ornamental and diplomatic governing class of this country. In order, perhaps, to mitigate the feeling of soreness created in the market by the peculiar manner in which the shares of an Australian mine lately bought up and re-sold at an enormous profit (if re-sold) by this London and Globe concern were allotted, the shares in this new British America affair were offered first to the London and Globe shareholders alone. Whether they took them or not we cannot say, but there is not much inducement to the public to take them. The whole thing appears to us to be flimsy in the highest degree—a mere attempt to utilise for an ignoble gain the sudden craze which has arisen about the gold deposits on the Yukon River in the far North-West. For certain properties and rights, for sundry mines "believed to be of great value and among the best in British Columbia," for the assets and goodwill of the Alaska Commercial Company, by no means a stupendous affair we should think, for sundry stores, for town site property in Dawson City, for "claims," which may be located by an exploring party sent out to explore the Sweetlaritska River and so on—a bundle of possibilities merely—this new concern is to give half a million of its shares, leaving one million to be subscribed in cash, the money to be paid up promptly in full on allotment. It is lamentable to find men in the position of the Marquis of Dufferin and Lord Loch acting as figure-heads and decoys for what is little better than a "wild-cat" venture like this. Experience never appears to teach such people.

Whether they are so completely ignorant of the ways of financiers as to always be an easy prey, or whether they are afflicted with poverty, and anxious to make money as gourds grow, is hardly worth while discussing. That they do lend themselves to this kind of finance is a lamentable fact. Just as surely as the earth fulfils its orbit round the sun will the day of reckoning arrive for companies of this kind; in the future it is bound to be precisely as it has been in the past. There never is any real variation in the history of bubble-company making. Fashions in it pass over us in waves and cycles, beginning modestly with small companies and comparatively moderate profits, then growing and growing until they ultimately expand into monstrous proportions. When the height of folly has been reached comes collapse.

We do not think that collapse is very far off now for some of our latest freaks in this line, for the public has not been subscribing of late to the great bulk of the monster creations of the financial imagination. We can tell that they have not, to some extent, by the lavish profusion with which prospectuses have been advertised. The inference is also tested by the attitude of the Stock Exchange, which finds that it cannot deal freely in the shares of the majority of these companies. There is "no market" for them, as the phrase runs, the said shares being held in large masses by that class of people described as underwriters, a class of which, unless we are much mistaken, Lord Dufferin has made himself a member, through underwriting 50,000 shares in this British America Corporation. Now, "underwriting" is a very nice business if you can be sure of selling the shares you have provisionally undertaken to purchase, either directly they have been allotted to you or before allotment. Commissions of 10, 15, 20, sometimes even 50 per cent. are earned by the mere signing of one's name, nothing more, unless it be the chance of an extra haul through sales to the gudgeon public at a premium now and then, but this operates best under the "call of shares" system.

Should the public take the shares, the underwriter just bags his commission, and does not have to risk a penny; but if the public fails to take the shares things are rather different. Then, instead of receiving money, the underwriting fraternity have to find it. And during the last two years, speaking moderately, a large proportion of underwritten issues of capital has never been sold to the public. "Who has got the shares?" may be asked in the market. "Oh, the underwriters," is the answer. Strive as they may, these enterprising fellows cannot escape from their liability. They have made themselves responsible for so many shares, and must take them up and find the money for them whether they like it or not, the general public, whose money they hoped to finger, having failed to do so. A question, therefore, now arises, "Where does all the money come from which enables the great body of underwriters of new companies in and around the Stock Exchange to keep an unbroken front to the market in spite of their numerous and continually increasing commitments?" We should not like to answer off-hand, but significant indications are not wanting that some of the more imprudent among the banks have committed themselves to this form of business enterprise too deeply for their profit, although we trust not too deeply as yet to imperil their solvency. It is impossible to particularise, but if the intelligent reader will note down for himself the names of those banks which appear most frequently upon prospectuses, not merely as occupying the humble position of custodian of the cash, but as issuer of the capital submitted for subscription, a very shrewd idea may soon be arrived at as to the banks which are most likely to have to write off more or less stupendous losses when reckoning day comes. A 6 per cent. bank rate for three months is all that is required to disclose the ravages of the promoter and underwriter manœuvres, and we are working towards that.

NEW SOUTH WALES GOVERNMENT THREE PER CENT. INSCRIBED STOCK.—Second issue of £1,500,000, offered at a minimum price of 99 per cent. The loan is repayable at par, October 1, 1935, and the proceeds are wanted for railway and other permanent public works. Interest due April and October, and tenders will be received at the Bank of England on Tuesday next. The issue will rank *pari passu* with the stock already in the market, which is quoted at about 103. Recent issues have been as under:—

Date.	Amount offered. £	Minimum price per cent.	Average price obtained per cent. £ s. d.	Interest per cent.
April, 1888	3,500,000	102	103 12 8	3½
July, 1889	3,500,000	102	102 8 0	3½
September, 1891	4,500,000	95	95 0 4½	3½
September, 1894	832,000	100	101 14 8	3½
October, 1895	4,000,000	94	96 18 3	3

The public debt of the Colony is about sixty-two millions and the debt per head of population rather over £48. New South Wales, however, has recently made more progress than the other Australian Colonies, and the outlook is not unpromising. The minimum of the new issue is placed rather low-looking, but underwriters like to see a good premium quoted before allotment.

CITY OF TORONTO CORPORATION LOAN.—Issue of £213,000 sterling Three-and-a-Half per Cent. General Consolidated Loan Debentures redeemable July 1, 1929. Tenders will be received at the City Treasurer's Office, City Hall, Toronto, up to January 25; purchase money payable 5 per cent. on allotment, balance on delivery; interest due January and July. Net debenture debt of city, including present renewal issue, £3,463,700; value of assessable property, £26,711,409; estimated value of property owned by city, £2,670,000. Estimated revenue for last year is £590,000, of which three-fourths comes from taxation. The population of the city is 200,000, so that the debenture debt comes to quite £17 per head. The city has several higher interest bearing issues falling due within the next few years, and at 106½, which is about the price the bonds may be expected to go at, they should be a passable investment.

THE BARCELONA TRAMWAYS COMPANY, LIMITED, offers at par an issue of £100,000 Four-and-a-Half per Cent. Redeemable Debenture Stock, being one half a total creation of £200,000, the whole of which will be a first charge, subject to an outstanding balance of 5 per cent. debentures, now amounting to £53,800. Interest is due February and August, and the stock can be redeemed at six months' notice at 105 not earlier than August 1, 1903, and not later than February 1, 1931, by a cumulative sinking fund of 2 per cent. by purchase or drawings. The money is wanted to convert the present system into an electric tramway, which work is now in progress, and is expected to be completed in time for the summer service this year. Remaining half of this stock is reserved for the redemption of the existing 5 per cent. debentures, and for further expenditure. Company was formed in 1872; has a share capital of £300,000, of which £70,000 is unissued, and operates 17½ miles of line, which will be shortly increased to 19 under various concessions, the earliest of which expires in 1931, and the rest in the following years up to 1937. Average net earnings for three years, 1894-6, were £12,840, or nearly double the amount which will be required for debenture interest, and the substitution of electric for animal traction should lead to additional profits. Although Spain is far from an ideal country in which to trust one's money, the debentures should provide a good enough investment.

CITY OF SANTOS IMPROVEMENTS COMPANY, LIMITED.—This company, which has an issued share capital of £135,000 in £10 shares, of which 10,000 are Seven per Cent. Non-Cumulative Preferred shares and 3,500 Deferred, is now offering for subscription an issue of 10,000 Six per Cent. Cumulative Preference shares of £10 each at par. Company was incorporated in 1880 to acquire a concession for fifty years from 1870 to supply the city of Santos with gas and water, and to establish and work tramways. The tramways were sold in 1890 for £80,000, and the money used chiefly in redeeming £75,000 debentures issued in 1890. Of the gas and water it has a monopoly, and it is claimed that Santos is now the principal shipping port in the world for the export of coffee. Population of the city has grown since 1880 from 12,000 to 36,000 persons, and as the present water supply cannot provide for more than 4,000 persons, a fresh contract has been made with the city, which has granted the company a new concession, expiring in 1930. Under this, the company undertakes to carry out works necessary to supply 70,000 persons; the supply to all dwellings is made compulsory, and the water rates charged are fixed on a gold basis by means of a sliding scale, according to the rate of exchange; and the Government further undertakes to pay the company annually £3,000 for public services. But the Government reserves the right to expropriate the company after eighteen years if it be for the public good, in which case the works, plant, &c., are to be taken over at a valuation in gold based on the actual expenditure incurred by the company on the same. The money now to be raised is for the construction of new works, which will require about £150,000, the balance to be raised by debentures. The company has not done over well in the past. For the fine year ended 1891 the deferred shares got 7 per cent., but for 1892 the preferred received 6 per cent., and for 1893 and 1894 only 3 per cent., for 1895 6 per cent., and for 1896 5 per cent. For a Brazilian security, the shares seem no great catch, and the existing preferred £10 shares, which are non-cumulative, can be bought for 8½.

Messrs. J. S. Morgan and Co. have, in conjunction with Messrs. J. P. Morgan and Co., of New York, taken a first step in the conversion of the maturing and high interest bearing bonds of the New York Central Railway into the new Three and a Half per Cent. Consolidated bonds. They offer to receive an amount not exceeding 20,000,000 dols. in First Mortgage Seven per Cent., First Mortgage Six per Cent. Extended, Four per Cent. Certificates, and Five and Four per Cent. Debentures for exchange on a fixed scale determined by the present value of the maturing bonds calculated on a 3½ per cent. basis, the New Three and a Half per Cent. to be accepted in payment at 103 per cent.

Company Reports and Balance-Sheets.

THAT renowned mining engineer Mr. Bainbridge stated lately when giving evidence in the case of Holland *v.* Hess, that "dividends are a very severe test of a mine." These words strike us as full of the deepest wisdom, and their truth is beautifully illustrated in the balance-sheet of the Eagle Hawk Consolidated Gold Mining Company, Limited, which reached our hands the other day. This company has a paid-up capital of £117,000 only, and it received not less than £19. 4s. 8d. last year for its gold. To attain this wonderful result the mere expenditure on wages, salaries, and directors' fees in Australia and London came to the good round sum of £5,634. At what rate of progression must this company move in order to reach the dividend-paying state? Its directors alone require £500 a year to solace them for their labours, and all the shareholders as yet get for their money is the "encouraging views" of Sir John McIntyre. Still gold at £19 per pennyworth seems dear.

E. W. TARRY & CO., LIMITED, is a company which supplies machinery and other mechanical requisites for mining companies in South Africa, and it appears to own a large and progressive business. The accounts made up for the year ended August 31 show that the gross profit came to £88,144, against £84,351, but expenses were higher in proportion, so that the net profit is only £38,302, compared with £42,619. In spite of this, shareholders get a dividend of 15 per cent., together with a bonus of 5 per cent., which absorbs £25,000, compared with £18,750 distributed a year ago. Another £10,000 is added to reserve and £1,000 to reserve against bad debts, but the balance remaining is only £14,596 against £19,794. In some respects the balance-sheet shows improvement. Sundry creditors have been reduced from £22,604 to £6,647, and the £10,000 temporary loan against security has disappeared, but £1,090 is written off bad debts reserve, though it does not naturally follow that the two items are connected. Amongst the assets, goods have increased £19,000; freehold properties, £21,000; and machinery, plant, and tools, £3,900; while book debts and bills receivable are down £8,700 at £42,229. A branch has been opened at Bulawayo. Good profits appear to be made, but the business must be to a certain extent speculative.

THE COLONIAL BANK.—The business of this old institution—the charter dates from 1836—continues to decline, and the total of the balance-sheet is now not much above four millions, being a reduction of a million in four years. For the first half of last year the bank made a net profit of only £18,511, or little more than 3 per cent. on the paid-up capital of £600,000. This compares with a profit in the previous year of £31,804, so the dividend has to be reduced from 5 to 3 per cent. The note circulation is £24,000 less at £409,000, while deposits are down £85,000 at £1,757,000, and bills payable and other liabilities £558,000 less at £1,233,000. On the other side, cash and investments are down distinctly, and there is a drop of just upon £200,000 in bills discounted and advances. We could hardly have expected a more favourable showing considering the depression in business in the West Indies, which has been naturally increased by the gloomy report of the Royal Commission appointed to enquire into the industrial condition of the Colony. The outlook for the self-helpless sugar planters, and therefore for the bank, is not at all promising. In the circumstances the directors are wisely seeking powers to do business elsewhere than in Jamaica and the other West Indian islands, and they are also endeavouring to get power to reduce the nominal value of the shares, which means a reduction in the uncalled liability, now amounting to £70 a share, in addition to shareholders being liable for the note circulation. This will be a great relief to those holding shares in the bank, and will help to moderate their anxiety regarding the future, but should not its accounts be overhauled first?

JOHN CROSSLEY & SONS, LIMITED, have had a comparatively bad year, and the dividend is put even lower than we ventured to suggest a year ago. Profits and dividends for the last four years will be gathered from the subjoined figures:—

	Year's Profits.	Transfer from Reserve No. 2.	Dividend per cent.	Balance Forward.
	£	£		£
1894	74,074	15,000	10	585
1895	84,225	5,000	10	713
1896	83,309	6,000	10	924
1897	66,897	4,000	7	544

In each of the four years the amount distributed in dividends has been in excess of the actual profits earned; and while it is true that Reserve Fund No. 2 was formed to equalise dividends, we are of opinion that it has been drawn upon too heavily. When a trading company makes a profit of £74,074, as Crossley's did in 1894, £89,000 is too much to distribute by way of dividend. This policy, however, is now at an end, for Reserve No. 2 has been used up, and this year's dividend will have to come entirely out of profits. No trading account is published, and the only items of interest given in the balance-sheet are, on the one side, liabilities, book debts, &c., which have declined from £226,000 to £191,000; and on the other, freeholds, plant, stock, book debts, minerals, &c., amounting to £1,700,000. This item would be better for some sub-division, but we are glad to see that these assets appear to have been written down by £57,000. The company has no doubt suffered from diminished trade in Yorkshire, which does not seem likely to improve at present, and the unfavourable character of the report has knocked the shares down about £2. At their present prices the preference shares yield nearly 3¾ per cent. and the ordinary 4⅜ per cent., which is not a brilliant return considering the prospects of the company, for if there had been no reserve to fall back upon the dividend on the ordinary shares for last year could not have exceed 6¼ per cent.

ORIENT STEAM NAVIGATION COMPANY.—As a reward for their brilliant services a faithful body of shareholders have decided that they could not do better than re-elect the former managers, Anderson, Anderson, & Co. and F. Green & Co., for a further term of ten years. One plucky shareholder mildly ventured to move that a committee be appointed to take over and investigate matters and report to the shareholders, and he had the boldness to assert that the board had never yet presented the accounts in accordance with the articles of association. Without a fellow-shareholder to support him, the poor man was promptly ruled out of order, and told by a well-known Q.C. that his remarks were a gross insult, and that the affairs of the company had been managed with "marked ability." Well, they may have been; but there is no getting away from the fact that its affairs have been in low water for a long time, and the dividend record since 1887 is not a picture to have hung up in board room. In that year there was no dividend; then 5 per cent. was distributed for 1888 and 1889, and 3 per cent. for 1890. In the next four years there was no dividend, but for 1895 and 1896 it was possible to squeeze out 2½ per cent. Thus for ten years the average dividend is less than 2 per cent., but an admiring body of shareholders are content to let the two managers go on taking 4 per cent. of the gross earnings for another ten years, thankful to receive any small return that may be left for them.

SIR HECTOR M. HAY, Bart., who has been associated with Messrs. Mocatta and Goldsmid for the last fifty-two years, has retired from the firm. It has taken into partnership Mr. John R. Villiers, who has for some time past signed per procuration.

THE announcement comes from Perth, Western Australia, that the Government intend contracting a loan of £1,000,000 in March next.

French Finance and Trade.

(From our Correspondent.)

ACTIVITY IN THE BOURSE—THE RUSSIAN CONVERSION—FRENCH RAILWAYS.

Paris, January 5.

The Liquidation of the "Valeurs" and of the "Fonds d'Etat" has been completed, with very few exceptions, quite to the advantage of the buyers. Every "Bourse-day" since the new year has been more and more animated. Some people were afraid at the opening to-day, that the "reports" (contangoes) might be raised, but these apprehensions did not prove to be well founded. The rate was between 3½ and 4½, according to the quality of the shares and of the "reported" people. These rates being really moderate, the liquidation is now well forward, and in a few days the payment of the "coupons" will set free a considerable amount of money ready for re-investment.

The general tone of the market is good, and the Bourse to-day has been very busy indeed. Our Rentes are firm; the Three per Cent. Perpetual was at 103·40 at the opening, and 103·35 a little later, closing at the same figure; cash price, 103·10. The Three and a Half, which had reached 10 yesterday, stand to-night at 10·20. The premiums (discounts) are still offered on a large scale, so that the d/25 finds buyers at 15 centimes difference from the "ferme." As we are at the 5th of the month, one may suppose that such sales are not judicious. These very vendors being mostly buyers of "ferme," incited by the last months' receipts, might be suddenly turned out by "run-about" vendors. I believe that such a position may be worked against them one of these days.

Our Banks are affected differently. The Banque de France stands at 3,550 cash, and 3,535 for account, showing falls of 25 and 30 francs in the last séance. There is no good reason for believing that the new arrangements introduced in the privilege charter will be profitable to the shareholders, and certainly the prices would have fallen lower had not the new governor been a much more able man than M. Georges Pallain. The Credit Lyonnais is the most active of the Credit Societies, ranging between 803 and 813 francs. Speculators expect some profit from the Vienna Municipal Loan, about which our great financial house is in negotiation, since the Deutsche Bank has not been conciliated. The Banque de Paris et de Pays Bas stands firmly at 892, and the Banque Internationale advances to 618. Société Générale is, at 532, quiet; so is the Comptoir d'Escompte at 586. The Comptoir announces that it redeems or converts the 5 per cent. debentures of the Transcaucasian Railway. The "conversion" is completed in 4 per cent. shares free from every Russian duty or tax.

The French railways are very firm:—Nord, 2,060; Lyon, 1,830; Midi, 1,450; Orléans, 1,840; Est, 1,090; Ouest, 1,210. The rise of our great companies has een a very remarkable one during 1897. The principal gains have been made by the Lyon, with a 180-francs advance on the quotations of December 31, 1896; and the Nord, which has gained 200 francs from one year to the other. These results accrue from the far better receipts of the companies. Though these have no immediate effect on the dividends (the Nord excepted, which is not under the régime of the "guaranteed interest"), they are generally considered as indicating an improved future. The P.L.M. Company has signed a new convention with the State, approved of last week by the Chamber of Deputies, by which the "compensation" of the two debts—that of the company and that of the State—against each other is allowed, so that the P.L.M. Company, which has not asked for guarantee for two years, will be able to realise all the receipts. You know that the sums given to the company by the Treasury for the completion of insufficient receipts are only "reimbursable advances," producing simple interest at 4 per cent., and constituting a "conditional" debt, exigible so far only as the further net results allow of it, after the yearly payment of the guaranteed revenue to the shareholders. The companies, on their side, are creditors of the State for the advance in money and work, made by them for the construction of the secondary lines since 1883, reimbursable by annual instalments.

For instance, the Lyon Company need never have put aside anything from its earnings beyond the forty-four million francs which are necessary to pay the yearly 55 francs dividend to the shareholders. To allow "compensation" to be made between the two debts, the company has given up the benefit derived from the "conditionality" of its debt; it agrees to the repayments to be made actually, and appropriated *partly* to the definitive reimbursement of its excess receipts to the State. The State has the advantage of certain payment. The full payment has been fixed at 150,897,478 francs.

Our industrial shares Bourse is very active. The General Traction Company, recently formed and introduced on the market, is being pushed on towards 125 francs; a good many electrical concessions have been granted to that syndicate. The General Omnibus Company's receipts for 1897 amount to 45,684,370 francs, an increase of 1,396,609 francs on the preceding year. The company are shortly to adopt mechanical traction for their 'buses. A good many new lines will be opened in 1898.

I give you the total amount of the credit operations during 1897—"Issues" or "introductions":—

	Francs.
Emprunt de l'Etat de Minas-Geraes 5 per cent.	50,700,000
25,000 obligations Compagnie Fives-Lille 4 per cent. ...	12,500,000
5,555 obligations Grand Hôtel 4 per cent.	2,777,500
Emprunt bulgare	30,000,000
7,200 act. Appontements de Pauillac	3,000,000
12,000 obligations Appontements de Pauillac	6,000,000
32,400 actions Oural-Volga à 595	19,278,000
150,000 actions Compagnie Générale de Traction ...	15,000,000
25,000 obligations Compagnie Générale de Traction ...	12,500,000
20,000 act. nouv. Thomson-Houston, émises à 750 ...	15,000,000
10,000 actions nouvelles Briansk émises à 1,000 ...	10,000,000
30,000 act. nouv. Banque Internationale émises à 580...	17,400,000
5,000 act. priv. Omnium Russe	3,150,000
30,000 obl. Omnium Russe	15,000,000
8,000 act. Forces Motrices du Rhône	4,000,000
16,000 oblig. 5 per cent. Forces Motrices du Rhône ...	8,000,000
11,500 oblig. Trignac...	5,750,000
2,000 actions Penarroya à 1,500	3,000,000
6,000 act. Toulouse à Boulogne-sur-Gesse	3,000,000
5,000 obligations Sels Gemmes	2,500,000
20,000 actions Mines d'Héraclée à 600 francs.	12,000,000
Fr.	250,555,500

I must add the participations of French capital in oreign loans, such as the Five per Cent. Hongrois Ponts de Fer, the Three and a Half per Cent. Autrichien (116,840,000 couronnes), the lettres de gage of the Banque Foncière (Russ.) del Noblesse, &c. I believe the total of investments amount to about 450 or 500 millions. These figures are interesting to compare with the annual hoarding which amounts in France to about a milliard francs at least. Does all the rest go to the *bas de laine*?

LOUIS DE TOURVILLE.

The Produce Markets.

GRAIN.

The markets opened dull yesterday week, sellers showing more disposition to deal, but buyers were cautious and waiting for "developments." They preserved this attitude during the week, and on Wednesday the market was inactive, with sellers and buyers alike indifferent. Though business was carried on slowly, prices were generally maintained. At Mark-lane, English wheat was in short supply, but buyers held off, reds offering up to 38s., and whites 39s. to 39s. 6d. Foreign was in slow request, and to induce business less money must have been taken. Flour was unaltered in value, but the trade was nominal. Maize was irregular in price and limited in demand. mixed American, 16s. 3d., ex ship; old mixed, 12s. 3d., ex quay; and Galatz-Bessarabian at 18s. ex quay. Barley was very quiet at 15s. 6d. ex ship, Odessa-Nikolaieff. Oats moved very slowly; common Petersburg, 16s. 3d., ex quay; Canadian white, 16s., ex ship; Canadian mixed, 15s. 9d.; and mixed American, 15s. 6d. to 15s. 9d. There was no improvement in the cargo market, and no cargo sales were reported. Californian, prompt, were obtainable at 37s. 3d., and Walla Walla, January, at 36s. Oregon, September, may be had at 39s., while for a handy cargo Manitoba, January shipment, 38s. 4½d. is bid; No. 2 Chicago, January 14-February offered at 36s. 6d.; Entre Rios, steamer, January 15-February, to be had at 35s. 6d.; for Santa Fé a bid of 34s. 6d. is solicited, and for a March-April steamer 34s. is wanted. In wheat futures at Liverpool the market was quiet at ⅛d. to ¼d. decline.

OFFICIAL CLOSING VALUES (100 lb. deliveries—January 6).

	Jan.	March.	May.	July.	Sept.
Red American Wheat	—	7·3⅞	7·2⅜	6·11⅝	6·6¼

In New York on Wednesday wheat opened easy, with ½ c. decline, under increased crop estimates, then revived on some covering, but again declined on a disappointing export demand, and closed weak, ⅜c. lower, spot weak; spring 101⅜c.

COTTON.

The Liverpool market was closed for several days this week for holidays. The spot market has been fairly active throughout. In American, good business has been done at rather easier rates. Brazilian and Surats remain dull without change. Egyptian in active demand at steady prices. Futures dull, and closed ½ point below Tuesday's prices. Wednesday's tenders at the Clearing House were 400 bales American and 250 bales Egyptian on new dockets.

NEW YORK CLOSING VALUES.

	Spot.	Jan.	Feb.	Mar.	April.	May.	June.	July.	Aug.	Sept.	Oct.
Wednesday ..	5 11/16	5·74	5·76	5·79	5·84	5·88	5·93	5·97	6·01	6·01	6·02

WOOL.

The total decrease in the importation of Colonial wool into Great Britain during 1897, as compared with 1896, is stated in Messrs. Brown and Eagle's circular to have amounted to 24,006 bales. The shipments direct from the Australian Colonies and Cape of Good Hope were 428,500 bales against 518,500 bales in 1896. The total arrivals of Colonial wool for the London sales in 1897 were 1,627,747 bales. There were sold here 1,323,130 bales. Messrs. Jacomb, Son, & Co., in their annual circular, state that "the general course of trade during the first half of 1897 bears striking contrast to that of the last six months, for whereas during the former period great excitement was experienced in the feverish heat of express deliveries to the United States in avoidance of an obstructive customs tariff there, the latter has been marked by the deadly dulness of one of the too often recurring disputes between employers and employed, leading to a general paralysis of many of the home industries. The hopes that were generally felt at the termination of 1896 that better prices for wool would be forthcoming in the year just passed have been disappointed, for at no time during the last twelve months has there been the much-needed spurt, either at home or on the Continent. The exception to this, however, is in the case of the U.S.A., as, anticipatory of higher protective duties, buyers from there, in the early months of the year, secured suitable wools with unprecedented eagerness, and, before the tariff arrangements had been settled, swept the board of all the best deep grown merino wools, and subsequently turned them over to great advantage; thus somewhat checkmating the expectations of our home manufacturing districts. Throughout the week the market has been rather cheerful, with a firmer tone. Further arrivals of River Plate sheepskins to the extent of 569 bales, chiefly Buenos Ayres produce under mark N in diamond, were offered by auction at Liverpool on Wednesday, and attracted a good attendance of buyers. Competition was active, and the whole of the offering was sold without change from the prices ruling on December 17. Matadero first—138½ lb. making 4⅝d.; 144½ lb., 4¼d.; 160 lb., 3⅝d.; second—134 lb., 4⅝d.; 149¾ lb., 4¼d.; 159¾ lb., 3¾d.; third—135¾ lb., 5d.; 130½ lb., 4⅝d.; fourth—141¼ lb., 4⅞d.; fifth—143 lb., 5d., all under mark N in diamond; and three-quarter woolled merino mark F.G.T.—106 lb., 4½d. to 4⅝d.; cross-bred half-woolled mark E F over U—77 lb., 4½d. per lb. The next Plate wool sale will be held on January 14.

METALS AND COAL.

There has been an active business in copper during the week, and on Wednesday trade was done in cash at £48. 8s. 9d., or 1s. 3d. above the quotation of the previous day. Subsequent transactions were, however, put through at £48. 7s. 6d. In the afternoon, however, cash rallied again to £48. 8s. 9d., and nearer the close advanced to £48. 10s., three months also hardening to £48. 17s. 6d. The close was firm at rates, making a rise of 2s. 6d. for cash, and 1s. 2d. for forward delivery.

SETTLEMENT PRICES.

	Jan. 5.	Dec. 29.	Dec. 22.	Dec. 15.	Dec. 8.	Dec. 1.
	£ s. d.	£ s. d.	£ s. d.	£ s. d.	£ s. d.	£ s. d.
Copper ..	48 10 0	48 5 0	48 2 6	48 7 6	48 10 0	

The iron market has been inactive, and little business has been done during the week.

SETTLEMENT PRICES.

	Jan. 5.	Dec. 29.	Dec. 22.	Dec. 15.	Dec. 8.	Dec. 1.
	s. d.	s. d.	s. d.	s. d.	s. d.	s. d.
Scotch	45 6	45 4½	45 6	45 0	45 0	
Cleveland ..	40 4½	40 3	40 6	40 1½	40 3	
Hematite ..	48 4½	48 4½	48 4½	47 10½	47 10¼	

In the coal market there has been little doing, and the demand has been insignificant. In the seaborne department the situation was practically unaltered so far as price is concerned, but only one cargo was sold, which, however, found a market without difficulty. Official quotations are unchanged, 17s. and 16s. being announced as the value of Hetton Wallsend and Hetton Lyons respectively—usual market terms in the pool. In the inland trade there was very little movement, and, with an absence of orders, there was in some cases evidence of a disposition to quote easier rates. Best West Yorkshire, 10s. to 10s. 6d.; Barnsley selected, 9s.; soft nuts 7s.; Sheffield silkstone, 8s. to 8s. 6d.; best Derby Blackshale, 9s. to 9s. 3d.; North Derby Tupton, 7s. 3d. to 7s. 6d.; Erewash brights and nuts, 7s. 6d. and 9s. 3d. respectively. Since Monday 15 coal-laden vessels have arrived in the Thames.

SUGAR.

The business done in sugar has been but moderate, though prices continue steady. Quotations:—Tate's cubes, No. 1, 15s.; No. 2, 14s. 1½d.; crushed, No. 1, 13s. 3d.; No. 2, 12s. 9d.; granulated, 13s. 3d.; yellow crystals, 12s. 6d.; Lyle's crystals, No. 1, 13s. 3d.; No. 3, 12s. 9d.; granulated, No. 1, 13s. 3d.; No. 2, 12s. 9d.; white, A, 12s. 9d.; B, 12s.; yellow crystallized, O and P, 12s. 6d. Foreign.—Granulated opened steady and ruled slow throughout the day, closing easy. Immediate D V sold at 11s. 1½d. and 11s. 0⅞d., combined to 11s. 0⅞d. Ready, Groningen, Glauzic, and E C H, 11s. 1⅛d. January, E C H and first marks, 11s. 1⅛d.; March, E C H, 11s. 3d.; March-April, first marks, 11s. 3d.; May-August, R A V, 11s. 6d.; first marks, 11s. 5¼d., and sellers, f.o.b. Hamburg.—Cubes—F M S, ready, sold at 12s. 6d.; January-March, 12s. 9d., sellers; Meyer, ready, 13s., accepted; January-March, 13s. 3d., sellers; Hansa, prompt, 12s. 4½d., f.o.b. Hamburg.—W S R and S and T, prompt, 13s. 4½d.; A S R and cut loaf, 13s. 3d., f.o.b. Amsterdam.—Cane sorts firm and in fair demand, but little offering; beet futures steadier at ¼d. advance.

TEA AND COFFEE.

Tuesday's tea auction comprised 26,300 packages Ceylon, and common to low medium, also fine, met with good competition, and realised firm prices; while broken Pekoes ruled weak, many lots being withdrawn. Wednesday's auctions comprised 3,650 packages of Indian and 720 Java, which met with a steady demand. Terminal markets unchanged. At the coffee auctions on Tuesday 5,868 bags were offered, and on Wednesday 1,832 packages passed slowly. Futures on Wednesday opened weak upon continued large receipts in Brazil, and, after fluctuating, closed flat at fully 1s. decline. Closing values:—March, 31s. 6d.; May, 32s.; September, 32s. 6d.; December, 33s. Contracts registered, 6,000 bags Santos.

HEMP AND JUTE.

Hemp has been quiet, but steady and firm in price. At auction on Wednesday 30 bales fully fair to good Mauritius sold at £19. 10s. to £20. 15s. Manila—50 bales superior current sold at £19, and 250 good seconds, afloat by sailer, at £15. 15s., further 500 bales being withdrawn at the price. For shipment 1,000 bales fair current, February-April, sailer, sold at £17. 7s. 6d.; 1,000 superior seconds ditto at £16. 15s.; and a small lot, per distant steamer, at £17 5s. For May-July sailer there are buyers of fair current at £17. 10s. Jute has been generally firm. On Wednesday 600 bales first marks, January-February, steamer, London, sold at £10. 5s., and rather buyers, sellers holding for £10. 7s. 6d.

THE Bombay correspondent of the *Standard* says that the plague is still increasing in that Presidency. "Outlying districts which were free from the pestilence a few weeks ago now furnish every week scores of hundreds of victims." A far more severe trial, he adds, will have to be borne this winter than last in that part of the Peninsula. This is most serious news, and the only consolation to be found in it is in the hope that the sufferings of the people of India may at least rouse public opinion at home to take cognisance of the utterly forlorn condition of the bulk of the population in that misgoverned dependency.

THE companies that remain faithful to the Harvey-North combination—the Arauco Company, the Tarapaca Waterworks, the San Pablo Nitrate, the Great Boulder Mines, and a few semi-private concerns—have removed their offices from the old domicile to 55-56, Bishopsgate-street Within. The Woolpack building, which had such a notoriety in the palmy days of the late Colonel North, has, therefore, well nigh lost its character as the home of the group. Only the Nitrate Railways Company remains, for many other companies flitted some time back when they were able to shake off the grip of the North coterie.

THE PROPERTY MARKET.

Business was only resumed on Wednesday after the holidays at the Auction Mart, and there is consequently little to say about the week's business. Several sales of importance have, however, been recently arranged by private treaty. Mr. William Houghton has thus disposed of 3½ acres of building land in Walthamstow for £6,000, upwards of £1,700 an acre, a remarkable price for land in this district. At Launceston the little White Hart Hotel was sold the other day by Mr. J. Kittow for £2,350. Messrs. Maple and Co., of Brighton and Eastbourne, have recently had some good sales of leasehold and freehold properties in these places, the total amounting to £8,000.

Mr. Alfred Richards, of Finsbury-circus, is to have some rather important sales of stocks and shares at the Mart on the 28th inst. There are £11,701 of "C" capital stock to be raised under the provisions of the Tottenham and Edmonton Gas Act, 1882, ranking for a standard dividend of 7 per cent.; 1,000 additional ordinary £10 shares of the Lowestoft Water and Gas Company, ranking for a maximum dividend of 7 per cent.; £5,000 of ordinary stock in the Guildford Gas Light and Coke Company, ranking for a standard dividend of 5 per cent.; new issue of £5,000 four per cent. perpetual debenture stock of the Southend Waterworks Company; £4,100 four per cent. perpetual debenture stocks of the Ascot District Gas Company; and £970 of ordinary stock in the Taunton Gas Light and Coke Company; and £300 original stock in the Brighton and Hove General Gas Company.

Messrs. Newton, Edwards, & Shephard also announce sales at the mart, on the 15th inst., of freehold and leasehold properties and ground rents.

A GREAT SAVINGS BANK.

The Glasgow Savings Bank claims to be the greatest in the Kingdom. At the annual meeting held the other day, it was reported that the business of last year had been greater than in any former year. The balance due to 198,273 depositors was £7,402,509. The number of new accounts opened during the year was 35,302. There was a free surplus of £135,668. The Lord Provost, who presided, remarked that the Bank represented the largest amount of money invested by the public of any city. One gratifying feature in Glasgow was the large number of penny banks allied with the Savings Bank. In and around Glasgow there were 250 of these banks in active operation, conducted entirely by voluntary effort. The transactions totalled £80,000, and the number of youthful depositors was 90,000. Another speaker stated that the unfortunate engineering dispute had not affected the bank to any material extent. It had probably occasioned some withdrawals, but the general prosperity of the city had made up all deficiencies. Glasgow still justifies her motto.

The London and General Bank.—Mr. S. Wheeler, the Official Receiver and Liquidator of the Balfour group of companies, has given notice to the creditors of the London and General Bank that an eighth dividend of 7d. in the pound will be payable on Thursday next. This will make a total of 17s. in the pound returned to the creditors of the bank. Neither in this company nor in any of the other unfortunate companies connected with the "Balfour group" will a single penny ever be available for the shareholders.

The Editor of "Willich's Tithe Commutation Tables" writes to the *Times* to say that as a result of the corn averages for the seven years to Christmas, 1897, published in the *London Gazette* of Tuesday evening—viz., wheat, 3s. 5¼d. per imperial bushel; barley, 3s. 1d. per imperial bushel; oats, 2s. 2d. per imperial bushel, each £100 of tithe rent-charge will for the year 1898 amount to £68. 14s. 11d. being on the commutation about 1½ per cent. less than last year The following statement shows the worth of £100 of tithe rent-charge for the last seven years:—For the year 1891, £76. 3s. 3¾d.; 1892, £75. 18s. 3¼d.; 1893, £74. 15s. 2¾d.; 1894, £74. 3s. 9½d.; 1895, £73. 13s. 0¼d.; 1896, £71. 9s. 6¾d.; 1897, £69. 17s. 11½d. The average value of £100 of tithe rent-charge for the sixty-two years which have elapsed since the passing of the Tithe Commutation Act of 1836 is £97. 9s. 11¾d.

Japan and China Mails.—A Post Office notice was issued Tuesday stating that mails for Japan and China will be dispatched from London, by way of Vancouver, during the next few months on the evenings of the undermentioned dates, which are all Fridays:—The 14th inst., February 11, March 11, and April 1. Mails will be made up in Ireland on the following day in each case. Parcel Mails for Japan will be made up at Liverpool in each case on the Saturday morning.

It is officially announced that the Spanish Government have consented to suspend the operation of the new regulations in respect to certificates of origin, which were to come into force on the 1st inst., until the 15th. Those interested in Spanish trade would do well, in the meantime, to inform themselves of the exact requirements of the new regulations.

According to Mr. Ottoman Haupt, the able Paris correspondent of the *Financial Times*, the total production of gold in 1897 will amount to £36,000,000; while the stocks of gold held by the leading banks and Treasuries of France, Austria, Russia, the United Sta es, and Japan will have increased by about £47,500,000. On this reckoning some £11,000,000 of the old stock of the metal will have been absorbed. We believe Mr. Haupt under-estimates the gold oduc ion of the past year, but still there can be no doubt that it is less than the absorption, and the Bank of England has suffered by this absorption more than any other institution of the kind in the world. It is 20 millions poorer now in gold than it was eighteen months ago.

LAST YEAR'S SHIPPING AND FREIGHTS.

Mr. John White's annual review of the shipbuilding trade, supplemented by Messrs. Angier Brothers' report on the freight markets, give us a very vivid notion of the state of these important industries during 1897. One thing on which Mr. White very properly insists is the prejudicial effect of the prolonged engineers' strike upon shipbuilding. At the beginning of the year orders were abundant, and most of the yards had booked enough to keep them going for twelve months. There is no slackening of the orders now; but much of the work on hand has been waiting completion for months, and cannot yet be got rid of. From present appearances there is no saying when the work can be finished, and so the orders offered cannot be placed here. Some of them have been placed abroad. Mr. White, without expressing any opinion on the pending dispute, has some very cogent remarks on the injury done to trade by these incessant labour quarrels. He says most truly:—"The loss incurred by these strikes is immeasurable. Not only is there the loss to the parties directly concerned, but the distrust created amongst customers as to when their orders will be executed through these incessant labour troubles causes many contracts to be placed abroad. The loss is therefore a national one, as other interests beyond the labour employed in building the ship and her machinery are involved in the production of every ship."

It was, therefore, only to be expected that there should be a diminution in the shipbuilding output of 1897 as compared with that of 1896. Mr. White gives the total at 1,122,824 tons gross register, comprising 712 steamers of 1,057,025 tons, and 222 sailing vessels of 65,799 tons. This is about 250,000 tons less than the output of 1896; and the loss may be ascribed to the engineers' quarrel. There still remains, however, a large addition to our mercantile marine; but in estimating the effect of this addition to our sailing power on the freight market we have to keep in mind the large amount of tonnage which is yearly removed from the British register. Last year the total so removed came to about 640,000 tons of steamers and 280,000 tons of sailing vessels, or 920,000 tons in all, so that the actual addition to the carrying capacity of our mercantile fleet is comparatively small, and it can hardly be said that the present tonnage is in excess of the demand. There is yet, therefore no danger of a shrinkage in freights.

As to the fate of these old ships removed from the register, some doubtless represent losses at sea; others become dilapidated in various ways. Some are sold abroad, and continue competitors for freights for a year or two, while some are broken up and their materials sold. The foreign output of shipping has, however, also increased during the year—a fact mainly attributable, as we have said, to the engineering quarrel. At the end of September last our yards had under construction 877,387 tons of steamers and 6,949 tons of sailing vessels, and the greater part of the steam tonnage is still on the stocks. While our yards are thus lying idle, however, other countries are going a-head of us. Germany, for example, made considerable strides in shipbuilding; the United States have considerably increased their production; and even Japan has been making progress in the same direction. All which facts ought surely to be very carefully noted and remembered by the men who are now refusing to work, hardly knowing why they so refuse.

In regard to freights, the famine and plague in India greatly restricted the export trade, and homeward rates were consequently very low. Cargoes from the Black Sea and the Danube were also smaller than usual owing to the floods in Roumania, which destroyed large portions of the crops. Homeward freights from the Argentine were likewise small, through the failure of the harvest. It is true the cattle and dead meat business continued brisk, but the home trade proved largely unremunerative, so that towards the middle of the year many vessels, after discharging their cargoes at the River Plate, made sail for the Gulf and other ports of the United States in order to load up for home. In fact, the excellent business done with North America quite made up for disappointments in other directions. "America," says Mr. White, "has been the salvation of the freight market, and rates have continued remarkably good considering the large amount of tonnage thrown on this market from the Eastern and other trades." Messrs. Angier Bros. endorse this opinion. Not only was the American business very large, but freight rates gradually improved to a comparatively high level, and a large trade was done almost up to the end of the year, being only checked by the approach of Christmas. Australian business was not on a large scale, homeward freights having been contracted by the short wool-clip. The effect of the increased production of the American mines and the cheaper cost of rail transport to the Atlantic seaboard brought about a considerable diminution of shipments of ore to the Mediterranean. On the whole, however, the outlook for the present year is decidedly hopeful.

The gold shipments from Australia to London during last year are valued at £12,150,000. This is exclusive of Queensland and New Zealand.

The West India and Panama Telegraph Company announces that the rate from Europe to Jamaica has been reduced since the 1st. of this month from 5s. 10d. to 3s. per word. Rates to stations east of Jamaica and to Demerara will be reduced to a like extent. This notable fall in prices is the result of the projection of the Direct West India Cable Company last November. The latter company has a moderate short-dated subsidy from the Government, and will work in union with the Halifax and Bermudas Cable Company. The fight thus commenced will lead to the West Indies obtaining more reasonable telegraphic rates, as 5s. 10d. per word to Jamaica seems an anachronism, when one can communicate with Melbourne for 4s. 10d. per word, and the rate to New York is no more than 1s. per word. Altogether it seems a pity that the reduction in rates did not come before the second route was projected.

CONSUMPTION OF INDIAN TEAS.

MESSRS. GOW, WILSON, & STANTON report in their annual circular that the Home consumption of tea reached a higher figure in 1897 than ever before, viz., about 232,000,000 lb., or an increase of 5,700,000 lb. This increase benefited the India and Ceylon tea-growers alone, and the total consumption of British-grown tea rose last year to 261,000,000 lb., or thereabouts. This is more than half the tea consumed in one year by the civilised world. As the increase in the supply was smaller than the increase of production, the danger of an over supply seems less than many apprehended. Wherever the English language is spoken the use of tea is expanding, and now Australia and North America are the two best markets for Indian tea outside the United Kingdom. Russia, which has so long stuck by the Chinese, is now using increased quantities of Ceylon tea. The total output this season of Indian tea is estimated at 151,000,000 lb., against 149,000,000 lb. last. The tendency has been towards lower rates; the outturn of Ceylon is expected to reach 117,000,000 lb., as compared with 108,000,000 lb. last year. The total deliveries of tea in London in 1896-7 were:—Indian, 126,165,318 lb.; Ceylon, 90,677,108 lb.; China, 39,777,957 lb.; and Java, 3,912,380 lb.

Messrs. W. J. & H. Thompson remark a noticeable feature in the growth of the demand for Indian and Ceylon tea from abroad. The China tea trade is declining with other countries and markets besides London; stocks abroad appear to be gradually shrinking in their dimensions, and traders in various parts of the world are turning to Calcutta and Colombo to supply the deficiency. Business with these new markets is not yet extensive, as the progress, though sure and continuous, is slow; but it is sufficient to affect sterling values of produce in London as well as in Calcutta and Colombo, and promises to have an important influence upon the prosperity of the tea industry in future years. Looking at the position of tea from the broadest point of view it would seem to be thoroughly sound. The dreaded over-production has not been realised, and there are signs that planters in India and Ceylon, who hold the key, are alive to the necessity of moderating the policy of excessive plucking, and of reverting to methods which give rather smaller but much finer crops. Values of produce have been steadily maintained, and stand to-day at a moderate level.

The London figures for 1896-7 are:—

		Imports. lb.	Delivery. lb.	Stock, Dec. 31. lb.
Indian tea	1896	125,400,000	124,650,000	54,145,000
"	1897	134,884,000	127,356,000	61,673,000
Ceylon tea	1896	89,992,000	85,450,000	18,355,000
"	1897	93,445,000	95,172,000	16,629,000
China and Java tea	1896	40,584,000	43,789,000	25,990,000
" "	1897	32,401,000	38,600,000	19,760,000

LESS gold coin by about £930,000, was issued from the Imperial Mints last year than the amount of old and worn coins withdrawn from circulation. But upon the two years 1896-7 the excess was the other way, £1,600,000 more gold coins having been issued than were withdrawn. The issue of silver was also considerably less active, but still about £600,000 in excess of the amount withdrawn. In regard to silver, the public should take note of the fact that the Bank of England will not now accept as good any silver coins with holes in them, but all worn or cracked coins which are not so completely defaced as to make it impossible to tell what they are will still be exchanged for new money.

EXCELLENT reports have been received concerning the Uruguay wheat crop, and the condition of maize is said to be very promising.

LAST year's operations at the Melbourne Mint were the largest since its opening in 1872. The value of the coin issued was £5,130,565, and of bullion, £213,439. The receipts of gold amounted to 1,380,364 oz.

THE Canadian Pacific Land Department sold, during 1897, 200,000 acres for 650,000 dols., as compared with 88,000 acres for 307,000 dols. in 1896—an increase beyond anything ever before experienced in the business of the Department.

ACCORDING to the report of the Labour Department of the Board of Trade for 1896, it seems that the total income of 100 of the principal trade unions, with a membership of 966,953, was £1,675,645, and the expenditure £1,239,230, the membership in 1895 having been 921,686, the income £1,573,925, and the expenditure £1,403,095. The funds in hand at the end of 1896 amounted to £2,168,989, against £1,732,574 in the previous year.

THE Washington Treasury are preparing fresh instructions to Customs officers to assess additional countervailing duties on French sugars, which receive indirect as well as direct bounties. There is no protection for the consumer in America.

THE Marquis Ito has not yet apparently succeeded in forming his new Cabinet. His first combination seems to have failed, and on Wednesday we were told from Yokohama that he was engaged in trying another.

MR. W. J. BRYAN, the Silver champion of the United States, has been on a visit to Mexico. He was received with "all the honours," was the guest of the nation, had the freedom of the capital conferred upon him, and had to deliver an address in Congress on the invitation of the Speaker! Even the President of the Republic did his best to make Mr. Bryan's stay in Mexico a pleasant one.

ACTING on the recommendation of the Indian Secretary, the Bombay, Baroda and Central India Railway Company are to apply to Parliament next session for powers to borrow any sums on bonds "not exceeding one-half of the capital of the company instead of one-third as provided by their Act of 1859." The money is wanted to construct and improve certain stations and generally to improve their undertaking.

Answers to Correspondents.

Questions about public securities will be answered week by week, in the REVIEW, on the following terms and conditions:—

A fee of FIVE shillings must be remitted for each question put, provided they are questions about separate securities. Should a private letter be required, then an extra fee of FIVE shillings must be sent to cover the cost of such letter, the fee then being TEN shillings for one query only, and FIVE shillings for every subsequent one in the same letter. While making this concession the EDITOR will feel obliged if private replies are as much as possible dispensed with. It is wholly impossible to answer letters sent merely "with a stamped envelope enclosed for reply."

Correspondents will further greatly oblige by so framing their questions as to obviate the necessity to name securities in the replies. They should *number* the questions, keeping a copy for reference, thus:—"(1) Please inform me about the present position of the Rowenzori Development Co. (2) Is a dividend likely to be paid soon on the capital stock of the Congo-Sudan Railway?"

Answers to be given to all such questions by simply quoting the numbers 1, 2, 3, and so on. The EDITOR has a rooted objection to such forms of reply as—"I think your Timbuctoo Consols will go up," or "Sell your Slowcoach and Draggem Bonds," because this kind of thing is open to all sorts of abuses. By the plan suggested, and by using a fancy name to be replied to, each query can be kept absolutely private to the inquirer, and no scope whatever be given to market munipulations. Avoid, as names to be replied to, common words, like "investor," "inquirer," and so on, as also "bear" or "bull." Detached syllables of the inquirer's name, or initials reversed, will frequently do as well as anything, so long as the answer can be identified by the inquirer.

The EDITOR further respectfully requests that merely speculative questions should as far as possible be avoided. He by no meant, sets himself up as a market prophet, and can only undertake so provide the latest information regarding the securities asked about. This he will do faithfully and without bias.

Replies cannot be guaranteed in the same week if the letters demanding them reach the office of the INVESTORS' REVIEW, Norfolk House, Norfolk-street, W.C., later than the first post on Wednesday mornings.

VERAX might retain his holding for the present. Traffics generally are good. There is little chance, however, of any dividend.

H. F. G.—We do not possess the particulars you require. If you will send the list we will examine it; meantime do nothing. There is no haste.

Next Week's Meetings.

MONDAY, JANUARY 10.

London Tramways Company .. .. 303, Camberwell New-road, noon

TUESDAY, JANUARY 11.

Belgian Mining Trust of South Africa .. Brussels, 2 p.m.

WEDNESDAY, JANUARY 12.

Chicago Great Western Railway Company (Gen. and ex-Gen.) .. .. Cannon-street Hotel, 2 p.m.
Leamington Tennis Court Company .. Club Room, Leamington, noon.
Oak Spinning .. .. Oldham, 7.30 p.m.
Union Bank of London .. .. .. 2, Princes-street, noon.

FRIDAY, JANUARY 14.

Blackpool and Fleetwood Tramroad (Ex. Gen.) .. .. Manchester, noon.
Dominion Atlantic Railway (Special) .. 6, Great Winchester-street, noon.
East and West India Dock .. .. Winchester House, 2 p.m.
English Sewing Cotton Four per Cent. First Mortgage Debentures .. Call of 50 per cent. = £375,000.
English Sewing Cotton, Preference .. Call of 5s. per share = £187,500.
English Sewing Cotton, Ordinary .. Call of 5s. per share = £187,500.
North and South Western Junction Railway .. .. Euston Station, noon.
Peel River Land and Mineral .. .. Palmerston Buildings, 1 p.m.

SATURDAY, JANUARY 15.

Watney & Co., Three and a Half per Cent. Debentures .. .. .. Call of 50 per cent. = £300,000.

DR. JAMESON, it is announced, recently paid a visit to Johannesburg. It was "secret" but friendly, and the Transvaal authorities were not alarmed. They did not scent a new conspiracy, but carefully watched the doctor and his friends while they were in the City.

OWING to the death of Mr. Walter Hayes Burns, new partnership arrangements have been made by Messrs. J. S. Morgan & Co., who have admitted as partners Mr. John Pierpont Morgan, jun., the son of their senior, and Mr. Walter Spencer Morgan Burns, the son of the late partner.

MESSRS. BROWN, SHIPLEY, & CO. announce that Mr. Lawrence Edlmann Chalmers, son of their Mr. Frederick Chalmers, and Mr. George Harrison Frazier have been admitted partners in their firms in London and the United States (Mr. G. H. Frazier continuing to reside in Philadelphia). Mr. Edward Clifton Brown, nephew of their Mr. A. H. Brown, has been authorised to sign for Messrs. Brown, Shipley, & Co. per procuration; and Mr. James Crosby Brown, son of their Mr. John Crosby Brown, has been authorised to sign for Messrs. Brown, Brothers, & Co. in Philadelphia.

CLERICAL, MEDICAL & GENERAL LIFE ASSURANCE SOCIETY.

Chief Office:
15, ST. JAMES'S SQUARE, LONDON, S.W.

ESTABLISHED 1824.

CHAIRMAN, RIGHT HON. SIR JOHN ROBERT MOWBRAY, BART., D.C.L., M.P.

Assets nearly 3½ MILLIONS Sterling.

The Clerical, Medical and General Life Assurance Society was Established in 1824 as a Proprietary Company with a Capital of Half-a-Million Sterling. Thus the Assured possess

THE ABSOLUTE GUARANTEE OF A WEALTHY PROPRIETARY

that every benefit, once granted, whether Sum Assured or Bonus Addition, will be fully and safely enjoyed.

VALUATION RATE OF INTEREST 2½ PER CENT. ONLY.

The Results of the 1897 Valuation showed—

1. INCREASED RESERVES.
2. INCREASED PROFITS.

THE TOTAL SURPLUS DIVIDED WAS

£515,346.

Which was larger by £86,896 than any previously distributed, and represented the **HIGHEST RATE OF PROFIT EVER DECLARED** by the Society.

The new Bonus Report, the new and full Prospectus, and every information on application.

15, ST. JAMES'S SQUARE, LONDON, S.W.

W. J. H. WHITTALL,
Actuary and Secretary.

CALEDONIAN INSURANCE COMPANY.

The Oldest Scottish Insurance Office.

FOUNDED 1805.

LIFE BONUS YEAR, 1897.

Ordinary Assurances completed before the closing of the books at the end of 1897 will rank for a Bonus at the Division of Profits to be made as at 31st December.

Subject to the approval of the Directors, the Books will be kept open till 11th January, 1898.

Fire Insurance at moderate rates, and on good security.

Head Office: 19, GEORGE ST., EDINBURGH.
LONDON: 82, King William Street, E.C.;
14, Waterloo Place, Pall Mall, S.W.

To Correspondents.

The EDITOR cannot undertake to return rejected communications.
Letters from correspondents must, in every case, be authenticated by the name and address of the writer.

SUBSCRIPTION PRICE, POST FREE:—

INVESTORS' REVIEW alone—

United Kingdom.		
Three Months.	Six Months.	One Year.
7s.	14s.	28s.
All Foreign Countries.		
7s. 6d.	15s.	30s.

INVESTORS' REVIEW and INVESTMENT INDEX together—

United Kingdom.		
Three Months.	Six Months.	One Year.
9s. 6d.	18s. 6d.	36s.
All Foreign Countries.		
9s. 10d.	19s. 6d.	38s. 6d.

Payable in Advance.

The INVESTMENT INDEX will continue for the present to be issued Quarterly, price 2s. net, and may be subscribed for separately, at 8s. 6d. per annum, or with the INVESTORS' REVIEW, as above.

Cheques and Postal Orders should be made payable to CLEMENT WILSON.

The INVESTORS' REVIEW can be obtained in Paris of Messrs. BOYOEAU ET CHEVILLET, 22, Rue de la Banque.
The Mining and Provincial Lists have been unavoidably left out.

The Investors' Review.

Money Market.

A transformation scene almost invariably takes place in the Money Market at the end of the year. On December 31 all is hunger and want, and on January 1 comes abundance. So was it last week, but the first view was that the ease of the early days of January could not last beyond the middle of the month. It would be for the good of many things if it did not, but we cannot be sure. The Bank of England, which is now managed with vigour and consistency, has a full bill-case for January, and ought to be able to obtain control of the rates outside again, after all the short loans and discounts have run off this week. On the other hand, banks in general are free from the dread of balance-sheet exhibits for some time—the monthly shows being now considerably dodged—and can lend with a free hand. By doing this they have already brought floating money down from 4 per cent. or more on December 31 to 1½ and 2 per cent. We do not see how the decline is to be stopped just yet.

Discount rates have, of course, gone down with money rates, and last night three months' bank bills were quoted at 2⅜ per cent. The worst of it is that foreign Exchanges no longer wear a threatening aspect, and the demand for gold for export has shrunk so much in the open market that bars may have to be sent to the Bank. A week ago the quotation for these was 77s. 11½d. per oz.; now it is a penny less. The half million in sovereigns taken out of the Bank for Buenos Ayres yesterday did stiffen the loan market slightly, and made the bill brokers hold back from reducing their deposit rates, but not the bullion market, with which it had nothing to do, representing, as it does, little other than an episode in the process of rehabilitating Argentine Government finance. In this process a good harvest out there, demanding coin to move it, may play a considerable part.

Such indications in current events appear, therefore, to point in the main to moderate rates and a quiet market for some little time, and not even the Bank's holding of January bills, unusually large though it be, may prevent some further shrinkage, although the low rates of last spring cannot come this year. The gold demand of last autumn was largely a credit-originated demand on account of Russia and Austria. The demand arising from Europe's short harvest has not yet come upon London direct, and if the United States buy their railroad securities freehandedly this year it may never come. If they intercept, as they have been doing, part of the Australian supply, we shall not miss it.

At the moment, however, the outlook is rather uncertain, and may change, like an April day, without warning. We must not forget that India is just now a point of danger for our markets more threatening than the United States. Something will have to be done soon to extricate Indian finances and commerce from their danger, and that something might take the shape of exports of gold bought here with money raised by loans. We hope no step of the kind will be taken, because gold is not what India requires. This possibility, however, should not be left out of account, nor yet that attached to developments in China under British patronage.

Yesterday's Bank return tells little. The Bank seems to have lent a million to the Government "for deficiency," but that does not help the market much.

"Other" deposits, which contain the current cash of the market, have barely increased £1,200,000 on the week, and the Bank's reserve is £21,000 less at £19,885,000, notwithstanding the increase of £768,000 in the coin and bullion. Notes have gone out against the gold come in, and the open market is not particularly flush.

BANK OF ENGLAND.

AN ACCOUNT pursuant to the Act 7 and 8 Vict., cap. 32, for the Week ending on Wednesday, January 5, 1898.

ISSUE DEPARTMENT.

	£		£
Notes Issued	45,988,060	Government Debt	11,015,100
		Other Securities	5,784,900
		Gold Coin and Bullion	29,188,060
		Silver Bullion	—
	£45,988,060		£45,988,060

BANKING DEPARTMENT.

	£		£
Proprietors' Capital	14,553,000	Government Securities	14,023,036
Rest	3,388,138	Other Securities	34,793,736
Public Deposits (including Exchequer, Savings Banks, Commissioners of National Debt, and Dividend Accounts)	9,190,843	Notes	17,851,015
Other Deposits	41,443,070	Gold and Silver Coin	2,033,992
Seven Day and other Bills	126,728		
	£68,701,779		£68,701,779

Dated January 6, 1898.

H. G. BOWEN, *Chief Cashier.*

In the following table will be found the movements compared with the previous week, and also the totals for that week and the corresponding return last year:—

Banking Department.

Last Year. Jan. 6		Dec. 29, 1897.	Jan. 5, 1898.	Increase.	Decrease.
£	Liabilities.	£	£	£	£
3,406,871	Rest	3,173,542	3,388,138	214,596	—
8,063,487	Pub. Deposits	9,402,537	9,190,843	—	211,694
46,839,007	Other do.	40,244,131	41,443,070	1,198,939	—
118,884	7 Day Bills	99,348	126,728	27,380	—
	Assets.			Decrease.	Increase.
15,717,867	Gov. Securities	13,024,159	14,023,036	—	998,877
32,516,540	Other do.	34,541,986	34,793,736	—	251,750
24,746,842	Total Reserve	19,906,413	19,885,007	21,406	—
				1,462,321	1,462,321
				Increase.	Decrease.
£		£	£	£	£
26,571,250	Note Circulation	27,347,080	28,137,045	789,965	—
45 p.c.	Proportion	40 p.c.	39⅜ p.c.	—	—
4 ,,	Bank Rate	3 ,,	3 ,,	—	—

Foreign Bullion movement for week £164,000 increase.

LONDON BANKERS' CLEARING.

Week ending	1897.	1896.	Increase.	Decrease.
	£	£	£	£
Dec. 1	171,792,000	166,125,000	5,667,000	—
,, 8	136,090,000	124,457,000	11,633,000	—
,, 15	161,483,000	165,735,000	—	4,252,000
,, 22	155,425,000	133,202,000	22,223,000	—
,, 29	105,382,000	132,437,000	—	27,055,000
Total from Jan. 1, 1897	7,491,281,000	7,574,853,000	—	83,572,000

Week ending	1898.	1897.	Increase.	Decrease.
	£	£	£	£
Jan. 5	222,654,000	174,376,000	48,278,000	—

BANK AND DISCOUNT RATES ABROAD.

	Bank Rate.	Altered.	Open Market.
Paris	2	March 14, 1895	2
Berlin	5	October 9, 1897	3¾
Hamburg	5	October 9, 1897	3¾
Frankfort	5	October 9, 1897	3¾
Amsterdam	3	April 13, 1897	2¾
Brussels	3	April 28, 1896	2¾
Vienna	4	January 22, 1896	3¾
Rome	5	August 27, 1895	3
St. Petersburg	6	August 26, 1896	5
Madrid	5	June 17, 1896	4
Lisbon	6	January 25, 1891	6
Stockholm	5	October 27, 1897	5
Copenhagen	5	August 3, 1897	5
Calcutta	10	January 6, 1898	—
Bombay	10	January 6, 1898	—
New York call money	2½ to 3	—	—

NEW YORK ASSOCIATED BANKS (dollar at 4s.).

	Jan. 1, 1898.	Dec. 25, 1897.	Dec. 18, 1897.	Jan. 2, 1897.
	£	£	£	£
Specie	20,946,000	20,880,000	20,854,000	15,968,000
Legal tenders	15,904,000	14,880,000	15,756,000	17,928,000
Loans and discounts	121,556,000	122,122,000	121,336,000	98,276,000
Circulation	3,104,000	3,141,800	3,150,000	3,980,000
Net deposits	115,012,000	133,826,000	133,978,000	106,158,000

Legal reserve is 25 per cent. of net deposits; therefore the total reserve (specie and legal tenders) exceeds this sum by £8,137,000, against an excess last week of £2,303,500.

BANK OF FRANCE (25 francs to the £).

	Jan. 6, 1898.	Dec. 30, 1897.	Dec. 23, 1897.	Jan. 7, 1897.
	£	£	£	£
Gold in hand	77,637,120	78,115,000	78,509,000	76,333,000
Silver in hand	48,265,040	48,230,360	48,469,280	49,045,000
Bills discounted	38,536,920	38,393,840	31,810,080	*33,136,000
Advances	16,336,600	15,199,760	14,810,840	—
Note circulation	154,505,080	152,362,080	147,565,800	150,898,000
Public deposits	12,962,760	12,640,600	10,958,500	8,491,000
Private deposits	21,616,560	20,691,400	19,925,760	24,045,000

Proportion between bullion and circulation 81⅞ per cent. against 82⅞ per cent. a week ago.

* Includes advances.

IMPERIAL BANK OF GERMANY (20 marks to the £).

	Dec. 31, 1897.	Dec. 23, 1897.	Dec. 15, 1897.	Dec. 31, 1896.
	£	£	£	£
Cash in hand	41,327,800	44,417,150	44,447,100	40,229,000
Bills discounted	38,438,900	33,140,950	31,157,400	*49,408,000
Advances on stocks	8,633,550	4,806,650	4,686,250	—
Note circulation	65,998,600	56,598,700	53,986,050	62,896,000
Public deposits	21,320,900	22,710,300	24,648,050	22,166,000

* Includes advances.

AUSTRIAN-HUNGARIAN BANK (1s. 8d. to the florin).

	Dec. 31, 1897.	Dec. 23, 1897.	Dec. 15, 1897.	Dec. 31, 1896.
	£	£	£	£
Gold reserve	30,315,750	30,395,833	30,738,333	22,517,000
Silver reserve	10,276,417	10,278,500	10,295,917	12,871,000
Foreign bills	1,572,333	1,657,166	1,915,500	—
Advances	2,319,333	2,181,166	2,084,500	—
Note circulation	58,325,583	55,857,583	53,546,500	60,626,000
Bills discounted	17,244,750	14,572,083	13,682,833	*26,233,000

* Includes advances.

NATIONAL BANK OF BELGIUM (25 francs to the £).

	Dec. 30, 1897.	Dec. 23, 1897.	Dec. 16, 1897.	Dec. 31, 1896.
	£	£	£	£
Coin and bullion	4,119,880	4,236,240	4,250,560	4,027,000
Other securities	18,033,000	17,426,040	17,114,760	17,099,000
Note circulation	19,488,760	19,114,840	19,077,360	18,869,000
Deposits	3,008,040	3,817,480	2,756,800	3,648,000

BANK OF SPAIN (25 pesetas to the £).

	Jan. 2, 1898.	Dec. 25, 1897.	Dec. 18, 1897.	Jan. 2, 1897.
	£	£	£	£
Gold	9,430,680	9,430,680	9,394,320	8,528,320
Silver	10,318,960	10,302,400	11,121,120	10,139,840
Bills discounted	20,646,040	20,482,240	18,988,040	8,731,640
Advances and loans	5,063,560	5,117,320	5,259,360	8,339,000
Notes in circulation	48,250,840	47,839,440	47,467,520	41,376,240
Treasury advances, coupon account	113,920	505,480	461,240	86,640
Treasury balances	nil	2,269,840	2,073,920	2,807,960

LONDON COURSE OF EXCHANGE.

Place.	Usance.	Dec. 28.	Dec. 30.	Jan. 4.	Jan. 6.
Amsterdam and Rotterdam	short	No post day.	12·2	12·1½	12·1½
Do. do.	3 months		12·3⅜	12·3⅜	12·3⅜
Antwerp and Brussels	3 months		25·41	25·40	25·40
Hamburg	3 months		20·62	20·60	20·60
Berlin and German B. Places	3 months		20·63	20·61	20·60
Paris	cheques		25·25	25·23¾	25·23¾
Do.	3 months		25·40	25·38¾	25·38¾
Marseilles	3 months		25·41	25·38¾	25·38¾
Switzerland	3 months		25·63¾	25·62	25·58¾
Austria	3 months		12·16¼	12·15	12·15
St. Petersburg	3 months		25$\frac{1}{16}$	25$\frac{1}{16}$	25$\frac{1}{16}$
Moscow	3 months		25	25	25
Italian Bank Places	3 months		26·76¼	26·75	26·75
New York	60 days		49	49	49
Madrid and Spanish B. P.	3 months		35½	35¼	35¼
Lisbon	3 months		35$\frac{5}{16}$	35⅜	35⅜
Oporto	3 months		35$\frac{5}{16}$	35⅜	35⅜
Copenhagen	3 months		18·38	18·38	18·38
Christiania	—		18·38	18·38	18·38
Stockholm	—		18·38	18·38	18·38

FOREIGN RATES OF EXCHANGE ON LONDON.

Place.	Usance.	Last week's.	Latest.	Place.	Usance.	Last week's.	Latest.
Paris	chqs.	25·23	25·22	Italy	sight	26·45	26·44
Brussels	chqs.	25·27	25·25½	Do. gold prem.	..	104·77	104·77
Amsterdam	short	12·08½	12·07½	Constantinople	3 mths	109·25	109·32
Berlin	short	20·38	20·38½	B. Ayres gd. pm.	..	174	167
Do.	3 mths	20·36½	20.40½	Rio de Janeiro	90 dys	7¼d.	6$\frac{11}{16}$d.
Hamburg	3 mths	20.21	20.26	Valparaiso	90 dys	17$\frac{11}{16}$d.	17$\frac{11}{16}$d.
Frankfort	short	20·37	20.38	Calcutta	T. T.	1/3$\frac{15}{16}$	1/3$\frac{15}{16}$
Vienna	short	12.00	12.00	Bombay	T. T.	1/3⅞	1/3$\frac{15}{16}$
St. Petersburg	3 mths	93.60	93·60	Hong Kong	T. T.	1/11⅛	1/10⅞
New York	60 dys	4·81½	4·82⅜	Shanghai	T. T.	2/8	2/7¼
Lisbon	sight	36d.	36d.	Singapore	T. T.	1/11¾	1/11⅜
Madrid	sight	33·58	33·50				

OPEN MARKET DISCOUNT RATES.

	Per cent.
One and two months remitted bills	2½—2⅝
Three months "	2⅝—2¾
Four months "	2⅝—2¾
Six months "	2¾
Three months first inland bills	2¾—2⅞
Four months "	2¾—3
Six months "	2¾—3

BANK AND SHORT LOAN RATES

	per cent
Bank of England minimum discount rates	3
" " short loan rates	—
Other banker's rate on deposits	1½
Bill brokers' deposit rate (call money)	2
" 7 and 14 days' notice money	2¼
Current market rates for 7 days' loans	1¾—2
" " for call loans	1¼—1¾

BY the retirement of Mr. G. E. Noble, one of the joint managers of the London branch, the Hong Kong and Shanghai Banking Corporation loses one of the oldest members of its staff. He joined the Kong Kong branch in January, 1866, or within a year of the formation of the bank. After serving for many years in the East, with chief command in Calcutta for five years, Mr. Noble became general manager, which post he filled for two years. Long residence in the East had, however, undermined his constitution, and he was compelled to relinquish the heavy burden, and subsequently became joint-manager. He has now joined the London committee of the corporation, so that his services will not be entirely lost. Mr. John Walter, who has been inspector of branches for the last six years, will fill the vacant post. The London office of the bank was opened concurrently with the head office at Hong Kong in October, 1865, and then consisted of two small rooms on the first floor in Gresham House with a staff composed of the agent, two clerks, and a boy, one of the clerks being Mr. G. H. Burnet, the present sub-manager in London. Since then the London office has been shifted to a large ground floor in Lombard-street, and the staff numbers seventy-five in all. At the start the bank had ten offices, and its first report showed notes and deposits totalling 3,000,000 dols. The offices now number twenty-five, and in the last balance-sheet the notes and deposits aggregated no less than 147,000,000 dols. Not a bad record in these degenerate days.

The Week's Stock Markets.

Stock markets, an experienced jobber remarked the other day, are of three sorts. First, there is the market where you can't deal because all the stocks have been absorbed by investors, and it is dreary waiting for "deceased estates." Secondly, there is the market where you can't deal because nobody wants to buy the rubbish offered. Those who hold it, hold hoping it will go up, and those who have it not could only be tempted to purchase at lower prices. This is a market hanging where Mahomet's coffin is supposed to be.

Finally, there is the manipulated market wherein securities move like awkward squads on parade at the bidding of groups, cliques, wire-pullers, syndicates, millionaires, apes of millionaires, underwriting forlorn hopes, &c. In this last, most of the recent activity lies. The public is buying Grand Trunks freely—bless it!—Argentine securities to a limited extent, and sundry miscellaneous fancies by fits, but it does not buy Rio Tintos, nor De Beers, nor mines of any sort to the least appreciable degree. Nor has it got much beyond the selling humour for United States railways. So the manipulated market is rather treacherous, and the range for speculating in many of the "securities" it embraces so limited as to justify this skit, "What price Snooks's Hope?" "There isn't a price. The market has gone for a drink." He who plays under such conditions, tosses knives whose sheaths are loose.

Although business has been curtailed by the New Year holidays the tone has been generally firm, with a fair amount doing. Interest has largely centred on the progress of affairs in the Far East, and hopes are high that our Government will out-trump its rivals. A sharp recovery is therefore apparent in the various Chinese bonds, and an English loan to China would be popular.

Consols were firm at the commencement of the week on cheaper money, but "bear" sales on the part of speculators caused a relapse. The possibility of a new Chinese loan, guaranteed by the British Government, also helped to weaken the price, as this would mean the absorbing of a large amount of floating credit. Indian and Colonial issues show no material change. A new three per cent. loan of £1,500,000 is announced by the New South Wales Government. Several of the leading Home Corporation stocks mark a rise on the week.

Highest and Lowest this Year.		Last Carrying over Price.	BRITISH FUNDS, &c.	Closing Price.	Rise or Fall.
113⅛	112⅞	—	Consols 2¾ p.c. (Money)...	112⅞	—
113$\frac{5}{16}$	113$\frac{1}{16}$	112¾	Do. Account (Feb. 2)	113	+ $\frac{1}{16}$
106⅛	106	106	2½ p.c. Stock red. 1905 ...	106⅛	—
349	347½	—	Bank of England Stock...	349	+ 1½
117	116¾	116¾	India 3½ p.c. Stk. red. 1931	116¾	—
109¼	109	109	Do. 3 p.c. Stk. red. 1948	109	—
96⅜	95⅞	96	Do. 2½ p.c. Stk. red. 1926	96	—

Home Railway stocks have been firm, the traffic returns being satisfactory on the whole. The principal feature has been the large dealings in Great Central issues, which were bought on the favourable reports concerning the London extension, and as the market was rather short of stock prices rose sharply. South Eastern was depressed at one time, it being rumoured that the dividend to be announced next week would not be more than 3¾ per cent., not 4 per cent., which was the rate the market was going for. Underground stocks again advanced, and it is said that a selling limit in Districts which has been hanging about for some time is now closed. North British drooped slightly, owing to the collision near Dunbar, but soon recovered.

Highest and Lowest this Year.		Last Carrying over Price.	HOME RAILWAYS.	Closing Price.	Rise or Fall.
182½	181½	181½	Brighton Def.	182½	+ ¾
58⅜	57⅝	57½	Caledonian Def.	58¼	+ ⅝
19¼	19	19	Chatham Ordinary	19¼	+ ⅜
72	66	67	Great Central Pref.	72	+6
25⅝	22¼	21¾	Do. Def.	23½	+1¾
123⅝	122½	122	Great Eastern	123⅝	+ ⅝
61	59½	59½	Great Northern Def.	61	+1½
177½	177	176	Great Western	177⅜	+ ⅜
47	46¾	47	Hull and Barnsley	47	—
156	152	148	Lanc. and Yorkshire	148½	—
135¼	133½	132¾	Metropolitan	135¼	+1½
31	30	29¾	Metropolitan District	30¾	+ ¾
88¼	87¾	87¾	Midland Pref.	88½	+ ⅜
94¾	94¼	94½	Do. Def.	94⅞	+ ⅜
90¾	90¼	90	North British Pref.	90¾	+ ½
46¼	45	44¾	Do. Def.	46¼	+1
180¼	179¼	178¾	North Eastern	180¼	—1
204⅝	204½	204	North Western	204⅝	—
115½	114⅝	115¼	South Eastern Def.	115	— ¼
98¾	96⅝	96	South Western Def.	98½	+1¾

Canadian Pacific Railway shares gave way on the publication of the traffic returns for last week, which did not come up to expectations. Grand Trunks were at one time pressed for sale, holders taking advantage of the good November statement to realise. There was only a temporary set-back, however, and a sharp recovery soon followed, the weekly traffic being much better than had been anticipated, and prices accordingly show a big rise since last week.

Highest and Lowest this Year.		Last Carrying over Price.	CANADIAN AND U.S. RAILWAYS.	Closing Prices.	Rise or Fall.
13⅜	13	13¼	Atchison Shares	13⅜	— ⅛
31¾	30⅞	31½	Do. Pref.	31½	— ⅜
12xd	11⅛	12¼	Central Pacific	11⅞	— ½
97⅞	95¾	98⅛	Chic. Mil. & St. Paul	97⅞	—
11⅞	11½	12	Denver Shares	11¾	+ ⅛
47½	46⅞	47	Do. Prefd.	47¼	+ ⅛
15⅛	14¾	15⅛	Erie Shares	14⅝	— ⅛
39¾	38	39½	Do. Prefd.	39¼	—
58½	56⅞	58	Louisville & Nashville	57¼	— ½
13⅛	12¾	13¼	Missouri & Texas	13⅛	+ ⅛
112½	108¼	110¾	New York Central	112½	+2
48¾	47¾	48¾	Norfolk & West. Prefd.	48⅝	—
61⅛	59⅞	61	Northern Pacific Prefd.	61⅛	+1⅛
16⅜	15⅞	16½	Ontario Shares	16⅜	+ ¼
59½	58⅞	58¾	Pennsylvania	59⅜	+ ⅝
11¾	11⅛	11⅞	Reading Shares	11¾	+ ⅜
33	30⅞	33¼	Southern Prefd.	32¾	—
27¼	26⅛	26½	Union Pacific	27½	+1
18¾	18	18½	Wabash Prefd.	18¾	+¼
28¼	27⅜	28¼	Do. Income Debs.	28¼	—
86⅜	83⅝	83½	Canadian Pacific	86¾	+3⅜
72½	69⅞	68¾	Grand Trunk Guar.	72½	+3½
61¼	57⅛	55¾	Do. 1st Pref.	60⅜	+4⅝
41⅛	37¼	36	Do. 2nd Pref.	40⅞	+4⅞
21	19¼	19	Do. 3rd Pref.	20⅞	+1⅞
105	104	104	Do. 4 p.c. Deb.	105	+1½

United States Railroad shares have been wobbly, despite the large increases in earnings again reported. Following the agreement between the Presidents of the Trunk lines and the Western connections, the East bound and West bound freight rates were restored on the 3rd inst. It is thought that most of the large increases in earnings was due to the pushing forward of cargoes before the advance in rates agreed upon came into force. Prices were also depressed by a report that the President of the Chicago, Milwaukee, and St. Paul road had said that the rates were so unsatisfactory that there was no profit in the competitive through business under present conditions. Other officials, however, who have been interviewed do not bear out this statement. The *Financial Chronicle* makes the gross earnings of seventy-five roads in the third week in December show an increase of 7·59 per cent. A report was circulated on this side that the Southern Pacific Company had defaulted, but this was found to apply only to the Central Pacific Government aided bonds, on which default was generally looked for. The November statement of the Pennsylvania Company was a very satisfactory one, the business of the road now outstripping all previous records. The Wabash Company announces that it has reduced its floating debt during the year by 400,000 dols. After being a dull market for the greater part of the week there was a much steadier tone apparent towards the close, owing to better prices coming to hand from Wall-street.

Among Foreign Government bonds the principal movements in the upward direction have been in Chinese descriptions, for reasons just given. Egyptian stocks advanced when it was announced that more troops were to be despatched to Egypt, and prices generally have been well supported by the firmer tendency exhibited on Continental Bourses. Among South American issues Argentine Government and the various Cedulas have been very firm, helped by the decline in the gold premium and the encouraging harvest prospects; Brazilian bonds weakened on the continued fall in the Rio Exchange, and Uruguayan stocks have lost part of the recent rise. As regards some of the other active counters, Spanish "fours" have been pressed for sale on Berlin account. A Reuters telegram from Madrid states that the Minister of the Colonies believes that he will be able to raise 100,000,000 pesetas by the sale of Cuban Mortgage Cedulas, while the Minister of Finance hopes to obtain a like sum by a fresh issue of Treasury bonds guaranteed by the Customs receipts. As the expenses of the campaign in Cuba only amount to 40,000,000 a month, these operations will furnish a sum sufficient to last until the re-opening of Parliament. Turkish groups have again attracted considerable attention, at higher prices, on talk of consolidating them. South American Rails have not maintained the rise registered during the earlier part of the week, one of the reasons given for the weakness of Argentine Railway stocks, being a three days' strike among the engineers.

Highest and Lowest this Year.		Last Carrying over Price.	FOREIGN BONDS.	Closing Price.	Rise or Fall.
93	92½	94¼	Argentine 5 p.c. 1886	92⅝	—1⅝
89⅜	89	89¼	Do. 6 p.c. Funding	89¼	— ¼
71½	71	71¾	Do. 5 p.c. B. Ay. Water	71¼	—1½
61	60	60⅝	Brazilian 4 p.c. 1889	60¼	— ⅜
68	67½	68	Do. 5 p.c. 1895	67½	— ½
63	62½	63	Do. 5 p.c. West Minas Ry.	62½	— ½
106½	106¼	106¼	Egyptian 4 p.c. Unified	106½	+ ¼
102½	102	102	Do. 3½ p.c. Pref.	102¼	—
102½	102	102½	French 3 p.c. Rente	102	+ ⅛
34½	34½	35	Greek 4 p.c. Monopoly	34½	—
93 7/16	93	94⅜	Italian 5 p.c. Rente	93⅜	+1
97	95¾	96½	Mexican 6 p.c. 1888	96¾	+1¼
20⅝	20¼	20¾	Portuguese 1 p.c.	20⅝	+ ⅝
60⅛	59⅛	61	Spanish 4 p.c.	60	— ⅞
45	43	42½	Turkish 1 p.c. "B"	45	+1⅞
25 1/16	24 11/16	24⅜	Do. 1 p.c. "C"	25 1/16	[illegible]
22	21 13/16	21⅞	Do. 1 p.c. "D"	22	[illegible]
42½	41¾	41	Uruguay 3½ p.c. Bonds	41¾	— ⅝

In the Miscellaneous section Coats's have been a very active market, and finish firm after displaying a rather weak tendency. A great deal of dissatisfaction has been expressed by the tardy way in which the allotments of the new English Sewing Cotton Company have been sent out, and the premium is now quoted at only 1⅜. Bank shares have moved up a bit, the dividends announced so far being quite up to expectations. Anglo-American Telegraph issues continue to attract attention

Highest and Lowest this Year.		Last Carrying over Price.	FOREIGN RAILWAYS.	Closing Price.	Rise or Fall.
20¼	20	20	Argentine Gt. West. 5 p.c. Pref.	20¼	+ ¼
103	103	103	Do. 6 p.c. 2nd Deb.	—	—
149½	149	148	B. Ay. Gt. Southern Ord..	149	—
76	75½	73½	B. Ay. and Rosario Ord...	75½	+1
11⅞	11 11/16	11⅝	B. Ay. Western Ord.	11¾	—
82½	80½	78½	Central Argentine Ord....	82	+2½
90	89¾	89½	Cordoba and Rosario 6 p.c. Deb.	90	—
94¼	94	93¾	Cord. Cent. 4 p.c. Deb. (Cent. Nth. Sec.)	94	—
60¼	58½	58	Do. Income Deb. Stk. ...	60	+2
19	18	18	Mexican Ord. Stk.	19	+1
75½	72	72	Do. 8 p.c. 1st Pref.	75	+3

and maintain last week's rise, but in Hudson Bays a slight set-back is apparent.

Brewery stocks have been rather dull in tone, and this also applies to Gas stocks. A feature has been the steady rise in Waterlow and Sons Deferred, and Prussian Petroleum continues on the up grade, and now stands at a big premium. Welsbach Gas ordinary shares, after slipping back to par, recovered slightly, but the preferred are still quoted at a small discount. John Crossley and Sons announce a dividend at the rate of 7 per cent., which goes against 10 per cent. last year, hence the weakness in the price of the shares.

Markets close with a very firm tendency, the principal movements being a further considerable advance in Canadian and Grand Trunk stocks, partly due to the glowing statements made by the High Commissioner for Canada last night. Americans have also to a lesser extent participated in the rise, and there is also a small "boom" in Mexican rails. The Home Railway market closes firm, with the exception of a slight reaction in Great Centrals.

Consols are unaltered on the week, and this also applies to most of the leading Indian and Colonial stocks. Foreign bonds leave off fairly steady, apart from Chinese bonds, which have again risen sharply. Among mines, Copper shares wind up with a further advance, but Kaffirs and Westralians exhibit no special feature.

MINING AND FINANCE COMPANIES.

The South African has been very inactive, but the tone remains steady, helped by a few buying orders from Paris, but there is no special feature to note. Among Western Australian ventures, Lake View Consols have been adversely affected by the absence of any news from the mine. Several others of the leading counters, notably Hannan's Brownhill and Ivanhoe have risen slightly, but business has been quiet, and does not seem to have been much helped by the reopening of the Adelaide Stock Exchange. There has been very little real business in the General Mining section. Copper shares advanced owing to the rise in the price of the metal, the Mount Lyell group and the other leading producers being chiefly influenced. Indians close firm, the monthly crushings being up to expectations.

ENGLISH RAILWAY TRAFFIC RETURNS.

Cleator and Workington.—Gross receipts for the five days ending December 31 amounted to £916, an increase of £214. Since the commencement of the half-year the total receipts amount to £26,560, showing a decrease of £1,223.

Cockermouth, Keswick, and Penrith.—Gross receipts for the six days ending December 31 amounted to £641. Total gross increase for the half-year, £1,925.

TRAMWAY AND OMNIBUS RECEIPTS.

Increases for past week:—Belfast, £239; Croydon, £90; Glasgow, £182; Lea Bridge, £156; London, £481; London & Deptford, £52; London Southern, £96; London General Omnibus, £685; London Road Car, £251; Metropolitan, £578; North Staffordshire, £36; Provincial, £103; Southampton, £37; South London, £51; Swansea, £3; Wolverhampton, £46; Woolwich & S. E. London, £65; Calcutta, £145.

Decreases for past week:—Sunderland, £7; Barcelona, £38; Bordeaux, £218; Calais, £34.

Anglo-Argentine, week ending December 2, £78 increase. Vienna Omnibus, week ending December 25, £363 increase. City of Buenos Ayres, week ending December 6, £402 increase. Melbourne, gross receipts for December, £36,000.

GOLD CRUSHINGS FOR DECEMBER.

BRILLIANT AND ST. GEORGE.—Last three weeks' crushings 1,725 tons of quartz yield 4,579 oz. of gold. Approximate value, £15,820.

CALIFORNIA MILLING AND MINING.—Ore milled, 3,200 tons. Estimated income, 4,392 dols.; estimated expenditure, 3,352 dols.; estimated profit for month, 1,040 dols.

ST. AGNES GOLD REEFS.—The clean-up to December 22 (thirteen days) was 200 tons quartz, yielding 163 oz. of gold. Average sample of tailings is under 5 dwt. per ton.

UTAH CONSOLIDATED.—Ore shipments during November and December:—Lot 16—48 tons gave 825·26 dols. Assay value, 14 per cent. copper, 4·12 dols. gold and 2·45 oz. silver. Lot 17 66 tons gave 1,031·59 dols. Assay value, 13·6 per cent. copper ·3·04 gold and 2·5 oz. silver. Lot 18—48 tons gave 875·09. Assay Value, 15·2 per cent. copper, 3·50 dols. gold, and 2·5 oz. silver. Lot 19—43 tons gave 615·47 dols. Assay value, 13·4 per cent. copper, 3·13 dols. gold and 2·25 oz. silver. Lot 20—44 tons gave 495·02 dols. Assay value, 12 per cent. copper, 2·18 gold, and 2·2 oz. silver. Lot 21—42 tons gave 575·69 dols. Assay value, 13·5 per cent. copper, 2·56 dols. gold, and 2·4 oz. silver. Lot 22 - 50 tons gave 1,107·32 dols. Assay value, 16·35 per cent. copper, 6·55 dols. gold, and 3 oz. silver Lot 23—117 tons gave 2,367·65 dols. Assay value, 16 8 per cent. copper, 3 dols. gold and 3·5 oz. silver.

MAYALL'S UNITED GOLD MINING COMPANY.—Clean-up for fifteen days to December 20, crushing 940 tons of ore for a yield of 350 oz. of gold.

THE IVANHOE GOLD MINING COMPANY crushed during the six months ended September 30 last 5,802 tons, yielding 15,250 oz. of gold.

THE GREAT BOULDER COMPANY crushed 1,183 tons during the fortnigh ending January 3, yielding 3,038 oz. of gold.

PESTARENA UNITED GOLD MINING COMPANY.—Return for December, 461 tons of ore produced 751 oz.

QUEENSLAND MENZIES GOLD MINING COMPANY.—Crushed 330 tons for 953 oz.

GLENROCK PREMIER MINE, NEW ZEALAND.—Have crushed 480 tons and obtained 321 oz. of gold. Cyanide 24 tons tailings produced 19 oz. gold; total, 340 oz. of gold, Value £1,300.

MOUNT YAGAHONG.—Summary for month of October: Ore on hand, 105 tons; ore raised and carted to battery, 300 tons. Ore milled during month, 196 tons.

AMALGAM recovered 460 oz. Retorted gold, 242 oz. 160 dwts.

EASTLEIGH.—Sixty stamps ran 24 days 15 hours; crushed 4,927 tons, yielded 577 oz. Cyanide treated, 4,030 tons; yielded 1,504 oz. Slimes treated, 780 tons yielded 263 oz. Total for month, 1,344 oz.

BURMAH RUBY MINES.—75,000 loads washed, producing rubies valued at Rs. 90,000.

CHAMPION REEF GOLD MINING COMPANY OF INDIA.—7,108 tons of stone produced 9,054 oz. of gold; 2,400 tons of tailings, 595 oz.; and 4,895 tons of tailings (cyanide process), 1,225 oz.

CITY OF LONDON GOLD MINES.—Return for thirty-two days: Crushed, 196 tons; produced, 209 oz.

COROMANDEL GOLD MINING COMPANY OF INDIA.—1,200 tons of stone produced 954 oz.; 900 tons of tailings (cyanide process) produced 50 oz.

CUE 1 GOLD MINE.—Crushed, 740 tons; obtained, 545 oz.

GOLDFIELDS OF MYSORE.—41 oz. of gold from 700 tons, sand cyanide process, and 269 oz. of gold from amalgamation.

GREAT BOULDER PROPRIETARY GOLD MINES.—Fortnight ended January 3: 1,183 tons of ore crushed for 3,038 oz.

MYSORE GOLD MINING COMPANY.—7,280 tons produced 11,002 oz.; 2,985 tons tailings, 745 oz.; and 1,820 tons of tailings (cyanide process), 322 oz.

MYSORE WEST AND MYSORE-WYNAAD, TANK BLOCK.—1,400 tons for 966 oz. of gold.

NUNDYDROOG COMPANY.—5,050 tons of quartz produced 4,934 oz.; 715 tons of tailings, 94 oz.; 2,900 tons (cyanide process), 312 oz.

OOREGUM GOLD MINING COMPANY OF INDIA.—5,831 tons of quartz produced 4,062 oz., and 4,475 tons tailings, 533 oz.

CONSOLIDATED MURCHISON GOLD MINES.—Crushed 292 tons; yield, 295 oz. gold.

PREMIER TATI MONARCH REEF COMPANY.—Crushed 1,830 tons; yield of gold, oz.; includes 840 tons at grass of low grade ore. Shipped two bars of gold worth £1,850.

MOUNT YAGAHONG GOLD MINING AND EXPLORATION COMPANY.—December crushing, 575 tons of ore, 612 oz. of gold, exclusive of tailings—about 10 dwt. per ton. Ore from new lode on the Mount Yagahong Lease is averaging nearly 30 dwt. per ton.

STANHOPE.—Last month's crushing yielded 1,089 oz. Decrease on November, 39 oz.

KOFFYFONTEIN.—Returns for December were 3,300 carats.

CONSOLIDATED MURCHISON.—Crushed, 292 tons; obtained, 295 oz. of gold.

MALAYAN (PAHANG) EXPLORATION.—December: 1,300 tons crushed; 618 oz. of gold; value, £2,100; twenty-two days; thirty stamps.

NEW GUADALCAZAR.—The production of quicksilver for the past month, according to a cable received from the mines, amounts to 8,400 lb., equal to 112 flasks.

HANNAN'S OROYA.—During last month mill worked twenty-six days; crushed, 766 tons; yielded, 275 oz. gold. (Average, 7 dwt. 4 gr. gold.)

IVANHOE GOLD CORPORATION.—Clean up for the three weeks ending December 31, results: 1,178 tons crushed; yield, 2,273 oz. gold.

LADY SHENTON.—Started December 11. Cleaned up December 24; 215 tons crushed; yield, 1,000 oz. Also 355 oz. obtained from plates. Mining costs 18s. per ton. Milling, £1. 1s. per ton.

BRITISH BROKEN HILL PROPRIETARY.—"Mill returns for the fortnight ending December 29, 1897:—4,092 tons crude ore produced 749 tons concentrates, which contain 455 tons lead and 18,956 oz. silver."

NIGEL DEEP.—Still improving "D" shaft, east drive. Assays average for month 98 dwt. over 6¾ in. West drive—57 dwt. over 9 in. "C" shaft—Samples over 6 in. gave 52 and 145 dwt.

PREMIER TATI MONARCH.—"Thirty stamps running twenty-four days; crushed 1,830 tons. Yield of retorted gold, 503 oz.; Includes 840 tons at grass of low-grade ore. Have shipped two bars of gold, worth £1,850." Increase on November, 184 oz.

MOUNT MALCOLM.—Cleaned up 31st ult. Mill working 214 hours (nine days); crushed 202 tons for 362 oz. Average Value of tailings, 17 dwt. (Office note—This makes total return for December 472 tons for 680 oz., exclusive of tailings. This clean up was made in order that the battery might start afresh with the New Year.)

JUMPERS.—From the report for November:—Working expenses—Mining, cost per ton, 9s. 8·83d.; hauling and pumping, 2s. 5·48d.; transport, 1s. 4·90d.; milling, 4s. 7·72d.; redemption, 3s. 0·00d.; cyaniding tailings and concentrates, 1s. 8·27d.; charges, 1s. 2·10d.—24s. 1·32d. Profit for month, £7,372. 7s. 9d., or 12s. 9·86d. per ton. Mine development, 582½ ft. Ore developed by the footage was 13,815 tons.

OOREGUM.—4,595 oz. from 5,831 tons, including 533 oz. from tailings.

NUNDYDROOG.—5,340 oz. from 5,050 tons, including 94 oz. from tailings and 312 oz. from cyanide.

COROMANDEL.—1,004 oz. from 1,200 tons, including 50 oz. from tailings.

GOLD FIELDS OF MYSORE.—310 oz.

CUE 1 MINE.—545 oz. from 740 tons.

CITY OF LONDON MINE.—209 oz. from 196 tons.

MYSORE GOLD MINING COMPANY.—Return of gold for the month of December, 7,280 tons of quartz, yielding 11,002 oz. of gold; 2,965 tons of tailings 745 oz. of gold; 1,820 tons of tailings (cyanide process), 322 oz. of gold; the total yield for the month, 12,069 oz. The return includes 265 oz. collected from slags.

CHAMPION REEF GOLD MINING COMPANY OF INDIA, LIMITED.—Last month's returns of gold, 7,108 tons of stone, yield 9,054 oz.; 2,400 tons of tailings, 595 oz.; 4,895 tons of tailings (cyanide process), 1,225 oz. of gold; total production for the month, 10,874 oz. of gold.

BURMA RUBY MINES.—Result for December was 75,000 loads washed, producing rubies valued at 4s., 90,000.

ENGLISH RAILWAYS.

Div. for half years. 1895	1896	1896	1897	Last Balance forward.	Amt. to pay 1 p.c. on Ord. for ½ yr.	Name.	Date.	Gross Traffic for week: Amt.	Inc. or dec. on 1897.	Inc. or dec. on 1896.	Gross Traffic for half-year to date: No. of weeks.	Amt.	Inc. or dec. on 1897.	Inc. or dec. on 1896.	Mileage.	Inc. on 1892.	Working Expenses.	Fixed Charges last ½ year.	Prop. add. Cap. Exp. this ½ year.
				£	£												%	£	£
10	10	10	10	6,805	4,906	Barry	Jan. 1	8,815	+410	+626	1	8,818	+410	+625	31	—	47·36	66,663	316,008
nil	nil	nil	nil	—	—	Brecon and Merthyr	Jan. 2	1,497	+13	—	1	1,497	+13	—	61	—	—	—	—
nil	nil	nil	nil	4,020	4,749	Cambrian	Jan. 2	4,294	+86	+561	2 days	703	+14	—	250	—	61·16	63,472	42,000
1½	1¾	1¾	2	1,034	3,150	City and South London	Jan. 2	1,050	−27	+33	1	1,050	−27	+33	3½	—	56·07	5,552	109,500
1	1	2	1½	4,823	13,210	Furness	Jan. 2	8,752	+25	+1,575	—	—	—	—	139	—	50·85	96,623	52,963
1¾	1	1½	2	2,116	27,463	Great Central (late M., S., & L.)	Jan. 2	35,543	−346	—	27	1,246,522	+30,722	—	352½	—	56·09	609,255	1,130,000
4	1½	4½	2	2,666	62,865	Great Eastern	Jan. 2	75,336	+7,661	+14,503	1	75,336	+7,661	+14,503	1,156	7	59·9	847,611	210,500
¾	1½	1½	¾	4,593	102,406	Great Northern	Jan. 2	87,031	+1,025	+7,763	1	87,031	+1,025	+7,768	1,071	8	62·28	640,779	1,002,250
7	4½	7½	4½	16,273	116,381	Great Western	Jan. 2	159640	−940	+4,380	27	5,321,290	+204,820	—	2,573	34	57·91	1,424,324	650,000
nil	nil	2	nil	24,449	16,425	Hull and Barnsley	Jan. 2	5,785	+16	+637	26	183,134	−1,790	+6,780	73	—	61·21	54,684	44,019
5½	5	5¾	5	21,423	83,704	Lancashire and Yorkshire	Jan. 2	85,244	+2,422	+8,187	26	2,554,024	+9,481	+111,544	555½	25½	55·01	682,671	387,592
8½	4½	8	4½	16,376	43,049	London, Brighton, & S. Coast	Jan. 1	54,345	+2,394	+1,779	1	54,345	+2,394	+1,779	477	—	54·91	328,273	199,675
nil	nil	nil	nil	1,561	56,296	London, Chatham, & Dover	Jan. 2	25,466	+247	+1,153	27	870,917	+13,261	+35,947	185	—	57·29	220,181	nil
7½	6½	8	6½	95,016	203,263	London and North Western	Jan. 2	207547	+1,991	+10,701	26	6,465,430	+174,572	+364,788	1,912	—	55·91	1,411,298	425,000
7¾	5	8½	5½	23,525	58,667	London and South Western	Jan. 2	63,492	+1,241	+5,656	1	63,492	+1,241	+5,656	941	6½	55·93	527,257	370,000
5¾	2½	6	2½	7,572	6,691	London, Tilbury, & Southend	Jan. 2	4,935	+426	+1,129	1	4,935	+426	+1,129	81	—	57·00	40,041	15,000
3	3½	3¾	3½	16,398	28,659	Metropolitan	Jan. 2	16,761	+608	+1,819	1	16,761	+608	+1,819	64	12	56·70	110,744	109,000
nil	nil	nil	nil	4,310	11,250	Metropolitan District	Jan. 2	8,522	+316	−22	1	8,522	+316	−22	13	—	45·32	159,412	23,150
6½	5	7	5½	18,336	174,175	Midland	Jan. 2	148210	+5,176	+17,703	1	148,210	+5,176	+17,703	1,354	15	57·47	1,213,866	650,000
6½	5½	7½	5½	22,374	135,568	North Eastern	Jan. 1	142543	+14,623	+27,339	26	4,127,560	+134,968	+205,091	1,597½	1½	58·70	791,956	372,790
7½	7½	7½	7½	6,213	10,102	North London	Jan. 2	8,895	−317	−118	1	8,895	−317	−118	12	—	51·65	51,329	4,000
4½	4	5	4	3,356	16,150	North Staffordshire	Jan. 2	15,716	+2,380	+3,091	1	15,716	+2,380	+3,091	312	—	55·27	118,148	19,605
8½	10	10	11	1,642	3,004	Rhymney	Jan. 1	4,010	−1,000	−669	1	4,010	−1,000	−669	71	—	40·68	22,049	16,700
6	3	6½	3½	4,516	50,915	South Eastern	Jan. 1	41,398	+144	+197	1	41,398	+144	+197	448	—	[illegible]	382,193	130,000
3½	3½	3½	3½	5,904	25,691	Taff Vale	Jan. 1	12,630	−2,915	−1,712	1	12,630	−2,958	−1,711	121	—	[illegible]	61,997	43,000

SCOTCH RAILWAYS.

5½	5	5	5½	15,350	77,570	Caledonian	Jan. 2	74,893	+ 3,013	+ 7,541	22	1,559,733	+ 22,937	+ 67,11[illegible]	851	86	50·30	556,914	375,966
5	5	5½	5	5,886	24,639	Glasgow and South-Western	" 1	27,579	− 261	+ 1,379	22	657,700	− 8,79[illegible]	+ 57,00[illegible]	363	8	55·14	221,120	180,556
3½	3½	3½	3½	1,291	4,600	Great North of Scotland	" 1	9,761	+ 696	+ 2,720	22	199,[illegible]33	+ 6,93[illegible]	+ 14,0[illegible]	[illegible]	16	[illegible]	92,173	60,000
[illegible]	3	nil	2	10,477	12,820	Highland	" 0	8,295	+ 47	+ 844	18	172,894	+ 5,373	+ 7,7[illegible]	479	27	[illegible]	78,976	84,000
1½	1	1½	1	3,703	45,819	North British	" 2	74,945	+ 2,064	+ 9,657	22	1,673,31[illegible]	+ 43,[illegible]	+ 67,1[illegible]	[illegible]	23	44·[illegible]	[illegible]1,766	190,009

IRISH RAILWAYS.

6½	6½	6½	6½	2,405	1,745	Belfast and County Down	Dec. 31	2,334	+ 662	+ 43½	26	70,761	+ 2,775	+ 4,931	70	—	—	56·49	17,665	38,000
6½	5½	6½	5½	—	4,284	Belfast and Northern Counties	" 31	4,081	− 142	+ 148	26	154,310	+ 1,257	+ 5,645	249	—	—	—	—	—
3	2	3	2½	1,418	1,200	Cork, Bandon, and S. Coast	Jan. 1	1,021	+ 102	+ 49	—	—	—	—	61	—	—	54·82	14,436	3,450
2	1½	nil	nil	—	3,500	Dublin, Wicklow, & Wexford		not received			—	—	—	—	144	—	—	—	—	—
6½	6½	6½	6½	21,537	17,709	Great Northern	Dec. 31	14,463	− 721	+ 2,676	26	441,0[illegible]	+ 22,527	+ 26,36[illegible]	402		5	54·02	87,068	16,000
5½	5½	5½	5½	12,037	24,855	Great Southern and Western	" 31	14,094	+ 106	+ 995	26	454,930	+ 13,195	+ 10,01[illegible]	[illegible]	13	33	55·78	72,800	35,140
4½	4	4	4	4,085	11,850	Midland Great Western	" 31	12,803	+ 1,289	—	—	—	—	—	[illegible]	—	—	53·19	82,845	2,600
nil	nil	nil	nil	229	2,822	Waterford and Central	" 31	866	+ 266	—	—	—	—	—	59	—	—	55·24	6,858	1,500
nil	nil	nil	nil	2,601	2,987	Waterford, Limerick & W.	" 31	3,414	− 18	− 483	—	—	—	—	342	—	—	58·70	43,076	8,869

INDIAN RAILWAYS.

Mileage. Total.	Increase on 1896.	Increase on 1895.	Name.	Gross Traffic for Week. Week ending	Amount.	In. or Dec. on 1896.	In. or Dec. on 1895.	Gross Traffic to Date. No. of Weeks.	Amount.	In. or Dec. on 1896.	In. or Dec. on 1895.
867	4	5	Bengal Nagpur	Dec. 18	Rs.1,12,000	−Rs.17,710	—	24	Rs.21,04,759	−Rs.160,286	—
818	63	63	Bengal and North-Western	Dec. 4	Rs.1,01,330	+Rs.2,765	+Rs.2,352	22	Rs.22,01,217	+Rs.109,425	+Rs.1,98,797
461	—	—	Bombay and Baroda	Dec. 25	£58,850	−£8,308	—	25	£1,315,551	−£40,173	—
1,884	2	13	East Indian	Dec. 31*	Rs.21,79,000	+Rs.2,15,000	—	26	Rs.2,92,18,000	+Rs.21,02,000	—
1,491	—	—	Great Indian Penin.	Dec. 31*	£100,458	+£1,754	—	26	£1,144,565	−£90,685	—
736	—	—	Indian Midland	Dec. 31*	Rs.2,70,680	+Rs.23,268	+Rs.41,080	26	Rs.28,15,251	+Rs.2,02,496	+Rs.3,41,606
840	—	—	Madras	Dec. 25	£16,968	−£917	—	25	£500,115	+£31,918	—
1,043	—	—	South Indian	Dec. 4	Rs.159,869	+Rs.4,432	—	22	Rs.37,99,[illegible]	+Rs.53,045	—

FOREIGN RAILWAYS.

Mileage. Total.	Increase on 1896.	Increase on 1895.	Name.	Gross Traffic for Week. Week ending	Amount.	In. or Dec. upon 1896.	In. or Dec. upon 1895.	Gross Traffic to Date. No. of Weeks.	Amount.	In. or Dec. upon 1896.	In. or Dec. upon 1895.
					£	£	£		£	£	£
370	—	—	Argentine Great Western	Dec. 31	5,504	+ 861	+ 2,349	26	137,908	− 13,190	+ 30,880
76½	—	—	Bahia and San Francisco	Dec. 11	2,439	+ 421	+ 21	24	56,132	+ 16,904	+ 17,064
234	57	84	Bahia Blanca and North West	Dec. 5	1,293	+ 473	+ 793	23	13,916	+ 307	—
75	—	—	Buenos Ayres and Ensenada	Jan. 2	3,244	− 1,476	− 464	24	—	—	—
420	—	—	Buenos Ayres and Pacific	Jan. 1	5,109	− 3,360	− 1,001	26	157,216	− 42,589	+ 4,874
914	1	3	Buenos Ayres and Rosario	Jan. 1	11,126	− 6,203	+ 1,019	—	—	—	—
1,469	66	68	Buenos Ayres Great Southern	Jan. 2	26,170	− 3,399	− 1,271	26	682,074	+ 48,374	+ 95,033
602	142	177	Buenos Ayres Western	Jan. 2	10,196	− 6,392	− 3,628	26	292,262	− 66,852	− 62,808
790	—	22	Central Argentine	Jan. 1	14,549	− 3,306	+ 1,350	—	—	—	—
197	—	—	Central Bahia	Oct. 31*	$83,031	− $6,258	—	10 mos.	$1,121,178	+ $175,344	—
271	—	—	Central Uruguay of Monte Video	Jan. 1	8,260	+ 2,644	+ 1,211	26	142,976	− 15,559	− 15,407
180	—	—	Cordoba and Rosario	Dec. 25	1,435	− 555	− 65	26	49,450	− 11,740	− 300
128	—	—	Cordoba Central	Dec. 26	$19,000	− $4,450	− $200	52	$1,434,120	− $257,510	− [illegible]
549	—	—	Do. Northern Extension	Dec. 26	$49,000	− $13,860	− $2,340	52	$3,378,870	− $961,590	− [illegible]
137	—	—	Costa Rica	Dec. 25	4,395	− 1,610	+ 3,606	41	246,036	+ 29,340	+ 45,163
99	—	—	East Argentine	Nov. 21	738	+ 117	− 216	47	31,614	− 3,149	− 884
386	—	6	Entre Rios	Jan. 1	1,728	+ 639	+ 817	26	28,477	+ 568	+ 932
555	—	24	Inter Oceanic of Mexico	Jan. 1	$53,900	+ $12,590	—	26	$1,389,040	+ $171,990	—
23	—	—	La Guaira and Caracas	Dec. 2	1,531	− 516	− 521	46	101,424	− 9,374	− 1,085
321	—	—	Mexican	Jan. 1	15,800	+ 1,200	+ 3,910	39	378,110	+ 20,760	+ 92,790
1,846	—	—	Mexican Central	Dec. 31‡	$193,000	+ $36,000	+ $111,541	26	$6,271,569	+ $976,383	+ $1,390,473
1,217	—	—	Mexican National	Dec. 31‡	$155,770	− $24,361	+ $18,900	26	$2,822,395	+ $201,113	+ $627,407
228	—	—	Mexican Southern	Dec. 31‡	$13,660	− $677	+ $2,529	26	$455,595	− $83,516	+ $132,996
205	—	—	Minas and Rio	Nov. 30	$179,485	+ $24,384	—	5 mos.	$996,637	+ $201,287	—
111	—	17	N. W. Argentine	Jan. 1	961	− 296	—	—	—	—	—
239½	—	—	Nitrate	Dec. 31†	21,583	+ 10,026	− 7,845	24	300,891	+ 39,505	− 79,428
390	—	—	Ottoman	Dec. 25	5,053	− 308	+ 1,399	26	242,768	+ 3,701	+ 39,447
77½	—	—	Recife and San Francisco	Oct. 30	4,656	− 194	+ 1,269	19	47,546	− 10,116	− 6,400
869	—	—	San Paulo	Nov. 28*	25,496	− 6,338	—	22	349,594	− 27,229	—
186	—	—	Santa Fe and Cordova	Jan. 1	1,067	− 1,045	+ 202	27	22,003	− 20,810	− 5,448

* For month ended. † For fortnight ended. ‡ Ten days ended

Dividends Announced.

B. C. Bushell, Watkins, & Co.—Interim dividend of 8 per cent. will be paid on ordinary shares.

Westlake's Brewery, Limited.—Dividend declared at rate of 8 per cent. per annum for six months ended September 30, 1897.

Benjamin Brooke & Co., Limited.—Interim dividend at rate of 10 per cent. per annum on ordinary shares has been distributed.

The Baraoora (Sylhet) Tea Company has paid an interim dividend at rate of 6 per cent. on ordinary shares.

London & Greenwich Railway have decided to recommend a dividend on ordinary stock at rate of £1. 8s. 3d. per cent., less income tax, payable on and after January 20, 1898.

Fowler Bros., Limited, recommend payment of dividend of 5 per cent. for year on ordinary shares, leaving balance of £10,491 which has been carried to reserve account, making a total in reserve of £23,669.

Nahor-Rani Tea Company.—Two and a Half per cent. interim dividend on ordinary shares declared.

Hitchings, Limited. — Seven per cent. interim on ordinary shares.

Langlaagte Estate and Gold Mining Company, Limited.—Dividend for first half-year ended December 31 at the rate of 30 per cent. per annum is announced.

Fletcher, Son, & Fearnall, Limited.—Interim dividend has been declared on preference shares at rate of 6 per cent. per annum for the six months ending December 31, 1897, and payable on January 1, 1898.

Mount Morgan Gold Mining Company, Limited.—A dividend of £25,000, being 6d. a share for month of December, was payable on January 3.

Palace Theatre, Limited. — Directors recommend interim dividend of 7 per cent., free of income tax, payable January 29 next.

Porges Randfontein Gold Mining Company, Limited.—A dividend of 10 per cent., equal to 2s. per share, for year ending December 31, has been declared.

Chenhall & Co., Limited. — A dividend of 6 per cent. on preference shares was declared for the year.

A. J. White ("Mother Seigel").—The quarterly dividend of 6 per cent. cumulative preference shares was posted January 1.

Union Bank of London.—Declared a dividend of 15s. 6d. per share, equal to 10 per cent. per annum, carrying forward about £22,000. Dividend of last year was at same rate, and £22,047 was carried forward.

Debenture Corporation.—Directors recommend a dividend at the rate of 8 per cent. on the ordinary shares for six months ended December 31, and a bonus of ½ per cent. for the year. £10,000 is added to reserve fund, and £4,206 carried forward.

Raffety Thornton & Co., Limited, will, on the 21st inst., recommend the payment of a dividend at the rate of 15 per cent. per annum for the six months ended December 31, making the interim dividend 10 per cent. for year. £2,000 is added to reserve and £4,502 carried forward.

London Improved Cab Company, Limited, will pay an interim dividend for the six months ended November 30, 1897, at the rate of 6 per cent. per annum, on January 25, 1898. £500 will be added to reserve account, and £1,077. 10s. 9d. carried forward

The Berkeley Hotel Company, Limited, have issued dividend warrants in payment of an interim dividend at the rate of 5 per cent. and 6 per cent. respectively on the first and second preference shares, and of 5 per cent. per annum on the ordinary shares.

Debenture Corporation Founders' Share Company.—1½ per cent. for 1897.

Lovell & Christmas.—At the rate of 10 per cent. per annum on ordinary shares.

Robert Arthur Theatres Company.—Fifteen per cent. per annum interim on ordinary shares.

London United Laundries, Limited, have declared an interim dividend at the rate of 6 per cent. per annum, for the half-year ended November 30, on the ordinary share capital.

Queensland Menzies Gold Mining Company.—A dividend of 6d. per share is announced.

Peel River Land Company.—Three per cent., making in all 5 per cent. for year.

Jackson's Stores.—Twelve and a half per cent. per annum interim on ordinary shares.

Clifford, Hawes, & Company, Limited.—A dividend at the rate of 6 per cent. has been declared on preference shares for the half-year ended January 1.

Lady Shenton Gold Mine.—A dividend of 1s. per share has been declared, payable on 19th inst., making 20 per cent. for the year.

London Tramways Company, Limited, show a net income of £41,193 against £35,833 for corresponding half-year of 1896, enabling dividend of 12s. 9d. to be paid on ordinary shares, and 10s. 3d. per certificate on the scrip certificates.

O. C. Hawkes, Limited.—A dividend of 5 per cent. on the preference shares has been declared.

Elmslie, Limited.—An interim dividend of 10 per cent. on the preference, and 5 per cent. on the ordinary shares.

United African Syndicate pay an interim dividend of 15 per cent. on the ordinary shares.

General Life Assurance.—A dividend at the rate of 10 per cent. per annum, and a bonus equal to an additional 5 per cent. per annum, are now payable.

London and Westminster Bank.—A dividend of 6¼ per cent for the half-year ending December 31 last, making 12½ per cent. for the year, carrying forward about £18,000. The dividend a year ago was 6 per cent., and balance carried forward, £7,910.

National Discount Company.—A dividend at the rate of 11 per cent. per annum; £4,300 carried forward. The dividend last year was at the same rate, and £4,777 was carried forward.

West Riding Union Banking Company.—The usual dividend of 8s. per share, making, with the distribution in July last, 8 per cent. per annum, leaving £5,242 carried to the reserve fund.

The New Investment Company.—An interim dividend at the rate of 5 per cent. per annum for the six months ending January 10, 1898.

The Financial Times.—The usual dividend at the rate of 25 per cent. per annum.

Sun (Fire) Insurance Office.—An interim dividend of 4s. per share, it being increased by 1s. per share at the expense of the final dividend payable in July with a view to more nearly equalising the half-yearly payments.

West Australian Joint Stock Trust and Finance Corporation.—Interim dividend at the rate of 20 per cent. per annum.

West Australian Loan and General Finance Corporation.—Dividend at the rate of 20 per cent. per annum for the past year.

Pawsons & Leafs.—Recommended a dividend of 3s. per share, and a bonus of 1s. 6d. per share (making a distribution for the year at the rate of 5 per cent.), carrying forward £38 248. This compares with a 3s. dividend, with £35,670 carried forward last year.

North and South Wales Bank.—Dividend for the half year ended 31st ultimo 10s. per share, with bonus of 6 per cent. per share, making the distribution for the year 15 per cent. Dividends same as last year.

The Bank of Bengal has declared a dividend of 10 per cent. for the first half-year, carried forward Rs.3,00,000, and placed to reserve Rs.3,50,000.

The Assets Founders' Share Company recommend a dividend for the year ending December 31, 1897, at the rate of 1¼ per cent. per annum.

The Assets Realisation Company propose to pay a final dividend on the ordinary shares for the six months ending December 31 last, at the rate of 12 per cent. per annum, making a total return of 10 per cent. for the year. They place £10,000 to the reserve fund.

Halifax and Huddersfield Union Banking Company, Limited.—£5,000 added to reserve fund. Dividend of 8s. per share for the half-year ending December 31, making a total of 8 per cent. per annum, free of income tax. Balance of £2,396 to be carried forward.

London and Midland Bank.—Dividend for past half-year at the rate of 16 per cent. per annum; bonus 1 per cent., making 17 per cent. for the year; transferring £40,000 to bank premises redemption fund, £5,000 to the officers' pension fund, and carrying forward £100,806. This compares with 16 per cent. last year, when £40,213 was carried forward.

Adelphi Bank, Limited.—Dividend at the rate of 8 per cent., carrying forward £5,000 to reserve fund. Last year dividend was at the rate of 7 per cent.

Ocean Marine Insurance Company.—Dividend of 2s. 6d. per share, and 5s. per share bonus, making, with interim already paid 10s. per share.

London Produce Clearing House—Dividend of 2s. 6d. per share on ordinary shares, and £8. 6s. 8d. per share on the Founder's shares, carrying forward £2,165.

Union Discount Company, London, recommend a dividend of 10 per cent. per annum, carrying forward £16,852. Last year dividend was at the rate of 9 per cent. with £22,107.

London and Yorkshire Bank.—Dividend of 10 per cent., £2,500 to bank premises account, £5,000 to reserve fund, and carrying forward £7,105. Last year dividend was at the rate of 9 per cent. with £5,819 carried forward.

London Joint Stock Bank.—A dividend of 10 per cent. per annum is declared, £10,000 is applied to Imperial Bank Purchase Account, £10,000 to Superannuation Allowance Fund, and £11,400 carried forward. Last year the dividend was at the same rate with £9,181 carried forward.

City Bank, Limited.—Dividend at the rate of 10 per cent. per annum, against 9 per cent. last year.

Stock Conversion and Investment Trust.—Dividends of 1s. 9d. per ordinary share, and 10s. per Founders share, carrying forward £5,391.

Fore Street Warehouse.—Dividend of 5s. 6d. per share, making 5 per cent. for the year, carrying forward £267.

DISCONTENT IN PERSIA.

Persia is said to be on the brink of revolution, and the discontent is worst in the district where Russian and British interests are most in conflict. According to the Berlin correspondent of the *Standard*, a dissolution of the central authority and the conversion of the provinces into independent states is anticipated. The cause of the discontent is said to be the extravagance of the new Shah, who has spent all the enormous accumulations of his predecessor, and overburdened the inhabitants with taxation. It is three months since Shiraz expelled its governor, and set up a triumvirate of its own. It pays tribute to the Shah, but that is all. If other districts do not follow this example it will not be the fault of the Shah apparently. Even the priests accuse him of incompetence.

According to the *Railway Age* of Chicago only 1,864 miles of new railroads were built in the States last year. This was but 164 miles more than the total for 1896, and is a very tiny figure compared with the glorious times of 1880 to 1890; but then, in that happy period, the American railroad constructor could draw any number of millions of money from England. Now English purse-strings are drawn tight, and this particular industry shrivels. We hope the purses will not be opened again in a hurry. American railroads require another ten years' starvation to settle down and consolidate, and for their managers to get some glimmering of what goes to make up common honesty.

Prices Quoted on the London Stock Exchange.

Throughout the INVESTORS' REVIEW middle prices alone are quoted, the object being to give the public the approximate current quotations of every security of any consequence in existence. On the markets the buying and selling prices are both given, and are often wide apart where stocks are seldom dealt in. Other particulars will be found in the INVESTMENT INDEX published quarterly—January, April, July, and October—in connection with this REVIEW, price 2s., by post 2s. 2d. Where dividends are paid only once a year, an *italic* type is used to distinguish them. The London Stock Exchange Official List is quoted in the REVIEW almost entire, only very insignificant issues, or bonds falling due within the next two or three years, being omitted. But the list is subdivided into the leading, or active, stocks, and those less frequently dealt in. The former will be found under the head of "Stock Markets," and with more details than it is possible to give for the bulk of securities. By retaining the file of the INVESTORS' REVIEW any subscriber can follow for himself the movements of securities from week to week, and the INVESTMENT INDEX will from time to time help to fill up deficiencies in the information.

Tea Companies and Mines and Mining Finance Stocks are placed in special lists.

Among the abbreviations used are the following:—S.F., Snk.Fd. *sinking fund*; Certs., *certificates*; Debs. or Dbs., *debentures*; Db. or D.Stk., *debenture stock*; Pf., Prf., or Pref., *preference*; Prefd. or Pfd., *preferred*; Dfd., *deferred*; L. or Ltd., *limited*; Sh., *share*; Ans., *annuities*; Cu. or Cm., *cumulative*; Gu. or Guar., *guaranteed*; Bds., *bonds*; S., Sr., or Ser., *series*; In., Ins., Insc. *inscribed*; Dr., Drgs., Drwgs., *drawings*; Stg., Strlg., *sterling*; Lia., *liable to*; Sp., Surp., *surplus*; Per., Perp. *perpetual*; Ln. *lien*; Lo. *loan*. Prices marked † signify they are *ex. div.*

The dates following the names of securities are the years of issue or of redemption. Where shares are not fully paid up, their nominal amount is given with the name so that investors may know the liability upon them.

BRITISH FUNDS, &c.

Rate.	Name.	Price.
2¾	2¾ p.c.'s (Childers') Red.. 1905	106½
3	Local Loans Stk. 1912	113
3	Metro. Police Deb. Stk. 1920	104
—	Red Sea Ind. Tel. Ann. 1908	9½
4	Canada Gv. "Intcl. Rly." 1903	109½
4	Do. do. .. 1908	113
4	Do. Bonds 1910	117
4	Do. Bonds 1913	119½
3	Egyptian Gov. Gar.	108½
3	Mauritius Ins. Stk. 1940	115
4	Turkish Guar. 1855	110
11½	Bank of Ireland Stk.	392½
3½	India Rupee Paper	60½
3½	Do. 1854-5	62½
3	Do. 1896-7 1916	52
3½	Isle of Man Deb.	106
3	Do. Deb. Stk... 1919-29	105

CORPORATION AND COUNTY STOCKS.

FREE OF STAMP DUTY.

Rate.	Name.	Price.
3½	Metropolitan Con. 1929	121
3	Do. 1941	114
2½	Do. 1920-49	101½
2½	L.C.C. Con. Stock 1920	80½
3½	Comm. of Sewers, Scp., S.F. 1905	106
3½	Corp. of Lond. Bds...1897-1902	100½
3	Do. 1897-1912	103
3½	Do., Debs. Scp. ...... S.F. 1916	106
—	Do., Deb. Stk. Scrip .. 1927-57	99½
3	Barnsley 1916-46	104
3	Barry 1914-46	100
3	Bath 1909-34	104
3	Batley 1914-44	101½
3½	Birmingham 1945	123
3	Do. 1947	113
2½	Do. 1926	99½
3	Blackburn 1930	105½
3	Bournemouth 1913-33	104
3½	Bradford 1945	120
3	Do. Deb. Stock .. 1954	111
3	Brighouse 1916-46	101
3½	Brighton 1946	120½
2½	Do. 1957	98
3	Burton-on-Trent 1913-43	102½
3	Cambridge 1913-43	104
3½	Cardiff 1935	119
3	Do. 1914-54	105
3	Cheltenham 1971	112
3	Chichester 1916-46	102
3½	Croydon	135½
3	Do. 1940	111½
3	Derby 1920-50	107
3	Devon C.C. 1917-33	106
3½	Dewsbury 1930	111
3	Do. 1930	105
3	Dorset County 1922-32	107
3	Douglas (I. of Man) 1926	101
3	Dover 1913-43	103
3½	Dublin 1944	111
3	Eastbourne 1920-40	105
3	Edinburgh 1924	107
2½	Do. 1929	98
2½	Exeter 1917-57	97
3	Glamorgan County 1914-34	104
3½	Glasgow 1914	110½
3	Do. 1921	106½
2½	Do. 1925-40	99
3	Gloster 1915-55	103
3	Grimsby 1913-45	104½
3	Hampshire County 1914-34	106½
3	Hanley 1913-43	104
3	Harrogate 1914-34	104
3	Hastings 1915-54	104
2½	Hertfordshire C.C. 1916-36	99†
3	Heston & Isleworth U.D.C. 1915-35	101
3	Huddersfield 1934	107
3½	Hull (1st Iss.)	131½
3	Inverness 1914-44	102
3	Ipswich 1952	111
3	Lancaster 1919-55	104
2½	Leeds 1927	98
3½	Leicester 1934	117
3	Lincoln 1919	104
3½	Liverpool	135

Corporation, &c. (*continued*) :—

Rate.	Name.	Price.
3	Manchester 1941	109
3	Mansfield 1915-45	100
3½	Middlesbro' .... 1909 (†	105½
3½	Do. 1911-13	104
3	Do. 1915	104
3	Middlesex C.C. 1915-35	106
3½	Newcastle 1936	118½
3½	Do. Irred.	129½
2½	Do. 1915-36	101
3	Newcastle-under-Lyme.. 1909-44	100
3	Newport (Mon.) 1915-55	104½
3	Norwich 1952	113
3	Nottingham	117
3	Oxford 1951	111
3	Penzance 1916-46	102½
3	Plymouth 1942	112
3	Pontypridd U.D.C. 1916-46	99
3	Poole 1915-45	102½
3½	Portsmouth ....1916 24 & 27	112
3	Do. 1913-33	107
3	Ramsey 1920-40	100
3	Ramsgate 1915-55	103
3½	Reading	135
3	Do. 1962	109
3½	Rhyl U.D.C. 1953	112
3	Richmond (Surrey) 1942	106
3	River Wear Debt Certs.	101
3	St. Helen's 1915-55	104½
3	Scarbro' 1915-50	102
2½	Sheffield 1925-57	97½
3	Shipley U.D.C. 1915-35	101
3	Somerset Co. 1923-33	107
3	South Shields 1925-45	104
2½	Southampton 1915-45	102
3	Southend-on-Sea 1916-46	102
3	Staffs C.C. 1915-35	106
3	Stockport 1914-54	103
3	Stockton 1939	105
3	Do. 1915-35	103½
3	Surrey Co. 1922-32	106½
3½	Swansea	132
3	Do. 1955	106
3	Taunton 1918 3-9-43	101
3	Tees Conserv. Deb. Stk. 1947	101
3	Thames Conserv. "A" Deb. Stk. 1954	102
	Do. "B" Deb. Stk. 1954	102
3	Torquay 1913-43	102½
3	Tunbridge Wells 1931	105
3	Tynemouth 1913	101
3	Wakefield 1929	105
3	Walsall 1932	108
3	West Bromwich 1930	108½
3½	West Ham 1929	111
3	Do. 1945	107
3	West Sussex C.C. 1915-35	107
3	Weston-s.-Mare Lcl. Bd. 1914-44	102
3	Weymouth & Melc. Regis 1918	101
3	Widnes 1913-55	102
3	Wigan 1921	108
3	Windsor 1918-55	103
3½	Wisbech 1947	115½
3½	Wolverhampton 1932	119½
3	Do. 1924-54	107½
3	York 1916-41	106

SUBJECT TO STAMP DUTY.

Rate.	Name.	Price.
3½	Belfast City & Dis. Watr. 1938	116
3	Do. Red Stk. 1953-6	108½
3½	Belfast 1924	104
4	Blackburn Con. Deb. Irred.	141½
3½	Do. do. Irred.	138½
3½	Bristol	133
3½	Burnley 1933	116
2½	Chesterfield Gas & Wtr. 1916-46	98
3½	Douglas Town 1921	105
3	Dover Harb. 1st Deb... 1956	105
3½	Hull (2nd iss.)	129½
4	Leeds Deb. 1927	125
3½	Do.	113½
3	Do. 1927	106½
3	Leicester 1919-44	106
4	Manchester	150
3	Do. 1928	105
4½	Middlesboro' Mrts. 1908	111†
3½	Newark-on-Trent .. 1901-41	96
3½	Sheffield 1898-1916	106
3½	Do. 1925-36	110½
3	Do. 1925	107
3½	Southampton .... S.F.	105
4½	Stockton Morts. 1908	111†
3½	Worcester 1950	111

COLONIAL AND PROVINCIAL GOVERNMENT SECURITIES.

Rate.	Name.	Price.
6	British Columbia .... 1907 (†	113½
4½	Do. Debs. .. 1917 (†	110½
3	British Guiana Imgtn. Bds.	90½
5	Canada, "Intercol. Rail," 1903	111½
4	Do. (Bonds) 1904-5-6-8	100
4	Do. Reduced 1910	111†
3½	Do. Bnds. 1910-34	109
4	Do. Loan 1910-35	112†
3	Do. Loan 1915	107†
6	Cape of G. Hope 1900	—
5	Do. 1900	—
4½	Do. red. by an. draw.	111
4½	Do. 1879	111
4	Do. 1881	108
4	Do. 1917-23	117
4½	Ceylon	110
4	Do.	108½
4½	Fiji Gov. Deb. Sink. Fd.	100½
4	Jamaica Sink. Fd. 1923	104
5	Manitoba Debs. 1910	113
5	Do. Ster. Bds. 1928	119
4	Do. Ster. Debs.	106
4	Mauritius, Cons. Debs. 1880....	103½
4½	Natal, Sink. Fd. 1919	120
4	Do. do. 1926	118
3½	Newfoundland Stg. Bds. 1941	99†
3½	Do. do. .. 1947	99†
3	Do. do.	99
5	New South Wales ..1857-1902 (†	104½
4	Do. 1903-5-8-9-10 (†	104½
5	New Zealand 1914	120
5	Do. Cnsls. 1 p.c. per an. Sink. Fd.	104
3½	Nova Scotia Debs.	104†
5	Quebec Prov. 1904-6	108½
4½	Do. (drgs.)	103†
5	Do. Strlg. Bds. 1912	115†
4	Do. Strlg. Bds. 1923	108†
4	Do. Strlg. Bds. 1934	110
4	Queensland 1913-15	108†
4½	St. Lucia Debs.	100
6	South Australia ....1897-1900 (†	103½
6	Do. 1901-1918	118†
5	Do. ....1911-1920 (†	115½
4	Do. 1899-1916	105†
4	Do. .... 1929 (†	110½
4	Do. 1916	109½
4	Do. 1917-18-24	112
6	Tasmania 1897-1901	104†
4	Do. 1908-11, 1913-14-20	108†
5	Trinidad Debs., an. drw. 1 p.c...	107
4	Victoria ....1899-1901 (†	101½
4½	Do. 1904	106†
4	Do. Rail. Loan 1907	106†
4	Do. Loans 1908-13	108
4½	West. Austr. 1 p.c. ac. Sink. Fd.	108
4	Do. do.	108

REGISTERED AND INSCRIBED STOCKS.

No stamp duty except for Canada 4 p.c. Reduced (½ per cent.).

Rate.	Name.	Price.
4	Antigua Insc. Stk. Red. 1919-44	111
3½	Barbados Insc. Stk. 1925-42	108
3	British Colum. Insc. Stk. 1941	102
4	British Guiana Insc. 1935	120
4	Canada Stk. Regd. ..1904-5-6-8	109
4	Do. 4 p.c. (late 5 p.c.) Regd. 1910	111
3½	Do. 3½ p.c. Stock Regd. 1909-34	109
4	Do. Ln. for 4 milln. stg. 1910-35	112
3	Do. Stk. Regd. 1938	107
2½	Do. Insc. 1947	93
4	Cape G. Hope Regd. .. 1917-23	118
4	Do. (Ln. of '83) Insc. .. 1923	119
4	Do. Cons. Stk. Insc. 1916-36	116
3½	Do. Consol. Insc. Stock 1929-49	114½
4	Ceylon Insc. Stock 1934	126
3	Do. 1940	107
4	Grenada Insc. Stock 1917-42	112
3½	Hong Kong Insc. Stock 1918-43	105½
4	Jamaica Insc. Stock 1934	122
—	Do. 1922-44	99
4	Mauritius Inscribed 1937	119†
4	Natal Consd. Stk. Insc. 1927	118
4	Do. 1937	122
3½	Do. Inscribed Stock .. 1914-39	107
4	Newfoundland Inscribed 1913-38	108
4	Do. 1935	113
4	Do. Consd. Stk. Ins. 1936	113
4	N. S. Wales Stock Insc. 1933	122
3½	Do. 1924	110
3½	Do. 1918	108
3	Do. 1935	103½

Colonial, &c. (*continued*) :—

Rate.	Name.	Price.
4	N. Zealnd. Con. Stk. Ins. 1929	116
3½	Do. 1940	109½
3	Do. Inscribed 1945	101½
3	Quebec (Prov.) Ins. Stk. 1937	95
4	Queensland Stock Insc. 1915-24	112½
3½	Do. 1921-4-30	105
3½	Do. 1945	109
—	Do. 1922-47	100
4	St. Lucia Insc. Stock .. 1919-44	112
4	S. Austrln. (1882-7) Reg. 1916-36	113½
3½	Do. In. Stk. Reg. 1939	110
3	Do. 1916-26	100
15/	Do. 1916	100
3½	Tasmanian Insc. Stock.. 1920-40	110
4	Do. 1920-40	115
4	Trinidad Insc. Stock 1917-42	112
—	Do. 1922-44	98
4	Victoria Rly. Loan '81, Inscribed Stock 1907	106
4	Victoria Insc. Stock 1908-13-15	108½
4	Victoria (1883) Ins. Stk. 1920	112
3½	Do. Inscribed Stock 1921-3-6	108
4	Do. do. 1911-26	109
4	W. Austral. Insc. Stock 1934	120
4	Do. 1911-31	113
3½	Do. 1915-35	107
3	Do. 1915-35	99
3	Do. 1926-36	99

FOREIGN STOCKS, BONDS, &c.

COUPONS PAYABLE IN LONDON.

Last Div.	Name.	Price.
36/	Argentine Ry. Loan 6 p.c. 1881	88
15/	Do. 5 p.c. 1884	80†
30/	Do. N. Cent. Ry. Ext. 5 p.c. 1887-8-9	67½†
30/	Do. 5 p.c. Trry. Convs. 1887	67½
3/4½	Do. 4½ p.c. Interl. Gld. 1888	[illegible]
27/	Do. 4½ p.c. Stlg. Extrl. 1888	[illegible]
10/6	Do. 3½ p.c. External .. 1889	[illegible]
4	Do. 4 p.c. Ry. Guar. Res.	[illegible]
4½	Brazilian 1883	[illegible]
4½	Do. Gold 1879	[illegible]
4½	Do. 1888	[illegible]
30/	Buenos Ayres 1882	80
6	Do. 1882-76	47
6	Bulgarian 1888	97
6	Do. Mort. Bonds 1892	[illegible]
4½	Chilian 1885	[illegible]
4½	Do. 1886	[illegible]
4½	Do. 1887	[illegible]
4½	Do. 1889	[illegible]
5	Do. 1892	[illegible]
4½	Do. 1893	[illegible]
4½	Do. 1895	[illegible]
5	Do. 1896	[illegible]
7	Chinese Silver 1894	[illegible]
6	Do. Gold 1895	[illegible]
6	Do. Apl. '95 by dwgs. 1901-1915	[illegible]
5	Do. Red. dwgs. in 36 yr. 1896	[illegible]
5	Do. Do. Regis. 1896	[illegible]
1½	Colmbn. 1½ to 3 p.c. Ext. Bds. 1896	[illegible]
6	Cordova, Prov. 1886	[illegible]
—	Do. Eng. Ass. Certs.	[illegible]
—	Do. 6 p.c. 1887-8	[illegible]
—	Do. Eng. Ass. Certs.	[illegible]
3	Costa Rica "A"	[illegible]
2½	Do. "B"	[illegible]
3	Danish Gold 1894	[illegible]
10/	Ecuador N. Ext. Bds. 4½ p.c. ascn. to 5 p.c.	[illegible]
3½	Egypt'n Ins. Stk. lia. Stp. Dty. 1890	[illegible]
4½	Do. State Domain 1878	[illegible]
4	Do. D. Sanieh, Red. .. 1905	[illegible]
6	Entre Rios 1886-8	[illegible]
6	Do. Fndg. Lo. Bds. 1891-1901	27
6	Do. do. Parana City	[illegible]
15/	Greek 1881	[illegible]
15/	Do. 1884	[illegible]
12/	Do. Rentes	[illegible]
15/	Do. (Piræus-Larissa Ry.)	[illegible]
7/6	Do. Fundg. Loan 1893	[illegible]
4	Guatemala Extl. Debt	[illegible]
6	Hawaiian .... (†	[illegible]
4	Hungarian Gold Rentes	[illegible]
3	Do. 1895	88
6	Italian Irriga. Guar. .... (†	111½
5	Do. Maremmana	92†
5	Japan 5 p.c.	105
5	Mexican (Nat. R. Tehuantp c.) ..	98†
6	Do. Extrl. 1890	86½†

Foreign Stocks, &c. (*continued*):—

Last Div.	Name.	Price.
6	Mexican Extrl. 1893	93½
5	Do. Intrnl. Cons. Slvr.	34½
5	Do. Intern. Rd. Bds. 2d. Ser.	34¼
4	Nicaragua 1886...............	40½
3½	Norwegian, red. 1937, or earlier	100
3	Do. do. 1965, do.	100
3½	Do. 3½ p.c. Bnds.	103
1	Paraguay 1p.c. ris. 3p.c. 1886-96	14†
5	Russian, 1822, £ Strlg.	149½
3	Do. 1859	92
4	Do. (Nicolas Ry.) 1867-9 ..	103
3	Do. Transcauc. Ry. 1882 ..	92
4	Do. Con. R. R. Bd. Ser. I., 1889 (†	103½
4	Do. Do. II., 1889 (†	103½
4	Do. Do. III., 1891 (†	102¼
3½	Do. Bonds .... (†	100½
4	Do. Ln. (Dvinsk and Vitbsk)	102
6	Salvador 1889...............	72½
—	S. Domingo 4s. Unified: .. 1950	60
6	San Luis Potosi Stg. 1889	92½
5	San Paulo (Brzl.), Stg. 1888	91½
6	Santa Fé 1883-4...............	33
—	Do. Eng. Ass. Certs. Dep...	32
5	Do. 1888..................	43
—	Do. Eng. Ass. Certs. Dpsit..	43
5	Do. (W. Cnt. Col. Rly.) Mrt.	22
5	Do. & Reconq. Rly. Mort...	22
5	Spanish Quicksilvr Mort. 1870 ..	102†
3½	Swedish 1880	103
3	Do. 1888	99
3	Do. Conversion Loan 1894..	100
5	Trans. Gov. Loan Red...1903-42	105†
59/	Tucuman (Prov.) 1888..........	69
4	Turkish, Secd. on Egypt. Trib.	103½
3½	Turkish, Egpt. Trib., Ott. Bd., '94	98
4	Do. Priority 1890..........	91
1	Do. Convted Series, "A"..	65½
5	Do. Customs Ln. 1886......	96½
5	Uruguay Bonds 1896	53†
3	Venzula New Con. Debt 1881....	38

COUPONS PAYABLE ABROAD.

Last Div.	Name.	Price.
7	Argent. Nat. Cedla. Sries. "B".	32½
5	Austrian Ster. Rnts., ex 10fl., 1870	85†
5	Do. do. do.	86
5	Do. Paper do. 1870	85
5	Do. do. do.	85
4	Do. Gld Rentes 1876	102
2½	Belgian eXchange 25 fr.	92†
3	Do. do.	101
3½	Danish Int., 1887, Rd. 1896	97½
3½	Do. '87, Red. by pur. or draw. fr. Dec., 1900	98½
2½	Dutch Certs. ex 12 gldrs.	87†
3	Do. Bonds	99
3	Do. Insc. Stk........	99
3½	French Rentes	105½
3	Do. 1878, '81-4., Red.	101
3	German Imp. Ln. 1891..........	96½
3	Do. do. 1892-3	96½
3	Do. do. 1890-4	96†
5	Japan Cons. Ln., '92, 3, & 5, Red.	47½
4	Prussian Consols	102†
3	" Cons. Stg. Ln. 1891....	97
4	Rumanian Bds. 1890	—
4	Do. do. 1891	—
4	Utd. States, 1877, Red. 1907	116
4	Do. 1895, 30 yrs........	131½
3½	Do. Maschsetts Gl. 1935	113½
3½	Do. Gold Bonds 1923	110½
2	Virginia Cpn. Bds., 3 p.c. from July, 1901	70

BRITISH RAILWAYS.

ORD. SHARES AND STOCKS.

Last Div.	Name.	Price.
10	Barry, Ord.	288½
4	Do. Prefd.	129
6	Do. Defd.	158½
5½	Caledonian, Ord............	158
3	Do. Prefd.	101
—	Do. Defd. Ord., No. 1	4⅞
—	Cambrian, Ord............	6½
—	Do. Coast Cons.	6½
24/	Cardiff Ry. Pref. Ord.	118
3/	Central Lond. £10 Ord. Sh.	10†
-/9½	Do. do. £6 paid......	5½†
3½d.	Do. Pref. Half-Shares..	1½†
1/6	Do. Def. do..........	4½†
2	City and S. London	67
—	East London, Cons.	7
1½	Furness	70½
—	Glasgow and S. West. Pfd.	84
—	Do. do. Dfd.	66
—	Great Central, Ord.... 1894	42
32/o	Do. London Exten.....	78
3½	Great N. of Scotland......	118
4	Great Northern, Prefd.	123½
—	Do. Consolidated "A"	56
—	Do. do. "B"	195½
2	Highland	79
4	Isle of Wight, Prefd.	122½
3	Do. Defd.	86½
—	Lancs. Derbys. and E. Cst.	5
4½	L. Brighton and S. C. Ord.	190
37/11	Do. New 70 p.c. pd.	186†
6	Do. Prefd. Ord.	201
7/6	Do. Contgt. Rights Certs.	19
5½	Lond. and S. Western Ord.	232½
4	Do. Preferred	138
2½	Lond., Tilb., and Southend	134½
—	Mersey, £20 shares	1
—	Metropolitan, New Ord. ..	129
2½	Do. Surplus Lands	98
4	North Cornwall, 4 p.c. Pref.	106½
7/6	Do. Deferred	27½
7½	North London..............	228½
4	North Staffordshire	131

British Railways (*continued*):—

Last Div.	Name.	Price.
1/6	Plymouth, Devenport, and S. W. Junc. £10	9
3/	Port Talbot £10 Shares ..	9½†
9d.	Rhondda Swns. B. £10 Sh.	6½
11	Rhymney, Cons.	277½
4	Do. Prefd.	129
—	Do. Defd.	157½
1½	Scarboro', Bridlington Junc.	47½
3½	South Eastern, Ord........	156
6	Do. Pref.	198
3½	Taff Vale	84
25/	Vale of Glamorgan ...... (†	132½
2/8½	Waterloo & City £10 shares	12½

LEASED AT FIXED RENTALS.

Last Div.	Name.	Price.
4	Birkenhead	151
5.19.0	East Lincnshire..........	215
5½	Hamsmith. & City Ord. ..	201½
4½	Lond. and Blackwll.	167½
4½	Do. £10 4½ p. c. Pref...	167
56/6	Lond. & Green. Ord........	104
5	Do. 5 p. c. Pref.	178½
5	Nor. and Eastn. £50 Ord...	92
6	Do. ..	109
3½	N. Cornwall 3½ p. c. Stk...	128½
4½	Nott. & Granthm. R. & C...	150
3½	Portptk. & Wigtn. Guar. Stk.	126
9	Vict. Stn. & Pimlico Ord. (†	317½
4½	Do. 4½ p. c. Pref... (†	163½
4/	West Lond. £20 Ord. Shs.	14½
4⅛	Weymouth & Portld.......	162½

DEBENTURE STOCKS.

Last Div.	Name.	Price.
3	Barry, Cons.	110†
4	Brecon & Mrthyr, New A	127½
4	Do. New B	103
4	Caledonian	155
4	Cambrian "A"	134½
4	Do. "B"	129½
4	Do. "C"	126½
4	Do. "D"	108½
3	Cardiff Rly.	105†
4	City and S. Lond.	139
3½	Cleator & Working Junc. (†	118½
3	Devon & Som. "A"	105½
16/3	Do. "B" 4 p. c.	36
—	Do. "C" 4 p. c.	10
4	E. Lond. and Ch. 4 p. c. A	139†
5/-	Do. 2nd B	65½
—	Do. 3rd Ch. 4 p. c. ..	20½
—	Do. 4th do.	9½
3½	Do. 1st (3½ p. c.) .. (†	128½
2½	Do. 2½ p.c. (Whitech. Exn).	87†
4	Forth Bridge	147†
4	Furness	145
4	Glasgow and S. Western ..	154
5	Gt. Central	—
4½	Do.	160½
4	Gt. Eastern	151
4	Gt. N. of Scotland..........	148½
3	Gt. Northern	118
4	Gt. Western	156†
4½	Do.	162†
4½	Do.	172†
5	Do.	192†
2½	Do.	99†
4	Highland	143½
3	Hull and Barnsley ...... (†	107½
3	Do. 2nd (3-4 p. c). (†	124½
4	Isle of Wight .... (†	142½
3	Do. Cent. "A"..	90½†
4½	Do. "B" .... (†	113½
4	Do. "C"	82½†
3	Lancs. & Yorkshire .... (†	117
4	Lancs. Derbys. & E. Cst. (†	124½
4	Lpool St. Hlen's & S. Lancs.	126†
4½	Ldn. and Blackwall .... (†	158½
4	Ldn. and Greenwich .... (†	148½
4	Lond., Brighton, &c.	151†
4½	Do.	170†
4½	Lond., Chath., &c., Arb. (†	159½
4½	Do. "B" (†	156½
4	Do.	139†
4	Do. 1883....	139†
3	Do.	106†
3	Lond. & N. Western	120
3	Lond. & S. Westn. "A" ..	118†
3	Do. Consld.	118†
4	Lond., Til., & Southend ..	150†
—	Mersey, 5 p. c. (Act, 1866)	65
4	Metropolitan	150†
4½	Do. .... (†	164½
3½	Do. .... (†	129½
6	Met. District	208½
4	Do. .... (†	138½
3	Midland	118†
4½	Mid-Wales "A" ...... (†	135½
4	Neath & Brecon 1st	128†
4	Do. "A 1" ..	118
3	North British	114
3	Do. 1893	111½
3½	N. Cornwall, Launcstn., &c.	128½
3	North Eastern............	118

Debenture Stocks (*continued*):—

Last Div.	Name.	Price.
4½	North London..............	168½
3	N. Staffordshire	115†
4	Plym. Devpt. & S.W. Jn. (†	133½
4	Rhondda and Swan. Bay (†	130½
4	Rhymney	147†
4	South-Eastern	151†
5	Do.	191†
3½	Do.	130†
3	Do.	115†
3	Taff Vale	112
4	Tottenham & For. Gate ..	146†
3	Vale of Glamorgan .... (†	106½
3	West Highld. (Gtd. by N.B.)	111½
4	Wrexham, Mold, &c. "A"	115½
4	Do. "B"	106½
4	Do. "C"	97½

GUARANTEED SHARES AND STOCKS.

Last Div.	Name.	Price.
4	Caledonian	152½
4	Do.	152
4	Forth Bridge	146†
4	Furness 1881	138
4	Glasgow & S. Western	15[illegible]
4	Do. St. Enoch, Rent	150½
6	Gt. Central	202½
4½	Do. 1st Pref.........	155½
3½	Do. Pref.	108
5	Do. Irred. S.Y. Rent	167½
4½	Do. do.	144½
4	Gt. Eastern, Rent	148
5	Do. Metropolitan..	182½
4	Do.	150
4	Gt. N. of Scotland........	141
4	Gt. Northern	152
5	Gt. Western, Rent........	191
5	Do. Cons.	191
4	Lancs. & Yorkshire	152
5	L., Brighton & S. C........	188
3½	L., Chat. & D. (Shrtlds.) (†	110½
4	L. & North Western	153
4	L. & South Western.. 1881	152
4½	Met. District, Ealing Rent	154
4½	Do. Fulham Rent	152
4	Do. Midland Rent	145
4	Do. Mid. & Dist. Guar.	136½
4	Midland, Rent............	153
4	Do. Cons.	153
3	Mid. & G. N. Jt., "A" Rnt (†	110½
3	N. British, Lien	111
4	Do. Cons. Pref. No. 1	147
3	N. Cornwall, Wadebrge. Gu.	108
4	N. Eastern	152
5	N. Staff. Trent & M. £20 Shs.	37½
3½	Nott. Suburban Ord.	126½
20/6	S. E. Perp. Ann.	36½†
4½	Do. 4½ p.c...........	166†
3½	S. Yorks. Junc. Ord. .. (†	118½
4½	W. Cornwall (G. W., Br., Ex., & S. Dev. Joint Rent	168½
3	W. Highl. Ord. Stk. (Gua., N.B.)..................	109½

PREFERENCE SHARES AND STOCKS.

DIVIDENDS CONTINGENT ON PROFIT OF YEAR.

Last Div.	Name.	Price.
5	Barry (First)	171½
4	Do. Consolidated......	140½
4	Caledonian Cons., No. 1 ..	149
4	Do. do. No. 2 ..	147
5	Do. do. 1878	183½
4	Do. Pref. 1884	146
4	Do. do. 1887 (Conv.)	155
—	Cambrian, No. 1 4 p.c. Pref.	72½
—	Do. No. 2 do.	37½
—	Do. No. 3 do.	19
—	Do. No. 4 do.	10
5	City & S. Lond. £10 shares	15½
—	Do. New	14
4	Furness, Cons. 1881	133½
4	Do. ......"A" 1881	131½
4	Do. ......"B" 1883	129½
4	Glasgow & S. Western....	147
4	Do. No. 2....	147
4	Do. 1888	146
4	Do. 1891	146
5	Gt. Central	168
4	Do.	136½
5	Do. Conv..... 1872	156½
5	Do. do. 1874	156½
5	Do. do. 1876	156½
5	Do. do. 1879	155½
5	Do. do. 1881	155½
4	Do. 1889	118½
4	Do. 1891	115½
5	Do. 1894	116
4	Gt. Eastern, Cons........	148
4	Do. 1886	146
4	Do. 1881	145½
4	Do. 1884	145
4	Do. 1887	145

Preference Shares, &c. (*continued*):—

Last Div.	Name.	Price.
4	Gt. Eastern, Cons..... 1888	144½
3½	Do. 1890	126½
3½	Do. 1891	125½
—	Do. (Int. fr. Jan '99) 1893	117½
4	Gt. North Scotland "A"..	136½
4	Do. "B"..	135½
4	Gt. Northern, Cons.	149
3	Do. 1896	109½
5	Gt. Western Cons........	189
—	Hull & Barnsley Red. at 115	110
4	Isle of Wight	135½
3	Lancs. & Yorkshire, Cons.	112
2/2½	Lanc. Drby & E.C. 5 p.c. £10	11
—	Do. 5 p.c. 2nd £10	10
5	Lond., Bright., &c., Cons.	187½
5	Do. 2nd Cons.	186½
4½	Lond., Chat. & Dov. Arbitr.	135
25/o	Do. 2nd Pref. 4½ p.c.	83
4	Lond. & N. Western......	152
4	Lond. & S. Western.. 1881	151
4	Do. 1884	150
3½	Do.	131
4	Lond., Tilbury & Southend	147
4	Do. Cons., 1887	146
4	Do 1891	146
—	Mersey, 5 p.c. Perp.	9½
4	Metropolitan, Perp.	148
4	Do. 1882	145½
4	Do. Irred.	145½
4	Do. 1887	145½
4	Do. New........	144½
4½	Do.	148½
3½	Do.	126½
3	Do. Guar.	104½
4	Metrop. Dist. Exten. 5 p.c.	111
4	Midland, Cons. Perpetual..	151
4	N. British Cons., No. 2 ..	142
4½	Do. Edin. & Glasgow	156½
5	Do. 1865	173½
5	Do. Conv. 1874	173½
4½	Do. 1875	156
4½	Do. Conv. 1875	156½
5	Do. do. 1879	172½
4	Do. do. 1884	139
4	Do. do. 1888	139
4	Do. do. 1890	139
4	Do. do. 1892	139
4	N. Eastern	151
4½	N. Lond., Cons....... 1866	179½
4½	Do. 2nd Cons. .. 1875	164½
3	N. Staffordshire	110
4½	Plym. Devpt. & S. W. Junc.	150½
9½d.	Port Talbot, &c., 4 p.c. £10 Shares, 4 paid	5
5/	Rhondda & Swansea Bay, 5 p.c. £10 Shares	13½
4	Rhymney, Cons.	144
4½	S. Eastern, Cons.	166†
5	Do. do. ...... (†	183½
4	Do. Vested Cos'.....	145
4	Do. 1891	144†
3½	Do. 1893	127
2	Do. 3 p.c. after July 1900	105
4	Taff Vale	143

INDIAN RAILWAYS.

Last Div.	Name.	Paid.	Price.
3½	Assam Bengal, Ld., (3½ p.c. till June 30, then 3 p.c.)	100	103†
4/	Barsi Light, Ld., £10 Shs.	10	10½
6	Bengal and N. West., Ld.	100	146½
4/	Do. £10 Shares	10	14
3/6	Do. 3½ p.c. Cum. Pf. Shs.	10	10½
8½d.	Do.	4	4½
2/3½	Bengal Central, Ld., £10 (3½ p.c. + ⅓th net earn)	5	5½
3	Bengal Dooars, Ld.	100	118
4	Bengal Nagpr., Lim. (gua. 4 p.c. + 4th sp. pfts.) ..	100	115
7½	Bombay, Baroda, and C. I. (gua. 5 p.c.)	100	223
36/1	Burma, Ld. (gua. 2½ p.c., and ½ p.c. add. till 1901)	100	105½
7'97d.	Do. £10 Shares	2½	2½
4	Delhi Umb. Kalka, Ld., Gua. 3½ p.c. + net earn.	100	119
4	Do. Deb. Stk., 1890 (1916)	100	113
9/10	Estn. Bengal, "A" An. 1957	—	25
9/	Do. "B" 1957	—	31
4	Do. Gua. Deb. Stock ..	100	144½
9/7½	East Ind. Ann. "A" (1953)	—	27
8/4½	Do. "C"	—	30
8/11½	Do. "B"	—	32
6⅟₁₀	Do. Def. Ann. Cap. (gua. 4 p.c. + ⅕th sp. pfts.)	—	148
115/9	East Ind. Def. Ann. "D"	—	154
4½	East Ind. Irred. Stock ..	100	166½
5	Gt. Indian Penin., Gua. 5 p.c. + ½ surplus profits..	100	174†
4	Do. Irred. 4 p.c. Deb. St.	100	146½
4	Indian Mid., Ld. (gua. 4 p.c. + ⅕th surplus pfts.)	100	115†
5	Madras Guar. + ½ sp. pfts.	100	169
4½	Do. do.	100	159
4½	Do. do.	100	149
4	Nilgiri, Ld., 1st Deb. Stk.	100	97†
4	Oude & Rohil. Db. Stk. Rd.	100	100
5⅟₁₀	Rohil. and Kumaon, Ld.	100	132
9/11	Scinde, Punj., and Delhi, "A" Ann., 1958	—	26
9/1	Do. "B" do. ..	—	31

Indian Railways (*continued*):—

Last Div.	Name.	Paid.	Price.
4/	South Behar, Ld., £10 shs.	10	10†
3½	Do. Deb. Stk. Red.	100	102
4½	South Ind., Gu. Deb. Stk.	100	166½
5	South Indian, Ld. (gua. 3 p.c., and ½ spls. profits)	100	120½
5	Sthn. Mahratta, Ld. (3½ p.c. & ¼th net earnings)	100	123
4	Do. Deb. Stk. Red.	100	124
3½	Southern Punjab, Ld.	100	115
3½	Do. Deb. Stk. Red.	—	107
5	Nizam's Gua. State, Ld. (†	100	114½
4	Do. Mort. Deb., 1936	100	109†
4	Do. do. Reg.	100	108†
17/3¼	Nizam's Gua. State, Ld., 3½ p.c. Mt. Deb. bearer	—	94½†
17/3¼	Do. Reg. do. ..	—	93½†
5	W. of India Porigese., Ld.	100	73½
5	Do. Deb. Stk., Red	100	100

RAILWAYS.—BRITISH POSSESSIONS.

Last Div.	Name.	Paid.	Close.
5	Atlantic & N.W. Gua. 1 Mt. Bds., 1937	100	126†
5/3	Buff. & L. Huron Ord. Sh.	10	13½
5½	Do. 1st Mt. Perp. Bds. 1879	100	142½
5½	Do. 2nd Mt. Perp. Bds.	100	142½
—	Calgary & Edmon. 6 p.c. 1st Mt. Stg. Bds. Red..	100	67
5	Canada Cent. 1st Mt. Bds. Red.	100	105
4	Can. Pacific Pref. Stk.....	100	100
5	Do. Strl. 1st Mt. Deb. Bds. 1915	100	119†
3½	Do. Ld. Grnt. Bds., 1938..	100	109†
3½	Do. Ld. Grnt. Ins. Stk. ..	100	109†
4	Do. Perp. Cons. Deb. Stk.	100	115
5	Do. Algoma Bch. 1st Mt. Bds., 1937	100	119†
2	Demerara, Original Stock	100	49
7	Do. Perp. Pref. Stk.......	100	157½
9½d.	Do. 4 p.c. Cum. Ext. Pref. £10 Shs.	4	5
—	Dominion Atlntc. Ord. Stk.	100	8½
25/	Do. 5 p.c. Pref. Stk.....	100	101
4	Do. 1st. Deb. Stk.......	100	110
4	Do. 2nd do. Red.	100	99†
—	EmuBay&Mt.Bischoff,Ld.	5	4½
4½	Do. Irred. Deb. Stk....	100	98†
nil.	Gd. Trunk of Canada, Stk.	100	7½
6	Do. 2nd. Equip. Mt. Bds.	100	130½
5	Do. Perp. Deb. Stk.......	100	141†
5	Do. Gt. Westn. Deb. Stk.	100	136
5	Do. Nthn. of Can. 1st Mt. Bds., 1902	100	103†
4	Do. do. Deb. Stk	100	102
5	Do. G. T. Geor. Bay & L. Erie 1 Mt., 1903	100	105
5	Do. Mid. of Can. Stl. 1st Mt. (Mid. Sec.) 1908	100	108
5	Do.do.Cons.1 Mt.Bds. 1912	100	107†
5	Do. Mont. & Champ. 1 Mt. Bds., 1902	100	102†
/2	Do. Welln., Grey & Brce. 7 p.c. Bds. 1 Mt.	100	108
4	Jamaica 1st Mtg. Bds. Red.	—	104
6	Manitoba & N. W., 6 p.c. 1st Mt. Bds., Red	100	41½
—	Do. Ldn. Bdhldrs. Certs.	—	43
5	Manitoba S. W. Col. 1 Mt. Bd., 1934 $1,000 price %	—	116
—	Mid. of W. Aust. Ld. 6 p.c. 1 Mt. Dbs., Red.	100	25
4	Do. Deb. Bds., Red.	100	103†
4	Nakusp & Slocan Bds., 1918	100	106†
3	Natal Zululand Ld. Debs.,	100	79½
5	N. Brunswick 1st Mt. Stg. Bds., 1934	100	121
4	Do. Perp. Cons. Deb. Stk.	100	113
—	N. Zealand Mid., Ld., 5 p.c 1st Mt. Debs...........	100	35
6	Ontario & Queb. Cap. Stk.	$100	153½
5	Do. Perm. Deb. Stk......	100	147½
—	Qu'Appelle, L. Lake & Sask. 6p.c. 1 Mt. Bds. Red.	100	38½
5	Queb. & L. S. John, 1st Mt. Bds., 1909	100	18½
5	Quebec Cent., Prior Ln. Bds., 1908	100	109
1½	Do. 5 p.c. Inc. Bds.	100	37
4	St. Lawr. & Ott. Stl. 1st Mt.	100	112
4	Shuswap & Okan., 1st Mt. Deb. Bds., 1915	100	70½†
5	Temiscouata, 5 p.c. Stl. 1st Deb. Bds., Red.........	100	9½†
5	Do. (S. Franc. Brch.) 5 p.c. Stl. 1 Mt. Db. Bds., 1920	100	12½
4	Toronto, Grey & B. 1st Mt.	100	110†
1/2½	Well. & Mana. £5 Shs. ..	1	1
5	Do. Debs., 1908	100	110
5	Do. 2nd Debs., 1908	100	109
5	Do. 3rd do., 1908	100	108
6	Atlan. & St. Law. Shs., 6 p.c.	100	167
5	Gd. Trunk Mt. Bds., 1934	100	107½
5	Michigan Air Line, 5 p.c. 1st Mt. Bds., 1902......	100	102
4	Minneap., S. P. & Slt. Ste. Mar, 1st Mt. Bds., 1938	$1000	99

AMERICAN RAILROAD STOCKS AND SHARES.

Last Div.	Name.	Paid.	Price.
6/	Alab. Gt. Sthn. A 6 p.c. Pref.	10l.	9†
3/	Do. do "B" Ord. ..	10l.	2
—	Alabma. N. Orl.-Tex. &c., "A" Pref.	10l.	½
—	Do. "B" Def.	10l.	¼
4½	Atlant. First Lsd. Ls. Rtl. Trust..................	Stk.	100
$2	Baltimore & Ohio Com. ..	$100	14
—	Baltimore Ohio S.W. Pref.	$100	6½
—	Chesap. & Ohio Com.	$100	23
—	Chic. Gt. West. 5 p.c. Pref. Stock "A"	$100	35½
—	Do. do. Scrip. In.......	—	32½
8/3	Do. 4 p.c. Deb. Stk.......	$100	70½
4	Do. Interest in Scrip	$100	67½
$4	Chic. Junc. Rl. & Un. Stk. Yds. Com.	$100	113½
6/2	Do. 6 p.c. Cum. Pref.	$100	112½
$3½	Chic. Mil. & St. P. Pref...	$100	146
7	Cleve. & Pittsburgh......	$50	87
$1½	Clev., Cincin., Chic., & St. Louis Com.	$100	—
—	Erie 4 p.c. Non-Cum. 1st Pf.	—	39
—	Do. 4 p.c. do. 2nd Pf.	—	20
—	Gt. Northern Pref.	$100	135
$2½	Illinois Cen. Lsd. Lines ..	$100	94
—	Kansas City, Pitts & G. ..	$100	26
$3	L. Shore & Mich. Sth. C. (†	$100	176½
—	Mex. Cen. Ltd. Com.	$100	6
—	Miss. Kan. & Tex. Pref...	$100	37½
—	N.Y., Pen. & O. 1st Mt. Tst. Ltd., Ord.	—	45½
4	Do. 1st Mort. Deb. Stk. ..	$100	93½
8	North Pennsylvania	$50	—
—	Northn. Pacific, Com.....	$100	21½
1½	Pitts. F. Wayne & Chic...	$100	175
—	Reading 1st Pref.	$50	26½
—	Do. 2nd Pref.	$50	14
—	S. Louis & S. Fran. Com.	$100	7½
—	Do. 2nd Pref.	$100	27
6	St. Louis Bridge 1st Pref...	$100	107
3	Do. 2nd Pref.	$100	50
6	Tunnel Rail. of St. Louis	$100	107
$1½	St. Paul, Min. and Man...	$100	127½
—	Southern, Com.	$100	9½
—	Wabash, Common........	$100	7½

AMERICAN RAILROAD BONDS. CURRENCY.

Last Div.	Name.		Price.
7	Albany & Susq. 1 Con. Mrt.	1906	122½
7	Allegheny Val. 1 Mt.......	1910	127½
5	Burling., Cedar Rap. & N. 1 Mt.	1906	100½
5	Canada Southern 1 Mt....	1908	108
5	Chic. & N. West. Sk. Fd. Db.	1933	117½
5	Do. Deb. Coupon	1921	112½
6	Chicago & Tomah	1905	112½
5	Chic. Burl. & Q. Skge. Fd.	1901	102½
4	Do. Nebraska Ext.......	—	100
6	Chic., Mil., & S. Pl., 1 Mt. S.W. Div...............	1909	117½
7	Do. (S. Paul Div.) 1 Mt.	1902	132½
5	Do. (La Cross & D.	1919	112½
7	Do. 1 Mt. (Hast. & Dak.)	1910	132
5	Do. Chic. & Mis. Riv. 1 Mt.	1926	112½
5	Chic., Rock Is. and Pac. 1 Mt. Ext.	1934	106½
6	Det., G. Haven & Mil. Equip	1918	110
6	Do. do. Cons. Mt.	1918	106½
6	Ill. Cent., 1 Mt., Chic. & S.	1898	102½
7	Indianap. & Vin., 1 Mt. ..	1908	125
6	Do. do. 2 Mt. ..	1900	104½
6	Lehigh Val., Cons. Mt.....	1923	112½
—	Mexic. Cent., Ln. 2 Cons. Inc.	—	7
7	N.Y. Cent. & H.R. Mt. Bonds	1903	119½
5	Do. Deb.	1904	112
6	Penns. Cons. S. F M.	1905	115
4	West Shore, 1 Mt.	2361	110

DITTO—GOLD.

Last Div.	Name.		Price.
6	Alabama Gt. Sthn. 1 Mt. ..	1908	107½
5	Do. Mid. 1	1928	94½
4	Allegheny Val. Gen. Mt. ..	1942	108½
4	Atch., Top., & S. Fé Gn. Mt.	1995	92½
3	Do. Adj. Mt.............	1995	60
5	Do. Equipt. Tmst.	—	103†
5	Atlantic & Dan. 1 Mt......	1950	92
5	Baltimore & Ohio..........	1925	80
5	Do. Speyer's Tst. Recpts.	1925	80
5	Do. Cons. Mt.	1988	97½
4½	Do. 4½ p.c. 1 Mt. Term.	1934	86
4½	Do. Brown Shipley's Dep. Cts.	—	84
5	Balt. Belt 5 p.c. 1 Mort.....	1990	—
4½	Balt. & Ohio S.W. 1 Mt. ..	1990	101
4½	Do. 4½ p.c. 1 Cons. Mt. 1893	1993	77½
4½	Do. Inc. Mt. 5 p.c. Cl. A	—	13
—	Do. do. Cl. B	—	19
5	Balt. & Ohio S.W. Term 5 p.c.	1942	9
6	Balt. & Pтmac (Mn. L.) 1 Mt.	1911	124½
6	Do. do. (Tunnel) 1 Mt.	1911	123
4	Beech Creek 1 Mt.	1936	107
5	Do 2 Mort.	1936	116
4	Carthage & Adiron. 1 Mt...	1981	107½

American Railroad Bonds—Gold (*continued*):—

Last Div.	Name.	Price.
5	Cent. of Georgia 1 Mort. .. 1945	119
5	Do. Cons. Mt. 1945	92½
5	Cent. of N. Jrsy. Gn. Mt... 1987	113
6	Central Pacific, 1 Mort. 1898	102½
—	Do. Speyer's Certs....... —	103½
5	Do. Land Grant 1900	102
5	Chesap. & Ohio 1st Cons. Mt. 1939	117
4½	Do. Gen. Mt............. 1992	85
6	Chic. & W. Ind. Gen. Mt. Skg. Fd. 1932	122
5	Chic. Mil. & St. Pl. (Chic. & L. Sup.) 1 Mt. 1921	115
5	Do. Chic. & Pac. W. 1921	117
5	Do. Wisc. & Minn. 1 Mt. 1921	115
5	Do. Terminal Mt. 1914	114½
4	Do. General Mt. 1989	107
5	Chic. St. L. & N. Orleans.. 1951	122½
4	Do. 1 Mort. (Memphis) .. 1951	102½
4	Clevel., Cin., Chic. & St. L., 1 Mt. (Cairo) 1939	90
4	Do. 1 Mt. (Cinc., Wab., & Mich.) 1991	90
4	Do. 1 Col. Tst. Mt. (S. Louis) 1990	97
4	Do. General Mt. 1993	82
4½	Clevel. & Mar. Mt. 1935	109
4½	Clevel. & Pittsburgh 1942	120½
4½	Do. Series B. 1942	119½
6	Colorado Mid. 1 Mt. 1936	66
—	Do. Bdhrs.' Comm. Certs. —	65
4	Dnvr. & R. Gde. 1 Cons. Mt. 1936	92
5	Do. Imp. Mort. 1928	89
4	Detroit & Mack. 1 Lien 1995	90
5	E. Tennes., Virg., & Grgia. Cons. Mt. 1956	112½
5	Elmira, Cort., & Nthn. Mt. 1914	97
4	Erie 1 Cons. Mt. Pr. Ln. .. 1996	93
3	Do. Gen. Lien 1996	73
6	Galvest., Harrish., &c., 1 Mt.	109
5	Georgia, Car. & N. 1 Mt. .. 1929	90†
4½	Gd. Rpds. & Inda. Ex. 1 Mt. 1941	110
5	Do. 1 Mt. (Muskegon) .. 1926	39½
3½	Illinois Cent. 1 Mt. 1951	103
4	Do. 1952	106
4	Do. Cairo Bdge. .. 1950	101
4	Do. 1953	104
4	Do. General Mort. .. 1904	100
—	Kans. City, Pitts. & G. 1 M. 1923	82
3½	L. Shore & Mich. Southern 1997	107
4½	Lehigh Val. N.Y. 1 Mt..... 1940	104
5	Lehigh Val. Term. 1 Mt. .. 1941	112½
5	Long Island 1931	114
5	Do. Deb. 1934	101
5	Do. (N. Shore Bch.) 1 Cons. Mt. 1932	96
6	Louisville & Nash. G. Mt .. 1930	119
6	Do. 2 Mt. Sk. Fd. (S. & N. Alabama........ 1910	108
6	Do. 1 Mt. N. Orl. & Mis. 1930	122
5	Do. 1 Mt. Coll. Tst. ... 1931	104½
4	Do. Unified 1940	88
4½	Do. Mobile & Montgy. 1 Mt. 1945	107½
4	Manhattan Cons. Mt. 1990	98
4	Mexican Cent. Cons. Mt. .. 1911	68†
—	Do. 1 Cons. Inc, ...	17
6	Mexican Nat. 1 Mt.......... 1927	106
3	Do. 2 Mt. 6 p.c. Inc. A 1917	57
—	Do. do. B.. 1917	—
3	Do. Matheson's Certs.	—
3	Michig. Cnt. (Battle Ck. & S.) 1 Mt. 1989	84
6	Minneap. & S. L. 1 Mt. Pacific Ext. 1921	120½
5	Do. 1 Consold. 1934	108½
4	Minne., Slt. S. M. & A. 1 Mt. 1926	100†
5	Minneapolis Westn. 1 Mt... 1911	105
4	Miss. Kans. & Tex. 1 Mt... 1990	89
4	Do. 2 do. 1990	65
4	Mobile & Birm. Mt. Inc.... 1945	38
5	Do. P. Lien 1945	88
4	Mohawk & Mal. 1 Mt....... 1991	108
5	Montana Cent. 1 Mt....... 1937	105
5	Nashv., Chattan., & S. L. 1 Cons. Mt............... 1928	104½
5	Nash., Flor., & Shff. Mt... 1937	92
4	N. Y. & Putnam 1 Cons. Mt. 1993	109
5	N. Y., Brooklyn, & Man. B. 1 Cons. Mt............ 1935	109
4	N. Y. Cent. & Hud. R. Deb. Certs. 1890 1905	106
4	Do. Ext. Debt. Certs.... 1905	106
7	N. Y., L. Erie, & W. 1 Cons. Mt. (Erie) 1920	143½
7	Do. 1 Con. Mt. Fd. Coup. 1920	142½
5	N. Y., Onto., & W. Cons. 1 Mt..................... 1939	110
4	Do. 4 p.c. Refund. Mt.. 1992	99
5	N. Y. & Rockaway B. 1 Mt. 1927	104½
6	Norfolk & West. Gn. Mt.... 1931	128
6	Do. Imp. & Ext....... 1934	120
4	Do. 1 Cons. Mt. ...... —	81
6	N. Pacific Gn. 1 Mt. Ld. Gt. 1921	120
4	Do. P. Ln. Rl. & Ld. Gt. —	98
3	Do. Gn. Ln. Rl. & Ld. Gt. —	60½
5	Oregon & Calif. 1 Mt....... 1927	76
5	Oregon Rl. & Nav. Col. Tst. —	—
5	Oreg. Sh. Line & Utah Col. Trst. 5 p.c. G. Bonds 1919	—
6	Panama Skg. Fd. Subsidy.. 1910	105½
4½	Pennsylvania Rlrd. 1913	115
4	Do. Equip. Tst. Ser. A.. 1914	105
4	Do. Cons. Mt............ 1943	115
4½	Penna. Company 1st Mort. 1921	115
5	Perkiomen 1 Mrt., 2nd ser.. 1918	90
4½	{ Pitts., C., C., & St. Ls. Con. Mt. G. B., Ser. A } 1940-2	115
4	Do. Cons. Mort., Ser. D.. 1945	105
6	Pittsbgh., Cle., & Toledo .. 1922	102½
4	Reading, Phil., & R. Genl. 1997	86
5	Richmond & Dan. Equip. .. 1909	99½
5	Rio Grande Junc. 1st Mort. 1939	90
4	Rio Grande West 1st Tst. Mt. 1939	83
6	St. Joseph & Gd. Island .. 1925	—
7	S. Louis Bridge 1st Mort. .. 1925	135½

American Railroad Bonds (*continued*):

Last Div.	Name.	Price.
5	S. Louis Mchts. Bdge. Term. 1st Mort.................. 1930	104½
4	S. Louis S. West 1st Mort.. 1989	75½
—	Do. 4 p.c. 2nd Mort. Inc. 1989	28½
—	S. Louis Term. Cupples Sta. & Prop. 1st. Mrt. 4½ p.c. 1908-17	100
4½	St. Paul, Minn., & Manit. 1933	109
6	Do. do. 1933	127
6	Shamokin, Sunbury, &c. 2 Mt. 1925	107
5	S. & N. Alabama Cons. Mt. 1936	95½
5	Southern 1 Cons. Coup. 1994	95
4	Do. E. Tennes Reorg. Lien .. 1938	86½
6	S. Pacific of Cal. 1 Mt... 1905-12	111
4½	Trml. Assn. of S. Louis 1 Mt. 1939	113½
5	Do. 1 Cons. Mt............ 1944	110
5	Texas & Pac. 1 Mt.......... 2000	100
—	Do. 5 p.c. 2 Mt. Income 2000	30
5	Toledo & Ohio Cent. 1 Mt. West. Div. 1935	103½
4½	Toledo., Walbon., Val., & Ohio 1 Mt. 1931-3	102½
6	Union Pacific 1 Mt. 1896-9	101½
5	Do. Coll. Tverst....	—
5	Union Pac., Linc., & Color. 1 Mt..................... 1918	—
4	United N. Jersey Gen. Mt... 1944	117½
6	Vicksbrg., Shrevept., & Pac. Pr. Ln. Mt. 1915	102½
5	Wabash 1 Mt. 1939	110
4	Wn. Pennsylvania Mt. 1928	108½
5	W. Virga. & Pittsbg. 1 Mt.. 1990	77½
5	Wheeling & L. Erie 1 Mt. (Wheelg. Div.) 5 p.c. 1928	75
5	Do. Extd. Imp. Mt. 1930	—
—	Do. do. Brown Shipley's Cts..	—
5	Willmar & Sioux Falls 1 Mt. 1938	110

STERLING.

Last Div.	Name.	Price.
6	Alabama Gt. Sthn. Deb..... 1906	105½
5	Do. Gen. Mort. .. 1907-8	98
5	Alabama, N. Orl., Tex. & Pac. 5 p.c. "A" Dbs... 1910-40	98
50/	Do. do. "B" do. 1910-40	46
—	Do. do. "C" do.	20
6-7	Allegheny Valley 1910	133½
4	Atlantic 1st Leased Line Perp...	100
6	Baltimore and Ohio 1902	107
6	Do. do. 1910	114
5	Do. do. 1877.........	90
—	Do. Morgan's Certs. ..	88½
4½	Do. do. 1933	76
6	Chicago & Alton Cons. Mt. 1903	111†
5	Chic. St. Paul & Kan. City Priority	105†
6	Eastn. of Massachusetts 1906	117½
5	Illinois Cent. Skg. Fd.	104
5	Do. 1905	108
3½	Do. 1950	100½
4	Do. 1 Mt. 1951	114
3	Do. 1 Mt. 1951	94
6	Louisville & Nash., M. C. & L. Div., 1 Mt. 1902	107
7	Do. 1 Mt. (Memphis & O.) 1901	111
47/4	Mexican Nat. "A" Certs. 5 p.c. Non. cum.	47
—	Do. "B" Certs.	10
6	N.Y. & Canada 1 Mt........ 1904	110½
6	N. York Cent. & H.R. Mort. 1903	112†
4½	N. York, Penna., & Ohio Pr. Ln. Extd. 1935	—
5	Do. Equip. Tst.	102
5	Do. 5 p.c. Equip. Tst. (1890)	102
6	Nrthn. Cent. Cons. Gen. Mt.	105†
6	Pennsylvania Gen. Mt. 1910	129†
6	Do. Cons. Skg. Fd. Mt. 1905	120†
3½	Do. Cons. Mt. 1945	106†
6	Phil. & Erie Cons. Mort.. 1920 (†	128½
6	Phil. & Reading Gen. Cons. Mort. 1911	128½
6	Do. Improvt. Mt. ...... —	—
6	Pittsbg. & Connells. Cons. 1926	108
—	Do. Morgan's Certs.	105½
4	St. Paul., Min., & Manitoba (Pac. Extn.) 1940	99†
6	S. & N. Alabama 1903	107½
6	Union Pacific, Omaha Bridge [illegible]	—
6	Un. N. Jersey & C. Gen. Mt. 1901	111

FOREIGN RAILWAYS.

Last Div.	Name.	Paid.	Price.
4/	Alagoas, Ltd., Shs.	20	6
5	Do. Deb. Stk., Red. ..	100	[illegible]
6	Antofagasta, Ltd., Stk. ..	100	77†
4	Do. Perp. Deb. Stk. ..	100	[illegible]
—	Arauco, Ld., Ord. Shs. ..	20	[illegible]
—	Do. 10 p.c. Cum. Pref.	10	[illegible]
20/	Argentine Gt. W., Ld.,	20	[illegible]
20/	Do. 5 p.c. Cum. Pref. Shs.	20	[illegible]
4	Do. 1 Deb. Stk. .... (†	100	103½
6/0/0	Do. 6 p.c. 2 Db. Stk. Assg.	100	—
6/0/0	Do. do. Non-Assg.	100	—
1/0/0	Argentine N.E., Ltd., 6 p.c. Cum. Pref. Stk. ..	100	[illegible]
—	Do. 5 p.c. Deb. Stk., Red.	100	30
2/	Arica and Tacna Shs. ..	20	[illegible]
10/	Bahia & San Fcisco., Ld.,	20	[illegible]
6/	Do. Timbo. Bch. Shs.	20	6
12/	Bahia, Blanca, & N.W. Ln. Prf. Cum. 6 p.c. ..	100	[illegible]
4	Do. 4 p.c. 1 Deb. Stk., Red.	100	[illegible]
6	Barranquilla R. & P., Ld., 6 p.c. 1 Deb. Stk., Red.	100	95†

Foreign Railways (*continued*):—

Last Div.	NAME.	Paid.	Price.
3/	Bilbao Riv. & Cantabn., Ltd., Ord.	3	5¾
—	Bolivar, Ltd., Shs.	10	1¾
6	Do. 6 p.c. Deb. Stk.	100	99½
—	Brazil Gt. Southn. Ltd., 7 p.c. Cum. Pref.	20	1½
6	Do. Perm. Deb. Stk	100	50
6½	B. Ayres Gt. Southn., Ld., Ord. Stk.	100	149½
5	Do. Pref. Stk.	100	139
4	Do. Deb. Stk.	100	118†
30/	B. Ayres & Ensen. Port., Ltd., Ord. Stk.	100	44
5	Do. Cum. 1 Pref. Stk.	100	108
6/0/0	Do. 6p.c.Con. Pref.Stk.	100	92
4	Do. Deb. Stk., Irred.	100	105†
9⅛	B. Ayres Northern, Ltd., Ord. Stk.	100	255½
12	Do. Pref. Stk.	100	315
6	Do. 5 p.c. Mt. Deb. Stk., Red.	100	112†
3/15/c	B. Ayres & Pac., Ld., 7 p.c. 1 Pref. Stk. (Cum.)	100	103
4	Do. 1 Deb. Stk.	100	102
5/5/0	Do. 4½ p.c. 2 Deb. Stk.	100	91
1	B Ayres & Rosario, Ltd., Ord. Stk.	100	76
—	Do. New, £20 Shs.	20	21¾
7/	Do. 7 p.c. Pref. Shs.	10	17¾
7/	Do. Sunchales Ext.	10	15
4	Do. Deb. Stk., Red.	100	109
12/	B. Ayres & Val. Trans., Ltd., 7 p.c. Cum. Pref.	20	6¾
—	Do. 4 p.c. "A" Deb. Stk., Red.	100	72½†
—	Do. 6 p.c. "B" Deb. Stk., Red.	100	45
6/	B. Ayres Westn. Ld. Ord.	10	11¾
3/	Do. Def. Shs	10	7¾
5	Do. 5 p.c. Pref.	10	13¼
4	Do. Deb. Stk	100	112†
6	Cent. Arg. Deb. Sk. Rd. [†	100	163½
4	Do. Deb. Stk. Rd	100	112†
6	Cent. Bahia L. Ord. Stk.	100	47½
6	Do. Deb. Stk., 1934	100	70
5	Do. Deb. Stk., 1937	100	61½
4/6	Cent. Uguy. East. Ext. L. Shs	10	5
5	Do. Perm. Stk.	100	108†
3/	Do. Nthn. Ext. L. Sh.	10	4
5	Do. Perm. Deb. Stk	100	101†
3	Do. of Montev. Ltd., Ord. Stk	100	81
6	Do. Perm. Deb. Stk	100	140
8/	Conde d'Eu, Ltd. Ord.	20	7
—	Cordba & Rosar., Ltd., 6 p.c. Pref. Shs.	100	47
4	Do. 1 Deb. Stk	100	96½
75/	Do. 6 p.c. Deb. Stk	100	90
—	Cordba Cent., Ltd., 5 p.c. Cu. 1 Pref. Stk	100	91
—	Do. 5 p.c. Non-Cum. 2 Pref. Stk	100	52½
5	Do. Deb. Stk	100	123
—	Costa Rica, Ltd., Shs.	10	4½
8/	Dna. Thrsa. Chris., Ltd., 7 p.c. Pref. Shs.	20	4†
20/	E. Argentine, Ltd	100	48
6	Do. Deb. Stk	100	106
—	Egyptn. Dltn. Lgt. Rys., Ltd., £10 Pref. Shs.	6	6
—	Entre Rios, L., Ord. Shs.	5	¾
—	Do. Cu. 5 p.c. Pref.	5	3
6/	Gt. Westn. Brazil, Ltd.,	20	12
6	Do. Perm. Deb. Stk	100	97½
6	Do. Extn. Deb. Stk	100	84½
—	Int.-Oceanic Mex., Ltd., 7 p.c. Pref.	10	1⅝
4	Do. Deb. Stk	100	82
42/6	Do. 7 p.c. "A" Deb. Sk.	100	52
—	Do. 7 p.c. "B" Deb. Sk.	100	25
5/	La Guaira & Carac.	10	7†
5	Do. 5 p.c. Deb. Sk. Red.	100	102
8/4	Lembg.-Czern.-Jassy	30	24½
1/	Lima, Ltd.	20	2¾
—	Manila Ltd. 7 p.c. Cu. Pf.	10	¾
20/6½	Mexican 2nd Pref. 6 p.c.	100	31
6	Do. Perp. Deb. Stk.	100	139
1/0/0	Mexican Sthrn., Ld., Ord.	100	21
—	Do. 4 p.c. 1 Db. Stk. Rd.	100	86
—	Do. 4 p.c. 2 do.	100	62
—	Mid. Urgy., Ltd.	100	20
5	Do. Deb. Stk.	100	60
12/	Minas & Rio, Ltd.	20	11½
5/2	Namur & Liege	20	13
11/6	Do. Pref.	20	29
5/	Natal & Na. Cruz, Ld., 7 p.c. Cum Pref.	20	7
—	Nitrate Ltd., Ord.	10	6½
—	Do. 7 p.c. Pr. Con. Or.	10	4¾
—	Do. Def. Conv. Ord.	10	1¾
7/	N.-E. Urgy., Ltd., Ord.	10	14½
7/	Do. 7 p.c. Pref.	10	15
—	N.-W. Argentine Ld., 7 p.c. Pref.	10	2¾
6	Do. 6 p.c. 1 Deb. Stk.	100	114†
—	Do. 2 Deb. Stk.	100	94
20/	N.W. Uruguay 6 p.c. 2 Pref. Stk.	100	16
—	Do. 5 p.c. 2 Pref. Stk.	100	7½
6	Do. 6 p.c. Deb. Stk.	100	74½
16/	Ottoman (Sm. Aid.)	20	16
—	Paraguay Cntl., Ld., 5 p.c. Perm. Deb. Stk.	100	11
—	Piræus, Ath., & Pelo.	275	1
5/	Pto. Alegre & N. Hambg. Ld., 7 p.c. Pref. Shs.	20	4½
6	Do. Mt. Deb. Stk. Red.	100	77½
—	Puerto Cabello & Val. Ld.	10	1¾
5	Recife & S. Francisco	100	72
14/	R. Claro S. Paulo, Ld., Sh.	10	21½
5	Do. Deb. Stk.	100	128†
7/	Royal Sardinian Ord.	10	11½

Foreign Railways (*continued*):—

Last Div.	NAME.	Paid.	Price.
7/	Royal Sardinian Pref.	10	12½
4	Ryl. Swedish, Lm. Db. Stk., Red.	100	10
5/	Sambre & Meuse	20	19
5/6	Do. Pref.	10	12
28/	San Paulo Ld.	20	36½
2/9½	Do. New Ord. £10 sh.	4	8¾
2/	Do. 5 p.c. Non.Cm.Pref.	10	12½
5½	Do. Deb. Stk. [†	100	136½
5	Do. 5 p.c. Deb. Stk.	100	128†
—	S. Fé & Cordova, Gt. Sthn., Ld., Shares	100	56
6	Do. Perp. Deb. Stk.	100	121†
3/2½	S. Austrian	20	7¼
10/	Sthn. Braz. R. Gde. do Sul, Ld.	20	8
6	Do. 6 p.c. Deb. Stk.	100	73
4	Swedish Centl., Ld., 4 p.c. Deb. Stk.	100	108
5	Do. Pref.	100	98½
1/9	Taltal, Ld.	5	2⅜
4/	Uruguay Nthn., Ld. 7 p.c. Pfd. Stk.	100	6
3½	Do. 5 p.c. Deb. Stk.	100	25†
—	Villa Maria & Rufino, Ld., 6 p.c. Pref. Shs.	100	20
4	Do. 4 p.c. 1 Deb. Stk.	100	72
6/0/0	Do. 6 p.c. 2 Deb. Stk.	100	44
5/9	West Flanders	8⅜	22
5/6	Do. 5½ p.c. Pref.	10	18
3/	Wstn. of Havana, Ld.	10	4¾

FOREIGN RAILWAY OBLIGATIONS

Per Cent.	NAME.	Price.
6	Alagoas Ld., 6 p.c. Deb., Rd.	85½
£1	Alcoy & Gandia, Ld., 5 p.c. Debs., Red.	25
5	Arauco., Ld., 5 p.c. 1st Mt., Rd.	68
6	Do. 6 p.c. Mt. Deb., Rd.	48½
6	Brazil G. Sthn., L., Mt. Dbs., Rd.	83
6	Do. Mt. Dbs. 1893, Rd.	52½
5½	Campos & Caran. Dbs., Rd.	76†
6	Central Bahia, L., Dbs., Rd.	93½
5½	Conde d'Eu, L., Dbs., Rd.	77†
6	Costa Rica, L., 1st Mt. Dbs., Rd.	110†
6	Do. 2nd Dbs., Rd.	96
5	Do. Prior Mt. Db., Rd.	107
6	Cucuta Mt. Dbs., Rd.	100†
5½	Donna Thrsa. Cris., L., Dbs., Rd.	75
3	Eastn. of France, £20 Dbs., Rd.	19
4	Egyptn. Delta Light, L., Db., Rd.	100
—	Espito. Santo & Cara. 5 p.c. Stl. Dbs., Rd.	38
4	Gd. Russian Nic., Rd.	101
5	Inter-Oceanic Mex., L., 5 p.c. Pr. Ln. Dbs., Rd.	104†
3	Ital. 3 p.c. Bds. A & B, Rd.	57½†
—	Ituana 6 p.c. Debs., 1918	72½
—	Leopoldina, 6 p.c. Dbs. £50 Bds.,	25
—	Do. do. Comms. Cert.	25
—	Do. 5 p.c. Stg. Dbs. (1888), Rd.	34
—	Do. do. Comm. Certs.	34
—	Do. 5 p.c. Stg. Dbs. (1890), Rd.	25
—	Do. do. Comms. Certs.	25
11/1	Macahé & Cam. 5 p.c. Dbs., Rd.	35
—	Do. do. Comms. Certs.	35
11/1	Do. (Cantagallo), 5 p.c., Red.	35
—	Do. do. Comm. Certs.	35
—	Manila Ltd., 6 p.c. Deb., Red.	22
6	Do. Prior Lien Mt., Rd.	103†
6	Do. Series "B," Rd.	78†
7	Matanzas & Sab., Rd.	101½
6	Minas & Rio, L., 6 p.c. Dbs., Rd.	100
5	Mogyana 5 p.c. Deb. Bds., Rd.	102
5	Moscow-Jaros., Rd.	105½
5½	Natal & Na. Cruz Ltd., 5½ p.c. Debs., Red.	88½
5	Nitrate, Ltd. Mt. Bds., Red.	88½†
3	Nthn. France, Red.	19†
4	N. of S. Af. Rep. (Trnsvl.) Gu. Bds. Red.	96
3	Nthn. of Spain £20 Pri. Obs. Red.	8½
6	Ottmn. (Smy to A.) (Kujk) Asnt. Debs., Red.	108½
6	Ottmn. (Seraik.) Asg. Debs. Red.	108½
6	Ottmn. (Seraik) Non-Asg. D., Rd	108½
5	Ottmn. Kuyjk. Ext. Red.	108
5	Ottmn. Serkeuy. Ext. Red.	103½
5	Ottmn. Tireh Ext. 1910	98
5	Ottmn. Debs, 1886, Red.	97½
5	Do. 1888, Red. 1935	97½†
5	Do. 1893, Red. 1935	96½
5	Ottmn. of Anlia. Debs., Rd.	91
5	Do. Ser. II.	89
4	Ottomn. Smyr. & Cas. Ext. Bds., Red.	82½
3	Paris, Lyon & Medit. (old sys., £20), Red.	19†
3	Paris, Lyon & Medit. (new sys., £20), Red.	19
50/	Piræus, At. & Pelp., 6 p.c. 1st Mt. Bds., Red.	88½
30/	Do. 5 p.c. Mt. Bds., Red.	61½†
4	Pretoria-Pietbg., Ltd., Red.	94†
7	Puerto Cab. & Val., Ltd., 1st Mt. Debs., Red.	95†
—	Rio de Jano. & Nthn., Ltd., 6 p.c. £100 Deb., Red.	25
—	Rio de Jano. (Gr. Para.), 5 p.c. 1st Mt. St. £100 Debs., Red.	24
3	Royal Sardinian, A, Rd. £20	12
3	Royal Sardinian, B., Rd. £20	12†

Foreign Rly. Obligations (*continued*):—

Per Cent.	NAME.	Price.
5	Ryl. Trns.-Afric. 5 p.c. 1st Mt. £100 Bds., Red.	61†
7	Sagua La Grande, B pRd.	98†
4	Sa. Fe & Cor. G.S., Ld. Pr Ln. Bds.	100†
5	Sa. Fe, 5 p.c. and Reg. Dbs.	79
3	South Austrian, £20 Red.	15½†
3	South Austrian, (Ser. X.)	15½
3	South Italian £20 Obs. (Ser. A to G), Red.	12½
3½	S. W. of Venez. (Barq.), Ltd., 7 p.c. 1st Mt. £100 Debs.	57½†
5	Taltal, Ltd., 5 p.c. 1st Ch. Debs., Red.	99†
5	Utd. Rwys. Havana, Red.	79†
3	Wtrn. of France, £20 Red.	19†
6	Wrn. B. Ayres St. Mt. Debs., 1902	111
6	Wrn. B. Ayres, Reg. Cert.	109
5	Do. Mt. Bds.	123†
6	Wtrn. of Havna., Ld, Mt. Dbs., Rd.	99
7	Wrn. Ry. San Paulo Red.	101
1	Wrn. Santa Fé, 7 p.c. Red.	39
4/7	Zafra & Huelva, 3 p.c. Red.	3

BANKS.

Div.	NAME.	Paid.	Price.
1/9½	Agra, Ltd.	6	3½
2/6	Anglo-Argentine, Ltd., £9	7	5½
8½ fls.	Anglo-Austrian	120f [illegible]	14
6/	Anglo-Californian, Ltd., £20 Shares	10	11
4/	Anglo-Egyptian, Ltd., £15	5	5½
3/6	Anglo-Foreign Bkg., Ltd.	7	8
2/	Anglo-Italian, Ltd.	5	7½
7/6	Bk. of Africa, Ltd., £18¾	6¼	10½
20/	Bk. of Australasia	40	53
8/	Bk. of Brit. Columbia	20	18½
25/	Bk. of Brit. N. America	50	65
7/6	Bk. of Egypt, Ltd., £25	12½	19
5/	Bk. of Mauritius, Ltd.	10	10
18/	Bk. of N. S. Wales	20	38
4 p.c.	Bk. of N. Zland. Gua. Stk.	100	103
6/	Bk. of Roumania, £20 Shs.	6	7½†
2/6	Tarapaca & Ldn., Ltd., £10	5	3½
—	Bque. Fse. de l'Afri. du S.	100f	3½
f. 12.50	Bque. Internatle. de Paris	20	24†
6/	Brit. Bk. of S. America, Ltd., £20 Shares	10	11½
16/	Capital & Ctîes., L., £50	10	39½
16/	Chart. of India, &c.	20	29
9/	City, Ltd., £40 Shares	10	20
18/	Colonial, £100 Shares	30	23
10/	Delhi and London, Ltd.	25	—
5/	German of London, Ltd.	10	11
25/	Hong-Kong & Shanghai	28½	41
4/	Imperl. of Persia	6½	3½†
10/	Imperl. Ottoman, £20 Shs	10	12⅜
9/	Intrnatl. of Ldn., Ld., £20	15	9
10/	Ionian, Ltd.	25	15
12/	Lloyds, Ltd., £50 Shs.	8	28½
10/	Ldn. & Brazil. Ltd., £20	10	18
44/	Ldn. & County, Ltd., £80	20	104
5/	Ldn. & Hanseatic, L., £20	10	11
20/	Ldn. & Midland, L., £60	12½	51
8/9	Ldn. & Provin., Ltd., £10	5	22
21/	Ldn. & Riv. Plate, L., £25	15	48½
2/1½	Ldn. & San Fcisco, Ltd.	7	4½
24/	Ldn. & Sth. West., L., £50	20	66½
24/	Ldn. & Westmins., L., £100	20	59½
3/	Ldn. of Mex. & S. Amer., Ltd., £10 Shs.	6	5½
15/	Ldn. Joint Stk., L., £100	15	35
9/7	Ldn., Paris & Amer., L. £20	16	26
1/7½	Merchant Bkg., L., £9	4	2½
6/3	Metropn, Ltd., £50 Shs.	5	14
9/	National, Ltd., £50 Shs.	10	20
4/3	Natl. of Mexico, $100 Shs.	$40	11½†
1/3	National of N. Z., L., £7½	2½	2½†
8/	National S. Afric. Rep.	20	14
21/	National Provcl. of Eng., Ltd., £75 Shs.	10½	49½
24/	Do. do. £60 Shs.	12	56
6/3	North Eastn., Ltd., £20 Shs	6	15
19/	Parr's, Ld., £100 Shs.	20	92
12/6	Prov. of Ireland, L., £100	12½	29
40/	Stand. of S. Afric., L., £100	25	66½
12/6	Union of Australia, L., £75	25	29½
4 p.c.	Do. do. Ins. Stk. Dep. 1900	100	103†
17/	Union of Ldn., Ltd., £100	15½	37

BREWERIES AND DISTILLERIES.

Div.	NAME.	Paid.	Price.
4½	Albion Prp. 1 Mt. Db. Sk.	100	108
4	All Saints', L., Db. Sk. Rd.	100	99
6	Allsopp, Ltd.	100	163
6	Do. Cum. Pref.	100	159†
4½	Do. Deb. Stk., Red.	100	117†
3½	Do. Deb. Stk., Red.	100	101†
4½	Alton & Co., L., Db., Rd	100	106
4½	Do. Mt. Bds., 1896	100	105
8/	Arnold, Perrett, Ltd.	10	7
6	Do. Cum. Pref.	10	10
4½	Do. 1 Mt. Db. Stk., Rd.	100	106†

Breweries, &c. (*continued*):—

Div.	NAME.	Paid.	Price.
5½	Arrol, A., & Sons, L., Cum. Pref. Shs.	10	10½
4½	Do. 1 Mt. Db. Stk., Rd.	100	106
6	Backus, 1 Mt. Db., Red.	100	59½
4	Barclay, Perk., L., Cu. Pf.	10	11½†
3½	Do. Mt. Db. Stk., Red.	100	110†
4/	Barnsley, Ltd.	10	10
6	Do. Cum. Pref.	10	12½
1/	Barrett's, Ltd.	2½	1½
5	Do. 5 p.c. Pref.	2½	2½
3/	Bartholomay, Ltd.	10	4½†
8	Do. Cum. Pref.	10	9½
6	Do. Deb.	100	103½
5	Bass, Ratcliff, Ltd., Cum. Pref. Stk. [†	100	147½
4½	Do. Mt. Db. Stk., Rd.	100	124†
4	Bell, John, Ltd., 1 Mt. Deb. Stk., Red.	100	102
5	Benskin's, L., Cum. Pref.	5	5½
4½	Do. 1 Mt. Db. Stk. Red.	100	110†
4½	Do. "B" Deb. Sk, Rd.	100	109†
5/	Bentley's Yorks., Ltd.	10	11½
6	Do. Cum. Pref.	10	12½
4½	Do. Mt. Debs., Red.	100	109†
4½	Do. do. 1 92, Red.	100	109†
—	Bieckert's, Ltd.	20	2
5	Do. Debs., Red.	100	55½†
—	Birmingham., Ltd., 6 p.c. Cum. Pref.	5	2½
4½	Do. Mt. Debs., Red.	50	40½
5½	Boardman's, Ld., Cm. Pf.	10	8½
4½	Do., Perp. 1 Mt. Db. Sk. †	100	103½
4½	Brakspear, L., 1 D. Stk. Rd	100	111
4	Brandon's, L., 1 D. Stk. R. †	100	103½
17/	Bristol (Georges) Ltd.	10	45
6	Do. Cum. Pref.	10	17½†
5	Do. Mt. Db. Sk. 1888 Rd. †	100	115½
—	Bristol United, Ltd.	10	36
6	Do. Cum. Pref.	10	16½†
4½	Do. Db. Sk. Rd.	100	126
5½	Buckley's, L., C. Pre-prf.	10	11
4½	Do. 1 Mt. Db. Stk. Rd. †	100	105½
4	Bullard & Sns, L., D. Sk. R.	100	107
6	Bushell, Watk., L., C. Pf.	10	13½†
4½	Do. 1 Mt. Db. Sk. Rd.	100	112
5	Camden, Ltd., Cum. Pref.	10	11½
4½	Do. 1 Mt. Db. Sk. Rd.	100	109
5½	Cameron, Ltd., Cm. Prf.	10	13
4½	Do. Mort Deb. Stk.	100	108
3½	Do. Perp Mt. Db. Sk.	100	100½
5	Cam'bell, J'stone, L., C. Pf.	5	5½
4½	Do. 4½ p.c. 1 Mt. Db. Sk.	100	104†
4	Campbell, Praed, L., Per. 1 Mort. Deb. Stk.	100	106
4	Cannon, L., Mt. Db. Stk.	100	110
4	Do. "B" Deb. Stk.	100	104
5	Castlemaine, L., 1 Mt. Db.	100	94†
3½	Charrington, Ltd., Mort. Deb. Stk. Red.	100	109
2/	Cheltnhm. Orig., Ltd.	5	7†
6	Do. Cum. Pref.	5	8†
4	Do. Debs. Red.	100	107
10	Chicago, Ltd.	10	4†
6	Do. Debs.	100	87½
—	Cincinnati, Ltd.	10	½
8	Do. Cum. Pref.	10	1½
10/	City of Baltimore	10	4†
16/	Do. 8 p.c. Cum. Pref	10	8†
14/	City of Chicago, Ltd.	10	1½
8	Do. Cum. Pref.	10	5½†
8	City of London, Ltd.	100	194½
5	Do. Cum. Pref.	100	140
4	Do. Mt. Deb. Stk., Rd.	100	118½
2/6	Colchester, Ltd.	5	4½
7	Do. Pref.	5	6½
4½	Do. Deb. Stk., Red.	100	109†
5	Combe, Ltd., Cum. Pref.	10	14½
4	Do. Mt. Db. Stk, Rd.	100	111
3½	Do. Perp. Deb. Stk.	100	107
5	Comm'cial, L., D. Sk., Rd.	100	107½
5	Courage, L., Cm. Pref. Shs.	100	139½
4	Do. Irr. Mt. Deb. Stk.	100	131
3½	Do. Irr. "B" Mt. Db. Sk.	100	106
6	Daniell & Sons, Ltd.	10	6⅜
7	Do. Cum. Pref.	10	12½
4½	Do. 1 Mt. Perp. Db. Sk.	100	108½
4½	Do. "B" Deb. Stk.	100	98½
5	Dartford, Ltd.	5	5½
5	Do. Cum. Pref.	5	5¾
4	Do. 1 Mt. Db. Sk. Rd.	100	101
4	Davenport, Ld., 1 D. Stk. †	100	101
10/	Denver United, Ltd.	10	3½
8	Do. Cum. Pref.	10	8½†
6	Do. Debs.	100	98½†
4½	Deuchar, L., 1 D. Sk., Rd.	100	108†
17/	Distillers, Ltd.	10	23
4½	Do. Mt. Db. Stk., Rd.	100	113
—	Dublin Distillers, Ltd.	5	1½
6/	Do. Cum. Pref.	5	4½
4½	Do. Irr. Deb. Stk.	100	[illegible]
5	Eadie, Ltd., Cum. Pref.	10	11
4	Do. Irr. 1 Mt. Db. Sk.	100	108½
10/	Edinbgh. Utd., Ltd.	10	13½
6	Do. Cum. Prf.	10	12½†
5	Do. 1 Mt. Dbs. †	100	110†
4	Eldridge, Pope, L. D. St. R.	100	110½
3/	Emerald & Phœnix, Ltd.	10	1
8	Do. Cum. Pref.	10	6½
6	Empress Ltd., C. Pf.	10	11
4½	Do. Mt. Deb. Stk.	100	101½
10/	Farnham, Ltd.	10	16
6	Do. Cum. Pref.	10	15†
4	Fenwick, L., 1 D. Sk., Rd.	100	103
4	Flower & Sons, Irr. D. Sk.	100	113
4	Friary, L., 1 Db. Stk., Rd. †	100	105
4	Do. 1 "A" Db. Sk., Rd.	100	102½
4½	Groves, L., 1 Db. Sk., Rd	100	110†
24	Guinness, Ltd.	100	590
6	Do. Cum. Prf. Stk.	100	195
5	Do. Deb. Stk., Red.	100	123½
5	Hall's Oxford L., Cm. Pf.	5	5½
6	Hancock, Ld., Cm. Pf. Ord.	10	14
7/	Do. Def. Ord.	10	17½

Breweries, &c. (*continued*) :—

Div.	Name.	Paid.	Price.
6	Hancock, Ld., Cum. Pref.	10	15½
4	Do. 1 Deb. Stk., Rd.	100	113
5	Hoare, Ltd. Cum. Pref.	10	13½
5	Do. "A" Cum. Pref.	10	12½
4	Do. Mt. Deb. Stk., Rd.	100	110†
3½	Do. do. do. Rd.	100	104†
4/6	Hodgson's, Ltd.	5	9½
5	Do. 1 Mt. Db., Red.	—	120½
4	Do. 2 Mt. Db., 1906	—	102
4½	Hopcraft & N., Ltd., 1 Mt. Deb. Stk., Red.	100	102†
5	Huggins, Ltd., Cm. Prf.	10	12½
4½	Do. 1st D. Stk. Rd.	100	112
4½	Do. "B" Db. Stk. Rd.	100	110
8/	Hull, Ltd.	10	17
7	Do. Cum. Pref.	10	15
4½	Ind, Coope, L., D.Sk., Rd.	100	119†
4	Do. "B" Mt. Db. Stk. Rd.	100	114
3/	Indianapolis, Ltd.	10	3½†
6	Do. Cm. Prf.	10	9†
5/	Jones, Frank, Ltd.	10	4
7½	Do. Cum. Pref.	10	8
5	Do. 1st Mort. Debs.	100	95½
4/	J. Kenward & Ct., Ltd.	5	5½
4½	Kingsbury, L., 1 D.Sk., Rd.	100	107½
4	Lacon, L., D. Stk., Red.	100	107†
4	Do. Irrd. "B" D. Sk.	100†	106½
4	Lascelles, Ltd.	5	10½
6	Do. Cum. Pref.	5	7½
5	Leney, Ltd., Cum. Pref.	10	11½
4	Do. 1 Mt. Db. Stk., Rd.	100	103
27	Lion, Ltd., £25 shares	17	48½
6	Do. New £10 shares	6	16½
6	Do. Perp. Pref.	20	31½
4	Do. B Mt. Db. Sk. Rd.	100	109
4½	Lloyd & Y., Ltd., 1 Mt. Deb. Stk., Rd.	100	97½†
4½	Locke & S., Ltd., Irr. 1st Mt. Deb. Stk.	100	100†
4½	Lovibond, Ltd., 1st Mt. Deb. Stk., Rd.	100	97½†
8/	Manchester, Ltd.	10	16
7	Do. Cum. Pref.	10	16½
5	Marston, J., L., Cm. Prf.	10	10½†
4	Do. 1 Mt. Db. Sk., Rd.	100†	101½
9/	Massey's Burnley, Ltd.	10	16
6	Do. Cum. Pref.	10	14½
4½	McCracken, Ltd., 1 Mt. Deb., 1908	100	64
5	McEwan, Ltd., Cm. Pref.	10	15½
5	Meux, Ltd., Cum. Pref.	10	14½
4	Do. Mt. Db. Stk. Red.	100	112
4½	Michell & A., Ltd., 1 Mt. Deb. Stk. Red.	100	105†
4½	MileEnd Dist. Db. Sk. Rd	100	108†
4/	Milwaukee & Chic., Ltd.	10	1½†
4/	Do. Cum. Pref.	10	6½†
4½	Mitchell, Toms, L., Db.	50	55†
6	Morgan, Ltd., Cum. Pref.	10	14½
20/	Nalder & Coll., Ltd	10	31
6	Do. Cum. Pref.	10	16
4½	Do. Deb. Red.	100	113
3/	New Beeston, Ltd.	5	4
2/9	Do. Cum. Pref.	5	4½
4	Do. Mt. Deb. Stk. Red.	100	96½
12/	Newcastle, Ltd.	10	19½†
6	Do. Cum. Pref.	10	14½†
5	Do. 1 Mt. Deb., 1911	100	110½
4	Do. "A" Deb. Stk. Red.	100	106
6/	New England, Ltd.	10	4½
8	Do. Cum. Pref.	10	9½
6	Do. Debs. Red.	100	102½
4	New London, L., 1 D.Sk.	100	103½
2/4½	New Westminster, Ltd.	4	9½
6	Do. Pref.	4	6½
5	New York, Ltd.	10	1
18/	Do. 8 p.c. Cum. Pref.	10	3½
6	Do. 1 Mt. Deb. Red.	100	83½
5	Noakes, Ld., Cum. Pref.	10	12
4	Do. 1 Mt. Db. Stk., Rd.	100	107
4½	Norfolk, L., "A" D.Sk. Rd.	100	106†
20/	Northampton, Ld.	10	16½†
7	Do. Cum. Pref.	10	15½
6	Do. Cum. Pref.	10	13
5	Do. 1 Mt. Per. Db. Sk.	100	127
4	Nth. East., L., 1 D.Sk. Rd.	100	100
4½	N. Worcesters, L., Per. 1 Mort. Deb. Stock	100	94½
6	Nottingham, L., Cm. Prf.	10	11
5	Do. 1 Mt. Deb. Stk., Red.	100	115
17/4	Do. "B" do. Red.	50(†	111½
6/	Ohlsson' Cape, Ld.	5	16†
7	Do. Cum. Pref.	5	8½
4½	Do. 2nd Cum. Pref.	5	5½
5	Do. Deb. Stk., Red.	100	112
4½	Oldfield, L., 1 Mt. Db. Stk.	100	102†
6	Page & Overt., L., Cm. Prf.	10	13
4½	Do. 1 Mt. Dbs., Red.	100	110
15/	Parker's Burslem, Ltd.	10	25½
6	Do. Cum. Pref.	10	15½
4	Do. 1 Mt. Db. Stk., Red.	100	111
4	Persse, Ld., 1 Mt. Db., Rd.	100	93†
4	Phipps, L., Irr. 1 Db. Stk.	100	115
5	Plymouth, L., Min. Cu. Pf.	10	13½
4½	Do. Mt. Deb. Stk., Red.	100	104½
4½	Pryor, Reid, L., 1 D.S., R.(†	100	104½
5	Reid's, Ld., Cm. Pref. Stk.	100	140½
4	Do. Mt. Deb. Stk., Red.	100	113
3½	Do. "B" Mt. Db. Stk., Rd.	100	103
5	Rhondda Val., L., Cu. Pf.	10	11†
4½	Do. 1 Mt. Deb. Stk., Rd.	100	109†
5	Robinson, Ld., Cum. Pref.	10	11½†
4½	Do. 1 Mt. Perp. Db. Stk.	100	112†
4/	Rochdale, Ltd.	10	5½
4½	Do. 1 Mt. Deb. Stk.	100	96½†
21/	Royal, Brentford, Ltd.	10	19½
6	Do. Cum. Pref.	10	14
4½	Do. 1 Mt. Dbs. Red	100	112
4/	St. Louis, Ltd.	10	4†
8	Do. Cum. Pref.	10	8½†
24/	St. Pauli, Ltd.	10	10†
7	Do. Cum. Pref.	10	11†
4½	Salt (T.), L., 1 Db. Sk. Rd.	100	110†
4½	Do. "B" Db. Stk. Red.	100	107†

Breweries, &c. (*continued*) :—

Div.	Name.	Paid.	Price.
6/7	San Francisco, Ltd.	10	½
8/	Do. 8 p.c. Cum. Pref.	10	½
4½	Savill Brs., L., D. Sk. Rd.	100	115†
4½	Scarboro., Ltd., 1 Db. Stk.	100	105
4	Shaw (Hy.), Ltd., 1 Mt. Db. Stk., Red.	100	104†
22/	Showell's, Ltd.	10	33
7	Do. Cum. Pref.	10	17½†
3/	Do. Gua. Shs.	5	7½†
4½	Do. Mt. Db. Stk., Red.	100	—
4	Simonds, L., 1 D. Sk., Rd.	100	111
5½	Simson & McP., L., Cu. Pf.	10	9½†
4½	Do. 1 Mt. Deb. Stk.	100	100
12/	Smith, Garrett, L., £20 Shs	10	15½
5	Do. Cum. Pref.	20	26†
4½	Do. Mt. Db. Stk., Red.	100	—
5	Smith's, Tadcster, L., CPf	10	11½
4½	Do. Deb. Stk., Red.	100	112†
4	Do. Deb. Stk., Red.	100	108†
4½	Star, L., 1 M. Db. Stk., Rd.	100	104
4	Steward & P., L., 1 D. Sk.	100	113
9/	Strettons Derby, Ltd.	10	13
6	Do. Cum. Pref.	10	13
4	Do. Irr. 1 Mt. Db. Stk.	100	101½
4½	Strong, Romsey, L., 1 D. S.	100	112
5	Stroud, L., Db. Sk., Rd.	100	111½
4½	Tadcaster To'er, L., D.Sk.	100	112
8/	Tamplin, Ltd	10	22
6	Do. Cum. Pref.	100	15
4	Do. "A" Db. Sk., Rd.	10	107
6	Thorne, Ltd., Cum. Pref.	10	14½
4	Do. Deb. Stk., Red.	100	103½
16/	Threlfall, Ltd.	10	49
6	Do. Cum. Pref.	10	17
5	Do. 1 Mt. Dbs., Red.	100	116†
4	Tollemache, L., D. Sk. Rd.	100	106
4	Truman, Hanb., D. Sk., R.	100	110†
3	Do. "B" Mt. Db. Sk., Rd.	100	94½
10/	United States, Ltd.	10	10½
8	Do. Cum. Pref.	10	12½
6	Do. 1 Mt. Deb.	100	107½
2/2½	Walker & H., Ld., Cm. Prf.	10	13½†
4½	Do. 1 Mt. Deb. Stk., Red.	100	107†
5	Walker, Peter, Ld. Cm. Prf.	10	13½†
4	Do. 1 Mt. Dbs. Red.	100	110†
4	Wallingford, L., D. Sk. Rd.	100	107
6	Watney, Ld., Cm. Prf. Sk.	100	170
5	Do. Mt. Db. Sk., Rd.	100	116½
4½	Do. "B" Mt. Db. Sk., Rd.	100	111†
5	Watney, D., Ld., Cm. Prf.	10	12½
4½	Do. 1 Mt. Db. Stk.	100	107
5	Wenlock Ltd., Pref.	10	12½
4	Do. 1 Mt. Db. Sk., Rd.	100	108
5	West Cheshire, L., Cu. Pf.	10	10½†
4	Do. Irred. 1 Mt. Db. Sk.	100	100†
4½	Whitbread, L., Cu. Pf. Sh.	100	125½
4	Do. Db. Stk., Red.	100	112
3½	Do. "B" Db. Stk., Rd.	100	103
9/	Wolverhmpton & D. Ld.	10	14½
6	Do. Cum. Pref.	10	13
4½	Do. 1 Mt. Dbs., Red.	100	108†
5½	Worthington, Ld., Cm. Prf.	10	15½
5½	Do. Cum. "B" Pref.	10	13½
4½	Do. Mt. Db. Sk., Rd.	100	113
3½	Do. Irr. "B" Db. Stk.	100	103
10/	Yates's Castle, Ltd.	10	12½
5	Do. Cum. Pref.	10	18½
5	Younger W., L., Cu. Pf. Sh.	100	131

CANALS AND DOCKS.

Last Div.	Name.	Paid.	Price.
4½	Alexandra Con. Stk. "B"	100	112½
4½	Do. 1 Prf Con. Stk. "A"	100	128½
4	Do. Perp. Deb. Stk.	100	132½
4	Birmingham Canal	100	146
—	E. & W. India Dock	100	23½
4	Do. Deb. Stk.	100	106
85/	Do. Def. Deb. Stk.	100	90
3½	Do. 1st Mt. Certs.	100	108
4	Do. Mt. Bds. (1885)	—	100
40/	G. Junction Ord. Shs.	100	151½
6/	Do. do. Pref.	10	19†
4½	King's Lynn Per. Db. Stk.	100	120½
2½	Leeds & Lpool Canal	100	67
2½	Lndn & St. Kath. Dks.	100	58
4½	Do. Pref.	100	138½
4½	Do. Pref., 1878	100	134½
4½	Do. Pref., 1882	100	130
4	Do. Deb. Stk.	100	135†
—	Mchester Ship C. 5 p.c. Pf.	10	1½
3½	Do. 1st Perp. Mt. Deb.	100	98†
—	Milford Dks. Db. Stk. "A"	100	21½
2	Millwall Dk.	100	61
5	Do. Perp. Pref.	100	146½
4½	Do. Pref.	100	108½
5	Do. New Per. Prf., 1887	100	128½
5	Do. Per. Deb. Stk.	100†	152½
4/	Newhaven Har.	10	14½†
2	N. Metropolitan	100	65
5	Sharpness Nw. Pf. "A" Sk.	100	144½
4	Do. Deb. Stk.	100	121½
4	Sheffield & S. Yorks Nav. 4½ p.c. Pref. Stk.	100	117½
36.43	Suez Canal	20	130†
5	Surrey Comcl. Dok., Ord.	100	149½
5	Do. Min. 4 p.c. Pref. "A"	110	152½
5	Do. Pref. "B"	100	150½
5	Do. do. "C"	100	150
5	Do. do. "D"	100	145½
4½	Do. Deb. Stk.	100	154½

COMMERCIAL, INDUSTRIAL, &c.

Last Div.	Name.	Paid.	Price.
5	Accles, L., 1 Mt. Db., Red.	100	87½
5/	Aërated Bread, Ltd.	1	11½
—	African Gold Recovery, 1L	1	½
2/	Aluminium, L., "A" Shs.	1	2½
4½	Do. 1 Mt. Db. Stk., Red.	100	99
5½	Amelia Nitr., L., 1 Mort. Deb., Red.	100	84½†
7	Anglo-Chil. Nitrate, Ltd., Cum. Pref.	10	7
4½	Do. Cons. Mt. Bds., Red.	100	78½
4½	Anglo-Russian Cotton, Ld., 1 Charge Debs., Red.	100	98†
3/9	Angus (G., & Co., L.), £10	7½	17
—	Apollinaris, Ltd.	10	12½
—	Do. 5 p.c. Cum. Pref.	10	10½
4	Do. Irred. Deb. Stock	100	107
5/	Appleton, French, & S., L.	5	1
3/	Argentine Meat Pres., L., 7 p.c. Pref.	10	2½
5	Argentine Refinry, Db. Rd.	100	96†
2/2	Armstrong, Whitw., Ltd.	1	3
4	Do. Cum. Pref.	5	6½
5	Artisans', Labr. Dwllgs., L.	100	127½
4½	Do. Non-Cm. Prf., 1879	100†	132½
4½	Do. do. 1884	100†	131½
—	Asbestos & Asbestic, Ltd.	10	9
5½	Ashley-grdns., L., C. Prf.	5	6½
4½	Do. 1 Mt. Deb. Stk.	100	115½
5/	Assam Rly. & Trdng., L., 8 p.c. Cum. Pref. "A"	10	15
—	Do. Deferrd. "B" Shs.	1	4½
—	Do. do. (ist.f.pd)	1	3½
8	Do. Cum. Pre-Prf. "A"	10	14½
6	Do. New Pref.	10	11½
5	Do. Debs., Red.	100	107†
5	Do. Red. Mort. Debs.	100	109
6	Aust'lian Pastrl, L., Cu. Pf.	10	7½†
6d.	Aylesbury Dairy, Ltd.	1	1½
4	Do. 4 p.c. Mt. Dbs.	100†	104½
20/	Babcock & Wilcox, Ltd.	10	31
6	Do. 6 p.c. Cm. Prf.	10	16½
8	Baker (Chs.), L., Cm. Pf.	5	8½
8	Do. "B," Cm. Pref.	5	½
8d.	Barker (John), Ltd.	1	3
5½	Do. Cum. Pref.	5	7½
4½	Do. Irred. 1 Mt. Db. Stk.	100	132†
2/6	Barnagore Jute, Ltd.	5	3½
5	Do. Cum. Pref.	5	4½
7½d.	Belgravia Dairy, Ltd.	1	1
5/	Bell (R.) & Co., Ltd.	5	½
1/	Bell's Asbestos, Ltd.	1	½
5	Do. Mt. Db. Bds., Rd.	100	105†
10/	Bengal Mills, Ltd.	10	11½
6/	Do. 5 p.c. Cum. Prf.	10	10½†
5	Benson (J. W.) L., Cm. Pf.	10	100
4	Do. Perp. Mt. Db. Stk.	100	10
6	Bergvik, L., 6 p.c. Cm. Pf.	10	12½
10/	Do. Dfd.	10	9
4½	Do. 1 Dbs., Red.	100	102½
8/	Birm'ham Vinegar, Ltd.	5	8
5	Do. Cum. Pref.	5	5½
4½	Do. 1 Mt. Db. Stk., Rd.	100	105†
3/9	Boake (A.) L., 5 p.c. Cu. Pf.	10	10½†
2/6	Bodega, Ltd.	5	8†
4½	Do. Mt. Deb. Stk., Rd.	100	111†
8/	Bottomley & Brs., Ltd.	10	6½
6/	Do. 6 p.c. Pt.	10	9½
8½d.	Bovril, Ltd.	1	1½
—	Do. Def.	1	½
6½d.	Do. Cum. Pref.	1	1½
4½	Do. Deb. Stk.	100	102
6/4½	Bradbury, Gretrex., Ltd., £10 share	8	14
5/	Do. 5 p.c. Cum. Pref.	10	13½
5/	Brewers' Sugar, L., 5 p.c. Cum. Pref.	10	10½
2/6	BrightonGrd. Hotel, Ld.	5	2½
4	Do. Mt. Db. Stk., Red.	100	102½
5	Bristol Hotel & Palm. Co., Ltd. 1st Mt. Red. Deb.	100	106†
9½d.	British & Bengton's. Tea Tr. Asc., Ltd.	1	1½
5	Do. Cum. Prf.	5	5½
—	British Deli & Lgkat. Tobacco, Ltd.	1	½
7	Do. Cum. Prf.	1	½
—	British Tea Table, Ltd.	1	2½
5½	Do. Cum. Pref.	1	1½
2/6	Brooke, Ben., & Co., Ltd., Cum. Pref.	5	5½†
7/6	Brooke, Bond & Co., Ltd.	5	20½†
6	Brown Brs., L., Cum. Pref.	5	6
6/	Browne & Eagle, Ltd.	10	13½
5/	Do. Cum. Pref.	10	13†
4	Do. Mrt. Db. Sk., Red.	100	109†
20/	Brunner, Mond, & Co., Lt.	10	39
7/	Do. £10 shares	3½	15
7	Do. Cum. Pref.	10	18
7	Do. £10 shares	5	9
7/6	Bryant & May, Ltd.	5	19½
2/	Bucknall, H., & Sons, Lt.	5	8
6	Do. Cum Pref.	5	8
4/	Burke, E. & J., Ltd.	5	7½
6	Do. Cum. Pref.	5	7½
6	Do. Irred. Deb. Stk.	100	155
1/	Burlington Htls. Co., Ltd	1	1½
5	Do. Cum. Pref.	1	1½†
4	Do. Perp. Deb. Stk.	100	104½
5	Bush, W. J., & Co., Ltd., Cum. Pref.	5	5½
4	Do. 1 Deb. Stk., Red.	100	103
5½	Callard, Stewart, & Watt, Ltd., Cum. Pref.	1	1½
4/	Callender's Cable L., Shs.	5	7½
4½	Do. 1 Deb. Stk., Red.	100†	108½
2/6	Campbell, R., & Sons, Lt.	3	1½
6	Cantareira Water, Bd., Rd	100	98½
5	Do. (2nd Issue)	100	92
4	Cartavio Sugar, Ltd., 6 p.c. 1st Debs., Red.	80	75½
4/6	Cassell & Co., Ltd., £10	9	17½
5	Causton, Sir J., & Sons, Ltd., Cum. Pref.	10	13½

Commercial, &c. (*continued*) :—

Last Div.	Name.	Paid.	Price.
4	Cent. Prod. Mkt. of B.A. 1st Mt. Str. Debs.	100	70
4	Chappell & Co., Ltd., Mt. Deb. Stk. Red	100	103
8	Chicago & N.W. Gran. Cum. Pref.	10	2½
8/	Chicago Packing & Prov.	10	6
8	Do. Cum. Pref.	10	9
6/	City Offices, Ltd	36½	13
3½	Do. Mt. Deb. Stk.	100	110½
9/7½	Cy. London Real Prop., Ltd., £25 shs.	19	19
7/6	Do. £12½ shs.	7½	13½
3½	Do. Deb. Stk. Red.	100	108½
3½	Do. Deb. Stk. Red.	100	106½
3	Do.	100	101½
4/	Cy. of Santos Imprvts., Ltd., 7 p.c. Pref.	10	8½
20/	Clay, Bock, & Co., Ltd.	10	8
8	Do. Cum. Pref.	10	11
6	Do. Mort. Deb.	100†	106½
20/	Coats, J. & P., Ltd.	10	61
6	Do. Cum. Pref.	10	18½
4½	Do. Deb. Stk. Red.	100†	111½
9½d.	Coburg Hotel, Ltd	1	1½
4	Do. Deb. Stk. Red.	100	102†
6	Colonial Consign & Dis., Ltd., Cum. Pref.	5	4½
4½	Do. 1st Mort. Debs.	100	97½
2/6	Colorado Nitrate, Ltd.	5	½
4/	Co. Gén. des Asphtes. de F., Ltd.	6	8½
5	Do. Non-Cm. Prf.	—	5½
5	Cook, J. W., & Co., Ltd., Cum. Pref.	5	5½
5	Cook, T., & Son, Egypt, Ltd., 1st Mt. Deb. Red.	100	110½
—	Cork Co., Ltd., 6 p.c. Cum. Pref.	5	2½
5	Cory, W., & Sn, L., Cu. Pf.	5	6
4	Do. 1st Deb. Stk. Red.	100	109
8½d.	Crisp & Co., Ltd	1	1½
5	Do. Cum. Pref.	1	1½†
3/	Crompton & Co., Ltd., 7 p.c. Cum. Pref.	5	2½
5	Do. 1st Mt. Reg. Deb.	—	80½
2/6	Crossley, J., & Sons, Ltd.	5	8
5	Do. Cum. Pref.	5	6½
3	Crystal Pal. Ord. "A" Stk.	100	8½
—	Do. "B" Red. Stk	100	1½
6	Do. 6 p.c. 1st 1887 Deb. Stk. Red.	100†	115½
20/	Do. 6 p.c. 2nd 1887 Deb. Stk. Red.	100	38½
—	Do. 6 p.c. 3rd 1887 Deb. Stk. Red.	100	15½
3	Do. 3 p.c. 1st 1895 Deb. Stk.	100	80½†
†) —	Daimler Motor, Ltd	10	5
4/	Dalgety & Co., £20 Shs.	5	5
4½	Do. Deb. Stk	100	120†
4	Do.	100	112
10½d.	De Keyser's Ryl. Htl., L.	10	11†
5	Do. Cum. Pref.	10	11½†
4	Do. Deb. Stk., Red.	100	109†
6	Denny, H., & Sons, Ltd., Cum. Pref.	10	14½†
3/6	Devas, Routledge & Co., L.	7	6½
5	Dickinson, J., & Co., L., Cum. Pref. Stk.	100	135
4½	Domin. Cottn. Mls., Ltd. Mt. Stg. Dbs.	100	98†
4/	Dorman, Long & Co., L.	5	4½
10/	Eastmans, Ltd	10	18½
8	Do. Cum. Pref.	10	10
6/	E. C. Powder, Ltd.	3	6½†
1/9½	Edison & Swn Utd. Elec. Ltd., "A" £5 Shs.	3	2½
2/9½	Do. fully-paid	5	5
4½	Ekman Pulp & Ppr. Co., Ltd., Mt. Deb., Red.	100	95½
1/1½	Electric Construc., Ltd.	2	2½
7	Do. Cum. Pref.	2	2½
10/	Eley Bros., Ltd.	10	30
10/	Elmore's Cop. Deptg., L.	1	½
—	Elmore's Wire Mnfg., L.	2	½
—	Elysée Pal. Hotel Co., L.	5/	½
—	Do. 5 p.c. £100 Db., Rd.	70	70†
8½d.	Evans, Ben., & Co., Ltd.	1	1
5	Do. 1 Mt. Db. Sk., Rd.	100	108†
8½d.	Evans., D. H., & Co., L.	1	1½
6	Do. Cum. Pref.	1	1½
4½	Do. 1 Mt. Db. Sk., Rd.	100	110†
2/1	*Evening News*, L., 5 p.c. Cum. Pref.	5	6½
5/3	Evered & Co., L., £10 Sh.	7	13½
7/6	Do.	10	18½
4	Fairbairn Pastoral Co., Aust., L., 1 Mt. Db., Rd.	100†	103†
6	Fairfield Shipbldg., Ltd., Cum. Pref.	10	10
4½	Do. Mort. Deb. Stk.	100	108½
—	Farmer & Co., Ld., 6 p.c. Cum. Pref.	10	13½
10	Field, J. C. & J., Ltd.	10	30
14/	Do. 7 p.c. Cum. Pref.	10	14
9d.	Fordham, W.B., & Sns, Ld.	1	2
3/6	Fore-st. Warehouse, Ltd.	11	10
4	Do. Regd. Debs., Rd.	100†	108½
2/6	Foster, M. B. & Sons, Ltd.	4	8½
5	Do. Pref.	10	13½
7/	Foster, Porter, & Co., L.	10½	17
4	Fowler, J., & Co. (Leeds), Ltd., 1 Mt. Deb., Red.	100†	100½
3/	Fraser & Chalmers, Ltd.	3	1½
4½	Free, Rodwell & Co., Ltd., Deb Stk.	100	108½
6½d.	Furness, T., & Co., Ltd., 5½ p.c. Cum. Pref.	1	1½
4½	Gartside & Co. (of Manchstr), L., 1 Mt. Db. Sk.	100	110†
5	Genl. Hydraul. Power, L.	100	[illegible]

Commercial, &c. (*continued*):—

Last Div.	Name.	Paid.	Price.
2/	Gillman & Spencer, Ltd.	5	2½
6	Do. Pref.	5	4½
5	Do. Mort. Debs.	50	48†
4	Goldsbro., Mort & Co., L., "A" Deb. Stk., Red.	100	72½†
—	Do. 3 p.c. "B" Inc. Deb. Stk., Red.	100	19
12/	Gordon Hotels, Ltd.	10	20½
5½	Do. Cum. Pref.	10	14½
4½	Do. Perp. Deb. Stk.	100†	136½
4	Do. do.	100†	123½
—	Greenwich Inld. Linoleum Co., Ltd.	1	⅛
7	Greenwood & Batley, Ltd., Cum. Pref.	10	10
7½d.	Hagemann & Co., Ltd., 6 p.c. Cum. Pref.	1	1½
—	Hammond, Ltd.	10	½
6/8	Do. 8 p.c. Cum. Pref.	10	2
6	Do. 6 p.c. Cum. Inc. Stk. Red.	100	52½
4	Hampton & Sons, Ltd., 4 p.c. 1 Mt. Db. St. Red.	100	105†
—	Hans Crescent Htl., L., 6 p.c. Cum. Pref.	5	3½
4	Do. 1 Mt. Deb. Stk.	100	85†
5	Harmsworth, Ld., Cm. Pf.	1	1 5/16
4/	Harrison, Barber, Ltd.	5	4½
1/	Harrod's Stores, Ltd.	1	5
2/6	Do. Cum. Pref.	5	7
5½	Hawaiian Comcl. & Sug. 1 Mt. Debs.	100	94½
5	Hazell, Watson, Ld., Cm. Pref.	10	12†
6/	Henley's Teleg., Ltd.	10	20½
7	Do. Pref. Shs.	10	19
4½	Do. Mt. Db. Stk., Rd.	100	112½
6	Henry, Ltd.	10	12½
5	Do. Cum. Pref.	10	13½
4½	Do. Mt. Debs., Red.	50	53
6	Hepworth, Ld., Cm. Prf.	10	11¼
5/	Herrmann, Ltd.	5	4½
—	Hildesheimer, Ltd.	3	1
9½d.	Holbrn. & Frasca, Ltd.	1	2
5	Do. Cum. Pref.	10	11½
4	Do. Deb. Stk.	100	113†
6	Home & Col. Stres, Ltd., Cum. Pref.	5	7½
6	Hood & M.'s Stres., Ltd., Cum. Pref.	1	¾
5/	Hook, C. T., Ltd.	10	4
7/2	Hornsby, Ltd., £10 Shs.	8	2½
5/6	Do. 6 p.c. Cm. Pf. Sk.	100	9
—	Hotchks. Ordn., Ltd.	10	⅜
—	Do. 7 p.c. Cm. Prf.	10	4½
5	Do. 1 Mt. Dbs., Rd.	100	97½†
6	Htl. Cecil, Ld., Cm. Prf.	5	4½
4	Do. 1 Mt. D. Sk., R.	100	105½
8/	Howard & Bulgh, Ltd.	10	36†
6	Do. Pref.	10	16†
4	Do. Deb. Stk., Red.	100	107†
4/	Howell, J., Ltd., £5 Shs.	4	9¼
1/	Howell & Js., Ld., £3½ Shs.	3	1
1/6	Humber, Ltd.	1	¾
6	Do. Cum. Pref.	1	1½
2/6	Hunter, Wilts., Ltd.	5	7
—	Hyam Clthg., Ltd., 5 p.c. Cum. Pref.	5	5½†
10/	Impl. Russn. Cotton, L.	5	5½†
5	Impd. Industl. Dwgs., Ld.	100	130½
6d.	Do. Defrd.	1	1½
£1	Impd. Wood Pave., Ltd.	10	16
5/	Ind. Rubber, Gutta Per. Telegraph Works, Ltd.	10	24
4	Do. 1 Mt. Debs., Red.	100	105
6	Intern. Tea, Cum. Pref.	5	6½
7½d.	Jays, Ltd.	1	1½
5½	Do. Cum. Pref.	5	6½
8½d.	Jones & Higgins, Ltd.	1	2½
4½	Do. 1 Mt. Db. Sk., Rd.	100	113
3/	Kelly's Directory, Ltd., 5 p.c. Cum. Pref.	10	12½†
—	Do. Mort. Db. Sk., Rd.	100	105†
—	Kent Coal Exprltn. Ltd.	1	¼
5½d.	King, Howmann, Ltd.	1	1½
4/	Kinloch & Co., Ltd.	5	8½
6	Do. Pref.	5	7
5	Lady's Pictorial Pub., Ltd., Cum. Pref.	5	5
—	La Guaira Harb., Ltd., 7 p.c. Deb. Stk.	100	—
—	Do. 2 Mt. 7 p.c. Deb. Bds., Red.	100	—
4/	Lagunas Nitrate, Ltd.	5	2½
—	Lagunas Syn., Ltd.	5	1½†
5	Do. 1 Mt. Debs., Red.	100	80
—	L. Copais Ld., 1 Mt. 6 p.c. Debs., Red.	100	35½
3/	Lautaro Nitrate, Ltd.	5	4½†
5	Do. 1 Mt. Debs., Red.	—	95½†
9/	Lawes Chem. L., £10 shs.	9	5½
14/	Do. N. Cm. Min. Pref.	10	12½
3/6	Leeds Forge, 7 p.c. Cm. Pf.	5	2½
5	Do. 1 Mt. Debs., Red.	50	42½
5	Lever Bros., L., Cm. Pf.	10	13†
6	Liberty, L., 6 p.c. Cm. Pf.	10	14½
60/	Liebig's, Ltd.	20	76
5	Lilley & Sk., L., Cm. Pf.	5	4½
3/	Linoleum Manftg., Ltd.	5	18½
3/	Linotype, Ltd., Pref.	5	4
4/	Do. Def.	5	7½
4/	Lister & Co., Ltd.	10	5
5	Do. Cum. Pref.	10	8½
5/	Liverpool. Nitrate	5	6½
5/0½	Liverpool. Warehsg., Ltd.	10	3½
5½	Do. Cum. Pref.	10	8½
4	Do. 1 Mt. Db. Stk., Rd.	100	105½
5½	Lockharts, Ltd., Cm. Pf.	1	1½
4/6	Ldn. & Til., Lightrage £10	9	5½
6/	Ldn. Comcl. Sale Rms., Ltd.	10	18
3	Do. 1 Mt. Deb. Stk., Red.	100	104
8/4½	London Nitrate, Ltd.	5	2
4/	London Nitrate, Ld. 8 p.c. Cm. Min. Pf.	5	3½
3/	London Pavilion, Ltd.	5	7½
1/6	†London. Produce Clg. Ho., Ltd., £10 Shares	2½	3½
4/	London Stereos., Ltd.	5	3
6/	Ldn. Un. Laun. L. Cm. Pf.	1	
8½d.	Louise, Ltd.	1	¾
5½	Do. Cum. Pref.	1	¾
6/	Lovell & Christmas, Ltd.	5	12½
6	Do. Cum. Pref.	5	7½
4	Do. Mt. Deb. Stk., Red.	100	108½
1/3	Lyons, Ltd.	1	2½
4½	Do. 1 Mt. Deb., Stk., Rd.	100	105½
10/	Machinery Trust, Ltd.	5	15
6	MacLellan, Ltd., Min. Cum. Pref.	10	6½
5	Do. 1 Mt. Debs., 1900	100	98½†
6/	McEwan, J. & Co, Ltd.	10	1½
6	Do. Mt. Debs., Red.	100	89½†
8	McNamara, L., Cm. Pref.	10	9†
7½d.	Maison Virot, Ltd.	1	1½†
3/	Do. 6 p.c. Cum. Pref.	5	4½†
15/	Manbré Sacc., L., Cm. Pf.	10	12†
15/	Mangan. Brze., L., £10 Shs.	6	15½
3/	Mason & Mason, Ltd.	5	3½
6	Do. Cum. Pref.	5	6
—	Maynards, Ltd.	1	¾
6	Do. Cum. Pref.	1	¾
9½d.	Mazawatee Tea, Ltd.	1	1½
5	Do. Cum. Pref.	5	5½
6	Mellin's Food Cum. Pref.	5	7
4½	Met. Ascn. Imp. Dwlgs. L.	100	109
3½	Do. 1 Mt. Deb. Stk.	100	97
5	Metro. Indus. Dwlgs., Ltd.	5	5
4	Do. do. Cum. Pref.	5	5½
5	Metro. Prop., L., Cm. Pf.	5	6½
4½	Do. 1st Mt. Debs. Stk.	100	110½
6	Mexican Cotton 1 Mt. Db.	100	97½
4½	Mid. Class Dwlgs., L., Db.†	100	120½
1/	Millars' Karri, Ltd.	1	2½
6	Do. Cum. Pref.	1	1½
15/	Milner's Safe, Ltd.	10	19
10/	Moir & Son, Ltd., Pref.	5	8
6	Morgan Cruc., L., Cm. Pf.	10	15
2/	Morris, B., Ltd.	3½	3½
—	Murray L. 5½ p.c. C. Pf.	5	108
—	Do. 4½ 1 Mt. Db. Sk. Rd.	100	
2/6	Natnl. Dwlgs., L., 5 p.c. Pf.	5	1
1/7½	Nat. Safe Dep., Ltd.	4	3½
6	Do. Cum. Pref.	1	1½
—	Native Guano, Ltd.	5	½
5	Nelson Bros., Ltd.	10	2½
5	Do. Deb. Stk., Red.	100	80½†
4/	Neuchtel Asph., Ltd.	10	10½
—	New Central Borneo, Ld.	1	1/16
—	New Darvel Tob., Ltd.	18/	⅜
2/4½	New Explosives, Ltd.	3	2½
5/3½	New Gd. Htl., Bham, L.	5	4
5	Do. Pref.	5	4½
4	Do. 1 Mt. Db. Stk., Rd.	100	98½
—	New Julia Nitrate, Ltd.	10/	1/16
2/	New Ldn. Borneo Tob., L.	16/	⅜
1/6	New Premier Cycle, Ltd.	1	⅞
—	Do. 6 p.c. Cum. Pref.	1	⅞†
—	Do. 4 p.c. 1 Mt. Db. Rd.	100	—†
1/	New Tamargl. Nitr., Ltd.	1	1/16
1/2½	Do. 8 p.c. Cum. Pref.	1	¾
6	Do. 6 p.c. 1 Mt. Dbs. Rd.	100	68
—	Newnes, G., L., Cm. Prf.	1	1½†
1/3	Nitr. Provision, Ltd.	2½	¼
24/	Nobel-Dynam., Ltd.	10	17½
—	North Brazn. Sugar, Ltd.	1	—
10/	Oakey, Ltd.	10	29
6	Do. Cum. Pref.	10	15½
4/	Paccha Jarp. Nitr., Ltd.	5	¾
5	Pac. Borax, L., 1 Db. Rd.	100	110†
—	Palace Hotel, Ltd.	10	6½
5½	Do. Cum. Pref.	10	9
4	Do. 1 Mt. Deb. Stk.	100	104
2/6	Palmer, Ltd.	5	1½
6	Do. Cum. Pref.	5	3½
9½d.	Paquin, Ltd.	1	1
6	Do. Cum. Pref.	5	4½†
5½	Parnall, Ltd., Cum. Pref.	1	¾
3/	Pawsons, Ltd., £10 Shs.	6	6½
4	Do. Mt. Debs., Red.	100	107†
6	Pearks, G. & T., Ltd., 6 p.c. Cum. Pref.	1	¾
1/2½	Pears, Ltd.	1	1½
6	Do. Cum. Pref.	10	14½
5	Do. Deb. Stk.	100	130†
5½	Pearson, C. A., L., Cu. Pf.	5	5
4/	Peebles, Ltd.	5	7½
5	Do. Cum. Pref.	5	6½
4½	Do. Mt. Deb. Stk. Red.	100	112
5½	Peek Bros., Ltd., 1 Cum. Pref., Nos. 1-60,000	5	6½
3½	Do. 3½ p.c. 1 Db. Stk.	100	101
7½d.	Pegamoid, Ltd.	1	⅞
4/	Phospho-Guano, Ltd.	5	2½
4/	Pillsbury-W. Fl. Mills, L.	10	2½
16/	Do. 8 p.c. Cum. Pref.	10	6½
6	Do. 1 Mort. Debs.	100	94½
7½d.	Plummer, Ltd.	1	1½
5	Do. Cum. Pref.	5	5½
15/	Price's Candle, Ltd.	16	40
6	Priest Marians, L., Cm. Pf.	1	1⅛
6	Pryce Jones, Ld., Cm. Pf.	5	7½
5	Do. Deb. Stk.	100	120½
10. 8d.	Pullman, Ltd.	1	1½†
6d.	Do. Cum. Pref.	1	1½
1/	Raleigh Cycle, Ltd.	1	15/16
6	Do. Cum. Pref.	1	⅞
5	Recife Drnge., Ld., 1 Mt. Debs., Red.	100	19
6	Redfern, Ltd., Cum. Prf.	10	14
5	Ridgways, Ltd., Cu. Pf.	5	5½
5/	R. Janeiro Cy. Imps., Ld.	25	10
5	Do. Debs.	100	80
5	Do. 1882-1893	100	77
11/	R. Jan. Fl. Mills, Ltd.	7	7½
5	Do. 1 Mt. Debs., Rd*	100	93†
10/	Riv. Plate Meat, Ltd.	5	3½
10	Do. Pref.	5	5
8½d.	Roberts, J. R., Ltd.	1	1½
5	Do. 1 Mt. Db. Sk., Rd.	100	112†
8½d.	Roberts, T. R., Ltd.	1	2½
5	Do. Cum. Pref.	1	1½
3/	Rosario Nit., Ltd.	5	3½
5	Do. Debs., Red.	100	103
5	Do. Huara, Debs. †	—	101½
1/	Rover Cycle, Ltd.	1	¾
6/	Ryl. Aquarium, Ltd.	5	4½
6	Do. Pref.	5	5½†
5	Ryl. Htl., Edin., Cm. Pf.	1	1½
1/2½	Ryl. Niger, Ltd., £10 Sh.	2	2½
6/	Do.	10	14½
3/	Ruston, Proctor, Ltd.	10	11
4½	Do. 1 Mort. Debs.	100	104†
6/	Sadler, Ltd.	12	7
—	Sal. Carmen Nit., Ltd.	5	4½
9d.	Salmon & Gluck., Ltd.	1	1½
2/	Salt Union, Ltd.	10	2½
14/	Do. 7 p.c. Pref.	10	9
4½	Do. Deb. Stk.	100	110†
4½	Do. "B" Deb. Sk., Rd. †	100	104½
2/6	San Donato Nit., Ltd.	5	¾
2/6	San Jorge Nit., Ltd.	5	3½
5/	San Pablo Nit., Ltd.	5	¾
2/	San Sebastn. Nit., Ltd.	5	¾
1/	Sanitas, Ltd.	1	2½
5/	Sa. Elena Nit., Ld.	5	½
10/	Sa. Rita Nit., Ltd.	5	2
10/	Savoy Hotel, Ltd.	10	19
7	Do. Pref.	10	16
4	Do. 1 Mt. Deb. Stk. †	100	112½
5	Do. Debs., Red. †	100	102½
5	Do. & Ldn. For. Htl., Ltd., 5 p.c. Debs. Red.	100	99†
1½d.	Schweppes, Ltd.	1	1½
—	Do. Def.	1	¾
5	Do. Cum. Pref.	1	1⅛
4	Do. Deb. Stk.	100	104
1/	Singer Cyc., Ltd.	1	11/16
5½	Do Cum. Pref.	1	11/16
—	Smokeless Pwdr., Ltd.	1	¼
5½d.	S. Eng. Dairies, Ltd., 6 p.c. Cum. Pref.	1	1½†
—	Sowler Thos. L.	1	
—	Do. 5½ Cm. Pf.	5	
5	Skinner LdCm. Pf.	10	
4	Do. 1 Mt. Ds. Sk. Rd.	100	
3/6	Spencer, Turner, & Co. Ltd.	5	8½
5	Do. Cum. Pref.	5	6½
5	Spicer, Ld., 5 p.c. Dbs. Rd.	100	65†
4/	Spiers & Pond, Ltd.	10	21½†
5	Do. 1 Mt. Debs., Red†.	100	116½
5	Do. "A" Db. Stk., Rd.	100	110†
5	Do. "B" 1 Db. Stk., Rd.	100	110
4	Do. Fd. "C" 1 Db. S., R.	100	102†
5/	Spratt's, Ltd	5	13
4	Do. Debs., 1914	—	104†
7/	Stewart & Clydesdale, L.	10	13
6	Do. Cum. Pref.	10	15
—	Swan & Edgar, L.	1	1½
1/3	Sweetmeat Automatic, L.	1	4
2/9	Teetgen, Ltd., Cum. Pref.	5	5½†
12/	Teleg. Construction., Ld.	12	37½
5	Do. Db. Bds., Rd. 1899	100	102½
3/0½	Tilling, Ld., 5½ p.c. Cm. Prf.	5	5½†
4	Do. 4 p.c. 1 Dbs., Rd.	—	103†
8½d.	Tower Tea, Ltd.	1	1½
5	Do. Cum. Pref.	5	5½
5	Travers, Ltd., Cum. Pref.	10	12½
4	Do. 1 Mt. Dbs., Rd.	100	101½
6	Tucuman Sug., 1 Dbs., Rd.	100	98†
4/	United Alkali, Ltd.	10	2½
7	Do. Cum. Pref.	10	9½
5	Do. Mt. Db. Stk., Rd.	100	109½
2½d.	United Horse Shoe, Ltd., Non-Cum. 8 p.c. Pref.	1	½
5	Un. Kingm. Tea, Cm. Prf.	5	4½
1/	Un. Lankat Plant., Ltd.	1	2½
2/	Un. Limmer Asphlte., Ld.	3	4½
5/	Val de Travers Asph., L.	10	14½
3/	V. den Bergh's, L., Cm. Prf.	5	6½
6	Walkers, Park., L., C. Pf.	10	4
4½	Do. 1 Mt. Debs., Red.	100	90½†
4/	Wallis, Thos. & Co., Ltd.	5	13½
6	Do. Cum. Pref.	5	8½
5½	Waring, Ltd., Cum. Pref.	5	5½
4½	Do. 1 Mt. Db. Sk., Red. †	100	109½
4½	Do. Irred. "B" Db. Stk.	100	103†
6/	Waterlow, Ltd.	10	
12/8	Do. Dfd. Ord.	15	
12/8	Do. Pref.	15	
9½	Do. Cum. Pref.	10	10½
10/	Waterlow Bros. & L., Ld.	10	
5	Waterlow, Dfd.	10	12½
9½d.	Welford, Ltd.	1	2
4½	Do. Debs., Red.	100	107†
4½d.	Welford's Surrey Dairies, L.	1	1½
7½d.	West London Dairy, Ltd.	1	1
4½	Wharncliffe Dwllgs, L., Pf.	10	11½
18/10	Do. 3 p.c. Irr. Mt. Db. Sk.	100	100
6d.	White, A. J., Ltd.	1	¾
6	Do. 6 p.c. Cum. Pref.	1	¾†
4	White, J. Bazley, Ltd., 1 Mort. Debs., Red.	100	94½†
5	White, R., Ltd., 1 Mort. Deb. Stock, Red.	100	106½
5/	White, Tomkins, Ltd.	10	12½
5	Do. Cum. Pref.	10	12
6	White, W. N., L., Cm. Pf.	1	1
2/6	Wickens, Pease & Co., L.	5	2
6	Wilkie, Ltd., Cum. Pref.	10	16†
3/6	Willans & Robinson, Ltd.	5	8
6	Do. Cum. Pref.	5	7
4½	Do. 1 Mt. Db. Stk., Red.	100	106
7½d.	Williamsons, L., Cm. Prf.	1	1½†
6	Winterbottm Black Cloth, Ltd., Cum. Prf.	10	15
3/	Yates, Ltd.	5	6½
6	Do. Cum. Pref.	5	6½†
1/6	Young's Paraffin, Ltd.	4	1½

CORPORATION STOCKS—COLONIAL AND FOREIGN.

Per Cent.	Name.	Paid.	Price.
6	Auckland City, '72 1904-24	100	118
6	Do. Cons., '79, Red. 1930	100	138½
5	Do. Deb. Ln., '83..1934-8	100	116†
6	Auckland Harb. Debs.	100	113
5	Do. 1917	100	111
5	Do. 1936	100	116
5½	Balmain Boro' 1914	—	117
5	Boston City (U.S.) †	100	100½
5	Do. 1902	100	104½
5	Brunswick Town 5. c. Debs. 1916-20	100	111†
15/	B. Ayres City 6 p.c.	100	51
4½	Do. 4½ p.c.	100	73
5	Cape Town, City of	100	113†
4	Do. 1943	100	113†
4	Chicago, City of, Gold 1915	—	107½
6	Christchurch 1926	100	128½
6	Cordoba City	100	86
5	Duluth (U.S.) Gold 1926	—	110†
6	Dunedin (Otago) 1925	100	124†
6	Do. 1906	100	113†
5	Do. Consols 1908	100	113
4	Durban Insc. Stk. 1944	1000	111
4	Essex Cnty., N. Jersey 1926	$100	113½
5	Fitzroy, Melbrne. 1916-19	100	108†
5	Gisborne Harbour 1915	100	110½
4	Greymouth Harbour 1925	100	111
4	Hamilton 1934	100	109
5	Hobart Town 1918-30	100	111
4	Do. 1940	100	104
4½	Invercargill Boro. Dbs. 1936	100	113
6	Kimberley Boro., S. A. Dbs.	—	104
4	Launceston Twn. Dbs. 1916	100	107
6	Lyttleton, N.Z., Harb. 1929	100	123†
4	Melbourne Bd. of Wks. 1921	100	109
5	Melb. City Debs. 1897-1907	100	107½
4	Do. Debs. 1908-27	100	113½
4	Do. Debs. 1915-20-22	100	108
5	Melbne. Harb. Bds., 1908-9	100	112†
4½	Do. do. 1915	100	110†
4	Do. do. 1918-21	100	106†
4½	Melbrne. Tms, Dbs. 1914-16	100	112†
4½	Do. Fire Brig. Db. 1921	100	109
5	Mexico City Stg.	100	89†
4	Moncton N. Bruns. City	100	104
4½	Montevideo	100	56
5	Montreal Stg.	100	103
5	Do. 1874	100	103
5	Do. 1879	100	104
3½	Do. 1933	100	104
3	Do. Perm. Deb. Stk.	100	98
4	Do. Cons. Deb. Stk. 1932	100	113
6	Napier Boro. Consolid. 1914	100	119†
5	Napier Harb. Debs. 1920	100	114†
5	Do. Debs. 1928	100	106†
6	New Plymouth Harb. Debs. 1909	100	107
6	New York City 1901	—	106†
3½	Do. 1910-26	—	105½
4½	Nth. Melbourne Debs. 1-600 1921	100	105†
5	Oamaru Boro. Cons. 1920	100	101†
6	Do. Harb. Bds. (Reg.)	100	74½
25/	Do. 6 p.c. (Bearer) 1919	100	35
6	Otago Harb. Deb. Reg.	100	103†
6	Do. 1877	100	107†
6	Do. 1881 1921	100	115†
5	Do. Debs. 1921	100	107†
5	Do. Cons. 1934	100	105†
6	Ottawa City	100	109
6	Do. 1904	100	115½
4½	Do. Debs. 1913	100	112
6	Port Elizabeth Waterworks	100	113½
5	Port Louis	100	108†
5	Prahran Debs. 1917	100	111
4	Do. Debs. 1919	100	103
6	Quebec C. Coupon. 1875 1905	100	112†
6	Do. do. 1878 1908	100	116†
4½	Do. Debs. 1914-18	100	107†
4	Do. Debs. 1923	200	107†
3½	Do. Cns. Rg. Stk., Red.	100	101†
5	Richmond (Melb.) Dbs. 1917	100	111†
4	Rio Janeiro City	100	59
4	Rome City	100	—
4	Do. 2nd to 8th Iss.	100	94
6	Rosario C.	100	26½
6	Do.	100	26½
4	St. Catherine (Ont.) 1926	100	103
4	St. John, N.B., Debs. 1934	—	104
4½	St. Kilda (Melb) Dbs. 1918-21	100	104†
4	St. Louis C. (Miss.) 1911	100	102
4	Do. 1913	100	103½
3·65	Do. 1915	—	107½
6	Santa Fé City Debs.	100	11
6	Santos City	100	97
6	Sofia City	100	84½
5	Sth. Melbourne Debs. 1915	100	111†
4½	Do. Debs. 1919	100	107†
5	Sydney City 1904	100	109†
4	Do. Debs. 1912-13	100	107†
4	Do. do. (1894) 1919	100	109†
7	Timaru Boro. 7 p.c. 1910	100	124½
5	Timaru Harb. Debs 1914†	100	106†
5	Do. Debs. 1916	100	106†
6	Toronto City Wtwks 1904-6	100	110
6	Do. Cons. Debs. 1898	100	101†
5	Do. G. Cns. Dbs. 1919-20	100	118†
4	Do. Strlg. 1922-8	100	107†
4	Do. Local Improv.	100	102†
3½	Do. 1929	100	105†
5½	Valparaiso	100	99†
4	Vancouver 1931	100	108
4	Do. 1932	100	109
6	Wanganui Harb. Dbs. 1905	100	110
6	Wellington Con. Deb. 1907	100	117†
6	Do. Improv., 1879	100	126
6	Do. Wtrwks. Dbs., 1880	100	126
4½	Do. Debs., 1893 1933	100	116
4½	Wellington Harb. 1907	100	106
4	Westport Harb. Dbs. 1925	100	111
6	Winnipeg City Deb. 1907	500	118†
5	Do. 1914	100	118

FINANCIAL, LAND, AND INVESTMENT.

Last Div.	Name.	Paid.	Price.
5	Agncy, Ld. & Fin. Aust., Ltd., Mt. Db. Stk., Rd.	100	82½†
6	Amer. Frehld. Mt. of Lon., Ld., Cum. Pref. Stk. ..	100	77½†
4½	Do. Deb. Stk., Red. ..	100	96
1/	Anglo-Amer. Db. Cor., L.	2	1
4	Do. Deb. Stk., Red (†	100	105½
5½	Ang.-Ceylon & Gen. Est., Ltd., Cons. Stk.	100	73½
6	Do. Reg. Debs., Red.	100	104½
—	Ang.-Fch. Explorn., Ltd.	1	3½
6	Do. Cum. Pref.	1	1½
—	Argent. Ld. & Inv., Ltd. £1 Shares	10/	nil
5	Do. Cum. Pref.	4	1½
—	Assets Fnders' Sh., Ltd.,	4	1½
4/	Assets Realiz., Ltd., Ord.,	5	9
5	Do. Cum. Pref.	5	6½†
21/	Austrln. Agricl £25 Shs.	21½	65½
—	Aust. N. Z. Mort., Ltd., £10 Shs.	1	1½d.
4½	Do. Deb. Stk., Red. ..	100	90½
4	Do. Deb. Stk., Red. ..	100	82½
4½	Australian Est. & Mt., L., 1 Mt. Deb. Stk., Red.	100	105
5	Do. "A" Mort. Deb. Stk., Red.	100	94†
2/6	Australian Mort., Ld., & Fin., Ltd. £25 Shs. ..	5	4½
1/6	Do. New, £25 Shs. ..	3	2½
4	Do. Deb. Stk.......	100	111†
3	Do. Do.	100	85†
4	Baring Est. 2 Mt. Debs., Red.	100	105†
5	Bengal Presidy. 1 Mort. Deb., Red.	100	105†
25/	British Amer. Ld. "A"	1	20
—	Do. "B"	24	6½
1/2½	Brit. & Amer. Mt., Ltd. £10 Shs.	2	1
5/	Do. Pref.	10	10
4	Do. Deb. Stk., Red. ..	100	100†
1/3	Brit. & Austrian Tst Ln., Ltd. £25 Shs.	2½	⅝
4½	Do. Perm. Debs., Red.	100	102½
1½d.	Brit. N. Borneo. £1 Shs.	15/	½
2½d.	Do.	1	1
—	Brit. S. Africa	1	3
5	Do. Mt. Deb., Red.	—	98
6	B. Aires Harb. Tst., Red.	100	97½
—	Canada Co.	1	25
—	Canada N. W. Ld., Ltd.	$25	85½
—	Do. Pref.	$100	85½
4	Canada Perm. Loan & Sav. Perp. Deb. Stk...	100	99½†
—	Curamalan Ld., 1 Mt. 7 p.c. Bds., Red.	—	—
2/4½	Deb Corp., Ld., £10 Shs	4	3½
5	Do. Cum. Pref.	10	11†
4	Do. Perp. Deb. Stk...	100	114†
—	Deb. Corp. Fders' Sh., Ld.	3	1
4/5⅛	Eastn. Mt. & Agncy, Ld., "A"	10	6½
4½	Do. Deb. Stk., Red.	100	100
5	Equitable Revers. In. Ltd.	100	—
—	Exploration, Ltd.	1	1½
1	Freehold Trst. of Austrla. Ltd. £10 Shs.	1	¾
4	Do. Perp. Deb. Stk...	100	103
—	Genl. Assets Purchase, Ltd., 5 p.c. Cum. Pref.	10	—
50/	Genl. Reversionary, Ltd.	100	—
3½	House Prop. & Inv.	100	83½
13/	Hudson's Bay	13	23
4	Impl. Col. Fin. & Agcy. Corp.	100	93½†
4½	Impl. Prop. Inv., Ltd., Deb. Stk., Red.	100	93½
2/6	Internatl. Fincial. Soc., Ltd. £7½ Shs.	2½	1½
4	Do. Deb. Stk., Red...	100	94½
—	Kent Coal Fin. & Dev., Ltd.	5/	⅛
1/9½	Ld. & Mtge. Egypt, Ltd. £18 Shs.	3	2½
5	Do. Debs., Red.	100	103
4½	Do. Debs., Red.	100	101
—	Ld. Corp. of Canada, Ltd.	1	⅝
4½	Ld. Mtge. Bk. of Texas Deb. Stk.	100	—
3½	Ld. Mtge. Bk. Victoria 4½ p.c. Deb. Stk.	100	75†
2/9⅜	Law Debent. Corp., Ltd., £10 Shs.	2	2
4½	Do. Cum. Pref., ...	10	12½
4	Do. Deb. Stk.	100	119
1/	Ldn. & Australasian Deb. Corp., Ltd., £4 Shs. ..	2	½
4½	Do. 4½ p.c. Mt. Deb. Stk., Red.	100	101
—	Ldn. & Middx. Frhld. Est. £2 Shs.	35/	
2/6	Lndn. & N. Y. Inv. Corp., Ltd.	5	2½†
5	Do. 5 p.c. Cum. Pref...	10	9†
1/6	Ldn. & Nth. Assets Corp., Ltd., £2 Shs.	1½	⅞
2/	Ldn. & N. Deb. Corp., L.	2	1½
4/	Ldn. & S. Afric. Explrn. L.	½	14
2/	Mtge. Co. of R. Plate, Ltd. £10 Shs.	2	3
4½	Do. Deb. Stk., Red...	100	112
4½	Morton, Rose Est., Ltd., 1st Mort. Debs.	—	99
—	Natal Land Col. Ltd. ..	10	6½
4/	Do. 8 p.c. Pref., 1870..	5	8½
5/6	Natl. Disct. L., £25 Shs.	5	10½
4½	New Impl. Invest., Ltd. Pref. Stk.	100	63½
—	New Impl. Invest., Ltd. Def. Stk.	100	9
4	N. Zld. Ln. & Mer. Agcy., Ltd. Prf. Ln. Deb. Stk	100	96

Financial, Land, &c. (*continued*):—

Last Div.	Name.	Paid.	Price.
16/	N. Zld. Ln. & Mer. Agcy., Ltd. 5 p.c. "A" Db. Sk.	100	42½
—	N. Zld. Ln. & Mer. Agcy., Ltd., 5 p.c. "B" Db. Stk.	100	4
2/6	N. Zld. Tst. & Ln. Ltd., £25 Shs.	5	1½
12/6	N. Zld. Tst. & Ln. Ltd., 5 p.c. Cum. Pref.	25	19†
—	N. Brit. Australsn. Ltd. ..	100	7½
—	Do. Irred. Guar.....	100	38½
5	Do. Mort. Debs.....	100	72½
4½	N. Queensld. Mort. & Inv., Ltd., Deb. Stk.	100	94
—	Oceana Co., Ltd.	—	—
4	Peel Riv., Ld. & Min. Ltd.	100	90
—	Peruvian Corp., Ltd.	100	2½
—	Do. 4 p.c. Pref.	100	9½
3	Do. 6 p.c. 1 Mt. Debs., Red.	100	40½
—	Queenld. Invest. & Ld. & Mort. Pref. Ord. Stk...	100	20
3/7	Queenld. Invest. & Ld. & Mort. Ord. Shs.	4	3½†
4	Queenld. Invest. & Ld. Mort. Perp. Debs.	100	90
3½	Raily. Roll Stk. Tst. Deb., 1903-6. .... (†	100	100½
50/	Reversiony. Int. Soc., Ltd.	100	—
2/8½	Riv. Plate Trst., Loan & Agcy., L., "A" £10 Shs.	2	4½
1/6	Riv. Plate Trst., Loan & Agcy., Ltd., Def. "B"	5	3½
4	Riv. Plate Trst., Loan & Agy., L., Db. Stk., Red.	100	107†
—	Santa Fé & Cord. Gt. South Land, Ltd.	20	5
—	Santa Fé Land	10	2½
2/	Scot. Amer. Invest., Ltd. £10 Shs.	2	2½
2½	Scot. Australian Invest., Ltd., Cons.	100	89½
6	Scot. Australian Invest., Ltd., Guar. Pref. .. (†	100	132½
5	Scot. Australian Invest., Ltd., Guar. Pref. .. (†	100	104½
4	Scot. Australian Invest., Ltd., 4 p.c. Perp. ‡Dbs. (†	100	105½
5	Sivagunga Zemdy., 1st Mort., Red.	100	99
20/	Sth. Australian	20	57½
3½	Stock Exchange Deb., Rd.	—	101½
—	Strait Develt., Ltd.	1	1/16
2/6	Texas Land & Mt., Ltd. £10 Shs.	2½	3
4½	Texas Land & Mt., Ltd., Deb. Stk., Red.	100	103
—	Transvaal Est. & Dev., L.	1	1/16
—	Transvaal Lands, Ltd., £1 Shs.	15/	½
—	Do. F. P.	1	¾
—	Transvaal Mort., Loan, & Fin., Ltd., £10 Shs. ..	2	⅛
2/	Tst & Agcy. of Austrlsa., Ltd., £10 Shs.	1	2½
7	Do. Old, fully paid ..	10	15½
5/7	Do. New, fully paid ..	10	12½
5	Do. Cum. Pref.	10	12½†
3/	Trust & Loan of Canada, £20 Shs.	5	4½
1/9½	Do. New £20 Shs....	3	2
—	Tst. & Mort. of Iowa, Ltd., £10 Shs.	2½	⅜
4½	Do. Deb. Stk. Red...	100	94½
—	Tst., Loan, & Agency of Mexico, Ltd., £10 Shs.	2	½
—	Trsts., Exors, & Sec. Ins. Corp., Ltd., £10 Shs..	7	1½
5/	Union Dsc., Ld., £10 Shs.	5	10½
—	Union Mort. & Agcy. of Aust., Ltd., £6 Shs. ..	2	—
—	Do. Pref. Stk	100	35
—	Do. 6 p. Pref. £6 Shs.	2	½
4½	Do. Deb. Stk	100	92½†
4	Do. Deb. Stk	100	85½†
5	Do. Deb. Stk. Red...	100	96†
1/6	U.S. Deb. Cor. Ltd., £8 Shs.	1	⅜
5½	Do. Cum. Pref. Stk..	100	102½
4½	Do. Irred. Deb. Stk..	100	109½
5	U.S. Tst. & Guar. Cor., Ltd., Pref. Stk	100	69½
6/	Van Dieman's	25	16
4	Walker's Prop. Cor., Ltd., Guar. 1 Mt. Deb. Stk..	100	119†
4½	Wstr. Mort. & Inv., Ltd., Deb. Stk.	100	90

FINANCIAL—TRUSTS.

Last Div.	Name.	Paid.	Price.
1/	Afric. City Prop., Ltd...	1	1½
6	Do. Cum. Pref.......	1	1½
4	Alliance Invt., Ltd., Cm. 4½ p.c. Prefd.	100	72½
—	Do. Defd	100	11½
4	Do. Deb. Stk. Red...	100	106½
5	Amrcn. Invt., Ltd., Prfd.	100	123½
5	Do. Defd.	100	87½
4	Do. Deb. Stk. Red...	100	117½
4	Army & Navy Invt., Ltd., 5 p.c. Prefd.	100	76½†
—	Do. Defd. Stk.	100	17½
4	Do. Deb. Stk.	100	106½
4	Atlas Investment, Ltd., Prefd. Stk.	100	70½
4½	Bankers' Invest., Ltd., Cum. Prefd.	100	104
—	Do. Defd	100	27½
4	Do. Deb. Stk	100	113†

Financial—Trusts (*continued*):—

Last Div.	Name.	Paid.	Price.
4/6	†Brewery & Comml. Inv., Ltd., £10 Shs.........	5	6
4	British Investment, Ltd., Cum. Prefd.	100	109½
5	Do. Defd.	100	102½
4	Do. Deb. Stk. .... (†	100	107½
6	Brit. Steam. Invst., Ltd., Prefd. .... (†	100	114½
—	Do. Defd...........	100	66½
4½	Do. Perp. Deb. Stk (†	100	120½
2/3	Car Trust Invst., Ltd., £10 Shs...............	2½	2½
5	Do. Pref	100	165½
4	Do. Deb. Stk., 1915..	100	106†
4	‡Clnl. Sec., Ltd., Prefd. (†	100	105½
—	Do. Defd.	100	46½
4	Consolidated, Ltd., Cum. 1st Pref.	100	94
4	Do. 5 p.c. Cm. 2nd do.	100	74½
—	Do. Defd.	100	114½
4½	Do. Deb. Stk.	100	113½
4½	Edinburgh Invest., Ltd., Cum. Prefd. Stk......	100	110½
4	Do. Deb. Stk. Red.	100	108½
5	Foreign, Amer. & Gen. Invt., Ltd., Prefd.	100	119
2	Do. Defd.	100	54½
4	Do. Deb. Stk.	100	116½
5	Foreign & Colonial Invt., Ltd., Prefd.	100	134½
4½	Do. Defd.	100	89½
4½	Gas, Water & Gen. Invt., Cum. Prefd. Stk.......	100	91½
—	Do. Defd. Stk.	100	33½
4	Do. Deb. Stk.	100	106†
5	Gen. & Com. Invt., Ltd., Prefd. Stk.............	100	105½
—	Do. Defd. Stk.	100	34½
4	Do. Deb. Stk.	100	110½
1/9	Globe Telegph. & Tst., Ltd.	10	11½
6	Do. do. Pref.	10	17½
4	Govt. & Genl. Invt., Ld., Prefd.	100	84½†
3½	Do. Defd.	100	40½
4½	Govts. Stk. & other Secs. Invt., Ltd., Prefd.	100	96½
—	Do. Defd.	100	27½
4½	Do. Deb. Stk.	100	110†
4	Do. do.	100	102†
4½	Guardian Invt., Ltd., Pfd.	100	91½
—	Do. Defd.	100	20½
4	Do. Deb. Stk.	100	106
5	Indian & Gen. Inv., Ltd., Cum. Prefd.	100	109½
2½	Do. Defd.	100	56
4½	Do. Deb. Stk.	100	120½
5	Indust. & Gen. Tst., Ltd., Unified	100	100
3½	Do. Deb. Stk. Red.	100	102½
4½	Internat. Invt., Ltd., Cm. Prefd.	100	72
—	Do. Defd.	100	9
4	Do. Deb. Stk.	100	104†
4	Invest. Tst. Cor. Ltd. Pfd.	100	103
4	Do. Defd.	100	83
4	Do. Deb. Stk. Red.	100	106†
25/	Ldn. Gen. Invest. Ltd., 5 p.c. Cum. Prefd.	100	111½
37/6	Do. Defd.	100	120
4½	Ldn. Scot. Amer. Ltd. Pfd.	100	103½
£3	Do. Defd.	100	59½
4	Do. Deb. Stk.	100	111†
4	Ldn. Tst., Ltd., Cum. Prfd. Stk.	100	104
4	Do. Defd. Stk.	100	73½
4	Do. Deb. Stk., Red.	100	109
3½	Do. Mt. Deb. Stk., Red.	100	101½
5	Mercantile Invt. & Gen., Ltd., Prefd.	100	108
2	Do. Defd.	100	47½
4	Do. Deb. Stk.	100	116½
4	Merchants, Ltd., Pref. Stk.	100	104
4	Do. Ord.	100	78
4	Do. Deb. Stk.	100	117
5	Municipal, Ltd., Prefd...	100	58½
—	Do. Defd.	100	18½
4½	Do. Debs.	100	113†
4½	Do. Debs. "B"...	100	100†
4½	Do. "C" Deb. Stk.	100	88½†
5	New Investment, Ltd. Ord.	100	97
5	Omnium Invest., Ltd., Pfd.	100	96½
£1	Do. Defd.....	100	27½
4	Do. Deb. Stk..	100	102†
4/	†Railway Deb. Tst. Ld., £20 Shs.	10	6½
5	Do. Debs., Red. ..	100	105½
4½	Do. Deb. Stk., 1911	100	105½
4	Do. do. 1927	100	109½
4	Railway Invst. Ltd., Prefd.	100	116
18/6	Do. Defd.	100	24
6/4½	Railway Share Trust & Agency "A"	8	6½
7½	Do. "B" Pref. Stk.	100	145
4½	River Plate & Gen. Invt., Ltd., Prefd.	100	106
£3	Do. Defd.	100	54½
5	Scot. Invst., Ltd., Pfd. Stk.	100	93½
1½	Do. Defd..	100	26½
4	Do. Deb. Stk.	100	108
4½	Sec. Scottish Invst., Ltd., Cum. Prefd.	100	90½
£2	Do. Defd. Stk.	100	32
4	Do. Deb. Stk.	100	106½
7/6	Sth. Africa Gold Tst., Ltd.	1	5½
6	Do. Cum. Pref.	1	1
5½	Do. 1st Debs., Red.	100	102†
9d.	†Stock Conv. & Invest., Ltd., £5 Shs.	1	1½
—	Do. do. 4½ p.c. Cm. Prf.	100	113
2½	Do. Ldn. & N. W. 1st. Charge Prefd.	100	116
4	Do do. 2nd Chge Prfd.	100	113
32/6	Do. do. Defd. Charge	100	31
3	Do. N. East. 1 Chge Pfd.	100	94

Financial—Trusts (*continued*):—

Last Div.	Name.	Paid.	Price.
37/6	Stock N. East Defd. Chge	100	39
6	Submarine Cables	100	138½
5	U.S. & S. Amer. Invest., Ltd., Prefd.	100	98
2	Do. Defd.	100	27½
4	Do. Deb. Stk.	100	104½

GAS AND ELECTRIC LIGHTING.

Last Div.	Name.	Paid.	Price.
10/6	Alliance & Dublin Con. 10 p.c. Stand.	10	24½
7/6	Do. 7 p.c. Stand...	10	17
5	Austln. Gas Lght. (Syd.) Debs. 1909	100	106†
5	Bay State of N. Jrsy. Sk. Fd. Tst. Bd., Red. ..	—	92½†
3/	Bombay, Ltd..........	5	7
2/4½	Do. New	4	5½
12	Brentford Cons.	100	302½
9	Do. New	100	239½
5	Do. Pref.	100	147½
4	Do. Deb. Stk. ..	100	136
11½	Brighton & Hove Gen. Cons. Stk.	100	277½
8½	Do. "A" Cons. Stk.	100	202½
5	Bristol 5 p.c. Max.	100	132½
22/6	British Gas Light, Ltd.	20	57
11/6	Bromley Gas Consumrs.' 10 p.c. Stand.	10	26
8/6	Do. 7 p.c. Stand...	10	21
—	Brush Electl. Enging., L.	—	2
2/	Do. 6 p.c. Pref.	—	2½
4½	Do. Deb. Stk.	100	111
4½	†Do. 2 Deb. Stk., Red.	100	101½
5/	B. Ayres (New), Ltd. ..	10	9½
4	Do. Deb. Stk., Rd. ..	—	98†
12/	Cagliari Gas & Wtr., Ltd.	20	31
8/	Cape Town & Dist. Gas Light & Coke, Ltd.	10	17
4½	Do. Pref.	10	12
6	Do. 1 Mt. Debs. 1910	50	60
3/	Charing Cross & Strand Elec. Sup., Ltd....	5	13
4½	Do. Cum. Pref.	5	6½
2/6	†Chelsea Elec. Sup., Ltd.	5	10½
4½	Do. Deb. Stk., Red.	100	113½
5	Chic. Edison Co. 1 Mt., Red.	$1000	108
14/	City of Ldn. Elec. Lht., L.	10	26½
—	Do. New	10	26
6/	Do. Cum. Pref.	10	17½
5	Do. Deb. Stk., Red. (†	100	131½
11½	Commercial, Cons.	100	340½
10½	Do. New	100	287½
4½	Do. Deb. Stk.	100	136
10	Continental Union, Ltd.	100	[illegible]
7	Do. Pref. Stk.	100	215½
—	County of Lon. & Brush Prov. Elec. Lg., Ltd.	10	13½
6	Do. Cum. Pref.	10	15½
14	Croydon Comcl. Gas, Ld., "A" Stk., 10 p.c. ..	100	317½
11	Do. "B" Stk., 7 p.c.	100	254½
5½	Crystal Pal. Dist. Ord. 5 p.c. Stk.	100	140
5	Do. Pref. Stk.	100	141½
14/	European, Ltd.	10	26½
10/6	Do.	7½	19
12½	Gas Light & Cke Cons. Stk., "A" Ord.	100	314½
4	Do. "B" (4 p.c. Max.)	100	118½
10	Do. "C," "D," & "E" (Pref.)	100	[illegible]
5	Do. "F" (Pref.)	100	[illegible]
7½	Do. "G" (Pref.)	100	[illegible]
7	Do. "H" (7 p.c. Max.)	100	[illegible]
10	Do. "J" (Pref.)......	100	[illegible]
6	Do. "K"	100	[illegible]
4	Do. Deb. Stk.	100	139
4½	Do. do.	100	165
6	Do. do.	100	207
8/	Hong Kong & China, Ld.	10	14½
—	†House to House Elec. Light Sup., Ltd. ..	5	9
7	Do. Cum. Pref.	5	11
10	Imperial Continental ..	100	219
3½	Do. Deb. Stk., Red ..	100	103
2/	Malta & Medit., Ltd. ..	5	6
5/	†Metrop. Elec. Sup., Ltd.	10	28
3/8	Do. New	10	18½
4½	Do. 1 Mt. Deb. Stk.	100	129
5	Metro. of Melbrne. Dbs. 1908-12	100	113
4½	Do. Debs.. 1918-22-4	100	110
10/	Monte Video, Ltd.	20	25
8/	†Notting Hill Elec. Lig., Ltd.	10	18
4/6	Oriental, Ltd.	5	[illegible]
4/0½	Do. New	[illegible]	[illegible]
10½d.	Do. do. 1879	1	[illegible]
3/6	Ottoman, Ltd.	5	[illegible]
—	Para, Ltd.	—	—
6	People's Gas Lt. & C. of Chic. 1 Mt.....1904	100	[illegible]
6	River Plate Elec. Lgt. & Trac., Ltd., 1 Deb. Stk.	—	[illegible]
112	Royal Elec. of Montreal	—	[illegible]
4½	Do. 1 Mt. Deb. ..	100	106
3/6	†St. James' & Pall Mall Elec. Light, Ltd. ..	5	17½
7	Do. Pref.	5	10½
4	Do. Deb. Stk., Red. †	100	[illegible]
10/	San Paulo, Ltd.	20	6½

Gas and Electric (*continued*):—

Last Div.	Name.	Paid.	Price.
10	Sheffield Unit. Gas Lt. "A"	100	251½
10	Do. "B"	100	251½
10	Do. "C"	100	251½
—	Sth. Ldn. Elec. Sup., Ld.	2	2¾
5¼	South Metropolitan	100	144½
3	Do. 3 p.c. Deb. Stk.	100	107½
12	Tottenham & Edmonton Gas Lt. & C., "A"	100	290
9	Do. "B"	100	210
7/	Tuscan, Ltd.	10	14†
5	Do. Debs., Red.	100	102
4/9	West Ham 10 p.c. Stan.	5	12
4/	Wstmnstr. Elec. Sup., Ld.	5	16¼

INSURANCE.

Last Div.	Name.	Paid.	Price.
4/	Alliance, £20 Shs.	44/	11½
10/	Alliance, Mar., & Gen., Ld., £100 Shs.	25	52
5/	Atlas, £50 Shs.	6	31½
8/	British & For. Marine, Ld., £20 Shs.	4	25
7½d.	British Law Fire, Ltd., £10 Shs.	1	1⅜
7/6	Clerical, Med., & Gen. Life, £25 Shs.	50/	16½
10/	Commercial Union, Ltd., £50 Shs.	5	44½
4	Do. "W. of Eng." Ter. Deb. Stk.	100	110½
60/	County Fire, £100 Shs.	80	185
2/6	Eagle, £50 Shs.	5	—
4/	Employrs' Liability, Ltd., £10 Shs.	2	4
—	Empress, Ltd., £5 Shs.	1	1½
21/	Equity & Law, £100 Shs.	6	22
7/6	General Life, £100 Shs.	5	15†
4½d.	Gresham Life, £5 Shs.	15/	2¼†
6/6	Guardian, Ld., £10 Shs.	5	12½
10/	Imperial, Ltd., £20 Shs.	5	32†
5/6	Imperial Life, £20 Shs.	4	7
6/	Indemnity Mutual Mar., Ltd., £15 Shs.	3	12
1/	Lancashire, £20 Shs.	2	5
7½d.	Law Acc. & Contin., Ltd., £5 Shs.	10/	⅜
5/	Law Fire, £100 Shs.	2½	18
4½d.	Law Guar. & Trust, Ltd., £10 Shs.	1	1⅛
6/	Law Life, £20 Shs.	2	5
2/9	Law Un. & Crown £10 Shs.	12/	7
14	Do. Deb. Stk., 1942	100	110½
14/6	Legal & General, £50 Shs.	8	15½
9d.	Lion Fire, Ltd., £8½ Shs.	1½	1
14/	Liverpool & London & Globe, Stk.	2	56½
10/	Do. Globe £1 Ann.	—	36
15/	London, £25 Shs.	12½	62½
4/	Lond. & Lanc. Fire, £25 Shs	2½	19½
2/	Lond. & Lanc. Life, £25 Shs	2	5†
10	Lond. & Prov. Mar., Ld., £10 Shs.	1	1½
2/	Lond. Guar. & Accident, Ltd., £5 Shs.	2	11½
10/	Marine, Ltd., £25 Shs.	4½	44½†
2/	Maritime, Ltd., £10 Shs.	2	4½
1/6	Merc. Mar., Ld., £10 Shs.	2½	2½
1/	National Marine, Ltd., £9 Shs.	1	½
10/	N. Brit. & Merc., £25 Shs.	6¼	43½
20/	Northern, £100 Shs.	10	82
60/	Norwich Union Fire, £100 Shs.	12†	128½
5/	Ocean Acc. & Guar., fy. pd.	5	19½
1/	Do. £5 Shs.	1	3½
2/6	Ocean, Marine, Ltd.	2½	9½
1/	Palatine, £10 Shs.	2	3¼
2/6	Pelican, £10 Shs.	1	3¼
12/	Phœnix, £50 Shs.	5	45
25/	Provident, £100 Shs.	10	36
3/	Railway Psngrs., £10 Shs.	2	8½
2/6	Rock Life, £5 Shs.	10/	4½
8	Royal Exchange	100	360†
18/	Royal, £20 Shs.	3	56
5/6	Sun, £10 Shs.	10/	12
3/9	Sun Life, £10 Shs.	7½	15†
4/	Thames & Mrsey. Marine, Ltd., £20 Shs.	2	11
9/	Union, £10 Shs.	4	24½†
3/6	Union Marine, £20 Shs.	2½	9½
12/	Universal Life, £100 Shs.	12	42†
2/	World Marine, £5 Shs.	2	1⅞

IRON, COAL, AND STEEL.

Last Div.	Name.	Paid.	Price.
	Barrow Hæm. Steel, Ltd.	7½	2½
9/	Do. 6 p.c. 2nd Pref.	7½	7
10/	Bolck., Vaugh. & C., Ld.	20	17
6/	Do. £8 liab.	12	9½
7/6	Brown, J. & Co., Ltd., £20 Shs.	15	19½
22/6	Consett Iron, Ld., £10 Shs.	7½	29½
4/	Do. 8 p.c. Cum. Pref.	5	11½
7/6	Ebbw Vale Steel, Iron & Coal, Ltd., £23 Shs.	20	6½
15/	General Mining Assn., Ld.	5½	7½
16/	Harvey Steel Co. of Gt. Britain, Ltd.	10	26½
5	Lehigh V. Coal 1 Mt. 5 p.c. Guar. Gd. Cp. Bds.	—	94
42/6	Nantyglo & Blaina Iron, Ltd., Pref.	862	94
1/	Nerbudda Coal & Iron, Ltd., £3 Shs.	56/	¾
6/	Newport Abrcrn. Bk. Vein Steam Coal, Ltd.	10	4¾
5/	New Sharlston Coll., Ltd. Pref	20	11
4½d.	Nw. Vancvr. Coal & Ld., L.	1	⅜
	North's Navigation Coll. (1889) Ltd.	5	2
	Do. 10 p.c. Cum. Pref.	5	7½
	Rhymney Iron, Ltd.	5	1¼
	Do. New, £5 Shs.	4½	⅜
5	Do. Mt. Debs., Red.	100	98†
5	Shelton Irn., Stl. & Cl. Co., Ltd., 1 Chg. Debs., Red.	100	97½†
10	Sth. Hetton Coal, Ltd.	100	173½
10/	Vickers & Maxim, Ltd.	10	—
5	Do. 5 p.c. Prfd. Stk.	100	133

SHIPPING.

Last Div.	Name.	Paid.	Price.
4/	African Stm. Ship, £20 Shs.	16	9½
5/	Do. Fully-paid	20	13½
5/	Amazon Steam Nav., Ltd.	12½	9½†
8/	Castle Mail Pakts., Ltd., £20 Shs.	14	15½
3½	Do. 1st Deb. Stk., Red.	100	101†
6/	China Mutual Steam, Ltd.	5	2¾
6	Do. Cum. Pref.	10	9½
10/	Cunard, Ltd.	20	3½
5/	Do. £20 Shs.	10	—
4½	Furness, Withy, & Co., Ltd., 1 Mt. Dbs., Red.	100	105
6/	General Steam	15	8¼
5/	Do. 5 p.c. Pref., 1874	10	9
5/	Do. 5 p.c. Pref., 1877	10	9
5/	Leyland & Co., Ltd.	10	15½
7/	Do. 7 p.c. Cum. Pref.	10	14½†
—	Do. 4½ p.c. Cum. Pre-Pf.	3	10½
4	Do. 1st Mt. Dbs., Red.	100	106½
2/6	Mercantile Steam, Ltd.	5	7½
6/4½	New Zealand Ship., Ltd.,	6	5
4	Do. Deb. Stk., Red.	100	104†
5/	Orient Steam, Ltd.	10	4½
5	P. & O. Steam, Cum. Prefd.	100	154½
19	Do. Defd.	100	232½
3½	Do. Deb. Stk.	100	118
5	Richelieu & Ont., 1st Mt. Debs., Red.	100	100
30/	Royal Mail, £100 Shs.	60	51
2/6	Shaw, Sav., & Alb., Ltd., "A" Pref.	5	5
5/	Do. "B" Ord.	5	3
8/	Union Steam, Ltd.	20	18½
4/	Do. New £20 Shs.	10	8
4	Do. Deb. Stk., Red.	100	107†
7/	Union of N.Z., Ltd.	10	9½
3/1½	Wilson's & Fur.-Ley., 5½ p.c. Cum. Pref.	10†	10½
4½	Do. 1 Mt. Db. Sk., Rd.	100†	102½

TELEGRAPHS AND TELEPHONES.

Last Div.	Name.	Paid.	Price.
4	African Direct, Ltd., Mort. Debs., Red.	100	102†
—	Amazon Telegraph, Ltd.	10	6½
14/	Anglo-American, Ltd.	100	63
28/	Do. 6 p.c. Prefd. Ord.	100	111
—	Do. Defd. Ord.	100	14
3/	Brazilian Submarine, Ltd.	10	16½
5	Do. Debs., 2 Series	100†	114½

Telegraphs and Telephones (*continued*):—

Last Div.	Name.	Paid.	Price.
4/	Chili Telephone, Ltd.	5	3½
82½	Conicial. Cable, $100 Shs.	—†	184½
4	Do. Stg. 500-yr. Deb. Stk. Red.	100	105†
2½d.	Consd. Telpehone Constr., &c., Ltd.	10/	¼
8/	Cuba Submarine, Ltd.	10	9
10/	Do. 10 p.c. Pref.	10	19
2/	Direct Spanish, Ltd.	5	4½
5/	Do. 10 p.c. Cum. Pref.	5	10½
4½	Do. Debs.	50†	103½
3/	Direct U.S. Cable, Ltd.	20	10½
2/6	Eastern, Ltd.	10	17½
3/	Do. 6 p.c. Cum. Pref.	10	18½
4	Do. Mt. Deb. Stk., Red.	100	131½
2/6	Eastern Exten., Aus., & China, Ltd.	10	18½
5	Do. (Aus. Gov. Sub.) Deb., Red.	100	101†
5	Do. do. Bearer	100†	101½
4	Do. Mort. Deb. Stk.	100	133½
5	Eastn. & S. Afric., Ltd., Mort. Deb. 1900	100	101†
5	Do. Bearer	100	102†
4	Do. Mort. Debs. 1909	100	104½
4	Do. Mort. Debs. (Maur. Subsidy)	25	109½
5/	Grt. Nthn. Copenhagen	10	26½†
5	Do. Debs., Ser. B., Red.	100	103½
12/6	Indo-European, Ltd.	25	53½
6	London Platino-Brazilian, Ltd., Debs. 1904	100	109
4/	Montevideo Telph., Ltd., 6 p.c. Pref.	5	2½
3/	National Telephone, Ltd.	5	6½
6/	Do. Cum. 1 Pref.	10	16
6/	Do. Cum. 2 Pref.	10	15
5	Do. Non-Cum. 3 Pref.	5	6½
3½	Do. Deb. Stk., Red.	100†	104½
4d.	Oriental Telephone, Ltd.	1	⅜
4	Pac. & Euro. Tlg. Dbs., Rd.	100†	106½
4/	Reuter's, Ltd.	8	8
5/	Un. Riv. Plate Telph., Ltd.	5	4
5	Do. Deb. Stk., Red.	100†	102½
—	West African Telg., Ltd.	10	5
5	Do. 5 p.c. Mt. Debs., Red.	100	104½
—	W. Coast of America, Ltd.	10	—
3/	Western & Brazilian, Ltd.	15	10
3/	Do. 5 p.c. Pref. Ord.	7½	7½
—	Do. Defd. Ord.	7½	3
4	Do. Deb. Stk., Red.	100†	105½
1/	W. India & Panama, Ltd.	10	¾
6/	Do. Cum. 1 Pref.	10	7½
6/	Do. Cum. 2 Pref.	10	6
5	Do. Debs., Red.	100†	106½
7	West. Union, 1 Mt. 1902 ($	1000	107½
6	Do. 6 p.c. Stg. Bds., Rd.	100	102½

TRAMWAYS AND OMNIBUS.

Last Div.	Name.	Paid.	Price.
1/6	Anglo-Argentine, Ltd.	5	3½
6/	Do. Deb. Stk.	100†	125½
4	Barcelona, Ltd.	10	13
5	Do. Deb., Red.	100	104½
6/6	Belfast Street Trams.	10	17
—	Blackpl. & Fltwd. Tram., £10 Shs.	8	9
4/	Bordeaux Tram. & O. Ltd.	10	12½
5	Do. Cum. Pref.	10	11
—	Brazilian Street Ry., Ltd.	2	½
—	British Elec. Trac., Ltd.	10	16¾
—	B. Ayres & Belg. Tram., Ltd., 6 p.c. Cum. Pref.	5	4
6	Do. 1 Deb. Stk.	100	92½†
—	B. Ayres. Gd. Nat., Ltd., 6 p.c 1 Deb. Bds., Red.	100	60
5½	Do. Pref. Debs., Red.	100	92½†
6d.	Calais, Ltd.	5	1
—	Calcutta, Ltd.	10	3½
—	Carthagena & Herr., Ltd.	10	3
5	Do. Deb., Red.	100	95
5	City of B'ham. Trams., Ltd., 5 p.c. Cum. Pref.	5	5½
4	Do. 1 Mort. Debs., Rd.	100	104½
3/9	City of B. Ayres, Ltd.	5	6½
2/3	Do. Ext. £5 Shs.	3	3½
6	Do. Deb. Stk.	100	150
9d.	Edinburgh Street Tram.	4	3
1/	Glasgow Tram. & Omni. Ltd., £9 Shs.	8	3½
3/7½	Imperial, Ltd.	6	1½
2/	Lond., Deptfd, & Greenwich, Prefd.	5	3
nil	Do. Defd.	5	1
10½	Lond. Gen. Omni., Ltd.	100	200
4	Do. Deb., Red.	100	113½

Tramways and Omnibus (*continued*):—

Last Div.	Name.	Paid.	Price.
6/	London Road Car	6	10½
5	London St. Rly. (Prov., Ont.), Mt. Debs.	100	112
4/9	London St. Trams.	—	3
7/6	†London Trams., Ltd.	10	11
6/	Do. Non-Cum. Pref.	10	11
5	Do. Mt. Db. Stk., Rd.	100	100½
5	Lynn & Boston 1 Mt. 1924 $	1000	107
5	Milwaukee Elec. Cons. Mt. $	1000	98½
5	Minneapolis St. 1 Cons. Mt $	1000	94†
5	Montreal St. Dbs., 1908	100	110
4½	Do. Debs., 1922	100	109
6/	Nth. Metropolitan	10	13
1/9½	Nth. Staffords., Ltd.	6	4
5/6	Provincial, Ltd.	10	6½
6/	Do. Cum. Pref.	10	13½†
5	St. Paul City, 1937 $	1000	94†
5	Do. Guar. Twin City Rap. Trans. $	1000	94†
5/	Southampton	10	7
3/	South London	10	5½
3/6	Sunderland, Ltd.	10	5
4½	Toronto 1 Mt., Red.	100	109
2/6	Tramways Union, Ltd.	5	7
4½	Do. Deb., Red.	100	109†
5/	Vienna Generla Omnibus.	5	6½
5	Do. 5 p.c. Mt. Deb., Red.	100	105
4/	Wolverhampton, Ltd.	10	6

WATER WORKS.

Last Div.	Name.	Paid.	Price.
8/	Antwerp, Ltd.	20	21½
6/	Cape Town District, Ltd.	5	5½
10½	Chelsea	100†	335½
5	Do. Pref. Stk.	100†	178½
4½	Do. Pref. Stk., 1875	100†	158½
4½	Do. Deb. Stk.	100	162½
5/	City St. Petersburg, Ltd.	13	11
4/6	Colne Valley	10	15
4	Do. Deb. Stock	100†	137½
£4	Consol. of Rosar., Ltd., 4 p.c. 1 Deb. Stk., Red.	100	90†
7½	East London	100	234
4½	Do. Deb. Stk.	100†	163½
3	Do. Deb. Stk., Red.	100	106†
37/6	Grand Junction (Max. 10 p.c.) "A"	50	124½
18/9	Do. "B"	25	—
18/9	Do. "C" (Max. 7½ p.c.)	25	57½
35/	Do. "D" (Max. 7 p.c.)	50	102½
4	Do. Deb. Stock	100	149½
13	Kent	100	364½
7	Do. New (Max. 7 p.c.)	100	217½
5/7½	Kimberley, Ltd.	7	4½
6	Do. Debs., Red.	100	102½
6	Do. Deb. Stk., Red.	100†	102½
10	Lambeth (Max. 10 p.c.)	100	305†
7	Do. (Max. 7½ p.c.), 50 & 25	—	227†
4	Do. Deb. Stock	100	148½
3	Do. Red. Deb. Stock	100	105
10/	Montevideo, Ltd.	20	16½
5	Do. 1 Deb. Stk.	100	108†
5	Do. 2 Deb. Stk.	100	103†
130/11	15] New River New	100	454½
4	Do. Deb. Stk.	100	153½
4	Do. Deb. Stk. "B"	100	153½
6/	Odessa, Ltd., "A" 6 p.c. Prefd.	20	—
nil	Do. "B" Deferred	20	—
4	Portland Con. Mt. "B," 1927	—	—
8/	Seville, Ltd.	20	12½
5/6	Southend "Addl." Ord.	10	17½
6	Southwark and Vauxhall	100	166½
6	Do. "D" Shares (7½ p.c. max.)	100	159½
5	Do. Pref. Stock	100	177½
4	Do. "A" Deb. Stock	100	145½
3	Staines Resvirs. Jt. Com. Gua. Deb. Stk., Red.	100	105†
7/	Tarapaca, Ltd.	10	9⅜
10	West Middlesex	100	317½
4½	Do. Deb. Stk.	100	163
3	Do. Deb. Stk.	100	107

UNITED STATES AND CANADIAN RAILWAYS.

Mileage. Total.	Increase on 1896.	Increase on 1895.	Name.	Gross Traffic for Week. Period Ending.	Amount.	In. or Dec. on 1896.	Gross Traffic to Date. No. of Weeks.	Amount.	In. or Dec. on 1896.
					dols.	dols.		dols.	dols.
310	—	—	Alabama Gt. South.	Dec. 7	38,597	+468	21	755,296	+22,553
6,547	103	156	Canadian Pacific	Dec. 31	797,000	+106,000	*	24,043,000	+3,374,000
6,169	—	469	Chicago, Mil., & St. Paul	Dec. 31	884,000	+68,000	26	18,430,700	+1,691,950
1,685	—	—	Denver & Rio Grande	Dec. 31	236,500	+71,800	24	4,329,700	+645,600
3,512	—	—	Grand Trunk, Main Line	Dec. 31*	£122,557	+£22,960	24	£2,264,971	+£147,301
335	—	—	Do. Chic. & Grand Trunk	Dec. 31	£21,309	+£21	24	£337,972	+£13,453
189	—	—	Do. Det., G. H. & Mil.	Dec. 31	£6,498	−£529	24	£108,877	+£554
2,938	—	—	Louisville & Nashville	Dec. 25	572,990	+16,254	24	11,190,121	+965,528
2,197	137	137	Miss., K., & Texas	Dec. 31	386,209	+56,607	24	7,044,461	+495,444
477	—	—	N. Y., Ontario, & W.	Dec. 31	97,021	+8,312	24	2,113,285	+61,763
1,570	—	—	Norfolk & Western	Dec. 31	156,000	−12,000	24	5,547,000	+460,000
3,499	336	—	Northern Pacific	Dec. 7	477,430	+162,966	*	19,566,681	+1,539,115
4,654	—	—	Southern	Dec. 21	434,000	+38,000	23	9,809,812	+479,446
1,979	—	—	Wabash	Dec. 31	337,000	+34,000	*	11,637,465	+193,034

* From January 1.

MONTHLY STATEMENTS.

Mileage. Total.	Increase on 1896.	Increase on 1895.	Name.	Net Earnings for Month. Month.	Amount.	In. or Dec. on 1896.	In. or Dec. on 1895.	Net Earnings to Date. No. of Months.	Amount.	In. or Dec. on 1896.	In. or Dec. on 1895.
					dols.	dols.	dols.		dols.	dols.	dols.
6,935	44	444	Atchison	October	3,695,379	+392,688	+630,197	4	12,927,404	+1,670,269	+3,088,713
1,970	—	—	Erie	October	3,269,293	+170,999	+102,830	10	27,387,757	+1,465,770	+2,211,338
3,127	—	239	Illinois Central	November	2,534,427	+664,861	+377,039	11	22,138,724	+2,451,949	+2,487,092
2,396	—	—	New York Central	November	3,900,753	+18,435	−300,993	11	41,934,547	+1,697,686	+1,616,507
3,407	—	—	Pennsylvania	October	5,996,778	+399,900	−266,500	10	52,785,348	+1,127,500	−324,600
1,055	—	—	Phil. & Reading	October	2,184,454	+91,523	−89,806	10	17,441,119	+149,794	−2,557,200

INDIAN AND CEYLON TEA COMPANIES.

Acres Planted.	Crop, 1896.	Paid up Capital.	Share.	Paid up.	Name.	Dividends. 1894.	1895.	1896.	Int. 1897.	Price.	Yield.	Reserve.	Balance Forward.	Working Capital.	Mortgages, Debs. or Pref. Capital not otherwise stated.
	lb.	£	£	£	INDIAN COMPANIES.							£	£	£	£
11,240	3,109,000	120,000	10	3	Amalgamated Estates	—	*	10	—	3½	6⅝	10,000	16,500	D52,990	—
		400,000	10	10	Do. Pref.	—	*	5	2½	10½	4¾				
10,223	3,387,100	187,160	20	20	Assam	20	20	20	5	62½	6½	55,000	1,730	D11,330	—
5,900	3,320,000	142,500	10	10	Assam Frontier	3	6	6	2½	9½	6½	—	286	90,000	82,500
		142,500	10	10	Do. Pref.	6	6	6	3	12	5				
2,087	865,550	66,745	5	5	Attaree Khat	12	12	8	3	7½	5¼	3,790	4,800	7,770	—
1,633	550,980	78,170	10	10	Borelli	4	4	5	—	9	5½	—	3,256	D170	—
1,689	880,000	60,825	5	5	British Indian	6	5	5	—	4¾	5¼	—	2,920	12,300	—
3,223	2,282,430	114,500	5	5	Brahmapootra	20	18	20	—	14½	6¾	23,440	—	41,600	—
3,904	1,634,000	76,500	10	10	Cachar and Dooars	*	8	7	—	9½	7¼	—	1,645	21,240	—
		76,500	10	10	Do. Pref.	*	6	6	3	12½	4¾				
3,946	2,002,370	72,010	1	1	Chargola	8	7	10	2½	1	10	3,000	3,300	—	—
		81,000	1	1	Do. Pref.	7	7	7	3½	1⅜	5				
1,971	968,090	33,000	5	5	Chubwa	10	8	10	3½	7½	6½	10,000	2,043	D5,400	—
		33,000	5	5	Do. Pref.	7	7	7	3½	7	5				
33,250	10,620,000	120,000	10	3	Cons. Tea and Lands	—		10	5	3⅜	7½	65,000	14,240	D191,674	—
		1,000,000	10	10	Do. 1st Pref.	—	*	5	2½	11	4½				
		400,000	10	10	Do. 2nd Pref.	—	*	7	3½	11¾	5½				
2,230	593,160	135,420	20	20	Darjeeling	5½	5½	6	—	24	5	5,552	1,565	1,700	—
2,114	456,580	60,000	10	10	Darjeeling Cons.	—		4/2	—	7½	2¾	—	1,820	—	—
		60,000	10	10	Do. Pref.	—	*	5	2½	9½	5				
6,600	2,973,050	150,000	10	10	Dooars	12½	12½	12½	2½	20½	6¼	45,000	300	D30,000	—
		75,000	10	10	Do. Pref.	7	7	7	3½	17½	3¾				
3,367	1,833,520	165,000	10	10	Doom Dooma	11¼	10	12½	5	23½	5¼	30,000	4,032	—	10,000
1,377	500,080	61,120	5	5	Eastern Assam	5	nil.	4	—	3½	5¾	—	1,790	—	10,000
4,038	1,529,380	85,000	10	10	East India and Ceylon	*	nil.	7	—	9½	7	—	1,710	—	—
		85,000	10	10	Do. Pref.	*	6	6	3	12½	4¾				
7,570	3,600,000	219,000	10	10	Empire of India	—	*	6/10	—	13½	—	15,000	—	27,000	—
		219,000	10	10	Do. Pref.	—	*	5	—	11½	4½				
1,180	647,600	94,060	10	10	Indian of Cachar	7	3½	3	—	6	5½	6,070	—	7,120	—
2,916	968,000	83,500	5	5	Jhanzie	10	10	10	4	8½	5½	14,500	1,070	2,700	—
7,980	3,467,000	250,000	10	10	Jokai	10	10	10	5	18½	5½	45,000	990	D7,000	—
		100,000	10	10	Do. Pref.	*	6	6	3	15½	3¾				
5,224	1,801,600	200,000	20	20	Jorehant	20	20	20	—	56	7	26,220	2,955	3,000	—
1,547	554,560	65,660	10	8	Lebong	15	15	15	5	17½	6½	9,000	2,150	6,650	—
5,082	1,843,700	100,000	10	10	Lungla	*	10	6	3	10	6	—	1,343	D21,000	—
		100,000	10	10	Do. Pref.	*	6	6	3	12½	4¾				
2,684	866,300	95,970	10	10	Majuli	7	5	5	2	7½	6½	—	2,606	560	—
1,300	226,000	91,840	1	1	Makum	—	—	2	—	1⅛	1¾	—	—	1,200	25,000
3,140	938,400	100,000	1	1	Moabund	—	—	*	—	1⅛	—	—	—	—	—
		50,000	1	1	Do. Pref.	—	—	*	2½	1	5				
1,080	510,000	79,590	10	10	Scottish Assam	7	7	7	—	11	6½	6,500	800	9,590	—
4,150	1,635,000	100,000	10	10	Singlo	*	8	5	—	13	5	—	300	D5,200	—
		80,000	10	10	Do. Pref.	*	6½	6½	3¼	14½	6¼				
					CEYLON COMPANIES.										
10,315	1,743,824	250,000	100	100	Anglo-Ceylon, & Gen.	—	*	5½	—	72	7	10,992	1,405	D72,844	166,980
2,759	685,741	50,000	10	10	Associated Tea	—	*	5	—	8	6¼	—	164	2,478	—
		60,000	10	10	Do. Pref.	—	*	6	—	11	5½				
8,227	3,763,000	167,380	10	10	Ceylon Tea Plantations	15	15	15	7	27½	5½	84,500	1,516	D30,819	—
		81,080	10	10	Do. Pref.	7	7	7	3½	17½	4				
5,700	1,542,700	55,960	5	3	Ceylon & Oriental Est.	5	8	7	—	2¾	7¼	—	230	D2,047	71,000
		46,000	5	5	Do. Pref.	6	6	6	3	5½	5½				
1,835	—	111,330	5	5	Dimbula Valley	—	*	10	2½	6½	7	—	—	1,733	6,030
		62,607	5	5	Do. Pref.	—	*	6	3	6½	4½				
10,535	3,715,000	298,250	5	5	Eastern Prod. & Est.	3	5	6½	2½	6½	4½	20,000	11,740	D17,797	102,800
3,118	646,160	150,000	10	10	Lanka Plantations	4	5	5	5	7½	6½	—	495	D11,300	14,700 Pref.
1,792	542,433	90,000	10	10	Imperial	—		5	—	9	5½	—	33	—	—
2,193	960,100	22,080	10	10	New Dimbula "A"	10	16	16	16	25	6	11,000	2,024	1,150	—
		55,710	10	10	Do. "B"	18	16	16	16	23½	6¾				
		8,400	10	10	Do. "C"	nil.	8	14	14	—	—				
2,459	564,000	100,000	10	10	Ouvah	6	8	6	2	10	6	4,000	1,151	D1,255	—
—	—	200,000	10	10	Nuwara Eliya	—	*	6	3	12	5	—	—	—	30,000
1,963	720,000	41,000	10	10	Scottish Ceylon	15	15	15	5	—	—	7,000	1,252	D3,970	—
		9,000	10	10	Do. Pref.	7	7	7	3½	—	—				
2,280	602,000	56,000	10	6	Standard	18	16	16	16	14½	6¼	9,000	800	D15,012	4,000

In working capital column D stands for debit.

* Company formed this year. † Interim dividends are given as actual distribution made.

Printed for the Proprietor by LOVE & WYMAN, LTD., Great Queen Street, London, W.C.; and Published by CLEMENT WILSON at Norfolk House, Norfolk Street, Strand, London, W.C.

The Investors' Review

Vol. I.—No. 2. New Series. FRIDAY, JANUARY 14, 1898. [Registered as a Newspaper.] Price 6d. By post, 6½d

CONTENTS

The Investors' Review.

Economic and Financial Notes and Correspondence.

A Call to Arms.

Much of the following letter has had to be deleted as being of too flattering a character to us, and more because less than respectful towards neighbours, but the advice it gives is too valuable to be ignored. We shall be glad indeed to do our part if only shareholders will do theirs. The difficulty lies in their lack of cohesion, and apathy. Most of them seem ashamed to own that they have been victimised; they never attend meetings when meetings are held; and they merely swear in private when a fresh infamy perpetrated at their expense comes to light.

To the Editor.

SIR,—There is but one thing to be said against the new departure announced by the INVESTORS' REVIEW: its light ought to be shed on the dark places of finance, not once in the week only, but once at least on every working day. There never was a time, within the recollection of City men of this present generation, when honest and independent financial journalism was more greatly needed than at present, and in none of the markets is fearless criticism more urgently required than in that wide field of speculation which comes under the category of mines.

There is one object alone which has only to be accomplished in order to ensure for the REVIEW a lasting place in the gratitnde of all who allowed themselves to be drawn into that maelstrom of speculation which eclipsed all previous phenomena of the kind a couple of years ago. Much of the paper for which the public gave their good money when they once got into the vortex, was found to be representative of interests in genuine properties managed by honest and capable men. Much, on the other hand, could only be regarded as counters in wild-cat ventures emanating from the cupidity of some of the choicest rascals north or south of the line; but betwixt and between these two distinct categories come a number of concerns which were sound enough in their inception, and have a basis of genuine value to rest upon, but have proved nothing but disappointing and ruinous in the hands of those by whom they are controlled. These people, notoriously ignorant of the first principles of mining and industrial direction, are manifestly indifferent to the duties and responsibilities that attach to them in respect of the issues they brought out. They are indifferent because they believe themselves beyond the reach of the arm of the law. Mere remonstrance evokes nothing but their derision and contempt. They introduced companies by the dozen and planted the British public with shares by the million. Never a prospectus did they issue; but they employed every species of advertisement, journalistic and social, to persuade the gullible public that they were giving away sovereigns for ten shillings. They sold, in many instances, every share that existed, in some instances shares that did not exist, and then—not satisfied with their plunder—they must needs plunge the companies into debt as deep as they could go, shut down the mines, and pursue every course that was calculated to make the too confiding shareholder believe that his senses had deceived him, and that his holding was not worth pence where he had acquired it for pounds. It will be a service to the community, an encouragement to honest men, and a wholesome example to those who live by force and fraud, if THE INVESTORS' REVIEW will drag these malefactors into the light of day, so that they may be known and exposed, and never be able to fatten upon the widow and the orphan again.

The first step to this end is that shareholders should be roused to action on their own behalf. They *must* act, and that soon, or the interests that are now in jeopardy will have to be placed in the list of "total loss." The game which the wreckers clearly propose to play is a game they have played before, with impunity and with eminent success. Will THE INVESTORS' REVIEW not signalise its new departure by rendering impossible that disregard of shareholders' interests which the law, or the absence of law, seems positively to encourage? There is no transaction in Transvaal shares, entered into in England, upon which the Chancellor of the Exchequer does not levy toll, and no light toll either, but the victim of this imposition looks to the law in vain for aid or recognition when he happens to need redress. The magnates who have had his money afford him no information concerning his property; they hold no meetings of English shareholders; they deny him the right of finding out the names of his partners, so that he may communicate with them on matters of mutual concern; they even refuse to let him have a copy of the Articles of Association; and the law as it stands says it can afford him no help in the matter.

The most effectual way to avoid the injury and the inconvenience which this state of affairs involves is, of course, to leave all such ventures alone; but that is a counsel of perfection for guidance in the future; and meantime I venture to hope that THE INVESTORS' REVIEW will emphasise the fact, for the benefit of its readers and the community at large, that the case is pre-eminently one in which Heaven will help those who help themselves. The snug Semites in the City, hidden by the millions which the too confiding British public have entrusted to their administration, will not feel quite so confident in their airs of lordly indifference and security if they have to face the ordeal of a meeting of angry shareholders every few weeks, and a careful regard for their own skins will inculcate the expediency of stopping short of the point at which the cup of shareholders' endurance must overflow. When the shareholder does rise in his wrath, he will be so completely and agreeably astonished by the results, that he will be inclined to kick himself for having remained so long supine. His lamb-like acquiescence is being used, not only as "an object lesson to the Transvaal Government," but as a means of filling once again the pockets that have been already filled at his expense. He has only to bestir himself to discover that the first and the last principle of successful speculation in mines is to be well assured of honest direction and good management of the mine itself.—I am, sir, your obedient servant,

ONE WHO UNDERSTANDS THE GAME

London: January 6, 1898.

THE MIDLAND RAILWAY OF WESTERN AUSTRALIA.

Yes, we shall be happy to further the course recommended in the subjoined letter :—

To the Editor.

Reform Club, Pall Mall, S.W.
January 12, 1898.

SIR,—Letters have appeared from time to time in financial papers from bondholders in the Midland Railway of Western Australia, and you have expressed a very strong opinion with regard to the directors, but no united action has ever been taken against them. I, for one, believe they are liable for any loss incurred, and have obtained a legal opinion to that effect, and if other bondholders will join me, am ready to try the issue.

If nothing is done soon, there will be little left for the bondholders.

I hope you will insert this letter in your influential paper.—Yours truly,

A BONDHOLDER.

CHATHAM AND DOVER EXTRAVAGANCE.

Stockholders in the London, Chatham, and Dover Railway should not be too sanguine about coming dividends on anything. The enterprising board of the undertaking has been spending money like the reckless men they are, and on the repair of Camberwell Station, of all places. True, the utmost economy has been exercised ; scraps of wood from old hoardings, packing-cases, and such like, to judge by their appearance, have been used in the building operations going on upon the platforms. So that there has been no waste. The outlay for paint, however, must be considerable, and the work has been in hand for the best part of a year, exhausting the energies of the staff, and causing serious inroads on the company's resources. If this sort of thing goes on, and the board should have the courage to undertake similar extravagant works at Brixton, Loughborough Junction, Walworth "Shoot," or the "Elephant," there is no saying what may happen. The day might even arrive again when the Arbitration Preference stock would have to go short of its full dividend. Stockholders, please take note, and have a care.

KLONDIKE—A HINT.

Astronomers tell us that they think the Northern hemisphere of this earth of ours enjoys an age of ice about once in every hundred thousand years. They cannot tell us, though, when the last ice age ended, nor are they yet sure whether we are receding from one or going towards it. It is a pity that the knowledge we possess is thus limited, because there might be hope for Klondike were we approaching that period in the cycle of a hundred thousand years when the summer north of the equator is at its longest. Under present conditions we do not see how the Canadian North-West, and especially this Klondike region, can possibly be permanently benefited by the gold so many deluded people are hoping to rake out of it. That some population may stick and struggle in parts of British Columbia is possible ; that the North-West, as a whole, can become a thickly-peopled, well-tilled part of the earth is, under present physical conditions, entirely, impossible. And about the gold itself we may say that fully 95 per cent. of the tales about it circulated in the Press are purely romantic.

GOLD-ABSORBING RHODESIA.

A seasonable warning was given the other day by the Bulawayo correspondent of the *Standard* to those who contemplate going out to Rhodesia in search of a fortune. The labour market, he said, is overstocked there. Bulawayo is filled with good carpenters, masons, bricklayers, plumbers, electricians, &c., some of whom are at work on small jobs at comparatively low rates of pay, some living "on their means," and some on "charity" work, provided by the Government at 5s. a day. He stated that no one should go out without enough money to keep him for at least a month, and a small sum will not do that, for food is extremely dear, and will remain so until a dry season comes, and enables heavier trains to be run over that wonderful Bulawayo Railway. It was the wet season when this correspondent wrote, and then flour cost £4 per 100-lb. bag ; Boer meal, £4. 10s. ; mealies, £3. 10s. ; mutton, 2s. to 2s. 6d. per lb. ; beef, 2s. 6d. to 3s. 6d. ; and bread 6d. per loaf, always less than a pound in weight, and varying in size with the price of flour. Butter was 3s. 6d. a pound ; tea, 3s. to 5s. ; potatoes, 1s. to 1s. 6d. ; fresh milk, 1s. to 3s. per bottle, and so on. The hope is expressed that a great improvement will set in once the mines get fully to work later on in the year ; but in the meantime people need be in no hurry to rush out. They should not arrive until April or May, the writer says ; and we may add if they arrive in too great numbers then they run considerable risk of starvation.

In a speech at the Salisbury Chamber of Mines, Rhodesia, Mr. J. Scott, a delegate from the Bulawayo Chamber, made some interesting remarks which have a certain suggestiveness, and add force to the above warning. After pointing out that, what with war and rinderpest, no work had been done on mining claims in Rhodesia for some eighteen months, he went on as follows :—

They found that the majority of mining properties in the country were held by large companies aggregating between £15,000,000 and £20,000,000 of nominal capital, while the working capital was not, he supposed, more than £1,500,000, and that £1,500,000 is all that we have to depend upon until we can show a gold-producing country, if we do not get a boom. We have a certain number of companies who can only be protected by the principle of concentration, or paying for their protection certificate. He thought if they got these companies to spend their money they must allow them to do it in the way most advantageous to their shareholders, and in a way where there was a chance of getting their mines into a gold-producing stage ; but if you pass a law that they would have to work a certain number of claims in certain districts, irrespective of merit, cost of labour, machinery and transport, probably they would lose their claims, and having got this enormous amount of money from the British public, it would be an injustice to us and them. The principle is, of course, that people who have claims should work them, but they should make an exception in the peculiar circumstances of this case. If you leave the law as to concentration, as it is applicable only to each district, the result will be that people would pay inspection certificate under the smaller tariff, which would not become due until 1898. It would affect no mine materially for people in one district, and would not operate in some districts until 1899. It would be a pity to keep to a law which would prevent companies devoting their money to where they wished, and force them to pay it to the Chartered Company for protection certificates. If they were starting a new country, they might insist upon every block of claims being worked to a certain extent, but this country was being developed by British capital, and if the British public, in their haste and greed to secure properties, have got more than they are able to work, they must make allowances in the circumstances. It would ensure an early production of gold, and that was the one thing they wanted to do. It would be best to spend £20,000 developing one mine to get an output, than in proving six. The best mines, with three or four exceptions, were held by the smaller companies, who did not own claims in other districts but one. The Willoughby was doing the best of their work on three mines. Negotiations were going on to divide the larger companies into separate smaller ones, and settle with the B.S.A. Company for their interests. Things would right themselves gradually. He instanced the Mashonaland Central, which had floated other companies, and reduced their holding to 400 claims.—*Rhodesian Times.*

Financial Crisis in Japan.

Japan is just now in the throes of a financial crisis, induced by the reckless speculation and company promotion of the past two years and precipitated in part by the adoption of that gold standard which was designed to avert it. Our friends appear to have miscalculated their commercial strength. Much of the large sum of money brought into the country after the war has gone to the effete West to pay for such expensive toys as battleships and other munitions of war; and the rest has been embarked upon more than doubtful ventures—railways, banks, merchant ships, and so on—most of which have by this time demonstrated their utter inability to make profits. The foreign capital that was to have been induced to try its luck in Yokohama and Osaka by the gold standard, has kept studiously away, and Japan's trade with silver-using countries, especially China, has fallen off. Meantime, the country finds itself saddled with a lot of unsaleable silver; the gold reserve is small and is rapidly disappearing; and every month's trade returns show a balance of imports over exports large enough to be a serious menace to a country situated as Japan is. Our mail advices tell us that —to say nothing of the mushroom banks which have gone under by the score—some of the leading institutions of Osaka have been compelled to suspend payment, while others have been kept going only through the aid extended by the Bank of Japan. Business house failures have also increased, and the general tightness of money is described as alarming. It has for some time been apparent to dispassionate observers that Nemesis would not long stay his coming. Now that he has paid his visit, the Japanese are beginning to realise what a panic is. It is to be feared that the worst is not yet over.

In this connection, some figures, published by the Department of Finance, showing the amounts of hard and paper money circulated in Japan in the past twenty-one years, should be interesting. In 1871 the total was 72,712,000 yen, equal to 2½ yen per head of the population. This was the period of "awakening." By 1880 the total had grown to 203,994,000 yen, equal to 5¼ yen per head; by 1890, to 205,483,260 yen, equal to a trifle over 5 yen per head; and by 1896 to 293,168,000 yen, equal to 6¾ yen. In September, 1897, the last month for which returns have been received, the total circulation was 296,747,000 yen, equal to about 7 yen per head. With few breaks, the total has gone up in the two decades, but the *per capita* distribution shows that the country is too poor to indulge in startling financial breaks.

Forsaken Crete.

Crete has, for the present, been apparently abandoned by the European Concert. The candidature of Prince George of Greece has been withdrawn. Indeed, it is now declared that it was never formally proposed by Russia. But though the other Powers would have adopted the Prince as Governor, Germany would not, and so the Prince is dismissed, as were Colonel Schaefer, M. Petrovitch, and others. Diplomatists have also, according to the Athens correspondent of the *Times*, discovered that there is no great hurry for the settlement of the Cretan question. It will "simplify matters" if the settlement is left over until the traces of war are effaced, the indemnity paid, and Thessaly evacuated. Mr. Balfour, at Manchester on Monday, suggested a further simplification of the business by "tossing up" for a Governor, as it had been found impossible to hit upon one that fulfils the high ideals of the Powers. This is pretty sarcasm, but affords no consolation to the miserable inhabitants of Crete, who are suffering both in purse and person by the state of anarchy in which the island is allowed to remain by the carelessness of Europe, and who may disturb at least the equanimity of the Powers at any moment by a new violent attempt to settle the question of Government for themselves.

The Ottoman Railway.

If the approval of the Council of Ministers at Constantinople is of any value, the Ottoman Railway is to be congratulated; for such approval has been unanimously granted to its demands to extend its line to Dinair. For years the company has been endeavouring to extend its system eastwards, and, in spite of the fact that it had years ago given up its guarantee, and that all subsequent extensions have been effected without Government aid, its reasonable proposals have been simply ignored. Meantime the Porte has been granting heavy subsidies to the German system in Asia Minor, known as the Anatolian Railway, whose avowed object is to draw the railway business of the Peninsula to itself.

Only by extending eastwards can the Ottoman Railway, the English Company, shake itself free from the encroaching power of the German financiers, who years ago bought up the Smyrna and Cassaba line, and thus obtained entrance into the most important part of Asia Minor. In the past we have not failed to criticise the financial methods of the Ottoman Railway Company, which have been infantile in their lack of foresight, but we have always deprecated the injustice of their treatment by the authorities at Constantinople. Let us hope a turn for the better has come, or is coming.

Needless to say the hungry Germans have not been idle, and have been credited with successfully obtaining an increase in the guarantee of the proposed extension fron Chai to Dinair. This is an extension of the Smyrna Kassaba line to the same point that the Ottoman Railway is aiming for, and where, it is hoped, the line which reaches the town first will have the best chance of securing the caravan trade from the interior. The difference between the policy of the two sets of railway builders must strike even the dull-witted Porte, but perhaps there it is only a matter of palm-oil. Turkish railway guarantees in the past have always been repudiated, and when the Germans have served the Turk's turn there may be a difficulty about the guarantee of the Anatolian system.

A Persian Coup d'Etat!

Of International troubles there seems no end just now. With China seething, Crete groaning, troubles in the Soudan, and England, France, and even Germany looking crosswise in West Africa, here we have the possibe addition of a *coup d'etat* in Persia! The present Shah has squandered the immense treasure left by his predecessor, and has been squeezing his subjects for taxes until they—quiet and peace-loving as they are—seem ready for revolt. One provincial Governorship has already become virtually independent, and others are following the example. The Shah is losing grip of the country; and Russia has taken prompt note of the state of affairs, and is apparently prepared for its absorption. Her first business will be to seize Khorassan; the rest may follow as opportunity offers.

THE SOUDAN EXPEDITION.

If there is mystery about the ultimate aim and object of the Soudan expedition, we are not to be permitted to know anything at all of its progress towards its goal. Newspaper correspondents are not to be allowed to accompany the force. An exception is to be made in favour of Reuter's agent, who is to act, apparently, as official chronicler of such information as the Sirdar wishes to be known. But this is not what the public wish to know. They want independent testimony as to the conduct of the expedition. It is not because there is any difficulty on the ground of military expediency. Sir H. Kitchener does not suggest that. It is the difficulty of transport that he fears. But newspaper correspondents, as a rule, find their own transport, without troubling the military authorities. There must be another reason. What is it? Are we going, not only to Khartoum, but beyond—to Fashoda, say, in order to checkmate the Marchand expedition?

GERMANY AND SUGAR BOUNTIES.

A month or two ago the German Finance Minister announced that, as the result of negotiations with other countries granting sugar bounties, he hoped to lay before the Reichsrath this session a measure dealing with this foolish and costly form of protection. Hopes were therefore entertained that some practical step was about to be taken for the abolition of the bounties. A semi-official statement just published in Berlin, however, seems to throw a considerable stream of cold water on these hopes and anticipations. Germany is favourable to the abolition, we are assured, and so is Austria-Hungary. That is so far satisfactory; but nothing is said of France; and all that has been done in the matter appears only to amount to this. The Belgian Government some time ago asked Germany whether she would be willing to take part in an International Conference on this sugar question, and Germany, having consulted with Austria, agreed. There the matter rests. Belgium has done nothing more, though her decision is expected very soon. But if it is only in favour of an International Conference, it means that we are practically no nearer the abolition of the sugar bounties than we are now. The taxpayers of the sugar bounty countries show great forbearance under the burden imposed upon them by their rulers in order to supply us with cheap sugar. But nothing can be done unless they themselves take action. Meantime, British Guiana has joined in the cry to the Government for countervailing duties, without which, it is declared in a memorial about to be presented to her Majesty and the House of Commons, that the colony must inevitably be ruined, and every one above the peasant class be driven out of it. The prospect thus pictured is no doubt very sad, but there is probably another side to the picture; and at any rate the House of Commons is not at all likely to listen just yet to this urgent cry and prayer.

THE SEALSKIN BILL IN OPERATION.

If the United States Customs officers aim at making the famous Sealskin Bill intolerable, they may possibly succeed in their object. They have been able to inflict a vast amount of annoyance on people about the Canadian border. If a Canadian goes out for a stroll, and happens to cross the border with a sealskin overcoat, or cap, or pair of gloves on, he is instantly pounced upon, and compelled to give up these useful and ornamental coverings—unless, indeed, he can produce a certificate from a United States Consul that his sealskins were not obtained by pelagic fishing. Tourists intent upon viewing the Niagara Falls, and crossing to the American side without thought of the character of their clothing, have had their sealskin coverings ruthlessly taken from them, and sent forth to bear the winter cold as they might. Ladies are the chief sufferers, and have been extremely forcible in the expression of their indignation. We may sympathise with them; but as the obnoxious law is enforced in the sacred cause of American monopoly, the United States Government are not likely to award them even sympathy.

DANISH NEUTRALITY.

It seems that the Government of Denmark have been making an appeal to the Powers to grant a guarantee of the permanent neutrality of Denmark. But the Powers refused; they declared it impossible. Why it should be impossible we do not altogether understand. Denmark is not in a position now to disturb the international equilibrium, and is not likely to rouse the cupidity of any of the Powers. There can be no thought of its further "partition," and there is small probability of a coalition with Norway and Sweden. Indeed, all three countries are desirous of securing this guarantee of permanent neutrality. They are peopled by industrious folk, who are steadily advancing in trade and commerce; and a guaranteed neutrality, which would enable them to continue their work undisturbed by the dread of war or other serious commotion, would surely be an unmixed benefit to the world.

SOUTH AFRICAN REPUBLIC RAILWAY BONDS.

For the second time the bank of Williams Deacon has stepped forward and purchased the coupons of the Northern Railroad of the South African Republic Four per Cent. bonds. The issue is for £1,500,000, and it is a notorious fact that the railway upon which the bonds have been issued has been in a comatose condition for more than a year past. Presumably the coupons are purchased on behalf of the Transvaal Government, which guaranteed the interest upon the bonds, but the fact that the line is not completed, long after the date agreed upon, raises the prospect of some embarrassing difficulties in the future. The matter, we believe, is before the Courts on the Continent, the company being a Belgian one, but the bulk of the money was, of course, found in Great Britain. No doubt seems to have been thrown upon the right of the bondholders to claim their interest under the guarantee, but it would certainly be more satisfactory if some statement were made from official sources, as there must be great disinclination to buy the bonds under present conditions. The issue was made by the Railway Share Trust and Agency Company, and surely that concern should be in a position to inform the public on the business.

NEW CABLE SCHEME.

The Pacific Cable scheme of Sir Sandford Fleming slumbers, probably because the Colonial Ministers of Finance do not see the fun of paying for the toy they wish to possess. In the interim, if intuition goes for anything, we have in an apparently inspired article in a leading journal, a new scheme for a cable connecting the outlying colonies with the Mother country. The scheme is admittedly the proposal of the Eastern Telegraph group of companies, and must be considered as the alternative of that powerful group to the Sandford Fleming Pacific scheme, which was conceived out of enmity to that system.

The projected cable of the Eastern Company would run from Cornwall to Gibraltar, from there to Capetown, *via* Sierra Leone and the Islands of St. Helena and Ascension, and from Capetown to Perth, West Australia, *via* the Mauritius and Christmas Isle, the latter an islet, to the south of Sumatra. In this way an all-British cable would be provided that would not have the fault of the tremendous stretch required by the Pacific route, and it would not, moreover, have to depend upon foreign companies, which the Sandford Fleming scheme has had to do. We have not, however, been told the cost of the projected cable, or how the money is to be provided. Apparently the Eastern Company is hankering after a subsidy, but one cannot be sure of that until the demand is made.

PAWNED GREECE.

There was no help for it we suppose. The Greeks committed the crime of making a mistake, or, if we are to believe the diplomatist who has been writing to *Truth*, they were betrayed into making war with Turkey in order to further the domestic schemes of their alien king. Their position now, however brought about, must cause some qualms of conscience to those who hounded them on to their fate a year ago. For the whole nation is put in commission and under the control of the six delegates composing it—one for each mitigating power. This Commission will administer the revenues assisted by a Greek company sitting in Athens, working under its absolute control. With the help of the collecting company the monopolies now in existence will be maintained and in all probability multiplied. All the money encashed by the Greek company will be paid over weekly to the Caisse of the Control and will be converted into gold within fifteen days. The power of issuing debt will be withdrawn from the figure-head Greek Government, and the Commission will take in hand the unification of the existing public debt, issue all further loans to cover floating debt, and, to a limited extent, for public purposes, and will reduce by degrees the 94,000,000 drachmas of paper money. Sentimentally it is a pity to see the very life of a nation thus pledged to its creditors; yet compensations may be given even to the unhappy Greek. In all probability the taxes will now be more ably and honestly collected and more carefully spent than they have ever been before. Democratic Governments are never distinguished either by the upright or economical administration of their finances. Greece, therefore, may emerge more solvent, possessed of better administrative methods, and possibly more able to rule itself, when it has cleared itself of the burdens now laid upon it.

CITY OF BUENOS AYRES SIX PER CENT. LOAN, 1888.

Messrs. Louis Cohen & Sons, who issued this loan, have the conspicuous merit of sticking to those who invested in it on the faith of their name. The negotiations have been long and difficult, but the firm would not give in, and the result is an arrangement as satisfactory as could be expected in the circumstances. Under it new Argentine Government four per cent. sterling bonds for 6,950,000 dols., or the equivalent in pounds sterling, will be issued par for par in exchange for the bonds of the City, interest on which has been paid in depreciated paper. In addition to the 4 per cent. interest the new bonds will enjoy a fund of ½ per cent. per annum from 1901, and a sum of £121,884 in bonds, equivalent to about 20 per cent. for every £100 in drawn bonds or coupons, will be handed to the agents for distribution. We trust the Argentine Government will prove able to keep this contract.

"INDIA" AS A WEEKLY NEWSPAPER.

We welcome *India* among the weeklies. It is a paper which the true Imperialist, as distinguished from the opera bouffe impostor, ought to know and read. A side of Indian affairs is presented to our eyes in it, which the ordinary organs of public opinion systematically ignore. We may not subscribe to all its opinions, but we assuredly shall have to give more attention in the future than we have done in the past to the native questions, its principal aim is to bring before the British public.

SCOTCH PARAFFIN.

In speaking of the new "Anchor" oil last week we forgot, and the lapse of memory is unpardonable, to mention the Scotch oil, which is a domestic product whose flash point is 105, and which ought not to be forgotten by the consumer. In the whole fifty years during which this oil has been on the market there has never, we believe, been an accident through its storage or use. And, by the bye, will the introducers of the "Anchor" oil, to whose enterprise every credit is due, see to it that the flash point of their article is kept up to 103. We are told that some of the cargo now on sale in Manchester goes off below the advertised temperature. Also the smell might be made a good deal less rank.

INDIAN CURRENCY ISSUE.

It is proposed to introduce a Bill to-day (Friday), into the Legislative Council in Calcutta, to enable the Government of India to issue currency, not only, as hitherto, against gold held by that Government in India, but also against gold held by the Secretary of State for India in this country. The object of this measure is to give the public the means of obtaining such issues immediately on payment of an equivalent sum in England, without having, as they now have, to wait for the arrival of gold in India.

Between April 1 and Saturday last the total receipts into the Exchequer amounted to £74,140,088, compared with £72,767,410 in the corresponding period of the last financial year; whilst the expenditure was £79,005,820, as against £78,437,853. On the latter day the Bank balances stood at £2,868,215; on the same day last year they were £1,297,106.

The Crisis in India.

So the Indian Government is going to copy the Japanese plan and issue notes in India against gold deposited with the Bank of England. This sounds nice, but we do not see how the plan is going to work. The Japanese Government had the advantage of being the owner of the gold it left in the hands of the Bank, but the Indian Government has no gold, only a multitude of debts. So it is the gold of other people that it wishes to see deposited in order that it may put more paper money in circulation in India. In other words, the artificial scarcity of money which has been created in India by the absurd policy of attempting to create a fixed exchange there, is to be utilised to compel bankers and merchants here to employ their own means in helping to make good the deficiency. We fancy they will be much more likely to send the gold out to India as hitherto and sell it in the bazaars at its market price. For how are they going to get this gold back again supposing they want it? Are they to have the power of expanding and contracting the Indian currency at their pleasure? If so, we should have two forces at work sometimes—the Government and the private trader or corporation. The lot of the people cannot fail to be a hard one under such a régime.

The truth is this silly proposition, which has come apparently from that refuge of all the cranks and nonentities of the race, the India Office, is put forward as a means of averting the storm now ready to burst over India. Many months ago we warned the British public that it was coming; but the only interest the bulk of us take in anything Indian is "Ranji's" latest score or catch at cricket. We have gone so soundly to sleep about the most dangerous portion of our Empire, that neither the brutalities of that mountain campaign —which has brought enough misery in its train to sensibly diminish our feeble hold on the allegiance of the natives—nor the sight of money at 12 per cent. in Calcutta and Bombay at the languid season of the business year, has the slightest effect in rousing us. "Why should it, India pays?" This is the legend which deceives us, the fact being that India is more than three-parts bankrupt, and that the day for the exhibition of her insolvency in the gaze of men is being hastened by the dementia of her British rulers. Having depleted the Treasuries by their extravagance and folly, having impoverished the people by their exactions, they conceived the noble idea that all would be put straight if only "a gold standard" could be introduced.

You know the story. Ever since the coinage of silver was suspended, matters have been going from bad to worse with the finances of the Indian Government and with Indian trade, but the stoppage of the coinage of silver is not alone responsible for the present critical state of affairs. The money difficulty merely serves to bring the other consequences of administrative folly to a head, and the position is such at the present time that if we at home do not put our hands in our pockets, and pretty deeply too, in order to relieve Indian finances from their embarrassment, the Government out there will have to make a composition with its creditors. That is the blunt fact. It is no use for us to dream and dream about India's wealth, about its marvellous development under our rule, and so on, for the truth is that India is very poor, and would be utterly bankrupt, save for the money we pour into it every year. Behold the secret of the rapidly succeeding loans its Government has issued and must continue to issue!

Within the last twelve months about ten millions sterling have been added to the debt of this British dependency, mainly, if not entirely, in London. The Indian railways have also been considerable borrowers. At this moment there is a floating debt of six million pounds in Indian Treasury bills on the London market, one million of which is now offered for renewal in three, six, or twelve months' bills, and not one penny of which could India pay out of her own resources.

By such devices it has been possible, year in and out, to lift off to some extent the weight of Indian Home Charges from Indian trade. Were these charges to be borne in full by that trade, India's available means could not stand the strain for three years. People here never think what the development of India, as we glibly call it, implies to the Indian people. Were the entire burden laid upon these people it would mean the remittance to Europe every year of from eighteen to nineteen million pounds in payment of Home Charges incurred by the Indian Government and by railway interest and dividend obligations to British investors; also it would mean the payment of all freights out and in upon the merchandise of India, which is almost exclusively conveyed to and fro in British ships. And a multitude of other items have to be provided for in the shape of money saved and profits earned all remitted home by British producers in India or British officials. All the profits of the tea-growing industry, for instance, come home to this country every year, and a large proportion of those of the cotton manufacturing industry; all the profits of gold mining, also, and a variety of small items of which no exact estimate could be formed.

Many years ago we made a somewhat minute investigation of the whole of these burdens, and came to the conclusion that they could not be less than thirty millions sterling a year all told. Probably the total is now considerably higher; but put it at only thirty millions still, and how does India stand? What is the power of her people as exhibited by her commerce with every part of the world to meet this charge? It can only be met by the excess of exports over imports, and for last year, the year ended June 30, 1897, this excess was just about fifteen million pounds, or, say, on a moderate estimate, one half of the full amount required. Sometimes it is less than this, sometimes more, but never by any chance is the surplus enough. People frequently talk as if the payment of the obligations of India to England was a mere matter of drawing Council bills. There is so much to pay, therefore so many bills on the Indian Treasuries are sold in the London market, and the thing is finished. But if there be no sufficient surplus of exports over imports to meet these bills, how are they to be paid? They cannot be paid, and the practical proof of India's inability to pay them has been abundantly given in recent years by the expedients to which the Government has resorted in order to avoid having to remit bills on the Presidency Treasuries for payment. Last year drawings were discontinued altogether for some considerable time, partly because there was no money in the Treasuries to draw against, partly owing to the insane folly of trying to create a gold standard for India out of nothing, and less than nothing. This gold standard will-o'-the-wisp appears to be the last effort of minds gone crazy, and to be destined to break down the entire structure of India's public credit. Well, it is no use arguing with Indian bureaucrats on this subject. Their minds move in a vicious circle, and only when too late will they wake up to the fact that in trying to reach the unattainable they have brought visible insolvency upon the Indian Empire.

Shall we have Dearer Money soon?

One of the dominant problems of the moment is the near future of the Money market. Is the rate of interest going up or down? Just now, of course, the market is in its usual sloppy condition. After dividends and interest payable in the beginning of the month have been distributed, short loans become cheap, and many people are ready to suppose that the cheapness will continue. In recent years, through a variety of causes, it has continued, the quietness of trade and the great increase in the production of gold being the chief. Will it continue cheap this year? We confess to have doubts on the point. A position materially altered in several respects has to be faced. To begin with, there is less money in the market than it has been accustomed to—we may say for the past three years; then the demands upon this money promise to be larger in the coming spring than for a long time back. We say nothing about such apparent pulls upon our supply of banking credit as the New South Wales and Western Australian loans, because these really bring money into the market instead of taking it away. The Governments of these Colonies borrow here in order to save themselves the necessity of remitting home, or in order to pay for railway and other materials ordered in this country. By acting thus they can keep their revenues for domestic expenditure, and plume themselves on their riches and the ease with which they carry their burdens. The subscription on Colonial loans, therefore, means that money is collected from all parts of the country to lie in banks until dispersed again by interest and other payments, and swell the amount of credit available on the London market.

But this year we shall be subject to demands upon our gold, and therefore to a reduction of a serious description in the credit handled by the market. The position of India is dealt with elsewhere, and we need only say here that if her finances are to be saved, at least ten millions sterling will have to be supplied to her, most of it within the next six months. Then it is highly probable that a Chinese loan may be issued before next May, and if that Empire obtains sixteen millions on our endorsement, some considerable portion of this will have to be sent to the East. This loan must be raised if China is not to become a prey to land-grabbers from Russia, Germany, France, and perhaps other countries, and if the full payment on her existing debt is to be kept up. Again, Europe has not yet paid for the grain it has required to import in order to make good the deficiencies of its harvest. The full weight of this debt may not be experienced until well on in the summer, but it is a factor to be kept in view as tending to increase the pressure upon our Money market. There are other sources of danger to us, more or less artificially created, which also have to be taken note of, such as further shipments of gold to Buenos Ayres to sustain the great financial scheme for restoring Argentine credit, and the demands of Russia in connection with the still incomplete establishment of her currency upon a gold basis.

Against such sources of exhaustion as we have indicated, we must not forget to place the great and steadily increasing output of gold from mines in all parts of the world. South Africa alone turned out more than 3,000,000 oz. of gold last year, and the yield of Australian mines and of Indian has been well sustained. A new source of supply of considerable magnitude may possibly develop in that region in Canada which lies at the back of the North Wind, but without counting this it may fairly be assumed that the entire gold production of the world in the year 1898 will approach £50,000,000. We may certainly assume that it will be over £45,000,000, and it is impossible to over-estimate the effect of this supply in mitigating the dangers our Money market may be threatened with. Should an export of gold to the United States occur in the coming spring, then, indeed, money might rise to 5 per cent. with us, but we see little prospect of this. It can only come if the British public loses its head once more about American railroad securities, and such a lamentable catastrophe is not yet in view. On the whole, then, we are disposed to think that although money will not be so cheap this year as it was for the greater part of 1897, and although it may become dearer next month and continue dearer for some time than it is now, we are in no danger of a 4 per cent. Bank rate, at least not before the end of the financial year. The collection of the taxes always tells against the market in February and March, and without that the ability with which the Bank of England is now conducted, and which has given it a strong independent hold over the market, should save us from further decline after the next week or two is over. A steady, firm market at moderate rates is what we have every reason to look for on all grounds. If rates were only stiff enough to check reckless speculation, the future, even the distant future, would not give cause for much anxiety, but it is to be feared that the new gold alone will keep the market free from anything approaching real stringency.

British Trade in 1897.

Taken as a whole, the foreign trade of the United Kingdom was fair last year. The gross value of it in and out was over 745 millions; and when we remember that prices have been low in most branches of trade, that we have had adverse circumstances to contend with, both in India and in the further East, and that for the latter half of the year the United States tariff has obstructed business, we may consider the sum total of the year's business almost encouraging. It is not quite so good, however, as we should like to see even in adverse circumstances.

The *Standard* of Monday drew attention to the remarkable increase in our imports of food and drink, and was quite justified in so doing. The gross value of this portion of our import trade has risen to nearly £180,000,000. The whole of this prodigious total is not retained for home consumption; but the greater part of it is, and it does not say much for our enterprise as farmers, cattle graziers, and dairymen, that we have required over ten millions' worth of live cattle, a millions' worth of sheep, and nearly six millions' worth of fresh beef from abroad last year, besides five millions' worth of fresh mutton, a millions' worth of fresh and salted pork, and preserved meats of various kinds amounting to another million and a half. Nor is it seemly that we should be dependent — upon France, Holland, and Denmark principally—for about sixteen millions' worth of butter, let alone two and a half millions' worth of margarine. We bought nearly six millions' worth of cheese last year, and over six millions' worth of foreign fruit, much of which might have been produced at home. And our imports of food grains have become altogether phenomenal. The value of the wheat and wheat flour received at our ports last year was nearly thirty-three millions, and grows with comparative regularity, good harvests and bad. Altogether the value of the cereals of every description imported by us in 1897 exceeded fifty-three and a half millions, almost the whole of which was retained for our own food.

We don't want to play alarmist in any sense, but we decidedly think that the soil of England, if properly cultivated, is capable of reducing to some extent this dependence upon the foreigner for our daily bread. Happily, there appears to be no danger of such a thing as a famine now anywhere by mere failure of crops. The Northern hemisphere came nearer to scarcity last year than it has done at any time since the United States began to feed Europe. But on our grain imports, at any rate, the short European harvest has left little trace; we have paid a little more for the grain, and that is about all. If the United States had us alone to look to to absorb their redundant crop of last year, they would be very poorly off. They have done better, in a sense, with their cattle than with their grain, so far as we are concerned. Turning to other sections of the trade returns, we find the imports of tea steadily increasing, those of coffee almost stationary, as also the imports of foreign spirits, although those of wine have gone up. We bought less sugar last year than in either of the two preceeding years, and got our supply materially cheaper. Raw products used in manufactures have also been on the whole cheap, without material variation in price. Cotton has decidedly fallen in the market, for a quantity less in weight by merely 275,000 cwt. on a gross import of about 15,700,000 cwt. in 1896 cost us four millions less in money.

With food still on the whole cheap, with raw materials not difficult to buy at moderate prices, our export trade ought, one might have hoped, to be showing expansion. Unhappily it does not, and this is where the most unsatisfactory element in these returns comes in. At no point can we just now say that our export business is progressive. We should not have the slightest objection to see imports mounting rapidly, especially imports of the raw materials used in our industries, were there visible, at the same time, a steady growth in the volume and value of our exports, but that is just what is not now visible. Our imports rose last year by nearly 9¾ millions to a total of 451¼ millions, and our exports fell off about £5,800,000—exports of British and Irish produce, *i.e.*—to £234,350,000; the difference between the two thus exceeded 215 millions, or, if we add the value of the re-exported foreign and colonial produce to that of strictly British exports, the balance against us is still 157 millions. Making allowance for the movements of bullion, which were but slightly against this country for the whole year, and for that unknown quantity, the value of ships built in British yards for foreign owners, we may still place the excess value of the imports over that of the exports at more than 150 millions. How do we find the means of paying such a large adverse trade balance? It is found, in part, from the earnings of our unrivalled mercantile marine and from the profits of our exports which are sold when they reach their destination at prices more or less higher than those at which they are entered at the port of departure. Probably also our imports are put down at the Custom House at a higher price than the invoice cost at the point of origin.

It would be ample to allow fifty millions for these earnings and differences in favour of the British trader both ways, and still there remains 100 millions to pay for which no visible means are provided. Of course, the real source of our power to go on thus lavishly spending more than we can afford lies in the interest received by us from our foreign investments, and in the revenue we draw from the debts incurred at our instance by India and from all those incurred by our many self-governing dependencies. Let any mishap take away a portion of the magnificent income which these investments afford and the nation must at once become pinched. We shall have a good deal to say from time to time on this aspect of our economic position, but for the present all we desire to do is to insist upon the necessity for greater energy in the development of our export business, which is dwindling at too many points. The United States, we know, have dealt a sharp blow at us; but that ought to stimulate us all the more to strike out elsewhere, and the gain we should receive in neutral fields from the self-immolating policy of the American Union ought to be made diligent use of, lest one of these days that Union should turn free-trader and catch us asleep. There is room for a larger trade in English goods with all South America, with China and Japan, and probably with Spain, Italy, Roumania, Mexico, Egypt, and perhaps Portugal. From our own dependencies there is not much to be hoped for; unless we lend them the money they cannot increase their trade with us to any large extent. Some of them, notably Canada, have deliberately slammed their door in our face, and it may not be long before they erect barriers against each other similar to those now standing between peoples of the same origin in North America.

It is a remarkable fact that the country to which the world primarily owes its railways and steam-engines should have been able to export only a million's worth of locomotives last year, and that the total value of the steam engines exported, including ocomotives, should have been little more than three millions. Our largest trade in this class of industrial product is in textile machinery; but even that was less last year than for some years back, owing to the dispute between the working engineers and their employers. Our exports of mining machinery also fell off, and this, in some respects the most valuable of our great industries, is threatened with decay. Our exports of cotton textiles also fell off last year with a large number of countries, and is not remarkably progressive at any point. China and Japan both took less goods from us. Turkey and Egypt took more, Belgium more, France and Germany less, Dutch India rather more, the United States more, Mexico less, Central America less, and most of the South American States decidedly less. Compensation was not found either in our possessions and dependencies, not even in South Africa. The same tendency was displayed by our woollen industry, which has suffered more than any other by the Dingley tariff; but on the whole, exports of woollen goods appear to stand their ground rather better than cotton. Still, it is not a progressive trade, and we cannot afford to allow it to decline further. We must make up our minds either to regain lost ground or conquer new. Linen manufactures have lost less than might have been expected, the total amount in yards exported to the United States being rather larger than in 1896, although smaller considerably than in 1895; but on the whole this is also a declining branch of business, and if we do not take care our foreign export trade may become a trade in "smalls" everywhere. In few directions do we now "hold the field."

Shipping "Rings."

Mr. Chamberlain succeeded the other day in ridding himself of the very unpleasant question of shipping rings which he is responsible for having brought into the full prominence it now enjoys. In that Blue Book of his on Great Britain's commercial relations with its Colonies, the operation of the British shipping rings is one of the agents expressly named as working to the detriment of British traders in competition with Germans, Americans, and others, and some very plain language is used condemnatory of them. Straightway the South African Mercantile Association, through its chairman, asks the Colonial Secretary to receive a deputation, with a view to a Select Committee of the House of Commons to investigate the whole matter. But the shipping interest is enormously powerful in the House, as Mr. Chamberlain knows, and the shipping interest is bitterly opposed to any public consideration of shipping rings—any public revelation of the little tricks of this big trade. So Mr. Chamberlain's secretary is instructed to reply "that, as this matter primarily concerns British trade and British merchants and shipowners, any representations to the Government should be made to the Board of Trade, to which department Mr. Chamberlain must refer the Association. No doubt he acted with strict propriety in this matter, and probably he was glad to shift the responsibility. But when he sent out his dispatch to the Colonial Governors, he told them he was "impressed with the extreme importance of securing as large a share as possible of the mutual trade of the United Kingdom and the Colonies for British producers and manufacturers," and that he therefore wished to investigate thoroughly the extent to which in each of the Colonies foreign imports are displacing British goods, and the causes thereof. When a chance presents itself of doing a real service to British manufacturers and traders by the unmasking of an abuse which has become a vile blot upon our commercial system, he quietly backs down from this high resolve, refers the aggrieved ones to that monument of ineptitude—the Board of Trade, and points out that if they please to take action on their own account there is nothing to prevent them from getting a member of Parliament to move for a committee of inquiry. He probably thought it superfluous to add in so many words what his remarks imply—that the Government would not encourage any private member to injure their friends the shipowners by ventilating this grievance. The Association is hopeful that good may result to its cause by the discussion of the question in the House of Commons, and that a committee will be appointed. We confess that we are not very sanguine on this last point; and if it were possible to secure full publicity for the whole question in any other way, we should not be sorry if the Government were to discourage the appointment of a committee of inquiry, for it is notorious that this institution exists now merely as a purgatory where inconvenient questions are tortured, and then left languishing; and it is a dead certainty that no legislation would ensue. But even a committee of inquiry would be able to throw some much-needed light on the dark ways of the shipping rings, and that would be a step at least in advance.

The Association which is moving for the committee concerns itself only with the abuses which have sprung up in the carrying trade to South Africa, and, whether it speaks for a large or for a small proportion of the South African traders of London, it has made out a case for inquiry, and has proved, in spite of Sir Donald Currie and those who are with him, that German shippers can send goods from interior points of their country to South Africa at considerably less than the English shipper can do from the port of departure, provided he ships them through and avoids making a bargain with the Hamburg owners, who are part and parcel of the South African Conference. Mr. H. H. Clarke, in his evidence before the Merchandise Marks Act Committee, gave some instances of the difference against British traders. Eleven cases of hardware, shipped through from Pinnebergen, are landed at Durban for the equivalent of £6. 13s. 9d., whereas the Conference rate from Hamburg or a British port is £10. 15s. 9d.—that is, £4. 2s. 9d. more. Now, something of this difference is due to the German preferential railway rates, for which no British shipowner can be held responsible, and it is argued for the Conference that it possessed no knowledge of what arrangement exists for the division of charge or revenue between the railways and the German steamship lines. But it knew of the existence of the arrangement, and it is an obvious rejoinder that British owners should have made no terms with the German lines until furnished with the information which was necessary to enable them see how far they were, protecting themselves—to say nothing of any supposititious protection for the British manufacturer. We were told that much advantage would accrue to British commercial interests, seeing that the sea-freight from foreign ports would be the same as from British. But this piece of optimism ignored the sea-freight arrangement under the through-rate system, and Mr. Clarke is authority for the assertion that this freight works out at from 5s. to 20s. per ton less than the rates at British ports on many classes of goods. It is impossible to believe that the special advantages admittedly possessed by German shippers through the tender solicitude of a paternal Government anxious to spoil the English can account for differences running in some cases to as much as 60 per cent. in favour of the German trader. In the case of steamship lines sailing from New York to South Africa, but owned by British firms in the "ring," there is a more direct and unequivocal discrimination. In that Blue Book on Colonial trade, which is Mr. Chamberlain's pride, we find the chief of the Customs Department at Cape Town stating that the rates of freight from the United States to South Africa "are actually lower than from the United Kingdom, notwithstanding that the distance is longer, and there is absolutely no return cargo." This does not, we understand, apply to all South African ports touched at by the steamers; but to East London the American rate is 5s., and to Port Natal, 7s. 6d. per ton under the lowest British rates. Then there is the China Steamship conference, which asks 47s. 6d. per ton for British cottons to Shanghai, while it carries American cottons transhipped at English ports for 17s. 6d. or 19s.; which again loads iron girders at Antwerp at 19s. per ton, and then goes to London and charges 25s. for British girders. An instance of the killing of independent enterprise by this body and by the Indian ring is afforded by the case of the Manchester Canal, which these two have materially contributed to ruin. We all know what happened to the Nippon Yusen Kaisha when it entered into competition on the Bombay-Japan route with the P. and O., the Austrian-Lloyds, and the Rubattino lines. Some further examples of discrimination in favour of foreigners may be found in the evidence given before the Commissioners on the operations of the Merchandise Marks Act above alluded to. The Holt line loads foreign iron at Amsterdam for Java at 14s. 2d. per ton, carries it to Liverpool and there loads British iron at 25s. per ton, plus 10 per cent. Examples of this kind of thing might easily be multiplied, but enough have been adduced to afford a prima facie justification of the charge that, in their anxiety to grab the earth, these iniquitous rings are doing their level best, with their eyes wide open, to aid the foreigner at the expense of their own countrymen. We indulge in no sentimental prate about patriotism — there is none of this weakness about your keen man of business. But shipping rings are in the position of renegades, and we are entitled to ask for some protection against them. Their methods do not amount to an illegality, and we suggest nothing that can operate in restraint of trade—quite the reverse, for it is the rings which operate in that way; and if some means could be devised to curb them somewhat, trade would be materially benefited. We might also, while we are about it, do something to compel our railway companies to deal equitably, and without discrimination, with British traders; but that is another matter. Meantime, would it not be well if we ceased to grow indignant at the contemplation of Yankee trusts and monopolies, and began to recognise that we ourselves are far from being free from that reproach?

The rebate abuse is intimately bound up with the existence of the rings. The rebate is, in fact, the trump card which the shipowner keeps up his sleeve to spoil the shipper who may essay to play the giddy goat with him. The ring keeps up rates, and incurs the shipper's displeasure; the rebate acts as the medium of reconciliation, and at the same time becomes the badge of servitude. For if the trader offers any of his patronage elsewhere, he forfeits the rebate of 10 per cent. which has been accumulating for months in the shipowner's cashbox in respect of his previous dealings with that gentleman. If this does not make the shipper a slave to the owner, we should be glad of duce to hat will more accurately define the relation.

against us is

the movemen.

against this cou ith an eye to the Transvaal Presidential election day, in reference to a recent despatch from Mr.

unknown quantity, doctrine of English Suzerainty in the Trans. nation.

Stock Market Notes and Comments.

Were a stockbroker to be asked in the curt way of the City, "how's business?" the chances are he would answer "nothing doing." This could not be true in a literal sense, because there are some three thousand people in the Stock Exchange living and apparently becoming rich on "doing nothing." What the broker really means is that there is not much volume of speculative business going on. Investment business has never been better than it is now, it's only drawback being the difficulty of finding securities to invest in. But it is speculation which "makes markets bum," and feeds the minds of the brokers and jobbers there with visions of sudden fortune. And speculation is in a curious position. We cannot say it is bad, because the movements in prices indicate plenty of life, but it is speculation conducted to a great extent by syndicates, combinations of financiers, arbitrageurs, and wire-pullers of all sorts, who are busy making prices move to attract the public. For the most part the public is looking on. Grand Trunk stocks are the only ones we know at the moment in which there is a daily widening public interest, a fine fat gamble developing. They are old favourites to which John Bull has been accustomed now for a generation and a half, and therefore a stir in them produces a very widespread interest. They have been under a long eclipse, and it took some little time to rouse attention, but once roused, people began to buy right and left, and we are now in for a good, old-fashioned inflation in the good, old-fashioned style. We know its symptoms well. All the dark lines have disappeared from the Trunk "spectrum"; it is bright throughout. Receipts are improving and will continue to improve for ever and a day; honest management has succeeded the reverse; economies have been introduced which will tell powerfully on net receipts. "The system never was in better order." Everything, in a word, is first-rate and prosperous, and the public believes it. All we can say is, do not believe it too long, good public. For some months to come, perhaps for the best part of this year, the roseate tints, now sending a glow through the hearts of all "bulls" as they gaze and buy, will continue to entice men on; but the world is not improving, not even in Canada, quite with the speed the Press would have us believe; and the day is not so far distant when the prudent holder will sell to the less prudent believer. It is a "faith-healing" process. If we might give a "tip" about this particular section of the market, it is to get ready for selling when the whole financial Press is singing in chorus "now is the time to buy." It does not all do this from corrupt motives, but merely because men, even journalists, are imitative animals. A few interested ones start the chant, others catch it up, and soon all are eagerly repeating the same bit of "gag."

But other sections of the market have risen quite as remarkably as Grand Trunk. Are the people not behind those movements also? Not yet, to any great extent. The Stock Exchange itself has dabbled pretty freely in United States Railway Shares, but up to now the outside public has sold more than it has bought. And the rise in prices, which has now got under weigh for the third time, is mostly a professional one, the work of houses here and in the United States who want to unload. We think, however, that the public is now going to buy these shares, and the probability, therefore, is that during the next six months they may see considerably higher prices than they do now. All we can say here, also, is the higher prices go the more sceptical let people become for the United States are by no means in the condition of prosperity, nor is railroad management there in that perfection of honesty which would justify a permanent investment on our part in such treacherous securities.

Argentine Railway and Government stocks, again, form another division of the market in which there has been great apparent activity, and the public has been buying the stocks of the railways steadily and quietly for a long time back, justifiably buying, too, although the quotations for some of them are now decidedly as high as they ought to be. The stocks of the Government, however, whether national or provincial, have likewise been hoisted by the financiers interested in preparing the way for handing over to the public the heavy risks they have incurred in keeping Argentine finance on its legs since the crisis of 1890. Outsiders, no doubt, are now joining to some extent in the movement, and helping these bankers and financiers; the more is the pity. But it is not a solid movement yet, except in the sense that those who conduct it command enormous wealth. So far as we can judge, the end sought is a unification of all the debts of the Republic in one low interest-bearing stock, with which shall be wrapped up new debt to the tune of anything you please from 10 to 20 millions sterling. The accumulated deficits of the Argentine Republic cannot at the present time be much less than ten millions. As far as the governing class goes there, nothing has been changed for the better since the crisis. Both Houses of the Legislature are just as spendthrift, just as incompetent, as any similar body in America. There is no such thing as economy known in the public offices of the country. Of course, population is increasing, more land is going under tillage, and the great foreign element, steadily increasing in the Republic, gives promise of stability, and perhaps of a higher order of public morality in the Government at a date far ahead. Possibly also the present and past operations of the financiers may in that long future be justified. The immediate outlook, though, is not very grand, and it will be quite prudent to discount the inspired language about "wonderful harvests," and all the rest of it, by at least 50 per cent.

There remains the mining market to touch on. Other sections may be left for a future day. In this department also there has been considerable movement—at least in the South African division—and there likewise the thing is worked and sustained by the financiers, trust companies, and speculative syndicates whose purpose it is to unload enormous quantities of shares on a foolish public. Already that public is nibbling, because it never can be brought to suspect a rising market. There are so many signs of greater prosperity to be spread out before it by a Press almost wholly in the direct or indirect control of these masters of the market. Every nerve is being strained also to make the output of gold from the Rand mines, and particularly from the Deep Levels, phenomenal in its riches. We shall have much to say on this matter as the weeks go by, but at present the subject cannot be pursued. To all, however, who are itching to buy, we say, weigh the facts, and wait before taking any step which may involve risk and disappointment, and perhaps bitter loss. Above all, remember that the Barnato fraternity, the Consolidated Goldfields and its group, the Robinson Bank and its group, with any number of trusts and share-punting combinations, have enormous piles of shares which they are anxious to sell at a profit.

Why are Great Central stocks going up—the old Sheffield that was? Because the company will require more money, and wants a good price for a new issue of stock. Is that a good reason for buying? We should say not. The "rig" is being overdone, and is quite African in its unscrupulousness, for the prospects of the company are not very good.

ENGLISH RAILWAY TRAFFIC RETURNS

Cleator and Workington.—Gross receipts for the eight days ending January 8 amounted to £945, a decrease of £248.

Cockermouth, Keswick, and Penrith.—Gross receipts for the nine days ending January 9 amounted to £877, an increase of £120.

East and West Yorkshire Union.—Gross receipts for the week ending January 7 amounted to £241, an increase of £27.

TRAMWAY AND OMNIBUS RECEIPTS.

Increases for past week:—Belfast, £240; Croydon, £94; Glasgow, £139; Lea Bridge, £148; London, £874; London & Deptford, £55; London Southern, £103; London General Omnibus, £2,213; London Road Car, £798; Metropolitan, £915; North Staffordshire, £4; Provincial, £162; Southampton, £1; South London, £165; Wolverhampton, £30; Woolwich & S. E. London, £36; Calais, £16.

Decreases for past week:—Barcelona, £38.

Anglo-Argentine, week ending December 9, £112 increase.

Vienna Omnibus, week ending January 1, £31 increase.

BIG LINEN-THREAD COMBINATION.

The *Belfast Evening Telegraph* of Wednesday states that a gigantic thread combination, in which the North of Ireland manufacturers are chiefly concerned, has been arranged, and that the agreement was signed in London by the following firms:—Barbour and Sons, Hilden, near Belfast, and America; the Marshall Thread Company, Paisley and New York; Finlayson, Bousfield, & Company, Paisley; and Knox & Company, Kilbirnie, Ayrshire, with several other smaller concerns. The combination will deal with linen thread tonly, and will, according to the Belfast journal equal in capital he Coats combination. The headquarters of the new firm will be in London.

It is reported that work has been begun on the extension of the Beira Railway, to Salisbury, in Rhodesia. Up to date 90 miles of permanent way material have been shipped from England.

The first instalment of relief for the Cubans from America has arrived at Havana, and has caused great dissatisfaction among the Spaniards, as the distribution of the relief may be used as a pretext for interference in Cuban affairs by the United States Consols and others.

What is supposed to have been the "mother lode' and quartz origin of the Klondyke placer goldfields is said to have been discovered. It was found 30 ft. below the surface. The ledge is 18 in. wide, and is generally sprinkled with free gold. It is added that the quartz seems to be immensely rich.

The revised return of Victorian gold for 1897 shows a total of 892,632 oz., the highest reached for fifteen years, and 10,546 oz. more than in 1896.

Messrs. Pixley & Abell state in their annual circular that during the past year the Bank of England did not receive a single bar of gold, owing to the great demand in other countries. By the middle of May about five millions had been sent to Japan; India took about two-and-a-half millions of small ingots for bazaar purposes; New York received about £600,000 in October, while the Continent, particularly Russia, bought largely throughout the year. This demand kept the price up to over 77s. 11d. per oz. standard, except for a short period, when it dropped to 77s. 9½d. per oz. £12,500,000 arrived in London from South Africa, being an increase of over £4,000,000 in the previous year, exclusive of 2,500,000 sovereigns from the Cape. With regard to silver, India bought about five-and-three-quarter millions as against under five millions in 1896. China wanted rather less than in 1896, and the Straits less than in any year since 1888. The fluctuations in price were greater than in 1896, when the variation was only 1⅛d., whereas last year it was 6 1/16d., the highest being at the commencement of the year; and dropping gradually as the months went by, till it reached the lowest of 23¾d. in August and again in September. On Japan adopting a gold standard many speculators were induced to sell bars for long delivery, and a rapid covering of sales caused prices to go up in the autumn until the announcement that the Indian mints would not be re-opened for the free coinage of silver. On the cessation of Council sales and renewed enquiries for the East, the prices became considerably higher towards the end of the year.

Critical Index to New Investments.

WESTERN AUSTRALIAN GOVERNMENT THREE PER CENT. INSCRIBED STOCK.—Issue of £1,000,000, being the first instalment of a loan of £2,500,000; minimum price, 95 per cent.; interest due January and July; principal repayable at par January 15, 1927. Loan is raised to provide a permanent water supply to Coolgardie goldfields. All the money is to be paid up by March 14, but payments may be made in full on January 21 at 2 per cent. discount. Recent issues of the Colony have been as under:—

Date.	Interest per cent.	Minimum price per cent.	Amount offered. £	Average price obtained per cent. £. s. d.
May, 1895	3½	99	750,000	103 1 4
April, 1896	3	98	750,000	100 16 8
May, 1897	3	95	1,000,000	95 0 10
January, 1897	3	98	1,100,000	98 3 11

Of the last-named stock, which was issued by the Government in payment for the properties of the West Australian Land Company, only £233,300 was taken at the time, but the balance was afterwards placed, partly through the London and Westminster Bank, at the minimum. The new issue raises the public debt of the Colony to about £8,000,000, and the debt per head of population, which may be estimated at 150,000, to over £53. This is an enormous figure for a Colony, the future of which depends entirely upon the permanence of its goldfields, and Coolgardie has as yet done precious little.

CHICHESTER CORPORATION THREE PER CENT. STOCK, redeemable at par February 27, 1946, or after February, 1916, on six months notice being given. Further issue of £55,000, offered for tender at a minimum of 100½ per cent., the object of the loan being to purchase the undertaking of the Chichester Waterworks Company for £49,848, and to improve the works at a cost of £5,190. Dividends due March and September. Rateable value of city, £48,935; total debt, including present issue, £118,368. The existing Three per Cent. Stock stands at 101, so the new issue is full priced. The issue, however, was well applied for, the total tendered being £124,670, at prices varying from £100. 10s. to £102. 10s.; but tenders at only sixpence over the minimum got 19 per cent. The average price obtained was nearly £101. 8s. 3d.

WESTMINSTER ELECTRIC SUPPLY CORPORATION, LIMITED, offer for subscription at par an issue of £200,000, out of a total of £250,000, first mortgage 3½ per cent. debentures, interest being payable January and July. The fully-paid share capital is £399,500, and the £5 shares are fetching £16 apiece. The business of the company has grown rapidly from 2,582,801 units generated in 1894, to 5,018,023 units in 1897, and the gross income has increased from £53,407 in 1894, to £70,511 in 1895, and to £87,986 in 1896, the dividends being respectively 5, 7, and 9 per cent. The accounts for last year are not yet completed. The present debentures will be a first charge on the whole of the assets, present and future, and they will be redeemable on March 1, 1920, or may be paid off before then at 5 per cent. premium on six months' notice given. In connection with the present issue the 5 per cent. and 4½ per cent. first mortgage debentures are to be paid off next March, and the balance of the money will be used in extending existing stations and in providing plant and machinery to meet increase of business. The Westminster is about the best of the electric lighting companies, and the debentures are amply secured, but 3½ per cent. is getting up to the gilt-edged level.

JOHANNESBURG WATERWORKS, ESTATE, AND EXPLORATION COMPANY, LIMITED.—Share capital £500,000 in £1 shares. Company now offer £250,000 5 per cent. mortgage debentures in bonds of £100 and £50 each, the whole to be redeemed by the end of 1925 at par, by a cumulative sinking fund commencing 1901, or by purchase thereafter if price is below par; and the company reserves the right of redeeming the whole from the end of 1911 at 3 per cent. premium on six months' notice. Applications at par will be received by the Johannesburg Consolidated Investment Company. Interest payable April and November. Present debenture capital £42,000 in first mortgage 7 per cent. debentures, redeemable by annual drawings, and the whole to be paid off by December 31, 1900. Issue is made simultaneously in Johannesburg and Capetown, and instalments may be paid up in advance at 2½ per cent. discount. Holders of existing 7 per cent. debentures can exchange into the new bonds receiving in addition a cash payment of 4 per cent. and a bonus of 1 per cent. The company was formed to work a concession to supply Johannesburg with water, and has since acquired the right to supply thirteen suburbs of the town, the population of both being 103,000. The company has eighty-five miles of main and distributing pipes, several large reservoirs, with a capacity of 323 million gallons, and extensive pumping and filtering machinery. It holds 83,334 £1 shares, out of 120,000, of the Zuurbekom Water Company, and has secured the right to take all the water that may be obtained at Zuurbekom at a price to be agreed upon. The whole of the plant laid down for this scheme and the works at Zuurbekom have been paid for and belong to the Johannesburg Waterworks Company, and the present issue is made to introduce further improvements in the present machinery, and to extend the works, for paying off floating debt amounting to £50,000, and for completing works, machinery, and laying down pipes from the Zuurbekom site; also for redeeming the 7 per cent. debentures. Profits for last four years were £20,770 in 1894; £36,078 in 1895; £29,585 (after paying £11,663 special services) in 1896; and £4,946 in 1897; while the dividend in 1894 was 6¼ per cent., and in the three following years 7½ per cent. Amount required for the service of this loan is £12,500 per annum, and for sinking fund, to commence in 1901 and within twenty-five years to pay off £250,000, is £6,857. The company is, of course, a Transvaal concern, and English investors would have no say in the management, but the share capital is large, and reasonable dividends are being paid, so the debentures should be a fair venture.

CANNING JARRAH TIMBER COMPANY (WESTERN AUSTRALIA), LIMITED.—Share capital, £250,000 in £1 shares, of which 83,333 shares and £166,667 in cash are taken by the International Trust and Finance Corporation, who are the vendors and promoters, and resell at a profit; and the company is also to take over at cost price valuation the stock of sawn timber, logs and stores, timber afloat and additional plant in transit. Remaining 166,667 shares and £75,000 five per cent. first mortgage debentures are offered at par. The debenture issue is part of a total of £100,000, redeemable in twenty years by annual drawings at 105 per cent., and are a first charge on the concession, railway, and lands in Perth and elsewhere. Interest is due June and December. Company buys a Government concession for an unexpired term of twenty years, a railway of about thirty miles, three saw mills, timber yard, and a plot of about 14 acres at Midland Junction. The auditors certify net profits for last three years to have averaged £11,678, and that last year's profits were £18,183, while another authority estimates future profits of the Canning business at £45,780 per annum, and the Donnybrook property is estimated to give a profit of £12,000. But still another authority goes one better, for the Conservator of Forests to the West Australian Government estimates the net profits obtainable from the sale of marketable timbers growing on the concession at £1,218,750 "if disposed of at the present price." Of the estimated revenue of £57,780, debenture interest will claim only £3,750. The point is how much reliance is to be placed in these estimates? And if they are reliable, why is such a promising property sold, and why are the directors satisfied to take only one-third of the purchase money in shares? The public have had several of these Jarrah undertakings offered to them of late, which suggests that competition is growing. We do not admire the thing.

PRINCES' HALL RESTAURANT, LIMITED. — Subscriptions are invited for 8,000 £5 shares at 10s. per share premium, as the business is to be extended at a cost of £30,000 by taking over a long lease of the fully licensed premises, 37 and 38, Jermyn-street, known as Rawlin's Hotel, together with part of 36, Jermyn-street, which premises are to be pulled down and a new building erected communicating with the present restaurant. This company was formed January, 1896 with a capital of £40,000, and, from May 15 that year to May 31, 1897, made a net profit of £7,112, and paid a dividend of 10 per cent. a further interim dividend at the same rate being paid this month. It appears that one of the directors lately acquired the new property and now lets the company have a long under-lease at a profit rental of £300 per annum to the director. It is proposed to fit up a Masonic Temple in order to cater for the banquets given by lodges. As these lodges are known to be wealthy, we should feel disposed to leave the new issue of shares to them.

The gold produced in New South Wales during 1897 amounted to 292,217 oz., a decrease of 3,854 oz. as compared with 1896, but the value showed an increase of £15,053.

A Bill is to be promoted in the coming session of Parliament for the incorporation of a company to construct a new railway, fifty miles in length, from Llanilaw, in Cardiganshire, to New Radnor.

In a recent interview with Senator Chandler, Mr. McKinley is said to have declared himself still firmly in favour of bimetallism. He further considered that the negotiations on the subject were only suspended in consequence of the condition of affairs in India. The President is to resume the negotiations as soon as the conditions are favourable.

Company Reports and Balance-Sheets.

CLERICAL, MEDICAL AND GENERAL LIFE ASSURANCE SOCIETY.—Last year, ended 30th June, this company issued 831 policies insuring £582,000, and, allowing for a small amount of re-assurances, this gave an addition of £19,710 to the annual net income, which rose to £277,600. The Society's total income was £410,600, claims paid took £220,367, the rate of interest earned was £3. 17s. 3d.—a fall of 1s. 6d. on the previous year—but the Company is one of those which values at 2½ per cent. only, so the margin is ample, as was proved by the fact that the valuation last year, on the strictest lines known, gave a surplus of £605,000, to divide among 11,761 participating policies.

THE MOUNT LYELL MINING AND RAILWAY COMPANY.—There is not a great deal of information in the report of the Board of this Company for the half-year ended September 30 last, but what there is is highly satisfactory. The first five furnaces and convertors put up and now in operation have done their work so well that the Directors are now duplicating them. Thus the output ought soon to be doubled. With only part of the five in full blast the last six months the Company was able to make a net profit of nearly £67,000, and two dividends each of 4s. per share have been paid; but the first one only on that portion of the capital then issued. In order to pay 4s. per share per quarter on the present capital, a net revenue of £200,000 will now be required over and above the sums necessary for writing down the cost of the property, plant, &c. Granted a continuance of the supply of ore on the same scale and of the same quality as that at present mined, we see no reason why this income should not be forthcoming, and a great deal more. But this Company must not be confounded with the Mount Lyell North.

UNION DISCOUNT COMPANY OF LONDON, LIMITED, made £139,554 gross last half year, including £15,184 brought forward. Deducting £75,258 for rebate, a handsome sum, and current expenses, the board has enough net profit to pay the 10 per cent. per annum dividend declared, leaving £16,853 for the new half-year. This is excellent and progressive, but we trust the board will rest satisfied with 10 per cent., for the reserve would bear increasing.

DEVAS ROUTLEDGE & COMPANY, LIMITED.—The old-established company of this name—it was formed in 1878—reports the satisfactory profit of £11,134 for the past year. Dividends equal to 6¼ per cent. for the year are declared, being the rate paid for years past, and the balance forward is increased from £4,907 to £5,934. The Company has a reserve of £15,000 invested in Consols, and its buildings stand for nothing in the balance-sheet. Unfortunately no attempt is made to supply a profit and loss account, which materially reduces the value of the information supplied.

PAWSON AND LEAFS, LIMITED.—During 1897 this Company had an important windfall in the shape of £3,900 received from letting its windows to view the Jubilee procession. Of this sum, £3,450 was devoted to paying a bonus of 1s. 6d. per share, and £450 went to the benefit of the ordinary accounts. Eliminating this exceptional revenue from the total, the net profit for the year is not satisfactory, as it amounts only to £15,928, as against £16,327 in 1895. The differenee, however, is accounted for by the increased charge for debenture interest, since the new buildings were completed, and this charge may prove less onerous when the portion unused by the company is fully let. Fortunately the concern has been paying dividends well within its means of late, and it is therefore able to announce the usual dividend of 5 per cent. in addition to the bonus previously alluded to, which is equal to 1½ per cent. more; and then the balance forward is increased £2,578 to a total of £38,248. This balance forward is really the company's reserve, and we are glad to see that it is now within £2,000 of the total at which it stood prior to the unfortunate absorption of Leaf's business.

THE DEBENTURE CORPORATION, LIMITED, continues a career which we frankly admit has hitherto been considerably more prosperous than we think it deserves to be, some of its business methods considered. Besides paying 7 per cent. for the year on the ordinary shares, the directors are able to give them a bonus of ½ per cent.; to hand £3,866 to the Founders' shares, to add £8,000 to reserve, and to carry forward £4,206. There is no information whatever in the report about any of the company's investments, but we fancy it has some trouble still with its Mauritius property. Its reserve, however, is now £210,000, and it has a large amount of cash in hand.

THE UNION BANK OF LONDON did not do so well as other London banks, the net profits for the six months being £96,831 against £98,938 in the corresponding period. But a larger amount was brought into the accounts so that the available total is slightly increased. The dividend is again at the rate of 10 per cent. per annum; £5,000 is, as usual, applied in reducing premises account, and £22,233 carried forward. The banks deposits are fully £250,000 lower, and are now below 15½ millions, while acceptances are still above 2 millions. On the other side, there is £414,000 less in bills, and £498,000 more in loans and advances. The cash is more than £200,000 larger, while money at call and notice is down £385,000, and investments have been reduced by £139,000. Beyond the larger amount out as loans and advances, these changes indicate diminished earning power.

THE LONDON AND MIDLAND BANK is still growing—we hope not beyond its strength. During the past year the paid-up capital has been increased to £1,467,000, and the reserve to £1,250,000, which is an excellent proportion. And good employment seems to be found for the extra capital, for the profits for the second half of the year come out at £177,085 compared with only £119,983 for the corresponding period, and the dividend of 8 per cent., and bonus of 1 per cent. makes 17 per cent. paid for the year against 16 per cent. for 1896. When the directors established the officers' pension fund a year ago they appropriated £10,000 to it, and this year they add £5,000; but they carry forward as much as £100,000, compared with £40,000. During the half-year the bank took over the business of the North-Western bank, and established half-a-dozen new branches, so that the balance-sheet figures are naturally swollen. Deposits at £21,725,000 are up nearly six millions, and a larger business is done in acceptances, while bills have increased from £1,667,000 to £2,759,000, and advances from £8,669,000 to £11,566,000. The stock of cash has risen from £2,297,000 to £3,174,000, and money at call from £1,294,000 to £2,191,000. Of the investments, Consols still stand at £1,211,124, but its other investments have increased from £2,129,619 to £3,248,158. Against its deposits the Bank holds cash, inclusive of call and notice money, and investments to the extent of 45 per cent., which, although slightly above the proportion held a year ago, is not so large as a bank of this description ought to hold.

MANCHESTER AND COUNTY BANK.—The accounts of this bank show substantial progress, after allowing for the absorption of the Bank of Bolton last year. Profits in the last half-year came to £83,671 as against £69,066 a year ago, but the Board has taken the opportunity to fulfil the promise to start a Superannuation Fund for the officers, and for this purpose has set aside the considerable sum of £10,000 out of revenue. Consequently, after paying the usual dividend at the rate of 15 per cent. per annum, no allocation is made to reserve, but the amount forward is raised by £5,236 to a total of £15,278.

NOTTINGHAM JOINT STOCK BANK.—A much increased profit is shown by this bank in the past year, but as it raised its distribution from 10 to 12½ per cent., the amounts placed to reserve and so forth are rather lower. Thus £1,000 is placed to reserve, as against £3,000 a year ago, and the amount forward is reduced from £2,275 to £1,235. The reduction of £1,000 in the Bank Premises account is at the usual figure. Current and deposit accounts are about £30,000 higher at £1,530,316, but a good deal of the cash received from the recent issue of shares has been used in discount and advances, the total of these being £137,000 higher at £1,327,674.

The London, Brighton, and South Coast Railway Company are seeking power next session to raise £1,000,000, and to borrow upon their capital £333,000, for the purpose of widening their railway on the western side from a point near the Victoria Station to within a few chains of Clapham Junction.

The Ottoman Government has made arrangements with a group of financiers representing the Ottoman Bank, the Deutsche Bank, and the Anatolian Railway Company, for a loan of £1,200,000, bearing interest at 7 per cent., the principal being guaranteed upon the Greek war indemnity.

A Bill to incorporate the Bideford and Clovelly Railway Company has been deposited. The proposed company seeks power to construct a railway of about ten miles, commencing in the parish of Abbotsham, by a junction with the authorised Bideford, Westward Ho! and Appledore Railway, and terminating at Clovelly.

In a recent conference with the Chamber of Commerce at East London, Cape Colony, Sir J. Gordon Sprigg stated that he thought they might have a much more advantageous mail service for South Africa, and that he intended to lay before Parliament next session proposals upon which tenders could be based.

By the Bill deposited by the Isle of Wight Railway Company Parliament is asked to sanction the acquisition by them of the undertaking of the Brading Harbour and Railway Company, which is one of the assets of the Liberator group of companies. The price to be paid has been agreed upon at £16,500.

The South Eastern Railway Company's Bill for next session seeking power to construct about eight miles of new lines, which, taken together, will form a duplication of their existing system from Deptford, through Lewisham, Lee, Bromley, and Chislehurst, to Orpington Station.

The *Engineering and Mining Journal* of New York thinks it "quite evident that the Klondike boom has collapsed." The American public, it is said, has got frightened at the number of illegitimate Company schemes which have been put forward in connection with the "boom." The feeling is far from being unknown in this country.

The Midland Railway Company have deposited Parliamentary Bills seeking powers for the construction of railways from Royston to Huddersfield, Halifax and Bradford. About thirty miles of new line are comprised in the proposal. For this purpose the Company proposes to raise a further sum of £3,600,000, £900,000 by debenture stock, and the remainder by the issue of New Preferred Converted and Deferred Converted Ordinary stock in equal proportions.

The London and North-Western Railway Company are to seek powers next session to provide and use steam vessels between Holyhead and Dublin, Kingstown, Greenore, and any place upon the Lough of Carlingford, and also between any places on the Lough. For this purpose the Company seek power to employ any capital not required for the purpose for which it was authorised.

We must not imagine that the new regulations which the Russian Government are going to put in force with a view to control the sale of spirituous liquors have anything benevolent about them; they are merely the outcome of a settled policy already put in operation over considerable areas of the Empire by which the entire monopoly of the manufacture and sale of intoxicants will be in the hands of the State. This policy is being ruthlessly pursued, and by its latest developments some 12,000 people are to be thrown out of employment, and cleared out of the cities to go back and probably die of starvation in their native place. A few thousand lives more or less makes no perceptible difference in Russia, and the multitude of the people have not yet taught their rulers to respect their existence. They will some day.

French Finance and Trade.

(From our Correspondent.)

THE BOURSE MORE ACTIVE—RAILWAY SHARES—THE INDUSTRIAL OUTLOOK.

Paris, January 12th.

The Chamber of Deputies has resumed most quietly, real politics being very quiet. Attention is entirely drawn towards that strange and mysterious Dreyfus-Esterhazy affair. Very few interpellations, happily, are to be be expected in the near future; so the Budget, it is hoped, may be finished at last, the Chamber having to be re-elected not later than April or May next. We, however, had at the end of last week two Bourse days far less good than the preceding ones. Of course, quotations remained sufficiently high, and the tone was generally firm, but transactions were again far too rare and difficult, the causes of that restriction in affairs, somewhat unexpected indeed, being at once the general weakness of domestic politics, and fickleness towards great external questions.

This week the market has begun to be satisfactory again, the different questions which worked against the revival of brisk speculation, seeming to enter into a better phase. The Græco-Turkish question, at least, is settled, except some particular points; the Cuban question seems to shape more favourably; in the Far East, our Bourse financiers cannot believe that the constant efforts made these two years by all European Powers towards a peaceful agreement, can end in failure, peace prevailing at the end everywhere but there. Finally, the monetary "tension," so much feared, did not reach the point expected, the dreaded money scarcity not coming to anything.

Yesterday, and still more to-day, we have enjoyed a far better market. The ease of the London fortnightly liquidation, and the news coming to us from over the Channel, had the best effect on speculators' minds. Some hold that the Bank rate would, perhaps, be shortly reduced again in London, and the rumour has contributed to create better feelings. To-day's Bourse, steadily improving, has been a little more active at last, and, as we write, after some realisations due to profit-taking, the general tone remains firm and the quotations high, with a fair amount of business.

As far as Rentes are concerned, the 3 per cent. has again recovered the round price of 103 francs, attaining 103·20, the current of the reinvestments beginning to tell. Many transactions on account were done at 103·25, and 103·27½. Uncovered, the option vendors begin to feel threatened, and are gradually closing. You remember we told you last week they would be obliged to do so. The 3½ is firm also, between 107·35 and 107·37½. There are some big revenue giving "Fonds d'Etat," which derive important benefits from the difficulty capitalists find in re-investing their ready money. Amongst them is now the Emprunt 5 per cent. Minas-Geraes, which was standing still at a little more than 60 francs till the other day, and has now reached 67 francs. But the low price of this stock was due to the liquidation of the syndicate formed in the middle of last year to hold and vend the loan, which was not a success. The half-yearly coupon, representing 12·50 francs net, will be detached on the 15th inst., so the price stands still again; but we think it will soon improve. In fact the Minas-Geraes Special State Budget has been concluded always with excess receipts, which have permitted the construction or subvention of more than 300 kilometres of railway and other public works. We think much better indeed of this stock than of the Federal Brazilian bonds, or of Spanish Funds. Our Credit Societies stand firm after having suffered from selling to secure profits. The *Banque de France* remains unchanged at 3,520 fr. The *Banque de Paris et des Pays Bas* is up 4 fr. to 894 fr., under the stimulus of the rise in Argentine funds. The *Banque de Paris et des Pays Bas* is said to be at the head of a Syndicate formed with the *Banque des Pays Autrichiens* and some other powerful Banking Corporations, in order to undertake the conversion of the Bulgarian Debt. They say the Syndicate has already submitted tenders to the Sofia Government for the emission of a 4½ per cent. loan, taken at 90 per cent. *Credit Lyonnais* are at 723 fr., after 720 fr.; the *Comptois National* at 592; the *Banque Internationale* at 617 fr., its recent increase of capital being well interpreted at a moment when industrial undertakings begin to enjoy a "boomlet"; *Société Générale* shares are in demand at 544; *Credit Foncier*, instead of falling, as yesterday, through "bull" realisations, stays at 665 fr.

The firmness continues in the shares of our great railway companies. We have not received yet the fifty-second week's earnings, but up to December 23, from January 1, 1897, they have aggregated 1,224,765,000 francs, instead of 1,189,896,000 francs during the corresponding period of 1896. This is nearly thirty-five million francs in favour of 1897. The Lyon shares are at 1835; Orleans, 1845; Nord, 2,050; Midi, 1425; Est, 1094; Ouest, 1219·50. The "*Banque foncière de la Noblesse*" *(Russ) obligations*, have not been allowed to be quoted in the official list; they, of course, have not been really issued to the public. The same difficulty has met the 3 per cent. Norwegian 1896, the 3½ per cent. Norwegian, 1895, and a good many foreign municipal loans, such as Christiania, Moscow, Odessa, &c. Our Government seems to be unwilling to allow any new admission at the Cote Officielle des Agents de Change of the Bourse to a foreign stock or bond without having obtained equivalent advantages for our foreign trade and commerce.

Most industrial shares continue their upward movement, and are standing firm. Suez shares leaped from 3·323 to 3·342, and the movement commenced some days ago does not seem to be exhausted. The Metaux Society shares have risen from 675-680 to 695, in conformity with the new arrangements settled between the manager, the well-known M. Secretan, and the Seciété d'Electro-Metallargie. The General Omnibus Company has attained 1,700, and the Paris Voitures Company, 780; this Company, under the able management of M. Bixio, is trying the last-invented electrical automotor systems. In 1897, the receipts were 21,033,055 for, against 19,778,063 in 1896. The dividend is expected to be 31 francs at least, instead of 28·50 for 1896. The French Thomson Houston Company should stand at 1,375, it having secured the contract to work the whole of the Nice and Riviera-Coast trams by electricity.

We hear that the Schneider (Creuzot) firm intends to build new iron and steel works at Cette, near Montpellier, on the side of the Thau Lake, communicating with the Mediterranean. These new works may cost some 30 million frs., and will be fitted for a yearly production of 200,000 tons of cast-iron. The situation seems to be a good one, adjoining the iron minerals of the Aude and of the Pyrénées.

The Exposition 1900 ticket *bons* have experienced a notable revival, and reach nearly 18 frs.; this firmness is accounted for by the scarcity of the stock, till now lying in the credit establishments which were the issuers. The public is thinking that the available *bons* are already scarce, and at this very moment comes the interdiction by the Government of sales of the chances of drawings without the *bons* themselves.

A decline of 136 pesetas has been experienced by the Madrid-Saragosse-Alicante Company's shares since the Tarragone-Barcelone-France Company, which it had decided to absorb, and to which it had lent in advance thirty million pesetas (by contract signed June 2, 1891), has suspended all payments. The "T. B. F." Company will be obliged to propose a very poor composition to its creditors, among which the Madrid-Saragosse is included.

The news reaches us from Berne that the Swiss Federal Council has sanctioned the agreement between the banks and the Jura-Simplon Railway Company to raise the necessary money for the boring of the Simplon tunnel.

Here are some statistics relating to the wine and cider productions in France during 1897. The total production amounts to 32,350,722 hectolitres, i.e., an average yield of 20 lect. per hectare. These figures are normal ones compared with the general average of the last ten years, 32,476,000 hectolitres. But the two immediately preceding years gave very different results: 1895, 26,688,000 hect. only; and 1896, 44,656,000. The cider production has been much worse, hard weather having prevailed last year on the coast, the growing-place of the apple-tree; 1897 gave 6,788,711 hectolitres only, that is, 1,285,677 hect. less than in 1896, and 7,534,496 hect. less than the general average production of the last ten years.

Apropos of beverage, the peculiar assembly which figures as the dignified Paris Municipal Council has taken steps for lowering the heavy octroi duties on those drinks which are supposed to be "hygienic." The intention must be good, but the money lost in that way has to be recovered in another. To cloak their responsibility our Municipal Councillors have invited *referendum* consultations in a new manner. All the Parisians who think they have ideas about taxes or duties are kindly invited to present notes or memoirs on the subject up to a given date, at which the propositions will be examined. Most of the memorials presented up to now are naturally Socialistic, more or less advocating a single tax, which should be personal and progressive, and be borne by both capital and revenue, and saying nothing about hygienic or noxious drinks.

LOUIS DE TOURVILLE.

The Produce Markets.

GRAIN.

The wheat market, both in spot and futures, opened quietly, and continued so throughout the week. Sellers tried to secure an advance on Saturday, but buyers did not respond; indeed they were rather indifferent; and so values remained unchanged. At Mark-lane on Wednesday English and foreign wheat were unchanged in value, and a poor business doing. Flour was slow and unaltered, while arrivals are still on a large scale. Maize steady, with a fair business at 16s. 6d. for American mixed, ex ship; old crop, 17s. 3d., ex quay; and Galatz-Bessarabian, 18s. 6d. Barley was firm at 15s. 6d. for Odessa-Nikolaieff, ex ship. Oats had a good sale at firm to rather higher rates for mixed American; common Petersburg, 15s. 3d. ex quay; Canadian white, 15s. 9d. to 16s. ex ship; Canadian mixed, 15s. 9d. to 16s.; mixed American, 16s. to 16s. 3d. At Liverpool spot parcels were firmly held, and in some instances sellers asked 7⅛d. per cental more money, but the demand was quiet. Red American futures gained ¼d. per cental at opening in unison with the advance in America, but later, after some minor fluctuations, weakened, owing to disappointing Paris advices together with an absence of support, and values at the second call were unchanged to ⅜d. per cental lower. The market then became steadier, and closed steady and ⅛d. to ¼d. per cental lower except September, which was ¼d. per cental higher. American Maize, mixed, on the spot, was in moderate demand at full prices. European steady and unchanged. American mixed options opened ¼d. per cental dearer owing to higher cables, but afterwards weakened, the values at second call being unchanged to ⅛d. dearer. The cargo market has been quiet, the only point of attraction being the Argentine. A steamer of 1,500 tons, La Plata, January-February, sold at 33s. 6d.; 2,300 tons Santa Fé, shipping or shipped, at 34s. 9d.; and 3,000 tons Rosario-Santa Fé, March-April, at 33s. February-March steamers are offered at 33s. 6d., and sailers at 34s. Californian prices are nominal—September, B.-L., obtainable at 37s. 9d., and November and prompt at 36s. Walla Walla, on passage, may be had at 35s. 3d. to 35s., and January-February at 34s. 9d. No. 2 red winter, destination wanted, is offered at 36s. 9d. Parcels quiet.

OFFICIAL CLOSING VALUES (100 lb. deliveries—January 12).

	Jan.	March.	May.	July.	Sept.
Red American Wheat	—	7·1½	7·0¾	6·9½	6·4½

In New York on Wednesday wheat opened easy, with ⅛c. fall, due to bearish cable news, then reacted on covering and better late cables; but declined sharply later under realising, and a disappointing export demand, and closed weak, with January ⅛c. up and other months unchanged to ⅜c. down. Spot weak. Spring, 102⅜c. Winter, 100⅝c. Sales, futures, 1,200,000 bushels. Spot, nil. Corn opened steady, but declined under predictions of increased receipts and colder weather, and closed weak at ¼c. fall. Spot easy. Western, 34½c. Sales, futures, 100,000 bushels. Spot, 50,000 bushels.

COTTON.

The spot demand has been fairly active during the week, closing steady on Wednesday with a better demand. In American a good business has been done, though at the previous day's reduction of 1/32d. Brazilian and Egyptian have been quietly steady. Surats were in limited demand at unchanged prices. Futures opened at a loss of ½ to 1 point owing to a "bearish" circular issued by Messrs. Neill Brothers, but, with local "bears" covering, about recovered the fall during the day. Business has been restricted throughout, but the undertone was very steady, the close being partially ½ point lower than Tuesday. Wednesday's tenders at the clearing-house were 200 bales American and 250 Egyptian on new dockets.

NEW YORK CLOSING VALUES.

	Spot.	Jan.	Feb.	Mar.	April.	May.	June.	July.	Aug.	Sept.	Oct.
Jan. 12 ..	5⅞	5·70	5·70	5·74	5·78	5·85	5·85	5·89	5·92	5·92	5·93

Messrs. Neill Bros., in their circular of the 11th inst., state:—"Mr. Henry Neill fully confirms his estimate at 11,000,000 bales, given in our circular of December 7. To us it appears, from the data received from himself and other correspondents, that his then figures may be rather large for Texas, but if so, and there is no certainty of it, the discrepancy may easily be made up in the other States, from several of which we have recently had still larger estimates than his, so we see no reason to make any change in the aggregate total, although the glowing reports we have had, especially from Alabama, Mississippi, Georgia, and the Carolinas would justify an increase on even his large figures!" They anticipate lower prices.

WOOL.

There has been rather an improved tone in the wool markets, and this has been fairly well maintained, during the week Messrs. Helmuth, Schwartze, & Co., in their annual report, seem to think that this improvement will continue, as it may fairly be assumed that no excessive stocks of goods remain in Europe, and with their disappearance "one of the main causes of last year's depressed trade is removed. The lowest estimates put the decrease which the Australasian clips have suffered from last year's unparalleled drought at 150,000 bales; the Cape will probably also show a distinct diminution and though there may be some increase in the River Plate States, its amount is not likely to be such as in any degree to counterbalance the huge deficit in the Colonies. In the matter of supplies, therefore, the article stands in as sound a position as can well be wished and an improvement in its value would appear to be only a matter of time." The first series of Colonial wool sales has been fixed to commence on Tuesday, January 18, and to close on Friday, February 4, thus allowing for sixteen selling days. The arrivals to date are as follows:—New South Wales, 30,200 bales; Queensland, 16,000; Victoria, 24,200; South Australia, 8,800; West Australia, 8,000; Tasmania, 100; New Zealand, 12,600; Cape and Natal, 39,100—total, 139,000 bales. Deducting about 54,000 which have been forwarded direct to Yorkshire and Continent, and adding old stock 32,000 bales, the total available amounts at present to 117,000 bales. Sheepskin sales will be held on Thursday and Friday next.

METALS AND COAL.

The improved tone in copper shown last week has continued this. Wednesday's sales amounted to about 1,200 tons. Opening rates marked a partial advance of 2s. 6d. on yesterday's close, and good buying on the part of leading operators caused a further improvement of a like sum during the morning; cash and three months starting at £48. 13s. 9d. and £49. 2s. 6d. respectively, and gradually rising to £48. 17s. 6d. and £49. 5s., while four months realised £49. 6s. 3d. and later £49. 7s. 6d. Early business at the afternoon session was very quiet, but towards the end the advance brought sellers forward, and on free offerings both cash and three months quickly fell to £48. 15s. and £49. 2s. 6d. respectively, at which prices the market closed with further sellers.

SETTLEMENT PRICES.

	Jan. 12 £ s. d.	Jan. 5. £ s. d.	Dec. 29. £ s. d.	Dec. 22. £ s. d.	Dec. 15. £ s. d.	Dec. 8. £ s. d.
Copper ..	48 17 6	48 10 0	48 5 0	48 2 6	48 7 6	48 10 0

There has been a steady business in the iron market. Scotch—45s. 9½d., 45s. 9d. cash; 40s. 10½d. one month; buyers, 45s. 9d. cash, 45s. 11½d. one month; sellers ½d. more. Cleveland—buyers 40s. 8d. cash, 40s. 10½d. one month; sellers 1½d. more. Cumberland hematite—buyers 48s. 8½d. cash, 48s. 11½d. one month; sellers ½d. more.

SETTLEMENT PRICES.

	Jan. 12. s. d.	Jan. 5. s. d.	Dec. 29. s. d.	Dec. 22. s. d.	Dec. 15. s. d.	Dec. 8. s. d.
Scotch.. ..	45 9	45 6	45 4½	45 6	45 0	45 0
Cleveland ..	40 7½	40 4½	40 3	40 6	40 1½	40 3
Hematite ..	48 9	48 4½	48 4½	48 4½	47 10½	47 10½

Little business has been done in coal, and no material alteration in value. Labour disputes threaten the stoppage of one or two collieries in the Barnsley district.

SUGAR.

Market quiet, and practically unchanged. Tate's cubes, No. 1, 14s. 10½d.; No. 2, 14s.; crystals, No. 1, 13s. 1½d.; No. 2, 12s. 7½d.; granulated, 13s. 3d.; yellow crystals, 12s. 6d., Lyle's crystals No. 1, 13s.; No. 3, 12s. 6d.; granulated, No. 1, 13s.; No. 2, 12s. 6d.; white, A, 12s. 9d.; B, 12s.; yellow crystallized, O and P, 12s. 6d. Foreign.—Granulated opened flat, and a moderate amount of business has been done at ⅜d. to 1½d. decline. Cane sugar steadier, with a better inquiry. Messrs. Tate's quotations:—Crystals, No. 1, 13s. 4½d.; small, 13s. 3d.; No. 2, 12s. 10½d.; granulated, standard, 12s. 7½d.; coarse, 13s. 3d.; fine, 13s. 4½d. Beet flat. January, 9s. 3d., v.; February, 9s. 4½d., s.; March, 9s. 5d., v.; April, 9s. 6d., v.; May, 9s. 6½d., b.; June, 9s. 7½d., b. Best futures weak at 1d. to 1½d. decline.

TEA AND COFFEE.

In coffee, spot market has been somewhat dull, and little business doing, prices remaining unchanged. At auction on Wednesday, 1,407 bags, consisting chiefly of ordinary qualities, met with slow competition at easy prices, except a parcel of good home trade, which sold readily at full rates. Savanilla, middling to good bold greenish coloury, slightly nipped, 72s. 6d. to 86s.; good ordinary dingy to fine ordinary bright greenish, 48s. 6d. to 59s. 6d.; ordinary mottled pale, 44s.; low brownish mixed, 31s.; peaberry, 80s. 6d.; Colombian, low middling greenish, 67s. 6d.; fine ordinary bright pale and green, 54s. to 55s.; common dingy mixed grayish, 40s. 6d. Nicaragua, ordinary foxy green, 40s. Futures dull at 3d. decline. About 3,000 bags Santos sold—March at 30s. 6d. and May at 30s. 9d. Closing values:—March, 30s. 6d.; May, 30s. 9d.; September, 31s. 6d.; and December, 31s. 9d. Contracts registered, 7,500 bags Santos. At Indian auction on Monday 43,088 packages of tea were offered.

This is the largest amount of Indian tea ever offered at auction in one day. It met with fair competition, and realised generally steady prices, the exception being in teas from 9d. to 1s. 2d., which were easier, the weakness being most noticeable in broken kinds. At auction on Wednesday 8,000 packages Indian sold, common leaf ruling steady; medium to fine broken easier. Terminals dull—Indian, type 1, January-February, quoted at 7$\frac{5}{16}$d.; March, 7$\frac{3}{8}$d.; type 2, January-February, 6$\frac{11}{16}$d.; March, 6$\frac{1}{8}$d.; Ceylon, January, 7$\frac{3}{4}$d.; China, January, 4$\frac{3}{4}$d.; February, 4$\frac{11}{16}$d.; March, 4$\frac{1}{2}$d.

HEMP AND JUTE.

Though quiet, hemp remained firm during the week. At auction on Wednesday 250 bales fair current Manilla and 250 fair seconds were withdrawn at £17. 15s. and £16 respectively. There are sellers of fair current at £17. 10s., December-February, sailer, £18, and February-April £18. 5s. 240 bales barely fair current on spot sold at £17, 140 good roping at £19, and 100 superior seconds at £16. 10s. Jute firm on the whole, good first months December, February, and January, March steamer held at £10. 5s.

THE CHINESE CRISIS.

Things seem to be settling down in China. From the quietness reigning during the week it could scarcely be supposed that a crisis existed. Even in money matters the Pekin Government appear to be in no hurry. The negotiations for a loan are progressing very slowly, in consequence of the dilatory tactics of the Chinese officials. The only announcement likely to arouse keen attention is that made yesterday by the *Times'* correspondent at Hong Kong, that an English gunboat had been sent to Hainan, towards which the French are supposed to be looking fondly. Mr. Balfour's explanation of English Ministerial policy, that what Great Britain wanted was not more territory but freedom for the development of trade, seems to have given entire satisfaction both in Germann and France. The Berlin journals declare that Germany asks for nothing more. Kiao-Chau, they insist, is meant only as a *point d'appui* for trade. There will be no exclusiveness—no great scheme of military fortification. The *Cologne Gazette* even hails with goodwill the efforts being made by England to secure the Chinese loan. This, it is urged, would be good not only for Germany but for all the Powers.

But, though a hand-to-hand policy with England in China would be acceptable to Germany, there is said to be a growing conviction that a hand-to-hand policy all the way to China is not so agreeable. Prince Henry, on his voyage to Kiao-Chau, has to call at seven coaling stations, all of which are English. So the Berlin *Post* urges the establishment of a direct route to the Indian Ocean through Austria, Turkey, and Asia Minor; such a route, it is contended, terminating at Bosra or at the Strait of Ormuz, would present far smaller technical difficulties than the Siberian Railway. But that is a matter for future consideration and discussion. If Germany can arrange for a new route England will offer no objection. What is eminently satisfactory for the present, is that Germany endorses England's policy in China and declares her own to be precisely similar, intending to make Kiao-Chau a trading port rather than a warlike stronghold. Austria, it is now stated, will send no warship to China, will seek no territory, but a wealthy Austrian is understood to have left for China, and contemplates playing there a similar rôle to that played by Mr. Cecil Rhodes in South Africa. So the rumour goes in Vienna. We need hardly add that it lacks confirmation. The subject of an Anglo-Japanese alliance is discussed in the Japanese Press, and the military party in Japan insists on Japan asserting herself in the present crisis. But there is nothing yet to indicate the approach of violence. For the present the outlook is perfectly quiet and peaceful. The Chinese crisis may almost be regarded as at an end.

Spain has been added to the list of countries entitled to the benefits of the Canadian reciprocal tariff to the 1st of August next.

AUSTRALIAN GOLD PRODUCTION.

The figures of Australian gold production in 1897, which have been cabled over this week, do not pretend to finality; but they may be accepted as approximately accurate, and they show that mining activity in the various Colonies—those at least from which returns have been received—was last year great and general. Victoria's 810,000 oz. compares with 805,087 oz. in 1896, and 740,086 oz. in 1895; Queensland's 794,000 oz. with 640,385 oz. and 631,682 oz.; New South Wales's 292,217 oz., with 296,072 oz. and 360,165 oz.; and Western Australia's 687,000 oz., with 281,265 oz. and 231,512 oz. Though the New South Wales yield represents a decrease in quantity as compared with 1896, there is an increase of £15,053 in the aggregate value; and, save for 1894-5-6, last year's figure for this colony is higher than that of any year since 1873. Having regard to recent progress in Gippsland, Victoria's increase of nearly 5,000 oz. falls below expectations; but it is possible that the increased output of this field has served to compensate for decreases on some of the older mining grounds. That we shall find out when the official returns are available six months hence.

Queensland's contribution for 1897 constitutes a record for that Colony, and brings it very near to the realisation of its most ardent desire—to surpass Victoria. Its previous best years were 1889, with 739,103 oz., and 1894, with 679,511 oz. In 1896 the yield of the Charters Towers mines was 36,056 oz. less than in the previous year, the falling off being accounted for by the large amount of exploratory and development work carried on. Advices from this district indicate that during the twelvemonths just closed the companies were meeting with their reward for this costly "dead labour," in the shape of an enhanced output. Much appears to have been done also in the development of those minor mining districts which are so numerous in Queensland. But the feature of the year was undoubtedly the big upward jump made by Western Australia. If this pushful young Colony continues to go ahead at this rate, it will before long beat the best accomplished by Victoria in its palmiest days. It would, however, be unsafe to prophesy that it *will* go ahead at this rate. It is young, and in their days, the other Colonies did equally remarkable things which were not long maintained. And at present, the gold production is small enough when placed by the capital of the Westralian companies floated in London in the past few years.

LONDON CHAMBER OF MINES.

The following statement may have some interest to those interested in mining affairs:—"Some months ago a number of gentlemen interested in mining in the Colonies registered the Australasian Chamber of Mines under licence of the Board of Trade. As many of the members were interested in Canadian mining, a Canadian Chamber was afterwards formed. These Chambers have now been merged into one body, which, with the consent of the Board of Trade, will be known in future as the Incorporated London Chamber of Mines. The object of this change is to make the name of the Chamber agree more fittingly with the scope of the Chamber's work, more especially in connection with the proposed International Mining, Metallurgical, and Machinery Exhibition which the Chamber proposes to hold in London next year. It is not to be supposed that this change of name will lessen the Chamber's interests in or relations with the Australasian Colonies." As to the proposed mining exhibition in London the subject is said to be exciting considerable interest in Australia, and the Premier of Queensland has promised £15,000 towards it. The site has not yet been determined upon.

A NEW METAL.

Washington advices announce the discovery of a new metal which may revolutionise the iron trade. It is asserted that, admixed with iron, the new metal renders cast-iron as tough and strong as wrought iron. The *Chronicle* correspondent tells us that Mr. Edison refuses to go into details now; but he is about to begin a series of experiments to determine the conditions most favourable to obtaining the best results.

It is stated from Brazil that an English syndicate will sign a contract for purchasing, for the sum of 18,000,000 dols., several plantations between Sarandy and Batataes; and that another syndicate is reported to be organising in London, with Dutch and American capital to twice that amount, for buying plantations in the west or north of San Paulo.

In West Australia, during the month of December, applications for 19,982 acres of land were approved under the terms of conditional purchase, besides 6,600 acres as homestead farms, and 2,300 acres as homestead leases, as well as 49,288 acres for timber licences, while 613,000 acres under the conditions of the Land Regulations as pastoral leases were also approved.

Notices of Books, &c.

Norman's Universal Cambist: With an Exposition of the World's Present Mechanism of the Interchanges of Things. By JOHN HENRY NORMAN, of the London Chamber of Commerce; Expert in the Science of, and Practice with, Money. London: Effingham Wilson.

Mr. Norman is a revolutionary as well as an enthusiast in the cause of currency reform. He dedicates his book "to the world's first man of science who in the future produces a science primer of money such as will compel the world to accept and teach it as truth." This book he means as a help towards that science, if it does not quite fulfil his own aspirations. He is ingenious, well-read in his subject, with probably clear ideas in his own mind, though in his exposition he is occasionally somewhat confusing and erratic. He pleads for simplicity, and has no patience with bimetallists. He condemns the tendency to abstraction in economic discussion, and quotes approvingly a statement by Professor I. K. Ingram that "the study of the economic phenomena of society ought to be systematically combined with that of the other aspects of social existence." Mr. Norman's ideal currency system would be "one metal intermediary for the whole world," in place of the varying intermediaries at present existing. "The abolition of monetary signs, and the use of one weight measure, would be the true Volapuk of money." If this one standard were gold, the fluctuations in the exchanges would be confined within a very narrow margin; the conditions of barter would be preserved, and no ready-reckoner of the world's exchanges would be required. The great difficulty, however, would be to get the world to agree upon a standard weight measure. Mr. Norman is much taken with the notion; he discusses the question with considerable acumen; but he is fain to admit that it is only an ideal, a thing that "may be in the distant future." Currency philosophers may debate it, though they are more likely to pick holes in the argument than to tend towards agreement. But practical financiers will be slow to tackle it. To them it would mean a tremendous revolution; and revolutions, even if producing great advantages, are not readily embraced by practical men. So Mr. Norman betakes himself to the practical work of elaborating and applying his decigrams to existing intermediaries; and insists that, with the aid of less than 60,000 figures, 756 tables of exchange, consisting of from 13,800 to 200,000 figures each, may be dispensed with. By means of his decigrams he seeks to convert "the monetary sign for a weight of gold (or silver) in one country into the monetary sign for the same weight of gold (or silver) in another country . . . . by means of the mint-issue weight of pure metal in each chief money of account of the world." Mr. Norman's book is decidedly ingenious, and should prove useful to those who can devote the necessary study to it.

The Law of Sales of Stocks and Shares: By CHARLES FRAMPTON STALLARD, B.A. London: Clement Wilson, Norfolk House, Norfolk-street.

Although at the present time nearly every one invests their earnings or savings in some security or other, very few persons have any ideas concerning their legal rights and liabilities. Mr. Stallard has furnished this information in the present book, which is both interesting and practical. The first part deals with the rules and customs of the Stock Exchange, following on which is a short statement of the law governing agency in the sale of stocks and shares. The two remaining portions of the work treat of the terms and discharge of the contract, the latter including the law relating to transfers and payment. It is certainly a volume to be perused by every investor who is not already acquainted with the legal part of the subject.

The Law of the Liability of Directors and Promoters. By R. STOREY DEANS, LL.B. London: Clement Wilson, Norfolk House, Norfolk-street.

The liability of company directors and promoters is stated clearly and briefly in this volume under three heads. First of all, to individuals dealing under this division with fraudulent prospectuses, notices, reports, and puffs in newspapers—under which heading the case of Andrews *v.* Mockford figures conspicuously. The author then shows how, and under what circumstances, a director or promoter may become liable to the company itself; and in the third part, discusses their liability in the winding-up for misfeasance and breach of trust. It is well-written, and the law concisely stated; but we should have liked to have seen a table of the cited cases with the dates of the decisions.

Answers to Correspondents.

Questions about public securities will be answered week by week, in the REVIEW, on the following terms and conditions:—

A fee of FIVE shillings must be remitted for each question put, provided they are questions about separate securities. Should a private letter be required, then an extra fee of FIVE shillings must be sent to cover the cost of such letter, the fee then being TEN shillings for one query only, and FIVE shillings for every subsequent one in the same letter. While making this concession the EDITOR will feel obliged if private replies are as much as possible dispensed with. It is wholly impossible to answer letters sent merely "with a stamped envelope enclosed for reply."

Correspondents will further greatly oblige by so framing their questions as to obviate the necessity to name securities in the replies. They should *number* the questions, keeping a copy for reference, thus:—"(1) Please inform me about the present position of the Rowenzori Development Co. (2) Is a dividend likely to be paid soon on the capital stock of the Congo-Sudan Railway?"

Answers to be given to all such questions by simply quoting the numbers 1, 2, 3, and so on. The EDITOR has a rooted objection to such forms of reply as—"I think your Timbuctoo Consols will go up," or "Sell your Slowcoach and Draggem Bonds," because this kind of thing is open to all sorts of abuses. By the plan suggested, and by using a fancy name to be replied to, each query can be kept absolutely private to the inquirer, and no scope whatever be given to market munipulations. Avoid, as names to be replied to, common words, like "investor," "inquirer," and so on, as also "bear" or "bull." Detached syllables of the inquirer's name, or initials reversed, will frequently do as well as anything, so long as the answer can be identified by the inquirer.

The EDITOR further respectfully requests that merely speculative questions should as far as possible be avoided. He by no meant, sets himself up as a market prophet, and can only undertake so provide the latest information regarding the securities asked about. This he will do faithfully and without bias.

Replies cannot be guaranteed in the same week if the letters demanding them reach the office of the INVESTORS' REVIEW, Norfolk House, Norfolk-street, W.C., later than the first post on Wednesday mornings.

H. F. G.—The board cannot be considered strong, prospectus is meagre. You will do well to leave the concern alone.

N. S.—You might wait a little longer. Company is reported to be interested in a scheme in connection with the opening up of the western country.

M. L. B.—I do not, as I anticipate the company will have a good deal of difficulty with its extension.

WAVERLEY.—Prefer Nos. 1 and 3; should not recommend investment of all the fund in this manner. Sinking Fund should be larger than you suggest.

To Correspondents.

The EDITOR cannot undertake to return rejected communications. Letters from correspondents must, in every case, be authenticated by the name and address of the writer.

The Investors' Review.

The Week's Money Market.

The market during the week has been struggling against its over-supply of funds. A good portion of the money obtained from the Bank of England on bills discounted before the turn of the year remains upon its hands, and was increased to a slight extent by the release of Japanese funds, and these floating supplies beat down the rates for short loans. The banker and bill-broker must turn their spare money-over, else their profits would be materially reduced, and consequently the rate for day to day money steadily slipped back each day until it is now no more than 1¼ per cent., as against 1½ to 2 per cent. a week ago. Weekly fixtures are likewise quoted lower at 1½ to 1¾ per cent., as compared with 1¾ to 2 per cent. last week. The increased ease caused some disturbance amongst the discount houses, and several meetings were held to discuss the advisability of putting down the allowances for money at "call" and "notice," but no action was taken.

Discount rates, however, have been fairly maintained throughout the week, and closed just a shade harder at 2⅜ to 2$\frac{7}{16}$ for three months' bank bills. The knowledge that the Treasury will be sweeping in outside balances directly, and that the bills held by the Bank of England are also daily maturing, encouraged a spirit of caution, which was heightened by the aggravation of the monetary stringency in India, although this development has not led to gold being purchased this week for that quarter. Undoubtedly bidding would have been brisk for the metal on that account, but the propounding of the gold-depositing scheme by the Indian Government caused intending exporters to hold their hand. Much was talked about the shipment of the metal to the Argentine Republic; but, after all, only £80,000 was taken, which, with the withdrawal last week, stated to be for South America, practically constitutes the withdrawals from the Bank during its financial week. As a matter of fact, we have reason for stating that a fair proportion of the £520,000 taken a week ago ostensibly for South America went to the Continent.

The Stock Exchange settlement found the market more inclined to lend to the "House," and fortnightly loans did not often exceed 3¼ to 3½ per cent. The Indian Government announced the renewal of the £1,000,000 of Sterling Treasury Bills, falling due on the 23rd inst., a course that was fully expected. The New South Wales Loan for £1,500,000 went at an average premium of £1. 8s. 4d. above the minimum of 99, but although this appears a moderate premium in these days of investment hunger, it compares very favourably with the previous issue of Three per Cents. by the same Colony in October, 1895, when only £96. 18s. 3d. per cent. was obtained.

There is nothing at all unusual in this week's Bank return. It shows that the market has paid off £1,624,000 due by it on "other" securities at the expense of a reduction of £1,073,000 in "other" deposits. Probably the change of credits from the control of the market to that of the Bank would have been considerably larger but for the readiness of the Bank to discount bills. The banking reserve has been increased by about £800,000 to £20,685,000 by the return of the cash drawn out at the end of the year. Nevertheless, it lost £587,000 in gold by export within the week ended on Wednesday.

BANK OF ENGLAND.

AN ACCOUNT pursuant to the Act 7 and 8 Vict., cap. 32, for the Week ending on Wednesday, January 5, 1898.

ISSUE DEPARTMENT.

	£		£
Notes Issued	46,060,965	Government Debt	11,015,100
		Other Securities	5,784,900
		Gold Coin and Bullion	29,260,965
		Silver Bullion	—
	£46,060,965		£46,160,965

BANKING DEPARTMENT.

	£		£
Proprietors' Capital	14,553,000	Government Securities......	14,023,036
Rest	3,423,887	Other Securities............	33,169,652
Public Deposits (including Exchequer, Savings Banks, Commissioners of National Debt, and Dividend Accounts)..................	9,391,449	Notes	18,558,575
Other Deposits	40,370,457	Gold and Silver Coin	2,126,303
Seven Day and other Bills..	138,773		
	£67,877,566		£67,877,566

Dated January 13, 1898.

H. G. BOWEN, *Chief Cashier.*

In the following table will be found the movements compared with the previous week, and also the totals for that week and the corresponding return last year:—

Banking Department.

Last Year. Jan. 13		Jan. 5, 1898.	Jan. 12, 1898.	Increase.	Decrease.
£	Liabilities.	£	£	£	£
3,406,871	Rest	3,388,138	3,423,887	35,749	—
8,063,487	Pub. Deposits....	9,190,843	9,391,449	200,606	—
46,839,007	Other do.	41,443,070	40,370,457	—	1,072,613
118,884	7 Day Bills	126,728	138,773	12,045	—
	Assets.			Decrease.	Increase.
15,717,867	Gov. Securities ..	14,023,036	14,023,036	—	—
32,516,540	Other do.	34,793,736	33,169,652	1,624,084	—
24,746,842	Total Reserve....	19,883,007	20,684,878	—	799,871
				1,872,484	1,872,484
				Increase.	Decrease.
£		£	£	£	£
26,571,250	Note Circulation.	28,137,045	27,502,390	—	634,655
45 p.c.	Proportion	39⅛ p.c.	41½ p.c.	—	—
4 "	Bank Rate	3 "	3 "	—	—

Foreign Bullion movement for week £587,000 out.

LONDON BANKERS' CLEARING.

Week ending	1897.	1896.	Increase.	Decrease.
	£	£	£	£
Dec. 1	171,792,000	166,125,000	5,667,000	—
" 8	136,090,000	124,457,000	11,633,000	—
" 15	161,483,000	165,735,000	—	4,252,000
" 22	155,425,000	133,202,000	22,223,000	—
" 29	105,382,000	132,437,000	—	27,055,000
Total from Jan. 1, 1897	7,491,281,000	7,574,853,000	—	83,572,000

Week ending	1898.	1897.	Increase.	Decrease.
	£	£	£	£
Jan. 5	222,654,000	174,376,000	48,278,000	—
Jan. 12	144,603,000	127,315,000	17,288,000	—

BANK AND DISCOUNT RATES ABROAD.

	Bank Rate.	Altered.	Open Market.
Paris	2	March 14, 1895	2
Berlin..	5	October 9, 1897	3¾
Hamburg	5	October 9, 1897	3¾
Frankfort	5	October 9, 1897	3¾
Amsterdam	3	April 13, 1897	2¾
Brussels	3	April 28, 1896	2
Vienna	4	January 22, 1896	3⅛
Rome..............................	5	August 27, 1895	3
St. Petersburg...................	6	August 26, 1896	5
Madrid	5	June 17, 1896	4
Lisbon	6	January 25, 1891	6
Stockholm	5	October 27, 1897	5
Copenhagen......................	5	August 3, 1897	5
Calcutta	11	January 11, 1898	—
Bombay	12	January 11, 1898	—
New York call money	2 to 2½	—	—

NEW YORK ASSOCIATED BANKS (dollar at 4s.).

	Jan. 6, 1898.	Jan. 1, 1898.	Dec. 25, 1897.	Jan. 9, 1897.
	£	£	£	£
Specie..........................	21,318,000	20,946,000	20,880,000	15,378,000
Legal tenders	17,414,000	15,964,000	14,880,000	20,822,000
Loans and discounts	121,956,000	121,556,000	122,122,000	98,224,000
Circulation	3,114,400	3,104,000	3,145,800	3,782,000
Net deposits	137,118,000	135,012,000	133,826,000	109,608,000

Legal reserve is 25 per cent. of net deposits; therefore the total reserve (specie and legal tenders) exceeds this sum by £4,452,500, against an excess last week of £8,157,000.

BANK OF FRANCE (25 francs to the £).

	Jan. 13, 1898.	Jan. 6, 1898.	Dec. 30, 1897.	Jan. 14, 1897.
	£	£	£	£
Gold in hand	77,326,960	77,637,120	78,115,000	76,199,000
Silver in hand	48,214,120	48,265,040	48,230,360	49,021,000
Bills discounted	38,258,760	38,536,920	38,303,840	*52,036,000
Advances	15,161,920	16,336,600	15,199,760	—
Note circulation	153,518,280	154,505,080	152,362,080	151,420,000
Public deposits	10,153,400	12,962,760	12,640,600	7,869,000
Private deposits	21,008,000	21,616,560	20,691,400	22,856,000

Proportion between bullion and circulation 81⅞ per cent. against 81½ per cent. a week ago.

* Includes advances.

IMPERIAL BANK OF GERMANY (20 marks to the £).

	Jan. 7 1898.	Dec. 31, 1897.	Dec. 23, 1897.	Jan. 7, 1897.
	£	£	£	£
Cash in hand	42,422,900	41,327,800	44,417,150	41,236,000
Bills discounted	33,625,850	38,438,900	33,140,950	*42,658,000
Advances on stocks	6,405,750	8,633,550	4,806,650	—
Note circulation	61,634,000	65,998,600	56,598,700	58,934,000
Public deposits	19,672,900	21,320,200	22,710,300	20,815,000

* Includes advances.

AUSTRIAN-HUNGARIAN BANK (1s. 8d. to the florin).

	Jan. 7, 1898.	Dec. 31, 1897.	Dec. 23, 1897.	Jan. 7, 1897.
	£	£	£	£
Gold reserve	30,363,833	30,315,750	30,395,833	30,295,000
Silver reserve	10,280,083	10,278,417	10,278,500	12,550,000
Foreign bills	1,592,166	1,572,333	1,657,166	—
Advances	2,229,666	2,319,333	2,181,166	—
Note circulation	56,636,000	58,325,583	55,857,583	63,876,000
Bills discounted	16,029,750	17,244,750	14,572,083	*23,270,000

* Includes advances.

NATIONAL BANK OF BELGIUM (25 francs to the £).

	Jan. 6, 1898.	Dec. 30, 1897.	Dec. 23, 1897.	Jan. 7, 1897.
	£	£	£	£
Coin and bullion	4,290,960	4,119,880	4,236,240	4,193,000
Other securities	8,541,280	18,033,000	17,426,040	16,852,000
Note circulation	19,542,560	19,488,760	19,124,840	19,209,000
Deposits	4,548,400	3,998,040	3,817,480	3,044,000

BANK OF SPAIN (25 pesetas to the £).

	Jan. 8, 1898.	Jan. 1, 1898.	Dec. 25, 1897.	Jan. 9, 1897.
	£	£	£	£
Gold	9,430,680	9,430,680	9,430,680	8,528,320
Silver	10,314,200	10,318,960	10,302,400	10,078,400
Bills discounted	20,394,120	20,646,040	20,482,240	8,424,160
Advances and loans	5,131,040	5,063,560	5,117,320	8,857,000
Notes in circulation	48,515,040	48,250,840	47,859,440	41,739,920
Treasury advances, coupon account	95,200	113,920	505,480	95,280
Treasury balances	39,760	nil	2,269,840	2,735,960

LONDON COURSE OF EXCHANGE.

Place.	Usance.	Jan. 4.	Jan. 6.	Jan. 11.	Jan. 13.
Amsterdam and Rotterdam	short	12·1¼	12·1½	12·1¼	12·1½
Do. do.	3 months	12·3⅜	12·3⅜	12·3⅜	12·3⅞
Antwerp and Brussels	3 months	25·40	25·40	25·40	25·40
Hamburg	3 months	20·60	20·60	20·61	20·60
Berlin and German B. Places	3 months	20·61	20·60	20·61	20·60
Paris	cheques	25·23¾	25·23¾	25·25	25·25
Do.	3 months	25·38¾	25·38¾	25·40	25·38¾
Marseilles	3 months	25·38¾	25·38¾	25·40	25·40
Switzerland	3 months	25·62	25·58¾	25·60	25·60
Austria	3 months	12·15	12·15	12·15	12·15
St. Petersburg	3 months	25⁵⁄₁₆	25⁵⁄₁₆	25⁵⁄₁₆	25⁵⁄₁₆
Moscow	3 months	25	25	25	25
Italian Bank Places	3 months	26·75	26·75	26·77½	26·77½
New York	60 days	49	49	49	49
Madrid and Spanish B. P.	3 months	35¼	35¼	35⁵⁄₁₆	35¼
Lisbon	3 months	35⅜	35⅜	35⅜	35⁵⁄₁₆
Oporto	3 months	35⅜	35⅜	35⅜	35⁵⁄₁₆
Copenhagen	3 months	18·38	18·38	18·38	18·38
Christiania	—	18·38	18·38	18·38	18·38
Stockholm	—	18·38	18·38	18·38	18·38

FOREIGN RATES OF EXCHANGE ON LONDON.

Place.	Usance.	Last week's.	Latest.	Place.	Usance.	Last week's.	Latest.
Paris	chqs.	25·22	25·22½	Italy	sight	26·44	26·46
Brussels	chqs.	25·25½	25·26	Do. gold prem.	..	104·77	104·85
Amsterdam	short	12·07½	12·06½	Constantinople	3 mths	109·32	109·05
Berlin	short	20·38½	20·38	B. Ayres gd. pm.	..	167	167
Do.	3 mths	20.40½	20·40	Rio de Janeiro	90 dys	6⁷⁄₃₂d.	6⅛
Hamburg	3 mths	20.26	20.25	Valparaiso	90 dys	17¹³⁄₁₆d.	17¾
Frankfort	short	20.38	20·37	Calcutta	T. T.	1/3¹⁵⁄₁₆	1/4¹⁄₁₆
Vienna	short	12.00	12.01	Bombay	T. T.	1/3¹⁵⁄₁₆	1/4
St. Petersburg	3 mths	93·60	93·75	Hong Kong	T. T.	1/10¾	1/11⅜
New York	60 dys	4·82½	4·82½	Shanghai	T. T.	2/7½	2/8
Lisbon	sight	36d.	35¹¹⁄₁₆	Singapore	T. T.	1/11⅜	1/11¾
Madrid	sight	33·50	33·58				

OPEN MARKET DISCOUNT.

	Per cent.
Thirty and sixty day remitted bills	2⅛—2¼
Three months ,,	2⅛—2 3/16
Four months ,,	2⅛—2¼
Six months ,,	2⅛—2¼
Three months fine inland bills	2¼—2½
Four months ,,	2½—3
Six months ,,	2¾—3

BANK AND DEPOSIT RATES.

	per cent
Bank of England minimum discount rates	3
,, ,, short loan rates	—
Banker's rate on deposits	1½
Bill brokers' deposit rate (call)	2
,, 7 and 14 days' notice	2¼
Current rates for 7 day loans	1¼—1¾
,, ,, for call loans	1½—1¾

The Week's Stock Markets.

Markets were dull towards the end of last week, due to some realisations in anticipation of the settlement, which commenced on Tuesday. When the account had been finally adjusted the tendency became distinctly firm in all departments, with the exception of Home Government Securities, although the latest prices in several instances are not the highest of the week. The account was somewhat heavier than a fortnight ago, but was easily arranged, rates being generally lower. The principal activity has been in Canadian and American Railway shares and Foreign Government stocks.

Consols have shown a drooping tendency, and "marked" as low as 112⅝ on Tuesday, after having touched 113 earlier in the week. Indian Government Securities have also declined, but there is a slight improvement in Rupee Paper, due to the further sharp rise in the Indian Exchanges.

Highest and Lowest this Year.	Last Carrying over Price.	BRITISH FUNDS, &c.	Closing Price.	Rise or Fall.
113½ 112⅝	—	Consols 2¾ p.c. (Money)...	112¹¹⁄₁₆	−³⁄₁₆
113⁵⁄₁₆ 112¹¹⁄₁₆	112⁷⁄₈	Do. Account (Feb. 2)	112¹³⁄₁₆	−³⁄₁₆
106⅛ 105½	106	2½ p.c. Stock red. 1905 ...	105⅝	−⅛
350 347½	—	Bank of England Stock...	350	+1
117 116½	116¾	India 3½ p.c. Stk. red. 1931	116½	−½
109½ 108½	109	Do. 3 p.c. Stk. red. 1948	108½	−½
96⅛ 95½	96	Do. 2½ p.c. Stk. red. 1926	95½	−½

Home Railway stocks have exhibited a firm tone, and business has been fairly active. Continuation rates were considerably lower, and all stocks, with the exception of South-Eastern Deferred, were scarcer for delivery than at the last account. On Chatham Ordinary and Great Central issues there was a backwardation; Great Eastern was continued at ⅛, Great Western at ⁵⁄₁₆, Midland Preferred at ⅛, North-Western at ⁵⁄₁₆, and South-Eastern Deferred at ¼ contango. Great Central stocks have again attracted most attention, and, owing partly to several misleading telegrams from Manchester, which gave the dividend as 4 per cent. on the Preferred, prices advanced rapidly. When it was found that the dividend was really at the rate of 2 per cent. on the Preferred (equal to 1 per cent. on the undivided Ordinary), there was a sharp decline in all the Great Central issues. A year ago the dividend was 3 per cent on the Preferred (or 1½ per cent. on the Ordinary) and practically the same amount has now been placed to reserve and carried forward. South-Eastern Deferred sprang up suddenly on Saturday and relapsed as quickly on Monday, on the manipulations of a clique. The Scottish stocks have been favourably influenced by rumours that the engineers in the North were preparing to desert the Union and return to work as non-unionists. The Caledonian and Glasgow and South-Western Companies announce a 20 per cent. reduction in passenger rates from Paisley and Glasgow, to take effect next month, and it is expected that the other competing lines will follow suit. All the traffic returns were considered satisfactory.

Highest and Lowest this Year.	Last Carrying over Price.	HOME RAILWAYS.	Closing Price.	Rise or Fall.
183⅞ 181½	182¼	Brighton Def.	183⅞	+1⅝
58⅞ 57⅝	58⅝	Caledonian Def.	58½	+ ¼
19¼ 19	19⅛	Chatham Ordinary	19⅛	− ⅛
77¼ 66	76	Great Central Pref.	74	+2
24⅝ 22½	23⅝	Do. Def.	23¼	− ¼
123⅝ 122⅜	123¼	Great Eastern	122¾	− ⅝
61⅞ 59½	60¼	Great Northern Def.	61	—
177½ 176¾	177	Great Western	176⅜	− ⅝
48 46¾	47½	Hull and Barnsley	47½	+ ½
148½ 148	148	Lanc. and Yorkshire	148	− ½
135¼ 133½	135	Metropolitan	135½	+ ¼
31 30	30½	Metropolitan District	30⅜	− ⅛
88⅜ 87¾	88¼	Midland Pref.	88¼	+ ⅛
95 94½	94¾	Do. Def.	94¾	—
92⅝ 90¼	92	North British Pref.	92¼	+1¾
47 45	46⅜	Do. Def.	46⅜	+ ⅛
180¾ 179¼	179¾	North Eastern	180¼	—
205¼ 204½	204¾	North Western	204½	− ⅛
116¼ 114⅝	115¼	South Eastern Def.	115⅝	+ ⅜
98¾ 96⅝	98	South Western Def.	98	− ½

United States Railroad shares have presented a straggling appearance, but after several ups and downs prices leave off with a considerable margin in favour of holders. Wall-street buying is principally responsible for the improvement, and the earnings published this week have helped to raise prices. The somewhat stale letters appearing in the *Times* on Monday, *re* the Silver campaign in the United States, created a mild sort of a "slump," but the effect soon wore off. There has again been some talk of the Union Pacific and the Chicago and North-Western Companies consolidating, but nothing definite is known on this side.

Union Pacific shares have also been largely bought on the report that the committee has secured control of the Oregon Short line and the Oregon Navigation Company; and a good traffic return for the first week in January is responsible for the rise in Chicago and Milwaukee. The East-bound railway freights despatched from Chicago during last week amounted to nearly 142,000 tons, as compared with about only 89,000 tons for the preceding week.

Canadian Pacific Railway shares have again attracted a good deal of attention, and large buying orders have come on the market from Germany. Grand Trunk Stocks continued their upward flight for a time, but the recent rapid rise has naturally been followed by a considerable amount of profit taking. The traffic return was again wonderfully good, although not up to market expectations.

Highest and Lowest this Year.	Last Carrying over Price.	CANADIAN AND U.S. RAILWAYS.	Closing Prices.	Rise or Fall.
13¾ 13	13½	Atchison Shares	13½	+ ⅛
32¾ 30⅜	32	Do. Pref.	31⅞	+ ⅜
12⅞ 11⅞	12½	Central Pacific	12⅜	+1
99¾ 95¼	98⅞	Chic. Mil. & St. Paul	99½	+1¼
13 11½	12	Denver Shares	12¾	+1
51 46⅝	48¼	Do. Prefd.	48¾xd	+2½
15¾ 14¾	15¼	Erie Shares	15¾	+ ⅜
40½ 38	39¾	Do. Prefd.	39¾	+ ½
60 56⅝	58½	Louisville & Nashville	58⅝	+1⅛
13½ 12¾	13¼	Missouri & Texas	13¼	+ ⅛
114¾ 108½	114	New York Central	115⅛	+3⅜
49¾ 47¾	49	Norfolk & West. Prefd.	49	+ ⅜
66⅞ 59⅞	64½	Northern Pacific Prefd.	65	+3⅞
17¼ 15⅞	16¾	Ontario Shares	16½	+ ⅛
60⅞ 58⅞	60	Pennsylvania	60	+ ⅜
12½ 11⅛	11¾	Reading Shares	11⅞	− ⅛
33¼ 30⅞	33	Southern Prefd.	33⅛	+ ⅞
32⅝ 26½	29¼	Union Pacific	31½	+4
20 18	19	Wabash Prefd.	19½	+ ¾
30¼ 27⅝	28½	Do. Income Debs.	30¼	+2
90¼ 83⅞	88⅞	Canadian Pacific	89	+2¼
73⅝ 69⅞	73	Grand Trunk Guar.	72⅝	+ ¼
67 57⅛	64½	Do. 1st Pref.	64¾	+3⅜
44 37¼	42½	Do. 2nd Pref.	41½	+ ⅝
23⅝ 19¾	22⅝	Do. 3rd Pref.	22	+1⅛
105¼ 104	105	Do. 4 p.c. Deb.	105	—

Among Foreign Government securities Chinese bonds advanced steadily, but became dull owing to a reported hitch in the arrangements for the new loan, and there has been a good demand for Argentine Government and the various Cedula issues. The gold premium at Buenos Ayres continues to decline, helped in that direction by the shipments of sovereigns from London for payment of wheat, and more gold is expected to go either from London or Paris. Greek bonds mark a substantial rise, on the proposed settlement of the Debt, it being further announced that the Government will receive authority to raise a loan sufficiently large to wipe out the 1897 deficit, and also to provide for the deficit of this year. Spanish Fours have recovered a little on more cheerful news from Cuba; Turkish groups maintain last week's rise, and, according to a Reuter's telegram, negotiations are now on foot for a new Turkish loan for £T400,000 to the Government against an increase of the guarantee for the railway between Eskishehr and Konieh. Uruguay bonds have been dull, the country being again on a verge of a revolution, despite the energetic action of President Cuestas. The Peruvian Corporation issues advanced in sympathy with the firmness of Argentine Govt. bonds.

Highest and Lowest this Year.	Last Carrying over Price.	FOREIGN BONDS.	Closing Price.	Rise or Fall.
94 92½	93½	Argentine 5 p.c. 1886	93¼	+ ⅛
91¼ 89	90¾	Do. 6 p.c. Funding	90½	+ 1¼
75⅝ 71	73¾	Do. 5 p.c. B. Ay. Water	74⅜	+ 3½
61 60	60¼	Brazilian 4 p.c. 1889	60¼	—
68 67½	67½	Do. 5 p.c. 1895	67½	—
63 62½	62½	Do. 5 p.c. West Minas Ry.	62½	—
106¾ 106¼	106⅝	Egyptian 4 p.c. Unified	106¾	+ ¼
102½ 102	102¼	Do. 3½ p.c. Pref.	102½	+ ¼
102½ 102	102	French 3 p.c. Rente	102½	+ ½
38 34½	36	Greek 4 p.c. Monopoly	38	+ 3½
93$\frac{5}{16}$ 93	93	Italian 5 p.c. Rente	93⅛	− ¼
98¼ 95¾	97¾	Mexican 6 p.c. 1888	97¾	+ 1
20¾ 20¼	20¾	Portuguese 1 p.c.	20½	− ⅛
61 59⅞	60¼	Spanish 4 p.c.	60⅜	+ ⅜
45 43	44⅜	Turkish 1 p.c. "B"	44½	− ½
25½ 24$\frac{7}{16}$	25¼	Do. 1 p.c. "C"	25$\frac{5}{16}$	+ ¼
22$\frac{5}{16}$ 21$\frac{13}{16}$	22	Do. 1 p.c. "D"	22$\frac{1}{16}$	+ $\frac{1}{16}$
42½ 41½	41½	Uruguay 3½ p.c. Bonds	41¾	—

Foreign railway stocks have shown great strength. Argentine and other South American companies leading the way. This week's traffic returns being more satisfactory. Mexican issues were buoyant, and it is confidently expected that the Mexican Government will grant powers to enable the company to raise rates.

Highest and Lowest this Year.	Last Carrying over Price.	FOREIGN RAILWAYS.	Closing Price.	Rise or Fall.
20½ 20	20¼	Argentine Gt. West. 5 p.c. Pref.	20½	+ ¼
155¼ 149	149½	B. Ay. Gt. Southern Ord.	155	+6
78 75½	77	B. Ay. and Rosario Ord.	77½	+2
12¼ 11$\frac{13}{16}$	11⅞	B. Ay. Western Ord.	12¼	+ ⅜
86 80½	84½	Central Argentine Ord.	85½	+3½
90 89½	89½	Cordoba and Rosario 6 p.c. Deb.	91	+1
95 93¾	94	Cord. Cent. 4 p.c. Deb. (Cent. Nth. Sec.)	94½	+ ½
61¾ 58½	60	Do. Income Deb. Stk.	61½	+1½
21¾ 18	21	Mexican Ord. Stk.	21¼	+2¼
79 72	78½	Do. 8 p.c. 1st Pref.	77	+2

In the Miscellaneous market business continues to spread, and transactions have been numerous. Movements in the upward direction are apparent in Aerated Bread shares, Anglo-Argentine Tramways, British Electric Traction, D. H. Evans, and Waterlow & Sons, Deferred. Telegraph stocks are firmer, notably Anglo-American. The satisfactory dividends announced by the leading banks, has caused an inquiry for their shares, and brewery debentures have been actively dealt in at higher prices. Hudson Bays have moved within narrow limits, Coats are about 1½ higher, and Apollinaris also marks a rise.

Markets close with an irregular tendency. Among Home Railway stocks, Brighton Deferred advanced sharply on dividend rumours, a 7 per cent. distribution being looked for to-morrow. South Eastern and Great

Eastern close firm, but Great Central issues and the Scotch stocks were slightly weaker. Canadian Pacific, and Grand Trunk descriptions show heavy falls just at the last, and United States Railroad shares are weaker, with the exception of New York Central. As regards Foreign Government securities, the Greek loans, leave off firm, but there is a slight get back in Argentine, and the Cedulas, Italian, Spanish, and Turkish groups.

Dividends Announced.

Austro-Hungarian Bank.—A dividend of 23 florins 60 kreutzers, for the second half of 1897, has been declared.

Badcock & Wilcox, Limited.—Interim dividend 10 per cent. per annum.

Bank of Victoria.—A cable has been received from the head office, Melbourne, stating that the directors propose to pay off in advance on 15th April a further Instalment of 20 per cent. of its deferred deposit receipts.

Bank of Liverpool.—Directors have declared the usual interim dividend of 12s. 6d. per share.

Bank of Madras.—For the past half-year a dividend is declared at the rate of 10 per cent. per annum, with a bonus of 1 per cent., carrying forward 226,000 rupees. The dividend is at the same rate as last year.

Bristol Brewery (Georges & Co.)—Dividend at rate of 15 per cent. per annum, and bonus of 6 per cent. per annum, making 19 per cent. for year against 17½ per cent. for 1896.

Beacon Gold Mines have declared a third interim dividend of 6d. per share.

British Columbia Development Association.—An interim dividend of 10 per cent. for the year is declared on the preference shares.

Capital and Counties Bank has declared dividend for the past six months at the rate of 16 per cent. per annum.

Debenture Corporation.—A dividend of 7 per cent. for the year is declared on the ordinary shares, with a bonus of ½ per cent., adding £8,000 to reserve, and carrying forward £4,206. The dividend last year was at the rate of 8 per cent., with ½ per cent. bonus.

De Keyser's Royal Hotel, Limited.—Dividend 7s. on ordinary shares, making 6½ per cent. for year; £3,472 carried forward.

Direct United States Cable Company.—Interim dividend of 3s. per share for quarter; £12,000 to reserve and £4,090 forward.

Distillers' Company.—Interim dividend of 8s. per share. Last year the dividend was at the same rate.

Great Boulder Proprietary Company.—Dividend of 6d. per share on the divided shares.

Great Central Railway Company.—Dividend for past half-year announced at rate of 2 per cent. per annum on preference ordinary stock. For corresponding half of 1896 the dividend on the undivided ordinary stock was at the rate of 1½ per cent. per annum; £7,000 is placed to reserve and £2,800 carried forward.

Great Northern Railway Company of United States.—Quarterly dividend declared of 1½ per cent. on preferred capital stock, and the regular quarterly dividend of 1½ per cent. on the capital stock of the St. Paul, Minneapolis and Manitoba Railway Company 6 per cent. guaranteed shares.

Halifax Joint Stock Banking Company announce a dividend at the rate of 10 per cent. per annum for half past year, carrying forward £7,119, the dividend being at the same rate as last year.

Liebig Extract of Meat Company.—Interim dividend of 20s. per share.

Lister & Co.—Directors recommend dividend at the rate of 2 per cent. to the ordinary shareholders, taking £4,874 from reserve.

Lloyds' Bank.—A dividend of 16s. per share is declared, being at the rate of 20 per cent., making a distribution for the year of 17½ per cent., adding £50,000 to reserve fund, placing £25,000 to premises account, carrying forward £32,000. The corresponding dividend last year was at the rate of 16½ per cent. per annum.

London and Greenwich Railway Company will pay dividends at rate of £1. 8s. 3d. per cent., out of an available balance of £12,326.

London and Provincial Bank.—It is proposed to pay a dividend at the rate of 17½ per cent., place £6,288 to reserve fund, to add £10,000 to reduction of premises account, £4,000 to pension fund, and to carry forward £21,773. Last year the dividend was at the rate of 17 per cent. per annum.

London and South Western Bank.—After placing £10,000 to reserve, writing £10,000 off premises account, a dividend at the rate of 10 per cent. is declared, and a bonus of 2 per cent., making, with the dividend and bonus paid in August, 13 per cent. for the year, carrying forward about £15,000. The dividend last year was at the rate of 10 per cent., with a bonus of 1 per cent., placing £20,000 to reserve, and carrying forward £15,000.

Manchester and County Bank.—After setting aside £10,000 towards officers' superannuation fund, a dividend at the rate of 15 per cent. per annum is declared, leaving £15,278 to be carried forward. The dividend remains the same as at the same period last year.

Manchester and Liverpool District Banking Company.—Dividend of 15s. declared and a bonus of 5s. per share, adding £15,000 to reserve, and carrying forward £19,249. The dividend and bonus were the same last year, with £21,438 carried forward.

Mercantile Bank of Lancashire.—After adding £3,000 to reserve fund, the directors recommend a dividend for past half year of £2. 10s. on the "A" share, and at the rate of 7½ per cent. per annum on the ordinary shares. The corresponding dividends were at the same rate.

Merchants' Marine Insurance.—Dividend of 1s. 6d. per share, making 6 per cent. per annum.

Redeem Tea Company.—Interim dividend of 2½ per cent. on ordinary shares.

New Tivoli, Limited.—Interim dividend for the past six months at the rate of 16 per cent. per annum, and a bonus of 2s. per share. Last year the dividend was at the same rate, with a bonus of 3s. per share.

North Eastern Banking.—Directors propose to pay a dividend of 6s. 6d. per share, and to carry forward £2,843. The corresponding dividend last year was at the rate of 10⅝ per cent.

North Metropolitan Tramway Company.—Six per cent. per annum dividend. Carried forward, £4,700.

Nottingham Joint Stock Bank.—Dividend at the rate of 15 per cent. per annum, and a bonus of 2½ per cent. The dividend last year was at the same rate.

Oldham Joint Stock Bank.—Recommend a dividend of 4s. per share, making with the interim dividend 10 per cent. for the year, being at the same rate as last year.

Provincial Bank of Ireland.—Dividend for the past six months at the rate of 10 per cent. per annum. The dividend last year was at the same rate and £9,765 was carried forward.

Royal Brewery, Brentford.—Interim dividend on the ordinary shares at the rate of 7 per cent. per annum, being at the same rate as last year.

Union Bank of London.—The directors have declared a dividend of 15s. 6d. per share, placed £5,000 to reduction of bank premises account, and carried forward £22,233. The dividend was at the same rate last year, with £22,047 carried forward.

Williams, Deacon, and Manchester and Salford Bank.—Dividend of 12s. per share, placing £20,000 to reserve fund, £15,000 to buildings depreciation fund, and carrying forward £20,927. Last year the dividend was at the rate of 12½ per cent., with £17,629 carried forward.

City and South London Railway Company.—Dividend at the rate of 1½ per cent. per annum for the half-year ended December 31, with £1,510 carried forward. Dividend same as last year.

Hong Kong and Shanghai Banking Corporation.—Dividend for the half-year ended December 31 of 25s. per share, adding 1,000,000 dol. to reserve fund (which will then stand at 8,000,000 dols.) and carrying forward about 300,000 dols.

Liverpool Union Bank.—Dividend of £1 per share is declared for the past half year, and a bonus of 10s. per share, making with the dividend already paid 12½ per cent. per annum.

GOLD MINING IN ONTARIO AND BRITISH COLUMBIA.

Mr. E. R. Rathbone delivered an interesting lecture on Tuesday evening at a meeting of the Royal Colonial Institute on "The Goldfields of Ontario and British Columbia." He had no doubt that the Dominion, taking advantage of the experience gained in other gold-mining countries, would be able to avoid many of the costly mistakes which had so frequently accompanied the first discovery of payable goldfields elsewhere. After alluding to the nature of alluvial and vein-gold mining, and explaining the methods, the lecturer said it was to hydraulic mining that British Columbia owed its principal production of alluvial gold at the present time. So far as could be ascertained from the Government reports of British Columbia and Ontario, the total gross value of gold derived from placer gold mining in British Columbia, principally from the district of Cariboo, and spread over a period of about forty years, amounted to something like £12,000,000 sterling. The greatest period of prosperity in this class of mining was apparently during the sixties, when the annual output ranged in value from about £500,000 to £1,000,000 sterling. During the past decade, however, it appears to have ranged only from £80,000 to £120,000. Doubtless in the next few years the gold production derived from placer mining within the Dominion would enormously increase owing to the recent discoveries in the North-Western Territories, on the Yukon and at Klondike. The amount of gold produced from vein-mining in British Columbia had, until quite recently, been hardly worthy of notice, and indeed even at the present time it was largely due to the production of one mine. Coming to mineral statistics and mining laws, Mr. Rathbone said there was no better method of illustrating the progress made in the mineral industry of a country than by the frequent and intelligent publication of its mineral statistics. The importance of the publication of facts and figures in order to draw the attention of the public to any newly-discovered goldfield could not well be exaggerated. Much useful work can be accomplished in this connection by the establishment of a Chamber of Mines. Having described the mining undertakings at work, the lecturer, in his concluding remarks, said it was in the nature of things that gold mining should be taken advantage of by ignorant and unprincipled persons to so exaggerate and confuse the minds of the investing public that it was often held in much disrepute. It was unfortunate that, whereas in nearly all other industries, some practical knowledge was considered as a necessary condition of success, yet in gold mining especially no such knowledge was demanded by the investing public, and any one, if he had only lived in a mining country, was supposed to have absorbed by contact a sufficient knowledge of mining to enable him to distinguish good properties from bad, and otherwise direct one of the most complicated of industries. It was also a drawback to mining that engineers were not obliged to qualify in some way in their profession; under present conditions it was competent for any jack-of-all-trades to suddenly pose as a mining engineer, whose opinion was seriously accepted by a gullible public so long as it was sufficiently favourable.

DR. CORNELIUS HERZ.

Now that the last of the Panama trials have been disposed of in France, Dr. Cornelius Herz, is trying to turn the tables on the French Government, for what he calls the persecution to which they subjected him. He has, through counsel, presented to the State Department at Washington, a claim for an indemnity in consideration of this "persecution," which he declares to have been illegal. It is urged that, though born in France of French parents, he is really an American, as, when three years old, his parents went to New York and obtained American citizenship. The claim demands that the State Department shall prefer a claim in full for the injury done to the name and health of Dr. Herz. Although a specific sum is not mentioned, the brief shows that Dr. Herz demanded a sum of 5,000,000 dols. in a letter which he addressed to the French President, which was never answered. The State Department has promised to consider the matter.

The exports of gold from Cape Colony, during December, amounted in value to £1,257,886, and the total exports for the past year to £10,991,926.

The *Heraldo* of Madrid states that the Minister of Finance has abandoned all idea of a credit operation based on any arrangement connected with the Almaden Mines.

PROPOSED NEW DEEP-SEA CABLE.

Sir Gordon Sprigg, the Cape Premier, told his constituents the other day that, while in England, he had discussed a project for laying a deep-sea cable to the Mother Country. The proposal is that the cable should go from England to Gibraltar, and thence *viâ* Sierra Leone, Ascension, and St. Helena to Cape Town, whence it would proceed overland to Durban, and from Durban be carried to Mauritius, and to Perth, Western Australia. The Premier added that should this scheme be carried out he would submit to Parliament that the Cape as its share should bear the cost of construction to Cape Town and Durban.

THE PROPERTY MARKET.

There has been renewed activity at the Auction Mart, and during the week some notable sales have been effected. The present home of the French Embassy at Albert-gate, Knightsbridge, held under lease from the Crown, has been bought by the French Government for something over £25,000. Messrs. Barker & Neale have sold to Mr. Stanley Leighton, M.P., the house occupied by the late Sir H. Havelock-Allan, 70, Chester-square. The price, however, is not stated. Messrs. H. E. Foster & Cranfield sold, at the Mart on Tuesday, a number of reversions at good prices. Among those was a moiety of a trust fund valued at £11,150, and one moiety in possession of five twenty-fourths, with the remaining moiety in reversion, of the York Hotel, &c., Albemarle-street, f., r. £2,758, life 52 years—£11,000. Messrs. G. B. Hilliard & Son sold the manor of Pebmarsh and Dagworth at £900; and that of North Weald, Essex, at £1,550. Mr. C. H. Brown had extensive sales of house property at the Mart yesterday. Among these were the houses 16 and 18, Dartmouth-street, Westminster, f., r. £180. 16s.—£2,310; 30, Great Chapel-street, f. r. £120—£3,030.

Only two lots were disposed of at Tokenhouse-yard on Monday, viz.: The Railway Tavern and Lyonsdown House, New Barnet, freehold properties, let at £80 and £30 a year, which were sold by Messrs. Rumball & Edwards for £3,400 and £410 respectively. The Donyland Brewery, Colchester, with twenty-eight tied-houses, offered by Messrs. Fenn & Co., was bought in at £120,000, the highest bid being £116,000.

Messrs. Hampson & Co. announce the sale, at the Mart, on the 17th inst., of a profit rental (£100 p.a.) on No. 25, King-street, Regent-street, W.; the town residence, 29, Duke-street, W.; a pair of leasehold houses at Camberwell; and residences at Maida-vale and Maidenhead.

The examinations (preliminary, intermediate, and final) of the Auctioneers' Institute will be held in London towards the end of March or the beginning of April. Forms of entry, which must be filled up and lodged with the secretary on or before March 1st, may now be obtained upon application at the Institute, 57 and 58, Chancery-lane, London, W.C.

The date of Mr. Alfred Richard's sale of stocks and shares at the Mart was incorrectly given in the last number of the INVESTORS' REVIEW as the 28th. It should have been the 25th.

THE BRINSMEAD CASE.

The case of the Queen *v.* Brinsmead was mentioned at the Old Bailey, where Mr. Justice Hawkins was presiding, on Tuesday, in reference to the question of the recognisances. It was stated by Mr. Carson, who appeared for some of the defendants, that an application was made on December 10 on behalf of three of these, for the removal of the trial to the Queen's Bench. The application was granted. Since then, Lomax, one of the defendants, had disappeared, but the other six defendants had done all that lay upon them in order to have the case tried in the superior Court. But the disappearance of Lomax had led to this—that the order of the Court had not been fully carried out. Under these circumstances he now applied on behalf of the remaining six defendants, that the original order might be superseded and a fresh order made for the removal of the trial of the six defendants to this Court. There was a good deal of discussion on the point. In the end Mr. Justice Hawkins said the Court would, in reference to three of the defendants, grant the rule asked for, but upon the condition that the trial should be actively commenced by the 25th of the present month, and that fresh recognisances should be entered into. This was accepted by Mr. Carson, who said the absent defendant would probably surrender, so as to facilitate the proceedings. Upon this, Mr. Justice Hawkins remarked that he would rather suppose that there would be a Bench warrant for him.

The name of Prince George of Greece as candidate for the Governorship of Crete has been formally withdrawn, in consequence of the opposition of Germany.

The gold exports from Western Australia during December amounted to 72,411 oz., valued at £275,211, as compared with 75,845 oz., valued at £288,211, during November, and 29,653 oz., valued at £112,683, in December, 1896.

The Glasgow and South-Western Railway announces a reduction of 20 per cent. in passenger rates between Glasgow and Paisley from February 1. This seems likely to be followed by the cutting of rates on the part of other companies.

Next Week's Meetings.

SATURDAY, JANUARY 15.

Watney & Co., Three and a Half per Cent. Debentures	Call of 50 per cent. = £300,000.

MONDAY, JANUARY 17.

Conde d' Eu Railway Company ..	Winchester House, noon.

TUESDAY, JANUARY 18.

Assets Founder Share Company ..	Worcester House, Walbrook, noon.
Assets Realisation Company	Worcester House, Walbrook, noon.
Buenos Ayres and Pacific Railway Company, 1st debentures	Winchester House, 2.30 p.m.
City Bank	5, Threadneedle-street, noon.
Lady Loch Gold Mines	Winchester House.
Lancashire and Yorkshire Bank	Manchester, noon.
London and Provincial Marine Insurance	2, Royal Exchange Buildings, noon.
North Mount Lyell Copper Company ..	Winchester House, 11.45 a.m.

WEDNESDAY, JANUARY 19.

Debenture Corporation	Cannon-street Hotel, noon.
London and Greenwich Railway Company	Winchester House, 12.30 p.m.
London and Provincial Bank	Cannon-street Hotel, 12.30 p.m.
London and Westminster Bank (Gen.) ..	Lothbury, 1 p.m.
Manchester and Liverpool District Bank	Manchester, noon.
Morton Rose Estate Debentures ..	6, Princes-street, E.C., noon.
National Discount	Cannon-street Hotel, noon.

THURSDAY, JANUARY 20.

Adelphi Bank	Liverpool, noon.
London Joint Stock Bank	Princes-street, E.C., noon.
Union Discount Company	Cannon-street Hotel, 12.30 p.m.

FRIDAY, JANUARY 21.

London and Midland Bank	Birmingham, 1 p.m.
Manchester and County Bank	66, King-street, Manchester, noon.
North-Eastern Banking	Newcastle-on-Tyne, noon.
Rafferty, Thornton, & Co.	42, Old Broad-street, 3 p.m.

It is stated that no new railways will be undertaken in India this year, but that Government will allot £7,000,000 to lines already under construction.

By his will, written in 1895, the late Sir Henry Doulton, of the firm of Doulton & Co., potters, left personal estate valued at £309,483.

For the first time for ten years the dividend of the Austro-Hungarian Bank is under 7 per cent.; consequently the two States do not participate in the net profits.

Canadian Pacific land sales for the past year show a great increase. For 1897 the figures are 200,000 acres, valued at 650,000 dols., while in 1896 88,000 acres were sold for 307,000 dols.

The Lands Department at Sydney is said to be arranging to withdraw large areas from pastoral lessees, and that about a million acres will thus be eventually available for occupation by farmers.

Germany has just appointed a Consul in Liberia, on the West Coast of Africa, an appointment which is regarded as significant. About three months ago the French established a new Consul at Monrovia.

The Ceylon Customs receipts of the past year, including port and harbour dues, which reach 903,455 rupees, amounted to 7,290,124 rupees, exceeding the receipts for 1896 by 757,000 rupees, and the receipts for 1895, the highest previous year, by 602,207 rupees.

It is announced from Berlin that the German Asiatic Bank has already arranged to establish a branch in the Chinese territory occupied by Germany. Other banks are preparing to follow the example.

The British Embassy is said to be quietly negotiating a series of treaties to extend the benefits of so much reciprocity as is obtainable under the Dingley tariff to British possessions in the West Indies.

Experiments are being made at the New South Wales Government farm in the growth of the ramie, or rhea plant, from the fibre of which various fabrics have already been produced by treatment in England. It is cautiously added that the industry is believed to offer great possibilities.

CRIPPLEGATE FIRE VERDICT.—The inquiry at the Guildhall by the City Coroner, Mr. Langham, into the cause of the Cripplegate fire was concluded on Wednesday, and the jury, after nearly five hours' deliberation, returned a verdict to the effect that the fire was not accidental, but was wilfully started by some person or persons unknown.

Tenders for £1,500,000 New South Wales Government 3 per cent. Stock were opened Tuesday at the Bank of England. The applications amounted to £3,908,400—at prices varying from £102 to £99 (the minimum). Tenders at £100. 3s. 6d. will receive about 31 per cent. of the amount applied for, those above that price being allotted in full. The average price obtained for the Stock is £100. 8s. 4d.

THE SUGAR BOUNTIES.—Mr. Czarnikow, in his weekly circular, dated yesterday, states that "a Sugar conference of European countries is shortly to be summoned to Brussels, and Austria, Germany, and Belgium are said to be actually agreed upon abolition of bounties, provided France will abolish both direct and indirect bounties. The latter proposal will meet with great opposition, unless England follows the example of America, or a formula can be invented and agreed to limit bounties strictly to home consumption."

Prices of Mine and Mining Finance Companies' Shares.

Shares £1 each, except where otherwise stated.

AUSTRALIAN.

Making-Up Price, Jan. 10.	Name.	Closing Price.	Making-Up Price, Jan. 10.	Name.	Closing Price.
2⅜	Aladdin	2½	8½	Hannan's Brownhill	7⅝ x
4½	Associated	4⅝	1⅞	Hannan's Oroya	1⅞
1	Do. Southern	⅞	16/9	Do. Proprietary	16/
17/9	Brilliant, £2	17/ x	1⅛	Do. Star	1
2⅛	Do. St. George's	2⅛	—	Ivanhoe, New	6⅛
20/6	British Broken Hill	21/3	1⅛	Kalgurli Mt. & Iron King, 18/	1⅛
6⅛	Do. Westralia	6⅛	6⅛	Kalgurli	6⅝
2	Broken Hill Proprietary	2⅛	2⅛	Lady Shenton	2⅛
2⅛	Brownhill Extended	1⅞	⅞	Lake View Cons.	10½
1⅞	Burbank's Birthday	1⅞	1⅛	Do. Extended	1½
1⅞	Central Boulder	1⅞	2⅛	Do. South	1½
7/9	Chaffers, 4/	7/9	2⅛	London & Globe Finance	2⅜
1	Colonial Finance, 15/	½pm	1⅛	London & W.A. Exploration	1⅛
⅞	Croesus S. United	⅞	⅞	Do. Investment	⅞
16/	Day Dawn Block	16/	⅞	Mainland Consols	⅞
1⅛	E. Murchison	1⅛	7/6	Mills' Day Dawn, 15/6	⅞
1	Gold Estates	1	1⅛	North Boulder, 10/	1⅛
7/6	Golden Arrow	7/	1⅛	North Kalgurli	1⅜
8⅛	Golden Horseshoe	8	1⅛	Northern Territories	1⅛
1⅛	Golden Link	1⅛	—	Peak Hill	2⅛
—	Great Boulder, 2/	1⅛	3	South Kalgurli	3
1⅛	Do. Main Reef, 10/	1⅛	2⅜	W. A. Goldfields	2
4⅛	Do. Perseverance	4⅛	2⅛	W. A. Joint Stock	2⅛ x
1	Do. South	1⅛	1⅛	W. A. Market Trust	1⅛
2⅛	Hainault	2⅛	1⅛	W. A. Loan & General Fin.	1⅛ x
2	Hampton Plains	1⅞	⅞	White Feather	⅞

SOUTH AFRICAN.

5⅜	Angelo	5⅜	1⅛	Langlaagte Block "B"	1⅛
1⅛	Aurora West	1⅛	3/3	Lisbon-Berlyn	3/3
1⅛	Bantjes	1⅛	2⅛	May Consolidated	2⅛
20/3	Barrett, 10/	12/6	4⅜	Meyer and Charlton	4⅜
3⅛	Bonanza	3⅛	3	Modderfontein	3⅛
⅞	Buffelsdoorn	⅞	⅞	Do. "B"	⅞
1⅛	Champ d'Or	1⅜	1⅛	New Bultfontein	1
6⅛	City and Suburban, £4	6⅛	4⅛	New Primrose	4⅜
3⅛	Comet (New)	3⅜	2⅛	Nigel	1⅞
1⅛	Con. Bultfontein	1	—	Nigel Deep	1⅛
5⅛	Con. Deep Level	5⅛	1⅛	North Randfontein	1⅛
14⅛	Crown Deep	14⅛	7⅛	Nourse Deep	7⅛
12⅛	Crown Reef	12⅛	1⅛	Porges-Randfontein	1⅛
28⅛	De Beers, £5	28⅛	2⅛	Princess	2⅛
4⅛	Driefontein	3⅛	34⅛	Rand Mines	34⅛
6⅛	Durban Roodepoort	6	2⅛	Randfontein	2⅛
4⅛	Do. Deep	4⅜	2⅛	Rietfontein	2⅛
5⅛	East Rand	5⅛	10⅛	Robinson Deep	11⅛
24	Ferreira	24	8⅛	Do. Gold, £5	8⅛
6⅛	Geldenhuis Deep	6⅛	1⅛	Do. Randfontein	1⅛
4⅛	Do. Estate	4⅛	1⅛	Roodepoort Central Deep	1⅛
1⅛	George Goch	1⅛	⅞	Do. Deep	2⅛
3	Ginsberg	3	7⅛	Rose Deep	7
2⅛	Glencairn	2⅛	3⅛	Salisbury	3⅜
2⅛	Glen Deep	2⅛	2⅛	Sheba	2⅛
10⅛	Goldfields Deep	10⅛	3⅛	Simmer and Jack, £5	3⅛
8⅛	Griqualand West	8⅛	4⅛	Transvaal Gold	4⅛
9⅛	Henry Nourse	9⅛	3⅛	Treasury	6⅛
8	Heriot	8	4⅛	United Roodepoort	3⅛
8	Jagersfontein	8⅜	1⅛	Van Ryn	1⅛
8⅛	Jubilee	8⅛	6⅛	Village Main Reef	6⅛
5⅛	Jumpers	5⅛	1⅛	Vogelstruis	1⅛
6	Jumpers Deep	6⅛	1⅛	Do. Deep	1⅛
2⅛	Kleinfontein	2⅛	9⅛	Wemmer	9⅛
4⅛	Knight's	4⅛	⅞	West Rand	⅞
2⅛	Lancaster	2⅛	6⅛	Wolhuter, £4	6⅛
4	Langlaagte Estate	3⅛	2⅛	Worcester	2⅛

RHODESIAN.

3⅛	Anglo-French Ex.	3⅛	1⅛	Mozambique	1⅛
2⅛	Barnato Consolidated	2⅛	1⅛	New African	1⅛
⅞	Bechuanaland Ex.	1	⅞	Oceana Consolidated	⅞
3⅛	Chartered B.S.A.	3⅛	2⅛	Orange Free State	2⅛
1⅛	Cassel Coal	1⅛	1⅛	Rhodesia, Ltd.	1⅛
⅞	Colenbrander	⅞	5⅛	Do. Exploration	6⅛
5⅛	Cons. Goldfields	5⅛	1⅛	Do. Goldfields	1⅛
1⅛	Do. Pref.	21/3 x	4	Robinson Bank	4
⅞	Estates Finance	⅞	5⅛	S. A. Gold Trust	4⅛
1⅛	Exploration	1⅛	1⅛	Tati Concessions	1⅛
1⅛	Henderson's Est.	1⅛	⅞	Transvaal Development	⅞
2⅛	Johannesburg Con. In.	2⅛	1⅛	Do. Goldfield	1⅛
1⅛	Do. Water	1⅛	4⅛	Do. Gold Mining	4⅛
2⅛	Mashonaland Agency	2⅛	⅞	United Rhodesia	⅞
⅞	Do. Central	⅞	1⅛	Willoughby	1⅛
7	Matabele Gold Reefs	7⅛	1⅛	Zambesia Explor.	1⅛

MISCELLANEOUS.

2⅛	Alamillos, £2	1⅛	1⅛	Mount Lyell, South	1⅛
4⅛	Anaconda, $25	5⅛	—	Mount Morgan	4⅛
20/	Balaghât, 18/	19/	5⅛	Mysore, 10s.	⅞
4⅛	Cape Copper, £2	4⅛	13/6	Mysore Goldfields	13/
5⅛	Champion Reef, 10s.	4⅛	11/	Do. Reefs, 17/	12/
2	Copiapo, £2	2⅛	15/	Do. West	8/
3⅛	Coromandel	3⅛ x	13/9	Do. Wynaad	7/
2⅛	Frontino & Bolivia	2⅛	2⅛	Namaqua, £2	2⅛
1⅛	Grand Central	1⅛	4⅛	Nundydroog	4⅛
1⅛	Hall Mines	1⅛	2⅛	Ooregum	3⅛
2⅛	Libiola, £5	2⅛	3⅛	Do. Pref.	3⅛
7⅛	Linares, £3	8	24⅛	Rio Tinto Def., £5	20⅛
3	Mason & Barry, £3	2⅛	6	Do. Pref. £5	6⅛
—	Mountain Copper, £5	5⅛	18/9	St. John del Rey	19 6
14	Mount Lyell, £3	13⅛	6⅛	Tharsis, £2	6⅛
⅞	Mount Lyell, North	1	2	Tolima "A," £5	3

MINING RETURNS.

ALASKA MEXICAN.—Bullion shipment, 30,193 dols.; ore milled, 14,322 tons; sulphurets treated, 291 tons. Bullion, 9,053 dols.

BLOCK B, LANGLAAGTE ESTATE GOLD MINING COMPANY.—Mill: ore crushed, 11,740 tons of 2,000 lb.; gold retorted, 3,044 oz. Tailings (cyanide process): 7,20· tons; gold recovered, 1,104 oz. Concentrates (Cyanide process): tons treated, 178; gold, 336 oz. Total, 4,484 oz.

DURBAN-ROODEPOORT GOLD MINING COMPANY.—Quartz milled, 10,440 tons produced 4,850 oz.; tailings treated, 7,960 tons produced 1,230 oz. Total, 6,080 oz.

GEORGE GOCH AMALGAMATED GOLD MINING COMPANY.—10,300 tons crushed, yielding 3,941 oz., and 1,238 oz. from tailings.

GLENCAIRN MAIN REEF GOLD MINING COMPANY.—6,099 oz. Profit, £10,600.

LANGLAAGTE ESTATE AND GOLD MINING COMPANY.—Ore crushed, 26,878 tons of 2,000 lb.; gold retorted, 6,033 oz. Tailings (cyanide process): tons treated, 16,650; gold recovered, 1,707 oz. Concentrates (cyanide process): tons treated, 750; gold recovered, 1,269 oz. Total, 9,009 oz.

LANGLAAGTE STAR GOLD MINING COMPANY.—Ore crushed, 5,310 tons of 2,000 lb.; gold retorted, 3,118 oz. Tailings (cyanide process): tons treated, 4,313; gold recovered, 902 oz. Total, 4,020 oz.

MAY CONSOLIDATED GOLD MINING COMPANY.—The yield of gold, 4,076 oz. from 14,489 tons crushed; cyanide, 2,010 oz. from 7,865 tons. Total, 6,086 oz.

NEW HERIOT GOLD MINING COMPANY.—Last month's crushings, 6,010 oz.

NORTH RANDFONTEIN GOLD MINING COMPANY.—Ore crushed, 6,167 tons of 2,000 lb.; gold retorted, 1,667 oz. Tailings (cyanide process): tons treated, 3,840; gold recovered, 687 oz. Total, 2,354 oz.

PORGES RANDFONTEIN GOLD MINING COMPANY.—Mill: ore crushed, 7,500 tons of 2,000 lb.; gold retorted, 3,117 oz. Tailings (cyanide process): tons treated, 5,70·; gold recovered, 980 oz.; Concentrates (cyanide process): treated, 98 tons; gold recovered, 403 oz. Total, 4,500 oz.

ROBINSON GOLD MINING COMPANY.—Crushed, 16,041 tons of ore; yielded, smelted gold, 11,042 oz.; from concentrates (by chlorination), 1,378 oz.; from tailings (cyanide process), 3,783 oz.; from slimes, 646 oz.; from concentrates bought (by chlorination), 3,835 oz.; total gold recovered, 20,683 oz.

ROBINSON RANDFONTEIN GOLD MINING COMPANY.—Ore crushed, 5,040 tons of 2,000 lb.; gold retorted, 2,525 oz. Tailings (cyanide process): tons treated, 4,085; gold recovered, 725 oz. Concentrates (cyanide process): tons treated, 31; gold recovered, 123 oz. Total, 3,373 oz.

TREASURY GOLD MINES.—Output for December, 5,317 tons yielded 3,770 oz.

VIOLET CONSOLIDATED GOLD MINING COMPANY during December crushed 4,965 tons. Total yield from all sources, 1,513 oz.

WEST RAND MINES crushed 3,965 tons, yielding 1,032 oz.; cyanide treated 2,888 tons, yielding 680 oz.

WITWATERSRAND GOLD MINING COMPANY.—Crushed 14,800 tons, yielding 3,813 oz. gold; 9,010 tons cyanide tailings treated, yielding 1,170 oz. gold.

WOLHUTER GOLD MINES.—Crushed 13,378 tons, producing 4,532 oz.; cyanide, 3,138 oz. Total, 7,670 oz.

ASSOCIATED GOLD MINES OF WEST AUSTRALIA.—Clean up from 1,750 tons ore produced 2,335 oz. gold.

MOUNTAIN MAID AND IRON PRINCE.—36 dwt. per ton from 19 tons. Iron Prince: crushed 4 tons picked ore which yielded 106 oz.

NORTH STAR.—Crushing for December 352 tons, yielded 564 oz.

CHAMPION REEF (Nannine, West Australia).—Crushed 730 tons, yield 173 oz. retorted gold.

VICTORY CHARTERS TOWERS.—Crushing for fortnight from No. 3 shaft, 88 tons, yield 314 oz. gold. Approximate value £1,067; profit £517.

WORCESTER.—Last month 2,615 tons were crushed, yielding 2,615 oz. gold.

AGAMEMNON.—285 tons of ore crushed, yielding 136 oz. of gold. Assay of tailings show a loss of 2¼ dwt.

BROKEN HILL PROPRIETARY COMPANY.—22,244 tons of ore produced 530 oz. of gold, 429,966 oz. of silver, 1,969 tons of lead, 63 tons antimonial lead, the copper matte containing 13 tons of copper and 31,004 oz. of silver.

CASSELL COAL.—December output, 22,300 tons. Profit, £3,600.

CHIAPAS.—During December the concentrating mill ran thirty days; 1,750 tons crushed, yielded 75 tons of concentrates. The stamp mill ran twenty-seven days crushing 1,550 tons tailings, yielding 158 oz. of gold.

EASTLEIGH MINES.—December crushing: 60-stamp mill ran twenty-four days: total output, 1,900 oz. of gold. Telegram adds: Labour short."

GELDENHUIS ESTATE.—Results for December: crushed 17,000 tons. Obtained from mill, 6,391 oz. of gold; from concentrates by cyanide, 838 oz.; and from tailings by cyanide, 2,232 oz. of gold. Total 9,461 oz. (November yield, 9,471 oz.)

GLYNN'S LYDENBURG.—Crushed during December 1,196 tons, obtaining 453 oz. of fine gold. Treated by cyanide 800 tons, yielding 298 oz. Total 751 oz. of fine gold, value £3,191. November yield 843 oz.

GOLCONDA.—"Have cleared up after a run of 10 hours. 10 stamps working. Crushed 370 tons yielding 850 oz. Assay of tailings 2 dwt. per ton."

GOLD FIELDS OF WEST AFRICA.—Cablegram: "Have crushed during December 900 tons of ore, which yielded 425 oz. of gold."

GRAND CENTRAL.—Thirty stamps, worked 29½ days. Crushed 3,100 tons of ore, yielding bullion valued at £6,304, and concentrates valued at £1,746. Expenses for month, £5,150; and profit, £2,900.

GREAT BOULDER PERSEVERANCE.—Milled, 780 tons; yield, 816 oz. Return by smelting, 601 oz.

HAURAKI.—Twenty-eight days, crushing 130 tons, yielding 445 oz. of gold, value £1,335.

HENRY NOURSE.—December result:—Mill working twenty-nine days. Crushed 8,650 tons, producing 4,861 oz. of gold; treated 6,500 by cyanide, producing 2,473 oz. Total, 7,334 oz. (November yield, 7,678 oz.)

HYDERABAD (DECCAN).—The output of coal from the Singareni collieries of the Hyderabad (Deccan) Company for the five weeks ended December 11 was 37,481 tons. The output for the preceding five weeks ending November 13 was 35,982 tons.

KALGOORLIE BANK OF ENGLAND GOLD.—Cablegram dated 7th inst. from Adelaide:—"Kalgoorlie Bank of England struck an important body of ore 300 ft. level, assaying 3 oz. per ton, width not yet determined. Further information by later cable."

KLERKSDORP GOLD AND DIAMOND.—December return:—1,031 oz. of gold, estimated value, £3,183, against 365 oz. for November.

LANCASTER.—Result for December:—Fifty stamps crushed 5,114 tons of ore, yielding 2,049 oz. of gold, from the mill. Assay of tailings, 3½ dwt. per ton, which have not yet been treated. The company short of native labour.

MENZIES MINING AND EXPLORATION (O'Driscoll's).—Stamps arrived. Will commence crushing about end of January. Last crushing 75 tons, yielding 85 oz. Mines look well.

MOUNT MORGAN.—Result for December was:—Tons chlorinated, 13,8·· producing 14,026 oz. of gold.

NEW RIETFONTEIN.—Cable dated January 7:—Started crushing to-day.

NEW ZEALAND CROWN MINES.—Cabled report for December:—"No. ·· level extended 39 ft.; No. 6 level 54 ft. Tons mined, 1,150. Tons crushed, ··· Value of bullion, £3,220. This return is for twenty-four days only, as the mill was stopped on December 24 for the Christmas holidays."

NIGEL.—Last month's yield from battery 1,168 oz., from cyanide 1,639 oz.

OTTO KOPJE.—Week ending 8th January, 6,004 loads, producing ·· carats. Note: Still treating top stuff to widen working face.

PAARL CENTRAL.—Mill crushed 6,673 tons, yielding 2,082 oz. of gold. Cyanide works treated 4,670 tons, yielding 1,203 oz. of gold. Total value £10,822.

ROODEPOORT UNITED.—Result for December: Crushed 7,225 tons, producing 3,447 oz., cyanide 967 oz. Total 4,414 oz.

SALISBURY.—Last month's crushing yielded 2,150 oz.

SPITZKOP.—Ore mined 837 tons. Tons crushed 808, producing 61 oz. Cyanide process 770 tons, yielding 156 oz. Estimated value £706, expenses, £940.

TRANSVAAL GOLDFIELDS.—3,742 tons crushed, yielding 2,228 oz.

ST. JOHN DEL REY.—Gold produced in December was valued at £17,168, being a yield of ·74 oz. per ton.

BRADFORD MANUFACTURING COMPANY, LIMITED.—Dividend for the six months ending December 31, 1897, at the rate of 12 per cent. per annum.

TRANSVAAL GOLD MINING ESTATES.—Result for December:—Crushed 8,912 tons; obtained 3,901 oz. of gold. By cyanide, 5,410 tons, yielding 680 oz. Value of month's output, £19,493.

WEMMER.—Result for December was:—Mill ran twenty-nine days; crushed 6,661 tons, yielding 4,380 oz.; 4,500 tons treated by cyanide yielded 928 oz., and from concentrates 151 tons caught, assaying 90 dwt. per ton. Total, 5,987 oz. of gold.

GELDENHUIS MAIN REEF.—Crushed 3,646 tons, yielding 661 oz., 2,120 treated by cyanide, yielded 394 oz. Total 1,055 oz. of gold. Profit for month £3. This unsatisfactory result is due to crushing poorer ore.

TREHARN MONTANA MINES.—A further interim dividend of 9d. per fully paid shares.

BALMORAL.—Return for December, 1,596 oz.; 60 stamps ran fourteen days. Delay caused by accident to machinery. (November yield, 2,659 oz.)

MINING AND FINANCE COMPANIES.

The account in the South African market was adjusted withou much difficulty. Rates, after opening stiff, eased off, and there was not much of an increase apparent in the speculative account. Generally speaking, the rate was about 8 to 10 per cent., slipping back in several instances to half that amount. "Chartereds" were continued at from 1½d. to 2½d., and Consolidated Goldfields at from 5 to 8 per cent. "Record" Rand outputs are now looked for almost as a matter of course, and pass practically unnoticed, the return published on Tuesday having little or no effect on prices Taking into consideration that there must have been a certain amount of interruption over the Christmas holidays, and that native labour is still reported scarce, the return is a good one, although a certain amount of the increase is due to the inclusion of a first crushing by the Nourse Deep Company. As regards Western Australian companies, the continuation rates ranged from 8 per cent. to 10 per cent. Business continues on a very small scale, cable interruptions being put forward as one excuse, but there is apparently very little backbone in the market. Among Copper shares Rio Tinto keep firm, and Indians are practically unaltered.

The Manchester Ship Canal receipts from all sources during 1897 show an advance of only £20,000.

In addressing his constituents in Cape Colony recently, Sir Gordon Sprigg, the Cape Premier, stated that the future policy of his Government comprised railway construction in the colony, irrigation works, and compulsory education of Europeans, declaring that, if these measures were not carried, he was prepared to appeal to the country.

There is a report in Southampton that a new German shipping company is to be formed to develop the trade on the West Coast of Africa, and that Southampton will be the English port for the new line.

Mr. Worthington, of Manchester, is about to start as a Government Commissioner, to inquire into the conditions of the local markets of South America. He is to be accompanied by Sir Vincent Barrington, on behalf of the Associated Chambers of Commerce.

ENGLISH RAILWAYS.

Div. for half years. 1895	1896	1896	1897	Last Balance forward.	Amt. to pay 1 p.c. on Ord. for ½ yr.	NAME.	Date.	Gross Traffic for week: Amt.	Inc. or dec. on 1897.	Inc. or dec. on 1896.	Gross Traffic for half-year to date: No. of weeks.	Amt.	Inc. or dec. on 1897.	Inc. or dec. on 1896.	Mileage.	Inc. on 1897.	Working Expenses.	Fixed Charges last ½ year.	Prop. add. Cap. Exp. this ½ year.
				£	£												%	£	£
10	10	10	10	6,805	4,906	Barry	Jan. 8	8,075	+610	−85	2	16,893	+1,011	+641	31	—	47·36	66,665	316,000
nil	nil	nil	nil	—	—	Brecon and Merthyr	Jan. 9	1,524	+15	+117	2	3,021	+28	+192	61	—	—	—	—
nil	nil	nil	nil	4,020	4,749	Cambrian	Jan. 9	3,887	−108	+260	*	4,590	−94	—	250	—	61·16	63,472	42,000
2½	1¾	1¾	2	1,034	3,150	City and South London	Jan. 9	1,124	+13	+104	2	2,174	−14	+137	3½	—	56·07	5,552	109,500
1	1	2	1½	4,823	13,210	Furness	Jan. 9			Not	re-	ceived.			139	—	50·85	96,623	52,96
2½	1	1½	2	2,416	27,463	Great Central (late M., S., & L.)	Jan. 9	40,683	+1,203	+550	1	40,683	+1,108	+550	352½	—	56·09	609,255	1,130,000
4	2½	4½	2	2,666	62,865	Great Eastern	Jan. 9	72,105	+712	+4,577	1	72,105	+712	+4,557	1,156	7	59·29	847,811	210,500
8	1½	1¼	¾	4,595	102,406	Great Northern	Jan. 9	86,300	+1,537	+1,721	2	173,331	+2,562	+9,489	1,071	8	62·28	640,779	1,091,250
7	4½	7½	4½	16,273	116,381	Great Western	Jan. 9	164320	+6,600	+8,670	1	164,320	+6,600	+8,670	2,575	14	57·94	1,484,324	650,000
nil	nil	2	nil	24,449	16,425	Hull and Barnsley	Jan. 9	6,463	−10	+443	1	6,463	−10	+443	73	—	61·21	54,064	44,019
5¼	5	5¾	5	21,423	83,704	Lancashire and Yorkshire	Jan. 9	85,467	+3,653	+9,157	1	85,467	+3,653	+9,157	555¼	25¼	55·01	602,671	387,521
8½	4½	8	4½	16,376	43,049	London, Brighton, & S. Coast	Jan. 8	45,237	+1,720	+3,474	2	99,582	+4,114	+5,253	477	—	54·91	398,273	199,675
nil	nil	nil	nil	1,561	56,296	London, Chatham, & Dover	Jan. 9	25,779	+875	+1,900	1	25,799	+875	+1,900	185	—	57·29	220,181	nil
7½	6½	8	6½	95,016	203,063	London and North Western	Jan. 9	210464	+1,849	+4,053	1	210,464	+1,849	+4,053	1,912	—	55·91	1,411,298	425,000
7½	5	8½	5½	23,525	58,667	London and South Western	Jan. 9	61,097	+2,246	+4,242	1	61,079	+2,246	+4,242	941	6½	55·93	527,257	370,000
5¼	2½	6	2½	7,572	6,691	London, Tilbury, & Southend	Jan. 9	4,753	+295	+1,011	2	9,688	+721	+1,440	81	—	57·00	40,041	15,000
3	3½	3⅞	3½	16,398	28,659	Metropolitan	Jan. 9	16,404	+427	+704	*	20,815	+654	—	64	12	56·70	110,744	109,000
nil	nil	nil	nil	4,380	11,250	Metropolitan District	Jan. 9	9,094	+504	+392	2	17,616	+820	+370	13	—	45·32	159,412	23,130
6½	5	7	5½	18,336	174,175	Midland	Jan. 9	176091	+2,311	+4,907	2	324,301	+7,487	+22,610	1,354¾	15½	57·47	1,213,866	650,000
6½	5½	7½	5½	22,374	135,568	North Eastern	Jan. 8	124263	+3,851	+10,207	1	124,263	+3,851	+10,207	1,597¾	1½	58·70	791,956	372,700
7½	7½	7½	7½	6,213	10,102	North London	Jan. 9			Not	re-	ceived.			12	—	51·66	51,329	4,000
4½	4	5	4	3,356	16,150	North Staffordshire	Jan. 9	15,166	+619	+227	2	30,882	+2,990	+3,318	312	—	55·27	118,142	19,625
8½	10	10	11	1,642	3,004	Rhymney	Jan. 8	4,634	+171	+59	2	8,644	−829	−610	71	—	49·68	29,049	10,700
6	3	6¾	3½	4,526	50,215	South Eastern	Jan. 8	45,213	+4,472	+8,186	*	46,725	+2,031	—	448	—	56·04	382,193	150,000
3½	3½	3½	3½	5,904	25,691	Taff Vale	Jan. 8	14,371	−145	−574	2	27,001	−3,103	−2,356	121	—	53·06	95,297	43,000

* From January 1.

SCOTCH RAILWAYS.

5¼	5	5	5¼	15,350	77,570	Caledonian	Jan. 9	57,306	+ 1,595	− 3,916	23	1,717,041	+ 24,532	+ 63,105	851¼	5	50·50	500,914	375,000
5	5	5½	5	5,886	24,639	Glasgow and South-Western	,, 8	23,584	+ 737	− 3,091	23	681,284	+ 9,516	+ 53,937	393½	8	55·12	221,120	180,556
3½	3½	3½	3½	1,291	4,600	Great North of Scotland	,, 8	7,897	+ 474	− 271	23	207,530	+ 7,412	+ 14,491	331	16	52·03	92,178	60,000
[illegible]	3	nil	2	10,477	12,820	Highland	,, 9	7,530	+ 490	+ 309	19	180,424	+ 5,863	+ 8,092	479½	27½	58·63	78,976	84,000
1½	1	1½	1	3,763	45,819	North British	,, 9	61,452	+ 2,410	− 8,029	23	1,734,764	+ 45,612	+ 89,170	1,230	23	44·65	821,756	126,000

IRISH RAILWAYS.

6½	6½	6½	6½	2,405	1,745	Belfast and County Down	Jan. 7	1,915	− 50	+ 40	—	1,915	− [illegible]	—	70	—	50·49	[illegible]	[illegible]
6½	5½	6½	5½	—	4,284	Belfast and Northern Counties	,, 7	4,461	+ 322	+ 528	*	4,461	− 298	—	249	—	—	—	—
3	2	3	2½	1,418	1,200	Cork, Bandon, and S. Coast	,, 8	1,155	+ 66	+ 113	*	1,403	− 49	—	103	—	54·82	14,436	5,450
6½	6½	6½	6½	21,537	17,709	Great Northern	,, 7	12,572	+ 205	+ 785	1	12,572	+ 205	+ 785	528	36	54·03	87,058	16,000
5½	5½	5½	5½	12,037	24,855	Great Southern and Western	,, 7	—	—	—	not	received	—	—	603	13	55·78	72,802	35,140
4½	4	4	4	4,085	11,850	Midland Great Western	,, 7	7,937	+ 95	—	—	—	—	—	538	—	53·12	82,845	2,600
nil	nil	nil	nil	229	2,822	Waterford and Central	,, 7	757	+ 111	—	—	—	—	—	59	—	53·24	6,858	1,500
nil	nil	nil	nil	2,601	2,987	Waterford, Limerick & W.	,, 7	2,796	+ 237	—	—	—	—	—	342	—	58·70	43,076	8,859

* From January 1.

INDIAN RAILWAYS.

Mileage. Total.	Increase on 1897.	Increase on 1896.	NAME.	GROSS TRAFFIC FOR WEEK. Week ending	Amount.	In. or Dec. on 1897.	In. or Dec. on 1896.	GROSS TRAFFIC TO DATE. No. of Weeks.	Amount.	In. or Dec. on 1897.	In. or Dec. on 1896.
867	4	5	Bengal Nagpur	Dec. 31	Rs.2.64.00	- Rs.30.344	+ Rs.53.365	26	Rs.24.58.259	- Rs.85.321	+ Rs.51.192
818	63	63	Bengal and North-Western ..	Dec. 11	Rs.1.05.450	+ Rs.768	+ Rs.7.303	24	Rs.23.46.261	+ Rs.69.007	+ Rs.1.85.714
461	—	—	Bombay and Baroda	Jan. 1	£60,225	- £5,195	- £12,213	27	£1,369,919	- £33,604	- £145,334
1,884	2	13	East Indian	Jan. 8	Rs.13.33.000	+ Rs.44.000	+ Rs.1.70000	—	—	—	—
1,491	—	—	Great Indian Penin.	Jan. 8	£56,806	+ £8,727	—	—	—	—	—
736	—	—	Indian Midland	Jan. 8	Rs.1.56.890	+ Rs.9,229	- Rs.33.676	—	—	—	—
840	—	—	Madras	Jan. 1	£21,725	+ £1,467	—	26	£502,185	+ £31.918	—
1,043	—	—	South Indian	Dec. 11	Rs.1.71.368	+ Rs.24.022	+ Rs.249	24	Rs.3.974.235	+ Rs.80.348	+ Rs.77.369

FOREIGN RAILWAYS.

Mileage. Total.	Increase on 1897.	Increase on 1896.	NAME.	GROSS TRAFFIC FOR WEEK. Week ending	Amount.	In. or Dec. upon 1897.	In. or Dec. upon 1896.	GROSS TRAFFIC TO DATE. No. of Weeks.	Amount.	In. or Dec. upon 1897.	In. or Dec. upon 1896.
					£	£	£		£	£	£
319	—	—	Argentine Great Western ..	Jan. 8§	—	—	—	—	—	—	—
762	—	—	Bahia and San Francisco ..	Dec. 11	2,439	+ 421	+ 21	24	56,137	+ 16,904	+ 17,004
234	57	84	Bahia Blanca and North West ..	Dec. 12	1,212	+ 212	—	24	17,128	+ 539	—
127	—	—	Buenos Ayres and Ensenada ..	Jan. 8	3,476	- 1,456	- 316	—	—	—	—
426	—	—	Buenos Ayres and Pacific ..	Jan. 8	5,392	- 1,178	- 812	27	162,608	- 44,477	+ 4,062
914	1	3	Buenos Ayres and Rosario ..	Jan. 8	16,278	+ 816	+ 3,834	—	—	—	—
1,469	66	68	Buenos Ayres Great Southern ..	Jan. 9	35,653	+ 2,193	+ 5,965	27	717,797	+ 50,767	+ 101,298
602	142	177	Buenos Ayres Western	Jan. 9	13,965	- 2,400	- 558	27	306,227	- 69,252	+ 63,378
845	55	77	Central Argentine	Jan. 8	20,186	+ 3,242	+ 5,310	—	—	—	—
397	—	—	Central Bahia	Oct. 31*	$83,051	- $6,238	- $36,002	10 mos.	$1,111,178	+ $175,344	+ $203,586
271	—	—	Central Uruguay of Monte Video	Jan. 8	8,600	+ 2,746	+ 1,305	27	151,576	- 12,013	- 24,012
180	—	—	Cordoba and Rosario	Jan. 2	1,685	- 605	- 270	27	51,135	- 22,345	- 570
128	—	—	Cordoba Central	Jan. 2	$20,000	- $5,230	+ $200	—	—	—	—
549	—	—	Do. Northern Extension	Jan. 2	$46,500	- $12,500	- $4,840	—	—	—	—
137	—	—	Costa Rica	Jan. 8‖	1,164	- 3,416	+ 213	—	—	—	—
99	—	—	East Argentine	Nov. 28	910	- 52	—	48	30,524	- 3,760	—
386	—	6	Entre Rios	Jan. 8	2,301	+ 949	+ 1,279	—	—	—	—
555	—	24	Inter Oceanic of Mexico	Jan. 8	$51,700	+ $1,650	+ $10,290	28	$1,440,740	+ $173,630	+ $304,140
23	—	—	La Guaira and Caracas	Dec. 9	1,231	- 1,078	—	48	109,654	- 10,453	—
321	—	—	Mexican	Jan. 8	$69,000	+ $3,500	—	—	—	—	—
1,846	—	—	Mexican Central	Jan. 8	$217,170	+ $3,292	+ $32,688	—	—	—	—
1,217	—	—	Mexican National	Jan. 8	$103,662	+ $10,447	—	—	—	—	—
228	—	—	Mexican Southern	Jan. 7	$11,000	+ $1,895	+ $1,631	41	$306,595	+ $15,411	+ $133,627
206	—	—	Minas and Rio	Nov. 30*	$179,485	+ $24,364	+ $66,853	5 mos.	$696,037	+ $201,987	+ $204,840
111	—	17	N. W. Argentine	Jan. 8	961	- 296	—	—	—	—	—
242	3	—	Nitrate	Dec. 31†	21,583	+ 10,026	- 7,845	26	239,891	- 23,495	- 142,522
320	—	—	Ottoman	Jan. 1	5,067	- 691	+ 413	26	225,167	+ 2,256	+ 21,872
77½	—	—	Recife and San Francisco ..	Nov. 13	5,431	+ 307	+ 860	20	52,074	- 9,983	- 5,092
86½	—	—	San Paulo	Dec. 12†	23,928	- 6,560	—	24	372,822	+ 27,099	—
186	—	—	Santa Fe and Cordova	Jan. 8	1,067	- 1,045	+ 202	27	22,993	- 20,819	- 5,448

* For month ended. † For fortnight ended. ‡ Ten days ended. ‖ Traffic suspended this week. § Traffic suspended for a time owing to floods.

UNITED STATES AND CANADIAN RAILWAYS.

Mileage. Total.	Increase on 1897.	Increase on 1896.	NAME.	GROSS TRAFFIC FOR WEEK. Period Ending.	Amount.	In. or Dec. on 1897.	GROSS TRAFFIC TO DATE. No. of Weeks.	Amount.	In. or Dec. on 1897.
					dols.	dols.		dols.	dols.
310	—	—	Alabama Gt. South.	Dec. 21	40,307	+ 1,770	23	1,595,268	+ 104,692
6,547	103	156	Canadian Pacific	Jan. 7	401,000	+ 81,000	—	—	—
6,169	—	469	Chicago, Mil., & St. Paul ..	Jan. 7	504,000	+ 100,000	27	19,314,000	+ 1,791,930
1,685	—	—	Denver & Rio Grande	Jan. 7	148,400	+ 45,400	27	4,478,100	+ 694,000
3,512	—	—	Grand Trunk, Main Line ..	Jan. 7	£68,117	+ £12,926	—	—	—
335	—	—	Do. Chic. & Grand Trunk	Jan. 7	£13,090	+ £1,172	—	—	—
189	—	—	Do. Det., G. H. & Mil. ..	Jan. 7	£3,221	+ £16	—	—	—
2,938	—	—	Louisville & Nashville	Jan. 7	381,000	+ 23,000	—	—	—
2,197	137	137	Miss., K., & Texas	Jan. 7	228,181	+ 30,051	27	7,272,642	+ 525,495
477	—	—	N. Y., Ontario, & W.	Jan. 7	47,071	+ 894	27	2,160,365	+ 62,675
1,570	—	—	Norfolk & Western	Jan. 7	221,000	+ 3,000	27	5,768,000	+ 463,000
3,499	336	—	Northern Pacific	Dec. 21	361,626	+ 5,013	*	20,368,143	+ 1,943,402
4,654	—	—	Southern	Jan. 7	347,000	+ 9,000	27	10,079,812	+ 514,448
1,979	—	—	Wabash	Jan. 7	205,000	+ 30,000	—	—	—

* From January 1.

MONTHLY STATEMENTS.

Mileage. Total.	Increase on 1896.	Increase on 1895.	NAME.	NET EARNINGS FOR MONTH. Month.	Amount.	In. or Dec. on 1896.	In. or Dec. on 1895.	NET EARNINGS TO DATE. No. of Months.	Amount.	In. or Dec. on 1896.	In. or Dec. on 1895.
					dols.	dols.	dols.		dols.	dols.	dols.
6,935	44	444	Atchison	November	1,373,663	+ 342,028	+ 360,334	11	7,880,450	+ 124,951	+ 2,850,604
1,970	—	—	Erie	November	819,192	+ 21,332	+ 52,579	11	7,880,994	+ 201,967	+ 791,296
3,127	—	239	Illinois Central*	November	2,534,427	+ 664,861	+ 377,039	11	22,138,724	+ 2,451,919	+ 2,487,092
2,396	—	—	New York Central*	November	3,900,753	+ 18,435	- 300,993	11	41,934,547	+ 1,697,686	+ 1,616,507
3,407	—	—	Pennsylvania	November	1,960,658	+ 164,400	- 48,400	11	18,867,671	+ 2,302,100	- 879,500
1,055	—	—	Phil. & Reading	November	2,924,717	- 170,084	—	11	8,447,110	+ 133,428	—

* Statements of gross traffic.

Prices Quoted on the London Stock Exchange.

Throughout the INVESTORS' REVIEW middle prices alone are quoted, the object being to give the public the approximate current quotations of every security of any consequence in existence. On the markets the buying and selling prices are both given, and are often wide apart where stocks are seldom dealt in. Other particulars will be found in the INVESTMENT INDEX published quarterly—January, April, July, and October—in connection with this REVIEW, price 2s., by post 2s. 2d. Where dividends are paid only once a year, an *italic* type is used to distinguish them. The London Stock Exchange Official List is quoted in the REVIEW almost entire, only very insignificant issues, or bonds falling due within the next two or three years, being omitted. But the list is subdivided into the leading, or active, stocks, and those less frequently dealt in. The former will be found under the head of "Stock Markets," and with more details than it is possible to give for the bulk of securities. By retaining the file of the INVESTORS' REVIEW any subscriber can follow for himself the movements of securities from week to week, and the INVESTMENT INDEX will from time to time help to fill up deficiencies in the information.

Tea Companies and Mines and Mining Finance Stocks are placed in special lists.

Among the abbreviations used are the following:—S.F. Snk. Fd. *sinking fund*; Certs., *certificates*; Debs. or Dbs., *debentures*; Db. or D.Stk., *debenture stock*; Pf., Prf., or Pref., *preference*; Prefd. or Pfd., *preferred*; Dfd., *deferred*; L. or Ltd., *limited*; Sh., *share*; Ans., *annuities*; Cu. or Cm., *cumulative*; Gu or Guar., *guaranteed*; Bds., *bonds*; S., Sr., or Ser., *series*; In., Ins., Insc., *inscribed*; Dr., Drgs., Drwgs., *drawings*; Stg., Strlg., *sterling*; Lia., *liable to*; Sp., Surp., *surplus*; Per., Perp., *perpetual*; Ln. *lien*; Lo. *loan*. Prices marked † signify they are *ex. div.*

The dates following the names of securities are the years of issue or of redemption. Where shares are not fully paid up, their nominal amount is given with the name so that investors may know the liability upon them.

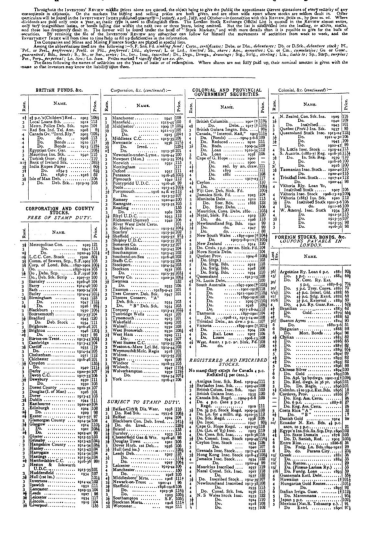

BRITISH FUNDS, &c.

Rate.	Name.	Price.
2¾	2¾ p.c.'s (Childers') Red.. 1905	106½
3	Local Loans Stk. 1912	113
3	Metro. Police Deb. Stk. 1920	104
—	Red Sea Ind. Tel. Ann. 1908	9½
4	Canada Gv. "Intcl. Rly." 1903	109½
4	Do. do. .. 1908	113
4	Do. Bonds 1910	117
4	Do. Bonds 1913	119½
3	Egyptian Gov. Gar.	108½
3	Mauritius Ins. Stk. 1940	115
4	Turkish Guar. 1855	110
11½	Bank of Ireland Stk.	392½
3½	India Rupee Paper	60½
3½	Do. 1854-5	62½
3	Do. 1896-7 1916	62
3½	Isle of Man Deb.	106
3	Do. Deb. Stk... 1919-29	105

CORPORATION AND COUNTY STOCKS.

FREE OF STAMP DUTY.

Rate.	Name.	Price.
3½	Metropolitan Con. 1929	121
3	Do. 1941	113
2½	Do. 1920-49	101½
2½	L.C.C. Con. Stock 1920	80½
3½	Comm. of Sewers, Scp., S.F. 1905	105
3½	Corp. of Lond. Bds... 1897-1902	100½
3	Do. 1897-1919	103
3½	Do, Debs. Scp. ...... S.F. 1916	106
—	Do., Deb. Stk. Scrip .. 1927-57	100
3	Barnsley 1916-46	104
3	Barry 1914-46	100
3	Bath 1909-34	104
3	Batley 1914-44	101½
3½	Birmingham 1945	123
3	Do. 1947	112½
2½	Do. 1926	99½
3	Blackburn 1930	106½
3	Bournemouth 1913-33	104
3½	Bradford 1945	120
3	Do. Deb. Stock .. 1954	111
3	Brighouse 1916-46	101
3½	Brighton 1946	120½
2½	Do. 1957	98
3	Burton-on-Trent 1913-43	102½
3	Cambridge 1913-43	104
3½	Cardiff 1935	119
3	Do. 1914-54	105
3	Cheltenham 1971	112
3	Chichester 1916-46	101
3	Croydon	135½
3	Do. 1940	111½
3	Derby 1920-50	107
3	Devon C.C. 1917-33	106
3½	Dewsbury 1930	111
3	Do. 1930	105
3	Dorset County 1922-32	107
3	Douglas (I. of Man) 1926	101
3	Dover 1913-43	103
3½	Dublin 1944	111
3	Eastbourne 1920-40	104
3	Edinburgh 1924	108
2½	Do. 1929	98
2½	Exeter 1917-57	97
3	Glamorgan County 1914-34	104
3	Glasgow 1914	110½
3	Do. 1921	106½
2½	Do. 1925-40	99
3	Gloster 1915-55	103
3	Grimsby 1913-45	104½
3	Hampshire County 1914-34	106½
3	Hanley 1913-43	104
3	Harrogate 1914-34	104
3	Hastings 1915-54	104
2½	Hertfordshire C.C. 1916-36	99†
3	Heston & Isleworth U.D.C. 1915-35	101
3½	Huddersfield 1934	107
3½	Hull (1st iss.)	131½
3	Inverness 1914-44	102
3	Ipswich 1952	111
3	Lancaster 1919-55	104
3	Leeds 1927	98
3½	Leicester 1934	117
3	Lincoln 1919	104
3½	Liverpool	135

Corporation, &c. (*continued*):—

Rate.	Name.	Price.
3	Manchester 1941	109
3	Mansfield 1915-45	100
3½	Middlesbro' .... 1909 (†	105½
3½	Do. 1911-13	105
3	Do. 1915	104†
3	Middlesex C.C. 1915-35	106
3½	Newcastle 1936	117½
3½	Do. Irred.	129½
2¾	Do. 1915-36	101
3	Newcastle-under-Lyme.. 1909-44	100
3	Newport (Mon.) 1915-55	104½
3	Norwich 1952	113
3	Nottingham	117
3	Oxford 1951	111
3	Penzance 1916-46	102½
3	Plymouth 1942	112
3	Pontypridd U.D.C. 1916-46	99
3	Poole 1915-45	102½
3½	Portsmouth ....1916 24 & 27	112
3	Do. 1913-33	107
3	Ramsey 1920-40	100
3	Ramsgate 1915-55	103
3	Reading	135
3	Do. 1962	109
3½	Rhyl U.D.C. 1953	112
3	Richmond (Surrey) 1942	106
3	River Wear Debt Certs.	101
3	St. Helen's 1915-55	104½
3	Scarbro' 1915-50	102
2½	Sheffield 1925-57	97½
3	Shipley U.D.C. 1915-35	101
3	Somerset Co. 1923-33	107
3	South Shields 1915-45	104
2¾	Southampton 1915-45	102
3	Southend-on-Sea 1916-46	102
3	Staffs C.C. 1915-35	106
3	Stockport 1914-54	103
3	Stockton 1932	105
3	Do. 1915-35	103½
3	Surrey Co. 1922-32	106½
3½	Swansea	132
3	Do. 1955	106
3	Taunton 1918 3-9-43	101
3	Tees Conserv. Deb. Stk. 1947	101
3	Thames Conserv. "A" Deb. Stk. 1954	103
3	Do. "B" Deb. Stk. 1954	103
3	Torquay 1913-43	102½
3	Tunbridge Wells 1931	105
3	Tynemouth 1913	101
3	Wakefield 1929	105
3	Walsall 1932	108
3	West Bromwich 1930	108½
3½	West Ham 1929	111
3	Do. 1945	107
3	West Sussex C.C. 1915-35	106
3	Weston-s.-Mare Lcl. Bd. 1914-44	102
3	Weymouth & Melc. Regis 1918	101
3	Widnes 1915-55	102
3	Wigan 1921	108
3	Windsor 1918-55	103
3	Wisbech 1947	115½
3½	Wolverhampton 1932	119½
3	Do. 1924-54	107½
3	York 1916-41	106

SUBJECT TO STAMP DUTY.

Rate.	Name.	Price.
3½	Belfast City & Dis. Watr. 1938	116
3	Do. Red Stk. 1953-6	108½
3	Belfast 1924	104
4	Blackburn Con. Deb. Irred.	141½
3½	Do. do. Irred.	129½
3½	Bristol	128½
3½	Burnley 1933	116
3½	Chesterfield Gas & Wtr. 1916-46	98
3½	Douglas Town 1921	105
3	Dover Harb. 1st Deb... 1936	105
3½	Hull (2nd iss.)	128½
4	Leeds Deb. 1927	125
3½	Do.	113½
3	Do. 1927	106½
3	Leicester 1919-44	106
4	Manchester	150
3	Do. 1928	105
4½	Middlesboro' Mrts. 1908	111†
4	Newark-on-Trent .. 1901-41	96
3½	Sheffield 1898-1916	106
3½	Do. 1925-36	114½
3	Do. 1925	105½
3½	Southampton .... S.F.	105½
4	Stockton Morts. 1908	111†
3½	Worcester 1950	111

COLONIAL AND PROVINCIAL GOVERNMENT SECURITIES.

Rate.	Name.	Price.
6	British Columbia........ 1907 (†	119½
4½	Do. Debs... 1917 (†	110½
3	British Guiana Imgtn. Bds.	99½
5	Canada, "Intercol. Rail," 1903	111½
4	Do. (Bonds) 1904-5-6-8	109
4	Do. Reduced 1910	111
3½	Do. Bnds. 1909-34	109
4	Do. Loan 1910-35	112
3	Do. Loan 1938	106
6	Cape of G. Hope 1900	—
5	Do. 1900	—
4½	Do. red. by an. draw.	111
4½	Do. 1879	111
4	Do. 1881	108
4	Do. 1917-23	117
4½	Ceylon	110
4	Do.	108½
4½	Fiji Gov. Deb. Sink. Fd.	100½
4	Jamaica Sink. Fd. 1923	104
5	Manitoba Debs 1910	113
5	Do. Ster. Bds. 1888	122
4	Do. Ster. Debs.	106
4	Mauritius, Cons. Debs. 1880....	103½
4½	Natal, Sink. Fd. 1919	120
4	Do. do. 1926	118
3½	Newfoundland Stg. Bds. 1941	99
3½	Do. do. .. 1947	99
3	Do. do.	88
5	New South Wales ..1897-1902 (†	104½
4	Do. 1903-5-8-9-10 (†	105½
5	New Zealand 1914	120
5	Do. Cnsls. 1 p.c. per an. Sink. Fd.	104
3½	Nova Scotia Debs.	104
5	Quebec Prov. 1904-6	108½
4½	Do. (drgs.)	103
5	Do. Strlg. Bds. 1912	115
4	Do. Strlg. Bds. 1928	108
4	Do. Strlg. Bds. 1934	110
4	Queensland 1913-15	108
4½	St. Lucia Debs.	100
6	South Australia ....1897-1900 (†	103½
6	Do. 1901-1918	118
5	Do. ......1911-1920 (†	115½
4	Do. 1899-1916	105
4	Do. .... 1929 (†	110½
4	Do. 1916	109½
4	Do. 1917-18-24	112
6	Tasmania 1897-1901	104
4	Do. 1908-11, 1913-14-20	108
5	Trinidad Debs., an. drw. 1 p.c...	107
4	Victoria ....1899-1901 (†	101½
4½	Do. 1904	106
4	Do. Rail. Loan 1907	106
4	Do. Loans 1908-13	108
4½	West. Austr. 1 p.c. ac. Sink. Fd.	108
4	Do. do.	108

REGISTERED AND INSCRIBED STOCKS.

No stamp duty except for Canada 4 p.c. Reduced (½ per Cent.).

Rate.	Name.	Price.
4	Antigua Insc. Stk. Red. 1919-44	111
3½	Barbados Insc. Stk. 1925-42	108
3	British Colum. Insc. Stk. 1941	103
3	British Guiana Insc. 1935	103
4	Canada Stk. Regd. ..1904-5-6-8	109
4	Do. 4 p.c. (late 5 p.c.) Regd. 1910	111
3½	Do. 3½ p.c. Stock Regd. 1909-34	108
3	Do. Ln. for 4 milln. stg. 1910-35	112
3	Do. Stk. Regd. 1938	106
3	Do. Insc. 1947	93½
3½	Cape G. Hope Regd. .. 1917-23	118
4	Do. (Ln. of '83) Insc. .. 1923	119
4	Do. Cons. Stk. Insc. 1916-36	116
3½	Do. Consol. Insc. Stock 1929-49	114½
4	Ceylon Insc. Stock 1934	126
3	Do. 1940	107
4	Grenada Insc. Stock.... 1917-42	112
3½	Hong Kong Insc. Stock 1918-43	106½
4	Jamaica Insc. Stock.... 1934	122
—	Do. 1922-44	99
4	Mauritius Inscribed 1937	119
4	Natal Consd. Stk. Insc. 1927	118
3	Do. 1937	122
4	Do. Inscribed Stock.. 1914-39	107
4	Newfoundland Inscribed 1913-38	108
3½	Do. 1935	113
4	Do. Consd. Stk. Ins. 1936	115
4	N. S. Wales Stock Insc. 1933	122
3½	Do. 1924	110
3½	Do. 1918	108
3	Do. 1935	102

Colonial, &c. (*continued*):—

Rate.	Name.	Price.
4	N. Zealnd. Con. Stk. Ins. 1929	116
3½	Do. 1940	109
3	Do. Inscribed.... 1945	101
3	Quebec (Prov.) Ins. Stk. 1937	95
4	Queensland Stock Insc. 1915-24	112½
3½	Do. 1921-4-30	106
3½	Do. 1945	109
—	Do. 1922-47	99
4	St. Lucia Insc. Stock .. 1919-44	113
4	S. Austrln. (1882-7) Reg. 1916-36	113½
3½	Do. In. Stk. Reg. 1939	110
3	Do. 1916-26	100
3/	Do. 1916	100
3½	Tasmanian Insc. Stock.. 1920-40	110
4	Do. 1920-40	115
4	Trinidad Insc. Stock.... 1917-42	112
—	Do. 1922-44	98
4	Victoria Rly. Loan '81, Inscribed Stock 1907	106
4	Victoria Insc. Stock 1908-13-19	109½
4	Victoria (1885) Ins. Stk. 1920	112
3½	Do. Inscribed Stock 1921-3-6	106
4	Do. do. 1911-26	109
4	W. Austral. Insc. Stock 1934	120
4	Do. 1911-31	113
3½	Do. 1915-35	107
3	Do. 1915-35	98
3	Do. 1916-36	98

FOREIGN STOCKS, BONDS, &c.

COUPONS PAYABLE IN LONDON.

Last Div.	Name.	Price.
36/	Argentine Ry. Loan 6 p.c. 1881	92½
15/	Do. 5 p.c. 1884	69½
30/	Do. N. Cent. Ry. Ext. 5 p.c. 1887-8-9	70½
30/	Do. 5 p.c. Trsy. Convs. 1887	70
5/4½	Do. 4½ p.c. Interl. Gld. 1888	66
27/	Do. 4½ p.c. Stlg. Extrl. 1888	68
10/6	Do. 3½ p.c. External .. 1889	50
4	Do. 4 p.c. Ry. Guar. Res....	62½
4½	Brazilian 1883	62
4½	Do. Gold 1879	66½
4½	Do. 1888	62
36/	Buenos Ayres 1824	90
6	Do. 1882-3-6	51
6	Bulgarian 1888	98
6	Do. Mort. Bonds 1892	96
4½	Chilian 1885	92
4½	Do. 1886	83
4½	Do. 1887	82
4½	Do. 1889	83½
5	Do. 1892	89
4½	Do. 1893	82
4½	Do. 1895	82
5	Do. 1896	88
7	Chinese Silver 1894	100
6	Do. Gold 1895	106
6	Do. Apl. '95 bydwgs. 1901-15 (†	109½
6	Do. Red. dwgs. in 36 yr. 1896	101
6	Do. Do. Regis. 1896	101
1½	Colmbn. 1 to 3 p.c. Ext. Bds. 1896	18
6	Cordova, Prov. 1886	27
—	Do. Eng. Ass. Certs.	26
—	Do. 6 p.c. 1887-8	27
—	Do. Eng. Ass. Certs.	26
3	Costa Rica "A"	32
2½	Do. "B"	17
3	Danish Gold 1894	99
10/	Ecuador N. Ext. Bds. 4½ p.c. ascn. to 5 p.c.	21
3½	Egypt'n Ins. Stk. lia. Stp. Dty. 1890	102
4½	Do. State Domain 1878	105
4	Do. D. Sanieh, Red. 1905	103½
4	Entre Rios 1886-8	34
6	Do. Fndg. Ln. Bds. 1894-1921	29
6	Do. do. Parana City	23½
15/	Greek 1881	36
15/	Do. 1884	35
12/	Do. Rentes	29
15/	Do. (Piræus-Larissa Ry.)	35
7/6	Do. Fundg. Loan 1893	39
4	Guatemala Extl. Debt	35½
6	Hawaiian .... (†	101½
4	Hungarian Gold Rentes	101½
4	Do. 1895	92
3	Italian Irriga. Guar. .... (†	112½
5	Do. Maremmana	93½
5	Japan 5 p.c.	102½
5	Mexican (Nat. R. Tehuantp c.)	91
5	Do Extrl. 1890	97½

Foreign Stocks, &c. (*continued*):—

Last Div.	Name.	Price.
6	Mexican Extrl. 1893	95½
5	Do. Intrnl. Cons. Slvr.	34½
5	Do. Intern. Rd. Bds. 2d. Ser.	34½
4	Nicaragua 1886	51
3½	Norwegian, red. 1937, or earlier	100
3	Do. do. 1965, do.	100
3½	Do. 3½ p.c. Bnds.	103
1	Paraguay 1p.c. ris. 3p.c. 1886-96	15½
5	Russian, 1822, £ Strlg.	149½
3	Do. 1859	92
4	Do. (Nicolas Ry.) 1867-9	103
3	Do. Transcauc. Ry. 1882	92
4	Do. Con. R. R. Bd. Ser. I., 1889	103½
4	Do. Do. II., 1889	103½
4	Do. Do. III., 1891	103½
3½	Do. Bonds	100½
4	Do. Ln. (Dvinsk and Vitbsk)	102
6	Salvador 1889	72½
—	S Domingo 4s. Unified .. 1980	65½
6	San Luis Potosi Stg. 1889	92½
5	San Paulo (Brzl.), Stg. 1888	91½
6	Santa Fé 1883-4	37
—	Do. Eng. Ass. Certs. Dep.	36
5	Do. 1888	48
—	Do. Eng. Ass. Certs. Dpsit.	48
5	Do. (W. Cnt. Col. Rly.) Mrt.	26
5	Do. & Reconq. Rly. Mort.	26
5	Spanish Quicksilvr Mort. 1870	102
3½	Swedish 1880	103
3	Do. 1888	100
3	Do. Conversion Loan 1894	100
5	Trans. Gov. Loan Red. ..1903-42	105†
59/	Tucuman (Prov.) 1888	69
4	Turkish, Secd. on Egypt. Trib.	103½
3½	Turkish, Egpt. Trib., Ott. Bd., '94	98½
4	Do. Priority 1890	92
1	Do. Convted Series, "A"	65½
5	Do. Customs Ln. 1886	96½
5	Uruguay Bonds 1896	52
3	Venzula New Con. Debt 1881	39

COUPONS PAYABLE ABROAD.

Last Div.	Name.	Price.
7	Argent. Nat. Cedla. Sries, "B".	37½
5	Austrian Ster. Rnts., ex 10fl., 1870	85
5	Do. do. do.	86
5	Do. Paper do. 1870	85
5	Do. do. do.	85
4	Do. Gld Rentes 1876	102
2½	Belgian exchange 25 fr.	92†
3	Do. do.	101
3½	Danish Int., 1887, Rd. 1896	97½
3½	Do. '87, Red. by pur. or draw. fr. Dec., 1900	98½
2½	Dutch Certs. ex 12 gldrs.	87†
3	Do. Bonds	99
3	Do. Insc. Stk.	99
3½	French Rentes	106
3	Do. 1878, '81-4., Red.	101½
3	German Imp. Ln. 1891	96½
3	Do. do. 1892-3	96½
3	Do. do. 1890-4	96
5	Japan Cons. Ln., '92, 3, & 5, Red.	48½
4	Prussian Consols	102
3	" Cons. Stg. Ln. 1891	97
4	Rumanian Bds. 1890	—
4	Do. do. 1891	—
4	Utd. States, 1877, Red. 1907	116
4	Do. 1895, 30 yrs.	131½
3½	Do. Maschsetts Gl. 1935	113½
3½	Do. Gold Bonds 1923	110½
2	Virginia Cpn. Bds., 3 p.c. from July, 1901	71

BRITISH RAILWAYS.

ORD. SHARES AND STOCKS.

Last Div.	Name.	Price.
10	Barry, Ord.	288½
4	Do. Prefd.	129
6	Do. Defd.	158½
5½	Caledonian, Ord.	159
3	Do. Prefd.	102
—	Do. Defd. Ord., No. 1	5
—	Cambrian, Ord.	6½
—	Do. Coast Cons.	6½
24/	Cardiff Ry. Pref. Ord.	118
3/	Central Lond. £10 Ord. Sh.	10
1/9½	Do. do. £6 paid	5½
3½d.	Do. Pref. Half-Shares	1½
1/6	Do. Def. do.	4½
2	City and S. London	70
—	East London, Cons.	7
1½	Furness	70½
—	Glasgow and S. West. Pfd.	86
	Do. do. Dfd.	70
	Great Central, Ord. ...1894	45½
32/0	Do. London Exten.	81
3½	Great N. of Scotland	119
4	Great Northern, Prefd.	124½
—	Do. Consolidated "A"	57
—	Do. do. "B"	195½
2	Highland	80
4	Isle of Wight, Prefd.	122½
2	Do. Defd.	86½
½	Lancs. Derbys. and E. Cst.	5
4½	L. Brighton and S. C. Ord.	190
37/11	Do. New 70 p.c. pd.	186
6	Do. Prefd. Ord.	202
7/6	Do. Contgt. Rights Certs.	19
5½	Lond. and S. Western Ord.	232½
4	Do. Preferred	138
2½	Lond., Tilb., and Southend	134½
—	Mersey, £20 shares	1
—	Metropolitan, New Ord.	131
2½	Do. Surplus Lands	98
4	North Cornwall, 4 p.c. Pref.	106½
17/6	Do. Deferred	27½
7½	North London	228½
4	North Staffordshire	130

British Railways (*continued*):—

Last Div.	Name.	Price.
1/6	Plymouth, Devenport, and S. W. Junc. £10	9
3/	Port Talbot £10 Shares	9½
9d.	Rhondda Swns. B. £10 Sh.	6½
11	Rhymney, Cons.	275½
4	Do. Prefd.	129
—	Do. Defd.	152½
1½	Scarboro', Bridlington Junc.	47½
3½	South Eastern, Ord.	156
6	Do. Pref.	198
3½	Taff Vale	84
25/	Vale of Glamorgan	132½
2/6½	Waterloo & City £10 shares	12½

LEASED AT FIXED RENTALS.

Last Div.	Name.	Price.
4	Birkenhead	151
5.19.0	East Lincnshire	215
5½	Hamsmith. & City Ord.	200½
4½	Lond. and Blackwll.	167½
4½	Do. £10 4½ p. c. Pref.	167
56/6	Lond. & Green. Ord.	104
5	Do. 5 p. c. Pref.	180½
5	Nor. and Eastn. £50 Ord.	92
6	Do.	109
3½	N. Cornwall 3½ p. c. Stk.	129½
4 5/7	Nott. & Granthm. R. & C.	150
3½	Portptk. & Wigtn. Guar. Stk.	126
9	Vict. Stn. & Pimlico Ord.	317½
4½	Do. 4½ p. c. Pref.	163½
4/	West Lond. £20 Ord. Shs.	14½
4 1/2	Weymouth & Portld.	162½

DEBENTURE STOCKS.

Last Div.	Name.	Price.
3	Barry, Cons.	110
4	Brecon & Mrthyr, New A	129
4	Do. New B	105
4	Caledonian	155
4	Cambrian "A"	134½
4	Do. "B"	130½
4	Do. "C"	126½
4	Do. "D"	110½
3	Cardiff Rly.	105
4	City and S. Lond.	139
3½	Cleator & Working Junc.	118½
3	Devon & Som. "A"	105½
16/3	Do. "B" 4 p. c.	36
—	Do. "C" 4 p. c.	10
4	E. Lond. and Ch. 4 p. c. A	139
5/-	Do. 2nd B	65½
—	Do. 3rd Ch. 4 p. c.	19½
—	Do. 4th do.	9½
3½	Do. 1st (3½ p. c.)	128½
2½	Do. 2½ p.c. (Whitech. Exn).	87
4	Forth Bridge	146
4	Furness	145
4	Glasgow and S. Western	154
5	Gt. Central	—
4½	Do.	161
4	Gt. Eastern	151
4	Gt. N. of Scotland	148½
3	Gt. Northern	118
4	Gt. Western	156
4½	Do.	162
4½	Do.	172
5	Do.	192
2½	Do.	100
4	Highland	143½
3	Hull and Barnsley	107
3	Do. 2nd (3-4 p. c).	124
4	Isle of Wight	144½
3	Do. Cent. "A"	92½
4½	Do. "B"	113½
4	Do. "C"	82½
3	Lancs. & Yorkshire	117
4	Lancs. Derbys. & E. Cst.	124½
4	Lpool St. Hlen's & S. Lancs	126
4½	Ldn. and Blackwall	159
4	Ldn. and Greenwich	148½
4	Lond., Brighton, &c.	152
4½	Do.	170
4½	Lond., Chath., &c., Arb.	160
4½	Do. "B"	156½
4	Do.	139
4	Do. 1883	139
3	Do.	106
3	Lond. & N. Western	120
3	Lond. & S. Westn. "A"	118
3	Do. Consld.	118
4	Lond., Til., & Southend	150
—	Mersey, 5 p. c. (Act, 1866)	65
4	Metropolitan	150
4½	Do.	164½
3½	Do.	129½
6	Met. District	206½
4	Do.	139½
3	Midland	118
4½	Mid-Wales "A"	137½
4	Neath & Brecon 1st	128
4	Do. "A 1"	119
3	North British	114
3	Do. 1893	111½
3½	N. Cornwall, Launcstn., &c.	128½
3	North Eastern	118

Debenture Stocks (*continued*):—

Last Div.	Name.	Price.
4½	North London	169½
3	N. Staffordshire	115
4	Plym. Devps. & S.W. Jn.	141½
4	Rhondda and Swan. Bay	130½
4	Rhymney	147
4	South-Eastern	151
5	Do.	191
3½	Do.	130
3	Do.	116
3	Taff Vale	112
4	Tottenham & For. Gate	146
3	Vale of Glamorgan	106½
3	West Highld. (Gtd. by N.B.)	111½
4	Wrexham, Mold, &c. "A"	115½
4	Do. "B"	106½
4	Do. "C"	97½

GUARANTEED SHARES AND STOCKS.

Last Div.	Name.	Price.
4	Caledonian	152½
4	Do.	152
4	Forth Bridge	146
4	Furness 1881	138
4	Glasgow & S. Western	151½
4	Do. St. Enoch, Rent	150½
6	Gt. Central	202½
4½	Do. 1st Pref.	155½
3½	Do. Pref.	108
5	Do. Irred. S.Y. Rent	167½
4½	Do. do.	144½
4	Gt. Eastern, Rent	148
5	Do. Metropolitan	182½
4	Do.	150
4	Gt. N. of Scotland	141
4	Gt. Northern	152
5	Gt. Western, Rent	191
5	Do. Cons.	191
4	Lancs. & Yorkshire	152
5	L., Brighton & S. C.	188
3½	L., Chat. & D. (Shrtlds.)	110½
4	L. & North Western	153
4	L. & South Western .. 1881	152
4½	Met. District, Ealing Rent	154
4½	Do. Fulham Rent	152
4	Do. Midland Rent	145
4	Do. Mid. & Dist. Guar.	136½
4	Midland, Rent	153
4	Do. Cons.	153
3	Mid. & G. N. Jt., "A" Rnt.	110½
3	N. British, Lien	111
4	Do. Cons. Pref. No. 1	147
3	N. Cornwall, Wadebrgs. Gu.	108
4	N. Eastern	152
5	N. Staff. Trent & M. £20 Shs.	37
3½	Nott. Suburban Ord.	126½
20/6	S. E. Perp. Ann.	364
4½	Do. 4½ p.c.	167
3½	S. Yorks. Junc. Ord.	118½
4½	W. Cornwall (G. W., Br., Ex., & S. Dev. Joint Rent	168½
3	W. Highl. Ord. Stk. (Gua. N.B.)	109½

PREFERENCE SHARES AND STOCKS.

DIVIDENDS CONTINGENT ON PROFIT OF YEAR.

Last Div.	Name	Price.
5	Barry (First)	171½
4	Do. Consolidated	140½
4	Caledonian Cons., No. 1	149
4	Do. do. No. 2	147
5	Do. do. 1878	183½
4	Do. Pref. 1884	147
4	Do. do. 1887 (Conv.)	156
—	Cambrian, No. 1 4 p. c. Pref.	72½
—	Do. No. 2 do.	37½
—	Do. No. 3 do.	19
—	Do. No. 4 do.	10
5	City & S. Lond. £10 shares	15½
—	Do. New	14
4	Furness, Cons. 1881	133½
4	Do. "A" 1882	131½
4	Do. "B" 1883	129½
4	Glasgow & S. Western	147
4	Do. No. 2	147
4	Do. 1888	146
4	Do. 1891	146
5	Gt. Central	168
4	Do.	136½
5	Do. Conv. 1872	156½
5	Do. do. 1874	156½
5	Do. do. 1876	156½
5	Do. do. 1879	156½
5	Do. do. 1881	156½
4	Do. 1889	118½
4	Do. 1891	136
5	Do. 1894	118½
4	Gt. Eastern, Cons.	168
4	Do. 1880	146
4	Do. 1882	145½
4	Do. 1884	145
4	Do. 1887	145

Preference Shares, &c. (*continued*):—

Last Div.	Name.	Price.
4	Gt. Eastern, Cons. 1888	144
3½	Do. 1890	126
3½	Do. 1893	125
—	Do. (Int. fr. Jan '99) 1897	117
4	Gt. North Scotland "A"	136
4	Do. "B"	135
4	Gt. Northern, Cons.	148
3	Do. 1896	108
5	Gt. Western Cons.	180
—	Hull & Barnsley Red. at 115	120
4	Isle of Wight	135
3	Lancs. & Yorkshire, Cons.	112
2/2½	Lanc. Drby & E.C. 5 p.c. £10	11
—	Do. 5 p.c. 2nd £10	10
5	Lond., Bright., &c., Cons.	187
5	Do. 2nd Cons.	186
4½	Lond., Chat. & Dov. Arbitr.	135
23/0	Do. 2nd Pref. 4½ p.c.	80
4	Lond. & N. Western	152
4	Lond. & S. Western ..1881	152
4	Do. 1884	150
3½	Do.	131
4	Lond., Tilbury & Southend	147
4	Do. Cons., 1887	147
4	Do 1891	146
—	Mersey, 5 p.c. Perp.	9
4	Metropolitan, Perp.	148
4	Do. 1882	145
4	Do. Irred.	145
4	Do. 1887	145
4	Do. New	144
4½	Do.	146
3½	Do.	126
3	Do. Guar.	104½
4	Metrop. Dist. Exten. 5 p.c.	112
4	Midland, Cons. Perpetual	151
4	N. British Cons., No. 2	142
4½	Do. Edin. & Glasgow	156½
5	Do. 1865	173½
5	Do. Conv. 1874	173½
4½	Do. 1875	136
4½	Do. Conv. 1875	156½
5	Do. do. 1879	172½
4	Do. do. 1884	140
4	Do. do. 1888	140
4	Do. do. 1890	140
4	Do. do. 1892	138½
4	N. Eastern	151
4½	N. Lond., Cons. 1866	179½
4½	Do. 2nd Cons. ..1875	164½
4	N. Staffordshire	110
4½	Plym. Devps. & S. W. Junc.	158½
5½d.	Port Talbot, &c., 4 p.c. £10 Shares, 4 paid	5
5/	Rhondda & Swansea Bay, 5 p.c. £10 Shares	13½
4	Rhymney, Cons.	244
4½	S. Eastern, Cons.	166
5	Do. do.	184½
4	Do. Vested Cos'.	146
4	Do. 1891	144
3½	Do. 1893	127
2	Do. 3 p.c. after July 1900	105
4	Taff Vale	143

INDIAN RAILWAYS.

Last Div.	Name.	Paid.	Price.
3½	Assam Bengal, Ld. (3½ p.c. till June 30, then 3 p.c.)	100	103
4/	Barsi Light, Ld., £10 Shs.	10	[illegible]
6	Bengal and N. West., Ld.	100	14[illegible]
4/	Do. £10 Shares	10	14
3/6	Do. 3½ p.c. Cum. Pf. Shs.	10	1[illegible]
5½d.	Do.	4	4
2/3½	Bengal Central, Ld., £10 (3½ p.c. + ⅓th net earn)	5	5
3	Bengal Dooars, Ld.	100	118
4	Bengal Nagpr., Lim. (gua. 4 p.c. + 4th sp. pfts.)	100	115
7½	Bombay, Baroda, and C. I. (gua. 5 p.c.)	100	223
36/1	Burma, Ld. (gua. 2½ p.c. and ½ p.c. add. till 1901)	100	105
7·97d.	Do. £10 Shares	2½	3
4	Delhi Umb. Kalka, Ld., Gua. 3½ p.c. + net earn.	100	119
4	Do. Deb. Stk., 1890 (1916)	100	11[illegible]
9/10	Estn. Bengal, "A" An. 1957	—	2[illegible]
9/	Do. "B" 1957	—	3[illegible]
4	Do. Gua. Deb. Stock	100	14[illegible]
9/7½	East Ind. Ann. "A" (1953)	—	[illegible]
8/4½	Do. "C"	—	[illegible]
8/11½	Do. "B"	—	
6½	Do. Def. Ann. Cap. (gua. 4 p.c. + ⅕th sp. pfts.)	—	15
115/9	East Ind. Def. Ann. "D"	—	15
4½	East Ind. Irred. Stock	100	16[illegible]
5	Gt. Indian Penin., Gua. 5 p.c. + ½ surplus profits	100	17[illegible]
4	Do. Irred. 4 p.c. Deb. St.	100	14[illegible]
4	Indian Mid., Ld. (gua. 4 p.c. + ¼th surplus pfts.)	100	11[illegible]
5	Madras Guar. + ½ sp. pfts.	100	16
4½	Do. do.	100	15
4½	Do. do.	100	14
4	Nilgiri, Ld., 1st Deb. Stk.	100	9
4	Oude & Rohil. Db. Stk. Rd.	100	1[illegible]
3⅓	Rohil. and Kumaon, Ld.	100	1
9/17	Scinde, Punj., and Delhi, "A" Ann., 1958	—	
9/1	Do. "B" do.	—	

Indian Railways (*continued*):—

Last Div.	Name.	Paid.	Price.
4/	South Behar, Ld., £10 shs.	10	10
3½	Do. Deb. Stk. Red.	100	103
4½	South Ind., Gu. Deb. Stk.	100	166½
5	South Indian, Ld. (gua. 3 p.c., and ½ spls. profits)	100	120½
5	Sthn. Mahratta, Ld. (3½ p.c. & ¼th net earnings)	100	123
4	Do. Deb. Stk. Red.	100	124
3½	Southern Punjab, Ld.	100	114
3½	Do. Deb. Stk. Red.	—	107
5	Nizam's Gua. State, Ld. (†	100	114½
4	Do. Mort. Deb., 1936	100	109
4	Do. do. Reg.	100	108
17/3	Nizam's Gua. State, Ld., 3½ p.c. Mt. Deb. bearer	—	94½
17/3	Do. Reg. do. ..	—	93½
5	W. of India Portgese., Ld.	100	72½
5	Do. Deb. Stk., Red	100	100

RAILWAYS.—BRITISH POSSESSIONS.

Last Div.	Name.	Paid.	Price.
5	Atlantic & N.W. Gua. 1 Mt. Bds., 1937	100	126†
5/.	Buff. & L. Huron Ord. Sh.	10	13½
5	Do. 1st Mt. Perp. Bds. 1879	100	142½
5	Do. 2nd Mt. Perp. Bds.	100	142½
—	Calgary & Edmon. 6 p.c. 1st Mt. Stg. Bds. Red..	100	69
5	Canada Cent. 1st Mt. Bds. Red.	100	105
4	Can. Pacific Pref. Stk.....	100	109
5	Do. Strl. 1st Mt. Deb. Bds. 1915	100	119
3½	Do. Ld. Grnt. Bds., 1938..	100	109
3½	Do. Ld. Grnt. Ins. Stk. ..	100	109
4	Do. Perp. Cons. Deb. Stk.	100	116½
5	Do. Algoma Bch. 1st Mt. Bds., 1937	100	121
2	Demerara, Original Stock	100	49
7	Do. Perp. Pref. Stk.......	100	157½
9/-	Do. 4 p.c. Cum. Ext. Pref. £10 Shs.	4	5
—	Dominion Atlntc. Ord. Stk.	100	31½
25/	Do. 5 p.c. Pref. Stk.....	100	101
4	Do. 1st. Deb. Stk.......	100	110
4	Do. 2nd do. Red.	100	99†
	EmuBay&Mt. Bischoff, Ld.	5	4½
4½	Do. Irred. Deb. Stk....	100	98†
nil	Gd. Trunk of Canada, Stk.	100	8½
6	Do. 2nd. Equip. Mt. Bds.	100	130½
5	Do. Perp. Deb. Stk.......	100	141†
5	Do. Gt. Westn. Deb. Stk.	100	136
5	Do. Nthn. of Can. 1st Mt. Bds., 1902	100	105
4	Do. do. Deb. Stk	100	103
5	Do. G. T. Geor. Bay & L. Erie 1 Mt., 1903	100	105
5	Do. Mid. of Can. Stl. 1st Mt. (Mid. Sec.) 1908	100	108
5	Do. do. Cons. 1 Mt. Bds. 1912	100	108
5	Do. Mont. & Champ. 1 Mt. Bds., 1902	100	104
/2	Do. Welln., Grey & Brce. 7 p.c. Bds. 1 Mt.	100	110
4	Jamaica 1st Mtg. Bds. Red.	—	104
6	Manitoba & N. W., 6 p.c. 1st Mt. Bds., Red	100	44½
—	Do. Ldn. Bdhldrs. Certs.	—	44½
5	Manitoba S. W. Col. 1 Mt. Bd., 1934 $1,000 price %	—	116
—	Mid. of W. Aust. Ld. 6 p.c. 1 Mt. Dbs., Red.	100	25
4	Do. Deb. Bds., Red.	100	103
4	Nakusp & Slocan Bds., 1918	100	106
3	Natal Zululand Ld. Debs.,	100	79½
5	N. Brunswick 1st Mt. Stg. Bds., 1934	100	122
4	Do. Perp. Cons. Deb. Stk.	100	114
—	N. Zealand Mid., Ld., 5 p.c. 1st Mt. Debs.	100	35
6	Ontario & Queb. Cap. Stk.	$100	153½
5	Do. Perm. Deb. Stk......	100	147½
—	Qu'Appelle, L. Lake & Sask. 6 p.c. 1 Mt. Bds. Red.	100	38½
5	Queb. & L. S. John, 1st Mt. Bds., 1909	100	18½
5	Quebec Cent., Prior Ln. Bds., 1908	100	109
1½	Do. 5 p.c. Inc. Bds.	100	39
4	St. Lawr. & Ott. Stl. 1st Mt.	100	112
4	Shuswap & Okan., 1st Mt. Deb. Bds., 1915	100	70½
5	Temiscouata, 5 p.c. Stl. 1st Deb. Bds., Red........	100	9½
5	Do. (S. Franc. Brch.) 5 p.c. Stl. 1 Mt. Db. Bds., 1910	100	12½
4	Toronto, Grey & B. 1st Mt.	100	111
2/2½	Well. & Mana. £5 Shs. ..	1	1
5	Do. Debs., 1908	100	110
5	Do. 2nd Debs., 1908	100	109
5	Do. 3rd do., 1908	100	108
6	Atlnn. & St. Law. Shs., 6 p.c.	100	167
5	Gd. Trunk Mt. Bds., 1934	100	107½
5	Michigan Air Line, 5 p.c. 1st Mt. Bds., 1902	100	104
4	Minneap., S. P. & Slt. Ste. Mar, 1st M. Bds., 1938	$1000	99½

AMERICAN RAILROAD STOCKS AND SHARES.

Last Div.	Name.	Paid.	Price.
6/	Alab. Gt. Sthn. A 6 p.c. Pref.	10*l.*	9
3/	Do. do "B" Ord. ..	10*l.*	2
—	Alabma. N. Orl.-Tex. &c., "A" Pref.	10*l.*	[illegible]
—	Do. "B" Def.	10*l.*	[illegible]
4½	Atlant. First Lsd. Ls. Rtl. Trust..................	Stk.	100
$2	Baltimore & Ohio Com. ..	$100	15
—	Baltimore Ohio S.W. Pref.	$100	6½
—	Chesap. & Ohio Com.	$100	23
—	Chic. Gt. West. 5 p.c. Pref. Stock "A"	$100	35½
—	Do. do. Scrip. In.......	—	32½
8/3	Do. 4 p.c. Deb. Stk.......	$100	72
4	Do. Interest in Scrip	$100	67½
$4	Chic. Junc. Rl. & Un. Stk. Yds. Com.	$100	115½
6/2	Do. 6 p.c. Cum. Pref.	$100	112½
$3½	Chic. Mil. & St. P. Pref...	$100	147½
7	Cleve. & Pittsburgh......	$10	87
$1½	Clev., Cincin., Chic., & St. Louis Com.	$100	—
—	Erie 4 p.c. Non-Cum. 1st Pf.	—	40
—	Do. 4 p.c. do. 2nd Pf.	—	21
—	Gt. Northern Pref.	$100	135
$2½	Illinois Cen. Lsd. Lines ..	$100	94
—	Kansas City, Pitts & G. ..	$100	21½
$3	L. Shore & Mich. Sth. C. (†	$100	176½
—	Mex. Cen. Ltd. Com.	$100	6
—	Miss. Kan. & Tex. Pref...	$100	37½
—	N.Y., Pen. & O. 1st Mt. Tst. Ltd., Ord.	—	45½
4	Do. 1st Mort. Deb. Stk. ..	$100	93½
8	North Pennsylvania	$50	—
—	Northn. Pacific, Com.....	$100	24½
1½	Pitts. F. Wayne & Chic...	$100	175
—	Reading 1st Pref.	$50	26½
—	Do. 2nd Pref.	$50	14½
—	S. Louis & S. Fran. Com.	$100	7½
—	Do. 2nd Pref.	$100	27
6	St. Louis Bridge 1st Pref..	$100	107
3	Do. 2nd Pref.	$100	50
6	Tunnel Rail. of St. Louis	$100	107
$1½	St. Paul, Min. and Man...	$100	127½
—	Southern, Com.	$100	9½
—	Wabash, Common........	$100	7½

AMERICAN RAILROAD BONDS. CURRENCY.

Last Div.	Name.	Price.
7	Albany & Susq. 1 Con. Mrt. 1906	122½
7	Allegheny Val. 1 Mt. 1910	127½
5	Burling., Cedar Rap. & N. 1 Mt. 1906	100½
5	Canada Southern 1 Mt. 1908	108
5	Chic. & N. West. Sk. Fd. Db. 1933	119½
5	Do. Deb. Coupon 1921	115½
6	Chicago & Tomah 1905	112½
5	Chic. Burl. & Q. Skge. Fd. 1901	102½
4	Do. Nebraska Ext...... —	100
6	Chic., Mil., & S. Pl., 1 Mt. S.W. Div.............. 1909	117½
7	Do. (S. Paul Div.) 1 Mt. 1902	132½
5	Do. (La Cross & D. 1919	112½
7	Do. 1 Mt. (Hast. & Dak.) 1910	132
5	Do. Chic. & Mis. Riv. 1 Mt. 1926	112½
5	Chic., Rock Is. and Pac. 1 Mt. Ext. 1934	106½
6	Det., G. Haven & Mil. Equip 1918	110
6	Do. do. Cons. Mt. 1918	105½
6	Ill. Cent., 1 Mt., Chic. & S. 1898	102½
7	Indianap. & Vin., 1 Mt. .. 1908	125
6	Do. do. 2 Mt. .. 1900	104½
6	Lehigh Val., Cons. Mt..... 1923	112½
—	Mexic. Cent., Ln. 2 Cons. Inc. —	7
7	N.Y. Cent. & H.R. Mt. Bonds 1903	119½
5	Do. Deb. 1904	112
6	Penns. Cons. S. F M. 1905	115
4	West Shore, 1 Mt. 2361	110

DITTO—GOLD.

Last Div.	Name.	Price.
6	Alabama Gt. Sthn. 1 Mt. .. 1908	107½
5	Do. Mid. 1 1928	94½
4	Allegheny Val. Gen. Mt. .. 1942	108½
4	Atch., Top., & S. Fé Gn. Mt. 1995	95½
3	Do. Adj. Mt............ 1995	61½
5	Do. Equipt. Tmst. ...... —	103†
5	Atlantic & Dan. 1 Mt. 1950	92
5	Baltimore & Ohio 1925	86½
5	Do. Speyer's Tst. Recpts. 1925	86½
5	Do. Cons. Mt. 1988	100
4½	Do. 4½ p.c. 1 Mt. Term. 1934	84
4½	Do. Brown Shipley's Dep. Cts. —	84
5	Balt. Belt 5 p.c. 1 Mort..... 1990	—
4½	Balt. & Ohio S.W. 1 Mt. .. 1990	102
4½	Do. 4½ p.c. 1 Cons. Mt. 1893 1993	77
2½	Do. Inc. Mt. 5 p.c. Cl. A —	31
—	Do. do. Cl. B —	12
5	Balt. & Ohio S.W. Term 5 p.c. 1942	99
6	Balt. & Ptmac (Mn. L.) 1 Mt. 1911	124½
6	Do. do. (Tunnel) 1 Mt. 1911	123
4	Beech Creek 1 Mt. 1936	107
5	Do 2 Mort. 1936	116
4	Carthage & Adiron. 1 Mt... 1981	107½

American Railroad Bonds—Gold (*continued*):—

Last Div.	Name.	Price.
5	Cent. of Georgia 1 Mort. ... 1945	119
5	Do. Cons. Mt. 1945	92½
5	Cent. of N. Jrsy. Gn. Mt... 1987	115
6	Central Pacific, 1 Mort. 1898	102½
—	Do. Speyer's Certs....... —	103½
5	Do. Land Grant 1900	102
5	Chesap. & Ohio 1st Cons. Mt. 1939	117
4½	Do. Gen. Mt............ 1992	85
6	Chic. & W. Ind. Gen. Mt. Skg. Fd. 1932	122
5	Chic. Mil. & St. Pl. (Chic. & L. Sup.) 1 Mt. 1921	115
5	Do. Chic. & Pac. W. 1921	117
5	Do. Wisc. & Minn. 1 Mt. 1921	115
5	Do. Terminal Mt. 1914	114½
4	Do. General Mt. 1989	107
5	Chic. St. L. & N. Orleans.. 1951	122½
4	Do. 1 Mort. (Memphis) .. 1951	102½
4	Clevel., Cin., Chic. & St. L. 1 Mt. (Cairo) 1939	90
4	Do. 1 Mt. (Cinc., Wab., & Mich.) 1991	90
4	Do. 1 Col. Tst. Mt. (S. Louis) 1990	98½
4	Do. General Mt. 1993	82
4½	Clevel. & Mar. Mt. 1935	110
4½	Clevel. & Pittsburgh 1942	120½
4½	Do. Series B. 1942	119½
6	Colorado Mid. 1 Mt. 1936	67
—	Do. Bdhrs.' Comm. Certs. —	67
4	Dnvr. & R. Gde. 1 Cons. Mt. 1936	93
5	Do. Imp. Mort............ 1928	89
4	Detroit & Mack. 1 Lien 1995	92½
5	E. Tennes., Virg., & Grgia. Cons. Mt. 1956	112½
5	Elmira, Cort., & Nthn. Mt. 1914	97
4	Erie 1 Cons. Mt. Pr. Ln. .. 1996	94
3	Do. Gen. Lien 1996	73
6	Galvest., Harrisb., &c., 1 Mt....	109
5	Georgia, Cnr. & N. 1 Mt. .. 1929	96
4½	Gd. Rpds. & Indn. Ex. 1 Mt 1941	110
5	Do. 1 Mt. (Muskegon) .. 1926	39½
3½	Illinois Cent. 1 Mt. 1951	103
4	Do. 1952	106
4	Do. Cairo Bdge. .. 1950	101
4	Do. 1953	104
4	Do. General Mort. .. 1904	100
—	Kans. City, Pitts. & G. 1 M. 1923	83
3½	L. Shore & Mich. Southern 1997	108
4½	Lehigh Val. N.Y. 1 Mt.... 1940	105
5	Lehigh Val. Term. 1 Mt. .. 1941	112½
5	Long Island 1931	114
5	Do. Deb.............. 1934	101
5	Do. (N. Shore Bch.) 1 Cons. Mt. 1932	96
6	Louisville & Nash. G. Mt.. 1930	120
6	Do. 2 Mt. Sk. Fd. (S. & N. Alabama 1910	108
6	Do. 1 Mt. N. Orl. & Mb. 1930	122
5	Do. 1 Mt. Coll. Tst. 1931	104½
4	Do. Unified 1940	88
4½	Do. Mobile & Montgy. 1 Mt. 1945	107½
4	Manhattan Cons. Mt. 1990	98
4	Mexican Cent. Cons. Mt. .. 1911	68
—	Do. 1 Cons. Inc, ...	18
6	Mexican Nat. 1 Mt.......... 1927	106
3	Do. 2 Mt. 6 p.c. Inc. A 1917	57
—	Do. do. B.. 1917	—
3	Do. Matheson's Certs.....	—
3	Michig. Cnt. (Battle Ck. & S.) 1 Mt. 1989	84
6	Minneap. & S. L. 1 Mt. Pacific Ext. 1921	120½
5	Do. 1 Consold. 1934	108½
4	Minne., Slt. S. M. & A. 1 Mt. 1926	100
5	Minneapolis Westn. 1 Mt... 1911	105
4	Miss. Kans. & Tex. 1 Mt... 1990	89
4	Do. 2 do. 1990	66
4	Mobile & Birm. Mt. Inc.... 1945	38
5	Do. P. Lien 1945	88
4	Mohawk & Mal. 1 Mt...... 1991	109
5	Montana Cent. 1 Mt....... 1937	105
5	Nashv., Chattan., & S. L. 1 Cons. Mt................ 1928	104½
5	Nash., Flor., & Shff. Mt... 1937	92
4	N. Y. & Putnam 1 Cons. Mt. 1993	109
5	N. Y., Brooklyn, & Man. B. 1 Cons. Mt.............. 1935	109
4	N. Y. Cent. & Hud. R. Deb. Certs. 1890 1905	106
4	Do. Ext. Debt. Certs.... 1905	106
7	N. Y., L. Erie, & W. 1 Cons. Mt. (Erie) 1920	149½
7	Do. 1 Con. Mt. Fd. Coup. 1920	142½
5	N. Y., Onto., & W. Cons. 1 Mt.................... 1939	110
4	Do. 4 p.c. Refund. Mt.. 1992	99
5	N. Y. & Rockaway B. 1 Mt. 1927	104½
6	Norfolk & West. Gn. Mt.... 1931	128
6	Do. Imp. & Ext........ 1934	120
4	Do. 1 Cons. Mt. ...... —	82
6	N. Pacific Gn. 1 Mt. Ld. Gt. 1921	120
4	Do. P. Ln. Rl. & Ld. Gt. —	99
3	Do. Gn. Ln. Rl. & Ld. Gt. —	64½
5	Oregon & Calif. 1 Mt....... 1927	76
5	Oregon Rl. & Nav. Col. Tst. —	—
5	Oreg. Sh. Line & Utah Col. Trst. 5 p.c. G. Bonds 1919	—
6	Panama Skg. Fd. Subsidy.. 1910	105½
4½	Pennsylvania Rlrd. 1913	115
4	Do. Equip. Tst. Ser. A.. 1914	106
4	Do. Cons. Mt........... 1943	115
4½	Penna. Company 1st Mort. 1921	116
5	Perkiomen 1 Mrt., 2nd ser.. 1918	90
4½	{ Pitts., C., C., & St. Ls. Con. Mt. G.B., Ser. A } 1940-2	115
4	Do. Cons. Mort., Ser. D.. 1945	105
6	Pittsbgh., Cle., & Toledo .. 1922	105½
4	Reading, Phil., & R. Genl. 1997	87
5	Richmond & Dan. Equip. .. 1909	99½
5	Rio Grande Junc. 1st Mort. 1939	90
4	Rio Grande West 1st Tst. Mt. 1939	84
6	St. Joseph & Gd. Island .. 1925	—
7	S. Louis Bridge 1st Mort .. 1929	135½

American Railroad Bond (*continued*):

Last Div.	Name.	Price.
5	S. Louis Mchts. Bdge. Term. 1st Mort.................. 1930	104½
4	S. Louis S. West 1st Mort.. 1989	75½
—	Do. 4 p.c. 2nd Mort. Inc. 1989	28½
—	S. Louis Term. Cupples Sta. & Prop. 1st. Mrt. 4½ p.c. 1902-17	100
4½	St. Paul, Minn., & Manit. 1933	109
6	Do. do. 1933	127
6	Shamokin, Sunbury, &c. 2 Mt. 1925	107
5	S. & N. Alabama Cons. Mt. 1936	95½
5	Southern 1 Cons. Coup. 1994	95
4	Do. E. Tennes Reorg. Lien .. 1938	96½
6	S. Pacific of Cal. 1 Mt... 1905-12	111
4½	Trml. Assn. of S. Louis 1 Mt. 1939	113½
5	Do. 1 Cons. Mt.......... 1944	110
5	Texas & Pac. 1 Mt.......... 2000	101½
—	Do. 5 p.c. 2 Mt. Income 2000	30
5	Toledo & Ohio Cent. 1 Mt. West. Div. 1935	103½
4½	Toledo., Walhon., Val., & Ohio 1 Mt. 1931-3	109½
6	Union Pacific 1 Mt. 1896-9	101½
5	Do. Coll. Tverst.....	—
5	Union Pac., Linc., & Color. 1 Mt. 1918	—
4	United N. Jersey Gen. Mt... 1944	117½
6	Vicksbrg., Shrevept., & Pac. Pr. Ln. Mt. 1915	102½
5	Wabash 1 Mt. 1939	110
4	Wn. Pennsylvania Mt. 1928	109½
5	W. Virga. & Pittsbg. 1 Mt.. 1990	79½
5	Wheeling & L. Erie 1 Mt. (Wheelg. Div.) 5 p.c. 1928	75
5	Do. Extd. Imp. Mt. 1930	—
—	Do. do. Brown Shipley's Cts...	—
5	Willmar & Sioux Falls 1 Mt. 1938	117

STERLING.

Last Div.	Name.	Price.
6	Alabama Gt. Sthn. Deb..... 1906	104½
5	Do. Gen. Mort. .. 1927-8	99
5	Alabama, N. Orl., Tex. & Pac. 5 p.c. "A" Dbs... 1910-40	99
50/	Do. do. "B" do. 1910-40	46
—	Do. do. "C" do.	20
6-7	Allegheny Valley 1910	133½
4	Atlantic 1st Leased Line Perp...	100
6	Baltimore and Ohio 1902	107
6	Do. do. 1910	115
5	Do. do. 1877........	92
—	Do. Morgan's Certs. ..	92½
4½	Do. do. 1933	78
6	Chicago & Alton Cons. Mt. 1903	111
5	Chic. St. Paul & Kan. City Priority	105
6	Eastn. of Massachusetts 1906	117½
5	Illinois Cent. Skg. Fd.	105
5	Do. 1905	108
3½	Do. 1950	100½
4	Do. 1 Mt. 1951	114
3	Do. 1 Mt. 1951	94
6	Louisville & Nash., M. C. & L. Div., 1 Mt. 1902	107
7	Do. 1 Mt. (Memphis & O.) 1901	111
47/4	Mexican Nat. "A" Certs. 5 p.c. Non. cum.	46
—	Do. "B" Certs.....	10
6	N.Y. & Canada 1 Mt....... 1904	111½
6	N. York Cent. & H.R. Mort. 1903	112
4½	N. York, Penns., & Ohio Pr. Ln. Extd. 1935	—
5	Do. Equip. Tst.	102
5	Do. 5 p.c. Equip. Tst. (1890)	102
6	Nrthn. Cent. Cons. Gen. Mt. ..	106
6	Pennsylvania Gen. Mt. 1910	128
6	Do. Cons. Skg. Fd. Mt. 1905	117
3½	Do. Cons. Mt.......... 1945	106
6	Phil. & Erie Cons. Mort.. 1920 (†	132½
6	Phil. & Reading Gen. Cons. Mort. 1911	126
6	Pittsbg. & Connells. Cons. 1926	110
—	Do. Morgan's Certs.....	110
4	St. Paul., Min., & Manitoba (Pac. Extn.) 1940	98
6	S. & N. Alabama 1903	107½
6	Union Pacific, Omaha Bridge 1896	—
6	Un. N. Jersey & C. Gen. Mt. 1901	111

FOREIGN RAILWAYS.

Last Div.	Name.	Paid.	Price.
4/	Alagoas, Ltd., Shs.	20	6
5	Do. Deb. Stk., Red. ..	100	56
6	Antofagasta, Ltd., Stk. ..	100	77
4	Do. Perp. Deb. Stk. ..	100	95
—	Arauco, Ld., Ord. Shs. ..	10	¼
—	Do. 10 p.c. Cum. Pref.	10	1½
20/	Argentine Gt. W., Ld.,	20	14½
20/	Do. 5 p.c. Cum. Pref. Shs.	20	20½
4	Do. 1 Deb. Stk. .... (†	100	102
6/0/0	Do. 6 p.c. 2 Db. Stk. Astg.	100	—
6/0/0	Do. do. Non-Astg.	100	—
1/0/0	Argentine N.E., Ltd., 6 p.c. Cum. Pref. Stk. ..	100	10
—	Do. 5 p.c. Deb. Stk., Red.	100	33½
2/	Arica and Tacna Shs. ..	20	1½
10/	Bahia & San Fcisco., Ld.,	20	12
6/	Do. Timbo. Bch. Shs.	20	5
12/	Bahia, Blanca, & N.W. Ln. Prf. Cum. 6 p.c. ..	100	61
4	Do. 4 p.c. 1 Deb. Stk., Red.	100	96
6	Barranquilla R. & P., Ld., 6 p.c. 1 Deb. Stk., Red.	100	95

Foreign Railways (*continued*):—

Last Div.	Name.	Paid.	Price.
3/	Bilbao Riv. & Cantabn., Ltd., Ord.	3	6
—	Bolivar, Ltd., Shs.	10	1½
6	Do. 6 p.c. Deb. Stk.	100	98½
—	Brazil Gt. Southn. Ltd., 7 p.c. Cum. Pref.	20	1¼
6	Do. Perm. Deb. Stk	100	80
6½	B. Ayres Gt. Southn., Ld., Ord. Stk.	100	153
5	Do. Pref. Stk.	100	140
4	Do. Deb. Stk.	100	118
30/	B. Ayres & Ensen. Port., Ltd., Ord. Stk.	100	82
5	Do. Cum. 1 Pref. Stk.	100	115
6/0/0	Do. 6p.c.Con. Pref.Stk.	100	97
4	Do. Deb. Stk., Irred.	100	105
9⅞	B. Ayres Northern, Ltd., Ord. Stk.	100	257½
12	Do. Pref. Stk.	100	315
6	Do. 5 p.c. Mt. Deb.Stk., Red.	100	112
3/15/0	B. Ayres & Pac., Ld., 7 p.c. 1 Pref. Stk. (Cum.)	100	106
4	Do. 1 Deb. Stk.	100	104
5/5/0	Do. 4½ p.c. 2 Deb. Stk.	100	94
1	B. Ayres & Rosario, Ltd., Ord. Stk.	100	77½
—	Do. New, £20 Shs.	20	21½
7/	Do. 7 p.c. Pref. Shs.	10	17½
7/	Do. Sunchales Ext.	10	15¾
4	Do. Deb. Stk., Red.	100	109
12/	B. Ayres & Val. Trans., Ltd., 7 p.c. Cum. Pref.	20	6¾
—	Do. 4 p.c. "A" Deb. Stk., Red.	100	73
—	Do. 6 p.c. "B" Deb. Stk., Red.	100	46
6/	B. Ayres Westn. Ld. Ord.	10	12½
3/	Do. Def. Shs.	10	8½
5	Do. 5 p.c. Pref.	10	13¼
4	Do. Deb. Stk.	100	112
6	Cent. Arg. Deb. Sk. Rd. (†	100	163½
4	Do. Deb. Stk. Rd.	100	112†
6	Cent. Bahia L. Ord. Stk.	100	48½
6	Do. Deb. Stk., 1934	100	74
5	Do. Deb. Stk., 1937	100	61
4/6	Cent. Uguy. East. Ext. L. Shs.	10	5½
5	Do. Perm. Stk.	100	108
3/	Do. Nthn. Ext. L. Sh.	10	4¼
5	Do. Perm. Deb. Stk.	100	102
3	Do. of Montev. Ltd., Ord. Stk.	100	84
6	Do. Perm. Deb. Stk.	100	141
8/	Conde d'Eu, Ltd. Ord.	20	7
—	Cordba & Rosar., Ltd., 6 p.c. Pref. Shs.	100	48
4	Do. 1 Deb. Stk.	100	97
75/	Do. 6 p.c. Deb. Stk.	100	91
—	Cordba Cent., Ltd., 5 p.c. Cu. 1 Pref. Stk.	100	95
—	Do. 5 p.c. Non-Cum. 2 Pref. Stk.	100	52½
5	Do. Deb. Stk.	100	124
—	Costa Rica, Ltd., Shs.	10	4
8/	Dna. Thrsa. Chris., Ltd., 7 p.c. Pref. Shs.	20	4
20/	E. Argentine, Ltd.	100	48
6	Do. Deb. Stk.	100	106
—	Egyptn. Dlta. Lgt. Rys., Ltd., £10 Pref. Shs.	6	8
—	Entre Rios, L., Ord. Shs.	5	½
—	Do. Cu. 5 p.c. Pref.	5	3½
6/	Gt. Westn. Brazil, Ltd.,	20	12
6	Do. Perm. Deb. Stk.	100	94½
6	Do. Extn. Deb. Stk.	100	84½
—	Int.-Oceanic Mex., Ltd., 7 p.c. Pref.	10	1½
4	Do. Deb. Stk.	100	83
42/6	Do. 7 p.c. "A" Deb. Sk.	100	58
—	Do. 7 p.c. "B" Deb. Sk.	100	27
5/	La Guaira & Carac.	10	7
5	Do. 5 p.c. Deb. Sk. Red.	100	102
8/4	Lembg.-Czern.-Jassy	30	24½
1/	Lima, Ltd.	20	2½
—	Manila Ltd. 7 p.c. Cu. Pf.	10	½
20/6½	Mexican 2nd Pref. 6 p.c.	100	35
6	Do. Perp. Deb. Stk.	100	139
1/0/0	Mexican Sthrn., Ld., Ord.	100	21
—	Do. 4 p.c. 1 Db. Stk. Rd.	100	86
—	Do. 4 p.c. 2 do.	100	62
—	Mid. Urgy., Ltd.	100	20
5	Do. Deb. Stk.	100	63
12/	Minas & Rio, Ltd.	20	11½
3/2	Namur & Liege	20	13
11/6	Do. Pref.	20	29
5/	Natal & Na. Cruz, Ld., 7 p.c. Cum Pref.	20	7
—	Nitrate Ltd., Ord.	10	6½
—	Do. 7 p.c. Pr. Con. Or.	10	5
—	Do. Def. Conv. Ord.	10	1½
7/	N.-E. Urgy., Ltd., Ord.	10	14½
7/	Do. 7 p.c. Pref.	10	15
—	N.-W. Argentine Ld., 7 p.c. Pref.	10	3
6	Do. 6 p.c. 1 Deb. Stk.	100	114
—	Do. 2 Deb. Stk.	100	94
20/	N.W. Uruguay 6 p.c. 1 Pref. Stk.	100	16
—	Do. 5 p.c. 2 Pref. Stk.	100	7½
6	Do. 6 p.c. Deb. Stk.	100	74½
16/	Ottoman (Sm. Ald.)	20	16
—	Paraguay Cntl., Ld., 5 p.c. Perm. Deb. Stk.	100	11
—	Piræus, Ath., & Pelo.	275	1
5/	Pto. Alegre & N. Hambg. Ld., 7 p.c. Pref. Shs.	20	4½
6	Do. Mt. Deb. Stk. Red.	100	77½
—	Puerto Cabello & Val. Ld.	10	1½
5	Recife & S. Francisco	100	73
14/	R. Claro S. Paulo, Ld., Sh.	10	21½
5	Do. Deb. Stk.	100	130
7/	Royal Sardinian Ord.	10	11½

Foreign Railways (*continued*):—

Last Div.	Name.	Paid.	Price.
7/	Royal Sardinian Pref.	10	12½
5/	Sambre & Meuse	20	19
5/6	Do. Pref.	10	12
28/	San Paulo Ld.	20	36½
2/9½	Do. New Ord. £10 sh.	4	8½
2/	Do. 5 p.c. Non.Cm. Pref.	10	12¼
5½	Do. Deb. Stk. (†	100	136½
5	Do. 5 p.c. Deb. Stk.	100	128
—	S. Fé & Cordova, Gt. Sthn., Ld., Shares	100	
6	Do. Perp. Deb. Stk.	100	57
3/2½	S. Austrian	20	121½
10/	Sthn. Braz. R. Gde. do S 1, Ld.	20	8
6	Do. 6 p.c. Deb. Stk.	100	73
4	Swedish Centl., Ld., 4 p.c. Deb. Stk.	100	108
5	Do. Pref.	100	98½
1/9	Taltal, Ld.	5	3
4/	Uruguay Nthn., Ld. 7 p.c. Pfd. Stk.	100	6
3½	Do. 5 p.c. Deb. Stk.	100	26
—	Villa Maria & Rufino, Ld., 6 p.c. Pref. Shs.	100	20
4	Do. 4 p.c. 1 Deb. Stk.	100	76
6/0/0	Do. 6 p.c. 2 Deb. Stk.	100	46
5/9	West Flanders	8½	22
5/6	Do. 5½ p.c. Pref.	10	18
3/	Wstn. of Havana, Ld.	10	4½

FOREIGN RAILWAY OBLIGATIONS

Per Cent.	Name.	Price.
6	Alagoas Ld., 6 p.c. Deb., Rd.	85½
£1	Alcoy & Gandia, Ld., 5 p.c. Debs., Red.	25
5	Arauco., Ld., 5 p.c. 1st Mt., Rd.	68
6	Do. 6 p.c. Mt. Deb., Rd.	48½
6	Brazil G. Sthn., L., Mt. Dbs., Rd.	83
6	Do. Mt. Dbs. 1893, Rd.	52½
5½	Campos & Caran. Dbs., Rd.	76
6	Central Bahia, L., Dbs., Rd.	83½
5½	Conde d'Eu, L., Dbs., Rd.	77
6	Costa Rica, L., 1st Mt. Dbs., Rd.	110
6	Do. 2nd Dbs., Rd.	96
5	Do. Prior Mt. Db., Rd.	107
6	Cucuta Mt. Dbs., Rd.	100
5½	Donna Thrsa. Cris., L., Dbs., Rd.	75
3	Eastn. of France, £20 Dbs., Rd.	19
4	Egyptn. Delta Light, L., Db., Rd.	100
—	Espito. Santo & Cara. 5 p.c. Stl. Dbs., Rd.	38
4	Gd. Russian Nic., Rd.	101
5	Inter-Oceanic Mex., L., 5 p.c. Pr. Ln. Dbs., Rd.	104
3	Ital. 3 p.c. Bds. A & B, Rd.	57½
—	Ituana 6 p.c. Debs., 1918	72½
—	Leopoldina, 6 p.c. Dbs. £50 Bds.,	24
—	Do. do. Comms. Cert.	24
—	Do. 5 p.c. Stg. Dbs. (1888), Rd.	34
—	Do. do. Comm. Certs.	34
—	Do. 5 p.c. Stg. Dbs. (1890), Rd.	24
—	Do. do. Comms. Certs.	24
11/2	Macahé & Cam. 5 p.c. Dbs., Rd.	34
—	Do. do. Comms. Certs.	34
11/2	Do. (Cantagallo), 5 p.c., Red.	34
—	Do. do. Comm. Certs.	34
—	Manila Ltd., 6 p.c. Deb., Red.	23
6	Do. Prior Lien Mt., Rd.	105
6	Do. Series "B," Rd.	79
7	Matanzas & Sab., Rd.	101½
6	Minas & Rio, L., 6 p.c. Dbs., Rd.	100
5	Mogyana 5 p.c. Deb. Bds., Rd.	102
5	Moscow-Jaros., Rd.	106
5½	Natal & Na. Cruz Ltd., 5½ p.c. Debs., Red.	88½
5	Nitrate, Ltd. Mt. Bds., Red.	89½
3	Nthn. France, Red.	19
4	N. of S. Af. Rep. (Trnsvl.) Gu. Bds. Red.	97
3	Nthn. of Spain £20 Pri. Obs. Red.	8½
6	Ottmn. (Smy to A.) (Kujk) Asst. Debs., Red.	108½
6	Ottmn. (Seraik.) Asg. Debs. Red.	108½
6	Ottmn. (Seraik) Non-Asg. D., Rd.	108½
5	Ottmn. Kuyjk. Ext. Red.	106
5	Ottmn. Serkeuy. Ext. Red.	103½
5	Ottmn. Tireh Ext. 1910	98
5	Ottmn. Debs, 1886, Red.	97½
5	Do. 1888, Red. 1935	97½
5	Do. 1893, Red. 1935	96½
5	Ottmn. of Anlia. Debs., Rd.	91
5	Do. Ser. II.	89
4	Ottomn. Smyr. & Cas. Ext Bds., Red.	82½
3	Paris, Lyon & Medit. (old sys., £20), Red.	19
3	Paris, Lyon & Medit. (new sys., £20), Red.	19
50/	Piræus, At. & Pelp., 6 p.c. 1st Mt. Bds., Red.	88½
30/	Do. 5 p.c. Mt. Bds., Red.	61½
4	Pretoria-Pietbg., Ltd., Red.	94
7	Puerto Cab. & Val., Ltd., 1st Mt. Debs., Red.	96
—	Rio de Jano. & Nthn., Ltd., 6 p.c. £100 Deb., Red.	24
—	Rio de Jano. (Gr. Para.), 5 p.c. 1st Mt. St. £100 Debs., Red.	24
3	Royal Sardinian, A, Rd. £20	12
3	Royal Sardinian, B., Rd £20	12

Foreign Rly. Obligations (*continued*):—

Per Cent.	Name.	Price.
5	Ryl. Trns.-Afric. 5 p.c. 1st Mt. £100 Bds., Red.	61†
7	Sagua La Grande, B pRd.	98†
4	Sa. Fe & Cor. G.S., Ld. Pr Ln. Bds.	100†
5	Sa. Fe, 5 p.c. 2nd Reg. Dbs.	79
3	South Austrian, £20 Red.	15½†
3	South Austrian, (Ser X.)	15½
3	South Italian £20 Obs. (Ser. A to G), Red.	12½
3½	S. W. of Venez. (Barq.), Ltd., 7 p.c. 1st Mt. £100 Debs.	57½†
5	Taltal, Ltd., 5 p.c. 1st Ch. Debs., Red.	89†
5	Utd. Rwys. Havana, Red.	79†
3	Wtrn. of France, £20 Red.	19†
6	Wrn. B. Ayres St. Mt. Debs., 1900	111
6	Wrn. B. Ayres, Reg. Cert.	109
5	Do. Mt. Bds.	123†
6	Wtrn. of Havna., Ld. Mt. Dbs., Rd.	98
7	Wrn. Ry. San Paulo Red.	101
1	Wrn. Santa Fé 7 p.c. Red.	39
4/7	Zafra & Huelva, 3 p.c. Red.	3

BANKS.

Div.	Name.	Paid.	Price.
1/9½	Agra, Ltd.	6	3½
4/2½	Anglo-Argentine, Ltd., £9	7	5½
8½ fls.	Anglo-Austrian	120 fl	14
6/	Anglo-Californian, Ltd., £20 Shares	10	11
4/	Anglo-Egyptian, Ltd. £15	5	5½
2/6	Anglo-Foreign Bkg., Ltd.	7	8
2/	Anglo-Italian, Ltd.	5	7½
7/6	Bk. of Africa, Ltd., £18¾	6¼	10½
20/	Bk. of Australasia	40	52
8/	Bk. of Brit. Columbia	20	19
25/	Bk. of Brit. N. America	50	65
7/6	Bk. of Egypt, Ltd., £25	12½	19
5/	Bk. of Mauritius, Ltd.	10	10
18/	Bk. of N. S. Wales	20	38
4 p.c.	Bk. of N. Zland. Gua. Stk.	100	103
6/	Bk. of Roumania, £20 Shs.	6	7½
2/6	Tarapaca & Ldn., Ltd., £10	5	3½
—	Bque. Fse. de l'Afri. du S.	100 f	3½
f.12.50	Bque. Internatle. de Paris	20	24
6/	Brit. Bk. of S. America, Ltd., £20 Shares	10	11
15/	Capital & Ctles., L., £50	10	40
16/	Chart. of India, &c.		29½
9/	City, Ltd., £40 Shares	10	20½
18/	Colonial, £100 Shares	30	21
10/	Delhi and London, Ltd.	25	—
5/	German of London, Ltd.	10	11
25/	Hong-Kong & Shanghai	62½	44
4/	Imperl. of Persia	6½	3½
10/	Imperl. Ottoman, £20 Shs	10	12½
9/	Internatl. of Ldn., Ld., £20	15	9½
10/	Ionian, Ltd.	25	15
12/	Lloyds, Ltd., £50 Shs.	8	29½
10/	Ldn. & Brazila. Ltd., £20	10	18
44/	Ldn. & County, Ltd., £50	20	105
5/	Ldn. & Hanseatic, L., £20	10	11
20/	Ldn. & Midland, L., £60	12½	53½
8/9	Ldn. & Provin., Ltd., £10	5	23
30/	Ldn. & Riv. Plate, L., £25	15	50
2/1½	Ldn. & San Fcisco, Ltd. z.	7	4½
24/	Ldn. & Sth. West., L., £50	20	68
24/	Ldn. & Westmins., L., £100	20	58½
3/	Ldn. of Mex. & S. Amer., Ltd., £10 Shs.	6	5½
15/	Ldn. Joint Stk., L., £100	15	34½
9/7	Ldn., Paris & Amer., L., £20	16	26
1/7½	Merchant Bkg., L., £9	4	2½
6/3	Metropn, Ltd., £50 Shs.	5	14
9/	National, Ltd., £50 Shs.	10	20
4/5	Natl. of Mexico, $100 Shs.	$40	12
1/3	National of N. Z., L., £7½	2½	2½
2/	National S. Afric. Rep.	10	14½
18/10½	National Provcl. of Eng., Ltd.; £75 Shs.	10½	49
21/7½	Do. do. £60 Shs.	12	55½
6/3	NorthEastn., Ltd., £20 Shs	6	15
19/	Parr's, Ld., £100 Shs.	20	92½
12/6	Prov. of Ireland, L., £100	12½	29
40/	Stand. of S. Afric., L., £100	25	68
12/6	Union of Australia, L., £75	25	29½
4 p.c.	Do. do. Ins. Stk. Dep. 1900	100	103
17/	Union of Ldn., Ltd., £100	15½	36

BREWERIES AND DISTILLERIES.

Div.	Name.	Paid.	Price.
4½	Albion Prp. 1 Mt. Db. Sk.	100	110
4	All Saints', L., Db. Sk. Rd.	100	99
6	Allsopp, Ltd.	100	164
6	Do. Cum. Pref.	100	158
4½	Do. Deb. Stk., Red.	100	117
3½	Do. Deb. Stk., Red.	100	100
4½	Alton & Co., L., Db., Rd.	100	106
4½	Do. Mt. Bds., 1896	100	105
8/	Arnold, Perrett, Ltd.	10	7
6	Do. Cum. Pref.	10	10
4½	Do. 1 Mt. Db. Stk., Rd.	100	106

Breweries, &c. (*continued*):—

Div.	Name.	Paid.	Price.
5½	Arrol, A., & Sons, L., Cum. Pref. Shs.	10	10½
4½	Do. 1 Mt. Db. Stk., Rd.	100	106
6	Backus, 1 Mt. Db., Red.	100	59½
4	Barclay, Perk., L., Cu. Pf.	10	11½
3½	Do. Mt. Db. Stk., Red.	100	110
4/	Barnsley, Ltd.	10	10½
6	Do. Cum. Pref.	10	12½
1/	Barrett's, Ltd.	2½	1½
1/3	Do. 5 p.c. Pref.	2½	2½
3/	Bartholomay, Ltd.	10	4½
8	Do. Cum. Pref.	10	9
6	Do. Deb.	100	103½
5	Bass, Ratcliff, Ltd., Cum. Pref. Stk. (†	100	147½
4½	Do. Mt. Db. Stk., Rd.	100	124
4	Bell, John, Ltd., 1 Mt. Deb. Stk., Red.	100	102
2/6	Benskin's, L., Cum. Pref.	5	5½
4½	Do. 1 Mt. Db. Stk. Red.	100	110
4½	Do. "B" Deb. Sk, Rd.	100	109
2/	Bentley's Yorks., Ltd.	10	11½
6	Do. Cum. Pref.	10	12½
4½	Do. Mt. Debs., Red.	100	109
4½	Do. do. 1 92, Red.	100	109
—	Bleckert's, Ltd.	20	2
5	Do. Debs., Red.	100	56½
—	Birmingham., Ld., 6 p.c. Cum. Pref.	5	2½
4½	Do. Mt. Debs., Red.	50	40½
5½	Boardman's, Ld., Cm. Pf.	10	8½
4½	Do., Perp. 1 Mt. Db. Sk.†	100	105½
4½	Brakspear, L., 1 D. Stk. Rd	100	111
4	Brandon's, L., 1 D. Stk. R.†	100	105½
17/	Bristol (Georges) Ltd.	10	47
6	Do. Cum. Pref.	10	17½
5	Do. Mt. Db. Sk. 1888 Rd.	100	115½
—	Bristol United, Ltd.	10	36
6	Do. Cum. Pref.	10	16½
4½	Do. Db. Sk. Rd.	100	126
5½	Buckley's, L., C. Pre-prf.	10	11
4½	Do. 1 Mt. Db. Stk. Rd.	100	106½
4	Bullard & Sns, L., D. Sk. R.	100	107
6	Bushell, Watk., L., C. Pf.	10	13½
4½	Do. 1 Mt. Db. Sk. Rd.	100	112
5	Camden, Ltd., Cum. Pref.	10	11½
4½	Do. 1 Mt. Db. Sk. Rd.	100	109
5½	Cameron, Ltd., Cm. Pf.	10	13
4½	Do. Mort. Deb. Stk.	100	108
3½	Do. Perp Mt. Db. Sk.	100	98½
5	Cam'bell, J'stone, L., C. Pf.	5	5½
4½	Do. 4½ p.c. 1 Mt. Db. Sk.	100	104
4	Campbell, Praed, L., Per. 1 Mort. Deb. Stk.	100	106
4	Cannon, L., Mt. Db. Stk.	100	110
4	Do. "B" Deb. Stk.	100	104
5	Castlemaine, L., 1 Mt. Db.	100	94
3½	Charrington, Ltd., Mort. Deb. Stk. Red.	100	109
2/	Cheltnhm. Orig., Ltd.	5	7
6	Do. Cum. Pref.	5	8
4	Do. Debs. Red.	100	107
10	Chicago, Ltd.	10	4
6	Do. Debs.	100	87½
—	Cincinnati, Ltd.	10	½
8	Do. Cum. Pref.	10	1½
17/	City of Baltimore	10	4
16/	Do. 8 p.c. Cum. Pref	10	8
14/	City of Chicago, Ltd.	10	1½
8	Do. Cum. Pref.	10	6½
8	City of London, Ltd.	100	195½
5	Do. Cum. Pref.	100	140
4	Do. Mt. Deb. Stk., Rd.	100	113½
2.6	Colchester, Ltd.	5	4½
7	Do. Pref.	5	6½
4½	Do. Deb. Stk., Red.	100	109
5	Combe, Ltd., Cum. Pref.	10	14½
4	Do. Mt. Db. Stk, Rd.	100	111
3½	Do. Perp. Deb. Stk.	100	107
5	Comm'cial, L., D. Sk., Rd.	100	107½
5	Courage, L., Cm. Pref. Shs.	100	139½
4	Do. Irr. Mt. Deb. Stk.	100	130
3½	Do. Irr. "B" Mt. Db. Sk.	100	105
6	Daniell & Sons, Ltd.	10	7
7	Do. Cum. Pref.	10	12½
4½	Do. 1 Mt. Perp. Db. Sk.	100	105½
4½	Do. "B" Deb. Stk.	100	98½
5	Dartford, Ltd.	5	5½
5	Do. Cum. Pref.	5	5½
4	Do. 1 Mt. Db. Sk. Rd.	100	101
4	Davenport, Ld., 1 D. Stk.†	100	101½
10/	Denver United, Ltd.	10	3½
8	Do. Cum. Pref.	10	8½
6	Do. Debs.	100	96½
4½	Deuchar, L., 1 D. Sk., Rd.	100	108
17/	Distillers, Ltd.	10	33½
4½	Do. Mt. Db. Stk., Rd.	100	115½
—	Dublin Distillers, Ltd.	5	1½
6/	Do. Cum. Pref.	5	4½
4½	Do. Irr. Deb. Stk.	100	—
5	Eadie, Ltd., Cum. Pref.	10	11½
4	Do. Irr. 1 Mt. Db. Sk.	100	108
10/	Edinbgh. Utd., Ltd.	10	13½
6	Do. Cum. Prf.	10	13½
5	Do. 1 Mt. Dbs.†	100	110½
4	Eldridge, Pope, L. D. Sk. R.	100	110½
3/	Emerald & Phœnix, Ltd.	10	1½
8	Do. Cum. Pref.	10	6
6	Empress Ltd., C. Pf.	10	11½
4½	Do. Mt. Deb. Stk.	100	101
10/	Farnham, Ltd.	10	16
6	Do. Cum. Pref.	10	15
4	Fenwick, L., 1 D. Sk., Rd.	100	105
4	Flower & Sons, Irr. D. Sk.	100	113
4	Friary, L., 1 Db. Stk., Rd.†	100	105½
4	Do. 1 "A" Db. Sk., Rd.	100	109
4½	Groves, L., 1 Db. Sk., Rd.	100	110
24	Guinness, Ltd.	100	580
6	Do. Cum. Prf. Stk.	100	182½
5	Do. Deb. Stk., Red.	100	123
6	Hall's Oxford L., Cm. Pf.	5	5½
7/	Hancock, Ld., Cm. Pf. Ord.	10	14
	Do. Def. Ord.	10	17½

Breweries, &c. (*continued*):—

Div.	Name.	Paid.	Price.
6	Hancock, Ld., Cum. Pref.	10	15½
4	Do. 1 Deb. Stk., Rd.	100	113
5	Hoare, Ltd. Cum. Pref.	10	13½
5	Do. "A" Cum. Pref.	10	12½
4	Do. Mt. Deb. Stk., Rd.	100	110
3½	Do. do. do. Rd.	100	104
4/6]	Hodgson's, Ltd.	5	9½
5	Do. 1 Mt. Db., Red.	—	120½
4	Do. 2 Mt. Db., 1906	—	102
4½	Hopcraft & N., Ltd., 1 Mt. Deb. Stk., Red.	100	102
5	Huggins, Ltd., Cm. Prf.	10	12¼
4½	Do. 1st D. Stk. Rd.	100	112
4½	Do. "B" Db. Stk. Rd.	100	110
8/	Hull, Ltd.	10	17
7	Do. Cum. Pref.	10	15
4½	Ind, Coope, L., D.Sk., Rd.	100	119
4	Do. "B" Mt. Db. Stk. Rd.	100	115
8	Indianapolis, Ltd.	10	3½
8	Do. Cm. Prf.	10	9
5/	Jones, Frank, Ltd.	10	4
7½	Do. Cum. Pref.	10	8
5	Do. 1st Mort. Debs.	100	95½
4/	J. Kenward & Ct., Ltd.	5	5½
4½	Kingsbury, L., 1 D.Sk., Rd	100	107½
4	Lacon, L., D. Stk., Red.	100	108
4	Do. Irrd. "B" D. Sk.	100†	107
4	Lascelles, Ltd.	5	10½
6	Do. Cum. Pref.	5	7½
5	Leney, Ltd., Cum. Pref.	10	11½
4	Do. 1 Mt. Db. Stk. Rd.	100	103
17	Lion, Ltd., £25 shares	17	49½
6	Do. New £10 shares	6	17
6	Do. Perp. Pref.	20	31
4	Do. B. Mt. Db. Sk. Rd.	100	109
4½	Lloyd & Y., Ltd., 1 Mt. Deb. Stk., Rd.	100	98½
4½	Locke & S., Ltd., Irr. 1st Mt. Deb. Stk.	100	100
4½	Lovibond, Ltd., 1st Mt. Deb. Stk., Rd.	100	100
8/	Manchester, Ltd.	10	16
7	Do. Cum. Pref.	10	16½
5	Marston, J., L., Cm. Prf.	10	10½
4	Do. 1 Mt. Db. Sk., Rd.	100†	101½
9/	Massey's Burnley, Ltd.	10	16
6	Do. Cum. Pref.	10	14½
4½	McCracken, Ltd., 1 Mt. Deb., 1908	100	64
5	McEwan, Ltd., Cm. Pref.	10	15½
5	Meux, Ltd., Cum. Pref.	10	14½
4	Do. Mt. Db. Stk. Red.	100	113
4½	Michell & A., Ltd., 1 Mt. Deb. Stk. Red.	100	105
4½	MileEndDist. Db. Sk. Rd.	100	108
14/	Milwaukee & Chic., Ltd.	10	1½
4/	Do. Cum. Pref.	10	6½
4½	Michell, Toms, L., Db.	50	55
6	Morgan, Ltd., Cum. Pref.	10	14½
10/	Nalder & Coll., Ltd.	10	31
6	Do. Cum. Pref.	10	16
4½	Do. Deb. Red.	100	113
4/	New Beeston, Ltd.	5	4
2/9	Do. Cum. Pref.	5	4½
4	Do. Mt. Deb. Stk. Red.	100	96½
12/	Newcastle, Ltd.	10	19½
6	Do. Cum. Pref.	10	14½
5	Do. 1 Mt. Deb., 1911	100	110½
4	Do. "A" Deb. Stk. Red.	100	106
6/	New England, Ltd.	10	5
8	Do. Cum. Pref.	10	9½
6	Do. Debs. Red.	100	102½
4	New London, L., 1 D.Sk.	100	103
2/4½	New Westminster, Ltd.	4	10
6	Do. Pref.	4	6½
5	New York, Ltd.	10	1
18/	Do. 8 p.c. Cum. Pref.	10	3½
6	Do. 1 Mt. Deb. Red.	100	83½
5	Noakes, Ld., Cum. Pref.	10	12
4	Do. 1 Mt. Db. Stk., Rd.	100	106
4½	Norfolk, L., "A" D.Sk. Rd.	100	106
10/	Northampton, Ld.	10	16½
7	Do. Cum. Pref.	10	15½
6	Do. Cum. Pref.	10	13
5	Do. 1 Mt. Per. Db. Sk.	100	127
4	Nth. East., L., 1 D.Sk. Rd.	100	101
4½	N. Worcesters., L. Per. 1 Mort. Deb. Stock	100	93½
6	Nottingham, L., Cm. Prf.	10	11
5	Do. 1 Mt. Deb. Stk., Red.	100	115
17/4	Do. "B" do. Red.	50	111½
6/	Ohlsson' Cape, Ld.	5	16
7	Do. Cum. Pref.	5	8½
4½	Do. 2nd Cum. Pref.	5	5½
5	Do. Deb. Stk., Red.	100	112
4½	Oldfield, L., 1 Mt. Db. Stk.	100	102
6	Page & Overt., L., Cm. Prf.	10	13½
4½	Do. 1 Mt. Dbs., Red.	100	110
15/	Parker's Burslem, Ltd.	10	25½
6	Do. Cum. Pref.	10	15½
4	Do. 1 Mt. Db. Stk., Red.	100	111
4	Persse, Ld., 1 Mt. Db. Rd.	100	93
4	Phipps, L., Irr. 1 Db. Stk.	100	115
5	Plymouth, L., Min. Cu. Pf.	10	13½
4½	Do. Mt. Deb. Stk., Red.	100	104½
4½	Pryor, Reid, L., 1 D.S., R.	100†	105½
5	Reid's, Ld., Cm. Pref. Stk.	100	140½
4	Do. Mt. Deb. Stk., Red.	100	113
3½	Do. "B" Mt. Db. Stk., Rd.	100	103
5	Rhondda Val., L., Cu. Pf.	10	11
4½	Do. 1 Mt. Deb. Stk., Rd.	100	109
5	Robinson, Ld., Cum. Pref.	10	11½
4½	Do. 1 Mt. Perp. Db. Stk.	100	112
4/	Rochdale, Ltd.	10	5½
4½	Do. 1 Mt. Deb. Stk.	100	96½
11/	Royal, Brentford, Ltd.	10	19½
6	Do. Cum. Pref.	10	14
4½	Do. 1 Mt. Dbs. Red	100	112
6/	St. Louis, Ltd.	10	4
8	Do. Cum. Pref.	10	8½
14/	St. Pauli, Ltd.	10	10
7	Do. Cum. Pref.	10	11½
4½	Salt (T.), L., 1 Db. Sk. Rd.	100	110
4½	Do "B" Db. Stk. Red.	100	108

Breweries, &c. (*continued*):—

Div.	Name.	Paid.	Price.
6/7	San Francisco, Ltd.	10	½
8/	Do. 8 p.c. Cum. Pref.	10	½
4½	Savill Brs., L., D. Sk. Rd.	100	115
4½	Scarboro., Ltd., 1 Db. Stk.	100	105
4	Shaw (Hy.), Ltd., 1 Mt. Db. Stk., Red.	100	104
22/	Showell's, Ltd.	10	32½
7	Do. Cum. Pref.	10	17½
3/	Do. Gua. Shs.	5	7½
4½	Do. Mt. Db. Stk., Red.	100	--
4	Simonds, L., 1 D.Sk., Rd.	100	111
5½	Simson & McP., L., Cu. Pf.	10	9½
4½	Do. 1 Mt. Deb. Stk.	100	100
12/	Smith, Garrett, L., £20 Shs	10	15½
5	Do. Cum. Pref.	20	26
4½	Do. Mt. Db. Stk., Red.	100	—
5	Smith's, Tadcster, L., CPf	10	11½
4½	Do. Deb. Stk., Red.	100	112
4	Do. Deb. Stk., Red.	100	108
4½	Star, L., 1 M. Db. Stk., Rd.	100	104
4	Steward & P., L., 1 D. Sk.	100	113
9/	Strettons Derby, Ltd.	10	13
6	Do. Cum. Pref.	10	13
4	Do. Irr. 1 Mt. Db. Stk.	100	101½
4½	Strong, Romsey, L., 1 D.S.	100	113
5	Stroud, L., Db. Sk., Rd.	100	111½
4½	Tadcaster To'er, L., D.Sk.	100	113
8/	Tamplin, Ltd.	10	22
6	Do. Cum. Pref.	100	15
4	Do. "A" Db. Sk., Rd.	10	107
6	Thorne, Ltd., Cum. Pref.	10	14½
4	Do. Deb. Stk., Red.	100	103½
16/	Threlfall, Ltd.	10	49
6	Do. Cum. Pref.	10	17
5	Do. 1 Mt. Dbs., Red.	100	116
4	Tollemache, L., D. Sk. Rd.	100	105
4	Truman, Hanb., D. Sk., R.	100	110
3	Do. "B" Mt. Db. Sk., Rd.	100	94
10/	United States, Ltd.	10	10½
8	Do. Cum. Pref.	10	12½
6	Do. 1 Mt. Deb.	100	107½
2/2½	Walker & H., Ld., Cm. Prf.	10	11½
4½	Do. 1 Mt. Deb. Stk., Red.	100	107
5	Walker, Peter, Ld. Cm. Prf.	10	13½
4	Do. 1 Mt. Dbs. Red.	100	110
4	Wallingford, L., D.Sk. Rd.	100	107
6	Watney, Ld., Cm. Prf. Sk.	100	170
5	Do. Mt. Db. Sk., Rd.	100	117½
4½	Do. "B" Mt. Db. Sk., Rd.	100	111
5	Watney, D., Ld., Cm. Prf.	10	12½
4½	Do. 1 Mt. Db. Stk.	100	107
5	Wenlock Ltd., Pref.	10	12½
4	Do. 1 Mt. Db. Sk., Rd.	100	108
5	West Cheshire, L., Cu. Pf.	10	10½
4	Do. Irred. 1 Mt. Db. Sk.	100	100
4½	Whitbread, L., Cu. Pf. Sh.	100	125½
4	Do. Db. Stk., Red.	100	112
3½	Do. "B" Db. Stk., Rd.	100	103
9/	Wolverhmpton & D. Ld.	10	15
6	Do. Cum. Pref.	10	13
4½	Do. 1 Mt. Dbs., Red.	100	108
5½	Worthington, Ld., Cm. Prf.	10	15½
5½	Do. Cum. "B" Pref.	10	13½
4½	Do. Mt. Db. Sk., Rd.	100	113
3½	Do. Irr. "B" Db. Stk.	100	103
10/	Yates's Castle, Ltd.	10	12½
5	Do. Cum. Pref.	10	11
5	Younger W., L., Cu. Pf. Sh.	100	138½

CANALS AND DOCKS.

Last Div.	Name.	Paid.	Price.
4½	Alexandra Con. Stk. "B"	100	112½
4½	Do. 1 Prf Con. Stk. "A"	100	128½
4	Do. Perp. Deb. Stk.	100	132½
4	Birmingham Canal	100	146
—	E. & W. India Dock	100	23½
4	Do. Deb. Stk.	100	109
85/	Do. Def. Deb. Stk.	100	91
3½	Do. 1st Mt. Certs.	100	109
4	Do. Mt. Bds. (1885)	—	101
40/	G. Junction Ord. Shs.	100	151½
6/	Do. do. Pref.	10	19
4½	King's Lynn Per. Db. Stk.	100	120½
2½	Leeds & L'pool Canal	100	67
2½	Lndn & St. Kath. Dks.	100	58½
4½	Do. Pref.	100	138½
4½	Do. Pref., 1878	100	134½
4½	Do. Pref., 1882	100	130
4	Do. Deb. Stk.	100	134
—	Mchester Ship C. 5 p.c. Pf.	10	1½
3½	Do. 1st Perp. Mt. Deb.	100	98
—	Milford Dks. Db. Stk. "A"	100	20
2	Millwall Dk.	100	61
5	Do. Perp. Pref.	100	145½
4½	Do. Pref.	100	108½
5	Do. New Per. Prf., 1887	100	128½
5	Do. Per. Deb. Stk.	100	152½
4/	Newhaven Har.	10	14½
2	N. Metropolitan	100	65
5	Sharpness Nw. Pf. "A" Sk.	100	144½
4	Do. Deb. Stk.	100	120½
4	Sheffield & S. Yorks Nav. 4½ p.c. Pref. Stk.	100	117½
36.432	Suez Canal	20	132½
5	Surrey Comcl. Dok., Ord.	100	149½
5	Do. Min. 4 p.c. Pref. "A"	110	152½
5	Do. Pref. "B"	100	150½
5	Do. do. "C"	100	150
5	Do. do. "D"	100	145½
4½	Do. Deb. Stk.	100	154½

COMMERCIAL, INDUSTRIAL, &c.

Last Div.	Name.	Paid.	Price.
5	Accles, L., 1 Mt. Db., Red.	100	87½
5/	Aërated Bread, Ltd.	1	12½
—	African Gold Recovery, L.	1	½
2/	Aluminium, L., "A" Shs.	1	2½
4½	Do. 1 Mt. Db. Stk., Red.	100	99
5½	Amelia Nitr., L., 1 Mort. Deb., Red.	100	34½†
7	Anglo-Chil. Nitrate, Ltd., Cum. Pref.	10	7
4½	Do. Cons. Mt. Bds., Red.	100	78½
4½	Anglo-Russian Cotton, Ld., 1 Charge Debs., Red.	100	98†
3/9	Angus (G., & Co., L.), £10	7½	17
6/	Apollinaris, Ltd.	10	13½
5/	Do. 5 p.c. Cum. Pref.	10	11½
4	Do. Irred. Deb. Stock	100	107
5/	Appleton, French, & S., L.	5	1
3/	Argentine Meat Pres., L., 7 p.c. Pref.	10	2½
5	Argentine Refinry, Db. Rd.	100	97
2/2	Armstrong, Whitw., Ltd.	1	3
4	Do. Cum. Pref.	5	6½
5	Artisans', Labr. Dwllgs., L.	100	127½
4½	Do. Non-Cm. Prf., 1879	100†	132½
4½	Do. do. 1884	100†	131½
—	Asbestos & Asbestic, Ltd.	10	9
5½	Ashley-grdns., L., C. Prf.	5	6½
4½	Do. 1 Mt. Deb. Stk.	100	115½
5/	Assam Rly. & Trdng., L., 8 p.c. Cum. Pref. "A"	10	15
—	Do. Deferrd. "B" Shs.	1	4½
—	Do. do. (iss. f. pd)	1	3½
8	Do. Cum. Pre-Prf. "A"	10	15
6	Do. New Pref.	10	11½
5	Do. Debs., Red.	100	107†
5	Do. Red. Mort. Debs.	100	109
6	Aust'lian Pastrl, L., Cu. Pf.	10	7½†
6d.	Aylesbury Dairy, Ltd.	1	1½
4	Do. 4 p.c. Mt. Dbs.	100†	104½
20/	Babcock & Wilcox, Ltd.	10	31
6	Do. 6 p.c. Cm. Prf.	10	17
8	Baker (Chs.), L., Cm. Pf.	5	8½
8	Do. "B" Cm. Pref.	5	7½
8d.	Barker (John), Ltd.	1	3
5½	Do. Cum. Pref.	5	7½
4½	Do. Irred. 1 Mt. Db. Stk.	100	133
2/6	Barnagore Jute, Ltd.	5	3½
5	Do. Cum. Pref.	5	4½
7½d.	Belgravia Dairy, Ltd.	1	1½
5/	Bell (R.) & Co., Ltd.	5	3½
1/	Bell's Asbestos, Ltd.	1	½
5	Do. Mt. Db. Bds., Rd.	100	103†
10/	Bengal Mills, Ltd.	10	11½
6/	Do. 5 p.c. Cum. Prf.	10	10½†
5	Benson (J.W.) L., Cm. Pf.	10	10½
4	Do. Perp. Mt. Db. Stk.	100	103½
6	Bergvik, L., 6 p.c. Cm. Pf.	10	12½
10/	Do. Dfd.	10	9
4½	Do. 1 Dbs., Red.	100	102½
5/	Birm'ham Vinegar, Ltd.	5	8½
5	Do. Cum. Pref.	5	5½
4½	Do. 1 Mt. Db. Stk., Rd.	100	105†
5/4	Boake (A.) L., 5 p.c. Cu. Pf.	10	10½†
2/6	Bodega, Ltd.	5	8†
4½	Do. Mt. Deb. Stk., Rd.	100	111†
8/	Bottomley & Brs., Ltd.	10	6½
6/	Do. 6 p.c. Pt.	10	9½
8½d.	Bovril, Ltd.	1	1½
—	Do. Def.	1	½
6½d.	Do. Cum. Pref.	1	1½
4½	Do. Deb. Stk.	100	103
6/4½	Bradbury, Gretrex., Ltd., £10 share	8	14
5/	Do. 5 p.c. Cum. Pref.	10	13½
5/	Brewers' Sugar, L., 5 p.c. Cum. Pref.	10	10½
2/6	BrightonGrd. Hotel, Ld.	5	3½
4	Do. Mt. Db. Stk., Red.	100	102½
5	Bristol Hotel & Palm. Co., Ltd. 1st Mt. Red. Deb.	100	107
9½d.	British & Bengton's. Tea Tr. Asc., Ltd.	1	1½
5	Do. Cum. Prf.	5	5½
—	British Deli & Lgkat. Tobacco, Ltd.	1	½
7	Do. Cum. Prf.	1	½
—	British Tea Table, Ltd.	1	2½
5½	Do. Cum. Pref.	1	1½
2/6	Brooke, Ben., & Co., Ltd., Cum. Pref.	5	5½†
7/6	Brooke, Bond & Co., Ltd.	5	20½†
6	Brown Brs., L., Cum. Pref.	5	6
6/	Browne & Eagle, Ltd.	10	14
5/	Do. Cum. Pref.	10	13†
4	Do. Mrt. Db. Sk., Red.	100	109†
20/	Brunner, Mond, & Co., Lt.	10	41
7/	Do. £10 shares	3½	16½
7	Do. Cum. Pref.	10	18
7	Do. £10 shares	5	8½
7/6	Bryant & May, Ltd.	5	20
2/	Bucknall, H., & Sons, Lt.	5	8
6	Do. Cum Pref.	5	8
4/	Burke, E. & J., Ltd.	5	7½
6	Do. Cum. Pref.	5	7½
6	Do. Irred. Deb. Stk.	100	155
1/	Burlington Htls. Co., Ltd	1	1½
5	Do. Cum. Pref.	1	1½†
4	Do. Perp. Deb. Stk.	100	104
5	Bush, W. J., & Co., Ltd., Cum. Pref.	5	5½
4	Do. 1 Deb. Stk., Red.	100	103
5½	Callard, Stewart, & Watt, Ltd., Cum. Pref.	1	1½
4/	Callender's Cable L., Shs.	5	8
4½	Do. 1 Deb. Stk., Red.	100†	100½
2/6	Campbell, R., & Sons, Lt.	3	1½
6	Cantareira Water, Bd., Rd	100	90½
5	Do. (2nd issue)	100	92
4	Cartavio Sugar, Ltd., 6 p.c. 1st Debs., Red.	90	78
4/6	Cassell & Co., Ltd., £10	9	18
5	Causton, Sir J., & Sons, Ltd., Cum. Pref.	10	13½

Commercial, &c. (*continued*):—

Last Div.	Name.	Paid.	Price.
4	Cent. Prod. Mkt. of B.A. 1st Mt. Str. Debs.	100	71½
4	Chappell & Co., Ltd., Mt. Deb. Stk. Red.	100	103
8	Chicago & N.W. Gran. Cum. Pref.	10	2½
8/	Chicago Packing & Prov.	10	6
8	Do. Cum. Pref.	10	9
6/	City Offices, Ltd.	36½	15
3½	Do. Mt. Deb. Stk.	100	108½
9/7½	Cy. London Real Prop., Ltd., £25 shs.	12	19
7/6	Do. £12½ shs.	7½	13½
3½	Do. Deb. Stk. Red.	100	108½
3½	Do. Deb. Stk. Red.	100	106½
3	Do.	100	101½
4/	Cy. of Santos Imprvts., Ltd., 7 p.c. Pref.	10	8½
20/	Clay, Bock, & Co., Ltd.	10	8
8	Do. Cum. Pref.	10	15
6	Do. Mort. Deb.	100†	106½
20/	Coats, J. & P., Ltd.	10	63
6	Do. Cum. Pref.	10	19
4½	Do. Deb. Stk. Red.	100†	111½
9½d.	Coburg Hotel, Ltd.	1	1½
4	Do. Deb. Stk. Red.	100	102†
6	Colonial Consign & Dis., Ltd., Cum. Pref.	5	4½
4½	Do. 1st Mort. Debs.	100	97½
2/6	Colorado Nitrate, Ltd.	5	½
4/	Co. Gén. des Asphtes. de F., Ltd.	6	6½
5	Do. Non-Cm. Prf.	—	5½
5	Cook, J. W., & Co., Ltd., Cum. Pref.	5	5½
5	Cook, T., & Son, Egypt, Ltd., 1st Mt. Deb. Red.	100	110½
3/	Cork Co., Ltd., 6 p.c. Cum. Pref.	5	2
5	Cory, W., & Sn, L., Cu. Pf.	5	6½
4	Do. 1st Deb. Stk. Red.	100	109
8½d.	Crisp & Co., Ltd	1	1½
5	Do. Cum. Pref.	1	1½†
3/	Crompton & Co., Ltd., 7 p.c. Cum. Pref.	5	2½
5	Do. 1st Mt. Reg. Deb.	—	88½
4/6	Crossley, J., & Sons, Ltd.	5	8½
5	Do. Cum. Pref.	5	6
3	Crystal Pal. Ord. "A" Stk.	100	9½
—	Do. "B" Red. Stk	100	2
6	Do. 6 p.c. 1st 1887 Deb. Stk. Red.	100†	115½
20/	Do. 6 p.c. 2nd 1887 Deb. Stk. Red.	100	41½
—	Do. 6 p.c. 3rd 1887 Deb. Stk. Red.	100	15½
3	Do. 3 p.c. 1st 1895 Deb. Stk.	100	90½†
—	Daimler Motor, Ltd.	10	5
4/	Dalgety & Co., £20 Shs.	5	5
4½	Do. Deb. Stk.	100	121†
4	Do.	100	112
3/10	De Keyser's Ryl. Htl., L.	10	12½
5	Do. Cum. Pref.	10	11½†
4	Do. Deb. Stk., Red.	100	109†
6	Denny, H., & Sons, Ltd., Cum. Pref.	10	15†
5/3	Devas, Routledge & Co., L.	7	8½
5	Dickinson, J., & Co., L., Cum. Pref. Stk.	100	125
4½	Domin. Cottn. Mls., Ltd. Mt. Stg. Dbs.	100	92†
4/	Dorman, Long & Co., L.	5	4½
10/	Eastmans, Ltd	10	2½
8	Do. Cum. Pref.	10	10½
2/6	E. C. Powder, Ltd	3	6
1/9½	Edison & Swn Utd. Elec. Ltd., "A" £5 Shs.	3	2½
2/9½	Do. fully-paid	5	5
4½	Ekman Pulp & Ppr. Co., Ltd., Mt. Deb., Red.	100	95
1/1½	Electric Construc., Ltd.	2	2½
7	Do. Cum. Pref.	2	3½
10/	Eley Bros., Ltd.	10	39
10/	Elmore's Cop. Deptg., L.	1	[illegible]
—	Elmore's Wire Mnfg., L.	2	½
—	Elysée Pal. Hotel Co., L.	5/	½
8/9	Do. 5 p.c. £100 Db., Rd.	70	70†
8½d.	Evans, Ben., & Co., Ltd.	1	1
5	Do. 1 Mt. Db. Sk., Rd.	100	104†
8½d.	Evans., D. H., & Co., L.	1	2½
6	Do. Cum. Pref.	1	1½
4½	Do. 1 Mt. Db. Sk., Rd.	100	110†
2/1	*Evening News*, L., 5 p.c. Cum. Pref.	5	5½
5/3	Evered & Co., L., £10 Sh.	7	13½
7/6	Do.	10	19½
4	Fairbairn Pastoral Co., Aust., L., 1 Mt. Db., Rd.	100†	102½
6	Fairfield Shipbldg., Ltd., Cum. Pref.	10	19½
4½	Do. Mort. Deb. Stk.	100	109½
—	Farmer & Co., Ld., 6 p.c. Cum. Pref.	10	13½
10	Field, J. C. & J., Ltd.	10	10
14/	Do. 7 p.c. Cum. Pref.	10	14
9d.	Fordham, W.B., & Sns. Ld.	1	2
5/6	Fore-st. Warehouse, Ltd.	11	10
4	Do. Regd. Debs., Rd.	100†	102
2/6	Foster, M. B. & Sons, Ltd.	4	5½
5	Do. Pref.	10	10½
7/	Foster, Porter, & Co., L.	10½	17
4	Fowler, J., & Co. (Leeds) Ltd., 1 Mt. Deb., Red.	100†	100½
1/	Fraser & Chalmers, Ltd.	3	1½
4½	Free, Rodwell & Co., Ltd. Deb Stk.	100	102½
6½d.	Furness, T., & Co., Ltd., 5½ p.c. Cum. Pref.	1	1†
4½	Gartside & Co. (of Manchstr), L., 1 Mt. Db. Sk.	100	110
5	Genl. Hydraul. Power, L.	100	260†

Commercial, &c. (*continued*):—

Last Div.	Name.	Paid.	Price.
2/	Gillman & Spencer, Ltd.	5	2¼
6	Do. Pref.	5	4¼
5	Do. Mort. Debs.	50	50
4	Goldsbro., Mort & Co., L., "A" Deb. Stk., Red.	100	72½
—	Do. 3 p.c. "B" Inc. Deb. Stk., Red.	100	17
12/	Gordon Hotels, Ltd.	10	20½
5½	Do. Cum. Pref.	10	14¾
4½	Do. Perp. Deb. Stk.	100	136½
4	Do. do.	100	123½
—	Greenwich Inld. Linoleum Co., Ltd.	1	⅜
7	Greenwood & Batley, Ltd., Cum. Pref.	10	10
7½d.	Hagemann & Co., Ltd., 6 p.c. Cum. Pref.	1	1⅛
—	Hammond, Ltd.	10	[illegible]
6/8	Do. 8 p.c. Cum. Pref.	10	2
6	Do. 6 p.c. Cum. Inc. Stk. Red.	100	52½
4	Hampton & Sons, Ltd., 4 p.c. 1 Mt. Db. St. Red.	100	104
	Hans Crescent Htl., L., 6 p.c. Cum. Pref.	5	3½
4	Do. 1 Mt. Deb. Stk.	100	85
5	Harmsworth, Ld., Cm. Pf.	1	1⅛
4/	Harrison, Barber, Ltd.	5	4½
1/	Harrod's Stores, Ltd.	1	5
2/6	Do. Cum. Pref.	5	7½
5½	Hawaiian Comcl. & Sug. 1 Mt. Debs.	100	94½
5	Hazell, Watson, Ld., Cm. Pref.	10	12
6/	Henley's Teleg., Ltd.	10	21
7	Do. Pref. Shs.	10	19
4½	Do. Mt. Db. Stk., Rd.	100	112½
6	Henry, Ltd.	10	12½
5	Do. Cum. Pref.	10	13¼
4½	Do. Mt. Debs., Red.	50	53
6	Hepworth, Ld., Cm. Prf.	10	11½
5/	Herrmann, Ltd.	5	4½
—	Hildesheimer, Ltd.	3	1
9½d.	Holbrn. & Frasca, Ltd.	1	2
5	Do. Cum. Pref.	10	11½
4	Do. Deb. Stk.	100	113
6	Home & Col. Stres, Ltd., Cum. Pref.	5	7½
6	Hood & M.'s Stres., Ltd., Cum. Pref.	1	¾
5/	Hook, C. T., Ltd.	10	4
7/2	Hornsby, Ltd., £10 Shs.	8	2¾
3/6	Do. 6 p.c. Cm. Pf. Sk.	100	90
14/	Hotchks. Ordn., Ltd.	10	¾
7/	Do. 7 p.c. Cm. Prf.	10	4¾
5	Do. 1 Mt. Dbs., Rd.	100	97½
6	Htl. Cecil, Ld., Cm. Prf.	5	4½
4	Do. 1 Mt. D. Sk., R.	100	105½
8/	Howard & Bulgh, Ltd.	10	36
6	Do. Pref.	10	16
4	Do. Deb. Stk., Red.	100	107
4/	Howell, J., Ltd., £5 Shs.	4	9½
1/	Howell & Js., Ld., £3½ Shs.	3	1
1/6	Humber, Ltd.	1	¾
6	Do. Cum. Pref.	1	1½
2/6	Hunter, Wilts., Ltd.	5	7
2/7	Hyam Clthg., Ltd., 5 p.c. Cum. Pref.	5	5½
10/	Impl. Russn. Cotton, L.	5	6½
5	Impd. Industl. Dwgs., Ld.	100	130½
6d.	Do. Defrd.	1	1½
£1	Impd. Wood Pave., Ltd.	10	16
5/	Ind. Rubber, Gutta Per. Telegraph Works, Ltd.	10	24
4	Do. 1 Mt. Debs., Red.	100	106
6	Intern. Tea, Cum. Pref.	5	6½
7½d.	Jays, Ltd.	1	1½
5½	Do. Cum. Pref.	5	6½
8½d.	Jones & Higgins, Ltd.	1	2½
4½	Do. 1 Mt. Db. Sk., Rd.	100	113
5/	Kelly's Directory, Ltd., 5 p.c. Cum. Pref.	10	12½
—	Do. Mort. Db. Sk., Rd.	100	106
—	Kent Coal Explrtn. Ltd.	1	¼
1½d.	King, Howmann, Ltd.	1	1¼
4/	Kinloch & Co., Ltd.	5	8½
6	Do. Pref.	5	7
5	Lady's Pictorial Pub., Ltd., Cum. Pref.	5	5
—	La Guaira Harb., Ltd., 7 p.c. Deb. Stk.	100	—
—	Do. 2 Mt. 7 p.c. Deb. Bds., Red.	100	—
4/	Lagunas Nitrate, Ltd.	5	2½
2/	Lagunas Syn., Ltd.	5	1½
5	Do. 1 Mt. Debs., Red.	100	80
—	L. Copais Ld., 1 Mt. 6 p.c. Debs., Red.	100	35½
3/	Lautaro Nitrate, Ltd.	5	4
5	Do. 1 Mt. Debs., Red.	—	5½
9/	Lawes Chem. L., £10 shs.	9	5½
14/	Do. N. Cm. Min. Pref.	10	12½
3/6	Leeds Forge, 7 p.c. Cm. Pf.	5	3
5	Do. 1 Mt. Debs., Red.	50	44½
5	Lever Bros., L., Cm. Pf.	10	13
6	Liberty, L., 6 p.c. Cm. Pf.	10	14½
60/	Liebig's, Ltd.	20	76
5	Lilley & Sk., L., Cm. Pf.	5	5½
3/	Linoleum Manftg., Ltd.	5	19
3/	Linotype, Ltd., Pref.	5	6
4/	Do. Def.	5	8
4/	[illegible]ster & Co., Ltd.	10	5
16/	[illegible]. Cum. Pref.	10	8½
—	Pa[illegible]ool. Nitrate	5	6½
	p.[illegible]l. Warehsg., Ltd.	10	3½
—	Pirmu[illegible]im. Pref.	10	8½
5/	Pto. Ale[illegible] Db. Stk., Rd.	100	105½
	Ld., 7 p[illegible]d., Cm. Pf.	1	1½
6	Do. Mt. [illegible]htrage £10	9	8½
—	Puerto Cabel[illegible]le Rms.		
5	Recife & S. Fn.	10	18
14/	R. Claro S. Paulo, Red.	100	104
5	Do. De[illegible]	5	2
7/	Royal Sardinian Or[illegible]		

Commercial, &c. (*continued*):—

Last Div.	Name.	Paid.	Price.
4/	London Nitrate, Ld. 8 p.c. Cm. Min. Pf.	5	3½
3/	London Pavilion, Ltd.	5	7½
1/6	†London. Produce Clg. Ho., Ltd., £10 Shares	2½	3½
4/	London Stereos., Ltd.	5	3
6/	Ldn. Un. Laun. L. Cm. Pf.	1	
8½d.	Louise, Ltd.	1	¾
5½	Do. Cum. Pref.	1	¾
5/	Lovell & Christmas, Ltd.	5	12
6	Do. Cum. Pref.	5	7½
4	Do. Mt. Deb. Stk., Red.	100	107½
1/3	Lyons, Ltd.	1	3
4½	Do. 1 Mt. Deb., Stk., Rd.	100	105½
10/	Machinery Trust, Ltd.	5	15½
6	MacLellan, Ltd., Min. Cum. Pref.	10	7
5	Do. 1 Mt. Debs., 1900	100	98½
6/	McEwan, J. & Co., Ltd.	10	1½
6	Do. Mt. Debs., Red.	100	89½
8	McNamara, L., Cm. Pref.	10	9
7½d.	Maison Virot, Ltd.	1	1½
2/7	Do. 6 p.c. Cum. Pref.	5	4½
5/	Manbré Sacc., L., Cm. Pf.	10	12
15/	Mangan Brze., L., £10 Shs.	6	15½
2/	Mason & Mason, Ltd.	5	3½
6	Do. Cum. Pref.	5	6
—	Maynards, Ltd.	1	¾
6	Do. Cum. Pref.	1	¾
9½d.	Mazawattee Tea, Ltd.	1	1½
5	Do. Cum. Pref.	5	6½
6	Mellin's Food Cum. Pref.	5	7
4½	Met. Ascn. Imp. Dwlgs. L.	100	109
3½	Do. 1 Mt. Deb. Stk.	100	97
5	Metro. Indus. Dwlgs., Ltd.	5	5
4	Do. do. Cum. Pref.	5	5½
5	Metro. Prop., L., Cm. Pf.	5	6½
4½	Do. 1st Mt. Debs. Stk.	100	110½
6	Mexican Cotton 1 Mt. Db.	100	97½
4½	Mid. Class Dwlgs., L., Db.	100	120½
1/	Millars' Karri, Ltd.	1	2
6	Do. Cum. Pref.	1	1¾
15/	Milner's Safe, Ltd.	10	19
10/	Moir & Son, Ltd., Pref.	5	9
6	Morgan Cruc., L., Cm. Pf.	10	15
2/	Morris, B., Ltd.	3½	3½
—	Murray L. 5½ p.c. C. Pf.	5	
—	Do. 4½ 1 Mt. Db. Sk. Rd.	100	108
2/6	Natnl. Dwlgs., L., 5 p.c. Pf.	5	1
1/7½	Nat. Safe Dep., Ltd.	4	3½
6	Do. Cum. Pref.	1	1½
—	Native Guano, Ltd.	5	¾
5/	Nelson Bros., Ltd.	10	2½
5	Do. Deb. Stk., Red.	100	80½
4/	Neuchtel Asph., Ltd.	10	11
—	New Central Borneo, Ld.	1	⅛
—	New Darvel Tob., Ltd.	18/	⅜
2/4½	New Explosives, Ltd.	3	2
5/1½	New Gd. Htl., Bham, L.	5	4
5½	Do. Pref.	5	4½
4	Do. 1 Mt. Db. Stk., Rd.	100	98½
—	New Julia Nitrate, Ltd.	10/	⅛
2/	New Ldn. Borneo Tob., L.	16/	¾
1/6	New Premier Cycle, Ltd.	1	1¼
—	Do. 6 p.c. Cum. Pref.	1	¾
—	Do. 4½ p.c. 1 Mt. Db. Rd	100	—
1/	New Tamargl. Nitr., Ltd	1	⅛
1/2½	Do. 8 p.c. Cum. Pref.	1	⅝
6	Do. 6 p.c. 1 Mt. Dbs. Rd.	100	68
3/7⅜d.	Newnes, G., L., Cm. Prf.	1	1½
1/3	Nitr. Provision, Ltd.	2½	¾
24/	Nobel-Dynam., Ltd.	10	17¾
—	North Brazn. Sugar, Ltd.	1	
10/	Oakey, Ltd.	10	30
6	Do. Cum. Pref.	10	15½
4/	Paccha Jazp. Nitr., Ltd.	5	¾
5	Pac. Borax, L., 1 Db. Rd.	100	110
—	Palace Hotel, Ltd.	10	6
5½	Do. Cum. Pref.	10	8½
4	Do. 1 Mt. Deb. Stk.	100	104
2/6	Palmer, Ltd.	5	1½
6	Do. Cum. Pref.	5	3½
9⅒d.	Paquin, Ltd.	1	1
6	Do. Cum. Pref.	5	4½
5½	Parnall, Ltd., Cum. Pref.	1	¾
3/	Pawsons, Ltd., £10 Shs.	6	6½
4	Do. Mt. Debs., Red.	100	107
6	Pearks, G. & T., Ltd., 6 p.c. Cum. Pref.	1	¾
1/2½	Pears, Ltd.	1	1¾
6	Do. Cum. Pref.	10	14½
5	Do. Deb. Stk.	100	130
5½	Pearson, C. A., L., Cu. Pf.	5	5
4/	Peebles, Ltd.	5	7½
5	Do. Cum. Pref.	5	6½
4½	Do. Mt. Deb. Stk. Red.	100	112
5½	Peek Bros., Ltd., 1 Cum. Pref., Nos. 1-60,000	5	6½
3½	Do. 3½ p.c. 1 Db. Stk.	100	101
7½d.	Pegamoid, Ltd.	1	⅞
4/	Phospho-Guano, Ltd.	5	2½
4/	Pillsbury-W. Fl. Mills, L.	10	2
16/	Do. 8 p.c. Cum. Pref.	10	6½
6	Do. 1 Mort. Debs.	100	94½
7½d.	Plummer, Ltd.	1	1½
5	Do. Cum. Pref.	5	5½
15/	Price's Candle, Ltd.	16	40
6	Priest Marians, L., Cm. Pf.	1	1⅛
6	Pryce Jones, Ld., Cm. Pf.	5	7½
5	Do. Deb. Stk.	100	120½
10.8d.	Pullman, Ltd.	1	1½
6d.	Do. Cum. Pref.	1	1½
1/	Raleigh Cycle, Ltd.	1	⅞
6	Do. Cum. Pref.	1	¾
5	Recife Drnge. Ld. 1 Mt. Debs., R	100	19
6	Redfern, Ltd. Cum. Prf.	10	14
5	Ridgways, Ltd., Cu. Pf.	5	5½
3/	R. Janeiro Cy. Imps., Ld.	25	10
5	Do. Debs.	100	80
5	Do. 1882-1893	100	79½
11/	R. Jan Fl. Mills, Ltd.	7	7½
5	Do. 1 Mt. Debs., Rd.	100	94

Commercial, &c. (*continued*):—

Last Div.	Name.	Paid.	Price.
10/	Riv. Plate Meat, Ltd.	5	3½
10	Do. Pref.	5	5
8½d.	Roberts, J. R., Ltd.	1	1½
5	Do. 1 Mt. Db. Sk., Rd.	100	112
8½d.	Roberts, T. R., Ltd.	1	2¾
5	Do. Cum. Pref.	1	1¾
3/	Rosario Nit., Ltd.	5	3½
5	Do. Debs., Red.	100	103
5	Do. Hunra, Debs.	—	101½
1/	Rover Cycle, Ltd.	1	¾
6/	Ryl. Aquarium, Ltd.	5	4½
6	Do. Pref.	5	5½
5	Ryl. Htl., Edin., Cm. Pf.	1	1½
1/2½	Ryl. Niger, Ltd., £10 Sh.	2	2½
6/	Do.	10	14½
3/	Ruston, Proctor, Ltd.	10	11
4½	Do. 1 Mort. Debs.	100	104
6/	Sadler, Ltd.	12	7
—	Sal. Carmen Nit., Ltd.	5	4½
9d.	Salmon & Gluck., Ltd.	1	1½
2/	Salt Union, Ltd.	10	2
14/	Do. 7 p.c. Pref.	10	8½
4½	Do. Deb. Stk.	100	110
4½	Do. "B" Deb. Sk., Rd.	100	104½
2/6	San Donato Nit., Ltd.	5	¾
2/6	San Jorge Nit., Ltd.	5	3½
5/	San Pablo Nit., Ltd.	5	¾
2/	San Sebastn. Nit., Ltd.	5	¾
1/	Sanitas, Ltd	1	2½
5/	Sa. Elena Nit., Ltd.	5	¾
10/	Sa. Rita Nit., Ltd.	5	2
10/	Savoy Hotel, Ltd.	10	19
7	Do. Pref.	10	16
4	Do. 1 Mt. Deb. Stk.	100	112½
5	Do. Debs., Red	100	102½
5	Do. & Ldn. For. Htl., Ld., 5 p.c. Debs. Red.	100	99
1½d.	Schweppes, Ltd.	1	1½
—	Do. Def.	1	1½
5	Do. Cum. Pref.	1	1⅛
4	Do. Deb. Stk.	100	105
1/	Singer Cyc., Ltd.	1	⅞
5½	Do. Cum. Pref.	1	¾
—	Smokeless Pwdr., Ltd.	1	¾
5½d.	S. Eng. Dairies, Ltd., 6 p.c. Cum. Pref.	1	1½
—	Sowler Thos. L.	1	1
—	Do. 5½ Cm. Pf	5	6½
3/6	Spencer, Turner, & Co. Ltd	5	8½
5	Do. Cum. Pref.	5	6½
5	Spicer, Ld., 5 p.c. Dbs. Rd.	100	65
4/	Spiers & Pond, Ltd.	10	21
5	Do. 1 Mt. Debs., Red.	100	116½
5	Do. "A" Db. Stk., Rd.	100	110
5	Do. "B" 1 Db. Stk., Rd.	100	110
4	Do. Fd. "C" 1 Db. S., R.	100	105
5/	Spratt's, Ltd	5	13
4	Do. Debs., 1914	—	104
5	Steiner Ld., Cm. Pf.	10	11½
4	Do. 1 Mt. Db. Sk. Rd.	100	106
7/	Stewart & Clydesdale, L.	10	13
6	Do. Cum. Pref.	10	15
—	Swan & Edgar, L.	1	1½
1/3	Sweetmeat Automatic, L.	1	¾
2/9	Teetgen, Ltd., Cum. Pref.	5	5½
12/	Teleg. Construction., Ld.	12	37½
5	Do. Db. Bds., Rd., 1899	100	102½
3/0½	Tilling, Ld. 5½ p.c. Cm. Prf.	5	6
4	Do. 4 p.c. 1 Dbs., Rd.		103
8½d.	Tower Tea, Ltd.	1	1½
5	Do. Cum. Pref.	5	5½
5	Travers, Ltd., Cum. Pref.	10	12½
4	Do. 1 Mt. Dbs., Rd.	100	101½
6	Tucuman Sug., 1 Dbs., Rd.	100	100
4/	United Alkali, Ltd.	10	2½
7	Do. Cum. Pref.	10	9½
5	Do. Mt. Db. Stk., Rd.	100	109½
9½d.	United Horse Shoe, Ltd., Non-Cum. 8 p.c. Pref.	1	⅝
5	Un. Kingm. Tea, Cm. Prf.	5	4½
1/	Un. Lankat Plant., Ltd.	1	2½
2/	Un. Limmer Asphlte., Ld.	3	4½
5/	Val de Travers Asph., L.	10	14½
3/	V. den Bergh's, Ltd., Cm. Pref.	5	6½
6	Walkers, Park., L., C. Pf.	10	4
4½	Do. 1 Mt. Debs., Red.	100	90½
4/	Wallis, Thos. & Co., Ltd.	5	1½
6	Do. Cum. Pref.	5	5½
5½	Waring, Ltd., Cum. Pref.	5	5½
4½	Do. 1 Mt. Db. Sk., Red.	100	109½
4½	Do. Irred. "B" Db. Stk.	100	103
12/	Waterlow, Dfd. Ord.	10	15½
12/	Do. Pref.	10	15
3½	Do. Cum. Pref.	10	11
10/	Waterlow Bros. & L., Ld.	10	10½
9½d.	Welford, Ltd.	1	2
4½	Do. Debs., Red.	100	107
4½d.	Welford's Surrey Dairies, Ltd.	1	1½
7½d.	West London Dairy, Ltd.	1	1
4½	Wharncliffe Dwllgs., L., Pf.	10	11½
18/10	Do. 3 p.c. Irr. Mt. Db. Sk.	100	96
6d.	White, A. J., Ltd.	1	¾
6	Do. 6 p.c. Cum. Pref.	1	¾
4	White, J. Bazley, Ltd., 1 Mort. Debs., Red	100	94½
5	White, R., Ltd., 1 Mort. Deb. Stock, Red.	100	108½
5/	White, Tomkins, Ltd	10	12½
5	Do. Cum. Pref.	10	12
6	White, W. N., L., Cm. Pf.	1	1
2/6	Wickens, Pease & Co., L.	5	2
6	Wilkie, Ltd., Cum. Pref.	10	16
3/6	Willans & Robinson, Ltd.	5	8
6	Do. Cum. Pref.	5	7
4½	Do. 1 Mt. Db. Stk., Red.	100	106
7½d.	Williamsons, L., Cm. Prf.	1	1½
6	Winterbottm Black Cloth, Ltd., Cum. Prf.	10	15
3/	Yates, Ltd.	5	6½
6	Do. Cum. Pref.	5	6½
	Young's Paraffin, Ltd.	4	1½

CORPORATION STOCKS—COLONIAL AND FOREIGN.

Per Cent.	Name.	Paid.	Price.
6	Auckland City, '72 1904-24	100	118
6	Do. Cons., '79, Red. 1930	100	138½
5	Do. Deb. Ln., '83..1934-8	100	116
6	Auckland Harb. Debs.	100	111½
5	Do. 1917	100	111
5	Do. 1936	100	116
5½	Balmain Boro' 1914	—	17
5	Boston City (U.S.)	100	109½
5	Do. 1902	100	104½
5	Brunswick Town 5 c. Debs. 1916-20	100	111
15/	B. Ayres City 6 p.c.	100	54
4½	Do. 4½ p.c.	100	76
5	Cape Town, City of	100	113
4	Do. 1943	100	113
4	Chicago, City of, Gold 1915	—	110
6	Christchurch 1926	100	128½
6	Cordoba City	100	117
5	Duluth (U.S.) Gold 1926	—	110
6	Dunedin (Otago) 1925	100	124
6	Do. 1926	100	113
5	Do. Consols 1908	100	113
4	Durban Insc. Stk. 1944	1000	111
4	Essex Cnty., N. Jersey 1926	100	113½
5	Fitzroy, Melbrne. 1916-19	100	108
5	Gisborne Harbour 1915	100	110½
4	Greymouth Harbour 1925	100	111
4	Hamilton 1934	100	109
5	Hobart Town 1918-30	100	116
4	Do. 1940	100	107
4½	Invercargill Boro. Dbs. 1936	100	113
6	Kimberley Boro., S.A. Dbs.	—	104
4	Launceston Twn. Dbs. 1916	100	107
6	Lyttleton, N.Z., Harb. 1929	100	123
4	Melbourne Bd. of Wks. 1921	100	109
5	Melb. City Debs. 1897-1907	100	107½
4	Do. Debs. 1908-27	100	113½
4	Do. Debs. 1915-20-22	100	108
5	Melbne. Harb. Bds., 1908-9	100	112
4½	Do. do. 1915	100	110
4	Do. do. 1918-21	100	106
4½	Melbrne. Tms. Dbs. 1914-16	100	112
4½	Do. Fire Brig. Db. 1921	100	109
5	Mexico City Stg.	100	89
4	Moncton N. Bruns. City	100	104
4½	Montevideo	100	57
5	Montreal Stg.	100	103
5	Do. 1874	100	103
5	Do. 1879	100	104
3½	Do. 1933	100	104
3	Do. Perm. Deb. Stk.	100	98
4	Do. Cons. Deb. Stk. 1932	100	113
6	Napier Boro. Consolid. 1914	100	119
5	Napier Harb. Debs. 1920	100	114
5	Do. Debs. 1928	100	105
6	New Plymouth Harb. Debs. 1909	100	107
6	New York City 1901	—	106
3½	Do. 1910-26	—	105½
4½	Nth. Melbourne Debs. 1-600 1921	100	105
5	Oamaru Boro. Cons. 1920	100	101
6	Do. Harb. Bds. (Reg.)	100	74½
25/	Do. 6 p.c. (Bearer) 1919	100	85
6	Otago Harb. Deb. Reg.	100	108
6	Do. 1877	100	107
6	Do. 1881 1921	100	118
5	Do. Debs. 1921	100	107
5	Do. Cons. 1934	100	105
6	Ottawa City	100	109
6	Do. 1904	100	115½
4½	Do. Debs. 1913	100	112
6	Port Elizabeth Waterworks	100	115½
5	Port Louis	100	108
5	Prahran Debs. 1917	100	111
4	Do. Debs. 1919	100	105
6	Quebec C. Coupon. 1875 1905	100	112
6	Do. do. 1878 1908	100	116
4½	Do. Debs. 1914-18	100	107
4	Do. Debs. 1923	100	107
3½	Do. Cns. Rg. Stk., Red.	100	101
5	Richmond (Melb.) Dbs. 1917	100	111
4	Rio Janeiro City	100	60
4	Rome City	100	—
4	Do. 2nd to 8th Iss.	100	[illegible]
6	Rosario C.	100	[illegible]
6	Do.	100	[illegible]
4	St. Catherine (Ont.) 1926	100	103
4	St. John, N.B., Debs. 1934	—	108
4½	St. Kilda (Melb) Dbs. 1918-21	100	104
4	St. Louis C. (Miss.) 1911	100	108
4	Do. 1913	100	108½
3·65	Do. 1915	—	107½
6	Santa Fé City Debs.	100	[illegible]
6	Santos City	100	97
6	Sofia City	100	86
5	Sth. Melbourne Debs. 1915	100	111
4½	Do. Debs. 1919	100	107
5	Sydney City 1904	100	103
4	Do. Debs. 1912-13	100	107
4	Do. do. (1894) 1919	100	109
7	Timaru Boro. 7 p.c. 1910	100	128½
5	Timaru Harb. Debs 1914	100	106
5	Do. Debs. 1916	100	106
6	Toronto City Wtrwks 1904-6	100	110
6	Do. Cons. Debs. 1898	100	102
5	Do. G. Cns. Dbs. 1919-20	100	112
4	Do. Stg. 1922-8	100	107
4	Do. Local Improv.	100	102
3½	Do. 1929	100	105
5½	Valparaiso	100	90
4	Vancouver 1931	100	108
4	Do. 1932	100	108
6	Wanganui Harb. Dbs. 1905	100	110
6	Wellington Con. Deb. 1907	100	117
6	Do. Improv., 1879	100	120
6	Do. Wtrwks. Dbs., 1880	100	120
4½	Do. Debs., 1893 1933	100	116
4½	Wellington Harb. 1907	100	108
4	Westport Harb. Dbs. 1925	100	111
6	Winnipeg City Deb. 1907	100	118
5	Do. 1914	100	118

FINANCIAL, LAND, AND INVESTMENT.

Last Div.	Name.	Paid.	Price.
5	Agncy, Ld. & Fin. Aust., Ltd., Mt. Db. Stk., Rd.	100	84½
6	Amer. Frehld. Mt. of Lon., Ld., Cum. Pref. Stk. ..	100	77½
4½	Do. Deb. Stk., Red. ..	100	96
1/	Anglo-Amer. Db. Cor., L.	2	1
4	Do. Deb. Stk., Red [†	100	107½
5½	Ang.-Ceylon & Gen. Est., Ltd., Cons. Stk.	100	73½
6	Do. Reg. Debs., Red.	100	104½
—	Ang.-Fch. Explorn., Ltd.	1	3⅛
6	Do. Cum. Pref.	1	1 1/16
—	Argent. Ld. & Inv., Ltd. £1 Shares	10/	nil
5	Do. Cum. Pref.	4	2
—	Assets Fnders 'Sh., Ltd.,	4	1⅝
4/	Assets Realiz., Ltd., Ord.,	5	9
5	Do. Cum. Pref.	5	6⅜
21/	Austrln. Agricl £25 Shs.	21½	65½
—	Aust. N. Z. Mort., Ltd., £10 Shs.	1	1½d.
4½	Do. Deb. Stk., Red. ..	100	90½
4	Do. Deb. Stk., Red. ..	100	82½
4½	Australian Est. & Mt., L., 1 Mt. Deb. Stk., Red.	100	105
5	Do. "A" Mort. Deb. Stk., Red.	100	96
2/6	Australian Mort., Ld., & Fin., Ltd. £25 Shs. ..	5	4¼
1/6	Do. New, £25 Shs. ..	3	2½
4	Do. Deb. Stk	100	111
3	Do. Do.	100	85
4	Baring Est. 2 Mt. Debs., Red.	100	105†
5	Bengal Presidy. 1 Mort. Deb., Red.	100	105†
25/	British Amer. Ld. "A"	1	20
—	Do. "B"	24	6½
1/2½	Brit. & Amer. Mt., Ltd. £10 Shs.	2	1
5/	Do. Pref.	10	10
4	Do. Deb. Stk., Red. ..	100	100†
1/3	Brit. & Austrlsn Tst Ln., Ltd. £25 Shs.	2½	⅜
4½	Do. Perm. Debs., Red.	100	102†
1½d.	Brit. N. Borneo. £1 Shs.	15/	1 1/16
2½d.	Do.	1	1
—	Brit. S. Africa	1	3 1/16
5	Do. Mt. Deb., Red.	—	99
6	B. Aires Harb. Tst., Red.	100	97½
—	Canada Co.	1	25
—	Canada N. W. Ld., Ltd.	$25	85½
—	Do. Pref.	$100	854
4	Canada Perm. Loan & Sav. Perp. Deb. Stk...	100	99½†
—	Curamalan Ld., 1 Mt. 7 p.c. Bds., Red.	—	—
2/4½	Deb Corp., Ld., £10 Shs	4	3½
5	Do. Cum. Pref.	10	11½
4	Do. Perp. Deb. Stk...	100	114†
—	Deb. Corp. Fders' Sh., Ld.	3	1
4/5 7/10	Eastn. Mt. & Agncy, Ld., "A"	10	6½
4½	Do. Deb. Stk., Red.	100	100
5	Equitable Revers. In. Ltd.	100	—
—	Exploration, Ltd.	1	1 1/16
t	Freehold Trst. of Austrla. Ltd. £10 Shs.	1	¾
4	Do. Perp. Deb. Stk...	100	102
—	Genl. Assets Purchase, Ltd., 5 p.c. Cum. Pref.	10	—
50/	Genl. Reversionary, Ltd.	100	—
3½	House Prop. & Inv.	100	85½
13/	Hudson's Bay	13	25
4	Impl. Col. Fin. & Agcy. Corp.	100	93½†
4½	Impl. Prop. Inv., Ltd., Deb. Stk., Red.	100	93½
2/6	Internatl. Fincial. Soc., Ltd. £7½ Shs.	2½	1½
4	Do. Deb. Stk., Red...	100	94½
—	Kent Coal Fin. & Dev., Ltd.	5/	⅛
1/9½	Ld. & Mtge. Egypt, Ltd. £18 Shs.	3	2¼
5	Do. Debs., Red.	100	103
4½	Do. Debs., Red.	100	101
—	Ld. Corp. of Canada, Ltd.	1	⅛
4½	Ld. Mtge. Bk. of Texas Deb. Stk.	100	—
3½	Ld. Mtge. Bk. Victoria 4½ p.c. Deb. Stk.	100	78
2/9½	Law Debent. Corp., Ltd., £10 Shs.	2	2
4½	Do. Cum. Pref., ...	10	12½
4	Do. Deb. Stk.	100	119
1/	Ldn. & Australasian Deb. Corp., Ltd., £4 Shs. ..	2	½
4½	Do. 4½ p.c. Mt. Deb. Stk., Red.	100	101
—	Ldn. & Middx. Frhld. Est. £2 Shs.	35/	
2/6	Lndn. & N. Y. Inv. Corp., Ltd.	5	3
5	Do. 5 p.c. Cum. Pref...	10	2½
1/6	Ldn. & Nth. Assets Corp., Ltd., £2 Shs.	1½	9
2/	Ldn. & N. Deb. Corp., L.	2	1½
4/	Ldn. & S. Afric. Explrn. L.	½	14¼
2/	Mtge. Co. of R. Plate, Ltd. £10 Shs.	2	3
4½	Do. Deb. Stk., Red...	100	113
4½	Morton, Rose Est., Ltd., 1st Mort. Debs.	—	99
—	Natal Land Col. Ltd. ..	10	6½
4/	Do. 8 p.c. Pref., 1870..	5	8¼
5/6	Natl. Disct. L., £25 Shs.	5	10¼
4½	New Impl. Invest., Ltd. Pref. Stk.	100	64½
—	New Impl. Invest., Ltd. Def. Stk.	100	9
4	N. Zld. Ln. & Mer. Agcy., Ltd. Prf. Ln. Deb. Stk	100	96

Financial, Land, &c. (*continued*):—

Last Div.	Name.	Paid.	Price.
16/	N. Zld. Ln. & Mer. Agcy., Ltd. 5 p.c. "A" Db. Sk.	100	42½
—	N. Zld. Ln. & Mer. Agcy., Ltd., 5 p.c. "B" Db. Stk.	100	4
2/6	N. Zld. Tst. & Ln. Ltd., £25 Shs.	5	1½
12/6	N. Zld. Tst. & Ln. Ltd., 5 p.c. Cum. Pref.	25	19†
—	N. Brit. Australsn. Ltd...	100	7½
—	Do. Irred. Guar.	100	34½
5	Do. Mort. Debs.	100	72½
4½	N. Queensld. Mort. & Inv., Ltd., Deb. Stk.	100	94
—	Oceana Co., Ltd.	—	—
4	Peel Riv., Ld. & Min. Ltd.	100	91
—	Peruvian Corp., Ltd.	100	2½
—	Do. 4 p.c. Pref.	100	9½
3	Do. 6 p.c. 1 Mt. Debs., Red.	100	41½
—	Queenld. Invest. & Ld. & Mort. Pref. Ord. Stk...	100	20
3/7	Queenld. Invest. & Ld. & Mort. Ord. Shs.	4	3½†
4	Queenld. Invest. & Ld. Mort. Perp. Debs.	100	90
3½	Raily. Roll Stk. Tst. Deb., 1903-6. .... [†	100	100½
50/	Reversiony. Int. Soc., Ltd.	100	—
2/8½	Riv. Plate Trst., Loan & Agcy., L., "A" £10 Shs.	2	4¼
1/6	Riv. Plate Trst., Loan & Agcy., Ltd., Def. "B"	5	3½
4	Riv. Plate Trst., Loan & Agy., L., Db. Stk., Red.	100	107†
—	Santa Fé & Cord. Gt. South Land, Ltd.	20	5
—	Santa Fé Land	10	2½
2/	Scot. Amer. Invest., Ltd. £10 Shs.	2	2¾
2½	Scot. Australian Invest., Ltd., Cons.	100	91½
6	Scot. Australian Invest., Ltd., Guar. Pref. .. [†	100	132½
5	Scot. Australian Invest., Ltd., Guar. Pref. .. [†	100	104½
4	Scot. Australian Invest., Ltd., 4 p.c. Perp. Dbs. [†	100	105½
5	Sivagunga Zemdy., 1st Mort., Red.	100	99
20/	Sth. Australian	20	57½
3½	Stock Exchange Deb., Rd.	—	101½
—	Strait Develt., Ltd.	1	1/16
2/6	Texas Land & Mt., Ltd. £10 Shs.	2½	3
4½	Texas Land & Mt., Ltd., Deb. Stk., Red.	100	103
—	Transvaal Est. & Dev., L.	1	1/16
—	Transvaal Lands, Ltd., £1 Shs.	15/	⅛
—	Do. F. P.	1	⅛
—	Transvaal Mort., Loan, & Fin., Ltd., £10 Shs. ..	2	⅛
2/	Tst & Agcy. of Austrlsa., Ltd., £10 Shs.	1	2¼
7	Do. Old, fully paid ..	10	15¼
5/7	Do. New, fully paid ..	10	12½
5	Do. Cum. Pref.	10	12¾
3/	Trust & Loan of Canada, £20 Shs.	5	4½
1/9½	Do. New £20 Shs. ...	3	2¼
—	Tst. & Mort. of Iowa, Ltd., £10 Shs.	2½	⅜
4½	Do. Deb. Stk. Red...	100	94½
—	Tst., Loan, & Agency of Mexico, Ltd., £10 Shs.	2	½
—	Trsts., Exors, & Sec. Ins. Corp., Ltd., £10 Shs..	7	1⅛
5/	Union Dsc., Ld., £10 Shs.	5	10¼
—	Union Mort. & Agcy. of Aust., Ltd., £6 Shs. ..	2	—
—	Do. Pref. Stk	100	35
—	Do. 6 p. Pref. £6 Shs.	2	¼
4½	Do. Deb. Stk	100	92½
4	Do. Deb. Stk	100	85½
5	Do. Deb. Stk. Red...	100	96
1/6	U.S. Deb. Cor. Ltd., £8 Shs.	1	⅛
5½	Do. Cum. Pref. Stk..	100	102½
4½	Do. Irred. Deb. Stk..	100	109½
5	U.S. Tst. & Guar. Cor., Ltd., Pref. Stk.	100	69½
6/	Van Dieman's	25	16
4	Walker's Prop. Cor., Ltd., Guar. 1 Mt. Deb. Stk..	100	109
4½	Wstr. Mort. & Inv., Ltd., Deb. Stk.	100	90

FINANCIAL—TRUSTS.

Last Div.	Name.	Paid.	Price.
1/	Afric. City Prop., Ltd ...	1	1⅛
6	Do. Cum. Pref.	1	1⅛
4	Alliance Invt., Ltd., Cm. 4½ p. c. Prefd.	100	73½
—	Do. Defd	100	11½
4	Do. Deb. Stk. Red...	100	106½
5	Amrcn. Invt., Ltd., Prfd.	100	123½
5	Do. Defd.	100	89½
4	Do. Deb. Stk. Red...	100	118½
4	Army & Navy Invt., Ltd.. 5 p.c. Prefd.	100	77½
—	Do. Defd. Stk.	100	17½
4	Do. Deb. Stk.	100	106½
4	Atlas Investment, Ltd., Prefd. Stk.	100	70½
4½	Bankers' Invest., Ltd., Cum. Prefd.	100	105
—	Do. Defd	100	27½
4	Do. Deb. Stk	100	113

Financial—Trusts (*continued*):—

Last Div.	Name.	Paid.	Price.
4/6	†Brewery & Comml. Inv., Ltd., £10 Shs.	5	6
4	British Investment, Ltd., Cum. Prefd.	100	109½
5	Do. Defd.	100	102½
4	Do. Deb. Stk. .... [†	100	107½
6	Brit. Steam. Invst., Ltd., Prefd. .... [†	100	116½
—	Do. Defd	100	66½
4½	Do. Perp. Deb. Stk [†	100	120½
2/3	Car Trust Invst., Ltd., £10 Shs.	2½	2
5	Do. Pref.	100	105½
4	Do. Deb. Stk., 1915..	100	106†
4	‡Clnl. Sec., Ltd., Prefd. [†	100	106½
—	Do. Defd.	100	46½
4	Consolidated, Ltd., Cum. 1st Pref.	100	94
4	Do. 5 p.c. Cm. 2nd do.	100	74½
—	Do. Defd.	100	14½
4½	Do. Deb. Stk.	100	113½
4½	Edinburgh Invest., Ltd., Cum. Prefd. Stk.	100	110½
4	Do. Deb. Stk. Red.	100	108½
5	Foreign, Amer. & Gen. Invt., Ltd., Prefd.	100	119
2	Do. Defd.	100	54½
4	Do. Deb. Stk.	100	117½
5	Foreign & Colonial Invt., Ltd., Prefd.	100	135½
4½	Do. Defd.	100	89½
4½	Gas, Water & Gen. Invt., Cum. Prefd. Stk.	100	91½
—	Do. Defd. Stk.	100	32½
4	Do. Deb. Stk.	100	106
5	Gen. & Com. Invt., Ltd., Prefd. Stk.	100	106½
—	Do. Defd. Stk.	100	34½
4	Do. Deb. Stk.	100	110½
1/9	Globe Telegph. & Tst., Ltd.	10	12
6	Do. do. Pref.	10	18
4	Govt. & Genl. Invt., Ld., Prefd.	100	84½
3½	Do. Defd.	100	40½
4½	Govts. Stk. & other Secs. Invt., Ltd., Prefd.	100	95½
—	Do. Defd.	100	28
4½	Do. Deb. Stk.	100	110
4	Do. do.	100	104
4½	Guardian Invt., Ltd., Pfd.	100	92½
—	Do. Defd.	100	20½
4	Do. Deb. Stk.	100	107
5	Indian & Gen. Inv., Ltd., Cum. Prefd.	100	109½
2½	Do. Defd.	100	55
4½	Do. Deb. Stk.	100	120½
5	Indust. & Gen. Tst., Ltd., Unified	100	100
3½	Do. Deb. Stk. Red.	100	102½
4½	Internat. Invt., Ltd., Cm. Prefd.	100	71½
—	Do. Defd.	100	9
4	Do. Deb. Stk.	100	104
4	Invest. Tst. Cor. Ltd. Pfd.	100	102
4	Do. Defd.	100	83
4	Do. Deb. Stk. Red.	100	105
25/	Ldn. Gen. Invest. Ltd., 5 p.c. Cum. Prefd.	100	111½
37/6	Do. Defd.	100	120
4½	Ldn. Scot. Amer. Ltd. Pfd.	100	104½
£3	Do. Defd.	100	59½
4	Do. Deb. Stk.	100	111
4	Ldn. Tst., Ltd., Cum. Prfd. Stk.	100	106
4	Do. Defd. Stk.	100	76½
4	Do. Deb. Stk., Red.	100	109
3½	Do. Mt. Deb. Stk., Red.	100	101½
5	Mercantile Invt. & Gen., Ltd., Prefd.	100	108
2	Do. Defd.	100	47½
4	Do. Deb. Stk.	100	116½
4	Merchants, Ltd., Pref. Stk.	100	104
4	Do. Ord.	100	79
4	Do. Deb. Stk.	100	117
5	Municipal, Ltd., Prefd...	100	56½
—	Do. Defd.	100	18½
4½	Do. Debs.	100	113
4½	Do. Debs. "B"	100	100
4½	Do. "C" Deb. Stk.	100	88½
5	New Investment, Ltd. Ord.	100	97
5	Omnium Invest., Ltd., Pfd.	100	95½
£1	Do. Defd.	100	27½
4	Do. Deb. Stk.	100	102
4/	†Railway Deb. Tst. Ld., £20 Shs.	10	7
5	Do. Debs., Red. ..	100	105½
4½	Do. Deb. Stk., 1911	100	105½
4	Do. do. 1927	100	109½
4	Railway Invst. Ltd., Prefd.	100	116
18/6	Do. Defd.	100	24
6/4½	Railway Share Trust & Agency "A"	8	6½
7½	Do. "B" Pref. Stk.	100	145
4½	River Plate & Gen. Invt., Ltd., Prefd.	100	105
£3	Do. Defd.	100	54½
5	Scot. Invst., Ltd., Pfd. Stk.	100	94½
1½	Do. Defd...	100	26½
4	Do. Deb. Stk.	100	108
4½	Sec. Scottish Invst., Ltd., Cum. Prefd.	100	90½
£2	Do. Defd. Stk.	100	32
4	Do. Deb. Stk.	100	106½
7/6	Sth. Africa Gold Tst., Ltd.	1	5
6	Do. Cum. Pref.	1	1
5½	Do. 1st Debs., Red.	100	102
9d.	†Stock Conv. & Invest., Ltd., £5 Shs.	1	1½
—	Do. do. 4½ p.c. Cm. Prf.	100	112
3½	Do. Ldn. & N. W. 1st Charge Prefd.	100	116
4	Do. do. 2nd Chge Prfd.	100	113
32/6	Do. do. Defd. Charge	100	33
3	Do. N. East. 1 Chge Pfd.	100	95

Financial—Trusts (*continued*):—

Last Div.	Name.	Paid.	Price.
37/6	Stock N. East Defd. Chge	100	42
6	Submarine Cables	100	138½
5	U.S. & S. Amer. Invest., Ltd., Prefd.	100	98
2	Do. Defd.	100	27½
4	Do. Deb. Stk.	100	104½

GAS AND ELECTRIC LIGHTING.

Last Div.	Name.	Paid.	Price.
10/6	Alliance & Dublin Con. 10 p.c. Stand.	10	24½
7/6	Do. 7 p.c. Stand...	10	17
5	Austln. Gas Lght. (Syd.) Debs. 1902	100	106†
5	Bay State of N. Jrsy. Sk. Fd. Tst. Bd., Red. ..	—	92½†
3/	Bombay, Ltd.	5	7
2/4½	Do. New	4	5½
12	Brentford Cons.	100	302½
9	Do. New	100	229½
9	Do. Pref.	100	147½
4	Do. Deb. Stk. ..	100	136
11½	Brighton & Hove Gen. Cons. Stk.	100	277½
8½	Do. "A" Cons. Stk.	100	202½
5	Bristol 5 p.c. Max.	100	132½
22/6	British Gas Light, Ltd.	20	57
11/6	Bromley Gas Consumrs.' 10 p.c. Stand.	10	26
8/6	Do. 7 p.c. Stand...	10	21
—	Brush Electl. Enging., L.	—	2
2/	Do. 6 p.c. Pref.	—	2½
4½	Do. Deb. Stk.	100	111
4½	†Do. 2 Deb. Stk., Red.	100	101½
5/	B. Ayres (New), Ltd. ..	10	9½
4	Do. Deb. Stk., Rd. ..	—	97
12/	Cagliari Gas & Wtr., Ltd.	20	31
8/	Cape Town & Dist. Gas Light & Coke, Ltd.	10	17
4½	Do. Pref.	10	12
6	Do. 1 Mt. Debs. 1910	50	60
3/	Charing Cross & Strand Elec. Sup., Ltd.	5	13
4½	Do. Cum. Pref.	5	6½
2/6	†Chelsea Elec. Sup., Ltd.	5	10½
4½	Do. Deb. Stk., Red.	100	113
5	Chic. Edison Co. 1 Mt., Red.	$1000	108
14/	City of Ldn. Elec. Lht., L.	10	26½
—	Do. New	10	26
6/	Do. Cum. Pref.	10	17½
5	Do. Deb. Stk., Red. [†	100	131½
13½	Commercial, Cons.	100	342½
10½	Do. New	100	257½
4½	Do. Deb. Stk.	100	156
10	Continental Union, Ltd.	100	252½
7	Do. Pref. Stk.	100	215½
—	County of Lon. & Brush Prov. Elec. Lg., Ltd.	10	14
6	Do. Cum. Pref.	10	15½
14	Croydon Comcl. Gas, Ld., "A" Stk., 10 p.c. ..	100	317½
11	Do. "B" Stk., 7 p.c.	100	254½
5¼	Crystal Pal. Dist. Ord. 5 p.c. Stk.	100	140
5	Do. Pref. Stk.	100	141½
14/	European, Ltd.	10	26½
10/6	Do.	7½	19
12¾	Gas Light & Ck' Cons. Stk., "A" Ord.	100	314½
4	Do. "B" (4 p.c. Max.)	100	115½
10	Do. "C," "D," & "E" (Pref.)	100	322½
5	Do. "F" (Pref.)	100	152½
7½	Do. "G" (Pref.)	100	224½
7	Do. "H" (7 p.c. Max.)	100	206½
10	Do. "J" (Pref.)	100	321½
6	Do. "K"	100	184½
4	Do. Deb. Stk.	100	139
4½	Do. do.	100	156
6	Do. do.	100	207
8/	Hong Kong & China, Ld.	10	14½
—	†House to House Elec. Light Sup., Ltd. ..	5	9½
7	Do. Cum. Pref.	5	11½
10	Imperial Continental ..	100	217½
3½	Do. Deb. Stk., Red ..	100	105½
2/	Malta & Medit., Ltd. ..	5	5½
5/	†Metrop. Elec. Sup., Ltd.	10	19
3/8	Do. New	10	18½
4½	Do. 1 Mt. Deb. Stk.	100	119†
5	Metro. of Melbrne. Dbs. 1908-12	100	113
4½	Do. Debs... 1918-22-4	100	110
10/	Monte Video, Ltd.	20	15½
8/	†Notting Hill Elec. Lig.. Ltd.	10	18
4/6	Oriental, Ltd.	5	8½
4/0½	Do. New	4½	7½
10½d	Do. do. 1876	1	1½
3/6	Ottoman, Ltd.	5	4½
—	Para, Ltd.	—	—
6	People's Gas Lt. & C. of Chic. 2 Mt. 1904	100	105½
6	River Plate Elec. Lgt. & Trac., Ltd., 1 Deb. Stk.	—	92½†
112	Royal Elec. of Montreal	—	146
4½	Do. 1 Mt. Deb. ..	100	106
3/6	†St. James' & Pall Mall Elec. Light, Ltd. ..	5	17½
7	Do. Pref.	5	10½
4	Do. Deb. Stk., Red. [†	100	102½
10/	San Paulo, Ltd.	10	16½

Gas and Electric (*continued*):—

Last Div.	Name.	Paid.	Price.
10	Sheffield Unit. Gas Lt. "A"	100	251½
10	Do. "B"	100	251½
10	Do. "C"	100	251½
—	Sth. Ldn. Elec. Sup., Ld.	2	2½
5½	South Metropolitan	100	144½
3	Do. 3 p.c. Deb. Stk.	100	107½
12	Tottenham & Edmonton Gas Lt. & C., "A"	100	290
9	Do. "B"	100	210
7/	Tuscan, Ltd.	10	14
5	Do. Debs., Red.	100	101½
4/9	West Ham 10 p.c. Stan.	5	12
4/	Wstmnstr. Elec. Sup., Ld.	5	16½

INSURANCE.

Last Div.	Name.	Paid.	Price.
4/	Alliance, £20 Shs.	44/	11½
10/	Alliance, Mar., & Gen., Ld., £100 Shs.	25	52
5/	Atlas, £50 Shs.	6	31½
8/	British & For. Marine, Ld., £20 Shs.	4	25
7½d.	British Law Fire, Ltd., £10 Shs.	1	1⅜
7/6	Clerical, Med., & Gen. Life, £25 Shs.	50/	16½
10/	Commercial Union, Ltd., £50 Shs.	5	45½
4	Do. "W. of Eng." Ter. Deb. Stk.	100	110½
60/	County Fire, £100 Shs.	80	185
2/6	Eagle, £50 Shs.	5	—
4/	Employrs' Liability, Ltd., £10 Shs.	2	4
—	Empress, Ltd., £5 Shs.	1	—
21/	Equity & Law, £100 Shs.	6	21
7/6	General Life, £100 Shs.	5	15
4½d.	Gresham Life, £5 Shs.	15/	2½
2/6	Guardian, Ld., £10 Shs.	5	12½
10/	Imperial, Ltd., £20 Shs.	5	32
3/6	Imperial Life, £20 Shs.	4	7
6/	Indemnity Mutual Mar., Ltd., £15 Shs.	3	12
1/	Lancashire, £20 Shs.	2	5
7½d.	Law Acc. & Contin., Ltd., £5 Shs.	10/	⅝
5/	Law Fire, £100 Shs.	2½	18
4½d.	Law Guar. & Trust, Ltd., £10 Shs.	1	1½
9/	Law Life, £20 Shs.	2	24½
2/9	Law Un. & Crown £10Shs.	12/	7
4	Do. Deb. Stk., 1942	100	110½
14/6	Legal & General, £50 Shs.	8	15½
9d.	Lion Fire, Ltd., £8½ Shs.	1½	1
14/	Liverpool & London & Globe, Stk	2	55½
10/	Do. Globe £1 Ann.	—	36
15/	London, £25 Shs.	12½	62
4/	Lond. & Lanc. Fire, £25Shs	2½	19½
2/	Lond. & Lanc. Life, £25Shs	2	5†
20	Lond. & Prov. Mar., Ld., £10 Shs.	1	1½
2/	Lond. Guar. & Accident, Ltd., £5 Shs.	2	11½
10/	Marine, Ltd., £25 Shs.	4½	44½†
2/	Maritime, Ltd., £10 Shs.	2	4½
1/6	Merc. Mar., Ld., £10 Shs.	2½	2½
1/	National Marine, Ltd., £9 Shs.	1	½
10/	N. Brit. & Merc., £25 Shs.	6¼	43½
20/	Northern, £100 Shs.	10	82
60/	Norwich Union Fire, £100 Shs.	12†	129½
5/	Ocean Acc. & Guar., fy. pd.	5	19½
1/	Do. £5 Shs.	1	3½
2/6	Ocean, Marine, Ltd.	2½	9½
1/	Palatine, £10 Shs.	2	3½
2/6	Pelican, £10 Shs.	1	3½
12/	Phœnix, £50 Shs.	5	45
25/	Provident, £100 Shs.	10	36
3/	Railway Passngrs., £10Shs.	2	8½
2/6	Rock Life, £5 Shs.	10/	4½
8	Royal Exchange	100	360†
18/	Royal, £20 Shs.	3	56
4/	Sun, £10 Shs.	10/	12
3/9	Sun Life, £10 Shs.	7½	15†
4/	Thames & Mrsey. Marine, Ltd., £20 Shs.	2	11
9/	Union, £10 Shs.	4	24½†
3/6	Union Marine, £20 Shs.	2½	9½
12/	Universal Life, £100 Shs.	12	42†
2/	World Marine, £5 Shs.	2	1½

IRON, COAL, AND STEEL.

Last Div.	Name.	Paid.	Price.
3/9	Barrow Hæm. Steel, Ltd.	7½	2½
9/	Do. 6 p.c. and Pref.	7½	7
10/	Bolck., Vaugh. & C., Ld.	20	17½
6/	Do. £8 liab.	12	10
7/6	Brown, J. & Co., Ltd., £20 Shs.	15	19½
22/6	Consett Iron, Ld., £10 Shs.	7½	30
4/	Do. 8 p.c. Cum. Pref.	5	11½
7/6	Ebbw Vale Steel, Iron & Coal, Ltd., £23 Shs.	20	6½
15/	General Mining Assn., Ld.	5½	7½
16/	Harvey Steel Co. of Gt. Britain, Ltd.	10	26
5	Lehigh V. Coal 1 Mt. 5 p.c. Guar. Gd. Cp. Bds.	—	97½
42/6	Nantyglo & Blaina Iron, Ltd., Pref.	862	96
1/	Nerbudda Coal & Iron, Ltd., £3 Shs.	56/	½
6/	Newport Abrcrn. Bk. Vein Steam Coal, Ltd.	10	4½
5/	New Sharlston Coll., Ltd. Pref.	20	11
4½d.	Nw. Vancvr. Coal & Ld., L.	1	⅛
3/6	North's Navigation Coll. (1889) Ltd.	5	2
10/	Do. 10 p.c. Cum. Pref.	5	7½
1/	Rhymney Iron, Ltd.	5	1½
	Do. New, £5 Shs.	4½	⅛
5	Do. Mt. Debs., Red.	100	98
5	Shelton Irn., Stl. & Cl. Co., Ltd., 1 Chg. Debs., Red.	100	97½
10	Sth. Hetton Coal, Ltd.	100	176½
	Vickers & Maxim, Ltd.	10	2½
	Do. 5 p.c. Prfd. Stk.	100	134

SHIPPING.

Last Div.	Name.	Paid.	Price.
4/	African Stm. Ship, £20 Shs.	16	9½
5/	Do. Fully-paid	20	13½
5/	Amazon Steam Nav., Ltd.	12½	9½
8/	Castle Mail Pakts., Ltd., £20 Shs.	14	15½
3½	Do. 1st Deb. Stk., Red.	100	101
6/	China Mutual Steam, Ltd.	5	2½
6	Do. Cum. Pref.	10	9½
10/	Cunard, Ltd.	20	10
5/	Do. £20 Shs.	10	4
4½	Furness, Withy, & Co., Ltd., 1 Mt. Dbs., Red.	100	105
6/	General Steam	15	8½
5/	Do. 5 p.c. Pref., 1874	10	9
5/	Do. 5 p.c. Pref., 1877	10	9
5/	Leyland & Co., Ltd.	10	15½
7/	Do. 7 p.c. Cum. Pref.	10	14½†
—	Do. 4½ p.c. Cum. Pre-Pf.	3	10½
4	Do. 1st Mt. Dbs., Red.	100	106½
2/6	Mercantile Steam, Ltd.	5	7½
6/4½	New Zealand Ship., Ltd.,	6	5
4	Do. Deb. Stk., Red.	100	104
5/	Orient Steam, Ltd.	10	4½
5	P. & O. Steam, Cum. Prefd.	100	155½
19	Do. Defd.	100	232½
3½	Do. Deb. Stk.	100	121
5	Richelieu & Ont., 1st Mt. Debs., Red.	100	100
30/	Royal Mail, £100 Shs.	60	51
2/6	Shaw, Sav., & Alb., Ltd., "A" Pref.	5	5
5/	Do. "B" Ord.	5	3½
8/	Union Steam, Ltd.	20	18½
4/	Do. New £20 Shs.	10	8
4	Do. Deb. Stk., Red.	100	107
7/	Union of N.Z., Ltd.	10	9½
3/1½	Wilson's & Fur.-Ley., 5½ p.c. Cum. Pref.	10†	10½
4½	Do. 1 Mt. Db. Sk., Rd.	100†	102½

TELEGRAPHS AND TELEPHONES.

Last Div.	Name.	Paid.	Price.
4	African Direct, Ltd., Mort. Debs., Red.	100	102
—	Amazon Telegraph, Ltd.	10	6½
14/	Anglo-American, Ltd.	100	62
28/	Do. 6 p.c. Prefd. Ord.	100	111
—	Do. Defd. Ord.	100	13½
3/	Brazilian Submarine, Ltd.	10	16½
5	Do. Debs., 2 Series	100†	114

Telegraphs and Telephones (*continued*):—

Last Div.	Name.	Paid.	Price.
4/	Chili Telephone, Ltd.	5	3½
$2½	Conmcial. Cable, $100 Shs.	—	184½
4	Do. Stg. 500-yr. Deb. Stk. Red.	100	106
2½d.	Consd. Telpehone Constr., &c., Ltd.	10/	⅛
8/	Cuba Submarine, Ltd.	10	8½
10/	Do. 10 p.c. Pref.	10	18½
2/	Direct Spanish, Ltd.	5	4½
5/	Do. 10 p.c. Cum. Pref.	5	10½
4½	Do. Debs.	50	103½
3/	Direct U.S. Cable, Ltd.	20	10½
2/6	Eastern, Ltd.	10	17½
3/	Do. 6 p.c. Cum. Pref.	10	18½
4	Do. Mt. Deb. Stk., Red.	100	132½
2/6	Eastern Exten., Aus., & China, Ltd.	10	18½
5	Do. (Aus. Gov. Sub.) Deb., Red.	100	101†
5	Do. do. Bearer	100	101½
4	Do. Mort. Deb. Stk.	100	133½
5	Eastn. & S. Afric., Ltd., Mort. Deb. 1900	100	101†
5	Do. Bearer	100	102†
4	Do. Mort. Debs. 1909	100	104½
4	Do. Mort. Debs. (Maur. Subsidy)	25	109½
5/	Grt. Nthn. Copenhagen	10	27
5	Do. Debs., Ser. B., Red.	100	102½
12/6	Indo-European, Ltd.	25	53½
6	London Platino-Brazilian, Ltd., Debs. 1904	100	108½
4/	Montevideo Telph., Ltd., 6 p.c. Pref.	5	2½
3/	National Telephone, Ltd.	5	6½
6/	Do. Cum. 1 Pref.	10	16
6/	Do. Cum. 2 Pref.	10	15
5	Do. Non-Cum. 3 Pref.	5	6½
3½	Do. Deb. Stk., Red.	100	104½
4d.	Oriental Telephone, Ltd.	1	½
4	Pac. & Euro. Tlg. Dbs., Rd.	100	106½
4/	Reuter's, Ltd.	8	8
5/	Un. Riv. Plate Telph., Ltd.	5	4½
5	Do. Deb. Stk., Red.	100	103½
6/	West African Telg., Ltd.	10	4½
5	Do. 5 p.c. Mt. Debs., Red.	100	104½
—	W. Coast of America, Ltd.	10	—
3/	Western & Brazilian, Ltd.	15	10
3/	Do. 5 p.c. Pref. Ord.	7½	7½
—	Do. Defd. Ord.	7½	3
4	Do. Deb. Stk., Red.	100	106½
1/	W. India & Panama, Ltd.	10	½
6/	Do. Cum. 1 Pref.	10	7½
6/	Do. Cum. 2 Pref.	10	6
5	Do. Debs., Red.	100	106½
7	West. Union, 1 Mt. 1900 $	1000	107½
6	Do. 6 p.c. Stg. Bds., Rd.	100	102½

TRAMWAYS AND OMNIBUS.

Last Div.	Name.	Paid.	Price.
1/6	Anglo-Argentine, Ltd.	5	3½
6/	Do. Deb. Stk.	100†	125½
4	Barcelona, Ltd.	10	13
5	Do. Deb., Red.	100	104½
6/6	Belfast Street Trams.	10	17
—	Blackpl. & Fltwd. Tram., £10 Shs.	8	9
4/	Bordeaux Tram. & O., Ltd.	10	12½
5	Do. Cum. Pref.	10	11½
—	Brazilian Street Ry., Ltd.	2	½
—	British Elec. Trac., Ltd.	10	17½
2/	B. Ayres & Belg. Tram., Ltd., 6 p.c. Cum. Pref.	5	4
6	Do. 1 Deb. Stk. †	100	102½
—	B. Ayres. Gd. Nat., Ltd., 6 p.c. 1 Deb. Bds., Red.	100	60
5½	Do. Pref. Debs., Red.	100	102
6d.	Calais, Ltd.	5	1
—	Calcutta, Ltd.	10	3½
—	Carthagena & Herr., Ltd.	10	3
5	Do. Deb., Red.	100	95
5	City of B'ham. Trams., Ltd., 5 p.c. Cum. Pref.	5	5½
4	Do. 1 Mort. Debs., Rd.	100	104½
3/9	City of B. Ayres, Ltd.	5	7
2/3	Do. Ext. £5 Shs.	3	4
6	Do. Deb. Stk.	100	150
9d.	Edinburgh Street Tram.	4	3
1/	Glasgow Tram. & Omni. Ltd., £9 Shs.	8	3½
3/7½	Imperial, Ltd.	6	12½
2/	Lond., Deptfd, & Greenwich, Prefd.	5	3
nil	Do. Defd.	5	1
10½	Lond. Gen. Omni., Ltd.	100	200
4	Do. Deb., Red.	100	113½

Tramways and Omnibus (*continued*):—

Last Div.	Name	Paid.	Price.
6/	London Road Car	6	10½
5	London St. Rly. (Prov., Ont.), Mt. Debs.	100	112
4/9	London St. Trams.	—	3
12/9	†London Trams., Ltd.	10	10½
6/	Do. Non-Cum. Pref.	10	10½
5	Do. Mt. Db. Stk., Rd.	100	100½
5	Lynn & Boston 1 Mt. 1924 $	1000	107
5	Milwaukee Elec. Cons. Mt. $	1000	97
5	Minneapolis St. 1 Cons. Mt $	1000	94
5	Montreal St. Dbs., 1908	100	110
4½	Do. Debs., 1922	100	109
6/	Nth. Metropolitan	10	13
1/9½	Nth. Staffords., Ltd.	6	4½
5/6	Provincial, Ltd.	10	6½
6/	Do. Cum. Pref.	10	13½
5	St. Paul City, 1937 $	1000	94
5	Do. Guar. Twin City Rap. Trans. $	1000	94
5/	Southampton	10	7
3/	South London	10	5½
3/6	Sunderland, Ltd.	10	5
4½	Toronto 1 Mt., Red.	100	109
2/6	Tramways Union, Ltd.	5	7
4½	Do. Deb., Red.	100	109
5/	Vienna Generla Omnibus.	5	6½
5	Do. 5 p.c. Mt. Deb., Red.	100	105
4/	Wolverhampton, Ltd	10	6½

WATER WORKS.

Last Div.	Name.	Paid.	Price.
8/	Antwerp, Ltd.	20	21½
6/	Cape Town District, Ltd.	5	5½
10½	Chelsea	100	337½
5	Do. Pref. Stk.	100	178½
4½	Do. Pref. Stk., 1875	100	158½
4½	Do. Deb. Stk.	100	162½
5/	City St. Petersburg, Ltd.	13	11
4/6	Colne Valley	10	15
4	Do. Deb. Stock	100	157½
£4	Consol. of Rosar., Ltd., 4 p.c. 1 Deb. Stk., Red.	100	90
7½	East London	100	234
4½	Do. Deb. Stk.	100	163½
3	Do. Deb. Stk., Red.	100	106
37/6	Grand Junction (Max. 10 p.c.) "A"	50	124½
18/9	Do. "B"	25	—
18/9	Do. "C" (Max. 7½ p.c.)	25	57½
35/	Do. "D" (Max. 7 p.c.)	50	102½
4	Do. Deb. Stock	100	149½
13	Kent	100	364½
7	Do. New (Max. 7 p.c.)	100	217½
6/7½	Kimberley, Ltd.	7	4½
6	Do. Debs., Red.	100	102½
6	Do. Deb. Stk., Red.	100	102½
10	Lambeth (Max. 10 p.c.)	100	306½
7	Do. (Max. 7½ p.c.), 50 & 25	—	227
4	Do. Deb. Stock	100	148½
3	Do. Red. Deb. Stock	100	105
10/	Montevideo, Ltd.	20	16½
5	Do. 1 Deb. Stk.	100	108½
5	Do. 2 Deb. Stk.	100	103½
130/11	15] New River New	100	454½
4	Do. Deb. Stk.	100	153½
4	Do. Deb. Stk. "B"	100	153½
6/	Odessa, Ltd., "A" 6 p.c. Prefd.	20	—
nil	Do. "B" Deferred	20	—
4	Portland Con. Mt. "B," 1927	—	—
8/	Seville, Ltd.	20	12½
5/6	Southend "Addl." Ord.	10	17½
6	Southwark and Vauxhall	100	166½
6	Do. "D" Shares (7½ p.c. max.)	100	159½
5	Do. Pref. Stock	100	177½
4	Do. "A" Deb. Stock	100	145½
3	Staines Resvirs. Jt. Com. Gua. Deb. Stk., Red.	100	105
7/	Tarapaca, Ltd.	10	9½
10	West Middlesex	100	317½
4½	Do. Deb. Stk.	100	163½
3	Do. Deb. Stk.	100	107

Prices Quoted on the Leading Provincial Exchanges.

ENGLISH.

In quoting the markets, B stands for Birmingham; Bl for Bristol; M for Manchester; L for Liverpool; and S for Sheffield.

CORPORATION STOCKS.

Chief Markets.	Int or Div.	Name.	Amount paid.	Price.
M	3½	Bolton, Red. 1935 ..	100	116
M	3½	Burnley, Red. 1933..	100	116
M	3½	Bury, Red. 1946	100	118
L	2¾	Liverpool, Red. 1925	100	102
B	3½	Longton, 1932	100	107
M	4	Oldham Prp. Db. Sk.	100	144
M	£1	Do. Gas & W. Ann.		35
S	4	Rotherham 4 p.c., Red. 1927...... [£	1 an	114
S	3	Do. Red. 1920..	100	104
M	3½	Runcorn Red. 1923..	100	105
S	2½	Sheffield Water Ann.	100	118
S	5	Do.	3 an	90
L	3½	Southport Red. 1936 {	5 an 100	112
L	5	Do. Red. 1914..	100	104
M	3	Todmorden, Red. 1914	100	103

RAILWAYS.

Chief Markets.	Int or Div.	Name.	Amount paid.	Price.
Bl	4½	Bridgewater Pref. ..	100	137½
M	4	Cleator & Workton.	100	78
M	4	Do. 1883 Pref. ..	100	111
L	4	Cockermth. K. & P.	100	116
L	6	Isle of Man	5	6⅛
L	5	Do. Pref.	5	6⅝
L	3	Liverpool Overhead	10	11½
L	4	Do. Deb. Stk. ..	100	109
L	5	Do. Pref.	10	16½
L	6	Maryport & Carlisle	100	169
S	6	Mid. Shef. & Roth. Pf.	100	234
Bl	35/	Neath & Brecon "A"	100	60
M	4½	Oldham, Ashton, &c.	10	17
Bl	5½	Penarth Harbour ..	100	184½
Bl	4	Do. Deb. Stk. ..	100	145
Bl	3½	Do. Deb. Stk. ..	100	127
Bl	½	Ross & Monmouth..	20	5⅛
Bl	6	Do. Pref.	20	43
M	3	Southport & Cheshire Deb. Stk.	100	105½
M	nil.	Do. Pref.	100	26
Bl	2½	West Somerset Gu...	100	97½
Bl	5	Wye Val. Deb. Stk.	100	162½

BANKS.

Chief Markets.	Int or Div.	Name.	Amount paid.	Price.
L	6/	Adelphi, L., £20 Shs.	10	16
L	20/	Bk of L'pool, L., £100 Sh	12½	39¼
B	4/6	Brmnghm. Dis. & C., Ltd., £20 Shs.....	4	10½
B	6/3	Co. of Staffs., L., £40	5	13
S	17½	Crompton & Evans, Ltd., £20 Shs	4	15
M	10/	Lancs. & Yorks, Ltd., £20 Shs.....	10	32½
L	20/	Livrpl. Union, Ltd., £100 Shs.	20	62
M	24/	Manchester & Co., Ltd., £100 Shs. ..	16	61½
M	20/	Mnchstr. & Livrpool. Dis., Ltd., £60 Shs.	10	52¾
M	1/6	Mer. of Lancashire, Ltd., £20 Shs.....	3	6⅛
L	14/	Nth. & Sth. Wales, Ltd., £40 Shs.....	10	35
B	5/	Notts Joint St., Ltd., £50 Shs..........	10	22¾
M	3/	Oldham Joint Stk., Ltd., £20 Shs.....	4	10
S	10	Sheffield Banking, Ltd., £50 Shs.....	17½	51½
S	10	Do. & Rotherham, Ltd., £50 Shs...	8	27
S	15	Do. & Hallamsh., Ltd., £100 Shs..	25	61⅝
S	10	Do. Union, Ltd., £40 Shs.........	10	25¼
M	12/	Union of Manchester, Ltd., £25 Shs.. ..	11	27½
M	10/	Williams, Deacon, &c. Ltd., £50 Shs.....	8	26½
Bl	20	Wilts & Dorset, Ltd., £50 Shs..........	10	50
S	10/	York City & Co., Ltd., £10 Shs.....	3	13

BREWERIES.

Chief Markets.	Int or Div.	Name.	Amount paid.	Price.
B	6	Ansell & Sons Pref.	10	15½
B	5	Do. Debs.	100	110†
L	7/	Bent's..............	10	18¾
L	6	Do. Cum. Pref...	10	14½
L	4½	Do. Deb. Stk. ..	100	110
L	13/6	Birkenhead, £5 paid	5	22
L	13/6	Do. £10 paid....	10	25
M	9/	Boddington's	9	21½
M	5	Do. Cum. Pref...	10	13¼
M	4	Do. Deb. Stk. ..	100	109
B	4½	Butler & Co. Db. Stk	100	110
M	6	Chesters' Cum. Pref.	10	13¾
M	4½	Do. Debs.	100	112½
S	17/	Clarkson's Ord.	10	25
S	6	Do. Cum. Prf. Stk.	10	14
M	4	Dutton & Co. Db. Sk.	100	104†
M	4½	Hardy's Crown Debs.	100	110½
B	6/	Holt	10	18½
B	5	Do. Cum. Pref. ..	10	12¾
B	4	Do. Debs.	100	107½
B	12	Lichfield	10	24
B	5	Do. Cum. Pref...	10	11¾
M	5½	Manchester Deb. Stk.	100	140½
B	14	Mitchell, H., & Co.	10	37½†
B	6	Do. Cum. Pref...	10	15¾
Bl	6	Oakhill Pref........	10	16¾

Breweries (*continued*):—

Chief Market.	Int. or Div.	Name.	Amount paid.	Price.
M	—	Springwell	10	10¾
M	7	Do. Pref.	10	13½
Bl	10	Stroud	10	17½
Bl	6	Do. Pref	10	14⅝
M	—	Taylor's Eagle......	10	11
M	7	Do. Cum. Pref ..	10	13½
M	5½	Do. Deb. Stk. ..	100	120½
S	10	Tennant Bros £20 shs	15	33½
S	10	Wheatley & Bates ..	10	14
S	6	Do. Cum. Pref.	10	13

CANALS AND DOCKS.

Chief Market.	Int. or Div.	Name.	Amount paid.	Price.
Bl	5	Hill's Dry Dk. &c. £20	18	8
M	4	Manc. Ship Canal 1st Mt. Deb. Stk.	100	104†
M	4	Do. 2nd do.	100	103†
L	36/3	Mersey Dck. & Harb.	an.	119½
L	35/	Do.	an.	114
M	—	Rochdale Canal	100	37½
B	35/	Staff. & Worc. Canal	100	75½
B	4½	Do. Deb. Stk....	100	137†
Bl	4	Swansea Harb....(†	100	114
B	27/6	Warwick & Birm. Cnl	100	66
B	12/6	Do. & Napton do.	100	21½

COMMERCIAL & INDUSTRIAL.

Chief Market.	Int. or Div.	Name.	Amount paid.	Price.
L	5	Agua Santa Mt. Debs	100	100½
M	—	Armitage, Sir E. & Sns Ltd..............	10	19
M	5	Do. Deb. 1910 ..	100	103
L	6	Ang. Chil. Nit. 1 Mt. Debs., 1919 ..	100	107
Bl	8½	Bath Stone Firms ..	10	19½
M	4/9½	Barlow & Jones, Ltd., £10 Shs.	8	10⅜
B	7/6	Birmgham. Ry. Car.	10	17
B	6	Do. Pref.	10	15½
B	5/	Do. Small Arms	5	18
M	£12	Blackpool Pier......	100	275
M	5	Do. Tower Debs.	50	54½
M	6/6	Do. Wi. Gar. & P.	5	4½
Bl	10	Bristl. & S. W. R. Wag. £20 Shs............	3	6½
Bl	8	Do. Wag. & Carri. £10 Shs..........	10	14½
M	7/	Crosses & Winkwth. Ltd...............	5	12¾
L	5	G. Angus & Co. Pref.	10	13½
Bl	10	Gloster. Carri. & W.	■	10
Bl	5	Gt. Wstn. Cttn., Ltd.	20	15¾
M	6	Hetherington, L. Prf.	10	8¾
M	4½	Do. Debs., 1910	100	96
B	1/4½	Hinks (J. & Son), Ltd.	1	1⅜
S	10/	Jessop & Sons, £50 Sh	30	26
S	10	Kayser, Ellsn. & Co. L.	5	10
S	6	Do. Pref.	5	7½
M	7/6	Kellner-Partgton., L.	5	14½
M	4½	Do. Debs., 1914..	100	105½
M	5	Kerr Thread, Ltd., Debs.............	100	99
B	17/	King's Norton Metal, £10 Shs..........	8½	18
M	6/	Lancashire & Yorks. Wagon, Ltd.	10	9¾
L	10/	Liverpool Exch., Ltd.	20	27½
L	35/	Do. Grain Stge, Ltd.	50	110
L	2/6	Do. Rubber, Ltd...	5	6¾
M	9d.	Manchester Bond. Whse., L., £10 Shs.	4½	2¾
M	3/9	Do. Comcial. Bldgs., Ltd., £10 Shs.	5	10⅝
M	3/9	Do. No. 2, £10 Shs.	5	10¾
M	2/3	Do. No. 3, £10 Shs.	5	7½
M	4/	Do. Corn, &c., Exchange, Ltd.	10	16½
M	4	Do. Debs.	100	125
M	8	Do. Ryl. Exchge, L.	100	245
B	5	Midland Rlwy. Car. Wgn., Ld., £20 Sh.	10	14½
B	59	Millers & Corys Dbs.	100	101
B	12/6	Mint, Brgham., Ltd.	5	7
B	5	Do. Debs.	25	107
B	10/	Nettlefolds, Ltd.....	10	46
B	5	Do. Pref.	10	15
S	9	Nth. Centrl. Wgn., L.	5	8½
B	10/	Patnt. Nut & Bolt, L.	10	28
B	5	Do. Pref.	10	14½
B	6d.	Perry & Co., Ltd. ..	1	1½
B	6d.	Do. Pref.	1	1½
S	10	Round, J., & Co., L., £10 Shs.	6	12½
S	10	Rodgers, J., & Sons, L.	100	218
M	18/9	Rylands & Sons, Ltd., £20	15	40½
M	2½	Do. paid up	20	45
M	4	Do. Debs. .. 1909	100	106
S	5	Sanderson Brs. & Co., Ltd Debs.	100	102
M	4½	Schwabe, S., & Co., Ltd., 1 Debs. 1914	100	104
S	7½	Sheffield Forge & Rolling, Ltd.	10	11
L	4	Southport Pier, Ltd.	100	92½
L	2½	Do. W. Gdns., Ltd.	5	3
Bl	5	Spillers & Bakers, Ltd, £10 Shs.	9	14¾
Bl	6	Do. Pref.	10	14½
B	5/	Union Rolling Stock, Ltd., £20 Shs.....	5	7½
M	5/	Victoria Pr., S'port, L.	5	4½
Bl	6	Western Wagon & Property, Ltd.....	6	10
S	10	Wostenholm, G., & Son, Ltd., £25 Shs.	20	27
S	6½	Yorksh. Wagon, Ltd.	2	2¾

FINANCIAL, TRUSTS, &c.

Chief Market.	Int. or Div.	Name.	Amount paid.	Price.
M	1/	Manchstr. Trst. £10 Shs...............	2	15/†
M	1/3	N. of Eng. T. Deb. & A., Ltd. £10 Shs.	2½	21/6
M	3½	Do. 1 Mt. Debs...	100	95½
L	5/	Pacific Ln. & Inv., L.	2½	2⅜
L	4	Do. Deb. Stk.....	100	102†
L	—	United Trst., L. Prfd.	100	72½
L	—	Do. Deferred....	100	63

GAS.

Chief Market.	Int. or Div.	Name.	Amount paid.	Price.
Bl	5	Bristol Gas (5 p.c. mx.)	100	130
Bl	4	Do. 1st Deb.	100	136†
S	10	Gt. Grimsby "C" ..	10	202
L	10	Liverpool Utd. "A"	100	258
L	7	Do. "B"......	100	191
L	4	Do. Deb.	100	135†
S	10	Sheffield Gas "A," "B," "C"	100	254
S	10	Do. "D." £6 Shs.	10	15
B	10½	Wolverhampton	100	220½
B	3	Do. 6 p.c. Pref...	100	170½

INSURANCE.

Chief Market.	Int. or Div.	Name.	Amount paid.	Price.
M	6	Equitable F. & Acc. £5 Shs.	1	38/
L	2/	Liverpool Mortgage £10 Shs.	2	1 5/16
M	2/	Mchester. Fire £20 Shs	2	7⅜
M	5/	National Boiler & G., Ltd., £10 Shs.	3	13⅜
L	2/	Reliance Mar., Ltd., £10 Shs.	2	4¾
L	2/	Sea, Ltd., £10 Shs...	2	10 [illegible]
L	8/	Stnd. Mar., L., £20 Sh.	4	8 [illegible]
L	1/	State Fire, L., £20 Sh.	1	2⅜

COAL, IRON, AND STEEL.

Chief Market.	Int. or Div.	Name.	Amount paid.	Price.
Bl.	7/6	Albion Stm. Coal ..	10	10⅜
M	16/	And. Knowles & S., Ltd., £37½ Shs. ..	22½	13½
M	5	Do. Mt. Debs. 1908	100	105†
Bl.	1/½	Ashton V. Iron	100	25
S		Bessemer, Ltd.	10	19½
S	5	Do. Pref.	10	13
S	7	Briggs, H., & Co., "A" £15 Shs.....	12½	15½
S	7	Do. "B" £15 Shs.	8½	9½
S	20	Brown Baley's, Stl., L.	10	28¾
S	5	Brown, J., & Co., Cum. Pref.	10	13⅜
S	£5	Cammell, Ch. & Co., Ltd., £100 Shs...	80	215
S	5	Do. "A" Pref. ..	20	33½
S	40/	Do. "B"	20	53¾
M	5	Chatterley Whitfield. Col., Debs., 1905..	100	100½
Bl	4	Davis, D., & Sons, Ld.	10	10¾
M	5	Evans, R., & Co., Ltd., Deb., 1910 [†	100	100½
S	12½	Fox, S., & Co., Ltd., £100 Shs.	80	178¼
Bl	10	Gt. Wstn. Col., L., "A"	5	10
Bl	5	Do. "B"	5	4⅝
Bl	3	Main Colliery, Ltd.	10	7
B	2/6	Muntz's Metal, Ltd.	5	7½
B	5	Do. Pref......	5	5⅛
M	1/8½	Nth. Lonsd. Iron and Steel, Ltd., £10 Sh.	8½	2⅜
Bl	6	North's Nav. Coll., Ltd., Debs.	100	104
S	60/	Parkgate Irn. & Stl., Ltd., £100 Shs. ..	75	68
M	6	Pearson & Knls., Ld., "A" Cum. Pref...	50	46
B	10/	Sandwell Pk. Col., L.	10	17
M	6/3	Sheepbridge Coal and Iron, Ltd., "A"	25	16½
M	2/6	Do. "B"	10	6½
M	5	Do. "C" Gua. Pf.	25	29¼
Bl	41	South Wales Coll., Ltd., "A"	17	8½
S	55/	Staveley Coal & Iron, Ltd., "A" £100 Sh.	60	79
S	55/	Do. "C"	60	80¾
M	1/10½	Tredegar Iron & Cl., Ld., "A" £10 Sh.	7½	2½
M	1½	Do. "B" Stk. ..	100	29½
M	2/	Wigan Cl. & Irn., Ld.	10	6
M	1/6	Do. £10 Shs.	7½	3½

SHIPPING.

Chief Market.	Int. or Div.	Name.	Amount paid.	Price.
Bl	6	Bristol St. Nav. Pref.	10	12
L	5/	Brit. & Af. St. Nav..	10	13½
L	3/3	British & Estn, Ltd.	6½	3
L	10/	Pacific Stm. Nav., L.	25	24½
L	10/	Wst. Ind. & Pac. St. Ltd., £25 Shs....	20	29

TRAMWAYS, &c.

Chief Market.	Int. or Div.	Name.	Amount paid.	Price.
B	9/	Brmngh. & Aston, L.	5	11
B	5/	Do. Mid., Ltd. ..	10	8
Bl	6/	Bristol Tr. & Car., Ltd..............	10	19¾
Bl	4/	Do. Debs.	100	121†
L	6	I. of Man Elec., L., Pref.	1	1½
M	15/	Manchester C. & T., L., "A" £20 Shs.	15	27½
M	10/	Do. "B"	10	18¾

WATER WORKS.

Chief Market.	Int. or Div.	Name.	Amount paid.	Price.
Bl	7	Bristol	25	59½
Bl	7	Do..............	20	46
Bl	58/	Do. 7 p.c. max. ..	100	157½
Bl	4½	Do. Pref.	20	32½†
Bl	5	Do. Pref.	10	18⅜
Bl	3½	Do. Deb.	100	127†
M	10	Fylde "A"........	100	335
M	7	Do. "B"	100	224
B	6	S. Staffs. Ord. "A"	100	168
B	—	Do. "B"	100	167
B	4	Do. Deb. Stk.	100	140†
B	5	Do. Pf "A" "B" "C"	100	165†
M	£3½	Stockport District ..	100	185
B	2/	Wolverhampton New	5	6¾

SCOTTISH.

In quoting the markets, E stands for Edinburgh, and G for Glasgow.

RAILWAYS.

Chief Market.	Int. or Div.	Name.	Nom. Amount	Price.
E	5½	Arbroath and Forfar	25	51
G	1½	Callander and Oban.	10	7½
G	4	Do. Deb. Stock	100	148
G	4½	Do. Pref.......	10	14½
G	4	Cathct. Dist. Deb. Stk.	100	148
E	5	Edin. and Bathgate .	100	181½
E	7	Forth & Clyde Junc.	100	225
G	4½	Lanarks. and Ayrsh.	10	14
G	4	Do. & Dumbartons.	10	14½
G	4	Do. Deb. Stk.	100	149

BANKS.

Chief Market.	Int. or Div.	Name.	Nom. Amount	Price.
G	12	Bank of Scotland ..	100	359½
G	20	British Linen	100	474†
G	8	Caledonian, Ltd.....	2½	97/6
G	—	Clydesdale, Ltd.	10	23½
G	16	Commercl. of Scot., L.	20	88½†
G	16	National of Scot. Ld.	100	413
G	7½	North of Scotland, L.	4	9¾
G	8	Royal of Scotland ..	100	230
G	12½	Town & County, Ltd.	7	21
G	11	Union of Scotland, L.	10	25¾

BREWERIES.

Chief Market.	Int. or Div.	Name.	Nom. Amount	Price.
E	5	Bernard, Thos. Pref.	10	11¼
E	5	Bernard, T. & J., Cum. Pref.........	10	12¾
G	10	Highland Distilleries	3½	10⅜

CANALS AND DOCKS.

Chief Market.	Int. or Div.	Name.	Nom. Amount	Price.
G	4	Clyde Nav. 4 p.c....	100	127½
G	3½	Do. 3½ p.c......	100	103½
G	3½	Greenock Harb. "A"	100	96½
G	1	Do. "B"	100	38½

MISCELLANEOUS.

Chief Market.	Int. or Div.	Name.	Nom. Amount	Price.
G	4½	Alexander & Co. Debs.	100	110½
G	5	Baird, H., & Sns. C. P.	10	13
E	10	Barry, Ostlere, & Co.	7½	12½
E	6	Do. Cum. Pref...	10	15⅛
G	5	Brown, Stewart, Deb.	100	78
E	7½	Broxburn Oil	8½	8¾
E	6	Do. Cum. Pref...	10	11 5/16
E	7	Edinburgh & Dist. Tram. Cum. Pref.	5	8¾
E	5	Gilroy, Sons, & Co. Debs.	100	99
G	3/	Glasgow Cot. Spin...	6	5
G	55/	Do. Royal Exchg.	46	110
G	—	Pumpherston Oil Pf.	10	8¾
E	7	Scottish Assam Tea	10	11½
E	5	Scottish Waggon....	10	13½
G	5	Stoddard & Co. Pref.	10	12¾

FINANCIAL, LAND, AND INVESTMENT.

Chief Market.	Int. or Div.	Name.	Nom. Amount	Price.
G	1/	Assets Co..........	1	47/
E	4½	Investors' Mort. Pref.	100	98¾
E	4	Do. Deb. Stk....	100	103½
E	4	Nthn. Inv. N. Zeal. Deb. Stk.	100	106
E	4	N. of Scot. Canadian Deb. Stk.	100	106
E	4½	Real & Deb. Corp. Deb. Stk.	100	106¾
E	6	Swan Land & Cattle Cum. Pref.	10	10½

INSURANCE.

Chief Market.	Int. or Div.	Name.	Amount paid.	Price.
G	12/	Caledonian F. & Life	5	35¾
G	4/6	City of Glasgow Life	2½	13¾
E	20/	Edinburgh Life	20	55
G	13/2	Life Ass. of Scotland	8⅓	34½
E	8	Nat. Guar. & Surety	2 1/?	48/6
G	17½	Scottish Union and National "A"....	1	95/
G	17½	Do. "B"	3⅛	17½

IRON, COAL, AND STEEL.

Chief Market.	Int. or Div.	Name.	Amount paid.	Price.
E	Nil.	Addie, Coll. Cm. Pref.	10	7½
E	12/6	Arniston Coal	8	14¾
E	5	Cairntable Gas Coal	8	86/
E	7½	Fife Coal	10	21
E	5	Do. Cum. Pref..	10	13¼
G	7	Merry & Cunghame. Cum. Pref........	10	15¼
G	5	Do. Debentures ..	100	103½
E	1/9	Niddrie & Benhar Cl.	1½	39/
G	5	Steel Com. of Scotlnd	—	
—		"A" Deb. Stk. ..	100	110
G	6	Do. and Mt. "B"	100	105
E	5/	Watson, John	8½	10½
E	6	Do. Cum. Pref..	7½	8⅞
E	12½	Wilson's & Cly. Coal	3	8¼

IRISH.

In quoting the markets, B stands for Belfast, and D for Dublin.

CORPORATION STOCKS.

Chief Market.	Int. or Div.	Name.	Amount paid.	Price.
B	3½	Belfast, 1921	100	113
B	3½	Do. 1912........	100	108½
B	3½	Do. 1924........	100	109½
B	3	Do. 1955........	100	106
B	3½	Do. Water Com...	100	117
B	3	Do. do.	100†	107½
B	3½	Do. Harbour Com.	100	113¾
D	3½	Rathmines & Rathgar	100	110
D	3½	Waterford Deb.	100	—

RAILWAYS.

Chief Market.	Int. or Div.	Name.	Amount Paid.	Price.
D	25/	Cork, Bandon, & S.C.	100	76
D	4	Do. Deb.........	100	—
D	4	Do. W. Cork Pref.	100	119
B	3½	Belfast & Northern..	100	161
B	4	Do. Deb.........	100	148½
B	4	Do. Pref.	100	145
B	6½	Belfast & C. Down..	100	167
B	4	Do. Deb.........	100	149
B	3	Do.	100	109
B	4½	Do. 4½ Pref. B...	100	153½
B	5	Do. Guar.	100	173½
D	Nil.	Dublin, Wick. & Wex.	100	25
D	4	Do. Deb.........	100	125½
D	4½	Do. Deb.........	100	130
D	6	Do. Guar.	100	160
D	4	Do. C. of Dub. Junc.	100	116
D	5	Do. 1860 Pref. ..	100	106
D	—	Do. 1864 Pref. ..	100	90
D	—	Do. 1865 Pref. ..	100	—
B	6½	Great Northern	100	183
B	4	Do. Deb.........	100	150
B	4	Do. Pref. B.	100	145½
B	5½	Gt. South & Western	100	144½
B	4	Do. Deb.	100	149½
B	4	Do. Guar.........	100	146
D	4	Midland Gt. Western	100	112
D	4	Do. Deb.	100	—
D	4½	Do. Deb.	100	—
D	4½	Do. Deb.	100	—
D	5	Do. Pref.	100	177
D	4	Do. Pref.	100	143
D	—	Waterford & Central	100	—
D	3	Do. Deb.	100	—
D	3½	Do. Pref.	100	—
D	4	Waterfd. L., & W. Db.	100	128†
D	4½	Do. Deb.	100	—
D	4	Do. Pref.	100	116
D	3½	Do. Pref.	100	90

BANKS.

Chief Market.	Int. or Div.	Name.	Amount paid.	Price.
B	50/	Belfast, Old, £125 Shs.	25	127
B	20/	Do. New, £125 Shs.	25	80½
D	2/	Hibernian, £20 Shs.	3	6¼
D	2/	Munster & Leinster £5 Shs.	2	8¼
B	11/	Northern, £50 Shs...		25½
D	13/	Royal, £50 Shs.	10	—
B	5/	Ulster, £15 Shs.	2½	12¼

BREWERIES AND DISTILLERIES.

Chief Market.	Int. or Div.	Name.	Amount paid.	Price.
D	10/	Castlebellingham & Drog.	10	15½
D	6	Do. Pref.	10	15½
D	4½	Do. Deb.	100	116
B	17/	Dunville & Co.......	10	29
B	6	Irish Distillery, Pref.	10	13
B	5	Do. Deb.	100	111
B	6	J. & J. M'Connell, Pf.	10	14½†
B	13/6	Mitchell & Co......	9	19½
B	5	Do. Deb.	10	11½†
D	4½	Phœnix Brew. Deb.	100	90
B	6/	Wm. Cowan........	10	12½
B	6	Do. Pref. ..	10	13½
B	8/	Young, King, & Co.	8	16

STEAM AND CANAL.

Chief Market.	Int. or Div.	Name.	Amount paid.	Price.
B	Nil	Belfast Steamship ..	50	35½
D	10/	British and Irish	50	—
D	15/	City of Dublin......	100	62
D	3½	Do. Deb.	100	104
D	30/	Dublin & Lpool. Bldg..	50	—
D	2/6	Dundalk & Newry..	10	—
D	3/6	Grand Canal........	10	11½
D	3	Do. Pref. ..	10	9½
D	3	Do. Deb. ..	100	99½
B	30/	Irish Shipowners....	100	60
B	3/6	Ulster Steamship....	5	5¼

MISCELLANEOUS.

Chief Market.	Int. or Div.	Name.	Amount paid.	Price.
D	3/1	Arnott & Co.	[illegible]	[illegible]
D	6	Do. Pref. ..	[illegible]	[illegible]
B	9/	Belfast Com. Bldgs.	[illegible]	[illegible]
B	52/6	Do. Ropework Co.	[illegible]	[illegible]
B	5	Do. do. Pref.	[illegible]	[illegible]
B	2/	Do. Discount Co..	[illegible]	[illegible]
B	5	Do. do. Pref.	[illegible]	[illegible]
B	10/	Brookfield Linen	[illegible]	[illegible]
B	Nil	Coey & Co.	[illegible]	[illegible]
B	5	Do. Deb.	[illegible]	[illegible]
B	4½	David Allen & S's Deb.	[illegible]	[illegible]
D	4/	Dublin Trams	[illegible]	[illegible]
D	6	Do. Pref.	[illegible]	[illegible]
D	4	Do. Deb. ...	[illegible]	[illegible]
B	5/	Edenderry Spinning .	[illegible]	[illegible]
B	25/	Falls Flax Spinning .	[illegible]	[illegible]
B	17/	Forster, Green, & Co.	[illegible]	[illegible]
B	9/	Island Spinning	[illegible]	[illegible]
B	6/	Jas. Lindsay & Co..	[illegible]	[illegible]
B	1/7½	John Arnott & Co...	[illegible]	[illegible]
B	4½	Do. Deb.	[illegible]	[illegible]
D	5/	Kinahan & Co.......	[illegible]	[illegible]
D	5½	Do. Pref.	[illegible]	[illegible]
D	4½	Do. Deb.	[illegible]	[illegible]
B	12/	Kirker & Co.	[illegible]	[illegible]
B	5/	Lenky, Kelly, & Lenky	[illegible]	[illegible]
B	6	Do. Pref.	[illegible]	[illegible]
B	2/4½	Lindsay Bros. Ltd...	[illegible]	[illegible]
B	4½	Do. Deb.	[illegible]	[illegible]
D	1/	National Assurance .	[illegible]	[illegible]
B	10/	Olley & Co.	[illegible]	[illegible]
D	1/1½	Patriotic Assurance..	[illegible]	[illegible]
B	3/7½	P. Johnston & Son, L.	[illegible]	[illegible]
B	10/	Robertson, F., & Co.	[illegible]	[illegible]
B	5	Ulster Marine Insur.	[illegible]	[illegible]
B	15/	York-street Flax	[illegible]	[illegible]
B	6	Do. Pref.......	[illegible]	[illegible]
B	4½	Do. Deb.......	100	[illegible]

INDIAN AND CEYLON TEA COMPANIES.

Acres Planted.	Crop, 1896.	Paid up Capital.	Share.	Paid up.	Name.	Dividends. 1894.	1895.	1896.	Int. 1897.	Price.	Yield.	Reserve.	Balance Forward.	Working Capital.	Mortgages, Debs., or Pref. Capital not otherwise stated.
	lb.	£	£	£	INDIAN COMPANIES.							£	£	£	£
11,240	3,109,000	120,000	10	3	Amalgamated Estates	—	*	10	5	3¾	6½	10,000	16,500	D52,950	—
		400,000	10	10	Do. Pref.	—	*	5	1½	10½	4¾				
10,223	3,387,100	187,160	20	20	Assam	20	20	20	5	62½	6¼	55,000	1,730	D11,330	—
5,900	3,310,000	142,500	10	10	Assam Frontier.........	3	6	6	—	9½	6¼	—	256	20,000	80,500
		142,500	10	10	Do. Pref.	6	6	6	3	12	5				
2,087	865,550	66,745	5	5	Attaree Khat	12	12	8	3	7½	5½	3,790	4,820	7,770	—
1,633	550,980	78,170	10	10	Borelli	4	4	5	—	9	5½	—	3,256	D270	6,500
1,689	880,000	60,825	5	5	British Indian	6	3	3	—	4¾	5½	—	2,000	12,300	18,500
3,223	2,282,430	114,500	5	5	Brahmapootra	20	15	20	6	14½	6¾	—	26,440	42,000	*
3,904	1,634,000	76,500	10	10	Cachar and Dooars	*	8	7	—	9⅞	7¼	—	1,645	21,040	*
		76,500	10	10	Do. Pref.	*	6	6	3	12½	4¾				
3,946	2,002,370	72,010	1	1	Chargola	8	7	10	2½	1	10	3,000	3,300	—	—
		81,000	1	1	Do. Pref.	7	7	7	3½	1¼	5				
2,971	968,090	33,000	5	5	Chubwa	10	8	10	3½	7	6½	10,000	2,043	D5,400	—
		33,000	5	5	Do. Pref.	7	7	7	3½	7	5				
33,250	10,620,000	120,000	10	3	Cons. Tea and Lands	—		10	5	3½	7½	65,000	14,240	D291,874	—
		2,000,000	10	10	Do. 1st Pref.	—	*	5	15	11	4½				
		400,000	10	10	Do. 2nd Pref.	—	*	7	17	11½	5½				
2,230	593,160	135,420	20	20	Darjeeling	5½	5½	6	—	24	5	5,558	1,965	1,700	—
2,114	456,580	60,000	10	10	Darjeeling Cons.........	—	—	4/2	—	7½	9½	—	1,800	—	—
		60,000	10	10	Do. Pref.	—	*	5	2½	9½	5				
6,600	2,973,050	150,000	10	10	Dooars	12½	12½	12½	2½	21	6¼	45,000	300	D30,000	—
		75,000	10	10	Do. Pref.	7	7	7	3½	17½	3½				
3,367	1,833,580	165,000	10	10	Doom Dooma	11¾	10	12½	5	23½	5½	30,000	4,032	—	[illegible]
1,377	500,080	61,120	5	5	Eastern Assam	½	nil.	4	—	3½	5½	—	1,790	—	[illegible]
4,038	1,529,380	85,000	10	10	East India and Ceylon	*	nil.	7	—	9½	7	—	1,710	—	—
		85,000	10	10	Do. Pref.	*	6	6	3	12½	4¾				
7,570	3,600,000	219,000	10	10	Empire of India	—	*	6/10	2½	13½	—	15,000	—	27,000	—
		219,000	10	10	Do. Pref.	—	*	5	2½	11½	4½				
1,180	647,600	94,060	10	10	Indian of Cachar	7	3½	3	—	6	5½	6,070	—	7,200	—
2,916	968,000	83,500	5	5	Jhanzie	10	10	10	4	8½	5½	14,500	1,070	2,700	—
7,980	3,467,000	250,000	10	10	Jokai	10	10	10	5	18	5½	45,000	990	D9,000	—
		100,000	10	10	Do. Pref.	*	6	6	3	15½	3¾				
5,224	1,801,600	100,000	20	20	Jorehaut	20	20	20	—	58	7	26,020	2,955	3,000	—
1,547	534,560	65,660	10	8	Lebong	1½	15	15	5	17½	6¾	9,000	2,130	5,490	—
5,082	1,843,700	100,000	10	10	Lungla	*	10	6	3	10	6	—	1,543	D21,000	—
		100,000	10	10	Do. Pref.	*	6	6	3	12½	4¾				
2,684	866,300	95,970	10	10	Majuli	7	5	5	—	7	7	—	2,606	960	—
1,300	216,000	91,840	1	1	Makum	—	—	2	—	1½	1½	—	—	1,000	[illegible]
3,140	938,400	100,000	1	1	Moabund	—	—	*	—	1	—	—	—	-	[illegible]
		50,000	1	1	Do. Pref.	—	—	*	2½	1	5				
2,080	520,000	79,590	10	10	Scottish Assam	7	7	7	—	11	6¼	6,500	800	9,990	—
4,150	1,635,000	100,000	10	10	Singlo	6	5	5	—	9½	4½	—	300	D3,200	—
		80,000	10	10	Do. Pref.	*	6½	6½	3½	13	5				
					CEYLON COMPANIES.										
10,315	1,743,824	250,000	100	100	Anglo-Ceylon, & Gen.	—	*	3½	—	72	7	20,998	1,405	D70,844	[illegible]
1,836	685,741	50,000	10	10	Associated Tea	—	*	5	—	8½	6¼	—	164	2,498	—
		60,000	10	10	Do. Pref.	—	*	6	—	11	5½				
10,390	3,763,000	167,380	10	10	Ceylon Tea Plantations ..	15	15	15	7	28	5½	84,900	1,516	D90,809	—
		81,080	10	10	Do. Pref.	7	7	7	17	17½	4				
5,720	1,549,700	55,960	5	3	Ceylon & Oriental Est.....	5	8	7	—	[illegible]	7¼	—	290	D2,047	[illegible]
		46,000	5	5	Do. Pref.	6	6	6	3	5½	5½				
2,157	801,609	111,330	5	5	Dimbula Valley	—	*	10	5	6½	7	—	—	5,735	[illegible]
		62,607	5	5	Do. Pref.	—	*	6	3	6½	4½				
11,496	3,775,000	298,250	5	5	Eastern Prod. & Est.	3	5	6¼	[illegible]	[illegible]	4½	20,000	12,740	D27,797	[illegible]
3,218	701,100	150,000	10	10	Lanka Plantations.........	4	5	5	15	7½	6¾	—	[illegible]	D11,300	[illegible]
2,193	960,200	22,080	10	10	New Dimbula "A"	10	16	16	—	25	6	12,000	2,004	2,190	—
		55,710	10	10	Do. "B"	18	16	16	—	24	6¾				
		8,400	10	10	Do. "C"	nil.	8	14	—	—	—				
2,570	570,360	100,000	10	10	Ouvah	6	8	6	*	10	6	4,000	7,731	D1,055	—
2,630	535,675	200,000	10	10	Nuwara Eliya	—	*	6	3	11½	5¼	—	—	—	[illegible]
1,780	720,800	41,000	10	10	Scottish Ceylon	15	15	15	5	23	6½	7,000	[illegible]	D3,070	—
		9,000	10	10	Do. Pref.	7	7	7	3½	16	4½				
2,450	602,000	56,000	10	6	Standard	19½	15	15	5	24½	6¼	9,000	800	D15,082	[illegible]

* Company formed this year. In working capital column D stands for debit. † Interim dividends are given as actual distribution made. ‡ *Total* div.

Printed for the Proprietor by Love & Wyman, Ltd., Great Queen Street, London, W.C.; and Published by Clement Wilson at Norfolk House, Norfolk Street, Strand, London, W.C.

The Investors' Review

Vol. I.—No. 3. New Series. FRIDAY, JANUARY 21, 1898. [Registered as a Newspaper.] Price 6d. By post, 6½d

The Investment Index,

A Quarterly Supplement to the "Investors' Review."

Price 2s. net. 8s. 6d. per annum, post free.

THE INVESTMENT INDEX is an indispensable supplement to the Investors' Review. A file of it enables investors to follow the ups and downs of markets, and each number gives the return obtainable on all classes of securities at recent prices, arranged in a most convenient form for reference. Appended to its tables of figures are criticisms on company balance sheets, State Budgets, &c., similar to those in the Investors' Review.

Regarding it, the *Speaker* says: "The Quarterly 'Investment Index' is probably the handiest and fullest, as it is certainly the safest, of guides to the investor."

"The compilation of securities is particularly valuable."—*Pall Mall Gazette.*

"Its carefully classified list of securities will be found very valuable."—*Globe.*

"At no time has such a list of securities been more valuable than at the present."—*Star.*

"The invaluable 'Investors' Index.'"—*Sketch.*

"A most valuable compilation."—*Glasgow Herald.*

Subscription to the "Investors' Review" and "Investment Index," 21s. per annum, post free.

CLEMENT WILSON,
29, PATERNOSTER ROW, LONDON, E.C.

CONTENTS

The Investors' Review.

Economic and Financial Notes and Correspondence.

THE NEW INDIAN JUGGLING.

For the life of us we cannot understand what the officials of the Government in Calcutta expect to gain by their last device for providing India with a currency. A long speech was made by Sir James Westland a week ago to-day, and we have read it. Without being able to guess what it all really means, it is easy to see that the Government is in a mess, which mess it sturdily refuses to ascribe to its own folly; but what we do not comprehend is the motive which dictates the latest proposal for escaping from the difficulties the Government has created for itself. As readers know, what seems now to be aimed at is to provide a "gold standard" in London for a silver and paper currency in India. Gold is to be deposited here, and, against it, silver notes and rupees will be issued in India to enable bankers there to buy bills on London, which they otherwise would not have the means to do, because the bureaucrats have stripped the dependency of money. This we understand; but how is the banker who operates in such a way to protect himself from losses by fluctuations in exchange? Sir James very justly said that at the present moment "the only effect of the rate of exchange upon the banker is to convince him that the less he remits to India the better for himself, for he is bringing out his money at the top of the market, but cannot possibly remit it on better rates, and he might have to do so on worst rates."

A

Just so. And does Sir James mean us to believe that keeping the gold in London will make any difference? That gold is used in India just as much as if it had been sent there, and the banker who speculates in exchange on the Government plan is not relieved from any of the substantial risks which he runs now if he sends out gold. It is pitiful to see men in charge of a great dependency peddling and muddling in this fashion, shutting their eyes to the facts, obstinately blinding themselves to the true economic position of India, and therefore hurrying that unhappy country towards a catastrophe.

"India is All Right."

But India is all right, said Sir Michael Hicks-Beach at Bristol. There is no more honest man in Parliament than the present Chancellor of the Exchequer, and he would not have said what he did had he not believed it. None the less is he and the country behind him being grossly deceived regarding the position of Indian finance. It may be quite true that the officials in India do not wish to appeal for help to us. They have got things into such a hopeless mess that they are naturally in terror at the prospect of investigation and discovery. None the less is India in sore need. Her famines, pestilence, and marauding expeditions on a grand scale beyond the frontier must have cost at least two hundred million rupees, and the Treasury has not two millions to pay with. Probably the misguiding men who preside over the unhappy peninsula nourish the hope of being able to resume their extravagant policy of railway extension, and thus procure the means to hide up the yawning deficit. They may have no hope except that of the ostrich. Perhaps it is just as well that the mess should be allowed to simmer and come to a head, since only through a breakdown and the prospect of impending ruin does it seem possible to induce the "imperial" British public to learn to take an intelligent interest in India. A large dole now would only enable the futile creatures, now masters of the destinies of 250 millions of people, to dribble on until remedy of any kind became impossible.

Midland Railway of Western Australia.

Debenture-holders in this unfortunate concern should take note of the following, and try to act together. They may depend upon it no means will be left untried to escape liability, assuming that it exists, a point upon which we are not in a position to give any opinion :—

Reform Club, Pall Mall, S.W.,
January 18, 1898.

Sir,—A meeting of the Midland Railway of Western Australia is to be held in about two months to consider a scheme for reconstruction to be proposed by Mr. A. Young, who has been appointed the receiver of the Company by the Six Per Cent. Debenture holders, and it will be well for the debenture-holders to consider before the meeting what their course ought to be.

Mr. Young quite ignores the liability of the directors to make good any deficiency or loss incurred by the debenture-holders through their neglect in not calling up the share capital, or from the misleading statements in the prospectus.

The first thing Mr. Young has to do is to ascertain what is the liability of the directors in this respect.

I have taken counsel's opinion and am informed that the directors are liable for all loss.—Yours faithfully, A Bondholder.

The Stock Conversion and Investment Trust.

Amongst Company Reports will be found reference to the Stock Conversion and Investment Trust, whose display for the past year is, we believe, the best ever made in its history. But we should like to draw attention to a glaring fault in the drawing up of its profit and loss account. All kinds of revenue of the Trust for the year are lumped together in the one item of: "By profit on investments, dividends, commission, transfer fees, interest, &c., £74,489." Now, to obtain any idea of the substantial character, or otherwise, of this revenue, this amalgamated total ought to have been split up into at least four separate items, so that the income from dividends, from profits upon realisations, and from commissions could be ascertained.

In the present form, all investigation into this matter from the side of the information supplied in the report leads to confusion rather than enlightenment. Thus the securities held by the Trust, including £34,369 loans on securities, amounted to £704,588, and form the whole of its assets outside cash. Nearly three-quarters of the amount is in Home Railway stocks, and so, if we allowed 5 per cent. interest upon the money as revenue from this source, our estimate would surely be a liberal one. Commission upon working the North Eastern and North Western Railways "split" stocks certainly should not exceed £2,500, and if this is added to 5 per cent. upon the investments we get an income of £37,600, or just about half of the amount, £74,489, returned as revenue for the year. Whether profits on selling stock, or sources of revenue of which we have no knowledge, provided the difference we have nothing to show, and perhaps the directors think that it is not necessary to explain the problem. But to the man who is inclined to buy the shares upon the strength of the 12½ per cent., such information is of prime importance. Profit from realisation of stocks is a most uncertain form of revenue, and if it provided last year anything like half the income, the probability of its continuance must be exceedingly doubtful.

Government and the Sugar Bounties.

Mr. Chamberlain was good enough at Liverpool to explain the general line of the policy Government has resolved upon in dealing with the distress and trade depression in the West Indies. Details are wanting; but enough was said to show that the policy proposed is right in the main, and, if properly carried out, will be helpful for the island, while involving no interference with freedom of trade. Mr. Chamberlain does not intend to fight the sugar bounties by countervailing duties, for the very sufficient reason that he does not believe they would be effectual. They would involve us in difficulties with powers with whom we have commercial treaties and most-favoured-nation clauses, while new duties would involve an expenditure altogether disproportionate to their amount. Finally, he considers it an unscientific way of attempting to benefit a trade of 260,000 tons per annum—the amount of the West Indian sugar output—by interfering with, and perhaps injuring, a trade of 1,500,000 tons, the amount of our sugar importation from other countries. Such a course must surely appear preposterous to any one. The Commission that inquired into the condition of the West Indies made certain recommendations, wise enough in themselves, and which the Government hoped to give effect to; but their action would be slow; and meanwhile something had to be done to save the Colony from ruin.

Government have, therefore, decided on giving a large grant in aid, which might enable the colonists to tide over the crisis until Continental nations shall have recognised the impolicy of the sugar bounties. This policy of a grant in aid was probably inevitable; but if spent in the reproductive interests of the colony at large, and not for the personal benefit of individuals, who may make use of the aid thus granted to turn their backs upon the colony, and so leave it poorer than before, may, on the whole, be advantageous. Mr. Chamberlain spoke as if he fully appreciated the danger involved; and if he takes care that the grant is used for stimulating the new industries suggested by the Commissioners, and in assisting the Colonists to help themselves, the West Indies may take a new lease of life—become in time even practically independent of the sugar-cane industry, with which their existence has always been too closely bound up.

By the bye, we hope the amiable and enterprising Secretary of State for the Colonies is in a position to be congratulated on the success of his own family enterprise in the West Indies. The Chamberlains in this case will be entitled to take a distinguished place among the men who have not sat themselves down and wept because sugar could only be produced by industry, intelligence, economy, and close attention to business. Thanks to the initiative of this Midland family, an industry was started in the Bahamas, by a company called the Andros Fibre Company, Ltd., and preparations made for the growth of a variety of agave, known as *Agave Rigida*, out of which a variety of hemp was to be manufactured of a quality deemed superior to Manila. So fine were the prospects of this new business that an issue of £200,000 in 5 per cent. mortgage debentures was made upon the personal guarantee of Messrs. Joseph, Austen and Neville Chamberlain in order to make the business grand. We have never heard how the thing got on, but feel perfectly certain that with such men in control it must have been an immense success. By this time all the debentures are no doubt paid off, and the company rich enough almost to keep the Lotus eaters of the Antilles out of their distress without calling upon us for any money at all.

THE DREYFUS AFFAIR.

At first sight the ferment in France, and especially in Paris, over this lamentable affair may seem to have nothing financial about it. Everything, however, touches the mundane interests represented by money at some point, and were it only for the race hatred it is bringing to the front, this turmoil deserves watching by everybody with any stake in the public securities of Europe. No one who has read only a fragment of the literature surrounding this case, without prejudice, can avoid the conviction that Captain Dreyfus was unjustly condemned, and after a perusal of the startling document, signed *Judex*, courageously published by M. Yves Guyot, last Sunday in the *Siècle*, it is impossible to resist the conclusion that the sentence was what we should describe in this country as a "put-up job," concocted apparently in hatred of the Jewish community in France, against whom a storm is undoubtedly gathering. *Judex* says that the judges who presided over the court-martial were about to acquit Captain Dreyfus because there was not sufficient evidence that the memorandum of which so much has been made, and which had really nothing in it, was in his handwriting. At the critical moment General Mercier, then Minister of War, entered the room and laid before them a letter containing the words "this scamp D—— is getting too exigent." He said this D—— signified "Dreyfus," and that the letter clearly proved Dreyfus to be in communication with enemies abroad. The sentence of acquittal was thereupon altered to one of condemnation, and Captain Dreyfus was degraded, tortured, and sent prisoner to a far away earthly hell, in a fashion which blasts the fair fame of the French Army in the sight of all civilised peoples, on evidence not only in itself vicious, but which, such as it was, had been withheld from his counsel. That this charge is true has been proved by the lame attempts at rebuttal which the military faction has since published in its organs. It speaks well for the real heart of the French people that a swelling tide of indignation has been rising up in the country which may yet be capable even of overcoming the prejudice which undoubtedly exists there against the Jews. We have no sympathy with that prejudice, but recognise that it may prove to be an agent of destruction in the Republic of the most powerful description, if not exorcised or beaten down by a display of right-minded public opinion. If this hatred of the Jew is so great amongst certain classes in France as to cause men, otherwise honourable, to perpetrate a deed so dastardly mean and cruel as this sentence on Captain Dreyfus, an Alsatian Jew; if formalism has so profoundly entered into the soul of the French politician as to make him incapable of sympathy with the wronged in spite of military cliques, clerical dictation and race antipathies, then the not distant future of France is calculated to fill her best friends everywhere with the profoundest anxiety.

REFORM OF THE COMPANY LAWS.

Sir Michael Hicks-Beach spoke very plainly at Swansea as to the necessity of reforming the law relating to public companies. But it seems to have been merely the expression of a "pious opinion," not the prelude to more stringent legislation. Indeed, although the Chancellor of the Exchequer insists that the existing law is a "deliberate encouragement to frauds upon the public," he is doubtful if Parliament, unless actually forced by public opinion, will tackle the question. Governments have submitted amending Bills, but they have been of no use, for House of Lords' lawyers are "not eager reformers." They are already responsible for whittling down the Company Acts; they are not likely to favour renewed stringency. It is, therefore, urges Sir Michael Hicks-Beach, a question for the public. Outside agitation must compel the Houses of Parliament to do their duty in this matter, and if, as the Chancellor of the Exchequer says, the existing law "deliberately encourages fraud," can Members of Parliament relieve themselves of responsibility for this fraud while deliberately neglecting to do anything to reform and amend this fraudulent law? Let us, however, by all means, have public agitation. There must be very few in this country who do not very much desire the reform aimed at. But how to begin it? The main sufferers by the action of existing Acts are hardly a united body, and as a rule would rather submit to loss than trouble themselves to agitate.

THE END OF THE ENGINEERS' STRIKE.

At last the engineers have acknowledged their folly. They have withdrawn the London strike notices for the forty-eight hours' week, and appeal to the Employers' Federation to stop the lock-out, which was only decided upon because of these strike notices. This, however, cannot be done at a moment's warning; and the employers naturally took time to review their posi-position, so as to be able to act in unison. Yesterday they announced their readiness to close the lock-out on receiving a formal acceptance of the terms arranged at the conference. That the men are heartily sick of the quarrel is evident from the numbers who have already applied for work on the employers' terms—whether as unionists or non-unionists, they do not seem to care much. "All's well that ends well," and we welcome this tardy repentance of the workmen as ending a quarrel which should never have been raised—which has only brought serious loss and injury to themselves, and probably inflicted irreparable damage on the trade of the country.

But are the workmen of the kind that learn by experience, or will they be equally ready, a few months or years hence, to fall into another trap set by their somewhat erratic leaders? We cannot say that we can feel much confidence in their future action. We all know how keen is the competition of our foreign commercial rivals. It is becoming keener and more telling every day; yet the workmen never seem to give a thought to the serious danger lurking in this tremendous rivalry. At a time when employers should be devoting their utmost energies to seeking new markets, or in devising means to hold their own in the markets they have—a task by no means easy—their workmen, instead of sympathising with them and helping them, try to thwart them in order to force them to reduce the present not unduly formidable working week by a few hours.

That this danger of foreign competition is no mere bogey is shown by the weekly newspaper called *London*—a journal devoted to municipal affairs, and not unsympathetic with the claims of workmen—which has been inquiring into the possible effects upon home trade of the large expenditure contemplated by many provincial bodies on the extension of their tramway and light railway systems. Millions will be spent in this way during the next few years. And here are some of the results as regards our home trade described in *London*:—

Liverpool City Council has accepted a tender for American rails, an American firm has the contract for equipping Plymouth electric tramways, and a Continental firm has secured the contract for Hull. Public authorities have to put work up to tender, and although they are not bound to accept the lowest tender, it is not likely that they will pay 20 per cent. more to home manufacturers. Our own manufacturers seem to be completely undersold. This question has another phase: It renders entirely nugatory the labour clauses introduced into contracts. Our town councils cannot bind foreign firms to trades-union conditions.

So that not only is the work lost to the home manufacturer, but the trade-union workman is placed at a disadvantage in carrying out the contract. But how is it that the foreign contractor is thus procuring a lodgment in the very heart and centre of England? Eight years ago England could produce steel rails cheaper than any other country. It certainly cannot do so now. As the above extract shows, the American manufacturer can undersell us at our own door. The Trade Unions may not be entirely to blame in this matter; but they must bear a large share in the responsibility. If they would give a little more thought to the difficulties with which employers have to contend, and a little less to the search for petty personal triumphs, trade and the workmen too would soon begin to feel the benefit in increasing work and better wages.

OUR POSITION IN THE SOUDAN.

Affairs in the Soudan are much more serious than was imagined. If the Kalifa were a "man of war," and alert at taking advantage of an enemy's weakness, our position would be critical. The *Standard* announces that it is in a position to state "authoritatively" that the despatch of British troops to the Soudan is "a purely defensive measure." The line held by the Egyptian army extends from Kassala to Dongola, thence northward to Assouan. Then, as the *Standard* points out, the Kalifa at Omdurman "occupies a position from which, if he has the courage to advance, he may strike with overwhelming force against any part" of the long line held by the comparatively small army of Egyptian fellaheen. It has been supposed that he would attack Berber, but that is not certain; and as he has a large choice, he may strike at any moment at any one of a dozen or so of posts which are but indifferently defended by Egyptian troops. Were they British soldiers, the position would be an extremely awkward one, and it is not sure that we could even then come out of it with victory. With only overmatched fellaheen, if the Khalifa were now to attack, we should almost certainly suffer defeat—a disaster which would involve us in another desperate struggle for the mastery in the Soudan. It is clear that Sirdar Kitchener cannot trust his Egyptian force; hence his demand for British troops. Then the Nile is very low, and the gunboats on it are useless for attack or defence; they can neither advance nor retire. Fortunately the Khalifa remains quiet; let us hope he will continue so. But how is it that the Sirdar has allowed himself to get into this perilous position? We have heard nothing recently but of triumphal progresses and town after town taken from the Khalifa. Did it never occur to our commander that he was extending his line too far to be safe? And now we must spend a great deal of money in preparing to defend the positions taken, and to avert disaster. There must have been very serious bungling somewhere. Who is to blame? Fortunately it was announced yesterday that Sir H. Kitchener has received sufficient reinforcements.

THE LATE MR. VILLIERS.

Mr. C. P. Villiers, whose death took place on Sunday evening last, in his ninety-seventh year, was known as "The Father of the House of Commons." He might equally truly have been called "The Father of Free Trade." It was he who first introduced it to the notice of the House of Commons. Every year for fifteen years he hammered at the subject in the House, running the serious risk of injuring himself and his cause by getting himself regarded as a bore. But, fortunately, he never fell to this level. His speeches on the subject were ever fresh, ever new, and remain to us as amongst the best store-houses of Free Trade facts in existence. It is idle to discuss whether Villiers, or

Cobden, or Bright, or Peel, did most in establishing Free Trade. The work of all four was essential; and without the assistance of the vigorous eloquence of Bright, and the shrewd commercial presentments of Cobden, Villiers might have gone on till Doomsday with his annual motions in the House of Commons without bringing Free Trade legislation a bit nearer. He had clear views on the subject, and explained them with great lucidity; but, convinced and confident as he was of the excellence of Free Trade principles, Villiers could never have become the popular advocate of them in the country. His was the hard dry nature of the old Whig. Intellectual conviction guided him, not popular sympathy. But his share in the great work was well and thoroughly done. He did little more. He was President of the Poor Law Board in Lord Palmerston's second Ministry, and carried a valuable Union Chargability Bill. But he never joined another Cabinet, and though Member for Wolverhampton to the last, his voice has not been heard in the House of Commons for probably thirty years.

THE AUSTRIAN OUTLOOK.

It is far from pleasant, and anything but reassuring. There has recently been no serious external sign of the nationalist fires seething underneath, and even the Government were hopeful for a time that their efforts at compromise would be crowned with success. But the meeting of the Bohemian Landtag must have rudely undeceived them. Neither Czechs nor Germans will hear of compromise. They are both fighting for the mastery, and nothing less than that will satisfy them. Concessions on the language question were proposed to the Diet, but these were in the direction of practical equality for both languages, and were scorned alike by both parties. Reconciliation in such circumstances seems impossible; and external pressure—that is, the influence of the Crown—is demanded as the only method of putting an end to the present deadlock. They will not allow the poor Emperor to play the rôle of constitutional monarch, much as he wishes to do so. It was bad enough to begin his jubilee year by suspending the Reichsrath; it will be worse still to follow that up by coercing Czechs and Germans alike into a policy of decent toleration towards one another. But there really does seem no help for it. Matters have also been somewhat complicated by the turn events have taken in Hungary. The Government there conducted the discussions on the *Ausgleich* with far more moderation and statecraft than the Austrian Ministers showed; but the passage of a Bill revising the relations between the Magyar peasants and their landlords has roused the passions of the former until riots have become unpleasantly frequent in the country districts. The peasants cannot hold public meetings; but they may gather together at balls, and great numbers of these have recently been held, at which there was more denunciation of the obnoxious measure referred to than dancing. The Socialists fan the agitation; and present appearances indicate the approach of a condition of unrest as great in Hungary as in Austria.

REPORTS OF COMPANY MEETINGS.

The subjoined letter illustrates the mischief pointed out by us in our first weekly number with regard to the reports of company meetings paid for as advertisements. It is for shareholders themselves to put a stop to this subtle form of corruption. Unless they forbid their directors to spend money in this way they may be quite sure it will continue to be spent, and more largely, it is probable, in the future than in the past. The public should always bear in mind that the pressure put upon the financial journal or journalist by monied interests of all descriptions, to be either silent or in some way to disseminate what is not true, is constant and almost over-powering. We are bound to say that the great London and provincial daily newspapers, not exclusively financial, have, as far as we can judge, kept clear of this kind of thing; but the day may come when they also will give way, such is the unremitting determination of the more shrewd class of financiers to work upon public opinion unseen and un-noticed.

(To the Editor).

SIR,—Your Editorial Notes in THE INVESTORS' REVIEW of the 7th inst., exposes a great wrong in allusion to the custom now followed in some public companies in issuing the published reports of their meetings.

Formerly the reporters from financial papers, who attended meetings, reported fairly and independently, not omitting the criticisms and suggestions of shareholders attending; and that was only just, for the annual meetings afford the only opportunity for publicity to the shareholders' grievances.

Now it appears to be the custom for the reporters to submit their reports for curtailment by the directors, omitting any unpleasant criticisms and suggestions by shareholders; or else they make their reports over to the officials of the company who engage them, who then strike out all the directors wish omitted, and issue curtailed reports from the offices.

In November, 1896, and again in November, 1897, as a large shareholder, I attended the annual meetings of an Australian Land Company, at which there was considerable adverse criticism and some useful suggestions offered by shareholders, all of which were, however, carefully omitted from the printed reports of the meetings issed from the office of the company to every shareholder. I am surprised that the directors could have issued such reports as representing all that took place at the meetings in question.—I am, Sir, yours faithfully,

A SUBSCRIBER TO THE "INVESTORS' REVIEW."

January 13, 1897.

METHODS OF STATING ACCOUNTS.

A glance at the reports of the Direct United States and Eastern Telegraph Companies brings out one radical difference in the method of stating their accounts. The Eastern puts down as a revenue charge the cost of repairs and renewal of cables, and only draws upon its reserve in order to provide funds for outlay that could clearly be put to capital account if the Board so wished. The Direct United States Company, on the other hand, charges against its reserve fund the cost of renewals and repairs during the half-year.

As a result its profit and loss account is given an undue appearance of prosperity, which is not altogether the best thing for a struggling Telegraph Company. To set aside £12,000 to reserve out of revenue in the half-year looks like opulence, but when we find that on the other side £10,325 is deducted for repairs and renewals of cable and depreciation of buildings, the poverty of the concern is displayed. Far better bring these items into the revenue account, and not allow shareholders and the public to imagine that after the dividends are paid, the sum of £12,000 is left for reserve.

THE LINEN THREAD COMBINE.

The wise man will not accept too literally the assertion that the combination of linen thread manufacturers is designed "to effect ecomonies in distribution only." Under the circumstances of the present case, economies that must be considerable should result from proper management; but this is only one of the objects in view. It has been stated that one purpose of the arrangement is to counteract the operations of the two-fold cotton-thread combine. This, however, seems scarcely reasonable. It is much more probable that the success of the movement in the cotton thread trade has suggested to a small group of leading linen thread men that the emulation of that movement in their line might prove equally profitable to them. Cotton thread is enabled to injure the sale of linen only with a very low range of prices, and cotton thread has gone up at least 25 per cent. in the last few years. The fact is that to all intents and purposes linen thread has its market unaffected by the cotton article; and it depends upon the various manufacturers in the trade whether their profits shall be large or small. The firms which have now "combined" have worked amicably for years past on the basis of identical price-lists, &c., and have dominated the market, because they are stronger than all their rivals put together. This arrangement, made ostensibly for "economies in distribution only," is undoubtedly, if it is anything at all, the first step in a process of absorption which has for its ultimate aim the control of prices by a handful of unscrupulous manufacturers; and in due time, if the combination has not misjudged its power, we shall see a big upward jump in the prices of linen thread.

BATTEN, CARNE, & CO.'S BANK.

A little bank down Land's End way—Batten, Carne, & Carne's Banking Company, Limited—sold its business to Messrs. Bolitho, the great Cornish bankers, in November, 1896, and produced a balance-sheet at that date showing a surplus of £126,195, "subject to realisation." Alas for the "realisation"! On the 9th inst. another balance-sheet made its appearance "for the year ended" on that date, and not only does it show no "surplus" whatever, but Messrs. Bolitho have had to lend the liquidators nearly £16,000 to enable them to pay off mortgage to "Ford's Trustees." The shareholders are not likely to receive a penny. How many more, we wonder, of these little county banks are in a similar condition, hugging properties at book values which probably never at any time represented the true value, and which lapse of time has rendered moth-eaten —and the interest-moth is very destructive when allowed to cumulate—and altogether worthless.

THE GROSVENOR HOTEL SCANDAL.

A preliminary canter was taken this week into the affairs of the Grosvenor and West-end Railway Terminus Hotel, in a libel action brought by one of the directors against a shareholder. This stage of the litigation surrounding the affairs of that company was brought to a termination by the withdrawal of a juror, without prejudice to any further litigation with regard to the affairs of the hotel. The present plaintiff was a nominee of a Mr. Drew, who, as was expressed in the course of the case, "ran the show," and the shares the plaintiff held in the company, by which he became qualified as a director, he held in trust for Mr. Drew. At this the Lord Chief Justice expressed surprise, and asked Mr. Newitt, the plaintiff, whether he did not think that it was a dishonourable thing to do, namely, to hold an office of trust without any real interest in the company. On being assured that it was done every day, he exclaimed, "Well, companies are bad enough, but they are not all so bad as that!" We are afraid it must be admitted that in many companies this form of "director" is far from uncommon, and the sooner the Legislature can see its way to protect the public from the appointment of such guardians of their interests the better.

ALGERIAN WINES.

Algeria, profiting by the prevalence of black-rot in French vineyards seventeen years ago, started vine-growing herself, and is now possessed of an industry which, our Consul at Algiers declares, has a great future before it. Algeria has now 125,000 hectares of land under vines, and is improving its expertness in vinification. A large portion of its crop, of course, goes to France, which, in 1895, took 2,920,482 hectolitres; but Germany, Belgium, Holland, and Denmark also take considerable quantities of the wine. Very little comes to Britain—only 258 hectolitres in 1895; but if the phylloxera is kept at bay by the planting of American vines, and the quality is improved, with experience and knowledge, Algeria may some day be one of our most important sources of wine supply.

The Chinese Loan.

On Monday last the *Times* gave some welcome, because authentic, particulars regarding the proposed loan to China to be made by the British Government. Some things were a little obscure, but the outlines of the proposal are clear enough, and prove that the capacity for far-seeing statesmanship has not left us. Our own commercial interests in China have unhappily been decaying for a good many years back, our trade with that great empire, even if the whole trade of Hong Kong be included in its total, being not now much more than £12,000,000 a year. In fact, recently it has been under that figure. The trade of India with China has also been decidedly non-progressive, although it still amounts to nearly 15 per cent. of the entire export and import business of our Indian dependency. Something had to be done to arrest this decay and stagnation. If we had decided to sit still and allow Russia and Germany to lay their hands upon the Chinese Customs control, to carry out schemes for railway building and for land absorption at their will and pleasure, there could be no doubt that within a measurable period of time we should have been excluded almost entirely from assisting in the commercial and industrial development of the Chinese Empire. The methods of our rivals on the Continent are utterly different from ours. They aim at exclusive trade privileges for themselves; we set up barriers against no man. The real question, then, now pending in China, is whether the method of selfish exclusion, or the method of free and open dealing which has been the glory of England, shall prevail.

Unquestionably our Government has taken the right course to secure the victory for us. The demands made on China have been moderate. We think some ports of refuge might reasonably have been demanded, and we should have liked to see the stipulation made that the control of the Empire's maritime customs should have been guaranteed to England for at least the whole of the fifty years during which the proposed loan of twelve millions sterling is to remain unpaid. But it was right, probably, to abstain from asking too much, and the important proviso that no part of the Valley of the Yangtse-kiang is to be alienated to a foreign Power is worth all the rest. Also the stipulation that the Burmah railway shall be allowed to run into Yun-nan may prove to be of the highest importance to our trade with South-Western China, and to the future of the British provinces of Burmah.

We are told that Russia and Germany are opposing these proposals, and can well believe it, for they do not love us and our free commercial ways. They ascribe to British greed, British unscrupulousness, and so forth, triumphs which are really due to the most enlightened, liberal, and unselfish mercantile policy the world has ever seen. But they may object as much as they please; we have the power of the purse, and, taken all in all, we have done most of any Western nation to secure the esteem and confidence of the rulers of China. They have suffered injustice at our hands, doubtless, and we have made wars upon them the causes of which were too slender to justify such a course. But we have never stooped to the meanness of the Germans, and seized and held Chinese ports to keep in perpetuity, because some missionaries have been maltreated or slain. Through our instrumentality China has a better Customs service at its open or "treaty" ports than any other Asiatic Power—better, probably, than that of most European Powers. The Chinese have every reason, therefore, to confide in us, and they know well that we have the power to stand by them even to war as Sir Michael Hicks-Beach said, were a war necessary to vindicate their independence and ours.

And we can find them cash. Were Russia and Germany to step forward and offer another loan they could not raise the money without our help. Close the London market to them and they are helpless, for Paris is so overloaded with the debts of its neighbours and with the burden which Russia has laid upon the French people that it alone could not find the money. Therein lies our true strength at the present juncture. We can not only find the money, were it twice twelve millions, but we can find it on less onerous terms than any of our competitors. Did our Government choose to directly guarantee this proposed loan it might be given to China at 3 per cent., and still leave at least a ½ per cent. per annum for sinking fund. From this point of view our position is supreme, and we ought to use our advantage to the uttermost, because we are working not merely in the interests of our own and of Indian commerce, but also in the interests of peace. Let Russia and Germany, one or both, secure the guidance of Chinese foreign affairs, and at no distant date war must break out. The Japanese would not submit to be excluded from China by arbitrary barriers and vexatious restrictions, nor can we. The end of any such dominance of our rivals must, therefore, be a war in which the Japanese and ourselves might have to fight Germany, Russia, and possibly misguided France. It is surely better that we should risk a few millions of our money in lending it to a country whose resources in many directions are still undeveloped, whose population is capable of bearing the light additional burden our help asks them to carry, than that all might be lost in a destructive conflict out of which Japan, at least, might not emerge capable of maintaining a civilising Government even if victorious. Modern finance has its good side in that it does make for peace in many ways, and in doing so helps man onwards towards a higher plane of existence by giving him time to develop the arts which can only thrive when the nations are at peace.

The Exploration Company, Limited.

This concern cannot be said to have lived up to its first reputation. Issued by the banking firm of Sir Samuel Scott & Co., it had the then Sir Horace Farquhar, partner of the Duke of Fife, upon its board and the Rothschilds took a large portion of its capital. No less than 7,200 out of the 148,000 shares at that time allotted were taken by members of this firm, and the then powerful firm of Barings took 4,800 shares. With these leaders pointing the way, there was no lack of enthusiasm on the part of the public and the issue of the company was therefore one of the most successfu of the time, although the unhealthy activity of 1888-90 had well-nigh run its course when the company was floated. Apart from the Central London Railway scheme, out of which it made considerable profit, its most notable achievement has sprung from the attention paid to the Deep Level mines of the Witwatersrand. Under the guidance of its then managing director, Mr. Hamilton Smith, a considerable stake was laid in this direction. In February, 1893, the larger part of the Geldenhuis Deep capital was offered by the Exploration Company at £1. 1s. per share, and the company also gave its shareholders the opportunity to subscribe for Rose Deep shares at a moderate figure. It had a large interest in the Consolidated Deep Levels and Jumpers Deep, and no doubt reaped considerable benefits from the interest taken in these directions.

The Rhodesian mirage did not pass unheeded by this concern, and under the lead of Mr. Rochfort Maguire, with Major Ricarde Seave as his lieutenant, the Goldfields of Mashonaland and Goldfields of Mazoe were floated. Needless to say, these ventures did not come up to the level of the Witwatersrand "Deeps," and the first one is quoted a bad market at 2s. to 3s. per £1 share, while the second lies amongst the rubbish that is not considered worthy of a price. About this time two auxiliary companies—the Transvaal and General Association and West Australian and General Association—were formed to act as company sausage-machines in the two countries mentioned, but, after an existence of a little more than two years, these concerns were absorbed by their parent, and under guise of this operation the said parent's capital was inflated almost beyond recognition. The original paid-up capital had been £30,000 in 148,000 Ordinary shares and 2,000 Founders' shares. In the new company, formed in 1896, shareholders in the original company received four fully-paid £1 shares for every three 4s. shares in the old, so that the £30,000 of original capital was magnified into £400,000, and of course nothing further was paid up. The Founders, as a solatium for the loss of their rights, were allowed to subscribe for 50,000 shares at par. Shareholders of the Transvaal and General Association received 250,000 new shares, being share for share; and the West Australian and General Association received 250,000 new shares for their £200,000 of capital, or five new shares for four old. In addition, 150,000 new £1 shares were offered to the shareholders of the old companies at £2 apiece. In this way a capitalisation of £1,100,000 was created, of which £200,000 represented fresh capital subscribed, and no less than £420,000 was mere paper and ink.

After this notable expansion the old managing directors, Messrs. Hamilton-Smith and J. Rochfort Maguire, retired, and Mr. Lukach became managing director alone. But the business just antecedent to this change and afterwards had not been well conceived, and the new Exploration Company does not bid fair to equal the glories of its progenitor. The Alaska group of mines—the Alaska Treadwell, the Alaska Mexican, and the Alaska United—have certainly proved a moderate success, but the shares, despite New-courtly assistance, are quoted little above the figures at which they were introduced to the market. And, by-the-bye, we might note that the Exploration Company in its operations does not favour the common method of issue heralded by a prospectus. Rather, it prefers to deal with syndicates and market dealers, who take "blocks" of shares at prices unknown to the public, and then, with the aid of the Exploration Company and its *entourage*, these dealers "make a market" for the newly-created securities, just as spiders weave a web. It is therefore extremely difficult to follow the group's course of operation. It may be working in the market long before the public has the faintest idea of the affair. Suddenly there bursts out a flood of enthusiastic praise of the new mining company in the financial press, dealings become active, nay, turbulent, and the public see the shares of the new-comer quoted at a premium. For a time this premium is maintained, and then drops down a little, when possibly the public, in a fit of ill-judged enthusiasm steps in and buys the shares. It foolishly imagines that if the Exploration Company and its allied dealers start the shares at a certain price, it must be good business to buy a little below that figure. But history does not say what the Exploration Company and its friends paid for the undertaking, and possibly great surprise would be expressed if the actual facts came out. As it is, every Exploration issue of recent years has been a source of loss to the public, for prices tend to fall as time goes on, and the more the public get bitten, the weaker, generally speaking, becomes the market.

We do not say that the subjoined list is a full statement of the mining issues of the Corporation in the past two years, for it is difficult to trace its windings. For instance, Mr. Dudley Ryder, who shares with Mr. Lukach the burden of service on the boards of many of the subservient undertakings, is connected with the Wentworth Extension and its offspring—the Lagoon Creek and Tambaroora Creek Companies—but we doubt whether the Exploration Company had any direct share in the production of that extremely nebulous group. Other of its allies are interested in a vast number of enterprises, in which it may have taken a hand, but we have no definite proof that it did so. We therefore confine our table to those mining companies that are believed to be true and acknowledged Exploration offspring, and the productions of the last few years may be taken as being included in the following list:—

Name.	Nominal Capital. £	Capital Issued. £	Capital Considered as Paid. £
Anaconda Copper	6,000,000	6,000,000	6,000,000
Aroha Gold Mines	100,000	100,000	60,000
Beacon Gold Mines	200,000	200,000	175,000
Consolidated Goldfields of New Zealand	225,000	185,000	185,000
Ejudina Gold Mines	100,000	100,000	75,000
Grand Central Mining	300,000	250,000	250,000
Lake George Mines	150,000	150,000	150,000
Norseman Gold Mine	250,000	200,000	200,000
New Australasian Gold Mines	80,000	75,000	60,000
New Zealand Crown Mines	200,000	200,000	200,000
New Zealand Exploration Co.	125,000	75,000	75,000
Progress Mines of New Zealand	250,000	250,000	200,000
Sulphide Corporation (Ashcroft's Process)	1,100,000	1,100,000	1,100,000

The Ejudina proved a terrible fiasco, and the property was sold at a knock-out price to the Triumph Leases, whose shares find no quotation amongst active mines. The Norseman is another West Australian property whose history has not been a success, while the New Australasian seems absolutely unknown to the market. The Sulphide Corporation was floated with great *éclat* in October, 1895, in order to try a process for treating sulphide ores, and also to take over the Central Broken Hill Mine. The mine has not developed well, while the process has not done all that was expected, and the shares, after running down to about 50 per cent. discount, have faded out of active lists. Four of the New Zealand group—the Aroha, New Zealand Crown, New Zealand Exploration, and Progress Mines of New Zealand—stand at heavy discounts or have no price at all, and only the Consolidated Goldfields of New Zealand stands at a premium, but then its shares were started at an absurdly high figure, and have been dropping almost ever since. The Anaconda shares, after passing through the hands of more than one syndicate, were started about £7 apiece, and on the whole their history has been one of declining quotations. At one time, we believe, they were quoted 7¾, but since the whole of the American proprietors' shares were quoted here, every rise has led to a break, as if shares were welling into the market from some hidden source. One reason for the latest decline was found in the bad news that came to hand early in December, and we begin to fear that this is only another case of a worked-out American mine foisted upon the British investor. The Grand Central is an almost exactly similar case. This company works eight gold and silver mines in Mexico that had formerly been operated by American capitalists, and when Capt. Mein, one of the representatives of the Exploration Company upon its board, went out to visit the property, he found the lode in the most important property far from what it had been represented. Hence there came a great break in the price of the shares, which has never been mended. In order to show the decaying tendency of the prices for the shares of these mines, we give the following table:—

	Price at or about Special Settlement.	Highest Price.	Present Price.
Anaconda Copper	6¼	7⅝	5 11/16
Aroha Gold Mines	1¼	1½	[illegible]
Beacon Gold Mines	1⅛	1	[illegible]
Consldtd. Goldfields of New Zealand	4	4⅜	2⅛
Grand Central Mining	2 1/16	3¼	1⅛
Lake George Mines	2 11/16	2⅝	2½
Norseman Gold Mine	1/16 pm.	2	[illegible]
New Zealand Crown	2 1/16	2¼	[illegible]
New Zealand Exploration	*	3⅜	[illegible]

* No price obtainable about this date.

We have chosen the special settlement granted by the Stock Exchange Committee as the initial quotation for the shares, because, no prospectus having been issued, in cases it is impossible to say when dealing assumed large proportions. Indeed, we fancy that often when special settlements were obtained, the activity of the shares was not very great, and that the highest price is more likely to fix the time when public interest was most pronounced. The Exploration Company will doubtless be undeterred by the misfortunes of the past—perhaps it has not suffered pecuniarily from the disasters—and it has, we believe, a string of undertakings with which it is quite ready to oblige the British public. There are such things as the Helena and 'Frisco Mining, the Oneida Gold Mine and Milling, the Steeple Rock Development Company, and the Tomboy Gold Mines, in which the company has a considerable stake it possibly means to market at the earliest opportunity. We should leave it to "explore" on its own account for a while—the mines, we mean, not British pockets.

Mr. Gage's Currency Proposals.

The reports of a Secretary of the United States Treasury are always valuable, and often interesting to read. A uniform plan has been adopted in framing the statistics appended to them, and the text preceding the figures is always packed with information. Greater interest, however, than usual attaches to this first report of Mr. Lyman Gage because he has embodied in it proposals for a reform in the United States currency. As most people know, the paper money of the United States is mainly of two kinds—one issued directly by the State, partly in greenbacks—a relic of the forced currency days of the Civil War—partly in "certificates" issued against deposits or purchases chiefly of silver—and the other bank-notes issued upon Government security. Metallic money of course there is in the country, but it is little used by the people, and substantially "money" in the States means paper. This might be all right if the holders of this paper money could be sure of changing it into the metal they want at any time. This is just what they cannot be. An ambiguity exists in regard to the liability of the Federal Government at Washington to redeem its promises to pay its greenbacks in gold. Mr. Gage explains this ambiguity in very clear language. "The earlier issues of our Government bonds were," he says, "payable in 'dollars.' With greenbacks a legal tender, with gold and silver on a substantial commercial parity, but both at a large premium over paper money, a similar question arose, What did 'dollars' mean? And in 1869, 'to remove all doubt upon the subject,' an Act was passed solemnly pledging the faith of the United States to the payment in coin or its equivalent of all its interest-bearing obligations, except when otherwise expressly provided in the law. The commercial disparity between our 'legal-tender dollars' and 'coin dollars' was not then essentially greater than the present commercial disparity between silver and gold. This Act of 1869 was judicious. To refund our outstanding bonds, now payable in coin, into bonds payable in gold, would strengthen and confirm the public credit and put us in a position to command the markets of the world for our securities on the most advantageous terms."

It will be seen from this that the United States Government is bound to pay its debts in coin merely; but there is nothing to bind it down that the coin shall be gold, it might be silver or any other metal the Administration might choose to select, and Mr. Gage is quite right in thinking that this ambiguity injures the credit of his country. He proposes to get over the defect by, in the first place, getting an Act passed to allow the interest-bearing debt to be refunded in 2½ per cent. bonds, the interest and principal of which shall be paid in gold coin. Then, in order to deal with the paper money, he proposes to set aside 125 million dollars in gold, to be used for the purpose of redeeming notes in the hands of the public. Besides this he would place in this fund all the silver dollars now held for the redemption of silver certificates and all the silver bullion bought under the Act of 1890. Along with these deposits of gold and silver he proposes to place 200 million dollars of the greenbacks withdrawn from circulation, the whole to be deposited in what he describes as the Issue and Redemption Division of the United States Treasury. His plan, in short, is a sort of copy of the Issue Department of the Bank of England, and the object he has in view is to, as it were, fence off the United States Treasury from the public. Coin and notes placed to this special reserve are not to be got at by the public, except by a circuitous route. Additional bank-notes are to take the place of greenbacks, and the paper money created by the banks is to be made expansive enough to meet all the requirements of the people without the necessity of falling back on the Treasury deposit. Mr. Gage's plan is highly ingenious, and, at the same time, it sounds to our ears like something coming almost from the dark ages of banking. At the foundation of the new scheme for giving plenty of money cheap to the American people is an extension of the existing banking law, which would enable small banks, with a minimum capital of £5,000, to start business in any place with a population of 2,000 or less.

Even tiny banks of this kind are to be allowed to issue notes. They can take their share in depositing with the Treasury, greenbacks, Treasury notes, or silver certificates to a total amount of 200 million dollars, against which the Comptroller of the Currency can hand out to them national bank-notes of an equal amount. After a time United States bonds are to be substituted for the greenbacks and other floating certificates of indebtedness first deposited; but that is a detail. On the top of the 200 millions of new paper money, this substitute for gold to the amount of 50 per cent. of the paid-up capital of the banks, they are to be allowed to issue an additional 25 per cent. in notes, without any specific security, but merely on their general assets. All this paper money is to enjoy a certain State guarantee, and to secure the Government against loss, a tax of 2 per cent. per annum is to be imposed upon the unsecured portion of the note issues, that on the secured portion being only one half of one per cent. In order further to prevent the improper multiplication of notes issuing banks are to be restricted as to the value of the notes they may create. No national bank-note is to be issued under 10 dollars (say £2). Such is briefly the outline of Mr. Gage's proposals, and the idea behind them appears to be found in the following sentence: "Paper money is the product of industrial, commercial, and financial evolution. Its economising effect in the use of metallic money precludes the idea of its abandonment until society shall relapse into anarchy." This sounds very fine, but it does not mean much, as a moment's thought should have convinced the man who wrote it, nor is it true. As a matter of fact, civilisation is rapidly rising above the necessity to employ paper money of the kind Mr. Gage had in his mind. It may be that credit is so primitive in the United States, and so precariously based, that individual banks issuing notes, their promises to pay cash on demand, are an absolute necessity for the community. We have got past that stage in England; whether for good or for evil it is not now necessary to enquire. In all our larger commerce, and in much of our retail, the employment of bank notes has been gradually reduced until the day does not seem distant when it may disappear altogether. With the disappearance of the bank note must come the complete severence of the Government from all interference with the credit machinery of the nation. Surely this is a good thing, a higher ideal to aim at than the one set forth by Mr. Gage. It has never been good for his country that its Government should be so closely identified, as it now is, with the embodiments of credit represented by banks. The one function, as we understand it, of Government towards money, should be to provide coin—coin of definite weight, unalterable fineness, and perfect manufacture. Beyond this it is always unsafe to go; all else should be left to private enterprise. It is so to a very large extent in England now; and credit is so refined with us that the bank note is very little required in the daily transactions of life, most of which are carried out by means of cheques. Dangers may, and do, lurk in this highly-refined system, but certainly it is better than the one suggested in the report before us. Mr. Gage's plan gets rid of no difficulty; it does not lessen the liability of the Government for the conduct of the banking and bank-note issuing business of the nation or for the convertibility of the paper money; nor does it in the very least release the Treasury from the responsibility of having coin on hand at all times to meet any sudden demand. Had the Secretary to the Treasury proposed that the bank-note circulation should be based upon coin held in reserve by the banks themselves, say to the amount of 50 per cent. of their issue, some kind of buttress might have been got together to stand between the Treasury and the demands of the people. But nothing of the kind is to be attempted. Upon the 25 millions sterling of gold there is to be erected a large superstructure of paper money, of credit, and that is all. This will not deliver the United States from the troubles they are now afflicted by, nor will it restore confidence to the European investors in the ability or willingness of the United States people and Government to meet their obligations honestly, in honest money. It is merely a shunting of the difficulty, one more refusal frankly and squarely to face the position. At one point only is there a good suggestion made. It is that a definite pledge should be given by the Government that its debts shall be paid in gold; but that is just the suggestion which evokes the greatest hostility in the United States. The majority of both Houses of the Legislature are decidedly opposed to any measure of uprightness such as this would be. They much prefer to leave the door open for fraud. From a practical point of view, however, it seems waste of time to discuss these proposals, for they stand small chance of becoming law. They are interesting merely as disclosing the views of a practical American banker remarkable amongst his *confrères* for his business intelligence and probity; remarkable also, we should say, for the limitations of his economic insight.

American Life Insurance Offices.

Those of our readers, and we know there are many, whose memories go back to the days when this Review was a quarterly magazine, may recollect that we took up a position of such distinct hostility to these insurance offices as to absolutely refuse to insert any of their advertisements. We maintain this attitude to-day, and are moved to re-emphasise it, partly by a flaming puff of one of the New York Life Offices which appeared in many English newspapers late last week. For it is our conviction that the methods of business followed by these offices—they are not "companies" in the English sense of the term, at least, only one of them is—are calculated ultimately to bring disaster upon their clients, before the magnitude of which the downfall of the Balfour Group of Companies will appear an event of no magnitude. In the second edition of a little book, "Plain Advice about Life Insurance," published by us, we set forth in a table, worked out by us from the official returns filed in the State of New York, that the ratio of their working expenses to premium income was monstrously high, even taking the whole life policy as a basis for the calculation. The New York Life Office, for instance, paid away in 1896 more than 27 per cent. of its entire premium income to secure and conduct its business, and the Equitable disbursed 25 per cent. Had we calculated this expenditure on the basis of the duration of policies under the endowment system, these percentages must have been very much higher, for the simple reason that 80 per cent. commission paid to an agent on the first premium weighs much more heavily on a ten years' contract, or a twenty years' one for that matter, than on a whole life contract. Not only is the expenditure too high, but the whole system of business is repulsive to British ideas of life insurance, and of fair play towards policy-holders.

On this latter point, we need say no more than that in no instance did the returns show that 10 per cent. of the policies contracted for in one year appear to live to become claims. Surely here is reason enough for distrusting these offices; but there is another, and, if possible, more emphatic one, the existence of which is, we say it with the utmost deliberation and distinctness, attributable to the Parliament of the United Kingdom. Through its apathy and indifference, this Parliament has permitted these offices to come to England and contract liabilities towards British subjects, the aggregate of which, at the present time, may be forty, and might be more than fifty millions sterling, without asking them to invest one single shilling of the money drawn in premiums from the British people within the control of trustees for British policy-holders. This is a most scandalous thing, for which we are bound one day to suffer. All the money furnished by the British policy-holders in these concerns goes to the United States, and is invested there by people absolutely irresponsible to the people here. British policy-holders in these offices have no voice in the management—no policy-holder has for that matter. The offices are, all of them, run on strictly autocratic principles. Who elects their president, who appoints their officers, nobody here knows or seems to care. The Germans were wiser and more vigilant than we have been, and would not allow any of these concerns to do business within the Empire unless they invested German money in approved German securities. Is it not possible to arouse our Parliament to do as much for us before it is too late? It may rest assured that a catastrophe must one day come as the result of its apathy and negligence, and it may not be long before it does come, for there are ominous symptoms beginning that, in spite of their outrageous puffery and illusory promises, recooked and redressed on every possible occasion, these insurance offices are slowly being found out. They cannot, in other words, fulfil their promises, in spite of their efforts after high interest, as exemplified by their investments in American railway ordinary shares and such like; and every year that passes, as successive series of short-term policies can be put to the test of experience, the imposture practised upon the credulous, and it may be greedy, British insurer will become more and more patent.

Already that wretched affair, the Mutual Reserve, which ought never to have been allowed to open an office in this country under any condition, has been pretty well found out. The turn of the other and more reputable concerns is about to come, in spite of their professions of being the "largest, best, and strongest life offices in the world." In actual fact we might go so far as to say that the ways of the most fourth-rate British office may soon be easily better than those of the best American ones known here. We shall have a good deal more to say on this subject from time to time, but for the present must be content with stating one or two facts. To illustrate these facts let us quote the following from the "Jubilee" prospectus of the Mutual Life Office of New York:—

The best company for the policy-holder is the company that will give him the best return for his money in the form of guarantees and options most suited to his requirements. . . . There is, however, a growing tendency on the part of the public to exact a definite pledge in regard to policy results, thereby encouraging insurance companies to compete for business by means of estimates. The evil of this practice has been so fully illustrated in the experience of some companies, that it cannot be too severely deprecated. . . . A man's character and service in the *past* is the accepted measure of the confidence to be reposed in him in respect to any *prospective* service, and the principle involved applies with equal force in the choice of an insurance company.

This is profession. Now for an actual fact. Experience shows that there is not the slightest justification for this unctuous boasting. Figures have been laid before us detailing actual results, which show that the bonuses recently given by this concern are miserably below those of good, or even middling, British offices. Two of its policies lately became entitled to bonuses. One was on a life aged thirty at entry, and the bonus in this case was something over 25s. per cent. per annum reversion, or about 9s. 6d. per annum in cash. The other life, aged fifty-nine, got a bonus of a little over £2. 6s. per cent. per annum in reversion, or about 31s. 6d. per cent. per annum in cash. Thus the extravagant expenditure of this office caused the strain to be heavier on the younger than on the older life, and there are at least twenty life offices in Great Britain each of which would have given the younger life 30s. per cent. per annum in reversion, and at least six who would have given between 34s. and 64s. per cent. This is an example of how "the best and cheapest" life insurance can be done by an American office at an annual expenditure of at least 34 per cent. of the premium income. Not much foresight is required, nor any very abtruse calculation, to enable us to reach the conviction that only a comparatively brief number of years will now have to pass until no bonuses at all can be forthcoming. A little longer still, and deficits must take the place of surpluses, unless the whole system of the business is root and branch reformed. We shall return to the whole subject at an early date, because the peril is great, and the mischief now being done incalculable.

Critical Index to New Investments.

CAPE OF GOOD HOPE CONSOLIDATED THREE PER CENT. STOCK.

The London and Westminster Bank will on Monday receive tenders, the minimum price being par, for an issue of £1,250,000 stock, interest being payable February 1 and August 1. It is repayable at par February 1, 1943, but it can be redeemed at par ten years earlier on twelve months' notice being given. More money is wanted for railway and harbour works now in progress, on which a considerable amount of ordinary revenue has already been spent, and the occasion is not missed to state that the net revenues received from the Government railways have, for some time past, been more than sufficient to pay the interest charge and sinking fund on the total debt of the Colony. Payments may be made in full under discount on February 1 at the liberal rate of 1 per cent. In 1894 half a million of Three per Cent. stock was offered for tender in Capetown and London, and it went at an average price of £100 1s. per cent. The Public Debt is near twenty-five millions, and the total population some two millions, of which it would not be too much to say only 25 per cent. are whites The loan is sure to go well, and hardly required the issue of favourable trade reports by the Agent General to help it.

LIVERPOOL CORPORATION STOCK.

Issue of £1,500,000 stock, being part of a proposed £2,500,000. Minimum price, 98 per cent; interest January 1 and July 1. Tenders received to-day at the Bank of England. Stock is redeemable at par at the option of the Corporation on and after January 1923. The money is wanted for various purposes, chief among which are tramways, waterworks, and electric lighting. The total debt of the Corporation for all purposes except waterworks is £4,369,265. Of this mortgages or temporary loans for £400,000 on account of the purchase of the electric supply undertaking, and £600,000 for the purchase of the tramways undertaking, will be paid off out of the proceeds of this issue. The rateable value of the City is £3,846,321. The Corporation owns a large estate, as well as other municipal property, and the average income from revenue-producing property during the past ten years has been £110,000 per annum, or more than sufficient to pay the interest on the present debt irrespective of rates. The waterworks debt is £4,424,251. The stock will no doubt be largely applied for by trustees and others who have to confine their investments to this class of security.

EAST INDIAN RAILWAY COMPANY.

At various dates from July, 1895, this company has emitted 2½ per cent. debentures having eight years to run, until the aggregate of such is £950,000. The directors now propose to issue another £600,000 of these bonds, bringing up their total to £1,550,000, and have fixed the minimum at which they will receive tenders on Wednesday next at £97 per £100. Two of the previous sales were effected at prices which illustrate the fluctuating condition of credit, excellent credit, of course, at its lowest dip. In June, 1895, £300,000 were sold at an average of 102⅝, having been offered at par as a minimum, and in February last year half a million offered at 99 sold at only 1s. 8½d. or so above that price on the average. The bonds, which are little better than long-dated bills with coupons have never been cheap.

TORQUAY CORPORATION.

Issue of £82,000 3 per cent. redeemable stock; interest due January and July. Stock redeemable at par December 11, 1943, but can be redeemed on six months' notice after December 11, 1913. Minimum price, £100½. Money wanted to redeem part of existing debt, and for various works, including water and electric lighting. Rateable value of borough, £137,000; population last census 25,534; total debt, £348,000. Four years ago similar stock was sold at an average price of £98. 4s. 11d. This time an average of £101. 6s. 11d. was secured, the applications reaching £236,800

ILLINOIS CENTRAL RAILROAD COMPANY.

Issue of 10,000,000 dols. Louisville division and terminal first mortgage 3½ per cent. gold bonds, due July 1, 1953; and 5,000,000 dols. St. Louis division and terminal first mortgage 3½ per cent. gold bonds, due July 1, 1951. Interest in each case due January 1 and July 1, and both issues are direct obligations of the Illinois Central Railroad Company. Bonds are offered at 98⅜ per cent., which at the present exchange is equivalent to 95 per cent. for sterling bonds, but 3 per cent. discount can be saved by paying up in full. Allowing for repayment at par, the bonds yield investors on this side £3. 14s. 4d. per cent. per annum. These are excellent gold bonds, and it is no small merit that they cannot be paid off for more than fifty years.

THE AMERICAN FISHERIES COMPANY.

This hails from New Jersey, viâ Dublin, and is formed to buy the principal works and steamers engaged in the Menhaden fisheries on the Atlantic coast of the United States, from the Fish Oil and Guano Syndicate, Limited, as well as patent rights for the treatment of fish and fish oils. Capital, 10,000,000 dols., in 5 dol. shares, of which 40,000 are 7 per cent. cumulative preferred, and the rest ordinary shares. The preferred, on which interest is payable, January and July, are offered over here at £1. 0s. 10d. per share, and subscribers for 100 shares have the option to also subscribe for fifty ordinary at par. The Stanley patents are to be bought, and paid for in ordinary shares, but no figures are given as to what the purchase price is to be either for these or the various businesses to be acquired. Annual sales for last five years certified at 1,007,621 dols., and experts say expenses of a catch of 600 million fish will not exceed 501,594 dols.; deduct preference interest, there remains 366,027 dols., which, by additional profits to be derived by the adoption of the new process, is to be increased to a net annual sum of 1,881,027 dols. for expenses, ordinary dividends, reserve, &c. There you are! Could anything be more promising? But beyond this, little information is given in the prospectus to guide investors over here. What annual profits, it may be asked, have been made in the past by the concerns brought into the combination, and what is being paid for the works, and steamers, and the patent rights? And how comes it that only half the capital is taken by the Yankees? Is it because they really are 'cute?

THOMAS BROWN & SONS, LIMITED.

This is a company formed to acquire, from last July, the business of general merchants, warehousemen, agents, and manufacturers, carried on by the vendors, under the styles of Thomas Brown at Glasgow, and of D. L. Brown & Company at Brisbane. The capital is £270,000 in £5 shares, equally divided into Ordinary and five-and-a-half per cent. cumulative preference shares. This is also an issue of £130,000 four-and-a-half first mortgage debenture stock, repayable at par May 15, 1923. Interest due May 15 and November 15, and the security is a fixed charge on the freehold properties and a floating charge on the other assets of the company. All the debebture stock and preference shares are offered for subscription at par. Sir James Garrick is a trustee, but this is not an unusual way for a former Agent General of a Colony to increase his income in these days. The company takes the profits from July 1 last, and pays vendors 5 per cent. interest on the purchase-money from that date, by which plan the company may be out of pocket, for all investors can tell. Some Brisbane valuer puts the value of the freehold land and warehouses in that city at £146,398, and the stock-in-trade in Brisbane and Glasgow is stated at £175,581, while book debts and bills receivable, "guaranteed by vendors," are put at £79,426. Deducting trade liabilities, £83,161, and putting in goodwill at £60,894, a good round sum of £400,000 is worked up as value of the property and assets. The purchase price is therefore fixed at this amount, of which £135,000 will be taken in shares. But no details about profits are given; all that the vendors have the courage to show is that the average net profits for the past seven years is £29,290. What about last year's profits? If these had been given, investors might have rubbed their eyes—or noses.

S. W. ARNOLD & SONS, LIMITED.

A company formed to acquire the business of Messrs. Arnold & Sons, of the Rowbarton Brewery, Taunton, to which will be joined the business of the West Somerset Brewery, Taunton, recently bought by this firm, who will continue to hold practically all the share capital, which amounts to £100,000. Applications are now invited for an issue of £60,000 First Mortgage Four per Cent. Debenture stock, at £102 per cent., interest being payable April 1 and October 1. The security is a first mortgage on the properties and plant, and a floating charge on the undertaking, and the stock will be redeemable after October 1, 1905, at 110 per cent., subject to six months' notice. The company is at liberty to create another £25,000 of this stock, which will rank *pari passu*, the proceeds to be applied only to the purchase of further properties. Mason & Son value the freehold Rowbarton Brewery and the West Somerset Brewery, and the seventy-two licensed houses and other properties, at £97,415, and the stock-in-trade, book debts, &c. at £20,461. The profits of the Rowbarton Brewery alone for the three years and nine months ending September 29 last are stated year by year, and give an average of £5,016 per annum. Mason and Son estimate the annual increase of profits from the West Somerset Brewery at £2,000, whereas the amount required to pay the interest on the present issue is only £2,400. The vendors who themselves promote the company, take £126,200 as the purchase price, including £51,200 in cash. No figures are given respecting the past profits of the West Somerset Brewery, but the debenture stock now offered appears to be well secured and a satisfactory brewing investment.

RUSSELL'S GRAVESEND BREWERY, LIMITED.

Share capital, £95,000, in £10 shares, 3,000 being preference, carrying as much as 6 per cent. interest. There is now offered an issue of £125,000 4 per cent. first mortgage debenture stock at 105 per cent., part of an authorised sum of £150,000. Stock can be redeemed after 1910 at 110 per cent.; interest due June and December. Company formed in 1893, and bought a thirty-five-year-old brewery, with a wine and spirit business. Properties and plant valued at £200,950, but there is no statement as to what profits have been. With the proceeds of this issue the £70,000 of 4½ per cent. debenture stock will be paid off, and the balance of the money is wanted to buy more public-houses. Whole of share capital is held by directors and friends, who now try to borrow too cheaply by a large issue of high-priced debentures, for which there is insufficient "cover."

THE WANDSBROUGH PAPER COMPANY, LIMITED.

Company buys the business of paper manufacturers and paper-bag manufacturers carried on for many years by Alfred Colmen, Wansbrough and Partners, at Watchet and Cheddar. Mills, plant, &c., are valued at £87,466, exclusive of stock, book-debts, and goodwill. Profits for 1894 were £6,781; for 1895, £7,659; and for 1896, £8,124; while for six months to June 30 last they were £5,955. The whole year's figures, we should have thought, might have been got out by this time. Of the purchase price of £135,000, stock represents £20,577, and goodwill £26,957. Share capital, £100,000 in £5 shares, half ordinary and half five and a half per cent. cumulative preference, which, with an issue of £55,000 four and a half per cent. first mortgage debenture stock, is offered at par. Interest due May and November. Debenture stock redeemable at 110 from January 1, 1915, on six months' notice. Only £3. 17s. 6d. will be called up on ordinary shares. Average profits for three and a half years, £8,148, leaves a margin of £2,923 after paying interest on debentures and preference shares, both of which appear to offer satisfactory investments.

THE MANSIONS PROPRIETARY, LIMITED (ST. ERMIN'S, WESTMINSTER.)

Authorised share capital is £100,000 all issued; the company now offers £75,000 of 4 per cent. first mortgage debenture stock at par, and this will only be allotted in multiples of £10. It is repayable at par at the end of 1937, or redeemable at £107 after 1901 on six months' notice. Interest due January 1 and July 1, and a sinking fund will be provided for the repayment of the stock by which the trustees may purchase in the open market. The stock will be secured by a trust deed vesting St. Ermin's and the furniture, fixtures, &c., which are valued at £152,975, in trustees, and the present issue is made to repay a mortgage loan to the company, amounting to £30,000, now charged upon St. Ermin's, and for improvements, furniture, and other purposes. It is the intention of the directors to continue the present policy of furnishing suites of apartments as the present tenancies expire, and to re-let them as furnished suites. We regard the affair as sound, and the debenture stock a moderately good 4 per cent. investment.

SPENCER, SANTO & CO., LIMITED.

Share capital, £300,000 in £1 shares, two-thirds being ordinary and the remainder 5½ per cent. cumulative preference shares, on which interest is due January 1 and July 1; 66,667 shares of each class are offered for subscription. The company is formed to buy two building estates, one at Felixstowe and one at Linford, near Tilbury, and to acquire the building business of Spencer, Santo, & Co. The prospectus contains very eulogistic accounts of both places, but all we are told about the business to be taken over is that the profit for thirteen months ending September last amounted to £9,420. The vendor undertakes to be chairman of the company for three years, and guarantees for this period a minimum net income of £10,500 each year. The purchase price is £150,000, of which £83,334 is to be cash! We regard this as a highly speculative and undesirable investment.

WEBB & ELLEN, LIMITED.

Capital, £100,000 in £1 shares, 60,000 being ordinary, and remainder 6 per cent. cumulative preference. All the latter, with 21,000 ordinary, are offered for subscription. Company buys and consolidates two businesses of tea, provision, and food produce merchants, carried on chiefly at Woolwich and Plumstead. Properties are valued at £45,268, which is the purchase price, but the vendors do not want more that £9,000 in shares. All we are told about past profits is that for the last three years they have been at the rate of £5,550. So they may have been; but this is insufficient information to appeal to the public upon, and, in the absence of further details, we should leave the shares to gentlemen engaged in the tea trade, who may know more about the businesses.

THE CENTRAL SUPPLY COMPANY, LIMITED.

This is an undertaking formed to acquire and carry on under one management, from a central depôt, a large number of businesses of provision merchants, general store-keepers, and contractors in various London districts. The capital is £200,000 in equal moieties of ordinary and 6 per cent. cumulative preference shares, but a portion only of each class is now offered. All that there is to judge of the value of the businesses is the chartered accountant's certificate, which says that the average aggregate sales amounted to £251,997 per annum, producing an average annual net profit of £17,105 before writing off any amount for amortisation of leases, interest on capital, and proprietors' drawings. Of the present issue £25,000 will remain for the purchase of stock-in-trade and book debts, and for working capital. The value of the thirty retail shops to be acquired, including good-will, but exclusive of stock-in-trade, is certified at £117,735. Mr. G. Hilderbrandt is to be managing director for five years, and the City Stores Syndicate, Limited, fix the purchase price at £90,000 in cash and shares, proportions not stated. Combination stores we have had, good and also bad, and although a mass of shops can be often worked together more cheaply than separately, it is not conceivable that a man would part with a good business unless the promoters paid him a high price for it. With these good businesses there are often roped in many concerns "with a past" and no hope of a future.

Company Reports and Balance-Sheets.

Williams Deacon and Manchester and Salford Bank are able to report a fair improvement. Profits for the year were larger by £10,000, and a bigger balance was brought in. Consequently, after paying the same dividend of 12½ per cent., and adding £20,000 to reserve, the amount set aside for Buildings Depreciation Fund is increased from £5,000 to £15,000. Deposits are down some £300,000, and there is an equal reduction in bills, but advances are up £270,000 to the lofty total of £5,834,000.

Yorkshire Banking Company, Limited.—In the half-year ended 31st ult. this company made a profit of £32,000, and it gave £41,516 for distribution, including a balance brought forward. Out of this a dividend of 17s. 6d. per share, or at the rate of 14 per cent. per annum, is declared, and £10,000 added to reserve, leaving £5,266 to go to the new half-year. The bank seems to have realised a large profit by the sale of some securities, and £60,000 of this profit is also added to reserve, raising its total to £300,000, which is decidedly good policy.

London Joint Stock Bank.—A satisfactory feature is an increase of £1,100,000 in the bank's deposits, especially as nearly £500,000 more is in bills discounted and loans, including money at call (these items are not yet given separately). Cash in hand is up £307,000, and about £100,000 more has been put in securities. Profits for the half-year were £12,000 better than in the corresponding period, but £10,000 of this is credited to Superannuation Allowance Fund, the dividend for the shareholders being kept at 10 per cent. per annum.

London and Westminster Bank.—An increase of £19,000 in the half-year's profits suggests that the new branches being opened have not yet proved expensive. Of this increase £14,000 is used in paying the higher dividend of 13 per cent. per annum, against 12 per cent. per annum distributed a year ago. Deposits are up £350,000, but there is a sharp falling off in bills discounted, and loans of £1,500,000, the total now being £14,616,000. Cash in hand and at the Bank of England is up £300,000, while £1,600,000 more is out at call and short notice.

Parr's Bank, Limited.—Including £56,365 brought forward, the net profit for the past half-year was £204,081. From this, two quarterly dividends at the rate of 19 per cent. per annum have to be deducted, absorbing £125,400. £20,000 is placed to Bank premises account, and £58,681 left to carry forward. The balance-sheet now exhibits big figures: Deposits, &c., £20,321,552, and a total liability to shareholders and the public of £26,134,201. Among the assets are bills discounted, £2,316,571, and loans and advances, £11,287,994, much about the usual proportion now a days. The bank possesses £1,000,000 of consols taken at 90, and is otherwise in an eminently comfortable-looking position.

The City Bank increased its profits by £11,000, and brought in a larger balance from June; so it puts its dividend up from 9 to 10 per cent., and still carries forward a rather larger balance. Deposits are nearly a million higher, and there is also a fair increase in acceptances. Investments have increased by £64,000, but cash is down £130,000. A good feature is an addition of £290,000 in bills discounted, and £700,000 in loans and advances. Bank premises have been written up from £164,000 to £190,000, owing to the opening of new branches. Directors of banks should be in no hurry to write up this item; it will be time enough when he branches pay.

The London and South-Western Bank continues to reap benefit from the numerous branches it opened some years ago, and the time has come when the board might be materially strengthened. Net profits for the half-year are returned at £53,586, against £41,102 a year ago, but this is after placing only £10,000 to reserve against £20,000 in the corresponding period. As a larger balance was brought in, the available total is increased from £51,731 to £67,509, so the bonus paid, in addition to the 10 per cent. dividend, is increased from 1 to 2 per cent., absorbing an extra £6,000. Deposits at £9,421,000 are nearly a million up, but, while bills discounted show little change, the amount out as loans and advances has risen £660,000 to close on 4½ millions. The reserve fund might with advantage be increased more rapidly,

City and South London Railway Company.—This company is making good progress. Its net profits for the past half year were £11,493, or, with the balance forward, £12,567. So a dividend at the rate of 13s. 4d. per cent. per annum is to be paid on the ordinary stock, and still £1,511 will be left to carry forward. We wish its line ran from Streatham to Waterloo or Blackfriars.

Great Central Railway Company.—Gross revenue for half year to December 31 was £45,324 more than in the corresponding half of 1896, and the working expenses were £49,458 more. It follows that the net revenue was less in spite of the increase in gross income. Allowing for other credits and debits, including an increase of £8,478 in the debenture interest, &c., the amount available for distribution is smaller by nearly £14,000. Hence the reduction in the Preferred ordinary stock dividend to 2¼ per cent., against 2½ per cent. a year ago. The expenditure on capital account in the half-year was £1,198,000, and another £1,200,000 is expected to be spent in the present half-year.

London, Brighton, & South Coast Railway Company.—In the directors' report for the past half year it is stated that, besides the 500 new goods waggons ordered in 1896, they have had to order 500 more, as well as 500 coal waggons and a dozen new goods break vans. In the six months the gross income was £1,523,548, and the working expenses £764,912, an increase of £55,573 in the one, and of £32,341 in the other. Fixed charges have also expanded £1,845. As elsewhere announced, the dividend on the undivided ordinary stock for the half year is to be at the rate of 8¼ per cent. per annum, which gives the deferred half of the divided stock 7 per cent. for the year. A balance of £26,243 is left to be carried forward. Sir Allan Sarle, who joined the audit department in 1849, and lately retired from the general managership, is recommended for a seat at the board. For the past half year the capital expenditure was £206,000, and for the current one it is put at £241,000.

Great Eastern Railway Company.—Last half-year the gross income was £2,724,480, an increase of £114,790 on the corresponding half of 1896. Working expenses, however, increased by £88,156, so that the net gain was nothing like so large as anticipated. In fact, the ratio of expenditure to gross receipts was 55·35 per cent. last half-year, against 54·41 per cent. the year before. Then fixed charges absorbed £7,651 more than in the corresponding half-year, so that the increase in the dividend on ordinary stock to 5 per cent. per annum was quite as much as was to be expected. The better gross income is attributed by the board to the growth of the suburban traffic, the better harvest, a successful fishing season and higher prices for grain. Some progress was likewise made by the Continental traffic, which gained £2,620 gross, in spite of the active Belgian competition. Excluding the £188,962 paid for the Walton Railways, &c., the capital outlay of the past half-year was £216,485. That for the half-year now current is estimated at £250,000.

Foster, Porter, & Co., Limited.—The net profits of this old-established wholesale drapery firm amounted last year to £17,010, which allowed of 16s. per share, or about 7½ per cent., being distributed in the way of dividend, and the addition of £1,011 to the amount forward. This latter sum constitutes the reserve of the undertaking, and now amounts to £21,050, all being employed in the business. There is very little variation in the amount of the stock and debtor items.

The National Discount Company, Limited.—It cannot be said that this company makes much progress, but that may be just as well. Progress as indicated by swelling bulk does not invariably mean prosperity either in banking or discount business. All that the National Discount Company was able to do last half-year was to pay the usual dividend at the rate of 11 per cent. per annum, to set aside £28,000 odd for rebate, and to carry forward about £4.400. There is nothing in the accounts to call for notice, only we should like to see this fine old company wake up a bit.

LISTER & COMPANY, LIMITED.—What can we say more about this astonishing concern, which still has a reserve, although that is now reduced to £64,000? It still also keeps its goodwill, patents, and trade-marks at the original valuation, although it did write £23,000 off properties, &c., last year, or say, £17,500 net, after deducting the additions. It made a profit, too, and the profit was actually almost £45,000, so that the preference share dividend was paid in full, thanks to Lord Masham's surrender of the £15,800 due on the debenture stock held by him. Perhaps some day the company might pull round a bit, but its story is thus far dreary enough, and last year's gloomier than that of the year before.

BURLINGTON HOTELS COMPANY.—A youthful disregard of the future is displayed by the board of this new company. Hotel-keeping is not a business devoid of risk, and yet this board distributes all but a mere fraction of its earnings. In the year, £59,782 was received from business done, of which £43,021 was absorbed by working expenses. The balance of £16,761 was employed in paying preference and debenture interest, and a dividend of 10 per cent. upon the ordinary, only the trifle of £1,536 being left to be carried forward. No building up of a reserve is attempted, and yet the fixed charges of this heavily capitalised company come to £9,650 per annum. This is not the way to build up a solid business, and we fear the future.

DIRECT UNITED STATES CABLE COMPANY.—In the past half year revenue was £2,497 higher than in the second half of 1896. Expenses in the same time were £93 lower, so that the sum to be dealt with was £2,590 more. Consequently, after distributing the two interim dividends amounting to 6s. per share, or at the usual rate of 3 per cent. per annum, the Board is able to set aside £12,000 to reserve, and carry £4,090 forward. The reserve also benefited by £5,604 received from interest upon investments, but had to bear the outlay of £8,325 upon repairs and renewals of cables, and £2,000 for depreciation upon certain buildings. It therefore only increased £7,279 to a total of £345,767, which is virtually invested in high class securities.

LAW DEBENTURE CORPORATION.—A very good profit—£39,395—is shown by this company in the past year. This allows of a dividend of 7 per cent. upon the Ordinary shares and £27. 12s. 11d. per £10 share upon the Founders', or a trifle over 275 per cent. The reserves of the company, however, have been increased £9,800 in the year, and now amount to £33,474. They still represent a small proportion upon the £952,000 of capital for a company doing a fairly hazardous business. The weakest point, however, of the report is that £10,742, or about 25 per cent. of the net profit, is derived from profit upon sales of securities—a flimsy reed to lean upon for any length of time.

MAZAWATTEE TEA COMPANY.—Profit on trading in the year was £2,425 higher, at £56,695, and after meeting administrative charges a balance of £51,198 remained. The sum of £12,000 is set aside to reserve, raising it to £24,000, and £2,175 is allowed for depreciation, which seems a fair amount. Dividends amounting to 8 per cent. are again declared upon the ordinary shares, and the amount forward is increased £1,203 to a total of £2,466. "Trade marks and goodwill" still stand in the balance-sheet at the enormous figure of £382,489, against which the reserve of £24,000 is a mere atom, and this reserve, too, is still wholly locked up in the business. For the present, however, the company is doing well, and tea vending in retail is evidently a much more prosperous business than we thought it.

THOMAS WALLIS & CO., LIMITED.—The bad weather of the two last months of 1897 are said to account for a falling off of £4,247, to a total of £42,116, in the net profits of the year. Rather strangely, the directors' fees only amount to about half what they were in 1896, and debenture interest took less, so that after meeting these charges and preference interest the disposable balance is only about £1,500 below that of a year ago. The usual sum of £10,000 is set aside to redeem debentures, £1,000 is written off the new stables, and dividends amounting to 10 per cent. for the year declared upon the Ordinary shares, which is the same distribution as that made for 1896. The debenture debt will now be reduced to £90,000, as against £150,000 at the inception of the company, and the steady reduction of the capital thus effected is a strong guarantee for the maintenance of dividends in the future.

BRYANT & MAY, LIMITED.—Only a balance-sheet is vouchsafed to shareholders in this concern, the board still deeming a profit and loss account to be an unnecessary appendage. One, therefore, cannot say very much about the reduction of £3,273 in the net profit of last year to the total of £66,999. Depreciation is apparently met by charging all additions to premises and plant to revenue, and in this way £8,016 was spent in 1897, which seems a fair proportion of the £281,500 set down as the value of the properties. The company has a splendid reserve of £160,000, entirely invested in high-class securities, but stock has risen £18,000 in the year, to the detriment of the liquid assets. Dividends amounting to 17½ per cent., or the same as for 1895 and 1896, were declared, the payment of which will cause the balance forward to be reduced by £3,000 to £2,755. It is remarkable that the company does not seem to have attempted to accumulate a fire insurance fund, for we presume its buildings and works are not covered in the usual way.

STOCK CONVERSION AND INVESTMENT TRUST.—For the year ending December 31 this Trust earned a net profit of £54,865, which allowed of dividends amounting to 12½ per cent. on the ordinary shares, of 10s. per share, or 1,000 per cent., on the founders' shares, and the carrying forward of £14,247 to the reserves of the company. After deducting £1,246 for losses, these reserves amount to £74,418, as against £400,900 of ordinary and preference capital, and £217,650 of loans and debentures. In 1896 the profit was £43,495, which allowed of 10 per cent. dividends on the ordinary, 600 on the founders', and the placing of £17,497 to the reserves. The improvement, therefore, is considerable, and, in fact, the past year is probably the best ever experienced by the Trust, for the 20 per cent. dividend paid in 1889 was a little peculiar. Unfortunately, the profit and loss account is very poor, and one cannot, therefore, speak with assurance as to the manner in which profits are made. The proposed reduction in the nominal amount of the capital will reduce the uncalled capital to £1 per share.

EASTERN TELEGRAPH COMPANY.—In spite of reductions of rates, the income of this company from telegraph business increased £7,006 in the half-year ended September 30 to a total of £418,758. Revenue from investments in Telegraph shares was also slightly larger, but expenses were about £15,000 higher at £150,569, mainly on account of an additional charge of £9,517 in respect of cable renewal and repairs. The net balance of £293,158 for the half-year was, therefore, only £6,582 less than in 1896. Of this, £105,000 was set aside to various reserves, £50,195 went in interest upon debenture and preference capital, and £100,000 was distributed in the usual interim dividends, amounting to 2½ per cent. for the half-year. The various reserves of the company now amount to £1,087,640, and although £67,287 was taken to pay for the new Vigo-Gibraltar cable now being laid, the company has increased its investments in securities in the year by no less than £290,000. The whole of this large sum, it may be interesting to note, has been invested in Home Railway prior charge stocks. The preference stock of the company is to be rendered less cumbrous by exchanging £18. 10s. of new 3¼ per cent. preference stock for every £10 share of existing 6 per cent. preference capital. There will be no increased charge by the operation, which is similar to that carried through by many of the railway companies, but the new preference will probably stand at par, and will form a cheap medium for raising fresh capital.

More Laplanders and reindeer are about to be sent out to Klondike with relief for the citizens of Dawson City.

Nine thousand cotton operators in New Bedford, Mass., have struck against a reduction in wages announced by the employers. The reduction affects 125,000 operatives in New England.

The Newfoundland Government are negotiating with Mr. Reid, who built the railway across the island, to work the railway system of the colony for an extended term of years.

Reports continue in circulation as to the discovery of placer gold in various rivers in Labrador. Prospecting parties are preparing to start, and no doubt a "gold boom" will follow. The geological formation of Labrador is said to be the same as that of Klondike. The ice conditions are undoubtedly similar.

In a speech at Swansea, Sir Michael Hicks-Beech declared that what Government wanted in China was not territorial acquisition, but an open door for the commerce of the world; and the Government were absolutely determined, even at the cost of war, if necessary, that the door should not be shut again to us.

According to the Paris *Temps*, Russia is still pressing the candidature of Prince George of Greece for the Governorship of Crete, advising the Sultan to accede to this in order to avoid fresh embarrassments certain to arise, and probably lead to the annexation of Crete and Greece. At least two of the Powers, however, are said to be opposed to the Prince's candidature.

Essex county, in the extreme south of Ontario, has taken to tobacco-growing, and has made a good thing of it. Owing to the profits made from last year's crop, the acreage under tobacco is to be largely increased. It is said that an acre of good land, if carefully tilled, will produce from 1,000 to 2,000 lb. of leaf, which sells at 4d. to 7d. per pound, thus giving a gross profit of £16. 13s. 3d. to £33. 6s. 6d. per acre, which is far better than the £5 to £7 per acre given by wheat.

Speaking at a dinner of the Swansea Chamber of Commerce on Monday night, the Chancellor of the Exchequer expressed himself strongly in favour of a reform of the law as to limited liability companies. In its present state it deliberately encouraged fraud on the public. Does the right hon. gentleman contemplate legislation in the coming session? If the present law encourages fraud, no time should be lost in altering it.

The French Government Savings Bank returns for 1895 were only issued on Monday—a much longer delay than we are accustomed to even in this country. The deposits amounted to 355 million francs, and the withdrawals to 342 million francs. The law reducing the interest and limiting deposits to 1,500 francs caused a falling-off in the deposits, and in the last five months of 1895 the withdrawals exceeded these by seven million francs, but the aggregate deposits have now again increased, though at a slackened pace.

A PROMOTER'S FAILURE.—The first meeting of the creditors under the failure of Fordyce Sheridan, barrister-at-law and company promoter, has just been held. Mr. Sheridan has been fifteen years in the promotion business. Mr. R. Raphael stated that the debtor had prepared accounts showing liabilities £56,956, and assets estimated to produce £17,475. These liabilities included a sum of £50,000 due to the debtor's wife, who had been advised to tender a proof for only £25,000 at the present time. A scheme was being prepared under which Mrs. Sheridan's claim would be entirely withdrawn. Other claims would be either modified or entirely withdrawn, and 20s. in the £ would be paid to the remaining creditors. In these circumstances the meeting was adjourned until the last day of February.

The Produce Markets.

GRAIN.

Business has been slow during the week, buyers continuing Indifferent, but prices were generally maintained, and at Mark-lane on Wednesday the tendency was distinctly firmer. The supplies of English wheat were moderate. White quality quoted at 34s. 6d. to 39s. 6d., and red 33s. up to 38s. 6d. Holders of foreign kinds also a shade firmer in their demands, and supplies sparingly offered. Quotations of Californian and Walla remain nominal. Red Winter, 39s.; Manitoba, 39s. 6d. to 40s. 3d.; and Russian, 34s. 3d. up to 38s. 3d. Flour fully maintained at last Monday's rates, and meets with moderate attention, the following being the quotations:—Town households, 31s.; whites, 34s.; American top patents, 32s.; bakers, 27s. to 28s.; Hungarian, 39s. to 40s. per sack. Grinding barley is rather firmer, with a steady demand, and very little malting on offer. Oats in fair supply at firm to rather dearer rates, and the supply of Canadian white short. American mixed quoted at 15s. 6d. to 15s. 9d. ex ship, according to position, and 40 lb. ditto 16s. ex ship, 16s. 6d. landed. Maize meets a quiet sale, but rates are very steady. Beans upheld at fully last Monday's rates, peas remaining very firm. At Liverpool spot parcels were firm, but the demand was small. Red American futures began nominally ¼d. per cental dearer, fluctuated a good deal during the morning, though in the afternoon there was a steadier feeling. At second call, however, values were irregular, ¼d. per cental lower to ⅛d. higher. The market afterwards moved within narrow limits, and closed ⅛d. to ¼d. per cental lower, excepting March which advanced ⅛d. per cental. In London the movement in American options was ignored on Wednesday, and the market opened with unchanged values, while buyers were rather cautious and reserved. There was altogether a lack of urgency, and the close was quiet. Maize also was quiet, though a fairly good figure was obtained for a February mixed American, with further sales at the price, buyers were 3d. worse. Options in wheat ⅜d. to ⅝d. lower, and maize ⅜d. to ½d. down.

OFFICIAL CLOSING VALUES (100 lb. deliveries—January 19).

	March.	May.	July.	Sept.
Red American Wheat	7·3¼	7·0¾	6·10	6·5

In New York the Wheat market has shown less fluctuation, with a decided tendency to firmness, and on Tuesday there was a slight advance, but the response from Liverpool was disappointing, and the advance was not maintained. At the opening, on Wednesday, there was a reaction, May starting ¼ c. lower; but after further moderate recessions the tone became firmer under repurchases by "bears." A fairly good export inquiry helped near months, but trading throughout the afternoon was dull and featureless, the market closing steady at ⅛ c. to ½ c. advance except for May, which remains unchanged. Maize opened steady, and continued firm throughout the day, in sympathy with Chicago and on large purchases for export. Flour and oats both steady at unchanged rates. Spot firm. Spring wheat, 103½ c.; winter, 102 c.

COTTON.

The spot market at Liverpool has been steady, with a fair demand and good business, chiefly in American, which was less pressed for sale, at previous rates. Brazilian remained quiet, unchanged. Egyptians record a somewhat larger demand, and Surats are idle. Futures opened at a further decline of ½ to 1 point and remained in this position throughout the day, with a moderate business passing. The close was barely steady at the opening fall. Wednesday's tenders at the Clearing-house were 600 bales American and 50 Egyptian on new dockets.

NEW YORK CLOSING VALUES.

	Spot.	Jan.	Feb.	Mar.	April.	May.	June.	July.	Aug.	Sept.	Oct.	Nov.
Jan. 19 ..	5⅞	5·66	5·63	5·68	5·72	5·75	5·79	5·82	5·85	5·86	5·88	5·90

WOOL.

The first series of colonial wool sales for this year commenced on Tuesday. Referring to these, Messrs. Jacomb, Son, & Co. state:—"The list of arrivals closed on the 14th inst., and the available total only amounts to 171,000 bales, as against 263,000 for the corresponding series last year. Three catalogues, comprising 7,277 bales, have been offered; these, though small, contained, however, a fairly representative assortment. The attendance from all quarters is a very large one, including several representatives from America. With brisk biddings nearly all the wools offered were sold at an average advance of 5 per cent. for merinos (including South Africans), while cross-breds show no change from the rates ruling at the close of last auctions." The third auction at Liverpool took place on Wednesday afternoon. The bidding was irregular, and the general tone poor. Good export yellow sell well, and some of the better whites are reported fairly steady, but all classes of wools suitable for the American trade sell with difficulty and at reduced values. Otherwise the wool markets show cheerfulness, and in London on Wednesday there was great animation, with advancing prices. Merinos now rule from 5 to 10 per cent., and cross-breds partially 5 per cent. above previous closing rates. America was again very active, and secured some of the finest merino grease—viz., Sidney, G R L Y's at 10½d., C W S Mungadals at 11d., and Dungalear at 9½d.; while the bulk of the good selection of scoureds were sold on Belgian account at full rates.

METALS AND COAL.

Copper has been steady from the outset, and, as a consequence of the prospects of an early close of the engineers' strike, prices have been advancing. On Monday the market opened firm, and 3s. 9d. dearer. On Tuesday there was a partial advance of 1s. 3d., while on Wednesday the rates were 2s. 6d. higher than the previous close. During the morning no less than 1,000 tons changed hands, quite 800 of which were for forward delivery and chiefly for three months at £49. 11s. 3d., cash realising £49. 5s. and four months £49. 12s. 6d. In addition to these bargains a fair business was concluded privately on the basis of £49. 5s. for the 1st, 2nd, and 3rd of February, and £49. 7s. 6d. for the 19th. At the afternoon session there was a slight set back to £49 10s. three months, and £49. 6s. 3d. one month, but buyers again came forward, and the latter price and £49. 7s. 6d. combined was paid for February 11, the close being firm at the opening advance.

SETTLEMENT PRICES.

	Jan. 19.			Jan. 12			Jan. 5.			Dec. 29.			Dec. 22.			Dec. 15.		
	£	s.	d.	£	s.	d.	£	s.	d.	£	s.	d.	£	s.	d.	£	s.	d.
Copper ..	49	5	0	48	17	6	48	10	0	48	5	0	48	2	6	48	7	6

In pig-iron at Glasgow a considerable business has been done with a firmer tone throughout. On Wednesday the market was decidedly oversold, and were the public to come in higher prices would be seen. Shorts are nervous. Scotch closed unchanged, while Cleveland rose 1d.

SETTLEMENT PRICES.

	Jan. 19.		Jan. 12.		Jan. 5.		Dec. 29.		Dec. 22.		Dec. 15.	
	s.	d.	s.	d.	s.	d.	s.	d.	s.	d.	s.	d.
Scotch.. ..	46	0	45	9	45	6	43	4½	45	6	45	0
Cleveland ..	40	10½	40	7½	40	4½	40	3	40	6	40	1½
Hematite ..	48	10½	48	9	48	4½	48	4½	48	4½	47	10½

There has been no special movement on the Coal Exchange, and no change in values, though the tendency is rather downwards than otherwise. There is a steady reduction in merchants' stocks, and an upward movement may not be far off.

SUGAR.

Market quiet, but steady, with no change in prices. British cubes and pieces are in fairly good demand at steady prices; crystals show a good inquiry for yellows, and a moderate trade in others. Prices firm. Foreign—Granulated has ruled flat at ⅜d. decline. Ready Z R M, O F, and G D sold at 10s. 10½d.; January, first marks, 10s. 10½d. and sellers; February, 10s. 11¼d., sellers; March-April, 10s. 11¾d., value; May-August, 11s. 2¼d., paid, and sellers f.o.b. Hamburg. February, P P Z, sold at 11s. to 10s. 11¾d., f.o.b. Stettin. Cubes—Hausa, prompt, 12s. 3d.; F M S, 12s. 3d.; Meyer, 12s. 10½d., f.o.b. Hamburg; W S R, prompt, 13s. 3d.; S and T, 13s.; A S R and cut loaf, 13s., f.o.b. Amsterdam. Crushed—Dutch, A S R, prompt, 12s. sellers, f.o.b. Amsterdam. Austrian, T T D and V, prompt, 11s. 10½d., f.o.b. Hamburg. French—crystals, super 3's, prompt, 11s. 6⅜d., c.i.f., sellers; Say's cubes, prompt, 13s., sellers; loaves, 12s.; fine granulated, 11s. 6d.; Lebaudy's fine granulated, 12s. 3d., f.o.b. Paris. No. 3 crystals in Paris close firmer but quiet—January, 31f. 62½c.; March-June, 32f. 25c. Cane sorts quiet at unaltered prices. Beet futures dull, and 1d. lower. January sold at 9s. 3d., 9s. 2½d.; February at 9s. 3d.; March at 9s. 4¼d.; April, 9s. 5½d. sellers, 9s. 4¾d. buyers; May sold at 9s. 5½d., 9s. 5¾d., 9s. 6d., 9s. 5¾d.; June at 9s. 6½d.; July, 9s. 7½d. sellers, 9s. 7d. buyers; August, sold at 9s. 8d.; September, 9s. 7½d. sellers, 9s. 7¼d. buyers; October-December, 9s. 6⅝d. sellers, 9s. 6¼d. buyers.

TEA AND COFFEE.

The market has ruled quiet, with a tendency to dulness. At auction on Tuesday 4,981 packages met with slow competition at irregular prices; common qualities, of which the bulk consisted, only a small part sold at easier prices, Jamaica being 1s. to 2s. lower, while good to fine sorts, especially Ceylon and Costa Rica, brought very full rates. Ceylon, good middling to fine bold blue, 107s. to 116s.; peaberry, 151s. At auction on Wednesday 1,825 packages were offered, Ceylon and Costa Rica selling readily at full rates, while common sorts are still slow of sale, and Jamaica again lower. Ceylon—good middling to fine bold blue, 114s. to 116s.; fine small, 94s.; peaberry, 128s. Costa Rica—good bold smooth greenish coloury, 94s. to 99s.; good middling dull green, 85s. 6d.; peaberry mixed flats, 87s. Columbian—low middling dingy green mixed, 65s. to 70s.; bold soft dark coloury mixed, 62s. 6d.; good to fine ordinary dingy green mixed, 49s. to 57s. Jamaica—bold common brownish to good dull coloury, 77s. to 88s. 6d.; low middling to middling mixed, 64s. to 72s.; ordinary greenish to fine ordinary dull green, 41s. to 52s.; peaberry, 60s. to 67s. 6d. Futures steady, but quiet. Tea also has been quiet, though there was fair competition at the auction on Tuesday of 21,200 packages Ceylon, all good quality, medium and orange Pekoes maintaining previous prices. 14,500 packages Indian were offered on Wednesday; but, although a few good qualities maintained previous rates, the bulk of common to good medium grades ruled easier. Terminals quiet. Indian, type 1, January, quoted at 7⅛d.; February, 7$\frac{3}{16}$d.; March, 7¼d.; type 2, January, 6$\frac{1}{16}$d.; February, 6$\frac{1}{16}$d.; March, 6¼d.; April, 6$\frac{5}{16}$d.; Ceylon, January, 7¾d.; China, January, 4⅞d.; February, 4⅞d.; March, 4$\frac{15}{16}$d.

HEMP AND JUTE.

In the early part of the week hemp was rather flat. Though prices were maintained, buyers were certainly not eager. There was more firmness towards the close. At auction on Wednesday, seventy bales Mauritius, good to prime, sold at £20. 15s. to £22; Manila, F.C., February-April, sailer, sold at £18. 10s.; and May-July at £18. 15s. Jute has throughout been dull, though rather steadier on Wednesday, when 500 bales long group, first marks, January-March, steamer, London, sold at £9. 12s. 6d., and 1,000 six good marks at £9. 15s.

PRICE OF WHEAT IN 1897.

According to Government returns the imperial average price of wheat last year showed a rise of 4s. a quarter—the average being 30s. 2d., against 26s. 2d. in 1896. The highest weekly average was 34s. 4d., and the lowest 26s. 6d., a fluctuation of 7s. 10d. a quarter. In 1896 the fluctuation was 11s. a quarter. Of barley, the average price in 1897 was 22s. 11d., a rise of only 7d. a quarter. The highest price attained was 29s. 10d., and the lowest 17s. 4d., or a fluctuation of 12s. 6d. a quarter, against a fluctuation of 13s. 5d. in 1896. During five weeks last year barley was below the price of oats, the latter, in the week ending August 7, being 1s. 2d. above barley. The average price of oats in 1897 was 16s. 11d. per quarter, or 2s. 2d. a quarter higher than in 1896, that year's average being 14s. 9d. The highest price in 1897 was 19s. a quarter, and the lowest 16s., showing a fluctuation of 3s. a quarter. In 1896 the fluctuation was 4s. 6d. The average price of wheat in 1857 was 56s. 4d.; in 1867, 64s. 5d.; in 1877, 56s. 9d.; in 1887, 32s. 6d.; and 1897, 30s. 2d. Willich's tables state that the septennial tithe rent-charge for 1898 will be £68 14s. 11d. for £100, or 1¼ per cent. less than last year. The average for 62 years from the commutation in 1836 is £97 9s. 11⅜d.

THE PROPERTY MARKET.

There is little being done at the Mart—less even than is usual at this dull period of the year. Messrs. J. R. Kemp & Co., of Albany-street, acting in conjunction with Messrs. Debenham, Tewson, & Co., have sold by private treaty the freehold of Paul's Wharf, on the River Thames, near the Cathedral. The property fronts the Thames and Upper Thames-street, and has an area of upwards of 13,600 square feet. The large buildings on part of the site date from before the Great Fire of London in 1666, from the ravages of which they narrowly escaped.

The lease of the St. George's Hall, Langham-place, W., together with the minor hall, 76, Mortimer-street—occupied by the London Academy of Music—and premises in Mark's-court, Great Portland-street, will be offered under the hammer, on the 24th inst., by Messrs. Elliott, Son, & Boyton.

Mr. Alfred Richards' sale at the Mart, on the 25th inst., comprises a number of important Gas and Water debentures and ordinary stocks and shares, including £11,701 of ordinary "C" capital stocks of the Tottenham and Edmonton Gas Light and Coke Company, £3,900 four per cent. perpetual debenture stock of the Ascot District Gas Company, and £5,000 ordinary stock of the Southend Water Works Company. Messrs. Hampson & Co. had a good deal on offer at the London Mart, on Monday, but did nothing. Perhaps the reserves were responsible for this.

On Tuesday, Messrs. Weston & Son sold, at the Mart, the Haverstock Arms, Haverstock-hill, freehold, rent £100, for £4,800. Beyond this the transactions of the day were small, the total realisation being only £7,640.

At Masons' Hall Tavern, on Tuesday, the free lease, with possession, of the White Horse, No. 100, High Holborn, immediately facing the Royal Music Hall, held for sixty-eight years, at a rent of £185 per annum, and subject to a mortgage of £21,000, was sold by Messrs. Fleuret, Sons, & Adams, for £32,000, the New London Brewery being the purchasers. Two smaller houses were also offered, but without result.

At Messrs. Edwin Fox & Bousfield's sale of stocks and shares at the Mart on Wednesday, the following prices were realised:—Epsom Grand Stand Association, £20 original shares, fully paid, £51; £6. 13s. 4d. "New Thirds" shares, fully paid, £17. 10s.; Sandown Park, Limited, £10 shares, fully paid, £12; Bushell, Watkins, & Co., Limited, Westerham Brewery, Kent, £10 ordinary shares, fully paid, £20. 15s.; £10 six per cent. cumulative preference shares, fully paid, £15; Freehold and Leasehold Investment Company, Limited, £10 shares, £5 paid, £4 and £3. 17s. 6d.; British Farmers' Association, Limited, £1 shares, fully paid, 16s.; Otis Steel Company, Limited, £10 preference shares, fully paid, £1. 5s.; London and Australasian Debenture Corporation, Limited, £6. 13s. 4d., founders' shares, fully paid, £1. 12s.; Municipal Trust Company, Limited, £1,500 deferred stock, £20 per cent.

The *Frankfürter Zeitung* mentions a rumour that the Schweizerischer Bankverein, Basle, proposes shortly to establish a branch in London. As a consequence, it is said the capital of the bank would be increased from 35,000,000 francs. to 50,000,000 francs. The report is not confirmed.

Negotiations have been taking place between a Rand house and the Imperial and Natal Governments with a view to the acquisition of certain lands on the north and south banks of the Sordwana River, on the boundary of Zululand and Amatongaland, with a view to the construction of a harbour at Sordwana Bay.

Another suggestion for crossing the Channel under the sea. It is to build a viaduct from shore to shore, some 50 ft. below the level of the lowest tides, on which a platform, containing the train, will be run by electricity, gripping the viaduct with steel legs. It is hardly likely that much more will be heard of this original idea.

The Manchester Ship Canal is progressing. The total traffic last year was 2,065,935 tons. In 1896 it was 1,826,237 tons, showing an increase in 1897 of 239,698 tons. The advantage 1896 had over 1895, however, was 474,866 tons, so that the progress can hardly be said to be uninterrupted. The revenue is stated at £204,414, against £179,834 in 1896.

THE PRODUCTION OF COPPER.

The copper statistics have an unhappy knack of disappointing those who place much trust in them, but the figures published as to the position on January 15 are worth a little attention. For one thing, the absorption of the metal has continued at a high level, and the stock of copper is estimated on January 15 to have been no more than 31,033 tons, or less than 200 tons above the lowest total of the three years just previous. Compared with January, 1895, the falling off in stocks is about 25,800 tons, or very nearly one-half, and this, in face of the diminished demand that must have occurred, in some quarters through the engineering strike, is a little remarkable.

Now, one must not take these statistics too seriously, as a strong speculative movement is proceeding in copper mining shares, and it is a great temptation for operators in such shares to work the copper market at the same time in order to encourage a rise in the shares. But even allowing for this circumstance, the recent reductions in the stocks may be considered as partially the result of natural causes, for the diminution in the supplies is mainly due to a falling off in United States exports. Thus in the last four months of 1897 the receipts from that quarter only came to 31,100 tons, as against 44,700 tons in the same months of 1896. Coinciding with the news that the Anaconda mine has been producing less in that time, it is possible that the actual surplus of the American copper market has been less, for, of course, home demands, especially in regard to electrical enterprises, have been very large.

The Anaconda production represents no mean proportion of the American output, its out-turn in the twelvemonths ended June 30 last having been put at 66,182 tons, or more than the whole exports from North America in 1895, which amounted to 65,321 tons. In the two subsequent years these exports increased largely, having been 124,224 tons in 1896 and 130,363 tons in 1897, despite the diminution in the last four months. It is possible that production may have been pressed forward rather sharply in the United States, especially in the case of the Anaconda Company, where a distinct motive existed for such an aim in the shape of the selling of the shares upon the London market. Thus the out-turn of the mine in 1893 was 40,723 tons, and in 1894 it was 49,340 tons. Then came a broken period of six months, owing to the mine being turned over to the new Anglicised company, which took place in July, 1895, and in that time 24,962 tons was produced, or about the level of the previous year. The twelvemonths that followed saw a jump in production to 53,518 tons, and this was followed by the "record" out-turn of 66,182 tons in the twelvemonths ended June 30 last. Is it not at least possible that this progress has been too rapid, and that the mine needed the rest that the management admit to have been given last half-year on account of alterations to furnaces and flues?

STOCKBROKER AND CLIENT.

A curious point was raised in a case heard in the Coventry County Court on Tuesday. Last summer Mr. Joseph Cash, of Coventry, directed Messrs. Whittendale & Watson, a firm of stockbrokers in Birmingham, to buy five hundred shares in the Coventry Stamping Company, Limited, which had just been formed to take over a business in which Mr. Cash was interested. Owing to some statements in the prospectus, however, the directors decided to return the subscribers' money, but, in the meantime, Messrs. Whittendale and Watson had purchased 300 shares at 3s. premium, and they claimed from Mr. Cash the difference of £48 15s. This Mr. Cash refused to pay, on the ground that the purchase was for the special settlement and no such settlement had taken place. The chairman of the Birmingham Stock Exchange and another member were called in support of plaintiff's case, and judgment was given for the plaintiffs for the amount claimed.

Mercantile Failure in London.—In connection with the failure of John Clark Forster, carrying on business as Ferguson & Forster, wholesale spice merchants and liquorice importers, at 11 and 12, Great Tower-street, and 6 and 7, Osborne-street, Whitechapel, E.C., the debtor has submitted a statement of his affairs. He returns his gross liabilities at £34,143, of which £18,212 are expected to rank for dividend, with assets estimated to produce £11,639. It appears that the business is an old-established one, and on the death of his uncle in 1870 the debtor succeeded to a share in it. Since October last he has traded alone. He ascribes his insolvency to interest on borrowed money, to interest on advances made against warrants for liquorice juice, to bad debts, and to the expenses of an abortive attempt to convert the business into a company. An adjudication of bankruptcy has been made and a trustee appointed.

The London Water Supply.—Sir A. Binnie, chief engineer to the London County Council, has this week been giving evidence before the Royal Commission on the water supply of London. The witness quoted figures to show how nearly there might be an approach to the absorption of the whole flow of the Thames during comparatively long periods in the drier half of the year, and that the whole flow of the River Lea was practically absorbed in dry weather. The Lea Conservators afforded no protection to the public, because they were entirely overshadowed by the water companies. The witness referred to the bitter complaints which had reached the County Council as to the shocking state of the Lea. He did not altogether accept the finding of Lord Balfour's Commission that the Thames and Lea were satisfactory sources of supply. He would not abandon the present sources of supply, but supplement them. At the sitting of the Commission on Tuesday, Sir A. Binnie said his opinion was that the existing supply would have to be supplemented in ten or fifteen years. He was in favour of obtaining an additional supply from Wales, at a first outlay of over £14,000,000, and an ultimate expenditure of £26,000,000.

ENGLISH RAILWAY TRAFFIC RETURNS

Cleator and Workington.—Gross receipts for the week ending January 15 amounted to £1,164, an increase of £89. Total from January 1, £2,109, a decrease of £159.

Cockermouth, Keswick, and Penrith.—Gross receipts for the week ending January 15 amounted to £840, an increase of £97. Total from January 1, £1,837, an increase of £217.

East London railway traffic for month of November amounted to £4,288, showing an increase of £244.

TRAMWAY AND OMNIBUS RECEIPTS.

Increases for past week :—Belfast, £276 ; Croydon, £81 ; Glasgow, £27 ; Lea Bridge, £124 ; London & Deptford, £56 ; London Southern, £109 ; London General Omnibus, £1,882 ; London Road Car, £677 ; Metropolitan, £915 ; North Staffordshire, none ; Provincial, £155 ; Southampton, none ; South London, £132 ; Swansea, £28 ; Wolverhampton, £10 ; Woolwich & S. E. London, £29.

Decreases for past week :—Barcelona, £38 ; Bordeaux, £7 ; Calais, £2.

Anglo-Argentine, 11 days ending December 20, £346 increase. Vienna Omnibus, week ending January 8, £264 increase.

Next Week's Meetings.

MONDAY, JANUARY 24.

Birmingham and District Counties Banking Company	Birmingham, 3.30. p.m.
Bradford Old Bank	Bradford, noon.
Folkestone Gas Light and Coke Company	Folkestone, 3 p.m.
Lancaster Banking	Lancaster, 11 a.m.
Reliance Marine Insurance	Liverpool, 11.30 a.m.
Robert Campbell & Sons	Winchester House, 2 p.m.

TUESDAY, JANUARY 25.

British and Eastern Shipping Company	Liverpool, noon.
Bryant & May	Cannon-street Hotel, 3 p.m.
Burlington Hotels	Buckingham Palace Hotel, 1 p.m.
Caledonian Railway	Glasgow, 1 p.m.
Direct United States Cable	Winchester House, 2 p.m.
Folkestone Waterworks Company	Folkestone, 3 p.m.
Lister & Co.	Bradford, noon.
Sea Insurance	Liverpool 2 p.m.

WEDNESDAY, JANUARY 26.

British Shipowners Company	Liverpool, noon.
Craven Bank	Skipton, 2 p.m.
Great Central Railway	Manchester, noon.
Halifax and Huddersfield Union Bank	Huddersfield, noon.
Halifax Joint Stock Bank	Halifax, 11 a.m.
Liverpool Union Bank	Liverpool, 1 p.m.
London, Brighton and South Coast Railway	London Bridge, 2 p.m.
Maritime Insurance Company	Liverpool, noon.
Mazawattee Tea	Cannon-street Hotel, 2 p.m.
Provincial Bank of Ireland	8, Throgmorton-avenue, 11.30 a.m.
Union Bank of Manchester	Manchester, 11 a.m.

THURSDAY, JANUARY 27.

Bass, Ratcliff, & Gretton 3½ per cent. "B" debentures	Call of 50 per cent. = £280,000.
Bradbury, Greatorex, & Co.	Aldermanbury, noon.
Cranbrook and Paddock Wood Railway	Cannon-street Hotel, 10.45 a.m.
Foster, Porter, & Co.	47, Wood-street, 11 a.m.
Mercantile Bank of Lancashire	Manchester, noon.
Metropolitan Bank (of England and Wales)	Birmingham, noon.
National Bank	13, Old Broad-street, 1 p.m.
New York, Pennsylvania, and Ohio First Mortgage Trust	Winchester House, 2 p.m.
Oldham Joint Stock Bank	Oldham, 1 p.m.
Parr's Bank	Cannon-street Hotel, 1 p.m.
River Plate and General Investment Trust	52, Moorgate-street, 2 p.m.
South-Eastern Railway	Cannon-street Hotel, noon.
York City and County Banking Company	York.

FRIDAY, JANUARY 28.

Buenos Ayres Northern Railway Company	Winchester House, noon.
City and South London Railway	Winchester House, noon.
Liverpool Mortgage Insurance	Liverpool, noon.
London and St. Katharine Docks	Cannon-street Hotel, 2 p.m.
Metropolitan Railway	Cannon-street Hotel, 12 p.m.
Royal Aquarium, &c. Society	Royal Aquarium, Westminster, noon.
Thomas Wallis & Co.	Holborn, 3 p.m.

SATURDAY, JANUARY 29.

Australian Mortgage and Agency Company	Edinburgh, noon.

A new omnibus company is to start business in London. It is to have 400 'buses, and 4,000 horses. It is to be hoped the vehicles will be an improvement upon those we already possess.

It appears from the report of Mr. Consul Boyle that the foreign trade of Denmark is chiefly with Great Britain and Germany. In 1896 we took £9,427,000 of the exports and contributed £4,348,000 of the imports, against Germany's £3,213,000 exports and £7,004,000 imports.

Mr. Hobbs, ex-colleague of Jabez Balfour in the Liberator business, has been released from prison on account of the state of his health. His victims will be interested in knowing that the ex-convict has arrived at the family seat, Norbury Hall, Streatham, and that "the family carriage met him at the railway station."

Answers to Correspondents.

Questions about public securities, and on all points in company law, will be answered week by week, in the REVIEW, on the following terms and conditions :—

A fee of FIVE shillings must be remitted for each question put, provided they are questions about separate securities. Should a private letter be required, then an extra fee of FIVE shillings must be sent to cover the cost of such letter, the fee then being TEN shillings for one query only, and FIVE shillings for every subsequent one in the same letter. While making this concession the EDITOR will feel obliged if private replies are as much as possible dispensed with. It is wholly impossible to answer letters sent merely "with a stamped envelope enclosed for reply."

Correspondents will further greatly oblige by so framing their questions as to obviate the necessity to name securities in the replies. They should *number* the questions, keeping a copy for reference, thus :—"(1) Please inform me about the present position of the Rowenzori Development Co. (2) Is a dividend likely to be paid soon on the capital stock of the Congo-Sudan Railway ?"

Answers to be given to all such questions by simply quoting the numbers 1, 2, 3, and so on. The EDITOR has a rooted objection to such forms of reply as—"I think your Timbuctoo Consols will go up," or "Sell your Slowcoach and Draggem Bonds," because this kind of thing is open to all sorts of abuses. By the plan suggested, and by using a fancy name to be replied to, each query can be kept absolutely private to the inquirer, and no scope whatever be given to market munipulations. Avoid, as names to be replied to, common words, like "investor," "inquirer," and so on, as also "bear" or "bull." Detached syllables of the inquirer's name, or initials reversed, will frequently do as well as anything, so long as the answer can be identified by the inquirer.

The EDITOR further respectfully requests that merely speculative questions should as far as possible be avoided. He by no means sets himself up as a market prophet, and can only undertake to provide the latest information regarding the securities asked about. This he will do faithfully and without bias.

Replies cannot be guaranteed in the same week if the letters demanding them reach the office of the INVESTORS' REVIEW, Norfolk House, Norfolk-street, W.C., later than the first post on Wednesday mornings.

Y. F.—1. Brazil is not a tempting field for investment at present ; we cannot advise a purchase. Financial position of company is not strong ; quite recently vendor was endeavouring to raise a loan on his shares. 2. The ordinary dividend was only paid by drawing on the reserve, and the last report was a melancholy affair. 3. I hear good accounts of the prospects of this company, but it is too speculative to be described as an investment.

The total number of street railways in the United States is 806, of which 698 are worked by electricity.

The Lanarkshire and Dumbartonshire Railway Company are applying for parliamentary powers for raising additional capital, not having enough to defray their outstanding liabilities, though the railway and works are nearly completed. They propose to create additional ordinary capital to an amount not exceeding £225,000, with power to raise £75,000 additional debenture stock. The bill deposited proposes to empower the Caledonian Railway Company to subscribe £147,000 of the total amount required.

It is suggested by a correspondent of the *Daily News* that Russia is the Power to which Dreyfus was accused of selling information. It was at first supposed to be Germany, and the prosecution was begun on this supposition. As the case proceeded, however, it was found that the Power involved was Russia, and, as Russia is France's ally, strict silence had to be observed on the subject. But is it possible that the French legal authorities would have started a prosecution of this sort without knowing what Power was involved in it?

MINING IN THE YUKON DISTRICT.—The Canadian Government have issued amended regulations respecting placer mining in the Yukon district. Every miner and the employee of every miner must take out a miner's certificate, the fee for which will be 10 dols., and in the case of a company 50 dols. or 100 dols., according to the amount of capital stock. The miner's licence confers the right to mine, fish, hunt, and cut timber. The general size of mining claims is 250 ft., and of discoverer's claims 500 ft. Every alternate ten claims are reserved by the Government. Sub-aqueous mining leases will be issued in five-mile sections at a fee of 100 dols. per mile per annum and the usual royalty. The fee for recording and renewing mining claims is 15 dols.

TRADE UNIONS IN GERMANY.—In the German Reichstag on Tuesday, during the debate on the estimates for the Imperial Home Office, Herr von Kardorff, after pointing out the growth of Social-Democracy, which had followed the repeal of the Anti-Socialist Law and the depression of agriculture, declared that advantage ought to be taken of England's experiences, and dilated on the danger of handing over millions of workmen to the Social Democrats through trade unions. Dr. Lieber declared that the Centre would agree to no settlement of the question of the right of combination that was not based on absolutely equal rights for both employers and employed. Herr Pachnicke (Freisinnige Volkspartei) said that his party regarded the right of combination as the first essential for the protection of the working classes. The struggle in the Reichstag on this subject is becoming keen.

"INVESTORS' REVIEW."

NOTICES.

BACK NUMBERS.

Less than a dozen complete sets now remain of the first four Quarterly Numbers of the "INVESTORS' REVIEW," so that the first Number of all can only be supplied in volume form, price **21s.** net. The Volume for 1893 is also composed of Quarterly Parts, and its price is the same. The seven Quarterly Parts from Number II. onwards can still be had separately, price 5s. net. For the succeeding four years down to December, 1897, the "REVIEW" is in Monthly Numbers.

All Monthly Numbers more than six months old will now be charged 1s. 6d. net, and all Half-yearly Volumes, 10s. 6d. net (by post, 2d. and 10d. extra for the Number or Volume).

Cloth Cases for binding the "REVIEW" and the "INDEX" are charged for as follows:—For Annual Volumes of the "REVIEW," 1s. 6d.; for Semi-annual Volumes, 1s. 3d.; and for Yearly Volumes of the "INDEX," also 1s. 3d. Postage, in all instances, 2d. extra.

SUBSCRIPTION PRICE, POST FREE:—

INVESTORS' REVIEW alone—

	Three Months.	Six Months.	One Year.
United Kingdom.	7s.	14s.	28s.
All Foreign Countries.	7s. 6d.	15s.	30s.

INVESTORS' REVIEW and INVESTMENT INDEX together—

	Three Months.	Six Months.	One Year.
United Kingdom.	9s. 6d.	18s. 6d.	36s.
All Foreign Countries.	9s. 10d.	19s. 6d.	38s. 6d.

Payable in Advance.

Cheques and Postal Orders should be made payable to CLEMENT WILSON.

The INVESTORS' REVIEW can be obtained in Paris of Messrs. BOYVEAU ET CHEVILLET, 22, Rue de la Banque.

Of all Newsagents and at all Railway Bookstalls in the United Kingdom, or remit to The PUBLISHER, Norfolk House, Norfolk-street, Strand, W.C.

CLEMENT WILSON'S PUBLICATIONS.

LEGAL EPITOMES FOR GENERAL USE.

Price 2s. 6d. Fcap 8vo, cloth.

No. I.

LAW OF SALES OF STOCKS AND SHARES. By CHARLES FRAMPTON STALLARD, M.A. (Oxon.), of Gray's Inn, late Holt Scholar, Barrister-at-Law.

"The law is clearly and concisely given, and the book should certainly assist those who are concerned in dealings with stocks and shares."—*Law Times.*

"Cannot fail to be of service to many who have dealings in stocks and shares."—*Bankers' Magazine.*

No. II.

LAW OF BANKS AND BANKERS. By W. DE BRACY HERBERT, M.A., LL.M., of the Inner Temple, Barrister-at-Law.

"A clear and readable exposition of the English law of Banker and Customer."—*Scotsman.*

"Clear and simple in its style . . . and appears to be absolutely accurate."—*Law Times.*

No. III.

LAW OF DIRECTORS' AND PROMOTERS' LIABILITIES. By R. STORRY DEANS, LL.B. (London), of Gray's Inn, Barrister-at-Law, sometime Holder of Inns of Court Studentship, Arden Scholar of Gray's Inn, &c.

"A clearly written and useful book upon a subject of general interest."—*Manchester Guardian.*

"It is well fitted to be of assistance to directors, promoters, and shareholders."—*Dundee Advertiser.*

No. IV.

Now Ready.

LAW OF FIXTURES AND REPAIRS AS BETWEEN LANDLORD AND TENANT. By W. DE BRACY HERBERT, M.A., LL.M., of the Inner Temple, Barrister-at-Law.

BOOKS BY A. J. WILSON.

Editor of the "Investors' Review" and "Investment Index."

Price in cloth, 1s. 6d. net (post free, 1s. 8d.); paper cover, 1s. net (post free, 1s. 2d.)

No. I.

PRACTICAL HINTS TO INVESTORS.

"The perusal of Mr. Wilson's handy book will repay those concerned in the matters treated of; and as an example in terse and incisive English it may be read by the student and admirer of style."—*Manchester City News.*

No. II.

Now Ready. New Edition, Entirely Rewritten.

PLAIN ADVICE ABOUT LIFE INSURANCE.

"Pregnant with plain meaning, and hits hard, straight from the shoulder, as a work by Mr. Wilson usually does."—*Westminster Gazette.*

"Frank and out-spoken, and affords much useful information and guidance."—*Glasgow Herald.*

CLEMENT WILSON,
Norfolk House, Norfolk Street, W.C.

To Correspondents.

The EDITOR cannot undertake to return rejected communications. Letters from correspondents must, in every case, be authenticated by the name and address of the writer.

The Investors' Review.

The Week's Money Market.

Ease in the market has made further progress this week. The discount houses on Friday last had to reduce their allowance for deposits by $\frac{1}{2}$ per cent. to $1\frac{1}{2}$ per cent. for money at "call," and $1\frac{3}{4}$ per cent. for money at "notice," and the course of rates since has proved the necessity of the step. Day to day money has these last few days been so plentiful that the "call" rate has gradually drooped to 1 per cent., and loans for a week command no more than $1\frac{1}{4}$ per cent. So the market has not yet felt the influence of the maturing of bills held by the Bank of England.

In these circumstances discount rates could no longer be maintained, although the most was made of "impending gold withdrawals to the River Plate," and other such rumours to try to keep the market up. Shipments to Argentina, however, have all along been fully expected on a moderate scale during January, and after all the matter is not one of first-class importance. Accordingly, the great ease in money had full play, and discount rates have fallen steadily throughout the week, so that three months' remitted bills can be melted at $2\frac{1}{8}$ to $2\frac{1}{4}$ per cent. as against $2\frac{3}{8}$ to $2\frac{7}{16}$ per cent. a week ago. Sixty days' paper has fallen to a like extent, but rather significantly the six months' rate has shown less weakness, declining only to about $2\frac{5}{8}$ per cent. Foreign exchanges have moved against this country to a trifling extent, in spite of the reduction in the German Bank's official premium, and the price for gold in the open market has risen $\frac{1}{2}$d. to 77s. 11d. per ounce. About £130,000 in gold arrived from Japan as a result of sales of yen in that country, sent from the Straits Settlement. At intervals more may filter in from this quarter, but at present no one attaches importance to the movement.

A factor contributing towards the market weakness was the low average rate at which the £1,000,000 of India Treasury Bills were renewed. The whole amount went in six months' bills at £2. 4s. 5d. per cent., and after this announcement on Monday the market gave up any serious attempt to maintain rates. An issue of £1,000,000 Western Australian three per cent. stock went at an average of £96. 6s. 4d. per cent., or £1. 6s. 4d. above the minimum. The last issue by the colony, which was also in three per cents., produced £95. 0s. 10d. per cent. This difference shows that the credit conditions are a shade less favourable.

In one sense the Bank return published yesterday indicates a reason for the greater cheapness of money, in another it does not. The Banking Reserve has increased £1,206,000 to £21,891,000, and a large reserve always helps to ease the market. On the other hand the market itself is really poorer, as the decrease of £1,485,000 in the "other" deposits which comprise the bankers' balances, proves these deposits are now down to £38,885,000, by no means a total to rely upon for prolonged ease. All the money back from circulation, and the above amount off the "other" deposits in addition, has gone to swell the Government balances which are greater by £2,056,000, and to enable the market to reduce "other" securities by £629,000.

SILVER.

The Silver Market has weakened considerably during the week, the price for immediate delivery dropping $\frac{5}{16}$d. to $26\frac{1}{8}$d. per oz. and for delivery two months hence by $\frac{5}{8}$d. to $25\frac{7}{8}$d. per oz. Support has been lost through the easing of the monetary position both in China and India. Whereas discount rates in China a few weeks back were over 30 per cent., they are now no higher than 5 to 6 per cent., as the arrangements to meet the requirements of the Chinese New Year, which falls on the 22nd inst., have been completed. The stringency had caused Mexican dollars to be bought up in the Straits and shipped to China, and thus left room for the new British dollar, which is being actively minted at Bombay. Silver, of course, had to be purchased for this operation, and these orders have recently played an important part in maintaining the quotation. Now that the Chinese exchanges have fallen so heavily, —$\frac{1}{2}$d. to 1d. in the week—this operation is no longer so profitable. In India the ease is only relative, but "forward" rates of exchange keep low, so that the worst of the pressure may be over for a time, Consequently the demand for remittance has diminished, and the India Council did not allot any drafts last Wednesday, the applications being only for $6\frac{1}{2}$ lacs, at low quotations. This, of course, militates against the demand for silver, and at the same time the Bombay market—the chief one in India for the metal—is disorganised owing to the flight of most of the dealers from the city in consequence of the outbreak of the plague.

BANK OF ENGLAND.

AN ACCOUNT pursuant to the Act 7 and 8 Vict., cap. 32, for the Week ending on Wednesday, January 19, 1898.

ISSUE DEPARTMENT.

	£		£
Notes Issued	46,773,525	Government Debt	11,015,100
		Other Securities	5,784,900
		Gold Coin and Bullion	29,973,525
		Silver Bullion	—
	£46,773,525		£46,773,525

BANKING DEPARTMENT.

	£		£
Proprietors' Capital	14,553,000	Government Securities......	14,023,036
Rest	3,432,713	Other Securities............	32,540,632
Public Deposits (including Exchequer, Savings Banks, Commissioners of National Debt, and Dividend Accounts)	11,447,213	Notes	19,748,130
Other Deposits	38,885,244	Gold and Silver Coin	2,142,661
Seven Day and other Bills..	136,289		
	£68,454,459		£68,454,459

Dated January 20, 1898.

H. G. BOWEN, *Chief Cashier.*

In the following table will be found the movements compared with the previous week, and also the totals for that week and the corresponding return last year :—

Banking Department.

Last Year. Jan. 20		Jan. 12, 1898.	Jan. 19, 1898.	Increase.	Decrease.
£	Liabilities.	£	£	£	£
3,406,871	Rest	3,423,887	3,423,713	8,826	—
8,063,487	Pub. Deposits....	9,391,449	11,447,213	2,055,764	—
46,839,007	Other do.	40,370,457	38,885,244	—	1,485,213
118,884	7 Day Bills	138,773	136,289	—	2,484
	Assets.			Decrease.	Increase.
15,717,867	Gov. Securities ..	14,023,036	14,023,036	—	—
32,516,540	Other do.	33,169,652	32,540,632	629,020	—
24,746,842	Total Reserve....	20,684,878	21,890,791	—	1,205,913
				2,693,610	2,693,610
				Increase.	Decrease.
£		£	£	£	£
26,571,250	Note Circulation.	27,502,390	27,025,395	—	476,995
45 p.c.	Proportion	$41\frac{1}{2}$ p.c.	$43\frac{3}{4}$ p.c.	—	—
4 „	Bank Rate	3 „	3 „	—	—

Foreign Bullion movement for week £90,000 out.

LONDON BANKERS' CLEARING.

Week ending	1897.	1896.	Increase.	Decrease.
	£	£	£	£
Dec. 1	171,792,000	166,125,000	5,667,000	—
„ 8	136,090,000	124,457,000	11,633,000	—
„ 15	161,483,000	165,735,000	—	4,252,000
„ 22	155,425,000	133,202,000	22,223,000	—
„ 29	105,382,000	132,437,000	—	27,055,000
Total for 1897	7,491,281,000	7,574,853,000	—	83,572,000
Week ending	**1898.**	**1897.**	**Increase.**	**Decrease.**
	£	£	£	£
Jan. 5	222,654,000	174,376,000	48,278,000	—
„ 12	144,603,000	127,315,000	17,288,000	—
„ 19	171,777,000	156,200,000	15,577,000	—

BANK AND DISCOUNT RATES ABROAD.

	Bank Rate.	Altered.	Open Market.
Paris	2	March 14, 1895	2
Berlin	4	January 20, 1898	3⅞
Hamburg	4	January 20, 1898	3⅞
Frankfort	4	January 20, 1898	3⅞
Amsterdam	3	April 13, 1897	2⅞
Brussels	3	April 28, 1896	2
Vienna	4	January 22, 1896	3½
Rome	5	August 27, 1895	3
St. Petersburg	6	August 26, 1896	5
Madrid	5	June 17, 1896	4
Lisbon	6	January 25, 1891	6
Stockholm	5	October 27, 1897	5
Copenhagen	5	August 3, 1897	5
Calcutta	11	January 11, 1898	—
Bombay	12	January 11, 1898	—
New York call money	2 to 2½	—	—

NEW YORK ASSOCIATED BANKS (dollar at 4s.).

	Jan. 13, 1898.	Jan. 6, 1898.	Jan. 1, 1898.	Jan. 16, 1897.
	£	£	£	£
Specie	21,728,000	21,318,000	20,946,000	15,564,000
Legal tenders	18,046,000	17,414,000	15,964,000	22,740,000
Loans and discounts	122,198,000	121,956,000	121,556,000	98,280,000
Circulation	3,018,200	3,114,400	3,104,000	3,748,800
Net deposits	138,322,000	137,118,000	135,012,000	111,478,000

Legal reserve is 25 per cent. of net deposits; therefore the total reserve (specie and legal tenders) exceeds this sum by £5,193,500, against an excess last week of £4,452,500.

BANK OF FRANCE (25 francs to the £).

	Jan. 20, 1898.	Jan. 13, 1898.	Jan. 6, 1898.	Jan. 14, 1897.
	£	£	£	£
Gold in hand	77,079,040	77,326,960	77,637,120	76,297,000
Silver in hand	48,295,120	48,214,120	48,265,040	49,137,000
Bills discounted	35,723,640	38,258,760	38,536,920	*50,757,000
Advances	14,804,320	15,161,920	16,336,600	—
Note circulation	153,064,640	153,518,280	154,505,080	150,804,000
Public deposits	9,377,000	10,153,400	12,962,760	7,950,000
Private deposits	20,073,840	21,008,000	21,616,560	22,459,000

Proportion between bullion and circulation 81¾ per cent. against 81⅞ per cent. a week ago.

* Includes advances.

IMPERIAL BANK OF GERMANY (20 marks to the £).

	Jan. 15, 1898.	Jan. 7 1898.	Dec. 31, 1897.	Jan. 15, 1897.
	£	£	£	£
Cash in hand	44,149,600	42,422,900	41,327,800	42,830,000
Bills discounted	29,132,350	33,625,850	33,438,900	*37,133,000
Advances on stocks	5,409,400	6,405,750	8,633,550	—
Note circulation	57,595,050	61,654,000	65,998,600	54,738,000
Public deposits	20,008,150	19,672,900	21,320,200	21,214,000

* Includes advances.

AUSTRIAN-HUNGARIAN BANK (1s. 8d. to the florin).

	Jan. 14, 1898.	Jan. 7, 1898.	Dec. 31, 1897.	Jan. 14, 1897.
	£	£	£	£
Gold reserve	30,375,416	30,363,833	30,315,750	30,331,000
Silver reserve	10,304,750	10,280,083	10,278,417	12,614,000
Foreign bills	1,372,583	1,592,166	1,572,333	—
Advances	2,039,166	2,229,666	2,319,333	—
Note circulation	54,545,000	56,636,000	58,325,583	61,341,000
Bills discounted	13,004,333	16,020,750	17,244,750	*20,582,000

* Includes advances.

NATIONAL BANK OF BELGIUM (25 francs to the £).

	Jan. 13, 1898.	Jan. 6, 1898.	Dec. 30, 1897.	Jan. 14, 1897.
	£	£	£	£
Coin and bullion	4,206,360	4,290,960	4,119,880	4,114,360
Other securities	17,744,800	18,541,280	18,033,000	16,926,280
Note circulation	19,837,400	19,542,560	19,488,760	19,300,080
Deposits	3,490,160	4,548,400	3,908,040	2,924,800

BANK OF SPAIN (25 pesetas to the £).

	Jan. 15, 1898.	Jan. 8, 1898.	Jan. 1, 1898.	Jan. 16, 1897.
	£	£	£	£
Gold	9,430,680	9,430,680	9,430,680	8,528,360
Silver	10,323,800	10,314,200	10,318,960	10,227,480
Bills discounted	20,291,640	20,39 ,120	20,646,040	8,438,600
Advances and loans	5,435,920	5,131,040	5,063,560	8,843,320
Notes in circulation	49,053,880	48,515,040	48,250,840	42,125,520
Treasury advances, coupon account	30,800	95,200	113,920	17,000
Treasury balances	70,520	30,760	nil	2,488,160

LONDON COURSE OF EXCHANGE.

Place.	Usance.	Jan. 11.	Jan. 13.	Jan. 18.	Jan. 20.
Amsterdam and Rotterdam	short	12·1¼	12·1¼	12·1¼	12·1¼
Do. do.	3 months	12·3⅞	12·3⅞	12·3½	12·3½
Antwerp and Brussels	3 months	25·40	25·40	25·35⅝	25·38¾
Hamburg	3 months	20·61	20·60	20·59	20·59
Berlin and German B. Places	3 months	20·61	20·60	20·59	20·59
Paris	cheques	25·25	25·25	25·23¾	25·23¾
Do.	3 months	25·40	25·38¾	25·37½	25·37½
Marseilles	3 months	25·40	25·40	25·38¾	25·38¾
Switzerland	3 months	25·60	25·60	25·57½	25·57½
Austria	3 months	12·15	12·15	12·13¾	12·13¾
St. Petersburg	3 months	25 3/16	25 3/16	25 3/16	25 3/16
Moscow	3 months	25	25	25	25
Italian Bank Places	3 months	26·77½	25·77½	26·75	26·75
New York	60 days	49	49	49 1/16	49 1/16
Madrid and Spanish B. P.	3 months	35 1/16	35¼	35 1/16	35⅝
Lisbon	3 months	35⅝	35 3/16	35⅝	35 3/16
Oporto	3 months	35⅝	35 3/16	35⅝	35 3/16
Copenhagen	3 months	18·38	18·38	18·38	18·37
Christiania	—	18·38	18·38	18·38	18·37
Stockholm	—	18·38	18·38	18·38	18·37

FOREIGN RATES OF EXCHANGE ON LONDON.

Place.	Usance.	Last week's.	Latest.	Place.	Usance.	Last week's.	Latest.
Paris	chqs.	25·22⅝	25·21½	Italy	sight	26·46	26·45
Brussels	chqs.	25·26	25·24	Do. gold prem.	..	104·85	104·90
Amsterdam	short	12·06½	12·06½	Constantinople.	3 mths	109·05	109·10
Berlin	short	20·38	20·38	B. Ayres gd. pm.	..	167	163
Do.	3 mths	20·27½	20·27	Rio de Janeiro	90 dys	6 11/16	6⅝
Hamburg	3 mths	20·25	20·26½	Valparaiso	90 dys	17 11/16	17⅞
Frankfort	short	20·37	20·37	Calcutta	T. T.	1/4 1/32	1/4 1/32
Vienna	short	12·01	12·00½	Bombay	T. T.	1/4	1/4
St. Petersburg	3 mths	93·75	93·75	Hong Kong	T. T.	1/11⅞	1/11
New York	60 dys	4·82⅞	4·82⅞	Shanghai	T. T.	2/8	2/7
Lisbon	sight	35 1/16	36	Singapore	T. T.	1/11⅞	1/11½
Madrid	sight	33·58	33·53				

OPEN MARKET DISCOUNT.

	Per cent.
Thirty and sixty day remitted bills	2⅞—3⅛
Three months "	2⅞—3⅛
Four months "	2⅞—3⅛
Six months "	2⅞
Three months fine inland bills	2⅞
Four months "	2⅞—3⅛
Six months "	2⅞—3

BANK AND DEPOSIT RATES.

	Per cent.
Bank of England minimum discount rate	3
" " short loan rates	—
Banker's rate on deposits	1½
Bill brokers' deposit rate (call)	1½
" 7 and 14 days' notice	1½
Current rates for 7 day loans	1½
" " for call loans	1

Stock Market Notes and Comments.

The past week on the Stock Exchange cannot be described as a lively one. Much of the speculative business has been of the "mark time" order. We have had no excitement and very little to do. Of course, the chief point of interest has been the Chinese loan, which many in the Market have talked about as if it were to be issued next week. Everybody is delighted that the British Government should have taken the line it has apparently done in this business. It is one that the poorest head in the Stock Exchange thinks it can comprehend in all its bearings, and members jingled the coins in their pockets with an increased sense of satisfaction as they thought and talked about how neatly John Bull has "dished" the Russians and the Germans. There can be no doubt at all that the loan will be subscribed with enthusiasm when it does come. Are not Consols falling almost daily in preparation for it? It would be a dreadful thing if the Post Office, after all, took the lot!

So far the market has been somewhat disappointed with the dividends on Home Railways. That on the Great Eastern Company's stock was specially looked upon as a blow to milleniumites or "bulls." We fear there are more of the same kind to come. "Ah, you pessimist!" crows the man in the market; and he is quite right from his own point of view. Traffic receipts have been astonishingly good all through the past year, but it by no means followed that the bulk of the gross increase will prove to be net gain, as many people assume. Even in the passenger traffic, which has been remarkably well maintained, the tendency is for mere working expenses to grow faster even than the receipts, and a great deal of the increase in the goods traffic is attributable to the very heavy imports of food, the freights upon which obtainable by the railways are not particularly remunerative. From this point of view it might be worth while for the "bulls" to consider whether great increases in gross receipts may not be a sign that the country is living on its capital. That is just a hint by the way, thrown out with a view to cause the speculators for the rise to refrain from transports of exultation. All our Home Railway stocks are now at very high prices indeed—prices which would crumble with great rapidity were anything of an adverse kind to arise. There is scarcely one Home Railway stock in the entire list which can be looked upon as a solid permanent investment; that is to say, the man who buys now as an investor buys not far from the top. The collapse of the engineers' conflict has given a stimulus to this section of the Stock Exchange, and has caused a demand to arise for the stocks and shares of the iron and engineering companies affected by that contest. In consequence of this, and given a continuance of low rates for money, prices seem likely to advance beyond their present points, yet we certainly cannot advise any outsider to buy "bulls" of any stock in the list. They are all dear, hardly even excepting the Metropolitan—looked upon, that is, as investments. Should the Metropolitan line be able to run its trains by electricity, then certainly the price of its stock will go considerably higher, quite irrespective of its intrinsic value.

Next to the Home Railway Market, the most interesting division of the Exchange just now is that for United States railways, and we have some difficulty in giving any definite opinion about its prospects. On the whole, our impression is that prices will go higher, in spite of the eccentricities of Senator Wolcott and of the Silver party behind him; in spite, also, of the fact that nothing is likely to be done by the present Congress to settle the currency difficulties. The main reason we have for leaning to this opinion is not found so much in the expansive traffic returns, although these have a considerable influence, as in the enormous financial interests whose prospect of gain rests upon a large advance in prices. It must not be forgotten that many big railway systems in the States have been reorganised of late years. In the process of reorganisation the stocks fall into the hands of finance houses in America and England at comparatively low prices and in enormous amounts. It is the object of these financiers to sell this "bankrupt stock" at a profit. They cannot do this very well in the States, and must consequently look to London, the one free market Europe has. At the present moment there are very heavy amounts in Northern Pacific, Norfolk and Western, Atchison, Southern, Union Pacific, Baltimore and Ohio, and other properties—either rehabilitated or about to be—in this way held ready for sale. Prices accordingly are bound to advance. They will fluctuate, of course, and timidly-wise people, who rush into the market and buy bits of this and that, will always be checking the upward movement by taking their profits; but the bent of the market will be steadily upward for months to come as far as we can see, and we hope it may be so, because the English public has still a good many millions sunk in these securities which it would be just as well to get home again on any favourable opportunity. We by no means advise buying for investment any of these stocks; in shares, least of all. As a speculation, many of them may be all very well, but even the speculator, after a little time, will often have to jump out nimbly if he is going to escape loss. This is not said because we have no belief in the distant future of the United States, or of these railroads. On the contrary, both country and railways may, in the course of another generation, make enormous strides towards wealth, but the near prospect beyond the effects of the past harvest is not good. There are too many ugly questions unsettled, and there is too little honest disposition to settle them, to make the United States just now a safe repository of British money, so far as its large corporations are concerned.

The speculation in Grand Trunk stocks goes merrily on, and is not in our opinion near breaking-down point yet. Therefore, holders since long ago, who are waiting patiently to escape and have done for ever with one of the most treacherous properties Englishmen have ever put money in, should wait a little longer. The fever cannot be at its height by any means, when we think of all the coming fury about Klondike and of how the peopling of the North West is to excite imaginations and tempt men to buy and buy. As a fact, too, the property is now in better case and better managed than it ever was at any previous period of its history.

About the Mining Market nothing need be said this week in the way of advice. We are told that preparations are being quietly made to start a "boom" in Rhodesian shares of all descriptions, and certainly it is badly wanted. Also we hear that there are two or three really promising mining properties within that vast territory, and we may be sure the most will be made of them to carry the prices of the swarms that are worth nothing as high as they can be made to go. It will be as well, then, to act here very cautiously; but does not this advice apply to all classes of mine shares, even the Rio Tinto and De Beers, which surely cannot be regarded as substantial investments of a high class at present figures? As a whole, however, the Mining Market has been very listless, and the dealing in it mostly professional, not exactly of that kind described in the Stock Exchange as "dog eat dog," but the pitch and toss of syndicates, all of which, although seeming to buy, are anxious to sell. Thanks to them, all the Mining markets, except that for Indian gold mines, resemble the island on which Sindbad camped, only to discover that he was on the back of a monster of the deep. They will slide from under you some day.

The Week's Stock Markets.

Business on the Stock Exchange has not been very active all the week, the principal features being the announcement of several of the Home Railway dividends, and a further considerable appreciation in Canadian Railway shares. Consols have been dull, and the disturbances in France caused a weakness on the Paris Bourse which reacted on markets generally.

In the market for Home Government securities Consols have been dull on the coming Chinese loan, and touched 112½ at one time. The Indian sterling loans have risen slightly, and rupee paper advanced early in the week in sympathy with firmer exchanges, but the price eased off on Wednesday when it was found that the Indian Council had made no allotment of drafts. Bank of Ireland stock rose 5 on a satisfactory dividend, and Bank of England stock is higher. Among Colonial stocks the new Cape loan is quoted about 3 premium; the New South Wales at 1½ premium; and the West Anstralian at 2⅛ premium.

Highest and Lowest this Year.	Last Carrying over Price.	BRITISH FUNDS, &c.	Closing Price.	Rise or Fall.
113⅛ 112½	—	Consols 2¾ p.c. (Money)...	112 13/16	+ ⅛
113 5/16 112 11/16	112 9/16	Do. Account (Feb. 2)	112 13/16	+ ⅛
106¼ 105¾	106	2½ p.c. Stock red. 1905 ...	106	+ ⅛
352½ 347½	—	Bank of England Stock...	352½	+ 2½
117 116¼	116¾	India 3½ p.c. Stk. red. 1931	116¾	+ ¼
109¼ 108½	109	Do. 3 p.c. Stk. red. 1948	108¾	+ ¼
96⅜ 95⅜	96	Do. 2½ p.c. Stk. red. 1926	95½	

The Home Railway market has presented a firm aspect for the greater part of the week, owing to the more hopeful outlook in the engineering trade, the strike being to all intents and purposes settled, and this, coupled with several satisfactory dividend announcements, has tended to keep prices steady. The distribution by the Brighton Company, at the rate of 8¼ p.c. on the Ordinary, compared with 8 per cent. a year ago, was quite up to market expectations. This gives a return of 7 per cent. on the deferred stock, against 6¾ per cent. for 1896, and despite a certain amount of realisations the recent sharp rise in the price of the deferred has been maintained. South Eastern Deferred advanced just before the dividend was announced, and relapsed as quickly when it was found that the distribution was at the rate of 6⅝ per cent. on the Ordinary (giving 3¾ per cent. on the Deferred against 3⅝ per cent for 1896). Great Eastern stock fell nearly 2 points, the dividend at the rate of 5 per cent., or only ¼ higher than last year, being less than had been anticipated. The dividend for the whole year is 3½ per cent., against 3¼ per cent. for 1896. The distribution made by the Metropolitan Company was quite up to expectations, viz., 3¾ per cent., and the fact that the company's Electric Traction Bill is to be discussed at a meeting next week also helped to keep the price steady. Scottish stocks were bought at one time from the North, on the understanding that large numbers of engineers were returning to work. After the excitement caused by the several dividend announcements had worn off, prices became dull, although traffic returns (with the sole exception of the Midland) were satisfactory.

Highest and Lowest this Year.		Last Carrying over Price.	HOME RAILWAYS.	Closing Price.	Rise or Fall.
185¾	181½	182½	Brighton Def.	185¾	+1¾
59½	57¾	58⅝	Caledonian Def.	58⅝	+ ¼
19⅝	19	19½	Chatham Ordinary	19¾	+ ⅛
77½	66	76	Great Central Pref.	72	−2
24⅜	22½	23½	Do. Def.	23½	—
124½	121½	123½	Great Eastern	123½	+ ½
61⅜	59½	60½	Great Northern Def.	60⅝	− ¼
179	176½	177	Great Western	178	+1¼
48½	46½	47½	Hull and Barnsley	48½	+ ¾
148¼	148	148	Lanc. and Yorkshire	148½	+ ½
136½	133½	135	Metropolitan	136	+ ½
31	30	30½	Metropolitan District	31	+ ¼
88⅜	87¾	88¼	Midland Pref.	88¾	+ ¼
95⅛	94½	94¾	Do. Def.	95	+ ¼
93½	90½	92	North British Pref.	92¾	+ ¼
47½	45	46¾	Do. Def.	46¾	+ ¼
181½	179½	179¾	North Eastern	180	− ¼
205¼	204½	204¾	North Western	205	+ ¼
117	114⅝	115¼	South Eastern Def.	116⅜	+ ⅜
98⅜	96⅜	95	South Western Def.	97½	− ½

United Stated Railroad shares have been rather more active. Towards the end of last week there was renewed buying of New York Central and Lake share issues, on the statement that closer relations were going to be entered into between the two roads, and other of the leading shares advanced on the publication of satisfactory traffic returns. Later, the tone became dull, due to the weakness of Wall-street, but a resumption of home and Continental buying caused a slight rally. Union Pacific issues have more than maintained last week's rise, the November traffic return just published being a very satisfactory one. Wall-street has been agitated by rumours of fresh rate-cutting in the West, followed by the statement that American warships had been ordered to Cuba; and as the clique which has lately been responsible for most of the buying has ceased operating, prices exhibit a ragged appearance. The weaker tendency was also partly due to the decision of the Finance Committee to report to the Senate in favour of Mr. Teller's resolution, which gives the Government the option of paying United States bonds in gold or silver.

Canadian Railways have again been much to the front, and Canadian Pacific shares have been favourably influenced by the report that the company is trying to obtain a lease of the Seattle, Lake Shore, and Eastern road.

Highest and Lowest this Year.		Last Carrying over Price.	CANADIAN AND U.S. RAILWAYS.	Closing Prices.	Rise or Fall.
13¾	13	13½	Atchison Shares	13½	− ⅛
32¼	30⅜	32	Do. Pref.	30⅜	−1
13½	11⅛	12½	Central Pacific	13	+ ⅛
99¾	95½	98⅜	Chic. Mil. & St. Paul	97⅜	−1⅛
13½	11½	12	Denver Shares	12⅞	+ ⅜
51	46⅜	48¼	Do. Prefd.	50	+1¼
15⅜	14½	15¼	Erie Shares	15¼	− ⅛
40½	38	39¾	Do. Prefd.	39	− ⅛
60	56⅜	58½	Louisville & Nashville	57⅜	− ⅛
13½	12½	13¼	Missouri & Texas	13⅛	− ⅛
117½	108½	114	New York Central	116	+ ⅛
49¾	47¾	49	Norfolk & West. Prefd.	49¼	+ ⅛
67½	59⅜	64½	Northern Pacific Prefd.	66¼	+1⅛
17½	15⅜	16¼	Ontario Shares	16⅜	+ ⅛
60⅜	58⅜	60	Pennsylvania	59½	− ⅛
12½	11⅛	11¾	Reading Shares	11⅜	− ⅛
33½	30¾	33	Southern Prefd.	31⅛	−1⅛
33½	26⅛	29½	Union Pacific	32¾	+1⅛
20½	18	19	Wabash Prefd.	19¼	− ⅛
30½	27⅞	28½	Do. Income Debs.	30½	
92⅜	83¾	88⅜	Canadian Pacific	92½	+3¼
78⅜	69⅜	73	Grand Trunk Guar.	78⅜	+5⅜
68½	57½	64½	Do. 1st Pref.	68½	+4⅛
49	37½	42½	Do. 2nd Pref.	49	+7⅛
24½	19¼	22⅜	Do. 3rd Pref.	24½	+2⅛
105½	104	105	Do. 4 p.c. Deb.	105½	+ ⅛

As regards Foreign Railway stocks there was a steady all-round rise for several days, and Argentine descriptions continued to find favour. Traffics generally were fair, but a little profit-taking towards the close has resulted in a slight set-back. Mexican Railway issues, notably the First Pref., advanced when the traffic returns appeared, showing an increase of 6,800 dols.

Highest and Lowest this Year.		Last Carrying over Price.	FOREIGN RAILWAYS.	Closing Price.	Rise or Fall.
20½	20	20½	Argentine Gt. West. 5 p.c. Pref.	20½	+ ⅛
157⅛	149	149⅛	B. Ay. Gt. Southern Ord.	155	+6
78½	75¼	77	B. Ay. and Rosario Ord.	76½	−1
12¼	11⅛	11¾	B. Ay. Western Ord.	12	− ⅛
87	80½	84½	Central Argentine Ord.	86	+ ⅛
92	86½	89⅛	Cordoba and Rosario 6 p.c. Deb.	91	+1
95½	93½	94	Cord. Cent. 4 p.c. Deb. (Cent. Nth. Sec.)	95	+ ⅛
61⅞	58½	60	Do. Income Deb. Stk.	60	−1⅛
21⅞	18	21	Mexican Ord. Stk.	21½	+2⅛
79	72	78½	Do. 8 p.c. 1st Pref.	78	+1

Foreign Government Securities have shown considerable strength, but the improvement in prices has not been quite maintained up to the close, the disturbances in France causing a set-back on the Paris Bourse. One of the principal features has been the demand for the loans of the Argentine Government, and the Cedula issues. The gold premium at Buenos Ayres has declined slightly, and a further shipment of gold from London has also been notified during the past week. Brazilian issues advanced owing to a rumour that a Belgian syndicate was being formed for the purpose of leasing with the Brazilian railways. The confirmation of the news of a loan from the British Government to China caused an advance in Chinese bonds, and Egyptian Unified, and Greek Bonds have also been inquired for.

Highest and Lowest this Year.		Last Carrying over Price.	FOREIGN BONDS.	Closing Price.	Rise or Fall.
94½	92½	93½	Argentine 5 p.c. 1886	93½	+ ⅛
92⅜	89	90¾	Do. 6 p.c. Funding	91⅛	+1
76¾	71	73¾	Do. 5 p.c. B. Ay. Water	75¾	+1⅛
61½	60	60½	Brazilian 4 p.c. 1889	61	+ ⅛
69	67½	67½	Do. 5 p.c. 1895	68⅞	+1⅛
64	62½	62½	Do. 5 p.c. West Minas Ry.	63½	+1
107	106½	106⅜	Egyptian 4 p.c. Unified	107	+ ⅛
102½	102	102¼	Do. 3½ p.c. Pref.	102½	− ⅛
102½	102	102	French 3 p.c. Rente	102⅛	
39	34½	36	Greek 4 p.c. Monopoly	38	
93$\frac{3}{16}$	92½	93	Italian 5 p.c. Rente	92¾	− ⅛
98¼	95⅞	97¾	Mexican 6 p.c. 1888	97½	+ ⅛
20¾	20½	20¾	Portuguese 1 p.c.	20⅜	− ⅛
61	59⅜	60½	Spanish 4 p.c.	60⅜	
45	43	44⅜	Turkish 1 p.c. "B"	44½	− ⅛
25⅜	24$\frac{7}{16}$	25¼	Do. 1 p.c. "C"	25⅜	+ $\frac{1}{16}$
22$\frac{5}{16}$	21$\frac{15}{16}$	22	Do. 1 p.c. "D"	22	− $\frac{1}{16}$
42¾	41½	41½	Uruguay 3½ p.c. Bonds	42¼	+ ⅛

The Miscellaneous market has presented a quieter appearance, although a fairly good demand continues for high-class industrial securities for investment purposes. A feature has been the recovery in the shares of the various iron and steel companies, due to the collapse of the strike among the engineers. Aerated Bread shares continue on the up grade. Electric lighting companies again mark substantial rises, the dividends announced so far comparing very favourably with those of a year ago. Among brewery stocks, Allsopp ordinary has risen sharply; Telegraph securities have been active at higher prices, and several tramway and omnibus stocks are quoted firmer, notably the General Omnibus. Russian Petroleum Ordinary is rather lower, owing to the resignation of the chairman of the comany. The long looked-for dividend on Bovril Deferred has at last appeared, but did not meet with approval, a 5 per cent. distribution being considered poor, and no mention was made of the amounts carried to reserve or forward. Colonial Bank shares rose £3 on Mr. Chamberlain's statement with regard to the West Indies.

MINES AND FINANCE COMPANIES.

There has been little or nothing doing in mining shares, and members are migrating from this market to others where business is more active. Prices of South African ventures have drooped, more especially of those companies dealt in on the Paris Bourse, and a dead set is being made at the Barnato group, which has apparently been left to take care of itself. De Beers Diamond shares, however, have not participated in the general dulness, rumours that the shares are to be split into Preference and Ordinary again cropping up. Among Western Australian companies, the higher-priced shares have met with most support, and there has been a little more business, helped by a few buying orders from Adelaide. Copper shares have been very active, especially Rio Tinto and Anaconda, on the firmness displayed in the price of the metal owing to the aspect of the engineers' dispute, and the general understanding of an improved statistical position. As regards miscellaneous mines, the advance in Wassau (Gold Coast) shares is a feature, a circular to the shareholders stating that a Government engineer is to leave at once for the Gold Coast to commence the construction of a railway from the Port of Secondee to the mining district. Indian mines continue firm.

Markets on the whole close with a firm tendency. Consols rose 1/8 just before the close; Canadian Railway stocks continued their upward flight; and United States issues were also firmer at the last, with the exception of a slight reaction in Louisville, New York Central, Southern and Wabash. Home Railway stocks closed strong, notably Brighton Deferred, Great Eastern, and South Eastern Deferred. In the Foreign market, business was on a very small scale, and the tone was dull. South African and Western Australian mines closed weak, but copper shares were again in good demand.

The reported discovery of the "Mother lode" at Klondike is declared by the *Times* Ottawa correspondent to be a *canard*. It is not the first of the sort about Klondike, nor is it likely to be the last.

The plague continues to spread in India, and there is no sign of its having yet received an effectual check. The Indian Government has telegraphed for eight more doctors, two more lady doctors, and twenty-five more lady nurses.

We are not surprised to hear that at the annual meeting of the Association of Chambers of Commerce, to be held in March next, a resolution will be put forward approving of trade unions, and other combinations of workmen, as long as they are used for the purpose for which they were originally created, but expressing the opinion that such purposes have been greatly exceeded, and have given place to constantly growing demands by trade unions, which, in face of the steadily increasing competition from foreign countries, constitutes a grave danger to the prosperity and the very existence of our national trade and industry; and asking for a Parliamentary inquiry into the whole working and tendency of trade unions. Such an inquiry would undoubtedly be of great importance. It is time we took into practical consideration how best to overcome the constant friction, which so severely handicaps our manufacturers in their struggle with foreign rivals.

Prices of Mine and Mining Finance Companies' Shares.

Shares £1 each, except where otherwise stated.

AUSTRALIAN.

Making-Up Price, Jan. 10.	NAME.	Closing Price.	Rise or Fall.	Making-Up Price, Jan. 10.	NAME	Closing Price.	Rise or Fall.
1 3/4	Aladdin	1 3/4	+ 1/16	1	Hampton Plains	1 1/2	
4 1/2	Associated	4 3/16		8 1/2	Hannan's Brownhill	7 7/8	+ 1/16
1	Do. Southern	15/16		1 3/16	Hannan's Oroya	1 1/16	− 1/16
17/9	Brilliant, £2	16/6	− 6d.	16/9	Do. Proprietary	16/	
2 1/4	Do. St. George's	2 1/4	+ 1/16	1 1/16	Do. Star	15/16	− 1/16
10/6	British Broken Hill	11/3		—	Ivanhoe, New	6 1/4	− 1/16
6 1/4	Do. Westralia	6 1/4		1 1/4	Kalgurli Mt. & Iron King, 18/	1 1/4	+ 1/16
2	Broken Hill Proprietary	2 1/16		6 11/16	Kalgurli	6 9/16	
—	Do. Junction	2		2 1/2	Lady Shenton	2 1/16	− 1/16
—	Do. Block 10	3 3/16		13/16	Lake View Cons.	10 1/8	− 1/8
1 1/4	Brownhill Extended	1 1/16	+ 1/16	1 3/16	Do. Extended	1 1/16	− 1/16
1 11/16	Burbank's Birthday	1 3/16	+ 1/16	2 1/16	Do. South	1 1/16	− 1/16
1 1/4	Central Boulder	1 1/16		2 1/4	London & Globe Finance	2 1/16	− 1/16
7/9	Chaffers, 4/	7/9		1 1/16	London & W.A. Exploration	1 1/4	− 1/16
1	Colonial Finance, 15/	1/2 pm		3/16	Do. Investment	3/8	− 1/16
3/8	Crœsus S. United	3/8		9/16	Mainland Consols	3/8	
16/	Day Dawn Block	16/6	+ 6d.	1 1/16	North Boulder, 10/	11/16	− 1/16
1 1/16	E. Murchison	1 1/4		1 1/4	North Kalgurli	1 1/4	
1	Gold Estates	15/16	− 1/16	1 1/4	Northern Territories	1 1/16	− 1/16
7/6	Golden Arrow	6/6	− 6d.	—	Peak Hill	2 3/16	+ 1/8
8 1/16	Golden Horseshoe	8 1/16		3	South Kalgurli	2 15/16	− 1/16
1 1/4	Golden Link	1 1/4		2 3/4	W. A. Goldfields	2 1/4	
—	Great Boulder, 2/	1 1/32	+ 1/32	2 11/16	W. A. Joint Stock	2 3/4	+ 1/16
1 3/8	Do. Main Reef, 10/	1 3/8	+ 1/32	1 5/16	W. A. Market Trust	1 1/4	+ 1/16
4 3/8	Do. Perseverance	4 1/16		1 3/8	W. A. Loan & General Fin.	1 3/8 x	
1	Do. South	1	− 1/16	15/16	White Feather	15/16	− 1/16
2 1/4	Hainault	2	− 1/16				

SOUTH AFRICAN.

Making-Up Price, Jan. 10.	NAME.	Closing Price.	Rise or Fall.	Making-Up Price, Jan. 10.	NAME	Closing Price.	Rise or Fall.
5 3/4	Angelo	5 11/16	− 1/16	3/3	Lisbon-Berlyn	3/3	
1 1/4	Aurora West	1 1/4	− 1/8	2 1/4	May Consolidated	2 1/4	
1 1/32	Bantjes	1 1/16		4 3/8	Meyer and Charlton	4 5/16	
10/3	Barrett, 10/	15/16	− 1/16	3	Modderfontein	3 3/8	
3 3/8	Bonanza	3 1/16	+ 1/16	3/4	Do. "B"	3/4	
3/4	Buffelsdoorn	11/16	− 1/16	1 1/16	New Bultfontein	11/16	− 1/16
1 1/16	Champ d'Or	1 3/8		4 3/4	New Primrose	4 1/4	− 1/8
6 1/4	City and Suburban, £4	6	− 1/8	2 1/16	Nigel	1 1/4	− 1/8
3 1/4	Comet (New)	3 1/4	− 1/8	—	Nigel Deep	1 1/16	+ 1/16
5 11/16	Con. Deep Level	5 5/8	− 1/16	1 1/16	North Randfontein	1 1/16	
14 1/4	Crown Deep	14 1/4		7 5/16	Nourse Deep	7	− 1/8
12 1/4	Crown Reef	12 3/8	− 1/8	1 1/16	Porges-Randfontein	1 1/16	
28 3/4	De Beers, £5	29 11/16	+ 5/16	2 1/16	Princess	2 1/4	
4 1/4	Driefontein	3 15/16	+ 1/16	34 1/4	Rand Mines	33 3/4	− 15/16
6 1/4	Durban Roodepoort	5 3/4	− 1/8	2 1/4	Randfontein	2	− 1/16
4 1/4	Do. Deep	4 1/4		2 3/4	Rietfontein	2 13/16	− 1/16
5 1/16	East Rand	5 1/16	− 1/8	10 3/4	Robinson Deep	11 3/8	
24	Ferreira	24 1/2	+ 1/2	8 1/4	Do. Gold, £5	8 1/4	
6 1/4	Geldenhuis Deep	6 1/4		1 1/4	Do. Randfontein	1 1/16	− 1/16
4 3/8	Do. Estate	4 1/4	− 1/8	1 13/16	Roodepoort Central Deep	1 3/4	− 1/16
1 1/4	George Goch	1 1/16		15/16	Do. Deep	2 3/8	− 1/16
3	Ginsberg	2 3/4	− 1/8	7 3/8	Rose Deep	7 1/16	+ 1/16
2 1/4	Glencairn	2 1/16	− 1/8	3 1/4	Salisbury	3 1/16	− 1/16
2 1/16	Glen Deep	2 3/4		2 1/16	Sheba	2 1/4	
10 1/4	Goldfields Deep	10 1/4	− 1/8	3 1/4	Simmer and Jack, £5	3 1/16	− 1/16
8 1/4	Griqualand West	8 1/4	− 1/8	4 1/16	Transvaal Gold	4 1/4	− 1/16
9 1/4	Henry Nourse	9 1/4	− 1/8	3 1/4	Treasury	3 1/4	
8	Heriot	7 3/4	− 1/8	4 1/4	United Roodepoort	4 1/4	+ 1/8
8	Jagersfontein	8 1/16	− 1/16	1 1/16	Van Ryn	1 1/16	
8 3/8	Jubilee	8 1/2	+ 1/8	6 1/16	Village Main Reef	6 1/16	− 1/16
5 3/4	Jumpers	5 1/2	− 1/8	1 1/4	Vogelstruis	1 1/16	+ 1/16
6	Jumpers Deep	6	− 1/8	1 1/16	Do. Deep	1 1/16	− 1/16
2 11/16	Kleinfontein	2 11/16	− 1/8	9 1/4	Wemmer	9 1/4	− 1/16
4 3/8	Knight's	4 1/4	− 1/8	11/16	West Rand	15/16	
2 1/16	Lancaster	2 1/16	− 1/16	6 3/8	Wolhuter, £4	6 11/16	− 1/16
4	Langlaagte Estate	3 7/8	− 1/8	2 3/4	Worcester	2 1/2	− 1/8
1 5/16	Langlaagte Block "B"	1 1/4					

LAND EXPLORATION AND RHODESIAN.

Making-Up Price, Jan. 10.	NAME.	Closing Price.	Rise or Fall.	Making-Up Price, Jan. 10.	NAME	Closing Price.	Rise or Fall.
3 3/8	Anglo-French Ex.	3 1/16	− 1/8	1 15/16	Mozambique	1 15/16	
2 1/16	Barnato Consolidated	2 1/4	− 1/8	1 11/16	New African	1 5/8	− 1/8
15/16	Bechuanaland Ex.	15/16	− 1/16	11/16	Oceana Consolidated	5/8	− 1/16
3 1/16	Chartered B.S.A.	3 1/4	− 1/16	2 1/2	Orange Free State	2 3/8	
1 1/4	Cassel Coal	1 1/16	− 1/16	1 1/4	Rhodesia, Ltd.	1 3/8	
3/4	Colenbrander	11/16		5 3/4	Do. Exploration	5 3/4	− 1/8
5 1/16	Cons. Goldfields	5 1/16	− 1/8	1 1/16	Do. Goldfields	1 1/16	− 1/16
1 1/32	Do. Pref.	21/3 x		4	Robinson Bank	4	
1 1/16	Exploration	1 1/16		5 3/8	S. A. Gold Trust	5 1/16	− 3/16
1 1/4	Henderson's Est.	1	− 1/16	1 1/16	Tati Concessions	1 3/8	− 1/16
2 1/16	Johannesburg Con. In.	2	− 1/8	5/8	Transvaal Development	5/8	− 1/16
1 1/4	Do. Water	1 1/16		4 5/16	Do. Gold Mining	4 1/4	− 1/8
2 1/4	Mashonaland Agency	2 1/4	− 1/8	1/4	United Rhodesia	3/8	
3/8	Do. Central	3/8	− 1/16	1 1/4	Willoughby	1 1/4	− 1/8
7	Matabele Gold Reefs	6 3/8	− 1/8	1 3/8	Zambesia Explor.	1 1/4	

MISCELLANEOUS.

Making-Up Price, Jan. 10.	NAME.	Closing Price.	Rise or Fall.	Making-Up Price, Jan. 10.	NAME	Closing Price.	Rise or Fall.
1 1/4	Alamillos, £2	1 1/16		13/6	Mysore Goldfields	13/6	+ /6
4 3/8	Anaconda, $25	5 1/16	+ 1/16	11/	Do. Reefs, 17/	11/6	− /6
10/	Balaghât, 18/	11/6	− /6	15/	Do. West	16/6	− 1/5
4 1/16	Cape Copper, £2	4 3/16	+ 1/16	13/9	Do. Wynaad	15 6	− 1/6
5 1/4	Champion Reef, 10s.	5 1/16	+ 1/8	2 1/16	Namaqua, £2	2 3/8	+ 1/16
2	Copiapo, £2	2 1/4	+ 1/16	4 3/8	Nundydroog	4 3/8	− 1/16
3 1/16	Coromandel	3 1/16		2 11/16	Ooregum	3 1/16	
2 3/4	Frontino & Bolivia	2 1/16	+ 1/16	3 1/4	Do. Pref.	3 1/16	+ 1/16
1 1/4	Hall Mines	1 1/16	+ 1/8	24 3/8	Rio Tinto Def., £5	27 1/4	+ 15/16
2 3/4	Libiola, £5	3	+ 1/4	6	Do. Pref. £5	6 1/4	
7 3/4	Linares, £3	8		18/9	St. John del Rey	19 6	
3	Mason & Barry, £3	3 3/8	+ 5/16	—	Taitipu	1	
—	Mountain Copper, £5	5 1/16		6 3/8	Tharsis, £2	7	+ 3/8
4	Mount Lyell, £3	13 1/4	− 1/4	2	Tolima "A," £5	3	
14	Mount Lyell, North	3 3/8		—	Waihi	4 3/8	
1 1/16	Mount Lyell, South	1	− 1/16	—	Waitekauri	1 1/16	
—	Mount Morgan	4 1/4	+ 1/16	—	Woodstock	1 3/8	
5 1/4	Mysore, 10s.	5 3/8	+ 1/16				

AFRICAN MINING RETURNS.

Dividends Declared in 1896	1897	1898	Capital Issued.	Nominal Amount of Share.	Name of Company.	Monthly Crushings. October. Tons.	Ozs.	Per ton, dwts.	November. Tons.	Ozs.	Per ton, dwts.	December. Tons.	Ozs.	Per ton, dwts.	Totals. Months.	Ozs.	Profits Declared. Oct.	Nov.	Dec.	Totals. Months.	—	Stamps now Working.
p.c.	p.c.	p.c.	£	£													£	£	£		£	
—	—	—	225,000	1	Angelo	12,271	5,880	9.6	12,062	5,809	9.6	12,340	5,844	9.4	10	52,525	13,463	13,140	12,591	10	113,141	60
—	—	—	130,000	1	Balmoral	13,180	2,970	4.4	12,550	2,719	4.3	—	1,596	—	6	10,964	2,536	2,811	—	—	—	60
—	75	—	200,000	1	Bonanza	10,984	7,911	14.4	10,551	6,960	13.2	12,265	7,886	12.8	12	93,142	16,431	15,510	16,272	12	215,816	40
—	—	—	550,000	1	Buffelsdoorn	29,237	4,008	2.7	—	3,598	—	—	3,752	—	—	—	—	—	—	—	—	100
—	—	—	133,000	1	Champ d'Or	—	3,671	—	—	3,888	—	—	3,368	—	—	—	—	—	—	—	—	50
5	15	—	1,360,000	4	City and Suburban	34,235	11,844	6.9	31,759	11,804	7.4	—	11,792	—	12	133,672	22,459	22,365	21,618	12	276,126	160
—	—	—	224,635	1	Comet	9,692	3,395	7.0	9,446	3,243	6.8	9,427	3,229	6.8	12	37,703	6,350	6,510	5,838	12	50,177	40
—	—	—	300,000	1	Crown Deep	27,420	10,209	7.4	—	10,997	—	38,030	14,034	7.4	5	48,000	17,250	18,220	21,000	5	70,906	200
210	170	—	120,000	1	Crown Reef	28,452	11,838	8.3	28,114	13,203	9.4	—	12,298	—	12	148,894	20,523	25,094	22,764	12	255,954	120
55	80	—	125,000	1	Durban Roodepoort	17,130	6,067	7.1	17,380	6,152	7.1	17,700	6,080	6.9	12	71,176	—	—	—	—	—	80
275	300	—	90,000	1	Ferreira	17,603	12,613	14.3	17,593	12,996	14.7	—	13,196	—	12	154,457	30,248	31,148	30,870	12	353,461	80
12½	45	—	200,000	1	Geldenhuis	16,848	9,414	10.6	16,440	9,471	11.5	—	9,461	—	9	82,290	16,198	16,386	—	8	119,069	120
—	30	—	280,000	1	Geldenhuis Deep	32,010	9,183	5.7	—	9,462	—	30,724	10,008	6.5	12	109,021	11,174	11,700	14,980	12	131,050	260
—	10	—	150,000	1	Gelden. Main Reef	5,605	1,666	5.3	5,408	1,509	5.6	5,766	1,055	3.6	12	19,453	2,268	1,436	3	12	21,674	30
—	—	—	325,000	1	George Goch	18,056	2,866	3.1	21,116	3,093	2.9	—	3,179	—	12	37,449	492	—	—	—	—	120
—	25	—	160,000	1	Ginsberg	9,326	3,434	7.3	8,948	2,862	6.4	—	2,476	—	12	36,879	7,569	6,500	3,705	12	73,148	40
—	—	—	500,000	1	Glencairn	26,570	6,266	4.7	27,190	6,543	4.8	—	6,699	—	6	32,453	9,346	10,097	10,600	5	45,989	110
30	125	—	125,000	1	Henry Nourse	14,915	7,859	10.4	14,842	7,678	10.2	15,150	7,334	9.7	12	91,373	17,614	16,475	16,150	12	176,731	60
85	100	—	111,864	1	Heriot	15,473	6,052	7.8	15,005	5,995	7.9	—	6,010	—	12	72,909	10,548	12,575	10,467	12	129,807	70
350	500	—	21,000	1	Johan. Pioneer	5,773	3,421	11.8	—	3,737	—	—	4,337	—	12	43,616	8,368	—	—	9	79,101	30
60	90	—	50,000	1	Jubilee	—	—	—	a11,828	3,638	6.1	—	3,073	—	12	30,824	—	—	—	9	38,329	50
30	60	—	100,000	1	Juinpers	11,250	5,749	10.2	11,500	5,872	10.2	12,300	5,646	9.2	12	61,789	7,150	7,370	7,150	12	64,561	100
—	—	—	175,000	1	Kimberley Roodp't.	5,557	1,370	4.9	5,827	1,365	4.7	—	1,182	—	12	14,618	1,121	—	—	—	—	40
—	—	—	231,250	1	Kleinfontein	21,724	5,381	5.0	19,903	5,172	5.2	—	5,133	—	9	43,572	5,729	5,125	5,676	9	42,493	95
—	—	—	311,960	1	Knight's	23,450	5,021	4.3	21,970	4,724	4.3	23,210	4,963	4.3	12	59,166	4,122	—	—	8	28,490	120
30	30	—	470,000	1	Langlaagte	46,939	11,844	5.0	40,085	10,126	5.0	44,278	9,679	4.3	12	128,249	—	—	—	—	—	200
—	—	—	550,000	1	Lang. Block B.	17,614	4,306	4.9	17,945	4,355	4.8	19,118	4,484	4.7	12	44,919	—	—	—	—	—	75
20	—	—	275,000	1	May Consolidated	19,310	4,626	4.8	21,957	5,401	5.0	22,354	6,066	5.4	12	50,140	920	4,110	6,002	12	25,931	100
20	50	—	85,000	1	Meyer and Charlton	13,414	3,704	5.5	14,110	3,696	5.2	—	3,171	—	12	40,074	5,220	5,175	5,345	12	58,386	80
—	—	—	949,620	4	Modderfontein	—	1,532	—	—	1,801	—	—	—	—	—	—	1,941	1,801	—	—	—	60
—	—	—	200,020	1	Nigel	6,383	2,501	7.8	—	2,803	—	—	2,803	—	—	—	—	—	—	—	—	25
—	—	—	300,000	1	Nth. Randfontein	8,313	2,193	5.3	9,854	2,574	5.2	10,007	2,354	4.7	11	25,407	—	—	—	—	—	60
—	—	—	400,000	1	Paarl Central	11,933	3,272	5.5	11,451	3,312	5.8	11,343	3,255	5.8	12	35,691	—	—	—	—	—	60
—	10	—	487,500	1	Porges Randfontein	15,749	4,707	6.0	13,635	4,526	6.6	13,318	4,502	6.7	12	48,990	—	—	—	—	—	60
—	50	—	300,000	1	Primrose	38,194	10,589	5.5	38,917	10,207	5.2	—	9,704	—	12	116,260	16,214	15,417	14,250	12	155,255	160
—	10	—	165,000	1	Princess Estate	9,191	3,042	6.6	9,092	3,028	6.6	—	2,979	—	12	34,763	3,260	2,958	2,600	12	33,111	40
—	—	—	270,000	1	Rietfontein	b	—	—	—	—	—	—	—	—	—	—	—	—	—	—	—	30
—	—	—	300,000	1	Rietfontein "A"	13,123	5,229	7.9	13,251	5,445	8.2	—	5,447	—	5	26,413	11,000	11,040	11,767	5	56,565	50
12	15	—	2,750,000	5	Robinson	31,621	18,692	11.8	31,186	18,728	12.0	—	20,663	—	12	220,615	35,500	37,000	42,000	12	431,591	120
—	—	—	175,000	1	Roodepoort Gold	5,557	1,370	4.9	5,827	1,365	4.7	—	1,182	—	12	14,618	1,121	1,018	—	—	—	40
25	40	—	150,000	1	Roodepoort United	11,696	4,432	7.6	11,657	4,378	7.5	—	4,414	—	12	49,907	7,305	7,175	7,455	12	74,181	70
—	—	—	400,000	1	Rose Deep	13,271	5,242	7.9	—	9,520	—	26,345	9,491	7.2	—	—	5,092	10,638	16,000	—	—	100
—	—	—	100,000	1	Salisbury	c	—	—	11,220	2,950	5.2	—	2,150	—	12	21,463	—	—	—	—	—	30
20	20	—	1,073,000	1	Sheba	7,240	7,168	19.8	8,946	10,032	22.4	9,500	9,005	18.9	12	107,129	—	—	—	—	—	120
—	—	—	4,700,000	5	Simmer and Jack	21,500	5,048	4.7	17,960	7,090	7.9	—	8,120	—	12	77,260	4,718	—	—	10	33,716	100
—	—	—	235,000	1	Spes Bona	9,031	2,287	5.0	9,298	1,931	4.2	—	2,001	—	11	23,771	9,287	1,303	—	—	—	40
—	15	—	35,000	1	Stanhope	4,465	1,180	5.3	4,360	1,150	5.3	—	1,069	—	12	11,560	—	—	—	—	—	20
—	—	—	604,225	1	Trans. G. M. Est.	15,680	5,557	7.7	14,569	5,748	7.9	14,322	4,581	6.4	—	—	13,740	—	—	—	—	75
—	—	—	540,000	4	Treasury	10,298	3,653	7.1	9,664	3,575	7.4	—	3,770	—	12	39,715	5,641	5,196	6,124	12	51,538	40
—	—	—	177,000	1	Van Ryn	19,396	3,852	4.0	18,022	3,710	4.0	19,290	4,008	4.1	12	46,729	—	—	—	—	—	80
—	—	—	170,000	1	Van Ryn West	14,260	2,816	4.0	13,209	2,958	4.4	14,260	3,938	5.5	9	22,513	—	—	—	—	—	80
75	100	—	80,000	1	Wemmer	11,692	6,557	11.2	10,650	6,083	11.4	11,161	5,987	10.7	12	67,741	13,894	12,435	12,215	12	124,062	50
—	—	—	400,000	1	West Rand	7,328	1,430	3.9	7,505	1,752	4.6	6,853	1,732	5.0	9	14,441	—	—	—	—	—	30
—	10	—	860,000	4	Wolhuter	23,573	7,060	6.7	22,873	7,540	6.6	—	7,670	—	12	89,771	12,641	10,817	10,681	12	115,721	100
55	30	—	95,722	1	Worcester	4,737	2,562	10.9	—	2,772	—	—	2,615	—	12	25,727	—	—	—	—	—	40

a For two months. b Mill restarted January 7. c Scarcity of water stopped milling.

MINING RETURNS.

St. John Del Rey.—Gold produce, January 1 to 11, £5,425, yield per ton, ·62 of an oz. troy.

Crescent Gold Mining.—Result of crushing for past month, 400 tons—84 oz.

British Broken Hill Proprietary.—For fortnight ended January 13, 2,095 tons crude ore produced, 383 tons concentrates, containing 220 tons lead and 8,914 oz. silver.

Brilliant and St. George.—Crushed during fortnight 950 tons for 2,252 oz.

Simmer and Jack.—5,591 oz. from mill and 2,529 oz. of gold from tailings by cyanide.

Geldenhuis Deep.—For December, 18,394 tons crushed; yield in smelted gold, 6,484 oz.; 12,330 tons of sand and concentrates treated by cyanide, Yield in smelted gold, 3,564 oz; total, 10,008 oz.

Bellevue Proprietary Company.—Tons crushed, 230; yield, 461 oz.

Hannan's Brownhill.—Lot 7: smelters' returns, 227 tons ore treated, yielding 1,339 oz. gold.

Robinson Gold Mines (W.A.).—Result of clean up, 610 oz. gold, making a total for the year of 7,391 oz. from 5,213 tons, exclusive of concentrates and tailings. Value, £28,100.

Wassan (Gold Coast) Mining Company.—During November the ten-stamp 750-lb. mill worked twenty-one days, and the twelve-stamp 550-lb. mill fourteen days. Ore crushed, 389 tons; produced 459½ oz. standard gold from 438 bar gold, which realised £1,795.

Wassan (Gold Coast) Mining Company.—For December, 606 oz. gold from 488 tons ore; twenty-two stamps worked nineteen days.

Moodie's.—Last month's return: 1,000 tons crushed, yielding 700 oz. gold.

Buffelsdoorn Estate and Gold Mining.—For December, 3,750 oz.

Le Champ d'Or French Gold Mining Company.—For December, crushed 5,300 tons, yielded 2,255 oz.; 4,015 tons treated cyanide yielded 1,113 oz. Total, 3,368 oz.

Regina (Canada) Gold Mine.—For December, 429 tons crushed, yielding 200 oz., including 55 oz. from cyanide.

Geldenhuis Main Reef Gold Mining Company.—3,646 tons crushed, yield 661 oz.; 2,120 tons treated by cyanide, yield 394 oz.

Great Boulder Proprietary.—Crushings for fortnight ended January 17: 1,740 tons, yielding 3,233 oz. gold.

Anglo-Mexican.—Output for December; crushed, 1,702 tons, 18,585 dols. (United States gold); cyanide plant: tons treated, 1,060; 14,800 dols.

Frank Smith Diamond Mines.—1,800 loads washed, producing 92 carats.

Gullewa.—During month 169 tons crushed, yielding 247 oz. gold.

Princess Royal (Cue).—Clean up from 140 tons gave 105 oz., exclusive of tailings.

Lake View South (W.A.).—Total amount crushed in twenty-six days, 1,500 tons. Clean up, 331 oz. Approximate total concentrates 50 tons, containing 383 oz., equalling 16 dwt. per ton.

Dividends Announced.

BANKS.

City Bank.—Dividend of 10 per cent. per annum. £15,529 carried forward. Previous year, 9 per cent.

Bradford Old Bank, Limited.—Dividend for the half-year to 31st ult. at the rate of 9 per cent. per annum. £4,138 carried forward.

Union Bank of Australia.—Dividend of 12s. 6d. per share, being at the rate of 5 per cent. per annum. About £24,500 carried forward.

Wilts and Dorset Bank.—20s. per share declared for half-year ended December last, and a payment of 10s. per share on the new shares.

West Riding Union Banking Company.—Profits for past year, £31,927. Final dividend declared of 8s. per share, making, with last interim dividend, 16s. for year. Balance of £5,242 placed to reserve, which will then amount to £50,007.

Metropolitan Bank (of England and Wales), Limited.—Dividend declared for the last half-year at the rate of 12½ per cent. per annum, free of income tax; £13,945 carried forward.

Parr's Bank, Limited.—Dividend recommended for past quarter at the rate of 19 per cent. per annum, and a further dividend at the same rate for the quarter ending March 31. £20,000 placed to bank premises account, and about £58,680 balance forward.

Wilkinson & Riddell.—Dividend for the past year of 5 per cent. on the preference shares, and 10 per cent. on the ordinary shares—the latter free of income tax, less the 5 per cent. interim paid August last.

Williams Deacon and Manchester and Salford Bank.—Dividend declared of 12½ per cent., £20,000 added to reserve fund, £15,000 to buildings depreciation fund, and £20,927 carried forward.

Foreign and Colonial Investment Trust.—5 per cent. per annum on pref. stock, and 5½ per cent. per annum, making 5 per cent. for year, on deferred stock, £12,911 placed to reserve, and £2,578 carried forward.

MARITIME INSURANCE.—2s. per share dividend recommended, free of income tax, making, with interim dividend of June 11 last, a total distribution at the rate of 11¼ per cent. for the year on the paid-up capital.

RELIANCE MARINE INSURANCE.—Dividend of 2s. per share, making, with interim dividend paid in July last, 10 per cent. for year.

LONDON AND COUNTY BANKING COMPANY.—Dividend 10 per cent. for half-year, and bonus of 1 per cent.; £25,000 written off premises account; £80,000 added to reserve, and £49,966 carried forward.

BANK OF EGYPT.—Dividend of 6 per cent. (making 9 per cent. for the year), and a bonus of 5s. per share, adding £5,000 to reserve fund, and carrying forward £4,734.

RAILWAY COMPANIES.

CITY AND SOUTH LONDON RAILWAY COMPANY.—The accounts for the half-year ended December 31 show a balance, after providing for the debenture interest and the dividend on the 5 per cent. preference shares, sufficient to allow the payment of a dividend on the consolidated ordinary stock at the rate of 1¾ per cent. per annum, carrying forward £1,510. The dividend for the corresponding period last year was at the rate of 1¾ per cent. per annum, the balance carried forward being £1,314.

SOUTH-EASTERN RAILWAY.—The accounts for the half-year ended December 31, 1897, subject to the completion of the audit, show a credit balance which admits of the following dividends on the ordinary stock:—At the rate of £6. 12s. 6d. per annum on the undivided stock; £6 per cent. per annum on the preferred ordinary stock; £3. 17s. 6d. per cent. upon the deferred ordinary stock for the year 1897; leaving a balance of about £4,000 to be carried forward.

BELFAST AND NORTHERN COUNTIES RAILWAYS.—Dividend on the ordinary stock at the rate of 6½ per cent. per annum for the half-year ended December 31. Upwards of £11,000 carried forward to next half-year's accounts.

GREAT EASTERN RAILWAY.—Payment of dividend on the ordinary shares at the rate of 5 per cent. per annum, as against 4½ per cent. per annum for second half of 1896. Balance forward about £51,000; previous year, £50,918.

LONDON, TILBURY, AND SOUTHEND RAILWAY COMPANY.—Dividend on ordinary stock for past half-year, 6¼ per cent. per annum, carrying forward £14,600. The dividend last year was at the rate of 6 per cent., with £820 carried forward. The increased amount carried forward is to provide for any payment to be made to the Great Eastern Railway Company in respect of the widening of the London and Blackwall Railway.

MISCELLANECUS.

BRENTFORD GAS.—Dividends recommended for the past half-year at the rate of £5, £12, and £9 per cent. per annum on the preference, consolidated, and new stock respectively.

ELECTRIC CONSTRUCTION COMPANY, LIMITED.—The transfer books for the ordinary shares will be closed from January 18 to 31 inclusive, for the payment of the second half of the dividend of 6 per cent. per annum declared on July 22 last.

GLOBE TELEGRAPH COMPANY.—Interim of 1s. 9d. per ordinary share.

GAS LIGHT AND COKE COMPANY.—Usual half-yearly dividend at the rate of 12¾ per cent. per annum.

EL MUNDO (MEXICO) GOLD MINING COMPANY, LIMITED.—Interim dividend of 6d. per share, payable February 1.

BRADFORD MANUFACTURING.—Directors recommend dividend for half-year ended December 31 last at the rate of 12 per cent. per annum.

BRILLIANT AND ST. GEORGE UNITED GOLD MINING COMPANY.—Directors have declared a dividend of 1s. per share, payable on the 22nd inst.

BURLINGTON HOTELS.—Dividend, at the rate of 10 per cent. per annum, will be posted on the 25th tnst.

DE KEYSER'S ROYAL HOTEL, LIMITED.—Directors recommend final dividend of 7s. per share, making, with interim dividend, 6½ per cent. for year. Balance forward £3,472.

HENRY & COMPANY (A. & S.).—Dividend on the Ordinary shares at the rate of 6 per cent. per annum, for the half year ended November 30 last, making 6 per cent. for year, as against 7 per cent. for previous year; £22,628 carried forward.

GEORGE NEWNES, LIMITED.—Interim dividend at the rate of 10 per cent. per annum, for the half year ended December 31, has been declared.

CAVE, AUSTIN, & COMPANY, LIMITED.—Dividend of 5 per cent., on both classes of shares, for six months ended September 30, 1897, representing, with previous dividend, 5 per cent. per annum for the first 15 months' trading. £1,550 also carried forward to reserve.

R. & J. HILL, LIMITED.—Interim dividend at the rate of 6 per cent. per annum will be paid on 24th inst. on the ordinary shares for period ending December 31, 1897.

ROBERT CAMPBELL & SONS, LIMITED.—Dividend of 2s. 6d. per share; £1,345 carried forward.

RUBBER TYRE MANUFACTURING.—Interim dividend for the past six months' trading of 10 per cent. per annum.

WELFORD & SONS, LIMITED.—Dividend at the rate of 12 per cent. per annum, making, with the interim dividend, 10 per cent. for the year.

HARROD'S STORES, LIMITED.—Dividend 15 per cent. for half-year on ordinary shares, making 20 per cent. for year. Reserve left at £251,720.

LONDON AND ST. KATHARINE DOCKS COMPANY.—A dividend at the rate of 1¼ per cent. for the past half-year, making 2½ per cent. for the year 1897, with £7,972 carried forward, as against 2¼ per cent. for the year 1896, with £3,116 forward.

EAST AND WEST INDIA DOCK COMPANY show balance of revenue account £70,663, as compared with £63,894 for the corresponding half of 1896. After paying fixed charges, a small balance is left, from which ½ per cent. on account of the arrears of interest on the deferred debenture stock will be paid.

LONDON ROAD CAR COMPANY.—Dividend recommended for half-year ended December 31 at the rate of 8 per cent. per annum. Balance left about £6,000, of which it is proposed to place £2,000 to a depreciation reserve fund, and carry forward about £4,000 to the credit of next half-year.

BELFAST STREET TRAMWAYS.—Directors recommend dividend at the rate of 6½ per cent. per annum, and a bonus of 1s. per share. About £800 carried forward. Previous year at the same rate.

BIRMINGHAM AND ASTON TRAMWAYS.—Dividend declared at the rate of 10 per cent. per annum for the six months ended December 31 last, as against 5 per cent. for corresponding period in 1896.

BIRMINGHAM AND MIDLAND TRAMWAYS.—Interim dividend at the rate of 5 per cent. per annum for six months ended December 31 last to all shareholders registered on the 12th inst.

ENGLISH RAILWAYS.

Div. for half years. 1895	1896	1896	1897	Last Balance forward.	Amt. to pay 1 p.c. on Ord. for ½ yr.	NAME.	Date.	Gross Traffic for week: Amt.	Inc. or dec. on 1897.	Inc. or dec. on 1896.	No. of weeks	Gross Traffic for half-year to date: Amt.	Inc. or dec. on 1897.	Inc. or dec. on 1896.	Mileage.	Inc. on 1897.	Working Expenses.	Fixed Charges last ½ year.	Prop. add. Cap. Exp. this ½ year.
				£	£												%	£	£
10	10	10	10	6,805	4,906	Barry	Jan. 15	9,450	−649	+1,430	3	26,243	+362	+1,063	31	—	47·36	66,665	316,008
nil	nil	nil	nil	—	—	Brecon and Merthyr	Jan. 16	1,724	+88	+118	3*	4,745	+116	+310	61	—	—	—	—
nil	nil	nil	nil	4,020	4,749	Cambrian	Jan. 16	4,263	+21	+443		8,853	−73	—	250	—	61·16	63,472	42,000
1½	1¾	1¾	2	1,034	3,150	City and South London	Jan. 16	2,085	None.	+81	3	3,259	−14	+218	3½	—	56·07	5,552	109,500
1	1	2	1½	4,823	13,210	Furness	Jan. 16								139	—	50·85	96,623	52,963
2¾	1	1½	2	2,416	27,463	Great Central (late M., S., & L.)	Jan. 16								352½	—	36·09	609,255	1,130,000
4	1½	4½	2	2,666	62,865	Great Eastern	Jan. 16	74,859	+1,815	—	2	146,964	+2,527	+18,583	1,156	7	59·29	847,811	210,500
⅝	1¼	1½	¼	4,595	102,406	Great Northern	Jan. 16	92,934	+3,382	—	3	266,285	+5,944	—	1,071	8	62·28	640,779	1,091,250
7	4¾	7¼	4¾	16,273	116,381	Great Western	Jan. 16	172590	+3,320	—	2	336,910	+9,920	+26,000	2,575	14	57·94	1,484,324	650,000
nil	nil	2	nil	24,449	16,425	Hull and Barnsley	Jan. 16	7,157	+252	—	2	13,622	+242	+2,454	73	—	61·21	54,684	44,019
5½	5	5¾	5	21,423	83,704	Lancashire and Yorkshire	Jan. 16	85,620	+666	—	2	171,087	+4,319	+17,720	555½	25½	55·01	662,671	387,522
8½	4¾	8	4¾	16,376	43,049	London, Brighton, & S. Coast	Jan. 15	44,784	+2,711	+3,408	3	144,366	+6,825	+8,661	477	—	54·91	398,273	199,675
nil	nil	nil	nil	1,561	56,296	London, Chatham, & Dover	Jan. 16	26,420	+1,094	—	2	52,195	+1,969	+3,625	185	—	57·19	220,181	nil
7½	6¼	8	6¼	95,016	203,063	London and North Western	Jan. 16	220918	+5,912	—	2	431,382	+7,761	+28,125	1,912	—	55·91	1,411,298	425,000
7¾	5	8¼	5½	23,525	58,667	London and South Western	Jan. 16	64,070	+2,184	—	2	125,167	+4,430	+8,476	941	6½	55·93	527,257	370,000
5¾	2¾	6	2¾	7,572	6,691	London, Tilbury, & Southend	Jan. 16	4,697	+248	+940	3*	14,385	+969	+3,080	81	—	57·00	40,041	15,000
3	3½	3¾	3½	16,398	28,659	Metropolitan	Jan. 16	16,581	+384	—		37,396	+1,038	—	64	12	56·70	110,744	109,000
nil	nil	nil	nil	4,300	11,250	Metropolitan District	Jan. 16	9,133	+353	—	2	18,232	+857	+1,016	13	—	45·32	159,412	23,150
6½	5	7	5½	18,336	174,175	Midland	Jan. 16	174259	−3,944	−2,502	3	408,560	+3,543	+20,106	1,354¼	15½	57·47	1,213,866	650,000
6¾	5½	7½	5½	22,374	135,568	North Eastern	Jan. 15	131861	+2,200	—	2	256,124	+6,051	+26,864	1,597¼	1¼	58·70	791,956	372,790
7½	7½	7½	7½	6,213	10,102	North London	Jan. 16								12	—	51·65	51,329	4,000
4½	4	5	4	3,356	16,150	North Staffordshire	Jan. 16	15,411	+873	None.	3	46,293	+3,872	+3,318	312	—	55·27	118,142	19,605
8½	10	10	11	1,642	3,004	Rhymney	Jan. 15	5,109	+102	+797	3*	13,754	−727	+188	71	—	40·68	29,049	16,700
6	3	6¾	3½	4,526	50,215	South Eastern	Jan. 15	39,422	+769	—		86,147	+2,501	—	448	—	56·04	382,193	150,000
3½	3½	3½	3½	5,004	21,601	Taff Vale	Jan. 15	16,620	+520	+375	3	43,627	−2,728	−1,827	121	—	53·06	95,907	43,000

* From January 1.

SCOTCH RAILWAYS.

5½	5	5	5½	15,350	77,570	Caledonian	Jan. 16	63,761	+ 2,578	+ 8,644	24	1,782,803	+ 27,110	+ 72,548	851½	5	50·50	566,914	373,966
5	5	5½	5	5,886	24,639	Glasgow and South-Western	,, 15	22,578	+ 353	+ 371	24	703,862	+ 9,869	+ 54,306	393½	8	55·12	221,100	180,556
3½	3½	3½	3½	1,291	4,500	Great North of Scotland	,, 15	7,474	+ 407	+ 809	24	215,004	+ 7,819	+ 15,300	331	15½	52·03	92,178	60,000
½	3	nil	2	10,477	12,820	Highland	,, 16	7,890	+ 699	+ 1,198	20	188,314	+ 6,562	+ 9,290	479¾	27¾	58·63	78,976	84,000
1¼	1	1¼	1	2,762	45,810	North British	,, 16	61,861	+ 1,913	+ 2,813	24	1,79[illegible],623	+ 47,525	+ 91,981	1,230	23	44·65	821,706	426,000

IRISH RAILWAYS.

6½	6½	6½	6½	2,405	1,745	Belfast and County Down ..	Jan. 14	2,011	+ 139	—	*	3,497	− [illegible]	—	[illegible]	—	[illegible]	17,[illegible]	[illegible]
6¼	5½	6½	5½	—	4,284	Belfast and Northern Counties	„ 14	4,391	+ 13	—	—	[illegible]	− [illegible]	—	249	—	—	—	—
3	2	3	2½	1,418	1,900	Cork, Bandon, and S. Coast ..	„ 15	1,348	+ 57	—	*	2,752	+ 6	—	103	—	14'82	14,436	5,450
6½	6½	6½	6½	21,537	17,709	Great Northern	„ 14	13,475	+ 422	+ 855	2	26,047	+ 617	+ 942	596	36	[illegible]	67,[illegible]	16,000
5½	5½	5½	5½	12,037	24,855	Great Southern and Western ..	„ 14	—	—	—	not received		—	—	603	13	[illegible]	72,[illegible]	35,140
4½	4	4	4	4,085	11,850	Midland Great Western ..	„ 14	8,807	+ 1,144	—	2	16,[illegible]	+ 1,9[illegible]	+ 1,535	538	—	[illegible]	[illegible]	2,600
nil	nil	nil	nil	229	2,822	Waterford and Central ..	„ 14	996	+ 104	—	2	1,753	+ [illegible]	—	59	—	[illegible]	6,658	1,500
nil	nil	nil	nil	2,601	2,987	Waterford, Limerick & W. ..	„ 14	3,666	+ 305	—	2	10,[illegible]	+ 1,[illegible]	—	350½	—	[illegible]	43,[illegible]	8,869

* From January 1.

FOREIGN RAILWAYS.

Mileage. Total.	Increase on 1897.	Increase on 1896.	Name.	Gross Traffic for Week. Week ending	Amount.	In. or Dec. upon 1897.	In. or Dec. upon 1896.	Gross Traffic to Date. No. of Weeks.	Amount.	In. or Dec. upon 1897.	In. or Dec. upon 1896.
					£	£	£		£	£	£
319	—	—	Argentine Great Western ..	—	—	—	—	—	—	—	—
76½	—	—	Bahia and San Francisco ..	Dec. 25	2,427	+ 356	+ 944	25	61,203	+ 17,515	+ 12,294
234	57	84	Bahia Blanca and North West ..	Dec. 19	1,242	+ 253	+ 397	25	18,370	+ 793	—
187	—	—	Buenos Ayres and Ensenada ..	Jan. 16	3,395	− 945	− 361	2	6,871	− 4,800	− 2,460
496	—	—	Buenos Ayres and Pacific ..	Jan. 15	7,469	− 554	+ 1,163	29	170,077	− 45,431	+ 5,245
914	1	3	Buenos Ayres and Rosario ..	Jan. 15	16,882	+ 1,041	+ 3,160	2	34,216	+ 559	+ 3,102
1,469	66	68	Buenos Ayres Great Southern ..	Jan. 16	37,316	+ 2,241	+ 6,716	29	755,043	+ 53,008	+ 107,930
602	142	177	Buenos Ayres Western	Jan. 16	14,521	− 2,748	− 522	29	300,748	− 70,000	− 63,960
845	55	77	Central Argentine	Jan. 15	20,017	+ 2,515	+ 1,409	2	42,616	+ 2,718	+ 2,084
107	—	—	Central Bahia	Oct. 31*	$83,051	− $6,253	− $36,002	10 mos.	$1,121,178	+ $175,344	+ $803,586
271	—	—	Central Uruguay of Monte Video	Jan. 15	8,845	+ 2,350	+ 2,251	29	160,421	− 10,423	− 21,762
180	—	—	Cordoba and Rosario	Jan. 9	2,465	− 80	+ 390	28	53,740	− 22,285	− 15
128	—	—	Cordoba Central	Jan. 9	$21,500	− $3,460	− $2,400	—	—	—	—
549	—	—	Do. Northern Extension	Jan. 9	$48,000	− $8,500	+ $570	—	—	—	—
137	—	—	Costa Rica	Jan. 15	3,881	+ 414	+ 2,252	2	5,178	− 3,6[illegible]3	+ 1,545
99	—	—	East Argentine	Dec. 5	831	− 2	− 112	49	33,355	− 3,762	− 1,414
386	—	6	Entre Rios	Jan. 15	2,478	+ 847	+ 1,265	—	—	—	—
555	—	24	Inter Oceanic of Mexico	Jan. 15	$62,800	+ $18,090	+ $21,700	29	$1,303,340	+ $101,720	+ $303,840
23	—	—	La Guaira and Caracas	Dec. 23	2,082	− 1,076	− 268	51	106,904	− 17,770	+ 2,045
321	—	—	Mexican	Jan. 15	$79,800	+ $6,800	—	2	$160,100	+ $790	—
1,846	—	—	Mexican Central	Jan. 15	$243,381	+ $8,637	+ $72,016	2	$460,351	+ $460,351	+ $104,774
1,217	—	—	Mexican National	Jan. 15	$110,457	+ $20,060	+ 34,103	2	$216,119	+ $39,537	+ $46,387
228	—	—	Mexican Southern	Jan. 14	$14,440	+ $3,453	+ $5,026	42	$581,255	+ $80,083	+ $139,873
206	—	—	Minas and Rio	Nov. 30*	$179,485	+ $24,354	+ $66,053	5 mos.	$996,637	+ $601,267	+ $204,840
111	—	17	N. W. Argentine	Jan. 15	960	− 870	− 114	2	1,921	− 2,448	− 880
242	3	—	Nitrate	Jan. 15†	17,354	− 1,604	− 12,327	—	—	—	—
390	—	—	Ottoman	Jan. 8	5,818	− 456	+ 2,160	2	10,885	− 1,137	+ 2,373
77½	—	—	Recife and San Francisco ..	Nov. 20	5,521	− 227	+ 674	21	57,594	− 10,871	− 5,049
86½	—	—	San Paulo	Dec. 12†	23,228	− 6,560	—	—	—	—	—
186	—	—	Santa Fe and Cordova	Jan. 15	2,090	− 915	+ 450	29	96,075	− 22,490	− 4,900

* For month ended. † For fortnight ended.

INDIAN RAILWAYS.

Mileage. Total.	Increase on 1897.	Increase on 1896.	Name.	Gross Traffic for Week. Week ending	Amount.	In. or Dec. on 1897.	In. or Dec. on 1896.	Gross Traffic to Date. No. of Weeks.	Amount.	In. or Dec. on 1897.	In. or Dec. on 1896.
867	4	5	Bengal Nagpur	Jan. 8	Rs.1,47,000	− Rs.56,295	− Rs.98,902	—	—	—	—
818	63	63	Bengal and North-Western ..	Dec. 11	Rs.1,05,450	+ Rs.768	+ Rs.7,303	24	Rs.23,46,281	− Rs.89,807	+ Rs.1,85,714
461	—	—	Bombay and Baroda	Jan. 15	£22,092	− £870	− £8,677	2	£47,667	− £6,963	− £19,193
1,884	2	13	East Indian	Jan. 15	Rs.11,37,000	− Rs.66,000	+ Rs.25,000	2	Rs.24,70,000	− Rs.1,83,000	− Rs.1,43,000
1,491	—	—	Great Indian Penin.	Jan. 15	£56,733	− £4,663	− £16,605	2	£122,550	− £9,750	− £70,931
736	—	—	Indian Midland	Jan. 15	Rs.1,41,390	− Rs.2,552	+ Rs.21,474	2	Rs.2,98,780	+ Rs.6,677	− Rs.12,209
840	—	—	Madras	Jan. 8	£20,533	+ £1,833	+ £2,991	—	—	—	—
1,043	—	—	South Indian	Dec. 18	Rs.153,191	+ Rs.3,769	− Rs.14,097	24	Rs.4,120,698	+ Rs.16,189	− Rs.49,184

UNITED STATES AND CANADIAN RAILWAYS.

Mileage. Total.	Increase on 1897.	Increase on 1896.	Name.	Gross Traffic for Week. Period Ending.	Amount.	In. or Dec. on 1897.	Gross Traffic to Date. No. of Weeks.	Amount.	In. or Dec. on 1897.
					dols.	dols.		dols.	dols.
310	—	—	Alabama Gt. South.	Dec. 28	48,002	− 1,495	24	1,643,270	+ 103,197
6,547	103	156	Canadian Pacific	Jan. 14	404,000	+ 79,000	2	805,000	+ 160,000
6,169	—	469	Chicago, Mil., & St. Paul ..	Jan. 14	541,000	+ 85,000	28	19,855,000	+ 1,876,950
1,685	—	—	Denver & Rio Grande	Jan. 14	150,000	+ 36,000	28	4,628,100	+ 732,000
3,512	—	—	Grand Trunk, Main Line ..	Jan. 14	£76,757	+ £13,004	2	£144,874	+ £25,930
335	—	—	Do. Chic. & Grand Trunk	Jan. 14	£15,131	+ £3,181	2	£28,221	+ £4,360
189	—	—	Do. Det., G. H. & Mil. ..	Jan. 14	£3,330	− £343	2	£6,551	− £329
2,938	—	—	Louisville & Nashville	Jan. 14	407,000	+ 37,000	2	788,009	+ 50,000
2,197	137	137	Miss., K., & Texas	Jan. 14	221,871	+ 23,392	28	6,969,018	+ 348,887
477	—	—	N. Y., Ontario, & W.	Jan. 14	67,640	+ 4,061	28	2,227,996	+ 66,738
1,570	—	—	Norfolk & Western	Jan. 7	221,000	+ 3,000	27	5,768,000	+ 463,000
3,499	336	—	Northern Pacific	Dec. 28	540,396	+ 132,360	32	20,997,633	+ 2,146,876
4,654	—	—	Southern	Jan. 14	382,000	+ 19,000	28	10,401,812	+ 546,448
1,979	—	—	Wabash	Jan. 14	229,000	+ 32,000	2	434,000	+ 62,000

MONTHLY STATEMENTS.

Mileage. Total.	Increase on 1896.	Increase on 1895.	Name.	Net Earnings for Month. Month.	Amount.	In. or Dec. on 1896.	In. or Dec. on 1895.	Net Earnings to Date. No. of Months.	Amount.	In. or Dec. on 1896.	In. or Dec. on 1895.
					dols.	dols.	dols.		dols.	dols.	dols.
6,935	44	444	Atchison	November	1,373,663	+ 342,028	+ 560,334	11	7,880,450	+ 124,951	+ 2,850,604
1,970	—	—	Erie	November	819,192	+ 21,332	+ 52,579	11	7,580,994	+ 201,967	+ 794,296
3,127	—	239	Illinois Central*	November	2,534,427	+ 664,661	+ 377,039	11	22,138,784	+ 2,451,949	+ 2,487,092
2,396	—	—	New York Central	November	3,900,753	+ 18,435	− 300,903	11	41,934,547	+ 1,697,686	+ 1,616,507
3,407	—	—	Pennsylvania	November	1,960,658	+ 164,400	− 48,400	11	18,867,671	+ 2,302,100	− 879,500
1,055	—	—	Phil. & Reading	November	2,924,717	− 179,084	—	11	8,447,110	+ 133,428	—

* Statements of gross traffic

Prices Quoted on the London Stock Exchange.

Throughout the INVESTORS' REVIEW middle prices alone are quoted, the object being to give the public the approximate current quotations of every security of any consequence in existence. On the markets the buying and selling prices are both given, and are often wide apart where stocks are seldom dealt in. Other particulars will be found in the INVESTMENT INDEX published quarterly—January, April, July, and October—in connection with this REVIEW, price 2s., by post 2s. 2d. Where dividends are paid only once a year, an *italic* type is used to distinguish them. The London Stock Exchange Official List is quoted in the REVIEW almost entire, only very insignificant issues, or bonds falling due within the next two or three years, being omitted. But the list is subdivided into the leading, or active, stocks, and those less frequently dealt in. The former will be found under the head of "Stock Markets," and with more details than it is possible to give for the bulk of securities. By retaining the file of the INVESTORS' REVIEW any subscriber can follow for himself the movements of securities from week to week, and the INVESTMENT INDEX will from time to time help to fill up deficiencies in the information.

Tea Companies and Mines and Mining Finance Stocks are placed in special lists.

Among the abbreviations used are the following:—S.F. Snk. Fd. *sinking fund*; Certs., *certificates*; Debs. or Dbs., *debentures*; Db. or D.Stk., *debenture stock*; Pf., Prf., or Pref., *preference*; Prefd. or Pfd., *preferred*; Dfd., *deferred*; L. or Ltd., *limited*; Sh., *share*; Ans., *annuities*; Cu. or Cm., *cumulative*; Gu or Guar., *guaranteed*; Bds., *bonds*; S., Sr., or Ser., *series*; In., Ins., Insc., *inscribed*; Dr., Drgs., Drwgs., *drawings*; Stg., Strlg., *sterling*; Lia., *liable to*; Sp., Surp., *surplus*; Per., Perp., *perpetual*; Ln. *lien*; Lo. *loan*.

The dates following the names of securities are the years of issue or of redemption. Where shares are not fully paid up, their nominal amount is given with the name so that investors may know the liability upon them.

BRITISH FUNDS, &c.

Rate.	Name.	Price.
2½	2½ p.c.'s (Childers') Red.. 1905	106½
3	Local Loans Stk. 1912	113¼
3	Metro. Police Deb. Stk. 1920	105½
—	Red Sea Ind. Tel. Ann. 1908	9½
4	Canada Gv. "Intcl. Rly." 1903	109½
4	Do. do. .. 1908	113
4	Do. Bonds 1910	117
4	Do. Bonds 1913	119½
3	Egyptian Gov. Gar.	103½
3	Mauritius Ins. Stk. 1940	115
4	Turkish Guar. 1855	111
c1½	Bank of Ireland Stk.	397½
3½	India Rupee Paper	60½
3½	Do. 1854-5	63½
3	Do. 1896-7 1916	54½
3½	Isle of Man Deb.	105
3	Do. Deb. Stk... 1919-29	105

CORPORATION AND COUNTY STOCKS.

FREE OF STAMP DUTY.

Rate.	Name.	Price.
3½	Metropolitan Con. 1929	121
3	Do. 1941	114
2½	Do. 1920-49	101½
2½	L.C.C. Con. Stock 1920	80½
3½	Comm. of Sewers, Scp., S.F. 1905	105
3½	Corp. of Lond. Bds... 1897-1902	100½
3	Do. 1897-1912	103
3½	Do., Debs. Scp. ...... S.F. 1916	106
—	Do., Deb. Stk. Scrip .. 1927-57	100
3	Barnsley 1916-46	104
3	Barry 1914-46	100
3	Bath 1909-34	104
3	Batley 1914-44	101½
3½	Birmingham 1945	123
5	Do. 1947	113
2½	Do. 1926	99½
3	Blackburn 1930	106½
3	Bournemouth 1913-33	104
3½	Bradford 1945	120
3	Do. Deb. Stock .. 1954	111
3	Brighouse............ 1916-46	101
3½	Brighton 1946	120½
2½	Do. 1957	98
3	Burton-on-Trent........ 1913-43	102½
3	Cambridge 1913-43	104
3½	Cardiff 1935	119
3	Do. 1914-54	105
3	Cheltenham............ 1971	112
3	Chichester 1916-46	102
3½	Croydon	135½
3	Do. 1940	111½
3	Derby 1920-50	107
3	Devon C.C.............. 1917-33	106
3½	Dewsbury 1930	111
3	Do. 1930	105
3	Dorset County 1922-32	107
3	Douglas (I. of Man) 1926	101
3	Dover 1913-43	103
3½	Dublin 1944	111
3	Eastbourne 1920-40	104
3	Edinburgh 1924	108
2½	Do. 1929	98
2½	Exeter 1917-57	97
3	Glamorgan County 1914-34	104
3½	Glasgow 1914	110½
3	Do. 1921	106½
2½	Do. 1925-40	99
3	Gloster 1915-55	103
3	Grimsby 1913-45	104½
3	Hampshire County 1914-34	106½
3	Hanley 1913-43	105
3	Harrogate 1914-34	104
3	Hastings 1915-54	104
2½	Hertfordshire C.C. 1916-36	99
3	Heston & Isleworth U.D.C. 1915-35	101
3	Huddersfield 1934	107
3½	Hull (1st iss.)	131½
3	Inverness 1914-44	102
3	Ipswich 1952	111
3	Lancaster 1919-55	104
2½	Leeds 1927	98
3½	Leicester 1934	117
3	Lincoln............... 1919	104
3½	Liverpool	135

Corporation, &c. (*continued*):—

Rate.	Name.	Price.
3	Manchester 1941	109
3	Mansfield............ 1915-45	100
3½	Middlesbro'............ 1909 (+	105½
3½	Do. 1911-13	105
3	Do. 1915	104
3	Middlesex C.C.......... 1915-35	106
3½	Newcastle 1936	118½
3½	Do. Irred.	129½
2½	Do. 1915-36	101
3	Newcastle-under-Lyme.. 1909-44	100
3	Newport (Mon.) 1915-55	104½
3	Norwich 1952	113
3	Nottingham	117
3	Oxford 1951	111
3	Penzance 1916-46	102½
3	Plymouth 1942	112
3	Pontypridd U.D.C. 1916-46	99
3	Poole............... 1915-45	102½
3½	Portsmouth.......1916 24 & 27	112
3	Do. 1913-33	106
3	Ramsey 1920-40	100
3	Ramsgate............ 1915-55	102
3	Reading	135
3	Do. 1962	108
3½	Rhyl U.D.C. 1953	112
3	Richmond (Surrey) 1942	106
3	River Wear Debt Certs.	101
3	St. Helen's 1915-55	104½
3	Scarbro' 1915-50	102
2½	Sheffield 1925-57	97½
3	Shipley U.D.C.......... 1915-35	101
3	Somerset Co. 1923-33	107
3	South Shields......... 1915-45	104
2½	Southampton 1915-45	102
3	Southend-on-Sea 1916-46	102
3	Staffs C.C. 1915-35	106
3	Stockport............ 1914-54	103
3	Stockton 1932	108
3	Do. 1915-35	103½
3	Surrey Co. 1922-32	106½
3½	Swansea	132
3	Do. 1955	106
3	Taunton 1918 3-9-43	101
3	Tees Conserv. Deb. Stk. 1947	101
3	Thames Conserv. "A" Deb. Stk. 1954	103
3	Do. "B" Deb. Stk. 1954	103
3	Torquay 1913-43	102½
3	Tunbridge Wells 1931	105
3	Tynemouth 1913	101
3	Wakefield............ 1929	105
3	Walsall............... 1932	108
3	West Bromwich......... 1930	108½
3½	West Ham 1929	111
3	Do. 1945	107
3	West Sussex C.C. 1915-35	106
3	Weston-s.-Mare Lcl. Bd. 1914-44	103
3	Weymouth & Melc. Regis 1918	101
3	Widnes............... 1915-55	102
3	Wigan 1921	108
3	Windsor 1918-55	103
3½	Wisbech 1947	115½
3½	Wolverhampton......... 1932	119½
3	Do. 1924-54	108
3	York 1916-41	106

SUBJECT TO STAMP DUTY.

Rate.	Name.	Price.
3½	Belfast City & Dis. Watr. 1938	116
3	Do. Red Stk. 1953-6	108½
3½	Belfast 1924	104
4	Blackburn Con. Deb. Irred.	141½
3½	Do. do. Irred...............	129½
3½	Bristol	133
3½	Burnley............... 1933	116
2½	Chesterfield Gas & Wtr. 1916-46	98
3½	Douglas Town 1921	105
3	Dover Harb. 1st Deb... 1956	105
3½	Hull (2nd iss.)	129½
4	Leeds Deb............. 1927	125
3½	Do.	113½
3	Do. 1927	106½
3	Leicester 1919-44	106
4	Manchester...............	150
3	Do. 1928	105
4½	Middlesboro' Mrts. 1908	111
3½	Newark-on-Trent .. 1901-41	96
3½	Sheffield 1898-1916	106
3½	Do. 1925-36	114½
3	Do. 1925	105½
3½	Southampton .... S.F.	105½
4½	Stockton Morts......... 1908	111
3½	Worcester.. 1950	111

COLONIAL AND PROVINCIAL GOVERNMENT SECURITIES.

Rate.	Name.	Price.
6	British Columbia........ 1907	119½
4½	Do. Debs. .. 1917	110½
3	British Guiana Imgtn. Bds.	99½
5	Canada, "Intercol. Rail," 1903	111½
4	Do. (Bonds) 1904-5-6-8	109
4	Do. Reduced 1910	111
3½	Do. Bnds. 1909-34	108
4	Do. Loan 1910-35	112
3	Do. Loan 1938	105
6	Cape of G. Hope 1900	—
5	Do. 1900	—
4½	Do. red. by an. draw.	111
4½	Do. 1879	111
4	Do. 1881	108
4	Do. 1917-23	117
4½	Ceylon	110
4	Do.	108½
4½	Fiji Gov. Deb. Sink. Fd.	100½
4	Jamaica Sink. Fd. 1923	104
5	Manitoba Debs.......... 1910	113
5	Do. Ster. Bds. 1888	122
4	Do. Ster. Debs.	106
4	Mauritius, Cons. Debs. 1880....	103½
4½	Natal, Sink. Fd......... 1919	120
4	Do. do. 1926	118
3½	Newfoundland Stg. Bds. 1941	100
3½	Do. do. .. 1947	100
3	Do. do.	88
5	New South Wales 1897-1902	105½
4	Do. 1903-5-8-9-10	105½
5	New Zealand 1914	118
5	Do. Cnsls. 1 p.c. per an. Sink. Fd.	103
3½	Nova Scotia Debs.	104
5	Quebec Prov. 1904-6	110
4½	Do. (drgs.)	103
5	Do. Strlg. Bds. 1912	115
4	Do. Strlg. Bds. 1928	109
4	Do. Strlg. Bds. 1934	110
4	Queensland 1913-15	108
4½	St. Lucia Debs...............	100
6	South Australia 1897-1900	103½
6	Do. 1901-1918	118
5	Do. 1911-1920	115½
4	Do. 1899-1916	105
4	Do. 1929	110½
4	Do. 1916	109½
4	Do. 1917-18-24	112
6	Tasmania 1897-1901	104
4	Do. 1908-11, 1913-14-20	108
5	Trinidad Debs., an. drw. 1 p.c...	107
4	Victoria 1899-1901	101½
4½	Do. 1904	106
4	Do. Rail. Loan 1907	106
4	Do. Loans 1908-13	108½
4½	West. Austr. 1 p.c. an. Sink. Fd.	108
4	Do. do.	106

REGISTERED AND INSCRIBED STOCKS.

No stamp duty except for Canada 4 p.c. Reduced (½ per cent.).

Rate.	Name.	Price.
4	Antigua Insc. Stk. Red. 1919-44	111
3½	Barbados Insc. Stk. 1925-42	108
3	British Colum. Insc. Stk. 1941	103
4	British Guiana Insc..... 1935	120
4	Canada Stk. Regd. ..1904-5-6-8	109
4	Do. 4 p.c. (late 5 p.c.) Regd. 1910	111
3½	Do. 3½ p.c. Stock Regd. 1909-34	108
4	Do. Ln. for 4 milln. stg. 1910-35	112
3	Do. Stk. Regd. 1938	106
2½	Do. Insc. 1947	93½
4	Cape G. Hope Regd. .. 1917-23	118
4	Do. (Ln. of '83) Insc. .. 1923	119
4	Do. Cons. Stk. Insc..... 1916-36	116
3½	Do. Consol. Insc. Stock 1929-49	115
4	Ceylon Insc. Stock 1934	124
3	Do. 1940	107
4	Grenada Insc. Stock.... 1917-42	112
3½	Hong Kong Insc. Stock 1918-43	105½
4	Jamaica Insc. Stock.... 1934	121
—	Do. 1922-44	99
4	Mauritius Inscribed 1937	119
4	Natal Consd. Stk. Insc. 1927	118
4	Do. 1937	122
3½	Do. Inscribed Stock.. 1914-39	107
4	Newfoundland Inscribed 1913-38	108
4	Do. 1935	113
4	Do. Consd. Stk. Ins. 1936	113
4	N. S Wales Stock Insc. 1933	122
3½	Do. 1924	110
3½	Do. 1918	108
3	Do. 1935	102

Colonial, &c. (*continued*):—

Rate.	Name.	Price.
4	N. Zealnd. Con. Stk. Ins. 1929	116½
3½	Do. 1940	109
3	Do. Inscribed 1945	101
3	Quebec (Prov.) Ins. Stk. 1937	95
4	Queensland Stock Insc. 1915-24	112½
3½	Do. 1921-4-30	106
3½	Do. 1945	109
—	Do. 1922-47	100
4	St. Lucia Insc. Stock .. 1919-44	112
4	S. Austrln. (1882-7) Reg. 1916-36	113½
3½	Do. In. Stk. Reg. 1939	110
3	Do. 1916-26	100
3/	Do. 1916	100
3½	Tasmanian Insc. Stock.. 1920-40	110
4	Do. 1920-40	115
4	Trinidad Insc. Stock..... 1917-42	112
—	Do. 1922-44	98½
4	Victoria Rly. Loan '81, Inscribed Stock 1907	106
4	Victoria Insc. Stock 1908-13-19	109½
4	Victoria (1883) Ins. Stk. 1920	112
3½	Do. Inscribed Stock 1921-3-6	106
4	Do. do. 1911-26	109
4	W. Austral. Insc. Stock 1934	120
4	Do. 1911-31	113
3½	Do. 1915-35	107
3	Do. 1915-35	98
3	Do. 1916-36	98

FOREIGN STOCKS, BONDS, &c.

COUPONS PAYABLE IN LONDON.

Last Div.	Name.	Price.
36/	Argentine Ry. Loan 6 p.c. 1881	92½
15/	Do. 5 p.c. 1884	72
30/	Do. N. Cent. Ry. Ext. 5 p.c. 1887-8-9	72
30/	Do. 5 p.c. Trsy. Convs. 1887	72
5/4½	Do. 4½ p.c. Interl. Gld. 1888	68
27/	Do. 4½ p.c. Stlg. Extrl. 1888	69
10/6	Do. 3½ p.c. External .. 1889	52
4	Do. 4 p.c. Ry. Guar. Res....	63½
4½	Brazilian 1883	63
4½	Do. Gold......... 1879	66½
4½	Do. 1888	63
36/	Buenos Ayres 1824	90
6	Do. 1882-3-6	51
6	Bulgarian 1888	98
6	Do. Mort. Bonds 1892	95
4½	Chilian 1885	82
4½	Do. 1886	83
4½	Do. 1887	82
4½	Do. 1889	83½
5	Do. 1892	89
4½	Do. 1893	82
4½	Do. 1895	82
5	Do. 1896	88
7	Chinese Silver 1894	102
6	Do. Gold 1895	106
6	Do. Apl. '95 by dwgs. 1901-15	109½
5	Do. Red. dwgs. in 36 yr. 1896	101
5	Do. Do. Regis. 1896	101
1½	Colmbn. 1½ to 3 p.c. Ext. Bds. 1896	18½
6	Cordova, Prov. 1886	27
—	Do. Eng. Ass. Certs.	26
—	Do. 6 p.c. 1887-8	27
—	Do. Eng. Ass. Certs.	26
3	Costa Rica "A"	32
2½	Do. "B"	27
3	Danish Gold 1914	100
10/	Ecuador N. Ext. Bds. 4½ p.c. ascn. to 5 p.c..............	21
3½	Egypt'n Ins. Stk. lia. Stp. Dty. 1890	102
4½	Do. State Domain 1878	105
4	Do. D. Sanieh, Red. .. 1905	103½
6	Entre Rios............... 1886-8	33
6	Do. Fndg. Ln. Bds. 1894-1921	29
6	Do. do. Parana City......	23½
15/	Greek 1881	36
15/	Do. 1884	36
12/	Do. Rentes..................	29
15/	Do. (Piræus-Larissa Ry.)	33
7/6	Do. Fundg. Loan 1893	40
4	Guatemala Extl. Debt..........	36
6	Hawaiian	101½
4	Hungarian Gold Rentes........	101½
3	Do. 1895	91
6	Italian Irriga. Guar.	112½
5	Do. Maremmana	93½
5	Japan 5 p.c.	102
5	Mexican (Nat. R. Tehuantp c.)..	92
	Do Extrl. 1890	97½

Foreign Stocks, &c. (*continued*):—

Last Div.	Name.	Price.
6	Mexican Extrl. 1893	95½
5	Do. Intrnl. Cons. Slvr.	34¼
5	Do. Intern. Rd. Bds. 2d. Ser.	34½
4	Nicaragua 1886	50
3½	Norwegian, red. 1937, or earlier	100
3	Do. do. 1965, do.	100
3½	Do. 3½ p.c. Bnds.	103
1	Paraguay 1p.c. ris. 3p.c. 1886-96	16
5	Russian, 1822, £ Strlg.	149½
3	Do. 1850	92
4	Do. (Nicolas Ry.) 1867-9	103
3	Do. Transcauc. Ry. 1882	92
4	Do. Con. R. R. Bd. Ser. I., 1889	103¼
4	Do. Do. II., 1889	103¼
4	Do. Do. III., 1891	104¼
3½	Do. Bonds	100½
4	Do. Ln. (Dvinsk and Vitbsk)	102
6	Salvador 1889	72½
—	S. Domingo 4s. Unified: 1980	66¼
6	San Luis Potosi Stg. 1889	93½
5	San Paulo (Brzl.), Stg. 1888	91½
6	Santa Fé 1883-4	37
—	Do. Eng. Ass. Certs. Dep.	36
5	Do. 1888	47
—	Do. Eng. Ass. Certs. Dpsit.	46
5	Do. (W. Cnt. Col. Rly.) Mrt.	26
5	Do. & Reconq. Rly. Mort.	26
5	Spanish Quickslvr Mort. 1870	102
3½	Swedish 1880	103
3	Do. 1888	101
3	Do. Conversion Loan 1894	101
5	Trans. Gov. Loan Red. 1903-49	106
50/	Tucuman (Prov.) 1888	69
4	Turkish, Secd. on Egypt. Trib.	103½
3½	Turkish, Egpt. Trib., Ott. Bd., '94	93½
4	Do. Priority 1890	94
1	Do. Convted Series, "A"	65½
5	Do. Customs Ln. 1886	97½
5	Uruguay Bonds 1896	54
3	Venzula New Con. Debt 1881	30

COUPONS PAYABLE ABROAD.

Last Div.	Name.	Price.
7	Argent. Nat. Cedla. Sries, "B".	37½
5	Austrian Ster. Rnts., ex 10fl., 1870	85
5	Do. do. do.	86
5	Do. Paper do. 1870	85
5	Do. do. do.	85
4	Do. Gld Rentes 1876	102
2½	Belgian exchange 25 fr.	92
3	Do. do.	101
3½	Danish Int., 1887, Rd. 1896	97½
3½	Do. '87, Red. by pur. or draw. fr. Dec., 1900	98½
2½	Dutch Certs. ex 12 gldrs.	87½
3	Do. Bonds	99
3	Do. Insc. Stk.	99
3½	French Rentes	106
3	Do. 1878, '81-4, Red.	101
3	German Imp. Ln. 1891	96½
3	Do. do. 1892-3	96¼
3	Do. do. 1890-4	96
5	Japan Cons. Ln., '92, 3, & 5, Red.	46½
4	Prussian Consols	102
3	,, Cons. Stg. Ln. 1891	97
4	Rumanian Bds. 1890	—
4	Do. do. 1891	—
4	Utd. States, 1877, Red. 1907	116
4	Do. 1895, 30 yrs.	131
3½	Do. Maschsetts Gl. 1935	113½
3½	Do. Gold Bonds 1923	110½
2	Virginia Cpn. Bds., 3 p.c. from July, 1901	71

BRITISH RAILWAYS.

ORD. SHARES AND STOCKS.

Last Div.	Name.	Price.
10	Barry, Ord.	288½
4	Do. Prefd.	129
6	Do. Defd.	158½
5¼	Caledonian, Ord.	160
3	Do. Prefd.	102
—	Do. Defd. Ord., No. 1	5
—	Cambrian, Ord.	6½
—	Do. Coast Cons.	6½
24/	Cardiff Ry. Pref. Ord.	118
3/	Central Lond. £10 Ord. Sh.	10
1/9¼	Do. do. £6 paid	5½
3½d.	Do. Pref. Half-Shares	1½
1/6	Do. Def. do.	4½
2	City and S. London	70
—	East London, Cons.	7
1½	Furness	72½
—	Glasgow and S. West. Pfd.	86
—	Do. do. Dfd.	71
—	Great Central, Ord. 1894	44
32/6	Do. London Exten.	81
3½	Great N. of Scotland	119
4	Great Northern, Prefd.	126
—	Do. Consolidated "A"	57
—	Do. do. "B"	195½
2	Highland	81
4	Isle of Wight, Prefd.	122½
1	Do. Defd.	86½
—	Lancs. Derbys. and E. Cst.	5
4½	L. Brighton and S. C. Ord.	191
38/11	Do. New 70 p.c. pd.	187
6	Do. Prefd. Ord.	202
7/6	Do. Contgt. Rights Certs.	20½
5½	Lond. and S. Western Ord.	232½
4	Do. Preferred	138
2½	Lond.; Tilb., and Southend	134½
—	Mersey, £20 shares	1
—	Metropolitan, New Ord.	131
2½	Do. Surplus Lands	99
4	North Cornwall, 4 p.c. Pref.	106½
7/6	Do. Deferred	27½
7½	North London	229½
	North Staffordshire	131

British Railways (*continued*):—

Last Div.	Name.	Price.
1/6	Plymouth, Devenport, and S. W. Junc. £10	9
3/	Port Talbot £10 Shares	9½
9d.	Rhondda Swns. B. £10 Sh.	6½
11	Rhymney, Cons.	275½
4	Do. Prefd.	128
—	Do. Defd.	152½
1½	Scarboro', Bridlington Junc.	47½
3½	South Eastern, Ord.	156
6	Do. Pref.	199
3½	Taff Vale	85
25/	Vale of Glamorgan	132½
2/8½	Waterloo & City £10 shares	12½

LEASED AT FIXED RENTALS.

Last Div.	Name.	Price.
4	Birkenhead	150
5.19.0	East Lincnshire	215
5½	Hamsmith. & City Ord.	200½
4½	Lond. and Blackwll.	167½
4½	Do. £10 4½ p. c. Pref.	167
56/6	Lond. & Green. Ord.	104
5	Do. 5 p. c. Pref.	180½
5	Nor. and Eastn. £50 Ord.	92
6	Do.	109
3½	N. Cornwall 3½ p. c. Stk.	128½
4½	Nott. & Granthm. R. & C.	150
3½	Portpik. & Wigtn. Guar. Stk.	126
9	Vict. Stn. & Pimlico Ord.	317½
4½	Do. 4½ p. c. Pref.	163½
4/	West Lond. £20 Ord. Shs.	14½
4½	Weymouth & Portld.	162½

DEBENTURE STOCKS.

Last Div.	Name.	Price.
3	Barry, Cons.	110
4	Brecon & Mrthyr, New A	129
4	Do. New B	105
4	Caledonian	155
4	Cambrian "A"	134½
4	Do. "B"	132½
4	Do. "C"	127½
4	Do. "D"	110½
3	Cardiff Rly.	106
4	City and S. Lond.	139
3½	Cleator & Working Junc.	118½
3	Devon & Som. "A"	105½
16/3	Do. "B" 4 p. c.	36
—	Do. "C" 4 p. c.	10
4	E. Lond. and Ch. 4 p. c. A	139
5/	Do. and B	65½
—	Do. 3rd Ch. 4 p. c.	19½
—	Do. 4th do.	9½
3½	Do. 1st (3½ p. c.)	128½
2½	Do. 2½ p.c. (Whitech. Exn).	88
4	Forth Bridge	146
4	Furness	145
4	Glasgow and S. Western	154
5	Gt. Central	—
4½	Do.	161
4	Gt. Eastern	151
4	Gt. N. of Scotland	148½
3	Gt. Northern	118
4	Gt. Western	156
4½	Do.	162
4½	Do.	173½
5	Do.	192
2½	Do.	101
4	Highland	143½
3	Hull and Barnsley	107
3	Do. and (3-4 p. c).	124
4	Isle of Wight	144½
3	Do. Cent. "A"	92½
4½	Do. "B"	115½
4	Do. "C"	82½
3	Lancs. & Yorkshire	117
4	Lancs. Derbys. & E. Cst.	124½
4	Lpool St. Hlen's & S. Lancs.	126
4½	Ldn. and Blackwall	159
4	Ldn. and Greenwich	149½
4	Lond., Brighton, &c.	152
4½	Do.	170
4½	Lond., Chath., &c., Arb.	160
4½	Do. "B"	156½
4	Do.	140
4	Do. 1883	140
3	Do.	106
3	Lond. & N. Western	119
3	Lond. & S. Westn. "A"	118
3	Do. Consld.	118
4	Lond., Til., & Southend	150
—	Mersey, 5 p. c. (Act, 1866)	65
4	Metropolitan	150
4½	Do.	164½
3½	Do.	129½
6	Met. District	208½
4	Do.	139
3	Midland	118
4½	Mid-Wales "A"	137½
4	Neath & Brecon 1st	128½
4	Do. "A 1"	121
3	North British	114
3	Do. 1893	111½
3½	N. Cornwall, Launcstn., &c.	128½
3	North Eastern	118

Debenture Stocks (*continued*):—

Last Div.	Name.	Price.
4½	North London	168
3	N. Staffordshire	115
4	Plym. Devpt. & S.W. Jn.	141½
4	Rhondda and Swan. Bay	130½
4	Rhymney	148
4	South-Eastern	151
5	Do.	191
3½	Do.	130
3	Do.	116
3	Taff Vale	112
4	Tottenham & For. Gate	146
3	Vale of Glamorgan	106½
3	West Highld. (Gtd. by N.B.)	111½
4	Wrexham, Mold, &c. "A"	115½
4	Do. "B"	106½
4	Do. "C"	97½

GUARANTEED SHARES AND STOCKS.

Last Div.	Name.	Price.
4	Caledonian	152½
4	Do.	152
4	Forth Bridge	146
4	Furness 1881	138
4	Glasgow & S. Western	151½
4	Do. St. Enoch. Rent	150½
6	Gt. Central	204½
4½	Do. 1st Pref.	156½
3½	Do. Pref.	108
5	Do. Irred. S.Y. Rent	167½
4½	Do. do.	144½
4	Gt. Eastern, Rent	148
5	Do. Metropolitan	182½
4	Do.	150
4	Gt. N. of Scotland	141
4	Gt. Northern	152
5	Gt. Western, Rent	191
5	Do. Cons.	191
4	Lancs. & Yorkshire	152
5	L., Brighton & S. C.	188
3½	L., Chat. & D. (Shrtlds.)	110½
4	L. & North Western	153
4	L. & South Western 1881	152
4½	Met. District, Ealing Rent	152
4½	Do. Fulham Rent	152
4	Do. Midland Rent	143½
4	Do. Mid. & Dist. Guar.	136½
4	Midland, Rent	153
4	Do. Cons.	153
3	Mid. & G.N. Jt., "A" Rnt.	110½
3	N. British, Lien	111
4	Do. Cons. Pref. No. 1	147
3	N. Cornwall, Wadebrge. Gu.	108
4	N. Eastern	152
5	N. Staff. Trent & M. £20 Shs.	36½
3½	Nott. Suburban Ord.	126½
20/6	S. E. Perp. Ann.	36½
4½	Do. 4½ p.c.	167
3½	S. Yorks. Junc. Ord.	118½
4½	W. Cornwall (G. W., Br., Ex., & S. Dev. Joint Rent	168½
3	W. Highl. Ord. Stk. (Gua., N.B.)	109½

PREFERENCE SHARES AND STOCKS.

DIVIDENDS CONTINGENT ON PROFIT OF YEAR.

Last Div.	Name	Price.
5	Barry (First)	171½
4	Do. Consolidated	140½
4	Caledonian Cons., No. 1	149
4	Do. do. No. 2	147
5	Do. do. 1878	183½
4	Do. Pref. 1884	147
4	Do. do. 1887 (Conv.)	155
—	Cambrian, No. 1 4 p.c. Pref.	72½
—	Do. No. 2 do.	37½
—	Do. No. 3 do.	19
—	Do. No. 4 do.	10
5	City & S. Lond. £10 shares	15½
—	Do. New	14
4	Furness, Cons. 1881	133½
4	Do. "A" 1881	131½
4	Do. "B" 1883	129½
4	Glasgow & S. Western	147
4	Do. No. 2	147
4	Do. 1888	147
4	Do. 1891	146
5	Gt. Central	168
4	Do.	136½
5	Do. Conv. 1872	157½
5	Do. do. 1874	157½
5	Do. do. 1876	157½
5	Do. do. 1879	156½
5	Do. do. 1881	156½
4	Do. 1889	118½
4	Do. 1891	116
4	Do. 1894	119½
4	Gt. Eastern, Cons.	148
4	Do. 1886	146
4	Do. 1881	145½
4	Do. 1884	145
4	Do. 1887	146

Preference Shares, &c. (*continued*):—

Last Div.	Name.	Price.
4	Gt. Eastern, Cons. 1888	144½
3½	Do. 1890	126½
3½	Do. 1893	120½
—	Do. (Int. fr. Jan '99) 1893	117½
4	Gt. North Scotland "A"	136½
4	Do. "B"	135½
4	Gt. Northern, Cons.	149
3	Do. 1896	108½
5	Gt. Western Cons.	189
—	Hull & Barnsley Red. at 115	110
4	Isle of Wight	135½
3	Lancs. & Yorkshire, Cons.	112
2/2½	Lanc. Drby & E.C. 5 p.c. £10	11
—	Do. 5 p.c. and £10	10
5	Lond., Bright., &c., Cons.	187½
5	Do. and Cons.	186½
4½	Lond., Chat. & Dov. Arbitr.	137
—	Do. 2nd Pref. 4½ p.c.	89
4	Lond. & N. Western	152
4	Lond. & S. Western 1881	151
4	Do. 1884	150
3½	Do.	132
4	Lond., Tilbury & Southend	147
4	Do. Cons., 1887	147
4	Do 1891	146
—	Mersey, 5 p.c. Perp.	94
4	Metropolitan, Perp.	148
4	Do. 1882	148½
4	Do. Irred.	146½
4	Do. 1887	146½
4	Do. New	144½
4½	Do.	148½
3½	Do.	128½
3	Do. Guar.	104½
4	Metrop. Dist. Exten. 5 p.c.	113
4	Midland, Cons. Perpetual	151
4	N. British Cons., No. 2	143
4½	Do. Edin. & Glasgow	156½
5	Do. 1865	173½
5	Do. Conv. 1874	173½
4½	Do. 1875	156
4½	Do. Conv. 1875	156½
5	Do. do. 1879	173½
4	Do. do. 1884	141
4	Do. do. 1888	141
4	Do. do. 1890	141
4	Do. do. 1892	141
4	N. Eastern	151
4½	N. Lond., Cons. 1866	180½
4½	Do. 2nd Cons. 1875	166½
3	N. Staffordshire	111
4½	Plym. Devpt. & S. W. Junc.	152½
5½d.	Port Talbot, &c., 4 p.c. £10 Shares, 4 paid	5
5/	Rhondda & Swansea Bay, 5 p.c. £10 Shares	13½
4	Rhymney, Cons.	144
4½	S. Eastern, Cons.	166
5	Do. do.	188½
4	Do. Vested Cos'.	146
4	Do. 1891	144
3½	Do. 1893	127
2	Do. 3 p.c. after July 1900	105
4	Taff Vale	143

INDIAN RAILWAYS.

Last Div.	Name.	Paid.	Price.
3½	Assam Bengal, Ld., (3½ p.c. till June 30, then 3 p.c.)	100	105
4/	Barsi Light, Ld., £10 Shs.	10	10½
6	Bengal and N. West., Ld.	100	147½
4/	Do. £10 Shares	10	14½
3.6	Do. 3½ p.c. Cum. Pf. Shs.	10	10½
£1 4d.	Do.	4	4½
2.3½	Bengal Central, Ld., £10 (3½ p.c. + ¼th net earn)	5	5½
3	Bengal Dooars, Ld.	100	118
4	Bengal Nagpr., Lim. (gua. 4 p.c. + 4th sp. pfts.)	100	115
7½	Bombay, Baroda, and C. I. (gua. 5 p.c.)	100	222
36/1	Burma, Ld. (gua. 2½ p.c. and ½ p.c. add. till 1901)	100	107½
1/	Do. £10 Shares	2½	3
4	Delhi Umb. Kalka, Ld., Gua. 3½ p.c. + net earn.	100	119
4	Do. Deb. Stk., 1897 (1916)	100	113
9/10	Eastn. Bengal, "A" An. 1957	—	28
9/	Do. "B" 1957	—	31
4	Do. Gua. Deb. Stock	100	144½
9/7½	East Ind. Ann. "A" (1953)	—	27
8/4½	Do. "C"	—	30
8/11½	Do. "B"	—	32
6½	Do. Def. Ann. Cap. (gua. 4 p.c. + ⅕th sp. pfts.)	—	150
115/0	East Ind. Def. Ann. "D"	—	156
4½	East Ind. Irred. Stock	100	166½
5	Gt. Indian Penin., Gua. 5 p.c. + ½ surplus profits	100	172
4	Do. Irred. 4 p.c. Deb. St.	100	146½
4	Indian Mid., Ld. (gua. 4 p.c. + ¼th surplus pfts.)	100	115
51/	Madras Guar. + ½ sp. pfts.	100	168
48/6	Do. do.	100	158
46/	Do. do.	100	148
4	Nilgiri, Ld., 1st Deb. Stk.	100	97
4	Oude & Rohil. Db. Stk. Rd.	100	101
5½	Rohil. and Kumaon, Ld.	100	132
9/11	Scinde, Punj., and Delhi, "A" Ann., 1958	—	29
9/1	Do. "B" do.	—	32

Indian Railways (*continued*):—

Last Div.	Name.	Paid.	Price.
4/	South Behar, Ld., £10 shs.	10	10
3½	Do. Deb. Stk. Red.	100	103
4½	South Ind., Gu. Deb. Stk.	100	166½
5	South Indian, Ld. (gua. 3 p.c., and ½ spls. profits)	100	120½
5	Sthn. Mahratta, Ld. (3½ p.c. & ¼th net earnings)	100	123
4	Do. Deb. Stk. Red.	100	124
3½	Southern Punjab, Ld.	100	113
3½	Do. Deb. Stk. Red.	—	107
5	Nizam's Gua. State, Ld. (†	100	114½
4	Do. Mort. Deb., 1936	100	109
4	Do. do. Reg.	100	108
17/3½	Nizam's Gua. State, Ld., 3½ p.c. Mt. Deb. bearer	—	94½
17/3½	Do. Reg. do. ..	—	93½
5	W. of India Portgese., Ld.	100	68
5	Do. Deb. Stk., Red	100	98

RAILWAYS.—BRITISH POSSESSIONS.

Last Div.	Name.	Paid.	Price.
5	Atlantic & N.W. Gua. 1 Mt. Bds., 1937	100	127
5/3	Buff. & L. Huron Ord. Sh.	10	13½
5½	Do. 1st Mt. Perp. Bds. 1879	100	143½
5½	Do. 2nd Mt. Perp. Bds.	100	143½
—	Calgary & Edmon. 6 p.c. 1st Mt. Stg. Bds. Red..	100	99½
5	Canada Cent. 1st Mt. Bds. Red.	100	105
4	Can. Pacific Pref. Stk.....	100	101½
5	Do. Strl. 1st Mt. Deb. Bds. 1915	100	119
3½	Do. Ld. Grnt. Bds., 1938..	100	109
3½	Do. Ld. Grnt. Ins. Stk. ..	100	109
4	Do. Perp. Cons. Deb. Stk.	100	117½
5	Do. Algoma Bch. 1st Mt. Bds., 1937	100	121
2	Demerara, Original Stock	100	*49
7	Do. Perp. Pref. Stk.......	100	157½
9½d.	Do. 4 p.c. Cum. Ext. Pref. £10 Shs.	4	5
—	Dominion Atlntc. Ord. Stk.	100	32½
25/	Do. 5 p.c. Pref. Stk......	100	101
4	Do. 1st. Deb. Stk.......	100	110
4	Do. 2nd do. Red.	100	99
4½	EmuBay&Mt.Bischoff,Ld.	5	4½
[illegible]	Do. Irred. Deb. Stk....	100	98½
nil.	Gd. Trunk of Canada, Stk.	100	9
6	Do. 2nd. Equip. Mt. Bds.	100	130½
5	Do. Perp. Deb. Stk.......	100	141
5	Do. Gt. Westn. Deb. Stk.	100	136
5	Do. Nthn. of Can. 1st Mt. Bds., 1902	100	105
4	Do. do. Deb. Stk	100	104
5	Do. G. T. Geor. Bay & L. Erie 1 Mt., 1903	100	105
5	Do. Mid. of Can. Stl. 1st Mt. (Mid. Sec.) 1908	100	108
5	Do. do. Cons. 1 Mt. Bds. 1912	100	108
5	Do. Mont. & Champ. 1 Mt. Bds., 1902	100	104
	Do. Welln., Grey & Brce. 7 p.c. Bds. 1 Mt.	100	110
4	Jamaica 1st Mtg. Bds. Red.	—	103
6	Manitoba & N. W., 6 p.c. 1st Mt. Bds., Red	100	44½
—	Do. Ldn. Bdhldrs. Certs.	—	44½
5	Manitoba S. W. Col. 1 Mt. Bd., 1934 $1,000 price %	—	119
—	Mid. of W. Aust. Ld. 6 p.c. 1 Mt. Dbs., Red.	100	25
4	Do. Deb. Bds., Red.	100	103
4	Nakusp & Slocan Bds., 1918	100	106
3	Natal Zululand Ld. Debs.,	100	79½
5	N. Brunswick 1st Mt. Stg. Bds., 1934	100	122
4	Do. Perp. Cons. Deb. Stk.	100	114
—	N. Zealand Mid., Ld., 5 p.c 1st Mt. Debs...........	100	35
6	Ontario & Queb. Cap. Stk.	$100	156½
5	Do. Perm. Deb. Stk......	100	147½
—	Qu'Appelle, L. Lake & Sask. 6 p.c. 1 Mt. Bds. Red.	100	40½
5	Queb. & L. S. John, 1st Mt. Bds., 1909	100	18½
5	Quebec Cent., Prior Ln. Bds., 1908	100	109
1½	Do. 5 p.c. Inc. Bds.	100	41
4	St. Lawr. & Ott. Stl. 1st Mt.	100	112
4	Shuswap & Okan., 1st Mt. Deb. Bds., 1915	100	70½
5	Temiscouata, 5 p.c. Stl. 1st Deb. Bds., Red.........	100	9½
5	Do. (S. Franc. Brch.) 5 p.c. Stl. 1 Mt. Db. Bds., 1910	100	12½
4	Toronto, Grey & B. 1st Mt.	100	112
1/2½	Well. & Mana. £5 Shs. ..	1	1
5	Do. Debs., 1908	100	110
5	Do. 2nd Debs., 1908	100	109
5	Do. 3rd do., 1908	100	108
6	Atlan. & St. Law. Shs., 6 p.c.	100	167
5	Gd. Trunk Mt. Bds., 1934	100	107½
5	Michigan Air Line, 5 p.c. 1st Mt. Bds., 1902	100	104
4	Minneap., S. P. & Slt. Ste. Mar, 1st M. Bds., 1938	$1000	100

AMERICAN RAILROAD STOCKS AND SHARES.

Last Div.	Name.	Paid.	Price.
6/	Alab. Gt. Sthn. A 6 p.c. Pref.	10/.	9
3/	Do. do "B" Ord. ..	10/.	2
—	Alabma. N. Orl.-Tex. &c., "A" Pref.	10/.	⅝
—	Do. "B" Def.	10/.	¼
4½	Atlant. First Lsd. Ls. Rtl. Trust..................	Stk.	100
$2	Baltimore & Ohio Com. ..	$100	13
—	Baltimore Ohio S.W. Pref.	$100	6½
—	Chesap. & Ohio Com.	$100	23½
—	Chic. Gt. West. 5 p.c. Pref. Stock "A"	$100	37½
—	Do. do. Scrip. In.......	—	35½
8/3	Do. 4 p.c. Deb. Stk.......	$100	71
4	Do. Interest in Scrip	$100	67½
$4	Chic. Junc. Rl. & Un. Stk. Yds. Com.	$100	113½
6/2	Do. 6 p.c. Cum. Pref.	$100	113½
$3½	Chic. Mil. & St. P. Pref...	$100	147½
7	Cleve. & Pittsburgh......	$10	87
$1½	Clev., Cincin., Chic., & St. Louis Com.	$100	—
—	Erie 4 p.c. Non-Cum. 1st Pf.	—	39
—	Do. 4 p.c. do. 2nd Pf.	—	21
—	Gt. Northern Pref.	$100	135
$2½	Illinois Cen. Lsd. Lines ..	$100	94
—	Kansas City, Pitts & G. ..	$100	22
$3	L. Shore & Mich. Sth. C. (†	$100	180
—	Mex. Cen. Ltd. Com.	$100	6
—	Miss. Kan. & Tex. Pref...	$100	37½
—	N.Y., Pen. & O. 1st Mt. Tst. Ltd., Ord.	—	45½
4	Do. 1st Mort. Deb. Stk. ..	$100	93½
8	North Pennsylvania	$50	—
—	Northn. Pacific, Com.	$100	27
1½	Pitts. F. Wayne & Chic...	$100	176
—	Reading 1st Pref.	$50	26
—	Do. 2nd Pref.	$50	14
—	S. Louis & S. Fran. Com.	$100	7½
—	Do. 2nd Pref.	$100	27
6	St. Louis Bridge 1st Pref..	$100	107
3	Do. 2nd Pref.	$100	50
6	Tunnel Rail. of St. Louis	$100	107
$1½	St. Paul, Min. and Man...	$100	127½
—	Southern, Com.	$100	9½
—	Wabash, Common.........	$100	7½

AMERICAN RAILROAD BONDS. CURRENCY.

Last Div.	Name.	Price.
7	Albany & Susq. 1 Con. Mrt. 1906	122½
7	Allegheny Val. 1 Mt. 1910	127½
5	Burling., Cedar Rap. & N. 1 Mt. 1906	100½
5	Canada Southern 1 Mt. 1908	111
5	Chic. & N. West. Sk. Fd. Db. 1933	119½
5	Do. Deb. Coupon 1921	115½
6	Chicago & Tomah 1905	112½
5	Chic. Burl. & Q. Skge. Fd. 1901	102½
4	Do. Nebraska Ext....... —	100
6	Chic., Mil., & S. Pl., 1 Mt. S.W. Div. 1909	117½
7	Do. (S. Paul Div.) 1 Mt. 1902	132½
5	Do. (La Cross & D. 1919	112½
7	Do. 1 Mt. (Hast. & Dak.) 1910	132
5	Do. Chic. & Mis. Riv. 1 Mt. 1926	112½
5	Chic., Rock Is. and Pac. 1 Mt. Ext. 1934	106½
6	Det., G. Haven & Mil. Equip 1918	110
6	Do. do. Cons. Mt. 1918	105½
6	Ill. Cent., 1 Mt., Chic. & S. 1898	102½
7	Indianap. & Vin., 1 Mt. .. 1908	125
6	Do. do. 2 Mt. .. 1900	104½
6	Lehigh Val., Cons. Mt..... 1923	112½
—	Mexic. Cent., Ln. 2 Cons. Inc. —	7
7	N.Y. Cent. & H.R. Mt. Bonds 1903	119½
5	Do. Deb. 1904	112
6	Penns. Cons. S. F M. 1905	115
4	West Shore, 1 Mt. 2361	110

DITTO—GOLD.

Last Div.	Name.	Price.
6	Alabama Gt. Sthn. 1 Mt. .. 1908	112
5	Do. Mid. 1 1928	94½
4	Allegheny Val. Gen. Mt. .. 1942	109
4	Atch., Top., & S. Fé Gn. Mt. 1995	93½
3	Do. Adj. Mt. 1995	60½
5	Do. Equipt. Tmst. ...... —	104½
5	Atlantic & Dan. 1 Mt. 1950	94½
5	Baltimore & Ohio 1925	90
5	Do. Speyer's Tst. Recpts. 1925	90
5	Do. Cons. Mt. 1988	100
4½	Do. 4½ p.c. 1 Mt. Term. 1934	84½
4½	Do. Brown Shipley's Dep. Cts. —	84½
5	Balt. Belt 5 p.c. 1 Mort..... 1990	—
4½	Balt. & Ohio S.W. 1 Mt. .. 1990	102
4½	Do. 4½ p.c. 1 Cons. Mt. 1893 1993	77
2½	Do. Inc. Mt. 5 p.c. Cl. A —	31
—	Do. do. Cl. B —	12
5	Balt. & Ohio S.W. Term 5 p.c. 1942	99½
6	Balt. & Ptmac (Mn. L.) 1 Mt. 1911	124½
6	Do. do. (Tunnel) 1 Mt. 1911	123
4	Beech Creek 1 Mt. 1936	107
5	Do 2 Mort. 1936	116
4	Carthage & Adiron. 1 Mt... 1981	107½

American Railroad Bonds—Gold (*continued*):—

Last Div.	Name.	Price.
5	Cent. of Georgia 1 Mort. .. 1945	117½
5	Do. Cons. Mt. 1945	92½
5	Cent. of N. Jrsy. Gn. Mt... 1987	115
6	Central Pacific, 1 Mort. 1898	102½
—	Do. Speyer's Certs...... —	104½
5	Do. Land Grant 1900	102
5	Chesap. & Ohio 1st Cons. Mt. 1939	117
4½	Do. Gen. Mt. 1992	85
6	Chic. & W. Ind. Gen. Mt. Skg. Fd. 1932	122
5	Chic. Mil. & St. Pl. (Chic. & L. Sup.) 1 Mt. 1921	115
5	Do. Chic. & Pac. W. 1921	119½
5	Do. Wisc. & Minn. 1 Mt. 1921	114½
5	Do. Terminal Mt. 1914	114½
4	Do. General Mt. 1989	107
5	Chic. St. L. & N. Orleans.. 1951	122½
4	Do. 1 Mort. (Memphis) .. 1951	102½
4	Clevel., Cin., Chic. & St. L, 1 Mt. (Cairo) 1939	90
4	Do. 1 Mt. (Cinc., Wab., & Mich.) 1991	90
4	Do. 1 Col. Tst. Mt. (S. Louis) 1990	98½
4	Do. General Mt. 1993	82
4½	Clevel. & Mar. Mt. 1935	110
4½	Clevel. & Pittsburgh 1942	120
4½	Do. Series B. 1942	119
6	Colorado Mid. 1 Mt. 1936	68
—	Do. Bdhrs.' Comm. Certs. —	68
4	Dnvr. & R. Gde. 1 Cons. Mt. 1936	93
5	Do. Imp. Mort. 1928	90
4	Detroit & Mack. 1 Lien 1995	92½
5	E. Tennes., Virg., & Grgia. Cons. Mt. 1956	114½
5	Elmira, Cort., & Nthn. Mt. 1914	99½
4	Erie 1 Cons. Mt. Pr. Ln. .. 1996	94
3	Do. Gen. Lien 1996	73
6	Galvest., Harrisb., &c., 1 Mt.	107½
5	Georgia, Car. & N. 1 Mt. .. 1929	96
4½	Gd. Rpds. & Inda. Ex. 1 Mt. 1941	111½
5	Do. 1 Mt. (Muskegon) .. 1926	39½
3½	Illinois Cent. 1 Mt. 1951	104½
4	Do. 1952	106
4	Do. Cairo Bdge. .. 1950	102
4	Do. 1953	105
4	Do. General Mort. .. 1904	100
—	Kans. City, Pitts. & G. 1 M. 1923	83
3½	L. Shore & Mich. Southern 1997	109
4½	Lehigh Val. N.Y. 1 Mt. 1940	105
5	Lehigh Val. Term. 1 Mt. .. 1941	112½
5	Long Island 1931	114
5	Do. Deb. 1934	101
5	Do. (N. Shore Bch.) 1 Cons. Mt. 1932	96
6	Louisville & Nash. G. Mt. .. 1930	120
6	Do. 2 Mt. Sk. Fd. (S. & N. Alabama........ 1910	108
6	Do. 1 Mt. N. Orl. & Mb. 1930	122½
5	Do. 1 Mt. Coll. Tst. 1931	106
4	Do. Unified 1940	88
4½	Do. Mobile & Montgy. 1 Mt. 1945	107½
4	Manhattan Cons. Mt. 1990	100
4	Mexican Cent. Cons. Mt. .. 1911	68½
—	Do. 1 Cons. Inc, ...	18
6	Mexican Nat. 1 Mt. 1927	106
3	Do. 2 Mt. 6 p.c. Inc. A 1917	57
—	Do. do. B.. 1917	—
	Do. Matheson's Certs.	—
3	Michig. Cnt. (Battle Ck. & S.) 1 Mt. 1989	84
6	Minneap. & S. L. 1 Mt. Pacific Ext. 1921	120½
5	Do. 1 Consold. 1934	108½
4	Minne., Slt. S. M. & A. 1 Mt. 1926	100
5	Minneapolis Westn. 1 Mt... 1911	105½
4	Miss. Kans. & Tex. 1 Mt... 1990	89
4	Do. 2 do. 1990	66
4	Mobile & Birm. Mt. Inc.... 1945	38
5	Do. P. Lien 1945	88
4	Mohawk & Mal. 1 Mt...... 1991	110
5	Montana Cent. 1 Mt....... 1937	108½
5	Nashv., Chattan., & S. L. 1 Cons. Mt. 1928	104½
5	Nash., Flor., & Shff. Mt... 1937	90
4	N. Y. & Putnam 1 Cons. Mt. 1993	110
5	N. Y., Brooklyn, & Man. B. 1 Cons. Mt. 1935	109
4	N. Y. Cent. & Hud. R. Deb. Certs. 1890 1905	106
4	Do. Ext. Debt. Certs.... 1905	106
7	N. Y., L. Erie, & W. 1 Cons. Mt. (Erie) 1920	149½
7	Do. 1 Con. Mt. Fd. Coup. 1920	142½
5	N. Y., Onto., & W. Cons. 1 Mt. 1939	110
4	Do. 4 p.c. Refund. Mt.. 1992	100
5	N. Y. & Rockaway B. 1 Mt. 1927	104½
6	Norfolk & West. Gn. Mt.... 1931	128
6	Do. Imp. & Ext........ 1934	119½
4	Do. 1 Cons. Mt. ...... —	82
6	N. Pacific Gn. 1 Mt. Ld. Gt. 1921	120
4	Do. P. Ln. Rl. & Ld. Gt. —	99½
3	Do. Gn. Ln. Rl. & Ld. Gt. —	64½
5	Oregon & Calif. 1 Mt....... 1927	77
5	Oregon Rl. & Nav. Col. Tst. —	—
5	Oreg. Sh. Line & Utah Col. Trst. 5 p.c. G. Bonds 1919	—
6	Panama Skg. Fd. Subsidy.. 1910	105½
4½	Pennsylvania Rlrd. 1913	115
4	Do. Equip. Tst. Ser. A.. 1914	106
4	Do. Cons. Mt. 1943	115
4½	Penna. Company 1st Mort. 1921	116
5	Perkiomen 1 Mrt., 2nd ser.. 1918	90
4½	Pitts., C., C., & St. L. Con. Mt. G.B., Ser. A 1940-2	115
4	Do. Cons. Mort., Ser. D.. 1945	105
6	Pittsbgh., Cle., & Toledo .. 1922	105½
4	Reading, Phil., & R. Genl. 1997	86½
5	Richmond & Dan. Equip. .. 1909	99½
5	Rio Grande Junc. 1st Mort. 1939	90
4	Rio Grande West 1st Tst. Mt. 1939	84
6	St. Joseph & Gd. Island .. 1925	—
7	S. Louis Brid e 1st Mort .. 1925	135½

American Railroad Bonds (*continued*):

Last Div.	Name.	Price.
5	S. Louis Mchts. Bdge. Term. 1st Mort. 1930	104½
4	S. Louis S. West 1st Mort.. 1989	75½
—	Do. 4 p.c. 2nd Mort. Inc. 1989	28½
—	S. Louis Term. Cupples Sta. & Prop. 1st. Mrt. 4½ p.c. 1902-17	100
4½	St. Paul, Minn., & Manit. 1933	110
6	Do. do. 1933	127½
6	Shamokin, Sunbury, &c. 2 Mt. 1925	107
5	S. & N. Alabama Cons. Mt. 1936	92½
5	Southern 1 Cons. Coup. 1994	95
4	Do. E. Tennes Reorg. Lien .. 1938	98
6	S. Pacific of Cal. 1 Mt... 1905-12	113½
4½	Trml. Assn. of S. Louis 1 Mt. 1939	113½
5	Do. 1 Cons. Mt.......... 1944	119
5	Texas & Pac. 1 Mt. 2000	102
—	Do. 5 p.c. 2 Mt. Income 2000	30
5	Toledo & Ohio Cent. 1 Mt. West. Div. 1935	103½
4½	Toledo., Walhon., Val., & Ohio 1 Mt. 1931-3	109½
6	Union Pacific 1 Mt. 1896-9	101½
5	Do. Coll. Tverst.....	—
5	Union Pac., Linc., & Color. 1 Mt. 1918	—
4	United N. Jersey Gen. Mt... 1944	117½
6	Vicksbrg., Shrevept., & Pac. Pr. Ln. Mt. 1915	102½
5	Wabash 1 Mt. 1939	110
4	Wn. Pennsylvania Mt. 1928	109½
5	W. Virga. & Pittsbg. 1 Mt. 1990	84
5	Wheeling & L. Erie 1 Mt. (Wheelg. Div.) 5 p.c. 1928	82½
5	Do. Extd. Imp. Mt ... 1930	—
—	Do. do. Brown Shipley's Cts...	—
5	Willmar & Sioux Falls 1 Mt. 1938	111

STERLING.

Last Div.	Name.	Price.
6	Alabama Gt. Sthn. Deb..... 1906	106
5	Do. Gen. Mort. .. 1927-8	99
5	Alabama, N. Orl., Tex. & Pac. 5 p.c. "A" Dbs... 1910-40	99
50/	Do. do. "B" do. 1910-40	46
—	Do. do. "C" do.	20
—	Allegheny Valley 1910	135½
4	Atlantic 1st Leased Line Perp...	100
6	Baltimore and Ohio 1902	108
6	Do. do. 1910	116
5	Do. do. 1877........	94½
—	Do. Morgan's Certs. ..	94
4½	Do. do. 1933	80
6	Chicago & Alton Cons. Mt. 1903	111
5	Chic. St. Paul & Kan. City Priority	105
6	Eastn. of Massachusetts 1906	117½
5	Illinois Cent. Skg. Fd.	106
5	Do. 1905	108
3½	Do. 1950	100½
4	Do. 1 Mt. 1951	114
3	Do. 1 Mt. 1951	94
6	Louisville & Nash., M. C. & L. Div., 1 Mt. 1902	107
7	Do. 1 Mt. (Memphis & O.) 1901	111
47/4	Mexican Nat. "A" Certs. 5 p.c. Non. cum.	46
—	Do. "B" Certs.	10
6	N.Y. & Canada 1 Mt. 1904	111½
6	N. York Cent. & H.R. Mort. 1903	112
4½	N. York, Penns., & Ohio Pr. Ln. Extd. 1935	—
5	Do. Equip. Tst.	102
5	Do. 5 p.c. Equip. Tst. (1890)	102
6	Nrthn. Cent. Cons. Gen. Mt. ..	106
6	Pennsylvania Gen. Mt. 1910	128
6	Do. Cons. Skg. Fd. Mt. 1905	117
3½	Do. Cons. Mt. 1945	106
6	Phil. & Erie Cons. Mort.. 1920 (†	132½
6	Phil. & Reading Gen. Cons. Mort. 1911	127
6	Pittsbg. & Connells. Cons. 1926	111
—	Do. Morgan's Certs.....	111
4	St. Paul., Min., & Manitoba (Pac. Extn.) 1940	98
6	S. & N. Alabama 1903	107½
6	Union Pacific, Omaha Bridge 1896	—
6	Un. N. Jersey & C. Gen. Mt. 1901	111

FOREIGN RAILWAYS.

Last Div.	Name.	Paid.	Price.
4/	Alagoas, Ltd., Shs.	20	6
5	Do. Deb. Stk., Red. ..	100	55
6	Antofagasta, Ltd., Stk. ..	100	78
4	Do. Perp. Deb. Stk. ..	100	95
—	Arauco, Ld., Ord. Shs. ..	10	½
—	Do. 10 p.c. Cum. Pref.	10	1½
20/	Argentine Gt. W., Ld.,	20	14½
20/	Do. 5 p.c. Cum. Pref. Shs.	20	20½
4	Do. 1 Deb. Stk. .... (†	100	104½
6/0/0	Do. 6 p.c. 2 Db. Stk. Astg.	100	—
6/0/0	Do. do. Non-Astg.	100	—
1/0/0	Argentine N.E., Ltd., 6 p.c. Cum. Pref. Stk. ..	100	13
—	Do. 5 p.c. Deb. Stk., Red.	100	35½
2/	Arica and Tacna Shs. ..	20	1½
10/	Bahia & San Fcisco., Ld.,	20	12
6/	Do. Timbo. Bch. Shs.	20	5
12/	Bahia, Blanca, & N.W. Ln. Prf. Cum. 6 p.c. ..	100	63
4	Do. 4 p.c. 1 Deb. Stk., Red.	100	96
6	Barranquilla R. & P., Ld., 6 p.c. 1 Deb. Stk., Red.	100	95

Foreign Railways (*continued*):—

Last Div.	Name.	Paid.	Price.
3/	Bilbao Riv. & Cantabn., Ltd., Ord.	3	6
—	Bolivar, Ltd., Shs.	10	1½
6	Do. 6 p.c. Deb. Stk.	100	99½
4/	Brazil Gt. Southn. Ltd., 7 p.c. Cum. Pref.	20	1¼
6	Do. Perm. Deb. Stk	100	50½
6½	B. Ayres Gt. Southn., Ld., Ord. Stk.	100	157
5	Do. Pref. Stk.	100	140
4	Do. Deb. Stk.	100	118
30/	B. Ayres & Ensen. Port., Ltd., Ord. Stk.	100	56
5	Do. Cum. 1 Pref. Stk.	100	115
6/0/0	Do. 6p.c.Con. Pref.Stk.	100	98
4	Do. Deb. Stk., Irred.	100	106
9⅛	B. Ayres Northern, Ltd., Ord. Stk.	100	257½
12	Do. Pref. Stk.	100	315
5	Do. 5 p.c. Mt. Deb. Stk., Red.	100	112
3/15/6	B. Ayres & Pac., Ld., 7 p.c. 1 Pref. Stk. (Cum.)	100	105
4	Do. 1 Deb. Stk.	100	105
5/5/0	Do. 4½ p.c. 2 Deb. Stk.	100	94
1	B Ayres & Rosario, Ltd., Ord. Stk.	100	77
—	Do. New, £20 Shs.	20	22½
7/	Do. 7 p.c. Pref. Shs.	10	17½
7/	Do. Sunchales Ext.	10	15½
4	Do. Deb. Stk., Red.	100	109
12/	B. Ayres & Val. Trans., Ltd., 7 p.c. Cum. Pref.	20	7
4 p.c.	Do. 4 p.c. "A" Deb. Stk., Red.	100	73
—	Do. 6 p.c. "B" Deb. Stk., Red.	100	48
6/	B. Ayres Westn. Ld. Ord.	10	12
3/	Do. Def. Shs	10	8
5	Do. 5 p.c. Pref.	10	13½
4	Do. Deb. Stk	100	112
6	Cent.Arg.Deb.Sk. Rd.	100	163½
4	Do. Deb. Stk. Rd	100	112
6	Cent. Bahia L. Ord. Stk.	100	51½
6	Do. Deb. Stk., 1934	100	77½
5	Do. Deb. Stk., 1937	100	61
4/6	Cent. Uguy. East. Ext. L. Shs	10	5½
5	Do. Perm. Stk	100	109
3/	Do. Nthn. Ext. L. Sh.	10	4½
5	Do. Perm. Deb. Stk	100	106
3	Do. of Montev. Ltd., Ord. Stk	100	86
6	Do. Perm. Deb. Stk	100	141
8/	Conde d'Eu, Ltd. Ord.	20	7½
—	Cordba & Rosar., Ltd., 6 p.c. Pref. Shs.	100	51
4	Do. 1 Deb. Stk	100	97
7½/	Do. 6 p.c. Deb. Stk	100	91
—	Cordba Cent., Ltd., 5 p.c. Cu. 1 Pref. Stk	100	94
—	Do. 5 p.c. Non-Cum. 2 Pref. Stk	100	50
5	Do. Deb. Stk	100	125
—	Costa Rica, Ltd., Shs.	10	4
8/	Dna. Thrsa. Chris., Ltd., 7 p.c. Pref. Shs.	20	4½
20/	E. Argentine, Ltd	100	47
6	Do. Deb. Stk	100	108
1/1	Egyptn. Dlta. Lgt. Rys., Ltd., £10 Pref. Shs.	6	8½
—	Entre Rios, L., Ord. Shs.	5	½
—	Do. Cu. 5 p.c. Pref.	5	3½
6/	Gt. Westn. Brazil, Ltd.	20	11½
6	Do. Perm. Deb. Stk	100	94½
6	Do. Extn. Deb. Stk	100	84½
—	Int.-Oceanic Mex., Ltd., 7 p.c. Pref.	10	1½
4	Do. Deb. Stk	100	83
42/6	Do. 7 p.c. "A" Deb. Sk.	100	59
—	Do. 7 p.c. "B" Deb. Sk.	100	23
5/	La Guaira & Carac	10	7
5	Do. 5 p.c. Deb. Sk. Red.	100	102
8/4	Lembg.-Czern.-Jassy	30	24½
1/	Lima, Ltd.	20	2½
—	Manila Ltd. 7 p.c. Cu. Pf.	10	½
20/6½	Mexican and Pref. 6 p.c.	100	35
6	Do. Perp. Deb. Stk.	100	139
1/0/0	Mexican Sthrn., Ld., Ord.	100	25
—	Do. 4 p.c. 1 Db.Stk. Rd.	100	87
—	Do. 4 p.c. 2 do.	100	63
—	Mid. Urgy., Ltd.	100	19½
5	Do. Deb. Stk	100	63
12/	Minas & Rio, Ltd.	20	11½
5/2	Namur & Liege	20	12½
11/6	Do. Pref.	20	28
5/	Natal & Na. Cruz, Ld., 7 p.c. Cum Pref.	20	7½
—	Nitrate Ltd., Ord.	10	6½
—	Do. 7 p.c. Pr. Con. Or.	10	5
—	Do. Def. Conv. Ord.	10	1½
7/	N.-E. Urgy., Ltd., Ord.	10	14½
7/	Do. 7 p.c. Pref.	10	15
—	N.-W. Argentine Ld., 7 p.c. Pref.	10	3½
6	Do. 6 p.c. 1 Deb. Stk.	100	114
—	Do. 2 Deb. Stk.	100	94
—	N.W. Uruguay 6 p.c. 1 Pref. Stk.	100	17
—	Do. 5 p.c. 2 Pref. Stk.	100	7½
6	Do. 6 p.c. Deb. Stk.	100	76½
16/	Ottoman (Sm. Ald.)	20	16
—	Paraguay Cntl., Ld., 5 p.c. Perm. Deb. Stk.	100	11
—	Piræus, Ath., & Pelo.	275	1
5/	Pto. Alegre & N. Hambg. Ld., 7 p.c. Pref. Shs.	20	4½
6	Do. Mt. Deb. Stk. Red.	100	77½
—	Puerto Cabello & Val. Ld.	10	1½
5	Recife & S. Francisco	100	74
14/	R. Claro S. Paulo, Ld., Sh.	10	21½
5	Do. Deb. Stk.	100	130
5/	Royal Sardinian Ord	10	11½
5/	Royal Sardinian Pref.	10	12½
5/	Sambre & Meuse	20	19
5/6	Do. Pref.	10	12
28/	San Paulo Ld.	20	37½
2/9½	Do. New Ord. £10 sh.	4	8½
2/	Do. 5 p.c. Non.Cm.Pref.	10	12½
5½	Do. Deb. Stk. †	100	136½
5	Do. 5 p.c. Deb. Stk	100	129
—	S. Fé & Cordova, Gt. Sthn., Ld., Shares	100	57
6	Do. Perp. Deb. Stk.	100	121
3/2½	S. Austrian	20	7½
10/	Sthn. Braz. R. Gde. do Sul, Ld.	20	9
6	Do. 6 p.c. Deb. Stk.	100	75
4	Swedish Centl., Ld., 4 p.c. Deb. Stk.	100	108
5	Do. Pref.	100	99
1/9	Taltal, Ld.	5	3
4/	Uruguay Nthn., Ld. 7 p.c. Pfd. Stk.	100	8
3½	Do. 5 p.c. Deb. Stk.	100	23
—	Villa Maria & Rufino, Ld., 6 p.c. Pref. Shs.	100	20
4	Do. 4 p.c. 1 Deb. Stk.	100	77
6/0/0	Do. 6 p.c. 2 Deb. Stk.	100	49
5/9	West Flanders	8½	22
5/6	Do. 5½ p.c. Pref.	10	18
3/	Wstn. of Havana, Ld.	10	5

FOREIGN RAILWAY OBLIGATIONS

Per Cent.	Name.	Price.
6	Alagoas Ld., 6 p.c. Deb., Rd.	85½
£1	Alcoy & Gandia, Ld., 5 p.c. Debs., Red.	25
5	Arauco., Ld., 5 p.c. 1st Mt., Rd.	68
6	Do. 6 p.c. Mt. Deb., Rd.	48½
6	Brazil G. Sthn., L., Mt. Dbs., Rd.	83
6	Do. Mt. Dbs. 1893, Rd.	52½
5½	Campos & Caran. Dbs., Rd.	76
6	Central Bahia, L., Dbs., Rd.	93½
5½	Conde d'Eu, L., Dbs., Rd.	77
6	Costa Rica, L., 1st Mt. Dbs., Rd.	110
6	Do. 2nd Dbs., Rd.	96
5	Do. Prior Mt. Db., Rd.	107
6	Cucuta Mt. Dbs., Rd.	100
5½	Donna Thrsa. Cris., L., Dbs., Rd.	75
3	Eastn. of France, £20 Dbs., Rd.	19
4	Egyptn. Delta Light, L., Db., Rd.	100
—	Espito. Santo & Cara. 5 p.c. Stl. Dbs., Rd.	38
4	Gd. Russian Nic., Rd.	101
5	Inter-Oceanic Mex., L., 5 p.c. Pr. Ln. Dbs., Rd.	104
3	Ital. 3 p.c. Bds. A & B, Rd.	57½
—	Ituana 6 p.c. Debs., 1918	72½
—	Leopoldina, 6 p.c. Dbs. £50 Bds.	24
—	Do. do. Comms. Cert.	24
—	Do. 5 p.c. Stg. Dbs. (1888), Rd.	35
—	Do. do. Comm. Certs.	35
—	Do. 5 p.c. Stg. Dbs. (1890), Rd.	24
—	Do. do. Comms. Certs.	24
—	Macahé & Cam. 5 p.c. Dbs., Rd.	35
—	Do. do. Comms. Certs.	35
—	Do. (Cantagallo), 5 p.c., Red.	35
—	Do. do. Comm. Certs.	35
—	Manila Ltd., 6 p.c. Deb., Red.	23
6	Do. Prior Lien Mt., Rd.	104
6	Do. Series "B," Rd.	79
7	Matanzas & Sab., Rd.	101½
6	Minas & Rio, L., 6 p.c. Dbs., Rd.	101
5	Mogyana 5 p.c. Deb. Bds., Rd.	102
5	Moscow-Jaros., Rd.	106
5½	Natal & Na. Cruz Ltd., 5½ p.c. Debs., Red.	88½
5	Nitrate, Ltd. Mt. Bds., Red.	90
3	Nthn. France, Red.	19
4	N. of S. Af. Rep. (Trnsvl.) Gu. Bds. Red.	97
3	Nthn. of Spain £20 Pri. Obs. Red.	8½
6	Ottmn. (Smy to A.)(Kujk) Asnt. Debs., Red.	108½
6	Ottmn. (Seraik.) Asg. Debs. Red.	108½
6	Ottmn. (Seraik.) Non-Asg. D., Rd	108½
5	Ottmn. Kuyjk. Ext. Red.	108
5	Ottmn. Serkeuy. Ext. Red.	103½
5	Ottmn. Tireh Ext. 1910	98
5	Ottmn. Debs, 1886, Red.	97½
5	Do. 1888, Red. 1935	96½
5	Do. 1893, Red. 1935	96½
5	Ottmn. of Anlia. Debs., Rd.	93
5	Do. Ser. II	89
4	Ottomn. Smyr. & Cas. Ext. Bds., Red.	82½
3	Paris, Lyon & Medit. (old sys., £20), Red.	19
3	Paris, Lyon & Medit. (new sys., £20), Red.	19
50/	Piræus, At. & Pelp., 6 p.c. 1st Mt. Bds., Red.	88½
3	Do. 5 p.c. Mt. Bds., Red.	61½
4	Pretoria-Pietbg., Ltd., Red.	94
7	Puerto Cab. & Val., Ltd., 1st Mt. Debs., Red.	95
—	Rio de Jano. & Nthn., Ltd., 6 p.c. £100 Deb., Red.	24
—	Rio de Jano. (Gr. Para.), 5 p.c. 1st Mt. St. £100 Debs., Red.	24
3	Roya Sardinian, A, Rd. £20	12
3	Roya Sardinian, B., Rd. £20	12
5	Ryl. Trns.-Afric. 5 p.c. 1st Mt. £100 Bds., Red.	61
7	Sagua La Grande, B pRd.	98
4	Sa. Fe & Cor. G.S., Ld. Pr. Ln. Bds.	101
5	Sa. Fe, 5 p.c. 2nd Reg. Dbs.	83
3	South Austrian, £20 Red.	15½
3	South Austrian, (Ser. X.)	15½
3	South Italian £20 Obs. (Ser. A to G), Red.	12½
3½	S.W. of Venez. (Barq.), Ltd., 7 p.c. 1st Mt. £100 Debs.	57½
5	Taltal, Ltd., 5 p.c. 1st Ch. Debs., Red.	99
5	Utd. Rwys. Havana, Red.	78
3	Wtrn. of France, £20 Red.	19
6	Wrn. B. Ayres St. Mt. Debs., 1900	111
6	Wrn. B. Ayres, Reg. Cert.	109
5	Do. Mt. Bds.	123
6	Wtrn. of Havna., Ld. Mt. Dbs., Rd.	102
7	Wrn. Ry. San Paulo Red.	101
—	Wrn. Santa Fé, 7 p.c. Red.	41
4/7	Zafra & Huelva, 3 p.c. Red.	3

BANKS.

Div.	Name.	Paid.	Price.
1/9½	Agra, Ltd.	6	2½
4/2½	Anglo-Argentine, Ltd., £9	7	5½
8½ fls.	Anglo-Austrian	120f	14
6/	Anglo-Californian, Ltd., £20 Shares	10	11
4/	Anglo-Egyptian, Ltd., £15	5	5½
3/6	Anglo-Foreign Bkg., Ltd.	7	8
2/	Anglo-Italian, Ltd.	5	7½
7/6	Bk. of Africa, Ltd., £18¾	6¼	11
20/	Bk. of Australasia	40	53
8/	Bk. of Brit. Columbia	20	19½
25/	Bk. of Brit. N. America	50	65
7/6	Bk. of Egypt, Ltd., £25	12½	19
5/	Bk. of Mauritius, Ltd.	10	10
18/	Bk. of N. S. Wales	20	38
4 p.c.	Bk. of N. Zland. Gua. Stk.	100	103
6/	Bk. of Roumania, £20 Shs.	6	7½
2/6	Tarapaca & Ldn., Ltd., £10	5	3½
—	Bque. Fse. de l'Afr. du S.	100f	3½
f.12.50	Bque. Internatle. de Paris	20	24
6/	Brit. Bk. of S. America, Ltd., £20 Shares	10	11
16/	Capital & Ctics., L., £50	10	39
16/	Chart. of India, &c.	20	30½
9/	City, Ltd., £40 Shares	10	20½
13/	Colonial, £100 Shares	30	23
10/	Delhi and London, Ltd.	25	—
3/	German of London, Ltd.	10	11
25/	Hong-Kong & Shanghai	28½	45
4/	Imperl. of Persia	6½	3½
10/	Imperl. Ottoman, £20 Shs	10	12½
9/	Intrnatl. of Ldn., Ld., £20	15	9½
10/	Ionian, Ltd.	25	15
12/	Lloyds, Ltd., £50 Shs.	8	29½
10/	Ldn. & Brazil, Ltd., £20	10	18
44/	Ldn. & County, Ltd., £80	20	105
5/	Ldn. & Hanseatic, L., £20	10	11
20/	Ldn. & Midland, L., £60	12½	54
8/9	Ldn. & Provin., Ltd., £10	5	23
30/	Ldn. & Riv. Plate, L., £25	15	51
2/1½	Ldn. & San Fcisco, Ltd.	7	4½
24/	Ldn. & Sth. West., L., £50	20	70
24/	Ldn. & Westmins., L., £100	20	59
3/	Ldn. of Mex. & S. Amer., Ltd., £10 Shs.	6	5½
15/	Ldn. Joint Stk., L., £100	15	34½
9/7	Ldn., Paris & Amer., L. £20	16	26
1/7½	Merchant Bkg., L., £9	4	2½
6/3	Metropn, Ltd., £50 Shs.	5	14
9/	National, Ltd., £50 Shs.	10	20
4/5	Natl. of Mexico, $100 Shs.	$40	12
1/3	National of N. Z., L., £7½	2½	2½
3/	National S. Afric. Rep.	10	14½
18/10½	National Provcl. of Eng., Ltd., £75 Shs.	10½	49
21/7½	Do. do. £60 Shs.	12	56½
6/3	North Eastn., Ltd., £20 Shs	6	15
19/	Parr's, Ld., £100 Shs.	20	93½
12/6	Prov. of Ireland, L., £100	12½	28½
40/	Stand. of S. Afric., L., £100	25	68½
12/6	Union of Australia, L., £75	25	30
4 p.c.	Do. do. Ins. Stk. Dep. 1900	100	103
15/6	Union of Ldn., Ltd., £100	15½	35

BREWERIES AND DISTILLERIES.

Div.	Name.	Paid.	Price.
4½	Albion Prp. 1 Mt. Db. Sk.	100	115
4	All Saints', L., Db. Sk. Rd.	100	99
6	Allsopp, Ltd	100	165
6	Do. Cum. Pref	100	158
4½	Do. Deb. Stk., Red.	100	117
3½	Do. Deb. Stk., Red.	100	101
4½	Alton & Co., L., Db., Rd	100	106
4½	Do. Mt. Bds., 1896	100	105
8/	Arnold, Perrett, Ltd.	10	7
6	Do. Cum. Pref.	10	10
4½	Do. 1 Mt. Db. Stk., Rd.	100	106
5½	Arrol, A., & Sons, L., Cum. Pref. Shs.	10	10½
4½	Do. 1 Mt. Db. Stk., Rd.	100	106
6	Backus, 1 Mt. Db., Red.	100	59½
4	Barclay, Perk., L., Cu. Pf.	10	11½
3½	Do. Mt. Db. Stk., Red.	100	111
—	Barnsley, Ltd.	10	11
6	Do. Cum. Pref.	10	13
1/	Barrett's, Ltd	2½	1½
1/3	Do. 5 p.c. Pref.	2½	2½
3/	Bartholomay, Ltd.	10	4½
8	Do. Cum. Pref.	10	8½
6	Do. Deb.	100	103½
5	Bass, Ratcliff, Ltd., Cum. Pref. Stk. †	100	147½
4½	Do. Mt. Db. Stk., Rd.	100	125
4	Bell, John, Ltd., 1 Mt. Deb. Stk., Red.	100	102
2/6	Benskin's, L., Cum. Pref.	5	5½
4½	Do. 1 Mt. Db. Stk Red.	100	110
4½	Do. "B" Deb. Sk. Rd.	100	109
7/	Bentley's Yorks., Ltd.	10	11
6	Do. Cum. Pref.	10	12½
4½	Do. Mt. Debs., Red.	100	109
4½	Do. do. 1 92, Red.	100	109
—	Bieckert's, Ltd.	20	2
5	Do. Debs., Red.	100	57½
—	Birmingham, Ltd., 6 p.c. Cum. Pref.	5	2½
4½	Do. Mt. Debs., Red.	50	40½
5½	Boardman's, Ld., Cm. Pf.	10	9
4½	Do., Perp. 1 Mt. Db. Sk. †	100	102½
4½	Brakspear, L., 1 D. Stk. Rd	100	111
4	Brandon's, L., 1 D. Stk. R. †	100	103½
17/	Bristol (Georges) Ltd.	10	47
6	Do. Cum. Pref.	10	28
5	Do. Mt. Db. Sk. 1886 Rd.	100	115½
—	Bristol United, Ltd.	10	36
6	Do. Cum. Pref.	10	16½
4½	Do. Db. Sk. Rd.	100	126
5½	Buckley's, L., C. Pre-pref.	10	11
4½	Do. 1 Mt. Db. Stk. Rd.	100	105½
4	Bullard & Sns, L., D. Sk. R.	100	107
6	Bushell, Watk., L., C. Pf.	10	13½
4½	Do. 1 Mt. Db. Sk. Rd.	100	112
5	Camden, Ltd., Cum. Pref.	10	11½
4½	Do. 1 Mt. Db. Sk. Rd.	100	109
5½	Cameron, Ltd., Cm. Pf.	10	13
4½	Do. Mort. Deb. Stk.	100	108
3½	Do. Perp. Mt. Db. Sk.	100	100½
5	Campbell, J stone, L., C. Pf.	5	5½
4½	Do. 4½ p.c. 1 Mt. Db. Sk.	100	104
4	Campbell, Praed, L., Per. 1 Mort. Deb. Stk.	100	105
4	Cannon, L., Mt. Db. Stk.	100	111
4	Do. "B" Deb. Stk.	100	104
5	Castlemaine, L., 1 Mt. Dbs.	100	94
3½	Charrington, Ltd., Mort. Deb. Stk. Red.	100	109
2/	Cheltnhm. Orig., Ltd.	5	7
6	Do. Cum. Pref.	5	8
4	Do. Debs. Red.	100	107
10/	Chicago, Ltd.	10	3½
6	Do. Debs.	100	87½
—	Cincinnati, Ltd.	10	½
8	Do. Cum. Pref.	10	1½
10/	City of Baltimore	10	4
10/	Do. 8 p.c. Cum. Pref	10	8
14/	City of Chicago, Ltd.	10	1½
8	Do. Cum. Pref.	10	6½
8	City of London, Ltd.	100	198
5	Do. Cum. Pref.	100	140
4	Do. Mt. Deb. Stk., Rd.	100	113½
2/6	Colchester, Ltd.	5	4½
7	Do. Pref.	5	6½
4½	Do. Deb. Stk., Red.	100	110
5	Combe, Ltd., Cum. Pref.	10	14½
4	Do. Mt. Db. Stk, Rd.	100	112
3½	Do. Perp. Deb. Stk.	100	107
5	Comm'cial, L., D. Sk., Rd.	100	107½
5	Courage, L., Cm. Pref. Shs.	100	139½
4	Do. Irr. Mt. Deb. Stk.	100	130
3½	Do. Irr. "B" Mt. Db. Sk.	100	106
6	Daniell & Sons, Ltd.	10	7
7	Do. Cum. Pref.	10	12
4½	Do. 1 Mt. Perp. Db. Sk.	100	108½
4½	Do. "B" Deb. Stk.	100	99½
10d.	Dartford, Ltd.	5	5½
10d.	Do. Cum. Pref.	5	5½
4	Do. 1 Mt. Db. Sk. Rd.	100	101
4	Davenport, Ld., 1 D. Stk. †	100	101½
10/	Denver United, Ltd.	10	3½
8	Do. Cum. Pref.	10	8½
6	Do. Debs	100	98½
4½	Deuchar, L., 1 D. Sk., Rd.	100	108
8/	Distillers, Ltd.	10	25½
4½	Do. Mt. Db. Stk., Rd.	100	115½
—	Dublin Distillers, Ltd.	5	1½
6/	Do. Cum. Pref.	5	4½
4½	Do. Irr. Deb. Stk.	100	—
5	Eadie, Ltd., Cum. Pref.	10	11½
4	Do. Irr. 1 Mt. Db. Sk.	100	108
10/	Edinbgh. Utd., Ltd.	10	13
6	Do. Cum. Prf.	10	13½
5	Do. 1 Mt. Dbs. †	100	110½
4	Eldridge, Pope, L. D. St. R.	100	110
3/	Emerald & Phœnix, Ltd.	10	1½
5	Do. Cum. Pref.	10	6
6	Empress Ltd., C. Pf.	10	11½
4½	Do. Mt. Deb. Stk.	100	101
10/	Farnham, Ltd.	10	15½
6	Do. Cum. Pref.	10	15
4	Fenwick, L., 1 D. Sk., Rd.	100	103
4	Flower & Sons, Irr. D. Sk.	100	113
4	Friary, L., 1 Db. Stk., Rd. †	100	105½
4	Do. 1 "A" Db. Sk., Rd	100	102
4½	Groves, L., 1 Db. Sk., Rd	100	110
24	Guinness, Ltd.	100	580
6	Do. Cum. Prf. Stk	100	193½
5	Do. Deb. Stk., Red.	100	123
6	Hall's Oxford L., Cm. Pf.	5	5½
6/	Hancock, Ld., Cm. Pf. Ord.	10	14
—	Do. Def. Ord.	10	17½

Breweries, &c. (*continued*) :—

Div.	Name.	Paid.	Price.
6	Hancock, Ld., Cum. Pref.	10	15½
4	Do. 1 Deb. Stk., Rd.	100	113
5	Hoare, Ltd. Cum. Pref.	10	13¼
5	Do. "A" Cum. Pref.	10	12¼
4	Do. Mt. Deb. Stk., Rd.	100	110
3½	Do. do. do. Rd.	100	104
4/6	Hodgson's, Ltd.	5	9½
5	Do. 1 Mt. Db., Red.	—	120½
4	Do. 2 Mt. Db., 1906	—	102
4½	Hopcraft & N., Ltd., 1 Mt. Deb. Stk., Red.	100	102
5	Huggins, Ltd., Cm. Prf.	10	12½
4½	Do. 1st D. Stk. Rd.	100	112
4½	Do. "B" Db. Stk. Rd.	100	110
8/	Hull, Ltd.	10	17
7	Do. Cum. Pref.	10	15
4½	Ind, Coope, L., D.Sk., Rd.	100	119
4	Do. "B" Mt. Db. Stk. Rd.	100	115
8	Indiannapolis, Ltd.	10	3½
8	Do. Cm. Prf.	10	9
5/	Jones, Frank, Ltd.	10	4
7½	Do. Cum. Pref.	10	8
5	Do. 1st Mort. Debs.	100	94½
4/	J. Kenward & Ct., Ltd.	5	5½
4½	Kingsbury, L., 1 D.Sk., Rd	100	107½
4	Lacon, L., D. Stk., Red.	100	108
4	Do. Irrd. "B" D. Sk.	100	107
4	Lascelles, Ltd.	5	10½
6	Do. Cum. Pref.	5	7½
5	Leney, Ltd., Cum. Pref.	10	11½
4	Do. 1 Mt. Db. Stk. Rd.	100	104
17/	Lion, Ltd., £25 shares	17	49½
6	Do. New £10 shares	6	17½
6	Do. Perp. Pref.	20	31
4	Do. B. Mt. Db. Sk. Rd.	100	110
4½	Lloyd & Y., Ltd., 1 Mt. Deb. Stk., Rd.	100	98½
4½	Locke & S., Ltd., Irr. 1st Mt. Deb. Stk.	100	100
4½	Lovibond, Ltd., 1st Mt. Deb. Stk., Rd.	100	99½
8/	Manchester, Ltd.	10	17½
7	Do. Cum. Pref.	10	17
5	Marston, J., L., Cm. Prf.	10	10½
4	Do. 1 Mt. Db. Sk., Rd.	100†	101½
9/	Massey's Burnley, Ltd.	10	16
6	Do. Cum. Pref.	10	14½
4½	McCracken, Ltd., 1 Mt. Deb., 1908	100	64
5	McEwan, Ltd., Cm. Pref.	10	15½
5	Meux, Ltd., Cum. Pref.	10	14½
4	Do. Mt. Db. Stk. Red.	100	113
4½	Michell & A., Ltd., 1 Mt. Deb. Stk. Red.	100	105
4½	MileEndDist.Db.Sk.Rd.	100	108
14/	Milwaukee & Chic., Ltd.	10	1½
4/	Do. Cum. Pref.	10	6½
4½	Michell, Toms, L., Db.	50	55
6	Morgan, Ltd., Cum. Pref.	10	14½
10/	Nalder & Coll., Ltd.	10	31
6	Do. Cum. Pref.	10	16
4½	Do. Deb. Red.	100	113
3/	New Beeston, Ltd.	5	4
2/9	Do. Cum. Pref.	5	4½
4	Do. Mt. Deb. Stk. Red.	100	95½
12/	Newcastle, Ltd.	10	19½
6	Do. Cum. Pref.	10	14½
5	Do. 1 Mt. Deb., 1911	100	110½
4	Do. "A" Deb. Stk. Red.	100	106
6/	New England, Ltd	10	5
8	Do. Cum. Pref.	10	9¾
6	Do. Debs. Red	100	103½
4	New London, L., 1 D.Sk.	100	103
7/2	New Westminster, Ltd.	4	9¾
2/4½	Do. Pref.	4	6½
5	New York, Ltd.	10	1
18/	Do. 8 p.c. Cum. Pref.	10	3½
6	Do. 1 Mt. Deb. Red.	100	83½
5	Noakes, Ld., Cum. Pref.	10	12
4	Do 1 Mt. Db. Stk., Rd.	100	106
4½	Norfolk, L., "A" D.Sk.Rd.	100	106
20/	Northampton, Ld.	10	17
7	Do. Cum. Pref.	10	15½
6	Do. Cum. Pref.	10	13
5	Do. 1 Mt. Per. Db. Sk.	100	127
4	Nth. East., L., 1 D.Sk.Rd.	100	101
4½	N. Worcesters., L. Per. 1 Mort. Deb. Stock	100	94½
6	Nottingham, L., Cm. Prf.	10	11
5	Do. 1 Mt. Deb. Stk., Red.	100	115
17/4	Do. "B" do. Red.	50	111½
6/	Ohlsson' Cape, Ld.	5	16
7	Do. Cum. Pref.	5	8½
4½	Do. 2nd Cum. Pref.	5	5½
5	Do. Deb. Stk., Red.	100	112
4½	Oldfield, L., 1 Mt. Db. Stk.	100	103
6	Page & Overt., L., Cm. Prf.	10	13½
4½	Do. 1 Mt. Dbs., Red.	100	110
10/	Parker's Burslem, Ltd.	10	25
6	Do. Cum. Pref.	10	15
4	Do. 1 Mt. Db. Stk., Red.	100	111
4	Persse, Ld., 1 Mt. Db. Rd.	100	93
4	Phipps, L., Irr. 1 Db. Stk.	100	115
5	Plymouth, L., Min. Cu. Pf.	10	13½
4½	Do. Mt. Deb. Stk., Red.	100	104½
4½	Pryor, Reid, L., 1 D.S., R.†	100	105½
5	Reid's, Ld., Cm. Pref. Stk.	100	140½
4	Do. Mt. Deb. Stk., Red.	100	113
3½	Do. "B" Mt. Db. Stk., Rd.	100	103
5	Rhondda Val., L., Cu. Pf.	10	11
4½	Do. 1 Mt. Deb. Stk., Rd.	100	109
5	Robinson, Ld., Cum. Pref.	10	11½
4½	Do. 1 Mt. Perp. Db. Stk.	100	112
4/	Rochdale, Ltd.	10	5½
4½	Do. 1 Mt. Deb. Stk.	100	96½
7/	Royal, Brentford, Ltd.	10	19
6	Do. Cum. Pref.	10	13½
4½	Do. 1 Mt. Dbs. Red	100	112
6/	St. Louis, Ltd.	10	4
8	Do. Cum. Pref.	10	8¾
14/	St. Pauli, Ltd.	10	10
7	Do. Cum. Pref.	10	11½
4½	Salt (T.), L., 1 Db. Sk. Rd.	100	111
4½	Do "B" Db. Stk. Red.	100	108

Breweries, &c. (*continued*) :—

Div.	Name.	Paid.	Price.
6/7	San Francisco, Ltd	10	½
8/	Do. 8 p.c. Cum. Pref.	10	¾
4½	Savill Brs., L., D. Sk. Rd.	100	116
4½	Scarboro., Ltd., 1 Db. Stk.	100	105
4	Shaw (Hy.), Ltd., 1 Mt. Db. Stk., Red.	100	104
22/	Showell's, Ltd.	10	32½
7	Do. Cum. Pref.	10	17½
3/	Do. Gua. Shs.	5	7½
4½	Do. Mt. Db. Stk., Red.	100	—
4	Simonds, L., 1 D. Sk., Rd.	100	111
5½	Simson & McP., L., Cu. Pf.	10	9½
4½	Do. 1 Mt. Deb. Stk.	100	100
12/	Smith, Garrett, L., £20 Shs	10	15½
5	Do. Cum. Pref.	20	26
4½	Do. Mt. Db. Stk., Red.	100	—
5	Smith's, Tadcster, L., CPf	10	11½
4½	Do. Deb. Stk., Red.	100	112
4	Do. Deb. Stk., Red.	100	108
4½	Star, L., 1 M. Db. Stk., Rd.	100	104
4	Steward & P., L., 1 D. Sk.	100	113
9/	Strettons Derby, Ltd.	10	12½
6	Do. Cum. Pref.	10	13
4	Do. Irr. 1 Mt. Db. Stk.	100	101½
4½	Strong, Romsey, L., 1 D.S.	100	114
5	Stroud, L., Db. Sk., Rd.	100	111½
4½	Tadcaster To'er, L., D.Sk.	100	112
8/	Tamplin, Ltd	10	22
6	Do. Cum. Pref.	100	15
4	Do. "A" Db. Sk., Rd.	10	107
6	Thorne, Ltd., Cum. Pref.	10	14½
4	Do. Deb. Stk., Red.	100	103½
16/	Threlfall, Ltd.	10	49
6	Do. Cum. Pref.	10	17
5	Do. 1 Mt. Dbs., Red.	100	116
4	Tollemache, L., D. Sk. Rd.	100	105
4	Truman, Hanb., D. Sk., R.	100	110
3	Do. "B" Mt. Db. Sk., Rd.	100	95
10/	United States, Ltd.	10	10½
8	Do. Cum. Pref.	10	12½
6	Do. 1 Mt. Deb	100	107½
6/	Walker & H., Ld., Cm. Prf.	10	11½
4½	Do. 1 Mt. Deb. Stk., Red.	100	107
5	Walker, Peter, Ld. Cm. Prf.	10	14
4	Do. 1 Mt. Dbs. Red.	100	111
4	Wallingford, L., D. Sk. Rd.	100	107
6	Watney, Ld., Cm. Prf. Sk.	100	170
5	Do. Mt. Db. Sk., Rd.	100	117½
4½	Do. "B" Mt. Db. Sk., Rd.	100	111
5	Watney, D., Ld., Cm. Prf.	10	12½
4½	Do. 1 Mt. Db. Stk.	100	108
5	Wenlock Ltd., Pref.	10	12½
4	Do. 1 Mt. Db. Sk., Rd.	100	107
5	West Cheshire, L., Cu. Pf.	10	10¾
4	Do. Irred. 1 Mt. Db. Sk.	100	100
4½	Whitbread, L., Cu. Pf. Sh.	100	125½
4	Do. Db. Stk., Red.	100	112
3½	Do. "B" Db. Stk., Rd.	100	103
9/	Wolverhmpton & D. Ld.	10	15
6	Do. Cum. Pref.	10	13
4½	Do. 1 Mt. Dbs., Red.	100	108
5½	Worthington, Ld., Cm. Prf.	10	15½
5½	Do. Cum. "B" Pref.	10	13½
4½	Do. Mt. Db. Sk., Rd.	100	113
3½	Do. Irr. "B" Db. Stk.	100	103
10/	Yates's Castle, Ltd.	10	12½
5	Do. Cum. Pref.	10	11
5	Younger W., L., Cu. Pf. Sh.	100	138½

CANALS AND DOCKS.

Last Div.	Name.	Paid.	Price.
4½	Alexandra Con. Stk. "B"	100	112½
4½	Do. 1 Prf Con. Stk. "A"	100	128½
4	Do. Perp. Deb. Stk.	100	132½
4	Birmingham Canal	100	146
—	E. & W. India Dock	100	23½
4	Do. Deb. Stk.	100	111
85/	Do. Def. Deb. Stk.	100	91
3½	Do. 1st Mt. Certs.	100	111
4	Do. Mt. Bds. (1885)	—	101
40/	G. Junction Ord. Shs.	100	151½
6/	Do. do. Pref.	10	19
4½	King's Lynn Per. Db. Stk.	100	120½
2½	Leeds & Lpool Canal	100	67
2½	Lndn & St. Kath. Dks.	100	57½
4½	Do. Pref.	100	138½
4½	Do. Pref., 1878	100	134½
4½	Do. Pref., 1882	100	130
4	Do. Deb. Stk.	100	134
—	Mchester Ship C. 5 p.c. Pf.	10	1½
3½	Do. 1st Perp. Mt. Deb.	100	98
—	Milford Dks. Db. Stk. "A"	100	20
2	Millwall Dk.	100	61
5	Do. Perp. Pref.	100	145½
4½	Do. Pref.	100	108½
5	Do. New Per. Prf., 1887	100	128½
5	Do. Per. Deb. Stk.	100	152½
4/	Newhaven Har.	10	14½
2	N. Metropolitan	100	65
5	Sharpness Nw. Pf. "A" Sk.	100	144½
4	Do. Deb. Stk.	100	120½
4	Sheffield & S. Yorks Nav. 4½ p.c. Pref. Stk.	100	117½
36.432	Suez Canal	20	134½
5	Surrey Comcl. Dok. Ord.	100	150½
5	Do. Min. 4 p.c. Pref. "A"	110	152½
5	Do. Pref. "B"	100	150½
5	Do. do. "C"	100	150
5	Do. do. "D"	100	145½
4½	Do. Deb. Stk.	100	154½

COMMERCIAL, INDUSTRIAL, &c.

Last Div.	Name.	Paid.	Price.
5	Accles, L., 1 Mt. Db., Red.	100	87½
5/	Aërated Bread, Ltd.	1	13
—	African Gold Recovery, L.	1	¾
2/	Aluminium, L., "A" Shs.	1	2½
4½	Do. 1 Mt. Db. Stk., Red.	100	99
5½	Amelia Nitr., L., 1 Mort. Deb., Red.	100	84½
7	Anglo-Chil. Nitrate, Ltd., Cum. Pref.	10	7½
4½	Do. Cons. Mt. Bds., Red.	100	82½
4½	Anglo-Russian Cotton, Ld., 1 Charge Debs., Red.	100	98
3/9	Angus (G., & Co., L.), £10	7½	17
6/	Apollinaris, Ltd.	10	13½
5/	Do. 5 p.c. Cum. Pref.	10	11½
4	Do. Irred. Deb. Stock	100	108
8/	Appleton, French, & S., L.	5	1
3/	Argentine Meat Pres., L., 7 p.c. Pref.	10	2½
5	Argentine Refinry, Db. Rd.	100	98
2/2	Armstrong, Whitw., Ltd.	1	3
4	Do. Cum. Pref.	5	6½
5	Artisans', Labr. Dwllgs., L.	100	127½
4½	Do. Non-Cm. Prf., 1879	100	132½
4½	Do. do. 1884	100	132½
—	Asbestos & Asbestic, Ltd.	10	9
5½	Ashley-grdns., L., C. Prf.	5	6½
4½	Do. 1 Mt. Deb. Stk.	100	115½
5/	Assam Rly. & Trdng., L., 8 p.c. Cum. Pref. "A"	10	15
—	Do. Deferrd. "B" Shs.	1	4½
—	Do. do. (iss. f. pd)	1	3½
8	Do. Cum. Pre-Prf. "A"	10	15
6	Do. New Pref.	10	11½
5	Do. Debs., Red.	100	107
5	Do. Red. Mort. Debs.	100	109
6	Aust'lian Pastrl, L., Cu. Pf.	10	7½
6d.	Aylesbury Dairy, Ltd.	1	1¼
4	Do. 4 p.c. Mt. Dbs.	100†	104½
20/	Babcock & Wilcox, Ltd.	10	32
6	Do. 6 p.c. Cm. Prf.	10	17
8	Baker (Chs.), L., Cm. Pf.	5	8¾
8	Do. "B," Cm. Pref.	5	7¾
8d.	Barker (John), Ltd.	1	3
5½	Do. Cum. Pref.	5	7½
4½	Do. Irred. 1 Mt. Db. Stk.	100	133
—	Barnagore Jute, Ltd.	5	3½
5	Do. Cum. Pref.	5	4½
7½d.	Belgravia Dairy, Ltd.	1	1½
5/	Bell (R.) & Co., Ltd.	5	3½
1/	Bell's Asbestos, Ltd.	1	¾
5	Do. Mt. Db. Bds., Rd.	100	103
10/	Bengal Mills, Ltd.	10	11½
6/	Do. 5 p.c. Cum. Prf.	10	10½
5	Benson (J.W.) L., Cm. Pf.	10	10½
4	Do. Perp. Mt. Db. Stk.	100	103½
6	Bergvik, L., 6 p.c. Cm. Pf.	10	12½
10/	Do. Dfd.	10	9
4½	Do. 1 Dbs., Red.	100	103½
5/	Birm'ham Vinegar, Ltd.	5	8½
5	Do. Cum. Pref.	5	5½
4½	Do. 1 Mt. Db. Stk., Rd.	100	105
5	Boake (A.) L., 5 p.c. Cu. Pf.	10	10½
2/6	Bodega, Ltd.	5	8
4½	Do. Mt. Deb. Stk., Rd.	100	111
8/	Bottomley & Brs., Ltd.	10	6½
6/	Do. 6 p.c. Pt.	10	9½
8½d.	Bovril, Ltd.	1	1½
—	Do. Def.	1	¾
6½d.	Do. Cum. Pref.	1	1½
4½	Do. Deb. Stk.	100	103
6/4½	Bradbury, Gretrex., Ltd., £10 share	8	14
5/	Do. 5 p.c. Cum. Pref.	10	13½
5/	Brewers' Sugar, L., 5 p.c. Cum. Pref.	10	10¾
2/6	BrightonGrd. Hotel, Ld.	5	3½
4	Do. Mt. Db. Stk., Red.	100	102½
5	Bristol Hotel & Palm. Co., Ltd. 1st Mt. Red. Deb.	100	107
9½d.	British & Bengton's. Tea Tr. Asc., Ltd.	1	1½
5	Do. Cum. Prf.	5	5½
—	British Deli & Lgkat. Tobacco, Ltd.	1	½
—	Do. Cum. Prf.	1	½
—	British Tea Table, Ltd.	1	2½
5½	Do. Cum. Pref.	1	1½
2/6	Brooke, Ben., & Co., Ltd., Cum. Pref.	5	5¾
7/6	Brooke, Bond & Co., Ltd.	5	20½
6	Brown Brs., L., Cum. Pref.	5	6
6/	Browne & Eagle, Ltd.	10	14
5	Do. Cum. Pref.	10	13
4	Do. Mrt. Db. Sk., Red.	100	109
20/	Brunner, Mond, & Co., Lt.	10	41
7/	Do. £10 shares	3½	16½
7	Do. Cum. Pref.	10	18
7	Do. £10 shares	5	8½
7/6	Bryant & May, Ltd.	5	20
2/	Bucknall, H., & Sons, Lt.	5	8
6	Do. Cum Pref.	5	8
4/	Burke, E. & J., Ltd.	5	7½
6	Do. Cum. Pref.	5	7½
6	Do. Irred. Deb. Stk.	100	155
1/	Burlington Htls. Co., Ltd	1	1½
5	Do. Cum. Pref.	1	1½
4	Do. Perp. Deb. Stk.	100	103½
5	Bush, W. J., & Co., Ltd., Cum. Pref.	5	5¾
4	Do. 1 Deb. Stk., Red.	100	104
5½	Callard, Stewart, & Watt, Ltd., Cum. Pref.	1	1½
4/	Callender's Cable L., Shs.	5	8
4½	Do. 1 Deb. Stk., Red.	100†	109½
—	Campbell, R., & Sons, Lt.	3	1½
6	CantareiraWater, Bd., Rd	100	99½
5	Do. (2nd issue)	100	92
4	Cartavio Sugar, Ltd., 6 p.c. 1st Debs., Red.	20	80
4/6	Cassell & Co., Ltd., £10	9	18
5	Causton, Sir J., & Sons, Ltd., Cum. Pref.	10	13¾

Commercial, &c. (*continued*) :—

Last Div.	Name.	Paid.	Price.
4	Cent. Prod. Mkt. of B.A. 1st Mt. Str. Debs.	100	77½
4	Chappell & Co., Ltd., Mt. Deb. Stk. Red	100	103
6/	Chicago & N.W. Gran. 8 p.c. Cum. Pref.	10	2½
—	Chicago Packing & Prov.	10	6
8	Do. Cum. Pref.	10	8
6/	City Offices, Ltd	36½	13
3½	Do. Mt. Deb. Stk.	100	108½
7/2½	Cy. London Real Prop., Ltd., £25 shs.	12	19
4/6	Do. £19½ shs.	7½	13½
3½	Do. Deb. Stk. Red.	100	108½
3½	Do. Deb. Stk. Red.	100	106½
3	Do.	100	101½
4/	Cy. of Santos Imprvts., Ltd., 7 p.c. Pref.	10	8½
20/	Clay, Bock, & Co., Ltd.	10	8
8	Do. Cum. Pref.	10	11
6	Do. Mort. Deb.	100	106½
20/	Coats, J. & P., Ltd.	10	62½
6	Do. Cum. Pref.	10	18
4½	Do. Deb. Stk. Red.	100	111½
9½d.	Coburg Hotel, Ltd	1	1½
4	Do. Deb. Stk. Red.	100	102
6	Colonial Consign & Dis., Ltd., Cum. Pref.	5	4¾
4½	Do. 1st Mort. Debs.	100	97½
—	Colorado Nitrate, Ltd.	5	½
4/	Co. Gén. des Asphtes. de F., Ltd.	6	6½
5	Do. Non-Cm. Prf.	—	5½
5	Cook, J. W., & Co., Ltd., Cum. Pref.	5	5½
5	Cook, T., & Son, Egypt. Ltd., 1st Mt. Deb. Red.	100	110½
—	Cork Co., Ltd., 6 p.c. Cum. Pref.	5	2
5	Cory, W., & Sn, L., Cu. Pf.	5	6
4	Do. 1st Deb. Stk. Red.	100	109
8½d.	Crisp & Co., Ltd	1	1½
5½	Do. Cum. Pref.	1	1¼
—	Crompton & Co., Ltd., 7 p.c. Cum. Pref.	5	2½
5	Do. 1st Mt. Reg. Deb.	—	88½
4/6	Crossley, J., & Sons, Ltd.	5	8½
5	Do. Cum. Pref.	5	6½
—	Crystal Pal. Ord. "A" Stk.	100	9½
—	Do. "B" Red. Stk	100	2
6	Do. 6 p.c. 1st 1887 Deb. Stk. Red.	100	116½
—	Do. 6 p.c. 2nd 1887 Deb. Stk. Red.	100	41½
—	Do. 6 p.c. 3rd 1887 Deb. Stk. Red.	100	15½
3	Do. 3 p.c. 1st 1895 Deb. Stk.	100	95½
—	Daimler Motor, Ltd	10	5
4/	Dalgety & Co., £20 Shs.	5	5
4½	Do. Deb. Stk	100	122
4	Do.	100	112
3/10	De Keyser's Ryl. Htl., L.	10	12½
5	Do. Cum. Pref.	10	11½
4	Do. Deb. Stk., Red.	100	109
6	Denny, H., & Sons, Ltd., Cum. Pref.	10	15
5/3	Devas, Routledge & Co., L.	7	8½
5	Dickinson, J., & Co., L., Cum. Pref. Stk.	100	125
4½	Domin. Cottn. Mls., Ltd. Mt. Stg. Dbs.	100	92
4/	Dorman, Long & Co., L.	5	4½
—	Eastmans, Ltd	10	2½
12/	Do. 8 p.c. Cum. Pref	10	10½
2/6	E. C. Powder, Ltd	3	6
1/9½	Edison & Swn Utd. Elec. Ltd., "A" £5 Shs.	3	2½
2/9½	Do. fully-paid	5	5
4½	Ekman Pulp & Ppr. Co., Ltd., Mt. Deb., Red	100	95
1/1½	Electric Construc., Ltd.	2	2¾
7	Do. Cum. Pref.	2	3½
10/	Eley Bros., Ltd.	10	39
—	Elmore's Cop. Deptg., L.	1	¾
—	Elmore's Wire Mnfg., L.	2	¾
—	Elysée Pal. Hotel Co., L.	5/	½
5 p.c.	Do. 5 p.c. £100 Db., Rd.	70	70
8½d.	Evans, Ben., & Co., Ltd.	1	1
5	Do. 1 Mt. Db. Sk., Rd.	100	104
8½d.	Evans., D. H., & Co., L.	1	2½
6	Do. Cum. Pref.	1	1½
4½	Do. 1 Mt. Db. Sk., Rd.	100	110
2/1	*Evening News*, L., 5 p.c. Cum. Pref.	5	5¾
5/3	Evered & Co., L., £10 Sh.	7	13½
7/6	Do.	10	19½
4	Fairbairn Pastoral Co., Aust., L., 1 Mt. Db., Rd.	100	102
6	Fairfield Shipbldg., Ltd., Cum. Pref	10	9½
4½	Do. Mort. Deb. Stk.	100	107½
—	Farmer & Co., Ld., 6 p.c. Cum. Pref.	10	13¾
10	Field, J. C. & J., Ltd.	10	10
14/	Do. 7 p.c. Cum. Pref.	10	14
9d.	Fordham, W.B., & Sns, Ld.	1	2
5/6	Fore-st. Warehouse, Ltd.	11	9½
4	Do. Regd. Debs., Rd.	100	102½
2/6	Foster, M. B. & Sons, Ltd.	4	5½
5	Do. Pref.	10	11
7/	Foster, Porter, & Co., L.	10½	17
4	Fowler, J., & Co. (Leeds), Ltd., 1 Mt. Deb., Red.	100	100½
3/	Fraser & Chalmers, Ltd.	3	1½
4½	Free, Rodwell & Co., Ltd., Deb Stk	100	102½
6½d.	Furness, T., & Co., Ltd., 5½ p.c. Cum. Pref.	1	1
4½	Gartside & Co. (of Manchstr), L., 1 Mt. Db. Sk.	100	110
5	Genl. Hydraul. Power, L.	100	260

Commercial, &c. (*continued*):—

Last Div.	Name.	Paid.	Price.
8/	Gillman & Spencer, Ltd.	5	2½
6	Do. Pref.	5	4½
5	Do. Mort. Debs.	50	50
4	Goldsbro., Mort & Co., L., "A" Deb. Stk., Red.	100	72½
—	Do. 3 p.c. "B" Inc. Deb. Stk., Red	100	17
12/	Gordon Hotels, Ltd.	10	20½
5½	Do. Cum. Pref.	10	14½
4½	Do. Perp. Deb. Stk.	100	136½
4	Do. do.	100	124½
—	Greenwich Inld. Linoleum Co., Ltd.	1	⅜
7	Greenwood & Batley, Ltd., Cum. Pref.	10	10
7½d.	Hagemann & Co., Ltd., 6 p.c. Cum. Pref.	1	1⅛
—	Hammond, Ltd.	10	⅜
—	Do. 8 p.c. Cum. Pref.	10	2
—	Do. 6 p.c. Cum. Inc. Stk. Red.	100	52½
4	Hampton & Sons, Ltd., 4 p.c. 1 Mt. Db. St. Red.	100	104
	Hans Crescent Htl., L., 6 p.c. Cum. Pref.	5	3½
4	Do. 1 Mt. Deb. Stk.	100	85
5	Harmsworth, Ld., Cm. Pf.	1	1⅛
4/	Harrison, Barber, Ltd.	5	4½
1/	Harrod's Stores, Ltd.	1	5
2/6	Do. Cum. Pref.	5	7½
5½	Hawaiian Comcl. & Sug. 1 Mt. Debs.	100	94½
5	Hazell, Watson, Ld., Cm. Pref.	10	12
6/	Henley's Teleg., Ltd.	10	21½
7	Do. Pref. Shs.	10	19
4½	Do. Mt. Db. Stk., Rd.	100	112½
6	Henry, Ltd.	10	12½
5	Do. Cum. Pref.	10	13½
4½	Do. Mt. Debs., Red.	50	53
6	Hepworth, Ld., Cm. Prf.	10	11½
6/	Herrmann, Ltd.	5	4½
—	Hildesheimer, Ltd.	3	1
9½d.	Holbrn. & Frasca, Ltd.	1	2
5	Do. Cum. Pref.	10	11½
4	Do. Deb. Stk.	100	113
6	Home & Col. Stres, Ltd., Cum. Pref.	5	7½
6	Hood & M.'s Stres., Ltd., Cum. Pref.	1	¾
—	Hook, C. T., Ltd.	10	4
7/2	Hornsby, Ltd., £10 Shs.	8	24
5/6	Do. 6 p.c. Cm. Pf. Sk.	100	90
—	Hotchks. Ordn., Ltd.	10	¾
—	Do. 7 p.c. Cm. Prf.	10	4½
5	Do. 1 Mt. Dbs., Rd.	100	95½
6	Htl. Cecil, Ld., Cm. Prf.	5	4½
4	Do. 1 Mt. D. Sk., R.	100	105½
8/	Howard & Bulgh, Ltd.	10	36
6	Do. Pref.	10	16
4	Do. Deb. Stk., Red.	100	107
4/	Howell, J., Ltd., £5 Shs.	4	9½
—	Howell & Js., Ld., £3½ Shs.	3	1
1/6	Humber, Ltd.	1	⅞
6	Do. Cum. Pref.	1	1⅛
2/6	Hunter, Wilts., Ltd.	5	7
2/7	Hyam Cltbg., Ltd., 5 p.c. Cum. Pref.	5	5½
10/	Impl. Russn. Cotton, L.	5	5½
5	Impd. Industl. Dwgs., Ld.	100	130½
6d.	Do. Defrd.	1	1¼
£1	Impd. Wood Pave., Ltd.	10	16
5/	Ind. Rubber, Gutta Per. Telegraph Works, Ltd.	10	24
4	Do. 1 Mt. Debs., Red.	100	105
6	Intern. Tea, Cum. Pref.	5	6½
7½d.	Jays, Ltd.	1	1½
5½	Do. Cum. Pref.	5	6½
8½d.	Jones & Higgins, Ltd.	1	2½
4½	Do. 1 Mt. Db. Sk., Rd.	100	113
5/	Kelly's Directory, Ltd., 5 p.c. Cum. Pref.	10	12½
—	Do. Mort. Db. Sk., Rd.	100	105
—	Kent Coal Explrtn. Ltd.	1	⅜
1½d.	King, Howmann, Ltd.	1	1½
4/	Kinloch & Co., Ltd.	5	8½
6	Do. Pref.	5	7
5	Lady's Pictorial Pub., Ltd., Cum. Pref.	5	5
—	La Guaira Harb., Ltd., 7 p.c. Deb. Stk.	100	—
—	Do. 2 Mt. 7 p.c. Deb. Bds., Red.	100	—
4/	Lagunas Nitrate, Ltd.	5	2½
2/	Lagunas Syn., Ltd.	5	1½
5	Do. 1 Mt. Debs., Red.	100	80
—	L. Copais Ld., 1 Mt. 6 p.c. Debs., Red.	100	35½
3/	Lautaro Nitrate, Ltd.	5	4
5	Do. 1 Mt. Debs., Red.	—	95½
9/	Lawes Chem. L., £10 shs.	9	5¼
14/	Do. N. Cm. Min. Pref.	10	13
—	Leeds Forge, 7 p.c. Cm. Pf.	5	3
5	Do. 1 Mt. Debs., Red.	50	44½
5	Lever Bros., L., Cm. Pf.	10	13
6	Liberty, L., 6 p.c. Cm. Pf.	10	15
60/	Liebig's, Ltd.	20	76
5	Lilley & Sk., L., Cm. Pf.	5	5¼
3/	Linoleum Manftg., Ltd.	5	19
3/	Linotype, Ltd., Pref.	5	5½
4/	Do. Def.	5	8½
—	Lister & Co., Ltd.	10	5
5	Do. Cum. Pref.	10	8½
5/	Liverpool. Nitrate	5	6½
—	Liverpool. Warehsg., Ltd.	10	3½
5½	Do. Cum. Pref.	10	8½
4	Do. 1 Mt. Db. Stk., Rd.	100	105½
5½	Lockharts, Ltd., Cm. Pf.	1	1½
4/6	Ldn. & Til., Lightrage £10	9	5½
6/	Ldn. Comcl. Sale Rms., Ltd.	10	18
4	Do. 1 Mt. Deb. Stk., Red.	100	104
—	London Nitrate, Ltd.	5	2

Commercial, &c. (*continued*):—

Last Div.	Name.	Paid.	Price.
4/	London Nitrate, Ld. 8 p.c. Cm. Min. Pf.	5	3½
3/	London Pavilion, Ltd.	5	8
1/6	†London Produce Clg. Ho., Ltd., £10 Shares	2½	3½
4/	London Stereos., Ltd.	5	3
6/	Ldn. Un. Laun. L. Cm. Pf.	1	
8½d.	Louise, Ltd.	1	⅜
5½	Do. Cum. Pref.	1	¾
5/	Lovell & Christmas, Ltd.	5	12
6	Do. Cum. Pref.	5	7½
4	Do. Mt. Deb. Stk., Red.	100	107
1/3	Lyons, Ltd.	1	2½
4½	Do. 1 Mt. Deb. Stk., Rd.	100	105½
10/	Machinery Trust, Ltd.	5	15½
6	MacLellan, Ltd., Min. Cum. Pref.	10	7½
5	Do. 1 Mt. Debs., 1900	100	98½
—	McEwan, J. & Co, Ltd.	10	1½
6	Do. Mt. Debs., Red.	100	89½
8	McNamara, L., Cm. Pref.	10	9
7½d.	Maison Virot, Ltd.	1	1½
2/7	Do. 6 p.c. Cum. Pref.	5	4½
5/	Manbré Sacc., L., Cm. Pf.	10	12
15/	Mangan Brre., L., £10 Shs.	6	15½
3/	Mason & Mason, Ltd.	5	3½
6	Do. Cum. Pref.	5	5½
—	Maynards, Ltd.	1	⅜
6	Do. Cum. Pref.	1	⅞
9½d.	Mazawattee Tea, Ltd.	1	1½
5	Do. Cum. Pref.	5	5½
6	Mellin's Food Cum. Pref.	5	7
4½	Met. Ascn. Imp. Dwlgs. L.	100	109
3½	Do. 1 Mt. Deb. Stk.	100	97
5	Metro. Indus. Dwlgs., Ltd.	5	5
4	Do. do. Cum. Pref.	5	5½
5	Metro. Prop., L., Cm. Pf.	5	6½
4½	Do. 1st Mt. Debs. Stk.	100	110½
6	Mexican Cotton 1 Mt. Db.	100	97½
4½	Mid. Class Dwlgs., L., Db.	100	120½
1/	Millars' Karri, Ltd.	1	2½
6	Do. Cum. Pref.	1	1½
15/	Milner's Safe, Ltd.	10	19
10/	Moir & Son, Ltd., Pref.	5	9
6	Morgan Cruc., L., Cm. Pf.	10	15
2/	Morris, B., Ltd.	3½	3½
—	Murray L. 5½ p.c. C. Pf.	5	5½
—	Do. 4½ 1 Mt. Db. Sk. Rd.	100	108
2/6	Natnl. Dwlgs., L., 5 p.c. Pf.	5	1
1/7½	Nat. Safe Dep., Ltd.	4	3½
6	Do. Cum. Pref.	1	1½
—	Native Guano, Ltd.	5	¾
5/	Nelson Bros., Ltd.	10	2½
5	Do. Deb. Stk., Red.	100	80½
4/	Neuchtel Asph., Ltd.	10	11
—	New Central Borneo, Ld.	1	⅛
—	New Darvel Tob., Ltd.	18/	1
2/4½	New Explosives, Ltd.	3	2
5/3½	New Gd. Htl., Bham, L.	5	4
5½	Do. Pref.	5	4½
4	Do. 1 Mt. Db. Stk., Rd.	100	98½
—	New Julia Nitrate, Ltd.	10/	½
2/	New Ldn. Borneo Tob., L.	16/	1
1/6	New Premier Cycle, Ltd.	1	1½
—	Do. 6 p.c. Cum. Pref.	1	⅜
—	Do. 4½ p.c. 1 Mt. Db. Rd	100	—
1/	New Tamargl. Nitr., Ltd	1	½
1/2½	Do. 8 p.c. Cum. Pref.	1	½
6	Do. 6 p.c. 1 Mt. Dbs. Rd.	100	68
3·78d.	Newnes, G., L., Cm. Prf.	1	1½
1/3	Nitr. Provision, Ltd.	2½	¾
24/	Nobel-Dynam., Ltd.	10	17½
—	North Brazn. Sugar, Ltd.	1	⅜
10/	Oakey, Ltd.	10	30
6	Do. Cum. Pref.	10	15½
4/	Paccha Jarp. Nitr., Ltd.	5	¾
5	Pac. Borax, L., 1 Db. Rd.	100	110
—	Palace Hotel, Ltd.	10	6
5½	Do. Cum. Pref.	10	9
4	Do. 1 Mt. Deb. Stk.	100	105
2/6	Palmer, Ltd.	5	1½
6	Do. Cum. Pref.	5	3½
9 1/10d.	Paquin, Ltd.	1	1
6	Do. Cum. Pref.	5	4½
5½	Parnall, Ltd., Cum. Pref.	1	⅜
3/	Pawsons, Ltd., £10 Shs.	6	6½
4	Do. Mt. Debs., Red.	100	107
6	Pearks, G. & T., Ltd., 6 p.c. Cum. Pref.	1	¾
1/2½	Pears, Ltd.	1	1½
6	Do. Cum. Pref.	10	14½
5	Do. Deb. Stk.	100	129
5½	Pearson, C. A., L., Cu. Pf.	5	5
4/	Peebles, Ltd.	5	7½
5	Do. Cum. Pref.	5	6½
4½	Do. Mt. Deb. Stk. Red.	100	112
5½	Peek Bros., Ltd., 1 Cum. Pref., Nos. 1-60,000	5	6½
3½	Do. 3½ p.c. 1 Db. Stk.	100	101
7½d.	Pegamoid, Ltd.	1	⅞
4/	Phospho-Guano, Ltd.	5	2½
4/	Pillsbury-W. Fl. Mills, L.	10	2
16/	Do. 8 p.c. Cum. Pref.	10	6½
6	Do. 1 Mort. Debs.	100	96½
7½d.	Plummer, Ltd.	1	1½
5	Do. Cum. Pref.	5	5½
15/	Price's Candle, Ltd.	16	40
6	Priest Marians, L., Cm. Pf.	1	1⅛
6	Pryce Jones, Ld., Cm. Pf.	5	7½
5	Do. Deb. Stk.	100	120½
10.8d.	Pullman, Ltd.	1	1½
6d.	Do. Cum. Pref.	1	1¼
1/	Raleigh Cycle, Ltd.	1	½
6	Do. Cum. Pref.	1	⅞
5	Recife Drnge. Ld. 1 Mt. Debs., R	100	19
6	Redfern, Ltd. Cum. Prf.	10	14
5	Ridgways, Ltd., Cu. Pf.	5	5½
5	R. Janeiro Cy. Imps., Ld.	25	9½
5	Do. Debs.	100	80
5	Do. 1882-1893	100	79
11/	R. Jan Fl. Mills, Ltd.	7	7
5	Do. 1 Mt. Debs., Rd.	100	94

Commercial, &c. (*continued*):—

Last Div.	Name.	Paid.	Price.
—	Riv. Plate Meat, Ltd.	5	3½
—	Do. Pref.	5	5
8½d.	Roberts, J. R., Ltd.	1	1½
5	Do. 1 Mt. Db. Sk., Rd.	100	112
8½d.	Roberts, T. R., Ltd.	1	2½
5	Do. Cum. Pref.	1	1½
3/	Rosario Nit., Ltd.	5	3½
5	Do. Debs., Red.	100	103
5	Do. Huara, Debs.	—	101½
1/	Rover Cycle, Ltd.	1	¾
6/	Ryl. Aquarium, Ltd.	5	4½
6	Do. Pref.	5	5½
5	Ryl. Htl., Edin., Cm. Pf.	1	1½
1/2½	Ryl. Niger, Ltd., £10 Sh.	2	2½
6/	Do.	10	14½
3/	Ruston, Proctor, Ltd.	10	11
4½	Do. 1 Mort. Debs.	100	104
6/	Sadler, Ltd.	12	7
—	Sal. Carmen Nit., Ltd.	5	4½
9d.	Salmon & Gluck., Ltd.	1	1½
2/	Salt Union, Ltd.	10	2
14/	Do. 7 p.c. Pref.	10	8½
4½	Do. Deb. Stk.	100	110
4½	Do. "B" Deb. Sk., Rd.	100	104½
—	San Donato Nit., Ltd.	5	⅜
2/6	San Jorge Nit., Ltd.	5	3½
—	San Pablo Nit., Ltd.	5	⅜
2/	San Sebastn. Nit., Ltd.	5	⅝
1/	Sanitas, Ltd	1	2½
—	Sa. Elena Nit., Ltd.	5	⅜
—	Sa. Rita Nit., Ltd.	5	2
10/	Savoy Hotel, Ltd.	10	19
7	Do. Pref.	10	16
4	Do. 1 Mt. Deb. Stk.	100	112½
5	Do. Debs., Red	100	102½
5	Do. & Ldn. For. Htl., Ltd., 5 p.c. Debs. Red.	100	99
1½d.	Schweppes, Ltd.	1	1½
—	Do. Def.	1	1½
5	Do. Cum. Pref.	1	1¼
4	Do. Deb. Stk.	100	105
1/	Singer Cyc., Ltd.	1	½
5½	Do Cum. Pref.	1	¾
—	Smokeless Pwdr., Ltd.	1	⅜
5½d.	S. Eng. Dairies, Ltd., 6 p.c. Cum. Pref.	1	1½
—	Sowler Thos. L.	1	1
—	Do. 5½ Cm. Pf	5	5½
3/6	Spencer, Turner, & Co. Ltd	5	8½
5	Do. Cum. Pref.	5	6½
5	Spicer, Ld., 5 p.c. Dbs. Rd.	100	65
4/	Spiers & Pond, Ltd.	10	21
5	Do. 1 Mt. Debs., Red.	100	116½
5	Do. "A" Db. Stk., Rd.	100	110
5	Do. "B" 1 Db. Stk., Rd.	100	110
4	Do. Fd. "C" 1 Db. S., R.	100	103
5/	Spratt's, Ltd	5	13½
4	Do. Debs., 1914	—	104
5	Steiner Ld., Cm. Pf.	10	11½
4	Do. 1 Mt. Db. Sk. Rd.	100	106
7/	Stewart & Clydesdale, L.	10	13½
6	Do. Cum. Pref.	10	15
—	Swan & Edgar, L.	1	1½
1/3	Sweetmeat Automatic, L.	1	4
2/9	Teetgen, Ltd., Cum. Pref.	5	6
12/	Teleg. Construction., Ld.	12	39½
5	Do. Db. Bds., Rd, 1899	100	103½
3/0½	Tilling, Ld. 5½ p.c. Cm. Prf.	5	6
4	Do. 4 p.c. 1 Dbs., Rd.	—	103
8½d.	Tower Tea, Ltd.	1	1½
5	Do. Cum. Pref.	5	5½
5	Travers, Ltd., Cum. Pref.	10	12½
4	Do. 1 Mt. Dbs., Rd.	100	101½
6	Tucuman Sug., 1 Dbs., Rd.	100	100
4/	United Alkali, Ltd.	10	2½
7	Do. Cum. Pref.	10	9½
5	Do. Mt. Db. Stk., Rd.	100	109½
2½d.	United Horse Shoe, Ltd., Non-Cum. 8 p.c. Pref.	1	½
5	Un. Kingm. Tea, Cm. Prf.	5	4½
1/	Un. Lankat Plant., Ltd.	1	2½
2/	Un. Limmer Asphlte., Ld.	3	4½
5/	Val de Travers Asph., L.	10	14½
3/	V. den Bergh's, Ltd., Cm. Pref.	5	6½
6	Walkers, Park., L., C. Pf.	10	4
4½	Do. 1 Mt. Debs., Red.	100	90½
4/	Wallis, Thos. & Co., Ltd.	5	13½
6	Do. Cum. Pref.	5	8½
5½	Waring, Ltd., Cum. Pref.	5	5½
4½	Do. 1 Mt. Db. Sk., Red.	100	109½
4½	Do. Irred. "B" Db. Stk.	100	103
12/	Waterlow, Dfd. Ord.	10	15½
12/	Do. Pref.	10	15
3½	Do. Cum. Pref.	10	11
10/	Waterlow Bros. & L., Ld.	10	10½
9½d.	Welford, Ltd.	1	2
4½	Do. Debs., Red.	100	107
4½d.	Welford's Surrey Dairies, Ltd.	1	1½
7½d.	West London Dairy, Ltd.	1	1
4½	Wharncliffe Dwllgs., L., Pf.	10	11½
18/10	Do. 3 p.c. Irr. Mt. Db. Sk.	100	96
6d.	White, A. J., Ltd.	1	⅜
6	Do. 6 p.c. Cum. Pref.	1	⅞
4	White, J. Bazley, Ltd., 1 Mort. Debs., Red	100	94½
5	White, R., Ltd., 1 Mort. Deb. Stock, Red.	100	106½
5/	White, Tomkins, Ltd.	10	12½
5	Do. Cum. Pref.	10	12
6	White, W. N., L., Cm. Pf.	1	1
2/6	Wickens, Pease & Co., L.	5	2
6	Wilkie, Ltd., Cum. Pref.	10	16
3/6	Willans & Robinson, Ltd.	5	8
6	Do. Cum. Pref.	5	7
4½	Do. 1 Mt. Db. Stk., Red.	100	106
7½d.	Williamsons, L., Cm. Prf.	1	1½
6	Winterbottm Black Cloth, Ltd., Cum. Prf.	10	15
3/	Yates, Ltd.	5	6½
6	Do. Cum. Pref.	5	6½
	Young's Paraffin, Ltd.	4	1½

CORPORATION STOCKS—COLONIAL AND FOREIGN.

Per Cent.	Name.	Paid.	Price.
6	Auckland City, '72 1904-24	100	118
6	Do. Cons., '79, Red. 1930	100	128½
5	Do. Deb. Ln., '83..1934-8	100	116
6	Auckland Harb. Debs.	100	111½
5	Do. 1917	100	112
5	Do. 1936	100	116
3½	Balmain Boro' 1914	—	117
5	Boston City (U.S.)	100	100½
5	Do. 1902	100	107½
5	Brunswick Town 5. C. Debs. 1916-20	100	111
15/	B. Ayres City 6 p.c.	100	65
4½	Do. 4½ p.c.	100	60
5	Cape Town, City of	100	113
4	Do. 1943	100	113
4	Chicago, City of, Gold 1915	—	110
6	Christchurch 1926	100	128½
6	Cordoba City	100	17
5	Duluth (U.S.) Gold 1926	—	110
6	Dunedin (Otago) 1925	100	124
6	Do. 1906	100	113
5	Do. Consols 1908	100	113
4	Durban Insc. Stk. 1944	1000	111
4	Essex Cnty., N. Jersey 1926	100	113½
5	Fitzroy, Melbrne. 1916-19	100	110
5	Gisborne Harbour 1915	100	110½
4	Greymouth Harbour 1925	100	111
4	Hamilton 1934	100	109
5	Hobart Town 1918-30	100	116
4	Do. 1940	100	107
4½	Invercargill Boro. Dbs. 1936	100	113
6	Kimberley Boro., S.A. Dbs.	—	104
4	Launceston Twn. Dbs. 1916	100	107
6	Lyttleton, N.Z., Harb. 1929	100	123
4	Melbourne Bd. of Wks. 1921	100	109
5	Melb. City Debs. 1897-1907	100	107½
4	Do. Debs. 1908-27	100	113½
4	Do. Debs. 1915-20-22	100	108
5	Melbne. Harb. Bds., 1908-9	100	112
4½	Do. do. 1915	100	110
4	Do. do. 1918-21	100	106
4½	Melbrne. Tms. Dbs. 1914-16	100	113
4½	Do. Fire Brig. Db. 1921	100	109
5	Mexico City Stg.	100	99½
4	Moncton N. Bruns. City	100	104
4½	Montevideo	100	57
5	Montreal Stg.	100	108
5	Do. 1874	100	104
5	Do. 1879	100	106
3½	Do. 1933	100	104
3	Do. Perm. Deb. Stk.	100	98
4	Do. Cons. Deb. Stk. 1932	100	113
6	Napier Boro. Consolid. 1914	100	119
5	Napier Harb. Debs. 1920	100	114
5	Do. Debs. 1928	100	108
6	New Plymouth Harb. Debs. 1909	100	107
6	New York City 1901	—	107½
3½	Do. 1910-26	—	108½
4½	Nth. Melbourne Debs. 1-600 1921	100	108
5	Oamaru Boro. Cons. 1920	100	101
6	Do. Harb. Bds. (Reg.)	100	74½
25/	Do. 6 p.c. (Bearer) 1919	100	35
6	Otago Harb. Deb. Reg.	100	103
6	Do. 1877	100	107
6	Do. 1881 1921	100	115
5	Do. Debs. 1921	100	107
5	Do. Cons. 1934	100	105
6	Ottawa City	100	109
6	Do. 1904	100	115½
4½	Do. Debs. 1913	100	112
6	Port Elizabeth Waterworks	100	113½
5	Port Louis	100	108
5	Prahran Debs. 1917	100	111
4	Do. Debs. 1919	100	105
6	Quebec C. Coupon. 1875 1905	100	112
6	Do. do. 1878 1908	100	116
4½	Do. Debs. 1914-18	100	107
4	Do. Debs. 1923	100	107
3½	Do. Cns. Rg. Stk., Red.	100	101
5	Richmond (Melb.) Dbs. 1917	100	111
4	Rio Janeiro City	100	61
4	Rome City	100	—
4	Do. 2nd to 8th Iss.	100	94
6	Rosario C.	100	26½
6	Do.	100	26½
4	St. Catherine (Ont.) 1926	100	103
4	St. John, N.B., Debs. 1934	—	104
4½	St. Kilda (Melb) Dbs. 1918-21	100	104
4	St. Louis C. (Miss.) 1911	100	104
4	Do. 1913	100	103½
3·65	Do. 1915	—	107
—	Santa Fé City Debs.	100	20
6	Santos City	100	98
6	Sofia City	100	86
5	Sth. Melbourne Debs. 1915	100	111
4½	Do. Debs. 1919	100	107
5	Sydney City 1904	100	109
4	Do. Debs. 1912-13	100	107
4	Do. do. (1894) 1919	100	109
7	Timaru Boro. 7 p.c. 1910	100	124½
5	Timaru Harb. Debs 1914	100	106
5	Do. Debs. 1916	100	106
6	Toronto City Wtwks 1904-6	100	110
6	Do. Cons. Debs. 1898	100	101
5	Do. G. Cns. Dbs. 1919-20	100	118
4	Do. Strlg. 1922-8	100	107
4	Do. Local Improv.	100	102
3½	Do. 1929	100	105
5½	Valparaiso	100	101
4	Vancouver 1931	100	108
4	Do. 1932	100	108
6	Wanganui Harb. Dbs. 1905	100	110
6	Wellington Con. Deb. 1907	100	117
6	Do. Improv., 1879	100	128
6	Do. Wtrwks. Dbs., 1880	100	128
4½	Do. Debs., 1893 1933	100	116
4½	Wellington Harb. 1907	100	106
4	Westport Harb. Dbs. 1905	100	111
6	Winnipeg City Deb. 1907	—	118
5	Do. 1914	100	119

FINANCIAL, LAND, AND INVESTMENT.

Last Div.	Name.	Paid.	Price.
5	Agncy, Ld. & Fin. Aust., Ltd., Mt. Db. Stk., Rd.	100	85½
6	Amer. Frehld. Mt. of Lon., Ld., Cum. Pref. Stk. ..	100	77½
4½	Do. Deb. Stk., Red. ..	100	96
1/	Anglo-Amer. Db. Cor., L.	2	1
4	Do. Deb. Stk., Red (†	100	107½
5½	Ang.-Ceylon & Gen. Est., Ltd., Cons. Stk.	100	70
6	Do. Reg. Debs., Red.	100	104½
—	Ang.-Fch. Explorn., Ltd.	1	3½
6	Do. Cum. Pref.	1	1⅛
—	Argent. Ld. & Inv., Ltd. £1 Shares	10/	nil
5	Do. Cum. Pref.	4	2
—	Assets Fnders' Sh., Ltd.,	4	1¾
4/	Assets Realiz., Ltd., Ord.,	5	9
5	Do. Cum. Pref.	5	6½
21/	Austrln. Agricl £25 Shs.	21½	65½
—	Aust. N. Z. Mort., Ltd., £10 Shs.	1	1½d.
4½	Do. Deb. Stk., Red. ..	100	90½
4	Do. Deb. Stk., Red. ..	100	82½
4½	Australian Est. & Mt., L., 1 Mt. Deb. Stk., Red.	100	105
5	Do. "A" Mort. Deb. Stk., Red.	100	96
2/6	Australian Mort., Ld., & Fin., Ltd. £25 Shs. ..	5	4½
1/6	Do. New, £25 Shs...	3	2½
4	Do. Deb. Stk.	100	112
3	Do. Do.	100	85
4	Baring Est. 2 Mt. Debs., Red.	100	105
5	Bengal Presidy. 1 Mort. Deb., Red.	100	105
25/	British Amer. Ld. "A"	1	20
—	Do. "B"	24	6½
1/2½	Brit. & Amer. Mt., Ltd. £10 Shs.	2	1
5/	Do. Pref.	10	10
4	Do. Deb. Stk., Red. ..	100	100
1/3	Brit. & Austrian Tst Ln., Ltd. £25 Shs.	2½	⅝
4½	Do. Perm. Debs., Red.	100	102
1½d.	Brit. N. Borneo. £1 Shs.	15/	½
2½d.	Do.	1	1
—	Brit. S. Africa	1	3½
5	Do. Mt. Deb., Red.	—	100
6	B. Aires Harb. Tst., Red.	100	97½
—	Canada Co.	1	25
—	Canada N. W. Ld., Ltd.	$25	85½
—	Do. Pref.	$100	854
4	Canada Perm. Loan & Sav. Perp. Deb. Stk...	100	99½
—	Curamalan Ld., 1 Mt. 7 p.c. Bds., Red.	—	92½
2/4½	Deb Corp., Ld., £10 Shs	4	3½
5	Do. Cum. Pref.	10	11½
4	Do. Perp. Deb. Stk...	100	114
—	Deb. Corp. Fders' Sh., Ld.	3	1
4/5 7/10	Eastn. Mt. & Agncy, Ld., "A"	10	6½
4½	Do. Deb. Stk., Red.	100	100
5	Equitable Revers. In. Ltd.	100	—
—	Exploration, Ltd.	1	1 1/16
1	Freehold Trst. of Austrla. Ltd. £10 Shs.	1	¾
4	Do. Perp. Deb. Stk...	100	102
—	Genl. Assets Purchase, Ltd., 5 p.c. Cum. Pref.	10	—
50/	Genl. Reversionary, Ltd.	100	—
3½	Holborn Vi. Land	100	107
3½	House Prop. & Inv.	100	85
13/	Hudson's Bay	13	24½
4	Impl. Col. Fin. & Agcy. Corp.	100	93½
4½	Impl. Prop. Inv., Ltd., Deb. Stk., Red.	100	93½
2/6	Internatl. Fincial. Soc., Ltd. £7½ Shs.	2¼	1½
4	Do. Deb. Stk., Red...	100	94½
1/9½	Ld. & Mtge. Egypt, Ltd. £18 Shs.	3	2½
5	Do. Debs., Red.	100	103
4½	Do. Debs., Red.	100	101
—	Ld. Corp. of Canada, Ltd.	1	⅜
4½	Ld. Mtge. Bk. of Texas Deb. Stk.	100	—
3½	Ld. Mtge. Bk. Victoria 4½ p.c. Deb. Stk.	100	78
2/9½	Law Debent. Corp., Ltd., £10 Shs.	2	2
4½	Do. Cum. Pref., ...	10	12½
4	Do. Deb. Stk.	100	118
1/	Ldn. & Australasian Deb. Corp., Ltd., £4 Shs. ..	2	½
4½	Do. 4½ p.c. Mt. Deb. Stk., Red.	100	101
—	Ldn. & Middx. Frhld. Est. £2 Shs.	35/	3
2/6	Lndn. & N. Y. Inv. Corp., Ltd.	5	2½
5	Do. 5 p.c. Cum. Pref...	10	9
1/6	Ldn. & Nth. Assets Corp., Ltd., £2 Shs.	1½	⅞
2/	Ldn. & N. Deb. Corp., L.	2	1¼
4/	Ldn. & S. Afric. Explrn. Ltd.	½	14½
2/	Mtge. Co. of R. Plate, Ltd. £10 Shs.	2	3
4½	Do. Deb. Stk., Red...	100	111
4½	Morton, Rose Est., Ltd., 1st Mort. Debs.	—	100
—	Natal Land Col. Ltd. ..	10	6½
4/	Do. 8 p.c. Pref., 1870..	5	8½
5/6	Natl. Disct. L., £25 Shs.	5	11
4½	New Impl. Invest., Ltd. Pref. Stk.	100	66½
—	New Impl. Invest., Ltd. Def. Stk.	100	9
4	N. Zld. Ln. & Mer. Agcy., Ltd. Prf. Ln. Deb. Stk	100	97

Financial, Land, &c. (*continued*):—

Last Div.	Name.	Paid.	Price.
16/	N. Zld. Ln. & Mer. Agcy., Ltd. 5 p.c. "A" Db. Stk.	100	42½
—	N. Zld. Ln. & Mer. Agcy., Ltd., 5 p.c. "B" Db. Stk.	100	4
2/6	N. Zld. Tst. & Ln. Ltd., £25 Shs.	5	1½
12/6	N. Zld. Tst. & Ln. Ltd., 5 p.c. Cum. Pref.	25	19
—	N. Brit. Australsn. Ltd...	100	7½
—	Do. Irred. Guar.	100	30½
5	Do. Mort. Debs.	100	72½
4½	N. Queensld. Mort. & Inv., Ltd., Deb. Stk.	100	94
—	Oceana Co., Ltd.	—	—
4	Peel Riv., Ld. & Min. Ltd.	100	93
—	Peruvian Corp., Ltd.	100	3
—	Do. 4 p.c. Pref.	100	10½
3	Do. 6 p.c. 1 Mt. Debs., Red.	100	43½
—	Queenld. Invest. & Ld. & Mort. Pref. Ord. Stk...	100	20
3/7	Queenld. Invest. & Ld. & Mort. Ord. Shs.	4	3½
4	Queenld. Invest. & Ld. Mort. Perp. Debs.	100	90
3½	Raily. Roll Stk. Tst. Deb., 1903-6. .... (†	100	100½
50/	Reversiony. Int. Soc., Ltd.	100	—
2/8½	Riv. Plate Trst., Loan & Agcy., L., "A" £10 Shs.	2	4½
1/6	Riv. Plate Trst., Loan & Agcy., Ltd., Def. "B"	5	3¾
4	Riv. Plate Trst., Loan & Agy., L., Db. Stk., Red.	100	107
—	Santa Fé & Cord. Gt. South Land, Ltd.	20	5
—	Santa Fé Land	10	2¾
2/	Scot. Amer. Invest., Ltd. £10 Shs.	2	2¾
2½	Scot. Australian Invest., Ltd., Cons.	100	91½
6	Scot. Australian Invest., Ltd., Guar. Pref. .. (†	100	134½
5	Scot. Australian Invest., Ltd., Guar. Pref. .. (†	100	102½
4	Scot. Australian Invest., Ltd., 4 p.c. Perp. Dbs. (†	100	105½
5	Sivagunga Zemdy., 1st Mort., Red.	100	99
20/	Sth. Australian..........	20	57½
3½	Stock Exchange Deb., Rd.	—	101½
—	Strait Develt., Ltd.	1	1/16
2/6	Texas Land & Mt., Ltd. £10 Shs.	2½	3
4½	Texas Land & Mt., Ltd., Deb. Stk., Red.	100	103
—	Transvaal Est. & Dev., L.	1	1/16
—	Transvaal Lands, Ltd., £1 Shs.	15/	½
—	Do. F. P.	1	½
—	Transvaal Mort., Loan, & Fin., Ltd., £10 Shs. ..	2	½
2/	Tst & Agcy. of Austrlsa., Ltd., £10 Shs.	1	2½
7	Do. Old, fully paid ..	10	15½
5/7	Do. New, fully paid ..	10	12½
5	Do. Cum. Pref.	10	12¾
3/	Trust & Loan of Canada, £20 Shs.	5	4½
1/9½	Do. New £20 Shs. ...	3	2½
—	Tst. & Mort. of Iowa, Ltd., £10 Shs.	2½	¾
4½	Do. Deb. Stk. Red...	100	94½
—	Tst., Loan, & Agency of Mexico, Ltd., £10 Shs.	2	½
—	Trsts., Exors, & Sec. Ins. Corp., Ltd., £10 Shs..	7	1⅜
5/	Union Dsc., Ld., £10 Shs.	5	10¼
—	Union Mort. & Agcy. of Aust., Ltd., £6 Shs. ..	2	—
—	Do. Pref. Stk.	100	35
—	Do. 6 p. Pref. £6 Shs.	2	½
4½	Do. Deb. Stk	100	92½
4	Do. Deb. Stk	100	85½
5	Do. Deb. Stk. Red...	100	96
1/6	U.S. Deb. Cor. Ltd., £8 Shs.	1	⅝
5½	Do. Cum. Pref. Stk .	100	102½
4½	Do. Irred. Deb. Stk ..	100	109½
5	U.S. Tst. & Guar. Cor., Ltd., Pref. Stk.	100	69½
6/	Van Diemen's	25	16
4	Walker's Prop. Cor., Ltd., Guar. 1 Mt. Deb. Stk..	100	109
4½	Wstr. Mort. & Inv., Ltd., Deb. Stk.	100	90

FINANCIAL—TRUSTS.

Last Div.	Name.	Paid.	Price.
1/	Afric. City Prop., Ltd...	1	1⅜
6	Do. Cum. Pref.	1	1
4	Alliance Invt., Ltd., Cm. 4½ p. c. Prefd.	100	73½
—	Do. Defd	100	11½
4	Do. Deb. Stk. Red...	100	106½
5	Amrcn. Invt., Ltd., Prfd.	100	123½
5	Do. Defd.	100	89½
4	Do. Deb. Stk. Red...	100	118½
4	Army & Navy Invt., Ltd., 5 p.c. Prefd.	100	77½
—	Do. Defd. Stk.	100	17½
4	Do. Deb. Stk.	100	104½
4	Atlas Investment, Ltd., Prefd. Stk.	100	70½
4½	Bankers' Invest., Ltd., Cum. Prefd.	100	105
—	Do. Defd	100	27½
4	Do. Deb. Stk	100	113
4/6	†Brewery & Comml. Inv., Ltd., £10 Shs.	5	6
4	British Investment, Ltd., Cum. Prefd.	100	109½
5	Do. Defd.	100	102½
4	Do. Deb. Stk. ....(†	100	107½
6	Brit. Steam. Invst., Ltd., Prefd. .... (†	100	117½
—	Do. Defd	100	68½
4½	Do. Perp. Deb. Stk (†	100	120½
2/3	Car Trust Invst., Ltd., £10 Shs.	2½	2
5	Do. Pref	100	105½
4	Do. Deb. Stk., 1915..	100	106
4	‡Clnl. Sec., Ltd., Prefd. (†	100	106½
—	Do. Defd.	100	47½
4	Consolidated, Ltd., Cum. 1st Pref.	100	95
4	Do. 5 p.c. Cm. 2nd do.	100	74½
—	Do. Defd.	100	14½
4½	Do. Deb. Stk.	100	114½
4½	Edinburgh Invest., Ltd., Cum. Prefd. Stk.	100	110½
4	Do. Deb. Stk. Red.	100	106½
5	Foreign, Amer. & Gen. Invt., Ltd., Prefd.	100	119
2	Do. Defd.	100	54½
4	Do. Deb. Stk.	100	117½
5	Foreign & Colonial Invt., Ltd., Prefd.	100	135½
4½	Do. Defd.	100	92
4½	Gas, Water & Gen. Invt., Cum. Prefd. Stk.	100	91½
—	Do. Defd. Stk.	100	32½
4	Do. Deb. Stk.	100	106
5	Gen. & Com. Invt., Ltd., Prefd. Stk.	100	106½
—	Do. Defd. Stk.	100	34½
4	Do. Deb. Stk.	100	110½
1/9	Globe Telegph. & Tst., Ltd.	10	12
6	Do. do. Pref.	10	18
4	Govt. & Genl. Invt., Ld., Prefd.	100	84½
3½	Do. Defd.	100	40½
4½	Govts. Stk. & other Secs. Invt., Ltd., Prefd.	100	95½
—	Do. Defd.	100	28
4½	Do. Deb. Stk.	100	110
4	Do. do.	100	104
4½	Guardian Invt., Ltd., Pfd.	100	92½
—	Do. Defd.	100	21½
4	Do. Deb. Stk.	100	104½
5	Indian & Gen. Inv., Ltd., Cum. Prefd.	100	109½
2½	Do. Defd.	100	55
4½	Do. Deb. Stk.	100	120½
5	Indust. & Gen. Tst., Ltd., Unified	100	100
3½	Do. Deb. Stk. Red.	100	102
4½	Internat. Invt., Ltd., Cm. Prefd.	100	72½
—	Do. Defd.	100	9
4	Do. Deb. Stk.	100	104
4	Invest. Tst. Cor. Ltd. Pfd.	100	102
4	Do. Defd.	100	83
4	Do. Deb. Stk. Red.	100	106
25/	Ldn. Gen. Invest. Ltd., 5 p.c. Cum. Prefd.	100	111½
37/6	Do. Defd.	100	120
4½	Ldn. Scot. Amer. Ltd. Pfd.	100	104½
£3	Do. Defd.	100	59½
4	Do. Deb. Stk.	100	111
4	Ldn. Tst., Ltd., Cum. Prfd. Stk.	100	106
4	Do. Defd. Stk.	100	76½
4	Do. Deb. Stk., Red.	100	108
3½	Do. Mt. Deb. Stk., Red.	100	101½
5	Mercantile Invt. & Gen., Ltd., Prefd.	100	108
2	Do. Defd.	100	47½
4	Do. Deb. Stk.	100	117½
4	Merchants, Ltd., Pref. Stk.	100	104
4	Do. Ord.	100	79
4	Do. Deb. Stk.	100	117
5	Municipal, Ltd., Prefd...	100	56½
—	Do. Defd.	100	18½
4½	Do. Debs.	100	113
4½	Do. Debs. "B"	100	100
4½	Do. "C" Deb. Stk.	100	98½
5	New Investment, Ltd. Ord.	100	97
5	Omnium Invest., Ltd., Pfd.	100	95½
£1	Do. Defd.	100	27½
4	Do. Deb. Stk.	100	102
4/	†Railway Deb. Tst. Ld., £20 Shs.	10	7
5	Do. Debs., Red. ..	100	105½
4½	Do. Deb. Stk., 1911	100	105½
4	Do. do. 1927	100	109½
4	Railway Invst. Ltd., Prefd.	100	116
18/6	Do. Defd.	100	24
6/4½	Railway Share Trust & Agency "A"	8	6½
7½	Do. "B" Pref. Stk.	100	142
4½	River Plate & Gen. Invt., Ltd., Prefd.	100	105
£3	Do. Defd.	100	54½
5	Scot. Invst., Ltd., Pfd. Stk.	100	94½
1½	Do. Defd...	100	26½
4	Do. Deb. Stk.	100	108
4½	Sec. Scottish Invst., Ltd., Cum. Prefd.	100	90½
£2	Do. Defd. Stk.	100	32
4	Do. Deb. Stk.	100	107½
7/6	Sth. Africa Gold Tst., Ltd.	1	5¼
6	Do. Cum. Pref.	1	1
5½	Do. 1st Debs., Red.	100	102
9d.	†Stock Conv. & Invest., Ltd., £5 Shs.	1	1⅜
—	Do. do. 4½ p.c. Cm. Prf.	100	112½
3½	Do. Ldn. & N. W. 1st. Charge Prefd.	100	116
4	Do do. 2nd Chge Prfd.	100	113
32/6	Do. do. Defd. Charge	100	33
3	Do. N. East. 1 Chge Pfd.	100	95
37/6	Stock N. East Defd. Chge	100	42
6	Submarine Cables	100	140½
5	U.S. & S. Amer. Invest., Ltd., Prefd.	100	98½
2	Do. Defd.	100	27½
4	Do. Deb. Stk.	100	104½

GAS AND ELECTRIC LIGHTING.

Last Div.	Name.	Paid.	Price.
10/6	Alliance & Dublin Con. 10 p.c. Stand.	10	24½
7/6	Do. 7 p.c. Stand...	10	17
5	Austln. Gas Lght. (Syd.) Debs. 1902	100	106
5	Bay State of N. Jrsy. Sk. Fd. Tst. Bd., Red. ..	—	92½
3/	Bombay, Ltd.	5	7
2/4½	Do. New	4	5½
12	Brentford Cons.	100	302½
9	Do. New	100	229½
5	Do. Pref.	100	147½
4	Do. Deb. Stk. ..	100	136
11½	Brighton & Hove Gen. Cons. Stk.	100	277½
8½	Do. "A" Cons. Stk.	100	202½
5	Bristol 5 p.c. Max.	100	132½
22/6	British Gas Light, Ltd.	20	57
11/6	Bromley Gas Consumrs.' 10 p.c. Stand.	10	26
8/6	Do. 7 p.c. Stand...	10	21
—	Brush Electl. Enging., L.	—	2½
2/	Do. 6 p.c. Pref.	—	2½
4½	Do. Deb. Stk.	100	111
4½	†Do. 2 Deb. Stk., Red.	100	101½
5/	B. Ayres (New), Ltd. ..	10	9½
4	Do. Deb. Stk., Rd. ..	—	97
12/	Cagliari Gas & Wtr., Ltd.	20	31
8/	Cape Town & Dist. Gas Light & Coke, Ltd.	10	17½
4½	Do. Pref.	10	12
6	Do. 1 Mt. Debs. 1910	50	60
3/	Charing Cross & Strand Elec. Sup., Ltd....	5	13
4½	Do. Cum. Pref.	5	6½
2/6	†Chelsea Elec. Sup., Ltd.	5	10½
4½	Do. Deb. Stk., Red.	100	113
5	Chic. Edison Co. 1 Mt., Red.	$1000	108
14/	City of Ldn. Elec. Lht., L.	10	28½
—	Do. New	10	27½
6/	Do. Cum. Pref.	10	17½
5	Do. Deb. Stk., Red. (†	100	131½
13½	Commercial, Cons.	100	342½
10½	Do. New	100	257½
4½	Do. Deb. Stk.	100	155
10	Continental Union, Ltd.	100	252½
7	Do. Pref. Stk.	100	217½
—	County of Lon. & Brush Prov. Elec. Lg., Ltd.	10	14
6	Do. Cum. Pref.	10	15½
14	Croydon Comcl. Gas, Ld., "A" Stk., 10 p.c...	100	317½
11	Do. "B" Stk., 7 p.c.	100	254½
5¼	Crystal Pal. Dist. Ord. 5 p.c. Stk.	100	140
5	Do. Pref. Stk.	100	141½
14/	European, Ltd.	10	26½
10/6	Do.	7½	19
12½	Gas Light & Ck Cons. Stk., "A" Ord.	100	314½
4	Do. "B" (4 p.c. Max.)	100	115½
10	Do. "C," "D," & "E" (Pref.)	100	322½
5	Do. "F" (Pref.)	100	152½
7½	Do. "G" (Pref.)	100	224½
7	Do. "H" (7 p.c. Max.)	100	206½
10	Do. "J" (Pref.).....	100	321½
6	Do. "K"	100	184½
4	Do. Deb. Stk.	100	139
4½	Do. do.	100	156
6	Do. do.	100	207
8/	Hong Kong & China, Ld.	10	14½
—	†House to House Elec. Light Sup., Ltd. ..	5	9½
7	Do. Cum. Pref.	5	11½
10	Imperial Continental ..	100	217½
3½	Do. Deb. Stk., Red ..	100	105½
2/	Malta & Medit., Ltd. ..	5	5½
5/	†Metrop. Elec. Sup., Ltd.	10	19
3/8	Do. New	10	18½
4½	Do. 1 Mt. Deb. Stk.	100	119½
5	Metro. of Melbrne. Dbs. 1908-12	100	113
4½	Do. Debs...1918-22-4	100	110
10/	Monte Video, Ltd.	20	15½
8/	†Notting Hill Elec. Ltg., Ltd.	10	18
4/6	Oriental, Ltd..........	5	8½
4/0½	Do. New	4½	7½
10½d.	Do. do. 1879	1	1½
3/6	Ottoman, Ltd.	5	4½
—	Para, Ltd.	—	—
6	People's Gas Lt. & C. of Chic. 2 Mt.....1904	100	105½
6	River Plate Elec. Lgt. & Trac., Ltd., 1 Deb. Stk.	—	92½†
112	Royal Elec. of Montreal	—	146
4½	Do. 1 Mt. Deb. ..	100	106
3/6	†St. James' & Pall Mall Elec. Light, Ltd. ..	5	17½
7	Do. Pref.	5	10½
4	Do. Deb. Stk., Red.†	100	102½
10/	San Paulo, Ltd.	10	16½

Gas and Electric (*continued*):—

Last Div.	Name.	Paid.	Price.
10	Sheffield Unit. Gas Lt. "A"	100	251½
10	Do. "B"	100	251½
10	Do. "C"	100	251½
—	Sth. Ldn. Elec. Sup., Ld.	2	3
5¼	South Metropolitan	100	144½
3	Do. 3 p.c. Deb. Stk.	100	106¼
12	Tottenham & Edmonton Gas Lt. & C., "A"	100	290
9	Do. "B"	100	210
7/	Tuscan, Ltd.	10	14
5	Do. Debs., Red.	100	101½
4/9	West Ham 10 p.c. Stan.	5	12
4/	Watmnstr. Elec. Sup., Ld.	5	16½

INSURANCE.

Last Div.	Name.	Paid.	Price.
4/	Alliance, £20 Shs.	44/	11½
20/	Alliance, Mar., & Gen., Ld., £100 Shs.	25	53
5/	Atlas, £50 Shs.	6	31½
8/	British & For. Marine, Ld., £20 Shs.	4	25
7½d.	British Law Fire, Ltd., £10 Shs.	1	1⅜
7/6	Clerical, Med., & Gen. Life, £25 Shs.	50/	16½
20/	Commercial Union, Ltd., £50 Shs.	5	46½
4	Do. "W. of Eng." Ter. Deb. Stk.	100	110½
60/	County Fire, £100 Shs.	80	185
2/6	Eagle, £50 Shs.	5	—
4/	Employers' Liability, Ltd., £10 Shs.	2	4
—	Empress, Ltd., £5 Shs.	1	—
21/	Equity & Law, £100 Shs.	6	21
7/6	General Life, £100 Shs.	5	15
4½d.	Gresham Life, £5 Shs.	15/	2½
2/6	Guardian, Ld., £10 Shs.	5	12½
20/	Imperial, Ltd., £20 Shs.	5	32
5/6	Imperial Life, £20 Shs.	4	7
6/	Indemnity Mutual Mar., Ltd., £15 Shs.	3	12
2/	Lancashire, £20 Shs.	2	5
7½d.	Law Acc. & Contin., Ltd., £5 Shs.	10/	¾
5/	Law Fire, £100 Shs.	2½	18
4½d.	Law Guar. & Trust, Ltd., £10 Shs.	1	1½
9/	Law Life, £20 Shs.	2	24½
2/9	Law Un. & Crown £10 Shs.	12/	7
4	Do. Deb. Stk., 1942	100	110½
14/6	Legal & General, £50 Shs.	8	15½
9d.	Lion Fire, Ltd., £8½ Shs.	1½	1
14/	Liverpool & London & Globe, Stk.	2	55½
20/	Do. Globe £1 Ann.	—	36
25/	London, £25 Shs.	12½	62
4/	Lond. & Lanc. Fire, £25 Shs.	2½	19½
2/	Lond. & Lanc. Life, £25 Shs.	2	5
10	Lond. & Prov. Mar., Ld., £10 Shs.	1	1½
2/	Lond. Guar. & Accident, Ltd., £5 Shs.	2	11½
40/	Marine, Ltd., £25 Shs.	4½	44½
2/	Maritime, Ltd., £10 Shs.	2	4½
1/6	Merc. Mar., Ld., £10 Shs.	2½	2½
1/	National Marine, Ltd., £9 Shs.	1	½
20/	N. Brit. & Merc., £25 Shs.	6½	43
20/	Northern, £100 Shs.	10	82
40/	Norwich Union Fire, £100 Shs.	12†	129½
5/	Ocean Acc. & Guar., fy. pd.	5	20½
1/	Do. £5 Shs.	1	4
2/6	Ocean, Marine, Ltd.	2½	9½
1/	Palatine, £10 Shs.	2	3½
2/6	Pelican, £10 Shs.	1	3½
42/	Phœnix, £50 Shs.	5	45
25/	Provident, £100 Shs.	10	36
3/	Railway Passngrs., £10 Shs.	2	8½
2/6	Rock Life, £5 Shs.	10/	4½
8	Royal Exchange	100	360
28/	Royal, £20 Shs.	3	56
4/	Sun, £10 Shs.	10/	11½
3/9	Sun Life, £10 Shs.	7½	15
4/	Thames & Mrsey. Marine, Ltd., £20 Shs.	2	11
9/	Union, £10 Shs.	4	24½
3/6	Union Marine, £20 Shs.	2½	9½
12/	Universal Life, £100 Shs.	12	42
2/	World Marine, £5 Shs.	2	1½

IRON, COAL, AND STEEL.

Last Div.	Name.	Paid.	Price.
3/9	Barrow Hæm. Steel, Ltd.	2½	2½
9/	Do. 6 p.c. and Pref.	7½	7
10/	Bolck., Vaugh. & C., Ld.	20	18
6/	Do. £8 liab.	12	10
7/6	Brown, J. & Co., Ltd., £20 Shs.	15	20½
22/6	Consett Iron, Ld., £10 Shs.	7½	30
4/	Do. 8 p.c. Cum. Pref.	5	11½
7/6	Ebbw Vale Steel, Iron & Coal, Ltd., £23 Shs.	20	7
15/	General Mining Assn., Ld.	5½	7½
16/	Harvey Steel Co. of Gt. Britain, Ltd.	10	26
5	Lehigh V. Coal 1 Mt. 5 p.c. Guar. Gd. Cp. Bds.	—	97½
42/6	Nantyglo & Blaina Iron, Ltd., Pref.	56a	96
1/	Nerbudda Coal & Iron, Ltd., £3 Shs.	56/	⅜
6/	Newport Abrcrn. Bk. Vein Steam Coal, Ltd.	10	4¾
5/	New Sharlston Coll., Ltd. Pref.	20	11
4½d.	Nw. Vancvr. Coal & Ld., L.	1	⅜
3/6	North's Navigation Coll. (1889) Ltd.	5	2
10/	Do. 10 p.c. Cum. Pref.	5	7½
1/	Rhymney Iron, Ltd.	5	1½
	Do. New, £5 Shs.	4½	½
5	Do. Mt. Debs., Red.	100	96½
5	Shelton Irn., Stl. & Cl. Co., Ltd., 1 Chg. Debs., Red.	100	98½
10	Sth. Hetton Coal, Ltd.	100	176½
	Vickers & Maxim, Ltd.	10	2¾
	Do. 5 p.c. Prfd. Stk.	100	134

SHIPPING.

Last Div.	Name.	Paid.	Price.
4/	African Stm. Ship, £20 Shs.	16	9½
5/	Do. Fully-paid	20	13½
5/	Amazon Steam Nav., Ltd.	12½	9½
8/	Castle Mail Pakts., Ltd., £20 Shs.	14	15½
3½	Do. 1st Deb. Stk., Red.	100	101
5/	China Mutual Steam, Ltd.	5	2½
6	Do. Cum. Pref.	10	9½
10/	Cunard, Ltd.	20	10
5/	Do. £20 Shs.	10	4
4½	Furness, Withy, & Co., Ltd., 1 Mt. Dbs., Red.	100	105
6/	General Steam	15	8½
5/	Do. 5 p.c. Pref., 1874	10	9
5/	Do. 5 p.c. Pref., 1877	10	9
5/	Leyland & Co., Ltd.	10	15½
7/	Do. 7 p.c. Cum. Pref.	10	14½
—	Do. 4½ p.c. Cum. Pre-Pf.	3	10½
4	Do. 1st Mt. Dbs., Red.	100	106½
2/6	Mercantile Steam, Ltd.	5	7½
6/4½	New Zealand Ship., Ltd.,	6	5
4	Do. Deb. Stk., Red.	100	104
5/	Orient Steam, Ltd.	10	4½
5	P. & O. Steam, Cum. Prefd.	100	155½
19	Do. Defd.	100	232½
3½	Do. Deb. Stk.	100	121
5	Richelieu & Ont., 1st Mt. Debs., Red.	100	100
30/	Royal Mail, £100 Shs.	60	51
2/6	Shaw, Sav., & Alb., Ltd., "A" Pref.	5	5
5/	Do. "B" Ord.	5	3½
8/	Union Steam, Ltd.	20	18½
4/	Do. New £20 Shs.	10	8
4	Do. Deb. Stk., Red.	100	107
7/	Union of N.Z., Ltd.	10	10
3/1½	Wilson's & Fur.-Ley., 5½ p.c. Cum. Pref.	10†	10½
4½	Do. 1 Mt. Db. Sk., Rd.	100†	102½

TELEGRAPHS AND TELEPHONES.

Last Div.	Name.	Paid.	Price.
4	African Direct, Ltd., Mort. Debs., Red.	100	102
—	Amazon Telegraph, Ltd.	10	6½
14/	Anglo-American, Ltd.	100	62
28/	Do. 6 p.c. Prefd. Ord.	100	111½
—	Do. Defd. Ord.	100	13½
3/	Brazilian Submarine, Ltd.	10	16½
5	Do. Debs., 2 Series	100†	114

Telegraphs and Telephones (*continued*):—

Last Div.	Name.	Paid.	Price.
4/	Chili Telephone, Ltd.	5	3½
$2	Comcial. Cable, $100 Shs.	—	187½
4	Do. Stg. 500-yr. Deb. Stk. Red.	100	106
2½d.	Consd. Telephone Constr., &c., Ltd.	10/	¼
8/	Cuba Submarine, Ltd.	10	8½
10/	Do. 10 p.c. Pref.	10	18½
2/	Direct Spanish, Ltd.	5	4½
5/	Do. 10 p.c. Cum. Pref.	5	10½
4½	Do. Debs.	50	104½
3/	Direct U.S. Cable, Ltd.	20	10½
2/6	Eastern, Ltd.	10	18
3/	Do. 6 p.c. Cum. Pref.	10	19
4	Do. Mt. Deb. Stk., Red.	100	132½
2/6	Eastern Exten., Aus., & China, Ltd.	10	19
5	Do. (Aus. Gov. Sub.) Deb., Red.	100	101
5	Do. do. Bearer	100	101½
4	Do. Mort. Deb. Stk.	100	133½
5	Eastn. & S. Afric., Ltd., Mort. Deb. 1900	100	101½
5	Do. Bearer	100	102½
4	Do. Mort. Debs. 1909	100	105½
4	Do. Mort. Debs. (Maur. Subsidy)	25	102½
5/	Grt. Nthn. Copenhagen	10	27½
5	Do. Debs., Ser. B., Red.	100	102½
12/6	Indo-European, Ltd.	25	53½
6	London Platino-Brazilian, Ltd., Debs. 1904	100	109½
4/	Montevideo Telph., Ltd., 6 p.c. Pref.	5	2½
3/	National Telephone, Ltd.	5	6½
6/	Do. Cum. 1 Pref.	10	16
6/	Do. Cum. 2 Pref.	10	15
5	Do. Non-Cum. 3 Pref.	5	6½
3½	Do. Deb. Stk., Red.	100	104½
4d.	Oriental Telephone, Ltd.	1	½
4	Pac. & Euro. Tlg. Dbs., Rd.	100	106½
4/	Reuter's, Ltd.	8	8
5/	Un. Riv. Plate Telph., Ltd.	5	4½
5	Do. Deb. Stk., Red.	100	103½
6/	West African Telg., Ltd.	10	4½
5	Do. 5 p.c. Mt. Debs., Red.	100	104½
—	W. Coast of America, Ltd.	10	—
3/	Western & Brazilian, Ltd.	15	10
3/	Do. 5 p.c. Pref. Ord.	7½	7½
—	Do. Defd. Ord.	7½	3
4	Do. Deb. Stk., Red.	100	105½
1/	W. India & Panama, Ltd.	10	½
6/	Do. Cum. 1 Pref.	10	7½
6/	Do. Cum. 2 Pref.	10	6
5	Do. Debs., Red.	100	106½
7	West. Union, 1 Mt. 1900 $	1000	107½
6	Do. 6 p.c. Stg. Bds., Rd.	100	102½

TRAMWAYS AND OMNIBUS.

Last Div.	Name.	Paid.	Price.
1/6	Anglo-Argentine, Ltd.	5	3½
6/	Do. Deb. Stk.	100	129½
4	Barcelona, Ltd.	10	13
5	Do. Deb., Red.	100	104½
6/6	Belfast Street Trams.	10	17
—	Blackpl. & Fltwd. Tram., £10 Shs.	8	9
4/	Bordeaux Tram. & O., Ltd.	10	13
5	Do. Cum. Pref.	10	11½
—	Brazilian Street Ry., Ltd.	2	½
—	British Elec. Trac., Ltd.	10	17½
2/	B. Ayres & Belg. Tram., Ltd., 6 p.c. Cum. Pref.	5	4
6	Do. 1 Deb. Stk. †	100	102½
—	B. Ayres. Gd. Nat., Ltd., 6 p.c. 1 Deb. Bds., Red.	100	60
5½	Do. Pref. Debs., Red.	100	92½
6d.	Calais, Ltd.	5	1
—	Calcutta, Ltd.	10	3½
—	Carthagena & Herr., Ltd.	10	3
5	Do. Deb., Red.	100	95
5	City of B'ham. Trams., Ltd., 5 p.c. Cum. Pref.	5	5½
4	Do. 1 Mort. Debs., Rd.	100	104½
3/9	City of B. Ayres, Ltd.	5	7
2/3	Do. Ext. £5 Shs.	3	4
6	Do. Deb. Stk.	100	150
9d.	Edinburgh Street Tram.	4	3
1/	Glasgow Tram. & Omni. Ltd., £9 Shs.	8	3½
3/7½	Imperial, Ltd.	6	12½
2/	Lond., Deptfd, & Greenwich, Prefd.	5	3½
nil	Do. Defd.	5	1
10½	Lond. Gen. Omni., Ltd.	100	206
4	Do. Deb., Red.	100	113½

Tramways and Omnibus (*continued*):—

Last Div.	Name	Paid.	Price.
6/	London Road Car	6	10½
5	London St. Rly. (Prov., Ont.), Mt. Debs.	100	112
4/9	London St. Trams.	—	3
12/9	†London Trams., Ltd.	10	11
6/	Do. Non-Cum. Pref.	10	10½
5	Do. Mt. Db. Stk., Rd.	100	100½
5	Lynn & Boston 1 Mt. 1924 $	1000	107
5	Milwaukee Elec. Cons. Mt. $	1000	97
5	Minneapolis St. 1 Cons. Mt. $	1000	94
5	Montreal St. Dbs., 1908	100	110
4½	Do. Debs., 1922	100	109
6/	Nth. Metropolitan	10	13
1/9½	Nth. Staffords., Ltd.	6	4½
5/6	Provincial, Ltd.	10	6½
6/	Do. Cum. Pref.	10	13½
5	St. Paul City, 1937 $	1000	94
5	Do. Guar. Twin City Rap. Trans. $	1000	94
5/	Southampton	10	7
7/	South London	10	8½
3/6	Sunderland, Ltd.	10	8½
4½	Toronto 1 Mt., Red.	100	109
2/6	Tramways Union, Ltd.	5	7
4½	Do. Deb., Red.	100	109
5/	Vienna General Omnibus.	5	6½
5	Do. 5 p.c. Mt. Deb., Red.	100	105
4/	Wolverhampton, Ltd.	10	6½

WATER WORKS.

Last Div.	Name.	Paid.	Price.
8/	Antwerp, Ltd.	20	21½
6/	Cape Town District, Ltd.	5	6½
17½	Chelsea	100	337½
5	Do. Pref. Stk.	100	178½
4½	Do. Pref. Stk., 1875	100	158½
4½	Do. Deb. Stk.	100	162½
5/	City St. Petersburg, Ltd.	13	11
4/6	Colne Valley	10	15
4	Do. Deb. Stock	100	137½
£4	Consol. of Rosar., Ltd., 4 p.c. 1 Deb. Stk., Red.	100	91
7½	East London	100	238
4½	Do. Deb. Stk.	100	163½
3	Do. Deb. Stk., Red.	100	105
27/6	Grand Junction (Max. 10 p.c.) "A"	50	124½
18/9	Do. "B"	25	
16/9	Do. "C" (Max. 7½ p.c.)	25	57½
35/	Do. "D" (Max. 7 p.c.)	50	102½
4	Do. Deb. Stock	100	149½
13	Kent	100	364½
7	Do. New (Max. 7 p.c.)	100	217½
6/7½	Kimberley, Ltd.	7	5
6	Do. Debs., Red.	100	104½
6	Do. Deb. Stk., Red.	100	104½
10	Lambeth (Max. 10 p.c.)	100	309½
7	Do. (Max. 7½ p.c.), 50 & 25	—	229½
4	Do. Deb. Stock	100	148½
3	Do. Red. Deb. Stock	100	105
10/	Montevideo, Ltd.	20	16½
5	Do. 1 Deb. Stk.	100	108½
5	Do. 2 Deb. Stk.	100	103½
130/11	15] New River New	100	454½
4	Do. Deb. Stk.	100	153½
4	Do. Deb. Stk. "B"	100	153½
—	Odessa, Ltd., "A" 6 p.c. Prefd.	20	—
nil	Do. "B" Deferred	20	—
4	Portland Con. Mt. "B," 1927	—	—
8/	Seville, Ltd.	20	18½
5/6	Southend "Addl." Ord.	10	17½
6	Southwark and Vauxhall	100	166½
6	Do. "D" Shares (7½ p.c. max.)	100	159½
5	Do. Pref. Stock	100	177½
4	Do. "A" Deb. Stock	100	147½
3	Staines Resvirs. Jt. Com. Gua. Deb. Stk., Red.	100	105
7/	Tarapaca, Ltd.	10	9½
10	West Middlesex	100	317½
4½	Do. Deb. Stk.	100	163½
3	Do. Deb. Stk.	100	107

Prices Quoted on the Leading Provincial Exchanges.

ENGLISH.

In quoting the markets, B stands for Birmingham; Bl for Bristol; M for Manchester; L for Liverpool; and S for Sheffield.

CORPORATION STOCKS.

Chief Market.	Int or Div.	Name.	Amount paid.	Price.
M	3½	Bolton, Red. 1935 ..	100	116
M	3½	Burnley, Red. 1933..	100	116
M	3½	Bury, Red. 1946	100	118
L	2½	Liverpool, Red. 1925	100	102
B	3½	Longton, 1932	100	106
M	4	Oldham Prp. Db. Sk.	100	144
M	£1	Do. Gas & W. Ann.		35
S	4	Rotherham 4 p.c., Red. 1927...... {£	1 an	114
S	3	Do. Red. 1920..	100	104
M	3½	Runcorn Red. 1923..	100	105
S	2¾	Sheffield Water Ann.	100	117¾
S	5	Do.	3 an	90
L	3½	Southport Red. 1936 {	5 an 100	112
L	3	Do. Red. 1914..	100	104
M	3	Todmorden, Red. 1914	100	103

RAILWAYS.

Chief Market.	Int or Div.	Name.	Amount paid.	Price.
Bl	4½	Bridgewater Pref. ..	100	137½
M	4	Cleator & Workton.	100	78
M	4	Do. 1883 Pref. ..	100	111
L	4	Cockermth. K. & P.	100	116
L	6	Isle of Man	5	6¼
L	5	Do. Pref.	5	6⅝
L	3	Liverpool Overhead	10	11 1/16
L	4	Do. Deb. Stk. ..	100	109
L	5	Do. Pref.	10	16½
L	6	Maryport & Carlisle	100	170
S	6	Mid. Shef. & Roth. Pf.	100	231
Bl	35/	Neath & Brecon "A"	100	60
M	4¾	Oldham, Ashton, &c.	10	17
Bl	5½	Penarth Harbour ..	100	184½
Bl	4	Do. Deb. Stk. ..	100	145
Bl	3½	Do. Deb. Stk. ..	100	127
Bl	½	Ross & Monmouth..	20	5⅜
Bl	6	Do. Pref.	20	43
M	3	Southport & Cheshire Deb. Stk.	100	105½
M	nil.	Do. Pref.	100	26
Bl	2½	West Somerset Gu...	100	97½
Bl	5	Wye Val. Deb. Stk.	100	164

BANKS.

Chief Market.	Int or Div.	Name.	Amount paid.	Price.
L	6/	Adelphi, L., £20 Shs.	10	16
L	14/	Bk of L'ool, L., £100 Sh	12½	38½
B	4/6	Brmnghm. Dis. & C., Ltd., £20 Shs.	4	10⅜
B	6/3	Co. of Staffs., L., £40	5	13
S	17½	Crompton & Evans, Ltd., £20 Shs	4	15
M	14/	Lancs. & Yorks, Ltd., £20 Shs.	10	32½
L	18/	Livrpl. Union, Ltd., £100 Shs.	20	60½
M	24/	Manchester & Co., Ltd., £100 Shs. ..	16	61½
M	20/	Mnchstr. & Livrpool. Dis., Ltd., £60 Shs.	10	52½
M	1/6	Mer. of Lancashire, Ltd., £20 Shs.	3	6⅛
L	16/	Nth. & Sth. Wales, Ltd., £40 Shs.	10	34½
	5/	Notts Joint St., Ltd., £50 Shs.	10	23
M	3/	Oldham Joint Stk., Ltd., £20 Shs.	4	10½
S	10-	Sheffield Banking, Ltd., £50 Shs.	17½	51½
S	10	Do. & Rotherham, Ltd., £50 Shs. ..	8	26⅝
S	15	Do. & Hallamsh., Ltd., £100 Shs. ..	25	61⅛
S	10	Do. Union, Ltd., £40 Shs.	10	24½
M	12/	Union of Manchester, Ltd., £25 Shs.. ..	11	26⅝
M	16/	Williams, Deacon, &c. Ltd., £50 Shs.	8	26
Bl	20	Wilts & Dorset, Ltd., £50 Shs.	10	50
S	10/	York City & Co., Ltd., £10 Shs.	3	14

BREWERIES.

Chief Market.	Int or Div.	Name.	Amount paid.	Price.
B	6	Ansell & Sons Pref.	10	15½
B	5	Do. Debs.	100	110
L	7/	Bent's	10	20½
L	6	Do. Cum. Pref...	10	14½
L	4½	Do. Deb. Stk. ..	100	110
L	13/6	Birkenhead, £5 paid	5	22
L	13/6	Do. £10 paid....	10	25
M	9/	Boddington's	9	21½
M	5	Do. Cum. Pref...	10	13½
M	4	Do. Deb. Stk. ..	100	109
B	4½	Butler & Co. Db. Stk	100	110½
M	6	Chesters' Cum. Pref.	10	13½
M	4½	Do. Debs.	100	112½
S	17/	Clarkson's Ord.	10	24½
S	6	Do. Cum. Prf. Stk.	10	15
M	4	Dutton & Co. Db. Sk.	100	103
M	4½	Hardy's Crown Debs.	100	110½
B	6/	Holt	10	19
B	5	Do. Cum. Pref...	10	12½
B	4	Do. Debs.	100	107½
B	12/6	Lichfield	10	24
B	5	Do. Cum. Pref...	10	11¾
M	5½	Manchester Deb. Stk.	100	140½
B	14	Mitchell, H., & Co.	10	37½
B	6	Do. Cum. Pref...	10	15¾
Bl	6	Oakhill Pref........	10	16½

Breweries (*continued*):—

Chief Market.	Int. or Div.	Name.	Amount paid.	Price.
M	—	Springwell	10	10¼
M	7	Do. Pref.	10	13½
Bl	10	Stroud	10	17½
Bl	6	Do. Pref	10	14½
M	—	Taylor's Eagle......	10	11
M	7	Do. Cum. Pref ..	10	13½
M	5½	Do. Deb. Stk. ..	100	120½
S	10	Tennant Bros £20 shs	15	33½
S	10	Wheatley & Bates ..	10	14
S	6	Do. Cum. Pref.	10	13

CANALS AND DOCKS.

Chief Market.	Int. or Div.	Name.	Amount paid.	Price.
Bl	3	Hill's Dry Dk. &c. £20	18	8
M	4	Manc. Ship Canal 1st Mt. Deb. Stk.	100	104
M	4	Do. and do.	100	103
L	36/3	Mersey Dck. & Harb.	an.	119½
L	35/	Do.	an.	114
M	—	Rochdale Canal	100	37½
B	35/	Staff. & Worc. Canal	100	75½
B	4½	Do. Deb. Stk....	100	137
Bl	4	Swansea Harb.... [†	100	114
B	27/6	Warwick & Birm. Cnl	100	66
B	12/6	Do. & Napton do.	100	21½

COMMERCIAL & INDUSTRIAL.

Chief Market.	Int. or Div.	Name.	Amount paid.	Price.
L	5	Agua Santa Mt. Debs	100	100½
M	—	Armitage, Sir E. & Sns Ltd.	10	19
M	5	Do. Deb. 1910 ..	100	103
L	6	Ang. Chil. Nit. 1 Mt. Debs., 1919 ..	100	108½
Bl	8½	Bath Stone Firms ..	10	19⅝
M	4/9½	Barlow & Jones, Ltd., £10 Shs.	8	10⅝
B	7/6	Birmgham. Ry. Car.	10	17
B	6	Do. Pref.	10	15½
B	5/	Do. Small Arms	5	18
M	£12	Blackpool Pier......	100	275½
M	5	Do. Tower Debs.	50	54½
M	6/6	Do. Wi. Gar. & P.	5	4½
Bl	10	Bristl. & S.W.R. Wag. £20 Shs.	3	6½
Bl	8	Do. Wag. & Carri. £10 Shs.	10	14½
M	7/	Crosses & Winkwth. Ltd.	5	12¾
L	5	G. Angus & Co. Pref.	10	13½
Bl	10	Gloster. Carri. & W.		10
Bl	5	Gt. Wstn. Cttn., Ltd.	20	15½
M	6	Hetherington, L. Prf.	10	9
M	4½	Do. Debs., 1910	100	96
B	75	Hinks (J. & Son), Ltd.	1	1½
S	10/	Jessop & Sons, £50 Sh	30	26⅝
S	10	Kayser, Ellsn. & Co. L.	5	10
S	6	Do. Pref.	5	7½
M	7/6	Kellner-Partgton., L.	5	14½
M	4½	Do. Debs., 1914	100	105½
M	5	Kerr Thread, Ltd., Debs.	100	99
B	17/	King's Norton Metal, £10 Shs.	8½	18
M	5/	Lancashire & Yorks. Wagon, Ltd.	10	9¾
L	10/	Liverpool Exch., Ltd.	20	27½
L	35/	Do. Grain Stge, Ltd.	50	110
L	2/6	Do. Rubber, Ltd...	5	7
M	9d.	Manchester Bond. Whse., L., £10 Shs.	4½	2¾
M	3/9	Do. Comcial. Bldgs., Ltd., £10 Shs.	5	10¾
M	3/9	Do. No. 2, £10 Shs.	5	10½
M	2/3	Do. No. 3, £10 Shs.	5	7½
M	4/	Do. Corn, &c., Exchange, Ltd.	10	16½
M	4	Do. Debs.	100	125
M	8	Do. Ryl. Exchge, L.	100	246½
B	5	Midland Rlwy. Car. Wgn., Ld., £20 Sh.	10	13½
B	59	Millers & Corys Dbs.	100	101
B	12/6	Mint, Brgham., Ltd.	5	7
B	5	Do. Debs.	25	107
B	10/	Nettlefolds, Ltd.....	10	46
B	5	Do. Pref.	10	15
S	9	Nth. Centrl. Wgn., L.	5	2½
B	10/	Paint. Nut & Bolt, L.	10	28½
B	5	Do. Pref.	10	14½
B	6d.	Perry & Co., Ltd. ..	1	1½
B	6d.	Do. Pref.	1	1¼
S	10	Round, J., & Co., L., £10 Shs.	6	12½
S	10	Rodgers, J., & Sons, L.	100	218
M	18/9	Rylands & Sons, Ltd., £20	15	40⅛
M	2½	Do. paid up	20	46
M	4	Do. Debs. ..1909	100	106
S	5	Sanderson Brs. & Co., Ltd. Debs.	100	102
M	4½	Schwabe, S., & Co., Ltd., 1 Debs. 1914	100	104
S	7½	Sheffield Forge & Rolling, Ltd.	10	11
L	—	Southport Pier, Ltd.	100	92½
L	2½	Do. W. Gdns., Ltd.	5	3½
Bl	5	Spillers & Bakers, Ltd, £10 Shs.	9	14½
Bl	6	Do. Pref.	10	14½
B	5/	Union Rolling Stock, Ltd., £20 Shs.....	5	7½
M	5/	Victoria Pr., S'port, L.	5	4⅝
Bl	8	Western Wagon & Property, Ltd.....	6	10
S	10	Wostenholm, G., & Son, Ltd., £25 Shs.	20	26¾
S	6½	Yorksh. Wagon, Ltd.	2	2½

FINANCIAL, TRUSTS, &c.

Chief Market.	Int. or Div.	Name.	Amount paid.	Price.
M	1/	Manchstr. Trst. £10 Shs.	2	14/6
M	1/3	N. of Eng. T. Deb. & A., Ltd. £10 Shs.	2½	21/6
M	3½	Do. 1 Mt. Debs...	100	95½
L	—	Pacific Ln. & Inv., L.	2½	2⅝
L	4	Do. Deb. Stk.....	100	102
L	—	United Trst., L. Prfd.	100	72½
L	—	Do. Deferred....	100	62½

GAS.

Chief Market.	Int. or Div.	Name.	Amount paid.	Price.
Bl	5	Bristol Gas (5 p.c. mx.)	100	130
Bl	4	Do. 1st Deb.	100	136
S	10	Gt. Grimsby "C" ..	10	202
L	10	Liverpool Utd. "A"	100	258
L	7	Do. "B"......	100	191
L	4	Do. Deb.	100	136
S	10	Sheffield Gas "A," "B," "C"	100	254
B	10½	Wolverhampton	100	222
B	3	Do. 6 p.c. Pref. ..	100	170½

INSURANCE.

Chief Market.	Int. or Div.	Name.	Amount paid.	Price.
M	6	Equitable F. & Acc. £5 Shs.	1	38/
L	—	Liverpool Mortgage £10 Shs.	2	1 5/16
M	2/	Mchester. Fire £20 Shs	2	7¾
M	5/	National Boiler & G., Ltd., £10 Shs.	3	13½
L	2/	Reliance Mar., Ltd., £10 Shs.	2	4¾
L	2/	Sea, Ltd., £10 Shs...	2	10 11/16
L	—	Stnd. Mar., L., £20 Sh.	4	8½
L	—	State Fire, L., £20 Sh.	1	2½

COAL, IRON, AND STEEL.

Chief Market.	Int. or Div.	Name.	Amount paid.	Price.
Bl.	7/6	Albion Stm. Coal ..	10	10¾
M	18/	And. Knowles & S., Ltd., £37½ Shs. ..	22½	13½
M	5	Do. Mt. Debs. 1908	100	105½
Bl.	1/½	Ashton V. Iron	100	25
S		Bessemer, Ltd.	10	19¾
S	5	Do. Pref.	10	13
S	7	Briggs, H., & Co., "A" £15 Shs.	12½	15½
S	7	Do. "B" £15 Shs.	8½	9½
S	20	Brown Baley's Stl., L.	10	28½
S	5	Brown, J., & Co., Cum. Pref.	10	13½
S	£5	Cammell, Ch. & Co., Ltd., £100 Shs...	80	216½
S	5	Do. "A" Pref. ..	20	33½
S	40/	Do. "B"	20	53½
M	5	Chatterley Whitfield. Col., Debs., 1905..	100	100½
Bl	4	Davis, D., & Sons, Ld.	10	9½
M	5	Evans, R., & Co., Ltd., Deb., 1910 [†	100	100½
S	12½	Fox, S., & Co., Ltd., £100 Shs.	80	178½
Bl	10	Gt. Wstn. Col., L., "A"	5	10
Bl	5	Do. "B"	5	4⅝
Bl	3	Main Colliery, Ltd.	10	7
B	2/6	Muntz's Metal, Ltd.	5	7½
B	5	Do. Pref.......	5	6⅛
M	2/6½	Nth. Lonsd. Iron and Steel, Ltd., £10 Sh.	8½	2½
Bl	6	North's Nav. Coll., Ltd., Debs.	100	107
S	60/	Parkgate Irn. & Stl., Ltd., £100 Shs. ..	75	68½
M	6	Pearson & Knls., Ld., "A" Cum. Pref...	50	46
B	10/	Sandwell Pk. Col., L.	10	17½
M	6/3	Sheepbridge Coal and Iron, Ltd., "A"	25	16⅝
M	2/6	Do. "B"	10	6½
M	5	Do. "C" Gua. Pf.	25	28½
Bl	4	South Wales Coll., Ltd., "A"	17	8½
S	55/	Staveley Coal & Iron, Ltd., "A" £100 Sh.	60	79½
S	55/	Do. "C"	60	80⅝
M	1/10½	Tredegar Iron & Cl., Ld., "A" £10 Sh.	7½	2½
M	1½	Do. "B" Stk. ..	100	29½
M	2/	Wigan Cl. & Irn., Ld.	10	6
M	1/6	Do. £10 Shs.	7½	3½

SHIPPING.

Chief Market.	Int. or Div.	Name.	Amount paid.	Price.
Bl	6	Bristol St. Nav. Pref.	10	11½
L	5/	Brit. & Af. St. Nav..	10	13½
L	—	British & Estn, Ltd.	6½	3
L	10/	Pacific Stm. Nav., L.	25	24
L	10/	Wst. Ind. & Pac. St. Ltd., £25 Shs.....	20	29½

TRAMWAYS, &c.

Chief Market.	Int. or Div.	Name.	Amount paid.	Price.
B	5/	Brmngh. & Aston, L.	5	11
B	5/	Do. Mid., Ltd. ..	10	8
Bl	6/	Bristol Tr. & Car., Ltd.	10	19¾
Bl	4/	Do. Debs.	100	121
L	6	I. of Man Elec., L., Pref.	1	1½
M	15/	Manchester C. & T, L., "A" £20 Shs.	15	27½
M	10/	Do. "B"	10	18¾

WATER WORKS.

Chief Market.	Int. or Div.	Name.	Amount paid.	Price.
Bl	7	Bristol	25	59½
Bl	7	Do..............	20	46
Bl	58/	Do. 7 p.c. max. ..	100	157½
Bl	4½	Do. Pref.	20	32½
Bl	5	Do. Pref.	10	18¾
Bl	3½	Do. Deb.	100	129½
M	10	Fylde "A"........	100	335
M	7	Do. "B"	100	224
B	6	S. Staffs. Ord. "A"	100	168
B	—	Do. "B"	100	167
B	4	Do. Deb. Stk.	100	140
B	5	Do. Pf "A" "B" "C"	100	165
M	£3½	Stockport District ..	100	185
B	2/	Wolverhampton New	5	6¾

SCOTTISH.

In quoting the markets, E stands for Edinburgh, and G for Glasgow.

RAILWAYS.

Chief Market.	Int. or Div.	Name.	Nom. Amount	Price.
E	6½	Arbroath and Forfar	25	51
G	1¾	Callander and Oban .	10	7½
G	4	Do. Deb. Stock	100	148
G	4½	Do. Pref.......	10	14½
G	4	Cathct. Dist. Deb. Stk.	100	148
E	5	Edin. and Bathgate .	100	181½
E	7	Forth & Clyde Junc.	100	226
G	4¾	Lanarks. and Ayrsh.	10	14
G	4	Do. & Dumbartons.	10	14½
G	4	Do. Deb. Stk.	100	149

BANKS.

Chief Market.	Int. or Div.	Name.	Nom. Amount	Price.
G	12	Bank of Scotland ..	100	358
G	20	British Linen	100	478
G	8	Caledonian, Ltd.....	2½	97/6
G	—	Clydesdale, Ltd.	10	23 11/16
G	16	Commercl. of Scot., L.	20	88½†
G	16	National of Scot. Ld.	100	413
G	7½	North of Scotland, L.	4	9¾
G	8	Royal of Scotland ..	100	230
G	12½	Town & County, Ltd.	7	20 11/16
G	11	Union of Scotland, L.	10	25⅝

BREWERIES.

Chief Market.	Int. or Div.	Name.	Nom. Amount	Price.
E	5	Bernard, Thos. Pref.	10	11½
E	5	Bernard, T. & J., Cum. Pref........	10	12¾
G	10	Highland Distilleries	2½	10½

CANALS AND DOCKS.

Chief Market.	Int. or Div.	Name.	Nom. Amount	Price.
G	4	Clyde Nav. 4 p.c....	100	127½
G	3½	Do. 3½ p.c.......	100	103½
G	3½	Greenock Harb. "A"	100	96½
G	1	Do. "B"	100	38½

MISCELLANEOUS.

Chief Market.	Int. or Div.	Name.	Nom. Amount	Price.
G	4½	Alexander & Co. Debs.	100	110½
G	5	Baird, H., & Sns. C.P.	10	12½
E	10	Barry, Ostlere, & Co.	7½	12½
E	6	Do. Cum. Pref...	10	15⅛
G	5	Brown, Stewart, Deb.	100	78
E	7½	Broxburn Oil	8½	8½
E	6	Do. Cum. Pref...	10	11 5/16
E	7	Edinburgh & Dist. Tram. Cum. Pref.	5	8 11/16
E	5	Gilroy, Sons, & Co. Debs.	100	99
G	3/	Glasgow Cot. Spin...	6	5
G	55/	Do. Royal Exchg.	46	110
G	—	Pumpherston Oil Pf.	10	8¾
E	7	Scottish Assam Tea	10	11½
E	5	Scottish Waggon....	10	13½
G	5	Stoddard & Co. Pref.	10	12½

FINANCIAL, LAND, AND INVESTMENT.

Chief Market.	Int. or Div.	Name.	Nom. Amount	Price.
G	1/	Assets Co...........	1	47/
E	4½	Investors' Mort. Pref.	100	98½
E	4	Do. Deb. Stk....	100	103½
E	4	Nthn. Inv. N. Zeal. Deb. Stk.	100	106½
E	4	N. of Scot. Canadian Deb. Stk.	100	106
E	4½	Real & Deb. Corp. Deb. Stk.	100	106½

INSURANCE.

Chief Market.	Int. or Div.	Name.	Amount paid.	Price.
G	12/	Caledonian F. & Life	5	36½
G	4/6	City of Glasgow Life	2½	13½
E	19/	Edinburgh Life	20	55
G	13/2	Life Ass. of Scotland	8¼	34½
E	8	Nat. Guar. & Surety	2	48/6
G	17½	Scottish Union and National "A"	1	96/
G	17½	Do. "B"	3¼	18

IRON, COAL, AND STEEL.

Chief Market.	Int. or Div.	Name.	Amount paid.	Price.
E	Nil.	Addie, Coll. Cm. Pref.	10	8
E	8/	Arniston Coal	8	14½
E	5	Cairntable Gas Coal	8	86/
E	7½	Fife Coal	10	21
E	5	Do. Cum. Pref.	10	13½
G	7	Merry & Cunghame. Cum. Pref.	10	15½
G	5	Do. Debentures	100	105
E	1/9	Niddrie & Benhar Cl.	1½	39/
G	5	Steel Com. of Scotlnd	—	
	—	"A" Deb. Stk.	100	110
G	6	Do. 2nd Mt. "B"	100	105
E	—	Watson, John	8½	10½
E	6	Do. Cum. Pref.	7½	8½
E	12½	Wilson's & Cly. Coal	3	8½

IRISH.

In quoting the markets, B stands for Belfast, and D for Dublin.

CORPORATION STOCKS.

Chief Market.	Int. or Div.	Name.	Amount paid.	Price.
B	3½	Belfast, 1921	100	113
B	3½	Do. 1912	100	108½
B	3½	Do. 1924	100	109½
B	3	Do. 1955	100	106
B	3½	Do. Water Com.	100	117
B	3	Do. do.	100†	107½
B	3½	Do. Harbour Com.	100	113½
D	3½	Rathmines & Rathgar	100	110½
D	3½	Waterford Deb.	100	—

RAILWAYS.

Chief Market.	Int. or Div.	Name.	Amount Paid.	Price.
D	25/	Cork, Bandon, & S.C.	100	76
D	4	Do. Deb.	100	—
D	4	Do. W. Cork Pref.	100	119
B	5½	Belfast & Northern	100	161
B	4	Do. Deb.	100	148½
B	4	Do. Pref.	100	143
B	6½	Belfast & C. Down	100	167
B	4	Do. Deb.	100	149
B	3	Do.	100	109
B	4½	Do. 4½ Pref. B.	100	153½
B	5	Do. Guar.	100	173½
D	Nil.	Dublin, Wick. & Wex.	100	25
D	4	Do. Deb.	100	125½
D	4½	Do. Deb.	100	130
D	6	Do. Guar.	100	163
D	4	Do. C. of Dub. Junc.	100	—
D	5	Do. 1860 Pref.	100	106
D	—	Do. 1864 Pref.	100	90
D	—	Do. 1865 Pref.	100	81
B	6½	Great Northern	100	183
B	4	Do. Deb.	100	150
B	4	Do. Pref. B.	100	145½
B	5½	Gt. South & Western	100	144½
B	4	Do. Deb.	100	149½
B	4	Do. Guar.	100	146
D	4	Midland Gt. Western	100	112
D	4	Do. Deb.	100	—
D	4½	Do. Deb.	100	150
D	4½	Do. Deb.	100	—
D	5	Do. Pref.	100	177
D	4	Do. Pref.	100	143
D	—	Waterford & Central	100	—
D	3	Do. Deb.	100	94½
D	3½	Do. Pref.	100	—
D	4	Waterfd. L., & W. Db.	100	128
D	4½	Do. Deb.	100	—
D	4	Do. Pref.	100	116
D	3½	Do. Pref.	100	90½

BANKS.

Chief Market.	Int. or Div.	Name.	Amount paid.	Price.
B	50/	Belfast, Old, £125 Shs.	25	127
B	20/	Do. New, £125 Shs.	25	50½
D	2/	Hibernian, £20 Shs.	5	6½
D	2/	Munster & Leinster £5 Shs.	2	8½
B	11/	Northern, £50 Shs.		[illegible]
D	13/	Royal, £50 Shs.	10	29½
B	5/	Ulster, £15 Shs.	2½	12½

BREWERIES AND DISTILLERIES.

Chief Market.	Int. or Div.	Name.	Amount paid.	Price.
D	10/	Castlebellingham & Drog.	10	15½
D	6	Do. Pref.	10	15½
D	4½	Do. Deb.	100	116
B	17/	Dunville & Co.	10	29
B	6	Irish Distillery, Pref.	10	13
B	5	Do. Deb.	100	111
B	6	J. & J. M'Connell, Pf.	10	14½
B	13/6	Mitchell & Co.	9	19½
B	5	Do. Deb.	10	11½
D	4½	Phœnix Brew. Deb.	100	—
B	6/	Wm. Cowan	10	12½
B	6	Do. Pref.	10	13½
B	8/	Young, King, & Co.	8	14

STEAM AND CANAL.

Chief Market.	Int. or Div.	Name.	Amount paid.	Price.
B	Nil	Belfast Steamship	90	35½
D	10/	British and Irish	90	—
D	15/	City of Dublin	100	63½
D	3½	Do. Deb.	100	104½
D	30/	Dublin & Lpool. Bldg.	50	—
D	2/6	Dundalk & Newry	10	4½
D	3/6	Grand Canal	10	11½
D	3	Do. Pref.	10	9½
D	3	Do. Deb.	100	—
B	30/	Irish Shipowners	100	60
B	3/6	Ulster Steamship	5	5½

MISCELLANEOUS.

Chief Market.	Int. or Div.	Name.	Amount paid.	Price.
D	3/1	Arnott & Co.	4	7½
D	6	Do. Pref.	4	6½
B	9/	Belfast Com. Bldgs.	10	11
B	50/6	Do. Ropework Co.	75	91½
B	5	Do. do. Pref.	10	12½
B	2/	Do. Discount Co.	3	45/
B	5	Do. do. Pref.	3	4½
B	10/	Brookfield Linen	25	17½
B	Nil	Cory & Co.	25	4
B	5	Do. Deb.	50	[illegible]
B	4½	David Allen & S's Deb.	100†	[illegible]
D	4/	Dublin Trams	10	[illegible]
D	6	Do. Pref.	10	[illegible]
D	4	Do. Deb.	100	[illegible]
B	5/	Edenderry Spinning	10	[illegible]
B	25/	Falls Flax Spinning	25	[illegible]
B	17/	Forster, Green, & Co.	10	[illegible]
B	2/	Island Spinning	[illegible]	[illegible]
B	8/	Jas. Lindsay & Co.	[illegible]	[illegible]
B	1/7½	John Arnott & Co.	4	[illegible]
B	4½	Do. Deb.	[illegible]	[illegible]
D	5/	Kinahan & Co.	[illegible]	—
D	5½	Do. Pref.	10	11½
D	4½	Do. Deb.	100	—
B	12/	Kirker & Co.	10	10
B	5/	Leahy, Kelly, & Leahy	5	[illegible]
B	6	Do. Pref.	[illegible]	[illegible]
B	2/4½	Lindsay Bros. Ltd.	[illegible]	[illegible]
B	4½	Do. Deb.	50	[illegible]
D	1/	National Assurance	[illegible]	—
B	10/	Olley & Co.	[illegible]	[illegible]
D	1/1½	Patriotic Assurance	[illegible]	[illegible]
B	3/7½	P. Johnston & Son, L.	[illegible]	[illegible]
B	10/	Robertson, F., & Co.	[illegible]	[illegible]
B	5	Ulster Marine Insur.	[illegible]	[illegible]
B	15/	York-street Flax	[illegible]	[illegible]
B	6	Do. Pref.	[illegible]	[illegible]
B	4½	Do. Deb.	100	[illegible]

INDIAN AND CEYLON TEA COMPANIES.

Acres Planted.	Crop, 1896.	Paid up Capital.	Share.	Paid up.	Name.	Dividends. 1894.	1895.	1896.	Int. 1897.	Price.	Yield.	Reserve.	Balance Forward.	Working Capital.	Mortgages, Debs. or Pref. Capital not otherwise stated.
	lb.	£	£	£	INDIAN COMPANIES.							£	£	£	£
11,240	3,109,000	120,000	10	3	Amalgamated Estates	—	*	10	5	3½	6½	10,000	16,500	D52,990	—
		400,000	10	10	Do. Pref.	—	*	5	15	10½	4½				
10,223	3,387,100	187,160	20	20	Assam	20	20	20	5	60	6½	55,000	1,730	D11,350	—
5,900	3,310,000	142,500	10	10	Assam Frontier	3	6	6	—	9½	6½	—	286	20,000	80,900
		142,500	10	10	Do. Pref.	6	6	6	3	12	5				
2,087	865,550	66,745	5	5	Attaree Khat	12	12	8	3	7½	5½	3,790	4,800	7,770	—
1,633	550,980	78,170	10	10	Borelli	4	4	5	—	8½	5½	—	3,056	D670	6,900 Pref.
1,689	880,000	60,825	5	5	British Indian	6	5	5	—	4½	5½	—	2,900	12,300	16,500 Pref.
3,223	2,282,430	114,500	5	5	Brahmapootra	20	18	20	6	14½	6½	—	28,440	41,600	•
3,904	1,634,000	76,500	10	10	Cachar and Dooars	*	8	7	—	9½	7½	—	1,645	21,240	•
		76,500	10	10	Do. Pref.	*	6	6	3	12½	4½				
3,946	2,000,370	72,010	1	1	Chargola	8	7	10	2½	1	10	3,000	3,300	—	—
		31,000	1	1	Do. Pref.	7	7	7	3½	1⅜	5				
1,971	968,090	33,000	5	5	Chubwa	10	8	10	3½	7	6½	10,000	2,043	D5,400	—
		33,000	5	5	Do. Pref.	7	7	7	3½	7	5				
33,250	10,620,000	120,000	10	3	Cons. Tea and Lands	—	*	10	5	4	7½	65,000	14,240	D191,674	—
		1,000,000	10	10	Do. 1st Pref.	—	*	5	15	11	4½				
		400,000	10	10	Do. 2nd Pref.	—	*	7	17	11½	5½				
2,230	593,160	135,420	20	20	Darjeeling	5½	5½	6	—	23½	5	5,552	1,365	1,700	—
2,114	456,580	60,000	10	10	Darjeeling Cons.	—	*	4/2	—	7½	2½	—	1,820	—	—
		60,000	10	10	Do. Pref.	—	*	5	2½	9½	5				
6,600	2,973,050	150,000	10	10	Dooars	12½	12½	12½	2½	21	6½	45,000	300	D32,000	—
		75,000	10	10	Do. Pref.	7	7	7	3½	17½	3½				
3,367	1,833,590	165,000	10	10	Doom Dooma	11½	10	12½	5	23½	5½	30,000	4,032	—	20,000
1,377	500,080	61,120	5	5	Eastern Assam	2	nil.	4	—	3½	5½	—	1,790	—	20,000
4,038	1,529,380	85,000	10	10	East India and Ceylon	2	nil.	7	—	9½	7	—	1,710	—	—
		85,000	10	10	Do. Pref.	*	6	6	3	12½	4½				
7,570	3,600,000	219,000	10	10	Empire of India	—	*	6/10	2	13½	—	15,000	—	27,000	—
		219,000	10	10	Do. Pref.	—	*	5	2½	11½	4½				
1,180	647,600	94,060	10	10	Indian of Cachar	7	3½	3	—	6	5½	6,070	—	7,120	—
2,916	968,000	83,500	5	5	Jhanzie	10	10	10	4	8½	5½	14,500	1,070	2,700	—
7,980	3,467,000	250,000	10	10	Jokai	10	10	10	5	18	5½	45,000	990	D9,000	—
		100,000	10	10	Do. Pref.	*	6	6	3	15½	3½				
5,224	1,801,600	100,000	20	20	Jorehant	20	20	20	—	58	7	26,220	2,955	3,000	—
1,547	554,560	65,660	10	8	Lebong	15	15	15	5	17½	6½	9,000	2,750	5,690	—
5,082	1,843,700	100,000	10	10	Lungla	8	10	6	3	10	6	—	1,543	D21,000	—
		100,000	10	10	Do. Pref.	*	6	6	3	12½	4½				
2,684	866,300	95,970	10	10	Majuli	7	5	5	—	7	7	—	2,606	560	—
1,300	216,000	91,840	1	1	Makum	—	—	2	—	1½	1½	—	—	1,800	25,000
3,140	938,400	100,000	1	1	Moabund	—	—	*	—	1	—	—	—	—	—
		50,000	1	1	Do. Pref.	—	—	*	2½	1	5				
2,080	510,000	79,590	10	10	Scottish Assam	7	7	7	—	11	6½	6,900	800	9,590	—
4,150	1,635,000	100,000	10	10	Singlo	6	8	5	1	9½	4½	—	300	D5,000	—
		80,000	10	10	Do. Pref.	*	6½	6½	3½	13	5				
					CEYLON COMPANIES.										
10,315	1,743,824	250,000	100	100	Anglo-Ceylon, & Gen.	—	*	5½	—	70	7½	10,992	1,405	D72,844	166,900
1,836	685,741	50,000	10	10	Associated Tea	—	*	5	—	8½	6½	—	164	2,478	—
		60,000	10	10	Do. Pref.	—	*	6	—	11	5½				
10,390	3,763,000	167,380	10	10	Ceylon Tea Plantations	15	15	15	7	27½	5½	84,900	1,516	D30,819	—
		81,080	10	10	Do. Pref.	7	7	7	17	17½	4				
5,722	1,542,700	55,260	5	3	Ceylon & Oriental Est.	5	8	7	—	2½	7½	—	230	D2,027	51,000
		46,000	5	5	Do. Pref.	6	6	6	3	5½	5½				
2,157	801,629	111,330	5	5	Dimbula Valley	—	*	10	5	6½	7	—	—	1,733	6,000
		62,607	5	5	Do. Pref.	—	*	6	3	6½	4½				
11,496	3,715,000	298,230	5	5	Eastern Prod. & Est.	3	5	6½	2½	6½	4½	20,000	11,740	D17,797	200,000
3,118	701,100	150,000	10	10	Lanka Plantations	4	5	5	15	7½	6½	—	495	D11,300	14,700 Pref.
2,193	960,100	22,080	10	10	New Dimbula "A"	10	16	16	—	25	6	11,000	2,024	1,750	—
		55,710	10	10	Do. "B"	18	16	16	—	23½	6½				
		6,400	10	10	Do. "C"	nil.	8	14	—	15	8½				
2,572	570,360	100,000	10	10	Ouvah	6	8	6	2	10	6	4,000	1,151	D1,255	—
2,630	535,675	200,000	10	10	Nuwara Eliya	—	*	6	3	11½	5	—	—	—	30,000
1,780	720,000	41,000	10	10	Scottish Ceylon	15	15	15	5	23	6½	7,000	1,252	D3,970	—
		9,000	10	10	Do. Pref.	7	7	7	3½	17	3½				
2,430	602,000	56,000	10	6	Standard	12½	15	15	5	14½	6½	9,000	800	D15,012	4,000

Working-Capital Column.—In working-capital column, D stands for *debit*.

* Company formed this year. † Interim dividends are given as actual distribution made. ‡ *Total* div.

Printed for the Proprietor by LOVE & WYMAN, LTD., Great Queen Street, London, W.C.; and Published by CLEMENT WILSON at Norfolk House, Norfolk Street, Strand, London, W.C.

The Investors' Review

Vol. I.—No. 4. New Series. FRIDAY, JANUARY 28, 1898. [Registered as a Newspaper.] Price 6d. By post, 6½d

The Investment Index,

A Quarterly Supplement to the "Investors' Review."

Price 2s. net. 8s. 6d. per annum, post free.

THE INVESTMENT INDEX is an indispensable supplement to the Investors' Review. A file of it enables investors to follow the ups and downs of markets, and each number gives the return obtainable on all classes of securities at recent prices, arranged in a most convenient form for reference. Appended to its tables of figures are criticisms on company balance sheets, State Budgets, &c., similar to those in the Investors' Review.

Regarding it, the *Speaker* says: "The Quarterly 'Investment Index' is probably the handiest and fullest, as it is certainly the safest, of guides to the investor."

"The compilation of securities is particularly valuable."—*Pall Mall Gazette.*

"Its carefully classified list of securities will be found very valuable."—*Globe.*

"At no time has such a list of securities been more valuable than at the present."—*Star.*

"The invaluable 'Investors' Index.'"—*Sketch.*

"A most valuable compilation."—*Glasgow Herald.*

Subscription to the "Investors' Review" and "Investment Index," 36s. per annum, post free.

CLEMENT WILSON,
NORFOLK HOUSE, NORFOLK STREET, LONDON, W.C.

CALEDONIAN INSURANCE COMPANY.

The Oldest Scottish Insurance Office.

LIFE ASSURANCE WITH AND WITHOUT MEDICAL EXAMINATION ON EXCEPTIONALLY LIBERAL TERMS.

Example of the Company's Threefold Option Investment Policy.

Entrant at age 26 may secure in return for an Annual Premium of only £30 the following benefits—

A. An Assurance of £1,000, payable if death occur before age 65;

B. An Endowment of £2,000 on attainment of age 65; or in lieu of B. one of the following options:

C. A paid-up Assurance of £2,800, commencing at age 65; or,

D. An Annuity after 65 of £108 : 11 : 8,* with a paid-up Assurance of £1,400 commencing at 65; or

E. An Annuity after 65 of £213 : 3 : 4,* without any paid-up Assurance.

* The Annuities quoted are for males, and are dependent on the present prices being still in force when age 65 is reached.

Fire Insurance at moderate rates and on good security.

Head Office: 19, GEORGE ST., EDINBURGH.

LONDON: 82, King William Street, E.C.;
14, Waterloo Place, Pall Mall, S.W.

CONTENTS

The Investors' Review.

Economic and Financial Notes and Correspondence.

THE STRUGGLE IN PEKIN.

There is a lull at present over the question of the British loan to China. Rumours still continue to circulate notwithstanding, and we must be careful not to excite ourselves about them. So far as things have gone the victory has been substantially with British diplomacy, and it is bound to remain with us if we stand quietly and firmly on our treaty rights. To fall into violence might be disastrous. Already our activity at Pekin has brought Germany to announce that Kiao-Chau is to be a free port, thus detaching her from Russia. This is a distinct gain and an acknowledgment of the equity of British contentions. It would have been a distinct violation of existing treaties with China had Germany laid hold of this place and constituted it an exclusive possession. In another way we have to some extent got the better of Russia, for in the eagerness her representative before the Emperor of China has displayed to prevent us from obtaining the opening of Ta-lien-wan as a treaty port, the intention has been disclosed to seize Manchuria and treat it as a sphere exclusively in the hands of Russia. By letting this out, Russia, we think, has put herself in an entirely false position, not only as against Great Britain, but in relation to the whole of Western Europe. No power, if the Western nations are alive to their interests, ought to be allowed to take possession of any portion of the territory of China and shut out the other European Powers from it. Our Ambassador ought, therefore, to bring this

Russian design into high relief, and hold fast to the righteousness of his position. No war is in prospect through our firmness. We stand for the common right of all nations to share in the trade and development of China, and so standing are unassailable.

While this dispute rages, any question of a loan is, of course, in abeyance. The loan, however, must come forward again because China must have money to pay off Japan with, and there is no country except ours, as we have said before, which can find the money. But it must not be found on too easy terms; we do not mean as regards interest, for that might very well be low, but as regards the concessions to be granted in exchange for the use of British credit. These concessions ought to be extensive, and as we ask no exclusive privileges, there can be no objection whatever to pacifying the Germans by allowing them to participate in the loan if they please, we taking strict care that the concessions obtained from China are to be the unalienable right of every nation trading with the Chinese Empire. With Germany detached, and possibly France, and with Japan behind us, Russia will be powerless for mischief.

GREEK FINANCE.

The first report of the International Commission appointed to control the finances of Greece has been issued, and proves a moderately-worded and sensible State paper. If the Commission goes on as it has begun, the creditors of Greece will by-and-by receive their own with usury. At present, of course, Greek finance is in considerable disorder; but as it stands, the Commissioners look for a revenue of over 85,500,000 drachmas, and by 1903 they expect an income exceeding 100,000,000. Of this the State is to be allowed to spend 63,250,000 in 1898. The rest goes principally to the creditors of Greece, but we do not yet know exactly what the holders of the foreign loans will receive. It cannot be very much, because a new loan of £5,000,000 is to be issued forthwith to provide the indemnity due to Turkey, and to fill other gaps. Greece is also, according to the Constantinople correspondent of the *Times*, to be allowed to borrow another £1,000,000, so that the total of the nominal amount of the Greek Debt will in a year or two's time be about £27,000,000. Of course, the new loans will be issued under favourable conditions, and the whole of the new £6,000,000, if obtained at 4 per cent., should not cost much more than a quarter of a million sterling for interest and sinking fund, but when that is paid the margin over for the other creditors must necessarily be small for some time to come. Both Greece and her creditors, therefore, must ultimately benefit materially from the strict control now to be exercised over her financial affairs.

INDIA SAVED.

At last the bill which is to ease the transaction of commercial affairs in India has become law. Thanks to it, Indian exporters may now buy exchange on London, when they cannot help themselves, at the lofty price of anything over 1s. 4$\frac{3}{32}$d. per rupee. The Government now in Calcutta will accept deposits of gold in London, and the India Council here will telegraph out to it to give rupees—silver and paper—to banks on the spot against this gold, so that there may be no lack of currency. This is capacity and statesmanlike foresight for you, and it is sure to be deeply appreciated by all Indian bankers and merchants. True we have not yet heard of any deposits of gold made for this purpose; true also is it that Indian exports are being choked as with a viper's grip by the artificially elevated rate of exchange; but these are passing inconveniences, sure to be removed by the high wisdom now made manifest. May we not, then, offer our profoundest admiration to those enlightened bureaucrats on the skill and resource they are displaying in steering India, not exactly through, but towards the most stupendous economic crisis in her history under British rule! "We are all tight and snug now," as the sparrow said when she built her nest in the house gutter.

THE LONDON JOINT STOCK BANK.

A suggestive and interesting little speech was made by Mr. James Stern, the chairman of this Bank, at its recent half-yearly meeting. He had a pleasant story to tell, business prosperous, staff not forgotten in the prosperity, branches being opened in suitable places, and so on. Thus far the directors have not thought it prudent to open branches outside London, and there should be plenty of scope within it yet for extension. Mr. Stern's observations on the effect of the enlarged supplies of gold are worth quoting because they endorse so heartily the doctrine of large reserves which we have almost wearied of preaching:—

About the year 1851, at the time of the Californian and Australian gold discoveries, a former Director of this Bank maintained the seeming paradox that the effect of a greater production of gold would be rather to raise than to lower the value of money, as he held that for every 20s. of gold produced, trade would increase 21s. This bold forecast, by the aid, however of the great waste and the vast expenditure of the Crimean War, was fully realised. While no one would venture to-day to anticipate a similar issue, we may fairly expect that an enlarged volume of trade and an enlarged volume of values will at least mitigate the effect of an enlarged production of gold, and that room will still be left for profitable banking, when based on prudent management and on well-established connection. With, too, the extension of the gold currency of the world, there must be an ever-widening sphere for London banking, so long as England retains her pre-eminence as the special, I might say, the only, home of free gold. This unique and leading position carries with it however, corresponding duties. For as it is evident that the wider the use of gold becomes, the greater may be the calls made on us, we are more than ever bound to see that our reserves (already not too large) are kept entirely in gold. It is on this sure foundation, and not on the unstable basis of treaties, that we must continue to stand; and while casting aside, as antiquated and obsolete, the permission given 50 years ago to hold part of our reserves in silver, which is quite out of harmony with the facts of to-day, we must more than ever insist that as our engagements are made in gold, so our ability to fulfil those engagements must be placed beyond all possibility even of suspicion, by our reserves being held in gold and in nothing but gold.

GOLDEN CEMENT CLAIMS.

In October, 1895, this Western Australian Company, with a fascinating name, was brought out with a great flourish of trumpets and a nominal capital of £200,000, one quarter of which was assigned as working capital. In a letter from the secretary, forwarded with the prospectus, it was stated that Messrs. Bewick, Moreing, & Co. had made an independent report upon the property, in which they estimated the ore in sight to be worth £2,500,000. Naturally such a statement, coming from such a quarter, led the public to apply for the shares, and they went, for a brief period, to a considerable premium on the market. None of the predictions and estimates of the prospectus have been justified, the report of the eminent Western Australian engineers least of all, and it is now, we fear, impossible to sell the shares at any price, their nominal quotation being 1s. to 2s. per £1 share. In these circumstances one of the unfortunate allottees has asked us to make a public demand for information about the property. Is there any paying ore in the "mine" at all? Has any of the capital remained unspent? What have the vendors done with the 90,000 shares taken by them in part payment for the "mining leases" over about thirty-two acres of land, leases which have given no return?

Perhaps the West Australian Venture Syndicate, the West Australian Mines Development Syndicate, the Anglo-German Exploration Company of Western Australia, and the Anglo-French Exploration Company of Western Australia, Limited, who united to invite subscriptions for 85,000 of the shares, will condescend, should they themselves still exist, to supply some information to the shareholders, since none seems to be extractable from the board itself. We fear there is very little to be hoped for, but even the brokers in London and Glasgow who put their names on the prospectus ought to do their utmost in the circumstances to recover some of the money of their clients. If they cannot do this, they might, at least, tell the public into whose pockets it went. Did the promoting syndicates pay dividends out of it and prate about the "prosperous condition of their business"?

The Curtin Davis Proprietary Company.

In September last* we spoke well of the manner in which this adventure had been handled and placed before the public. From our language many seem to have inferred that we spoke in terms of praise about the mine itself. That was not the case, we are happy to say, for the mine has not turned out at all according to expectations. The ore found in it has been difficult to extract, and is not worth much when got out. This is unfortunate, and if the directors had behaved as mine directors usually do, the shareholders would have had to lament the loss of their money. Happily we are still able to commend the board, which is composed of the same people who developed and brought out the Mount Lyell mine. Instead of rushing into large expenditure for plant and machinery before they tested the property, the directors in Melbourne kept the money in hand until they had made a thorough examination, and as soon as they obtained proof of the disappointing character of the property, they, on their own responsibility, and with their own means, bought a half interest in the Colebrook Company, which interest, less amount expended in improving it, they have transferred without cost to the shareholders of the Curtin Davis Company. This seems to us honourable and straightforward conduct, and we trust the Colebrook property will amply compensate the Curtin Davis shareholders for any disappointment their original possession may have caused them.

Mortgage Company of the River Plate.

As will be seen in our Company Report and Balance-Sheet columns, the Mortgage Company of the River Plate had an excellent time of it last year. But while a 10 per cent. dividend, with £15,000 to reserve, will naturally satisfy shareholders, we cannot forbear to point out that the liabilities of the company have risen rapidly of late. Two years ago, with the same amount of paid-up share capital as now—£200,000—the Debenture bonds and Debenture stock totalled £545,070, whereas the total of this form of debt is now £689,514. Possibly the "loans on mortgages," which form the bulk of the assets of the company, may be more liquid than they were a couple of years ago, for properties on hand have been reduced by nearly two-thirds in the interval; yet £3 10s. of Debentures to every £1 of paid-up share capital is not a happy combination.

Experience of Land Mortgage Companies in Canada, in the United States, in Australia, in New Zealand, and in the River Plate itself is dead against this excess of borrowed to paid-up share capital. While everything smiles it is a fat time for the shareholders, who rake in fine dividends from the profit margin upon the loan business of the concern; but the high dividends thus attained serve to attract other capital into the business, and when a bad time comes, as it does with great regularity in these new countries, the interest upon the debt becomes a serious burden. So far this company has fared well, but it should be borne in mind that until recently the proportion of borrowed money to share capital was usually 2½ to 1. As it is, the charge for interest now nearly equals the net profits of the concern, much as they have risen of late.

The remedy is, of course, to call up more share capital, say £1 per share, which would mean £100,000, without taking into account any aid from premiums, and with the proceeds pay off some of the Debenture bonds as they mature. It will very likely be urged that £517,766 of the Debenture debt is in Debenture stock that does not mature for a good many years, if at all, but although this circumstance would certainly guard the company against a sudden demand for the return of principal, the dead-weight of the interest charge cannot be avoided. Many Mortgage Companies have congratulated themselves upon the conversion of Terminable Debentures into Debenture stock, but such a change does not take away the danger of carrying too much dead-weight of debt.

Municipal Trust Company.

It is doubtless a wise step of the Municipal Trust Company to proceed to the reduction of its capital. Unfortunately many of its assets have permanently deteriorated, whilst the majority of the holdings have no market, so that the Trust cannot hope to benefit much from the steady appreciation in prices upon the Stock Exchange. The holding of United States Municipal, County, and Water and Light bonds has, we believe, proved more disastrous than the most bitter critic of such investments could have imagined some years back, and a confession of the parlous condition of affairs was absolutely necessary. But to suggest that the Preference capital should be written down 20 per cent. seems to us a very strong measure.

For one thing, before such a proposal can be even considered, a detailed statement as to the present revenue, probable revenue in the future, and condition of securities in default, should be rendered to the shareholders. Even then it seems to us that the Deferred

* Investors' Review, monthly issue, No. 53, vol. 10.

stock ought to bear the whole of the loss, as it would have gained the whole of the surplus revenue had any existed. There is, however, the difficulty that the charge of 5 per cent. upon the Preference capital is too heavy for the company to bear, and to meet this we would suggest that a better arrangement might be found in reducing the Deferred capital by 60 per cent., and at the same time cutting down the interest upon the Preferred stock from 5 to 4 per cent. In this way revenue would be relieved, and, should it grow again, the surplus above the 4 per cent. required for the Preferred stock might be divided equally between the Preferred and Deferred stock. We are afraid, though, that there would not be much difficulty about this division.

The Future of Rhodesia.

Mr. Rhodes's estimate of the future of Rhodesia is the reverse of roseate if a *Chronicle* correspondent has correctly reported our "African pro-consul's" statements. Mr. Rhodes is said to have declared that Rhodesia can never be self-supporting. It is no agricultural country; neither food for the settlers, nor fodder for the cattle can be raised in the colony. It must stand or fall by its gold—and its coal. But both are as yet to seek. At least no proof is forthcoming that they exist in quantities sufficient to found a State on. Says Mr Rhodes—"When the railway has brought up our machinery from the coast, and we have discovered good coal in Rhodesia, and if we can get the natives to work in our mines, we ought to be able to pay dividends." Here, however, we have nothing but "oughts" and "ifs," not much to make an impression even on "Imperial" financiers. Of course, gold may be found, coal may be discovered, and natives may be induced to work in the mines; but by the time these not very hopeful hypotheses are fulfilled—if they ever be—would there be earnable a dividend sufficient to give a return for the sacrifices of shareholders? All that can now be said is, that whatever may be the expectations or dreams of Mr. Rhodes, there is as yet no tangible proof of their probable realisation. The only thing the confiding shareholder has received is an abundant stock of hope deferred, and his heart may well be sick to death long before his "dividend" is in sight. Without an agricultural backbone to keep it erect, it would require an enormous output of both gold and coal to make Rhodesia worth its salt. Mr. Rhodes wants no immigrants but capitalists; but without agriculture, and with gold and coal things that have only entered into the "study of imagination," on what could their capital be bestowed with utility and profit?

Agriculture at the Cape.

The "Agricultural and Live Stock Returns" of Cape Colony for 1896-7 are valuable as presenting us with a comparatively accurate picture of the present economic condition of the colony. Agriculture has long—may be said to have always been—its weak point; for the farms are mainly worked by Boers; and whatever else may be said of the Dutch in South Africa, they are not devotees of modern agricultural methods. They dislike change. Such farming as their ancestors have been accustomed to, they consider "good enough for them." It provides them with something more than a mere subsistence; and to the Cape farmer, as a rule, the fuss and fret and forceful push of the modern agriculturist, with his complicated machinery, are personally distasteful and even irritating. For long the Cape formed the main source of our wool supply; but it has allowed itself to be outdone by more careful and energetic competitors. Cape farmers have still large numbers of sheep—the total is given at 14,000,000 in these returns—and last year the colony produced 43,000,000 lb. of wool; but only a comparatively small portion of it, we fear, commanded the top price of the market here. The number of ostriches returned—237,000—strikes us as rather small, though we have not the statistics of previous years to refer to for comparison. In a country with so vast a pastoral area 2,250,000 head of cattle seems a meagre possession; and even that small number must now be infinitely less by reason of the ravages of the rinderpest. Of horses the colony only boasts the ownership of 357,000, while of goats it has 5,000,000, though of what commercial value these may be there is nothing to show.

In the matter of cereals, the agriculturists of the colony can scarcely be said to have yet awakened from the long sleep of years—almost ages. These returns tell us that in the year under review about 81,000 muids of wheat (a muid being equivalent to some three bushels) were sown in an area which is about twice the size of Great Britain! There may be exceptional difficulties of climate to contend against; but whatever these may be, surely if wheat is worth sowing at all, it is worth sowing in much larger quantities than are stated here. The produce of those 81,000 muids sown was 1,400,000 muids, and of this total nearly one-half was lost through rust, drought, and other causes. Barley was rather more successful, for though only 22,000 muids were sown, the total produced was 320,000 muids, of which 250,000 muids were safely harvested. 63,000 muids of mealies were sown, 920,000 muids saved, and 375,000 muids lost. But, though the losses seem very great, colonial experts regard the net product satisfactory enough to encourage a much larger cultivation. There are plenty of markets waiting for the corn to be produced. The real want of the Cape agriculturist seems to be energy, mental alertness, and readiness to grapple with difficulties of soil and climate—as well as a willingness to adopt the new methods and machinery which even the peasants of many parts of Russia have begun to work, or are preparing to do so. The vine industry seems improving. Cape wines have so far recovered the character they lost through careless manufacture and bad vinification; but still the growers have been thus far beaten in the competition for English markets by their shrewder and more energetic Australian rivals. The vines in Cape Colony numbered, in 1896, 86,000,000, 5,000,000 having been planted in that year. Unfortunately, 7,000,000 were destroyed in the same year by the phylloxera—a considerable loss, but, if that wretched pest can be checked, far from an irrecoverable one. There is no reason to fear that, with careful management on the part of the growers, and increased skill in wine manufacture, the export of wines may not become an important source of income for the Cape.

The Mazawattee Tea Company.

A correspondent sends the following defence of this company's finance. We plead guilty to the "retail" error, having been led thereto by the packet tea system worked through agents. But we cannot assume a penitent attitude in regard to the company's balance-sheet. When most of the capital of any company is represented by goodwill and trade marks, a day must some time come when this capital will be wanted and not found unless profits are meanwhile accumulated to replace it. For money paid on account of goodwill and money clean gone out of a business cannot possibly be capital in a company and available for it :—

To the Editor.

January 22, 1898.

SIR,—I see you notice this company's report; but there is a mistake in it. You do not yet know quite what the Mazawattee Company is. You say tea vending *in retail* is evidently a much more prosperous business than you thought it. The Mazawattee Company never sells an ounce of tea in retail, they are exclusively wholesale, and never directly or indirectly get any *retailers'* profit. You speak about the goodwill being enormous, which I grant, though I do not say it is too much, that remains to be seen, and when you say the £24,000 of reserve is a "mere atom," to some extent I am with you, but not altogether. It represents more than 6 per cent. of the "enormous goodwill" put back into the business in *two* years.

I can see no reason in investing the reserve separately, while it can be usefully employed in the business. It seems to me rather a farce to imagine you are better off by having £24,000 Consols in a cupboard, while you have £382,000 goodwill figuring as an asset on the other side. However, that is matter of opinion. I hope to see the company add a bit more to the reserve fund, and then begin scoring the "goodwill" out.

I should not give 50 per cent. premium for the shares myself until they have shown their capacity to put by £12,000 a year for, say, *five* years at least, but the public must do as they like—they make the price of Mazawattee—there is not, and never has been, any "support" given by the vendors.

If they can go on paying 8 per cent. and putting by £12,000 a year, you will very soon alter your opinion as to the goodwill being too large; but I am not a prophet, and will not say they are going to prosper.

THE IMPERIAL CONTINENTAL WATERWORKS, LIMITED.

Appended is an effective rejoinder to the letter which appeared in our issue of the 7th inst. :—

To the Editor.

Genoa, January 18, 1898.

SIR,—I trust you will allow me to reply, as shortly as possible, to a letter, dated 28th ult., from Mr. George F. Deacon, enclosed in one from the Secretary of the Imperial Continental Waterworks, Limited, which appeared in your number of 7th inst.

I need not reply to the Secretary's official communication, because it is based on Mr. Deacon's letter. I cannot hope to persuade him that I am not opposed to this scheme from interested motives; or that the "steel mains" which are "being shipped" are likely to meet the fate of the cast-iron pipes shipped for the Genoa Waterworks Company, Limited; or that his company may not reasonably hope to make £51,000 a year out of Genoa, "without encroaching on the parts supplied" by the existing companies. It stands to reason that if a valuable unsupplied area existed in Genoa, it would be eagerly competed for by the Genoese companies; but I cannot expect him, as Secretary, to acknowledge this. He may, however, be surprised to learn that, as against his estimate of £51,000, the two companies (the Nicolai and the Gorzente), who serve an area inhabited by about 367,000 persons, encash from them, for water supplied for domestic purposes, about £28,000 a year—say, rather more than 1s. 6d. per head of the population.

As to Mr. Deacon's letter, I see in the first place :—

1. That he disclaims responsibility for a very rash statement in the Company's prospectus, which he whittles down, on his own account, to what seems at first sight an innocent expression of opinion. It is, however, calculated to mislead any one who does not know Genoa. The "population lying next to the company's proposed reservoir," which has at present "no adequate public supply," is contained in the villages of Cavassolo and Doria, and in Staglieno, the well-known suburb of Genoa where the cemetery lies. Some few thousand people live in these places (perhaps 10,000 in all), the chief group being Staglieno near the entrance to which are the Gorzente mains, which will be extended into Staglieno as soon as it is worth while. It is absurd to talk of this area as if it could give an important contribution to the company's expected £51,000 a year.

2. Mr. Deacon says that the Gorzente Company cannot increase their supply, because "their concession only permits the withdrawal of 250 litres per second."

For his information, allow me to state that during 1897 the average quantity drawn by the Gorzente Company from its reservoirs was 424·24 litres per second, besides about 30 litres spring water, tapped by the tunnel through which the water flows.

Of this quantity 47·92 litres per second, on an average throughout the year, was run to waste at Isoverde, after driving the company's electric plant, as it was not required in Genoa. As these requirements are increasing the quantity carried to Genoa will be increased this year. It is quite safe to assume that the Gorzente Company know what they are about, and that as they take more than 250 litres they have the right to do so. Mr. Deacon probably does not know that they own the chief part of the 4,200 acres of barren hillside which constitute their gathering ground, and can therefore, independently of their concession, dispose of the water that falls on their land.

3. Mr. Deacon says that the authorities do not allow the Gorzente Company's lower reservoir to be filled, and suggests or implies that although this reservoir may have held 475 million gallons "on an occasion" in 1892, it would not be safe to work it normally at this figure. I beg to assure him that it is worked normally and continuously at anything up to 500 million gallons. It contains about 450 million gallons just now, and is supplying Genoa, while the upper reservoir is standing full (800 million gallons).

4. Mr. Deacon says that I have "omitted to mention the Bisagno area," which is to form part of the proposed gathering ground.

I did not include the Bisagno, because Mr. Deacon, in his report of July 20 last, says that "the position of the proposed reservoir on the Bisagno was open to objection on account of pollution from the village of La Presa." Mr. Deacon very wisely gave up the Bisagno altogether for the present (besides being polluted, it is completely controlled by the intakes for the Municipal aqueduct), and stated that "about 240,000 persons" could be supplied "from the Concasca alone." I pointed out that the Concasca was far too small for such a supply, and Mr. Deacon now tells me that I must take in the Bisagno!

5. As to the letter addressed to the company by fifty-two residents, it would be more to the purpose to tell us how much the residents have subscribed; £100,000 were reserved for subscription in Italy; has any "leading citizen" in Genoa subscribed £50?

6. Finally, I venture to point out to Mr. Deacon that, although "from a physical point of view" he may fairly claim that his areas were originally the best, he must not forget that the world has moved along since these "gathering grounds" were created.

When the Municipal aqueduct was built, hundreds of years ago, the Italian engineers rightly went to the nearest source for good water, and took up the Concasca and the Bisagno.

Since then Genoa has grown immensely, and these sources have become insufficient and objectionable; the Italian engineers had to look about for a further supply, which led them to tap the Scrivia and the Gorzente. Does Mr. Deacon think they would not have preferred nearer gathering grounds? or that they do not know their own hills? or that they are not capable engineers? If these questions must be answered in the negative, I fear it must be assumed that Mr. Deacon's plan will not do.—I am, Sir, your obedient servant,

FREDK. A. G. BROWN.

TEA COMPANY'S TABLES.

Complaint has been made that in our standing table of tea companies we do not state the item of working capital correctly. Our object in showing this item is to set forth the resources of the company outside its estates, and we arrived at the amount by deducting the value of the estates, factories, &c. from the share and debenture capital. In several cases, especially where large reserves exist that have been employed upon the development of the estates, their value considerably exceeds that of the capital, and so a *debit* balance is brought out. In order to prevent misapprehension on this head, we have carefully included the amount of the reserve and balance forward in the table, so that any one can deduct these items from the *debit* working balance, and thus arrive at a fair estimate of the position. On the other hand, if we deducted the reserve, and then showed the amount in the table, it would lead to erroneous conclusions, for it would almost invariably be counted twice over.

SWEATING ON THE GREAT EASTERN RAILWAY.

Apropos of the 5 per cent. per annum dividend declared by the directors of this railway, an Eastern Counties correspondent writes to tell us how the thing is done. He gives a concrete example which is calculated to dispel the wonder that railway servants should be discontented. At Wisbech station for three or four months back the clerks in the Great Eastern goods office have been working from 9 a.m. till from 9 to 10 p.m., with an hour for dinner and a few minutes for tea; also they have to work eight hours every Sunday, receiving only six days' wages from their taskmasters for the whole seven days. Last Sunday week, when the clerks had at length risen in protest, they were given one day's extra wage for eleven hours' work. Our correspondent adds:—"A 5 per cent. dividend is of course very satisfactory to the shareholders, but I think many of those people who receive this dividend would not feel quite so comfortable in their minds if they knew the kind of sweating that is going on, and presumably by no means confined to Wisbech." We are not so sure about the consciences of the dividend receivers as our correspondent appears to be, but the truth had better out.

UNREST IN ITALY.

Things are not by any means in a satisfactory condition in Italy. Bread-riots have been frequent; on Tuesday the Government found it judicious to reduce the duties on grain by 2½ lire; but on Wednesday they took the most serious step of all—they decided to increase the effective winter strength of the Army from 140,000 men to 180,000. In Rome and the principal cities throughout the kingdom the police service has been strengthened; so that Ministers evidently regard the probabilities of grave disorder to be very great. The harvest in Italy was this year a good deal below the average, but that in itself would not account for the widespread and still extending distress, nor all the hunger which is impelling the poorer inhabitants of the cities to try to steal the bread which they cannot buy. The truth is Italy has long been grievously overtaxed. Vast sums were sunk in mad African expeditions, while her partnership with Germany and Austria in the Triple Alliance is more costly than Italian finances can stand. If the unrest and rioting of the past week or two continues, it may become a very serious thing for the Italian monarchy. There is no doubt that the Jesuits are in earnest, for their own ends, in encouraging a Republican agitation among the Catholic population. It is probable that the Pope himself is cognisant of their aims, if he does not cordially sympathise with them. In the first instance, this Jesuit agitation is aimed directly at King Humbert. Its main object is revolutionary; and the bread rioters are unconsciously helping the ecclesiastical agitators.

DEBENTURE-HOLDERS' SECURITY.

A hard blow was struck this week against the holders of Debentures in Castell & Brown, Limited, in particular, and Debenture-holders in general, concerning their security. The question was raised whether the bankers of the company who had advanced money on the security of its title-deeds were entitled to priority over the Debenture-holders, notwithstanding that the property to which those deeds related was comprised in the Debentures, and the company was prohibited expressly from charging such property in priority to the charge created by the Debentures. Of course, in the present case, although the Debentures were prior in date, the bank at the date of its charges had no notice, express or implied, of the prior incumbrance. Mr. Justice Romer has held that the bank was entitled to a declaration that their charge had priority to the Debentures of the company. This decision, undoubtedly, will reduce the value of this class of security, for companies will in this way be able to create a charge on their property which will take precedence of Debentures, although the money advanced on those securities was expressly lent on the stipulation that no prior charge should be created.

The scientists seem perfectly satisfied with the results of their observations of the total eclipse of the sun in India; so do the natives on the whole, with a difference. To them it is a sign and presage of the downfall of the British Raj. But they are no doub "pessimist" Hindoos, who resent heavy taxation, restricted trade and artificially-created scarcity of money. Still, even Indian Jingoes might usefully reflect on the significant fact that the Indian native's first notion is to associate the dreaded phenomenon of the solar eclipse with the oppression of the British Raj.

Mr. Commissioner Kerr's advice to a disappointed mining shareholder who appeared before him to answer a summons for the payment of some share calls, was to have nothing to do with any gold company. The defendant shareholder pleaded that he had been misled by misrepresentation in the prospectus, but the Commissioner could not see that there had been misrepresentation; he "had been entrapped in exactly the same way as a good many other silly members of the British public were." The defendant lost the suit, but gained this further advice: "Never believe a director again for the rest of your life." What a tremendous "pessimist" Mr. Commissioner Kerr must be! That, we believe, is the proper way to label a cautious adviser nowadays.

According to the directors' report, the profits of the Queensland National Bank for the past year amounted to only £8,000. The low rate of interest and the losses caused in the colony by severe drought are said to have seriously restricted the directors, and the report, under the circumstances, is said to be regarded as satisfactory. It is a poor satisfaction.

Mr. W. A. Carlyle, provincial mineralogist, estimates that the total output of the British Columbia mines will amount to $10,000,000 for the past year. In 1895 the output was $5,655,302, and in 1896 $7,146,420.

King Humbert has signed a decree reducing the Italian customs tariff on cereals from 7·50 lire to 5 lire until April 30. The decree came into force on Tuesday last.

The *Speaker* has just entered on its ninth year of publication. It has done much for the furtherance of Liberal principles, and has lost none of its vigour and freshness; nay, it is aiming with new energy at a further extension of its usefulness, and is soon to devote special attention to the great constitutional question of the House of Lords, on which a number of well-known writers will contribute a series of articles. We wish the *Speaker* every success.

A clandestine printing establishment in London has been issuing forged certificates of the Two and a Half per Cent. 1896 Tontine as well as Paris bonds. The plot was discovered by Scotland-yard, which at once communicated with the French authorities.

Trade in Japan is said to be suffering seriously from the scarcity of money. Traders have little or nothing to pay for the goods which the importers have for distribution.

The following are the returns of the gold yield for the various districts of Victoria during the year 1897:—Ararat, 32,833 oz.; Ballarat, 178,910 oz.; Buchworth, 123,785 oz.; Castlemain, 62,608 oz.; Gippsland, 112,658 oz.; Maryborough, 59,601 oz.; Sandhurst, 200,323 oz.; unspecified, 42,047 oz. The dividends paid amounted to £532,294.

Herr Johannes Trojan, the editor of the *Kladderadatsch*, has been sent to a fortress for two months for the audacious caricature of the Emperor which appeared in his paper. It is *lèse majesté*. The imperial reputation cannot stand a joke.

The average production of French wine during the last ten years has been about 730,700,000 gallons. The amount for last year was 727,791,245.

The Vienna Bourse Committee and the Bankers' Union have memorialised the Minister of Commerce against the decree permitting Savings Banks—official institutions—entering into Bourse speculations not entailing any risk.

Fermenting France.

However much our minds may be preoccupied with the affairs of Empire in the far East, we must not quite take our eyes off France. Events are happening there which bear an ominous aspect from many points of view. It may not be that we are on the eve of another French Revolution, but the symptoms are assuredly those which past revolutions have always been heralded by. A great social ferment has broken out, not in Paris only, but all over the country, and even in Algiers, and this ferment bears a singular resemblance to the outbursts which preceded the Revolution of 1789. Essentially the cause is the same. Hunger is at the bottom of it. While a certain section of the French people have been growing richer, and displaying their wealth with more and more ostentation every year, the great mass of them have been growing poorer. Oppressive taxation is stripping them ; discontent, bred of this poverty, with its pinching want, has been festering in the cities of the Republic these many years back, and its existence has been only too well known to those in authority, many of whom have been living in fear, trying to avert the evil day by yielding sometimes to unjust demands, and by coddling and bribery more or less secret.

It is this element of discontent among what are called the masses which gives significance to the Dreyfus affair. Democracies in the bulk are never enlightened ; they suffer, and know not the cause of their suffering. It is so in France ; but true as this may be the popular instinct generally causes social movements to concentrate upon some point not unconnected with the real cause of the suffering. In the present instance all the ferment has arisen over the degraded Captain Dreyfus, and France is apparently divided into two camps because of the unjust condemnation passed upon this Jewish officer, formerly in the French Army. In its essence, as we pointed out last week, this question is a simple one enough. It impugns the honour of the French Army in a sense, and, much more, the just spirit of the officers composing the secret court-martial by which Captain Dreyfus was condemned. This at first trivial-looking question might easily have been settled by a revision of the sentence before a Civil Tribunal ; and it would have been so settled had France possessed an administration of able and enlightened men—of men not cowards before the military organisation which is still, it appears, the one master France has—instead of one apparently made up of martinets and ciphers. It has not been settled, and around it has come to rage a great tempest of angry passions, expressive of all the concentrated hate of the down-trodden. The multitude has taken up the cries "Down with the Jew," "Save the honour of the Army from the Jew," "Save France from the Jew," and amid the din thus raised the voice of those calling for righteousness in high places is lost.

Out of the miserable tragedy of a mock trial, and, as we believe, an unjust condemnation, France has awakened to find herself in the midst of a dangerous crisis, the ugliest which has threatened the Third Republic since its foundation amid the national disasters of 1870-1.

Why should the nation in its masses suddenly rage so furiously against the Jew as to threaten not only the Republic with overthrow, but all Europe with convulsions, and the French people with one more blighting military dictatorship? It is, we believe, because to the mind of the country's multitude, the Jew is the living embodiment of that tyranny of France which has proved to be more blood-draining to the modern democracy than the tyranny of the old *régime* was to the slaves who lived before the first Revolution. No doubt the personal qualities of the Jews as a race, and a long down-trodden race, have served to inflame the prejudices which go to foment popular hate ; but in the main the Jew is held accursed because he seems to be for ever riveting fetters of debt round the limbs of every workman in France; because he seems to control public opinion through his all-grasping power over the Press, to set up ministries and pull them down again in furtherance of his financial combinations; because when any great financial scandal comes to light, such as that of the never-forgotten Panama Canal, the Jew is found to be the bribing agent, the universal corrupter, the man who degrades Frenchmen by employing some of them to buy the souls and consciences of their brethren—deputies, journalists, even preachers and monks. For it is the concrete example, such as that of the Panama Canal, which sinks deepest into the minds of the unlettered common people and peasants throughout the land, and a hate thus born is nourished there against these conspirators, as they are called, which is as likely as not to be quenched only in blood.

The people do not see that, however degraded many of the Jews may be in their moral standards, they would be perfectly powerless to do any harm were it not for the eagerness of their victims. If we behold the people ready always to fall into the snares laid for them, surely it is not the Jew so much as Frenchmen of pure descent who must stand accused of having caused France to be so weighted with debt of every description that she can hardly now stagger along beneath her load. The French people have attempted, and continue to attempt, public works all over the country which do not pay the cost of construction. The merchants of France have insisted upon excessive subsidies to their mercantile marine. French agriculturists have combined with the sugar boilers to lay a monstrous bounty for their own benefit upon the backs of the people in order that beet-root cultivation and sugar manufacturing may flourish. It is monopoly and privilege everywhere, and the man with the gun standing over all. If the Jew steps in and, by his superior abilities in finance, smoothes the way for carrying out the nefarious plots of Frenchmen against Frenchmen, can he be blamed any more than those with whom they originated? And if he does take care to fence himself by buying the Press of Paris until there seems to be hardly a journal published in it entirely free from some controlling interest in finance, is he more to be blamed than the Frenchman who prides himself on the purity of his blood and sells his conscience and his pen to the best payer? All this may be quite just, and is, but it will not alter the fact that the passions of the French people are now at fever heat against the race by whom they believe themselves to have been enslaved and brought to their present misery ; nor does it lessen the danger that out of the present turmoil and excitement a passionate movement of revolt may spring which will sweep away Jew and bureaucrats and Parliamentary Government in one great tempest of destruction. At this moment, we imagine, it is only the

Army, that plague spot of French life, which stands between France and a new season of anarchy. If the Army fails to maintain order all will be lost, and yet the triumph of the Army must mean the destruction of liberty. We confess to have our doubts about the capacity of the French Army to do good of any kind. For one thing, it has no great leader, and that, perhaps, is well for France; but what is not well is that it appears to have no higher *morale* now than it had when Napoleon III. was betrayed into launching his enervated and undisciplined battalions against the solid masses of a reawakened German nation. If the Army, such as it is, and with its insolent pretensions that override the civil liberties of its citizens, fail to maintain order all may fail, and chaos come again in France. We are on the way towards some upheaval, most assuredly. It may be that the present ferment will die out, and M. Méline has still time, perhaps, to vindicate individual rights before all the world, and in so doing to calm the passions now at fever heat. But if he delays much longer popular passions will grow hotter and hotter, breaking out, now here, now there, between to-day and the coming General Election. If not calmed before that election takes place, some four months hence, polling day may be the signal for a new upheaval, the waves of which will disturb every civilised Government on the earth's surface. What hope of good can we have in a nation which is willing to see its liberties trampled under foot by an insolent military caste, if only in their destruction its mad thirst for insane revenge can be gratified by the persecution of the Jew? With all his faults the Jew, at least, is on the side of civil liberty and the majesty of equity, not on the side of brute force. Is France once more to become the prey of this force? We wait her answer with anxiety.

Syndicates and the Liverpool Loan.

Two loans were announced last week which have met with a curiously different fate at the hands of the public. The Corporation of Liverpool offered a million and a half of Two and a Half per Cent. stock, at a minimum of 98, through the agency of the Bank of England. When the tenders came to be opened, it was found that only about one-third of the amount had been applied for. In rivalry with this domestic issue, the London and Westminster Bank offered a million and a quarter of Cape of Good Hope Three per Cent. stock at a minimum of 100, and this was apparently rushed after with such eagerness that the applications amounted to 4,654,300, at prices ranging from 100 up to 105. Why should this remarkable difference be exhibited in the apparent treatment of these two securities by the investing public? Of the two, prudent people should certainly give the preference to the domestic stock. Liverpool is one of the great ports of the world, the greatest export centre of the United Kingdom; its Corporation is very wealthy, possesses enormous and highly-valuable properties, and is able, one would suppose, to offer as good security for the money borrowed by it as the County Council of London, whose Two and a Half per Cent. stock stands at 102. At the best, the Cape of Good Hope cannot be regarded as being in a position to offer more than a second-class security. Its continued power to pay on the present very heavy debt contracted by it, depends not upon its own resources, which are scanty and poorly developed, but upon the gold of the Transvaal and Rhodesia and the diamonds of Kimberley, won from territory stolen from the Orange Free State. No appreciable progress has been made by the Cape in agricultural or pastoral industries. It has developed no great trade in any domestic product. Were the supplies of diamonds and gold to become less abundant there would be a reduction in the through traffic of the Cape railways, and should either precious mineral cease to be forthcoming it is highly improbable that the purely domestic traffic of the Cape railways would be sufficient to meet their working expenses. As it is, and assuming a continued increase rather than a diminution of the output of gold and precious stones, the railways of the Cape are threatened, as we have more than once pointed out of late in this Review, with formidable competition both from Natal and from points in Portuguese territory. Should it ever happen, as has been rumoured, that the Delagoa Bay Railway passes into British hands, the continuance of that railway into Rhodesia cannot fail to divert the great bulk of such traffic as that territory may afford to the much shorter route thereby opened up to the sea.

Considerations of this kind ought to have been well enough known to the market, and yet it apparently dashed after this Cape security with frantic haste, and left the gilt-edged Liverpool one out in the cold. Again we ask, why should this be so? The answer is simple enough. As things are now managed in the City of London these monster subscriptions so frequently brought before the eyes of newspaper readers are not made by the investing public at all, they are the work of syndicates. A few men get up these syndicates, arrange a price at which the new emission is to be applied for, and rush about the City and obtain subscriptions to the new loan from underwriters. Sometimes there are two or three of these syndicates working in opposition to each other, and when that is the case the subscription price may have to be pitched high in order to secure an allotment. Generally, however, they agree by laying their heads together. Underwriters are given half the broker's commission, plus the chances of unloading the stock at a profit upon the investors. In the competition thus manufactured intrinsic quality has no weight. The end looked at is the immediate market premium, and it is the business of the brokers and bankers interested in these operations to keep the quotation for the as yet unissued scrip of the new stock slightly above the price at which they propose to tender. Frequently, in the days which elapse between the issue of a prospectus and the hour for opening the tenders, the premium on the unissued stock is run up considerably above the price the syndicate means to subscribe at. But it is always let down again near that price about tendering time. In this way the enthusiasm of the underwriting phalanx is stimulated, and at the same time the desire on the part of rival syndicates to outbid each other is damped in sufficient time to cause some of them to pause.

In the light of this explanation it is only necessary to say that one syndicate wrote for the Cape Loan twice over, that syndicates swarmed over it in fact, and that the Liverpool Loan was not underwritten at all, or only to a very small extent. The fact is, Liverpool is not just now popular on the Stock Exchange. On a previous occasion when the Corporation made an issue of new stock it was managed badly. London did not get the chances it expected out of that operation, and disappointed brokers, with their supporters, made all sorts of charges of unfairness against the method of allotment, and particularly against the Corporation for having handled the issue itself in Liverpool instead of leaving it to be done in London City. So this new emission was, in a sense, boycotted by the market, but as far as it was subscribed, the buyers were probably, for the most part, individuals and institutions whose intention it is to keep what they bought. In this respect, therefore, Liverpool is in a far better position than Cape Colony, for the Cape Loan is held by groups of people whose only purpose is to sell it by degrees at a profit to themselves as investors give them the opportunity. The loan, in a word, is not placed: it is only held in suspense; and the same is true of all these Colonial issues whose astonishing subscription lists week by week dazzle the public. The New South Wales Loan issued the other day is still mostly in the hands of its underwriters. So are the Western and South Australian Loans, and if we could get a peep under the surface we should most likely find that there are considerable amounts of all the Colonial loans floated in London for years back still in the hands of the middlemen composing the syndicates which climbed over each other in their haste to "get a bit." Indeed, we have had repeated proofs that this is the case, and none is more significant than the condition of the Colonial Market in the Stock Exchange. When any tremor passes through it, or when money threatens to get a little dearer than usual, Colonial stocks of all descriptions have an awkward knack of becoming unsaleable. Dealers in them are paralysed by the load of unplaced stock lying behind them or on their backs, and simply dare not buy. This is the position, and it discloses a most unwholesome inflation. Unfortunately, we see no way of remedying it, except the drastic way of such a collapse among the underwriters as might eventually kill the practice for many a day. In all such operations, it is hardly necessary to say, the public are never considered. No chance is given to any private investor to purchase these securities at a reasonable price: the whole market is held up against him. It is overburdened by sellers, and yet these sellers can keep prices up because they command an unlimited amount of banking credit, and can hold many millions of stock in pawn to wait for the unwary investor in search of a security in which to place his money. If we had a 5 per cent. bank rate, with money in the open market about as dear, and with Stock Exchange loans running at 6 per cent. to 7 per cent. for a matter of three or four months, then the whole artificial fabric of the syndicates would crumble and come to pieces, enabling the public, in all probability, to pick up many a stock from 10 per cent. to 15 per cent. cheaper than it can be bought to-day. The moral of this is, do not let these fancy subscriptions deceive you as to the quality of any security. Look at everything carefully, and if investigation does not warrant confidence, do not buy.

Parliament meets on February 8. Ministerial and Opposition leaders have this week issued the usual letters to their supporters.

The £10 fully-paid shares of the Great Horseless Carriage Company changed hands on Saturday at 6s.

The Monetary Circulation in France.

(FROM A FRENCH CORRESPONDENT.)

France is more fully supplied with monetary "tokens," metallic currency as well as notes, than any country in Europe, or probably in the world. Without guaranteeing the accuracy of the figures, we give the following estimate by an American statistician of the stocks of money per head of population in 1896:—

	Gold. $	Silver. $	Uncovered Notes. $	Total. $
United States	9·35	8·78	5·90	24·03
France	20·10	12·82	2·55	35·47
England...	14·86	3·10	2·84	20·80
Germany	12·91	3·96	2·41	19·28
Italy	3·25	1·26	5·45	9·96

Those in France who see in the abundance of the precious metals a sign of wealth ought to be satisfied, yet this is not the case with every Frenchman. As Baron de Courcel said, at a conference held at the Foreign Office on July 15 last, "Our population, notably our agricultural population, finds that it has not at its disposal sufficient resources in currency—in metallic currency." All are not, however, of that opinion, any more than all are agreed to regard the maintenance of a low fixed rate of discount as an ideal, at the same time that gold is quoted at a premium for exportation—a premium which last year reached 4 per cent. Discount fluctuations are frequent in England and in Germany. Rates there are apparently higher than that of the Bank of France; yet we may say that commercial and industrial affairs are more active with these rivals of France than with herself. People do not concern themselves either in England or Germany with the decadence of the mercantile marine, for in these countries there is progress; the total emissions of new capital in London exceed £160,000,000 per annum, those of Berlin £80,000,000, while those of Paris hardly reach £18,000,000. France suffers from a sort of economic anæmia for which the Protectionist and fiscal régime to which she submits is in great part responsible.

Monetary statistics are always ticklish to handle; for you have to deal not only with tangible facts, such as the amount of cash in banks or the number of notes issued, but to estimate the amount of money in circulation and in the pockets of the public. M. de Foville estimated in 1892 the amount of gold money in France at £180,000,000, that of silver at £88,000,000 in five-franc pieces. M. Ottomar Haupt's estimate for 1896 is as follows, reckoning 25 francs to the £:—

Gold coin and bars at the Bank	£76,000,000
Gold coin in circulation	104,000,000
French five-franc pieces at the Bank	33,000,000
Foreign " " " " "	16,200,000
French " " " in circulation ...	75,200,000
Foreign " " " " " ...	4,800,000
French fractional currency	10,400,000
Bronze money	2,600,000
Uncovered bank-notes	28,000,000
Total	£350,200,000

Since January 24, 1893, the maximum fiduciary issue of the Bank of France has been fixed at four milliards (£160,000,000). The new law increases it to five milliards (£200,000,000). The average circulation was 3,445 millions of francs in 1893, 3,476 in 1894, 3,526 millions in 1895, 3,607 millions in 1896, and 3,710 millions in the autumn of 1897. The average reserve of the Bank was:—

	Gold.	Silver.	Total.
1893	1,684 millions	1,271 millions	2,956 millions
1894	1,821 "	1,262 "	3,083 "
1895	2,047 "	1,243 "	3,291 "
1896	1,978 "	1,244 "	3,222 "
1897	1,959 "	1,206 "	3,166 "

In the month of September, 1897, there were at the Bank 465 millions in foreign five-franc silver pieces. At various times there has been, on a given day, an inventory taken in France of the composition of the effective cash in the Government Treasuries and in the tills of some of the principal finance houses. These have served as a guide to indicate the monetary condition of the country at certain intervals. Such inventories have been made in 1878, 1885, 1891, and, lastly, by order of M. Cothery, on September 15, 1897. On this last occasion every public office handling money was embraced in the inquest — Treasury-payers-general, private receivers, collectors, receivers of indirect taxes, customs licences and registration fees, and all post and telegraph offices. Altogether 26,000 Government *Caisses* were included in the investigation, besides the Bank of France, the Bank of Algeria, the Crédit Foncier of France, the Crédit Lyonnais, the Société Générale, the Comptoir d'Escompte, the Crédit Industriel et Commercial, with their numerous branches. The summation embraced (1) bank-notes, (2) money in gold, (3) silver five-franc pieces, (4) smaller silver coins, and (5) bronze or copper coins. This monetary census gave the following results :—

	Francs.	Proportion.
Bank-notes	173,358,020 ...	82·21 per cent.
Gold coins	23,199,640 ...	11·10 "
Five-franc pieces ...	9,311,370 ...	4·45 "
Fractional moneys ...	2,968,875 ...	1·42 "
Bronze or copper coins	243,650 ...	0·82 "
	209,081,555 ...	100 "

It is interesting to place these figures beside those previously obtained :—

	1885.	Proportion per cent.	1891.	Proportion per cent.
Bank-notes	35,737,720 ...	67·63 ...	97,100,165 ...	80·51
Gold moneys	11,860,430 ...	22·44 ...	16,365,080 ...	17·57
Five-franc pieces	5,247,885 ...	9·93 ...	9,311,370 ...	5·92
	52,846,035		120,593,275	

The results of the 1878 inquiry not being comparable have been left out. What is most clearly established by these figures, as M. Fournier observes, is that the bank-note is more and more taking the place of the gold and silver money, which is consequently tending more and more to accumulate in the Bank of France. "We might even go so far," he adds, "as to infer that the stock of metallic money in France is on the decline rather than on the increase."

At Paris in 1897 the circulation was found to be as follows :—Notes, 89·86 per cent. ; gold, 7·61 per cent. ; silver five-franc pieces, 1·66 per cent.; subsidiary silver coins, 0·84 per cent.; copper, 0·03 per cent. There is 9½ per cent. more of notes in Paris than in the Provinces ; but this city stands 5 per cent. below the average in gold, 4 per cent. below in five-franc pieces, and 0·80 per cent. in small moneys. The Parisian does not care much for the "crown pieces"—the five-franc coins. If we may judge by the results of the examination of 1898 the circulation of foreign coins in France is on the decline. On the one hand the proportion of foreign gold coins to the entire monetary circulation of francs has been as follows at the successive dates given. The increase shown in the later years is chiefly attributable to an influx of Italian gold pieces, the proportion of which has risen from 3·95 per cent. to 4·54 per cent.

	Per Cent.		Per Cent.
1878	12·88	1891	11·36
1885	10·36	1897	12·57

On the other hand, foreign silver money (five-francs) shows the following percentages, at successive dates, to the entire silver circulation of the country :—

	National Pieces.	Foreign Pieces.
1878	67·99	32·01
1885	71·34	28·76
1891	68·48	31·52
1897	87·63	12·37

The decrease in this latter case is quite remarkable, and, in order to emphasise it, we place in Juxtaposition the totals for 1878 and 1897 .—

	1878.		1897.
Italian five-franc pieces ...	959,560	...	798,020
Belgian " " " ...	933,029	...	226,515
Greek " " " ...	19,640	...	41,730
Swiss " " " ...	30,460	...	15,180
	1,982,085		1,151,645

The explanation of this great diminution is to be found in the action of the Bank of France in withdrawing, as far as possible, all but French pieces from circulation. Here are the total of foreign five-franc pieces in the coffers of the Bank at the two dates given :

	1878.	1891.
Belgian, five-franc pieces	266,292,000	190,324,000
Italian " "	184,806,000	132,805,000
Swiss " "	4,548,000	2,933,000
Greek " "	9,970,000	4,372,000
	465,616,000	330,394,000

As regards the coins of smaller denomination, the divisional moneys, the inquiry showed that French coins represented 84·54 per cent. ; Belgian, 7·88 per cent. ; Greek, 2·10 per cent. ; and Swiss, 4·48 per cent. Italy, we know, has withdrawn her coins of less denomination than five francs, which, in 1897, represented 28·78 of the total of such coins.

At the end of the report upon this monetary census a very curious table is given, showing the different kinds of money handled in the offices of the State and in banks and their branches. We reproduce it here in its entirety, by reason of its importance from the point of view of the movements of bank-notes and of specie :—

	Bank-notes. Fr.	Specie. Fr.	Totals. Fr.
Public Offices in France and Algeria	60,675,215	23,956,118	84,631,333
Bank of France :			
Paris	28,916,770	2,318,495	31,235,765
Branches (above reserves)	45,804,875	5,478,916	51,244,791
Comptoir d'Escompte :			
Paris	4,883,600	442,180	4,925,780
Branches	4,916,000	233,817	5,149,817
Crédit Lyonnais :			
Paris	3,494,600	4,494,610	3,980,210
Branches	6,042,880	1,121,496	7,164,376
Société Générale :			
Paris	3,904,750	378,058	4,282,808
Branches	11,824,340	1,203,026	13,117,366
Crédit Foncier de France	384,150	21,073	405,223
Crédit Industriel et Commercial	1,499,750	16,612	1,516,362
Banque de l'Algérie	1,411,000	9,130	1,421,330
Totals.....................	173,358,020	35,733,536	209,081,556

M. Fournier considers that this table confirms his opinion that the stock of coined money in France must be diminishing rather than increasing, in consequence of the enormous circulation of Bank of France notes. The public, unconsciously in a sense, reject silver and even gold, finding paper more convenient. It would, therefore, appear that the accumulations of gold in the pockets of the public, or rather in the "old stockings" of the small hoarder, are on the decline. The people carry their savings more to the savings banks, or allow the ordinary banks to draw it away from them, keeping much less cash lying idle by them than was formerly their habit.

That Council of Foreign Bondholders Again.

Monarchs may die or get deposed, empires may blaze up and disappear, the fashion of my lady's gown change each week; but the Council of Foreign Bondholders is ever the same, its purpose unalterable as the laws of the Medes. And this purpose is expressed in the Bill of the venerable and excellent Sir John Lubbock, now to be laid before Parliament. We have already discussed this Bill, and need now only, as the tub orator said, "observe in abbrevious language" that it, if carried as drafted, would give to twenty-one men the property and right of 540 others, now possessed of a common title. There are other peculiarities, such as the complete elimination of the right of bondholders to protect their own interests by having seats on the Council; but in order to bring the monstrous character of this Bill into relief it is necessary to recall the history of this singularly perverted institution. The story is rather a long one, but it is also highly suggestive, and will repay careful perusal.

The Corporation of Foreign Bondholders was founded by holders of Foreign bonds for their own protection and for that of other holders, who were to pay for services rendered. As all holders of Foreign bonds were not members of the Corporation, it was founded on a system providing for the earning and distribution of profits among those who subscribed the funds with which it began its operations. The Council only was declared to be composed of those who should and would render gratuitous services. As a Royal Charter—which had been set out in the prospectus as to be obtained—could not be had, and as this was becoming known, and led to the withdrawal of many who had subscribed, recourse was hurriedly had to the Board of Trade for a licence under the Limited Liability Act without the word "Limited." The plea under which the licence was obtained was that the Association was not for purposes of profit. In this respect the promoters sacrificed the subscribers in that the application was not made known to them; they had no option of withdrawal, but were only informed of the fact when the licence had been obtained. It was important to move before the project should be dangerously crippled by the further withdrawal of funds. Those who withdrew realised the absurdity of undertaking risk except with the prospect of profit. The haste used in registration under limited liability may have been to prevent further withdrawals, but it established conditions which did not bind the Council, depriving permanent members of any rights, privileges or powers except the right of voting at meetings of the Corporation.

On Mr. Gerstenberg's death, the gratuitous services of the Council came to an end. Several money votes were made by the Council to certain of its members, illegally, as they afterwards ascertained. Eventually resolutions were carried by which payments to the Council were authorised and have ever since been made. Whether those payments vitiate the licence of the Board of Trade and whether, in consequence of their having been made, the penalty of unlimited liability has or has not been incurred is still undetermined.

When the resolutions authorising payments to the Council were passed, a question since that time in discussion and never settled, cropped up. Permanent members asked why, if the gratuitous principle had broken down *quâ* the Council, they should be debarred from a participation in the profits which were used to pay the members of the Council and to build up a fund for people who had not contributed support for the Council supposed to be engaged in the protection of interests out of which no fund had been raised? The inquiry practically was why 580 men who had founded, with their own moneys, the association charged with the protection of the whole body holding foreign loans, should abandon their right to the assets of that association when the council in charge of the funds had themselves lapsed from their resolve to render "gratuitous services," the more so as the great body of bondholders abstained from making any contributions to the Support Fund.

Sir John Lubbock's own arguments on this point are very instructive. He in 1876—March 6—was emphatic on the subject of "gratuitous services" to be rendered by the Council. Subsequently to 1880, he has been equally emphatic in the opposite sense, when it had become a question of applying the doctrine adopted by the Council to the permanent members, by whom some interest, some privileges, some powers, were asked for. Tact and a high degree of art has since been manifested in the way of presenting the matter through the Press to the public.

So much for past history. We shall deal next week with the fruits brought forth by the anomalous and irresponsible body thus created. Meanwhile, independent certificate holders had better rally in support both of their own interests and of those of foreign bondholders at large.

The Resources of Canada.

In his search for fresh openings for his talents and other people's money, the company promoter has during the last year or two looked with an unusually favourable eye upon Canada. There was no particular reason why he should not have bestowed his attentions upon this country years ago in preference to some others of much less promise which he has exploited for all—and more than—they are worth; and, as it is, he comes into the field rather late in the day. 'Cute Yankees saw the potentialities of the Dominion while he was engaged elsewhere, and, with their customary energy, sailed right in and took full advantage of all the opportunities that offered. It is a fact, which the Canadians are the first to admit, that the progress made in the past decade or two in the development of the material resources of their country is attributable in large measure to the steady influx of American capital and the introduction of American appliances, agricultural and mineral. This has been more particularly the case, perhaps, in the matter of mining in British Columbia, though it applies also to the same industry in its varied forms in other provinces; and it is a consideration which should not be forgotten in connection with the present activity in the flotation of Canadian — and especially British Columbian — ventures. Now that he has come to recognise the Dominion as a likely field of operations, our friend the promoter is moving around with a feverish cheerfulness, which seems to indicate that he intends to make up for lost time. Herein lies further food for reflection, for hurry is inconsistent with caution, and the man who is not cautious in the taking up of the mining properties offered to him is prone to make mistakes—for which, oftener than not, the investing public has to pay. We do not mean to imply that all the mines of any account in Canada are under the control of Americans, but at the same time it is undoubted that a large proportion of them are in American hands, and that much of what is now being offered to British investors ranks as sweepings, which can be readily placed in the United Kingdom because of our lax Company Laws, and because the English promoter (taken in the lump) is a notorious and unscrupulous scoundrel, and the English investor not a person of superlative wisdom.

This by way of precaution. At the same time, it is indubitable that the resources of Canada are immense, and the indications go to show that progress in the years immediately to come will be more considerable and more rapid than in any previous period. Population, production, and wealth are growing; the spread of railway and water communication is opening out for cultivation vast tracts of land which have hitherto remained idle, or have at most been worked for local requirements; and the investment of foreign capital is causing the mineral output to increase by leaps and bounds. A few figures will suffice to show how real has been the advance made in the past few years. The value of the import and export trade in the year 1896 was 239,025,000 dols., against 218,608,000 dols. in 1890 and 174,401,200 dols. in 1880. While the imports show a tendency to diminish, the exports are going up every year, and in 1896 accounted for 121,013,800 dols. of the whole, compared with 96,749,100 dols. in 1890, and 87,911,500 dols. in 1880. The value of the minerals produced in the calendar year 1896 was 22,610,000 dols., against 16,763,300 dols. in 1890, and 10,221,255 dols. in 1886; and of the animal and agricultural products exported in the fiscal year 1895-6, 48,791,300 dols., against 35,443,600 dols. in 1889-90 (a bad year), and 38,866,300 dols. in 1879-80. Fishery exports in 1880 were valued at 6,579,600 dols.; in 1890, at 8,461,900 dols.; and in 1896 at 11,077,700 dols. The railways in operation in 1880 measured 6,891 miles; by 1890 the length had increased to 13,256 miles; and by 1896 to 16,270 miles. The gross earnings, which in 1880 had reached 23,561,450 dols., stood in 1890 at 46,844,000 dols., and in 1896 at 50,545,600 dols. Clearing House transactions in 1896 represent an increase of 24 per cent. on the figures of 1890, and as showing the improvement in the condition of the people generally, it may be added that the aggregate of deposits with the various savings banks in 1896 reached 61,259,100 dols., against 51,921,500 dols. in 1890, and 17,734,000 dols. in 1880.

Having regard to the area and possibilities of the country, these several groups of figures cannot be regarded as remarkable, but on the basis of population —5,083,400, being at the rate of 1·4 inhabitant per square mile—they afford plenty of ground for satisfaction and plenty of hope for the early future; and, any way, whatever the causes which have conspired to retard the settlement and development of the country, they furnish indisputable evidence of solid progress, such as it is. It remains for the Dominion, with the aid of outsiders, to improve upon this record, and to remove the obstacles which still exist to curtail commercial intercourse.

Apart from the general indications of increased prosperity and stability which are apparent in the figures we have quoted above, the Dominion is chiefly interesting to the English investor for its minerals, and (if we leave out Klondike until we receive definite evidence of what that much-advertised district is going to do) there is no part of the country which has attracted so much notice and so much money as British Columbia. The bulk of the gold, silver, and lead annually mined comes from that province; the big rise in the output of copper is due to the development of the Kootenay mines; and, as soon as the Crow's Nest Pass Railroad is completed, coal in large quantities will be added to the list. At the same time, the provision of good fuel at 2 dols. per ton at the pit's mouth in the province cannot fail to give a great fillip to the gold-mining industry, which at present is compelled to draw most of its supplies from South Wales, and to pay for them as much as 15 dols. per ton. West Kootenay is about as liberally financed as its excellent prospects warrant; but East Kootenay remains to be exploited to the full. Moreover, the geological surveyors have shown that the province is scattered all over with valuable deposits, which have not yet been touched; and, even if the vocation of these gentlemen be not accepted as sufficient guarantee of their capacity, there is no doubting the proof afforded by recent discoveries at considerable distances from Kootenay. Among the metals now mined in Canada, gold leads with an output valued at 2,780,100 dols. in 1896, silver following with 2,149,500 dols., nickel with 1,189,000 dols., copper with 1,021,960 dols., lead with 721,160 dols. and iron with 191,560 dols. Among non-metals, coal accounts for 7,226,462 dols. out of 1896's total of 22,610,000 dols., and petroleum for 1,155,647 dols.

Under all these several heads, there has been unbroken progress since 1886, and the prospects for the immediate future are promising even for iron, the production of which has been retarded hitherto by the impossibility of competing with other ores in foreign markets, and by the limited number of furnaces at Home. Under the influence of a bounty of two dollars per ton, the furnaces have increased in number and in capacity, and in 1896 they turned out 53,900 tons, against 25,697 tons in 1890; while the proportion of Home to foreign iron consumed in Canada was 59·2 per cent., against 22·7 per cent. The country boasts very extensive deposits of iron ores—magnetic, hematite, chromic, &c.—in many localities from ocean to ocean, and those of Nova Scotia rank in quality with the best Swedish. The bulk of the present coal output is furnished by Nova Scotia, which yielded 2,503,700 tons in 1896, against 1,002,260 tons for British Columbia, and 237,300 tons for the other provinces. The Nova Scotian beds are exceptionally thick, running in some places to 70 ft.; and there are other valuable deposits awaiting development in the Rocky Mountains as well as in the Crow's Nest Pass and in other parts. It would be interesting to pursue this question of Canada's mineral wealth as part of the wide subject of Canada's resources in general; but space is lacking, and we must be content with having touched it briefly. We have probably said enough to show that, with proper management and steady aid from the British investor, the country is capable of much better things than it has heretofore given us. But it must be understood that belief in a country is quite consistent with disbelief in some of the ventures designed ostensibly for the benefit of that country. This reiterated precaution is all the more necessary because it is extremely probable that the company-monger will shortly increase his activity with choice Canadian properties for his stock-in-trade.

American Life Insurance Offices.

II.

Englishmen are led to believe by the literature placed in their hands and by the *vivâ voce* statements of agents, that the profits of American life offices not only surpass those of English and Scottish offices, but stand so exceptionally above all things of the kind as to make their policies investments of the highest order. This is the language all these concerns hold, but by none of them is the art of puffing carried to heights quite so lofty as by the Mutual Life of New York, whose ten years' career on this side of the water has been as successful as that of the most popular of American "Revival" preachers. Indeed, the literature emitted by this concern has an unctuous perfervency about it which forcibly reminds its students of those meteoric "evangelists" from across the Atlantic who from time to time favour us with their presence, and enjoy "a high old time" at our expense. And it has been so highly successful that the company now probably enjoys a gross income of nearly £350,000 a year from its British policies.

We should be glad to see a separate statement of these policies drawn up on the same lines as the returns furnished to the State of New York, but unhappily our Board of Trade is as powerless to order the production of such a statement as to stop the tide at London Bridge. After the catastrophe we have no doubt at all that the powers conferred upon it by our sapient lawmakers will be stupendous, but it has none now. Failing this help, we must be satisfied with what figures we can procure, and those published in our "Plain Advice," applicable to the entire business of these offices, are damning enough.

A few tiny facts, though, are available even in London, and we gave some of them a week ago—the actual results on two policies which had become entitled to a bonus distribution—and now invite the reader to put these results alongside a boast such as the following, which we extract from the *British Bulletin* for December, 1890, a paper issued by this concern :—

The following are examples of bonuses actually declared and payable during 1889, in Five-Year Distribution Policies, issued in 1884.

The actual results in every one of these policies, and on *every policy* whose distribution period has been reached in the Mutual Life of New York, are better than the company's estimates. No better reason or argument can be shown for preferring distribution policies of this company to those of all others. . . . . *The bonuses range* from £1 19s. 1d. to £3 12s. 7d. *per cent.* per annum according to age, on Whole-Life Policies of only *five years' standing*.

So enamoured was the office of this fine display, that in its prospectus for that same year its managers burst forth in this style :—

ESTIMATES OF THE MUTUAL OF NEW YORK.

On the ground that some of the American companies have failed to realise their estimates, objection has been made to the practice of quoting profits. This objection can have no possible application to the estimates of the Mutual of New York, which are not only based on entirely different data from those of the companies referred to, but have in every case been fully vindicated by results. The evidence of this is seen in the fact, that the distribution policies maturing in 1889 have, in every case, exceeded the estimates upon which they were issued five years ago. This is not only proof of the soundness of the data upon which the company's calculations are based, but indisputably points to the conclusion that, with the fuller operation of the survivorship principle, under the long term distribution, the more liberal results anticipated on these policies will be fully realised.

We have already given the results in the case of two policies taken out on the strength of this emphatic language. They were nearly 40 per cent. smaller than the "estimates" placed before the public in the prospectus just quoted, and our contention all along has been that this must be so. Only by grabbing an undue proportion of "lapses," and by shedding off in other objectionable ways liabilities contracted on extravagant terms, can these concerns maintain a monstrous rate of current expenditure and pay bonuses of any sort to the few policies which survive.

The excuse, by-the-bye, which these alien enterprises, with no roots but merely suckers, in British soil, always proffer for the ghastly extravagance of their expenses is "the volume of their new business." It is an excuse which has no relevancy except on the supposition, which is the truth, that the bulk of the policies issued by them never live to become old. The scale on which "new business" is introduced every year has been so nearly uniform for a long time back that, had the bulk secured in any one year survived even the short period necessary to entitle policy-holders to some sort of surrender value, the expenses ratio ought to have been nothing like 20 per cent. of the gross premium income, let alone 25 per cent. to 35 per cent. But, as a matter of fact, exceptional results, unexampled profits, and all the other unusual benefits alleged to flow towards the blessed holders of policies in these offices, can only be enjoyed by a small survival of the numbers who enter by the gilded doors. Were the remnant to actually get these excessive profits, there would be nothing very surprising in the fact in existing circumstances. If, notwithstanding all "lapses" and "surrenders," the benefits reaped by the few whose policies exist long enough to become entitled to them are not only smaller than those provided by many third-class British offices, and also tending rapidly to diminish, what other conclusion can we arrive at except that these American offices are moving steadily towards the day of deficits? They have great power, large accumulations of funds—which accumulations we hope to analyse some day—and if they decided, even at this late day, to reform and bring themselves into line with conservative life insurance business everywhere, they might recover public confidence. To go on as they are doing is to render a far-reaching catastrophe absolutely certain.

As we write the annual report of the New York Life Insurance Company for the year 1897 falls into our hands. It is a mere puff of the usual type. Never was such a business done, never such prosperity seen, no company could do as much, the oldest and best international company, and so on. Yes; but the expenses of the business last year were about 26·4 per cent. of the premium income as shown by the summary of business done which accompanies the report. When we get the official accounts from Albany we shall probably find the percentage higher—it was over 27 per cent.

1896—and we insist that no insurance company in the world can do fairly by its clients and live at this wasteful rate. And that the New York Life is not doing as a British company would is demonstrated by the fact that its percentage of lapses to new policies in 1896 was 43 per cent., as compared with 36·6 per cent. for the Equitable of the United States, and 45·7 per cent. for the Mutual. The hardship and loss to individuals these figures imply cannot be measured.

Critical Index to New Investments.

BRITISH GUIANA GOVERNMENT THREE PER CENT. INSCRIBED STOCK.

Tenders will to-day be opened at the offices of the Crown Agents for the Colonies for an issue of £150,000 stock, the minimum price being fixed at 96½ per cent. Loan is secured on the general revenue and assets of the Government of the Colony, and the principal is repayable at par February 1, 1945, by a sinking fund of 1 per cent. per annum, to be formed in this country under the management of the Crown Agents, but the Government has the option of redemption at par from February 1, 1923, on six months' notice being given. Interest is due February and August. In April, 1896, a similar amount of Three per Cent. stock was placed at an average price of £101 5s. 4d.

LEICESTER CORPORATION TWO AND A HALF PER CENT. STOCK.

This Corporation invites tenders for £450,000 of this stock, and the minimum price asked is 95 per cent. The stock is to be redeemed within 60 years, and the whole is to be paid up on June 21 next. Three months' interest on full allotments will be paid on July 1 next. Tenders must be delivered to Town Clerk, Town Hall, Leicester, before 12 noon on February 3; or at Pares's and Leicester Banks, Leicester; or Smith Payne & Smith, or London and Westminster Banks, in London, before 4 p.m. on February 2. On December 31 the entire Municipal and Sanitary debt, exclusive of the capital of the gas and water undertakings and for electric lighting, was £1,115,562, while the Corporation estate is estimated to be worth at least that amount. The minimum of 95 per cent. is moderate as things go, and the whole issue should be placed without difficulty, recent fiascos notwithstanding.

WEST RIDING BONDS.

The County Council of the West Riding of Yorkshire is desirous of borrowing £102,500 at 2¾ per cent. for General County purposes, in bonds of £100 each, consisting of 325 bonds, thirteen of which will be repaid on March 31 in each year during the period of twenty-five years; and 700 bonds, twenty-five of which will be repaid on March 31 in each year during a period of twenty-eight years. Interest due March and September. The rateable value of the Administrative County is £7,157,022, while the outstanding debt is £318,000. It requires two people to arrange a loan, and at the price offered we should think that the lender may be some time in coming forward.

IRISH PROPRIETARY OIL FIELDS OF GASPE, CANADA, LIMITED.

The capital of this enterprise is £100,000 in £1 shares, of which 66,667 shares are offered for subscription, the remainder with £32,667 in cash being taken by the vendors, the London and Dublin Finance Corporation, Limited, who are the promoters and are selling at a profit. Company is formed to buy property in the oil belt at Gaspé, in the Province of Quebec, and especially with a view to supplying oils to the Irish market. Why the Irish market? The prospectus contains many general statements about millions of gallons of oil here and there, and millions sterling of profits, but we do not find anything tangible about the property to be acquired by this company. It is true that several extracts from reports of the officers of the Government Geological Survey of Canada accompany the prospectus, but these are upon the whole district of Gaspé, and it seems a little curious that the dates of these reports are not mentioned. Before recommending these shares we should like to know how many hundreds of miles the property is away from the nearest railway station, and if the nearest refinery is nearly a thousand miles away; also if in the wells which have been drilled sufficient oil has been found to secure the success of the company, and why the vendors are trying to sell the property. In the absence of this knowledge the shares ought not to be touched.

PERTH (WESTERN AUSTRALIA) LAND CORPORATION, LIMITED.

Company is going to buy land in Perth which may be considered suitable for building purposes. We should imagine it is really formed to buy from the Perth Mining and Trading Syndicate of Western Australia, Limited, 533 acres of land in South Perth, and the vendors are to receive £50,000, two-thirds being in cash. The capital is £100,000, in £1 shares, of which 80,000 are offered for subscription. Some very gassy statements are contained in the prospectus regarding the value of land out there which makes one think one is buying land in Park-lane, or Belgravia. The Syndicate guarantee 5 per cent. interest for the twelve months upon the amount paid up on the shares, which the purchase price should allow them to do very comfortably. But——

ARNOLD J. VAN DEN BERGH, LIMITED.

Company is formed to buy a steam cooperage and some wood factories in Rotterdam and Cleves. Share capital, £60,000 in £1 shares, which are taken by the vendor in payment of the whole of the purchase money. There is now offered an issue of £60,000 Five per Cent. Debenture stock at par, interest due January and July; stock repayable in 1925, but can be redeemed after 1907 by annual drawings at 105 per cent., or by purchase in the market. The money is wanted to pay off mortgages and for completing further extension, and the security consists of freehold property and plant valued by Weatherall & Green, of Chancery-lane, at £81,444, stock-in-trade and book debts amounting to £31,626, and the new money after paying mortgage. "It is not considered prudent, for business purposes, to disclose the actual profits, but accountants certify profits for 1895 and 1896 to have been nearly double the amount necessary for the payment of interest on the present issue," so we may presume they were something under £6,000. But this is before charging depreciation, salaries of managing directors, and interest on capital borrowed or otherwise. The issue seems to us a poor sort of affair.

LONDON ELECTRICAL CAB COMPANY, LIMITED.

The public are offered the balance of 86,388 shares of the total share capital of £150,000. They are £1 shares and are issued at 22s. 6d. each. Company was formed in November, 1896, and it is quite true, as stated, that their cabs are now a familiar object in the streets of London. But as the shares already issued can be bought at par, or under, we fail to see where the pleasure of paying a premium comes in.

JOHN HAWLEY, LIMITED.

Company is formed to buy the watch and cycle manufacture business carried on under the style of John Hawley & Son, and the Hawley Cycle Manufacturing Company at Coventry and at Hatton-garden, London. A local valuer puts the value of the property to be acquired at £3,000, and the stock, plant, and machinery was of the estimated value of £10,423 at the date of the last stock-taking, whenever that was. But in addition to all this, the company will acquire the patents and the trade-mark, and will also take over book-debts amounting to £3,750. A Coventry accountant explains, or professes to do so, what he found on examining the books. Purchase price, £25,000. Capital, £40,000. Business appears to have been worked up for the express purpose of selling it.

HOULDER BROTHERS & CO., LIMITED.

This is the well-known steamship firm, of London, Liverpool Glasgow, and South America, who are willing to sell their business for £225,000, of which £100,000 will be in Ordinary shares, £33,330 in Preference, and the remainder in cash. Subscriptions are invited for £66,670 Five and a Half per Cent. Cumulative Preference shares of £5 each, and £125,000 Four and a Half per Cent. First Mortgage Debenture stock at par. The latter is redeemable, at the option of the company, from January 1, 1905, at 105 per cent., on six months' notice, and interest is payable January and July. Business was established in 1853, and its expansion and certain family settlements render the present a favourable opportunity for converting the concern into a limited liability company. Including £100,000 for goodwill, the assets at the end of last year amounted to £225,980, of which

£15,345 are book debts guaranteed; £15,023 general investments in connection with the business, and £25,000 shares in the Pacific Islands Company, guaranteed by vendors. Profits for four years are given, those for 1893 being £22,055, for 1894, £26,735; for 1895, £20,347; and for 1896, £31,018; while the vendors are able to say that the profits for last year, which will not be ready before April, will exceed those for 1896. While not at all enamoured with investments in shipping companies, owing to the risks run, there seems to be in this case a large margin—£13,914—after meeting interest on the Debenture stock. We hope it will turn out so.

Company Reports and Balance-Sheets.

SOUTH-EASTERN RAILWAY COMPANY.—The gross revenue for the six months ended December 31 last was £1,436,786, being £76,084 more than in the second half of 1896, and the expenditure was £745,546, or £63,336 more, or nearly 86 per cent. of the increase in receipts. Such a heavy proportion is attributed to the larger number of trains run, higher wages in the traffic departments, and the afternoon service between London and Boulogne. It follows that the net revenue was greater by £12,748 only, at £691,240. Adding the balance brought forward, £4,527, the amount left for dividend, after paying all fixed charges, was £336,730, out of which a dividend at the rate of 6⅝ per cent. per annum has been declared. This gives the Preferred Ordinary stock its full 6 per cent., and leaves 3⅜ per cent. for the Deferred Ordinary for the year 1897. The dividends are payable this day week. All classes of passenger traffic show increases, which are, of course, largest in the third class. By still greater liberality in the higher fares no doubt the expansion in first and second class coaching traffic will be more rapid. In the half-year just closed the capital expenditure was £480,360, as the board is at last widening the line between Charing Cross and London Bridge. In the current half-year it is put down at £250,000. No less than £7,206 was paid in law and Parliamentary charges last half-year, and the accounts are full of the usual trivial items which we never have been able to recognise as prudently chargeable to capital at all. But while dividends go up shareholders will always be happy.

EAST LONDON RAILWAY COMPANY.—In the past half-year this company earned £26,066 gross, being £1,115 more than in the corresponding half of 1896. The company's net income is the rent of £14,500 paid to it by the lessee companies, and out of this the interest on the Whitechapel extension (2½ per cent.) debt and on the First and Second-class "A" Debenture stocks, together with 5s. per cent. on the Class "B" Debenture stock, has been paid. At last the Great Eastern Company has decided to build the hoist at Spitalfields for the goods and mineral traffic there. Sir Charles Scotter has been re-elected standing arbitrator for the current year.

PRESCOTT, DIMSDALE, CAVE, TUGWELL & CO., LIMITED.—Although a limited company Messrs. Prescott still issue no report or profit and loss account; and they are quite right from their point of view, because the shareholders are still presumably the old partners in the various private firms out of whose amalgamation the company arose. At the same time, we cannot see what harm the issue of a profit and loss account can possibly do to a bank, whose position towards the public is altogether different from that of an ordinary manufacturing or industrial business, conducted, it may be, under the Limited Liability Act by its private owners. However, we get a balance-sheet, and it is, in some ways, a decidedly strong one. The total to which it amounts is £5,281,000, and of this nearly £600,000 is cash in hand and at the Bank of England, while nearly a million more is invested in securities, mostly of the highest class. Including money at call and notice and bills discounted the cash and other liquid assets amount to over £2,000,000, which is a very good proportion indeed.

DANIELL & SONS' BREWERIES, LIMITED.—All branches of revenue showed an improvement in the year ended November 30 last, and expenses were only a trifle higher, so that the net revenue of £25,032 was £4,361 above that of the preceding twelve months. After meeting Debenture and Preference interest, the balance permitted of a dividend of 3 per cent. on the Ordinary shares, the placing of £1,000 to reserve for depreciation, the writing off £1,239 from expenses of "B" Debenture issue, and the adding of £1,912 to the balance forward. Apparently there is improvement all round, but it should be remembered that the reserve is not an ordinary reserve, but one against depreciation, and this company will have to add to the amount yearly set aside very much if it is going to place itself in line with average brewery companies. There ought to be room to do something more, as Debenture interest should be less this year, and the Debenture issue expense item ought to be wiped out by next November.

ROYAL AQUARIUM, &C., LIMITED.—After a long struggle this company has worked itself into the comfortable position of being able to declare a bonus of 1 per cent., in addition to a dividend of 5 per cent. for the year 1897. Such prosperity would not have been dreamed of a few years back, and from what we have seen of the reports it is in a fair measure due to the prudent husbanding of resources. In this way a balance forward or reserve of £18,577 has been accumulated, of which £13,449 has been invested in securities. Many alterations and improvements have been written off in past years out of revenue, and the credit of the company has so improved that the interest on the mortgage of £80,000 was reduced last year from 4½ per cent. to 3¾ per cent. It therefore stands with a fixed charge of £5,250 for preference and debenture interest, upon gross profits which amount to about £20,000. There is thus a fair margin for those contingencies that sometimes arise in a pleasure-catering business.

MORTGAGE COMPANY OF THE RIVER PLATE.—The profit for last year amounted to £33,706, and compares very favourably with previous years. Accordingly the Board is able to declare dividends amounting to 10 per cent. on the shares and place £15,000 to reserve. The reserve will then amount to £100,000, and is practically held in Consols and cash. A very good sign is the realisation of £30,873 from properties held, that is foreclosed upon, and as no properties had to be taken over in the year, the amount of such holding has been reduced to £43,300 as against £114,738 two years ago. The Company appears to have increased its loans very much.

BUENOS AYRES NORTHERN RAILWAY COMPANY.—It is a wise proceeding for this company to merge itself into the capital of the company that guarantees its revenue. At present the stocks of the Buenos Ayres Northern Railway are difficult to deal in and unwieldy in price, but the proposed conversion of the Ordinary and Preference stocks into Three and a Half per Cent. Debenture stock of the Central Argentine Railway Company will remove these disadvantages. In order to carry the project through, the latter railway will have to issue about £1,000,000 of the Three and a Half per Cent. Debenture stock, so that the amount will be large enough to give the stock a fair market. No doubt, for the Central Argentine, the lease of this company was not arranged on the best terms, being settled just at the "boomy" time of 1888, and as a result it has to give £357 of new Debenture stock for each £100 of Preference, and £280 of new Debenture stock for each £100 of Ordinary. The leasing of the line rendered the entrance of the Central Argentine Railway into Buenos Ayres secure, and the charge of £35,000 that it implied is not probably a severe burden now, considering that it saved the lessee the cost of a new line built through that populous city. So the Central Argentine may not have lost much or anything by the arrangement, great as the advantage has been to the shareholders of the Buenos Ayres Northern. The £275,000 of Four per Cent. and Five per Cent. Debenture stock will be undisturbed, but both are redeemable on January 1, 1900, the former at par and the latter at 110, when the Central Argentine Railway Company will be able to effect a little saving on its rent-charge.

METROPOLITAN RAILWAY COMPANY.—In the half-year ended December 31 last, this railway earned £412,825, at a cost of £180,103, so that the net income was £232,723. The receipts were thus £20,658 larger, and expenses rose £12,446. The extra money was consequently earned at a cost of 60 per cent., whereas the proportion of expenses to gross income in the entire earnings was about 43½ per cent. Still the net income was £191,000 in round figures, and admitted the payment of a dividend at the rate of 3¾ per cent. per annum on the ordinary stock, leaving £17,133 to be carried forward, as against £13,214 a year ago. There is nothing to say about the traffic of this line and not much about its prospects beyond what everybody knows. From the fact that the Board has deposited a Bill in Parliament to obtain powers to work the line by electricity, it is inferred that this important reform will be made at an early date; and everyone knows that great things are expected when the new railway into London, the Great Central, is open for traffic, as it is expected to be by the end of this year. Besides its ordinary railway stock, this company has a Lands stock, the revenue from which increases but slowly. There was, however, £36,510 available for dividends on this stock at the end of the half-year, and a dividend at the rate of 2¾ per cent. has been declared upon it. The Company's capital outlay was about £630,000 last half-year, and is estimated at rather over a quarter of a million in the current half-year, the increase arising chiefly from the necessity of providing for the Central Company's traffic.

GAS LIGHT AND COKE COMPANY.—The Board of this company is still struggling against that inevitable reduction in dividend. Revenue from sale of gas increased in the past half-year by about £30,000, but this was swallowed up in increased expenses, and residuals brought in £7,290 less. Worst of all, the company had no balance in hand to fall back upon, and so, after meeting prior charges, the net balance of £302,483 was insufficient by £74,519 to meet the statutory dividend at the rate of 12¾ per cent. per annum. This sum was taken from reserve, and thus the fund will be reduced to £48,483, in order that the statutory dividend might be distributed. It is a sorry performance, for the Board first dissipated a balance forward amounting to the huge sum of £256,000, and has now reduced its reserve from £132,357 to £48,483 in its idolatry of its fetish—the statutory dividend; and, meanwhile, its neighbour in South London goes on steadily paying dividends below its minimum and yet flourishes. The current year may be a bit better for the Gas Light and Coke Company, as the price of coal may easily be lower, while residuals appear at last to have taken a turn for the better. But we are doubtful whether that £74,519 will be made up.

RIVER PLATE AND GENERAL INVESTMENT TRUST COMPANY.—The turn in the value of many South American securities has not brought increased revenue to this company, as its income of £20,641 for last year was £1,244 below that of 1896. It was, however, sufficient to permit of the 4½ per cent. interest being paid upon the Preferred stock, the distribution of 3 per cent. on the Deferred stock, and the addition of £165 to the balance forward. A glance through the investments discloses the fact that the Trust holds large blocks of securities that have improved in value considerably of late, and the time must be approaching when it may be able to shake itself free of some of its old "lock-ups." In spite of steady writing off of losses, the reserve stands at £24,022, while the only prior charge is a £20,000 loan from bankers, so that fair improvement may be expected. But if realisations are effected upon favourable terms, the question is, what will be done with the proceeds? For some of the new investments do not seem very hopeful.

GOVERNMENTS STOCK AND OTHER SECURITIES INVESTMENT COMPANY.—With £1,274,863 invested in securities and advances on stocks, the total income of this company last year amounted to £41,658, or nearly 3½ per cent. As three-fourths of the share and debenture capital bears interest at 4 or 4½ per cent., principally the latter, the Deferred stock came off badly, and only 1 per cent. could be squeezed out for its dividend for the year. A profit of £4,525, derived from profit upon securities realised, was more than counterbalanced by a loss of £5,972, so that the reserve declined to £42,961. The securities held by the company are a poor lot, and it has about £27,000 in American Water and Irrigation bonds, which are a source of some trouble, being very much akin to the securities of Messrs. Coffin & Stanton, of ill-favoured memory. The worst sign, perhaps, as to the capacity of the board is the continued tendency to go heavily into small concerns. Thus in the last few years there has appeared amongst its investments £7,000 of Grand Hotel Monte Carlo debentures, £19,100 of Grierson, Oldham, & Co. debentures, £9,500 of J. B. Cramer & Co. Debentures, and £3,900 of New Trinidad Lake Asphalt Company debentures. These do not seem to our mind hopeful investments, and it looks as if this Trust will go from bad to worse.

HARROD'S STORES, LIMITED.—The happy proprietors of this business seem to have no cause to growl at the increase in the capital to £421,400 during the past year by the issue of 100,000 £1 Ordinary shares, part of 140,000 authorised. These shares were sold at £2 10s. premium; so that the Company got, as it were, a quarter of a million for nothing. No wonder, then, other things being favourable, that the net profit of the year was £89,313. At least, it should have been that, but wasn't, really, because £17,935 was lost on the "Jubilee sites" speculation. Also, interest had to be paid on money spent on land and buildings under construction; and so, with one thing and another, including £3,380 taken to equalise dividends, the reserve fund, first augmented by the quarter of a million received in share premiums, had to be depleted by £30,000 odd in order to leave the above-mentioned profit intact. This is modern finance, and all very good while it lasts; so good, that it enables the Board to bring the dividend on the Ordinary shares up to 20 per cent. for 1897, leaving still £28,400, which goes to the Founders' shares, par value £1,400. These founders, therefore, receive a dividend of over £2,000 per cent., which is not so bad in these times. And no less than £15,300 has been written off property valued in the books at about £650,000.

FRIENDS' PROVIDENT INSTITUTION.—For the year closed "on the 20th of the eleventh month," 1897, this mutual office of the Society of Friends did a modestly progressive insurance business, which resulted in a new premium income of £8,006, but the annuity business was a trifle smaller. The mortality involving claims, although higher than in the previous year, was still well within "expectation" as measured by the Institution's mortality-table. By the quinquennial valuation just completed, and the report of which has yet to be issued, £290,000 was found to be available for division among policy-holders. Loss and depreciation on securities held have been provided for at a cost of £20,366, and £5,000 has been added to the investments reserve fund, making it £10,891. The expenses of conducting the business last year were less than 9½ per cent. of the premium income, the average rate earned on investments was £4 0s. 5d. per cent., and the accumulated funds now stand at £2,646,391.

UNITED LANKAT PLANTATIONS COMPANY, LIMITED.—No less than £60,580 in net profit was made by this prosperous Company in the year ended October 31 last, out of which its directors have been able to pay two dividends of 5 per cent. each and a bonus of 5 per cent., making 15 per cent. in all, on the Ordinary shares, and to carry £25,000 to reserve, still leaving £2,845 to be carried forward, as against £125 brought in. The general reserve now stands at £60,000, and the fund for depreciation on leases at £7,918. At the date of the balance-sheet the Company had £85,000 on deposit. Truly a most satisfactory exhibit.

MARTIN'S BANK, LIMITED.—The fourteenth report of this bank discloses a net profit of £23,918 for the half-year to December 31 last, inclusive, of £4,858 brought forward. Of this, £15,000 is appropriated to a dividend at the rate of 6 per cent. per annum. £2,500 is added to the reserve, and £6,418 left to carry forward. The bank owes £2,521,000 on current and other accounts, and has £1,320,000 of this in hand either in cash, money on the short loan market, or approved securities. It holds bills to the amount of £556,000, and had loans outstanding aggregating £999,000.

RHYMNEY RAILWAY.—The gross income for the December half-year was £124,311, being £1,336 more than in the corresponding period. Of this £54,437 was net, and after meeting preferential charges a dividend at the rate of 10 per cent. per annum is given to the Ordinary stock. This leaves £2,237 to be carried forward, against £1,642 brought in. Expenses were 50·11 per cent. of gross receipts, compared with 51·29 per cent. a year ago. Only £9,000 was spent on capital account in the half-year. The directors state that both the Cardiff Railway Company and the Barry Railway Company are promoting extensions inimical to the Rhymney property, and appear to consider the action of the Cardiff Company in particular something very like a breach of faith. Both Bills are to be opposed.

RYLANDS & SONS, LIMITED, have had a comparatively poor half-year, like many other Manchester firms. The profits for the second of 1897 came to only £82,875; against £117,866 in the corresponding half, and £110,888 in 1895. The usual dividend at the rate or 12½ per cent. is to be paid, but to do this £10,874 is taken from the reserve, so that the directors apparently consider the falling-off in profits only temporary. This will reduce the rererve to £489,125, while the insurance fund remains at £106,245. Sundry liabilities stand in the balance-sheet at £893,496, while the properties figure for £1,021,456, and stock, investments, and cash for £3,295,434; but these weighty items tell nothing about the business. In place of Mr. John Edmonson, retired, Mr. John E. Sunderland, who has for thirty years purchased the raw cotton required at the company's factories, has been elected a director. He might suggest a few more details being given in the balance-sheet.

LONDON & INDIA DOCKS JOINT COMMITTEE.—The two undertakings which form this combination have not done so well in the second half of last year as was anticipated. As regards tonnage they make a good show, as the amount which entered their docks during the past half-year was larger by 147,182 tons than in the corresponding six months, whereas the increase in the entire tonnage entering the docks of London was only 98,194 tons, so that they have secured what some one else had lost. But the increase in the total revenue of the Joint Committee was only £671, while there was a net saving in expenses of £1,720, wages being down £12,000, and expenses in the engineer's department up £7,000. The dividends of both companies we gave last week, and the only further point to notice is a satisfactory increase in the stock of goods warehoused. The East and West India Company's share of the profits only just sufficed—the margin being £301—to meet the interest on the Deferred Debenture stock, but the company will be in a much easier position when the court sanctions the scheme of arrangement, in anticipation of which the Four per Cent. Debenture stock has been rising almost daily.

LIVERPOOL UNION BANK, LIMITED.—A gross profit of £106,492 resulted from the business of 1897, after rebating bills on hand at 5 per cent. Expenses took £27,874, leaving £78,618 as net gain. To this the balance of £14,552 brought forward has to be added, making the sum available for distribution £93,170. Ten per cent. dividend (half in July, half now), and a bonus of 2½ per cent., absorbs £75,000, and £2,316 goes to pay income-tax and a balance of £15,854 left to go to the new year. The balance-sheet shows a total of £4,549,390, of which £2,590,000 is due to depositors, &c. The bank holds £1,024,000 in bills, and is strong otherwise. Its contingent loan liability in acceptances is rather heavy.

MESSRS. BARCAY & Co's balance-sheet, dated December 31, shows that the amount due on deposit, current, and other accounts is no less than £28,290,000, showing the substantial increase, compared with a year ago, of £2,750,000, but of this probably £2,000,000 is due to the absorption of the business of Messrs. Wood & Co., of Newcastle-on-Tyne last August. The addition to advances and bills discounted is £1,3000,000. Of course there is no balance-sheet.

MESSRS. COUTTS & Co.'s balance sheet, dated January 18, 1898, shows an aggregate of £8,306,707 of which £7,369,707 represent amount of current and deposit accounts. Nearly £5,000,000 of this is represented by cash, money lent in the Market, and British Government and other high-class investments. Bills discounted and loans are put in one item.

The Produce Markets.

GRAIN.

There has been very little fluctuation in wheat, but the tone throughout has been firm, and the tendency is upward. The demand has been good, and the supply not over-abundant. At Mark Lane, however, the attendance has not been very large, and the market for English wheat has been rather indifferent, though prices have been maintained at the following quotations:—English white, 34s. 6d. to 39s. 6d.; red, 34s. to 37s. Foreign descriptions, on the other hand, remain very firm, and rather stiffer rates are demanded, but not obtained. Californian nominal. Manitoba, 41s. asked, landed. Walla Walla, 38s. 6d. to 39s. Russian nominal, 3d. to 6d. more being asked; and of red winter, none offering. Flour, although steady in tone, meets a dull trade. Town household, 31s.; whites, 34s.; American first patents, 32s. 6d. ex store; and bakers, 27s. 6d. to 28s.; with Hungarian at 39s. to 40s. Maize on spot is fairly firm, although prices are not quotably dearer. Flat, 17s., landed; Odessa, 18s. Oats continue in short supply, and the tone remains firm, while occasionally higher rates are asked, and the cargo market for wheat maintains a steady tone, with a quiet demand. Californians, for shipment, are not offered. The Muskoka, 15,913 qr. Californian, arrived at Queenstown, is offered at 38s. 3d.; and for December, b.l., 37s. 3d. is asked. For Walla Walla, November, buyers, 36s. 3d.; January, sellers, 35s. 3d. No. 1 hard Manitoba, February, 39s. 3d.; and No. 2 red winter, afloat, 37s. 6d. La Plata sorts are more freely offered. Steamers, January-February, 35s.; and February-March, 34s. 6d. Sailers, 34s. 6d. to 34s. Parcels quiet. White Karachi, March-April, sold at 34s. 6d. for Hull.

Maize is rather dearer. At Liverpool wheat futures opened ⅛ dearer, and after moderate fluctuations, became steady at ⅛d. to ¼d. advance. Maize steady, ¼d. dearer.

Wheat options were irregular, with March 1d. higher. Maize is partially ⅛d. better, with sales for June and November.

Barley, oats, and beans, steady with fair business, and prices unchanged.

Spot trade on the whole good, and parcels firmly held.

OFFICIAL CLOSING VALUES (100 lb. deliveries—January 26).

	March.	May.	July.	Sept.
Red American Wheat	7'7⅞	7'4⅞	7'1⅞	6'7⅞

New York wheat has been firm throughout, and towards the end of the week prices advanced, and the advance was maintained on

Wednesday. A selling movement by local operators caused a reaction before noon, after which the market slowly improved in the absence of any selling pressure. Towards the close the recovery was more rapid, "bears" covering freely, followed by general speculative buying, induced by war rumours cabled from Europe and considerable export demand for forward shipment. The market closed strong, with current month ¼c. lower, but other positions ⅛c. to 1c. higher.

COTTON.

Spot market has been quiet during the week, with more doing on Wednesday, and a firmer tone. American have met a fair inquiry, resulting in a moderate business, and quotations were raised 1/32d. (middling 3 1/32d.). Brazilian continued quiet, unchanged. Egyptian were in better demand, but prices continue to favour buyers. Surats remain quite neglected. Futures opened ½ to 1 point dearer in sympathy with better American cables, and further improved slightly on "bears" covering, but with realisations reacted fractionally. The afternoon brought no further developments, and after a moderate business the market closed steady, with quotations generally 1 point higher. Prices fluctuated considerably on Wednesday, but closed steady, 2 to 4 points up. Spot quiet, 1/16d. dearer.

NEW YORK CLOSING VALUES.

	Spot.	Jan.	Feb.	Mar.	April.	May.	June.	July.	Aug.	Sept.	Oct.	Nov.
Jan. 26 ..	5 11/16	5·72	5·71	5·75	5·78	5·81	5·84	5·87	5·90	5·90	5·91	5·93

WOOL.

There has been great animation in wools throughout the week, and keen competition at the sales. Regarding these Messrs. Jacomb, Son Company state in their circular: "The attendance of buyers continues to be a very full one, and competition from all quarters is more keen and even in its distribution than has lately been the case. America is not allowed to monopolise all the good wools, and this m re widespread demand is no doubt accentuated by the justifiable anticipations that the Clip of the year will not by any means be large enough to go round, especially as regards merino growths. At the present time shipments of wool from all Australasian Colonies show a reduction of some 200,000 bales, as compared with the corresponding period last year. Doubtless some of this reduction is due to a later season, but the most recent estimates put the deficiency of the output at upwards of 160,000 bales. This deficiency, following that of 1896, is serious enough, but the effects of it are still further increased by the greater shrinkage in the yield of much of the wools of this year. Improved advices of the woollen industries in general, coupled with the above, have contributed to a firm strengthening in the tone of the market, and the average general appreciation in values for all sorts of merino wools is now 10 per cent. above December last, and cross-breds have also advanced fully 5 per cent. Cape and Natal greasies of the better sorts sold quite 10 per cent. dearer, some choice lots realising 8½d., while scoureds again reached 1s. 5½d. The latter with Natal grease were taken for Germany, while Cape grease went chiefly to the home trade.

METALS AND COAL.

Metal markets fairly firm. The close of the engineers' strike having been discounted, it has made little difference to business yet. Copper has been easy, with rather a downward tendency. On Tuesday prices went down 3s. 9d., but recovered somewhat on Wednesday, though closing 1s. 3d. less. For mid-February, £49 was registered; three months passing at £49 5s.; and later, £49 3s. 9d. Business was almost wholly confined to the morning session, the only later transactions noted being in cash on Monday at £48 16s. 3d.; and near the end £48 17s. 6d. for one week.

SETTLEMENT PRICES.

	Jan. 26 £ s. d.	Jan. 19. £ s. d.	Jan. 12 £ s. d.	Jan. 5. £ s. d.	Dec. 29. £ s. d.	Dec. 22. £ s. d.
Copper ..	48 17 6	49 5 0	48 17 6	48 10 0	48 5 0	48 2 6

Pig-iron has been very quiet—dull indeed—all the week with very little business doing.

SETTLEMENT PRICES.

	Jan. 26. s. d.	Jan. 19. s. d.	Jan. 12. s. d.	Jan. 5. s. d.	Dec. 29. s. d.	Dec. 22. s. d.
Scotch	46 0	46 0	45 9	45 6	45 4½	45 6
Cleveland ..	40 10½	40 10½	40 7½	40 4½	40 3	40 6
Hematite ..	47 0	48 10½	48 9	48 4½	48 4½	48 4½

There is little to report of the coal market, in which there has been a total absence of animation, and unless a spell of colder weather comes the outlook for dealers will be somewhat discouraging. Best West Yorks are quoted 10s. to 10s. 3d.; Barnsley selected, 8s. 6d.; soft nuts, 7s.; Sheffield silkstone, 7s. 6d. to 8s.; best Derby blackshale, 9s. to 9s. 3d.; North Derby Tupton, 7s. to 7s. 3d.; Erewash brights and nuts, 7s. 6d. and 8s. 3d. respectively.

SUGAR.

Cane sorts have been quiet all the week, and beet futures dull until Wednesday, when there was more steadiness. January, 9s. 1d. sellers, 9s. buyers; February sold at 9s. 0¾d.; March, 9s. 2d.; April, 9s. 3d. sellers, 9s. 2d. buyers; May sold at 9s. 3¾d., 9s. 3½d., 9s. 3¼d.; June at 9s. 4½d., 9s. 4¼d.; July, 9s. 5¼d. sellers, 9s. 5d. buyers: August sold at 9s. 6¼d.; September, 9s. 5¾d. sellers, 9s. 5d. buyers; October-December, 9s. 4¾d. sellers, 9s. 4½d. buyers; London Produce Clearing-house prices for 88 per cent.: January, 9s. 0½d.; February, 9s. 1d.; March, 9s. 1¾d.; April, 9s. 2½d.; May, 9s. 3¼d.; June, 9s. 4½d.; July, 9s. 5¼d.; August, 9s. 6¼d.; September, 9s. 5½d.; October-December, 9s. 4¾d. Spot quotations. Refined.—British cubes fairly active at full rates; pieces quiet but steady; and crystals in better demand at late quotations. Foreign.—Granulated opened dull, but shortly after a steady tone prevailed, especially for ready. The close, however, is barely steady and business only moderate. Immediate O F sold at 10s. 9d. and 10s. 8¼d. combined; ready E C H, 10s. 9d. and 10s. 8¼d. combined; Groningen, 10s. 9d; January, first marks, 10s. 9d. and 10s. 8¼d. combined, sellers; February, eight best first marks, sold at 10s. 9d.; March-April, first marks, 10s. 9d., sellers; May-August, 11s. paid and sellers, f.o.b. Hamburg. Cubes.—Hansa, prompt, 12s. 1½d., sellars,; F M S, 12s.; Meyer, 12s. 7½d., f.o.b. Hamburg; W S R, prompt, 12s 10½d.; S and T, 12s 9d.; A S R, and cut loaf, 12s. 9d., f.o.b. Amsterdam. Crushed.—Dutch A S R, prompt, sold at 11s. 10½d., f.o.b. Amsterdam; Austrian, T T D and V, prompt, 11s. 9d., f.o.b. Hamburg. The demand in New York was slow.

In his current circular, Mr. Czernikow says:—"For the time being legitimate trading seems to be at a standstill, but the fact remains that the consumption of the world is proceeding on a satisfactory scale, and the general position of the article is quite unchanged, and in fact perfectly sound. According to statistics so far to hand, the supplies before us during the next six or seven months will hardly prove excessive, and in view of increased consumption during the summer months, the present wave of depression may be expected to speedily give way to a more encouraging tone."

TEA AND COFFEE.

Coffee has been for the most part dull, except in the finer sorts. Wednesdays auctions comprised 2,603 bags, and all good qualities sold readily at very full rates, while common descriptions still continue dull of sale. East India bold common dull green to fine blue, 91s. 6d. to 108s.; low to good middling, 71s. to 95s.; small, 57s. to 63s.; peaberry, 98s. 6d. to 110s. Costa Rica fine to very fine bold deep blue, 107s. 6d. to 112s. 6d.; good to fine bold smooth greenish coloury, 94s. 6d. to 105s. 6d.; middling to fine middling, 77s. 6d. to 96s. 6d.; fine ordinary to low middling dark green mixed, 62s. to 69s.; small common mixed to very fine blue, 46s. to 92s. 6d.; peaberry common mixed to fine, 64s. 6d. to 108s. 6d. Futures irregular, and prices barely steady. Sales, 3,000 bags Santos. Santos: January, 29s. 9d.; March, 29s. 9d.; May, 30s. 3d.; July, 30s. 6d.; September, 30s. 9d.; December, 31s. 3d. Tea has generally been steady, with moderate sales. At auction on Wednesday 8,500 packages Indian sold at fairly steady prices for good quality medium to fine grades; while common leaf again tended in favour of buyers. Terminals dull and unaltered.

HEMP AND JUTE.

Hemp rather quiet in early part of week, but prices steady. There was more strength on Tuesday, which was maintained on Wednesday, when higher prices were demanded. This rather checked business. 500 bales fair current Manila, May-July sailer, sold at £19 and buyers. February-April, £18 15s., value. Jute steady, but quiet. London on Wednesday:—500 bales equal to R. F. C., near steamer, sold at £13 2s. 6d. 1,000 red H B, February-March steamer, £10. 1,000 Parliament excluding Dutt M, March-April, £9 17s. 6d., and sellers. To Hamburg, 1,000 red C S and Sikdar, near steamer, £10 2s. 6d. 2,000 J M N in heart Nos. 1-3, January-March, Cape, £11 15s.

THE PROPERTY MARKET.

More activity is being shown at the Mart, and on Monday the day's sales showed a total of £29,135. For the most part, however, it consisted of small properties. The Gorridge estate in Streatham-lane, Mitcham, comprising rather over 69 acres, was, however, an exception, and for it Messrs. Weatherell & Green obtained £21,000, or over £300 an acre. There seems to be a steady rise in the value of building land near London. Messrs. Elliott, Son, & Boyton and W. A. Blakemore met with considerable success with a number of metropolitan and suburban properties, for which there was a ready demand. Mr. Alfred Richards announces for next Wednesday sales of several freehold properties in northern suburbs.

There was still more activity at the Mart on Tuesday, when the total of the day's sales amounted to £61,205. The greater part of this was contributed by Mr. Alfred Richards, who disposed of a number of stocks and shares at good prices. £1,000 Lowestoft Water and Gas £10 Additional Ordinary shares went at £15,158; £1,000 Taunton Gas Ordinary stock brought £1,748; Ascot Gas £3,900 Four per Cent. Perpetual Debenture stock fetched £4,105; £5,000 Guildford Gas Ordinary stock, £6,257; and £5,300 Ordinary "C" Capital stock Tottenham and Edmonton Gas realised £11,867. Mr. Prichard's total was £47,000. A great variety of house property was also disposed of at good prices, Messrs. J. & R. Kemp & Co. and A. Phillips being the principal dealers.

At Masons' Hall Tavern on Tuesday the lease for about thirty-six and a half years at a rental of £120 per annum of the Devonshire Arms in Denman-street, Piccadilly, together with the goodwill, was disposed of by Mr. S. H. Baker for £11,000. Messrs. Belton & Sons sold a freehold rental of £100 per annum on the Middleton Arms in Mansfield-street, Kingsland-road, for £3,000; an improved rental of £65 a year on the King's Head, Westmoreland-street, Marylebone, with a reversion for eight years, for £1,910; and a freehold public-house known as The Ship, in Bacon-street, Bethnal Green-road, for £2,000. The lease and goodwill of the Globe Tavern, at the corner of Charles-street and Hatton-garden, Holborn, was withdrawn by Mr. Matthew Miles at £30,000.

Messrs. Thos. Carter & Company, of Blackpool, have issued a detailed list of the property sales effected during the past year, and estimate that the gross auction sales throughout the Fylde district produced a total of £583,000, out of which sum they claim that £414,000 passed through their hands.

St. George's Hall, Langham-place, with an unexpired lease of five years, at ground rents amounting to £796 per annum, and having an estimated rental value of £2,431, was withdrawn at Messrs. Elliott, Son, & Boyton's sale, on Tuesday, at £2,900.

Messrs. Jones, Lang, & Company have sold by private contract the newly-erected building known as Bush-lane House, Bush-lane, Cannon-street, E.C. The property produces a yearly rental of about £5,000.

The best sale at the Mart on Wednesday was effected by Messrs. Physick & Lowe, who obtained £3,900 for a leasehold residence, No. 35, Upper Hamilton-terrace, St. John's Wood.

THE CHINESE EMPEROR'S ADVISERS.

Now that China is so much to the fore, it may not be amiss to take a glance at the sort of men on whom the Emperor has to rely for advice in his present sore straits. A correspondent of the *North China Herald* seems to have had exceptional opportunities of tudying these gentlemen, and he has not been highly impressed by a single one of them. Prince Kung takes the lead in the Cabinet, or Grand Council, consisting of five members. At one time he had a great reputation, directed China's foreign affairs successfully for twenty years, but was driven into retirement by the anti-foreign party, and was only recalled by the Empress-Dowager when she saw the ship of state was on the rocks. He is now old, in bad health, and deeply disgusted with the treatment he has received. Such advice as he gives the Emperor can hardly be regarded as enlightened. Prince Li is another member of the Grand Council, and Chancellor of the Board of Astronomy. What time he may devote to the study of the stars is not known, but he apparently gives no time to the consideration of mundane affairs outside Pekin. He is a nonentity. Weng-Tung-ho, the Emperor's private tutor, was violently anti-foreign until surprised by the victory of the Japanese over China. He seems then to have given some study to the subject, and when Prince Kung is absent, the Emperor consults him, though to no great purpose. Tung-ho is ignorant of statecraft, and has no advice worth listening to. Kang-Li is also of the antediluvian order. On the outbreak of the war with Japan he presented arms and ammunition to the Pekin field force and a large sum of money to the Emperor, and straightway was promoted to high office. It was he who ordered the soldiers to practise drill with bows and arrows, while insisting that those who did use foreign guns should use clay bullets, and not waste money on lead. Chien Ying-pu has, we are informed, no prejudice against foreigners, but he knows nothing about them or their affairs, and has no experience of anything outside Pekin.

Such are the "advisers" who may speak direct to the Emperor A select lot, apparently useful in leading a young ruler in the wrong path if so disposed. Two of these hold office also at the Ministry of War, which consists of four members. Prince Ching is the third of this squad, has never been out of Pekin, knows nothing of the world, and though "fair-minded" is very narrow. Jung Lu is probably the moving spirit of the War Office. He has spent most of his life in military posts at Pekin, and prefers remaining there to taking part in campaigns. But he is bold though unenlightened, and urges his Majesty to repel the foreigner, and throw himself upon the patriotism of the people, not reflecting, apparently, that this is asking the Emperor to lean on a broken reed. There remains the Tsung-li-Yamen, or Office of Foreign Affairs. Here the Emperor has our friends Princes Kung and Ching, Jung Lu, and Weng-Tung-ho to advise him. Chinese Mandarins ought to be many-sided, they have to give advice on so many and diverse subjects. At the Foreign Office we also find Li-Hung-Chang, our old and far-travelled friend, whom somebody has described as "gifted with no mean intelligence, and with a double dose of Chinese cunning; . . . too much of a sceptic to allow prejudices or principles of any kind to stand in his way." He is ever ready with his advice—readier than the Emperor, unfortunately, is to take it. The other members of the Tsung-li-Yamen—four or five of them—are not worth mentioning. They seem to have been promoted to the Foreign Office because they knew nothing of foreigners or foreign affairs. They have hardly ever been out of Pekin. One was in this country for the Jubilee, but experience has not taught him anything. He is an accomplished weathercock, without any policy of his own. Another—Wu Ting-fen—entered the office with hopes as a reformer, but found that the wrong tack, and retired disgusted in September last to "repair his ancestral tombs." It is possible that he may be so employed for the remainder of his life. With such advisers, it is a matter of astonishment that China should be so far from ruin as it is. One word as to the Dowager-Empress, a much more important personage, in many ways, than the Emperor himself. She revises the advice given by "Ministers," and if she finds or thinks it wrong, comes down upon the advisers like a whirlwind, and "boxes their ears all round until they kneel before her with their foreheads on the ground, in genuine awe, to receive her gracious commands." A vigorous woman, evidently; but then she enjoys supreme command. The Emperor would not think of disputing the orders of his mother. Prince Kung, himself of Royal lineage, has frequent rows with the Dowager, but he has generally to yield with his head on the ground.

Dividends Announced.

BANKS.

COMMERCIAL OF SYDNEY.—Dividend declared at the rate of 8 per cent. per annum, and £15,407 carried forward. Reserve fund remains at £1,010,000.

BANK OF EGYPT.—9 per cent. for the year ended December 31 (of which an interim dividend of 3 per cent. was paid in July last), and also a bonus of 5s. per share.

BANK OF VICTORIA.—Dividend proposed on Preference shares at the rate of 5 per cent. per annum. £58,689 to be carried forward.

DERBY & DERBYSHIRE BANKING COMPANY.—14 per cent. per annum for half-year, with a bonus of 1s. 3d. per share.

LONDON TRADING.—5 per cent. per annum for the last half-year.

KNARESBOROUGH & CLARE.—Payment of dividend of 10s. per share for the half-year ended December 31, making, with the interim dividend paid in last July, 17½ per cent. for the year.

LANCASTER.—In addition to the interim dividend of 12s. per share already paid, a further dividend of 14s. per share has been declared, free of income-tax, and £4,000 carried forward.

MARTIN'S BANK, LIMITED.—Dividend at the rate of 6 per cent. per annum, £2,500 to be placed to reserve fund, and £6,418 carried forward.

COMMERCIAL OF AUSTRALIA, LIMITED.—At the half-yearly meeting to be held at Melbourne on February 3, a dividend at the rate of 2 per cent. per annum, will be declared on the Preference shares, £30,000 carried to assets trust special reserve account, and £6,350 carried forward.

LIVERPOOL UNION.—Dividend declared at the rate of 10 per cent. per annum, and bonus of 2½ per cent.; balance forward, £15,854.

UNION CREDIT, LIMITED.—Dividend at the rate of 4 per cent. per annum upon the Preference share capital.

CUMBERLAND UNION.—Dividend of 4 per cent., making, with that already paid, 8 per cent. for the year. £1,150 carried forward.

LONDON AND HANSEATIC BANK.—Dividend 9s. per share for half-year, which includes 5s. interim, paid July 1; £8,593 carried forward.

MERCHANT BANKING COMPANY.—Dividend for last half-year at the rate of 6 per cent. per annum, making, with the dividend paid in July, 5 per cent. for the year.

MISCELLANEOUS.

BRIGHTON GRAND HOTEL.—3½ per cent. for the year 1897. The dividend in 1896 was 2½ per cent.

HARROD'S STORES.—15 per cent. dividend on the Ordinary shares for half-year ended December 31, which, together with interim dividend of 5 per cent. paid in August last, will make 20 per cent. for year.

HARROD'S STORES FOUNDERS' SHARES.—30 per cent. dividend for year.

ELEY BROTHERS.—25s. per share in addition to the interim dividend of 5 per cent. paid in July.

LONDON & ST. KATHARINE DOCK.—Dividend on the capital stock at the rate of 1½ per cent. for the past half-year, making 2½ per cent. for 1897, with £7,972 carried forward, as against 2¼ per cent. for 1896, with £3,116 carried forward.

NORTH BORNEO CIGAR SYNDICATE.—Dividend proposed at the rate of 12½ per cent. for the past year.

WALKER & HOMFRAYS, LIMITED.—Dividend at the rate of 8 per cent. per annum on the Ordinary shares, and a balance of £275 carried forward.

UNITED LANKAT PLANTATION.—5 per cent., together with bonus of 5 per cent., making, with interim dividend paid last July, 15 per cent. for year ended October 31. Previous year, 10 per cent.

MORTGAGE COMPANY OF THE RIVER PLATE.—After paying dividend of 10 per cent. per year, and adding £15,000 to reserve, balance is left of £6,364.

ROYAL AQUARIUM, LIMITED.—Five shillings per share dividend, and 1s. per share bonus, equal to 6 per cent. per annum, are proposed, with £3,998 added to balance forward. Previous year, 6 per cent.

LINOTYPE COMPANY.—Dividend at the rate of 10 per cent. per annum on the Deferred Ordinary shares, and of 6 per cent. per annum on the Preferred Ordinary for half-year ended December 31. Corresponding period of 1896, dividend on Deferred at the rate of 7½ per cent., and on Preferred of 6 per cent.

PATENT NUT AND BOLT.—Usual dividend of 10 per cent. and a bonus of 5s. per share.

LONDON PAVILION, LIMITED.—Directors recommend dividend at the rate of 14 per cent. per annum for half-year ended December 31, and a bonus of 1s. per share.

CAMBRIDGE MUSIC HALL, LIMITED.—Dividend warrants at the rate of 7 per cent. per annum to all shareholders have been posted.

AUSTRALIAN AGRICULTURAL COMPANY will recommend an interim dividend of 20s. per share at the half-yearly meeting, which will be held on February 24.

HUNTERS, THE TEAMEN, LIMITED.—Interim dividend at the rate of 10 per cent. per annum for the half-year ended December 31.

ALEX. FERGUSON & CO.—Interim dividend at the rate of 6 per cent. per annum on the Preference shares, and at the rate of 10 per cent. on the Ordinary.

COLONIAL ESTATES AND INVESTMENTS.—Interim dividend at the rate of 10 per cent. per annum for the year ended December 31 upon the Ten per Cent. Cumulative Preference shares.

ANGLO-AMERICAN TELEGRAPH, LIMITED.—Balance dividends recommended of 19s. 6d. per cent. on the Ordinary Consolidated stock, and £1 19s. per cent. on the Preferred for 1897; making with dividends already paid £3 per cent. on the Ordinary Consolidated and £6 per cent on the Preferred stock.

LLANDUDNO PIER.—Dividend recommended of 12½ per cent.; £1,500 added to reserve; £1.000 placed to alterations and extensions account, and £1,113 carried forward.

GLASGOW TRAMWAY AND OMNIBUS.—Dividend for the past six months at the rate of 1s. per share, £1,000 added to reserve, and £499 carried forward.

MERCANTILE STEAMSHIP.—10 per cent. for past year as against 7½ per cent. in 1896.

WELFORD'S SURREY DAIRIES.—Balance dividend proposed at the rate of 10 per cent. per annum, making 8·4 per cent. for the year ended December 31.

THRELFALL'S BREWERY.—Interim dividend at the rate of 6 per cent. per annum on the Preference shares, and 15 per cent. per annum on the Ordinary shares.

HOLBORN AND FRASCATI.—Balance dividend recommended by directors on the Ordinary shares at the rate of 8 per cent. per annum, and a bonus of 2 per cent. for the year, subject to income-tax.

SOUTH AFRICAN GOLD TRUST.—Five shillings per share dividend on the Ordinary shares, being at the rate of 25 per cent. per annum. Balance forward, £369,437.

A. M. PEEBLES & SON, LIMITED.—Interim dividend on Ordinary shares, 8½ per cent. per annum, against 8 per cent. a year ago.

NEW SHARLSTON COLLIERIES COMPANY recommend a dividend for the year ended December 31 of 5s. per share.

NATIONAL TELEPHONE COMPANY.—The following dividends for past half-year are declared: At the rate of 6 per cent. per annum on the First and Second Preferences; at the rate of 5 per cent. on the Third Preferences; and at the rate of 6 per cent. on the Ordinary shares; carrying forward £40,000 to reserve and £9,000 to next account.

INSURANCE.

LONDON & PROVINCIAL MARINE.—10 per cent. per annum for the half-year.

LION FIRE.—3 per cent. for the past year.

LIVERPOOL MORTGAGE.—5 per cent. per annum.

THAMES & MERSEY MARINE.—Payment of 6s. per share, being 2s. per share dividend and 4s. bonus; making with interim dividend paid in July last 10s. per share for the year ended December 31, 1897.

UNION MARINE.—Payment of 4s. per share, making, with the interim dividend of 3s. 6d. per share paid in July last, a distribution for the year of 7s. 6d. per share.

RAILWAYS.

BARRY.—Dividend for past half-year at the rate of 10 per cent per annum. £2,707 carried forward. Last half of 1896 dividend at same rate, and £1,900 carried forward.

LONDON TILBURY & SOUTHEND.—Dividend on the Ordinary stock for the past half-year of £6 5s. per cent. per annum, carrying forward about £4,600. For corresponding period of 1896 the dividend was at the rate of £6 per cent. per annum with a balance of £820 carried forward.

LONDON CHATHAM & DOVER.—£2 5s. per cent. for the past half-year in the Arbitration Preference stock.

GREAT NORTHERN OF IRELAND.—Dividend for past half-year at the rate of 6¾ per cent. per annum, with balance of £38,776 carried forward, as against 6¾ per cent. and £38,101 carried forward in second half of 1896.

RHYMNEY.—Dividend at the rate of 10 per cent. per annum to be paid on the Ordinary stock for the last half-year, leaving a balance of £2,237. Last half of 1896, 10 per cent. dividend and balance of £482.

MIDLAND GREAT WESTERN OF IRELAND.—4½ per cent per annum on the Consolidated Stock for the half-year ended December 31. Balance forward, £11,200.

GREAT SOUTHERN & WESTERN.—Dividend for past half-year at the rate of 5½ per cent. per annum, with £30,339 carried forward, as against 5¼ per cent. per annum and £28,575 forward in corresponding half of 1896.

LANCASHIRE & YORKSHIRE.—Distribution for past half-year at the rate of 5¼ per cent. per annum, carrying forward about £21,000. A year ago the dividend was 5¾ and £29,190 carried forward.

LONDON AND SOUTH-WESTERN RAILWAY.—The directors recommend a dividend for the half-year ended December 31, 1897, at the rate of 8½ per cent. per annum on the original Ordinary stock, the full dividend at the rate of 4 per cent. per annum for the half-year on the Preferred Converted Ordinary stock, and 3 per cent. for the whole year on the Deferred Converted Ordinary stock. The dividends of 8½ per cent. on the undivided Ordinary stock, and 3 per cent. on the Deferred Ordinary stock, compare with 8¼ per cent. and 2⅝ per cent. respectively for the corresponding periods of 1896, and the balance of net revenue carried forward is £23,038, as against £24,805 at this time last year.

NORTH LONDON RAILWAY COMPANY.—The accounts for the half-year show, after placing £7,000 to reserve (as compared with £3,500 in 1896), a balance sufficient to admit of the declaration of a dividend on the Ordinary stock at the rate of 7½ per cent. per annum. About £7,000 is carried forward against £4,714 in the corresponding period of the previous year.

BLACKWALL RAILWAY COMPANY.—Dividend for past half-year at the usual rate of 4½ per cent. per annum.

METROPOLITAN DISTRICT RAILWAY COMPANY.—2⅝ per cent. per annum on Five per Cent. Preference stock against 2¼ per cent. at the corresponding period.

NORTH EASTERN RAILWAY COMPANY.—Dividend for past half-year 7 per cent. against 7¼ per cent. for corresponding period.

Next Week's Meetings.

SATURDAY, JANUARY 29.	
Australasian Mortgage and Agency Company	Edinburgh, noon.
MONDAY, JANUARY 31.	
Colchester, Stour Valley, Sudbury, and Halstead Railway	Cannon-street Hotel, 12.15 p.m.
East London Railway	Cannon-street Hotel, noon.
Enfield Gas Company	Enfield, 6.30 p.m.
Mersey Railway Company	Worcester House, Walbrook, 2 p.m.
Union Bank of Australia	71, Cornhill, 1 p.m.
Welsbach Incandescent Gas Ord. ..	Call of 15s. per share = £740,381.
Welsbach Incandescent Gas Pref. ..	Call of £3 15s. per share = £852,881.
TUESDAY, FEBRUARY 1.	
Alabama, New Orleans, Texas, and Pacific Junction Railway	Cannon-street Hotel, 12.30 p.m.
Daniell & Sons' Brewery	Great Eastern Hotel, Liverpool-street, 12.30 p.m.
East and West India Dock	Winchester House, 2 p.m.
Great Eastern Railway	Cannon-street Hotel, noon
London and Blackwall Railway	Fenchurch-street Station, 1 p.m.
London Cemetery	29, New Bridge-street, noon.
Merchants' Marine Insurance	37, Cornhill, 12.30 p.m.
Mortgage Company of River Plate ..	Winchester House, 2 p.m.
Munster and Leinster Bank	Cork, 1 p.m.
WEDNESDAY, FEBRUARY 2.	
Central London Railway	16, Great George-street, S.W., noon.
City of London Brewery	Cannon-street Hotel, 1 p.m.
Ely and St. Ives Railway	Hamilton House, Bishopsgate-street, 1 p.m.
Forth Bridge	Great George-street, S.W.
General Land Drainage and Improvement	9, Bridge-street, S.W., 2.30 p.m.
Union Marine Insurance	Liverpool, 3 p.m.
Williams, Deacon, and Manchester and Salford Bank	Manchester, noon.
THURSDAY, FEBRUARY 3.	
Harrod's Stores	Brompton-road, 3 p.m.
London and County Banking Company	Cannon-street Hotel, 1 p.m.
London, Tilbury, and Southend Railway	Cannon-street Hotel, noon.
Northern and Eastern Railway	Liverpool-street Station, 2.40 p.m.
FRIDAY, FEBRUARY 4.	
Barry Railway	Cardiff, 2.30 p.m.
Gas Light and Coke Company	Horseferry-road, Westminster.
Rhymney Railway	Cardiff, 1 p.m.
Vale of Glamorgan Railway	Cardiff, 3 p.m.
Victoria Station and Pimlico	57, Moorgate-street, 3.30 p.m.
SATURDAY, FEBRUARY 5.	
Harrow and Uxbridge Railway	12, Victoria-street, Westminster, 10 a.m.
Whitechapel and Bow Railway	12, Victoria-street, Westminster, 10.15 a.m.

Answers to Correspondents.

Questions about public securities, and on all points in company law, will be answered week by week, in the REVIEW, on the following terms and conditions:—

A fee of FIVE shillings must be remitted for each question put, provided they are questions about separate securities. Should a private letter be required, then an extra fee of FIVE shillings must be sent to cover the cost of such letter, the fee then being TEN shillings for one query only, and FIVE shillings for every subsequent one in the same letter. While making this concession the EDITOR will feel obliged if private replies are as much as possible dispensed with. It is wholly impossible to answer letters sent merely "with a stamped envelope enclosed for reply."

Correspondents will further greatly oblige by so framing their questions as to obviate the necessity to name securities in the replies. They should *number* the questions, keeping a copy for reference, thus:—"(1) Please inform me about the present position of the Rowenzori Development Co. (2) Is a dividend likely to be paid soon on the capital stock of the Congo-Sudan Railway?"

Answers to be given to all such questions by simply quoting the numbers 1, 2, 3, and so on. The EDITOR has a rooted objection to such forms of reply as—"I think your Timbuctoo Consols will go up," or "Sell your Slowcoach and Draggem Bonds," because this kind of thing is open to all sorts of abuses. By the plan suggested, and by using a fancy name to be replied to, each query can be kept absolutely private to the inquirer, and no scope whatever be given to market munipulations. Avoid, as names to be replied to, common words, like "investor," "inquirer," and so on, as also "bear" or "bull." Detached syllables of the inquirer's name, or initials reversed, will frequently do as well as anything, so long as the answer can be identified by the inquirer.

The EDITOR further respectfully requests that merely speculative questions should as far as possible be avoided. He by no means sets himself up as a market prophet, and can only undertake to provide the latest information regarding the securities asked about. This he will do faithfully and without bias.

Replies cannot be guaranteed in the same week if the letters demanding them reach the office of the INVESTORS' REVIEW, Norfolk House, Norfolk-street, W.C., later than the first post on Wednesday mornings.

R. K.—Sorry cannot assist you. Please read notes above. Will return your P.O.

IRON.—No reliable information is obtainable; the shares are placed on the market by means of newspaper puffs, and the quoted price is maintained by the clique interested in the company. I think you will be happier without any shares.

Notice to Subscribers.

Complaints are continually reaching us that the INVESTORS' REVIEW cannot be obtained at this and the other railway bookstall, that it does not reach Scotch and Irish cities till Monday, and that it is not delivered in the City till Saturday morning.

We publish on Friday in time for the REVIEW to be at all Metropolitan bookstalls by at latest 4 p.m., and we believe that it is there then, having no doubt that Messrs. W. H. Smith & Son do their best, but they have such a mass of papers to handle every day that a fresh one may well look almost like a personal enemy and be kept in short supply unless the reading public shows unmistakably that it is wanted. A little perseverance, therefore, in asking for the INVESTORS' REVIEW is all that should be required to remedy this defect.

All London newsagents can be in a position to distribute the paper on Friday afternoon if they please, and here also the only remedy is for subscribers to insist upon having it as soon as published. Arrangements have been made that all our direct City subscribers shall have their copies before 4 p.m. on Friday. As for the provinces, we can only say that the paper is delivered to the forwarding agents in ample time to be in every English and Scotch town, and in Dublin and Belfast, likewise, early on Saturday morning. Those despatched by post from this office can be delivered by the first London mail on Saturday in every part of the United Kingdom.

Cheques and Postal Orders should be made payable to CLEMENT WILSON.

The INVESTORS' REVIEW can be obtained in Paris of Messrs. BOYVEAU ET CHEVILLET, 22, Rue de la Banque.

To Correspondents.

The EDITOR cannot undertake to return rejected communications. Letters from correspondents must, in every case, be authenticated by the name and address of the writer.

The Investors' Review.

The Week's Money Market.

The inevitable turn in the Money Market has proved more decisive than the conditions of affairs a week ago would have led many to expect. Heavy payments on account of the revenue, and the fact that the maturing India Bills were chiefly held by the Government Departments, or by the Bank, materially reduced floating supplies of cash, and of course the Bank of England is steadily drawing money in as the bills held by it run off. The effect of these influences was accentuated by the Stock Exchange settlement, and the rate for day to day money has steadily advanced, until it is now quoted 2 to 2½ per cent. as against 1 per cent. a week ago. "Fixtures" for a week or more also command 2 to 2½ per cent., as compared with 1¼ per cent. yesterday week. So sudden a swing round, occasioned, as it apparently has been, by the shifting of a mere million or two of floating credits, emphasises the mistake the market made in allowing rates to slip away so quickly and so far; but the market is always apt to reason from its most recent experience. "What happened last year will happen this," it says, and is often quite wrong.

Discount rates have also naturally hardened, and 2⅝ to 2¾ per cent. is quoted for three months' choice bills, with 2⅝ per cent. for sixty-day paper, and 2⅝ per cent. for six months' bills. This means an advance of about ½ per cent. in the week, and yet general conditions cannot be said to have altered much. Foreign exchanges have moved rather in our favour for the German Exchange is 1½ to 2 pfge. up, and the Russian rate is ·10 copecs higher at 97·85. The demand for gold on Russian account, therefore, promises to diminish, and already the quotation for the metal in the open market is lower at 77s. 10⅝d., but we have yet to deal with the Austrian demand, as the Vienna exchange has been steadily falling for months, and is now only 11·99. Austria, however, is not the strong buyer that Russia proved to be last year, and so conditions are more favourable in this respect. The hardening in rates must, therefore, be ascribed entirely to internal needs, and as these are likely to be pressing for a time, the only surprise is that the previous case should have been so pronounced.

The Stock Exchange settlement disclosed a relatively light account, but the reduction of cash supplies in the market caused bankers to charge 3¼ to 3½ per cent. for loans to the "House" as against 3 to 3½ per cent. on the previous occasion. A rush was made for the £1,250,000 of Cape Three per Cent. stock, and the average price obtained was £102 18s. 9d. per cent. as against £100 1s. per cent. netted for the previous issue. But grumbling goes on because almost the whole issue was absorbed by a syndicate. We rather wish the syndicate joy of it, for the turn upward in the value of money will render its speculation less profitable than was expected. A different fate befell the other issues of the week. Of the £1,500,000 of Liverpool Three and a Half per Cent. stock only £508,400 was subscribed last Friday, and although the lists were kept open until Wednesday not more than an additional £100,000 was applied for, and the balance had to be withdrawn. The East Indian Railway with its issue of £600,000 Two and a Half per Cent. Eight Year debentures fared even worse, for only £92,400 was subscribed at 1s. 3d. above the minimum of 97 per cent. A syndicate will, it is believed, be got together to take over the balance. The ill-success of both issues is partly the result of the rapid change in market conditions, for a week earlier might have seen both readily subscribed. But the Indian debentures are very dear.

This week's Bank returns lets us see that the process of draining the market of its balances continues. Again there is an increase in the banking reserve amounting to £863,000, so that its total is now up to £22,753,000. But the open market gets no good of this money whatever, because it has had to meet bills falling due at the Bank to the extent of £645,000, as is shown by the decrease of that amount in the "other" securities, now down to £13,896,000. Also the tax-gatherer has been busy, and the "public" deposits, which contain the Government balances have risen on the week £1,646,000, making their total now £13,093,000. In consequence of these two demands upon its means the market is, actually, and in spite of the increase in the reserve, poorer by £1,406,000 than it was seven days ago and the total of the "other" deposits is now only £37,479,000. The gold withdrawn for export this week was £262,000, all supplied from the internal circulation, which has contracted no less than £1,124,000. Notes have come back to the amount of £415,000, and gold to the amount of £709,000, including the above-mentioned sum in sovereigns sent abroad.

SILVER.

As the end of the month is near, and silver cannot therefore be arranged to be brought over from America, and other distant quarters, before the usual settling time, the price of "spot" silver has hardened to a moderate extent, and the quotation is firm at 26$\frac{3}{16}$d. per oz. For delivery two months hence the quotation is also higher at 25$\frac{15}{16}$d., but the demand is not so keen as for prompt delivery. India continues to be the best market for the metal, much of the proceeds having gone into the Bombay Mint to be coined into dollars for the Straits. According to the official reports of the Russian Government, the market is likely to lose at an early date the support it has received at times from purchases of the metal from that quarter.

The Russian currency scheme is about complete, and this means that the minting of subsidiary silver coins will slacken. The Indian banks have seen a further improvement in their balances, and the consequent ease has lessened the demand for Council Drafts, so that only eleven lacs were applied for last Wednesday, nothing above 1s. 3⅜d. for bills and 1s. 3$\frac{13}{32}$d. for transfers being offered. The Council did not allot, and only 19 lacs of specials have since been sold. Its position, therefore, is getting a weak one, for it has sold only £5,736,000 up to date, which implies that it ought to dispose of nearly £4,500,000 in the next two months, an amount quite beyond the power of the market to absorb.

BANK OF ENGLAND.

AN ACCOUNT pursuant to the Act 7 and 8 Vict., cap. 32, for the Week ending on Wednesday, January 26, 1898.

ISSUE DEPARTMENT.

	£		£
Notes Issued	47,095,590	Government Debt	11,015,100
		Other Securities	5,784,900
		Gold Coin and Bullion	30,295,590
		Silver Bullion	—
	£47,095,590		£47,095,590

BANKING DEPARTMENT.

	£		£
Proprietors' Capital	14,553,000	Government Securities	14,023,076
Rest	3,434,090	Other Securities	31,895,784
Public Deposits (including Exchequer, Savings Banks, Commissioners of National Debt, and Dividend Accounts)	13,093,079	Notes	20,485,185
Other Deposits	37,478,834	Gold and Silver Coin	2,268,216
Seven Day and other Bills	113,218		
	£68,672,221		£68,672,221

Dated January 27, 1898.

H. G. BOWEN, *Chief Cashier.*

In the following table will be found the movements compared with the previous week, and also the totals for that week and the corresponding return last year :—

Banking Department.

Last Year. Jan. 27		Jan. 19, 1898.	Jan. 26, 1898.	Increase.	Decrease.
£	Liabilities.	£	£	£	£
3,469,357	Rest	3,432,713	3,434,090	1,377	—
9,588,998	Pub. Deposits	11,447,213	13,093,079	1,645,866	—
45,224,325	Other do.	38,885,244	37,478,834	—	1,406,410
146,738	7 Day Bills	136,289	113,218	—	23,071
	Assets.			Decrease.	Increase.
14,235,117	Gov. Securities	14,023,036	14,023,036	—	—
38,473,069	Other do.	32,540,632	31,895,784	644,848	—
28,274,230	Total Reserve	21,890,791	22,753,401	—	862,610
				2,292,091	2,292,091
				Increase.	Decrease.
£		£	£	£	£
23,631,880	Note Circulation	27,025,395	26,610,335	—	415,060
53⅝ p.c.	Proportion	43⅞ p.c.	44⅞ p.c.	—	—
3½ „	Bank Rate	3 „	3 „	—	—

Foreign Bullion movement for week £262,000 out.

LONDON BANKERS' CLEARING.

Week ending	1897.	1896.	Increase.	Decrease.
	£	£	£	£
Dec. 1	171,792,000	166,125,000	5,667,000	—
„ 8	136,090,000	124,457,000	11,633,000	—
„ 15	161,483,000	165,735,000	—	4,252,000
„ 22	155,425,000	133,202,000	22,223,000	—
„ 29	105,382,000	132,437,000	—	27,055,000
Total for 1897	7,491,281,000	7,574,853,000	—	83,572,000

Week ending	1898.	1897.	Increase.	Decrease.
	£	£	£	£
Jan. 5	222,654,000	174,376,000	48,278,000	—
„ 12	144,603,000	127,315,000	17,288,000	—
„ 19	171,777,000	156,200,000	15,577,000	—
„ 26	134,247,000	118,667,000	15,580,000	—

BANK AND DISCOUNT RATES ABROAD.

	Bank Rate.	Altered.	Open Market.
Paris	2	March 14, 1895	2
Berlin	4	January 20, 1898	2⅞
Hamburg	4	January 20, 1898	3
Frankfort	4	January 20, 1898	3⅛
Amsterdam	3	April 13, 1897	2⅞
Brussels	3	April 28, 1896	2
Vienna	4	January 22, 1896	3⅞
Rome	5	August 27, 1895	3
St. Petersburg	6	August 26, 1896	4⅛
Madrid	5	June 17, 1896	4
Lisbon	6	January 25, 1891	6
Stockholm	5	October 27, 1897	5
Copenhagen	4	January 20, 1898	4
Calcutta	11	January 11, 1898	—
Bombay	12	January 11, 1898	—
New York call money	1½ to 2	—	—

NEW YORK ASSOCIATED BANKS (dollar at 4s.).

	Jan. 22, 1898.	Jan. 15, 1898.	Jan. 8, 1898.	Jan. 23, 1897.
	£	£	£	£
Specie	22,130,000	21,728,000	21,318,000	15,826,000
Legal tenders	19,850,000	18,046,000	17,414,000	23,760,000
Loans and discounts	124,694,000	122,198,000	121,956,000	98,068,000
Circulation	2,918,800	3,018,800	3,114,400	3,696,000
Net deposits	149,894,000	138,322,000	137,118,000	112,696,000

Legal reserve is 25 per cent. of net deposits; therefore the total reserve (specie and legal tenders) exceeds this sum by £6,256,500, against an excess last week of £5,193,500.

BANK OF FRANCE (25 francs to the £).

	Jan. 27, 1898.	Jan. 20, 1898.	Jan. 13, 1898.	Jan. 28, 1897.
	£	£	£	£
Gold in hand	77,180,000	77,079,040	77,306,960	76,371,000
Silver in hand	48,396,440	48,295,120	48,214,120	49,174,000
Bills discounted	36,077,040	35,723,640	38,258,760	*51,000,000
Advances	14,487,400	14,804,320	15,161,900	—
Note circulation	151,761,800	153,064,640	153,518,280	150,[illegible]
Public deposits	9,[illegible],440	9,377,000	10,153,400	9,[illegible]
Private deposits	21,786,760	20,073,840	21,008,000	22,76[illegible]

Proportion between bullion and circulation 82¾ per cent. against 81½ per cent. a week ago.

* Includes advances.

IMPERIAL BANK OF GERMANY (20 marks to the £).

	Jan. 22, 1898.	Jan. 15, 1898.	Jan. 7, 1898.	Jan. 23, 1897.
	£	£	£	£
Cash in hand	45,757,850	44,149,600	42,482,900	44,[illegible]
Bills discounted	28,219,750	29,132,350	33,625,850	*35,036,000
Advances on stocks	4,710,600	5,409,400	6,405,750	—
Note circulation	54,813,750	57,595,050	61,634,000	52,000,000
Public deposits	22,169,810	20,008,150	19,672,900	23,[illegible]

* Includes advances.

AUSTRIAN-HUNGARIAN BANK (1s. 8d. to the florin).

	Jan. 22, 1898.	Jan. 14, 1898.	Jan. 7, 1898.	Jan. 23, 1897.
	£	£	£	£
Gold reserve	30,334,000	30,375,416	30,363,833	30,356,000
Silver reserve	10,331,416	10,304,750	10,280,083	12,637,000
Foreign bills	1,344,000	1,372,583	1,392,166	—
Advances	2,048,583	2,039,166	2,220,666	—
Note circulation	57,760,000	54,545,000	56,636,000	[illegible]
Bills discounted	12,865,083	13,994,333	16,029,750	*[illegible]

* Includes advances.

NATIONAL BANK OF BELGIUM (25 francs to the £).

	Jan. 20, 1898.	Jan. 13, 1898.	Jan. 6, 1898.	Jan. 21, 1897.
	£	£	£	£
Coin and bullion	4,[illegible],120	4,[illegible]	4,[illegible]	4,[illegible]
Other securities	17,603,080	17,744,800	18,541,280	[illegible]
Note circulation	19,537,100	19,837,400	19,340,[illegible]	19,[illegible]
Deposits	3,690,840	3,490,360	4,548,400	3,077,000

BANK OF SPAIN (25 pesetas to the £).

	Jan. 22, 1898.	Jan. 15, 1898.	Jan. 8, 1898.	Jan. 26, 1897.
	£	£	£	£
Gold	9,430,680	9,430,680	9,430,680	[illegible]
Silver	10,480,400	10,323,800	10,374,800	[illegible]
Bills discounted	20,217,840	20,192,640	20,390,120	[illegible]
Advances and loans	5,439,800	5,435,920	5,131,040	9,145,[illegible]
Notes in circulation	49,089,120	49,053,880	48,525,040	[illegible]
Treasury advances, coupon account	38,920	30,800	95,800	[illegible]
Treasury balances	151,400	70,520	39,760	[illegible]

LONDON COURSE OF EXCHANGE.

Place.	Usance.	Jan. 18.	Jan. 20.	Jan. 25.	Jan. 27.
Amsterdam and Rotterdam	short	12·1¾	12·1¾	12·1½	[illegible]
Do. do.	3 months	12·3½	12·3½	12·3½	[illegible]
Antwerp and Brussels	3 months	25·35⅝	25·36¼	25·38¾	25·40
Hamburg	3 months	20·59	20·59	20·59	[illegible]
Berlin and German B. Places	3 months	20·59	20·59	20·60	20·[illegible]
Paris	cheques	25·23¾	25·23¾	25·23¾	[illegible]
Do.	3 months	25·37½	25·37½	25·37½	[illegible]
Marseilles	3 months	25·38¾	25·38¾	[illegible]	[illegible]
Switzerland	3 months	25·57½	25·57½	[illegible]	[illegible]
Austria	3 months	12·13¾	12·13¾	12·13¾	[illegible]
St. Petersburg	3 months	25[illegible]	25[illegible]	25[illegible]	[illegible]
Moscow	3 months	25	[illegible]	[illegible]	[illegible]
Italian Bank Places	3 months	26·75	26·75	26·77½	[illegible]
New York	60 days	49[illegible]	49[illegible]	49[illegible]	[illegible]
Madrid and Spanish B. P.	3 months	35[illegible]	35[illegible]	33[illegible]	[illegible]
Lisbon	3 months	35[illegible]	35[illegible]	33[illegible]	[illegible]
Oporto	3 months	35[illegible]	35[illegible]	[illegible]	[illegible]
Copenhagen	3 months	18·38	18·37	18·37	18·37
Christiania	—	18·38	18·37	18·37	18·37
Stockholm	—	18·38	18·37	18·37	18·37

FOREIGN RATES OF EXCHANGE ON LONDON.

Place.	Usance.	Last week's.	Latest.	Place.	Usance.	Last week's.	Latest.
Paris	chqs.	25·22½	25·20	Italy	sight	26·45	26·49
Brussels	chqs.	25·24	25·22½	Do. gold prem.	..	104·90	105
Amsterdam	short	12·06½	12·06½	Constantinople	3 mths	109·20	109·05
Berlin	short	20·38	20·40½	B. Ayres gd. pm.	..	163	159·50
Do.	3 mths	20·27	20·28	Rio de Janeiro	90 dys	6[illegible]	6[illegible]
Hamburg	3 mths	20·26½	20·26½	Valparaiso	90 dys	17[illegible]	17[illegible]
Frankfort	short	20·37	20·41	Calcutta	T. T.	1/3[illegible]	1/3[illegible]
Vienna	short	12·00½	12·00	Bombay	T. T.	1/4	1/3[illegible]
St. Petersburg	3 mths	93·75	93·85	Hong Kong	T. T.	1/11	1/10[illegible]
New York	60 dys	4·84[illegible]	4·84[illegible]	Shanghai	T. T.	2/7	2/7
Lisbon	sight	36	35[illegible]	Singapore	T. T.	1/11[illegible]	1/11[illegible]
Madrid	sight	33·53	33·07				

OPEN MARKET DISCOUNT.

	Per cent.
Thirty and sixty day remitted bills	$2\frac{5}{8}$
Three months "	$2\frac{1}{2}$—$2\frac{5}{8}$
Four months "	$2\frac{3}{4}$
Six months "	$2\frac{3}{4}$
Three months fine inland bills	3
Four months "	3
Six months "	3—$3\frac{1}{4}$

BANK AND DEPOSIT RATES.

	Per cent.
Bank of England minimum discount rate	3
" " short loan rates	3
Banker's rate on deposits	$1\frac{1}{2}$
Bill brokers' deposit rate (call)	$1\frac{1}{2}$
" 7 and 14 days' notice	$1\frac{3}{4}$
Current rates for 7 day loans	$2\frac{1}{2}$
" " for call loans	$2\frac{1}{2}$—$2\frac{3}{4}$

Stock Market Notes and Comments.

Markets are still without much character. We have had a settlement this week, and its features are similar to those which have gone before it these many months past. The account never seems to alter much. The same people carry over about the same amount of stock fortnight after fortnight, sometimes paying a little more for the money, sometimes a little less. Speculation, in other words, is not exactly dead, but half suffocated, or else hid away in banks, and not seen on account days at all. Prices have been run up to such heights that there is now no inducement offered to the general public to engage in extensive operations. In many departments, also, the market itself is overburdened by the loads of unmarketable stuff carried partly by it, but still more by the finance establishments outside. A large amount of general business in small investments keeps going on, but it is increasingly difficult to transact, and a kind of feeling pervades markets that a clearance of some sort is required to give room and fresh opportunities.

Under such conditions it is waste of time to enter into details about the position in Home Railway stocks, the more so as we shall presently have to discuss their accounts for the half-year just closed; and there is not much more scope in regard to Foreign Government bonds which are tossed between market and market it may be, but which are dealt in only to a very modest extent by the British public. The only centres of interest just now are the American Railway Market and the "Kaffir Circus," or South African Mining Market; and as regards United States and Canadian Railways, what can we say more than was said last week? Did we hold any of these securities we should be in no haste to sell, and, equally, if we did not possess any we should be slow to buy. At the same time it is safe to say that both United States and Canadian Railway securities promise considerable advances in prices between now and next May. The promise might be treated almost as a certainty but for the position of the Money Market, which is not quite so comfortable as it might be. Still, and that notwithstanding, markets look like going up, but speculators are of the "jump in and jump out" class, which gives movements no stability.

Before passing on to speak of South African shares, a word of caution may be given in regard to the securities of Electric Lighting Companies because these are the popular fancy of the moment. Unquestionably the bulk of these securities are excellent investments, and it is quite possible that those amongst them not now receiving any dividend may, in a few years time, prove remunerative. We have no word to say against their prospects, but what we do wish to insist upon is that the very best security in the world may be bought too dear, and we think electric light shares are getting to be that. There can be no profit in the long run in buying, at a high premium, a share now yielding nothing at all, and not much in buying those that give the purchaser less than 4 per cent. That is, at least, the view we hold, and, holding it, think investors should be very careful not to commit themselves too deeply at current figures.

Now, as regards the South African Market, what is its position? Prices are high for almost all the shares embraced in it, and some of the most conspicuous among them keep moving up, or rather get frequent jerks up, and then slip back again. Who stand behind the movement? Not the public, readers may be very sure. It is entirely a manipulated market, and ought to offer no temptation to anybody with money to lose, least of all to speculators who have no money, but who buy hoping to make some. The man who invests in any, even the best shares in this department, takes upon himself a great risk for a small chance of return. The man who merely speculates falls into the position of a tributary to the large firms who control the market. Each fortnight as Contango Day comes round these firms graciously lend the money to the speculative buyer at from 6 per cent. to 10 per cent. or more. It is an excellent business for them, they have sold him shares in their possession which the speculative buyer is unable to pay for, shares that may have cost them nothing at all, and they get 6 per cent. or more on the price he has agreed to give. In addition, the buyer has to pay his broker at every account some small commission for the trouble of carrying over his shares, and the only chance of his escaping from this position without loss rests in a sharp advance in prices. There is no public, however, rushing into the market to produce this advance; shares are merely screwed up and up by the finance houses to try and attract the public. But prices will not be driven far up by these houses for two good reasons. One is that there are hundreds of thousands of people throughout the three kingdoms who are sitting upon shares, bought by them in the folly of 1895, who would immediately sell were a favourable opportunity provided; the other is that it becomes expensive to the financier to have to hand over differences every account to the speculators in his grasp whom he now bleeds slowly to death. Hence the inert and sluggish condition of this market, which is so entirely in the hands of a few firms and companies that there can be little or no free dealing in it. A man buys and cannot sell again. Directly any number of people attempt to sell, prices are lowered and there is "no market."

Such is the general position, and it ought to keep every sane man from coming near the alluring traps artfully baited for his undoing. Next week, we shall commence the publication of some papers dealing fully and impartially with the prospects of the "deep level" companies on the Rand, and, therefore, abstain from saying more now, except this: it is these deep level shares which the financiers are most anxious to sell, and in order to sell them at great profit to themselves they have got almost the entire financial Press of London into their control. Either they have started gutter rags of their own, or bought up prepondering interests in journals of more or less repute, or they have subsidised papers by advertisements, or they have bribed individual writers, or intimidation has been practiced to reduce the straightforward writer to silence. No stone has been left unturned to prevent the truth from reaching the ears of the public, and delusive estimates of future profit have appeared in quarters where they were least to be expected. There is no infamy, one may say, which the South African group of market controllers have stuck at, or will stick at, in order to attain their end. This being so, the public will do well to be doubtful of what they see about Rand "deep levels," even in places esteemed the most incorruptible and respectable.

Talking about South African Markets naturally leads one to think of Western Australia, but really it is difficult to say much about the market for shares of companies working, or supposed to be working, in that territory. Elsewhere, however, in this number we deal with them, and give a table showing the results thus far attained by some of the companies. It is not particularly encouraging. The number which either give or promise profit to shareholders is infinitesimal compared with the multitude of worthless companies which have been wholly or partially traded off upon the simple public as frauds pure and simple. If the South African Market is doctored and controlled by a few great potentates of finance this Western Australian one may be said to be manipulated by a few financial skallywags. Therefore it resembles a quagmire rather than a balloon, and those who venture into it stand a good chance of being smothered. There is not a gold mine share in it worth buying to-day by any sensible man, as far as we can discover.

As regards the future, generally, it seems probable that prices will continue strong. There is nothing in sight calculated to seriously depress them apart from the turmoil in France which has not yet come to its height, and the formidable body of banking credit brought to bear upon the maintenance of quotations is so powerful that there is almost no limit to the extent to which the present inflation may be carried. Consequently we still look for hard markets, advancing rather than recoiling, but the more they bound up the more difficult it is becoming for the investor to thread his way and find a safe spot in which to plank down his money.

The Week's Stock Markets.

There was an almost general decline in prices on the Stock Exchange towards the close of last week, owing chiefly to realisations in view of the settlement which commenced on Monday last; but part of the fall is of course, due to the unsettled political outlook. Although there has been very little increase in the volume of business, the tone became firmer when the account had been finally adjusted. Consols have fallen slightly owing to the hardening tendency of the discount market, and the Indian sterling loans are also rather easier. Home Corporation stocks show moderate declines in several instances, due to the failure of the last Liverpool Corporation issue.

Highest and Lowest this Year.		Last Carrying over Price.	BRITISH FUNDS, &c.	Closing Price.	Rise or Fall.
113⅛	112½	—	Consols 2¾ p.c. (Money)...	112⅜	− 1/16
113 1/16	112⅜	112 5/16	Do. Account (Feb. 2)	112 1/16	− ⅛
106¼	105¾	106	2½ p.c. Stock red. 1905 ...	105⅜	− ⅛
358	347½	—	Bank of England Stock...	357½	+ 5
117	116⅜	116¾	India 3½ p.c. Stk. red. 1931	116½	+ ⅛
109½	108¼	109	Do. 3 p.c. Stk. red. 1948	108½	+ ¼
96⅜	95⅜	96	Do. 2½ p.c. Stk. red. 1926	95⅜	

The Home Railway Market was under a cloud for several days, the half-yearly reports of the South-Eastern and Great Eastern Companies being viewed unfavourably, owing to the large increase shown in working expenses, coupled with the proposed issue of new capital by the latter company. Then the announcement of a dividend of only 5¼ per cent. by the Lancashire & Yorkshire Company (which is worse by ½ per cent. than for the corresponding period, and with £8,000 less carried forward), also helped to depress the market. The Chatham dividend was up to expectations, the First Preference receiving in full, and the carry forward shows an increase of about £8,000. Prices became firmer when it was found that stock was, as a rule, scarce for delivery, and the finer weather and good traffics also helped to raise quotations. Continuation rates ruled lower than a fortnight since, with the exception of Brighton Deferred, on which the rate rose from ¼ to ⅜ per cent. On North-Western the contango was ⅜ per cent. (easing off to ¼ per cent.), on North-Eastern ⅛ per cent., on Great Western ¼ to ⅜ per cent, and on Midland ⅛ to ¼ per cent. Great Central and Great Eastern were carried over "even," and in the latter case a slight backwardation was reported quite at the last. South-Western Deferred has had a sharp set-back, and the dividend of 8⅓ per cent. (giving 3 per cent. on the Deferred for the year, against 2⅝ per cent. for 1896) caused a further decline. Central London shares have attracted some attention on the publication of the report. Most of the traffic returns show good increases, but the Midland again lags behind.

Highest and Lowest this Year.		Last Carrying over Price.	HOME RAILWAYS.	Closing Price.	Rise or Fall.
186	178⅞xd	185¼	Brighton Def.	178⅞xd	—
59½	57⅜	58¼	Caledonian Def.	58⅝	— ⅜
19⅜	19	19⅝	Chatham Ordinary	19⅛	— ⅛
77½	66	71	Great Central Pref.	70xd	—
24⅝	22¼	23	Do. Def.	22⅝	— ⅜
124½	120¼	122¼	Great Eastern	120⅝	+ ⅜
61½	59½	60	Great Northern Def.	60½	— ⅜
179	170½	177½	Great Western	178¼	+ ⅜
48½	46⅜	47¼	Hull and Barnsley	47¼	—1
148¾	147	147½	Lanc. and Yorkshire	148½	— ⅜
136½	133½	135¼	Metropolitan	135½	— ⅜
31	30	30⅜	Metropolitan District	30⅜	— ⅜
88⅜	87⅜	88¼	Midland Pref.	88¼	— ⅜
95⅜	93⅞	94	Do. Def.	93⅞	—1⅜
93½	90½	92½	North British Pref.	92½	— ⅜
47½	45	46⅝	Do. Def.	46⅝	— ⅜
181½	179½	180	North Eastern	180½	+ ⅜
205¼	204½	204½	North Western	205	—
117	114⅜	115⅝	South Eastern Def.	116½	— ½
98⅜	95½	95½	South Western Def.	96	—1⅜

United States R.R. shares exhibited a weak tendency for the greater part of the week, under the influence of New York selling, but when London turned round and bought on Tuesday a recovery set in. Wall Street has since bought rather freely, principally New York Central, Lake Shore, and Ontario shares. Actual consolidation between the New York Central and Lake Shore roads is now talked of, but no official statement has yet been published. The Vanderbilt group has engaged most of the time and attention of "insiders," and the announcement of the election of Mr. Chauncey Depew to a seat on the Board of the New York-Ontario Company has also helped to raise the price of their shares. All the roads again publish good traffic returns.

Large dealings have again taken place in Canadian Pacific and Grand Trunk stocks, and prices have fluctuated rather wildly. Canadian Pacific shares fell sharply, selling orders coming from Montreal, when it was announced that the Northern Pacific Company had succeeded in outbidding them, and so securing the control of the Seattle, Lake Shore, & Eastern Road; but a very satisfactory traffic return helped to pull the price up again. Grand Trunk stocks were adversely affected early in the week by a certain amount of profit taking, but the upward movement has apparently not yet spent itself.

Highest and Lowest this Year.		Last Carrying over Price.	CANADIAN AND U.S. RAILWAYS.	Closing Prices.	Rise or Fall.
13⅞	12⅜	12¾	Atchison Shares	13⅜	+ ⅜
32¾	29⅞	29⅞	Do. Pref.	31⅞	+ ⅞
14½	11⅜	13⅜	Central Pacific	14⅜	+1⅛
99¾	95½	96⅞	Chic. Mil. & St. Paul	98½	+1
13½	11½	12¼	Denver Shares	13½	+ ⅜
51	46⅜	48½	Do. Prefd.	50⅜	+ ⅞
15⅝	14⅛	14⅞	Erie Shares	15⅛	— ⅜
40½	37½	37½	Do. Prefd.	40	+1
60	56⅜	57	Louisville & Nashville	58⅜	+1
14½	12⅛	12⅝	Missouri & Texas	14¼	+1⅜
121½	108½	116½	New York Central	121½	+5⅜
49¾	47¾	48	Norfolk & West. Prefd.	49	— ⅜
67¾	59⅜	65¼	Northern Pacific Prefd.	67¼	+ ⅞
19	15⅛	17	Ontario Shares	18⅞	+2⅛
60½	58⅛	59	Pennsylvania	59½	—
12½	10½	11	Reading Shares	11⅝	+ ⅜
33½	30¼	30⅞	Southern Prefd.	32	+ ⅜
34½	26⅛	31⅝	Union Pacific	34⅜	+1⅜
20½	18	18½	Wabash Prefd.	19¼	—
30½	27⅜	28¼	Do. Income Debs.	29¼	—1
92¾	83¾	91	Canadian Pacific	91⅜	— ⅜
78½	69⅛	77	Grand Trunk Guar.	76⅜	—1⅜
69½	57⅜	68	Do. 1st Pref.	68	— ⅜
50⅜	37¼	48½	Do. 2nd Pref.	48⅜	— ⅜
25½	19¼	24	Do. 3rd Pref.	25⅛	+ ⅜
105½	104	105¼	Do. 4 p.c. Deb.	105¼	— ⅜

The Foreign Market has been steady to firm. Despite the rather unsettled aspect of affairs in the far East;

and the disturbances in the French Chamber attracted little or no attention. The Reuter's telegram published on Saturday concerning the relations between Argentina and Chile caused a decline in the bonds of these Republics, but later news regarding the boundary dispute was of a less alarming description, and the President has officially denied the rumours lately current in reference to international difficulties. The steady fall in the gold premium at Buenos Ayres has tended to strengthen prices, but business continues on a very small scale. Continuation rates were ½ to 1 per cent. lower at the settlement, Russian bonds being continued at from 1 to 2 per cent., Greek and Spanish at 2 to 4 per cent., Italian Rentes at about 4 per cent., and Argentine and Turkish groups at about 4½ per cent. Turkish issues were pressed for sale from Paris, a rumour going the round there that a note had been forwarded to the Sultan from France and Russia regarding the state of affairs in Crete. Ottoman Bank shares weakened on the reported resignation of Sir R. H. Lang, but the rumour turned out to be pure fiction. Italian and Spanish both show some recovery from the lowest points of the week, and Greek bonds are firm on the publication of the report of the International Commission of Control over Greek finances.

Highest and Lowest this Year.		Last Carrying over Price.	FOREIGN RAILWAYS.	Closing Price.	Rise or Fall.
20¾	20	20¼	Argentine Gt. West. 5 p.c. Pref.	20¼	− ¼
158	149	155	B. Ay. Gt. Southern Ord.	158	+3
78½	75½	77	B. Ay. and Rosario Ord.	78	+1½
12¼	11⅛	11¼	B. Ay. Western Ord.	12	
87½	80½	85¾	Central Argentine Ord.	87	+1
92	89¾	89½	Cordoba and Rosario 6 p.c. Deb.	91	
95½	93¾	94½	Cord. Cent. 4 p.c. Deb. (Cent. Nth. Sec.)	94½	− ½
61¾	58½	59	Do. Income Deb. Stk.	60	
24	18	21	Mexican Ord. Stk.	23¾	+2¾
83	72	78	Do. 8 p.c. 1st Pref.	82½	+4½

Among Foreign Railway stocks a feature was the rise of 12½ and 10 in the Ordinary and Preference stocks respectively, of the Buenos Ayres Northern Company, the report stating that a proposal had been received from the Central Argentine Company for taking over their line. Prices of other Central and South American companies have moved up and the tendency is firm. Continuation rates ruled at from 5 to 5½ per cent. Mexican railway stocks were neglected all the week, but rose sharply on Wednesday, when the traffic return appeared.

Highest and Lowest this Year.		Last Carrying over Price.	FOREIGN BONDS.	Closing Price.	Rise or Fall.
94½	92½	93	Argentine 5 p.c. 1886	92¾	− ¾
92⅝	89	91½	Do. 6 p.c. Funding	91½	− ¼
76¾	71	75½	Do. 5 p.c. B. Ay. Water	76	+ ½
61½	60	61	Brazilian 4 p.c. 1889	61	
69	67½	68¾	Do. 5 p.c. 1895	69	+ ½
64	62½	64	Do. 5 p.c. West Minas Ry.	64	+ ½
107½	106½	107	Egyptian 4 p.c. Unified	107½	+ ¼
102½	102	102⅜	Do. 3½ p.c. Pref.	102½	+ ¼
102½	102	102¼	French 3 p.c. Rente	102	− ½
39¾	34½	39	Greek 4 p.c. Monopoly	39	+ 1
93 3/16	92⅝	92⅞	Italian 5 p.c. Rente	92⅞	
98¼	95¾	97½	Mexican 6 p.c. 1888	97¾	+ ¼
20¾	20	20	Portuguese 1 p.c.	20⅛	− ⅛
61½	59⅞	60⅝	Spanish 4 p.c.	61¼	+ ⅞
45	43	44½	Turkish 1 p.c. "B"	44¾	+ ⅜
26	24 1/16	25⅜	Do. 1 p.c. "C"	26	+ ⅝
22¾	21 13/16	22	Do. 1 p.c. "D"	22⅜	+ ⅜
42¾	41½	42	Uruguay 3½ p.c. Bonds	42½	+ ½

In the Miscellaneous Market the shares of the various electric lighting companies have again attracted most attention, and a large amount of business has been transacted at considerably higher prices than those ruling last week. The directors of the New English Sewing Cotton Company are apparently quite indifferent to outside criticisms, and go on slowly doling out letters of regret, but allotments are still vainly looked for. Among Brewery stocks, Allsopp has fallen sharply, and recovered, on various dividend rumours, an increase of 1 per cent. being now generally expected. City of London Ordinary stock has risen considerably, but there is a set-back of 10 points in Guinness. Linotype shares were offered at one time, but on the announcement of a dividend at the rate of 10 per cent. on the Deferred, there was a recovery. Colonial Bank shares again advanced, London General Omnibus Debenture is 4 higher, and Aerated Bread shares have also shown great strength; but Salt Union issues close weak, and among Telegraph companies Anglo-American stocks are slightly lower, the dividend not being quite up to what the more sanguine operators had looked for.

MINING AND FINANCE COMPANIES.

There has been little or nothing doing in South African ventures, apart from the arranging of the accounts, and prices have been marked down day after day, helped in that direction by sales from Paris and the Cape. Towards the close a very slight improvement is apparent, but the little buying that took place was professional. The "carry over" was easily arranged, rates ruling rather higher than last time, at about 5 to 7 per cent. East Rands were continued at about those rates, De Beers at 9d. to 1s. 3d., and Chartered at about 2½d. to 3½d. Western Australian companies have also shared in the general dulness, a little buying from Adelaide giving a slightly firmer tone before the close. The general rate for continuing West Australian shares was slightly stiffer at from 8 to 10 per cent. Among Miscellaneous Mines, Indians were dull, in sympathy with a sharp drop in Nundydroog, which was due to the announcement by that company of a flood in the mine. Wassan (Gold Coast) shares continue in request. Copper securities advanced at one time, when sales on Paris account ceased, but there has been a slight reaction, on a resumption of selling orders.

The principal features noticeable at the close of the week are a sharp fall in Canadian Pacific and Grand Trunk stocks, and a further considerable advance in Mexican Railway stocks. United States Railroad shares close with a very firm tendency, Lake Shore again leading the way. Home Railway issues were rather dull, with the exception of South-Western Deferred, Great Northern Preferred, and South-Eastern Deferred, which close firm. Among Foreign Government bonds there was a sharp rally in Spanish Fours and Turkish Groups, Italian Rentes, and Argentina Cedulas all finish strong. Rupee paper suddenly rose ¾, and Bank of England stock marks a further rise.

ENGLISH RAILWAY TRAFFIC RETURNS

Cleator and Workington.—Gross receipts for the week ending January 22 amounted to £959, a decrease of £60. Total receipts from January 1, £3,068, a decrease of £219.

Cockermouth, Keswick, and Penrith.—Gross receipts for the week ending January 22 amounted to £820, an increase of £89. Total receipts for three weeks £2,658, an increase of £305.

East and West Yorkshire Union.—Gross receipts for the week ending January 14 amounted to £280, an increase of £78. Total receipts for two weeks £548, an increase of £105.

TRAMWAY AND OMNIBUS RECEIPTS.

Increases for past week :—Belfast, £391; Croydon, £123; Glasgow, £51; Lea Bridge, £217; London, £1,693; London & Deptford, £121; London Southern, £159; London General Omnibus, £4,096; London Road Car, £1,331; Metropolitan, £2,261; North Staffordshire, 31; Provincial, £560; Southampton, £68; South London, £309; Sunderland, £97; Swansea, £27; Wolverhampton, £50; Woolwich & S. E. London, £82; Bordeaux, £118; Calais, £28; Calcutta, £217.

Decreases for past week :—

Anglo-Argentine, week ending December 27, £37 increase. Vienna Omnibus, week ending January 15, £131 increase.

The National Sound Money Conference at Indianapolis have approved the plan of monetary reform adopted by the committee at the former conference.

WEST AUSTRALIAN MINE CRUSHINGS.

Capital Issued.	Property.	Goldfields.	Name of Company.	1895.		1896.		1897.		Total since Crushing Commenced.	
£	Acres.			Tons.	Oz.	Tons.	Oz.	Tons.	Oz.	Tons.	Oz.
61,426	108	Murchison	Agamemnon	—	—	—	—	1,329	1,433	8,355	4,685
97,007	129	Mount Margaret	Arrow Brownhill	—	—	—	—	378	339	378	339
425,000	156	Kalgoorlie	Associated G. M. of W. A.	—	—	—	—	12,332	26,842	12,332	26,842
150,007	106	Coolgardie	Big Blow	104	44	134	72	355	140	613	256
250,000	65	N. E. Coolgardie	Black Flag Proprietary	—	—	—	—	9,955	3,205	9,953	3,205
150,000	39	Coolgardie	Burbank's Birthday Gift	157	622	1,614	7,296	6,184	13,019	7,955	20,937
250,000	51	Murchison	Champion Reef	—	—	—	—	9,283	4,687	9,283	4,687
64,660	132	Pilbarra	Consolidated G. M. of W. A.	178	206	733	686	753	884	1,635	1,732
113,000	119	Murchison	Consolidated Murchison	7,274	4,168	12,970	6,989	6,247	4,779	26,491	15,936
100,000	12	Murchison	Cue No. 1	—	—	2,040	1,903	6,692	4,692	8,732	6,595
92,197	42	Murchison	Cue Victory	—	—	—	—	1,870	1,322	2,008	1,427
233,500	94	Dundas	Desirable Proprietary Gold	—	—	287	1,326	2,105	1,772	—	—
122,830	77	Mount Margaret	Diorite King	—	—	—	—	333	923	333	923
230,000	117	East Murchison	East Murchison United	—	—	1,467	2,576	10,717	17,291	12,184	19,867
54,139	40	Yalgoo	Emerald Reward	1,082	1,334	419	410	408	477	2,104	3,512
65,000	12	Murchison	Emperor Gold	14	94	137	108	897	755	—	—
85,000	84	Murchison	Golconda	1,230	2,092	2,213	4,995	1,335	3,240	4,780	10,327
182,380	60	N. E. Coolgardie	Golden Arrow	—	—	—	—	707	579	707	579
100,000	24	Kalgoorlie	Golden Horse Shoe	—	—	57	32	1,513	6,336	1,967	6,368
175,000	24	Kalgoorlie	Great Boulder Perseverance	—	—	1,410	4,550	12,189	23,416	13,599	27,966
160,000	85	Kalgoorlie	Great Boulder Proprietary	4,291	26,663	16,729	55,949	29,463	83,292	50,483	165,904
500,000	114	Coolgardie	Great Dyke and Orizaba	—	—	—	—	3,100	1,136	3,100	1,136
105,000	42	Yalgoo	Gullewa	—	—	117	217	1,218	1,784	1,335	2,001
143,807	60	N. E. Coolgardie	Half-Mile Reef	—	—	—	—	1,453	1,075	1,453	1,075
85,000	20	Kalgoorlie	Hannan's Brownhill	—	—	1,002	3,241	4,071	27,134	5,073	30,295
140,000	36	Kalgoorlie	Hannan's Oroya	—	—	—	—	2,435	1,177	2,441	1,229
75,000	27	Kalgoorlie	Hannan's Reward	—	—	—	—	2,264	1,453	2,264	1,453
225,000	29	North Coolgardie	Hick's Gold Mine	—	—	—	—	705	831	770	936
321,054	134	Pilbarra and Kalgoorlie	Imperial W. A. Corporation	30	119	140	520	1,129	1,140	1,299	1,780
1,000,000	94	Kalgoorlie	Ivanhoe	1,757	3,036	3,367	10,636	14,951	29,322	20,075	42,994
150,000	42	Kalgoorlie	Kalgoorlie Mint and Iron King	200	689	518	1,298	1,060	2,058	1,768	4,326
50,000	38	Murchison	Lady Mary Amalgamated	22	41	1,472	1,241	977	969	2,571	2,676
260,000	36	North Coolgardie	Lady Shenton	—	—	1,749	7,078	4,842	17,206	6,591	24,284
250,000	48	Kalgoorlie	Lake View Consols	3,377	10,428	5,900	17,244	25,943	90,093	35,476	[illegible]
119,444	52	Coolgardie	Lindsay's Consolidated	—	—	—	—	2,580	1,581	2,580	1,581
699,999	67	Coolgardie	Londonderry	245	1,425	907	873	347	545	1,499	10,803
150,000	37	Murchison	Mainland Consols	—	8,250	1,372	6,111	2,206	3,769	3,578	18,130
100,000	44	North Coolgardie	Menzies Alpha Leases	—	—	53	380	467	1,393	520	1,773
224,125	156	North Coolgardie	Menzies Consolidated	—	—	—	—	5,958	5,800	5,958	5,800
193,100	44	North Coolgardie	Menzies Crusoe	—	—	3,244	6,957	4,191	6,594	7,435	13,551
99,585	16	North Coolgardie	Menzies Golden Age	—	—	50	329	195	800	245	1,122
173,821	91	North Coolgardie	Menzies Gold Reefs Proprietary	—	—	2,272	3,891	2,428	3,608	4,830	7,486
200,000	102	Mount Margaret	Mount Malcolm Proprietary	—	—	—	—	1,814	1,591	1,814	1,594
85,000	84	Murchison	Mount Yagahong	—	—	341	684	3,392	2,734	3,740	3,418
160,000	120	Murchison	Murchison New Chum	—	12,303	1,330	2,473	439	701	1,769	14,880
180,000	90	North Coolgardie	Ninety-Mile Proprietary	—	—	1,038	845	1,684	948	2,722	1,793
200,000	164	Dundas	Norseman Gold	—	—	—	—	2,479	2,852	2,479	2,850
120,000	19	Kalgoorlie	North Boulder	—	—	890	2,081	5,134	10,350	6,024	12,431
115,000	143	Mount Margaret	North Star	—	—	—	—	3,435	3,753	3,435	3,753
123,114	78	Pilbarra	Pilbarra United	63	146	308	517	65	96	436	759
62,100	24	Murchison	Polar Star Proprietary	—	—	98	393	267	478	365	871
25,799	36	Coolgardie	Premier Gold	—	—	2,240	4,611	3,997	4,647	6,237	9,258
65,003	12	Murchison	Princess Royal (Cue)	30	96	220	432	2,350	2,354	2,620	2,882
31,387	19½	N. Coolgardie	Queensland Menzies	—	—	177	1,215	3,828	14,844	4,005	16,059
78,984	51	N. E. Coolgardie	Robinson (W.A.)	—	—	642	1,071	5,230	7,391	5,892	8,462
75,000	22	Pilbarra	Stray Shot and Excelsior	100	190	403	972	146	135	—	—
—	168	Mount Margaret	Sons of Gwalia	—	—	—	—	4,687	6,891	4,687	6,891
80,540	18	N. E. Coolgardie	Waldon's Find	—	—	—	—	409	526	409	526
110,993	72	Murchison	Weld-Hercules	—	—	—	—	1,250	1,066	1,250	1,066
200,000	98	Coolgardie	Westralia and East Extension	—	—	—	—	7,641	8,075	7,641	8,075
140,300	48	N. E. Coolgardie	White Feather Main Reef	—	—	—	—	4,035	2,712	4,035	2,712
75,000	66	N. E. Coolgardie	White Feather Reward	489	1,037	2,389	4,795	7,365	4,520	10,243	10,352

WEST AUSTRALIAN MINES.

From the returns issued by the West Australian Chamber of Mines it appears that the gold exports from the colony during the past year amounted to 674,993 oz., compared with 281,265 oz. in the previous year; 231,413 oz. in 1895; 207,131 oz. in 1894; 110,891 oz. in 1893, and only 59,548 oz. in 1892. Since the early days of gold returns in 1886 down to the close of last year Western Australia has exported 1,641,500 oz., representing in value £4,500,000 so that the colony's claim to be one of the great goldfields of the world has some justification. Shareholders, however, who have put enormous sums of money into West Australian mining ventures, and more particularly into the pockets of promoters, have so far received back but an extremely small modicum in dividends, and the important question of the permanency of the reefs has yet to be settled. What is now termed the Kalgoorlie field, upon which are the Great Boulder, Lake view, Ivanhoe, and Hannan's Brownhill, has turned out decidedly rich, but beyond the Great Boulder, and to a smaller extent the Ivanhoe, none even of these Kalgoorlie mines have up to the present returned much in the shape of dividends to their shareholders, while, on the other hand, many undertakings have had to go through the process of reconstruction, mainly owing to the inadequacy of the original working capital because of the greed of the promoters. Amongst the reconstructions during the past eighteen months are many well-known companies, including the Arrow Brownhill, the Big Blow, Blackett's Gold Mines, the Black Flag Proprietary, the Black Flag Consolidated, the Champion Reef (Nannine), the Consolidated Gold Mines of West Australia, the Consolidated Murchison, the Consuello, the Cue Victory, the Empress of Coolgardie, the Gem of Cue, the Gladiators, the Gleeson's Success, the Golconda, the Golden Arrow, the Hannan's North, the Hicks' Gold, the Hit or Miss, the Kalgoorlie Mint and Iron King, the Lady Loch, the McCulloch Coolgardie, the Menzies Gold Estates, the Menzies Pioneers, the Mount Burgess Gold, the Mount Jackson, the Mount Magnet; the New Arrow Proprietary, the Water Trust, Mining, and Public Crushing; the Murchison Goldfields, the Polar Star Proprietary (formerly Murchison Gift), the Abbott's Gold, the Sam's Wealth of Nations, the Waldon's Find, the West Australian Gold Concessions, and the White Feather Main Reef. Surprise will probably be expressed at this number of reconstructions, but, as a matter of fact, the cases mentioned refer only to companies who have, mostly during the past two years, had to undergo this process after having started crushing, and there are many others which had to reconstruct before this period—English companies, of course.

From what can be judged, there are many more to go through the process. Even from the Great Boulder Proprietary Company itself, the yield of gold per ton crushed during the last eight months has steadily diminished from 3 oz. 4 dwt. in May, to 2 oz. 9 dwt. at the end of December, though we are not, of course, suggesting any reconstruction in this case—at least, not at present—only calling attention to the decline in the richness of the ore dealt with. But there are numerous instances where the fall in the yield is a serious matter, such as the Black Flag Proprietary, Burbank's Birthday Gift, Champion Reef, East Murchison, Emerald Reward, Emperor Gold, Hannan's Reward, Mount Magnet, North Boulder, Robinson, and White Feather Reward, and Main Reef Companies. Unless things improve soon, most of these look like coming round with the hat before long, while the West Australian Proprietary Cement Leases Company is abandoning its present property and is to have a fresh one provided by the Venture Corporation, Limited, the promoting syndicate. It would be a good thing if vendors kept new properties in stock to hand over in the event of failure. Fortunately the public on this side has not risked a heavy stake in the game, and the present elevated level of many of the better-known shares is due to operations by the Adelaide market and the finance jugglers over here. This has not been a difficult matter, far easier than getting the British public to relieve them of their holding at the outrageous prices quoted. When the Government of Western Australia has squandered a few millions in providing the mining district with water, and when railways and other modern appliances have further reduced the cost of working, it will be time enough to take a hand in the speculation.

MINING RETURNS.

BRILLIANT BLOCK GOLD MINING.—Crushed during the month 1,343 tons of quartz for 461 oz. gold.

HIGHLAND CHIEF.—Crushed 161 tons, yield 46 oz. retorted gold.

OTTOS KOPJE.—During week ended 20th inst. 6,122 loads crushed, 166 carats produced, including one stone of 11 carats.

WESTRALIA AND EAST EXTENSION.—Twenty stamps running 439 hours crushed 1,306 tons, yielding 856 oz. gold.

LAKE GEORGE MINES.—5,174 tons crude ore treated, yielding 350 tons of matte and bullion, containing 703 oz. gold, 28,860 oz. silver, and 114·64 tons copper.

PEHANG CORPORATION.—December return as follows: Jeram Lumping Mill, 1,140 tons of stone crushed, producing 70 tons of block tin. Jeram Batang Mill, 1,050 tons crushed, producing 12 tons of tin.

BELLVUE PROPRIETARY.—140 tons crushed for yield of 300 oz.

LINDSAY CONSOLIDATED.—Crushed 260 tons, yield 60 oz. gold, exclusive of tailings.

ROSE DEEP.—For December, tons crushed, 14,728; yield from mill, 5,694 oz. gold; 11,577 tons of sand and concentrates treated by cyanide, yield, 2,797 oz.

IVANHOE GOLD CORPORATION.—Clean up for two weeks: 790 tons crushed, yielding 1,426 oz. gold.

ALADDIN'S LAMP.—340 tons crushed, yielding 575 oz.

DAY DAWN P.O.—Crushing for fortnight ended January 22: No. 3 Shaft, 380 tons, 672 oz.

ORO PRETO GOLD MINES OF BRAZIL.—5,116 tons of ore produced 1,511 oz. of gold. Lower tonnage on account of the holidays. Ore delivered at mill this month showing some improvement.

MENZIES CONSOLIDATED.—Crushed 455 tons, each of 2,240 lb. of ore. The total yield is 601 oz. of smelted gold.

ALASKA TREADWELL.—Bullion shipment, $50,782; ore milled, 18,010 tons. Sulphurets treated, 280 tons; bullion from same, $14,176.

CROWN DEEP.—For December: Tons crushed, 21,000; yield in smelted gold from mill, 7,006 oz. Tons of sand and concentrates treated by cyanide, 17,030; yield in gold from same, 7,038 oz.

DAY DAWN BLOCK.—Tons crushed, 1,780; yield 2,362 oz. gold, including tailings.

THE MOUNT LYELL MINING AND RAILWAY COMPANY, LIMITED.—From December 16 to January 12, inclusive, a total quantity of 7,617 tons of ore has been treated, 6,792 tons from open cuts, assaying before treatment—copper 3·95 per cent., silver 3·08 oz., gold ·161 oz. per ton. 825 tons from No. 4 tunnel assaying before treatment—copper 8·42 per cent., silver 7·33 oz. per ton, gold ·037 oz. per ton. The converters have produced during the same period 318 tons blister copper, containing copper 315 tons, silver 24,255 oz., gold 1,374 oz. London office note:—The decreased results in the above returns are explained as being owing to a partial interruption in the operations in consequence of great bush fires, with excessive drought.

CROWN DEEP.—Results for December:—Tons crushed by 160 stamps working 28 days, 21,000, yield in smelted gold from mill, 7,006 oz.; tons of sand and concentrates treated by cyanide works, 17,030, yield in smelted gold, 7,028 oz. Profits for month, £20,882.

VICTORY (Charters Towers).—Crushed 105 tons for 418 oz. Approximate value, £1,421. Profit, £671.

PEAK HILL.—432 tons of ore crushed for a return of 1,863 oz. of smelted gold.

BURBANK'S BIRTHDAY GIFT.—After 344 tons were crushed, the clean-up gave 550 oz. free gold, exclusive of tailings.

WEALTH OF NATIONS.—Crushed 520 tons, yielding 310 oz. of gold.

LEICESTER CONSOLIDATED DIAMOND MINES.—Washed 197 loads from the mine, 3,725 loads, lumps, and hopperings, producing 126 carats.

HYDERABAD (DECCAN) COMPANY.—The output of coal for the last two years from the Lingareni Coalfield is reported as follows:—1896, 262,660 tons; 1897, 365,550 tons; Increase, 102,870 tons. The output during December, 1897, was 34,903 tons, being the largest quantity yet attained in any one month.

THE BROKEN HILL PROPRIETARY, BLOCK 10, COMPANY, LIMITED.—Dividend No. 56, of 2s. per share, payable February 16. The result of working to date has been under estimated returns. We consider it prudent to reduce dividend for the present.

NEW ROAD TO KLONDIKE.

A Toronto correspondent of the *Times* states that the Dominion Government has signed a contract with a large firm of railway contractors for the construction of a railway 150 miles long from Glenora, on the Stickeen River, to Teslin Lake, from which there is continuous navigation for river steamboats, to Klondike and all points in the Yukon district. The contractors have undertaken to complete the line by next September. This will secure a practically all-Canadian route direct to the goldfields, and it has been obtained without any cost in money to the country, the company receiving a large grant of mineral lands by way of assistance to the enterprise.

Prices of Mine and Mining Finance Companies' Shares.

Shares £1 each, except where otherwise stated.

AUSTRALIAN.

Making-Up Price, Jan. 24	Name.	Closing Price.	Rise or Fall.	Making-Up Price, Jan. 24	Name	Closing Price.	Rise or Fall.
1 3/4	Aladdin	1 3/4		1 1/2	Hampton Plains	1 1/16	− 1/16
4 1/16	Associated	3 7/8	− 1/16	7 3/8	Hannan' Brownhill	7 5/16	− 1/16
1/16	Do. Southern	1/16		1 1/16	Hannan's Oroya	1	− 1/16
16/	Brilliant, £2	16/	− 6d.	15/9	Do. Proprietary	15/6	− 6d.
2 1/2	Do. St. George's	2 1/2		1	Do. Star	13/16	
11/	British Broken Hill	11/3		—	Ivanhoe, New	6 1/4	
6	Do. Westralia	6 1/4		15/16	Kalgurli Mt. & Iron King, 18/	7/8	− 1/8
2 1/16	Broken Hill Proprietary	2	1/16	6 1/2	Kalgurli	5 13/16	− 5/8
—	Do. Junction	2		2 1/16	Lady Shenton	2 1/4	+ 1/16
—	Do. Block 10	3 3/8	− 1/8	10 1/16	Lake View Cons.	10 1/4	+ 1/8
1 3/4	Brownhill Extended	1 5/8	− 1/16	1 1/2	Do. Extended	1 1/16	− 1/8
1 11/16	Burbank's Birthday	1 11/16	+ 1/16	1 1/16	Do. South	1 1/16	
1 1/4	Central Boulder	1 1/16		2 1/16	London & Globe Finance	2 1/16	− 1/8
7/9	Chaffers, 4/	7/−	9d.	1 1/4	London & W.A. Exploration	1 1/4	− 1/8
1/16	Colonial Finance, 15/	1/2 pm		5/8	Do. Investment	5/8	
1/16	Crœsus S. United	3/8		15/16	Mainland Consols	15/16	− 1/16
16/	Day Dawn Block	16/3	− 3d.	[illegible]	North Boulder, 10/	[illegible]	− 1/16
1 1/16	E. Murchison	1 1/16	− 1/16	1 1/2	North Kalgurli	1 3/8	+ 1/16
13/16	Gold Estates	13/16		1 1/16	Northern Territories	1 1/4	− 1/16
6/6	Golden Arrow	6/	− 6d.	—	Peak Hill	2 13/16	+ 1/8
8 3/8	Golden Horseshoe	8 1/16		2 13/16	South Kalgurli	2 3/4	− 1/16
1 1/2	Golden Link	1 1/16	− 1/16	2 1/4	W. A. Goldfields	2 1/16	− 1/16
—	Great Boulder, 2/	23/	− 1 1/2	2 1/4	W. A. Joint Stock	2 1/16	− 1/16
1 1/4	Do. Main Reef, 10/	1 1/4	− 3/32	1 1/4	W. A. Market Trust	1 1/4	
4 1/2	Do. Perseverance	4 1/16	− 1/4	1 3/4	W. A. Loan & General Fin.	1 11/16	− 1/16
1	Do. South	1		3/8	White Feather	1/16	
1 13/16	Hainault	1 3/8	− 1/8				

SOUTH AFRICAN

Making-Up Price, Jan. 24	Name	Closing Price	Rise or Fall	Making-Up Price, Jan. 24	Name	Closing Price	Rise or Fall
5 1/4	Angelo	5 3/8	+ 1/16	3/	Lisbon-Berlyn	3/	− 3d
1 1/16	Aurora West	1 1/16	− 1/16	2 1/16	May Consolidated	2 1/4	
1 1/16	Bantjes	1 1/16		4 1/4	Meyer and Charlton	4 5/16	
11/	Barrett, 10/	11/	− 3d.	3 1/4	Modderfontein	3 1/4	
3 1/4	Bonanza	3 1/4	− 1/16	3/8	Do. "B"	3/4	
13/16	Buffelsdoorn	7/8	− 1/16	1	New Bultfontein	1	+ 1/16
1 1/16	Champ d'Or	1 3/8		4 1/4	New Primrose	4 1/4	− 1/8
5 3/4	City and Suburban, £4	5 1/2	− 1/8	1 11/16	Nigel	1 3/4	
3 1/4	Comet (New)	3 1/4		—	Nigel Deep	1 1/4	+ 1/16
5 3/4	Con. Deep Level	5 3/4		1	North Randfontein	1	− 1/16
14	Crown Deep	14	− 1/4	6 3/4	Nourse Deep	6 3/4	− 1/8
12	Crown Reef	12	− 1/4	1 1/4	Porges-Randfontein	1 1/16	− 1/8
29 3/4	De Beers, £5	29 13/16	+ 1/4	2 1/4	Princess	2 1/4	
3 15/16	Driefontein	4	+ 1/16	33 1/2	Rand Mines	33 3/8	− 1/8
5 7/8	Durban Roodepoort	5 7/8		1 13/16	Randfontein	2	
4 1/16	Do. Deep	4 1/4	− 1/4	2 1/2	Rietfontein	2 1/4	− 1/16
5 1/2	East Rand	5 1/4	+ 1/4	11 1/4	Robinson Deep	11 1/4	− 1/8
24	Ferreira	24 1/2	+ 1/2	8 1/2	Do. Gold, £5	8 1/2	
6 3/4	Geldenhuis Deep	7	+ 1/4	1 1/16	Do. Randfontein	1 5/8	− 1/16
4 1/16	Do. Estate	4 1/16	+ 1/16	1 1/4	Roodepoort Central Deep	1 1/4	
1 1/2	George Goch	1 1/2	+ 1/16	2 13/16	Do. Deep	1 3/4	
3	Ginsberg	3	+ 1/8	7	Rose Deep	7 1/4	+ 1/16
2 1/4	Glencairn	2 1/16		3 1/4	Salisbury	3 1/4	− 1/16
2 13/16	Glen Deep	3	+ 1/8	2 11/16	Sheba	2 1/2	
9 3/4	Goldfields Deep	10 1/4	− 1/8	3 1/4	Simmer and Jack, £5	3 1/4	+ 1/16
8 11/16	Griqualand West	8 3/4		4 1/16	Transvaal Gold	4 1/16	− 1/16
9 1/2	Henry Nourse	9 1/2		3 3/8	Treasury	3 3/8	− 1/8
7 1/4	Heriot	7 3/8	− 1/4	4 1/16	United Roodepoort	4 1/4	
8 1/2	Jagersfontein	8 1/4	− 1/16	1 1/16	Van Ryn	1 1/16	
9	Jubilee	8 1/2	− 1/2	6 1/16	Village Main Reef	6 1/4	− 1/16
5 1/4	Jumpers	5 7/8		1 3/4	Vogelstruis	1 5/8	+ 1/16
5 1/4	Jumpers Deep	5 1/8	− 1/8	1 1/4	Do. Deep	1 1/16	− 1/8
2 11/16	Kleinfontein	2 1/4	+ 1/16	8 3/8	Wemmer	9	− 1/8
3 15/16	Knight's	4 1/16	− 1/16	1 1/4	West Rand	1/16	
2 1/2	Lancaster	2 3/8	− 1/16	6 3/8	Wolhuter, £4	6 3/8	− 1/16
3 3/8	Langlaagte Estate	3 1/4		2 3/8	Worcester	2 3/8	− 1/8
1 1/2	Langlaagte Block "B"	1 1/4					

LAND EXPLORATION AND RHODESIAN.

Making-Up Price, Jan. 24	Name	Closing Price	Rise or Fall	Making-Up Price, Jan. 24	Name	Closing Price	Rise or Fall
3	Anglo-French Ex.	3 1/16		1 13/16	Mozambique	1 3/4	− 1/16
2 1/4	Barnato Consolidated	2 1/16	− 1/16	1 1/2	New African	1 1/2	
7/8	Bechuanaland Ex.	7/8	− 1/16	13/16	Oceana Consolidated	13/16	− 1/16
3	Chartered B.S.A.	3 1/4		2 1/4	Orange Free State	2 1/4	+ 1/8
1 1/16	Cassel Coal	1 1/16		1 1/16	Rhodesia, Ltd.	1 1/16	− 1/16
3/4	Colenbrander	3/4	− 1/16	5 1/4	Do. Exploration	5 1/4	
4 3/8	Cons. Goldfields	4 1/16	− 1/8	1 1/16	Do. Goldfields	1 1/4	− 1/16
1 1/16	Do. Pref.	21/	− 3d	4	Robinson Bank	4	
1 13/16	Exploration	1 3/4	− 1/16	5	S. A. Gold Trust	5 1/16	− 1/4
1 1/8	Henderson's Est.	1		1 1/4	Tati Concessions	1 1/4	− 1/8
2	Johannesburg Con. In.	2		1/16	Transvaal Development	1/16	− 1/16
1 1/4	Do. Water	1 1/16		4 1/16	Do. Gold Mining	4 1/16	− 1/16
2 3/8	Mashonaland Agency	2 1/16	− 1/16	11/16	United Rhodesia	3/4	
13/16	Do. Central	7/8		1 1/16	Willoughby	1 1/16	− 1/16
6 3/8	Matabele Gold Reefs	6 1/4	− 1/8	1 1/2	Zambesia Explor.	1 1/4	− 1/8

MISCELLANEOUS.

Making-Up Price, Jan. 24	Name	Closing Price	Rise or Fall	Making-Up Price, Jan. 24	Name	Closing Price	Rise or Fall
1 1/2	Alamillos, £2	1 3/8	+ 1/16	13/3	Mysore Goldfields	15/	+ 1/6
5 3/8	Anaconda, $25	5 3/8	− 1/16	12/	Do. Reefs, 17/	12/	+ /6
11/3	Balaghât, 18/	11/	− /6	17/	Do. West	18/	+ 1/6
4 11/16	Cape Copper, £2	4 11/16	− 1/8	16/	Do. Wynaad	16/	+ /6
5	Champion Reef, 10s.	5	− 1/16	2 1/16	Namaqua, £2	2 1/16	− 1/16
2 1/16	Copiapo, £2	2 1/16	− 1/16	4 1/16	Nundydroog	3 3/4	− 1/4
3 1/4	Coromandel	3 1/4	− 1/16	2 13/16	Ooregum	3	− 1/16
1 3/8	Frontino & Bolivia	2 1/4	− 1/16	3 7/8	Do. Pref.	3 7/8	− 1/16
1 1/4	Hall Mines	1 1/16		27 1/4	Rio Tinto Def., £5	27 1/2	+ 1/4
2 11/16	Libiola, £5	2 3/8	− 1/8	6 3/8	Do. Pref. £5	6 1/4	
7 7/8	Linares, £3	8		19/	St. John del Rey	19 6	
3 3/8	Mason & Barry, £3	3 3/8	+ 1/16	15/16	Taitipu	7/8	− 1/8
5 1/2	Mountain Copper, £5	5 1/16	− 1/8	7 3/8	Tharsis, £2	7 1/4	+ 1/8
13 3/4	Mount Lyell, £3	14	+ 1/4	2 1/2	Tolima "A," £5	3	
3 11/16	Mount Lyell, North	3 1/16	− 1/16	4 1/16	Waihi	4 1/16	− 1/16
7/8	Mount Lyell, South	7/8	− 1/8	1 3/8	Waitekauri	1 1/2	− 1/16
4 7/8	Mount Morgan, 17s. 6d.	4 7/8		1 1/4	Woodstock (N.Z.)	1 1/16	− 1/16
5 1/2	Mysore, 10s.	5 1/4	− 1/8				

THE POSITION OF THE IMPERIAL CONTINENTAL GAS COMPANY.

After running all over Europe Dr. Lueger, the Burgomaster of Vienna, has at last induced the Deutsche Bank to arrange a loan of thirty million florins, which will bear 4 per cent. interest, and be issued at 98 per cent. The anti-Semitic Burgomaster denies that he has entered into any engagement in regard to the tramways, in which the Deutsche Bank and its colleagues in the Syndicate are deeply interested, but no credence is given to this denial, as it was precisely on this point that the negotiations with the same group fell through some months ago. It is, however, a very moot point whether this large sum will be handed over to Dr. Lueger simply for the purpose of fighting the Imperial Continental Gas Association. The worthy Burgomaster is a little bit *tête montée* about capitalists, and Jewish capitalists in particular, and because the late Sir Julian Goldsmid was the prime mover in the Imperial Continental Gas Association, he has steadily opposed the renewal of the concession for lighting Vienna by gas at present held by the Association, and which expires in 1899. But this concession only applies to old Vienna and its million of inhabitants, and the Association has contracts with no less than twenty-seven of its suburbs, which run up to dates between 1903 and 1917. As many of these suburbs have since been incorporated in the Vienna Municipality, the Doctor endeavoured in the Law Courts to prove that the contracts were thereby broken, and that these agreements fall in in 1899.

His first appeal to the Courts has led to a thorough defeat. But, of course, he has power to make two appeals yet, although his prospects of reversing the decision are not very promising. It is, therefore, quite possible that the Deutsche Bank has only agreed to a loan upon Dr. Lueger undertaking to come to terms with the Association. Like every demagogue, the worthy Doctor is a poor Minister of Finance, and he must by this time be at his wit's end to know how to carry on the financial part of his operations. The gas works so far erected by him will only serve as a necessary adjunct to the existing plant of the English company; and now that he has lost the suburbs, representing one-third of the population, the prospects of an entirely new undertaking are not very bright. A compromise on these lines is, therefore, by no means out of the question. Meantime the Association is in a very strong position to meet any loss of business at Vienna, although its business in that city is important. Thus, in spite of carrying on gas undertakings at no less than twenty-eight places on the Continent, the profits of the Vienna business represent one-third of the total. The Association, however, has taken time by the forelock and reduced its dividend from 12 to 10 per cent., utilising the money thus saved in adding to its reserves. Taking the accounts for the year ended September 30 last, we find the profits came to £497,403, and the 10 per cent. dividend took £380,000. There was added to a contingency fund no less than £154,000 in that time, and £87,800 was written off for depreciation, while the reserve fund increased by £10,441. Now, the reserve increases automatically, as its total of £392,441 is invested in Consols, and the interest received from these is added each half-year. The depreciation fund now amounts to £999,099, and is held in English, Indian, Colonial, and foreign securities, the interest upon which must represent at least £40,000 per annum. The contingency fund stands now at £761,342, and is not specially invested, but is practically held in a liquid form, as the Association has large amounts in cash, bills, and a trifle of £250,000 in London and North-Western Railway stock at its command. The effect of a loss of the Vienna business may therefore be said to have been discounted, and anything short of that result must be looked upon as gain.

An agreement has been concluded with Natal and Cape Colony for a reduced railway tariff to the Transvaal for over-sea goods equivalent to a reduction of 20s. per ton. The arrangement comes into force on March 1.

Rodriques must be a queer little island to live on. It boasts of 2,635 inhabitants, including, besides natives, settlers from Mauritius, Madagascar, India, China, Europe, Leychelles, and Réunion traders, agriculturists. The character of these "samples" seem doubtful, for last year there were forty-six criminal convictions, or one for every fifty-seven nhabitants. The revenue for 1896 was Rs.8,310—a decrease of Rs.2,062—while the expenditure rose to no less than Rs.24,479, an increase of Rs.1,378. If this goes on, Rodriques must quickly accumulate a national debt of very respectable dimensions.

WAR OFFICE ECONOMIES.

Who says the War Office is not economically conducted—that its officials are not thriftily parsimonious of the nation's money? Mr. St. John Brodrick denies the impeachment, and, being Under-Secretary for War, he ought to know the facts. Here is one of the facts, as related by himself:—Eleven years ago, as we all know, was an anxious time in the Soudan. General Gordon had been murdered, Khartoum had fallen, and there was no saying what the redoubtable Mahdi might not do, or attempt to do. Soon after the disaster at Khartoum, General Sir Redvers Buller entered Lord Wolseley's apartments at Korti, very sleepy, and told him he could not write his War Office report as he had not been in bed for three days. His Lordship suggested that a bottle of champagne might assist him. Sir Redvers tried it, and the report was written. Sir Wilfrid Lawson may be sceptical about the effects of the champagne, but even he must admire the economic vigilance of the storekeeper or steward, who, while sending the bottle to the wearied General, carefully noted its price and the cost of "transport" to Sir Redvers' lodgings, and kept his mind and glittering eye on the account until it was safely landed at the London War Office. Here it lay for eight months, awaiting the return of Sir Redvers Buller to his staff duties. Then it was presented and, no doubt, paid. This official was—is still, let us hope—a jewel. How many seven and sixpences may he not have saved to the nation, even in the very midst of "war's alarms"? Of course, there are cynics who grimly smile at this, and who suggest there are officials who, while strictly watchful of champagne bottles, will let thousands of pounds slip through their fingers unnoted. But then cynical people will say anything.

NOTICES.

To holders of our Certificates of Deposit for Union Pacific First Mortgage Six per Cent. bonds, Union Pacific Extended Sinking Fund Eight per Cent. bonds, and to holders of Union Pacific Six per Cent. Purchase Money Certificates.——The Union Pacific Reorganisation Committee having acquired the main line of the Union Pacific Railroad at foreclosure sales, announces that it is preparing to deliver at an early date to the holders of its above-named certificates, in exchange for such certificates, the new securities applicable thereto respectively. Such holders of our Certificates of Deposit, and of the Committee's Six per Cent. Purchase Money Certificates who desire to have the new securities delivered to them in London, are requested to deposit their certificates with the Bank of Montreal on or before February 1, 1898, and receive in exchange therefor a temporary receipt entitling the holder to such new securities, which will be delivered, when received by us, free of charge against the surrender of such temporary receipts.—For the Bank of Montreal (Signed), A Lang, manager, 22, Abchurch-lane, E.C., January 24, 1898.

The English Association of American Bond and Shareholders, Limited, notifies that it is prepared to receive for payment the following coupons of its certificates:—Coupon No. 24 for half-yearly dividend of 3 per cent. on Bald Eagle Valley R.R. shares; Coupon No. 23 for half-yearly dividend of 3 per cent. on Lake Shore and Michigan Southern R.R. shares; Coupon No. 19 for quarterly dividend of 1¼ per cent. on Central Railroad of New Jersey shares; and Coupon No. 21 for quarterly dividend of 1½ per cent. on St. Paul, Minneapolis, and Manitoba R.R. shares.

VARIOUS TRAFFIC RETURNS, &c.

UNITED STATES AND CANADIAN RAILWAYS.

Baltimore and Ohio South-Western.—Second week of January, $127,012; increase, $9,951. Aggregate from July 1, $3,716,191; increase, $378,556.

Mobile and Birmingham.—Fourth week of December, $17,357; increase, $7,180. Aggregate from July 1, 177,853; decrease, $30,409. Net earnings for November were $14,301, an increase of $2,845; total for five months, $11,152, a decrease of $43,901. Ratio working expenses, 64·24 per cent. compared with 66·66 per cent.

Quebec Central.—Fourth week of December, $10,459; increase, $507. Aggregate from January 1, $457,543; increase, $60,437.

INDIAN AND FOREIGN RAILWAYS.

Nizam's State Railways.—Receipts for six months ending December 31 show an increase of Rs. 2,53,502.

Mexican National Railway.—1,217 miles open. Approximate earnings for third week in January, $M. 106,271; increase, $6,249.

Chicago Great Western Railway.—Third week of January, $86,520; increase, $13,321. Aggregate from July 1, $3,065,493; increase, $491,486.

A Russo-Belgian company is in course of formation for the development of commercial relations between European Russia and Siberia. The chief object will be the export of Siberian raw products and the import of manufactured goods from Moscow and elsewhere.

The Greek Army.—The first part of the Crown Prince's report on the Greek campaign in Thessaly has been presented to the Minister of War at Athens. It is a remarkable document; but it is unnecessary to quote from it, as it is but a long and detailed conformation of what has been said before—this namely, that the Greek Government entered upon the war without plan of operations or preparations; that there were no reserves to fall back upon in case of defeat, and no attempt made by the fleet to create a diversion. Such an army was doomed to disaster from the first. The wonder is not that it did so little, but that it did anything at all.

The wheat harvest in Uruguay is estimated to yield about 280,000 metric tons, of which about 170,000 tons will probably be available for export.

THE MENZIES GOLDEN RHINE GOLD MINES, LIMITED.

On Wednesday, January 20, before Mr. Justice Wright, there came on for hearing the petition which was recently presented by one of the shareholders for the winding-up of the Menzies Golden Rhine Gold Mines (W.A.), Limited. From the statements of counsel, it appears that the Company was incorporated on February 18, 1896, with a nominal capital of £130,000 in shares of £1 each, the object for which the Company was formed being, according to the prospectus, the acquisition of certain alleged gold mines, called the Menzies Golden Rhine Gold Mines, which said "mines" have since turned out to be worthless. The nominal vendor to the Company was Mr. Charles Christopher Braithwaite, but it was alleged by the petitioner, and practically admitted by the respondent, that the Company was, in fact, promoted by Mr. John Waddington, and that he was the real vendor of the said properties to the Company; the name of the said C. C. Braithwaite (who is a brother-in-law of Mr. Waddington) being used for the purpose of concealing the fact that he, the said John Waddington, was the vendor.

For this wonderful property the consideration paid to the said John Waddington was the sum of £105,000, partly in cash and partly in shares. No definite particulars were forthcoming as to the actual price given by the said John Waddington for the properties, but it appeared that the sum realised by the original vendors (Messrs. Jersoe & Gregory), who transferred direct to the Company, was £4,000 only. In these circumstances, the petitioner desired that a winding-up order should be made with a view of subsequent proceedings being taken against the said John Waddington to set aside the sale to the Company, and to obtain the return of the consideration paid to him. His Lordship was of opinion that the petitioner had made out a *prima facie* case for the winding-up, but, in view of a suggestion which had been made by Mr. Waddington that he should have an opportunity of offering to the shareholders, free of expense, another property in substitution for that originally transferred by him to the Company, his Lordship directed the petition to stand over until March 9 next, so as to afford Mr. Waddington an opportunity of laying a scheme before the shareholders. He, however, intimated that, unless before that date the shareholders were satisfied with Mr. Waddington's proposal, a winding-up order would be made.

In our opinion the Judge acted with great forbearance.

ENGLISH RAILWAYS.

Div. for half years. 1896	1896	1897	1897	Last Balance forward.	Amt. to pay 1 p.c. on Ord. for ½ yr.	NAME.	Date.	Gross Traffic for week: Amt.	Inc. or dec. on 1897.	Inc. or dec. on 1896.	No. of weeks	Gross Traffic for half-year to date: Amt.	Inc. or dec. on 1897.	Inc. or dec. on 1896.	Mileage.	Inc. on 1897.	Working	Prior Charges last ½ year.	Prop. add Cap. Exp. this ½ year.
				£	£												%	£	£
10	10	10	10	6,805	4,996	Barry	Jan.22	9,101	+243	−2	4	35,444	+605	+1,061	31	—	47·36	66,665	316,008
nil	nil	nil	nil	—	—	Brecon and Merthyr	Jan.23	1,749	+19	+51	4	6,494	+135	+361	61	—	—	—	—
nil	nil	nil	nil	4,020	4,749	Cambrian	Jan.23	4,154	+111	+457	*	13,007	+38	—	250	—	61·16	63,472	42,000
1¾	1¾	2	1¾	1,510	3,150	City and South London ..	Jan.23	1,075	−39	+81	4	4,334	−53	+299	3½	—	56·67	5,552	124,000
1	2	1½		4,803	13,210	Furness	Jan.23	8,896	+376	+1,036	*	26,629	+410	—	139	—	50·85	96,623	52,963
1	1½	2		2,207	27,470	Great Central (late M., S., & L.)	Jan.23	12,785	+104	+2,493	3	125,165	+1,384	+8,544	358½	—	57·17	697,386	1,200,000
1½	4½	2	5	51,283	62,865	Great Eastern	Jan.23	78,393	+3,675	+7,581	3	225,357	+6,202	+25,334	1,156	7	55·35	860,138	250,000
3	5½	3		4,595	102,406	Great Northern	Jan.23	94,098	+2,381	+8,070	4	360,383	+8,525	+24,318	1,071	8	62·28	640,779	1,092,250
4½	7½	4½		16,273	116,381	Great Western	Jan.23	173080	+6,250	+8,270	3	509,990	+18,170	+33,860	2,575	14	57·94	1,484,324	650,000
nil	2	nil		24,449	16,425	Hull and Barnsley	Jan.23	6,116	−99	+687	3	19,738	+143	+2,547	73	—	61·21	54,684	44,019
5	5¾	5		21,423	83,704	Lancashire and Yorkshire ..	Jan.23	89,722	+3,386	+4,876	3	260,809	+7,705	+23,108	555½	25½	55·01	662,671	387,520
4¼	8	4½	3½	26,213	42,049	London, Brighton, & S. Coast	Jan.22	43,901	+3,272	+2,998	4	188,267	+10,097	+11,649	476½	—	50·20	407,042	240,735
nil	nil	nil	nil	7,561	56,296	London, Chatham, & Dover ..	Jan.23	26,942	+1,867	+2,706	3	79,141	+3,836	+6,135	185	—	57·29	220,181	nil
6½	8	6½		95,016	203,061	London and North Western ..	Jan.23	192736	+5,677	+13,897	3	654,118	+13,378	+40,444	1,912	—	55·91	1,411,098	405,000
5	8¾	8¾		23,525	58,667	London and South Western ..	Jan.23	65,438	+4,694	+5,781	3	190,605	+9,124	+14,144	941	6½	55·93	587,757	370,000
2¾	6	2½	6¼	7,572	6,691	London, Tilbury, & Southend	Jan.23	4,672	+449	+846	4	19,037	+1,428	+3,926	81	—	57·00	40,041	15,000
3½	3¾	3¾	3¾	17,133	26,409	Metropolitan	Jan.23	16,409	+336	+1,312	*	53,805	+1,374	—	64	12	43·63	148,047	254,000
nil	nil	nil	nil	4,370	11,250	Metropolitan District	Jan.23	9,091	+339	+309	3	27,323	+1,196	+1,432	13	—	45·32	159,412	23,150
5	7	5¼		18,336	174,175	Midland	Jan.23	187447	−2,906	+13,428	4	638,007	+637	+33,606	1,354¾	15¼	57·47	1,213,866	650,000
5½	7¼	5¾		22,374	135,568	North Eastern	Jan.22	143911	+4,940	+8,147	3	420,035	+10,991	+35,994	1,597¾	—	58·70	791,056	372,790
7½	7¾	7½		6,213	10,102	North London	Jan.23			Not recd			+ not	recvd.	12	—	51·65	51,329	4,000
4	5			3,356	16,150	North Staffordshire	Jan.23	15,861	+990	+798	4	62,154	4,862	+4,116	312	—	55·27	118,142	19,605
10	10	11		1,642	3,004	Rhymney	Jan.22	5,264	+473	+611	4	19,019	−252	+800	71	—	49·68	29,049	16,700
3	6⅝	3½	6⅝	4,034	50,215	South Eastern	Jan.22	38,733	+2,727	+3,755	*	124,921	+4,857	—	448	—	51·88	380,763	250,000
3½	3½	3½		5,904	25,691	Taff Vale	Jan.22	15,969	−714	−70	4	59,596	−3,442	−1,897	121	—	53·06	95,297	43,000

* From January 1.

SCOTCH RAILWAYS.

5	5	5¼	—	15,350	77,570	Caledonian	Jan.23	68,808	+ 4,197	+ 2,837	25	1,851,011	+ 31,307	+ 75,979	851½	5	50·50	366,914	373,966
5	5½	5	—	5,886	24,639	Glasgow and South-Western	,, 22	23,374	+ 386	+ 102	25	727,236	+ 10,255	+ 54,610	393½	8	55·12	221,190	180,556
3½	3½	3½	—	1,291	4,600	Great North of Scotland	,, 22	7,731	+ 354	+ 1,492	25	222,735	+ 8,173	+ 16,609	331	15½	52·03	92,178	60,000
3	nil	2	—	10,477	12,820	Highland	,, 23	7,807	+ 711	+ 608	21	195,921	+ 7,273	+ 10,809	479¾	27¾	58·63	78,976	84,000
1	1¼	1	—	3,763	45,819	North British	,, 23	64,333	+ 1,900	+ 1,896	25	1,862,958	+ 49,495	+ 94,102	1,230	23	44·65	821,766	426,009

IRISH RAILWAYS.

6½	6½	6½	—	2,405	1,745	Belfast and County Down ..	Jan. 21	2,088	+ 214	+ 370	*	6,015	− 153	—	76½	—	56·49	17,665	38,000
5½	6½	5½	—	—	4,284	Belfast and Northern Counties	,, 21	5,397	+ 238	+ 298	*	14,247	− 47	—	249	—	—	—	—
2	3	2	—	1,418	1,200	Cork, Bandon, and S. Coast ..	,, 22	1,935	+ 13	+ 45	*	3,988	+ 24	—	103	—	54·89	14,436	5,450
6½	6¾	6½	—	21,537	17,709	Great Northern	,, 21	13,645	+ 600	+ 1,271	3	39,692	+ 1,227	+ 2,213	528	36	54·03	87,068	16,000
5½	5½	5½	—	12,037	24,855	Great Southern and Western ..	,, 21	—	—	—	not	received	—	—	603	13	55·78	72,802	35,140
4	4	4	—	4,085	11,850	Midland Great Western ..	,, 21	8,658	+ 654	+ 71	*	95,462	+ 1,893	—	538	—	53·12	80,845	9,600
nil	nil	nil	nil	229	2,822	Waterford and Central ..	,, 21	809	+ 108	+ 272	*	2,562	+ 323	—	59½	—	53·24	6,858	1,500
nil	nil	nil	nil	2,601	2,987	Waterford, Limerick & W. ..	,, 21	3,506	+ 200	+ 491	*	20,300	+ 1,439	—	350½	—	58·70	43,076	8,869

* From January 1.

FOREIGN RAILWAYS.

Mileage.			Name.	Gross Traffic for Week.				Gross Traffic to Date.			
Total.	Increase on 1897.	Increase on 1896.		Week ending	Amount.	In. or Dec. upon 1897.	In. or Dec. upon 1896.	No. of Weeks.	Amount.	In. or Dec. upon 1897.	In. or Dec. upon 1896.
					£	£	£		£	£	£
319	—	—	**Argentine Great Western** ..	Jan. 14	6,751	+ 2,048	+ 2,692	28	145,582	− 13,965	+ 31,789
76½	—	—	**Bahia and San Francisco** ..	Dec. 25	2,427	+ 356	+ 944	25	61,203	+ 17,515	+ 18,294
234	57	84	Bahia Blanca and North West ..	Dec. 26	875	− 80	——	26	19,245	+ 712	——
127	—	—	Buenos Ayres and Ensenada ..	Jan. 23	3,497	− 976	− 727	3	11,561	− 3,908	− 2,200
420	—	—	Buenos Ayres and Pacific ..	Jan. 22	6,803	− 1,524	+ 74	30	176,880	− 46,955	+ 5,319
914	1	3	Buenos Ayres and Rosario ..	Jan. 22	17,516	+ 3,224	+ 4,143	3	51,742	+ 3,783	+ 7,244
2,469	66	68	Buenos Ayres Great Southern ..	Jan. 23	36,714	+ 1,099	+ 7,053	29	791,557	+ 54,107	+ 114,985
602	142	177	Buenos Ayres Western	Jan. 23	13,250	− 2,949	− 1,192	29	333,998	− 74,949	− 65,152
845	55	77	Central Argentine..	Jan. 22	22,245	+ 5,155	+ 2,108	3	64,861	+ 7,873	+ 4,192
207	—	—	Central Bahia	Oct. 31*	$83,051	− $6,258	− $16,002	10 mos.	$1,121,178	+ $175,344	+ $203,586
271	—	—	Central Uruguay of Monte Video	Jan. 22	9,026	+ 2,682	+ 2,733	29	150,447	− 7,741	− 29,028
180	—	—	Cordoba and Rosario	Jan. 16	2,790	+ 190	− 10	29	56,539	− 22,095	− 48
128	—	—	Cordoba Central	Jan. 16	$24,000	− $3,470	− $3,400	2	$51,700	− $12,840	− $15,360
349	—	—	Do. Northern Extension	Jan. 16	$49,500	− $9,000	− $4,400	2	$110,790	− $30,030	− $23,380
137	—	—	Costa Rica..	Jan. 15	3,881	+ 414	+ 2,252	2	5,178	− 3,633	+ 1,545
99	—	—	East Argentine	Dec. 5	831	− 2	− 112	49	33,355	− 3,762	− 1,024
386	—	6	Entre Rios..	Jan. 15	2,478	+ 897	+ 1,285	—	——	——	——
555	—	24	Inter Oceanic of Mexico.. ..	Jan. 22	$69,800	+ $24,400	+ $25,900	30	$1,572,440	+ $216,120	+ $390,840
23	—	—	La Guaira and Caracas	Dec. 23	2,082	− 1,076	− 268	51	106,924	− 11,770	+ 2,045
321	—	—	Mexican	Jan. 22	$81,200	+ $8,700	——	3	$241,300	+ $9,450	——
1,846	—	—	**Mexican Central**	Jan. 22	$253,586	+ $14,806	+ $62,382	3	$714,137	+ $26,735	+ $167,096
1,217	—	—	Mexican National	Jan. 22	$106,271	+ $6,049	+ $18,680	3	$322,390	+ $15,786	+ $65,088
228	—	—	Mexican Southern	Jan. 21	$13,780	+ $3,999	+ $6,332	43	$537,035	+ $93,082	+ $146,252
205	—	—	**Minas and Rio**	Nov. 30*	$179,485	+ $24,384	+ $66,883	5 mos.	$996,637	+ $201,287	+ $204,840
211	—	17	N. W. Argentine	Jan. 15	960	− 870	− 134	2	1,921	− 2,448	− 880
242	3	—	Nitrate	Jan. 15†	17,354	− 1,604	− 12,326	—	——	——	——
320	—	—	Ottoman	Jan. 15	5,528	− 1,652	+ 1,728	3	16,413	− 2,809	+ 4,301
77½	—	—	Recife and San Francisco ..	Nov. 27	5,872	+ 122	+ 605	22	63,466	− 10,149	− 4,405
86½	—	—	**San Paulo**	Dec. 26†	23,002	− 3,560	——	2	46,230	− 10,120	——
186	—	—	Santa Fe and Cordova	Jan. 22	2,070	− 699	+ 170	30	26,145	− 23,119	− 4,730

* For month ended. † For fortnight ended.

INDIAN RAILWAYS.

Mileage.			Name.	Gross Traffic for Week.				Gross Traffic to Date.			
Total.	Increase on 1897.	Increase on 1896.		Week ending	Amount.	In. or Dec. on 1897.	In. or Dec. on 1896.	No. of Weeks.	Amount.	In. or Dec. on 1897.	In. or Dec. on 1896.
867	4	5	Bengal Nagpur	Jan. 15	Rs.1.98.000	− Rs.40.353	− Rs.37.094	2	Rs.2.45.000	− Rs.1.96.648	− Rs.165.997
818	63	63	Bengal and North-Western ..	Dec. 18	Rs.1.15.230	+ Rs.14.624	+ Rs.26.383	25	Rs.24.65.908	+ Rs.1.08.418	+ Rs.20.16.294
461	—	—	Bombay and Baroda	Jan. 22	£23,100	− £1,430	− £9,475	3	£70,767	− £2,395	− £38,668
1,884	2	13	East Indian	Jan. 22	Rs.14.12.000	+ R.2.88.000	+ Rs.13.13.000	3	Rs.38.82.000	+ Rs.7.66.000	+ Rs.22.70.000
2,492	—	—	Great Indian Penin.	Jan. 22	£56,888	− £5,209	− £20,330	3	£179,438	− £14,960	− £91,283
736	—	—	Indian Midland	Jan. 22	Rs.1.39.720	+ Rs.10.584	+ Rs.26.460	3	Rs.4.38.000	+ Rs.17.260	+ Rs.14.264
840	—	—	Madras	Jan. 22	£17,692	− £275	+ £183	3	£58,470	− £493	− £4,059
1,043	—	—	South Indian	Dec. 18	Rs.1.53.191	+ Rs.3.769	− Rs.14.027	25	Rs.41.29.698	+ Rs.86.389	− Rs.49.124

UNITED STATES AND CANADIAN RAILWAYS.

Mileage.			Name.	Gross Traffic for Week.			Gross Traffic to Date.		
Total.	Increase on 1897.	Increase on 1896.		Period Ending.	Amount.	In. or Dec. on 1897.	No. of Weeks.	Amount.	In. or Dec. on 1897.
					dols.	dols.		dols.	dols.
310	—	—	**Alabama Gt. South.**	Jan. 7	37,215	+ 10,734	—	—	—
6,547	103	156	Canadian Pacific	Jan. 21	396,000	+ 81,000	3	1,201,000	+ 241,000
6,169	—	469	**Chicago, Mil., & St. Paul** ..	Jan. 21	554,000	+ 66,000	29	20,409,000	+ 1,942,950
1,685	—	—	**Denver & Rio Grande**	Jan. 21	137,000	+ 30,000	29	4,765,100	+ 762,700
3,512	—	—	**Grand Trunk, Main Line** ..	Jan. 21	£74,030	+ £7,266	3	£218,904	+ £33,196
335	—	—	Do. Chic. & Grand Trunk	Jan. 21	£14,048	+ £2,679	3	£42,269	+ £7,039
189	—	—	Do. Det., G. H. & Mil...	Jan. 21	£3,535	− £310	3	£10,086	− £639
2,938	—	—	**Louisville & Nashville**	Jan. 21	409,000	+ 38,000	3	1,197,009	+ 88,000
2,197	137	137	**Miss., K., & Texas**	Jan. 21	223,099	+ 7,840	29	7,741,004	+ 556,727
477	—	—	N. Y., Ontario, & W.	Jan. 21	66,391	+ 3,667		2,294,387	+ 70,405
1,570	—	—	Norfolk & Western	Jan. 14	220,000	− 18,000	29	5,968,000	+ 443,000
3,499	336	—	Northern Pacific	Jan. 14	313,000	+ 80,000	28	690,000	+ 186,000
4,654	—	—	Southern	Jan. 21	399,000	+ 26,000	29	10,800,812	+ 572,448
1,979	—	—	Wabash	Jan. 21	208,000	+ 18,000	3	642,000	+ 80,000

MONTHLY STATEMENTS.

Mileage.			Name.	Net Earnings for Month.				Net Earnings to Date.			
Total.	Increase on 1896.	Increase on 1895.		Month.	Amount.	In. or Dec. on 1896.	In. or Dec. on 1895.	No. of Months.	Amount.	In. or Dec. on 1896.	In. or Dec. on 1895.
					dols.	dols.	dols.		dols.	dols.	dols.
6,935	44	444	Atchison	December	986,000	+ 52,000	—	12	8,966,480	+ 176,951	—
2,970	—	—	Erie..	November	819,192	+ 21,332	+ 52,579	11	7,880,994	+ 201,967	+ 792,296
3,127	—	239	Illinois Central*	November	2,534,427	+ 664,861	+ 377,039	11	22,138,724	+ 2,451,949	+ 2,487,092
2,396	—	—	New York Central*	November	3,900,753	+ 18,435	− 300,993	[illegible]	41,984,547	+ 1,697,686	+ 1,616,507
3,407	—	—	Pennsylvania	November	1,960,658	+ 164,400	− 48,400	11	18,867,671	+ 2,302,100	− 879,300
1,055	—	—	Phil. & Reading.*	December	1,947,585	+ 208,345	—	12	21,313,421	—	—

* Statements of gross traffic.

Prices Quoted on the London Stock Exchange.

Throughout the INVESTORS' REVIEW middle prices alone are quoted, the object being to give the public the approximate current quotations of every security of any consequence in existence. On the markets the buying and selling prices are both given, and are often wide apart where stocks are seldom dealt in. Other particulars will be found in the INVESTMENT INDEX published quarterly—January, April, July, and October—in connection with this REVIEW, price 2s., by post 2s. 2d. Where dividends are paid only once a year, an *italic* type is used to distinguish them. The London Stock Exchange Official List is quoted in the REVIEW almost entire, only very insignificant issues, or bonds falling due within the next two or three years, being omitted. But the list is subdivided into the leading, or active, stocks, and those less frequently dealt in. The former will be found under the head of "Stock Markets," and with more details than it is possible to give for the bulk of securities. By retaining the file of the INVESTORS' REVIEW any subscriber can follow for himself the movements of securities from week to week, and the INVESTMENT INDEX will from time to time help to fill up deficiencies in the information.

Tea Companies and Mines and Mining Finance Stocks are placed in special lists.

Among the abbreviations used are the following:—S.F. Snk. Fd. *sinking fund*; Certs., *certificates*; Debs. or Dbs., *debentures*; Db. or D.Stk., *debenture stock*; Pf., Prf., or Pref., *preference*; Prefd. or Pfd., *preferred*; Dfd., *deferred*; L. or Ltd., *limited*; Sh., *share*; Ans., *annuities*; Cu. or Cm., *cumulative*; Gu or Guar., *guaranteed*; Bds., *bonds*; S., Sr., or Ser., *series*; In., Ins., Insc., *inscribed*; Dr., Drgs., Drwgs., *drawings*; Stg., Strlg., *sterling*; Lia., *liable to*; Sp., Surp., *surplus*; Per., Perp., *perpetual*; Ln. *lien*; Lo. *loan*.

The dates following the names of securities are the years of issue or of redemption. Where shares are not fully paid up, their nominal amount is given with the name so that investors may know the liability upon them.

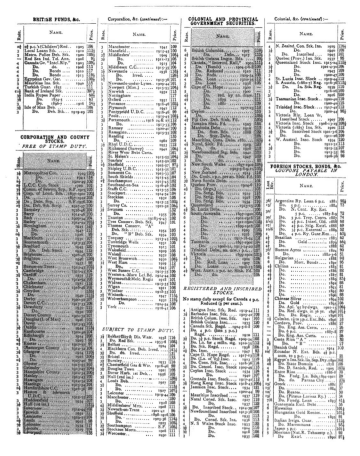

BRITISH FUNDS, &c.

Rate.	Name.		Price.
2¾	2¾ p.c.'s (Childers') Red..	1905	106
3	Local Loans Stk.	1912	113½
3	Metro. Police Deb. Stk.	1920	105½
—	Red Sea Ind. Tel. Ann.	1908	9¼
4	Canada Gv. "Intcl. Rly."	1903	109½
4	Do. do. ..	1908	113
4	Do. Bonds	1910	117
4	Do. Bonds	1913	119½
3	Egyptian Gov. Gar.		108½
3	Mauritius Ins. Stk.	1940	115
4	Turkish Guar. 1855		111
c1½	Bank of Ireland Stk.		397½
3½	India Rupee Paper		60½
3½	Do. 1854-5		63
3	Do. 1896-7	1916	54½
3½	Isle of Man Deb.		106
3	Do. Deb. Stk...	1919-29	105

CORPORATION AND COUNTY STOCKS.

FREE OF STAMP DUTY.

Rate.	Name.		Price.
3½	Metropolitan Con.	1929	120½
3	Do.	1941	114
2½	Do.	1920-49	102
2½	L.C.C. Con. Stock	1920	101
3½	Comm. of Sewers, Scp., S.F.	1905	105
3½	Corp. of Lond. Bds.	1897-1902	100½
3	Do.	1897-1912	103
3½	Do., Debs. Scp. ...... S.F.	1936	106
2½	Do., Deb. Stk. Scrip ..	1927-57	100
3	Barnsley	1916-46	104
3	Barry	1914-46	100
3	Bath	1909-34	104
3	Batley	1914-44	101½
3½	Birmingham	1945	122
3	Do.	1947	113
2½	Do.	1926	99
3	Blackburn	1930	107
3	Bournemouth	1913-33	104
3½	Bradford	1945	120
3	Do. Deb. Stock ..	1954	112
3	Brighouse	1916-46	100
3½	Brighton	1946	120½
2½	Do.	1957	98
3	Burton-on-Trent	1913-43	102½
3	Cambridge	1913-43	104
3½	Cardiff	1935	119
3	Do.	1914-54	105
3	Cheltenham	1971	112
3	Chichester	1916-46	102
3½	Croydon		135½
3	Do.	1940	111½
3	Derby	1920-50	107
3	Devon C.C.	1917-33	106
3½	Dewsbury	1930	111
3	Do.	1930	105
3	Dorset County	1922-32	107
3	Douglas (I. of Man)	1926	101
3	Dover	1913-43	103
3½	Dublin	1944	113½
3	Eastbourne	1920-40	104
3	Edinburgh	1924	108
2½	Do.	1929	98
2½	Exeter	1917-57	97
3	Glamorgan County	1924-34	104
3½	Glasgow	1914	110½
3	Do.	1921	106½
2½	Do.	1925-40	99
3	Gloster	1915-55	103
3	Grimsby	1913-45	104½
3	Hampshire County	1914-34	106½
3	Hanley	1913-43	105
3	Harrogate	1914-34	104
3	Hastings	1915-54	104
2½	Hertfordshire C.C.	1916-36	99
3	Heston & Isleworth U.D.C.	1915-35	101
3	Huddersfield	1934	107
3½	Hull (1st iss.)		131½
3	Inverness	1914-44	102
3	Ipswich	1952	111
3	Lancaster	1919-55	104
2½	Leeds	1927	98
3½	Leicester	1934	117
3	Lincoln	1919	104
3½	Liverpool		135

Corporation, &c. (*continued*):—

Rate.	Name.		Price.
3	Manchester	1941	109
3	Mansfield	1915-45	100
3½	Middlesbro'	1909	105½
3½	Do.	1911-13	105
3	Do.	1915	104
3	Middlesex C.C.	1915-35	106
3½	Newcastle	1936	118½
3½	Do. Irred.		129½
2½	Do.	1915-36	101
3	Newcastle-under-Lyme..	1909-44	101
3	Newport (Mon.)	1915-55	104½
3	Norwich	1952	113
3	Nottingham		117
3	Oxford	1951	111
3	Penzance	1916-46	102½
3	Plymouth	1942	112
3	Pontypridd U.D.C.	1916-46	99
3	Poole	1915-45	102½
3½	Portsmouth 1916	24 & 27	112
3	Do.	1913-33	106
3	Ramsey	1920-40	100
3	Ramsgate	1915-55	102
3	Reading		135
3	Do.	1962	109
3½	Rhyl U.D.C.	1953	112
3	Richmond (Surrey)	1942	106½
3	River Wear Debt Certs.		101
3	St. Helen's	1915-55	104½
3	Scarbro'	1915-50	102
2½	Sheffield	1925-57	97½
3	Shipley U.D.C.	1915-35	101
3	Somerset Co.	1923-33	107
3	South Shields	1915-45	104
2½	Southampton	1915-45	102
3	Southend-on-Sea	1916-46	102
3	Staffs C.C.	1915-35	106
3	Stockport	1914-54	104
3	Stockton	1932	105
3	Do.	1915-35	103½
3	Surrey Co.	1922-32	106½
3½	Swansea		132
3	Do.	1955	106
3	Taunton	1918 3-9-43	102
3	Tees Conserv. Deb. Stk.	1947	101
3	Thames Conserv. "A" Deb. Stk.	1954	103
3	Do. "B" Deb. Stk.	1954	103
3	Torquay	1913-43	102½
3	Tunbridge Wells	1931	105
3	Tynemouth	1913	101
3	Wakefield	1929	105
3	Walsall	1932	108
3	West Bromwich	1930	108½
3¼	West Ham	1929	112
3	Do.	1945	107
3	West Sussex C.C.	1915-35	106
3	Weston-s.-Mare Lcl. Bd.	1914-44	102
3	Weymouth & Melc. Regis	1918	101
3	Widnes	1915-55	102
3	Wigan	1921	108
3	Windsor	1918-55	103
3½	Wisbech	1947	115½
3½	Wolverhampton	1932	119½
3	Do.	1924-54	108
3	York	1916-41	106

SUBJECT TO STAMP DUTY.

Rate.	Name.		Price.
3½	Belfast City & Dis. Watr.	1938	116
3	Do. Red Stk.	1953-6	108½
3¼	Belfast	1924	104
4	Blackburn Con. Deb. Irred.		141½
3½	Do. do. Irred.		131
3½	Bristol		133
3½	Burnley	1933	116
2½	Chesterfield Gas & Wtr.	1916-46	98
3½	Douglas Town	1921	105
3	Dover Harb. 1st Deb...	1956	105
3½	Hull (2nd iss.)		129½
4	Leeds Deb.	1927	125
3½	Do.		113½
3	Do.	1927	107½
3	Leicester	1919-44	106
4	Manchester		150
3	Do.	1928	105
4½	Middlesboro' Mrts.	1908	111
3½	Newark-on-Trent ..	1901-41	96
3½	Sheffield	1898-1916	106
3½	Do.	1925-36	114½
3	Do.	1925	105½
3½	Southampton	S.F.	105½
4½	Stockton Morts.	1908	111
3½	Worcester..	1950	111

COLONIAL AND PROVINCIAL GOVERNMENT SECURITIES.

Rate.	Name.		Price.
6	British Columbia	1907	118½
4½	Do. Debs...	1917	110½
3	British Guiana Imgtn. Bds.		99½
5	Canada, "Intercol. Rail,"	1903	111½
4	Do. (Bonds)	1904-5-6-8	109
4	Do. Reduced	1910	111
3½	Do. Bnds.	1909-34	108
4	Do. Loan	1910-35	112
3	Do. Loan	1938	105
6	Cape of G. Hope	1900	—
5	Do.	1900	—
4½	Do. red. by an. draw.		111
4½	Do. 1879		111
4	Do. 1881		109
4	Do.	1917-23	118
4½	Ceylon		110
4	Do.		108½
4½	Fiji Gov. Deb. Sink. Fd.		100½
4	Jamaica Sink. Fd.	1923	104
5	Manitoba Debs	1910	113
5	Do. Ster. Bds.	1888	122
4	Do. Ster. Debs.		106
4	Mauritius, Cons. Debs. 1880....		103½
4½	Natal, Sink. Fd.	1919	120
4	Do. do.	1926	118
3½	Newfoundland Stg. Bds.	1941	100
3½	Do. do. ..	1947	100
3	Do. do.		88
5	New South Wales	1897-1900	104½
4	Do.	1903-5-8-9-10	105½
5	New Zealand	1914	118
5	Do. Cnsls. 1 p.c. per an. Sink. Fd.		105
3½	Nova Scotia Debs.		104
5	Quebec Prov.	1904-6	110
4½	Do. (drgs.)		103
5	Do. Strlg. Bds.	1912	115
4	Do. Strlg. Bds.	1928	109
4	Do. Strlg. Bds.	1934	110
4	Queensland	1913-15	108
4½	St. Lucia Debs.		100
6	South Australia	1897-1900	103½
6	Do.	1901-1918	118
5	Do.	1911-1920	115½
4	Do.	1899-1916	105
4	Do.	1929	110½
4	Do.	1916	109½
4	Do.	1917-18-24	112
6	Tasmania	1897-1901	104
4	Do. 1908-11,	1913-14-20	108
5	Trinidad Debs., an. drw. 1 p.c...		107
4	Victoria	1899-1901	101½
4½	Do.	1904	106
4	Do. Rail. Loan	1907	106
4	Do. Loans	1908-13	108½
4½	West. Austr. 1 p.c. ac. Sink. Fd.		108
4	Do. do.		106

REGISTERED AND INSCRIBED STOCKS.

No stamp duty except for Canada 4 p.c. Reduced (½ per cent.).

Rate.	Name.		Price.
4	Antigua Insc. Stk. Red.	1919-44	111
3½	Barbados Insc. Stk.	1925-42	108
3	British Colum. Insc. Stk.	1941	103
4	British Guiana Insc.	1935	120
4	Canada Stk. Regd. ..	1904-5-6-8	109
4	Do. 4 p.c. (late 5 p.c.) Regd.	1910	111
3½	Do. 3½ p.c. Stock Regd.	1909-34	108
4	Do. Ln. for 4 milln. stg.	1910-35	112
3	Do. Stk. Regd.	1938	106
2½	Do. Insc.	1947	93
4	Cape G. Hope Regd. ..	1917-23	118
4	Do. (Ln. of '83) Insc. ..	1923	119
4	Do. Cons. Stk. Insc.	1916-36	116
3½	Do. Consol. Insc. Stock	1929-49	115
4	Ceylon Insc. Stock	1934	124
3	Do.	1940	107
4	Grenada Insc. Stock	1917-42	112
3½	Hong Kong Insc. Stock	1918-43	106½
4	Jamaica Insc. Stock	1934	121
—	Do.	1922-44	99
4	Mauritius Inscribed	1937	119
4	Natal Consd. Stk. Insc.	1927	118
4	Do.	1937	122
3½	Do. Inscribed Stock..	1914-39	107
4	Newfoundland Inscribed	1913-38	108
4	Do.	1935	113
4	Do. Consd. Stk. Ins.	1936	113
4	N. S Wales Stock Insc.	1933	122
3½	Do.	1924	110
3½	Do.	1918	108
3	Do.	1935	102

Colonial, &c. (*continued*):—

Rate.	Name.		Price.
4	N. Zealnd. Con. Stk. Ins.	1929	116½
3½	Do.	1940	109
3	Do. Inscribed	1945	101
3	Quebec (Prov.) Ins. Stk.	1937	95
4	Queensland Stock Insc.	1915-24	112½
3½	Do.	1921-4-30	106
3½	Do.	1945	109
3	Do.	1922-47	100
4	St. Lucia Insc. Stock ..	1919-44	112
4	S. Austrln. (1882-7) Reg.	1916-36	113½
3½	Do. In. Stk. Reg.	1939	110
3	Do.	1916-26	100
3/	Do.	1916	100
3½	Tasmanian Insc. Stock..	1920-40	110
4	Do.	1920-40	115
4	Trinidad Insc. Stock	1917-42	112
3	Do.	1922-44	98½
4	Victoria Rly. Loan '81, Inscribed Stock	1907	106
4	Victoria Insc. Stock	1908-13-19	109½
4	Victoria (1885) Ins. Stk.	1920	112
3½	Do. Inscribed Stock	1921-3-6	106
4	Do. do.	1911-26	109
4	W. Austral. Insc. Stock	1934	120
4	Do.	1911-31	113
3½	Do.	1915-35	107
3	Do.	1915-35	98
3	Do.	1926-36	98

FOREIGN STOCKS, BONDS, &c.

COUPONS PAYABLE IN LONDON.

Last Div.	Name.		Price.
36/	Argentine Ry. Loan 6 p.c.	1881	92½
15/	Do. 5 p.c.	1884	73
30/	Do. N. Cent. Ry. Ext. 5 p.c.	1887-8-9	72
30/	Do. 5 p.c. Trsy. Convs.	1887	74
5/4½	Do. 4½ p.c. Interl. Gld.	1888	68
27/	Do. 4½ p.c. Stlg. Extrl.	1888	69
10/6	Do. 3½ p.c. External ..	1889	52
4	Do. 4 p.c. Ry. Guar. Res		63½
4½	Brazilian	1883	62
4½	Do. Gold	1879	66½
4½	Do.	1888	62
36/	Buenos Ayres	1824	90
6	Do.	1882-3-6	51
6	Bulgarian	1888	98
6	Do. Mort. Bonds	1892	95
4½	Chilian	1885	81
4½	Do.	1886	82
4½	Do.	1887	81
4½	Do.	1889	83½
5	Do.	1892	88
4½	Do.	1893	81
4½	Do.	1895	80
5	Do.	1896	88
7	Chinese Silver	1894	102
6	Do. Gold	1895	106
6	Do. Apl. '95 by dwgs.	1901-15	109½
5	Do. Red. dwgs. in 36 yr.	1896	101½
5	Do. Do. Regis.	1896	101
1½	Colmbn. 1½ to 3 p.c. Ext. Bds.	1896	18
6	Cordova, Prov.	1886	27
—	Do. Eng. Ass. Certs.		26
—	Do. 6 p.c.	1887-8	27
—	Do. Eng. Ass. Certs.		26
3	Costa Rica "A"		32
2½	Do. "B"		27
3	Danish Gold	1914	100
10/	Ecuador N. Ext. Bds. 4½ p.c. ascn. to 5 p.c.		21
3½	Egypt'n Ins. Stk. lia. Sep. Dty.	1890	102
4½	Do. State Domain	1878	106
4	Do. D. Sanieh, Red. ..	1905	103½
6	Entre Rios	1886-8	33
6	Do. Fndg. Ln. Bds.	1894-1921	29
6	Do. do. Parana City		23½
15/	Greek	1881	37
15/	Do.	1884	37
10/	Do. Rentes		30
15/	Do. (Piræus-Larissa Ry.)		34
7/6	Do. Fundg. Loan	1893	41½
4	Guatemala Extl. Debt		35
6	Hawaiian		101½
4	Hungarian Gold Rentes		101½
3	Do.	1893	91
6	Italian Irriga. Guar.		112½
5	Do. Maremmana		93½
5	Japan 5 p.c.		101½
5	Mexican (Nat. R. Tehuantp c.) ..		92
5	Do Extrl.	1890	97½

Foreign Stocks, &c. (*continued*) :—

Last Div.	Name.	Price.
6	Mexican Extrl. 1893	95½
5	Do. Intrnl. Cons. Slvr.	34½
5	Do. Intern. Rd. Bds. 2d. Ser.	34
4	Nicaragua 1886	50
3½	Norwegian, red. 1937, or earlier	100
3	Do. do. 1965, do.	100
3½	Do. 3½ p.c. Bnds.	103
1	Paraguay 1 p.c. ris. 3 p.c. 1886-96	16
5	Russian, 1822, £ Strlg.	149½
3	Do. 1850	92
4	Do. (Nicolas Ry.) 1867-9	103
3	Do. Transcauc. Ry. 1882	92
4	Do. Con. R. R. Bd. Ser. I., 1889	103½
4	Do. Do. II., 1889	103½
4	Do. Do. III., 1891	104½
3½	Do. Bonds	100½
4	Do. Ln. (Dvinsk and Vitbsk)	102
6	Salvador 1889	72½
—	S Domingo 4s. Unified 1980	65½
6	San Luis Potosi Stg. 1889	93½
5	San Paulo (Brzl.), Stg. 1888	91½
6	Santa Fé 1883-4	37
—	Do. Eng. Ass. Certs. Dep.	36
5	Do. 1888	47
—	Do. Eng. Ass. Certs. Dpsit.	46
5	Do. (W. Cnt. Col. Rly.) Mrt.	26
5	Do. & Reconq. Rly. Mort.	26
5	Spanish Quickslvr Mort. 1870	102
3½	Swedish 1880	103
3	Do. 1888	101
3	Do. Conversion Loan 1894	101
5	Trans. Gov. Loan Red. 1903-42	105
59/	Tucuman (Prov.) 1888	69
4	Turkish, Secd. on Egypt. Trib.	103½
3½	Turkish, Egpt. Trib., Ott. Bd., '94	98½
4	Do. Priority 1890	94
1	Do. Convted Series, "A"	65½
5	Do. Customs Ln. 1886	97½
5	Uruguay Bonds 1896	54
3	Venzula New Con. Debt 1881	39

COUPONS PAYABLE ABROAD.

Last Div.	Name.	Price.
7	Argent. Nat. Cedla. Sries, "B"	37½
5	Austrian Ster. Rnts., ex 10fl., 1870	85
5	Do. do. do.	86
5	Do. Paper do. 1870	85
5	Do. do. do.	85
4	Do. Gld Rentes 1876	102
2½	Belgian exchange 25 fr.	92
3	Do. do.	101
3½	Danish Int., 1887, Rd. 1896	97½
3½	Do. '87, Red. by pur. or draw. fr. Dec., 1900	98½
2½	Dutch Certs. ex 12 gldrs.	87
3	Do. Bonds	99
3	Do. Insc. Stk.	99
3½	French Rentes	106
3	Do. 1878, '81-4., Red.	101
3	German Imp. Ln. 1891	96½
3	Do. do. 1892-3	96½
3	Do. do. 1890-4	96
5	Japan Cons. Ln., '92, 3, & 5, Red.	48½
36/9	Prussian Consols	102
3	" Cons. Stg. Ln. 1891	97
4	Rumanian Bds. 1890	—
4	Do. do. 1891	—
4	Utd. States, 1877, Red. 1907	116
4	Do. 1895, 30 yrs.	131½
3½	Do. Maschsetts Gl. 1935	113½
3½	Do. Gold Bonds 1923	110½
2	Virginia Cpn. Bds., 3 p.c. from July, 1901	72

BRITISH RAILWAYS.

ORD. SHARES AND STOCKS.

Last Div.	Name.	Price.
10	Barry, Ord.	286½
4	Do. Prefd.	129
6	Do. Defd.	157½
5½	Caledonian, Ord.	161
3	Do. Prefd.	102
—	Do. Defd. Ord., No. 1	5½
[illegible]	Cambrian, Ord.	6½
—	Do. Coast Cons.	6½
24/	Cardiff Ry. Pref. Ord.	118
3/	Central Lond. £10 Ord. Sh.	10
1/9½	Do. do. £6 paid	6
3½d.	Do. Pref. Half-Shares	1½
1/6	Do. Def. do	4½
2	City and S. London	70
—	East London, Cons.	7
1½	Furness	72½
—	Glasgow and S. West. Pfd.	85
—	Do. do. Dfd.	72½
—	Great Central, Ord. 1894	44½
32/6	Do. London Exten.	82
3½	Great N. of Scotland	122
4	Great Northern, Prefd.	125
—	Do. Consolidated "A"	57
—	Do. do. "B"	195½
2	Highland	84
4	Isle of Wight, Prefd.	122½
1	Do. Defd.	86½
—	Lancs. Derbys. and E. Cst.	5
4½	L. Brighton and S. C. Ord.	191
37/11	Do. New 70 p.c. pd.	188
6	Do. Prefd. Ord.	202
7/6	Do. Contgt. Rights Certs.	20½
5½	Lond. and S. Western Ord.	232½
4	Do. Preferred	138
2½	Lond., Tilb., and Southend	134½
—	Mersey, £20 shares	1
—	Metropolitan, New Ord.	131
2½	Do. Surplus Lands	99
4	North Cornwall, 4 p.c. Pref.	106½
-/6	Do. Deferred	27½
7½	North London	229½
	North Staffordshire	132

British Railways (*continued*) :—

Last Div.	Name.	Price.
1/6	Plymouth, Devenport, and S. W. Junc. £10	9
3/	Port Talbot £10 Shares	9½
9d.	Rhondda Swns. B. £10 Sh.	6½
11	Rhymney, Cons.	277½
4	Do. Prefd.	128
—	Do. Defd.	155½
—	Scarboro', Bridlington Junc.	47½
3½	South Eastern, Ord.	156
6	Do. Pref.	199
3½	Taff Vale	85
25/	Vale of Glamorgan	120½
2/8½	Waterloo & City £10 shares	13

LEASED AT FIXED RENTALS.

Last Div.	Name.	Price.
4	Birkenhead	150
5.19.0	East Lincnshire	215
5½	Hammsmith. & City Ord.	200½
4½	Lond. and Blackwll.	167½
4½	Do. £10 4½ p. c. Pref.	167
56/6	Lond. & Green. Ord.	104
5	Do. 5 p. c. Pref.	180½
5	Nor. and Eastn. £50 Ord.	92
6	Do.	109
3½	N. Cornwall 3½ p. c. Stk.	129½
4⅞	Nott. & Granthm. R. & C.	150
3½	Portptk. & Wigtn. Guar. Stk.	126
9	Vict. Stn. & Pimlico Ord.	317½
4½	Do. 4½ p. c. Pref.	163½
4/	West Lond. £20 Ord. Shs.	14½
4⅛	Weymouth & Portld.	162½

DEBENTURE STOCKS.

Last Div.	Name.	Price.
3	Barry, Cons.	110
4	Brecon & Mrthyr, New A	129
4	Do. New B	105
4	Caledonian	155
4	Cambrian "A"	134½
4	Do. "B"	132½
4	Do. "C"	127½
4	Do. "D"	110½
3	Cardiff Rly.	105
4	City and S. Lond.	139
3½	Cleator & Working Junc.	118½
3	Devon & Som. "A"	105½
16/3	Do. "B" 4 p. c.	36
—	Do. "C" 4 p. c.	10
4	E. Lond. and Ch. 4 p. c. A	139
5/	Do. 2nd B	65½
—	Do. 3rd Ch. 4 p. c.	19½
—	Do. 4th do.	9½
3½	Do. 1st (3½ p. c.)	128½
2½	Do. 2½ p.c. (Whitech. Exn).	88
4	Forth Bridge	146
4	Furness	145
4	Glasgow and S. Western	154
5	Gt. Central	—
4½	Do.	161
4	Gt. Eastern	151
4	Gt. N. of Scotland	148½
3	Gt. Northern	117
4	Gt. Western	156
4½	Do.	162
4½	Do.	173½
5	Do.	192
2½	Do.	101
4	Highland	143½
3	Hull and Barnsley	107
3	Do. 2nd (3-4 p. c).	124
4	Isle of Wight	144½
3	Do. Cent. "A"	92½
4½	Do. "B"	115½
4	Do. "C"	82½
3	Lancs. & Yorkshire	116
4	Lancs. Derbys. & E. Cst.	124½
4	Lpool St. Hlen's & S. Lancs.	126
4½	Ldn. and Blackwall	159
4	Ldn. and Greenwich	149½
4	Lond., Brighton, &c.	152
4½	Do.	170½
4½	Lond., Chath., &c., Arb.	160
4½	Do. "B"	158½
4	Do.	140
4	Do. 1883	140
3	Do.	106
3	Lond. & N. Western	119
3	Lond. & S. Westn. "A"	118
3	Do. Consld.	118
4	Lond., Til., & Southend	150
—	Mersey, 5 p. c. (Act, 1866)	65
4	Metropolitan	150
4½	Do.	164½
3½	Do.	129½
6	Met. District	209½
4	Do.	139
3	Midland	118
4½	Mid-Wales "A"	137½
4	Neath & Brecon 1st	129
4	Do. "A 1"	121
3	North British	114
3	Do. 1893	111½
3½	N. Cornwall, Launcstn., &c.	128½
3	North Eastern	117

Debenture Stocks (*continued*) :—

Last Div.	Name.	Price.
4½	North London	168
3	N. Staffordshire	115
4	Plym., Devpt. & S.W. Jn.	141½
4	Rhondda and Swan. Bay	130½
4	Rhymney	148
4	South-Eastern	151
5	Do.	191
3½	Do.	130
3	Do.	116
3	Taff Vale	111
4	Tottenham & For. Gate	146
3	Vale of Glamorgan	105½
3	West Highld. (Gtd. by N. B.)	111½
4	Wrexham, Mold, &c. "A"	115½
4	Do. "B"	106½
4	Do. "C"	97½

GUARANTEED SHARES AND STOCKS.

Last Div.	Name.	Price.
4	Caledonian	152½
4	Do.	152
4	Forth Bridge	146
4	Furness 1881	138
4	Glasgow & S. Western	151½
4	Do. St. Enoch, Rent	150½
6	Gt. Central	204½
4½	Do. 1st Pref.	156½
3½	Do. Pref.	108
5	Do. Irred. S.Y. Rent	167½
4½	Do. do.	144½
4	Gt. Eastern, Rent	148
5	Do. Metropolitan	182½
4	Do.	150
4	Gt. N. of Scotland	141
4	Gt. Northern	152
5	Gt. Western, Rent	191
5	Do. Cons.	191
4	Lancs. & Yorkshire	152
5	L., Brighton & S. C.	188
3½	L., Chat. & D. (Shrlds.)	110½
4	L. & North Western	155
4	L. & South Western 1881	152
4½	Met. District, Ealing Rent	152
4½	Do. Fulham Rent	152
4	Do. Midland Rent	143½
4	Do. Mid. & Dist. Guar.	136½
4	Midland, Rent	153
4	Do. Cons.	153
3	Mid. & G.N. Jt., "A" Rnt.	110½
3	N. British, Lien	111
4	Do. Cons. Pref. No. 1	147
3	N. Cornwall, Wadebrge. Gu.	108
4	N. Eastern	152
5	N. Staff. Trent & M. £50 Shs.	36½
3½	Nott. Suburban Ord.	126½
20/6	S. E. Perp. Ann.	36½
4½	Do. 4½ p.c.	167
3½	S. Yorks. Junc. Ord.	118½
4½	W. Cornwall (G. W., Br., Ex., & S. Dev. Joint Rent	168½
3	W. Highl. Ord. Stk. (Gua., N.B.)	109½

PREFERENCE SHARES AND STOCKS.

DIVIDENDS CONTINGENT ON PROFIT OF YEAR.

Last Div.	Name	Price.
5	Barry (First)	171½
4	Do. Consolidated	140½
4	Caledonian Cons., No. 1	149
4	Do. do. No. 2	148
5	Do. do. 1878	183½
4	Do. Pref. 1884	147
4	Do. do. 1887 (Conv.)	155
—	Cambrian, No. 1 4 p.c. Pref.	72½
—	Do. No. 2 do.	37½
—	Do. No. 3 do.	19
—	Do. No. 4 do.	10
5	City & S. Lond. £10 shares	15½
—	Do. New	14
4	Furness, Cons. 1881	133½
4	Do. "A" 1881	131½
4	Do. "B" 1883	129½
4	Glasgow & S. Western	147
4	Do. No. 2	147
4	Do. 1888	147
4	Do. 1891	146
5	Gt. Central	169½
4	Do.	136½
5	Do. Conv. 1872	157½
5	Do. do. 1874	157½
5	Do. do. 1876	157½
5	Do. do. 1879	156½
5	Do. do. 1881	156½
4	Do. 1889	119½
4	Do. 1891	116
5	Do. 1894	119½
4	Gt. Eastern, Cons.	148
4	Do. 1886	146
4	Do. 1881	145½
4	Do. 1884	145
4	Do. 1887	145

Preference Shares, &c. (*continued*) :—

Last Div.	Name.	Price.
4	Gt. Eastern, Cons. 1888	144½
3½	Do. 1890	126½
3½	Do. 1891	125½
—	Do. (Int. fr. Jan '99) 1893	117½
4	Gt. North Scotland "A"	136½
4	Do. "B"	136½
4	Gt. Northern, Cons.	149
3	Do. 1896	109½
5	Gt. Western Cons.	189
—	Hull & Barnsley Red. at 115	110
4	Isle of Wight	136½
3	Lancs. & Yorkshire, Cons.	112
2/3½	Lanc. Drby & E.C. 5 p.c. £10	11
—	Do. 5 p.c. 2nd £10	10
5	Lond., Bright., &c., Cons.	187½
5	Do. 2nd Cons.	186½
4½	Lond., Chat. & Dov. Arbitr.	137
25/	Do. 2nd Pref. 4½ p.c.	89
4	Lond. & N. Western	152
4	Lond. & S. Western 1881	152
4	Do. 1884	150
3½	Do.	132
4	Lond., Tilbury & Southend	147
4	Do. Cons., 1887	147
4	Do 1891	146
—	Mersey, 5 p.c. Perp.	9½
4	Metropolitan, Perp.	148
4	Do. 1882	145½
4	Do. Irred.	145½
4	Do. 1887	143½
4	Do. New	144½
4½	Do.	149½
3½	Do.	126½
3	Do. Guar.	104½
4	Metrop. Dist. Exten. 5 p.c.	113
4	Midland, Cons. Perpetual	151
4	N. British Cons., No. 2	143
4½	Do. Edin. & Glasgow	156½
5	Do. 1865	173½
5	Do. Conv. 1874	173½
4½	Do. 1875	156
4½	Do. Conv. 1875	156½
5	Do. do. 1879	173½
4	Do. do. 1884	141
4	Do. do. 1888	141
4	Do. do. 1890	141
4	Do. do. 1892	141
4	N. Eastern	151
4½	N. Lond., Cons. 1866	180½
4½	Do. 2nd Cons. 1875	166½
3	N. Staffordshire	111
4½	Plym., Devpt. & S. W. Junc.	152½
9½d.	Port Talbot, &c., 4 p.c. £10 Shares, 4 paid	5
5/	Rhondda & Swansea Bay, 5 p.c. £10 Shares	13½
4	Rhymney, Cons.	144
4½	S. Eastern, Cons.	167
5	Do. do.	184½
4	Do. Vested Cos'.	145
4	Do. 1891	144
3½	Do. 1893	127
2	Do. 3 p.c. after July 1900	105
4	Taff Vale	143

INDIAN RAILWAYS.

Last Div.	Name.	Paid.	Price.
3½	Assam Bengal, Ld., (3½ p.c. till June 30, then 3 p.c.)	100	103
4/	Barsi Light, Ld., £10 Shs.	10	10
6	Bengal and N. West., Ld.	100	147
4/	Do. £10 Shares	10	14
3/6	Do. 3½ p.c. Cum. Pf. Shs.	10	10
8½d.	Do.	4	4
2/3½	Bengal Central, Ld., £10 (3½ p.c. + ¼th net earn.)	5	5
3	Bengal Dooars, Ld.	100	118
4	Bengal Nagpr., Lim. (gua. 4 p.c. + 4th sp. pfts.)	100	115
7½	Bombay, Baroda, and C. I. (gua. 5 p.c.)	100	218
36/1	Burma, Ld. (gua. 2½ p.c. and ½ p.c. add. till 1901)	100	108
1/7	Do. £10 Shares	2½	3
4	Delhi Umb. Kalka, Ld., Gua. 3½ p.c. + net earn.	100	119
4	Do. Deb. Stk., 1890 (1926)	100	113
9/10	Eastn. Bengal, "A" An. 1957	—	26
9/	Do. "B" 1957	—	31
4	Do. Gua. Deb. Stock	100	144
9/7½	East Ind. Ann. "A" (1953)	—	27
8/4½	Do. "C"	—	30
8/11½	Do. "B"	—	32
6⅛	Do. Def. Ann. Cap. (gua. 4 p.c. + ¼th sp. pfts.)	—	150
115/9	East Ind. Def. Ann. "D"	—	156
4½	East Ind. Irred. Stock	100	166
5	Gt. Indian Penin., Gua. 5 p.c. + ½ surplus profits	100	169
4	Do. Irred. 4 p.c. Deb. St.	100	146
4	Indian Mid., Ld. (gua. 4 p.c. + ¼th surplus pfts.)	100	115
51/	Madras Guar. + ½ sp. pfts.	100	166
48/6	Do. do.	100	155
46/	Do. do.	100	14[illegible]
4	Nilgiri, Ld., 1st Deb. Stk.	100	9[illegible]
4	Oude & Robil. Db. Stk. Rd.	100	10[illegible]
3⅞	Robil. and Kumaon, Ld.	100	1[illegible]
9/11	Scinde, Punj., and Delhi, "A" Ann., 1958	—	2[illegible]
9/1	Do. "B" do.	—	3[illegible]

Indian Railways (*continued*):—

Last Div.	Name.	Paid.	Price.
4	South Behar, Ld., £10 shs.	100	100
3½	Do. Deb. Stk. Red.	100	103
4½	South Ind., Gu. Deb. Stk.	100	166½
5	South Indian, Ld. (gua. 3 p.c., and ⅓ spls. profits)	100	120½
5	Sthn. Mahratta, Ld. (3½ p.c. & ¼th net earnings)	100	122
4	Do. Deb. Stk. Red.	100	124
3½	Southern Punjab, Ld....	100	113
3½	Do. Deb. Stk. Red.	—	107
5	Nizam's Gua. State, Ld. (†	100	114½
4	Do. Mort. Deb., 1936	100	110
4	Do. do. Reg.	100	108
17/3½	Nizam's Gua. State, Ld., 3½ p.c. Mt. Deb. bearer	—	94½
17/3½	Do. Reg. do. ..	—	93½
5	W. of India Portgese., Ld.	100	68½
5	Do. Deb. Stk., Red	100	98

RAILWAYS.—BRITISH POSSESSIONS.

Last Div.	Name.	Paid.	Price.
5	Atlantic & N.W. Gua. 1 Mt. Bds., 1937	100	127
5/3	Buff. & L. Huron Ord. Sh.	10	13½
5½	Do. 1st Mt. Perp. Bds. 1879	100	143½
5½	Do. 2nd Mt. Perp. Bds.	100	143½
—	Calgary & Edmon. 6 p.c. 1st Mt. Stg. Bds. Red..	100	79½
5	Canada Cent. 1st Mt. Bds. Red.	100	105
4	Can. Pacific Pref. Stk.....	100	102½
5	Do. Strl. 1st Mt. Deb. Bds. 1915	100	119
3½	Do. Ld. Grnt. Bds., 1938..	100	109
3½	Do. Ld. Grnt. Ins. Stk. ..	100	109
4	Do. Perp. Cons. Deb. Stk.	100	118
5	Do. Algoma Bch. 1st Mt. Bds., 1937	100	121
2	Demerara, Original Stock	100	49
7	Do. Perp. Pref. Stk.......	100	157½
9½d.	Do. 4 p.c. Cum. Ext. Pref. £10 Shs.	4	5
—	Dominion Atlntc. Ord. Stk.	100	32½
25/	Do. 5 p.c. Pref. Stk.....	100	101
4	Do. 1st. Deb. Stk.......	100	110
4	Do. 2nd do. Red.	100	99
—	Emu Bay & Mt. Bischoff, Ld.	5	4½
4½	Do. Irred. Deb. Stk....	100	98
nil.	Gd. Trunk of Canada, Stk.	100	9½
6	Do. 2nd. Equip. Mt. Bds.	100	130½
5	Do. Perp. Deb. Stk... ...	100	141
5	Do. Gt. Westn. Deb. Stk.	100	136
5	Do. Nthn. of Can. 1st Mt. Bds, 1902	100	105
4	Do. do. Deb. Stk	100	104
5	Do. G. T. Geor. Bay & L. Erie 1 Mt., 1903	100	105
5	Do. Mid. of Can. Stl. 1st Mt. (Mid. Sec.) 1908	100	108
5	Do. do. Cons. 1 Mt. Bds. 1912	100	108
5	Do. Mont. & Champ. 1 Mt. Bds., 1902	100	104
	Do. Welln., Grey & Brce. 7 p.c. Bds. 1 Mt.	100	111
4	Jamaica 1st Mtg. Bds. Red.	—	103½
—	Manitoba & N. W., 6 p.c. 1st Mt. Bds., Red......	100	—
—	Do. Ldn. Bdhldrs. Certs.	—	—
5	Manitoba S. W. Col. 1 Mt. Bd., 1934 $1,000 price %	—	120
—	Mid. of W. Aust. Ld. 6 p.c. 1 Mt. Dbs., Red.	100	25
4	Do. Deb. Bds., Red.	100	103
4	Nakusp & Slocan Bds., 1918	100	106
3	Natal Zululand Ld. Debs.,	100	79½
5	N. Brunswick 1st Mt. Stg. Bds., 1934	100	124
4	Do. Perp. Cons. Deb. Stk.	100	115
—	N. Zealand Mid., Ld., 5 p.c 1st Mt. Debs..........	100	35
6	Ontario & Queb. Cap. Stk.	$100	156½
5	Do. Perm. Deb. Stk......	100	147½
—	Qu'Appelle, L. Lake & Sask. 6 p.c. 1 Mt. Bds. Red.	100	45½
5	Queb. & L. S. John, 1st Mt. Bds., 1909	100	27½
5	Quebec Cent., Prior Ln. Bds., 1908	100	109
1½	Do. 5 p.c. Inc. Bds.	100	42
4	St. Lawr. & Ott. Stl. 1st Mt.	100	113
4	Shuswap & Okan., 1st Mt. Deb. Bds., 1915	100	70½
5	Temiscouata, 5 p.c. Stl. 1st Deb. Bds., Red.........	100	9½
5	Do. (S. Franc. Brch.) 5 p.c. Stl. 1 Mt. Db. Bds., 1910	100	12½
4	Toronto, Grey & B. 1st Mt.	100	114
1/2½	Well. & Mana. £5 Shs. ..	1	1
5	Do. Debs., 1908	100	110
5	Do. 2nd Debs., 1908....	100	109
5	Do. 3rd do., 1908	100	108
6	Atlan. & St. Law. Shs., 6 p.c.	100	167
5	Gd. Trunk Mt. Bds., 1934	100	107½
5	Michigan Air Line, 5 p.c. 1st Mt. Bds., 1902......	100	104
4	Minneap., S. P. & Slt. Ste. Mar, 1st M. Bds., 1938	$1000	100

AMERICAN RAILROAD STOCKS AND SHARES.

Last Div.	Name.	Paid.	Price.
6/	Alab. Gt. Sthn. A 6 p.c. Pref.	10/.	9
—	Do. do "B" Ord. ..	10/.	2
—	Alabma. N. Orl.-Tex. &c., "A" Pref.	10/.	[illegible]
—	Do. "B" Def.	10/.	[illegible]
4½	Atlant. First Lsd. Ls. Rll. Trust..................	Stk.	100
$2	Baltimore & Ohio Com. ..	$100	13
—	Baltimore Ohio S.W. Pref.	$100	6
—	Chesap. & Ohio Com.	$100	22
—	Chic. Gt. West. 5 p.c. Pref. Stock "A"...........	$100	37½
—	Do. do. Scrip. In.......	—	35½
8/3	Do. 4 p.c. Deb. Stk.......	$100	71½
4	Do. Interest in Scrip	$100	67½
$4	Chic. Junc. Rl. & Un. Stk. Yds. Com.	$100	116½
$1½	Do. 6 p.c. Cum. Pref.	$100	113½
$3½	Chic. Mil. & St. P. Pref...	$100	147½
7	Cleve. & Pittsburgh......	$10	87
$1½	Clev., Cincin, Chic., & St. Louis Com.	$100	—
—	Erie 4 p.c. Non-Cum. 1st Pf.	—	38½
—	Do. 4 p.c. do. 2nd Pf.	—	20
—	Gt. Northern Pref.	$100	135
$2½	Illinois Cen. Lsd. Lines ..	$100	96
—	Kansas City, Pitts & G. ..	$100	21
$3	L. Shore & Mich. Sth. C.	$100	182½
—	Mex. Cen. Ltd. Com.	$100	6
—	Miss. Kan. & Tex. Pref...	$100	37½
1	N.Y., Pen. & O. 1st Mt. Tst. Ltd., Ord.	—	45½
4	Do. 1st Mort. Deb. Stk. ..	$100	93½
8	North Pennsylvania	$50	—
—	Northn. Pacific, Com.....	$100	28
1½	Pitts. F. Wayne & Chic...	$100	176
—	Reading 1st Pref.	$50	25½
—	Do. 2nd Pref.	$50	13½
—	S. Louis & S. Fran. Com.	$100	7½
—	Do. 2nd Pref.	$100	27
6	St. Louis Bridge 1st Pref..	$100	107
3	Do. 2nd Pref.	$100	50
6	Tunnel Rail. of St. Louis	$100	107
$1½	St. Paul, Min. and Man...	$100	127½
—	Southern, Com.	$100	9½
—	Wabash, Common.........	$100	7½

AMERICAN RAILROAD BONDS. CURRENCY.

Last Div.	Name.	Price.
7	Albany & Susq. 1 Con. Mrt. 1906	122½
7	Allegheny Val. 1 Mt...... 1910	127½
5	Burling., Cedar Rap. & N. 1 Mt. 1906	102½
5	Canada Southern 1 Mt..... 1908	111
5	Chic. & N. West. Sk. Fd. Db. 1933	119½
5	Do. Deb. Coupon 1921	115½
6	Chicago & Tomah 1905	112½
5	Chic. Burl. & Q. Skg. Fd. 1901	102½
4	Do. Nebraska Ext....... —	100
6	Chic., Mil., & S. Pl., 1 Mt. S.W. Div.............. 1909	117½
7	Do. (S. Paul Div.) 1 Mt. 1902	132½
5	Do. (La Cross & D. 1919	112½
7	Do. 1 Mt. (Hast. & Dak.) 1910	132
5	Do. Chic. & Mis. Riv. 1 Mt. 1926	112½
5	Chic., Rock Is. and Pac. 1 Mt. Ext. 1934	108
6	Det., G. Haven & Mil. Equip 1918	110
6	Do. do. Cons. Mt. 1918	105½
6	Ill. Cent., 1 Mt., Chic. & S. 1898	—
7	Indianap. & Vin., 1 Mt. .. 1908	125
6	Do. do. 2 Mt. .. 1900	104½
6	Lehigh Val., Cons. Mt.... 1923	112½
—	Mexic. Cent., Ln. 2 Cons. Inc. —	7
7	N.Y. Cent. & H.R. Mt. Bonds 1903	119½
5	Do. Deb. 1904	112
6	Penns. Cons. S. F M. 1905	115
4	West Shore, 1 Mt. 2361	110

DITTO—GOLD.

Last Div.	Name.	Price.
6	Alabama Gt. Sthn. 1 Mt. .. 1908	112
5	Do. Mid. 1 1928	94½
4	Allegheny Val. Gen. Mt. .. 1942	109
4	Atch., Top., & S. Fé Gn. Mt. 1995	94
3	Do. Adj. Mt............ 1995	60½
5	Do. Equipt. Tmst. ...... —	104½
5	Atlantic & Dan. 1 Mt...... 1950	94½
5	Baltimore & Ohio.......... 1925	90½
5	Do. Speyer's Tst. Recpts. 1925	90½
5	Do. Cons. Mt. 1988	100
4½	Do. 4½ p.c. 1 Mt. Term. 1934	84½
4½	Do. Brown Shipley's Dep. Cts. —	84½
5	Balt. Belt 5 p.c. 1 Mort..... 1990	—
4½	Balt. & Ohio S.W. 1 Mt. .. 1990	102
4½	Do. 4½ p.c. 1 Cons. Mt. 1893 1993	76½
—	Do. Inc. Mt. 5 p.c. Cl. A —	30
—	Do. do. Cl. B —	11
5	Balt. & Ohio S.W. Term 5 p.c. 1942	99½
6	Balt. & Ptmac (Mn. L.) 1 Mt. 1911	124½
6	Do. do. (Tunnel) 1 Mt. 1911	124½
4	Beech Creek 1 Mt. 1936	106½
5	Do 2 Mort. 1936	116
4	Carthage & Adiron. 1 Mt... 1981	107½

American Railroad Bonds—Gold (*continued*):—

Last Div.	Name.	Price.
5	Cent. of Georgia 1 Mort. .. 1945	117½
5	Do. Cons. Mt. 1945	92½
5	Cent. of N. Jrsy. Gn. Mt... 1987	115
6	Central Pacific, 1 Mort. 1898	102½
6	Do. Speyer's Certs. ...... —	105
5	Do Land Grant 1900	102
5	Chesap. & Ohio 1st Cons. Mt. 1939	117
4½	Do. Gen. Mt............ 1992	85
6	Chic. & W. Ind. Gen. Mt. Skg. Fd. 1932	122
5	Chic. Mil. & St. Pl. (Chic. & L. Sup.) 1 Mt. 1921	114½
5	Do. Chic. & Pac. W. 1921	119½
5	Do. Wisc. & Minn. 1 Mt. 1921	114½
5	Do. Terminal Mt. 1914	114½
4	Do. General Mt. 1989	107
5	Chic. St. L. & N. Orleans.. 1951	122½
4	Do. 1 Mort. (Memphis) .. 1951	102½
4	Clevel, Cin., Chic. & St. L. 1 Mt. (Cairo)............ 1939	90
4	Do. 1 Mt. (Cinc., Wab., & Mich.) 1991	90
4	Do. 1 Col. Tst. Mt. (S. Louis) 1990	98½
4	Do. General Mt. 1993	84
4½	Clevel. & Mar. Mt. 1935	111½
4½	Clevel. & Pittsburgh 1942	122½
4½	Do. Series B. 1942	122½
—	Colorado Mid. 1 Mt. 1936	68
—	Do. Bdhrs.' Comm. Certs. —	68
4	Dnvr. & R. Gde. 1 Cons. Mt. 1936	95
5	Do. Imp. Mort........... 1928	91
4	Detroit & Mack. 1 Lien 1995	92½
5	E. Tennes., Virg., & Grgia. Cons. Mt. 1956	114½
5	Elmira, Cort., & Nthn. Mt. 1914	99½
4	Erie 1 Cons. Mt. Pr. Ln. .. 1996	94
3	Do. Gen. Lien 1996	72
6	Galvest., Harrisb., &c., 1 Mt.	107½
5	Georgia, Car. & N. 1 Mt. .. 1929	96
4½	Gd. Rpds & Indn. Ex. 1 Mt. 1941	111½
5	Do. 1 Mt. (Muskegon) .. 1926	39½
3½	Illinois Cent. 1 Mt. 1951	104½
4	Do. 1952	107
4	Do. Cairo Bdge. .. 1950	102
4	Do. 1953	105
4	Do. General Mort. .. 1904	102½
—	Kans. City, Pitts. & G. 1 M. 1923	83
3½	L. Shore & Mich. Southern 1997	109
4½	Lehigh Val. N.Y. 1 Mt.... 1940	105
5	Lehigh Val. Term. 1 Mt. .. 1941	112½
5	Long Island 1931	114½
5	Do. Deb.......... 1934	101
5	Do. (N. Shore Bch.) 1 Cons. Mt. 1932	96
6	Louisville & Nash. G. Mt.. 1930	120
6	Do. 2 Mt. Sk. Fd. (S. & N. Alabama......... 1910	108
6	Do. 1 Mt. N. Orl. & Mb. 1930	122½
5	Do. 1 Mt. Coll. Tst. 1931	106
4	Do. Unified 1940	88
4½	Do. Mobile & Montgy. 1 Mt. 1945	107½
4	Manhattan Cons. Mt. 1990	100
4	Mexican Cent. Cons. Mt. .. 1911	68½
—	Do. 1 Cons. Inc, ...	18
6	Mexican Nat. 1 Mt......... 1927	106½
3	Do. 2 Mt. 6 p.c. Inc. A 1917	57
—	Do. do. B.. 1917	—
3	Do. Matheson's Certs.....	—
3	Michig. Cnt. (Battle Ck. & S.) 1 Mt. 1989	84
6	Minneap. & S. L. 1 Mt. Pacific Ext. 1921	120½
5	Do. 1 Consold. 1934	110
4	Minne., Slt. S. M. & A. 1 Mt. 1926	101
5	Minneapolis Westn. 1 Mt... 1911	105½
4	Miss. Kans. & Tex. 1 Mt... 1990	90
4	Do. 2 do. 1990	66
4	Mobile & Birm. Mt. Inc.... 1945	38
5	Do. P. Lien 1945	88
4	Mohawk & Mal. 1 Mt...... 1991	110
5	Montana Cent. 1 Mt....... 1937	111½
5	Nashv., Chattan., & S. L. 1 Cons. Mt............... 1928	104½
5	Nash., Flor., & Shff. Mt... 1937	90
4	N. Y. & Putnam 1 Cons. Mt. 1993	110
5	N. Y., Brooklyn, & Man. B. 1 Cons. Mt............. 1935	109
4	N. Y. Cent. & Hud. R. Deb. Certs. 1890 1905	107
4	Do. Ext. Debt. Certs.... 1905	107
7	N. Y., L. Erie, & W. 1 Cons. Mt. (Erie) 1920	149½
7	Do. 1 Con. Mt. Fd. Coup. 1920	147½
5	N. Y., Onto., & W. Cons. 1 Mt..................... 1939	110
4	Do. 4 p.c. Refund. Mt.. 1992	102
5	N. Y. & Rockaway B. 1 Mt. 1927	104½
6	Norfolk & West. Gn. Mt.... 1931	128
6	Do. Imp. & Ext......... 1934	118½
4	Do. 1 Cons. Mt........ —	82
6	N. Pacific Gn. 1 Mt. Ld. Gt. 1921	120
4	Do. P. Ln. Rl. & Ld. Gt. —	99½
3	Do. Gn. Ln. Rl. & Ld. Gt. —	63½
5	Oregon & Calif. 1 Mt....... 1927	81
5	Oregon Rl. & Nav. Col. Tst. —	—
—	Oreg. Sh. Line & Utah Col. Trst. 5 p.c. G. Bonds 1915	47½
6	Panama Skg. Fd. Subsidy.. 1910	105½
4½	Pennsylvania Rlrd. 1913	115½
4	Do. Equip. Tst. Ser. A.. 1914	106
4	Do. Cons. Mt.......... 1943	115
4½	Penna. Company 1st Mort. 1921	116½
5	Perkiomen 1 Mrt., 2nd ser.. 1918	90
4½	{Pitts., C., C., & St. Ls. Con. Mt. G.B., Ser. A} 1940-2	115
4	Do. Cons. Mort., Ser. D.. 1945	105
6	Pittsbgh., Cle., & Toledo .. 1922	105½
4	Reading, Phil., & R. Genl. 1997	86½
5	Richmond & Dan. Equip. .. 1909	99½
5	Rio Grande Junc. 1st Mort. 1939	90
4	Rio Grande West 1st Tst. Mt. 1939	84½
6	St. Joseph & Gd. Island .. 1925	—
7	S. Louis Brid e 1st Mort .. 1928	135½

American Railroad Bonds (*continued*):

Last Div.	Name.	Price.
5	S. Louis Mchts. Bdge. Term. 1st Mort................. 1930	104½
4	S. Louis S. West 1st Mort.. 1989	75½
—	Do. 4 p.c. 2nd Mort. Inc. 1989	27½
—	S. Louis Term. Cupples Sta. & Prop. 1st. Mrt. 4½ p.c. 1912-17	101
4½	St. Paul, Minn., & Manit. 1933	110
6	Do. do. 1933	127½
6	Shamokin. Sunbury, &c. 2 Mt. 1925	107
5	S. & N. Alabama Cons. Mt. 1936	92½
5	Southern 1 Cons. Coup. 1994	95
4	Do. E. Tennes Reorg. Lien .. 1938	98
6	S. Pacific of Cal. 1 Mt... 1905-12	113
4½	Trml. Assn. of S. Louis 1 Mt. 1939	113½
5	Do. 1 Cons. Mt.......... 1944	109
5	Texas & Pac. 1 Mt......... 2000	102
—	Do. 5 p.c. 2 Mt. Income 2000	32½
5	Toledo & Ohio Cent. 1 Mt. West. Div. 1935	103½
4½	Toledo., Walhon., Val., & Ohio 1 Mt. 1931-3	111½
6	Union Pacific 1 Mt. 1896-9	102½
5	Do. Coll. Tverst.....	—
—	Union Pac., Linc., & Color. 1 Mt. 1918	—
4	United N. Jersey Gen. Mt... 1944	117½
6	Vicksbrg., Shrevept., & Pac. Pr. Ln. Mt. 1915	102½
5	Wabash 1 Mt. 1939	110
4	Wn. Pennsylvania Mt. 1928	109½
5	W. Virga. & Pittsbg. 1 Mt. 1990	84
5	Wheeling & L. Erie 1 Mt. (Wheelg. Div.) 5 p.c. 1928	82½
5	Do. Extd. Imp. Mt 1930	—
—	Do. do. Brown Shipley's Cts..	—
5	Willmar & Sioux Falls 1 Mt. 1938	111

STERLING.

Last Div.	Name.	Price.
6	Alabama Gt. Sthn. Deb..... 1906	106
5	Do. Gen. Mort. .. 1927-8	100
5	Alabama, N. Orl., Tex. & Pac. 5 p.c. "A" Dis... 1910-40	99
50/	Do. do. "B" do. 1910-40	47
—	Do. do. "C" do.	19
—	Allegheny Valley 1910	135
4	Atlantic 1st Leased Line Perp...	100
6	Baltimore and Ohio 1902	108
6	Do. do. 1910	116
5	Do. do. 1877........	95½
—	Do. Morgan's Certs. ..	95
4½	Do. do. 1933	81
6	Chicago & Alton Cons. Mt. 1903	111
5	Chic, St. Paul & Kan. City Priority	105
6	Eastn. of Massachusetts 1906	117½
5	Illinois Cent. Skg. Fd.	105
5	Do. 1905	108
3½	Do. 1950	100½
4	Do. 1 Mt. 1951	114
3	Do. 1 Mt. 1951	94
6	Louisville & Nash., M. C. & L. Div., 1 Mt. 1902	107
7	Do. 2 Mt. (Memphis & O.).................. 1901	111
47/4	Mexican Nat. "A" Certs. 5 p.c. Non. cum.	47
—	Do. "B" Certs....	10
6	N.Y. & Canada 1 Mt....... 1904	111½
6	N. York Cent. & H.R. Mort. 1903	112
4½	N. York, Penns., & Ohio Pr. Ln. Extd. 1935	—
5	Do. Equip. Tst.	102
5	Do. 5 p.c. Equip. Tst. (1890)	102
6	Nrthn. Cent. Cons. Gen. Mt. ..	106
6	Pennsylvania Gen. Mt. 1910	129
6	Do. Cons. Skg. Fd. Mt. 1905	117
3½	Do. Cons. Mt. 1945	107
6	Phil. & Erie Cons. Mort .. 1920	134½
6	Phil. & Reading Gen. Cons. Mort. 1911	127
6	Pittsbg. & Connells. Cons. 1926	112
—	Do. Morgan's Certs....	112
4	St. Paul., Min., & Manitoba (Pac. Extn.) 1940	98
6	S. & N. Alabama 1903	107½
6	Union Pacific, Omaha Bridge 1896	—
6	Un. N. Jersey & C. Gen. Mt. 1901	112½

FOREIGN RAILWAYS.

Last Div.	Name.	Paid.	Price.
4/	Alagoas, Ltd., Shs.	20	6
5	Do. Deb. Stk., Red. ..	100	55
6	Antofagasta, Ltd., Stk. ..	100	81
4	Do. Perp. Deb. Stk. ..	100	95
—	Arnuco, Ld., Ord. Shs. ..	10	¼
—	Do. 10 p.c. Cum. Pref.	10	1½
20/	Argentine Gt. W., Ld.,	20	14½
20/	Do. 5 p.c. Cum. Pref. Shs.	20	20½
4	Do. 1 Deb. Stk. .... (f	100	104½
6/o/o	Do. 6 p.c. 2 Db. Stk. Astg.	100	—
6/o/o	Do. do. Non-Astg.	100	—
1/o/o	Argentine N.E., Ltd., 6 p.c. Cum. Pref. Stk. ..	100	12
—	Do. 5 p.c. Deb. Stk., Red.	100	35
2/	Arica and Tacna Shs. ..	20	1½
10/	Bahia & San Fcisco., Ld.,	20	12
6/	Do. Timbo. Bch. Shs.	20	5½
12/	Bahia, Blanca, & N.W. Ln. Prf. Cum. 6 p.c. ..	100	62½
4	Do. 4 p.c. 1 Deb. Stk., Red.	100	96
6	Barranquilla R. & P., Ld., 6 p.c. 1 Deb. Stk., Red.	100	95

Foreign Railways (*continued*):—

Last Div.	Name.	Paid.	Price.
3/	Bilbao Riv. & Cantabn., Ltd., Ord.	3	6
—	Bolivar, Ltd., Shs.	10	1¼
6	Do. 6 p.c. Deb. Stk.	100	99½
4/	Brazil Gt. Southn. Ltd., 7 p.c. Cum. Pref.	20	1¼
6	Do. Perm. Deb. Stk	100	50½
6½	B. Ayres Gt. Southn., Ld., Ord. Stk.	100	157
5	Do. Pref. Stk.	100	140
4	Do. Deb. Stk.	100	118
30/	B. Ayres & Ensen. Port., Ltd., Ord. Stk.	100	56
5	Do. Cum. 1 Pref. Stk.	100	119
6/0/0	Do. 6p.c.Con. Pref.Stk.	100	98
4	Do. Deb. Stk., Irred.	100	107
9 1/8	B. Ayres Northern, Ltd., Ord. Stk.	100	270
12	Do. Pref. Stk.	100	325
5	Do. 5 p.c. Mt. Deb. Stk., Red.	100	113
3/15/0	B. Ayres & Pac., Ld., 7 p.c. 1 Pref. Stk. (Cum.)	100	104
4	Do. 1 Deb. Stk.	100	106
5/5/0	Do. 4½ p.c. 2 Deb. Stk.	100	94
1	B. Ayres & Rosario, Ltd., Ord. Stk.	100	78
—	Do. New, £20 Shs.	20	22½
7/	Do. 7 p.c. Pref. Shs.	10	17¾
7/	Do. Sunchales Ext.	10	15¾
4	Do. Deb. Stk., Red.	100	109
12/	B. Ayres & Val. Trans., Ltd., 7 p.c. Cum. Pref.	20	7
4 p.c.	Do. 4 p.c. "A" Deb. Stk., Red.	100	73
—	Do. 6 p.c. "B" Deb. Stk., Red.	100	48
6/	B. Ayres Westn. Ld. Ord.	10	12
3/	Do. Def. Shs	10	8
5	Do. 5 p.c. Pref.	10	13½
4	Do. Deb. Stk	100	112
6	Cent. Arg. Deb. Sk. Rd.	100	163½
4	Do. Deb. Stk. Rd	100	112
6	Cent. Bahia L. Ord. Stk.	100	51½
6	Do. Deb. Stk., 1934	100	77½
5	Do. Deb. Stk., 1937	100	61
4/6	Cent. Uguy. East. Ext. L. Shs.	10	6
5	Do. Perm. Stk.	100	109
3/	Do. Nthn. Ext. L. Sh.	10	4½
5	Do. Perm. Deb. Stk.	100	106
3	Do. of Montev. Ltd., Ord. Stk.	100	86
6	Do. Perm. Deb. Stk.	100	142
8/	Conde d'Eu, Ltd. Ord.	20	8
—	Cordba & Rosar., Ltd., 6 p.c. Pref. Shs.	100	50
4	Do. 1 Deb. Stk	100	97
75/	Do. 6 p.c. Deb. Stk.	100	90
—	Cordba Cent., Ltd., 5 p.c. Cu. 1 Pref. Stk	100	91
—	Do. 5 p.c. Non-Cum. 2 Pref. Stk	100	49
5	Do. Deb. Stk	100	125
—	Costa Rica, Ltd., Shs.	10	4
8/	Dna. Thrsa. Chris., Ltd., 7 p.c. Pref. Shs.	20	4½
20/	E. Argentine, Ltd	100	47
6	Do. Deb. Stk	100	108
1/1	Egyptn. Dlta. Lgt. Rys., Ltd., £10 Pref. Shs.	6	8½
—	Entre Rios, L., Ord. Shs.	5	1
—	Do. Cu. 5 p.c. Pref.	5	3½
6/	Gt. Westn. Brazil, Ltd.,	20	11½
6	Do. Perm. Deb. Stk.	100	94½
6	Do. Extn. Deb. Stk.	100	84½
—	Int.-Oceanic Mex., Ltd., 7 p.c. Pref.	10	1½
4	Do. Deb. Stk	100	83½
42/6	Do. 7 p.c. "A" Deb. Sk.	100	58½
—	Do. 7 p.c. "B" Deb. Sk.	100	28½
5/	La Guaira & Carac	10	7
5	Do. 5 p.c. Deb. Sk. Red.	100	102
8/4	Lembg.-Czern.-Jassy	30	24½
1/	Lima, Ltd.	20	2½
—	Manila Ltd. 7 p.c. Cu. Pf.	10	½
20/6½	Mexican 2nd Pref. 6 p.c.	100	36
6	Do. Perp. Deb. Stk.	100	142
2/0/0	Mexican Sthrn., Ld., Ord.	100	25
—	Do. 4 p.c. 1 Db. Stk. Rd.	100	87
—	Do. 4 p.c. 2 do.	100	63
—	Mid. Urgy., Ltd.	100	19½
5	Do. Deb. Stk.	100	63
12/	Minas & Rio, Ltd.	20	12½
5/2	Namur & Liege	20	12½
11/6	Do. Pref.	20	28
5/	Natal & Na. Cruz, Ld., 7 p.c. Cum Pref.	20	7½
—	Nitrate Ltd., Ord.	10	6½
—	Do. 7 p.c. Pr. Con. Or.	10	4½
—	Do. Def. Conv. Ord.	10	1½
7/	N.-E. Urgy., Ltd., Ord.	10	14½
7/	Do. 7 p.c. Pref.	10	15
—	N.-W. Argentine Ld., 7 p.c. Pref.	10	3½
6	Do. 6 p.c. 1 Deb. Stk.	100	114
—	Do. 2 Deb. Stk.	100	94
—	N.W. Uruguay 6 p.c. 1 Pref. Stk.	100	17
—	Do. 5 p.c. 2 Pref. Stk.	100	7½
6	Do. 6 p.c. Deb. Stk.	100	77½
16/	Ottoman (Sm. Aid.)	20	16½
—	Paraguay Cntl., Ld., 5 p.c. Perm. Deb. Stk.	100	11
—	Piræus, Ath., & Pelo.	275	1
5/	Pto. Alegre & N. Hambg. Ld., 7 p.c. Pref. Shs.	20	4½
6	Do. Mt. Deb. Stk. Red.	100	77½
—	Puerto Cabello & Val. Ld.	10	1½
5	Recife & S. Francisco	20	74
14/	R. Claro S. Paulo, Ld., Sh.	10	22
5	Do. Deb. Stk.	100	130
5/	Royal Sardinian Ord.	10	11½
5/	Royal Sardinian Pref.	10	12½
5/	Sambre & Meuse	20	19
5/6	Do. Pref.	10	12
28/	San Paulo Ld.	20	38½
2/9½	Do. New Ord. £10 sh.	4	8½
2/	Do. 5 p.c. Non.Cm.Pref.	10	12½
5½	Do. Deb. Stk. †	100	136
5	Do. 5 p.c. Deb. Stk.	100	128
—	S. Fé & Cordova, Gt. Sthn., Ld., Shares	100	56
6	Do. Perp. Deb. Stk.	100	121
3/2½	S. Austrian	20	7½
10/	Sthn. Braz. R. Gde. do Sul, Ld.	20	9
6	Do. 6 p.c. Deb. Stk.	100	76
4	Swedish Centl., Ld., 4 p.c. Deb. Stk.	100	108
5	Do. Pref.	100	99
1/9	Taltal, Ld.	5	3
4/	Uruguay Nthn., Ld. 7 p.c. Pfd. Stk.	100	8
3½	Do. 5 p.c. Deb. Stk.	100	29
—	Villa Maria & Rufino, Ld., 6 p.c. Pref. Shs.	100	20
4	Do. 4 p.c. 1 Deb. Stk.	100	76
6/0/0	Do. 6 p.c. 2 Deb. Stk.	100	49
5/9	West Flanders	8½	22
5/6	Do. 5½ p.c. Pref.	10	18
3/	Wstn. of Havana, Ld.	10	5

FOREIGN RAILWAY OBLIGATIONS

Per Cent.	Name.	Price.
6	Alagoas Ld., 6 p.c. Deb., Rd.	85½
—	Alcoy & Gandia, Ld., 5 p.c. Debs., Red.	25
5	Arauco, Ld., 5 p.c. 1st Mt., Rd.	67½
6	Do. 6 p.c. Mt. Deb., Rd.	48½
6	Brazil G. Sthn., L., Mt. Dbs., Rd.	83
6	Do. Mt. Dbs. 1893, Rd.	52½
5½	Campos & Caran. Dbs., Rd.	76
6	Central Bahia, L., Dbs., Rd.	83½
5½	Conde d'Eu, L., Dbs., Rd.	77
6	Costa Rica, L., 1st Mt. Dbs., Rd.	110
6	Do. 2nd Dbs., Rd.	95
5	Do. Prior Mt. Db., Rd.	107
6	Cucuta Mt. Dbs., Rd.	100
5½	Donna Thrsa. Cris., L., Dbs., Rd.	75
3	Eastn. of France, £20 Dbs., Rd.	19
4	Egyptn. Delta Light, L., Db., Rd.	100
—	Espito. Santo & Cara. 5 p.c. Stl. Dbs., Rd.	38
4	Gd. Russian Nic., Rd.	103
5	Inter-Oceanic Mex., L., 5 p.c. Pr. Ln. Dbs., Rd.	104
3	Ital. 3 p.c. Bds. A & B, Rd.	57½
—	Ituana 6 p.c. Debs., 1918	72½
—	Leopoldina, 6 p.c. Dbs. £50 Bds.,	24
—	Do. do. Comms. Cert.	24
—	Do. 5 p.c. Stg. Dbs. (1888), Rd.	35
—	Do. do. Comm. Certs.	35
—	Do. 5 p.c. Stg. Dbs. (1890), Rd.	24
—	Do. do. Comms. Certs.	24
—	Macahé & Cam. 5 p.c. Dbs., Rd.	35
—	Do. do. Comms. Certs.	35
—	Do. (Cantagallo), 5 p.c., Red.	35
—	Do. do. Comm. Certs.	35
—	Manila Ltd., 6 p.c. Deb., Red.	24
6	Do. Prior Lien Mt., Rd.	106
6	Do. Series "B," Rd.	79
7	Matanzas & Sab., Rd.	101½
6	Minas & Rio, L., 6 p.c. Dbs., Rd.	98
5	Mogyana 5 p.c. Deb. Bds., Rd.	102
5	Moscow-Jaros., Rd.	107½
5½	Natal & Na. Cruz Ltd., 5½ p.c. Debs., Red.	88½
5	Nitrate, Ltd. Mt. Bds., Red.	91½
3	Nthn. France, Red.	19
4	N. of S. Af. Rep. (Trnsvl.) Gu. Bds. Red.	97
3	Nthn. of Spain £20 Pri. Obs. Red.	8½
6	Ottmn. (Smy to A.) (Kujk) Asnt. Debs., Red.	109
6	Ottmn. (Seraik.) Asg. Debs. Red.	109
6	Ottmn. (Seraik.) Non-Asg. D., Rd	109
5	Ottmn. Kuyjk. Ext. Red.	109
5	Ottmn. Serkeuy. Ext. Red.	104
5	Ottmn. Tireh Ext. 1910	99
5	Ottmn. Debs, 1886, Red.	98
5	Do. 1888, Red. 1935	99
5	Do. 1893, Red. 1935	97
5	Ottmn. of Anlia. Debs., Rd.	93
5	Do. Ser. II.	89
4	Ottomn. Smyr. & Cas. Ext. Bds., Red.	82½
3	Paris, Lyon & Medit. (old sys., £20), Red.	19
3	Paris, Lyon & Medit. (new sys., £20), Red.	19
50/	Piræus, At. & Pelp., 6 p.c. 1st Mt. Bds., Red.	88½
3	Do. 5 p.c. Mt. Bds., Red.	61½
4	Pretoria-Pietbg., Ltd., Red.	94
7	Puerto Cab. & Val., Ltd., 1st Mt. Debs., Red.	95
—	Rio de Jano. & Nthn., Ltd., 6 p.c. £100 Deb., Red.	24
—	Rio de Jano. (Gr. Para.), 5 p.c. 1st Mt. St. £100 Debs., Red.	24
3	Royal Sardinian, A, Rd. £20	12
3	Royal Sardinian, B., Rd. £20	12
5	Ryl. Trns.-Afric. 5 p.c. 1st Mt. £100 Bds., Red.	61
7	Sagua La Grande, B pRd.	98
4	Sa. Fe & Cor. G. S., Ld. Pr. Ln. Bds.	102
5	Sa. Fe, 5 p.c. 2nd Reg. Dbs.	81
3	South Austrian, £20 Red.	15½
3	South Austrian, (Ser. X.)	15½
3	South Italian £20 Obs. (Ser. A to G), Red.	12½
3½	S. W. of Venez. (Barq.), Ltd., 7 p.c. 1st Mt. £100 Debs.	57½
5	Taltal, Ltd., 5 p.c. 1st Ch. Debs., Red.	99
5	Utd. Rwys. Havana, Red.	78
3	Wtrn. of France, £20 Red.	19
6	Wrn. B. Ayres St. Mt. Debs., 1900	111
6	Wrn. B. Ayres, Reg. Cert.	109
5	Do. Mt. Bds.	122
6	Wtrn. of Havna., Ld. Mt. Dbs., Rd.	102
7	Wrn. Ry. San Paulo Red.	101
—	Wrn. Santa Fé, 7 p.c. Red.	40
4/7	Zafra & Huelva, 3 p.c. Red.	3

BANKS.

Div.	Name.	Paid.	Price.
1/9½	Agra, Ltd.	6	3½
4/2½	Anglo-Argentine, Ltd., £9	7	5¼
8½ fls.	Anglo-Austrian	120fl.	14
6/	Anglo-Californian, Ltd., £20 Shares	10	11
4/	Anglo-Egyptian, Ltd., £15	5	6
3/6	Anglo-Foreign Bkg., Ltd.	7	8
2/	Anglo-Italian, Ltd.	5	7½
7/6	Bk. of Africa, Ltd., £18¾	6¼	11
20/	Bk. of Australasia	40	54½
8/	Bk. of Brit. Columbia	20	20
25/	Bk. of Brit. N. America	50	65
7/6	Bk. of Egypt, Ltd., £25	12½	19
5/	Bk. of Mauritius, Ltd.	10	10
18/	Bk. of N. S. Wales	20	38
4 p.c.	Bk. of N. Zland. Gua. Stk.	100	103
6/	Bk. of Roumania, £20 Shs.	6	7½
2/6	Tarapaca & Ldn., Ltd., £10	5	3½
—	Bque. Fse. de l'Afri. du S.	100f	3½
f. 12.50	Bque. Internatle. de Paris	20	24
6/	Brit. Bk. of S. America, Ltd., £20 Shares	10	10½
16/	Capital & Ctics., L., £50	10	39
16/	Chart. of India, &c.	20	30½
9/	City, Ltd., £40 Shares	10	20½
18/	Colonial, £100 Shares	30	24
10/	Delhi and London, Ltd.	25	—
5/	German of London, Ltd.	10	11
25/	Hong-Kong & Shanghai	28½	44½
4/	Imperl. of Persia	6½	3½
10/	Imperl. Ottoman, £20 Shs	10	12½
9/	Intrnatl. of Ldn., Ld., £20	15	10
10/	Ionian, Ltd.	25	15
12/	Lloyds, Ltd., £50 Shs.	8	29½
10/	Ldn. & Brazil. Ltd., £20	10	18
44/	Ldn. & County, Ltd., £80	20	104½
5/	Ldn. & Hanseatic, L., £20	10	11
20/	Ldn. & Midland, L., £60	12½	54
8/9	Ldn. & Provin., Ltd., £10	5	23
39/	Ldn. & Riv. Plate, L., £25	15	52
2/1½	Ldn. & San Fcisco, Ltd.	7	4½
24/	Ldn. & Sth. West., L., £50	20	71
24/	Ldn. & Westmins., L., £100	20	59
3/	Ldn. of Mex. & S. Amer., Ltd., £10 Shs.	6	5½
15/	Ldn. Joint Stk., L., £100	15	34½
9/7	Ldn., Paris & Amer., L. £20	16	26
1/7½	Merchant Bkg., L., £9	4	2½
6/3	Metropn, Ltd., £50 Shs.	5	14
9/	National, Ltd., £50 Shs.	10	20
4/3	Natl. of Mexico, $100 Shs.	$40	12
1/3	National of N. Z., L., £7½	2½	2½
8/	National S. Afric. Rep.	10	14½
18/10½	National Provcl. of Eng., Ltd., £75 Shs.	10½	49
21/7½	Do. do. £60 Shs.	12	55½
6/3	NorthEastn., Ltd., £20 Shs	6	15
19/	Parr's, Ld., £100 Shs.	20	93½
12/6	Prov. of Ireland, L., £100	12½	28½
40/	Stand. of S. Afric., L., £100	25	68
12/6	Union of Australia, L., £75	25	30
4 p.c.	Do. do. Ins. Stk. Dep. 1900	100	103
15/6	Union of Ldn., Ltd., £100	15½	35

BREWERIES AND DISTILLERIES.

Div.	Name.	Paid.	Price.
4½	Albion Prp. 1 Mt. Db. Sk.	100	115
4	All Saints', L., Db. Sk. Rd.	100	99
6	Allsopp, Ltd	100	166
6	Do. Cum. Pref	100	160
4½	Do. Deb. Stk., Red.	100	117
3½	Do. Deb. Stk., Red.	100	102
4½	Alton & Co., L., Db., Rd	100	106
4½	Do. Mt. Bds., 1896	100	105
8/	Arnold, Perrett, Ltd.	10	7
6	Do. Cum. Pref.	10	10
4½	Do. 1 Mt. Db. Stk., Rd.	100	106

Breweries, &c. (*continued*):—

Div.	Name.	Paid.	Price.
5½	Arrol, A., & Sons, L., Cum. Pref. Shs.	10	1[illegible]
4½	Do. 1 Mt. Db. Stk., Rd.	100	10[illegible]
6	Backus, 1 Mt. Db., Red.	100	5[illegible]
4	Barclay, Perk., L., Cu. Pf.	10	1[illegible]
3½	Do. Mt. Db. Stk., Red.	100	11[illegible]
—	Barnsley, Ltd.	10	1[illegible]
6	Do. Cum. Pref.	10	1[illegible]
1/	Barrett's, Ltd	2½	[illegible]
1/3	Do. 5 p.c. Pref.	2½	[illegible]
3/	Bartholomay, Ltd.	10	[illegible]
8	Do. Cum. Pref.	10	[illegible]
6	Do. Deb.	100	10[illegible]
5	Bass, Ratcliff, Ltd., Cum. Pref. Stk. †	100	147
4½	Do. Mt. Db. Stk., Rd.	100	125
4	Bell, John, Ltd., 1 Mt. Deb. Stk., Red.	100	102
2/6	Benskin's, L., Cum. Pref.	5	5
4½	Do. 1 Mt. Db. Stk Red.	100	—
4½	Do. "B" Deb. Sk, Rd.	100	—
7/	Bentley's Yorks., Ltd.	10	11
6	Do. Cum. Pref.	10	12
4½	Do. Mt. Debs., Red.	100	109
4½	Do. do. 1 92, Red.	100	10[illegible]
—	Bieckert's, Ltd.	20	2
5	Do. Debs., Red.	100	57
—	Birmingham., td., 6 p.c. Cum. Pref.	5	2
4½	Do. Mt. Debs., Red.	90	40
5½	Boardman's, Ld., Cm. Pf.	10	9
4½	Do., Perp. 1 Mt. Db. Sk. †	100	102
4½	Brakspear, L., 1 D. Stk. Rd	100	111
4	Brandon's, L., 1 D. Stk. R. †	100	103
17/	Bristol (Georges) Ltd.	10	47
6	Do. Cum. Pref.	10	18
5	Do. Mt. Db. Sk. 1888 Rd.	100	115
—	Bristol United, Ltd.	10	36
6	Do. Cum. Pref.	10	16
4½	Do. Db. Sk. Rd.	100	126
5½	Buckley's, L., C. Pre-prf.	10	11
4½	Do. 1 Mt. Db. Stk. Rd.	100	105
4	Bullard & Sns, L., D. Sk. R.	100	107
6	Bushell, Watk., L., C. Pf.	10	13
4½	Do. 1 Mt. Db. Sk. Rd.	100	112
5	Camden, Ltd., Cum. Pref.	10	11
4½	Do. 1 Mt. Db. Sk. Rd.	100	109
5½	Cameron, Ltd., Cm. Pf.	10	13
4½	Do. Mort Deb. Stk.	100	108
3½	Do. Perp Mt. Db. Sk.	100	100
5	Cam'bell, J'stone, L., C. Pf.	5	5
4½	Do. 4½ p.c. 1 Mt. Db. Sk.	100	105
4	Campbell, Praed, L., Per. 1 Mort. Deb. Stk.	100	106
4	Cannon, L., Mt. Db. Stk.	100	111
4	Do. "B" Deb. Stk.	100	104
5	Castlemaine, L., 1 Mt. Db.	100	94
3½	Charrington, Ltd., Mort. Deb. Stk. Red.	100	109
2/	Cheltnhm. Orig., Ltd.	5	7
6	Do. Cum. Pref.	5	8
4	Do. Debs. Red.	100	107
10/	Chicago, Ltd.	10	3
6	Do. Debs.	100	87
—	Cincinnati, Ltd.	10	
8	Do. Cum. Pref.	10	1
10/	City of Baltimore	10	4
16/	Do. 8 p.c. Cum. Pref	10	8
14/	City of Chicago, Ltd.	10	1
8	Do. Cum. Pref.	10	6
8	City of London, Ltd.	100	205
5	Do. Cum. Pref.	100	140
4	Do. Mt. Deb. Stk., Rd.	100	113
2/6	Colchester, Ltd.	5	4
7	Do. Pref.	5	6
4½	Do. Deb. Stk., Red.	100	110
5	Combe, Ltd., Cum. Pref.	10	14
4	Do. Mt. Db. Stk, Rd.	100	112
3½	Do. Perp. Deb. Stk.	100	107
5	Comm'cial, L., D. Sk., Rd.	100	107
5	Courage, L., Cm. Pref. Shs.	100	13[illegible]
4	Do. Irr. Mt. Deb. Stk.	100	130
3½	Do. Irr. "B" Mt. Db. Sk.	100	106
6	Daniell & Sons, Ltd.	10	7
7	Do. Cum. Pref.	10	12
4½	Do. 1 Mt. Perp. Db. Sk.	100	10[illegible]
4½	Do. "B" Deb. Stk.	100	99
10d.	Dartford, Ltd.	5	5
10d.	Do. Cum. Pref.	5	5
4	Do. 1 Mt. Db. Sk. Rd.	100	101
4	Davenport, Ld., 1 D. Stk. †	100	101
10/	Denver United, Ltd.	10	3
8	Do. Cum. Pref.	10	8
6	Do. Debs.	100	9[illegible]
4½	Deuchar, L., 1 D. Sk., Rd.	100	10[illegible]
8/	Distillers, Ltd.	10	2[illegible]
4½	Do. Mt. Db. Stk., Rd.	100	11[illegible]
—	Dublin Distillers, Ltd.	5	
6/	Do. Cum. Pref.	5	
4½	Do. Irr. Deb. Stk.	100	—
5	Eadie, Ltd., Cum. Pref.	10	1[illegible]
4	Do. Irr. 1 Mt. Db. Sk.	100	10[illegible]
10/	Edinbgh. Utd., Ltd.	10	1[illegible]
6	Do. Cum. Pf.	10	1[illegible]
5	Do. 1 Mt. Dbs. †	100	11[illegible]
4	Eldridge, Pope, L. D. St. R.	100	11[illegible]
3/	Emerald & Phœnix, Ltd.	10	
8	Do. Cum. Pref.	10	
6	Empress Ltd., C. Pf.	10	1[illegible]
4½	Do. Mt. Deb. Stk.	100	10[illegible]
10/	Farnham, Ltd.	10	1[illegible]
6	Do. Cum. Pref.	10	1[illegible]
4	Fenwick, L., 1 D. Sk., Rd.	100	10[illegible]
4	Flower & Sons, Irr. D. Sk.	100	11[illegible]
4	Friary, L., 1 Db. Stk., Rd. †	100	10[illegible]
4	Do. 1 "A" Db. Sk., Rd.	100	1[illegible]
4½	Groves, L., 1 Db. Sk., Rd.	100	11[illegible]
24	Guinness, Ltd.	100	5[illegible]
6	Do. Cum. Prf. Stk.	100	1[illegible]
5	Do. Deb. Stk., Red.	100	12[illegible]
6	Hall's Oxford L., Cm. Pf.	5	
6/	Hancock, Ld., Cm. Pf. Ord.	10	1[illegible]
	Do. Def. Ord.	10	1[illegible]

Breweries, &c. (*continued*) :—

Div.	Name.	Paid.	Price.
6	Hancock, Ld., Cum. Pref.	10	15½
4	Do. 1 Deb. Stk., Rd.	100	113
5	Hoare, Ltd. Cum. Pref.	10	13½
5	Do. "A" Cum. Pref.	10	12½
4	Do. Mt. Deb. Stk., Rd.	100	111
3½	Do. do. do. Rd.	100	104
4/6	Hodgson's, Ltd.	5	9¾
5	Do. 1 Mt. Db., Red	—	120½
4	Do. 2 Mt. Db., 1906	—	102
4½	Hopcraft & N., Ltd., 1 Mt. Deb. Stk., Red.	100	102
5	Huggins, Ltd., Cm. Prf.	10	12½
4½	Do. 1st D. Stk. Rd.	100	112
4½	Do. "B" Db. Stk. Rd.	100	110
8/	Hull, Ltd.	10	17
7	Do. Cum. Pref.	10	15
4½	Ind, Coope, L., D.Sk., Rd.	100	119
4	Do. "B" Mt. Db. Stk. Rd.	100	115
8/	Indianapolis, Ltd.	10	3½
8	Do. Cm. Prf.	10	9
5/	Jones, Frank, Ltd.	10	4
7½	Do. Cum. Pref.	10	8
5	Do. 1st Mort. Debs.	100	94½
4/	J. Kenward & Ct., Ltd.	5	5½
4½	Kingsbury, L., 1 D.Sk., Rd	100	107½
4	Lacon, L., D. Stk., Red.	100	109
4	Do. Irrd. "B" D. Sk.	100	107
4/	Lascelles, Ltd.	5	10½
6	Do. Cum. Pref.	5	7½
5	Leney, Ltd., Cum. Pref.	10	11½
4	Do. 1 Mt. Db. Stk. Rd.	100	104
17/	Lion, Ltd., £25 shares	17	50½
6/	Do. New £10 shares	6	17½
6	Do. Perp. Pref.	20	31
4	Do. B. Mt. Db. Sk. Rd.	100	110
4½	Lloyd & Y., Ltd., 1 Mt. Deb. Stk., Rd.	100	98½
4½	Locke & S., Ltd., Irr. 1st Mt. Deb. Stk.	100	100
4½	Lovibond, Ltd., 1st Mt. Deb. Stk., Rd.	100	102½
8/	Manchester, Ltd.	10	17½
7	Do. Cum. Pref.	10	17
5	Marston, J., L., Cm. Prf.	10	10½
4	Do. 1 Mt. Db. Sk., Rd.	100	101½
9/	Massey's Burnley, Ltd.	10	16
6	Do. Cum. Pref.	10	14½
4½	McCracken, Ltd., 1 Mt. Deb., 1908	100	64
5	McEwan, Ltd., Cm. Pref.	10	15½
5	Meux, Ltd., Cum. Pref.	10	14½
4	Do. Mt. Db. Stk. Red.	100	113
4½	Michell & A., Ltd., 1 Mt. Deb. Stk. Red	100	105
4½	MileEndDist. Db. Sk. Rd.	100	108
14/	Milwaukee & Chic., Ltd.	10	1½
4/	Do. Cum. Pref.	10	6¾
4½	Michell, Toms, L., Db.	50	55
6	Morgan, Ltd., Cum. Pref.	10	14½
10/	Nalder & Coll., Ltd.	10	31
6	Do. Cum. Pref.	10	16
4½	Do. Deb. Red.	100	113
3/	New Beeston, Ltd.	5	4
2/9	Do. Cum. Pref.	5	4½
4	Do. Mt. Deb. Stk. Red.	100	95½
12/	Newcastle, Ltd.	10	20
6	Do. Cum. Pref.	10	14¾
5	Do. 1 Mt. Deb., 1911	100	110½
4	Do. "A" Deb. Stk. Red.	100	107
6/	New England, Ltd	10	5
8	Do. Cum. Pref.	10	9¾
6	Do. Debs. Red	100	102½
4	New London, L., 1 D.Sk.	100	103
7/2	New Westminster, Ltd.	4	10
2/4½	Do. Pref.	4	6½
—	New York, Ltd.	10	1
—	Do. 8 p.c. Cum. Pref.	10	3½
6	Do. 1 Mt. Deb. Red.	100	83½
5	Noakes, Ld., Cum. Pref.	10	12
4	Do. 1 Mt. Db. Stk., Rd.	100	106
4½	Norfolk, L., "A" D.Sk. Rd.	100	106
10/	Northampton, Ld.	10	17
7	Do. Cum. Pref.	10	15½
6	Do. Cum. Pref.	10	13
5	Do. 1 Mt. Per. Db.Sk.	100	127
4	Nth.East., L., 1 D.Sk.Rd.	100	101
4½	N. Worcesters., L. Per. 1 Mort. Deb. Stock	100	94½
6	Nottingham, L., Cm. Prf.	10	11¼
5	Do. 1 Mt. Deb. Stk., Red.	100	115
17/4	Do. "B" do. Red.	50	111½
6/	Ohlsson' Cape, Ld.	5	16½
7	Do. Cum. Pref.	5	8½
4½	Do. 2nd Cum. Pref.	5	5¾
5	Do. Deb. Stk., Red.	100	112
4½	Oldfield, L., 1 Mt. Db. Stk.	100	103
6	Page & Overt., L., Cm. Prf.	10	13½
4½	Do. 1 Mt. Dbs., Red.	100	110
10/	Parker's Burslem, Ltd.	10	25½
6	Do. Cum. Pref.	10	15
4	Do. 1 Mt. Db. Stk., Red.	100	113
4	Persse, Ld., 1 Mt. Db. Rd.	100	93
4	Phipps, L., Irr. 1 Db. Stk.	100	115
5	Plymouth, L., Min. Cu. Pf.	10	13½
4½	Do. Mt. Deb. Stk., Red.	100	104½
4½	Pryor, Reid, L., 1 D.S., R.	100	105½
5	Reid's, Ld., Cm. Pref. Stk.	100	140½
4	Do. Mt. Deb. Stk., Red.	100	113
3½	Do. "B" Mt. Db. Stk., Rd.	100	103
5	Rhondda Val., L., Cu. Pf.	10	11
4½	Do. 1 Mt. Deb. Stk., Rd.	100	109
5	Robinson, Ld., Cum. Pref.	10	11½
4½	Do. 1 Mt. Perp. Db. Stk.	100	112
4/	Rochdale, Ltd.	10	5½
4½	Do. 1 Mt. Deb. Stk.	100	96½
7	Royal, Brentford, Ltd.	10	19
	Do. Cum. Pref.	10	14
4½	Do. 1 Mt. Dbs. Red	100	112
6/	St. Louis, Ltd.	10	4
8	Do. Cum. Pref.	10	8¾
14/	St. Pauli, Ltd.	10	10
7	Do. Cum. Pref.	10	11½
4½	Salt (T.), L., 1 Db. Sk. Rd.	100	111
4½	Do "B" Db. Stk. Red.	100	108

Breweries, &c. (*continued*) :—

Div.	Name.	Paid.	Price.
6/7	San Francisco, Ltd.	10	½
8/	Do. 8 p.c. Cum. Pref.	10	½
4½	Savill Brs., L., D. Sk. Rd.	100	116
4½	Scarboro., Ltd., 1 Db. Stk.	100	104
4	Shaw (Hy.), Ltd., 1 Mt. Db. Stk., Red.	100	104
22/	Showell's, Ltd.	10	32½
7	Do. Cum. Pref.	10	17½
3/	Do. Gua. Shs.	5	7½
4½	Do. Mt. Db. Stk., Red.	100	—
4	Simonds, L., 1 D. Sk., Rd.	100	111
5½	Simson & McP., L., Cu. Pf.	10	9½
4½	Do. 1 Mt. Deb. Stk.	100	100
12/	Smith, Garrett, L., £20 Shs	10	15½
5	Do. Cum. Pref.	20	26
4½	Do. Mt. Db. Stk., Red.	100	—
5	Smith's, Tadcster, L., CPf	10	11½
4½	Do. Deb. Stk., Red.	100	112
4	Do. Deb. Stk., Red.	100	108
4½	Star, L., 1 M. Db. Stk., Rd.	100	104
4	Steward & P., L., 1 D. Sk.	100	113
9/	Strettons Derby, Ltd.	10	13
6	Do. Cum. Pref.	10	13
4	Do. Irr. 1 Mt. Db. Stk.	100	104½
4½	Strong, Romsey, L., 1 D. S.	100	114
5	Stroud, L., Db. Sk., Rd.	100	111½
4½	Tadcaster To'er, L., D.Sk.	100	112
8/	Tamplin, Ltd	10	22
6	Do. Cum. Pref.	100	15
4	Do. "A" Db. Sk., Rd.	10	107
6	Thorne, Ltd., Cum. Pref.	10	14½
4	Do. Deb. Stk., Red.	100	104½
16/	Threlfall, Ltd.	10	49
6	Do. Cum. Pref.	10	17
5	Do. 1 Mt. Dbs., Red.	100	116
4	Tollemache, L., D. Sk. Rd.	100	105
4	Truman, Hanb., D. Sk., R.	100	110
3	Do. "B" Mt. Db. Sk., Rd.	100	95
10/	United States, Ltd.	10	10
8	Do. Cum. Pref.	10	12½
6	Do. 1 Mt. Deb	100	107½
6/	Walker & H., Ld., Cm. Prf.	10	11½
4½	Do. 1 Mt. Deb. Stk., Red.	100	107
5	Walker, Peter, Ld. Cm. Prf.	10	14
4	Do. 1 Mt. Dbs. Red.	100	111
4	Wallingford, L., D.Sk. Rd.	100	107
6	Watney, Ld., Cm. Prf. Sk.	100	170
5	Do. Mt. Db. Sk., Rd.	100	117½
4½	Do. "B" Mt. Db. Sk., Rd.	100	111
5	Watney, D., Ld., Cm. Prf.	10	12½
4½	Do. 1 Mt. Db. Stk.	100	108
5	Wenlock Ltd., Pref.	10	12½
4	Do. 1 Mt. Db. Sk., Rd.	100	107
5	West Cheshire, L., Cu. Pf.	10	10½
4	Do. Irred. 1 Mt. Db. Sk.	100	100
4½	Whitbread, L., Cu. Pf. Sh.	100	124½
4	Do. Db. Stk., Red.	100	112
3½	Do. "B" Db. Stk., Rd.	100	103
9/	Wolverhmpton & D. Ld.	10	15½
6	Do. Cum. Pref.	10	13
4½	Do. 1 Mt. Dbs., Red.	100	108
5½	Worthington, Ld., Cm. Prf.	10	15½
5½	Do. Cum. "B" Pref.	10	13½
4½	Do. Mt. Db. Sk., Rd.	100	113
3½	Do. Irr. "B" Db. Stk.	100	103
10/	Yates's Castle, Ltd.	10	12½
5	Do. Cum. Pref.	10	11
5	Younger W., L., Cu. Pf. Sh.	100	138½

CANALS AND DOCKS.

Last Div.	Name.	Paid.	Price.
4	Birmingham Canal	100	146
—	E. & W. India Dock	100	22½
4	Do. Deb. Stk.	100	112
85/	Do. Def. Deb. Stk.	100	90
3½	Do. 1st Mt. Certs.	100	111
4	Do. Mt. Bds. (1885)	—	101
40/	G. Junction Ord. Shs.	100	151½
6/	Do. do. Pref.	10	19
4½	King's Lynn Per. Db. Stk.	100	120½
2½	Leeds & Lpool Canal	100	68
2½	Lndn & St. Kath. Dks.	100	57½
4½	Do. Pref.	100	138½
4½	Do. Pref., 1878	100	134½
4½	Do. Pref., 1882	100	130
4	Do. Deb. Stk.	100	134
—	Mchester Ship C. 5 p.c. Pf.	10	1½
3½	Do. 1st Perp. Mt. Deb.	100	98
—	Milford Dks. Db. Stk. "A"	100	20
2	Millwall Dk.	100	61
5	Do. Perp. Pref.	100	145½
4½	Do. Pref.	100	108½
5	Do. New Per. Prf., 1887	100	128½
5	Do. Per. Deb. Stk.	100	152½
4/	Newhaven Har.	10	14½
2	N. Metropolitan	100	65
5	Sharpness Nw. Pf. "A" Sk.	100	144½
4	Do. Deb. Stk.	100	120½
4	Sheffield & S. Yorks Nav. 4½ p.c. Pref. Stk.	100	117½
36.432	Suez Canal	20	135½
5	Surrey Comcl. Dok., Ord.	100	150½
5	Do. Min. 4 p.c. Pref. "A"	110	152½
5	Do. Pref. "B"	100	150½
5	Do. do. "C"	100	150
5	Do. do. "D"	100	145½
4½	Do. Deb. Stk.	100	154½

COMMERCIAL, INDUSTRIAL, &c.

Last Div.	Name.	Paid.	Price.
5	Accles, L., 1 Mt. Db., Red.	100	87½
5/	Aërated Bread, Ltd.	1	13
2	African Gold Recovery, L.	1	⅜
2/	Aluminium, L., "A" Shs.	1	2½
4½	Do. 1 Mt. Db. Stk., Red.	100	99
5½	Amelia Nitr., L., 1 Mort. Deb., Red.	100	84½
7/	Anglo-Chil. Nitrate, Ltd., Cum. Pref.	10	7½
4½	Do. Cons. Mt. Bds., Red.	100	82½
4½	Anglo-Russian Cotton, Ld., 1 Charge Debs., Red.	100	99
3/9	Angus (G., & Co., L.), £10	7½	17
6/	Apollinaris, Ltd.	10	13
5/	Do. 5 p.c. Cum. Pref.	10	11½
4	Do. Irred. Deb. Stock	100	108
6/	Appleton, French, & S., L.	5	¾
3/	Argentine Meat Pres., L., 7 p.c. Pref.	10	2½
5	Argentine Refinry, Db. Rd.	100	98
2/2	Armstrong, Whitw., Ltd.	1	3
4	Do. Cum. Pref.	5	6½
5	Artisans', Labr. Dwllgs., L.	100	129½
4½	Do. Non-Cm. Prf., 1879	100	132½
4½	Do. do. 1884	100	132½
—	Asbestos & Asbestic, Ltd.	10	9
2/7½	Ashley-grdns., L., C. Prf.	5	6½
4½	Do. 1 Mt. Deb. Stk.	100	115½
5/	Assam Rly. & Trdng., L., 8 p.c. Cum. Pref. "A"	10	15
—	Do. Deferrd. "B" Shs.	1	4½
—	Do. do. (iss. f. pd)	1	3½
8/	Do. Cum. Pre-Prf. "A"	10	15
6/	Do. New Pref.	10	11½
5	Do. Debs., Red.	100	107
5	Do. Red. Mort. Debs.	100	109
6	Aust'lian Pastrl, L., Cu. Pf.	10	7½
6d.	Aylesbury Dairy, Ltd.	1	1½
4	Do. 4 p.c. Mt. Dbs.	100	104½
20/	Babcock & Wilcox, Ltd.	10	32
6	Do. 6 p.c. Cm. Prf.	10	16½
8	Baker (Chs.), L., Cm. Pf.	5	8¾
8	Do. "B," Cm. Pref.	5	7¾
8d.	Barker (John), Ltd.	1	2¾
5½	Do. Cum. Pref.	5	7½
4½	Do. Irred. 1 Mt. Db. Stk.	100	133
—	Barnagore Jute, Ltd.	5	3½
5	Do. Cum. Pref.	5	4½
7½d.	Belgravia Dairy, Ltd.	1	1½
5/	Bell (R.) & Co., Ltd.	5	3½
1/	Bell's Asbestos, Ltd.	1	¾
5	Do. Mt. Db. Bds., Rd.	100	103
10/	Bengal Mills, Ltd.	10	11½
6/	Do. 5 p.c. Cum. Prf.	10	10½
2/5	Benson (J.W.) L., Cm. Pf.	10	10½
12/4	Do. Perp. Mt. Db. Stk.	100	103½
6	Bergvik, L., 6 p.c. Cm. Pf.	10	12½
10/	Do. Dfd.	10	9
4½	Do. 1 Dbs., Red.	100	103½
5/	Birm'ham Vinegar, Ltd.	5	9½
5	Do. Cum. Pref.	5	5½
4½	Do. 1 Mt. Db. Stk., Rd.	100	105
5	Boake (A.) L., 5 p.c. Cu. Pf.	10	10½
2/6	Bodega, Ltd.	5	8
4½	Do. Mt. Deb. Stk., Rd.	100	111
8/	Bottomley & Brs., Ltd.	10	6½
6/	Do. 6 p.c. Pt.	10	9½
8½d.	Bovril, Ltd.	1	1 1/16
—	Do. Def.	1	⅜
6¾d.	Do. Cum. Pref.	1	1½
4½	Do. Deb. Stk.	100	103
6/4½	Bradbury, Gretrex., Ltd., £10 share	8	14
5/	Do. 5 p.c. Cum. Pref.	10	13½
5/	Brewers' Sugar, L., 5 p.c. Cum. Pref.	10	10½
2/6	Brighton Grd. Hotel, Ld.	5	3½
4	Do. Mt. Db. Stk., Red.	100	102½
5	Bristol Hotel & Palm. Co., Ltd. 1st Mt. Red. Deb.	100	107
9½d.	British & Bengton's. Tea Tr. Asc., Ltd.	1	1½
5	Do. Cum. Prf.	5	5½
—	British Deli & Lgkat. Tobacco, Ltd.	1	½
—	Do. Cum. Prf.	1	¾
—	British Tea Table, Ltd.	1	2½
5½	Do. Cum. Pref.	1	1½
2/6	Brooke, Ben., & Co., Ltd., Cum. Pref.	5	5⅝
7/6	Brooke, Bond & Co., Ltd.	5	20½
6	Brown Brs., L., Cum. Pref.	5	6
6/	Browne & Eagle, Ltd.	10	14
5	Do. Cum. Pref.	10	13
4	Do. Mrt. Db. Sk., Red.	100	109
20/	Brunner, Mond, & Co., Lt.	10	41
7/	Do. £10 shares	3½	16½
7	Do. Cum. Pref.	10	18
7	Do. £10 shares	5	8½
7/6	Bryant & May, Ltd.	5	20
2/	Bucknall, H., & Sons, Lt.	5	8
6	Do. Cum Pref.	5	8
4/	Burke, E. & J., Ltd.	5	7½
6	Do. Cum. Pref.	5	7½
6	Do. Irred. Deb. Stk.	100	155
1/	Burlington Htls. Co., Ltd	1	1½
5	Do. Cum. Pref.	1	1½
4	Do. Perp. Deb. Stk.	100	104½
2/4	Bush, W. J., & Co., Ltd., Cum. Pref.	5	5¾
36/8	Do. 1 Deb. Stk., Red.	100	104
5½	Callard, Stewart, & Watt, Ltd., Cum. Pref.	1	1½
4/	Callender's Cable L., Shs.	5	8
4½	Do. 1 Deb. Stk., Red.	100	109½
—	Campbell, R., & Sons, Lt.	3	2½
6	Cantareira Water, Bd., Rd	100	99½
5	Do. (2nd issue)	100	92
4	Cartavio Sugar, Ltd., 6 p.c. 1st Debs., Red.	90	80
4/6	Cassell & Co., Ltd., £10	9	18
5	Causton, Sir J., & Sons, Ltd., Cum. Pref.	10	13½

Commercial, &c. (*continued*) :—

Last Div.	Name.	Paid.	Price.
4	Cent. Prod. Mkt. of B.A. 1st Mt. Str. Debs.	100	77½
4	Chappell & Co., Ltd., Mt. Deb. Stk. Red	100	104
6/	Chicago & N.W. Gran. 8 p.c. Cum. Pref.	10	2½
—	Chicago Packing & Prov.	10	6
8	Do. Cum. Pref.	10	9
6/	City Offices, Ltd	36½	13
3½	Do. Mt. Deb. Stk.	100	108½
7/2½	Cy. London Real Prop., Ltd., £25 shs.	12	19
4/6	Do. £12½ shs.	7½	13½
3½	Do. Deb. Stk. Red.	100	108½
3½	Do. Deb. Stk. Red.	100	105½
3	Do.	100	101½
4/	Cy. of Santos Imprvts., Ltd., 7 p.c. Pref.	10	8½
20/	Clay, Bock, & Co., Ltd.	10	8
8	Do. Cum. Pref.	10	11
6	Do. Mort. Deb.	100	106½
20/	Coats, J. & P., Ltd.	10	62½
6	Do. Cum. Pref.	10	18
4½	Do. Deb. Stk. Red.	100	111½
9½d.	Coburg Hotel, Ltd	1	1½
4	Do. Deb. Stk. Red.	100	102
6	Colonial Consign & Dis., Ltd., Cum. Pref.	5	4½
4½	Do. 1st Mort. Debs.	100	97½
—	Colorado Nitrate, Ltd.	5	½
4/	Co. Gén. des Asphtes. de F., Ltd.	6	6½
5	Do. Non-Cm. Prf.	—	5½
5	Cook, J. W., & Co., Ltd., Cum. Pref.	5	5¾
5	Cook, T., & Son, Egypt, Ltd., 1st Mt. Deb. Red.	100	110½
—	Cork Co., Ltd., 6 p.c. Cum. Pref.	5	2½
5	Cory, W., & Sn, L., Cu. Pf.	5	6
4	Do. 1st Deb. Stk. Red.	100	109
8½d.	Crisp & Co., Ltd	1	1½
5½	Do. Cum. Pref.	1	1½
—	Crompton & Co., Ltd., 7 p.c. Cum. Pref.	5	2½
5	Do. 1st Mt. Reg. Deb.	—	88½
4/6	Crossley, J., & Sons, Ltd.	5	8½
5	Do. Cum. Pref.	5	6½
—	Crystal Pal. Ord. "A" Stk.	100	9½
—	Do. "B" Red. Stk	100	2
6	Do. 6 p.c. 1st 1887 Deb. Stk. Red.	100	116½
—	Do. 6 p.c. 2nd 1887 Deb. Stk. Red.	100	42½
—	Do. 6 p.c. 3rd 1887 Deb. Stk. Red.	100	16½
3	Do. 3 p.c. 1st 1895 Deb. Stk.	100	95½
—	Daimler Motor, Ltd.	10	5
4/	Dalgety & Co., £20 Shs.	5	5½
4½	Do. Deb. Stk.	100	122
4	Do.	100	113
3/10	De Keyser's Ryl. Htl., L.	10	12½
5	Do. Cum. Pref.	10	11½
4	Do. Deb. Stk., Red.	100	109
6	Denny, H., & Sons, Ltd., Cum. Pref.	10	15
5/3	Devas, Routledge & Co., L.	7	8½
5	Dickinson, J., & Co., L., Cum. Pref. Stk.	100	125
4½	Domin. Cottn. Mls., Ltd. Mt. Stg. Dbs.	100	93
6/	Dorman, Long & Co., L.	5	4½
—	Eastmans, Ltd	10	2¾
12/	Do. 8 p.c. Cum. Pref.	10	10½
2/6	E. C. Powder, Ltd	3	5½
1/9½	Edison & Swn Utd. Elec. Ltd., "A" £5 Shs.	3	2¾
2/9½	Do. fully-paid	5	5
4½	Ekman Pulp & Ppr. Co., Ltd., Mt. Deb., Red.	100	95
1/1½	Electric Construc., Ltd.	2	2¾
7	Do. Cum. Pref.	2	3½
10/	Eley Bros., Ltd.	10	40
—	Elmore's Cop. Deptg., L.	1	⅛
—	Elmore's Wire Mnfg., L.	2	⅛
—	Elysée Pal. Hotel Co., L.	5/	½
5 p.c.	Do. 5 p.c. £100 Db., Rd.	70	70
8½d.	Evans, Ben., & Co., Ltd.	1	1
5	Do. 1 Mt. Db. Sk., Rd.	100	104
8½d.	Evans, D. H., & Co., L.	1	2½
6	Do. Cum. Pref.	1	1½
4½	Do. 1 Mt. Db. Sk., Rd.	100	110
2/1	*Evening News*, L., 5 p.c. Cum. Pref.	5	5¾
5/3	Evered & Co., L., £10 Sh.	7	13½
7/6	Do.	10	19½
4	Fairbairn Pastoral Co., Aust., L., 1 Mt. Db., Rd.	100	102
6	Fairfield Shipbldg., Ltd., Cum. Pref.	10	9½
4½	Do. Mort. Deb. Stk.	100	107½
—	Farmer & Co., Ld., 6 p.c. Cum. Pref.	10	13¾
10	Field, J. C. & J., Ltd.	10	10
14/	Do. 7 p.c. Cum. Pref.	10	14
9d.	Fordham, W.B., & Sns, Ld.	1	2
5/6	Fore-st. Warehouse, Ltd.	11	9¾
4	Do. Regd. Debs., Rd.	100	102½
2/6	Foster, M. B. & Sons, Ltd.	4	5½
5	Do. Pref.	10	11½
7/	Foster, Porter, & Co., L.	10½	17
4	Fowler, J., & Co. (Leeds), Ltd., 1 Mt. Deb., Red.	100	100½
3/	Fraser & Chalmers, Ltd	3	1½
4½	Free, Rodwell & Co., Ltd., Deb Stk.	100	104½
6½d.	Furness, T., & Co., Ltd., 5½ p.c. Cum. Pref.	1	1
4½	Gartside & Co. (of Manchstr), L., 1 Mt. Db. Sk.	100	110
5	Genl. Hydraul. Power, L.	100	260

Commercial, &c. (*continued*):—

Last Div.	Name.	Paid.	Price.
2/	Gillman & Spencer, Ltd.	5	2¼
6	Do. Pref.	5	4¾
5	Do. Mort. Debs.	50	51
4	Goldsbro., Mort & Co., L., "A" Deb. Stk., Red.	100	72½
—	Do. 3 p.c. "B" Inc. Deb. Stk., Red	100	17
12/	Gordon Hotels, Ltd.	10	20¼
5½	Do. Cum. Pref.	10	14¾
4½	Do. Perp. Deb. Stk.	100	136½
4	Do. do.	100	124½
—	Greenwich Inld. Linoleum Co., Ltd.	1	⅛
7	Greenwood & Batley, Ltd., Cum. Pref.	10	10
7½d.	Hagemann & Co., Ltd., 6 p.c. Cum. Pref.	1	1½
—	Hammond, Ltd.	10	⅛
—	Do. 8 p.c. Cum. Pref.	10	2
—	Do. 6 p.c. Cum. Inc. Stk. Red.	100	52½
4	Hampton & Sons, Ltd., 4 p.c. 1 Mt. Db. St. Red.	100	104
	Hans Crescent Htl., L., 6 p.c. Cum. Pref.	5	3½
4	Do. 1 Mt. Deb. Stk.	100	85
5	Harmsworth, Ld., Cm. Pf.	1	1⅛
4/	Harrison, Barber, Ltd.	5	4½
1/	Harrod's Stores, Ltd.	1	5
2/6	Do. Cum. Pref.	5	7½
5½	Hawaiian Comcl. & Sug. 1 Mt. Debs.	100	94½
5	Hazell, Watson, Ld., Cm. Pref.	10	12
6/	Henley's Teleg., Ltd.	10	21½
7	Do. Pref. Shs.	10	19
4½	Do. Mt. Db. Stk., Rd.	100	112½
6	Henry, Ltd.	10	12½
5	Do. Cum. Pref.	10	13½
4½	Do. Mt. Debs., Red.	50	53
6	Hepworth, Ld., Cm. Prf.	10	11½
5/	Herrmann, Ltd.	5	4½
—	Hildesheimer, Ltd.	3	1½
9½d.	Holbrn. & Frasca, Ltd.	1	2
5	Do. Cum. Pref.	10	11¾
4	Do. Deb. Stk.	100	113
6	Home & Col. Stres, Ltd., Cum. Pref.	5	7½
6	Hood & M.'s Stres., Ltd., Cum. Pref.	1	¾
—	Hook, C. T., Ltd.	10	4
7/2	Hornsby, Ltd., £10 Shs.	8	3
5/6	Do. 6 p.c. Cm. Pf. Sk.	100	90
—	Hotchks. Ordn., Ltd.	10	¾
—	Do. 7 p.c. Cm. Prf.	10	4½
5	Do. 1 Mt. Dbs., Rd.	100	95½
6	Htl. Cecil, Ld., Cm. Prf.	5	4¾
4	Do. 1 Mt. D. Sk., R.	100	105½
8/	Howard & Bulgh, Ltd.	10	35
6	Do. Pref.	10	16
4	Do. Deb. Stk., Red.	100	107
4/	Howell, J., Ltd., £5 Shs.	4	9¾
—	Howell & Js., Ld., £3½ Shs.	3	1
1/6	Humber, Ltd.	1	¾
6	Do. Cum. Pref.	1	1¼
2/6	Hunter, Wilts., Ltd.	5	7
2/7	Hyam Clthg., Ltd., 5 p.c. Cum. Pref.	5	5½
10/	Impl. Russn. Cotton, L.	5	5½
5	Impd. Industl. Dwgs., Ld.	100	130½
6d.	Do. Defrd.	1	1½
£1	Impd. Wood Pave., Ltd.	10	16
5/	Ind. Rubber, Gutta Per. Telegraph Works, Ltd.	10	23½
4	Do. 1 Mt. Debs., Red.	100	106
6	Intern. Tea, Cum. Pref.	5	6½
7½d.	Jays, Ltd.	1	1½
5½	Do. Cum. Pref.	5	6¾
8½d.	Jones & Higgins, Ltd.	1	2½
4½	Do. 1 Mt. Db. Sk., Rd.	100	113
5/	Kelly's Directory, Ltd., 5 p.c. Cum. Pref.	10	12¾
—	Do. Mort. Db. Sk., Rd.	100	106
—	Kent Coal Explrtn. Ltd.	1	⅛
5½d.	King, Howmann, Ltd.	1	1½
4/	Kinloch & Co., Ltd.	5	8½
6	Do. Pref.	5	7
5	Lady's Pictorial Pub., Ltd., Cum. Pref.	5	5
—	La Guaira Harb., Ltd., 7 p.c. Deb. Stk.	100	—
—	Do. 2 Mt. 7 p.c. Deb. Bds., Red.	100	—
4/	Lagunas Nitrate, Ltd.	5	2¾
2/	Lagunas Syn., Ltd.	5	1½
5	Do. 1 Mt. Debs., Red.	100	80½
—	L. Copais Ld., 1 Mt. 6 p.c. Debs., Red.	100	35½
3/	Lautaro Nitrate, Ltd.	5	4
5	Do. 1 Mt. Debs., Red.	—	98½
9/	Lawes Chem. L., £10 shs.	9	5½
14/	Do. N. Cm. Min. Pref.	10	13
—	Leeds Forge, 7 p.c. Cm. Pf.	5	2¾
5	Do. 1 Mt. Debs., Red.	50	44½
5	Lever Bros., L., Cm. Pf.	10	13
6	Liberty, L., 6 p.c. Cm. Pf.	10	15
60/	Liebig's, Ltd.	20	76
5	Lilley & Sk., L., Cm. Pf.	5	5½
3/	Linoleum Manftg., Ltd.	5	19
3/	Linotype, Ltd., Pref.	5	5¾
4/	Do. Def.	5	8½
—	Lister & Co., Ltd.	10	5
5	Do. Cum. Pref.	10	8½
5/	Liverpool. Nitrate	5	6½
—	Liverpool. Warehsg., Ltd.	10	3½
5½	Do. Cum. Pref.	10	8½
4	Do. 1 Mt. Db. Stk., Rd.	100	105½
5½	Lockharts, Ltd., Cm. Pf.	1	1¼
4/6	Ldn. & Til., Lightrage £10	9	5¾
6/	Ldn. Comcl. Sale Rms., Ltd.	10	18
3	Do. 1 Mt. Deb. Stk., Red.	100	104
—	London Nitrate, Ltd.	5	2

Commercial, &c. (*continued*):—

Last Div.	Name.	Paid.	Price.
4/	London Nitrate, Ld. 8 p.c. Cm. Min. Pf.	5	3½
3/	London Pavilion, Ltd.	5	8
1/6	London Produce Clg. Ho., Ltd., £10 Shares	9½	3¾
6/	London Stereos., Ltd.	5	3
6d.	Ldn. Un. Laun. L. Cm. Pf.	1	¾
8½d.	Louise, Ltd.	1	¾
5½	Do. Cum. Pref.	1	¾
5/	Lovell & Christmas, Ltd.	5	12¼
6	Do. Cum. Pref.	5	7½
4	Do. Mt. Deb. Stk., Red.	100	107
1/3	Lyons, Ltd.	1	2½
4½	Do. 1 Mt. Dsb., Stk., Rd.	100	106½
10/	Machinery Trust, Ltd.	5	15
6	MacLellan, Ltd., Min. Cum. Pref.	10	7½
5	Do. 1 Mt. Debs., 1900	100	98½
—	McEwan, J. & Co, Ltd.	10	1½
6	Do. Mt. Debs., Red.	100	89½
8	McNamara, L., Cm. Pref.	10	9
7½d.	Maison Virot, Ltd.	1	1½
2/7	Do. 6 p.c. Cum. Pref.	5	4½
4/	Manbré Sacc., L., Cm. Pf.	10	12
15/	Mangan Brze., L., £10 Sbs.	6	15½
3/	Mason & Mason, Ltd.	5	3½
6	Do. Cum. Pref.	5	5¾
—	Maynards, Ltd.	1	¾
6	Do. Cum. Pref.	1	¾
9½d.	Mazawattee Tea, Ltd.	1	1½
5	Do. Cum. Pref.	5	5½
6	Mellin's Food Cum. Pref.	5	7
4½	Met. Ascn. Imp. Dwlgs. L.	100	109
3½	Do. 1 Mt. Deb. Stk.	100	97
5	Metro. Indus. Dwlgs., Ltd.	5	5
4	Do. do. Cum. Pref.	5	5½
5	Metro. Prop., L., Cm. Pf.	5	6½
4½	Do. 1st Mt. Debs. Stk.	100	110½
6	Mexican Cotton 1 Mt Db	100	97½
4½	Mid. Class Dwlgs., L., Db.	100	120½
1/	Millars' Karri, Ltd.	1	2½
6	Do. Cum. Pref.	1	1¼
5/	Milner's Safe, Ltd.	10	19½
10/	Moir & Son, Ltd., Pref.	5	9
6	Morgan Cruc., L., Cm. Pf.	10	15
2/	Morris, B., Ltd.	3½	3¾
—	Murray L. 5½ p.c. C. Pf.	5	5¾
—	Do. 4½ 1 Mt. Db. Sk. Rd.	100	103
2/6	Natnl. Dwlgs., L., 5 p.c. Pf.	5	1
1/7½	Nat. Safe Dep., Ltd.	4	3½
6	Do. Cum. Pref.	1	1½
—	Native Guano, Ltd.	5	¾
5/	Nelson Bros., Ltd.	10	2½
5	Do. Deb. Stk., Red.	100	80½
4/	Neuchtel Asph., Ltd.	10	11
—	New Central Borneo, Ld.	1	—
—	New Darvel Tob., Ltd.	18/	1½
2/4½	New Explosives, Ltd.	3	2
5/3¾	New Gd. Htl., Bham, L.	5	4
5½	Do. Pref.	5	4½
4	Do. 1 Mt. Db. Stk., Rd.	100	98½
—	New Julia Nitrate, Ltd.	10/	⅛
—	New Ldn. Borneo Tob., L.	16/	¾
1/6	New Premier Cycle, Ltd.	1	⅛
6	Do. 6 p.c. Cum. Pref.	1	¾
4½	Do. 4½ p.c. 1 Mt. Db. Rd	100	—
1/	New Tamargl. Nitr., Ltd	1	⅛
1/2½	Do. 8 p.c. Cum. Pref.	1	⅜
6	Do. 6 p.c. 1 Mt. Dbs. Rd.	100	68
3⅞d.	Newnes, G., L., Cm. Prf.	1	1½
1/3	Nitr. Provision, Ltd.	2½	¾
24/	Nobel-Dynam., Ltd.	10	17¾
—	North Brazn. Sugar, Ltd.	1	¾
10/	Oakey, Ltd.	10	30
6	Do. Cum. Pref.	10	16
4/	Paccha Jarp. Nitr., Ltd.	5	½
5	Pac. Borax, L., 1 Db. Rd.	100	110
—	Palace Hotel, Ltd.	10	6
5½	Do. Cum. Pref.	10	9
4	Do. 1 Mt. Deb. Stk.	100	106
2/6	Palmer, Ltd.	5	1½
6	Do. Cum. Pref.	5	3½
9⅛d.	Paquin, Ltd.	1	1
6	Do. Cum. Pref.	5	4¾
5½	Parnall, Ltd., Cum. Pref.	1	¾
3/	Pawsons, Ltd., £10 Shs.	6	6½
4	Do. Mt. Debs., Red.	100	107
6	Pearks, G. & T., Ltd., 6 p.c. Cum. Pref.	1	¾
1/2½	Pears, Ltd.	1	1¾
6	Do. Cum. Pref.	10	14½
5	Do. Deb. Stk.	100	129
5½	Pearson, C. A., L., Cu. Pf.	5	5
4/	Peebles, Ltd.	5	7½
5	Do. Cum. Pref.	5	6½
4½	Do. Mt. Deb. Stk. Red.	100	112
5½	Peek Bros., Ltd., 1 Cum. Pref., Nos. 1-60,000	5	6½
3½	Do. 3½ p.c. 1 Db. Stk.	100	103½
7½d.	Pegamoid, Ltd.	1	⅝
4/	Phospho-Guano, Ltd.	5	2¾
4/	Pillsbury-W. Fl. Mills, L.	10	2
16/	Do. 8 p.c. Cum. Pref.	10	6¾
6	Do. 1 Mort. Debs.	100	95½
7½d.	Plummer, Ltd.	1	1½
5	Do. Cum. Pref.	5	5½
15/	Price's Candle, Ltd.	16	40
6	Priest Marians, L., Cm. Pf.	1	1⅛
6	Pryce Jones, Ld., Cm. Pf.	5	7½
5	Do. Deb. Stk.	100	120½
10.8d.	Pullman, Ltd.	1	1½
6d.	Do. Cum. Pref.	1	1½
11⅛d.	Raleigh Cycle, Ltd.	1	⅞
6	Do. Cum. Pref.	1	¾
5	Recife Drnge. Ld. 1 Mt. Debs., R	100	19
6	Redfern, Ltd. Cum. Prf.	10	14
5	Ridgways, Ltd, Cu. Pf.	5	5¾
5/	R. Janeiro Cy. Imps., Ld.	25	9½
5	Do. Debs.	100	84½
5	Do. 1882-1893	100	83½
11/	R. Jan Fl. Mills, Ltd.	7	7
5	Do. 1 Mt. Debs., Rd.	100	94

Commercial, &c. (*continued*):—

Last Div.	Name.	Paid.	Price.
—	Riv. Plate Meat, Ltd.	5	3½
—	Do. Pref.	5	5
8½d.	Roberts, J. R., Ltd.	1	1½
5	Do. 1 Mt. Db. Sk., Rd.	100	112
8½d.	Roberts, T. R., Ltd.	1	2¾
5	Do. Cum. Pref.	1	1¾
3/	Rosario Nit., Ltd.	5	3½
5	Do. Debs., Red.	100	103
5	Do. Hunra. Debs.	—	101½
1/	Rover Cycle, Ltd.	1	¾
6/	Ryl. Aquarium, Ltd.	5	4½
6	Do. Pref.	5	6
5	Ryl. Htl., Edin., Cm. Pf.	1	1½
1/2½	Ryl. Niger, Ltd., £10 Sh.	2	2½
6/	Do.	10	14½
3/	Ruston, Proctor, Ltd.	10	11
4½	Do. 1 Mort. Debs.	100	104
6/	Sadler, Ltd.	11	7
—	Sal. Carmen Nit., Ltd.	5	4½
9d.	Salmon & Gluck, Ltd.	1	1¼
2/	Salt Union, Ltd.	10	1½
14/	Do. 7 p.c. Pref.	10	8½
4½	Do. Deb. Stk.	100	108½
4½	Do. "B" Deb. Sk., Rd.	100	104½
—	San Donato Nit., Ltd.	5	¾
2/6	San Jorge Nit., Ltd.	5	3½
—	San Pablo Nit., Ltd.	5	¾
2/	San Sebastn. Nit., Ltd.	5	¾
1/	Sanitas, Ltd	1	2¾
—	Sa. Elena Nit., Ltd.	5	¾
—	Sa. Rita Nit., Ltd.	5	2
10/	Savoy Hotel, Ltd.	10	19
7	Do. Pref.	10	16
4	Do. 1 Mt. Deb. Stk.	100	112½
5	Do. Debs., Red	100	102½
5	Do. & Ldn. For. Htl., Ltd., 5 p.c. Debs. Red.	100	99
1½d.	Schweppes, Ltd.	1	1⅛
—	Do. Def.	1	1¼
5	Do. Cum. Pref.	1	1⅛
4	Do. Deb. Stk.	100	106
1/	Singer Cyc., Ltd.	1	⅞
5½	Do Cum. Pref.	1	⅞
—	Smokeless Pwdr., Ltd.	1	⅛
5½d.	S. Eng. Dairies, Ltd., 6 p.c. Cum. Pref.	1	1½
—	Sowler Thos. L.	1	1
—	Do. 5½ Cm. Pf.	5	5¾
3/6	Spencer, Turner, & Co. Ltd	5	6½
5	Do. Cum. Pref.	5	6½
5	Spicer, Ld., 5 p.c. Dbs. Rd.	100	66
4/	Spiers & Pond, Ltd.	10	21
5	Do. 1 Mt. Debs., Red.	100	116½
5	Do. "A" Db. Stk., Rd.	100	110
5	Do. "B" 1 Db. Stk., Rd.	100	110
4	Do. Fd. "C" 1 Db. S., R.	100	103
5/	Spratt's, Ltd	5	13½
4	Do. Debs., 1914	—	105
5	Steiner Ld., Cm. Pf.	10	11¾
4	Do. 1 Mt. Db. Sk. Rd.	100	106
7/	Stewart & Clydesdale, L.	10	13½
6	Do. Cum. Pref.	10	15
—	Swan & Edgar, L.	1	1¼
1/3	Sweetmeat Automatic, L.	1	¼
2/9	Teetgen, Ltd., Cum. Pref.	5	5½
12/	Teleg. Construction., Ld.	12	40½
5	Do. Db. Bds., Rd., 1899	100	103½
3/0½	Tilling, Ld. 5½ p.c. Cm. Prf.	5	6
4	Do. 4 p.c. 1 Dbs., Rd.	—	103
8½d.	Tower Tea, Ltd.	1	1¾
5	Do. Cum. Pref.	5	5½
5	Travers, Ltd., Cum. Pref.	10	12½
4	Do. 1 Mt. Dbs., Rd.	100	101½
6	TucumanSug., 1 Dbs., Rd.	100	100
4/	United Alkali, Ltd.	10	2½
7	Do. Cum. Pref.	10	9½
5	Do. Mt. Db. Stk., Rd.	100	111½
2½d.	United Horse Shoe, Ltd., Non-Cum. 8 p.c. Pref.	1	⅝
5	Un. Kingm. Tea, Cm. Prf.	5	5
1/	Un. Lankat Plant., Ltd.	1	2½
2/	Un. Limmer Asphlte., Ld.	3	4½
5/	Val de Travers Asph., L.	10	14¾
3/	V. den Bergh's, Ltd., Cm. Pref.	5	6½
6	Walkers, Park., L., C. Pf.	10	4
4½	Do. 1 Mt. Debs., Red.	100	90½
4/	Wallis, Thos. & Co., Ltd.	5	14
6	Do. Cum. Pref.	5	8¾
5½	Waring, Ltd., Cum. Pref.	5	5½
4½	Do. 1 Mt. Db. Sk., Red.	100	111½
4½	Do. Irred. "B" Db. Stk.	100	104
12/	Waterlow, Dfd. Ord.	10	15½
12/	Do. Pref.	10	15½
—	Do. Cum. Pref.	10	10½
10/	Waterlow Bros. & L., Ld.	10	9½
9½d.	Welford, Ltd.	1	2½
4½	Do. Debs., Red.	100	107
4½d.	Welford's Surrey Dairies, Ltd.	1	1½
7½d.	West London Dairy, Ltd.	1	1
4½	Wharncliffe Dwllgs., L., Pf.	10	12
18/10	Do. 3 p.c. Irr. Mt. Db. Sk.	100	96
6d.	White, A. J., Ltd.	1	¾
6	Do. 6 p.c. Cum. Pref.	1	⅞
4	White, J. Bazley, Ltd., 1 Mort. Debs., Red	100	96½
5	White, R., Ltd., 1 Mort. Deb. Stock, Red.	100	106½
5/	White, Tomkins, Ltd	10	12¾
5	Do. Cum. Pref.	10	12½
6	White, W. N., L., Cm. Pf.	1	1
2/6	Wickens, Pease & Co., L.	5	2
6	Wilkie, Ltd., Cum. Pref.	10	16
3/6	Willans & Robinson, Ltd.	5	8
6	Do. Cum. Pref.	5	7
4½	Do. 1 Mt. Db. Stk., Red.	100	107
7½d.	Williamsons, L., Cm. Prf.	1	1½
6	Winterbottm. Book Cloth, Ltd., Cum. Prf.	10	15
3/	Yates, Ltd.	5	6½
6	Do. Cum. Pref.	5	6½
—	Young's Paraffin, Ltd.	4	1¼

CORPORATION STOCKS—COLONIAL AND FOREIGN.

Per Cent.	Name.	Paid.	Price.
6	Auckland City, '72 1904-24	100	118
6	Do. Cons., '79, Red. 1930	100	138½
5	Do. Deb. Ln., '83..1934-8	100	116
6	Auckland Harb. Debs.	100	111½
5	Do. 1917	100	112
5	Do. 1936	100	116
5½	Balmain Boro' 1914	—	117
5	Boston City (U.S.)	100	100½
5	Do. 1909	100	107½
5	Brunswick Town 5. c. Debs. 1916-20	100	111
15/	B. Ayres City 6 p.c.	100	61
4½	Do. 4½ p.c.	100	79
5	Cape Town, City of	100	113
4	Do. 1943	100	113
4	Chicago, City of, Gold 1915	—	110
6	Christchurch 1926	100	128½
—	Cordoba City	100	17
5	Duluth (U.S.) Gold 1926	—	110
6	Dunedin (Otago) 1925	100	127½
6	Do. 1906	100	113
5	Do. Consols 1908	100	113
4	Durban Insc. Stk. 1944	1000	111
4	Essex Cnty., N. Jersey 1926	$100	112½
5	Fitzroy, Melbrne. 1916-19	100	110
5	Gisborne Harbour 1915	100	110½
4	Greymouth Harbour 1925	100	111
4	Hamilton 1934	100	109
5	Hobart Town 1918-30	100	116
4	Do. 1940	100	107
4½	Invercargill Boro. Dbs. 1936	100	113
6	Kimberley Boro., S.A. Dbs.	—	104
4	Launceston Twn. Dbs. 1916	100	107
6	Lyttleton, N.Z., Harb. 1929	100	123
4	Melbourne Bd. of Wks. 1921	100	109
5	Melb. City Debs. 1897-1907	100	107½
4	Do. Debs. 1908-27	100	113½
4	Do. Debs. 1915-20-22	100	108
5	Melbne. Harb. Bds., 1908-9	100	112
4½	Do. do. 1915	100	110
4	Do. do. 1918-21	100	106
4½	Melbrne. Tms. Dbs. 1914-16	100	113
4½	Do. Fire Brig. Db. 1921	100	109
5	Mexico City Stg.	100	90
4	Moncton N. Bruns. City	100	104
4½	Montevideo	100	57
5	Montreal Stg.	100	109
5	Do. 1874	100	104
5	Do. 1879	100	106
3½	Do. 1933	100	104
3	Do. Perm. Deb. Stk.	100	98
4	Do. Cons. Deb. Stk. 1932	100	113
6	Napier Boro. Consolid. 1914	100	119
5	Napier Harb. Debs. 1920	100	114
5	Do. Debs. 1928	100	105
6	New Plymouth Harb. Debs. 1909	100	107
6	New York City 1901	—	107½
3½	Do. 1910-26	—	105½
4½	Nth. Melbourne Debs. 1-600 1921	100	108
5	Oamaru Boro. Cons. 1920	100	101
6	Do. Harb. Bds. (Reg.)	100	79½
25/	Do. 6 p.c. (Bearer) 1919	100	36
6	Otago Harb. Deb. Reg.	100	108
6	Do. 1877	100	107
6	Do. 1881 1921	100	115
5	Do. Debs. 1921	100	107
5	Do. Cons. 1934	100	105
6	Ottawa City	100	109
6	Do. 1904	100	115½
4½	Do. Debs. 1913	100	112
6	Port Elizabeth Waterworks	100	113
5	Port Louis	100	108
5	Prahran Debs. 1917	100	111
4	Do. Debs. 1919	100	108
6	Quebec C. Coupon. 1875 1905	100	122
6	Do. do. 1878 1908	100	116
4½	Do. Debs. 1914-18	100	107
4	Do. Debs. 1903	100	107
3½	Do. Cns. Rg. Stk., Red.	100	101
5	Richmond (Melb.) Dbs. 1917	100	113
4	Rio Janeiro City	100	62
4	Rome City	100	—
4	Do. 2nd to 8th Iss.	100	98
—	Rosario C.	100	26
—	Do.	100	26
4	St. Catherine (Ont.) 1926	100	103
4	St. John, N.B., Debs. 1934	—	104
4½	St. Kilda (Melb) Dbs. 1918-21	100	104
4	St. Louis C. (Miss.) 1911	100	104
4	Do. 1913	100	104
3·65	Do. 1915	—	110
—	Santa Fé City Debs.	100	20
6	Santos City	100	98
6	Sofia City	100	86
5	Sth. Melbourne Debs. 1915	100	111
4½	Do. Debs. 1919	100	107
5	Sydney City 1904	100	109
4	Do. Debs. 1912-13	100	107
4	Do. do. (1894) 1919	100	109
7	Timaru Boro. 7 p.c. 1910	100	124
5	Timaru Harb. Debs 1914	100	106
5	Do. Debs. 1926	100	106
6	Toronto City Wtwks 1904-6	100	11
6	Do. Cons. Debs. 1898	100	101
5	Do. G. Cns. Dbs. 1919-20	100	11
4	Do. Strlg. 1922-8	100	10
4	Do. Local Improv.	100	10
3½	Do. 1929	100	105
5½	Valparaiso	100	10
4	Vancouver 1931	100	10
4	Do. 1932	100	10
6	Wanganui Harb. Dbs. 1905	100	11
6	Wellington Con. Deb. 1907	100	11
6	Do. Improv., 1879	100	1
6	Do. Wtrwks. Dbs., 1880	100	1
4½	Do. Debs., 1893 1933	100	1
4½	Wellington Harb. 1907	100	1
4	Westport Harb. Dbs. 1925	100	11
6	Winnipeg City Deb. 1907	—	11
5	Do. 1914	100	11

FINANCIAL, LAND, AND INVESTMENT.

Last Div.	Name.	Paid.	Price.
5	Agncy, Ld. & Fin. Aust., Ltd., Mt. Db. Stk., Rd.	100	87½
6	Amer. Frehld. Mt. of Lon., Ld., Cum. Pref. Stk.	100	79½
4½	Do. Deb. Stk., Red.	100	96
1/	Anglo-Amer. Db. Cor., L.	2	1
4	Do. Deb. Stk., Red [†	100	107½
5½	Ang.-Ceylon & Gen. Est., Ltd., Cons. Stk.	100	70
6	Do. Reg. Debs., Red.	100	106½
—	Ang.-Fch. Explorn., Ltd.	1	3
6	Do. Cum. Pref.	1	1 1/16
—	Argent. Ld. & Inv., Ltd. £1 Shares	10/	nil
5	Do. Cum. Pref.	4	2
—	Assets Fnders' Sh., Ltd.,	4	2
4/	Assets Realiz., Ltd., Ord.,	5	9
5	Do. Cum. Pref.	5	6¾
21/	Austrln. Agricl. £25 Shs.	21½	65½
—	Aust. N. Z. Mort., Ltd., £10 Shs.	1	1¾d.
4½	Do. Deb. Stk., Red.	100	90½
4	Do. Deb. Stk., Red.	100	82½
4½	Australian Est. & Mt., L., 1 Mt. Deb. Stk., Red.	100	105
5	Do. "A" Mort. Deb. Stk., Red.	100	97
2/6	Australian Mort., Ld., & Fin., Ltd. £25 Shs.	5	4½
1/6	Do. New, £25 Shs.	3	2½
4	Do. Deb. Stk.	100	112
3	Do. Do.	100	85
5	Baring Est. 2 Mt. Debs., Red.	100	105
5	Bengal Presidy. 1 Mort. Deb., Red.	100	105
25/	British Amer. Ld. "A"	1	20
—	Do. "B"	24	6½
1/2¾	Brit. & Amer. Mt., Ltd. £10 Shs.	2	¾
5/	Do. Pref.	10	10
4	Do. Deb. Stk., Red.	100	100
1/3	Brit. & Austrlsn Tst Ln., Ltd. £25 Shs.	2½	⅝
4½	Do. Perm. Debs., Red.	100	102
1½d.	Brit. N. Borneo. £1 Shs.	15/	1½
2½d.	Do.	1	1
—	Brit. S. Africa	1	3½
5	Do. Mt. Deb., Red.	—	100
6	B. Aires Harb. Tst., Red.	100	97½
12/6	Canada Co.	1	25
—	Canada N. W. Ld., Ltd.	$25	$5½
—	Do. Pref.	$100	$54
4	Canada Perm. Loan & Sav. Perp. Deb. Stk.	100	99½
—	Curamalan Ld., 1 Mt. 7 p.c. Bds., Red.	—	92½
2/4½	Deb Corp., Ld., £10 Shs	4	3½
5	Do. Cum. Pref.	10	11½
4	Do. Perp. Deb. Stk.	100	114
—	Deb. Corp. Fders' Sh., Ld.	3	1
4/5 7/10	Eastn. Mt. & Agncy, Ld., "A"	10	6½
4½	Do. Deb. Stk., Red.	100	100
5	Equitable Revers. In. Ltd.	100	—
2/	Exploration, Ltd.	1	1 1/16
1	Freehold Trst. of Austria. Ltd. £10 Shs.	1	¾
4	Do. Perp. Deb. Stk.	100	102
—	Genl. Assets Purchase, Ltd., 5 p.c. Cum. Pref.	10	—
90/	Genl. Reversionary, Ltd.	100	—
3½	Holborn Vi. Land	100	107
3½	House Prop. & Inv.	100	84½
23/	Hudson's Bay	13	24½
4	Impl. Col. Fin. & Agcy. Corp.	100	93½
4½	Impl. Prop. Inv., Ltd., Deb. Stk., Red.	100	93½
2/6	Internatl. Fincial. Soc., Ltd. £7½ Shs.	2½	1½
4	Do. Deb. Stk., Red.	100	94½
1/9½	Ld. & Mtge. Egypt, Ltd. £18 Shs.	3	2¼
5	Do. Debs., Red.	100	103
4½	Do. Debs., Red.	100	101
—	Ld. Corp. of Canada, Ltd.	1	⅝
4½	Ld. Mtge. Bk. of Texas Deb. Stk.	100	—
3½	Ld. Mtge. Bk. Victoria 4½ p.c. Deb. Stk.	100	78
2/9½	Law Debent. Corp., Ltd., £10 Shs.	2	2
4½	Do. Cum. Pref.,	10	12½
4	Do. Deb. Stk.	100	118
1/	Ldn. & Australasian Deb. Corp., Ltd., £4 Shs.	2	½
4½	Do. 4½ p.c. Mt. Deb. Stk., Red.	100	101
—	Ldn. & Middx. Frhld. Est. £2 Shs.	35/	3½
2/6	Lndn. & N. Y. Inv. Corp., Ltd.	5	2½
5	Do. 5 p.c. Cum. Pref.	10	9
1/6	Ldn. & Nth. Assets Corp., Ltd., £2 Shs.	1½	¾
2/	Ldn. & N. Deb. Corp., L.	2	1⅝
4/	Ldn. & S. Afric. Explrn. Ltd.	½	14
2/	Mtge. Co. of R. Plate, Ltd. £10 Shs.	2	3½
4½	Do. Deb. Stk., Red.	100	111
4½	Morton, Rose Est., Ltd., 1st Mort. Debs.	—	100
6/	Natal Land Col. Ltd.	10	6½
4/	Do. 8 p.c. Pref., 1870	5	8½
3/6	Natl. Disct. L., £25 Shs.	5	11
4½	New Impl. Invest., Ltd. Pref. Stk.	100	66½
	New Impl. Invest., Ltd. Def. Stk.	100	9
4	N. Zld. Ln. & Mer. Agcy., Ltd. Prf. Ln. Deb. Stk	100	97

Financial, Land, &c. (*continued*):—

Last Div.	Name.	Paid.	Price.
16/	N. Zld. Ln. & Mer. Agcy., Ltd. 5 p.c. "A" Db. Sk.	100	42½
—	N. Zld. Ln. & Mer. Agcy., Ltd., 5 p.c. "B" Db. Stk.	100	4
2/6	N. Zld. Tst. & Ln. Ltd., £25 Shs.	5	1¼
12/6	N. Zld. Tst. & Ln. Ltd., 5 p.c. Cum. Pref.	25	19
—	N. Brit. Australsn. Ltd.	100	7½
—	Do. Irred. Guar.	100	30½
5	Do. Mort. Debs.	100	77½
4½	N. Queensld. Mort. & Inv., Ltd., Deb. Stk.	100	94
—	Oceana Co., Ltd.	—	—
4	Peel Riv., Ld. & Min. Ltd.	100	92
—	Peruvian Corp., Ltd.	100	2¾
—	Do. 4 p.c. Pref.	100	10
3	Do. 6 p.c. 1 Mt. Debs., Red.	100	42½
—	Queensld. Invest. & Ld. & Mort. Pref. Ord. Stk.	100	20
3/7	Queensld. Invest. & Ld. & Mort. Ord. Shs.	4	3½
4	Queensld. Invest. & Ld. Mort. Perp. Debs.	100	90
3½	Raily. Roll Stk. Tst. Deb., 1903-6. [†	100	100½
50/	Reversiony. Int. Soc., Ltd.	100	—
2/8½	Riv. Plate Trst., Loan & Agcy., L., "A" £10 Shs.	2	4⅜
1/6	Riv. Plate Trst., Loan & Agcy., Ltd., Def. "B"	5	3¾
4	Riv. Plate Trst., Loan & Agy., L., Db. Stk., Red.	100	107
—	Santa Fé & Cord. Gt. South Land, Ltd.	20	5
—	Santa Fé Land	10	2⅜
2/	Scot. Amer. Invest., Ltd. £10 Shs.	2	2¾
2½	Scot. Australian Invest., Ltd., Cons.	100	91½
6	Scot. Australian Invest., Ltd., Guar. Pref. [†	100	134½
5	Scot. Australian Invest., Ltd., Guar. Pref. [†	100	102½
4	Scot. Australian Invest., Ltd., 4 p.c. Perp. Dbs. [†	100	105½
5	Sivagunga Zemdy., 1st Mort., Red.	100	99
20/	Sth. Australian	20	57½
3½	Stock Exchange Deb., Rd.	—	101½
—	Strait Develt., Ltd.	1	5/16
2/6	Texas Land & Mt., Ltd. £10 Shs.	2½	3
4½	Texas Land & Mt., Ltd., Deb. Stk., Red.	100	104
—	Transvaal Est. & Dev., L.	1	1/16
—	Transvaal Lands, Ltd., £1 Shs.	15/	⅜
—	Do. F. P.	1	½
—	Transvaal Mort., Loan, & Fin., Ltd., £10 Shs.	2	⅛
2/	Tst & Agcy. of Austrlsa., Ltd., £10 Shs.	1	2½
7/5	Do. Old, fully paid	10	15½
5/7	Do. New, fully paid	10	12½
5	Do. Cum. Pref.	10	12¾
3/	Trust & Loan of Canada, £20 Shs.	5	4½
1/9½	Do. New £20 Shs.	3	2¼
—	Tst. & Mort. of Iowa, Ltd., £10 Shs.	2½	¾
4½	Do. Deb. Stk. Red.	100	94½
—	Tst., Loan, & Agency of Mexico, Ltd., £10 Shs.	2	¼
—	Trsts., Exors, & Sec. Ins. Corp., Ltd., £10 Shs.	7	1⅝
5/	Union Dsc., Ld., £10 Shs.	5	11
—	Union Mort. & Agcy. of Aust., Ltd., £6 Shs.	2	—
6	Do. Pref. Stk.	100	35
—	Do. 6 p. Pref. £6 Shs.	2	¼
4½	Do. Deb. Stk.	100	92½
4	Do. Deb. Stk.	100	85½
5	Do. Deb. Stk. Red.	100	96
1/6	U.S. Deb. Cor. Ltd., £8 Shs.	1	⅝
5½	Do. Cum. Pref. Stk.	100	102½
4½	Do. Irred. Deb. Stk.	100	110
5	U.S. Tst. & Guar. Cor., Ltd., Pref. Stk.	100	69½
6/	Van Dieman's	25	16
4	Walker's Prop. Cor., Ltd., Guar. 1 Mt. Deb. Stk.	100	109
4½	Wstr. Mort. & Inv., Ltd., Deb. Stk.	100	90

FINANCIAL—TRUSTS.

Last Div.	Name.	Paid.	Price.
1/	Afric. City Prop., Ltd	1	1½
6	Do. Cum. Pref.	1	1
4	Alliance Invt., Ltd., Cm. 4½ p. c. Prefd.	100	77½
—	Do. Defd	100	11½
4	Do. Deb. Stk. Red.	100	106½
5	Amrcn. Invt., Ltd., Prfd.	100	123½
5	Do. Defd.	100	92½
4	Do. Deb. Stk. Red.	100	118½
4	Army & Navy Invt., Ltd., 5 p.c. Prefd.	100	77½
—	Do. Defd. Stk.	100	17½
4	Do. Deb. Stk.	100	104½
4	Atlas Investment, Ltd., Prefd. Stk.	100	70½
4½	Bankers' Invest., Ltd., Cum. Prefd.	100	105
1/0/0	Do. Defd	100	27½
4	Do. Deb. Stk	100	113

Financial—Trusts (*continued*):—

Last Div.	Name.	Paid.	Price.
4/6	†Brewery & Comml. Inv., Ltd., £10 Shs.	5	6
4	British Investment, Ltd., Cum. Prefd.	100	109½
5	Do. Defd.	100	102½
4	Do. Deb. Stk.	100	107½
6	Brit. Steam. Invst., Ltd., Prefd.	100	117½
3/0/0	Do. Defd	100	69½
4½	Do. Perp. Deb. Stk	100	120½
2/3	Car Trust Invst., Ltd., £10 Shs.	2½	2
5	Do. Pref.	100	105½
4	Do. Deb. Stk., 1915	100	106
4	‡Clnl. Sec., Ltd., Prefd. [†	100	107½
2	Do. Defd.	100	48
4	Consolidated, Ltd., Cum. 1st Pref.	100	95½
4	Do. 5 p.c. Cm. 2nd do.	100	74½
—	Do. Defd.	100	14½
4½	Do. Deb. Stk.	100	113½
4½	Edinburgh Invest., Ltd., Cum. Prefd. Stk.	100	110½
4	Do. Deb. Stk. Red.	100	106½
5	Foreign, Amer. & Gen. Invt., Ltd., Prefd.	100	119½
2	Do. Defd.	100	54½
4	Do. Deb. Stk.	100	117½
5	Foreign & Colonial Invt., Ltd., Prefd.	100	135½
4½	Do. Defd.	100	94
4½	Gas, Water & Gen. Invt., Cum. Prefd. Stk.	100	93
3	Do. Defd. Stk.	100	32½
4	Do. Deb. Stk.	100	106
5	Gen. & Com. Invt., Ltd., Prefd. Stk.	100	106½
2	Do. Defd. Stk.	100	35½
4	Do. Deb. Stk.	100	111½
1/9	Globe Telegph. & Tst., Ltd.	10	12¼
6	Do. do. Pref.	10	18
4	Govt. & Genl. Invt., Ld., Prefd.	100	84½
3½	Do. Defd.	100	42½
4½	Govts. Stk. & other Secs. Invt., Ltd., Prefd.	100	94½
1	Do. Defd.	100	28
4½	Do. Deb. Stk.	100	110
4	Do. do.	100	104
4½	Guardian Invt., Ltd., Pfd.	100	92½
—	Do. Defd.	100	21½
4	Do. Deb. Stk.	100	105½
5	Indian & Gen. Inv., Ltd., Cum. Prefd.	100	109½
2½	Do. Defd.	200	55½
4½	Do. Deb. Stk.	200	120½
5	Indust. & Gen. Tst., Ltd., Unified	100	100½
3½	Do. Deb. Stk. Red.	100	102½
4½	Internat. Invt., Ltd., Cm. Prefd.	100	72½
—	Do. Defd.	100	9
4	Do. Deb. Stk.	100	104
4	Invest. Tst. Cor. Ltd. Pfd.	100	102
4	Do. Defd.	100	83½
4	Do. Deb. Stk. Red.	100	106
25/	Ldn. Gen. Invest. Ltd., 5 p.c. Cum. Prefd.	100	110½
37/6	Do. Defd.	100	120
4½	Ldn. Scot. Amer. Ltd. Pfd.	100	104½
£3	Do. Defd.	100	59½
4	Do. Deb. Stk.	100	111
4	Ldn. Tst., Ltd., Cum. Prfd. Stk.	100	105
4	Do. Defd. Stk.	100	76½
4	Do. Deb. Stk., Red.	100	107
3½	Do. Mt. Deb. Stk., Red.	100	103
5	Mercantile Invt. & Gen., Ltd., Prefd.	100	110
2	Do. Defd.	100	47½
4	Do. Deb. Stk.	100	117½
4	Merchants, Ltd., Pref. Stk.	100	104½
4	Do. Ord.	100	80
4	Do. Deb. Stk.	100	117
5	Municipal, Ltd., Prefd.	100	56½
—	Do. Defd.	100	18½
4½	Do. Debs.	100	113
4½	Do. Debs. "B"	100	99½
4½	Do. "C" Deb. Stk.	100	88½
5	New Investment, Ltd. Ord.	100	94½
5	Omnium Invest., Ltd., Pfd.	100	95½
1	Do. Defd.	100	27½
4	Do. Deb. Stk.	100	102
4/	†Railway Deb. Tst. Ld., £20 Shs.	10	7
5	Do. Debs., Red.	100	107½
4½	Do. Deb. Stk., 1911	100	105½
4	Do. do. 1927	100	109½
4	Railway Invst. Ltd., Prefd.	100	116
18/6	Do. Defd.	100	25
6/4½	Railway Share Trust & Agency "A"	8	6½
7½	Do. "B" Pref. Stk.	100	142
4½	River Plate & Gen. Invt., Ltd., Prefd.	100	107
£3	Do. Defd.	100	54½
5	Scot. Invst., Ltd., Pfd. Stk.	100	94½
1½	Do. Defd.	100	26½
4	Do. Deb. Stk.	100	108
4½	Sec. Scottish Invst., Ltd., Cum. Prefd.	100	90½
£3	Do. Defd. Stk.	100	32
4	Do. Deb. Stk.	100	107½
7/6	Sth. Africa Gold Tst., Ltd.	1	5½
6	Do. Cum. Pref.	1	1
5½	Do. 1st Debs., Red.	100	102
9d.	†Stock Conv. & Invest., Ltd., £5 Shs.	1	1½
4½	Do. do. 4½ p.c. Cm. Prf.	100	112½
3½	Do. Ldn. & N. W. 1st. Charge Prefd.	100	116
4	Do do. 2nd Chge Prfd.	100	113
32/6	Do. do. Defd. Charge	100	32
3	Do. N. East. 1 Chge Pfd.	100	95

Financial—Trusts (*continued*):—

Last Div.	Name.	Paid.	Price.
37/6	Stock N. East Defd. Chge	100	42
6	Submarine Cables	100	142½
5	U.S. & S. Amer. Invest., Ltd., Prefd.	100	98½
2	Do. Defd.	100	29½
4	Do. Deb. Stk.	100	105½

GAS AND ELECTRIC LIGHTING.

Last Div.	Name.	Paid.	Price.
10/6	Alliance & Dublin Con. 10 p.c. Stand.	10	24½
7/6	Do. 7 p.c. Stand.	10	17
5	Austln. Gas Lght. (Syd.) Debs. 1902	100	106
5	Bay State of N. Jrsy. Sk. Fd. Tst. Bd., Red.	—	92½
3/	Bombay, Ltd.	5	7
2/4½	Do. New	4	5½
12	Brentford Cons.	100	302½
9	Do. New	100	229½
5	Do. Pref.	100	147½
4	Do. Deb. Stk.	100	136
11½	Brighton & Hove Gen. Cons. Stk.	100	277½
8½	Do. "A" Cons. Stk.	100	202½
5	Bristol 5 p.c. Max.	100	132½
22/6	British Gas Light, Ltd.	20	57
11/6	Bromley Gas Consumrs.' 10 p.c. Stand.	10	26
8/6	Do. 7 p.c. Stand.	10	21
—	Brush Electl. Enging., L.	—	2½
6	Do. 6 p.c. Pref.	—	2½
4½	Do. Deb. Stk.	100	111
4½	Do. 2 Deb. Stk., Red.	100	103½
5/	B. Ayres (New), Ltd.	10	10
4	Do. Deb. Stk., Rd.	—	97
12/	Cagliari Gas & Wtr., Ltd.	20	31
8/	Cape Town & Dist. Gas Light & Coke, Ltd.	10	17½
4½	Do. Pref.	10	12
6	Do. 1 Mt. Debs. 1910	50	60
3/	Charing Cross & Strand Elec. Sup., Ltd.	5	14½
4½	Do. Cum. Pref.	5	6½
2/6	Chelsea Elec. Sup., Ltd.	5	11
4½	Do. Deb. Stk., Red.	100	113
5	Chic. Edison Co. 1 Mt., Red.	$1000	108
14/	City of Ldn. Elec. Lht., L.	10	30½
—	Do. New	10	30
6/	Do. Cum. Pref.	10	17½
5	Do. Deb. Stk., Red. [†	100	131½
13½	Commercial, Cons.	100	342½
10½	Do. New	100	257½
4½	Do. Deb. Stk.	100	155½
14	Continental Union, Ltd.	100	252½
11	Do. Pref. Stk.	100	216½
—	County of Lon. & Brush Prov. Elec. Lg., Ltd.	10	15½
6	Do. Cum. Pref.	10	16
14	Croydon Comcl. Gas, Ld., "A" Stk., 10 p.c.	100	317½
11	Do. "B" Stk., 7 p.c.	100	254½
5½	Crystal Pal. Dist. Ord. 5 p.c. Stk.	100	138½
5	Do. Pref. Stk.	100	141½
14/	European, Ltd.	10	26½
10/6	Do.	7½	19
12¾	Gas Light & Ck Cons. Stk., "A" Ord.	100	316½
4	Do. "B" (4 p.c. Max.)	100	115½
10	Do. "C," "D," & "E" (Pref.)	100	322½
5	Do. "F" (Pref.)	100	152½
7½	Do. "G" (Pref.)	100	224½
7	Do. "H" (7 p.c. Max.)	100	206½
10	Do. "J" (Pref.)	100	321½
6	Do. "K"	100	189½
4	Do. Deb. Stk.	100	139½
4½	Do. do.	100	157½
6	Do. do.	100	207½
8/	Hong Kong & China, Ld.	10	14½
—	†House to House Elec. Light Sup., Ltd.	5	10½
7	Do. Cum. Pref.	5	11½
10	Imperial Continental	100	218½
3½	Do. Deb. Stk., Red	100	105½
2/	Malta & Medit., Ltd.	5	5½
5/	†Metrop. Elec. Sup., Ltd.	10	20
3/8	Do. New	10	19½
4½	Do. 1 Mt. Deb. Stk.	100	119½
5	Metro. of Melbrne. Dbs. 1908-12	100	113
4½	Do. Debs. 1918-22-4	100	110
10/	Monte Video, Ltd.	20	15½
8/	†Notting Hill Elec. Ltg., Ltd.	10	18½
4/6	Oriental, Ltd.	5	8½
4/0½	Do. New	4½	7½
10½d.	Do. do. 1879	1	1½
3/6	Ottoman, Ltd.	5	4½
—	Para, Ltd.	—	—
6	People's Gas Lt. & C. of Chic. 2 Mt. 1904	100	105½
5	River Plate Elec. Lgt. & Trac., Ltd., 1 Deb. Stk.	—	92½
8½	Royal Elec. of Montreal	—	146
4½	Do. 1 Mt. Deb.	100	106
3/6	†St. James' & Pall Mall Elec. Light, Ltd.	5	18½
7	Do. Pref.	5	10½
4	Do. Deb. Stk., Red. †	100	102½
10/	San Paulo, Ltd.	10	16½

Gas and Electric (*continued*):—

Last Div.	Name.	Paid.	Price.
10	Sheffield Unit. Gas Lt. "A"	100	251½
10	Do. "B"	100	251½
10	Do. "C"	100	251½
—	Sth. Ldn. Elec. Sup., Ld.	2	3
5¼	South Metropolitan	100	146½
3	Do. 3 p.c. Deb. Stk.	100	106½
12	Tottenham & Edmonton Gas Lt. & C., "A"	100	290
9	Do. "B"	100	210
7/	Tuscan, Ltd.	10	14
5	Do. Debs., Red.	100	101½
4/9	West Ham 10 p.c. Stan.	5	12
4/	Wstmnstr. Elec. Sup., Ld.	5	17½

INSURANCE.

Last Div.	Name.	Paid.	Price.
4/	Alliance, £20 Shs.	44/	11½
10/	Alliance, Mar., & Gen., Ld., £100 Shs.	25	53
5/	Atlas, £50 Shs.	6	32
8/	British & For. Marine, Ld., £20 Shs.	4	25
7½d.	British Law Fire, Ltd., £10 Shs.	1	1⅝
7/6	Clerical, Med., & Gen. Life, £25 Shs.	50/	16½
10/	Commercial Union, Ltd., £50 Shs.	5	46½
4	Do. "W. of Eng." Ter. Deb. Stk.	100	110½
60/	County Fire, £100 Shs.	80	185
2/6	Eagle, £50 Shs.	5	—
4/	Employrs' Liability, Ltd., £10 Shs.	2	4
—	Empress, Ltd., £5 Shs.	1	—
21/	Equity & Law, £100 Shs.	6	21
7/6	General Life, £100 Shs.	5	15
4½d.	Gresham Life, £5 Shs.	15/	2½
2/6	Guardian, Ld., £10 Shs.	5	12½
10/	Imperial, Ltd., £20 Shs.	5	32
5/6	Imperial Life, £20 Shs.	4	7
6/	Indemnity Mutual Mar., Ltd., £15 Shs.	3	12
1/	Lancashire, £20 Shs.	2	5½
7½d.	Law Acc. & Contin., Ltd., £5 Shs.	10/	⅜
5/	Law Fire, £100 Shs.	2½	18
4½d.	Law Guar. & Trust, Ltd., £10 Shs.	1	1¼
9/	Law Life, £20 Shs.	2	24½
2/9	Law Un. & Crown £10 Shs.	12/	7
4	Do. Deb. Stk., 1942	100	110½
14/6	Legal & General, £50 Shs.	8	15½
9d.	Lion Fire, Ltd., £6½ Shs.	1½	1
14/	Liverpool & London & Globe, Stk.	2	55½
10/	Do. Globe £1 Ann.	—	36
15/	London, £25 Shs.	12½	62½
4/	Lond. & Lanc. Fire, £25 Shs	2½	19½
2/	Lond. & Lanc. Life, £25 Shs	2	5
10	Lond. & Prov. Mar., Ld., £10 Shs.	1	1½
2/	Lond. Guar. & Accident, Ltd., £5 Shs.	2	11½
10/	Marine, Ltd., £25 Shs.	4½	44½
2/	Maritime, Ltd., £10 Shs.	2	4½
1/6	Merc. Mar., Ld., £10 Shs.	2½	2½
1/	National Marine, Ltd., £9 Shs.	1	½
10/	N. Brit. & Merc., £25 Shs.	6¼	43
20/	Northern, £100 Shs.	10	82
40/	Norwich Union Fire, £100 Shs.	12†	129½
5/	Ocean Acc. & Guar., fy. pd.	5	20½
1/	Do. £5 Shs.	1	4
2/6	Ocean, Marine, Ltd.	2½	9½
1/	Palatine, £10 Shs.	2	3½
2/6	Pelican, £10 Shs.	1	3¼
12/	Phœnix, £50 Shs.	5	45
25/	Provident, £100 Shs.	10	36
3/	Railway Passngrs., £10 Shs.	2	8½
2/6	Rock Life, £5 Shs.	10/	4½
8	Royal Exchange	100	360
18/	Royal, £20 Shs.	3	55½
4/	Sun, £10 Shs.	10/	11½
3/9	Sun Life, £10 Shs.	7½	15
4/	Thames & Mrsey. Marine, Ltd., £20 Shs.	2	11½
9/	Union, £10 Shs.	4	24½
3/6	Union Marine, £20 Shs.	2½	9½
12/	Universal Life, £100 Shs.	12	42
2/	World Marine, £5 Shs.	2	1½

IRON, COAL, AND STEEL.

Last Div.	Name.	Paid.	Price.
3/9	Barrow Hæm. Steel, Ltd.	7½	2½
9/	Do. 6 p.c. 2nd Pref.	7½	7½
10/	Bolck., Vaugh. & C., Ld.	20	18
6/	Do. £8 liab.	12	10
7/6	Brown, J. & Co., Ltd., £20 Shs.	15	20½
22/6	Consett Iron, Ld., £10 Shs.	7½	30
4/	Do. 8 p.c. Cum. Pref.	5	11½
7/6	Ebbw Vale Steel, Iron & Coal, Ltd., £23 Shs.	20	7
15/	General Mining Assn., Ld.	5½	7½
16/	Harvey Steel Co. of Gt. Britain, Ltd.	10	26
5	Lehigh V. Coal 1 Mt. 5 p.c. Guar. Gd. Cp. Bds.	—	97½
42/6	Nantyglo & Blaina Iron, Ltd., Pref.	$62	96
1/	Nerbudda Coal & Iron, Ltd., £3 Shs.	56/	⅛
6/	Newport Abercrn. Bk. Vein Steam Coal, Ltd.	10	4½
5/	New Sharlston Coll., Ltd. Pref.	20	11
4½d.	Nw. Vancvr. Coal & Ld., L.	1	⅛
3/6	North's Navigation Coll. (1889) Ltd.	5	2
10/	Do. 10 p.c. Cum. Pref.	5	7½
1/	Rhymney Iron, Ltd.	5	1½
	Do. New, £5 Shs.	4½	[illegible]
5	Do. Mt. Debs., Red.	100	96½
5	Shelton Irn., Stl. & Cl. Co., Ltd., 1 Chg. Debs., Red.	100	98½
10	Sth. Hetton Coal, Ltd.	100	176½
	Vickers & Maxim, Ltd.	10	3
	Do. 5 p.c. Prfd. Stk.	100	133½

SHIPPING.

Last Div.	Name.	Paid.	Price.
4/	African Stm. Ship, £20 Shs.	16	9½
5/	Do. Fully-paid	20	13½
5/	Amazon Steam Nav., Ltd.	19½	9½
8/	Castle Mail Pakts., Ltd., £20 Shs.	14	15½
3½	Do. 1st Deb. Stk., Red.	100	101
6/	China Mutual Steam, Ltd.	5	2½
6	Do. Cum. Pref.	10	9½
10/	Cunard, Ltd.	20	10
5/	Do. £20 Shs.	10	4
4½	Furness, Withy, & Co., Ltd., 1 Mt. Dbs., Red.	100	105
6/	General Steam	15	8½
5/	Do. 5 p.c. Pref., 1874	10	9
5/	Do. 5 p.c. Pref., 1877	10	9
5/	Leyland & Co., Ltd.	10	15½
7/	Do. 7 p.c. Cum. Pref.	10	14½
—	Do. 4½ p.c. Cum. Pre-Pf.	3	10½
4	Do. 1st Mt. Dbs., Red.	100	106½
2/6	Mercantile Steam, Ltd.	5	7½
6/4½	New Zealand Ship., Ltd.,	6	5
4	Do. Deb. Stk., Red.	100	104
5/	Orient Steam, Ltd.	10	4½
5	P. & O. Steam, Cum. Prefd.	100	155½
19	Do. Defd.	100	232½
3½	Do. Deb. Stk.	100	121
5	Richelieu & Ont., 1st Mt. Debs., Red.	100	101
30/	Royal Mail, £100 Shs.	60	51
2/6	Shaw, Sav., & Alb., Ltd., "A" Pref.	5	5½
5/	Do. "B" Ord.	5	3½
8/	Union Steam, Ltd.	20	18½
4/	Do. New £20 Shs.	10	8½
4	Do. Deb. Stk., Red.	100	107
7/	Union of N.Z., Ltd.	10	10
3/1½	Wilson's & Fur.-Ley., 5½ p.c. Cum. Pref.	10	10½
4½	Do. 1 Mt. Db. Sk., Rd.	100	105½

TELEGRAPHS AND TELEPHONES.

Last Div.	Name.	Paid.	Price.
4	African Direct, Ltd., Mort. Debs., Red.	100	102
—	Amazon Telegraph, Ltd.	10	6½
14/	Anglo-American, Ltd.	100	62
28/	Do. 6 p.c. Prefd. Ord.	100	111½
—	Do. Defd. Ord.	100	13
3/	Brazilian Submarine, Ltd.	10	16½
5	Do. Debs., 2 Series	100	114

Telegraphs and Telephones (*continued*):—

Last Div.	Name.	Paid.	Price.
4/	Chili Telephone, Ltd.	5	3½
$2½	Comcial. Cable, $100 Shs.	—	189½
4	Do. Stg. 500-yr. Deb. Stk. Red.	100	106
2½d.	Consd. Telpehone Constr., &c., Ltd.	10/	⅛
8/	Cuba Submarine, Ltd.	10	8½
10/	Do. 10 p.c. Pref.	10	18½
2/	Direct Spanish, Ltd.	5	4½
5/	Do. 10 p.c. Cum. Pref.	5	10½
4½	Do. Debs.	50	104½
3/	Direct U.S. Cable, Ltd.	20	10½
2/6	Eastern, Ltd.	10	18½
3/	Do. 6 p.c. Cum. Pref.	10	19½
4	Do. Mt. Deb. Stk., Red.	100	132½
2/6	Eastern Exten., Aus., & China, Ltd.	10	19
5	Do. (Aus. Gov. Sub.) Deb., Red.	100	101
5	Do. do. Bearer	100	101½
4	Do. Mort. Deb. Stk.	100	133½
5	Eastn. & S. Afric., Ltd., Mort. Deb. 1900	100	101
5	Do. Bearer	100	101½
4	Do. Mort. Debs. 1909	100	106½
4	Do. Mort. Debs. (Maur. Subsidy)	25	109½
5/	Grt. Nthn. Copenhagen	10	27½
5	Do. Debs., Ser. B., Red.	100	102½
12/6	Indo-European, Ltd.	25	53½
6	London Platino-Brazilian, Ltd., Debs. 1904	100	109½
4/	Montevideo Telph., Ltd., 6 p.c. Pref.	5	2½
3/	National Telephone, Ltd.	5	6½
6/	Do. Cum. 1 Pref.	10	16
6/	Do. Cum. 2 Pref.	10	15
5	Do. Non-Cum. 3 Pref.	5	6½
3½	Do. Deb. Stk., Red.	100	106½
4d.	Oriental Telephone, Ltd.	1	[illegible]
4	Pac. & Euro. Tlg. Dbs., Rd.	100	106½
4/	Reuter's, Ltd.	8	8
5/	Un. Riv. Plate Telph., Ltd.	5	4½
5	Do. Deb. Stk., Red.	100	103½
6/	West African Telg., Ltd.	10	4½
5	Do. 5 p.c. Mt. Debs., Red.	100	104½
—	W. Coast of America, Ltd.	10	—
3/	Western & Brazilian, Ltd.	15	10
3/	Do. 5 p.c. Pref. Ord.	7½	7½
—	Do. Defd. Ord.	7½	3
4	Do. Deb. Stk., Red.	100	106
1/	W. India & Panama, Ltd.	10	½
6/	Do. Cum. 1 Pref.	10	7½
6/	Do. Cum. 2 Pref.	10	6
5	Do. Debs., Red.	100	106½
7	West. Union, 1 Mt. 1900 $	1000	107½
6	Do. 6 p.c. Stg. Bds., Rd.	100	102½

TRAMWAYS AND OMNIBUS.

Last Div.	Name.	Paid.	Price.
1/6	Anglo-Argentine, Ltd.	5	3½
6	Do. Deb. Stk.	100	129½
4	Barcelona, Ltd.	10	13
5	Do. Deb., Red.	100	104½
6/6	Belfast Street Trams.	10	17
—	Blackpl. & Fltwd. Tram., £10 Shs.	8	9
4/	Bordeaux Tram. & O., Ltd.	10	13
5	Do. Cum. Pref.	10	11½
—	Brazilian Street Ry., Ltd.	2	⅛
—	British Elec. Trac., Ltd.	10	17½
—	B. Ayres & Belg. Tram., Ltd., 6 p.c. Cum. Pref.	5	4
6	Do. 1 Deb. Stk. †	100	102½
—	B. Ayres. Gd. Nat., Ltd., 6 p.c. 1 Deb. Bds., Red.	100	60
5½	Do. Pref. Debs., Red.	100	92½
6d.	Calais, Ltd.	5	1
—	Calcutta, Ltd.	10	3½
—	Carthagena & Herr., Ltd.	10	3
5	Do. Deb., Red.	100	90
5	City of B'ham. Trams., Ltd., 5 p.c. Cum. Pref.	5	5½
4	Do. 1 Mort. Debs., Rd.	100	104½
3/9	City of B. Ayres, Ltd.	5	7½
2/3	Do. Ext. £5 Shs.	3	4
6	Do. Deb. Stk.	100	150
9d.	Edinburgh Street Tram.	4	3½
1/	Glasgow Tram. & Omni. Ltd., £9 Shs.	8	3½
3/7½	Imperial, Ltd.	6	13
2/	Lond., Deptfd., & Greenwich, Prefd.	5	3½
nil	Do. Defd.	5	1
10½	Lond. Gen. Omni., Ltd.	100	205
4	Do. Deb., Red.	100	117½

Tramways and Omnibus (*continued*):—

Last Div.	Name	Paid.	Price.
6/	London Road Car	6	1[illegible]
5	London St. Rly. (Prov., Ont.), Mt. Debs.	100	11[illegible]
4/9	London St. Trams.	—	
12/9	London Trams., Ltd.	10	1[illegible]
6/	Do. Non-Cum. Pref.	10	1[illegible]
5	Do. Mt. Db. Stk., Rd.	100	10[illegible]
5	Lynn & Boston 1 Mt. 1924 $	1000	10[illegible]
5	Milwaukee Elec. Cons. Mt. $	1000	9[illegible]
5	Minneapolis St. 1 Cons. Mt. $	1000	9[illegible]
5	Montreal St. Dbs., 1908	100	11[illegible]
4½	Do. Debs., 1922	100	10[illegible]
6/	Nth. Metropolitan	10	1[illegible]
1/0½	Nth. Staffords., Ltd.	6	
5/6	Provincial, Ltd.	10	
6/	Do. Cum. Pref.	10	1[illegible]
5	St. Paul City, 1937 $	1000	[illegible]
5	Do. Guar. Twin City Rap. Trans. $	1000	8[illegible]
5/	Southampton	10	
3/	South London	10	
3/6	Sunderland, Ltd.	10	
4½	Toronto 1 Mt., Red.	100	10[illegible]
2/6	Tramways Union, Ltd.	5	
4½	Do. Deb., Red.	100	10[illegible]
5/	Vienna General Omnibus.	5	
5	Do. 5 p.c. Mt. Deb., Red.	100	10[illegible]
4/	Wolverhampton, Ltd.	10	

WATER WORKS.

Last Div.	Name.	Paid.	Price.
8/	Antwerp, Ltd.	20	[illegible]
6/	Cape Town District, Ltd.	5	[illegible]
10½	Chelsea	100	[illegible]
5	Do. Pref. Stk.	100	[illegible]
4½	Do. Pref. Stk., 1875	100	[illegible]
4½	Do. Deb. Stk.	100	[illegible]
5/	City St. Petersburg, Ltd.	13	[illegible]
4/6	Colne Valley	10	[illegible]
4	Do. Deb. Stock	100	[illegible]
£4	Consol. of Rosar., Ltd., 4 p.c. 1 Deb. Stk., Red.	100	[illegible]
7½	East London	100	[illegible]
4½	Do. Deb. Stk.	100	[illegible]
3	Do. Deb. Stk., Red.	100	[illegible]
37/6	Grand Junction (Max. 10 p.c.) "A"	50	[illegible]
18/9	Do. "B"	25	[illegible]
18/9	Do. "C" (Max. 7½ p.c.)	25	[illegible]
35/	Do. "D" (Max. 7 p.c.)	50	[illegible]
4	Do. Deb. Stock	100	[illegible]
13	Kent	100	[illegible]
7	Do. New (Max. 7 p.c.)	100	[illegible]
6/7½	Kimberley, Ltd.	7	[illegible]
6	Do. Debs., Red.	100	[illegible]
6	Do. Deb. Stk., Red.	100	[illegible]
10	Lambeth (Max. 10 p.c.)	100	[illegible]
7½	Do. (Max. 7½ p.c.), 50 & 25	—	[illegible]
4	Do. Deb. Stock	100	[illegible]
3	Do. Red. Deb. Stock	100	[illegible]
10/	Montevideo, Ltd.	20	[illegible]
5	Do. 1 Deb. Stk.	100	[illegible]
5	Do. 2 Deb. Stk.	100	[illegible]
130/11	15] New River New	100	[illegible]
4	Do. Deb. Stk.	100	[illegible]
4	Do. Deb. Stk. "B"	100	[illegible]
—	Odessa, Ltd., "A" 6 p.c. Prefd.	20	[illegible]
nil	Do. "B" Deferred	20	[illegible]
4	Portland Con. Mt. "B," 1927	—	[illegible]
8/	Seville, Ltd.	20	[illegible]
5/6	Southend "Addl." Ord.	10	[illegible]
6	Southwark and Vauxhall	100	[illegible]
6	Do. "D" Shares (7½ p.c. max.)	100	[illegible]
5	Do. Pref. Stock	100	[illegible]
4	Do. "A" Deb. Stock	100	[illegible]
3	Staines Resvirs. Jt. Com. Gua. Deb. Stk., Red.	100	[illegible]
7/	Tarapaca, Ltd.	10	[illegible]
10	West Middlesex	100	[illegible]
4½	Do. Deb. Stk.	100	[illegible]
3	Do. Deb. Stk.	100	[illegible]

Prices Quoted on the Leading Provincial Exchanges.

ENGLISH.

In quoting the markets, B stands for Birmingham; Bl for Bristol; M for Manchester; L for Liverpool; and S for Sheffield.

CORPORATION STOCKS.

Chief Market.	Int or Div.	Name.	Amount paid.	Price.
M	3½	Bolton, Red. 1935 ..	100	116
M	3½	Burnley, Red. 1933..	100	116
M	3½	Bury, Red. 1946	100	118
L	2¾	Liverpool, Red. 1925	100	102½
B	3½	Longton, 1932	100	106
M	4	Oldham Prp. Db. Sk.	100	144
M	£1	Do. Gas & W. Ann.		35
S	4	Rotherham 4 p.c., Red. 1927...... [£	1 an	114
S	3	Do. Red. 1920..	100	104
M	3½	Runcorn Red. 1923..	100	105
S	2¾	Sheffield Water Ann.	100	117½
S	5	Do.	3 an	90
L	3½	Southport Red. 1936 {	5 an 100	112
L	3	Do. Red. 1914..	100	104
M	3	Todmorden, Red. 1914	100	103

RAILWAYS.

Chief Market.	Int or Div.	Name.	Amount paid.	Price.
Bl	4½	Bridgewater Pref. ..	100	137½
M	4	Cleator & Workton.	100	78
M	4	Do. 1883 Pref. ..	100	111
L	4	Cockermth. K. & P.	100	116
L	4	Isle of Man	5	6¼
L	5	Do. Pref.	5	6⅝
L	3	Liverpool Overhead	10	11 1/16
L	4	Do. Deb. Stk. ..	100	109
L	5	Do. Pref.	10	16½
L	6	Maryport & Carlisle	100	170
S	6	Mid. Shef. & Roth. Pf.	100	231
Bl	35/	Neath & Brecon "A"	100	60
M	4½	Oldham, Ashton, &c.	10	17
Bl	5½	Penarth Harbour ..	100	184½
Bl	4	Do. Deb. Stk. ..	100	145
Bl	3½	Do. Deb. Stk. ..	100	127
Bl	½	Ross & Monmouth..	20	5⅞
Bl	6	Do. Pref.	20	43
M	3	Southport & Cheshire Deb. Stk.	100	105½
M	nil.	Do. Pref.	100	26
Bl	2½	West Somerset Gu...	100	97½
Bl	5	Wye Val. Deb. Stk.	100	164

BANKS.

Chief Market.	Int or Div.	Name.	Amount paid.	Price.
L	5/	Adelphi, L., £20 Shs.	10	16
L	12/6	Bk of L'pool, L., £100 Sh	12½	38¾
B	5/6	Brmnghm. Dis. & C., Ltd., £20 Shs.....	4	10⅞
B	6/3	Co. of Staffs., L., £40	5	13
S	17½	Crompton & Evans, Ltd., £20 Shs	4	14⅜
M	14/	Lancs. & Yorks, Ltd., £20 Shs.....	10	32½
L	18/	Livrpl. Union, Ltd., £100 Shs.	20	60½
M	24/	Manchester & Co., Ltd., £100 Shs. ..	16	61½
M	20/	Mnchstr. & Livrpool. Dis., Ltd., £60 Shs.	10	52¾
M	1/6	Mer. of Lancashire, Ltd., £20 Shs.....	3	6⅛
L	16/	Nth. & Sth. Wales, Ltd., £40 Shs.....	10	34¾
	5/	Notts Joint St., Ltd., £50 Shs..........	10	23
M	3/	Oldham Joint Stk., Ltd., £20 Shs.....	4	10⅛
S	10	Sheffield Banking, Ltd., £50 Shs.....	17½	51½
S	10	Do. & Rotherham, Ltd., £50 Shs....	8	26⅜
S	15	Do. & Hallamsh., Ltd., £100 Shs..	25	61
S	10	Do. Union, Ltd., £40 Shs.........	10	25
M	12/	Union of Manchester, Ltd., £25 Shs.. ..	11	26¾
M	10/	Williams, Deacon, &c. Ltd., £50 Shs.....	8	25⅜
Bl	20	Wilts & Dorset, Ltd., £50 Shs.........	10	49
S	10/	York City & Co., Ltd., £10 Shs.....	3	14

BREWERIES.

Chief Market.	Int or Div.	Name.	Amount paid.	Price.
	6	Ansell & Sons Pref.	10	15¼
	5	Do. Debs.	100	110
	7/	Bent's	10	20
	6	Do. Cum. Pref...	10	14⅜
	4½	Do. Deb. Stk. ..	100	111
	13/6	Birkenhead, £5 paid	5	22
	13/6	Do. £10 paid....	10	25
	9/	Boddington's	9	21¼
	5	Do. Cum. Pref...	10	13½
	4	Do. Deb. Stk. ..	100	109
	4½	Butler & Co. Db. Stk	100	111
	6	Chesters' Cum. Pref.	10	13¾
	4½	Do. Debs.	100	112½
	17/	Clarkson's Ord.	10	24¾
	6	Do. Cum. Prf. Stk.	10	15
	4	Dutton & Co. Db. Sk.	100	103
	4½	Hardy's Crown Debs.	100	111
	6/	Holt	10	19¼
	5	Do. Cum. Pref...	10	12¼
	4	Do. Debs.	100	107½
	12/6	Lichfield	10	24
	5	Do. Cum. Pref...	10	11¾
	5½	Manchester Deb. Stk.	100	141
	14	Mitchell, H., & Co.	10	37½
	6	Do. Cum. Pref...	10	15⅜
	6	Oakhill Pref........	10	16½

Breweries (*continued*):—

Chief Market.	Int. or Div.	Name.	Amount paid.	Price.
M	—	Springwell	10	10¾
M	7	Do. Pref.	10	13¼
Bl	9	Stroud	10	17
Bl	6	Do. Pref......	10	14½
M	—	Taylor's Eagle......	10	11
M	7	Do. Cum. Pref ..	10	13⅛
M	5½	Do. Deb. Stk. ..	100	120½
S	10	Tennant Bros £20 shs	15	33½
S	10	Wheatley & Bates ..	10	14
S	6	Do. Cum. Pref.	10	12⅜

CANALS AND DOCKS.

Chief Market.	Int. or Div.	Name.	Amount paid.	Price.
Bl	8	Hill's Dry Dk. &c. £20	18	8
M	4	Manc. Ship Canal 1st Mt. Deb. Stk.	100	104
M	4	Do. 2nd do.	100	103
L	36/3	Mersey Dck. & Harb.	an.	119¼
L	35/	Do.	an.	114
M	10/	Rochdale Canal	100	37¼
B	35/	Staff. & Worc. Canal	100	75½
B	4½	Do. Deb. Stk....	100	137
Bl	4	Swansea Harb......	100	114
B	27/6	Warwick & Birm. Cnl	100	66
B	12/6	Do. & Napton do.	100	21½

COMMERCIAL & INDUSTRIAL.

Chief Market.	Int. or Div.	Name.	Amount paid.	Price.
L	5	Agua Santa Mt. Debs	100	100
M	—	Armitage, Sir E. & Sns Ltd............	10	19
M	4	Do. Deb. 1910 ..	100	103
L	6	Ang. Chil. Nit. 1 Mt. Debs., 1919 ..	100	108½
Bl	8½	Bath Stone Firms ..	10	19⅝
M	4/9½	Barlow & Jones, Ltd., £10 Shs.	8	10⅜
B	7/6	Birmgham. Ry. Car.	10	17
B	6	Do. Pref.	10	15⅛
B	5/	Do. Small Arms	5	18
M	£12	Blackpool Pier......	100	275½
M	5	Do. Tower Debs.	50	54½
M	6/6	Do. Wi. Gar. & P.	5	4⅝
Bl	10	Bristl. & S. W. R. Wag. £20 Shs..........	3	6⅛
Bl	8	Do. Wag. & Carri. £10 Shs..........	10	14⅛
M	7/	Crosses & Winkwth. Ltd..............	5	12⅜
L	5	G. Angus & Co. Pref.	10	13⅝
Bl	10	Gloster. Carri. & W.		10
Bl	5	Gt. Wstn. Cttn., Ltd.	20	15¾
M	6	Hetherington, L. Prf.	10	9⅝
M	4½	Do. Debs., 1910	100	96
B	75	Hinks (J. & Son), Ltd.	1	1⅜
S	10/	Jessop & Sons, £50 Sh	30	26½
S	10	Kayser, Ellsn. & Co. L.	5	10
S	6	Do. Pref.	5	7½
M	7/6	Kellner-Partgton., L.	5	14½
M	4½	Do. Debs., 1914..	100	105½
M	5	Kerr Thread, Ltd., Debs..............	100	99
B	17/	King's Norton Metal, £10 Shs..........	8½	18¼
M	5/	Lancashire & Yorks. Wagon, Ltd.	10	10
L	10/	Liverpool Exch., Ltd.	20	27½
L	35/	Do. Grain Stge, Ltd.	50	110
L	2/6	Do. Rubber, Ltd...	5	7
M	9d.	Manchester Bond. Whse., L., £10 Shs.	4½	2¾
M	3/9	Do. Comcial. Bldgs., Ltd., £10 Shs.	5	10⅜
M	3/9	Do. No. 2, £10 Shs.	5	10⅛
M	2/3	Do. No. 3, £10 Shs.	5	7¼
M	4/	Do. Corn, &c., Exchange, Ltd.	10	16½
M	4	Do. Debs.	100	125
M	8	Do. Ryl. Exchge, L.	100	246½
B	5	Midland Rlwy. Car. Wgn., Ld., £20 Sh.	10	14½
B	59	Millers & Corys Dbs.	100	101
B	18/6	Mint, Brgham., Ltd.	5	7
B	5	Do. Debs.	25	107
B	10/	Nettlefolds, Ltd.....	10	46
B	5	Do. Pref.	10	15
S	9	Nth. Centrl. Wgn., L.	5	8¼
B	10/	Patnt. Nut & Bolt, L.	10	28½
B	5	Do. Pref.	10	14⅛
B	6d.	Perry & Co., Ltd. ..	1	29/6
B	6d.	Do. Pref.	1	1¼
S	10	Round, J., & Co., L., £10 Shs.	6	12⅝
S	10	Rodgers, J., & Sons, L.	100	218
M	18/9	Rylands & Sons, Ltd., £20	15	40¾
M	2/6	Do. paid up	20	46
M	4	Do. Debs. .. 1909	100	106
S	5	Sanderson Brs. & Co., Ltd Debs.	100	102
M	4½	Schwabe, S., & Co., Ltd., 1 Debs. 1914	100	104
S	7½	Sheffield Forge & Rolling, Ltd.	10	11
L	—	Southport Pier, Ltd.	100	92½
L	2½	Do. W. Gdns., Ltd.	5	3⅜
Bl	5	Spillers & Bakers, Ltd, £10 Shs.	9	14½
Bl	6	Do. Pref.	10	14¼
B	5/	Union Rolling Stock, Ltd., £20 Shs....	5	7½
M	5/	Victoria Pr., S'port, L.	5	4⅜
Bl	8	Western Wagon & Property, Ltd.....	6	9⅞
S	10	Wostenholm, G., & Son, Ltd., £25 Shs.	20	26¾
S	6½	Yorksh. Wagon, Ltd.	2	2⅜

FINANCIAL, TRUSTS, &c.

Chief Market.	Int. or Div.	Name.	Amount paid.	Price.
M	1/	Manchstr. Trst. £10 Shs..............	2	14/6
M	1/3	N. of Eng. T. Deb. & A., Ltd. £10 Shs.	2½	21/6
M	3½	Do. 1 Mt. Debs...	100	95½
L	—	Pacific Ln. & Inv., L.	2½	3
L	4	Do. Deb. Stk.....	100	102
L	—	United Trst., L. Prfd.	100	72½
L	—	Do. Deferred....	100	62½

GAS.

Chief Market.	Int. or Div.	Name.	Amount paid.	Price.
Bl	5	Bristol Gas (5 p.c. mx.)	100	130
Bl	4	Do. 1st Deb.	100	137
S	10	Gt. Grimsby "C" ..	10	202
L	10	Liverpool Utd. "A"	100	258
L	7	Do. "B"......	100	191
L	4	Do. Deb.	100	136
S	10	Sheffield Gas "A," "B," "C"	100	253
B	10½	Wolverhampton	100	222
B	3	Do. 6 p.c. Pref...	100	170½

INSURANCE.

Chief Market.	Int. or Div.	Name.	Amount paid.	Price.
M	6	Equitable F. & Acc. £5 Shs.	1	39/
L	—	Liverpool Mortgage £10 Shs.	2	1⅞
M	2/	Mchester. Fire £20 Shs	2	7⅛
M	5/	National Boiler & G., Ltd., £10 Shs.	3	13½
L	2/	Reliance Mar., Ltd., £10 Shs.	2	4⅜
L	2/	Sea, Ltd., £10 Shs...	2	10⅞
L	—	Stnd. Mar., L., £20 Sh.	4	8⅝
L	—	State Fire, L., £20 Sh.	1	2⅛

COAL, IRON, AND STEEL.

Chief Market.	Int. or Div.	Name.	Amount paid.	Price.
Bl.	7/6	Albion Stm. Coal ..	10	10⅞
M	—	And. Knowles & S., Ltd., £37½ Shs. ..	22½	13½
M	5	Do. Mt. Debs. 1908	100	105½
Bl.	1/½	Ashton V. Iron	100	25
S		Bessemer, Ltd.	10	19½
S	5	Do. Pref.	10	13
S	7	Briggs, H., & Co., "A" £15 Shs.....	12½	15½
S	7	Do. "B" £15 Shs.	8½	9⅞
S	20	Brown Baley's. Stl., L.	10	29½
S	5	Brown, J., & Co., Cum. Pref.	10	13¼
S	5	Cammell, C. & Co., Ltd.	85	12⅜
S	5	Do. Pref.	5	36½
M	5	Chatterley Whitfield. Col., Debs., 1905..	100	100½
Bl	4	Davis, D., & Sons, Ld.	10	9¾
M	5	Evans, R., & Co., Ltd., Deb., 1910 ..	100	100½
S	12½	Fox, S., & Co., Ltd., £100 Shs.	80	178½
Bl	10	Gt. Wstn. Col., L., "A"	5	10
Bl	5	Do. "B"	5	4⅝
Bl	3	Main Colliery, Ltd.	10	7
B	2/6	Muntz's Metal, Ltd.	5	7⅝
B	5	Do. Pref......	5	6⅛
M	2/6½	Nth. Lonsd. Iron and Steel, Ltd., £10 Sh.	8½	2½
Bl	6	North's Nav. Coll., Ltd., Debs.	100	107
S	60/	Parkgate Irn. & Stl., Ltd., £100 Shs. ..	75	68
M	6	Pearson & Knls., Ld., "A" Cum. Pref...	50	46
B	10/	Sandwell Pk. Col., L.	10	17⅜
M	6/3	Sheepbridge Coal and Iron, Ltd., "A"	25	17¾
M	2/6	Do. "B"	10	6½
M	5	Do. "C" Gua. Pf.	25	28½
Bl	4	South Wales Coll., Ltd., "A"	17	8½
S	55/	Staveley Coal & Iron, Ltd., "A" £100 Sh.	60	79¾
S	55/	Do. "C"	60	80¾
M	1/10½	Tredegar Iron & Cl., Ld., "A" £10 Sh.	7½	2⅞
M	1½	Do. "B" Stk. ..	100	29½
M	2/	Wigan Cl. & Irn., Ld.	10	6
M	1/6	Do. £10 Shs.	7½	3½

SHIPPING.

Chief Market.	Int. or Div.	Name.	Amount paid.	Price.
Bl	6	Bristol St. Nav. Pref.	10	11⅞
L	5/	Brit. & Af. St. Nav..	10	13¼
L	—	British & Estn, Ltd.	6½	3
L	10/	Pacific Stm. Nav., L.	25	24
L	10/	Wst. Ind. & Pac. St. Ltd., £25 Shs....	20	29½

TRAMWAYS, &c.

Chief Market.	Int. or Div.	Name.	Amount paid.	Price.
B	5/	Brmngh. & Aston, L.	5	11
B	5/	Do. Mid., Ltd...	10	8
Bl	6/	Bristol Tr. & Car., Ltd................	10	20½
Bl	4/	Do. Debs.	100	121
L	6	I. of Man Elec., L., Pref.	1	1½
M	15/	Manchester C. & T, L., "A" £20 Shs.	15	27½
M	10/	Do. "B"	10	18¾

WATER WORKS.

Chief Market.	Int. or Div.	Name.	Amount paid.	Price.
Bl	7	Bristol	25	61
Bl	7	Do................	20	46½
Bl	58/	Do. 7 p.c. max. ..	100	157½
Bl	4½	Do. Pref.	20	32½
Bl	5	Do. Pref.	10	18⅝
Bl	3½	Do. Deb.	100	129½
M	10	Fylde "A"........	100	335
M	7	Do. "B"	100	224
B	6	S. Staffs. Ord. "A"	100	168
B	—	Do. "B"	100	167
B	4	Do. Deb. Stk.	100	140
B	5	Do. Pf "A" "B" "C"	100	165
M	£3⅜	Stockport District ..	100	185½
B	2/	Wolverhampton New	5	6½

SCOTTISH.

In quoting the markets, E stands for Edinburgh, and G for Glasgow.

RAILWAYS.

Chief Market.	Int. or Div.	Name.	Nom. Amount	Price.
E	6⅛	Arbroath and Forfar	25	51
G	2	Callander and Oban.	10	7½
G	4	Do. Deb. Stock	100	148
G	4½	Do. Pref.......	10	14½
G	4	Cathct. Dist. Deb. Stk.	100	148
E	5	Edin. and Bathgate .	100	181½
E	7	Forth & Clyde Junc.	100	226
G	4	Lanarks. and Ayrsh.	10	14
G	4	Do. & Dumbartons.	10	14 9/16
G	4	Do. Deb. Stk.	100	149

BANKS.

Chief Market.	Int. or Div.	Name.	Nom. Amount	Price.
G	12	Bank of Scotland ..	100	357½
G	16	British Linen	100	478
G	8	Caledonian, Ltd.....	2½	97/6
G	10	Clydesdale, Ltd.	10	24
G	16	Commercl. of Scot., L.	20	88½†
G	16	National of Scot. Ld.	100	415
G	8	Royal of Scotland ..	100	230
G	12½	Town & County, Ltd.	7	20 13/16
G	11	Union of Scotland, L.	10	25⅛

BREWERIES.

Chief Market.	Int. or Div.	Name.	Nom. Amount	Price.
E	5	Bernard, Thos. Pref.	10	11½
E	5	Bernard, T. & J., Cum. Pref.........	10	12¾
G	20	Highland Distilleries	2½	10⅛

CANALS AND DOCKS.

Chief Market.	Int. or Div.	Name.	Nom. Amount	Price.
G	4	Clyde Nav. 4 p.c....	100	126½
G	3½	Do. 3½ p.c......	100	103½
G	3½	Greenock Harb. "A"	100	96½
G	1	Do. "B"	100	38½

MISCELLANEOUS.

Chief Market.	Int. or Div.	Name.	Nom. Amount	Price.
G	4½	Alexander & Co. Debs.	100	110½
G	5	Baird, H., & Sns. C. P.	10	12½
E	10	Barry, Ostlere, & Co.	7½	12½
E	6	Do. Cum. Pref...	10	15 5/16
G	5	Brown, Stewart, Deb.	100	84
E	7½	Broxburn Oil	8½	8¾
E	6	Do. Cum. Pref...	10	11 5/16
E	7	Edinburgh & Dist. Tram. Cum. Pref.	5	8 11/16
E	5	Gilroy, Sons, & Co. Debs.	100	99
G	3/	Glasgow Cot. Spin...	6	5 1/16
G	55/	Do. Royal Exchg.	46	110
G	—	Pumpherston Oil Pf.	10	8¾
E	7	Scottish Assam Tea	10	11½
E	5	Scottish Waggon....	10	13½
G	5	Stoddard & Co. Pref.	10	12 1/16

FINANCIAL, LAND, AND INVESTMENT.

Chief Market.	Int. or Div.	Name.	Nom. Amount	Price.
G	1/	Assets Co...........	1	47/
E	4½	Investors' Mort. Pref.	100	99½
E	4	Do. Deb. Stk....	100	103½
E	4	Nthn. Inv. N. Zeal. Deb. Stk.	100	107
E	4	N. of Scot. Canadian Deb. Stk.	100	106
E	4½	Real & Deb. Corp. Deb. Stk.	100	106½

INSURANCE.

Chief Market.	Int. or Div.	Name.	Amount paid.	Price.
G	12/	Caledonian F. & Life	5	36¾
G	4/6	City of Glasgow Life	2½	13⅞
E	19/	Edinburgh Life	20	55
G	13/1	Life Ass. of Scotland	8⅓	34½
E	8	Nat. Guar. & Surety	2	48/6
G	17½	Scottish Union and National "A"....	1	96/6
G	17½	Do. "B"	3¾	18

IRON, COAL, AND STEEL.

Chief Market.	Int. or Div.	Name.	Amount paid.	Price.
E	Nil.	Addie, Coll. Cm. Pref.	10	8
E	8/	Arniston Coal	8	14½
E	5	Cairntable Gas Coal	8	86/
E	7½	Fife Coal	10	21
E	5	Do. Cum. Pref..	10	13½
G	7	Merry & Cunghame. Cum. Pref........	10	15¼
G	5	Do. Debentures ..	100	105½
E	1/9	Niddrie & Benhar Cl.	1½	40/
G	5	Steel Com. of Scotlnd	—	
	—	"A" Deb. Stk. ..	100	110
G	6	Do. and Mt. "B"	100	105
E	—	Watson, John	8½	10¼
E	6	Do. Cum. Pref..	7½	8¾
E	12½	Wilson's & Cly. Coal	3	9½

IRISH.

In quoting the markets, B stands for Belfast, and D for Dublin.

CORPORATION STOCKS.

Chief Market.	Int. or Div.	Name.	Amount paid.	Price.
B	3½	Belfast, 1921	100	113
B	3⅝	Do. 1912........	100	108½
B	3½	Do. 1924........	100	109½
B	3	Do. 1955........	100	106
B	3½	Do. Water Com...	100	117
B	3	Do. do.	100†	107½
B	3½	Do. Harbour Com.	100	113½
D	3½	Rathmines & Rathgar	100	110¼
D	3½	Waterford Deb.	100	—

RAILWAYS.

Chief Market.	Int. or Div.	Name.	Amount Paid.	Price.
D	25/	Cork, Bandon, & S.C.	100	76
D	4	Do. Deb.........	100	—
D	4	Do. W. Cork Pref.	100	119
B	5½	Belfast & Northern..	100	161
B	4	Do. Deb.........	100	148½
B	4	Do. Pref.	100	143
B	6½	Belfast & C. Down..	100	167
B	4	Do. Deb.........	100	149
B	3	Do.	100	109
B	4½	Do. 4½ Pref. B...	100	153½
B	5	Do. Guar.	100	173½
D	Nil.	Dublin, Wick. & Wex.	100	25
D	4	Do. Deb.........	100	125½
D	4½	Do. Deb.........	100	130
D	6	Do. Guar.	100	163
D	4	Do. C. of Dub. Junc.	100	—
D	5	Do. 1860 Pref. ..	100	106
D	—	Do. 1864 Pref. ..	100	90
D	—	Do. 1865 Pref. ..	100	81
B	6½	Great Northern	100	183
B	4	Do. Deb.........	100	150
B	4	Do. Pref. B.	100	145½
B	5½	Gt. South & Western	100	144½
B	4	Do. Deb.	100	149½
B	4	Do. Guar.........	100	146
D	4	Midland Gt. Western	100	112
D	4	Do. Deb.	100	—
D	4½	Do. Deb.	100	150
D	4½	Do. Deb.	100	—
D	5	Do. Pref.	100	177
D	4	Do. Pref.	100	143
D	—	Waterford & Central	100	—
D	3	Do. Deb.	100	94½
D	3½	Do. Pref.	100	—
D	4	Waterfd. L., & W. Db.	100	128
D	4½	Do. Deb.	100	—
D	4	Do. Pref.	100	116
D	3½	Do. Pref.	100	90½

BANKS.

Chief Market.	Int. or Div.	Name.	Amount paid.	Price.
B	50/	Belfast, Old, £125 Shs.	25	127
B	20/	Do. New, £125 Shs.	25	50½
D	2/	Hibernian, £20 Shs.	5	6½
D	2/	Munster & Leinster £5 Shs.	2	5½
B	11/	Northern, £50 Shs...		26½
D	13/	Royal, £50 Shs.	10	29½
B	5/	Ulster, £15 Shs.	2½	12½

BREWERIES AND DISTILLERIES.

Chief Market.	Int. or Div.	Name.	Amount paid.	Price.
D	10/	Castlebellingham & Drog	10	15½
D	6	Do. Pref.	10	15½
D	4½	Do. Deb.	100	116
B	17/	Dunville & Co.......	10	29
B	6	Irish Distillery, Pref.	10	13
B	5	Do. Deb.	100	111
B	6	J. & J. M'Connell, Pf.	10	14½†
B	13/6	Mitchell & Co.......	9	19½
B	5	Do. Deb.	10	11½†
D	4½	Phœnix Brew. Deb.	100	—
B	6/	Wm. Cowan........	10	12½
B	6	Do. Pref. ..	10	13½
B	8/	Young, King, & Co.	8	14

STEAM AND CANAL.

Chief Market.	Int. or Div.	Name.	Amount paid.	Price.
B	Nil	Belfast Steamship ..	50	35½
D	10/	British and Irish	50	—
D	15/	City of Dublin......	100	63½
D	3½	Do. Deb.	100	104½
D	30/	Dublin & Lpool. Bldg.	50	—
D	2/6	Dundalk & Newry...	10	4½
D	3/6	Grand Canal........	10	11½
D	3	Do. Pref. ..	10	9½
D	3	Do. Deb. ..	100	—
B	30/	Irish Shipowners....	100	60
B	3/6	Ulster Steamship....	5	6½

MISCELLANEOUS.

Chief Market.	Int. or Div.	Name.	Amount paid.
D	3/1	Arnott & Co.	4
D	6	Do. Pref. ..	4
B	9/	Belfast Com. Bldgs.	10
B	52/6	Do. Ropework Co.	75
B	5	Do. do. Pref.	10
B	2/	Do. Discount Co..	3
B	5	Do. do. Pref.	5
B	10/	Brookfield Linen....	25
B	Nil	Coey & Co.	25
B	5	Do. Deb.	50
B	4½	David Allen & S's Deb.	100†
D	4/	Dublin Trams	10
D	6	Do. Pref.....	10
D	4	Do. Deb....	100
B	5/	Edenderry Spinning .	10
B	25/	Falls Flax Spinning .	25
B	17/	Forster, Green, & Co.	20
B	9/	Island Spinning	7½
B	8/	Jas. Lindsay & Co..	8
B	1/7½	John Arnott & Co...	4
B	4½	Do. Deb.........	50
D	5/	Kinahan & Co.......	10
D	5½	Do. Pref........	10
D	4½	Do. Deb........	100
B	12/	Kirker & Co.	10
B	5/	Leahy, Kelly, & Leahy	5
B	6	Do. Pref........	5
B	2/4½	Lindsay Bros. Ltd...	5
B	4½	Do. Deb........	50
D	1/	National Assurance .	2½
B	10/	Olley & Co.	5
D	1/1½	Patriotic Assurance..	2½
B	3/7½	P. Johnston & Son, L.	6
B	10/	Robertson, F., & Co.	8
B	5	Ulster Marine Insur.	5/
B	15/	York-street Flax	25
B	6	Do. Pref........	10
B	4½	Do. Deb........	100

INDIAN AND CEYLON TEA COMPANIES.

Acres Planted.	Crop, 1896.	Paid up Capital.	Share.	Paid up.	Name.	Dividends. 1894.	Dividends. 1895.	Dividends. 1896.	Int. 1897.	Price.	Yield.	Reserve.	Balance Forward.	Working Capital.	Mortgage Debs., or Pref. Capital not otherwise stated.
	lb.	£	£	£	INDIAN COMPANIES.							£	£	£	£
11,240	3,109,000	120,000	10	3	Amalgamated Estates	—	*	10	5	3¾	8½	10,000	16,500	D52,950	—
		400,000	10	10	Do. Pref.	—	*	5	15	1⅞	4⅛				
10,223	3,387,100	187,160	20	20	Assam	20	20	20	5	61	6½	55,000	1,730	D11,350	—
5,900	3,310,000	142,500	10	10	Assam Frontier...........	3	6	6	—	9½	6¼	—	286	20,000	82,500
		142,500	10	10	Do. Pref.	6	6	6	3	12	5				
2,087	865,550	66,745	5	5	Attaree Khat	12	10	8	3	7½	5½	3,790	4,820	7,770	—
1,633	550,980	78,170	10	10	Borelli	4	4	5	—	8½	5¾	—	3,256	D270	6,500 Pref.
1,689	880,000	60,825	5	5	British Indian	6	5	5	—	4½	5½	—	2,920	12,300	16,900 Pr
3,223	2,282,430	114,500	5	5	Brahmapootra	20	18	20	6	14½	7	—	28,440	41,600	
3,904	1,634,000	76,500	10	10	Cachar and Dooars	*	8	7	—	9½	7½	—	1,645	21,240	
		76,500	10	10	Do. Pref.	*	6	6	3	12½	4¾				
3,946	2,002,370	72,010	1	1	Chargola	8	7	10	2½	1	10	3,000	3,300	—	—
		81,000	1	1	Do. Pref.	7	7	7	3½	1⅛	5				
1,972	968,090	33,000	5	5	Chubwa	10	8	10	3½	7	7½	10,000	2,043	D5,400	—
		33,000	5	5	Do. Pref.	7	7	7	3½	7	5				
33,250	10,620,000	120,000	10	3	Cons. Tea and Lands	—		10	5	4	7½	65,000	14,240	D191,674	—
		1,000,000	10	10	Do. 1st Pref.	—	*	5	15	11	4½				
		400,000	10	10	Do. 2nd Pref.	—	*	7	17	11½	5½				
2,230	593,280	135,420	20	20	Darjeeling..............	5½	5½	6	—	23½	5	5,552	1,565	1,700	—
2,114	456,580	60,000	10	10	Darjeeling Cons..........	—		4/2	—	7½	—	—	1,880	—	—
		60,000	10	10	Do. Pref.	—	*	5	2½	9½	5				
6,600	2,973,050	150,000	10	10	Dooars	12½	12½	12½	7½	21	6¼	45,000	300	D32,000	—
		75,000	10	10	Do. Pref.	7	7	7	3½	17½	4				
3,367	1,833,520	165,000	10	10	Doom Dooma	11½	10	12½	5	23	5½	30,000	4,032	—	20,00
1,377	500,080	61,120	5	5	Eastern Assam	⅝	nil.	4	—	3½	5½	—	1,790	—	10,00
4,038	1,529,380	85,000	10	10	East India and Ceylon	¾	nil.	7	—	9½	7	—	1,710	—	—
		85,000	10	10	Do. Pref.	*	6	6	3	12	5				
7,570	3,600,000	219,000	10	10	Empire of India	—	*	6/10	2	12½	—	15,000	—	27,000	—
		219,000	10	10	Do. Pref.	—	*	5	2½	11½	4½				
1,180	647,600	94,060	10	10	Indian of Cachar	7	3½	3	—	5½	5½	6,070	—	7,120	—
2,916	968,000	83,500	5	5	Jhanzie	10	10	10	4	8½	5½	14,500	1,070	2,700	—
7,980	3,467,000	250,000	10	10	Jokai	10	10	10	5	18	5½	45,000	990	D9,000	—
		100,000	10	10	Do. Pref.	*	6	6	3	15½	3¾				
5,224	1,801,600	100,000	20	20	Jorehant	20	20	20	—	58	7	26,220	2,955	3,000	—
1,547	554,560	65,660	10	8	Lebong	15	15	15	5	17½	6½	9,000	2,150	8,690	—
5,082	1,843,700	100,000	10	10	Lungla		10	6	3	10	6	—	1,543	D21,000	—
		100,000	10	10	Do. Pref.	*	6	6	3	12½	4⅞				
2,684	866,300	95,970	10	10	Majuli	7	5	5	—	7	7	—	2,606	560	—
1,300	216,000	91,840	1	1	Makum	—	—	2	—	1½	1½	—	—	1,200	25,00
3,140	938,400	100,000	1	1	Moabund	—	—	*	—	1	—	—	—	—	—
		50,000	1	1	Do. Pref.	—	—	*	2½	1	5				
1,080	510,000	79,590	10	10	Scottish Assam	7	7	7	—	11	6½	6,500	800	9,590	—
4,150	1,635,000	100,000	10	10	Singlo..................		8	5	1	9½	4½	—	300	D5,200	—
		80,000	10	10	Do. Pref.	*	6½	6½	3½	13	5				
					CEYLON COMPANIES.										
10,315	1,743,824	250,000	100	100	Anglo-Ceylon, & Gen.	—	*	5½	—	70	7½	10,992	1,405	D72,844	166,5
1,836	685,741	50,000	10	10	Associated Tea	—	*	5	—	8½	5½	—	164	2,478	—
		60,000	10	10	Do. Pref.	—	*	6	—	11	5½				
10,390	3,763,000	167,380	10	10	Ceylon Tea Plantations ..	15	15	15	7	27½	5½	84,500	1,516	D30,819	—
		81,080	10	10	Do. Pref.	7	7	7	17	17	4½				
5,722	1,542,700	55,260	5	3	Ceylon & Oriental Est....	5	8	7	—	2½	7½	—	230	D2,047	71,0
		46,000	5	5	Do. Pref.	6	6	6	3	5	6				
2,157	801,629	111,330	5	5	Dimbula Valley	—	*	10	5	6½	7	—	—	1,733	6,
		62,607	5	5	Do. Pref.	—	*	6	3	6½	4½				
11,496	3,715,000	298,250	5	5	Eastern Prod. & Est.	3	5	6½	2½	6½	4½	20,000	11,740	D17,797	102,5
3,118	701,100	150,000	10	10	Lanka Plantations.......	4	5	5	15	7½	6½	—	495	D11,300	14,700
2,193	960,100	22,080	10	10	New Dimbula "A"	10	16	16	—	25	6	11,000	2,024	1,150	—
		55,710	10	10	Do. "B"	18	16	16	—	23½	6½				
		8,400	10	10	Do. "C"	nil.	8	14	—	15	8½				
2,572	570,360	100,000	10	10	Ouvah	6	8	6	2	9½	6½	4,000	1,151	D1,253	—
2,630	535,675	200,000	10	10	Nuwara Eliya	—	*	6	3	11½	5½	—	—	—	30,0
1,720	720,200	41,000	10	10	Scottish Ceylon	15	15	15	5	23	6½	7,000	1,252	D3,970	—
		9,000	10	10	Do. Pref.	7	7	7	3½	17	5½				
2,450	602 000	56,000	10	6	Standard	12½	15	15	5	14½	6½	9,000	800	D14,022	4,0

* Company formed this year.

Working-Capital Column.—In working-capital column, D stands for *debit*.

† Interim dividends are given as actual distribution made.

‡ *Total* div.

Printed for the Proprietor by Love & Wyman, Ltd., Great Queen Street, London, W.C.; and Published by Clement Wil
at Norfolk House, Norfolk Street, Strand, London, W.C.

The Investors' Review

Vol. I.—No. 5. New Series. FRIDAY, FEBRUARY 4, 1898. [Registered as a Newspaper.] Price 6d. By post, 6½d

The Investment Index,

A Quarterly Supplement to the "Investors' Review."

Price 2s. net. 8s. 6d. per annum, post free.

THE INVESTMENT INDEX is an indispensable supplement to the Investors' Review. A file of it enables investors to follow the ups and downs of markets, and each number gives the return obtainable on all classes of securities at recent prices, arranged in a most convenient form for reference. Appended to its tables of figures are criticisms on company balance sheets, State Budgets, &c., similar to those in the Investors' Review.

Regarding it, the *Speaker* says: "The Quarterly 'Investment Index' is probably the handiest and fullest, as it is certainly the safest, of guides to the investor."

"The compilation of securities is particularly valuable."—*Pall Mall Gazette.*

"Its carefully classified list of securities will be found very valuable." —*Globe.*

"At no time has such a list of securities been more valuable than at the present."—*Star.*

"The invaluable 'Investors' Index.'"—*Sketch.*

"A most valuable compilation."—*Glasgow Herald.*

. Subscription to the "Investors' Review" and "Investment Index," 36s. per annum, post free.

CLEMENT WILSON,
NORFOLK HOUSE, NORFOLK STREET, LONDON, W.C.

CONTENTS

The Investors' Review.

Economic and Financial Notes and Correspondence.

THE MEETING OF PARLIAMENT.

On Tuesday next the Parliamentary Session of 1898 begins. Is there anything to hope for from it? Will the men of tongue now assembling guard the nation's interests, watch jealously over the spending of its money, insist upon knowing the real and not merely the official truth about India, about the Soudan campaign, about Uganda, about China, about the "Chartered" Company; pry into affairs all round, and exhibit an enlightened Imperial spirit? We may safely predict that it will do none of these things. Party fights there will be, hot and noisy, and about as real as the pillow-fights of school boys; and party votes without end. But competence in affairs, disinterested patriotism, earnest application to the nation's business—these are qualities the thinking portion of the electorate has almost ceased to look for in the rank and file, or in most leaders also for that matter, of any party in the political arena.

Which one among all the 670 gentlemen of the House of Commons, who may be presumed to be at the post of duty next Tuesday, could take up either the Army or Navy estimates and go through them with an intelligent perception of their import? Not one. We do not blame them; the accounts, as now presented, are unfathomable by mortal man, and in all likelihood intended so to be. Chaotic heaps of figures revealing nothing, under which the truth is buried—truth about wastes and peculations and downright robberies beyond number, are flung on the table of the House and at sight of them most men flee. They are not to be blamed for that, but they are worthy of the deepest censure, because they have none of them the backbone to insist upon having the accounts presented in a form as clear as the balance-sheet, say, of a respectable company when laid before its board of directors.

Our members of Parliament are in a very real sense directors of some of the biggest businesses in the world—dockyards, ordnance factories, powder factories, clothing establishments, food and fodder depôts, horse-coping businesses, and so on, and they positively know nothing whatever about the industries and commerce they are popularly supposed to control. Knowing nothing, they allow every imaginable abuse to grow and flourish under their very eyes. All they can do is to vote away the nation's money as the wasters in the permanent departments demand it, gabbling over votes involving millions as a formalist gabbles his prayers, and caring less apparently about the misery the waste of these millions may lay upon millions of their constituents than about the management of the House Kitchens. When debates do arise over estimates they are always trivial debates, often ludicrously so; and the intelligent voter looks on and wonders how it will all end. Will King Demos grow weary one day of sending amiable philanthropists, shrewd pushing lawyers, unscrupulous or light-headed demagogues, retired merchants, worthy but fat, mingled with a trooping array of guinea-pig directors, fraudulent company promoters, and gamblers of every shade and degree to be his representative in Parliament and look after his affairs?

China and the Powers.

So far as we can make out, the British position in China is not necessarily weakened by the withdrawal of our demand that Ta-lien-wan should be opened as a treaty port. It must always be remembered that the strength of this position lies in our limiting our demands to "equal rights with every other Power." While Germany contemplated erecting Kiau-Chow into an exclusively German *entrepôt*, we had the right to regard this aggression as an infringement of existing treaties; but when Germany gave way and announced that Kiau-Chow would be an open port we had, and could have, nothing further to say. In like manner the pretensions of Russia to exclusive possession of Port Arthur, and to exclusive privileges over Manchuria, were offensive to us, contrary to treaty, and inimical to the interests of every European Power. But Russia, it is declared, has followed the example of Germany in announcing that Port Arthur will be free, and, as we gather, under the control of the Chinese Maritime Customs Service. If this be the case there remains no necessity whatever for our insisting upon the opening of Ta-lien-wan, and all that is doubtful is whether we should have given way without securing more substantial concessions in other directions. Possibly, however, this may have been done. We have only very imperfect information about what is going on at Pekin, and must guard against hasty judgments, however much we may dread that our Government is being jockeyed out of its supreme position in the country.

There still remains the question of the loan, over which, as was expected, the haggling is immense. Here also it appears to us no harm can come by admitting Germany, Russia, and France to participate in the guarantee if they are so minded. We have joined on other occasions with Continental Powers to guarantee loans, notably loans to Holland, Turkey, and Egypt, and no harm has come of the co-partnery. In like manner, it follows almost as a matter of course that if all the Powers are to have "equal rights" in China, all may claim to have equal share in the responsibilities assumed. If it gratifies the vanity, pride, or whatever you like to call it, of the Powers now worrying around the proposed loan to China to be admitted as participants in its guarantee, there is no reason why their wishes should not be met. We still retain the master position because the bulk of the money must be found here. On Wednesday we were told that the Disconto Bank, Deutsche Bank, together with several firms in Berlin and Petersburg, have joined in providing a loan of a hundred million roubles to China; and we say let them do so by all means, but they have got to find that money outside England, and it will take them all their time to do it, unless it be raised by bills discounted on the London market. Supposing that loan floated, Germany and Russia are really no better off in China than they are now, providing always that we hold fast by our "treaty rights." In this our strength lies quite as much as in our fleet, although a strong fleet must be kept in Chinese waters to secure respect for them. And the more strength we show, the more determined we appear to let no one get before us either with ports opened, concessions, or anything else, the safer will peace be. To talk about war is folly. There ought to be no war, and if war does break out it will be due to gross mismanagement either in Pekin or in Downing-street.

President McKinley and Silver.

Too much must not be made here of the ambiguity of Mr. McKinley's language at the National Banquet a week ago in New York. In saying that it is the duty of the National Government "to regulate the value of its money by the highest standards of commercial honesty and national honour," he probably went as far as his position allowed him. To say right off, that the standard money in the United States shall be gold money, would have caused such a division among his supporters as no party man could encounter. Readers know very well our opinion regarding the position of the United States in the matter of its currency. Nothing could be weaker or more unsatisfactory. It is a position calculated to bring a great disaster upon the country. At the same time, it is not an immediate disaster, and were the country to be governed economically and wisely in other respects, there is no particular reason why the disaster should ever come. The root of the weakness is in extravagance.

Suppose the worst, however, and that, after a brief spell of prosperity created by last year's good harvest, the United States should fall back into a condition of semi-insolvency—a condition forcing its Government to suspend the redemption of its paper money in gold altogether—it does not follow that the railway and other corporate securities of the Union should also dishonour their definite obligation to pay in gold. Great hardship there would be, and also here and there default, but we believe the country to be great enough and intrinsically wealthy enough to insure payment of the interest upon every well-secured obligation created within it. Also, we believe that there is a spirit of righteousness among the people of the United States which would assert itself were they once face to face with a great national danger. It must never be forgotten that the best side of the American people is not usually visible to us. To an extraordinary degree they are a patient, law-abiding, and industrious people. If they go astray on false economic by-paths and inflict injury upon themselves, or allow it to be inflicted, by cruelly devised tariffs, by monstrous steals like the Pensions Fund and the universal malversations of a corrupt political class, it is not because they are themselves in sympathy with dishonesty in high places, but because they are not yet fully aroused from their indifference. Let a crisis of a dangerous kind stir them up, and we should lose all faith in the future of democratic communities if we did not believe that the American people would rise to the occasion and set the wrong right.

The Railway Share Debenture and Trusts.

Mr. C. C. Macrae is to be congratulated on the manner in which he has piloted the twin trusts—the Railway Share Trust and Agency and the Railway Debenture Trust—past the shoals and quicksands of the past. To be able now to say that both these Trusts have a surplus value in their assets over liabilities, or very nearly so in the one case, is proof of considerable tact and foresight. There is, however, one matter which we cannot refrain from alluding to, and that is the manner in which the revenue of the Railway Share Trust and Agency is reported. This is simply stated as "gross profits, £66,078." Now, the total investments and loans of the Trust come to £832,073, and such a profit represents a little over 8 per cent. upon this total. It is impossible to imagine that such a return is obtained in these days from interest upon investments alone, and the revenue must be assisted from other sources. Would it not, therefore, be as well to divide up the revenue, so as to distinguish the sources, or the main sources? If profit on realisations or commissions upon new issues constitute a fair proportion of the amount, such a matter is of vital importance to shareholders, or intending shareholders, because such profits only assume importance at times like the present, and cannot be looked upon as stable revenue. To grant such information is very usual, and now that the Railway Share Trust has been lifted clear of its old disrepute, the reform might well be instituted.

United States Pension Scandal.

We are glad to see the New York *Commercial Chronicle* is at last taking this subject seriously in hand. In a very interesting article published by it on the 15th ult. it gives the history of the growth of this fraud upon the American people. According to this, in 1866, the first full year after the close of hostilities, the pension expenditure was only $15,000,000, and at the beginning of 1872 General James A. Garfield declared "that we may reasonably expect that the expenses for pensions will hereafter steadily decrease, unless our legislation should be unwarrantably extravagant." Yet in 1878 the pension expenditure had risen to $61,000,000, in 1882 to a hundred millions, and so it continued to mount up until in the fiscal year 1893 the monstrous total of $159,357,000 was attained. The money obtained by dishonest taxation, and dissipated in this way, was at this last date, therefore, nearly five times the amount which General Garfield, twenty-one years before, had declared to be the maximum under honest and economic administration. What can we say of a democracy which allows an infamy of this kind to be perpetrated upon it without serious protest, without shock, apparently, to its moral sense? We can only think that a people content to endure a thing of this kind deserves a master and not liberty; a master like John Rockefeller.

But it will not endure for long masters of this type. Of this we may feel sure. All we dread is that the infamy might last long enough to renew the smouldering antagonism between North and South. The treatment the conquering North has bestowed all through upon the South since the close of the Civil War has been brutally selfish in the extreme. One may almost say that all progress has been denied to the South by the fiscal policy of the Republican Party—the victorious party. Southern ports have been left to languish for want of trade—only in recent years have railway systems been formed and extended in a way calculated to develop those ports. But high tariffs have forced, and still force, the bulk of the foreign trade of the Republic to pass through Northern ports, and, above all, through the dominant port of New York. The handicap this means to the South is of a weight unmeasurable, and therefore progress in the South—the fairest, and naturally fattest, portion of the Union—has been slow. Its maltreatment at the hands of the "machine" politicians of the North has only to be continued long enough to raise a new rebellion.

The Indian Frontier Shambles.

Sir William Lockhart, Commander-in-Chief Designate of India, holds the opinion that "the campaign against the Afridis must be renewed in the spring." Of course. Our heroic and "patriotic" native army of India must have further lessons in the chivalrous act of waiting until the miserable wives and children of the hillmen have crept back to their huts in order that they may be mercifully and safely shot down in their sleep from a distance. British "honour" is in this way so nobly vindicated. The Afridis will not submit this winter, Sir William thinks, but his generous spirit is much comforted by the thought that "severe loss of life has already been inflicted on them, and their country terribly devastated." How noble and generous a profession is that of the warrior! How he steels his heart against the wail of the hungry and the dying, and gloats over the thought that the weak and defenceless shall be left shelterless among the mountains!

What good comes to us, to any one in India, in the border lands beyond the frontier, through the exercise of all this cruelty? Good? Who spoke of good? It is necessary to "punish" these "rebels" for daring to defend their homes against the British invaders; or if not, no matter. Soldiers are made to fight, and as well fight the mountain tribes as anybody else. It keeps the hand in, and enables a few survivors to wear the Victoria Cross. "Only, confound it, we never supposed these beggars could fight so well." Having surprised us in this respect, "British pluck" demands that we should now go in and win, although the winning should cost us India. Beautiful all this, is it not? And we now wait for Parliament to ecstacise itself over these "heroes." Hip, hip!

THE LEHIGH VALLEY RAILWAY.

We are much given in this country to plume ourselves upon the excellent management of our railway companies. There are no others like them in the world, we assert, and the assertion may be partly true; but we are by no means perfect; and if other United States railroad corporations take the same course as the *Commercial Chronicle* points out that this Lehigh Valley Company is now taking, the time is not far distant when we shall have to hide our diminished heads, and confess that, compared to them, we have managed our iron highways with reckless extravagance, often amounting almost to open dishonesty. A new management, it appears, has taken hold of the Lehigh Valley Company, and has been putting its accounts in order—and one thing it has done has been to revalue its rolling stock. This revaluation disclosed the fact that the book value of the stock was nearly $6,000,000 above its true value, engine and passenger cars alone exceeding their book value by rather more than half a million dollars. Deducting this from the ascertained loss the company has written off more than $5,000,000 from its capital account on that head alone. Not only so, but $1,500,000 charged to capital on improvements has also been written off, and a sinking fund has been instituted to provide against the exhaustion of the coal mines owned by the company. Nor is this all. The costs of all improvements made on the collieries during the year have been charged to working expenses and the interest on the Lehigh Valley Coal Company's bonds has now been made a direct charge on the income of the railroad, instead of merely on its profit and loss account. Interest and rents accrued but not due are now entered in the balance-sheet, and liabilities of a floating kind are classed as "current," "deferred," or "contingent," according to their character. If this system of clear book-keeping is maintained, as we have no doubt it will be, and spreads to other railroads in the Union, as it must in time, there cannot be the slightest doubt that the position of these great Corporations will soon be decidedly superior to our own so far as their capital account is concerned, Who ever heard of an English railway company revaluing its working stock and writing it down? We go on here in the happy-go-lucky style of charging everything to capital that can be charged, and write off nothing from capital spent in the past, however necessary it might be; and the consequence is that the dead weight of capital upon our railroads, as we have preached for many years, is steadily piling up until it must one day cause even the very best among them to fall into a doubtful position. We commend this American example to British boards of directors.

FRANCE AND THE SUGAR BOUNTIES.

It would seem as if Mr. Chamberlain were right in his anticipation that the forthcoming International Conference at Brussels would lead to the abolition of the sugar bounties. Germany has already pretty plainly shown her readiness—her anxiety, indeed—to give up these vexatious imposts. The French Chamber of Deputies is now to have an opportunity of formulating its opinion on the subject if so inclined, M. Castelin having given notice of his intention to introduce a Bill for the suppression of the bounties in France at any date that may be fixed by the Brussels Conference. It is not improbable that he may have given this notice with a view to the coming elections, but even so it indicates his opinion, as at least a political expert, that the proposed abolition would be popular with French constituencies; and of that, we believe, there need be little doubt. Frenchmen are getting to understand the sugar bounties. They are tiring of taxing themselves for the supply of cheap sugar to England. Even manufacturers, for whose benefit the bounties were imposed, have discovered that they are not the unmixed blessing they expected. M. Paul Leroy-Beaulieu estimates that for France alone the cost of these bounties for the current year will probably exceed £4,500,000. The only wonder is that French taxpayers have been content to bear this burden so long; that they have not long ago insisted on the passage of a much more drastic law than that to be proposed by M. Castelin, careless of what other nations might do.

By the way, the British Consul at Odessa, in his recently issued report on the agriculture of that district—in which, we may note, he tells us that there will be a severe wheat famine in Southern Russia this year—gives a valuable hint to the West Indian sugar growers as to how they may help themselves in spite of the sugar bounties. The West India Commission showed us that by the crude methods of manufacturing sugar practised in the West Indies, the growers lost about a fourth of their yearly produce—about 2,000 lbs. of sugar per acre being left in the canes after crushing. Now in Russia this enormous waste is avoided by having the presence and advice of a practical chemist while the sugar is being manufactured. In Russia, again, the utmost care is taken to grow only the best varieties of beets reared from selected seed. In Barbados and British Guiana they are trying to improve their canes by growin better varieties from seed; but the West Indian planters go on in the old ruts—losing 25 per cent. of th sugar by bad crushing, and depending on their old canes as if they were inexhaustible and not to b improved upon. Here is a hint, also, for Mr. Chamber lain in the application of his grant-in-aid. Let it b utilised so far, at least, in instructing the planters in th most modern methods of crushing, and in providin seed for the growth of better canes. He will thus b rendering the Island a signal service of permanen value. The planters might have thought of it them selves had they been as alert, intelligent, and energeti as they ought to have been. The present misery (their position is, in fact, little owing to foreign bountie

Since writing the foregoing we have received fro Mr. E. K. Muspratt, President of the Financial Refor Association, a letter containing a trenchant criticism (the whole system of grants-in-aid. We regret th we have not space to give the letter, though we entire agree in its general drift and tenor. As a rule the grants are bad in themselves, and ought not to l encouraged. We had considerable searchings heart before coming to the conclusion that, in the ca of the West Indies, some financial assistance, appli in ways suggested by the majority of the Sug Commission, might be desirable, if not necessary. B our support was given on strictly conditional terms. mere dole to the planters, without a careful supe vision of its expenditure, would be wholly pernicious worse than waste. Better for the colony that it we thrown into the sea. We have no great sympathy wi the sugar-growers. It is certainly not the bo that have injured their business; it is mainly their own lack of energy and intelligence in facing the competition which other cane-growing colonies have been forcing upon them. But a little temporary assistance at the right moment may help in the reformation of even our prodigal sons, and so set them on their feet again. This the grant-in-aid may be made to do. It may also be used—nay, ought to be chiefly used—in the encouragement of peasant proprietorships and in the fostering of new industries. In this way only can the grant be made of use to the colony at large, and it ought to be given for the benefit of the colony, not for the private advantage of certain individuals. If Mr. Chamberlain arranges to administer the grant on some such lines, we still think it may be of signal service to the islands; but if doled out to individuals, without a thought as to how it is spent, it would be money wasted. Thus administered it would assist in hastening the ruin of our West Indian colonies.

AFTER THE STRUGGLE.

The engineers' strike is over, and the men are presenting themselves for work faster than the employers can find it for them. So many of the vacancies have been filled up by non-union men—some establishments having no vacancies left at all—that it is probable many of the men must remain unemployed for some time yet. But we are glad to see that employers are showing not the slightest trace of vindictive feeling, and we have no doubt that every man who has gone through this prolonged struggle, fighting his hardest for the side he believed in, will find employment without undue delay, either in his old workshop or in some new one, where no grudge will be borne him for the part he may have taken in the long-contested battle. The hatchet seems to be buried on both sides—certainly on that of the employers; for one of them at least has written to the *Daily News* suggesting practical help for the workmen who may have had to run in debt owing to the length of the struggle and the meagreness of the assistance rendered by the union to the strikers. The employer backs up his suggestion by a cheque for £100. We mention the circumstance only as emphasising the fact that the employers are putting ill-feeling from them, as men prepared to work cordially with their workmen. And this cordial spirit of co-operation is now needed more than ever, and on both sides, too. Both have lost heavily, but the workmen more seriously than the masters; the loss to the workers we have seen estimated at three millions sterling. It is probably more rather than less. To make up that loss alone should be inducement enough to make them work in cordial goodwill with their employers; but if the necessity of coping with the rivalry of foreign nations is taken into account, how tremendous is the inducement to work closely together in aiming at the same end—the securing of England's lead in the trade and commerce of the world.

In this connection it may be of use to call the attention of British manufacturers, as well as workmen, to some interesting bits of news retailed in a recent number of a journal called *American Trade*, the organ of the National Association of Manufacturers of the United States. There is something, for example, of novelty in the announcement that a Pittsburg company has an order in hand for 24 tons of malleable iron for a Sheffield firm, and that "the company's business from London, Birmingham, and Sheffield has increased rapidly for the past eighteen months." American cotton manufactures, although higher in price than British goods, are said to be cutting these out in the Chinese markets. Large Russian contracts for hydraulic machinery have been secured by a Cincinnati firm; the Czar is getting an electric launch built in New York; South Africa is taking quantities of valves, machine fittings, and leather belting; tools in large number are being shipped to France; considerable shipments of aluminium have lately been made to Japan, Germany, Italy, Austria, and Sweden; 5,000 tons of Alabama pig-iron were recently despatched for Kobe and Yokohama. These are only a few of the samples boasted of in the American trade journal. Of course the best is made of them, and it may be that English firms are doing business with the extent of which they are perfectly satisfied. Still, it is interesting to know what our cousins are doing; and if the knowledge teaches nothing else, it seems to suggest that this is not a time for our own producers to be quarrelling among themselves, but rather to be working in cordial co-operation for their own benefit and the improvement of the trade of the country.

THE STATE OF THE ARMY.

Sir Charles Dilke is writing a series of papers in the *Daily Mail* which should be read by every tax-payer. His object, of course, is to emphasise the necessity for more men, more horses, more artillery, and so on, and possibly he is right. Before, however, sanctioning any further outlay, the nation has a right to know what becomes of the money already devoted to these purposes. Year by year, the cost of the Army grows until it threatens to become an intolerable burden to us. Yet, if we may believe Sir Charles, the machine provided by the money grows more and more imperfect. The first question, therefore, which has to be answered is who steals the money? That millions are stolen and squandered by corrupt and incompetent management every day of our lives is a fact about which there can be no doubt whatever. Will the reader ponder this matter and stir up his M.P. about it; and meanwhile try to grasp the significance of the following passage from Sir Charles Dilke's article in yesterday's *Daily Mail*:—

This condition of the Royal Artillery constitutes the most absolutely disgraceful charge which can easily be proved, and it deserves, therefore, some further attention. In other countries horses are not counted as fit for war under six years of age. We count them at five. We have only in the whole of our British establishment of cavalry and artillery and mounted infantry together, 10,000 horses between five and thirteen years of age: and the number of such horses, and the total number of horses in the artillery, taken by itself, have greatly decreased in recent years. In the last twenty years, for example (but the decrease has been steady, and has lasted more than twenty years), the horses of our artillery of all ages have declined from 6,000 to very little over 4,000 in number; and in the meantime the Army has increased; while it must be remembered that for the militia and volunteers there has never been any horse or field artillery at all. The horses required for the artillery at home are nearly 8,000, or double the total number of all ages, fit or not fit for war, which are maintained. The deficiency of cavalry horses is even more startling than the deficiency in artillery. The cavalry at home would require, for war, between 9,000 and 10,000 horses, and they possess about 3,600 horses between six and fourteen years of age.

The deficiency in the regular Army as regards artillery and cavalry, of course, cannot be supplied from militia or volunteers. As regards infantry, it is admitted by the Government that the deficiency of the militia in men is great, and in officers great and increasing—having grown from a deficiency of 591 officers in 1896 to a deficiency of 641 officers in 1897. The militia, indeed, though an excellent, is very much—as far as numbers go—a paper force. There are over 17,000 men required to complete the establishment. There are 14,000 men absent. There are over 31,000 men who are liable to Army service, and they are the best men in the militia, and the result is there are, according to Sir A. Haliburton's figures, 68,000, and according to mine only 58,000, men left for the militia, who are very short of officers, and who include a certain number of men who have fradulently enlisted in more than one regiment, and who are counted twice.

"Sea Interests of the German Empire."

We know how the German Emperor hankers after a great Navy; how at Kiel he assumed, not without some success, the character of Bombastes Furioso, in order to rouse German enthusiasm on the subject; how the occupation of Kiao-Chau was used as a naval object lesson with the same aim, though this squib has since been somewhat damped; and now we know, with the help of an excellent summary from the British Commercial Attaché at Berlin, how the German Government, in its sober moments, regards the subject of the "Sea Interests of the German Empire." The story is interesting though it must be remembered that the figures are those of the German Government, and are misleading in some important respects. From 1872 to 1897 the German population increased by 30 per cent., while the foreign trade improved by 60 per cent. The improvements in over-sea trade from 1873 to 1895, were for North America, 128 per cent.; for Mexico, Central and South America, 480 per cent.; for East and West Indies 480 per cent., and for Australia 475 per cent. In 1896 the tonnage of German shipping at Hamburg exceeded that of the English for the first time, the German tonnage being 2,914,913, and the English 2,734,528. Since 1871 the German Mercantile Marine has more than tripled its capabilities, and since 1880 has more than doubled them. German shipbuilding has kept pace with the increase of the Mercantile Marine. There has, at the same time, been a considerable consolidation of internal affairs; and while foreign luxuries have increased, Germany depends less upon foreign capital than ever before. Her high sea fisheries have greatly increased; there is more regular employment for the home population, and emigration has greatly diminished. These statistics, as we have said, are so far misleading. The fact that the Hanseatic towns were added to the German Customs Union is ignored, and this vitiates the figures while greatly reducing the 60 per cent. increase claimed in German foreign trade. In fact, the increase is only something like 9 per cent. The increase, however, is still fair. It is for the protection of this expanding foreign trade that the Government declare an increase in the Navy necessary. If the Germans could be sure that the chief object was the peaceful development of trade and commerce, we dare say they would cordially sympathise with the Government aspirations; but is it so?

The Copper Statistics.

Up to the end of January these show the remarkable decrease of 2,209 tons in the stocks, and their total now stands at 29,746 tons. This is by far the lowest total recorded in the past eight years, and the decline is a little puzzling to those who hear so much of increased production by the mines. The "bulls" of the metal and of copper shares ascribe the decline to the general expansion of consumption, especially in regard to electrical enterprises, but if this is the case it is astonishing that the metal market is not stronger, for the present price of £49 7s. 6d. per ton for copper compares with £51 2s. 6d. a year ago when the stock stood at 32,307 tons. Whatever the reason may be, the decline in the visible supplies has been pronounced, and in the following table we set forth the leading figures for the last few years:—

Jan. 31.	Total Supplies. tons.	Total Deliveries. tons.	Stock. tons.	Price per ton. £.
1892	7,808	6,480	57,462	44⅝
1893	11,773	9,011	58,507	45⅝
1894	11,947	12,090	47,152	41¼
1895	12,840	12,656	54,848	40¼
1896	15,639	15,328	46,128	43⅜
1897	15,687	18,307	32,307	51⅛
1898	15,158	17,367	29,746	49

The most striking feature in this table is the growth of deliveries which have kept ahead, almost continuously, of the increase in production. Taking the figures by themselves one would imagine that the demand for the time being is in excess of supply, but we must not forget that we are dealing with a market which at times developes great speculative activity, and so the statistics must be treated with caution. In any case, the opening out of new mines and the extension of operations by the older concerns are going on apace, so that the moderation with which the market pitches the price of the metal may be well advised, hidden stocks or none.

A Well-drawn Report.

A word of praise is due to the East-End Dwellings Company for the manner in which the Board draws up its report. The company works a number of blocks of industrial dwellings, and the report not only states the giveceipts and expenses of each block in detail, but it togets also full particulars of the cost of the properties, hold prher with the length of the leases upon the lease-in each operty, and the amount of depreciation allowed the comp-ase. In spite of this wealth of information, other company seems to prosper, and it would be well if The stringent ies of a like class would follow its example. Act compelling regulations of the last Building Societies' the amount of such societies to give schedules showing produced, have property in band and the revenue it the good societies, lly had a beneficial influence upon increase of informati nd it by no means follows that an of a company. Yet on is harmful to the market value harbour this notion. the majority of boards seems to

Disappearing China Teas.

British growers of teas are congratulating themselves upon the fact that, although the consumption of tea in the United Kingdom last year was the largest ever known, the proportion of Chinese growth in the amount consumed was the smallest ever known. Thus with 231,399,778 lb. of tea used in this country in 1897, only 17,242,247 lb. came from the Chinese producer, and no less than 210,000,000 lb. were supplied by the British-owned plantations in India and Ceylon. This brings out a percentage of 91 per cent. of British grown tea to 7 per cent. of Chinese growth, the balance being made up of Javan and Japanese teas. In 1896 the Chinese percentage was 9 per cent., and in 1895 it was 12 per cent., while if we only go back ten years, we find its percentage no less than 49 per cent., and in 1866 it represented 5 per cent. of our consumption. The largest consumption of Chinese teas in this Kingdom in one year was, we believe, in 1876, when 123,364,000 lb. were used. Last year, as we have stated, little more than one-eighth of this amount was taken by the British consumers. Glad as we are to see India and Ceylon coming to the front in the way here shown, we yet cannot help regretting that China should have been driven so rapidly to the wall. Her people have not yet had time to find a new industry to take the place of the one they have lost, and must suffer much in consequence.

A BREWERY RARA AVIS.

The report of the Bristol Brewery, Georges & Co., Limited, dealt with in the usual column, is like no other brewery company. Instead of swelling out its debenture issues, these have been kept stationary for years past, and their total only amounts to £162,000, as against £280,000 of preference, and £320,000 of ordinary share capital. Fresh money needed for extending the business has been found out of revenue, and consequently the balance-sheet is one of the strongest we have seen. The truth is this Board was wise in its generation, and acquired control of an enormous number of public-houses a long time back, obtaining the money by issues of share capital at good premiums, which were put to reserve. Since then the money for development upon a moderate scale has been found by deductions for depreciation, which in the last three years have led to a reduction in the balance-sheet value of the brewery premises, plant, &c., by £40,000, and enabled the properties to be increased by about £67,000.

MR. BLAKE AND THE "CHARTERED."

We hope the shareholders in the British South Africa Company, as well as the public in general, have made due note of Mr. J. Y. F. Blake's charges against it on many counts, and about all in regard to its treatment of the natives now under its sway. There was a letter of this gentleman's in yesterday's *Times* reiterating these charges in reply to Mr. Selous, and he winds up with the suggestion that the committee of last session should be re-appointed to investigate them. Will the public take up this demand and insist upon knowing the truth, or is everybody so bewitched by the tawdry "Imperialism" under which the company's misdeeds have been hidden, as to be willing that lapse of time alone may bring the truth to light? Before deciding the electorate should remember that the official report of Sir Richard Martin substantially bears Mr. Blake's testimony out, and that however ready men may be to lose their money, as they have irretrievably lost it to a few noble and other marauders, the nation at large cannot afford to rest under the stigma of accusations that would have made the spadassins of Cortez blush with shame.

MORE GOLD DISCOVERIES.

The dark and dreary places of the earth—sterile in everything else—are all, apparently, being lighted up by gold. Let us hope that the avaricious and the sanguine will not be too eager to rush upon disappointment. Recent letters from Dawson City—written in December last—speak in anything but an enthusiastic way of the prospects there; but the preparations for the spring rush to Klondike are on a gigantic scale. It will, apparently, be greater than anything seen before, throwing the Californian scramble and the Ballarat rush completely into the shade. But the curiosity of the gold-seeker has been further pricked by a comparatively modest discovery in Siberia. If this should prove well-founded, and the search show fruitful results, the rush thither will be chastened by the paternal admonitions of the Czar and his Government. But here, again, we have Labrador. A Canadian Company went there to establish a saw-mill, and they are said to have found gold in such quantities that it is presumed the saw-mill was forgotten. At all events, an expedition is to be fitted out for purposes of exploration and exploitation. It is not impossible that gold may yet lurk in Labrador; for it is on record that, in 1565, Admiral Frobisher, when in search of the North-West passage, discovered gold in such quantities that in three years he brought to England seventeen shiploads of the precious metal. If gold is still to be found in any quantity there, it is not a little surprising that it should not have attracted attention long ago. Then, again, on the Liard River, near its confluence with the Mackenzie River, we are told of a rich find of placer gold. The news comes from the Hudson's Bay Company's factor at Fort Simpson, and may, therefore, be trustworthy. We may hear of gold in Greenland next.

THE LAKE GEORGE MINES.

The latest aspirant to fame of the Exploration Company's group of mines—the Lake George Mines—is proposing to issue more capital. "In order to repay advances made by the agents of the company in Melbourne," 30,000 shares will be issued *pro rata* to the shareholders at 30s. apiece. By the side of the market quotation of 2⅝ for the shares, the offer looks a generous one, but it must be remembered that this quotation is probably about as unreal as most others created in the approved manner of the Exploration Company. It is quite the most modern way of paying a dividend to issue shares at a substantial reduction upon the market quotation, but the champion of this new policy—the British South Africa Company—has a sorry record, despite the fustian patriotism in which it is arrayed. It would be interesting to learn what working capital has been assigned to the Lake George Mines at the start, and also the terms upon which the "advances" were made by the agents. We presume the agents are Gibbs Bright, & Co., but of this we cannot be certain owing to the mystery that veils the inception of this new wonder. If Gibbs, Bright, & Co. are the agents, we may be sure that the terms were not light. The new issue is "guaranteed" in case it is not taken up by the shareholders, and we should like to know what the terms of this guarantee are. It is usual nowadays to publish this information, but "Lake George" is not meant, it would appear, to be usual in anything.

BARON CIGARETTES.

The active manner in which the Exchange Telegraph Company quotes the shares of the Baron Cigarette Company upon its tape, is now explained by the appearance of the report. This document is likely to give an outsider such an unduly favourable opinion of the shares that he might easily buy them in a fit of generous enthusiasm. Not only does the concern declare a dividend of 7½ per cent., but it writes £10,000 off its patents, and carries £11,336 forward. But the profit and loss account runs for sixteen and a half months, while the dividend is apparently only paid for a year, so that the return on the period involved is only a little over 5 per cent. Then of the £29,673 net profit, no less than £19,022 is produced by the sale of the South American and Cuban patent rights, and the company has taken £7,245 in shares of the company that bought these rights. After writing £10,000 off the "Patents," their value in the balance-sheet still stands at £91,679, and they constitute the only important assets, outside debtors and stock, the company has to set against the £115,000 of share capital.

The San Paulo Railway.

Some time back we went carefully into the position of the San Paulo Railway, and showed that while its monopoly is rather arbitrary its legal position was unquestioned. Much of the opposition to its paramount position, however, should have died away since then, for the fall in the Brazilian exchange has led to a serious drop in its charges, and it is now busily engaged in doubling its line, which will mean that traffic can be handled more freely. Those behind the Mogyana Railway Company, virtually, we believe the Paulista Railway Company, are still endeavouring to make use of the authorisation to build lines whereby San Paulo and Santos would be connected by a circuitous route. It must be circuitous because the monopoly of the San Paulo states that no company can build a line running in the same direction as its own for about twenty miles on either side of its line. The new project evidently proposes a line that will run at some distinct angle to the San Paulo, whilst within its monopoly area, and then parallel to this company's road when once outside this area. Such a scheme was peddled all round Europe some years back by the Paulista Railway Company without success, and the doubtful undertaking, one would have thought, should receive little support here now, where the whole of the capital of the San Paulo company is held. Too often, however, in ignorance one group of British capitalists is induced to enter into contest with another, just to satisfy the desire of bankers and brokers to pocket a smart commission.

Advertisements.

The subjoined letter raises a question of too much importance to be dealt with in a note. Therefore, what we have to say upon the subject will be found in the leader, headed "Concerning Advertisements," on another page. Unquestionably a moral responsibility is involved in the character of the advertisements newspapers insert. We define elsewhere how we have attempted to recognise this responsibility :—

Sir,—As a small investor who looks to your review for counsel and warning, may I be allowed to question the advisability of admitting such an advertisement as appeared on the back of the cover of your last number? The "Mount Lyell field" is an interesting subject, but information conveyed in such a manner is open to suspicion, and careless readers are apt to overlook the boundary that separates the advertisement pages from the editorial columns —Yours, Robert Cornish.

Sir J. Gordon Sprigg met the demand of the Dutch farmers for protection for their cattle by declaring it useless, as there is no marketable stock to protect. He was willing, if the Orange Free State would concur, that the meat duty should be suspended for three months until Parliament could deal with this question.

Queensland seems prospering agriculturally. The total number of acres under cultivation last year was 364,000, against 323,000 in 1896. 93,700 acres of sugar-cane were planted, and the produce of 83,500 acres was crushed, yielding 105,000 tons of sugar. There were 54,000 acres under wheat, producing 313,000 bushels, as compared with 36,000 acres in 1896, and 801,000 bushels.

Rand Deep Level Mines: An Investigation.—I.

The "Kaffir" Market has recently excited a certain amount of attention owing to the commencement of gold production by a number of the deep level mines, and the near approach of others to the same stage. During the past two years, in spite of the economical and political troubles in the Transvaal, considerable progress has been made in developing and equipping these properties; the money in the majority of cases having been found by the South African financiers controlling the companies. Six deep levels are now crushing, the Geldenhuis Deep, Rose Deep, Village Main Reef, Nourse Deep, Bonanza, and Crown Deep; while five others, the Jumpers Deep, Langlaagte Deep, Durban Deep, Glen Deep, and Robinson Deep, are expected to start during the next three or four months. The Simmer and Jack Proprietary, which is partly an outcrop and partly a deep level, has also commenced work with an increased reduction plant. Viewed from a mining standpoint, the returns from the deep levels now producing appear to be fairly satisfactory; but if examined in relation to the high prices ruling for the shares, there is nothing to warrant an excess of enthusiasm. On the other hand, it is difficult to understand on what grounds the present high level of valuations can be maintained, unless, indeed, purchasers are satisfied with a prospective return of only 4 or 5 per cent. on their money. Prices are again nearing the point which they reached during the insane "boom" of 1895, when the most absurd predictions were indulged in as to the richness of the mines, followed, it will be remembered, by the disastrous collapse which commenced three months before the Jameson raid, and compassed the ruin of many thousands of speculators. The lowest water-mark in the "Kaffir" Market was touched in April of last year, when, owing to the persistent shrinkage of values brought about partly by alarm at the political situation in the Transvaal, and partly, no doubt, by interested operators, a semi-panic occurred. Rand Mines, which in 1895 went as high as 44, and at the Jameson raid stood at 21¼, fell to 16⅛. Since that time a steady but gradual appreciation has taken place in all Kaffir mining shares, in which deep levels have taken a prominent place. Rand Mines are now quoted at about 3½.

In April, 1897, the seventeen deep level mines dealt in on the London Stock Exchange bore a market valuation of fourteen and a-half millions sterling; to-day these same shares are appraised at £29,000,000, a rise of 100 per cent. The appreciation in the shares of South African Trust Companies, whose principal holdings consist of deep levels, is even more pronounced. Six of these concerns, in April, 1897, were valued at £13,500,000; to-day they are standing in at approximately £29,750,000; a rise of 120 per cent.

Is this large increase in values warranted by the prospective dividend capacities and lives of the companies? One thing we know, the movement has not been a natural one arising from a public demand for such securities, it has been created by fictitious buying and other manœuvres directed by the South African financial houses which control the "Kaffir Circus." For if there is one thing certain about the deep level market, it is that so far the public have withstood all temptations and refrained from joining in the gamble. If it is wise it will continue to do so. The prices now reached are fanciful and unhealthy, and although the mines may be temporarily manipulated to give some semblance of stability to the structure, sooner or later the inevitable collapse will occur, and things again find their natural level. That there can be no two opinions as to the prices of deep level shares being unduly inflated a merely cursory examination will serve to show.

The seventeen deep level mines dealt in on the London Stock Exchange bear a market valuation of, roughly, £29,000,000. These companies are in debt to the tune of £2,000,000, and will require at least an additional £3,000,000 to prepare them for the producing stage, bringing up their total valuation to £34,000,000. Now it is only reasonable to expect a prospective annual return of at least 12 per cent. on this sum. Out of this, be it remembered, amortisation against the exhaustion of the mines has to be provided for, which, if the average life be twenty years, will leave only about 8 per cent. as actual interest. So that, not taking into account the item of deferred interest while the mines are in the preliminary stage of preparation, there should, within a reasonable period, be a probability of these seventeen companies being able to earn annual dividends aggregating £4,080,000, to justify the present level of prices. Can they possibly do this? In 1896, the twenty-two outcrop mines of the Central, or richest part of the Rand, distributed 11s. 6d. for every ton of ore crushed. The average for the whole of the fields for the same year was only 7s. In 1897, the dividends declared work out at 12s. 6d. per ton, including such rich mines as the Robinson, Ferreira, Crown Reef, and City and Suburban on the one hand, and poor mines which made no distribution on the other. The seventeen deep level mines are distributed more or less along the whole length of the fields; and, therefore, even allowing for improved economic conditions, it is improbable that they will be capable of earning an average distributable profit of more than 15s. per ton; while, as a matter of fact, the actual results are likely to be much lower. To earn £4,080,000, at the rate of 15s. for every ton of ore, will necessitate the treatment of 6,500,000 tons annually, and to do this 3,700 stamps will have to be employed. If the profit should only amount to 12s. 6d. per ton—which is far more probable—4,300 stamps will be required. When it is stated that fifty Witwatersrand outcrop mines, the majority of which have been in existence for nine or ten years, and occupy the whole length of the fields, are to-day only utilising 3,500 stamps, it will be recognised that there is not the remotest chance of the seventeen deep levels being able to carry out this condition—at any rate for a good many years to come. It is not estimated by their most sanguine advocates that they will have more than 2,200 stamps working even after the lapse of three or four years, and, as with the outcrop properties, many of the deep levels are pretty sure to prove failures, 1,800 stamps will probably prove to be nearer the actual number. The average return on the present valuations of the shares is, therefore, necessarily limited, and with 1,800 or 2,000 stamps can only be extremely small. This alone should demonstrate that ruling prices for deep levels are artificial and absurdly inflated.

There is an old saying, "Convince a woman against her will and she will hold the same opinion still," and this is also very true of the speculator in mining shares. He will tell you, "I do not care a brass farthing what interest I am likely to get on any varied assortment of shares during the next two or three years; show me that a rise is justified, or, rather, probable, in any particular share, and I am game for a gamble." It is in deference to such arguments that we now propose to descend to a little more detail and examine the prospects and positions of a few typical deep level mines. One of the most insidious, although certainly one of the most fallacious, of all the decoys which are being utilised to induce the public to buy deep level shares at inflated values, is the so-called comparison of the "selling price per claim" of deep levels and outcrops. The *modus operandi* is somewhat as follows: First of all, the selling price per claim of an outcrop mine is ascertained by taking the total market valuation of the company and dividing into it the number of claims owned, the result being the "selling price per claim." (A Transvaal mining claim, it must be explained, is equal to about one and a hal English acres, and the dimensions of all Transvaa mines are expressed in so many claims.) Thus, the Geldenhuis Estate Company possesses about forty unworked claims, its capital is £200,000, and the current price of the shares is 4⅜. The market valuation of the mine is, consequently, £875,000, and the "selling price per claim" is roughly £22,000. The market value of a certain unit, in which the size of the capital and area of the productive part of the property are both taken into account, being found, it is then apparently an easy matter to draw comparisons with other mines, including deep levels. So the deep level advocate proceeds to point out that, with Geldenhuis Deep shares standing at 6¾, the mine is only selling at £10,000 per claim (vide map issued with Consolidated Gold Fields 1897 report), and as the claims of the deep level contain as much gold as the claims of the adjacent outcrop company—the Geldenhuis Estate—the former is greatly under-valued. He then leaves it to be assumed, *q.e.d.*, that Geldenhuis Deep shares are worth exactly double their market price, *i.e.*, £13½. What surprises us most of all in connection with this ingenious method of calculation is not so much its fallaciousness, which we shall deal with by-and-by, but that the engineers of some of the deep level Trust Companies, who are supposed to be solely concerned in looking after the engineering and mechanical wants of the mines, should make it part of their business to disseminate statements of this description in order to influence the share market. In fact, it almost comes to this, that a South African mining engineer is not judged so much by his engineering ability as by his skill in advertising the wares of his employers.

Let us see where the conclusion at which we are invited to arrive leads to. The Geldenhuis mine in 1897 paid dividends of 15 and 30 per cent.—in all 45 per cent.—and is stated to have another ten years' supply of reef remaining. Presupposing, that the rate of the last half-yearly dividend is maintained during 1898, a purchaser, after allowing for amortisation, by setting aside a portion of each year's dividend and investing it at 2½ per cent. compound interest, would receive 5 per cent. on his money. Treating Geldenhuis deep shares in the same way, it will be found that last year one dividend of 30 per cent. was paid; but we are told that more stamps are shortly to be started, and that working full power (200 stamps), in 1898, 65 per cent. will be earned, and that on this basis the mine will last twenty years. Accepting this prediction—for, of course, we cannot substantiate it—a purchaser of the shares at 13¾, after providing for the amortisation of his capital as before, would receive rather under 1 per cent. on the investment. The fallacy lies in the explanation that, whereas in one case the whole of the profit will be won in ten years, in the other it will take twenty years to recover; and that deep level claims contain considerably less gold-bearing ore than those on or near the outcrop. This last reason is an important factor which is generally overlooked. In order that the reader may understand how it arises, it will be necessary to enter into technical detail. The Rand reefs, as some people know, do not go down into the earth perpendicularly, but are inclined at varying angles. Near the surface the incline is fairly steep, but lower down the reef flattens out, thus rendering deep level mining possible. As the mining limits of a claim go down horizontally, it follows that when the dip of the reef is steep there is a greater inclined surface of reef within its boundaries than where the reef is flatter. In the outcrops the reefs incline at from 45 deg. up to 80 deg.; while in the deep levels the average is about 30 deg. The ore contents of a claim in which the reef inclines at 65 deg. are double those of a claim with a reef dipping 30 deg. As a rough-and-ready rule, it may be taken that four deep level claims contain about the same quantity of reef as three outcrop claims. Sometimes, however, the proportion is three to one, as the Henry Nourse and Nourse Deep. The fallacy of comparing the market valuations of outcrop and deep level claims will thus be at once grasped.

Geldenhuis Deep shares, even at 6⅞—taking for granted all the conditions mentioned—would only give an anticipated yield of 5½ per cent. We have purposely taken a very moderate example of this method of calculation for illustration. The deep level advocate goes a great deal further than this. He compares the "selling price per claim" of a mine undeveloped and unequipped, and which will probably require the application of £500,000 hard cash, and three or four years' work, before it can even hope to produce gold, much less earn a profit, with that of a dividend-paying outcrop company, and then gravely propounds his theory that the deep level shares are "comparatively cheap speculations." Loss of interest on capital during the three or four years the mine is being prepared, the extra expense of equipment, the large cost of exposing big bodies of reef, and the difference in the ore contents of the claims, are all conveniently ignored. In fact, this advertising dodge —for it is nothing better—is as shallow as many of the preposterous puffs setting forth the claims of certain medical nostrums which daily meet the eye.

It is as hopeless a task to endeavour to judge the value of a Rand mining share from its declared profits, or even by its dividends. The Rand formation is not much different to other gold reefs in one respect; it varies greatly in its gold contents, good and poor zones being alternately met with in the same mine. It has frequently happened that when a mine has apparently settled down to a calm dividend-paying career, a poor zone is met with, and down fall the profits and away disappear the dividends, the public invariably finding itself loaded up with the shares. A good zone is found again, and the mine returns to its previous respectable pinnacle. Examples may be mentioned in such mines as the New Primrose, Glencairn, Meyer and Charlton, Geldenhuis Estate, Jumpers, and Roodepoort United.

Sometimes other factors also intervene, but the fact remains that to rely upon even a "good" Witwatersrand mine to return regular dividends is an extremely rash thing, while to base future profits on a single year's good returns would be the height of folly. Speculators who in 1895 bought Primrose shares at £8 on the strength of the dividend of 50 per cent. declared in that year, and on the expectations of a larger one the following year, must have been disagreeably surprised when 1896 came round and not a single penny was distributed. Early in 1897 fresh capital had to be raised, and immediately afterwards 20 per cent. was paid out of the profits "thus released." The Jumpers Mine paid 55 per cent. both in 1894 and 1895, and the shares went as high as 8⅝. In 1896 no dividend was forthcoming, and the price gradually fell to 2¾. True, last year 60 per cent. was distributed, but who is to know how long it will last? It would be possible to multiply these examples and proceed through the whole list of Rand mining shares; for out of about thirty-five outcrop mines which have at different times paid dividends, only eleven have made declarations during each of the last four successive years, while of these eleven, only three mines can boast of never having had a set-back in the amount distributed. In some cases these vagaries are due to fluctuations in the values of the ore bodies, in others to bad management, to neglect of development, and last, but not least, to the picking of the mines to produce good returns when the markets were booming. We shall deal at length with this "eye-picking" part of the subject next week.

Concerning Advertisements.

A letter to be found among our "Economic Notes and Correspondence" raises a question which has been often debated in the office of this REVIEW, and on which, therefore, some definition of the views and policy finally adopted may seem desirable. If readers will pardon us, we promise to bore them on the subject only this once.

The ideal financial newspaper would, perhaps, be one which contained no advertisements of any kind, but that ideal is unattainable while those who write and produce such papers have to earn bread and salt by their labour. Advertisements being, then, an essential part of a newspaper, without which no really useful journal could be published under existing conditions, the question at once arises, how far is a newspaper proprietor justified in having the advertisements sent to him for insertion edited? That there is a moral responsibility attached to the publication of advertisements is undeniable. We have ourselves recognised it in refusing to insert those of American life insurance offices and all forms of "bucket-shop" advertisements, usurers' advertisements, and the puff paragraph, thereby voluntarily surrendering a considerable revenue which other advertisements may be slow in making good. And this step helps towards a definition of the extent of the responsibility, by acknowledging that a newspaper proprietor has not the freedom to insert any advertisement which, from his previous knowledge of the facts, he has reason to believe is calculated to do an injury to his readers.

The proprietor must have this previous knowledge though, it seems to us. To go further and demand that he shall subject every advertisement collected by his advertisement manager to a strict analysis and censorship before inserting it is not only not fair but wholly impracticable. Moreover, such a course would lay upon the proprietor a moral responsibility of another kind quite too formidable to be endorsed: the responsibility of guaranteeing the statements contained in every advertisement he published to be genuine and in accordance with fact; this and nothing less. Surely neither our correspondent nor the public would have us go so far as that. We shall decline to take this responsibility, anyway. To merely suggest that it should be taken is to confound advertising and editorial functions in a manner which could not fail to delight, as it might very well serve to justify, all those owners and conductors of papers who habitually sell their editorial pages to the liar for so much cash.

In laying down the lines on which the INVESTORS' REVIEW is to be conducted, the utmost care has been taken to keep separate the editorial department from the advertising. So far has this separation been carried that no paragraph paid for, either directly or indirectly, as an advertisement can possibly get into those parts of the paper for which the Editor is responsible. A practice, for instance, has grown up and become quite a matter of course, under which paragraphs, generally of a more, rather than less, laudatory character, are drawn up about prospectuses sent to papers to be advertised, and these paragraphs are expected to be placed in the editorial columns as expressions of independent editorial opinion. Often the advertisement is not ordered for insertion except on the understanding that the paragraph shall also appear. Words need not be wasted upon this unwholesome custom. It should be sufficient for us to state that nothing of the kind can occur in the INVESTORS' REVIEW under any circumstances. The very finest security, in common with those of meaner sorts, will be treated there strictly on its merits, and without any reference whatever to whether an advertisement has been ordered or not.

Still further. While declining to be fettered in criticism of new ventures, we have also taken reasonable care that things really bad, but of whose quality we have no previous knowledge, shall not even be advertised. This has been done by instructing the advertisement manager to enter into relations with the more respectable class of advertising agents alone; with firms, that is, who have themselves reputations at stake. And, even in regard to these, his efforts are rather to be directed to the securing of those business advertisements of the highest repute, which benefit paper and advertiser alike by their presence, than to picking up prospectuses. If, in spite of these orders and precautions, things that are unworthy sometimes slip through, we really must decline to be held responsible, unless the unworthy things are endorsed and commended by us. Then, indeed, we shall deserve to lose the confidence of the investing public.

May we be allowed to add in regard to this Crotty advertisement, that it came to us from a respectable source, that it was not even read by the editor until after he saw it on the back page of the cover of this paper, and that now, when he has glanced through it, he does not see that it was a thing to be off-hand refused by his agent on his own responsibility. It is, no doubt, an extravagantly worded puff of the Mount Lyell mineral region and the Mount Lyell Mine, and Mr. Crotty is obviously interested in making the most of the wealth supposed to lie there; but is the average reader such a fool as not to know the value of the language the advertiser uses? We hope not, and whether or not, it was none of our business to say this Mr. Crotty is, or is not, to be trusted. For all we can tell at present, he may be quite justified in what he says. We know nothing about him yet in short; but, acting simply on the rule of conduct stated above, consigned to the waste-paper basket the editorial paragraph sent with the advertisement for insertion. If the public asks more than this at our hands, then it must raise the circulation of the INVESTORS' REVIEW to at least 50,000 copies a week. When this is done, perhaps we can—although that is doubtful—adopt a course impossible now, when all we can do is to make our subscribers and readers perfectly safe on one point: no advertisement inserted in the REVIEW shall ever be viewed in the light of a bribe either to secure silence or influence speech, nor will any advertisement be inserted if we have a reasonable foreknowledge that it is in furtherance of an imposture or a fraud. To take even this stand costs more than the casual newspaper reader has any idea of. Happily we already have a tolerably distinct assurance that he appreciates our position and the sacrifice it implies. And should he have a doubt about the quality of any wares displayed before him in the advertisement section of the paper, he can always rely upon us to solve those doubts to the best of our power, undeterred by any selfish consideration whatever. Have we said enough now to make our position clear?

American Life Insurance Offices.

III.

In this article we propose to put to the test of actual experience the modern American art of prophesy as illustrated in the literature of the Mutual Life Office of New York. We select it because the facts concerning it happen to be in our hands, and from no special hostility to it more than the others. To our thinking they are all alike guilty of a cultivation of methods of business repulsive to the most indiscriminating sense of equity and fair dealing as between man and man. At best they carry on the life-insuring traffic as if it were a form of pitch and toss, a gaming table for which they hold the bank. And it is an ignoble play they arrange, a play altogether unworthy of upright and honourable men. The best class of Americans would themselves be the first to condemn it if they knew what went on; and in all that has to be said, readers we hope will never forget that there is a better America than that represented by the agents of the United States Life Offices which "have" "boomed" and bribed their way into the pockets of so many of the Queen's subjects. Individual Americans we know and have known who are, and alas, have been, among the select of the earth; but men of this stamp are not a numerous class, and are rarely to be met with in the ranks of those citizens of the great Republic of the West who come here intent to do business with us. The average pushing American is not usually endowed with a keen moral sense on his own account; as an agent of a corporation he has, as often as not, no apparent moral sense of any sort. Provided he succeeds, all is well. Now suffer us to proceed with our story.

In 1896, the Mutual of New York put into the hands of its agents a leaflet for circulation amongst intending insurers setting forth the results of twenty policies, taken out under different tables, and at different ages in 1886, the distribution periods of which had been reached in 1896. The leaflet is not marked "private" or for "agents' use only" and is therefore intended to have the widest possible circulation. These examples of policies are prefaced by the following commentary:—

"It has been frequently alleged by the agents of rival companies that the "Former Results" made use of in the Illustration Books of this Company would probably not be again realised.

As a conclusive answer to such allegations, we submit to you with great satisfaction the following statement of results now declared on Ten Year Distribution Policies issued in 1886, none for longer periods (fifteen or twenty years) having yet matured.

In view of these results we reaffirm the statement that the deferred distribution system of dividends is the most profitable and equitable for the policy holders."

Then follows a schedule of policies with their results called "Cash dividend" and a column added called "Former results," these "former results" being *considerably less*, as will be seen by comparison, than the "cash dividends" distributed.

	Actual Results in 1896.*				Illustration Book.	
No. of Policy.	Age at Issue.	Amount of Policy.	Cash Dividend.	Per Cent. per Annum of Premium.	Former Result.	Per Cent. per Annum of Premium.
			Ordinary Life.			
		£	£ s. d.	per cent.	£ s. d.	per cent.
282,672	28	1,000	73 13 7	33·3	64 10 0	29·2
283,650	29	1,000	75 8 5	33·0	66 9 2	29·1
283,406	31	800	63 5 7	32·9	57 2 8	29·8
282,380	36	500	45 10 0	32·5	42 17 6	30·6
282,190	43	500	58 13 7	32·5	57 2 1	31·6
283,774	46	400	52 15 11	32·4	51 7 0	31·5
			Life, Ten Payments.			
278,529	29	600	71 15 5	25·4	65 3 6	23·1
281,171	39	1,000	152 9 2	25·8	144 10 10	24·5
291,819	44	1,600	280 14 0	25·1	253 2 8	24·0
			Life, Fifteen Payments.			
284,530	34	1,000	110 15 0	27·7	94 16 8	23·7
			Life, Twenty Payments.			
283,674	26	1,000	83 18 5	29·3	71 15 0	25·1
			Ten Year Endowments.			
287,438	25	200	45 4 3	21·3	30 5 8	14·3
283,299	28	200	45 14 1	21·4	30 9 4	14·3
291,252	30	200	46 0 10	21·5	30 9 4	14·3
293,249	36	1,000	237 1 2	21·9	164 14 2	15·3
283,681	41	400	98 13 1	22·5	71 11 8	16·3
287,466	49	200	54 17 3	24·0	48 10 8	21·2
			Twenty Year Endowments.			
286,356	22	1,000	120 12 7	24·9	101 0 0	20·9
285,094	40	300	42 13 3	26·8	34 6 3	21·6
285,846	41	1,000	145 9 5	27·1	113 5 0	21·5

* Converted from dollars at the rate of £1 equalling $5.

Any intelligent man reading these examples will naturally assume—and that he should do so is clearly the intention of the company—that the profits distributed on these policies were larger than was expected by the assured, that, in fact, they exceeded the "estimates" put before the assured in 1886—in those days, readers must note, the company rejoiced in the free use of the word "estimates"—by as much as the amount shown in the column marked "Cash dividend" exceeds that in the one marked "Former results."

Let us look, then, at the "estimates" taken from the agent's rate-book in use at that time—1886—and append them to each age, as given in each class of policy, and leave the reader to judge what would be thought of any first-class, or *fourth*-class for that matter, English Office which indulged in such jokes at its clients' expense.

ORDINARY LIFE.

Age at which Policy is taken out.	Sums Assured.	Estimated Surplus.
28	£1,000	£96 0 0
29	1,000	98 0 0
31	800	81 8 0
36	500	59 10 0
43	500	76 0 0
46	400	68 16 0
	LIFE—10 PAYMENTS.	
29	£600	£88 16 0
39	1,000	185 0 0
44	1,600	337 12 0
	LIFE—15 PAYMENTS.	
34	£1,000	£139 0 0
	LIFE—20 PAYMENTS.	
26	£1,000	£109 0 0
	TEN YEAR ENDOWMENTS.	
25	£200	£51 12 0
28	200	52 8 0
30	200	52 16 0
36	1,000	271 0 0
41	400	112 16 0
49	200	62 4 0
	TWENTY YEAR ENDOWMENT.	
22	£1,000	£147 0 0
40	300	52 4 0
41	1,000	178 0 0

In 1886 the word "surplus" was the equivalent for the "cash dividend" of 1896, and this juicy-looking phrase has since been supplanted by "Former results." The necessity for this legerdemain in nomenclature—a "sliding scale" in phrases—serves to reveal to what straits the company has been driven to in order to hide its shrinking bonus from prospective clients.

By leaps and bounds and year after year has the profligate expenditure of this company encroached on its profits, until it has left them depleted and almost imponderable. So rapid, indeed, have been the ravages that the company has found it necessary to recall and revise its agents' rate-book no less than *three times* since 1890. These "estimates," alias "illustrations," alias "adaptations," alias "former results," have gone through three distinct periods of pruning to bring them where they stand to-day—the last of these being effected in January, 1898. Some idea may be formed of the merciless manner in which the Yankee whittler's knife has been plied by taking the first half-dozen examples furnished in the leaflet of 1896 mentioned above, and placing side by side the "surpluses" displayed by the Mutual in its agents' rate-books at various dates.

Age.	Agent's rate-book in use in 1890. Ordinary Life. Amt. policy.	Surplus.	Agent's rate-book in use 1892. Ordinary Life. Surplus.	Agent's rate-book in use 1895. Ordinary Life. Surplus.	Agent's rate-book in use 1898. Ordinary Life. Surplus.
	£	£ s. d.	£ s. d.	£ s. d.	£ s. d.
28	1,000	96 0 0	66 0 0	64 10 0	57 5 0
29	1,000	98 0 0	68 0 0	66 9 2	58 17 0
31	800	82 8 0	59 4 0	57 2 8	49 17 4
36	500	59 10 0	45 0 0	42 17 6	36 10 0
43	500	76 0 0	63 0 0	57 2 1	48 11 0
46	400	68 16 0	58 16 0	51 7 0	44 11 0

This sort of thing reminds one of the White Queen's promise of jam in "Alice in Wonderland": "Jam yesterday, and jam to-morrow, but never jam to-day." Or it is as in "Through the Looking Glass," everything wrong way round. Thanks to us, the public and the not too grateful British life offices may now acquire some knowledge of the truth by looking at things backwards. And in course of time holders of these foreign life policies may, at their own expense, accumulate a valuable mass of evidence calculated to elucidate the difference between individual and corporate standards of morality. In England, let us hasten to assure the American gentlemen who "run" these alien life insurance "shows," we have not yet in a general way attained to that excellence in the art of duping here disclosed, although we have, it must be frankly admitted, a few native productions which could "give them points and beat them easy." The great majority of British life offices, however, are still short-sighted enough to strive to make their performances surpass their promises, and even when they succeed seldom indulge in extravagant boasts about it. To the American belongs the peculiar glory of not only failing but vaunting his failure more loudly than other folk boast of success.

Mr. Herbert Spencer and other observing philosophers maintain that the physiognomies of native-born white-skinned citizens of the American Republic, as generations pass, assume more and more the contour of those of the Red Indians whom they have supplanted. But the Red Indian with all his fine qualities—*vide* Hiawatha and other romances—never attained to the elevation in corporate emancipation from moral considerations revealed to us in the successive stages of this "Mutual" of New York Life Office's progress. Well may we stand in doubt where the mutuality comes in. Officers, agents, and Press engaged in this tragic business remind us of Jack Spratt and his wife. They among them consume the fat and the lean, and the policy-holder will soon probably have nothing left for his share but the clean platter.

The Mutual is evidently preparing the minds of its agents for a still further reduction of "surplus." This, at least, is the view suggested by a circular issued from the head office in Cornhill, dated November 27, 1897, in which the following passages occur:—

"It is not expected that this change in rates"—meaning the advance in rates from January, 1898, on young and middle-aged lives—"will produce any unfavourable effect upon the cash surrender values available at end of the distribution periods, ... the only difference being that of such total surrender value the 1898 policy would have a larger portion labelled 'reserve' than the 1897 policy, the *balance* in each case being labelled 'surplus.'"

In order to appreciate this curious reserved generosity, the public must bear in mind that it is this "balance" labelled "surplus," which has been steadily shrinking since 1890, until now there is well-nigh nothing but a skeleton left. Simultaneously with this American vanishing process the "balance" labelled "surplus" in the British offices has been steadily rising, in the face of diminishing returns from interest; a result in their case due, no doubt, to economy of management which, so far as her life offices known to us are concerned, in America is a lost art.

At an early date we hope to present our readers with an analysis of the investments of these American offices by way of "round-off" to the story. All we need add at present, therefore, is that a preliminary examination appears to indicate that the bulk of the money is well enough invested in United States securities. But why cannot policy-holders here take steps to find out the truth for themselves? If they combined and brought pressure to bear on these alien organisations, insisting on an actuarial investigation by men of their own selection, and on the investment of British policy-money in the names of British trustees, they might possibly still be in time to avert the disaster with which they are threatened, and that not distantly threatened either.

Critical Index to New Investments.

HOVIS-BREAD FLOUR COMPANY, LIMITED.

For £223,410, including £173,910 in cash, the vendors offer their business to the public, but we fear it cannot be looked upon as a generous action. The title sufficiently explains the business which has been carried on by S. Fitton & Son since 1893. The capital is fixed at £225,000 in £5 shares, of which 17,050 ordinary and £18,050 Six per Cent. Cumulative preference shares are offered for subscription. Chatteris, Nichols & Company certify net profits for three years ended September 30, 1897, at £15,370, £18,864, and £22,798 respectively, or an average of £19,010. This is before charging rent of freehold property, interest on capital, management, or income tax. The two last years' profits show 10 per cent. on the ordinary shares, but what would they show after deducting management expenses, &c.? The undertaking seems to us much over-capitalised.

BENSKIN'S WATFORD BREWERY, LIMITED.

This is a considerable enlargement of the old company of the same name, which was formed in 1894, and had a share and debenture capital amounting to £300,007, all the shares being held by the vendors. The new company now comes forward with a share capital of £620,000, of which half consists of £1 Ordinary shares, and half of £5 of Four per Cent. Cumulative Preference shares. There is also created £600,000 First Mortgage Irredeemable stock, interest on the latter being payable January 1 and July 1, and on the preference shares, March 31 and September 30. The new company takes over the old one, and acquires the businesses known as the Kings Langley Brewery, the Kingsbury (St. Albans) Brewery, Healey's King-street Brewery, Watford, and an agency at Woburn Sands, by which absorption 130 licensed houses are added to the houses already possessed by the old company. The latter, which is the promoter, has fixed the purchase price at £1,220,000, of which £310,000 will be taken in the whole of the ordinary shares, £150,000 in preference shares, £427,000 in debenture stock, and £333,000 in cash. All that the public are asked to subscribe for is 32,000 preference shares at 5s. premium, and £173,000 debenture stock at par. Of the present Debenture issue £339,000 goes in paying off the "A" and "B" debentures in the old company, £80,000 in paying off existing mortgages, and £181,000 in providing the purchase money of the additional businesses. Security consists of specific mortgage on properties in Benskin's, as per balance-sheet September 30, £521,043; and on properties included in recent purchases, costing about £300,000; also floating charge on general assets of Benskin's £146,897, and of the new businesses £40,000, representing a total security of £1,007,940. Benskin's profits for year ended September 30, were £43,821; rents from new properties acquired will be over £4,000, and profits from additional trade from the 130 new houses are estimated at £18,000. This gives a total of £66,000, of which debenture interest will want £24,000, and preference dividend £15,500. So far as earnings to meet interest go they seem ample, but we should have preferred a separate valuation and statement of profits made by the companies taken over. To buy licensed houses now must mean buying at very high prices, and nothing is known about these businesses outside their own immediate circle. The Old Benskin was, we think, a much better brewery investment than the new one.

CHICAGO, ROCK ISLAND, & PACIFIC RAILWAY COMPANY.

Speyer Brothers, of New York, having bought from the company $52,000,000 New General Mortgage Four per Cent. Ninety-year Gold bonds, interest payable January 1 and July, issued for the purpose of retiring various Five per Cent. and Seven per Cent. bonds, the London, New York and Frankfort firms offer until February 17, $25,000,000 of them to holders of the Five per Cent. First Mortgage, Extension, and Collateral bonds, and the Five per Cent. Debenture bonds in exchange for their existing holding at the price of 103½ per cent. and accrued interest, New York terms. Holders will no doubt willingly accept the new bonds on the terms offered, as ninety years is a good long period, and it is provided in the new mortgage that none of the existing bonds shall be extended at maturity, so that after their retirement the new bonds will be a first mortgage on all the railroad property and real estate of the company. The capital stock on March 31 was $46,156,000, and bonded debt $62,712,000; the net income for the year ended on that date $4,765,121 and the bond interest $2,321,525. The annual saving in interest will be $496,621.

KENILWORTH SUGAR ESTATES, LIMITED.

Under the auspices of the Gas, Water and General Investment Trust, this undertaking is brought out to buy 10,000 acres of freehold land situated on the Mississippi, believed to comprise some of the best sugar land in the State of Louisiana, and to erect thereon a sugar factory. Of the share capital of £160,000, in £5 shares, the vendor takes all the £80,000 of ordinary, with £45,000 in cash and subscriptions are now asked at par for £80,000 of Six per Cent. Cumulative Preference capital, and for an issue of £60,000, part of £80,000, Five per Cent. First Mortgage Debenture stock. Interest due January and July. The debenture stock, which is a specific first mortgage on the freehold property, plant, &c., is redeemable on six months' notice at 110 after January 1, 1900. A net profit of £18,620 is spoken of, or £10,820 above the amount required for debenture and preference interest. For all that, we are not drawn to the issue, and it is quite customary for American investments offered over here not to live up to their promise of their early youth. Suppose the sugar tariff abolished, what then?

GROSVENOR MANSIONS COMPANY, LIMITED.

Issue at par of £50,000 Four and a quarter per Cent. First Mortgage debentures, interest due January and July; share capital £120,000, of which £62,500 remains unissued. Debentures are redeemable at par, January 1, 1960, and are a first and only mortgage on properties, valued at £91,000, in Victoria-street, Westminster. Lease expires June 24, 1961, but redemption of debentures is secured by a sinking fund policy with Sun Life Society. Deducting ground rent from rental of £11,300—apparently if everything is let—there will remain £7,300 per annum, or three times the amount required for interest and sinking fund. As this class of business in the West End usually does well, the debentures should form a safe investment.

ANGLO-MEXICAN COLONIZATION AND TRADING COMPANY, LIMITED.

The capital of £150,000 in £1 shares is divided into 70,000 "A" and 80,000 "B" shares, ranking equally for dividend. Subscriptions are invited for 100,000 shares. Company buys from vendor 43,000 acres of freehold land and 60,000 acres freehold from the Mexican Government, and, of course, intends to promote subsidiary companies. Purchase price £80,000, including 50,000 "A" shares and the rest cash. It is estimated that the profits from developing only 2,000 acres will be sufficient to pay at least 25 per cent. on the capital, in addition to profits to be derived from subsidiary companies. If 2,000 acres will yield 25 per cent. on the capital, the yield on 103,000 acre. on the same basis works out at £1,931,250. Such a dazzling prospect doubtless induces the vendors to sell.

BRANDRAM BROTHERS & CO., LIMITED.

Here is an opportunity to take an interest in a firm of saltpetre and brimstone refiners and white lead manufacturers. Out of a capital of £150,000 in £10 shares, half ordinary and half Five per Cent. Cumulative Preference, investors can apply for the latter, all the ordinary, along with £75,000 in cash, going to the vendors. Preference interest due March and September. Total assets are valued at £102,169, of which lease, machinery, and plant represent £43,226, and stock-in-trade £45,000, which seems a little heavy. Profits appear a little funny. For 1894 they were £10,232; for 1895, £10,748; and for 1896, £8,408. Why this drop, and why are no figures given for 1897? Business is old-established — over 100 years—but no reason is given why the vendors want to withdraw their money. Can it be that the business is getting less profitable?

HENRY HEATH, LIMITED.

This is a firm of hatters of Oxford-street, which is formed with a share capital of £50,000, wholly taken by the vendor, along with £50,000 in cash. The public are invited to subscribe at par for an issue of £45,000 Four and a Half per Cent. First Mortgage Debenture stock. It is redeemable after January 1, 1918, on six months' notice, at 105, and interest is payable January and July. The security is the buildings on land held on lease having seventy years unexpired to run; and these premises, with plant, &c., seem very fully valued by Harry Higgs & Company at £47,856. Then there is stock-in-trade, probably including some old-fashioned "toppers," taken at manufacturer's cost price, £15,000, and book debts guaranteed, £4,568. Net profits per annum for three years ended December, 1897, are certified to have been considerably in excess of amount required for interest on the debentures. Even assuming properties are not over-valued, they very little exceed the proposed debenture issue, and the absence of any profit figures makes lending these hatters the money they ask for risky.

BOURNEMOUTH THREE PER CENT. REDEEMABLE STOCK.

An issue of £33,382 of this stock, bringing the total debt of the Borough up to about £266,000, is offered for tender at a minimum price of 101 by Messrs. Glyn, Mills & Co., acting for the Wilts and Dorset Banking Co. Bournemouth is a growing place, but also an overbuilt one and poor. Still, it had a revenue of £74,382 in the year ended March 31, 1897.

Company Reports and Balance-Sheets.

BARING BROS. & CO.—For 1897 accounts show a net profit of £99,503 or including balance brought forward, £110,149. Dividends on the preference shares, absorb £55,000; on the ordinary shares, £45,000, a very handsome return on their capital value of £25,000. Balance carried forward, £10,149, the reserve fund remaining at £100,000. No profit and loss account is published.

NEW IMPERIAL INVESTMENT COMPANY.—After replacing £600 taken in the previous year from reserve, the revenue of this company was insufficient by the amount of £1,327 to meet the full interest upon the Preferred Stock. As income improved after the accounts were made upon December 31, the directors recommended the payment of the full interest of 4½ per cent., carrying forward the excess payment as a kind of suspense charge upon the current year. It is a mean-looking result after years of uphill work, and yet we might have imagined that the company had surmounted its worst troubles were it not for the manner in which the new investments of the concern are being made. A perusal of the list of holdings, although it shows many securities that are permanently depreciated, also exhibits a fair number upon which there has been considerable improvement of late, both in respect of income and market valuation. The company, indeed, gained £5,964 from sales of securities in the past year, which it added to reserve, less £3,000 written off a hopeless investment. But we note amongst the new investments £7,200 of New Trinidad Lake Asphalt debentures, £4,000 of North-Eastern Breweries debentures, £6,670 of Hans Crescent Hotel Preference shares, and £2,500 of Hood & Moore's Preference shares. Now these blocks look very much like the outcome of underwriting operations, and if the reformed corporation is going largely in for this kind of business, the outcome can only be another reorganisation on a worse plane than the last.

CITY OF LONDON BREWERY COMPANY.—In the last five years this well-managed concern swelled its balance-sheet by £891,000, or about 50 per cent., chiefly by purchases of public-houses and granting loans on mortgage. Net profit in the same time rose from £114,932 to £153,641, or an increase of about 35 per cent., so that, despite the great reduction in interest, which has helped brewers so much of late years, net profits do not keep up to the level of the old days. The board, however, make the best use of the profits thus earned, placing £16,594 to leaseholds depreciation, £15,000 to reserve, and £5,000 to brewery improvements, before declaring dividends amounting to 10½ per cent. on the ordinary capital. After all this, it is possible to increase the balance forward a little to £4,528. The reserve will now amount to £204,045, of which £94,045 is represented by premiums upon new capital recently issued. Only £50,000 of the amount is invested in high-class securities, and the rest is employed in the business, and yet, as we have shown, net profits have relatively diminished, which shows how keen competition in this line of business has become.

THE RAILWAY DEBENTURE TRUST COMPANY.—The exhibit of this company was hardly so good as that of its sister Trust, but steady improvement was shown in its case. Profits for the year came to £110,989, being the highest for the last five years at least, and this enabled the dividend to be raised from 4 per cent. to 4½ per cent. Better still, the amount put to reserve was increased to £12,500, and its total now stands at £117,500, as against an ascertained depreciation upon the value of the investments of £110,345. The assets of the company would, therefore, have been comfortably in equilibrium with the liabilities, were it not for the fact that it has to carry as an asset the curious item of £77,028 for "difference between par and issue price of debentures and Four per Cent. Debenture stock." This item is being written down steadily, but at the rate the wiping out is going on all the present shareholders will be dead and buried before it disappears. It would therefore be a wise policy to tackle this item before increasing the dividend much, for this year the company promises to do better than last. The large debenture debt and liability upon the shares must act as a drag upon the price of these latter.

RAILWAY SHARE TRUST AND AGENCY.—The profits of this concern in the past year amounted to £66,078, being the best reported for a number of years. After payment of preference interest and administrative charges, the sum of £9,832 was put to reserve, the dividend on the "A," or ordinary shares was increased by 1 per cent. to 5 per cent., and the amount carried forward was raised £2,558 to £18,000. The valuation of the company's securities brought out a surplus of £20,167, which, added to the amount placed from revenue, makes a reserve of £30,000. Including the balance forward, the reserves therefore come to £48,000 upon a sum of £777,000 invested, but shareholders must not expect too much from the board, for it was only in 1894 that £194,260 had to be written off the capital by an order of the Court, so as to meet depreciation in the investments. Reserves ought, therefore, to be studiously attended to, so that the company may not be caught in a weak position on the rebound.

HYAM, WHOLESALE CLOTHING COMPANY, LIMITED.—We do not like the first report of this company, for while the profits of the whole year were taken into the revenue account, dividends were only paid for a trifle over six months. Certainly interest was paid to the vendor for the rest of the year, but this was at a low rate, and so the company had an unnaturally good showing. For the year the profit on trading was returned as £14,615, and after deducting £3,490, being interest paid to vendor, and directors' remuneration at the high figure of £1,412, the available balance of £9,720 remained. This allowed £750 to be set aside for leasehold redemption, £583 for depreciation and machinery, or about 10 per cent., £2,031 to reserves, and the remainder was employed in paying the preference interest at the rate of 5 per cent., and a dividend for the half-year on the ordinary shares at the rate of 10 per cent. per annum, the small sum of £295 being carried forward. Now, by the device of only paying interest to vendor for the first half-year the company gained £2,151, which virtually represents the allocation to reserve. As the allowances for leasehold redemption and depreciation were, we presume, absolute necessities, if the company had not gained this "finance" profit, either the 10 per cent. dividend on the ordinary shares could not have been declared, or nothing could have been placed to reserve. We wonder which course this board would have taken.

ANGLO-AMERICAN TELEGRAPH COMPANY.—The revenue of the past half-year showed the satisfactory increase of £6,540, and expenses were only £371 higher. The increased receipts follow upon a steady advance in the last few years as the traffic of last half-year came to £176,102, as against £142,975 in the second half of 1894. The company was able to declare dividends which brought up the distribution for the year to 3 per cent. on the ordinary stock and 6 per cent. on the preferred stock. The preferred stock thus received its full interest, but the over-sanguine folk who looked for a distribution on the deferred stock were disappointed, for the balance left over after doing this was only £209. Indeed, if the balance had been large, we doubt if the board would have acted wisely in dividing upon the deferred stock. The renewal or reserve fund has to bear the cost of cable used in repairs, and owing to this circumstance, although it nominally receives £12,000 each half-year from revenue plus the interest upon the securities held, amounting to £10,127 last half-year, the net addition in the six months was only £11,073. This is slow progress towards the £1,000,000 to which the board desire to build up the Renewal Fund, for its present total is £706,086.

MOBILE AND BIRMINGHAM RAILROAD COMPANY.—This United States railroad tells a satisfactory tale of its second year of working as a reorganised concern. In the twelve months ended June 30 last gross earnings increased $64,097, working expenses took only $30,898 more, and so the net revenue was $33,199 higher. The total of the latter came to $69,350, and after meeting the interest on the Prior Lien bonds, 2 per cent. was distributed on the First Mortgage bonds, and $13,350, or $9,452 more than was brought in, was carried forward. All classes of traffic showed increases, and a good deal of the expenditure was claimed to be really in the nature of improvements, which may well be the case, as working expenditure came to 80·72 of the receipts. A good deal, however, remains to be done in this respect, for, in spite of the attention devoted to it, the rolling stock seems to require considerable renovation. Car Trust notes are being redeemed, and only a small amount remain out. The effect of the good report thus shown has been quite upset by the outbreak of yellow fever in the second half of last year, during a good part of which traffic was thoroughly disorganised. The board, therefore, does not dare to pay more than the interest upon Prior Lien bonds, although at the same time it expresses the hope that the loss of traffic may not prove so severe as imagined. This may be so if the yellow fever does not reappear in the current year.

EAST END DWELLINGS COMPANY.—With £210,386 sunk in industrial dwellings, this company earned a profit of £10,305, after paying mortgage interest, and all other charges. A dividend of 5 per cent. was declared upon the ordinary shares, and £3,396 was added to reserve. In the profit, however, was £620 received in premiums upon new shares, but, of course, the large assignment to reserve more than covered this amount. The reserve would then have stood at £10,396, but the company having lost certain actions that arose out of the erection of its buildings, the expenses thus incurred amounting to £396, were written off this item. Mortgage debt stands at £57,636, only representing 25 per cent of the capital, and the reserve constitutes 5 per cent. of the amount. Altogether the record is a good one.

BARON CIGARETTE MACHINE COMPANY.—The report of this concern for the sixteen and a half months ended December 31 last reads very much like a neat circular to help the selling of shares. Out of £45,769 put down as receipts in that time, no less than £19,022 was ascribed as from sale of patent rights in South America and Cuba. Expenses came to £16,101, and the net profit of £29,673 was reported, out of which £10,000 was written off the cost of patents. A dividend of 7½ per cent. on the share capital absorbed £8,337, and £11,336 was left to be carried forward. As the capital amounts to £115,000, we presume the dividend was only for a year, although sixteen and a half months' receipts were taken into the profit and loss account. The balance brought forward must not be considered liquid, as £7,265 in shares of the company which bought the South American and Cuban patents were taken as part payment.

REVERSION INVESTMENT CORPORATION, LIMITED.—A very modest affair and modestly conducted. In its two years of life it has written off preliminary expenses, commenced a reserve fund with £500, and paid 6 per cent. for 1897 on its share capital of £14,000. As long as it does not rely too much on deposits, and it has only £5,330 of them now, it should go on and prosper.

LONDON, CHATHAM, AND DOVER RAILWAY.—This always wonderful company can boast of an increase in its receipts for the past half-year of about £21,000, obtained at a cost of rather less than £11,000 in its working expenses. The additional business, in fact, was secured at very little more than the average cost of working its entire traffic, which was 50·64 per cent., as compared with 50·61 per cent. in the second half of 1896. The gross receipts were £882,168, and the working expenses £446,790. After meeting debenture interest, rents, and so on, the company was able to pay 2¼ per cent. for the half-year, being the full dividend on the arbitration preference stock, and had £72,295 left to carry forward, as against £64,543 the year before. This company's year ends on June 30, so that this balance would seem to promise full protection for the arbitration preference stock at that date. When we look into the accounts, however, matters are not quite so satisfactory. The company spent nearly £84,000 on capital account last half-year, and it still makes no provision whatever for writing down its excessive expenditure on docks, steamboats, &c., an expenditure now standing in the books at £1,061,000. One very urgent reason why something should be done in this direction is found in the fact that the steamboat traffic really does not pay. It is worked at a cost of nearly 74½ per cent. of the gross receipts, and the net revenue amounts to only 1½ per cent. on the capital spent. But all through the accounts this company shows pinching, and there can be no doubt at all that at least another 5 per cent. of the gross income ought to be spent in meeting current working charges and in keeping the line in decent repair, in order to bring it up to anything like the standard of neighbouring lines.

NORTH STAFFORDSHIRE RAILWAY COMPANY.—The peculiarity of this company's accounts for the half-year ending December 31 is that the increase and working expenses exceed by £2,000 the increase in gross receipts, so that the company would apparently have been rather better off if it had had no increase in its traffic at all. Of course, this is not exactly the way to judge, because the added expenditure is really chargeable to the entire traffic of the half-year and not alone to the increase in that traffic. Wages, locomotive-power, rolling-stock repairs, traffic expenses, rates and taxes, compensation, everything, in fact, shows an increase compared with the second half of 1896, and the consequence is a reduction in the dividend of ¼ per cent. per annum, the rate being 4¾ per cent., as against 5 per cent. a year ago. In most other respects the position of the company appears to be eminently satisfactory. It spent very little on capital account, less than £19,000 in fact last half-year. It has engaged in no new enterprises and has a clean-looking balance-sheet. The figures in the report, however, more and more indicate the general tendency in railway business for working expenses to expand. Dividends are payable on and after February 19.

BELFAST AND COUNTY DOWN RAILWAY COMPANY.—This small but good company also discloses in its report for the December half of the year that the increase in working expenses exceeds the increase in gross receipts, being £3,282 against £2,764. The net revenue of £27,303 was therefore slightly smaller than that for the second half of 1896. The company spent £31,478 on capital account last half year, nearly £1,300 of which is on working stock and the rest on lines opened for traffic. It has started a new hotel at Newcastle, but we do not find the cost of it stated in the accounts. The dividend at the rate of 6½ per cent. on the ordinary stock is payable on the 28th inst.

LONDON, TILBURY, AND SOUTHEND RAILWAY.—No railway has done better than this little company last half-year. Its gross receipts rose by £17,412 to £186,267, and its expenses £8,215 to £97,930, with the result that the net profit was nearly £9,000 larger than in the second half of 1896. The increase in the traffic was obtained at a cost of about 47 per cent. in expenses. To put the matter roughly, after meeting all prior charges, the directors are able to pay a dividend at the rate of 6¼ per cent. per annum as against a 6 per cent. rate a year ago, and have £14,502 to carry forward compared with £820 in December, 1896. Only £28,487 was spent on capital account last half-year and the company appears to have no ambitious schemes on hand. As it is obtaining a closer connection with the Midland and is in other ways extending its hold over traffic in a district where it has no rival, we see no reason why its future should not be still more prosperous. Dividend payable to-day.

TAFF VALE RAILWAY COMPANY.—In the December half of 1897 this company's gross receipts amounted to £394,945, being £9,750 more than in the corresponding half-year. Working expenses, however, increased £8,014, so that the company is affected very little by the larger income. In fact, the total working expenses for the half-year were 55·9 per cent., as against 54·2 per cent. for the December half of 1896. Capital expenditure last half-year was nearly £63,000, included in which is the curious item, £282, representing an increased value in third-class coaching stock. It looks finiking bookkeeping to put a tiny amount like this, which it must be very difficult to ascertain, into the capital account. The dividend payable on the ordinary stock is at the rate of 3¼ per cent. per annum, equivalent to 8½ per cent. per annum on the old ordinary stock, and is at the same rate as twelve months ago. A slightly larger balance, £2,315 against £1,816, is carried forward. The dividend is payable on the 12th inst.

THE SHEFFIELD BANKING COMPANY, LIMITED, does not give a profit and loss account, so we cannot say much about its doings for 1897. The report itself is as slender as it well can be. It tells us that the profit was £45,430, out of which a dividend of 12½ per cent. is paid on the share capital of £33,425; 5 per cent. of it last July. The income-tax is also paid, £1,500 written off the value of bank premises, and £1,428 added to the surplus fund, which is now raised to £166,427. The total in the balance-sheet comes to £3,351,721, and of this amount £1,068,143 is absorbed in advances on current accounts and loans on securities. Bills of exchange stand for over £402,816. Cash in hand and money lent for short periods are all in one item, but the bank appears to be quite strong enough to warrant its directors in giving shareholders fuller information.

THE BRADFORD MANUFACTURING COMPANY, LIMITED, paid 10 per cent. for the year 1897, and had a balance of £274 to carry forward. It is a small company, but seems to be well managed. Only £16,277, the value of trade marks and goodwill, had better be written down. It represents nearly half the capital of the company.

BRISTOL BREWERY (GEORGES & CO.), LIMITED.—The prosperity of this remarkable undertaking continues, and the net profit of £80,451 for last year compares with £73,927 in 1896. The dividend is therefore increased by 1⅓ per cent. to 19 per cent.; £14,000 is written off the brewery premises, and £1,600 is put to dividend equalisation fund, which will then stand at £13,960. In addition there is a general reserve of £158,319, and a special reserve of £20,665 to meet the premium of 15 per cent. payable upon the £140,000 of Five per Cent. Debenture stock which matures next year. Furthermore there is a hidden reserve of over £80,000 in the reduced valuation of premises and general plant. If any brewing company should maintain its dividend this one ought, for its total debenture debt is only £162,000, as against £600,000 of share capital, and after the debentures are converted the charges in regard to them will not be more than £6,000, against a gross profit of over £105,000 a year.

LION BREWERY COMPANY.—After placing £3,445 to reserve, the disposable balance of this company allows of a dividend and bonus of 14 per cent. for the past year on the ordinary shares. The reserve also benefited by £4,555 received in premiums upon the "B" Debenture stock recently issued, and its total now stands at £153,200. Depreciation was allowed for to the extent of £27,215, and repairs came to £8,779. By recent additions, the total of the debenture debt and deposits amount to £558,000, as against only £383,000 of share capital, whereas two years ago the debentures and deposits only totalled £203,000, with the same amount of share capital.

LANCASHIRE AND YORKSHIRE RAILWAY COMPANY.—Earnings for half-year to December 31 last, was £2,573,000 or £28,568 up, and working expenses were £52,704 to £1,459,000. Here likewise the gross gain was much more than swallowed up in the fresh expenses, and the net revenue fell off £24,000 to £1,114,000. At the same time fixed and general interest charges rose £8,700 and helped to bring down the amount available for dividends, &c. to £865,000. Out of this the dividend at the rate of 5¼ per cent. per annum will be paid to the ordinary stockholders on the 10th inst. Capital expenditure amounted to nearly £210,000 for the half year which was less than authorised, but this is exclusive of £126,000 spent on lines under construction, and of the Thre per Cent. Debenture stock issued against the cancelled securities of absorbed lines. All these together make the nominal addition to the capital for the half-year about £698,000

METROPOLITAN DISTRICT RAILWAY COMPANY.—Last six months saw an addition of £5,884 to the gross receipts of this company, making them £217,000. Working expenses rose only £2,761 to £105,860, so that the profit was actually £3,122 up at £111,472. Debenture stock interest, rent charges, &c., all paid, left but £48,907, out of which the guaranteed stock gets £24,276, leaving enough to give the preference stock a dividend at the rate of 2¾ per cent. per annum, and still £4,000 remains for the new half-year. The dividend is payable on the 19th inst. Extensions are projected to Harrow, Uxbridge, and Bow, so the board does not lack enterprise. Shareholders, unfortunately, never benefit much by this enterprise. Capital expenditure last half-year was only to £14,227, but there is a good time coming.

MIDLAND GREAT WESTERN RAILWAY OF IRELAND COMPANY.—Gross receipts came to £288,115 last half-year and working expenses to £144,375; when debenture interest and rent charge stocks were met, £90,000 odd was left for dividends, including £4,085 brought forward. The ordinary stock gets 2¼ per cent. for the half-year, a rise of ½ per cent. per annum in the rate, and £11,372 is left to carry to the current half-year. Traffic income rose £8,466, all from merchandise and cattle. Capital expenditure was only £6,753 in the six months.

LLOYDS BANK, LIMITED, has grown into great figures, the total of its balance-sheet having risen now to a total of £40,760,000, and its debt on deposits to £37,112,000. Of this, £4,642,000 is held in cash, £4,095,000 in bills of exchange, and £18,962,000 is wrapped up in advances. The investments are £3,870,000 only and are all in one item. For the year closed 31st December, the net profit is put at £464,361 out of which 17½ per cent. has been paid on the share capital, £50,000 added to reserve, £25,000 written off bank premises, and £32,686 carried forward. Income-tax was paid in addition. Comparison with previous figures is impossible, because the bank is amalgamating at such a rate. Last year it absorbed the County of Gloucester Bank and Williams & Co. of Chester. The reserve fund is now £1,200,000, thanks principally to premiums on new shares issued in consequence of the amalgamation.

THE LONDON AND COUNTY BANKING COMPANY can look back on the half-year's working with considerable satisfaction. It is the biggest bill-buying bank in the kingdom, but on this occasion the bill case is much lighter than it was a year ago, so only £33,000 has to be set aside for rebate against £51,000 at the end of 1896. Thanks partly to this the improvement in the half-year's profits is as much, £61,726. The usual £25,000 is transferred to premises account, but the addition of £10,000 to the Provident Fund is not repeated this half-year. What is more satisfactory is that £80,000 is added to the reserve, raising it to £1,080,000, and this is the first addition made to it out of profits for some years past. Even now, it stands at only 54 per cent. of the paid-up capital, and will well bear further strengthening out of profits, not premiums on new shares. Shareholders receive the same dividend of 10 per cent. for the half-year, but this time a bonus of 1 per cent. is added, which makes the distribution for the year 22 per cent.—the best since 1891. As to the main items in the balance-sheet deposits are up only £376,000 and acceptances still over £2,000,000, are rather less, while investments show a similar increase to the deposits. Bills discounted, at £10,705,000, are down £1,734,000, but advances have swollen by £1,850,000 to the fine round total of £14,634,000.

The UNION BANK OF AUSTRALIA accounts, made up to August 31 last, show considerable shrinkage in business and profits. The note circulation is smaller, while the deposits have diminished as much as £1,822,000 and bills payable are down nearly £400,000. Amongst the assets, specie on hand and cash balances have dropped £450,000, and money at call and notice £965,000. Investments against the reserve remain intact, but the bank's other investments in stocks have been reduced by £363,000. Bills receivable are £210,000 less, and bills discounted and advances show a reduction of £247,000. This is a truly melancholy tale. Although the half-year's gross profits declined from £168,268 to £54,889, expenses, strangely enough, show an increase under all heads, even including income-tax, and amounted to £117,453 against £109,431, so that the half-year's net profits come out at only £37,436 as compared with £58,837. The dividend is kept at the rate of 5 per cent. per annum, but a year ago £10,000 was applied in reduction of bank premises account, and there is nothing of this on the present occasion. Unless a speedy change for the better sets in, shareholders should be prepared for a reduction in dividend, and possibly something besides—the reverse of a "bonus."

BANK OF BRITISH COLUMBIA.—This institution is making a little progress in the recovery of lost ground. Profits for the second half of last year were only £738 better than in the corresponding half of 1896, and £459 less was brought forward, but by curtailing expenses a balance of £18,351 is obtained, compared with £14,922, so the directors are able to raise their dividend from 4 to 5 per cent. per and annum, to carry forward £4,000 more. The note circulation has grown a little, deposits are virtually unaltered, and bills payable are up £200,000, while bills discounted and advances show the moderate increase of £77,000. With the development of the mining industry the bank should do better still before long, but it ought to be one of the first duties of the directors to rebuild the reserve fund, which, in order to meet losses, was recently reduced from £285,000 to £100,000.

BANK OF EGYPT.—All Anglo-Egyptian banks last year, it seems, did not do well. This one made a profit of only £29,971, or £5,000 less than during 1896. Dividend is 9 per cent. for the year, with a bonus of 5s. per share, and £5,000 is added to reserve, as in 1896, but the balance forward is reduced from £7,263 to £4,734. This will make the reserve £120,000, which is still slightly less than half the paid-up capital. Deposits show a welcome increase of nearly 29 per cent. to £547,000.

THE BANK OF CALCUTTA continues to grow steadily. Net profits for the second half of last year were Rs. 129,123, or Rs. 10,000 more than in the corresponding period. Only Rs. 12,500 is used in paying a dividend at the rate of 5 per cent. of ordinary shares, but as much as Rs. 100,000 is added to reserve, which in the three years of the bank's existence has been built up to Rs. 475,000, or nearly half the paid-up capital. Deposits are up Rs. 700,000, at nearly 63½ lacs, of which over 61 lacs is employed in loans, &c., bills discounted amounting to only Rs. 110,930.

LONDON AND SOUTH WESTERN RAILWAY COMPANY.—None of our larger railway corporations are doing better, one year with another, than the South Western. It did well last half-year although an increase of £100,000 in its gross receipts resulted in a net gain of only about £17,000. Working expenses increased about £84,000, and debenture interest, &c., by about £5,500, so the company shows the same results as its neighbours, working expenses expanding at a more rapid ratio than gross income. Notwithstanding this it was able to work its traffic in the past half-year for less than 52 per cent. of the gross receipts. This is really better than it appears, because the steamboat traffic of the company is conducted at very little profit, less than £3,000 in fact last year on a gross income of about £102,000. Dock receipts also are not so fat as they might be, and come only to about 1½ per cent. on the capital expenditure. It follows that the railway by itself is worked with great economy, and this economy enabled the company to pay 7 per cent. for the whole year 1896, or ⅛ per cent. more than in the previous year on its common stock. Gross receipts came to £2,331,000, including steamboat and dock receipts, and gross expenditure to £1,306,000. The company we see has obtained sanction from its shareholders to issue £600,000 new stock with its attendant borrowing power of £200,000, and last half year the capital expenditure came to £376,000 of which about £62,000 was for new plant, quays, &c. at the Southampton Docks and £107,000 on new working stock. Steamboats stand in the capital account of the company for £650,000, and the Southampton Docks up to the present have cost £2,655,000. Renewal and insurance on the steamboats seem to be fairly well provided for, but is not the capital item for steamers one to write down, if not by degrees to wipe out altogether? The New Waterloo and City Railway is expected to be opened early for traffic, and will lead to a general exodus from the South-Eastern Company's Charing Cross and Cannon-street line, perhaps one of the most miserable bits of road in the three kingdoms. The dividend will be payable on the 22nd inst.

HULL AND BARNSLEY RAILWAY AND DOCK COMPANY.—Gross receipts fell off on this line £267 last half-year, and working expenses increased £5,165, so the net revenue was naturally poorer by £4,000. Adding the balance brought from June the divisible amount was £53,000 odd, out of which an additional ½ per cent. is paid to the Three per Cent. Second Debenture stock, and a dividend at the rate of 1¾ per cent. on the ordinary stock. The usual regrets are expressed in the report that the half-year was not better, and the blame is laid on the decreased imports of grain into Hull, and on the engineers dispute. With all its adversities, however, the company was able to spend £54,226 on capital account last half-year. Dividends will be paid on the 17th inst.

THE AUSTRALIAN JOINT-STOCK BANK COMPANY, LIMITED.—With nearly £9,000,000 nominal at their command the directors of this bank contrived in the half-year ended December 31 to make a net profit of £1,725, after deducting £783 for rebate. We do not think that anything more need be said.

STUCKEY'S BANKING COMPANY.—Balance-sheet for 1897 shows similar changes to what is seen in many other banker's accounts, the directors having apparently taken advantage of high prices to sell securities and lend the money to bill-brokers. Investments have been reduced by £133,000, while loans at call and short notice have increased from £200,000 to £435,000. Deposits have risen £103,000 and now exceed £6,000,000, but bills discounted and advances are a trifle less.

THE DEVON AND CORNWALL BANKING COMPANY made a profit last year of £43,166, or a trifle more than in 1896, and having only a small capital of £200,000 is able to pay its shareholders a dividend and bonus of £4 per share, or 20 per cent. They are, however, £100 shares, with only £20 paid up, and the directors have apparently given up the idea of adding anything to the guaranteed fund, which stands at £200,000, or equal to the paid-up capital. Balance-sheet figures show no remarkable change compared with a year ago, but bank premises have been written up by £6,900 to £82,972, and only £3,000 is allowed out of profits in reduction of the estate. The directors are resolved not to let the grass grow under them, and have taken advantage of the lessened banking accommodation in the county of Dorset through the failure of a local private bank and the amalgamation of another, to open three new branches besides some new agencies, so competition is not likely to be reduced.

THE NORTHAMPTONSHIRE UNION BANK has a paid-up capital of £300,000, and a guarantee fund of £236,000, and the latter is to be steadily built up to the level of the former. Profits for 1897 were £46,416, against £41,815, but the dividend is kept at the substantial figure of 12 per cent. for the year. Although issuing annual reports the directors at the end of each half-year make appropriations to the guaranteed fund and to bank premises account. The amount added to the former fund is £6,000 in the year compared with only £2,977 in 1896, while premises are reduced by £1,000 to the moderate figure of £28,193. Deposits show a fair improvement, and now amount to over 2½ millions, but the bank has been selling some of its securities, the present total of £750,000 being nearly £100,000 less than a year ago. Cash and bills are slightly higher, but the extra money has gone in advances, &c., which at £1,862,000 show an increase of over £200,000.

MERCANTILE STEAMSHIP COMPANY.—Like most other steamship undertakings this company did very well last year, the profits on voyages completed being £48,820 against £37,127 in the previous year, and £29,859 in 1895. Home expenses are never a heavy item, and after providing for them the directors are in a position to raise the dividend from 7s. 6d. per share, which has been paid for several years, to 10s., or 10 per cent., and to carry forward the larger balance of £1,915. The improvement is mainly due to the large export business from the United States, for during the greater part of the year Indian, China and Pacific freights were exceptionally low, and it was not until the last three months that any considerable improvement took place. In 1895 only £10,000 was added to the depreciation fund, and in 1896 £20,000, but this time £25,000 is added. Taking advantage of the low prices the directors have had several new boats built and consequently the book value of the fleet has been rising until it now figures at £242,900, while the gross tonnage is 38,054 tons, and the depreciation and insurance funds stand at £53,525, which is not at all a bad position. It is a feature of this company to reward its captains if they navigate without accident for two consecutive years, and this time the increased number of seven have earned the extra gratuity. Captains, we should have thought, needed no such inducement.

Mr. Walter Beverley, sitting as arbitrator between the Brighouse Corporation and Mr. David Walshaw, regarding the purchase of a small bit of property, ordered the Corporation to pay £96 11s. and full costs. The full costs, it is stated, will amount to over £300. If arbitration is peaceful it seems it can be expensive.

In the United States there are 14,000 miles of electric tramway; in the United Kingdom, 80!

At Tuesday's sitting of the Royal Commission on the London water supply, Mr. H. E. Haward, Comptroller of the London County Council, contended that the water companies' shareholders have received premiums in addition to their dividends, and that the reduction of the water rates of some of them has been unduly postponed in consequence of the creation of unnecessary capital.

A Bill to increase the subvention to the North German Lloyd from £220,000 to £295,000 per annum, has been submitted to the German Reichsrath. In consideration of this increased subvention the company undertakes to open a regular fortnightly service of steamers to Eastern Asia.

The Produce Markets.

GRAIN.

Mark-lane has been poorly attended recently, and the business also has been poor. Prices, however, have shown no essential variation. English white wheat was quoted on Wednesday at 35s. to 40s., and red 34s. to 38s. Dulness has prevailed in foreign, and on Monday there was a drop of 6d. in some cases, though as a rule previous rates were maintained. Walla Walla quoted 39s. to 39s. 6d., and hard Manitoba 41s. to 41s. 6d. per qr. Flour moved with a slow tone, but values lately current were upheld. Town whites 34s., and households 31s. Country makes, 26s. to 31s. American patents 30s. to 32s. per sack. Barley was in limited request at previous rates. Grinding quoted 17s. ex quay. Oats were slow of sale, and American mixed clipped were quoted 15s. 9d. to 16s. ex ship. Maize was steadily held, but slow. At Liverpool spot parcels were firm with a fair inquiry. Red American futures opened unchanged to ½d. per cental lower on disappointing cables, weakened on free offers, but subsequently sellers diminished, and fair buying brought about a reaction. The market closed quiet and unchanged to ½d. per cental lower. There has been a dull tone in the London cargo market, with a tendency in buyers' favour. No sales were reported on Wednesday, but a La Plata sailer of 800 tons, prompt shipment, sold on Tuesday at 35s. 3d., and the Marion Chilcott, 11,400 qrs. Walla Walla, November 10, changed hands on the Continent at about 36s. 7½d. For a cargo of blue Stem, January, 36s. 6d. is said to be obtainable. Californian, September, is offered at 38s. 3d., and December-january at 37s. 6d. Wheat options irregular and ½d. down to ½d. up. Maize unchanged at ⅜ down. Contracts registered—96,000 centals wheat and 24,000 centals maize.

Barley quiet. Odessa-Nikolaieff-Crimean. February-March, is offered at 16s. 6d. Danubian, prompt, at 16s., and four options, March-May, at 15s. 6d. Parcels slow. Odessa-Nikolaieff, prompt, sellers, 16s. to 16s. 3d. Oats 1½d. to 3d. lower. Mixed American clipped, January-February, sold at 15s.; March, sellers, 14s. 9d. to 14s. 10½d. Beans quiet. Saide, prompt, quoted 29s. to 30s.

OFFICIAL CLOSING VALUES (100 lb. deliveries—February 2).

	March.	May.	July.	Sept.
Red American Wheat	7 9¼	7 4⅞	7 1¼	6 5⅞

New York wheat has shown considerable fluctuation, with a tendency downwards. On Wednesday it opened steadily ⅛ c. up, and for a time advanced on foreign buying and better cables, but went down later, and closed weak, ½ c. to 1⅝ c. lower; spot weak. Spring, 108⅜ c.; winter 103⅜ c. Sales, futures, 4,100,000 bushels. Spot, 40,000 bales. Receipts, Atlantic, 117,000 bushels; same day, last year, 20,000 bushels. Corn also declined. Chicago unsteady, and closed easy, with September and December unchanged, nearer deliveries, ⅝ c. to 2 c. down.

COTTON.

Spot market firm throughout the week, but without change in values, though on Wednesday, with a more active business in American cotton, sellers grew firmer. Egyptians were in fair demand, with values steadily maintained. There is still no demand for Surats. Futures opened ½ point lower, and varied but little until late in the afternoon, when increased offerings on disappointing American cables induced further concessions, the close being quiet at a fall of ½ to 1 point. The sales were estimated at 12,000 bales, including 500 on speculation and for export. In New York there was more fluctuation, and prices, which went upward in the early part of the week, declined later, and on Wednesday closed 1 to 2 points lower. Spot quiet. Manchester lacked buoyancy, but there was a fair inquiry, though at lower prices than sellers would accept. Yarn quotations little changed.

NEW YORK CLOSING VALUES.

	Spot.	Feb.	Mar.	April.	May.	June.	July.	Aug.	Sept.	Oct.	Nov.
Feb. 2 ..	5 11/32	5.69	5.72	5.75	5.79	5.82	5.85	5.89	5.89	5.91	5.92

WOOL.

The first series of sales of colonial wool for the current year ended on Wednesday. At these sales, Messrs. Jacomb, Son & Co. state in their circular, "157,361 bales out of the available total have been catalogued, and only a very small proportion bought in. Of the quantity sold 70,000 bales have been taken for foreign account, including about 10,000 for the U.S.A. Some 19,500 bales are held over for future sale. Since our last report there has been no cessation of the keenness of demand from all sides, and the only variation in price has been in the case of some of the lower and coarser cross-breds, either greasy or scoured, which do not quite maintain the best prices of the series. The average quotation as compared with the closing rates of last Series is for—Merino wools, 10 per cent. advance; cross-breds, fine, 5 per cent. advance; cross-breds, medium and coarse, par. The improvement in Cape and Natal wools is not so marked as in the case of Australasian. The general tendency of demand having been towards fine wools, the appreciation in values in many of such is not limited to 10 per cent. and exceptionally high prices have been realised for some of the best scoured and greasy clothings. In comparison with prices of last season's wool present rates show marked improvement, and the sales close with very firm tone." The second series of sales will commence on March 15. The general tone of the wool markets has been firm, with an increasing demand.

METALS AND COAL.

There has been some fluctuation in copper during the week, with a tendency upward, though the close on Wednesday was easier, with the tendency rather downward. Sales for cash were effected at £49 3s. 9d.; one month sold at £49 5s., and three months' at £49 8s. 9. At the close there were further sellers at these rates.

SETTLEMENT PRICES.

	Feb. 2.	Jan. 26	Jan. 19.	Jan. 12	Jan. 5.	Dec. 29.
	£ s. d.	£ s. d.	£ s. d.	£ s. d.	£ s. d.	£ s. d.
Copper ..	49 [illegible] 6	48 17 6	49 5 0	48 17 6	48 10 0	48 5 0

The dulness in pig-iron continues, though on Wednesday there was rather more doing. The bulk of the business, however, was of a jobbing character, being confined to members of the ring, and those who bought at opening in the hope of an upward turn, sold out in the afternoon at a loss. Sales amounted to 30,000 tons, and Scotch fell 1d., and hematite 2d., while Cleveland gained ½d. per ton.

SETTLEMENT PRICES.

	Feb. 2.	Jan. 26.	Jan. 19.	Jan. 12.	Jan. 5.	Dec. 29.
	s. d.	s. d.	s. d.	s. d.	s. d.	s. d.
Scotch	45 7½	46 0	46 0	45 9	45 6	45 4½
Cleveland ..	40 6	40 10½	40 10½	40 7½	40 4½	40 3
Hematite ..	48 6	47 0	48 10½	48 9	48 4½	48 4½

There is as yet no real improvement in the coal trade, though dealers are looking forward to a considerable demand following the close of the engineers' strike. This increased demand has not, however, begun. The attendance at the London Coal Exchange on Wednesday was small, and business was limited. The seaborne department was very inactive, and a cargo of Yorkshire coal which was on offer did not find a buyer. The gale, however, is delaying the movements of the boats, and there is a prospect of lighter deliveries. The official quotations stand at 17s. and 16s., usual terms in the Pool for Hetton Wallsend and Lyons respectively. Since Monday 12 cargoes have come to hand.

SUGAR.

No improvement is noticeable in the tone of the sugar market, which continues disappointingly dull. In their monthly circular, Messrs. W. Connal & Co. say :—"The advance of 6d. per cwt., which took place during the last days of December, and which then gave promise, not only of being maintained, but also of being enhanced with the opening of the year, has since been lost, and first products Beet, which on December 31 commanded 9s. 7½d., are to-day quoted at 9s. 1½d., f.o.b., Hamburg, basis 88 per cent. analysis. The abnormally mild season has left the navigation of Continental rivers free, and has permitted uninterrupted arrivals, in Hamburg and other shipping ports, of both raw and refined sugars, a great part of which would not, under ordinary circumstances, have been available for export until March or April, and as buyers have thus had ample supplies from which to select, they have been successful in gradually reducing prices. The decline which has taken place in the American markets has likewise had an unfavourable influence in European centres." Sales at Mincing-lane on Wednesday were small. German 88 per cent. sold—May at 9s. 3⅞d., and August at 9s. 6¼d. f.o.b. Hamburg. Cane sorts continue very quiet and business unimportant. The market for home refined remains slow and business limited. Tate's cubes sold at 14s. 9d.; second quality, 13s. 10½d.; No. 1 crushed, 13s.; No. 2 ditto, 12s. 6d.; granulated, 13s. 3d.; yellow crystallised, 12s.; No. 1 crystals (in Liverpool), 13s. 1½d.; No. 2 ditto, 12s. 9d.; Standard Liverpool granulated, 12s. 6d.; Lyle's No. 1 granulated, 12s. 9d.; No. 2 ditto, 12s.; No. 1 crystals, 12s. 9d.; No. 3 ditto, 12s.; A white, 12s. 6d.; B, 11s. 9d.; O and P Crystals, 11s. 9d. Pieces and crystals remain dull—yellow crystals at 11s. 6d. to 11s. 10½d.; Fowler's golden syrup, 11s. 6d.; German granulated continues slow, ready at easy prices, forward steady.

TEA AND COFFEE.

There is some tendency to improvement in tea, though not as yet very decided. Messrs. Gow, Wilson, and Stanton give us the movements of tea in London during the first eight months of the season. Although the deliveries during January are a trifle under those of last year, the clearance from the commencement of the season show an increase. Only 35,861 packages of Indian were brought forward; this resulted in a steady market for all descriptions. A few closing invoices have already been catalogued. The official telegram from the Indian Tea Association, Calcutta, gives the total exports to the United Kingdom from April 1 to date as 130,450,000 against 127,640,000 for the same period last season. The week's auction of Ceylon was heavy, comprising 33,095 packages, and although meeting with good attention from buyers, some slight reduction was noticeable in values, especially in medium teas, which were distinctly weaker. Only 875 packages of Java were brought to auction, comprising selections from three different estates; the teas were mostly sold with fair competition at rates current last week. 1,913 packages are advertised for sale next week.

The demand for coffee has been poor during the week, but at some of the auction sales there was good competition. At the auction on Wednesday, however, the uninteresting supply of 1,901 packages, chiefly consisting of common sorts, met with scarcely any demand, and only a small part sold at prices again lower, excepting a small parcel of Ceylon, which brought full rates. Ceylon—good middling to good bold dull green, 106s. 6d. to 113s.; small, 96s.; peaberry, 141s.; Guatemala—low middling to middling dull gray mixed pales, 68s. to 70s.; Salvador—middling dull coloury, 72s.; small mixed, 33s. 6d.; peaberry, 95s.; Ecuador—fine ordinary pale greenish, 40s. 6d. to 42s.

HEMP AND JUTE.

Hemp throughout has been quiet but firm, sellers of F. C. Manila near at hand, at £18; March-May, sailer, £19; and May-July, £19 2s. 6d. At auction 100 bales sold—good current, £18 to £18 10s.; and choice, £23 5s.; while 250 fair seconds were bought in.

Jute still quiet, but steadily held: Good group first marks, £9 17s. 6d., with buyers at £9 15s.

Dividends Announced.

BANKS.

LONDON AND COUNTY BANK.—10 per cent. for the last half-year and a bonus of 1 per cent., balance forward £49,966. The current and deposit accounts now stand at £41,527,000, against £41,151,000 a year ago.

LONDON AND HANSEATIC BANK.—Final dividend for second half of 1897 of 9s. per share, making with interim dividend 14s. per share or 7 per cent. for the year. £8,594 to be carried forward.

PARE'S LEICESTERSHIRE.—6¼ per cent. dividends on the two classes of shares, making 12½ per cent. for the year. £7,308 carried forward.

MERCHANT BANKING COMPANY.—Directors recommend the payment of a further dividend of 3 per cent., making a distribution of 5 per cent. for the year. Balance of £6,630 to be carried forward.

MANX BANK.—Payment of dividend of 6 per cent. per annum. £750 to be placed to reserve, £400 to depreciation, and balance of £26 to be carried forward.

LEICESTERSHIRE BANKING.—Two dividends of 10s. each are paid, being 10 per cent. for 1897. £8,000 is added to reserve fund, and £5,000 applied in reduction of bank premises, and £3,658 carried forward.

RAILWAYS.

NORTH-EASTERN.—Dividend at the rate of 7 per cent. per annum for the past half year, as against 7¼ a year ago.

METROPOLITAN DISTRICT.—Dividend for past half-year at the rate of 2¼ per cent. per annum on the preference. Second half of 1896, 2½ per cent.

NORTH STAFFORDSHIRE.—Dividend for the half-year ended December 31 at the rate of 4¾ per cent. per annum. £4,765 carried forward. For the corresponding half of 1896 the distribution was at the rate of 5 per cent., and £3,098 was carried forward.

HULL AND BARNSLEY.—Payment of additional interest for the whole year at the rate of ½ per cent. per annum to the Second debenture stock holders. Full dividend of 4 per cent. recommended on preference stock, together with a dividend for the half year on the ordinary stock at the rate of 1¾ per cent., carrying forward a balance of £8,952. For the corresponding period of 1896 the distribution on the Ordinary stock was at the rate of 2 per cent. per annum, with £10,285 forward.

TAFF VALLEY.—Dividend for half-year ended December 31 at the rate of 3½ per cent. per annum. £4,000 placed to reserve, and £2,315 carried forward. For the corresponding half of 1896 the dividend was the same, £3,000 was placed to reserve, and £1,816 carried forward.

LONDON AND BLACKWALL.—Dividend for last half of 1897 at the usual rate of 4½ per cent. per annum.

ISLE OF WIGHT.—Interest at the rate of 4 per cent. per annum on the preferred ordinary stock for half-year ended December 31, and a distribution at the rate of 5 per cent. per annum on the deferred ordinary stock. £1,800 to be carried forward.

GREAT NORTHERN RAILWAY.—Dividend may be declared at the rate of £5 per cent. per annum on the ordinary capital of the company, giving for the half-year £2 per cent. to the preferred converted ordinary stock, £2 per cent. to the deferred converted ordinary stock, £3 per cent. to the "B" stock, and £2 per cent. to the "A" stock. These rates will make the dividend for the whole year as follows, viz.:—£4 per cent. to the preferred converted Ordinary stock, £2. 5s. per cent. to the deferred converted ordinary stock, £6 per cent. to the "B" stock, and £2 5s. per cent. to the "A" stock, carrying forward £15,094.

MISCELLANEOUS.

A. M. PEEBLES & SON, LIMITED.—8½ per cent. per annum interim on the ordinary shares, against 8 per cent. per annum a year ago.

BARON CIGARETTE MACHINE COMPANY.—Dividend of 7½ per cent. per annum; £11,336 carried forward.

MACHINERY TRUST, LIMITED.—20 per cent. per annum for the past half-year, with £7,891 carried forward, against £5,257 last year.

M. HYAM WHOLESALE CLOTHING COMPANY.—10 per cent. per annum on the ordinary shares for the past half year.

CHARING CROSS AND STRAND ELECTRICITY SUPPLY CORPORATION, LIMITED.—Dividend for the half-year ended December 31, 1897, at the rate of 8 per cent. per annum, making, with the interim dividend distributed for the half-year ended June 30, 1897, at the rate of 6 per cent. per annum, a dividend payable for the year 1897 of 7 per cent. on the ordinary share capital. This compares with a dividend of 6 per cent. for the year 1896.

MOUNT MORGAN GOLD MINING.—Dividend declared of £25,000, being 6d. a share for the month of January.

BREWERY AND COMMERCIAL INVESTMENT TRUST.—Dividend on the ordinary shares at the rate of 6 per cent. per annum for the half-year ended December 31. Payable on the 15th inst.

GORDON HOTELS, LIMITED.—Warrants will be posted on the 12th for an interim dividend at the rate of 8 per cent. per annum on the ordinary shares and of 5½ per cent. on the preference.

ROBERT ROBERTS & CO.—Dividend for 1897 at the rate of 5 per cent. on the Preference shares and 6 per cent. on the Ordinary shares.

SANITAS COMPANY, LIMITED.—Payment of a final dividend of 1s. and a bonus of 9d. per share bringing up the total distribution for the year to 13¾ per cent. on the fully-paid shares numbered from 1 to 50,000, and a final dividend and bonus of 1s. 2½d. on the shares numbered from 50,001 to 60,000.

NATIONAL TELEPHONE COMPANY.—Dividend for the past half-year at the rate of 6 per cent. per annum on the amounts paid up on the ordinary shares; £40,000 placed to reserve and about £9,000 carried forward.

LONDON GENERAL OMNIBUS COMPANY.—Directors propose dividend at the rate of 8 per cent. per annum for the past half-year and a bonus of £1 5s. per cent. (equal to 10½ per cent. per annum), to add £10,000 to general reserve fund, and to carry forward about £15,000.

J. W. BENSON, LIMITED.—5 per cent. on the ordinary shares of the company.

HOME AND COLONIAL STORES, LIMITED.—Dividend at the rate of 5s. per share, making, with interim dividend already paid on the ordinary shares, 12½ per cent. for the year 1897.

PORTSEA ISLAND BUILDING SOCIETY.—A final dividend of 1s. 1½d. in the £, making a total dividend of 10s. 1½d. in the £, is being paid by direction of Lord Macnaghten, the arbitrator appointed under the Portsea Island Building Society (Arbitration) Act, 1893. The return thus being made will bring the total distribution up to about £412,000.

LIBERTY & COMPANY.—Dividend declared at the rate of 6 per cent. per annum on the six per cent. cumulative preference shares for the six months ended January 31.

BIRMINGHAM RAILWAY CARRIAGE AND WAGON, LIMITED.—12½ per cent. per annum on the ordinary capital for the half-year ended December 31, making a dividend of 10 per cent. for the year 1897.

FREEHOLD AND LEASEHOLD INVESTMENT COMPANY.—Interim dividend at the rate of 5 per cent. per annum on the share capital.

BOND'S (BRISTOL) BREWERY, LIMITED.—5 per cent. for the twelve months ended November 30 last.

JAMES W. COOK & COMPANY, LIMITED.—3s. 6d. per share for the half-year ended December 31, making, with interim dividend paid in July last, a total dividend for the year of 7s. per share on the ordinary share capital.

ANGELO GOLD MINES, LIMITED.—25 per cent., less tax, declared.

BULLOCK, LADE, & COMPANY, LIMITED.—Interim dividend on the ordinary shares for the half-year ended 31st ult., at the rate of 10 per cent. per annum.

BEACON GOLD MINES, LIMITED.—A third interim dividend of 6d. per share, free of income tax.

SWEETMEAT AUTOMATIC DELIVERY COMPANY, LIMITED.—Interim dividend for the quarter ended December 31 last at the rate of 20 per cent. per annum, as compared with 15 per cent. for corresponding period of 1896.

HARRISON, BARBER, & COMPANY.—Dividend recommended at the rate of 4 per cent. per annum for 1897, £1,000 to be placed to general reserve, £1,000 to reserve for depreciation, and £550 carried forward.

CUBA SUBMARINE TELEGRAPH, LIMITED.—Dividend on the ordinary shares at the rate of 6 per cent. per annum, tax free, for the half-year ended December 31.

J. B. BROOKS & COMPANY, LIMITED.—Interim dividends at the rate of 5 per cent. per annum to be declared on the preference and ordinary shares (the latter free of income tax) for the half-year ended 28th inst.

W. LEVY & SONS.—Dividend declared on the ordinary shares, which, including the interim paid in July last, makes in all 7 per cent. for the year.

MOSER MACHINE.—15s. per share for 1897, and £2,500 placed to a reserve fund account, leaving a balance of £664 to be carried forward.

GREAT WESTERN RAILWAY.—Dividend is announced for the past half-year at the rate of 7¼ per cent. per annum, carrying forward £31,300. For the corresponding period the dividend was at the same rate with £42,800 carried forward.

OTTOMAN RAILWAY (Smyrna to Aidin).—Dividend of 22s. per share for half-year ended December 31, carrying forward £11,000.

GREAT WESTERN OF BRAZIL RAILWAY.—Week ending December 25, $36,532; increase $11,240, aggregate to date $1,360,577; decrease $298.574.

It may be interesting to know that, in the opinion of the United States Board of General Appraisers, a trade mark is not a decoration. The Collector of Customs had given his opinion that it was.

The London School Board estimate that the total amount they will require on loan from the London County Council for the eighteen months up to September 30, 1899, will be £900,000.

Basing their estimates for this year on the basis of last year's revenue, the Transvaal Government believe that, after providing for the necessary expenditure, there should be a credit balance at the end of the year of about £400,000. Provision for projected railways and public works is to be made by a State loan.

A workmen's conference has solemnly resolved that the proposed Victoria Embankment tramway must be opposed, because it would "seriously interfere" with the marshalling of working-class processions. If that is the worst that can be said against the proposed new tram line, people may come to think it not so perverse a project after all.

Parcels left at railway stations "till called for" may be regarded as left at the owner's risk. In a case heard at the Windsor County Court, a parcel that had been left at the railway-station booking office for three days had been carried off by thieves, who broke into the place. The Judge dismissed the claim for payment against the railway company on the ground that, as a reasonable time had elapsed for the delivery of the parcel after its reception at the station, the company simply held the position of warehousers, and were not liable for its loss.

A receiving order has been made in the London Bankruptcy Court against Henry Beckwith, described as of Finsbury Circus-buildings, Finsbury-circus, secretary to a public company. The amount of the liabilities not announced.

Answers to Correspondents.

Questions about public securities, and on all points in company law, will be answered week by week, in the REVIEW, on the following terms and conditions:—

A fee of FIVE shillings must be remitted for each question put, provided they are questions about separate securities. Should a private letter be required, then an extra fee of FIVE shillings must be sent to cover the cost of such letter, the fee then being TEN shillings for one query only, and FIVE shillings for every subsequent one in the same letter. While making this concession the EDITOR will feel obliged if private replies are as much as possible dispensed with. It is wholly impossible to answer letters sent merely "with a stamped envelope enclosed for reply."

Correspondents will further greatly oblige by so framing their questions as to obviate the necessity to name securities in the replies. They should *number* the questions, keeping a copy for reference, thus:—"(1) Please inform me about the present position of the Rowenzori Development Co. (2) Is a dividend likely to be paid soon on the capital stock of the Congo-Sudan Railway?"

Answers to be given to all such questions by simply quoting the numbers 1, 2, 3, and so on. The EDITOR has a rooted objection to such forms of reply as—"I think your Timbuctoo Consols will go up," or "Sell your Slowcoach and Draggem Bonds," because this kind of thing is open to all sorts of abuses. By the plan suggested, and by using a fancy name to be replied to, each query can be kept absolutely private to the inquirer, and no scope whatever be given to market munipulations. Avoid, as names to be replied to, common words, like "investor," "inquirer," and so on, as also "bear" or "bull." Detached syllables of the inquirer's name, or initials reversed, will frequently do as well as anything, so long as the answer can be identified by the inquirer.

The EDITOR further respectfully requests that merely speculative questions should as far as possible be avoided. He by no means sets himself up as a market prophet, and can only undertake to provide the latest information regarding the securities asked about. This he will do faithfully and without bias.

Replies cannot be guaranteed in the same week if the letters demanding them reach the office of the INVESTORS' REVIEW, Norfolk House, Norfolk-street, W.C., later than the first post on Wednesday mornings.

COL.—Seem likely to hold their price for the present, as there has recently been a fair demand for shares, and the underwriters who had to take up, I understand, about 75 per cent. must be nearly sold out. The contracting company was formed the year before, and is fairly strong financially. Their terms were more favourable to themselves perhaps than they might have been, but they have had a lot of difficult work to carry through. It is impossible to say how the earnings will turn out, but in the long run they ought to be good, and yield a fair return, though difficulties may arise at the start, in which case the price will probably recede.

CAROLUS.—Ordinary are quoted 1½-⅝, and seem to me dear at the price. Your quotation from the chairman's speech I do not understand, as certainly the figures you mention are in the balance-sheet as an asset. Gross profits are below those of 1896, about £1,600, not quite so much as you say. Preference are quoted 1$\frac{3}{16}$-$\frac{5}{16}$. In the criticism you refer to you will find these described as a fair investment, and they ought to be so still, though probably there is not much chance of any further increase in the capital value. Shareholders should, I think, insist on more detail in the balance-sheet. Stocks and Sundry Debtors should be separate items. Another improvement would be the appearance of a liquid asset representing the reserve.

OLICANA AND J.P.—Cannot reply to your questions in these columns. See Rule II. I will write you in a day or two.

A. Z. B.—Can you send me copy of balance sheet and accounts? Company does not publish them.

R. K.—I must apologise for overlooking your first question last week. If you can get in under your selling price you might do so, but there is no haste to re-purchase at the moment; intrinsically the value is very small, but speculatively another upward turn is quite probable.

B. M. C. Joss.—I am sorry, but I must ask you to read above rules

---

The revenue of Western Australia during January was £226,747 against £202,580 for January, 1897.

The *Standard's* New York Correspondent, quoting from the Treasury figures, shows that the January deficit amounts to $7,901,484, the largest for this generation. This makes the year's deficit $51,901,823; or 8,000,000 above that of the previous year. The correspondent adds that the popular response to the Teller incident is such that Congress will take another forward step rather than make a campaign upon Mr. Dingley's surplus as the issue.

The shareholders of the Salt Union recently adopted at a private meeting a resolution appointing a committee of seven, with power to add to their number, to approach the directors in a friendly spirit, and to take such other steps as they might deem advisable for "improving the management and prospects of the company's business." The following gentlemen were elected to serve on the committee: Messrs. J. W. Brett, Edward Edmondson, James Head, J. B. Hunter, William S. McDowell, Thomas R. Royden, and Frederick Walker.

Notice to Subscribers.

Complaints are continually reaching us that the INVESTORS' REVIEW cannot be obtained at this and the other railway bookstall, that it does not reach Scotch and Irish cities till Monday, and that it is not delivered in the City till Saturday morning.

We publish on Friday in time for the REVIEW to be at all Metropolitan bookstalls by at latest 4 p.m., and we believe that it is there then, having no doubt that Messrs. W. H. Smith & Son do their best, but they have such a mass of papers to handle every day that a fresh one may well look almost like a personal enemy and be kept in short supply unless the reading public shows unmistakably that it is wanted. A little perseverance, therefore, in asking for the INVESTORS' REVIEW is all that should be required to remedy this defect.

All London newsagents can be in a position to distribute the paper on Friday afternoon if they please, and here also the only remedy is for subscribers to insist upon having it as soon as published. Arrangements have been made that all our direct City subscribers shall have their copies before 4 p.m. on Friday. As for the provinces, we can only say that the paper is delivered to the forwarding agents in ample time to be in every English and Scotch town, and in Dublin and Belfast, likewise, early on Saturday morning. Those despatched by post from this office can be delivered by the first London mail on Saturday in every part of the United Kingdom.

Cheques and Postal Orders should be made payable to CLEMENT WILSON.

The INVESTORS' REVIEW can be obtained in Paris of Messrs. BOYVEAU ET CHEVILLET, 22, Rue de la Banque.

ADVERTISEMENTS.

All Advertisements are received subject to approval, and should be sent in not later than 5 p.m. on Thursdays.

For tariff and particulars of positions open apply to the Advertisement Manager, Norfolk House, Norfolk-street, W.C.

THE STOCK EXCHANGE.—NOTICE.
NO MEMBER OF THE STOCK EXCHANGE is ALLOWED to ADVERTISE for business purposes, or to issue circulars to persons other than his own principals.

Persons who advertise as Brokers or Share Dealers are not Members of The Stock Exchange, or under the control of the Committee.

A List of Members of The Stock Exchange who are Stock and Share Brokers may be seen at the Bartholomew-lane entrance of the Bank of England, or obtained on application to EDWARD SATTERTHWAITE,
Secretary to the Committee of the Stock Exchange.
Committee Room, The Stock Exchange, London, E.C.

ESTABLISHED 1824.

CLERICAL, MEDICAL AND GENERAL

LIFE ASSURANCE SOCIETY.

Chief Office:

15, ST. JAMES'S SQUARE, LONDON, S.W.

CHAIRMAN, RIGHT HON. SIR JOHN ROBERT MOWBRAY, BART., D.C.L., M.P.

Assets nearly 3½ MILLIONS Sterling.

VALUATION RATE OF INTEREST 2½ PER CENT. ONLY.

The Results of the 1897 Valuation showed—

1. INCREASED RESERVES.
2. INCREASED PROFITS.

THE TOTAL SURPLUS DIVIDED WAS

£515,346.

Which was larger by £86,896 than any previously distributed, and represented the

HIGHEST RATE OF PROFIT EVER DECLARED by the Society.

The Bonus Report, (1897), Prospectus, Forms of Proposal, and every information on application.

W. J. H. WHITTALL, Actuary and Secretary.

15, ST. JAMES'S SQUARE, LONDON, S.W.

To Correspondents.

The EDITOR cannot undertake to return rejected communications. Letters from correspondents must, in every case, be authenticated by the name and address of the writer.

The Investors' Review.

The Week's Money Market.

A little slackening in the pressure was the distinguishing feature of the Money Market in the past seven days. Directly the Stock Exchange Settlement was over, short loans were in less request, and at one time no more than 2 to 2½ per cent. was bid for day-to-day money; but payment to the bank of maturing bills and a few "calls" in the Industrial share market caused an inquiry last Monday and Tuesday, which compelled the market to re-borrow all the money it had repaid the Bank, and sent up the rate outside to 2½ to 2¾ per cent, since when it has slipped back to 2 to 2¼ per cent. A little Japanese money is said to have been released during the time, while on Wednesday it is understood that the Government settled for stock that it had purchased, the latter reason being the chief cause of the ease then ensuing. The discount houses raised their allowances on Friday last by ½ per cent. to 2 per cent. for money at "call," and 2¼ per cent. for "notice" money.

This reduction in the demand for money has caused discount rates to weaken to a moderate extent, and three months' bank bills are quoted 2⅝ per cent., as against 2¾ to 2⅞ per cent a week ago. The market, however, is working upon a narrow margin, and it is felt that the slightest demand above the ordinary would cause it to tend upwards. In all probability the Chinese Loan will be issued shortly, for the payment of the £12,000,000 to Japan is due in the first week in May, so that the amount ought to be in hand before that time. When this payment is made a fair proportion is likely to remain for an indefinite period under the control of the Japanese Government, and will, therefore, be lost to the market. With revenue collections growing in importance, and bills maturing at the Bank of England steadily throughout the month, the ease is not likely to go much further. Although both the Russian and German exchanges have moved further in our favour, and the Indian exchange has dropped to a point that removes the chances of exports to that quarter as a pure exchange operation, the demand for gold has been well maintained. At 77s. 10¼d. the Cape arrival of over £500,000 in raw gold was disposed of to Austria; and since then the price has risen to 77s. 11d.

East Indian Railway Two and a Half per Cent. debentures were taken up this week by a syndicate, but the terms were altered, their duration being fixed at three years instead of eight years, and, consequently, they gained a better price—rumour says 98¾ per cent.

Consols "Pay Day" had the effect of stiffening money rates a little on Wednesday morning, but the release of Government money through its operation more than effaced its effect. One public issue of the week was £150,000 in British Guiana Three per Cent. Inscribed stock, which received a lukewarm welcome, applications not amounting to twice the sum required. Allotments were made at £96 13s. per cent., or only 3s. per cent. above the minimum, and the average rate did not rise above £96 16s. 4d. per cent. In April, 1896, a similar amount yielded an average of £101 5s. 4d. per cent.

Yesterday's Bank return discloses a continuance of the process which has been going on now since the new year. The Bank is taking in money from the market as its loans thereto and bills held fall due, and accordingly the "other" securities fell off £440,000 within the week to £31,456,000. At the same time the Government is piling in the revenue and "public" deposits therefore rose £1,305,000 to £14,398,000, notwithstanding the Treasury disbursements at the end of January. Thanks to these two influences the "other" deposits have declined £1,800,000, and are now only £35,678,000, a total by no means comfortably large to encounter the spring and summer with. The return of coin from circulation has been almost balanced by the efflux of notes, so that the reserve of the banking department has been altered only £21,000. It has increased that amount to £22,774,000. Altogether the drift of these figures is in the direction of dearer money, but the dearness need not be prolonged nor yet amount to much. Its principal source is the heaping up of money in the hands of the Government, whose balances are now £3,732,000 larger than they were a year ago at the same date, larger, in fact, than they usually are towards the end of March. This pile must be dispersed soon; and as it is, the market will be placed in funds. Probably the delay in the delivery of armour-plates and machinery for the new war vessels in course of construction accounts for much of the accumulation. The engineering dispute, however, is now a thing of the past and work kept back so long will now be pressed forward.

SILVER.

Just as the end of the month came the price of bars was pushed up to 26⅛d. per oz., but directly the speculative engagements at that point were undone, the quotation weakened, and has fallen to 26d. per oz. At this price the tendency is in favour of sellers, while the gradual working off of the speculative "bear" position takes away a great support from the market. The Indian price of the metal has remained practically stationary throughout the week although the exchanges have dropped from 16d. to 15 11/16d. in the time, so that there is less inclination than ever on the part of our great dependency to take the metal. Chinese rates have also dropped ⅛d. to ⅜d. on the week. Apparently the India Council is becoming nervous as to its ability to dispose of its drafts, and on Wednesday broke down its price for bills to 1s. 3 11/16d., although the bulk of the applications were at 1s. 3⅞d. Its policy is bound to lead to a further decline, as the market now knows that it has to deal with an eager seller. Late last week much amusement was created in the Rupee paper market—a market distinctly peculiar to itself—by some foolish bidding from outsiders. Evidently led away by Lord George Hamilton's speech to believe that something magical would be done in aid of Indian currency, buyers demanded the paper with such vehemence that in a very short space of time the quotation run up from 63⅛ to 65 Needless to say, Lord George meant nothing, and with a weak exchange the price for the delusive paper has dropped back to 63½ to 63⅝. Arbitrage dealers netted a nice profit, and the India Council sold a number of "specials" to cover the operations, and the market is left with the knowledge that the paper is in weak hands.

BANK OF ENGLAND.

AN ACCOUNT pursuant to the Act 7 and 8 Vict., cap. 32, for the Week ending on Wednesday, February 2, 1898.

ISSUE DEPARTMENT.

	£		£
Notes Issued	47,397,425	Government Debt	11,015,100
		Other Securities	5,784,900
		Gold Coin and Bullion	30,597,425
		Silver Bullion	—
	£47,397,425		£47,397,425

BANKING DEPARTMENT.

	£		£
Proprietors' Capital	14,553,000	Government Securities	14,003,036
Rest	3,463,958	Other Securities	31,455,746
Public Deposits (including Exchequer, Savings Banks, Commissioners of National Debt, and Dividend Accounts)	14,398,388	Notes	20,437,315
Other Deposits	35,678,498	Gold and Silver Coin	2,336,762
Seven Day and other Bills	139,015		
	£68,232,859		£68,232,859

Dated February 2, 1898.

H. G. BOWEN, *Chief Cashier.*

In the following table will be found the movements compared with the previous week, and also the totals for that week and the corresponding return last year:—

Banking Department.

Last Year. Feb. 3.		Jan. 26, 1898.	Feb. 2, 1898.	Increase.	Decrease.
£	Liabilities.	£	£	£	£
3,501,695	Rest	3,434,090	3,463,958	29,868	—
10,665,700	Pub. Deposits	13,093,079	14,398,388	1,305,309	—
43,020,319	Other do.	37,478,834	35,678,498	—	1,800,336
159,186	7 Day Bills	113,218	139,015	25,797	—
	Assets.			Decrease.	Increase.
14,770,976	Gov. Securities	14,023,036	14,003,036	20,000	—
28,884,481	Other do.	31,895,784	31,455,746	440,038	—
28,244,443	Total Reserve	22,753,401	22,774,077	—	20,676
				1,821,012	1,821,012
				Increase.	Decrease.
£		£	£	£	£
25,863,555	Note Circulation	25,610,335	26,960,110	342,775	—
52½ p.c.	Proportion	44⅞ p.c.	45⅜ p.c.	—	—
3 „	Bank Rate	3 „	3 „	—	—

Foreign Bullion movement for week £75,000 in.

LONDON BANKERS' CLEARING.

Week ending	1897.	1896.	Increase.	Decrease.
	£	£	£	£
Dec. 1	171,792,000	166,125,000	5,667,000	—
„ 8	136,090,000	124,457,000	11,633,000	—
„ 15	161,483,000	165,735,000	—	4,252,000
„ 22	155,425,000	133,202,000	22,223,000	—
„ 29	105,382,000	132,437,000	—	27,055,000
Total for 1897	7,491,281,000	7,574,853,000	—	83,572,000

Week ending	1898.	1897.	Increase.	Decrease.
	£	£	£	£
Jan. 5	222,654,000	174,376,000	48,278,000	—
„ 12	144,603,000	127,315,000	17,288,000	—
„ 19	171,777,000	156,200,000	15,577,000	—
„ 26	134,247,000	118,667,000	15,580,000	—
Feb. 2	194,544,000	174,498,000	20,056,000	—

BANK AND DISCOUNT RATES ABROAD.

	Bank Rate.	Altered.	Open Market.
Paris	2	March 14, 1895	1⅞
Berlin	4	January 20, 1898	2⅞
Hamburg	4	January 20, 1898	2⅞
Frankfort	4	January 20, 1898	3
Amsterdam	3	April 13, 1897	2⅞
Brussels	3	April 28, 1896	2
Vienna	4	January 22, 1896	3⅞
Rome	5	August 27, 1895	3
St. Petersburg	5½	January 23, 1898	5
Madrid	5	June 17, 1896	4
Lisbon	6	January 25, 1891	6
Stockholm	5	October 27, 1897	5
Copenhagen	4	January 20, 1898	4
Calcutta	11	January 11, 1898	—
Bombay	12	January 11, 1898	—
New York call money	1½ to 2	—	—

NEW YORK ASSOCIATED BANKS (dollar at 4s.).

	Jan. 29, 1898.	Jan. 22, 1898.	Jan. 15, 1898.	Jan. 30, 1897.
	£	£	£	£
Specie	22,618,000	22,130,000	21,728,000	15,936,000
Legal tenders	20,628,000	19,830,000	18,046,000	26,060,000
Loans and discounts	125,174,000	124,624,000	122,198,000	97,754,000
Circulation	2,893,800	2,918,800	3,018,200	3,600,000
Net deposits	144,496,000	142,894,000	138,322,000	122,666,000

Legal reserve is 25 per cent. of net deposits; therefore the total reserve (specie and legal tenders) exceeds this sum by £7,224,800, against an excess last week of £6,256,500

BANK OF FRANCE (25 francs to the £).

	Feb. 3, 1898.	Jan. 27, 1898.	Jan. 20, 1898.	Feb. 4, 1897.
	£	£	£	£
Gold in hand	77,076,800	77,182,000	77,079,040	76,442,000
Silver in hand	48,380,640	48,356,440	48,295,120	49,232,000
Bills discounted	37,871,600	36,637,640	35,723,640	*47,872,000
Advances	14,826,920	14,487,400	14,804,320	—
Note circulation	154,375,600	151,361,200	153,064,640	150,606,000
Public deposits	8,136,360	9,622,440	9,377,000	8,102,000
Private deposits	20,032,240	21,786,760	20,072,840	20,484,000

Proportion between bullion and circulation 81½ per cent. against 82⅞ per cent. a week ago.

* Includes advances.

FOREIGN RATES OF EXCHANGE ON LONDON.

Place.	Usance.	Last week's.	Latest.	Place.	Usance.	Last week's.	Latest.
Paris	chqs.	25·22	25·22	Italy	sight	26·49	26·52
Brussels	chqs.	25·25½	25·26½	Do. gold prem.	..	105	105·12½
Amsterdam	short	12·06½	12·05¾	Constantinople	3 mths	109·05	109·17
Berlin	short	20·40½	20·42½	B. Ayres gd. pm.	..	159·50	151·70
Do.	3 mths	20·28	20·30	Rio de Janeiro	90 dys	6 11/16	6 11/16
Hamburg	3 mths	20.26½	20·29	Valparaiso	90 dys	17⅞	17⅞
Frankfort	short	20·41	20·43	Calcutta	T. T.	1/3 31/32	1/3 31/32
Vienna	short	12.00	12·00½	Bombay	T. T.	1/3 31/32	1/3 31/32
St. Petersburg	3 mths	93.85	93·90	Hong Kong	T. T.	1/10⅝	1/10⅝
New York	60 dys	4·82½	4·82½	Shanghai	T. T.	2/7	2/6¾
Lisbon	sight	35 11/32	36	Singapore	T. T.	1/11 5/16	1/10½
Madrid	sight	33·67	33·50				

IMPERIAL BANK OF GERMANY (20 marks to the £).

	Jan. 31, 1898.	Jan. 22, 1898.	Jan. 15, 1898.	Jan. 30, 1897.
	£	£	£	£
Cash in hand	45,672,450	45,757,850	44,149,600	43,904,000
Bills discounted	28,435,050	28,219,750	29,132,350	*35,652,000
Advances on stocks	4,385,300	4,110,600	5,409,400	—
Note circulation	54,542,300	54,813,750	57,595,050	52,479,000
Public deposits	21,798,550	27,169,840	20,008,150	22,853,000

* Includes advances.

AUSTRIAN-HUNGARIAN BANK (1s. 8d. to the florin).

	Jan. 31, 1898.	Jan. 22, 1898.	Jan. 14, 1898.	Jan. 30, 1897.
	£	£	£	£
Gold reserve	30,272,833	30,354,000	30,375,416	30,330,000
Silver reserve	10,352,166	10,331,416	10,304,750	12,646,000
Foreign bills	1,403,916	1,344,000	1,372,583	—
Advances	1,907,000	1,946,583	2,039,166	—
Note circulation	52,318,333	52,780,000	54,545,000	59,872,000
Bills discounted	12,058,000	12,865,083	13,994,333	*19,107,000

* Includes advances.

NATIONAL BANK OF BELGIUM (25 francs to the £).

	Jan. 27, 1898.	Jan. 20, 1898.	Jan. 13, 1898.	Jan. 28, 1897.
	£	£	£	£
Coin and bullion	4,200,280	4,286,120	4,206,360	4,084,000
Other securities	17,888,360	17,625,080	17,744,800	16,873,000
Note circulation	19,756,480	19,557,120	19,837,400	19,366,000
Deposits	3,721,040	3,092,840	3,490,360	2,957,000

BANK OF SPAIN (25 pesetas to the £).

	Jan. 29, 1898.	Jan. 22, 1898.	Jan. 15, 1898.	Jan. 30, 1897.
	£	£	£	£
Gold	9,430,680	9,430,680	9,430,680	8,528,360
Silver	10,568,320	10,480,400	10,323,800	10,379,760
Bills discounted	21,656,840	20,217,840	20,291,640	8,336,400
Advances and loans	4,735,200	5,439,200	5,435,920	9,282,040
Notes in circulation	49,391,760	49,089,120	49,053,880	42,167,640
Treasury advances, coupon account	108,840	38,920	30,800	388,720
Treasury balances	329,280	151,400	70,520	2,714,440

LONDON COURSE OF EXCHANGE.

Place.	Usance.	Jan. 25.	Jan. 27.	Feb. 1.	Feb. 3.
Amsterdam and Rotterdam	short	12·1½	12·1½	12·1½	12·1½
Do. do.	3 months	12·3½	12·3½	12·3½	12·3½
Antwerp and Brussels	3 months	25·38¾	25·40	25·41	25·41
Hamburg	3 months	20·59	20·61	20·62	20·62
Berlin and German B. Places	3 months	20·60	20·61	20·62	20·62
Paris	cheques	25·23¾	25·23¾	25·25	25·25
Do.	3 months	25·37½	25·37½	25·38¾	25·38¾
Marseilles	3 months	25·38¾	25·38¾	25·38¾	25·38¾
Switzerland	3 months	25·58¾	25·58¾	25·60	25·60
Austria	3 months	12·13¾	12·13¾	12·13¾	12·13¾
St. Petersburg	3 months	25 1/16	25 1/16	25 1/16	25 1/16
Moscow	3 months	25	25	25	25
Italian Bank Places	3 months	26·77½	26·78¾	26·80	26·82½
New York	60 days	49 1/16	49 1/16	49 1/16	49 1/16
Madrid and Spanish B. P.	3 months	35½	35½	35 1/16	35⅜
Lisbon	3 months	35½	35 1/16	35 1/16	35⅜
Oporto	3 months	35½	35 1/16	35 1/16	35⅜
Copenhagen	3 months	18·37	18·37	18·37	18·37
Christiania	—	18·37	18·37	18·37	18·37
Stockholm	—	18·37	18·37	18·37	18·37

OPEN MARKET DISCOUNT.

		Per cent.
Thirty and sixty day remitted bills		2⅝
Three months	"	2 9/16—2⅝
Four months	"	2¾—2⅞
Six months	"	2¾—2⅞
Three months fine inland bills		2¾—3
Four months	"	2¾—3
Six months	"	2⅞—3

BANK AND DEPOSIT RATES.

	Per cent.
Bank of England minimum discount rate	3
" " short loan rates	3
Banker's rate on deposits	1½
Bill brokers' deposit rate (call)	2
" 7 and 14 days' notice	2¼
Current rates for 7 day loans	2½
" " for call loans	2—2½

Stock Market Notes and Comments.

There is still nothing to say about the large divisions of the Stock Market, apart from the one devoted to the United States "rails." It continues to display much activity, and prices have been advancing during the past week in a feverish manner. Each advance, that is to say, has been followed by that kind of reaction which indicates sales effected by timid speculators for the rise, or by old holders of securities, who sell out thankful to escape with part of their money. For all that, the volume of business done in this department is becoming larger, and more and more of the speculatively inclined are joining in the play. We are in fact setting back to quite old-fashioned times in these securities. The finance houses who manage the market have arranged everything with a view to a fine outburst during the coming spring which will enable them to unload great masses of bonds and shares upon the British speculator and speculative investor, and, perhaps, 10 per cent. of what we acquire may turn out a bargain; but experience has painfully taught us that the remainder will be purchased at prices involving ultimately more or less considerable loss.

Even the securities of the Vanderbilt companies may not be quite worth buying for investment. Just now they are all the fashion, especially in Wall-street, and unquestionably the purchase of the Lake Shore Line by the New York Central, combined with the reorganization of the New York Central Company's bonded debt, gives a solid ground for the advance in the prices of these stocks on the market. Amalgamations also are very likely to be the fashion among United States railroad corporations in the future, just as they once were in England, and, within limits, ought to have an excellent effect upon the intrinsic qualities of the resulting new securities. Quite true as this is, and true also as it may be that American railroad management is gradually attaining to a higher moral standard in the United States, caution is none the less advisable in touching any of these securities at present prices for investment. Of a speculation in them we can say little, the speculator knows his chances, and if he thinks that there is a prospect within the next six months, as is probable enough, of a much further general advance in quotations, he must take the risk of buying on the probabilities with his eyes open. But there is one class of these securities that we think decidedly dangerous; in fact we may say two classes First, the Grainger roads of the North-West, which are now being lauded to the skies in the most extravagant language by railway officials, offer, in our opinion, only dangerous pit-falls to the buyer. Their present prosperity, such as it is, depends upon a condition of circumstances which might not recur again for another ten years. There has not only been a large harvest in the North-West, but it is possible to market this harvest, or part of it, at excellent prices. Traffic has consequently been stimulated all over these roads, and upon the top of the prosperity thus created has come the madness about the gold discoveries in the far North-West and in British Columbia. Throughout the first half of this year, therefore, it is highly probable that the earnings of all roads situated in the line of the rush to Klondike, Kootenay, and other uninhabitable regions in the bleak north-west, will be much in excess of those in any recent year. Advantage will be taken of the prosperity to shower predictions upon the British public of splendid dividends to come and everlasting prosperity, aye, and thumping dividends will be paid. Prices also will be manipulated to great heights all in the old style, and then, when the people who manage this kind of thing have sold out, the usual collapse will ensue. No sensible man should be drawn into buying any of these securities, except as a passing speculation offering him a chance of conveying some of his neighbours' money into his own pocket. To buy for investment on the faith of a continuance of the present exceptional conditions is to court loss.

Another class of American railroad securities to be fought shy of, we must repeat, consists of the new bonds and shares manufactured in the course of the reorganisation of such properties as the Atchison, Topeka Santa Fé, Norfolk and Western, Louisville and Nashville, the Union Pacific, and, later on, the Baltimore and Ohio. These roads, to begin with, are all in the middle States, the south-west or south—in that portion of the Union which still lies crushed in the grasp of the north. Prosperity, therefore, comes to the railroads of that region at best but slowly, and some of them, it is to be feared, are still in the hands of individuals unscrupulous enough to be classed with common thieves. That great efforts will be made, and are being made, to elevate the prices of the new securities created in the reorganisation process now being applied to these properties, goes without saying; but we are really not able to recommend the public to join even in the speculation for the rise which is now being artificially manufactured in the new issues of some of these properties. The worst of all such speculation is that those who begin it seldom know where to stop.

Elsewhere, in the Stock Exchange, large markets are singularly dead, some of them, like that for Home Railways, have got into a condition where further advances can scarcely be engineered, and where a fall is to be dreaded and averted by every means known to the market. How would our magnificent banking deposits look were all Home Railroad ordinary and preference stocks, or for that matter all extravagantly priced industrial stocks, to be sheared down by but a mere 10 to 15 per cent.? A relapse of that kind is too horrible to contemplate, and, therefore, at all hazards prices must be sustained. The dealers, however, in such markets remind one of the old joke about the sailor in the Crimean War who shouted to a comrade in the neighbourhood of the trenches before Sebastopol, "Bill I have caught a Tartar." "Bring him along then," Bill answered. "I can't," replied Jack, "he wont let me." They can neither work prices up nor let them down. There is no large amount of stock passing from hand to hand because the market is swept bare by investors, by the multitudes of people who are ekeing out their incomes with the margins between what they get in dividends on the stocks they hold and what they pay their bankers in interest. The market is thus caught in a vice, and will probably be more or less dull and uninteresting until something comes to send prices back to reasonable limits.

It is quite unnecessary to enlarge upon the subject of mines this week, for they are also a kind of desert, and such speculation as there is outside the United States railroad market, spends its energies in rushes upon individual securities not in the mining market at all, but in the miscellaneous or industrial market. No doubt considerable activity has been displayed during the past week in Rio Tinto copper mine shares and in De Beers diamond mine shares, but this has been quite factitious. The public have not been handling these shares. They are tossed backwards and forwards between finance houses in London and Paris, and this week Paris has been the buyer. Why it should take De Beers shares by the thousand at £30 a piece it passes our understanding to guess, and its avidity for Rio Tinto's is not much more explicable. We know, of course, that the stock of copper is low, and that the Rothchilds and their associates are still busy in the endeavour to get control of the entire copper production of the world, that supplies from the United States have fallen off, and that consumption is steadily expanding. All this, however, and much more, does not justify prices for Rio Tinto new ordinary and preference shares equivalent to about, together, £34 for the old £10 share. We shall probably have another "copper smash" some day, and the public is wise in standing by and looking on with its hands in its pockets. Nothing is more pleasant at times to the cool observer than the sight of expert finance houses scalping each other.

Amongst miscellaneous issues there are only two calling for notice this week. The shares of the Hudson Bay Company and the "stock" of the Welsbach Incandescent Gas Company. As regards the former, which have been run up to £27 a share, there is not much to be said. Gold is at the bottom of it, and as a matter, of course, gold in Klondike, gold on the Mackenzie River, gold, for all we can tell, at the bottom of every bush and tussock in the wilderness. Given gold, whether in the actuality or in the imagination, and there is no limit to the price which a share touched by the glint of it is capable of attaining. Speculators say these shares will go to £30, £40, £50, according to the heat their minds have got into. The maddest of them may be justified for all we can tell, and a few years hence these very shares might be looked upon as dear at £10.

About "Welsbach's" we are in doubt; that is, we cannot be sure that the public is playing with them to any extent at all. As some readers may know the "stock" now quoted at 24 to 25 premium is the product of amalgamations upon which we have several times sharply commented. Presumably, therefore, it is still very largely in the hands of the men or groups who carried the operation to a conclusion. The price can be put where these people please by a judicious use of the usual machinery the Stock Exchange for the purpose. Intrinsically, however, and so far as the volume of its capital is concerned, this company has to be regarded in the light of a bubble, and all the tales about contracts with the South Metropolitan Company, contracts with Vienna, and such like, ought to be disbelieved except on proof furnished. We quite admit that the mantle this company furnishes is capable of raising the illuminated power of gas and also of saving its consumption. It is not, however, the only device of the kind in the world; it is shockingly dear, and fragile to a degree, which causes many people to abandon its use after a trial because of the trouble it gives. So imperfect is the article supplied that we may be quite sure it will at no distant date be superseded by something better; and even if the company should acquire all the new important inventions of this sort it does not follow that it can continue able to pay excessive dividends. Something will have to be paid for whatever invention threatens competition, and the price of the mantle, as every article supplied by the company, must presently come down. Patents, the public should never forget, do not last for ever, nor can inventions of any description be long kept secret. Taking all things into account, and remembering that the capital to begin with is mostly represented by nothing but patents, this stock is not the thing for people with money to touch. Buyers now stand an excellent chance of contemplating their purchase a little later on with lighter pockets.

The Week's Stock Markets.

Business on the Stock Exchange remains restricted, the only really active market being the one for United States Railroad shares. Home Railway stocks have attracted very little attention, and the Foreign market has been quite idle.

Consols were steady until the "carry over" on Monday, when the price gave way, the continuation rate which opened at 1½-2 per cent. rising to 2¼-¾ per cent. The Indian sterling loans have been neglected, but one of the features of the week has been the sudden inquiry for Rupee Paper. This was attributed to the speech made by Lord Geo. Hamilton on Thursday last. Bank of England stock has again advanced, and several of the leading Home Corporation' stocks are quoted higher.

Highest and Lowest this Year.		Last Carrying over Price.	BRITISH FUNDS, &c.	Closing Price.	Rise or Fall.
113⅛	112¼	—	Consols 2¾ p.c. (Money)...	112⅝	—
113 5/16	112 7/16	112⅝	Do. Account (Mar. 1)	112 11/16	+ ⅛
106¼	105¾	106	2½ p.c. Stock red. 1905 ...	106	+ ⅛
363	347½	—	Bank of England Stock...	362	+4½
117	115⅝	116½	India 3½ p.c. Stk. red. 1931	116¼	− ⅛
109½	108⅛	108¼	Do. 3 p.c. Stk. red. 1948	108½	− ⅛
96⅜	95	95½	Do. 2½ p.c. Stk. red. 1926	95	

Towards the end of last week Home Railway issues were depressed by disappointing dividend announcements made by the Great Northern and North Eastern companies, but the tone has hardened up since under the influence of a fair amount of investment business. Traffic returns were again good, and a recovery set in, lead by the "heavy" stocks, when it was found that the engineers were going back to work in double quick time. The North Eastern dividend is at the rate of 7 per cent., or ½ per cent. lower than last time, while the distribution made by the Great Northern Company, is at the rate of 5 per cent. on the ordinary, as compared with 5¼ per cent. The stocks of both these companies fell sharply when the dividends were made known, and Midland and North-Western were also weaker in anticipation of a reduction in their dividends. Holders of Metropolitan stock were disappointed at the statement made by the chairman of the company at the meeting held last Friday, he not being able to hold out any hope of the immediate adoption of electric traction. The Hull and Barnsley dividend at the rate of 1¾ per cent., or only ¼ per cent. worse than last year, was well received, and caused a recovery in the price. There has been considerable activity in Central London shares, and Chatham issues have also been largely bought on the satisfactory increase week by week in the traffic receipts.

Highest and Lowest this Year.		Last Carrying over Price.	HOME RAILWAYS.	Closing Price.	Rise or Fall.
186	177⅞	185½	Brighton Def.	178½	— ¼
59½	57⅜	58⅞	Caledonian Def.	58½	— ⅜
20⅝	19	19⅝	Chatham Ordinary	20	+ ⅜
77½	66	71	Great Central Pref.	70½	+ ½
24⅝	22¼	23	Do. Def.	22⅞	— ¼
124½	119¾	122¼	Great Eastern	120⅞	— ⅛
61½	58	60	Great Northern Def.	58¼	—2
179⅝	176¾	177½	Great Western	177⅞	— ¼
49¼	46¾	47¼	Hull and Barnsley	47½	+ ¼
148¾	147	147½	Lanc. and Yorkshire	148¾	+ ⅝
136¼	133½	135¼	Metropolitan	135	— ½
31	30	30⅝	Metropolitan District	30	— ¼
88¾	87¾	88¼	Midland Pref.	88	— ¼
95⅝	92¾	94	Do. Def.	93⅜	— ¾
93¼	90¼	92¼	North British Pref.	92¼	— ¼
47½	45	46¾	Do. Def.	46⅝	— ⅜
181½	178¼	180	North Eastern	180	— ½
205¼	204¼	204½	North Western	204¾	— ¼
117	114⅝	115¾	South Eastern Def.	115⅝	— ¼
98¾	95¼	95½	South Western Def.	97	+1

United States Railroad shares have shown more life and activity than for months past. Wall-street operators for the rise were apparently satisfied by Mr. McKinley's utterances, but as a set-off there came Mr. Teller's resolution to the Senate. The New York Central Company's proposal to issue $100,000,000 Three and a Half per Cent. debentures, and to take over the whole of the Lake Shore capital, and work the two systems under one management, caused a big rise in both companies' shares. The New York Central Company offers $200 in Three and a Half per Cent. bonds for each $100 Lake Shore share, and it is ultimately intended to include all the Vanderbilt lines under one system.

Louisville and Nashville shares have been in good demand on the statement that a scheme for refunding the bonded debt was on the *tapis* and nearing completion. Northern Pacific advanced on the publication of a 1 per cent. dividend on the preferred, and Chesapeake and Ohio were inquired for, on the possibility of the line being included in the New York Central combination. The usual tabular statement of the *Financial Chronicle* shows an increase of 14.13 per cent. in the gross earnings of sixty-seven roads for the third week in January. The Denver and Rio Grande Company has made arrangements for refunding over $6,000,000 of Seven per Cent. bonds due in 1900, into Four and a Half Consolidated bonds, and this has caused an advance in the company's issues. The rise in Ontario shares was traced to a rumour to the effect that this road was also eventually going to be absorbed by the Vanderbilt combination, and Reading Fours advanced sharply on the purchase by a London Syndicate of $6,000,000 of the bonds.

Canadian Pacific Railway shares have had many ups and downs during the week, and the December statement showing a net increase of $129,000 did not do much more than steady the price for a time. Grand Trunk stocks have also fluctuated rather wildly, but the net result was to leave quotations until yesterday in very much the same position as at the end of last week.

Among foreign railways there has been a steady rise in Uruguayan issues, but other South American descriptions have been dull although the traffic returns were good. The Mexican company's stocks advanced sharply early in the week, chiefly on the extreme narrowness of the market, and it was thought at one time that the clique which has been handling Grand Trunk Stocks had turned its attention to the old Mexican Railway. They used to trot in one team. The rise was, however, quite ephemeral, and prices soon slipped back.

Highest and Lowest this Year.		Last Carrying over Price.	CANADIAN AND U.S. RAILWAYS.	Closing Prices.	Rise or Fall.
13¾	12¾	12¾	Atchison Shares	13¼	− ¼
32¾	29½	29¾	Do. Pref.	31¼	—
15⅝	11⅛	13¾	Central Pacific	15⅛	+ ⅜
99¾	95¼	96¾	Chic. Mil. & St. Paul	98⅞	− ¾
14⅜	11½	12¼	Denver Shares	13⅛	+ ¾
52⅝	46⅝	48½	Do. Prefd.	52⅛	+2
15⅞	14⅛	14¾	Erie Shares	15⅛	− ⅛
41	37½	37½	Do. Prefd.	40½	+ ⅜
62¾	56⅝	57	Louisville & Nashville	61⅜	+2⅜
14¾	12⅝	12¾	Missouri & Texas	13⅜	− ⅜
122¾	108½	116½	New York Central	122¼	+ ¾
51⅜	47¾	48	Norfolk & West. Prefd.	51	+2
70¼	59⅜	65¼	Northern Pacific Prefd.	69½	+2¼
19½	15⅞	17	Ontario Shares	18⅝	—
61½	58⅞	59	Pennsylvania	60⅛	+1½
12½	10¾	11	Reading Shares	11⅜	+ ⅛
33¼	30⅞	30¾	Southern Prefd.	32¼	+ ¼
37½	26⅜	31¼	Union Pacific	36⅜	+1¼
20¼	18	18½	Wabash Prefd.	19¼	—
30¼	27¾	28¼	Do. Income Debs.	29¼	—
92¾	83¾	91	Canadian Pacific	90	−1¾
78½	69⅞	77	Grand Trunk Guar.	76	− ¾
69½	57⅛	68	Do. 1st Pref.	66	−2
50⅛	37¼	48½	Do. 2nd Pref.	47⅞	− ¼
25¼	19¼	24	Do. 3rd Pref.	23½	− ⅜
105½	104	105¼	Do. 4 p.c. Deb.	105¼	—

Foreign Government securities have not been actively dealt in, and prices show slight irregular movements. Argentine bonds have exhibited a weak tendency in spite of the steady fall in the gold premium at Buenos Ayres. Brazilian issues also weakened on the announcement that martial law has been extended until the 23rd inst., and the Government has also stated that it is determined not to lease the Central Railway. Venezuela bonds fell 2, as the agents have not received the instalment due on the 26th inst. As regards "Internationals," the little business that has been transacted has been on account of Paris. Spanish Fours mark an advance on the receipt of more satisfactory news from Cuba, but Italian Rente declined on German sales. The settlement on the Paris Bourse was carried out without difficulty, and rates of continuation were light.

Highest and Lowest this Year.		Last Carrying over Price.	FOREIGN RAILWAYS.	Closing Price.	Rise or Fall.
20¼	20	20¼	Argentine Gt. West. 5 p.c. Pref.	20½	
158	149	155	B. Ay. Gt. Southern Ord..	157	−1
78½	75½	77	B. Ay. and Rosario Ord...	77½	−½
12¼	11⁹⁄₁₆	11¾	B. Ay. Western Ord.	12	
87¼	80½	85¾	Central Argentine Ord....	85½	
92	89½	89½	Cordoba and Rosario 6 p.c. Deb.	91	−1½
95½	93¾	94½	Cord. Cent. 4 p.c. Deb. (Cent. Nth. Sec.)	94½	
61¾	58½	59	Do. Income Deb. Stk. ...	59½	−½
25¾	18	21	Mexican Ord. Stk.	24	+¾
83½	72	78	Do. 8 p.c. 1st Pref.	82	−½

In the Miscellaneous section business has been on a very small scale, quite half the transactions taking place in the shares of a few of the leading favourites for the time being. Hudson's Bay shares have been one of the most prominent, on the news of a rich find of "placer" gold on the Mackenzie River, but whether in their own territory or not, is still unknown. The rise in Welsbach Gas stocks has also been a failure, one report being that the company has obtained a contract to light the city of Vienna, but the buying, apart from a few orders from Vienna, has been professional. Anglo-American telegraph stocks have moved up a little, and tramway companies shares have been active at higher prices. The buying of electric lighting issues has nearly ceased for the present, but the recent sharp rise does not seem to have been followed by any appreciable amount of profit taking. Owing to rumours of a fresh issue of capital, British Electric Traction Ordinary again advanced, it being expected that holders will get a prior allotment on advantageous terms of any new capital offered. Gas Light "A" stock has slipped back day by day, holders evidently not liking the large reduction in the reserve disclosed in the half-yearly report. Among brewery companies City of London is £5 higher, the dividend just announced being quite up to expectations.

Highest and Lowest this Year.		Last Carrying over Price.	FOREIGN BONDS.	Closing Price.	Rise or Fall.
94½	92¼	93	Argentine 5 p.c. 1886......	92¾	
92⅛	89	91¼	Do. 6 p.c. Funding	91	−¼
76¾	71	75½	Do. 5 p.c. B. Ay. Water	75¾	−¼
61⅝	60	61	Brazilian 4 p.c. 1889	61½	+½
69⅞	66½xd	68¾	Do. 5 p.c. 1895	66¾xd	+¼
65	62½	64	Do. 5 p.c. West Minas Ry..................	64½	+½
107½	106¼	107	Egyptian 4 p.c. Unified...	107¾	+⅜
102⅝	102	102⅜	Do. 3½ p.c. Pref. ...	102½	
103	102	102¼	French 3 p.c. Rente	102½	+½
39¾	34½	39	Greek 4 p.c. Monopoly...	39	
93⁹⁄₁₆	92½	92⅞	Italian 5 p.c. Rente	92½	−1⅜
99½	95¾	97½	Mexican 6 p.c. 1888	99¼	+1½
20¾	20	20	Portuguese 1 p.c.	20⅝	+⅝
62	59⅞	60⅝	Spanish 4 p.c.	62	+¾
45⅛	43	44¼	Turkish 1 p.c. "B"	44⅞	+⅛
26⁷⁄₁₆	24⁷⁄₁₆	25⅝	Do. 1 p.c. "C"	26¼	+¾
22⁷⁄₁₆	21¹³⁄₁₆	22	Do. 1 p.c. "D"	22¼	−⅛
42¾	41xd	42	Uruguay 3½ p.c. Bonds...	41xd	−⅛

MINES AND MINE FINANCE COMPANIES.

South African ventures have presented an inanimate appearance for the greater part of the week, and apart from a steady rise which has taken place in De Beers Diamond shares, there is hardly any change of importance to chronicle. Ferreira was about the one solitary exception, a sharp rise being marked, due to dividend anticipations. The Paris Bourse gave a little support on Wednesday, but it met with hardly any response on this side. Western Australian companies had received very little better treatment, the most prominent feature being a moderate rise in Lady Shenton. Among Indian shares Nundydroog has further declined on some fresh particulars coming to hand concerning the flood in the mine, and other Indians have been dull in sympathy. Copper shares, on the other hand, have shown great strength, owing to the further reduction in the visible supply of the metal, and the Mount Lyell group and Rio Tintos mark a substantial rise on the week.

Except for a foolish rise in Chatham stocks, markets closed flat. Grand Trunk and Canadian Pacific Railway shares fell heavily just at the last. United States Railroad shares were also generally easier, although there were one or two exceptions, notably Baltimore and Ohio, Denver and Norfolk, and Western issues. Home Railway stocks closed dull led by a fall in Great Western which was due to the dividend declaration. Among Foreign Government bonds, apart from a further rise in Spanish and a slight recovery in Argentine and Mexican descriptions, the tone was weak. Hudson's Bay shares reacted sharply before the finish. The settlement begins on Monday for mines and on Tuesday for all other securities, and people are realising in time.

THE PROPERTY MARKET.

The market has continued fairly active, but sales at the Mart have for the most part been confined to bricks and mortar. Outside, we had, at Mr. Stevens' rooms, a novelty in the shape of a sale of Egyp mummies — royal ones, two kings and a queen — a King o Egypt, a King of Syria, and a Queen of Babylon. But the demand was small and the bidding slow. Mummies are not things exactly suitable for household decoration. The lot was in the end knocked down to Mr. Cross, of Liverpool, the animal dealer, for seventy-five guineas. The travelling showman will now be able to utilise the mummies. The next two lots, consisting of rolled Egyptian mummies in coffins, were bought for Horniman's Museum. A Peruvian mummy, curled up in a glass case, with her plaited hair in an excellent state of preservation, will also adorn the same museum. She cost twenty-seven guineas. Lot 237, consisting o an antique Egyptian mummy, said to be 4,000 years old, was bough by a dealer for thirty-four guineas.

Debenham, Tewson, & Company sold at the Mart the freehold premises, 43, Borough High-street, for £5,950. Mr. Stonehewer disposed of some properties at Tottenham, the total for the day being about £8,700.

At the Mason's Hall Tavern Messrs. Tabernacle & Son sold a re building lease for eighty-one years, with possession at Midsummer 1904, of the Dundee Arms, Artillery-street, Horsleydown, subject to a ground rent of £150 per annum, and an expenditure of £5,000 for £9,525. Messrs. J. J. Orgill, Marks, & Orgill, also sold the "Morning Star," a freehold off-licensed house in St. James's-roa Forest Gate, with possession in 1903, £2,100; five freehold house Nos. 88 to 96 even, St. James's-road, let on weekly tenancie amounting to £132 12s. per annum, £1,420; the "Estcourt Arms, Dawes-road, Fulham, freehold, to which is attached an off-licenc for the sale of beer, with reversion at Christmas, 1899, £3,260.

The chief sale at the Mart on Wednesday was that of the Ho and Grapes public-house in the Broadway, Westminster, for whic Messrs. Rushworth and Stevens obtained £8,500. Messrs. Furbe Price and Furber sold some leasehold houses in Sinclair-road, Ke sington, and two small leaseholds in Battersea were disposed of Mr. Harold Griffin, the day's transactions amounting to a little ov £10,800.

Messrs. Edwin Fox and Bousfield had a rather important sale stocks and shares at the Mart on Wednesday, at which the followi prices were realised:—Sandown Park, Limited, £10 shares, ful paid, £12; Folkestone Racecourse Company, Limited, £1 shar fully-paid, 20s. and 21s.; Langham Hotel Company, Limited, £ shares, £6 paid, £13 to £13 10s.; B. C. Bushell, Watkins & C Limited, Westerham Brewery, £10 ordinary shares fully-paid, £ £10 Six per Cent. Cumulative Preference shares, fully-paid in the same company, £15; Gillman & Spencer, Limited, £5 Six per Ce Preference shares, fully-paid, £4 10s.; New River Three per Ce Debenture stock "C," £110 to £111 10s. per cent.; Australas Automatic Weighing Machine Company, Limited, £1 shares, fu paid, 6s. and 6s. 6d.

A TAX ON TITLES.—King James I. of England, as we know, dr a thriving trade in the sale of knighthoods. Some Italian deput looking to the woeful straits the Government are in for mo have apparently seriously suggested the imposition of a tax on ti The Government have not yet said that they will even consider subject; but, in the present hunger-driven condition of Italy, knows how soon the question may be pressed within the spher practical politics by the clamour of the starving crowd, to wh bread seems becoming an almost unpurchasable luxury, so he burdened are they by the taxation deemed necessary by her r to maintain Italy in her precarious international position?

According to a despatch from Louisville, a Liverpool syndic about to build an immense tobacco manufactory in that city. upon it will be begun in the early spring. It is said that about men will be employed in the factory.

The latest news from the Soudan is that the Dervishes evacuating Metemmeh and retiring on Omdurman, where Khalifa is throwing up entrenchments.

M. Dubois de l'Estang, the French Financial Commissioner consented to open negotiations with the French capitalists in in connection with the indemnity loan.

ANOTHER REVOLUTION IN TELEGRAPHY.

A further revolution in telegraphy seems near at hand. The "Telescriptor" may supersede the telephone. It is also a type-printing machine. The merchant may have it at his elbow in his office, and can easily read the message it conveys, and, without rising from his seat, reply to it at once. If he is out, the message awaits his return, and can then be attended to. Another advantage of the "telescriptor" is that it prints at both ends, so that the sender can see whether his message is being correctly sent, and has the copy before him for reference when the reply is forthcoming. It is automatic in its action, and trouble both to sender and receiver will thus be reduced to a minimum. Another invention is the zerograph, different in its method of working, but practically achieving the same results as the telescriptor, though more fitted for long-distance working. The zerograph is being tested at the Post Office; and, if found as good as their inventors represent them, no doubt both machines will be acquired by our great postal and telegraphic monopoly. If so, it is to be hoped the authorities will show more enlightenment than they usually do in placing the advantages of the new machines at the disposal of the mercantile community.

MINING RETURNS.

DAY DAWN P.C.—Crushings for fortnight ended January 26. No. 1 shaft, 263 tons for 475 oz.

HIGHLAND CHIEF.—Crushed 277 tons yield retorted gold 91 oz.

ST. JOHN DEL REY.—January 12 to 22. Gold produced, £3,970. Yield per ton, ·48 of an oz. troy.

OTTO KOPJE.—For week ended January 27, 5,725 loads washed, 184 carats.

EASTLEIGH.—For December. Crushed 4,540 tons, yielding 522 oz.; tailings, 3,475 tons, yielding 1,172 oz. Slimes, 750 tons, 170 oz.

BAYLEY'S UNITED GOLD MINES have forwarded 1 ton 4 cwt. arsenical pyrites, worth altogether 460 oz. gold.

BONNIE DUNDEE GOLD.—A trial crushing of 25 tons has yielded 30 oz. gold.

LONDONDERRY.—Cleaned up after crushing 330 tons for a yield of 652 oz.

PESTARENA UNITED.—Return for January: 463 tons of ore produced 575 oz. gold.

HAURAKI ASSOCIATED.—Crushed 90 tons for return of 290 oz., value £800.

FRANK SMITH DIAMOND.—1,980 loads washed, producing 69 carats.

GREAT BOULDER PROPRIETARY.—Return for fortnight ended January 31:—Crushed 1,416 tons of ore, producing 3,366 oz. of gold.

MYSORE REEFS (Kangundy).—956 tons of ore crushed, yielding 603 oz. retorted gold.

MYSORE WEST AND WYNAAD.—For January, 1,500 tons produced 516 oz.

MIKADO.—Result of last clean-up: 462 oz. of gold from 509 tons, exclusive of tailings.

GLENROCK PREMIER MINE.—410 tons crushed, producing 372 oz. gold.

PRINCESS ROYAL (Cue).—Clean-up from 150 tons gave 114 oz.

IVANHOE.—Clean-up for two weeks, 1,333 oz. of gold; 766 tons crushed. Total clean-up for month, 2,760 oz. of gold; 1,555 tons crushed. Tailings assay 11 dwt. of gold per ton.

BRITISH BROKEN HILL PROPRIETARY.—Returns for fortnight ended January 27: 3,173 tons crude ore produced 566 tons concentrates, containing 344 tons lead and 24,513 oz. silver.

ASSOCIATED GOLD MINES OF W.A.—Wallaroo, to January 28, 315 tons yielded 1,050 oz. gold. Dry Creek, to January 21, 951 tons yielded 3,583 oz. gold. Net proceeds amounting to £13,203.

CHAMPION REEF (Nannim, W.A.).—560 tons crushed; yield, 101 oz. retorted gold.

CHAMPION EXTENDED AND HOME RULE.—Clean up from 425 tons gave 283 oz. of gold.

GREAT EASTERN COLLIERIES.—Output for January, 23,800 tons.

LEICESTER CONSOLIDATED DIAMOND.—From the mine, 1,685, and from floors, 5,550 loads washed, producing 237 carats.

STANHOPE GOLD.—Last month's crushings yielded 1,058 oz.

CHAMPION REEF GOLD MINING COMPANY OF INDIA.—7,108 tons of stone produced 9,104 oz. of gold, 2,430 tons of tailings produced 607 oz., and 4,785 tons of tailings (cyanide process) produced 1,245 oz. of gold.

GOLDFIELDS OF MYSORE.—During month of January 700 tons and treated by cyanide produced 50 oz. of gold; 209 oz. of gold were obtained from amalgamation.

OOREGUM GOLD MINING COMPANY OF INDIA.—Return for month of January is as follows:—5,761 tons of quartz produced 3,632 oz. of gold: 4,780 tons of tailings produced 488 oz. of gold.

NOTICES.

Letters of allotment in Arnold J. Van den Bergh, Limited, have been posted.

The board of John Barker & Company, Limited, have resolved to increase the Ordinary share capital by £40,000 by the issue of 40,000 of the unissued shares of £1 each. They will be offered at £2 10s. each to ordinary shareholders on the register on February 10 at the rate of one new share for every complete four old shares held.

LONDON AND SOUTH WESTERN BANK, LIMITED.—In consequence of the retirement of Mr. G. T. Goodinge from the general managership of the London and South Western Bank—he having been elected to a seat on the board—the directors have appointed Mr. John Williams, the present assistant manager, and Mr. Robert Woodhams, the manager of the Fleet-street Branch, to be joint general managers of the bank.

Izzet Bey, sometime a favourite of the Sultan, has fallen from his high estate; he has been arrested for high treason. The crime, however, seems really to have been committed by his son, who was accused of complicity with the Young Turkey party, but escaped across the frontier, carrying with him considerable sums of money and important documents containing secrets of State.

The Belgian Government have decided to reduce to 15fr. the excise dues on refined sugar from October 1, 1899.

The Brazilian Government announce their firm determination not to lease the Central Railway.

Jamaica and the West Indies have been brought into communication with Great Britain by cables independent of foreign control. The new route is by way of Halifax, Nova Scotia; thence by submarine cable to Bermuda and Jamaica.

The Liverpool Cotton Association have adopted the new arbitration scheme on American docket cotton, and the system is thus assimilated with that of New York and Bremen.

Prices of Mine and Mining Finance Companies' Shares.

Shares £1 each, except where otherwise stated.

AUSTRALIAN.

Making-Up Price, Jan. 24.	NAME.	Closing Price.	Rise or Fall.	Making-Up Price, Jan. 24.	NAME	Closing Price.	Rise or Fall.
1 3/8	Aladdin	1 3/8		1 1/2	Hampton Plains	1 1/2	+ 1/16
4 3/16	Associated	4 5/16	+ 1/16	7 3/4	Hannan's Brownhill	8 1/4	+ 1/16
15/16	Do. Southern	15/16		1 1/16	Hannan's Oroya	1 1/8	+ 1/8
16/	Brilliant, £2	16/		15/9	Do. Proprietary	16/	+ 6d.
2 1/4	Do. St. George's	2 1/4		1	Do. Star	1	+ 1/16
11/	British Broken Hill	12/	+ 9d.	—	Ivanhoe, New	6 1/2	
6	Do. Westralia	6 1/4		11/16	Kalgurli Mt. & Iron King, 18/	13/16	+ 1/16
2 1/16	Broken Hill Proprietary	2		6 3/8	Kalgurli	6 1/2	+ 1/16
—	Do. Junction	1 3/8	− 1/8	2 3/16	Lady Shenton	2 11/16	+ 1/16
—	Do. Block 10	3 3/4		10 5/16	Lake View Cons.	10 3/16	− 1/16
1 3/4	Brownhill Extended	1 5/8	− 1/8	1 1/4	Do. Extended	1 1/16	
1 11/16	Burbank's Birthday	1 5/8	− 1/16	1 3/16	Do. South	1 1/4	+ 1/16
1 1/4	Central Boulder	1 5/16	+ 1/16	2 1/16	London & Globe Finance	2 1/16	− 1/8
7/9	Chaffers, 4/	7/3	+ 3d.	1 1/4	London & W.A. Exploration	1 1/4	
1/2	Colonial Finance, 15/	1/4 pm		3/4	Do. Investment	3/4	− 1/8
3/8	Crœsus S. United	3/8		5/8	Mainland Consols	5/8	
16/	Day Dawn Block	16/6	+ 3d.	7/8	North Boulder, 10/	3/4	− 1/8
1 1/16	E. Murchison	1 1/8	+ 1/16	1 5/8	North Kalgurli	1 5/8	
15/16	Gold Estates	7/8	− 1/16	1 1/16	Northern Territories	1 3/16	+ 1/16
6/6	Golden Arrow	6/6	+ 6d.	—	Peak Hill	2 1/16	− 1/8
8 5/8	Golden Horseshoe	8 13/16	+ 1/4	2 13/16	South Kalgurli	2 15/16	+ 1/16
1 3/8	Golden Link	1 3/16		2 1/4	W. A. Goldfields	2 1/4	+ 1/16
—	Great Boulder, 2/	24/	+ 1	2 3/8	W. A. Joint Stock	2 1/2	+ 1/16
1 1/4	Do. Main Reef, 10/	1 7/16	+ 3/16	1 1/4	W. A. Market Trust	1 3/16	− 1/16
4 3/8	Do. Perseverance	4 1/2	+ 1/16	1 1/4	W. A. Loan & General Fin.	1 3/8	+ 1/16
1	Do. South	1		3/8	White Feather	3/8	− 1/16
1 11/16	Hainault	2	+ 1/8				

SOUTH AFRICAN

Making-Up Price, Jan. 24.	NAME.	Closing Price.	Rise or Fall.	Making-Up Price, Jan. 24.	NAME	Closing Price.	Rise or Fall.
5 5/8	Angelo	5 11/16	+ 1/16	3/	Lisbon-Berlyn	3/	
1 1/16	Aurora West	1 1/8	− 1/16	2 3/16	May Consolidated	2 1/4	
1 3/16	Bantjes	1 1/16		4 1/4	Meyer and Charlton	4 5/16	
11/	Barrett, 10/	11/	− 3d.	3 1/2	Modderfontein	3 1/2	
3 3/8	Bonanza	3 9/16	+ 1/16	5/8	Do. "B"	3/4	
13/16	Buffelsdoorn	13/16	+ 1/16	1	New Bultfontein	15/16	− 1/16
1 1/16	Champ d'Or	1 1/8		4 1/4	New Primrose	4 1/4	
5 3/4	City and Suburban, £4	5 13/16	+ 1/8	1 11/16	Nigel	1 5/8	− 1/16
3 1/4	Comet (New)	3 1/2	+ 1/4	—	Nigel Deep	1 1/4	
5 1/4	Con. Deep Level	5 3/4		1	North Randfontein	1	
14	Crown Deep	13 7/8	− 1/8	6 1/4	Nourse Deep	6 3/4	+ 1/2
12	Crown Reef	12		1 3/8	Porges-Randfontein	1 1/2	+ 1/8
29 5/8	De Beers, £5	30 3/16	+ 1/2	2 1/4	Princess	2 1/4	
3 13/16	Driefontein	4 1/16	+ 1/16	33 1/2	Rand Mines	33 7/8	+ 3/8
5 3/8	Durban Roodepoort	5 3/8		1 15/16	Randfontein	2	
4 1/16	Do. Deep	4 3/16	+ 1/16	2 3/8	Rietfontein	2 13/16	+ 1/16
5 3/8	East Rand	5 7/16	+ 1/16	11 1/4	Robinson Deep	11 1/4	− 1/4
24	Ferreira	26 1/2	+ 2	8 3/4	Do. Gold, £5	8 3/4	+ 1/8
6 3/4	Geldenhuis Deep	6 1/2	− 1/4	1 1/16	Do. Randfontein	1 3/16	+ 1/16
4 5/16	Do. Estate	4 7/16	+ 1/8	1 1/2	Roodepoort Central Deep	1 1/16	− 1/16
1 1/4	George Goch	1 1/4		2 13/16	Do. Deep	2 7/8	
3	Ginsberg	2 15/16	− 1/16	7	Rose Deep	7 1/16	− 1/16
2 1/4	Glencairn	2 1/16		3 1/4	Salisbury	3 1/16	− 1/16
2 11/16	Glen Deep	2 5/8	− 1/8	2 1/2	Sheba	2 1/2	
9 3/4	Goldfields Deep	10 1/2		3 3/8	Simmer and Jack, £5	3 1/2	+ 1/8
8 1/2	Griqualand West	8 1/2		4 1/16	Transvaal Gold	4 1/16	− 1/8
9 1/2	Henry Nourse	9 1/2		3 5/8	Treasury	3 3/4	
7 1/2	Heriot	7 11/16	+ 1/16	4 3/16	United Roodepoort	4 1/4	
8 3/8	Jagersfontein	8 3/8	+ 1/8	1 5/16	Van Ryn	1 3/8	
9	Jubilee	8 3/4		6 3/16	Village Main Reef	6 1/4	− 1/8
5 3/8	Jumpers	5 1/16	− 1/16	1 3/8	Vogelstruis	1 3/8	
5 5/8	Jumpers Deep	5 5/8		1 1/16	Do. Deep	1 1/16	
2 11/16	Kleinfontein	2 3/4		8 3/8	Wemmer	8 1/4	− 1/8
3 11/16	Knight's	4	− 1/16	17/32	West Rand	7/8	− 1/16
2 3/8	Lancaster	2 7/16	+ 1/16	6 3/8	Wolhuter, £4	6 3/8	
3 3/8	Langlaagte Estate	3 1/4		2 3/8	Worcester	2 3/8	
1 1/8	Langlaagte Block "B"	1 1/8					

LAND EXPLORATION AND RHODESIAN.

Making-Up Price, Jan. 24.	NAME.	Closing Price.	Rise or Fall.	Making-Up Price, Jan. 24.	NAME	Closing Price.	Rise or Fall.
3	Anglo-French Ex.	3 1/16		1 15/16	Mozambique	1 7/8	
2 1/4	Barnato Consolidated	2 1/2	+ 3/16	1 5/8	New African	1 3/4	
3/8	Bechuanaland Ex.	3/8		13/16	Oceana Consolidated	13/16	
3	Chartered B.S.A.	3 1/4	+ 1/8	2 1/4	Orange Free State	2 1/4	
1 1/16	Cassel Coal	1 1/16		1 3/16	Rhodesia, Ltd.	1 1/4	− 1/16
3/4	Colenbrander	3/4		5 3/4	Do. Exploration	5 5/8	− 1/8
4 7/8	Cons. Goldfields	5	+ 1/16	1 3/16	Do. Goldfields	1 1/4	
1 1/16	Do. Pref.	21/		4	Robinson Bank	3 3/4	− 1/4
1 11/16	Exploration	1 11/16	+ 1/16	5	S. A. Gold Trust	5 1/16	
1 1/8	Henderson's Est.	1 11/16	− 1/16	1 3/8	Tati Concessions	1 1/4	
2	Johannesburg Con. In.	15/16	− 1/16	15/16	Transvaal Development	15/16	
1 1/8	Do. Water	1 1/16		4 1/16	Do. Gold Mining	4 1/4	− 1/16
2 1/4	Mashonaland Agency	2 1/8	− 1/16	11/16	United Rhodesia	11/16	− 1/16
15/16	Do. Central	13/16	− 1/16	1 1/16	Willoughby	1 1/4	+ 1/16
6 3/8	Matabele Gold Reefs	6 5/8	+ 1/8	1 1/8	Zambesia Explor.	1 1/4	

MISCELLANEOUS.

Making-Up Price, Jan. 24.	NAME.	Closing Price.	Rise or Fall.	Making-Up Price, Jan. 24.	NAME	Closing Price.	Rise or Fall.
1 1/2	Alamillos, £2	1 1/4	− 1/8	13/3	Mysore Goldfields	14/6	− /6
5 3/8	Anaconda, $25	5 3/8		12/	Do. Reefs, 17/	12/6	+ /6
11/3	Balaghât, 18/	10/6	− /6	17/	Do. West	15/	− 3/
4 15/16	Cape Copper, £2	5	+ 1/16	16/	Do. Wynaad	13/	− 3/
5	Champion Reef, 10s.	5		2 9/16	Namaqua, £2	2 5/8	+ 1/16
2 1/16	Copiapo, £2	2 1/4	+ 1/16	4 1/16	Nundydroog	3 7/8	− 1/8
3 1/4	Coromandel	3 1/4		2 13/16	Ooregum	2 13/16	− 1/16
1 3/8	Frontino & Bolivia	2 1/16	− 1/16	3 1/2	Do. Pref.	3 3/8	− 1/8
1 1/2	Hall Mines	1 1/16		27 1/4	Rio Tinto Def., £5	26 1/2	+ 1
2 11/16	Libiola, £5	2 3/8		6 1/2	Do. Pref. £5	6 1/2	
7 1/2	Linares, £3	8		19/	St. John del Rey	19/6	− /6
3 3/8	Mason & Barry, £3	3 3/8	+ 1/16	11/16	Taitipu	15/16	+ 1/16
5 3/8	Mountain Copper, £5	5 1/4	− 1/16	7 3/8	Tharsis, £2	7 1/16	+ 1/16
13 3/4	Mount Lyell, £3	14 3/8	+ 5/8	2 7/8	Tolima "A," £5	3	
3 11/16	Mount Lyell, North	3 3/4	+ 1/16	4 5/16	Waihi	4 3/8	− 1/16
1/2	Mount Lyell, South	18/	+ 6d	1 1/4	Waitekauri	1 3/8	
4 7/8	Mount Morgan, 17s. 6d.	4 1/16	− 1/16	1 1/4	Woodstock (N.Z.)	1 3/16	
5 1/4	Mysore, 10s.	5 1/4					

THE GREAT EASTERN AND THEIR WORKMEN.

Lord Claud Hamilton, presiding at the half-yearly meeting of the Great Eastern Railway Company, entered into an explanation and defence of their dealings with their workmen. The company were about to commence the erection of cottages for their workmen at two centres in their district, as well as in the suburbs of London. Many of the men also rented allotments on the unused land of the company. They had an invaluable boon in the privilege tickets and in the free passes they had on their annual holiday, for which they received wages. They had at Stratford a mechanics' institute, erected nearly 50 years ago at the cost of the company, which the company had maintained ever since, and which they were about to extend. This institute had been the means of sending out into many parts of the world men trained in the company's workshops; and in their locomotive and carriage and wagon shops their superintendent, when engaging new hands, always gave the preference to sons of Great Eastern men. Their savings bank was open to all their men, their wives, and children, and had an invested sum of £250,000, on which the company allowed 4 per cent. interest. There were also their superannuation, pension supplemental, and pension funds, their provident society, and their accident fund. The latter was about to be abolished on account of the new Government Workmen's Compensation Act. So valuable had their accident fund been to the men during the past seventeen years that he hoped, with the proprietors' sanction, to be able to start a new fund outside of the Act, the practical result of which would be to combine all the benefits offered by their existing fund and those contained in the Government Act into one scheme, entailing only a very small weekly contribution on the part of the men. His lordship also referred to their Pension Bill, for which they were to apply for the sanction of Parliament. This Bill would place the pension fund upon the basis of the guarantee of the company instead of upon the actuarial basis. The public, added his lordship, had to consider a good deal more than what they heard and read in regard to wages and hours.

RAILWAY TRAFFIC RETURNS.

MOBILE AND BIRMINGHAM RAILWAY COMPANY.—Gross earnings for second week of January, $9,920; increase, $3,341.

ALGECIRAS (GIBRALTAR) RAILWAY COMPANY.—Receipts for the week ended January 22, 18,430 pesetas; increase, 1,020 pesetas. Aggregate for twenty-nine weeks to January 22, 601,519 pesetas; increase, 8,393 pesetas.

ALABAMA GREAT SOUTHERN RAILWAY COMPANY.—Traffic receipts for month of December, $177,000; increase, $12,000.

CINCINNATI SOUTHERN RAILWAY COMPANY.—Traffic return for month of December, $340,000; increase, $36,000.

QUEBEC CENTRAL.—Second of January, $4,446; decrease, $463. Aggregate from January 1, $8,581; decrease, $443.

BAHIA AND SAN FRANCISCO RAILWAY COMPANY (Timbo Branch).—Traffic receipts for week ended January 8, £377; increase £86.

CENTRAL URUGUAY EASTERN EXTENSION RAILWAY.—Traffic for week ended January 30, £2,240; increase £1,069.

CENTRAL URUGUAY NORTHERN EXTENSION RAILWAY.—Week ending January 30, £562; decrease £206.

WESTERN RAILWAY OF HAVANA.—Week ended January 29, £1,960; increase £427. Aggregate from July 1, £53,405; increase £5,633.

WESTERN OF SANTE FE RAILWAY.—Traffic receipts for week ending January 29, $40,000; increase $3,000.

VILLA MARIA AND RUFFINS RAILWAY.—Receipts for week ended January 29, $3,571; increase $96. Aggregate from January 1, $14,943; increase, $678.

BENGAL DOOARS RAILWAY COMPANY.—Traffic receipts for six months to December 31, Rs. 174,209, against Rs. 166,709 for the same period last year.

BENGAL CENTRAL RAILWAY COMPANY.—Traffic receipts for eight days ended January 8, Rs.18,802; decrease, Rs.4,005

WEST OF INDIA PORTUGUESE RAILWAY.—Return for eight days to January 8, Rs.4,805; increase, Rs.231.

SOUTHERN MAHRATTA RAILWAY.—Traffic for first eight days in January, Rs.1,11,487; decrease Rs.17,110.

H. H. THE NIZAM'S GUARANTEED STATE RAILWAYS COMPANY.—Traffic for eight days to January 8, Rs.83,231; increase, Rs.1,532.

DELHI UMBALLA KALKA RAILWAY COMPANY.—Traffic return for week ended January 22, Rs.71,500; increase, Rs.50,700. Total from commencement of half-year, Rs.124,900; increase, Rs.55,400.

CLEATOR AND WORKINGTON.—Gross receipts for the week ending January 9 amounted to £1,037, a decrease of £24. Total receipts from January 1, £4,105, a decrease of £243.

COCKERMOUTH, KESWICK, AND PENRITH.—Gross receipts for the week ending January 29 amounted to £825, an increase of £126. Total receipts for four weeks £3,483, an increase of £432.

EAST AND WEST YORKSHIRE UNION.—Gross receipts for the week ending January 14 amounted to £280, an increase of £78. Total receipts for two weeks £548, an increase of £105.

Mr. E. G. Thorpe Goodinge has just resigned the general managership of the London and South-Western Bank, with which he has been connected for thirty-five years.

Between the first of April and the 29th ult. the total receipts into the Exchequer amounted to £82,091,020, compared with £80,378,514 in the corresponding period of the last financial year; and the expenditure to £83,381,881, as against £82,687,599.

Next Week's Meetings.

SATURDAY, FEBRUARY 5.

Harrow and Uxbridge Railway ...	12, Victoria-street, Westminster, 10 a.m.
Whitechapel and Bow Railway ...	12, Victoria-street, Westminster, 10.15 a.m.

MONDAY, FEBRUARY 7.

A. & S. Henry & Co....	Manchester, noon.
East End Dwellings	27, Chancery-lane, 2 p.m.
Edinburgh Street Tramways ...	Edinburgh, noon.
Eley Brothers...	Cannon-street Hotel, 1 p.m.
Glasgow Tramway and Omnibus ...	Glasgow
Metropolitan District Railway ...	Westminster Palace Hotel, 1 p.m.
M. Hyam Wholesale Clothing Co. ...	Cannon-street Hotel, noon.
Ocean Marine Insurance	2 and 3, Old Broad-street, noon.
Reversion Investment Corporation	3, Chancery-lane, 4 p.m.
Southend Gas	Winchester House, 2 p.m.

TUESDAY, FEBRUARY 8.

Belfast and County Down Railway..	Belfast, noon.
Dublin United Tramways	Dublin, 2 p.m.
Hull, Barnsley and West Riding, &c., Railways	Winchester House, noon.
London Necropolis	2, Lancaster-place, 2.30 p.m.
Railway Debenture Trust	Cannon-street Hotel, noon.
Railway Share Trust and Agency ...	Cannon-street Hotel, 11.30 a.m.
Taff Vale Railway	Bristol, 2 p.m.
Texas Land and Cattle	Dundee, 1 p.m.

WEDNESDAY, FEBRUARY 9.

Cork, Bandon, and South-Coast Railway	Cork, noon.
Kent Waterworks	Cannon-street Hotel, noon.
Lake George Mines	11, Cornhill, 2 p.m.
Lancashire and Yorkshire Railway .	Manchester, noon.
Leicester Banking	Leicester, noon.
National Mutual Life Assurance ...	39, King-street, 2 p.m.
Newhaven Harbour	London Bridge Station, 1 p.m.
New Imperial Investment	Winchester House, 2.30 p.m.

THURSDAY, FEBRUARY 10.

Bank of Egypt	26, Old Broad-street, noon.
East Lincolnshire Railway	King's Cross Station, 12.30.
Great Western Railway	Paddington.
London and Hanseatic Bank ...	38, Lombard-street, noon.
London and Provincial Marine Insurance	Winchester House, 2 p.m.
London and South Western Railway	Waterloo Station, noon.
Merchant Banking	112, Cannon-street, 12.30 p.m
Midland Great Western of Ireland Railway	Dublin, 1 p.m.
Natal Land and Colonization Company	41, Threadneedle-street, 1 p.m.
South Eastern Railway	Cannon-street Hotel, noon.
Waterloo and City Railway... ...	Waterloo Station, 2 p.m.

FRIDAY, FEBRUARY 11.

Belfast Street Tramways	7, Poultry, noon.
Brentford Gas...	Charing Cross Hotel, 2 p.m.
Cardiff Railway (Spec.)	Queen Anne's Gate.
Great Northern Railway (Spec.) ...	King's Cross, noon.
North Eastern Railway	York, noon.

SATURDAY, FEBRUARY 12.

Great Southern and Western Railway Company	Dublin, noon.

TRAMWAY AND OMNIBUS RECEIPTS.

Increases for past week:—Belfast, £389; Bristol, £606; Croydon, £107; Glasgow, £64; Lea Bridge, £165; London, £1,448; London & Deptford, £95; London Southern, £133; London General Omnibus, £3,270; London Road Car, £1,249; Metropolitan, £1,762; North Staffordshire, 32; Provincial, £323; Southampton, £39; South London, £254; South Staffordshire, £73; Sunderland, £163; Swansea, £32; Wolverhampton, £25; Woolwich & S. E. London, £60; Bordeaux, £13; Calais, £3; Calcutta, £178.

Decreases for past week:—

Anglo-Argentine, week ending January 3, £285 increase; Buenos Ayres Grand National, week ending January 1, $5,756 incease; Vienna Omnibus, week ending January 15, £131 increase; Buenos Ayres & Belgrano of month of December, £4,858 gross, an increase of £513.

Food is again becoming seriously dear in Bulawayo. Mealies, which two months ago were sold at 30s. a bag, now cost 70s. The rains have been heavy, and transport consequently extremely difficult.

About 300 architects, surveyors, civil engineers, professors, and theatre managers have, it seems, formed themselves into what is called a British Fire Protection Committee. A laudable object, but how are the committee to proceed in attaining it? The reading and discussion of papers may be excellent entertainment, but it is hardly business.

Yet another gold discovery. This time it is in the Hay, Buffalo, and other rivers which run into the Great Slave Lake, in the district of Prince Albert in Canada. The discovery, it seems, was made by a party going into the direction of the Yukon river. Of course, prospectors are now preparing to start for the district.

A Winnipeg telegram states that the clearings of the Winnipeg banks had increased by $20,000,000 last year to a total of 82,000,000.

LONDON AND NORTH-WESTERN RAILWAY PENSION SCHEME.

This is good of the company—the right line to take. Mr. E. Garrity, financial secretary to the Amalgamated Society of Railway Servants, in an interview with a Press representative, made a statement in regard to the extinction of the London and North-Western Insurance Fund and the Workmen's Compensation Act. He said that Mr. L. H. Viner, the secretary to the London and North-Western Insurance Society, has issued a circular to the employés of his company reminding them that the arrangements entered into between the members of the insurance society and the company which have been in operation under the Employers' Liability Act since January 1, 1881, will cease and the agreements become null and void from and after July 8, 1898, which will render the winding-up and reconstruction of the present insurance society a legal necessity. Mr. Viner, therefore, invites the members to lose no time if they are desirous of continuing the existence of the insurance society in arranging with their employers for establishing a new system of mutual insurance. Mr. Garrity, on behalf of the amalgamated society, had no hesitation in recommending the men to have nothing whatever to do with the proposals of the company. He believed the scheme would be on a profit-sharing system which might be based on the following lines:—1. The rates of pay which are now in force to be considered the standard rate of pay, and to remain unchanged unless and until the annual amount of net profit earned exceeds 4 per cent. upon the amount of capital expended in the construction of the line, and in the provision of rolling stock and appliances necessary to equip the railway as a going concern, when the profit-sharing scheme will come into operation. 2. The profit fund to be the balance of the revenue account which would remain after providing a sum sufficient to pay 4 per cent. upon the total capital expenditure. 3. A bonus of 1s. 8d. in the pound of their standard wages to be paid to all railway employés included in the scheme in respect of every 1 per cent. of additional net profit equal to 1d. in the pound o standard wages for every 1s. of additional net profits over and above 4 per cent.

Lord Palmerston once declared that dirt was only matter in the wrong place. A certain Mr. W. Higgins Jacob seems to think dirt is in its right place in the streets. He objects to the constant watering. It "creates fog, dirt, influenza, and diphtheria." Who would have ht it?

ENGLISH RAILWAYS.

Div. for half years. 1896	1896	1897	1897	Last Balance forward.	Amt. to pay 1 p.c. on Ord. for ½ yr.	NAME.	Date.	Gross Traffic for week: Amt.	Inc. or dec. on 1897.	Inc. or dec. on 1896.	Gross Traffic for half-year to date: No. of weeks	Amt.	Inc. or dec. on 1897.	Inc. or dec. on 1896.	Mileage.	Inc. on 1897.	Working	Prior Charges last ½ year.	Prop. add Cap. Exp. this ½ year.
				£	£												%	£	£
10	10	10		6,805	4,906	Barry	Jan. 29	9,383	+379	+3,105	5	44,827	+584	+5,066	31	—	47·36	66,665	316,008
nil	nil	nil	nil	—	—	Brecon and Merthyr	Jan. 30	1,542	+6	−16	5	8,036	+142	+345	61	—	—	—	—
nil	nil	nil	nil	4,020	4,749	Cambrian	Jan. 30	4,573	+131	+689	*	17,580	— +169	—	250	—	61·16	63,472	42,000
1¾	1¾	2	1¾	1,510	3,130	City and South London	Jan. 30	1,059	−42	+68	5	5,393	−95	+367	3½	—	56·67	5,552	124,000
1	2	1½		4,823	13,220	Furness	Jan. 30	8,667	+101	+98	*	35,296	+521	+720	139	—	50·85	96,623	52,963
1	1½	½	1	2,207	27,470	Great Central (late M., S., & L.)	Jan. 30	41,786	+1,109	+1,494	4	166,951	+2,493	+10,038	352½	—	57·17	627,386	1,200,000
3½	4¾	2	5	51,283	62,865	Great Eastern	Jan. 30	76,301	+2,607	+5,972	4	301,658	+8,811	+30,861	1,156	7	55·35	860,138	250,000
3	5½	3		4,595	102,406	Great Northern	Jan. 30	93,643	+2,020	+8,455	5	454,026	+10,545	+32,773	1,071	8	62·28	640,779	1,091,250
4¾	7½	4¾		16,273	116,381	Great Western	Jan. 30	170000	+6,290	+11,400	4	679,990	+22,460	+39,050	2,582	21	57·94	1,484,324	650,000
nil	2	nil	1¾	8,951	16,487	Hull and Barnsley	Jan. 30	5,846	−691	−230	4	25,584	−548	+2,968	73	—	58·21	70,290	52,920
5	5¾	5	5½	21,495	83,704	Lancashire and Yorkshire	Jan. 30	88,777	+4,616	+5,382	4	340,586	+12,321	+27,039	555½	25	56·70	674,745	451,976
4¾	8	4¾	8½	26,243	43,049	London, Brighton, & S. Coast	Jan. 31	43,485	+4,586	+1,639	5	231,752	+14,683	+13,288	476½	—	50·20	407,042	240,735
nil	nil	nil	nil	72,294	56,296	London, Chatham, & Dover	Jan. 30	25,736	+1,490	+1,812	4	104,877	+5,326	+7,947	185½	—	50·65	367,873	nil
6½	8	6½		95,016	203,061	London and North Western	Jan. 30	227354	+6,149	+16,526	4	881,472	+19,527	+60,939	1,911½	—	55·91	1,411,298	425,000
5	8½	8½	8½	23,038	59,367	London and South Western	Jan. 30	63,613	+2,372	+4,634	4	254,218	+11,496	+18,100	941	6½	51·75	523,740	389,000
2¾	6	2½	6½	14,592	6,691	London, Tilbury, & Southend	Jan. 30	4,683	+574	+970	5	23,740	+1,992	+4,896	81	—	52·57	39,590	15,000
3½	3¾	3¾	3¾	17,133	26,409	Metropolitan	Jan. 30	16,183	+434	+1,419	*	60,988	+1,808	—	64	12	43·63	148,047	254,000
nil	nil	nil	nil	4,006	11,250	Metropolitan District	Jan. 30	8,822	+355	+635	4	36,145	+1,551	+1,472	13	—	48·70	119,663	38,450
5	7	5½		18,336	174,175	Midland	Jan. 30	185727	−4,829	+20,170	5	871,734	−4,192	+53,776	1,354¾	15½	57·47	1,213,866	650,000
6¾	7½	5¾		22,374	135,568	North Eastern	Jan. 29	141715	+9,042	+4,741	4	541,750	+20,033	+41,045	1,597¾	—	58·70	791,956	372,790
7½	7½	7½		6,213	10,102	North London	Jan. 30			Not recd			not	recvd.	12	—	51·66	51,329	4,000
4	5	4	4¾	4,745	16,150	North Staffordshire	Jan. 30	16,262	+2,510	+1,472	5	78,416	+7,372	+5,588	312	—	55·27	118,142	19,605
10	10	11		1,642	3,004	Rhymney	Jan. 29	5,644	+627	+1,126	5	24,662	+375	+1,926	71	—	49·68	29,049	16,700
3	6¾	3½	6¾	4,054	50,215	South Eastern	Jan. 29	37,994	+4,600	+4,124	*	162,915	+9,078	—	448	—	51·88	380,763	250,000
3½	3½	3½	3½	2,315	25,961	Taff Vale	Jan. 29	16,008	+63	+1,944	5	75,604	−3,379	+47	121	—	54·90	94,800	92,000

* From January 1.

SCOTCH RAILWAYS.

5	5	5½	—	15,350	77,570	Caledonian	Jan. 30	72,245	+ 2,446	+ 6,894	26	1,923,256	+ 33,753	+ 82,872	851⅓	5	50·50	566,914	375,966
5	5½	5	—	5,886	24,639	Glasgow and South-Western	„ 29	23,082	+ 977	− 190	26	750,318	+ 11,232	+ 54,420	393½	—	55·12	221,120	180,556
3½	3½	3½	—	1,291	4,600	Great North of Scotland	„ 29	7,418	+ 1,431	+ 814	26	230,153	+ 9,604	+ 17,808	331	15½	52·03	92,178	60,000
3	nil	2	—	10,477	12,820	Highland	„ 30	7,761	+ 1,209	+ 697	22	203,682	+ 8,482	+ 12,355	479¾	27½	58·63	78,976	84,000
1	1½	1	—	3,763	45,819	North British	„ 30	65,441	+ 3,393	+ 3,004	26	1,928,399	+ 52,818	+ 97,106	1,230	23	44·65	821,766	426,009

IRISH RAILWAYS.

6½	6½	6½	—	5,466	1,790	Belfast and County Down	Jan. 28	2,113	+ 369	+ 333	*	8,129	+ 213	—	76½	—	55·58	17,690	10,000
5½	6½	5½	—	—	4,284	Belfast and Northern Counties	„ 28	4,545	+ 107	+ 150	*	18,794	+ 60	—	249	—	—	—	—
2	3	2	—	1,418	1,200	Cork, Bandon, and S. Coast	„ 29	855	− 162	− 351	*	4,844	− 138	—	103	—	54·82	14,436	5,450
6½	6¾	6½	—	21,537	17,709	Great Northern	„ 28	13,781	+ 1,591	+ 1,094	4	53,473	+ 2,818	—	528	36	54·03	87,068	16,000
5½	5½	5½	—	12,037	24,855	Great Southern and Western	„ 28	—	—	—	not	received	—	—	603	13	55·78	72,802	35,140
4	4	4	4½	11,372	11,850	Midland Great Western	„ 28	8,780	+ 113	− 364	*	34,242	+ 2,006	—	538	—	50·31	83,129	1,800
nil	nil	nil	nil	229	2,822	Waterford and Central	„ 28	824	+ 136	—	*	3,386	+ 469	—	59½	—	53·24	6,858	1,500
nil	nil	nil	nil	2,601	2,987	Waterford, Limerick & W.	„ 28	4,341	+ 264	+ 280	*	24,641	+ 1,703	—	350½	—	58·70	43,076	8,869

* From January 1.

FOREIGN RAILWAYS.

Mileage. Total.	Increase on 1897.	Increase on 1896.	Name.	Gross Traffic for Week. Week ending	Amount.	In. or Dec. upon 1897.	In. or Dec. upon 1896.	Gross Traffic to Date. No. of Weeks.	Amount.	In. or Dec. upon 1897.	In. or Dec. upon 1896.
					£	£	£		£	£	£
319	—	—	Argentine Great Western	Jan. 28	7,094	+ 1,275	+ 2,396	29	156,583	− 14,111	+ 33,611
76½	—	—	Bahia and San Francisco	Jan. 8	2,780	+ 1,161	+ 1,011	—	—	—	—
234	57	84	Bahia Blanca and North West	Jan. 2	1,124	+ 93	—	27	20,369	+ 805	—
74	—	—	Buenos Ayres and Ensenada	Jan. 30	3,298	− 589	− 1,161	4	13,985	− 4,265	− 4,135
426	—	—	Buenos Ayres and Pacific	Jan. 29	7,311	− 1,671	+ 822	31	184,190	− 48,627	+ 6,140
914	1	3	Buenos Ayres and Rosario	Jan. 29	18,196	+ 5,272	+ 2,436	4	69,918	+ 9,055	+ 9,680
1,499	98	68	Buenos Ayres Great Southern	Jan. 30	39,807	+ 4,234	+ 8,651	30	831,564	+ 58,341	+ 123,636
602	142	177	Buenos Ayres Western	Jan. 30	15,870	− 692	+ 194	30	349,868	− 75,641	− 64,958
845	55	77	Central Argentine	Jan. 29	22,054	+ 4,835	− 422	4	86,915	+ 12,708	+ 3,770
197	—	—	Central Bahia	Nov. 31*	$71,637	− $29,321	− $26,571	11 mos.	$1,192,815	+ $146,023	+ $177,015
271	—	—	Central Uruguay of Monte Video	Jan. 29	7,354	+ 2,790	+ 860	30	176,801	− 4,951	− 18,168
180	—	—	Cordoba and Rosario	Jan. 23	3,015	+ 615	− 120	30	59,545	− 21,480	− 165
128	—	—	Cordoba Central	Jan. 23	$24,500	+ $3,500	− $1,900	3	$73,700	− $9,340	− $17,280
549	—	—	Do. Northern Extension	Jan. 23	$48,000	− $2,510	− $4,440	3	$158,790	− $32,540	− $27,820
137	—	—	Costa Rica	Jan. 29	5,065	− 1,936	− 2,164	4	15,565	− 5,950	+ 679
99	—	—	East Argentine	Dec. 12	926	+ 114	− 80	50	34,281	− 3,648	− 1,094
386	—	6	Entre Rios	Jan. 29	2,774	+ 1,457	− 319	30	38,748	+ 4,884	+ 5,977
555	—	24	Inter Oceanic of Mexico	Jan. 29	$70,200	+ $13,960	+ $25,900	31	$1,640,580	+ $228,080	+ $350,840
23	—	—	La Guaira and Caracas	Dec. 23	2,082	− 1,076	− 268	51	106,904	− 11,770	+ 2,045
321	—	—	Mexican	Jan. 29	$77,500	+ $11,900	—	4	$318,800	+ $20,950	—
1,846	—	—	Mexican Central	Jan. 22	$253,586	+ $14,806	+ $62,382	3	$714,137	+ $26,735	+ $167,056
1,217	—	—	Mexican National	Jan. 22	$106,271	+ $6,249	+ $18,680	3	$322,390	+ $45,786	+ $65,068
228	—	—	Mexican Southern	Jan. 31‡	$19,046	− $2,979	+ $5,787	44	$556,081	+ $90,104	+ $141,992
105	—	—	Minas and Rio	Dec. 31*	$177,973	+ $6,511	—	6 mos.	$1,174,610	+ $207,798	—
94	—	17	N. W. Argentine	Jan. 29	1,024	− 509	− 167	4	4,104	− 3,017	− 956
242	3	—	Nitrate	Jan. 31†	18,229	− 1,458	− 8,723	4	55,563	− 3,062	− 21,050
320	—	—	Ottoman	Jan. 22	5,955	− 968	+ 1,740	4	22,368	+ 3,777	2,248
77½	—	—	Recife and San Francisco	Dec. 4	6,845	− 329	+ 2,346	23	69,311	− 11,680	− 3,179
86½	—	—	San Paulo	Dec. 26†	23,009	− 3,960	—	2	46,230	− 10,120	—
186	—	—	Santa Fe and Cordova	Jan. 29	3,518	+ 481	+ 1,000	31	31,733	− 22,638	− 3,730

* For month ended. † For fortnight ended. ‡ For ten days.

INDIAN RAILWAYS.

Mileage. Total.	Increase on 1897.	Increase on 1896.	Name.	Gross Traffic for Week. Week ending	Amount.	In. or Dec. on 1897.	In. or Dec. on 1896.	Gross Traffic to Date. No. of Weeks.	Amount.	In. or Dec. on 1897.	In. or Dec. on 1896.
867	4	5	Bengal Nagpur	Jan. 22	Rs.1.33.000	− Rs.39.628	− Rs.36.500	3	Rs.3.78.000	− Rs.1.66.476	− Rs2.03.497
818	63	63	Bengal and North-Western	Dec. 31*	Rs.2.15.440	+ Rs.30.293	+ Rs.69.429	26	Rs.2.673.413	+ Rs.1.31.182	+ Rs2.78.194
461	—	—	Bombay and Baroda	Jan. 22	£23,100	− £1,430	− £9,475	3	£70,767	− £8,395	− £38,668
2,884	2	13	East Indian	Jan. 29	Rs.12.44.000	− R.25.000	+ Rs.35.000	4	Rs.51.26.000	+ Rs.2.41.000	+ Rs2.05.000
1,491	—	—	Great Indian Penin.	Jan. 29	£60,803	− £3,200	− £21,474	4	£240,241	− £17,761	− £112,757
736	—	—	Indian Midland	Jan. 29	Rs.1.36.290	+ Rs.2.450	+ Rs.28.386	4	Rs.5.74.295	+ Rs.19.713	+ Rs.42.655
840	—	—	Madras	Jan. 22	£17,692	− £275	+ £183	3	£58,470	− £493	− £4,059
1,043	—	—	South Indian	Dec. 18	Rs.1.53.191	+ Rs.3.769	− Rs.14.027	25	Rs.41.29.698	+ Rs.86.389	− Rs.49.124

* For 13 days.

UNITED STATES AND CANADIAN RAILWAYS.

Mileage. Total.	Increase on 1897.	Increase on 1896.	Name.	Gross Traffic for Week. Period Ending.	Amount.	In. or Dec. on 1897.	Gross Traffic to Date. No. of Weeks.	Amount.	In. or Dec. on 1897.
					dols.	dols.		dols.	dols.
310	—	—	Alabama Gt. South.	Jan. 7	37,215	+ 10,734	—	—	—
6,547	103	156	Canadian Pacific	Jan. 21	396,000	+ 82,000	3	1,201,000	+ 241,000
6,169	—	469	Chicago, Mil., & St. Paul	Jan. 31	762,000	+ 100,000	30	21,171,000	+ 2,042,950
1,685	—	—	Denver & Rio Grande	Jan. 21	137,000	+ 30,000	29	4,765,100	+ 762,000
3,512	—	—	Grand Trunk, Main Line	Jan. 41	£99,826	+ £14,514	4	£318,730	+ £47,710
335	—	—	Do. Chic. & Grand Trunk	Jan. 31	£18,349	+ £2,966	4	£60,618	+ £10,005
189	—	—	Do. Det., G. H. & Mil.	Jan. 31	£4,332	− £216	4	£14,418	− £855
2,938	—	—	Louisville & Nashville	Jan. 21	409,000	+ 38,000	3	1,197,009	+ 88,000
2,197	137	137	Miss., K., & Texas	Jan. 21	223,099	+ 7,840	29	7,741,004	+ 556,727
477	—	—	N. Y., Ontario, & W.	Jan. 21	66,391	+ 3,667	29	2,294,387	+ 70,405
1,570	—	—	Norfolk & Western	Jan. 21	257,000	+ 64,000	29	6,245,000	+ 509,000
3,499	336	—	Northern Pacific	Jan. 21	307,000	+ 87,000	3	927,000	+ 273,000
4,654	—	—	Southern	Jan. 21	399,000	+ 26,000	29	10,800,812	+ 572,448
1,979	—	—	Wabash	Jan. 21	208,000	+ 18,000	3	642,000	+ 80,000

MONTHLY STATEMENTS.

Mileage. Total.	Increase on 1896.	Increase on 1895.	Name.	Net Earnings for Month. Month.	Amount.	In. or Dec. on 1896.	In. or Dec. on 1895.	Net Earnings to Date. No. of Months.	Amount.	In. or Dec. on 1896.	In. or Dec. on 1895.
					dols.	dols.	dols.		dols.	dols.	dols.
6,935	44	444	Atchison	December	986,000	+ 52,000	—	12	8,966,480	+ 176,951	[illegible]
6,547	103	106	Canadian Pacific	December	1,053,000	+ 129,000	—	12	10,304,000	+ 2,296,000	[illegible]
[illegible]	[illegible]	[illegible]	Erie	November	819,[illegible]	+ 21,332	+ 52,579	11	7,880,994	+ 201,967	+ [illegible]
3,127	—	239	Illinois Central	November	2,534,497	+ 664,861	+ 377,039	11	22,138,724	+ [illegible]	+ [illegible]
2,396	—	—	New York Central*	December	3,674,592	+ 36,424	− 346,255	12	45,609,139	+ 1,524,110	+ 1,270,290
3,407	—	—	Pennsylvania	November	1,960,658	+ 164,400	− 48,400	11	18,867,671	+ 2,302,100	− 879,500
1,055	—	—	Phil. & Reading.*	December	1,947,585	+ 208,345	—	16	11,886,164	+ 668,603	—

* Statements of gross traffic.

Prices Quoted on the London Stock Exchange.

Throughout the INVESTORS' REVIEW middle prices alone are quoted, the object being to give the public the approximate current quotations of every security of any consequence in existence. On the markets the buying and selling prices are both given, and are often wide apart where stocks are seldom dealt in. Other particulars will be found in the INVESTMENT INDEX published quarterly—January, April, July, and October—in connection with this REVIEW, price 2s., by post 2s. 2d. Where dividends are paid only once a year, an *italic* type is used to distinguish them. The London Stock Exchange Official List is quoted in the REVIEW almost entire, only very insignificant issues, or bonds falling due within the next two or three years, being omitted. But the list is subdivided into the leading, or active, stocks, and those less frequently dealt in. The former will be found under the head of "Stock Markets," and with more details than it is possible to give for the bulk of securities. By retaining the file of the INVESTORS' REVIEW any subscriber can follow for himself the movements of securities from week to week, and the INVESTMENT INDEX will from time to time help to fill up deficiencies in the information.

Tea Companies and Mines and Mining Finance Stocks are placed in special lists.

Among the abbreviations used are the following:—S. F. Snk. Fd. *sinking fund*; Certs., *certificates*; Debs. or Dbs., *debentures*; Db. or D.Stk., *debenture stock*; Pf., Prf., or Pref., *preference*; Prefd. or Pfd., *preferred*; Dfd., *deferred*; L. or Ltd., *limited*; Sh., *share*; Ans., *annuities*; Cu. or Cm., *cumulative*; Gu or Guar., *guaranteed*; Bds., *bonds*; S., Sr., or Ser., *series*; In., Ins., Insc., *inscribed*; Dr., Drgs., Drwgs., *drawings*; Stg., Strlg., *sterling*; Lia., *liable to*; Sp., Surp., *surplus*; Per., Perp., *perpetual*; Ln., *lien*; Lo. *loan*.

The dates following the names of securities are the years of issue or of redemption. Where shares are not fully paid up, their nominal amount is given with the name so that investors may know the liability upon them.

BRITISH FUNDS, &c.

Rate.	Name.	Price.
2¾	2¾ p.c.'s (Childers') Red.. 1905	106½
3	Local Loans Stk. 1912	113½
3	Metro. Police Deb. Stk. 1920	105½
—	Red Sea Ind. Tel. Ann. 1908	8½
4	Canada Gv. "Intcl. Rly." 1903	109½
4	Do. do. .. 1908	113
4	Do. Bonds 1910	117
4	Do. Bonds 1913	119½
3	Egyptian Gov. Gar.	108½
3	Mauritius Ins. Stk. 1940	115
4	Turkish Guar. 1855	109
11½	Bank of Ireland Stk.	392½
3½	India Rupee Paper	61½
3½	Do. 1854-5	64
3	Do. 1896-7 1916	57½
3½	Isle of Man Deb.	104
3	Do. Deb. Stk... 1919-29	103

CORPORATION AND COUNTY STOCKS.

FREE OF STAMP DUTY.

Rate.	Name.	Price.
3½	Metropolitan Con. 1929	120½
3	Do. 1941	114
2½	Do. 1920-49	101½
2½	L.C.C. Con. Stock 1920	100½
3½	Comm. of Sewers, Scp., S.F. 1905	105
3½	Corp. of Lond. Bds...1897-1902	100½
3	Do. 1897-1912	103
3½	Do, Debs. Scp. ...... S.F. 1916	106
2½	Do., Deb. Stk. Scrip .. 1927-57	100
3	Barnsley 1916-46	105
3	Barry 1914-46	100
3	Bath 1909-34	104
3	Batley 1914-44	101½
3½	Birmingham 1945	124
3	Do. 1947	113
2½	Do. 1926	99
3	Blackburn 1930	107
3	Bournemouth 1913-33	104
3½	Bradford 1945	120
3	Do. Deb. Stock .. 1954	112
3	Brighouse.............. 1916-46	100
3½	Brighton 1946	120½
2½	Do. 1957	98
3	Burton-on-Trent........ 1913-43	102½
3	Cambridge 1913-43	104
3½	Cardiff 1935	119
3	Do. 1914-54	105
3	Cheltenham............ 1971	112
3	Chichester 1916-46	102
3½	Croydon	135½
3	Do. 1940	111½
3	Derby 1920-50	107
3	Devon C.C.............. 1917-33	106½
3½	Dewsbury 1930	111
3	Do. 1930	105
3	Dorset County 1922-32	107
3	Douglas (I. of Man) 1926	101
3	Dover 1913-43	103½
3½	Dublin 1944	113½
3	Eastbourne 1920-40	105
3	Edinburgh 1924	108
2½	Do. 1929	98
2½	Exeter 1917-57	97
3	Glamorgan County 1914-34	104
3½	Glasgow 1914	110½
3	Do. 1921	106½
2½	Do. 1925-40	99
3	Gloster 1915-55	103
3	Grimsby 1913-45	103½
3	Hampshire County 1914-34	105½
3	Hanley 1913-43	105
3	Harrogate 1914-34	104
3	Hastings 1915-54	104
2½	Hertfordshire C.C. 1916-36	99
3	Heston & Isleworth U.D.C. 1915-35	101
3	Huddersfield 1934	107
3½	Hull (1st iss.)	131½
3	Inverness 1914-44	102
3	Ipswich 1952	111
3	Lancaster.............. 1919-55	104
2½	Leeds 1927	98
3½	Leicester 1934	117
3	Lincoln.............. 1919	104
3½	Liverpool	135

Corporation, &c. (*continued*):—

Rate.	Name.	Price.
3	Manchester 1941	110
3	Mansfield.......... 1915-45	100
3½	Middlesbro'.......... 1909	105½
3½	Do. 1911-13	105
3	Do. 1915	104
3	Middlesex C.C.......... 1915-35	106
3½	Newcastle 1936	118½
3½	Do. Irred.	129½
2½	Do. 1915-36	101
3	Newcastle-under-Lyme.. 1909-44	101
3	Newport (Mon.) 1915-55	104½
3	Norwich 1952	113
3	Nottingham	117
3	Oxford 1951	111
3	Penzance 1916-46	102½
3	Plymouth 1942	112
3	Pontypridd U.D.C. 1916-46	99
3	Poole.......... 1915-45	102½
3½	Portsmouth........1916 24 & 27	112
3	Do. 1913-33	106
3	Ramsey 1920-40	100
3	Ramsgate.......... 1915-55	102
3	Reading	135
3	Do. 1962	109
3½	Rhyl U.D.C. 1953	112
3	Richmond (Surrey) 1942	106½
3	River Wear Debt Certs.	101
3	St. Helen's 1915-55	104½
3	Scarbro' 1915-50	102
2½	Sheffield 1925-57	97½
3	Shipley U.D.C. 1915-35	101
3	Somerset Co. 1923-33	107
3	South Shields.......... 1915-45	104
2½	Southampton 1915-45	102
3	Southend-on-Sea 1916-46	102
3	Staffs C.C. 1915-35	105
3	Stockport.......... 1914-54	104
3	Stockton 1932	105
3	Do. 1915-35	103½
3	Surrey Co. 1922-32	106½
3½	Swansea	132
3	Do. 1955	106
3	Taunton 19183-9-43	102
3	Tees Conserv. Deb. Stk. 1947	101
3	Thames Conserv. "A" Deb. Stk. 1954	103
3	Do. "B" Deb. Stk. 1954	103
3	Torquay 1913-43	102½
3	Tunbridge Wells 1931	105
3	Tynemouth 1913	101
3	Wakefield.......... 1929	105
3	Walsall.......... 1932	108
3	West Bromwich.......... 1930	108½
3½	West Ham 1929	112
3	Do. 1945	107
3	West Sussex C.C. 1915-35	106
3	Weston-s.-Mare Lcl.Bd. 1914-44	102
3	Weymouth&Melc. Regis 1918	101
3	Widnes.......... 1915-55	102
3	Wigan 1921	108
3	Windsor 1918-55	103
3½	Wisbech 1947	115½
3½	Wolverhampton 1932	118½
3	Do. 1924-54	108
3	York 1916-41	106

SUBJECT TO STAMP DUTY.

Rate.	Name.	Price.
3½	Belfast City & Dis. Watr. 1938	116
3	Do. Red Stk. 1953-6	105
3½	Belfast 1924	104
4	Blackburn Con. Deb. Irred.	141½
3½	Do. do. Irred..........	131
3½	Bristol	133
3½	Burnley.......... 1933	116
2½	Chesterfield Gas & Wtr. 1916-46	98
3½	Douglas Town 1921	105
3	Dover Harb. 1st Deb... 1956	105
3½	Hull (2nd iss.)	129½
4	Leeds Deb.......... 1927	125
3½	Do.	113½
3	Do. 1927	107½
3	Leicester 1919-44	106
4	Manchester..........	150
3	Do. 1928	105
4½	Middlesboro' Mrts. 1908	111
3½	Newark-on-Trent .. 1901-41	96
3½	Sheffield 1898-1916	106
3½	Do. 1925-36	114½
3	Do. 1925	105½
3½	Southampton .... S.F.	105½
4½	Stockton Morts.......... 1908	111
3½	Worcester.. 1950	111

COLONIAL AND PROVINCIAL GOVERNMENT SECURITIES.

Rate.	Name.	Price.
6	British Columbia........ 1907	119½
4½	Do. Debs... 1917	110½
3	British Guiana Imgtn. Bds.	99½
5	Canada, "Intercol. Rail," 1903	111½
4	Do. (Bonds) 1904-5-6-8	109
4	Do. Reduced 1910	111
3½	Do. Bnds. 1909-34	107
4	Do. Loan 1910-35	112
3	Do. Loan 1938	106
6	Cape of G. Hope 1900	—
5	Do. 1900	—
4½	Do. red. by an. draw.	111
4½	Do. 1879	111
4	Do. 1881	109
4	Do. 1917-23	118
4½	Ceylon	110
4	Do.	108½
4½	Fiji Gov. Deb. Sink. Fd.	102½
4	Jamaica Sink. Fd. 1923	104
5	Manitoba Debs.......... 1910	113
5	Do. Ster. Bds. 1888	122
4	Do. Ster. Debs.	106
4	Mauritius, Cons. Debs. 1880....	103½
4½	Natal, Sink. Fd........ 1919	120
4	Do. do. 1926	118
3½	Newfoundland Stg. Bds. 1941	100
3½	Do. do. .. 1947	100
3	Do. do.	88
5	New South Wales 1897-1902	104½
4	Do. 1903-5-8-9-12	105½
5	New Zealand 1914	118
5	Do. Cnsls. 1 p.c. per an. Sink. Fd.	103
3½	Nova Scotia Debs.	104
5	Quebec Prov. 1904-6	110
4½	Do. (drgs.)	103
5	Do. Strlg. Bds. 1912	115
4	Do. Strlg. Bds. 1928	110
4	Do. Strlg. Bds. 1934	110
4	Queensland 1913-15	108
4½	St. Lucia Debs..........	100
6	South Australia 1897-1900	103½
6	Do. 1901-1918	118
5	Do. 1911-1920	115½
4	Do. 1899-1916	105
4	Do. 1929	110½
4	Do. 1916	109½
4	Do. 1917-18-24	114
6	Tasmania 1897-1901	104
4	Do. 1908-11, 1913-14-20	108
5	Trinidad Debs., an. drw. 1 p.c...	108
4	Victoria 1899-1901	101½
4½	Do. 1904	106
4	Do. Rail. Loan 1907	106
4	Do. Loans 1908-13	108½
4½	West. Austr. 1 p.c. ac. Sink. Fd.	108
4	Do. do.	106

REGISTERED AND INSCRIBED STOCKS.

No stamp duty except for Canada 4 p.c. Reduced (½ per cent.).

Rate.	Name.	Price.
4	Antigua Insc. Stk. Red. 1919-44	109
3½	Barbados Insc. Stk. 1925-42	109
3	British Colum. Insc. Stk. 1941	104
4	British Guiana Insc..... 1935	120
4	Canada Stk. Regd. ..1904-5-6-8	109
4	Do. 4 p.c. (late 5 p.c.) Regd. 1910	111
3½	Do. 3½ p.c. Stock Regd. 1909-34	107
4	Do. Ln. for 4 milln. stg. 1910-35	112
3	Do. Stk. Regd. 1938	106
2½	Do. Insc. 1947	93
4	Cape G. Hope Regd. .. 1917-23	118
4	Do. (Ln. of '83) Insc. .. 1923	119
4	Do. Cons. Stk. Insc..... 1916-36	116
3½	Do. Consol. Insc. Stock 1929-49	115
4	Ceylon Insc. Stock 1934	124
3	Do. 1940	107
4	Grenada Insc. Stock.... 1917-42	112
3½	Hong Kong Insc. Stock 1918-43	105½
4	Jamaica Insc. Stock.... 1934	121
—	Do. 1922-44	99
4	Mauritius Inscribed 1937	119
4	Natal Consd. Stk. Insc. 1927	118
4	Do. 1937	122
3½	Do. Inscribed Stock.. 1914-39	107
4	Newfoundland Inscribed 1913-38	108
4	Do. 1935	114
4	Do. Consd. Stk. Ins. 1936	114
4	N. S. Wales Stock Insc. 1933	122
3½	Do. 1924	110
3½	Do. 1918	106
3	Do. 1935	101½

Colonial, &c. (*continued*):—

Rate.	Name.	Price.
4	N. Zealnd. Con. Stk. Ins. 1929	116½
3½	Do. 1940	109
3	Do. Inscribed.... 1945	101
3	Quebec (Prov.) Ins. Stk. 1937	95
4	Queensland Stock Insc. 1915-24	112½
3½	Do. 1921-4-30	106
3½	Do. 1945	109
3	Do. 1922-47	99½
4	St. Lucia Insc. Stock .. 1919-44	112
4	S. Austrln. (1882-7) Reg. 1916-36	114
3½	Do. In. Stk. Reg. 1939	110
3	Do. 1916-26	100
3/	Do. 1916	100
3½	Tasmanian Insc. Stock.. 1920-40	110
4	Do. 1920-40	115
4	Trinidad Insc. Stock.... 1917-42	112
3	Do. 1922-44	98½
4	Victoria Rly. Loan '81, Inscribed Stock 1907	106
4	Victoria Insc. Stock 1908-13-19	109½
4	Victoria (1885) Ins. Stk. 1920	112
3½	Do. Inscribed Stock 1921-3-6	106
4	Do. do. 1911-26	109
4	W. Austral. Insc. Stock 1934	120
4	Do. 1911-31	113
3½	Do. 1915-35	107
3	Do. 1915-35	98
3	Do. 1916-36	98

FOREIGN STOCKS, BONDS, &c.

COUPONS PAYABLE IN LONDON.

Last Div.	Name.	Price.
36/	Argentine Ry. Loan 6 p.c. 1881	92½
15/	Do. 5 p.c. 1884	73
30/	Do. N. Cent. Ry. Ext. 5 p.c. 1887-8-9	72
30/	Do. 5 p.c. Trsy. Convs. 1887	74
5/4½	Do. 4½ p.c. Interl. Gld. 1888	69
27/	Do. 4½ p.c. Stlg. Extrl. 1888	69
10/6	Do. 3½ p.c. External .. 1889	52
4	Do. 4 p.c. Ry. Guar. Res....	63
4½	Brazilian 1883	62
4½	Do. Gold 1879	66½
4½	Do. 1888	63
30/	Buenos Ayres 1824	90
6	Do. 1882-3-6	51
6	Bulgarian 1888	95
6	Do. Mort. Bonds 1892	95
4½	Chilian 1885	80
4½	Do. 1886	81
4½	Do. 1887	80
4½	Do. 1889	82½
5	Do. 1892	88
4½	Do. 1893	80
4½	Do. 1895	80
5	Do. 1896	87
7	Chinese Silver 1894	102
6	Do. Gold 1895	106
6	Do. Apl. '95 by dwgs. 1901-15	109½
5	Do. Red. dwgs. in 36 yr. 1896	101
5	Do. Do. Regis. 1896	101
1½	Colmbn. 1½ to 3 p.c. Ext. Bds. 1896	18
6	Cordova, Prov. 1886	29
—	Do. Eng. Ass. Certs.	27
—	Do. 6 p.c. 1887-8	29
—	Do. Eng. Ass. Certs.	27
3	Costa Rica "A"	32
2½	Do. "B"	27
3	Danish Gold 1914	100
10/	Ecuador N. Ext. Bds. 4½ p.c. ascn. to 5 p.c.	23
3½	Egypt'n Ins. Stk. lia. Stp. Dty. 1890	102
4½	Do. State Domain 1878	106½
4	Do. D. Sanieh, Red. .. 1905	103½
6	Entre Rios.......... 1886-8	37
6	Do. Fndg. Ln. Bds. 1894-1921	30
6	Do. do. Parana City......	23½
15/	Greek 1881	36
15/	Do. 1884	36
12/	Do. Rentes..........	29
15/	Do. (Piræus-Larissa Ry.)	34
7/6	Do. Fundg. Loan 1893	42½
4	Guatemala Extl. Debt..........	35
6	Hawaiian	101½
4	Hungarian Gold Rentes..........	101½
3	Do. 1895	91
6	Italian Irriga. Guar.	112½
5	Do. Maremmana	93½
5	Japan 5 p.c.	101½
5	Mexican (Nat. R. Tehuantp c.)..	92
	Do. Extrl. 1890	99

Foreign Stocks, &c. (*continued*):—

Last Div.	Name.	Price.
6	Mexican Extrl. 1893	98
5	Do. Intrnl. Cons. Slvr.	34
5	Do. Intern. Rd. Bds. 2d. Ser.	33½
4	Nicaragua 1886	50
3½	Norwegian, red. 1937, or earlier	100
3	Do. do. 1963, do.	99
3½	Do. 3½ p.c. Bnds.	103
1	Paraguay 1p.c. ris. 3p.c. 1886-96	17
5	Russian, 1822, £ Strlg.	149½
3	Do. 1859	93
4	Do. (Nicolas Ry.) 1867-9	103
3	Do. Transcauc. Ry. 1882	92
4	Do. Con. R. R. Bd. Ser. I., 1889	103½
4	Do. Do. II., 1889	103½
4	Do. Do. III., 1891	104½
3½	Do. Bonds	100½
4	Do. Ln. (Dvinsk and Vitbsk)	102
6	Salvador 1889	74½
—	S. Domingo 4s. Unified .. 1980	65½
6	San Luis Potosi Stg. 1889	93½
5	San Paulo (Brzl.), Stg. 1888	91½
6	Santa Fé 1883-4	42
—	Do. Eng. Ass. Certs. Dep.	41
5	Do. 1888	53
—	Do. Eng. Ass. Certs. Dpsit.	52
5	Do. (W. Cnt. Col. Rly.) Mrt.	29
5	Do. & Reconq. Rly. Mort.	29
5	Spanish Quicksilvr Mort. 1870	103
3½	Swedish 1880	103
3	Do. 1888	100
53	Do. Conversion Loan 1894	101
45	Trans. Gov. Loan Red. ..1903-42	105
13/	Tucuman (Prov.) 1888	69
	Turkish, Secd. on Egypt. Trib.	104
½	Turkish, Egpt. Trib., Ott. Bd., '94	99
4	Do. Priority 1890	94
1	Do. Convted Series, "A"	65½
5	Do. Customs Ln. 1886	97½
5	Uruguay Bonds 1896	54
3	Venzula New Con. Debt 1881	37½

COUPONS PAYABLE ABROAD.

Last Div.	Name.	Price.
7	Argent. Nat. Cedla. Sries, "B"	39
5	Austrian Ster. Rnts., ex 10fl., 1870	85
5	Do. do. do.	86
5	Do. Paper do. 1870	84
5	Do. do. do.	85
4	Do. Gld Rentes 1876	102
2½	Belgian exchange 25 fr.	92
3	Do. do.	101
3½	Danish Int., 1887, Rd. 1896	97½
3½	Do. '87, Red. by pur. or draw. fr. Dec., 1900	98½
2½	Dutch Certs. ex 12 gldrs.	87
3	Do. Bonds	100
3	Do. Insc. Stk.	99
3½	French Rentes	106½
3	Do. 1878, '81-4., Red.	101
3	German Imp. Ln. 1891	96½
3	Do. do. 1892-3	96½
3	Do. do. 1890-4	96
5	Japan Cons. Ln., '92, 3, & 5, Red.	48½
36/9	Prussian Consols	102
3	" Cons. Stg. Ln. 1891	97
4	Rumanian Bds. 1890	—
4	Do. do. 1891	—
4	Utd. States, 1877, Red. 1907	116
4	Do. 1895, 30 yrs.	131½
3½	Do. Maschsetts Gl. 1935	113½
3½	Do. Gold Bonds 1923	110½
2	Virginia Cpn. Bds., 3 p.c. from July, 1901	72

BRITISH RAILWAYS.

ORD. SHARES AND STOCKS.

Last Div.	Name.	Price.
10	Barry, Ord.	286½
4	Do. Prefd.	129
6	Do. Defd.	157½
3½	Caledonian, Ord.	160
3	Do. Prefd.	102½
—	Do. Defd. Ord., No. 1	5½
	Cambrian, Ord.	6½
—	Do. Coast Cons.	6½
24/	Cardiff Ry. Pref. Ord.	118
3/	Central Lond. £10 Ord. Sh.	10
1/9½	Do. do. £6 paid	6
3½d.	Do. Pref. Half-Shares	1½
1/6	Do. Def. do.	4½
2	City and S. London	70
—	East London, Cons.	7
1½	Furness	71½
—	Glasgow and S. West. Pfd.	85
—	Do. do. Dfd.	69
—	Great Central, Ord. 1894	42
32/0	Do. London Exten.	79
3½	Great N. of Scotland	123
4	Great Northern, Prefd.	125
—	Do. Consolidated "A"	54
—	Do. do. "B"	195½
2	Highland	89½
4	Isle of Wight, Prefd.	122½
1	Do. Defd.	86½
—	Lancs. Derbys. and E. Cst.	4½
6½	L. Brighton and S. C. Ord.	187
37/11½	Do. New 20 p.c. pd.	188
6	Do. Prefd. Ord.	199
10/	Do. Contgt. Rights Certs.	20½
5½	Lond. and S. Western Ord.	232½
4	Do. Preferred	138
2½	Lond., Tilb., and Southend	135½
—	Mersey, £20 shares	1
—	Metropolitan, New Ord.	131
2½	Do. Surplus Lands	99
4	North Cornwall, 4 p.c. Pref.	106½
7/6	Do. Deferred	27½
7½	North London	229½
	North Staffordshire	132

British Railways (*continued*):—

Last Div.	Name.	Price.
1/6	Plymouth, Devenport, and S. W. Junc. £10	9
3/	Port Talbot £10 Shares	9½
9d.	Rhondda Swns. B. £10 Sh.	6½
11	Rhymney, Cons.	277½
4	Do. Prefd.	128
—	Do. Defd.	155½
—	Scarboro', Bridlington Junc.	47½
3½	South Eastern, Ord.	156
6	Do. Pref.	199
3½	Taff Vale	85
25/	Vale of Glamorgan	129½
2/6½	Waterloo & City £10 shares	13½

LEASED AT FIXED RENTALS.

Last Div.	Name.	Price.
4	Birkenhead	150
5.19.0	East Lincnshire	215
5½	Hamsmith. & City Ord.	197½
4½	Lond. and Blackwll.	167½
4½	Do. £10 4½ p. c. Pref.	167
50/6	Lond. & Green. Ord.	102
5	Do. 5 p. c. Pref.	180½
5	Nor. and Eastn. £50 Ord.	92
6	Do.	109
3½	N. Cornwall 3½ p. c. Stk.	129½
4⁷⁄₁₀	Nott. & Granthm. R. & C.	150
3½	Portptk. & Wigtn. Guar. Stk.	126
9	Vict. Stn. & Pimlico Ord.	317½
4½	Do. 4½ p. c. Pref.	163½
4/	West Lond. £20 Ord. Shs.	14½
4⁷⁄₁₀	Weymouth & Portld.	162½

DEBENTURE STOCKS.

Last Div.	Name.	Price.
3	Barry, Cons.	110
4	Brecon & Mrthyr, New A	129
4	Do. New B	105
4	Caledonian	154
4	Cambrian "A"	134½
4	Do. "B"	132½
4	Do. "C"	127½
4	Do. "D"	110½
3	Cardiff Rly.	105
4	City and S. Lond.	139
3½	Cleator & Working Junc.	118½
3	Devon & Som. "A"	105½
16/3	Do. "B" 4 p. c.	36
—	Do. "C" 4 p. c.	10
4	E. Lond. 2nd Ch. 4 p. c. A	139
5/	Do. 2nd B	66½
—	Do. 3rd Ch. 4 p. c.	19½
—	Do. 4th do.	9½
3½	Do. 1st (3½ p. c.)	128½
2½	Do. 2½ p.c. (Whitech. Exn)	88
4	Forth Bridge	146
4	Furness	145
4	Glasgow and S. Western	151
5	Gt. Central	—
4½	Do.	161
4	Gt. Eastern	151
4	Gt. N. of Scotland	148½
3	Gt. Northern	117
4	Gt. Western	156
4½	Do.	162
4½	Do.	173½
5	Do.	192
2½	Do.	100
4	Highland	143½
3	Hull and Barnsley	107
3	Do. 2nd (3-4 p. c).	124
4	Isle of Wight	144½
3	Do. Cent. "A"	92½
4½	Do. "B"	115½
4	Do. "C"	82½
3	Lancs. & Yorkshire	116
4	Lancs. Derbys. & E. Cst.	124½
4	Lpool St. Hlen's & S. Lancs.	126
4½	Ldn. and Blackwall	159
4	Ldn. and Greenwich	149½
4	Lond., Brighton, &c.	152
4½	Do.	170½
4½	Lond., Chath., &c., Arb.	160
4½	Do. "B"	158½
4	Do.	140
4	Do. 1883	140
3	Do.	107
3	Lond. & N. Western	118
3	Lond. & S. Westn. "A"	118
3	Do. Conald.	118
4	Lond., Til., & Southend	150
—	Mersey, 5 p. c. (Act, 1866)	65
4	Metropolitan	150
4½	Do.	164½
3½	Do.	129½
6	Met. District	209½
4	Do.	139
3	Midland	118
4½	Mid-Wales "A"	137½
4	Neath & Brecon 1st	129
4	Do. "A 1"	121
3	North British	114
	Do. 1893	111½
3½	N. Cornwall, Launcstn., &c.	128½
3	North Eastern	117

Debenture Stocks (*continued*):—

Last Div.	Name.	Price.
4½	North London	168
3	N. Staffordshire	115
4	Plym. Devpt. & S.W. Jn.	141½
4	Rhondda and Swan. Bay	130½
4	Rhymney	148
4	South-Eastern	152
5	Do.	191
3½	Do.	130
3	Do.	116
3	Taff Vale	111
4	Tottenham & For. Gate	146
3	Vale of Glamorgan	105½
3	West Highld. (Gtd. by N.B.)	111½
4	Wrexham, Mold, &c. "A"	115½
4	Do. "B"	106½
4	Do. "C"	97½

GUARANTEED SHARES AND STOCKS.

Last Div.	Name.	Price.
4	Caledonian	150½
4	Do.	152
4	Forth Bridge	146
4	Furness 1881	138
4	Glasgow & S. Western	151½
4	Do. St. Enoch. Rent	150½
6	Gt. Central	202
4½	Do. 1st Pref.	153½
3½	Do. Pref.	106
5	Do. Irred. S.Y. Rent	166½
4½	Do. do.	141½
4	Gt. Eastern, Rent	148
5	Do. Metropolitan	182½
4	Do.	148
4	Gt. N. of Scotland	141
4	Gt. Northern	152
5	Gt. Western, Rent	189
5	Do. Cons.	191
4	Lancs. & Yorkshire	152
5	L., Brighton & S. C.	186
3½	L., Chat. & D. (Shrhlds.)	110½
4	L. & North Western	155
4	L. & South Western.. 1881	152
4½	Met. District, Ealing Rent	152
4½	Do. Fulham Rent	152
4	Do. Midland Rent	143½
4	Do. Mid. & Dist. Guar.	136½
4	Midland, Rent	153
4	Do. Cons.	153
3	Mid. & G.N. Jt., "A" Rnt.	110½
3	N. British, Lien	110
4	Do. Cons. Pref. No. 1	148
3	N. Cornwall, Wadebrge. Gu.	108
4	N. Eastern	152
5½	N. Staff. Trent & M. £20 Shs.	36½
3½	Nott. Suburban Ord.	126½
20/6	S. E. Perp. Ann.	36½
4½	Do. 4½ p.c.	168
3½	S. Yorks. Junc. Ord.	118½
4½	W. Cornwall (G. W., Br., Ex., & S. Dev. Joint Rent	168½
3	W. Highl. Ord. Stk. (Gua., N.B.)	107½

PREFERENCE SHARES AND STOCKS.

DIVIDENDS CONTINGENT ON PROFIT OF YEAR.

Last Div.	Name	Price.
5	Barry (First)	171½
4	Do. Consolidated	141½
4	Caledonian Cons., No. 1	149
4	Do. do. No. 2	148
5	Do. do. 1878	183½
4	Do. Pref. 1884	147
4	Do. do. 1887 (Conv.)	156
—	Cambrian, No. 1 4 p. c. Pref.	74½
—	Do. No. 2 do.	39½
—	Do. No. 3 do.	19
—	Do. No. 4 do.	10
5	City & S. Lond. £10 shares	15½
—	Do. New	14
4	Furness, Cons. 1881	134½
4	Do. ....."A" 1881	131½
4	Do. ....."B" 1883	129½
4	Glasgow & S. Western	148½
4	Do. No. 2	147
4	Do. 1888	147
4	Do. 1891	146
5	Gt. Central	167½
4	Do.	134½
5	Do. Conv. 1872	154½
5	Do. do. 1874	154½
5	Do. do. 1876	154½
5	Do. do. 1879	153½
5	Do. do. 1881	153½
4	Do. 1889	117½
4	Do. 1891	113½
5	Do. 1894	116½
4	Gt. Eastern, Cons.	146
4	Do. 1886	145
4	Do. 1881	144
4	Do. 1884	143
4	Do. 1887	143

Preference Shares, &c. (*continued*):—

Last Div.	Name.	Price.
4	Gt. Eastern, Cons. 1888	143
3½	Do. 1890	124½
3½	Do. 1893	123½
—	Do. (Int. fr. Jan '99) 1893	117½
4	Gt. North Scotland "A"	136½
4	Do. "B"	136½
4	Gt. Northern, Cons.	[illegible]
3	Do. 1896	[illegible]
5	Gt. Western Cons.	189
—	Hull & Barnsley Red. at 115	110
4	Isle of Wight	136½
3	Lancs. & Yorkshire, Cons.	112
2/2½	Lanc. Drby & E.C. 5 p.c. £10	11
—	Do. 5 p.c. 2nd £10	10
5	Lond., Bright., &c., Cons.	186½
5	Do. 2nd Cons.	185½
4½	Lond., Chat. & Dov. Arbitr.	137
2½/	Do. 2nd Pref. 4½ p.c.	90
4	Lond. & N. Western	152
4	Lond. & S. Western.. 1881	152
4	Do. 1884	150
3½	Do.	132
4	Lond., Tilbury & Southend	148
4	Do. Cons., 1887	148
4	Do 1891	147
—	Mersey, 5 p.c. Perp.	9½
4	Metropolitan, Perp.	148
4	Do. 1882	145½
4	Do. Irred.	145½
4	Do. 1887	145½
4	Do. New	144½
4½	Do.	149½
3½	Do.	126½
3	Do. Guar.	104½
4	Metrop. Dist. Exten 5 p.c.	113
4	Midland, Cons. Perpetual	151
4	N. British Cons., No. 2	143
4½	Do. Edin. & Glasgow	156½
5	Do. 1865	178½
5	Do. Conv. 1874	173½
4½	Do. 1875	156
4½	Do. Conv. 1875	156½
5	Do. do. 1879	173½
4	Do. do. 1884	141
4	Do. do. 1888	141
4	Do. do. 1890	141
4	Do. do. 1892	141
4	N. Eastern	151
4½	N. Lond., Cons. 1866	187½
4½	Do. 2nd Cons. .. 1875	166½
3	N. Staffordshire	111
4½	Plym. Devpt. & S. W. Junc.	159½
9½d.	Port Talbot, &c., 4 p.c. £10 Shares, 4 paid	3
5/	Rhondda & Swansea Bay, 5 p.c. £10 Shares	13½
4	Rhymney, Cons.	144
4½	S. Eastern, Cons.	167
5	Do. do.	184½
4	Do. Vested Cos'.	145
4	Do. 1891	145
3½	Do. 1893	127
2	Do. 3 p.c. after July 1900	105
4	Taff Vale	143

INDIAN RAILWAYS.

Last Div.	Name.	Paid.	Price.
3½	Assam Bengal, Ld., (3½ p.c. till June 30, then 3 p.c.)	100	105
4/	Barsi Light, Ld., £10 Shs.	10	10½
6	Bengal and N. West., Ld.	100	148½
4/	Do. £10 Shares	10	14½
3/6	Do. 3½ p.c. Cum. Pf. Shs.	10	10½
8½d.	Do.	4	4½
2/3½	Bengal Central, Ld., £10 (3½ p.c. + ½th net earn)	5	5½
3	Bengal Dooars, Ld.	100	138
4	Bengal Nagpr., Lim. (gua. 4 p.c. + 4th sp. pfts.)	100	135
7½	Bombay, Baroda, and C. I. (gua. 5 p.c.)	100	227
36/1	Burma, Ld. (gua. 2½ p.c. and ½ p.c. add. till 1901)	100	111½
1/7	Do. £10 Shares	8½	5½
4	Delhi Umb. Kalka, Ld., Gua. 3½ p.c. + net earn.	100	121
4	Do. Deb. Stk., 1890 (1926)	100	133
9/10	Estn. Bengal, "A" An. 1957	—	26
9/	Do. "B" 1957	—	31
4	Do. Gua. Deb. Stock	100	144½
9/7½	East Ind. Ann. "A" (1953)	—	27
8/4½	Do. "C"	—	30
8/11½	Do. "B"	—	30
6⅓	Do. Def. Ann. Cap. (gua. 4 p.c. + ½th sp. pfts.)	—	151
115/9	East Ind. Def. Ann. "D"	—	157
4½	East Ind. Irred. Stock	100	164½
5	Gt. Indian Penin., Gua. 5 p.c. + ½ surplus profits	100	170
4	Do. Irred. 4 p.c. Deb. St.	100	164½
4	Indian Mid., Ld. (gua. 4 p.c. + ½th surplus pfts.)	100	118
51/	Madras Guar. + ½ sp. pfts.	100	[illegible]
48/6	Do. do.	100	[illegible]
46/	Do. do.	100	[illegible]
4	Nilgiri, Ld., 1st Deb. Stk.	100	[illegible]
4	Oude & Robil. Db. Stk. Rd.	100	[illegible]
5⅓	Rohil. and Kumaon, Ld.	100	[illegible]
9/11	Scinde, Punj., and Delhi, "A" Ann., 1958	—	29
9/1	Do. "B" do.	—	31

Indian Railways (*continued*):—

Last Div.	NAME.	Paid.	Price.
4	South Behar, Ld., £10 shs.	100	100
3½	Do. Deb. Stk. Red.	100	103
4½	South Ind., Gu. Deb. Stk.	100	166½
5	South Indian, Ld. (gua. 3 p.c., and ½ spls. profits)	100	120½
5	Sthn. Mahratta, Ld. (3½ p.c. & ¼th net earnings)	100	121
4	Do. Deb. Stk. Red.	100	124
3½	Southern Punjab, Ld.....	100	113
3½	Do. Deb. Stk. Red.	—	107
5	Nizam's Gua. State, Ld. (†	100	114½
4	Do. Mort. Deb., 1936	100	110
4	Do. do. Reg.	100	108
17/3½	Nizam's Gua. State, Ld., 3½ p.c. Mt. Deb. bearer	—	94½
17/3½	Do. Reg. do. ..	—	93½
5	W. of India Portgese., Ld.	100	68½
5	Do. Deb. Stk., Red	100	98

RAILWAYS.—BRITISH POSSESSIONS.

Last Div.	NAME.	Paid.	Price.
5	Atlantic & N.W. Gua. 1 Mt. Bds., 1937	100	127
5/3	Buff. & L. Huron Ord. Sh.	10	13½
5½	Do. 1st Mt. Perp. Bds. 1879	100	143½
5½	Do. 2nd Mt. Perp. Bds.	100	143½
—	Calgary & Edmon. 6 p.c. 1st Mt. Stg. Bds. Red..	100	79½
5	Canada Cent. 1st Mt. Bds. Red.	100	105
4	Can. Pacific Pref. Stk.....	100	102½
5	Do. Strl. 1st Mt. Deb. Bds. 1915	100	119
3½	Do. Ld. Grnt. Bds., 1938..	100	109
3½	Do. Ld. Grnt. Ins. Stk. ..	100	109
4	Do. Perp. Cons. Deb. Stk.	100	119
5	Do. Algoma Bch. 1st Mt. Bds., 1937	100	121
2	Demerara, Original Stock	100	49
7	Do. Perp. Pref. Stk.....	100	157½
9½d.	Do. 4 p.c. Cum. Ext. Pref. £10 Shs.	4	6½
—	Dominion Atlntc. Ord. Stk.	100	32½
25/	Do. 5 p.c. Pref. Stk.....	100	101
4	Do. 1st. Deb. Stk.......	100	110
4	Do. 2nd do. Red.	100	99
—	EmuBay&Mt.Bischoff,Ld.	5	4½
4½	Do. Irred. Deb. Stk....	100	98
nil.	Gd. Trunk of Canada, Stk.	100	9½
6	Do. 2nd. Equip. Mt. Bds.	100	130½
5	Do. Perp. Deb. Stk......	100	141
5	Do. Gt. Westn. Deb. Stk.	100	134
5	Do. Nthn. of Can. 1st Mt. Bds., 1902	100	106
4	Do. do. Deb. Stk	100	103
5	Do. G. T. Geor. Bay & L. Erie 1 Mt., 1903	100	104
5	Do. Mid. of Can. Stl. 1st Mt. (Mid. Sec.) 1908	100	108
5	Do.do.Cons.1 Mt.Bds. 1912	100	108
5	Do. Mont. & Champ. 1 Mt. Bds., 1902	100	104
	Do. Welln., Grey & Brce. 7 p.c. Bds. 1 Mt.	100	111
4	Jamaica 1st Mtg. Bds. Red.	—	103½
—	Manitoba & N. W., 6 p.c. 1st Mt. Bds., Red	100	—
—	Do. Ldn. Bdhldrs. Certs.	—	—
5	Manitoba S. W. Col. 1 Mt. Bd., 1934 $1,000 price %	—	120
—	Mid. of W. Aust. Ld. 6 p.c. 1 Mt. Dbs., Red.	100	25
4	Do. Deb. Bds., Red.	100	103
4	Nakusp & Slocan Bds., 1918	100	106
3	Natal Zululand Ld. Debs.,	100	79½
5	N. Brunswick 1st Mt. Stg. Bds., 1934	100	122
4	Do. Perp. Cons. Deb. Stk.	100	116
—	N. Zealand Mid., Ld., 5 p.c 1st Mt. Debs..........	100	35
6	Ontario & Queb. Cap. Stk.	$100	156½
5	Do. Perm. Deb. Stk......	100	147½
—	Qu'Appelle, L. Lake & Sask. 6p.c. 1 Mt. Bds. Red.	100	46½
5	Queb. & L. S. John, 1st Mt. Bds., 1909	100	27½
5	Quebec Cent., Prior Ln. Bds., 1908	100	107
1½	Do. 5 p.c. Inc. Bds.	100	41
4	St. Lawr. & Ott. Stl. 1st Mt.	100	113
4	Shuswap & Okan., 1st Mt. Deb. Bds., 1915	100	70½
5	Temiscouata, 5 p.c. Stl. 1st Deb. Bds., Red.........	100	9½
5	Do. (S. Franc. Brch.) 5 p.c. Stl. 1 Mt. Db. Bds., 1910	100	12½
4	Toronto, Grey & B. 1st Mt.	100	114
1/2½	Well. & Mana. £5 Shs. ..	1	1
5	Do. Debs., 1908	100	110
5	Do. 2nd Debs., 1908	100	109
5	Do. 3rd do., 1908	100	108
6	Atlan. & St. Law. Shs., 6 p.c.	100	167
5	Gd. Trunk Mt. Bds., 1934	100	110½
5	Michigan Air Line, 5 p.c. 1st Mt. Bds., 1902	100	104
4	Minneap., S. P. & Slt. Ste. Mar, 1st M. Bds., 1938	$1000	100½

AMERICAN RAILROAD STOCKS AND SHARES.

Last Div.	NAME.	Paid.	Price.
6/	Alab. Gt. Sthn. A 6 p.c. Pref.	10/.	9
—	Do. do "B" Ord. ..	10/.	2
—	Alabma. N. Orl.-Tex. &c., "A" Pref.	10/.	½
—	Do. "B" Def.	10/.	¼
4½	Atlant. First Lsd. Ls. Rtl. Trust..................	Stk.	100
$2	Baltimore & Ohio Com. ..	$100	16
—	Baltimore Ohio S.W. Pref.	$100	6
—	Chesap. & Ohio Com.	$100	22
—	Chic. Gt. West. 5 p.c. Pref. Stock "A"	$100	37½
—	Do. do. Scrip. In.......	—	35½
8/3	Do. 4 p.c. Deb. Stk........	$100	71½
4	Do. Interest in Scrip	$100	67½
$4	Chic. Junc. Rl. & Un. Stk. Yds. Com.	$100	116½
$1½	Do. 6 p.c. Cum. Pref.	$100	116½
$3½	Chic. Mil. & St. P. Pref...	$100	147½
7	Cleve. & Pittsburgh	$10	87
$1½	Clev., Cincin., Chic., & St. Louis Com.	$100	—
—	Erie 4 p.c. Non-Cum. 1st Pf.	—	41
—	Do. 4 p.c. do. 2nd Pf.	—	21
—	Gt. Northern Pref.	$100	146
$2½	Illinois Cen. Lsd. Lines ..	$100	97½
—	Kansas City, Pitts & G. ..	$100	22
$3	L. Shore & Mich. Sth. C.	$100	197½
—	Mex. Cen. Ltd. Com.	$100	6
—	Miss. Kan. & Tex. Pref...	$100	41½
1	N.Y., Pen. & O. 1st Mt. Tst. Ltd., Ord.	—	47½
4	Do. 1st Mort. Deb. Stk. ..	$100	92½
8	North Pennsylvania	$50	—
—	Northn. Pacific, Com.....	$100	29
1½	Pitts. F. Wayne & Chic...	$100	176
—	Reading 1st Pref.	$50	27
—	Do. 2nd Pref.	$50	14½
—	S Louis & S. Fran. Com.	$100	7½
—	Do. 2nd Pref.	$100	27
6	St. Louis Bridge 1st Pref..	$100	107
3	Do. 2nd Pref.	$100	50
6	Tunnel Rail. of St. Louis	$100	107
$1½	St. Paul, Min. and Man...	$100	127½
—	Southern, Com.	$100	9½
—	Wabash, Common........	$100	7½

AMERICAN RAILROAD BONDS. CURRENCY.

Last Div.	NAME.	Price.
7	Albany & Susq. 1 Con. Mrt. 1906	122½
7	Allegheny Val. 1 Mt....... 1910	127½
5	Burling., Cedar Rap. & N. 1 Mt. 1906	109½
5	Canada Southern 1 Mt..... 1908	111
5	Chic. & N. West. Sk. Fd. Db. 1933	120½
5	Do. Deb. Coupon 1921	115½
6	Chicago & Tomah 1905	112½
5	Chic. Burl. & Q. Skg. Fd. 1901	102½
4	Do. Nebraska Ext....... —	102
6	Chic., Mil., & S. Pl., 1 Mt. S.W. Div.............. 1909	117½
7	Do. (S. Paul Div.) 1 Mt. 1902	132½
5	Do. (La Cross & D. 1919	112½
7	Do. 1 Mt. (Hast. & Dak.) 1910	132
5	Do. Chic. & Mis. Riv. 1 Mt. 1926	112½
5	Chic., Rock Is. and Pac. 1 Mt. Ext. 1934	108
6	Det., G. Haven & Mil. Equip 1918	110
6	Do. do. Cons. Mt. 1918	104½
6	Ill. Cent., 1 Mt., Chic. & S. 1898	—
7	Indianap. & Vin., 1 Mt. .. 1908	125
6	Do. do. 2 Mt. .. 1906	104½
6	Lehigh Val., Cons. Mt. 1923	112½
—	Mexic. Cent., Ln. 2 Cons. Inc. —	7
7	N.Y. Cent. & H.R. Mt. Bonds 1903	119½
5	Do. Deb. 1904	112
6	Penns. Cons. S. F M. 1905	115
4	West Shore, 1 Mt. 2361	110

DITTO—GOLD.

Last Div.	NAME.	Price.
6	Alabama Gt. Sthn. 1 Mt. ..1908	112
5	Do. Mid. 1 1928	96
4	Allegheny Val. Gen. Mt. ..1942	110
4	Atch., Top., & S. Fé Gn. Mt. 1995	96
3	Do. Adj. Mt.............1995	62½
5	Do. Equipt. Tmst. ...... —	104½
5	Atlantic & Dan. 1 Mt.......1950	94½
5	Baltimore & Ohio..........1925	94½
5	Do. Speyer's Tst. Recpts. 1925	92½
5	Do. Cons. Mt. 1988	99½
4½	Do. 4½ p.c. 1 Mt. Term. 1934	85
4½	Do. Brown Shipley's Dep. Cts. —	85
5	Balt. Belt 5 p.c. 1 Mort.....1990	—
4½	Balt. & Ohio S.W. 1 Mt. ..1990	102
4½	Do. 4½ p.c. 1 Cons. Mt. 1893 1993	76½
—	Do. Inc. Mt. 5 p.c. Cl. A —	30
—	Do. do. Cl. B —	11
5	Balt. & Ohio S.W. Term 5 p.c. 1942	99½
6	Balt. & Ptmac (Mn. L.) 1 Mt. 1911	127½
6	Do. do. (Tunnel) 1 Mt. 1911	126
4	Beech Creek 1 Mt. 1936	106½
5	Do 2 Mort. 1936	116
4	Carthage & Adiron. 1 Mt...1981	109

American Railroad Bonds—Gold (*continued*):—

Last Div.	NAME.	Price.
5	Cent. of Georgia 1 Mort. ..1945	117½
5	Do. Cons. Mt. 1945	92½
5	Cent. of N. Jrsy. Gn. Mt...1987	116
6	Central Pacific, 1 Mort. 1898	102½
6	Do. Speyer's Certs....... —	102½
5	Do Land Grant 1900	102
5	Chesap. & Ohio 1st Cons. Mt. 1939	119
4½	Do. Gen. Mt............1992	86
6	Chic. & W. Ind. Gen. Mt. Skg. Fd. 1932	122
5	Chic. Mil. & St. Pl. (Chic. & L. Sup.) 1 Mt. 1921	114½
5	Do. Chic. & Pac. W. 1921	119½
5	Do. Wisc. & Minn. 1 Mt. 1921	114½
5	Do. Terminal Mt. 1914	114½
4	Do. General Mt. 1989	108
5	Chic. St. L. & N. Orleans..1951	122½
4	Do. 1 Mort. (Memphis) ..1951	102½
4	Clevel, Cin., Chic. & St. L. 1 Mt. (Cairo)............1939	90
4	Do. 1 Mt. (Cinc., Wab., & Mich.) 1991	98
4	Do. 1 Col. Tst. Mt. (S. Louis) 1990	98½
4	Do General Mt. 1993	84
4½	Clevel. & Mar. Mt. 1935	111½
4½	Clevel. & Pittsburgh 1942	122½
4½	Do. Series B. 1942	124½
—	Colorado Mid. 1 Mt. 1936	68
—	Do. Bdhrs.' Comm. Certs. —	68
4	Dnvr. & R. Gde. 1 Cons. Mt. 1936	97
5	Do. Imp. Mort...........1928	95
4	Detroit & Mack. 1 Lien 1995	92½
5	E. Tennes., Virg., & Grgia. Cons. Mt. 1956	114½
5	Elmira, Cort., & Nthn. Mt. 1914	99½
4	Erie 1 Cons. Mt. Pr. Ln. ..1996	94
3	Do. Gen. Lien 1996	73½
6	Galvest., Harrisb., &c., 1 Mt.....	107½
5	Georgia, Car. & N. 1 Mt. ..1929	96
4½	Gd Rpds & Inda. Ex 1 Mt. 1941	111½
5	Do. 1 Mt. (Muskegon) ..1926	39½
3½	Illinois Cent. 1 Mt. 1951	104½
4	Do. 1952	107
4	Do. Cairo Bdge. ..1950	102
4	Do. 1953	105
4	Do. General Mort. ..1904	102½
—	Kans. City, Pitts. & G. 1 M. 1923	83
3½	L. Shore & Mich. Southern 1997	109
4½	Lehigh Val. N.Y. 1 Mt.....1940	106
5	Lehigh Val. Term. 1 Mt. ..1941	112½
5	Long Island 1931	122½
5	Do. Deb...........1934	102
5	Do. (N. Shore Bch.) 1 Cons. Mt. 1932	96
6	Louisville & Nash. G. Mt..1930	121
6	Do. 2 Mt. Sk. Fd. (S. & N. Alabama........1910	108
6	Do. 1 Mt. N. Orl. & Mb. 1930	122½
5	Do. 1 Mt. Coll. Tst. ...1931	107½
4	Do. Unified 1940	89
4½	Do. Mobile & Montgy. 1 Mt. 1945	107½
4	Manhattan Cons. Mt. 1990	100
4	Mexican Cent. Cons. Mt. ..1911	70
—	Do. 1 Cons. Inc, ...	18
6	Mexican Nat. 1 Mt.........1927	107½
3	Do. 2 Mt. 6 p.c. Inc. A 1917	58
—	Do. do. B..1917	—
3	Do. Matheson's Certs.....	—
3	Michig. Cnt. (Battle Ck. & S.) 1 Mt. 1989	84
6	Minneap. & S. L. 1 Mt. Pacific Ext. 1921	120½
5	Do. 1 Consold. 1934	110
4	Minne., Slt. S. M. & A. 1 Mt. 1926	102
5	Minneapolis Westn. 1 Mt...1911	105½
4	Miss. Kans. & Tex. 1 Mt...1990	93
4	Do. 2 do. 1990	68
4	Mobile & Birm. Mt. Inc....1945	38
5	Do. P. Lien 1945	88
4	Mohawk & Mal. 1 Mt......1991	110
5	Montana Cent. 1 Mt. 1937	111½
5	Nashv., Chattan., & S. L. 1 Cons. Mt................1928	104½
5	Nash., Flor., & Shff. Mt...1937	90
4	N. Y. & Putnam 1 Cons. Mt. 1993	110
5	N. Y., Brooklyn, & Man. B. 1 Cons. Mt..............1935	110
4	N. Y. Cent. & Hud. R. Deb. Certs. 1890 1905	107
4	Do. Ext. Debt. Certs....1905	107
7	N. Y., L. Erie, & W. 1 Cons. Mt. (Erie) 1920	149½
7	Do. 1 Con. Mt. Fd. Coup. 1920	147½
5	N. Y., Onto., & W. Cons. 1 Mt.....................1939	110
4	Do. 4 p.c. Refund. Mt..1992	102
5	N. Y. & Rockaway B. 1 Mt. 1927	104½
6	Norfolk & West. Gn. Mt....1931	128
6	Do. Imp. & Ext.........1934	120
4	Do. 1 Cons. Mt. .... —	84
6	N. Pacific Gn. 1 Mt. Ld. Gt. 1921	120
4	Do. P. Ln. Rl. & Ld. Gt. —	100
3	Do. Gn. Ln. Rl. & Ld. Gt. —	64½
5	Oregon & Calif. 1 Mt.......1927	84
5	Oregon Rl. & Nav. Col. Tst. —	—
—	Oreg. Sh. Line & Utah Col. Trst. 5 p.c. G. Bonds 1919	47½
6	Panama Skg. Fd. Subsidy..1910	105½
4½	Pennsylvania Rlrd. ....191.	115½
4	Do. Equip. Tst. Ser. A..191.	106
4	Do. Cons. Mt...........194.	115
4½	Penna. Company 1st Mort. 192.	116½
5	Perkiomen 1 Mrt., 2nd ser..191.	90
4*	{ Pitts., C., C., & St. Ls. Con. Mt. G. B., Ser. A } 1940-.	116
4	Do. Cons. Mort., Ser. D..194.	105
6	Pittsbgh., Cle., & Toledo ..192.	105
4	Reading, Phil., & R. Genl. 199.	89
5	Richmond & Dan. Equip. ..190.	99
5	Rio Grande Junc. 1st Mort. 193.	94
4	Rio Grande West 1st Tst. Mt. 193.	86
6	St. Joseph & Gd. Island ..192.	—
7	S. Louis Bridge 1st Mort ..192.	137½

American Railroad Bonds (*continued*):

Last Div.	NAME.	Price.
5	S. Louis Mchts. Bdge. Term. 1st Mort....................1930	107½
4	S. Louis S. West 1st Mort..1989	77½
—	Do. 4 p.c. 2nd Mort. Inc. 1989	30
—	S. Louis Term. Cupples Sta. & Prop. 1st. Mrt. 4½ p.c. 1902-17	102
4½	St. Paul, Minn., & Manit. 1933	110
6	Do. do. 1933	127½
6	Shamokin, Sunbury, &c. 2 Mt. 1925	107
5	S. & N. Alabama Cons. Mt. 1936	95½
5	Southern 1 Cons. Coup. 1994	96
4	Do. E. Tennes Reorg. Lien ..1938	100
6	S. Pacific of Cal. 1 Mt...1905-12	114
4½	Trml. Assn. of S. Louis 1 Mt. 1939	113½
5	Do. 1 Cons. Mt..........1944	109
5	Texas & Pac. 1 Mt..........2000	103½
—	Do. 5 p.c. 2 Mt. Income 2000	35½
5	Toledo & Ohio Cent. 1 Mt. West. Div. 1935	105½
4½	Toledo., Walhon., Val., & Ohio 1 Mt. 1931-3	111½
6	Union Pacific 1 Mt. 1896-9	102½
5	Do. Coll. Trust.	—
—	Union Pac., Linc., & Color. 1 Mt. 1918	—
4	United N. Jersey Gen. Mt...1944	117½
6	Vicksbrg., Shrevept., & Pac. Pr. Ln. Mt. 1915	102½
5	Wabash 1 Mt. 1939	110
4	Wn. Pennsylvania Mt. 1928	109½
5	W. Virga. & Pittsbg. 1 Mt. 1990	84
5	Wheeling & L. Erie 1 Mt. (Wheelg. Div.) 5 p.c. 1928	82½
5	Do. Extd. Imp. Mt 1930	—
—	Do. do. Brown Shipley's Cts...	—
5	Willmar & Sioux Falls 1 Mt. 1938	111

STERLING.

Last Div.	NAME.	Price.
6	Alabama Gt. Sthn. Deb.....1906	106
5	Do. Gen. Mort. ..1927-8	100
5	Alabama, N. Orl., Tex. & Pac. 5 p.c. "A" Dbs...1910-40	99
55/	Do. do. "B" do. 1910-40	51
—	Do. do. "C" do.	19
—	Allegheny Valley 1910	135
4	Atlantic 1st Leased Line Perp...	98
6	Baltimore and Ohio 1902	109
6	Do. do. 1910	117
5	Do. do. 1877.........	96
—	Do. Morgan's Certs. ..	96
4½	Do. do. 1933	82
6	Chicago & Alton Cons. Mt. 1903	111
5	Chic. St. Paul & Kan. City Priority	105
6	Eastn. of Massachusetts....1906	117½
5	Illinois Cent. Skg. Fd.	105
5	Do. 1905	108
3½	Do. 1950	100½
4	Do. 1 Mt. 1951	114
3	Do. 1 Mt. 1951	94
6	Louisville & Nash., M. C. & L. Div., 1 Mt. 1902	104½
7	Do. 1 Mt. (Memphis & O.)......................1901	111
47/4	Mexican Nat. "A" Certs. 5 p.c. Non. cum.	49
—	Do. "B" Certs......	11
6	N.Y. & Canada 1 Mt.......1904	111½
6	N. York Cent. & H.R. Mort. 1903	112
4½	N. York, Penns., & Ohio Pr. Ln. Extd. 1935	—
5	Do. Equip. Tst.	103½
5	Do. 5 p.c. Equip. Tst. (1890)	103½
6	Nrthn. Cent. Cons. Gen. Mt. ..	106
6	Pennsylvania Gen. Mt. 1910	129
6	Do. Cons. Skg. Fd. Mt. 1905	117
3½	Do. Cons. Mt. 1945	107
6	Phil. & Erie Cons. Mort ..1920	134½
6	Phil. & Reading Gen. Cons. Mort. 1911	127
6	Pittsbg. & Connells. Cons. 1926	112
—	Do. Morgan's Certs.....	112
4	St. Paul., Min., & Manitoba (Pac. Extn.) 1940	98
6	S. & N. Alabama 1903	107½
6	Union Pacific, Omaha Bridge 1896	—
6	Un. N. Jersey & C. Gen. Mt. 1901	112½

FOREIGN RAILWAYS.

Last Div.	NAME.	Paid.	Price.
4/	Alagoas, Ltd., Shs.......	20	6
5	Do. Deb. Stk., Red. ..	100	53
6	Antofagasta, Ltd., Stk. ..	100	81
4	Do. Perp. Deb. Stk. ..	100	94
—	Arauco, Ld., Ord. Shs. ..	10	½
—	Do. 10 p.c. Cum. Pref.	10	1½
20/	Argentine Gt. W., Ld.,	20	15
20/	Do. 5 p.c. Cum. Pref. Shs.	20	20½
4	Do. 1 Deb. Stk. .... (†	100	105
6/0/0	Do. 6 p.c. 2 Db. Stk. Astg.	100	—
6/0/0	Do. do. Non-Astg.	100	—
1/0/0	Argentine N.E., Ltd., 6 p.c. Cum. Pref. Stk. ..	100	12
—	Do. 5 p.c. Deb. Stk., Red.	100	35
2/	Arica and Tacna Shs. ..	20	1½
10/	Bahia & San Fcisco., Ld.,	20	11½
6/	Do. Timbo. Bch. Shs.	20	5½
12/	Bahia, Blanca, & N.W. Ln. Prf. Cum. 6 p.c. ..	100	61½
4	Do. 4 p.c. 1 Deb. Stk., Red.	100	96
6	Barranquilla R. & P., Ld., 6 p.c. 1 Deb. Stk., Red.	100	

Foreign Railways (*continued*):—

Last Div.	Name.	Paid.	Price.
3/	Bilbao Riv. & Cantabn., Ltd., Ord.	3	6
—	Bolivar, Ltd., Shs.	10	1¾
6	Do. 6 p.c. Deb. Stk.	100	99½
4/	Brazil Gt. Southn. Ltd., 7 p.c. Cum. Pref.	20	1½
6	Do. Perm. Deb. Stk	100	47½
6½	B. Ayres Gt. Southn., Ld., Ord. Stk.	100	157
5	Do. Pref. Stk.	100	140
4	Do. Deb. Stk.	100	118
30/	B. Ayres & Ensen. Port., Ltd., Ord. Stk.	100	57
5	Do. Cum. 1 Pref. Stk.	100	119
6/0/0	Do. 6p.c.Con. Pref.Stk.	100	98
4	Do. Deb. Stk., Irred.	100	103
9⅛	B. Ayres Northern, Ltd., Ord. Stk.	100	270
12	Do. Pref. Stk.	100	325
5	Do. 5 p.c. Mt. Deb. Stk., Red.	100	113
3/15/0	B. Ayres & Pac., Ld., 7 p.c. 1 Pref. Stk. (Cum.)	100	104
4	Do. 1 Deb. Stk.	100	105
5/5/0	Do. 4½ p.c. 2 Deb. Stk.	100	94
1	B Ayres & Rosario, Ltd., Ord. Stk.	100	77½
—	Do. New, £20 Shs.	20	22½
7/	Do. 7 p.c. Pref. Shs.	10	17½
7/	Do. Sunchales Ext.	10	15½
4	Do. Deb. Stk., Red.	100	109
12/	B. Ayres & Val. Trans., Ltd., 7 p.c. Cum. Pref.	20	7
4	Do. 4 p.c. "A" Deb. Stk., Red.	100	73
—	Do. 6 p.c. "B" Deb. Stk., Red.	100	48
6/	B. Ayres Westn. Ld. Ord.	10	12
3/	Do. Def. Shs.	10	7½
5	Do. 5 p.c. Pref.	10	13½
4	Do. Deb. Stk.	100	112
6	Cent. Arg. Deb. Sk. Rd.	100	163½
4	Do. Deb. Stk. Rd	100	112
6	Cent. Bahia L. Ord. Stk.	100	51½
6	Do. Deb. Stk., 1934	100	74½
5	Do. Deb. Stk., 1937	100	58
1/6	Cent. Uguy. East. Ext. L. Shs.	10	6½
5	Do. Perm. Stk.	100	109
3/	Do. Nthn. Ext. L. Sh.	10	4½
5	Do. Perm. Deb. Stk	100	106
3	Do. of Montev. Ltd., Ord. Stk	100	92
6	Do. Perm. Deb. Stk	100	142
10/	Conde d'Eu, Ltd. Ord.	20	7½
—	Cordba & Rosar., Ltd., 6 p.c. Pref. Shs.	100	50
4	Do. 1 Deb. Stk	100	97
75/	Do. 6 p.c. Deb. Stk.	100	91
—	Cordba Cent., Ltd., 5 p.c. Cu. 1 Pref. Stk.	100	91
—	Do. 5 p.c. Non-Cum. 2 Pref. Stk.	100	51
5	Do. Deb. Stk.	100	125
—	Costa Rica, Ltd., Shs.	10	4
8/	Dna. Thrsa. Chris., Ltd., 7 p.c. Pref. Shs.	20	4½
20/	E. Argentine, Ltd	100	47
6	Do. Deb. Stk	100	108
1/1	Egyptn. Dlta. Lgt. Rys., Ltd., £10 Pref. Shs.	6	8½
—	Entre Rios, L., Ord. Shs.	5	¾
—	Do. Cu. 5 p.c. Pref.	5	3½
6/	Gt. Westn. Brazil, Ltd.,	20	11½
6	Do. Perm. Deb. Stk	100	90
6	Do. Extn. Deb. Stk.	100	80½
—	Int.-Oceanic Mex., Ltd., 7 p.c. Pref.	10	1½
4	Do. Deb. Stk	100	87
42/6	Do. 7 p.c. "A" Deb. Sk.	100	64
—	Do. 7 p.c. "B" Deb. Sk.	100	32
5/	La Guaira & Carac	10	7
5	Do. 5 p.c. Deb. Sk. Red.	100	102
8/4	Lembg.-Czern.-Jassy	30	25
1/	Lima, Ltd.	20	2½
—	Manila Ltd. 7 p.c. Cu. Pf.	10	½
20/6½	Mexican 2nd Pref. 6 p.c.	100	39
6	Do. Perp. Deb. Stk.	100	147
1/0/0	Mexican Sthrn., Ld., Ord.	100	29
—	Do. 4 p.c. 1 Db. Stk. Rd.	100	85
—	Do. 4 p.c. 2 do.	100	63
—	Mid. Urgy., Ltd.	100	20
5	Do. Deb. Stk	100	63
12/	Minas & Rio, Ltd.	20	12½
5/2	Namur & Liege	20	12½
11/6	Do. Pref	20	28
5/	Natal & Na. Cruz, Ld., 7 p.c. Cum Pref.	20	7½
—	Nitrate Ltd., Ord.	10	6½
—	Do. 7 p.c. Pr. Con. Or.	10	4½
—	Do. Def. Conv. Ord.	10	1½
7/	N.-E. Urgy., Ltd., Ord	10	15
7/	Do. 7 p.c. Pref.	10	15½
—	N.-W. Argentine Ld., 7 p.c. Pref.	10	3½
6	Do. 6 p.c. 1 Deb. Stk.	100	114
—	Do. 2 Deb. Stk.	100	94
—	N.W. Uruguay 6 p.c. 1 Pref. Stk.	100	17
—	Do. 5 p.c. 2 Pref. Stk.	100	7½
6	Do. 6 p.c. Deb. Stk.	100	77½
16/	Ottoman (Sm. Aid.)	20	16½
—	Paraguay Cntl., Ld., 5 p.c. Perm. Deb. Stk.	100	11
—	Piræus, Ath., & Pelo.	275	1
5/	Pto. Alegre & N. Hambg. Ld., 7 p.c. Pref. Shs.	20	4½
6	Do. Mt. Deb. Stk. Red.	100	77½
—	Puerto Cabello & Val. Ld.	10	1½
5	Recife & S. Francisco	20	75
14/	R Claro S. Paulo, Ld., Sh.	10	22
5	Do. Deb. Stk.	100	130
	Royal Sardinian Ord	10	11½

Foreign Railways (*continued*):—

Last Div.	Name.	Paid.	Price.
5/	Royal Sardinian Pref.	10	12½
5/	Sambre & Meuse	20	19
5/6	Do. Pref.	10	12
28/	San Paulo Ld.	20	36
2/9½	Do. New Ord. £10 sh.	4	8½
2/	Do. 5 p.c. Non. Cm. Pref.	10	12½
5½	Do. Deb. Stk.	100	136
5	Do. 5 p.c. Deb. Stk	100	128
—	S. Fé & Cordova, Gt. Sthn., Ld., Shares	100	56
6	Do. Perp. Deb. Stk.	100	121
3/2½	S. Austrian	20	7½
10/	Sthn. Braz. R. Gde. do Sul, Ld.	20	9
6	Do. 6 p.c. Deb. Stk.	100	77
4	Swedish Centl., Ld., 4 p.c. Deb. Stk.	100	108
5	Do. Pref.	100	99
1/9	Taltal, Ld.	5	3
—	Uruguay Nthn., Ld. 7 p.c. Pfd. Stk.	100	8
3½	Do. 5 p.c. Deb. Stk.	100	29
—	Villa Maria & Rufino, Ld., 6 p.c. Pref. Shs.	100	20
4	Do. 4 p.c. 1 Deb. Stk.	100	76
6/0/0	Do. 6 p.c. 2 Deb. Stk.	100	49
5/9	West Flanders	8½	22
5/6	Do. 5½ p.c. Pref.	10	18
3/	Wstn. of Havana, Ld.	10	5

FOREIGN RAILWAY OBLIGATIONS

Per Cent.	Name.	Price.
6	Alagoas Ld., 6 p.c. Deb., Rd.	83½
—	Alcoy & Gandia, Ld., 5 p.c. Debs., Red.	25
5	Arauco., Ld., 5 p.c. 1st Mt., Rd.	67½
—	Do. 6 p.c. Mt. Deb., Rd.	48½
6	Brazil G. Sthn., L., Mt. Dbs., Rd.	89½
6	Do. Mt. Dbs. 1891, Rd.	48½
5½	Campos & Caran. Dbs., Rd.	76
6	Central Bahia, L., Dbs., Rd.	90½
5½	Conde d'Eu, L., Dbs., Rd.	77
6	Costa Rica, L., 1st Mt. Dbs., Rd.	110
6	Do. 2nd Dbs., Rd.	95
5	Do. Prior Mt. Db., Rd.	107
6	Cucuta Mt. Dbs., Rd.	100
5½	Donna Thrsa. Cris., L., Dbs., Rd.	75
3	Eastn. of France, £20 Dbs., Rd.	19
4	Egyptn. Delta Light, L., Db., Rd.	100
—	Espito. Santo & Cara. 5 p.c. Stl. Dbs., Rd.	38
4	Gd. Russian Nic., Rd.	102
5	Inter-Oceanic Mex., L., 5 p.c. Pr. Ln. Dbs., Rd.	104
3	Ital. 3 p.c. Bds. A & B, Rd.	57½
—	Ituana 6 p.c. Debs., 1918	72½
—	Leopoldina, 6 p.c. Dbs. £50 Bds.,	26
—	Do. do. Comms. Cert.	26
—	Do. 5 p.c. Stg. Dbs. (1888), Rd.	36
—	Do. do. Comm. Certs.	36
—	Do. 5 p.c. Stg. Dbs. (1890), Rd.	26
—	Do. do. Comms. Certs.	26
—	Macahé & Cam. 5 p.c. Dbs., Rd.	36
—	Do. do. Comms. Certs.	36
—	Do. (Cantagallo), 5 p.c., Red.	36
—	Do. do. Comm. Certs.	36
—	Manila Ltd., 6 p.c. Deb., Red.	24
6	Do. Prior Lien Mt., Rd.	105
6	Do. Series "B," Rd.	79
7	Matanzas & Sab., Rd.	101½
6	Minas & Rio, L., 6 p.c. Dbs., Rd.	101
5	Mogyana 5 p.c. Deb. Bds., Rd.	103
5	Moscow-Jaros., Rd.	107½
5½	Natal & Na. Cruz Ltd., 5½ p.c. Debs., Red.	88½
5	Nitrate, Ltd. Mt. Bds., Red.	90
3	Nthn. France, Red.	19
4	N. of S. Af. Rep. (Trnsvl.) Gu. Bds. Red.	97
3	Nthn. of Spain £20 Pri. Obs. Red.	8½
6	Ottmn. (Smy to A.)(Kujk) Asnt. Debs., Red.	109
6	Ottmn. (Seraik.) Asg. Debs. Red.	109
6	Ottmn. (Seraik.) Non-Asg. D., Rd	109
5	Ottmn. Kuyjk. Ext. Red.	109
5	Ottmn. Serkeuy. Ext. Red.	104
5	Ottmn. Tireh Ext. 1910	99
5	Ottmn. Debs, 1886, Red.	98
5	Do. 1888, Red. 1935	99
5	Do. 1893, Red. 1935	97
5	Ottmn. of Anlia. Debs., Rd.	93
5	Do. Ser. II	89
4	Ottomn. Smyr. & Cas. Ext. Bds., Red.	81
3	Paris, Lyon & Medit. (old sys., £20), Red.	19
3	Paris, Lyon & Medit. (new sys., £20), Red.	19
50/	Piræus, At. & Pelp., 6 p.c. 1st Mt. Bds., Red.	88½
5	Do. 5 p.c. Mt. Bds., Red.	61½
4	Pretoria-Pietbg., Ltd., Red.	94
7	Puerto Cab. & Val., Ltd., 1st Mt. Debs., Red.	96
—	Rio de Jano. & Nthn., Ltd., 6 p.c. £100 Deb., Red.	26
—	Rio de Jano. (Gr. Para.), 5 p.c. 1st Mt. St. £100 Debs., Red.	26
3	Royal Sardinian, A, Rd. £20	12
3	Royal Sardinian, B., Rd. £20	12

Foreign Rly. Obligations (*continued*):—

Per Cent.	Name.	Price.
5	Ryl. Trns.-Afric. 5 p.c. 1st Mt. £100 Bds., Red.	61
7	Sagua La Grande, B ... Rd.	98
4	Sa. Fe & Cor. G.S., Ld. Pr. Ln. Bds.	102
5	Sa. Fe, 5 p.c. 2nd Reg. Dbs.	81
3	South Austrian, £20 Red.	15½
3	South Austrian, (Ser X.)	15½
3	South Italian £20 Obs. (Ser. A to G), Red.	12½
3½	S. W. of Venez. (Barq.), Ltd., 7 p.c. 1st Mt. £100 Debs.	57½
5	Taltal, Ltd., 5 p.c. 1st Ch. Debs., Red.	99
5	Utd. Rwys. Havana, Red.	82½
3	Wtrn. of France, £20 Red.	19
6	Wrn. B. Ayres St. Mt. Debs., 1902	111
6	Wrn. B. Ayres, Reg. Cert.	109
5	Do. Mt. Bds.	122
6	Wtrn. of Havna., Ld, Mt. Dbs., Rd.	102
7	Wrn. Ry. Sao Paulo Red.	101
—	Wrn. Santa Fé, 7 p.c. Red.	42
4/7	Zafra & Huelva, 3 p.c. Red.	3

BANKS.

Div.	Name.	Paid.	Price.
1/9½	Agra, Ltd.	6	3½
4/2½	Anglo-Argentine, Ltd., £9	7	5½
8½ fls.	Anglo-Austrian	120f	14
6/	Anglo-Californian, Ltd., £20 Shares	10	11
4/	Anglo-Egyptian, Ltd., £15	5	6
3/6	Anglo-Foreign Bkg., Ltd.	7	8
2/	Anglo-Italian, Ltd.	5	7½
7/6	Bk. of Africa, Ltd., £18¾	6¼	11
20/	Bk. of Australasia	40	56
8/	Bk. of Brit. Columbia	20	20
25/	Bk. of Brit. N. America	50	65
7/6	Bk. of Egypt, Ltd., £25	12½	19
5/	Bk. of Mauritius, Ltd.	10	10
18/	Bk. of N. S. Wales	20	38½
4 p.c.	Bk. of N. Zland. Gua. Stk.	100	103
6/	Bk. of Roumania, £20 Shs.	6	7½
2/6	Tarapaca & Ldn., Ltd., £10	5	3½
—	Bque. Fse. de l'Afri. du S.	100f	3½
f.12.50	Bque. Internatle. de Paris	20	24
6/	Brit. Bk. of S. America, Ltd., £20 Shares	10	10½
15/	Capital & Ctiés., L., £50	10	39
16/	Chart. of India, &c.	20	30½
10/	City, Ltd., £40 Shares	10	20½
18/	Colonial, £100 Shares	30	23
20/	Delhi and London, Ltd.	25	—
5/	German of London, Ltd.	10	11
25/	Hong-Kong & Shanghai	28½	45
4/	Imperl. of Persia	6½	3½
10/	Imperl. Ottoman, £20 Shs.	10	12½
9/	Intrnatl. of Ldn., Ld., £20	15	11
10/	Ionian, Ltd.	25	15
12/	Lloyds, Ltd., £50 Shs.	8	30
10/	Ldn. & Braziln. Ltd., £20	10	18
44/	Ldn. & County, Ltd., £30	20	104½
5/	Ldn. & Hanseatic, L., £20	10	11
22/6	Ldn. & Midland, L., £60	12½	53½
8/9	Ldn. & Provin., Ltd., £10	5	22½
39/	Ldn. & Riv. Plate, L., £25	15	54
2/1½	Ldn. & San Fcisco, Ltd.	7	4½
24/	Ldn. & Sth. West., L., £50	20	72
24/	Ldn. & Westmins., L., £100	20	57
3/	Ldn. of Mex. & S. Amer., Ltd., £10 Shs.	6	5½
15/	Ldn. Joint Stk., L., £100	15	34
9/7	Ldn., Paris & Amer., L. £20	16	26
1/7½	Merchant Bkg., L., £9	4	2½
6/3	Metropn, Ltd., £30 Shs.	5	13½
9/	National, Ltd., £50 Shs.	10	19½
4/5	Natl. of Mexico, $100 Shs.	$40	12
1/3	National of N. Z., L., £7½	2½	2½
8/	National S. Afric. Rep.	10	14½
18/10½	National Provcl. of Eng., Ltd., £75 Shs.	10½	49½
21/7½	Do. do. £60 Shs.	12	56
6/6	North Eastn., Ltd., £20 Shs	6	15
19/	Parr's, Ld., £100 Shs.	20	93½
12/6	Prov. of Ireland, L., £100	12½	28½
40/	Stand. of S. Afric., L., £100	25	68
12/6	Union of Australia, L., £75	25	30
4 p.c.	Do. do. Ins. Stk. Dep. 1900	100	103
15/6	Union of Ldn., Ltd., £100	15½	35

BREWERIES AND DISTILLERIES.

Div.	Name.	Paid.	Price.
4½	Albion Prp. 1 Mt. Db. Sk.	100	115
4	All Saints', L., Db. Sk. Rd.	100	99
6	Allsopp, Ltd	100	166
6	Do. Cum. Pref	100	160
4½	Do. Deb. Stk., Red.	100	117
3½	Do. Deb. Stk., Red.	100	103
4½	Alton & Co., L., Db., Rd	100	106
4½	Do. Mt. Bds., 1896	100	105
8/	Arnold, Perrett, Ltd.	10	7
6	Do. Cum. Pref.	10	10
4½	Do. 1 Mt. Db. Stk., Rd.	100	106

Breweries, &c. (*continued*):—

Div.	Name.	Paid.	Price.
5½	Arrol, A., & Sons, L., Cum. Pref. Shs.	10	10½
4½	Do. 1 Mt. Db. Stk., Rd.	100	106
6	Backus, 1 Mt. Db., Red.	100	89½
4	Barclay, Perk., L., Cu. Pf.	10	11½
3½	Do. Mt. Db. Stk., Red.	100	111
—	Barnsley, Ltd.	10	11
6	Do. Cum. Pref.	10	13
1/	Barrett's, Ltd	2½	1½
1/3	Do. 5 p.c. Pref.	2½	2½
3/	Barthelomay, Ltd.	10	4
8	Do. Cum. Pref.	10	8½
6	Do. Deb.	100	102½
5	Bass, Ratcliff, Ltd., Cum. Pref. Stk. †	100	147½
4½	Do. Mt. Db. Stk., Rd.	100	126
4	Bell, John, Ltd., 1 Mt. Deb. Stk., Red.	100	108
2/6	Benskin's, L., Cum. Pref.	5	5½
4½	Do. 1 Mt. Db. Stk Red.	100	—
4½	Do. "B" Deb. Sk, Rd.	100	—
7/	Bentley's Yorks., Ltd.	10	11
6	Do. Cum. Pref.	10	12½
4½	Do. Mt. Debs., Red	100	100
4½	Do. do. 1 92, Red.	100	100
—	Bieckert's, Ltd.	20	2
5	Do. Debs., Red.	100	57½
—	Birmingham., Ld., 6 p.c. Cum. Pref.	5	3½
4½	Do. Mt. Debs., Red.	30	40½
5½	Boardman's, Ld., Cm. Pf.	10	8½
4½	Do., Perp. 1 Mt. Db. Sk. †	100	102½
4½	Brakspear, L., 1 D. Stk. Rd	100	109
4	Brandon's, L., 1 D. Stk. R. †	100	108½
17/	Bristol (Georges) Ltd.	10	47
6	Do. Cum. Pref.	10	18
5	Do. Mt. Db. Sk. 1888 Rd.	100	115½
—	Bristol United, Ltd.	10	[illegible]
6	Do. Cum. Pref.	10	16½
4½	Do. Db. Sk. Rd.	100	128
5½	Buckley's, L., C. Pre-prf.	10	11
4½	Do. 1 Mt. Db. Stk. Rd.	100	106½
4	Bullard & Sns, L., D. Sk. R.	100	107
6	Bushell, Watk., L., C. Pf.	10	13½
4½	Do. 1 Mt. Db. Sk. Rd.	100	112
5	Camden, Ltd., Cum. Pref.	10	11½
4½	Do. 1 Mt. Db. Sk. Rd.	100	109
5½	Cameron, Ltd., Cm. Pf.	10	13½
4½	Do. Mort. Deb. Stk.	100	108
3½	Do. Perp. Mt. Db. Sk.	100	100½
5	Cam'bell, J'stone, L., C. Pf.	5	5
4½	Do. 4½ p.c. 1 Mt. Db. Sk.	100	105
4	Campbell, Praed, L., Per. 1 Mort. Deb. Stk.	100	106
4	Cannon, L., Mt. Db. Stk.	100	109
4	Do. "B" Deb. Stk.	100	105
5	Castlemaine, L., 1 Mt. Db.	100	94
3½	Charrington, Ltd., Mort. Deb. Stk. Red.	100	107
2/	Cheltnhm. Orig., Ltd.	5	7
6	Do. Cum. Pref.	5	8
4	Do. Debs. Red.	100	107
10/	Chicago, Ltd.	10	3½
6	Do. Debs.	100	87½
—	Cincinnati, Ltd.	10	½
8	Do. Cum. Pref.	10	1½
10/	City of Baltimore	10	4
16/	Do. 8 p.c. Cum. Pref	10	8
14/	City of Chicago, Ltd.	10	1½
8	Do. Cum. Pref.	10	6½
8	City of London, Ltd.	100	210½
5	Do. Cum. Pref.	100	140
4	Do. Mt. Deb. Stk., Rd.	100	112½
2/6	Colchester, Ltd.	5	4½
7	Do. Pref.	5	6½
4½	Do. Deb. Stk., Red.	100	110
5	Combe, Ltd., Cum. Pref.	10	14½
4	Do. Mt. Db. Stk, Rd.	100	112
3½	Do. Perp. Deb. Stk.	100	107
5	Comm'cial, L., D. Sk., Rd.	100	108½
5	Courage, L., Cm. Pref. Shs.	100	139½
4	Do. Irr. Mt. Deb. Stk.	100	130
3½	Do. Irr. "B" Mt. Db. Sk.	100	106
6	Daniell & Sons, Ltd.	10	7
7	Do. Cum. Pref.	10	12
4½	Do. 1 Mt. Perp. Db. Sk.	100	108½
4½	Do. "B" Deb. Stk.	100	99
10d.	Dartford, Ltd.	5	4½
10d.	Do. Cum. Pref.	5	5½
4	Do. 1 Mt. Db. Sk. Rd.	100	101
4	Davenport, Ld., 1 D. Stk. †	100	101½
10/	Denver United, Ltd.	10	3½
8	Do. Cum. Pref.	10	8½
6	Do. Debs.	100	96½
4½	Deuchar, L., 1 D. Sk., Rd.	100	107
8/	Distillers, Ltd.	10	24
4½	Do. Mt. Db. Stk., Rd.	100	115½
—	Dublin Distillers, Ltd.	5	1½
6/	Do. Cum. Pref.	5	4½
4½	Do. Irr. Deb. Stk.	100	—
5	Eadie, Ltd., Cum. Pref.	10	11½
4	Do. Irr. 1 Mt. Db. Sk.	100	108
10/	Edinbgh. Utd., Ltd.	10	13
6	Do. Cum. Prf.	10	13½
5	Do. 1 Mt. Dbs. †	100	110½
4	Eldridge, Pope, L. D. St. R.	100	110
3/	Emerald & Phœnix, Ltd.	10	1½
8	Do. Cum. Pref.	10	6
6	Empress Ltd., C. Pf.	10	11½
4½	Do. Mt. Deb. Stk.	100	105
10/	Farnham, Ltd.	10	15½
6	Do. Cum. Pref.	10	15
	Fenwick, L., 1 D. Sk., Rd.	100	103
	Flower & Sons, Irr. D. Sk.	100	111
4	Friary, L., 1 Db. Stk., Rd. †	100	105½
4	Do. 1 "A" Db. Sk., Rd	100	102
4½	Groves, L., 1 Db. Sk., Rd	100	108
24	Guinness, Ltd.	100	590
6	Do. Cum. Prf. Stk.	100	192½
3	Do. Deb. Stk., Red.	100	123
6	Hall's Oxford L., Cm. Pf.	5	5½
6/	Hancock, Ld., Cm. Pf. Ord.	10	14
	Do. Def. Ord.	10	17½

Breweries, &c. (*continued*) :—

Div.	Name.	Paid.	Price.
6	Hancock, Ld., Cum. Pref.	10	15½
4	Do. 1 Deb. Stk., Rd.	100	113
5	Hoare, Ltd. Cum. Pref.	10	13½
5	Do. "A" Cum. Pref.	10	12½
4	Do. Mt. Deb. Stk., Rd.	100	111
3½	Do. do. do. Rd.	100	104
4/6	Hodgson's, Ltd.	5	9¾
5	Do. 1 Mt. Db., Red.	—	120½
4	Do. 2 Mt. Db., 1906	—	102
4½	Hopcraft & N., Ltd., 1 Mt. Deb. Stk., Red.	100	102
5	Huggins, Ltd., Cm. Prf.	10	12½
4½	Do. 1st D. Stk. Rd.	100	112
4½	Do. "B" Db. Stk. Rd.	100	110
8/	Hull, Ltd.	10	17
7	Do. Cum. Pref.	10	15
4½	Ind, Coope, L., D.Sk., Rd.	100	119
4	Do. "B" Mt. Db. Stk. Rd.	100	115
8/	Indianapolis, Ltd.	10	3½
8	Do. Cm. Prf.	10	9
5/	Jones, Frank, Ltd.	10	4
7½	Do. Cum. Pref.	10	8
5	Do. 1st Mort. Debs.	100	94½
4/	J. Kenward & Ct., Ltd.	5	5¾
4½	Kingsbury, L., 1 D.Sk., Rd	100	—
4	Lacon, L., D. Stk., Red.	100	109
4	Do. Irrd. "B" D. Sk.	100	107
4/	Lascelles, Ltd.	5	10¾
6	Do. Cum. Pref.	5	7½
5	Leney, Ltd., Cum. Pref.	10	11½
4	Do. 1 Mt. Db. Stk. Rd.	100	104
17/	Lion, Ltd., £25 shares	17	50½
6/	Do. New £10 shares	6	17½
6	Do. Perp. Pref.	20	31
4	Do. B. Mt. Db. Sk. Rd.	100	110
4½	Lloyd & Y., Ltd., 1 Mt. Deb. Stk., Rd.	100	98½
4½	Locke & S., Ltd., Irr. 1st Mt. Deb. Stk.	100	100
4½	Lovibond, Ltd., 1st Mt. Deb. Stk., Rd.	100	102½
8/	Manchester, Ltd.	10	17½
7	Do. Cum. Pref.	10	17
5	Marston, J., L., Cm. Prf.	10	10¾
4	Do. 1 Mt. Db. Sk., Rd.	100	101½
9/	Massey's Burnley, Ltd.	10	16
6	Do. Cum. Pref.	10	14½
4½	McCracken, Ltd., 1 Mt. Deb., 1908	100	64
5	McEwan, Ltd., Cm. Pref.	10	15
5	Meux, Ltd., Cum. Pref.	10	14½
4	Do. Mt. Db. Stk. Red.	100	111
4½	Michell & A., Ltd., 1 Mt. Deb. Stk. Red	100	105
4½	MileEndDist. Db. Sk. Rd.	100	108
—	Milwaukee & Chic., Ltd.	10	1½
4/	Do. Cum. Pref.	10	6¾
4½	Michell, Toms, L., Db.	50	55
6	Morgan, Ltd., Cum. Pref.	10	14½
10/	Nalder & Coll., Ltd.	10	32
6	Do. Cum. Pref.	10	16
4½	Do. Deb. Red.	100	113
3/	New Beeston, Ltd.	5	4½
2/9	Do. Cum. Pref.	5	4¾
4	Do. Mt. Deb. Stk. Red.	100	96½
12/	Newcastle, Ltd.	10	20
6	Do. Cum. Pref.	10	15
5	Do. 1 Mt. Deb., 1911	100	110½
4	Do. "A" Deb. Stk. Red.	100	105
6/	New England, Ltd	10	5
8	Do. Cum. Pref.	10	9¾
6	Do. Debs. Red	100	104½
4	New London, L., 1 D.Sk.	100	104
7/2	New Westminster, Ltd	4	10½
2/4½	Do. Pref.	4	6½
—	New York, Ltd.	10	1
—	Do. 8 p.c. Cum. Pref.	10	3½
6	Do. 1 Mt. Deb. Red.	100	83½
5	Noakes, Ld., Cum. Pref.	10	12
4	Do. 1 Mt. Db. Stk., Rd.	100	106
4½	Norfolk, L., "A" D.Sk. Rd.	100	106
10/	Northampton, Ld.	10	17
7	Do. Cum. Pref.	10	15½
6	Do. Cum. Pref.	10	13
5	Do. 1 Mt. Per. Db.Sk.	100	127
4	Nth. East., L., 1 D.Sk. Rd.	100	102
4½	N. Worcesters., L. Per. 1 Mort. Deb. Stock	100	93½
6	Nottingham, L., Cm. Prf.	10	11½
5	Do. 1 Mt. Deb. Stk., Red.	100	112
17/4	Do. "B" do. Red.	50	111½
6/	Ohlsson' Cape, Ld.	5	16½
7	Do. Cum. Pref.	5	8½
4½	Do. 2nd Cum. Pref.	5	5¾
5	Do. Deb. Stk., Red.	100	112
4½	Oldfield, L., 1 Mt. Db. Stk.	100	104
6	Page & Overt., L., Cm. Prf.	10	13½
4½	Do. 1 Mt. Dbs., Red.	100	108
10/	Parker's Burslem, Ltd.	10	25½
6	Do. Cum. Pref.	10	15
4	Do. 1 Mt. Db. Stk., Red.	100	113
4	Persse, Ld., 1 Mt. Db. Rd.	100	93
4	Phipps, L., Irr. 1 Db. Stk.	100	115
5	Plymouth, L., Min. Cu. Pf.	10	13½
4½	Do. Mt. Deb. Stk., Red.	100	104½
4½	Pryor, Reid, L., 1 D.S., R.	100	105½
5	Reid's, Ld., Cm. Pref. Stk.	100	137½
4	Do. Mt. Deb. Stk., Red.	100	111
3½	Do. "B" Mt. Db. Stk., Rd.	100	103
5	Rhondda Val., L., Cu. Pf.	10	11
4½	Do. 1 Mt. Deb. Stk., Rd.	100	109
5	Robinson, Ld., Cum. Pref.	10	11½
4½	Do. 1 Mt. Perp. Db. Stk.	100	112
4/	Rochdale, Ltd.	10	5½
4½	Do. 1 Mt. Deb. Stk.	100	96½
7	Royal, Brentford, Ltd.	10	19
	Do. Cum. Pref.	10	14
4½	Do. 1 Mt. Dbs. Red	100	112
6/	St. Louis, Ltd.	10	4
8	Do. Cum. Pref.	10	8¾
14/	St. Pauli, Ltd.	10	10
7	Do. Cum. Pref.	10	12
4½	Salt (T.), L., 1 Db. Sk. Rd.	100	111
4½	Do "B" Db. Stk. Red.	100	108

Breweries, &c. (*continued*) :—

Div.	Name.	Paid.	Price.
6/7	San Francisco, Ltd.	10	¼
8/	Do. 8 p.c. Cum. Pref.	10	¾
4½	Savill Bra., L., D. Sk. Rd.	100	117
4½	Scarboro., Ltd., 1 Db. Stk.	100	104
4	Shaw (Hy.), Ltd., 1 Mt. Db. Stk., Red.	100	104
22/	Showell's, Ltd.	10	32½
7	Do. Cum. Pref.	10	17½
3/	Do. Gun. Shs.	5	7½
4½	Do. Mt. Db. Stk., Red.	100	—
4	Simonds, L., 1 D. Sk., Rd.	100	111
5½	Simson & McP., L., Cu. Pf.	10	9½
4½	Do. 1 Mt. Deb. Stk.	100	100
12/	Smith, Garrett, L., £20Shs	10	15¾
5	Do. Cum. Pref.	20	26
4½	Do. Mt. Db. Stk., Red.	100	—
5	Smith's, Tadcster, L., CPf	10	11¾
4½	Do. Deb. Stk., Red.	100	112
4	Do. Deb. Stk., Red.	100	108
4½	Star, L., 1 M. Db. Stk., Rd.	100	104
4	Steward & P., L., 1 D. Sk.	100	113
9/	Strettons Derby, Ltd.	10	13½
6	Do. Cum. Pref.	10	13
4	Do. Irr. 1 Mt. Db. Stk.	100	104½
4½	Strong, Romsey, L., 1 D.S.	100	114
5	Stroud, L., Db. Sk., Rd.	100	111½
4½	Tadcaster To'er, L., D.Sk.	100	112
8/	Tamplin, Ltd	10	22
6	Do. Cum. Pref.	100	15
4	Do. "A" Db. Sk., Rd.	10	107
6	Thorne, Ltd., Cum. Pref.	10	14½
4	Do. Deb. Stk., Red.	100	104½
15/	Threlfall, Ltd.	10	49
6	Do. Cum. Pref.	10	16½
5	Do. 1 Mt. Dbs., Red.	100	116
4	Tollemache, L., D. Sk. Rd.	100	105
4	Truman, Hanb., D. Sk., R.	100	110
3	Do. "B" Mt. Db. Sk., Rd.	100	95
10/	United States, Ltd.	10	9
8	Do. Cum. Pref.	10	12
6	Do. 1 Mt. Deb.	100	107½
6/	Walker & H., Ld., Cm. Prf.	10	11½
4½	Do. 1 Mt. Deb. Stk., Red.	100	107
5	Walker, Peter, Ld. Cm. Prf.	10	14
4	Do. 1 Mt. Dbs. Red.	100	111
4	Wallingford, L., D.Sk. Rd.	100	107
6	Watney, Ld., Cm. Prf. Sk.	100	170
5	Do. Mt. Db. Sk., Rd.	100	117
4½	Do. "B" Mt. Db. Sk., Rd.	100	111
5	Watney, D., Ld., Cm. Prf.	10	12½
4½	Do. 1 Mt. Db. Stk.	100	108
5	Wenlock Ltd., Pref.	10	12
4	Do. 1 Mt. Db. Sk., Rd.	100	108
5	West Cheshire, L., Cu. Pf.	10	10¾
4	Do. Irred. 1 Mt. Db. Sk.	100	100
4½	Whitbread, L., Cu. Pf. Sh.	100	124½
4	Do. Db. Stk., Red.	100	112
3½	Do. "B" Db. Stk., Rd.	100	101
9/	Wolverhmpton & D. Ld.	10	16
6	Do. Cum. Pref.	10	13
4½	Do. 1 Mt. Dbs., Red.	100	108
5½	Worthington, Ld., Cm. Prf.	10	15½
5½	Do. Cum. "B" Pref.	10	13½
4½	Do. Mt. Db. Sk., Rd.	100	113
3½	Do. Irr. "B" Db. Stk.	100	104
10/	Yates's Castle, Ltd.	10	12½
5	Do. Cum. Pref.	10	11
5	Younger W., L., Cu. Pf. Sh.	100	137½

CANALS AND DOCKS.

Last Div.	Name.	Paid.	Price.
4	Birmingham Canal	100	146
—	E. & W. India Dock	100	21½
4	Do. Deb. Stk.	100	112
85/	Do. Def. Deb. Stk.	100	90
3½	Do. 1st Mt. Certs.	100	111
4	Do. Mt. Bds. (1885)	—	101
40/	G. Junction Ord. Shs.	100	151½
6/	Do. do. Pref.	10	19
4½	King's Lynn Per. Db. Stk.	100	117½
2½	Leeds & Lpool Canal	100	68
2½	Lndn & St. Kath. Dks.	100	58
4½	Do. Pref.	100	138½
4½	Do. Pref., 1878	100	134½
4½	Do. Pref., 1882	100	130
4	Do. Deb. Stk.	100	135
—	Mchester Ship C. 5 p.c. Pf.	10	1½
3½	Do. 1st Perp. Mt. Deb.	100	98
—	Milford Dks. Db. Stk. "A"	100	20
2	Millwall Dk.	100	61
5	Do. Perp. Pref.	100	145½
4½	Do. Pref.	100	108½
5	Do. New Per. Prf., 1887	100	128½
5	Do. Per. Deb. Stk.	100	152½
4/	Newhaven Har.	10	14½
2	N. Metropolitan	100	65
5	Sharpness Nw. Pf. "A" Sk.	100	144½
4	Do. Deb. Stk.	100	120½
4	Sheffield & S. Yorks Nav. 4½ p.c. Pref. Stk.	100	117½
36.432	Suez Canal	20	135½
5	Surrey Comcl. Dck., Ord.	100	150½
5	Do. Min. 4 p.c. Pref. "A"	110	152½
5	Do. Pref. "B"	100	150½
5	Do. do. "C"	100	150
5	Do. do. "D"	100	145½
4½	Do. Deb. Stk.	100	154½

COMMERCIAL, INDUSTRIAL, &c.

Last Div.	Name.	Paid.	Price.
5	Accles, L., 1 Mt. Db., Red.	100	87½
5/	Aërated Bread, Ltd.	1	12¾
2	African Gold Recovery, L.	1	¾
2/	Aluminium, L., "A" Shs.	1	2½
4½	Do. 1 Mt. Db. Stk., Red.	100	99
5½	Amelia Nitr., L., 1 Mort. Deb., Red.	100	84½
7/	Anglo-Chil. Nitrate, Ltd., Cum. Pref.	10	7½
4½	Do. Cons. Mt. Bds., Red.	100	82½
4½	Anglo-Russian Cotton, Ld., 1 Charge Debs., Red.	100	99
11/3	Angus (G., & Co., L.), £10	7½	17
6/	Apollinaris, Ltd.	10	12¾
5/	Do. 5 p.c. Cum. Pref.	10	11½
4	Do. Irred. Deb. Stock	100	108
6/	Appleton, French, & S., L.	5	½
3/	Argentine Meat Pres., L., 7 p.c. Pref.	10	2½
5	Argentine Refinry, Db. Rd.	100	98
2/2	Armstrong, Whitw., Ltd.	1	3
4	Do. Cum. Pref.	5	6½
5	Artisans', Labr. Dwllgs., L.	100	130½
4½	Do. Non-Cm. Prf., 1879	100	132½
4½	Do. do. 1884	100	132½
—	Asbestos & Asbestic, Ltd.	10	9
2/7½	Ashley-grdns., L., C. Prf.	5	6½
4½	Do. 1 Mt. Deb. Stk.	100	115½
5/	Assam Rly. & Trdng., L., 8 p.c. Cum. Pref. "A"	10	15
—	Do. Deferrd. "B" Shs.	1	4½
—	Do. do. (iss. f. pd)	1	3½
8/	Do. Cum. Pre-Prf. "A"	10	15
6/	Do. New Pref.	10	11½
5	Do. Debs., Red.	100	107
5	Do. Red. Mort. Debs.	100	109
6	Aust'lian Pastrl, L., Cu. Pf.	10	7½
6d.	Aylesbury Dairy, Ltd.	1	1½
4	Do. 4 p.c. Mt. Dbs.	100†	104½
20/	Babcock & Wilcox, Ltd.	10	32
6	Do. 6 p.c. Cm. Prf.	10	16½
8	Baker (Chs.), L., Cm. Pf.	5	8¾
8	Do. "B" Cm. Pref.	5	7¾
8d.	Barker (John), Ltd.	1	2¾
5½	Do. Cum. Pref.	5	7½
4½	Do. Irred. 1 Mt. Db. Stk.	100	132
—	Barnagore Jute, Ltd.	5	3½
5	Do. Cum. Pref.	5	4¾
7½d.	Belgravia Dairy, Ltd.	1	1½
5/	Bell (R.) & Co., Ltd.	5	3½
1/	Bell's Asbestos, Ltd.	1	¾
5	Do. Mt. Db. Bds., Rd.	100	103
10/	Bengal Mills, Ltd.	10	11½
6/	Do. 5 p.c. Cum. Prf.	10	10½
2/5	Benson (J. W.) L., Cm. Pf.	10	10½
12/4	Do. Perp. Mt. Db. Stk.	100	103½
6	Bergvik, L., 6 p.c. Cm. Pf.	10	12½
10/	Do. Dfd.	10	9
4½	Do. 1 Dbs., Red.	100	103½
5/	Birm'ham Vinegar, Ltd.	5	10
5	Do. Cum. Pref.	5	5½
4½	Do. 1 Mt. Db. Stk., Rd.	100	105
5	Bonke (A.) L., 5 p.c. Cu. Pf.	10	10½
2/6	Bodega, Ltd.	5	8
4½	Do. Mt. Deb. Stk., Rd.	100	111
8/	Bottomley & Brs., Ltd.	10	6½
6/	Do. 6 p.c. Pt.	10	9½
8½d.	Bovril, Ltd.	1	1 1/16
—	Do. Def.	1	¾
6¾d.	Do. Cum. Pref.	1	1½
4½	Do. Deb. Stk.	100	103
6/4½	Bradbury, Gretrex., Ltd., £10 share	8	14
5/	Do. 5 p.c. Cum. Pref.	10	13½
5/	Brewers' Sugar, L., 5 p.c. Cum. Pref.	10	10¾
2/6	Brighton Grd. Hotel, Ld.	5	3½
4	Do. Mt. Db. Stk., Red.	100	102½
5	Bristol Hotel & Palm. Co., Ltd. 1st Mt. Red. Deb.	100	107
9½d.	British & Bengton's. Tea Tr. Asc., Ltd.	1	1½
5	Do. Cum. Prf.	5	5½
—	British Deli & Lgkat. Tobacco, Ltd.	1	1
—	Do. Cum. Prf.	1	¾
—	British Tea Table, Ltd.	1	2½
5½	Do. Cum. Pref.	1	1½
2/6	Brooke, Ben., & Co., Ltd., Cum. Pref.	5	5¾
7/6	Brooke, Bond & Co., Ltd.	5	20½
6	Brown Brs., L., Cum. Pref.	5	6
6/	Browne & Eagle, Ltd.	10	14
5	Do. Cum. Pref.	10	13
4	Do. Mrt. Db. Sk., Red.	100	109
20/	Brunner, Mond, & Co., Lt.	10	42
7/	Do. £10 shares	3½	16½
7	Do. Cum. Pref.	10	18
7	Do. £10 shares	5	8½
10/	Bryant & May, Ltd.	5	19½
2/	Bucknall, H., & Sons, Lt.	5	8
6	Do. Cum Pref.	5	8
4/	Burke, E. & J., Ltd.	5	7½
6	Do. Cum. Pref.	5	7½
6	Do. Irred. Deb. Stk.	100	155
1/	Burlington Htls. Co., Ltd	1	1½
5	Do. Cum. Pref.	1	1½
4	Do. Perp. Deb. Stk.	100	104½
2/4	Bush, W. J., & Co., Ltd., Cum. Pref.	5	5¾
36/8	Do. 1 Deb. Stk., Red.	100	104
5½	Callard, Stewart, & Watt, Ltd., Cum. Pref.	1	1½
4/	Callender's Cable L., Shs.	5	8½
4½	Do. 1 Deb. Stk., Red.	100†	109½
—	Campbell, R., & Sons, Lt.	3	2½
6	Cantareira Water, Bd., Rd	100	99
5	Do. (2nd Issue)	100	92
4	Cartavio Sugar, Ltd., 6 p.c. 1st Debs., Red.	80	80
4/6	Cassell & Co., Ltd., £10	9	18
5	Causton, Sir J., & Sons, Ltd., Cum. Pref.	10	13½

Commercial, &c. (*continued*) :—

Last Div.	Name.	Paid.	Pr.
4	Cent. Prod. Mkt. of B.A. 1st Mt. Str. Debs.	100	77½
4	Chappell & Co., Ltd., Mt. Deb. Stk. Red.	100	102
6/	Chicago & N.W. Gran. 8 p.c. Cum. Pref.	10	2½
—	Chicago Packing & Prov.	10	6
8	Do. Cum. Pref.	10	10
6/	City Offices, Ltd	3(½	13
3½	Do. Mt. Deb. Stk.	100	108½
7/2½	Cy. London Real Prop., Ltd., £25 shs.	12	19
4/6	Do. £12½ shs.	7½	13½
3½	Do. Deb. Stk. Red.	100	108½
3½	Do. Deb. Stk. Red.	100	106½
3	Do.	100	101½
4/	Cy. of Santos Imprvts., Ltd., 7 p.c. Pref.	10	8½
20/	Clay, Bock, & Co., Ltd.	10	8
8	Do. Cum. Pref.	10	11
6	Do. Mort. Deb.	100	106½
20/	Coats, J. & P., Ltd.	10	61½
6	Do. Cum. Pref.	10	18
4½	Do. Deb. Stk. Red.	100	111½
9½d.	Coburg Hotel, Ltd	1	1½
4	Do. Deb. Stk. Red.	100	102
6	Colonial Consign & Dis., Ltd., Cum. Pref.	5	4½
4½	Do. 1st Mort. Debs.	100	97½
—	Colorado Nitrate, Ltd.	5	¾
4/	Co. Gén. des Asphtes. de F., Ltd	6	6½
5	Do. Non-Cm. Prf.	—	5½
5	Cook, J. W., & Co., Ltd., Cum. Pref.	5	5¾
5	Cook, T., & Son, Egypt, Ltd., 1st Mt. Deb. Red.	100	110½
—	Cork Co., Ltd., 6 p.c. Cum. Pref.	5	2½
5	Cory, W., & Sn, L., Cu. Pf.	5	6
4	Do. 1st Deb. Stk. Red.	100	109
8½d.	Crisp & Co., Ltd	1	1¾
5½	Do. Cum. Pref.	1	1½
—	Crompton & Co., Ltd., 7 p.c. Cum. Pref.	5	
5	Do. 1st Mt. Reg. Deb.	—	11
4/6	Crossley, J., & Sons, Ltd.	5	
5	Do. Cum. Pref.	5	
—	Crystal Pal. Ord. "A" Stk.	100	
—	Do. "B" Red. Stk	100	2
6	Do. 6 p.c. 1st 1887 Deb. Stk. Red.	100	116½
—	Do. 6 p.c. 2nd 1887 Deb. Stk. Red.	100	47½
—	Do. 6 p.c. 3rd 1887 Deb. Stk. Red.	100	16½
3	Do. 3 p.c. 1st 1895 Deb. Stk.	100	95½
—	Daimler Motor, Ltd	10	5
4/	Dalgety & Co., £20 Shs.	5	5½
4½	Do. Deb. Stk	100	123
4	Do.	100	114
7/	De Keyser's Ryl. Htl., L.	10	13
5	Do. Cum. Pref.	10	11½
4	Do. Deb. Stk., Red.	100	100
6	Denny, H., & Sons, Ltd., Cum. Pref.	10	15
5/3	Devas, Routledge & Co., L.	7	8½
5	Dickinson, J., & Co., L., Cum. Pref. Stk.	100	123
4½	Domin. Cottn. Mls., Ltd. Mt. Stg. Dbs.	100	97
6/	Dorman, Long & Co., L.	5	4½
—	Eastmans, Ltd.	10	3
12/	Do. 8 p.c. Cum. Pref.	10	10½
2/6	E. C. Powder, Ltd	3	5½
1/9½	Edison & Swn Utd. Elec. Ltd., "A" £5 Shs.	3	2¾
2/9½	Do. fully-paid	5	5
4½	Ekman Pulp & Ppr. Co., Ltd., Mt. Deb., Red.	100	95
1/1½	Electric Construc., Ltd.	2	2½
7	Do. Cum. Pref.	2	3½
10/	Eley Bros., Ltd.	10	40
—	Elmore's Cop. Deptg., L.	1	¾
—	Elmore's Wire Mnfg., L.	2	½
—	Elysée Pal. Hotel Co., L.	5/	
5 p.c.	Do. 5 p.c. £100 Db., Rd.	70	70
8½d.	Evans, Ben., & Co., Ltd.	1	1
5	Do. 1 Mt. Db. Sk., Rd.	100	104
8½d.	Evans, D. H., & Co., L.	1	2½
6	Do. Cum. Pref.	1	1½
4½	Do. 1 Mt. Db. Sk., Rd.	100	111
2/1	*Evening News*, L., 5 p.c. Cum. Pref.	5	5¾
5/3	Evered & Co., L., £10 Sh.	7	13½
7/6	Do.	10	19½
4	Fairbairn Pastoral Co., Aust., L., 1 Mt. Db., Rd.	100	102
6	Fairfield Shipbldg., Ltd., Cum. Pref.	10	10
4½	Do. Mort. Deb. Stk.	100	107½
6/	Farmer & Co., Ld., 6 p.c. Cum. Pref.	10	13¾
10	Field, J. C. & J., Ltd.	10	10
14/	Do. 7 p.c. Cum. Pref.	10	14
9d.	Fordham, W.B., & Sns, Ld.	1	2
5/6	Fore-st. Warehouse, Ltd.	11	9½
4	Do. Regd. Debs., Rd.	100	103½
2/6	Foster, M. B. & Sons, Ltd.	4	5½
5	Do. Pref.	10	11½
7/	Foster, Porter, & Co., L.	10½	17
4	Fowler, J., & Co. (Leeds), Ltd., 1 Mt. Deb., Red.	100	100½
3/	Fraser & Chalmers, Ltd.	3	1¾
4½	Free, Rodwell & Co., Ltd., Deb Stk.	100	104½
6¼d.	Furness, T., & Co., Ltd., 5½ p.c. Cum. Pref.	1	1
4½	Gartside & Co. (of Manchstr), L., 1 Mt. Db. Sk.	100	110
5	Genl. Hydraul. Power, L.	100	[illegible]

Commercial, &c. (continued):—

Last Div.	Name.	Paid.	Price.
2/	Gillman & Spencer, Ltd.	5	2½
6	Do. Pref.	5	4½
5	Do. Mort. Debs.	50	51
4	Goldsbro., Mort & Co., L., "A" Deb. Stk., Red.	100	72½
—	Do. 3 p.c. "B" Inc. Deb. Stk., Red.	100	17
22/	Gordon Hotels, Ltd.	10	21¼
5½	Do. Cum. Pref.	10	14¼
4½	Do. Perp. Deb. Stk.	100	136½
4	Do. do.	100	124½
—	Greenwich Inld. Linoleum Co., Ltd.	1	⅜
7	Greenwood & Batley, Ltd., Cum. Pref.	10	10
7½d.	Hagemann & Co., Ltd., 6 p.c. Cum. Pref.	1	1⅛
—	Hammond, Ltd.	10	¼
—	Do. 8 p.c. Cum. Pref.	10	2
—	Do. 6 p.c. Cum. Inc. Stk. Red.	100	52½
4	Hampton & Sons, Ltd., 4 p.c. 1 Mt. Db. St. Red.	100	106
	Hans Crescent Htl., L., 6 p.c. Cum. Pref.	5	3½
4	Do. 1 Mt. Deb. Stk.	100	85
5	Harmsworth, Ld., Cm. Pf.	1	1⅝
4/	Harrison, Barber, Ltd.	5	4¼
1/	Harrod's Stores, Ltd.	1	5
2/6	Do. Cum. Pref.	5	7½
5½	Hawaiian Comcl. & Sug. 1 Mt. Debs.	100	94½
5	Hazell, Watson, Ld., Cm. Pref.	10	12
6/	Henley's Teleg., Ltd.	10	22
7	Do. Pref. Shs.	10	19½
4½	Do. Mt. Db. Stk., Rd.	100	112½
6	Henry, Ltd.	10	12½
5	Do. Cum. Pref.	10	13½
4½	Do. Mt. Debs., Red.	50	53
6	Hepworth, Ld., Cm. Prf.	10	11½
6/	Herrmann, Ltd.	5	4½
—	Hildesheimer, Ltd.	3	1½
9½d.	Holbrn. & Frasca, Ltd.	1	2½
5	Do. Cum. Pref.	10	12½
4	Do. Deb. Stk.	100	113
6	Home & Col. Stres, Ltd., Cum. Pref.	5	7½
6	Hood & M.'s Stres., Ltd., Cum. Pref.	1	¾
—	Hook, C. T., Ltd.	10	4
7/2	Hornsby, Ltd., £10 Shs.	8	3
5/6	Do. 6 p.c. Cm. Pf. Sk.	100	90
—	Hotchks. Ordn., Ltd.	10	¾
—	Do. 7 p.c. Cm. Prf.	10	4½
5	Do. 1 Mt. Dbs., Rd.	100	95½
6	Htl. Cecil, Ld., Cm. Prf.	5	4½
4	Do. 1 Mt. D. Sk., R.	100	105½
8/	Howard & Bulgh, Ltd.	10	35
6	Do. Pref.	10	16
4	Do. Deb. Stk., Red.	100	107
4/	Howell, J., Ltd., £5 Shs.	4	9½
—	Howell & Js., Ld., £3½ Shs.	3	1
2/6	Humber, Ltd.	1	⅞
6	Do. Cum. Pref.	1	⅞
2/6	Hunter, Wilts., Ltd.	5	7
2/7	Hyam Clthg., Ltd., 5 p.c. Cum. Pref.	5	5¼
20/	Impl. Russn. Cotton, L.	5	5¼
5	Impd. Industl. Dwgs., Ld.	100	130½
6d.	Do. Defrd.	1	1¼
£1	Impd. Wood Pava., Ltd.	10	15
5/	Ind. Rubber, Gutta Per. Telegraph Works, Ltd.	10	23
4	Do. 1 Mt. Debs., Red.	100	105
6	Intern. Tea, Cum. Pref.	5	6½
7½d.	Jays, Ltd.	1	1½
5½	Do. Cum. Pref.	5	6½
8½d.	Jones & Higgins, Ltd.	1	2½
4½	Do. 1 Mt. Db. Sk., Rd.	100	113
5/	Kelly's Directory, Ltd., 5 p.c. Cum. Pref.	10	12½
4	Do. Mort. Db. Sk., Rd.	100	105
	Kent Coal Explrtn. Ltd.	1	½
5½d.	King, Howmann, Ltd.	1	1¼
4/	Kinloch & Co., Ltd.	5	8¼
6	Do. Pref.	5	7
5	Lady's Pictorial Pub., Ltd., Cum. Pref.	5	5
—	La Guaira Harb., Ltd., 7 p.c. Deb. Stk.	100	—
—	Do. 2 Mt. 7 p.c. Deb. Bds., Red.	100	—
4/	Lagunas Nitrate, Ltd.	5	2½
2/	Lagunas Syn., Ltd.	5	1½
5	Do. 1 Mt. Debs., Red.	100	80
—	L. Copais Ld., 1 Mt. 6 p.c. Debs., Red.	100	35½
3/	Lautaro Nitrate, Ltd.	5	4
5	Do. 1 Mt. Debs., Red.	—	98
9/	Lawes Chem. L., £10 shs.	9	5½
14/	Do. N. Cm. Min. Pref.	10	13
—	Leeds Forge, 7 p.c. Cm. Pf.	5	2½
5	Do. 1 Mt. Debs., Red.	50	44½
5	Lever Bros., L., Cm. Pf.	10	13
6	Liberty, L., 6 p.c. Cm. Pf.	10	14½
60/	Liebig's, Ltd.	20	76
5	Lilley & Sk., L., Cm. Pf.	5	5½
3/	Linoleum Manfg., Ltd.	5	23
3/	Linotype, Ltd., Pref.	5	5½
4/	Do. Def.	5	8
4/	Lister & Co., Ltd.	10	4½
5	Do. Cum. Pref.	10	8½
5/	Liverpool Nitrate	5	6½
—	Liverpool Warehsg., Ltd.	10	3½
5½	Do. Cum. Pref.	10	8½
4	Do. 1 Mt. Db. Stk., Rd.	100	105½
5½	Lockharts, Ltd., Cm. Pf.	1	1½
4/6	Ldn. & Til., Lightrage £10	9	5½
6/	Ldn. Comcl. Sale Rms., Ltd.	10	18
—	Do. 1 Mt. Deb. Stk., Red.	100	104
3	London Nitrate, Ltd.	5	2

Commercial, &c. (continued):—

Last Div.	Name.	Paid.	Price.
4/	London Nitrate, Ld. 8 p.c. Cm. Min. Pf.	5	3½
3/	London Pavilion, Ltd.	5	8
1/6	London, Produce Clg. Ho., Ltd., £10 Shares	2½	4
4/	London Stereos., Ltd.	5	3
6d.	Ldn. Un. Laun. L. Cm. Pf.	1	½
8½d.	Louise, Ltd.	1	½
5½	Do. Cum. Pref.	1	¾
5/	Lovell & Christmas, Ltd.	5	12
6	Do. Cum. Pref.	5	7½
4	Do. Mt. Deb. Stk., Red.	100	107
1/3	Lyons, Ltd.	1	2½
4½	Do. 1 Mt. Deb. Stk., Rd.	100	106½
10/	Machinery Trust, Ltd.	5	15
4½	Do. 4½ Deb. Stk.	100	105
6	MacLellan, L., Min. C. Pf.	10	7½
5	Do. 1 Mt. Debs., 1900	100	98½
—	McEwan, J. & Co., Ltd.	10	1½
6	Do. Mt. Debs., Red.	100	89½
8	McNamara, L., Cm. Pref.	10	9
7½d.	Maison Virot, Ltd.	1	1½
2/7	Do. 6 p.c. Cum. Pref.	5	4½
5/	Manbré Sacc., L., Cm. Pf.	10	12
15/	Mangan Brze., L., £10 Shs.	6	15½
3/	Mason & Mason, Ltd.	5	3½
6	Do. Cum. Pref.	5	5½
—	Maynards, Ltd.	1	¾
6	Do. Cum. Pref.	1	¾
9½d.	Mazawattee Tea, Ltd.	1	1½
5	Do. Cum. Pref.	5	5½
6	Mellin's Food Cum. Pref.	5	7
4½	Met. Ascn. Imp. Dwlgs. L.	100	109
3½	Do. 1 Mt. Deb. Stk.	100	97
5	Metro. Indus. Dwlgs., Ltd.	5	5
4	Do. do. Cum. Pref.	5	5½
5	Metro. Prop., L., Cm. Pf.	5	6½
4½	Do. 1st Mt. Debs. Stk.	100	110½
6	Mexican Cotton 1 Mt Db	100	97
4½	Mid. Class Dwlgs., L., Db.	100	120½
1/	Millars' Karri, Ltd.	1	2½
6	Do. Cum. Pref.	1	1½
5/	Milner's Safe, Ltd.	10	19½
[illegible]	Moir & Son, Ltd., Pref.	5	9
6	Morgan Cruc., L., Cm. Pf.	10	15
2/	Morris, B., Ltd.	3½	3½
—	Murray L. 5½ p.c. C. Pf.	5	5½
—	Do. 4½ 1 Mt. Db. Sk. Rd.	100	108
2/6	Natnl. Dwlgs., L., 5 p.c. Pf.	5	1
1/7½	Nat. Safe Dep., Ltd.	4	3½
6	Do. Cum. Pref.	1	1½
—	Native Guano, Ltd.	5	
5/	Nelson Bros., Ltd.	10	2½
5	Do. Deb. Stk., Red.	100	80½
4/	Neuchtel Asph., Ltd.	10	11
—	New Central Borneo, Ld.	1	—
10d.	New Darvel Tob., Ltd.	13/	1½
2/4½	New Explosives, Ltd.	3	2
5/3½	New Gd. Htl., Bham, L.	5	4
5½	Do. Pref.	5	4½
4	Do. 1 Mt. Db. Stk., Rd.	100	95½
—	New Julia Nitrate, Ltd.	10/	½
—	New Ldn. Borneo Tob., L.	16/	½
1/6	New Premier Cycle, Ltd.	1	½
6	Do. 6 p.c. Cum. Pref.	1	½
4½	Do. 4½ p.c. 1 Mt. Db. Rd	100	—
—	New Tamargl. Nitr., Ltd	1	½
—	Do. 8 p.c. Cum. Pref.	1	¾
6	Do. 6 p.c. 1 Mt. Dbs. Rd.	100	65½
3·78d.	Newnes, G., L., Cm. Prf.	1	1½
1/3	Nitr. Provision, Ltd.	2½	½
24/	Nobel-Dynam., Ltd.	10	18
—	North Brazn. Sugar, Ltd.	1	½
10/	Oakey, Ltd.	10	30
6	Do. Cum. Pref.	10	16
4/	Paccha Jazp. Nitr., Ltd.	5	1
5	Pac. Borax, L., 1 Db. Rd.	100	110
—	Palace Hotel, Ltd.	10	6
5½	Do. Cum. Pref.	10	9
4	Do. 1 Mt. Deb. Stk.	100	106
2/6	Palmer, Ltd.	5	1½
6	Do. Cum. Pref.	5	3½
9[illegible]d.	Paquin, Ltd.	1	1
6	Do. Cum. Pref.	5	4½
5½	Parnall, Ltd., Cum. Pref.	1	¾
4/6	Pawsons, Ltd., £10 Shs.	6	6½
4	Do. Mt. Debs., Red.	100	107
6	Pearks, G. & T., Ltd., 6 p.c. Cum. Pref.	1	¾
1/2½	Pears, Ltd.	1	1½
6	Do. Cum. Pref.	10	14½
5	Do. Deb. Stk.	100	129
5½	Pearson, C. A., L., Cu. Pf.	5	5
4/	Peebles, Ltd.	5	8
5	Do. Cum. Pref.	5	6½
4½	Do. Mt. Deb. Stk. Red.	100	112
5½	Peek Bros., Ltd., 1 Cum. Pref., Nos. 1-60,000	5	6½
3½	Do. 3½ p.c. 1 Db. Stk.	100	103½
7½d.	Pegamoid, Ltd.	1	¾
—	Phospho-Guano, Ltd.	5	2½
—	Pillsbury-W. Fl. Mills, L.	10	2
16/	Do. 8 p.c. Cum. Pref.	10	6½
6	Do. 1 Mort. Debs.	100	95½
7½d.	Plummer, Ltd.	1	1½
5	Do. Cum. Pref.	5	5½
15/	Price's Candle, Ltd.	16	40
6	Priest Marians, L., Cm. Pf.	1	1½
6	Pryce Jones, Ld., Cm. Pf.	5	7½
5	Do. Deb. Stk.	100	120½
10.8d.	Pullman, Ltd.	1	1½
6d.	Do. Cum. Pref.	1	1½
11[illegible]	Raleigh Cycle, Ltd.	1	½
6	Do. Cum. Pref.	1	¾
—	Recife Drnge. Ld. 1 Mt. Debs., R	100	19
6	Redfern, Ltd. Cum. Prf.	10	14
5	Ridgways, Ltd., Cu. Pf.	5	5½
—	R. Janeiro Cy. Imps., Ld.	25	9½
5	Do. Debs.	100	90
5	Do. 1882-1893	100	90
11/	R. Jan Fl. Mills, Ltd.	7	7
5	Do. 1 Mt. Debs., Rd.	100	94

Commercial, &c. (continued):—

Last Div.	Name.	Paid.	Price.
—	Riv. Plate Meat, Ltd.	5	3½
—	Do. Pref.	5	5
8½d.	Roberts, J. R., Ltd.	1	1½
5	Do. 1 Mt. Db. Sk., Rd.	100	112
8½d.	Roberts, T. R., Ltd.	1	2½
5	Do. Cum. Pref.	1	1½
3/	Rosario Nit., Ltd.	5	3½
5	Do. Debs., Red.	100	103
5	Do. Hunra. Debs.	—	101½
1/	Rover Cycle, Ltd.	1	¾
6/	Ryl. Aquarium, Ltd.	5	5½
6	Do. Pref.	5	6
5	Ryl. Htl., Edin., Cm. Pf.	1	1½
1/2½	Ryl. Niger, Ltd., £10 Sh.	2	2½
6/	Do.	10	14½
3/	Ruston, Proctor, Ltd.	10	11
4½	Do. 1 Mort. Debs.	100	104
6/	Sadler, Ltd.	12	7
—	Sal. Carmen Nit., Ltd.	5	4
9d.	Salmon & Gluck., Ltd.	1	1½
2/	Salt Union, Ltd.	10	1½
14/	Do. 7 p.c. Pref.	10	8
4½	Do. Deb. Stk.	100	108½
4½	Do. "B" Deb. Sk., Rd.	100	104½
—	San Donato Nit., Ltd.	5	¾
2/6	San Jorge Nit., Ltd.	5	3½
—	San Pablo Nit., Ltd.	5	¾
2/	San Sebastn. Nit., Ltd.	5	¾
1/	Sanitas, Ltd	1	2½
—	Sa. Elena Nit., Ltd.	5	¾
—	Sa. Rita Nit., Ltd.	5	2
10/	Savoy Hotel, Ltd.	10	19
7	Do. Pref.	10	16
4	Do. 1 Mt. Deb. Stk.	100	112½
5	Do. Debs., Red	100	102½
5	Do. & Ldn. For. Htl., Ltd., 5 p.c. Debs. Red.	100	99
1½d.	Schweppes, Ltd.	1	1⅛
—	Do. Def.	1	¾
5	Do. Cum. Pref.	1	1½
4	Do. Deb. Stk.	100	106
1/	Singer Cyc., Ltd.	1	¾
5½	Do Cum. Pref.	1	¾
—	Smokeless Pwdr., Ltd.	1	¾
5½d.	S. Eng. Dairies, Ltd., 6 p.c. Cum. Pref.	1	1½
—	Sowler Thos. L.	1	1
—	Do. 5½ Cm. Pf.	5	5½
3/6	Spencer, Turner, & Co. Ltd	5	8½
5	Do. Cum. Pref.	5	6½
5	Spicer, Ld., 5 p.c. Dbs. Rd.	100	65
4/	Spiers & Pond, Ltd.	10	20½
5	Do. 1 Mt. Debs., Red.	100	116½
5	Do. "A" Db. Stk., Rd.	100	110
5	Do. "B" 1 Db. Stk., Rd.	100	110
4	Do. Fd. "C" 1 Db. S., R.	100	103
5/	Spratt's, Ltd	5	13½
4	Do. Debs., 1914	—	105
5	Steiner Ld., Cm. Pf.	10	11½
4	Do. 1 Mt. Db. Sk. Rd.	100	106
7/	Stewart & Clydesdale, L.	10	15
6	Do. Cum. Pref.	10	15½
—	Swan & Edgar, L.	1	1½
1/3	Sweetmeat Automatic, L.	1	4
2/9	Teetgen, Ltd., Cum. Pref.	5	5½
12/	Teleg. Construction., Ld.	12	40½
5	Do. Db. Bds., Rd., 1899	100	103½
3/0½	Tilling, Ld. 5½ p.c. Cm. Prf.	5	6
4	Do. 4 p.c. 1 Dbs., Rd.	—	103
8½d.	Tower Tea, Ltd.	1	1½
5	Do. Cum. Pref.	5	5½
5	Travers, Ltd., Cum. Pref.	10	12½
4	Do. 1 Mt. Dbs., Rd.	100	103
6	Tucuman Sug., 1 Dbs., Rd.	100	100
4/	United Alkali, Ltd.	10	2½
7	Do. Cum. Pref.	10	9½
5	Do. Mt. Db. Stk., Rd.	100	111½
2½d.	United Horse Shoe, Ltd., Non-Cum. 8 p.c. Pref.	1	¾
5	Un. Kingm. Tea, Cm. Prf.	5	5
1/	Un. Lankat Plant., Ltd.	1	2½
2/	Un. Limmer Asphlte., Ld.	3	4½
5/	Val de Travers Asph., L.	10	14½
3/	V. den Bergh's, Ltd., Cm. Pref.	5	6½
6	Walkers, Park., L., C. Pf.	10	4
4½	Do. 1 Mt. Debs., Red.	100	90½
4/	Wallis, Thos. & Co., Ltd.	5	14
6	Do. Cum. Pref.	5	8½
5½	Waring, Ltd., Cum. Pref.	5	5½
4½	Do. 1 Mt. Db. Sk., Red.	100	111½
4½	Do. Irred. "B" Db. Stk.	100	104
12/	Waterlow, Dfd. Ord.	10	15½
12/	Do. Pref.	10	15½
—	Do. Cum. Pref.	10	10½
10/	Waterlow Bros. & L., Ld.	10	9½
9½d.	Welford, Ltd.	1	2½
4½	Do. Debs., Red.	100	107
4½d.	Welford's Surrey Dairies, Ltd.	1	1½
7½d.	West London Dairy, Ltd.	1	1
4½	Wharncliffe Dwllgs, L., Pf.	10	12
18/10	Do. 3 p.c. Irr. Mt. Db. Sk.	100	96
6d.	White, A. J., Ltd.	1	½
6	Do. 6 p.c. Cum. Pref.	1	½
4	White, J. Bazley, Ltd., 1 Mort. Debs., Red	100	96½
5	White, R., Ltd., 1 Mort. Deb. Stock, Red.	100	104½
5/	White, Tomkins, Ltd	10	12½
5	Do. Cum. Pref.	10	12½
6	White, W. N., L., Cm. Pf.	1	1
2/6	Wickens, Pease & Co., L.	5	2
6	Wilkie, Ltd., Cum. Pref.	10	16
3/6	Willans & Robinson, Ltd.	5	8½
6	Do. Cum. Pref.	5	7
4½	Do. 1 Mt. Db. Stk., Red.	100	107
7½d.	Williamsons, L., Cm. Prf.	1	1½
6	Winterbottm. Book Cloth, Ltd., Cum. Prf.	10	15
3/	Yates, Ltd.	5	6½
6	Do. Cum. Pref.	5	6½
	Young's Paraffin, Ltd.	4	1½

CORPORATION STOCKS-COLONIAL AND FOREIGN.

Per Cent.	Name.	Paid.	Price.
6	Auckland City, '72 1904-24	100	118
6	Do. Cons., '79, Red. 1930	100	128½
5	Do. Deb. Ln., '83..1934-8	100	116
6	Auckland Harb. Debs.	100	111½
5	Do. 1917	100	112
5	Do. 1936	100	116
5½	Balmain Boro' 1914	—	117
5	Boston City (U.S.)	100	100½
5	Do. 1902	100	107½
5	Brunswick Town 5 c. Debs. 1916-20	100	111
15/	B. Ayres City 6 p.c.	100	61
4½	Do. 4½ p.c.	100	79
5	Cape Town, City of	100	113
4	Do. 1943	100	113
4	Chicago, City of, Gold 1915	—	110
6	Christchurch 1926	100	128½
—	Cordoba City	100	17
5	Duluth (U.S.) Gold 1926	—	110
6	Dunedin (Otago) 1925	100	127½
6	Do. 1906	100	113
5	Do. Consols 1908	100	113
4	Durban Insc. Stk. 1944	100	111
4	Essex Cnty., N. Jersey 1926	100	114½
5	Fitzroy, Melbrne. 1916-19	100	110
5	Gisborne Harbour 1915	100	110½
4	Greymouth Harbour 1925	100	111
4	Hamilton 1934	100	108
5	Hobart Town 1918-30	100	116
4	Do. 1940	100	107
4½	Invercargill Boro. Dbs. 1936	100	113
6	Kimberley Boro., S. A. Dbs.	—	104
4	Launceston Twn. Dbs. 1916	100	107
6	Lyttleton, N.Z., Harb. 1929	100	128
4	Melbourne Bd. of Wks. 1921	100	109
5	Melb. City Debs. 1897-1907	100	107½
4	Do. Debs. 1908-27	100	113½
4	Do. Debs. 1915-20-22	100	108
5	Melbne. Harb. Bds., 1908-9	100	112
4½	Do. do. 1915	100	110
4	Do. do. 1918-21	100	106
4½	Melbrne. Tms. Dbs. 1914-16	100	113
4½	Do. Fire Brig. Db. 1921	100	109
5	Mexico City Stg.	100	91½
4	Moncton N. Bruns. City	100	104
4½	Montevideo	100	57
5	Montreal Stg.	100	108
5	Do. 1874	100	108
5	Do. 1879	100	106
3½	Do. 1933	100	104
3	Do. Perm. Deb. Stk.	100	98
4	Do. Cons. Deb. Stk. 1932	100	113
6	Napier Boro. Consolid. 1914	100	119
5	Napier Harb. Debs. 1920	100	115
5	Do. Debs. 1928	100	108
6	New Plymouth Harb. Debs. 1909	100	108
6	New York City 1901	—	107½
3½	Do. 1910-26	—	106½
4½	Nth. Melbourne Debs. 1-600 1921	100	105
5	Oamaru Boro. Cons. 1920	100	101
6	Do. Harb. Bds. (Reg.)	100	74
25/	Do. 6 p.c. (Bearer) 1919	100	35
6	Otago Harb. Deb. Reg.	100	105
6	Do. 1877	100	107
6	Do. 1881 1921	100	115
5	Do. Debs. 1921	100	107
5	Do. Cons. 1934	100	105
6	Ottawa City	100	109
6	Do. 1904	100	115½
4½	Do. Debs. 1913	100	112
6	Port Elizabeth Waterworks	100	113½
5	Port Louis	100	108
5	Prahran Debs. 1917	100	111
4	Do. Debs. 1919	100	105
6	Quebec C. Coupon. 1875 1905	100	112
6	Do. do. 1878 1908	100	116
4½	Do. Debs. 1914-18	100	108
4	Do. Debs. 1923	100	107
3½	Do. Cns. Rg. Stk., Red.	100	101
5	Richmond (Melb.) Dbs. 1917	100	113
4	Rio Janeiro City	100	59
4	Rome City	100	—
4	Do. 2nd to 8th Iss.	100	94
—	Rosario C.	100	26½
—	Do.	100	26½
4	St. Catherine (Ont.) 1926	100	103
4	St. John, N.B., Debs. 1934	—	104
4½	St. Kilda (Melb) Dbs. 1918-21	100	104
4	St. Louis C. (Miss.) 1911	100	104
4	Do. 1913	100	104½
3·65	Do. 1915	—	110
—	Santa Fé City Debs.	100	20
6	Santos City	100	95
6	Sofia City	100	86
5	Sth. Melbourne Debs. 1915	100	111
4½	Do. Debs. 1919	100	107
5	Sydney City 1904	100	109
4	Do. Debs. 1912-13	100	107
4	Do. do. (1894) 1919	100	109
7	Timaru Boro. 7 p.c. 1910	100	126
5	Timaru Harb. Debs 1914	100	106
5	Do. Debs. 1916	100	106
6	Toronto City Wtwks 1904-6	100	110
6	Do. Cons. Debs. 1898	100	101
5	Do. G. Cns. Dbs. 1919-20	100	118
4	Do. Strlg. 1922-8	100	107
4	Do. Local Improv.	100	102
3½	Do. 1929	100	106
5½	Valparaiso	100	101
4	Vancouver 1931	100	109
4	Do. 1932	100	108
6	Wanganui Harb. Dbs. 1905	100	110
6	Wellington Con. Deb. 1907	100	117
6	Do. Improv., 1879	100	126
6	Do. Wtrwks. Dbs., 1880	100	126
4½	Do. Debs., 1893 1933	100	116
4½	Wellington Harb. 1907	100	106
4	Westport Harb. Dbs. 1925	100	111
6	Winnipeg City Deb. 1907	—	118
5	Do. 1914	100	119

FINANCIAL, LAND, AND INVESTMENT.

Last Div.	Name.	Paid.	Price.
5	Agency, Ld. & Fin. Aust., Ltd., Mt. Db. Stk., Rd.	100	89½
6	Amer. Frehld. Mt. of Lon., Ld., Cum. Pref. Stk. ..	100	79½
4½	Do. Deb. Stk., Red. ..	100	96
1/	Anglo-Amer. Db. Cor., L.	2	1
4	Do. Deb. Stk., Red †	100	106½
5½	Ang.-Ceylon & Gen. Est., Ltd., Cons. Stk.	100	68
6	Do. Reg. Debs., Red.	100	106½
—	Ang.-Fch. Explorn., Ltd.	1	3
6	Do. Cum. Pref.	1	11/16
—	Argent. Ld. & Inv., Ltd. £1 Shares	10/	nil
5	Do. Cum. Pref.	4	2
1/	Assets Fnders.' Sh., Ltd.,	4	1⅜
6/	Assets Realis., Ltd., Ord.,	5	8¾
5	Do. Cum. Pref.	5	6¾
21/	Austrln. Agricl £25 Shs.	21½	65½
—	Aust. N. Z. Mort., Ltd., £10 Shs.	1	1½d.
4½	Do. Deb. Stk., Red. ..	100	90½
4	Do. Deb. Stk., Red. ..	100	82½
4½	Australian Est. & Mt., L., 1 Mt. Deb. Stk., Red.	100	105
5	Do. "A" Mort. Deb. Stk., Red.	100	97
2/6	Australian Mort., Ld., & Fin., Ltd. £25 Shs. ..	5	4½
1/6	Do. New, £25 Shs. ..	3	2¼
4	Do. Deb. Stk.	100	112
3	Do. Do.	100	85
5	Baring Est. 2 Mt. Debs., Red.	100	105
5	Bengal Presidy. 1 Mort. Deb., Red.	100	106
25/	British Amer. Ld. "A"	1	20
—	Do. "B"	24	6½
1/2½	Brit. & Amer. Mt., Ltd. £10 Shs.	2	¾
5/	Do. Pref.	10	10
4	Do. Deb. Stk., Red. ..	100	100
1/3	Brit. & Austrlan Tst Ln., Ltd. £25 Shs.	2½	⅝
4½	Do. Perm. Debs., Red.	100	103
1½d.	Brit. N. Borneo. £1 Shs.	15/	11/16
2½d.	Do.	1	1
—	Brit. S. Africa	1	3½
5	Do. Mt. Deb., Red.	—	98
6	B. Aires Harb. Tst., Red.	100	97½
12/6	Canada Co.	1	26
—	Canada N. W. Ld., Ltd.	$25	$5½
—	Do. Pref.	$100	$54
4	Canada Perm. Loan & Sav. Perp. Deb. Stk. ..	100	99½
—	Curamalan Ld., 1 Mt. 7 p.c. Bds., Red.	—	92½
3/7½	Deb Corp., Ld., £10 Shs	4	3½
5	Do. Cum. Pref.	10	11¼
4	Do. Perp. Deb. Stk. ..	100	114
9d.	Deb. Corp. Fders' Sh., Ld.	3	1
4/5 1/10	Eastn. Mt. & Agncy, Ld., "A"	10	6½
4½	Do. Deb. Stk., Red.	100	100
5	Equitable Revers. In. Ltd.	100	—
2/	Exploration, Ltd.	1	1½
1	Freehold Trst. of Austrla. Ltd. £10 Shs.	1	¾
4	Do. Perp. Deb. Stk. ..	100	102
—	Genl. Assets Purchase, Ltd., 5 p.c. Cum. Pref.	10	—
50/	Genl. Reversionary, Ltd.	100	—
3½	Holborn Vi. Land	100	105
3½	House Prop. & Inv.	100	84½
13/	Hudson's Bay	13	27
4	Impl. Col. Fin. & Agcy. Corp.	100	93½
4½	Impl. Prop. Inv., Ltd., Deb. Stk., Red.	100	91½
2/6	Internatl. Fincial. Soc., Ltd. £7½ Shs.	2½	1¼
4	Do. Deb. Stk., Red. ..	100	96½
1/9½	Ld. & Mtge. Egypt, Ltd. £18 Shs.	3	2¼
5	Do. Debs., Red.	100	103
4½	Do. Debs., Red.	100	101
—	Ld. Corp. of Canada, Ltd.	1	⅛
4½	Ld. Mtge. Bk. of Texas Deb. Stk.	100	—
3½	Ld. Mtge. Bk. Victoria 4½ p.c. Deb. Stk.	100	78
2/9½	Law Debent. Corp., Ltd., £10 Shs.	2	2
4½	Do. Cum. Pref., ...	10	12¼
4	Do. Deb. Stk.	100	118
1/	Ldn. & Australasian Deb. Corp., Ltd., £4 Shs. ..	2	½
4½	Do. 4½ p.c. Mt. Deb. Stk., Red.	100	101
—	Ldn. & Middx. Frhld. Est. £2 Shs.	35/	3¼
2/6	Lndn. & N. Y. Inv. Corp., Ltd.	5	2¼
5	Do. 5 p.c. Cum. Pref. ..	10	9
1/6	Ldn. & Nth. Assets Corp., Ltd., £2 Shs.	1½	⅝
2/	Ldn. & N. Deb. Corp., L.	2	1⅛
4/	Ldn. & S. Afric. Explrn. Ltd.	½	14
2/	Mtge. Co. of R. Plate, Ltd. £10 Shs.	2	3¼
4½	Do. Deb. Stk., Red. ..	100	111
4½	Morton, Rose Est., Ltd., 1st Mort. Debs.	—	101
6/	Natal Land Col. Ltd. ..	10	6½
4/	Do. 8 p.c. Pref., 1870 ..	5	8½
5/6	Natl. Disct. L., £25 Shs.	5	11
4½	New Impl. Invest., Ltd. Pref. Stk.	100	66½
—	New Impl. Invest., Ltd. Def. Stk.	100	9
4	N. Zld. Ln. & Mer. Agcy., Ltd. Prf. Ln. Deb. Stk	100	97

Financial, Land, &c. (*continued*):—

Last Div.	Name.	Paid.	Price.
16/	N. Zld. Ln. & Mer. Agcy., Ltd. 5 p.c. "A" Db. Sk.	100	42½
—	N. Zld. Ln. & Mer. Agcy., Ltd., 5 p.c. "B" Db. Stk.	100	4
2/6	N. Zld. Tst. & Ln. Ltd., £25 Shs.	5	1½
12/6	N. Zld. Tst. & Ln. Ltd., 5 p.c. Cum. Pref.	25	19
—	N. Brit. Australsn. Ltd. ..	100	7½
—	Do. Irred. Guar.	100	32½
5	Do. Mort. Debs.	100	82½
4½	N. Queensld. Mort. & Inv., Ltd., Deb. Stk.	100	94
—	Oceana Co., Ltd.	—	—
6	Peel Riv., Ld. & Min. Ltd.	100	90
—	Peruvian Corp., Ltd.	100	3
—	Do. 4 p.c. Pref.	100	10
3	Do. 6 p.c. 1 Mt. Debs., Red.	100	43
—	Queenld. Invest. & Ld. & Mort. Pref. Ord. Stk. ..	100	20
3/7	Queenld. Invest. & Ld. & Mort. Ord. Shs.	4	3½
4	Queenld. Invest. & Ld. Mort. Perp. Debs.	100	90
3½	Raily. Roll Stk. Tst. Deb., 1903-6	100	100½
50/	Reversiony. Int. Soc., Ltd.	100	—
2/8½	Riv. Plate Trst., Loan & Agcy., L., "A" £10 Shs.	2	4½
1/6	Riv. Plate Trst., Loan & Agcy., Ltd., Def. "B"	5	3⅛
4	Riv. Plate Trst., Loan & Agy., L., Db. Stk., Red.	100	108
—	Santa Fé & Cord. Gt. South Land, Ltd.	20	5
—	Santa Fé Land	10	2½
2/	Scot. Amer. Invest., Ltd. £10 Shs.	2	2¾
2½	Scot. Australian Invest., Ltd., Cons.	100	91½
6	Scot. Australinn Invest., Ltd., Guar. Pref.	100	134½
5	Scot. Australian Invest., Ltd., Guar. Pref.	100	102½
4	Scot. Australian Invest., Ltd., 4 p.c. Perp. Dbs.	100	105½
5	Sivagunga Zemdy., 1st Mort., Red.	100	101
20/	Sth. Australian	20	55½
3½	Stock Exchange Deb., Rd.	—	101½
—	Strait Develt., Ltd.	1	3/16
2/6	Texas Land & Mt., Ltd. £10 Shs.	2½	3
4½	Texas Land & Mt., Ltd., Deb. Stk., Red.	100	105
—	Transvaal Est. & Dev., L.	1	11/16
—	Transvaal Lands, Ltd., £1 Shs.	15/	½
—	Do. F. P.	1	¾
—	Transvaal Mort., Loan, & Fin., Ltd., £10 Shs. ..	2	⅛
2/	Tst & Agcy. of Austrlsa., Ltd., £10 Shs.	1	2½
7/5	Do. Old, fully paid ..	10	15½
5/7	Do. New, fully paid ..	10	12½
5	Do. Cum. Pref.	10	12¼
3/	Trust & Loan of Canada, £20 Shs.	5	4½
1/9½	Do. New £20 Shs.	3	2¼
—	Tst. & Mort. of Iowa, Ltd., £10 Shs.	2½	⅜
4½	Do. Deb. Stk. Red. ..	100	92½
—	Tst., Loan, & Agency of Mexico, Ltd., £10 Shs.	2	¼
—	Trsts., Exors, & Sec. Ins. Corp., Ltd., £10 Shs. ..	7	1⅜
5/	Union Dsc., Ld., £10 Shs.	5	10¼
—	Union Mort. & Agcy. of Aust., Ltd., £6 Shs. ..	2	—
6	Do. Pref. Stk	100	35
—	Do. 6 p. Pref. £6 Shs.	2	½
4½	Do. Deb. Stk	100	92½
4	Do. Deb. Stk	100	85½
5	Do. Deb. Stk. Red. ..	100	96
1/6	U.S. Deb. Cor. Ltd., £8 Shs.	1	⅝
5½	Do. Cum. Pref. Stk ..	100	102½
4½	Do. Irred. Deb. Stk ..	100	108
5	U.S. Tst. & Guar. Cor., Ltd., Pref. Stk	100	71½
6/	Van Dieman's	25	16
4	Walker's Prop. Cor., Ltd., Guar. 1 Mt. Deb. Stk.	100	109
4½	Wstr. Mort. & Inv., Ltd., Deb. Stk.	100	92½

FINANCIAL—TRUSTS.

Last Div.	Name.	Paid.	Price.
1/	Afric. City Prop., Ltd ...	1	1½
6	Do. Cum. Pref.	1	1
4	Alliance Invt., Ltd., Cm. 4½ p. c. Prefd.	100	77½
—	Do. Defd	100	11½
4	Do. Deb. Stk. Red. ..	100	106½
5	Amrcn. Invt., Ltd., Prfd.	100	123½
5	Do. Defd.	100	92½
4	Do. Deb. Stk. Red. ..	100	118½
4	Army & Navy Invt., Ltd., 5 p.c. Prefd.	100	79½
—	Do. Defd. Stk.	100	17½
4	Do. Deb. Stk.	100	104½
4	Atlas Investment, Ltd., Prefd. Stk.	100	70½
4½	Bankers' Invest., Ltd., Cum. Prefd.	100	105
1/0/0	Do. Defd	100	29½
4	Do. Deb. Stk	100	113

Financial—Trusts (*continued*):—

Last Div.	Name.	Paid.	Price.
4/6	Brewery & Comml. Inv., Ltd., £10 Shs.	5	6
4	British Investment, Ltd., Cum. Prefd.	100	109½
5	Do. Defd.	100	102½
4	Do. Deb. Stk.	100	107½
6	Brit. Steam. Invst., Ltd., Prefd.	100	117½
3/0/0	Do. Defd	100	70½
4½	Do. Perp. Deb. Stk ..	100	120½
2/3	Car Trust Invst., Ltd., £10 Shs.	2½	2
5	Do. Pref	100	105½
4	Do. Deb. Stk., 1915 ..	100	106
4	‡Clnl. Sec., Ltd., Prefd. †	100	107½
2	Do. Defd.	100	48
4	Consolidated, Ltd., Cum. 1st Pref.	100	95½
4	Do. 5 p.c. Cm. 2nd do.	100	74½
—	Do. Defd.	100	14½
4½	Do. Deb. Stk.	100	111½
4½	Edinburgh Invest., Ltd., Cum. Prefd. Stk.	100	110½
4	Do. Deb. Stk. Red.	100	106½
5	Foreign, Amer. & Gen. Invt., Ltd., Prefd.	100	119½
2	Do. Defd.	100	54½
4	Do. Deb. Stk.	100	117½
5	Foreign & Colonial Invt., Ltd., Prefd.	100	135½
4½	Do. Defd.	100	96
4½	Gas, Water & Gen. Invt., Cum. Prefd. Stk.	100	93
2	Do. Defd. Stk.	100	32½
4	Do. Deb. Stk.	100	106
5	Gen. & Com. Invt., Ltd., Prefd. Stk.	100	106½
2	Do. Defd. Stk.	100	35½
4	Do. Deb. Stk.	100	111½
1/9	Globe Telegph. & Tst., Ltd.	10	12½
6	Do. do. Pref.	10	18
4	Govt. & Genl. Invt., Ld., Prefd.	100	84½
3½	Do. Defd.	100	42½
4½	Govts. Stk. & other Secs. Invt., Ltd., Prefd.	100	94½
1	Do. Defd.	100	28
4½	Do. Deb. Stk.	100	110
4	Do. do.	100	104
4½	Guardian Invt., Ltd., Pfd.	100	92½
—	Do. Defd.	100	21½
4	Do. Deb. Stk.	100	105½
5	Indian & Gen. Inv., Ltd., Cum. Prefd.	100	109½
2½	Do. Defd.	100	55
4½	Do. Deb. Stk.	100	120½
5	Indust. & Gen. Tst., Ltd., Unified	100	101½
3½	Do. Deb. Stk. Red.	100	102½
4½	Internat. Invt., Ltd., Cm. Prefd.	100	72½
—	Do. Defd.	100	11
4	Do. Deb. Stk.	100	104
4	Invest. Tst. Cor. Ltd. Pfd.	100	102
4	Do. Defd.	100	83
4	Do. Deb. Stk. Red.	100	106
25/	Ldn. Gen. Invest. Ltd., 5 p.c. Cum. Prefd.	100	110½
37/6	Do. Defd.	100	120
4½	Ldn. Scot. Amer. Ltd. Pfd.	00	104½
£3	Do. Defd.	100	59½
4	Do. Deb. Stk.	100	111
4	Ldn. Tst., Ltd., Cum. Prfd. Stk.	100	105
4	Do. Defd. Stk.	100	76½
4	Do. Deb. Stk., Red.	100	107
3½	Do. Mt. Deb. Stk., Red.	100	104
5	Mercantile Invt. & Gen., Ltd., Prefd.	100	112
2	Do. Defd.	100	52½
4	Do. Deb. Stk.	100	117½
4	Merchants, Ltd., Pref. Stk.	100	105½
4	Do. Ord.	100	81
4	Do. Deb. Stk.	100	117
6	Municipal, Ltd., Prefd. ..	100	56½
—	Do. Defd.	100	18½
4½	Do. Debs.	100	113
4½	Do. Debs. "B"	100	99½
4½	Do. "C" Deb. Stk.	100	88½
5	New Investment, Ltd. Ord.	100	91½
5	Omnium Invest., Ltd., Pfd.	100	95½
1	Do. Defd.	100	27½
4	Do. Deb. Stk.	100	102
4/	†Railway Deb. Tst. Ld., £20 Shs.	10	7½
5	Do. Debs., Red. ..	100	107½
4½	Do. Deb. Stk., 1911	100	105½
4	Do. do. 1927	100	107½
4	Railway Invst. Ltd., Prefd.	100	117
13/6	Do. Defd.	100	25
6/4½	Railway Share Trust & Agency "A"	8	6½
7½	Do. "B" Pref. Stk.	100	143
4½	River Plate & Gen. Invt., Ltd., Prefd.	100	107
£3	Do. Defd.	100	54½
5	Scot. Invst., Ltd., Pfd. Stk.	100	95½
1½	Do. Defd. ..	100	26½
4	Do. Deb. Stk.	100	108
4½	Sec. Scottish Invst., Ltd., Cum. Prefd.	100	90½
£2	Do. Defd. Stk.	100	32
4	Do. Deb. Stk.	100	107½
7/6	Sth. Africa Gold Tst., Ltd.	1	5
6	Do. Cum. Pref	1	1
5½	Do. 1st Debs., Red.	100	102
1/9	Stock Conv. & Invest., Ltd., £5 Shs.	1	1⅜
4½	Do. do. 4½ p.c. Cm. Prf.	100	112½
3½	Do. Ldn. & N. W. 1st. Charge Prefd.	100	116½
4	Do do. 2nd Chge Prfd.	100	113
32/6	Do. do. Defd. Charge	100	32½
3	Do. N. East. 1 Chge Pfd.	100	95

Financial—Trusts (*continued*):—

Last Div.	Name.	Paid.	Price.
37/6	Stock N. East Defd. Chge	100	41
6	Submarine Cables	100	142½
5	U.S. & S. Amer. Invest., Ltd., Prefd.	100	98½
2	Do. Defd.	100	29½
4	Do. Deb. Stk.	100	105½

GAS AND ELECTRIC LIGHTING.

Last Div.	Name.	Paid.	Price.
10/6	Alliance & Dublin Con. 10 p.c. Stand.	10	25½
7/6	Do. 7 p.c. Stand. ..	10	17
5	Austln. Gas Lght. (Syd.) Debs. 1902	100	106
5	Bay State of N. Jrsy. Sk. Fd. Tst, Bd., Red. ..	—	92½
3/	Bombay, Ltd.	5	7
2/4½	Do. New	4	5½
12	Brentford Cons.	100	302½
9	Do. New	100	229½
5	Do. Pref.	100	147½
4	Do. Deb. Stk. ..	100	136
11½	Brighton & Hove Gen. Cons. Stk.	100	277½
8½	Do. "A" Cons. Stk.	100	202½
5	Bristol 5 p.c. Max.	100	132½
22/6	British Gas Light, Ltd.	20	57
11/6	Bromley Gas Consumrs.' 10 p.c. Stand.	10	26
8/6	Do. 7 p.c. Stand. ..	10	21
—	Brush Electl. Enging., L.	—	2½
6	Do. 6 p.c. Pref.	—	2¼
4½	Do. Deb. Stk.	100	111
4½	Do. 2 Deb. Stk., Red.	100	103½
5/	B. Ayres (New), Ltd. ..	10	10
4	Do. Deb. Stk., Rd. ..	—	97
12/	Cagliari Gas & Wtr., Ltd.	20	31
8/	Cape Town & Dist. Gas Light & Coke, Ltd.	10	17½
4½	Do. Pref.	10	12¼
6	Do. 1 Mt. Debs. 1910	50	60
3/	Charing Cross & Strand Elec. Sup., Ltd.	5	14½
4½	Do. Cum. Pref.	5	6¼
2/6	Chelsea Elec. Sup., Ltd.	5	11½
4½	Do. Deb. Stk., Red.	100	113
5	Chic. Edison Co. 1 Mt., Red.	$1000	108
14/	City of Ldn. Elec. Lht., L.	10	30
—	Do. New	10	29½
6/	Do. Cum. Pref.	10	18
5	Do. Deb. Stk., Red. †	100	131½
13½	Commercial, Cons.	100	342½
10½	Do. New	100	257½
4½	Do. Deb. Stk.	100	155½
14	Continental Union, Ltd.	100	252½
11	Do. Pref. Stk.	100	216½
—	County of Lon. & Brush Prov. Elec. Lg., Ltd.	10	16
6	Do. Cum. Pref.	10	16
14	Croydon Comcl. Gas, Ld., "A" Stk., 10 p.c. ..	100	317½
11	Do. "B" Stk., 7 p.c.	100	254½
5½	Crystal Pal. Dist. Ord. 5 p.c. Stk.	100	138½
5	Do. Pref. Stk.	100	141½
8/	European, Ltd.	10	26
6/	Do.	7½	13½
12¾	Gas Light & Ck Cons. Stk., "A" Ord.	100	311½
4	Do. "B" (4 p.c. Max.)	100	115½
10	Do. "C," "D," & "E" (Pref.)	100	322½
5	Do. "F" (Pref.)	100	152½
7½	Do. "G" (Pref.)	100	224½
7	Do. "H" (7 p.c. Max.)	100	206½
10	Do. "J" (Pref.)	100	321½
6	Do. "K"	100	189
4	Do. Deb. Stk.	100	139½
4½	Do. do.	100	157½
6	Do. do.	100	207½
8/	Hong Kong & China, Ld.	10	14½
—	†House to House Elec. Light Sup., Ltd. ..	5	11
7	Do. Cum. Pref.	5	11½
10	Imperial Continental ..	100	218½
3½	Do. Deb. Stk., Red ..	100	105½
2/	Malta & Medit., Ltd. ..	5	5½
5/	Metrop. Elec. Sup., Ltd.	10	20½
3/8	Do. New	10	20
4½	Do. 1 Mt. Deb. Stk.	100	119
5	Metro. of Melbrne. Dbs. 1908-12	100	113
4½	Do. Debs. .. 1918-22-4	100	110
10/	Monte Video, Ltd.	20	15½
8/	†Notting Hill Elec. Ltg., Ltd.	10	18½
4/6	Oriental, Ltd.	5	8½
4/0½	Do. New	4½	7½
10½d.	Do. do. 1879	1	1⅛
3/6	Ottoman, Ltd.	5	4¾
—	Para, Ltd.	—	—
6	People's Gas Lt. & C. of Chic. 2 Mt. 1904	100	106½
5	River Plate Elec. Lgt. & Trac., Ltd., 1 Deb. Stk.	—	92½
8½	Royal Elec. of Montreal	—	146
4½	Do. 1 Mt. Deb. ..	100	106
3/6	†St. James' & Pall Mall Elec. Light, Ltd. ..	5	18½
7	Do. Pref.	5	10½
4	Do. Deb. Stk., Red. †	100	102½
10/	San Paulo, Ltd.	10	16½

Gas and Electric (*continued*):—

Last Div.	Name.	Paid.	Price.
10	Sheffield Unit. Gas Lt. "A"	100	251½
10	Do. "B"	100	251½
10	Do. "C"	100	251½
—	Sth. Ldn. Elec. Sup., Ld.	2	3
5½	South Metropolitan	100	146½
3	Do. 3 p.c. Deb. Stk.	100	106½
12	Tottenham & Edmonton Gas Lt. & C., "A"	100	290
9	Do. "B"	100	210
7/	Tuscan, Ltd.	10	14
5	Do. Debs., Red.	100	101½
4/9	West Ham 10 p.c. Stan.	5	12
4/	Wstmnstr. Elec. Sup., Ld.	5	18½

INSURANCE.

Last Div.	Name.	Paid.	Price.
4/	Alliance, £20 Shs.	44/	11½
10/	Alliance, Mar., & Gen., Ld., £100 Shs.	25	53
2/	Atlas, £50 Shs.	6	32
8/	British & For. Marine, Ld., £20 Shs.	4	25½
7½d.	British Law Fire, Ltd., £10 Shs.	1	1½
7/6	Clerical, Med., & Gen. Life, £25 Shs.	50/	16½
10/	Commercial Union, Ltd., £50 Shs.	5	46
4	Do. "W. of Eng." Ter. Deb. Stk	100	110½
60/	County Fire, £100 Shs.	80	185
2/6	Eagle, £50 Shs.	5	—
4/	Employrs' Liability, Ltd., £10 Shs.	2	4½
—	Empress, Ltd., £5 Shs.	1	—
21/	Equity & Law, £100 Shs.	6	21
7/6	General Life, £100 Shs.	5	15
4½d.	Gresham Life, £5 Shs.	15/	2½
2/6	Guardian, Ld., £10 Shs.	5	12
10/	Imperial, Ltd., £20 Shs.	5	31½
5/6	Imperial Life, £20 Shs.	4	7
6/	Indemnity Mutual Mar., Ltd., £15 Shs.	3	12½
1/	Lancashire, £20 Shs.	2	5
7½d.	Law Acc. & Contin., Ltd., £5 Shs.	10/	½
5/	Law Fire, £100 Shs.	2½	18
4½d.	Law Guar. & Trust, Ltd., £10 Shs.	1	1½
9/	Law Life, £20 Shs.	2	24½
2/9	Law Un. & Crown £10Shs.	12/	7
4	Do. Deb. Stk., 1942	100	110½
14/6	Legal & General, £50Shs.	8	15½
9d.	Lion Fire, Ltd., £8½ Shs.	1½	1
14/	Liverpool & London & Globe, Stk.	2	55½
10/	Do. Globe £1 Ann.	—	36
15/	London, £25 Shs.	12½	63
4/	Lond. & Lanc. Fire, £25Shs	2½	19½
2/	Lond. & Lanc. Life, £25Shs	2	5
10	Lond. & Prov. Mar., Ld., £10 Shs.	1	1½
2/	Lond. Guar. & Accident, Ltd., £5 Shs.	2	12
10/	Marine, Ltd., £25 Shs.	4½	44½
2/	Maritime, Ltd., £10 Shs.	2	4½
1/6	Merc. Mar., Ld., £10 Shs.	2½	2½
1/	National Marine, Ltd., £9 Shs.	1	½
10/	N. Brit. & Merc., £25 Shs.	6½	43
20/	Northern, £100 Shs.	10	82
40/	Norwich Union Fire, £100 Shs.	12†	129½
5/	Ocean Acc. & Guar., fy. pd.	5	20½
1/	Do. £5 Shs.	1	4
2/6	Ocean, Marine, Ltd.	2½	9½
1/	Palatine, £10 Shs.	2	3½
2/6	Pelican, £10 Shs.	1	3½
12/	Phœnix, £50 Shs.	5	45
25/	Provident, £100 Shs.	10	36
3/	Railway Passngrs., £10Shs.	2	8½
2/6	Rock Life, £5 Shs.	10/	4½
8	Royal Exchange	100	360
18/	Royal, £20 Shs.	3	55½
4/	Sun, £10 Shs.	10/	11½
3/9	Sun Life, £10 Shs.	7½	15
4/	Thames & Mrsey. Marine, Ltd., £20 Shs.	2	11½
9/	Union, £10 Shs.	4	24½
3/6	Union Marine, £20 Shs.	2½	9½
12/	Universal Life, £100 Shs.	12	42
2/	World Marine, £5 Shs.	2	1½

IRON, COAL, AND STEEL.

Last Div.	Name.	Paid.	Price.
3/9	Barrow Hæm. Steel, Ltd.	7½	2½
9/	Do. 6 p.c. 2nd Pref.	7½	7½
10/	Bolck., Vaugh. & C., Ld.	20	18
6/	Do. £8 liab.	12	10
7/6	Brown, J. & Co., Ltd., £20 Shs.	15	21
22/6	Consett Iron, Ld., £10 Shs.	7½	30
4/	Do. 8 p.c. Cum. Pref.	5	11½
7/6	Ebbw Vale Steel, Iron & Coal, Ltd., £23 Shs.	20	7½
15/	General Mining Assn., Ld.	5½	7½
16/	Harvey Steel Co. of Gt. Britain, Ltd.	10	26
5	Lehigh V. Coal 1 Mt. 5 p.c. Guar. Gd. Cp. Bds.	—	99½
42/6	Nantyglo & Blaina Iron, Ltd., Pref.	860	96
1/	Nerbudda Coal & Iron, Ltd., £3 Shs.	56/	$\frac{1}{16}$
6/	Newport Abrcrn. Bk. Vein, Steam Coal, Ltd.	10	4½
5/	New Sharlston Coll., Ltd. Pref.	20	11
4½d.	Nw. Vancvr. Coal & Ld., L.	1	½
3/6	North's Navigation Coll. (1889) Ltd.	5	2
10/	Do. 10 p.c. Cum. Pref.	5	7½
1/	Rhymney Iron, Ltd.	5	1½
	Do. New, £5 Shs.	4½	½
5	Do. Mt. Debs., Red.	100	97½
5	Shelton Irn., Stl. & Cl. Co., Ltd., 1 Chg. Debs., Red.	100	98½
10	Sth. Hetton Coal, Ltd.	100	176½
	Vickers & Maxim, Ltd.	10	3
	Do. 5 p.c. Prfd. Stk.	100	133½

SHIPPING.

Last Div.	Name.	Paid.	Price.
4/	African Stm. Ship, £20 Shs.	16	9½
5/	Do. Fully-paid	20	13½
5/	Amazon Steam Nav., Ltd.	19½	9½
8/	Castle Mail Pakts., Ltd., £20 Shs.	14	15½
3½	Do. 1st Deb. Stk., Red.	100	101
6/	China Mutual Steam, Ltd.	5	3
6	Do. Cum. Pref.	10	9½
10/	Cunard, Ltd.	20	10
5/	Do. £20 Shs.	10	4
4½	Furness, Withy, & Co., Ltd., 1 Mt. Dbs., Red.	100	105
6/	General Steam	15	8½
5/	Do. 5 p.c. Pref., 1874	10	9
5/	Do. 5 p.c. Pref., 1877	10	9
5/	Leyland & Co., Ltd.	10	15½
7/	Do. 7 p.c. Cum. Pref.	10	14½
2/11	Do. 4½ p.c. Cum. Pre-Pf.	3	10½
4	Do. 1st Mt. Dbs., Red.	100	106½
2/6	Mercantile Steam, Ltd.	5	7½
6/4½	New Zealand Ship., Ltd.,	6	5
4	Do. Deb. Stk., Red.	100	104
5/	Orient Steam, Ltd.	10	4½
5	P. & O. Steam, Cum. Prefd.	100	156½
19	Do. Defd.	100	232½
3½	Do. Deb. Stk.	100	121
5	Richelieu & Ont., 1st Mt. Debs., Red.	100	101
30/	Royal Mail, £100 Shs.	60	51
2/6	Shaw, Sav., & Alb., Ltd., "A" Pref.	5	5½
5/	Do. "B" Ord.	5	3½
8/	Union Steam, Ltd.	20	18½
4/	Do. New £20 Shs.	10	8½
4	Do. Deb. Stk., Red.	100	107
7/	Union of N.Z., Ltd.	10	10
5½	Wilson's & Fur.-Ley., 5½ p.c. Cum. Pref.	10	10½
4½	Do. 1 Mt. Db. Sk., Rd.	100	105½

TELEGRAPHS AND TELEPHONES.

Last Div.	Name.	Paid.	Price.
4	African Direct, Ltd., Mort. Debs., Red.	100	102
—	Amazon Telegraph, Ltd.	10	6½
14/	Anglo-American, Ltd.	100	63
28/	Do. 6 p.c. Prefd. Ord.	100	113
—	Do. Defd. Ord.	100	13½
3/	Brazilian Submarine, Ltd.	10	17
5	Do Debs., 2 Series	100	114

Telegraphs and Telephones (*continued*):—

Last Div.	Name.	Paid.	Price.
4/	Chili Telephone, Ltd.	5	3½
8½	Comcial. Cable, $100 Shs.	—	180½
4	Do. Stg. 500yr. Deb. Stk. Red.	100	107
2½d.	Consd. Telpehone Constr., &c., Ltd.	10/	½
8/	Cuba Submarine, Ltd.	10	8½
10/	Do. 10 p.c. Pref.	10	18½
2/	Direct Spanish, Ltd.	5	4½
5/	Do. 10 p.c. Cum. Pref.	5	10½
4½	Do. Debs.	50	104½
3/	Direct U.S. Cable, Ltd.	20	10½
2/6	Eastern, Ltd.	10	18½
3/	Do. 6 p.c. Cum. Pref.	10	19½
4	Do. Mt. Deb. Stk., Red.	100	132½
2/6	Eastern Exten., Aus., & China, Ltd.	10	19
5	Do. (Aus. Gov. Sub.) Deb., Red.	100	101
5	Do. do. Bearer	100	101½
4	Do. Mort. Deb. Stk.	100	131½
5	Eastn. & S. Afric., Ltd., Mort. Deb. 1900	100	101
5	Do. Bearer	100	101½
4	Do. Mort. Debs. ..1909	100	103½
4	Do. Mort. Debs. (Maur. Subsidy)	25	109½
5/	Grt. Nthn. Copenhagen	10	27½
5	Do. Debs., Ser. B., Red.	100	102½
12/6	Indo-European, Ltd.	25	53½
6	London Platino-Brazilian, Ltd., Debs. 1904	100	03½
4/	MonteVideo Telph., Ltd., 6 p.c. Pref.	5	2½
3/	National Telephone, Ltd.	5	6½
6/	Do. Cum. 1 Pref.	10	16
6/	Do. Cum. 2 Pref.	10	15
5	Do. Non-Cum. 3 Pref.	5	6½
3½	Do. Deb. Stk., Red.	100	106½
4d.	Oriental Telephone, Ltd.	1	½
4	Pac. & Euro. Tlg. Dbs., Rd.	100	106½
4/	Reuter's, Ltd.	8	8½
5/	Un. Riv. Plate Telph., Ltd.	5	4½
5	Do. Deb. Stk., Red.	100	103½
6/	West African Telg., Ltd.	10	4½
5	Do. 5 p.c. Mt. Debs., Red.	100	104½
—	W. Coast of America, Ltd.	10	—
3/	Western & Brazilian, Ltd.	15	10½
3/	Do. 5 p.c. Pref. Ord.	7½	7½
—	Do. Defd. Ord.	7½	3½
4	Do. Deb. Stk., Red.	100	106
1/	W. India & Panama, Ltd.	10	½
6/	Do. Cum. 1 Pref.	10	8
6/	Do. Cum. 2 Pref.	10	6
5	Do. Debs., Red.	100	106½
7	West. Union, 1 Mt. 1902($	1000	107½
6	Do. 6 p.c. Stg. Bds., Rd.	100	102½

TRAMWAYS AND OMNIBUS.

Last Div.	Name.	Paid.	Price.
1/6	Anglo-Argentine, Ltd.	5	4
6	Do. Deb. Stk	100	132
4	Barcelona, Ltd.	10	12½
5	Do. Deb., Red.	100	102½
6/6	Belfast Street Trams.	10	17
—	Blackpl. & Fltwd. Tram., £10 Shs.	8	10
4/	Bordeaux Tram. & O., Ltd.	10	13½
5	Do. Cum. Pref.	10	11½
—	Brazilian Street Ry., Ltd.	2	½
—	British Elec. Trac., Ltd.	10	18½
—	B. Ayres & Belg. Tram., Ltd., 6 p.c. Cum. Pref.	5	4½
6	Do. 1 Deb. Stk. †	100	102½
—	B. Ayres. Gd. Nat., Ltd., 6 p.c 1 Deb. Bds., Red.	100	60
5½	Do. Pref. Debs., Red.	100	94½
6d.	Calais, Ltd.	5	1
—	Calcutta, Ltd.	10	3½
—	Carthagena & Herr., Ltd.	10	3
5	Do. Deb., Red.	100	90
5	City of B'ham. Trams., Ltd., 5 p.c. Cum. Pref.	5	6
4	Do. 1 Mort. Debs., Rd.	100	105½
3/9	City of B. Ayres, Ltd.	5	7½
2/3	Do. Ext. £3 Shs.	3	4
6	Do. Deb. Stk.	100	150
9d.	Edinburgh Street Tram.	4	3½
1/	Glasgow Tram. & Omni. Ltd., £9 Shs.	8	3½
3/7½	Imperial, Ltd.	6	14
2/	Lond., Deptfd, & Greenwich, Prefd.	5	3½
nil	Do. Defd.	5	1
10½	Lond. Gen. Omni., Ltd.	100	205
4	Do. Deb., Red.	100	117½

Tramways and Omnibus (*continued*):—

Last Div.	Name	Paid.	Price.
6/	London Road Car	6	10½
5	London St. Rly. (Prov., Ont.), Mt. Debs.	100	112
4/9	London St. Trams.	—	3
12/6	London Trams., Ltd.	10	10½
6/	Do. Non-Cum. Pref.	10	10½
5	Do. Mt. Db. Stk., Rd.	100	100½
5	Lynn & Boston 1 Mt. 1924	$ 1000	107
5	Milwaukee Elec. Cons. Mt.	$ 1000	98
5	Minneapolis St. 1 Cons. Mt	$ 1000	94
5	Montreal St. Dbs., 1908	100	110
4½	Do. Debs., 1922	100	107
6/	Nth. Metropolitan	10	17½
1/4½	Nth. Staffords., Ltd.	6	4½
5/6	Provincial, Ltd.	10	7
6/	Do. Cum. Pref.	10	13½
5	St. Paul City, 1937	$ 1000	94
5	Do. Guar. Twin City Rap. Trans.	$ 1000	91
5/	Southampton	10	7
3/	South London	10	5½
3/6	Sunderland, Ltd.	10	6
4½	Toronto 1 Mt., Red.	100	109
2/6	Tramways Union, Ltd.	5	7
4½	Do. Deb., Red.	100	109
5/	Vienna General Omnibus.	5	6½
5	Do. 5 p.c. Mt. Deb., Red.	100	105
4/	Wolverhampton, Ltd.	10	6½

WATER WORKS.

Last Div.	Name.	Paid.	Price.
8/	Antwerp, Ltd.	20	21½
6/	Cape Town District, Ltd.	5	6½
17¼	Chelsea	100	337½
5	Do. Pref. Stk.	100	178½
4½	Do. Pref. Stk., 1875	100	158½
4½	Do. Deb. Stk.	100	162½
5/	City St. Petersburg, Ltd.	13	11
4/6	Colne Valley	10	15
4	Do. Deb. Stock	100	137½
£4	Consol. of Rosar., Ltd., 4 p.c. 1 Deb. Stk., Red.	100	91
7½	East London	100	235
4½	Do. Deb. Stk.	100	163½
3	Do. Deb. Stk., Red.	100	106
37/6	Grand Junction (Max. 10 p.c.) "A"	50	124½
18/9	Do. "B"	25	
18/9	Do. "C" (Max. 7½ p.c.)	25	57½
35/	Do. "D" (Max. 7 p.c.)	50	102½
4	Do. Deb. Stock	100	149½
13	Kent	100	364½
7	Do. New (Max. 7 p.c.)	100	217½
5/7½	Kimberley, Ltd.	7	5
6	Do. Debs., Red.	100	102½
6	Do. Deb. Stk., Red.	100	104½
10	Lambeth (Max. 10 p.c.)	100	309½
7½	Do. (Max. 7½ p.c.), 50 & 25	—	229½
4	Do. Deb. Stock	100	148½
3	Do. Red. Deb. Stock	100	106
10/	Montevideo, Ltd.	20	16½
5	Do. 1 Deb. Stk.	100	108½
5	Do. 2 Deb. Stk.	100	103½
130/11	15] New River New	100	454½
4	Do. Deb. Stk.	100	153½
4	Do. Deb. Stk. "B"	100	153½
—	Odessa, Ltd., "A" 6 p.c. Prefd.	20	—
nil	Do. "B" Deferred	20	—
4	Portland Con. Mt. "B," 1927	..	—
8/	Seville, Ltd.	20	12½
5/6	Southend "Addl." Ord.	10	17½
6	Southwark and Vauxhall	100	166½
6	Do. "D" Shares (7½ p.c. max.)	100	162
5	Do. Pref. Stock	100	177½
4	Do. "A" Deb. Stock	100	148½
3	Staines Resvirs. Jt. Com. Gua. Deb. Stk., Red.	100	105
7/	Tarapaca, Ltd.	10	9½
10	West Middlesex	100	319½
4½	Do. Deb. Stk.	100	164½
3	Do. Deb. Stk.	100	107

Prices Quoted on the Leading Provincial Exchanges.

ENGLISH.

In quoting the markets, B stands for Birmingham; Bl for Bristol; M for Manchester; L for Liverpool; and S for Sheffield.

CORPORATION STOCKS.

Chief Market.	Int or Div.	Name.	Amount paid.	Price.
M	3½	Bolton, Red. 1935 ..	100	116
M	3½	Burnley, Red. 1933..	100	116
M	3½	Bury, Red. 1946	100	118
L	2½	Liverpool, Red. 1925	100	102½
B	3½	Longton, 1932	100	106
M	4	Oldham Prp. Db. Sk.	100	144
M	£1	Do. Gas&W.Ann.		34½
S	4	Rotherham 4 p.c., Red. 1927...... {£	1 an	114
S	3	Do. Red. 1920..	100	104
M	3½	Runcorn Red. 1923..	100	105
S	2½	Sheffield Water Ann.	100	117½
S	3	Do.	3 an	90
L	3½	Southport Red. 1936	5 an 100	110
L	3	Do. Red. 1914..	100	102½
M	3	Todmorden, Red. 1914	100	104

RAILWAYS.

Chief Market.	Int or Div.	Name.	Amount paid.	Price.
Bl	4½	Bridgewater Pref. ..	100	137½
M	4	Cleator & Workton.	100	78
M	4	Do. 1883 Pref. ..	100	111
L	4	Cockermth. K. & P.	100	116
L	4	Isle of Man	5	6½
L	5	Do. Pref.	5	6¾
L	3	Liverpool Overhead	10	11½
L	4	Do. Deb. Stk. ..	100	109
L	5	Do. Pref.	10	16½
L	6	Maryport & Carlisle	100	170
S	6	Mid.Shef.& Roth.Pf.	100	231
Bl	55/	Neath & Brecon "A"	100	60
M	4½	Oldham, Ashton. &c.	10	17
Bl	5½	Penarth Harbour ..	100	184½
Bl	4	Do. Deb. Stk. ..	100	145
Bl	3½	Do. Deb. Stk. ..	100	127
Bl	¾	Ross & Monmouth..	20	5½
Bl	6	Do. Pref.	20	43
M	3	Southport & Cheshire Deb. Stk.	100	104½
M	nil.	Do. Pref.	100	26
Bl	2½	West Somerset Gu...	100	97½
Bl	5	Wye Val. Deb. Stk.	100	164

BANKS.

Chief Market.	Int or Div.	Name.	Amount paid.	Price.
L	5/	Adelphi, L., £20 Shs.	10	16
L	12/6	Bk of L'ool, L., £100 Sh	12½	38½
B	5/6	Brmnghm. Dis. & C., Ltd., £20 Shs.....	4	11
B	6/3	Co. of Staffs., L., £40	5	13
S	17½	Crompton & Evans, Ltd., £20 Shs	4	14½
M	14/	Lancs. & Yorks, Ltd., £20 Shs.....	10	31½
L	18/	Livrpl. Union, Ltd., £100 Shs.	20	60½
M	24/	Manchester & Co., Ltd., £100 Shs. ..	16	61
M	20/	Mnchstr. & Livrpool. Dis., Ltd., £60 Shs.	10	51½
M	1/6	Mer. of Lancashire, Ltd., £20 Shs.....	3	6½
L	16/	Nth. & Sth. Wales, Ltd., £40 Shs.....	10	34½
	5/	Notts Joint St., Ltd., £50 Shs..........	10	23
M	4/	Oldham Joint Stk., Ltd., £20 Shs.....	4	10½
S	10	Sheffield Banking, Ltd., £50 Shs.....	17½	50½
S	10	Do. & Rotherham, Ltd., £50 Shs...	8	26½
S	15	Do. & Hallamsh., Ltd., £100 Shs..	25	61
S	10	Do. Union, Ltd., £40 Shs.........	10	25
M	12/	Union of Manchester, Ltd., £25 Shs.. ..	11	27½
M	10/	Williams, Deacon, &c. Ltd., £50 Shs.....	8	25½
Bl	20	Wilts & Dorset, Ltd., £50 Shs..........	10	49
S	10/	York City & Co., Ltd., £10 Shs.....	3	14

BREWERIES.

Chief Market.	Int or Div.	Name.	Amount paid.	Price.
B	6	Ansell & Sons Pref.	10	15½
B	5	Do. Debs.	100	110
L	7/	Bent's	10	19½
L	6	Do. Cum. Pref...	10	14½
L	4½	Do. Deb. Stk. ..	100	111
L	13/6	Birkenhead, £5 paid	5	22
L	13/6	Do. £10 paid....	10	25
M	9/	Boddington's	9	21½
M	5	Do. Cum. Pref...	10	13
M	4	Do. Deb. Stk. ..	100	109
B	4½	Butler & Co. Db. Stk	100	110½
M	6	Chesters' Cum. Pref.	10	13½
M	4½	Do. Debs.	100	112½
S	17/	Clarkson's Ord.	10	24½
S	6	Do. Cum. Prf. Stk.	10	15
M	4	Dutton & Co. Db.Sk.	100	103
M	4½	Hardy's Crown Debs.	100	111
B	6/	Holt	10	19½
B	5	Do. Cum. Pref...	10	12½
B	4	Do. Debs.	100	107½
B	12/6	Lichfield	10	24
B	5	Do. Cum. Pref...	10	11½
M	5½	Manchester Deb. Stk.	100	141
B	14	Mitchell, H., & Co.	10	37½
B	6	Do. Cum. Pref...	10	15½
Bl	6	Oakhill Pref........	10	16½

Breweries (*continued*):—

Chief Market.	Int. or Div.	Name.	Amount paid.	Price.
M	5/	Springwell	10	10½
M	7	Do. Pref.	10	13½
Bl	9	Stroud	10	17
Bl	6	Do. Pref	10	14½
M	6/	Taylor's Eagle......	10	11
M	7	Do. Cum. Pref ..	10	13½
M	5½	Do. Deb. Stk. ..	100	120½
S	10	Tennant Bros £20 shs	15	33½
S	10	Wheatley & Bates ..	10	14
S	6	Do. Cum. Pref.	10	12½

CANALS AND DOCKS.

Chief Market.	Int. or Div.	Name.	Amount paid.	Price.
Bl	5	Hill's Dry Dk. &c. £20	18	8
M	4	Manc. Ship Canal 1st Mt. Deb. Stk.	100	104
M	4	Do. 2nd do.	100	103
L	36/3	Mersey Dck. & Harb.	an.	118½
L	35/	Do.	an.	113
M	10/	Rochdale Canal	100	37½
B	35/	Staff. & Worc. Canal	100	75½
B	4½	Do. Deb. Stk....	100	137
Bl	4	Swansea Harb......	100	114
B	27/6	Warwick & Birm. Cnl	100	66
B	12/6	Do. & Napton do.	100	21½

COMMERCIAL & INDUSTRIAL.

Chief Market.	Int. or Div.	Name.	Amount paid.	Price.
L	5	Agua Santa Mt. Debs	100	100
M	8/	Armitage, Sir E. & Sns Ltd.............	10	19
M	4	Do. Deb. 1910 ..	100	103
L	6	Ang. Chil. Nit. 1 Mt. Debs., 1919 ..	100	108½
Bl	8½	Bath Stone Firms ..	10	19½
M	4/9½	Barlow & Jones, Ltd., £10 Shs.	8	10½
B	7/6	Birmgham. Ry. Car.	10	18
B	6	Do. Pref.	10	15½
B	16/8	Do. Small Arms	5	18
M	£12	Blackpool Pier......	100	275½
M	5	Do. Tower Debs.	50	54½
M	3/	Do. Wi. Gar. & P.	5	4½
Bl	10	Bristl. & S.W.R. Wag. £20 Shs..........	3	6½
Bl	8	Do. Wag. & Carri. £10 Shs..........	10	14½
M	7/	Crosses & Winkwth. Ltd..............	5	12½
L	5	G. Angus & Co. Pref.	10	13½
Bl	7	Gloster. Carri. & W.		10
Bl	5	Gt. Wstn. Cttn., Ltd.	20	15½
M	6	Hetherington, L. Prf.	10	9½
M	4½	Do. Debs., 1910	100	99½
B	7½d.	Hinks (J. & Son), Ltd.	1	27/6
S	10/	Jessop & Sons, £50 Sh	30	27½
S	10	Kayser, Ellsn. & Co. L.	5	10½
S	6	Do. Pref.	5	7½
M	7/6	Kellner-Partgton., L.	5	14½
M	4½	Do. Debs., 1914 .	100	105½
M	5	Kerr Thread, Ltd., Debs.............	100	99
B	17/	King's Norton Metal, £10 Shs..........	8½	18½
M	5/	Lancashire & Yorks. Wagon, Ltd.	10	9½
L	10/	Liverpool Exch., Ltd.	20	27½
L	45/	Do. Grain Stge, Ltd.	50	108
L	2/6	Do. Rubber, Ltd...	5	7
M	9d.	Manchester Bond. Whse., L., £10 Shs.	4½	2½
M	3/9	Do. Comcial. Bldgs., Ltd., £10 Shs.	5	10½
M	3/9	Do. No. 2, £10 Shs.	5	10½
M	2/3	Do. No. 3, £10 Shs.	5	7½
M	4/	Do. Corn, &c., Exchange, Ltd.	10	16½
M	4	Do. Debs.	100	125
M	8	Do. Ryl. Exchge, L.	100	246½
B	19/	Midland Rlwy. Car. Wgn., Ld., £20 Sh.	10	14½
Bl	5	Millers & Corys Dbs.	100	100½
B	12/6	Mint, Brgham., Ltd.	5	7
B	5	Do. Debs.	25	107
B	10/	Nettlefolds, Ltd.....	10	46
B	5	Do. Pref.	10	15
S	9	Nth. Centrl. Wgn., L.	5	9
B	10/	Patnt. Nut & Bolt, L.	10	28½
B	5	Do. Pref.	10	14½
B	6d.	Perry & Co., Ltd. ..	1	29/6
B	6d.	Do. Pref.	1	28/
S	10	Round, J., & Co., L., £10 Shs.	6	12½
S	10	Rodgers, J., & Sons, L.	100	218
M	18/9	Rylands & Sons, Ltd., £20	15	40½
M	2/6	Do. paid up	20	46
M	4	Do. Debs. .. 1909	100	106
S	5	Sanderson Brs. & Co., Ltd, Debs.	100	102
M	4½	Schwabe, S., & Co., Ltd., 1 Debs. 1914	100	104
S	7½	Sheffield Forge & Rolling, Ltd.	10	11½
L	—	Southport Pier, Ltd.	100	92½
L	2½	Do. W. Gdns., Ltd.	5	3½
Bl	5	Spillers & Bakers, Ltd, £10 Shs.	9	14½
Bl	6	Do. Pref.	10	14½
B	5/	Union Rolling Stock, Ltd., £20 Shs.....	5	7½
M	5/	Victoria Pr., S'port, L.	5	4½
Bl	8	Western Wagon & Property, Ltd.....	6	9½
S	10	Wostenholm, G., & Son, Ltd., £25 Shs.	20	26½
S	6½	Yorksh. Wagon, Ltd.	2	2½

FINANCIAL, TRUSTS, &c.

Chief Market.	Int. or Div.	Name.	Amount paid.	Price.
M	1/	Manchstr. Trst. £10 Shs.............	2	12/6
M	1/3	N. of Eng. T. Deb. & A., Ltd. £10 Shs.	2½	21/9
M	3½	Do. 1 Mt. Debs...	100	95½
L	—	Pacific Ln. & Inv., L.	2½	3
L	4	Do. Deb. Stk.....	100	102
L	—	United Trst., L. Prfd.	100	72½
L	—	Do. Deferred....	100	62½

GAS.

Chief Market.	Int. or Div.	Name.	Amount paid.	Price.
Bl	5	Bristol Gas (5 p.c. mx.)	100	130
Bl	4	Do. 1st Deb.	100	137
S	10	Gt. Grimsby "C" ..	10	202
L	10	Liverpool Utd. "A"	100	258
L	7	Do. "B"......	100	192
L	4	Do. Deb.	100	136
S	10	Sheffield Gas "A," "B," "C"	100	253
B	10½	Wolverhampton	100	222
B	3	Do. 6 p.c. Pref...	100	170½

INSURANCE.

Chief Market.	Int. or Div.	Name.	Amount paid.	Price.
M	6	Equitable F. & Acc. £5 Shs.	1	39/
L	—	Liverpool Mortgage £10 Shs.	2	1½
M	2/	Mchester. Fire £20 Shs..............	2	8
M	5/	National Boiler & G., Ltd., £10 Shs.	3	13½
L	2/	Reliance Mar., Ltd., £10 Shs.	2	4½
L	2/	Sea, Ltd., £10 Shs...	2	10⅝
L	—	Stnd. Mar., L., £20 Sh.	4	8½
L	—	State Fire, L., £20 Sh.	1	2½

COAL, IRON, AND STEEL.

Chief Market.	Int. or Div.	Name.	Amount paid.	Price.
Bl.	7/6	Albion Stm. Coal ..	10	10½
M	—	And. Knowles & S., Ltd., £37½ Shs. ..	22½	13½
M	5	Do. Mt. Debs. 1908	100	105½
Bl.	1/½	Ashton V. Iron	100	25
S		Bessemer, Ltd.	10	19½
S	5	Do. Pref.	10	15
S	7	Briggs, H., & Co., "A" £15 Shs.....	12½	15½
S	7	Do. "B" £15 Shs.	8½	9½
S	20	Brown Baley's. Stl., L.	10	29½
S	5	Brown, J., & Co., Cum. Pref.	10	13½
S	5	Cammell, C. & Co., Ltd.............	85	12½
S	5	Do. Pref.	5	6½
M	5	Chatterley Whitfield. Col., Debs., 1905..	100	100½
Bl	4	Davis, D., & Sons, Ld.	10	9½
M	5	Evans, R., & Co., Ltd., Deb., 1910 ..	100	100½
S	12½	Fox, S., & Co., Ltd., £100 Shs.	80	178½
Bl	10	Gt. Wstn. Col., L., "A"	5	10
Bl	5	Do. "B"	5	4½
Bl	3	Main Colliery, Ltd.	10	7
B	2/6	Muntz's Metal, Ltd.	5	7½
B	5	Do. Pref.......	5	6½
M	2/6½	Nth. Lonsd. Iron and Steel, Ltd., £10 Sh.	8½	2½
Bl	6	North's Nav. Coll., Ltd., Debs.	100	105
S	60/	Parkgate Irn. & Stl., Ltd., £100 Shs. ..	75	69½
M	6	Pearson & Knls., Ld., "A" Cum. Pref...	50	46
B	10/	Sandwell Pk. Col., L.	10	17½
M	6/3	Sheepbridge Coal and Iron, Ltd., "A"	25	17½
M	2/6	Do. "B"	10	6½
M	5	Do. "C" Gua. Pf.	25	28½
Bl	4	South Wales Coll., Ltd., "A"	17	8½
S	55/	Staveley Coal & Iron, Ltd., "A" £100 Sh.	60	79½
S	55/	Do. "C"	60	80½
M	1/10½	Tredegar Iron & Cl., Ld., "A" £10 Sh.	7½	25
M	1½	Do. "B" Stk. ..	100	29½
M	2/	Wigan Cl. & Irn., Ld.	10	6
M	1/6	Do. £10 Shs.	7½	3½

SHIPPING.

Chief Market.	Int. or Div.	Name.	Amount paid.	Price.
Bl	6	Bristol St. Nav. Pref.	10	11½
L	5/	Brit. & Af. St. Nav..	10	13½
L	3/10½	British & Estn, Ltd.	6½	2½
L	10/	Pacific Stm. Nav., L.	25	24
L	10/	Wst. Ind. & Pac. St. Ltd., £25 Shs....	20	29½

TRAMWAYS, &c.

Chief Market.	Int. or Div.	Name.	Amount paid.	Price.
B	5/	Brmngh. & Aston, L.	5	11
B	5/	Do. Mid., Ltd...	10	8
Bl	6/	Bristol Tr. & Car., Ltd..............	10	20½
Bl	4/	Do. Debs.	100	121
L	6	I. of Man Elec., L., Pref.	1	1½
M	15/	Manchester C. & T., L., "A" £20 Shs.	15	27½
M	10/	Do. "B"	10	18½

WATER WORKS.

Chief Market.	Int. or Div.	Name.	Amount paid.	Price.
Bl	7	Bristol	25	62
Bl	7	Do..............	20	46½
Bl	58/	Do. 7 p.c. max. ..	100	157½
Bl	4½	Do. Pref.	20	32½
Bl	5	Do. Pref.	10	18½
Bl	3½	Do. Deb.	100	129½
M	10	Fylde "A"	100	335
M	7	Do. "B"	100	224
B	6	S. Staffs. Ord. "A"	100	168
B	—	Do. "B"	100	167
B	4	Do. Deb. Stk.	100	140
B	5	Do. Pf "A" "B" "C"	100	165
M	£3½	Stockport District ..	100	184½
B	2/	Wolverhampton New	5	6½

SCOTTISH.

In quoting the markets, E stands for Edinburgh, and G for Glasgow.

RAILWAYS.

Chief Market.	Int. or Div.	Name.	Nom. Amount	Price.
E	6½	Arbroath and Forfar	25	51
G	2	Callander and Oban.	10	7½
G	4	Do. Deb. Stock	100	148
G	4½	Do. Pref.......	10	14½
G	4	Cathct. Dist. Deb. Stk.	100	148
E	5	Edin. and Bathgate .	100	181½
E	7	Forth & Clyde Junc.	100	226
G	4	Lanarks. and Ayrsh.	10	14
G	4	Do. & Dumbartons.	10	14½
G	4	Do. Deb. Stk.	100	149

BANKS.

Chief Market.	Int. or Div.	Name.	Nom. Amount	Price.
G	12	Bank of Scotland ..	100	357½
G	16	British Linen	100	478
G	8	Caledonian, Ltd.....	2½	97/6
G	10	Clydesdale, Ltd.	10	24
G	16	Commercl. of Scot., L.	20	88½†
G	16	National of Scot. Ld.	100	417
G	8	Royal of Scotland ..	100	231
G	11	Union of Scotland, L.	10	26

BREWERIES.

Chief Market.	Int. or Div.	Name.	Nom. Amount	Price.
E	5	Bernard, Thos. Pref.	10	10½
E	5	Bernard, T. & J., Cum. Pref.........	10	12½
G	20	Highland Distilleries	3½	10½

CANALS AND DOCKS.

Chief Market.	Int. or Div.	Name.	Nom. Amount	Price.
G	4	Clyde Nav. 4 p.c....	100	126
G	3½	Do. 3½ p.c.......	100	103½
G	3½	Greenock Harb. "A"	100	99
G	2	Do. "B"	100	38½

MISCELLANEOUS.

Chief Market.	Int. or Div.	Name.	Nom. Amount	Price.
G	4½	Alexander & Co. Debs.	100	110½
G	5	Baird, H., & Sns. C.P.	10	12½
E	10	Barry, Ostlere, & Co.	7½	12½
E	6	Do. Cum. Pref...	10	15
G	5	Brown, Stewart, Deb.	100	84
E	7½	Broxburn Oil	8½	8½
E	6	Do. Cum. Pref...	10	11⅝
E	7	Edinburgh & Dist. Tram. Cum. Pref.	5	8⅝
E	5	Gilroy, Sons, & Co. Debs............	100	99
G	3/	Glasgow Cot. Spin...	6	5½
G	55/	Do. Royal Exchg.	46	110
G	—	Pumpherston Oil Pf.	10	8½
E	7	Scottish Assam Tea	10	11½
E	5	Scottish Waggon....	10	13½
G	5	Stoddard & Co. Pref.	10	12½

FINANCIAL, LAND, AND INVESTMENT.

Chief Market.	Int. or Div.	Name.	Nom. Amount	Price.
G	1/	Assets Co..........	1	47/
E	4½	Investors' Mort. Pref.	100	99½
E	4	Do. Deb. Stk....	100	103½
E	4	Nthn. Inv. N. Zeal. Deb. Stk.	100	107
E	4	N. of Scot. Canadian Deb. Stk.	100	106
E	4½	Real & Deb. Corp. Deb. Stk.	100	106½

INSURANCE.

Chief Market.	Int. or Div.	Name.	Amount paid.	Price.
G	12/	Caledonian F. & Life	5	36½
G	4/6	City of Glasgow Life	2½	13¾
E	19/	Edinburgh Life	20	55
G	13/1	Life Ass. of Scotland	8¼	34½
E	8	Nat. Guar. & Surety	2	49/
G	17½	Scottish Union and National "A"....	1	96/
G	17½	Do. "B"	3¾	18

IRON, COAL, AND STEEL.

Chief Market.	Int. or Div.	Name.	Amount paid.	Price.
E	Nil.	Addie, Coll. Cm. Pref.	10	8
E	8/	Arniston Coal	8	14
E	5	Cairntable Gas Coal	8	86/
E	7½	Fife Coal	10	21
E	5	Do. Cum. Pref..	10	13¼
G	7	Merry & Cunghame. Cum. Pref........	10	15¼
G	5	Do. Debentures ..	100	105¾
E	1/9	Niddrie & Benhar Cl.	1½	40/
G	5	Steel Com. of Scotlnd	—	
	—	"A" Deb. Stk. ..	100	113
G	6	Do. and Mt. "B"	100	105
E	—	Watson, John	8¼	10¼
E	6	Do. Cum. Pref..	7½	8¾
E	19½	Wilson's & Cly. Coal	3	9

IRISH.

In quoting the markets, B stands for Belfast, and D for Dublin.

CORPORATION STOCKS.

Chief Market.	Int. or Div.	Name.	Amount paid.	Price.
B	3½	Belfast, 1921	100	112
B	3¾	Do. 1912........	100	108¾
B	3½	Do. 1924........	100	109¼
B	3	Do. 1955........	100	106
B	3½	Do. Water Com...	100	117½
B	3	Do. do.	100	106¼
B	3½	Do. Harbour Com.	100	114
D	3½	Rathmines & Rathgar	100	110¼
D	3½	Waterford Deb.	100	—

RAILWAYS.

Chief Market.	Int. or Div.	Name.	Amount Paid.	Price.
D	25/	Cork, Bandon, & S.C.	100	76
D	4	Do. Deb.........	100	—
D	4	Do. W. Cork Pref.	100	119
B	5½	Belfast & Northern..	100	162
B	4	Do. Deb.........	100	147
B	4	Do. Pref.	100	142
B	6½	Belfast & C. Down..	100	160
B	4	Do. Deb.........	100	147½
B	3	Do.	100	109
B	4½	Do. 4½ Pref. B...	100	153½
B	5	Do. Guar.	100	173½
D	Nil.	Dublin, Wick. & Wex.	100	25
D	4	Do. Deb.........	100	124½
D	4½	Do. Deb.........	100	130
D	6	Do. Guar.	100	163
D	4	Do. C. of Dub. Junc.	100	—
D	5	Do. 1860 Pref. ..	100	116¼
D	—	Do. 1864 Pref. ..	100	100
D	—	Do. 1865 Pref. ..	100	—
B	6½	Great Northern	100	182
B	4	Do. Deb.........	100	148
B	4	Do. Pref. B.	100	145½
B	5½	Gt. South & Western	100	147½
B	4	Do. Deb.	100	147¾
B	4	Do. Guar.........	100	146
D	4	Midland Gt. Western	100	115
D	4	Do. Deb.	100	—
D	4½	Do. Deb.	100	151½
D	4½	Do. Deb.	100	—
D	5	Do. Pref.	100	177
D	4	Do. Pref.	100	142¾
D	—	Waterford & Central	100	—
D	3	Do. Deb.	100	94½
D	3½	Do. Pref.	100	115
D	4	Waterfd. L., & W. Db.	100	127½
D	4½	Do. Deb.	100	—
D	4	Do. Pref.	100	119
D	3½	Do. Pref.	100	90½

BANKS.

Chief Market.	Int. or Div.	Name.	Amount paid.	Price.
B	50/	Belfast, Old, £125 Shs.	25	127
B	20/	Do. New, £125 Shs.	25	51½
D	2/	Hibernian, £25 Shs.	5	6⅞
D	2/	Munster & Leinster £5 Shs.	2	5⅝
B	11/	Northern, £50 Shs...		27½
D	13/	Royal, £50 Shs.	10	29¾
B	5/	Ulster, £15 Shs.	2½	12⅞

BREWERIES AND DISTILLERIES.

Chief Market.	Int. or Div.	Name.	Amount paid.	Price.
D	10/	Castlebellingham & Drog	10	15¼
D	6	Do. Pref.	10	15¼
D	4½	Do. Deb.	100	116
B	17/	Dunville & Co.......	10	29⅞
B	6	Irish Distillery, Pref.	10	13
B	5	Do. Deb.	100	111
B	6	J. & J. M'Connell, Pf.	10	15
B	13/6	Mitchell & Co.......	9	19¼
B	5	Do. Deb.	10	11½
D	4½	Phœnix Brew. Deb.	100	—
B	6/	Wm. Cowan........	10	13
B	6	Do. Pref. ..	10	13½
B	8/	Young, King, & Co.	8	14

STEAM AND CANAL.

Chief Market.	Int. or Div.	Name.	Amount paid.	Price.
B	Nil	Belfast Steamship ..	50	35½
D	10/	British and Irish	50	—
D	15/	City of Dublin......	100	63½
D	3½	Do. Deb.	100	105
D	30/	Dublin & Lpool. Bldg.	50	76
D	2/6	Dundalk & Newry..	10	4½
D	3/6	Grand Canal........	10	11⅝
D	3	Do. Pref. ..	10	9¾
D	3	Do. Deb. ..	100	97½
B	30/	Irish Shipowners....	100	60
B	3/6	Ulster Steamship....	5	6

MISCELLANEOUS.

Chief Market.	Int. or Div.	Name.	Amount paid.	Price.
D	3/1	Arnott & Co.	4	[illegible]
D	6	Do. Pref. ..	4	[illegible]
B	8/	Belfast Com. Bldgs.	10	11
B	52/6	Do. Ropework Co.	75	[illegible]
B	5	Do. do. Pref.	10	[illegible]
B	2/	Do. Discount Co..	3	[illegible]
B	5	Do. do. Pref.	5	[illegible]
B	10/	Brookfield Linen....	25	17
B	Nil	Coey & Co.	25	[illegible]
B	5	Do. Deb.	50	[illegible]
B	4½	David Allen & S's Deb.	100	[illegible]
D	4/	Dublin Trams	10	[illegible]
D	6	Do. Pref....	10	[illegible]
D	4	Do. Deb....	100	—
B	5/	Edenderry Spinning .	10	9
B	25/	Falls Flax Spinning .	25	15
B	17/	Forster, Green, & Co.	10	[illegible]
B	9/	Island Spinning	7½	[illegible]
B	8/	Jas. Lindsay & Co..	8	[illegible]
B	1/7½	John Arnott & Co...	4	[illegible]
B	4½	Do. Deb.........	50	97
D	5/	Kinahan & Co.......	10	—
D	5½	Do. Pref.........	10	118
D	4½	Do. Deb.........	100	[illegible]
B	12/	Kirker & Co.	10	10
B	5/	Leahy, Kelly, & Leahy	5	[illegible]
B	6	Do. Pref.........	5	[illegible]
B	2/4½	Lindsay Bros. Ltd...	5	[illegible]
B	4½	Do. Deb.........	50	[illegible]
D	1/	National Assurance .	2½	—
B	10/	Olley & Co.	5	[illegible]
D	1/1½	Patriotic Assurance..	2½	[illegible]
B	3/7½	P. Johnston & Son, L.	6	[illegible]
B	10/	Robertson, F., & Co.	8	[illegible]
B	10	Ulster Marine Insur.	5/	[illegible]
B	15/	York-street Flax	25	34
B	6	Do. Pref.........	20	15
B	4½	Do. Deb.........	100	119

INDIAN AND CEYLON TEA COMPANIES.

Acres Planted.	Crop, 1896.	Paid up Capital.	Share.	Paid up.	Name.	Dividends 1894.	Dividends 1895.	Dividends 1896.	Int. 1897.	Price.	Yield.	Reserve.	Balance Forward.	Working Capital.	Mortgages, Debs. or Pref. Capital not otherwise stated.
	lb.	£	£	£	INDIAN COMPANIES.							£	£	£	£
11,240	3,109,000	120,000	10	3	Amalgamated Estates	—	*	10	5	3¾	8¼	10,000	16,500	D52,950	—
		400,000	10	10	Do. Pref.	—	*	5	†5	10½	4¾				
10,223	3,387,100	187,160	20	20	Assam	20	20	20	5	60	6¾	55,000	1,730	D11,350	—
5,900	3,310,000	142,500	10	10	Assam Frontier..........	3	6	6	—	9	6¾	—	286	20,000	82,500
		142,500	10	10	Do. Pref.	6	6	6	3	12	5				
2,087	865,550	66,745	5	5	Attaree Khat	12	12	8	3	7¼	5¼	3,790	4,820	7,770	—
1,633	550,980	78,170	10	10	Borelli	4	4	5	—	8¾	5¾	—	3,256	D270	6,500 Pref.
1,689	880,000	60,825	5	5	British Indian	6	5	5	—	4½	5¾	—	2,920	12,300	16,500 Pref.
3,223	2,282,430	114,500	5	5	Brahmapootra	20	18	20	6	14	7	—	28,440	41,600	-
3,904	1,634,000	76,500	10	10	Cachar and Dooars	*	8	7	—	9½	7¾	—	1,645	21,240	-
		76,500	10	10	Do. Pref.	*	6	6	3	12½	4¾				
3,946	2,002,370	72,010	1	1	Chargola	8	7	10	2½	1	10	3,000	3,300	—	—
		81,000	1	1	Do. Pref.	7	7	7	3½	1⅛	5½				
1,971	968,090	33,000	5	5	Chubwa	10	8	10	3½	7	7¼	10,000	2,043	D5,400	—
		33,000	5	5	Do. Pref.	7	7	7	3½	7	5				
33,250	10,620,000	120,000	10	3	Cons. Tea and Lands	—	*	10	5	3¾	7½	65,000	14,240	D191,674	—
		1,000,000	10	10	Do. 1st Pref.	—	*	5	†5	11	4¾				
		400,000	10	10	Do. 2nd Pref.	—	*	7	†7	11¾	5¾				
2,230	593,160	135,420	20	20	Darjeeling..............	5½	5½	6	—	23	5	5,552	1,565	1,700	—
2,114	456,580	60,000	10	10	Darjeeling Cons..........	—	—	4/2	—	7½	—	—	1,820	—	—
		60,000	10	10	Do. Pref.	—	*	5	2½	9½	5				
6,600	2,973,050	150,000	10	10	Duoars	12½	12½	12½	2½	21	6¼	45,000	300	D32,000	—
		75,000	10	10	Do. Pref.	7	7	7	3½	17½	4				
3,367	1,833,520	163,000	10	10	Doom Dooma	11¾	10	12½	5	22¾	5½	30,000	4,032	—	10,000
1,377	500,080	61,120	5	5	Eastern Assam	5	nil.	4	—	3	5¾	—	1,790	—	10,000
4,038	1,529,380	85,000	10	10	East India and Ceylon	5	nil.	7	—	9½	7	—	1,710	—	—
		85,000	10	10	Do. Pref.	*	6	6	3	12	5				
7,570	3,600,000	219,000	10	10	Empire of India	—	*	6/10	2	12½	—	15,000	—	27,000	—
		219,000	10	10	Do. Pref.	—	*	5	2½	11½	4½				
1,180	647,600	94,060	10	10	Indian of Cachar	7	3½	3	—	5½	5½	6,070	—	7,120	—
2,916	968,000	83,500	5	5	Jhanzie	10	10	10	4	8¾	5¾	14,500	1,070	2,700	—
7,980	3,467,000	250,000	10	10	Jokai	10	10	10	5	18	5½	45,000	990	D9,000	—
		100,000	10	10	Do. Pref.	*	6	6	3	15¼	3¾				
5,224	1,801,600	100,000	20	20	Jorehaut	20	20	20	—	58	7	36,220	2,955	3,000	—
1,547	554,560	65,660	10	8	Lebong	15	15	15	5	17½	6¾	9,000	2,150	8,650	—
5,082	1,843,700	100,000	10	10	Lungla	5	10	6	3	9½	6	—	1,543	D21,000	—
		100,000	10	10	Do. Pref.	*	6	6	3	12	4¾				
2,684	866,300	95,970	10	10	Majuli	7	5	5	—	7	7	—	2,606	560	—
1,300	216,000	91,840	1	1	Makum	—	—	2	—	1⅛	1¾	—	—	1,200	25,000
3,140	938,400	100,000	1	1	Moabund	—	—	*	—	1	—	—	—	-	—
		50,000	1	1	Do. Pref.	—	—	*	2½	1	5				
1,080	510,000	79,590	10	10	Scottish Assam	7	7	7	—	11	6¼	6,500	800	9,590	—
4,150	1,635,000	100,000	10	10	Singlo..............	5	8	5	1	9½	4½	—	300	D5,200	—
		80,000	10	10	Do. Pref.	*	6½	6½	3½	13	5				
					CEYLON COMPANIES.										
10,315	1,743,824	250,000	100	100	Anglo-Ceylon, & Gen.	—	*	5½	—	70	7¾	10,992	1,405	D72,844	166,520
1,836	685,741	50,000	10	10	Associated Tea	—	*	5	—	8½	5¾	—	164	2,478	—
		60,000	10	10	Do. Pref.	—	*	6	—	11	5¾				
10,390	3,763,000	167,380	10	10	Ceylon Tea Plantations ..	15	15	15	7	27¾	5¾	84,500	1,516	D30,819	—
		81,080	10	10	Do. Pref.	7	7	7	†7	17½	4¾				
5,722	1,542,700	55,960	5	3	Ceylon & Oriental Est.....	5	8	7	—	2¾	7¾	—	230	D2,047	71,000
		46,000	5	5	Do. Pref.	6	6	6	3	5	6				
2,157	801,629	111,330	5	5	Dimbula Valley	—	*	10	5	6¼	7	—	—	1,733	6,250
		62,607	5	5	Do. Pref.	—	*	6	3	6¼	4¾				
11,496	3,715,000	298,250	5	5	Eastern Prod. & Est.	3	5	6¼	2½	6½	4¾	20,000	11,740	D17,797	100,500
3,118	701,100	150,000	10	10	Lanka Plantations........	4	5	5	†5	7¾	6¾	—	495	D11,300	14,700 Pref.
2,193	960,100	22,080	10	10	New Dimbula "A"	10	16	16	—	25	6	11,000	2,024	1,150	—
		55,710	10	10	Do. "B"	18	16	16	—	23½	6¾				
		8,400	10	10	Do. "C"	nil.	8	14	—	15	8¾				
2,572	570,360	100,000	10	10	Ouvah	6	8	6	2	9½	6½	4,000	1,151	D1,255	—
2,030	535,675	200,000	10	10	Nuwara Eliya	—	*	6	3	11¾	5¾	—	—	—	30,000
1,720	720,200	41,000	10	10	Scottish Ceylon	15	15	15	5	23	6¾	7,000	1,252	D3,970	—
		9,000	10	10	Do. Pref.	7	7	7	3½	16½	3¾				
2,450	602,000	56,000	10	6	Standard	12½	15	15	5	14¾	6¾	9,000	800	D14,018	4,000

Working-Capital Column.—In working-capital column, D stands for *debit*.

* Company formed this year. † Interim dividends are given as actual distribution made. ‡ *Total* div.

Printed for the Proprietor by LOVE & WYMAN, LTD., Great Queen Street, London, W.C.; and Published by CLEMENT WILSON at Norfolk House, Norfolk Street, Strand, London, W.C.

The Investors' Review

Vol. I.—No. 6. New Series. FRIDAY, FEBRUARY 11, 1898. [Registered as a Newspaper.] Price 6d. By post, 6½d

The Investment Index,

A Quarterly Supplement to the "Investors' Review."

Price 2s. net. 8s. 6d. per annum, post free.

THE INVESTMENT INDEX is an indispensable supplement to the Investors' Review. A file of it enables investors to follow the ups and downs of markets, and each number gives the return obtainable on all classes of securities at recent prices, arranged in a most convenient form for reference. Appended to its tables of figures are criticisms on company balance sheets, State Budgets, &c., similar to those in the Investors' Review.

Regarding it, the *Specker* says: "The Quarterly 'Investment Index' is probably the handiest and fullest, as it is certainly the safest, of guides to the investor."

"The compilation of securities is particularly valuable."—*Pall Mall Gazette.*

"Its carefully classified list of securities will be found very valuable."—*Globe.*

"At no time has such a list of securities been more valuable than at the present."—*Star.*

"The invaluable 'Investors' Index.'"—*Sketch.*

"A most valuable compilation."—*Glasgow Herald.*

Subscription to the "Investors' Review" and "Investment Index," 36s. per annum, post free.

CLEMENT WILSON,
NORFOLK HOUSE, NORFOLK STREET, LONDON, W.C.

"INVESTORS' REVIEW."

NOTICES.

BACK NUMBERS.

Less than a dozen complete sets now remain of the first four Quarterly Numbers of the "INVESTORS' REVIEW," so that the first Number of all can only be supplied in volume form, price **21s.** net. The Volume for 1893 is also composed of Quarterly Parts, and its price is the same. The seven Quarterly Parts from Number II. onwards can still be had separately, price 5s. net. For the succeeding four years down to December, 1897, the "REVIEW" is in Monthly Numbers.

All Monthly Numbers more than six months old will now be charged 1s. 6d. net, and all Half-yearly Volumes, 10s. 6d. net (by post, 2d. and 10d. extra for the Number or Volume).

Cloth Cases for binding the "REVIEW" and the "INDEX" are charged for as follows:—For Annual Volumes of the "REVIEW," 1s. 6d.; for Semi-annual Volumes, 1s. 3d.; and for Yearly Volumes of the "INDEX," also 1s. 3d. Postage, in all instances, 2d. extra.

Volume I. (July, 1895—April, 1896) and Volume II. (July, 1896—April, 1897) of the "INVESTMENT INDEX" now ready, price 9s. 6d. each, net (post free, 10s.).

CONTENTS

The Investors' Review.

Economic and Financial Notes and Correspondence.

STALEMATE IN CHINA.

Lord Salisbury's statement in the House of Lords on Tuesday night may appear satisfactory to all except those who know anything about the affairs in the Far East. He made it clear enough that the port of Ta-lien-wan, over which so much fuss has been made, was used merely as an engine of diplomacy for the purpose of clearing up an ambiguous position. But is this position cleared up? We doubt it much. Both Russia and Germany had seized the places on the Chinese coast, with the apparent intention of converting them into exclusive depôts for their own ships of war and commerce. It was quite on the cards that France would follow their example, and therefore the British Government was under the necessity of taking steps to oblige these Powers to declare themselves. Our Ambassador at Pekin put forward our treaty rights in opposition to the exclusive attitude of Germany and Russia, and suggested the opening of Ta-lien-wan as a treaty port. The move was excellent, and it has resulted in "Stalemate." "We shall make our ports free," quoth the Powers, and Lord Salisbury thankfully accepts. "A free port is better than a treaty port," he told the House of Lords. That doctrine, with all respect to him, is mischievous nonsense. A treaty port means a port whose commerce is regulated by the European maritime customs service of China, a service which guarantees equal rights to all comers. A "free port" means whatsoever Germany or Russia pleases—free while we watch and grumble, closed when our attention is elsewhere. At other points in the game we also seem to have come off second best. Our treaty rights have been recognised in form and undermined in reality. The equality of all the Powers before the Chinese is broken, and the patch-up now come to might very easily be the prelude to a fight. Well may the *Standard* speak out against such an exhibition of "fustian and funk."

The fuss about the loan to China, on the other hand, appears a little misplaced, and it is quite conceivable that China may not require a loan so soon as was expected; and, when she does want it, we can, if we like, prevent her from getting it if she does not take it of us. Of course, the attempt of the Pekin Government to raise an internal loan will only have laughable results, because John Chinaman has no reason to trust the officials of the Empire. But suppose it fail, and suppose China obtain no money from anywhere, may not this be exactly what Japan just now wants? We have left Japan too much out of sight in all our recent splutterings about our "rights," our capacities to "enforce" them, and the rest of the stage gag in the Far East. It has been almost forgotten that Japanese interests have been more vitally touched by the great Continental Powers even than ours, and that Japan has the strongest ground for resenting the presence of Russia and Germany as naval powers in Chinese waters. By that presence the position has been completely altered since the Treaty of Shimonosaki was signed, and it is now more than probable that Japan would not surrender Wei-hai-wei, even were the entire indemnity due to her paid. Her Government might say, and say with very good reason, "we cannot give up this place while Powers who have shown themselves at a critical period in our history enemies to us remain in possession of Port Arthur and Kiau-Chau."

What were the terms of the treaty of peace in regard to the indemnity? Japan was to hold Wei-hai-wei until all the money was paid, and the ultimate date of payment was 1902. Between May, 1898, when the last instalment of the second portion of the indemnity, amounting to about £2,500,000, falls due, and May, 1902, China has to pay Japan nearly £17,000,000, including interest. Power, however, was reserved to her to escape the interest charges, and to release the occupied port by paying up the final instalment in full next May. Hence the desirability of obtaining a loan of £12,000,000 between now and then. The money for the instalment due in May being already provided, it would just take China about £12,000,000 to pay out Japan in advance, and release Wei-hai-wei. If, however, Japan will not surrender this port, there can be no urgent necessity for China to pay the money, and it is quite on the cards that the two Powers may so arrange matters that China will be released from part of her money obligations under the treaty of peace, in exchange for the continued occupancy of Wei-hai-hei by Japan. Certainly, this is an arrangement which would suit us admirably, for our one friend, at present, in the distant East is, undoubtedly, Japan.

The Army and National Expenditure.

We give the following pregnant sentences, which formed the concluding portion of Sir William Harcourt's speech in the opening debate on the Address in reply to the Queen's Speech. The right hon. gentleman was discussing the proposals for increased expenditure on the Army; and his denunciation of this constant addition to the national expenditure is a weighty warning which ought to be profoundly considered by every reasonable and responsible person in this country. "You have had great and cumulative surpluses without any relief to the taxpayer," said Sir William. This is true; and there is no sign that the Government is yet giving a thought to the relief of the taxpayer, or, indeed, of doing anything whatever to check this steadily increasing drain on the vital resources of the nation. If some step in this direction is not taken soon, it may come too late:—

I have felt it my duty before to raise a note of warning as to the expenditure of this country. The Government, or at least some of them, enter upon these estimates with imperfect information. One of them says that there has been no addition to the Army for thirty years, whereas, as a matter of fact, there has been an addition of over 100,000 men, 30,000 to the colours and 80,000 reserve. There has been, moreover, an increase in the expenditure on the Army of 50 per cent., for the estimates have risen from £12,000,000 to £18,000,000; and if you add to that the military defences of the Empire and the increase in the Indian Army, the addition to the expenditure on the Army has been enormous. (Hear, hear.) The additions to naval and military expenditure together since 1870 have been £19,000,000 a year. I would ask the House and the Chancellor of the Exchequer to bear in mind these figures. The additions in a time of nominal peace to the naval and military expenditure of this country are greater than the charge on the national debt for the accumulated wars of two centuries. (Hear, hear.) I have always warned the House of the growth in expenditure. It is growing, not in arithmetical but in geometrical progression. The growth in the expenditure of this country has been in the last thirty years £27,000,000, and if you choose to add to it, as you ought, the money you take out of the Exchequer to give in local subsidies, the amount is £35,000,000. The resources of this country are vast, but they are not inexhaustible. You have a great revenue founded on a sound commercial and monetary basis. The yield is abundant, and I am glad to know that the Chancellor of the Exchequer will have a large surplus (hear, hear); and you have this remarkable fact, that in the third year of cumulative surpluses you are told you are going to have unprecedented estimates. You have, for the first time in the financial history of this country, this phenomenon, that you have had great and cumulative surpluses without any relief to the taxpayer. (Hear, hear.) You will have a great revenue, but you will have great demands upon it, demands for the Army, demands for the Navy, for Ireland, for the West Indies, and I know not what besides. When the Chancellor of the Exchequer comes to satisfy these demands I think he will regret those £2,000,000 which he threw away on the Agricultural Rates Bill ("Oh, oh," and cheers), a dole given out of the Exchequer upon the false pretence now known to everybody to be false, that the land of England was going out of cultivation. We now find Minister after Minister getting up and saying that there never was such a delusion, and that that was not what they meant. They were perfectly shocked, and the chairman of the Commission said that the profession of agriculture was a more agreeable and, on the whole, a more profitable calling than any other trade. Well, sir, you have a splendid revenue if you administer it wisely and well, but if you abuse it by squandering your resources, by giving doles to favoured industries, by unnecessary frontier wars and Soudan expeditions, it is my firm belief that you will exhaust the springs on which the life of your Empire depends. (Cheers.)

The Vanishing Concert.

There is at present rather a lull in the excitement which Russian diplomacy had caused in connection with the candidature of Prince George of Greece for the governorship of Crete. There were ominous prophecies about the break up of the European Concert—which could hardly be regarded as an irreparable calamity—and there were very real indications that the "understanding" between Austria and Russia was no longer binding, if it has not already come to an untimely end. It has become tolerably clear that the two countries cannot agree in their policy in the Balkans. Both want the same thing—dominating influence in that particular part of the world, and, of course, only one can be successful in achieving her purpose. For the present, however, the battle is over the governorship of Crete. Austria has adopted a *non-possumus* attitude; Russia, until the other day, was vigorously active in forcing forward the candidature of Prince George; but during the last day or two she has slackened her energy in that direction, and has, indeed, postponed further action for the present. Russia's immediate purpose, it would seem, is first to get the Turks out of Thessaly. With this view apparently she has joined with England and France in guaranteeing the Greek indemnity loan; and, having paid out Turkey, will insist on the evacuation of Thessaly. This accomplished, the candidature of Prince George will be revived, and, no doubt, insisted upon. Meanwhile Lord Salisbury informs us that, though the Turkish troops will not be called upon to withdraw from Crete, no reinforcements shall be allowed to land, and he hopes to see those remaining take their departure in no very long time. But as all this action is being taken by only three out of the six members of the Concert, it may, we presume, be taken for granted that the famous—or notorious—European Areopagus is already practically at an end. Indeed, the Russian official communication, published yesterday, looks very much like a determination to withdraw from it altogether, unless she can have her way about the new Governor-General of Crete.

THE "CHARTERED" COMPANY AND ITS VANISHING BOARD.

In view of last Monday's announcement that the Duke of Fife and Lord Farquhar have retired from the board of the British South African Company, it is desirable that the Government should be pressed to give fuller information in regard to the dealings of the members of this board on the Stock Exchange. In June, 1896, we drew attention to the shareholdings of the Duke of Fife, the Duke of Abercorn, Mr. Rhodes, and some other directors of the company at different dates, and it may be of interest to quote part of what we then said here :—

So far as we have got names, a comparison of the later list with the list of 1893 seems to indicate pretty clearly that the leading spirits of the company have been unloading. The 1893 list appears to have shown that Cecil Rhodes held about 772,000 shares at that date, including those received by him for his large slice of the United Concessions Company's capital. According to the figures given in the *Chronicle*, his holding last July was reduced to less than 52,000 shares. What has become of the 700,000 odd, we have no means of knowing; but a series of lists might enable us to trace them to some extent. Perhaps they have gone abroad as "bearer" certificates. Sir Horace Farquhar, one of the directors of the company, appeared to possess about 16,000 shares in 1893, and in July, 1895, this, on the testimony of the *Chronicle*, was reduced to 6,358. The Duke of Fife, another director, is exhibited as holding 16,850 at the first date, and only 3,855 at the later date. If these gentlemen realised on the "boom" of last summer and autumn, their fortunes must have been substantially increased by the operation. The chairman of the company, however,—the Duke of Abercorn—appears to have held steadily to his investment almost with the tenacity of an enthusiast; for he realised between the two dates only about 3,200 of his shares, *i.e.*, he held 8,600 shares in 1893 and 5,419 in July, 1895, if we can believe the copyists.—INVESTORS' REVIEW, vol. vii., pp. 355, 356.

These figures indicated that the members of the board had been selling heavily to the public, trading upon the legend that the company was doing a great work in extending the borders of the Empire. Now that the board is falling to pieces it is not fair that transactions like these should be quietly hushed up. Lord Farquhar (then Sir Horace) has told a *Daily Mail* interviewer that he has too much to do now to be able to attend to the Chartered Company's affairs, which moreover—and this seems contradictory—do not now require any looking after. "The time of trouble has passed," quoth he, "and the company is now free from cares"—*vide* Mr. Cecil Rhodes on this point as quoted below. And is Lord Farquhar free from shares? Why cannot the House of Commons order the share lists of various dates to be published in parallel columns, so that all may see how money has been passing from the pockets of the public to those inside the magic circle? It may, of course, be that these gentlemen have not really parted with all the shares they seem to have sold; they may have turned their shares into bearer certificates and stuck to them. We are willing to give them the benefit of the doubt, but the matter must be cleared up.

This is the more necessary because the great master conjurer of them all, Mr. Cecil Rhodes, has now adopted the tone regarding the territory of the "Chartered" Company which cannot fail to have a most disastrous influence on the price of "Chartered" shares and the shares of the host of companies created under its patronage. There is something pathetic in the story told by Mr. Gambier Bolton in last Saturday's *Daily News*. The great conjurer of empires by share emissions, wielder of millions, is afraid to trot on horseback lest the motion should cause his heart to stop; the triumphant conqueror of the Stock Exchange, of the British Government, and of Mr. Chamberlain, is now grey and white haired with anxiety, all the buoyancy gone out of him, and gloomy forebodings taking the place of the boastful language indulged in not so many months before. A week later, though, the same paper shows us the man in his old character—boisterously confident, and, having got his million safe, full of mockery at British philanthrophy plus 5 per cent. But his candour to Mr. Bolton interests us most. Just read the pith of that melancholy tale :—

He didn't scruple to admit that Rhodesia at present is practically worthless from the agricultural point of view, what with horse and mule sickness of two kinds, tsetse fly, and rinderpest or cattle-plague, scab, locusts, drought, and above all the scarcity of native labour. And, even from a mining point of view, owing to the want of labour. It was almost pathetic to hear him hurl anathemas against Exeter Hall and the Aborigines' Protection Society. Those bodies, and Sir Richard Martin's report on the subject, have stopped forced labour. As for the ordinary emigrant—he is the last person they want in Rhodesia. So long as food for man and grain for animals have to be brought into the country the cost of living *must* be enormous—far higher than any wages would provide for. No—the only sort of emigrant Mr. Rhodes wants is the capitalist—capital, capital. Capital — to develop the mines — to buy the crushing machinery—the extraction of more gold from the earth. Now that he has got his railroad to Buluwayo, Mr. Rhodes's fear is of a rush of poor people from the old country, to find no work, no food, only cold, heat, fever, and plagues of all sorts. It is for its gold, upon whose presence Mr. Rhodes stakes his reputation, and upon its usefulness as land over which his Cairo cable can run. Then, if he hadn't annexed it, some one else would, and that would never have done.

And, meanwhile, what is to happen?

Well, Mr. Rhodes said that when the two railways are open they would be able to get up the heavy machinery from the coast necessary to crush the quartz, and then, supposing they could get the natives to work, they might be able to pay dividends—in time.

The natives won't work unless they're made. They say they don't want the white man's money. They lived without it *before* he came to their country, they can do so now. They are mostly warriors, and fighting and hunting are all they care for. "Look at them!" exclaimed Mr. Rhodes, raging; "there they sit—great, able-bodied men, squatting round their huts week after week, plotting and scheming, loafing, eating, and sleeping; and the country going to rack and ruin for want of the labour which they alone can give us, if we are to work our mines and farms profitably. Exeter Hall and the Aborigines' Protection Society have dealt us—and me personally—the worst blow that has ever fallen on this country, and if things go wrong from this cause on their heads must be the blame." These are almost Mr. Rhodes's own words.

With all his faults Mr. Cecil Rhodes has the merit of being frank to brutality. He never minces matters and only in the Jameson raid episode could he be said ever to have been guilty of ambiguities of speech. The statements here reported are therefore in the highest degree interesting. They admit that slave labour was part of the means by which Rhodesian mines were to be developed, and they admit the practical worthlessness of the country for anything except minerals. To do him justice still further, Mr. Rhodes never said that it was anything else. And he may plead that forced, or slave, labour is no worse in Rhodesia than in the Transvaal and Kimberley, where it exists as a practical institution, with Exeter Hall silent. But what a contrast the master's blunt outspokenness is to the "all trouble over" optimism of Lord Farquhar. Have his Lordship and the Duke of Fife sold out in despair? What is the truth about this "Chartered" Company with its globular capital, its absence of accounts, the complete silence in which its affairs have been wrapped since we turned its balance-sheets inside out in April, 1896? No accounts of any kind have been published of a later date than March, 1895. Is Parliament going to allow this sort of thing to continue, while one by one or two by two the rats slink off and leave the nation to face unknown responsibilities, perhaps enormous debts?

The Managers of the Stock Exchange and Sir Henry Burdett, K.C.B.

We are rather sorry for Sir Henry Burdett; he has given himself away so very badly in the correspondence with the trustees and managers of the Stock Exchange which he has just published. His object in instituting this correspondence was to get these gentlemen to give him a pension, and in his argument in support of his petition he cites the settled custom in the City of London in the case of highly-placed officials of the Bank of England, the Corporation, and other wealthy bodies. But surely this is nothing to the purpose. The real question is, What was Sir Henry's contract? Recognising, perhaps, the weakness of this argument, he proceeded in a long memorandum to set forth his services, and to furnish medical certificates intended to prove that his resignation was forced upon him by ill-health, the result of over-work in the service of the Stock Exchange. He claims to have conceived and produced the book now known as "Burdett's Official Intelligence," the capital value of which, he says, at a moderate computation, "cannot be less than £30,000." We should be sorry to give £3,000 for it. As a result of his labours, he further claims to have added £3,800 per annum to the resources of the managers, and in return for seventeen years devoted to these arduous labours he thinks he should have a pension.

When Sir Henry's resignation was first made public, this pension question was considerably agitated at his own instance. We made inquiries then among members of the "House" of the highest standing, and the result was to force upon us the conclusion that the voluntarily-retiring secretary to the Share and Loan Department was not entitled to any pension. For many years, we were told, if not for the whole period of his service, his income was four thousand guineas per annum, enough, surely, to enable him to provide a retiring competency for himself? And, as regards his over-work, what many of the members pointed out to us was that Sir Henry had not obtained his K.C.B.-ship by serving the Committee of General Purpose and editing its "Official Intelligence." If he was over-worked, they said, it must be because so much of his time and energy were absorbed by philanthropic labours in connection with hospitals, the editing of his periodical named *The Hospital*, the writing of letters of great length to the newspapers on benevolent objects, and in the compilation of a fearful and wonderful "Life of the Prince of Wales," or because he laboured so hard in whipping up subscriptions for his Nurses Benevolent Fund—a curious "blend" of philanthropy and hard-hearted business.

In short, instead of finding Sir Henry popular with the majority of the members of the House, as he seems himself to imagine he was, we discovered a considerable feeling of resentment to be widely prevalent at the way in which he had used his position as the servant of the Committee to push himself forward socially. This being so, he ought not to be surprised at the cold reception given by the managers to his request for a retiring allowance. Even had they been disposed at one time to grant his request they would have probably changed their minds when they found Sir Henry becoming a director of such a company as the Welsbach Incandescent Gas Company.

In the light of this correspondence one can understand now why the managers decided to give Sir Henry's successor a fixed salary of only £1,500 per annum. Our view is that they made a mistake in cutting down the pay after this fashion, and we have spoken somewhat sharply about it. Our remarks were directed against the policy, by no means against the man selected, whom we do not know but of whom we hear nothing but good. It seemed to us that to give so small a salary was to belittle an office the highest in importance in connection with the Stock Exchange so far as the public is concerned, the occupant of which is subject at times to great temptations; and this view seems still the right one to take. At the same time we are disposed to fully forgive the trustees and managers after reading this correspondence. Their plain intention is to have a servant, henceforth, and not a would-be dictator.

Brewing Profits.

The brewing business is a wonderful one, and its powers to produce profits seem at times almost unfathomable. The Holt Brewery Company, for instance, was started as a modest concern in 1887, and did remarkably well. About 1894 its board dissipated the reserve of £45,000 by transforming it into sixty-two preference shares, which were distributed amongst the shareholders. Then, in 1896, a scheme was proposed whereby the £195,000 of preference and debenture capital was converted into a debenture issue of £250,000, the difference between the two amounts merely representing bonuses of capital. For the ordinary shares a still greater watering was proposed, for each £10 share received three Five per Cent. Preference shares of £10 each, and two £10 ordinary shares. In this way, £285,000 of share and debenture capital was swollen out into £700,000 without the proprietors subscribing another penny. One would have thought that such a pronounced expansion would have paralysed the concern, and yet in the two last years the company has met its fixed charges, paid 8 per cent. dividends upon the bloated ordinary capital, and set aside £25,000 to reserve. Of course, the company has been exceedingly well managed all through, but it is only in a monopoly industry such as brewing has become that such a result is possible.

GERMANY'S IMPERIAL DEBT.

In his report to the Foreign Office on the estimates of the German Empire for 1898-99, Mr. Spring Rice, Second Secretary of the British Embassy at Berlin, lets us see that Germany, the youngest daughter of Imperialism, is showing singular vigour in qualifying herself for a position of Imperial "respectability" among the nations by steadily accumulating a big debt. Your only pattern for ambitious States is the spendthrift rake, who does not "feel his feet" in the world until he has got through his limit of ordinary expenditure, entered on the glories of "extraordinary expenditure," and has tapped the beautiful system of loans, on which he manages for a long time to subsist in comfort and even luxury. In 1870 the Germanic Confederation had a paltry debt of £13,000,000, but that has been practically paid off. In 1877 the Imperial debt was only £800,000—a wretched pittance for an Empire that would be great. But so vigorously did her rulers set to remedying this defect in a well-regulated Empire, that in 1887 the amount had risen to £24,000,000, and in the present year the Germanic debt stands at the handsome figure of £107,500,000. Not bad for twenty years. Though it will doubtless yet be improved, Germany's position as a borrower is already tolerably secure; and where she formerly borrowed at 4 per cent. she now pays on the larger portion of her debt only 3½, while new loans are issued at 3 per cent. There could not be a better testimonial to her rising respectability. But Prussia is yet far ahead of the Empire with a thumping debt of £300,000,000; only much of that was borrowed for railway construction, and her railways yield Prussia about £25,000,000 a year. The other German States have all debts of a fairly respectable amount, Baden standing at the bottom of the list with a poor £16,000,000. But in every State the railways yield enough profit, at least, to pay the interest on its debt. On the Imperial debt, however, the interest has to be paid out of the taxes, and patriotic Germans seem proud to bear this rapidly-growing burden. Still, German revenue steadily increases; it has doubled since 1886, but if accumulation of debt goes on at the rate it has been doing, it must become a serious burden for the Empire.

STORM IN A TEA-POT.

There is not to be war—even a war of tariffs—between Germany and the United States. Prominent men in both countries seem, however, to have had the San Jose plant-bug fever very badly for a day, or perhaps two. But steam was promptly worked off in words, and sanity and mental sobriety have resumed their sway. Mr. Dingley was especially fierce in denouncing the conduct of Germany in prohibiting the importation of some Californian fresh fruit. He ridiculed the suggestion that the prohibition was enforced because of dread of the plant-bug scourge. It was an evasion of commercial treaties—at least, a straining of their legal provisions. But the Washington Minister of Agriculture kept his head cool. Fruit diseases, he explained to the Cabinet, could be carried by fruit, and become operative at great distances. At any rate, Prussia was within her rights in enforcing the prohibition. On the other hand, Germany has issued an official explanation of the reasons which induced her to act as she did. That San Jose bug is clearly an abominable pest. In itself an insignificant little sinner, it has such a tremendous power of reproduction that, from spring to autumn in a single year, one individual may multiply the species to the extent of 3,000 millions. We are all interested in keeping such a vigorously fruitful little monster at bay. Its depredations, says the German *Imperial Gazette*, have now to be combated from Chile to British Columbia. It must be kept out of Europe at all cost—even the cost of Mr. Dingley's indignation. It is worse than the grape phylloxera, whose ravages in European vineyards are now estimated at several milliards of marks—a trifle of £100,000,000 sterling or so. The San Jose plant-bug may not have got a working lodgment—a perceptible hold—in California or other fruit districts in America; but, after the phylloxera, poor old Europe had much better be over-cautious than remiss in keeping a watchful eye and powerful microscopes on the movements of a possible visitor, so minute yet so energetic. And the United States, so nicely "protected" from all adverse competitive trade-winds, need not grumble at Germany taking drastic measures against the importation of so lively a pest. Consider the precautions America has taken against pelagic seal fishing—altogether without reason, as now appears!

MR. KRUGER'S RE-ELECTION.

It never was really in doubt for a moment. Mr. Schalk Burger, his strongest-looking opponent, is a man of comparatively poor presence, and totally without the prestige of the aged statesman, whom we shall be wise if we treat still with reasonable respect. That his policy is reactionary is true enough, and it is also tone that there is an element of corruption in the service of the State which his defeat might, perhaps have done something to remove. For all that, constitutional means of obtaining reforms ought not to be abandoned, and it is only to do mischief, to indulge in threats, as some of the Outlanders' organs in the Press of South Africa are already doing. The tiny numbers of the poll, 18,457 all told, giving a majority of 9,048 to Krüger over Burger, and of 7,105 over Burger and Joubert combined, constitutes the most powerful and convincing of all arguments for an enlargement of the franchise. It is impossible that all the powers of the State can long remain in the hands of such a small and isolated group in the community. The figures bid the aliens agitate and persevere.

BRITISH AND FOREIGN COMPETITION.

There were several points worth consideration in Mr. Henry Birchenough's lecture at the Royal Colonial Institute on Tuesday evening, though there was, perhaps, a little too much of Jingo spread-eagleism about it. "Empire-building" is no doubt a pretty phrase, but a more modest coinage would have suited quite as well. Mr. Birchenough, on the whole, treated his subject with quiet moderation. In reference to our foreign trade rivals, he reminds us that in twelve years the German Empire had increased six-fold, and the French Empire four-fold. An increase in trade competition was therefore inevitable. We fear, however, that English traders were at first surprised by it, and for a time, at least, partly paralysed by it. In some measure they seem now recovering, and taking steps to regain some of their lost ground. A complete recovery in this respect is impossible; no exertion can replace us in the position our traders occupied until ten or twenty years ago. The virtual monopoly we then possessed is gone for ever; but we still retain a predominant position. If we can maintain this predominant position it is all we can look for, and to do that will require steady push and vigorous persistence. Germany, Mr. Birchenough regards as our great rival of the present; the United States of the future. In this he is probably not far wrong; for it may be that Germany places too much reliance on the "cheap and showy goods," which take the eye for a time, but can scarcely be relied upon in themselves to build up a great and enduring trade. Doubtless, Germany's exports are just now increasing by leaps and bounds; but as to this, Mr. Clavell Tripp pertinently remarks, in this month's *Nineteenth Century*, that "it would be interesting to know if the profits of German trade are increasing in the same ratio." Our traders should be ready to supply the "cheap and showy goods" where they are wanted; but it would be suicidal to neglect for these the more substantial wares which have given English traders name and fame, and which must still be a prime element in consolidating them in that "predominant position" which has replaced their whilom monopoly.

The English Sewing Cotton Company, Limited.

An intimation has been sent round by a newsagent that the Press, making known the fact that the well-known firm of R. F. & J. Alexander, Limited, thread manufacturers, of Glasgow and Barcelona, have been absorbed by the new English Sewing Cotton Company, Limited, lately formed with the sanction, we may say, of the all-powerful J. & P. Coates, Limited. The Alexander Company's capital is about £600,000 in debentures and preference and ordinary shares, and control has been obtained by the purchase of the ordinary shares so that the combination of all English and Scotch makers of sewing cotton articles the Coates' Company is now complete. We regret it, and the public will in turn, we fear, regret it, but there is no stopping these things. We shall now see whether a domestic monopoly is able to keep out competition from abroad without the help of a tariff on imported threads.

Gas Light and Coke Company.

After exhausting their enormous balance forward, and the best part of their reserve, the directors of this concern make a further confession of incompetence, by stating that they will raise the price of gas. Now, the 2s. 10d. per 1,000 ft., at present charged throughout the greater portion of the company's district, is 7d. per 1,000 ft. above that of the South Metropolitan Gas Company; or, say, 6d. per 1,000 ft. more than the natural difference as settled by the price of gas which rules the statutory dividends of the two companies. If the South Metropolitan charges 2s. 3d., the Gas Light and Coke ought to charge 2s. 6d., and 4d. upon this price, taking into account the enormous business, is a very serious matter. Yet, rather than submit to a little further reduction in dividend, the board intends to make this difference all the greater, and so encourage the natural enemy, the electric light. With vestries opening electric lighting undertakings in various parts of its district, this is the only thing the board feels able to do to rise to the situation! Of course, it will be answered that electric lighting does not hurt the gas companies, but we beg to differ on this point. Otherwise, how is it that the South Metropolitan Company in these seven years ended June 30 last increased its sale by 33 per cent., while the Gas Light and Coke only increased its sale by 7¾ per cent. Last half-year, too, the increase of the South Metropolitan was 6 per cent. as against 2 per cent. by the Gas Light and Coke. Every 1d. per 1,000 feet in the price of gas is a serious consideration in the struggle, and yet Colonel Makins and his board go on blindly worshipping at the shrine of that statutory dividend.

A Prosperous Electric Undertaking.

The progress of the electric lighting companies supplying the London districts must have exceeded the anticipations of their promoters. For instance, the Westminster Electric Supply Corporation was only formed in 1888, and, of course, had to lay the very foundations of its business, so that it was not until 1892 that a dividend—and this at the moderate rate of 3½ per cent.—could be declared. Since then progress has been by "leaps and bounds," culminating in the 12 per cent. dividend for last year, set forth in our reports. In the last three years the amount of electric current sold has doubled, and still the growth of new connections remains important. It should be remembered, too, that these electric light companies do not have a whole district to themselves like the gas companies, while there is always the old-established gas consumption to contend with. But then the electric lighting companies north of the Thames have been inconceivably blessed by having the Gas Light and Coke Company managed by its present board.

Before leaving the Westminster Electric Supply Corporation, we might mention that the conversion of the founders' shares, which was carried out last year, has proved a great success. At the time, we spoke hopefully of the operation, but never imagined that one short year would actually prove its efficacy. The £500 of founders' shares had the right to claim one quarter of the profits after the ordinary had received 7 per cent. To get rid of this irritating charge, the founders were allowed last year to subscribe £60,000 of share capital at par, which, as the shares stood at double their nominal price, gave them a bonus of £60,000, and for this they extinguished their founders' rights. The new shares meant an addition of 20 per cent. to the share capital, so that the increased burden was very considerable. Yet we find the ordinary shareholders actually gained last year by this arrangement. Thus the divisible balance was £49,461, and 7 per cent. on the old capital would have taken £23,765. Then, allowing £2,400 as interest upon the £60,000 subscribed by the founders, we have a net balance of £23,296, of which one quarter would have represented £5,824. Now to pay the 12 per cent. upon the £60,000 of new share capital required £7,200, but £2,400 must be deducted as interest upon the new money provided, and so the actual founders' charge only came to £3,800, as against £5,824, which would have been demanded under the old system.

THE MASSACRE OF THE INNOCENTS.

We are glad to note that the meetings of the subsidiary companies of the London and Globe Corporation are not passing off without discussion. It is a neat device of the Corporation, having sucked out the blood of these victims, to propose that they obliterate themselves in a new corporation with a capital upon a gorgeous scale. Indeed, we have every reason to believe that the arrangement, if carried through as originally suggested, might lead to the London and Globe netting a handsome profit on the operation, but we cannot be certain on this point as we have not been amongst the unfortunate receivers of the proposals. At three of the meetings the consideration of the resolutions was adjourned for a fortnight, so that there is plenty of time to thrash out the matter yet before coming to a decision.

A CHANGE FOR THE BETTER.

We must say that the London and Middlesex Freehold Estate Company is a great improvement on its predecessor, the London Financial Association. The latter, almost throughout its career, was an object of mingled pity and contempt. Formed in 1863, when a good deal of bad financial business was being done, it only paid one dividend—1¼ per cent. in 1873—on its huge paid-up capital of £1,443,375. Badly financed, the affair was for a long time loaded down with debt, and in 1880 it had £210,000 of debentures, and a mortgage of £246,929 upon its property. In 1885, the paid-up capital was written down to £658,692, but this did not lead to much improvement, although the debt was much reduced, and finally, in 1896, a rigid reconstruction took place, which brought down the paid-up capital to its present total of £121,122. All debt has been repaid, and so the estates are the absolute property of the shareholders. Realisations have proceeded upon a fair scale, and the last balance-sheet showed liquid assets amounting to about £20,000, after paying the dividend of 5 per cent. The knife had to be ruthlessly applied, but the result is a company much healthier in every respect.

THE IMPERIAL CONTINENTAL WATERWORKS, LIMITED.

The following letter has been "left to our impartiality" by the board of this company, and we insert it with pleasure, only hoping that the discussion will not be prolonged, or run either to lengthy letters or a personal wrangle :—

To the Editor.

London, February 9, 1898.

SIR,—My directors did not trouble you last week with any comments on Mr. Brown's (the director of the Gorzente Works) "effective" rejoinder, which you published on 28th ultimo, because Mr. Deacon (to whose letter to my board it purported to reply) has been away from London, and will not return till next week; and also because it scarcely seemed to them to require much notice.

While Mr. Brown evades all the important points with which he was confronted, he, with charming candour, makes two astounding confessions, viz., 1st. That his company violates their concession by taking much more water than it is legally entitled to, for does not the "barren hill side" to which he refers, form part of the hydrographic basin from which it is entitled to draw 250 litres per second, and uses the curious argument that "as they take it, they have the right to do so." 2nd. That his company also violates or has violated the prohibition of the authorities by filling their dam to above five metres of the sill, and thus endangering the lives of those who live below it.

Mr. Brown states that the two companies which, as he says, serve an area inhabited by 367,000 persons, encash £28,000 per annum from water sold for domestic purposes, which amounts to 1s. 6d. per head.

The inference which he clearly wishes to be drawn is that the whole 367,000 persons are supplied with water.

Now we, of course, possess and have studied the documents connected with these two companies, including balance-sheets and tariffs, and these last clearly show that, calculated on the basis of even their minimum charges, an enormous number of inhabitants cannot possibly receive water from them. Other people besides Mr Brown know Genoa and its requirements, and irrespective of the letter signed, in three days, by fifty-two of the leading citizens, on being shown his first letter, we assert that it is a matter of general knowledge that the water supply of the City and its environs is insufficient in quantity and inferior in quality.

In reply to Mr. Brown I may say that possibly the reason why his company went to its present source of supply may be found in the fact that its choice was limited. They only applied for their Concession in 1871 (see page 11 of their book), while the best areas, viz., those possessed by this company were bespoken in 1869.

In conclusion, I may point out that discussion and argument is somewhat difficult with a gentleman who appears to attach no importance to laws, authorities, or the validity of concession.

It has been I think, however, shown that Mr. Brown's statements are refuted by the facts, by the laws, by his own company's Engineer-in-Chief, and by himself; and we leave it, with confidence, to the common sense of your readers to decide whether it was not a legitimate inference that he is (as he himself puts it) "opposed to the scheme from interested motives."

I am, Sir,
Your obedient servant,
For the Imperial Continental Waterworks, Limited.
ERNEST J. R. DODD,
Secretary.

P.S.—Mr. Deacon on his return to London will have Mr. Brown's letter laid before him by my board, when probably he may answer Mr. Brown's letter, so far as he himself is concerned. E. J. R. D.

LONDON AND GLOBE CORPORATION.

We hope shareholders in the various mining companies which this corporation proposes to amalgamate, will not, at the meeting to-day, accept the scheme too hastily. No information is given them about their properties, and they should certainly demand good reasons before their consent is given. It is not so long ago since Mainland Consols were over £4 for the £1 share, on reports sanctioned by the directors, that the mine was extraordinarily valuable. Some of the shares, in others of the companies, were also at high prices in those glorious days. We know "want of water" was the excuse for their non-success, but that is not sufficient to explain why such high prices were given in cash and shares to the vendors, or why all the working capital has disappeared. The whole scheme, now being driven through, looks like an attempt to hide away some very bad bargains for which those who bought the shares have to suffer. We notice also, two or three companies which are not quoted on the market, are to be included in the new Exploration Company. Who hold the shares in these? Directors should explain. If they do not—well, we shall think a lot.

LONDON MERCHANTS AND THE SUGAR BOUNTIES.

It was right that the London Chamber of Commerce should have its say on the subject of the sugar bounties; but little was said at the recent meeting of the Chamber either for the enlightenment of the public or to influence Parliament on the question. The resolution passed properly denounced the bounties and formally demanded their abolition—a beautifully academic sentiment, to which everybody could assent, and everybody at the meeting referred to did assent, with the exception of one solitary individual, whose name has unfortunately been lost to the world through the remissness of the reporters. But what better are we for the formal repetition, even by London merchants, of a demand which has been so often made during the last dozen years or so? It should have been made, not "at large" at public meetings, or to the English Parliament, but to the Governments that, foolishly for themselves, insist on supplying us with cheap sugar at the cost of their own taxpayers. It is worthy of note, however, that the speakers who supported the resolution were all more or less openly in favour of meeting the foreign bounties by countervailing duties at home—that is, by filching money from the English taxpayers for the benefit of a few sugar-refiners, in order that they may be saved the trouble of exercising their ingenuity or putting forth their energy in coping with a difficulty experienced by almost every trade in this country. It never seems to occur to these Protectionist orators that their favourite countervailing duties are but taxes on the general community for the benefit of a comparatively small number of lazy and unenterprising traders. We can quite understand the annoyance felt by the Protectionists at the London Chamber of Commerce when reminded by one speaker that sugar-refining was of much less importance to England than the confectionery and jam business, which, in 1894, gave employment to 54,000 persons, while sugar-refining in the same year only afforded work for 4,500. Mr. Henry Coke denounced this as "frivolous," supported in his denunciations by those inarticulate but stentorian cheers which seem about the only "arguments" which Sir Howard Vincent can command. But we cannot see where the frivolity comes in. This frivolousness seems shown rather by those who wish to cripple the confectionery industry, built up by men of energy and business aptitude, for the benefit of sugar-refiners suffering mainly from the lack of those qualities which are at the foundation of success in business. The demand for countervailing duties against sugar bounties is about as rational as would be an agitation for the re-enactment of the Corn Laws.

The Insurances Corporation v. Bird.

Last week the action brought by the Insurances Corporation, Limited, and its directors, against Messrs. Bird, a firm of solicitors, and also against one of its shareholders, for libel and conspiracy, terminated by the plaintiffs consenting to judgment being entered for the defendants with costs, without a shot being fired. The learned counsel who appeared for the Corporation and its directorate said that this decision was arrived at owing to the technical difficulties which might arise, but he was met with an assurance on the part of the defendants that, while accepting judgment on the legal aspect of the case, they were prepared with a full answer on the facts. We wonder if this is the last we shall hear of this concern; but it may not be out of place to recall a few facts relating to it. It was one of twins given birth to by the Contract Agency, its brother being the Merchants' Fire Office, Limited. In February last year, that company entered upon a voluntary liquidation. The Insurances Corporation was started with the modest capital of £1,000,000, but an unappreciative public only came forward with £100,000 in response to the £250,000 offered for subscription by the directors. At the beginning of last year a meeting was held to consider the report of an Investigation Committee, which had been appointed at the instigation of some shareholders.

By the articles of association all directors, except the original ones, had to hold £2,000 in shares. At that meeting it was admitted that the joint board held the magnificent number of 310 shares between them. It was also stated that the balance at the bank was the huge sum of £2,525 on deposit at 2 per cent., that the Corporation had issued policies to the amount of £82,170, and that the premiums earned had reached £675. What the property insured could have been surpasses understanding, as this premium works out at the average of about 16s. 6d. per £100! If this was the condition of this Corporation at the beginning of 1897, we can well imagine that an investigation at the commencement of 1898, unless an extraordinary change had taken place, would hardly be welcome. Another fact with regard to the history of this insurance scheme is curious. The Corporation was promoted, as we have stated, by the Contract Agency, the acting member of which was a Mr. T. Fenwick, who was a member of the board of the corporation and also of the Merchants' Fire Office. The Agency had a call for a certain period of the balance of the first issue of the shares. Messrs. T. Fenwick & Co. have during the last year issued broadcast prospectuses offering these shares at anything from £2 to 5s. premium, though it is only fair to say that this action has been repudiated by the directors of the Corporation, and Mr. T. Fenwick has since retired from the board. We should have been much interested in a thorough investigation of the affairs of this Corporation, and we trust there may be one before very long.

The American Seal Fishing Folly.

From the report and joint statement of conclusions signed by the British, Canadian, and United States delegates respecting the fur seal fishery in the Behring Sea, it would appear that the alarm raised as to the extermination of the fur-seal was entirely groundless. There has undoubtedly been a diminution in the herd on Pribyloff Island, but it is far from involving or threatening the extermination of the species; it has not been caused by the pelagic fishing, an industry which is declared to have been conducted in an orderly manner, and in a spirit of acquiescence in the limitations imposed by law. Indeed, the decrease in the pelagic industry is greater than in the herd on the island, while the chief cause of the heavy mortality among the seal pups is a parasitic worm only just discovered. But there are other causes. They may starve by straying from their mothers; and they are often "squelched" by their fighting fathers. To all appearance, however, the pelagic fishing is not in the slightest degree responsible for the decrease. The sudden zeal of the United States lawmakers against this orderly industry was not only excessive, but premature, as well as unreasonable. They ought to have waited for the report of the investigating Commission, whose conclusions are endorsed by the delegates of the United States, as well as by the delegates for Canada and Great Britain. Now that it has been shown that the law as to pelagic fishing was passed under the influence of groundless panic and mistaken inferences, the only reasonable course for the Washington Congress is to repeal the obnoxious Act, and to return the numberless sealskin garments of which the United States Customs officers have been despoiling foreign ladies who ventured to cross the American border without the indispensable "certificate," that the seals from which their cloaks were made were not caught in the open sea. It is not a dignified position for a legislative to have placed itself in; but there would be still less dignity in hesitating about promptly undoing the mischief they have worked by legislating hurriedly under the influence of inexcusable panic and false impressions.

THE NEW YORK LIFE INSURANCE COMPANY.

In the flaming advertisements setting forth the wonderful things accomplished by this Life Office last year, it is stated that the company "has set aside a special reserve of £3,332,495 in order to place the whole of its reserve on a 3 per cent. basis, but after carrying into effect this most important operation—an operation by which its reserves are enormously strengthened—it is still able to show a net surplus over all liabilities of no less than £3,534,178." We should just like to ask one question about this statement. Has the valuation on a 3 per cent. basis been made upon the gross premiums of the company or upon the net? It used to be the fashion in the bad old times for British companies to value future increment upon their gross premiums, oblivious of the fact that a more or less large percentage of them went in working expenses. Does the New York Life continue that bad custom? Perhaps its controllers will allow a British actuary of repute to examine their books and report upon the point. It is of the highest importance in measuring such statements as we have quoted, especially in the case of a concern like this, one-quarter at least of whose premium income never enters its treasury at all, except to come out again in payment of working expenditure.

THE CURTIN DAVIS MINE.

The subjoined letter comes to us with the Liverpool post-mark. Its writer, we are glad to think, has been too much ashamed of it to send name or address. But it is too pretty an appreciation to be kept in the dark, aud so we print it here, its insinuations in no way affecting us. Let it serve as a warning to readers to elevate no frail and fallible human being into an 'idol":—

TO THE EDITOR.

DEAR SIR,—In this week's issue of THE INVESTORS' REVIEW you say speaking of "The Curtin Davis Proprietary Company"; "In September last we spoke well of the manner in which this adventure had been handled and placed before the public. From our language many seem to have inferred that we spoke in terms of praise about the mine itself. That was not the case, we are happy to say," &c.

Permit me to remark that it was the case, and as you seem to have forgotten your words, and may not have a copy of your REVIEW for September conveniently to hand, I shall, with all respect, take the liberty of quoting them to you.

After dexterously opening your article on "The Curtin Davis Proprietary Company" by a paragraph of praise about the Mount Lyell Mine, you continue in the following style:—"But the Mount Lyell is not the only mine of *great potentialities* in that region of Tasmania. We have before us the report of a meeting of shareholders in a neighbouring property, the Curtin Davis, held in Melbourne on May 31 last, Mr. William Knox in the chair; and at this meeting *a number of statements were made calculated to inspire a strong belief in the possibilities of this copper mine likewise.*"

That these statements were worthy of credence you yourself vouch for by speaking of them as "calculated to inspire *a strong belief.*" The whole tenor of the article is to the same effect, that what was said by the chairman could be relied on, as your main point is the responsible character and caution of the directors.

You go on to say:—"Whatever there is of a speculative sort about the venture, other than the risks inherent in all mining undertakings, is to be found in the arrangements the directors have made to gain control of another mine in the same range of mountains, some three and a half miles further on; but even this has been gone about with caution, and in a way which does not involve the Curtin Davis Company in any large expenditure. If the same caution is displayed here in joining these Colonial adventures, a great industry may spring up in Tasmania which will prove of immense benefit, not only to the Colony, but to the whole range of industries dependent upon copper."

I think I have quoted sufficiently from your article to show from your own words that you did speak "in terms of praise about the mine itself."

From the remainder of the article, too lengthy to quote, it may be clearly inferred, for your remarks will bear no other interpretation that you were of opinion that the Curtin Davis mine was to be a means of depriving the Rothschilds of their monopoly in copper.

But now, unfortunately, comes the worst part, which can hardly be written without a blush. At the meeting of shareholders to which you refer, no authoritative statements were made to "inspire a strong belief in the possibilities of this copper mine likewise." On the contrary, the chairman informed the meeting that at his recent visit to the mine he was not at all pleased with it, and had *countermanded his orders for expensive machinery.*

The report was disappointing in the extreme, and the chairman to give him his due, held out no false hopes.

The acquisition of the Colebrook mine, to which you took exception with such alluring *naiveté*, is the only thing that has saved the shareholders from absolute disaster.

For the future, resume your character of a canny Scot, and never deny what you have written. It can do no good. Your reasons for praising the Curtin Davis, and your allusions to statements that were never made, can only be guessed.—I remain, my dear Shattered Idol, yours faithfully, VERY SAD.

THE DUNLOP DISPUTE.

An interesting phase of the dispute between the cycle trade and the Dunlop Tyre Company has been reached. It is well known that the company, in its efforts to attain a paramount position somewhat upon the lines of, the Standard Oil Company of the United States, has been trying to induce makers to pledge themselves to sell tyres only supplied by that company by a system of heavy rebates. Needless to say there are other good tyres in the market, notably the Fleuss tyres, which are not included in this arrangement, and a number of the cycle makers rufused to be "tied" to the Dunlop oligarchy. Furthermore, they approached the Board of Trade, and after stating the facts, asked that Board to compel the Dunlop Company to issue licences. Before assenting to the petition, which was otherwise favourably received, Sir Courtenay Boyle desired the opinion of a representative body of cyclists, and accordingly appealed to the Cyclist Touring Club. Two of the officials of that important club thereupon interviewed Mr. Arthur Ducros, and the facts elicited in that interview showed the monopoly-instincts of the company in all their nakedness. The council of the Cyclist Touring Club accordingly reported to the Board of Trade against the company, and strongly urged that body to do all in its power to checkmate the attempted monopoly.

The Governor of the Bank of England was rather severely injured on Monday by being thrown out of a carriage he was driving. The pony took fright at a motor car, and ran into a lamp-post.

British Foreign Trade in January.

The figures for this month of the foreign trade of the United Kingdom do not indicate much one way or another. The gross value of the imports came to £39,916,491, and of the exports £19,231,404, imports being about £141,000 more and exports about £555,000 less than in January, 1897. Imports thus continue to advance and exports to recede, as is shown by the fact that the increase in the former compared with January, 1896, is £1,442,000, and the decrease in the latter £1,915,000. Unquestionably this is a serious fact, if the tendency does not show some change soon; and as regards imports it is made all the more serious because living animals, grain, bacon and hams, fresh beef, preserved meats, fresh and salted pork, dead rabbits, fish, potatoes, condensed milk, hops, lard, and unrefined sugar contribute in a more or less constant and important degree to sustain the total, while raw materials used in our manufactures, such as pig lead, raw cotton, flax, hemp, jute, silk, and wool, show a more or less pronounced tendency to decline. In the case of cotton the decline is to some extent attributable to lower prices, but wool has fallen off in value nearly £1,000,000 compared with January, 1897, and over £200,000 compared with January, 1896, without material alteration in price. We must not press the inference too far from the figures of one month only.

Exports, however, are also unsatisfactory in several respects, showing real elasticity at no point if we except coal. We are not even exporting larger quantities of raw materials like wool, and our exports of such important commodities as cotton yarn and twist barely appear to hold their own. France, Italy, Greece, Egypt, Dutch India, China, Mexico and Central America, West Africa, and Australasia all took smaller consignments of cotton piece goods last January than in January, 1897. And compensation for the decline revealed in these quarters was not quite found elsewhere, although India, on the whole, bought much more freely. The month's total shows a larger decrease on 1896 than on 1897; and the same holds good of jute yarn and manufactures, although in regard to the latter the United States and Australasia may be said to account for the whole decrease. Linen manufactures, again, appear to be steadily declining both in quantities and values in our export tables. The United States took, it is true, only about £14,000 worth less last month than in January, 1897, but the decrease on January, 1896, is fully £100,000 and no other country has helped us in any material way to make this loss good. Canada took £3,000 worth more last month than in the same month a year ago but nearly £8,500 worth less than in January, 1896. The Argentine Republic is not increasing its demands, nor Australasia, nor the Foreign West Indies, nor France, and from Germany the trade continues to be rather insignificant and by no means progressive.

Our silk trade is too small to require anything like analysis, but it seems to be in rather better case than any of those just mentioned. The decline, however, in woollen goods of all descriptions is serious. On a total of about £8,600,000 the shrinkage in one month, comparing last January with the January before, is fully £500,000, and as against January, 1896, the decline is £1,500,000. This sort of thing cannot go on without serious searchings of heart on the part of the manufacturing community. One naturally looks for a poor return in the metal trades, all of which have suffered more or less from the conflict between the working engineers and their employers, but, on the whole, this department shows up wonderfully well. Hardware and cutlery, cutlery being now shown in detail for the first time—in fact, the whole return has been carefully revised and is clearly edited with great care—are considerably down last month compared with previous years, but not so pig, bar, and other iron, railroad iron, hoops, galvanised iron, tinplates, cast iron, or steel. The total in this section is larger than in either of the two preceding Januaries, but the falling off in machinery amounts to £400,000, being £1,071,781 this January as against £1,477,778 the year before. No doubt the exports of machinery, one of the most important and profitable branches of our domestic industry, will soon pick up again. It is not necessary to go through the accounts further, all the items tell much the same story. There is either very slight progress or some recoil, with the grand result stated at the beginning. The only consolation one can turn to is the fact that the raw exports of Foreign and Colonial merchandise amounted to £4,682,661 last month, which was nearly £530,000 more than in January, 1897. During January the movements of bullion resulted in a net export of £427,497 in gold and £124,435 in silver.

Rand Deep Level Mines: An Investigation.—II.

We come now to a branch of this subject which is of the utmost importance to all holders of shares in Transvaal mining companies. Are these mines worked, say, as the Indian ones are, or mainly for Stock Exchange purposes? We fear the reply must be given that the Rand mines of all kinds are from time to time undoubtedly stripped of their rich ore, and, if further testimony is required on this point, it is only necessary to interview half-a-dozen Rand mine managers to obtain direct confirmation. When a new manager takes charge of a property it is quite a common thing for him to proclaim that his predecessor has taken out all the rich rock developed and left the poorer stuff behind, making it extremely difficult until some more rich reef has been exposed to keep up the output to its normal level. Evidence of this is to be found in the back columns of any of the Johannesburg papers.

Situated adjacent to these dividend-paying outcrop mines are the deep level properties which are now being so prominently brought before the investing public. The question is whether the deep levels will be different to the outcrops, and prove free from the sins of their parents? Will picking out the rich ore to justify high prices for the shares ever be resorted to in the case of the deep levels? Human nature is weak, and the commercial morality of mining men is avowedly set upon a very low pedestal; and where there is temptation there will come offence.

One thing is certain, the facilities for picking out the richer ore in the deep level mines are even greater than in the outcrop mines. The deep level mines now crushing, or about to crush, have been in course of preparation—development is the technical term—for the past four, five, and six years. During this period enormous sums of money have been spent in sinking shafts, and exposing vast quantities of the gold bearing reefs, and to-day the majority of companies are in a position to continue milling for the next three or four years without doing another stroke of development work. For instance, the Simmer and Jack has from 850,000 to 1,000,000 tons of ore exposed; the Geldenhuis Deep, 800,000 tons; the Jumpers Deep, 530,000 tons; the Rose Deep, 520,000 tons; the Crown Deep, 400,000 tons; the Nourse Deep 300,000 tons; and so on. But all the ore in a mine is not of the same value. Any one who is acquainted with the Rand is well aware of the fact, that not only are there poor and rich zones, but also poor and rich reefs. Taking the fields from one end to the other, there are, roughly speaking, four principal reefs—the North Reef, Main Reef, Main Reef Leader, and South Reef. One of these—generally the South Reef, sometimes the North Reef—is invariably richer than any of the others, and if crushed by itself will give a high yield. Should this selection of the rich ore be adopted and persisted in, the mine would in a comparatively short space of time be deprived of all its better grade ore and be left gutted. While the rich reef is being crushed large profits can be shown, and unless the true position of affairs is generally known, an altogether false idea is gained of the value of the mine. To show how the different reefs vary in richness, we give a few instances extracted from the companies' own reports :—

NOURSE DEEP.

Tons developed.		Reef.		Assay value.
175,000	......	South Reef	......	16½ dwt. per ton.
115,000	......	Middle Reef	......	8¾ "
Nil.	......	Main Reef	......	Unpayable.

It will be seen that if the simple operation of only extracting South Reef be pursued, unnaturally high results could easily be obtained; but the limit to which picking can be carried does not stop here. The whole of the 175,000 tons of South Reef is not of an equal grade, part of it may assay, say, 1 oz., some of it 15 dwt., some 10 dwt., and some 8 dwt. This fact is not shown in the official reports, but the manager of the outcrop mine, the Henry Nourse, which has identically the same reefs, appears to be more confiding. He states that of 240,000 tons South Reef ore developed in his mine 138,000 tons assay 15 dwt. per ton; 62,000 tons from 9 to 15 dwt.; and 38,000 below 9 dwt. In the Nourse Deep precisely the same variation in the values occurs.

At the Crown Deep mine the South Reef assays 1 oz. 17 dwt. per ton, the Main Reef Leader 1 oz. 8 dwt. per ton, and the Main Reef itself, being very poor, has not been developed. Some parts of the South Reef are extremely rich. At the Langlaate Deep the South Reef assays 1 oz. per ton, while the Main Reef Leader only gives 12 dwt. A larger proportion of South Reef is consequently being developed. Under such conditions it will be recognised that with the immense quantity of ore developed it is a very easy matter to pick the mines, and this, as things are now situated, could probably go on for a year or even longer without the returns falling off and the device being discovered. These tactics have been adopted by the same people with the outcrop mines in the past, and it would be making a large draft on the credulity of our readers if we asked them to believe that they will not be again resorted to when it is desired to "off-load" deep level shares on the public. Prices are unnaturally inflated, the controlling firms are supporting these prices, and it remains to be seen whether they can justify them in any other manner to the speculating fools who go over and over again to the fire.

And already there is evidence in support of this selection-of-ore habit which should not be neglected, in view of the possibly coming outburst of speculation in these deep level mines. Deep level engineers are never tired of affirming that the reefs in the deep levels are of about the same value as those in the outcrops; but even these hysterically-inclined optimists have not suggested they are richer. How, then, do they account for the fact that while the average recovery from the New Primrose during the past two years has only been £1 9s. per ton, at the Rose Deep, its deep level, the ore is yielding an average of £2 3s. 9d. per ton after only three months' crushing! At the Geldenhuis Estate, in a similar manner, the average yield during the past two years has been £1 11s. 7d. per ton; while at the Geldenhuis Deep it has risen to £1 17s. per ton. Is it that the deep mines are better, or is it that an undue proportion of rich reef is being extracted?

Take this other illustration. When the deep level mines were being developed estimates were made by the engineers, arrived at by sampling and fire assays, of the recovery that would be obtained from the reefs. As most people who have at any time been interested in mining shares are aware, such estimates are proverbially optimistic; and therefore what can be more astonishing than to find that the actual crushing results from the deep levels exceed the estimates. Were the Rand engineers pessimistic in their forecast, because if they were, it is the first time they have ever erred in this direction? Or is it, as we suspect, that an undue proportion of rich reef is being milled, a factor not accounted for when the estimates were compiled. It will be interesting to examine a few of the engineers' reports in this direction.

The consulting engineer of the Nourse Deep put the average value of the reef at 10 dwt. fine gold, or 40s. per ton. This recovery was expected when the mill had got into running order, and included the probable extraction from the slimes. The first crushing from this mine—and first crushings are generally poor owing to absorption of gold by the plates, and from other causes—shows a recovery at the rate of 46s.; while had the whole of tailings produced been treated it would have been nearer 52s. per ton. This without treating the slimes, the plant for which is not yet erected.

At the Rose Deep it was estimated that the ore with sorting would, including the extraction from slimes, give a recovery of 10 dwt. fine gold, equal to 40s. per ton. During the three months the crushing has been carried on, the actual recovery has averaged 43s. 9d. per ton, without any gold being taken from the slimes. Bearing in mind what has already been said about the generality of such forecasts these results are remarkable. Does this not look as if the ore is being picked?

A clue which seems to shed some light on the matter, astonishing to relate, is to be found in some of the deep level yearly reports. As has been explained at the Nourse Deep two reefs are being exploited, a rich south reef and a poorer middle reef. In the last annual report of the mine the following precise statement is made :—

This latter grade (speaking of the fire assays) would indicate, with, say, 20 per cent. sorting, a recovery of 10 dwt. fine gold per ton. As it is intended to exclude most of the middle reef ore for the present, it is confidently expected that the rate of the yield can be *graded up* to about 12 dwt., or, say, 48s. per ton.

Again, a little further on in the same report, is to be found the following :—

> It was expected that milling operations would commence in about welve months ; but, owing to the desire to increase the development in the south reef as much as possible, the construction of the reduction plant was not pushed.

That this is not an isolated instance of the tactics of these deep level magnates in "*grading-up*" the value of the ore may also be judged from the following extract from another annual report, that of the Jumpers Deep, Limited (1897), a mine which is soon to commence crushing :—

> The assay value of the ore on this basis works out at 11½ dwt., which indicates a recovery for the entire development of about 7 dwt. fine gold per ton, but by careful working of the mine, and allowing for waste rock, &c., it is estimated that when crushing operations are fairly under way, the rate of gold can be *graded up* to about 11 or 12 dwt., or say 45s. to 50s. per ton.

The exact meaning of such phraseology as "grading up," "excluding poorer reefs," and "careful working" must be left to the reader ; but if this is not a *prima-facie* admission on the part of "deep-level manufacturers" that it is their intention to pick the rich eyes out of the mines, we cannot conceive what is. Therefore, to attempt to predict the future of deep levels based on the present outputs from the mines, as is being done day after day by the "uninterested" South African and financial Press, is the height of absurdity.

After such handling of the mines one is not surprised to discover that even the accounts of the deep level companies are arranged so as to make it appear that the profits are far larger than they actually are. As may be imagined, to develop the enormous bodies of ore the mines have in sight has cost very large sums of money, and with the deep levels this expenditure will be found in every case charged to "capital account." The Simmer and Jack has spent £180,000 in this way, the Jumpers Deep £165,000, the Nourse Deep £180,000, Geldenhuis Deep £110,000, Rose Deep £200,000, and Crown Deep £200,000. Besides these amounts, heavy expenditure has been incurred on shafts, also debited to capital account, Simmer and Jack having spent £150,000, the Nourse Deep £80,000, the Jumpers Deep £77,000, the Geldenhuis Deep £50,000, the Rose Deep £50,000, and the Crown Deep £82,000. It is apparent that the cost of sinking shafts and putting in levels to expose the reef bodies cannot properly be looked upon as an asset. It is not convertible, and when the mine is exhausted is valueless. On the other hand, it would be inconvenient to debit the whole of these initial expenses to profit and loss account *en bloc*. Consequently it is the custom with the Rand outcrop mining companies as the reef is milled to write off from the "development account" an amount proportionate to the quantity of ore extracted, charging it to the current expenses account.

When the mine is worked out the whole of the development account is thus wiped out. The initial cost of shaft sinking is similarly obliterated by writing off annually a certain percentage for depreciation. By this method the expenses are fairly portioned over each ton of ore treated. The deep levels, however, in their anxiety to show low working costs and large profits, have ignored all such minor considerations, and are drawing on their ore reserves without writing anything off their profits for the original cost of developing the ore. They have even gone further than this. In one case, at the Geldenhuis Deep, such items as directors' fees, salaries, licences, office expenses, debenture interest, interest on loans, &c., have also been debited to capital account, while a loss made as the result of the first three months' crushing has been dealt with in the same way, the whole being treated as an asset. By this means last year was started with a clean profit and loss sheet, and a dividend of 30 per cent. declared at the end of twelve months out of the profits shown on paper.

To convince the sceptical it will, perhaps, be necessary to quote chapter and verse. The Geldenhuis Deep up to the end of 1894 spent £13,200 for directors' fees, office expenses, interest, cost of debenture issue, &c. During 1895 it crushed during three months, and made a loss for the year of £20,300. Consequently, at the beginning of 1896 there should have been £33,500 standing to the debit of profit-and-loss account. The directors, however, transferred the whole of this sum to capital account, and treated it as an asset. Thus, in 1896, the books of the company showed a clean profit-and-loss account. During 1896 a paper profit of £3,700 was made ; but this was only arrived at by failing to debit the expenses account with the cost of developing the ore extracted. The quantity of ore developed during the year was 26,700 tons less than that milled, while no charge was made to profit-and-loss account for reef taken from the "surface dumps" (stuff that had already been mined and lay on the ground). During 1897, regular monthly profits were announced, redemption of development account, cost of shaft sinking, depreciation on machinery, directors' fees, &c., not being charged up ; and in December a dividend of 30 per cent., absorbing £84,000, was declared. This may be a very fine method of advertising deep levels, but it is not book-keeping. In a similar manner the Rose Deep working expenses for December are officially declared at only £1 1s. 5d. per ton ; but in the statement issued there is nothing to show that the cost of developing the ore is being charged out of profits. In these circumstances, it is impossible to ascertain the actual cost of working in the deep level mines, and the much-vaunted claim that the mines can be operated as cheaply as, or cheaper than, the outcrops must be received with the greatest reserve. The profits declared month by month are evidently entirely deceptive, and must not be accepted as genuine returns on which to base any calculations as to the dividend-earning capacities of the mines.

Another very specious device requisitioned to advertise "deep levels" is to incorporate an extensive area of mining ground into one company, thus giving it theoretically a much longer "life" than an "outcrop" property. The argument is used that it is preferable to hold shares in deep levels, with prospective lives of twenty-five years, than shares in outcrops mines with lives of only ten years. Unfortunately, however, for the validity of this contention, when all the necessary funds for the equipment of the deep mines have been raised, the capitals of the deep levels will be nearly as large in proportion as those of the outcrops. Then it must be borne in mind that although the surface area of the deeps is extensive, the mines are really not so large as they appear to be, owing to the fact that the ore contents of the deep claims are considerably less than those nearer the outcrop. For instance, a Henry Nourse claim contains three times as much gold-bearing reef as a Nourse Deep claim, and consequently, in comparing the two companies, the area of the deep level must be divided by three. The Henry Nourse, with a capital of £125,000, owns twenty-three claims "now being worked," and thirty-eight claims "not being worked" (*vide* Gold Fields Deep diagram compiled by E. V. Melville), making sixty-one claims in all. The Nourse Deep has at present an issued capital of £450,000, and owns 259 deep claims, equal in contents to about eighty-six outcrop claims. To earn an appreciable dividend on the present market valuation of the stock (quoted at $7\frac{1}{4}$), it will be necessary to erect at least another 100 stamps, rendering the raising of further money necessary, entailing an addition to the capital. We are aware that part of the Henry Nourse mine consists of dip ground; but even making allowance for this, it is difficult to understand where the deep level scores an advantage. The large capitals of the deep levels, and the huge valuations ruling for their shares, will necessitate operations being carried on upon a very large scale. This means the sinking of immense sums of money in the erection of plant and in initial development so that the capitals of the deep levels, large as they are to-day, and heavily in debt beyond as many of the companies are, will be considerably heavier when the regular producing stage is arrived at. The following table giving the present capitals of some of the deep levels, and their adjoining outcrop mines, indicates how heavily the deeps are loaded even to day in this respect :—

Deep Levels.		Corresponding Outcrops.	
Company.	Capital.	Company.	Capital.
Simmer and Jack...	£4,700,000	——	——
Simmer and Jack East *...............	600,000	Geldenhuis Estate	£200,000
Langlaagte Deep *	650,000	Langlaagte.........	470,000
Glen Deep *	550,000	May................	275,000
Nourse Deep.........	450,000	Henry Nourse ...	125,000
Nigel Deep	450,000	Nigel	200,000
Rose Deep *	400,000	New Primrose ...	300,000
Jumpers Deep * ...	407,391	Jumpers	100,000
Durban Deep *......	291,000	Durban	125,000

* In debt.

A Sham Council of "Foreign Bondholders."

Yes, sham it is and sham it is apparently meant to remain. How many members of the Lubbock-charmed "Council" now regularly voting as they are ordered in Moorgate-street are holders of foreign bonds? Is Sir John Lubbock himself interested in any, or many, of the loans whose more or less bogus "committees" he plays chairman to? A parade has been made of the Privy Councillors, the members of our great banking firms, of railway directors, and of Members of Parliament upon the Council. What Sir John Lubbock said on that subject is true enough, and nothing to the purpose. He is surrounded by men of great attainments, men of note, men of social standing and of influence in Governmental and political circles. But Sir John is an adept at throwing dust into people's eyes. It is diamond dust and its glitter entrances. It is, however, dust after all. Sir John's notables are men without whom his Uruguay arrangement would not have passed muster. Guatemala, where twice the overdue coupons have been abstracted from bondholders; Ecuador, where utter ignorance and neglect have sacrificed bondholders; Costa Rica, where Mr. Kattengall and the Council walked off with every penny of the cash paid by the Government; Portugal, where the Council issued and ceased to issue certificates of claim for unpaid dues; Columbia, where a better arrangement was in course of negotiation: every one of these cases shows that if Sir John Lubbock's Council were consulted it knew little of the business it was engaged in, while if it accepted his *dicta*, the duty it had undertaken was grossly neglected.

The practice of co-opting members of the Council may have been adopted with the best purposes. In effect, it has been a complete failure so far as the protection of bondholders is concerned. Witness the compromises made by the Council during many past years, which have resulted in the destruction of the security that was sought when the Corporation of Foreign Bondholders was formed.

On the default of Portugal, the price of Portuguese bonds fell 20 or 30 per cent. in a few weeks. No effort had been made by preventive action to avert this catastrophe. Costa Rica is a case where the blunder of 1884 was repeated eleven years later. Experience carried no reflection, taught no wisdom, and the result proved calamitous. Again and again the Council has proved that it did not rightly appreciate the duties it had undertaken. Speculators buy from discomfited investors the bonds for which they had paid hard cash. The French purchased the Turkish bonds sold by disheartened English supporters of the political Ottoman Empire, and at the lowest prices; Germans acquired the depreciated Central and South American bonds, realised by us at a ruinous price; and a handful of English ornamental persons, at meetings called by the Council, voted away the property of others who looked in vain for protection at the hands of the Council of Foreign Bondholders.

Had the certificates of permanent membership of the Corporation of Foreign Bondholders been confined to holders of foreign bonds, as was resolved by the Council in 1873-4, the Council would have been controlled by the members of the Corporation. In 1883-4, thirty-six certificates of permanent membership were stated by a speaker at one of the meetings to have remained unclaimed. The same speaker foresaw that the number of unclaimed certificates would increase, and would be bought up by some clique, who would deal with the assets of the Corporation as they might think well.* At meetings from 1880 to the present day,

* As illustrating the way the certificates of the permanent memberships are trafficked with in secret by the Council of Foreign Bondholders, we append here a list of the new names which have been put upon the register since February, 1897. The great majority appear to be those of personal friends of Sir John Lubbock. Why were these certificates not sold openly to foreign bondholders, and to the highest bidder? A return ought to be obtained of the price paid for each, and considering the methods employed by the secretary, methods exposed by us in our monthly issue for September last, the manner in which they come into the Council's hands for disposal ought also to be investigated:—Benwell, J.P.; Bristowe, Arthur Lynn, 27, Austin Friars; Callard, G. S. Esmond, 3 and 4, Great Winchester-street; Campbell, A. J., 55, Old Broad-street; Campbell, Lord Archibald, Coombe Hall Farm, Morbiton; Clark, Edward, Stock Exchange, E.C.; Collins, Mrs. L. M., 38, Porchester-terrace, W.; Davidson, Theodore, Elmfield, Sidcup, Kent; Evans, W. Freke, 35, Gloucester-place, Hyde Park, W.; Gardner, Samuel, 13, Copthall-court; Grimston, H. S., 22, Ryder-street, W.; Gunyon, J. E., North Cray, Foot's Cray, Kent; Hamilton, J. F., 25, Ladbrooke Gardens, W.; Harvey, Richard M., 7, Mincing-lane, E.C.; Holland, R. M., 68, Lombard-street, E.C.; Kennedy, A. E. R., Bartholomew House, E.C.; Konstam, Mrs. Teresina, 142, Ebury-street, Eaton Square, W.; Lambert, Streeter, 24, Kensington Gore, W.; Landau, H., 5, Copthall-buildings, E.C.; Lidderdale, Right Hon. W., Bank of England; Lowenadler, F.

a Bill has been spoken of, and proposed, to give the certificate holders the rights and interest they pretend to in the operations of the Council.

Sir John Lubbock replies to the demand for these rights by a Bill to disestablish the permanent members of the Corporation, to give the assets of the Corporation to some twenty-one of their number, to deprive the remainder of every right they have or should possess, and to perpetuate a Council that is not representative of the English holders of foreign bonds. Meanwhile, the holders of foreign bonds are dazed. They suppose the eminent men whom Sir John Lubbock has introduced to the Council equal, in the domain of foreign loans, to the position they occupy in their own sphere, and stand aghast at the way in which their interests are played with or thrown aside. In any case, no single holder of foreign bonds has spoken out, except in the recent case of the Province of Buenos Ayres, when Mr. Bruce Gardyne challenges Sir John Lubbock to call a public meeting of bondholders. Sir John does not seem fond of public meetings. He loves to move in his own circle!

In this case the Council is as inept as in others. It makes no sign; consequently, and unless steps are taken by some other body, the Province of Buenos Ayres—as well able to meet its debt as the City of London itself—will escape upon a private arrangement between the Central Government and the Province, whitewashed because it is aided by the Council of Foreign Bondholders to clear itself by passing a brush over the balance it owes, or will owe, to its sterling bondholders.

The Council has been readily listened to when its mouthpiece stated that £100 a year each to twenty men of eminence, and £1,200 a year to its president were relatively small sums. But the Council is eminently unjust in seeking to deprive those who took the risk of establishment upon their hands of the increment of value in the assets of the Corporation. The Council has not contented bondholders because it has not protected their interests; it is out of touch with what concerns those interests. There is not upon the Council one man who is intimately acquainted with negotiations for foreign loans.

And now this inept body comes forward with a Bill. The proposed Bill was authorised owing to tactics which did not give any opportunity for a discussion upon merits, and the requisite statutory majority could not have been obtained had not secrecy been observed and those tactics adopted. There is one way of obtaining what is desired, and one way only, by reorganisation under limited liability. Banks, insurance offices, institutions of the highest station and credit, have organised or reorganised under limited liability. All that has been said in this case in opposition to limited liability is sheer nonsense. Leave a sufficient capital sum for the continuance of business. Form strong committees of bondholders, and give them the power of nomination to the Council. Let the bondholders in sections and in turn give a support vote to the Council, and then a strong Council understanding its work will be found protecting efficiently the interests of the English holders of foreign bonus, against the wire-pulling and intrigue of houses in the loan-mongering line and everybody else. The first step in effecting this reform is to offer combined and strenuous opposition to the Bill now before Parliament.

(Trumner & Co.), 4, Fenchurch-street, E.C.; Macfadyen, J., 47, Harrington Gardens, S.W.; Malcolm, Ronald, 1, Princes Gardens, W.; Marjoribanks, C. J., 22, Hans-road, S.W.; Morice, W. F., 23, Old Broad-street, E.C.; Mortimer, Stanley, 75, Old Broad-street, E.C.; Neild, Fredk., 2, Coleman-street, E.C.; Passmore, F. B., Suffolk House, Laurence Pountney Hill, E.C.; Pawle, Geo. S., 1, Cushion-court, Old Broad-street; Phipps, W. W., 8, Great Tower-street, E.C.; Pollok, Joseph, Stock Exchange, E.C.; Pritchard, J. Mostyn, 31, Throgmorton-street, E.C.; Robertson, H. M., Stock Exchange, E.C.; Rose, C. D., 6, Princes-street, E.C.; Rosenfeld, Sidney (Lazurus & Rosenfeld), 314, Bevis Marks, E.C.; Ryder, J. H. D., 59, Strand, W.C.; Salt, J. C., 72, Lombard-street, E.C.; Scott, Edward Henry, exors. of; Shannon, F. A., 7, Westbourne-terrace, W.; Sherrington, W. Staunton, 10, New-court, Carey-street, E.C.; Simmonds, Fredk. Henry, Government and General Investment Company, 10, Tokenhouse-yard, E.C.; Smith, E. C., Crichtons, Romford; Smith, Reginald Abel, 1, Lombard-street, E.C.; Smith, Niemann, Clevedon, Lewisham Hill; Spens, Nathaniel, 12 and 13, Nicholas-lane, E.C.; Stiebel, I., (no address given): Touch, G. A. (Industrial and General Trust Company), 8, Princes-street, E.C.; Tuke, W. M., Saffron Walden, Essex; Van Raalte, M., 22, Austin Friars, E.C.; Welby, The Lord, C.C.B., 11, Stretton-street, Piccadilly; Wells, H. W., Wallingford Bank, Wallingford; Wigan, J. A. Graham, Kentish Bank, Maidstone; Wilson, W. J., Bartholomew House, E.C.; Wodehouse, Col., K.R.B., 12, Stanhope Gardens, S.W.

American Affairs.

(FROM A CHICAGO CORRESPONDENT.)

I desire to congratulate you most sincerely on the appearance of your first weekly number and on finally having reached a stage at which your calls on readers will be frequent enough to become well known to the great army interested in financial matters.

There appears to be but little which is new with us. I doubt if anything of moment is done in currency reform at this session. The majority are disinclined to act, or take up in earnest so important a financial question, until the situation under the new tariff act is more fully determined. They also fear making mistakes just at this time. Then, too, there is quite a desire among the people for quiet. One will often hear something like "Better let well enough alone. We are doing very well, and don't want to be disturbed now. Better wait awhile," &c., &c., and I am inclined to believe it is as well to be more steady on our pegs, and, in the meantime, consider and discuss the new propositions before they are taken up by Congress.

Senator Wolcott's recent speech has done him no good, and was, I think, most unfortunate for himself. For a man, in such a speech as his was to be, to first cover the President with fulsome praise, claiming him as a partisan, and then lampoon him over Mr. Gage's shoulders, was such transparent demagoguery, that it became ridiculous, and naturally weakened the whole speech.

There is much satisfaction among the people over so many of our securities coming home, and it is coupled with a feeling that liquidation of debt owing to other countries should now progress rapidly. The return of our obligations in 1893 was an object lesson not soon to be forgotten. A few days ago I heard it put substantially in this way: "Even if our currency were all one could desire, and there was no longer danger from that source, Europe is constantly threatened with disturbance, and no one can tell when the holders of our bonds and stocks will need to realise, and so give us trouble. Better develop less rapidly, pay our debts, and be in a position to make the most out of opportunities. We are too rich to justify being in debt to other countries."

Your engineers' strike has enabled us to introduce considerable machinery into England, which is claimed to possess superior merit. A great engine-building concern in Milwaukee has, I am told, booked large

English orders for engines regarded as superior for certain uses, but which England would not try until the strike occurred. The builders believe that as soon as in use large orders will follow, but I don't see much in it, as the English can build like them, and surely some of the shops will adopt the improvements if really valuable.

General business is going very satisfactorily. The trouble about wages in the New England cotton mills is, I think, the beginning of a piece of "poetic justice" in which the prime movers of emancipation, and greatest disturbers of the Southern States, are to be the sufferers. Living is much cheaper, and wages, since the war, much lower, in the South than in the North. Cotton mills in the South have done very well indeed, although up to this time their chief production has been most largely of the coarser fabrics, which yield the smallest profits. When the South goes in for finer goods, as it no doubt soon will, New England cannot compete any better than it can now in the coarser, as the South has almost every advantage, except capital, the one thing which can be moved there without expense.

I firmly believe that the next quarter of a century will see the most of our cotton mills on the highlands of Tennessee and other Southern States. It is right among the cotton plantations, the climate is very fine and very healthy, people can live cheaply, and are accustomed to do so, and there is practically no end of people to draw on for such work. The only hope I can see for New England cotton in this race is free trade, and manufacturing largely for export.

The surplus of ready money in the West continues large, but no doubt it will be put in use before very long. I wish you could make up your mind to a vacation, come to Chicago, and take up railways under the changed conditions, growing out of the consolidation of weak, unprofitable lines into the various great systems, which has been going on so long, but just now reaching the fairly completed stages, with whatever it implies. I would like to do it if competent, but the most I could do would be to arouse attention, and spoil originality for others.

We are at sea on the Chinese question, as now presented, and are wondering what you will all make of it. Our cue will be to let you fight it out, and take the chances of getting our share—"Monroe doctrine," you know. I was greatly impressed by an article of last autumn, by some Frenchman, entitled "Who will exploit China?" more so, perhaps, because it brought so vividly to mind what my old friend Governor Jewel said to me after his return from Russia, to which he was our minister in Grant's time.

He, in answer to queries, said in substance: "The Russians are great diplomats, and, like the Jesuits, plan for the far distant future as much as the present. While an outlet to the Mediterranean is one of their greatest ambitions, I believe they regard the opening up of Siberia, and control on the Pacific Coast, as of much greater importance. Russia does not expect to extend her possessions westward, nor does she want detached dependencies; did not want Alaska, but did want us to have it, and would like to see us in control of all the North American Pacific coast. Asia offers Russia great opportunities, and, with Siberia opened up by a railway through to the Pacific, she would be largely master of the situation. There are, no doubt, several reasons for the Russian friendship for the United States, which I believe is very genuine. They believe in but two kinds of Government: absolute monarchy, and a republic for which the people are properly prepared, and that the geographical positions and policies of Russia and the United States furnish a good guarantee against confliction of interests."

We get an occasional Cuban shake up, but are beginning to believe the end is near—that Spain has pretty nearly exhausted her resources for keeping up the fight, and that it will end before very long. Cuba has been a source of great annoyance and expense. We do not want it, but do want the island peaceful and productive. Hawaii hangs in the balance, and no one can guess the turn. The new Chinese question may, however, make annexation more probable. L. B. S.

Critical Index to New Investments.

UNITED ORDNANCE AND ENGINEERING COMPANY, LIMITED.

With this is incorporated the business of Easton, Anderson & Goolden, Limited. Share capital is £275,000, ordinary £1 shares, and £275,000, Five and a Half per Cent. Cumulative Preference shares of £1 each, and there is also offered £250,000 First Mortgage Four and a Half per Cent. Debenture stock. By a fault in drawing up the prospectus, the issue price of the stock is not mentioned, but it is presumably par, nor do we see at what dates the interest is due. The debenture stock is redeemable at 105 after January 1, 1908, on six months' notice being given, and it is secured by a first mortgage on the freeholds and fixed plant, as well as a floating charge on the other assets. The company which is a Hooley promotion, is formed to manufacture and sell guns, gun carriages, ammunition and war material, and to carry on business as electrical, hydraulic, mining and general engineers; to acquire a licence to manufacture and sell the Schneider-Canet artillery, and to take over the business of Easton, Anderson & Goolden, Limited, engineers, of Erith and London. Fuller, Horsey, Sons & Cassell, value the freehold engineering works and plant of Easton, Anderson, & Golden, at £202,257, exclusive of goodwill, and W. B. Peat & Co. certify that the stocks and stores and other assets on June 30 last (some time back) were valued in the books of the company at £154,955. Peat's certificate might have been dispensed with, for there is nothing in it; anyone can certify what assets stand at in books. That does not guide one to an estimate of their proper value. Sir W. G. Pearce and Mr. Francis Elgar sell the Schneider licence to Mr. Ernest Terah Hooley for £50,000, and this gentleman sells the licence and properties to the company for £550,000 in cash. Two points seem to be missing—what profits Easton Anderson, & Golden have made in the past, and what Mr. Hooley gave for their business.

As a matter of history we may mention that a company called Easton & Anderson, Limited, was formed in 1888 to take over a business of engineers and shipbuilders carried on under the same name at Erith and London. The capital was £250,000 in £100 shares, of which £206,000 was issued as ordinary, and the balance in 5 per cent. preference shares. What the company did, or whether it made any profits, was not made public. Six years later a company was brought out called the Easton, Anderson, & Goolden, Limited, which took over the 1888 company, as well as the business of W. T. Goolden & Co. The capital this time was put at £200,000 in £10 shares, half ordinary and half 6 per cent. preference, all the ordinary being allotted, and £59,860 of the preference. In May, last year, an issue of £150,000 four and half per cent. first mortgage debenture stock was offered through Messrs. Hoare & Co., at par, and besides this an issue of £30,000 second mortgage debenture stock was made. Investors, we believe, showed no undue anxiety to subscribe the capital, and several trust companies were left to "hold the baby" between them, as their list of investments showed. Any merit there may be in the undertaking now formed it is difficult to find, and we certainly see no security for the preference capital, because Easton Anderson & Goolden have not the courage to disclose what their real position is. The capital, too, like that of all Mr. Hooley's companies, is vast.

DAVID THOM, DOMEIER & CO., LIMITED.

Company acquires the soap, oil, tallow and glycerine business established in 1848 of David Thom & Co., of Manchester, and the business of Domeier & Co., established in 1865, which has been for many years connected with Thom & Co. The profits of the two businesses for four years are given by the chartered accountants and look remarkably fine; but the certificate is very loosely drawn, and is not at all likely to create confidence in the mind of an investor. The assets are a varied assortment, including goodwill, trade marks and trade secrets, but, strangely enough, their valuation is not given in the prospectus. The capital is £180,000 in £5 shares, divided equally into ordinary and six per cent. cumulative preference shares, and for this very choice collection the vendors are willing to accept a mere £147,459 in cash, thus showing a decided preference to sovereigns over shares. In addition to this the company undertakes certain liabilities incurred on November 20, 1897. This is mysterious; but the hand of the philanthropist is so clearly seen throughout the whole affair that we hope the generosity of the vendors will be appreciated in its proper light.

BALLARD & CO., LIMITED.

Company is formed to buy the business of brewers and maltsters carried on by Henry George Beeman for twenty years under the style of Ballard & Co., of Lewes, Sussex. Capital, £80,000 in £10 shares, in equal parts of ordinary and 5 per cent. cumulative preference shares. There is also an issue of £80,000 four per cent. first mortgage debenture stock at par; interest due April and October, and stock is redeemable after October 1, 1915, at 110. Purchase price is £150,000, including all the share capital, and £70,000 in cash, so that only £10,000 out of the debenture issue will be available for buying new properties. Profits for 1895 were £5,950; for 1896, £6,366; and for 1897, £7,088, which are small enough for such a capitalisation. Collins, Tootell, & Co. value the properties at £115,000, and many of the licensed houses have been acquired in recent years, probably at high prices. The security, for only 4 per cent., seems hardly sufficient.

ARMY AND NAVY PROPERTIES, LIMITED.

The vendor, Frederick Dawkins, transfers to the company various properties around Charing Cross and in Victoria-street, S.W., for £144,000, being the full sum at which they are valued by Joseph Hibbard & Sons. Accountants certify gross annual rental value at £16,572, of which 80 per cent., they say, was fully let. Properties are held on leases having seventy-three to ninety-four years unexpired, at ground-rents amounting to £2,595 per annum. Authorised capital, £100,000, in 10,000 Five per Cent. Cumulative Preference shares of £5 each and 50,000 ordinary shares of £1 each. The whole of the preference shares, which are repayable at 5s. premium by Sun Insurance Company, under a Redemption Sinking Fund policy, are offered at par, and allottees of preference shares are graciously permitted to take ten ordinary shares at par for every ten preference allotted. Of the purchase price £80,000 is represented by a mortage on the properties, and the rest is taken in cash. Consequently while the vendor gets all this money with one hand, with the other he holds a mortgage over the properties for an amount which may not be much under their selling value, so that the security for the preference shares dwindles near to vanishing point.

BRITISH ELECTRIC TRACTION COMPANY, LIMITED.

Company was formed in November 1896 to take over the business of the Pioneer Company, and to develop electric traction. Share capital is £600,000, of which one-half in £10 shares is already issued and quoted about 8 premium. The company is now issuing through the Electric and General Investment Company the other half of the capital in Six per cent. preference shares of £1 each. They are offered at 50s. premium so that they return a purchaser 4½ per cent. interest due February and August. Sir Charles Rivers Wilson is chairman of the board, and a large number of undertakings are said to be engaging the attention of the directors. As this class of business is very much to the front just now, the shares should be a tolerably good investment, though not in any way cheap.

GLENCAIRN MAIN REEF GOLD MINING COMPANY.

Through the "Johnnies" Investment Company this undertaking offers an issue of £140,000 6 per cent. first mortgage debentures of £50 each at par. They will be secured by a first mortgage on all the landed property, buildings &c., of the Company, will be repayable at 102 in seven annual drawings of £20,000 each, commencing May 1st, 1901, or by purchases if below par, and holders will have option until February 7th, 1900, of converting them into ordinary shares at 70s. per share. Interest is due May and November. Issued share capital is £500,000, but no dividend has been paid since the end of 1895, when the capital was less than half what it is now. On the one hand, the interest is tempting; the option to exchange into shares would be valuable were any rich ore to be come across, and it is a well-known fact that many debentures issued by African mine undertakings have turned out remarkably remunerative. The Glencairn, however, is certainly not a rich mine, and although the present issue is made to pay off debt incurred in alterations and improvements, the mine itself seems some long way off resuming dividends. Still, 6 per cent., with repayment at 2 premium, and the chance of something rich being found, makes the debentures a speculative venture, not entirely without a tempting side, even though it is one of the Barnato group.

VENESTA, LIMITED.

Investors will probably not rush to take shares in this venture. The capital is £100,000, the present issue being 60,000 shares of £1 each, of which 20,000 shares are allotted to the vendors, the Venesta Syndicate, Limited, in full payment of the purchase money. Venesta boards, which are used for making boxes, tea-chests, &c., are manufactured by cementing together with a patent waterproof composition two or more thicknesses of veneer. Experiments are said to have been highly successful, the only difficulty being the supply to satisfy the demand. To meet this difficulty arrangements have been made with a Russian firm by which a continuous supply will be obtained, and this firm is about to form its business into a company to work harmoniously. The capital of the Russian Company is to be £160,000, and the directors of Venesta, Limited, intend to apply for £32,000 of shares, the Russian Company in return applying for 5,000 shares in Venesta, Limited. This is all very pretty, but the whole affair seems so up in the clouds that none but those in the trade would probably care to take shares.

THE UNITED RAILWAYS OF THE HAVANA AND REGLA WAREHOUSES, LIMITED.

This company has been created with a share capital of £1,540,000, all of it in £10 preferred shares except the odd 40,000 deferred shares. In addition there will be a debt of £2,000,000; £1,600,000 of it is in 5 per cent. consolidated irredemable debenture stock, and the remaining £400,000 in new 5 per cent. prior lien irredeemable debenture stock, of which £350,000 is offered now by Messrs. J. Henry Schröder & Co. at 98. The motives for creating this new English company seem to be twofold—to get out this prior lien stock, and to detach the railway and the warehouses—in themselves excellent properties—from the Commercial Bank of Havana, with whose chequered fortunes they are now too closely identified. Holders of the existing 5 per cent. bonds of the Bank and Railway Company will be allowed to exchange into the new consolidated debenture stock, and the prior lien stock will be offered to the public. Of course, the priority of this new stock can only be established if the old bonds of 1890—redeemable at 105—are converted. Apart from this passing defect, the bond seems good enough, and the railway, with its warehouses, ought to be a fair investment when Cuba is quiet again. As it is, the lines of the company have suffered much since 1894, and the receipts for the past year fell to £327,434 against £524,652 in the former year. To be sure, the net revenue, even then, is brought out at £150,000, or more than enough for the interest on both classes of new bonds; but the net income cannot be very clearly defined under present conditions of working. The prior lien bonds, however, ought to be all right.

BUENOS AYRES AND BELGRANO ELECTRIC TRAMWAYS COMPANY.

The objects of this company are to acquire and amalgamate the concessions, lines, and properties of the old Buenos Ayres and Belgrano Tramway Company, and the concession recently granted to Charles Bright for an electric tramway between Buenos Ayres and Belgrano. The share capital of the new company is £850,000 in £5 shares, of which 40,000 are "A" 6 per cent. cumulative preference, 30,000 "B" 6 per cent. cumulative preference, and 100,000 ordinary shares. There is also created £320,000, 5 per cent. debenture stock which is redeemable after 1,910 at 115, or at par on January 1, 1930. There is now offered for subscription £260,000 debenture stock, and £200,000 "A" 6 per cent. cumulative preference shares. Interest is payable January and July. In November last the former company obtained permission to use the overhead system for the greater portion of its lines, the grant being for ninety-nine years, after which the lines and rolling stock revert to the municipality; but Mr. Bright has now obtained a concession for an electric tramway between Buenos Ayres and Belgrano by another route, the concession being for sixty years, after which the lines and rolling stock revert to the municipality without payment. For the Buenos Ayres and Belgrano Company's concessions and properties, the new company pays £168,000 in 5 per cent. debenture stock, or cash; £137,500 "B" preference shares and £107,500 ordinary shares; and for the Bright concession and properties, together with the vendor's guarantee of subscription of the "A" shares, and such amount of debenture stock as may be required for the purposes of the company, and for paying off such of the holders of the existing 6 per cent. debenture stock of the old company as do not elect to take new debenture stock, £38,000 in cash and the balance of the ordinary shares, and the actual cost plus 10 per cent. of work done, materials, rolling-stock, &c. This means a very large blowing out of the capital, for whereas the old company had a share and debenture capital of £377,500, the share and debenture capital of the new company, when it is all issued, will be £1,170,000. Naturally, a large sum will be required to equip the tramways with electricity, but the old company seems to be getting very liberal treatment, for it was a none too successful undertaking. In the first year of its existence 6 per cent. was paid on the ordinary shares, and in the two following years 15 per cent.; but for 1889 the dividend descended to 8 per cent., and only 3 per cent. was paid in 1890 on the preference shares. For the next two years nothing was paid on either class of share, while for 1893 1½ per cent., and for 1894 and 1895 2 per cent., was distributed on account of arrears on the preference capital; but for 1896 there was no dividend at all. The passenger traffic between Buenos Ayres and Belgrano is carried by the railways, and it remains to be seen if the new company will draw this traffic to itself after possibly a long period of competition. Under these circumstances the future of the Electric Tramways Company with its inflated capital looks none too promising.

CICERO & PROVISO STREET RAILWAY COMPANY.

Messrs. Van Oss & Co. offer for sale at par $1,700,000 5 per cent. consolidated mortgage gold bonds, redeemable May 1, 1915, of the Cicero and Proviso Street Railway Company. Interest is due May and November and principal and interest is guaranteed by the West Chicago Street Railway Company. The bonds are part of a total of $2,500,000, some of which are reserved for future requirements, and after 1904, when $250,000 6 per cent. bonds mature they will have first mortgage rights on the property. The system is leased for fifty years to the West Chicago Street Railroad Company and each bond has endorsed upon it the absolute guarantee of this company. It is claimed that the West Chicago company is one of the leading tramway companies in the United States, that it owns and operates 259 miles of street railways, almost the whole of which is worked by electricity. Its funded debt is $10,800,000, and its common stock is $13,189,000. Upon the latter, dividends are regularly paid, those for the last three years being 6 per cent. The issue, one-fourth of which has been subscribed by investment and insurance companies in Great Britain, would seem to offer a fair 5 per cent. investment to those who are not afraid of American securities. The guarantor company appears to be in a pretty robust condition, and it is upon its progress that investors will have to keep their eye.

Company Reports and Balance-Sheets.

DANIELL & SONS' BREWERIES, LIMITED.—In our notice of this company's report in THE INVESTORS' REVIEW of January 28, the dividend on the ordinary shares was, by mistake, stated at 3 per cent.; it should have been 4 per cent. The amount carried forward was given as £1,912; it should have been £2,441.

THE GREAT NORTHERN RAILWAY COMPANY.—Gross receipts, £2,751,657; expenses, £1,686,944; proportion of expenses to receipts, 61·3 per cent. In its report for the last six months of 1897 the board of this company makes it very plain why the dividend on its various ordinary stocks has fallen off. Out of the gross increase of £105,000 in the receipts, little more than £4,000 remained to add to net revenue: the balance was all swallowed up in working expenses. Even the slight amount left did nothing to help the ordinary stock, because the amount of capital upon which the company has to pay dividends is half-year by half-year increasing. We make the net increase in the preferential charges compared with a year ago to be about £13,000, and therefore the balance available for dividends on the ordinary stocks tends to diminish, and the capital expenditure goes on steadily year by year. In the past six months it amounted to about £660,000, exclusive of the £391,250 issued to cancel the Royston and Hitchin rent charge. In the current half-year it is estimated that three-quarters of a million will be spent on capital account, and a Bill is to be laid before the proprietors for their sanction which will involve the raising of another £2,500,000 of capital. The proprietors might note these things, and ponder them. After paying a dividend at the rate of 5 per cent. per annum on each £100 of each original ordinary stock, a balance of £15,000 is left to be carried forward, as against £8,000 brought in a year ago; but, owing to the rapid growth of capital charges, this additional balance will count for nothing in helping to eke out the dividend for the current half-year. What with expenses and capital charges, the outlook for the ordinary stock holder, and especially for the deferred ordinary stock holder, in this railway does not appear to us very satisfactory in the near future. The dividends are payable on the 22nd inst.

THE NORTH-EASTERN RAILWAY COMPANY.—Gross receipts, £4,225,698; expenses, £2,454,408; ratio of expenses to income, 58 per cent. The directors in this case also have precisely the same story to tell as their neighbours. Gross receipts rose nearly £133,000, but expenditure increased more than £137,000, consequently the net receipts were actually nearly £4,500 less than in the corresponding half of 1896. This result, the directors state, is mainly due to advanced wages in several grades, to increase in the number of men employed necessitated by shortened hours of labour, and to the larger expenditure upon coal and materials in the locomotive and permanent way departments. It appears to us that this kind of extension in working charges is bound to go on. There is as little finality in it as in the capital account, which in the case of this company expands somewhat less rapidly than in some other instances, but still £325,000 was spent in the half-year just closed. A Bill is before Parliament involving the creation of powers to raise another £2,800,000. In time this capital must tell upon the company's power to pay a high dividend on its ordinary stock. The dividend now due falls short by a ¼ per cent. per annum compared with a year ago, and is only at the rate of 7 per cent. on the consolidated stock. It will be payable on the 19th inst.

THE GREAT WESTERN RAILWAY COMPANY.—Gross receipts, £5,243,967; expenses, £2,931,727; ratio of expenses to receipts, 55·9 per cent. For the half-year to December 31 the gross increase in the receipts was £233,777, and in the expenses £199,093. The increased expenses, therefore, swallowed up 85 per cent. of the increase in gross receipts. Still, this company did rather better than either the Great Northern or the North-Eastern, but it was unable to increase the dividend on its ordinary stock, which remains at the rate of 7½ per cent. per annum, and the balance carried forward is only £31,351, against £42,884, so that the whole of the additional receipts and more have been consumed in meeting fresh charges on capital account. An addition of £1,500,000 has been made to the consolidated ordinary stock during 1897, and the net result of the capital charges is that about £36,000 more has been required to pay the same dividends on preference and ordinary stocks as a year ago. Within the past six months the company spent £626,441 in new capital, £218,000 of it on working stock, and the expenditure for the current half-year is put roundly at £800,000. The company is going into some extensive commitments in connection with Irish railways; but how far this, if carried through, may add to the preferential burdens, we cannot yet say. It may be that they will involve, in the long run, no extra charge at all. Ireland should benefit by having such a wealthy and powerful corporation as the Great Western behind it; but the company's capital expenditure in England is by no means nearing an end, for the estimated amount of it in the future is £4,415,000, and improvements, additions, and expansions are continually going on. Each half-year's addition to capital, taken by itself, looks small for a company whose gross receipts exceed £10,000,000 per annum; still, they eat into the net revenue steadily and irretrievably. The dividends will be payable on the 16th inst.

NORTH LONDON RAILWAY COMPANY.—Gross income, £270,955; expenditure, £137,921; percentage of expenses to income, 50·90. These figures show an increase of £6,850 in the receipts, and of £3,916 in the expenses, so that the company has obtained its new business at almost a normal outlay. It is a company in the happy position of possessing an almost closed capital account, since only £2,666 was spent on this head last half-year. After paying debenture interest and adding £7,000 to the reserve fund, against £3,500 in the corresponding half of 1896, the company is able to cover its preferential dividends and to give the usual 3¾ per cent. for the half-year on its ordinary stock, making up the year's dividends to the accustomed 7½ per cent. The balance carried forward, however, is, at £7,061, about £650 less than in the second half of 1896. The balance-sheet has a very satisfactory appearance, and there was £140,474 in cash at the company's credit when it was drawn up. The dividend is payable on the 19th inst.

GREAT SOUTHERN AND WESTERN RAILWAY COMPANY OF IRELAND.—Gross receipts, £458,965; expenses, £231,024; ratio of expenses to receipts, 50·3. Out of the net revenue of £196,628 all the preference dividends are met, and a dividend at the rate of 5½ per cent. per annum is declared on the ordinary stock, £3,000 added to reserve, and a balance of £30,339 carried forward. Traffic receipts increased £12,223, and working expenses £6,661. The company spent £24,488 on capital account in the half-year, and looks to expend £304,386 in future years. In the balance-sheet the reserve fund of £23,000, together with superannuation fund of £77,877, stand against an amount of £162,366 at the debit of capital account. The dividends are payable on March 1.

TOTTENHAM AND HAMPSTEAD RAILWAY COMPANY.—This little property, controlled by the Midland, earned enough last half-year to pay a dividend at the rate of 8½ per cent. per annum on its ordinary stock, leaving about £10 more to carry forward than it had in the second half of 1896. It spent only £207 on capital account in the half-year.

LLOYDS BANK, LIMITED.—The secretary of this bank sends us the following letter, and we have to express our regret that the two mistakes referred to should have been allowed to creep into this paper :—' I am directed to call attention to some grave mistakes in your paragraph (page 164, issue of February 4) with respect to this bank's recently issued report. It is there stated that our investments amount to £3,870,000 only, and are all in one item. Both these assertions are, as you will see upon reference to the report, quite erroneous, as the investments are clearly set out by us in *two items*, and amount, together, to close upon £8,000,000. You have obviously overlooked a most important line — Consols, &c., £4,000,000 odd—and the error, and the inference based upon it, are serious and misleading. I have also to mention that the reserved fund has not been increased by premiums on new shares as you suggest, and the report does not warrant such a surmise, the fact being that the adjustments of capital and reserves of the two banks which we have acquired during the past year have, as mentioned by the directors, increased our own share capital by £260,000, and the reserved fund by £150,000. So recently as September last we had occasion to write you respecting a mistake in THE INVESTORS' REVIEW with respect to this bank, and it is unfortunate that a much greater one should have been suffered to appear after so short an interval.

TRAMWAYS UNION COMPANY.—An old-established company which works tramways at Bremen, Bucharest, and Madrid. Like other companies working abroad, it has not kept up the farce of denying the leasehold character of the business, and so is accumulating sinking funds both to redeem debentures and the share capital. Considerable expenditure has taken place during the past year in the three cities, chiefly in Madrid, which is being supplied with an electric installation. The company has therefore issued £150,000 of Five per Cent. "B" debentures in the year. After setting aside £2,440 to debenture fund, and £1,026 towards repayment of share capital, the net revenue amounted to £12,366, which allowed a distribution of 5 per cent. upon the share capital, and the carrying forward of £351. There is a dividend equalisation reserve of £5,000, but the capital reserve of £10,575 was last year absorbed by special improvements at Bremen.

WESTMINSTER ELECTRIC SUPPLY CORPORATION.—This is one of the best, if not the best electric lighting company in London, and its record for the past year is remarkably good. Its revenue of £107,366 showed an increase of £20,734, or about 23 per cent. over that of the preceding year. Expenses naturally increased, but only moderately, and the net profit of £49,585 permitted of a dividend of 12 per cent., and the carrying forward of £3,119. Larger sums were allowed for repairs and depreciation, and the various reserves of this comparatively new company amount to £59,878, and the result is seen in its balance-sheet, where evidence of comfortable circumstances is patent. During the year 4,355,781 Board of Trade units of current were sold for the equivalent of 290,561 lamps of eight-candle power, as against 3,503,054 Board of Trade units sold in the preceding twelve months for an equivalent of 249,318 lamps of eight-candle power. There are now on circuit 292,883 lamps of eight-candle power, and applications have been received for a further 10,886. The company is about to repay £100,000 of Four and a Half per Cent. and Five per Cent. debentures, and therefore issued £200,000 of Three and a Half per Cent. debenture stock, partly, of course, to meet further expenditure.

LONDON AND MIDDLESEX FREEHOLD ESTATES COMPANY.—This is the old London Financial Association of unholy memory under a new name, with its share capital reduced to sensible dimensions. Consequently it appears to be doing better, and in the past year earned a net profit of £16,094. Most of this, however, was obtained from profit on the sale of land and investments, and the board, therefore, prudently distribute only about a third of the amount in a dividend of 5 per cent. upon the shares, carrying forward no less than £10,038. Comfortable sayings are uttered in regard to some of the "lock-ups" of the old company, and those who have stood by it throughout may yet win back a part of their loss.

NATIONAL MORTGAGE AND AGENCY OF NEW ZEALAND. — This company did a trifle better in the past year, for it was able to pay the usual dividend of 5 per cent., and carry forward £962 more than it brought in. Although another £1 per share has been called up of late, the debentures issued are about the same in amount as they were a year ago. The company, we are glad to see, has reduced the issue of guaranteed mortgages by two-thirds in the same period, for such mortgages are a most unsatisfactory sort of security. The new money has apparently gone to swell the investments and liquid assets, so that the position ought to have improved, but no clue is given as to the nature of the investments. The debenture interest, however, is still a serious charge, representing, as it does, two-thirds of the net profits earned in the year.

BRIGHTON GRAND HOTEL COMPANY.—After a stormy past the affairs of this company have improved of late, and for last year the profit of £4,299 was £1,314 above that of 1896. A dividend of 3½ per cent. was declared, as against 2½ per cent. in 1896, and still worse announcements earlier. The company, however, is not yet in a firm position, and we should like to see more regard paid to depreciation in its accounts. Thus "furniture and plant" stand at £47,874 both in last year's and this year's report, and yet we should imagine that in the interval they had somewhat depreciated. The consolidation of the various debenture issues into one stock was a wise proceeding, but at the same time the expenses in this connection, put at £1,873, ought to be written out of the balance-sheet The allowance for repairs appears to be good.

BRENTFORD GAS COMPANY.—Net profits last half-year were slightly higher at £38,103, but the balance brought in was smaller, and after paying debenture interest the surplus of £58,729 was a little less than a year ago. The usual dividends at the rate of 12 per cent. per annum on the consolidated stock and at the rate of 9 per cent. per annum on the new stock were declared, leaving about £25,000 to be carried forward. The sale of gas increased in the half-year by 9 per cent.

HOLT BREWERY COMPANY.—Net profits last year amounted to £55,028, or an increase of £4,723 over the previous twelve months. Dividends amounting to 8 per cent. were declared upon the ordinary shares, and £15,000 was added to reserve. The latter fund will then amount to £25,000, being the result of two years' accumulations since the company was reconstructed. Depreciation to the extent of £6,969 was allowed for, which seems low, while repairs only came to £1,451, the value of the properties being returned as £769,325.

ANDREW KNOWLES & SONS, LIMITED.—This colliery company announces that in the past year there was no improvement in the prices of coal, and no alteration in colliers' wages. The output of the year was somewhat reduced by an accident, which caused a stoppage at one of the company's collieries for about six months. Net profit for the year amounted to £16,226, which allowed of a dividend of 15s. 9d. per share, or 3½ per cent., as against 18s. per share in 1896. To do this the balance forward was reduced £3,461. The company seems to have no reserves worth speaking of, and although £12 10s. per share was written off capital in 1895-6, the balance-sheet has not even now a prepossessing look.

CRYSTAL PALACE DISTRICT GAS COMPANY.—The great aid received in the past by this company from residuals is now rather a misfortune, as their prices have fallen so much of late. To pay the June dividend of 5½ per cent. no less than £3,669 had to be withdrawn from the reserve fund, and in the past half-year the net revenue only came to £11,652. This implies that £4,416 will have to be withdrawn from the same fund if the dividend of 5½ per cent. is now to be paid, and evidently it is the intention of the board to favour such a proposal. After this deduction the reserve will amount to £32,166, which means that the company can go on for some years without reducing its dividend. It is stated that revenue has borne the cost of improvement of plant which will be productive in the near future, and the district is a promising one, so that this company, with its low charge of 2s. 7d. per 1,000 feet, ought soon to bring its accounts into equilibrium.

BRISTOL UNITED BREWERIES.—The absorption by this company of the brewing concern of D. Sykes & Co. has produced a strong-looking combination. When the amount due on the shares is paid up, the capital should consist of £440,000, with £220,000 of debenture stock, £37,552 of mortgages, and a reserve of £130,000. The percentage of borrowed money to share capital will, therefore, be good, while the reserve represents 20 per cent. of the total share debenture and mortgage capital. The profit and loss account of last year was confused by the arrangements in connection with the amalgamation, but the net revenue sufficed to pay dividends and bonus on the ordinary shares amounting to 15 per cent. for the year. It would be a vast improvement if the allowances for repairs, depreciation, and bad debts, were stated in the profit and loss account. No less than £40,271 of the reserve is invested in securities.

SOUTH METROPOLITAN GAS COMPANY.—Thanks to an increase of over 6 per cent. in the sale of gas, this company was able to pay its usual dividend of 5½ per cent. out of revenue, and to carry the small balance of £1,802 forward. The reserve fund will, therefore, stand at £94,872, and in addition there is an insurance fund of £44,864, and a leasehold renewal fund of £16,846. Each fund is credited with interest each half-year, so that they grow automatically. To earn its revenue, the company, of course, had to put forth great efforts, and the increase in meters, private, company-owned, and automatic, and stoves and fires used by its clients came to nearly 10 per cent.

NATIONAL TELEPHONE COMPANY.—Gross income for the half-year ending December 31, amounted to £507,602 ; net, £178,457, increases of £67,624 and £23,473 respectively. Working expenses are 61·33, increase ·06. Addition to reserve, £40,000, making it £510,671. Dividends on ordinary, 6 per cent., free of income tax. On capital account, £267,375 has been expended for additional exchanges, private and underground lines, &c., and further extensions are anticipated, but no estimate of the amount is given.

WILTS AND DORSET BANKING COMPANY.—A net profit for the year of £113,398 is shown in the report, including £8,576 brought forward, which compares with £108,577 for 1896, when £7,027 was brought in. The usual dividend of 20 per cent. is distributed, and 10s. per share interest is paid on new shares, leaving £8,398 to go forward. The figures of the balance-sheet have been swollen by the new capital raised so that comparison is of little use. Deposits have risen from £7,499,000 to £9,444,000, and bills discounted and loans from £3,581,000 to £5,079,000, which is a heavy total, and might be divided. The premium on the new shares has been added to the reserve, raising it to £700,000, the whole of which stands in Consols at 90. The bank is evidently going ahead, for another half-million of capital is to be raised on such terms as the directors may think fit, and not divided, as previous issues have been, amongst the shareholders. During the year two amalgamations have been effected, and three new branches have been opened, besides several agencies.

CRYSTAL PALACE COMPANY.—A hitherto unexplained advance of considerable dimensions has recently taken place in the prices of the various stocks of the company, but the annual report sheds some light. In this it is stated that a movement has been started for improving the financial position of the company, and it is hoped that by the day of the meeting (next Thursday) the negotiations, which are now pending, will be in a sufficiently advanced stage to be reported to the proprietors. We await the scheme with considerable interest, but think it prudent not to expect too much. In other respects the annual statement is as doleful as usual. Gross receipts came to £134,704, and all but £9,851 was absorbed in expenses. After providing for First Debenture stocks there remains £58 to be added to the previous balance of £239 standing at the credit of the Second Debenture Stock Interest Account, and thus £1,330,175 of stock goes without interest. The year's receipts owing to the Handel Festival are £13,000 more than in the previous year, but the net revenue is the lowest for very many years past. The number of season tickets sold was only 9,140, being also the lowest for many years, but the daily admissions by payment amounting to 1,171,532 were larger than they have been since 1890. The imperial Victorian Exhibition failed to attract any great additional number of visitors; and there was a great falling off in the receipts from the Handel Festival because it was held so soon after Jubilee day. There is a well-grounded idea that everything at the Palace has to be paid for; yet we find that there were given during the year free, gratis, and for nothing 365 concerts, 553 popular entertainments, 25 firework displays, 20 special fetes and choral festivals and 10 bird, cat, dog, flower, fruit and other shows, besides additional attractions. In spite of all this and of the Handel gathering, the directors did not manage, as was intended, to write off any portion of the £5,500 in respect of repairs to main building in suspense, which has consequently again to be carried forward. The old out-of-the-way Palace seems to be sorely in need of a vigorous push from some quarter to give it a fresh start, but we certainly do not approve of the suggestion of surrounding vestries that such a "white elephant" should be bought up with ratepayers money.

LONDON ROAD CAR COMPANY.—The report for the second half of last year does not show the improvement we expected. Receipts came to £171,934, against £160,438 in the corresponding period, but expenses were £154,865, against £143,229, so that the profit, amounting to £17,068, was actually £141 less than a year ago. The continued growth of the concern is seen in the fact that the number of horses in stock was 4,287, compared with 3,964; the average number of cars working 356, against 334, and the number of people carried over 29 millions, against 27 millions. But while the weekly average traffic receipts per car were £17 14s. 8d., or 2s. 8d. more than in 1896, the weekly average expenses were £16 11s. 3¼d., being an increase of almost 5s. Expenses under all headings were larger, the cost of feeding per horse per week rising from 7s. 10½d. to 8s. 1½d. Although the company made no larger profit the dividend is raised from 7 to 8 per cent. per annum, and in place of the £3,000 added last year to general reserve, a sum of £2,000 is set aside towards starting a depreciation fund, and a slightly smaller balance is carried forward. The dividends and bonus for the whole year amount to 9 per cent., so that at their present price of 11 the shares yield still 5 per cent.

THE GERMAN BANK OF LONDON made a gross profit last year of £40,414, inclusive of £3,416 brought forward, and a net profit of £27,044. A dividend of 10s. per share, or 5 per cent., is paid for the year for the fifth time in succession, and £4,000 is added to the reserve against £3,000 last year. With this addition it will amount to only £84,000, compared with a fully-paid capital of £400,000. Current accounts of the bank do not exceed £206,470, but its acceptances stand for the remarkably large total of £1,007,564. On the other side bills discounted and advances amount to £1,425,461, but the bank appears to hold no investments. The position seems somewhat unique, but not necessarily unsatisfactory.

NATIONAL PROVIDENT INSTITUTION.—This Mutual Life Office issued 1855 new policies last year insuring £652,400 and yielding £27,490 in new premiums, £11,736 was also received for annuities amounting to £782. Altogether the premium income was £414,788, and the total income, exclusive of £17,299 credited as "balance on revaluation of assets" £635,400. Claims took £316,581, including bonuses, and expenses, exclusive of income-tax and commission, came to £47,419 or little more than 11·3 per cent. of the premium income. After meeting all charges and applying £58,676 in reduction of premiums, there is a balance of £176,329 to be added to the funds, making their total £5,233,418. The quinquennial valuation shows favourable results and gives a total surplus on the five years as at November 20 last of £775,585 of which £714,390 is divided, £7,000 added to the superannuation fund, and £61,195 placed to the insurance fund as undividend surplus.

GLYN, MILLS, CURRIE & Co's balance-sheet, dated January 31 last, comes to a total of £14,267,069. Cash in hand and at the bank stands at £1,597,675; money at call and notice at £2,335,600; investment, including £1,666,667 Consols at 90, at £2,846,605; and stock company with unlimited liability, there is no profit and loss bills, loans, &c., at £7,308,190. Of course, being a private joint-account. There is a contingent liability of £1,072,375 on acceptances.

ROBARTS, LUBBOCK & Co.—The balance-sheet of this private banking firm, dated January 31, shows current and deposit accounts amounting to £3,803,969. Cash in hand, and at Bank of England, came to £770,461, and bills discounted and advances to £1,709,434.

The gold output on the lowlands of the Amur, in Eastern Siberia, is steadily increasing. During 1897 the washings realised 132 poods as against 81 poods in 1896.

Answers to Correspondents.

Questions about public securities, and on all points in company law, will be answered week by week, in the REVIEW, on the following terms and conditions:—

A fee of FIVE shillings must be remitted for each question put, provided they are questions about separate securities. Should a private letter be required, then an extra fee of FIVE shillings must be sent to cover the cost of such letter, the fee then being TEN shillings for one query only, and FIVE shillings for every subsequent one in the same letter. While making this concession the EDITOR will feel obliged if private replies are as much as possible dispensed with. It is wholly impossible to answer letters sent merely "with a stamped envelope enclosed for reply."

Correspondents will further greatly oblige by so framing their questions as to obviate the necessity to name securities in the replies. They should *number* the questions, keeping a copy for reference, thus:—"(1) Please inform me about the present position of the Rowenzori Development Co. (2) Is a dividend likely to be paid soon on the capital stock of the Congo-Sudan Railway?"

Answers to be given to all such questions by simply quoting the numbers 1, 2, 3, and so on. The EDITOR has a rooted objection to such forms of reply as—"I think your Timbuctoo Consols will go up," or "Sell your Slowcoach and Draggem Bonds," because this kind of thing is open to all sorts of abuses. By the plan suggested, and by using a fancy name to be replied to, each query can be kept absolutely private to the inquirer, and no scope whatever be given to market manipulations. Avoid, as names to be replied to, common words, like "investor," "inquirer," and so on, as also "bear" or "bull." Detached syllables of the inquirer's name, or initials reversed, will frequently do as well as anything, so long as the answer can be identified by the inquirer.

The EDITOR further respectfully requests that merely speculative questions should as far as possible be avoided. He by no means sets himself up as a market prophet, and can only undertake to provide the latest information regarding the securities asked about. This he will do faithfully and without bias.

Replies cannot be guaranteed in the same week if the letters demanding them reach the office of the INVESTORS' REVIEW, Norfolk House, Norfolk-street, W.C., later than the first post on Wednesday mornings.

A VICTIM.—Your further communications received. I doubt if the gentleman you name would consent to act; it would be better to get a shareholder. I am glad you have done so much. These companies do not send me notices of their meetings, hence the omission; the only ones I had information about are to be held to-day, and I understand some protest will be made. Unless the opposition is strong it will be difficult to get any satisfaction.

H. B.—The original prospectus was not very attractive, and for some time the preference shares, which alone were offered for public subscription, were in the hands of underwriters. A good dividend has helped to raise the market price, and presumably they have taken advantage of it, as they are now dealt in fairly easily and at a good premium. There is also a fair market in the ordinary, which were taken by the vendors in part payment. The price is too high to make them a tempting purchase.

A. Z. B.—I hope to have some news for you in a day or two.

W. H. S.—Your letter has been forwarded.

EXON.—I do not consider the rates offered sufficiently tempting to induce you to consent to the locking up of your money for so long. There is no cause for alarm, but if anything did happen you would be unable to help yourself, as you have not a marketable security. It would be better to accept a little interest and have something you could sell if there were need.

From 1890 to 1897 inclusive, 218 trains were "held up" by train robbers in the United States, resulting in death to seventy-eight people, and the wounding of sixty-seven others. The American Government seems to look helplessly on, and takes no steps in seriously attempting to stop these desperate outrages. Yet it does seem high time that something was done.

The United States War Department are taking steps to control the disorderly crowd now heading for the Alaskan Goldfields. Persons inadequately supplied with provisions will be refused admission altogether.

The new White Star steamer, "Cymric," just out of the builders' hands, is said to be the largest cargo carrying steamer in the world. Her length is 600 ft.; her beam 64 ft., and depth 42 ft.

The affairs of a "financial investor," of the name of E. Bunn, have been placed in the hands of the Official Receiver, to be wound up in bankruptcy, but the gentleman himself has not yet surrendered under the proceedings. This financial investor seems to have had expansive methods of business. He is described as of London, Ipswich, Manchester, Balham, and Brighton. He accepted deposits at the rate of five per cent., with bonuses as circumstances permitted. How much was paid in these respects does not appear; but at the meeting of creditors the assets were said to be of "doubtful value."

The Queensland gold returns for January are as follow:—Charters Towers, 35,900 tons crushed, yielding 26,400 oz.; Mount Morgan, 12,600 tons crushed, yielding 14,600 oz.; Gympie, 800 tons, yielding 1,800 oz.; Croydon, 1,800 tons, yielded 1,500 oz.; other fields, 4,600 tons, yielded 5,800 oz.; alluvial yielded 1,800 oz.; total, 49,900 oz.

THE SUBSCRIPTION LIST WILL BE CLOSED ON OR BEFORE WEDNESDAY, THE 16th FEBRUARY

United Railways of the Havana and Regla Warehouses, Limited.

Incorporated under the Companies Acts, 1862 to 1893.

(INTERNATIONAL COMPANY).

SHARE CAPITAL { 140,000 Preferred—£10 each - - £1,400,000 } **£1,540,000**
{ 14,000 Deferred—£10 each - - 140,000 }

DEBENTURE STOCKS—£400,000 Five per Cent. "A" Irredeemable Debenture Stock.
£1,600,000 Five per Cent. Consolidated Irredeemable Debenture Stock.

Issue of £350,000 (part of a total of £400,000) Five per cent. "A" Irredeemable Debenture Stock.

This "A" Stock ranks in priority to all other Issues of the English Company, and is secured upon its whole property and undertaking, but as regards the Railways subject to any of the Bonds of 1890 for the time being unconverted.

The valuable Dock-warehouses (Wharves), Ferries, Lands, and Appurtenances, which formed no part of the security for the Bonds of 1890, are specially charged to secure the Five per Cent. "A" Debenture Stock.

No charge can be created *pari passu* or in priority to this Debenture Stock without the assent of three-fourths of the Holders.

Conversion of the £1,566,900 existing Five per Cent. Bonds (1890) of the United Railways of the Havana into Five per Cent. Consolidated Irredeemable Debenture Stock of this Company.

Trustees for the Five per Cent. "A" Irredeemable Debenture Stock:
Sir HENRY C. BURDETT, K.C.B. ALEXANDER YOUNG, Esq.

Trustees for the Consolidated Irredeemable Debenture Stock and Voting Trustees:
Baron SCHRODER. J. NAPIER HIGGINS, Esq., Q.C. WALPOLE GREENWELL, Esq.

Messrs. J. HENRY SCHRODER & CO. offer for public subscription the above-named £350,000 Five per Cent. "A" Irredeemable Debenture Stock, which they have contracted for.

The price of issue is £98 for £100 Stock, payable as follows:—

£ 5 on application.
35 ,, allotment.
35 ,, the 15th March.
23 ,, the 14th April.
£98

Interest at 5 per cent. per annum, from the date of the above Instalments, to 1st July, 1898, will be paid on that date.

Allottees will have the option of paying up in full on allotment, or on the date of any subsequent instalment, under discount at the rate of 2 per cent. per annum. The failure to pay any instalment when due renders all previous payments liable to forfeiture.

In case no allotment is made the deposit will be returned forthwith.

Scrip Certificates will be issued in due course in exchange for the Allotment Letter and receipt for the amount due on allotment.

CONVERSION OF THE EXISTING 5 PER CENT. BONDS (1890) OF THE UNITED RAILWAYS OF THE HAVANA.

Holders of these Bonds are entitled to receive Consolidated Irredeemable Debenture Stock of the English Company in exchange for the Bonds of 1890 to the same amount.

The bonds must be delivered to Messrs. J. Henry Schröder & Co., with all unpaid coupons, including the coupon due 1st July next. The interest on the Debenture stock will run from the 1st January last.

Applications for conversion should be lodged forthwith.

The Share Capital of the Old Company, $7,000,000 gold, say equal to £1,400,000, is held by about 900 shareholders, and there will be issued in respect thereof the Preferred shares of this Company to that amount.

United Railways of the Havana and Regla Warehouses, Limited (International Company), has been formed to acquire from the Old Company, named Banco Del Comercio Ferrocarriles Unidos De La Habana y Almacenes De Regla, the well-known system forming the United Railways of the Havana, which has for over forty years past been owned and worked under perpetual concessions. In 1889 the two local Companies which owned the system were amalgamated into the Old Company. This Company also acquires from the Old Company the Dock-warehouses at the Regla Terminus in the harbour of Havana (where the Sugar, Tobacco and other products of the zone served by the Railways, as well as merchandise arriving by sea are stored); also valuable lands adjoining the Main Havana Station in the centre of the City, at Tallapiedra, and elsewhere near the City.

It was not considered advisable by this Company that the Bank of Commerce, the business of which hitherto formed an integral part of Old Company, should be taken over.

For some time past efforts have been made to convert the Railway and Warehouse business into an English Company. With this object, Mr. Underdown, who has now accepted the position of Chairman of this Company, entered, on 30th October last, into a Contract with the Old Company, the benefit of which he transfers to this Company, upon the terms and conditions of the Contract hereinafter mentioned. It is considered that the undertaking, administered under new regulations by an experienced Board of Directors, will have a much enhanced value, and the financial results be greatly improved.

The Five per cent. "A" Irredeemable Debenture Stock, of which £350,000 is now offered, together with the Deferred Shares, have been created to carry out this operation, to clear the Railway of its floating debt, to put the Railway and Rolling Stock in good order (which have naturally suffered to a certain extent, but not seriously, by the political disturbances), to provide working capital, and a reserve fund specially set aside to supplement the earnings of the properties, so that under all circumstances the service of the Debenture Stocks in the early period of resuscitation of the regular traffics may be fully assured.

It is one of the conditions of the transfer of the property that the Railways shall be taken over subject to any of the Bonds of 1890 for the time being unconverted. In that year, £1,600,000 Five Per Cent. Bonds were created in order to extinguish the then existing Bonds of the Bay of Havana and of the Havana Railways, and for further extensions. The latter Bonds have all been redeemed, with the exception of £51,300 of the issue of 1886 (against which £50,000 of the Bonds of 1890 are held by Messrs. J. Henry Schröder & Co.), and these will shortly be redeemed.

The Five per Cent. Consolidated Irredeemable Debenture Stock of £1,600,000 is created chiefly for the purpose of converting the above-mentioned existing Bonds of 1890, and holders of these Bonds are now entitled to exchange them for this Irredeemable Debenture Stock of the Company.

It is pointed out to the Bondholders of 1890 that the advantages they will obtain by conversion will be the following:—

(1) They will become entitled to an Irredeemable Debenture Stock of an English Company (secured by a Trust Deed) carrying interest at 5 per cent. in place of a Bond of a Foreign Company bearing that interest, but which is liable to be paid off at any time at 105, thereby preventing it rising to any much higher price.

(2) This Debenture Stock, though subject to the Five per Cent. "A" Debenture Stock, has more security than the Bonds of 1890, having a charge on the valuable Warehouses and Lands above mentioned, which the Bonds do not possess.

(3) It is believed that, under the management of an English Company, the Share Capital will earn a substantial dividend, whereby the 5 per cent. Consolidated Debenture Stock will have a value far beyond the 105 per cent. at which the existing Bonds are liable to be redeemed.

(4) A very substantial voting power at General Meetings of the Company is secured for the Trustees of this Debenture Stock, so as to render any infringement of the rights of the Debenture Stockholders impossible.

The Statement, furnished by the London Agency of the Old Company, gives particulars of the properties acquired by this Company, together with a return of the revenues derived from the Railways and the Warehouses for the last seven years. It will be seen therefrom that the net revenue of the Regla Warehouses alone during that period has averaged £18,798 per annum, an amount in excess of the sum required to pay the interest on the Five per Cent. "A" Debenture Stock—

The net revenue from the Railways and Warehouses averages per annum ... ... (after deducting the £36,767 mentioned in the report).		£196,179
The interest on the £350,000 "A" Debenture stock requires per annum	£17,500	
The interest on the Consolidated Debenture stock requires per annum	£80,000	
		£97,500
Showing a surplus of		98,679
The net revenue of 1897 from the railways and warehouses amounts to ... (after deducting a similar sum of £36,767).		122,104

The reports now being received from Cuba indicate a growing amelioration of the political situation, and that a steady resumption of the cultivation of crops has been going on for some considerable time, and this is evidenced by the circumstance that whereas at this time last year only 16 sugar factories were said to be at work, 83 factories are now reported to be working, while other industries are also improving.

The entire Share Capital of this Company is to be issued credited as fully-paid up under the terms of the Agreement below mentioned, the proprietors of the Shares of the Old Company receiving in respect of their Shares the Preferred Shares of this Company, they retaining the Banking business and premises as a separate concern.

The Preferred Shares are entitled to a Cumulative Preferential Dividend of 3 per cent.; then the Deferred Shares receive a like Dividend, any further profits being divided without distinction of class. When the Deferred Shares have received 3 per cent. Dividend in two consecutive financial years, all Shares will become Ordinary Shares.

The forms of the Deed of Trust securing the Five per Cent. "A" Debenture Stock, and of the Deed of Trust securing the Five per Cent. Consolidated Debenture Stock, containing provisions as to the exercise of voting power by the Trustees, both of which deeds provide for convening meetings of Debenture Stockholders whereby a prescribed majority can bind a minority; copy of Agreement dated the 9th day of February, 1898, and made between the Company of the first part, E. M. Underdown, as transferor, of the second part, and Messrs. J. Henry Schröder & Co. of the third part, in which the above-mentioned Contract of 30th October last, as well as other matters, are set out, can, together with the Memorandum and Articles of Association of the Company, be seen at the Offices of the Solicitors, 57½, Old Broad Street, London, E.C.

Applications for quotations on the Stock Exchange will be made in due course.

Prospectuses and Forms of Application and for Conversion may be obtained at the Offices of Messrs. Henry Schroder & Co., No. 145, Leadenhall Street, E.C., from Messrs. W. Greenwell & Co., No. 2 Finch Lane, E.C., and from Messrs. Jourdan & Pawle, No. 1, Cushion Court, E.C.

London, 11th February, 1898.

Directors.

*E. M. UNDERDOWN, Q.C., Chairman.
Sir HENRY MATHER JACKSON, Bart.
CHARLES J. CATER SCOTT, Esq.
GERALD P. TORRENS, Esq.
*Exmo A. G. DE BUSTAMANTE, Marques del Solar.

Solicitors.

Messrs. NORTON, ROSE, NORTON & Co., 57½, Old Broad Street, E.C.

Bankers.

THE LONDON AND WESTMINSTER BANK LIMITED, Lothbury, E.C.

Secretary and Offices.

ROBERT A. McLEAN, 1, Queen Victoria Street, E.C.

Local Board in Havana.

*Exmo Marques de ARGUELLES.
*Exmo Don ARTURO AMBLARD.
*Don LUCIANO RUIZ.
JOHN ALLAN McLEAN.

*These gentleman are connected with the old Company or interested in the contract above mentioned.

Notice to Subscribers.

Complaints are continually reaching us that the INVESTORS' REVIEW cannot be obtained at this and the other railway bookstall, that it does not reach Scotch and Irish cities till Monday, and that it is not delivered in the City till Saturday morning.

We publish on Friday in time for the REVIEW to be at all Metropolitan bookstalls by at latest 4 p.m., and we believe that it is there then, having no doubt that Messrs. W. H. Smith & Son do their best, but they have such a mass of papers to handle every day that a fresh one may well look almost like a personal enemy and be kept in short supply unless the reading public shows unmistakably that it is wanted. A little perseverance, therefore, in asking for the INVESTORS' REVIEW is all that should be required to remedy this defect.

All London newsagents can be in a position to distribute the paper on Friday afternoon if they please, and here also the only remedy is for subscribers to insist upon having it as soon as published. Arrangements have been made that all our direct City subscribers shall have their copies before 4 p.m. on Friday. As for the provinces, we can only say that the paper is delivered to the forwarding agents in ample time to be in every English and Scotch town, and in Dublin and Belfast, likewise, early on Saturday morning. Those despatched by post from this office can be delivered by the first London mail on Saturday in every part of the United Kingdom.

Cheques and Postal Orders should be made payable to CLEMENT WILSON.

The INVESTORS' REVIEW can be obtained in Paris of Messrs. BOYVEAU ET CHEVILLET, 22, Rue de la Banque.

To Correspondents.

The EDITOR cannot undertake to return rejected communications.
Letters from correspondents must, in every case, be authenticated by the name and address of the writer.

The Investors' Review.

The Week's Money Market.

The scarcity of floating balances in the market has been fully disclosed in the past seven days. There was little in the way of "calls" or issues to disturb the equilibrium, and the amounts falling due to be repaid to the Bank of England were only moderate; yet the arrangements in connection with the distribution of the Railway dividends and the settlement of a moderate-sized Stock Exchange account, were quite sufficient to create a keen demand for short loans. Probably all the money repaid to the Bank, and a little more besides, had to be borrowed, with the consequence that day to day loans are quoted 2¾ to 3 per cent., as compared with 2¼ to 2½ per cent. a week ago. Seven-day market loans have also risen from 2½ per cent. to 2¾ per cent.

This greater demand for, or greater scarcity of money has placed the bill market at rather a disadvantage, and discounts have not moved up in consonance, and bills have to be discounted at rates that are often below those paid for money. There has, however, been a mild upward movement here, for sixty day and three months' bills are both quoted 2 11/16 to 2¾ per cent., as against 2⅝ per cent. a week ago. It is difficult, however, to establish an advance, as it is felt that the tightness of money is in a great measure due to the high total of the Public Deposits, which now stand at 15½ millions. An average total for these deposits at this time of year is about nine to ten millions, so that there is the prospect that some of this money may be released when least expected. The failure of the Chinese Loan proposals has taken away another motive for caution, but we have reason to believe that if Japan only receives 2½ millions next May, a loan for that country will be imminent. The Paris exchange has moved steadily in our favour throughout the week and is now about par, but it is a temporary change due to Stock Exchange commitments. On the other hand, the Russian rate has fallen ·05 to 93·90, but the price of gold is dull at about 77s. 10¾d. per ounce.

The Stock Exchange Settlement showed a somewhat heavier account, and loans for the fortnight were quoted hard at 3½ per cent., while those who borrowed after the first day had to pay 3¾ per cent. A small issue of Bournemouth 3 per cent. stock received fair attention, and the £33,382 offered was applied for more than three times over. Tenders at £102 0s. 6d., or £1 0s. 6d. above the minimum, received in full. The East Indian Railway Loan was arranged upon the terms mentioned last week, original subscribers having the right to take the modified terms—a very fair arrangement.

Little has to be said this week about the figures of the Bank return. It is still the familiar story of taxes eating into market balances, and the market, therefore, forced to lean upon the Bank. "Public" deposits have increased £1,049,000 within the week, and "other" securities are up £873,000. The market did not borrow all the tax-collectors took from it, because £471,000 in coin and notes came in from circulation, raising the banking reserve to that extent—it is now £23,246,000—and adding £283,000 to the "other" deposits. But the market is poor, and promises to remain poor these six weeks to come.

SILVER.

There has been little change on the week in this market. For a time the price of bars for immediate shipment was pushed up to 26¼d. per oz., but their selling at once became prominent, and the quotation dropped to 26 1/16d. The two-months' forward price has moved in unison at a ¼d. below that for "spot." Better applications were received for the India Council drafts on Wednesday, if the total demanded is solely taken into account, for the amount offered was nearly covered twice, but many of the applications were at rates that could not be entertained, and the Council did not quite sell its complement. Rupee paper has been quieter, but the opening of a "bull" campaign by M. Ottomar Haupt caused the price to recover to 63¼, after having been 63⅛. Indian exchanges have improved 1/16d. to 3/32d. on the week, as the Money Markets there are growing tighter once again. Chinese rates, however, keep dull.

BANK OF ENGLAND.

AN ACCOUNT pursuant to the Act 7 and 8 Vict., cap. 32, for the Week ending on Wednesday, February 9, 1898.

ISSUE DEPARTMENT.

	£		£
Notes Issued	47,379,625	Government Debt	11,015,100
		Other Securities	5,784,900
		Gold Coin and Bullion	30,579,625
		Silver Bullion	—
	£47,379,625		£47,379,625

BANKING DEPARTMENT.

	£		£
Proprietors' Capital	14,553,000	Government Securities	13,999,565
Rest	3,472,459	Other Securities	32,329,262
Public Deposits (including Exchequer, Savings Banks, Commissioners of National Debt, and Dividend Accounts)	15,447,084	Notes	20,779,390
Other Deposits	35,901,137	Gold and Silver Coin	2,466,286
Seven Day and other Bills	140,823		
	£69,574,503		£69,574,503

Dated February 9, 1898.

H. G. BOWEN, *Chief Cashier.*

In the following table will be found the movements compared with the previous week, and also the totals for that week and the corresponding return last year:—

Banking Department.

Last Year. Feb. 10.		Feb. 2, 1898.	Feb. 9, 1898.	Increase.	Decrease.
£	Liabilities.	£	£	£	£
3,509,006	Rest	3,463,958	3,472,459	8,501	—
13,175,053	Pub. Deposits	14,398,388	15,447,084	1,048,696	—
40,699,405	Other do.	35,678,498	35,901,137	222,639	—
146,614	7 Day Bills	139,015	140,823	1,808	—
	Assets.			Decrease.	Increase.
14,767,630	Gov. Securities	14,003,036	13,999,565	3,471	—
28,456,015	Other do.	31,455,746	32,329,262	—	873,516
28,859,433	Total Reserve	22,774,077	23,245,676	—	471,599
				1,345,115	1,345,115
				Increase.	Decrease.
£		£	£	£	£
25,644,360	Note Circulation	26,960,110	26,600,235	—	359,875
53½ p.c.	Proportion	45⅛ p.c.	45¼ p.c.	—	—
3 "	Bank Rate	3 "	3 "	—	—

Foreign Bullion movement for week £101,000 out.

LONDON BANKERS' CLEARING.

Week ending	1898.	1897.	Increase.	Decrease.
	£	£	£	£
Jan. 5	222,654,000	174,376,000	48,278,000	—
" 12	144,603,000	127,315,000	17,288,000	—
" 19	171,777,000	156,200,000	15,577,000	—
" 26	134,247,000	118,667,000	15,580,000	—
Feb. 2	194,544,000	174,498,000	20,056,000	—
" 9	137,204,000	129,209,000	8,995,000	—

BANK AND DISCOUNT RATES ABROAD.

	Bank Rate.	Altered.	Open Market.
Paris	2	March 14, 1895	1⅞
Berlin	4	January 20, 1898	2⅞
Hamburg	4	January 20, 1898	2⅞
Frankfort	4	January 20, 1898	2⅞
Amsterdam	3	April 13, 1897	2⅜
Brussels	3	April 28, 1896	2
Vienna	4	January 22, 1896	3⅝
Rome	5	August 27, 1895	3
St. Petersburg	5½	January 23, 1898	5
Madrid	5	June 17, 1896	4
Lisbon	6	January 25, 1891	6
Stockholm	5	October 27, 1897	5
Copenhagen	4	January 20, 1893	4
Calcutta	11	January 11, 1898	—
Bombay	12	January 11, 1898	—
New York call money	1 to 1½	—	—

NEW YORK ASSOCIATED BANKS (dollar at 4s.).

	Feb. 5, 1898.	Jan. 29, 1898.	Jan. 22, 1898.	Feb. 6, 1897.
	£	£	£	£
Specie	22,818,000	22,618,000	22,130,000	15,912,000
Legal tenders	20,830,000	20,628,000	19,850,000	23,444,000
Loans and discounts	126,772,000	125,174,000	124,694,000	99,302,000
Circulation	2,878,400	2,803,800	2,918,800	3,358,000
Net deposits	146,766,000	144,496,000	142,894,000	113,792,000

Legal reserve is 25 per cent. of net deposits; therefore the total reserve (specie and legal tenders) exceeds this sum by £6,956,500, against an excess last week of £7,224,800

BANK OF FRANCE (25 francs to the £).

	Feb. 10, 1898.	Feb. 3, 1898.	Jan. 27, 1898.	Feb. 11, 1897.
	£	£	£	£
Gold in hand	77,030,000	77,076,800	77,162,070	76,443,000
Silver in hand	47,323,020	48,360,640	48,356,440	49,193,000
Bills discounted	31,058,200	37,871,600	36,637,640	*45,912,000
Advances	14,538,600	14,826,020	14,467,400	—
Note circulation	150,463,880	154,375,600	151,161,800	148,728,000
Public deposits	8,192,520	6,136,360	9,672,440	10,030,000
Private deposits	19,178,120	20,012,240	21,756,760	18,114,000

Proportion between bullion and circulation 83⅜ per cent. against 81⅓ per cent. a week ago.

* Includes advances.

FOREIGN RATES OF EXCHANGE ON LONDON.

Place.	Usance.	Last week's.	Latest.	Place.	Usance.	Last week's.	Latest.
Paris	chqs.	25·22	25·24½	Italy	sight	26·52	26·60
Brussels	chqs.	25·20½	25·27½	Do. gold prem.	..	105·12½	105·40
Amsterdam	short	12·05½	12·06½	Constantinople	3 mths	109·17	109·25
Berlin	short	20·42½	20·42	B. Ayres gd. pm.	..	153·70	161·30
Do.	3 mths	20·30	20·25	Rio de Janeiro	90 dys	6 11/16	6⅞
Hamburg	3 mths	20·29	20·27½	Valparaiso	90 dys	17⅝	17⅝
Frankfort	short	20·43	20·42	Calcutta	T. T.	1/3 11/16	1/3 13/16
Vienna	short	12·00½	12·01	Bombay	T. T.	1/3 11/16	1/3¾
St. Petersburg	3 mths	93·90	93·90	Hong Kong	T. T.	1/10⅝	1/10¾
New York	60 dys	4·82¾	4·83½	Shanghai	T. T.	2/6⅛	2/6⅜
Lisbon	sight	36	36	Singapore	T. T.	1/10⅛	1/10⅜
Madrid	sight	33·50	33·66				

IMPERIAL BANK OF GERMANY (20 marks to the £).

	Feb. 7, 1898.	Jan. 31, 1898.	Jan. 22, 1898.	Feb. 6, 1897.
	£	£	£	£
Cash in hand	46,313,150	45,672,450	45,757,850	44,284,000
Bills discounted	26,713,000	25,433,050	22,219,750	*32,386,000
Advances on stocks	4,129,450	4,185,000	4,110,600	—
Note circulation	52,827,050	54,542,350	54,613,750	50,498,000
Public deposits	21,538,300	21,755,550	22,169,850	22,202,000

* Includes advances.

AUSTRIAN-HUNGARIAN BANK (1s. 8d. to the florin).

	Feb. 7, 1898.	Jan. 31, 1898.	Jan. 22, 1898.	Feb. 6, 1897.
	£	£	£	£
Gold reserve	30,347,656	30,272,833	30,254,000	30,557,000
Silver reserve	10,445,417	10,352,116	10,331,416	12,643,000
Foreign bills	1,732,333	1,403,916	1,344,000	—
Advances	1,587,250	1,700,000	1,046,563	—
Note circulation	52,299,333	52,318,333	52,780,000	59,979,000
Bills discounted	11,761,416	12,253,200	12,855,083	*15,224,000

* Includes advances.

NATIONAL BANK OF BELGIUM (25 francs to the £).

	Feb. 3, 1898.	Jan. 27, 1898.	Jan. 20, 1898.	Feb. 4, 1897.
	£	£	£	£
Coin and bullion	4,427,280	4,220,230	4,286,120	4,279,000
Other securities	17,631,560	17,888,360	17,625,080	16,835,000
Note circulation	19,209,160	19,756,480	19,557,120	18,864,000
Deposits	4,109,120	3,721,910	3,792,840	3,525,000

BANK OF SPAIN (25 pesetas to the £).

	Feb. 5, 1898.	Jan. 29, 1898.	Jan. 22, 1898.	Feb. 6, 1897.
	£	£	£	£
Gold	9,495,120	9,433,680	9,430,680	8,528,360
Silver	10,616,720	10,568,320	10,480,400	10,462,000
Bills discounted	21,840,600	21,656,840	20,217,840	8,111,120
Advances and loans	4,873,000	4,735,200	5,439,200	9,255,520
Notes in circulation	49,902,430	49,321,760	49,069,120	42,713,680
Treasury advances, coupon account	211,680	108,840	38,920	448,040
Treasury balances	454,280	329,960	151,400	2,343,400

LONDON COURSE OF EXCHANGE.

Place.	Usance.	Feb. 1.	Feb. 3.	Feb. 8.	Feb. 10.
Amsterdam and Rotterdam	short	12·1½	12·1½	12·1½	12·1½
Do. do.	3 months	12·3¾	12·3½	12·3½	12·3½
Antwerp and Brussels	3 months	25·41	25·41	25·42½	25·42½
Hamburg	3 months	20·62	20·62	20·62	20·62
Berlin and German B. Places	3 months	20·62	20·62	20·62	20·62
Paris	cheques	25·25	25·25	25·26½	25·26½
Do.	3 months	25·38¾	25·38¾	25·38¾	25·38¾
Marseilles	3 months	25·38¾	25·38¾	25·40	25·40
Switzerland	3 months	25·60	25·60	25·60	25·60
Austria	3 months	12·13½	12·13¾	12·15	12·16½
St. Petersburg	3 months	25 1/32	25 1/32	25 1/32	25 1/32
Moscow	3 months	25	25	25	25
Italian Bank Places	3 months	26·80	26·82½	26·87½	26·90
New York	60 days	49 1/16	49 1/16	49	49
Madrid and Spanish B. P.	3 months	35 1/16	35⅛	35½	35½
Lisbon	3 months	35 1/16	35⅛	35⅛	35 1/16
Oporto	3 months	35 1/16	35⅛	35⅛	35 1/16
Copenhagen	3 months	18·37	18·37	18·37	18·37
Christiania	—	18·37	18·37	18·37	18·37
Stockholm	—	18·37	18·37	18·37	18·37

OPEN MARKET DISCOUNT.

	Per cent.
Thirty and sixty day remitted bills	2¾—2⅞
Three months „	2$\frac{13}{16}$—2⅞
Four months „	2¾
Six months „	2¾
Three months fine inland bills	3
Four months „	3
Six months „	3—3¼

BANK AND DEPOSIT RATES.

	Per cent.
Bank of England minimum discount rate	3
„ „ short loan rates	3
Banker's rate on deposits	1½
Bill brokers' deposit rate (call)	2
„ 7 and 14 days' notice	2¼
Current rates for 7 day loans	2½—2¾
„ „ for call loans	2½—2¾

Stock Market Notes and Comments.

We have had a settlement on the Stock Exchange this week and, as usual now, it leaves things much where they were. A certain number of people have lent money and a larger number have borrowed it, and neither lenders nor borrowers have made very much by the operation. At least intermediate lenders have not. Banks, of course, continue to do very well, and the men who take risks on mine shares, getting their 7 per cent. to 10 per cent. or 12 per cent. for their money, are also becoming richer, and, as long as they feel no anxiety about the fate of their capital can continue to possess comfortable minds. But to the general body of those who gamble or take risks on the Stock Exchange times are not propitious. The "House" has been making money in American securities, but, at the same time, its commitments therein have been rapidly on the increase. Notwithstanding all that the financial press here and in America pour forth about "the unprecedented prosperity," which has arrived for all American Railroads, the more staid section of the British public refuses to be moved, or is moved only to sell. Ask any old-fashioned investment broker, and he will answer that his clients have taken no share in producing the recent advance in United States and Canadian Railways. If they have done anything at all it has been to realise previous holdings. This being so, the middleman, or financier, and the Stock Exchange itself, together with an increasing number of those who take moderate risks by joining in current market movements, are alone responsible for the advance in prices. Consequently the "account" in "American rails" to be settled this week proves to be larger than previous accounts and required more money to carry it.

Judging by previous experience this is a good sign for the future. That is to say, markets are almost certain to go higher in order to enable those now "in" to sell out. The movement in both United States and Canadian securities is thus, in our opinion, far from being exhausted. We are told that the Canadian Pacific Railroad Company has earned about 5½ per cent. on its own common stock for the past year, and will pay a 4 per cent. dividend. The traffic receipts of the Northern Pacific Company are increasing at such a pace that dividends appear to be in sight on the common stock of that company likewise, even should nothing be done in the way of selling its lands, which extend to an area about as great as that of all England. Elsewhere we have traffic receipts improving, even the anthracite coal properties appear to be doing rather better in spite of the handicap placed upon them by the artificial restrictions under which they carry on business. This being the view, we think it a pity that old holders of any of these securities should part with them just yet. In dealing with market chances the present is not the time to take the intrinsic merits of these properties into consideration. It may be quite true, and probably is, that in four or five years from now another crop of bankruptcies and reorganizations, revelations of huge floating debts, of lines allowed to run down in order to keep up appearances by paying dividends not earned, and so forth will be upon us, but it would be very foolish to sell stocks at the existing stage of the rise merely on this distant probability. The immediate future is favourable all over the American continent, and it does not seem to us that the forces behind the markets and operating for higher prices are in danger of being exhausted for another six months at the very least.

In other sections of the Stock Exchange the position does not seem to us quite so favourable. It is a very significant fact that Liverpool and Leicester, let alone the East Indian Railway Company, should have been unable to place their loans at the very fine rates of interest offered. Market influences were doubtless at work to spoil the subscriptions to some of these issues, but after all these have been weighed and allowed for we fear it must be concluded that the true cause of failure lay in the higher rates for money now current. Credit is a most sensitive thing. There can be no doubt at all that, intrinsically, these three borrowers are just as able to fulfil their engagements now as they were when money in the Market was floating about at 1 per cent. But money is now scarce at 2½ to 3½ per cent., and therefore loans which would have been snapped up when credit was "cheap" are left alone when it becomes moderately dear. Does not this fact prove that it is not the intrinsic quality of any security which determines the price at which it can be sold, but the condition of the floating credit in the money market. And this in its turn indicates to us that the true standard of the ability of any borrower to raise money is to be found not in the borrower's position but in the facility buyers of a security find for pawning it. Investors pure and simple, satisfied with a 2½ per cent. return upon their money, should be just as ready to buy Liverpool or Leicester stock, offered to them under par, when money in the open market is 2½ per cent. or more, as when it is 1½ per cent. or less. They want permanent security with moderate income, but they form a very small class. The larger proportion even of investors desire to increase their incomes by holding more stock than they can pay for, and they can only hold this stock at profit to themselves when there is a margin between what they give for the money borrowed to carry it with and what the investment yields. Wipe out this margin and the motive for buying is immediately gone. Syndicates above all are paralysed. Perhaps those Colonies of ours, who are so continually coming to us for money, will take note of this aspect of the question and plume themselves less upon the excellent position of their "credit" in London. Were the Bank of England rate 5 per cent. there is not one of them that could borrow a penny at anything like the rates prolonged cheap money here has accustomed them to.

This consideration should not be left out of sight either by that wide-spread community which has been putting money of its own, and of Banks, into Home Railway ordinary stocks for the last two or three years. Not only ought these people to be warned by the rise in money rates, but also by the decline in dividends upon the stocks they hold. Surely both circumstances combined should make everyone with money to invest hold back from these stocks at present. What profit can there be in purchasing any Home Railway stock, even the best, at prices which yield the buyer very little more than 3 per cent. to 3¼ per cent. now, and which may in a year or two return very much less? Expenses are increasing rapidly upon our Home Railways, especially upon those whose stocks are called "heavy," namely the North-Eastern, the North-Western, the Great Western, and the Midland, as will be seen from the analysis of the companies' reports in this and previous numbers of the REVIEW. The increased expenditure has generally swept away nearly the whole of the increase of the revenue, and in some instances even more than that increase. A tendency is thus revealed which is not nearly at an end, and the fact is that two main influences are at work in this direction. One is the greater restrictions put upon the companies as to the hours of labour, coupled with the necessity for advancing wages; the other is the compulsion of circumstances which is driving the companies to carry on their business at a lower scale of charges.

This is an old story to us, and we are not going to enlarge upon it here, but there can be no question at all that railway freights must tend downwards and fall to a very considerably lower plane if we are going to revive our export trade. No inland manufacturer can hope to compete successfully against the productions of Germany, for example, which are carried to the sea, and often over the sea, at much lower charges than English railways habitually levy. In spite of themselves, these railways must grant rebates to allow them to meet the competition. A market committed to extravagant prices for we may say, all our Home Railway stocks, cannot be expected to pay much attention to considerations like these, but the investing public should do so, and above all that class of public which invests speculatively. We can see no good foundation on which to build higher prices for the great bulk of our railway ordinary stocks just now. On the contrary it appears to us that they are much more likely in the near future to fall back than to advance. We are told, of course, that there is "really no stock in the market"; that it is all held by investors; and this is from the jobber's point of view quite true; but how much stock have these so-called investors pledged with their bankers and what interest are they paying for the money they have borrowed? We cannot answer the question and only throw it out to be meditated over.

It is quite possible, now that the loan to China has been, for a time at any rate, lifted off the Market, that we shall see a renewed attempt made to force prices up, and were the Government in a position to buy Consols to a large amount the rise in them which would be the consequence of this buying could not fail to stimulate prices for all classes of good securities. We hardly think, however, that the Government can do much in this way beyond its usual Sinking Fund purchases. Therefore the market promises to lie much where it is, with small gambles going on in odd corners, such as the one in progress this week in Russian Petroleum Oil shares and in Welsbach stock. A general movement outside the American market does not appear probable. There is not enough impulse from the outside public. If speculation breaks out at one point, that point appears to exhaust the entire energy of the speculating community. Look how dead the "Kaffir Circus" has been since American Railways have become the fashion. No amount of puffing, or of fine returns from crushings, &c., stimulates it in the very least. Now and again financiers come in and bid for a few shares, causing prices to go up a little, but there is no echo to their bidding, and when they leave off, carrying away perhaps a few thousand more shares to lock up in their strong boxes, prices sagg back again, and the market is as dormant as before. So it will go on until something happens to, in colloquial language, skake out the holders at high prices, by whom most divisions of the Stock Exchange are now bolstered up. And something will happen soon in the South African market, we believe. The upset looks like beginning in Paris, so please, good public, stand back and look on.

The Week's Stock Markets.

The approach of the Settlement, which began on Tuesday, had the usual effect on markets, and business has been on a small scale. All the Continental Bourses have exhibited a feeling of uneasiness at the present aspect of the Cretan question, and the abandonment of the Chinese loan has also helped to weaken prices. United States Railroad shares have again been the one really active market, and although a good deal of profit taking has occurred, prices generally mark a substantial rise on the week in this department. Consols declined at one time to 112$\frac{5}{16}$, and then rallied in spite of the firmer tendency displayed by the money market. Indian Government loans have weakened, but there has been rather more business in Colonial Government issues. Bank of England stock, after establishing a record price, has re-acted somewhat, and there is a fall of 2½ in Bank of Ireland stock. Home Corporation issues have hardly moved, and the Leicester issue fiasco passed almost unnoticed.

Highest and Lowest this Year.		Last Carrying over Price.	BRITISH FUNDS, &c.	Closing Price.	Rise or Fall.
113½	112¼	—	Consols 2¾ p.c. (Money)...	112$\frac{5}{16}$	− $\frac{1}{16}$
113$\frac{5}{16}$	112$\frac{7}{16}$	112⅝	Do. Account (Mar. 1)	112⅜	− $\frac{1}{16}$
106¼	105½	106	2½ p.c. Stock red. 1905 ...	106	—
363	347½	—	Bank of England Stock...	360	− 2
117	115¾	116½	India 3½ p.c. Stk. red. 1931	116	− ½
109½	108	108½	Do. 3 p.c. Stk. red. 1948	108¼	− ¼
96⅜	94⅞	95½	Do. 2½ p.c. Stk. red. 1926	95	—

The Home Railway Market was flat for the first half of the week, and inclined to brighten up in the latter half. Prices went all to pieces when the Midland dividend was announced as ½ per cent. worse than for 1896, that is, 6½ against 7 per cent., although curiously enough the price least affected at the time was Midland deferred. Then a decided "slump" occurred in Great Northern stocks, owing to the paragraph in the report relating to fresh capital powers. The North Western dividend of 7¾ per cent. (making 7½ per cent. for the whole year as comapred with 7½ per cent. for 1896) was received with equanimity by the market, the way having been paved for the appearance of a lower distribution by previous announcements of a disappointing character. Prices became firmer when goods traffic returns were posted, and the account disclosed a scarcity of stock. On London and North Western there was a "back" of ¼ per cent. paid. South Eastern deferred went to nearly "even," but on Brighton deferred the rate rose to ¼ per cent., and on Great Western ¼ to ⅜ was charged. Great Eastern was continued at about $\frac{1}{16}$, the stock being still scarce for delivery. On balance the principal movements in the upward direction have been in South Eastern, South Western, and Chatham issues, while on the other hand the Scottish section has been rather dull, and Great Northern deferred has only partly recovered the earlier fall.

Highest and Lowest this Year.		Last Carrying over Price.	HOME RAILWAYS.	Closing Price.	Rise or Fall.
186	177⅜	178	Brighton Def.	178⅝	+ ⅛
59¼	57⅞	57¾	Caledonian Def.	58⅛	− ⅜
20⅜	19	20	Chatham Ordinary	20⅜	+ ⅜
77½	66	70	Great Central Pref.	71	+ ½
24⅜	22¼	22½	Do. Def.	22¼	—
124½	119⅞	120	Great Eastern	120¼	+ ⅛
61¼	56	56¾	Great Northern Def.	57½	− ¼
179⅜	176⅜	178	Great Western	178½	+ ⅜
49¼	46½	47½	Hull and Barnsley.........	46½x.d.	+ ⅜
149¼	146½	148¾	Lanc. and Yorkshire	146½x.d.	+ ⅜
136¼	133¼	135	Metropolitan	133½x.d.	+ ⅜
31	29½	30	Metropolitan District......	29½	− ¼
88⅜	87½	87¾	Midland Pref.	87⅜	− ¼
95⅜	92⅞	93½	Do. Def.	93¾	+ ¼
93¼	90¼	91½	North British Pref.	91⅜	− ½
47½	45	45¾	Do. Def.	46⅛	− ⅜
181½	178⅜	179½	North Eastern...............	180	—
205½	204¼	204½	North Western	204⅜	—
117½	113	116¾	South Eastern Def.	113⅜	+ 1¼
98¾	95½	97	South Western Def.	97½	+ ½

United States Railroad shares have again been very active, and substantial rises are apparent in several of the leading company's issues. The Erie Company has definitely concluded arrangements for the purchase of the New York Susquehanna and Western Road on advantageous terms, and it is reported that they will shortly conclude the sale of a block of first preferred stock to pay for the Susquehanna stock acquired. The President of the New York Ontario Road says that the whole of the outstanding 5 per cent. shares will be refunded on June 1 at 105 into 4 per cents., thereby affecting a saving of about $40,000 per annum. Pennsylvania shares have also been in renewed request on a proposal to issue 3 per cent. bonds to retire existing issues.

The Northern Pacific Company is negotiating a sale of lands which will enable them to pay off the whole of the outstanding "Firsts." As regards continuation rates, 4 to 5 per cent. was generally paid, but Chicago and Milwaukee was scarce for delivery and the rate was not more than 3½ per cent. Later advices from New York and lower quotations caused a set-back on this side, in several instances, and Wall-street operators have been getting nervous over the renewed discussion of foreign politics in Congress.

Highest and Lowest this Year.	Last Carrying over Price.	CANADIAN AND U.S. RAILWAYS.	Closing Prices.	Rise or Fall.
14 1/16 12¾	13¾	Atchison Shares	13¾	+ ⅞
34 29½	33	Do. Pref.	32⅝	+1⅛
15⅝ 11⅞	14¾	Central Pacific	14½	− ¼
99¾ 95¼	99	Chic. Mil. & St. Paul	98½	—
14¾ 11½	13¾	Denver Shares	14	+ ⅜
54¼ 46⅝	53¼	Do. Prefd.	53¾	+1¼
16⅝ 14⅛	16¼	Erie Shares	16	+ ⅛
43¾ 37½	42¼	Do. Prefd.	43¾	+3¼
62½ 56⅝	61½	Louisville & Nashville	61½	—
14½ 12⅜	13⅞	Missouri & Texas	13⅞	—
122¾ 108½	121½	New York Central	121	−1¼
57¼ 47¼	50¼	Norfolk & West. Prefd.	55¼xd	+5¼
70⅛ 59⅝	69¾	Northern Pacific Prefd.	68¾xd	+ ½
19½ 15⅞	18¼	Ontario Shares	18⅛	− ⅛
62½ 58⅞	62	Pennsylvania	61½	+ ½
12½ 10¾	11⅜	Reading Shares	11¼	− ⅛
33½ 30⅞	32⅞	Southern Prefd.	32½	+1¼
37⅛ 26⅛	34¾	Union Pacific	35	−1⅛
20¼ 18	19½	Wabash Prefd.	19¼	—
30½ 27¾	29½	Do. Income Debs.	29¼	+ ¼
92¾ 83¾	90½	Canadian Pacific	90¾	+ ¾
78⅛ 69⅞	76¼	Grand Trunk Guar.	76⅛	+ ⅞
69⅝ 57⅛	67½	Do. 1st Pref.	67⅞	+1⅛
50⅞ 37¼	49	Do. 2nd Pref.	49¼	+1¾
25⅛ 19¾	24½	Do. 3rd Pref.	24¼	+ ¾
105¾ 104	104½	Do. 4 p.c. Deb.	104¼	− ½

A considerable fall occurred in Canadian railway stocks towards the close of last week, on rumours from Montreal of a disagreement between the Canadian Pacific and Grand Trunk lines on a question of rate cutting. Prices, however, have since recovered, and it is now stated that amicable terms have been agreed upon. Contango rates on Grand Trunk first and second preferences ruled at about ⅛ per cent., and on the guaranteed at ⅛ to 3/16 per cent., or rather heavier than at the last account. Foreign Government bonds, with one or two exceptions, are lower on the week. Chinese issues were, of course, adversely affected by the failure of the proposed loan. Spanish "fours" have been depressed by a rapid rise in the exchange, coupled with alarmist telegrams from Cuba, although President McKinley professes to regard the position of affairs between Spain and the United States as quite satisfactory. Italian rente hardened up at one time, but the price gave way under the influence of a heavier contango. There has been a good deal of buying of Egyptian securities, and Turkish groups and Greek bonds are firmer in view of the new loan guaranteed by the three great Powers. It is reported that negotiations are pending for the refunding of the whole of the Gold Debt of the Mexican Government. The present debt amounts to $100,000,000, bears interest at the rate of 6 per cent., and is redeemable in July. The proposal is to place it on a 4½ per cent. basis. Among South American descriptions Brazilian bonds have hardened up slightly, in spite of a weaker exchange, but Argentine stocks of the Cedulas have exhibited a dull tendency, although the gold premium has again moved in favour of holders.

Highest and Lowest this Year.	Last Carrying over Price.	FOREIGN BONDS.	Closing Price.	Rise or Fall.
94½ 92⅛	92½	Argentine 5 p.c. 1886	92½	− ¼
92⅝ 89	90½	Do. 6 p.c. Funding	90½	− ⅛
76¾ 71	75¼	Do. 5 p.c. B. Ay. Water	75½	− ¼
61¾ 60	61⅛	Brazilian 4 p.c. 1889	61¼	− ¼
69⅞ 66	67	Do. 5 p.c. 1895	66¼	− ½
65 62½	64¼	Do. 5 p.c. West Minas Ry.	64	− ¼
108¼ 106¼	107¾	Egyptian 4 p.c. Unified	108¼	+ ⅝
103¾ 102	103	Do. 3½ p.c. Pref.	103½	+1
103 102	102	French 3 p.c. Rente	102⅛	—
41 34½	39½	Greek 4 p.c. Monopoly	40½	+1½
93 9/16 92¼	92½	Italian 5 p.c. Rente	92 11/16	+ 3/16
100 95¾	99	Mexican 6 p.c. 1888	98¾	− ¼
20⅞ 20	20⅜	Portuguese 1 p.c.	20⅜	—
62½ 59⅞	61¼	Spanish 4 p.c.	61 3/16	−1⅛
45⅛ 43	43½	Turkish 1 p.c. "B"	44¼	− ⅝
26 7/16 24 7/16	25¾	Do. 1 p.c. "C"	26⅛	− ⅛
22 7/16 21 13/16	22⅜	Do. 1 p.c. "D"	22 7/16	+ 1/16
42¾ 40	40½	Uruguay 3½ p.c. Bonds	40½	− ½

Chilian bonds drooped when it was announced that the Government had climbed down and accepted the proposals made by Peru for the settlement of the question relating to the provinces of Arica and Tacna now held by Chile.

Continuation rates ranged from 3 to 4 per cent., or practically the same as those ruling at the last account, but Egyptian, Italian, and Portuguese were continued on slightly heavier terms.

Foreign Railways have attracted very little attention, and rises and falls are about evenly balanced. San Paulo shares have recovered their recent fall, and the London and Brazilian Bank announces that it has decided not to proceed for the present with the issue of debentures of the Mogyana Company for the purpose of the extension, which the San Paulo Company objected to. Mexican Railway stocks have hardly moved.

Highest and Lowest this Year.	Last Carrying over Price.	FOREIGN RAILWAYS.	Closing Price.	Rise or Fall.
20¼ 20	20¼	Argentine Gt. West. 5 p.c. Pref.	20½	+ ¼
158¼ 149	156½	B. Ay. Gt. Southern Ord.	158	+1
78½ 75½	77	B. Ay. and Rosario Ord.	77	− ½
12¼ 11 11/16	11⅞	B. Ay. Western Ord.	12	—
87¼ 80½	85	Central Argentine Ord.	85	− ¼
92 89¾	90½	Cordoba and Rosario 6 p.c. Deb.	91	—
95½ 93¾	94½	Cord. Cent. 4 p.c. Deb. (Cent. Nth. Sec.)	94½	—
61¾ 58¼	58½	Do. Income Deb. Stk.	59	− ½
25¼ 18	23¾	Mexican Ord. Stk.	24	—
83½ 72	82	Do. 8 p.c. 1st Pref.	82	—

In the Miscellaneous market the principal activity has again centred in Welsbach Gas stocks, and after several heavy falls on successive days a move in the upward direction occurred. A feature of the week is a big rise in General Hydraulic Power, the dividend just announced being 1½ per cent. better than a year ago, but a proposed fresh issue of capital has, no doubt, added a considerable value to the old stock in the shape of "rights." Among Brewery companies the interim dividend of 14 per cent. on Guinness ordinary, against 12 per cent. last year, is responsible for an advance of twenty points in the price. The Allsopp dividend is about due, and as is usually the case just before the declaration, the market is a very sensitive one, and the price has jumped about a good deal. Crystal Palace pebentures have been enquired for, but holders seem inclined to keep what they have got, and wait the course of events. Some mysterious selling of Spiers & Pond shares has been going on, and among gas stocks Gas Light "A" has again been pressed for sale, although a slightly firmer tone is apparent towards the close. Holders of British Electric Traction shares were a little disgusted when they found that the new issue of preference shares was being offered to the public at 25 per cent. premium, and nothing was said about a priorallotment being made to existing shareholders.

Mining and Finance Companies.

The South African market has been idle with no very decided tendency, and a general absence of business. The account was easily arranged, rates being quoted about as usual, or 6 to 10 per cent. as a general rule. Chartered shares were unaffected by the resignations of the Duke of Fife and Lord Farquhar from the board; in fact, the price hardened up slightly afterwards. In De Beers, which have been taken up on Paris account, the continuation rate was only 3 per cent., but the price has, nevertheless, weakened. Among Western Australian ventures there has been no business to speak of, Lady Shenton shares being about the only ones much mentioned. Copper shares have not maintained last week's rise, but Indians have met with a fair amount of support, the monthly returns being up to expectations.

Home Railway stocks finish up the week with a steady tone, especially for Brighton deferred, Metropolitan, and Chatham issues. Canadian Pacific shares closed dull, but Grand Trunk stocks, after several violent fluctuations, finally left off well above last week's level. United States Railroad shares were rather ragged, but closed generally above the worst. Foreign government bonds, apart from a set-back at the last in Brazilian issues, were quiet but steady.

The Produce Markets.

GRAIN.

Business at Mark-lane has been quiet throughout the week, though firm, yet sales, on the whole, were limited. White was quoted on Wednesday at 36s. to 40s., and red, 34s. to 38s. Foreign descriptions, as a rule, were held for full current values, but buyers, on the other hand, were far from eager for business, only moderate sales resulting. Californian was quoted 38s. 9d. ex store; and Walla-Walla, 38s. 6d.; Manitoba, 40s. to 40s. 9d. ex ship. The demand for flour has been generally poor and with more liberal arrivals late values are with some difficulty upheld. Town whites, 34s.; and households, 31s.; whilst country brands vary from 26s. to 31s. according to grade; American patents, 30s. to 32s.; and Bakers, 27s. to 28s.; Hungarian, 38s. to 40s.; French 31. Barley generally dull, and actual sales were on a small scale, but prices were well maintained. Grinding quoted 17s. 3d. to 17s. 6d. landed. Oats were in steady request at about late values. American mixed were quoted 15s. 7½d. ex ship. Maize did not move very actively, but a steady tone prevailed. Beans and peas remain firmly held. The cargo section for wheat ruled quiet, but holders required previous prices for all descriptions. Prompt Californian offered at 36s. 9d., whilst for afloat 37s. to 38s. 6d. is asked. Walla-Walla, prompt shipment, held for 35s. 3d. to 35s. 9d., and afloat from 35s. 9d. to 37s. There has been some fluctuation in the cargo market, but, as a rule, business has been quiet, with no change in rates. For some days sellers held back, but on Wednesday they were more disposed to meet buyers, who, however, evinced considerable indifference. The only sale reported was a steamer of 1,750 tons, Rosario-Santa Fé, February, which changed hands at about 35s. 4½d. The Eddystone, No. 2 red winter, from New Orleans, 15,000 qr., arrived at Falmouth, is offered at 37s. Californian, September, is obtainable at 38s. 6d., and December at 37s. 3d., and prompt shipment at 36s. 6d. to 36s. 9d. Oregon is offered at 37s. Walla-Walla, November, at 36s. 9d. to 37s., and prompt at 35s. 6d. Maize held at 3d. advance, but buyers do not respond. Wheat options ¼d. to ¾d. up. Maize unchanged to ½d. dearer. Contracts registered—Wheat, 32,800 centals; maize, 14,400. Barley quiet and unchanged. Oats quiet, with prices favouring buyers. In the Liverpool spot parcels have been firm throughout the week, with a moderate business. Red American futures opened at ½d. per cental advance and, after weakening slightly, strengthened on good buying, together with light offerings. Later, the market was inactive, but near the close it became firmer, finishing steady at the highest of the day, ¾d. to 1d. per cental dearer. Sales, 350,000 centals.

Official Closing Values (100 lb. deliveries—February 9).

	March.	May.	July.	Sept.
Red American Wheat	7'8¾	7'4¼	7'1⅛	6'6⅜

In New York spot parcels have been firm throughout the week, and prices well maintained. In futures there has been considerable fluctuation, with a rather downward tendency. Wheat opened on Wednesday ⅜c. higher for May with a steady tone, and with firmer cables from Liverpool further improved. Local "bears" were active buyers to cover during the first hour, with something of a squeeze developing on March delivery. A reaction followed on a "bear" raid, based on large North-Western receipts and private cables from Argentine indicating an exportable surplus thence of 37,000,000 bushels, against previous highest pointers of 35,000,000, the cable further mentioning that the weather had much improved and that offerings were increasing. In the afternoon values rallied well, partly owing to foreign buying orders and on reports of a good export business again in progress at outputs, the sales being estimated at 25 boatloads. Near the close the market again broke on renewed "bear" pressure, and the final tone was easy, with near positions ⅜c. better, May unchanged, and July ¼c. lower. On the kerb a further fall of ⅛c. occurred.

COTTON.

There has been more activity in the spot market, and prices have been firmly maintained throughout the week. On Tuesday there was a rise of $\frac{1}{16}$d. on American, at which rate a good business was done. Thus late news maintained on Wednesday with a still larger business. Brazilian and Surats have continued dull at late rates. Egyptian have been in active demand, and quotations are raised $\frac{1}{16}$d. (F. G. F. Brown, 4¼d.). Futures opened unchanged, but, with little offering, improved 1 point during early trading. This was subsequently lost and regained several times on active trading, and during the last half-hour American buying orders lent support, the market closing steady at partially ½ point advance on the day. In New York the market has been quiet but firm, prices going rapidly upwards for the first few days; but on Wednesday the opening was only one point higher, though there was a further advance on shorts cornering, encouraging cables, strong reports from southern spot markets, prediction of decreased movement, more favourable Fall River accounts, and better outlook in dry, goods district. Market closed firm, 13 to 17 points up. Spot quiet, $\frac{1}{16}$c. dearer. Middling upland, 6¼c. Sales, 164,200 bales.

New York Closing Values.

	Spot.	Feb.	Mar.	April.	May.	June.	July.	Aug.	Sept.	Oct.	Nov.
Feb. 9 ..	6¼	6'01	6'04	6'08	6'12	6'15	6'18	6'21	6'20	6'21	6'22

WOOL.

The tone of the market continues fairly firm, but the business done is not large. The arrivals to date for the second series of sales (commencing March 15) include:—New South Wales, 54,414 bales; Queensland, 5,093; Victoria, 31,937; South Australia, 876; West Australia, 438; New Zealand, 6,182; Cape and Natal, 15,001. Total, 113,941 bales, of which about 35,000 (24,000 Australasian and 11,000 Cape) have been forwarded direct to manufacturing centres. In Bradford business is confined to actual requirements, while in Leeds the market is reported as about an average, and in Leicester the tone is described as strong and confident, with a regular and healthy turnover, in all the leading description of both home and colonial produce at full quotations.

METALS AND COAL.

Copper has been firm during the week, though on Wednesday the opening was rather easier, £49 2s. 6d. being accepted for Monday, and then £49 1s. 3d. for cash. There were, however, ready buyers of the latter at the price, and an improvement soon took place, the close of the first session showing an advance of 1s. 3d. over the best figures of previous day, cash making £49 3s. 9d. and three months £49 10s. Further dealings took place in cash and three months during the early afternoon without further change from these prices until £49 5s. was paid for the former. The price was not maintained, and the market closed with a bargain at £49 3s. 9d. and £49 6s. 3d., and 7s. 6d. combined for three months, which is about 1s. 3d. better on the day. Sales, 800 tons.

Settlement Prices.

	Feb. 9.			Feb. 2.			Jan. 26.			Jan. 19.			Jan. 12.			Jan. 5.		
	£	s.	d.	£	s.	d.	£	s.	d.	£	s.	d.	£	s.	d.	£	s.	d.
Copper ..	49	5	0	49	2	6	48	17	6	49	5	0	48	17	6	48	10	0

Practically nothing can be said about pig-iron. Market dull and slow throughout the week, and little doing. At Glasgow on Wednesday a prominent "bear" sold fully 20,000 tons on Wednesday forenoon, but buying was as good as the selling. Nevertheless, prices closed weak at an all-round fall of 1½d. per ton. Sales, 40,000 tons.

Settlement Prices.

	Feb. 9.		Feb. 2.		Jan. 26.		Jan. 19.		Jan. 12.		Jan. 5.	
	s.	d.	s.	d.	s.	d.	s.	d.	s.	d.	s.	d.
Scotch	45	7½	45	7½	46	0	46	0	45	9	45	6
Cleveland ..	40	4½	40	6	40	10½	40	10½	40	7½	40	4½
Hematite ..	48	7½	48	6	47	0	48	10½	48	9	48	4½

Attendance at the London Coal Exchange is improving, and signs of increased animation have been shown, but they have not lead to any great accession of business, the seaborne market again disappointing. In the inland market there has been a slight revival of trade.

SUGAR.

The Market is still dull, especially in beetroot descriptions. Cane rather better, though still rather quiet. German .88 per cent. sold—February at 9s. 2d.; April at 9s. 3½d.; May at 9s. 4½d.; June 9s. 4½d.; and July at 9s. 6½d. f.o.b. Hamburg. The market for home refined is quiet, and sales generally moderate. Pieces at previous prices. Crystals unaltered. Yellow sold at 11s. 7½d. to 11s. 10½d. Stoved goods quiet, and sales moderate. Tate's cubes at 14s. 9d.; second quality, 13s. 10½d.; No. 1 crushed, 13s.; No. 2 ditto, 12s. 6d.; granulated, 13s. 3d.; yellow crystallised, 12s.; No. 1 crystals (in Liverpool), 13s. 1½d.; No. 2 ditto, 12s. 9d.; Standard Liverpool granulated, 12s. 6d.; Lyle's No. 1 granulated, 12s. 9d.; No. 2 ditto, 12s.; No. 1 crystals, 12s. 9d.; No. 3 ditto 12s.; A white, 12s. 6d.; B, 11s. 9d.; O and P crystals, 12s.

TEA AND COFFEE.

Coffee generally quiet, though good qualities commanded full rates. Tuesday's auctions comprised 3,326 bags, about half being East India, and all good qualities sold with good competition at firm prices. Wednesday's auctions comprised 1,561 packages, and all good to fine qualities, especially East India, sold with brisk competition at very full prices; while common descriptions continue extremely slow. East India, bold dull grey to fine bright deep blue, 101s. to 111s. 6d.; low to fine middling, 79s. 6d. to 103s.; smalls, 58s. to 74s.; peaberry, 97s. to 125s. Jamaica, low to good middling bright grey, 70s. 6d. to 88s. 6d.

In tea there has been practically no change during the week. At auction on Tuesday 28,000 packages Ceylon sold; and all grades with the exception of leaf for price marked a decline. Quality generally continues to show deterioration. Terminals slow and unchanged. 5,800 packages, Indian, sold on Wednesday with a good demand at steady prices. Terminals quiet. Good common black Congou: February, 4¼d.; March, 4⅜d.; April, 4$\frac{7}{16}$d. Indian—Type 1: February, 6$\frac{11}{16}$d.; March, 7d.; April, 7$\frac{1}{16}$d. Indian—Type 2: February, 6$\frac{7}{16}$d.; March, 6½d.; April, 6⅝d.; May, 6⅝d. Ceylon: February, 7½d.

HEMP AND JUTE.

Hemp dull throughout the week. Baltic still neglected, though sellers of spot are easier. For arrival the tone is firm. But buyers hold off. Manila, F. C., near, £18, value; 250 bales May-July, sailer, sold at £19. Jute dull, only beginning to show a little firmness on Wednesday. First marks, January-March steamer, London, £9 17s. 6d., sellers, with buyers at £9 15s. "Entries" at Calcutta for first week of February, 112,000 bales, against 42,000 in the same period last year; total to 7th inst., 2,876,000, against 2,241,000 a year ago, being 96,000 bales more than total of previous season.

Dividends Announced.

MISCELLANEOUS.

GEORGE WILSON & CO., LEICESTER.—Warrants for the half-year's dividend on the 6 per cent. preference shares were posted on the 1st inst.

BROWNE & EAGLE, LIMITED. — Further dividend on the ordinary shares of 10s., making 8 per cent. for the year, free of income tax.

SOUTH LONDON DAIRIES.—Interim dividend of 7½d. per £1 share for the half-year ended January 1 on the ordinary shares.

NEW BRITISH RUBBER.—Warrants posted for the 6 per cent. dividend on the preference shares.

W. T. HENLEY'S TELEGRAPH WORKS.—Dividend at the rate of 12 per cent. per annum on the ordinary shares, including the interim of 3 per cent. paid in September.

QUEEN HOTEL, HARROGATE.—Usual dividend of 10 per cent. for the year; £1,000 placed to reserve.

CHARLES CLIFFORD & SON.—Interim at the rate of 6 per cent. per annum on the preference and 10 per cent. per annum on the ordinary shares.

H. J. FRANCIS & COMPANY.—Further dividend of 7½ per cent., making, with the interim dividend, 10 per cent. for the year ended December 31 last.

HOLT BREWERY COMPANY, LIMITED.—Dividends equal to 8 per cent. are declared on the ordinary shares, £15,000 placed to reserve, and £5,457 carried forward.

PATENT VICTORIA STONE.—Five per cent. for the half-year ended December 31, which, with the interim paid in July last, will make 10 per cent. for 1897, £5,257 to be carried forward.

GRANTHAM WATERWORKS.—Five per cent. for the half-year ended December 31.

GRANTHAM GAS.—Five per cent. on the old shares and 3½ per cent. on the new shares for the half-year ended December 31.

BARON CIGARETTE MACHINE, LIMITED.—7½ per cent. dividend has been declared.

LORD GEORGE SANGER.—Warrants for an interim dividend at the rate of 10 per cent. per annum will be posted on the 14th. The dividend will be calculated from October 23, 1897, to December 31, 1897.

WESTMINSTER PALACE HOTEL.—Interim dividend of 5s. per share on account of the year ending June 30 next.

ARTHUR GUINNESS, SON, & CO.—Interim dividend at the rate of 14 per cent. per annum on the ordinary stock for the six months ended December 31.

WAIHI GOLD MINING COMPANY, LIMITED.—Dividend of 2s. per share on the old shares, and at the rate of 5 per cent. on the new shares, payable March 1.

SALMON & GLUCKSTEIN.—Dividend proposed at the rate of 7½ per cent. per annum on the full capital of the company, £8,096 to be placed to depreciation, £1,365 to preliminary expenses not entirely extinguished, and £10,166 to be carried forward.

EDISON AND SWAN UNITED ELECTRIC LIGHT COMPANY, LIMITED.—Dividend on account of the current year at the rate of 5 per cent. per annum, less tax, on the "A" shares of the company, in respect of the half-year ended December 31, 1897. This will work out at 1s. 6d. per share on the partly-paid £5 shares (£3 paid), and 2s. 6d. per share on the fully-paid £5 shares, less tax.

WARING AND GILLOW, LIMITED.—Dividend of 10 per cent. on the ordinary shares for the past year and the transfer of £10,000 to reserve fund.

TELEGRAPH CONSTRUCTION AND MAINTENANCE COMPANY, LIMITED.—Dividend of 10 per cent. (£1 4s. per share) in addition to the 5 per cent. already paid, making 15 per cent. for the year 1897.

MUNTZ'S METAL COMPANY.—Payment of a dividend out of the profits of the past year at the rate of 7½ per cent. per annum on the ordinary shares and 5 per cent. on the preference shares, carrying forward a balance of about £2,000.

GIRLS' PUBLIC DAY SCHOOL.—Dividend at the rate of 4 per cent., and £688 to be carried forward.

Stock Conversions and Investment Trust notifies that the balance over on its North-Western Railway deferred charge stock, to be carried forward to June 30 next, is equal to 2¼ per cent., against 2⅝ a year ago, and that on its North-Eastern deferred charge stock 2⅜ per cent. against 2⅛.

MILLWALL DOCK COMPANY.—Dividend on the ordinary shares at the rate of £3 15s. per cent. per annum. Balance forward, £292.

WORCESTER EXPLORATION AND GOLD MINING COMPANY, LIMITED.—A dividend of 15 per cent., payable in South Africa on March 9, has been declared.

MARBEESA IRON ORE.—Further dividend of 2s. per share, making, with interim dividend paid, 10s. for year. £535 forward.

WEST AUSTRALIAN MARKET TRUST.—Interim dividend at the rate of 15 per cent. per annum for six months ended January 30.

SOUTH LONDON TRAMWAYS.—Dividend of 5s. per share is declared on the ordinary shares, making 8s. for the year, adding £1,000 to reserve fund, carrying forward £1,485.

BANKS.

BRITISH NORTH AMERICA.—2½ per cent. (payable April 4), £10,000 to be placed to reserve and £3,726 carried forward.

INSURANCE.

NORTHERN ACCIDENT.—Dividend of 8 per cent. as against 7 per cent. last year; £3,000 placed to reserve and £1,485 carried forward.

RAILWAYS.

FURNESS.—Dividend at the rate of 2 per cent. for the half-year ended December 31.

MIDLAND.—Dividend at the rate of 2½ per cent. per annum on the preferred ordinary stock, and at the rate of 4 per cent. per annum on the deferred converted ordinary stock, being equal to 6¼ per cent. on the former ordinary stock. Balance carried forward is £38,000.

LONDON & NORTH-WESTERN.—Dividend at the rate of 7⅞ per cent. per annum. The dividend for the half-year ended December 31, 1896, was at the rate of £8 per cent. per annum.

MARYPORT & CARLISLE.—Dividend at the rate of 6½ per cent. per annum for the half-year ended December 31. For the corresponding period of 1896 the dividend was at the rate of 6 per cent. per annum.

ISLE OF WIGHT.—Dividends at the rate of 5 per cent. for the half-year on the deferred converted ordinary stock; balance of £1,844 to be carried forward.

RHONDDA AND SWANSEA BAY.—Payment recommended of usual dividend on the preference shares for the half-year at the rate of 5 per cent. £512 to be carried forward.

BREWERIES.

EMERALD AND PHŒNIX.—8s. per share on the preference shares for the half-year ended November 30.

CANNON.—8 per cent. for the half-year on the ordinary shares, making a total of 16 per cent. for the year, which absorbs £56,000. £3,000 added to reserve and £250 carried forward.

MINING RETURNS.

CONSOLIDATED MURCHISON.—Crushed 503 tons for 507 oz. gold.

GIBRALTAR CONSOLIDATED.—For January: 920 tons inclusive 280 tons low grade, 1,055 oz.; concentrates, 280 oz.; tailings, 103 oz.

BAYLEY'S UNITED GOLD MINES.—For four weeks ended January 27: cyanide plant treated 869 tailings, yielding 1,015 oz. gold.

BIG BLOW.—Crushed 150 tons for 70 oz. gold.

HALL MINES, LIMITED, BRITISH COLUMBIA.—Twenty-seven days, twelve hours' smelting:—5,675 tons of ore smelted, yielding 372 tons matte, containing (approximately) 157 tons copper, 109,070 oz. silver, 338 oz. gold.

MOUNT USHER.—Crushed 238 tons of ore, yielding 183 oz. gold.

NINE REEFS COMPANY.—Result of the first clea up from stamps mill: 1,300 tons milled, amalgamation on plates yielded 121 oz. gold.

ROBINSON GOLD MINES OF W.A.—During January crushed 650 tons, yielding 439 oz., exclusive of concentrates and tailings.

NORSEMAN.—For January 630 tons crushed yielding 444 oz. smelted gold.

NUNDYDROOG.—4,620 tons of quartz produced 4,349 oz.; 800 tons of tailings, 106 oz.; and 3,232 tons of tailings (cyanide) produced 337 oz.

QUEENSLAND MENZIES.—287 tons for 857 oz. A trial crushing of 17 tons from the south winze gives a return of 287 oz.

UNITED IVY REEF.—January output, 720 oz.; crushed, 1,100 tons.

MOUNT MALCOLM.—470 tons crushed for 440 oz., exclusive of tailings.

ACHILLES GOLDFIELDS.—Twenty-two days' crushing: 700 tons, 393 oz.

BONNIE DUNDEE.—Crushed 179 tons from Victory Reef for 216 oz.

BRILLIANT.—3,150 tons of stone have been crushed for a yield of 2,800 oz.

BROKEN HILL PROPRIETARY.—24,571 tons ore were treated for the four weeks ended February 3. The output from the refinery was 3,541 oz. gold (estimated), 387,792 oz. silver, 2,238 tons lead, and 65 tons antimonial lead (estimated); the copper matte contained 39 tons copper (estimated) and 34,584 oz. silver (estimated).

BURMA RUBY MINES.—Result for January was 76,000 loads washed, producing rubies valued at Rs. 1,04,000.

MONTANA.—Output for January: gold, 2,340 oz.; silver, 7,600 oz.; from 6,700 tons of ore.

NEW KLEINFONTEIN.—For last month: Tons crushed, 10,984; ounces recovered from mill, 3,921; tons treated by cyanide, 7,228; ounces recovered, 1,242.

NIGEL GOLD.—Last month's crushings yielded: Battery, 1,299 oz.; and cyanide, 1,532 oz.

SALISBURY GOLD.—Crushing for January yielded 2,400 oz.

SHEBA GOLD.—During January: 8,400 tons of ore crushed for 3,795 oz.; 3,360 tons of tailings, 1,387 oz.; 174 tons of concentrates, 1,218 oz. Total, 6,400 oz.

MOUNT MORGAN.—Tons chlorinated, 12,166; gold returned, 14,191 oz.

INVERELL DIAMOND FIELDS.—1,834 carats of diamonds, washed by hand from 147 loads. This gives an average of 12½ carats per load.

GLYNN'S LYDENBURG.—For January—from mill: crushed, 1,290 tons; obtained, 453 oz. of fine gold; from cyanide: 840 tons; yield, 330 oz. of fine gold.

LANCASTER GOLD MINING COMPANY.—For January: Crushed, 7,098 tons of ore, yielding 3,185 oz.

WORCESTER EXPLORATION AND GOLD MINING COMPANY.—Result for last month's crushing yielded 2,739 oz.

ANGELO GOLD MINES.—For January: Tons crushed, 6,998; ounces recovered from mill, 3,362; tons treated by cyanide, 5,659; ounces recovered, 2,501.

NEW COMET.—For January: Tons crushed, 5,311; ounces recovered from mill, 1,982; tons treated by cyanide, 4,396; ounces recovered, 1,249.

BARRETT.—January: Gold, 770 oz. from 2,436 tons; estimated value, £2,600.

COROMANDEL GOLD MINING COMPANY OF INDIA.—100 tons of stone produced 885 oz. gold; 800 tons of tailings (cyanide) produced 76 oz. gold.

CUE I GOLD MINE.—820 tons for 565 oz.

HENRY NOURSE.—For January, 8,750 tons for 4,917 oz. cyanide, 6,450 tons treated yielding 2,691 oz.

ST. AGNES GOLD REEFS.—Cleaned up 340 tons yielding 160 oz. gold.

CHIAPAS during January crushed 1,650 tons of ore, yielding 70 tons of concentrates. The stamp mill crushed 1,450 tons of failings, yielding 174 oz. gold.

FERREIRA GOLD.—Results for January: Crushed, 10,400 tons; bar gold extracted, 7,914 oz.; concentrates, 240 tons; assay value of concentrates, 6 oz. fine gold per ton. Cyanide works: Bullion from tailings, 2,859 oz.

GRAND CENTRAL crushed 5,100 tons, yielding bullion $32,400, and concentrates estimated to yield $14,000.

JUBILEE GOLD.—Last month's return: 2,390 oz., obtained from 5,852 tons crushed; tailings yielded 700 oz.

NEW GUADALCAZAR QUICKSILVER.—Production for the past month amounted to 9,100 lb.=121⅓ flasks.

PIGG'S PEAK DEVELOPMENT.—Mill return for the month gives results of ore crushed 2,850 tons for 302 oz.; cyanided, 2,550 tons for 430 oz.; gross yield, 732 oz.

PREMIER TATI MONARCH REEF COMPANY.—Crushings for January: 1,810 tons of ore crushed, yield of gold 706 oz.

ST. JOHN DEL REY MINING.—Gold produce for January, £13,375; yield per ton, 0·51 of an ounce troy.

VAN RYN.—For January: Tons milled, 11,542; number of ounces recovered, 2,725. Cyanide works: Number of tons treated, 8,400; ounces recovered, 1,464.

VIOLET CONSOLIDATED.—January: Tons crushed, 5,431; total yield, 954 oz.

WEMMER GOLD.—Result during January: Mill crushed 6,466 tons, yielding 4,410 oz. Cyanide plant: 4,375 tons treated, yielding 956 oz.; and from concentrates, 157 tons caught, assaying 90 dwt. per ton. Total, 6,072 oz.

BALMORAL MAIN REEF.—January production, 2,318 oz.

CONSOLIDATED MAIN REEF MINES AND ESTATE.—3,500 tons crushed, including 1,300 from dump, produced 1,129 oz. Cyanide: 1,080 tons treated, producing 159 oz.

CROWN DEEP.—For January: Tons crushed, 22,082; yield in smelted gold from mill, 6,869 oz.; tons of sand and concentrates treated by cyanide works, 20,180 oz.; yield in smelted gold, 6,560 oz.

ROSE DEEP.—For January: Tons crushed, 14,706; yield in smelted gold from mill, 5,955 oz.; tons of sand and concentrates treated by cyanide, 12,352; yield, 3,711 oz.

DAY DAWN BLOCK AND WYNDHAM GOLD.—For the fortnight ended February 5: Tons crushed, 1,190, yielding 1,310 oz., including tailings. Have shipped 5,820 oz. of bullion.

DE LAMAR.—Return for January: Crushed, 4,100 tons; bullion produced in the mill, $36,180.

DURBAN-ROODEPOORT.—Results for January: Quartz milled, 10,290 tons for 4,910 oz., and tailings treated, 6,545 tons for 1,195 oz.; total, 6,105 oz.

FRANK SMITH DIAMOND.—2,100 loads washed, producing 86 carats.

GEORGE GOCH AMALGAMATED GOLD MINING COMPANY.—January: 8,010 tons crushed, yielding 1,908 oz. gold, and 1,160 oz. from tailings.

GOLD REEFS OF WEST AFRICA.—Have crushed during January 180 tons of ore, which yielded about 315 oz. of gold.

GINSBERG.—January production, 2,475 oz.

GLENCAIRN MAIN REEF.—Production for January, 6,749 oz.

HANNAN'S REWARD.—Results for January: Lode crushed, 216 tons, yield, 43 oz.; also cement crushed, 256 tons, yield, 103 oz.

JUMPERS.—Crushed, 11,500 tons; obtained from mill, 3,902 oz.; obtained from concentrates by cyanide, 505 oz.; obtained from tailings by cyanide, 1,000 oz.—total, 5,407 oz.

KLERKSDORP GOLD AND DIAMOND.—Results of crushing for January, 875 oz. of gold of the estimated value of £2,525.

LEICESTER CONSOLIDATED DIAMOND.—From the mine, 1,925; floors, 5,200; loads washed producing 187 carats.

LISBON-BERLYN.—For January: Ore mined, 2,150 tons; ore crushed, 2,100 tons; treated by cyanide, 1,900 tons; fine gold recovered, 767 oz.

MEYER AND CHARLTON.—Result for January: Crushed 9,021 tons, producing 2,674 oz.; extracted from tailings, 1,236 oz.; total, 3,910 oz.

NEW PRIMROSE.—Production for January, 9,137 oz.

NEW SPES BONA.—January production, 2,037 oz.

REGINA (CANADA) GOLD MINE.—For January, 465 tons crushed, yielding 136 oz. gold.

RIETFONTEIN A.—January production, 5,545 oz.

ROODEPOORT UNITED MAIN REEF.—Result for January:—Crushed 7,056 tons, producing 3,201 oz.; cyanide, 1,222 oz.; total, 4,423 oz.

SIMMER AND JACK PROPRIETARY MINES.—26,010 tons crushed yielded 10,163 oz. of gold.

SULPHIDE CORPORATION (ASHCROFT'S PROCESS).—"Have shipped 104 tons of silver lead bullion, containing 5,500 oz. silver."

TREASURY.—Output for January:—5,533 tons yielded 3,585 oz.

VAN RYN WEST MINING COMPANY.—Tons milled, 8,710; ounces recovered, 3,130; cyanide works—tons treated, 6,720; ounces recovered, 1,333; total, 4,463 oz.

WITWATERSRANDT (KNIGHT'S).—Mill ran twenty-three days, crushing 14,600 tons, yielding 4,070 oz. gold; 9,690 tons cyanide tailings treated, yielding 1,145 oz. gold.

CROWN REEF GOLD MINES.—Crushed during January, 15,971 tons, yielding 7,919 oz. of gold. Obtained by cyanide 3,643 oz.

VILLAGE MAIN REEF.—40 stamps ran 26 days, crushed 5,370 tons, yielding 3,098 oz.

PRINCESS ESTATE GOLD MINING.—Result for January: crushed 5,025 tons, producing 1,905 oz. of gold. Extracted from tailings, 932 oz. Total, 2,837 oz. of gold. December yield, 2,979 oz.

WEST RAND MINES.—Mill ran 29 days, crushing 3,815 tons, yielding 1,076 oz. of gold. Cyanide treated 3,064 tons, yielding 313 oz.

ASSOCIATED OF WESTERN AUSTRALIA.—Treated at mill, 2,000 tons, yielding 2,108 oz. of smelted gold.

Next Week's Meetings.

SATURDAY, FEBRUARY 12.

Great Southern and Western Railway (of Ireland)	Dublin, noon.

MONDAY, FEBRUARY 14.

Bristol Brewery, Georges & Company	Bristol, 12.30 p.m.
Crœsus South United Gold Mines...	Winchester House, noon.
Hibernian Bank	Dublin, noon.
Isle of Wight Railway	Westminster Palace Hotel, 2 p.m.
Leslie Steamship	Aberdeen, 3 p.m.
Lloyds Bank	Birmingham.
Peak Hill Gold Fields	Winchester House, 2.30 p.m.
Rhondda and Swansea Bay	Swansea, 1 p.m.
South African Gold Trust	Cannon Street Hotel, 12.30 p.m.

TUESDAY, FEBRUARY 15.

Andrew Knowles & Sons	Manchester, noon.
Clergy Mutual Assurance (Spec.) ...	2 and 3, Sanctuary, 2.30 p.m.
Colne Valley Water	Charing Cross Hotel, noon.
Fife Coal	Leven, 11.45 a.m.
Liverpool United Gas	Liverpool, 2 p.m.
North Staffordshire Railway ...	Stoke-on-Trent, 2.30 p.m.
Tramways Union	Winchester House, noon.
Wandsworth and Putney Gas, Light, and Coke	North-street, Wandsworth, 5 p.m.

WEDNESDAY, FEBRUARY 16.

Baring Brothers & Co.	8, Bishopsgate-street Within, 3 p.m.
Brown & Eagle	Winchester House, noon.
Coventry Electric Tramways ...	4, Bank Buildings, 2.30 p.m.
Daveniere & Co.	Guildhall Tavern, 2.45 p.m.
Edinburgh and Bathgate Railway ...	Edinburgh.
Great Northern Railway (Ireland)...	Dublin, noon.
Law Guarantee and Trust	47, Chancery-lane, 2 p.m.
London, Chatham, and Dover Railway	Cannon-street Hotel, noon.
National Mortgage and Agency of New Zealand	Winchester House, 3 p.m.
Norwich Electric Tramways ...	4, Bank Buildings, 2.30 p.m.
Port Talbot Railway and Docks ...	Westminster Palace Hotel, noon.
Provident Clerks' Mutual Life Assurance	Cannon-street Hotel, 6 p.m.
South Metropolitan Gas	Bridge House Hotel, 2 p.m.
Westminster Electric Supply ...	Eccleston-street, S.W., 11 a.m.

THURSDAY, FEBRUARY 17.

City Offices	34, Old Broad-street, noon.
City of York Tramways	York, noon.
Colne Valley and Halstead Railway	3, Throgmorton-avenue, 1 p.m.
Crystal Palace...	Cannon-street Hotel, noon.
Leicestershire Banking	Leicester, noon.
Leicester Tramways	Leicester, 3 p.m.
Linoleum Manufacturing	6, Old Bailey, noon.
Manchester Ship Canal	Manchester, 11 a.m.
National Telephone	Cannot-street Hotel, 1 p.m.
North London Railway	Euston Station, 1 p.m.

FRIDAY, FEBRUARY 18.

Bombay, Baroda, and Central India Railway	Cannon-street Hotel, 1 p.m.
Crystal Palace Gas	Albion Tavern, 3 p.m.
Dublin and Lucan Steam Trams ...	Dublin, 1 p.m.
Furness Railway	14, Great George-street, S.W., noon.
Lancashire, Derby and East Coast Railway	Westminster Palace Hotel, 3 p.m.
London and North-Western Railway	Euston Station, noon.
Millwall Dock	Cannon-street Hotel, 1 p.m.
North Metropolitan Railway and Canal	138, Leadenhall-street, noon.
South London Tramway	Winchester House, noon.

NOTICES.

The Right Hon. the Earl of Denbigh has been elected a director of the Equitable Life Assurance Society, in the place of Major-General C. A. Sim, deceased.

The Leicester loan has had much the same fate as the Liverpool one. The Corporation asked for tenders for £450,000 two and a half per cent. redeemable stock, the minimum price being 95 per cent. The tenders received only amounted to £125,158. The average price obtained was £95 4s. 5d. The remainder of the stock is now on sale at the minimum price, applications to be sent to the Town Clerk at Leicester.

Asked in the German Imperial Diet on Wednesday as to the state of the negociations with England as to a commercial Treaty, Herr von Bülow stated that at present he could only say that "the main lines of the proposals which we intend to address to England have been determined by consultations between the departments concerned. We have sent these proposals to London, and we are now awaiting the answer."

RAILWAY TRAFFIC RETURNS.

ALGECIRAS (GIBRALTAR) RAILWAY.—Traffic for week ended January 29, Ps. 18,600; increase, Ps. 2,335. Aggregate from July 1, Ps. 620,119; increase, Ps. 10,728.

WESTERN RAILWAY OF HAVANA.—Receipts for week ended February 5, £2,000; increase, £210. Aggregate from July 1, £55,405; increase, £5,873.

ROHILKUND AND KUMAON RAILWAY.—Traffic for eight days ended January 8, £5,906; decrease, £305.

SOUTHERN MAHRATTA RAILWAY.—Receipts for week ending January 15, Rs.99,278; decrease Rs.2,811.

PERUVIAN CORPORATION RAILWAYS.—Receipts for January, $276,325; increase $16,250.

GREAT NORTHERN RAILWAY OF MINNESOTA.—Traffic receipts for month of January, $1,367,000; increase $335,500.

QUEBEC CENTRAL PAILWAY.—Receipts for third week of January, $7,492; increase $943. Aggregate from January 1, $16,074; increase $499.

MOBILE AND BIRMINGHAM RAILROAD.—Traffic for third week of January, $10,933; increase, $3,240. Aggregate from July 1, $207,741; decrease, $20,390.

MANILA RAILWAY.—Traffic receipts for week ended February 5, $20,990; increase, $7,848. Aggregate from January 1st, $89,890; increase, $5,163.

ASSAM BENGAL RAILWAY.—Traffic for thirteen days ended December 31, Rs. 46,499; increase, Rs. 25,019.

NORTH-WESTERN OF URUGUAY RAILWAY.—Receipts for month of January, $13,200; increase, $1,793.

BILBAO RIVER AND CANTABRIAN RAILWAY.—Receipts for January, £9,050; increase, £337.

DOMINION ATLANTIC RAILWAY.—Receipts for month of January, $32,409; decrease, $789.

PUERTO CABELLO AND VALENCIA RAILWAY.—Traffic for eight days ended December 31, £781; increase, £6.

VILLA MARIA AND RUFFINO RAILWAY.—Traffic for week ending February 5, $3,438; decrease, $2,329. Aggregate from January 1, $17,916; decrease, $2,678.

CENTRAL URUGUAY NORTHERN EXTENSION RAILWAY.—Week ending February 5, £1,570; increase, £144. Aggregate from July 1, £36,837; increase, £2,129.

CENTRAL URUGUAY EASTERN EXTENSION RAILWAY.—Traffic for week ending February 5, £493; decrease, £131. Aggregate from July 1, £20,130; decrease, £1,747.

BURMA RAILWAYS.—Receipts for eight days to January 8, Rs. 2,08,166; decrease, Rs. 59,343.

WESTERN RAILWAY OF HAVANA.—Traffic receipts for week ended February 5, £2,000; increase, £210.

ARGENTINE GREAT WESTERN RAILWAY.—Receipts for week ended £7,378; increase, £2,395.

WEST OF INDIA PORTUGUESE RAILWAY.—Week ending January 15, Rs. 3,712; increase, Rs. 669.

CHICAGO GREAT WESTERN RAILWAY.—Traffic for ten days ended January 31, $120,758; increase, $17,916.

BENGAL CENTRAL RAILWAY.—Traffic for week ending January 15, Rs. 17,226; increase, Rs. 1,135.

BALTIMORE AND NORTH-WESTERN RAILWAY.—Return for week ended January 31, $146,488; decrease, $7,620.

ATLANTIC AND DANVILLE RAILWAY.—Return for month of January, $43,660; increase, $2,796.

BALTIMORE AND OHIO SOUTH-WESTERN RAILWAY.—Traffic for fourth week of January, $146,488; decrease, $7,620. Aggregate from July 1, $3,974,763; increase, $378,947.

ALABAMA GREAT SOUTHERN RAILWAY COMPANY.—Traffic receipts for month of December, $177,000; increase, $12,000.

CINCINNATI SOUTHERN RAILWAY COMPANY.—Traffic return for month of December, $340,000; increase, $36,000.

BENGAL DOOARS RAILWAY COMPANY.—Traffic receipts for eight days ending January 8, Rs. 2,700, against Rs. 5,810 for the same period last year.

H. H. THE NIZAM'S GUARANTEED STATE RAILWAYS COMPANY.—Traffic for seven days ending January 15, Rs. 66,058; decrease, Rs. 2,372. Total from January 1, Rs. 149,282; decrease, Rs. 840.

CLEATOR AND WORKINGTON.—Gross receipts for the week ending February 5 amounted to £1,033, an increase of £13. Total receipts from January 1, £5,138, a decrease of £230.

COCKERMOUTH, KESWICK, AND PENRITH.—Gross receipts for the week ending February 5 amounted to £842, an increase of £123. Total receipts for five weeks £4,325, an increase of £556.

TRAMWAY AND OMNIBUS RECEIPTS.

Increases for past week:—Belfast, £165; Croydon, £76; Glasgow, £121; Lea Bridge, £147; London & Deptford, £70; London Southern, £107; London General Omnibus, £2,539; London Road Car, £844; Metropolitan, £1,347; North Staffordshire, £10; Provincial, £116; Southampton, £2; South London, £167; Wolverhampton, £21; Woolwich & S. E. London, £37; Calais, £13.

Decrease for past week:—Bordeaux, £104.

Anglo-Argentine, week ending January 10, £147 increase; Buenos Ayres Grand National, week ending January 1, $5,756 increase; Vienna Omnibus, week ending January 29, £241 increase; Buenos Ayres & Belgrano, month of December, £4,858 gross, an increase of £513.

There is a considerable agitation in Canada just now for the government inspection of private banks.

Mr. Charles Steel, general manager of the Highland Railway, has been appointed successor to Sir Henry Oakley as general manager of the Great Northern Railway.

Prices of Mine and Mining Finance Companies' Shares.

Shares £1 each, except where otherwise stated.

AUSTRALIAN.

Making-Up Price, Feb. 7.	Name.	Closing Price.	Rise or Fall.	Making-Up Price, Feb. 7.	Name	Closing Price.	Rise or Fall.
1¾	Aladdin	2 11/16	− 1/16	1¼	Hampton Plains	1 1/16	− 1/16
4½	Associated	4½	+ 1/16	7⅞	Hannan' Brownhill	8 1/16	− 1/16
1	Do. Southern	1 1/16	+ ⅛	1 1/16	Hannan's Oroya	1 1/16	− 1/16
16/	Brilliant, £2	15/6	− /6	15/9	Do. Proprietary	15/6	− 6d.
2½	Do. St. George's	2½		1	Do. Star	1 1/16	+ 1/16
11/6	British Broken Hill	12/		—	Ivanhoe, New	6½	
6	Do. Westralia	6½		11/16	Kalgurli (Mt. & Iron King, 18/	11/16	
2	Broken Hill Proprietary	2 1/16	+ 1/16	6 1/16	Kalgurli	6⅛	− ⅛
—	Do. Junction	1¼		3 1/16	Lady Shenton	3¼	+ 1/16
—	Do. Block 10	3½		10½	Lake View Cons.	10½	− 1/16
1 1/16	Brownhill Extended	1½		1 1/16	Do. Extended	1 1/16	
1 1/16	Burbank's Birthday	1⅛	+ ⅛	1⅜	Do. South	1 1/16	+ 1/16
1 1/16	Central Boulder	1¼	+ ⅛	2 1/16	London & Globe Finance	2	− 1/16
⅜	Chaffers, 4/	7/3		1	London & W.A. Exploration	1 1/16	− 1/16
1	Colonial Finance, 15/	¼pm		⅜	Do. Investment	⅜	
6/	Crœsus S. United	5/16	− 1/16	5/16	Mainland Consols	¼	− 1/16
16/6	Day Dawn Block	16/6		11/16	North Boulder, 10/	1	+ ⅛
1 1/16	E. Murchison	1 1/16	− 1/16	1⅛	North Kalgurli	2 1/16	+ 1/16
⅞	Gold Estates	15/16	+ 1/16	1⅛	Northern Territories	2 3/16	+ 1/16
6/6	Golden Arrow 19/	6/	− /6	—	Peak Hill	3	+ 1/16
8⅝	Golden Horseshoe	8⅝	− 1/16	2⅜	South Kalgurli	2⅜	− 1/16
1⅛	Golden Link	1 1/16		2½	W. A. Goldfields	2½	
—	Great Boulder, 2/	23/6	− /6	2 1/16	W. A. Joint Stock	2 1/16	+ 1/16
1⅜	Do. Main Reef, 10/	1 1/16	− ⅛	1 1/16	W. A. Market Trust	1 1/16	
4½	Do. Perseverance	4½	+ ⅛	1⅜	W. A. Loan & General Fin.	1⅜	+ 1/16
1	Do. South	1		⅛	White Feather	⅛	
2	Hainault	2					

SOUTH AFRICAN

Making-Up Price, Feb. 7.	Name.	Closing Price.	Rise or Fall.	Making-Up Price, Feb. 7.	Name	Closing Price.	Rise or Fall.
5 11/16	Angelo	5 11/16	− ¼	3/	Lisbon-Berlyn	3/	
1 5/16	Aurora West	1¼		2 1/16	May Consolidated	2½	
1 5/16	Bantjes	1 5/16		4⅜	Meyer and Charlton	4 11/16	
11/6	Barrett, 10/	10/6	− 6d.	3⅝	Modderfontein	3 11/16	+ 1/16
3 11/16	Bonanza	3 11/16		⅞	Do. "B"	⅞	
15/16	Buffelsdoorn	⅞	− 1/16	15/16	New Bultfontein	15/16	
1 5/16	Champ d'Or	1⅜		4½	New Primrose	4½	
5 11/16	City and Suburban, £4	5 11/16		1 11/16	Nigel	1 11/16	
3 5/16	Comet (New)	3⅜	− ⅛	—	Nigel Deep	1¼	
5⅝	Con. Deep Level	5⅝		1	North Randfontein	1	
13⅜	Crown Deep	13⅜		6⅜	Nourse Deep	6⅜	− ⅛
12	Crown Reef	12		1 1/16	Porges-Randfontein	1 1/16	− 1/16
30½	De Beers, £5	30	− 5/16	33½	Rand Mines	33¼	− ⅛
4 1/16	Driefontein	4 1/16		2	Randfontein	2	
5 11/16	Durban Roodepoort	5 11/16	+ 1/16	2⅜	Rietfontein	2⅜	− 1/16
4 5/16	Do. Deep	4 5/16		11½	Robinson Deep	11½	
5 11/16	East Rand	5 11/16	− ⅛	8½	Do. Gold, £5	8½	
25½	Ferreira	26½	− ½	1 1/16	Do. Randfontein	1⅜	− 1/16
6⅞	Geldenhuis Deep	7	+ ¼	1⅛	Roodepoort Central Deep	1 1/16	
4 11/16	Do. Estate	4 11/16	+ ⅛	7¼	Rose Deep	7 1/16	
1¼	George Goch	1⅛		3 1/16	Salisbury	3 1/16	
3	Ginsberg	2½	− 1/16	2⅜	Sheba	2½	− ⅛
2½	Glencairn	2½	− 1/16	3 11/16	Simmer and Jack, £5	3 11/16	− 1/16
2⅜	Glen Deep	2⅜		4⅛	Transvaal Gold	4 1/16	
10 1/16	Goldfields Deep	10⅛		3⅜	Treasury	3½	
8½	Griqualand West	8½		4 1/16	United Roodepoort	4½	
9½	Henry Nourse	9½		1 1/16	Van Ryn	1 5/16	
7⅝	Heriot	7⅝	− 1/16	6 5/16	Village Main Reef	6½	+ ⅛
8⅜	Jagersfontein	8½	− ⅛	1 11/16	Vogelstruis	1⅜	
8½	Jubilee	8⅜		1	Do. Deep	1	− 1/16
5⅞	Jumpers	5½	+ 1/16	8⅜	Wemmer	8½x	+ ⅛
6	Jumpers Deep	5⅞		⅞	West Rand	⅞	
2 11/16	Kleinfontein	2 11/16	− 1/16	6⅜	Wolhuter, £4	6½	− ⅛
3 5/16	Knight's	3¼	− ⅛	2⅜	Worcester	2⅜	
2 5/16	Lancaster	2⅜	+ 1/16				
3¾	Langlaagte Estate	3¾					
1⅜	Langlaagte Block "B"	1⅜	− ⅛				

LAND EXPLORATION AND RHODESIAN.

Making-Up Price, Feb. 7.	Name.	Closing Price.	Rise or Fall.	Making-Up Price, Feb. 7.	Name	Closing Price.	Rise or Fall.
3 1/16	Anglo-French Ex.	3	− 1/16	6⅜	Matabele Gold Reefs	6 3/16	− 1/16
2 5/16	Barnato Consolidated	2⅛	− ⅛	2⅛	Mozambique	2⅛	+ ⅛
⅞	Bechuanaland Ex.	⅞		1⅜	New African	1⅜	
3 5/16	Chartered B.S.A.	3¼	− ⅛	⅞	Oceana Consolidated	⅞	+ 1/16
1 1/16	Cassel Coal	1 1/16		1½	Rhodesia, Ltd.	1 5/16	− 1/16
¾	Colenbrander	¾		5½	Do. Exploration	5½	− ⅛
4 11/16	Cons. Goldfields	4 11/16	− 1/16	1 5/16	Do. Goldfields	1⅛	
1 1/16	Do. Pref.	20/6	− /6	3⅜	Robinson Bank	3⅜	
1¼	Exploration	1⅜	+ 1/16	5	S. A. Gold Trust	5	− 1/16
2⅜	Geelong	2⅜		1¼	Tati Concessions	1¼	
1⅛	Henderson's Est.	1	+ 1/16	5/16	Transvaal Development	5/16	
1 11/16	Johannesburg Con. In.	1 11/16		4⅛	Do. Gold Mining	4⅛	
1⅛	Do. Water	1 1/16	− ⅛	11/16	United Rhodesia	11/16	
2⅛	Mashonaland Agency	2⅛		1⅛	Willoughby	1⅛	
11/16	Do. Central	11/16		1⅜	Zambesia Explor.	1⅜	

MISCELLANEOUS.

Making-Up Price, Feb. 7.	Name.	Closing Price.	Rise or Fall.	Making-Up Price, Feb. 7.	Name	Closing Price.	Rise or Fall.
1¼	Alamillos, £2	1⅜	+ ⅛	15/	Mysore Goldfields	14/6	
5½	Anaconda, $25	5⅜	− ⅛	11/9	Do. Reefs, 17/	10/	− ⅛
10/	Balaghât, 18/	10/	− /6	15/	Do. West	15/	
4 11/16	Cape Copper, £2	4⅝	− ⅛	14/	Do. Wynaad	13/6	+ /6
4 11/16	Champion Reef, 10s.	5		2 5/16	Namaqua, £2	2 5/16	− 1/16
2 5/16	Copiapo, £2	2 1/16	− 1/16	3 11/16	Nundydroog	3 11/16	+ 1/16
3⅜	Coromandel	3⅜		2⅛	Ooregum	2 5/16	
2⅜	Frontino & Bolivia	2⅜	+ 1/16	3⅞	Do. Pref.	3⅞	
1 5/16	Hall Mines	1 1/16		27½	Rio Tinto Def., £5	28 1/16	− 1/16
2 11/16	Libiola, £5	2½	− ⅛	6½	Do. Pref. £5	6½	
7½	Linares, £3	7½	− ⅛	18/6	St. John del Rey	18/6	− 1/
3½	Mason & Barry, £3	3½	+ ⅛	18/	Taitipu	1 1/16	+ ⅛
5⅞	Mountain Copper, £5	5⅞	+ ⅛	7⅜	Tharsis, £2	7 1/16	− ⅛
14½	Mount Lyell, £3	14½	− ½	2½	Tolima "A," £5	3	
3 11/16	Mount Lyell, North	3½	− ⅛	4 5/16	Waihi	4 5/16	− 1/16
⅞	Mount Lyell, South	17/6	− 6d.	1¼	Waitekauri	1⅜	
4½	Mount Morgan, 17s. 6d.	4 1/16		1¼	Woodstock (N.Z.)	1 1/16	+ ⅛
5 5/16	Mysore, 10s.	5⅜	+ ⅛				

MR. SUTHERST'S COMPANIES.

The action for libel brought by Mr. Sutherst, the whilom 'bus trike leader, against Mr. Hess of the *African Critic*, now the *Critic*, has terminated in a verdict for the defendant. The action is interesting from the light that it throws on the "gentle art of company promoting." Mr. Sutherst is a barrister, and in addition to that profession has carried on of recent years the business of a financier and company promoter. In that capacity he assisted in the promotion of a concern called "The African Contracts Corporation, Limited." This was registered in September, 1895. Hearing that a Mr. Regan had a property in Mashonaland for sale, said to be gold-bearing, he entered into a contract to buy it of him, together with some Transvaal property, for £40,000 in cash and shares, and paid him a deposit of £5,000. Mr. Sutherst then sold what he had bought to the syndicate for £10,000 in cash, and £20,000 in shares. In October, 1895, "Charterland Consolidated" was registered, and the syndicate sold those properties to them for £150,000. Favourable reports as to the estates had been received, but after the sale to the Charterland, on further reports coming, the shareholders' money was returned, and the company entered into liquidation. The Lord Chief Justice expressed surprise that the reports had not been verified before the shares had been offered to the shareholders; but as in this case the money was returned, our only comment must be that these shareholders were exceedingly lucky, and we wish that the same could be said of those who have placed money in other companies. One of the plaintiff's admissions in cross-examination is truly delightful—namely, "Of all his companies the 'Pulp' Company was the best of the lot, but it had not paid a dividend for five years." That is certainly not surprising if his companies are brought out in the way that the African Contracts Corporation and the Charterland Consolidated, according to the reports of the recent action, saw the light.

The average expenses of the war in Cuba, is estimated at 300,000,000 pesetas half-yearly.

The output of pig-iron in the United States during 1897 is stated at 9,652,000 tons.

It is stated from Paris that the French Government objects to take part in the Brussels Sugar Bounty Conference, unless it is intended to arrive at an international agreement with a view to suppressing the direct bounty on exports. M. Méline would not, however, be inclined to modify the internal trade regulations of France, and he is understood to be determined to reserve full liberty of action in regard to the maintenance of the law of July 29, 1884, and the bonus to manufacturers. This is not a very hopeful outlook for the Conference.

On account of the revolution in Nicaragua, the American warship "Alert" has landed troops at San juan del Sur, which is held by the rebels, in order to protect the Consulate.

The export of cereals from Russia for the week ended the 5th inst. amounted to a total of 3,848,000 poods against 4,157,000 in the previous week.

The shareholders of the Banco del Commercio of Buenos Ayres are stated to have accepted the arrangements made with the London Bank of Mexico and South America. There is no amalgamation of the two concerns, it is said, only a sort of working agreement.

INDIAN AND CEYLON TEA COMPANIES.

Acres Planted.	Crop, 1896.	Paid up Capital.	Share.	Paid up.	Name.	Dividends. 1894.	1895.	1896.	Int. 1897.	Price.	Yield.	Reserve.	Balance Forward.	Working Capital.	Mortgages, Debs. or Pref. Capital not otherwise stated.
	lb.	£	£	£	INDIAN COMPANIES.							£	£	£	£
11,240	3,109,000	120,000	10	3	Amalgamated Estates	—	*	10	5	3⅝	8¼	10,000	16,500	D52,950	—
		400,000	10	10	Do. Pref.	—	*	5	‡5	[illegible]	4¼				
10,223	3,387,100	187,160	20	20	Assam	20	20	20	5	60	6¾	55,000	1,730	D11,350	—
5,900	3,310,000	142,500	10	10	Assam Frontier	3	6	6	—	9	6½	—	186	20,000	82,500
		142,500	10	10	Do. Pref.	6	6	6	3	11½	5¼				
2,087	865,550	66,745	5	5	Attaree Khat	12	12	8	3	7¾	5¼	3,790	4,820	7,770	—
1,633	550,980	78,170	10	10	Borelli	4	4	5	—	8½	5¾	—	3,368	D270	6,500 Pref.
1,689	880,000	60,825	5	5	British Indian	6	5	5	—	4½	5¾	—	2,920	12,300	16,500 Pref.
3,223	2,282,430	114,500	5	5	Brahmapootra	20	15	20	6	14	7	—	26,440	41,600	
3,904	1,634,000	76,500	10	10	Cachar and Dooars	*	6	7	—	10	7½	—	1,645	21,240	
		76,500	10	10	Do. Pref.	*	6	6	3	12	4¾				
3,946	2,001,370	72,010	1	1	Chargola	8	7	10	2½	1½	10¾	3,000	3,300	—	—
		71,000	1	1	Do. Pref.	7	7	7	3½	1¼	5½				
1,971	968,890	33,000	5	5	Chubwa	10	8	10	3½	6½	7½	10,000	2,043	D5,406	—
		33,000	5	5	Do. Pref.	7	7	7	3½	7	5				
33,250	10,620,000	120,000	10	3	Cons. Tea and Lands	—	*	10	5	3½	7¼	65,000	14,240	D191,674	—
		1,000,000	10	10	Do. 1st Pref.	—	*	5	‡5	11¾	4¼				
		400,000	10	10	Do. 2nd Pref.	—	*	7	‡7	11⅞	5¾				
2,230	593,160	135,400	20	20	Darjeeling	5½	5½	6	—	23	5	5,552	1,565	1,700	—
2,114	456,580	60,000	10	10	Darjeeling Cons.	—	*	4½	—	7½	—	—	1,820	—	—
		60,000	10	10	Do. Pref.	—	*	5	2½	9½	5				
6,600	2,973,050	150,000	10	10	Dooars	12½	12½	12½	2½	21	6¼	45,000	300	D32,000	—
		75,000	10	10	Do. Pref.	7	7	7	3½	17¼	4				
3,367	1,833,520	165,000	10	10	Doom Dooma	11½	10	12½	5	22	5¾	30,000	4,032	—	10,000
1,377	500,080	61,120	5	5	Eastern Assam	5	nil.	4	—	3½	5¾	—	1,790	—	10,000
4,038	1,529,380	85,000	10	10	East India and Ceylon	*	nil.	7	—	9½	7	—	1,710	—	—
		85,000	10	10	Do. Pref.	*	6	6	3	12½	4¾				
7,570	3,600,000	219,000	10	10	Empire of India	—	*	6,10	2	12½	—	15,000	—	27,000	—
		219,000	10	10	Do. Pref.	—	*	5	2½	11½	4½				
1,180	647,600	94,060	10	10	Indian of Cachar	7	3½	3	—	5½	5½	6,070	—	7,120	—
2,916	968,000	53,500	5	5	Jhanzie	10	10	10	4	8½	5¾	14,500	1,070	2,700	—
7,980	3,467,000	250,000	10	10	Jokai	10	10	10	5	16	5½	45,000	590	D9,000	—
		100,000	10	10	Do. Pref.	*	6	6	3	15½	3¾				
5,224	1,801,600	100,000	20	20	Jorehaut	20	20	20	—	57½	7	36,220	2,955	3,000	—
1,547	554,560	65,660	10	8	Lebong	15	15	15	5	17	6¾	9,000	2,150	8,650	—
5,082	1,843,700	100,000	10	10	Langla	*	10	6	3	9½	6	—	1,543	D21,000	—
		100,000	10	10	Do. Pref.	*	6	6	3	12	4¾				
2,684	866,300	95,970	10	10	Majuli	7	5	5	—	7	7	—	2,606	560	—
1,300	216,000	91,840	1	1	Makum	—	—	2	—	1⅛	1¾	—	—	1,200	25,000
3,140	938,400	100,000	1	1	Moabund	—	—	*	—	1	—	—	—	-	—
		50,000	1	1	Do. Pref.	—	—	*	2½	1	5				
1,080	510,000	79,590	10	10	Scottish Assam	7	7	7	—	11	6¼	6,500	800	9,590	—
4,150	1,635,000	100,000	10	10	Singlo	*	8	5	1	9½	4¾	—	300	D5,200	—
		80,000	10	10	Do. Pref.	*	6½	6½	3½	13½	4¾				
					ÇEYLON COMPANIES.										
10,315	1,743,824	250,000	100	100	Anglo-Ceylon, & Gen.	—	*	5½	—	68	7¾	10,992	1,405	D72,844	166,500
1,836	685,741	50,000	10	10	Associated Tea	—	*	5	—	8½	5¾	—	164	2,478	—
		60,000	10	10	Do. Pref.	—	*	6	—	11	5½				
10,390	3,763,000	167,360	10	10	Ceylon Tea Plantations	15	15	15	7	28	5¼	84,500	1,316	D30,819	—
		81,080	10	10	Do. Pref.	7	7	7	‡7	17½	4¼				
3,722	1,542,700	55,760	5	3	Ceylon & Oriental Est.	5	8	7	—	2½	7½	—	230	D2,047	71,000
		46,000	5	5	Do. Pref.	6	6	6	3	5	6				
2,157	801,629	111,330	5	5	Dimbula Valley	—	*	10	5	6½	6¼	—	—	1,733	6,250
		62,607	5	5	Do. Pref.	—	*	6	3	6½	4½				
11,496	3,715,000	298,850	5	5	Eastern Prod. & Est.	3	5	6½	2½	6½	4½	20,000	11,740	D17,797	102,500
3,118	701,100	150,000	10	10	Lanka Plantations	4	5	5	‡5	7½	6¾	—	495	D11,300	14,700 Pref.
2,193	960,100	22,080	10	10	New Dimbula "A"	10	16	16	—	25	6	11,000	2,024	1,150	—
		55,710	10	10	Do. "B"	18	16	16	—	23½	6¾				
		8,400	10	10	Do. "C"	nil.	8	14	—	15	8½				
2,570	500,360	200,000	10	10	Ouvah	6	8	6	2	9½	6¼	4,000	1,151	D1,255	—
2,630	606,075	200,000	10	10	Nuwara Eliya	—	*	6	3	11½	5½	—	—	—	30,000
1,290	736,800	41,000	10	10	Scottish Ceylon	15	15	15	5	24	6¼	7,000	2,252	D3,970	—
		9,000	10	7	Do. Pref.	7	7	7	3½	16½	3¾				
2,450	600,000	80,000	10	6	Standard	12½	15	15	5	14½	6¾	9,000	800	D14,011	4,000

Working Capital Column.—In working-capital column, D stands for *debit*.

* Company formed this year. † Interim dividends are given as actual distribution made. ‡ *Total* div.

THE PROPERTY MARKET.

On the whole the week has been a dull one at the Mart, and no great properties have changed hands. Yesterday week the total of the day's sales amounted to £9,368. Reversionary interests, life policies, and gas shares formed the staple supply, only one small property figuring in the returns. Some freehold ground rents at Hampstead and Harrow were bought in, as even gilt-edged securities are not worth more than their equivalent value in gold. A three-days' sale of engravings, left by the late Hon. Ashley Ponsonby, concluded on Wednesday at Messrs. Christie's, the amount realised being £3,875. Wednesday's sales at the Mart only realised £3,873. The more important lots failed to find purchasers.

Mr. Alfred Richards has another important sale of gas and water debenture and ordinary stocks and shares, at the Mart, on Monday next. There are included in the list, stocks and shares of the Crays Gas Company, Maidenhead Gas Company, Great Yarmouth Water Works Company, Henfield Gas and Coke Company, Limited, Whitechurch and District (Hants) Gas Company, Limited, Goring and Streatley District Gas and Water Company, Portsea Island Gas Light Company.

Merry Hall, Ashtead, near Epsom Downs, a freehold property with 30 acres, for sale on the 21st inst., is recommended by Messrs. Wootton & Green, the auctioneers, as specially adapted for the rearing of racehorses. The winner of the Grand National of seven years ago was trained here.

The estate of Melsetter, with an area of about 40,971 acres, has been sold at Edinburgh for £52,000.

There is terrible distress among the peasantry of the central and south-eastern provinces of Russia. It is said to be worse than during the famine of 1891. The peasants in Tamboff are feeding their half-starved cattle on thatch from the roofs of their houses, and are ready to sell their last cow or pig for a few kopeks. "Hunger, typhus, and other illnesses are making rapid headway," says the *Times* St. Petersburg correspondent. Hunger is probably the most incurable of these "illnesses."

The Governor General of Algeria has had a tidy little bill for 2½ million francs sent in to him as the proper costs of the recent raids upon the Jews during the excitement of the Dreyfus agitation. A hundred thousand pounds, or thereabouts, is a big sum to pay for a popular outburst of splenetic rage.

93,395 oz. of gold, valued at £354,900, were exported from Western Australia during the month of January, as against 72,411 oz., of the value of £275,164, in December.

Is this a triumph of British diplomacy at Pekin? Acceding to Sir Robert Hart's request, the Tsung-li-Yamen has appointed Mr. Robert Bredon Deputy Inspector General of Customs, but with the proviso, as the *Times* Shanghai correspondent states, that the chief authority is "not to be delegated." Just so. The proviso is doubtless for the satisfaction of Russia.

The directors of the Highland Railway Company announce a further issue of £100,000 three and a half per cent. preference stock, to be offered to the ordinary shareholders at 3 per cent. premium.

It is estimated that about 250,000 people—women as well as men—will be on their way to Klondike as soon as the roads open in the spring.

ENGLISH RAILWAYS.

Div. for half years. 1896	1896	1897	1897	Last Balance forward.	Amt. to pay 1 p.c. on Ord. for ½ yr.	Name.*	Date.	Gross Traffic for week: Amt.	Inc. or dec. on 1897.	Inc. or dec. on 1896.	No. of weeks.	Gross Traffic for half-year to date: Amt.	Inc. or dec. on 1897.	Inc. or dec. on 1896.	Mileage.	Inc. on 1897.	Working	Prior Charges last ½ year.	Prop. add Cap. Exp. this ½ year.
				£	£												%	£	£
10	10	10		6,805	4,906	Barry	Feb. 5	8,207	+601	+983	6	53,034	+1,585	+6,049	31	—	47·36	66,665	316,008
nil	nil	nil	nil	—	—	Brecon and Merthyr	Feb. 6	1,416	+89	−142	6	9,452	+231	+203	61	—	—	—	—
nil	nil	nil	nil	4,020	4,749	Cambrian	Feb. 6	3,743	+26	+346	*	21,323	+195	—	250	—	61·16	63,472	42,000
1½	1¾	2	1¾	1,510	3,150	City and South London ..	Feb. 6	1,063	−60	+91	6	6,456	−155	+459	3½	—	56·67	5,552	124,000
1	2	1½		4,823	13,210	Furness	Feb. 6	8,535	+386	+854	*	43,831	+907	+9,255	139	—	50·85	96,623	52,963
1	1½	½	1	2,207	27,470	Great Central (late M., S., & L.)	Feb. 6	40,868	+2,003	+3,318	5	207,819	+4,486	+11,655	352½	—	57·17	627,386	1,200,000
1½	4¾	2	5	51,283	62,865	Great Eastern	Feb. 6	76,574	+1,717	+4,222	5	378,232	+10,528	+37,106	1,156	7	55·35	860,138	250,000
3	5¾	3	5	15,094	102,496	Great Northern	Feb. 6	89,987	+5,882	+5,109	6	544,013	+16,427	+37,882	1,071	8	61·36	641,485	750,000
4½	7½	4¾	7½	31,350	121,981	Great Western	Feb. 6	167330	+10,840	+10,780	5	847,320	+33,300	+47,780	2,582	21	51·44	1,486,272	800,000
nil	2	nil	1¾	8,951	16,487	Hull and Barnsley	Feb. 6	6,251	−764	+227	5	31,835	−1,312	+3,141	73	—	58·21	70,290	52,920
5	5¾	5	5½	21,495	83,704	Lancashire and Yorkshire ..	Feb. 6	89,634	+5,384	+3,615	5	439,220	+17,705	+33,278	555½	25	56·70	674,745	451,976
4¾	8	4¾	8½	26,243	43,049	London, Brighton, & S. Coast	Feb. 5	46,323	+5,956	+5,338	6	278,075	+20,635	+18,576	476¾	—	50·20	407,042	240,735
nil	nil	nil	nil	72,294	56,296	London, Chatham, & Dover ..	Feb. 6	24,982	+1,678	+2,136	5	129,859	+7,004	+10,083	185¼	—	50·65	367,873	nil
6½	8	6½		95,016	203,063	London and North Western ..	Feb. 6	217089	+13,731	+9,564	5	1,098,561	+33,258	+67,220	1,911¼	—	55·91	1,411,298	425,000
5	8½	8½	8½	23,038	59,367	London and South Western ..	Feb. 6	63,791	+8,450	+6,566	5	318,009	+19,946	+22,912	941	6½	51·75	513,740	389,000
2¾	6	2½	6¼	14,592	6,691	London, Tilbury, & Southend	Feb. 6	4,462	+607	+939	6	28,202	+2,599	+5,565	81	—	52·57	39,590	15,000
3½	3¾	3¾	3¾	17,133	26,409	Metropolitan	Feb. 6	15,752	+260	+1,312	*	85,740	+2,068	—	64	12	43·63	148,047	254,000
nil	nil	nil	nil	4,006	11,250	Metropolitan District	Feb. 6	8,403	+203	+178	5	44,548	+1,754	+1,738	13	—	48·70	119,663	38,450
5	7	5½		18,336	174,175	Midland	Feb. 6	176054	−327	+5,109	6	1,047,788	−4,519	+58,885	1,354¾	15½	57·47	1,213,866	650,000
5¾	7½	5¾	7	22,374	138,189	North Eastern	Feb. 5	141464	+5,935	+4,613	5	683,214	+25,968	+46,435	1,597¾	—	58·82	795,077	436,004
7½	7½	7½	7½	7,061	10,102	North London	Feb. 6			Not recd			not	recvd.	12	—	50·90	49,973	7,600
4	5	4	4½	4,745	16,150	North Staffordshire	Feb. 6	15,384	−306	−127	6	93,800	+7,006	+5,461	312	—	55·27	118,142	19,605
10	10	11		1,642	3,004	Rhymney	Feb. 5	5,429	+813	+1,329	6	30,092	+1,189	+3,256	71	—	49·68	29,049	16,700
3	6⅜	3½	6⅜	4,054	50,215	South Eastern	Feb. 5	43,095	+4,941	+6,826	*	206,010	+14,699	—	448	—	51·88	380,763	250,000
3½	3½	3½	3½	2,315	25,961	Taff Vale	Feb. 5	15,228	+597	+2,147	6	90,832	−2,782	+2,194	121	—	54·90	94,800	92,000

* From January 1.

SCOTCH RAILWAYS.

5	5	5½	—	15,350	77,570	Caledonian	Feb. 6	65,606	+ 4,196	+ 3,696	1	65,606	+ 4,196	+ 3,696	851½	5	50·50	566,914	375,966
5	5½	5	—	5,886	24,639	Glasgow and South-Western	„ 5	25,331	+ 652	+ 1,688	1	25,331	+ 652	+ 1,688	393½	—	55·12	221,120	180,556
3½	3½	3½	—	1,291	4,600	Great North of Scotland	„ 5	7,624	+ 1,327	+ 898	1	7,624	+ 1,327	+ 898	331	15½	52·03	92,178	60,000
3	nil	2	—	10,477	12,820	Highland	„ 6	7,642	+ 616	+ 371	23	211,324	+ 9,098	+ 12,933	479¾	27¾	58·63	78,976	,000
1	1½	1	—	3,763	45,819	North British	„ 6	64,478	+ 2,443	+ 2,256	1	64,478	+ 2,443	+ 2,256	1,230	23	44·65	821,766	426,009

IRISH RAILWAYS.

6½	6½	6½	—	5,466	1,790	Belfast and County Down ..	Feb. 4	1,843	+ 163	+ 137	*	9,973	+ 377	—	76½	—	55·58	17,690	10,000
5½	6½	5½	—	—	4,284	Belfast and Northern Counties	„ 4	4,997	+ 704	+ 221	*	23,791	+ 764	—	249	—	—	—	—
2	3	2	—	1,418	1,200	Cork, Bandon, and S. Coast ..	„ 5	649	− 618	—	*	5,493	− 756	—	103	—	54·82	14,436	5,450
6½	6¾	6½	—	21,537	17,709	Great Northern	„ 4	13,434	+ 1,126	+ 1,151	5	66,907	+ 3,944	+ 4,448	528	36	54·03	87,068	16,000
5½	5½	5½	5½	12,037	24,855	Great Southern and Western ..	„ 4	—	—	—	not	received	—	—	603	13	51·45	72,[illegible]	46,582
4	4	4	4½	11,372	11,850	Midland Great Western ..	„ 4	9,913	+ 987	+ 1,146	5	44,155	+ 2,993	—	538	—	50·31	83,129	1,800
nil	nil	nil	nil	229	2,822	Waterford and Central ..	„ 4	[illegible],036	+ 288	—	*	4,422	+ 747	—	59½	—	51·24	6,858	1,500
nil	nil	nil	nil	2,601	2,987	Waterford, Limerick & W. ..	„ 4	3,938	+ 450	+ 405	*	38,579	+ 2,153	—	350½	—	53·70	43,076	8,869

* From January 1.

FOREIGN RAILWAYS.

Mileage. Total.	Increase on 1897.	Increase on 1896.	Name.	Gross Traffic for Week. Week ending	Amount.	In. or Dec. upon 1897.	In. or Dec. upon 1896.	Gross Traffic to Date. No. of Weeks.	Amount.	In. or Dec. upon 1897.	In. or Dec. upon 1896.
					£	£	£		£	£	£
319	—	—	Argentine Great Western	Jan. 28	7,094	+ 1,975	+ 2,396	29	156,583	− 14,111	+ 33,611
76½	—	—	Bahia and San Francisco	Jan. 8	2,780	+ 1,161	+ 1,011	—	——	——	——
234	57	84	Bahia Blanca and North West	Jan. 9	730	− 312	+ 239	28	21,099	+ 473	——
74	—	—	Buenos Ayres and Ensenada	Feb. 6	3,992	− 369	——	5	17,977	− 4,634	——
426	—	—	Buenos Ayres and Pacific	Feb. 5	8,172	+ 515	+ 1,257	31	192,362	− 48,112	+ 7,397
914	1	3	Buenos Ayres and Rosario	Feb. 5	18,081	+ 4,058	+ 2,692	5	88,019	+ 13,113	+ 12,372
1,499	98	68	Buenos Ayres Great Southern	Feb. 6	40,700	+ 5,654	+ 11,386	31	872,264	+ 63,995	+ 135,022
602	142	177	Buenos Ayres Western	Feb. 6	17,258	+ 2,512	+ 2,068	31	367,156	− 73,129	− 63,070
845	55	77	Central Argentine	Feb. 5	23,415	+ 4,959	+ 800	5	110,330	+ 17,667	+ 4,572
197	—	—	Central Bahia	Nov. 31*	$71,637	− $29,321	− $26,571	11 mos.	$1,192,815	+ $146,023	+ $177,015
271	—	—	Central Uruguay of Monte Video	Feb. 5	7,224	+ 1,318	+ 780	31	184,025	− 3,633	− 17,379
180	—	—	Cordoba and Rosario	Jan. 30	3,090	+ 565	− 285	31	62,750	− 20,800	− 385
128	—	—	Cordoba Central	Jan. 30	$24,000	+ $1,020	− $1,700	4	899,700	− 88,320	− 818,960
549	—	—	Do. Northern Extension	Jan. 30	$45,500	− $15,020	− $10,500	4	$204,290	− $47,560	− $37,320
237	—	—	Costa Rica	Jan. 29	5,065	− 1,936	− 2,164	4	15,565	− 5,950	+ 679
99	—	—	East Argentine	Dec. 26	914	+ 69	——	51	36,169	——	——
386	—	6	Entre Rios	Feb. 5	2,608	+ 1,228	+ 970	31	41,356	+ 6,112	+ 6,947
555	—	24	Inter Oceanic of Mexico	Jan. 29	$64,700	+ $12,680	+ $22,900	31	$1,705,280	+ $240,700	+ $401,450
23	—	—	La Guaira and Caracas	Dec. 23	2,082	− 1,076	− 268	51	106,904	− 11,770	+ 2,045
321	—	—	Mexican	Feb. 5	$80,500	+ $11,500	——	5	$399,300	+ $32,450	——
2,846	—	—	Mexican Central	Jan. 31‡	$363,368	− $19,836	+ $89,389	4	$1,077,505	+ 86,839	+ $256,545
2,217	—	—	Mexican National	Jan. 31‡	$141,423	+ $27,850	+ $13,832	4	$463,813	+ $73,636	+ $58,592
228	—	—	Mexican Southern	Feb. 7	$12,475	− $1,495	+ $1,133	45	$568,556	+ $88,609	+ $153,114
206	—	—	Minas and Rio	Dec. 31*	$177,973	+ $6,511	——	6 mos.	$1,174,610	+ $207,798	——
94	—	17	N. W. Argentine	Jan. 29	1,024	− 509	− 163	4	4,104	− 3,017	− 956
242	3	—	Nitrate	Jan. 31†	18,229	− 1,458	− 8,723	4	35,383	− 3,062	− 21,050
320	—	—	Ottoman	Jan. 29	5,965	− 1,890	+ 1,750	4	27,333	− 5,666	+ 7,213
77½	—	—	Recife and San Francisco	Dec. 11	6,263	+ 1,127	+ 847	24	75,574	− 10,533	− 2,333
86½	—	—	San Paulo	Dec. 26†	23,002	− 3,560	——	2	46,230	− 10,120	——
186	—	—	Santa Fe and Cordova	Jan. 29	3,568	+ 481	+ 1,000	31	31,733	− 22,638	− 3,730

* For month ended. † For fortnight ended. ‡ For ten days.

INDIAN RAILWAYS.

Mileage. Total.	Increase on 1897.	Increase on 1896.	Name.	Gross Traffic for Week. Week ending	Amount.	In. or Dec. on 1897.	In. or Dec. on 1896.	Gross Traffic to Date. No. of Weeks.	Amount.	In. or Dec. on 1897.	In. or Dec. on 1896.
862	—	—	Bengal Nagpur	Feb. 5	Rs.1,43,000	− Rs.10,360	− Rs.29,417	5	Rs.6,83,000	− Rs.1,66,617	− Rs.253,095
818	63	63	Bengal and North-Western	Dec. 31*	Rs.2,15,440	+ Rs.30,293	+ Rs.69,429	26	Rs.2,673,410	+ Rs.1,31,182	+ Rs.2,78,194
461	—	—	Bombay and Baroda	Feb. 5	£22,183	− £4,781	− £11,493	5	£115,133	− £17,096	− £62,149
1,884	2	13	East Indian	Jan. 29	Rs.12,44,000	− R.25,000	+ Rs.35,000	4	Rs.51,26,000	+ Rs.7,41,000	+ Rs.2,05,000
2,491	—	—	Great Indian Penin.	Feb. 5	£65,368	+ £604	− £19,205	5	£305,609	− £17,158	− £131,962
736	—	—	Indian Midland	Jan. 29	Rs.1,36,290	+ Rs.2,450	+ Rs.28,386	4	Rs.5,74,295	+ Rs.19,713	+ Rs.42,655
840	—	—	Madras	Jan. 22	£17,692	− £275	+ £163	3	£58,470	− £493	− £4,059
1,043	—	—	South Indian	Jan. 8	Rs.1,82,221	− Rs.19,062	− Rs.14,097	—	——	——	——

* For 13 days.

UNITED STATES AND CANADIAN RAILWAYS.

Mileage. Total.	Increase on 1897.	Increase on 1896.	Name.	Gross Traffic for Week. Period Ending.	Amount.	In. or Dec. on 1897.	Gross Traffic to Date. No. of Weeks.	Amount.	In. or Dec. on 1897.
					dols.	dols.		dols.	dols.
6,547	103	156	Canadian Pacific	Jan. 31*	472,000	+110,000	4	1,673,000	+360,000
6,169	—	469	Chicago, Mil., & St. Paul	Feb. 7	570,000	+42,000	5	2,930,801	+402,220
1,685	—	—	Denver & Rio Grande	Jan. 31*	195,600	+41,600	30	4,960,700	+803,600
3,512	—	—	Grand Trunk, Main Line	Feb. 7	£65,723	+£3,002	5	£384,453	+£50,712
335	—	—	Do. Chic. & Grand Trunk	Feb. 7	£12,475	+£2,094	5	£73,091	+£12,099
189	—	—	Do. Det., G. H. & Mil.	Feb. 7	£3,128	−£450	5	£17,546	−£1,305
2,938	—	—	Louisville & Nashville	Jan. 31*	575,000	+79,000	4	1,772,000	+167,000
2,197	137	137	Miss., K., & Texas	Jan. 31*	327,948	+3,656	30	8,068,952	+960,383
477	—	—	N. Y., Ontario, & W.	Jan. 31*	87,298	+13,868	30	2,382,685	+84,273
1,570	—	—	Norfolk & Western	Jan. 31*	188,000	+11,000	30	6,433,000	+694,000
3,499	336	—	Northern Pacific	Jan. 31*	474,000	+183,000	4	1,401,000	+456,000
1,223	—	—	St. Louis S. Western	Jan. 31*	165,000	+38,000	—	—	—
4,654	—	—	Southern	Jan. 31*	532,000	+39,000	30	11,332,812	+609,448
1,979	—	—	Wabash	Jan. 31*	300,000	+26,000	4	942,000	+106,000

* For ten days ended.

MONTHLY STATEMENTS.

Mileage. Total.	Increase on 1896.	Increase on 1895.	Name.	Net Earnings for Month. Month.	Amount.	In. or Dec. on 1896.	In. or Dec. on 1895.	Net Earnings to Date. No. of Months.	Amount.	In. or Dec. on 1896.	In. or Dec. on 1895.
					dols.	dols.	dols.		dols.	dols.	dols.
6,935	44	444	Atchison	December	986,000	+52,000	—	12	8,966,420	+176,951	—
6,547	103	106	Canadian Pacific	December	1,053,000	+129,000	—	12	10,304,000	+2,196,000	—
1,685	—	—	Denver & Rio Grande	December	273,000	+57,121	−8,253	6	1,786,320	+249,850	−50,604
1,970	—	—	Erie	December	605,798	+100,620	—	12	8,466,792	+302,587	—
3,127	—	239	Illinois Central*	December	2,555,393	+458,872	+349,241	12	24,723,399	+2,940,108	+2,909,052
2,396	—	—	New York Central*	January	3,505,000	+365,000	+27,034	—	—	—	—
477	—	—	New York Ontario, & W.	December	87,176	+14,635	+12,602	6	701,475	+4,958	+44,430
3,407	—	—	Pennsylvania	December	1,664,297	+26,100	−35,400	12	20,532,068	+2,328,300	+849,000
1,055	—	—	Phil. & Reading*	December	1,947,585	+208,345	—	6	11,886,164	+668,603	—

* Statements of gross traffic.

Prices Quoted on the London Stock Exchange.

Throughout the INVESTORS' REVIEW middle prices alone are quoted, the object being to give the public the approximate current quotations of every security of any consequence in existence. On the markets the buying and selling prices are both given, and are often wide apart where stocks are seldom dealt in. Other particulars will be found in the INVESTMENT INDEX published quarterly—January, April, July, and October—in connection with this REVIEW, price 2s., by post 2s. 2d. Where dividends are paid only once a year, an *italic* type is used to distinguish them. The London Stock Exchange Official List is quoted in the REVIEW almost entire, only very insignificant issues, or bonds falling due within the next two or three years, being omitted. But the list is subdivided into the leading, or active, stocks, and those less frequently dealt in. The former will be found under the head of "Stock Markets," and with more details than it is possible to give for the bulk of securities. By retaining the file of the INVESTORS' REVIEW any subscriber can follow for himself the movements of securities from week to week, and the INVESTMENT INDEX will from time to time help to fill up deficiencies in the information.

Tea Companies and Mines and Mining Finance Stocks are placed in special lists.

Among the abbreviations used are the following:—S.F. Snk. Fd. *sinking fund*; Certs., *certificates*; Debs. or Dbs., *debentures*; Db. or D.Stk., *debenture stock*; Pf., Prf., or Pref., *preference*; Prefd. or Pfd., *preferred*; Dfd., *deferred*; L. or Ltd., *limited*; Sh., *share*; Ans., *annuities*; Cu. or Cm., *cumulative*; Gu or Guar., *guaranteed*; Bds., *bonds*; S., Sr., or Ser., *series*; In., Ins., Insc., *inscribed*; Dr., Drgs., Drwgs., *drawings*; Stg., Strlg., *sterling*; Lia., *liable to*; Sp., Surp., *surplus*; Per., Perp., *perpetual*; Ln. *lien*; Lo. *loan*.

The dates following the names of securities are the years of issue or of redemption. Where shares are not fully paid up, their nominal amount is given with the name so that investors may know the liability upon them.

BRITISH FUNDS, &c.

Rate.	Name.		Price.
2¾	2¾ p.c.'s (Childers') Red..	1905	106½
3	Local Loans Stk.	1912	113
3	Metro. Police Deb. Stk.	1920	105½
—	Red Sea Ind. Tel. Ann.	1908	8½
4	Canada Gv. "Intcl. Rly."	1903	109½
4	Do. do. ..	1908	113
4	Do. Bonds	1910	117
4	Do. Bonds	1913	119½
3	Egyptian Gov. Gar.		107½
3	Mauritius Ins. Stk.	1940	115
4	Turkish Guar. 1855		109
11½	Bank of Ireland Stk.		390
3½	India Rupee Paper		62½
3½	Do. 1854-5		63½
3	Do. 1896-7	1916	57½
3½	Isle of Man Deb.		104
3	Do. Deb. Stk...	1919-29	103

CORPORATION AND COUNTY STOCKS.

FREE OF STAMP DUTY.

Rate.	Name.		Price.
3½	Metropolitan Con.	1929	120½
3	Do.	1941	114
2½	Do.	1920-49	101½
2½	L.C.C. Con. Stock	1920	100
3½	Comm. of Sewers, Scp., S.F.	1905	105
3½	Corp. of Lond. Bds...	1897-1902	100½
3	Do.	1897-1919	103
3½	Do, Debs. Scp. ...... S.F.	1916	106
2½	Do., Deb. Stk. Scrip ..	1927-57	100
3	Barnsley	1916-46	105
3	Barry	1914-46	100
3	Bath	1909-34	104
3	Batley	1914-44	101½
3½	Birmingham	1945	124
3	Do.	1947	113
2½	Do.	1926	99
3	Blackburn	1930	107
3	Bournemouth	1913-33	103
3½	Bradford	1945	120
3	Do. Deb. Stock ..	1954	112
3	Brighouse..........	1916-46	100
3½	Brighton	1946	120½
2½	Do.	1957	98
3	Burton-on-Trent..........	1913-43	102½
3	Cambridge	1913-43	104
3½	Cardiff	1935	119
3	Do.	1914-54	105
3	Cheltenham..........	1971	112
3	Chichester	1916-46	102
3½	Croydon		135½
3	Do.	1940	111½
3	Derby	1920-50	107
3	Devon C.C..........	1917-33	106½
3½	Dewsbury	1930	111
3	Do.	1930	105
3	Dorset County	1922-32	107
3	Douglas (I. of Man)	1926	101
3	Dover	1913-43	103½
3½	Dublin	1944	113½
3	Eastbourne	1920-40	105
3	Edinburgh	1924	108
2½	Do.	1929	98
2½	Exeter	1917-57	97
3	Glamorgan County	1914-34	104
3½	Glasgow	1914	110½
3	Do.	1921	106½
2½	Do.	1925-40	99
3	Gloster	1915-55	103
3	Grimsby	1913-45	103½
3	Hampshire County	1914-34	105½
3	Hanley	1913-43	105
3	Harrogate	1914-34	104
3	Hastings	1915-54	105
2½	Hertfordshire C.C.	1916-36	99
3	Heston & Isleworth U.D.C.	1915-35	101
3	Huddersfield	1934	107
3½	Hull (1st iss.)		131½
3	Inverness	1914-44	102
3	Ipswich	1952	111
3	Lancaster..........	1919-55	104
2½	Leeds	1927	98
3½	Leicester	1934	117
3	Lincoln..........	1919	104
3½	Liverpool..........		135

Corporation, &c. (*continued*):—

Rate.	Name.		Price.
3	Manchester	1941	110
3	Mansfield..........	1915-45	100
3½	Middlesbro'..........	1909	105½
3½	Do.	1911-13	105
3	Do.	1915	104
3	Middlesex C.C..........	1915-35	106
3½	Newcastle	1936	118½
3½	Do. Irred.		129½
2½	Do.	1915-36	101
3	Newcastle-under-Lyme..	1909-44	101
3	Newport (Mon.)	1915-55	104½
3	Norwich	1952	113
3	Nottingham		117
3	Oxford	1951	111
3	Penzance	1916-46	102½
3	Plymouth	1942	112
3	Pontypridd U.D.C.	1916-46	99
3	Poole..........	1915-45	102½
3½	Portsmouth........1916	24 & 27	112
3	Do.	1913-33	107
3	Ramsey	1920-40	100
3	Ramsgate..........	1915-55	102
3	Reading		135
3	Do.	1962	109
3½	Rhyl U.D.C.	1953	112
3	Richmond (Surrey)	1942	106½
3	River Wear Debt Certs.		101
3	St. Helen's	1915-55	104½
3	Scarbro'	1915-50	102
2½	Sheffield	1925-57	97½
3	Shipley U.D.C.	1915-35	101
3	Somerset Co.	1923-33	107
3	South Shields..........	1915-45	104
2½	Southampton	1915-45	102
3	Southend-on-Sea	1916-46	102
3	Staffs C.C.	1915-35	105
3	Stockport..........	1914-54	104
3	Stockton !..........	1932	105
3	Do.	1915-35	104
3	Surrey Co.	1922-32	106½
3½	Swansea		132
3	Do.	1955	106
3	Taunton	1918 3-9-43	102
3	Tees Conserv. Deb. Stk.	1947	101
3	Thames Conserv. "A" Deb. Stk..........	1954	103
3	Do. "B" Deb. Stk.	1954	103
3	Torquay	1913-43	102½
3	Tunbridge Wells	1931	105
3	Tynemouth	1913	101
3	Wakefield..........	1929	105
3	Walsall..........	1932	108
3	West Bromwich........	1930	108½
3½	West Ham	1929	112
3	Do.	1945	107
3	West Sussex C.C.	1915-35	106
3	Weston-s.-Mare Lcl Bd.	1914-44	102
3	Weymouth & Melc. Regis	1918	101
3	Widnes..........	1915-55	102
3	Wigan	1921	108
3	Windsor	1918-55	104
3½	Wisbech	1947	115½
3½	Wolverhampton	1932	118½
3	Do.	1924-54	108
3	York	1916-41	107

SUBJECT TO STAMP DUTY.

Rate.	Name.		Price.
3½	Belfast City & Dis. Watr.	1938	116
3	Do. Red Stk.	1953-6	106
3½	Belfast	1924	104
4	Blackburn Con. Deb. Irred.		141½
3½	Do. do. Irred..........		131
3½	Bristol		133
3½	Burnley..........	1933	116
2½	Chesterfield Gas & Wtr.	1916-46	98
3½	Douglas Town	1921	105
3	Dover Harb. 1st Deb...	1956	105½
3½	Hull (2nd iss.)		129½
4	Leeds Deb..........	1927	125
3½	Do.		113½
3	Do.	1927	107½
3	Leicester	1919-44	106
4	Manchester..........		150
3	Do.	1928	105
4½	Middlesboro' Mrts.	1908	111
3½	Newark-on-Trent ..	1901-41	96
3½	Sheffield..........	1898-1916	106
3½	Do.	1925-36	114½
3	Do.	1925	105½
3½	Southampton	S.F.	105½
4½	Stockton Morts.........	1906	112
3½	Worcester..	1950	111

COLONIAL AND PROVINCIAL GOVERNMENT SECURITIES.

Rate.	Name.		Price.
6	British Columbia........	1907	119½
4½	Do. Debs...	1917	111½
3	British Guiana Imgtn. Bds.		99½
5	Canada, "Intercol. Rail,"	1903	111½
4	Do. (Bonds)	1904-5-6-8	109
4	Do. Reduced	1910	111
3½	Do. Bnds.	1909-34	107
4	Do. Loan	1910-35	112
3	Do. Loan	1938	106
6	Cape of G. Hope	1900	—
5	Do.	1900	—
4½	Do. red. by an. draw.		111
4½	Do. 1879		111
4	Do. 1881		109
4	Do.	1917-23	118
4½	Ceylon		110
4	Do.		108½
4½	Fiji Gov. Deb. Sink. Fd.		102½
4	Jamaica Sink. Fd.	1923	104
5	Manitoba Debs..........	1910	113
5	Do. Ster. Bds.	1888	122
4	Do. Ster. Debs.		106
4	Mauritius, Cons. Debs. 1880...		103½
4½	Natal, Sink. Fd.........	1919	120
4	Do. do.	1926	118
3½	Newfoundland Stg. Bds.	1941	100
3½	Do. do. ..	1947	100
3	Do. do.		88
5	New South Wales	1897-1902	104½
4	Do.	1903-5-8-9-10	105½
5	New Zealand	1914	118
5	Do. Cnsls. 1 p.c. per an. Sink. Fd.		104
3½	Nova Scotia Debs.		104
5	Quebec Prov.	1904-6	110
4½	Do. (drgs.)		104
5	Do. Strlg. Bds.	1919	115
4	Do. Strlg. Bds.	1928	110
4	Do. Strlg. Bds.	1934	110
4	Queensland	1913-15	108
4½	St. Lucia Debs..........		100
6	South Australia	1897-1900	103½
6	Do.	1901-1918	118
5	Do.	1911-1920	115½
4	Do.	1899-1916	105
4	Do.	1929	110½
4	Do.	1916	109½
4	Do.	1917-18-24	114
6	Tasmania	1897-1901	104
4	Do. 1908-11,	1913-14-20	108
5	Trinidad Debs., an. drw. 1 p c...		108
4	Victoria	1899-1901	101½
4½	Do.	1904	106
4	Do. Rail. Loan	1907	106
4	Do. Loans	1908-13	108½
4½	West. Austr. 1 p.c. an. Sink. Fd.		108
4	Do. do.		106

REGISTERED AND INSCRIBED STOCKS.

No stamp duty except for Canada 4 p.c. Reduced (1 per cent.).

Rate.	Name.		Price.
4	Antigua Insc. Stk. Red.	1919-44	109
3½	Barbados Insc. Stk.	1925-42	109
3	British Colum. Insc. Stk.	1941	104
4	British Guiana Insc.....	1935	120
4	Canada Stk. Regd. ..	1904-5-6-8	109
4	Do. 4 p.c. (late 5 p.c.) Regd.	1910	111
3½	Do. 3½ p.c. Stock Regd.	1909-34	107
4	Do. Ln. for 4 milln. stg.	1910-35	112
3	Do. Stk. Regd.	1938	106
2½	Do. Insc.	1947	93
4	Cape G. Hope Regd. ..	1917-23	118
4	Do. (Ln. of '83) Insc. ..	1923	119
4	Do. Cons. Stk. Insc....	1916-36	116
3½	Do. Consol. Insc. Stock	1929-49	115
4	Ceylon Insc. Stock	1934	124
3	Do.	1940	107
4	Grenada Insc. Stock....	1917-42	112
3½	Hong Kong Insc. Stock	1918-43	105½
4	Jamaica Insc. Stock....	1934	121
—	Do.	1922-44	99
4	Mauritius Inscribed	1937	119
4	Natal Consd. Stk. Insc.	1927	118
4	Do.	1937	122
3½	Do. Inscribed Stock..	1914-39	107
4	Newfoundland Inscribed	1913-38	108
4	Do.	1935	114
4	Do. Consd. Stk. Ins.	1936	114
4	N. S Wales Stock Insc.	1933	122
3½	Do.	1924	110
3½	Do.	1918	106
3	Do.	1935	101½

.Colonial, &c. (*continued*):—

Rate.	Name.		Price.
4	N. Zealnd. Con. Stk. Ins.	1929	116½
3½	Do.	1940	109
3	Do. Inscribed....	1945	101
3	Quebec (Prov.) Ins. Stk.	1937	95
4	Queensland Stock Insc.	1915-24	112½
3½	Do.	1921-4-30	106
3½	Do.	1945	109
3	Do.	1922-47	99½
4	St. Lucia Insc. Stock ..	1919-44	112
4	S. Austrln. (1882-7) Reg.	1916-36	114
3½	Do. In. Stk. Reg.	1939	110
3	Do.	1916-26	100
3/	Do.	1916	100
3½	Tasmanian Insc. Stock..	1920-40	110
4	Do.	1920-40	116
4	Trinidad Insc. Stock....	1917-42	112
3	Do.	1922-44	98½
4	Victoria Rly. Loan '81, Inscribed Stock	1907	106
4	Victoria Insc. Stock	1908-13-19	109½
4	Victoria (1885) Ins. Stk.	1920	112
3½	Do. Inscribed Stock	1921-3-6	106
4	Do. do.	1911-26	109
4	W. Austral. Insc. Stock	1934	120
4	Do.	1911-31	113
3½	Do.	1915-35	107
3	Do.	1915-35	98
3	Do.	1916-30	98

FOREIGN STOCKS, BONDS, &c.

COUPONS PAYABLE IN LONDON.

Last Div.	Name.		Price.
36/	Argentine Ry. Loan 6 p.c.	1881	92½
15/	Do. 5 p.c.	1884	72
30/	Do. N. Cent. Ry. Ext. 5 p.c.	1887-8-9	71½
30/	Do. 5 p.c. Trsy. Convs.	1887	73
5/4½	Do. 4½ p.c. Interl. Gld.	1888	68
27/	Do. 4½ p.c. Stlg. Extrl.	1888	68
10/6	Do. 3½ p.c. External ..	1889	51
4	Do. 4 p.c. Ry. Guar. Res....		63
4½	Brazilian	1883	62
4½	Do. Gold..........	1879	68½
4½	Do.	1888	63
36/	Buenos Ayres	1824	90
6	Do.	1882-3-6	50
6	Bulgarian	1888	94
6	Do. Mort. Bonds	1892	94
4½	Chilian	1885	79
4½	Do.	1886	80
4½	Do.	1887	79
4½	Do.	1889	82½
5	Do.	1892	87
4½	Do.	1893	79
4½	Do.	1895	79
5	Do.	1896	86
7	Chinese Silver	1894	101
6	Do. Gold	1895	106
6	Do. Apl. '95 by dwgs.	1901-15	109½
5	Do. Red. dwgs. in 36 yr.	1896	101
5	Do. Do. Regis.	1896	101
1½	Colmbn. 1½ to 3 p.c. Ext. Bds.	1896	18
6	Cordova, Prov.	1886	28
—	Do. Eng. Ass. Certs.		27
—	Do. 6 p.c.	1887-8	28
—	Do. Eng. Ass. Certs.		27
3	Costa Rica "A"		32
2½	Do. "B"		27
3	Danish Gold	1914	100
10/	Ecuador N. Ext. Bds. 4½ p.c. ascn. to 5 p.c..........		23
3½	Egypt'n Ins. Stk. lia. Stp. Dty.	1900	102
4½	Do. State Domain	1878	105½
4	Do. D. Sanieh, Red. ..	1905	104½
6	Entre Rios..........	1880-8	30
6	Do. Fndg. Ln. Bds.	1894-1921	40
6	Do. do. Parana City......		27½
15/	Greek	1881	37
15/	Do.	1884	37
12/	Do. Rentes..........		30
15/	Do. (Piræus-Larissa Ry.)		34
7/6	Do. Fundg. Loan	1893	42½
4	Guatemala Extl. Debt..........		35
6	Hawaiian		101½
4	Hungarian Gold Rentes........		101½
3	Do.	1895	91
6	Italian Irriga. Guar.		112½
5	Do. Maremmana		83½
5	Japan 5 p.c.		102
5	Mexican (Nat. R. Tehuantp c.)..		86½
5	Do Extl.	1893	99

Foreign Stocks, &c. (*continued*) :—

Last Div.	Name.	Price.
6	Mexican Extrl. 1893	98½
5	Do. Intrnl. Cons. Slvr.	37½
5	Do. Intern. Rd. Bds. 2d. Ser.	37½
4	Nicaragua 1886	50
3½	Norwegian, red. 1937, or earlier	100
3	Do. do. 1965, do.	100
3½	Do. 3½ p.c. Bnds.	103
1	Paraguay 1p.c. ris. 3p.c. 1886-96	17
5	Russian, 1822, £ Strlg.	149½
3	Do. 1859	93
4	Do. (Nicolas Ry.) 1867-9	103
3	Do. Transcauc. Ry. 1882	92
4	Do. Con. R. R. Bd. Ser. I., 1889	104
4	Do. Do. II., 1889	104
4	Do. Do. III., 1891	103½
3½	Do. Bonds	101
4	Do. Ln. (Dvinsk and Vitbsk)	102
6	Salvador 1889	76
—	S Domingo 4s. Unified .. 1980	65½
6	San Luis Potosi Stg. 1889	93½
5	San Paulo (Brzl.), Stg. 1888	91½
6	Santa Fé 1883-4	38
—	Do. Eng. Ass. Certs. Dep.	36½
5	Do. 1888	49
—	Do. Eng. Ass. Certs. Dpsit.	48
5	Do. (W. Cnt. Col. Rly.) Mrt.	28
5	Do. & Reconq. Rly. Mort.	28
5	Spanish Quickslvr Mort. 1870	103
3½	Swedish 1880	103
3	Do. 1888	100
53	Do. Conversion Loan 1894	101
45	Trans. Gov. Loan Red...1903-42	105
50/	Tucuman (Prov.) 1888	69
	Turkish, Secd. on Egypt. Trib.	104½
	Turkish, Egpt. Trib., Ott. Bd., '94	99½
4½	Do. Priority 1890	93
1	Do. Convted Series, "A"	65½
5	Do. Customs Ln. 1886	97½
5	Uruguay Bonds 1896	53
3	Venzula New Con. Debt 1881	37½

COUPONS PAYABLE ABROAD.

Last Div.	Name.	Price.
7	Argent. Nat. Cedla. Sries. "B".	37½
5	Austrian Ster. Rnts., ex 10fl., 1870	85
5	Do. do. do.	86
5	Do. Paper do. 1870	84
5	Do. do. do.	85
4	Do. Gld Rentes 1876	103
2½	Belgian exchange 25 fr.	92
3	Do. do.	101
3½	Danish Int., 1887, Rd. 1896	97½
3½	Do. '87, Red. by pur. or draw. fr. Dec., 1900	98½
2½	Dutch Certs. ex 12 gldrs.	87
3	Do. Bonds	100
3	Do. Insc. Stk.	98
3½	French Rentes	106½
3	Do. 1878, '81-4., Red.	101
3	German Imp. Ln. 1891	96½
3	Do. do. 1892-3	96½
3	Do. do. 1890-4	96
5	Japan Cons. Ln., '92: 3, & 5, Red.	47
36/9	Prussian Consols	102
3	" Cons. Stg. Ln. 1891	97
4	Rumanian Bds. 1890	—
4	Do. do. 1891	—
4	Utd. States, 1877, Red. 1907	116
4	Do. 1895, 30 yrs.	131½
3½	Do. Maschsetts Gl. 1935	113½
3½	Do. Gold Bonds 1923	110½
2	Virginia Cpn. Bds., 3 p.c. from July, 1901	72

BRITISH RAILWAYS.

ORD. SHARES AND STOCKS.

Last Div.	Name.	Price.
10	Barry, Ord.	286½
4	Do. Prefd.	129
6	Do. Defd.	157½
5¼	Caledonian, Ord.	160
3	Do. Prefd.	102½
—	Do. Defd. Ord., No. 1	5½
	Cambrian, Ord	6½
—	Do. Coast Cons.	6½
24/	Cardiff Ry. Pref. Ord.	118
3/	Central Lond. £10 Ord. Sh.	10½
1/9½	Do. do. £6 paid	6
3½d.	Do. Pref. Half-Shares	1½
1/6	Do. Def. do.	4½
2	City and S. London	70
—	East London, Cons.	7
1½	Furness	68
—	Glasgow and S. West. Pfd.	85
—	Do. do. Dfd.	69
—	Great Central, Ord 1894	42
32/6	Do. London Exten.	79
3½	Great N. of Scotland	124
4	Great Northern, Prefd.	124½
—	Do. Consolidated "A"	64
—	Do. do. "B"	195½
2	Highland	89½
4	Isle of Wight, Prefd.	122½
1	Do. Defd.	86½
—	Lanca. Derbys. and E. Cst.	4½
8½	L. Brighton and S. C. Ord.	187
37/11½	Do. New 70 p.c. pd.	188
6	Do. Prefd. Ord.	199
20/	Do. Contgt. Rights Certs.	20½
5½	Lond. and S. Western Ord.	232½
4	Do. Preferred	138
2½	Lond., Tilb., and Southend	135½
—	Mersey, £20 shares	1
—	Metropolitan, New Ord.	131
2½	Do. Surplus Lands	98
4	North Cornwall, 4 p.c. Pref.	106½
7/6	Do. Deferred	27½
7½	North London	231
	North Staffordshire	132

British Railways (*continued*) :—

Last Div.	Name.	Price.
1/6	Plymouth, Devenport, and S. W. Junc. £10	9
3/	Port Talbot £10 Shares	9½
9d.	Rhondda Swns. B. £10 Sh.	6
11	Rhymney, Cons.	277½
4	Do. Prefd.	128
—	Do. Defd.	155½
—	Scarboro', Bridlington Junc.	47½
3½	South Eastern, Ord	156
6	Do. Pref.	199
3½	Taff Vale	85
25/	Vale of Glamorgan	129½
2/6½	Waterloo & City £10 shares	13½

LEASED AT FIXED RENTALS.

Last Div.	Name.	Price.
4	Birkenhead	150
5.14.0	East Lincnshire	215
5½	Hamsmith. & City Ord.	197½
4½	Lond. and Blackwll.	167½
4½	Do. £10 4½ p. c. Pref.	167
56/6	Lond. & Green. Ord.	102
5	Do. 5 p. c. Pref.	180½
5	Nor. and Eastn. £50 Ord.	92
6	Do.	109
3½	N. Cornwall 3½ p. c. Stk.	129½
4⅔	Nott. & Granthm. R. & C.	150
3½	Portptk. & Wigtn. Guar. Stk.	126
9	Vict. Stn. & Pimlico Ord.	317½
4½	Do. 4½ p. c. Pref.	163½
4/	West Lond. £72 Ord. Shs.	14½
4⅜	Weymouth & Portld.	162½

DEBENTURE STOCKS.

Last Div.	Name.	Price.
4	Alexandra Dks. & Ry.	132½
3	Barry, Cons.	110
4	Brecon & Mrthyr, New A	129
4	Do. New B	105
4	Caledonian	154
4	Cambrian "A"	134½
4	Do. "B"	132½
4	Do. "C"	127½
4	Do. "D"	110½
3	Cardiff Rly.	105
4	City and S. Lond.	139
3½	Cleator & Working Junc.	118½
3	Devon & Som. "A"	105½
16/3	Do. "B" 4 p. c.	36
—	Do. "C" 4 p. c.	10
4	E. Lond. 2nd Ch. 4 p. c. A	139
6/	Do. 2nd B	66½
—	Do. 3rd Ch. 4 p. c.	19½
—	Do. 4th do.	9½
3½	Do. 1st (3½ p. c.)	128½
2½	Do. 2½ p.c. (Whitech. Exn).	88
4	Forth Bridge	146
4	Furness	145
4	Glasgow and S. Western	151
5	Gt. Central	—
4½	Do.	161
4	Gt. Eastern	151
4	Gt. N. of Scotland	148½
3	Gt. Northern	117
4	Gt. Western	155
4½	Do.	162
4½	Do.	173½
5	Do.	192
2½	Do.	100
4	Highland	143½
3	Hull and Barnsley	107
3	Do. 2nd (3-4 p. c).	124
4	Isle of Wight	144½
3	Do. Cent. "A"	92½
4½	Do. "B"	115½
4	Do. "C"	82½
3	Lancs. & Yorkshire	116
4	Lancs. Derbys. & E. Cst.	124½
4	Lpool St. Hlen's & S. Lancs.	126
4½	Ldn. and Blackwall	159
4	Ldn. and Greenwich	149½
4	Lond., Brighton, &c.	152
4½	Do.	170½
4½	Lond., Chath., &c., Arb.	160
4½	Do. "B"	158½
4	Do.	140
4	Do. 1883	139
3	Do.	107
3	Lond. & N. Western	118
3	Lond. & S. Westn. "A"	118
3	Do. Consld.	118
4	Lond., Til., & Southend	150
—	Mersey, 5 p. c. (Act, 1866)	65
4	Metropolitan	150
4½	Do.	164½
3½	Do.	129½
6	Met. District	209½
4	Do.	139
4	Midland	118
4½	Mid-Wales "A"	137½
4	Neath & Brecon 1st	129
4	Do. "A 1"	121
3	North British	114
3	Do. 1893	111½
3½	N. Cornwall, Launcstn., &c.	128½

Debenture Stocks (*continued*) :—

Last Div.	Name.	Price.
4	North Eastern	117
4½	North London	167
3	N. Staffordshire	115
4	Plym. Devpt. & S.W. Jn.	141½
4	Rhondda and Swan. Bay	130½
4	Rhymney	148
4	South-Eastern	152
5	Do.	191
3½	Do.	130
3	Do.	116
3	Taff Vale	111
4	Tottenham & For. Gate	146
3	Vale of Glamorgan	105½
3	West Highld. (Gtd. by N. B.)	111½
4	Wrexham, Mold, &c. "A"	115½
4	Do. "B"	106½
4	Do. "C"	97½

GUARANTEED SHARES AND STOCKS.

Last Div.	Name.	Price.
4	Caledonian	150½
4	Do.	152
4	Forth Bridge	146
4	Furness 1881	138
4	Glasgow & S. Western	151½
4	Do. St. Enoch, Rent	150½
6	Gt. Central	202
4½	Do. 1st Pref.	153½
3½	Do. Pref.	106
5	Do. Irred. S.Y. Rent	166½
4½	Do. do.	141½
4	Gt. Eastern, Rent	148
5	Do. Metropolitan	182½
4	Do.	148
4	Gt. N. of Scotland	141
4	Gt. Northern	152
5	Gt. Western, Rent	189
5	Do. Cons.	191
4	Lancs. & Yorkshire	152
5	L., Brighton & S. C.	186
3½	L., Chat. & D. (Shrtlds.)	110½
4	L. & North Western	153
4	L. & South Western .. 1881	152
4½	Met. District, Ealing Rent	152
4½	Do. Fulham Rent	152
4	Do. Midland Rent	143½
4	Do. Mid. & Dist. Guar.	136½
4	Midland, Rent	153
4	Do. Cons.	153
3	Mid. & G. N. Jt., "A" Rnt.	109½
3	N. British, Lien	110
4	Do. Cons. Pref. No. 1	148
3	N. Cornwall, Wadebrge. Gu.	108
4	N. Eastern	152
5	N. Staff. Trent & M. £20 Shs.	36½
3½	Nott. Suburban Ord.	126½
20/6	S. E. Perp. Ann.	36½
4½	Do. 4½ p.c.	168
3½	S. Yorks. Junc. Ord.	118½
4½	W. Cornwall (G. W., Br., Ex., & S. Dev. Joint Rent	168½
3	W. Highl. Ord. Stk. (Gua., N.B.)	107½

PREFERENCE SHARES AND STOCKS.

DIVIDENDS CONTINGENT ON PROFIT OF YEAR.

Last Div.	Name	Price.
4½	Alexandra Dks. & Ry. "A"	128½
5	Barry (First)	171½
4	Do. Consolidated	141½
4	Caledonian Cons., No. 1	149
4	Do. do. No. 2	148
5	Do. do. 1878	183½
4	Do. Pref. 1884	147
4	Do. do. 1887 (Conv.)	155
—	Cambrian, No. 1 4 p.c. Pref.	74½
—	Do. No. 2 do.	39½
—	Do. No. 3 do.	19
—	Do. No. 4 do.	10
5	City & S. Lond. £10 shares	15½
—	Do. New	14
4	Furness, Cons. 1881	134½
4	Do. "A" 1881	131½
4	Do. "B" 1883	129½
4	Glasgow & S. Western	148½
4	Do. No. 2	147
4	Do. 1888	147
4	Do. 1891	146
5	Gt. Central	167½
4	Do.	134½
5	Do. Conv. 1872	154½
5	Do. do. 1874	154½
5	Do. do. 1876	154½
5	Do. do. 1879	153½
5	Do. do. 1881	153½
4	Do. 1889	117½
4	Do. 1891	112
5	Do. 1894	116½
4	Gt. Eastern, Cons.	146
4	Do. 1886	145
4	Do. 1881	144
4	Do. 1884	143

Preference Shares, &c. (*continued*) :—

Last Div.	Name.	Price.
4	Gt. Eastern, Cons. 1887	143
4	Do. 1888	143
3½	Do. 1890	124½
3½	Do. 1893	123½
—	Do. (Int. fr. Jan '99) 1893	117½
4	Gt. North Scotland "A"	136½
4	Do. "B"	135½
4	Gt. Northern, Cons.	148
3	Do. 1896	109½
5	Gt. Western Cons.	189
—	Hull & Barnsley Red. at 115	110
4	Isle of Wight	136½
3	Lancs. & Yorkshire, Cons.	112
2/2½	Lanc. Drby & E.C. 5 p.c. £10	11
—	Do. 5 p.c. 2nd £10	10
5	Lond., Bright., &c., Cons.	185½
5	Do. 2nd Cons.	184½
4½	Lond., Chat. & Dov. Arbitr.	136½
25/	Do. 2nd Pref. 4½ p.c.	95
4	Lond. & N. Western	158
4	Lond. & S. Western .. 1881	151
4	Do. 1884	150
3½	Do.	131
4	Lond., Tilbury & Southend	148
4	Do. Cons., 1887	148
4	Do 1891	147
—	Mersey, 5 p.c. Perp.	9½
4	Metropolitan, Perp.	148
4	Do. 1882	145½
4	Do. Irred.	145½
4	Do. 1887	145½
4	Do. New	144½
4½	Do.	149½
3½	Do.	124½
3	Do. Guar.	104½
4	Metrop. Dist. Exten 5 p.c.	113
4	Midland, Cons. Perpetual	151
4	N. British Cons., No. 2	143
4½	Do. Edin. & Glasgow	156½
5	Do. 1865	173½
5	Do. Conv. 1874	173½
4½	Do. 1873	156
4½	Do. Conv. 1875	156½
5	Do. do. 1879	173½
4	Do. do. 1884	141
4	Do. do. 1888	141
4	Do. do. 1890	141
4	Do. do. 1892	141
4	N. Eastern	150
4½	N. Lond., Cons. 1866	181½
4½	Do. 2nd Cons. .. 1875	166½
3	N. Staffordshire	111
4½	Plym. Devpt. & S. W. Junc.	152½
9½d.	Port Talbot, &c., 4 p.c. £10 Shares, 4 paid	5
5/	Rhondda & Swansea Bay, 5 p.c. £10 Shares	13½
4	Rhymney, Cons.	144
4½	S. Eastern, Cons.	167
5	Do. do.	184½
4	Do. Vested Cos'	145
4	Do. 1891	145
3½	Do. 1893	127
2	Do. 3 p.c. after July 1900	105
4	Taff Vale	143

INDIAN RAILWAYS.

Last Div.	Name.	Paid.	Price.
3½	Assam Bengal, Ld., (3½ p.c. till June 30, then 3 p.c.)	100	103
4/	Barsi Light, Ld., £10 Shs.	10	10½
6	Bengal and N. West., Ld.	100	148½
4/	Do. £10 Shares	10	14½
3/6	Do. 3½ p.c. Cum. Pf. Shs.	10	10½
8½d.	Do.	4	4½
2/3½	Bengal Central, Ld., £10 (3½ p.c. + ⅛th net earn)	5	5½
3	Bengal Dooars, Ld.	100	118
4	Bengal Nagpr., Lim. (gua. 4 p.c. + 4th sp. pfts.)	100	115
7½	Bombay, Baroda, and C. I. (gua. 5 p.c.)	100	216
36/1	Burma, Ld. (gua. 2½ p.c. and ½ p.c. add. till 1901)	100	111½
1/7	Do. £10 Shares	2½	3½
4	Delhi Umb. Kalka, Ld., Gua. 3½ p.c. + net earn.	100	121
4	Do. Deb. Stk., 1890 (1926)	100	113
9/10	Estn. Bengal, "A" An. 1957	—	36
9/	Do. "B" 1957	—	31
4	Do. Gua. Deb. Stock	100	144½
9/7½	East Ind. Ann. "A" (1953)	—	32
8/4½	Do. "C"	—	30
8/11½	Do. "B"	—	32
6⅛	Do. Def. Ann. Cap. (gua. 4 p.c. + ⅕th sp. pfts.)	—	188
115/9	East Ind. Def. Ann. "D"	—	158
4½	East Ind. Irred. Stock	100	164½
5	Gt. Indian Penin., Gua. 5 p.c. + ½ surplus profits	100	172
4	Do. Irred. 4 p.c. Deb. St.	100	164½
4	Indian Mid., Ld. (gua. 4 p.c. + ¼th surplus pfts.)	100	115
51/	Madras Guar. + ½ sp. pfts.	100	157
48/6	Do. do.	100	157
46/	Do. do.	100	147
4	Nilgiri, Ld., 1st Deb. Stk.	100	97
4	Oude & Rohil. Db. Stk. Rd.	100	201
5⅞	Rohil. and Kumaon, Ld.	100	132
9/11	Scinde, Punj., and Delhi, "A" Ann., 1958	—	35
9/1	Do. "B" do.	—	31

Indian Railways (*continued*):—

Last Div.	Name.	Paid.	Price.
4	South Behar, Ld., £10 shs.	100	100
3½	Do. Deb. Stk. Red.	100	103
4½	South Ind., Gu. Deb. Stk.	100	166½
5	South Indian, Ld. (gua. 3 p.c., and ½ spls. profits)	100	120½
5	Sthn. Mahratta, Ld. (3½ p.c. & ¼th net earnings)	100	121
4	Do. Deb. Stk. Red.	100	124
3½	Southern Punjab, Ld.	100	113
3½	Do. Deb. Stk. Red.	—	107
5	Nizam's Gua. State, Ld. (†	100	114½
4	Do. Mort. Deb., 1936	100	110
4	Do. do. Reg.	100	108
17/3½	Nizam's Gua. State, Ld., 3½ p.c. Mt. Deb. bearer	—	95½
17/3½	Do. Reg. do. ..	—	94½
5	W. of India Portgese., Ld.	100	68½
5	Do. Deb. Stk., Red	100	98

RAILWAYS.—BRITISH POSSESSIONS.

Last Div.	Name.	Paid.	Price.
5	Atlantic & N.W. Gua. 1 Mt. Bds., 1937	100	127
5/3	Buff. & L. Huron Ord. Sh.	10	13½
5½	Do. 1st Mt. Perp. Bds. 1879	100	143½
5½	Do. 2nd Mt. Perp. Bds.	100	143½
—	Calgary & Edmon. 6 p.c. 1st Mt. Stg. Bds. Red..	100	77½
5	Canada Cent. 1st Mt. Bds. Red.	100	105
4	Can. Pacific Pref. Stk.	100	102
5	Do. Strl. 1st Mt. Deb. Bds. 1915	100	119
3½	Do. Ld. Grnt. Bds., 1938..	100	100
3½	Do. Ld. Grnt. Ins. Stk. ..	100	108
4	Do. Perp. Cons. Deb. Stk.	100	110
5	Do. Algoma Bch. 1st Mt. Bds., 1937	100	121
2	Demerara, Original Stock	100	49
7	Do. Perp. Pref. Stk.	100	157½
9½d.	Do. 4 p.c. Cum. Ext. Pref. £10 Shs.	4	6½
—	Dominion Atlntc. Ord. Stk.	100	32½
25/	Do. 5 p.c. Pref. Stk.	100	101
4	Do. 1st. Deb. Stk.	100	110
4	Do. 2nd do. Red.	100	100
—	EmuBay&Mt.Bischoff, Ld.	5	4½
4½	Do. Irred. Deb. Stk. ...	100	98
nil.	Gd. Trunk of Canada, Stk.	100	9
6	Do. 2nd. Equip. Mt. Bds.	100	130½
5	Do. Perp. Deb. Stk.	100	141
5	Do. Gt. Westn. Deb. Stk.	100	134
5	Do. Nthn. of Can. 1st Mt. Bds, 1902	100	105
4	Do. do. Deb. Stk	100	103
5	Do. G. T. Geor. Bay & L. Erie 1 Mt., 1903	100	104
5	Do. Mid. of Can. Stl. 1st Mt. (Mid. Sec.) 1908	100	109
5	Do. do. Cons. 1 Mt. Bds. 1912	100	109
5	Do. Mont. & Champ. 1 Mt. Bds., 1902	100	104
	Do. Welln., Grey & Brce. 7 p.c. Bds. 1 Mt.	100	111
4	Jamaica 1st Mtg. Bds. Red.	—	103½
—	Manitoba & N. W., 6 p.c. 1st Mt. Bds., Red	100	—
—	Do. Ldn. Bdhldrs. Certs.	—	—
5	Manitoba S. W. Col. 1 Mt. Bd., 1934 $1,000 price %	—	120
—	Mid. of W. Aust. Ld. 6 p.c. 1 Mt. Dbs., Red.	100	25
4	Do. Deb. Bds., Red.	100	103
4	Nakusp & Slocan Bds., 1918	100	106
3	Natal Zululand Ld. Debs.,	100	79½
5	N. Brunswick 1st Mt. Stg. Bds., 1934	100	122
4	Do. Perp. Cons. Deb. Stk.	100	116
—	N. Zealand Mid., Ld., 5 p.c. 1st Mt. Debs.	100	35
6	Ontario & Queb. Cap. Stk.	$100	156½
5	Do. Perm. Deb. Stk	100	147½
—	Qu'Appelle, L. Lake & Sask. 6 p.c. 1 Mt. Bds. Red.	100	46½
5	Queb. & L. S. John, 1st Mt. Bds., 1909	100	25½
5	Quebec Cent., Prior Ln. Bds., 1908	100	107
1½	Do. 5 p.c. Inc. Bds.	100	41
4	St. Lawr. & Ott. Stl. 1st Mt.	100	113
4	Shuswap & Okan., 1st Mt. Deb. Bds., 1915	100	70½
5	Temiscouata, 5 p.c. Stl. 1st Deb. Bds., Red.	100	9½
5	Do. (S. Franc. Brch.) 5 p.c. Stl. 1 Mt. Db. Bds., 1910	100	12½
4	Toronto, Grey & B. 1st Mt.	100	113
1/2½	Well. & Mana. £5 Shs. ..	1	1
5	Do. Debs., 1908	100	110
5	Do. 2nd Debs., 1908	100	109
5	Do. 3rd do., 1908	100	108
6	Atlan. & St. Law. Shs., 6 p.c.	100	167
5	Gd. Trunk Mt. Bds., 1934	100	116½
5	Michigan Air Line, 5 p.c. 1st Mt. Bds., 1902	100	104
4	Minneap., S. P. & Slt. Ste. Mar, 1st M. Bds., 1938	$1000	100

AMERICAN RAILROAD STOCKS AND SHARES.

Last Div.	Name.	Paid.	Price.
6/	Alab. Gt. Sthn. A 6 p.c. Pref.	10/.	9
—	Do. do "B" Ord. ..	10/.	2
—	Alabma. N. Orl.-Tex. &c., "A" Pref.	10/.	½
—	Do. "B" Def.	10/.	½
4½	Atlant. First Lsd. Ls. Rtl. Trust	Stk.	100
$2	Baltimore & Ohio Com. ..	$100	18
—	Baltimore Ohio S.W. Pref.	$100	7
—	Chesap. & Ohio Com.	$100	25
—	Chic. Gt. West. 5 p.c. Pref. Stock "A"	$100	37½
—	Do. do. Scrip. In.	—	36½
8/3	Do. 4 p.c. Deb. Stk.	$100	71½
4	Do. Interest in Scrip	$100	67½
$4	Chic. Junc. Rl. & Un. Stk. Yds. Com.	$100	121½
$1½	Do. 6 p.c. Cum. Pref.	$100	118½
$3½	Chic. Mil. & St. P. Pref. ..	$100	147½
7	Cleve. & Pittsburgh	$50	87
$1½	Clev., Cincin., Chic., & St. Louis Com.	$100	—
—	Erie 4 p.c. Non-Cum. 1st Pf.	—	42½
—	Do. 4 p.c. do. 2nd Pf.	—	22
—	Gt. Northern Pref.	$100	160
$2½	Illinois Cen. Lsd. Lines ..	$100	97½
—	Kansas City, Pitts & G. ..	$100	24
$3	L. Shore & Mich. Sth. C.	$100	197½
—	Mex. Cen. Ltd. Com.	$100	6
—	Miss. Kan. & Tex. Pref. ..	$100	41½
1	N.Y., Pen. & O. 1st Mt. Tst. Ltd., Ord.	—	47½
4	Do. 1st Mort. Deb. Stk. ..	$100	92½
6	North Pennsylvania	$50	—
—	Northn. Pacific, Com.	$100	27½
1¾	Pitts. F. Wayne & Chic. ..	$100	176
—	Reading 1st Pref.	$50	26½
—	Do. 2nd Pref.	$50	14½
—	S. Louis & S. Fran. Com.	$100	7½
—	Do. 2nd Pref.	$100	27
6	St. Louis Bridge 1st Pref. .	$100	107
3	Do. 2nd Pref.	$100	50
6	Tunnel Rail. of St. Louis	$100	107
$1½	St. Paul, Min. and Man. ..	$100	135½
—	Southern, Com.	$100	9½
—	Wabash, Common	$100	7½

AMERICAN RAILROAD BONDS. CURRENCY.

Last Div.	Name.		Price.
7	Albany & Susq. 1 Con. Mrt.	1906	122½
7	Allegheny Val. 1 Mt.	1910	127½
5	Burling., Cedar Rap. & N. 1 Mt.	1906	109½
5	Canada Southern 1 Mt.	1908	111
5	Chic. & N. West. Sk. Fd. Db.	1933	120½
5	Do. Deb. Coupon	1921	115½
6	Chicago & Tomah	1905	112½
5	Chic. Burl. & Q. Skg. Fd.	1901	102½
4	Do. Nebraska Ext.	—	102
6	Chic., Mil., & S. Pl., 1 Mt. S.W. Div.	1909	117½
7	Do. (S. Paul Div.) 1 Mt.	1902	132½
5	Do. (La Cross & D.	1919	112½
7	Do. 1 Mt. (Hast. & Dak.)	1910	132
5	Do. Chic. & Mis. Riv. 1 Mt.	1926	112½
5	Chic., Rock Is. and Pac. 1 Mt. Ext.	1934	108
6	Det., G. Haven & Mil. Equip	1918	110
6	Do. do. Cons. Mt.	1918	104½
6	Ill. Cent., 1 Mt., Chic. & S.	1898	—
7	Indinnap. & Vin., 1 Mt. ..	1908	125
6	Do. do. 2 Mt. ..	1900	104½
6	Lehigh Val., Cons. Mt.	1923	112½
—	Mexic. Cent., Ln. 2 Cons. Inc.	—	7
7	N.Y. Cent. & H.R. Mt. Bonds	1903	119½
5	Do. Deb.	1904	112
6	Penns. Cons. S. F M.	1905	119½
4	West Shore, 1 Mt.	2361	110

DITTO—GOLD.

Last Div.	Name.		Price.
6	Alabama Gt. Sthn. 1 Mt. ..	1908	112
5	Do. Mid. 1	1928	95
4	Allegheny Val. Gen. Mt. ..	1942	110
4	Atch., Top., & S. Fé Gn. Mt.	1995	96½
3	Do. Adj. Mt.	1995	65
5	Do. Equipt. Tmst.	—	104½
5	Atlantic & Dan. 1 Mt.	1950	94½
5	Baltimore & Ohio	1925	102
5	Do. Speyer's Tst. Recpts.	1925	102
5	Do. Cons. Mt.	1988	104
4½	Do. 4½ p.c. 1 Mt. Term.	1934	85
4½	Do. Brown Shipley's Dep. Cts.	—	85
5	Balt. Belt 5 p.c. 1 Mort.	1990	90
4½	Balt. & Ohio S.W. 1 Mt. ..	1990	104
4½	Do. 4½ p.c. 1 Cons. Mt. 1893	1993	79
—	Do. Inc. Mt. 5 p.c. Cl. A	—	31
—	Do. do. Cl. B	—	12
5	Balt. & Ohio S. W. Term 5 p.c.	1942	99½
6	Balt. & Ptmac (Mn. L.) 1 Mt.	1911	127½
6	Do. do. (Tunnel) 1 Mt.	1911	126
4	Beech Creek 1 Mt.	1936	108
5	Do 2 Mort.	1936	116
4	Carthage & Adiron. 1 Mt. ..	1981	100

American Railroad Bonds—Gold (*continued*):—

Last Div.	Name.		Price.
	Cent. of Georgia 1 Mort. ..	1945	117½
	Do. Cons. Mt.	1945	92½
	Cent. of N. Jrsy. Gn. Mt. ..	1987	117
	Central Pacific, 1 Mort.	1898	102½
	Do. Speyer's Certs.	—	106
	Do. Land Grant	1900	102
	Chesap. & Ohio 1st Cons. Mt.	1939	119
4½	Do. Gen. Mt.	1992	86
6	Chic. & W. Ind. Gen. Mt. Skg. Fd.	1932	122
5	Chic. Mil. & St. Pl. (Chic. & L. Sup.) 1 Mt.	1921	114½
5	Do. Chic. & Pac. W.	1921	119½
5	Do. Wisc. & Minn. 1 Mt.	1921	114½
5	Do. Terminal Mt.	1914	114½
4	Do. General Mt.	1989	108
5	Chic. St. L. & N. Orleans ..	1951	122½
4	Do. 1 Mort. (Memphis) ..	1951	102½
4	Clevel., Cin., Chic. & St. L., 1 Mt. (Cairo)	1939	90
4	Do. 1 Mt. (Cinc., Wab., & Mich.)	1991	98
4	Do. 1 Col. Tst. Mt. (S. Louis)	1990	88½
4	Do. General Mt.	1993	84
4½	Clevel. & Mar. Mt.	1935	112
4½	Clevel. & Pittsburgh	1942	122½
4½	Do. Series B.	1942	124½
—	Colorado Mid. 1 Mt.	1936	68
—	Do. Bdhrs.' Comm. Certs.	—	68
4	Dnvr. & R. Gde. 1 Cons. Mt.	1936	98
5	Do. Imp. Mort.	1928	95
4	Detroit & Mack. 1 Lien	1995	92½
5	E. Tennes., Virg., & Grgia. Cons. Mt.	1956	114½
5	Elmira, Cort., & Nthn. Mt.	1914	99½
4	Erie 1 Cons. Mt. Pr. Ln. ..	1996	95½
3	Do. Gen. Lien	1996	75
6	Galvest., Harrisb., &c., 1 Mt.		107½
5	Georgia, Car. & N. 1 Mt. ..	1929	96
4½	Gd. Rpds & Indn. Ex. 1 Mt.	1941	111½
5	Do. 1 Mt. (Muskegon) ..	1926	39½
3½	Illinois Cent. 1 Mt.	1951	104½
4	Do.	1952	107
4	Do. Cairo Bdge. ..	1950	103
4	Do.	1953	105
4	Do. General Mort. ..	1904	102½
—	Kans. City, Pitts. & G. 1 M.	1923	83
3½	L. Shore & Mich. Southern	1997	109
4½	Lehigh Val. N.Y. 1 Mt.	1940	106
5	Lehigh Val. Term. 1 Mt. ..	1941	112½
5	Long Island	1931	122½
5	Do. Deb.	1934	102
5	Do. (N. Shore Bch.) 1 Cons. Mt.	1932	96
6	Louisville & Nash. G. Mt. ..	1930	122
6	Do. 2 Mt. Sk. Fd. (S. & N. Alabama	1910	168
6	Do. 1 Mt. N. Orl. & Mb.	1930	122½
5	Do. 1 Mt. Coll. Tst.	1931	107½
4	Do. Unified	1940	91
4½	Do. Mobile & Montgy. 1 Mt.	1945	107½
4	Manhattan Cons. Mt.	1990	100
4	Mexican Cent. Cons. Mt. ..	1911	70
—	Do. 1 Cons. Inc, ...		18
6	Mexican Nat. 1 Mt.	1927	108
3	Do. 2 Mt. 6 p.c. Inc. A	1917	58
—	Do. do. B.	1917	—
3	Do. Matheson's Certs.		—
3	Michig. Cnt. (Battle Ck. & S.) 1 Mt.	1989	86
6	Minneap. & S. L. 1 Mt. Pacific Ext.	1921	120½
5	Do. 1 Consold.	1934	110
4	Minne., Sit. S. M. & A. 1 Mt.	1926	101
5	Minneapolis Westn. 1 Mt. ..	1911	105½
4	Miss. Kans. & Tex. 1 Mt. ..	1990	94
4	Do. 2 do.	1990	67
4	Mobile & Birm. Mt. Inc.	1945	38
5	Do. P. Lien	1945	88
4	Mohawk & Mal. 1 Mt.	1991	110
5	Montana Cent. 1 Mt.	1937	111½
5	Nashv., Chattan., & S. L. 1 Cons. Mt.	1928	104½
	Nash., Flor., & Shff. Mt. ..	1937	92
	N. Y. & Putnam 1 Cons. Mt.	1993	110
5	N. Y., Brooklyn, & Man. B. 1 Cons. Mt.	1935	110
4	N. Y. Cent. & Hud. R. Deb. Certs. 1890	1905	107
4	Do. Ext. Debt. Certs. ...	1905	107
7	N. Y., L. Erie, & W. 1 Cons. Mt. (Erie)	1920	149½
7	Do. 1 Con. Mt. Fd. Coup.	1920	147½
5	N. Y., Onto., & W. Cons. 1 Mt.	1939	110
4	Do. 4 p.c. Refund. Mt. ..	1992	102
5	N. Y. & Rockaway B. 1 Mt.	1927	104½
6	Norfolk & West. Gn. Mt. ...	1931	128
6	Do. Imp. & Ext.	1934	120
4	Do. 1 Cons. Mt.	—	87
6	N. Pacific Gn. 1 Mt. Ld. Gt.	1921	122
4	Do. P. Ln. Rl. & Ld. Gt.	—	100
3	Do. Gn. Ln. Rl. & Ld. Gt.	—	65
5	Oregon & Calif. 1 Mt.	1927	84
5	Oregon Rl. & Nav. Col. Tst.	—	—
—	Oreg. Sh. Line & Utah Col. Trst. 5 p.c. G. Bonds	1919	50
6	Panama Skg. Fd. Subsidy ..	1910	105½
4½	Pennsylvania Rlrd.	1913	115½
4	Do. Equip. Tst. Ser. A ..	1914	106
4	Do. Cons. Mt.	1943	115
4½	Penna. Company 1st Mort.	1921	116½
5	Perkiomen 1 Mrt., 2nd ser. ..	1918	90
4½	{ Pitts., C., C., & St. Ls. Con. Mt. G. B., Ser. A }	1940-2	116
4	Do. Cons. Mort., Ser. D ..	1945	105
6	Pittsbgh., Cle., & Toledo ..	1922	105½
4	Reading, Phil., & R. Genl.	1997	89½
5	Richmond & Dan. Equip. ..	1909	99½
5	Rio Grande Junc. 1st Mort.	1939	94
4	Rio Grande West 1st Tst. Mt.	1939	86
6	St. Joseph & Gd. Island ..	1925	—
7	S. Louis Bridge 1st Mort ..	1928	137½

American Railroad Bonds (*continued*):

Last Div.	Name.		Price.
5	S. Louis Mchts. Bdge. Term. 1st Mort.	1930	104½
4	S. Louis S. West 1st Mort. ..	1989	77½
—	Do. 4 p.c. 2nd Mort. Inc.	1989	30
—	S. Louis Term. Cupples Sta. & Prop. 1st. Mrt. 4½ p.c.	1902-17	102
4½	St. Paul, Minn., & Manit.	1933	110
6	Do. do.	1933	127½
6	Shamokin, Sunbury, &c. 2 Mt.	1925	107
5	S. & N. Alabama Cons. Mt.	1936	95½
5	Southern 1 Cons. Coup.	1994	96
4	Do. E. Tennes Reorg. Lien ..	1938	100
6	S. Pacific of Cal. 1 Mt. ..	1905-12	114
4½	Trml. Assn. of S. Louis 1 Mt.	1939	113½
5	Do. 1 Cons. Mt.	1944	109
5	Texas & Pac. 1 Mt.	2000	103½
—	Do. 5 p.c. 2 Mt. Income	2000	35½
5	Toledo & Ohio Cent. 1 Mt. West. Div.	1935	105½
4½	Toledo., Walhon., Val., & Ohio 1 Mt.	1931-3	111
6	Union Pacific 1 Mt.	1896-9	102½
5	Do. Coll. Trust.		—
—	Union Pac., Linc., & Color. 1 Mt.	1918	—
4	United N. Jersey Gen. Mt. ..	1944	117½
6	Vicksbrg., Shrevept., & Pac. Pr. Ln. Mt.	1915	102½
5	Wabash 1 Mt.	1939	112
4	Wn. Pennsylvania Mt.	1928	109½
5	W. Virgn. & Pittsbg. 1 Mt.	1990	87
5	Wheeling & L. Erie 1 Mt. (Wheelg. Div.) 5 p.c.	1928	87
5	Do. Extd. Imp. Mt	1930	—
—	Do. do. Brown Shipley's Cts. ..		—
5	Willmar & Sioux Falls 1 Mt.	1938	111

STERLING.

Last Div.	Name.		Price.
6	Alabama Gt. Sthn. Deb.	1906	107½
5	Do. Gen. Mort. ..	1927-8	100
5	Alabama, N. Orl., Tex. & Pac. 5 p.c. "A" Dbs. ..	1910-40	99
55/	Do. do. "B" do.	1910-40	52
—	Do. do. "C" do.		19
—	Allegheny Valley	1910	136
4	Atlantic 1st Leased Line Perp. ..		98
6	Baltimore and Ohio	1902	109
6	Do. do.	1910	118
5	Do. do. 1877		97½
—	Do. Morgan's Certs. ..		97½
4½	Do. do.	1933	82
6	Chicago & Alton Cons. Mt.	1903	111
5	Chic. St. Paul & Kan. City Priority		105
6	Eastn. of Massachusetts	1906	117½
5	Illinois Cent. Skg. Fd.		105
5	Do.	1905	108
3½	Do.	1950	100½
4	Do. 1 Mt.	1951	114
3	Do. 1 Mt.	1951	94
6	Louisville & Nash., M. C. & L. Div., 1 Mt.	1902	104½
7	Do. 1 Mt. (Memphis & O.)	1901	111
47/4	Mexican Nat. "A" Certs. 5 p.c. Non. cum.		48
—	Do. "B" Certs.		11
6	N.Y. & Canada 1 Mt.	1904	111½
6	N. York Cent. & H.R. Mort.	1903	112
4½	N. York, Penns., & Ohio Pr. Ln. Extd.	1935	—
5	Do. Equip. Tst.		103½
5	Do. 5 p.c. Equip. Tst. (1890)		103½
6	Nrthn. Cent. Cons. Gen. Mt. ..		106
6	Pennsylvania Gen. Mt.	1910	129
6	Do. Cons. Skg. Fd. Mt.	1905	117
3½	Do. Cons. Mt.	1945	107
6	Phil. & Erie Cons. Mort ..	1920	134½
6	Phil. & Reading Gen. Cons. Mort.	1911	127
6	Pittsbg. & Connells. Cons.	1926	112
—	Do. Morgan's Certs.		112
4	St. Paul, Min., & Manitoba (Pac. Extn.)	1940	99
6	S. & N. Alabama	1903	107½
6	Union Pacific, Omaha Bridge	1896	—
6	Un. N. Jersey & C. Gen. Mt.	1901	112½

FOREIGN RAILWAYS.

Last Div.	Name.	Paid.	Price.
4/	Alagoas, Ltd., Shs.	20	6
5	Do. Deb. Stk., Red. ..	100	53
6	Antofagasta, Ltd., Stk. ..	100	80
4	Do. Perp. Deb. Stk. ..	100	94
—	Arauco, Ld., Ord. Shs. ..	10	¼
—	Do. 10 p.c. Cum. Pref.	10	1½
20/	Argentine Gt. W., Ld.,	20	15
20/	Do. 5 p.c. Cum. Pref. Shs.	20	20½
4	Do. 1 Deb. Stk.	100	105
1/0/0	Argentine N.E., Ltd., 6 p.c. Cum. Pref. Stk. ..	100	12
—	Do. 5 p.c. Deb. Stk., Red.	100	35
2/	Arica and Tacna Shs. ..	20	1½
10/	Bahia & San Fcisco., Ld.,	20	11½
6/	Do. Timbo. Bch. Shs.	20	5½
12/	Bahia, Blanca, & N.W. Ln. Prf. Cum. 6 p.c. ..	100	60½
4	Do. 4 p.c. 1 Deb. Stk., Red.	100	96
6	Barranquilla R. & P., Ld., 6 p.c. 1 Deb. Stk. Red.	100	95

Foreign Railways (*continued*):—

Last Div.	Name.	Paid.	Price.
3/	Bilbao Riv. & Cantabn., Ltd., Ord.	3	6
—	Bolivar, Ltd., Shs.	10	1¼
6	Do. 6 p.c. Deb. Stk.	100	99½
—	Brazil Gt. Southn. Ltd., 7 p.c. Cum. Pref.	20	1½
6	Do. Perm. Deb. Stk	100	47½
6½	B. Ayres Gt. Southn., Ld., Ord. Stk.	100	158
5	Do. Pref. Stk.	100	140
4	Do. Deb. Stk.	100	117½
30/	B. Ayres & Ensen. Port., Ltd., Ord. Stk.	100	53
5	Do. Cum. 1 Pref. Stk.	100	119
6/0/0	Do. 6p.c. Con. Pref. Stk.	100	98
4	Do. Deb. Stk., Irred.	100	103
9 7/8	B. Ayres Northern, Ltd., Ord. Stk.	100	270
12	Do. Pref. Stk.	100	325
5	Do. 5p.c. Mt. Deb. Stk., Red.	100	113
3/15/0	B. Ayres & Pac., Ld., 7 p.c. 1 Pref. Stk. (Cum.)	100	104
4	Do. 1 Deb. Stk.	100	105
5/5/0	Do. 4½ p.c. 2 Deb. Stk.	100	94
1	B. Ayres & Rosario, Ltd., Ord. Stk.	100	77
—	Do. New, £20 Shs.	20	22½
7/	Do. 7 p.c. Pref. Shs.	10	17½
7/	Do. Sunchales Ext.	10	15½
4	Do. Deb. Stk., Red.	100	109
12/	B. Ayres & Val. Trans., Ltd., 7 p.c. Cum. Pref.	20	7
4	Do. 4 p.c. "A" Deb. Stk., Red.	100	72
—	Do. 6 p.c. "B" Deb. Stk., Red.	100	48
6/	B. Ayres Westn. Ld. Ord.	10	12
3/	Do. Def. Shs.	10	7½
5	Do. 5 p.c. Pref.	10	13½
4	Do. Deb. Stk	100	112
6	Cent. Arg. Deb. Sk. Rd.	100	162½
4	Do. Deb. Stk. Rd	100	112
6	Cent. Bahia L. Ord. Stk.	100	51½
6	Do. Deb. Stk., 1934	100	74½
5	Do. Deb. Stk., 1937	100	58
1/6	Cent. Uguy. East. Ext. L. Shs.	10	6½
5	Do. Perm. Stk.	100	109
3/	Do. Nthn. Ext. L. Sh.	10	4½
5	Do. Perm. Deb. Stk.	100	106
3	Do. of Montev. Ltd., Ord. Stk.	100	90
6	Do. Perm. Deb. Stk.	100	142
10/	Conde d'Eu, Ltd. Ord.	20	7½
—	Cordba & Rosar., Ltd., 6 p.c. Pref. Shs.	100	50
4	Do. 1 Deb. Stk	100	97½
25/	Do. 6 p.c. Deb. Stk	100	91
—	Cordba Cent., Ltd., 5 p.c. Cu. 1 Pref. Stk	100	93
—	Do. 5 p.c. Non-Cum. 2 Pref. Stk	100	54
5	Do. Deb. Stk	100	125
—	Costa Rica, Ltd., Shs.	10	4
8/	Dna. Thrsa. Chris., Ltd., 7 p.c. Pref. Shs.	20	4½
20/	E. Argentine, Ltd	100	46
6	Do. Deb. Stk	100	108
1/1	Egyptn. Dlta. Lgt. Rys., Ltd., £10 Pref. Shs.	6	8½
—	Entre Rios, L., Ord. Shs.	5	1
—	Do. Cu. 5 p.c. Pref.	5	3½
6/	Gt. Westn. Brazil, Ltd.,	20	11½
6	Do. Perm. Deb. Stk	100	90½
6	Do. Extn. Deb. Stk	100	70½
—	Int.-Oceanic Mex., Ltd., 7 p.c. Pref	10	1⅜
4	Do. Deb. Stk	100	87
42/6	Do. 7 p.c. "A" Deb. Sk.	100	65
—	Do. 7 p.c. "B" Deb. Sk.	100	33
5/	La Guaira & Carac.	10	7
5	Do. 5 p.c. Deb. Sk. Red.	100	102
8/4	Lembg.-Czern.-Jassy	30	25
1/	Lima, Ltd.	20	2½
—	Manila Ltd. 7 p.c. Cu. Pf.	10	⅜
20/6½	Mexican and Pref. 6 p.c.	100	38
6	Do. Perp. Deb. Stk.	100	146
1/0/0	Mexican Sthrn., Ld., Ord.	100	27
—	Do. 4 p.c. 1 Db. Stk. Rd.	100	85
—	Do. 4 p.c. 2 do.	100	63
—	Mid. Urgy., Ltd.	100	20
5	Do. Deb. Stk.	100	63
12/	Minas & Rio, Ltd.	20	12½
5/2	Namur & Liege	20	12½
11/6	Do. Pref	20	28
5/	Natal & Na. Cruz, Ld., 7 p.c. Cum Pref.	20	8½
—	Nitrate Ltd., Ord.	10	6
—	Do. 7 p.c. Pr. Con. Or.	10	4½
—	Do. Def. Conv. Ord.	10	1
7/	N.-E. Urgy., Ltd., Ord.	10	15
7/	Do. 7 p.c. Pref.	10	15½
—	N.-W. Argentine Ld., 7 p.c. Pref.	10	3½
6	Do. 6 p.c. 1 Deb. Stk.	100	114
—	Do. 2 Deb. Stk.	100	94
—	N.W. Uruguay 6 p.c. 1 Pref. Stk.	100	17
—	Do. 5 p.c. 2 Pref. Stk.	100	7½
6	Do. 6 p.c. Deb. Stk.	100	78½
16/	Ottoman (Sm. Aid.)	20	16½
—	Paraguay Cntl., Ld., 5 p.c. Perm. Deb. Stk.	100	11
—	Piræus, Ath., & Pelo.	275	1½
5/	Pto. Alegre & N. Hambg. Ld., 7 p.c. Pref. Shs.	20	4½
6	Do. Mt. Deb. Stk. Red.	100	77½
—	Puerto Cabello & Val. Ld.	10	1½
5	Recife & S. Francisco	100	77
24/	R. Claro S. Paulo, Ld., Sh.	10	22½
5	Do. Deb. Stk.	100	131
	Royal Sardinian Ord.	10	11½
5/	Royal Sardinian Pref.	10	12½
5/	Sambre & Meuse	20	19
5/6	Do. Pref.	10	12
28/	San Paulo Ld.	20	37
2/9½	Do. New Ord. £10 sh.	4	8½
2/	Do. 5 p.c. Non. Cm. Pref.	10	12½
5½	Do. Deb. Stk.	100	137
5	Do. 5 p.c. Deb. Stk.	100	128
—	S. Fé & Cordova, Gt. Sthn., Ld., Shares	100	57
6	Do. Perp. Deb. Stk.	100	121
3/2½	S. Austrian	20	7½
10/	Sthn. Braz. R. Gde. do Sul, Ld.	20	9
6	Do. 6 p.c. Deb. Stk.	100	77
4	Swedish Centl., Ld., 4 p.c. Deb. Stk.	100	109
5	Do. Pref.	100	100
1/9	Taltal, Ld.	5	3
—	Uruguay Nthn., Ld. 7 p.c. Pfd. Stk.	100	8
3½	Do. 5 p.c. Deb. Stk.	100	30
—	Villa Maria & Rufino, Ld., 6 p.c. Pref. Shs.	100	20
4	Do. 4 p.c. 1 Deb. Stk.	100	76
6/0/0	Do. 6 p.c. 2 Deb. Stk.	100	49
5/0	West Flanders	8½	22
5/6	Do. 5½ p.c. Pref.	10	18
3/	Wstn. of Havana, Ld.	10	5

FOREIGN RAILWAY OBLIGATIONS

Per Cent.	Name.	Price.
6	Alagoas Ld., 6 p.c. Deb., Rd.	87½
—	Alcoy & Gandia, Ld., 5 p.c. Debs., Red.	25
5	Arauco, Ld., 5 p.c. 1st Mt., Rd.	67½
—	Do. 6 p.c. Mt. Deb., Rd.	48½
6	Brazil G. Sthn., L., Mt. Dbs., Rd.	83½
6	Do. Mt. Dbs. 1891, Rd.	48½
5½	Campos & Caran. Dbs., Rd.	76
6	Central Bahia, L., Dbs., Rd.	90½
5½	Conde d'Eu, L., Dbs., Rd.	78
6	Costa Rica, L., 1st Mt. Dbs., Rd.	109
6	Do. 2nd Dbs., Rd.	95
5	Do. Prior Mt. Db., Rd.	107
6	Cucuta Mt. Dbs., Rd.	104
5½	Donna Thrsa. Cris., L., Dbs., Rd.	75
3	Eastn. of France, £20 Dbs., Rd.	19½
4	Egyptn. Delta Light, L., Db., Rd.	100
—	Espito. Santo & Cara. 5 p.c. Stl. Dbs., Rd.	38
4	Gd. Russian Nic., Rd.	102
5	Inter-Oceanic Mex., L., 5 p.c. Pr. Ln. Dbs., Rd.	104
3	Ital. 3 p.c. Bds. A & B, Rd	57½
—	Ituana 6 p.c. Debs., 1918	72½
—	Leopoldina, 6 p.c. Dbs. £50 Bds.,	26
—	Do. do. Comms. Cert.	26
—	Do. 5 p.c. Stg. Dbs. (1883), Rd.	36
—	Do. do. Comm. Certs.	36
—	Do. 5 p.c. Stg. Dbs. (1890), Rd.	26
—	Do. do. Comms. Certs.	26
—	Macahé & Cam. 5 p.c. Dbs., Rd.	36
—	Do. do. Comms. Certs.	36
—	Do. (Cantagallo), 5 p.c., Red.	36
—	Do. do. Comm. Certs.	36
—	Manila Ltd., 6 p.c. Deb., Red.	24
6	Do. Prior Lien Mt., Rd.	105
6	Do. Series "B," Rd.	79
7	Matanzas & Sab., Rd.	101½
6	Minas & Rio, L., 6 p.c. Dbs., Rd.	102
5	Mogyana 5 p.c. Deb. Bds., Rd.	103
5	Moscow-Jaros., Rd.	107½
5½	Natal & Na. Cruz Ltd., 5½ p.c. Debs., Red.	88½
5	Nitrate, Ltd. Mt. Bds., Red.	88½
3	Nthn. France, Red.	19½
4	N. of S. Af. Rep. (Trnsvl.) Gu. Bds. Red.	97
3	Nthn. of Spain £20 Pri. Obs. Red.	9
6	Ottmn. (Smy to A.)(Kujk) Aant. Debs., Red.	109
6	Ottmn. (Seraik.) Asg. Debs. Red.	109
6	Ottmn. (Seraik.) Non-Asg. D., Rd	109
5	Ottmn. Kuyjk. Ext. Red.	109
5	Ottmn. Serkeuy. Ext. Red.	104
5	Ottmn. Tireh Ext. 1910	99
5	Ottmn. Debs, 1886, Red.	98
5	Do. 1888, Red. 1935	99
5	Do. 1893, Red. 1935	99
5	Ottmn. of Anlia. Debs., Rd.	93
5	Do. Ser. II	89
4	Ottomn. Smyr. & Cas. Ext. Bds., Red.	83½
3	Paris, Lyon & Medit. (old sys., £20), Red.	19
3	Paris, Lyon & Medit. (new sys., £20), Red.	19½
50/	Piræus, At. & Pelp., 6 p.c. 1st Mt. Bds., Red.	88½
3	Do. 5 p.c. Mt. Bds., Red.	61½
4	Pretoria-Pietbg., Ltd., Red.	94
7	Puerto Cab. & Val., Ltd., 1st Mt. Debs., Red.	96
—	Rio de Jano. & Nthn., Ltd., 6 p.c. £100 Deb., Red.	26
—	Rio de Jano. (Gr. Para.), 5 p.c. 1st Mt. St. £100 Debs., Red.	26
3	Royal Sardinian, A, Rd. £20	12
3	Royal Sardinian, B., Rd. £20	12
5	Ryl. Trns.-Afric. 5 p.c. 1st Mt. £100 Bds., Red.	61
7	Sogua La Grande, B pRd.	98
4	Sa. Fe & Cor. G.S., Ld. Pr Ln. Bds.	103
5	Sa. Fe, 5 p.c. 2nd Reg. Dbs.	81
3	South Austrian, £20 Red.	15½
3	South Austrian, (Ser X.)	15½
3	South Italian £20 Obs. (Ser. A to G), Red.	12½
3½	S.W. of Venez (Barq.), Ltd., 7 p.c. 1st Mt. £100 Debs.	57½
5	Taltal, Ltd., 5 p.c. 1st Ch. Debs., Red.	99
5	Utd. Rwys. Havana, Red.	87½
3	Wstn. of France, £20 Red.	19½
6	Wrn. B. Ayres St. Mt. Debs., 1902	111
6	Wrn. B. Ayres, Reg. Cert.	109
5	Do. Mt. Bds.	122
6	Wtrn. of Havna., Ld, Mt. Dbs., Rd.	102
7	Wrn. Ry. San Paulo Red.	101
—	Wrn. Santa Fé, 7 p.c. Red.	42
4/7	Zafra & Huelva, 3 p.c. Red.	3

BANKS.

Div.	Name.	Paid.	Price.
1/9½	Agra, Ltd.	6	3½
4/2½	Anglo-Argentine, Ltd., £9	7	5½
8½ Rs.	Anglo-Austrian	120f	14
6/	Anglo-Californian, Ltd., £20 Shares	10	11½
4/	Anglo-Egyptian, Ltd., £15	5	6
3/6	Anglo-Foreign Bkg., Ltd.	7	8
2/	Anglo-Italian, Ltd.	5	7½
7/6	Bk. of Africa, Ltd., £18¾	6¼	11
20/	Bk. of Australasia	40	56
8/	Bk. of Brit. Columbia	20	20½
25/	Bk. of Brit. N. America	50	66
7/6	Bk. of Egypt, Ltd., £25	12½	19
5/	Bk. of Mauritius, Ltd.	10	10
18/	Bk. of N. S. Wales	20	38½
4 p.c.	Bk. of N. Zland. Gua. Stk.	100	103
6/	Bk. of Roumania, £20 Shs.	6	7½
2/6	Tarapaca & Ldn., Ltd., £10	5	3½
—	Bque. Fse. de l'Afri. du S.	100f	3½
f.12.50	Bque. Internatle. de Paris	20	24
6/	Brit. Bk. of S. America, Ltd., £20 Shares	10	11
16/	Capital & Cties., L., £50	10	39
16/	Chart. of India, &c.	20	30½
10/	City, Ltd., £40 Shares	10	20
18/	Colonial, £100 Shares	30	23
10/	Delhi and London, Ltd.	25	—
5/	German of London, Ltd.	10	11
25/	Hong-Kong & Shanghai	28½	45
4/	Imperl. of Persia	6½	3½
10/	Imperl. Ottoman, £20 Shs	10	12½
9/	Intrnatl. of Ldn., Ld., £20	15	11½
20/	Ionian, Ltd.	25	15
12/	Lloyds, Ltd., £50 Shs.	8	30½
10/	Ldn. & Braziln. Ltd., £20	10	18
44/	Ldn. & County, Ltd., £80	20	104½
5/	Ldn. & Hanseatic, L., £20	10	11
22/6	Ldn. & Midland, L., £60	12½	53
8/9	Ldn. & Provin., Ltd., £10	5	22½
39/	Ldn. & Riv. Plate, L., £25	15	54
2/1½	Ldn. & San Fcisco, Ltd.	7	4½
24/	Ldn. & Sth. West., L., £50	20	72
26/	Ldn. & Westmins., L., £100	20	56½
3/	Ldn. of Mex. & S. Amer., Ltd., £10 Shs.	6	5½
15/	Ldn. Joint Stk., L., £100	15	34
9/7	Ldn., Paris & Amer., L. £20	16	26
1/7½	Merchant Bkg., L., £9	4	2½
6/3	Metropn, Ltd., £50 Shs.	5	13½
9/	National, Ltd., £50 Shs.	10	19½
4/5	Natl. of Mexico, $100 Shs.	$40	13
1/3	National of N. Z., L., £7½	2½	2½
3/	National S. Afric. Rep.	10	14½
18/10½	National Provcl. of Eng., Ltd., £75 Shs.	10½	50
21/7½	Do. do. £60 Shs.	12	56½
6/6	North Eastn., Ltd., £20 Shs	6	14½
19/	Parr's, Ld., £100 Shs.	20	93½
12/6	Prov. of Ireland, L., £100	12½	28½
40/	Stand. of S. Afric., L., £100	25	68
12/6	Union of Australia, L., £75	25	30
4 p.c.	Do. do. Ins. Stk. Dep. 1900	100	103
15/6	Union of Ldn., Ltd., £100	15½	35½

BREWERIES AND DISTILLERIES.

Div.	Name.	Paid.	Price.
4½	Albion Prp. 1 Mt. Db. Sk.	100	115
4	All Saints', L., Db. Sk. Rd.	100	99
6	Allsopp, Ltd	100	164
6	Do. Cum. Pref	100	160
4½	Do. Deb. Stk., Red.	100	117
3½	Do. Deb. Stk., Red.	100	103
4½	Alton & Co., L., Db., Rd	100	106
4½	Do. Mt. Bds., 1896	100	105
—	Arnold, Perrett, Ltd.	10	7
6	Do. Cum. Pref.	10	10
4½	Do. 1 Mt. Db. Stk., Rd.	100	106

Breweries, &c. (*continued*):—

Div.	Name.	Paid.	Price.
5½	Arrol, A., & Sons, L., Cum. Pref. Shs.	10	10½
4½	Do. 1 Mt. Db. Stk., Rd.	100	106
6	Backus, 1 Mt. Db., Red.	100	59½
4	Barclay, Perk., L., Cu. Pf.	10	11½
3½	Do. Mt. Db. Stk., Red.	100	111
—	Barnsley, Ltd.	10	11
6	Do. Cum. Pref.	10	13
1/	Barrett's, Ltd	2½	1½
1/3	Do. 5 p.c. Pref.	2½	2½
3/	Bartholomay, Ltd.	10	4
8	Do. Cum. Pref.	10	9
6	Do. Deb.	100	102½
5	Bass, Ratcliff, Ltd., Cum. Pref. Stk. (†)	100	147½
4½	Do. Mt. Db. Stk., Rd.	100	126
4	Bell, John, Ltd., 1 Mt. Deb. Stk., Red.	100	102
2/6	Benskin's, L., Cum. Pref.	5	—
4½	Do. 1 Mt. Db. Stk Red.	100	—
4½	Do. "B" Deb. Sk, Rd.	100	—
7/	Bentley's Yorks., Ltd.	10	11
6	Do. Cum. Pref.	10	12½
4½	Do. Mt. Debs., Red.	100	109
4½	Do. do. 1 92, Red.	100	109
—	Bieckert's, Ltd.	20	2
5	Do. Debs., Red.	100	56
—	Birmingham., Ltd., 6 p.c. Cum. Pref.	5	2½
4½	Do. Mt. Debs., Red.	50	40½
5½	Boardman's, Ld., Cm. Pf.	10	8½
4½	Do., Perp. 1 Mt. Db. Sk. †	100	103½
4½	Brakspear, L., 1 D. Stk. Rd	100	109
4	Brandon's, L., 1 D. Stk. R. †	100	103½
17/	Bristol (Georges) Ltd.	10	47
6	Do. Cum. Pref.	10	18
5	Do. Mt. Db. Sk. 1888 Rd.	100	115½
—	Bristol United, Ltd.	10	36½
6	Do. Cum. Pref.	10	16½
4½	Do. Db. Sk. Rd.	100	126
5½	Buckley's, L., C. Pre-prf.	10	11
4½	Do. 1 Mt. Db. Stk. Rd.	100	105½
4	Bullard & Sns, L., D. Sk. R.	100	107
6	Bushell, Watk., L., C. Pf.	10	13½
4½	Do. 1 Mt. Db. Sk. Rd.	100	112
5	Camden, Ltd., Cum. Pref.	10	11½
4½	Do. 1 Mt. Db. Sk. Rd.	100	109
5½	Cameron, Ltd., Cm. Pf.	10	13½
4½	Do. Mort Deb. Stk.	100	108
3½	Do. Perp Mt. Db. Sk.	100	100½
5	Cam'bell, J'stone, L., C. Pf.	5	5
4½	Do. 4½ p.c. 1 Mt. Db. Sk.	100	106
4	Campbell, Praed, L., Per. 1 Mort. Deb. Stk.	100	106
4	Cannon, L., Mt. Db. Stk.	100	109
4	Do. "B" Deb. Stk.	100	105
5	Castlemaine, L., 1 Mt. Db.	100	94
3½	Charrington, Ltd., Mort. Deb. Stk. Red.	100	107
2/	Cheltnhm. Orig., Ltd.	5	7
6	Do. Cum. Pref.	5	8
4	Do. Debs. Red.	100	107
—	Chicago, Ltd.	10	3½
6	Do. Debs.	100	87½
—	Cincinnati, Ltd.	10	1
8	Do. Cum. Pref.	10	1½
10/	City of Baltimore	10	4
16/	Do. 8 p.c. Cum. Pref	10	8
14/	City of Chicago, Ltd.	10	1½
8	Do. Cum. Pref.	10	6½
8	City of London, Ltd.	100	210½
5	Do. Cum. Pref.	100	140
4	Do. Mt. Deb. Stk., Rd.	100	112½
2/6	Colchester, Ltd.	5	4½
7	Do. Pref.	5	6½
4½	Do. Deb. Stk., Red.	100	110
5	Combe, Ltd., Cum. Pref.	10	14½
4	Do. Mt. Db. Stk, Rd.	100	112
3½	Do. Perp. Deb. Stk.	100	107
5	Comm'cial, L., D. Sk., Rd.	100	108½
5	Courage, L., Cm. Pref. Shs.	100	139½
4	Do. Irr. Mt. Deb. Stk.	100	130
3½	Do. Irr. "B" Mt. Db. Sk.	100	106
6	Daniell & Sons, Ltd.	10	7½
7	Do. Cum. Pref.	10	12
4½	Do. 1 Mt. Perp. Db. Sk.	100	108½
4½	Do. "B" Deb. Stk.	100	99
10d.	Dartford, Ltd.	5	4½
10d.	Do. Cum. Pref.	5	5½
4	Do. 1 Mt. Db. Sk. Rd.	100	101
4	Davenport, Ld., 1 D. Stk. †	100	102½
10/	Denver United, Ltd.	10	3½
8	Do. Cum. Pref.	10	8½
6	Do. Debs.	100	98½
4½	Deuchar, L., 1 D. Sk., Rd.	100	108
8/	Distillers, Ltd.	10	24
4½	Do. Mt. Db. Stk., Rd.	100	115½
—	Dublin Distillers, Ltd.	5	1½
6/	Do. Cum. Pref.	5	4½
4½	Do. Irr. Deb. Stk.	100	—
5	Eadie, Ltd., Cum. Pref.	10	11½
4	Do. Irr. 1 Mt. Db. Sk.	100	108
17/	Edinbgh. Utd., Ltd.	10	13
6	Do. Cum. Prf.	10	13½
5	Do. 1 Mt. Dbs. †	100	110½
4	Eldridge, Pope, L. D. St. R.	100	110
3/	Emerald & Phoenix, Ltd.	10	1½
8	Do. Cum. Pref.	10	6
6	Empress Ltd., C. Pf.	10	11½
4½	Do. Mt. Deb. Stk.	100	105
10/	Farnham, Ltd.	10	15½
6	Do. Cum. Pref.	10	15
4	Fenwick, L., 1 D. Sk., Rd.	100	108
4	Flower & Sons, Irr. D. Sk.	100	111
4	Friary, L., 1 Db. Stk., Rd. †	100	105½
4	Do. 1 "A" Db. Sk., Rd	100	102
4½	Groves, L., 1 Db. Sk., Rd	100	110
24	Guinness, Ltd.	100	610
6	Do. Cum. Prf. Stk.	100	[illegible]
5	Do. Deb. Stk., Red.	100	123
6	Hall's Oxford L., Cm. Pf.	5	6½
6/	Hancock, Ld., Cm. Pf. Ord.	10	14
	Do. Def. Ord.	10	17½

Breweries, &c. (*continued*) :—

Div.	Name.	Paid.	Price.
6	Hancock, Ld., Cum. Pref.	10	15½
4	Do. 1 Deb. Stk., Rd.	100	113
5	Hoare, Ltd. Cum. Pref.	10	13½
5	Do. "A" Cum. Pref.	10	12½
4	Do. Mt. Deb. Stk., Rd.	100	111
3½	Do. do. do. Rd.	100	104
4/6	Hodgson's, Ltd.	5	9¾
5	Do. 1 Mt. Db., Red.	—	120½
4	Do. 2 Mt. Db., 1906	—	102
4½	Hopcraft & N., Ltd., 1 Mt. Deb. Stk., Red.	100	103
5	Huggins, Ltd., Cm. Prf.	10	12½
4½	Do. 1st D. Stk. Rd.	100	112
4½	Do. "B" Db. Stk. Rd.	100	111
8/	Hull, Ltd.	10	17
7	Do. Cum. Pref.	10	15
4½	Ind, Coope, L., D. Sk., Rd.	100	119
4	Do. "B" Mt. Db. Stk. Rd.	100	115
8/	Indianapolis, Ltd.	10	3½
8	Do. Cm. Prf.	10	9
5/	Jones, Frank, Ltd.	10	4
7½	Do. Cum. Pref.	10	8
5	Do. 1st Mort. Debs.	100	94½
4/	J. Kenward & Ct., Ltd.	5	5½
4½	Kingsbury, L., 1 D. Sk., Rd	100	—
4	Lacon, L., D. Stk., Red.	100	110
4	Do. Irrd. "B" D. Sk.	100	107
4/	Lascelles, Ltd.	5	10¾
6	Do. Cum. Pref.	5	7½
5	Leney, Ltd., Cum. Pref.	10	11½
4	Do. 1 Mt. Db. Stk. Rd.	100	104
17/	Lion, Ltd., £25 shares	17	50½
6/	Do. New £10 shares	6	17½
6	Do. Perp. Pref.	20	31
4	Do. B. Mt. Db. Sk. Rd.	100	110
4½	Lloyd & Y., Ltd., 1 Mt. Deb. Stk., Rd.	100	98½
4½	Locke & S., Ltd., Irr. 1st Mt. Deb. Stk.	100	100
4½	Lovibond, Ltd., 1st Mt. Deb. Stk., Rd.	100	102½
8/	Manchester, Ltd.	10	17½
7	Do. Cum. Pref.	10	17½
5	Marston, J., L., Cm. Prf.	10	10¾
4	Do. 1 Mt. Db. Sk., Rd.	100	101½
9/	Massey's Burnley, Ltd.	10	16
6	Do. Cum. Pref.	10	14½
4½	McCracken, Ltd., 1 Mt. Deb., 1908	100	62½
5	McEwan, Ltd., Cm. Pref.	10	15
5	Meux, Ltd., Cum. Pref.	10	14½
4	Do. Mt. Db. Stk. Red.	100	111
4½	Michell & A., Ltd., 1 Mt. Deb. Stk. Red.	100	105
4½	MileEndDist. Db. Sk. Rd.	100	108
—	Milwaukee & Chic., Ltd.	10	1½
4/	Do. Cum. Pref.	10	6½
4½	Michell, Toms, L., Db.	50	55
6	Morgan, Ltd., Cum. Pref.	10	14½
10/	Nalder & Coll., Ltd.	10	32
6	Do. Cum. Pref.	10	16
4½	Do. Deb. Red.	100	113
3/	New Beeston, Ltd.	5	5½
2/9	Do. Cum. Pref.	5	5
4	Do. Mt. Deb. Stk. Red.	100	97½
12/	Newcastle, Ltd.	10	20
6	Do. Cum. Pref.	10	15
5	Do. 1 Mt. Deb., 1911	100	110½
4	Do. "A" Deb. Stk. Red.	100	105
6/	New England, Ltd	10	5
8	Do. Cum. Pref.	10	9¾
6	Do. Debs. Red.	100	104½
4	New London, L., 1 D. Sk.	100	105
7/2	New Westminster, Ltd.	4	10½
2/4½	Do. Pref.	4	6½
—	New York, Ltd.	10	1
—	Do. 8 p.c. Cum. Pref.	10	3¾
6	Do. 1 Mt. Deb. Red.	100	83½
5	Noakes, Ld., Cum. Pref.	10	12
4	Do. 1 Mt. Db. Stk., Rd.	100	106
4½	Norfolk, L., "A" D. Sk. Rd.	100	106
10/	Northampton, Ld.	10	17
7	Do. Cum. Pref.	10	15½
6	Do. Cum. Pref.	10	13
5	Do. 1 Mt. Per. Db. Sk.	100	127
4	Nth. East., L., 1 D. Sk. Rd.	100	102
4½	N. Worcesters., L. Per. 1 Mort. Deb. Stock	100	93½
6	Nottingham, L., Cm. Prf.	10	11½
5	Do. 1 Mt. Deb. Stk., Red.	100	112
17/4	Do. "B" do. Red.	50	111½
6/	Ohlsson' Cape, Ld.	5	16½
7	Do. Cum. Pref.	5	8¾
4½	Do. 2nd Cum. Pref.	5	5½
5	Do. Deb. Stk., Red.	100	114
4½	Oldfield, L., 1 Mt. Db. Stk.	100	105
6	Page & Overt., L., Cm. Prf.	10	13½
4½	Do. 1 Mt. Dbs., Red.	100	108
10/	Parker's Burslem, Ltd.	10	25½
6	Do. Cum. Pref.	10	15
4	Do. 1 Mt. Db. Stk., Red.	100	113
4	Persse, Ld., 1 Mt. Db. Rd.	100	95½
4	Phipps, L., Irr. 1 Db. Stk.	100	115
5	Plymouth, L., Min. Cu. Pf.	10	13½
4½	Do. Mt. Deb. Stk., Red.	100	104½
4½	Pryor, Reid, L., 1 D.S., R.(†	100	105½
5	Reid's, Ld., Cm. Pref. Stk.	100	137½
4	Do. Mt. Deb. Stk., Red.	100	111
3½	Do. "B" Mt. Db. Stk., Rd	100	103
5	Rhondda Val., L., Cu. Pf	10	11
4½	Do. 1 Mt. Deb. Stk., Rd.	100	109
5	Robinson, Ld., Cum. Pref.	10	11½
4½	Do. 1 Mt. Perp. Db. Stk.	100	112
4/	Rochdale, Ltd.	10	5½
4½	Do. 1 Mt. Deb. Stk.	100	96½
7	Royal, Brentford, Ltd.	10	19
	Do. Cum. Pref.	10	14½
4½	Do. 1 Mt. Dbs. Red	100	112
6/	St. Louis, Ltd.	10	4
8	Do. Cum. Pref.	10	8¾
14/	St. Pauli, Ltd.	10	10
7	Do. Cum. Pref.	10	12
4½	Salt (T.), L., 1 Db. Sk. Rd.	100	111
	Do "B Db. Stk. Red.	100	108

Breweries, &c. (*continued*) :—

Div.	Name.	Paid.	Price.
6/7	San Francisco, Ltd.	10	⅜
8/	Do. 8 p.c. Cum. Pref.	10	½
4½	Savill Brs., L., D. Sk. Rd.	100	117
4½	Scarboro., Ltd., 1 Db. Stk.	100	104
4	Shaw (Hy.), Ltd., 1 Mt. Db. Stk., Red.	100	104
22/	Showell's, Ltd.	10	32½
7	Do. Cum. Pref.	10	17½
3/	Do. Gua. Shs.	5	7½
4½	Do. Mt. Db. Stk., Red.	100	—
4	Simonds, L., 1 D. Sk., Rd.	100	111
5½	Simson & McP., L., Cu. Pf.	10	9½
4½	Do. 1 Mt. Deb. Stk.	100	100
12/	Smith, Garrett, L., £20 Shs	10	15½
5	Do. Cum. Pref.	20	26
4½	Do. Mt. Db. Stk., Red.	100	—
5	Smith's, Tadcster, L., C Pf	10	11½
4½	Do. Deb. Stk., Red.	100	112
4	Do. Deb. Stk., Red.	100	108
4½	Star, L., 1 M. Db. Stk., Rd.	100	104
4	Steward & P., L., 1 D. Sk.	100	113
9/	Strettons Derby, Ltd.	10	13
6	Do. Cum. Pref.	10	13
4	Do. Irr. 1 Mt. Db. Stk.	100	104½
4½	Strong, Romsey, L., 1 D. S.	100	114
5	Stroud, L., Db. Sk., Rd.	100	111½
4½	Tadcaster To'er, L., D. Sk.	100	112
8/	Tamplin, Ltd	10	22
6	Do. Cum. Pref.	100	15
4	Do. "A" Db. Sk., Rd.	10	107
6	Thorne, Ltd., Cum. Pref.	10	14½
4	Do. Deb. Stk., Red.	100	104½
15/	Threlfall, Ltd.	10	48
6	Do. Cum. Pref.	10	16½
5	Do. 1 Mt. Dbs., Red.	100	116
4	Tollemache, L., D. Sk. Rd.	100	105
4	Truman, Hanb., D. Sk., R.	100	110
3	Do. "B" Mt. Db. Sk., Rd.	100	95
10/	United States, Ltd.	10	9½
8	Do. Cum. Pref.	10	12
6	Do. 1 Mt. Deb.	100	107½
6/	Walker & H., Ld., Cm. Prf.	10	11½
4½	Do. 1 Mt. Deb. Stk., Red.	100	107
5	Walker, Peter, Ld. Cm. Prf.	10	14½
4	Do. 1 Mt. Dbs. Red.	100	111
4	Wallingford, L., D. Sk. Rd.	100	107
6	Watney, Ld., Cm. Prf. Sk.	100	170
5	Do. Mt. Db. Sk., Rd.	100	117½
4½	Do. "B" Mt. Db. Sk., Rd.	100	111
3½	Do. Mt. Db. Stk.	100	101
5	Watney, D., Ld., Cm. Prf.	10	12½
4½	Do. 1 Mt. Db. Stk.	100	108
5	Wenlock Ltd., Pref.	10	12½
4	Do. 1 Mt. Db. Sk., Rd.	100	108
5	West Cheshire, L., Cu. Pf.	10	10½
4	Do. Irred. 1 Mt. Db. Sk.	100	100
4½	Whitbread, L., Cu. Pf. Sh.	100	124½
4	Do. Db. Stk., Red.	100	112
3½	Do. "B" Db. Stk., Rd.	100	101
9/	Wolverhmpton & D. Ld.	10	16
6	Do. Cum. Pref.	10	13
4½	Do. 1 Mt. Dbs., Red.	100	108
5½	Worthington, Ld., Cm. Prf.	10	15½
5½	Do. Cum. "B" Pref.	10	13½
4½	Do. Mt. Db. Sk., Rd.	100	113
3½	Do. Irr. "B" Db. Stk.	100	104
10/	Yates's Castle, Ltd.	10	12½
5	Do. Cum. Pref.	10	11
5	Younger W., L., Cu. Pf. Sh.	100	137½

CANALS AND DOCKS.

Last Div.	Name.	Paid.	Price.
4	Birmingham Canal	100	146
—	E. & W. India Dock	100	21½
4	Do. Deb. Stk.	100	112
85/	Do. Def. Deb. Stk.	100	90
3½	Do. 1st Mt. Certs.	100	111
4	Do. Mt. Bds. (1885)	—	101
40/	G. Junction Ord. Shs.	100	151½
6/	Do. do. Pref.	10	19
4½	King's Lynn Per. Db. Stk.	100	117½
2½	Leeds & Lpool Canal	100	71
2½	Lndn & St. Kath. Dks.	100	58½
4½	Do. Pref.	100	138½
4½	Do. Pref., 1878	100	134½
4½	Do. Pref., 1882	100	130
4	Do. Deb. Stk.	100	135
—	Mchester Ship C. 5 p.c. Pf.	10	1½
3½	Do. 1st Perp. Mt. Deb.	100	98
—	Milford Dks. Db. Stk. "A"	100	20
2	Millwall Dk.	100	61
5	Do. Perp. Pref.	100	145½
4½	Do. Pref.	100	108½
5	Do. New Per. Prf., 1887	100	128½
5	Do. Per. Deb. Stk.	100	152½
4/	Newhaven Har.	10	14½
2	N. Metropolitan	100	65
5	Sharpness Nw. Pf. "A" Sk.	100	144½
4	Do. Deb. Stk.	100	120½
4	Sheffield & S. Yorks Nav. 4½ p.c. Pref. Stk.	100	117½
36.432	Suez Canal	20	135½
5	Surrey Comcl. Dok., Ord.	100	150½
5	Do. Min. 4 p.c. Pref. "A"	110	152½
5	Do. Pref. "B"	100	150½
5	Do. do. "C"	100	150
5	Do. do. "D"	100	145½
4½	Do. Deb. Stk.	100	154½

COMMERCIAL, INDUSTRIAL, &c.

Last Div.	Name.	Paid.	Price.
5	Accles, L., 1 Mt. Db., Red.	100	84½
5/	Aërated Bread, Ltd.	1	12¾
—	African Gold Recovery, L.	1	½
2/	Aluminium, L., "A" Shs.	1	2½
4½	Do. 1 Mt. Db. Stk., Red.	100	99
5½	Amelia Nitr., L., 1 Mort. Deb., Red.	100	84½
7/	Anglo-Chil. Nitrate, Ltd., Cum. Pref.	10	7½
4½	Do. Cons. Mt. Bds., Red.	100	82½
4½	Anglo-Russian Cotton, Ld., 1 Charge Debs., Red.	100	98
11/3	Angus (G., & Co., L.), £10	7½	17
6/	Apollinaris, Ltd.	10	13
5/	Do. 5 p.c. Cum. Pref.	10	11½
4	Do. Irred. Deb. Stock	100	108
6/	Appleton, French, & S., L.	5	½
3/	Argentine Meat Pres., L., 7 p.c. Pref.	10	2½
5	Argentine Refinry, Db. Rd.	100	98
2/2	Armstrong, Whitw., Ltd.	1	3½
4	Do. Cum. Pref.	5	6½
5	Artisans', Labr. Dwllgs., L.	100	130½
4½	Do. Non-Cm. Prf., 1879	100	132½
4½	Do. do. 1884	100	132½
—	Asbestos & Asbestic, Ltd.	10	8½
2/7½	Ashley-grdns., L., C. Prf.	5	6½
4½	Do. 1 Mt. Deb. Stk.	100	115½
5/	Assam Rly. & Trdng., L., 8 p.c. Cum. Pref. "A"	10	15½
—	Do. Deferrd. "B" Shs.	1	4½
—	Do. do. (iss. f. pd)	1	3½
8/	Do. Cum. Pre-Prf. "A"	10	15
6/	Do. New Pref.	10	11½
5	Do. Debs., Red.	100	107
5	Do. Red. Mort. Debs.	100	109
6	Aust'lian Pastrl, L., Cu. Pf.	10	7½
6d.	Aylesbury Dairy, Ltd.	1	1½
4	Do. 4 p.c. Mt. Dbs.	100†	104½
20/	Babcock & Wilcox, Ltd.	10	32
6	Do. 6 p.c. Cm. Prf.	10	16½
8	Baker (Chs.), L., Cm. Pf.	5	9
8	Do. "B," Cm. Pref.	5	8
8d.	Barker (John), Ltd.	1	2¾
5½	Do. Cum. Pref.	5	7½
4½	Do. Irred. 1 Mt. Db. Stk.	100	132
—	Barnagore Jute, Ltd.	5	3
5	Do. Cum. Pref.	5	4¾
7½d.	Belgravia Dairy, Ltd.	1	1½
5/	Bell (R.) & Co., Ltd.	5	3½
1/	Bell's Asbestos, Ltd.	1	½
5	Do. Mt. Db. Bds., Rd.	100	103
10/	Bengal Mills, Ltd.	10	11½
6/	Do. 5 p.c. Cum. Prf.	10	10½
2/5	Benson (J. W.) L., Cm. Pf.	10	10½
12/4	Do. Perp. Mt. Db. Stk.	100	103½
6	Bergvik, L., 6 p.c. Cm. Pf.	10	12½
10/	Do. Dfd.	10	9
4½	Do. 1 Dbs., Red.	100	103½
5/	Birm'ham Vinegar, Ltd.	5	10
5	Do. Cum. Pref.	5	5¾
4½	Do. 1 Mt. Db. Stk., Rd.	100	107
5	Boake (A.) L., 5 p.c. Cu. Pf.	10	10½
2/6	Bodega, Ltd.	5	8
4½	Do. Mt. Deb. Stk., Rd.	100	111
8/	Bottomley & Brs., Ltd.	10	6½
6/	Do. 6 p.c. Pt.	10	9½
8½d.	Bovril, Ltd.	1	1 1/16
—	Do. Def.	1	5/16
6½d.	Do. Cum. Pref.	1	1 1/16
4½	Do. Deb. Stk.	100	103
6/4½	Bradbury, Gretrex., Ltd., £10 share	8	14
5/	Do. 5 p.c. Cum. Pref.	10	13½
5/	Brewers' Sugar, L., 5 p.c. Cum. Pref.	10	10¾
2/6	BrightonGrd. Hotel, Ld.	5	3½
4	Do. Mt. Db. Stk., Red.	100	102½
5	Bristol Hotel & Palm. Co., Ltd. 1st Mt. Red. Deb.	100	107½
9½d.	British & Bengton's Tea Tr. Asc., Ltd.	1	1½
5	Do. Cum. Prf.	5	5½
—	British Deli & Lgkat. Tobacco, Ltd.	1	1½
—	Do. Cum. Prf.	1	¾
—	British Tea Table, Ltd.	1	2¾
5½	Do. Cum. Pref.	1	1⅜
2/6	Brooke, Ben., & Co., Ltd., Cum. Pref.	5	5¾
7/6	Brooke, Bond & Co., Ltd.	5	20½
6	Brown Brs., L., Cum. Pref.	5	6
6/	Browne & Eagle, Ltd.	10	14
5	Do. Cum. Pref.	10	13
4	Do. Mrt. Db. Sk., Red.	100	109
20/	Brunner, Mond, & Co., Lt.	10	43
7/	Do. £10 shares	3½	17
7	Do. Cum. Pref.	10	18½
7	Do. £10 shares	5	8½
10/	Bryant & May, Ltd.	5	19½
2/	Bucknall, H., & Sons, Lt.	5	8
6	Do. Cum Pref.	5	8
4/	Burke, E. & J., Ltd.	5	7½
6	Do. Cum. Pref.	5	7½
6	Do. Irred. Deb. Stk.	100	155
1/	Burlington Htls. Co., Ltd	1	1½
5	Do. Cum. Pref.	1	1⅛
4	Do. Perp. Deb. Stk.	100	105½
2/4	Bush, W. J., & Co., Ltd., Cum. Pref.	5	5¾
36/8	Do. 1 Deb. Stk., Red.	100	104
5½	Callard, Stewart, & Watt, Ltd., Cum. Pref.	1	1½
4/	Callender's Cable L., Shs.	5	9
4½	Do. 1 Deb. Stk., Red.	100	109½
—	Campbell, R., & Sons, Lt.	3	2½
6	Cantareira Water, Bd., Rd	100	99½
5	Do. (2nd issue)	100	92
4	Cartavio Sugar, Ltd., 6 p.c. 1st Debs., Red.	20	80
4/6	Cassell & Co., Ltd., £10	9	18
5	Causton, Sir J., & Sons, Ltd., Cum. Pref.	10	13½

Commercial, &c. (*continued*) :—

Last Div.	Name.	Paid.	Price.
4	Cent. Prod. Mkt. of B.A. 1st Mt. Str. Debs.	100	77½
4	Chappell & Co., Ltd., Mt. Deb. Stk. Red.	100	102
6/	Chicago & N.W. Gran. 8 p.c. Cum. Pref.	10	2½
—	Chicago Packing & Prov.	10	6
8	Do. Cum. Pref.	10	10½
6/	City Offices, Ltd	36½	13
3½	Do. Mt. Deb. Stk.	100	108½
7/2½	Cy. London Real Prop., Ltd., £25 shs.	12	19
4/6	Do. £12½ shs.	7½	13½
3½	Do. Deb. Stk. Red.	100	108½
3½	Do. Deb. Stk. Red.	100	106½
3	Do.	100	101½
4/	Cy. of Santos Imprvts., Ltd., 7 p.c. Pref.	10	8½
20/	Clay, Bock, & Co., Ltd.	10	8
8	Do. Cum. Pref.	10	11
6	Do. Mort. Deb.	100	106½
20/	Coats, J. & P., Ltd.	10	61½
6	Do. Cum. Pref.	10	18
4½	Do. Deb. Stk. Red.	100	111½
9½d.	Coburg Hotel, Ltd	1	1⅛
4	Do. Deb. Stk. Red.	100	102
6	Colonial Consign & Dis., Ltd., Cum. Pref.	5	4½
4½	Do. 1st Mort. Debs.	100	97½
—	Colorado Nitrate, Ltd.	5	¾
4/	Co. Gén. des Asphtes. de F., Ltd.	6	6½
5	Do. Non-Cm. Prf.	—	5½
5	Cook, J. W., & Co., Ltd., Cum. Pref.	5	5⅝
5	Cook, T., & Son, Egypt, Ltd., 1st Mt. Deb. Red.	100	110½
—	Cork Co., Ltd., 6 p.c. Cum. Pref.	5	2½
5	Cory, W., & Sn, L., Cu. Pf.	5	6
4	Do. 1st Deb. Stk. Red.	100	109
8½d.	Crisp & Co., Ltd	1	1⅜
5½	Do. Cum. Pref.	1	1½
—	Crompton & Co., Ltd., 7 p.c. Cum. Pref.	5	2½
5	Do. 1st Mt. Reg. Deb.	—	88½
4/6	Crossley, J., & Sons, Ltd.	5	8½
5	Do. Cum. Pref.	5	6½
—	Crystal Pal. Ord. "A" Stk.	100	9½
—	Do. "B" Red. Stk	100	2
6	Do. 6 p.c. 1st 1887 Deb. Stk. Red.	100	117½
—	Do. 6 p.c. 2nd 1887 Deb. Stk. Red.	100	58½
—	Do. 6 p.c. 3rd 1887 Deb. Stk. Red.	100	22½
3	Do. 3 p.c. 1st 1895 Deb. Stk.	100	96½
—	Daimler Motor, Ltd.	10	5
4/	Dalgety & Co., £20 Shs.	5	5½
4½	Do. Deb. Stk	100	123
4	Do.	100	114
7/	De Keyser's Ryl. Htl., L.	10	13½
5	Do. Cum. Pref.	10	11½
4	Do. Deb. Stk., Red.	100	110
6	Denny, H., & Sons, Ltd., Cum. Pref.	10	15
5/3	Devas, Routledge & Co., L.	7	8¾
5	Dickinson, J., & Co., L., Cum. Pref. Stk.	100	123
4½	Domin. Cottn. Mls., Ltd. Mt. Stg. Dbs.	100	97
6/	Dorman, Long & Co., L.	5	4⅝
—	Eastmans, Ltd	10	3
12/	Do. 8 p.c. Cum. Pref.	10	10½
2/6	E. C. Powder, Ltd	3	5½
1/9½	Edison & Swn Utd. Elec. Ltd., "A" £5 Shs.	3	2¾
2/9½	Do. fully-paid	5	4½
4½	Ekman Pulp & Ppr. Co., Ltd., Mt. Deb., Red.	100	95
1/1½	Electric Construc., Ltd.	2	2¾
7	Do. Cum. Pref.	2	3½
10/	Eley Bros., Ltd.	10	40
—	Elmore's Cop. Deptg., L.	1	½
—	Elmore's Wire Mnfg., L.	2	½
—	Elysée Pal. Hotel Co., L.	5/	
5 p.c.	Do. 5 p.c. £100 Db., Rd.	70	70
8½d.	Evans, Ben., & Co., Ltd.	1	1
5	Do. 1 Mt. Db. Sk., Rd.	100	104
8½d.	Evans., D. H., & Co., L.	1	2
6	Do. Cum. Pref.	1	1⅛
4½	Do. 1 Mt. Db. Sk., Rd.	100	111
2/1	*Evening News*, L., 5 p.c. Cum. Pref.	5	5¾
5/3	Evered & Co., L., £10 Sh.	7	13½
7/6	Do.	10	19½
4	Fairbairn Pastoral Co., Aust., L., 1 Mt. Db., Rd.	100	102
6	Fairfield Shipbldg., Ltd., Cum. Pref.	10	10
4½	Do. Mort. Deb. Stk.	100	107½
6/	Farmer & Co., Ld., 6 p.c. Cum. Pref.	10	13½
10	Field, J. C. & J., Ltd.	10	10
14/	Do. 7 p.c. Cum. Pref.	10	14
9d.	Fordham, W. B., & Sns, Ld.	1	2
5/6	Fore-st. Warehouse, Ltd.	11	9½
4	Do. Regd. Debs., Rd.	100	103½
2/6	Foster, M. B. & Sons, Ltd.	4	5½
5	Do. Pref.	10	11½
7/	Foster, Porter, & Co., L.	10½	17
4	Fowler, J., & Co. (Leeds), Ltd., 1 Mt. Deb., Red.	100	102½
3/	Fraser & Chalmers, Ltd.	3	1½
4½	Free, Rodwell & Co., Ltd., Deb Stk.	100	105½
6½d.	Furness, T., & Co., Ltd., 5½ p.c. Cum. Pref.	1	1
4½	Gartside & Co. (of Manchstr), L., 1 Mt. Db. Sk.	100	110
5	Genl. Hydraul. Power, L.	100	290

Commercial, &c. (*continued*):—

Last Div.	Name.	Paid.	Price.
8/	Gillman & Spencer, Ltd.	5	2½
6	Do. Pref.	5	4¼
5	Do. Mort. Debs.	50	51
4	Goldsbro., Mort & Co., L., "A" Deb. Stk., Red.	100	72½
—	Do. 3 p.c. "B" Inc. Deb. Stk., Red	100	17
12/	Gordon Hotels, Ltd.	10	21¾
5½	Do. Cum. Pref.	10	14¾
4½	Do. Perp. Deb. Stk.	100	137½
4	Do. do.	100	124½
—	Greenwich Inld. Linoleum Co., Ltd.	1	⅜
7	Greenwood & Batley, Ltd., Cum. Pref.	10	10
7½d.	Hagemann & Co., Ltd., 6 p.c. Cum. Pref.	1	1⅛
—	Hammond, Ltd.	10	¾
—	Do. 8 p.c. Cum. Pref.	10	2
—	Do. 6 p.c. Cum. Inc. Stk. Red.	100	52½
4	Hampton & Sons, Ltd., 4 p.c. 1 Mt. Db. St. Red.	100	105
	Hans Crescent Htl., L., 6 p.c. Cum. Pref.	5	3½
4	Do. 1 Mt. Deb. Stk.	100	85
5	Harmsworth, Ld., Cm. Pf.	1	1⅛
4/	Harrison, Barber, Ltd.	5	4¼
1/	Harrod's Stores, Ltd.	1	5½
2/6	Do. Cum. Pref.	5	7⅛
5½	Hawaiian Comcl. & Sug. 1 Mt. Debs.	100	94½
5	Hazell, Watson, Ld., Cm. Pref.	10	12
6/	Henley's Teleg., Ltd.	10	23
7	Do. Pref. Shs.	10	19¼
4½	Do. Mt. Db. Stk., Rd.	100	112½
6	Henry, Ltd.	10	12½
5	Do. Cum. Pref.	10	13¼
4½	Do. Mt. Debs., Red.	50	53
6	Hepworth, Ld., Cm. Prf.	10	11¼
6/	Herrmann, Ltd.	5	4½
—	Hildesheimer, Ltd.	3	1½
9½d.	Holbrn. & Frasca, Ltd.	1	2½
5	Do. Cum. Pref.	10	12½
4	Do. Deb. Stk.	100	113
6	Home & Col. Stres, Ltd., Cum. Pref.	5	7½
6	Hood & M.'s Stes., Ltd., Cum. Pref.	1	¾
—	Hook, C. T., Ltd.	10	6
7/2	Hornsby, Ltd., £10 Shs.	8	3½
5/6	Do. 6 p.c. Cm. Pf. Sk.	100	90
—	Hotchks. Ordn., Ltd.	10	¾
—	Do. 7 p.c. Cm. Prf.	10	4½
5	Do. 1 Mt. Dbs., Rd.	100	95½
6	Htl. Cecil, Ld., Cm. Prf.	5	4¼
4	Do. 1 Mt. D. Sk., R.	100	105½
8/	Howard & Bulgh, Ltd.	10	36
6	Do. Pref.	10	16
4	Do. Deb. Stk., Red.	100	107
4/	Howell, J., Ltd., £5 Shs.	4	9½
—	Howell & Js., Ld., £3½ Shs.	3	⅜
1/6	Humber, Ltd.	1	[illegible]
6	Do. Cum. Pref.	1	[illegible]
2/6	Hunter, Wilts., Ltd.	5	7
2/7	Hyam Clthg., Ltd., 5 p.c. Cum. Pref.	5	5½
10/	Impl. Russn. Cotton, L.	5	5½
5	Impd. Industl. Dwgs., Ld.	100	130½
6d.	Do. Defrd.	1	1¼
£1	Impd. Wood Pave., Ltd.	10	16
5/	Ind. Rubber, Gutta Per. Telegraph Works, Ltd.	10	22½
4	Do. 1 Mt. Debs., Red.	100	105
6	Intern. Tea, Cum. Pref.	5	6¼
7½d.	Jays, Ltd.	1	1⅜
5½	Do. Cum. Pref.	5	6½
8½d.	Jones & Higgins, Ltd.	1	2¼
4½	Do. 1 Mt. Db. Sk., Rd.	100	113
5/	Kelly's Directory, Ltd., 5 p.c. Cum. Pref.	10	12¾
4	Do. Mort. Db. Sk., Rd.	100	105
—	Kent Coal Explrtn. Ltd.	1	⅜
5½d.	King, Howmann, Ltd.	1	1½
4/	Kinloch & Co., Ltd.	5	8¾
6	Do. Pref.	5	7
5	Lady's Pictorial Pub., Ltd., Cum. Pref.	5	5
—	La Guaira Harb., Ltd., 7 p.c. Deb. Stk.	100	—
—	Do. 2 Mt. 7 p.c. Deb. Bds., Red.	100	—
4/	Lagunas Nitrate, Ltd.	5	2½
2/	Lagunas Syn., Ltd.	5	1¼
5	Do. 1 Mt. Debs., Red.	100	80
—	L. Copais Ld., 1 Mt. 6 p.c. Debs., Red.	100	35½
3/	Lautaro Nitrate, Ltd.	5	4½
5	Do. 1 Mt. Debs., Red.	—	98
9/	Lawes Chem. L., £10 shs.	9	5½
14/	Do. N. Cm. Min. Pref.	10	13
—	Leeds Forge, 7 p.c. Cm. Pf.	5	2½
5	Do. 1 Mt. Debs., Red.	50	44½
5	Lever Bros., L., Cm. Pf.	10	13
6	Liberty, L., 6 p.c. Cm. Pf.	10	14¾
60/	Liebig's, Ltd.	20	76
5	Lilley & Sk., L., Cm. Pf.	5	5½
3/	Linoleum Manftg., Ltd.	5	24
3/	Linotype, Ltd., Pref.	5	5½
4/	Do. Def.	5	8
4/	Lister & Co., Ltd.	10	4
5	Do. Cum. Pref.	10	8½
5/	Liverpool. Nitrate	5	6½
—	Liverpool. Warehsg., Ltd.	10	3½
5½	Do. Cum. Pref.	10	8½
4	Do. 1 Mt. Db. Stk., Rd.	100	105½
5½	Lockharts, Ltd., Cm. Pf.	1	1⅛
4/6	Ldn. & Til. Lightrage £10	9	5⅛
6/	Ldn. Comcl. Sale Rms., Ltd.	10	18
—	Do. 1 Mt. Deb. Stk., Red.	100	104
3	London Nitrate, Ltd.	5	2

Commercial, &c. (*continued*):—

Last Div.	Name.	Paid.	Price.
4/	London Nitrate, Ld. 8 p.c. Cm. Min. Pf.	5	3½
3/	London Pavilion, Ltd.	5	8
1/6	London. Produce Clg. Ho., Ltd., £10 Shares	2½	3½
4/	London Stereos., Ltd.	5	3
6d.	Ldn. Un. Laun. L. Cm. Pf.	1	⅜
8½d.	Louise, Ltd.	1	⅝
5½	Do. Cum. Pref.	1	⅝
5/	Lovell & Christmas, Ltd.	5	12
6	Do. Cum. Pref.	5	7½
4	Do. Mt. Deb. Stk., Red.	100	107
1/3	Lyons, Ltd.	1	2½
4½	Do. 1 Mt. Deb., Stk., Rd.	100	106½
10/	Machinery Trust, Ltd.	5	15
4½	Do. 4½ Deb. Stk.	100	105
6	MacLellan, L., Min. C. Pf.	10	7½
5	Do. 1 Mt. Debs., 1900	100	101½
—	McEwan, J. & Co., Ltd.	10	1¼
6	Do. Mt. Debs., Red.	100	89½
8	McNamara, L., Cm. Pref.	10	9
7½d.	Maison Virot, Ltd.	1	1½
2/7	Do. 6 p.c. Cum. Pref.	5	4½
5/	Manbré Sacc., L., Cm. Pf.,	10	12
15/	Mangan Brze., L., £10 Shs.	6	15½
3/	Mason & Mason, Ltd.	5	3½
6	Do. Cum. Pref.	5	5½
—	Maynards, Ltd.	1	⅝
6	Do. Cum. Pref.	1	⅝
9½d.	Mazawattee Tea, Ltd.	1	1⅜
5	Do. Cum. Pref.	5	5½
6	Mellin's Food Cum. Pref.	5	7
4½	Met. Ascn. Imp. Dwlgs. L.	100	110
3½	Do. 1 Mt. Deb. Stk.	100	97
5	Metro. Indus. Dwlgs., Ltd.	5	5
4	Do. do. Cum. Pref.	5	5½
5	Metro. Prop., L., Cm. Pf.	5	6½
4½	Do. 1st Mt. Debs. Stk.	100	110½
6	Mexican Cotton 1 Mt. Db.	100	97½
4½	Mid. Class Dwlgs., L., Db.	100	120½
1/	Millars' Karri, Ltd.	1	2½
6	Do. Cum. Pref.	1	1⅜
8/	Milner's Safe, Ltd.	10	19½
10/	Moir & Son, Ltd., Pref.	5	9
6	Morgan Cruc., L., Cm. Pf.	10	15
2/	Morris, B., Ltd.	3½	3½
—	Murray L. 5½ p.c. C. Pf.	5	5½
—	Do. 4½ 1 Mt. Db. Sk. Rd.	100	108
2/6	Natnl. Dwlgs., L., 5 p.c. Pf.	5	1
1/7½	Nat. Safe Dep., Ltd.	4	3½
6	Do. Cum. Pref.	1	1⅛
—	Native Guano, Ltd.	5	⅜
5/	Nelson Bros., Ltd.	10	2½
5	Do. Deb. Stk., Red.	100	80½
4/	Neuchtel Asph., Ltd.	10	11
—	New Central Borneo, Ld.	1	—
10d.	New Darvel Tob., Ltd.	18/	1½
2/4	New Explosives, Ltd.	3	2
5/3	New Gd. Htl., Bham, L.	5	4
5½	Do. Pref.	5	4½
4	Do. 1 Mt. Db. Stk., Rd.	100	96½
—	New Julia Nitrate, Ltd.	10/	½
—	New Ldn. Borneo Tob., L.	16/	⅜
1/6	New Premier Cycle, Ltd.	1	½
6	Do. 6 p.c. Cum. Pref.	1	⅝
4½	Do. 4½ p.c. 1 Mt. Db. Rd	100	—
—	New Tamargl. Nitr., Ltd	1	½
—	Do. 8 p.c. Cum. Pref.	1	⅜
6	Do. 6 p.c. 1 Mt. Dbs. Rd.	100	65½
3·78d.	Newnes, G., L., Cm. Prf.	1	1⅛
1/3	Nitr. Provision, Ltd.	2½	¾
24/	Nobel-Dynam., Ltd.	10	18
—	North Brazn. Sugar, Ltd.	1	½
10/	Oakey, Ltd.	10	31
6	Do. Cum. Pref.	10	16
4/	Paccha Jarp. Nitr., Ltd.	5	1
5	Pac. Borax, L., 1 Db. Rd.	100	110
—	Palace Hotel, Ltd.	10	5
5½	Do. Cum. Pref.	10	9
4	Do. 1 Mt. Deb. Stk.	100	106
2/6	Palmer, Ltd.	5	1½
6	Do. Cum. Pref.	5	3½
9⅛d.	Paquin, Ltd.	1	1
6	Do. Cum. Pref.	5	4½
5½	Parnall, Ltd., Cum. Pref.	1	⅝
4/6	Pawsons, Ltd., £10 Shs.	6	6½
4	Do. Mt. Debs., Red.	100	107
6	Pearks, G. & T., Ltd., 6 p.c. Cum. Pref.	1	⅞
1/2½	Pears, Ltd.	1	1⅜
6	Do. Cum. Pref.	10	14½
5	Do. Deb. Stk.	100	129
5½	Pearson, C. A., L., Cu. Pf.	5	5
4/	Peebles, Ltd.	5	8
5	Do. Cum. Pref.	5	6½
4½	Do. Mt. Deb. Stk. Red.	100	112
5½	Peek Bros., Ltd., 1 Cum. Pref., Nos. 1-60,000	5	6½
3½	Do. 3½ p.c. 1 Db. Stk.	100	103½
7½d.	Pegamoid, Ltd.	1	⅝
—	Phospho-Guano, Ltd.	5	2½
—	Pillsbury-W. Fl. Mills, L.	10	2
16/	Do. 8 p.c. Cum. Pref.	10	6½
6	Do. 1 Mort. Debs.	100	96½
7½d.	Plummer, Ltd.	1	1⅛
5	Do. Cum. Pref.	5	5½
15/	Price's Candle, Ltd.	16	40
6	Priest Marians, L., Cm. Pf.	1	1⅛
6	Pryce Jones, Ld., Cm. Pf.	5	7½
5	Do. Deb. Stk.	100	120½
10.8d.	Pullman, Ltd.	1	1⅛
6d.	Do. Cum. Pref.	1	1⅛
11⅛	Raleigh Cycle, Ltd.	1	⅜
6	Do. Cum. Pref.	1	¾
—	Recife Drnge. Ld. 1 Mt. Debs., R	100	19
6	Redfern, Ltd. Cum. Prf.	10	14
5	Ridgways, Ltd., Cu. Pf.	5	5½
—	R. Janeiro Cy. Imps., Ld.	25	9½
5	Do. Debs.	100	87½
5	Do. 1889-1893	100	87½
11/	R. Jan Fl. Mills, Ltd.	7	7
5	Do. 1 Mt. Debs., Rd.	100	94

Commercial, &c. (*continued*):—

Last Div.	Name.	Paid.	Price.
—	Riv. Plate Meat, Ltd.	5	3½
—	Do. Pref.	5	5
8½d.	Roberts, J. R., Ltd.	1	1¼
5	Do. 1 Mt. Db. Sk., Rd.	100	112
8½d.	Roberts, T. R., Ltd.	1	2¼
5	Do. Cum. Pref.	1	1⅛
3/	Rosario Nit., Ltd.	5	3½
5	Do. Debs., Red.	100	104
5	Do. Huara, Debs.	—	102½
1/	Rover Cycle, Ltd.	1	⅝
6/	Ryl. Aquarium, Ltd.	5	5½
6	Do. Pref.	5	6
5	Ryl. Htl., Edin., Cm. Pf.	1	1⅛
1/2½	Ryl. Niger, Ltd., £10 Sh.	2	2½
6/	Do.	10	14½
3/	Ruston, Proctor, Ltd.	10	11
4½	Do. 1 Mort. Debs.	100	104
6/	Sadler, Ltd.	12	7
—	Sal. Carmen Nit., Ltd.	5	4½
9d.	Salmon & Gluck., Ltd.	1	1½
2/	Salt Union, Ltd.	10	2
14/	Do. 7 p.c. Pref.	10	8½
4½	Do. Deb. Stk.	100	108½
4½	Do. "B" Deb. Sk., Rd.	100	104½
—	San Donato Nit., Ltd.	5	⅝
2/6	San Jorge Nit., Ltd.	5	3½
—	San Pablo Nit., Ltd.	5	⅝
2/	San Sebastn. Nit., Ltd.	5	⅝
1/	Sanitas, Ltd	1	2½
—	Sa. Elena Nit., Ltd.	5	⅝
—	Sa. Rita Nit., Ltd.	5	2
10/	Savoy Hotel, Ltd.	10	19
7	Do. Pref.	10	16
4	Do. 1 Mt. Deb. Stk.	100	112½
5	Do. Debs., Red	100	102½
5	Do. & Ldn. For. Htl., Ltd., 5 p.c. Debs. Red.	100	99
1½d.	Schweppes, Ltd.	1	1⅛
—	Do. Def.	1	⅝
5	Do. Cum. Pref.	1	1⅛
4	Do. Deb. Stk.	100	107
1/	Singer Cyc., Ltd.	1	½
5½	Do. Cum. Pref.	1	⅝
—	Smokeless Pwdr., Ltd.	1	⅛
5½d.	S. Eng. Dairies, Ltd., 6 p.c. Cum. Pref.	1	1½
—	Sowler Thos. L.	1	1
—	Do. 5½ Cm. Pf.	5	5½
3/6	Spencer, Turner, & Co. Ltd	5	8½
5	Do. Cum. Pref.	5	6½
5	Spicer, Ld., 5 p.c. Dbs. Rd.	100	65
4/	Spiers & Pond, Ltd.	10	19
5	Do. 1 Mt. Debs., Red.	100	116½
5	Do. "A" Db. Stk., Rd.	100	110
5	Do. "B" 1 Db. Stk., Rd.	100	110
4	Do. Fd. "C" 1 Db. S., R.	100	103
5/	Spratt's, Ltd	5	13½
4	Do. Debs., 1914	—	105
5	Steiner Ld., Cm. Pf.	10	11½
4	Do. 1 Mt. Db. Sk. Rd.	100	106
7/	Stewart & Clydesdale, L.	10	14½
6	Do. Cum. Pref.	10	15½
—	Swan & Edgar, L.	1	1⅛
1/3	Sweetmeat Automatic, L.	1	4
2/9	Teetgen, Ltd., Cum. Pref.	5	5½
12/	Teleg. Construction., Ld.	12	40½
5	Do. Db. Bds., Rd., 1899	100	103½
3/0½	Tilling, Ld. 5½ p.c. Cm. Prf.	5	6
4	Do. 4 p.c. 1 Dbs., Rd.	—	103
8½d.	Tower Tea, Ltd.	1	1⅜
5	Do. Cum. Pref.	5	5½
5	Travers, Ltd., Cum. Pref.	10	12½
4	Do. 1 Mt. Dbs., Rd.	100	103
6	Tucuman Sug., 1 Dbs., Rd.	100	100
4/	United Alkali, Ltd.	10	2½
7	Do. Cum. Pref.	10	9½
5	Do. Mt. Db. Stk., Rd.	100	111½
2½d.	United Horse Shoe, Ltd., Non-Cum. 8 p.c. Pref.	1	⅝
5	Un. Kingm. Tea, Cm. Prf.	5	5
1/	Un. Lankat Plant., Ltd.	1	2½
2/	Un. Limmer Asphlte., Ld.	3	4½
5/	Val de Travers Asph., L.	10	14½
3/	V. den Bergh's, Ltd., Cm. Pref.	5	6½
6	Walkers, Park., L., C. Pf.	10	4
4½	Do. 1 Mt. Debs., Red.	100	90½
4/	Wallis, Thos. & Co., Ltd.	5	1¼
6	Do. Cum. Pref.	5	8½
5½	Waring, Ltd., Cum. Pref.	5	5½
4½	Do. 1 Mt. Db. Sk., Red.	100	111½
4½	Do. Irred. "B" Db. Stk.	100	104
12/	Waterlow, Dfd. Ord.	10	15½
12/	Do. Pref.	10	15½
—	Do. Cum. Pref.	10	10½
10/	Waterlow Bros. & L., Ld.	10	9
9½d.	Welford, Ltd.	1	2½
4½	Do. Debs., Red.	100	107
4½d.	Welford's Surrey Dairies, Ltd.	1	1⅛
7½d.	West London Dairy, Ltd.	1	1
4½	Wharncliffe Dwllgs, L., Pf.	10	12
18/10	Do. 3 p.c. Irr. Mt. Db. Sk.	100	96
6d.	White, A. J., Ltd.	1	⅜
6	Do. 6 p.c. Cum. Pref.	1	⅝
4	White, J. Bazley, Ltd., 1 Mort. Debs., Red.	100	96½
5	White, R., Ltd., 1 Mort. Deb. Stock, Red.	100	104½
5/	White, Tomkins, Ltd.	10	12¾
5	Do. Cum. Pref.	10	12½
6	White, W. N., L., Cm. Pf.	1	1
2/6	Wickens, Pease & Co., L.	5	2
6	Wilkie, Ltd., Cum. Pref.	10	16
3/6	Willans & Robinson, Ltd.	5	8½
6	Do. Cum. Pref.	5	7
4½	Do. 1 Mt. Db. Stk., Red.	100	107
7½d.	Williamsons, L., Cm. Prf.	1	1¼
6	Winterbottm. Book Cloth, Ltd., Cum. Prf.	10	15
3/	Yates, Ltd.	5	6½
6	Do. Cum. Pref.	5	6½
	Young's Paraffin, Ltd.	4	1½

CORPORATION STOCKS—COLONIAL AND FOREIGN.

Per Cent.	Name.	Paid.	Price.
6	Auckland City, '72 1904-24	100	118
6	Do. Cons., '79, Red. 1930	100	138½
5	Do. Deb. Ln., '83..1934-8	100	117
6	Auckland Harb. Debs.	100	111½
5	Do. 1917	100	112
5	Do. 1936	100	116
5½	Balmain Boro' 1914	—	117
5	Boston City (U.S.)	100	102½
5	Do. 1902	100	107½
5	Brunswick Town 5 c. Debs. 1916-20	100	111
15/	B. Ayres City 6 p.c.	100	61
4½	Do. 4½ p.c.	100	79
5	Cape Town, City of	100	113
4	Do. 1943	100	114
4	Chicago, City of, Gold 1915	—	110
6	Christchurch 1926	100	128½
—	Cordoba City	100	17½
5	Duluth (U.S.) Gold 1926	—	110
6	Dunedin (Otago) 1925	100	127½
6	Do. 1906	100	113
5	Do. Consols 1908	100	113
4	Durban Insc. Stk. 1944	100	111
4	Essex Cnty., N. Jersey 1926	100	114½
5	Fitzroy, Melbrne. 1916-19	100	110
5	Gisborne Harbour 1915	100	110½
4	Greymouth Harbour 1925	100	111
4	Hamilton 1934	100	109
5	Hobart Town 1918-30	100	116
4	Do. 1940	100	107
4½	Invercargill Boro. Dbs. 1936	100	113
6	Kimberley Boro., S.A. Dbs.	—	104
4	Launceston Twn. Dbs. 1916	100	107
6	Lyttleton, N.Z., Harb. 1929	100	125
4	Melbourne Bd. of Wks. 1921	100	109
5	Melb. City Debs. 1897-1907	100	107½
4½	Do. Debs. 1908-27	100	113½
4	Do. Debs. 1915-20-22	100	108
5	Melbne. Harb. Bds., 1908-9	100	112
4½	Do. do. 1915	100	110
4	Do. do. 1918-21	100	106
4½	Melbrne. Tms. Dbs. 1914-16	100	113
4½	Do. Fire Brig. Db. 1921	100	109
5	Mexico City Stg.	100	92
4	Moncton N. Bruns. City	100	104
4½	Montevideo	100	58
5	Montreal Stg.	100	104
5	Do. 1874	100	104
5	Do. 1879	100	106
3½	Do. 1933	100	104
3	Do. Perm. Deb. Stk.	100	98
4	Do. Cons. Deb. Stk. 1932	100	113
6	Napier Boro. Consolid. 1914	100	119
5	Napier Harb. Debs. 1920	100	115
5	Do. Debs. 1928	100	106
6	New Plymouth Harb. Debs. 1909	100	108
6	New York City 1901	—	107½
3½	Do. 1910-26	—	106½
4½	Nth. Melbourne Debs. 1-600 1921	100	105
5	Oamaru Boro. Cons. 1920	100	101
6	Do. Harb. Bds. (Reg.)	100	74
25/	Do. 6 p.c. (Bearer) 1919	100	35
6	Otago Harb. Deb. Reg.	100	103
6	Do. 1877	100	107
6	Do. 1881 1921	100	115
5	Do. Debs. 1921	100	107
5	Do. Cons. 1934	100	105
6	Ottawa City	100	109
6	Do. 1904	100	115½
4½	Do. Debs. 1913	100	112
6	Port Elizabeth Waterworks	100	113½
5	Port Louis	100	108
5	Prahran Debs. 1917	100	111
4	Do. Debs. 1919	100	103
6	Quebec C. Coupon. 1875 1905	100	112
6	Do. do. 1878 1908	100	116
4½	Do. Debs. 1914-18	100	108
4	Do. Debs. 1923	100	107
3½	Do. Cns. Rg. Stk., Red.	100	101
5	Richmond (Melb.) Dbs. 1917	100	113
4	Rio Janeiro City	100	59
4	Rome City	100	—
4	Do. 2nd to 8th Iss.	100	94
—	Rosario C.	100	26½
—	Do.	100	26½
4	St. Catherine (Ont.) 1926	100	103
4	St. John, N.B., Debs. 1934	—	104
4½	St. Kilda (Melb) Dbs. 1918-21	100	104
4	St. Louis C. (Miss.) 1911	100	104
4	Do. 1913	100	104½
3·65	Do. 1925	—	110
—	Santa Fé City Debs.	100	21
6	Santos City	100	95
6	Sofia City	100	86
5	Sth. Melbourne Debs. 1915	100	111
4½	Do. Debs. 1929	100	107
5	Sydney City 1904	100	109
4	Do. Debs. 1912-13	100	107
4	Do. do. (1894) 1919	100	109
7	Timaru Boro. 7 p.c. 1910	100	126½
5	Timaru Harb. Debs 1914	100	106
5	Do. Debs. 1916	100	106
6	Toronto City Wtrwks. 1904-6	100	110
6	Do. Cons. Debs. 1898	100	101
5	Do. G. Cns. Dbs. 1919-20	100	118
4	Do. Strlg. 1922-8	100	107
4	Do. Local Improv.	100	102
3½	Do. 1929	100	105
5½	Valparaiso	100	101
4	Vancouver 1931	100	109
4	Do. 1932	100	107
6	Wanganui Harb. Dbs. 1905	100	110
6	Wellington Con. Deb. 1907	100	117
6	Do. Improv., 1879	100	126
6	Do. Wtrwks. Dbs., 1880	100	126
4½	Do. Debs., 1893 1933	100	116
4½	Wellington Harb. 1907	100	106
4	Westport Harb. Dbs. 1925	100	111
6	Winnipeg City Deb. 1907	—	118
5	Do. 1914	100	119

FINANCIAL, LAND, AND INVESTMENT.

Last Div.	Name.	Paid.	Price.
5	Agency, Ld. & Fin. Aust., Ltd., Mt. Db. Stk., Rd.	100	90½
6	Amer. Frehld. Mt. of Lon., Ld., Cum. Pref. Stk.	100	79½
4½	Do. Deb. Stk., Red.	100	96
1/	Anglo-Amer. Db. Cor., L.	2	1
4	Do. Deb. Stk., Red	100	106½
5½	Ang.-Ceylon & Gen. Est., Ltd., Cons. Stk.	100	68
6	Do. Reg. Debs., Red.	100	106½
—	Ang.-Fch. Explorn., Ltd.	1	3
6	Do. Cum. Pref.	1	11/16
—	Argent. Ld. & Inv., Ltd. £1 Shares	10/	nil
5	Do. Cum. Pref.	4	2
1/	Assets Fnders.' Sh., Ltd.	4	1⅜
6/	Assets Realiz., Ltd., Ord.	5	8½
5	Do. Cum. Pref.	5	6½
21/	Austrln. Agricl £25 Shs.	21½	65½
—	Aust. N. Z. Mort., Ltd., £10 Shs.	1	1½d.
4½	Do. Deb. Stk., Red.	100	90½
4	Do. Deb. Stk., Red.	100	82½
4½	Australian Est. & Mt., L., 1 Mt. Deb. Stk., Red.	100	106
5	Do. "A" Mort. Deb. Stk., Red.	100	97
2/6	Australian Mort., Ld., & Fin., Ltd. £25 Shs.	5	4½
1/6	Do. New, £25 Shs.	3	2½
4	Do. Deb. Stk.	100	112
3	Do. Do.	100	85
5	Baring Est. 2 Mt. Debs., Red.	100	105
5	Bengal Presidy. 1 Mort. Deb., Red.	100	106
25/	British Amer. Ld. "A"	1	20
—	Do. "B"	24	6½
1/2½	Brit. & Amer. Mt., Ltd. £10 Shs.	2	¾
5/	Do. Pref.	10	10
4	Do. Deb. Stk., Red.	100	100
1/3	Brit. & Austrlsn Tst Ln., Ltd. £25 Shs.	2½	⅝
4½	Do. Perm. Debs., Red.	100	103
1½d.	Brit. N. Borneo. £1 Shs.	15/	1⅛
2½d.	Do.	1	1
—	Brit. S. Africa	1	3½
5	Do. Mt. Deb., Red.	—	97
6	B. Aires Harb. Tst., Red.	100	99
12/6	Canada Co.	1	26
—	Canada N. W. Ld., Ltd.	$25	35½
—	Do. Pref.	$100	$54
4	Canada Perm. Loan & Sav. Perp. Deb. Stk.	100	99½
—	Curamalan Ld., 1 Mt. 7 p.c. Bds., Red.	—	92½
3/7½	Deb Corp., Ld., £10 Shs	4	3½
5	Do. Cum. Pref.	10	11½
4	Do. Perp. Deb. Stk.	100	116
9d.	Deb. Corp. Fders' Sh., Ld.	3	1
4/5⅒	Eastn. Mt. & Agncy, Ld., "A"	10	6½
4½	Do. Deb. Stk., Red.	100	100
5	Equitable Revers. In. Ltd.	100	—
2/	Exploration, Ltd.	1	1⅛
1	Freehold Trst. of Austrla. Ltd. £10 Shs.	1	¾
4	Do. Perp. Deb. Stk.	100	102
—	Genl. Assets Purchase, Ltd., 5 p.c. Cum. Pref.	10	—
50/	Genl. Reversionary, Ltd.	100	—
3½	Holborn Vi. Land	100	105
3½	House Prop. & Inv.	100	84½
13/	Hudson's Bay	13	25
4	Impl. Col. Fin. & Agcy. Corp.	100	93½
4½	Impl. Prop. Inv., Ltd., Deb. Stk., Red.	100	91½
2/6	Internatl. Fincial. Soc., Ltd. £7½ Shs.	2½	1½
4	Do. Deb. Stk., Red.	100	97½
1/9½	Ld. & Mtge. Egypt, Ltd. £18 Shs.	3	2½
5	Do. Debs., Red.	100	103
4½	Do. Debs., Red.	100	101
—	Ld. Corp. of Canada, Ltd.	1	⅛
4½	Ld. Mtge. Bk. of Texas Deb. Stk.	100	—
3½	Ld. Mtge. Bk. Victoria 4½ p.c. Deb. Stk.	100	78
2/9½	Law Debent. Corp., Ltd., £10 Shs.	2	2
4½	Do. Cum. Pref.,	10	12½
4	Do. Deb. Stk.	100	118
1/	Ldn. & Australasian Deb. Corp., Ltd., £4 Shs.	2	½
4½	Do. 4½ p.c. Mt. Deb. Stk., Red.	100	101
—	Ldn. & Middx. Frhld. Est. £2 Shs.	35/	3½
2/6	Ldn. & N. Y. Inv. Corp., Ltd.	5	2½
5	Do. 5 p.c. Cum. Pref.	10	9
1/6	Ldn. & Nth. Assets Corp., Ltd., £2 Shs.	1½	¾
2/	Ldn. & N. Deb. Corp., L.	2	1⅛
4/	Ldn. & S. Afric. Explrn. Ltd.	½	14
2/	Mtge. Co. of R. Plate, Ltd. £10 Shs.	2	3½
4½	Do. Deb. Stk., Red.	100	111
4½	Morton, Rose Est., Ltd., 1st Mort. Debs.	—	101
6/	Natal Land Col. Ltd.	10	6½
4/	Do. 8 p.c. Pref., 1870	5	8¼
5/6	Natl. Disct. L., £25 Shs.	5	11
4½	New Impl. Invest., Ltd. Pref. Stk.	100	65½
—	New Impl. Invest., Ltd. Def. Stk.	100	9
4	N. Zld. Ln. & Mer. Agcy., Ltd. Prf. Ln. Deb. Stk.	100	97

Financial, Land, &c. (*continued*):—

Last Div.	Name.	Paid.	Price.
16/	N. Zld. Ln. & Mer. Agcy., Ltd. 5 p.c. "A" Db. Sk.	100	42½
—	N. Zld. Ln. & Mer. Agcy., Ltd., 5 p.c. "B" Db. Stk.	100	4
2/6	N. Zld. Tst. & Ln. Ltd., £25 Shs.	5	1½
12/6	N. Zld. Tst. & Ln. Ltd., 5 p.c. Cum. Pref.	25	19
—	N. Brit. Australsn. Ltd.	100	7½
—	Do. Irred. Guar.	100	32½
5	Do. Mort. Debs.	100	82½
4½	N. Queensld. Mort. & Inv., Ltd., Deb. Stk.	100	94
—	Oceana Co., Ltd.	—	—
6	Peel Riv., Ld. & Min. Ltd.	100	90
—	Peruvian Corp., Ltd.	100	3
—	Do. 4 p.c. Pref.	100	10
3	Do. 6 p.c. 1 Mt. Debs., Red.	100	43
—	Queenld. Invest. & Ld. Mort. Pref. Ord. Stk.	100	20
3/7	Queenld. Invest. & Ld. Mort. Ord. Shs.	4	4
4	Queenld. Invest. & Ld. Mort. Perp. Debs.	100	90
3½	Raily. Roll Stk. Tst. Deb., 1903-6	100	100½
50/	Reversiony. Int. Soc., Ltd.	100	—
2/8½	Riv. Plate Trst., Loan & Agcy., L., "A" £10 Shs.	2	4⅜
1/6	Riv. Plate Trst., Loan & Agcy., Ltd., Def. "B"	5	3¾
	Riv. Plate Trst., Loan & Agy., L., Db. Stk., Red.	100	108
—	Santa Fé & Cord. Gt. South Land, Ltd.	20	5
—	Santa Fé Land	10	2⅜
2/	Scot. Amer. Invest., Ltd. £10 Shs.	2	2¾
2½	Scot. Australian Invest., Ltd., Cons.	100	89½
6	Scot. Australian Invest., Ltd., Guar. Pref.	100	135½
5	Scot. Australian Invest., Ltd., Guar. Pref.	100	105½
4	Scot. Australian Invest., Ltd., 4 p.c. Perp. Dbs.	100	105½
5	Sivagunga Zemdy., 1st Mort., Red.	100	101
20/	Sth. Australian	20	55½
3½	Stock Exchange Deb., Rd.	—	101½
—	Strait Develt., Ltd.	1	5/16
2/6	Texas Land & Mt., Ltd. £10 Shs.	2½	3
4½	Texas Land & Mt., Ltd., Deb. Stk., Red.	100	105
—	Transvaal Est. & Dev., L.	1	11/16
—	Transvaal Lands, Ltd., £1 Shs.	15/	⅜
—	Do. F. P.	1	½
—	Transvaal Mort., Loan, & Fin., Ltd., £10 Shs.	2	⅛
2/	Tst & Agcy. of Austrlsa., Ltd., £10 Shs.	1	2½
7/5	Do. Old, fully paid	10	15½
5/7	Do. New, fully paid	10	12½
5	Do. Cum. Pref.	10	12¾
3/	Trust & Loan of Canada, £20 Shs.	5	4½
1/9½	Do. New £20 Shs.	3	2½
—	Tst. & Mort. of Iowa, Ltd., £10 Shs.	2½	¾
4½	Do. Deb. Stk. Red.	100	92½
—	Tst., Loan, & Agency of Mexico, Ltd., £10 Shs.	2	½
—	Trsts., Exors, & Sec. Ins. Corp., Ltd., £10 Shs.	7	1½
5/	Union Dsc., Ld., £10 Shs.	5	11
—	Union Mort. & Agcy. of Aust., Ltd., £6 Shs.	2	—
6	Do. Pref. Stk.	100	35
—	Do. 6 p. Pref. £6 Shs.	2	½
4½	Do. Deb. Stk	100	92½
4	Do. Deb. Stk	100	85½
5	Do. Deb. Stk. Red.	100	96
1/6	U.S. Deb. Cor. Ltd., £8 Shs.	1	⅛
5½	Do. Cum. Pref. Stk.	100	102½
4½	Do. Irred. Deb. Stk	100	108
5	U.S. Tst. & Guar. Cor., Ltd., Pref. Stk.	100	71½
6/	Van Dieman's	25	16
4	Walker's Prop. Cor., Ltd., Guar. 1 Mt. Deb. Stk.	100	109
4½	Wstr. Mort. & Inv., Ltd., Deb. Stk.	100	92½

FINANCIAL—TRUSTS.

Last Div.	Name.	Paid.	Price.
1/	Afric. City Prop., Ltd	1	1⅛
6	Do. Cum. Pref.	1	1
4	Alliance Invt., Ltd., Cm. 4½ p. c. Prefd.	100	80½
—	Do. Defd	100	12½
4	Do. Deb. Stk. Red.	100	106½
5	Amrcn. Invt., Ltd., Prfd.	100	123½
5	Do. Defd.	100	92½
4	Do. Deb. Stk. Red.	100	117½
4	Army & Navy Invt., Ltd., 5 p.c. Prefd.	100	79½
—	Do. Defd. Stk.	100	17½
4	Do. Deb. Stk.	100	104½
4	Atlas Investment, Ltd., Prefd. Stk.	100	70½
4½	Bankers' Invest., Ltd., Cum. Prefd.	100	105
1/0/0	Do. Defd	100	29½
4	Do. Deb. Stk	100	113

Financial—Trusts (*continued*):—

Last Div.	Name.	Paid.	Price.
4/6	Brewery & Comml. Inv., Ltd., £10 Shs.	5	6
4	British Investment, Ltd., Cum. Prefd.	100	109½
5	Do. Defd.	100	102½
4	Do. Deb. Stk.	100	108½
6	Brit. Steam. Invst., Ltd., Prefd.	100	116½
3/0/0	Do. Defd	100	70½
4½	Do. Perp. Deb. Stk	100	120½
2/3	Car Trust Invst., Ltd., £10 Shs.	2½	2
5	Do. Pref.	100	105½
4	Do. Deb. Stk., 1915	100	106
4	Clnl. Sec., Ltd., Prefd.	100	108½
2	Do. Defd.	100	49
4	Consolidated, Ltd., Cum. 1st Pref.	100	95½
4	Do. 5 p.c. Cm. 2nd do.	100	72½
—	Do. Defd.	100	14½
4½	Do. Deb. Stk.	100	111½
4½	Edinburgh Invest., Ltd., Cum. Prefd. Stk.	100	110½
4	Do. Deb. Stk. Red.	100	106½
5	Foreign, Amer. & Gen. Invt., Ltd., Prefd.	100	119½
2	Do. Defd.	100	54½
4	Do. Deb. Stk.	100	117½
5	Foreign & Colonial Invt., Ltd., Prefd.	100	134½
4½	Do. Defd.	100	99½
4½	Gas, Water & Gen. Invt., Cum. Prefd. Stk.	100	93
3	Do. Defd. Stk.	100	32½
4	Do. Deb. Stk.	100	106
5	Gen. & Com. Invt., Ltd., Prefd. Stk.	100	106½
2	Do. Defd. Stk.	100	37½
4	Do. Deb. Stk.	100	111½
1/9	Globe Telegph. & Tst., Ltd.	10	12½
6	Do. do. Pref.	10	18
4	Govt. & Genl. Invt., Ld., Prefd.	100	84½
3½	Do. Defd.	100	42½
4½	Govts. Stk. & other Secs. Invt., Ltd., Prefd.	100	94½
1	Do. Defd.	100	28
4½	Do. Deb. Stk.	100	110
4	Do. do.	100	104
4½	Guardian Invt., Ltd., Pfd.	100	92½
—	Do. Defd.	100	22½
4	Do. Deb. Stk.	100	105
5	Indian & Gen. Inv., Ltd., Cum. Prefd.	100	108½
2½	Do. Defd.	100	55
4½	Do. Deb. Stk.	100	120½
5	Indust. & Gen. Tst., Ltd., Unified	100	102½
3½	Do. Deb. Stk. Red.	100	102½
4½	Internat. Invt., Ltd., Cm. Prefd.	100	73½
—	Do. Defd.	100	11
4	Do. Deb. Stk.	100	104
4	Invest. Tst. Cor. Ltd. Pfd.	100	102
4	Do. Defd.	100	85½
4	Do. Deb. Stk. Red.	100	107
25/	Ldn. Gen. Invest. Ltd., 5 p.c. Cum. Prefd.	100	110½
37/6	Do. Defd.	100	120
4½	Ldn. Scot. Amer. Ltd. Pfd.	100	104½
£3	Do. Defd.	100	59½
4	Do. Deb. Stk.	100	112
4	Ldn. Tst., Ltd., Cum. Prfd. Stk.	100	105
4	Do. Defd. Stk.	100	76½
4	Do. Deb. Stk., Red.	100	107
3½	Do. Mt. Deb. Stk., Red.	100	104
5	Mercantile Invt. & Gen., Ltd., Prefd.	100	112
2	Do. Defd.	100	52½
4	Do. Deb. Stk.	100	117½
4	Merchants, Ltd., Pref. Stk.	100	105½
4	Do. Ord.	100	81
4	Do. Deb. Stk.	100	117
6	Municipal, Ltd., Prefd.	100	56½
—	Do. Defd.	100	18½
4½	Do. Debs.	100	113
4½	Do. Debs. "B"	100	99½
4½	Do. "C" Deb. Stk.	100	88½
5	New Investment, Ltd. Ord.	100	94½
5	Omnium Invest., Ltd., Pfd.	100	89½
1	Do. Defd.	100	26½
4	Do. Deb. Stk.	100	102
4/	Railway Deb. Tst. Ld., £20 Shs.	10	7½
5	Do. Debs., Red.	100	107½
4½	Do. Deb. Stk., 1911	100	105½
4	Do. do. 1927	100	107½
4	Railway Invst. Ltd., Prefd.	100	117
18/6	Do. Defd.	100	24
6/4½	Railway Share Trust & Agency "A"	8	6⅜
7½	Do. "B" Pref. Stk.	100	144½
4½	River Plate & Gen. Invt., Ltd., Prefd.	100	107
£3	Do. Defd.	100	54½
5	Scot. Invst., Ltd., Pfd. Stk.	100	95½
1½	Do. Defd.	100	26½
4	Do. Deb. Stk.	100	108
4½	Sec. Scottish Invst., Ltd., Cum. Prefd.	100	90½
£3	Do. Defd. Stk.	100	32
4	Do. Deb. Stk.	100	107½
7/6	Sth. Africa Gold Tst., Ltd.	1	5
6	Do. Cum. Pref	1	1
5½	Do. 1st Debs., Red.	100	102
1/9	Stock Conv. & Invest., Ltd., £5 Shs.	1	1½
4½	Do. do. 4½ p.c. Cm. Prf.	100	112½
3½	Do. Ldn. & N. W. 1st. Charge Prefd.	100	116½
4	Do do. 2nd Chge Prfd.	100	113
33/0	Do. do. Defd. Charge	100	32½
3	Do. N. East. 1 Chge Pfd.	100	95
37/6	Stock N. East Defd. Chge	100	41
6	Submarine Cables	100	142½
5	U.S. & S. Amer. Invest., Ltd., Prefd.	100	91½
2	Do. Defd.	100	29½
4	Do. Deb. Stk.	100	105½

GAS AND ELECTRIC LIGHTING.

Last Div.	Name.	Paid.	Price.
10/6	Alliance & Dublin Con. 10 p.c. Stand.	10	25½
7/6	Do. 7 p.c. Stand.	10	17
5	Austln. Gas Lght. (Syd.) Debs. 1909	100	106
5	Bay State of N. Jrsy. Sk. Fd. Tst. Bd., Red.	—	92½
3/	Bombay, Ltd.	5	7
2/4½	Do. New	4	5½
12	Brentford Cons.	100	302½
9	Do. New	100	229½
5	Do. Pref.	100	147½
4	Do. Deb. Stk.	100	136
11½	Brighton & Hove Gen. Cons. Stk.	100	277½
8½	Do. "A" Cons. Stk.	100	202½
5	Bristol 5 p.c. Max.	100	132½
22/6	British Gas Light, Ltd.	20	57
11/6	Bromley Gas Consumrs.' 10 p.c. Stand.	10	26
8/6	Do. 7 p.c. Stand.	10	21
—	Brush Electl. Enging., L.	—	2½
6	Do. 6 p.c. Pref.	—	2½
4½	Do. Deb. Stk.	100	111
4½	Do. 2 Deb. Stk., Red.	100	103½
5/	B. Ayres (New), Ltd.	10	10
4	Do. Deb. Stk., Rd.	—	98
12/	Cagliari Gas & Wtr., Ltd.	20	31
8/	Cape Town & Dist. Gas Light & Coke, Ltd.	10	17½
4½	Do. Pref.	10	12½
6	Do. 1 Mt. Debs. 1910	50	60
3/	Charing Cross & Strand Elec. Sup., Ltd.	5	14½
4½	Do. Cum. Pref.	5	6½
2/6	Chelsea Elec. Sup., Ltd.	5	11½
4½	Do. Deb. Stk., Red.	100	113
5	Chic. Edison Co. 1 Mt., Red.	$1000	108
14/	City of Ldn. Elec. Lht., L.	10	29
—	Do. New	10	28
6/	Do. Cum. Pref.	10	18
5	Do. Deb. Stk., Red.	100	131½
13½	Commercial, Cons.	100	342½
10½	Do. New	100	257½
4½	Do. Deb. Stk.	100	155½
14	Continental Union, Ltd.	100	252½
11	Do. Pref. Stk.	100	216½
—	County of Lon. & Brush Prov. Elec. Lg., Ltd.	10	16
6	Do. Cum. Pref.	10	16
14	Croydon Comcl. Gas, Ld., "A" Stk., 10 p.c.	100	317½
11	Do. "B" Stk., 7 p.c.	100	254½
5¼	Crystal Pal. Dist. Ord. 5 p.c. Stk.	100	138½
5	Do. Pref. Stk.	100	141½
8/	European, Ltd.	10	26
6/	Do.	7½	18½
12¾	Gas Light & Ck Cons. Stk., "A" Ord.	100	308
4	Do. "B" (4 p.c. Max.)	100	115½
10	Do. "C," "D," & "E" (Pref.)	100	322½
5	Do. "F" (Pref.)	100	152½
7½	Do. "G" (Pref.)	100	224½
7	Do. "H" (7 p.c. Max.)	100	206½
10	Do. "J" (Pref.)	100	322½
6	Do. "K"	100	189½
4	Do. Deb. Stk.	100	139½
4½	Do. do.	100	157½
6	Do. do.	100	207½
8/	Hong Kong & China, Ld.	10	14½
—	House to House Elec. Light Sup., Ltd.	5	11
7	Do. Cum. Pref.	5	11½
10	Imperial Continental	100	224½
3½	Do. Deb. Stk., Red	100	105½
2/	Malta & Medit., Ltd.	5	5½
5/	Metrop. Elec. Sup., Ltd.	10	20½
3/8	Do. New	10	20
4½	Do. 1 Mt. Deb. Stk.	100	119
5	Metro. of Melbrne. Dbs. 1908-12	100	113
4½	Do. Debs. 1918-22-4	100	110
10/	Monte Video, Ltd.	20	15½
8/	Notting Hill Elec. Ltg., Ltd.	10	18½
4/6	Oriental, Ltd.	5	8½
4/0½	Do. New	4½	7½
10d½.	Do. do. 1870	1	1½
3/6	Ottoman, Ltd.	5	5
—	Para, Ltd.	—	—
6	People's Gas Lt. & C. of Chic. 2 Mt. 1904	100	105½
5	River Plate Elec. Lgt. & Trac., Ltd., 1 Deb. Stk.	—	92½
$2	Royal Elec. of Montreal	—	146
4½	Do. 1 Mt. Deb.	100	106
3/6	St. James' & Pall Mall Elec. Light, Ltd.	5	19
7	Do. Pref.	5	10½
4	Do. Deb. Stk., Red.	100	105½
10/	San Paulo, Ltd.	10	16½

Gas and Electric (*continued*):—

Last Div.	Name.	Paid.	Price.
10	Sheffield Unit. Gas Lt. "A"	100	251½
10	Do. "B"	100	251½
10	Do. "C"	100	251½
—	Sth. Ldn. Elec. Sup., Ld.	2	3
5½	South Metropolitan	100	146½
3	Do. 3 p.c. Deb. Stk.	100	106½
12	Tottenham & Edmonton Gas Lt. & C., "A"	100	290
9	Do. "B"	100	210
7/	Tuscan, Ltd.	10	14
5	Do. Debs., Red.	100	101½
4/9	West Ham 10 p.c. Stan.	5	12
4/	Wstmnstr. Elec. Sup., Ld.	5	18½

INSURANCE.

Last Div.	Name.	Paid.	Price.
4/	Alliance, £20 Shs.	44/	11½
10/	Alliance, Mar., & Gen., Ld., £100 Shs.	25	53
5/	Atlas, £50 Shs.	6	32
8/	British & For. Marine, Ld., £20 Shs.	4	26
7½d.	British Law Fire, Ltd., £10 Shs.	1	1½
7/6	Clerical, Med., & Gen. Life, £25 Shs.	50/	16½
20/	Commercial Union, Ltd., £50 Shs.	5	45½
4	Do. "W. of Eng." Ter. Deb. Stk.	100	110½
60/	County Fire, £100 Shs.	80	185
5/	Eagle, £50 Shs.	5	—
4/	Employrs' Liability, Ltd., £10 Shs.	2	4½
—	Empress, Ltd., £5 Shs.	1	—
21/	Equity & Law, £100 Shs.	6	21
7/6	General Life, £100 Shs.	5	15
4½d.	Gresham Life, £5 Shs.	15/	2½
2/6	Guardian, Ld., £10 Shs.	5	12
10/	Imperial, Ltd., £20 Shs.	5	31½
2/6	Imperial Life, £20 Shs.	4	7
6/	Indemnity Mutual Mar., Ltd., £15 Shs.	3	12½
1/	Lancashire, £20 Shs.	2	5
7½d.	Law Acc. & Contin., Ltd., £5 Shs.	10/	¾
5/	Law Fire, £100 Shs.	2½	18
4½d.	Law Guar. & Trust, Ltd., £10 Shs.	1	1½
9/	Law Life, £20 Shs.	2	24½
2/9	Law Un. & Crown £10Shs.	12/	7
4	Do. Deb. Stk., 1942	100	110½
14/6	Legal & General, £50Shs.	8	15½
9d.	Lion Fire, Ltd., £8½ Shs.	1½	1
14/	Liverpool & London & Globe, Stk	2	55
10/	Do. Globe £1 Ann.	—	36
15/	London, £25 Shs.	12½	63
4/	Lond. & Lanc. Fire, £25Shs	2½	19½
2/	Lond. & Lanc. Life, £25Shs	2	5
10	Lond. & Prov. Mar., Ld., £10 Shs.	1	1½
2/	Lond. Guar. & Accident, Ltd., £5 Shs.	2	12
10/	Marine, Ltd., £25 Shs.	4½	44½
2/	Maritime, Ltd., £10 Shs.	2	4½
1/6	Merc. Mar., Ld., £10 Shs.	2½	2½
1/	National Marine, Ltd., £9 Shs.	1	½
10/	N. Brit. & Merc., £25 Shs.	6¼	43
20/	Northern, £100 Shs.	10	82
40/	Norwich Union Fire, £100 Shs.	12†	128½
5/	Ocean Acc. & Guar., fy. pd.	5	20½
1/	Do. £5 Shs.	1	4
2/6	Ocean, Marine, Ltd.	2½	10
1/	Palatine, £10 Shs.	2	3½
2/6	Pelican, £10 Shs.	1	3½
12/	Phoenix, £50 Shs.	5	45
25/	Provident, £100 Shs.	10	36
3/	Railway Passngrs., £10Shs.	2	8½
2/6	Rock Life, £5 Shs.	10/	4½
8	Royal Exchange	100	360
18/	Royal, £20 Shs.	3	55½
4/	Sun, £10Shs.	10/	11½
3/9	Sun Life, £10 Shs.	7½	15
4/	Thames & Mrsey. Marine, Ltd., £20 Shs.	2	11½
9/	Union, £10 Shs.	4	24½
3/6	Union Marine, £20 Shs.	2½	9½
12/	Universal Life, £100 Shs.	12	42
2/	World Marine, £5 Shs.	2	1½

IRON, COAL, AND STEEL.

Last Div.	Name.	Paid.	Price.
3/9	Barrow Hæm. Steel, Ltd.	7½	2½
9/	Do. 6 p.c. 2nd Pref.	7½	7½
10/	Bolck., Vaugh. & C., Ld.	20	17½
6/	Do. £8 liab.	12	9½
7/6	Brown, J. & Co., Ltd., £20 Shs.	15	21
22/6	Consett Iron, Ld., £10 Shs.	7½	30
4/	Do. 8 p.c. Cum. Pref.	5	11½
7/6	Ebbw Vale Steel, Iron & Coal, Ltd., £27 Shs.	20	7½
15/	General Mining Assn., Ld.	5½	7½
16/	Harvey Steel Co. of Gt. Britain, Ltd.	10	26
5	Lehigh V. Coal 1 Mt. 5 p.c. Guar. Gd. Cp. Bds.	—	98
42/6	Nantyglo & Blaina Iron, Ltd., Pref.	86a	96
1/	Nerbudda Coal & Iron, Ltd., £3 Shs.	56/	1/16
—	Newport Abrcrn. Bk. Vein Steam Coal, Ltd.	10	4½
5/	New Sharlston Coll., Ltd. Pref	20	11
4½d.	Nw. Vancvr. Coal & Ld., L.	1	½
3/6	North's Navigation Coll. (1889) Ltd.	5	2½
10/	Do. 10 p.c. Cum. Pref.	5	7½
—	Rhymney Iron, Ltd.	5	1½
	Do. New, £5 Shs.	4½	½
5	Do. Mt. Debs., Red.	100	97½
5	Shelton Irn., Stl. & Cl. Co., Ltd., 1 Chg. Debs., Red.	100	98½
10	Sth. Hetton Coal, Ltd.	100	176½
	Vickers & Maxim, Ltd.	10	3
	Do. 5 p.c. Prfd. Stk.	100	133½

SHIPPING.

Last Div.	Name.	Paid.	Price.
4/	African Stm. Ship, £20 Shs.	16	9½
5/	Do. Fully-paid	20	13½
2/	Amazon Steam Nav., Ltd.	12½	9½
8/	Castle Mail Pakts., Ltd., £20 Shs.	14	15½
3½	Do. 1st Deb. Stk., Red.	100	101
6/	China Mutual Steam, Ltd.	5	3
6	Do. Cum. Pref.	10	9½
10/	Cunard, Ltd.	20	10
5/	Do. £20 Shs.	10	4
4½	Furness, Withy, & Co., Ltd., 1 Mt. Dbs., Red.	100	105
6/	General Steam	15	8½
5/	Do. 5 p.c. Pref., 1874	10	9
5/	Do. 5 p.c. Pref., 1877	10	9
5/	Leyland & Co., Ltd.	10	15½
7/	Do. 7 p.c. Cum. Pref.	10	14½
2/11	Do. 4½ p.c. Cum. Pre-Pf.	3	10½
4	Do. 1st Mt. Dbs., Red.	100	106½
2/6	Mercantile Steam, Ltd.	5	7½
6/4½	New Zealand Ship., Ltd.,	6	5
4	Do. Deb. Stk., Red.	100	104
5/	Orient Steam, Ltd.	10	4½
5	P. & O. Steam, Cum. Prefd.	100	156½
19	Do. Defd.	100	232½
3½	Do. Deb. Stk.	100	121
5	Richelieu & Ont., 1st Mt. Debs., Red.	100	101
30/	Royal Mail, £100 Shs.	60	51
2/6	Shaw, Sav., & Alb., Ltd., "A" Pref.	5	5½
5/	Do. "B" Ord.	5	3½
8/	Union Steam, Ltd.	20	19
4/	Do. New £20 Shs.	10	9
4	Do. Deb. Stk., Red.	100	107
7/	Union of N.Z., Ltd.	10	10
5½	Wilson's & Fur.-Ley., 5½ p.c. Cum. Pref.	10	10½
4½	Do. 1 Mt. Db. Sk., Rd.	100	106½

TELEGRAPHS AND TELEPHONES.

Last Div.	Name.	Paid.	Price.
4	African Direct, Ltd., Mort. Debs., Red.	100	102
—	Amazon Telegraph, Ltd.	10	6½
14/	Anglo-American, Ltd.	100	63
28/	Do. 6 p.c. Prefd. Ord.	100	113½
—	Do. Defd. Ord.	100	13½
3/	Brazilian Submarine, Ltd.	10	17
5	Do Debs., 2 Series	100	114

Telegraphs and Telephones (*continued*):—

Last Div.	Name.	Paid.	Price.
4/	Chili Telephone, Ltd.	5	3½
$2½	Comcial. Cable, $100 Shs.	—	189½
4	Do. Stg. 500-yr. Deb. Stk. Red.	100	107
2½d.	Consd. Telpehone Constr., &c., Ltd.	10/	½
8/	Cuba Submarine, Ltd.	10	8½
10/	Do. 10 p.c. Pref.	10	18
2/	Direct Spanish, Ltd.	5	4½
5/	Do. 10 p.c. Cum. Pref.	5	10½
4½	Do. Debs.	50	104½
3/	Direct U.S. Cable, Ltd.	20	11
2/6	Eastern, Ltd.	10	18½
3/	Do. 6 p.c. Cum. Pref.	10	19½
4	Do. Mt. Deb. Stk., Red.	100	132½
2/6	Eastern Exten., Aus., & China, Ltd.	10	19
5	Do. (Aus. Gov. Sub.) Deb., Red.	100	101
5	Do. do. Bearer	100	101½
4	Do. Mort. Deb. Stk.	100	131½
5	Eastn. & S. Afric., Ltd., Mort. Deb. 1900	100	101
5	Do. Bearer	100	101½
4	Do. Mort. Debs. 1909	100	103½
4	Do. Mort. Debs. (Maur. Subsidy)	25	109½
5/	Grt. Nthn. Copenhagen	10	27½
5	Do. Debs., Ser. B., Red.	100	102½
12/6	Indo-European, Ltd.	25	53½
6	London Platino-Brazilian, Ltd., Debs. 1904	100	109½
4/	Montevideo Telph., Ltd., 6 p.c. Pref.	5	2½
3/	National Telephone, Ltd.	5	6½
6/	Do. Cum. 1 Pref.	10	16
6/	Do. Cum. 2 Pref.	10	15
5	Do. Non-Cum. 3 Pref.	5	6½
3½	Do. Deb. Stk., Red.	100	106½
4d.	Oriental Telephone, Ltd.	1	½
4	Pac. & Euro. Tlg. Dbs., Rd.	100	106½
4/	Reuter's, Ltd.	8	8½
5/	Un. Riv. Plate Telph., Ltd.	5	4½
5	Do. Deb. Stk., Red.	100	103½
6/	West African Telg., Ltd.	10	4½
5	Do. 5 p.c. Mt. Debs., Red.	100	104½
—	W. Coast of America, Ltd.	10	—
3/	Western & Brazilian, Ltd.	15	10½
3/	Do. 5 p.c. Pref. Ord.	7½	7½
—	Do. Defd. Ord.	7½	3½
4	Do. Deb. Stk., Red.	100	106
1/	W. India & Panama, Ltd.	10	½
6/	Do. Cum. 1 Pref.	10	8
6/	Do. Cum. 2 Pref.	10	6
5	Do. Debs., Red.	100	106½
7	West. Union, 1 Mt. 1900 ($	1000	107½
6	Do. 6 p.c. Stg. Bds., Rd.	100	102½

TRAMWAYS AND OMNIBUS.

Last Div.	Name.	Paid.	Price.
1/6	Anglo-Argentine, Ltd.	5	4½
6	Do. Deb. Stk.	100	132½
4	Barcelona, Ltd.	10	12½
5	Do. Deb., Red.	100	102½
6/6	Belfast Street Trams.	10	17
—	Blackpl. & Fltwd. Tram., £10 Shs.	8	11
4/	Bordeaux Tram. & O., Ltd.	10	13½
5	Do. Cum. Pref.	10	11½
—	Brazilian Street Ry., Ltd.	2	½
—	British Elec. Trac., Ltd.	10	17½
—	B. Ayres & Belg. Tram., Ltd., 6 p.c. Cum. Pref.	5	4½
6	Do. 1 Deb. Stk.	100	104½
—	B. Ayres. Gd. Nat., Ltd., 6 p.c. 1 Deb. Bds., Red.	100	60
5½	Do. Pref. Debs., Red.	100	94½
6d.	Calais, Ltd.	5	1
—	Calcutta, Ltd.	10	3½
—	Carthagena & Herr., Ltd.	10	3
5	Do. Deb., Red.	100	90
5	City of B'ham. Trams., Ltd., 5 p.c. Cum. Pref.	5	6
4	Do. 1 Mort. Debs., Rd.	100	106½
3/9	City of B. Ayres, Ltd.	5	7½
2/3	Do. Ext. £5 Shs.	3	4½
6	Do. Deb. Stk.	100	150
9d.	Edinburgh Street Tram.	4	3½
1/	Glasgow Tram. & Omni. Ltd., £9 Shs.	8	3½
3/7½	Imperial, Ltd.	6	14½
2/	Lond., Deptfd, & Greenwich, Prefd.	5	3½
nil	Do. Defd.	5	1
10½	Lond. Gen. Omni., Ltd.	100	206
4	Do. Deb., Red.	100	117½

Tramways and Omnibus (*continued*):—

Last Div.	Name.	Paid.	Price.
6/	London Road Car	6	11
5	London St. Rly. (Prov., Ont.), Mt. Debs.	100	112
4/9	London St. Trams.	—	3
12/9	London Trams., Ltd.	10	10½
6/	Do. Non-Cum. Pref.	10	10½
5	Do. Mt. Db. Stk., Rd.	100	100½
5	Lynn & Boston 1 Mt. 1924 $	1000	107
5	Milwaukee Elec. Cons. Mt. $	1000	99½
5	Minneapolis St. 1 Cons. Mt $	1000	96
5	Montreal St. Dbs., 1908	100	110
4½	Do. Debs., 1922	100	107
6/	Nth. Metropolitan	10	13½
1/9½	Nth. Staffords., Ltd.	6	4½
5/6	Provincial, Ltd	10	7
6/	Do. Cum. Pref.	10	13½
5	St. Paul City, 1937 $	1000	94
5	Do. Guar. Twin City Rap. Trans. $	1000	94
5/	Southampton	10	7
3/	South London	10	5½
7/6	Sunderland, Ltd.	10	6
4½	Toronto 1 Mt., Red.	100	109
2/6	Tramways Union, Ltd.	5	7
4½	Do. Deb., Red.	100	109
5/	Vienna General Omnibus.	5	6½
5	Do. 5 p.c. Mt. Deb., Red.	100	105
4/	Wolverhampton, Ltd.	10	6½

WATER WORKS.

Last Div.	Name.	Paid.	Price.
8/	Antwerp, Ltd.	20	22
6/	Cape Town District, Ltd.	5	6½
10½	Chelsea	100	337½
5	Do. Pref. Stk.	100	178½
4½	Do. Pref. Stk., 1875	100	158½
4½	Do. Deb. Stk.	100	162½
5/	City St. Petersburg, Ltd.	13	11
4/6	Colne Valley	10	15½
4	Do. Deb. Stock	100	137½
£4	Consol. of Rosar., Ltd., 4 p.c. 1 Deb. Stk., Red.	100	91
7½	East London	100	235
4½	Do. Deb. Stk.	100	163½
3	Do. Deb. Stk., Red.	100	106
37/6	Grand Junction (Max. 10 p.c.) "A"	50	124½
18/9	Do. "B"	25	
18/9	Do. "C" (Max. 7½ p.c.)	25	57½
35/	Do. "D" (Max. 7 p.c.)	50	102½
4	Do. Deb. Stock	100	149½
13	Kent	100	364½
7	Do. New (Max. 7 p.c.)	100	217½
5/7½	Kimberley, Ltd.	7	5
6	Do. Debs., Red.	100	102½
6	Do. Deb. Stk., Red.	100	104½
10	Lambeth (Max. 10 p.c.)	100	309½
7½	Do. (Max. 7½ p.c.), 50 & 25	—	220½
4	Do. Deb. Stock	100	148½
3	Do. Red. Deb. Stock	100	105
10/	Montevideo, Ltd.	20	16½
5	Do. 1 Deb. Stk.	100	108½
5	Do. 2 Deb. Stk.	100	103½
130/11	15] New River New	100	454½
4	Do. Deb. Stk.	100	153½
4	Do. Deb. Stk. "B"	100	153½
—	Odessa, Ltd., "A" 6 p.c. Prefd.	20	—
nil	Do. "B" Deferred	20	—
4	Portland Con. Mt. "B," 1927	—	—
8/	Seville, Ltd.	20	12½
5/6	Southend "Addl." Ord.	10	17
6	Southwark and Vauxhall	100	167
6	Do. "D" Shares (7½ p.c. max.)	100	162
5	Do. Pref. Stock	100	177
4	Do. "A" Deb. Stock	100	140
3	Staines Resvirs. Jt. Com. Gua. Deb. Stk., Red.	100	105
7/	Tarapaca, Ltd.	10	9
10	West Middlesex	100	319
4½	Do. Deb. Stk.	100	164
3	Do. Deb. Stk.	100	107

Printed for the Proprietor by Love & Wyman, Ltd., Great Queen Street, London, W.C.; and Published by Clement Wilson at Norfolk House, Norfolk Street, Strand, London, W.C.

The Investors' Review

Vol. I.—No. 7.
New Series.

FRIDAY, FEBRUARY 18, 1898.

[Registered as a Newspaper.]

Price 6d.
By post, 6½d

CONTENTS

The Investors' Review.

Banking Prosperity and Market Inflation.

The half-year just passed was a good one for British banks. So say all bank chairmen at shareholders' meetings, and it is the fact. Rates for money were more favourable to the lender throughout the larger half of the six months, banks paid less for their deposits and obtained more from those who borrowed these deposits. Profits and dividends were consequently better on the average, and in some instances money saved from revenue was actually added to reserves; therefore bank shares have advanced to prices never seen before in the history of British banking. All sorts and conditions of men are gravely and persistently buying these shares for investment, with never a passing glance at the formidable liability most of them carry, and, by the law of averages which sways and evens down all human affairs, they must one day pay for their forgetfulness. In stating that profits have been good because the Money market is more favourable to the dealer therein, it should be plain to the least critical mind that the whole case is not thus comprehended. Pass outside banking business and, at most points, we fail to discover substantial grounds for this well-being. The country's trade did not expand last year, has not been expanding for years back, except on the import side—a side which may either indicate increasing national wealth, or increasing national thriftlessness, according as it represents increased returns from money invested abroad, or increased sales of foreign investments formerly held here. If the excess of imports, in other words, do not represent increased profits on exported merchandise or the increased command of British capital over foreign sources of production, then they must be paid for by the export of some portion of our already accumulated capital.

We believe that the nation is, and for some considerable time back has been, spending or wasting part of its accumulated capital, but this injurious proceeding may, while it lasts, be a stimulus to banking business, and a source of profit to the banks. Grant that it is so, and the fact remains that our trade, whether foreign or domestic, has not in itself been sufficiently expansive to demand important additional assistance from banking credit in carrying it on. And the decline in agriculture is too well known to require to be dwelt upon. The sources of recent extraordinary banking prosperity must therefore be found outside commerce, and it is so found as we shall proceed to explain. In order to be able to follow what we have to say, the reader must first make himself master of the following summary table compiled from the December balance-sheets of a number of London and country English Banks, the smallest of whose aggregate liabilities to shareholders and the public—and therefore aggregate assets—amount to three millions and upwards. The list is not complete partly because completeness is not necessary for the purpose in view, partly because some of the country banks have not yet sufficiently recognised the INVESTORS' REVIEW to send it their reports.

Name of Bank.	Cash in hand and at the Bank of England.	Bills of Exchange.	Percentage of Cash and Bills to total amount.	Advances and Loans.	Total assets.	Percentage of advances and loans to total assets.	Contingent liabilities on acceptances.
Bi'mgham. Disct. Counties*	681,000	—	—	3,052,000	5,682,000	—	—
City	948,000	1,611,000	21·6	5,521,000	12,236,000	45·1	1,906,000
Craven	92,000	124,000	5·6	2,301,000	3,693,000	62·3	—
Halifax Joint Stock*	390,000	891,000	32·6	2,184,000	3,716,000	58·7	—
Lanc. & Yorks†	796,000	397,000	23·8	2,671,000	4,585,000	58·3	—
Liverpool Union*	442,000	1,024,000	32·1	1,493,000	4,549,000	32·8	809,000
Lloyds	4,642,000	4,095,000	21·3	18,962,000	40,760,000	46·5	408,000
Lon. & County	5,424,000	10,705,000	—	14,615,000	46,057,000	—	2,047,000
Lon. & Midland	3,174,000	2,759,000	23·4	11,567,000	25,248,000	45·8	572,000
Lon. Joint Stock	2,770,000	—	—	§13,194,000	21,265,000	—	1,462,000
Lon. & Provincial	777,000	—	—	§6,350,000	10,565,000	—	—
L. & S.-Western	1,277,000	633,000	18	4,483,000	10,638,000	42·1	—
London and Westminster	4,119,000	—	—	§14,616,000	30,192,000	—	231,000
Manchester and Liverpool	1,741,000	—	—	§10,843,000	18,643,000	—	908,000
Metropolitan	585,000	761,000	16·8	4,456,000	7,973,000	55·8	—
Nat. Provincial	6,459,000	—	—	26,709,000	54,484,000	—	—
National (Irish)‡	1,568,000	3,964,000	40·8	4,110,000	13,555,000	45·09	—
N. & S.-Wales†	1,882,000	1,843,000	39·7	3,593,000	9,376,000	38·3	315,000
Nottingham and Notts	318,000	159,000	15·6	1,606,000	3,051,000	34·7	—
Paris	3,053,000	2,317,000	20·6	11,288,000	26,134,000	43·3	2,760,000
Prov. of Ireland*	488,000	—	—	3,250,000	5,880,000	—	—
William Deacon and M'chester and Salford	1,670,000	1,961,000	27·3	5,835,000	13,274,000	43·8	250,000
York City and County†	1,116,000	678,000	20·06	5,692,000	8,929,000	63·8	—
Yorkshire†	651,000	—	—	2,981,000	5,593,000	—	—

* Includes call money with London banks. † Includes call and notice money.
‡ Liability on inter-circulation in Ireland, £1,077,000.
§ Bills and advances in one item.

A few years ago such a table as the above could scarcely have been compiled, so imperfect were the balance-sheets bank boards thought fit to lay before shareholders. And even now there is a residuum of banks which adhere to the old fashion, so that in the case of the London and Westminster, the London Joint Stock, the National Provincial, and some others, we have had to leave the cash and bills column blank. Even the statutory returns hung up in their offices do not give bills separately as they used to do. Why they cannot put the figures in their half-yearly or yearly balance sheets is one of those oddities of the directorial mind which it is useless to discuss. But, assuming that the proportion of bills to advances held by these banks represents about the average, we find that in no single instance do bills and cash in hand and at the Bank of England represent 50 per cent. of the assets. In bills alone the total held is not seldom below 10 per cent. of the aggregate assets. On the other hand, the proportion of advances and loans, exclusive of the money lent at call and short notice in the market, ranges between 30 and 60 per cent. of the total assets, and is usually nearer the higher percentage than the lower. Out of the total assets amounting to about £370,000,000 shown by the above table, at a very liberal estimate not £30,000,000 is represented by bills of exchange.

This fact surely has an important bearing on the point now under discussion. We do not wish to push the inference too far, and to allege roundly that all these advances represent loans granted for more or less lengthened fixed periods on the security of stocks and shares, for this would not be true. Banking business in most districts may, and frequently does, consist of a multitude of small advances to traders and financiers, made either on specific securities lodged, mortgages, and so on, or on personal guarantees; and business of this kind has always been held to be legitimate for the banker. But, allowing for everything of this kind, the inference is none the less fair that the higher profitableness of the banking business of the three kingdoms has arisen to an increasing extent of late from the enlargement of their more or less direct business with the Stock Exchange. Some of these banks, indeed, openly state that this is so in their balance-sheets, or at least put the matter in a way which makes this a fair and reasonable inference.

But the statement does not rest on inference alone. Invite the testimony of any experienced member of the Stock Exchange, and he will tell you that the method of conducting speculative business has completely changed there within the present generation. Formerly, the speculative account, as it is called, was carried on mainly within the Exchange itself. Jobbers there, and brokers in command of capital, lent money to the speculative buyers of securities from fortnight to fortnight, and by doing so knew not only the extent of the speculative account open in any particular security, but the quality of it as well. Prudent men with this knowledge could protect themselves when they saw some particular movement becoming dangerous. To-day the Stock Exchange has neither this knowledge nor the business on which it was based. It may have itself to blame for the change, and to some extent has, for it is in great need of an overhaul and reform; but, if its own bad methods and want of proper government gave the opportunity, the banks undoubtedly were eager to take it, and the business which was the market's is now in great part theirs.

When a man possessed of any means or credit at all now buys a stock to hold for the rise, he arranges with his banker to pay for it, and it is at once lifted off the market. So long as it is a rising market, as it has in the main been for the past seven years, all goes beautifully, the buyer is richer, the banker is doing an excellent business. But reverse the process, and what then? Then the banks will stand in the breach where the Stock Exchange used to stand in times of crisis, and with nothing to lean upon except the capacity of the individual customer to make losses good. This is a very different position from the old one, where the jobber and the broker and the client, all three, stood between the bank and loss, and it is made worse by the fact that the extent of the speculative account open in any class of security is now altogether unascertainable. No one banker knows what his neighbour is doing. The "advances" set down in our table tell us nothing definite. To put 50, 100, or 200 millions of them down to Stock Exchange commitments would be mere guess work. But the changed position of the banker and his own absolute ignorance are plain enough. For many years back the banks have been busy, "letting each other in and out" of commitments on the Stock Exchange speculatively entered into, and the rising markets have made the trade thus done profitable to them all.

Concurrently with this gradual change in the relation of banks to the Stock Market we have had an unprecedented development in the art of company-mongering, in the creation of new "marketable securities." How far have the banks, in their eagerness to make high profits, committed their resources to this kind of business? Again we cannot say. We can only infer that the extravagant capitalisation of new or transmogrified businesses with which the past few years have made us familiar, and the extreme prices to which securities of all descriptions have risen, have not come about without the help of credit. Bank deposits and advances mount concurrently, lagging trade and low prices for raw and manufactured products notwithstanding, in a way which suggests inflation, for the simple reason that only through the extension of their business in the direction of the Stock Exchange could anything of the kind have come about. And if there be inflation, if banks have been drawn into partnership with loan syndicates, with company promoters, with speculators for the rise of every hue and degree, what will be their position, the position of their shareholders and creditors, when the inevitable reaction comes? This is a subject worth pondering over, and we shall leave those most interested to meditate on it for the present.

Shipping Bounties and Shipping "Rings."

From time to time a grumble arises in the newspapers over the charges of the shipping companies conducting our trade between India and the Far East and the Australasian Colonies. These die away, producing no result. What may be called a conspiracy of silence is maintained on the part of all shipping interests, and there is no redress. We propose to let a little daylight in upon this dark place.

Perhaps our Indian dependency suffers more than any other part of the Empire from this scourge; but at present we have not sufficient facts about the Indian trade to go into the matter in detail. Many months ago we gave some particulars of the way passengers were overcharged and roughly fed on the steamers of the P. and O. Company, but we are still without particulars in regard to the freight charges of the shipping firms composing the Eastern ring. We trust, however, that some public-spirited merchants, with the genuine interests of the Empire at heart, will come forward with the particulars, now that they know these columns are open to them. In the meantime the following complaint from Singapore, which the *Financial News* copied from the *Straits Times*, will give some idea of the feeling prevalent in trade circles :—

A correspondent of the *Straits Times* complains bitterly of the action of the shipping ring, the leading spirit of which, he says, is the P. and O. Company, from whose offices the business of the ring is transacted. The action of the ring in keeping up freights, he declares, is giving both Belgian and German merchants undue advantages in trade with the Straits Settlements.

"An instance may be given," he writes, "where a firm, last year, had an order for a quantity of iron for shipment to Java. It was found that if the order were executed from the Continent the rate of freight would be 14s. 2d. per ton, although the cargo would have to be loaded at Amsterdam, then brought to Birkenhead, and there transhipped to the Java steamer. If, on the other hand, the iron were got from England, the rate of freight by the same steamer would be 25s. and 10 per cent., and this in spite of the fact that the Amsterdam to Birkenhead voyage would be saved, and also the consequent transhipment. Inquiries made a few months ago showed that very much the same condition of affairs still prevailed, the freight asked from Amsterdam being 20s., and that from Liverpool 30s. per ton.

"It may be asked why the British merchant does not ship his goods by outside steamers or by any line which will accept a reasonable rate of freight. The reply to that is that, half-yearly or annually, the Shipping Conference make a return of 10 per cent. on freights paid to all merchants who make a declaration that they have not during such period shipped by any steamer outside of the Conference. Besides, opportunities of shipment by tramp steamers are very infrequent now, the Conference having succeeded in practically driving off all competition. Were the case otherwise, and were there any competition to speak of, it is unlikely that the Conference would be able to do as they have succeeded in doing during the last few weeks. A notification was issued by the chairman of the Conference in Singapore, intimating an advance in homeward rates of freight, the advance in some cases amounting to as much as 75 per cent. No reasonable person would complain of a material advance in freights if these were at the figure ruling about eighteen months ago, when ordinary Singapore bag goods could be shipped hence to London at about 5s. per ton. But up till a few weeks ago the Conference had their rates fixed on a scale which must have allowed ample remuneration to steamers, and it is this scale which has now been so enormously and so unreasonably enhanced.

"The result of this most recent action of the Conference can hardly fail to be disastrous to Singapore merchants. Indeed, it looks as if the object in view were to do all the harm possible to the trade of the colony. There are certain articles of produce shipped from the Straits Settlements which only find an outlet in European markets by reason of their cheapness. Some of these articles are very low-priced, the freight forming a good share of the cost to those on the other side, and this cheapness, which almost alone enables them to sell, will very largely disappear when high rates of freights have to be paid. Nor will merchants be able to take advantage of cheaper opportunities of shipping by sailing vessels; for it is in contemplation by the Conference to exclude from the benefit of any rebate all those who ship by a sailer instead of by a Conference steamer."

The correspondent suggests that something may be done in the way of limiting the action of the ring by Straits and British merchants approaching the Imperial Government with a demand that all subsidies should be withdrawn from the P. and O. Company.

This correspondent points to the true source of the mischief. It lies in the subsidies, the monstrously high subsidies, bestowed upon certain shipping companies, which, to all appearance, can do with the Post Office what they please, and over whose excessive bounties Parliament has no more real control than the writer of this article. According to the *Finance Accounts of the United Kingdom* for the year ended March 31, last, the public revenue of the United Kingdom was charged with £726,607 for "packet services." Of this money nearly one-half is admittedly dead loss to the British revenue. On this Eastern trade for instance, the loss last year was to us alone £165,000. The total amount of the subsidies bestowed upon the P. and O. Company for carrying these eastern mails was £265,000, of which India paid £60,600, Ceylon £1,400, the Strait Settlements £6,000, and Hong Kong £6,000, but the total receipts from postage came to less than £30,000, so the entire loss came to more than £200,000, assuming the postages from our dependencies home to be as large as that from England out. The service is therefore a monstrous loss to the Home Government and to the British dependencies sharing with us the burden of these iniquitous subsidies. Our trade with North America is much larger than with all the East put together, at any rate the receipts from American postage were fully £8,000 more last year than those from the whole postage of the East, and yet the charge for carrying these American mails was little more than £100,000, and the loss on this service only £62,500. This, of course, is exclusive of the Canada and China service, which can only be described as a disgusting job, perpetrated in the interests of sham Imperialists possessed of a fine eye to the main chance. We pay £60,000 per annum subsidy for that Pacific-China service, £15,000 of it coming from Canada, and the net receipts of the postage on that service in 1896-7, the last year for which we have figures, were estimated at £1,900. The actual loss, therefore, to the British Government on this job was over £43,000. Except to maintain shipping combinations by which the trade of the country can be throttled there is no reason whatever for the payment of such monstrous sums for any part of the over-sea mail service of the Empire. They are pernicious bounties which have done mischief in all directions, and not least in stimulating foreign nations to pay still heavier subsidies to their mercantile marine in order that they might enter into closer competition with us.

But let us see how the thing works; and, in order to clear the way, we ask the readers to peruse the following notices issued by the firms and companies composing the ring, together with the stipulations as to rebate circulated to shippers by the German companies who have been coerced into joining the combination. These documents are rather long, but they give the key to the system under which the trader is bound hand and foot, and totally unable to help himself :—

AUSTRALIAN REBATES.

For the Six Months ending June 30, 1897.

January 1, 1898.

To Messrs.

Annexed we beg to hand you a list of our shipments by the steamers and sailers loaded by you during the six months ending June 30, 1897, and we hereby declare that, with the exception of shipments by the British India Company's steamers to Queensland, and by the sailing ships loaded by the Australian Mutual Shipping Company, Limited, to Melbourne, Sydney, and Newcastle, neither we nor those for whom we have acted have, during the twelve months ending December 31, 1897, shipped or been interested, directly or indirectly, in any shipments, by steamers or sailers, direct or by transhipment, from the United Kingdom to ports in New South Wales, Victoria, South Australia, and Queensland, other than those loaded by—

The Peninsular & Oriental Co.
The Orient Steam Navigation Co., Limited.
The Messageries Maritimes.
Messrs. Anderson, Anderson, & Co.
" Aitken, Lilburn, & Co.
" Bethell, Gwyn, & Co.
" Birt, Potter, & Hughes.
The Colonial Line.
Messrs. Devitt & Moore.
" J. Dowie & Co.
" Gracie Beazley & Co.
" F. Green & Co.
" Houlder Brothers & Co.
Messrs. Ismay, Imrie, & Co.
" Thos. Law & Co.
" McIlwraith, McEacharn, & Co., Limited.
" Marwood & Christian.
" Wm. Milburn & Co.
" Geo. Thompson & Co.
" Trinder, Anderson, & Co.

and that neither we, nor those for whom we have acted, have as yet returned or allowed any portion in any shape or form, either directly or indirectly, of the rebates claimed under this declaration.

This declaration must be signed by a partner of the firm claiming the rebate, or by some one holding the firm's procuration. } Signature __________ Address __________

This claim is only valid if presented within three months of the date when the rebate falls due.

This declaration to be made out for each line of vessels separately, and to be sent in to the respective agents.

A similar "contract" is in our hands relative to the Western Australian trade, but we need only give the names of the companies and firms constituting the "ring" by which this contract is enforced :—

The Peninsular & Oriental Co.
The Orient Steam Navigation Co., Limited.
West Australian Steam Navigation Co., Limited, via Singapore.
Trinder, Anderson, & Co.
Bethell, Gwyn, & Co.
W. Marden.
Anderson, Anderson, & Co.
Birt, Potter, & Hughes.
T. Law & Co., from Glasgow.
James Dowie & Co. } from Liverpool.
Marwood & Christian } from Liverpool.

Now comes the most important document of all—made in Germany. It is a circular emitted by the Norddeutscher Lloyd and the Deutsch-Australische Dampfschiffe-Gesellschaft, and contains the stipulations regulating the gracious concession of rebates to all shippers who obey the mandate and constitute themselves perpetual slaves of the "ring" :—

NOTICE TO SHIPPERS.

Shippers to all ports of Australasia are hereby informed that as from January 1, 1897, and until further notice, and subject to the conditions and terms set out herein, the undersigned will pay to the shippers by the Norddeutscher Lloyd, Bremen, the Deutsch-Australische Dampfschiffs-Gesellschaft, and by sailing vessels put on the berth and or approved in writing by Rob. M. Sloman, jun., Hamburg, a rebate of 10 per cent. on the net freight (*i.e.*, exclusive of primage) received by them from such shippers.

The said rebate to be computed every six months up to June 30 and December 31 in each year, and to be payable six months after such respective dates to those shippers only who, until the date at which the rebate shall become payable, shall have made their shipments from the Continent between Hamburg and Havre, both inclusive, exclusively by steamers despatched by the said companies and (or by sailing vessels put on the berth and) or approved in writing by Rob. M. Sloman, jun.; and provided that such shippers, either as principals or as agents, have not directly or indirectly made or been interested in any shipments to any of the aforesaid ports by steamers or sailing ships other than those set forth herein, and also provided that the statement of claim for such rebate shall be made in the annexed form within twelve months of the date of shipment to the undernamed firms.

If required, the firm claiming rebate has to declare whether they are acting for own account or on instructions and for account of others; in the latter case, the signature of the principals resp. the firm owning the goods can be asked for.

Shipments to other ports of Australasia than South Australia, Victoria, and New South Wales by steamers (and or sailing vessels which do not load on the Continent) limits as above and sailing vessels despatched from Antwerp by Mr. C. W. Twelves for Australia will not invalidate, claims for the above rebate. The circular dated June, 1896, referring to Western Australia to remain in force.

Norddeutscher Lloyd.
Deutsch-Australische Dampfschiffs-Gesellschaft.
Rob. M. Sloman, Jr.

The reader will observe that the key to the position lies in the rebate system, and this system has been evolved out of the long struggle carried on intermittently by ship-broker after ship-broker, and by strong ship-owning firms, against the combination, backed by subsidies or bounties, which in the case of the P. & O. Company alone amounted last year to £376,750. The strong members of the ring are able always to coerce the interloper. The P. & O. Company itself can carry goods at freights which yield no profit at all, and still pay large dividends out of its grants from the various Governments tributary to it. Being strong through these grants, it simply orders freights down, when any competitor enters the field, to a point which causes the said competitor to run his vessels at a loss. Then, when the bold interloper has been well trounced, if it be worth while, the would-be independent rival is admitted into the combination, and allowed to share in what plunder can be extracted out of the unfortunate shipper. We use the word "plunder' advisedly, for nothing could savour more of the legendary robbers of the Rhine than the rebate system, under which freights are now levied by monopolists whose power rests upon the unwarrantable bounties paid by the British Government.

It is not enough, of course, to merely coerce the ship-owner; the trader must also be brought to heel, and this is done effectually by the rebate system. All the shipping firms in the "ring" carry the goods consigned to them at identical charges, and bind those who ship these goods to send nothing by any outside channel. Whatever member of the "ring" a shipper trades with is of small matter, but it is war to the knife and destruction to any man who ventures to go to any ship not within the combination. Swift punishment then falls upon him. He is deprived of his 10 per cent. discount on all goods shipped for the previous six, ten, it might even be twelve months. The rebate, in other words, is not deducted and paid over on each shipment. On the contrary, as the interesting notice to shippers which we print shows, it is computed for six months up to June 30 and December 31 each year, and it is not payable until six months after each half-year has expired. Often it is not paid even then, and as we have said, should any trader be found guilty of sending goods by an independent channel he 'stands to lose the whole of the rebates due to him on the business of at least six months previous, and he might be fined for any period of time up to twelve months. That such a system should be permitted to exist at the end of this nineteenth century, with its boasted progress in "liberty," and so on, is a startling fact; but it does exist, and the British Parliament, by its weakness, its readiness to do the bidding of the permanent officials, its subservience to shipowners, and its general helplessness, is mainly responsible for the evil. It is an evil which is garotting our foreign trade; above all, our trade with India and the further East, and with Australasia. But you will find the men most responsible for its institution and maintenance the loudest, usually, in boasting about the "greatness of the Empire," "the necessity for British interests to be supreme in the world," and so on, and so on. And the cloudy-headed multitude thinks them "first-class patriots." To doubt the wisdom or expediency of paying the shamefully excessive bounties we have mentioned is to be in the language of these ardent Imperialists, "a Little Englander." But they share with the Germans, these same immaculate Imperial patriots, and where they cannot do that they allow our trade to escape us and pass to the foreigner. Oh, British public, what an ass you are!

How Rand Deep Levels are Financed.

We now propose to investigate the financial and mining prospects of the most important of the deep level trust companies, especially in relation to the prices at which their shares now stand. But before doing so it may be as well to briefly review the conclusions arrived at in the two previous papers. It has been seen that to pay dividends of 8 per cent. on the present market valuations of the seventeen leading Rand deep levels would require an annual sum of £4,080,000, to earn which would necessitate the employment of at least 4,300 stamps. That this task is impossible of accomplishment is shown—(1) by the fact that these companies only contemplate erecting 2,200 stamps, the majority of which will not be crushing for two or three years; (2) by a comparison with the outcrops. In 1897 the fifty-five producing outcrop mines, under which the deeps are situated, only distributed dividends amounting to £2,500,000. From this it is evident that the prices ruling for deep levels are most absurdly inflated. The reader has likewise been warned against the ingenious devices being utilised to induce the unwary to buy these shares at high figures, and the remarkable difference between the gold contents for outcrop and deep level claims has been commented upon.

We have expressed a very strong belief that in the case of those deep levels now crushing, in order to show high returns, the "rich eyes" of the mines are being picked out; while, by actual reference to the published reports of at least one company, it has been proved that even the accounts are manipulated to show larger profits than are being earned. That we do not stand alone in the view that the mines are being picked is shown by some of the Johannesburg exchanges which arrived by last mail. One of them speaks of a "growing suspicion locally that the Rose Deep returns are being unduly forced," while a correspondent from the same quarter writes that he has "corroborated this idea in a very well-informed quarter." Even the *South African Mining Journal*, an organ of the deep level group, offers unconscious testimony in the same direction. In a note on the Rose Deep it states that the ore is being "drawn from six different levels." Why should this be done to supply only 100 stamps, unless a rich "chute" is being followed down from one level to another?

It now only remains to show why these very questionable tactics to rig the shares and delude outsiders are being adopted; and the reason is not far to seek. With the groups who control the deep levels it is probably a matter of dire necessity—a matter of financial life or death. The truth is that these mines have cost a great deal more to open up and equip than was ever anticipated. The engineers' estimates in nearly every case have proved greatly at fault. There is hardly a deep level which, in addition to its already enormous capitalisation, is not deeply in debt and heavily loaded with debentures. Even such a company as the Rose Deep, which recently raised an additional £200,000 working capital, is said to be still in debt to the tune of £150,000, and requires more money. The Simmer and Jack has spent about £1,000,000, and has had to sacrifice its subsidiary shares to meet its engagements. The Simmer East has a debenture charge of £500,000; the Knights Deep, £400,000; the Robinson Deep £300,000; the Durban Deep, Witwatersrand Deep, and Vogelstruis Deep, each £200,000; the Geldenhuis Deep, £160,000; while many other companies are plunged in debt to the extent of several hundred thousand pounds. These facts are carefully hidden from view. A contemporary recently estimated that close on £10,000,000 sterling will be wanted to bring all the deep levels of the Rand to the producing stage. Where is all this money to be obtained?

The public, so far, has certainly shown no disposition to provide it, and therefore the controlling groups and deep level trust companies have had to fall back on their own resources. This is why a year ago the Gold Fields was compelled to double its ordinary capital, and the Rand Mines to raise £1,000,000 by debentures. These, however, are merely flea-bites to what is to come. The credit of the Goldfields group is now pledged up to the hilt; for a company, which in 1897 was only able to pay a scrip dividend, and has no better prospects for the coming year, can hardly hope to place a further issue of debentures or shares on anything like reasonable terms. But the money has to be found, and the only apparent method of salvation left is to obtain it by selling some of the shares in the more advanced "deeps" at the highest possible prices. That is why it is that "pools" have been formed to keep up the market, that is why the "eyes" of the mines are being picked out, the profits manipulated, and the praises of deep levels sung in the vampire press far and wide. The fool is asked, nay begged, to buy deep levels. But the trick is too obvious, and has been badly managed, prices were rushed up too fast, and big outputs and profits have been followed too quickly by share and debenture creations. So the attempt has obviously failed, and the result is absolute stagnation in the "Kaffir Circus." The manipulators have for once overreached themselves; they were too greedy.

Now let us turn to some of these trust companies and see how they stand examination individually. The two principal deep level manufacturing groups are the Rand Mines, Limited, and the Consolidated Gold Fields of South Africa, which, together, hold an autocratic sway over fully 80 per cent. of the mines. These groups float a deep level company, provide its working capital and auditors, act as its bankers, secretaries, engineers, machinery suppliers, agents and directors; advertise its merits in their own financial and so-called social press, and finally endeavour to sell its shares to the public at immense profits to themselves. They are as much manufacturers and vendors of deep levels as the "Pears" Company is a manufacturer and vendor of soap; and they advertise their wares on an even more lavish scale. There are many ramifications of the Gold Fields group; there is the parent, the Consolidated Gold Fields of South Africa—to give it its full title—and several subsidiary or baby concerns, such as the South African Gold Trust, Gold Fields Deep, Belgian Mining Trust, and Trust Français, all managed, directly or indirectly, by the same people. The two groups, Rand Mines and Gold Fields, own together about 70 per cent. of the shares of the entire deep levels of the Central Rand, and how all these mines are severally and jointly interested is shown by a table which we have compiled, giving the particulars of each company's holdings.

A TABLE
SHOWING
THE DEEP LEVEL HOLDINGS OF THE SOUTH AFRICAN TRUST COMPANIES.

—	Central Nigel Deep.	Crown Deep.	Durban Roodepoort Deep.	Geldenhuis Deep.	Glen Deep.	Jumpers Deep.	Jupiter.	Knights Central.	Knights Deep.	Langlaagte Deep.
Barnato Mines	—	—	—	—	—	38,900	—	—	—	—
Belgian Mining Trust	—	—	—	—	—	—	—	—	—	—
Consolidated Deep Levels	—	—	—	—	—	66,[illegible]	—	—	—	—
Consolidated Goldfields of South Africa	68,500	—	—	—	62,000	—	130,000	82,000	120,000	—
Goldfields Deep	—	—	—	—	177,062	—	164,459	—	134,750	—
Rand Mines	—	194,050	59,000	114,763	228,001	296,941	—	—	—	648,700
Simmer and Jack Proprietary	—	—	—	—	—	—	—	—	—	—
South African Gold Trust	5,000	—	—	—	—	—	—	10,000	10,000	—
Trust Francais	20,000	—	—	—	10,000	—	—	5,000	5,000	—
Total Shares	93,500	194,050	59,000	114,763	477,063	401,861	294,459	97,000	268,350	648,700
Capitals of Companies in Shares	200,000	a 250,000	300,000	114,763	a 500,000	407,391	467,000	412,719	413,093	650,000

—	Nigel Deep.	Nourse Deep.	Rand Victoria.	Robinson Deep.	Rose Deep.	Simmer and Jack.	Simmer and Jack East.	Simmer and Jack West.	South Rand Mine.	Witwatersrand Deep.
Barnato Mines	—	—	—	—	—	—	—	—	—	—
Belgian Mining Trust	2,426	—	—	—	—	21,000	3,000	—	—	—
Consolidated Deep Levels	—	—	—	—	51,182	—	—	—	—	18,760
Consolidated Goldfields of South Africa	110,500	—	81,000	—	—	690,500	47,000	28,000	70,000	—
Goldfields Deep	—	—	176,084	300,000	55,200	—	39,225	21,604	—	—
Rand Mines	—	290,382	—	—	127,735	—	—	9,771	215,500	—
Simmer and Jack Proprietary	—	—	133,690	—	30,000	—	211,349	196,366	—	—
South African Gold Trust	26,000	—	—	5,000	—	55,000	25,000	5,000	—	1,000
Trust Francais	20,000	—	—	—	—	40,000	20,000	—	—	—
Total Shares	158,926	290,382	390,774	305,000	264,117	806,500	345,574	260,041	285,500	19,760
Capitals of Companies in Shares	d 300,000	b 274,934	650,000	400,000	c 355,000	c 940,000	a 550,000	300,000	300,000	351,000

a Since issued 50,000 additional shares. b Since issued 75,066 additional shares. c Since issued 45,000 additional shares. d Since reconstructed. e £5 shares.

Another 15 per cent. of these shares is held by private individuals and syndicates connected with the same groups, leaving, at the outside, only 15 per cent. distributed amongst the public. With such a large controlling interest in the mines it will be understood how it has been possible to manipulate and maintain prices at their present level. Indeed, to "sell a bear" would be to play as much into the hands of these houses as to actually buy the shares. The only safe course is to leave them entirely alone.

Not only, however, do these Trust Companies possess large interests in the deep levels, but they hold each other's shares to a remarkable extent. For instance, the Consolidated Gold Fields holds half the Gold Fields Deep capital, which company in its turn owns three-quarters of the Robinson Deep mine. The Gold Fields holds shares in the Trust Français and Trust Belgian; the Trust Français holds shares in the Gold Fields, Gold Fields Deep, and Trust Belgian; the Trust Belgian holds shares in the Trust Français, Gold Fields, and Gold Fields Deep; the Gold Trust holds shares in the Gold Fields Deep and Consolidated Gold Fields, and so on. In fact, the whole fabric is a most complicated one, and unless by some miraculous means it can be placed on a satisfactory financial footing it will one day come tumbling to the ground like a pack of cards.

Trust Companies.	Holdings.			
	Belgian Mining Trust.	Consolidated Gold Fields.	Gold Fields Deep.	Trust Français.
Belgian Mining Trust	—	20,000	18,000	27,557
Consolidated Gold Fields of South Africa	21,000	—	322,500	105,000
South African Gold Trust	—	100,000	50,000	—
Trust Français	—	19,000	30,000	—

As all these concerns are public companies, and the shareholders expect a return on their money, it is not only necessary from time to time to dispose of some of the shareholdings in the mines to provide for the capital calls of less developed properties, but funds have to be regularly found to pay dividends, and thus prevent the whole structure from collapsing. It is, consequently, vital to the existence of these trusts that such conditions shall be created as will enable them to sell their portions of their assets at big profits, and that endeavours are being made to induce the public to become the receptacle is evident from what has been said. There are not wanting signs that an energetic campaign is shortly to be entered upon with that object. The public mind is being prepared by means of inflated outputs, fictitious profits, and dividends paid partly out of capital; while the Press organs of the groups scattered throughout England and the Continent are engaged in singing pæans of praise on the deep levels. The market is supported by carefully conducted "pools," and prices have been worked up to a giddy height. In three or four months' time several other deep levels will commence crushing; and, the result, as we have shown, with their enormous ore reserves, can be made to exhibit apparently large profits, at any rate for a period. Deep level dividends will be declared, marvellously rich strikes announced, and a certain amount of activity created in the market to induce the public to bite. But will it do so? A hard lesson was learned in 1894 and 1895; which has surely not yet been forgotten? So far the voice of temptation has not been listened to, but there are many fools in the world, and time is a blurrer of memory as well as of grief. With a large section of the English Press at the command of these Deep Level magnates—and our readers would open their eyes wide if they knew some of those we include in this category—it is hoped to work wonders. A raid is now being prepared on the pockets of the English and Continental speculating public, beside which previous exploits will pale into insignificance.

The London and Globe Juggle.

The almost forgotten Mr. Barnato does not fail in humble imitators, and it is now becoming a rule of mining finance, when in difficulty "play an amalgamation." Modest arrangements of this kind often take place, but the proposal of the London and Globe Corporation in respect of its subsidiary companies is something above the ordinary kind. For one thing the capital involved is £2,000,000, and it is a striking fact that out of the twelve mining companies issued by this Corporation everyone is a failure, and yet the Corporation itself has apparently waxed fat and opulent in a market sense. The poor unfortunate subsidiary concerns having come to an end, or practically so, of their minute working capitals, the London and Globe says, "amalgamate into one big company at a composition of 10s. in the £, find £500,000 more capital, and we will run the show again." In other words, it has asked the shareholders of thirteen companies to amalgamate into one, called "the Standard Exploration," the exchange being made on the basis of one new share for every two old shares. Fresh capital to the extent of £500,000 is to be raised, of which £250,000 is to be guaranteed by the London and Globe, but this benefit is hedged with the proviso that the new concern must take £200,000 capital of the British America Corporation — the latest monstrosity perpetrated by this London and Globe affair itself. Now there are remarkable differences in the positions of the thirteen companies thus invited into the new "blind pool." The shares of six of them are held largely, if not wholly, by the public, those of six more are held almost exclusively by the London and Globe Corporation, its creatures, and allies, and the capital of the odd one is probably held half-and-half by the "insides" and the "out." The names and capitals of these companies are as follows:—

Held by Public.	Nom. capital. £	Held by Promoters.	Nom. capital. £
Golden Crown	100,000	Wealth of Nations Extended	175,000
Mainland Consols	150,000	Duke Gold Mine	150,000
Wealth of Nations	200,000	Hannan's Golden Dream	150,000
Paddington Consols	175,000	Paddington South	150,000
Hannan's Golden Group	175,000	Mahara Royal	150,000
Hannan's Golden Treasure	150,000	Karaka	150,000

Austin Friars Syndicate......£105,000.

Of course the separation here made is not absolute, and possibly some of the public may have Wealth of Nations Extended, while the promoters may have some Mainland Consols, but the general position is as described. Now for one thing, the Austin Friars Syndicate is a finance company, and what has that to do with the working of a number of mines? Then the Mahara Royal and Karaka own properties in New Zealand, while the rest are in Western Australia, so that the two gorgeously named companies are a poor acquisition to the group from a mere business point of view.

The gravest objection to the scheme, however, lies in the fact that through the proposed new Standard Exploration Company, the London and Globe Corporation, will be able to unload its otherwise unmarketable scrip upon the public. If the scheme went through, the quotation on the new shares, product of the fusion and confusion, would cover all these wretched productions that the public would not touch even in the height of its folly. It would be just the same then as with the shares held by Americans in the Anaconda mine. These were quoted with the rest, and can be sold on this side under the protection of the moderate amount originally offered to, and to some extent held, by, the British public. For a nice profitable chance of this kind the London and Globe Corporation pays nothing at all. But as a matter of simple business morality, the scheme ought not to be allowed to go through. One has only to refer to the Barnato amalgamation to see the effect of such an arrangement. Prior to that operation, which allowed Barnato Brothers and their friends to unload unsavoury holdings upon the public, Johannesburg Consolidated Investment shares stood at 4; they are now 1⅞ with every prospect of slipping lower.

But, of course, something must be done, for here are a number of companies that have run out of cash, and whose precarious position, owing to the small acreage and problematic nature of their grounds, requires every form of economy that could be obtained by amalgamation. To amalgamate in some form is better than to reconstruct singly, and therefore we think the shareholders of those companies in which the public have a large interest would do well to coalesce and act together after each has examined its position as to debts and working capital in hand, if any. But in doing this, the London and Globe should be given the go-by along with its precious British America Corporation. Owing to its gross mismanagement and extravagance the companies it has launched, or tried to, have been brought to this pass, and it will be far better to be rid of the pack of market operators who surround it and start clear with possibly a fair chance of doing some sound mining work. To those who only look to the market, such advice will be foolishness, but if the public coolly sits down to further endow those who have lost its money with power to strip it of more, then it will only have itself to blame should the financier wax more and more rapacious.

Economic and Financial Notes and Correspondence.

The Indian Debate in the Commons.

It is not possible to compliment the House of Commons on its Indian debate. An excuse may perhaps be found for the poor display made in the terms of Mr. Lawson-Walton's amendment, but that does not justify the exhibition made of themselves by the present and the late Secretary of State for India. These two gentlemen, Lord George Hamilton and Sir Henry Fowler, brought the discussion down to the level of a squabble between two guinea-pig directors, quarrelling over a subject of which neither had more than a perfunctory or superficial knowledge. It is pitiable to think that India should be perishing while such men, in essaying to play the *rôle* of statesmen, literally slang each other and come down to the level of draymen shouting to each other, "You did," "I did not," "It was you." This display went on, amazing mankind, and plague is spreading in India, and her finances rapidly getting into a tangle from which a composition in bankruptcy will alone release them.

Except as a manifestation of the most inveterate bungling on the part of the prominent officials and military party, now together destroying our Indian Empire, this frontier war is, in itself, a matter of secondary importance. The true question which ought to be to the front about India is the position of her finances, but directly these are touched upon, the inquirer is always diverted from his purpose and involved, if possible, in a despicable wrangle about "standards of value"; "Shall India have a gold standard?" "Ought the mints to be re-opened again?" and so on, mostly idiotic drivel. Such discussions are, in their way, quite as useful, though, to the bureaucrats as a fireworks display like the debate on Mr. Walton's amendment; they obscure the real question at issue and prevent the British public from realising the imminent danger threatening our greatest dependency.

Sir William Harcourt did for a brief period lift the debate to a considerable extent above the low level to which it was dragged down by Lord George Hamilton, and his denunciaton of Sir George White for coming forward and interfering in his capacity as Commander-in-Chief with the Civil Government of India was thoroughly well deserved. As we have often declared it is the dominance of this pestilent military spirit in the Government of India which is at the root of the mischief. The substance of the Indian people has been thereby wasted to an extent no man can measure. Year by year the masses of them fall into more abject poverty. Every few years millions die of hunger, and still this policy of military activity, of wars indulged in like games of chess, is blindly followed. Strategic railways and useless fortifications, built with borrowed money, the interest on which India is unable to pay, are multiplied on any pretext or none, until no thinking man can do other than tremble at the prospect before the nation. But Mr. Balfour, the leader of the Government in the House of Commons, knows nothing of this any more than his colleague, Lord George Hamilton, any more than Mr. H. Fowler. On that matter the ignorance he displayed on Tuesday night is enough to make the heart sick. What can come to a great, and, as we boast, Imperial people, when such flippant amateurs as Mr. Balfour lead in the counsels of the State.

An Indian Administrative Scandal.

By way of calling attention to the kind of thing that goes on in India at the present time without the slightest attention being paid to it either by Parliament or the British public, we mention a correspondence which has taken place between Sir William Wedderburn, M.P., and Lord George Hamilton, the Secretary of State for India. From this correspondence we learn that two native gentlemen of Poona, the Sirdar brothers Natu, were imprisoned about the middle of last year and have been kept in prison ever since without trial. Sir William drew Lord George Hamilton's attention to this scandalous proceeding, and points out that it was unwarranted by law, and that the Bombay Government had taken possession of a large amount of valuable personal property belonging to the Natu family, and asks for attachments to be removed and this property restored. Of course he gets no satisfaction, his first letter is dated November 4, 1897, and on January 5 last he writes again to point out that he has had no reply to his first letter, and that the brothers had then been in custody for about six months. The usual official acknowledgment reaches him on January 11, and at length on February 8 he gets a reply from which we make the following extract.

2. You are no doubt aware that the regulation under which Sirdar B. K. Natu and his brother are detained, for the reasons of State specified in the Preamble, can only be put in force as regards "individuals against whom there may not be sufficient ground to institute any judicial proceedings, or when such proceeding may not be adapted to the nature of the case, or may for other reasons be unadvisable or improper."

The Government of Bombay, therefore, by putting the regulation in force against the brothers Natu, have clearly indicated the view which they take of the advisability of instituting judicial proceedings against them; and I am to inform you, in reply to your question, that there is no present intention of bringing them to trial.

3. As regards the grounds on which Sirdar B. R. Natu and his brother are detained, I am directed to inform you that they have no relevancy whatever to the correspondence mentioned in your letter. The Government of Bombay are in possession of information which has convinced them that such detention is necessary in order to secure her Majesty's dominions from internal commotion, and that it must, in the opinion of the Government, be continued until they are satisfied that the public tranquility would not be endangered by the release of the brothers Natu.

4. Finally, you represent that Regulation XXV of 1827 gives no power to attach the personal effects of persons detained under its provisions. On this point the Government of Bombay has taken legal advice, and has issued orders for the release of such items in the list of property attached as cannot legally be dealt with under the Regulation.

This scarcely appears to be the conduct of a Government which is sure of its position. What on earth are the officials afraid of if the brothers Natu had nothing, and it is perfectly well-known that they had nothing, to do with the murder of Mr. Rand?

A Wail from Sydney.

Rather gloomy views are expressed by the Sydney *Daily Telegraph* about the trade of New South Wales for 1897, and about the prospects for the current year. At least they would be called "gloomy" and "pessimistic," and all the rest of it, if first uttered by us. Both imports and exports of merchandise for the year showed increases—imports being £606,362 larger at £15,283,824, and exports £472,441 larger at £11,999,191, but "practically the whole of the increase in the exports of merchandise has been in re-exports, leaving the exports of domestic produce in 1897 very much at the same level as in 1896." This is sad, and we are not much exhilarated in mind by the information that the imports of gold were only £85,028, against an export of £907,145. Adding the net exports of gold to the exports of merchandise, we find that last year the colony still imported nearly 2½ millions worth more than it exported.

Herein lies the seriousness of the position. This colony, like all its neighbours, has to remit a large sum every year to meet its debt charges in London. On the public debt alone the annual charge is now over 2½ millions, most of which is due here, and there are numerous interest and dividend charges payable on company debentures, and on share capital held here. How in the world can these charges, amounting, say, to three millions altogether, be covered at the same time that the export trade of the colony, all told, is insufficient in value to pay for current imports? We advise colonial statisticians to set their wits to work to solve this conundrum. To our dull, plain mind there appears but one sure method of solving the difficulty—borrowing more money in London. If the colonists can show us another way, we shall rejoice to be educated.

Bavarian Trade and United States Tariffs.

Bavarian trade, generally prosperous in 1896 and 1897, has suffered considerably in one respect. Hitherto the United States has been one of the chief outlets for Bavarian manufactures; but now it is closed to her owing to the highly protective tariffs to which our transatlantic cousins submit with so much humility. Hence some loss to Bavarian trade; but the Bavarians do not clamour for a war of tariffs in order to punish these short-sighted Americans; they prefer peace and the search for new markets. As one result, the trade with England and her colonies has considerably increased; arrangements have been made with Spain for a minimum tariff for German goods; and a commercial treaty has been concluded with Japan. Before Kiao-Chau was probably heard of, German merchants had combined to send a commercial mission to the Far East to discover what articles of German manufacture are most in demand there. Better this enterprise, surely, than the querulous cry to Government for "countervailing duties" to which we have become so uncomfortably accustomed. It is not all prosperity, however, even in Bavaria. The textile trade has suffered greatly from depression, and speculative building has been so feverishly active in the Munich district for some time that, unless it is promptly checked, a crisis is feared which may prove serious. One other fact is worthy of note. Although there is a tendency to a reduction of hours in factories, and in some cases the fifty-four hours week has been adopted, the general day's work is from ten to eleven hours, and in handwork establishments eleven to twelve hours. It is worthy of note, too, that Sunday rest is now enforced by the State, without any of the harm to industry which its opponents prophesied.

Trade in Chile.

1897 opened badly for trade in Chile; how it may have ended we do not yet know, as the report sent by the British Consul at Valparaiso only deals with the first six months of the year. During this period imports fell £949,665 below the same period of 1896—£5,071,840 against £6,021,505. The largest portion of this decrease is claimed by Valparaiso, but most of the ports are sufferers; indeed, there are only four which show a slight increase. Nor is this decline altogether owing to bad trade. In the sugar trade, for example, the decrease is mostly owing to the development of native sugar refineries, which are proving so successful that the decline in the imports of refined sugar must continue, and will steadily become more marked. So with the imports of timber. Though partially owing to depression in the building trade, it is largely due to the development of the native industry; and as the years pass by, the decline in timber imports is sure to grow greater. Still, trade in Chile was undoubtedly bad in the first half of last year. It is also shown by the diminution in the exports from £6,185,868 in the first half of 1896 to £4,270,346 in the opening six months of 1897. The decrease has been especially notable in nitrates and wheat. There was, however, an increase in the exports of coal, wool, and gold bars; while the exports of tanned hides were more than doubled in the six months referred to. It would thus seem that, probably, Chilian trade is only temporarily and not very seriously afflicted. As to the imports in 1896, it seems that Great Britain obtained 40·83 per cent. of them, Germany coming next with 27·10 per cent. But there is this significant contrast between the two: while Britain stood at the top, her percentage of the trade was 5·72 less than in 1895, while Germany had increased her shipments from £2,739,015 in 1895 to £3,179,483 in 1896. The trade with the United States also showed a marked increase in 1896, though her percentage of the whole was only 9·18. Thus, though Great Britain is still far ahead of her chief rivals, it would almost seem that she has got on the "down-grade" unless she can in some way win back her lost ground. That is not much as yet; but if she goes on losing, even by inches, while her rivals win by half-inches, Great Britain's supremacy is doomed all the same.

Dublin United Tramways Company (1896) Limited.

Mr. Chas. Eason, jun., and the Hon. Mr. Nugent expressed strong dissatisfaction with the management and accounts of this company at the meeting of shareholders held in Dublin on the 8th inst. They seem to us to have had good reason. The report and accounts are not clear, and, as regards the latter, it is to be noted that the auditors give a most guarded certificate, very different from the one the same men gave to the old Dublin United Tramways Company in July, 1896. Of course the pretext is that this new company only deals with the moneys received from the two old companies it has bought up, and has itself no details to supply. This is the line taken by the English companies which bought up American Breweries, and shareholders in such have acquired painful experience as to its cogency. "Legally," the chairman said "we are not bound to give this information," and they thought it might place the directors "in a great difficulty" with the Corporation "if they showed their hand too freely." This is nonsense if the business is being fairly and squarely conducted, but in law the board is, we fear, unassailable. If its articles of association permit it to cover up its operation and to issue a skeleton balance sheet, shareholders are powerless. But we doubt whether the law allows any limited company to conceal its share list from scrutiny whatever its deed of incorporation may authorise. It seems no share list has been filed with the Registrar of Joint Stock Companies. The attention of the Board of Trade ought to be drawn to this, as it seems to us, violation of the statute.

The United States and Spain.

It almost seemed for a day or two this week as if only war could soothe the offended dignity of the United States, stung by some indiscreet and indefensible comments made by the Spanish Ambassador at Washington in a letter to Senor Canalejas. The letter, no doubt, was a private one, but it was somehow obtained and published by an enemy; and, as it contained some severe strictures on President McKinley, Senor Dupuy de Lôme at once acknowledged the serious nature of his error by tendering his resignation, which was immediately accepted by the Spanish Cabinet. This, however, did not satisfy American Jingoes. They insisted that the Spanish Government ought to make an ample apology for what they declared to be a national insult offered to the United States. If apology was refused, they "would know the reason why," and the American Government was urged to prompt and decisive action in the matter. The object of the Jingoes was, of course, to force on war on any pretext in the interests of Cuba. Fortunately, however, President McKinley was not to be forced in the matter. He has already warned Spain of the danger lurking in the continuance of the war in Cuba. The Spanish authorities will do well to heed this warning. There is in America a strong financial as well as political interest in the Cuban question. An influential syndicate is ready for the exploitation of the island, and if its pacification is not secured soon, the time may come more quickly than is expected when the Executive Government will be unable to resist the pressure put upon them for intervention in Cuba, perhaps for its immediate purchase or annexation.

Lloyd's Bank, Limited.

As we owe this bank an *amende* for having twice blundered over its reports, and because the facts are interesting in themselves, we print the following extract from the speech of Mr. Thomas Salt, the retiring chairman, delivered at the fortieth shareholders' general meeting held in Birmingham on Monday last:—

Referring to the changes of the last ten years, Mr. Salt expressed a hope that first-class banks would, while maintaining a courteous rivalry, not resort to vulgar competition, but work together in friendship and harmony. In announcing his retirement from the chairmanship, on account of age and infirmity, he quoted the figures of the first balance-sheet he signed in 1886, in comparison with those of the last report, showing that in those eleven years the capital had advanced from £750,000 to £2,040,000, the reserve fund from £360,000 to £1,200,000, and the total assets from eleven millions to forty millions, or nearly quadrupled.

Openings in Hudson's Bay Territory.

We must revise our notions about Hudson's Bay Territory. It is not a bit cut out of the Arctic regions. Moose Bay is in a latitude further south than London, and even the more northern portion is not colder than the north of Scotland. What more is wanted? The bay does not freeze across in winter, and there is free navigation during five months of the year, or thereabouts. The Hudson Bay route would bring the North-West as near to Europe as to Quebec. It offers the best route to the goldfields there. There is gold in various parts of the territory; gipsum, iron, copper, silver, and lead are believed to be not uncommon. "No end" of good land is available for tillage. In one area as large as England a Scotchman—not the one of Polar fame—and a few dozen Indian families have the land to themselves. Why are they left undisturbed in their solitude? What is the Hudson's Bay Company thinking about? Is there not room for a spring rush there as well as to Klondike?

The French Mercantile Navy.

Even lavish Government subventions have failed in placing the French Mercantile Marine in a healthy condition. Since 1881, about £24,000,000 have been paid by Government in shipping subventions—more than the total value of the French Merchant Navy—yet the child thus carefully nurtured continues puny and stunted. It grows, but it is steadily falling further behind its vigorous English and German rivals in strength and activity. Ten years ago, the French Mercantile Marine was next—though at a long distance—to the British. But in 1895—the latest period for which we have official figures—Germany had completely outstripped France. During those ten years France had only increased her tonnage by 142,346 tons, while Great Britain's was improved by 3,391,784 tons, and Germany's by 678,475 tons. Even Norway showed a far more sturdy growth, for her tonnage increase was considerably more than double that of France. During last year French yards turned out only two large steamers of a total tonnage of 6,500, while Germany turned out thirty-three steamers of an aggregate of 63,000 tons. It is thus that protective duties—call them by what name you will—throw blight on every trade to which they are applied. Frenchmen are beginning to appreciate this in connection with the sugar bounties; when will they show a like appreciation of the fact that an expenditure of £24,000,000 in subventions has not encouraged native shipbuilding, but rather dwarfed and stunted its growth, and must end in so enfeebling it that it will probably not have energy enough to continue the struggle for existence?

It appears, however, that French ships can compete, with some seeming success, with British vessels in the carrying trade to French ports. In Rouen, for instance, our Consul points out that, since 1892, when a more protective French tariff was enforced, British shipping frequenting that port has declined both in number of ships and in total registered tonnage. In the three years previous to 1892 the British flag was represented at Rouen by a yearly average of 1,000 ships, the tonnage of which reached close upon 450,000 registered tons. Since 1892 there has been a gradual decline, until last year the figures fell to 700 British ships of 363,627 tons. Though much of this decline is attributed to the French protective tariff, yet there are other causes at work. There is more international competition in the sea-carrying trade. Swedish and Norwegian ships are supplanting British ships in the timber trade. It is the same in the wine trade to Rouen; British vessels hardly take any part in it now, while Swedish and Norwegian ships engaged in it have increased in number. But the French themselves have been the chief gainers. French ships are also entering into competition with British in conveying English coal to Rouen. Our Consul thinks it is only the navigation bounty that enables the French to engage in this competition, and even with that aid they find it difficult. They are now clamouring for increased bounties. If they succeed in this agitation, they may possibly supplant a few more English colliers, but the inevitable process of enervation will again set in, and their last state will be worse than their first. There is never much energy in the begging trader.

THE VALUE OF STATE RAILWAYS.

Prussia seems to find her railways a paying speculation. For their construction she had incurred a debt of £351,183,539, but this debt has been reduced to £261,500,000 out of profits earned. But that is not all. In the 13 years from 1882 to 1895 the excess of receipts over expenditure had been £198,368,576. After paying interest on the debt, and devoting £600,000 to meeting deficits in the State expenditure, there was a surplus of £77,560,332, of which sum £47,359,000 was applied to general State purposes, and £26,138,000 in paying off the State debt. As to passenger traffic, the Prussian experience seems to be similar to our own; the cheapest class produces the largest revenue. The first class gives 18 per cent. of the total, the second 23·93 per cent., and the third 40·25 per cent. But a fourth class has been introduced in recent years, and, although it is not yet universal, it is rapidly gaining upon the third class. Last year it supplied 23·93 per cent. of the income from passengers. Altogether Prussia makes a very good thing out of her railways. The danger is that Governments may come to dip too often and too deeply into their teeming coffers to make up deficits caused by reckless State expenditure. It would not be surprising if, at a push, they were made to contribute towards building up the Imperial Navy, or in paying the cost of an unpopular war.

MR. SUTHERST AGAIN!

From the rôle of a libelled company promoter, bringing his action for words imputing falsification of facts in a prospectus, to a bankrupt moving to expunge proofs against his estate, is, indeed, a far cry, but Mr. Sutherst has within the short space of five days played both these parts, and both unsuccessfully. We noted that in his cross-examination in the libel suit he estimated his assets at £395,875. We can imagine the hopes of his present creditors rising high at this information, only cruelly to be dashed to the ground on learning that that amount consisted entirely of shares and interests in companies, presumably of his own promotion.

SIMMERING CRETE.

The European Concert seems at last to have given up Crete as hopeless. They cannot get the six Powers to agree on anything, so the latest suggestion is that the business may be relegated to a committee of two Powers to choose some temporary governor for the island; or, if even two cannot come to an agreement on this terribly knotty point, that they may patch up "some semblance" of an autonomous régime, as the *Standard's* Constantinople correspondent puts it. It is said that the ambassadors have arranged to meet again soon for the discussion of this notable suggestion. The story may be true or it may not. It is impossible to say. Anything may happen in Crete, and at any moment. But the fact that such a suggestion has been put forward, even in the shape of a rumour, in Constantinople, is surely very fair evidence of the futility of the Concert's action throughout. There is nothing to indicate that Russia has definitively withdrawn the candidature of Prince George of Greece; but there are some signs that Russian diplomatists would not be disappointed if the Cretans were once more to take their fate in their hands and inaugurate a revolution. It would probably be successful. A *coup d'état* would find Prince George ready to land; and the distracted Powers that could not agree to anything while peace reigned might be promptly brought to accept an arrangement made in spite of them, at the cost of more fighting and further loss of life. Strange that this European Areopagus should only be brought into harmony by revolution!

Industrial Revolution in Sweden.

A kind of industrial revolution has been going on in Sweden during the last few years. She is giving up the export of raw material, and taking to manufacturing instead. In some things the Swede has already almost a monopoly. Of such are bicycle tubes, which are exported all over the world; steel bands rolled by cold process, umbrella frames, steel bones for corsets, and other things. The value of Swedish iron and steel is well known; but a few years ago it would have seemed absurd to speak of Sweden as a competitor with England in its manufacture. But a total change has come about in this respect: Sweden is a manufacturing competitor of England, and a tolerably successful one too. Good technical teaching has greatly helped in the development of the Swedish metal industry. It has a large supply of excellent skilled labour at a wage rate of from 3½d. to 5d. an hour. Few strikes occur, and the average hours of labour are sixty a week. Another notable thing remarked in the Foreign Office report is that, while Great Britain does the largest trade of any nation with Sweden, it imports from that country £8,000,000 worth of goods, and sends back only £5,500,000 worth; thus a balance of £2,500,000 stands against Great Britain in the transaction. Germany, on the other hand, imports £2,500,000 worth from Sweden, but returns goods worth no less than £6,500,000, thus leaving a balance of £4,000,000 in Germany's favour. More than that, about half the goods imported from Sweden to Britain were sent over in Swedish or Norwegian ships. England is therefore twice hit in the transaction; while in Sweden, as everywhere else, the German commercial traveller is ubiquitous, and the English ditto almost non-existent. British merchants and manufacturers will have to look to it, or suffer more.

A Long Expected Amalgamation.

This is a week of amalgamation proposals, but no one will be surprised that it is suggested the London and Northern Assets Corporation and the London and Northern Debenture Corporation should combine. Both have the same people on the board, both have the same office and secretary, and both have had misfortune. It is now proposed that the Debenture Company buy up the Assets Company by giving £13 in its shares for every £15 in shares of the Assets Company. The founders are to be practically extinguished by bonuses which perhaps are generous, but at the same time do not amount to much in the total.

As the one company is slightly better off than the other the arrangement seems a fair one, if the assets are identical in both cases. Of this, however, we cannot be sure, and it would be just as well if the character of these investments were disclosed. No list of them has ever been furnished to our knowledge, and only occasionally allusion is made to them by name, when necessity, generally a liquidation, compels the delicate matter to be touched upon. In the Board we have no faith, for Sir J. W. Maclure, Mr. J. M. Maclean, and Sir Joseph Renals, are not amongst those who, in our opinion, bring strength to a directorate. Therefore, now that this board has confessed to its failings, it ought to go a step further and show the nature of the assets remaining to these unfortunate concerns. Otherwise, how can the shareholders put that faith in the future they are expected to hold?

Mr. Bottomley's Amalgamation.

Envious of the London and Globe display of financial sleight of share-juggling, Mr. Bottomley is preparing to charm the world of mining finance with a tip-top amalgamation of his own. Having in the course of a few years formed four company-distilling corporations—the Associated Gold Mines, the Associated Southern, the North-West Associated, and the Auxiliary Associated—and these having produced on an average about one mine company a-piece, the distinguished originator of them all now proposes that they amalgamate into one "big concern." Is it not magnificent? To talk about the Duke of York and his 20,000 men is nothing beside this. The only sad point is that the amalgamation did not come off before the companies were floated, or it may be that Mr. Bottomley, with his *fin de siècle* methods, hopes, in the future, to even excel his present proposal. To the man who can put up the pieces of paper known as Northern Territories shares to 3¼ a-piece, everything is possible, in a market sense, until he is found out. After that the tale may be rather different, as the Barnatos, and others of their kind, found out not so very many months ago.

The Gold Production of North America.

According to Mr. John J. Valentine, the able President of the Wells, Fargo Express Company, the total output of gold in the States and Territories west of the Missouri River, including British Columbia, was last year $69,830,599, and of silver $37,184,034, say £14,000,000 of the one, and £7,450,000 of the other. To these totals Mexico added about £1,800,000 in gold and £12,145,000 in silver = $8,500,000 and $60,683,000 respectively. The Mexican production of silver, therefore, more than made good the decline in the United States and Canadian output of the same metal. But the North American production of gold, as Mr. Valentine points out, was last year the largest in its history. If his estimate of the world's production for the same period, which he puts at the "surprisingly large" total of approximately 240 million dollars, about £49,000,000, is correct, then the United States and British Columbian properties of the total, was about 29·590. This year it is to be presumed the British Columbian contribution will be larger, and, of course, there is Klondike. Ontario also yields a little gold now and may yield more. What shall we do with all the yellow metal? Dissipate it in wars, or what?

The Salt Union, Limited.

The dismal announcement is made that no dividend will be paid on the ordinary shares for the past year, and that holders of seven per cent. preference shares will get only 1¼ per cent., while a year ago the full interest was paid on the preference capital, and 1 per cent. on the ordinary shares. It is impossible to judge the true position until the directors' report and accounts are issued, but there is no getting away from the fact that whereas last year £90,000 was distributed in dividends, on this occasion the company divides only £12,500, which is actually less than the balance carried forward a year ago. We have for several years past called attention annually to the crisis gathering around the Company's affairs, and have been scoffed at for our pains. However, here it is, and the position of the debenture stock holders is serious. Altogether the share capital of the concern amounts to £3,000,000, and the A and B Debenture Stocks to £1,200,0000, while, on the other side, the properties, works, plant, and goodwill stood in the last balance-sheet at £3,439,952; but owing to the wretched earning power of the undertaking no proper allowance has been possible for depreciation, and we doubt if the real value of this item is much more than half its present figure. A reconstruction scheme is inevitable, and the more severe it is the more hope there will be for the future. Indeed, well done, it may put new life in the company, which has had to work too much under thrall of the vendors by whom it was created.

CRYSTAL PALACE RE-ORGANISATION SCHEME.

According to the *Daily Mail* of yesterday the proposal is to reduce the present capital of this unfortunate company, amounting to £1,591,000, to a total of £605,000, of which £250,000 will be in 3½ per cent. debentures, £150,000 in 4½ B shares, £105,000 in 5 per cent. accumulative preference shares, £95,000 in preferred ordinary, and £5,000 in deferred ordinary shares. This looks needlessly elaborate, but of course there are a variety of interests to be considered. The old capital embracing no less than three descriptions of debenture stocks besides an ordinary stock, and a B stock which does not represent anything, but whose nominal amount is £802,140. The main object of the proposed re-organisation is, apparently, to find fresh working capital to the amount of £100,000. It would seem that Messrs. J. Lyons & Co., Limited, who are to be appointed the caterers to the new company, and Messrs. Ind, Coope & Co., the brewers, are to take "a substantial interest" in the new scheme, and, really, we do not see why they should not find the new money. No share or debenture-holder in the old company has any motive to provide a penny of it. The history of the company has been one long monotony of disappointment, and the promise for the future is not appreciably better than for the past. But if refreshment caterers and brewers think they can put new life into a decaying concern they ought to be made welcome to try.

A SHAM COUNCIL OF "FOREIGN BONDHOLDERS."

Subjoined is a letter on this subject. It was impossible for us to make distinctions in printing the names, but none the less is this disclaimer of any "friendship" for Sir John Lubbock, *qua* Chairman of the Council, valuable. The suggestion made is also pertinent :—

To the Editor.

London, February 16, 1898.

SIR,—In a note at the foot of your article on the above subject in last week's REVIEW, you publish the names of recent purchasers of Certificates in the Council of Foreign Bondholders who have been put upon the register since February, 1897, and remark that "the great majority appear to be those of personal friends of Sir John Lubbock." You further say, "Why were these certificates not sold openly to foreign bondholders and to the highest bidder?"

On behalf of several members of the Stock Exchange, including myself, whose names appear in the list you have published, it is only fair to your readers to acquaint them with our intentions in obtaining possession, not through the medium of the secretary to the corporation, of some of those certificates.

Among the names you have quoted, including one member at least of the original founders of the corporation, may be seen those of gentlemen whose only object in obtaining certificates at some cost and considerable trouble has been to rescue this corporation from becoming a by-word to investors in foreign bonds for all time. Members of the Stock Exchange who are certificate holders have voluntarily subscribed a large sum of money among themselves, to oppose the present Bill before Parliament. We do so on public grounds: we live by the public, and are prepared to defend their interests in times like the present at our own cost. Our action at the present crisis is sufficient evidence that our monetary interest in the corporation and its future is altogether laid aside. Speaking personally, I can only trust that Parliament will appoint a small commission to enquire into the whole position and status of the corporation. In that case I feel assured that the funds accumulated by this institution would never be handed over in the form of an "open cheque" to a self-elected and irresponsible body of mutual friends, calling themselves a Council of Foreign Bondholders.—Yours faithfully,

[I enclose my card.] "STOCK EXCHANGE."

Critical Index to New Investments.

MARSHALL & SNELGROVE, LIMITED.

For family reasons the business is turned into a private limited company, the whole of the issued share capital, £500,000, being taken by the late and former partners. But the public is asked to subscribe for an issue of £225,000 first mortgage 4½ per cent. debenture stock, part of a total of £300,000, at 106 per cent. Interest is due February and August, and the stock is repayable at par on February 20, 1948, but it can be paid off at 110 in 1911 on six months' notice given. This famous old business dates from 1837, and the assets and goodwill are acquired by the company for £625,000, payable as to £125,000 in cash, and the whole of the share capital. Apart from goodwill the security for the debenture stock consists of leases, London and Scarborough, £130,000; horses, carts, fittings, &c., £32,596; stock £283,086 and debtors, cash and bills receivable, £318,195, making a total of £763,878, from which £101,823 has to be deducted, representing trade and other creditors, so that the total security is valued at £662,055. There is no freehold property, but the main London premises are held on leases for terms of sixty years from Lady-day next; the period of the Scarborough lease is not stated, and the lease of the premises at Leeds is about to expire, the business being transferred to the Scarborough branch. It is clear, too, from the figures that a very large proportion of the firm's business must be carried on on credit. It is not considered necessary to disclose the figures of the profits, but accountants certify that in each of the last nineteen years the profits have been sufficient to pay the interest on the present issue of debenture stock more than four times over. The company will maintain a policy with the Law Life Assurance Society to repay the amount of the stock at the end of fifty years, but we nevertheless consider the security offered for the debenture issue is not so good as it looks, though, of course, there should be no fear about the payment of interest while the business keeps up at its present level.

SHROPSHIRE BREWERY COMPANY, LIMITED.

The share capital of this company is £140,000, in £10 shares, of which 9,000 are five per cent. cumulative preference, and the rest ordinary. There is also an issue of £140,000 four per cent. irredeemable first mortgage debenture stock, which with 7,850 preference shares, is offered for subscription at par. The balance of the preference shares are held in reserve for future issue, while the whole of the ordinary are taken by the directors, tenants, and customers. Company is formed to purchase and enlarge the business of Wm. Hall & Co., brewers, maltsters, and wine and spirit merchants of Wem and Shrewsbury, there being besides the breweries, forty-nine freehold and fourteen leasehold houses, with forty freehold shops and houses. Profits for last three years are certified at £11,704, £11,749, and £14,355. Nothing has been written off for depreciation, because it is claimed that properties and plant have been maintained out of revenue. The entire properties are valued at £239,631 and there are book debts due to the business, and guaranteed by vendors, amounting to £11,000, while the purchase price is £253,500, including all the ordinary shares and £203,500 in cash, which is more than twenty years purchase of the average profits of the previous three years, and seems a pretty stiff figure. Against these average profits of £12,603 for the three years debenture stock interest and preference dividend stand for £9,525 which leaves a very fair margin. But this is not the time for the prudent investor to place his money in brewery issues, and, looking to the future, we can only regard the stock and shares offered as second-class investments.

LEEDS AND BATLEY BREWERIES, LIMITED.

This company acquires as going concerns the businesses of R. H. Sykes & Co., Limited, at the Soothill Brewery, Batley, with which was recently incorporated the Atlas Brewery, Batley, and Cutler's

Saville Green Brewery, Leeds, the total number of licensed houses being 74, of which 61 are freehold. The share capital is £225,000 in £1 shares, including 100,000 ordinary and 125,000 5½ per cent cumulative preference, all of which are offered for subscription, with an issue of £200,000 4½ per cent. irredeemable first mortgage debenture stock, the price asked for the latter being 105. Interest is due January and July. Profits of both breweries for three years are given separately, and show steady progress, and last year's profits with rents from various "publics" and cottages came to £15,031, while the value of the properties and assets is certified at £341,397. From the additional houses acquired by the company a further profit of £11,450 per annum is expected to be earned, making a total of £26,481, of which the debenture interest and preference dividend will require £15,875. Assuming these profits are earned there will be a surplus of £10,606 for the ordinary shares, administration, &c., so that on this estimate the debenture stock and preference shares appear to be a fair risk, always bearing in mind that we consider the best of the time is over for brewery investments. The purchase price is high—£414,000 in addition to the premium on the debenture stock, which together represents sixteen years' purchase on the actual and estimated additional profit. We notice too that the middle-men, who style themselves the Sykes and Cutler Reconstruction Syndicate, and who, of course, are selling at a profit, take all this money in cash.

AUSTRALASIAN UNITED STEAM NAVIGATION COMPANY.

For the purpose of retiring existing five per cent. terminable debentures and loans, and to provide for the cost of new steamers the company is endeavouring to issue £300,000 four per cent. debenture stock at par. It is repayable at par July 1, 1928, or may be redeemed on six months' notice at 105 any time after July 1, 1908. The stock is secured upon freehold wharves, offices, and warehouse property at Brisbane at cost £122,102; leasehold wharf properties £47,179, and steamers of the value of £280,719, which three items fit into the round sum of £450,000. These steamers cost the company £468,271, and have been written down at 7 per cent. per annum, which appears a fair allowance for depreciation, though whether sufficient it is not possible to say. The value of the security is always to exceed by 50 per cent. the amount of the debenture stock from time to time outstanding, and the stock is to be a general floating charge over the remaining fleet and assets, except the uncalled capital, which is probably the best security the company possesses. The undertaking was formed in 1887 to amalgamate two companies engaged in the Australian coasting trade, and of the subscribed capital of £445,200, there is uncalled £101,580. The value of the fleet, properties, &c., is £570,408, while the entire debts, including terminable debentures and cost of two new steamers just delivered, amount to £252,600. Not a figure is given showing what profits have been in the past, and the accountant's certificate, after mentioning that in 1893 and 1894 losses were made owing to competition, makes the general statement that average profits have been greatly in excess of the amount required to pay the interest on the proposed issue. This we should imagine will not attract investors.

AVONDALE HOTEL AND RESTAURANT, AND HATCHETT'S RESTAURANT, LIMITED.

The vendor having purchased the hotel and restaurant for a sum not mentioned is willing to turn them over to the public for £205,000 in cash and £75,000 in ordinary shares. The freehold premises are valued by Douglas Young & Co., at £198,500; and the furniture, fittings and stock at £12,500, making a total of £211,000. The profits of Hatchett's, we are told, have varied but little during the three years ended June 30th, 1897, and therefore they are given in the lump sum of £9,303, and as to the Avondale we are only told that during the 6½ months to October 31st, last, the business done amounted to £8,804. There are also three shops included in the purchase, the rents of which amount to £1,900. The share capital is £200,000 in £5 shares, one half being ordinary and the other 6 per cent. cumulative preference, and there is an issue of £125,000 4 per cent. first mortgage debenture stock, which, with the preference shares, is offered at par. Three-fourths of the ordinary shares go to the vendor, and the balance is held for future issue. The debenture stock is redeemable on six months' notice at 110, and the interest is payable January and July, while the preference dividend is due quarterly from April 5. In subscribing for the preference shares or debenture stock there seems some risk; better wait awhile until it is seen what sort of a business can be worked up.

AMAZONAS RUBBER ESTATES, LIMITED.

The object of this Company is to acquire and develop an India-rubber estate in Teffé, in the State of Amazonas, Brazil, covering about 137 English square miles. Estate is held in perpetuity, and some highly-coloured reports about the property accompany prospectus. Demand for rubber is said to have increased enormously during the last few years, and a table is supplied giving the exports from Para for thirty years, but it only brings us down to 1895. We should have preferred to have seen the figures for the last two years. The capital is £300,000 in £1 shares, comprising 150,000 ordinary and 150,000 7 per cent. cumulative preference shares, entitled to 25 per cent. of the balance of net profits after 10 per cent. has been paid on the ordinary shares. An estimated net profit of £105,000 is ventured upon, of which the preference interest would require only £10,500. The purchase price is £250,000, of which three-fifths is to be cash. It is impossible to judge of such a concern as this over here. All we can say is that the names of the directors inspire confidence, that the concern is highly speculative, and that those who care to take shares, must do so on their own responsibility. But we may point out that the cycle industry, which has so largely increased the demand for rubber, is now in a very depressed condition.

Company Reports and Balance-Sheets.

London and North Western Railway Company.—Gross receipts £6,697,578, expenses £3,812,364, ratio of expenses to receipts nearly 57 per cent. For the half-year the income was £191,984 larger, and the working expenses £262,826 larger, therefore the result of the heavier business done was a decrease of nearly £71,000, or, taking in miscellaneous receipts, of over £69,000 in the net income. A larger balance, however, had been brought forward so that the net decrease in the amount available for dividends was only £57,221, so stockholders will receive a dividend at the rate of 7¾ per cent. per annum, as against 8 per cent. a year ago. This, surely, is a most disappointing result but it is only what other reports have exhibited in a more or less marked way for the last half of 1897. In traffic expenses alone this company spent £116,000 more last half-year than in the corresponding half of 1896. Locomotive power cost about £70,000 more, maintenance of way about £18,000 more, carriage and waggon repairs about £38,000 more and compensation for accident and loss on passengers and goods, which reached the very heavy figure of £49,215, was £4,000 larger than in the December half of the preceding year. Fixed charges also tend to advance, although not at a rapid pace, and altogether the causes of the decrease in the dividends are not by any means occult. Capital expenditure within the half-year was only £482,891, of which £125,000 was on working stock; but the future estimates under this head amount to £4,324,541, of which £600,000 is estimated to be spent in the current half-year—£150,000 of it on additional working stock. More than half the future expenditure is to be on lines open for traffic, and the company has several Bills before Parliament involving considerable fresh capital expenditure. Great, rich, and powerful as this company is, we think its stockholders should take note of the tendency of a continuance of these two influences, growing working expenses and considerable capital outlay, to reduce the return upon their investments. The dividend is payable on the 25th inst.

Midland Railway Company.—Gross receipts for December half of 1897, £5,349,476; working expenses, £2,978,305; ratio of expenses to receipts, 57·59 per cent. The increase in the receipts was £153,448, and in the expenses £224,537, so that here, likewise, the net income available for dividends was less in spite of the large increase in gross income. As, at the same time, there was more stock to pay dividends upon, it followed that the ordinary stockholder got less by ½ per cent than in the corresponding half of 1896—6½ per cent. per annum against 7. The preference charges have risen about £18,000 within the year, and there has also been an increase of nearly £600,000 in the amount of ordinary stock to pay upon—we do not mean in the duplicated stock but the old ordinary stock. Expenses have risen on the same lines with this company as with its neighbours. Maintenance of way, &c., cost about £44,000 more, locomotive power about £70,000 more, traffic expenses about £100,000 more, and compensation about £5,500 more. This last was a large increase upon a total of less than £21,000 for the second half of 1896. As usual, the capital expenditure of this company continues rather high, and amounted to £1,036,930 in the half-year just closed—£121,000 of it on working stock, and £739,000 of it on lines open for traffic. The estimated future expenditure is under £3,000,000, and for the current half-year only £650,000, but this company, like its neighbours, must go on boring its way into new districts, and we have no doubt at all that future years will see fresh capital powers secured, and fresh additions made to the capital account. The dividend will be payable on the 26th inst.

National Provident Institution.—In our notice of this company's report in the last number of the Investor's Review, by the misplacement of a comma it read as if the expenses, exclusive instead of inclusive of commission, were a little more than 11·3 per cent. It should have read, "expenses and commission, exclusive of income tax," &c.

London and Northern Debenture Corporation.—Retrenchment is at last the word in regard to this concern, and in order to save expenses, it proposes to swallow up its twin—the London and Northern Assets Corporation. Before doing this a kind of "spring-clean" has been conducted, which results in a statement that the securities show a depreciation of £17,985. To partly fill this void the board takes the £5,132 credited as net revenue for the past year, the reserve of £6,550, and the £835 brought in, and after allowing £301 received for forfeited shares, the net deficiency is set forth as £5,165. There is of course no dividend, and the only suggestion is that this company absorbs its partner, and thus saves expenses in the future.

LONDON AND NORTHERN ASSETS CORPORATION.—In view of absorption by its twin brother, the board of this concern has been trying to put its affairs in order. First it works out a profit of £5,026 upon revenue, and then proceeds to value the assets, and in this operation produces a considerable deficiency. Accordingly £1,061 is written off leasehold property, £16,432 off investments, and £202 off office furniture, or a total of £17,695. To partly meet this sum the net revenue of £5,026, the balance brought in of £575, and the reserve of £4,100 are absorbed, leaving a debit balance of £7,993. Of course, no dividend is paid, and shareholders can only look forward to the future.

SOUTH LONDON TRAMWAYS.—The steady policy of allowing substantial sums for depreciation and repairs and renewals out of revenue has gradually caused this company to work at a better profit. In the half-year ended December 31, the gross receipts amounted to £46,361, and after working expenses had been met, including £6,777 for repairs and renewals, and £1,129 for depreciation, the net revenue came to £9,385. Adding £2,258 brought forward, the free balance permitted of £1,000 being put to reserve, a dividend of 5s. per share, making 4 per cent. for the year, and the carrying forward of a balance of £1,485. It is not a brilliant result after all, but the balance-sheet and capital account show distinct improvement compared with some years back.

EMPIRE PALACE, LIMITED.—For a company of this kind the report is particularly good. The profit and loss account gives a fair statement of the expenses, and the balance-sheet shows that properties are lightly capitalised. With a paid-up share capital of £31,250, the net profits of the past year came to £21,282, after allowing £8,029 for depreciation, £3,181 for renewals and repairs, and £430 for leasehold redemption. The board were therefore able to distribute 10s. 6d. per 15s. share, and 7s. per 10s. share in dividends, or very nearly 70 per cent. Such a result is only due to good management and the liberal way in which depreciation and repairs are allowed for out of revenue. Still, the business is by its nature speculative, and we should like to see some kind of a reserve created. The sinking fund is certainly invested, but that is ear-marked for leasehold redemption, and otherwise, when the dividends are paid, the company seems to be in debt, for £10,479 owing to creditors will only have about £4,000 of liquid assets against it.

BRITISH LAND COMPANY.—By steady repayments this company has reduced its debenture debt to practically vanishing point, for only £900 is outstanding. Deposits have also been reduced, so that only £2,185 of these exist, bearing interest at 2½ per cent. The whole of the property, therefore, belongs to the £300,000 of share capital, and the balance-sheet looks remarkably well. The chief assets consist of £160,605 in freehold land, buildings, leasehold offices, and ground rents; £71,211 as balance unpaid on land sold; £30,538 in advances on buildings; and £55,000 in India stock and on deposit at bank. Apparently, there is no reserve, but the percentage of liquid assets is particularly good. The profit in the past year amounted to £16,144 which allowed of a dividend of 5 per cent., and the carrying of a slightly larger balance. This is a vast improvement on the results of a few years back.

WHARNCLIFFE DWELLINGS COMPANY.—Last year this company earned a net profit of £7,136, which, after paying debenture and preference interest, allowed of a dividend of 3 per cent. on the deferred or ordinary shares, the placing of £500 to reserve, and the carrying forward of £266. The concern was not in possession of its properties for the whole of last year, and at the same time the debenture charge was only £850, as against £3,000 in the current twelve months. It is, therefore, difficult to give an opinion about its results. At the same time the amount of information supplied is very meagre, and we might refer the board to the East End Dwellings Company if they are in difficulty to know how to start improvement.

SOUTHAMPTON TRAMWAYS COMPANY.—In the past half-year the company earned a net revenue of £2,436, or about the same as in the corresponding period. Out of this £1,000 was written off reconstruction account, and a dividend of 5s. per share declared. The Corporation have given notice of their desire to purchase the undertaking, and offered the sum of £40,000. The directors considered this quite inadequate, and declined the offer, so that the matter will now go to arbitration. If this price was for the whole undertaking as it stands, the proposed payment would have left very little for the ordinary shareholders, as there are £16,650 of debentures and £15,000 of preference shares.

JOHN MOIR & SON, LIMITED.—With larger sales the profit of this company diminished, owing to the higher price of raw material, and the net revenue of £5,319, compares with £6,195 a year ago, although only £1,000 had been reserved for depreciation as against £2,000 in 1896. The balance for 1897, however, permits of a dividend of 10 per cent., or the same as last year, the placing of £276 to reserve, and the carrying forward of £2,323. Thus, the prudent policy of last year has been fully endorsed, and with less profits the company pays the same dividend, and increases its amount forward slightly. The reserve will now amount to £14,000, and the depreciation fund to £22,000, but they are both in the business, although they make the liquid assets good.

CHARING CROSS AND STRAND ELECTRICITY SUPPLY CORPORATION.—This company last year increased its lamps connected by 53·7 per cent. and the output in units from the stations was larger by 33⅓ per cent. than in 1896. Net earnings came to £18,907, and after paying interest, 7 per cent. in dividend was paid upon the ordinary shares, the amount forward being increased slightly to £3,014. The sum of £5,247 was added to the depreciation fund, and after deducting a little for leasehold depreciation, that fund stands at £13,000. There is also a share premium account of £9,608, which makes the reserves £22,608, and the employment of this money has enabled the company to carry out works of the value of £357,770, although only £324,000 of capital has been raised. It is in this way that solid concerns are formed, and shareholders will learn to bless the Legislature that forced the Official Auditor and his inquisitive ways upon the electric-lighting companies.

CANNON BREWERY COMPANY.—With £360,000 more of money employed, this company's profit of £115,958 for last year was £6,661 less than in 1896. Debenture and deposit interest required about the same amount as a year ago, but preference interest was £4,698 more, and consequently the available balance was only £59,250, as against £71,376 a year ago. In spite of this heavy reduction the dividend of 16 per cent. was maintained, and the allocation to reserve was reduced to the paltry sum of £3,000, only £250 being carried forward. The reserve therefore amounts to £46,796, against £1,854,000 of share capital, £1,200,000 of debenture stock, and £541,370 of deposits, loans and trade creditors. Verily a morsel of bread to a cataract of sack.

SPENCER, TURNER, & BOLDERO, LIMITED.—Like most of the other companies of this class, the firm earned less profit last year, the total being £40,110 against £45,862 in the preceding twelve months, and £52,014 in 1895. No special cause is assigned in the report for the serious falling off in profit. A dividend of 8 per cent. for the year is declared. £10,000 is placed to general reserve, and £17,532 is carried forward. The reserve will then amount to £35,000, and with the balance forward, forms a substantial fund for contingencies. It is rather ominous, however, to find the stock up £10,000 in view of the poor results of the last two years.

PERRY & COMPANY, LIMITED—The huge watering of the capital of this concern does not seem to have limited its power to distribute dividends. After paying preference and debenture interest, a dividend and bonus equivalent to 7½ per cent. is declared upon the ordinary shares, £10,000 is placed to reserve, and £6,161 is carried forward. The debentures only amount to £10,500, and are being steadily redeemed. The amount of liquid assets is good.

FURNESS RAILWAY COMPANY.—Gross receipts for the December half of the year, £251,806; working expenses, £125,599; increase in receipts, £10,619; increase in expenses, about £8,000; proportion of expenses to receipts, 50·2 per cent. Unlike some of its great neighbours, this little railway has been able to retain nearly £2,500 of the increase in its receipts as net revenue, but it is not in a position to pay a larger dividend on its ordinary stock. The rate is again 2 per cent. per annum, for the half-year, but the balance carried forward is about £2,500 more than that left from the second half of 1896. Nothing in the accounts of the company calls for particular remark. There has been very little expenditure on capital account, less than £37,000 within the six months, and future commitments are small. In their report the directors complain that the Boness Urban District Council has prevented the enlargement of the company's pier at Boness, on Windermere, and the grumble appears to be justified. The dividend warrants will be posted on February 25.

LONDON GENERAL OMNIBUS COMPANY, LIMITED.—One year with another the characteristics of this company are wonderfully stereotyped. There is the same curious expansion in the capital account the same droll certificate from the chartered accountants, and much the same slenderness of net income. In the half year ended December 31, 1897, the company's gross receipts were £541,261, an increase of £42,390. Expenses, however, amounted to £493,438, which was £50,587 more than in the corresponding half year, and consequently the net revenue was really less. Working expenses, in fact, took 94·45 per cent. of the gross income. Still the directors were able to declare a dividend at the rate of 8 per cent. per annum, and a bonus of 25s. per share, making the total distribution equal to 10½ per cent. per annum; and they had £15,054 left to carry forward. When we turn to the accounts this result does not look quite so pleasant. To be sure these accounts are, as we have said, quite of the usual kind, but their significance is none the less serious because that is so. For example, we find that going back two years leaseholds, &c., have been written up about £96,000. Of this freehold property accounts for nearly £39,000. We should very much like to know what justification there is for this continuous increase. It is extremely unusual, not to say unprecedented, for leasehold property to increase in value, especially short leasehold property, as the great bulk of that possessed by this company is. Then, along with this peculiar expansion in the capital value of freeholds and leaseholds—or the extremely rapid acquisition of further properties, we cannot say which, the report giving not the slightest information—we have to note a decline in the company's investments. At the end of 1806 these amounted to £183,034, and at the end of last year to £152,757, so that there is a decrease of nearly £30,000 on this head, the company having sold within the year some of its India stock, not an imprudent step perhaps. But what has been done with the money? Has it been used to buy new freehold and leasehold properties, or what? We ask these questions but do not for a moment imagine that any intelligible answer is likely to be forthcoming. But stockholders, however, get good dividends and are quite happy. The warrants for the present dividends will be posted on March 2.

MARYPORT AND CARLISLE RAILWAY COMPANY.—Gross receipts for the December half-year, £54,123; expenses, £26,859; proportion of expenses to receipts, 50·54 per cent. The gross revenue was £2,653 larger, and the expenditure about £870 larger. The net revenue was £27,265, exclusive of £1,446 brought forward, which enables the directors to pay a dividend at the rate 6½ per cent., leaving £1,528 to be carried forward. The company only spent £1,000 on capital account in the half-year, and appears to contemplate no further outlay under this head.

BRECON AND MERTHYR TYDFIL JUNCTION RAILWAY COMPANY.—Gross receipts for the December half-year, £46,426; expenditure, £26,352; proportion of expenses to receipts, 56·05 per cent. These figures show an increase of £2,487 in the income, and of £1,823 in the expenses so that £664 was left as net gain. On the extra traffic the total of the net revenue came to £20,097, which is sufficient to pay all fixed charges including full interest on the debenture stocks, and to write £1,013 off the debit balance brought forward from the previous half year.

HOLBORN AND FRASCATI, LIMITED.—The net profits of this company for 1897, after payment of debenture interest, directors' fees, and all other expenses, amounted to £32,419. Adding the balance brought forward, the amount available for a distribution is £35,039, out of which the preference dividend has been met and a dividend of 8 per cent., together with a bonus of 2 per cent. has been paid on the ordinary shares, £5,000 has been transferred to a reserve fund and £7,539 is left to carry forward. This is a very good result for a company so heavily capitalized as this is, and we notice that another £1,900 has been added to the leasehold redemption fund, together with the interest on a like sum previously invested in the company's own 4 per cent. perpetual debenture stock.

THE BREWERS' SUGAR COMPANY, LIMITED.—After deducting the cost of all repairs, directors' fees, management salaries, and all other expenses, this company made a net profit in 1897 of £28,180. This enables the directors to pay the preference dividend, a dividend of 7 per cent. upon the ordinary shares, to place £2,500 to depreciation account, £5,000 to reserve, still leaving £7,071 to be carried forward. The balance sheet looks well, and if the reserve and depreciation funds continue to be added to in a similar manner the company should have a long career of prosperity.

THE MINES AND BANKING CORPORATION, LIMITED.—This is a small company with a capital of £86,000 only, and borrowed money amounting to £27,696. On these limited resources a gross profit of fully £10,500 was made last year. Adding £2,000 brought forward the company had £12,535 available, out of which all expenses have been paid, and a dividend of 5 per cent. for the year upon the ordinary shares. This leaves £4,410 to be carried forward, which might be made the nucleus of a reserve.

THE MERCHANTS' TRUST, LIMITED.—The net revenue of this company for the year 1897, after placing £7,292 to reserve account, came to £41,505, to the £27,793 brought forward has to be added. This gives £69,298 all told of net, of which both the preference and ordinary stocks have received 4 per cent. for the year, leaving £30,131 to go to the new year. The board has written £45,537 off the cost of investments, which leaves the reserve fund at £50,000, which, they significantly add, "can be similarly appropriated hereafter if necessary."

MILLWALL DOCK COMPANY.—The present position of the company is not particularly promising. The number of vessels entering the docks during the past half-year was twelve more than in 1896, but the tonnage was less by 27,884 tons due entirely to the continued reduction in grain imports from Russia. The net receipts, however, increased by £385, and a dividend at the rate of 3¾ per cent. is declared on the ordinary stock. The company is heavily weighted with prior charges, and out of the £46,405 divided as much as £35,161 is absorbed in paying debenture and preference interest, so the prospect for the ordinary stockholder is none too good. The most satisfactory feature in the half-year's business is an increase of 54 per cent. in the American arrivals, which has largely offset the continued falling off in the Russian business. This has now gone on so long that the directors are becoming convinced it will be permanent, and it is thought that American oats will take the place of those from Russia. Unfortunately for the Millwall, its interest in American imports is very much less than in those from Russia as the former are brought in the large liners, which are so big that they have to use the docks lower down the river. Consequently, the company is looking out for fresh business.

MAPLE & CO., LIMITED.—Still another issue of capital is announced by this company, and we may as well say frankly that we do not like it. Only the other day a paltry £100,000, in preference shares was emitted, and realised a premium of 10s. per share, which premium, amounting to £50,000, was added to the company's reserve. Now the proposal is to create an additional £250,000 ordinary £1 shares, to be called "C" shares, which existing ordinary shareholders shall have the right, for a month after the confirmatory meeting, to subscribe for at par in the proportion of one new share for every two existing shares. Then, in order to enable the said shareholders to pay for this new issue, a quarter of a million is to be drawn from the general reserve fund, and given to them by way of a bonus of 10s. per share. No balance-sheet has as yet been issued by this company, but in the circular announcing the dividend of 10½ per cent. for the second half of 1897, completing the year, and making the total dividend for the past twelve months 15½ per cent, it is stated that the total reserve stands at £303,594, with the £50,000 added to it from premiums obtained on the preference share issue. All this is thoroughly vicious finance, and augurs no good for the future of the company, great and apparently prosperous though its business now is.

The Produce Markets.

GRAIN.

There has been no great stir in the market during the week, but the outlook is more cheerful, and at Mark-lane on Wednesday English wheat was held for 6d. advance, which was partially paid. There was a similar rise in foreign, and it was obtained in some cases, though buyers were not eager. There was little doing in flour. Maize was in fair demand at 3d. more money—American mixed, 16s. 3d., ex ship; old, 17s., ex quay; and Galatz-Bessarabian at 18s. Barley was slow at unaltered rates—Odessa-Nikolaieff, ex ship, 16s. 6d. to 16s. 9d.; and Danubian at 16s. 3d. to 16s. 6d. Oats 3d. dearer—mixed American, 15s. 9d. to 16s., ex ship; and Canadian white at 17s., ex quay. Spot parcels at Liverpool were firmly held for full prices to a further advance of ½d. Red American futures opened on Wednesday without change, but improved on free buying, but receding somewhat when the demand had been satisfied. Afterwards the market again hardened, and closed firm, at a rise of ¼d. to ⅜d. Sales, 450,000 centals. March, 8s. to 8s. 0⅜d.; May, 7s. 6d. to 7s. 6½d.; July, 7s. 2¼d. to 7s. 1¾d.; September, 6s. 7d. to 6s. 7½d.; December, 7s. East Indian shipments steady but quiet. Wheat cargoes continue firm, but the demand is quiet. Walla-Walla off coast, 37s. 9d. bid, but holders are not offering. Californian due, 27s. 9d., sellers. London cargo market quiet on the whole, but on Wednesday opened steady on American advices, and prices occasionally 3d. better. Trade, however, was not active, though the close was firm on stronger cables. Walla Walla shipping was sold at 35s.; also two steamers, about 2,200-2,500 tons each, Rosario-Santa Fe, February-March shipment changed hands on the Continent at 35s. 6d. and 35s. 9d. For 2,750 tons loading 36s. 3d. is asked. Californian September, is obtainable at 38s. 9d. to 39s., and for prompt shipment at 36s. 9d. Wheat options irregular. Maize firm. Barley rather slow. Oats 3d. higher.

OFFICIAL CLOSING VALUES (100 lb. deliveries—February 16).

	March.	May.	July.	Sept.
Red American Wheat	8·0¾	7·6¼	7·2¾	6·7¼

In New York the wheat market ruled rather easy in the beginning of the week, but gradually hardened. On Wednesday it opened ½ c. dearer for May, with "bears" eager to cover, partly owing to the news that twenty-nine boat loads had been sold to Lisbon late day, and that the Portuguese import duty on wheat had been reduced. After the initial spurt trading became erratic, and consisted mostly of "scalping" business, and in the afternoon the market became quiet. Local feeling is generally "bearish," and the "short" party is restrained from aggressive operations only by the fear of being caught by Chicago manipulators. Late in the session the market became again active and rising, partly owing to reports that Liverpool "short" sellers were buying No. 2 red winter wheat for early shipment. The closing tone was strong and prices 1 c. to 2⅛ c. dearer. On the kerb buying continued, and a further advance of 1 c. was paid, May delivery touching $1·00⅛. Sales, 5,500,000 bushels. The close in maize was firm, at a rise of ⅛ c. to ⅜ c. Flour in moderate request, but firm.

COTTON.

The spot market was firm in end of last week, and on Monday there was an easier feeling but fair activity. Tuesday was quieter, but on Wednesday there was a revival and holders were less easy to deal with. American in fair request at hardening rates. Brazilian ruled dull and Egyptian quiet at steady prices. Surats continued idle at late values. Futures opened 1½ point higher, and sellers were more reserved; business was chiefly covering, and the market was quiet with but little variation in the course of the forenoon. American opening cables coming lower, offerings increased, and under considerable realizations receded 1 to 1½ point, the close being quiet but steady at ½ to 1 point net gain. Wednesday's tenders at the Clearing-house were 400 bales American on new dockets. In New York the tendency, early in the week, was towards higher rates, but the improvement did not last, and on Wednesday the market, 1 to 4 points lower, declined further under disappointing cables, heavy interior receipts, and active local selling. The market, however, closed steady generally 5 points lower. Spot easy. Middling upland, 6¼c. Sales, 117,500 bales.

NEW YORK CLOSING VALUES.

	Spot.	Feb.	Mar.	April.	May.	June.	July.	Aug.	Sept.	Oct.	Nov.
Feb. 16 ..	6¼	5·93	5·95	5·98	6·02	6·05	6·08	6·12	6·10	6·10	6·12

WOOL.

The market has been rather unsettled. In consequence of local failures, operations in Bradford were conducted with caution. Staplers were at first content to wait, keeping up prices in the meantime, but this was found impossible, and on Monday sales of higher qualities of crossbreds were reported at very near the lowest point yet touched. There was, however, a fair demand. In the London wool market a good inquiry exists on home and Continental account, and some fair sized parcels have changed hands at late rates. Arrivals to date for the second series (commencing March 15th) are as follows:—New South Wales, 59,381 bales; Queensland, 7,654; Victoria, 39,240; South Australia, 1,371; West Australia, 502; New Zealand, 12,130; Cape and Natal, 20,419—total, 140,717 bales, of which about 48,000 (34,000 Australasian and 14,000 Cape) have been forwarded direct. The week's imports total 28,964 bales, and comprise Sydney, 10,074; Melbourne, 4,374; Queensland, 1,392; Adelaide, 400; New Zealand, 6,003; Cape and Natal, 3,598; Buenos Ayres, 73; Marseilles, 457; Batum, 224; Basra, 2,155; and sundries, 214. Messrs. Schwartze & Co. will probably offer on the 28th inst. about 2,700 bales of damaged China sheep's wool, salved ex *Cromarty*, and probably about 700 bales sound China wool out of same ship on the above date.

METALS AND COAL.

There has been great activity and firmness in the copper market throughout the week, and a sustained advance in price. On Tuesday £50 per ton was paid at the opening for three months' delivery, a figure that has not been recorded for nearly a year past. On Wednesday, however, the tendency was more easy, and values closed 1s. 3d. lower than the previous day for cash, and 2s. 6d. to 3s. 9d. for three months. About 700 tons sold during the morning—cash at £49 10s. and £49 11s. 3d., one week and mid-March £49 11s. 3d., March 10 £49 12s. 6d., April 18 and 24 £49 15s., and three months £49 17s. 6d., £49 16s. 3d.; while in the afternoon cash realized £49 10s., and three months £49 15s. and 16s. 3d. combined, and £49 15s. The mid-monthly copper statistics showed further diminution in the visible supply of copper, which has dropped from 29,145 to 29,076 tons, while the price since the 31st of last month has improved 12s. 6d. per ton. The shipments from America declined very considerably in January, as also those from Spain and Portugal, and the total supplies for the month were about 500 tons less than in January last year. The falling off in the supplies was, however, counteracted by a decline of nearly 1,000 tons in the deliveries. The demand for copper in the near future is likely to be considerably greater.

SETTLEMENT PRICES.

	Feb. 16.	Feb. 9.	Feb. 2.	Jan. 26	Jan. 19.	Jan. 12
	£ s. d.	£ s. d.	£ s. d.	£ s. d.	£ s. d.	£ s. d.
Copper ..	49 10 0	49 5 0	49 2 6	48 17 6	49 5 0	48 17 6

The pig-iron market has been very active. There have been good ship-building and engineers' trade reports, and though several attempts were made to break the rise in price, they were unsuccessful. On Wednesday, 30,000 tons changed hands. Scotch maintained previous price; Cleveland rose 1d.

SETTLEMENT PRICES.

	Feb. 16.	Feb. 9.	Feb. 2.	Jan. 26.	Jan. 19.	Jan. 12.
	s. d.	s. d.	s. d.	s. d.	s. d.	s. d.
Scotch	45 7½	45 7½	45 7½	46 0	46 0	45 9
Cleveland ..	40 7½	40 4½	40 6	40 10½	40 10½	40 7½
Hematite ..	48 9	48 7½	48 6	47 0	48 10½	48 9

Hardly any business is doing in coal. The recent improvement in the outlook has almost entirely disappeared, and from those who are unable to accept them there are frequent complaints of the existence of special prices in all departments of the trade. For seaborne coal the demand was decidedly inactive, only one cargo being offered, which is not to be loaded until the end of the week; but no transactions were reported, and apparently it would not be possible to effect sales except at easy rates. The official quotations continue at 17s. and 16s., usual terms in the pool for Hetton Wallsend and Lyons respectively.

SUGAR.

Cane sugar has been steady throughout the week, with a tendency to increase in price. British cubes and pieces quiet for the most part, but had an increased demand on Wednesday, when speculative beetroot advanced ½d. Crystals have a good inquiry for yellows, and white is in fair request at late quotations—Tate's cubes, No. 1, 14s. 9d.; No. 2, 13s. 10½d.; crushed, No. 1, 13s.; No. 2, 12s. 6d.; granulated, 13s. 3d.; yellow crystals, 12s. 1½d.; Lyle's crystals, No. 1, 13s.; No. 3, 12s. 3d.; granulated No. 1 13s.; No. 2, 12s. 3d.; white, A, 12s. 9d.; B, 12s.; yellow crystallised, O and P, 12s. Foreign.—Granulated firm, with a good business at ¾d. advance.

Mr. Czarynkow says the unsatisfactory feature in United Kingdom remains the continuous low values of refined, but as the spring advance this will doubtless adjust itself. In the States, also, there were complaints of the slow sale of refiners' produce, which is, after all, nothing unusual at this period of the year, and must in a few weeks be succeeded by more activity.

TEA AND COFFEE.

There was good competition at the tea auction during the week, 23,200 packages Indian sold on Monday. On Tuesday 23,000 packages Ceylon were offered, and nearly all sold, buyers easily supplying their wants at last week's prices. Pekoes about 6d.—occasionally ruled ¼d. cheaper. Terminals continue dull, Messrs. Gow, Wilson & Stanton state, that "the quantity of Ceylon tea exported direct to markets other than the United Kingdom continues year by year to substantially increase. The expansion which has taken place during the last seven years is shown in the following table:—

1897.	1896.	1895.	1894.	1893.	1892.	1891.
lb.	lb.	lb.	lb.	lb.	lb.	lb.
17,124,508	14,205,051	12,186,532	9,243,070	18,905,987	6,338,582	4,529,433

Another week of small auctions has added strength to the Indian tea market, an improved tone being shown for all descriptions and prices generally marking a distinct advance. Although the auction of Ceylon tea was lighter, prices were irregular and frequently slightly lower; the quality of offerings continues poor."

There has been a steady business in coffee, and good sorts sold at auction brought full prices. Other sorts slow. Costa Rica fine medium to fine bold bright hard blue, 105s. 6d. to 108s. 6d.; fair small mixed, 55s. 6d.; peaberry, 117s. Columbian good to fine bold blue, 85s. to 93s. 6d.; low middling hard faded gray to good middling colouring, 63s. to 86s.; low middling to middling mottled pale, 60s. to 66s. 6d.; small mixed, 41s. to 45s. 6d.; peaberry, 80s. to 101s. Futures steady at 3d. advance.

Messrs. W. J. & H. Thompson state that Java and China teas were very quiet, with only small transactions. About 200 packages of Natal tea sold in auction at 5½d. to 7½d. per lb.

HEMP AND JUTE.

Hemp firm throughout the week. At auction on Wednesday 80 bales fine quality sold at £22 10s. and 70 bales third Quillot were bought in at £27. To arrive, 500 bales F.C. December-January steamer, sold at £19; 500 February-April, sailer, £19 2s. 6d.; 500 March-May, £19 5s.; 1,000 May-July, £19 7s. 6d.; 1,000 good seconds, February-March, steamer, at £17 10s. Jute dull, prices generally unaltered. For shipment 1,000 bales first marks, February-April, steamer, London, sold at £9 15s.; 500 Pal P.N. group, January-March, steamer, Hamburg, £10 15s. The "entries" at Calcutta to date were 225,000 bales.

THE PROPERTY MARKET.

A good deal more business has been done at the Mart this week, though mainly in the disposal of bricks and mortar. Even these, however, were greatly superseded on Monday by gas and water stocks and shares, offered by Mr. Alfred Richards, which account for £12,088 out of the £14,813 total for the day. £3,500 new ordinary stock, Grays Gas, went for £4,255; £2,500 4 per cent. debenture stocks of the Great Yarmouth Water Company brought £3,038; 179 £10 shares of Whitchurch and District (Hunts.) Gas brought £2,198, and seventy-five £10 new ordinary shares Great Yarmouth brought £995.

The Bijou Theatre and Concert Hall at Llandudno, known as the St. George's Hall, was sold a few days ago, by Messrs. M. Dew & Sons, for £7,000.

A freehold residence, known as Shortlands, at Ash, Surrey, with stabling, pleasure grounds, paddock, &c., the whole covering an area of about 3¼ acres, has been sold by Messrs. Nash & Son, at Farnham, for £2,020.

Mr. Alfred Richards announces for Monday next at the London Mart, sales of freehold and leasehold properties in Wood Green, Hornsey, and South Hackney.

£47,370 was the handsome total of the sales at the Mart on Tuesday. There was an unusually good lot of securities offered, and the demand for them was encouraging. Messrs. Debenham, Tewson, & Company sold some freehold ground rents in Moor-lane, City, for £5,650. Another lot of theirs consisted of freehold premises in Drury-lane, with an area of 1,500 ft., which went at £3,050. Three acres of building land in Hartington-road, Chiswick, were bought at £2,500, or about £830 an acre. Messrs. Green & Son, of Hammersmith, disposed of a number of freehold ground rents at good prices, the principal lot being £168 15s. per annum, secured on property in Muriel-street, Caledonian-road, with reversion in twenty-three and a half years, which realised £8,600. Mr. Joseph Stower was successful with all his lots, save one; and Messrs. Brodie, Timbs, & Company made a clear book, with one very small exception. Freehold houses in Soho, offered by Messrs. Robins, Snell, & Gore, changed hands at satisfactory prices. It was altogether a good day's work.

There were also large sales at Mason's Hall Tavern. The free lease and goodwill of a well-known house in the south of London, the Alfred's Head, in Newington-causeway, with a term of fifty-five years at the annual rent of £300, was sold, after brisk competition, by Mr. W. Rolfe for £50,000; and the Camden Head, Islington Green, held on a lease for nineteen years at £100 per annum, was disposed of by Messrs. Belton & Sons for £12,010. Local veto does not seem to have yet affected the market value of public-houses.

The Mart was very animated on Wednesday, and the value of the sales reached the high total of £92,710. The main inducement attracting buyers was Messrs. Debenham, Tewson & Co.'s sale of the first portion of the properties of the Land Securities Company, in liquidation, comprising houses, shops, and building land at Wimbledon. One lot of leasehold houses in Cromwell-road, with a ground rent of £201 10s. went for £8,070. Another, consisting of freehold houses in the same road, fetched £8,060; a third lot in the same road brought £9,160; and a fourth, leasehold, £8,120. The houses 276 to 288 Haydon's-road, went for £2,510; houses 292 to 308, Haydon's-road, brought £4,980; houses 42 to 74, Haydon's-park-road went for £3,700; and 13 to 47 odd, in same road, fetched £4,750. A lot of leasehold houses in Gap-road brought £7,200; and 7 a. 3 r. 12 p. freehold building land sold at £5,500. The ninety lots offered sold for a total of £68,890. Some landed estate lots at Worplesdon, Surrey, were sold by Messrs. Daniel Smith, Son & Oakley at excellent prices—Hurst Farm, consisting of rather over seventy acres, freehold, going at £3,100.

MINING RETURNS.

CROWN REEF.—Crushed by 120-stamp mill, 15,971 tons, yield 7,919 oz. smelted gold; from cyanide 3,643 oz.; from slimes (for December and January) 548 oz.

LE CHAMP D'OR.—Crushed 5,359 tons in 29 days, yield 225 oz.; cyanide, 3,630 tons treated, yielding 968 oz.

MOODIE'S GOLD MINING AND EXPLORATION. — Tons crushed, 1,100; yield, 660 oz.

NATAL COLLIERIES AND DURBAN COALING STATION.—Output for December, 2,020 tons.

PALMAREJO.—Crushed 1,950 tons; panned 1,750 tons, producing $43,500.

PRINCESS ESTATE.—For January: Crushed 5,025 tons, producing 1,905 oz.; 932 oz. from tailings.

VILLAGE MAIN REEF.—Crushed 5,370 tons, yielding 3,098 oz. gold from battery.

LAKE VIEW CONSOLS.—Clear-up for January:—40 stamps (new mill) working 650 hours crushed 5,026 tons, yielding 4,576 oz. of gold; tail ings assay 14 dwt. per ton. Cyanide return.—3,527 tons treated, yielding 2,607 oz. of gold; tailings assay, 2 dwt. per ton; concentrates, 20 tons, value 371 oz of gold.

West Rand.—Crushed 3,815 tons, yielded 1,076 oz.; cyanide treated 3,064 tons, yielded 813 oz.

Windsor Gold.—3,930 tons yielded 1,271 oz. from plates; 671 oz. from cyanide treatment.

York.—For January: crushed 5,163 tons, yielding 2,302 oz.

Buffelsdoorn.—Production for January, 3,607 oz.

Bonanza.—From mill: crushed 6,102 tons, obtained 5,161 oz. gold. From cyanide and slimes: treated 5,525 tons, yielding 2,875 oz. gold.

Village Main Reef.—5,370 tons, yielding 3,098 oz.; cyanide process portion of tailings: 1,140 tons produced 401 oz.

Geldenhuis crushed 16,823 tons; yield from mill 6,392 oz., from concentrates by cyanide, 935 oz., from tailings, 2,126 oz., and from slimes, 635 oz. gold.

Geldenhuis Main Reef.—January returns:—3,634 tons crushed, yield 751 oz.; 2,100 tons treated by cyanide, yield 559 oz. Profit for month, £566.

Alaska Mexican.—Bullion shipment, $30,940; ore milled, 14,936 tons; sulphurets treated, 275 tons; bullion from sulphurets, $8,376.

Block B Langlaagte.—Ore crushed, 12,213 tons of 2,000 lb.; gold retorted, 3,182 oz. Tailings, cyanide process, 6,750 tons yield 1,185 oz. Concentrates, cyanide process, 166 tons, yield 342 oz.

City and Suburban.—Last month's crushings yielded 11,032 oz.

Langlaagte.—Production for January:—Mill.—Ore crushed, 22,195 tons of 2,000 lb.; gold retorted, 5,754 oz. Tailings, cyanide process.—Tons treated, 14,850 of 2,000 lb.; gold recovered, 1,472 oz. Concentrates, cyanide process.—Tons treated, 650 of 2,000 lb.; gold recovered, 1,466 oz. Total gold recovered, 8,692 oz.

Langlaagte Star.—Production for January:—Mill.—Ore crushed, 5,292 tons of 2,000 lb.; gold retorted, 3,097 oz. Tailings, cyanide process.—Tons treated, 4,381 of 2,000 lb.; gold recovered, 934 oz. Total gold recovered, 4,031 oz.

North Randfontein.—Production for January:—Mill.—Ore crushed, 5,856 tons of 2,000 lb.; gold retorted, 1,223 oz. Tailings, cyanide process.—Tons treated, 3,840 of 2,000 lb.; gold recovered, 518 oz. Concentrates, cyanide process.—Tons treated, 105 of 2,000 lb.; gold recovered, 203 oz.

Nourse Deep.—Results for January: Tons crushed by 60 stamps, 7,350; yield in smelted gold, 3,780 oz.; tons of sands and concentrates treated by cyanide works, 5,673 oz.; yield in smelted gold, 1,619 oz.

Paarl Central Gold Exploration.—Results for January:—From mill.—Crushed 5,520 tons, yielding 1,653 oz. From cyanide works.—Treated 4,084 tons, yielding 882 oz.

Porges Randfontein.—Production for January:—Mill.—Ore crushed, 6,655 tons of 2,000 lb.; gold retorted, 2,807 oz. Tailings, cyanide process.—Tons treated, 4,950 of 2,000 lb.; gold recovered, 714 oz. Concentrates, cyanide process.—Tons treated, 87 of 2,000 lb.; gold recovered, 480 oz.

Robinson Randfontein.—For January:—Mill.—Ore crushed, 5,242 tons of 2,000 lb.; gold retorted, 2,632 oz. Tailings, cyanide process.—Tons treated, 4,410 of 2,000 lb.; gold recovered, 570 oz. Concentrates, cyanide process. Tons treated, 48 of 2,000 lb.; gold recovered, 139 oz.

Transvaal.—For January:—Mill—Crushed 9,027 tons, obtained 3,934 oz. of fine gold. From cyanide works—Treated, 5,005 tons; yield (for December as well as January), 2,666 oz.

Wolhuter.—Result for January, 7,559 oz. gold.

May Consolidated.—During January 14,069 tons crushed; yield, 4,213 oz. Cyanide—8,380 tons; yield, 2,296 oz.

Wassan.—For December:—Ore crushed, 488 tons, producing 608 oz. bar gold, equal 634 oz. standard gold, which, together with 174 oz. from skimmings, realised £2,545. Returns for January:—736 oz. bar gold from 503 tons of ore.

Sons of Gwalia.—January:—Crushed, 1,260 tons; yield, 1,577 oz.; tailings, 25 dwt.

Paarl Central.—5,520 tons crushed, yielding 1,635 oz. gold. Cyanide—4,084 tons treated, yielding 882 oz. gold. Total value, £8,322. (Note.—The mill only ran twenty-three days.)

St. Augustine.—541 loads yielded 36 carats.

Transvaal Coal Trust.—Output 12,700 tons. Profit £500.

Crescent.—For past month 600 tons, 66 oz.

St. John del Rey.—For ten days of February, £3,245 gold produce; yield per ton ·42 of an oz. troy.

Waihi.—3,900 tons treated; bullion produced £14,750.

Mount Macolm.—Crushed 470 tons for 444 oz; tailings 13 dwt.

Great Boulder.—For fortnight, 30 stamps crushed 1,428 tons of ore; yield, 3,293 oz. gold.

Cassel Coal.—Output for January, 20,600 tons; profit, £3,000.

Caylloma Silver.—17,550 oz., troy, silver in export ore; 17,500 oz., troy, silver in bullion.

New Australian Broken Hill Consols.—Two tons, 3,500 oz. silver.

New Zealand Crown.—For January, 1,400 tons mined; 1,481 tons crushed; value of bullion, £3,041.

Robinson.—For January, mill crushed 14,940 tons; yield in smelted gold, 10,029 oz.; from concentrates (by chlorination), 1,503 oz.; from tailings (cyanide), 3,117 oz.; from slimes, 925 oz.; from own ore, 15,574 oz.; from concentrates bought, 1,396 oz.; total gold recovered, 16,970 oz.

Wentworth Goldfields.—Five weeks' return, 840 tons of ore crushed; yield, 845 oz.

Eaglehawk Consolidated.—Trial crushing, 30 tons, yielded 1 oz. 9 dwt. per ton.

Melbourne Democrat.—Crushed 18 tons first-class ore for 75 oz.; 530 tons mullock for 145 oz.

Frank Smith Diamond.—3,050 loads washed producing 189 carats.

Leicester Consolidated Diamond.—From the mine 2,000 loads, and from floors 5,500 loads, washed producing 213 carats.

Anglo-Mexican.—Crushed 1,630 tons, $28,973 (U.S. gold), 27 days run. Cyanide—tons treated, 1,035, $10,569 (U.S. gold).

Brilliant and St. George.—2,121 tons of quartz crushed for 3,630 oz. of gold; approximate value, £12,500.

Great Boulder Perseverance.—Milled 1,040 tons, yielding 933 oz.

Hannan's Oroya.—Crushed 832 tons of ore, yielded 374 oz. gold. Mill worked 25 days.

Westralia and Eastern Extension.—Twenty stamps running 615 hours crushed 1,882 tons. Yield of smelted gold, 1,236 oz.

Geldenhuis Deep.—Return for month of January:—190 stamps crushed 20,700 tons, yielding 7,201 oz. of gold. Treated by cyanide 15,190 tons, yielding 4,042 oz. Yield in smelted gold from slimes 250 oz. Total, 11,493 oz. of gold.

Next Week's Meetings.

Monday, February 21.

Aberdeen and Glasgow Steam Shipping	Birmingham, 2 p.m.
Anglo Foreign Banking (Gen.) ...	2, Bishopsgate-street, noon.
British Yukon Mining and Trading	53, Old Broad-street, 11.30 a.m.
Charing Cross and Strand Electricity Supply	15, Maiden-lane, W.C.
Dublin, Wicklow, and Wexford Railway	Dublin, 1 p.m.
Inter-oceanic of Mexico Railway ...	Winchester House, 2 p.m.
Kay & Company	Worcester, 1 p.m.
Municipal Trust (Ex. Gen.)	2, Great Winchester-street, noon.
National Temperance Land and Building (Gen.)	Guildhall Tavern, 7 p.m.
Prairie Cattle	Edinburgh, noon.
West India and Pacific Steamship...	Liverpool.
Wharncliffe Dwellings	16, Great George-street, S.W., 1 p.m.

Tuesday, February 22.

Atlantic 1st Leased Lines	Winchester House, 2 p.m.
Australian Agricultural (Spec.) ...	" " 1 p.m.
Cork, Blackrock, and Passage Ry. ...	Cork, 2.30 p.m.
Glasgow Cotton Spinning	Glasgow, 2 p.m.
John Moir & Son	Winchester House, 1.30 p.m.
London and County Banking ...	21, Lombard-street, 1 p.m.
London and North Western Railway (Spec.)	Euston Station, 1 p.m.
Perry & Company	Birmingham, 3 p.m.
South Wales Mineral Railway Company	Westminster Palace Hotel, 10 a.m.

Wednesday, February 23.

General Hydraulic Power	Winchester House, 2.30 p.m.
German Bottle Seal (Gen.)	8, Great Winchester-street, 2.30 p.m.
Isle of Wight Central Railway (Gen.)	3, Lothbury, 1 p.m.
Law Life Assurance	187, Fleet-street, 1 p.m.
Maryport and Carlisle Railway ...	Maryport, noon.
Mines and Banking Corporation ...	Winchester House, 3 p.m.

Thursday, February 24.

A. & S. Henry & Company (Ex. Gen.)	Manchester, 11 a.m.
Ascot District Gas (Gen.)	46, Cannon-street, noon.
Brewers' Sugar Trust	Greenock, 3 p.m.
Brighton Grand Hotel (Gen.) ...	Cannon-street Hotel, noon.
Bromley Gas Consumers	Bromley, 6 p.m.
Civil Service Supply Association ...	Cannon-street Hotel, 6 p.m.
London General Omnibus (Gen.) ...	6, Finsbury-square, 2 p.m.
Mathinna Union	18, Finsbury-circus, 4 p.m.
Mercantile Invest. and General Trust	Winchester House, noon.
New Shariston Collieries (Gen.) ...	Cannon-street Hotel, 1.30 p.m.
New Zealand Mort. and Invest. (Gen.)	11, Queen Victoria-street, 2 p.m.
Ross and Monmouth Ry. (Gen.) ...	Ross, 1.30 p.m.
South Hetton Coal	39, Lombard-street, 1 p.m.
South Staffordshire Waterworks ...	Birmingham, 1 p.m.
Spencer, Turner, & Boldero... ...	Lisson Grove, 3 p.m.

Friday, February 25.

Barnet Gas	Albion Tavern, 12.30 p.m.
British Land (Gen.)	Cannon-street Hotel, 3 p.m.
Didcot, Newbury, and Southampton Railway	Westminster Palace Hotel, noon.
Hornsey Gas	63, Chancery-lane, 3 p.m.
Merchants' Trust (Gen.)	Cannon-street Hotel, 2 p.m.
Milford Docks (Gen. and Spec.) ...	Winchester House, noon.
National Provident Institution ...	Cannon-street Hotel, noon.
Neath and Brecon Railway (Gen.)...	Charing Cross Hotel, 2.30 p.m.
West Ham Gas (Gen and Ex.-Gen.)..	Stratford, 5 p.m.

Saturday, February 26.

Cambrian Railway (Gen.)	Manchester, noon.
Tottenham and Edmonton Gas Light and Coke	Tottenham, 3 p.m.

Mr. Curzon stated in the House of Commons on Monday that Government proposed to advise Parliament to grant £75,000 to meet expenses in connection with the British section of the Paris Exhibition of 1900.

Washington is still a little disturbed about Germany's exclusion of American beef, fruits, and horses. The House of Representatives on Monday passed a resolution calling for the official correspondence with Germany on the subject.

Railway Traffic Returns.

CLEATOR AND WORKINGTON.—Gross receipts for the week ending February 12 amounted to £984, a decrease of £93. Total receipts from January 1, £6,122, a decrease of £323.

COCKERMOUTH, KESWICK, AND PENRITH.—Gross receipts for the week ending February 12 amounted to £830, an increase of £42. Total receipts for six weeks £5,156, an increase of £598.

ROHILKUND AND KUMAON RAILWAY.—Traffic for week ended January 15, Rs. 6,312; decrease, Rs. 654. Aggregate from January 1, Rs. 12,220; decrease, Rs. 959.

BURMA RAILWAYS.—Receipts for week ending January 15, Rs. 1,88,195; decrease, Rs. 35,363. Aggregate from January 1, Rs. 3,96,361; decrease, Rs. 94,706.

WEST OF INDIA PORTUGUESE RAILWAY.—Week ending January 22, Rs. 4,283; increase, Rs. 1,842.

BENGAL CENTRAL RAILWAY.—Traffic for week ending January 22, Rs. 20,373; increase, Rs. 2,200. Total from January 1, Rs. 56,401; decrease, Rs. 670.

BENGAL DOOARS RAILWAY COMPANY.—Traffic receipts for week ending January 15, Rs. 3,610, against Rs. 4,886.

H. H. THE NIZAM'S GUARANTEED STATE RAILWAYS COMPANY.—Traffic for seven days ending January 22, Rs. 79,723, increase, Rs. 4,980. Total from January 1, Rs. 229,005; increase, Rs. 4,140.

GREAT NORTHERN RAILWAY OF MINNESOTA.—Traffic receipts for month of January, $1,367,000; increase, $335,500.

QUEBEC CENTRAL RAILWAY.—Receipts for third week of January, $7,492; increase $943. Aggregate from January 1, $16,074; increase $499.

MOBILE AND BIRMINGHAM RAILROAD.—Traffic for third week of January, $10,933; increase, $3,240. Aggregate from July 1, $207,741; decrease, $20,390.

DOMINION ATLANTIC RAILWAY.—Receipts for month of January, $32,409; decrease, $789.

BALTIMORE AND NORTH-WESTERN RAILWAY.—Return for week ended January 31, $146,488; decrease, $7,620.

ATLANTIC AND DANVILLE RAILWAY.—Return for month of January, $43,660; increase, $2,796.

BALTIMORE AND OHIO SOUTH-WESTERN RAILWAY.—Traffic for fourth week of January, $146,488; decrease, $7,620. Aggregate from July 1, $3,974,763; increase, $378,947.

ALABAMA GREAT SOUTHERN RAILWAY COMPANY.—Traffic receipts for month of December, $177,000; increase, $12,000.

CINCINNATI SOUTHERN RAILWAY COMPANY.—Traffic return for month of December, $340,000; increase, $36,000.

ALABAMA AND VICKSBURG RAILWAY.—Receipts for month of January, $74,000; increase, $20,000.

VICKSBURG, SHREVEPORT, AND PACIFIC RAILWAY.—Gross receipts for month of January, $67,000; increase, $15,000.

ALGECIRAS (GIBRALTAR) RAILWAY.—Traffic for week ended January 29, Ps. 18,600; increase, Ps. 2,335. Aggregate from July 1, Ps. 620,119; increase, Ps. 10,728.

WESTERN RAILWAY OF HAVANA.—Receipts for week ended February 5, £2,000; increase, £210. Aggregate from July 1, £55,405 increase, £5,873.

PERUVIAN CORPORATION RAILWAYS.—Receipts for January, $276,325; increase, $16,250.

MANILA RAILWAY.—Traffic receipts for week ended February 12, $20,339; increase, $5,239. Aggregate from January 1, $100,229; increase, $30,402.

NORTH-WESTERN OF URUGUAY RAILWAY.—Receipts for month of January, $13,200; increase, $1,793.

BILBAO RIVER AND CANTABRIAN RAILWAY.—Receipts for January, £9,050; increase, £337.

VILLA MARIA AND RUFINO RAILWAY.—Traffic for week ending February 12, $5,237; decrease, $950. Aggregate from January 1, $23,153; decrease, $3,628.

CENTRAL URUGUAY NORTHERN EXTENSION RAILWAY.—Week ending February 5, £1,570; increase, £144. Aggregate from July 1, £36,837; increase, £2,129.

CENTRAL URUGUAY EASTERN EXTENSION RAILWAY.—Traffic for week ending February 5, £493; decrease, £131. Aggregate from July 1, £20,130; decrease, £1,747.

SAN PAULO BRAZILIAN RAILWAY.—Gross receipts for the three weeks ended January 16, £29,990; decrease, £7,066.

WEST FLANDERS RAILWAY.—Gross receipts for week ending February 13, £1,891; increase, £83. Total from January 1, £12,503; increase, £481.

GREAT WESTERN OF BRAZIL RAILWAY.—Traffic for week ending January 8th, $44,127; increase, $2,817. Aggregate receipts to date $76,266; increase, $7,506.

TRAMWAY AND OMNIBUS RECEIPTS.

Increases for past week:—Belfast, £79; Croydon, £64; Glasgow, £139; Lea Bridge, £98; London & Deptford, £40; London Southern, £87; London General Omnibus, £1,037; London Road Car, £403; Metropolitan, £513; North Staffordshire, £28; Provincial, £63; South London, £69; Wolverhampton, £10; Woolwich & S. E. London, £7.

Decrease for past week:—Bordeaux, £51; Calais, £2; Southampton, £2.

Anglo-Argentine, week ending January 17, £114 increase; Vienna Omnibus, week ending February 5, £291 increase.

The success of the spring crops in Northern and Central India are said to have been assured by an excellent rainfall. It is pleasant to hear of the success of anything besides official blundering being assured in India.

Answers to Correspondents.

Questions about public securities, and on all points in company law, will be answered week by week, in the REVIEW, on the following terms and conditions:—

A fee of FIVE shillings must be remitted for each question put, provided they are questions about separate securities. Should a private letter be required, then an extra fee of FIVE shillings must be sent to cover the cost of such letter, the fee then being TEN shillings for one query only, and FIVE shillings for every subsequent one in the same letter. While making this concession the EDITOR will feel obliged if private replies are as much as possible dispensed with. It is wholly impossible to answer letters sent merely "with a stamped envelope enclosed for reply."

Correspondents will further greatly oblige by so framing their questions as to obviate the necessity to name securities in the replies. They should *number* the questions, keeping a copy for reference, thus:—"(1) Please inform me about the present position of the Rowenzori Development Co. (2) Is a dividend likely to be paid soon on the capital stock of the Congo-Sudan Railway?"

Answers to be given to all such questions by simply quoting the numbers 1, 2, 3, and so on. The EDITOR has a rooted objection to such forms of reply as—"I think your Timbuctoo Consols will go up," or "Sell your Slowcoach and Draggem Bonds," because this kind of thing is open to all sorts of abuses. By the plan suggested, and by using a fancy name to be replied to, each query can be kept absolutely private to the inquirer, and no scope whatever be given to market manipulations. Avoid, as names to be replied to, common words, like "investor," "inquirer," and so on, as also "bear" or "bull." Detached syllables of the inquirer's name, or initials reversed, will frequently do as well as anything, so long as the answer can be identified by the inquirer.

The EDITOR further respectfully requests that merely speculative questions should as far as possible be avoided. He by no means sets himself up as a market prophet, and can only undertake to provide the latest information regarding the securities asked about. This he will do faithfully and without bias.

Replies cannot be guaranteed in the same week if the letters demanding them reach the office of the INVESTORS' REVIEW, Norfolk House, Norfolk-street, W.C., later than the first post on Wednesday mornings.

"A BONDHOLDER."—Will the writer of the letters signed thus in Nos. 2 and 3 (January 14 and 21) kindly forward his address. I regret it has been mislaid.

EXPRESS.—1. I will write you in reply to this question. 2. A fair second-class bond, but the finances of the guaranteeing company are complicated and rather mysterious. This guarantor is a kind of trust which controls several roads in the north-western part of the country. There are signs of considerable activity in that region, so these companies are likely to do well. 3. I never like to recommend this class of share as a permanent investment; the huge capital liability must not be forgotten. The yield is liable to considerable fluctuations in bad times. 4. The amount of capital behind these debentures is small, and the dividend on the ordinary shares was reduced last year from 10 per cent. to 8 per cent.

H. G.—1. Very speculative. Present price seems much inflated, and the market is certainly manipulated. 2. Yes.

Y. F.—So far the Government has paid its guarantee, which is the company's sole source of income. The road does not pay its working expenses. Bonds are bought, not drawn, the money coming from the guarantee. How long interest will be paid depends entirely on the ability or desire of the Government to meet its engagements. I do not think there is much chance of an improvement in the immediate future.

W. A. C.—You have a disagreeable loss at present prices, and I do not like to urge you to sell, but I have never had a high opinion of the management of the company. Generally the market is in a spiritless condition, and prices threaten to drag. On the other hand, a large mill is at work, and the monthly profits declared have been very fair. Should any activity show itself in the market a rise in your shares might be engineered, but that will not happen just yet. My own feeling is that you should not hold long.

A.N.Y.—Company is said to own some very promising properties, but the whole business is very speculative. Those controlling it are clever, but you must be prepared for a loss if you buy. There is no possibility of calculating the "worth" of the shares.

J. H. S.—I am sorry I have not been able to forward your letter yet owing to the loss of the "copy," but I hope to receive the address shortly.

A Special Commission is now sitting in St. Petersburg to consider the question as to the importation of foreign goods into Siberia by the Kara Sea duty free. It was so before, and the Siberian merchants and traders urge that it should be so again, as by the abolition of the privilege they had lost a valuable market for the export of their cereals, which were taken by British vessels trading with Siberian ports when their goods were admitted free of duty. The Moscow Exchange, however, oppose this arrangement, which they consider detrimental to Russian commerce. Russia herself, these enlightened gentlemen contend, can supply all essential requisites for the people of Siberia. Poor Siberia!

It is stated that the Admiralty contemplate the immediate commissioning of the first-class cruiser *Terrible* for service with the Chinese fleet.

CLEMENT WILSON'S PUBLICATIONS.

LEGAL EPITOMES FOR GENERAL USE.

Price 2s. 6d. Fcap 8vo, cloth.

No. I.

LAW OF SALES OF STOCKS AND SHARES. By CHARLES FRAMPTON STALLARD, M.A. (Oxon.), of Gray's Inn, late Holt Scholar, Barrister-at-Law.

"The law is clearly and concisely given, and the book should certainly assist those who are concerned in dealings with stocks and shares."—*Law Times.*

"Cannot fail to be of service to many who have dealings in stocks and shares."—*Bankers' Magazine.*

No. II.

LAW OF BANKS AND BANKERS. By W. DE BRACY HERBERT, M.A., LL.M., of the Inner Temple, Barrister-at-Law.

"A clear and readable exposition of the English law of Banker and Customer."—*Scotsman.*

"Clear and simple in its style . . . and appears to be absolutely accurate."—*Law Times.*

No. III.

LAW OF DIRECTORS' AND PROMOTERS' LIABILITIES. By R. STORRY DEANS, LL.B. (London), of Gray's Inn, Barrister-at-Law, sometime Holder of Inns of Court Studentship, Arden Scholar of Gray's Inn, &c.

"A clearly written and useful book upon a subject of general interest."—*Manchester Guardian.*

"It is well fitted to be of assistance to directors, promoters, and shareholders."—*Dundee Advertiser.*

No. IV.

Now Ready.

THE LAW OF FIXTURES AND REPAIRS AS BETWEEN LANDLORD AND TENANT. By W. DE BRACY HERBERT, M.A., LL.M., of the Inner Temple, Barrister-at-Law.

"Explains the law on the question plainly and concisely, but, at the same time, with accuracy, and will prove serviceable to property-owners, agents, and tenants."—*Manchester Guardian.*

"An excellent handbook."—*Yorkshire Post.*

BOOKS BY A. J. WILSON.

Editor of the "Investors' Review" and "Investment Index."

Price in cloth, 1s. 6d. net (post free, 1s. 8d.); paper cover, 1s. net (post free, 1s. 2d.)

No. I.

PRACTICAL HINTS TO INVESTORS.

"The perusal of Mr. Wilson's handy book will repay those concerned in the matters treated of; and as an example in terse and incisive English it may be read by the student and admirer of style."—*Manchester City News.*

No. II.

Now Ready. New Edition, Entirely Rewritten.

PLAIN ADVICE ABOUT LIFE INSURANCE.

"Pregnant with plain meaning, and hits hard, straight from the shoulder, as a work by Mr. Wilson usually does."—*Westminster Gazette.*

"Frank and out-spoken, and affords much useful information and guidance."—*Glasgow Herald.*

A GLOSSARY OF COLLOQUIAL, SLANG, AND TECHNICAL TERMS, in use on the Stock Exchange and in the Money Market. Edited by A. J. WILSON. Price 3s.

"A good deal of useful information is here presented in a very handy form."—*Times.*

"The work is a most useful one, and admirable in many respects."—*Pall Mall Gazette.*

"The book fills a gap among works of reference."—*Morning Post.*

"A book that will be found useful in the offices of a large class of business houses."—*Scotsman.*

"The explanations will be found helpful to all who wish to have a clear understanding of the language of the money and stock markets."—*Dundee Advertiser.*

THE ENGLISH AND THE DUTCH IN SOUTH AFRICA. A Historical Restrospect. By HARTLEY WITHERS. One Vol. crown 8vo, price 3s. 6d.

"Those who are prepared for a study of the historical conditions of the problem of the day will find abundant satisfaction in this modest volume."—*Daily News.*

"The salient facts of the English and Dutch occupation are set out in a very compact and impressive fashion."—*Liverpool Post.*

"Everyone who desires in a small compass to obtain a strong and comprehensive grasp of the situation cannot do better than follow Mr. Withers in his rapid but careful sketch of the history of the Dutch Huguenot population, known to the man in the street as the 'Boer.'"—*Banker's Magazine.*

CLEMENT WILSON,

Norfolk House, Norfolk Street, W.C.

Mr. T. Fisher Unwin's Selected List.

Crown 8vo, cloth, price 7s. 6d.

TOURGUENEFF

AND HIS FRENCH CIRCLE:

A Series of Letters to Flaubert, George Sand, Emile Zola, Guy de Maupassant, Gambetta, and others.

Edited by H. HALPERINE-KAMINSKY, and Translated, with Preface, by Miss ETHEL ARNOLD.

THE TIMES.

"The work has been admirably translated into English by Miss Ethel Arnold. . . . The preface contains much sound criticism very felicitously expressed. . . . The merit of the rendering is attested by the easy and idiomatic flow, and by the close correspondence it establishes between the style and man. . . . In a word, Miss Arnold has treated the book exactly in the right spirit."

THE SCOTSMAN.

"The English version is well done. . . . It is likely to be read with interest by a wide circle."

THE DAILY MAIL.

"They are well and spiritedly translated."

NOW READY.

MY LIFE IN TWO HEMISPHERES.

By Sir CHARLES GAVAN DUFFY.

In 2 vols. with a Photogravure Portrait to each, price 32s.

*** This work contains letters from John Stuart Mill, Cardinal Newman, Thomas Carlyle, Mrs. Carlyle, Richard Cobden, Father Mathew, Leigh Hunt, John Bright, Robert Lowe (Lord Sherbrooke), Sir Emerson Tennant, Sir Arthur Helps, H. E. Childers, John Forster, William Allingham, Clarence Mangan, and from eminent Political Men in Ireland and Australia too numerous to specify.

The Daily News.—"These volumes may serve for a history, not only of a man and of a movement, but of a whole nation in one of its most stirring periods . . . Sir Charles Duffy surveys the entire field of Imperial Politics, and there are few men of the first importance whom he is not able to estimate as personal forces."

The Daily Chronicle.—"A bright, refreshing narrative, full of valuable information, replete with admirable stories, and abounding in thoughtful and suggestive reflections."

The Newcastle Daily Leader.—"We commend Sir C. Duffy's graphic and vigorous pages to all who are sincerely desirous to know the ins and outs of the Irish questions."

NOW READY.

THE GLADSTONE COLONY: an Unwritten Chapter of Australian History.

By JAMES FRANCIS HOGAN, M.P., Author of "The Irish in Australia," "The Australian in London," "Robert Lowe, Viscount Sherbrooke," &c. With a Prefatory Note by the Right Hon. W. E. GLADSTONE. Demy 8vo, cloth, 7s. 6d.

ABRIDGED CONTENTS.—Prefatory Note; The Genesis of the Gladstone Colony; Some Preliminary Proposals; Constitution of the New Colony; Mr. Gladstone Enunciates his Land Property; The Founding of the Colony; The Veto of Earl Grey; The Vindication of Colonel Barney; The Growth and Development of Gladstone; Experiences of a Pioneer Squatter; The Great Gold Rush; The Correspondence of Sir Maurice O'Connell; A Grievous Error of the Gladstones; Major De Winton; Oldest Living Gladstonian; The Gladstone of To-day; Mr. Gladstone's "True Principles of Colonisation"; Mr. Gladstone and the Colonies; A Couple of Colonial Lectures.

SIR THOMAS MAITLAND. By W. FREWEN LORD.

(Vol. 2 of "Builders of Greater Britain.") Frontispiece and Maps, cloth, 5s.

The Pall Mall Gazette.—"Written in a bright and spirited style, this study of Sir Thomas Maitland furnishes a fascinating chapter in the history of the making of the empire."

SIR JAMES Y. SIMPSON. By H. LAING GORDON.

(Vol. 3 of "Masters of Medicine.") Illustrated, cloth, 3s. 6d.

The Glasgow Herald.—"The book, we repeat, should be widely read, and especially by Scotsmen."

THE PEOPLES AND POLITICS OF THE FAR EAST.

By HENRY NORMAN. Over Sixty Illustrations and Four Maps. Third Edition. Cloth, 21s.

WILD NATURE WON BY KINDNESS.

By Mrs. BRIGHTWEN. Many Illustrations. New Edition (the Eighth). Cloth, 1s. 6d.

HOW TO BE HAPPY THOUGH MARRIED.

By Rev. E. J. HARDY, M.A. New Edition, completing the Fiftieth Thousand. Cloth, 3s. 6d.

THE GREEN CLOTH LIBRARY

New Volumes. 6s. each.

JOHN OLIVER HOBBES.	**The School for Saints.**
LORD ERNEST HAMILTON.	**The Outlaws of the Marches.**
DR. WEIR MITCHELL.	**Hugh Wynne.**
BENJAMIN SWIFT.	**The Tormentor.**
GEORGE BARTRAM.	**The People of Clopton.**
OLIVE SCHREINER.	**Trooper Peter Halket.**

A Set of Prospectuses, Catalogues, and Lists, containing descriptive details of books in every class of English Literature, will be sent post free to any address on receipt of card. If desired, arrangements can be made for intending purchasers to view any book at the local booksellers.

London: T. FISHER UNWIN, Paternoster Square, E.C.

Notice to Subscribers.

Complaints are continually reaching us that the INVESTORS' REVIEW cannot be obtained at this and the other railway bookstall, that it does not reach Scotch and Irish cities till Monday, and that it is not delivered in the City till Saturday morning.

We publish on Friday in time for the REVIEW to be at all Metropolitan bookstalls by at latest 4 p.m., and we believe that it is there then, having no doubt that Messrs. W. H. Smith & Son do their best, but they have such a mass of papers to handle every day that a fresh one may well look almost like a personal enemy and be kept in short supply unless the reading public shows unmistakably that it is wanted. A little perseverance, therefore, in asking for the INVESTORS' REVIEW is all that should be required to remedy this defect.

All London newsagents can be in a position to distribute the paper on Friday afternoon if they please, and here also the only remedy is for subscribers to insist upon having it as soon as published. Arrangements have been made that all our direct City subscribers shall have their copies before 4 p.m. on Friday. As for the provinces, we can only say that the paper is delivered to the forwarding agents in ample time to be in every English and Scotch town, and in Dublin and Belfast, likewise, early on Saturday morning. Those despatched by post from this office can be delivered by the first London mail on Saturday in every part of the United Kingdom.

Cheques and Postal Orders should be made payable to CLEMENT WILSON.

The INVESTORS' REVIEW can be obtained in Paris of Messrs. BOYVEAU ET CHEVILLET, 22, Rue de la Banque.

ADVERTISEMENTS.

All Advertisements are received subject to approval, and should be sent in not later than 5 p.m. on Thursdays.

For tariff and particulars of positions open apply to the Advertisement Manager, Norfolk House, Norfolk-street, W.C.

The Investment Index,

A Quarterly Supplement to the "Investors' Review."

Price 2s. net. 8s. 6d. per annum, post free.

THE INVESTMENT INDEX is an indispensable supplement to the Investors' Review. A file of it enables investors to follow the ups and downs of markets, and each number gives the return obtainable on all classes of securities at recent prices, arranged in a most convenient form for reference. Appended to its tables of figures are criticisms on company balance sheets, State Budgets, &c., similar to those in the Investors' Review.

Regarding it, the *Speaker* says: "The Quarterly 'Investment Index' is probably the handiest and fullest, as it is certainly the safest, of guides to the investor."

"The compilation of securities is particularly valuable."—*Pall Mall Gazette.*

"Its carefully classified list of securities will be found very valuable."—*Globe.*

"At no time has such a list of securities been more valuable than at the present."—*Star.*

"The invaluable 'Investors' Index.'"—*Sketch.*

"A most valuable compilation."—*Glasgow Herald.*

Subscription to the "Investors' Review" and "Investment Index," 36s. per annum, post free.

CLEMENT WILSON,

NORFOLK HOUSE, NORFOLK STREET, LONDON, W.C.

To Correspondents.

The EDITOR cannot undertake to return rejected communications. Letters from correspondents must, in every case, be authenticated by the name and address of the writer.

The Investors' Review.

The Week's Money Market.

Poor Money Market! it has been living from hand to mouth during the past seven days. Each day has seen fair sums maturing for repayment at the Bank of England, and the market has endeavoured to meet these so far as its resources would permit, but never got free. Some days it paid-off half the amount falling due, on others it had to re-borrow the whole, and in the end the reduction of its indebtedness to the fountain of credit was not very important. At the same time the payment of the railway dividends caused a little dislocation of funds, and one or two "calls" of importance fell due in the week. Day to day money has accordingly kept tight at 2¾ to 3 per cent. during the greater part of the time, and loans for seven days have ruled about 2¾ per cent.

The sudden break in the quotation for gold from 77s. 10¾d. to just a trifle over the Bank's buying price of 77s. 9d. per oz., has naturally brought an easier tone to the discount market. We have good reason for stating that the great demand on account of the Continent has ceased, whether permanently or temporarily it is yet too early to say, but there are signs that the diminution in the bidding arises from causes likely to be permanent. Austria and Russia have each accumulated a large sum in gold at a costly price—a price that must have been a great strain upon their exchequers, and they must now have every reason to hold their hands. Even if another Japanese Loan is raised here, the sum obtained will only prevent gold filtering away from that country; while, if an internal loan is floated in Japan, as is spoken of in some quarters, that measure will only intensify the exports of gold from Japan. Probably, therefore, our market will have to face no drain of importance during the current six months, and, in this case, gold will soon begin to accumulate at the Bank of England once again. Such a prospect would have caused a sharp decline in discount rates, if the news had come at any other season, but, at the moment, the Government has in its Treasury more of the resources of the market than it can afford to spare, and, consequently, it is bound to act with caution. The discount rate for three months choice bills has, therefore, only declined to 2⅝ to 2$\frac{11}{16}$ per cent., as against 2$\frac{1}{16}$ to 2¾ per cent. a week ago, but longer dated paper is weak at 2½ to 2⅝ per cent. When Government disbursements on a large scale will take place it is hard to say. Some money may easily come out at the next Consols settlement, and when it does occur, the market will become much easier, very likely suddenly easier. It seems a pity that the action of the collector of the taxes on the Money Market should be so oppressive as it often is at the beginning of the year, but we must put up with it. This year the lock-up of credit in the Government balances has been much worse than usual.

No relief has yet come to the Money Market by the release of Government balances. On the contrary, the Bank Return published yesterday disclosed a further increase of £1,431,000 in the "public" deposits which contain the whole of the Treasury and departmental moneys, and the total now amounts to £16,878,000. It is quite possible that this accumulation may be continued for several weeks longer, for in 1896 it went on until the third week in March, when the total attained the rare height of £19,175,000. Should no relief come at the end of the present month by the payment of accounts by the Government, then the market has a very unpleasant prospect before it, because it is becoming steadily poorer. This week the "other" deposits, which comprise the balances of other banks, are again less by £838,000, at £35,123,000, and although the Reserve has increased £632,000 to £23,878,000 through the return of coin and notes from circulation, the market actually owes £5,453 more on "other" securities than it did last week. The total of these "other" securities is still £32,329,000 as against less than £27,000,000 in the first week of December last, and £28,635,000 in the third week of February last year. The Market is, therefore, heavily in the Bank's debt still and cannot escape from this position until the taxes now piled up to such an unusual amount begin to be paid out again.

SILVER.

A weak tone has prevailed in this market since we last wrote. The wearing away of the over-sold account is shown by the fact that the "spot" price now rules only $\frac{1}{16}$d. above that for delivery two months ahead. The normal divergence between the two quotations is about ⅛d., so that matters are almost in equilibrium, and, the market has therefore lost all the support it has obtained during the past four or five months from its over-sold condition. Perhaps, partly on account of this fact, buyers have been reluctant throughout, and, after some days of waiting, sellers had to break the price by ¼d. per oz. to 25$\frac{13}{16}$d. per oz. for "spot" in order to find a purchaser. At this price a little reaction occurred to 25⅞d. per oz., based to a slight degree upon a cable from New York, stating that a movement is on foot to combine the silver smelters in the States. Efforts in this direction have been made before, and if this movement should have a better result than the others, the American silver-mine owners will earn the thanks of producers in Australasia, Mexico, and other places, at severe cost to themselves. The India Council allotment must be considered poor for this time of year, the applications being only 4 lacs above the 40 lacs offered, while allotments were made at $\frac{1}{16}$d. lower than a week ago. Chinese exchanges have fallen ¼d. to ⅜d. during the week.

BANK OF ENGLAND.

AN ACCOUNT pursuant to the Act 7 and 8 Vict., cap. 32, for the Week ending on Wednesday, February 16, 1898.

ISSUE DEPARTMENT.

	£		£
Notes Issued	47,858,275	Government Debt	11,015,100
		Other Securities	5,784,900
		Gold Coin and Bullion	31,058,275
		Silver Bullion	—
	£47,858,275		£47,858,275

BANKING DEPARTMENT.

	£		£
Proprietors' Capital	14,553,000	Government Securities	13,994,565
Rest	3,493,103	Other Securities	32,334,715
Public Deposits (including Exchequer, Savings Banks, Commissioners of National Debt, and Dividend Accounts)	16,878,427	Notes	21,442,220
Other Deposits	35,122,986	Gold and Silver Coin	2,435,589
Seven Day and other Bills	159,573		
	£70,207,089		£70,207,089

Dated February 16, 1898.

H. G. BOWEN, *Chief Cashier.*

In the following table will be found the movements compared with the previous week, and also the totals for that week and the corresponding return last year :—

Banking Department.

Last Year. Feb. 17.		Feb. 9, 1898.	Feb. 16, 1898.	Increase.	Decrease.
£	Liabilities.	£	£	£	£
3,529,266	Rest	3,472,459	3,493,103	20,644	—
15,093,026	Pub. Deposits	15,447,084	16,878,427	1,431,343	—
40,188,702	Other do.	35,961,137	35,122,986	—	838,151
170,669	7 Day Bills	140,823	159,573	18,750	—
	Assets.			Decrease.	Increase.
14,088,858	Gov. Securities	13,999,565	13,994,565	5,000	—
28,635,374	Other do.	32,329,262	32,334,715	—	5,453
29,810,431	Total Reserve	23,245,676	23,877,809	—	632,133
				1,475,737	1,475,737
				Increase.	Decrease.
£		£	£	£	£
25,472,965	Note Circulation	26,600,235	26,416,055	—	184,180
53⅛ p.c.	Proportion	43⅜ p.c.	p.c.	—	—
3 ,,	Bank Rate	3 ,,	3 ,,	—	—

Foreign Bullion movement for week £56,000 in.

LONDON BANKERS' CLEARING.

Week ending	1898.	1897.	Increase.	Decrease.
	£	£	£	£
Jan. 5	222,654,000	174,376,000	48,278,000	—
,, 12	144,603,000	127,315,000	17,288,000	—
,, 19	171,777,000	156,200,000	15,577,000	—
,, 26	134,247,000	118,667,000	15,580,000	—
Feb. 2	194,544,000	174,498,000	20,056,000	—
,, 9	137,204,000	129,209,000	8,995,000	—
,, 16	184,403,000	162,163,000	22,245,000	—

BANK AND DISCOUNT RATES ABROAD.

	Bank Rate.	Altered.	Open Market.
Paris	2	March 14, 1895	1¾
Berlin	4	January 20, 1898	2⅞
Hamburg	4	January 20, 1898	2¾
Frankfort	4	January 20, 1898	2¾
Amsterdam	3	April 13, 1897	2½
Brussels	3	April 28, 1896	2
Vienna	4	January 22, 1896	3¾
Rome	5	August 27, 1895	3
St. Petersburg	5½	January 23, 1898	5
Madrid	5	June 17, 1896	4
Lisbon	6	January 25, 1891	6
Stockholm	5	October 27, 1897	5
Copenhagen	4	January 20, 1898	4
Calcutta	11	January 11, 1898	—
Bombay	12	January 11, 1898	—
New York call money	1½ to 1¾	—	—

NEW YORK ASSOCIATED BANKS (dollar at 4s.).

	Feb. 12, 1898.	Feb. 5, 1898.	Jan. 29, 1898.	Feb. 13, 1897.
	£	£	£	£
Specie	22,954,000	22,318,000	22,615,000	16,038,000
Legal tenders	20,424,000	20,630,000	20,622,000	22,692,000
Loans and discounts	127,668,000	126,772,000	125,174,000	100,074,000
Circulation	2,783,000	2,378,400	2,193,800	3,344,800
Net deposits	147,730,000	146,780,000	144,495,000	113,615,000

Legal reserve is 25 per cent. of net deposits; therefore the total reserve (specie and legal tenders) exceeds this sum by £5,488,000, against an excess last week of £6,036,900.

BANK OF FRANCE (25 francs to the £).

	Feb. 17, 1898.	Feb. 10, 1898.	Feb. 3, 1898.	Feb. 11, 1897.
	£	£	£	£
Gold in hand	77,166,520	77,080,000	77,076,800	76,645,000
Silver in hand	48,319,680	48,323,920	48,360,640	49,274,000
Bills discounted	29,691,080	31,058,200	37,271,600	*40,856,000
Advances	14,626,160	14,838,600	14,826,920	—
Note circulation	147,163,880	150,463,880	154,375,600	147,377,000
Public deposits	8,140,720	8,100,520	6,136,360	9,642,000
Private deposits	19,014,960	19,425,320	20,332,240	19,939,000

Proportion between bullion and circulation 84½ per cent. against 83⅜ per cent. a week ago.

*** Includes advances.**

FOREIGN RATES OF EXCHANGE ON LONDON.

Place.	Usance.	Last week's.	Latest.	Place.	Usance.	Last week's.	Latest.
Paris	chqs.	25·24½	25·27	Italy	sight	26·60	26·56
Brussels	chqs.	25·27½	25·29	Do. gold prem.	..	105·40	105·17
Amsterdam	short	12·06½	12·06	Constantinople	3 mths	109·25	109·30
Berlin	short	20·42	20·42	B. Ayres gd. pm.	..	161·50	167·00
Do.	3 mths	20·29	20·29½	Rio de Janeiro	90 dys	6½	6$\frac{11}{16}$
Hamburg	3 mths	20·28½	20·28½	Valparaiso	90 dys	17⅝	17⅝
Frankfort	short	20·42	20·42	Calcutta	T. T.	1/3$\frac{15}{16}$	1/3$\frac{15}{16}$
Vienna	short	12·01	12·01½	Bombay	T. T.	1/3¾	1/3¾
St. Petersburg	3 mths	93·90	93·90	Hong Kong	T. T.	1/10¾	1/10½
New York	60 dys	4·83½	4·83½	Shanghai	T. T.	2/6½	2/5⅞
Lisbon	sight	36	35⅞	Singapore	T. T.	1/10⅝	1/10$\frac{5}{16}$
Madrid	sight	33·66	33·58				

IMPERIAL BANK OF GERMANY (20 marks to the £).

	Feb. 7, 1898.	Jan. 31, 1898.	Jan. 22, 1898.	Feb. 6, 1897.
	£	£	£	£
Cash in hand	46,313,100	45,672,450	45,757,850	44,834,000
Bills discounted	26,750,000	28,435,050	26,219,750	*32,330,000
Advances on stocks	4,129,450	4,325,300	4,110,600	—
Note circulation	52,827,050	54,542,300	54,813,750	50,498,000
Public deposits	21,535,500	21,795,550	27,169,800	22,202,000

* Includes advances.

AUSTRIAN-HUNGARIAN BANK (1s. 8d. to the florin).

	Feb. 7, 1898.	Jan. 31, 1898.	Jan. 22, 1898.	Feb. 6, 1897.
	£	£	£	£
Gold reserve	30,347,666	30,272,833	30,354,000	30,557,000
Silver reserve	10,345,417	10,352,166	10,331,416	12,043,000
Foreign bills	1,382,333	1,403,916	1,344,000	—
Advances	1,887,250	1,907,000	1,946,583	—
Note circulation	52,209,333	52,316,333	52,780,000	50,979,000
Bills discounted	11,763,416	12,038,000	12,865,083	*15,234,000

* Includes advances.

NATIONAL BANK OF BELGIUM (25 francs to the £).

	Feb. 10, 1898.	Feb. 3, 1898.	Jan. 27, 1898.	Feb. 11, 1897.
	£	£	£	£
Coin and bullion	4,234,880	4,422,080	4,200,280	4,146,280
Other securities	17,204,420	17,601,560	17,888,360	16,183,440
Note circulation	19,348,560	19,209,160	19,736,480	18,777,680
Deposits	3,396,160	4,109,520	3,721,040	2,842,520

BANK OF SPAIN (25 pesetas to the £).

	Feb. 12, 1898.	Feb. 5, 1898.	Jan. 29, 1898.	Feb. 13, 1897.
	£	£	£	£
Gold	9,500,920	9,495,120	9,430,680	8,528,360
Silver	10,651,800	10,616,720	10,568,320	10,743,320
Bills discounted	21,855,320	21,846,600	21,636,840	8,155,240
Advances and loans	4,869,680	4,873,600	4,735,200	9,232,560
Notes in circulation	50,062,440	49,902,480	49,391,760	42,691,120
Treasury advances, coupon account	310,400	211,680	108,840	306,560
Treasury balances	547,840	454,280	329,280	2,036,000

LONDON COURSE OF EXCHANGE.

Place.	Usance.	Feb. 8.	Feb. 10.	Feb. 15.	Feb. 17.
Amsterdam and Rotterdam	short	12·1½	12·1½	12·1½	12·1½
Do. do.	3 months	12·3⅜	12·3⅜	12·3⅜	12·3½
Antwerp and Brussels	3 months	25·42½	25·42½	25·42½	25·43¾
Hamburg	3 months	20·62	20·62	20·62	20·62
Berlin and German B. Places	3 months	20·62	20·62	20·62	20·62
Paris	cheques	25·26½	25·26½	25·26¼	25·27½
Do.	3 months	25·38¾	25·38¾	25·40	25·41¼
Marseilles	3 months	25·40	25·40	25·41¼	25·41¼
Switzerland	3 months	25·60	25·60	25·60	25·60
Austria	3 months	12·15	12·16½	12·16¼	12·16½
St. Petersburg	3 months	25 1/16	25 1/16	25 1/16	25 1/16
Moscow	3 months	25	25	25	25
Italian Bank Places	3 months	26·87½	26·90	26·87½	26·87½
New York	60 days	49	49	49	49
Madrid and Spanish B. P.	3 months	35¼	35¼	35½	35 3/16
Lisbon	3 months	35⅝	35 9/16	35⅞	35⅞
Oporto	3 months	35⅝	35 11/16	35⅞	35⅞
Copenhagen	3 months	18·37	18·37	18·37	18·38
Christiania	—	18·37	18·37	18·38	18·38
Stockholm	—	18·37	18·37	18·38	18·38

OPEN MARKET DISCOUNT.

	Per cent.
Thirty and sixty day remitted bills	2 11/16—2¾
Three months ,,	2⅝—2 11/16
Four months ,,	2½—2⅝
Six months ,,	2½
Three months fine inland bills	2⅞—3
Four months ,,	2⅞—3
Six months ,,	2⅞—3

BANK AND DEPOSIT RATES.

	Per cent.
Bank of England minimum discount rate	3
,, ,, short loan rates	3
Banker's rate on deposits	1½
Bill brokers' deposit rate (call)	2
,, 7 and 14 days' notice	2¼
Current rates for 7 day loans	2¾
,, ,, for call loans	2¾—3

Stock Market Notes and Comments.

There is really not a great deal to say this week about the Stock Exchange; most departments of it remain in a somewhat paralysed condition. The public is not doing anything except to invest its savings, and not a great deal even of that. Such speculation as goes on is either between the London Market and foreign markets or between the leaders of the often-mentioned groups and combinations who make a show of business, anxious to get the public to come and buy their wares. Only one interesting point has to be noted in regard to investment stocks, and that is the selling of Colonial securities and of Home railway debenture and preference stocks by some of the banks,—at least it is inferred that the banks have been selling their own stock, not throwing out stock pawned with them by those who have been living on interest "margins." It has not been extensive selling, but just enough to indicate what a real and prolonged pressure for money would bring about. On most of what has been sold the sellers ought to have realised handsome profits, but small as the total business of this kind has been, it is singular how it has weakened the Market and made jobbers shy of dealing.

Regarding the great departments of the Stock Exchange, Home Railway ordinary stocks, United States and Canadian Railroad securities, and the miscellaneous market we can really say nothing fresh.

Up to the present the disappointing yields of English railway ordinary stocks for the past half-year, have not had much influence upon prices. Buying has merely stopped; the speculator has no motive to purchase for the rise nor has the investor any temptation to put money into securities which a year hence may not, at current prices, yield 3 per cent. The speculation in American railroad shares also has paused on account of the difficulties which have again arisen between the United States and Spain about Cuba. The source of the latest squabble was the publication of a brutally frank private letter of the Spanish minister at Washington, and we really cannot see that anything serious ought to arise out of this doubtless regrettable incident. Had President McKinley been a magnanimous man, he would have passed the matter over without notice of any kind, seeing that the letter was in no sense official. Being, however, essentially a small and commonplace man, a sort of quarrel has arisen which has given alarmists plenty of scope for inflammatory writing, and offers such a splendid opportunity to disseminate lies more or less grotesque, that even the lamentable accident to the United States cruiser *Maine* in Havana Harbour, was made use of to depress the market. In the result, the buying which was spreading on this side has paused, if not stopped altogether, and we must wait for the little tempest of doubts to blow over before this market resumes activity.

Of Foreign Government stocks we have also no particulars of an interesting kind to give, they are still so very little dealt in between London and Paris, as London will not buy most of these stocks on any terms, and Paris has lost taste for them since its inhabitants have seen red-handed revolution raising its head in their midst over this scandalous Dreyfus miscarriage of justice, and the still more scandalous behaviour of the Administration and the military faction. Well may M. Guyot dub M. Méline "Father Ruin." What is going to happen in France no man can forecast, but prudent men will be inclined to prepare for the worst, and in the tempest which seems brewing, surely the man who deserves sympathy far more than execration is the Jew. His wealth mainly consists in mortgages upon human labour, of one kind or another, the value of which would be extremely likely to disappear when the forces of disorder gain the upper hand. That he himself would receive maltreatment is a matter of no doubt at all, so little has the world progressed.

After all, however, this French question does not immediately and directly touch us. The most interesting, because most dangerous, section of our Stock Markets just now is the "Kaffir Circus." We hardly know what is going to happen there, but it is plain enough that it cannot remain in its present torpid condition without producing disastrous consequences in some directions. That the public will lose, and lose heavily, when the shares of Transvaal "outcrop" mining companies sink to their true level is unquestionable; but we are inclined to think that the financiers now stand to lose more even than the public, and the thought is comforting. In all our long experience of the City, we have never known any gigantic imposture carried through with more ruthlessness, with a greater disregard to every consideration, not merely of morality, but of business fair-play, than the "rig" of this South African Market. For some years the men engaged in developing it, and in enticing the British public to buy their wares at extravagant prices had everything their own way. The public went mad about "gold in the Transvaal"; sober citizens of all degrees of wealth lost their heads in the furore, and obscure and needy adventures by the dozen sprang suddenly into the position of millionaires possessing untold wealth. For the last eighteen months now at least the stream has been been running rather the other way, and it is a consolation to think that when the balance is ultimately struck a good deal of the wealth acquired in the days of the nation's madness, by men unscrupulous enough often to rob their own mothers, will have gone back again into the hands of some at least of those from whom it was originally drawn. In other words, since the public ceased to buy South African shares the occupation of these millionaires of yesterday has consisted in what is called "supporting the market." They have had to be the buyers in order to sustain prices, and in this position they have been obliged to take back again at high figures large numbers of the shares they had previously parted with. Being wealthy they have been able to do this up to now with considerable success; indications, however, now point to the conclusion that they think they have had enough of it and for some time the market has been dwindling, without life.

In our opinion it must continue to dwindle unless the speculative British public is foolish enough to take to selling "bears." That, as we point out elsewhere in reference to the Deep Level shares not yet placed with the public, would, indeed, be madness, and playing the game of the financier to perfection. To sell what a man has not got is nineteen cases out of twenty a profitless operation, even when the security sold may not be worth one-tenth of its quoted price. Still, where a market is large and free the bear now and again may "make a haul" if he follows the market downwards, and knows when to stop. The African Market, however, is not "free" by any means, and the prudent man who loves peace of mind with his crust will give it the go-by.

Were a large "bear" account to be opened in these South African mine shares prices would immediately be put up against the bear, and he would have to buy back at a loss, his money going into the pockets of the manipulators behind the market to enable them to write down the cost of the shares in their books, and, on a rising market, it is certain that a proportion of new buyers would come forward, so that the houses now loaded to the ceiling with unsaleable scrip might escape with the bulk of their ill-gotten gains. The only thing for the public to do, then, is to do nothing. Those who possess these South African shares ought, in our opinion, to sell them when they get an opportunity,—quietly, steadily, never in fevered haste. Those who do not possess them should neither buy nor sell. Let the market be left completely to itself.

We quite believe that this advice may occasionally seem bad, because there is plenty of strength still with those who have made this market, so far as outcrop mines go, and they can put prices up somewhat, if they like, but ultimately, we have no doubt whatever, our opinion will be amply justified. Even in regard to the very best looking properties in all the Rand there is not one which can be called reasonable in price, measured by the quotation for its shares on the market to-day. Every advance in price, however, ought to be taken advantage of by holders to escape.

Just look at the position of the "Chartered" Company; its shares are quoted at 3 and have remained comparatively steady in spite of the absence of all accounts for three years now, and in spite of the depressing opinions enunciated by Mr. Cecil Rhodes. The "vamosing" of two directors has had no appreciable influence, nor yet the intimation that the Colonial Office intends to take over the administration of the country while leaving the Company responsible for the finances. There can be but one explanation of this market indifference, and it is that large masses of the shares are in the hands of finance houses who dare not sell. Doubtless, the public also possesses immense quantities, but the public is mostly "in" at much higher prices, and holders in that unfortunate position never sell unless forced to. They hug their losses and groan. The movements of the market are, therefore, governed by the action of the groups which have flourished in the past by playing upon it, and since these groups, judging by the stagnation of prices, cannot now operate, we may be quite sure that evil is on the way, not good. They cannot effect an advance, these worthies, and they dare not allow a fall. In our opinion there will be no real healthy activity in any part of the Stock Markets until all the great mass of rubbish accumulated in the South African part of it has been cleared away. At every other point speculation is spasmodic. It flutters up, now in one security, now in another, to die away again, exhausted before its energy has been half developed. There is no more anxious business to be found in the United Kingdom at the present time than that of the Stock Exchange jobber.

The Week's Stock Markets.

General dulness and an all-round absence of business have been the chief characteristics of the past week on the Stock Exchange, but it was not until after the news arrived of the loss of the United States cruiser, *Maine*, in Cuban waters that falls assumed any very serious dimensions. Markets then became very weak, but the actual transactions were not considerable. Consols advanced steadily, and touched 113 on Saturday, due partly to purchases by the Government broker for Sinking Fund purposes, followed by a certain amount of "bear" closing. The price has since slipped back under the influence of a hardening tendency in the "short" money market.

Highest and Lowest this Year.		Last Carrying over Price.	BRITISH FUNDS, &c.	Closing Price.	Rise or Fall.
113½	112½	—	Consols 2¾ p.c. (Money)...	112⅝	+ 1/16
113 5/16	112 7/16	112⅜	Do. Account (Mar. 1)	112¾	—
106¼	105½	106	2½ p.c. Stock red. 1905 ...	106	—
363	347½	—	Bank of England Stock...	356½	−3½
117	115¾	116½	India 3½ p.c. Stk. red. 1931	116½	+ ¼
109½	108	108½	Do. 3 p.c. Stk. red. 1948	108½	+ ¼
96⅛	94¾	95½	Do. 2½ p.c. Stk. red. 1926	95	—

The Home Railway market was firm at the close of last week, and prices advanced for several days on end but the flatness of the American market had an unfavourable effect on Home Railways, and the latest quotations show an almost general shrinkage on the week. Traffic returns were good, that of the Midland Company especially, the big increase shown in that company's takings this week giving them a balance on the right side for the half-year up to date. The stocks of the Southern lines and Great Northern issues have been the weakest in the whole list, but on the other hand there has again been a good inquiry for Central London shares. City and South London stock drooped when a new issue of ordinary stock, to the extent of about £225,000, was announced. There has been a steady decline in the preference and debenture stocks of the leading lines.

Highest and Lowest this Year.		Last Carrying over Price.	HOME RAILWAYS.	Closing Price.	Rise or Fall.
186	177½	178	Brighton Def.	177¾	−1½
59½	57⅛	57¾	Caledonian Def.	57⅛	−⅜
20⅝	19	20	Chatham Ordinary	20⅛	−⅛
77½	66	70	Great Central Pref.	70	−1
24¾	22½	22⅜	Do. Def.	22½	—
124½	119¾	120	Great Eastern	121½	+⅜
61½	55½	56⅜	Great Northern Def.	55¾	−1⅜
179¼	176½	178	Great Western	178	−¼
49½	45¾	47½	Hull and Barnsley	46½	−¼
149½	146½	148½	Lanc. and Yorkshire	147¾	−1½
136¼	133½	135	Metropolitan	133½	—
31	29	30	Metropolitan District	29½	−½
88¾	87½	87¾	Midland Pref.	87½	−½
95⅜	92¾	93½	Do. Def.	93	−½
93½	90½	91½	North British Pref.	92	+½
47½	45	45⅞	Do. Def.	45⅞	−⅜
181½	178⅞	179½	North Eastern	179¾	−¼
205½	204½	204½	North Western	204½	−⅜
117⅛	112⅜	116¾	South Eastern Def.	112⅜	−1
98¾	95½	97	South Western Def.	97½	—

United States Railroad shares, after several ups and downs, finally show nothing but falls on the week. The resignation of the Spanish Ambassador at Washington led to a good deal of selling, but speculative purchases by professional operators again raised prices

All previous advances were, however, soon lost, when the semi-official statement appeared that President McKinley was going to communicate with Congress on Cuban affairs; and the mysterious blowing-up of the United States ironclad *Maine* in Cuban waters on Wednesday was the excuse for the general slump which immediately followed. One or two items of interest have to be noticed, one being that the Louisville Company has sold $12,500,000 of Collateral Trust Gold bonds to retire the 7 per cents. maturing in April. It is stated that Northern Pacific stockholders will receive rights to subscribe to the new securities of the syndicate about to be formed to purchase that company's lands. At the foreclosure sale of the Kansas Pacific line, the Union Pacific Reorganisation Committee's bid of $6,303,000 was accepted.

Highest and Lowest this Year.		Last Carrying over Price.	CANADIAN AND U.S. RAILWAYS.	Closing Prices.	Rise or Fall.
14 5/16	12¾	13¾	Atchison Shares	13¼	− ½
34	29½	33	Do. Pref.	31⅝	−1¼
15⅝	11⅛	14¾	Central Pacific...............	14¼	− ¼
99¾	95¼	99	Chic. Mil. & St. Paul......	97⅜	−1⅜
14¼	11½	13¾	Denver Shares	13½	− ½
54¼	46⅝	53¼	Do. Prefd.	52¼	−1½
16⅝	14¼	16¼	Erie Shares	15½	− ½
44⅝	37¼	42¼	Do. Prefd.	42¼	−1⅜
62½	56⅝	61⅝	Louisville & Nashville ...	60¾	− ¾
14½	12¾	13⅞	Missouri & Texas	13½	− ⅜
122¾	108¼	121½	New York Central	120¼	− ¼
57¼	47¼	56⅝	Norfolk & West. Prefd....	54	−1¼
70¼	59⅝	69¾	Northern Pacific Prefd....	67⅜	−1⅜
19½	15⅝	18¼	Ontario Shares	17⅜	− ⅞
62½	58⅝	62	Pennsylvania	60¾	− ⅝
12½	10¼	11¾	Reading Shares	10⅝	− ⅜
34¼	30⅞	32¼	Southern Prefd.	32⅜	− ⅜
37⅛	26⅜	34¾	Union Pacific	34¼	− ½
20¼	18	19½	Wabash Prefd.	18½	− ½
30¼	27⅜	29½	Do. Income Debs....	29	− ½
92¾	83½	90½	Canadian Pacific...........	89⅞	− ⅝
78½	69⅝	76¼	Grand Trunk Guar.	76¼	− ⅜
69½	57⅛	67½	Do. 1st Pref.	68¼	+ ¾
50⅝	37¼	49	Do. 2nd Pref.	48⅝	− ⅜
25¼	19¼	24½	Do. 3rd Pref.	24¼	− ¼
105¾	104	104½	Do. 4 p.c. Deb.	104¾	—

Canadian Railway stocks have presented a very lively appearance all the week, the negotiations between the management of the Canadian Pacific and Grand Trunk Railways regarding the disputed rates having had an unsatisfactory ending, but this has been partly off set by the publication of a very favourable half-yearly statement by the latter company. The Canadian Pacific dividend of 2½ per cent. (making 4 per cent. for the year, against 2 per cent. last year) was what the market had looked for, and the traffic returns were also up to expectations; but the latest quotations are lower than those ruling at the end of last week, in sympathy with the general dulness.

Highest and Lowest this Year.		Last Carrying over Price.	FOREIGN BONDS.	Closing Price.	Rise or Fall.
94½	91¼	92½	Argentine 5 p.c. 1886......	92	− ½
92⅝	89	90½	Do. 6 p.c. Funding	90⅞	+ ⅜
76¾	71	75¼	Do. 5 p.c. B. Ay. Water	74⅞	− ⅜
61¾	60	61⅛	Brazilian 4 p.c. 1889	60¼	−1
69⅞	65	67	Do. 5 p.c. 1895	65¼	−1
65	62½	64¼	Do. 5 p.c. West Minas Ry...................	63¾	− ¼
108¾	106¼	107¾	Egyptian 4 p.c. Unified...	108½	+ ¼
104¾	102	103	Do. 3½ p.c. Pref. ...	104½	+1
103	102	102	French 3 p.c. Rente	102½	—
41½	34½	39½	Greek 4 p.c. Monopoly...	41½	+1
93 9/16	92¼	92½	Italian 5 p.c. Rente	93 3/16	+ ½
100	95¾	99	Mexican 6 p.c. 1888	98¾	—
20⅞	20	20⅜	Portuguese 1 p.c.	20⅜	—
62⅝	59⅞	61½	Spanish 4 p.c.	61 3/16	—
45⅛	43	43¾	Turkish 1 p.c. "B"	44½	+ ¼
26 7/16	24 7/16	25¾	Do. 1 p.c. "C"	26⅛	—
22 7/16	21 13/16	22⅜	Do. 1 p.c. "D"	22 3/16	− ⅛
43⅜	40	40½	Uruguay 3½ p.c. Bonds...	42⅝	+ 2⅛

Business has been on a small scale in the Foreign Market owing to the existence of political difficulties, and speculators are unwilling to increase their commitments. Among South American issues the feature has been the rise in Uruguayan bonds, the *coup d'état* in Monte Video being looked upon as an improvement in the political situation.

Argentine descriptions also hardened up, but a rather sharp rise in the gold premium at Buenos Ayres has since had a weakening effect. Brazilian bonds are also easier, and Guatemala 4 per cent. fell on the news of the assassination of the President. Among "internationals" Spanish Fours gave way owing to the strained relations between Spain and the United States, and sales from Paris have also taken place. Greek bonds have shown great strength, the formal notification of assent to the scheme of arrangement with the bondholders being expected within the next few days from all the Powers. Egyptian issues have registered a considerable rise during the week, and Russian 4 per cent. and 3½ per cent. are higher on influential Paris buying. The rise in the latter case was due to rumours of a new Russian loan, or at any rate the conversion of existing loans, and the belief is also gaining ground that the proposed tax on Foreign Government Securities has been abandoned.

Among foreign railways, Buenos Ayres and Ensenada issues have risen sharply, but heavy sales of Central Argentine stock have depressed the price of that security. A good traffic return was responsible for a slight advance in Mexican issues and Interoceanic of Mexico debentures have been inquired for.

Highest and Lowest this Year.		Last Carrying over Price.	FOREIGN RAILWAYS.	Closing Price.	Rise or Fall.
20¾	20	20½	Argentine Gt. West. 5 p.c. Pref.	20¾	+ ¼
158¼	149	156½	B. Ay. Gt. Southern Ord..	156	−2
78½	75½	77	B. Ay. and Rosario Ord...	76½	− ½
12¼	11 1/16	11¼	B. Ay. Western Ord.........	11¾	− ¼
87¼	80½	85	Central Argentine Ord....	83	−2
92	89½	90½	Cordoba and Rosario 6 p.c. Deb.	91	—
95½	93¾	94½	Cord. Cent. 4 p.c. Deb. (Cent. Nth. Sec.)	94½	—
61¾	57	58½	Do. Income Deb. Stk. ...	57½	−1½
25⅝	18	23¾	Mexican Ord. Stk.	23¼	− ¼
83½	72	82	Do. 8 p.c. 1st Pref.	82¼	+ ½

In the Miscellaneous market, Allsopp Brewery Stock has been very much to the front. The price rose sharply when the interim dividend was announced at the rate of 7 per cent., but most of the rise has since been lost, and a fresh issue of capital is now talked of. Guinness rose 10 one day, only to fall as much the next, the market evidently being very limited, and North Worcestershire Brewery debentures have had a sharp relapse. There has been a shake out in Salt Union issues, the directors' announcement of a paltry 1¼ per cent. dividend on the preference shares, when at least the full dividend had been looked for, causing a good deal of surprise. Last year the ordinary received 2 per cent., so that things have pretty rapidly gone from bad to worse. General Hydraulic Power stock has moved up another 10 points, and a batch of satisfactory reports has helped to raise the prices of most of the leading trust companies. The scheme formulated by the directors of the Crystal Palace Company, has not been favourably received, and holders of the junior debentures have been throwing their stock on the market. Spiers & Pond shares show some recovery from last week's fall, and it is now announced that the company has succeeded in renewing their contract with the Chatham and Dover Railway, but only at an increased figure. The tale that they were going to enter the field against the companies now engaged in the light refreshment business, has been promptly denied by the directors. Hudson's Bay shares have had a set back, as there has been no confirmatory news regarding the reported gold discoveries in the company's territory. Electric lighting companies have again attracted buyers, the dividend of 10 per cent. announced by the City of London directors giving an additional fillip to this section of the market.

Mining and Finance Companies.

The daily report from the South African market has been little or nothing doing, and a dull tendency, and prices accordingly show only slightly irregular movements. The resignation of the chairman of the South African Gold Trust, when the shareholders declined to sanction the proposal for increasing the directors' fees, was followed by a drop in the price of the shares. As regards Western Australian ventures, rises or falls from day to day have generally been limited to about $\frac{1}{16}$ or $\frac{1}{8}$, and the net result is to leave prices in about the same position as at the end of last week. The "Bottomley" group has been much talked about, but apart from the engineering of a rise in Northern Territories, not much has happened. Copper shares have risen in sympathy with an advance in the price of the metal, and the statistics for the past fortnight showed that deliveries were again in excess of supplies. Indian shares have hardly moved.

Just at the last there was a partial recovery in United States Railroad shares on New York and provincial buying, but there is still an unbroken list of falls compared with last week. Home Railway stocks also closed slightly firmer, notably Lancashire and Yorkshire and Great Eastern, but Great Central issues left off weak. Among Foreign Government stocks a recovery is apparent in Spanish and Italian, but South American descriptions were again pressed for sale. Consols and Indian Government Securities eventually established a slight rise on the week, but a further set back in Bank of England stock has taken place.

THE BRITISH LINEN TRADE.

Belfast rejoices in the possession of an excellent institution whose object is the encouragement of flax cultivation in Ireland. Its name is the Flax Supply Association, and its members include practically all the important spinners and manufacturers in Ulster. The association has worked strenuously during more than a quarter of a century to fulfil the purpose of its being by the grant to farmers of high-class seed, by the dissemination of useful knowledge, by the offer of prizes, and by other similar works. In spite, however, of its best endeavours, the acreage under flax is gradually contracting. In 1880, the land under this crop in Ireland was 157,534 acres. In 1893, it was as low as 67,487 acres. When, in the following year, there was a sudden increase (due to a good return and high prices) to 101,081 acres, it was thought that matters had reached their worst, and were beginning to mend again. But in the following year the acreage fell to 95,203 acres; in 1896 it was only 72,253 acres; and last year only about 60,000 acres were in cultivation.

Flax is a notoriously unstable, as well as unpleasant crop, but its cultivation, taken one year with another, is highly profitable. The Irish article ranks next in quality after Belgian and Dutch, and one might suppose that it would be sure of its market and its full average price by virtue of production in the centre of the largest linen manufacturing district in the world. Such an assumption, it seems, would be erroneous. What with large imports of the cheap flax of Russia, and growing imports of the high grade flax of Belgium, the Irish fibre no longer commands the respectful attention of buyers. The average Ulster yield in 1896 was 24 stones per acre, which compares with nearly 33 stones in Austria-Hungary, 30 stones in Belgium, 43 stones in France, 37 stones in Germany, 32 stones in Holland, 22 stones in Italy, and about 17 stones in Russia. It is somewhat singular that in Leinster, Connaught and Munster, which now grow less than 500 acres among them, this crop does not make progress, for each of these provinces is good for a steady yield of from 30 to 38 stones.

The number of flax spindles in operation in the United Kingdom, including doubling spindles, is about 1,200,000, compared with 1,473,000 in 1875 and 1,588,000 in 1868. The decrease, it may be observed, has been most noticeable in England and Wales, where the number has fallen away from 440,000 to about 100,000; but Ireland also shows a decrease from 894,000 in 1868, to 869,000 in 1897. A diminution in the actual number of spindles does not, however, argue of itself a decline in productive capacity. A falling off in spindles may, on the contrary, go hand in hand with an enhanced output. The spindles in existence to-day are probably capable of an output as large as the total of 1868. The better part of our annual production is for export, and having regard to all the circumstances, it would not be unreasonable to look for a present foreign trade at least equal to, if not greater than, that of twenty or thirty years ago. Last year we shipped abroad 18,364,200 lbs. of linen yarn of the declared value of £976,658. For 1876, the quantity was 22,278,259 lbs., valued at £1,449,513; for 1866, 33,608,171 lbs., valued at £2,374,132; and for 1864, 40,177,150 lbs., valued at £2,991,969. But perhaps compensation for diminished shipments of linen yarn is to be found in increased shipments of linen cloth? We are the more entitled to ask this as—apart from their improved capacity—the number of power looms in work to-day is 31,484 compared with 24,300 in 1885, and 20,152 in 1875. Piece goods exports in 1865 amounted to 247,186,459 yards, of the value of £9,156,990; in 1875 to 204,573,172 yards, value £7,272,920; in 1885 to 149,468,600 yards value £4,961,093; in 1895, 203,587,600 yards value £5,351,025; in 1896, 174,208,000 yards value £5,030,966; and in 1897, 164,574,600 yards value £4,774,310. The values, it should be stated, include linen thread, which cannot be expressed in the same terms as piece goods. These figures show that while we have improved in regard to linen manufactures in recent years, we are still behind the averages of two or three decades ago; and it is apparent that our trade under this head offers no consolation for the falling off in yarns.

The most striking feature of our linen industry is the heavy volume of yarn imports. We have seen that the average annual shipment for the six years 1891–6 was 16,278,300 lbs. Our annual average import in the same time was as high as 20,106,510 lbs. Last year saw a decrease as compared with the two previous years, the figures being 15,907,161 lbs. for 1897, 20,069,122 lbs. for 1896, and 25,658,917 lbs. for 1895. There has, on this basis, been a very commendable decrease since 1895, when high-water mark was reached, while imports from other countries—Germany, France, and Holland—have diminished again, our receipts from Belgium have gone up steadily. In 1877 the figure stood at 4,942,785 lbs.; in 1886 it was 5,864,748 lbs.; in 1890, 12,485,017 lbs.; and in 1896, 16,517,027 lbs. For manufactured linens we do not trouble the foreigner much. The value of our imports of this commodity in 1896 was no more than £381,930 against £432,556 in 1890, and £308,022 in 1886, but such as the obligation is, we are indebted again in a large measure to Belgium, which sends us nearly one half of the whole, Germany being second with about one fourth. We are enabled, in fact, to supply practically all our home and foreign demand for piece goods by the aid of our own looms. But in the matter of yarns, it seems that we send abroad nearly all we make, and go to the Continent for what we need for our own consumption. The same anomaly may be observed by any one who chooses to take a glance at our woollen trade.

EAST AND WEST INDIA DOCKS.

The new scheme prepared under the Railway Companies Act, 1867, by the East and West India Dock Company has been confirmed in the Chancery Division before Mr. Justice Romer. Under the proposed scheme power is given to issue £750,000 Three per Cent. Prior Lien Debenture stock, of which £462,024 would be absorbed by being substituted for £94,700 existing Three and a Half per Cent. Debentures for £323,600 existing Three and a Half per Cent. First Mortgage certificates, leaving a balance of £287,976 available for further issue for the purposes of advances to the joint committee on account of new works. In the place of the present Four per Cent. Debenture stock, amounting to £2,297,980, £3 per Cent. Consolidated Debenture stock of a like amount, and £620,456 Four per Cent. Preference stock are to be issued. For the mortgages of 1885, £593,600 Consolidated Debenture stock, and for £293,896 Deferred Debenture Stock, £317,408 Four per Cent. Preference stock are to be provided.

Lord William Nevill pleaded guilty at the Central Criminal Court on Tuesday to a charge of unlawfully and fraudulently inducing Mr. Spender Clay to affix his name to certain promissory notes, to be dealt with as valuable securities. He was sentenced to five years' penal servitude.

The receipts on account of revenue from April 1, 1897, when there was a balance of £9,867,133, to February 12, 1898, were £88,825,114, against £86,973,541 in the corresponding period of the preceding financial year, which began with a balance of £8,975,201. The net expenditure was £86,315,451, against £85,638,806 to the same date in the previous year.

The Sugar Tax was discussed in the German Reichstag on Tuesday. It is noteworthy that every speaker expressed himself favourable to the abolition of the sugar bounties and the repeal of the consumption tax. Then why should Germany not act independently and at once rid herself of these stupid fiscal burdens?

Dividends Announced.

MISCELLANEOUS.

WEST AUSTRALIAN MARKET TRUST, LIMITED.—Interim dividend at the rate of 15 per cent. per annum for the six months ended January 30.

MERCHANTS' TRUST, LIMITED.—Dividend for the past half-year at the rate of 4 per cent. per annum on the preferred, and at the same rate on the ordinary stock, making 4 per cent. for the year ended January 31. £30,311 carried forward, as against £27,793 last year.

SPENCER, TURNER, & BOLDERO.—Dividend at the rate of 9 per cent. per annum, less tax, for the half-year ended January 15, making 8 per cent. for the year on the ordinary shares. Warrants will be posted on March 3.

BRUSH ELECTRICAL ENGINEERING.—Interim dividend at the rate of 6 per cent. on the preference shares for the half-year ended December 31 last, payable March 15.

MERCANTILE INVESTMENT AND GENERAL TRUST COMPANY.—Dividends at the rate of 5 per cent. per annum on the preferred stock, and at the rate of 3 per cent. per annum on the deferred, for the half-year ended January 31. £5,000 to be transferred to reserve fund, and a balance carried forward of about £8,800.

INDIA RUBBER, GUTTA PERCHA, AND TELEGRAPH WORKS.—Dividend recommended of 15s. per share, making 10 per cent. for the year, and leaving £13,173 to be carried forward.

SILVERTON TRAMWAY COMPANY.—2s. per share has been declared payable on March 1.

SOUTH STAFFORDSHIRE BLUE BRICK COMPANY.—Dividend at the rate of 10 per cent. per annum for the year ended December 31.

MORGAN & COMPANY.—Payment of 6 per cent. per annum for the year 1897. £3,000 carried forward.

BORDEAUX TRAMWAYS AND OMNIBUS COMPANY.—10s. per share, free of tax, on the ordinary shares, payable on March 10.

SALT UNION, LIMITED.—1¼ per cent. for the past year on the 7 per cent. preferred stock.

CAR TRUST INVESTMENT COMPANY, LIMITED.—Interim dividends at the rate of 5 per cent. per annum on the preference stock and 7 per cent. per annum on the ordinary shares.

W. B. FORDHAM & SONS, LIMITED.—Final dividend at the rate of 12½ per cent. per annum for the half-year ended December 31, making with the interim dividend 10 per cent. for the year.

CITY OF LONDON ELECTRIC LIGHTING COMPANY, LIMITED.—Payment of the following dividends:—On ordinary shares Nos. 40,001 to 80,000 £1 per share for the year, and on ordinary shares Nos. 80,001 to 90,000 10s. 7d. per share for the year, being a distribution at the rate of 10 per cent. for the year ended December 31.

MINES INVESTMENT CORPORATION, LIMITED.—Warrants for the dividend of 15 per cent. on the ordinary shares have been posted.

BROKEN HILL PROPRIETARY BLOCK 10 COMPANY, LIMITED.—Warrants for dividend No. 56 of 2s. per share have been posted.

ROBERT ROBERTS & COMPANY, LIMITED.—Six per cent. on the ordinary shares recommended.

BRILLIANT AND ST. GEORGE UNITED GOLD MINING COMPANY.—One shilling per share dividend payable on Tuesday, 22nd inst.

FIFE COAL.—Six per cent. for the half-year ended December 31, which, with the interim dividend of 3¾ per cent. paid for the first half-year, makes 10 per cent. per annum.

BARNET DISTRICT GAS AND WATER COMPANY.—Dividends at the rate of 9 per cent. per annum on the "A" and "C" stocks, 8 per cent. per annum on the "B" stock, and £6 6s. per cent. on the "D" capital gas and water stocks.

NEW PRIMROSE GOLD MINING COMPANY, LIMITED.—Warrants for dividend, No. 15, 6s. per share less tax, have been posted.

COUNTY OF LONDON AND BRUSH PROVINCIAL ELECTRIC LIGHTING.—For the six months ended December 31, a dividend is declared at the rate of 6 per cent. per annum on the preference shares, carrying forward £10,000 to next account.

ARGUS PRINTING COMPANY.—Dividend of 8 per cent. is declared for the year, carrying forward £1,529.

REVERSION PURCHASE COMPANY.—Dividend on the old shares at the rate of 5 per cent. per annum.

BREWERIES.

SAMUEL ALLSOPP & SONS, LIMITED.—Interim dividend for the past half-year at the rate of 7 per cent. per annum, as against 6 per cent. at the last half of 1896.

WASHINGTON COMPANY, LIMITED.—Interim dividends at the rate of 8 per cent. per annum on the preference shares, and 6 per cent. per annum on the ordinary shares for the half-year ended December 31. Payable March 1.

RAILWAYS.

COCKERMOUTH, KESWICK, AND PENRITH.—Dividend at the rate of 5 per cent. per annum for the half-year ended December 31.

CANADIAN PACIFIC.—2½ per cent. on the common stock and 2 per cent. on the preferred for the second half of 1897.

By 176 votes to 55 the Italian Chamber of Deputies has adopted the Bill guaranteeing the circulation of the banks of issue.

China has paid up promptly the pecuniary claim made by France for the kidnapped Tonquinois. No doubt France expected "better things."

There is a possible rival to Klondike; and in Nova Scotia too! Gold-mining has been carried on there with success for years; but a discovery just made near Whycocomagh promises more remarkable results than any yet seen in the colony.

Prices of Mine and Mining Finance Companies' Shares.

Shares £1 each, except where otherwise stated.

AUSTRALIAN.

Making-Up Price, Feb. 7.	Name.	Closing Price.	Rise or Fall.	Making-Up Price, Feb. 7.	Name	Closing Price.	Rise or Fall.
1 3/8	Aladdin	1 5/16		1 1/8	Hampton Plains	1	− 1/16
4 1/2	Associated	4 1/2	− 1/16	7 3/8	Hannan' Brownhill	7 5/16	− 1/8
1	Do. Southern	1	− 3/16	1 1/16	Hannan's Oroya	15/16	− 1/8
16/	Brilliant, £2	14/	− 1/6	15/9	Do. Proprietary	15/	− 6d.
2 1/2	Do. St. George's	2 1/2		1	Do. Star	13/16	− 1/8
11/6	British Broken Hill	12/		—	Ivanhoe, New	6 1/4	
2	Broken Hill Proprietary	2 1/4	+ 1/16	15/16	Kalgurli Mt. & Iron King, 12/	15/16	
—	Do. Junction	1 1/8		6 1/16	Kalgurli	5 3/4	− 1/4
—	Do. Block 10	3 1/2		3 1/16	Lady Shenton	2 15/16	− 1/16
1 1/16	Brownhill Extended	1 1/4	− 1/8	10 1/4	Lake View Cons.	10 3/16	− 1/16
1 13/16	Burbank's Birthday	1 5/8		1 1/16	Do. Extended	1 1/16	
1 1/16	Central Boulder	1 1/4	− 3/8	1 1/16	Do. South	1 1/16	− 1/8
5/8	Chaffers, 4/	6/6	− /9	2 1/16	London & Globe Finance	2	
1	Colonial Finance, 15/	1/2 pm		1	London & W. A. Exploration	15/16	− 1/8
6/	Crœsus S. United	3/4	+ 1/16	3/4	Do. Investment	3/4	
16/6	Day Dawn Block	16/3	− /3	1/16	Mainland Consols	3/8	− 1/8
1 1/16	E. Murchison	1 1/16		15/16	North Boulder, 10/	3/8	− 1/8
5/8	Gold Estates	11/16		1 3/8	North Kalgurli	2	− 1/16
6/6	Golden Arrow 19/	5/	− 1/	1 1/4	Northern Territories	3 1/2	+ 11/16
8 3/4	Golden Horseshoe	8 1/2	− 1/8	—	Peak Hill	3 1/16	+ 1/16
1 1/2	Golden Link	1 1/16	− 1/8	2 3/4	South Kalgurli	2 1/2	− 1/4
—	Great Boulder, 2/	22/6	− 1/	2 1/2	W. A. Goldfields	2 1/4	− 1/8
1 3/8	Do. Main Reef, 10/	1 1/2	− 1/16	2 1/16	W. A. Joint Stock	2 1/16	+ 1/16
4 1/2	Do. Perseverance	3 3/4	− 1/8	1 1/16	W. A. Market Trust	1 1/16	
1	Do. South	1		1 1/4	W. A. Loan & General Fin.	1 1/4	− 1/16
2	Hainault	1 15/16	− 1/16	1/4	White Feather	3/8	+ 1/8

SOUTH AFRICAN

Making-Up Price, Feb. 7.	Name.	Closing Price.	Rise or Fall.	Making-Up Price, Feb. 7.	Name	Closing Price.	Rise or Fall.
5 13/16	Angelo	5 13/16		3/	Lisbon-Berlyn	2/9	− 3d
1 1/16	Aurora West	1 3/16	+ 1/16	2 1/16	May Consolidated	2 1/2	
1 3/16	Bantjes	1 1/16	− 1/8	4 1/4	Meyer and Charlton	4 1/16	− 1/8
11/6	Barrett, 10/	10/6		3 3/4	Modderfontein	3 3/4	+ 1/16
3 13/16	Bonanza	3 3/4	− 1/16	15/16	New Bultfontein	15/16	
15/16	Buffelsdoorn	15/16	− 1/16	4 1/4	New Primrose	4	− 1/8
1 1/16	Champ d'Or	1 1/4	− 1/8	1 13/16	Nigel	1 13/16	
5 1/16	City and Suburban, £4	5 1/8	− 1/16	—	Nigel Deep	1 1/4	
3 1/16	Comet (New)	3 1/16	− 1/16	1	North Randfontein	1	
5 1/4	Con. Deep Level	5 1/2	− 1/4	6 3/4	Nourse Deep	6 3/4	− 1/8
13 1/2	Crown Deep	13 1/4	− 1/4	1 1/16	Porges-Randfontein	1 1/16	− 1/8
12	Crown Reef	12 1/2	+ 1/2	33 1/2	Rand Mines	32 1/16	− 1 1/16
30 1/4	De Beers, £5	30 1/4	+ 1/4	2	Randfontein	1 13/16	− 1/16
4 1/16	Driefontein	3 1/4	− 1/16	2 3/8	Rietfontein	2 3/8	− 1/8
5 13/16	Durban Roodepoort	6	+ 1/16	11 1/4	Robinson Deep	10 1/4	− 1/8
4 1/16	Do. Deep	4 1/2	− 3/16	8 1/4	Do. Gold, £5	8 1/4	− 1/4
5 13/16	East Rand	4 11/16	− 1/4	1 1/16	Do. Randfontein	1 13/16	+ 1/16
26 1/2	Ferreira	25 1/2	− 1/2	1 1/4	Roodepoort Central Deep	1 1/4	− 1/16
6 1/2	Geldenhuis Deep	6 1/2	− 1/8	7 1/4	Rose Deep	6 1/4	− 1/16
4 11/16	Do. Estate	4 1/2	− 3/16	3 1/16	Salisbury	3 1/4	− 1/16
1 1/2	George Goch	1 1/2	− 1/8	2 1/4	Sheba	2 1/4	− 1/8
3	Ginsberg	2 3/8		3 3/16	Simmer and Jack, £5	3 1/16	− 1/8
2 1/4	Glencairn	2 3/16	− 1/16	4 1/4	Transvaal Gold	3 3/4	− 1/16
2 3/8	Glen Deep	2 1/4	− 1/8	3 3/4	Treasury	3 1/2	− 1/8
10 3/16	Goldfields Deep	9 1/2	− 1/4	4 3/16	United Roodepoort	4 1/2	− 1/8
8 1/2	Griqualand West	8 1/2		1 13/16	Van Ryn	1 13/16	+ 1/8
9 1/4	Henry Nourse	8 15/16	− 1/16	6 3/16	Village Main Reef	5 1/2	− 1/4
7 3/4	Heriot	7 1/16	− 1/16	1 13/16	Vogelstruis	1 1/2	− 1/8
8 1/4	Jagersfontein	8 1/4		1	Do. Deep	11/16	− 1/16
8 1/4	Jubilee	8 1/8	− 1/8	8 3/4	Wemmer	8 1/2	
5 3/8	Jumpers	5 1/16	− 1/16	1/4	West Rand	1/4	
6	Jumpers Deep	5 3/4	− 1/4	6 1/2	Wolhuter, £4	6 1/4	− 1/8
2 13/16	Kleinfontein	2 11/16	− 1/8	2 3/8	Worcester	2 1/4	− 1/8
3 13/16	Knight's	3 3/4	− 1/8				
2 3/16	Lancaster	2 1/16	− 3/16				
3 3/4	Langlaagte Estate	3 3/8	− 1/8				
1 1/2	Langlaagte Block "B"	1 1/2	− 1/8				

LAND EXPLORATION AND RHODESIAN.

Making-Up Price, Feb. 7.	Name.	Closing Price.	Rise or Fall.	Making-Up Price, Feb. 7.	Name	Closing Price.	Rise or Fall.
3 1/16	Anglo-French Ex.	2 7/8	− 1/8	6 3/8	Matabele Gold Reefs	6 1/4	− 1/16
2 1/16	Barnato Consolidated	2 1/2	− 1/8	2 1/4	Mozambique	2 1/16	− 1/16
3/4	Bechuanaland Ex.	13/16	− 1/16	1 1/2	New African	1 1/16	− 1/16
3 3/16	Chartered B.S.A.	3	− 1/8	3/4	Oceana Consolidated	15/16	− 1/16
1 1/16	Cassel Coal	15/16	− 1/8	1 1/4	Rhodesia, Ltd.	1 1/16	
3/4	Colenbrander	5/8	− 1/8	5 1/4	Do. Exploration	5 1/4	− 1/8
4 13/16	Cons. Goldfields	4 5/8	− 3/16	1 13/16	Do. Goldfields	1 1/16	− 1/16
1 1/16	Do. Pref.	1/0	+ /6	3 1/2	Robinson Bank	3 1/4	− 1/8
1 1/4	Exploration	1 1/4		5	S. A. Gold Trust	4 3/4	− 1/8
2 1/2	Geelong	2 1/2		1 1/4	Tati Concessions	2 1/16	+ 1/16
1 1/4	Henderson's Est.	1		15/16	Transvaal Development	3/4	− 1/16
1 13/16	Johannesburg Con. In.	1 13/16	− 1/8	15/16	United Rhodesia	15/16	
1 1/2	Do. Water	1 1/16	− 1/8	1 1/4	Willoughby	1 1/16	− 1/16
2 1/2	Mashonaland Agency	2		1 1/8	Zambesia Explor.	1	− 1/8
15/16	Do. Central	15/16	− 1/8				

MISCELLANEOUS.

Making-Up Price, Feb. 7.	Name.	Closing Price.	Rise or Fall.	Making-Up Price, Feb. 7.	Name	Closing Price.	Rise or Fall.
1 1/4	Alamillos, £2	1 1/4	− 1/8	15/	Mysore Goldfields	14/6	
5 1/4	Anaconda, $25	5 1/16	+ 1/16	11/9	Do. Reefs, 17/	10/9	+ /9
10/	Balaghât, 18/	10/6	+ /6	15/	Do. West	15/6	+ /6
4 13/16	Cape Copper, £2	4 3/4		14/	Do. Wynaad	13/6	
4 13/16	Champion Reef, 10s.	4 11/16	− 1/16	2 3/16	Namaqua, £2	2 3/16	
2 1/16	Copiapo, £2	2 1/16	+ 1/16	3 13/16	Nundydroog	3 13/16	
3 3/4	Coromandel	3 1/16	− 1/16	2 3/4	Ooregum	2 11/16	
2 1/2	Frontino & Bolivia	2 1/16	− 1/16	3 1/2	Do. Pref.	3 1/2	− 1/8
1 1/16	Hall Mines	1 1/16		27 1/2	Rio Tinto Def., £5	28 13/16	+ 1/8
2 13/16	Libiola, £5	2 13/16	+ 1/16	6 1/2	Do. Pref. £5	6 1/2	
7 3/4	Linares, £3	8	− 1/4	18/6	St. John del Rey	18/9	+ /3
3 1/2	Mason & Barry, £3	3 3/4	+ 1/8	12/	Taitipu	13/16	− 1/8
5 1/2	Mountain Copper, £5	5 3/4	+ 1/4	7 1/2	Tharsis, £2	7 3/4	+ 1/16
14 3/4	Mount Lyell, £3	11 1/2	− 1/4	2 3/4	Tolima "A," £5	3	
3 13/16	Mount Lyell, North	3 1/2		4 1/16	Waihi	4 3/4	+ 1/16
1/2	Mount Lyell, South	10/	+ /6	1 1/4	Waitekauri	1 13/16	+ 1/16
4 1/2	Mount Morgan, 17s. 6d.	4 1/2	− 1/16	1 1/2	Woodstock (N.Z.)	1 1/4	− 1/16
5 1/16	Mysore, 10s.	[illegible]	[illegible]				

AFRICAN MINING RETURNS.

Dividends Declared in 1896	1897	1898	Capital Issued.	Nominal Amount of Share.	Name of Company.	Monthly Crushings. November. Tons.	November. Oz.	November. Dwt. per ton.	December. Tons.	December. Oz.	December. Dwt. per ton.	January. Tons.	January. Oz.	January. Dwt. per ton.	Totals. Months.	Totals. Ozs.	Profits Declared. Nov.	Dec.	Jan.	Totals. Months.	Totals. —	Stamps now Working.
p.c.	p.c.	p.c.	£	£													£	£	£		£	
—	—	25	225,000	1	Angelo	12,062	5,809	9.6	12,340	5,844	9.4	12,657	5,863	9.3	10	52,525	13,140	12,591	12,636	10	113,141	60
—	—	—	130,000	1	Balmoral	12,550	2,719	4.3	7,340	1,596	4.3	—	2,318	—	6	10,964	2,811	—	1,456	—	—	60
—	75	—	200,000	1	Bonanza	10,551	6,980	13.2	12,265	7,886	12.8	11,627	8,036	13.8	12	93,148	15,510	18,272	18,430	12	215,816	40
—	—	—	550,000	1	Buffelsdoorn ..	—	3,598	—	31,635	3,730	2.3	—	3,607	—	—	—	—	—	—	—	—	110
—	—	--	133,000	1	Champ d'Or ..	8,589	3,888	9.0	7,315	3,368	9.2	8,989	3,193	7.0	—	—	—	—	—	—	—	50
5	15	—	1,360,000	4	City and Suburban	31,759	11,804	7.4	33,409	11,792	7.0	—	11,032	—	12	133,672	22,365	21,658	18,553	12	226,126	160
—	—	—	224,635	1	Comet	9,446	3,243	6.8	9,427	3,229	6.8	9,707	3,231	6.6	12	37,703	6,510	5,838	4,814	12	50,177	40
—	—	—	300,000	1	Crown Deep ..	29,662	10,997	7.4	38,030	14,034	7.4	42,262	13,429	6.3	5	48,002	18,220	21,000	17,000	5	70,906	180
110	170	—	120,000	1	Crown Reef.. ..	28,114	13,203	9.4	26,730	12,298	9.2	—	12,110	—	12	148,894	25,094	22,764	22,379	12	255,954	120
55	80	—	125,000	1	Durban Roodepoort	17,380	6,152	7.1	17,700	6,080	6.9	16,635	6,105	7.2	12	71,176	—	—	—	—	—	80
275	300	—	90,000	1	Ferreira	17,593	12,996	14.7	18,453	13,196	14.3	—	12,213	—	12	154,457	31,148	30,870	27,775	12	353,461	80
12½	45	—	200,000	1	Geldenhuis Estate..	16,440	9,471	11.5	29,450	9,461	6.4	—	10,088	—	9	82,290	16,586	15,900	17,475	8	119,069	120
—	30	—	280,000	1	Geldenhuis Deep ..	29,840	9,462	6.3	30,724	10,008	6.5	35,890	11,493	6.3	12	109,023	11,700	14,980	16,500	12	131,059	160
—	10	—	150,000	1	Gelden. Main Reef	5,408	1,509	5.6	5,766	1,055	3.6	5,734	1,310	4.6	12	19,453	1,436	3	566	12	21,674	30
—	—	—	325,000	1	George Goch ..	21,116	3,093	2.9	17,731	3,179	3.6	—	3,068	—	12	37,449	—	—	—	—	—	120
—	25	—	160,000	1	Ginsberg	8,948	2,862	6.4	8,789	2,476	5.6	—	2,475	—	12	36,879	6,500	3,705	4,335	12	73,148	40
—	—	—	300,000	1	Glencairn	27,190	6,543	4.8	27,980	6,699	4.8	—	6,749	—	6	32,453	10,097	10,645	11,107	5	45,989	110
30	125	—	125,000	1	Henry Nourse ..	14,842	7,678	10.2	15,150	7,334	9.7	15,200	7,608	10.0	12	91,373	16,475	16,190	14,571	12	176,731	60
85	100	—	111,864	1	Heriot	15,005	5,995	7.9	15,950	6,010	7.5	—	5,832	—	12	72,909	12,575	10,467	10,030	12	129,807	70
350	500	—	21,000	1	Johan. Pioneer ..	5,541	3,737	13.5	5,278	4,337	16.4	—	3,723	—	12	43,618	—	—	—	9	79,101	30
60	90	—	50,000	1	Jubilee	a11,828	3,638	6.1	8,745	3,073	7.0	—	3,090	—	12	30,824	—	—	—	9	38,329	50
30	60	—	100,000	1	Jumpers	11,500	5,872	10.2	12,300	5,646	9.2	—	5,407	—	12	61,789	7,370	7,150	6,160	12	64,561	100
—	—	—	231,250	1	Kleinfontein ..	19,903	5,172	5.2	18,543	5,133	5.5	18,212	5,163	5.6	9	43,578	5,125	5,676	5,441	9	42,493	95
—	—	—	311,980	1	Knight's	21,970	4,724	4.3	23,210	4,983	4.3	24,290	5,215	4.3	12	59,106	—	—	—	8	28,420	120
30	30	—	470,000	1	Langlaagte Estate..	40,083	10,126	5.0	41,278	9,029	4.3	37,695	8,692	5.1	12	128,849	—	—	—	—	—	175
—	—	—	550,000	1	Lang. Block B. ..	17,945	4,355	4.8	19,118	4,484	4.7	19,129	4,709	4.9	12	44,919	—	—	—	—	—	75
—	—	—	250,000	1	Langlaagte Star ..	—	3,926	—	9,623	4,090	8.3	9,673	4,031	8.3	—	—	—	—	—	—	—	30
20	—	—	275,000	1	May Consolidated	21,987	5,401	5.0	22,354	6,086	5.4	22,399	6,509	5.8	12	59,340	4,110	6,002	—	12	25,931	100
20	50	—	85,000	1	Meyer and Charlton	14,110	3,696	5.2	15,264	3,871	5.7	—	3,910	—	12	45,074	5,175	5,345	5,348	12	58,386	80
—	—	—	949,620	4	Modderfontein ..	—	1,801	—	—	—	—	—	—	—	—	—	—	—	—	—	—	60
—	—	—	200,000	1	Nigel	6,090	2,803	8.0	6,570	2,803	8.5	—	2,831	—	—	—	—	—	—	—	—	25
—	—	—	300,000	1	Nth. Randfontein..	9,854	2,574	5.2	10,007	2,354	4.7	9,801	1,944	3.9	11	23,407	—	—	—	—	—	40
—	—	—	400,000	1	Paarl Central ..	11,451	3,312	5.8	11,343	3,285	5.8	9,604	2,535	5.3	12	35,691	—	—	—	—	—	60
—	10	—	487,500	1	Porges Randfontein	13,635	4,526	6.6	13,318	4,502	6.7	11,692	3,981	6.8	12	48,909	—	—	—	—	—	60
—	50	—	300,000	1	Primrose	38,917	10,207	5.2	37,581	9,704	5.1	—	9,137	—	12	116,280	15,417	14,161	12,463	12	155,255	160
—	10	—	165,000	1	Princess Estate ..	9,092	3,028	6.6	8,611	2,979	6.8	—	2,837	—	12	34,701	2,938	2,614	2,250	12	33,111	40
—	—	—	270,000	1	Rietfontein	b—	—	—	—	—	—	—	—	—	—	—	—	—	—	—	—	50
—	—	—	300,000	1	Rietfontein "A" ..	13,251	5,445	8.2	13,202	5,235	7.9	—	5,545	—	5	26,413	11,940	11,767	11,145	5	56,565	50
12	15	—	2,750,000	5	Robinson	31,186	18,728	12.0	31,792	16,847	10.6	—	c15,574	—	12	229,653	37,000	42,000	36,500	12	431,591	120
—	—	—	600,000	1	Robinson R'dfontein	—	2,769	—	9,184	3,373	7.3	9,700	3,341	6.9	—	—	—	—	—	—	—	35
—	—	—	175,000	1	Roodepoort Gold ..	5,827	1,365	4.7	5,405	1,182	4.4	—	1,266	—	11	14,618	1,018	—	—	—	—	40
25	40	—	150,000	1	Roodepoort United	11,657	4,378	7.5	12,321	4,414	7.1	—	4,423	—	12	49,807	7,375	7,455	7,240	12	74,121	70
—	—	—	400,000	1	Rose Deep	26,795	9,520	7.1	26,345	9,491	7.2	27,058	9,666	7.1	—	—	15,658	16,900	15,900	—	—	100
—	—	—	100,000	1	Salisbury	11,220	2,950	5.2	8,366	2,150	5.1	—	2,400	—	12	23,483	—	—	—	—	—	50
20	20	—	1,075,000	1	Sheba	8,946	10,032	22.4	9,500	9,005	18.9	11,760	6,400	10.9	12	107,129	—	—	—	—	—	120
—	—	—	4,700,000	5	Simmer and Jack ..	17,960	7,090	7.9	35,080	8,120	4.6	26,010	10,163	7.8	12	77,260	—	—	—	10	53,716	100
—	—	—	235,000	1	Spes Bona	9,298	1,931	4.2	9,259	2,001	4.5	—	2,037	—	11	23,771	1,303	771	—	—	—	40
—	15	—	35,000	1	Stanhope	4,360	1,150	5.3	4,565	1,069	4.7	—	1,058	—	12	11,808	—	—	—	—	—	20
—	—	—	604,225	1	Trans. G. M. Est...	14,569	5,748	7.9	14,322	4,581	6.4	14,032	6,600	9.4	—	—	18,072	12,305	—	—	—	75
—	—	—	540,000	4	Treasury	9,664	3,575	7.4	11,664	3,770	6.5	—	3,585	—	12	39,735	5,196	6,124	5,876	12	52,538	40
—	—	—	177,000	1	Van Ryn	18,622	3,710	4.0	19,290	4,002	4.1	19,942	4,189	4.2	12	46,729	—	—	—	—	—	80
—	—	—	170,000	1	Van Ryn West ..	13,299	2,958	4.4	14,260	3,938	5.5	15,430	4,463	5.8	9	22,833	—	—	9,018	—	—	80
75	100	—	80,000	1	Wemmer	10,650	6,083	11.4	11,161	5,987	10.7	10,998	6,072	11.0	12	67,748	12,435	12,215	13,190	12	124,062	50
—	—	—	400,000	1	West Rand	7,505	1,752	4.6	6,853	1,732	5.0	6,879	1,889	5.5	9	14,441	—	—	—	—	—	30
—	10	—	860,000	4	Wolhuter	22,873	7,540	6.6	22,718	7,670	6.7	—	7,559	—	12	89,771	10,817	10,681	10,823	12	118,721	100
55	30	15	95,722	1	Worcester	—	2,772	—	5,140	2,615	7.8	—	2,739	—	12	25,727	—	—	—	—	—	40
—	—	—	90,000	1	York	—	—	—	6,545	1,849	5.6	5,163	2,209	8.9	—	—	—	—	—	—	—	40

a For two months. *b* Mill restarted January 7. *c* Exclusive of yield from Concentrates bought—3,835 oz. in December and 1,396 oz. in January.

SOUTH AFRICAN CRUSHINGS.

For the first time the output for January embraces the whole of the South African Republic, and amounts to 336,577 oz. The Rand output itself is 313,826 oz., or 3,114 oz. more than the December yield, which, however, is not particularly satisfactory, and for this reason. After a rest of nearly three years the Village Main Reef Company has resumed working, and a crushing of 5,370 tons gave a return of 3,098 oz. of gold. Cyanide work also proceeded, but the result has not been yet disclosed. Another addition to the companies producing is the Consolidated Main Reef, which obtained 1,288 oz. Now, if these two yields are deducted from the total output there is an actual decrease compared with the December crushings. In a few instances, too, more stamps were in use, and in such cases an increased yield was obtained, especially in the case of the Simmer and Jack. The Lancaster again did well, and fair increases were shown by the Geldenhuis Deep and Knight's Companies, but the Crown Deep and Ferreira yields fell off distinctly, and the heavy reduction in the Sheba output is explained by a footnote that low. grade ore was crushed. In the return of the Transvaal Gold Mining Estates Company, the yield from the central cyanide works was for December as well as for January. Complaint of shortage of native labour is again made by some of the companies.

Gold found on the United States side of the Yukon territory! Those preparing for the rush to Klondike had better slacken their pace and consider whether it may not be wiser to cross the boundary. A certain Mr. Fritz Behnson announced to his brother that in one day in the rock crevices he picked up $50,000 worth in coarse gold. The brother is invited to go thither quickly, and with unspeakable generosity takes time before starting to tell the world, through the newspapers, of the great find!

The Colonial Office report for 1896-97 will rather surprise those who have heard of Basutoland only in connection with tribal disputes and rinderpest. For the twelve months ending March 31 last year dutiable goods were imported to the value of £135,560, against £104,858 in the previous year, an increase of £30,702. The figures of exports are only given to December 31, 1896, and for the twelve months ending then amounted to £160,277, against £139,496 in the previous year. But in these returns the period of the rinderpest devastation is not included, and so we cannot realise yet the economic results of the loss sustained. But the High Commissioner, considering the disturbing effect of the cattle plague on the native mind, thinks Sir Godfrey Lagden and his assistants may be congratulated on having got through the trying time without more serious trouble than they have had.

The Companies Bill, an old visitor to the House of Lords, was read a second time by that august assembly on Monday night, and then referred to a Select Committee. Mr. Faithfull Begg is now engaged in drafting a Bill on this subject, not caring, apparently, to trust in the House of Lords and its Select Committee.

LOANS TO LOCAL BODIES.

As, from a question put by Mr. Arthur O'Connor in the House of Commons on Monday, there seems to be some uncertainty as to the rates for local loans, it may be as well to give the information the Secretary to the Treasury conveyed to the House in his reply. Mr. Hanbury stated that loans in respect of allotments, burial grounds, lunatic asylums, and small holdings were advanced on the security of local rates, and the rates of interest were accordingly those prescribed by the Treasury minute under the Public Works Loan Act of last year—namely, where the period of repayment does not exceed thirty years, 2¾ per cent.; where the period exceeds thirty but does not exceed forty years, 3 per cent; where the period exceeds forty but does not exceed fifty years, 3¼ per cent. The advances by the Public Works Loan Commissioners at 2¾ per cent. interest from the passing of the Public Works Loan Act of last year, up to the 31st ult.. amounted in England and Wales to £505,328, and in Scotland to £17,830, a total of £523,158.

The "Farmer Party" in Natal have been snubbed by the Upper House of the legislature. They coerced the Government into presenting a Bill imposing duties on imported frozen meat. The Lower House passed the measure, the Upper Chamber threw it out.

MAIL SUBSIDIES IN GERMANY.

Germany is well satisfied with the results of her mail subsidies. In the discussion of the Subsidy Bill in the Reichstag on Tuesday, Herr von Podbielski, Secretary of State in the Department of Railways, Posts, and Telegraphs, pointed out that Germany had already advanced from the fourth to the second place in the carrying trade of the world. It would be rather unfortunate for the Government, however, if they accept it as proved that this advance is mainly owing to subventions. It was natural that the significance of the occupation of Kiao-Chau should be dwelt upon, as well as the prominent position held by Germany in the Postal Union, for the maintenance of which, it was urged, the present mail connections were inadequate. According to Herr Freze, the competition of the Siberian Railway would affect Western Europe but little so long as the mail steamers offered a sufficiently fast and frequent service.

Shanghai, it seems, is feeling considerable alarm at the breaking off of the loan negotiations at Pekin. In Shanghai they would give China perfect assurance of protection if she would place herself unreservedly in Great Britain's hands.

The West Australian Government Geologist has been visiting the goldfields there, and has returned to Perth enthusiastic. He reports that the possibilities of deep alluvial mining are very great, and that there is abundance of promisingly rich unoccupied ground outside leases available for alluvial workers.

ENGLISH RAILWAYS.

Div. for half years.				Last Balance forward.	Amt. to pay 1 p.c. on Ord. for ½ yr.	NAME.	Date.	Gross Traffic for week			Gross Traffic for half-year to date.				Mileage.	Inc. on 1897.	Working	Prior Charges last ½ year.	Prop. add Cap. Exp. this ½ year.
1896	1896	1897	1897					Amt.	Inc. or dec. on 1897.	Inc. or dec. on 1896.	No. of weeks	Amt.	Inc. or dec. on 1897.	Inc. or dec. on 1896.					
				£	£												%	£	£
10	10	10		6,805	4,906	Barry	Feb 12	8,926	+794	+1,099	7	61,060	+2,389	+7,148	31	—	47·36	66,665	316,008
nil	nil	nil	nil	—	—	Brecon and Merthyr	Feb 13	1,474	+7	−77	7	10,926	+238	+125	61	—	—	—	—
nil	nil	nil	nil	4,020	4,749	Cambrian	Feb 13	3,878	+23	+425	*	25,201	+218	—	250	—	61·16	63,472	42,000
3½	1¾	2	1¾	1,510	3,150	City and South London	Feb 13	1,058	−4	+109	7	7,514	−159	+568	3½	—	56·67	5,552	124,000
1	2	1½	2	7,893	13,210	Furness	Feb 13	8,995	+513	+1,210	*	52,826	+1,420	+10,778	139	—	49·88	97,423	20,910
2	1½	½	1	2,207	27,470	Great Central (late M., S., & L.)	Feb 13	41,549	+740	+2,275	6	249,368	+5,245	+15,654	352½	—	57·17	627,386	1,200,000
1½	4¾	2	5	51,283	62,865	Great Eastern	Feb 13	77,914	+6,411	+8,127	6	456,146	+6,939	+42,938	1,156	7	55·35	860,138	250,000
3	5¼	3	5	15,094	102,496	Great Northern	Feb 13	94,471	+3,109	+8,962	7	638,484	+19,536	+46,844	1,071	8	61·36	641,485	750,000
4¾	7½	4¾	7½	31,350	121,981	Great Western	Feb 13	165450	+530	+7,350	6	978,940	+33,830	+22,850	2,582	21	51·44	1,486,272	800,000
nil	2	nil	1¾	8,951	16,487	Hull and Barnsley	Feb 13	6,696	−332	+693	6	38,531	−1,644	+3,813	73	—	58·21	70,090	52,920
5	5¾	5	5½	21,495	83,704	Lancashire and Yorkshire	Feb 13	88,541	+3,105	+2,858	6	528,061	+20,810	+36,103	555½	25	56·70	674,745	451,976
4¾	8	4¾	8½	26,243	43,049	London, Brighton, & S. Coast	Feb 12	42,572	+1,909	+1,178	7	320,647	+22,548	+19,804	476½	—	50·20	407,042	240,735
nil	nil	nil	nil	72,294	56,296	London, Chatham, & Dover	Feb 13	25,082	+670	+1,295	6	154,951	+7,674	+11,328	185½	—	50·65	367,873	nil
6½	8	6½	7½	82,535	204,068	London and North Western	Feb 13	220290	+4,785	+12,567	6	1,318,853	+38,043	+79,987	1,911½	—	56·92	1,404,534	600,000
5	8½	8¼	8½	23,038	59,367	London and South Western	Feb 13	64,283	+2,176	+3,310	6	382,292	+22,122	+29,970	941	6½	51·75	513,740	389,000
2¾	6	2¾	6½	14,592	6,691	London, Tilbury, & Southend	Feb 13	4,650	+70	+936	7	32,852	+2,669	+6,771	81	—	52·57	39,390	15,000
3½	3¾	3½	3¾	17,133	26,409	Metropolitan	Feb 13	15,871	+303	+1,401	*	101,611	+2,373	—	64	12	43·63	148,047	254,000
nil	nil	nil	nil	4,006	11,250	Metropolitan District	Feb 13	8,422	+224	+567	6	52,970	+1,978	+1,935	13	—	48·70	119,663	38,450
5	7	5½	6½	38,143	174,582	Midland	Feb 13	185168	+11,204	+16,398	7	1,230,956	+6,685	+75,583	1,354¾	15½	57·59	1,216,582	650,000
5½	7½	5¾	7	22,374	138,189	North Eastern	Feb 12	134091	−2,513	+16,764	6	817,305	+23,455	+43,675	1,597¾	—	58·82	795,077	436,004
7½	7½	7½	7½	7,061	10,102	North London	Feb 13			Not recd			not	recvd.	12	—	50·90	49,973	7,600
4	5	4	4½	4,745	16,150	North Staffordshire	Feb 13	15,764	+1,139	−1,837	7	109,564	+8,205	+7,298	312	—	55·27	118,142	19,605
10	10	11		1,642	3,004	Rhymney	Feb 12	4,803	−206	+466	7	34,895	+983	+3,722	71	—	49·68	29,049	16,700
3	6⅝	3½	6⅝	4,054	50,215	South Eastern	Feb 12	38,011	+1,639	+3,336	*	244,021	+16,338	—	448	—	51·88	380,763	250,000
3½	3½	3½	3½	2,315	25,961	Taff Vale	Feb 12	15,793	+1,660	+1,022	7	106,625	−1,122	+3,216	121	—	54·90	94,800	92,000

* From January 1.

SCOTCH RAILWAYS.

5	5	5½	—	15,330	77,570	Caledonian	Feb 13	66,868	− 1,867	+ 5,724	2	132,474	+ 2,329	+ 2,442	851½	5	50·50	566,914	375,966
5	5½	5	—	5,886	24,639	Glasgow and South-Western	„ 12	26,269	+ 857	+ 2,444	2	51,600	+ 1,506	+ 5,070	393½	—	55·12	221,120	180,536
3½	3½	3½	—	1,291	4,600	Great North of Scotland	„ 12	7,304	+ 55	+ 578	2	14,928	+ 1,382	+ 1,322	331	15½	52·03	92,178	60,000
3	nil	2	—	10,477	12,820	Highland	„ 13	8,088	+ 716	− 299	24	219,412	+ 9,814	+ 13,008	479¾	27¾	58·63	78,976	,000
1	1½	1	—	3,763	45,819	North British	„ 13	65,125	+ 1,544	+ 1,951	2	129,603	+ 3,987	+ 354	1,230	23	44·65	821,766	426,009

IRISH RAILWAYS.

6½	6½	6½	—	5,466	1,790	Belfast and County Down	Feb. 11	1,920	+ 56	+ 154	*	11,893	+ 433	—	76½	—	55·58	17,690	10,000
5½	6½	5½	—	—	4,284	Belfast and Northern Counties	„ 11	4,773	+ 129	+ 670	*	28,564	+ 893	—	249	—	—	—	—
2	3	2	—	1,418	1,200	Cork, Bandon, and S. Coast	„ 12	1,162	+ 23	− 51	*	6,636	− 732	—	103	—	54·82	14,436	5,450
6½	6¾	6½	—	21,537	17,709	Great Northern	„ 11	13,275	+ 444	+ 1,004	6	80,182	+ 4,388	+ 5,002	528	36	54·03	87,068	16,000
5½	5½	5½	5½	30,339	24,855	Great Southern and Western	„ 11	—	—	—	not	received	—	—	603	13	51·45	72,802	46,582
4	4	4	4½	11,372	11,850	Midland Great Western	„ 11	8,853	+ 1,027	+ 849	6	53,008	+ 4,020	+ 3,209	538	—	50·31	83,129	1,800
nil	nil	nil	nil	229	2,822	Waterford and Central	„ 11	849	+ 77	—	*	5,271	+ 844	—	59½	—	53·24	6,858	1,500
nil	nil	nil	nil	1,936	2,987	Waterford, Limerick & W.	„ 11	4,030	+ 327	+ 541	*	42,579	+ 2,580	—	350½	—	57·83	42,617	7,075

* From January 1.

FOREIGN RAILWAYS.

Mileage. Total.	Increase on 1897.	Increase on 1896.	Name.	Gross Traffic for Week. Week ending	Amount.	In. or Dec. upon 1897.	In. or Dec. upon 1896.	Gross Traffic to Date. No. of Weeks.	Amount.	In. or Dec. upon 1897.	In. or Dec. upon 1896.
					£	£	£		£	£	£
319	—	—	Argentine Great Western ..	Feb. 5	7,378	+ 2,371	+ 3,101	31	163,961	− 11,979	+ 36,712
76½	—	—	Bahia and San Francisco ..	Jan. 22	2,420	+ 472	+ 743	3	7,935	+ 2,762	+ 2,463
234	48	84	Bahia Blanca and North West ..	Jan. 16	1,204	+ 118	+ 541	29	22,304	+ 592	—
74	—	—	Buenos Ayres and Ensenada ..	Feb. 13	3,955	− 171	—	6	21,932	− 4,825	—
426	—	—	Buenos Ayres and Pacific ..	Feb. 12	7,241	− 1,284	− 313	32	199,603	− 49,396	+ 7,084
914	1	3	Buenos Ayres and Rosario ..	Feb. 12	18,578	+ 6,833	+ 883	6	106,587	+ 19,046	+ 13,235
1,499	30	68	Buenos Ayres Great Southern ..	Feb. 13	32,143	+ 1,201	+ 5,184	32	910,407	+ 65,196	+ 141,206
600	107	177	Buenos Ayres Western	Feb. 13	13,120	− 1,619	− 3,479	32	380,276	− 74,748	− 60,349
845	55	77	Central Argentine..	Feb. 13	23,601	+ 7,046	− 2,631	6	133,931	+ 24,713	+ 1,941
297	—	—	Central Bahia	Nov. 31*	$71,637	− $29,321	− $26,571	11 mos.	$1,192,815	+ $146,023	+ $177,015
271	—	—	Central Uruguay of Monte Video	Feb. 13	6,459	+ 1,200	+ 164	32	190,524	− 2,433	− 17,215
128	—	—	Do. Eastern Extension	Feb. 12	1,745	+ 599	+ 270	32	38,582	+ 2,728	− 2,662
182	—	—	Do. Northern Extension	Feb. 12	545	− 68	− 301	32	20,675	− 1,813	− 5,136
280	—	—	Cordoba and Rosario	Feb. 6	3,145	+ 1,055	− 355	32	65,895	− 19,745	− 680
128	—	—	Cordoba Central	Feb. 6	$24,500	− $1,200	− $2,150	5	$124,900	− $9,580	− $21,130
549	—	—	Do. Northern Extension	Feb. 6	$41,500	− $16,270	− $8,050	5	$245,790	− $63,830	− $46,370
137	—	—	Costa Rica..	Feb. 12	6,623	− 1,944	− 275	—	—	—	—
99	—	—	East Argentine	Dec. 31	352	+ 67	—	52	36,721	− 3,474	—
366	—	6	Entre Rios..	Feb. 12	1,966	+ 752	+ 6	32	43,262	+ 6,864	+ 6,932
555	—	24	Inter Oceanic of Mexico.. ..	Jan. 29	$64,700	+ $12,620	+ $22,900	31	$1,703,280	+ $240,700	+ $401,450
23	—	—	La Guaira and Caracas	Dec. 23	2,082	− 1,076	− 268	51	106,904	− 17,770	+ 2,045
321	—	—	Mexican	Feb. 12	$78,000	+ $11,500	—	6	$487,300	+ $43,950	—
1,846	—	—	Mexican Central	Feb. 7	$238,422	− $12,428	+ $35,726	5	$1,315,927	− $5,529	+ $292,271
1,217	—	—	Mexican National	Feb. 7	$111,239	− $3,690	− $36,759	5	$575,052	—	—
228	—	—	Mexican Southern	Feb. 14	$12,330	− $2,169	+ $1,232	46	$581,666	+ $87,220	+ $155,136
105	—	—	Minas and Rio	Dec. 31*	$177,973	+ $6,511	—	6 mos.	$1,174,610	+ $207,798	—
94	—	17	N. W. Argentine	Feb. 12	993	− 498	− 412	6	6,067	− 3,424	− 1,588
242	3	—	Nitrate	Feb. 15	15,312	− 1,823	− 4,776	6	40,893	− 4,885	—
320	—	—	Ottoman	Feb. 5	4,672	− 2,266	− 395	5	40,895	− 7,933	+ 6,818
77½	—	—	Recife and San Francisco ..	Dec. 18	6,266	− 786	+ 967	25	82,861	− 10,189	− 365
86¼	—	—	San Paulo	Dec. 26†	23,002	− 3,560	—	2	46,230	− 10,120	—
186	—	—	Santa Fe and Cordova	Feb. 5	2,964	+ 693	+ 12	31	34,717	− 21,745	− 3,718
110	—	—	Western of Havana	Feb. 12	1,805	− 90	+ 1,430	32	57,210	+ 5,783	− 4,515

* For month ended. † For fortnight ended.

INDIAN RAILWAYS.

Mileage. Total.	Increase on 1897.	Increase on 1896.	Name.	Gross Traffic for Week. Week ending	Amount.	In. or Dec. on 1897.	In. or Dec. on 1896	Gross Traffic to Date. No. of Weeks.	Amount.	In. or Dec. on 1877.	In. or Dec. on 1896.
862	—	—	Bengal Nagpur	Feb. 5	Rs.1,43,000	− Rs.10,360	− Rs.29,412	5	Rs.6,83,000	− Rs.1,66,617	− Rs.253,095
818	63	63	Bengal and North-Western ..	Jan. 15	Rs.1,22,780	+ Rs.12,420	+ Rs.15,490	2	Rs.2,65,160	+ Rs.18,013	− Rs.7,044
461	—	—	Bombay and Baroda	Feb. 5	£22,183	− £4,781	− £11,493	5	£115,133	− £17,096	− £62,149
1,884	2	13	East Indian	Feb. 12	Rs.12,58,000	+ R.80,000	+ Rs.27,000	6	Rs.76,37,000	+ Rs.3,03,000	+ Rs.2,60,000
1,491	—	—	Great Indian Penin.	Feb. 12	£64,726	+ £3,934	− £18,146	6	£370,335	− £8,990	− £151,209
736	—	—	Indian Midland	Feb. 12	Rs.1,33,700	+ Rs.3,324	+ Rs.29,318	6	Rs.8,90,523	+ Rs.30,795	+ Rs.104,783
840	—	—	Madras	Feb. 5	£18,317	− £1,100	− £1,925	5	£97,337	− £35	− £7,263
1,043	—	—	South Indian	Jan. 15	Rs.1,33,347	+ Rs.4,763	− Rs.1,161	2	Rs.3,15,563	− Rs.15,198	− Rs.92,631

UNITED STATES AND CANADIAN RAILWAYS.

Mileage Total.	Increase on 1897.	Increase on 1896.	Name.	Gross Traffic for Week. Period Ending.	Amount.	In. or Dec. on 1897.	Gross Traffic to Date. No. of Weeks.	Amount.	In. or Dec. on 1897.
					dols.	dols.		dols.	dols.
917	—	—	Baltimore & Ohio S. Western ..	Feb. 5	123,446	+11,605	31	3,974,763	+267,106
6,547	103	156	Canadian Pacific	Feb. 7	385,000	+53,000	5	2,058,000	+413,000
922	—	—	Chicago Great Western	Feb. 7	96,614	+405	31	3,262,865	+510,007
6,169	—	469	Chicago, Mil., & St. Paul ..	Feb. 14	593,000	+80,000	6	3,523,801	+482,220
1,685	—	—	Denver & Rio Grande	Feb. 7	139,000	+27,000	31	5,099,700	+830,600
3,512	—	—	Grand Trunk, Main Line ..	Feb. 14	£67,287	+£9,347	6	£451,740	+£60,059
335	—	—	Do. Chic. & Grand Trunk	Feb. 14	£15,196	+£3,539	6	£88,289	+£15,638
189	—	—	Do. Det., G. H. & Mil..	Feb. 14	£2,881	−£642	6	£20,427	−£1,947
2,938	—	—	Louisville & Nashville	Feb. 7	430,000	+48,000	5	2,202,000	+715,000
2,197	137	137	Miss., K., & Texas	Feb. 7	200,274	−30,709	31	8,269,226	+529,674
477	—	—	N. Y., Ontario, & W.	Feb. 7	54,766	−1,569	31	2,437,451	+82,704
1,570	—	—	Norfolk & Western	Feb. 7	183,000	−900	31	6,616,000	+693,100
3,499	336	—	Northern Pacific	Feb. 7	372,000	+140,000	5	1,773,000	+598,000
1,223	—	—	St. Louis S. Western	Feb. 7	111,000	+21,000	5	584,700	—
4,654	—	—	Southern	Feb. 7	408,000	+37,000	31	11,740,812	+646,448
1,979	—	—	Wabash	Feb. 7	238,426	+25,000	5	1,180,426	+131,000

MONTHLY STATEMENTS.

Mileage. Total.	Increase on 1896.	Increase on 1895.	Name.	Net Earnings for Month. Month.	Amount.	In. or Dec. on 1896.	In. or Dec. on 1895.	Net Earnings to Date. No. of Months.	Amount.	In. or Dec. on 1896.	In. or Dec. on 1895.
					dols.	dols.	dols.		dols.	dols.	dols.
6,935	44	444	Atchison	December	986,000	+52,000	—	12	8,966,480	+176,951	—
6,547	103	106	Canadian Pacific	December	1,053,000	+129,000	—	12	10,304,000	+2,196,000	—
1,685	—	—	Denver & Rio Grande	December	273,000	+57,121	−8,253	6	1,786,320	+249,850	−50,604
1,970	—	—	Erie..	December	605,798	+100,620	—	12	8,486,792	+302,587	—
3,127	—	239	Illinois Central*	December	2,555,393	+458,872	+349,241	12	24,723,399	+2,940,108	+2,909,052
2,396	—	—	New York Central*	January	3,505,000	+365,000	+27,034	—	—	—	—
477	—	—	New York Ontario, & W. ..	December	87,176	+14,635	+12,602	6	701,475	+4,958	+44,430
3,407	—	—	Pennsylvania	December	1,664,297	+26,100	−35,400	12	20,532,068	+2,328,300	+849,200
1,055	—	—	Phil. & Reading*	December	1,047,585	+208,345	—	6	11,886,164	+668,602	—

* Statements of gross traffic.

Prices Quoted on the London Stock Exchange.

Throughout the INVESTORS' REVIEW middle prices alone are quoted, the object being to give the public the approximate current quotations of every security of any consequence in existence. On the markets the buying and selling prices are both given, and are often wide apart where stocks are seldom dealt in. Other particulars will be found in the INVESTMENT INDEX published quarterly—January, April, July, and October—in connection with this REVIEW, price 2s., by post 2s. 2d. Where dividends are paid only once a year, an *italic* type is used to distinguish them. The London Stock Exchange Official List is quoted in the REVIEW almost entire, only very insignificant issues, or bonds falling due within the next two or three years, being omitted. But the list is subdivided into the leading, or active, stocks, and those less frequently dealt in. The former will be found under the head of "Stock Markets," and with more details than it is possible to give for the bulk of securities. By retaining the file of the INVESTORS' REVIEW any subscriber can follow for himself the movements of securities from week to week, and the INVESTMENT INDEX will from time to time help to fill up deficiencies in the information.

Tea Companies and Mines and Mining Finance Stocks are placed in special lists.

Among the abbreviations used are the following:—S.F. Snk. Fd. *sinking fund*; Certs., *certificates*; Debs. or Dbs., *debentures*; Db. or D.Stk., *debenture stock*; Pf., Prf., or Pref., *preference*; Prefd. or Pfd., *preferred*; Dfd., *deferred*; L. or Ltd., *limited*; Sh., *share*; Ans., *annuities*; Cu. or Cm., *cumulative*; Gu or Guar., *guaranteed*; Bds., *bonds*; S., Sr., or Ser., *series*; In., Ins., Insc., *inscribed*; Dr., Drgs., Drwgs., *drawings*; Stg., Strlg., *sterling*; Lia., *liable to*; Sp., Surp., *surplus*; Per., Perp., *perpetual*; Ln. *lien*; Lo. *loan*.

The dates following the names of securities are the years of issue or of redemption. Where shares are not fully paid up, their nominal amount is given with the name so that investors may know the liability upon them.

BRITISH FUNDS, &c.

Rate.	Name.	Price.
2¾	2¾ p.c.'s (Childers') Red.. 1905	106
3	Local Loans Stk. 1912	113
3	Metro. Police Deb. Stk. 1920	105½
—	Red Sea Ind. Tel. Ann. 1908	8¾
4	Canada Gv. "Intcl. Rly." 1903	109½
4	Do. do. .. 1908	113
4	Do. Bonds 1910	117
4	Do. Bonds 1913	119½
3	Egyptian Gov. Gar.	108
3	Mauritius Ins. Stk. 1940	115
4	Turkish Guar. 1855	109
10½	Bank of Ireland Stk.	390
3½	India Rupee Paper	62½
3½	Do. 1854-5	63½
3	Do. 1896-7 1916	57½
3½	Isle of Man Deb.	104
3	Do. Deb. Stk... 1919-29	103

CORPORATION AND COUNTY STOCKS.

FREE OF STAMP DUTY.

Rate.	Name.	Price.
3½	Metropolitan Con. 1929	120½
3	Do. 1941	113
2½	Do. 1920-49	101½
2½	L.C.C. Con. Stock 1920	100
3½	Comm. of Sewers, Scp., S.F. 1905	105
3½	Corp. of Lond. Bds...1897-1902	100½
3	Do. 1897-1912	103
3½	Do., Debs. Scp. ...... S.F. 1916	106
2½	Do., Deb. Stk. Scrip .. 1927-57	100
3	Barnsley 1916-46	105
3	Barry 1914-46	100
3	Bath 1909-34	104
3	Batley 1914-44	101½
3½	Birmingham 1945	124
3	Do. 1947	113
2½	Do. 1926	99
3	Blackburn 1930	107
3	Bournemouth 1913-33	104
3½	Bradford 1945	120
3	Do. Deb. Stock .. 1954	112
3	Brighouse.............. 1916-46	100
3½	Brighton 1946	120½
2½	Do. 1957	98
3	Burton-on-Trent.......... 1913-43	102½
3	Cambridge 1913-43	104
3½	Cardiff 1935	119
3	Do. 1914-54	105
3	Cheltenham.......... 1971	112
3	Chichester 1916-46	102
3½	Croydon	135½
3	Do. 1940	111½
3	Derby 1920-50	107
3	Devon C.C.............. 1917-33	106½
3½	Dewsbury 1930	111
3	Do. 1930	105
3	Dorset County 1922-32	107
3	Douglas (I. of Man) 1926	101
3	Dover 1913-43	103½
3½	Dublin 1944	113½
3	Eastbourne 1910-40	105
3	Edinburgh 1924	108
2½	Do. 1927	98
2½	Exeter 1917-57	97
3	Glamorgan County 1914-34	104
3½	Glasgow 1914	110½
3	Do. 1921	106½
2½	Do. 1925-40	99
3	Gloster 1915-55	103
3	Grimsby 1913-45	103½
3	Hampshire County 1914-34	105½
3	Hanley 1913-43	105
3	Harrogate 1914-34	104
3	Hastings 1915-54	105
2½	Hertfordshire C.C. 1916-36	99
3	Heston & Isleworth U.D.C. 1915-35	101
3	Huddersfield 1934	107
3½	Hull (1st iss.)	131½
3	Inverness 1914-44	102
3	Ipswich 1952	111
3	Lancaster.............. 1919-55	104
2½	Leeds 1927	98
3½	Leicester 1934	117
3	Lincoln.............. 1919	104
[illegible]	Liverpool	[illegible]

Corporation, &c. (*continued*):—

Rate.	Name.	Price.
3	Manchester 1941	110
3	Mansfield.......... 1915-45	100
3½	Middlesbro'.......... 1909	105½
3½	Do. 1911-13	105
3	Do. 1915	104
3	Middlesex C.C.......... 1915-35	106
3½	Newcastle 1936	118½
3½	Do. Irred.	129½
2½	Do. 1915-36	101
3	Newcastle-under-Lyme.. 1909-44	101
3	Newport (Mon.) 1915-55	104½
3	Norwich 1952	113
3	Nottingham	117
3	Oxford 1951	111
3	Penzance 1916-46	102½
3	Plymouth 1942	112
3	Pontypridd U.D.C. 1916-46	99
3	Poole.......... 1915-45	102½
3½	Portsmouth........1916 24 & 27	112
3	Do. 1913-33	107
3	Ramsey 1920-40	100
3	Ramsgate.......... 1915-55	102
3	Reading	135
3	Do. 1962	109
3½	Rhyl U.D.C. 1953	112
3	Richmond (Surrey) 1942	106½
3	River Wear Debt Certs.	101
3	St. Helen's 1915-55	103
3	Scarbro' 1915-50	102
2½	Sheffield 1925-57	97½
3	Shipley U.D.C.......... 1915-35	101
3	Somerset Co. 1923-33	107
3	South Shields.......... 1915-43	104
2¾	Southampton 1915-45	102
3	Southend-on-Sea 1916-46	102
3	Staffs C.C. 1915-35	105
3	Stockport.......... 1914-54	104
3	Stockton 1932	106
3	Do. 1915-35	104
3	Surrey Co. 1922-32	106½
3½	Swansea	132
3	Do. 1955	106
3	Taunton 1918 3-9-43	102
3	Tees Conserv. Deb. Stk. 1947	101
3	Thames Conserv. "A" Deb. Stk.......... 1954	103
3	Do. "B" Deb. Stk. 1954	103
3	Torquay 1913-43	102½
3	Tunbridge Wells 1931	105
3	Tynemouth 1913	101
3	Wakefield.......... 1929	103
3	Walsall.......... 1932	108
3	West Bromwich.......... 1930	108½
3½	West Ham 1929	112
3	Do. 1945	107
3	West Sussex C.C. 1915-35	106
3	Weston-s.-Mare Lcl. Bd. 1914-44	102
3	Weymouth & Melc. Regis 1918	101
3	Widnes.......... 1915-55	102
3	Wigan 1921	108
3	Windsor 1918-55	104
3½	Wisbech 1947	115½
3½	Wolverhampton 1932	118½
3	Do. 1924-54	107
3	York 1916-41	107

SUBJECT TO STAMP DUTY.

Rate.	Name.	Price.
3½	Belfast City & Dis. Watr. 1938	116
3	Do. Red Stk. 1953-6	106
3½	Belfast 1924	104
4	Blackburn Con. Deb. Irred.	141½
3½	Do. do. Irred..........	131
3½	Bristol	133
3½	Burnley.......... 1933	114
2½	Chesterfield Gas & Wtr. 1916-46	98
3½	Douglas Town 1921	105
3	Dover Harb. 1st Deb... 1956	104½
3½	Hull (2nd iss.)	129½
4	Leeds Deb. 1927	125
3½	Do.	115½
3	Do. 1927	107½
3	Leicester 1919-44	106
4	Manchester..........	150
3	Do. 1928	105
4½	Middlesboro' Mrts. 1908	111
3½	Newark-on-Trent .. 1901-41	96
3½	Sheffield 1898-1916	104
3½	Do. 1925-36	112½
3	Do. 1925	104½
3½	Southampton .... S.F.	106
4½	Stockton Morts.......... 1908	112
[illegible]	W[illegible]	[illegible]

COLONIAL AND PROVINCIAL GOVERNMENT SECURITIES.

Rate.	Name.	Price.
6	British Columbia........ 1907	119½
4½	Do. Debs... 1917	111½
3	British Guiana Imgtn. Bds.	99½
5	Canada, "Intercol. Rail," 1903	111½
4	Do. (Bonds) 1904-5-6-8	108
4	Do. Reduced........ 1910	111
3½	Do. Bnds. 1909-34	107
4	Do. Loan 1910-35	111
3	Do. Loan 1938	106
6	Cape of G. Hope 1900	—
5	Do. 1900	—
4½	Do. red. by an. draw.	111
4½	Do. 1879	111
4	Do. 1881	109
4	Do. 1917-23	118
4½	Ceylon	110
4	Do.	106½
4½	Fiji Gov. Deb. Sink. Fd.	102½
4	Jamaica Sink. Fd. 1923	103
5	Manitoba Debs.......... 1910	113
5	Do. Ster. Bds. 1888	122
4	Do. Ster. Debs.	106
4	Mauritius, Cons. Debs. 1880....	103½
4½	Natal, Sink. Fd......... 1919	120
4	Do. do. 1926	118
3½	Newfoundland Stg. Bds. 1941	100
3½	Do. do. .. 1947	100
3	Do. do.	88
5	New South Wales 1897-1902	104½
4	Do. 1903-5-8-9-12	105½
5	New Zealand 1914	118
5	Do. Cnsls. 1 p.c. per an. Sink. Fd.	104
3½	Nova Scotia Debs.	104
5	Quebec Prov. 1904-6	110
4½	Do. (drgs.)	104
5	Do. Strlg. Bds. 1912	115
4	Do. Strlg. Bds. 1928	110
4	Do. Strlg. Bds. 1934	110
4	Queensland 1913-15	108
4½	St. Lucia Debs..........	100
6	South Australia 1897-1900	103½
6	Do. 1901-1918	118
5	Do. 1911-1920	115½
4	Do. 1899-1916	105
4	Do. 1929	110½
4	Do. 1916	109½
4	Do. 1917-18-24	114
6	Tasmania 1897-1901	104
4	Do. 1908-11, 1913-14-20	108
5	Trinidad Debs., an. drw. 1 p c...	108
4	Victoria 1899-1901	101½
4½	Do. 1904	106
4	Do. Rail. Loan 1907	106
4	Do. Loans 1908-13	108½
4½	West. Austr. 1 p.c. ac. Sink. Fd.	108
4	Do. do.	106

REGISTERED AND INSCRIBED STOCKS.

No stamp duty except for Canada 4 p.c. Reduced (½ per cent.).

Rate.	Name.	Price.
4	Antigua Insc. Stk. Red. 1919-44	109
3½	Barbados Insc. Stk. 1925-42	109
3	British Colum. Insc. Stk. 1941	104
4	British Guiana Insc..... 1935	120
4	Canada Stk. Regd. ..1904-5-6-8	108
4	Do. 4 p.c. (late 5 p.c.) Regd. 1910	111
3½	Do. 3½ p.c. Stock Regd. 1909-34	107
4	Do. Ln. for 4 milln. stg. 1910-35	111
3	Do. Stk. Regd. 1938	106
2½	Do. Insc. 1947	93
4	Cape G. Hope Regd. .. 1917-23	111
4	Do. (Ln. of '83) Insc. .. 1923	119
4	Do. Cons. Stk. Insc..... 1916-36	116
3½	Do. Consol. Insc. Stock 1929-49	115
4	Ceylon Insc. Stock 1934	124
3	Do. 1940	107
4	Grenada Insc. Stock.... 1917-42	112
3½	Hong Kong Insc. Stock 1918-43	105½
4	Jamaica Insc. Stock.... 1934	121
—	Do. 1922-44	99
4	Mauritius Inscribed 1937	119
4	Natal Consd. Stk. Insc. 1927	118
4	Do. 1937	122
3½	Do. Inscribed Stock.. 1914-39	107
4	Newfoundland Inscribed 1913-38	108
4	Do. 1935	114
4	Do. Consd. Stk. Ins. 1936	114
4	N. S. Wales Stock Insc. 1933	122
3½	Do. 1924	110
3½	Do. 1918	106

Colonial, &c. (*continued*):—

Rate.	Name.	Price.
4	N. Zealnd. Con. Stk. Ins. 1929	116½
3½	Do. 1940	109
3	Do. Inscribed.... 1945	101
3	Quebec (Prov.) Ins. Stk. 1937	95
4	Queensland Stock Insc. 1915-24	112½
3½	Do. 1921-4-30	106
3½	Do. 1945	109
3	Do. 1922-47	99½
4	St. Lucia Insc. Stock .. 1919-44	112
4	S. Austrln. (1882-7) Reg. 1916-36	114
3½	Do. In. Stk. Reg. 1939	110
3	Do. 1916-26	100
3/	Do. 1916	100
3½	Tasmanian Insc. Stock.. 1920-40	110
4	Do. 1920-40	116
4	Trinidad Insc. Stock.... 1917-42	110
3	Do. 1922-44	98½
4	Victoria Rly. Loan '81, Inscribed Stock 1907	106
4	Victoria Insc. Stock 1908-13-19	109
4	Victoria (1885) Ins. Stk. 1920	112
3½	Do. Inscribed Stock 1921-3-6	106
4	Do. do. 1911-26	109
4	W. Austral. Insc. Stock 1934	120
4	Do. 1911-31	113
3½	Do. 1915-35	107
3	Do. 1915-35	98
3	Do. 1916-36	98

FOREIGN STOCKS, BONDS, &c.

COUPONS PAYABLE IN LONDON.

Last Div.	Name.	Price.
36/	Argentine Ry. Loan 6 p.c. 1881	90½
15/	Do. 5 p.c. 1884	72
30/	Do. N. Cent. Ry. Ext. 5 p.c. 1887-8-9	71½
30/	Do. 5 p.c. Trsy. Convs. 1887	72
5/4½	Do. 4½ p.c. Interl. Gld. 1888	68
27/	Do. 4½ p.c. Stlg. Extrl. 1888	68
10/6	Do. 3½ p.c. External .. 1889	51
4	Do. 4 p.c. Ry. Guar. Res....	62½
4½	Brazilian 1883	62
4½	Do. Gold.......... 1879	68½
4½	Do. 1888	63
36/	Buenos Ayres 1824	90
6	Do. 1882-3-6	80
6	Bulgarian 1888	94
6	Do. Mort. Bonds 1892	94
4½	Chilian 1883	78
4½	Do. 1886	79
4½	Do. 1887	78
4½	Do. 1889	82½
5	Do. 1892	87
4½	Do. 1893	78
4½	Do. 1895	79
5	Do. 1896	86
7	Chinese Silver 1894	101
6	Do. Gold 1895	106
6	Do. Apl. '95 by dwgs. 1901-15	109½
5	Do. Red. dwgs. in 36 yr. 1896	101
5	Do. Do. Regis. 1896	101
1½	Colmbn. 1½ to 3 p.c. Ext. Bds. 1896	18
6	Cordova, Prov. 1886	28
—	Do. Eng. Ass. Certs.	27
—	Do. 6 p.c. 1887-8	28
—	Do. Eng. Ass. Certs.	27
3	Costa Rica "A"	32
2½	Do. "B"	27
3	Danish Gold 1914	100
10/	Ecuador N. Ext. Bds. 4½ p.c. ascn. to 5 p.c.	21
3½	Egypt'n Ins. Stk. lia. Stp. Dty. 1890	102
4½	Do. State Domain 1878	106
4	Do. D. Sanieh, Red. .. 1905	105½
6	Entre Rios.......... 1886-8	38
6	Do. Fndg. Ln. Bds. 1894-1921	32½
6	Do. do. Parana City......	27½
15/	Greek 1881	38
15/	Do. 1884	38
12/	Do. Rentes..........	31
15/	Do. (Piræus-Larissa Ry.)	36
17/6	Do. Fundg. Loan 1893	46
	Guatemala Extl. Debt..........	33
4	Hawaiian	101½
6	Hungarian Gold Rentes........	101½
4	Do. 1895	91
3	Italian Irriga. Guar.	112½
6	Do. Maremmana	93½
5	Japan 5 p.c.	102½
5	Mexican (Nat. R. Tehuantp c.)..	96½

Foreign Stocks, &c. (*continued*) :—

Last Div.	Name.	Price.
6	Mexican Extrl. 1893	96½
5	Do. Intrnl. Cons. Slvr.	39
5	Do. Intern. Rd. Bds. 2d. Ser.	37½
4	Nicaragua 1886	50
3½	Norwegian, red. 1937, or earlier	100
3	Do. do. 1965, do.	100
3½	Do. 3½ p.c. Bnds.	103
1	Paraguay 1p.c. ris. 3p.c. 1886-96	17
5	Russian, 1822, £ Strlg.	151
3	Do. 1859	93
4	Do. (Nicolas Ry.) 1867-9	104
3	Do. Transcauc. Ry. 1882	94
4	Do. Con. R. R. Bd. Ser. I., 1889	104
4	Do. Do. II., 1889	104
4	Do. Do. III., 1891	103½
3½	Do. Bonds	101½
4	Do. Ln. (Dvinsk and Vitbsk)	103
6	Salvador 1889	76
—	S Domingo 4s. Unified .. 1980	65½
6	San Luis Potosi Stg. 1889	94½
5	San Paulo (Brzl.), Stg. 1888	91½
6	Santa Fé 1883-4	39
—	Do. Eng. Ass. Certs. Dep.	37½
5	Do. 1888	50
—	Do. Eng. Ass. Certs. Dpsit.	49
5	Do. (W. Cnt. Col. Rly.) Mrt.	29
5	Do. & Reconq. Rly. Mort.	29
5	Spanish Quicksilvr Mort. 1870	103
3½	Swedish 1880	103
3	Do. 1888	100
53	Do. Conversion Loan 1894	101
45	Trans. Gov. Loan Red...1903-42	106
59/	Tucuman (Prov.) 1888	68
	Turkish, Secd. on Egypt. Trib.	104½
½	Turkish, Egpt. Trib., Ott. Bd., '94	100
4	Do. Priority 1890	93
1	Do. Convted Series, "A"	65½
5	Do. Customs Ln. 1886	97½
5	Uruguay Bonds 1896	55
3	Venzula New Con. Debt 1881	35½

COUPONS PAYABLE ABROAD.

Last Div.	Name.	Price.
7	Argent. Nat. Cedla. Sries, "B"	37½
5	Austrian Ster. Rnts., ex 10fl., 1870	85
5	Do. do. do.	86
5	Do. Paper do. 1870	84
5	Do. do. do.	86
4	Do. Gld Rentes 1876	103
2½	Belgian exchange 25 fr.	92
3	Do. do.	101
3½	Danish Int., 1887, Rd. 1896	97½
3½	Do. '87, Red. by pur. or draw. fr. Dec., 1900	98½
2½	Dutch Certs. ex 12 gldrs.	87
3	Do. Bonds	100
3	Do. Inac. Stk.	99
3½	French Rentes	105½
3	Do. 1878, '81-4., Red.	101
3	German Imp. Ln. 1891	97
3	Do. do. 1892-3	96½
3	Do. do. 1890-4	96
5	Japan Cons. Ln., '99, 3, & 5, Red.	47
36/9	Prussian Consols	102
3	" Cons. Stg. Ln. 1891	97
4	Rumanian Bds. 1890	—
4	Do. do. 1891	—
4	Utd. States, 1877, Red. 1907	116
4	Do. 1895, 30 yrs.	131½
3½	Do. Maschsetts Gl. 1935	113½
3½	Do. Gold Bonds 1923	110½
2	Virginia Cpn. Bds., 3 p.c. from July, 1901	72

BRITISH RAILWAYS.

ORD. SHARES AND STOCKS.

Last Div.	Name.	Price.
10	Barry, Ord.	281½
4	Do. Prefd.	127
6	Do. Defd.	152½
5½	Caledonian, Ord.	160
3	Do. Prefd.	102½
—	Do. Defd. Ord., No. 1	5½
	Cambrian, Ord	6½
—	Do. Coast Cons.	6½
24/	Cardiff Ry. Pref. Ord.	118
3/	Central Lond. £10 Ord. Sh.	10½
1/9½	Do. do. £6 paid	6½
3½d.	Do. Pref. Half-Shares	1½
1/6	Do. Def. do.	4½
1½	City and S. London	69
—	East London, Cons.	7
1½	Furness	68½
—	Glasgow and S. West. Pfd.	85
—	Do. do. Dfd.	68
—	Great Central, Ord. 1894	42
32/0	Do. London Exten.	79
3½	Great N. of Scotland	125
4	Great Northern, Prefd.	123
—	Do. Consolidated "A"	52
—	Do. do. "B"	195½
2	Highland	87½
4	Isle of Wight, Prefd.	122½
1	Do. Defd.	86½
—	Lancs. Derbys. and E. Cst.	4½
8½	L. Brighton and S. C. Ord.	187
37/11½	Do. New 70 p.c. pd.	188
6	Do. Prefd. Ord.	199
30/	Do. Contgt. Rights Certs.	20½
5½	Lond. and S. Western Ord.	233½
4	Do. Preferred	138
6½	Lond., Tilb., and Southend	132½
—	Mersey, £20 shares	1
—	Metropolitan, New Ord.	131
2½	Do. Surplus Lands	97
4	North Cornwall, 4 p.c. Pref.	106½
7/6	Do. Deferred	27½
7½	North London	231½
	North Staffordshire	133

British Railways (*continued*) :—

Last Div.	Name.	Price.
1/6	Plymouth, Devenport, and S. W. Junc. £10	9
3/	Port Talbot £10 Shares	8½
9d.	Rhondda Swns. B. £10 Sh.	6½
10	Rhymney, Cons.	272½
4	Do. Prefd.	126
—	Do. Defd.	149½
6½	Scarboro', Bridlington Junc.	47½
6½	South Eastern, Ord	153
6	Do. Pref.	194
3½	Taff Vale	84
25/	Vale of Glamorgan	127½
2/2½	Waterloo & City £10 shares	14

LEASED AT FIXED RENTALS.

Last Div.	Name.	Price.
4	Birkenhead	150
5.19.0	East Lincnshire	215
5½	Hamsmith. & City Ord.	197½
4½	Lond. and Blackwll.	165
4½	Do. £10 4½ p. c. Pref.	165
56/6	Lond. & Green. Ord.	104
5	Do. 5 p. c. Pref.	180½
5	Nor. and Eastn. £50 Ord.	90
6	Do.	107
3½	N. Cornwall 3½ p. c. Stk.	128½
4½	Nott. & Granthm. R. & C.	150
3½	Portptk. & Wigtn. Guar. Stk.	126
9	Vict. Stn. & Pimlico Ord.	317½
4½	Do. 4½ p. c. Pref.	163½
4/	West Lond. £20 Ord. Shs.	14½
4½	Weymouth & Portld.	160½

DEBENTURE STOCKS.

Last Div.	Name.	Price.
4	Alexandra Dks. & Ry.	132½
3	Barry, Cons.	110
4	Brecon & Mrthyr, New A	129
4	Do. New B	106
4	Caledonian	153
4	Cambrian "A"	134½
4	Do. "B"	132½
4	Do. "C"	128½
4	Do. "D"	110½
3	Cardiff Rly.	105
4	City and S. Lond.	139
3½	Cleator & Working Junc.	118½
3	Devon & Som. "A"	105½
16/3	Do. "B" 4 p. c.	36
—	Do. "C" 4 p. c.	10
4	E. Lond. 2nd Ch. 4 p. c. A	137
8/	Do. 2nd B	67½
—	Do. 3rd Ch. 4 p. c.	19½
—	Do. 4th do.	9½
3½	Do. 1st (3½ p. c.)	128½
2½	Do. 2½ p.c. (Whitech. Exn).	88
4	Forth Bridge	146
4	Furness	144
4	Glasgow and S. Western	150
5	Gt. Central	—
4½	Do.	160½
4	Gt. Eastern	149
4	Gt. N. of Scotland	148½
3	Gt. Northern	115
4	Gt. Western	154
4½	Do.	162
4½	Do.	172
5	Do.	191
2½	Do.	100
4	Highland	143½
3	Hull and Barnsley	107
3	Do. 2nd (3-4 p. c).	124
4	Isle of Wight	144½
3	Do. Cent. "A"	92½
4½	Do. "B"	115½
4	Do. "C"	82½
3	Lancs. & Yorkshire	115
4	Lancs. Derbys. & E. Cst.	124½
4	Lpool St. Hlen's & S. Lancs.	126
4½	Ldn. and Blackwall	159
4	Ldn. and Greenwich	149½
4	Lond., Brighton, &c.	152
4½	Do.	170½
4½	Lond., Chath., &c., Arb.	160
4½	Do. "B"	158½
4	Do.	140
4	Do. 1883	139
3	Do.	107
3	Lond. & N. Western	117
3	Lond. & S. Westn. "A"	117
3	Do. Consld.	117
4	Lond., Til., & Southend	150
—	Mersey, 5 p. c. (Act, 1866)	66
4	Metropolitan	150
4½	Do.	164½
3½	Do.	129½
6	Met. District	209½
4	Do.	139
3	Midland	116
4½	Mid-Wales "A"	137½
4	Neath & Brecon 1st	129
4	Do. "A 1"	121
3	North British	113
3	Do. 1893	111½
3½	N. Cornwall, Launcstn., &c.	128½

Debenture Stocks (*continued*) :—

Last Div.	Name.	Price.
3	North Eastern	116
4½	North London	167
3	N. Staffordshire	114
4	Plym. Devpt. & S.W. Jn.	141½
4	Rhondda and Swan. Bay	130½
4	Rhymney	148
4	South-Eastern	152
5	Do.	190
3½	Do.	130
3	Do.	116
3	Taff Vale	111
4	Tottenham & For. Gate	146
3	Vale of Glamorgan	106½
3	West Highld. (Gtd. by N. B.)	110½
4	Wrexham, Mold, &c. "A"	115½
4	Do. "B"	106½
4	Do. "C"	97½

GUARANTEED SHARES AND STOCKS.

Last Div.	Name.	Price.
4	Caledonian	150½
4	Do.	151
4	Forth Bridge	146
4	Furness 1881	138
4	Glasgow & S. Western	150
4	Do. St. Enoch, Rent	150
6	Gt. Central	202
4½	Do. 1st Pref.	153½
3½	Do. Pref.	106
5	Do. Irred. S.Y. Rent	166½
4½	Do. do.	140½
4	Gt. Eastern, Rent	147
5	Do. Metropolitan	182½
4	Do.	147
4	Gt. N. of Scotland	141
4	Gt. Northern	151
5	Gt. Western, Rent	187
5	Do. Cons.	189
4	Lancs. & Yorkshire	150
5	L., Brighton & S. C.	186
3½	L., Chat. & D. (Shrtlds.)	110½
4	L. & North Western	155
4	L. & South Western 1881	152
4½	Met. District, Ealing Rent	152
4½	Do. Fulham Rent	152
4	Do. Midland Rent	143½
4	Do. Mid. & Dist. Guar.	135½
4	Midland, Rent	152
4	Do. Cons.	152
3	Mid. & G.N. Jt., "A" Rnt.	109½
3	N. British, Lien	110
4	Do. Cons. Pref. No. 1	148
3	N. Cornwall, Wadebrge. Gu.	108
4	N. Eastern	151
5	N. Staff. Trent & M. £20 Shs.	36½
3½	Notl. Suburban Ord.	126½
20/6	S. E. Perp. Ann.	36½
4½	Do. 4½ p.c.	167
3½	S. Yorks. Junc. Ord.	118½
4½	W. Cornwall (G. W., Br., Ex., & S. Dev. Joint Rent	166½
3	W. Highl. Ord. Stk. (Gua., N.B.)	107½

PREFERENCE SHARES AND STOCKS.

DIVIDENDS CONTINGENT ON PROFIT OF YEAR.

Last Div.	Name	Price.
4½	Alexandra Dks. & Ry. "A"	128½
5	Barry (First)	169½
4	Do. Consolidated	139½
4	Caledonian Cons., No. 1	148
4	Do. do. No. 2	147
5	Do. do. 1878	181½
4	Do. Pref. 1884	146
4	Do. do. 1887 (Conv.)	155
—	Cambrian, No. 1 4 p.c. Pref.	74½
—	Do. No. 2 do.	39½
—	Do. No. 3 do.	19
—	Do. No. 4 do.	10
5	City & S. Lond. £10 shares	15½
—	Do. New	14
4	Furness, Cons. 1881	134½
4	Do. "A" 1881	131½
4	Do. "B" 1883	129½
4	Glasgow & S. Western	148
4	Do. No. 2	147
4	Do. 1888	147
4	Do. 1891	146
5	Gt. Central	167½
4	Do.	134½
5	Do. Conv. 1872	154½
5	Do. do. 1874	154½
5	Do. do. 1876	154½
5	Do. do. 1879	153½
5	Do. do. 1881	152½
4	Do. 1889	115½
4	Do. 1891	110½
5	Do. 1894	115½
4	Gt. Eastern, Cons.	145
4	Do. 1886	144
4	Do. 1881	144
4	Do. 1884	143

Preference Shares, &c. (*continued*) :—

Last Div.	Name.	Price.
4	Gt. Eastern, Cons. 1887	143
4	Do. 1888	143
3½	Do. 1890	124½
3½	Do. 1893	123½
—	Do. (Int. fr. Jan '99) 1893	117½
4	Gt. North Scotland "A"	136½
4	Do. "B"	135½
4	Gt. Northern, Cons.	148
3	Do. 1896	108½
5	Gt. Western Cons.	188
36/11	Hull & Barnsley Red. at 115	108
4	Isle of Wight	135½
3	Lancs. & Yorkshire, Cons.	110
2/2½	Lanc. Drby & E.C. 5 p.c. £10	10½
—	Do. 5 p.c. 2nd £10	10
5	Lond., Bright., &c., Cons.	185
5	Do. 2nd Cons.	184
4½	Lond., Chat. & Dov. Arbitr.	137
2/	Do. 2nd Pref. 4½ p.c.	96
4	Lond. & N. Western	151
4	Lond. & S. Western ..1881	150
4	Do. 1884	149
3½	Do.	131
4	Lond., Tilbury & Southend	146
4	Do. Cons., 1887	146
4	Do 1891	145
—	Mersey, 5 p.c. Perp.	—
4	Metropolitan, Perp.	145
4	Do. 1882	143½
4	Do. Irred.	143½
4	Do. 1887	143½
4	Do. New	143½
4½	Do.	144½
3½	Do.	124½
3	Do. Guar.	102½
2½	Metrop. Dist. Exten 5 p.c.	111½
4	Midland, Cons. Perpetual	150
4	N. British Cons., No. 2	142
4½	Do. Edin. & Glasgow	156½
5	Do. 1865	173½
5	Do. Conv. 1874	173½
4½	Do. 1875	156
4½	Do. Conv. 1875	156½
5	Do. do. 1879	173½
4	Do. do. 1884	141
4	Do. do. 1888	141
4	Do. do. 1890	141
4	Do. do. 1892	140
4	N. Eastern	149
4½	N. Lond., Cons. 1866	178½
4½	Do. 2nd Cons. ..1875	165½
3	N. Staffordshire	111
4½	Plym. Devpt. & S. W. Junc.	152½
9½d.	Port Talbot, &c., 4 p.c. £10 Shares, 4 paid	5
5/	Rhondda & Swansea Bay, 5 p.c. £10 Shares	13½
4	Rhymney, Cons.	142
4½	S. Eastern, Cons.	166
5	Do. do.	184
4	Do. Vested Cos'.	145
4	Do. 1891	145
3½	Do. 1893	127
2	Do. 3 p.c. after July 1900	105
4	Taff Vale	143

INDIAN RAILWAYS.

Last Div.	Name.	Paid.	Price.
3½	Assam Bengal, Ld., (3½ p.c. till June 30, then 3 p.c.)	100	103
4/	Barsi Light, Ld., £10 Shs.	10	10½
6	Bengal and N. West., Ld.	100	148½
4/	Do. £10 Shares	10	14½
3/6	Do. 3½ p.c. Cum. Pf. Shs.	10	10½
5½d.	Do.	4	4½
2/3½	Bengal Central, Ld., £10 (3½ p.c. + ½th net earn)	5	5½
3	Bengal Dooars, Ld.	100	118
4	Bengal Nagpr., Lim. (gua. 4 p.c. + 4th sp. pfts.)	100	115
7½	Bombay, Baroda, and C. I. (gua. 5 p.c.)	100	214
36/1	Burma, Ld. (gua. 2½ p.c. and ½ p.c. add. till 1901)	100	111½
1/7	Do. £10 Shares	2½	3½
4	Delhi Umb. Kalka, Ld., Gua. 3½ p.c. + net earn.	100	121
4	Do. Deb. Stk., 1890 (1916)	100	113
9/10	Estn. Bengal, "A" An. 1957	—	26
9/	Do. "B" 1957	—	31
4	Do. Gua. Deb. Stock	100	144½
9/7½	East Ind. Ann. "A" (1953)	—	28
8/4½	Do. "C"	—	30
8/11½	Do. "B"	—	32
6½	Do. Def. Ann. Cap. (gua. 4 p.c. + ½th sp. pfts.)	—	155
115/9	East Ind. Def. Ann. "D"	—	161
4½	East Ind. Irred. Stock	100	166½
5	Gt. Indian Penin., Gua. 5 p.c. + ½ surplus profits	100	173
4	Do. Irred. 4 p.c. Deb. St.	100	146½
4	Indian Mid., Ld. (gua. 4 p.c. + ½th surplus pfts.)	100	115
51/	Madras Guar. + ½ sp. pfts.	100	167
48/6	Do. do.	100	157
46/	Do. do.	100	147
4	Nilgiri, Ld., 1st Deb. Stk.	100	97
4	Oude & Robil. Db. Stk. Rd.	100	101
5½	Robil. and Kumaon, Ld.	100	132
9/11	Scinde, Punj., and Delhi, "A" Ann., 1958	—	26
9/1	Do. "B" do.	—	31

Indian Railways (*continued*) :—

Last Div.	Name.	Paid.	Price.
4	South Behar, Ld., £10 shs.	100	100
3½	Do. Deb. Stk. Red.	100	103
4½	South Ind., Gu. Deb. Stk.	100	166½
5	South Indian, Ld. (gua. 3 p.c., and ½ spls. profits)	100	121½
5	Sthn. Mahratta, Ld. (3½ p.c. & ½th net earnings)	100	121
4	Do. Deb. Stk. Red.	100	124
3½	Southern Punjab, Ld.	100	113
3½	Do. Deb. Stk. Red.	—	107
5	Nizam's Gua. State, Ld. (†	100	114½
4	Do. Mort. Deb., 1936	100	110
4	Do. do. Reg.	100	108
17/3½	Nizam's Gua. State, Ld., 3½ p.c. Mt. Deb. bearer	—	95½
17/3½	Do. Reg. do. ..	—	94½
5	W. of India Porigese., Ld.	100	68½
5	Do. Deb. Stk., Red	100	98

RAILWAYS.—BRITISH POSSESSIONS.

Last Div.	Name.	Paid.	Price.
5	Atlantic & N.W. Gua. 1 Mt. Bds., 1937	100	127
5/3	Buff. & L. Huron Ord. Sh.	10	13½
5½	Do. 1st Mt. Perp. Bds. 1879	100	143½
5½	Do. 2nd Mt. Perp. Bds.	100	143½
—	Calgary & Edmon. 6 p.c. 1st Mt. Stg. Bds. Red..	100	76½
5	Canada Cent. 1st Mt. Bds. Red.	100	105
4	Can. Pacific Pref. Stk.....	100	102½
5	Do. Strl. 1st Mt. Deb. Bds. 1915	100	119
3½	Do. Ld. Grnt. Bds., 1938..	100	109
3½	Do. Ld. Grnt. Ins. Stk. ..	100	108
4	Do. Perp. Cons. Deb. Stk.	100	119
5	Do. Algoma Bch. 1st Mt. Bds., 1937	100	122
2	Demerara, Original Stock	100	49
7	Do. Perp. Pref. Stk.....	100	157½
9½d.	Do. 4 p.c. Cum. Ext. Pref. £10 Shs.	4	6½
—	Dominion Atlntc. Ord. Stk.	100	32½
25/	Do. 5 p.c. Pref. Stk......	100	101
.	Do. 1st. Deb. Stk.......	100	110
.	Do. 2nd do. Red.	100	100
—	Emu Bay & Mt. Bischoff, Ld.	5	4½
4½	Do. Irred. Deb. Stk....	100	98
nil.	Gd. Trunk of Canada, Stk.	100	8½
6	Do. 2nd. Equip. Mt. Bds.	100	130½
5	Do. Perp. Deb. Stk......	100	141
5	Do. Gt. Westn. Deb. Stk.	100	133
5	Do. Nthn. of Can. 1st Mt. Bds, 1902	100	106
4	Do. do. Deb. Stk	100	103
5	Do. G. T. Geor. Bay & L. Erie 1 Mt., 1903	100	104
5	Do. Mid. of Can. Stl. 1st Mt. (Mid. Sec.) 1908	100	109
5	Do. do. Cons. 1 Mt. Bds. 1912	100	110
5	Do. Mont. & Champ. 1 Mt. Bds., 1902	100	104
	Do. Welln., Grey & Brce. 7 p.c. Bds. 1 Mt.	100	111
4	Jamaica 1st Mtg. Bds. Red.	—	104
—	Manitoba & N. W., 6 p.c. 1st Mt. Bds., Red	100	—
—	Do. Ldn. Bdhldrs. Certs.	—	—
5	Manitoba S. W. Col. 1 Mt. Bd., 1934 $1,000 price %	—	120
—	Mid. of W. Aust. Ld. 6 p.c. 1 Mt. Dbs., Red.	100	25
4	Do. Deb. Bds., Red.	100	103
4	Nakusp & Slocan Bds., 1918	100	106
3	Natal Zululand Ld. Debs.,	100	79½
5	N. Brunswick 1st Mt. Stg. Bds., 1934	100	122
4	Do. Perp. Cons. Deb. Stk.	100	116
—	N. Zealand Mid., Ld., 5 p.c. 1st Mt. Debs...........	100	35
6	Ontario & Queb. Cap. Stk.	$100	156½
5	Do. Perm. Deb. Stk......	100	147½
—	Qu'Appelle, L. Lake & Sask. 6 p.c. 1 Mt. Bds. Red.	100	45½
5	Queb. & L. S. John, 1st Mt. Bds., 1909	100	25½
5	Quebec Cent., Prior Ln. Bds., 1908	100	107
1½	Do. 5 p.c. Inc. Bds.	100	41
4	St. Lawr. & Ott. Stl. 1st Mt.	100	113
4	Shuswap & Okan., 1st Mt. Deb. Bds., 1915	100	72½
5	Temiscouata, 5 p.c. Stl. 1st Deb. Bds., Red.........	100	9½
5	Do. (S. Franc. Brch.) 5 p.c. Stl. 1 Mt. Db. Bds., 1910	100	12½
4	Toronto, Grey & B. 1st Mt.	100	113
1/2½	Well. & Mana. £5 Shs. ..	1	1
5	Do. Debs., 1908........	100	110
5	Do. 2nd Debs., 1908....	100	109
5	Do. 3rd do., 1908	100	108
6	Atlnn. & St. Law. Shs., 6 p.c.	100	167
5	Gd. Trunk Mt. Bds., 1934	100	116½
5	Michigan Air Line, 5 p.c. 1st Mt. Bds., 1902......	100	104
4	Minneap., S. P. & Slt. Ste. Mar, 1st M. Bds., 1938	$1000	100

AMERICAN RAILROAD STOCKS AND SHARES.

Last Div.	Name.	Paid.	Price.
6/	Alab. Gt. Sthn. A 6 p.c. Pref.	10*l.*	9
—	Do. do "B" Ord. ..	10*l.*	2
—	Alabma. N. Orl.-Tex. &c., "A" Pref.	10*l.*	½
—	Do. "B" Def.	10*l.*	¼
4½	Atlant. First Lsd. Ls. Rtl. Trust..................	Stk.	102
$2	Baltimore & Ohio Com. ..	$100	18
—	Baltimore Ohio S.W. Pref.	$100	7
—	Chesap. & Ohio Com.	$100	24
—	Chic. Gt. West. 5 p.c. Pref. Stock "A"	$100	35½
—	Do. do. Scrip. In.......	—	32½
8/3	Do. 4 p.c. Deb. Stk.......	$100	71½
4	Do. Interest in Scrip	$100	67½
$4	Chic. Junc. Rl. & Un. Stk. Yds. Com.	$100	119½
$1½	Do. 6 p.c. Cum. Pref.	$100	118½
$3½	Chic. Mil. & St. P. Pref...	$100	150
7	Cleve. & Pittsburgh	$10.	86½
$1½	Clev., Cincin, Chic., & St. Louis Com.	$100	—
—	Erie 4 p.c. Non-Cum. 1st Pf.	—	43½
—	Do. 4 p.c. do. 2nd Pf.	—	22
—	Gt. Northern Pref.	$100	155
$2½	Illinois Cen. Lsd. Lines ..	$100	99
—	Kansas City, Pitts & G. ..	$100	24
$3	L. Shore & Mich. Sth. C.	$100	197½
—	Mex. Cen. Ltd. Com.	$100	6
—	Miss. Kan. & Tex. Pref...	$100	41½
2½	N.Y., Pen. & O. 1st Mt. Tst. Ltd., Ord.	—	50
4	Do. 1st Mort. Deb. Stk. ..	$100	93½
2	North Pennsylvania	$50	—
—	Northn. Pacific, Com.....	$100	27½
1½	Pitts. F. Wayne & Chic...	$100	176
—	Reading 1st Pref.	$50	26
—	Do. 2nd Pref.	$50	14
—	S. Louis & S. Fran. Com.	$100	7½
—	Do. 2nd Pref.	$100	27
6	St. Louis Bridge 1st Pref..	$100	107
3	Do. 2nd Pref.	$100	50
6	Tunnel Rail. of St. Louis	$100	107
$1½	St. Paul, Min. and Man...	$100	137½
—	Southern, Com.	$100	9½
—	Wabash, Common........	$100	7½

AMERICAN RAILROAD BONDS. CURRENCY.

Last Div.	Name.	Price.
7	Albany & Susq. 1 Con. Mrt. 1906	122½
7	Allegheny Val. 1 Mt. 1910	127½
5	Burling., Cedar Rap. & N. 1 Mt. 1906	109½
5	Canada Southern 1 Mt. 1908	111
5	Chic. & N. West. Sk. Fd. Db. 1933	120½
5	Do. Deb. Coupon 1921	115½
6	Chicago & Tomah 1905	112½
5	Chic. Burl. & Q. Skg. Fd. 1901	102½
4	Do. Nebraska Ext....... —	102
6	Chic., Mil., & S. Pl., 1 Mt. S.W. Div............... 1909	117½
7	Do. (S. Paul Div.) 1 Mt. 1902	132½
5	Do. (La Cross & D. 1919	112½
7	Do. 1 Mt. (Hast. & Dak.) 1910	132
5	Do. Chic. & Mis. Riv. 1 Mt. 1926	112½
5	Chic., Rock Is. and Pac. 1 Mt. Ext. 1934	108
6	Det., G. Haven & Mil. Equip 1918	110
6	Do. do. Cons. Mt. 1918	104½
6	Ill. Cent., 1 Mt., Chic. & S. 1898	—
7	Indianap. & Vin., 1 Mt. .. 1908	125
6	Do. do. 2 Mt. .. 1900	104½
6	Lehigh Val., Cons. Mt..... 1923	112½
—	Mexic. Cent., Ln. 2 Cons. Inc. —	7
7	N.Y. Cent. & H.R. Mt. Bonds 1903	119½
5	Do. Deb. 1904	109½
6	Penns. Cons. S. F M. 1905	119½
4	West Shore, 1 Mt. 2361	110

DITTO—GOLD.

Last Div.	Name.	Price.
6	Alabama Gt. Sthn. 1 Mt. .. 1908	112
5	Do. Mid. 1 1928	96
4	Allegheny Val. Gen. Mt. .. 1942	108
4	Atch., Top., & S. Fé Gn. Mt. 1995	96
3	Do. Adj. Mt.............. 1995	65
5	Do. Equipt. Tmst. ...... —	104½
5	Atlantic & Dan. 1 Mt....... 1950	94½
5	Baltimore & Ohio........... 1925	100
5	Do. Speyer's Tst. Recpts. 1925	100
5	Do. Cons. Mt. 1988	104
4½	Do. 4½ p.c. 1 Mt. Term. 1934	85
4½	Do. Brown Shipley's Dep. Cts. —	85
5	Balt. Belt 5 p.c. 1 Mort..... 1990	90
4½	Balt. & Ohio S.W. 1 Mt. .. 1990	105
4½	Do. 4½ p.c. 1 Cons. Mt. 1893 1993	81
—	Do. Inc. Mt. 5 p.c. Cl. A —	31
—	Do. do. Cl. B —	11
5	Balt. & Ohio S.W. Term 5 p.c. 1942	99½
6	Balt. & Ptmac (Mn. L.) 1 Mt. 1911	127½
6	Do. do. (Tunnel) 1 Mt. 1911	126
4	Beech Creek 1 Mt. 1936	109
5	Do 2 Mort. 1936	116
4	Carthage & Adiron. 1 Mt... 1981	109

American Railroad Bonds—Gold (*continued*) :—

Last Div.	Name.	Price.
5	Cent. of Georgia 1 Mort. .. 1945	117½
5	Do. Cons. Mt. 1945	92½
5	Cent. of N. Jrsy. Gn. Mt... 1987	118
6	Central Pacific, 1 Mort. 1898	102½
6	Do. Speyer's Certs. ...... —	106
5	Do. Land Grant 1900	102
5	Chesap. & Ohio 1st Cons. Mt. 1939	119
4½	Do. Gen. Mt............. 1992	84
6	Chic. & W. Ind. Gen. Mt. Skg. Fd. 1932	120
5	Chic. Mil. & St. Pl. (Chic. & L. Sup.) 1 Mt. 1921	114½
5	Do. Chic. & Pac. W. 1921	119½
5	Do. Wisc. & Minn. 1 Mt. 1921	114½
5	Do. Terminal Mt. 1914	114½
4	Do. General Mt. 1989	108
5	Chic. St. L. & N. Orleans.. 1951	122½
4	Do. 1 Mort. (Memphis) .. 1951	105½
4	Clevel, Cin., Chic. & St. L. 1 Mt. (Cairo) 1939	90
4	Do. 1 Mt. (Cinc., Wab., & Mich.) 1991	98
4	Do. 1 Col. Tst. Mt. (S. Louis) 1990	98½
4	Do General Mt. 1993	84
4½	Clevel. & Mar. Mt. 1935	112
4½	Clevel. & Pittsburgh 1942	122½
4½	Do. Series B. 1942	124½
—	Colorado Mid. 1 Mt. 1936	63
—	Do. Bdhrs.' Comm. Certs. —	68
4	Dnvr. & R. Gde. 1 Cons. Mt. 1936	97
5	Do. Imp. Mort.......... 1928	95
4	Detroit & Mack. 1 Lien 1995	92½
5	E. Tennes., Virg., & Grgia. Cons. Mt. 1956	114½
5	Elmira, Cort., & Nthn. Mt. 1914	99½
4	Erie 1 Cons. Mt. Pr. Ln. .. 1996	95½
3	Do. Gen. Lien 1996	76
6	Galvest., Harrisb., &c., 1 Mt.	107½
5	Georgia, Car. & N. 1 Mt. .. 1929	96
4½	Gd Rpds & Inda. Ex. 1 Mt. 1941	112½
5	Do. 1 Mt. (Muskegon) .. 1926	39½
3½	Illinois Cent. 1 Mt. 1951	104½
4	Do. 1952	107
4	Do. Cairo Bdge. .. 1950	103
4	Do. 1953	105
4	Do. General Mort. .. 1904	102½
—	Kans. City, Pitts. & G. 1 M. 1923	83
3½	L. Shore & Mich. Southern 1997	109
4½	Lehigh Val. N.Y. 1 Mt..... 1940	107
5	Lehigh Val. Term. 1 Mt. .. 1941	112½
5	Long Island 1931	122½
5	Do. Deb........... 1934	102
5	Do. (N. Shore Bch.) 1 Cons. Mt. 1932	96
6	Louisville & Nash. G. Mt.. 1930	122
6	Do. 2 Mt. Sk. Fd. (S. & N. Alabama.......... 1910	168
6	Do. 1 Mt. N. Orl. & Mb. 1930	122½
5	Do. 1 Mt. Coll. Tst. ... 1931	109
4	Do. Unified 1940	93
4½	Do. Mobile & Montgy. 1 Mt. 1945	105½
4	Manhattan Cons. Mt. 1990	100
4	Mexican Cent. Cons. Mt. .. 1911	69½
—	Do. 1 Cons. Inc, ...	17
6	Mexican Nat. 1 Mt.......... 1927	108
3	Do. 2 Mt. 6 p.c. Inc. A 1917	58
—	Do. do. B.. 1917	10
3	Do. Matheson's Certs.....	—
3	Michig. Cnt. (Battle Ck. & S.) 1 Mt. 1989	88
6	Minneap. & S. L. 1 Mt. Pacific Ext. 1921	120½
5	Do. 1 Consold. 1934	110
4	Minne., Slt. S. M. & A. 1 Mt. 1926	101
5	Minneapolis Westn. 1 Mt... 1911	105½
4	Miss. Kans. & Tex. 1 Mt... 1990	93
4	Do. 2 do. 1990	65
4	Mobile & Birm. Mt. Inc.... 1945	33
5	Do. P. Lien.............. 1945	88
4	Mohawk & Mal. 1 Mt...... 1991	108
5	Montana Cent. 1 Mt....... 1937	111½
5	Nashv., Chattan., & S. L. 1 Cons. Mt................. 1928	104½
5	Nash., Flor., & Shff. Mt... 1937	97
4	N. Y. & Putnam 1 Cons. Mt. 1993	110
5	N. Y., Brooklyn, & Man. B. 1 Cons. Mt.............. 1935	110
4	N. Y. Cent. & Hud. R. Deb. Certs. 1890 1905	107
4	Do. Ext. Debt. Certs.... 1905	107
7	N. Y., L. Erie, & W. 1 Cons. Mt. (Erie) 1920	146
7	Do. 1 Con. Mt. Fd. Coup. 1920	143
5	N. Y., Onto., & W. Cons. 1 Mt........................ 1939	110
4	Do. 4 p.c. Refund. Mt.. 1992	100
5	N. Y. & Rockaway B. 1 Mt. 1927	102½
6	Norfolk & West. Gn. Mt.... 1931	128
6	Do. Imp. & Ext......... 1934	120
4	Do. 1 Cons. Mt........ —	86
6	N. Pacific Gn. 1 Mt. Ld. Gt. 1921	122
4	Do. P. Ln. Rl. & Ld. Gt. —	100
3	Do. Gn. Ln. Rl. & Ld. Gt. —	65
5	Oregon & Calif. 1 Mt....... 1927	83
5	Oregon Rl. & Nav. Col. Tst. —	—
—	Oreg. Sh. Line & Utah Col. Trst. 5 p.c. G. Bonds 1919	50
6	Panama Skg. Fd. Subsidy.. 1910	105½
4½	Pennsylvania Rlrd. 1913	115½
4	Do. Equip. Tst. Ser. A.. 1914	104
4	Do. Cons. Mt............ 1943	115
4½	Penna. Company 1st Mort. 1921	116½
5	Perkiomen 1 Mrt., 2nd ser.. 1918	91½
4½	{ Pitts., C., C., & St. Ls. Con. Mt. G. B., Ser. A } 1940-2	115
4	Do. Cons. Mort., Ser. D.. 1945	105
6	Pittsbgh., Cle., & Toledo .. 1922	105½
4	Reading, Phil., & R. Genl. 1997	89½
5	Richmond & Dan. Equip. .. 1909	93½
5	Rio Grande Junc. 1st Mort. 1936	94
4	Rio Grande West 1st Tst. Mt. 1939	86
6	St. Joseph & Gd. Island .. 1925	—
7	S. Louis Bridge 1st Mort [illegible]	[illegible]

American Railroad Bonds (*continued*) :

Last Div.	Name.	Price
5	S. Louis Mchts. Bdge. Term. 1st Mort.................. 1930	104½
4	S. Louis S. West 1st Mort.. 1989	77½
—	Do. 4 p.c. 2nd Mort. Inc. 1989	30
—	S. Louis Term. Cupples Sta. & Prop. 1st. Mrt. 4½ p.c. 1902-17	102
4½	St. Paul, Minn., & Manit. 1933	110
6	Do. do. 1933	127½
6	Shamokin, Sunbury, &c. 2 Mt. 1925	107
5	S. & N. Alabama Cons. Mt. 1936	98½
5	Southern 1 Cons. Coup. 1994	97
4	Do. E. Tennes Reorg. Lien .. 1938	98½
6	S. Pacific of Cal. 1 Mt.. 1905-12	114
4½	Trml. Assn. of S. Louis 1 Mt. 1939	113½
5	Do. 1 Cons. Mt.......... 1944	109
5	Texas & Pac. 1 Mt.......... 2000	103½
—	Do. 5 p.c. 2 Mt. Income 2000	35½
5	Toledo & Ohio Cent. 1 Mt. West. Div. 1935	105½
4½	Toledo., Walhon., Val., & Ohio 1 Mt. 1931-3	111½
6	Union Pacific 1 Mt. 1896-9	102½
5	Do. Coll. Trust.	—
—	Union Pac., Linc., & Color. 1 Mt. 1918	—
4	United N. Jersey Gen. Mt... 1944	119½
6	Vicksbrg., Shrevept., & Pac. Pr. Ln. Mt. 1915	102½
5	Wabash 1 Mt. 1939	112
4	Wn. Pennsylvania Mt. 1928	109½
5	W. Virga. & Pttsbg. 1 Mt. 1990	87
5	Wheeling & L. Erie 1 Mt. (Wheelg. Div.) 5 p.c. 1928	90½
5	Do. Extd. Imp. Mt 1930	—
—	Do. do. Brown Shipley's Cts..	—
5	Willmar & Sioux Falls 1 Mt. 1938	111

STERLING.

Last Div.	Name.	Price
6	Alabama Gt. Sthn. Deb..... 1906	104½
5	Do. Gen. Mort. .. 1927-8	100
5	Alabama, N. Orl., Tex. & Pac. 5 p.c. "A" Dbs... 1910-40	99
55/	Do. do. "B" do. 1910-40	51
—	Do. do. "C" do.	19
—	Allegheny Valley 1910	136
4	Atlantic 1st Leased Line Perp...	98
6	Baltimore and Ohio 1902	109
6	Do. do. 1910	118
5	Do. do. 1877........	97½
—	Do. Morgan's Certs. ..	97½
4½	Do. do. 1933	86
6	Chicago & Alton Cons. Mt. 1903	111
5	Chic. St. Paul & Kan. City Priority	105
6	Eastn. of Massachusetts 1906	117½
5	Illinois Cent. Skg. Fd.	105
5	Do. 1905	108
3½	Do. 1950	100½
4	Do. 1 Mt. 1951	114
3	Do. 1 Mt. 1951	94
6	Louisville & Nash., M. C. & L. Div., 1 Mt. 1902	104½
7	Do. 1 Mt. (Memphis & O.) 1901	111
47/4	Mexican Nat. "A" Certs. 5 p.c. Non. cum.	47
—	Do. "B" Certs.	10
6	N.Y. & Canada 1 Mt. 1904	111½
6	N. York Cent. & H.R. Mort. 1903	112
4½	N. York, Penns., & Ohio Pr. Ln. Extd. 1935	—
5	Do. Equip. Tst.	103½
5	Do. 5 p.c. Equip. Tst. (1890)	103½
6	Nrthn. Cent. Cons. Gen. Mt. ..	106
6	Pennsylvania Gen. Mt. 1910	129
6	Do. Cons. Skg. Fd. Mt. 1905	117
3½	Do. Cons. Mt.......... 1945	106
6	Phil. & Erie Cons. Mort .. 1920	134½
6	Phil. & Reading Gen. Cons. Mort. 1911	127
6	Pittsbg. & Connells. Cons. 1926	114
—	Do. Morgan's Certs....	114
4	St. Paul., Min., & Manitoba (Pac. Extn.) 1940	99
6	S. & N. Alabama 1903	107½
6	Union Pacific, Omaha Bridge 1896	—
6	Un. N. Jersey & C. Gen. Mt. 1901	112½

FOREIGN RAILWAYS.

Last Div.	Name.	Paid.	Price.
4/	Alagoas, Ld., Shs.	20	6
5	Do. Deb. Stk., Red. ..	100	54½
6	Antofagasta, Ltd., Stk. ..	100	79
4	Do. Perp. Deb. Stk. ..	100	94
—	Arauco, Ld., Ord. Shs. ..	10	½
—	Do. 10 p.c. Cum. Pref.	10	1½
20/	Argentine Gt. W., Ld.,	20	15½
20/	Do. 5 p.c. Cum. Pref. Shs.	20	20½
4	Do. 1 Deb. Stk.	100	105
1/0/0	Argentine N.E., Ltd., 6 p.c. Cum. Pref. Stk. ..	100	12
—	Do. 5 p.c. Deb. Stk., Red.	100	34½
2/	Arica and Tacna Shs. ..	20	1½
10/	Bahia & San Fcisco., Ld.,	20	11½
6/	Do. Timbo. Bch. Shs.	20	5½
12/	Bahia, Blanca, & N.W. Ln. Prf. Cum. 6 p.c. ..	100	60½
4	Do. 4 p.c. 1 Deb. Stk., Red.	100	96
6	Barranquilla R. & P., Ld., [illegible] Deb. Stk. [illegible]	100	94

Foreign Railways (*continued*) :—

Last Div.	Name.	Paid.	Price.
3/	Bilbao Riv. & Cantabn., Ltd., Ord.	3	6
—	Bolivar, Ltd., Shs.	10	1¾
6	Do. 6 p.c. Deb. Stk.	100	93½
—	Brazil Gt. Southn. Ltd., 7 p.c. Cum. Pref.	20	1¾
6	Do. Perm. Deb. Stk	100	47½
6½	B. Ayres Gt. Southn., Ld., Ord. Stk.	100	157
5	Do. Pref. Stk.	100	140
4	Do. Deb. Stk.	100	117½
30/	B. Ayres & Ensen. Port., Ltd., Ord. Stk.	100	64
5	Do. Cum. 1 Pref. Stk.	100	122
6/0/0	Do. 6p.c.Con. Pref.Stk.	100	104
4	Do. Deb. Stk., Irred.	100	111
10⅛	B. Ayres Northern, Ltd., Ord. Stk.	100	265
12½	Do. Pref. Stk.	100	320
5	Do. 5 p.c. Mt. Deb.Stk., Red.	100	113
3/15/0	B. Ayres & Pac., Ld., 7 p.c. 1 Pref. Stk. (Cum.)	100	104
4	Do. 1 Deb. Stk.	100	105
5/5/0	Do. 4½ p.c. 2 Deb. Stk.	100	94
1	B Ayres & Rosario, Ltd., Ord. Stk.	100	76½
—	Do. New, £20 Shs.	20	22½
7/	Do. 7 p.c. Pref. Sh.	10	17½
7/	Do. Sunchales Ext.	10	15½
4	Do. Deb. Stk., Red.	100	109
12/	B. Ayres & Val. Trans., Ltd., 7 p.c. Cum. Pref.	20	7
4	Do. 4 p.c. "A" Deb. Stk., Red.	100	72
—	Do. 6 p.c. "B" D. b. Stk., Red.	100	48
6/	B. Ayres Westn. Ld. Ord.	10	11¾
3/	Do. Def. Shs.	10	7½
5	Do. 5 p.c. Pref.	10	13½
4	Do. Deb. Stk	100	111½
6	Cent. Arg. Deb.Sk. Rd.	100	161½
4	Do. Deb. Stk, Rd	100	112
6	Cent. Bahia L. Ord. Stk.	100	51½
6	Do. Deb. Stk., 1934	100	74½
5	Do. Deb. Stk., 1937	100	58
1/6	Cent. Uguy. East. Ext. L. Shs.	10	6½
5	Do. Perm. Stk.	100	109
3/	Do. Nthn. Ext. L. Sh.	10	4¾
5	Do. Perm. Deb. Stk.	100	106
3	Do. of Montev. Ltd., Ord. Stk	100	88
6	Do. Perm. Deb. Stk	100	143
10/	Conde d'Eu, Ltd. Ord.	20	7½
—	Cordba & Rosar., Ltd., 6 p.c. Pref. Shs.	100	50
4	Do. 1 Deb. Stk.	100	93½
75/	Do. 6 p.c. Deb. Stk.	100	91
—	Cordba Cent., Ltd., 5 p.c Cu. 1 Pref. Stk	100	93
—	Do. 5 p.c. Non-Cum. 2 Pref. Stk.	100	54
5	Do. Deb. Stk	100	125
—	Costa Rica, Ltd., Shs.	10	3½
8/	Dna. Thrsa. Chris., Ltd., 7 p.c. Pref. Shs.	20	4½
20/	E. Argentine, Ltd.	100	45
6	Do. Deb. Stk	100	108
2/1	Egyptn. Dlta. Lgt. Rys. Ltd., £10 Pref. Shs.	8	8½
—	Entre Rios, L., Ord. Shs.	5	1
—	Do. Cu. 5 p.c. Pref.	5	3½
6/	Gt. Westn. Brazil, Ltd.	20	11½
6	Do. Perm. Deb. Stk	100	99½
6	Do. Extn. Deb. Stk.	100	70½
—	Int.-Oceanic Mex., Ltd. 7 p.c. Pref.	10	1¾
4	Do. Deb. Stk	100	89
42/6	Do. 7 p.c. "A" Deb. Sk.	100	70
—	Do. 7 p.c. "B" Deb. Sk.	100	36
5/	La Guaira & Carac.	10	7
5	Do. 5 p.c. Deb. Sk. Red.	100	102
8/4	Lembg.-Czern.-Jassy	30	25
1/	Lima, Ltd.	20	2½
—	Manila Ltd. 7 p.c. Cu. Pf.	10	⅛
20/6½	Mexican 2nd Pref. 6 p.c.	100	33
6	Do. Perp. Deb. Stk.	100	146
1/0/0	Mexican Sthrn., Ld., Ord	100	27
—	Do. 4 p.c. 1 Db.Stk. Rd	100	85
—	Do. 4 p.c. 2 do.	100	63
—	Mid. Urgy., Ltd.	100	20
5	Do. Deb. Stk.	100	63
12/	Minas & Rio, Ltd.	20	12½
5/2	Namur & Liege	20	12½
11/6	Do. Pref.	20	20
4/	Natal & Na. Cruz, Ld., 7 p.c. Cum Pref.	20	8½
32/0	Nitrate Ltd., Ord.	10	5½
3½	Great... Do. 7 p.c. Pr. Con. Or.	10	4
4	Great ... Def. Conv. Ord.	10	⅜
—	Do. Urgy., Ltd., Ord.	10	15
—	Do. 7 p.c. Pref.	10	15½
8	Highland ... gentine Ld., 7		
4	Isle of Wight, ...	10	3½
4	Do. Defd. ... Deb. Stk.	100	114
—	Lancs. Derbys. and ...	100	94
8½	L. Brighton and S. C ... p.c.		
37/11½	Do. New 70 p.c. pd.	100	17
6	Do. Prefd. Ord.	100	7½
10/	Do. Contgt. Rights Certs.	100	70½
5½	Lond. and S. Western Ord.	235	16½
4	Do. Preferred	138	
6½	Lond., Tilb., and Southend	132½	11
—	Mersey, £20 shares	1	
—	Metropolitan, New Ord.	131	
2½	Do. Surplus Lands	97	4
4	North Cornwall, 4 p.c. Pref.	106½	4
7/6	Do. Deferred	27½	3
7½	North London	231½	3
	North Staffordshire	133	3½

Foreign Railways (*continued*) :—

Last Div.	Name.	Paid.	Price.
5/	Royal Sardinian Pref.	10	12½
5/	Sambre & Meuse	20	19
5/6	Do. Pref.	10	12½
28/	San Paulo Ld.	20	37
2/9½	Do. New Ord. £10 sh.	4	8½
9/	Do. 5 p.c. Non.Cm.Pref.	10	12½
5½	Do. Deb. Stk.	100	137
5	Do. 5 p.c. Deb. Stk.	100	128
—	S. Fé & Cordova, Gt. Sthn., Ld., Shares	100	57
6	Do. Perp. Deb. Stk.	100	125
3/2½	S. Austrian	20	7½
10/	Sthn. Braz. R. Gde. do Sul, Ld.	20	8½
6	Do. 6 p.c. Deb. Stk.	100	77
4	Swedish Centl., Ld., 4 p.c. Deb. Stk.	100	109
5	Do. Pref.	100	100
1/9	Taltal, Ld.	5	2½
—	Uruguay Nthn., Ld. 7 p.c. Pfd. Stk.	100	8
3½	Do. 5 p.c. Deb. Stk.	100	30
—	Villa Maria & Rufino, Ld., 6 p.c. Pref. Shs.	100	20
4	Do. 4 p.c. 1 Deb. Stk.	100	75
6/0/0	Do. 6 p.c. 2 Deb. Stk.	100	49
5/0	West Flanders	8½	22
5/6	Do. 5½ p.c. Pref.	10	18
3/	Wstn. of Havana, Ld.	10	5

FOREIGN RAILWAY OBLIGATIONS

Per Cent.	Name.	Price.
6	Alagoas Ld., 6 p.c. Deb., Rd.	88½
—	Alcoy & Gandia, Ld., 5 p.c. Debs., Red.	25
5	Arauco., Ld., 5 p.c. 1st Mt., Rd.	67½
—	Do. 6 p.c. Mt. Deb., Rd.	47½
6	Brazil G. Sthn., L., Mt. Dbs., Rd.	80½
6	Do. Mt. Dbs. 1893, Rd.	41½
5½	Campos & Caran. Dbs., Rd.	77
6	Central Bahia, L., Dbs., Rd.	90½
5½	Conde d'Eu, L., Dbs., Rd.	78
6	Costa Rica, L., 1st Mt. Dbs., Rd.	109
6	Do. 2nd Dbs., Rd.	94
5	Do. Prior Mt. Db., Rd.	107
6	Cucuta Mt. Dbs., Rd.	106
5½	Donna Thrsa. Cris., L., Dbs., Rd.	75
3	Eastn. of France, £20 Dbs., Rd.	19½
4	Egyptn. Delta Light, L., Db., Rd.	100
—	Espito. Santo & Cara. 5 p.c. Stl. Dbs., Rd.	38
	Gd. Russian Nic., Rd.	102
4	Inter-Oceanic Mex., L., 5 p.c. Pr. Ln. Dbs., Rd.	104
3	Ital. 3 p.c. Bds. A & B, Rd	57½
—	Ituana 6 p.c. Debs., 1918	74
—	Leopoldina, 6 p.c. Dbs. £50 Bds.	26
—	Do. do. Comms. Cert.	26
—	Do. 5 p.c. Stg. Dbs. (1888), Rd.	36
—	Do. do. Comm. Certs.	36
—	Do. 5 p.c. Stg. Dbs. (1890), Rd.	26
—	Do. do. Comms. Certs.	26
—	Macahé & Cam. 5 p.c. Dbs., Rd.	36
—	Do. do. Comms. Certs.	36
-	Do. (Cantagallo), 5 p.c., Red.	36
—	Do. do. Comm. Certs.	36
—	Manila Ltd., 6 p.c. Deb., Red.	24
6	Do. Prior Lien Mt., Rd.	106
6	Do. Series "B," Rd.	79
7	Matanzas & Sab., Rd.	101½
6	Minas & Rio, L., 6 p.c. Dbs., Rd.	103
5	Mogyana 5 p.c. Deb. Bds., Rd.	103
5	Moscow-Jaros., Rd.	107½
5½	Natal & Na. Cruz Ltd., 5½ p.c. Debs., Red.	83½
5	Nitrate, Ltd. Mt. Bds., Red.	87
3	Nthn. France. Red.	19½
4	N. of S. Af. Rep. (Trnsvl.) Gu. Bds. Red.	98
3	Nthn. of Spain £20 Pri. Obs. Red.	9
6	Ottmn. (Smy to A.) (Kujk) Asnt. Debs., Red.	109
6	Ottmn. (Seraik.) Asg. Debs. Red.	109
6	Ottmn. (Seraik) Non-Asg. D., Rd	109
5	Ottmn. Kuyjk. Ext. Red.	109
5	Ottmn. Serkeuy. Ext. Red.	104
5	Ottmn Tireh Ext. 1910	99
5	Ottmn. Debs. 1886, Red.	98
5	Do. 1888, Red. 1935	99
5	Do. 1893, Red. 1935	99
5	Ottmn. of Anla. Debs., Rd.	93
5	Do. Ser. II.	89
4	Ottomn. Smyr. & Cas. Ext Bds., Red.	83½
3	Paris, Lyon & Medit. (old sys. £20), Red.	19
3	Paris, Lyon & Medit. (new sys., £20), Red.	19½
50/	Piræus, At. & Pelp., 6 p.c. 1st Mt. Bds., Red.	88½
3	Do. 5 p.c. Mt. Bds., Red.	61½
4	Pretoria-Pietbg., Ltd., Red.	93
-	Puerto Cab. & Val., Ltd., 1st Mt. Debs., Red.	96
-	Rio de Jano. & Nthn., Ltd., 6 p.c. £100 Deb., Red.	26
	Rio de Jano. (Gr. Para.), 5 p.c. 1st Mt. St. £100 Debs., Red.	26
	... Sardinian ... Rd. Com.	12

Foreign Rly. Obligations (*continued*) :—

Per Cent.	Name.	Price.
5	Ryl. Trns.-Afric. 5 p.c. 1st Mt. £100 Bds., Red.	61
7	Sagua La Grande, B pRd.	98
4	Sa. Fe & Cor. G.S., Ld. Pr Ln. Bds.	103
5	Sa. Fe, 5 p.c. 2nd Reg. Dbs.	81
3	South Austrian, £20 Red.	15½
3	South Austrian, (Ser X.)	15½
3	South Italian £20 Obs. (Ser. A to G), Red.	12½
3½	S. W. of Venez. (Barq.), Ltd., 7 p.c. 1st Mt. £100 Debs.	57½
5	Taltal, Ltd., 5 p.c. 1st Ch. Debs., Red.	99
5	Utd. Rwys. Havana, Red.	95
3	Wtrn. of France, £20 Red.	19½
6	Wrn. B. Ayres St. Mt. Debs., 1902	111
6	Wrn. B. Ayres, Reg. Cert.	109
5	Do. Mt. Bds.	122
6	Wtrn. of Havna., Ld, Mt. Dbs., Rd.	102
7	Wrn. Ry. San Paulo Red.	101
—	Wrn. Santa Fé, 7 p.c. Red.	43
4/7	Zafra & Huelva, 3 p.c. Red.	3

BANKS.

Div.	Name.	Paid.	Price.
1/9½	Agra, Ltd.	6	3½
4/2½	Anglo-Argentine, Ltd., £7	7	5½
8½ fl.	Anglo-Austrian	120 fl	14
6/	Anglo-Californian, Ltd., £20 Shares	10	11½
4/	Anglo-Egyptian, Ltd., £15	5	6
3/6	Anglo-Foreign Bkg., Ltd.	7	8
2/	Anglo-Italian, Ltd.	5	7½
7/6	Bk. of Africa, Ltd., £18½	6½	11
20/	Bk. of Australasia	40	56
10/	Bk. of Brit. Columbia	20	21½
25/	Bk. of Brit. N. America	50	66
7/6	Bk. of Egypt, Ltd., £25	12½	19
5/	Bk. of Mauritius, Ltd.	10	10
18/	Bk. of N. S. Wales	20	38½
4 p.c.	Bk. of N. Zland. Gua. Stk.	100	103
6/	Bk. of Roumania, £20 Shs.	6	7½
2/6	Tarapaca & Ldn., Ltd., £10	5	3½
—	Bque. Fse. de l'Afri. du S.	100 f	3½
f. 12.50	Bque. Internatle. de Paris	20	24
6/	Brit. Bk. of S. America, Ltd., £20 Shares	10	11
15/	Capital & Ctles., L., £50	10	39
16/	Chart. of India, &c.	20	31½
10/	City, Ltd., £40 Shares	10	20
18/	Colonial, £100 Shares	30	23
10/	Delhi and London, Ltd.	25	—
5/	German of London, Ltd.	10	10½
25/	Hong-Kong & Shanghai	28⅛	45
4/	Imperl. of Persia	6⅛	3½
10/	Imperl. Ottoman, £20 Sh.	10	12½
9/	Internatl. of Ldn., Ld., £20	15	12
10/	Ionian, Ltd.	25	15
12/	Lloyds, Ltd., £50 Shs.	8	30½
10/	Ldn. & Braziln. Ltd., £20	10	18
44/	Ldn. & County, Ltd., £80	20	102½
5/	Ldn. & Hanseatic, L., £20	10	11
22/6	Ldn. & Midland, L., £60	12½	53
8/9	Ldn. & Provin., Ltd., £10	5	22½
39/	Ldn. & Riv. Plate, L., £25	15	54
2/1½	Ldn. & San Fcisco, Ltd.	7	4½
28/	Ldn. & Sth. West., L., £50	20	70
26/	Ldn. & Westmins., L., £100	20	56
3/	Ldn. of Mex. & S. Amer., Ltd., £10 Shs.	6	5½
15/	Ldn. Joint Stk., L., £100	15	34
9/7	Ldn., Paris & Amer., L. £20	16	26
2/4½	Merchant Bkg., L., £9	4	2½
6/3	Metropn, Ltd., £50 Shs.	5	14
9/	National, Ltd., £50 Shs.	10	19½
4/5	Natl. of Mexico, $100 Shs.	$40	13
1/3	National of N. Z., L., £7½	2½	2½
3/	National S. Afric. Rep.	10	14½
18/10½	National Provcl. of Eng., Ltd., £75 Shs.	10½	50½
21/7½	Do. do. £60 Shs.	12	57½
6/6	North Eastn., Ltd., £20 Shs	6	14½
19/	Parr's, Ld., £100 Shs.	20	92½
12/6	Prov. of Ireland, L., £100	12½	28½
40/	Stand. of S. Afric., L., £100	25	68
12/6	Union of Australia, L., £75	25	29
4 p.c.	Do. do. Ins. Stk. Dep. 1900	100	103
15/6	Union of Ldn., Ltd., £100	15½	35½

BREWERIES AND DISTILLERIES

Div.	Name.	Paid.	Price.
4½	Albion Prp. 1 Mt. Db. Sk.	100	115
4	All Saints', L., Db.Sk.Rd.	100	99
6	Allsopp, Ltd.	100	165
6	Do. Cum. Pref.	100	161
4½	Do. Deb. Stk., Red.	100	117
3½	Do. Deb. Stk., Red.	100	103
4½	Alton & Co., L., Db., Rd	100	106
4½	Do. Mt. Bds., 1896	100	105
—	Arnold, Perrett, Ltd.	10	6
6	Do. Cum. Pref.	10	10

Breweries, &c. (*continued*) :—

Div.	Name.	Paid.	Price.
5½	Arrol, A., & Sons, L., Cum. Pref. Shs.	10	10½
4½	Do. 1 Mt. Db. Stk., Rd.	100	106
6	Backus, 1 Mt. Db., Red.	100	86½
4	Barclay, Perk., L., Cu. Pf.	10	11½
3½	Do. Mt. Db. Stk., Red.	100	111
—	Barnsley, Ltd.	10	11
6	Do. Cum. Pref.	10	13
1/	Barrett's, Ltd	2½	1½
1/3	Do. 5 p.c. Pref.	2½	2½
3/	Bartholomay, Ltd.	10	4
8	Do. Cum. Pref.	10	9
6	Do. Deb.	100	102½
5	Bass, Ratcliff, Ltd., Cum. Pref. Stk.	100	147½
4½	Do. Mt. Db. Stk., Rd.	100	126
4	Bell, John, Ltd., 1 Mt. Deb. Stk., Red.	100	102
2/6	Benskin's, L., Cum. Pref.	5	—
4½	Do. 1 Mt. Db. Stk Red.	100	—
4½	Do. "B" Deb. Sk, Rd.	100	—
7/	Bentley's Yorks., Ltd.	10	11
6	Do. Cum. Pref.	10	12½
4½	Do. Mt. Debs., Red.	100	109
4½	Do. do. 1 92, Red.	100	109
—	Bieckert's, Ltd.	20	2
5	Do. Debs., Red.	100	57
—	Birmingham., td., 6 p. c. Cum. Pref.	5	2½
4½	Do. Mt. Debs., Red.	50	40½
5½	Boardman's, Ld., Cm. Pf.	10	8½
4½	Do., Perp. 1 Mt. Db. Sk.†	100	103½
4½	Brakspear, L., 1 D. Stk. Rd	100	109
4	Brandon's, L., 1 D. Stk. R.†	100	103½
17/	Bristol (Georges) Ltd.	10	47
6	Do. Cum. Pref.	10	13
5	Do. Mt. Db. Sk. 1888 Rd.	100	115½
—	Bristol United, Ltd.	10	36½
6	Do. Cum. Pref.	10	16½
4½	Do. Db. Sk. Rd.	100	126
5½	Buckley's, L., C. Pre-pref.	10	11
4½	Do. 1 Mt. Db. Stk. Rd.	100	106½
4	Bullard & Sns, L., D. Sk. R.	100	108
6	Bushell, Watk., L., C. Pf.	10	14
4½	Do. 1 Mt. Db. Sk. Rd.	100	112
5	Camden, Ltd., Cum. Pref.	10	11½
4½	Do. 1 Mt. Db. Sk. Rd.	100	109
5½	Cameron, Ltd., Cm. Prf.	10	13½
4½	Do. Mort Deb. Stk.	100	108
3½	Do. Perp Mt. Db. Sk.	100	100½
5	Cambell, J'stone, L., C. Pf.	5	8
4½	Do. 4½ p.c. 1 Mt. Db. Sk.	100	108
4	Campbell, Praed, L., Per. 1 Mort. Deb. Stk.	100	107
4	Cannon, L., Mt. Db. Stk.	100	109
4	Do. "B" Deb. Stk.	100	105
5	Castlemaine, L., 1 Mt. Db.	100	94
3½	Charrington, Ltd., Mort. Deb. Stk. Red.	100	107
2/	Cheltnhm. Orig., Ltd.	5	7
6	Do. Cum. Pref.	5	8
4	Do. Debs. Red.	100	107
—	Chicago, Ltd.	10	3½
6	Do. Debs.	100	87½
—	Cincinnati, Ltd.	10	½
8	Do. Cum. Pref.	10	1½
10/	City of Baltimore	10	4
16/	Do. 8 p.c. Cum. Pref	10	8
14/	City of Chicago, Ltd.	10	1½
8	Do. Cum. Pref.	10	6½
13	City of London, Ltd.	100	205½
5	Do. Cum. Pref.	100	138
4	Do. Mt. Deb. Stk., Rd.	100	112½
2/6	Colchester, Ltd.	5	5
7	Do. Pref.	5	7
4½	Do. Deb. Stk., Red.	100	110
5	Combe, Ltd., Cum. Pref.	10	14½
4	Do. Mt. Db. Stk, Rd.	100	112
3½	Do. Perp. Deb. Stk.	100	107
5	Comm'cial, L., D. Sk., Rd.	100	108½
5	Courage, L., Cm. Pref. Shs.	100	130½
4	Do. Irr. Mt. Deb. Stk.	100	130
3½	Do. Irr. "B" Mt. Db. Sk.	100	106
8	Daniell & Sons, Ltd.	10	6½
7	Do. Cum. Pref.	10	12
4½	Do. 1 Mt. Perp. Db. Sk.	100	108½
4½	Do. "B" Deb. Stk.	100	100
10d.	Dartford, Ltd.	5	4½
10d.	Do. Cum. Pref.	5	5½
4	Do. 1 Mt. Db. Sk. Rd	100	101
4	Davenport, Ld., 1 D. Stk.†	100	108½
10/	Denver United, Ltd.	10	3½
8	Do. Cum. Pref.	10	8½
6	Do. Debs.	100	98½
4½	Deuchar, L., 1 D. Sk., Rd.	100	108
2/	Distillers, Ltd.	10	24
4½	Do. Mt. Db. Stk., Rd.	100	115½
—	Dublin Distillers, Ltd.	5	1½
6/	Do. Cum. Pref.	5	4½
4½	Do. Irr. Deb. Stk.	100	—
5	Eadie, Ltd., Cum. Pref.	10	11½
4	Do. Irr. 1 Mt. Db. Sk.	100	108
10/	Edinbgh. Utd., Ltd.	10	13
6	Do. Cum. Prf.	10	13½
5	Do. 1 Mt. Dbs.†	100	110½
4	Eldridge, Pope, L. D. St. R.	100	109
3/	Emerald & Phœnix, Ltd.	10	1½
8	Do. Cum. Pref.	10	7
6	Empress Ltd., C. Pf.	10	11½
4½	Do. Mt. Deb. Stk.	100	106
10/	Farnham, Ltd.	10	15½
6	Do. Cum. Pref.	10	15
4	Fenwick, L., 1 D. Sk., Rd.	100	103
4	Flower & Sons, Irr. D. Sk.	100	111
4	Friary, L., 1 Db. Stk., Rd.†	100	103½
4	Do. 1 "A" Db. Sk., Rd	100	102
4½	Groves, L., 1 Db. Sk., Rd	100	110
24	Guinness, Ltd.	100	600
6	Do. Cum. Prf. Stk.	100	196½
5	Do. Deb. Stk., Red.	100	123
6	Hall's Oxford L., Cm. Pf.	5	5½
6/	Hancock, Ld., Cm. Pf. Ord.	10	14

Breweries, &c. (*continued*) :—

Div.	Name.	Paid.	Price.
6	Hancock, Ld., Cum. Pref.	10	14
4	Do. 1 Deb. Stk., Rd.	100	113
5	Hoare, Ltd. Cum. Pref.	10	13½
5	Do. "A" Cum. Pref.	10	12½
4	Do. Mt. Deb. Stk., Rd.	100	111
3½	Do. do. do. Rd.	100	104
4/6	Hodgson's, Ltd.	5	9½
5	Do. 1 Mt. Db., Red.	—	120½
4	Do. 2 Mt. Db., 1906	—	102
4½	Hopcraft & N., Ltd., 1 Mt. Deb. Stk., Red.	100	103
5	Huggins, Ltd., Cm. Prf.	10	12½
4½	Do. 1st D. Stk. Rd.	100	113
4½	Do. "B" Db. Stk. Rd.	100	111
8/	Hull, Ltd.	10	17
7	Do. Cum. Pref.	10	15
4½	Ind, Coope, L., D.Sk., Rd.	100	119
4	Do. "B" Mt. Db. Stk. Rd.	100	115
8/	Indianapolis, Ltd.	10	3½
8	Do. Cm. Prf.	10	9
5/	Jones, Frank, Ltd.	10	3½
7½	Do. Cum. Pref.	10	8
5	Do. 1st Mort. Debs.	100	94½
4/	J. Kenward & Ct., Ltd.	5	5½
4½	Kingsbury, L., 1 D.Sk., Rd	100	—
4	Lacon, L., D. Stk., Red.	100	110
4	Do. Irrd. "B" D. Sk.	100	107
4/	Lascelles, Ltd.	5	10½
6	Do. Cum. Pref.	5	7½
5	Leney, Ltd., Cum. Pref.	10	11½
4	Do. 1 Mt. Db. Stk. Rd.	100	104
17/	Lion, Ltd., £25 shares	17	50½
6/	Do. New £10 shares	6	17½
6	Do. Perp. Pref.	20	32
4	Do. B. Mt. Db. Sk. Rd.	100	110
4½	Lloyd & Y., Ltd., 1 Mt. Deb. Stk., Rd.	100	98½
4½	Locke & S., Ltd., Irr. 1st Mt. Deb. Stk.	100	100
4½	Lovibond, Ltd., 1st Mt. Deb. Stk., Rd.	100	102½
30/4	Lucas & Co., Ld., Deb. Stk.	100	107
8/	Manchester, Ltd.	10	18½
7	Do. Cum. Pref.	10	17½
5	Marston, J., L., Cm. Prf.	10	10½
4	Do. 1 Mt. Db. Sk., Rd.	100	101½
9/	Massey's Burnley, Ltd.	10	16
6	Do. Cum. Pref.	10	14½
4½	McCracken, Ltd., 1 Mt. Deb., 1908	100	62½
5	McEwan, Ltd., Cm. Pref.	10	15
5	Meux, Ltd., Cum. Pref.	10	14½
4	Do. Mt. Db. Stk. Red.	100	111
4½	Michell & A., Ltd., 1 Mt. Deb. Stk. Red	100	106
4½	Mile End Dist. Db. Sk. Rd.	100	108
—	Milwaukee & Chic., Ltd.	10	1½
4/	Do. Cum. Pref.	10	6½
4½	Michell, Toms, L., Db.	50	55
6	Morgan, Ltd., Cum. Pref	10	14½
10/	Nalder & Coll., Ltd.	10	32
6	Do. Cum. Pref.	10	16
4½	Do. Deb. Red.	100	113
3/	New Beeston, Ltd.	5	5
2/9	Do. Cum. Pref.	5	5
4	Do. Mt. Deb. Stk. Red.	100	97½
12/	Newcastle, Ltd.	10	20
6	Do. Cum. Pref.	10	15
5	Do. 1 Mt. Deb., 1911	100	110½
4	Do. "A" Deb. Stk. Red.	100	105
6/	New England, Ltd	10	5
8	Do. Cum. Pref.	10	9½
6	Do. Debs. Red	100	104½
4	New London, L., 1 D.Sk.	100	105
7/2	New Westminster, Ltd.	4	10½
2/4½	Do. Pref.	4	6½
—	New York, Ltd.	10	1
—	Do. 8 p.c. Cum. Pref.	10	4
6	Do. 1 Mt. Deb. Red.	100	80½
5	Noakes, Ld., Cum. Pref.	10	12
4	Do. 1 Mt. Db. Stk., Rd.	100	106
4½	Norfolk, L., "A" D.Sk. Rd	100	106
10/	Northampton, Ld.	10	16½
7	Do. Cum. Pref	10	15½
6	Do. Cum. Pref	10	13
5	Do. 1 Mt. Per. Db. Sk.	100	127
4	Nth. East., L., 1 D. Sk. Rd.	100	102
4½	N. Worcesters., L. Per. 1 Mort. Deb. Stock	100	89½
6	Nottingham, L., Cm. Prf.	10	11½
5	Do. 1 Mt. Deb. Stk., Red.	100	112
17/4	Do. "B" do. Red.	50	111½
6/	Ohlsson' Cape, Ld.	5	16½
7	Do. Cum. Pref.	5	8½
4½	Do. 2nd Cum. Pref.	5	5½
5	Do. Deb. Stk., Red.	100	114
4½	Oldfield, L., 1 Mt. Db. Stk.	100	105
6	Page & Overt., L., Cm. Prf.	10	13½
4½	Do. 1 Mt. Dbs., Red.	100	108
10/	Parker's Burslem, Ltd.	10	25½
6	Do. Cum. Pref.	10	15
4	Do. 1 Mt. Db. Stk., Red.	100	113
4	Persse, Ld., 1 Mt. Db. Rd.	100	95½
4	Phipps, L., Irr. 1 Db. Stk.	100	115
5	Plymouth, L., Min. Cu. Pf.	10	14
4½	Do. Mt. Deb. Stk., Red.	100	104½
4½	Pryor, Reid, L., 1 D.S., R.(†)	100	105½
5	Reid's, Ld., Cm. Pref. Stk.	100	137½
4	Do. Mt. Deb. Stk., Red.	100	111
3½	Do. "B" Mt. Db. Stk., Rd	100	103
5	Rhondda Val., L., Cu. Pf	10	11
4½	Do. 1 Mt. Deb. Stk., Rd.	100	109
5	Robinson, Ld., Cum. Pref.	10	11½
4½	Do. 1 Mt. Perp. Db. Stk.	100	112
4/	Rochdale, Ltd.	10	5½
4½	Do. 1 Mt. Deb. Stk.	100	96½
7	Royal, Brentford, Ltd.	10	19½
	Do. Cum. Pref.	10	14½
4½	Do. 1 Mt. Dbs. Red	100	112
6/	St. Louis, Ltd.	10	3½
8	Do. Cum. Pref.	10	8½
14/	St. Pauli, Ltd.	10	10
7	Do. Cum. Pref.	10	12½
4½	Salt (T.), L., 1 Db. Sk. Rd.	100	111

Breweries, &c. (*continued*) :—

Div.	Name.	Paid.	Price.
4½	Salt (T.), "B" Db. Stk. Red	100	108
—	San Francisco, Ltd.	10	½
—	Do. 8 p.c. Cum. Pref.	10	¼
4½	Savill Brs., L., D. Sk. Rd.	100	117
4½	Scarboro., Ltd., 1 Db. Stk.	100	103
4	Shaw (Hy.), Ltd., 1 Mt. Db. Stk., Red.	100	104
22/	Showell's, Ltd.	10	32½
7	Do. Cum. Pref.	10	17½
3/	Do. Gua. Shs.	5	7½
4½	Do. Mt. Db. Stk., Red.	100	—
4	Simonds, L., 1 D. Sk., Rd.	100	111
5½	Simson & McP., L., Cu. Pf.	10	9½
4½	Do. 1 Mt. Deb. Stk.	100	100
5/	Smith, Garrett, L., £20 Shs	10	15½
5	Do. Cum. Pref.	20	26
4½	Do. Mt. Db. Stk., Red.	100	—
5	Smith's, Tadcaster, L., C Pf	10	11½
4½	Do. Deb. Stk., Red.	100	112
4	Do. Deb. Stk., Red.	100	108
4½	Star, L., 1 M. Db. Stk., Rd.	100	104
4	Steward & P., L., 1 D. Sk.	100	113
9/	Strettons Derby, Ltd.	10	13
6	Do. Cum. Pref.	10	13
4	Do. Irr. 1 Mt. Db. Stk.	100	104½
4½	Strong, Romsey, L., 1 D.S.	100	115
5	Stroud, L., Db. Sk., Rd.	100	111½
4½	Tadcaster To'er, L., D.Sk.	100	113
8/	Tamplin, Ltd	10	22
6	Do. Cum. Pref.	100	15
4	Do. "A" Db. Sk., Rd.	20	107
6	Thorne, Ltd., Cum. Pref.	10	14½
4	Do. Deb. Stk., Red.	100	104½
15/	Threlfall, Ltd.	10	48
6	Do. Cum. Pref.	10	16½
5	Do. 1 Mt. Dbs., Red.	100	116
4	Tollemache, L., D. Sk. Rd.	100	105
4	Truman, Hanb., D. Sk., R.	100	110
3	Do. "B" Mt. Db. Sk., Rd.	100	95
10/	United States, Ltd.	10	9½
8	Do. Cum. Pref.	10	12
6	Do. 1 Mt. Deb.	100	107½
6/	Walker & H., Ld., Cm. Prf.	10	11½
4½	Do. 1 Mt. Deb. Stk., Red.	100	107
5	Walker, Peter, Ld. Cm. Prf.	10	14½
4	Do. 1 Mt. Dbs. Red.	100	111
4	Wallingford, L., D. Sk. Rd.	100	107
6	Watney, Ld., Cm. Prf. Sk.	100	170
5	Do. Mt. Db. Sk., Rd.	100	117½
4½	Do. "B" Mt. Db. Sk., Rd.	100	111
3½	Do. Mt. Db. Stk.	100	101
5	Watney, D., Ld., Cm. Prf.	10	12½
4½	Do. 1 Mt. Db. Stk.	100	108
5	Wenlock Ltd., Pref.	10	12½
4	Do. 1 Mt. Db. Sk., Rd.	100	108
5	West Cheshire, L., Cu. Pf.	10	10½
4	Do. Irred. 1 Mt. Db. Sk.	100	100
4½	Whitbread, L., Cu. Pf. Sh.	100	124½
4	Do. Db. Stk., Red.	100	112
3½	Do. "B" Db. Stk., Rd.	100	101
9/	Wolverhmpton & D. Ld.	10	16½
6	Do. Cum. Pref.	10	13½
4½	Do. 1 Mt. Dbs., Red.	100	108
5½	Worthington, Ld., Cm. Prf.	10	15½
5½	Do. Cum. "B" Pref.	10	13½
4½	Do. Mt. Db. Sk., Rd.	100	113
3½	Do. Irr. "B" Db. Stk.	100	104
10/	Yates's Castle, Ltd.	10	13½
5	Do. Cum. Pref.	10	11
5	Younger W., L., Cu. Pf. Sh.	100	137½

CANALS AND DOCKS.

Last Div.	Name.	Paid.	Price.
4	Birmingham Canal	100	145½
—	E. & W. India Dock	100	21½
4	Do. Deb. Stk.	100	110
50/	Do. Def. Deb. Stk.	100	89
3½	Do. 1st Mt. Certs.	100	110
4	Do. Mt. Bds. (1885)	—	100
40/	G. Junction Ord. Shs.	100	151½
6/	Do. do. Pref.	10	19
4½	King's Lynn Per. Db. Stk.	100	117½
2½	Leeds & Lpool Canal	100	72
2½	Lndn & St. Kath. Dks.	100	57½
4½	Do. Pref.	100	136½
4½	Do. Pref., 1878	100	132½
4½	Do. Pref., 1882	100	128
4	Do. Deb. Stk.	100	135
—	Mchester Ship C. 5 p.c. Pf.	10	1½
3½	Do. 1st Perp. Mt. Deb.	100	98
—	Milford Dks. Db. Stk. "A"	100	21½
2	Millwall Dk.	100	61
5	Do. Perp. Pref.	100	145½
4½	Do. Pref.	100	108½
5	Do. New Per. Prf., 1887	100	128½
5	Do. Per. Deb. Stk.	100	152½
4/	Newhaven Har.	10	14½
2	N. Metropolitan	100	65
5	Sharpness Nw. Pf. "A" Sk.	100	144½
4	Do. Deb. Stk.	100	120½
4	Sheffield & S. Yorks Nav. 4½ p.c. Pref. Stk.	100	117½
36.432	Suez Canal	20	135½
5	Surrey Comcl. Dok., Ord.	100	150½
5	Do. Min. 4 p.c. Pref. "A"	110	152½
5	Do. Pref. "B"	100	150½
5	Do. do. "C"	100	150
5	Do. do. "D"	100	145½
4½	Do. Deb. Stk.	100	154½

COMMERCIAL, INDUSTRIAL, &c.

Last Div.	Name.	Paid.	Price.
5	Accles, L., 1 Mt. Db., Red.	100	84½
5/	Aërated Bread, Ltd.	1	12½
—	African Gold Recovery, L.	1	¼
2/	Aluminium, L., "A" Shs.	1	2½
4½	Do. 1 Mt. Db. Stk., Red.	100	99
5½	Amelia Nitr., L., 1 Mort. Deb., Red.	100	84½
7/	Anglo-Chil. Nitrate, Ltd., Cum. Pref.	10	7½
4½	Do. Cons. Mt. Bds., Red.	100	82½
4½	Anglo-Russian Cotton, Ld., 1 Charge Debs., Red.	100	98
11/3	Angus (G., & Co., L.), £10	7½	17
6/	Apollinaris, Ltd.	10	12½
5/	Do. 5 p.c. Cum. Pref.	10	11½
4	Do. Irred. Deb. Stock	100	108
6/	Appleton, French, & S., L.	5	½
3/	Argentine Meat Pres., L., 7 p.c. Pref.	10	2½
5	Argentine Refinry, Db. Rd.	100	98
2/2	Armstrong, Whitw., Ltd.	1	3½
4	Do. Cum. Pref.	5	6½
5	Artisans', Labr. Dwllgs., L.	100	131½
4½	Do. Non-Cm. Prf., 1879	100	132½
4½	Do. do. 1884	100	132½
—	Asbestos & Asbestic, Ltd.	10	8½
2/7½	Ashley-grdns., L., C. Prf.	5	6½
4½	Do. 1 Mt. Deb. Stk.	100	115½
5/	Assam Rly. & Trdng., L., 8 p.c. Cum. Pref. "A"	10	15½
—	Do. Deferrd. "B" Shs.	1	4½
—	Do. do. (iss. f. pd)	1	3½
8/	Do. Cum. Pre-Prf. "A"	10	15
6/	Do. New Pref.	10	11½
5	Do. Debs., Red.	100	107
5	Do. Red. Mort. Debs.	100	109
6	Aust'lian Pastrl, L., Cu. Pf.	10	7½
6d.	Aylesbury Dairy, Ltd.	1	1½
4	Do. 4 p.c. Mt. Dbs.	100	104½
10/	Babcock & Wilcox, Ltd.	10	32
6	Do. 6 p.c. Cm. Prf.	10	16½
8	Baker (Chs.), L., Cm. Pf.	5	9
8	Do. "B," Cm. Pref.	5	8
8d.	Barker (John), Ltd.	1	2½
5½	Do. Cum. Pref.	5	7½
4½	Do. Irred. 1 Mt. Db. Stk.	100	132
—	Barnagore Jute, Ltd.	5	3
5	Do. Cum. Pref.	5	4½
7½d.	Belgravia Dairy, Ltd.	1	1½
5/	Bell (R.) & Co., Ltd.	5	3½
1/	Bell's Asbestos, Ltd.	1	¾
5	Do. Mt. Db. Bds., Rd.	100	103
10/	Bengal Mills, Ltd.	10	11½
6/	Do. 5 p.c. Cum. Prf.	10	10½
2/5	Benson (J.W.) L., Cm. Pf.	10	10½
12/4	Do. Perp. Mt. Db. Stk.	100	103½
6	Bergvik, L., 6 p.c. Cm. Pf.	10	12½
10/	Do. Dfd.	10	9
4½	Do. 1 Dbs., Red.	100	103½
5/	Birm'ham Vinegar, Ltd.	5	10
5	Do. Cum. Pref.	5	5½
4½	Do. 1 Mt. Db. Stk., Rd.	100	107
5	Boake (A.) L., 5 p.c. Cu. Pf.	10	10½
2/6	Bodega, Ltd.	5	8
4½	Do. Mt. Deb. Stk., Rd.	100	111
8/	Bottomley & Brs., Ltd.	10	6½
6/	Do. 6 p.c. Pt.	10	9½
8½d.	Bovril, Ltd.	1	1
1/0½	Do. Def.	1	½
6½d	Do. Cum. Pref.	1	1
4½	Do. Deb. Stk.	100	103
5/	Bradbury, Gretrex., Ltd., £10 share	8	14
5/	Do. 5 p.c. Cum. Pref.	10	13½
5/	Brewers' Sugar, L., 5 p.c. Cum. Pref.	10	10½
2/6	Brighton Grd. Hotel, Ld.	5	3½
4	Do. Mt. Db. Stk., Red.	100	102½
5	Bristol Hotel & Palm. Co., Ltd. 1st Mt. Red. Deb.	100	107½
9½d.	British & Bengton's. Tea Tr. Asc., Ltd.	1	1½
5	Do. Cum. Prf.	5	5½
—	British Deli & Lgkat. Tobacco, Ltd.	1	1½
—	Do. Cum. Prf.	1	½
—	British Tea Table, Ltd.	1	2½
5½	Do. Cum. Pref.	1	1½
2/6	Brooke, Ben., & Co., Ltd., Cum. Pref.	5	5½
7/6	Brooke, Bond & Co., Ltd.	5	20½
6	Brown Brs., L., Cum. Pref.	5	6
6/	Browne & Eagle, Ltd.	10	14
5	Do. Cum. Pref.	10	13
4	Do. Mrt. Db. Sk., Red.	100	109
20/	Brunner, Mond, & Co., Lt.	10	43
7/	Do. £10 shares	3½	17
7	Do. Cum. Pref.	10	18½
7	Do. £10 shares	5	8½
10/	Bryant & May, Ltd.	5	19½
2/	Bucknall, H., & Sons, Lt.	5	8
6	Do. Cum Pref.	5	8
4/	Burke, E. & J., Ltd.	5	7½
6	Do. Cum. Pref.	5	7½
6	Do. Irred. Deb. Stk.	100	155
1/	Burlington Htls. Co., Ltd	1	1½
5	Do. Cum. Pref.	1	1½
4	Do. Perp. Deb. Stk.	100	105½
2/4	Bush, W. J., & Co., Ltd., Cum. Pref.	5	5½
36/8	Do. 1 Deb. Stk., Red.	100	104
5½	Callard, Stewart, & Watt, Ltd., Cum. Pref.	1	1½
4/	Callender's Cable L., Shs.	5	9½
4½	Do. 1 Deb. Stk., Red.	100	111½
—	Campbell, R., & Sons, Lt.	3	2½
6	Cantareira Water, Bd., Rd	100	99½
5	Do. (2nd issue)	100	92
4	Cartavio Sugar, Ltd., 6 p.c. 1st Debs., Red.	20	80
4/6	Cassell & Co., Ltd., £10	9	18½
5	Causton, Sir J., & Sons, Ltd., Cum. Pref.	10	13½

Commercial, &c. (*continued*) :—

Last Div.	Name.	Paid.	Price.
4	Cent. Prod. Mkt. of B.A. 1st Mt. Str. Debs.	100	79
4	Chappell & Co., Ltd., Mt. Deb. Stk. Red	100	102
6/	Chicago & N.W. Gran. 8 p.c. Cum. Pref.	10	2½
—	Chicago Packing & Prov.	10	6
8	Do. Cum. Pref.	10	10½
6/	City Offices, Ltd	36½	13
7½	Do. Mt. Deb. Stk.	100	108½
7/2½	Cy. London Real Prop., Ltd., £25 shs.	12	19
4/6	Do. £12½ shs.	7½	13½
3½	Do. Deb. Stk. Red.	100	108½
3½	Do. Deb. Stk. Red.	100	106½
3	Do.	100	101½
4/	Cy. of Santos Imprvts., Ltd., 7 p.c. Pref.	10	8½
20/	Clay, Bock, & Co., Ltd.	10	8
8	Do. Cum. Pref.	10	11
6	Do. Mort. Deb.	100	106½
20/	Conts, J. & P., Ltd.	10	61½
6	Do. Cum. Pref.	10	18
4½	Do. Deb. Stk. Red.	100	111½
9½d.	Coburg Hotel, Ltd	1	1½
4	Do. Deb. Stk. Red.	100	102
6	Colonial Consign & Dis., Ltd., Cum. Pref.	5	4½
4½	Do. 1st Mort. Debs.	100	97½
—	Colorado Nitrate, Ltd.	5	¼
4/	Co. Gén. des Asphtes. de F., Ltd.	6	6½
5	Do. Non-Cm. Prf.	—	5½
5	Cook, J. W., & Co., Ltd., Cum. Pref.	5	5½
5	Cook, T., & Son, Egypt, Ltd., 1st Mt. Deb. Red.	100	110½
—	Cork Co., Ltd., 6 p.c. Cum. Pref.	5	2½
5	Cory, W., & Sn, L., Cu. Pf.	5	6½
4	Do. 1st Deb. Stk. Red.	100	100
8½d.	Crisp & Co., Ltd	1	1½
5½	Do. Cum. Pref.	1	1½
—	Crompton & Co., Ltd., 7 p.c. Cum. Pref.	5	2½
5	Do. 1st Mt. Reg. Deb.	—	88½
4/6	Crossley, J., & Sons, Ltd.	5	8½
5	Do. Cum. Pref.	5	6½
—	Crystal Pal. Ord. "A" Stk.	100	8½
—	Do. "B" Red. Stk	100	1½
6	Do. 6 p.c. 1st 1887 Deb. Stk. Red.	100	117½
—	Do. 6 p.c. 2nd 1887 Deb. Stk. Red.	100	50½
—	Do. 6 p.c. 3rd 1887 Deb. Stk. Red.	100	10½
3	Do. 3 p.c. 1st 1895 Deb. Stk.	100	95½
—	Daimler Motor, Ltd	10	5
4/	Dalgety & Co., £20 Shs.	5	5½
4½	Do. Deb. Stk.	100	123
4	Do.	100	115
7/	De Keyser's Ryl. Htl., L.	10	13½
5	Do. Cum. Pref.	10	11½
4	Do. Deb. Stk., Red.	100	110
6	Denny, H., & Sons, Ltd., Cum. Pref.	10	15
5/3	Devas, Routledge & Co. L.	7	6½
5	Dickinson, J., & Co., L., Cum. Pref. Stk.	100	123
4½	Domin. Cottn. Mls., Ltd. Mt. Stg. Dbs.	100	97
6/	Dorman, Long & Co., L.	5	4½
—	Eastmans, Ltd	10	3
12/	Do. 8 p.c. Cum. Pref.	10	10½
2/6	E. C. Powder, Ltd	3	5½
1/6	Edison & Swn Utd. Elec. Ltd., "A" £5 Shs.	3	2½
2/5	Do. fully-paid	5	4½
4½	Ekman Pulp & Ppr. Co., Ltd., Mt. Deb., Red.	100	95
1/1½	Electric Construc., Ltd.	2	2½
7	Do. Cum. Pref.	2	3½
2½/	Eley Bros., Ltd.	10	39
—	Elmore's Cop. Deptg., L.	1	½
—	Elmore's Wire Mnfg., L.	2	½
—	Elysée Pal. Hotel Co., L.	5/	
5 p.c.	Do. 5 p.c. £100 Db., Rd.	70	70
8½d.	Evans, Ben., & Co., Ltd.	1	1
5	Do. 1 Mt. Db. Sk., Rd.	100	104
8½d.	Evans, D. H., & Co., L.	1	2
6	Do. Cum. Pref.	1	1½
4½	Do. 1 Mt. Db. Sk., Rd.	100	111
2/1	*Evening News*, L., 5 p.c. Cum. Pref.	5	5½
5/3	Evered & Co., L., £10 Sh.	7	13½
7/6	Do.	10	19½
4	Fairbairn Pastoral Co. Aust., L., 1 Mt. Db., Rd.	100	102
6	Fairfield Shipbldg., Ltd., Cum. Pref.	10	10
4½	Do. Mort. Deb. Stk.	100	107½
6/	Farmer & Co., Ld., 6 p.c. Cum. Pref.	10	13½
10	Field, J. C. & J., Ltd.	10	10
14/	Do. 7 p.c. Cum. Pref.	10	14
9d.	Fordham, W.B., & Sns, Ld.	1	2
5/6	Fore-st. Warehouse, Ltd.	11	9½
4	Do. Regd. Debs., Rd.	100	103½
2/6	Foster, M. B. & Sons, Ltd.	4	5½
4	Do. Pref.	10	11½
9	Foster, Porter, & Co., L.	10	16½
4	Fowler, J., & Co. (Leeds) Ltd., 1 Mt. Deb., Red.	100	103½
3/	Fraser & Chalmers, Ltd.	3	1½
4½	Free, Rodwell & Co., Ltd., Deb Stk.	100	105½
6½d.	Furness, T., & Co., Ltd., 5½ p.c. Cum. Pref.	1	1
4½	Gartside & Co. (of Manchstr), L., 1 Mt. Db. Sk.	100	110
5	Genl. Hydraul. Power, L.	100	300

Commercial, &c. (*continued*):—

Last Div.	Name.	Paid.	Price.
2/	Gillman & Spencer, Ltd.	5	2½
6	Do. Pref.	5	4½
5	Do. Mort. Debs.	50	51
4	Goldshrn., Mort & Co., L., "A" Deb. Stk., Red.	100	72½
—	Do. 3 p.c. "B" Inc. Deb. Stk., Red.	100	17
8/	Gordon Hotels, Ltd.	10	21
5½	Do. Cum. Pref.	10	14½
4½	Do. Perp. Deb. Stk.	100	137½
4	Do. do.	100	124½
—	Greenwich Inld. Linoleum Co., Ltd.	1	½
7	Greenwood & Batley, Ltd., Cum. Pref.	10	10
7½d.	Hagemann & Co., Ltd., 6 p.c. Cum. Pref.	1	1½
—	Hammond, Ltd.	10	½
—	Do. 8 p.c. Cum. Pref.	10	2
—	Do. 6 p.c. Cum. Inc. Stk. Red.	100	52½
4	Hampton & Sons, Ltd., 4 p.c. 1 Mt. Db. St. Red.	100	105
	Hans Crescent Htl., L., 6 p.c. Cum. Pref.	5	3
4	Do. 1 Mt. Deb. Stk.	100	85
5	Harmsworth, Ld., Cm. Pf.	1	1⅛
4/	Harrison, Barber, Ltd.	5	4½
3/	Harrod's Stores, Ltd.	1	4½
2/6	Do. Cum. Pref.	5	7½
5½	Hawaiian Comcl. & Sug. 1 Mt. Debs.	100	94½
5	Hazell, Watson, Ld., Cm. Pref.	10	12
6/	Henley's Teleg., Ltd.	10	23
7	Do. Pref. Shs.	10	19½
4½	Do. Mt. Db. Stk., Rd.	100	114½
6	Henry, Ltd.	10	12½
5	Do. Cum. Pref.	10	13½
4½	Do. Mt. Debs., Red.	50	55
6	Hepworth, Ld., Cm. Prf.	10	11½
—	Herrmann, Ltd.	1	½
—	Hildesheimer, Ltd.	3	1½
9½d.	Holbrn. & Frasca, Ltd.	1	2½
5	Do. Cum. Pref.	10	12½
4	Do. Deb. Stk.	100	113
6	Home & Col. Stres, Ltd., Cum. Pref.	5	7½
6	Hood & M.'s Stses., Ltd., Cum. Pref.	1	½
—	Hook, C. T., Ltd.	10	6
7/2	Hornsby, Ltd., £10 Shs.	8	3½
5/6	Do. 6 p.c. Cm. Pf. Sk.	100	90
—	Hotchks. Ordn., Ltd.	10	½
—	Do. 7 p.c. Cm. Prf.	10	4
5	Do. 1 Mt. Dbs., Rd.	100	93½
6	Htl. Cecil, Ld., Cm. Prf.	5	4½
4	Do. 1 Mt. D. Sk., R.	100	106½
8/	Howard & Bulgh, Ltd.	10	35
6	Do. Pref.	10	15
4	Do. Deb. Stk., Red.	100	107
5/	Howell, J., Ltd., £5 Shs.	4	9½
—	Howell & Js., Ld., £3½ Shs.	3	⅛
1/6	Humber, Ltd.	1	[illegible]
6	Do. Cum. Pref.	1	1½
2/6	Hunter, Wilts., Ltd.	5	7
2/7	Hyam Clthg., Ltd., 5 p.c. Cum. Pref.	5	5½
10/	Impl. Russn. Cotton, L.	5	6
4	Impl. Industl. Dwgs., Ld.	100	123½
6d.	Do. Defrd.	1	1½
25/	Impd. Wood Pave., Ltd.	10	15
5/	Ind. Rubber, Gutta Per. Telegraph Works, Ltd.	10	22½
4	Do. 1 Mt. Debs., Red.	100	105
6	Intern. Tea, Cum. Pref.	5	6½
7½d.	Jays, Ltd.	1	1½
5½	Do. Cum. Pref.	5	6½
8½d.	Jones & Higgins, Ltd.	1	2½
4½	Do. 1 Mt. Db. Sk., Rd.	100	113
5/	Kelly's Directory, Ltd., 5 p.c. Cum. Pref.	10	12½
4	Do. Mort. Db. Sk., Rd.	100	105
—	Kent Coal Explrtn. Ltd.	1	½
9½d.	King, Howmann, Ltd.	1	1½
4/	Kinloch & Co., Ltd.	5	8½
6	Do. Pref.	5	7
5	Lady's Pictorial Pub., Ltd., Cum. Pref.	5	5
—	La Guaira Harb., Ltd., 7 p.c. Deb. Stk.	100	—
—	Do. 2 Mt. 7 p.c. Deb. Bds., Red.	100	—
4/	Lagunas Nitrate, Ltd.	5	2
2/	Lagunas Syn., Ltd.	5	1½
5	Do. 1 Mt. Debs., Red.	100	80½
—	L. Copais Ld., 1 Mt. 6 p.c. Debs., Red.	100	35½
3/	Lautaro Nitrate, Ltd.	5	4½
5	Do. 1 Mt. Debs., Red.	—	100
9/	Lawes Chem. L., £10 shs.	9	5½
14/	Do. N. Cm. Min. Pref.	10	13
—	Leeds Forge, 7 p.c. Cm. Pf.	5	2½
5	Do. 1 Mt. Debs., Red.	50	44½
5	Lever Bros., L., Cm. Pf.	10	13
6	Liberty, L., 6 p.c. Cm. Pf.	10	14½
20/	Liebig's, Ltd.	20	75
5	Lilley & Sk., L., Cm. Pf.	5	5½
3/	Linoleum Manfig., Ltd.	5	23
3/	Linotype, Ltd., Pref.	5	6
4/	Do. Def.	5	8
4/	Lister & Co., Ltd.	10	4
5	Do. Cum. Pref.	10	8½
5/	Liverpool Nitrate	5	6½
—	Liverpool Warehsg., Ltd.	10	3½
5½	Do. Cum. Pref.	10	8½
4	Do. 1 Mt. Db. Stk., Rd.	100	105½
5½	Lockharts, Ltd., Cm. Pf.	1	1½
4/6	Ldn. & Til., Lightrage £10	9	5½
6/	Ldn. Comcl. Sale Rms., Ltd.	10	18
—	Do. 1 Mt. Deb. Stk., Red.	100	104
3	London Nitrate, Ltd.	5	2

Commercial, &c. (*continued*):—

Last Div.	Name.	Paid.	Price.
4/	London Nitrate, Ld. 8 p.c. Cm. Min. Pf.	5	3½
8/	London Pavilion, Ltd.	5	7
2/6	London Produce Clg. Ho., Ltd., £10 Shares	2½	3½
4/	London Stereos., Ltd.	5	3
6d.	Ldn. Un. Laun. L. Cm. Pf.	1	½
8½d.	Louise, Ltd.	1	½
5½	Do. Cum. Pref.	1	½
5/	Lovell & Christmas, Ltd.	5	12
6	Do. Cum. Pref.	5	7½
4	Do. Mt. Deb. Stk., Red.	100	107
1/3	Lyons, Ltd.	1	3
4½	Do. 1 Mt. Deb., Stk., Rd.	100	108½
10/	Machinery Trust, Ltd.	5	15
4½	Do. 4½ Deb. Stk.	100	105
6	MacLellan, L., Min. C. Pf.	10	7½
5	Do. 1 Mt. Debs., 1900	100	101½
—	McEwan, J. & Co., Ltd.	10	1½
6	Do. Mt. Debs., Red.	100	89½
8	McNamara, L., Cm. Pref.	10	9
7½d.	Maison Virot, Ltd.	1	1½
2/7	Do. 6 p.c. Cum. Pref.	5	4½
4/	Manbré Sacc., L., Cm. Pf.	10	12
10/	Mangan Brze., L., £10 Shs.	6	15½
2/	Mason & Mason, Ltd.	5	3½
6	Do. Cum. Pref.	5	5½
—	Maynards, Ltd.	1	½
6	Do. Cum. Pref.	1	½
9½d.	Mazawattee Tea, Ltd.	1	1½
5	Do. Cum. Pref.	5	5½
6	Mellin's Food Cum. Pref.	5	7
4½	Met. Ascn. Imp. Dwlgs. L.	100	110
3½	Do. 1 Mt. Deb. Stk.	100	97
5	Metro. Indus. Dwlgs., Ltd.	5	6
4	Do. do. Cum. Pref.	5	5½
5	Metro. Prop., L., Cm. Pf.	5	6½
4½	Do. 1st Mt. Debs. Stk.	100	110½
6	Mexican Cotton 1 Mt. Db.	100	97½
4½	Mid. Class Dwlgs., L., Db.	100	120½
1/	Millars' Karri, Ltd.	1	2½
6	Do. Cum. Pref.	1	1½
5/	Milner's Safe, Ltd.	10	20½
10/	Moir & Son, Ltd., Pref.	5	9
6	Morgan Cruc., L., Cm. Pf.	10	15
2/	Morris, B., Ltd.	3½	3½
—	Murray L. 5½ p.c. C. Pf.	5	5½
—	Do. 4½ 1 Mt. Db. Sk. Rd.	100	108
2/6	Natnl. Dwlgs., L., 5 p.c. Pf.	5	1
1/7½	Nat. Safe Dep., Ltd.	4	3½
6	Do. Cum. Pref.	1	1½
—	Native Guano, Ltd.	5	½
5/	Nelson Bros., Ltd.	10	2½
5	Do. Deb. Stk., Red.	100	80½
4/	Neuchtel Asph., Ltd.	10	11
—	New Central Borneo, Ld.	1	—
10d.	New Darvel Tob., Ltd.	18/	1½
2/4½	New Explosives, Ltd.	3	2
5/3½	New Gd. Htl., Bham, L.	5	4
5½	Do. Pref.	5	4½
4	Do. 1 Mt. Db. Stk., Rd.	100	95½
—	New Julia Nitrate, Ltd.	10/	1/16
—	New Ldn. Borneo Tob., L.	16/	½
1/5	New Premier Cycle, Ltd.	1	½
6	Do. 6 p.c. Cum. Pref.	1	½
4½	Do. 4½ p.c. 1 Mt. Db. Rd	100	—
—	New Tamargl. Nitr., Ltd	1	1/16
—	Do. 8 p.c. Cum. Pref.	1	½
6	Do. 6 p.c. 1 Mt. Dbs. Rd.	100	65½
3/7½d.	Newnes, G., L., Cm. Pf.	1	1½
1/3	Nitr. Provision, Ltd.	2½	½
24/	Nobel-Dynam., Ltd.	10	17½
—	North Brazn. Sugar, Ltd.	1	½
12/	Oakey, Ltd.	10	31
6	Do. Cum. Pref.	10	16
4/	Paccha Jazp. Nitr., Ltd.	5	½
5	Pac. Borax, L., 1 Db. Rd.	100	110
—	Palace Hotel, Ltd.	10	5½
5½	Do. Cum. Pref.	10	9
4	Do. 1 Mt. Deb. Stk.	100	106
2/6	Palmer, Ltd.	5	1½
6	Do. Cum. Pref.	5	3½
9½d.	Paquin, Ltd.	1	½
6	Do. Cum. Pref.	5	4½
5½	Parnall, Ltd., Cum. Pref.	1	½
4/6	Pawsons, Ltd., £10 Shs.	6	6½
4	Do. Mt. Debs., Red.	100	107
6	Pearks, G. & T., Ltd., 6 p.c. Cum. Pref.	1	½
1/2½	Pears, Ltd.	1	1½
6	Do. Cum. Pref.	10	14½
5	Do. Deb. Stk.	100	129
5½	Pearson, C. A., L., Cu. Pf.	5	5½
4/3	Peebles, Ltd.	5	7½
5	Do. Cum. Pref.	5	6½
4½	Do. Mt. Deb. Stk. Red.	100	110
5½	Peek Bros., Ltd., 1 Cum. Pref., Nos. 1-60,000	5	6½
3½	Do. 3½ p.c. 1 Db. Stk.	100	103½
7½d.	Pegamoid, Ltd.	1	½
—	Phospho-Guano, Ltd.	5	2½
—	Pillsbury-W. Fl. Mills, L.	10	2
16/	Do. 8 p.c. Cum. Pref.	10	6½
6	Do. 1 Mort. Debs.	100	96½
7½d.	Plummer, Ltd.	1	1½
5	Do. Cum. Pref.	5	5½
15/	Price's Candle, Ltd.	16	40
6	Priest Marians, L., Cm. Pf.	1	1½
6	Pryce Jones, Ld., Cm. Pf.	5	7½
5	Do. Deb. Stk.	100	120½
10.8d.	Pullman, Ltd.	1	1½
6d.	Do. Cum. Pref.	1	1½
1 1/10	Raleigh Cycle, Ltd.	1	⅞
6	Do. Cum. Pref.	1	½
—	Recife Drnge. Ld. 1 Mt. Debs., R	100	19
6	Redfern, Ltd. Cum. Prf.	10	14
5	Ridgways, Ltd., Cu. Pf.	5	5½
—	R. Janeiro Cy. Imps., Ld.	25	9½
5	Do. Debs.	100	88½
5	Do. 1889-1893	100	88½
11/	R. Jan Fl. Mills, Ltd.	7	7
5	Do. 1 Mt. Debs., Rd.	100	94

Commercial, &c. (*continued*):—

Last Div.	Name.	Paid.	Price.
—	Riv. Plate Meat, Ltd.	5	3½
—	Do. Pref.	5	5
8½d.	Roberts, J. R., Ltd.	1	1½
5	Do. 1 Mt. Db. Sk., Rd.	100	112
8½d.	Roberts, T. R., Ltd.	1	2½
5	Do. Cum. Pref.	1	1½
3/	Rosario Nit., Ltd.	5	3½
5	Do. Debs., Red.	100	104
5	Do. Huara, Debs.	—	102½
1/	Rover Cycle, Ltd.	1	½
6/	Ryl. Aquarium, Ltd.	5	5
6	Do. Pref.	5	6
5	Ryl. Htl., Edin., Cm. Pf.	1	1½
1/2½	Ryl. Niger, Ltd., £10 Sh.	2	2½
6/	Do.	10	14½
3/	Ruston, Proctor, Ltd.	10	11
4½	Do. 1 Mort. Debs.	100	104
6/	Sadler, Ltd.	12	7
—	Sal. Carmen Nit., Ltd.	5	4½
9d.	Salmon & Gluck., Ltd.	1	1½
2/	Salt Union, Ltd.	10	1½
14/	Do. 7 p.c. Pref.	10	6½
4½	Do. Deb. Stk.	100	106
4½	Do. "B" Deb. Sk., Rd.	100	102½
—	San Donato Nit., Ltd.	5	½
2/6	San Jorge Nit., Ltd.	5	3½
—	San Pablo Nit., Ltd.	5	½
2/	San Sebastn. Nit., Ltd.	5	½
1/	Sanitas, Ltd	1	2½
—	Sa. Elena Nit., Ltd.	5	½
—	Sa. Rita Nit., Ltd.	5	2
10/	Savoy Hotel, Ltd.	10	19
7	Do. Pref.	10	16
4	Do. 1 Mt. Deb. Stk.	100	112½
5	Do. Debs., Red	100	102½
5	Do. & Ldn. For. Htl., Ltd., 5 p.c. Debs. Red.	100	99
1½d.	Schweppes, Ltd.	1	1⅛
—	Do. Def.	1	½
5	Do. Cum. Pref.	1	1½
4	Do. Deb. Stk.	100	109
1/	Singer Cyc., Ltd.	1	½
5½	Do. Cum. Pref.	1	½
—	Smokeless Pwdr., Ltd.	1	½
5½d.	S. Eng. Dairies, Ltd., 6 p.c. Cum. Pref.	1	1½
—	Sowler Thos. L.	1	1½
—	Do. 5½ Cm. Pf.	5	5½
3/6	Spencer, Turner, & Co. Ltd	5	8½
5	Do. Cum. Pref.	5	6½
5	Spicer, Ld., 5 p.c. Dbs. Rd.	100	65
4/	Spiers & Pond, Ltd.	10	21
5	Do. 1 Mt. Debs., Red.	100	116½
5	Do. "A" Db. Stk., Rd.	100	110
5	Do. "B" 1 Db. Stk., Rd.	100	110
4	Do. Fd. "C" 1 Db. S., R.	100	103
5/	Spratt's, Ltd	5	13½
4	Do. Debs., 1914	—	105
5	Steiner Ld., Cm. Pf.	10	11
4	Do. 1 Mt. Db. Sk. Rd.	100	106
7/	Stewart & Clydesdale, L.	10	14½
6	Do. Cum. Pref.	10	15½
—	Swan & Edgar, L.	1	1½
1/3	Sweetmeat Automatic, L.	1	4
2/9	Teetgen, Ltd., Cum. Pref.	5	6
12/	Teleg. Construction., Ld.	12	40½
5	Do. Db. Bds., Rd., 1899	100	103½
3/0½	Tilling, Ld. 5½ p.c. Cm. Prf.	5	6½
4	Do. 4 p.c. 1 Dbs., Rd.	—	104
8½d.	Tower Tea, Ltd.	1	1½
5	Do. Cum. Pref.	5	5½
5	Travers, Ltd., Cum. Pref.	10	12½
4	Do. 1 Mt. Dbs., Rd.	100	103
6	TucumanSug., 1 Dbs., Rd.	100	100
4/	United Alkali, Ltd.	10	2½
7	Do. Cum. Pref.	10	9½
5	Do. Mt. Db. Stk., Rd.	100	111½
2½d.	United Horse Shoe, Ltd., Non-Cum. 8 p.c. Pref.	1	½
5	Un. Kingm. Tea, Cm. Prf.	5	5
2/	Un. Lankat Plant., Ltd.	1	2½
2/	Un. Limmer Asphlte., Ld.	3	4½
5/	Val de Travers Asph., L.	10	15
3/	V. den Bergh's, Ltd., Cm. Pref.	5	6½
6	Walkers, Park., L., C. Pf.	10	4
4½	Do. 1 Mt. Debs., Red.	100	90½
6/	Wallis, Thos. & Co., Ltd.	5	1½
6	Do. Cum. Pref.	5	8½
5½	Waring, Ltd., Cum. Pref.	5	5½
4½	Do. 1 Mt. Db. Sk., Red.	100	111½
4½	Do. Irred. "B" Db. Stk.	100	104
12/	Waterlow, Dfd. Ord.	10	15½
12/	Do. Pref.	10	15
—	Do. Cum. Pref.	10	10½
10/	Waterlow Bros. & L., Ld.	10	9
1/2½	Welford, Ltd.	1	2½
4½	Do. Debs., Red.	100	107
4½d.	Welford's Surrey Dairies, Ltd.	1	1½
7½d.	West London Dairy, Ltd.	1	1
4½	Wharncliffe Dwllgs, L., Pf.	10	12
18/10	Do. 3 p.c. Irr. Mt. Db. Sk.	100	96
6d.	White, A. J., Ltd.	1	½
6	Do. 6 p.c. Cum. Pref.	1	½
4	White, J. Bazley, Ltd., 1 Mort. Debs., Red.	100	96½
5	White, R., Ltd., 1 Mort. Deb. Stock, Red.	100	104½
5/	White, Tomkins, Ltd.	10	12½
5	Do. Cum. Pref.	10	12½
6	White, W. N., L., Cm. Pf.	1	1
2/6	Wickens, Pease & Co., L.	5	2
6	Wilkie, Ltd., Cum. Pref.	10	16
3/6	Willans & Robinson, Ltd.	5	8½
6	Do. Cum. Pref.	5	7
4½	Do. 1 Mt. Db. Stk., Red.	100	107
7½d.	Williamsons, L., Cm. Prf.	1	1½
6	Winterbottm. Book Cloth, Ltd., Cum. Prf.	20	15
3/	Yates, Ltd.	5	6½
6	Do. Cum. Pref.	5	6½
	Young's Paraffin, Ltd.	4	1½

CORPORATION STOCKS—COLONIAL AND FOREIGN.

Per Cent.	Name.	Paid.	Price.
6	Auckland City, '72 1904-24	100	118
6	Do. Cons., '79, Red. 1930	100	138½
5	Do. Deb. Ln., '83, 1934-8	100	117
6	Auckland Harb. Debs.	100	111½
5	Do. 1917	100	112
5	Do. 1936	100	116
5½	Balmain Boro'. 1914	—	117
5	Boston City (U.S.)	100	102½
5	Do. 1902	100	107½
5	Brunswick Town 5 c. Debs. 1916-20	100	111
15/	B. Ayres City 6 p.c.	100	61
4½	Do. 4½ p.c.	100	77
5	Cape Town, City of	100	113
4	Do. 1943	100	114
4	Chicago, City of, Gold 1915	—	110
6	Christchurch 1926	100	128½
—	Cordoba City	100	17½
5	Duluth (U.S.) Gold 1926	—	110
6	Dunedin (Otago) 1925	100	127½
6	Do. 1906	100	113
5	Do. Consols 1908	100	113
4	Durban Insc. Stk. 1944	100	111
4	Essex Cnty., N. Jersey 1926	100	114½
5	Fitzroy, Melbrne. 1916-19	100	110
5	Gisborne Harbour 1915	100	110½
4	Greymouth Harbour 1925	100	111
4	Hamilton 1934	100	109
5	Hobart Town 1918-30	100	116
4	Do. 1940	100	107
4½	Invercargill Boro. Dbs. 1936	100	113
6	Kimberley Boro., S.A. Dbs.	—	104
4	Launceston Twn. Dbs. 1916	100	107
6	Lyttleton, N.Z., Harb. 1929	100	125
4	Melbourne Bd. of Wks. 1921	100	109
5	Melb. City Debs. 1897-1907	100	107½
4½	Do. Debs. 1908-27	100	113½
4	Do. Debs. 1915-20-22	100	108
5	Melbne. Harb. Bds., 1908-9	100	112
4½	Do. do. 1915	100	110
4	Do. do. 1918-21	100	106
4½	Melbrne. Tms. Dbs. 1914-16	100	113
4½	Do. Fire Brig. Db. 1921	100	109
5	Mexico City Stg.	100	92½
4	Moncton N. Bruns. City	100	104
4½	Montevideo	100	60
5	Montreal Stg.	100	104
5	Do. 1874	100	104
5	Do. 1879	100	106
3½	Do. 1933	100	104
3	Do. Perm. Deb. Stk.	100	98
4	Do. Cons. Deb. Stk. 1932	100	113
6	Napier Boro. Consolid. 1914	100	119
5	Napier Harb. Debs. 1920	100	115
5	Do. Debs. 1928	100	106
6	New Plymouth Harb. Debs. 1909	100	108
6	New York City 1901	—	107½
3½	Do. 1910-26	—	105½
4½	Nth. Melbourne Debs. 1-600 1921	100	106
5	Oamaru Boro. Cons. 1920	100	101
6	Do. Harb. Bds. (Reg.)	100	74
25/	Do. 6 p.c. (Bearer) 1919	100	35
6	Otago Harb. Deb. Reg.	100	103
6	Do. 1877	100	107
6	Do. 1881 1921	100	115
5	Do. Debs. 1921	100	107
5	Do. Cons. 1934	100	106
6	Ottawa City	100	111
6	Do. 1904	100	115½
4½	Do. Debs. 1913	100	112
6	Port Elizabeth Waterworks	100	113½
5	Port Louis	100	111
5	Prahran Debs. 1917	100	111
4	Do. Debs. 1919	100	103
6	Quebec C. Coupon. 1875 1905	100	112
6	Do. do. 1878 1908	100	116
4½	Do. Debs. 1914-18	100	108
4	Do. Debs. 1923	100	108
3½	Do. Cns. Rg. Stk., Red.	100	101
5	Richmond (Melb.) Dbs. 1917	100	113
4	Rio Janeiro City	100	59
4	Rome City	100	—
4	Do. 2nd to 8th Iss.	100	94
—	Rosario C.	100	26½
—	Do.	100	26½
4	St. Catherine (Ont.) 1926	100	103
4	St. John, N.B., Debs. 1934	—	104
4½	St. Kilda (Melb) Dbs. 1918-21	100	104
4	St. Louis C. (Miss.) 1911	100	104
4	Do. 1913	100	104½
3.65	Do. 1915	—	110
—	Santa Fé City Debs.	100	21
6	Santos City	100	95
6	Sofia City	100	86
5	Sth. Melbourne Debs. 1915	100	111
4½	Do. Debs. 1919	100	107
5	Sydney City 1904	100	109
4	Do. Debs. 1912-13	100	107
4	Do. do. (1894) 1919	100	109
7	Timaru Boro. 7 p.c. 1910	100	126½
5	Timaru Harb. Debs 1914	100	106
5	Do. Debs. 1916	100	106
6	Toronto City Wtwks 1904-6	100	110
6	Do. Cons. Debs. 1898	100	101
5	Do. G. Cns. Dbs. 1919-20	100	118
4	Do. Strlg. 1922-8	100	107
4	Do. Local Improv.	100	102
3½	Do. 1929	100	105
5½	Valparaiso	100	101
4	Vancouver 1931	100	109
4	Do. 1932	100	108
6	Wanganui Harb. Dbs. 1905	100	110
6	Wellington Con. Deb. 1907	100	117
6	Do. Improv., 1879	100	126
6	Do. Wtrwks. Dbs., 1880	100	126
4½	Do. Debs., 1893 1933	100	116
4½	Wellington Harb. 1907	100	106
4	Westport Harb. Dbs. 1925	100	111
6	Winnipeg City Deb. 1907	—	118
5	Do. 1914	100	119

FINANCIAL, LAND, AND INVESTMENT.

Last Div.	Name.	Paid.	Price.
5	Agncy, Ld. & Fin. Aust., Ltd., Mt. Db. Stk., Rd.	100	90½
6	Amer. Frehld. Mt. of Lon., Ld., Cum. Pref. Stk.	100	82½
4½	Do. Deb. Stk., Red.	100	96
1/	Anglo-Amer. Db. Cor., L.	2	1
4	Do. Deb. Stk., Red	100	106½
5½	Ang.-Ceylon & Gen. Est., Ltd., Cons. Stk.	100	68
6	Do. Reg. Debs., Red.	100	106½
—	Ang.-Fch. Explorn., Ltd.	1	3
6	Do. Cum. Pref.	1	1½
—	Argent. Ld. & Inv., Ltd. £1 Shares	10/	nil
5	Do. Cum. Pref.	4	2
1/	Assets Fnders.' Sh., Ltd.,	4	1⅞
6/	Assets Realiz., Ltd., Ord.,	5	9
5	Do. Cum. Pref.	5	6½
21/	Austrln. Agricl £25 Shs.	21½	65½
—	Aust. N. Z. Mort., Ltd., £10 Shs.	1	1½d.
4½	Do. Deb. Stk., Red.	100	90½
4	Do. Deb. Stk., Red.	100	82½
4½	Australian Est. & Mt., L., 1 Mt. Deb. Stk., Red.	100	106
5	Do. "A" Mort. Deb. Stk., Red.	100	97
2/6	Australian Mort., Ld., & Fin., Ltd. £25 Shs.	5	4½
1/6	Do. New, £25 Shs.	3	2½
4	Do. Deb. Stk	100	112
3	Do. Do.	100	85
5	Baring Est. 2 Mt. Debs., Red.	100	105
5	Bengal Presidy. 1 Mort. Deb., Red.	100	106
25/	British Amer. Ld. "A"	1	20
—	Do. "B"	24	6½
1/2½	Brit. & Amer. Mt., Ltd. £10 Shs.	2	¾
5/	Do. Pref.	10	10
4	Do. Deb. Stk., Red.	100	101
1/3	Brit. & Austrlsn Tst Ln., Ltd. £25 Shs.	2½	⅝
4½	Do. Perm. Debs., Red.	100	103
1½d.	Brit. N. Borneo. £1 Shs.	15/	1⅛
2½d.	Do.	1	1
—	Brit. S. Africa	1	3
5	Do. Mt. Deb., Red.	—	97½
6	B. Aires Harb. Tst., Red.	100	100
12/6	Canada Co.	1	26
—	Canada N. W. Ld., Ltd.	$25	$5½
—	Do. Pref.	$100	$54
4	Canada Perm. Loan & Sav. Perp. Deb. Stk.	100	99½
—	Curamalan Ld., 1 Mt. 7 p.c. Bds., Red.	—	92½
3/7½	Deb Corp., Ld., £10 Shs	4	3½
5	Do. Cum. Pref.	10	11½
4	Do. Perp. Deb. Stk.	100	116
9d.	Deb. Corp. Fders' Sh., Ld.	3	1
4/5⅛	Eastn. Mt. & Agncy, Ld., "A"	10	6½
4½	Do. Deb. Stk., Red.	100	100
5	Equitable Revers. In. Ltd.	100	—
2/	Exploration, Ltd.	1	1⅜
1	Freehold Trst. of Austrla. Ltd. £10 Shs.	1	⅝
4	Do. Perp. Deb. Stk.	100	102
—	Genl. Assets Purchase, Ltd., 5 p.c. Cum. Pref.	10	—
50/	Genl. Reversionary, Ltd.	100	—
3½	Holborn Vi. Land	100	105
3½	House Prop. & Inv.	100	86½
13/	Hudson's Bay	13	23½
4	Impl. Col. Fin. & Agcy. Corp.	100	94½
4½	Impl. Prop. Inv., Ltd., Deb. Stk., Red.	100	91½
2/6	Internatl. Fincial. Soc., Ltd. £7½ Shs.	2½	1½
4	Do. Deb. Stk., Red.	100	97½
1/9½	Ld. & Mtge. Egypt, Ltd. £18 Shs.	3	2½
5	Do. Debs., Red.	100	103
4½	Do. Debs., Red.	100	101
—	Ld. Corp. of Canada, Ltd.	1	⅝
4½	Ld. Mtge. Bk. of Texas Deb. Stk.	100	—
3½	Ld. Mtge. Bk. Victoria 4½ p.c. Deb. Stk.	100	78
2/9½	Law Debent. Corp., Ltd., £10 Shs.	2	2
4½	Do. Cum. Pref.,	10	12
4	Do. Deb. Stk.	100	119
1/	Ldn. & Australasian Deb. Corp., Ltd., £4 Shs.	2	½
4½	Do. 4½ p.c. Mt. Deb. Stk., Red.	100	101
—	Ldn. & Middx. Frhld. Est. £2 Shs.	35/	3½
2/6	Lndn. & N. Y. Inv. Corp., Ltd.	5	2
5	Do. 5 p.c. Cum. Pref.	10	9
1/6	Ldn. & Nth. Assets Corp., Ltd., £2 Shs.	1½	⅝
2/	Ldn. & N. Deb. Corp., L.	2	1¼
4/	Ldn. & S. Afric. Explrn. Ltd.	½	14
2/	Mtge. Co. of R. Plate, Ltd. £10 Shs.	2	3½
4½	Do. Deb. Stk., Red.	100	112
4½	Morton, Rose Est., Ltd., 1st Mort. Debs.	—	101
6/	Natal Land Col. Ltd.	10	6½
4/	Do. 8 p.c. Pref., 1870	5	8½
5/6	Natl. Disct. L., £25 Shs.	5	10½
4½	New Impl. Invest., Ltd. Pref. Stk.	100	61½
—	New Impl. Invest., Ltd. Def. Stk.	100	9
4	N. Zld. Ln. & Mer. Agcy., Ltd. Prf. Ln. Deb. Stk.	100	97

Financial, Land, &c. (*continued*):—

Last Div.	Name.	Paid.	Price.
16/	N. Zld. Ln. & Mer. Agcy., Ltd. 5 p.c. "A" Db. Sk.	100	42½
—	N. Zld. Ln. & Mer. Agcy., Ltd., 5 p.c. "B" Db. Stk.	100	4
2/6	N. Zld. Tst. & Ln. Ltd., £25 Shs.	5	1¼
12/6	N. Zld. Tst. & Ln. Ltd., 5 p.c. Cum. Pref.	25	19
—	N. Brit. Australsn. Ltd.	100	7½
—	Do. Irred. Guar.	100	32½
5	Do. Mort. Debs.	100	82½
4½	N. Queensld. Mort. & Inv., Ltd., Deb. Stk.	100	95
—	Oceana Co., Ltd.	—	—
6	Peel Riv., Ld. & Min. Ltd.	100	89
—	Peruvian Corp., Ltd.	100	2⅞
—	Do. 4 p.c. Pref.	100	10½
3	Do. 6 p.c. 1 Mt. Debs., Red.	100	43½
—	Queenld. Invest. & Ld. Mort. Pref. Ord. Stk.	100	20
3/7	Queenld. Invest. & Ld. Mort. Ord. Shs.	4	4
4	Queenld. Invest. & Ld. Mort. Perp. Debs.	100	90
3½	Raily. Roll Stk. Tst. Deb., 1903-6	100	100½
50/	Reversiony. Int. Soc., Ltd.	100	—
2/8¾	Riv. Plate Trst., Loan & Agcy., L., "A" £10 Shs.	2	4½
1/6	Riv. Plate Trst., Loan & Agcy., Ltd., Def. "B"	5	3½
	Riv. Plate Trst., Loan & Agy., L., Db. Stk., Red.	100	108
—	Santa Fé & Cord. Gt. South Land, Ltd.	20	5
—	Santa Fé Land	10	2½
2/	Scot. Amer. Invest., Ltd. £10 Shs.	2	2¾
2½	Scot. Australian Invest., Ltd., Cons.	100	85½
6	Scot. Australian Invest., Ltd., Guar. Pref.	100	135½
5	Scot. Australian Invest., Ltd., Guar. Pref.	100	106½
4	Scot. Australian Invest., Ltd., 4 p.c. Perp. Dbs.	100	105½
5	Sivagunga Zemdy., 1st Mort., Red.	100	101
20/	Sth. Australian	20	54½
3½	Stock Exchange Deb., Rd.	—	101½
—	Strait Develt., Ltd.	1	5/16
2/6	Texas Land & Mt., Ltd. £10 Shs.	2½	3
4½	Texas Land & Mt., Ltd., Deb. Stk., Red.	100	105
—	Transvaal Est. & Dev., L.	1	11/16
—	Transvaal Lands, Ltd., £1 Shs.	15/	½
—	Do. F. P.	1	¾
—	Transvaal Mort., Loan, & Fin., Ltd., £10 Shs.	2	½
2/	Tst & Agcy. of Austrlsa., Ltd., £10 Shs.	1	2½
7/5	Do. Old, fully paid	10	15½
5/7	Do. New, fully paid	10	12½
5	Do. Cum. Pref.	10	12½
3/	Trust & Loan of Canada, £20 Shs.	5	4½
1/9½	Do. New £20 Shs	3	2½
—	Tst. & Mort. of Iowa, Ltd., £10 Shs.	2½	¾
4½	Do. Deb. Stk. Red.	100	92½
—	Tst., Loan, & Agency of Mexico, Ltd., £10 Shs.	2	¼
—	Trsts., Exors, & Sec. Ins. Corp., Ltd., £10 Shs.	7	1½
5/	Union Dsc., Ld., £10 Shs.	5	11
—	Union Mort. & Agcy. of Aust., Ltd., £6 Shs.	2	—
6	Do. Pref. Stk	100	35
—	Do. 6 p. Pref. £6 Shs.	2	½
4½	Do. Deb. Stk	100	92½
4	Do. Deb. Stk	100	85½
5	Do. Deb. Stk. Red.	100	96½
1/6	U.S. Deb. Cor. Ltd., £8 Shs.	1	⅝
5½	Do. Cum. Pref. Stk	100	102½
4½	Do. Irred. Deb. Stk.	100	108½
5	U.S. Tst. & Guar. Cor., Ltd., Pref. Stk.	100	71½
6/	Van Dieman's	25	16
4	Walker's Prop. Cor., Ltd., Guar. 1 Mt. Deb. Stk.	100	109
4½	Wstr. Mort. & Inv., Ltd., Deb. Stk.	100	92½

FINANCIAL—TRUSTS.

Last Div.	Name.	Paid.	Price.
1/	Afric. City Prop., Ltd	1	1⅜
6	Do. Cum. Pref.	1	1
4	Alliance Invt., Ltd., Cm. 4½ p. c. Prefd.	100	80½
—	Do. Defd	100	13½
4	Do. Deb. Stk. Red.	100	106½
5	Amron. Invt., Ltd., Prfd.	100	123½
5	Do. Defd.	100	92½
4	Do. Deb. Stk. Red.	100	117½
4	Army & Navy Invt., Ltd., 5 p.c. Prefd.	100	80½
—	Do. Defd. Stk.	100	17½
4	Do. Deb. Stk.	100	104½
4	Atlas Investment, Ltd., Prefd. Stk.	100	70½
4½	Bankers' Invest., Ltd., Cum. Prefd.	100	105
1/0/0	Do. Defd	100	29½
4	Do. Deb. Stk	100	113

Financial—Trusts (*continued*):—

Last Div.	Name.	Paid.	Price.
3/	Brewery & Comml. Inv., Ltd., £10 Shs.	5	6
4	British Investment, Ltd., Cum. Prefd.	100	109½
5	Do. Defd.	100	104½
4	Do. Deb. Stk.	100	108½
6	Brit. Steam. Invst., Ltd., Prefd.	100	116½
3/0/0	Do. Defd	100	70½
4½	Do. Perp. Deb. Stk	100	120½
2/3	Car Trust Invst., Ltd., £10 Shs.	2½	2
5	Do. Pref.	100	105½
4	Do. Deb. Stk., 1915	100	106
4	Clnl. Sec., Ltd., Prefd.	100	108½
2	Do. Defd.	100	49
4	Consolidated, Ltd., Cum. 1st Pref.	100	94½
4	Do. 5 p.c. Cm. 2nd do.	100	72½
—	Do. Defd.	100	14½
4½	Do. Deb. Stk.	100	111½
4½	Edinburgh Invest., Ltd., Cum. Prefd. Stk.	100	110½
4	Do. Deb. Stk. Red.	100	106½
5	Foreign, Amer. & Gen. Invt., Ltd., Prefd.	100	119½
2	Do. Defd.	100	56½
4	Do. Deb. Stk.	100	117½
5	Foreign & Colonial Invt., Ltd., Prefd.	100	134½
5½	Do. Defd.	100	97½
4½	Gas, Water & Gen. Invt., Cum. Prefd. Stk.	100	94
2	Do. Defd. Stk.	100	32½
4	Do. Deb. Stk.	100	106
5	Gen. & Com. Invt., Ltd., Prefd. Stk.	100	107½
2	Do. Defd. Stk.	100	37½
4	Do. Deb. Stk.	100	111½
1/9	Globe Telegph. & Tst., Ltd.	10	12½
6	Do. do. Pref.	10	18½
4	Govt. & Genl. Invt., Ld., Prefd.	100	84½
3½	Do. Defd.	100	42½
4½	Govts. Stk. & other Secs. Invt., Ltd., Prefd.	100	92½
1	Do. Defd.	100	27
4½	Do. Deb. Stk.	100	110
4	Do. do.	100	104
4½	Guardian Invt., Ltd., Pfd.	100	92½
—	Do. Defd.	100	21½
4	Do. Deb. Stk.	100	105
5	Indian & Gen. Inv., Ltd., Cum. Prefd.	100	108½
2½	Do. Defd.	100	55
4½	Do. Deb. Stk.	100	120½
5	Indust. & Gen. Tst., Ltd., Unified	100	102½
3½	Do. Deb. Stk. Red.	100	102½
4½	Internat. Invt., Ltd., Cm. Prefd.	100	73½
—	Do. Defd.	100	11
4	Do. Deb. Stk.	100	104
4	Invest. Tst. Cor. Ltd. Pfd.	100	103
4	Do. Defd.	100	87
4	Do. Deb. Stk. Red.	100	107
25/	Ldn. Gen. Invest. Ltd., 5 p.c. Cum. Prefd.	100	110½
37/6	Do. Defd.	100	120
4½	Ldn. Scot. Amer. Ltd. Pfd.	100	104½
£3	Do. Defd.	100	59½
4	Do. Deb. Stk.	100	112
4	Ldn. Tst., Ltd., Cum. Prfd. Stk.	100	104
4	Do. Defd. Stk.	100	76½
4	Do. Deb. Stk., Red.	100	107
3½	Do. Mt. Deb. Stk., Red.	100	104
5	Mercantile Invt. & Gen., Ltd., Prefd.	100	114
2	Do. Defd.	100	53½
4	Do. Deb. Stk.	100	117½
4	Merchants, Ltd., Pref. Stk.	100	105½
4	Do. Ord.	100	81
4	Do. Deb. Stk.	100	117
5	Municipal, Ltd., Prefd.	100	56½
—	Do. Defd.	100	18½
4½	Do. Debs.	100	113
4½	Do. Debs. "B"	100	99½
4½	Do. "C" Deb. Stk.	100	88½
5	New Investment, Ltd. Ord.	100	95½
5	Omnium Invest., Ltd., Pfd.	100	91½
1	Do. Defd.	100	26½
4	Do. Deb. Stk.	100	104
5/	Railway Deb. Tst. Ld., £20 Shs.	10	7½
5	Do. Debs., Red.	100	107½
4½	Do. Deb. Stk., 1911	100	105½
4	Do. do. 1927	100	107½
4	Railway Invst. Ltd., Prefd.	100	117
18/6	Do. Defd.	100	24
8/	Railway Share Trust & Agency "A"	8	6½
7½	Do. "B" Pref. Stk.	100	144½
4½	River Plate & Gen. Invt., Ltd., Prefd.	100	105
£3	Do. Defd.	100	50½
5	Scot. Invst., Ltd., Pfd. Stk.	100	95½
1½	Do. Defd.	100	26½
4	Do. Deb. Stk.	100	108
4½	Sec. Scottish Invst., Ltd., Cum. Prefd.	100	90½
£2	Do. Defd. Stk.	100	32
4	Do. Deb. Stk.	100	107½
7/6	Sth. Africa Gold Tst., Ltd.	1	4½
6	Do. Cum. Pref	1	1
5½	Do. 1st Debs., Red.	100	102
1/9	Stock Conv. & Invest., Ltd., £5 Shs.	1	1¼
4½	Do. do. 4½ p.c. Cm. Prf.	100	113½
3½	Do. Ldn. & N. W. 1st. Charge Prefd.	100	116½
4	Do do. 2nd Chge Prfd.	100	113
32/6	Do. do. Defd. Charge	100	32½
3	Do. N. East. 1 Chge Pfd.	100	95

Financial—Trusts (*continued*):—

Last Div.	Name.	Paid.	Price.
37/6	Stock N. East Defd. Chge	100	41
6	Submarine Cables	100	142½
5	U.S. & S. Amer. Invest., Ltd., Prefd.	100	99½
2	Do. Defd.	100	29½
4	Do. Deb. Stk.	100	105½

GAS AND ELECTRIC LIGHTING.

Last Div.	Name.	Paid.	Price.
10/6	Alliance & Dublin Con. 10 p.c. Stand.	10	25½
7/6	Do. 7 p.c. Stand.	10	17
5	Austln. Gas Lght. (Syd.) Debs. 1902	100	106
5	Bay State of N. Jrsy. Sk. Fd. Tst. Bd., Red.	—	92½
3/	Bombay, Ltd.	5	7
2/4½	Do. New	4	5½
12	Brentford Cons.	100	302½
9	Do. New	100	229½
5	Do. Pref.	100	147½
4	Do. Deb. Stk.	100	136
11½	Brighton & Hove Gen. Cons. Stk.	100	277½
8½	Do. "A" Cons. Stk.	100	202½
5	Bristol 5 p.c. Max.	100	132½
22/6	British Gas Light, Ltd.	20	57
11/6	Bromley Gas Consumrs.' 10 p.c. Stand.	10	26
8/6	Do. 7 p.c. Stand.	10	21
[illegible]	Brush Electl. Enging., L.	—	2½
6	Do. 6 p.c. Pref.	—	2½
4½	Do. Deb. Stk.	100	111
4½	Do. 2 Deb. Stk., Red.	100	103½
5/	B. Ayres (New), Ltd.	10	10
4	Do. Deb. Stk., Rd.	—	98
12/	Cagliari Gas & Wtr., Ltd.	20	31
8/	Cape Town & Dist. Gas Light & Coke, Ltd.	10	17½
4½	Do. Pref.	10	12½
6	Do. 1 Mt. Debs. 1910	50	60
3/	Charing Cross & Strand Elec. Sup., Ltd.	5	14½
4½	Do. Cum. Pref.	5	6½
2/6	Chelsea Elec. Sup., Ltd.	5	12
4½	Do. Deb. Stk., Red.	100	116
5	Chic. Edison Co. 1 Mt., Red.	$1000	108
14/	City of Ldn. Elec. Lht., L.	10	29
—	Do. New	10	28
6/	Do. Cum. Pref.	10	18
5	Do. Deb. Stk., Red.	100	131½
13½	Commercial, Cons.	100	342½
10½	Do. New	100	257½
4½	Do. Deb. Stk.	100	155½
14	Continental Union, Ltd.	100	251½
11	Do. Pref. Stk.	100	216½
—	County of Lon. & Brush Prov. Elec. Lg., Ltd.	10	16
6	Do. Cum. Pref.	10	16
14	Croydon Comcl. Gas, Ld., "A" Stk., 10 p.c.	100	317½
11	Do. "B" Stk., 7 p.c.	100	254½
5½	Crystal Pal. Dist. Ord. 5 p.c. Stk.	100	138½
5	Do. Pref. Stk.	100	141½
8/	European, Ltd.	10	26
6/	Do.	7½	18½
12½	Gas Light & Ck Cons. Stk., "A" Ord.	100	299½
4	Do. "B" (4 p.c. Max.)	100	122½
10	Do. "C," "D," & "E" (Pref.)	100	319½
5	Do. "F" (Pref.)	100	152½
7½	Do. "G" (Pref.)	100	222½
7	Do. "H" (7 p.c. Max.)	100	203½
10	Do. "J" (Pref.)	100	318½
6	Do. "K"	100	187½
4	Do. Deb. Stk.	100	139½
4½	Do. do.	100	157½
6	Do. do.	100	207½
8/	Hong Kong & China, Ld.	10	14½
—	House to House Elec. Light Sup., Ltd.	5	11
7	Do. Cum. Pref.	5	11½
10	Imperial Continental	100	222½
3½	Do. Deb. Stk., Red	100	104½
2/	Malta & Medit., Ltd.	5	5½
5/	Metrop. Elec. Sup., Ltd.	10	20½
3/8	Do. New	10	20
4½	Do. 1 Mt. Deb. Stk.	100	129
5	Metro. of Melbrne. Dbs. 1908-12	100	113
4½	Do. Debs. 1918-22-4	100	110
10/	Monte Video, Ltd.	20	15½
8/	Notting Hill Elec. Lig., Ltd.	10	19
4/6	Oriental, Ltd.	5	8½
4/0½	Do. New	4½	7½
10½d.	Do. do. 1879	1	1½
3/6	Ottoman, Ltd.	5	5
—	Para, Ltd.	—	—
6	People's Gas Lt. & C. of Chic. 2 Mt. 1904	100	105½
5	River Plate Elec. Lgt. & Trac., Ltd., 1 Deb. Stk.	—	92½
$2	Royal Elec. of Montreal	—	146
4½	Do. 1 Mt. Deb.	100	108
11/	St. James' & Pall Mall Elec. Light, Ltd.	5	19
7	Do. Pref.	5	10½
4	Do. Deb. Stk., Red.	100	108½
10/	San Paulo, Ltd.	10	16½

Gas and Electric (*continued*):—

Last Div.	Name.	Paid.	Price.
10	Sheffield Unit. Gas Lt. "A"	100	251½
10	Do. "B"	100	251½
10	Do. "C"	100	251½
—	Sth. Ldn. Elec. Sup., Ld.	2	3
5¼	South Metropolitan	100	147½
3	Do. 3 p.c. Deb. Stk.	100	106½
12	Tottenham & Edmonton Gas Lt. & C., "A"	100	290
9	Do. "B"	100	210
7/	Tuscan, Ltd.	10	14
5	Do. Debs., Red.	100	101½
4/9	West Ham 10 p.c. Stan.	5	12
4/	Wstmnstr. Elec.Sup., Ld.	5	18½

INSURANCE.

Last Div.	Name.	Paid.	Price.
4/	Alliance, £20 Shs.	44/	11½
10/	Alliance, Mar., & Gen., Ld., £100 Shs.	25	53
5/	Atlas, £50 Shs.	6	32
8/	British & For. Marine, Ld., £20 Shs.	4	25½
7½d.	British Law Fire, Ltd., £10 Shs.	1	1½
7/6	Clerical, Med., & Gen. Life, £25 Shs.	50/	16½
10/	Commercial Union, Ltd., £50 Shs.	5	45½
4	Do. "W. of Eng." Ter. Deb. Stk.	100	110½
60/	County Fire, £100 Shs.	80	195
5/	Eagle, £50 Shs.	5	—
4/	Employrs' Liability, Ltd., £10 Shs.	2	4½
—	Empress, Ltd., £5 Shs.	1	—
21/	Equity & Law, £100 Shs.	6	22
7/6	General Life, £100 Shs.	5	15
4½d.	Gresham Life, £5 Shs.	15/	2½
2/6	Guardian, Ld., £10 Shs.	5	12
10/	Imperial, Ltd., £20 Shs.	5	31
5/6	Imperial Life, £20 Shs.	4	6½
6/	Indemnity Mutual Mar., Ltd., £15 Shs.	3	12½
1/	Lancashire, £20 Shs.	2	5
7½d.	Law Acc. & Contin., Ltd., £5 Shs.	10/	¾
5/	Law Fire, £100 Shs.	2½	18
4½d.	Law Guar. & Trust, Ltd., £10 Shs.	1	1½
9/	Law Life, £20 Shs.	2	24½
2/9	Law Un. & Crown £10Shs.	10/	7
4	Do. Deb. Stk., 1949	100	110½
14/6	Legal & General, £50 Shs.	8	15½
9d.	Lion Fire, Ltd., £6½ Shs.	1½	½
14/	Liverpool & London & Globe, Stk.	2	55
10/	Do. Globe £1 Ann.	—	36
15/	London, £25 Shs.	12½	63½
4/	Lond. & Lanc. Fire, £25Shs	2½	19½
2/	Lond. & Lanc. Life, £25Shs	2	5
10	Lond. & Prov. Mar., Ld., £10 Shs.	1	1½
2/	Lond. Guar. & Accident, Ltd., £5 Shs.	2	12
10/	Marine, Ltd., £25 Shs.	4½	44½
2/	Maritime, Ltd., £10 Shs.	2	4½
1/6	Merc. Mar., Ld., £10 Shs.	2½	2½
1/	National Marine, Ltd., £9 Shs.	1	½
10/	N. Brit. & Merc., £25 Shs.	6½	43
20/	Northern, £100 Shs.	10	82
40/	Norwich Union Fire, £100 Shs.	12½	128½
5/	Ocean Acc. & Guar., fy. pd.	5	21½
1/	Do. £5 Shs.	1	¼
7/6	Ocean, Marine, Ltd.	2½	9½
1/	Palatine, £10 Shs.	2	3½
2/6	Pelican, £10 Shs.	1	3½
12/	Phœnix, £50 Shs.	5	45
25/	Provident, £100 Shs.	10	36
3/	Railway Passngrs., £10Shs.	2	8½
2/6	Rock Life, £5 Shs.	10/	4½
8	Royal Exchange	100	360
18/	Royal, £20 Shs.	3	56
4/	Sun, £10 Shs.	10/	11½
3/9	Sun Life, £10 Shs.	7½	15
6/	Thames & Mrsey. Marine, Ltd., £20 Shs.	2	10½
9/	Union, £10 Shs.	4	24½
4/	Union Marine, £20 Shs.	2½	9
12/	Universal Life, £100 Shs.	12	42
2/	World Marine, £5 Shs.	2	1½

IRON, COAL, AND STEEL.

Last Div.	Name.	Paid.	Price.
3/9	Barrow Hæm. Steel, Ltd.	7½	2½
9/	Do. 6 p.c. and Pref.	7½	7½
10/	Bolck., Vaugh. & C., Ld.	20	17½
6/	Do. £8 liab.	12	10
7/6	Brown, J. & Co., Ltd., £20 Shs.	15	20½
7/6	Consett Iron, Ld., £10 Shs.	7½	29½
4/	Do. 8 p.c. Cum. Pref.	5	11
7/6	Ebbw Vale Steel, Iron & Coal, Ltd., £23 Shs.	20	7½
15/	General Mining Assn., Ld.	5½	7½
8/	Harvey Steel Co. of Gt. Britain, Ltd.	10	27
5	Lehigh V. Coal 1 Mt. 5 p.c. Guar. Gd. Cp. Bds.	—	98
42/6	Nantyglo & Blaina Iron, Ltd., Pref.	£62	96
1/	Nerbudda Coal & Iron, Ltd., £3 Shs.	56/	1⁄16
—	Newport Abercrn. Bk. Vein Steam Coal, Ltd.	10	4½
5/	New Sharlston Coll., Ltd. Pref	20	10½
4½d.	Nw. Vancvr. Coal & Ld., L.	1	½
3/6	North's Navigation Coll. (1889) Ltd.	5	2½
10/	Do. 10 p.c. Cum. Pref.	5	7½
—	Rhymney Iron, Ltd.	5	1½
	Do. New, £5 Shs.	4½	½
5	Do. Mt. Debs., Red.	100	98½
5	Shelton Irn., Stl. & Cl. Co., Ltd., 1 Chg. Debs., Red.	100	99½
10	Sth. Hetton Coal, Ltd.	100	177½
	Vickers & Maxim, Ltd.	10	3
	Do. 5 p.c. Prfd. Stk.	100	132½

SHIPPING.

Last Div.	Name.	Paid.	Price.
4/	African Stm. Ship, £20 Shs.	16	9½
5/	Do. Fully-paid	20	13½
5/	Amazon Steam Nav., Ltd.	12½	9½
8/	Castle Mail Pakts., Ltd., £20 Shs.	14	15½
3½	Do. 1st Deb. Stk., Red.	100	101
6/	China Mutual Steam, Ltd.	5	3
6	Do. Cum. Pref.	10	9½
10/	Cunard, Ltd.	20	10
5/	Do. £20 Shs.	10	4
4½	Furness, Withy, & Co., Ltd., 1 Mt. Dbs., Red.	100	105
6/	General Steam	15	8½
5/	Do. 5 p.c. Pref., 1874	10	9
5/	Do. 5 p.c. Pref., 1877	10	9
5/	Leyland & Co., Ltd.	10	15½
7/	Do. 7 p.c. Cum. Pref.	10	14½
2/11	Do. 4½ p.c. Cum. Pre-Pf.	3	10½
4	Do. 1st Mt. Dbs., Red.	100	106½
7/6	Mercantile Steam, Ltd.	5	7½
6/4½	New Zealand Ship., Ltd.	6	5
4	Do. Deb. Stk., Red.	100	104
5/	Orient Steam, Ltd.	10	4½
5	P. & O. Steam, Cum. Prefd.	100	156½
19	Do. Defd.	100	232½
3½	Do. Deb. Stk.	100	121
5	Richelieu & Ont., 1st Mt. Debs., Red.	100	101
30/	Royal Mail, £100 Shs.	60	51
2/6	Shaw, Sav., & Alb., Ltd., "A" Pref.	5	5½
5/	Do. "B" Ord.	5	3½
8/	Union Steam, Ltd.	20	19½
4/	Do. New £20 Shs.	10	9
4	Do. Deb. Stk., Red.	100	107
7/	Union of N.Z., Ltd.	10	10
5½	Wilson's & Fur.-Ley., 5½ p.c. Cum. Pref.	10	10½
4½	Do. 1 Mt. Db. Sk., Rd.	100	106½

TELEGRAPHS AND TELEPHONES.

Last Div.	Name.	Paid.	Price.
4	African Direct, Ltd., Mort. Debs., Red.	100	102
—	Amazon Telegraph, Ltd.	10	6½
19/6	Anglo-American, Ltd.	100	61
39/	Do. 6 p.c. Prefd. Ord.	100	110½
—	Do. Defd. Ord.	100	12½
3/	Brazilian Submarine, Ltd.	10	17
5	Do. Debs., 2 Series	100	114

Telegraphs and Telephones (*continued*):—

Last Div.	Name.	Paid.	Price.
4/	Chili Telephone, Ltd.	5	3½
$2½	Comcial. Cable, $100 Shs.	—	189½
4	Do. Stg. 500-yr. Deb. Stk. Red.	100	107
2½d.	Consd. Telpehone Constr., &c., Ltd.	10/	¼
8/	Cuba Submarine, Ltd.	10	8
10/	Do. 10 p.c. Pref.	10	18
2/	Direct Spanish, Ltd.	5	4½
5/	Do. 10 p.c. Cum. Pref.	5	10½
4½	Do. Debs.	50	104½
3/	Direct U.S. Cable, Ltd.	20	11
2/6	Eastern, Ltd.	10	18½
3/	Do. 6 p.c. Cum. Pref.	10	19½
4	Do. Mt. Deb. Stk., Red.	100	132½
2/6	Eastern Exten., Aus., & China, Ltd.	10	19
5	Do. (Aus. Gov. Sub.) Deb., Red.	100	101
5	Do. do. Bearer	100	101½
4	Do. Mort. Deb. Stk.	100	131½
5	Eastn. & S. Afric., Ltd., Mort. Deb. 1900	100	101
5	Do. Bearer	100	101½
4	Do. Mort. Debs. 1909	100	103½
4	Do. Mort. Debs. (Maur. Subsidy)	25	109½
5/	Grt. Nthn. Copenhagen	10	28½
5	Do. Debs., Ser. B., Red.	100	103½
12/6	Indo-European, Ltd.	25	53½
6	London Platino-Brazilian, Ltd., Debs. 1904	100	109½
4/	Montevideo Telph., Ltd., 6 p.c. Pref.	5	2½
3/	National Telephone, Ltd.	5	7
6/	Do. Cum. 1 Pref.	10	16
6/	Do. Cum. 2 Pref.	10	15
5	Do. Non-Cum. 3 Pref.	5	6½
3½	Do. Deb. Stk., Red.	100	106½
4d.	Oriental Telephone, Ltd.	1	½
4	Pac. & Euro. Tlg. Dbs., Rd.	100	106½
4/	Reuter's, Ltd.	8	8½
5/	Un. Riv. Plate Telph., Ltd.	5	4½
5	Do. Deb. Stk., Red.	100	103½
6/	West African Telg., Ltd.	10	4½
5	Do. 5 p.c. Mt. Debs., Red.	100	104½
—	W. Coast of America, Ltd.	10	—
3/	Western & Brazilian, Ltd.	15	10½
3/	Do. 5 p.c. Pref. Ord.	7½	7½
—	Do. Defd. Ord.	7½	3½
4	Do. Deb. Stk., Red.	100	106
1/	W. India & Panama, Ltd.	10	½
6/	Do. Cum. 1 Pref.	10	8½
6/	Do. Cum. 2 Pref.	10	6
5	Do. Debs., Red.	100	106½
7	West. Union, 1 Mt. 1900 ($	1000	107
6	Do. 6 p.c. Stg. Bds., Rd.	100	102

TRAMWAYS AND OMNIBUS.

Last Div.	Name.	Paid.	Price.
1/6	Anglo-Argentine, Ltd.	5	4
6	Do. Deb. Stk.	100	132½
4	Barcelona, Ltd.	10	12½
5	Do. Deb., Red.	100	102½
6/6	Belfast Street Trams.	10	17
—	Blackpl. & Fltwd. Tram., £10 Shs.	8	11½
4/	Bordeaux Tram. & O., Ltd.	10	13½
5	Do. Cum. Pref.	10	11½
—	Brazilian Street Ry., Ltd.	2	½
—	British Elec. Trac., Ltd.	10	17½
—	B. Ayres & Belg. Tram., Ltd., 6 p.c. Cum. Pref.	5	4½
6	Do. 1 Deb. Stk.	100	105½
—	B. Ayres. Gd. Nat., Ltd., 6 p.c. 1 Deb. Bds., Red.	100	60
5½	Do. Pref. Debs., Red.	100	95½
1/	Calais, Ltd.	5	1
—	Calcutta, Ltd.	10	3½
—	Carthagena & Herr., Ltd.	10	3
5	Do. Deb., Red.	100	90
5	City of B'ham. Trams., Ltd., 5 p.c. Cum. Pref.	5	6
4	Do. 1 Mort. Debs., Rd.	100	106½
3/9	City of B. Ayres, Ltd.	5	7½
2/3	Do. Ext. £5 Shs.	3	4½
6	Do. Deb. Stk.	100	150
1/4	Edinburgh Street Tram.	4	3½
1/	Glasgow Tram. & Omni. Ltd., £9 Shs.	8	3½
3/7½	Imperial, Ltd.	6	15
2/	Lond., Deptfd, & Greenwich, Prefd.	5	3½
nil	Do. Defd.	5	1
10½	Lond. Gen. Omni., Ltd.	200	205
4	Do. Deb., Red.	100	117

Tramways and Omnibus (*continued*):—

Last Div.	Name.	Paid.	Price.
6/	London Road Car	6	11
5	London St. Rly. (Prov., Ont.), Mt. Debs.	100	112
4/9	London St. Trams.	—	3
12/9	London Trams., Ltd.	10	10
6/	Do. Non-Cum. Pref.	10	10½
5	Do. Mt. Db. Stk., Rd.	100	100½
5	Lynn & Boston 1 Mt. 1924 $	1000	107
5	Milwaukee Elec. Cons. Mt. $	1000	100½
5	Minneapolis St. 1 Cons. Mt $	1000	96
5	Montreal St. Dbs., 1908	100	110
4½	Do. Debs., 1922	100	107
6/	Nth. Metropolitan	10	13½
1/9½	Nth. Staffords., Ltd.	6	4½
5/6	Provincial, Ltd.	10	7
6/	Do. Cum. Pref.	10	13½
5	St. Paul City, 1937 $	1000	94
5	Do. Guar. Twin City Rap. Trans. $	1000	94
5/	Southampton	10	7
3/	South London	10	6
7/6	Sunderland, Ltd.	10	6
4½	Toronto 1 Mt., Red.	100	107
2/6	Tramways Union, Ltd.	5	7
4½	Do. Deb., Red.	100	109
5/	Vienna General Omnibus.	5	6½
5	Do. 5 p.c. Mt. Deb., Red.	100	105
4/	Wolverhampton, Ltd.	10	6½

WATER WORKS.

Last Div.	Name.	Paid.	Price.
8/	Antwerp, Ltd.	20	22
6/	Cape Town District, Ltd.	5	6½
10½	Chelsea	100	337½
5	Do. Pref. Stk.	100	178½
4½	Do. Pref. Stk., 1875	100	158½
4½	Do. Deb. Stk.	100	168½
5/	City St. Petersburg, Ltd.	13	11
4/6	Colne Valley	10	15½
4	Do. Deb. Stock	100	137½
£4	Consol. of Rosar., Ltd., 4 p.c. 1 Deb. Stk., Red.	100	91
7½	East London	100	235
4½	Do. Deb. Stk.	100	163½
3	Do. Deb. Stk., Red.	100	106
37/6	Grand Junction (Max. 10 p.c.) "A"	50	124½
18/9	Do. "B"	25	
18/9	Do. "C" (Max. 7½ p.c.)	25	57½
35/	Do. "D" (Max. 7 p.c.)	50	102½
4	Do. Deb. Stock	100	149½
13	Kent	100	350½
7	Do. New (Max. 7 p.c.)	100	215½
6/7½	Kimberley, Ltd.	7	5
6	Do. Debs., Red.	100	102½
6	Do. Deb. Stk., Red.	100	105½
10	Lambeth (Max. 10 p.c.)	100	308½
7½	Do. (Max. 7½ p.c.), 50 & 25	—	232½
4	Do. Deb. Stock	100	148½
3	Do. Red. Deb. Stock	100	105
10/	Montevideo, Ltd.	20	16½
5	Do. 1 Deb. Stk.	100	108½
5	Do. 2 Deb. Stk.	100	103½
132/9	New River New	100	449½
4	Do. Deb. Stk.	100	152½
4	Do. Deb. Stk. "B"	100	152½
—	Odessa, Ltd., "A" 6 p.c. Prefd.	20	—
nil	Do. "B" Deferred	20	—
4	Portland Con. Mt. "B," 1927	—	—
8/	Seville, Ltd.	20	12½
5/6	Southend "Addl." Ord.	10	17½
6	Southwark and Vauxhall	100	167½
6	Do. "D" Shares (7½ p.c. max.)	100	164½
5	Do. Pref. Stock	100	177½
4	Do. "A" Deb. Stock	100	148½
3	Staines Resvirs. Jt. Com. Gua. Deb. Stk., Red.	100	105
7/	Tarapaca, Ltd.	10	9½
10	West Middlesex	100	319½
4½	Do. Deb. Stk.	100	164½
3	Do. Deb. Stk.	100	107

Prices Quoted on the Leading Provincial Exchanges.

ENGLISH.

In quoting the markets, B stands for Birmingham; Bl for Bristol; M for Manchester; L for Liverpool; and S for Sheffield.

CORPORATION STOCKS.

Chief Market.	Int or Div.	Name.	Amount paid.	Price.
M	3½	Bolton, Red. 1935 ..	100	116
M	3½	Burnley, Red. 1933..	100	116
M	3½	Bury, Red. 1946	100	118
L	2¾	Liverpool, Red. 1925	100	102½
B	3½	Longton, 1932	100	106
M	4	Oldham Prp. Db. Sk.	100	144
M	£1	Do. Gas & W. Ann.		34½
S	4	Rotherham 4 p.c., Red. 1927...... [£	1 an	114
S	3	Do. Red. 1920..	100	104
M	3½	Runcorn Red. 1923..	100	105
S	2¾	Sheffield Water Ann.	100	117½
S	3	Do.	3 an	90
L	3½	Southport Red. 1936 {	5 an 100	110
L	3	Do. Red. 1914..	100	102½
M	3	Todmorden, Red. 1914	100	104

RAILWAYS.

Chief Market.	Int or Div.	Name.	Amount paid.	Price.
Bl	4½	Bridgewater Pref. ..	100	137½
M	4	Cleator & Workton.	100	78
M	4	Do. 1883 Pref. ..	100	111
L	4	Cockermth. K. & P.	100	116
L	4	Isle of Man	5	6¾
L	5	Do. Pref.	5	6⅝
L	3	Liverpool Overhead	10	11
L	4	Do. Deb. Stk. ..	100	109
L	5	Do. Pref.	10	16
L	6	Maryport & Carlisle	100	170
S	6	Mid. Shef. & Roth. Pf.	100	231
Bl	35/	Neath & Brecon "A"	100	60
M	4½	Oldham, Ashton, &c.	10	17
Bl	5½	Penarth Harbour ..	100	182½
Bl	4	Do. Deb. Stk. ..	100	145
Bl	3½	Do. Deb. Stk. ..	100	127
Bl	¾	Ross & Monmouth..	20	5¾
Bl	6	Do. Pref.	20	43
M	3	Southport & Cheshire Deb. Stk.	100	104½
M	nil.	Do. Pref.	100	26
Bl	2½	West Somerset Gu...	100	97½
Bl	5	Wye Val. Deb. Stk.	100	164

BANKS.

Chief Market.	Int or Div.	Name.	Amount paid.	Price.
L	6/	Adelphi, L., £20 Shs.	10	16
L	12/6	Bk of L'ool, L., £100 Sh	12½	39¾
B	5/6	Brmnghm. Dis. & C., Ltd., £20 Shs.....	4	10¾
B	6/3	Co. of Staffs., L., £40	5	13¼
S	17½	Crompton & Evans, Ltd., £20 Shs	4	14¾
M	14/	Lancs. & Yorks, Ltd., £20 Shs.....	10	31¾
L	18/	Livrpl. Union, Ltd., £100 Shs.	20	60½
M	24/	Manchester & Co., Ltd., £100 Shs. ..	16	61½
M	20/	Mnchstr. & Livrpool. Dis., Ltd., £60 Shs.	10	51½
M	1/6	Mer. of Lancashire, Ltd., £20 Shs.....	3	6½
L	16/	Nth. & Sth. Wales, Ltd., £40 Shs.....	10	34¾
	5/	Notts Joint St., Ltd., £50 Shs..........	10	23
M	4/	Oldham Joint Stk., Ltd., £20 Shs.....	4	10½
S	10	Sheffield Banking, Ltd., £50 Shs.....	17½	50½
S	10	Do. & Rotherham, Ltd., £50 Shs...	8	26
S	15	Do. & Hallamsh., Ltd., £100 Shs..	25	61¾
S	10	Do. Union, Ltd., £40 Shs.........	10	25
M	12/	Union of Manchester, Ltd., £25 Shs.. ..	11	28
M	10/	Williams, Deacon, &c. Ltd., £50 Shs....	8	25¾
Bl	20	Wilts & Dorset, Ltd., £50 Shs..........	10	49
S	10/	York City & Co., Ltd., £10 Shs.....	3	13¾

BREWERIES.

Chief Market.	Int or Div.	Name.	Amount paid.	Price.
B	6	Ansell & Sons Pref.	10	15½
B	5	Do. Debs.	100	110
L	7/	Bent's..............	10	19½
L	6	Do. Cum. Pref...	10	14¾
L	4½	Do. Deb. Stk. ..	100	111
L	13/6	Birkenhead, £5 paid	5	22
L	13/6	Do. £10 paid...	10	25
M	9/	Boddington's	9	20¾
M	5	Do. Cum. Pref...	10	13¼
M	4	Do. Deb. Stk. ..	100	109
B	4½	Butler & Co. Db. Stk	100	110½
M	6	Chesters' Cum. Pref.	10	13¼
M	4½	Do. Debs.	100	112½
S	17/	Clarkson's Ord.	10	24½
S	6	Do. Cum. Prf. Stk.	10	14¾
M	4	Dutton & Co. Db. Sk.	100	104
M	4½	Hardy's Crown Debs.	100	111
B	6/	Holt	10	18¾
B	5	Do. Cum. Pref...	10	12¾
B	4	Do. Debs.	100	108½
B	12/6	Lichfield	10	24
B	5	Do. Cum. Pref...	10	11¾
M	5½	Manchester Deb. Stk.	100	141
B	14	Mitchell, H., & Co.	10	37½
B	6	Do. Cum. Pref...	10	15½
Bl	6	Oakhill Pref........	10	16¾

Breweries (*continued*):—

Chief Market.	Int. or Div.	Name.	Amount paid.	Price.
M	5/	Springwell	10	10¾
M	7	Do. Pref.	10	13½
Bl	9	Stroud	10	17
Bl	6	Do. Pref......	10	14½
M	6/	Taylor's Eagle......	10	11
M	7	Do. Cum. Pref ..	10	13½
M	5½	Do. Deb. Stk. ..	100	120½
S	10	Tennant Bros £20 shs	15	34
S	10	Wheatley & Bates ..	10	14½
S	6	Do. Cum. Pref.	10	12¾

CANALS AND DOCKS.

Chief Market.	Int. or Div.	Name.	Amount paid.	Price.
Bl	5	Hill's Dry Dk. &c. £20	18	9
M	4	Manc. Ship Canal 1st Mt. Deb. Stk.	100	104
M	4	Do. 2nd do.	100	102½
L	36/3	Mersey Dck. & Harb.	an.	118½
L	35/	Do.	an.	116
M	10/	Rochdale Canal	100	37½
B	35/	Staff. & Worc. Canal	100	76
B	4½	Do. Deb. Stk....	100	137
Bl	4	Swansea Harb......	100	114
B	27/6	Warwick & Birm. Cnl	100	66½
B	12/6	Do. & Napton do.	100	23

COMMERCIAL & INDUSTRIAL.

Chief Market.	Int. or Div.	Name.	Amount paid.	Price.
L	5	Agua Santa Mt. Debs	100	100
M	8/	Armitage, Sir E. & Sns Ltd..............	10	19
M	4	Do. Deb. 1910 ..	100	103
L	6	Ang. Chil. Nit. 1 Mt. Debs., 1919 ..	100	109½
Bl	8½	Bath Stone Firms ..	10	20
M	4/9½	Barlow & Jones, Ltd., £10 Shs.	8	10¾
B	7/6	Birmgham. Ry. Car.	10	18
B	6	Do. Pref.	10	16½
B	16/8	Do. Small Arms	5	17½
M	£12	Blackpool Pier......	100	277½
M	5	Do. Tower Debs.	50	54½
M	3/	Do. Wi. Gar. & P.	5	4¾
Bl	10	Bristl. & S. W. R. Wag. £20 Shs..........	3	6
Bl	8	Do. Wag. & Carri. £10 Shs..........	10	14¾
M	7/	Crosses & Winkwth. Ltd..............	5	12¹⁄₁₆
L	5	G. Angus & Co. Pref.	10	13¾
Bl	7	Gloster. Carri. & W.		10½
Bl	5	Gt. Wstn. Cttn., Ltd.	20	15½
M	6	Hetherington, L. Prf.	10	8¾
M	4½	Do. Debs., 1910	100	99¾
B	7½d.	Hinks (J. & Son), Ltd.	1	27/6
S	10/	Jessop & Sons, £50 Sh	30	28
S	10	Kayser, Ellsn. & Co. L.	5	10½
S	6	Do. Pref.	5	7½
M	7/6	Kellner-Partgton., L.	5	14½
M	4½	Do. Debs., 1914	100	105½
M	5	Kerr Thread, Ltd., Debs.	100	101
B	17/	King's Norton Metal, £10 Shs..........	8½	18½
M	5/	Lancashire & Yorks. Wagon, Ltd.	10	9¾
L	10/	Liverpool Exch., Ltd.	20	27¾
L	45/	Do. Grain Stge, Ltd.	50	108
L	2/6	Do. Rubber, Ltd...	5	7
M	9d.	Manchester Bond. Whse., L., £10 Shs.	4½	2¾
M	3/9	Do. Comcial. Bldgs., Ltd., £10 Shs.	5	10½
M	3/9	Do. No. 2, £10 Shs.	5	10¾
M	2/3	Do. No. 3, £10 Shs.	5	7½
M	4/	Do. Corn, &c., Exchange, Ltd.	10	16¾
M	4	Do. Debs.	100	125
M	8	Do. Ryl. Exchge, L.	100	246½
B	19/	Midland Rlwy. Car. Wgn., Ld., £20 Sh.	10	14½
Bl	5	Millers & Corys Dbs.	100	100½
B	12/6	Mint, Brgham., Ltd.	5	8½
B	5	Do. Debs.	25	107
B	10/	Nettlefolds, Ltd.....	10	48
B	5	Do. Pref.	10	15
S	9	Nth. Centrl. Wgn., L.	5	8¾
B	15/	Patnt. Nut & Bolt, L.	10	26
B	5	Do. Pref.	10	14½
B	6d.	Perry & Co., Ltd. ..	1	29/
B	6d.	Do. Pref.	1	27/6
S	10	Round, J., & Co., L., £10 Shs.	6	12¾
S	10	Rodgers, J., & Sons, L.	100	218
M	18/9	Rylands & Sons, Ltd., £20	15	39½
M	2/6	Do. paid up	20	45
M	4	Do. Debs. ..1909	100	106
S	5	Sanderson Brs. & Co., Ltd, Debs.	100	102
M	4½	Schwabe, S., & Co., Ltd., 1 Debs. 1914	100	104
S	7½	Sheffield Forge & Rolling, Ltd.	10	11½
L	—	Southport Pier, Ltd.	100	88
L	2½	Do. W. Gdns., Ltd.	5	3½
Bl	5	Spillers & Bakers, Ltd, £10 Shs.	9	14¾
Bl	6	Do. Pref.	10	14½
B	5/	Union Rolling Stock, Ltd., £20 Shs.....	5	7½
M	5/	Victoria Pr., S'port, L.	5	4¾
Bl	8	Western Wagon & Property, Ltd.....	6	9¾
S	10	Wostenholm, G., & Son, Ltd., £25 Shs.	20	25
S	6½	Yorksh. Wagon, Ltd.	2	2¾

FINANCIAL, TRUSTS, &c.

Chief Market.	Int. or Div.	Name.	Amount paid.	Price.
M	1/	Manchstr. Trst. £10 Shs..............	2	13/9
M	1/3	N. of Eng. T. Deb. & A., Ltd. £10 Shs.	2½	22/
M	3½	Do. 1 Mt. Debs...	100	95½
L	—	Pacific Ln. & Inv., L.	2½	3
L	4	Do. Deb. Stk.....	100	102
L	—	United Trst., L. Prfd.	100	72½
L	—	Do. Deferred....	100	62½

GAS.

Chief Market.	Int. or Div.	Name.	Amount paid.	Price.
Bl	5	Bristol Gas (5 p.c. mx.)	100	130½
Bl	4	Do. 1st Deb.	100	137
S	10	Gt. Grimsby "C" ..	10	202
L	10	Liverpool Utd. "A"	100	258
L	7	Do. "B"......	100	192
L	4	Do. Deb.......	100	136
S	10	Sheffield Gas "A," "B," "C"	100	253
B	10½	Wolverhampton	100	225
B	3	Do. 6 p.c. Pref...	100	170½

INSURANCE.

Chief Market.	Int. or Div.	Name.	Amount paid.	Price.
M	6	Equitable F. & Acc. £5 Shs.	1	39/
L	—	Liverpool Mortgage £10 Shs.	2	1⅞
M	2/	Mchester. Fire £20 Shs..............	2	8
M	5/	National Boiler & G., Ltd., £10 Shs.	3	13¾
L	2/	Reliance Mar., Ltd., £10 Shs.	2	4⁹⁄₁₆
L	2/	Sea, Ltd., £10 Shs...	2	10⅛
L	—	Stnd. Mar., L., £20 Sh.	4	8⅞
L	—	State Fire, L., £20 Sh.	1	2⅛

COAL, IRON, AND STEEL.

Chief Market.	Int. or Div.	Name.	Amount paid.	Price.
Bl.	7/6	Albion Stm. Coal ..	10	11½
M	—	And. Knowles & S., Ltd., £37½ Shs. ..	22½	13½
M	5	Do. Mt. Debs. 1908	100	105½
Bl.	1/½	Ashton V. Iron	100	26
S		Bessemer, Ltd.	10	19½
S	5	Do. Pref.	10	12¾
S	7	Briggs, H., & Co., "A" £15 Shs.....	12½	15¾
S	7	Do. "B" £15 Shs.	8½	9¾
S	20	Brown Baley's. Stl., L.	10	29½
S	5	Brown, J., & Co., Cum. Pref.	10	13½
S	5	Cammell, C. & Co., Ltd.	85	12½
S	5	Do. Pref.	5	6⅝
M	5	Chatterley Whitfield. Col., Debs., 1905..	100	100½
Bl	4	Davis, D., & Sons, Ld.	10	9¾
M	5	Evans, R., & Co., Ltd., Deb., 1910 ..	100	100½
S	12½	Fox, S., & Co., Ltd., £100 Shs.	80	176
Bl	10	Gt. Wstn. Col., L., "A"	5	10
Bl	5	Do. "B"	5	4¹⁄₁₆
Bl	3	Main Colliery, Ltd.	10	7
B	2/6	Muntz's Metal, Ltd.	5	7½
B	5	Do. Pref.......	5	6⅝
M	2/6½	Nth. Lonsd. Iron and Steel, Ltd., £10 Sh.	8½	2½
Bl	6	North's Nav. Coll., Ltd., Debs.	100	105
S	60/	Parkgate Irn. & Stl., Ltd., £100 Shs. ..	75	70
M	6	Pearson & Knls., Ld., "A" Cum. Pref...	50	46
B	10/	Sandwell Pk. Col., L.	10	16¾
M	6/3	Sheepbridge Coal and Iron, Ltd., "A"	25	17½
M	2/6	Do. "B"	10	7
M	5	Do. "C" Gua. Pf.	25	28¾
Bl	4	South Wales Coll., Ltd., "A"	17	7½
S	55/	Staveley Coal & Iron, Ltd., "A" £100 Sh.	60	80½
S	55/	Do. "C"	60	81
M	1/10½	Tredegar Iron & Cl., Ld., "A" £10 Sh.	7½	2¾
M	1½	Do. "B" Stk. ..	100	29½
M	2/	Wigan Cl. & Irn., Ld.	10	6½
M	1/6	Do. £10 Shs.	7½	3½

SHIPPING.

Chief Market.	Int. or Div.	Name.	Amount paid.	Price.
Bl	6	Bristol St. Nav. Pref.	10	11¾
L	5/	Brit. & Af. St. Nav..	10	14
L	3/10½	British & Estn, Ltd.	6½	2⅞
L	10/	Pacific Stm. Nav., L.	25	24½
L	10/	Wst. Ind. & Pac. St. Ltd., £25 Shs....	20	20½

TRAMWAYS, &c.

Chief Market.	Int. or Div.	Name.	Amount paid.	Price.
B	5/	Brmngh. & Aston, L.	5	11¼
B	5/	Do. Mid., Ltd...	10	7¾
Bl	6/	Bristol Tr. & Car., Ltd..............	10	20¾
Bl	4/	Do. Debs.	100	121
L	6	I. of Man Elec., L., Pref.	1	1½
M	15/	Manchester C. & T., L., "A" £20 Shs.	15	27¾
M	10/	Do. "B"	10	19¾

WATER WORKS.

Chief Market.	Int. or Div.	Name.	Amount paid.	Price.
Bl	7	Bristol	25	62
Bl	7	Do..............	20	46½
Bl	58/	Do. 7 p.c. max. ..	100	157½
Bl	4½	Do. Pref.	20	32½
Bl	5	Do. Pref.	10	18½
Bl	3½	Do. Deb.	100	129½
M	10	Fylde "A"........	100	335
M	7	Do. "B"	100	224
B	6	S. Staffs. Ord. "A"	100	168
B	—	Do. "B"	100	167
B	4	Do. Deb. Stk.	100	140
B	5	Do. Pf "A" "B" "C"	100	165
M	£3¾	Stockport District ..	100	184½
B	2/	Wolverhampton New	5	6¾

SCOTTISH.

In quoting the markets, E stands for Edinburgh, and G for Glasgow.

RAILWAYS.

Chief Market.	Int. or Div.	Name.	Nom. Amount	Price.
E	6½	Arbroath and Forfar	25	51
G	2	Callander and Oban.	10	7½
G	4	Do. Deb. Stock	100	148
G	4½	Do. Pref.......	10	14½
G	4	Cathct. Dist. Deb. Stk.	100	148
E	5	Edin. and Bathgate .	100	179½
E	7	Forth & Clyde Junc.	100	226
G	4	Lanarks. and Ayrsh.	10	14
G	4	Do. & Dumbartons.	10	14½
G	4	Do. Deb. Stk.	100	149

BANKS.

Chief Market.	Int. or Div.	Name.	Nom. Amount	Price.
G	12	Bank of Scotland ..	100	357½
G	16	British Linen	100	480
G	8	Caledonian, Ltd.....	2½	95/6
G	10	Clydesdale, Ltd.	10	23½
G	16	Commercl. of Scot., L.	20	88½
G	16	National of Scot. Ld.	100	421
G	8	Royal of Scotland ..	100	233
G	11	Union of Scotland, L.	10	26½

BREWERIES.

Chief Market.	Int. or Div.	Name.	Nom. Amount	Price.
E	5	Bernard, Thos. Pref.	10	10¾
E	5	Bernard, T. & J., Cum. Pref........	10	13
G	20	Highland Distilleries	3½	10¾

CANALS AND DOCKS.

Chief Market.	Int. or Div.	Name.	Nom. Amount	Price.
G	4	Clyde Nav. 4 p.c....	100	125½
G	3½	Do. 3½ p.c.......	100	105
G	3¾	Greenock Harb. "A"	100	100
G	2	Do. "B"	100	40

MISCELLANEOUS.

Chief Market.	Int. or Div.	Name.	Nom. Amount	Price.
G	4½	Alexander & Co. Debs.	100	110½
G	5	Baird, H., & Sns. C. P.	10	12½
E	10	Barry, Ostlere, & Co.	7½	12½
E	6	Do. Cum. Pref...	10	15⅛
G	5	Brown, Stewart, Deb.	100	84
E	7½	Broxburn Oil	8½	8½
E	6	Do. Cum. Pref...	10	11⅛
E	7	Edinburgh & Dist. Tram. Cum. Pref.	5	8⅝
E	5	Gilroy, Sons, & Co. Debs.	100	99
G	3/	Glasgow Cot. Spin...	6	5¾
G	55/	Do. Royal Exchg.	46	110
G	—	Pumpherston Oil Pf.	10	8¾
E	7	Scottish Assam Tea	10	11½
E	5	Scottish Waggon....	10	12½
G	5	Stoddard & Co. Pref.	10	12⅝

FINANCIAL, LAND, AND INVESTMENT.

Chief Market.	Int. or Div.	Name.	Nom. Amount	Price.
G	1/	Assets Co...........	1	47/
E	4½	Investors' Mort. Pref.	100	99½
E	4	Do. Deb. Stk....	100	103½
E	4	Nthn. Inv. N. Zeal. Deb. Stk.	100	107
E	4	N. of Scot. Canadian Deb. Stk.	100	106
E	4½	Real & Deb. Corp. Deb. Stk.	100	107½

INSURANCE.

Chief Market.	Int. or Div.	Name.	Amount paid.	Price.
G	12/	Caledonian F. & Life	5	36
G	4/6	City of Glasgow Life	2½	13
E	19/	Edinburgh Life	20	55
G	13/1	Life Ass. of Scotland	8⅓	34½
E	8	Nat. Guar. & Surety	2	50/
G	17½	Scottish Union and National "A"....	1	97/
G	17½	Do. "B"	3⅓	18

IRON, COAL, AND STEEL.

Chief Market.	Int. or Div.	Name.	Amount paid.	Price.
E	Nil.	Addie, Coll. Cm. Pref.	10	8
E	8/	Arniston Coal	8	14
E	2½	Cairntable Gas Coal	8	86/
E	7½	Fife Coal	10	21
E	5	Do. Cum. Pref..	10	13½
G	7	Merry & Cunghame. Cum. Pref........	10	15½
G	5	Do. Debentures ..	100	106½
E	1/9	Niddrie & Benhar Cl.	1½	41/
G	5	Steel Com. of Scotlnd.	—	
	—	"A" Deb. Stk. ..	100	113
G	6	Do. and Mt. "B"	100	105
E	—	Watson, John	8½	10½
E	6	Do. Cum. Pref..	7½	8½
E	12½	Wilson's & Cly. Coal	3	8¾

IRISH.

In quoting the markets, B stands for Belfast, and D for Dublin.

CORPORATION STOCKS.

Chief Market.	Int. or Div.	Name.	Amount paid.	Price.
B	3½	Belfast, 1921	100	112
B	3½	Do. 1912	100	108½
B	3½	Do. 1924	100	109½
B	3	Do. 1955	100	106
B	3½	Do. Water Com...	100	117½
B	3	Do. do.	100	106
B	3½	Do. Harbour Com.	100	114
D	3½	Rathmines & Rathgar	100	110½
D	3½	Waterford Deb.	100	—

RAILWAYS.

Chief Market.	Int. or Div.	Name.	Amount Paid.	Price.
D	30/	Cork, Bandon, & S.C.	100	—
D	4	Do. Deb.	100	139½
D	4	Do. W. Cork Pref.	100	—
B	5½	Belfast & Northern..	100	163½
B	4	Do. Deb.	100	145
B	4	Do. Pref.	100	141
B	6½	Belfast & C. Down..	100	166
B	4	Do. Deb.	100	147
B	3	Do.	100	107½
B	4½	Do. 4½ Pref. B...	100	153½
B	5	Do. Guar.	100	172½
D	Nil.	Dublin, Wick. & Wex.	100	29½
D	4	Do. Deb.	100	125
D	4½	Do. Deb.	100	130
D	6	Do. Guar.	100	163
D	4	Do. C. of Dub. Junc.	100	—
D	5	Do. 1860 Pref. ..	100	114
D	—	Do. 1864 Pref. ..	100	101½
D	—	Do. 1865 Pref. ..	100	85
B	6½	Great Northern	100	182
B	4	Do. Deb.	100	147
B	4	Do. Pref. B.	100	145½
B	5½	Gt. South & Western	100	147
B	4	Do. Deb.	100	146½
B	4	Do. Guar.	100	145
D	4	Midland Gt. Western	100	112½
D	4	Do. Deb.	100	146½
D	4½	Do. Deb.	100	151½
D	4½	Do. Deb.	100	—
D	5	Do. Pref.	100	—
D	4	Do. Pref.	100	—
D	—	Waterford & Central	100	15½
D	3	Do. Deb.	100	105
D	3½	Do. Pref.	100	—
D	4	Waterfd. L., & W. Db.	100	127½
D	4½	Do. Deb.	100	—
D	4	Do. Pref.	100	128
D	3½	Do. Pref.	100	93

BANKS.

Chief Market.	Int. or Div.	Name.	Amount paid.	Price.
B	50/	Belfast, Old, £125 Shs.	25	125
B	20/	Do. New, £125 Shs.	25	60½
D	2/	Hibernian, £20 Shs.	5	6½
D	2/	Munster & Leinster £5 Shs.	2	5½
B	11/	Northern, £50 Shs...		27½
D	13/	Royal, £50 Shs.	10	29½
B	5/	Ulster, £15 Shs.	2½	12⅛

BREWERIES AND DISTILLERIES.

Chief Market.	Int. or Div.	Name.	Amount paid.	Price.
D	10/	Castlebellingham & Drog.	10	16½
D	6	Do. Pref.	10	16
D	4½	Do. Deb.	100	116
B	17/	Dunville & Co.......	10	29½
B	6	Irish Distillery, Pref.	10	13
B	5	Do. Deb.	100	110
B	6	J. & J. M'Connell, Pf.	10	15½
B	13/6	Mitchell & Co.......	9	20
B	5	Do. Deb.	10	11½
D	4½	Phœnix Brew. Deb.	100	—
B	6/	Wm. Cowan	10	13½
B	6	Do. Pref. ..	10	13½
B	8/	Young, King, & Co.	8	14

STEAM AND CANAL.

Chief Market.	Int. or Div.	Name.	Amount paid.	Price.
B	Nil	Belfast Steamship ..	50	35½
D	10/	British and Irish	50	—
D	15/	City of Dublin	100	63½
D	3½	Do. Deb.	100	105
D	30/	Dublin & Lpool. Bldg.	50	75
D	2/6	Dundalk & Newry..	10	4½
D	3/6	Grand Canal	10	12½
D	3	Do. Pref. ..	10	9½
D	3	Do. Deb. ..	100	99
B	30/	Irish Shipowners	100	63
B	3/	Ulster Steamship	5	5½

MISCELLANEOUS.

Chief Market.	Int. or Div.	Name.	Amount paid.	Price.
D	3/1	Arnott & Co.	4	7½
D	6	Do. Pref. ..	4	6½
B	8/	Belfast Com. Bldgs.	10	11
B	37/6	Do. Ropework Co.	75	90
B	5	Do. do. Pref.	10	13½
B	2/	Do. Discount Co..	3	43/
B	5	Do. do. Pref.	5	4½
B	10/	Brookfield Linen....	25	17½
B	Nil	Coey & Co.	25	4
B	5	Do. Deb.	50	49
B	4½	David Allen & S's Deb.	100	106½
D	4/	Dublin Trams	10	19½
D	6	Do. Pref.....	10	18½
D	4	Do. Deb.....	100	—
B	3/	Edenderry Spinning .	10	9
B	25/	Falls Flax Spinning .	25	15
B	17/	Forster, Green, & Co.	10	22
B	9/	Island Spinning	7½	7½
B	8/	Jas. Lindsay & Co..	8	16½
B	1/7½	John Arnott & Co...	4	4½
B	4½	Do. Deb........	50	56
D	5/	Kinahan & Co.......	10	11½
D	5½	Do. Pref........	10	11½
D	4½	Do. Deb........	100	109½
B	12/	Kirker & Co.	10	10
B	5/	Leahy, Kelly, & Leahy	5	8½
B	6	Do. Pref........	5	7⅛
B	2/4½	Lindsay Bros. Ltd...	8	7½
B	4½	Do. Deb........	50	56½
D	1/	National Assurance .	2½	38/6
B	10/	Olley & Co.	5	7⅛
D	1/1½	Patriotic Assurance..	2½	30/3
B	3/7½	P. Johnston & Son, L.	6	6½
B	10/	Robertson, F., & Co.	8	23½
B	10	Ulster Marine Insur.	5/	6/6
B	15/	York-street Flax	25	33½
B	6	Do. Pref........	10	15⅛
B	4½	Do. Deb........	100	120½

INDIAN AND CEYLON TEA COMPANIES.

Acres Planted.	Crop, 1897.	Paid up Capital.	Share.	Paid up.	Name.	Dividends. 1894.	1895.	1896.	Int. 1897.	Price.	Yield.	Reserve.	Balance Forward.	Working Capital.	Mortgages, Debs. or Pref. Capital not otherwise stated.
	lb.	£	£	£	INDIAN COMPANIES.							£	£	£	£
11,240	3,128,000	120,000	10	3	Amalgamated Estates	—	*	10	5	3¾	8¼	10,000	16,500	D52,950	—
		400,000	10	10	Do. Pref.	—	*	5	1½	10⅛	4¾				
10,223	3,560,000	187,160	20	20	Assam	20	20	20	5	61	6½	55,000	1,730	D11,350	—
5,900	3,278,000	142,500	10	10	Assam Frontier	1	6	6	—	9	6½	—	286	20,000	82,500
		142,500	10	10	Do. Pref.	6	6	6	3	11¼	5¼				
2,087	839,000	66,745	5	5	Attaree Khat	12	12	8	3	7¾	5¼	3,790	4,820	7,770	—
1,633	583,000	78,170	10	10	Borelli	4	4	5	—	8½	5¾	—	3,256	D270	6,500 Pref.
1,689	812,000	60,825	5	5	British Indian	6	5	5	—	4½	5½	—	2,920	12,300	16,500 Pref.
3,223	2,247,000	114,500	5	5	Brahmapootra	20	18	20	6	14	7	—	28,440	41,600	·
3,904	1,617,000	76,500	10	10	Cachar and Dooars	*	8	7	—	10	7½	—	1,645	21,240	·
		76,500	10	10	Do. Pref.	*	6	6	3	12½	5				
3,946	2,083,000	72,010	1	1	Chargola	8	7	10	2½	1	10½	3,000	3,300	—	—
		81,000	1	1	Do. Pref.	7	7	7	3½	1⅛	5½				
1,971	942,000	33,000	5	5	Chubwa	10	8	10	3½	6½	7¾	10,000	2,043	D5,400	—
		33,000	5	5	Do. Pref.	7	7	7	3½	7	5				
33,250	11,500,000	120,000	10	3	Cons. Tea and Lands	—	*	10	5	3½	7½	65,000	14,240	D191,674	—
		1,000,000	10	10	Do. 1st Pref.	—	*	5	1½	11¼	4½				
		400,000	10	10	Do. 2nd Pref.	—	*	7	1¾	12	5¾				
2,230	617,000	135,420	20	20	Darjeeling	5½	5½	6	—	23	5	5,552	1,565	1,700	—
2,114	445,000	60,000	10	10	Darjeeling Cons.	—	—	4/2	—	7½	—	—	1,820	—	—
		60,000	10	10	Do. Pref.	—	*	5	2½	9⅞	5				
6,600	3,518,000	150,000	10	10	Dooars	12½	12½	12½	2½	21	6¼	45,000	300	D32,000	—
		75,000	10	10	Do. Pref.	7	7	7	3½	17	4¼				
3,367	1,811,000	165,000	10	10	Doom Dooma	11¼	10	12½	5	22	5½	30,000	4,032	—	10,000
1,377	582,000	61,120	5	5	Eastern Assam	½	nil.	4	—	3	6½	—	1,790	—	10,000
4,038	1,675,000	85,000	10	10	East India and Ceylon	*	nil.	7	—	9	7½	—	1,710	—	—
		85,000	10	10	Do. Pref.	*	6	6	3	12½	4¾				
7,570	3,363,000	219,000	10	10	Empire of India	—	*	6/10	2	12¼	—	15,000	—	27,000	—
		219,000	10	10	Do. Pref.	—	*	5	2½	11¼	4¼				
1,180	540,000	94,060	10	10	Indian of Cachar	7	3½	3	—	5¾	5¼	6,070	—	7,120	—
2,916	824,000	83,500	5	5	Jhanzie	10	10	10	4	8¾	5¾	14,500	1,070	2,700	—
7,980	3,680,000	250,000	10	10	Jokai	10	10	10	5	18	5½	45,000	990	D9,000	—
		100,000	10	10	Do. Pref.	*	6	6	3	15¾	3¾				
5,224	1,563,000	100,000	20	20	Jorehaut	20	20	20	—	60	6½	36,220	2,955	3,000	—
1,547	504,000	65,660	10	8	Lebong	15	15	15	5	17	6¾	9,000	2,150	8,650	—
5,082	1,709,000	100,000	10	10	Lungla	1½	10	6	3	9½	6½	—	1,543	D21,000	—
		100,000	10	10	Do. Pref.	*	6	6	3	11¾	5				
2,684	885,000	95,970	10	10	Majuli	7	5	5	—	7	7	—	2,606	560	—
1,300	380,000	91,840	1	1	Makum	—	—	2	—	1⅛	1¾	—	—	1,200	25,000
3,140	770,000	100,000	1	1	Moabund	—	—	*	—	1	—	—	—	—	—
		50,000	1	1	Do. Pref.	—	—	*	2½	1	5				
1,080	482,000	79,590	10	10	Scottish Assam	7½	7	7	—	11	6½	6,500	800	9,590	—
4,150	1,456,000	100,000	10	10	Singlo	7½	8	5	1	9¼	4¾	—	300	D5,200	—
		80,000	10	10	Do. Pref.	*	6½	6½	3¼	12¾	5				
	Crop, 1896.				CEYLON COMPANIES.										
7,970	1,743,824	250,000	100	100	Anglo-Ceylon, & Gen.	—	*	5½	—	68	7¾	10,992	1,405	D72,844	166,520
1,836	685,741	50,000	10	10	Associated Tea	—	*	5	—	8¾	5¾	—	164	2,478	—
		60,000	10	10	Do. Pref.	—	*	6	—	11	5½				
10,390	4,000,000§	167,380	10	10	Ceylon Tea Plantations ..	15	15	15	7	27¾	5½	84,500	1,516	D30,819	—
		81,080	10	10	Do. Pref.	7	7	7	1¾	17¾	4¼				
5,722	1,542,700	55,260	5	3	Ceylon & Oriental Est....	5	8	7	—	2¾	7½	—	230	D2,047	71,000
		46,000	5	5	Do. Pref.	6	6	6	3	5	6				
2,157	801,629	111,330	5	5	Dimbula Valley	—	*	10	5	6½	7	—	—	1,733	6,250
		62,607	5	5	Do. Pref.	—	*	6	3	6½	4¾				
11,496	3,715,000	298,250	5	5	Eastern Prod. & Est.	3	5	6½	2½	6¾	4¾	20,000	11,740	D17,797	102,500
3,118	701,100	150,000	10	10	Lanka Plantations	4	5	5	1½	7½	6¾	—	495	D11,300	14,700 Pref.
2,193	1,050,000§	22,080	10	10	New Dimbula "A"	10	16	16	—	25	6	11,000	2,024	1,150	—
		55,710	10	10	Do. "B"	18	16	16	—	23½	6¾				
		8,400	10	10	Do. "C"	nil.	8	14	—	15	8¾				
2,572	570,360	100,000	10	10	Ouvah	6	8	6	2	9¾	6¼	4,000	1,151	D1,255	—
2,630	535,075	200,000	10	10	Nuwara Eliya	—	*	6	3	11¾	5¼	—	—	—	30,000
1,720	720,200	41,000	10	10	Scottish Ceylon	15	15	15	5	24	6¼	7,000	1,252	D3,970	—
		9,000	10	10	Do. Pref.	7	7	7	3½	16¼	3¾				
2,450	750,000§	56,000	10	6	Standard	12½	15	15	5	14¼	6¾	9,000	800	D14,012	4,000

Working-Capital Column.—In working-capital column, D stands for *debit*.

* Company formed this Year. † Interim dividends are given as actual distribution made. ‡ *Total* div. § Crop 1897.

Printed for the Proprietor by LOVE & WYMAN, LTD., Great Queen Street, London, W.C.; and Published by CLEMENT WILSON at Norfolk House, Norfolk Street, Strand, London, W.C.

The Investors' Review

EDITED BY A. J. WILSON.

Vol. I.—No. 8. New Series. FRIDAY, FEBRUARY 25, 1898. [Registered as a Newspaper.] Price 6d. By post, 6½d

The Investment Index,

A Quarterly Supplement to the "Investors' Review."

Price 2s. net. 8s. 6d. per annum, post free.

THE INVESTMENT INDEX is an indispensable supplement to the Investors' Review. A file of it enables investors to follow the ups and downs of markets, and each number gives the return obtainable on all classes of securities at recent prices, arranged in a most convenient form for reference. Appended to its tables of figures are criticisms on company balance sheets, State Budgets, &c., similar to those in the Investors' Review.

Regarding it, the *Specker* says: "The Quarterly 'Investment Index' is probably the handiest and fullest, as it is certainly the safest, of guides to the investor."

"The compilation of securities is particularly valuable."—*Pall Mall Gazette.*

"Its carefully classified list of securities will be found very valuable."—*Globe.*

"At no time has such a list of securities been more valuable than at the present."—*Star.*

"The invaluable 'Investors' Index.'"—*Sketch.*

"A most valuable compilation"—*Glasgow Herald.*

Subscription to the "Investors' Review" and "Investment Index," 36s. per annum, post free.

CLEMENT WILSON,
NORFOLK HOUSE NORFOLK STREET, LONDON, W.C.

CALEDONIAN
INSURANCE COMPANY.

The Oldest Scottish Insurance Office.

LIFE ASSURANCE WITH AND WITHOUT MEDICAL EXAMINATION ON EXCEPTIONALLY LIBERAL TERMS.

Example of the Company's Threefold Option Investment Policy.

Entrant at age 26 may secure in return for an Annual Premium of only £30 the following benefits—

A. An Assurance of £1,000, payable if death occur before age 65;

B. An Endowment of £2,000 on attainment of age 65; or in lieu of B. one of the following options:

C. A paid-up Assurance of £2,800, commencing at age 65; or,

D. An Annuity after 65 of £106 : 11 8,* with a paid-up Assurance of £1,400 commencing at 65; or

E. An Annuity after 65 of £213 : 3 : 4,* without any paid-up Assurance.

* The Annuities quoted are for males, and are dependent on the present prices being still in force when age 65 is reached.

Fire nsurance at moderate rates and on good security.

Head Office: 19, GEORGE ST., EDINBURGH.
LONDON: 82, King William Street, E.C.;
14, Waterloo Place, Pall Mall, S.W.

CONTENTS

When the weekly issue of this REVIEW *was originally decided upon it was considered expedient to withdraw the Editor's name, and make the paper altogether anonymous. This course was most agreeable to the Editor, who has no desire for personal notoriety, and appeared to be most consonant with journalistic usages.*

Unfortunately, the INVESTORS' REVIEW *has not an exclusive use of either of the words composing its name, and consequently quite a number of papers—many of them mere "bucket-shop" circulars, others ephemera of the mining markets—have taken the words "investor," "investment," and employed them to form titles colourably like the* INVESTORS' REVIEW. *For this reason principally it has been decided to restore the Editor's name to the cover and title of the paper, where it will henceforth appear as formerly on the monthly issue.*

The Investors' Review.

The Opening of China.

The news from China during the last few days has been the best we have heard for a long time. At last a loan has been definitely arranged for. It is to amount to £16,000,000, and will be issued conjointly by the Hong Kong and Shanghai Banking Corporation and the German Asiatic Bank. Germany has, therefore, succeeded in her endeavour to become partaker with England in the financial affairs of the Chinese Empire. We can have no objection to this. If Germany has the the capital to embark in this loan, and in the many Chinese enterprises which are bound to follow it, we shall be rejoiced to have her company, so long as she plays fair and seeks no exclusive advantage. In another respect this loan is much better arranged than any of those projected under the guarantee of one or more of the European Powers. It is to have no European guarantee, but will be issued on the security of taxes to be collected under new arrangements, whereby China will be bound up much more fully to European traders. The present Maritime Customs receipts allow no free balance for the service of any further loan; hence China had either to open up her territory to foreign trade, in order to secure further resources, or the loan had to be issued by the endorsement of a European Power or Powers, who, in return for affording the needed security, would have demanded exclusive privileges. China has chosen the better way, and we congratulate her Government upon having done so. The great resources of the Empire will now stand a chance to be developed for the good of the Chinese themselves.

Following this assertion of independence, the Chinese Government has decided to open inland ports at an early date, and this is a far more advantageous concession to England than the right to build a railway through Yun-nan, valuable though that may be in time. Most valuable of all is the promise made—which we trust will be duly ratified by a formal treaty—that no portion of the Yang-taze Valley shall ever be alienated to any other Power. We ought to be supreme as merchants in that valley, whatever comes, and if the ominous phrase, "sphere of influence," is going to become the fashion with the Powers who are bent on subdividing the Chinese Empire for their trade, if not for their governing, our "sphere" should emphatically be the territory drained by this immense river. Of immediate practical importance is the news that all the inland waters of China shall be open to navigation by steamers, whether foreign or native owned, within four months from now. Should this mean, as we hope it does, that the vexatious local dues and arbitrary "squeezes" of the provincial Governments are to be done away with, so that steamers may trade in any part of the Empire they can reach without restriction or the payment of duties other than those enforced in the treaty ports, then, indeed, an immense expansion in our business with the Far East should be at hand. We may very well leave the Russians to exploit Manchuria, and Germany to dredge and fortify Kiau-Chou; the heart of the Empire is henceforward open to our enterprise, and to that of the whole world.

It would, however, be best for us to assume no attitude of jealousy or rivalry towards any other Power. There is enough in China for all, and there ought to be no 'land-grabbing" of any sort. Heaven knows we have enough of the earth on our hands without China, or any part of it, to administer. And it should be sufficient for us there to be insured, as we now are, that so long as our trade overtops that of any other European nation, an Englishman shall preside over the administration of the Imperial Maritime Customs Service. This also we have, it seems, secured, and altogether Lord Salisbury and his Minister in Pekin have come we l out of this business. While to us, who knew only the floating rumours of the day, all seemed as good as lost, England was holding her own, and winning, winning, too, by ways of peace, not by shaking "the mailed fist." So may it always be.

We must not leave the subject without a good word for the Hong-Kong and Shanghai Bank. It is by this powerful institution that the loan has really been obtained. The Chinese know it and have had its help on many occasions, and they feel that they have always been honourably dealt with by it. What new candidates for their favour might do, or give, they cannot be sure of, but they can trust the Hong-Kong Bank. Had it, pleased, therefore, we believe it might have kept the loan to itself, but its managers have shown wisdom in allowing the Germans to have a share in the issue. If the Russians and the French desire to participate and have any money, there is no particular reason why they should not do so. Certainly their absence ought to give rise to no jealousy, for not one of these countries, nor all of them together, could have done what the Hong-Kong and Shanghai Bank has undertaken. Russia's terms and demands probably helped to cast the Chinese into our hands, and it is best so for all concerned.

West Africa and Jingo Folly.

The Marquis of Salisbury must have felt considerably annoyed at the irrepressible efforts of his restless colleague in the Colonial Office to keep himself advertised, and hence his snub to that gentleman in the House of Lords on Tuesday. On Friday night last a little comedy seems to have been arranged between Mr. Chamberlain and his friend Sir Charles Dilke, the effect of which might have been to seriously embroil this country with France. Mr. Chamberlain, in the small hours of the morning, read two telegrams he had received from the Governor of Lagos and the Acting-Governor of the Gold Coast, which set forth that some encroachment on what was claimed to be British territory, appeared to have been made by no less than a French-led tremendous Singalese army of thirty men. In themselves these telegrams were perfectly trumpery so far as information went, and bearing in mind the still undetermined frontier separating the British from the French territory in an ill-known region. Read as they were, however, at the close of a long sitting of the House, they bore the aspect of important news and produced quite a flutter in the City next day. Paris kept its head and remained undisturbed, and now the whole thing turns out to be either a mistake or a Gold Coast rumour of no worth. At the very worst it was not a matter of importance enough to go to war about or to threaten war upon.

We are quite prepared to believe that the officials, both French and British, away in the upper regions of the Niger have been endeavouring to checkmate each other, and that the French in particular are now trying an aggressive policy, partly with the view to divert attention from the critical state of affairs at home. It is not, however, to be for a moment supposed that these marchings and sparrings will be allowed to go so far as to bring the two Powers into open conflict, and we must never be too ready to believe all the rumours arriving from that far-off country. The French deny that they are in Sokoto, or anywhere near it with troops, and it may well be that all we hear about the "occupation" of this place and that is wild exaggeration. It must not be forgotten that the Royal Niger Company, whose conquests and responsibilities the nation is apparently about to take over and pay an enormous price for, has not been particularly scrupulous in the past. It, too, has been stealing a march here and there, annexing, making treaties with ignorant savages, and so on. The fault is thus not all on one side by any means, unless we are to believe that a divine mission has been given to us to steal all those parts of the world unable to defend themselves against our aggression. At all events, let us keep cool and not be led away by the screamings of the evening Press in particular. It, as usual, is busy degrading journalism by its outrageous sensationalism. From this sweeping assertion, though, we must emphatically exempt the *Westminster Gazette*, which has not only kept its reason but given to the public (on Wednesday last) an admirably sensible, temperate and conciliatory statement of the French side of the case, written by the London correspondent of the *Figaro*.

If nothing else will sober us, let the people who have money to lose consider for a moment what the effect would be upon their investments were war really to break out between England and France. How would holders of bank shares stand, for instance? In all probability before the war had been carried on for a month the strain upon the finances of this country would be so severe that large loans would have to be issued which could only be placed were other securities sold. But there is no one to buy these other securities. We English no longer hold foreign bonds to any extent, which might be sent abroad to neutral countries to raise money. Our wealth consists in domestic, and what may be called Imperial, securities. There are none of these that the Continent or America would buy to any large extent. Foreigners would not take our Colonial stocks nor our Indian, and only our Home Railway securities, perhaps, could go abroad in volume. But wherever we sold, and whatever, prices would have to be much lower than they are now, perhaps 20 per cent. lower on an average. Where would our banks be with such an all-round depreciation to reckon with? They lend on these stocks on margins of from 5 per cent. to 10 per cent., and most of those who borrow would, in a crisis, be quite unable to increase this margin. Depositors, in the general decline, would be sure to take alarm about one bank or another, and on the top of a Stock Exchange crisis we should have a bank panic. This is not the language of exaggeration, it is simply a common-sense inference from the facts surrounding a very inflated position. Well may the Marquis of Salisbury be a man of peace. No responsible statesman would venture to act so as to provoke a declaration of war against us by any great Power, with such prospects immediately ahead of him. It may be all very well to indulge in little wars in all the ends of the earth, and to waste our surplus in conquering territories which we cannot keep or utilise for any good purpose; or in subduing tribes which we can never hope to govern. But a great war is another matter. We have given a bond, with heavy penalties attached, to engage in no such war. That being so, had we not better moderate our transports and deal with such miserable disputes as this about the Niger Hinterland like sensible men of business instead of blood-thirsty fanatics?

American Life Offices:—More "Brilliant Results."

The British agents of the Equitable Life Assurance Society of the United States—the only one of the American companies known here which has a share capital, such share capital amounting to only $100,000, in $100 shares, which sell now and then at prices exceeding $1,000 each—have recently favoured us with its figures for 1897, showing total assets of £49,349,321, no less than £10,508,995 of which is called "surplus." Of course, these figures for 1897 display a large increase on those for 1896, and, equally of course, there is an increase in the total income. It is not difficult either to produce handsome surpluses by the American method when the returns published in the United States show that nearly 37 per cent. of each year's business never comes to maturity in any form, and that upwards of 60 per cent. of the policies taken out in any one year appear either to lapse altogether, or to be surrendered in exchange for new paid-up policies, generally representing but a miserable fragment of the original contract. Little more than 13½ per cent. of this office's new business, for example, appears to live to become "claims." Under such circumstances it is easy to appear flourishing, or ought to be. As a matter of fact, however, in spite of their enormous advantages in such directions none of these American companies are really doing well, or fulfilling their promises.

We have recently had put into our hands a careful analysis of the estimates and results published by, or obtained from, this company, drawn up by the Scottish Widows' Fund Office. That office was apparently compelled to enter the lists against this foreign concern in self-defence, and it would have been a good thing for British insurants if more of our Home offices had followed its example. Before dealing with the figures contained in this document, it may be well to give the following quotation extracted from the returns made by the Equitable Company of the United States to the Board of Trade in 1892:—

> The Society has not agreed in any of its policies to give cash surrender values—the law of the State of New York favouring a continuance of assurances rather than their termination—but it definitely agrees in most of its policies (not Tontine) to give paid-up policies (if applied for within a reasonable time after lapse), provided three annual premiums have been paid, and the amount of the paid-up policy, in case the original policy is on the ordinary whole-life plan with continuing premiums, is never less than two-thirds of the amount which the full net value of the original policy, taken as a net single premium, would buy. . . . In the case of limited-premium policies for the whole of life, and generally in the case of endowment assurance policies, the amount of the paid-up policy is represented by that proportion of the sum orginally assured which the number of full annual premiums paid bears to the number of annual payments, or their equivalent originally stipulated for.
>
> In the case of full Tontine policies no cash or paid-up values are given, until the Tontine period has been completed. In the case of semi-Tontine and free Tontine policies, paid-up assurance is given during the Tontine period, the same as to a corresponding non-Tontine policy, without reversionary additions.

To this it may be useful to add the following extract from the pleadings of the company in an action against it, heard in 1881:—

> The policy holder is not a partner, he is not a creditor, he is not a member of the company; he is a person who holds an agreement to receive a certain sum on a certain day. The fund produced by the payment of all the premiums does not in any sense belong to the policy holders, but belongs exclusively to the company.

This attitude and these claims of the American company cannot be too widely known because they make it perfectly plain to all policy-holders, and especially to all British policy-holders, that there is no redress whatever for them should anything happen to prevent such claims as do mature from being promptly paid. Of the capacity of all these companies to maintain their solvency we shall have more to say another day when we come to deal with the character of their investments. Let us now give some figures of the same description as those published by us some weeks back in reference to the Mutual Society of New York. Here, to begin with, is a table showing the estimates "in 1873, 1879, and 1884-5, of cash surplus on Tontine Assurances of £1,000 taken at the ordinary life rate"; together with "figures from 'tables to illustrate the advantages of Tontine policies based on the results of Tontine policies maturing in 1889' and later years."

Year when published.	Age at Entry, 25. Tontine Period. 15 years.	Age at Entry, 25. Tontine Period. 20 years.	Age at Entry, 35. Tontine Period. 15 years.	Age at Entry, 35. Tontine Period. 20 years.	Age at Entry, 45. Tontine Period. 15 years.	Age at Entry, 45. Tontine Period. 20 years.
	£	£	£	£	£	£
1873	277	538	385	764	591	1,254
1879	208	403	289	573	433	940
1884-5	154	336	210	474	323	777
1889	140	302	191	427	294	699
1890	140	282	191	398	294	652
1891	126	282	172	398	264	652
1892	112	252	152	356	235	584
1893	112	247	152	349	235	571
1894	105	233	143	329	220	538
1895	98	215	134	304	205	497

These figures, as the compiler of the Scottish Widows' Fund circular points out, reveal to us how small and beautifully less the yield upon the "Tontine" policies of this company have been growing. The figures for 1889 and later years, with the exception of those for the twenty years' period opposite 1889 and 1890, "are believed to be actual results, as they correspond with known assurances maturing in those years." They were supplied to agents, "and by them used as estimates, notwithstanding—or shall we say in consequence of—a prefatory note, from which the following is extracted and, in part, italicised":—

Calculations based on the experience of the past under policies which have matured in the Society's general class of Tontine assurance issued chiefly in the United States, show approximately the surplus profits which would be payable with such policies, *if they had been issued in the past and matured to-day*. While the results of the future must necessarily depend upon the experience of the future, *figures based on past experience furnish the best attainable data upon which to judge of the management of the Society and the value of its policies.*

Just so, and most true, though not perhaps quite in the sense we are expected to receive the truth. To illustrate still further, here is a table illustrating the "progress" of this equitable company, with another class of policy issued by it, viz.: the ordinary 'whole life" policy. It displays exactly similar characteristics to the "Tontine," or fixed term of years table; and "the 'Contribution System,' by which the dividends of this company are settled, produces curious results. For instance, in 1886 a life which had entered at thirty, five years previously, got 7s. 10d. less than a life of the same age and standing in 1883, while the ten-year-old policy-holder got within a penny as much as he of 1883, and the policy-holder of fifteen and twenty years standing got more."

Reversionary Bonus Addition on Ordinary Life Policies for £100.

Year of Valuation.	Age at Entry, 30. Age of Policy. 5 years. £ s. d.	Age at Entry, 30. 10 years. £ s. d.	Age at Entry, 30. 15 years. £ s. d.	Age at Entry, 30. 20 years. £ s. d.	Age at Entry, 40. Age of Policy. 5 years. £ s. d.	Age at Entry, 40. 10 years. £ s. d.	Age at Entry, 40. 15 years. £ s. d.	Age at Entry, 40. 20 years. £ s. d.
1876	1 10 0	1 17 10	1 19 0	—	1 13 8	2 2 0	2 3 5	—
1880	1 7 10	1 12 1	1 13 1	1 12 8	1 10 10	1 15 7	1 19 5	1 16 1
1883	1 7 10	1 10 1	1 11 9	1 11 4	1 10 10	1 15 7	1 15 3	1 13 0
1886	1 0 0	1 10 0	1 12 0	1 12 0	1 2 0	1 12 0	1 12 0	1 16 0
1889	0 18 0	1 4 0	1 10 0	1 8 0	1 0 0	1 6 0	1 12 0	1 12 0
1892	0 17 10	1 2 6	1 6 4	1 7 10	0 19 9	1 4 9	1 9 0	1 11 2

This declining scale, as exhibited in the above table, is tolerably rapid, if capricious; but in the case of whole term assurances at the ordinary life rate, with a fifteen year Tontine period attached, the results, always, be it noted, on the descending scale are even more capricious and rapid, as the subjoined table will make plain enough:—

Whole Term Assurances at the Ordinary Life Rate—Fifteen Years Tontine Period.

Year of Entry.	Number, Name, or Authority.	Age at Entry.	Sum originally Assured.	Cash Values at end of Period. Assurance and Surplus. Estimate.	Assurance and Surplus. Result.	Surplus only. Estimate.	Surplus only. Result.	Surplus only. Per cent of estimate.
			£	£	£	£	£	
1869	Policy No. 40,603	38	1,000	663	490	430	257	59·8
1871	Policy No. 63,699	41	5,000	3,735	2,644	2,428	1,337	55·1
1873	P. Matthew	45	1,500	1,539	1,018	1,040	540	51·9
1874	Policy No. 91,178	28	1,000	458	305	305	152	49·8
1875	J. E. (Glasgow)	49	1,000	1,070	710	730	366	50·1
1876	Policy No. 202,017	41	500	374	240	243	109	45·0
1878	Dundee Telegraph	48	800	821	427	554	221	40·0

It seems only necessary to add to this the following caustic observation contained in the circular before us:—

Mr. Peter Matthew, of Dundee, an agent of the company, was so delighted with the result of his venture that he wrote a letter, which was published by the company, contrasting it, *not with the estimate of 1873* (done above for him), but with the surrender value of an ordinary policy of the "Scottish Widows' Fund," which, unlike a Tontine policy, had all along a cash surrender value, and for ten of the fifteen years had carried a larger amount of assurance. The owner of Policy No. 91,178, also a Dundee man, gave a letter which bears a strong family likeness to other letters published by the company. When he signed it, can he have known that the cash value offered him for the assurance and surplus exactly corresponded with the 1874 estimate of surplus alone?

Getting such poor results, results continually and swiftly diminishing, one might suppose that the funds of the society would mount with unusual rapidity, but they do nothing of the kind; nor is this surprising when we note that at least one-fourth of the premium income is absorbed in the current expenditure of the company. If unwarrantable promises are made at the same time that expenses run to an excessive figure, and if the yield upon good investments is declining, the result can only be one thing—increasing poverty; and that this company is becoming poorer, in spite of its parade of £49,000,000 odd of assets, is demonstrated by the fact that in all the years of its existence —and it was established originally in 1859—it has only accumulated funds equal to between six and seven years' premium income to meet liabilities, which expand at a far more rapid pace, notwithstanding "sheddings-off" of all kinds. The last figures we have, as was shown in the second edition of "Plain Advice about Life Insurance," namely those for 1896, indicated that exactly six and a half years' premium income was in hand. This is miserable poverty compared with the position of English and Scotch Insurance Offices of good standing. Not one of these home offices have less than eight or nine years' premium income in hand. Many have from twelve to fifteen or sixteen years' premium income in hand, and some more than that. The consequence is that their strength grows on the whole in proportion to their liabilities, while each large increase in the liabilities of American concerns, such as this, results in a diminished capacity on the part of the contracting company or society to fulfil its promises. In order to live, these concerns must resort to subterfuges unworthy of honourable corporations, let alone of individuals with any shred of righteousness in them as between man and man.

Before leaving the subject for this week, might we venture to impress upon the home offices the necessity of being up and doing against these alien corporations. Surely they cannot be unaware of the fact that should anything happen to an American life office or to a British office conducted on the same lines, life insurance business of all descriptions would suffer to an extent impossible to estimate. And in this connection one might ask, what are British offices doing with their insurance Press? It is a large Press, and it is, for the most part, a prostituted Press, ready to sell its praises for a fee—shameless in its venality. Happily, in one sense, it is a Press of which the public which takes out policies, or which is invited to take policies out, knows nothing. With one or two exceptions it might, so far as the "general reader" is concerned, just as well be written in Chinese as in English, but what it is in its turpitude and impotence the insurance offices have made it—at a heavy outlay per annum to themselves. They act towards it as if they all had something to conceal, and which blackmailers must be paid not to disclose; or as if they could not get on without hired eulogists and defamers. Is this degrading position worthy of the wealthiest corporations of the kind in the world? If a collapse comes among unscrupulous, weak and extravagant institutions will it not be in the power of the public, which has lost, to turn and say, "You never warned us; you have behaved as if all were tarred with the same brush?"

The Grosvenor Hotel Case.

The action brought against the directors, manager of the Grosvenor Hotel, and Mr. Richard Collins Drew, for damages for fraudulent conspiracy, has at length terminated, after a protracted hearing of nine days, in a verdict for the plaintiffs. The evidence went to show that for years fraud and corruption had reigned supreme in the management of that hotel, and the jury indicated by their verdict that they believed that evidence, except the charge against Drew of falsifying weights, which they held "not proven."

The charges were, shortly, as follows: (1) That the directors, William C. Hale, J. T. Drew, Owen Reynolds, and E. J. Newitt were the mere nominees of R. C. Drew; (2) that the goods bought for the hotel were obtained, without tenders, from firms associated with and nominated by R. C. Drew; and (3) that by buying up shares R. C. Drew had secured the control of the company, and in fact "bossed the whole show."

The history of the case is quite Gilbertian in its way The hotel was incorporated in 1858 with a capital of £130,000 in shares of £10, and up to February, 1896. £111,220 had been issued and paid in full. In 1878, R. C. Drew began to buy shares in this company and managed to secure a large number at a low price. Now this gentleman up to September, 1890, was the owner of a half share in a butcher's business carried on under the name of Cowell & Drew, and from that date to July, 1896, he was the sole owner. In June, 1892, he bought the businesses of Craft & Co., poultrymen, and Grimmond & Co., grocers and fuel merchants, having in November, 1887, acquired that of Rush & Co., laundrymen. In passing it may be said that in July, 1896, he sold these four businesses to one J. Jervis, and these two gentlemen brought out the company of Cowell, Craft, & Co., to take these undertakings over, with a capital of £150,000. Mr. Drew is the managing director of this concern.

The next move was to secure a complacent directorate. Mr. Hale was appointed a director in 1878, Drew supplying the qualifying shares, and three days after his election was appointed chairman at £200 a year. This gentleman held his post till January this year. In 1881 Newitt was elected to the board, and "has been unanimously elected ever since." For this director, too, the beneficent Drew found the shares. This impartial and independent gentleman admitted he had never had a sixpence in the company himself, and that he knew Drew had a preponderating influence to carry what he wanted at the general meetings. The same year another valuable addition was made to the board in the person of one Owen Reynolds, Drew's brother-in-law. Needless to say the kindly Drew found for this gentleman also his qualifying shares. In 1892 the remaining member of this board commenced to take his seat in the person of J. T. Drew, a nephew of R. C. Drew. This gentleman, owing to differences with his fond uncle, was dismissed from his employment, and did not appear at the trial. His shares, needless to say, were found by his uncle.

These were the four directors who were to safeguard the interests of the minority of the shareholde. Between June, 1879, and December, 1895, the hotel paid to Cowell & Drew some £110,565 for meat; to Craft & Co., £35,798 for provisions; and £23,743 to Rush & Co. for laundry work. From 1882 to 1895 about £52,977 was paid to Grimmond & Co. for coa and grocery. The tales of the sweetbreads and bullocks heads must be present to the minds of all readers of the daily papers, and they were quite on a par with the coal and laundry transactions. Grimmond & Co. bought Welsh coal at 22s. per ton in 1890, and passed it in, in the fulness of their hearts, to the hotel at 28s. 6d., and other coals at a proportionate figure! Then, to assist the hotel, Rush & Co. took 60s. per thousand for the washing lest it should go elsewhere and pay 40s. And so the merry game went on, and we were not astonished to read that the profits of the hotel began to dwindle, and, instead of a profit of £91,134, which is the usual 40 per cent. profit on provisions set against the cost, on £227,811 expended during the last twelve years there was a considerable loss.

It will not be out of place to consider shortly the connection of this happy little family with some other places of public refreshment. Hale, until a year ago, was chairman and director of the St. James's Hotel, Drew finding the shares. Then comes Newitt, company director by profession, who is a gentleman certainly not devoid of humour. "A director should not be a shareholder. It is, in my opinion, wrong that he should be.' Thus testified Mr. Newitt in the witness box. He lately brought a libel action against Mr. Spokes, the plaintiff in this action, and in his evidence stated he was a director also in the Agricultural Hotel Company, the Star and Garter Hotel Company, the Tavistock Hotel Company, the Royal Hotel, Southend, Company, and the London and County Hotels Company. We should much like to know whether he has a sixpence of interest in any of those companies, barring, of course his director's fees. We are inclined to think not. What lucky hotels to have such a director. Till a week or two ago he was director of the Salisbury Hotel also, but failed to be re-elected by one vote. We condole with the Salisbury. For Owen Reynolds we feel something akin to pity. Besides being a director of the Grosvenor he held shares for Drew in the Salisbury, Long's, and the St. James's Hotels, but was not quite sure about the Star and Garter. On it being suggested to him that he was a mere puppet in Drew's hands, all he could reply was, "I do not care what you choose to call me." There is something really pathetic in that answer.

One word for the cheery-hearted auditor, John Steer Wills. He really could not remember when he was appointed auditor, or how long he had held the post. He could remember nothing, except that he also audited the books of Cowell & Drew, Grimmond & Co., and Rush & Co.

Such was the body of gentlemen who "safeguarded" the interests of Richard Collins Drew and the other shareholders. By the verdict of the jury they have been found guilty of fraudulent conspiracy with R. C. Drew, and the various charges of fraud which have been brought against them; though the manager Zeder, who received a £100 Christmas-box from Drew, and in return presented Mrs. Drew with a piece of plate, valued at about £25, at the festive season, has only been found guilty of fraudulent conspiracy to "a far lesser degree." We sincerely hope that this matter will not be allowed to remain where it is, and that in the public interest further proceedings will be taken. If we are not greatly mistaken, this hotel is not the only victim of corruption. There are certain others we could name where an investigation such as has just taken place would bring kindred facts to light. Next week we shall deal further with one or two concerns of Mr. Richard Collins Drew.

Economic and Financial Notes and Correspondence.

The Sad Plight of France.

One does not know what to be most amazed at in this Dreyfus-Esterhazy-Zola business; the overbearing insolence of the soldiers, the grovelling subserviency of the Civil Authorities, or the open contempt for justice—or fair play in any shape—exhibited by the judge in Court. The result of the trial was a foregone conclusion, given the conditions, but if there be any manliness left in the French people the monstrous travesty of justice which has ended in the sentence of M. Zola to a year's imprisonment is the beginning of the end for a good many impostures in France.

First to go, we trust, will be the pernicious military legend which, created under the brigand Napoleon, has poisoned the minds of Frenchmen for three generations. They now have revealed to them what militarism means in all its hideousness—contempt for law, brutal disregard of the common rights of citizenship, a clannishness which admits neither of criticism nor of interference from outside the uniformed and trained hordes of man-slayers. This kind of diseased self-importance is becoming more and more rampant among the soldiers of all countries—we ourselves are falling more and more under its domination, and in Germany the "mere civilian"—the man by whose labours the sword and gun owner is furnished and, sustained—is as dirt beneath the feet of the military caste. Will France, after the illustration of this spirit she has just received, arise and cast the demon forth, earning the gratitude of mankind? Alas, not yet. *La Gloire* still fascinates her fools and makes them an easy prey.

Next to the revelation of the soldier's notions of duty and obedience to the laws, France has witnessed the impotence of her so-called Government before these soldiers; and worse still, if that be possible, before the lawless mobs who have been stirred up to persecute the Jews, and to threaten the lives of all who ventured to stand up for even-handed dealing, as between man and man. To such an excess has the weakness of M. Mélines Ministry gone that certain miserable fanatics, clearly priest-driven, have been allowed to come from Algiers, fresh from murder and outrage, their handiwork though not done by their hands, to stir up in Paris race hatred and "a second St. Bartholomew against the Jews." "You cannot believe it?" It is true, nevertheless, and as infamous as true.

Can the just, intelligent, and thoughtful Frenchman—he forms the majority of the nation even now—do ought to sweep this impotence aside, and secure for the country a Government strong enough to put down alike military and mob lawlessness—they are really at bottom the same thing—with a firm hand? The coming elections will perhaps answer, but we regretfully confess that we do not look forward to them with any large measure of hope. The immediate future seems to be much more bodeful of revolution than of regeneration—revolution ending in one more military dictatorship and the triumph of fanatical clericalism, with, possibly enough, an expulsion of the Jews. No nation can retain its honour and self-respect and tolerate even, let alone condone, a trampling under foot of the liberties of its citizens such as the Zola trial has laid bare to the gaze of mankind.

The Great Nile Reservoirs.

No more pleasant news has been published for a long time than that which told the British public of the signing of the contract for the construction of a great dam across the Nile at Assouan. The terms of this contract are honourable alike to the Egyptian Government and to British enterprise. Of all firms in the world probably Messrs. John Aird & Co. alone have the means and power to carry out such a work satisfactorily. This firm is to build a great barrage across the Nile at Philæ, taking care of the ruins there, and also apparently a lesser dam at Assiout; and will complete the work in five years without asking the Egyptian Government in the meantime for one penny towards the cost.

As readers of Sir Alfred Milner's interesting and valuable book on "England in Egypt" may remember, works of this description have been urged upon the Egyptian Government for many years, and since the English took control of that country repeated surveys have been made and schemes formulated, all of which have been baulked by the obstinate opposition of the French. There is money lying idle in the Egyptian Treasury, the surpluses of many Budgets, which might have been most profitably employed in building these great reservoirs, in which it is calculated that nearly twenty million millions of cubic metres of water will be stored, capable of irrigating and bringing into a high state of fertility enormous areas of land now sandy desert, and therefore of increasing the revenue of the State by three or four hundred thousand pounds per annum, at least. To all proposals, however, that the accumulated revenue surplus should be used in this way the French have opposed an emphatic negative.

Now an English firm of contractors comes forward and offers to build these dams for a deferred payment extending over thirty years, the first instalment to become due when the works have been completed, not before. How much will have to be spent on this great undertaking we do not yet know. Sir Alfred Milner put £5,000,000 down as the possible cost of the works he sketched out, but then, if we remember aright, his plan embraced even larger areas than those the Assouan reservoir will fertilise. It is quite possible, however, that before both barrages are finished Messrs. John Aird & Co. will be £1,500,000 or £2,000,000 out of pocket. We congratulate them on the magnificent enterprise which has prompted them to enter into such obligations. These are the triumphs that outweigh a thousand military victories and bring benefit to mankind. But we trust that the passion for conquests now so dominant with all civilising powers may not in the meantime so load the Egyptian people with burdensome obligations as to neutralise the benefit this great work is sure to convey to hundreds and thousands of labouring men.

THE INCREASE IN THE ARMY.

Many times have we warned the British public that it would have to pay dearly for its Imperialism, and the bill is now beginning to come in. The new Army Estimates are out for 1898-9, and they show an increase of fully £2,000,000 on those for this year, now almost ended. As usual, the figures are mixed up and disguised, so that it is difficult to discover the truth, but an excellent summary of the totals appeared in last Monday's *Daily News*. The writer of that summary points out that the increase is not £880,000, as it appears to be in the bulky Yellow Book misleadingly called "Army Estimates for 1898-9." It is not even £1,646,000, as Lord Lansdowne's memorandum on the Estimates admits it would be but for an arrangement which casts £766,000 into a supplementary estimate for 1897-8.

The net original estimates for 1897-8, including the supplementary estimate of £200,000 for South Africa, was £18,340,500, but the original estimates and supplementary estimates for the year ending in March next, including the above-mentioned £766,000, Volunteer pay allowances, &c., in all £1,290,000, plus the estimates for the coming year, amount together to £38,851,000. Deduct the above-mentioned net estimate for 1897-8 from the total of the two years and the difference is £20,510,500. This is the real amount of the increased expenditure at present provided for the coming year, only part of it is to be thrown on this year's revenue, and it is the highest total in time of peace of this generation. In normal years the expenditure on the Army was from £14,500,000 to £18,000,000, with rare exceptions, any time since 1872 and down to 1896. Before that date it was occasionally under £14,000,000. Judging by the new programme now laid before Parliament, we may look upon £20,000,000 in the future as the minimum, for the Army is about to be increased by, ultimately, 25,000 men. A year ago a modest 9,000 extra was all that was demanded. Already the needs of Empire require 16,000 to be added to this. Next year we may see the estimate again enlarged—must see it, in fact, if we are going to continue our policy of little wars in Asia and Africa—and, after a few years, we shall probably have conscription in some form established.

Once again we say we hope the country likes the prospect. For the present the conscription policy has apparently been dropped in regard to the regular forces, but an agitation for applying it to the militia has been started, and, in one form or other, compulsory military service is inevitable in the near future if continent-swallowing Imperialism is to be the prevailing policy of our Government. For the present we shall say no more, for it is useless to go into the question of the cost of this army, measured by its size and strength. Unless the accounts presented to Parliament are re-modelled in an intelligent manner by conscientious men it will remain impossible for any human being to say how much of the money patiently found every year by the helpless taxpayer is made away with, giving no return whatever to the nation. We may say, however, that this costly unreformed and unreformable army of ours, with the wars its establishment and maintenance render a necessity if its existence is to be justified at all, will mean to the Home taxpayer at no distant date a shilling income tax in time of profound peace. What it may mean in time of war no man can forecast. But it is a subject that will have to be meditated upon, how far this nation—with its stagnant industries, fed from the Exchequer more than from foreign expansion, with its unprofitable agriculture, dependent as it is upon continual additions to the debt of its dependencies—would be able to stand an annual expenditure of twice the present amount for three years running. If, in short, the nation is exhausting its reserve financial strength in time of peace, how is it going to encounter a great conflict such as many among us now talk of waging against France?

RAND DEEP LEVELS.

We print the following eulogy on the Wernher-Beit group of Deep Levels, because it is fair that both sides should be heard. Readers, however, will note that it contains assertion and prophesy, not facts and analyses, as our articles did. An experienced public, too, should know that nothing is so delusive and ensnaring as high and advancing market prices for shares in mining enterprises not yet at maturity. The market argument is always "You cannot possibly buy this magnificent property too dear." Common sense answers, "The purchase of the unknown and unknowable is, generally speaking, too costly at any price." We know very well that the Rand Mines group of Deep Levels has been incomparably better financed than the Goldfields group, and have often said as much. This does not alter the fact that the financiers of the Rand Mines group now desire the public to purchase on their own valuation, as expressed in market prices created by them, shares in mines whose day of performance is more or less distant. All we say to the public is "wait and see." Nothing can be lost by doing this; much may be saved. Men with the faith of Mr. Hicks will surely be most delighted to hold "Rose Deeps," at present or higher prices, until the dividends bring them their money back with usury :—

To the Editor.

DEAR SIR,—In view of the fact that the above mines are now coming so much to the front, and your articles dealing with their prospects being so interesting, I have no doubt you will open your valuable paper to fair criticism on this subject. As one who has been interested in Transvaal mining for some years, it seems to me a mistake to deal with, say, twenty mines at once, and strike an average from the results. We all know by now which part of the Rand is richest.

You surely would not in dealing with outcrop mines add the profit, say, of the Henry Nourse and Knight's, together and then point out that the profit on the total capital of the two mines is very small; then why put the Nourse Deep and Knight's Deep in the same category. The Deep Levels must be classified, just as are the outcrops, *i.e.*, rich, medium grade, or poor. Of the twenty Deep Levels mentioned in your plan last week, four are not marketable and need not be dealt with; of the others eight, in my opinion, should be put in Class I., and eight in Class II. Class I. would comprise :—

	Group.
Crown Deep	Rand Mines.
Durban ditto	Ditto.
Geldenhuis ditto	Ditto.
Glen ditto	Ditto.
Jumper ditto	Ditto.
Nourse ditto	Ditto.
Robinson ditto	Goldfields.
Rose ditto	Rand Mines.
Class II.	Group.
Knight's Central	Goldfields.
Knight's Deep	Ditto.
Langlaate ditto	Rand Mines.
Niger ditto	Goldfields.
Simmer and Jack...	Ditto.
Simmer East	Ditto.
Simmer West	Ditto.
Witwatersand Deep	

Now, sir, on examining these lists, it will be at once seen that in Class I. the Rand Mines control seven mines, and the Goldfields one; but in Class II. the latter group control no less than six companies to the one by the Rand Mines, and this mine, the Langlaate Deep, will, according to latest information, prove to be a first-class mine.

My object in pointing out the difference in these mines (and this classification on a broad basis can scarcely be disputed) is to point out the difference between the Rand Mines and the Goldfields groups. These corporations cannot well be compared, and that you should write of them jointly is indeed surprising.

The Rand Mines practically control every good deep level mine except the Robinson Deep.

The Goldfields were interested in Rose Deep and Glen Deep, but have been selling their interest as fast as possible.

I quite agree with your remarks as applied to the Goldfields group, and if it were not for the Robinson Deep, which mine will probably save them, "the whole fabric might come tumbling to the ground like a pack of cards," as you suggest. The finance of the Rand Mine group is, on the other hand, in my opinion, magnificent. The way in which each of these huge concerns is financed and brought to the crushing and profit-earning stage is very fine, and that, sir, without the help of the public in nearly every case.

It seems a pity that your readers in these days of difficulty in finding remunerative investments should be frightened from taking an interest in some of the finest mines in the world, which will, beyond doubt, or anything that can be brought forward to the contrary, yield at present prices a very handsome rate of interest. By all means keep people from buying shares like those in Class II. (except as a speculation), which cannot be dividend-paying, in nearly every case, for three or four years. A great deal has been written of late on this subject. The *Financial Times*, for instance, had a slashing article against Rose Deep when they stood at 5¾. No doubt the readers of such nonsense as was then written left these shares alone, only to see them advance steadily to 7¼. Messrs. Wernher, Beit & Co. have given us good dividend-paying out-crops in the past, and I am confident that they will repeat this in their Deep Levels, and my advice, Mr. Editor, although it differs a little from yours, is to invest (not gamble) without hesitation in any of the mines in Class I.—Apologising for the length of this letter, I remain, yours faithfully,

ALFRED HICKS.

The Stock Exchange,
February 21, 1898.

BRITISH INSURANCE COMPANIES IN ARGENTINA.

A law has recently been passed by the Argentine Congress, in virtue of which every insurance company doing business in the Republic must make a deposit—in the case of a fire company of $300,000, and in that of marine or life office of $150,000—which money must be invested in a bond of a new internal loan to be taken at the price of 80, such loan, we understand, to bear only 3½ per cent. interest. At this price the bonds are quite 15 per cent. above the value they would fetch in the open market. The project is therefore one of robbery or blackmail unworthy of a civilised Government. The law ought to be protested against, not only by the insurance offices acting in concert, but by the British Minister in Buenos Ayres. It is really too bad that English capital invested abroad should be subjected to unprincipled raids of this kind on the part of needy and unscrupulous Governments. The opinion of lawyers in River Plate seems to be that the new law is unconstitutional, and the view is also expressed here that it is contrary to existing treaties between England and Argentina. What the constitutional aspect of the question may be is not of much importance. When a foreigner is to be plundered it is easy for Argentine politicians to strain the constitution or ignore it. If, however, we have treaty rights that enable us to prevent an imposition of this sort they ought to be at once put in force. Unless something is done, and done promptly, British insurance companies and offices will have seriously to consider whether it would not be advisable for them to take steps to withdraw altogether from the Argentine Republic.

THE PUSHING ELECTRIC LIGHT.

The London Electric Supply Corporation has been mentioned by us in previous articles on this subject as working in certain West-end districts. It is not generally known, however, that its central station for years has been at Deptford, and that the company possesses the right to supply the light in many of the South London parishes through which its mains pass. Although the oldest company in London, it has not hitherto attempted to serve these districts to any important extent, doubtless in consequence of the low charges of the great gas company that works there. The production of energy has cheapened of late years, and, as other electric lighting companies are turning their attention to South London, the old-established company has begun to move.

Of course it was essential to tariff the charge for energy upon as moderate a scale as possible in order to compete with the 2s. 3d. per 1,000 feet charged by the South Metropolitan Gas Company for its illuminant. Accordingly it is proposed that the ordinary rate shall be 6d. per unit, with a sliding-scale of rebates to 5d. per unit, presumably granted to large consumers. Such a rate works well North of the Thames, as it is practically equivalent to the high charge of the Gas Light and Coke Company; but evidently it is doubted whether canny shopkeepers and householders in South London will think the light cheap enough at this rate, and so what may be termed a fancy tariff has been evolved in order to attract consumers. They can take the energy under a sliding scale based upon their maximum demand, which is calculated, not upon the number of lamps installed, but upon the maximum number in use simultaneously. Upon this basis, the reduction will take the form of a discount or rebate to those consumers whose use of the electric light exceeds a two-hours' daily average of their maximum demand throughout the year; all excess current so used by them will be charged at half-price, that is, 3d. per unit. The arrangement seems involved, but is certainly better than others on the same lines, which were based upon the number of lamps installed. The same company has also made arrangements whereby wires and fittings can be supplied and installed by the National Electric Free Wiring Company, at a rental of ¾d. per unit. This last innovation is a great step in advance, and will lead to the introduction of the new illuminant into many houses and places of business where the initial cost of installation would have prevented its use.

THE IMPERIAL INSTITUTE.

Trouble seems gathering round the Imperial Institute. Some of the colonies are getting tired of contributing to its support, and Victoria now refuses to continue its annual subscription. Such a reaction was bound to come. The Institute has from the first been much more of a show place or a club, than a business establishment. Sir Walter Peace, the Agent-General for Natal, complains that the Institute is in no sense of the word Imperial, while the colonial exhibits in it are not arranged on a business basis. Who ever thinks of visiting the Institute for the purpose of acquiring information about the colonies or of examining the "exhibits" there laid out? It has not become a centre of interest for people connected with the colonies; they seem to avoid it. It is more a lounge for idlers—and even they are not numerous, except at the occasional evening entertainments—than an attraction to busy men of commerce. We do not see what can be done to save the Institute. If the other colonies cease their contributions, it must perforce be shut up. Victoria, New South Wales, and South Australia are in favour of renting a large building in the City for the display and distribution of colonial samples; and such a place would be infinitely more useful to the colonies than the establishment known as the Imperial Institute. It is too far from the City, and useless for business purposes.

KLONDIKE PROMOTIONS.

That the unscrupulous company promoter is always ready with his schemes to catch the public fancy was amply demonstrated by the late Jubilee promotions. Now it appears that Klondike is the name to conjure with, and to extract money by from the pockets of a gullible public. One of these delightful schemes, called the Central Klondike Gold Mining and Trading Company, Limited, has been described by the chairman, the Senior Official Receiver in Company Winding-up, at the meeting of its shareholders and creditors, as one of the most sordid cases of downright fraud that had ever come under his notice. We abstain from any comment on this concern as yet, as we understand that it is to become the subject of further enquiry, but we shall await the issue with interest.

THE REPORT OF THE COUNCIL OF FOREIGN BONDHOLDERS.

This has just appeared for the year 1897, but in a very defective shape, inasmuch as it is minus the appendices giving details of the dealing of the Council with the various defaulting States it is supposed to have in charge. Why these appendices should not come out now, as formerly, along with the report we do not understand. The date of their appearance has been gradually receding until it reached August last year; by and by at this pace they need not come out at all, and perhaps that is the intention. A deal of expense would be saved by their suppression and also much troublesome criticism.

Little can be said about the accounts which accompany the present report, but we think one curious feature ought to be explained to the shareholders in the Corporation at the meeting, and that is, why advances made in prosecuting claims, &c., have declined at the same time that reserves against those advances have gone up. In 1895 these advances amounted to £6,700, in 1896 to £7,700, and in 1897 to only £5,050. To an ordinary person this seems the reverse of what should have happened, considering the cost of dealing with slippery Governments. But if advances have fallen off reserves have mounted; they were only £9,000 in 1894, and are now £14,800, nearly three times the apparent sum risked. It will be very interesting to know how this has happened.

Space does not allow us to comment at length on the discrepancies in the report; but some of them should be mentioned. Why does the Council give itself airs about Argentina? The Rothschild Committee that deals with the debts of that Republic is not a Committee of the Council, and, so far as we know, never asked the Council's opinion or advice. In regard to the Buenos Ayres loans, the Council occupies even a more humiliating position, for it has not only failed to protect bondholders, but it has acted all along as the humble and obedient servant of the firms that issued these loans, and by whom the interests of creditors have been shamefully and systematically neglected. It has, in short, played into the debtors' hands and ignored the creditors. As to Ecuador, again, we might repeat what has been said in this REVIEW on former occasions: no service has been rendered to the bondholders by the Committee the Council has set up to watch over Ecuador bondholders' interests—unless it be a service to have obligingly assisted Ecuador to get rid of its debt through successive defaults. The story of Costa Rica is also well known—£26,662 10s. to Mr. Kattengall and £5,000 to the Council, proceeds of approving an unjust debt settlement, against which we protested strongly at the time; no cash left for the bondholders who have been induced to accept 50 per cent. on the "B" bond and 60 per cent. on the "A," with interest cut down by one-half as well. No wonder the Costa Rica Government can boast of a surplus of a million dollars. It is the same story throughout, and we think it too monotonously sad to be prolonged. On another occasion we hope to say something more about Sir John Lubbock's Bill now before Parliament.

MORE INDIAN FINANCE.

Lord George Hamilton, in the debate raised on the motion of Mr. Samuel Smith last Tuesday, made a statement with regard to the present state of Indian finance which deserves to be put on record as the first official version of the truth. Truth has many stages of elaboration in Indian affairs, and five or ten years hence it may be possible, by piecing this fragment and that together, to reach an intelligible whole. But the subjoined fragment will some day possess a certain historical interest. Quoth the noble lord :—

We received in the month of December a six months' estimate, that is, of course, for the present year 1897-98. Taking the exchange at 1s. 3d. per rupee it shows a deficit of six crores, 63 lakhs of rupees. The figures include 361 lakhs in addition to some sterling expenditure on account of the expeditions to the frontier ; 180 lakhs excess expenditure in relief works, and various items which balance one another. Of course a deficit of 663 lakhs is a very large deficit, but unsatisfactory as it is as regards the year to which it relates it is in one sense not unsatisfactory as regards the future. The famine expenditure, which is an extraordinary expenditure, is estimated at 540 lakhs, and taking the frontier war at 400 lakhs and other extraordinary expenditure at 12 lakhs, we get a total of 952 lakhs. But the total deficit is only 663 lakhs. The normal revenue, therefore, will meet 289 lakhs of the expenditure of this particular year of abnormal expenditure ; or, in other words, in a normal year there will probably be a considerable surplus of income over expenditure. Having got these figures we telegraphed to the Indian Government to get more accurate information as regarded the past. We sent the following telegram :—" Your telegram of December 7. Budget forecast. Please let me know by telegram for the information of her Majesty's Government whether the present financial condition of India and prospects for coming year are such as to justify anticipation that all necessary expenditure can be met without additional taxation or unduly increasing the indebtedness." To this we received the following reply :—" Financial position. Twenty years' accounts up to March, 1898, show a surplus of ordinary revenue amounting to 45 crores, against extraordinary expenditure on war of 21 crores, famine relief 8½ crores, railway construction, charged to revenue, 13½ crores ; showing a net surplus for the twenty years, after meeting these charges, of two crores." They go on to say, without committing themselves to figures, that they are fully confident that a substantial surplus can be forecasted for the next ensuing year, that no additional taxation will be imposed, but that as the examination of the figures both of revenue and expenditure is not complete they do not wish to commit themselves to it. In addition we got this further information from the Indian Government :—" Official telegram to-day succinctly states the facts bearing on the financial position, and warrants our considering external assistance unnecessary." Why, therefore, should we override the Indian Government and force this assistance upon them? There are most conclusive reasons why we should not do so.

No reason in the world why we should help India provided India can pay her way. But she cannot, and all this talk about "surpluses," past and to come, is —Lord George must really bear with the expression— so much juggling with words. Most of the figures he was given by the Indian Government to reel off for the discomfiture of its critics were figures built upon the foundation of an artificial and unreal rate of exchange. How is it that the rupee is kept at 1s. 3d. or 1s. 4d. or any neighbouring figure? Simply by suspending in part the payment of the home charges for which the Indian Government is liable. Not two-thirds of these charges are provided for this financial year. Lay them in full any year on the trade of India, without counterpoise in the shape of large fresh loans raised here on Indian account, and the rupee could not long be kept from declining to 6d. or less. What is the use of gabbling about "surpluses," "growth," or "recovery" of revenue and so forth before a position like this?

Some Notable English Railway Statistics for 1897.

These figures should really have been in last week. Also they ought to be more elaborate, as we used to make them in the monthly. But elaborate tables are not required to point our moral, which is that capital expenditure and working expenditure are together slowly undermining the productiveness of the ordinary stock to investors. We have brought this point before readers in almost every railway company's report analysed by us during the past month, and the following table merely serves to bring our conclusions before the eye in a concrete fashion. Over thirteen millions sterling of new capital was spent by these fourteen railways last year, and an increase of nearly two a half millions in gross income gave little more than £200,000 more net. At the same time additional preferential dividend and interest charges took £164,000 more, and another £27,000 is now required to maintain the dividends on ordinary stocks. These figures, be it noted, are for the whole year. Had those for the second half of it only been taken the outcome would have been much worse :—

	Capital expenditure in 1897.	Increase or decrease in gross revenue.	Increase or decrease in working expenses.	Increase or decrease in prior charges and interest.	Increase in amount required to pay 1 p. on ord. stock.
	£	£	£	£	£
Brighton	292,842	+84,091	+65,221	−2,330	+4,474
Chatham	184,514	+37,019	+19,236	+9,063	—
Great Central	2,371,725	+63,862	+78,254	+15,448	nil.
Great Eastern	627,726	+297,197	+160,641	+21,237	nil.
Great Northern	1,499,608	+204,527	+138,491	+36,654	nil.
Great Western	2,311,779	+383,645	+332,054	+10,480	+11,800
Lanc. & York	995,820	+52,580	+75,715	+24,631	nil.
Metropolitan	147,399	+45,534	+23,786	−700	nil.
Metrop. District	14,840	+16,032	+5,469	−303	—
Midland	1,695,009	+403,176	+408,480	+24,888	+3,581
North-Eastern	580,638	+283,733	+260,066	−10,513	+5,803
North-Western	905,173	+359,533	+403,028	−435	+1,020
South-Eastern	607,601	+95,574	+120,212	+6,607	nil.
South-Western	852,181	+201,349	+140,717	+15,393	+1 000
	13,086,908	2,459,867	2,251,301	164,491	27,068

Good News for "Chartered" Shareholders.

It is not of much present importance whether Rhodesia is to have one Administrative Council, or two, or a score, under Mr. Chamberlain's new plan ; nor yet whether the Commander of the Forces of the Crown is to cease to be a "Deputy Commissioner." The form of the new Government is quite secondary to the fact that the proposal as a whole means, if carried through, the incorporation of the Chartered Company's estate into a dominion of the Crown at no distant date. A continuance of a "board of directors," with nothing to direct except mining claims and licences, not likely to be profitable in the majority of instances, is nothing short of absurd, if not highly dangerous. This board will first grumble at the expense the company is put to on Government account, and then begin to agitate and to formulate claims with a view to being bought out at the highest possible price by the British taxpayer.

How any responsible British Minister could propose, apparently in all seriousness, to enter into intimate relations with such a company as this—a bubble of the worst type throughout its history, a thing conceived in cruelty and fraud and carried out from first to last in cold-blooded indifference to everything except the personal enrichment of the group that organised it—baffles our comprehension. But we have no doubt at all that the scheme will be allowed to pass the present Parliament, the worst the country has had since 1832, and that within a very few years we shall be told that from ten or fifteen millions must be found to buy out "vested interests" created in the first instance by the simple process of manufacturing shares and distributing them gratis. Is the scheme to be forced through without so much as a disclosure of the present financial position of the Company?

THE TERMS AND SECURITY OF THE NEW CHINESE LOAN.

Neither seems to be absolutely fixed. We believe, however, that the loan will be a 4½ per cent. one, issued probably about 90, with the usual provision for redemption by sinking fund. Half of it may be offered in Germany and half here, and the underwriting of it is already completed, the subscribers receiving 2 per cent. commission. The loan has, of course, been taken in taels by the Hong-Kong Bank. As regards security, it seems that there is still a surplus of about three to four hundred thousand pounds left over from the Customs revenue after providing for the loans already issued. This is taking the Haikwan tael at 2s. 9d., which is about its present exchange value. Were silver to fall much further in price this surplus might disappear, but for the present it goes some way towards meeting the fresh charge imposed by the new loan. Then there will be the Salt Dues and some portion of the Li-Kin, or Inland Customs Dues, which are to be henceforth collected direct by Europeans. Should difficulty be experienced with the one or the other, then the Pekin Government will have to hurry forward the opening of fresh ports so as to increase the income from the Maritime Customs. Until we are sure that the security is ample, the new loan will be regarded as rather inferior to the ones now in the hands of the public, but there is no reason to doubt that, by one channel or another, it will be amply provided for.

BUSH FIRES IN AUSTRALIA.

No special correspondent or news agency has thought it worth while to tell us anything of the terrible devastation wrought in several districts of the Colony of Victoria by a series of bush fires unprecedented in extent and length of duration. They broke out in the end of last year and the beginning of this, and when the mail left about January 16 they were still burning in parts where anything was left to consume. The fires seem to have first made their appearance in Thorpdale, an important agricultural centre, a good day's journey distant from Melbourne. Here there were about fifty homesteads, and every one of these have been destroyed, with every bit of furniture the two hundred inhabitants owned. No human lives have been lost, but scarcely a horse or cow or pig has been left in the district: they have all been roasted. The produce of the recent harvest—a very abundant one—has been swept clean away. Scarcely a blade of grass has been left; so that where here and there cattle have escaped destruction, they are being sold because there is nothing with which to feed them.

The land for probably fifty miles or so has been laid waste. It consisted of prosperous farms for the most part, with a number of "selections" which were being brought under cultivation, and large areas of forest trees. These fed the flames, and kept them travelling for miles, spreading destruction everywhere around. At one township only a fowl-house was left; at another men and women by persistent effort kept the fire at bay for three weeks, only to be foiled in the end by a sudden change of wind throwing the flames back upon them, and compelling them to seek safety in flight. Scenes more strangely weird we have rarely read of. The roads are everywhere blocked, and it is impossible to attempt their clearance until the fires have burned out. The Government have sent a number of tents for the houseless inhabitants. Hurried arrangements were being made when the mail left to send food as well; for of that there was little or none. Grass seed will have to be supplied also; for there is now only a blackened desert where, a month or two ago, there were only fruitful farms. Many an industrious colonist will have to begin life anew with diminished strength, his capital gone, and with the abiding dread that a like visitation may be repeated any summer just as he has garnered his crops, and is waiting for transport to the nearest markets.

THE DUBLIN UNITED TRAMWAYS COMPANY, LIMITED.

The following refers to a matter of public importance. It is a shame that bills of the kind here described are allowed to slip through Parliament and become law:—

SIR,—I enclose a copy of a letter of mine which appears in the Dublin papers of to-day, and also a memorandum relating to the tramways compiled from the Return just issued by the Board of Trade. I thank you for your notice in your paper of last week—there is just one slight error in it, arising from the similarity of the names of the Old and New Dublin Tramway Company. The Dublin United Tramways Company (1896) has filed its list of shareholders. It was the Dublin United Tramways Company, which by a clause in its Act of Parliament was exempted from the obligation to furnish a list of shareholders to the registrar of Joint Stock Companies, and I think it is the duty of the Board of Trade to examine Tramway Bills, and see that no such clause is inserted, as I presume we all agree it is a matter of public importance that the list of shareholders should be accessible in this way.

Yours faithfully,
CHARLES EASON (junior).

THE NATIONAL TELEPHONE COMPANY.

"Create a monopoly and go and hang yourself" is a saying the truth of which appears to be well illustrated by the action of the National Telephone Company in the City. It has a most oppressive tariff therein for the use of its instruments, viz., £20 each, but it is graciously pleased to reduce this tariff by 15 per cent. to £17 if its customers will consent to sign a hard-and-fast agreement with it for five years.

Those who will neither sign away their freedom thus nor pay the higher scale are threatened with the loss of the service, and in one instance known to us the wires were actually disconnected. It would be highly interesting to learn the motive for these oppressive ongoings. Does the company expect to make a hard bargain with the nation for its business, or to entrench itself against the County Council, or what?

CITY OF LONDON ELECTRIC COMPANY.

Unlike other electric lighting companies, this company has a sliding scale fixed in the Act of Parliament which regulates its working. The clause reads as follows:—

If the balance of receipts over expenditure shown by the undertakers' annual accounts for any year ending December 31, ... exceeded a cumulative profit of 10 per cent. on the amount of the capital for the time being employed in the undertaking, the price of energy to private consumers charged otherwise than by agreement should be reduced for the year ensuing after the next following 25th day of March, at the rate of one halfpenny per unit for each 1 per cent. over the 10 per cent. so shown by the accounts.

This seems to imply that when dividends exceed 10 per cent. the price of energy must be reduced, but a good deal of importance lies in the reading of the word "cumulative." If that means that dividends in past years below 10 per cent. can be made up before the price of energy is reduced, the company will have yet some time before the sliding scale comes into force, as there is a considerable balance in favour of the company on account of dividends distributed below 10 per cent., but its exact percentage cannot easily be stated owing to the differing amounts of capital in existence.

A Little Hotel Issue.

A curious commentary upon the Grosvenor Hotel case is furnished by the share list of the Hans Crescent Hotel Company, issued in July, 1896. The only share list furnished at Somerset House contains the following as the largest shareholders :—

	No. of Shares. Pref.	Ord.
Belgravia Estate, Limited	5,433	1,151
D. H. Evans	680	200
Hans Place Hotel Company, Limited	800	17,393
S. Marler	1,600	—
New Imperial Investment	1,358	—
S. J. Waring	500	—
Stephens, Bastow, & Company, Limited	1,000	—
Total	11,371	18,774
Total share capital	16,000	20,000

Now, the whole of the ordinary shares and one-third of the preference went to the vendors as part payment, and apparently the first-named holdings come within this category. Messrs. S. J. Waring & Sons furnished the hotel, and Stephens, Bastow, & Company built it, so that the public who hold the balance of shares cannot have much influence compared with the insiders. At the same time the poor subscription accounts for the weakness in the market price. Ought such a company to have gone to allotment?

The Salt Union, Limited.

Various reasons are put forward in the directors' report to account for the further drop in profits. The continued decline in the demand for manufactured salt in the chemical and allied industries, and the imposition and reimposition of fiscal duties in countries to which British salt is exported increased the competition amongst salt manufacturers in the United Kingdom, rendering decrease in tonnage coincident with decrease in price. The rise in the rates of freight for sea-borne salt continued, and further limited the profits derivable from the sale and consignment of salt; the effect of which was particularly noticeable in the Indian market, which was also adversely affected by war, famine, and plague. Finally, the fishing on the East coast of Scotland, and on various parts of the English coast, was much less successful than usual, causing considerable decline in the quantity of salt used for fish-curing purposes. All this is, of course, very unfortunate, but the company is not suffering only from one year's bad trade, for it has been going downhill right away from the start, and, as will be seen from the following figures, the decline has been pretty rapid :—

Year.	Salt Delivered.	Gross Revenue.	Net Profits.	Dividend on Ordinary Shares.
	Tons.	£	£	Per Cent.
1889	1,770,000	562,968	368,512	10
1890	1,629,000	524,200	306,447	7
1891	1,478,000	435,799	243,911	5
1892	1,354,000	384,774	215,919	5
1893	1,240,000	256,292	176,860	3
1894	1,284,000	319,527	170,482	2½
1895	1,217,000	314,208	162,154	2
1896	1,066,000	295,868	145,292	1
1897	1,014,000	210,489	66,823	0

The past year has of course been disastrous, and not only is there nothing for the ordinary shareholders, but only 1¼ per cent. for holders of 7 per cent. preference shares, so that the long impending crisis in the company's affairs may be said to have been reached. Unfortunately it is not only loss of profit that has to be lamented, but the financial position of the concern calls for immediate attention. Over-capitalisation was the chief initial fault, and in 1895 an issue of £200,000 "B" debenture stock increased the prior charges, while all the time profits were diminishing. In 1892 the company had a reserve fund of £117,500, of which only £60,333 was represented by investments, but although the reserve still stands in the balance-sheet for the same amount, investments have fallen to £21,564, and this money is in the company's own debenture stocks

The worst item, however, is that relating to properties and works, plant, and goodwill which stood in the 1890 accounts at £3,365,498, and beyond a small appropriation out of profits, has had nothing written off from it by way of depreciation; on the contrary, it has been written up to £3,457,364. Then we find surplus freehold estates have risen in the seven years from £90,830 to £106,297; and shares in other salt trading companies from £116,128 to £138,168, which we should think is a very questionable valuation. The item steamers, barges, flats and appliances, has certainly been reduced from £183,639 to £163,791 since 1890, but rolling stock figures for £130,697 against £132,170, stocks of salt at £81,677 against £51,069, and stocks of fuel and material at £50,683 against £47,957. The balance-sheet wants thorough overhauling, so that it can be seen how the company really stands.

We are not disposed to blame the present directors for the present condition of affairs; the blame is due to the vendors and the original directors, many of whom have disappeared from the board, who saddled or crippled the undertaking at the start with heavy encumbrances. For instance, the balance-sheet shows that so far £135,035 has been spent in the acquisition of distribution agencies and covenants with vendors, but this does not seem to have helped profits much, nor has the steady expenditure every year on new works. Neither are we disposed to support the persons who have come forward as a shareholders' committee and would no doubt like to get a footing in the management. The existing directors should bring forward a scheme of reconstruction and be given another opportunity of making the affair a success before outsiders are called in. But the position must be faced at once as the margin between profits and debenture interest is vanishing.

Critical Index to New Investments.

ALBION (BURTON-ON-TRENT) BREWERY, LIMITED.

Issue of £110,000 four per cent. perpetual mortgage "A" debenture stock at par; interest due May and November. Share capital is £140,000 all issued to the vendors, except eighty-seven shares, and there is in existence an issue of £180,000 four and a-half per cent. perpetual first mortgage debenture stock, standing at about 115. By the present issue the company will have twice as much debenture stock as share capital, but it must be admitted that it is an exceptional undertaking. It was formed in 1896 to acquire the brewery, with 153 licensed houses, 121 unlicensed houses, stores, and cottages, and about 119 acres of freehold and long leasehold building and other land. The whole of the licensed houses are now leased for twenty-one years to Thomas Salt & Co., Limited; the brewery is let on favourable terms for seventy-nine years, and the whole of the company's other property is let to produce a good rental. With a view to further increasing its income contracts have been entered into for the acquisition of fifty-five additional licensed houses which are to be leased to Ind Coope & Co., Limited, for twenty-one years, and it is to complete the purchase of these properties that the present issue of debenture stock is made. It is secured by an absolute specific first mortgage on properties valued at £101,607; and a fixed charge after the existing debenture stock on the brewery and general undertaking valued at £149,143 net. The rents and royalties receivable from the two large firms and other tenants are calculated to produce £20,170 per annum, of which the first debenture stock interest will absorb £8,100, and the stock now offered £4,400, so that the margin of £7,670 per annum should make the stock a fair investment.

SCHIBAIEFF PETROLEUM COMPANY, LIMITED.

Share capital is £750,000 in 75,000 6 per cent. cumulative preference shares of £5 each, and 375,000 ordinary shares of £1 each. The object of this company is to buy all the [illegible]

March 31 last in a petroleum business carried on at Baku, Moscow, and elsewhere by a Russian private limited liability company known as Messrs. S. M. Schibaieff & Co. The Russian company was established in 1884, and has a share capital of about £265,000. Mr. Redwood supplies a well-varnished report on the properties to be taken over, and Turquand, Youngs & Co. say that the balance-sheets and profit and loss accounts, as given to them, show net profits of £29,032 for 1894-5; of £59,523 for 1895-6; and of £55,501 for 1896-7. It is claimed that besides the capital some £300,000 has been spent out of profits on the construction and development of the business and there are other assets amounting to £116,000. Even so we fail to see why the capital is to be blown out to such an extent, nor do we learn why the concern is to be sold. Are these Russian companies being got rid of because of the efforts being made over here to raise the flash point? The vendors, who are the promoters, and are selling at a profit—this we can well understand—have fixed the purchase price at £640,000, of which only £20,000 is to be in shares. Is this, then, their measure of belief in the future of the undertaking? For the three years dealt with by Turquand, Youngs, the average profits are £48,019, but, assuming that the net profits of £55,500 for the last of the three years are maintained, we much doubt if, after paying directors' fees and London office expenses, they would show more than 7 per cent. on the ordinary shares, which is certainly not in our opinion, a return commensurate with the risks run.

THE "ERA" INCANDESCENT OIL LAMP COMPANY LIMITED.

Company is formed to acquire British, foreign and colonial letters patent for Graetz's incandescent Oil Lamp. The inventions acquired by the Company enable the Welsbach system of incandescent lighting to be used in connection with oil lamps burning ordinary petroleum just in the same manner as it is now used with gas. We were under the impression that the Welsbach company made out that it was the owner of this patent, but this is evidently not so. The connection lies in the fact that the "Era" lamp has been fully tested by the Incandescent Gas Light Company, now being amalgamated with the Welsbach Company, and it has taken an exclusive licence from this country for Great Britain at a rate of royalty not stated, but under this licence it has had manufactured 20,000 "Era" lamps, which will shortly be placed on the market. The capital of the company is £60,000 in £1 shares, which seems moderate, but the purchase price is £50,000, of which £10,000 will be in shares. As an investment, it is early to judge of the merits of the concern, but there is always a certain risk run in taking shares in a company dependent only on a patent.

PREMIER TRAWLING AND FISH-CARRYING COMPANY, LIMITED.

The idea of this venture is to buy ten steam trawlers belonging to Richard Simpson & Co., Limited, and the benefit and advantage (or otherwise) of contracts entered into for the construction of thirty-four more steam fishing vessels. For the twelve months commencing November, 1896, the profits of this firm are certified at £8,259, but the valuation of A. & W. Dudgeon (we presume the name is spelt right) counts for little, because the value of the vessels in use, and under construction are all piled up together with goodwill and various other items. It will probably come as a surprise that the share capital is £200,000 in £1 shares, half ordinary and half 6 per cent cumulative preference, besides an issue at par of £150,000 4½ per cent. first mortgage debenture stock, redeemable in 1910 at 105. And the surprise will, no doubt, be increased by the fact that the vendors, the Fisheries Syndicate, Limited, who are the promoters, and, it is needless to say, are selling at a profit—substantial, we should imagine—are asking £170,000 as the purchase price, including £103,334 in cash. Not satisfied with this, the company is to pay £161,800 for the new boats, besides paying extra for fishing gear. The proposal seems to have some flavour of fish, and it would pay the vendors splendidly.

Company Reports and Balance-Sheets.

MERCANTILE INVESTMENT AND GENERAL TRUST.—A further improvement is seen in the position of this concern. Revenue increased but slightly, so that the net income of £82,009 was only £1,776 above that of 1896. This permitted of the payment of preference and debenture interest, and a dividend of 3 per cent. upon the deferred stock. In addition, £5,000 was placed to reserve, and the balance carried forward was £4,500 higher. The reserve also benefited by the net result from realisations of investments to the tune of £48,073, against which £19,683 was absorbed by writing down the value of certain securities which were permanently depreciated. Its total, therefore, amounts to £103,892, and it is specially invested in high-class securities. The securities, which have a cost value in the books of £3,113,149, are too numerous for a careful analysis, but they contain many stocks and shares which are improving in value. Further realisations of bank shares (the weak point of the trust) have been effected, and two hopeless affairs, £2,000 of David Martineau & Sons' debentures and £5,000 of Standard Bank of Australia shares, have been written clean off. The trust issue a statement of securities purchased and sold in the year, and we must say that a perusal of these does not heighten our sense of the prudence of the management.

LONDON AND AUSTRALASIAN DEBENTURE CORPORATION.—In some ways the affairs of this company show improvement. The terminal debentures have been wiped out, the loan against securities reduced to £1,100, and the investment reserve raised to £2,625 by additions from profit on sales. Revenue also improved, and after payment of a dividend of 2½ per cent., the balance forward was increased by £1,400 to £2,961. All this appears favourable for a company whose share capital amounts to £100,700, and whose debenture debt is £50,000, especially as it is stated that the valuation of the company's *quoted* (we presume officially quoted) investments shows a considerable appreciation upon the figures at which they stand in the books. Unfortunately, however, the whole of this pretty picture is blurred by the fact that the company has a lock-up of £52,318 in shares of the Australian Cities Investment Corporation, and a further liability on account of these shares of £22,422. The Australian company is in difficulties, and has had to make terms with its creditors, and some scheme of rearrangement seems to lie in the future. The whole character of the balance-sheet which only runs into £165,571, is rendered uncertain by the anxieties which surround this one investment, and we are afraid that all the hard work of late years in putting the affairs of this concern into order may be rendered migratory by the bad results of this one *coup*.

TEMPERANCE PERMANENT BUILDING SOCIETY.—This society keeps up its high record, and with £921,354 invested in mortgages on house property, no less than £630,000 is in mortgages which do not exceed £500 a piece. Another £153,000 is in mortgages between £500 and £1,000 a piece, so that only £140,000 is left for larger mortgages which partake of a financial character. Thus the main object of the society is well adhered to, and the wisdom of this policy is seen in the small amount of properties in possession, for these only number four, which stand in the books for £15,890. Even these are a source of profit, for they yield a net income equal to 9¾ per cent. upon the money advanced, and the larger portion of this income is being used to write down their capital value. The profits on working the society allowed of the usual dividend of 5½ per cent. on the original shares, and the carrying of £2,977 to reserve, raising that fund to £61,554. It is a pity, however, that liquid assets are not accumulated to a greater extent, for there is only £20,377 of consols and Staffordshire County stock, against £237,674 of deposits, and it looks as if most of the cash will be dissipated in the dividends. A strong society like this ought to have its reserve invested outside its business.

SCOTTISH AMERICAN INVESTMENT COMPANY.—A company with a prosperous record, but which seems to divide its profits well up to the hilt. Even profit on securities sold is treated as ordinary revenue, and of the net revenue of £50,609, no less than £50,000 is absorbed in paying the dividend of 10 per cent., leaving only the odd £609 to be carried forward. At the same time the company must be well managed, for with investments to the value of £2,696,008 in the balance-sheet, it is stated that the market value is considerably above that amount. There is also a reserve fund of £300,000. But nothing whatever is set forth in the report that discloses the character or nature of those investments. Clearly real estate mortgages form a part of its business, and yet there is nothing said about property held as a result of foreclosure. Yet the debentures and debenture stock of the concern amount to £1,933,000, as against £516,799 of paid-up share capital, and the amount required for interest last year was £74,191, or three-fifths of the sum received in interest on investments. Altogether a company of mysterious silences that do not encourage prudent folk to touch it.

CITY OF LONDON ELECTRIC LIGHTING COMPANY.—The progress of this company goes on at a remarkably rapid pace. With a capital expenditure of £1,283,720, or only £82,000 more than the preceding year, the gross revenue of 1897 was £186,836, or £38,300 more than in 1896. This shows that past outlays have by no means borne their full fruit. Expenditure came to £81,685, so that the net revenue was £105,151, as compared with £79,527 in 1896. The growth of gross revenue was therefore 20 per cent., while that of net was no less than 32 per cent., as against increased capital outlay of less than 7 per cent. Out of the net income the board set aside £17,000 for depreciation, £3,528 for reserve, and £1,338 towards the wiping out of a small suspense account. The balance, after meeting fixed charges, permitted of a dividend on the ordinary shares of 10 per cent., as compared with 7 per cent. in the preceding twelve months. Unfortunately, the company continues its confusing system of using proceeds of premiums to meet a part of the depreciation charges, and in this way keeps down its working charges at an artificially low level. The increase in the number of customers and lamps connected last year were well up to the level of the two preceding years, but the number applied for and waiting connection, was, not unnaturally, less than a year ago.

CIVIL SERVICE SUPPLY ASSOCIATION.—In spite of the granting of permanent tickets to subscribers of five years' standing, this association turned over a little less last year than in the preceding twelve months. The profit for the second half of the year was just a trifle lower at £129,011, which allowed of the usual dividend of 12s. per £10 of capital, the placing of £2,000 to reserve, and the carrying forward of £4,942. The sum of 9d. per £10 of capital is returned as interest upon the reserve. Repairs and depreciation are allowed for on a liberal scale, and rather more is written off premises as these have been considerably added to in the year.

CAMBRIAN RAILWAYS COMPANY.—Gross receipts for half-year ended December 31, £161,293, expenses £98,326, proportion of expenses to receipts, 60·8 per cent. The income for the half-year rose £5,196, but the expenditure was £6,705 greater, therefore the net revenue is £1,508 less than in the corresponding period of 1896. The company, however, is able to pay full interest on the A, B, C, and D debenture stocks, and a sum of £3,979 is left to carry forward. During the six months £17,908 was spent on capital account, £11,820 of it on working expenses stock. Interest warrants will be posted on the 28th inst.

COCKERMOUTH, KESWICK AND PENRITH RAILWAY.—Gross receipts for second half of 1897, £26,029, working expenses £15,288, proportion of expenses to receipts 57·7 per cent. The traffic gave an increase of £1,769, and expenses rose only £1,004. The net revenue therefore benefited to a small extent, and the directors were able to declare a dividend at the rate of 5 per cent. on the ordinary stock, leaving £178 to carry to the new half year. Only £405 was spent on capital account during the half-year and this little company appears to be in quite a comfortable position.

WEST CLARE RAILWAY COMPANY, LIMITED.—Gross receipts were £6,814 in the half-year ended October 31 last, and expenses came to £6,197, this left only £617 as net revenue, as against £1,286 in October 1896, so the net revenue is down about £669. The traffic appears to be sadly non-progressive, and is smaller than in the corresponding half of either of the two previous years.

SOUTH CLARE RAILWAY COMPANY, LIMITED.—Gross receipts for the half-year ended October 31, £3,804; expenses, £3,585; net revenue, £219. Here also the figures are lower than those of the corresponding half of 1896 and 1895. Expenses have also been reduced slightly compared with 1896, but are higher than those of the half-year ended October 1895. Passenger traffic has fallen off most conspicuously, and live stock traffic is also less. Both these little companies justify eloquently to the depressed condition of the districts they serve. Pity it does not attract the English tourist more, for County Clare is full of beauty.

KENSINGTON & KNIGHTSBRIDGE ELECTRIC LIGHTING COMPANY.—Small as the area of this company is, it has shown considerable expansion in business during the year. The number of customers increased from 1,325 to 1,620, and the number of lamps connected from 119,955 of 8 c.p. to 137,953 of 8 c.p. Net revenue during the year amounted to £14,647, and after paying debenture and preference interest the balance permits of the distribution of 10 per cent. upon the ordinary shares, as against 7 per cent. for the preceding year. The sum of £8,061 is placed to the renewal fund, which is increased thereby to £20,497, and there is also a depreciation fund account for works on leasehold account which now amounts to £1,435. Of the sum of £2,079 received in premiums upon new capital, £558 has been devoted towards wiping out the balance of cost of conversion of debentures, and the remainder has been written off the purchase price of a small electrical undertaking bought up some time ago. The company therefore grows in strength each year, and has already expended £22,707 upon the undertaking in excess of capital raised.

H. E. RANDALL, LIMITED.—This bootselling company earned last year a gross profit of £11,628, including £604 from profit on Jubilee windows. The sum of £1,400 is allowed for depreciation, and £739 is devoted to wiping off balance of preliminary expenses, and after debenture interest and other charges have been met, the sum of £7,461 remains, but of this the preference interest required £2,400, and the ordinary shares receive distributions equal to 10 per cent. for the year, which absorb £3,000, leaving £2,178 to be carried forward. It is a good showing in a way, but the auditors can only sign their report "subject to any necessary provision being made against the expiration of leases of shops." That seems to imply that no provision has been made for such a contingency, which is an important one for the company. We also note that the indebtedness of the concern is very large. In addition to £30,000 of debentures, there was £18,390 owing to sundry creditors, and £4,382 for bills payable. These for a business which is eminently of a ready-money character seems unduly large.

THE PRUDENTIAL ASSURANCE COMPANY, LIMITED.—A "valuation report" issued by this company—we have not seen its full accounts yet; they come to hand shyly—for the year 1897, states that the result is a surplus of £811,663, including £213,568 brought forward. This is on the "ordinary" life and annuity businesses, both of which have attained large proportions with great rapidity. In the industrial, or burial money branch, the business continues tremendous, and there is a valuation surplus at the end of the year amounting to £870,162 notwithstanding the fact that the company has granted free policies for £1,600,000 in lieu of discontinued assurances, "and to provide for the increase in the sums assured given to industrial policy holders." This is only just, and the company is well able to go still further in the same direction, for its industrial fund now amounts to £13,668,034, and its ordinary life and annuities funds, £15,134,804, or together, £28,802,838, a magnificent total.

THE COUNTY FIRE OFFICE.—Deducting re-insurance, the net premium income of this company for 1897 was £274,631, an increase of £3,321 on 1896. Losses by fire took £99,828, or about 36·4 per cent. of the net premium income; and expenses and commission, £91,419, or about 33·3 per cent. Adding interest and dividends, £20,698, the balance left to be carried forward is £103,662. The company has a paid-up capital of £254,560, and upon this a dividend of £12 per share, or 15 per cent., has been paid for the year—£3 of it in September last, and £9 now. This will leave £28,478 to be added to the reserve fund, which will, therefore, now stand at £366,430.

LAW LIFE ASSURANCE SOCIETY.—At the seventy-fourth annual general meeting of this society, held on the 23rd inst., Mr. Charles Stewart in the chair, the report was presented, and showed that 504 new policies, assuring £690,378, or, deducting re-assurances, £526,561, had been effected during the year. The total net premium income for the year was £248,472, the net renewal premium income showing an increase for the sixth year in succession. The expenses of management (including commission) were £11 16s. 4d. per cent. of the total net premium income. The net claims by death amounted to £294,429, which amount was about £77,000 less than the expected amount, and the total fuuds at the end of the year amounted to £4,918,288, an increase of £108,360. Interest on the society's invested funds averaged £4 1s. 4d. per cent., without deducting income-tax. The society has a well-distributed and first-class list of investments.

THE TELEGRAPH CONSTRUCTION AND MAINTENANCE COMPANY has not done so well as in the preceding year, and its profits are not so good as they used to be. Last year they came to £61,131 against £88,300 in 1896, £32,589 in 1895, and £91,921 in 1894. The amount brought forward is, however, £21,000 larger, so that the available total is only £6,000 less. The dividend of 15 per cent., to which it was lowered in 1895, is repeated, and the substantial balance of £33,841 carried forward. The company's works are said to have been actively employed, and, therefore, it may be presumed from the smaller profits that the work done has been less remunerative. The figures of the balance-sheet are of the usual heavy description. Property, plant, stocks, and leases have been further written down to £329,163; but debts owing by the company, £586,814, debts owing to the company, £379,053, and sundry securities, £539,633, all show increases compared with a year ago. Of what real value these sundry securities are we know not, but we notice they have increased by £69,000 since 1893, and probably they are not very marketable.

BERGVIK COMPANY.—Further recovery appears to have been made during the past year, though in the absence of a balance sheet from the Swedish Company, it is impossible to be too sure. This company, we are told, wrote £11,321 off cost of buildings and works, against only £5,263 a year ago, when, however, it also wrote £2,676 off the pulp factory. It has also added £10,000 to reserve, raising it to £30,000, and has redeemed £3,611 of its 4½ per cent. debentures, which are thus reduced to £33,333. After doing all this by way of strengthening itself, it hands over £50,000 to the English undertaking, being the amount of dividend declared by the Swedish Company, and with this sum the directors over here wipe out the balance of £7,600, representing bonuses on debentures redeemed under the conversion scheme, and set aside £6,200 for redemption of debentures; while from the remainder they pay the 6 per cent. preference shares, and increase the dividend on the deferred shares from 10s. to 12s., or from 5 to 6 per cent. The company has benefited from the strength of the wood market, and now that nothing will be required in future for redemption of debenture bonuses, it would be a good opportunity to start a reserve fund.

JOHN OAKEY & SONS, LIMITED, make knife polish, and became a public company nearly five years ago, with a share capital of £225,000 in £10 shares, 10,000 being 6 per cent. preference, now fetching 16, and 12,500 ordinary, which are dealt in above 31. We do not remember to have seen a copy of the directors' report before, but have obtained one for the past year which discloses a most satisfactory position. The company has a capital reserve of £3,734, and a general reserve of £22,500, the whole of which is in Consols and Colonial Government securities. Sundry creditors do not stand for more than £13,056, while debtors represent £35,185. Stocks on hand figure at the moderate total of £28,531, and plant, &c., at £19,751. Freehold land and buildings are down for £60,748, and goodwill for £82,455. Another £5,000 is to be now added to reserve and invested, but in the absence of a working account we do not know what amount is allowed for depreciation, or whether anything is being written off goodwill. The net profits for the past year were £27,317, of which the ordinary shareholders get £15,625 in the shape of a dividend of 10 per cent, and a bonus of 2½ per cent., which is the same distribution as was made a year ago. At their present price the return on the shares is very moderate.

NEW EXPLOSIVES COMPANY.—There is little reason for elation over the result of the year's working, the profit being only £2,601, compared with £4,155, and under these circumstances the dividend is lowered from 4 to 2½ per cent. There is no cause to complain of the amount of business, the output in tonnage exceeding that of 1896 by 25 per cent., but the increased trade had to be done at a reduced rate of profit. The new factory, the completion of which was delayed by a local strike and the lock-out in the engineering trade, has at length been completed, and now that the whole of the debentures have been placed, practically with members of the company, the concern should be in a more comfortable position, and be able to render a better account of itself next year.

BANK OF BRITISH NORTH AMERICA.—The report for the past half-year shows a gratifying improvement, the profits, with £8,323 brought forward, being £39,435, as compared with £26,018 a year ago, when £5,252 was brought in. The dividend is therefore raised from 20s. to 25s. a share, and £10,000 is added to the reserve, raising to £285,000. Deposits and current accounts have recovered from £2,066,000 to £2,310,000.

The Produce Markets.

GRAIN.

The week opened firmly, with a general advance in the price of wheat of 6d. to 1s. The strength and activity of the American markets, of course, greatly influenced the English. By Tuesday, however, business had become more dull, and at Mark-lane on Wednesday buyers held off, but sellers were firm, and Monday's advance was maintained. Flour was unaltered in value, but the movement was slow. Maize was in poor demand at unchanged rates; mixed American, ex ship, 16s. to 16s. 3d.; old crop, 17s., ex quay; and Galatz-Bessarabian at 18s. Barley had a quiet sale; Odessa-Nikolaieff, 16s. to 16s. 9d., ex ship; and Danubian at 16s. 3d. to 16s. 6d. Oats were disappointing in the demand. Mixed American, ex ship, are obtainable at 15s. 7½d. to 15s. 9d. Arrivals:—Wheat, 22,340 qr.; maize, 27,510 qr.; flour, 24,960 sacks; and oats, 27,510 qr. At Liverpool the course of the market was somewhat similar, with a good spot demand in the early part of the week; but on Wednesday, though rates were maintained, the tendency was in buyers' favour. Red American futures, which opened the week at a slight rise, receded on Wednesday ½d. to ⅝d.; but the decline was checked in the afternoon by firmer advices from Paris. The market closed steady ¾d. to 1¼d. cental lower. Sales, 350,000 centals, comprising March, 8s. 0½d. to 7s. 11⅝d.; May, 7s. 7¼d. to 7s. 6⅝d.; July, 7s. 3¾d. to 7s. 3¼d.; September, 6s. 7⅝d. to 6s. 7¼d.; December, 6s. 6½d. to 6s. 6d. East Indian shipments:—Cargoes quiet and easier. Walla Walla, February, sold at 36s., and La Plata, February-March, sailer, at the same price. The London cargo market has not been very brisk, and there has been little fluctuation. On Wednesday near-at-hand cargoes were not pressed for sale, while for distant shipments there is little or no inquiry. The break in the American option market has produced an uncertain feeling, and the close is quiet and easy. Options were ½d. to ⅝d. down with business for March, June, and September. Maize ⅛d. to ½d. lower. Barley firm, but not much offering. Oats quiet. Beans unaltered.

OFFICIAL CLOSING VALUES (100 lb. deliveries—February 23).

	March.	May.	July.	Sept.	Dec.
Red American Wheat	7·11⅝	7·6¼	7·3¼	6·7⅞	6·6½

In New York the wheat market has been rather easy throughout the week. On Wednesday it opened 1⅝ c. lower, recovered a little later, but closed ⅞ c. to 1¼ c. down. Spot easy. *Bradstreet's* figures show decrease in supplies East Rockies of 989,000 bushels on week. Spring, 115⅝ c.; winter, 108⅞. Sales: futures, 4,100,000 bushels; spot, 120,000 bushels. Receipts: Atlantic (two days), 217,000 bushels; last year (three days), 227,000 bushels. This season, 45,643,000 bushels; last season, 31,847,000 bushels. Clearances (two days), 275,000 bushels; last year (three days), 246,000 bushels. This season, 46,433,000 bushels; lost season, 27,324,000 bushels. Flour steady.

COTTON.

The spot market at Liverpool has ruled rather dull during the week, though on Tuesday and Wednesday there was rather more activity at steady prices. On Wednesday a fair business was done in American at firmer rates. Brazilian and Surats quiet at late rates. Egyptians were in limited request at steady prices. Futures opened unchanged and with little offering, and, "bears" covering, hardened 2 points in the forenoon. Subsequently there was little change of note, and, after a small business, the close was steady at a rise of 2½ to 3 points.

In New York cotton ruled dull, with prices generally down until Wednesday, when market opened firmer, 10 to 11 points higher on better cables, light interior receipts, more peaceful political situation abroad, active covering, and investment buying. Advance was partially lost later under liquidation, and market closed quiet, 7 to 9 points up. Spot dull. Middling upland, 6¼c. Sales, 197,500 bales.

NEW YORK CLOSING VALUES.

	Spot.	Feb.	Mar.	April.	May.	June.	July.	Aug.	Sept.	Oct.	Nov.	Dec.
Feb. 23 ..	6¼	6·02	6.03	6·04	6·08	6·11	6·14	6·17	6·16	6·15	6·15	6·18

WOOL.

No decided improvement is reported in the wool markets; but dealers believe that prices have touched their lowest level, and hold out for some advance. But buyers do not respond, and the consequence is that the volume of the business remains small. At the London Wool Exchange the attendance at the low wool sales was good, but the bidding was dull, and but little was sold at a fall of ¼d. per lb. on Tuesday, and another ¼d. to ½d. on Wednesday. German houses were the principal buyers, and a few lots here and there fell to home account. The China camels' hair and sheep's wool experienced a particularly slow sale, a few parcels selling at about unchanged rates, but the cashmere was all withdrawn. Spanish black unwashed wools, after bids of 3½d., were taken in, but the seven bales of super Cape mohair sold well at 12½d. to 15½d.

METALS AND COAL.

There has been great activity in copper during the week, and prices have gone up daily until there was an increase on the week of 7s. to 10s. On Wednesday about 800 tons were disposed of, and throughout the day the tone was extremely firm. Cash realised £49 17s. 6d., March dates up to the 14th £49 17s. 6d. and £49 18s. 9d.; May 10 and three months, £50 2s. 6d., and four months £50 3s. 9d. and £50 5s. The market was quieter during the afternoon, when an additional 300 tons changed hands. Cash and early dates £49 17s. 6d. and £49 18s. 9d.; three months and June 2 at £50 3s. 9d.

SETTLEMENT PRICES.

	Feb. 23.	Feb. 16.	Feb. 9.	Feb. 2.	Jan. 26	Jan. 19.
	£ s. d.	£ s. d.	£ s. d.	£ s. d.	£ s. d.	£ s. d.
Copper ..	49 17 6	49 10 0	49 5 0	49 2 6	48 17 6	49 5 0

Tin has also shown considerable activity, with several rises in price. Card sales on Wednesday, at £64 1s. 3d.; March dates up to the middle of the month at £64 2s. 6d. and 64s. 5s. The pig-iron market has been strong in tone on the whole, with ocassional hesitation in consequence of unsustained war rumours. On Tuesday Scotch rose 3½d., and Cleveland 2d.; but on Wednesday there was a downward tendency, though the market closed 1½d. higher on the day.

SETTLEMENT PRICES.

	Feb. 23.	Feb. 16.	Feb. 9.	Feb. 2.	Jan. 26.	Jan. 19.
	s. d.	s. d.	s. d.	s. d.	s. d.	s. d.
Scotch	46 3	45 7½	45 7½	45 7½	46 0	46 0
Cleveland ..	40 10½	40 7½	40 4½	40 6	40 10½	40 10½
Hematite ..	49 1½	48 9	48 7½	48 6	47 0	48 10½

SUGAR.

There has been a decided improvement in the tone of the market, stocks are firmly held, and the tendency has been rather upward if anything. Refined British cubes were on Wednesday in better demand at full values; crushed 3d. dearer; in pieces a good trade was done at steady rates, and crystals have a moderate enquiry; prices unchanged. Quotations—Tate's cubes, No. 1, 14s. 10½d.; No. 2, 14s.; crushed, No. 1, 13s. 6d.; No. 2, 13s.; granulated, 13s.; yellow crystals, 12s. 3d.; Lyle's crystals, No. 1, 13s. 3d.; No. 2, 12s. 6d.; granulated, No. 1, 13s.; No. 2, 12s. 3d.; whites, A, 12s. 9d.; B, 12s.; yellow crystallised, O and P, 12s. 3d. Foreign.—Granulated opened firm at ¾d. advance, but closed quieter with the improvement partially lost. Ready G D and Groningen sold at 11s. 1½d.; Z R M, 11s. 0¾d. March, first marks, 11s. 0¾d.; April, 11s. 1½d. and sellers; May-August, 11s. 4½d. to 11s. 3¾d. and buyers, f.o.b. Hamburg. Cubes—F M S, prompt, sold at 12s. 1½d.; Meyer, 12s. 9d.; Hansa, 12s. 1½d., sellers, f.o.b. Hamburg; W S R, prompt, held for 13s. 1½d.; S and T, 12s. 10½d.; A S R and cut loaf, 12s. 9d., f.o.b. Amsterdam. Cane kinds steady but quiet. Beet futures firm at ½d. to ¾d. advance.

TEA AND COFFEE.

Messrs. Gow, Wilson, & Stanton state in their tea report that "exports from Calcutta direct to consuming countries show encouraging increases, those to Australia and New Zealand being particularly hopeful. It is evident that this important market is gradually following the example of Great Britain in displacing its China consumption by teas grown in India and Ceylon. Under the influence of continued moderate auctions the Indian market has been gradually gaining strength, and the improved tone noticed last week was fully maintained for all grades. The auction of Ceylon tea comprised 17,280 packages, but passed without any improvement in quotations, which were irregular and sometimes below those reported last week. During the last few weeks some invoices of garden tea have been brought forward from Natal; the teas were of fair make in leaf, but rather thin in cup, and consequently only low average prices were realised. Java was not represented. 202 packages are catalogued for the next fortnight."

The coffee auctions have been well attended, and there was a keen competition at full rates for all good to fine sorts. On Wednesday the auctions comprised 3,194 packages, more than half consisting of East India, which met with a good demand and realised firm prices; Ceylon sold steadily; Guatemala easy; Colombian about steady; and Jamaica again lower. Ceylon—low middling to bold green, 92s. to 115s.; peaberry, 102s. East India—bold common dull grey to fine dull coloury, 95s. to 112s.; low middling to good middling, 74s. to 94s. 6d.; smalls common to bold, 51s. to 75s.; peaberry, 91s. to 109s. Guatemala—good middling soft blue mixed, 81s. Colombian—bold rough faded-grey, 72s. to 73s.; low middling to bold faded green mixed, 59s. to 67s. 6d. Jamaica—middling to bold dull grey, 71s. 6d. to 86s.; common medium to bold brownish mixed, 57s. to 72s.; good ordinary, mixed broken to very fine ordinary greenish, 37s. to 51s. 6d.; peaberry brownish, 68s.

HEMP AND JUTE.

Up to Monday, hemp remained firm, with good demand and sparingly offered, but on that day there were large receipts, and the market eased considerably; Manila, F. C., February-April, sailer, £19 5s., and May-July, £19 7s. 6d., sellers. Imports during past week, 3,250 bales. Jute dull for the most part, with rather a downward tendency. First marks, according to group, February-March steamer, £19 12s. 6d. to £19 15s. sellers.

Mr. William Tuke, a director of the West Australian Eldorado Syndicate, shot himself through the head at his office in Gracechurch-street a few days ago. He seemed in his usual health on arriving at the office, and no suspicion of anything wrong was entertained until a shot was heard in his private room. He was removed to Guy's Hospital, where he died without regaining consciousness.

An amended offer has been sent by the London Syndicate to the Canadian Government for the construction of the Yukon railway. It proposes to build from Pyramid Harbour to Rink Rapids, a distance of 288 miles, for a land grant in alternate sections of one mile square for a distance of ten miles on each side of the railway from the boundary to the Rapids, a total of 1,248,000 acres, or it will build from the Stickeen to Teslin Lake for 1,000,000, or 2,750,000 acres less than Messrs. Mackenzie & Mann claims.

The Afrikander Bond Congress at Cape Town have come to the conclusion that there ought to be a tax on foreign dividends. Surely they should rather insist on the Government ceasing to borrow.

The Transvaal revenue for January last amounted to £84,000, as compared with £117,000 for January, 1897.

Notice to Subscribers.

Complaints are continually reaching us that the INVESTORS REVIEW cannot be obtained at this and the other railway bookstall, that it does not reach Scotch and Irish cities till Monday, and that it is not delivered in the City till Saturday morning.

We publish on Friday in time for the REVIEW to be at all Metropolitan bookstalls by at latest 4 p.m., and we believe that it is there then, having no doubt that Messrs. W. H. Smith & Son do their best, but they have such a mass of papers to handle every day that a fresh one may well look almost like a personal enemy and be kept in short supply unless the reading public shows unmistakably that it is wanted. A little perseverance, therefore, in asking for the INVESTORS' REVIEW is all that should be required to remedy this defect.

All London newsagents can be in a position to distribute the paper on Friday afternoon if they please, and here also the only remedy is for subscribers to insist upon having it as soon as published. Arrangements have been made that all our direct City subscribers shall have their copies before 4 p.m. on Friday. As for the provinces, we can only say that the paper is delivered to the forwarding agents in ample time to be in every English and Scotch town, and in Dublin and Belfast, likewise, early on Saturday morning. Those despatched by post from this office can be delivered by the first London mail on Saturday in every part of the United Kingdom.

Cheques and Postal Orders should be made payable to CLEMENT WILSON.

The INVESTORS' REVIEW can be obtained in Paris of Messrs. BOYVEAU ET CHEVILLET, 22, Rue de la Banque.

ADVERTISEMENTS.

All Advertisements are received subject to approval, and should be sent in not later than 5 p.m. on Thursdays.

For tariff and particulars of positions open apply to the Advertisement Manager, Norfolk House, Norfolk-street, W.C.

To Correspondents.

The EDITOR cannot undertake to return rejected communications. Letters from correspondents must, in every case, be authenticated by the name and address of the writer.

The Investors' Review.

The Week's Money Market.

The Money Market has had a worse time during the past seven days than in the preceding week. Not only have all loans from the Bank of England been renewed upon maturity, but a large sum has been borrowed in addition, as is indicated by the increase of £2,711,000 in the "other securities" of the Bank Return. The pressure has been in a measure accentuated by the payment of the railway dividends which have occasioned considerable transfers of cash; but the large borrowings from the Bank have probably left balances over in places, for, in spite of yesterday being Stock Exchange "Pay Day," there was a little more money about. Day to day loans, therefore, closed about 2½ to 3 per cent., although on most other days the higher rate was usual. Seven day market loans have moved up to the same quotation.

Discount rates have hardened in spite of the cessation of the Continental demand for gold, for although the last shipment was taken, that arriving to-morrow will go into the Bank. The market, indeed, has been swept so completely clear of floating balances, that it could no longer continue to discount at terms distinctly below what money was costing it. The upward movement was further accentuated by the rather unexpected announcement that an Anglo-German Loan for £16,000,000 has been arranged with China. The operation, however satisfactory from a financial and diplomatic point of view, comes at an awkward time for the market, for the desire to pay off Japan quickly must force on the issue almost at once. On the other hand, the market does not know when it will get back any large percentage of the eight millions, or so, of its usual balances now held by the Government, while its indebtedness to the Bank of England harasses its actions from day to day. It is urged that the Loan may cause shipments of gold from Berlin to this side, and the sharp advance of late in the German exchanges supports this view, but the last big Chinese loan did not see Berlin's quota taken up, and payment for what was subscribed was spread over a considerable time by dint of credits raised in London. Bankers and bill brokers have, therefore, declined to work upon the old terms, and three months' short bills are quoted 2¾ to 2⅞ per cent. as against 2⅝ to 2{11/16} a week ago. Longer dated paper, however, keeps dulls at about 2⅝ per cent.

Although the Stock Exchange settlement disclosed a rather lighter account open, loans to the "House" were quoted hard at 3½ to 3¾, with most business doing at the higher figure. The issue of Treasury bills for £1,500,000 to be tendered for to-day, only replaces a like amount maturing, but such bills of late have been found to be owned chiefly by the Government departments. Competition is not, therefore, likely to be keen on the part of the market, and it will not be surprising if the bulk again falls into official hands. The Bank of England displeased some people yesterday by granting loans into March. It would only discount bills running over the end of the month, and brokers are loth to part with bills on its terms.

The Bank return issued yesterday revealed very heavy borrowings at the Bank, whose advances on "other" deposits have gone up £2,711,361 to £35,046,076. Thanks to the money thus procured, and to £605,941 added to the reserve of the banking department through the return of coins and a few notes from circulation, the market has been able to add £1,639,507 to the "other" deposits, notwithstanding the increase of £1,716,363 in the "public" deposits, which now amount to £18,594,790—a most unusual total at this time of year. The market has had to procure cash to pay railway dividends, and at the same time to meet the drain set up by the tax collector. No wonder, then, that money has been "tight" all the week; but the extreme height to which the "public" deposits have now mounted must imply Government disbursements at an early date. On March 19, 1896, the Government balances reached a total of £19,175,000. With the exception of the four Wednesdays of that month, the aggregate has never been so high as it is now.

SILVER.

The practical disappearance of the "bear" position in this market has been signalised by a further drop of $\frac{1}{8}$d. in the "spot" price to 25$\frac{11}{16}$d. per ounce. Although Indian exchanges have risen $\frac{1}{16}$d. to $\frac{1}{8}$d. in the week, the movement is solely the result of tighter money markets there which resulted in a rise in the Bank rates by 1 per cent. to 12 per cent. for Bengal, and 13 per cent. for Bombay; and so the fall in the "bazaar" price of silver has neutralised the change. Sellers of the white metal have therefore had to reduce their price, and at the lower level the tone is none too good. The two months' forward rice has ruled about $\frac{1}{8}$d. below the "spot" price. The announcement about the Chinese loan did not have any effect, as it is known that no silver will be taken on its account. Japan, which will receive the great bulk of the issue, if disposed to ship bullion would certainly take gold, while, if any balance remains over for China, it will be cheapest to use it to meet interest requirements in Europe. The monetary stringency in India enabled the India Council to sell its drafts freely, and it has sold without being too ready to raise its price. By this policy it has disposed of no less than seventy lacs yesterday and to-day. With the Bank of Bombay rate at the record level of 13 per cent., the strain upon traders must be very great.

BANK OF ENGLAND.

AN ACCOUNT pursuant to the Act 7 and 8 Vict., cap. 32, for the Week ending on Wednesday, February 23, 1898.

ISSUE DEPARTMENT.

	£		£
Notes Issued	48,371,080	Government Debt	11,015,100
		Other Securities	5,784,900
		Gold Coin and Bullion	31,571,080
		Silver Bullion	—
	£48,371,080		£48,371,080

BANKING DEPARTMENT.

	£		£
Proprietors' Capital	14,553,000	Government Securities	13,994,565
Rest	3,482,523	Other Securities	35,046,076
Public Deposits (including Exchequer, Savings Banks, Commissioners of National Debt, and Dividend Accounts)	18,594,790	Notes	22,017,615
Other Deposits	36,762,493	Gold and Silver Coin	2,466,135
Seven Day and other Bills	131,585		
	£73,524,391		£73,524,391

Dated February 23, 1898.

H. G. BOWEN, *Chief Cashier.*

In the following table will be found the movements compared with the previous week, and also the totals for that week and the corresponding return last year:—

Banking Department.

Last Year. Feb. 24.		Feb. 16, 1898.	Feb. 23, 1898.	Increase.	Decrease.
£	Liabilities.	£	£	£	£
3,532,991	Rest	3,493,103	3,482,523	—	10,580
16,233,795	Pub. Deposits	16,878,427	18,594,790	1,716,363	—
40,283,304	Other do.	35,122,986	36,762,493	1,639,507	—
152,459	7 Day Bills	159,573	131,585	—	27,988
	Assets.			Decrease.	Increase.
15,088,858	Gov. Securities	13,994,565	13,994,565	—	—
29,401,361	Other do.	32,334,715	35,046,076	—	2,711,361
30,265,330	Total Reserve	23,877,809	24,483,750	—	605,941
				3,355,870	3,355,870
				Increase.	Decrease.
£		£	£	£	£
25,563,940	Note Circulation	26,416,055	26,353,465	—	62,590
53$\frac{7}{8}$ p.c.	Proportion	45$\frac{5}{8}$ p.c.	44$\frac{3}{8}$ p.c.	—	—
3 ,,	Bank Rate	3 ,,	3 ,,	—	—

Foreign Bullion movement for week £68,000 in.

LONDON BANKERS' CLEARING.

Week ending	1898.	1897.	Increase.	Decrease.
	£	£	£	£
Jan. 5	222,654,000	174,376,000	48,278,000	—
,, 12	144,603,000	127,315,000	17,288,000	—
,, 19	171,777,000	156,200,000	15,577,000	—
,, 26	134,247,000	118,667,000	15,580,000	—
Feb. 2	194,544,000	174,498,000	20,056,000	—
,, 9	137,204,000	129,209,000	8,995,000	—
,, 16	184,403,000	162,168,000	22,235,000	—
,, 23	132,450,000	131,777,000	673,000	—

BANK AND DISCOUNT RATES ABROAD.

	Bank Rate.	Altered.	Open Market.
Paris	2	March 14, 1895	1$\frac{7}{8}$
Berlin	3	February 20, 1898	2$\frac{3}{4}$
Hamburg	3	February 20, 1898	2$\frac{3}{4}$
Frankfort	3	February 20, 1898	2$\frac{3}{4}$
Amsterdam	3	April 13, 1897	2$\frac{1}{4}$
Brussels	3	April 28, 1896	2
Vienna	4	January 22, 1896	3$\frac{3}{4}$
Rome	5	August 27, 1895	3
St. Petersburg	5$\frac{1}{2}$	January 23, 1898	5
Madrid	5	June 17, 1896	4
Lisbon	6	January 25, 1891	6
Stockholm	5	October 27, 1897	5
Copenhagen	4	January 20, 1893	4
Calcutta	12	February 24, 1898	—
Bombay	13	February 24, 1898	—
New York call money	1$\frac{1}{2}$ to 1$\frac{3}{4}$	—	—

NEW YORK ASSOCIATED BANKS (dollar at 4s.).

	Feb. 19, 1898.	Feb. 12, 1898.	Feb. 5, 1898.	Feb. 20, 1897.
	£	£	£	£
Specie	23,366,000	22,994,000	22,812,000	16,564,000
Legal tenders	18,698,000	20,428,000	20,830,000	23,204,000
Loans and discounts	129,384,000	127,968,000	126,772,000	99,750,000
Circulation	2,755,600	2,783,000	2,678,400	3,322,000
Net deposits	147,712,000	147,736,000	146,766,000	114,534,000

Legal reserve is 25 per cent. of net deposits; therefore the total reserve (specie and legal tenders) exceeds this sum by £5,136,000, against an excess last week of £6,488,000.

BANK OF FRANCE (25 francs to the £).

	Feb. 24, 1898.	Feb. 17, 1898.	Feb. 10, 1898.	Feb. 25, 1897.
	£	£	£	£
Gold in hand	77,303,760	77,186,520	77,080,000	76,659,000
Silver in hand	48,512,280	48,319,680	48,323,920	49,317,000
Bills discounted	29,853,200	29,891,080	31,038,200	*45,796,000
Advances	14,562,600	14,696,160	14,838,600	—
Note circulation	148,445,960	149,163,880	150,483,880	146,594,000
Public deposits	7,985,080	8,140,720	8,106,520	10,206,000
Private deposits	21,089,240	19,004,960	19,428,320	20,579,000

Proportion between bullion and circulation 84$\frac{7}{8}$ per cent. against 84$\frac{3}{8}$ per cent. a week ago.

* Includes advances.

FOREIGN RATES OF EXCHANGE ON LONDON.

Place.	Usance.	Last week's.	Latest.	Place.	Usance.	Last week's.	Latest.
Paris	chqs.	25·27	25·28	Italy	sight	26·56	26·61
Brussels	chqs.	25·29	25·31$\frac{1}{4}$	Do. gold prem.	..	105·17	105·20
Amsterdam	short	12·06	12·07$\frac{1}{2}$	Constantinople	3 mths	109·30	109·15
Berlin	short	20·42	20·44	B. Ayres gd. pm.	..	167·00	167·30
Do.	3 mths	20·29$\frac{1}{2}$	20·31	Rio de Janeiro	90 dys	6$\frac{11}{16}$	6$\frac{11}{16}$
Hamburg	3 mths	20·28$\frac{1}{2}$	20.30	Valparaiso	90 dys	17$\frac{7}{8}$	17$\frac{7}{8}$
Frankfort	short	20·42	20·44	Calcutta	T. T.	1/3$\frac{31}{32}$	1/4
Vienna	short	12·01$\frac{1}{2}$	12.01$\frac{1}{2}$	Bombay	T. T.	1/3$\frac{7}{8}$	1/3$\frac{31}{32}$
St. Petersburg	3 mths	93·90	93·95	Hong Kong	T. T.	1/10$\frac{1}{2}$	1/10$\frac{3}{4}$
New York	60 dys	4·83$\frac{1}{2}$	4·83$\frac{1}{2}$	Shanghai	T. T.	2/5$\frac{1}{8}$	2/5$\frac{3}{8}$
Lisbon	sight	35$\frac{5}{8}$	35$\frac{5}{8}$	Singapore	T. T.	1/10$\frac{1}{16}$	1/10$\frac{3}{16}$
Madrid	sight	33·58	33·80				

IMPERIAL BANK OF GERMANY (20 marks to the £).

	Feb. 15, 1898.	Feb. 7, 1898.	Jan. 31, 1898.	Feb. 13, 1897.
	£	£	£	£
Cash in hand	47,570,800	46,313,100	45,672,450	45,393,000
Bills discounted	25,612,000	26,750,000	28,435,050	*30,695,000
Advances on stocks	4,158,600	4,129,450	4,385,300	—
Note circulation	50,645,450	52,827,050	54,542,300	48,650,000
Public deposits	23,319,900	21,535,500	21,798,550	23,501,000

* Includes advances.

AUSTRIAN-HUNGARIAN BANK (1s. 8d. to the florin).

	Feb. 15, 1898.	Feb. 7, 1898.	Jan. 31, 1898.	Feb. 13, 1897.
	£	£	£	£
Gold reserve	30,324,417	30,347,666	30,272,833	30,661,000
Silver reserve	10,371,500	10,345,417	10,352,166	12,669,000
Foreign bills	1,318,917	1,382,333	1,403,916	—
Advances	1,850,333	1,887,250	1,907,000	—
Note circulation	51,074,417	52,209,333	52,318,333	58,383,000
Bills discounted	10,502,250	11,763,416	11,058,000	*16,137,000

* Includes advances.

NATIONAL BANK OF BELGIUM (25 francs to the

	Feb. 17, 1898.	Feb. 10, 1898.	Feb. 3, 1898.	Feb. 18, 1897.
	£	£	£	£
Coin and bullion	4,311,040	4,234,880	4,422,080	4,240,000
Other securities	17,011,600	17,204,480	17,601,560	16,224,000
Note circulation	19,145,960	19,348,560	19,209,160	18,486,000
Deposits	3,495,440	3,396,560	4,109,520	3,208,000

BANK OF SPAIN (25 pesetas to the £).

	Feb. 19, 1898.	Feb. 12, 1898.	Feb. 5, 1898.	Feb. 20, 1897.
	£	£	£	£
Gold	9,517,560	9,500,920	9,495,120	8,528,360
Silver	10,712,600	10,651,800	10,616,720	10,888,640
Bills discounted	21,763,160	21,855,320	21,846,600	8,020,360
Advances and loans	4,805,800	4,869,680	4,873,600	9,229,000
Notes in circulation	49,856,480	50,062,440	49,902,480	42,470,440
Treasury advances, coupon account	236,240	310,400	211,680	420,480
Treasury balances	887,400	347,840	454,280	2,370,080

LONDON COURSE OF EXCHANGE.

Place.	Usance.	Feb. 15.	Feb. 17.	Feb. 22.	Feb. 24.
Amsterdam and Rotterdam	short	12·1⅞	12·1⅞	12·1⅞	12·1⅞
Do. do.	3 months	12·3⅞	12·3⅞	12·3⅞	12·3⅞
Antwerp and Brussels	3 months	25·42½	25·43¾	25·45	25·46¼
Hamburg	3 months	20·62	20·62	20·62	20·63
Berlin and German B. Places	3 months	20·62	20·62	20·62	20·63
Paris	cheques	25·26¼	25·27½	25·28¾	25·30
Do.	3 months	25·40	25·41¼	25·43¾	25·42½
Marseilles	3 months	25·41¼	25·41¼	25·43¾	25·41¼
Switzerland	3 months	25·60	25·60	25·60	25·62½
Austria	3 months	12·16½	12·16½	12·16½	12·15
St. Petersburg	3 months	25⅛	25⅛	25⅛	25⅛
Moscow	3 months	25	25	25	25
Italian Bank Places	3 months	26·87½	26·87½	26·87½	26·91¼
New York	60 days	49	49	49	49
Madrid and Spanish B. P.	3 months	35¼	35⅛	35⅛	35
Lisbon	3 months	35¼	35¼	35	35
Oporto	3 months	35¼	35¼	35	35
Copenhagen	3 months	18·37	18·38	18·38	18·38
Christiania	—	18·38	18·38	18·38	18·38
Stockholm	—	18·38	18·38	18·38	18·38

OPEN MARKET DISCOUNT.

	Per cent.
Thirty and sixty day remitted bills	2⅞—2⅞
Three months "	2⅞
Four months "	2⅞—2⅞
Six months "	2⅞
Three months fine inland bills	3
Four months "	3
Six months "	2⅞—3

BANK AND DEPOSIT RATES.

	Per cent.
Bank of England minimum discount rate	3
" " short loan rates	3
Banker's rate on deposits	1½
Bill brokers' deposit rate (call)	2
" 7 and 14 days' notice	2¼
Current rates for 7 day loans	2½
" " for call loans	2½—3

Stock Market Notes and Comments.

The past week has been rather lively on the Stock Exchange. Markets generally are interesting when "bears" are having innings, and thanks to Mr. Chamberlain and two or three American railroad bosses, they had a fine time of it in the end of last and beginning of the present week. It is not often that two scares come together, as they have done on the present occasion. The Secretary of State for the Colonies did his best to terrify everybody last Saturday by the portentous manner in which he foreshadowed a possible row with France over territory in West Africa, territory, it is pretty certain, quite useless to either country. He really, we may surmise, thought only of "dishing Salisbury." Last week too, we had formidable telegrams from Montreal announcing a tremendous outbreak of hostilities between the Canadian Pacific and Grand Trunk Railways; and from New York came messages telling us that the entire railway system of the North-West was practically in a state of hostility. Rates were being "cut" not only for the Klondike traffic so-called, but for local traffic also. As by magic, the whole prospect had suddenly changed.

They are really very funny fellows these American railroad managers. Being quite free from any control by shareholders or boards of directors, either in America or here, they make war or peace in all probability according as it suits their bets on the Stock Exchange. Not many weeks ago all the news from across the water was of peace and abundance. Such a thing as "rate cutting" was never to be heard of again; prophecies of coming dividends were freely given forth, and we were told that a long era of prosperity lay before the United States, and, therefore, before any one who bought their depreciated railroad securities. Having succeeded by these flowery statements in drawing speculative people, both in America and here, into considerable purchases of such securities, and having probably unloaded very freely to these purchasers, the railroad bosses suddenly resolved to have 'a fight.'" No sooner said than done. A "desperate conflict" immediately arose by cable, and prices went tumbling down faster than they had risen. How much those behind the working of this system of market plundering may have made in this latest raid it is impossible to estimate; but in a general way it is known that no surer path to the millionaire's heaven can be found than that of the management of a big American railroad. What the rights or the wrongs are of the present dispute it is hardly worth while to ask. Who began the struggle it is equally useless to know. The North-Western roads of the States, by the voice of their controllers, say the Canadian Pacific started the cutting, and the Canadian Pacific managers retort that it was begun by the Grand Trunk, and by others of its neighbours. On the other hand, Grand Trunk poses as a victim of the overbearing tendencies of its great rival and insists that the dispute is essentially insignificant and local. Of the three classes of virtuous protesters we are on the whole inclined to believe the Grand Trunk. It has too often been "put upon" of late years not to seem fair game still, but, being now well managed, it should be able to give a better account of itself in the fight than it has hitherto done. The rise in its stocks though must have been an irresistible temptation, and we are told that Montreal "went bear," before the last news came, for more than it was worth.

Of more importance to the British holder of the securities involved in this struggle is the question how long will it last? That, we suppose, will depend to a considerable extent on how far the "bear" account opened before the conflict broke out has been closed. It is not in the nature of 'bear" accounts such as this to be kept open, very long, and we consequently believe that the struggle will be as brief as it may be sharp. Within the next two or three weeks, in all probability, the whole thing will be over, and markets run full tide upwards again. This, however, is merely an outsider's view. We watch the play and try to discover the influences at work, but have no inside experience or knowledge of it whatsoever. It interests us much as watching a gaming-table does, and the opinion we express is only valuable as being the result of many years' observation. Times and again this sort of thing has occurred, the general mass of players have lost their money, and the few have become rich.

Whether the limit of time we have ventured to give will see the end of this episode or not, holders of United States and Canadian railroad securities may be quite sure of one thing; the present is not the right time for them to sell. They should never yield to manufactured scares whose almost avowed object it is to get them to throw away their securities. Those who play for a small profit ought rather to be buyers than sellers now, and what has taken place is a testimony to the prudence of the advice given by us week after week in this column—not to go for large profits in these securities, however true it may be that the broad, general tendency of the market for them is upward. Breaks of the kind witnessed this week are sure to occur at more or less frequent intervals, as speculators in control of the railroads, or in touch with the management, see their chance of gathering in a few more million dollars at the expense of the weak "bull." No man, consequently, ought to buy more of any of these securities than he can hold on to through the severest of such spasms. The man who buys more than he can carry in a storm invariably ends by losing what money he may have, and very often loses a great deal more than he can afford. It is the height of folly to put the hand out further than it can be drawn back.

The political and railroad flurries had comparatively little effect upon the settlement which was successfully concluded last night, with rather fewer messes than might have been expected. There would have been more but for the customary patchings-up; but, after all, the market stood up to its losses very well. Naturally, the differences to be paid by the operators for the rise have been heavier in all departments, but the fall was not so severe as might have been expected, because the public is not widely committed in a speculative way at present on the Exchange itself. A certain amount of weakly-held stock was flung on the market and absorbed without difficulty, and the way is now open for a fresh rise, or nearly so. The settlement in mines was the hardest—harder even than an American or Canadian railway—because of the high rates for money, and the steady decline in the price of "Kaffir" shares. Even this, however, passed off without apparent strain, and prices were put up again at once in the mechanical way which indicates a market still well in the grasp of the financiers by whom it has been brought to its present position. Home securities have not fallen much because there is no account in them carried over fortnight by fortnight in the Stock Exchange; at least, none of any importance. Even Consols dropped less than ten shillings on Mr. Chamberlain's lugubrious utterance, a fact which ought to disappoint him as a lover of theatrical effect.

The chief trouble of the settlement, apart from the differences which had been found on American railroad shares, and on South African mines, has been the dearness of money. That, however, will not last much longer. Perhaps by the middle of March our own Government's payments will be going out sufficiently fast to send rates of interest down and make borrowing more easy. By the end of next month at the longest there is every appearance of cheaper money. No doubt, should both an Indian and a Chinese loan be issued next month, or early in April, they would do something to sustain rates, but they would not control credit in the effective way the Government now does by holding the taxes. Short of fresh scares, however, the prospect is by no means a bad one for holders of securities, but scares are things that come unawares, like measles, mumps, and whooping-cough.

The Week's Stock Markets.

The feeling of uneasiness produced by the aspect of affairs in West Africa caused a dull tone to prevail in Stock Markets towards the close of last week, but it was not until Saturday that a "slump" really occurred. Mr. Chamberlain's statement in the House of Commons on Friday night caused so much uneasiness that prices came down with a run. A partial rally occurred on Tuesday in all departments, due to the bears repurchasing, and it was soon found that the public was not throwing stock on the market. Heavy sales on the part of Wall-street operators then caused a collapse in United States Railroad shares, the forced closing of weak accounts being the principal reason for the decline, but Wall-street operators evidently intend waiting the outcome of the Cuban business before in any way increasing their commitments. The "war of rates" between the Canadian Pacific and other roads also helped to further depress prices, and a dull tone spread to all markets. The settlement of the account has absorbed a good deal of attention, but it was easily arranged, although one or two failures are rather looked for in the "Kaffir Circus," and several operators will want helping over.

Consols were but little affected by the political "scare," and remained remarkably steady through it all, and the appearance of the Government broker as a buyer finally caused a sharp upward movement; but the latest price is not quite the highest of the week. The Indian sterling loans have been rather pressed for sale (the weakness being due to rumours of an approaching loan), and the dull tone has also spread to Colonial Government securities.

Highest and Lowest this Year.	Last Carrying over Price.	BRITISH FUNDS, &c.	Closing Price.	Rise or Fall.
113⅛ 112	—	Consols 2¾ p.c. (Money)...	112 11/16	+ 1/16
113 1/16 112¼	112⅝	Do. Account (Mar. 1)	112¾	—
106¼ 105½	106	2½ p.c. Stock red. 1905 ...	106	—
363 347½	—	Bank of England Stock...	355	– 1½
117 115½	116½	India 3½ p.c. Stk. red. 1931	116	– ½
109½ 107½	108½	Do. 3 p.c. Stk. red. 1948	108½	– ¼
96⅜ 94½	95½	Do. 2½ p.c. Stk. red. 1926	94½	– ¼

Home Railway stocks suffered more than any other by the political scare, and prices dropped heavily, more especially for Brighton "A," Metropolitan, South-Eastern deferred, and the Scotch stocks. Those that gave way most, however, took the lead in the subsequent advance, and in several cases more than recovered the amount of the fall. Continuation rates at the settlement were about the same as last time, Midland, North Eastern, and South Eastern deferred being continued at ⅛ to ¼, Metropolitan and Great Western at ¼, London and North Western at 3/16, and Brighton deferred at ⅜ to ½ per cent. Great Eastern stock was again scarce for delivery, the rate varying from ⅛ "backwardation" to "even." There has been a steady and continuous fall in the premier securities of the leading companies. Traffic returns were all satisfactory, comparing as they do with large takings last year.

Highest and Lowest this Year.	Last Carrying over Price.	HOME RAILWAYS.	Closing Price.	Rise or Fall.
186 174	175¼	Brighton Def.	176⅜	– 1
59¼ 55½	56¾	Caledonian Def.	57	– ⅝
20⅞ 19	19¾	Chatham Ordinary	20⅛	—
77¼ 66	70	Great Central Pref.	70	—
24⅝ 21⅞	22	Do. Def.	22	– ½
124½ 119¾	121	Great Eastern	121½	+ ⅜
61⅜ 53⅞	54⅞	Great Northern Def.	53¼x.d.	– ½
179⅞ 173⅞	176¾	Great Western	174¼x.d.	– ¼
49¼ 45½	46	Hull and Barnsley.........	46¼	—
149¼ 146½	147¼	Lanc. and Yorkshire......	147½	– ¼
136⅛ 130⅞	131	Metropolitan	132½	– 1
31 28¼	28¾	Metropolitan District......	28⅞	– ⅜
88⅞ 85½	86¾	Midland Pref.	85¾x.d.	– ½
95⅞ 90¼	92	Do. Def.	90½x.d.	– ¼
93¼ 90¼	91½	North British Pref.	91½	– ½
47½ 43⅞	44¾	Do. Def.	45¼	– ¼
181½ 176	179¼	North Eastern...............	176½x.d.	+ ¼
205½ 199¾	203½	North Western	202¼x.d.	– ¼
117⅞ 110	110⅝	South Eastern Def.	111⅝	– ¼
98⅜ 93¾	97	South Western Def.	94 x.d.	– ½

United States Railroad shares were rather firmer in price for a brief period, but suffered in common with all other departments last Saturday. The various rumours current respecting the *Maine* disaster, and the rate war between the Canadian Pacific, Northern Pacific, and Great Northern roads, have been quite enough in themselves to knock prices down all round, and, despite one or two short-lived rallies, the result of the week's operations is that quotations leave off generally lower. Tuesday being Washington's birthday, did not tend to help matters, Wall-street operators closing their commitments before the holiday, and home realisations in view of the settlement here also helped to depress prices. The account was easily arranged, and stock was more plentiful than a fortnight ago, but rates reached a slightly higher level, viz., 4½ to 5½ per cent. The telegrams from Montreal, on Saturday, announcing further "rate cutting" by the Canadian Pacific Company, were followed by heavy selling orders, and Canadian Pacific shares fell about $7, but recovered a little of the lost ground afterwards. The Grand Trunk Company being also implicated, although only to a minor extent, that company's stocks declined somewhat sharply, and then a partial rally followed.

Highest and Lowest this Year.		Last Carrying over Price.	CANADIAN AND U.S. RAILWAYS.	Closing Prices.	Rise or Fall.
14 3/16	12	12½	Atchison Shares	12	−1¼
34	28¼	29¾	Do. Pref.	28¼	−3⅜
15⅝	11⅞	13⅜	Central Pacific...............	13	−1¼
99¾	94¼	97¼	Chic. Mil. & St. Paul......	95⅜	−2
14¼	11½	12¾	Denver Shares	12½	−1⅛
54¼	46⅝	50	Do. Prefd.	48½	−3¾
16⅞	14¼	14¾	Erie Shares	14½	−1
44⅞	37¼	40½	Do. Prefd.	40¼	−2⅜
62½	55½	57¼	Louisville & Nashville ...	56½	−3⅛
14½	12	12½	Missouri & Texas	12	−1½
122¾	108¼	118	New York Central	115¼	−5¼
57¼	47¾	51	Norfolk & West. Prefd....	49¼	−4¾
70½	59⅛	64½	Northern Pacific Prefd....	62½	−4⅛
19½	15⅜	16½	Ontario Shares	15⅛	−1¾
62½	58⅛	59¾	Pennsylvania	59½	−1¼
12½	10⅛	10¼	Reading Shares	10⅛	− ¾
34¼	29⅛	30½	Southern Prefd.	29½	−3⅛
37⅛	26⅛	31½	Union Pacific	30¼	−4
20¼	17	17¼	Wabash Prefd.	17	−1½
30¼	26⅞	27½	Do. Income Debs....	27	−2
92¾	83¾	84½	Canadian Pacific............	84¾	−5½
78½	69⅛	73	Grand Trunk Guar.	73¾	−2½
69⅛	57⅛	64½	Do. 1st Pref.	65¼	−3⅛
50½	37¼	44¾	Do. 2nd Pref.	44¾	−3⅛
25½	19¼	21½	Do. 3rd Pref.	21¼	−2¼
105¾	102½	103¼	Do. 4 p.c. Deb.	103¼	−1¼

In the Foreign market prices were marked down steadily day after day, during the earlier part of the week, but the firmness of the foreign Bourses was finally reflected on the London market and a more cheerful tone prevailed. The various Chinese loans advanced on the news from Berlin that a loan for £16,000,000 sterling had been arranged. Spanish 4 per cent. have been pressed for sale, chiefly on Paris account, due to the vague notification by the Bank of Spain to the effect that the April coupons would be paid as usual, but that the bank could not pledge itself as to the future. Greek bonds have been fairly steady, and Italian rentes, after being very weak, rallied. Among South American issues Argentine descriptions fell sharply, and partly recovered; but Uruguayan 3½ per cents. have exhibited great strength on the announcement of a remittance for the debt service, coupled with the general improvement in the political situation at Monte Video. Continuation rates were slightly firmer than on the last occasion Argentine stocks being carried over at from 3 to 5 per, cent., and other South American issues at from 4 to 6 per cent., the general rate ranging from 3¾ to 4¼ per cent.

Highest and Lowest this Year.		Last Carrying over Price.	FOREIGN BONDS.	Closing Price.	Rise or Fall.
94½	89	90¾	Argentine 5 p.c. 1886......	90¾	−1¼
92⅜	88½	90	Do. 6 p.c. Funding	90	− ⅛
76¾	71	73¾	Do. 5 p.c. B. Ay. Water	73¾	−1⅛
61¾	59½	60¼	Brazilian 4 p.c. 1889	60¼	—
69⅜	64¾	65¼	Do. 5 p.c. 1895	65¼	—
65	62⅛	64	Do. 5 p.c. West Minas Ry..................	64	+ ¼
108¾	106¼	108¼	Egyptian 4 p.c. Unified...	108¼	− ¼
104¾	102	104¼	Do. 3½ p.c. Pref. ...	104¼	− ¼
103	102	102¼	French 3 p.c. Rente	102⅛	—
41½	34½	40½	Greek 4 p.c. Monopoly...	40⅛	−1
93 1/16	92¼	92⅛	Italian 5 p.c. Rente	93⅛	− 1/16
100	95¾	98	Mexican 6 p.c. 1888	98¼	− ¾
20¾	19¼	20½	Portuguese 1 p.c.	19⅛	− ¾
62½	59⅛	61	Spanish 4 p.c.	59 11/16	−1⅛
45¼	43	44	Turkish 1 p.c. "B"	44¼	− ¼
26 1/16	24 1/16	25¾	Do. 1 p.c. "C"	25⅛	− ¼
22 1/16	21 13/16	22	Do. 1 p.c. "D"	22⅛	− 1/16
43⅜	40	43	Uruguay 3½ p.c. Bonds...	43⅜	+ ⅜

Foreign Railway stocks shared in the general weakness, and the publication of a batch of good traffic returns only acted as a temporary check to the downward trend of prices. Argentine issues have been the principal sufferers, but the Mexican, Mexican Central, and Interoceanic companies have also lost ground considerably.

Highest and Lowest this Year.		Last Carrying over Price.	FOREIGN RAILWAYS.	Closing Price.	Rise or Fall.
20¾	20	20¼	Argentine Gt. West. 5 p.c. Pref.	20⅛	− ⅛
158¼	149	153	B. Ay. Gt. Southern Ord..	154	−2
78½	73	74½	B. Ay. and Rosario Ord...	75½	−1
12¼	11½	11⅜	B. Ay. Western Ord.	11½	—
87¼	80½	81½	Central Argentine Ord....	83	—
92	89½	90½	Cordoba and Rosario 6 p.c. Deb.	90	−1
95⅛	92⅛	92⅛	Cord. Cent. 4 p.c. Deb. (Cent. Nth. Sec.)	93⅛	−1
61⅞	54	54	Do. Income Deb. Stk. ...	55	−2½
25½	18	22½	Mexican Ord. Stk.	23¼	− ½
83½	72	80	Do. 8 p.c. 1st Pref.	82¼	− ¼

The Miscellaneous market has been the firmest in the Stock Exchange, although some of the leading favourites have been adversely affected by the weakness in other departments. Electric Lighting companies have again attracted buyers, several more satisfactory reports coming to hand, and Notting Hill shares were especially firm on the publication of a dividend of 6 per cent. Russian Petroleum ordinary marks a further substantial rise, but Salt Union issues have again declined heavily. Hudson Bay shares dropped several points and then recovered, despite a contango of 1s. 9d. Welsbach Gas stocks have met with little or no support, and a small amount of profit taking was quite enough to put down the price several points. Allsopp ordinary stock jumped from 160 to 164 and back again, otherwise few changes have occurred in brewery issues. Several insurance companies' shares mark declines. Among telegraph companies Cuba Submarine has slipped back a little. A feature in gas stocks was a big rise in Croydon "A" and "B."

Heavy selling of United States railroad shares was the principal feature at the close of the week, various wild rumours about the *Maine* disaster being circulated, and stock was almost unsaleable for a time, but the last prices are ½ to 3 dollars above the lowest of the week. Canadian railway issues closed dull in sympathy, and the Grand Trunk traffic return was looked upon as unsatisfactory. Home railway stocks left off fairly steady, and Mexican railway issues registered a rise just before the close. Among foreign government bonds Spanish 4 per cents. closed very weak, and Argentine and Uruguay bonds also fell sharply.

Mining and Finance Companies.

South African ventures have been very depressed all the week, the action of President Kruger in dismissing Chief Justice Kotze being looked upon as an unsatisfactory sort of start to his new term of office. Towards the close there has been a slight rise owing to Paris taking a few shares off the London market, but the difficulties of several operators disclosed at the settlement have tended to check any very decided rally. In Western Australian companies, Lady Shenton and Northern Territories have attracted most attention, but there has been very little real business. Continuation rates were about as usual, 7 to 9 per cent. on "Kaffirs," and from that up to 12 per cent. on "Westralians." Indian and copper shares show a slightly harder tendency towards the last, after dragging heavily for days.

Mr. Labouchere is to move, in Committee on the Army Estimates, to reduce the number of the men by 13,367.

Japan, having pressed China to renew a previous assurance that Russia would withdraw from Port Arthur after the winter, the Chinese Government appealed to the Russian Government, and the latter explained that the warships would have to remain longer than was at first proposed. The Chinese look upon this as an intimation that the Russian occupation is meant to be permanent. Of course. Did anybody suppose it was meant to be anything else?

Dividends Announced.

MISCELLANEOUS.

JOHN OAKEY & SONS, LIMITED.—Final dividend on the ordinary shares of 5 per cent. for the half-year ended December 31, together with a bonus of 2½ per cent. making 12½ per cent. for the year.

COUNTY OF LONDON AND BRUSH PROVINCIAL ELECTRIC LIGHTING COMPANY.—Dividend on the preference shares for the six months ended December 31 at the rate of 6 per cent. per annum. £10,000 carried forward.

LONDON STREET TRAMWAYS COMPANY.—Distribution of 12s. 6d. per share out of the amount standing to the credit of revenue account from the making of the company to October 14, and from the revenue reserves.

PLANET BUILDING SOCIETY.—3½ per cent. has been declared.

ARGUS PRINTING COMPANY, LIMITED.—Dividend at the rate of 8 per cent. has been declared, £1,250 being placed to a special reserve account, and £1,529 carried forward.

JOHN HUNTER, WILTSHIRE & CO.—5s. 6d. per share tax free, being at the rate of 11 per cent. per annum for the six months ended December 31, making, with the interim dividend paid in August, 8 per cent. for the year. £700 to be placed reserve fund; £1,000 to be written off business purchase account; and £1,316 carried forward.

LIBERTY & CO.—Dividend at the rate of 12 per cent. per annum on the ordinary shares for the year ended January 31.

DRURY-LANE THEATRE ROYAL.—Interim of 10 per cent. on the paid-up capital.

INTERNATIONAL INVESTMENT TRUST.—Usual dividend at the rate of 4½ per cent. per annum on the preferred stock for the half-year ended January 31.

E. & S. JAY, LIMITED, GRENOBLE.—Dividend declared for the year 1897 at the rate of 6 per cent. per annum on the preference and ordinary shares.

CIVIL SERVICE SUPPLY ASSOCIATION.—A distribution at the rate of 12s. in respect of every ten £1 shares. £2,000 placed to reserve, and £4,942 carried forward.

BRILLIANT GOLD MINING COMPANY.—6d. per share has been declared.

HART & LEVY, LIMITED.—Final dividend on the ordinary shares at the rate of 8 per cent. per annum for the half-year ended December 31. £1,500 to reserve and £588 carried forward.

AFRICAN CITY PROPERTIES' TRUST, LIMITED.—Dividend of 1s. 6d. per share on the ordinary shares, which, with the interim dividend paid in September last, makes 2s. 6d. per share, or 12½ per cent. for the year. £5,800 placed to reserve and balance forward of £6,896.

KAFFIRS CONSOLIDATED INVESTMENT AND LAND COMPANY, LIMITED.—Warrants for the usual monthly dividend of 3d. per share have been posted.

H. E. RANDALL, LIMITED.—From an available balance of £7,461, the preference dividends are paid and a further dividend recommended at the rate of 12 per cent. on the ordinary shares, making 10 per cent for the year and leaving £2,178 to be carried forward.

CASSELL & CO., LIMITED.—5 per cent. for the half-year, making, with the interim dividend paid in September last, a distribution for 1897 of 7½ per cent.

BOLCKOW, VAUGHAN, & CO.—Dividend at the rate of 5 per cent. per annum for the year ended December 31st last, less the interim dividend paid in September; £25,000 to be placed to reserve, £43,500 to be spent on new plant, and £60,800 carried forward.

GLASGOW EVENING NEWS.—A dividend of 12½ per cent. has been paid for the past year and a large sum carried to reserve.

SURREY COMMERCIAL DOCK COMPANY.—Directors recommend a dividend of £2 10s. per cent. on the ordinary stock, and on the preference stock "A," making, with the interim dividend alreadty paid, 5 per cent. for the year, and in addition a bonus of £1 per cen.

STATE FIRE INSURANCE.—Dividend declared at the rate of 5 per cent. per annum.

EAST LONDON WATERWORKS.—A dividend at the rate of 8 pe cent. per annum is declared for the past half-year, leaving a balance of £19,627 to be carried forward.

MOUNT LYELL MINING AND RAILWAY COMPANY.—Dividend is declared of 4s. per share.

BANKS.

ANGLO-CALIFORNIAN.—Further dividend of 6s. per share, making, with interim dividend paid in September last, 6 per cent. for the year. £9,252 to be carried forward.

CREDIT ANSTALT.—Dividend of 17 florins per share, 250,000 florins to be placed to reserve and 275,000 florins to be distributed as bonus to directors and staff.

ANGLO-FOREIGN, LIMITED.—Share warrant coupon No. 50 will be payable at 5s. per share on and after Monday 28th inst.

BANK OF AFRICA.—Distribution to be recommended of £31,500 for dividend and bonus (equal to 12 per cent. per annum), £10,000 to reserve fund, £1,500 to pension fund, and about £9,500 to be carried forward.

RAILWAYS.

NEATH AND BRECON.—After payment in full of the first "A 1" and debentures there is sufficient to pay a dividend for the year of £2 5s. on the "A 2" debentures. This compares with £1 5s. in 1896 on the latter.

GREAT NORTH OF SCOTLAND.—Dividend on the ordinary stock for the half-year to January 31 will be at the rate of 4 per cent. per annum, carrying forward £3,000. For corresponding period of 1896-7 the distribution was at the rate of 3½ per cent. with £2,791 forward.

BREWERIES.

COLCHESTER BREWING COMPANY, LIMITED.—Usual interim dividend of 3s. 6d. per share on the preference shares, and an interim dividend of 2s. per share on the ordinary shares for the half-year ended December 31.

INDEMNITY MUTUAL MARINE ASSURANCE.—A dividend of 6s. per share is recommended.

MINING RETURNS.

PAHANG CORPORATION.—Jeram Lumpong: 1,235 tons of stone crushed, producing 70 tons of black tin. Jeram Batang: 1,110 tons crushed, producing 10 tons of black tin.

WILD HERCULES.—200 tons of ore yielded 135 oz. retorted gold.

HIGHLAND CHIEF.—Crushed 275 tons, yield 109 oz. of retorted gold.

OTTOO KOPJE DIAMOND.—5,921 loads washed, 180 carats won, including one stone each of 11½ and 9½ carats.

BRILLIANT BLOCK.—Crushed during month, 1,153 tons of quartz, for a yield of 455 oz. gold.

LAKE GEORGE MINES.—A shipment is announced of 140 tons of matter, containing 182 oz. of gold, 11,235 oz. of silver, and 42 tons of copper.

ROYAL SOVEREIGN.—73 tons of ore crushed, yielding 168 oz. of gold.

CONSOLIDATED MURCHISON.—Crushed, 481 tons; obtained, 493 oz.

CROWN DEEP.—For January:—Tons crushed by stamps, 22,082; yield in smelted gold, 6,869 oz.; tons of sands and concentrates treated by cyanide 20,180; yield in smelted gold 6,560 oz.—total, 13,429 oz.

MYSORE WEST AND MYSORE-WYNAAD CONSOLIDATED.—1898:—The mill ran 788 hours, crushed 1,500 tons, and yielded 516 oz. of bar gold.

NOURSE DEEP.—For January:—Tons crushed by stamps, 7,350; yield in smelted gold from mill, 3,780 oz.; tons of sands and concentrates treated by cyanide, 5,673; yield in smelted gold, 1,619 oz.—total, 5,399 oz.

ROSE DEEP.—For January:—Tons crushed by stamps, 14,706; yield in smelted gold, 5,955 oz.; tons of sands and concentrates treated by cyanide, 12,352; yield in smelted gold, 3,711 oz.—total, 9,666 oz.

LADY SHENTON.—Tons crushed 552. Yield, 1,518 ozs. smelted gold.

IVANHOE.—Clean up for two weeks, 1,354 ozs. of gold from 793 tons of ore crushed. Tailings assay 17 dwts. per ton.

MOUNT LYELL MINING AND RAILWAY COMPANY.—From January 13 to February 9 inclusive a total quantity of 8,873 tons of ore has been treated, 7,259 tons from open cuts assaying before treatment:—copper, 3·32 per cent.; silver, 4·24 oz. per ton; gold, ·237 oz. per ton—1,613 tons from No. 4 tunnel assaying before treatment:—copper, 7·41 per cent.; silver, 10·07 oz. per ton; gold, ·067 oz. per ton. The converters have produced during the same period 366 tons blister copper containing:—copper, 361 tons; silver, 37,217 oz.; gold, 1,740 oz.

DAY DAWN BLOCK AND WYNDHAM GOLD.—Result for fortnight ended February 19:—Tons crushed, 1,290; yield of gold, 1,602 oz., including tailings.

BURBANK'S BIRTHDAY GIFT.—Crushed, 373 tons; yield, 505 oz. free gold, exclusive of tailings.

VICTORY, CHARTERS TOWERS.—Crushed for the fortnight from No. 3 shaft, 119 tons for 495 oz. of gold. Approximate value, £1,650. Profit, £900.

OURO PRETO.—5,466 tons of ore produced 1,425 oz. of gold.

HYDERABAD (DECCAN).—The output of coal from the Singareni Collieries for the four weeks ended January 29, was 29,992 tons. The output for 1897 gave an average per month of 28,042 tons.

NEW AUSTRALIAN BROKEN HILL CONSOLS.—One ton, three cwts., containing 4,200 oz. of silver.

JUBILEE.—Quartz mined, 15,253 tons; development, 862½ ft. Tons crushed, 13,109. Cyanide works.—Bullion recovered, 1,969 oz., 14 dwts. Ore reserve.—Ore at grass, 1,993 tons. Cash profit per quarter, £10,098. Expenditure on capital account, £1,546.

FRANK SMITH DIAMOND.—3,900 loads washed, producing 180 carats, including one stone of 34 carats.

ST. AUGUSTINE.—1,450 loads washed yielded 66 carats, value £120.

ST. JOHN DEL REY.—Gold produce 11th to 19th February £3,100. Yield per ton ·40 of an oz. troy.

GREAT BOULDER PROPRIETARY.—The West Australian Bank has shipped 3,293 oz. of gold per steamer *Occana*, estimated value, £13,500.

According to the *Frankfürter Zeitung*, the Sultan has explained to the German Ambassador at Constantinople that he takes a favourable view of the proposal that two Powers—presumably France and Italy—should undertake the pacification of Crete by the instrumentality of their own officials. No doubt; all the more if, as is stated, his Majesty believes that such a step would remove the burning question of the governorship from troubling him for a long time. But *would* it remove this burning question?

The Attorney-General of Queensland has ordered the prosecution of the late directors and auditors of the Queensland National Bank.

WEALTH OF NATIONS.

A very condensed report of the meeting held on the 11th inst. has been sent to the shareholders in this company. None of the hostile criticism has been printed. Doubtless the chairman was prudent in himself moving the motion for a committee after the result of the meetings of other companies in the proposed group, and it is to be hoped the gentlemen chosen will get some good reasons for the proposed absorption of their company. Accounts to September 30, 1897, are also published, showing a cash balance of over £20,000. This, we gather from the chairman, has since been reduced to £16,000. With this money in hand, if amalgamation is decided upon, they ought to have more equitable treatment. It seems cool that shares in this company with some cash left should be offered on exactly the same terms as shares in another concern with a large debt. Whether amalgamation should be accepted is a question for the committee. If the property is as good as the directors believe, would it not be better to keep clear of the London & Globe scheme? One point we would emphasise—the amalgamation, if agreed to, should not include companies which have had no existence outside the offices of their promoters.

Railway Traffic Returns.

ALGECIRAS (GIBRALTAR) RAILWAY.—Traffic for week ended February 12, Ps. 21,780; increase, Ps. 1,940. Aggregate from July 1 Ps. 661,409; increase, Ps. 11,703.

BENGAL CENTRAL RAILWAY.—Traffic for week ending January 29, Rs. 30,266; increase, Rs. 12,132. Total from January 1, Rs. 86,667; increase, Rs. 11,462.

BENGAL DOOARS RAILWAY COMPANY.—Traffic receipts for week ending January 15, Rs. 3,610, against Rs. 4,886.

BURMA RAILWAYS.—Receipts for week ending January 22, Rs. 2,01,858; decrease, Rs. 32,494. Aggregate from January 1, Rs. 598,219; decrease, Rs. 127,200.

CLEATOR AND WORKINGTON.—Gross receipts for the week ending February 19 amounted to £998, a decrease of £180. Total receipts from January 1, £7,120, a decrease of £503.

COCKERMOUTH, KESWICK, AND PENRITH.—Gross receipts for the week ending February 12 amounted to £830, an increase of £42. Total receipts for six weeks £5,156, an increase of £598.

GREAT WESTERN OF BRAZIL RAILWAY.—Traffic for week ending January 15th, $51,912; increase, $4,446. Aggregate receipts to date $128,172; increase, $11,952.

H. H. THE NIZAM'S GUARANTEED STATE RAILWAYS COMPANY.—Traffic for seven days ending January 22, Rs. 79,723, increase, Rs. 4,980. Total from January 1, Rs. 229,005; increase, Rs. 4,140.

MOBILE AND BIRMINGHAM RAILROAD.—Traffic for fourth week of January, $12,827; increase, $6,053. Aggregate from July 1, $220,568; decrease, $14,336.

MANILA RAILWAY.—Traffic receipts for week ended February 19, $20,055; increase, $2,732. Aggregate from January 1, $130,284; increase, $33,134.

QUEBEC CENTRAL RAILWAY.—Receipts for fourth week of January, $5,334; decrease $1,200. Aggregate from July 1, $29,207; decrease $799.

ROHILKUND AND KUMAON RAILWAY.—Traffic for week ending January 22, Rs. 4,966; decrease, Rs. 497. Aggregate from January 1, Rs. 17,186; decrease, Rs. 807.

VILLA MARIA AND RUFINO RAILWAY.—Traffic for week ending February 19, $3,988; decrease, $1,930. Aggregate from January 1, $27,141; decrease, $5,558.

WEST FLANDERS RAILWAY.—Gross receipts for week ending February 20, £2,074; increase, £99. Total from January 1, £14,837; increase, £587.

WEST OF INDIA PORTUGUESE RAILWAY.—Week ending January 29, Rs. 4,900; increase, Rs. 2,157.

BOLIVAR RAILWAY.—Receipts for month of January, £1,443; decrease, £1,449. Aggregate for seven months, £10,239; decrease, £5,658.

ASSAM-BENGAL RAILWAY.—Traffic for eight days ended January 8, Rs. 26,223; increase, Rs. 1,994.

ANTOFAGASTA (CHILI) AND BOLIVIA RAILWAY.—Traffic receipts for month of January, $304,000; decrease, $110,000.

MIDLAND URUGUAY RAILWAY.—Receipts for month of January, £3,617; increase, £718.

PUERTO CABELLO AND VALENCIA RAILWAY.—Traffic receipts for week ending January 14, £881; decrease, £154.

TRAMWAY AND OMNIBUS RECEIPTS.

Increases for past week:—Belfast, £108; Calais, £34; Calcutta, £183; Croydon, £68; Glasgow, £169; Lea Bridge, £119; London & Deptford, £21; London Southern, £43; London General Omnibus, £1,037; London Road Car, £403; London Southern, £43; Metropolitan, £534; North Staffordshire, none; South London, £18; Sunderland, £21; Swansea, £14; Woolwich & S. E. London, £4.

Decrease for past week:—Barcelona, £125; Bordeaux, £83; Provincial, £8; Southampton, £8; Wolverhampton, £9.

Anglo-Argentine, week ending January 24, £257 increase; Vienna Omnibus, week ending February 5, £291 increase.

City of Buenos Ayres, week ending January 24, £664 increase,

Answers to Correspondents.

Questions about public securities, and on all points in company law, will be answered week by week, in the REVIEW, on the following terms and conditions:—

A fee of FIVE shillings must be remitted for each question put, provided they are questions about separate securities. Should a private letter be required, then an extra fee of FIVE shillings must be sent to cover the cost of such letter, the fee then being TEN shillings for one query only, and FIVE shillings for every subsequent one in the same letter. While making this concession the EDITOR will feel obliged if private replies are as much as possible dispensed with. It is wholly impossible to answer letters sent merely "with a stamped envelope enclosed for reply."

Correspondents will further greatly oblige by so framing their questions as to obviate the necessity to name securities in the replies. They should *number* the questions, keeping a copy for reference, thus:—"(1) Please inform me about the present position of the Rowenzori Development Co. (2) Is a dividend likely to be paid soon on the capital stock of the Congo-Sudan Railway?"

Answers to be given to all such questions by simply quoting the numbers 1, 2, 3, and so on. The EDITOR has a rooted objection to such forms of reply as—"I think your Timbuctoo Consols will go up," or "Sell your Slowcoach and Draggem Bonds," because this kind of thing is open to all sorts of abuses. By the plan suggested, and by using a fancy name to be replied to, each query can be kept absolutely private to the inquirer, and no scope whatever be given to market manipulations. Avoid, as names to be replied to, common words, like "investor," "inquirer," and so on, as also "bear" or "bull." Detached syllables of the inquirer's name, or initials reversed, will frequently do as well as anything, so long as the answer can be identified by the inquirer.

The EDITOR further respectfully requests that merely speculative questions should as far as possible be avoided. He by no means sets himself up as a market prophet, and can only undertake to provide the latest information regarding the securities asked about. This he will do faithfully and without bias.

Replies cannot be guaranteed in the same week if the letters demanding them reach the office of the INVESTORS' REVIEW, Norfolk House, Norfolk-street, W.C., later than the first post on Wednesday mornings.

J. H. S.—Your letter was forwarded on the 23rd inst.

E. H. W.—I have received your letter, and will endeavour to send some suggestions.

C. J.—Divide the money among several banks—Scotch or English, avoiding any that offer exceptionally large rates of interest, which is never a good sign. Bank of England notes are legal tender under all circumstances.

Next Week's Meetings.

MONDAY, FEBRUARY 28.

Holborn and Frascati Restaurant ...	Holborn Restaurant, 3 p.m.
Rossendale Valley Tramways ...	61, Gracechurch-street, 3.30 p.m.
Scottish Employers' Liability Insurance	Aberdeen, 1 p.m.
South Yorkshire Junction Railway...	23, Queen Victoria-street, 3 p.m.
Tunbridge Wells Gas...	Tunbridge Wells, 7 p.m.

TUESDAY, MARCH 1.

Bank of British North America ...	3, Clement's-lane, 12.30 p.m.
Crescent Gold Mining Company ...	6, Queen-street-place, 3 p.m.
Hull, Barnsley, and West Riding Junction Railway (Spec.)	Winchester House, 2 p.m.
John Oakey & Sons	Albion Tav., Aldersgate-st., 12.30 p.m.
Junior Army and Navy Stores ...	St. Martin's Town Hall, 2.30 p.m.
Legal and General Life Assurance ...	10, Fleet-street, 2 p.m.
Marbella Iron Ore	78, Queen Victoria-street, 2 p.m.
M. B. Foster & Sons	242, Marylebone-road, 11 a.m.

WEDNESDAY, MARCH 2.

Barcelona Tramways...	Winchester House, noon
City of London Electric Lighting ...	Ditto, 2.30 p.m.
London and Australasian Deb. Corp.	Ditto, 2 p.m.
Nine Reefs Company	6, Queen-street-place, 11.30 a.m.
Oriental Gold Mining of India ...	Ditto. 12.30 p.m.

THURSDAY, MARCH 3.

International Bank of London ...	Winchester House, noon.
Kensington and Knightsbridge Electric	1, Gt. George-street, S.W., 5 p.m.
London Street Tramways	Cannon-street Hotel, 1 p.m.
Prudential Assurance	142, Holborn Bars, 2 p.m.

FRIDAY, MARCH 4.

Pontypool Gas and Water (Gen.) ...	Pontypool, 2.30 p.m
Scottish Temperance Life Assurance	Glasgow, 1 p.m.

SATURDAY, MARCH 5.

Town and County Bank	Aberdeen, 12.30 p.m.

The Select Committee on Money Lending has resumed its sittings at Westminster. Mr. T. W. Russell has been re-elected chairman. It is now to concentrate its attention upon legal points and possible remedies.

To those about to leave for Klondike. Do not apply to Canadian insurance offices for life insurance. They will refuse it.

GOVERNMENT AND THE CHARTERED COMPANY.

Mr. Chamberlain's memoranda of proposed alterations in the administrative powers of the Chartered Company were published yesterday. Their effect seems to be that all administrative work will be carried through or controlled by the Crown and its own officers. No responsibility toward the debenture or share holder will be assumed by the Crown: that is to remain with the board of directors. Life directors are to be withdrawn, and the whole board elected by the shareholders. Any director or official may be removed from office by the Secretary of State, and is not eligible for re-election without his consent.

Financially, the company does not seem to benefit much, as the greater part of the cost of administration is to be borne by it.

THE PROPERTY MARKET.

The animation of last week—which closed with a total of sales of £189,858, as compared with £94,787 in the same week last year—at the London Mart has been continued during the present. On Monday the day's sales amounted to £36,087. The chief feature of the day, however, seemed to be the unpopularity of big breweries. The Biggleswade Brewery, with 109 tied houses, was put in at £80,000, and the biddings rose to £132,500, when, as no further offer was made, the auctioneer withdrew the property at £160,000. The Wolverhampton Brewery, with fifty-three licensed houses attached, was withdrawn at £76,000. The Old Lion Brewery, at Tipton, with its following of twenty-three public and beer-houses, did, however, find a purchaser at £27,500. Mr. Alfred Thomas was the auctioneer. Other properties offered were of minor interest, but the bidding was brisk. Two freehold houses in Blythwood-road, Crouch Hill, went for £1,500, while another freehold property at Kingston Hill, Surrey, brought £1,520.

No. 6, Seamore-place, which was for many years the residence of the late Lord Monk-Bretton, has been sold by Messrs. William Grogan & Boyd. The property is freehold, and the price secured is stated to approach £40,000.

The produce of Tuesday's sales at the Mart was £26,755, and business thus continues fairly good. Messrs. W. W. Read & Co. were the principal operators, and there was keen competition for their principal lot, a freehold ground rent of £200 per annum on premises in Lombard-street, with reversion to the rack-rent in thirty-six years. It went for £12,200, which is sixty-one years' purchase. The same firm disposed of a number of freeholds at Stratford at the satisfactory total of £7,000. Messrs. Segrave, Browett, & Taylor sold a freehold house in Betterton-street, Long Acre, rent £55, at £1,015; while Herring, Son, & Daw disposed of one at Streatham at £1,360. A third, of £12 10s., went for £780. The remaining lots were of minor importance.

Messrs. Debenham, Tewson, & Co. resumed their sale of the assets of the Land Securities Company, Limited, in liquidation, at the Mart, on Wednesday. Only one lot failed to go off, and the remaining lots brought a total of £12,615. Messrs. Robert Tidey & Son cleared a long list of brick and mortar investments, but the other sales were not of a very important class. The total amount realised for the day was £20,675.

There was an interesting sale of local shares at Sheffield on Tuesday, under the auspices of Messrs. Nicholson, Greaves, Barker, & Hastings. Among the prices obtained were:—Sheffield Union Bank, £60 shares, £10 paid, £25 and £25 2s. 6d.; Sheffield and Rotherham Bank, £50 shares, £8 paid, £26 5s.; Sheffield and Hallamshire Bank, £100 shares, £25 paid, £64 7s. 6d.; Sheffield Forge and Rolling Mill Company, £10 shares, fully-paid, £11 5s.

On Tuesday, at the Thatched House Hotel, Manchester, Messrs. C. W. Provis & Son offered for sale fifteen freehold dwelling-houses in Vernon-street, Ardwick, subject to a chief rent of £35 4s. 6d., and producing a gross annual rental of £219 14s. The property realised £2,030.

NOTICES.

EAST AND WEST INDIA DOCK COMPANY.—Notice is given that for the purpose of carrying out the conversions of securities under the new scheme of arrangement of the East and West India Dock Company, the Registers of the Debentures, First Mortgage Certificates, East and West India Dock Debenture Stock, Mortgages and Deferred Debenture Stock, will be closed from March 1 to 21, inclusive. Up to and including February 28, the company will receive transfers of the old description of securities. While the registers are closed the company will not receive any transfers except for ordinary stock. On the re-opening of the registers the company will only recognise transfers for the new description of stocks created by the scheme. The new certificates will be ready for issue or exchange on March 22. The interest which has accrued on the old securities from January 1 to February 12, 1898 (the date of confirmation of the scheme) will be paid on March 22, when the registers are re-opened.—J. G. BROODBANK, Secretary.

The Customs returns of New South Wales for 1897 show that the imports amounted in value to £21,744,350, an increase on 1896 of £1,182,840, and the exports to £23,602,991, an increase of £592,642. The exports thus exceed the imports by £572,642.

Prices of Mine and Mining Finance Companies' Shares.

Shares £1 each, except where otherwise stated.

AUSTRALIAN.

Making-Up Price, Feb. 21.	Name.	Closing Price.	Rise or Fall.	Making-Up Price, Feb. 21.	Name	Closing Price.	Rise or Fall.
1 5/16	Aladdin	1 3/8	− 1/16	15/16	Hampton Plains	1	
3 15/16	Associated	4	− 1/8	7 3/4	Hannan's Brownhill	7 3/4	− 1/16
15/16	Do. Southern	1 1/8	+ 1/8	1/2	Hannan's Oroya	7/16	
14/	Brilliant, £2	14/6	+ /6	13/6	Do. Proprietary	1	+ 1/4
2 1/2	Do. St. George's	2 1/2		11/16	Do. Star	11/16	
12/	British Broken Hill	12/		—	Ivanhoe, New	6 1/16	+ 1/16
2 1/2	Broken Hill Proprietary	2 1/2		15/16	Kalgurli Mt. & Iron King, 18/	15/16	
—	Do. Junction	1 1/2		5 3/4	Kalgurli	5 5/8	− 1/8
—	Do. Block 10	3 1/4	− 1/4	3 1/4	Lady Shenton	2 1/2	
1 3/16	Brownhill Extended	1 1/8	− 1/8	9 5/8	Lake View Cons.	9 5/8	− 3/16
1 3/16	Burbank's Birthday	1 1/16	− 1/16	1	Do. Extended	1	− 1/16
1 1/16	Central Boulder	1 1/16	− 1/16	1 1/16	Do. South	1 1/4	− 1/16
5/6	Chaffers, 4/	5/6	− 1/	1 15/16	London & Globe Finance	2	
1/4	Colonial Finance, 15/	3/8 pm	+ 1/8	13/16	London & W. A. Exploration	3/4	− 1/16
—	Crœsus S. United	3/8	+ 1/8	13/16	Do. Investment	11/16	− 1/16
16/	Day Dawn Block	15/9	− /6	5/16	Mainland Consols	1/4	
1	E. Murchison	1 1/16		11/16	North Boulder, 10/	11/16	− 1/16
3/8	Gold Estates	5/16		1 1/2	North Kalgurli	1 3/8	− 1/8
4/6	Golden Arrow 19/	4/6	− /6	3 7/8	Northern Territories	4	+ 1/8
7 3/4	Golden Horseshoe	7 11/16	− 1/16	2 3/4	Peak Hill	2 5/8	− 1/16
15/16	Golden Link	1	− 1/16	2 1/4	South Kalgurli	2 1/16	− 1/16
1	Great Boulder, 2/	22/9	+ /3	1 15/16	W. A. Goldfields	2	
1 3/16	Do. Main Reef, 10/	1 1/16	− 1/8	2 1/16	W. A. Joint Stock	2 1/16	
3 1/2	Do. Perseverance	3 1/4	− 1/4	1 1/2	W. A. Market Trust	1 5/8	+ 1/8
15/16	Do. South	1		2	W. A. Loan & General Fin.	2 1/4	+ 1/8
1 3/4	Hainault	2 1/16	+ 1/8	1/16	White Feather	3/8	

SOUTH AFRICAN.

Making-Up Price, Feb. 21.	Name.	Closing Price.	Rise or Fall.	Making-Up Price, Feb. 21.	Name	Closing Price.	Rise or Fall.
5 3/8	Angelo	5 1/4	− 1/16	3 5/8	Langlaagte Estate	3 5/8	− 1/8
1 3/16	Aurora West	1 1/8	− 1/16	2/6	Lisbon-Berlyn	2/9	
15/16	Bantjes	1 1/16		2 1/2	May Consolidated	2 1/2	
10/	Barrett, 10/	10/6		4 1/16	Meyer and Charlton	4 3/16	
3 3/4	Bonanza	3 13/16	+ 1/16	3 1/4	Modderfontein	3 1/4	− 1/8
7/8	Buffelsdoorn	15/16		15/16	New Bultfontein	7/8	− 1/16
1 1/4	Champ d'Or	1 1/4		3 3/4	New Primrose	4	
5 1/16	City and Suburban, £4	5 1/4		1 5/8	Nigel	1 5/8	− 1/16
3 1/2	Comet (New)	3 1/4	− 1/16	—	Nigel Deep	—	
5 1/2	Con. Deep Level	5 3/8	− 1/8	3/8	North Randfontein	—	
13	Crown Deep	13 1/8	+ 1/8	6	Nourse Deep	6 1/4	− 1/8
12 1/2	Crown Reef	12 1/4	− 1/4	1 1/4	Porges-Randfontein	1 1/16	
29 1/2	De Beers, £5	29 1/4	− 1/4	30 1/2	Rand Mines	31 1/2	− 15/16
3 3/8	Driefontein	3 1/2	+ 1/8	1 3/16	Randfontein	1 1/16	
5 3/4	Durban Roodepoort	5 5/8	− 1/8	2 1/2	Rietfontein	2 1/4	− 1/8
3 15/16	Do. Deep	4	− 1/8	10	Robinson Deep	10 3/8	− 1/8
4 1/16	East Rand	4 3/8	− 1/16	8 3/4	Do. Gold, £5	8 1/4	
25 1/2	Ferreira	25 1/2	− 1/2	1 1/2	Do. Randfontein	1 1/4	− 1/16
6 1/4	Geldenhuis Deep	6 1/2	+ 1/4	1 3/16	Roodepoort Central Deep	1 1/16	− 1/16
4 3/8	Do. Estate	4 13/16	+ 1/16	6 5/8	Rose Deep	6 3/8	− 1/4
1 1/16	George Goch	1 1/16	− 1/16	3	Salisbury	3	− 1/4
2 1/8	Ginsberg	2 1/16	− 1/16	2 1/16	Sheba	2 3/16	+ 1/16
2	Glencairn	2 1/16	− 1/8	3 1/16	Simmer and Jack, £5	3 1/4	− 1/16
2 1/2	Glen Deep	2 1/2		3 3/8	Transvaal Gold	3 5/8	− 1/8
9 1/4	Goldfields Deep	9 1/16	− 1/16	3	Treasury	3 3/8	− 1/8
8 13/16	Griqualand West	8 1/2		4	United Roodepoort	4	− 1/8
8 1/4	Henry Nourse	8 1/2	+ 1/16	1 15/16	Van Ryn	1 13/16	− 1/8
7 3/4	Heriot	7 1/16	− 1/4	5 5/8	Village Main Reef	5 3/4	+ 1/8
8	Jagersfontein	8	− 1/4	1 13/16	Vogelstruis	1 7/8	+ 1/8
8 1/2	Jubilee	8 1/4	− 1/4	3/4	Do. Deep	11/16	− 1/8
5 3/4	Jumpers	5 1/2	− 1/16	8 1/16	Wemmer	8 1/2	
5 3/4	Jumpers Deep	5 5/8	− 1/8	1/2	West Rand	1/2	
2 3/4	Kleinfontein	2 1/16	− 1/8	6 1/2	Wolhuter, £4	6 3/8	
3 3/8	Knight's	3 3/8		2 3/8	Worcester	2 1/2	
2 1/16	Lancaster	2 1/16					

LAND EXPLORATION AND RHODESIAN.

Making-Up Price, Feb. 21.	Name.	Closing Price.	Rise or Fall.	Making-Up Price, Feb. 21.	Name	Closing Price.	Rise or Fall.
2 1/2	Anglo-French Ex.	2 3/8	− 1/8	3/8	Mashonaland Central	3/8	− 1/16
2	Barnato Consolidated	2	− 1/8	6 1/2	Matabele Gold Reefs	6 1/2	− 1/8
3/4	Bechuanaland Ex.	11/16		2 1/16	Mozambique	2 3/16	
2 7/8	Chartered B.S.A.	2 3/4	− 1/8	1 1/2	New African	1 1/16	
13/16	Cassel Coal	13/16		1 1/4	Oceana Consolidated	13/16	
3/8	Clark's Cons.	5/16		1 1/2	Rhodesia, Ltd.	1 1/8	
5/16	Colenbrander	5/16	− 1/16	4 1/2	Do. Exploration	4 3/8	− 1/8
4 1/16	Cons. Goldfields	4 1/4		1	Do. Goldfields	1 1/16	
1 1/16	Do. Pref.	21/6	+ /6	3 1/2	Robinson Bank	3 1/2	+ 1/8
1 13/16	Exploration	1 11/16	− 1/16	4 1/16	S. A. Gold Trust	4 1/4	− 1/8
2 1/2	Geelong	2 1/4		1 1/16	Tati Concessions	2 1/16	
13/16	Henderson's Est.	11/16	− 1/16	3/4	Transvaal Development	13/16	+ 1/16
1 1/4	Johannesburg Con. In.	1 13/16		1/16	United Rhodesia	5/16	− 1/8
1 1/16	Do. Water	1 1/16		1 1/16	Willoughby	1 1/4	− 1/16
1 15/16	Mashonaland Agency	2		13/16	Zambesia Explor.	3/4	− 1/8

MISCELLANEOUS.

Making-Up Price, Feb. 21.	Name.	Closing Price.	Rise or Fall.	Making-Up Price, Feb. 21.	Name	Closing Price.	Rise or Fall.
1 1/2	Alamillos, £2	1 1/2		14/	Mysore Goldfields	12/6	− 2/
5 1/2	Anaconda, $25	5 1/16	− 1/4	10/	Do. Reefs, 17/	9/	− 1/9
10/	Balaghât, 18/	10/	− /6	15/	Do. West	15/	− /6
4 1/2	Cape Copper, £2	4 1/4	− 1/8	12/3	Do. Wynaad	12/	− 1/6
4 13/16	Champion Reef, 10s.	4 13/16		2 1/2	Namaqua, £2	2 1/16	− 1/8
2 1/2	Copiapo, £2	2 1/2	− 1/16	3 3/8	Nundydroog	3 3/8	− 1/16
3 1/16	Coromandel	3 1/8	− 1/16	2 1/2	Ooregum	2 13/16	
2 1/16	Frontino & Bolivia	2 1/16	+ 1/8	3 1/2	Do. Pref.	3 1/2	
1 3/16	Hall Mines	1 1/16		28 1/2	Rio Tinto Def., £5	28 1/16	− 1/2
2 1/2	Libiola, £5	2 1/4	− 1/16	6 1/2	Do. Pref. £5	6 1/2	
7 3/4	Linares, £3	8		18/6	St. John del Rey	18/9	
3 1/2	Mason & Barry, £3	3 1/2		18/9	Taitipu	3/8	− 1/16
5 1/2	Mountain Copper, £5	5 1/16	− 1/16	7 1/2	Tharsis, £2	7 5/8	
13 1/2	Mount Lyell, £3	14	− 1/4	2 1/2	Tolima "A," £5	3	
3 1/2	Mount Lyell, North	3 1/16	+ 1/16	4 1/8	Waihi	4 1/16	− 1/16
1	Mount Lyell, South	17/6	− /6	1 1/2	Waitekauri	2	+ 1/16
4 1/16	Mount Morgan, 17s. 6d.	4 1/16	+ 1/16	1 1/16	Woodstock (N.Z.)	1 1/2	
5 3/4	Mysore, 10s.	5 1/16					

WEST AUSTRALIAN MINE CRUSHINGS.

Capital Issued.	Property.	Goldfields.	Name of Company.	November.		December.		January.		Total since Crushing Began.		Cash distributions in '97.
£	Acres.			Tons.	Oz.	Tons.	Oz.	Tons.	Oz.	Tons.	Oz.	£
61,426	108	Murchison	Agamemnon	255	202	380	270	600	350	8,957	5,037	—
97,007	129	Mount Margaret ..	Arrow Brownhill	156	159	162	134	—	—	378	339	—
425,000	156	Kalgoorlie	Associated G. M. of W. A. ..	2,498	4,499	1,750	2,355	3,246	6,741	16,614	36,220	—
155,000	100	Coolgardie	Bayley's United	613	912	772	872	869	1,015	13,257	64,644	—
150,007	166	Coolgardie	Big Blow	57	28	125	65	150	70	763	327	—
150,000	65	N. E. Coolgardie ..	Black Flag Proprietary	281	75	—	—	—	—	9,955	3,205	—
150,000	39	Coolgardie	Burbank's Birthday Gift	750	1,325	630	1,108	961	1,558	8,916	22,496	15,000
150,000	51	Murchison	Champion Reef	1,200	443	730	175	560	101	9,843	4,788	—
64,660	132	Pilbarra	Consolidated G. M. of W. A. ..	60	68	—	—	69	112	1,733	1,888	—
113,000	112	Murchison	Consolidated Murchison	1,012	1,106	862	380	812	821	27,303	16,757	—
100,000	12	Murchison	Cue No. 1	422	371	740	545	820	565	9,552	7,160	—
92,297	42	Murchison	Cue Victory	250	151	—	—	494	325	2,364	1,647	—
122,830	77	Mount Margaret ..	Diorite King	68	95	60	182	64	58	397	981	—
130,000	117	East Murchison	East Murchison United	1,325	1,860	1,950	2,100	1,410	1,630	13,631	21,497	7,500
54,139	40	Yalgoo	Emerald Reward	—	—	230	218	—	—	2,104	3,512	—
85,000	84	Murchison	Golconda	345	845	370	850	—	—	4,780	10,327	—
162,380	60	N. E. Coolgardie ..	Golden Arrow	70	53	68	83	—	—	707	579	—
100,000	24	Kalgoorlie	Golden Horse Shoe	—	—	—	—	—	—	—	—	—
175,000	24	Kalgoorlie	Great Boulder Perseverance ..	894	1,676	1,022	1,417	1,040	933	14,639	28,899	35,000
160,000	85	Kalgoorlie	Great Boulder Proprietary ..	2,704	6,965	2,575	6,509	2,756	6,599	53,239	172,503	160,000
60,000	24	Coolgardie	Great Boulder Main Reef ..	520	970	648	1,634	730	1,200	4,277	10,445	—
105,000	42	Yalgoo	Gullewa	190	263	75	126	169	247	1,504	2,248	—
85,000	20	Kalgoorlie	Hannan's Brownhill	121	496	210	1,696	963	2,285	6,036	32,580	42,500
140,000	36	Kalgoorlie	Hannan's Oroya	639	288	776	275	832	374	3,273	1,603	—
75,000	27	Kalgoorlie	Hannan's Reward	473	159	452	165	472	146	3,736	1,600	—
1,000,000	24	Kalgoorlie	Ivanhoe	1,867	3,656	2,595	4,891	1,555	2,760	21,630	45,754	18,225
160,000	36	North Coolgardie ..	Lady Shenton	500	1,512	415	1,961	552	1,518	7,143	25,145	24,000
250,000	48	Kalgoorlie	Lake View Consols	6,445	8,552	7,988	8,615	8,573	7,554	40,452	103,776	125,000
119,444	52	Coolgardie	Lindsay's Consolidated	205	140	418	216	682	182	3,262	1,763	—
699,999	67	Coolgardie	Londonderry	100	195	330	652	—	—	1,829	11,430	—
224,125	156	North Coolgardie ..	Menzies Consolidated	761	731	455	601	748	644	7,161	7,065	—
193,100	44	North Coolgardie ..	Menzies Crusoe	167	134	185	199	330	244	7,765	13,795	—
173,811	91	North Coolgardie ..	Menzies Gold Reefs Proprietary	125	130	—	—	50	154	4,750	7,473	—
200,000	192	Mount Margaret ..	Mount Malcolm Proprietary ..	270	318	202	360	470	444	1,684	2,044	—
85,000	84	Murchison	Mount Yagahong	385	471	575	612	—	—	3,740	3,418	—
200,000	164	Dundas	Norseman Gold	612	648	680	410	630	444	3,109	3,296	—
120,000	19	Kalgoorlie	North Boulder	507	524	577	738	1,241	575	7,265	13,006	8,250
115,000	143	Mount Margaret ..	North Star	424	356	352	564	408	388	3,843	4,739	—
25,799	36	Coolgardie	Premier Gold	380	354	378	253	710	484	7,325	9,995	5,375
65,003	12	Murchison	Princess Royal (Cue)	460	444	550	499	290	219	2,910	3,101	—
31,387	19½	N. Coolgardie	Queensland Menzies	312	827	330	953	304	1,144	4,309	17,203	26,400
78,984	51	N. E. Coolgardie ..	Robinson (W.A.)	495	470	660	610	650	439	6,542	8,902	7,898
—	168	Mount Margaret ..	Sons of Gwalia	800	993	840	1,213	1,260	1,377	5,947	8,468	—
900,000	98	Coolgardie	Westralia and East Extension ..	1,634	1,723	1,611	1,339	1,306	856	8,947	8,931	—
140,300	48	N. E. Coolgardie ..	White Feather Main Reef ..	750	410	880	252	698	341	4,733	3,054	—

THE NEWFOUNDLAND RAILWAYS.

An important contract has been concluded between the Newfoundland Government and Mr. Reid, the builder of the railway across the island. According to this, Mr. Reid, or his representative, is to work the entire railway system of 650 miles, for 50 years, receiving a grant of 2,500 acres of land per mile. He is to pay $1,000,000 now, and $6,000,000 more at the end of the period. He also buys St. John's Dock for $350,000, and the Government telegraph lines for $125,000, and undertakes, in consideration of a subsidy of $100,000 for 30 years, to build seven mail steamers to ply in the great bays, and for a payment of $140,000 to build an electric railway in St. John's, and pave the main streets with granite. A wonderful contract, which seems, at least, good for Mr. Reed. It is, however, very highly thought of in the colony.

New South Wales is devoting increased energy to bringing forth her wealth of coal. Last year the output amounted to 4,417,600 tons, exceeding the production of 1896 by nearly 500,000 tons.

Messrs. E. Morewood & Company, of the South Wales Tinplate Works, Llanelly, have been compelled to ask the indulgence of their creditors, in consequence, as they say, of losses from strikes and the depression in the tinplate industry. The firm has maintained an exceptionally high position for many years, and employed about 1,200 hands at the Llanelly works, and 700 at Cwmbwrla. It was converted into a limited liability company last year, with a capital of £168,750.

The Victorian gold yield for January was 43,760 oz., showing an increase on the output in the same month last year of 16,085 oz.

The redemption of the Swiss railways by the State has been carried on the referendum by an unexpectedly large majority. The numbers were—for the proposal, 384,146; against, 177,130.

Roumanian receipts and expenditure, according to the Finance Minister's Budget statement, balance at 222,000,000 francs, as compared with 215,000,000 francs last year. The Minister has also introduced a Bill for the conversion of 446,634,000 francs worth of the State debt.

Ominous rumours come from Cleveland, Ohio, that an effort is being made by the Carnegie Iron Company to form a trust controlling the entire pig-iron of the country.

Frenchmen seem incorrigible on the subject of bounties. They are restive about the sugar bounties, and seem inclined to join in the Conference which will probably result in their abolition. Yet here we have the Budget Committee calmly recommending a 60 cent. per kilo bounty on cotton, 400 francs per par of silk spun from French cocoons, and 340 francs for silk spun from foreign cocoons. The bounties are to remain in force for ten years—if the taxpayers do not kick against them before that.

There can be no doubt that Germany is showing great activity in preparing for the exploitation of whatever mineral wealth there may be in its leasehold property around Kiao-Chau. It has already concessions for two railways, and negotiations for others are still in progress. Besides these, the German Asiatic Bank is also active in negotiation. Coal mines and the flotation of subsidiary companies for various undertakings in China are its especial care. It seems intended to pay particular attention to the opening up of the coal mines in the locality. A German official, who has been to Kiao-Chau, during a recent lecture in Berlin declared Chinese coal far superior to Japanese, and Germany meant soon to export coal to Japan. What if the Japanese were to refuse belief in its superiority?

The Madras Government reports that the total public works expenditure to the end of the famine will amount to 71 lakhs. This is more than was previously estimated—60 lakhs being the amount then allotted to the Public Works Department, while the Civil Department had 33 lakhs. This may possibly be slightly reduced; but the Government, "in the uncertainty of the Public Works system of accounting," is "reluctantly forced" to an estimate of 100 lakhs. Just so. The "uncertainty" of public ways of accounting is very general—and generally ends in sending the balance to the wrong side.

There may be no hitch in the negotiations for the Sugar Bounties Conference, but it does not look as if these negotiations were going quite smoothly. There is, however, we are assured, "no question of an indefinite postponement of the Conference."

It is stated in Berlin that the Imperial Postal Department has concluded a contract for a regular fortnightly mail steamship service between Shanghai and Kiao-Chau, the steamers also going on to Chifu and Ta-ku.

The profits of the Vienna Crediteurstalt last year amounted to 4,936,000 fl., as compared with 5,224,000 fl. in 1896. The directors propose a dividend of 17 fl. per share.

NEW BOOKS RECEIVED.

We have to acknowledge receipt of a number of extremely interesting official publications from New South Wales. One is a "Statistical Account of the Seven Colonies of Australasia, 1895-96," by L. A. Coghlan. It traces the progress of the Colonies mainly since 1861, although in some instances the information extends back to the very beginning of settlement. At the close of the year 1861, the population of Australasia, excluding the uncivilised native races, amounted to 1,265,898; in 1895 it had increased to 4,238,369. The tonnage of shipping entered and cleared rose from 1,076,856 in 1861 to 6,859,936 in 1895; while inter-Colonial shipping rose from 1,751,628 in 1861 to 11,309,401 in 1895. The value of imports and exports taken together in 1861 was £35,061,282; in 1895 it reached £67,606,523, or very nearly double. The volume of trade between the Colonies in 1861 amounted in value to £17,166,925, rose to £60,114,797 in 1891, and fell to £47,231,360 in 1895. The deposits in banks and saving institutions now amount to £130,246,495.

Another work by Mr. Coghlan, published officially, is "The Wealth and Progress of New South Wales, 1895-96." It is in two closely-packed volumes, and gives an interesting outline of the progress of the Colony. The volume of "The Wealth and Progress of New South Wales" for 1896-7 has likewise been sent us. We have also received "New South Wales: The Mother Colony of the Australias," with maps and many illustrations; and the "New South Wales Statistical Register."

We have received copies of Messrs. Mathieson's handbooks and traffic tables, which show the same care and comprehensiveness of get-up as have always characterised these useful little works of reference. Panton Ham's "Universal Interest Tables" (Effingham Wilson) are also on our table. They are on the decimal system, and the interest may be calculated for any number of days, on any sum of any current coinage of the world.

"Queensland Past and Present: an Epitome of its Resources and Development," is another compact Colonial compilation, which gives in brief compass a vivid picture of Queensland, geographical, commercial, and social. The author is Mr. Thornhill Weedon, compiler of general statistics.

A copy of a "Handbook of the Workmen's Compensation Act, 1897," (Cardiff: *Western Mail*), by M. Roberts-Jones, has reached us. It is the fifth edition of a useful little work, in which the effect and general bearing of the Act in question are simply and lucidly explained. The author makes several suggestions as to the improvement of the Act in the interests of workmen, especially in encouraging "friendly schemes" of compensation in connection with Friendly Societies.

ENGLISH RAILWAYS.

Div. for half years.				Last Balance forward.	Amt. to pay 1 p.c. on Ord. for ½ yr.	NAME.	Date.	Gross Traffic for week				Gross Traffic for half-year to date.			Mileage.	Inc. on 1897.	Working	Prior Charges last ½ year.	Prop. add Cap. Exp. this ½ year.
1896	1896	1897	1897					Amt.	Inc. or dec. on 1897.	Inc. or dec. on 1896.	No. of weeks	Amt.	Inc. or dec. on 1897.	Inc. or dec. on 1896.					
				£	£												%	£	£
10	10	10	10	2,707	5,094	Barry	Feb 19	8,613	−1,730	+1,068	8	70,573	+640	+8,216	31	—	8·89	60,665	316,853
nil	nil	nil	nil	—	—	Brecon and Merthyr	Feb 20	1,385	+36	−153	8	12,312	+275	−27	61	—	—	—	—
nil	nil	nil	nil	3,979	4,749	Cambrian	Feb 20	4,374	−162	+626	*	29,575	+56	—	250	—	60·96	63,148	40,000
1½	1½	2	1½	1,510	3,150	City and South London	Feb 20	7,051	+7	+83	8	8,565	−152	+651	3½	—	56·67	5,552	124,000
1	2	1½	2	7,895	13,210	Furness	Feb 20	8,945	+110	+1,160	*	61,771	+1,530	—	139	—	49·83	97,423	20,910
1	1½	½	1	2,207	27,470	Great Central (late M., S., & L.)	Feb 20	42,166	+109	+3,557	7	291,534	+5,354	+18,546	352½	—	57·17	627,386	1,200,000
1½	4¾	2	5	51,283	62,865	Great Eastern	Feb 20	78,183	+2,325	+8,106	7	534,309	+19,264	+51,064	1,156	7	55·35	800,138	250,000
3	5¾	3	5	15,094	102,496	Great Northern	Feb 20	92,935	+1,167	+8,409	8	731,419	+20,703	+55,253	1,071	8	61·36	641,485	750,000
4½	7½	4¾	7½	31,350	121,981	Great Western	Feb 20	168780	+6,630	+14,330	7	1,181,550	+40,460	+67,360	2,582	21	51·44	1,486,272	800,000
nil	2	nil	1½	8,931	16,487	Hull and Barnsley	Feb 20	5,718	−617	−332	7	44,049	−2,261	+3,978	73	—	58·21	70,290	52,920
5	5¾	5	5½	21,495	83,704	Lancashire and Yorkshire	Feb 20	92,312	+3,019	+6,172	7	620,373	+23,829	+42,429	555½	25	56·70	674,745	451,076
4¾	8	4¾	8½	26,243	43,049	London, Brighton, & S. Coast	Feb 19	42,968	+3,454	+4,024	8	363,615	+26,002	+23,828	476½	—	50·20	407,042	240,735
nil	nil	nil	nil	72,294	56,296	London, Chatham, & Dover	Feb 20	25,309	+622	+2,306	7	180,250	+8,296	+13,634	185½	—	50·65	367,873	nil
6½	8	6½	7¾	89,535	204,068	London and North Western	Feb 20	222089	+4,606	+14,049	7	1,540,042	+42,649	+94,351	1,911½	—	56·92	1,404,534	600,000
5	8½	8½	8½	23,038	59,367	London and South Western	Feb 20	64,391	+3,047	+5,195	7	446,683	+25,169	+33,388	941	6½	51·75	513,740	389,000
2½	6	2½	6½	14,592	6,691	London, Tilbury, & Southend	Feb 20	4,740	+344	+1,149	8	37,592	+3,013	+7,920	81	—	52·37	39,590	15,000
3½	3¾	3¾	3¾	17,133	26,409	Metropolitan	Feb 20	15,959	+373	+1,524	*	117,570	+2,746	—	64	12	43·63	148,047	254,000
nil	nil	nil	nil	4,006	11,250	Metropolitan District	Feb 29	8,448	+422	+592	7	61,418	+2,400	+2,478	13	—	48·70	119,663	38,450
5	7	5½	6½	38,143	174,582	Midland	Feb 20	180154	+3,252	+10,356	8	1,413,110	+9,937	+85,939	1,354¾	15½	57·59	1,216,582	650,000
5½	7½	5¾	7	22,374	138,189	North Eastern	Feb 19	143546	+327	+6,037	7	960,851	+23,782	+54,208	1,597¾	—	58·82	795,077	436,004
7½	7½	7½	7½	7,061	10,102	North London	Feb 20			Not recd			not	recvd.	12	—	50·90	49,973	7,600
4	5	4	4½	4,745	16,150	North Staffordshire	Feb 20	15,543	+447	+1,364	8	125,109	+8,652	+8,662	312	—	55·27	118,142	19,605
10	10	11		1,642	3,004	Rhymney	Feb 19	5,350	+318	+892	8	40,245	+1,301	+4,614	71	—	49·68	29,049	16,700
3	6⅝	3½	6⅝	4,054	50,215	South Eastern	Feb 19	39,322	+2,688	+4,885	*	283,343	+18,709	—	448	—	51·88	380,763	250,000
3½	3½	3½	3½	2,315	25,961	Taff Vale	Feb 19	14,898	−1,429	−271	8	121,523	−2,551	+3,045	121	—	54·90	94,800	92,000

* From January 1.

SCOTCH RAILWAYS.

5	5	5¼	—	15,350	77,570	Caledonian	Feb 20	66,991	− 1,649	+ 3,942	3	199,465	+ 679	+ 8,290	851½	5	50·50	566,914	375,966
5	5½	5	—	5,886	24,639	Glasgow and South-Western	" 19	26,824	+ 45	+ 3,246	2	78,424	+ 1,554	+ 8,069	393½	—	55·12	221,120	180,556
3½	3½	3½	—	1,291	4,600	Great North of Scotland	" 19	7,458	− 358	+ 584	3	22,380	+ 1,024	+ 1,906	331	15½	52·03	92,178	60,000
3	nil	2	—	10,477	12,820	Highland	" 20	8,014	+ 24	− 296	25	227,426	+ 9,838	+ 12,635	479¾	27¾	58·63	78,976	,000
1	1½	1	—	3,763	45,819	North British	" 20	65,603	+ 1,757	+ 2,586	2	195,206	+ 5,744	+ 2,783	1,230	23	44·65	821,766	426,009

IRISH RAILWAYS.

6½	6½	6½	—	5,466	1,700	Belfast and County Down	Feb. 18	2,046	+ 13	+ 206	*	13,940	+ 446	—	76½	—	55·58	17,690	10,000
5½	6½	5½	—	—	4,284	Belfast and Northern Counties	" 18	4,748	+ 271	− 361	*	33,311	+ 1,164	—	249	—	—	—	—
2	3	2	—	1,418	1,200	Cork, Bandon, and S. Coast	" 19	1,263	+ 10	− 29	*	7,920	− 722	—	103	—	54·82	14,436	5,450
6½	6½	6½	—	21,537	17,709	Great Northern	" 18	13,454	+ 693	+ 835	7	93,636	+ 5,081	+ 5,837	528	36	54·03	87,068	16,000
5½	5½	5½	5½	30,339	24,855	Great Southern and Western	" 18	—	—	—	not	received	—	—	603	13	51·45	72,602	46,582
4	4	4	4½	11,372	11,850	Midland Great Western	" 18	9,483	+ 1,090	+ 1,136	7	62,491	+ 5,110	+ 4,688	538	—	50·31	83,129	1,800
nil	nil	nil	nil	229	2,822	Waterford and Central	" 18	885	+ 30	—	*	6,156	+ 874	—	59½	—	53·24	6,858	1,500
nil	nil	nil	nil	1,936	2,987	Waterford, Limerick & W.	" 18	3,928	+ 368	+ 266	*	46,507	+ 2,840	—	350½	—	57·83	42,617	7,075

* From January 1.

FOREIGN RAILWAYS.

Mileage. Total.	Increase on 1897.	Increase on 1896.	Name.	Gross Traffic for Week. Week ending	Amount.	In. or Dec. upon 1897.	In. or Dec. upon 1896.	Gross Traffic to Date. No. of Weeks.	Amount.	In. or Dec. upon 1897.	In. or Dec. upon 1896.
					£	£	£		£	£	£
319	—	—	Argentine Great Western	Feb. 20	6,394	+ 575	+ 1,391	33	177,433	− 9,730	− 39,998
76½	—	—	Bahia and San Francisco	Jan. 22	2,420	+ 472	+ 743	3	7,935	+ 2,362	+ 2,465
234	48	84	Bahia Blanca and North West	Jan. 23	1,081	+ 98	+ 279	30	23,385	+ 690	—
74	—	—	Buenos Ayres and Ensenada	Feb. 20	3,379	− 106	− 1,017	7	25,311	− 4,931	− 6,361
426	—	—	Buenos Ayres and Pacific	Feb. 19	7,623	− 395	+ 409	33	207,226	− 49,791	+ 8,493
914	1	3	Buenos Ayres and Rosario	Feb. 19	19,195	+ 5,783	+ 5,127	7	125,782	+ 25,729	+ 18,376
2,499	30	68	Buenos Ayres Great Southern	Feb. 20	40,320	+ 3,328	+ 7,851	33	950,727	+ 68,524	+ 248,057
602	107	177	Buenos Ayres Western	Feb. 20	14,034	− 646	+ 290	33	394,310	− 75,394	− 66,059
845	55	77	Central Argentine	Feb. 19	22,110	+ 6,659	+ 2,388	7	156,041	+ 31,372	+ 4,329
297	—	—	Central Bahia	Dec. 31*	$214,389	− $4,688	+ $22,144	12 mos.	$1,307,205	+ $141,334	+ $196,159
271	—	—	Central Uruguay of Monte Video	Feb. 19	6,765	+ 926	+ 1,392	33	197,269	− 1,907	− 15,815
228	—	—	Do. Eastern Extension	Feb. 19	1,504	− 20	+ 352	33	40,086	+ 2,708	− 2,314
182	—	—	Do. Northern Extension	Feb. 19	428	+ 83	− 279	33	21,100	− 1,898	− 5,418
280	—	—	Cordoba and Rosario	Feb. 13	2,585	+ 400	− 1,525	33	68,480	− 19,325	− 2,015
328	—	—	Cordoba Central	Feb. 13	$19,000	− $6,580	− $7,240	6	$143,200	− $16,100	− $28,370
549	—	—	Do. Northern Extension	Feb. 13	$33,000	− $29,840	− $19,500	6	$278,790	− $93,670	− $64,832
237	—	—	Costa Rica	Feb. 18	6,623	− 1,944	− 275	—	—	—	—
99	—	—	East Argentine	Jan. 9‡	709	− 128	− 493	—	—	—	—
386	—	6	Entre Rios	Feb. 19	2,445	+ 1,176	+ 970	33	45,707	+ 8,040	+ 7,822
555	—	24	Inter Oceanic of Mexico	Feb. 19	$64,800	+ $13,300	+ $23,010	33	$1,834,680	+ $265,760	+ $448,100
23	—	—	La Guaira and Caracas	Jan. 21	2,016	− 646	− 304	3	5,633	− 7,125	− 2,056
321	—	—	Mexican	Feb. 19	$89,000	+ $14,000	—	7	$576,300	+ $59,950	—
1,846	—	—	Mexican Central	Feb. 14	$267,266	+ $16,167	+ $92,923	6	$1,583,193	+ $10,638	+ $385,194
1,217	—	—	Mexican National	Feb. 14	$119,057	+ $12,383	+ $29,558	6	$694,109	+ $89,709	+ $114,314
228	—	—	Mexican Southern	Feb. 21	$12,640	− $1,796	+ $2,923	47	$594,306	+ $85,424	+ $158,059
206	—	—	Minas and Rio	Dec. 31*	$177,973	+ $6,511	—	6 mos.	$1,174,610	+ $207,798	—
94	—	17	N. W. Argentine	Feb. 19	1,077	− 293	− 16	7	7,144	− 3,643	− 1,599
242	3	—	Nitrate	Feb. 15†	15,312	− 1,823	− 4,776	6	40,295	− 4,885	—
320	—	—	Ottoman	Feb. 12	3,866	− 835	− 1,481	6	35,871	− 8,768	+ 5,335
77½	—	—	Recife and San Francisco	Dec. 25	5,559	+ 563	+ 1,389	26	88,420	− 9,726	+ 1,024
86½	—	—	San Paulo	Dec. 26†	23,002	− 3,560	—	2	46,230	− 10,120	—
186	—	—	Santa Fe and Cordova	Feb. 19	4,315	+ 1,731	+ 1,588	32	41,813	− 19,954	− 2,318
110	—	—	Western of Havana	Feb. 19	1,705	− 106	+ 1,345	33	58,915	+ 5,677	− 3,170

* For month ended. † For fortnight ended. ‡ For nine days ended.

INDIAN RAILWAYS.

Mileage. Total.	Increase on 1897.	Increase on 1896.	Name.	Gross Traffic for Week. Week ending	Amount.	In. or Dec. on 1897.	In. or Dec. on 1896	Gross Traffic to Date. No. of Weeks.	Amount.	In. or Dec. on 1897.	In. or Dec. on 1896.
862	—	—	Bengal Nagpur	Feb. 12	Rs.1.43.000	− Rs. 5.867	− Rs.13.862	6	Rs.8.26.000	− Rs.1.72.485	− R.2.66.960
818	63	63	Bengal and North-Western	Jan. 22	Rs.1.28.680	+ Rs.22.911	− Rs. 4.432	3	Rs.3.03.840	+ Rs.40.924	− R.1.01.476
461	—	—	Bombay and Baroda	Feb. 19	£22,641	− £2,807	− £11,059	6	£158,858	− £25,024	− £83,347
1,884	2	13	East Indian	Feb. 19	Rs.12.91.000	+ R.1.54.000	+ Rs1.41.000	7	Rs.89.28.000	+ Rs.4.37.000	+ Rs4.03.000
1,491	—	—	Great Indian Penin.	Feb. 19	£65,881	+ £8,533	− £18,114	7	£437,297	− £3,610	− £168,041
736	—	—	Indian Midland	Feb. 19	Rs.1.31.760	− Rs.7.613	+ Rs.34.645	7	Rs.9.82.281	+ Rs.23.179	+ Rs1.39.426
840	—	—	Madras	Feb. 12	£18,700	− £1,833	− £733	6	£116,037	− £1873	− £8,000
1,043	—	—	South Indian	Jan. 22	Rs.1.35.294	− Rs.20.384	− Rs.36.178	3	Rs.4.52.736	− Rs.33.708	− R.1.24.926

UNITED STATES AND CANADIAN RAILWAYS.

Mileage Total.	Increase on 1897.	Increase on 1896.	Name.	Gross Traffic for Week. Period Ending.	Amount.	In. or Dec. on 1897.	Gross Traffic to Date. No. of Weeks.	Amount.	In. or Dec. on 1897.
					dols.	dols.		dols.	dols.
917	—	—	Baltimore & Ohio S. Western	Feb. 14	126,474	+9,597	32	4,224,683	+400,149
6,547	103	156	Canadian Pacific	Feb. 14	375,000	+52,000	6	2,433,000	+463,000
922	—	—	Chicago Great Western	Feb. 14	102,002	+1,933	32	3,386,938	+478,553
6,169	—	469	Chicago, Mil., & St. Paul	Feb. 21	574,000	+49,000	6	4,097,801	+531,220
1,685	—	—	Denver & Rio Grande	Feb. 14	137,000	+26,300	32	5,236,700	+858,900
3,512	—	—	Grand Trunk, Main Line	Feb. 21	£66,748	+£2,596	7	£518,488	+£62,655
335	—	—	Do. Chic. & Grand Trunk	Feb. 21	£14,630	+£3,059	7	£102,919	+£18,697
189	—	—	Do. Det., G. H. & Mil.	Feb. 21	£3,206	−£735	7	£23,633	−£2,682
2,938	—	—	Louisville & Nashville	Feb. 14	430,000	+43,000	6	2,632,000	+758,000
2,197	137	137	Miss., K., & Texas	Feb. 14	223,354	−4,420	32	8,482,580	+525,254
477	—	—	N. Y., Ontario, & W.	Feb. 14	65,724	+8,178	32	2,503,175	+90,882
1,570	—	—	Norfolk & Western	Feb. 14	215,000	+27,000	32	6,821,000	+720,000
3,499	336	—	Northern Pacific	Feb. 14	322,000	+82,000	6	2,095,000	+680,000
1,223	—	—	St. Louis S. Western	Feb. 14	104,000	+19,000	6	688,700	+117,100
4,654	—	—	Southern	Feb. 14	430,000	+25,000	32	1,217,822	+1,094,448
1,979	—	—	Wabash	Feb. 14	241,000	+30,000	6	1,421,496	+372,000

MONTHLY STATEMENTS.

Mileage. Total.	Increase on 1896.	Increase on 1895.	Name.	Net Earnings for Month. Month.	Amount.	In. or Dec. on 1896.	In. or Dec. on 1895.	Net Earnings to Date. No. of Months.	Amount.	In. or Dec. on 1896.	In. or Dec. on 1895.
					dols.	dols.	dols.		dols.	dols.	dols.
6,935	44	444	Atchison	December	986,000	+52,000	—	12	8,966,480	+176,951	—
6,547	103	106	Canadian Pacific	December	1,053,000	+129,000	—	12	10,304,000	+2,196,000	—
1,685	—	—	Denver & Rio Grande	December	273,000	+37,121	−8,253	6	1,786,320	+249,830	−30,604
1,970	—	—	Erie	December	605,798	+100,620	—	12	8,486,792	+300,587	—
3,127	—	239	Illinois Central*	December	2,555,393	+458,872	+349,241	12	24,723,399	+2,940,108	+2,909,052
2,396	—	—	New York Central*	January	3,505,000	+365,000	+27,034	—	—	—	—
477	—	—	New York Ontario, & W.	December	87,176	+14,635	+12,602	6	701,475	+4,958	+44,430
3,407	—	—	Pennsylvania	December	1,664,297	+26,100	−35,400	12	20,532,068	+2,328,300	+849,200
1,055	—	—	Phil. & Reading*	December	1,947,585	+208,345	—	6	11,886,164	+668,603	—

* Statements of gross traffic.

Prices Quoted on the London Stock Exchange.

Throughout the Investors' Review middle prices alone are quoted, the object being to give the public the approximate current quotations of every security of any consequence in existence. On the markets the buying and selling prices are both given, and are often wide apart where stocks are seldom dealt in. Other particulars will be found in the Investment Index published quarterly—January, April, July, and October—in connection with this Review, price 2s., by post 2s. 2d. Where dividends are paid only once a year, an *italic* type is used to distinguish them. The London Stock Exchange Official List is quoted in the Review almost entire, only very insignificant issues, or bonds falling due within the next two or three years, being omitted. But the list is subdivided into the leading, or active, stocks, and those less frequently dealt in. The former will be found under the head of "Stock Markets," and with more details than it is possib e to gi e for the bulk of securities. By retaining the file of the Investors' Review any subscriber can follow for himself the movements of securities from week to week, and the Investment Index will from time to time help to fill up deficiencies in the information.

Tea Companies and Mines and Mining Finance Stocks are placed in special lists.

Among the abbreviations used are the following:—S. F. Snk. Fd. *sinking fund*; Certs., *certificates*; Debs. or Dbs., *debentures*; Db. or D.Stk., *debenture stock*; Pf., Prf., or Pref., *preference*; Prefd. or Pfd., *preferred*; Dfd., *deferred*; L. or Ltd., *limited*; Sh., *share*; Ans., *annuities*; Cu. or Cm., *cumulative*; Gu or Guar., *guaranteed*; Bds., *bonds*; S., Sr., or Ser., *series*; In., Ins., Insc., *inscribed*; Dr., Drgs., Drwgs., *drawings*; Stg., Strlg., *sterling*; Lia., *liable to*; Sp., Surp., *surplus*; Per., Perp., *perpetual*; Ln. *lien*; Lo. *loan*.

The dates following the names of securities are the years of issue or of redemption. Where shares are not fully paid up, their nominal amount is given with the name so that investors may know the liability upon them.

BRITISH FUNDS, &c.

Rate.	Name.	Price.
2¾	2¾ p.c.'s (Childers') Red.. 1905	106
3	Local Loans Stk. 1912	113
3	Metro. Police Deb. Stk. 1920	105½
—	Red Sea Ind. Tel. Ann. 1908	8½
4	Canada Gv. "Intcl. Rly." 1903	109½
4	Do. do. .. 1908	113
4	Do. Bonds 1910	117
4	Do. Bonds 1913	119½
3	Egyptian Gov. Gar.	103
3	Mauritius Ins. Stk. 1940	115
4	Turkish Guar. 1855	109
31½	Bank of Ireland Stk.	392½
3½	India Rupee Paper	62½
3½	Do. 1854-5	63½
3	Do. 1896-7 1916	57½
3½	Isle of Man Deb.	104
3	Do. Deb. Stk... 1919-29	103

CORPORATION AND COUNTY STOCKS.

FREE OF STAMP DUTY.

Rate.	Name.	Price.
3½	Metropolitan Con. 1929	120
3	Do. 1941	113
2½	Do. 1920-49	101½
2½	L.C.C. Con. Stock 1920	100
3½	Comm. of Sewers, Scp., S.F. 1905	105
3½	Corp. of Lond. Bds... 1897-1902	100½
3	Do. 1897-1912	103
3½	Do., Debs. Scp. ...... S.F. 1916	106
2½	Do., Deb. Stk. Scrip .. 1927-57	100
3	Barnsley 1916-46	105
3	Barry 1914-46	101
3	Bath 1909-34	104
3	Batley 1914-44	101½
3½	Birmingham 1945	124
3	Do. 1947	112
2½	Do. 1926	99
3	Blackburn 1930	107
3	Bournemouth 1913-33	104
3½	Bradford 1945	120
3	Do. Deb. Stock .. 1954	112
3	Brighouse.............. 1916-46	100
3½	Brighton 1946	120½
2½	Do. 1957	98
3	Burton-on-Trent........ 1913-43	102½
3	Cambridge 1913-43	104
3½	Cardiff 1935	119
3	Do. 1914-54	105
3	Cheltenham.......... 1971	112
3	Chichester 1916-46	101
3½	Croydon	135½
3	Do. 1940	111½
3	Derby 1920-50	107
3	Devon C.C.......... 1917-33	106½
3½	Dewsbury 1930	111
3	Do. 1930	105
3	Dorset County 1922-32	107
3	Douglas (I. of Man) 1926	101
3	Dover 1913-43	103½
3½	Dublin 1944	113½
3	Eastbourne 1920-40	105
3	Edinburgh 1924	108
2½	Do. 1927	98
2½	Exeter 1917-57	97
3	Glamorgan County 1914-34	104
3½	Glasgow 1914	110½
3	Do. 1921	106½
2½	Do. 1925-40	99
3	Gloster 1915-55	103
3	Grimsby 1913-45	103½
3	Hampshire County 1914-34	106½
3	Hanley 1913-43	105
3	Harrogate 1914-34	104
3	Hastings 1915-54	105
2½	Hertfordshire C.C. 1916-36	99
3	Heston & Isleworth U.D.C. 1915-35	101
3	Huddersfield 1934	107
3½	Hull (1st iss.)	131½
3	Inverness 1914-44	102
3	Ipswich 1952	111
3	Lancaster.......... 1919-55	104
2½	Leeds 1927	98
3½	Leicester 1934	115½
3	Lincoln.......... 1919	104
3½	Liverpool..........	135

Corporation, &c. (*continued*):—

Rate.	Name.	Price.
3	Manchester 1941	110
3	Mansfield.......... 1915-45	100
3½	Middlesbro'.......... 1909	105½
3½	Do. 1911-13	105
3	Do. 1915	104
3	Middlesex C.C.......... 1915-35	106
3½	Newcastle 1936	118½
3½	Do. Irred.	129½
2½	Do. 1915-36	101
3	Newcastle-under-Lyme.. 1909-44	101
3	Newport (Mon.) 1915-55	104½
3	Norwich 1952	112½
3	Nottingham	117
3	Oxford 1951	111
3	Penzance 1916-46	102½
3	Plymouth 1942	112
3	Pontypridd U.D.C. 1916-46	99
3	Poole.......... 1915-45	102½
3½	Portsmouth........1916 24 & 27	112
3	Do. 1913-33	107
3	Ramsey 1920-40	100
3	Ramsgate.......... 1915-55	102
3	Reading	135
3	Do. 1962	109
3½	Rhyl U.D.C. 1953	112
3	Richmond (Surrey) 1942	106½
3	River Wear Debt Certs.	101
3	St. Helen's 1915-55	102½
3	Scarbro' 1915-50	102
2½	Sheffield 1925-57	97½
3	Shipley U.D.C.......... 1915-35	101
3	Somerset Co. 1923-33	107
3	South Shields.......... 1915-45	104
2½	Southampton 1915-45	102
3	Southend-on-Sea 1916-46	102
3	Staffs C.C. 1915-35	105
3	Stockport.......... 1914-54	104
3	Stockton 1932	106
3	Do. 1915-35	104
3	Surrey Co. 1922-32	106½
3½	Swansea	132
3	Do. 1955	106
3	Taunton 19183-9-43	102
3	Tees Conserv. Deb. Stk. 1947	101
3	Thames Conserv. "A" Deb. Stk. 1954	103
3	Do. "B" Deb. Stk. 1954	103
3	Torquay 1913-43	102½
3	Tunbridge Wells 1931	105
3	Tynemouth 1913	101
3	Wakefield.......... 1929	103
3	Walsall.......... 1932	108
3	West Bromwich.......... 1930	108½
3½	West Ham 1929	112
3	Do. 1945	107
3	West Sussex C.C. 1915-35	106
3	Weston-s.-Mare Lcl Bd. 1914-44	102
3	Weymouth & Melc. Regis 1918	101
3	Widnes.......... 1915-55	102
3	Wigan 1921	108
3	Windsor 1918-55	104
3½	Wisbech 1947	115½
3½	Wolverhampton 1932	118½
3	Do. 1924-54	107
3	York 1916-41	107

SUBJECT TO STAMP DUTY.

Rate.	Name.	Price.
3½	Belfast City & Dis. Watr. 1938	116
3	Do. Red Stk. 1953-6	106
3½	Belfast 1924	104
4	Blackburn Con. Deb. Irred.	141½
3½	Do. do. Irred..........	131
3½	Bristol	130½
3½	Burnley.......... 1933	114
2½	Chesterfield Gas & Wtr. 1916-46	98
3½	Douglas Town 1921	105
3	Dover Harb. 1st Deb... 1956	104½
3½	Hull (2nd iss.)	129½
4	Leeds Deb.......... 1927	125
3½	Do.	115½
3	Do. 1927	107½
3	Leicester 1919-44	106
4	Manchester..........	150
3	Do. 1928	105
4½	Middlesboro' Mrts. 1908	111
3½	Newark on-Trent .. 1901-41	96
3½	Sheffield 1898-1916	105½
3½	Do. 1925-36	114
3	Do. 1925	104½
3½	Southampton .... S.F.	106
4½	Stockton Mrts.......... 1908	112
3½	Worcester.. 1950	111

COLONIAL AND PROVINCIAL GOVERNMENT SECURITIES.

Rate.	Name.	Price.
6	British Columbia........ 1907	119½
4½	Do. Debs... 1917	111½
3	British Guiana Imgtn. Bds.	99½
5	Canada, "Intercol. Rail," 1903	111½
4	Do. (Bonds) 1904-5-6-8	108
4	Do. Reduced........ 1910	109
3½	Do. Bnds. 1909-34	105½
4	Do. Loan 1910-35	110
3	Do. Loan 1938	105
6	Cape of G. Hope........ 1900	—
5	Do. 1900	—
4½	Do. red. by an. draw.	111
4½	Do. 1879	111
4	Do. 1881	109
4	Do. 1917-23	118
4½	Ceylon	110
4	Do.	106½
4½	Fiji Gov. Deb. Sink. Fd.	102½
4	Jamaica Sink. Fd. 1923	103
5	Manitoba Debs.......... 1910	113
5	Do. Ster. Bds. 1888	122
4	Do. Ster. Debs.	106
4	Mauritius, Cons. Debs. 1880....	103½
4½	Natal, Sink. Fd........ 1919	120
4	Do. do. 1926	117
3½	Newfoundland Stg. Bds. 1941	100
3½	Do. do. .. 1947	100
3	Do. do.	88
5	New South Wales 1897-1902	104½
4	Do. 1903-5-8-9-12	105½
5	New Zealand 1914	118
5	Do. Cnsls. 1 p.c. per an. Sink. Fd.	104
3½	Nova Scotia Debs.	104
5	Quebec Prov. 1904-6	110
4½	Do. (drgs.)	104
5	Do. Strlg. Bds. 1919	115
4	Do. Strlg. Bds. 1928	110
4	Do. Strlg. Bds. 1934	110
4	Queensland 1913-15	108
4½	St. Lucia Debs..........	100
6	South Australia 1897-1900	103½
6	Do. 1901-1918	118
5	Do. 1911-1920	115½
4	Do. 1899-1916	105
4	Do. 1929	110½
4	Do. 1916	109½
4	Do. 1917-18-24	114
6	Tasmania 1897-1901	104
4	Do. 1908-11, 1913-14-20	108
5	Trinidad Debs., an. drw. 1 p c...	108
4	Victoria 1899-1901	101½
4½	Do. 1904	105
4	Do. Rail. Loan 1907	105
4	Do. Loans 1908-13	107
4½	West. Austr. 1 p.c. ac. Sink. Fd.	108
4	Do. do.	106

REGISTERED AND INSCRIBED STOCKS.

No stamp duty except for Canada 4 p.c. Reduced (½ per cent.).

Rate.	Name.	Price.
4	Antigua Insc. Stk. Red. 1919-44	109
3½	Barbados Insc. Stk. 1925-42	108
3	British Colum. Insc. Stk. 1941	104
4	British Guiana Insc..... 1935	120
4	Canada Stk. Regd. ..1904-5-6-8	108
4	Do. 4 p.c. (late 5 p.c.) Regd. 1910	109
3½	Do. 3½ p.c. Stock Regd. 1909-34	105½
4	Do. Ln. for 4 milln. stg. 1910-35	110
3	Do. Stk. Regd. 1938	105
2½	Do. Insc. 1947	93
4	Cape G. Hope Regd. .. 1917-23	118
4	Do. (Ln. of '83) Insc. .. 1923	119
4	Do. Cons. Stk. Insc.... 1916-36	116
3½	Do. Consol. Insc. Stock 1929-49	115
4	Ceylon Insc. Stock 1934	124
3	Do. 1940	107
4	Grenada Insc. Stock.... 1917-42	112
3½	Hong Kong Insc. Stock 1918-43	105½
4	Jamaica Insc. Stock.... 1934	121
—	Do. 1922-44	99
4	Mauritius Inscribed 1937	119
4	Natal Consd. Stk. Insc. 1927	117
4	Do. 1937	122
3½	Do. Inscribed Stock.. 1914-39	107
4	Newfoundland Inscribed 1913-38	108
4	Do. 1935	114
4	Do. Consd. Stk. Ins. 1936	114
4	N. S Wales Stock Insc. 1933	122
3½	Do. 1924	110
3½	Do. 1918	106
3	Do. 1935	101

Colonial, &c. (*continued*):—

Rate.	Name.	Price.
4	N. Zealnd. Con. Stk. Ins. 1929	116½
3½	Do. 1940	109
3	Do. Inscribed.... 1945	100½
3	Quebec (Prov.) Ins. Stk. 1937	95
4	Queensland Stock Insc. 1915-24	112½
3½	Do. 1921-4-30	106
3½	Do. 1945	109
3	Do. 1922-47	99
4	St. Lucia Insc. Stock .. 1919-44	112
4	S. Austrln. (1882-7) Reg. 1916-36	114
3½	Do. In. Stk. Reg. 1939	110
3	Do. 1916-26	100
3/	Do. 1916	100
3½	Tasmanian Insc. Stock.. 1920-40	110
4	Do. 1920-40	116
4	Trinidad Insc. Stock.... 1917-42	110
3	Do. 1922-44	98½
4	Victoria Rly. Loan '81, Inscribed Stock 1907	105
4	Victoria Insc. Stock 1908-13-19	109
4	Victoria (1885) Ins. Stk. 1920	112
3½	Do. Inscribed Stock 1921-3-6	105
4	Do. do. 1911-26	108
4	W. Austrnl. Insc. Stock 1934	120
4	Do. 1911-31	112
3½	Do. 1915-35	107
3	Do. 1915-35	98
3	Do. 1916-36	98

FOREIGN STOCKS, BONDS, &c.

COUPONS PAYABLE IN LONDON.

Last Div.	Name.	Price.
36/	Argentine Ry. Loan 6 p.c. 1881	90½
15/	Do. 5 p.c. 1884	71
30/	Do. N. Cent. Ry. Ext. 5 p.c. 1887-8-9	70
30/	Do. 5 p.c. Trsy. Convs. 1887	71
5/4½	Do. 4½ p.c. Interl. Gld. 1888	68
27/	Do. 4½ p.c. Stlg. Extrl. 1888	69
10/6	Do. 3½ p.c. External .. 1889	50
4	Do. 4 p.c. Ry. Guar. Res....	62
4½	Brazilian 1883	61
4½	Do. Gold.......... 1879	68½
4½	Do. 1888	62
36/	Buenos Ayres 1824	90
6	Do. 1882-3-6	48
6	Bulgarian 1888	95
6	Do. Mort. Bonds 1892	95
4½	Chilian 1885	78
4½	Do. 1886	79
4½	Do. 1887	78
4½	Do. 1889	82½
5	Do. 1892	87
4½	Do. 1893	78
4½	Do. 1895	79
5	Do. 1896	86
7	Chinese Silver 1894	102
6	Do. Gold 1895	106
6	Do. Apl. '95 by dwgs. 1901-15	110
5	Do. Red. dwgs. in 36 yr. 1896	102
5	Do. Do. Regis. 1896	102
1½	Colmbn. 1½ to 3 p.c. Ext. Bds. 1896	18
6	Cordova, Prov. 1886	27
—	Do. Eng. Ass. Certs.	26
—	Do. 6 p.c. 1887-8	27
—	Do. Eng. Ass. Certs.	26
3	Costa Rica "A"	32
2½	Do. "B"	27
3	Danish Gold 1914	98
10/	Ecuador N. Ext. Bds. 4½ p.c. ascn. to 5 p.c.	21
3½	Egypt'n Ins. Stk. lia. Stp. Dty. 1890	102
4½	Do. State Domain 1878	105½
4	Do. D. Sanieh, Red. .. 1905	105½
6	Entre Rios.......... 1886-8	36
6	Do. Fndg. Ln. Bds. 1894-1921	32
6	Do. do. Parana City......	27½
15/	Greek 1881	38
15/	Do. 1884	38
12/	Do. Rentes..........	31
15/	Do. (Piræus-Larissa Ry.)	36
7/6	Do. Fundg. Loan 1893	46
4	Guatemala Extl. Debt..........	34
6	Hawaiian	102½
4	Hungarian Gold Rentes........	102½
4	Do. 1895	91½
3	Italian Irriga. Guar.	112½
6	Do. Maremmana	94½
5	Japan 5 p.c.	102
5	Mexican (Nat. R. Tehuantp c.)..	96½
5	Do Extrl. 1890	96½

Foreign Stocks, &c. (*continued*):—

Last Div.	Name.	Price.
6	Mexican Extrl. 1893	98½
5	Do. Intrnl. Cons. Slvr.	39
5	Do. Intern. Rd. Bds. 2d. Ser.	39
4	Nicaragua 1886................	50
3½	Norwegian, red. 1937, or earlier	100
3	Do. do. 1965, do.	93
3½	Do. 3½ p.c. Bnds.	103
1	Paraguay 1p.c. ris. 3p.c. 1886-96	17
5	Russian, 1822, £ Strlg.	151½
3	Do. 1859	93
4	Do. (Nicolas Ry.) 1867-9 ..	104
3	Do. Transcauc. Ry. 1882 ..	94
4	Do. Con. R. R. Bd. Ser. I., 1889 ..	104
4	Do. Do. II., 1889 ..	104
4	Do. Do. III., 1891 ..	103½
3½	Do. Bonds	101½
4	Do. Ln. (Dvinsk and Vitbsk)	103
6	Salvador 1889................	67½
—	S Domingo 4s. Unified .. 1980	65½
6	San Luis Potosi Stg. 1889	94½
5	San Paulo (Brzl.), Stg. 1888	91½
6	Santa Fé 1883-4................	37
—	Do. Eng. Ass. Certs. Dep...	35½
5	Do. 1888	48
—	Do. Eng. Ass. Certs. Dpsit..	47
5	Do. (W. Cnt. Col. Rly.) Mrt.	27
5	Do. & Reconq. Rly. Mort...	27
5	Spanish Quickslvr Mort. 1870 ..	103
3½	Swedish 1880	103
3	Do. 1888	99
53	Do. Conversion Loan 1894..	101
45	Trans. Gov. Loan Red...1903-42	105
59/	Tucuman (Prov.) 1888..........	69
	Turkish, Secd. on Egypt. Trib.	104½
3½	Turkish, Egpt. Trib., Ott. Bd., '94	100
4	Do. Priority 1890..........	93
1	Do. Convted Series, "A"..	65½
5	Do. Customs Ln. 1886......	97½
5	Uruguay Bonds 1896	55
3	Venzula New Con. Debt 1881....	35½

COUPONS PAYABLE ABROAD.

Last Div.	Name.	Price.
7	Argent. Nat. Cedla. Sries, "B".	36
5	Austrian Ster. Rnts., ex 10fl., 1870	85
5	Do. do. do.	86
5	Do. Paper do. 1870	84
5	Do. do. do.	86
4	Do. Gld Rentes 1876	103
2½	Belgian exchange 25 fr.	92
3	Do. do.	101
3½	Danish Int., 1887, Rd. 1896	97½
3½	Do. '87, Red. by pur. or draw. fr. Dec., 1900	98½
2½	Dutch Certs. ex 12 gldrs.	87
3	Do. Bonds	100
3	Do. Insc. Stk.........	99
3½	French Rentes	106½
3	Do. 1878, '81-4., Red.	101
3	German Imp. Ln. 1891..........	97
3	Do. do. 1892-3	97
3	Do. do. 1890-4	96
5	Japan Cons. Ln., '92, 3, & 5, Red.	47
36/9	Prussian Consols	102
3	" Cons. Stg. Ln. 1891....	97
4	Rumanian Bds. 1890	—
4	Do. do. 1891	—
4	Utd. States, 1877, Red. 1907	116
4	Do. 1895, 30 yrs.......	131½
3½	Do. Maschsetts Gl. 1935	113½
3½	Do. Gold Bonds 1923	110½
3½	Virginia Cpn. Bds., 3 p.c. from July, 1901	72

BRITISH RAILWAYS.

ORD. SHARES AND STOCKS.

Last Div.	Name.	Price.
10	Barry, Ord.	281½
4	Do. Prefd.	127
6	Do. Defd.	152½
5½	Caledonian, Ord..........	158
3	Do. Prefd.	100½
2½	Do. Defd. Ord., No. 1	5⅞
—	Cambrian, Ord..........	6⅞
—	Do. Coast Cons.	6¾
32/	Cardiff Ry. Pref. Ord.	117
3/	Central Lond. £10 Ord. Sh.	10½
1/9½	Do. do. £6 paid......	6½
3½d.	Do. Pref. Half-Shares..	1¼
1/6	Do. Def. do..........	4¾
1½	City and S. London	67
	East London, Cons.	7
1½	Furness	68½
—	Glasgow and S. West. Pfd.	85
—	Do. do. Dfd.	67
—	Great Central, Ord....1894	40½
32/6	Do. London Exten.....	77
3½	Great N. of Scotland......	124
4	Great Northern, Prefd.....	120
—	Do. Consolidated "A"	52
—	Do. do. "B"	194½
4	Highland	87½
4	Isle of Wight, Prefd.	122½
4	Do. Defd.	85½
2½	Lancs. Derbys. and E. Cst.	
8½	L. Brighton and S. C. Ord.	186
37/11½	Do. New all pd........	186
6	Do. Prefd. Ord.	196½
10/	Do. Contgt. Rights Certs.	80½
5½	Lond. and S. Western Ord.	232½
4	Do. Preferred	138
6½	Lond., Tilb., and Southend	132½
—	Mersey, £20 shares	1
—	Metropolitan, New Ord. ..	129
2½	Do. Surplus Lands....	96
4	North Cornwall, 4 p.c. Pref.	106½
7/6	Do. Deferred	27½
7½	North London............	231½
3	North Staffordshire	133

British Railways (*continued*):—

Last Div.	Name.	Price.
1/6	Plymouth, Devenport, and S. W. Junc. £10	9
3/	Port Talbot £10 Shares ..	8½
9d.	Rhondda Swns. B. £10 Sh.	5½
10	Rhymney, Cons...........	272½
4	Do. Prefd.	125
—	Do. Defd.	149½
6½	Scarboro', Bridlington Junc.	47½
6½	South Eastern, Ord.........	152
6	Do. Pref.	193
3½	Taff Vale	83
25/	Vale of Glamorgan........	127½
2/6½	Waterloo & City £10 shares	14

LEASED AT FIXED RENTALS.

Last Div.	Name.	Price.
4	Birkenhead	149
5.19.0	East Lincnshire...........	215
5½	Hamamith. & City Ord. ..	192½
4½	Lond. and Blackwll.	164
4½	Do. £10 4½ p. c. Pref...	163½
56/6	Lond. & Green. Ord........	102
5	Do. 5 p. c. Pref.	180½
5	Nor. and Eastn. £50 Ord...	90
6	Do. ..	107
3½	N. Cornwall 3½ p. c. Stk...	128½
4⅕	Nott. & Granthm. R.& C...	150
3½	Portptk.& Wigtn.Guar.Stk.	126
9	Vict. Stn. & Pimlico Ord...	317½
4½	Do. 4½ p. c. Pref....	163½
4/	West Lond. £20 Ord. Shs.	14½
4⅕	Weymouth & Portld.......	160½

DEBENTURE STOCKS.

Last Div.	Name.	Price.
4	Alexandra Dks. & Ry.	132½
3	Barry, Cons.	109
4	Brecon & Mrthyr, New A	129
4	Do. New B	105
4	Caledonian	153
4	Cambrian "A"	134½
4	Do. "B"	132½
4	Do. "C"	128½
4	Do. "D"	110½
3	Cardiff Rly.	105
4	City and S. Lond.	139
3½	Cleator & Working Junc...	118½
3	Devon & Som. "A"	105½
16/3	Do. "B" 4 p. c.	36
—	Do. "C" 4 p. c.	10
4	E. Lond. and Ch. 4 p. c. A	137
8/	Do. and B	67½
—	Do. 3rd Ch. 4 p. c. ..	19½
—	Do. 4th do.	9½
3½	Do. 1st (3½ p. c.)	128½
2½	Do. 2½ p.c.(Whitech.Exn)	88
4	Forth Bridge	146
4	Furness	142½
4	Glasgow and S. Western ..	151
5	Gt. Central	—
4½	Do.	159½
4	Gt. Eastern	149
4	Gt.N.of Scotland..........	148½
3	Gt. Northern	115
4	Gt. Western	153½
4½	Do.	161½
4½	Do.	171½
5	Do.	190
2½	Do.	100
4	Highland	143½
3	Hull and Barnsley	106
3	Do. 2nd (3-4 p. c)...	124
4	Isle of Wight	144½
3	Do. Cent. "A"..	92½
4½	Do. "B"	115½
4	Do. "C"	82½
3	Lancs. & Yorkshire	115
4	Lancs. Derbys. & E. Cst...	123½
4	Lpool St.Hlen's & S.Lancs.	126
4½	Ldn. and Blackwall	159
4	Ldn. and Greenwich......	149½
4	Lond., Brighton, &c.	151
4½	Do.	169
4½	Lond., Chath., &c., Arb...	159
4½	Do. "B"..	158½
4	Do.	140
4	Do. 1883....	138
3	Do.	107
3	Lond. & N. Western......	117
3	Lond. & S. Westn. "A"..	116
3	Do. Consld.	116
4	Lond., Til., & Southend ..	149½
—	Mersey, 5 p. c. (Act, 1866)	65
4	Metropolitan	150
4½	Do.	164½
3½	Do.	128½
6	Met. District	209½
4	Do.	139
3	Midland	116
4½	Mid-Wales "A"	137½
4	Neath & Brecon 1st	129
4	Do. "A 1" ..	121
3	North British	113
3	Do. 1893	111½
3½	N. Cornwall, Launcstn., &c.	128½

Debenture Stocks (*continued*):—

Last Div.	Name.	Price.
3	North Eastern............	115
4½	North London............	167
3	N. Staffordshire	114
4	Plym. Devpt. & S.W. Jn...	141½
4	Rhondda and Swan. Bay..	130½
4	Rhymney	148
4	South-Eastern............	151½
5	Do.	188½
3½	Do.	130
3	Do.	116
3	Taff Vale	111
4	Tottenham & For. Gate ..	146
3	Vale of Glamorgan	106½
3	West Highld.(Gtd.by N.B.)	110½
4	Wrexham, Mold, &c. "A"	115½
4	Do. "B"	102½
4	Do. "C"	97½

GUARANTEED SHARES AND STOCKS.

Last Div.	Name.	Price.
4	Caledonian	150½
4	Do.	149
4	Forth Bridge	146
4	Furness 1881	137½
4	Glasgow & S. Western	149
4	Do. St. Enoch, Rent	149
6	Gt. Central	202
4½	Do. 1st Pref.	153½
3½	Do. Pref.	106
5	Do. Irred. S.Y. Rent	166½
4½	Do. do.	140½
4	Gt. Eastern, Rent	147
5	Do. Metropolitan..	182½
4	Do.	147
4	Gt. N. of Scotland........	141
4	Gt. Northern	150
5	Gt. Western, Rent	185½
5	Do. Cons.	187½
4	Lancs. & Yorkshire	149
5	L., Brighton & S. C.......	183½
3½	L., Chat. & D. (Shrtlds.)..	110½
4	L. & North Western	152
4	L. & South Western.. 1881	151
4½	Met. District, Ealing Rent	152
4½	Do. Fulham Rent	152
4	Do. Midland Rent	143½
4	Do. Mid. & Dist. Guar.	133½
4	Midland, Rent............	151½
4	Do. Cons.	151½
3	Mid.&G.N. Jt., "A" Rnt..	109½
3	N. British, Lien	108
4	Do. Cons.Pref.No. 1	146
3	N.Cornwall, Wadsbrge. Gu.	108
4	N. Eastern	150
5	N. Staff. Trent & M. £20Shs.	36½
3½	Nott. Suburban Ord.	126½
20/6	S. E. Perp. Ann.	36½
4½	Do. 4½ p.c............	165½
3½	S. Yorks. Junc. Ord.	118½
4½	W. Cornwall (G. W., Br., Ex., & S. Dev. Joint Rent	166½
3	W. Highl. Ord. Stk. (Gua., N.B.)................	106½

PREFERENCE SHARES AND STOCKS.

DIVIDENDS CONTINGENT ON PROFIT OF YEAR.

Last Div.	Name	Price.
4½	Alexandra Dks. & Ry. "A"	128½
5	Barry (First)	169½
4	Do. Consolidated......	139½
4	Caledonian Cons., No. 1 ..	147½
4	Do. do. No. 2 ..	147
5	Do. do. 1878	181½
4	Do. Pref. 1884	146
4	Do. do. 1887(Conv.)	155
—	Cambrian, No. 1 4 p.c. Pref.	74½
—	Do. No. 2 do.	39½
—	Do. No. 3 do.	19
—	Do. No. 4 do.	10
5	City & S. Lond. £10 shares	15½
—	Do. New	14
4	Furness, Cons. 1881	134½
4	Do. ......"A" 1881	131½
4	Do. ......"B" 1883	129½
4	Glasgow & S. Western	147
4	Do. No. 2....	146
4	Do. 1888	144½
4	Do. 1892	143½
5	Gt. Central	167½
4	Do.	134½
5	Do. Conv..... 1872	154½
5	Do. do. 1874	154½
5	Do. do. 1876	154½
5	Do. do. 1879	153½
5	Do. do. 1881	153½
4	Do. 1889	115½
4	Do. 1891	110½
5	Do. 1894	114½
4	Gt. Eastern, Cons.........	144
4	Do. 1886	143
4	Do. 1881	143
4	Do. 1884	143

Preference Shares, &c. (*continued*):—

Last Div.	Name.	Price.
4	Gt. Eastern, Cons.... 1887	143
4	Do. 1888	143
3½	Do. 1890	122½
3½	Do. 1893	120½
—	Do. (Int. fr. Jan '99) 1893	117½
4	Gt. North Scotland "A"..	136½
4	Do. "B"..	135½
4	Gt. Northern, Cons.	147½
3	Do. 1896	108½
5	Gt. Western Cons.........	186½
36/11	Hull & Barnsley Red. at 115	108
4	Isle of Wight	135½
3	Lancs. & Yorkshire, Cons.	109
2/2½	Lanc. Drby & E.C. 5 p.c. £10	10½
—	Do. 5 p.c. 2nd £10	9
5	Lond., Bright., &c., Cons.	181½
5	Do. 2nd Cons.	180½
4½	Lond., Chat. & Dov. Arbitr.	155½
25/	Do. 2nd Pref. 4½ p.c.	94
4	Lond. & N. Western......	150
4	Lond. & S. Western.. 1881	149
4	Do. 1884	147½
3½	Do.	130
4	Lond., Tilbury & Southend	146
4	Do. Cons., 1887	146
4	Do 1891	145
—	Mersey, 5 p.c. Perp.	—
4	Metropolitan, Perp.	143½
4	Do. 1882	143½
4	Do. Irred.	143½
4	Do. 1887	143½
4	Do. New........	143½
4½	Do.	146½
3½	Do.	124½
3	Do. Guar.	102½
2½	Metrop. Dist. Exten 5 p.c.	111
4	Midland, Cons. Perpetual..	149
4	N. British Cons., No. 2 ..	141
4½	Do. Edin. & Glasgow	156½
5	Do. 1865	172½
5	Do. Conv..... 1874	172½
4½	Do. 1875	156
4½	Do. Conv. 1875	156½
5	Do. do. 1879	172½
4	Do. do. 1884	141
4	Do. do. 1888	141
4	Do. do. 1890	141
4	Do. do. 1892	140
4	N. Eastern	147½
4½	N. Lond., Cons........1866	178½
4½	Do. 2nd Cons. .. 1875	164½
3	N. Staffordshire	110½
4½	Plym. Devpt. & S. W. Junc.	152½
9½d.	Port Talbot, &c., 4 p.c. £10 Shares, 4 paid	5
5/	Rhondda & Swansea Bay, 5 p.c. £10 Shares	13½
4	Rhymney, Cons...........	142
4½	S. Eastern, Cons.	163½
5	Do. do.	181½
4	Do. Vested Cos'.....	145
4	Do. 1891	146
3½	Do. 1893	126
2	Do. 3 p.c. after July 1900	105
4	Taff Vale	143

INDIAN RAILWAYS.

Last Div.	Name.	Paid.	Price.
3½	Assam Bengal, Ld., (3½ p.c. till June 30, then 3 p.c.)	100	105
4/	Barsi Light, Ld., £10 Shs.	10	10½
6	Bengal and N. West., Ld.	100	148½
4/	Do. £10 Shares	10	14½
3/6	Do. 3½ p.c. Cum. Pf. Shs.	10	10½
8½d.	Do.	4	4½
2/3½	Bengal Central, Ld., £10 (3½ p.c. + ½th net earn)	5	5½
3	Bengal Dooars, Ld.	100	118
4	Bengal Nagpr., Lim. (gua. 4 p.c. + 4th sp. pfts.) ..	100	115
7½	Bombay, Baroda, and C. I. (gua. 5 p.c.)	100	209
36/1	Burma, Ld. (gua. 2½ p.c. and ½ p.c. add. till 1901)	100	110½
1/7	Do. £10 Shares	2½	3½
4	Delhi Umb. Kalka, Ld., Gua. 3½ p.c. + net earn.	100	121
4	Do. Deb.Stk., 1890 (1926)	100	113
9/10	Estn. Bengal, "A" An. 1957	—	26
9/	Do. "B" 1957	—	31
4	Do. Gua. Deb. Stock ..	100	144½
9/7½	East Ind. Ann. "A" (1953)	—	28
8/4½	Do. "C"	—	30
8/11½	Do. "B"	—	32
6⅝	Do. Def. Ann. Cap. (gua. 4 p.c. + ½th sp. pfts.)	—	155
115/9	East Ind. Def. Ann. "D"	—	161
4½	East Ind. Irred. Stock ..	100	166½
5	Gt. Indian Penin., Gua. 5 p.c. + ½ surplus profits..	100	170
4	Do. Irred. 4 p.c. Deb. St.	100	146½
4	Indian Mid., Ld. (gua. 4 p.c. + ½th surplus pfts.)	100	115
51/	Madras Guar. + ½ sp. pfts.	100	167
48/6	Do. do.	100	157
46/	Do. do.	100	147
4	Nilgiri, Ld., 1st Deb.Stk.	100	97
4	Oude & Rohil. Db.Stk. Rd.	100	108
5⅕	Rohil. and Kumaon, Ld.	100	132
9/11	Scinde, Punj., and Delhi, "A" Ann., 1958	—	30
9/1	Do. "B" do. ..	—	31

Indian Railways (*continued*) :—

Last Div.	Name.	Paid.	Price.
4	South Behar, Ld., £10 shs.	100	100
3½	Do. Deb. Stk. Red.	100	103
4½	South Ind., Gu. Deb. Stk.	100	166½
5	South Indian, Ld. (gua. 3 p.c., and ½ spls. profits)	100	121½
5	Sthn. Mahratta, Ld. (3½ p.c. & ½th net earnings)	100	120
4	Do. Deb. Stk. Red.	100	124
3½	Southern Punjab, Ld.	100	112
3½	Do. Deb. Stk. Red.	—	107
5	Nizam's Gua. State, Ld. (†	100	114½
4	Do. Mort. Deb., 1936	100	110
4	Do. do. Reg.	100	108
17/3½	Nizam's Gua. State, Ld., 3½ p.c. Mt. Deb. bearer	—	95½
17/3½	Do. Reg. do. ..	—	94½
5	W. of India Portgese., Ld.	100	68½
5	Do. Deb. Stk., Red	100	98

RAILWAYS.—BRITISH POSSESSIONS.

Last Div.	Name.	Paid.	Price.
5	Atlantic & N.W. Gua. 1 Mt. Bds., 1937	100	127
5/3	Buff. & L. Huron Ord. Sh.	10	13½
5½	Do. 1st Mt. Perp. Bds. 1879	100	143½
5½	Do. 2nd Mt. Perp. Bds.	100	143½
—	Calgary & Edmon. 6 p.c. 1st Mt. Stg. Bds. Red..	100	74½
5	Canada Cent. 1st Mt. Bds. Red.	100	105
4	Can. Pacific Pref. Stk.....	100	102
5	Do. Strl. 1st Mt. Deb. Bds. 1915	100	118
3½	Do. Ld. Grnt. Bds., 1938..	100	108
3½	Do. Ld. Grnt. Ins. Stk. ..	100	108
4	Do. Perp. Cons. Deb. Stk.	100	117
5	Do. Algoma Bch. 1st Mt. Bds., 1937	100	122
2	Demerara, Original Stock	100	49
7	Do. Perp. Pref. Stk.......	100	157½
9½d.	Do. 4 p.c. Cum. Ext. Pref. £10 Shs.	4	6½
—	Dominion Atlntc. Ord. Stk.	100	35½
25/	Do. 5 p.c. Pref. Stk.....	100	101
4	Do. 1st. Deb. Stk.......	100	110
4	Do. 2nd do. Red.	100	100
—	EmuBay&Mt.Bischoff,Ld.	5	4½
4½	Do. Irred. Deb. Stk....	100	98
nil.	Gd. Trunk of Canada, Stk.	100	8½
6	Do. 2nd. Equip. Mt. Bds.	100	131½
5	Do. Perp. Deb. Stk......	100	140½
5	Do. Gt. Westn. Deb. Stk.	100	131½
5	Do. Nthn. of Can. 1st Mt. Bds., 1902	100	106
4	Do. do. Deb. Stk	100	103
5	Do. G. T. Geor. Bay & L. Erie 1 Mt., 1903	100	104
5	Do. Mid. of Can. Stl. 1st Mt. (Mid. Sec.) 1908	100	108
5	Do. do. Cons. 1 Mt. Bds. 1912	100	108
5	Do. Mont. & Champ. 1 Mt. Bds., 1902	100	104
	Do. Welln., Grey & Brce. 7 p.c. Bds. 1 Mt.	100	111
4	Jamaica 1st Mtg. Bds. Red.	—	104
—	Manitoba & N. W., 6 p.c. 1st Mt. Bds., Red	100	—
—	Do. Ldn. Bdhldrs. Certs.	—	—
5	Manitoba S. W. Col. 1 Mt. Bd., 1934 $1,000 price %	—	120
—	Mid. of W. Aust. Ld. 6 p.c. 1 Mt. Dbs., Red.	100	25
4	Do. Deb. Bds., Red.	100	103
4	Nakusp & Slocan Bds., 1918	100	106
3	Natal Zululand Ld. Debs.,	100	79½
5	N. Brunswick 1st Mt. Stg. Bds., 1934	100	122
4	Do. Perp. Cons. Deb. Stk.	100	114
—	N. Zealand Mid., Ld., 5 p.c 1st Mt. Debs...........	100	35
6	Ontario & Queb. Cap. Stk.	$100	157½
5	Do. Perm. Deb. Stk......	100	145½
—	Qu'Appelle, L. Lake & Sask. 6 p.c. 1 Mt. Bds. Red.	100	43½
5	Queb. & L. S. John, 1st Mt. Bds., 1909	100	25½
5	Quebec Cent., Prior Ln. Bds., 1908	100	107
5½	Do. 5 p.c. Inc. Bds.	100	40
4	St. Lawr. & Ott. Stl. 1st Mt.	100	113
4	Shuswap & Okan., 1st Mt. Deb. Bds., 1915	100	76
5	Temiscouata, 5 p.c. Stl. 1st Deb. Bds., Red.........	100	9½
5	Do. (S. Franc. Brch.) 5 p.c. Stl. 1 Mt. Db. Bds., 1910	100	12½
4	Toronto, Grey & B. 1st Mt.	100	113
1/2½	Well. & Mana. £5 Shs. ..	1	1
5	Do. Debs., 1908........	100	110
5	Do. 2nd Debs., 1908....	100	109
5	Do. 3rd do., 1908	100	108
6	Atlan. & St. Law. Shs., 6 p.c.	100	167
5	Gd. Trunk Mt. Bds., 1934	100	116½
5	Michigan Air Line, 5 p.c. 1st Mt. Bds., 1902......	100	104
4	Minneap., S. P. & Slt. Ste. Mar, 1st M. Bds., 1938	$1000	98

AMERICAN RAILROAD STOCKS AND SHARES.

Last Div.	Name.	Paid.	Price.
6/	Alab. Gt. Sthn. A 6 p.c. Pref.	10/.	9
—	Do. do "B" Ord. ..	10/.	2
—	Alabma. N. Orl.-Tex. &c., "A" Pref.	10/.	½
—	Do. "B" Def.	10/.	½
4½	Atlant. First Lsd. Ls. Rtl. Trust.................	Stk.	102
$2	Baltimore & Ohio Com. ..	$100	17
—	Baltimore Ohio S.W. Pref.	$100	7
—	Chesap. & Ohio Com.	$100	22½
—	Chic. Gt. West. 5 p.c. Pref. Stock "A"	$100	32½
—	Do. do. Scrip. In.......	—	30½
8/3	Do. 4 p.c. Deb. Stk.......	$100	70
4	Do. Interest in Scrip	$100	67½
$4	Chic. Junc. Rl. & Un. Stk. Yds. Com.	$100	119½
$1½	Do. 6 p.c. Cum. Pref.	$100	118½
$3½	Chic. Mil. & St. P. Pref...	$100	152½
7	Cleve. & Pittsburgh......	$10	86½
$1½	Clev., Cincin., Chic., & St. Louis Com.	$100	—
—	Erie 4 p.c. Non-Cum. 1st Pf.	—	41
—	Do. 4 p.c. do. 2nd Pf.	—	20
—	Gt. Northern Pref.	$100	155
$2½	Illinois Cen. Lsd. Lines ..	$100	99
—	Kansas City, Pitts & G. ..	$100	24
$3	L. Shore & Mich. Sth. C.	$100	197½
—	Mex. Cen. Ltd. Com.	$100	6
—	Miss. Kan. & Tex. Pref...	$100	40
2½	N.Y., Pen. & O. 1st Mt. Tst. Ltd., Ord.	—	50
4	Do. 1st Mort. Deb. Stk. ..	$100	93½
8	North Pennsylvania	$50	—
—	Northn. Pacific, Com.....	$100	24
1½	Pitts. F. Wayne & Chic...	$100	176
—	Reading 1st Pref.	$50	24½
—	Do. 2nd Pref.	$50	13
—	S. Louis & S. Fran. Com.	$100	7
—	Do. 2nd Pref.	$100	26
6	St. Louis Bridge 1st Pref..	$100	107
3	Do. 2nd Pref.	$100	50
6	Tunnel Rail. of St. Louis	$100	107
$1½	St. Paul, Min. and Man...	$100	136
—	Southern, Com.	$100	9½
—	Wabash, Common........	$100	7½

AMERICAN RAILROAD BONDS. CURRENCY.

Last Div.	Name.	Price.
7	Albany & Susq. 1 Con. Mrt. 1906	122½
7	Allegheny Val. 1 Mt....... 1910	127½
5	Burling., Cedar Rap. & N. 1 Mt. 1906	109½
5	Canada Southern 1 Mt..... 1908	111
5	Chic. & N. West. Sk. Fd. Db. 1933	120½
5	Do. Deb. Coupon 1921	115½
6	Chicago & Tomah 1905	112½
5	Chic. Burl. & Q. Skg. Fd. 1901	102½
4	Do. Nebraska Ext....... —	102
6	Chic., Mil., & S. Pl., 1 Mt. S.W. Div............... 1909	117½
7	Do. (S. Paul Div.) 1 Mt. 1902	132½
5	Do. (La Cross & D. 1919	112½
7	Do. 1 Mt. (Hast. & Dak.) 1910	132
5	Do. Chic. & Mis. Riv. 1 Mt. 1926	112½
5	Chic., Rock Is. and Pac. 1 Mt. Ext. 1934	108
6	Det., G. Haven & Mil. Equip 1918	110
6	Do. do. Cons. Mt. 1918	104½
6	Ill. Cent., 1 Mt., Chic. & S. 1898	—
7	Indianap. & Vin., 1 Mt. .. 1908	125
6	Do. do. 2 Mt. .. 1900	104½
6	Lehigh Val., Cons. Mt..... 1923	112½
—	Mexic. Cent., Ln. 2 Cons. Inc. —	7
7	N.Y. Cent. & H.R. Mt. Bonds 1903	119½
5	Do. Deb. 1904	109½
6	Penns. Cons. S. F M. 1905	119½
4	West Shore, 1 Mt. 2361	110

DITTO—GOLD.

Last Div.	Name.	Price.
6	Alabama Gt. Sthn. 1 Mt. ..1908	112
5	Do. Mid. 1 1928	96
4	Allegheny Val. Gen. Mt. ..1942	108
4	Atch., Top., & S. Fé Gn. Mt. 1995	95
3	Do. Adj. Mt. 1995	63½
5	Do. Equipt. Tmst. ...... —	104½
5	Atlantic & Dan. 1 Mt.......1950	94½
5	Baltimore & Ohio..........1925	100
5	Do. Speyer's Tst. Recpts. 1925	100
5	Do. Cons. Mt. 1988	104
4½	Do. 4½ p.c. 1 Mt. Term. 1934	85
4½	Do. Brown Shipley's Dep. Cts. —	85
5	Balt. Belt 5 p.c. 1 Mort.....1990	90
4½	Balt. & Ohio S.W. 1 Mt. ..1990	105
4½	Do. 4½ p.c. 1 Cons. Mt. 1893 1993	80
—	Do. Inc. Mt. 5 p.c. Cl. A —	31
—	Do. do. Cl. B —	11
5	Balt. & Ohio S.W. Term 5 p.c. 1942	99½
6	Balt. & Ptmac (Mn. L.) 1 Mt. 1911	127½
6	Do. do. (Tunnel) 1 Mt. 1911	126
4	Beech Creek 1 Mt. 1936	109
5	Do 2 Mort. 1936	116
4	Carthage & Adiron 1 Mt...1981	109

American Railroad Bonds—Gold (*continued*) :—

Last Div.	Name.	Price.
5	Cent. of Georgia 1 Mort. ...1945	117½
5	Do. Cons. Mt. 1945	92½
5	Cent. of N. Jrsy. Gn. Mt...1987	118
6	Central Pacific, 1 Mort. 1898	102½
6	Do. Speyer's Certs....... —	106
5	Do. Land Grant 1900	102
5	Chesap. & Ohio 1st Cons. Mt. 1939	119
4½	Do. Gen. Mt. 1992	84
6	Chic. & W. Ind. Gen. Mt. Skg. Fd. 1932	120
5	Chic. Mil. & St. Pl. (Chic. & L. Sup.) 1 Mt. 1921	114½
5	Do. Chic. & Pac. W. 1921	119½
5	Do. Wisc. & Minn. 1 Mt. 1921	114½
5	Do. Terminal Mt. 1914	114½
4	Do. General Mt. 1989	108
5	Chic. St. L. & N. Orleans..1951	122½
4	Do. 1 Mort. (Memphis) ..1951	105½
4	Clevel., Cin., Chic. & St. L., 1 Mt. (Cairo) 1939	90
4	Do. 1 Mt. (Cinc., Wab., & Mich.) 1991	98
4	Do. 1 Col. Tst. Mt. (S. Louis) 1990	98½
4	Do. General Mt. 1993	84
4½	Clevel. & Mar. Mt. 1935	112
4½	Clevel. & Pittsburgh 1942	122½
4½	Do. Series B. 1942	124½
—	Colorado Mid. 1 Mt. 1936	68
—	Do. Bdhrs.' Comm. Certs. —	68
4	Dnvr. & R. Gde. 1 Cons. Mt. 1936	97
5	Do. Imp. Mort...........1928	93
4	Detroit & Mack. 1 Lien 1995	92½
5	E. Tennes., Virg., & Grgia. Cons. Mt. 1956	114½
5	Elmira, Cort., & Nthn. Mt. 1914	102½
4	Erie 1 Cons. Mt. Pr. Ln. ..1996	94
3	Do. Gen. Lien 1996	75
6	Galvest., Harrisb., &c., 1 Mt.....	107½
5	Georgia, Car. & N. 1 Mt. ..1929	96
4½	Gd. Rpds. & Inda. Ex. 1 Mt. 1941	112½
5	Do. 1 Mt. (Muskegon) ..1926	39½
3½	Illinois Cent. 1 Mt. 1951	104½
4	Do. 1952	107
4	Do. Cairo Bdge. ..1950	103
4	Do. 1953	106
4	Do. General Mort. ..1904	102½
—	Kans. City, Pitts. & G. 1 M. 1923	83
3½	L. Shore & Mich. Southern 1997	109
4½	Lehigh Val. N.Y. 1 Mt.....1940	106
5	Lehigh Val. Term. 1 Mt. ..1941	112½
5	Long Island 1931	122½
5	Do. Deb...........1934	102
5	Do. (N. Shore Bch.) 1 Cons. Mt. 1932	96
6	Louisville & Nash. G. Mt. .1930	122
6	Do. 2 Mt. Sk. Fd. (S. & N. Alabama........1910	108
6	Do. 1 Mt. N. Orl. & Mb. 1930	122½
5	Do. 1 Mt. Coll. Tst. 1931	109
4	Do. Unified 1940	91
4½	Do. Mobile & Montgy. 1 Mt. 1945	105½
4	Manhattan Cons. Mt. 1990	100
4	Mexican Cent. Cons. Mt. ..1911	68
—	Do. 1 Cons. Inc, ...	16
6	Mexican Nat. 1 Mt.........1927	108
3	Do. 2 Mt. 6 p.c. Inc. A 1917	58
—	Do. do. B..1917	10
3	Do. Matheson's Certs.....	—
3	Michig. Cnt. (Battle Ck. & S.) 1 Mt. 1989	88
6	Minneap. & S. L. 1 Mt. Pacific Ext. 1921	120½
5	Do. 1 Consold. 1934	110
4	Minne., Slt. S. M. & A. 1 Mt. 1926	100
5	Minneapolis Westn. 1 Mt...1911	105½
4	Miss. Kans. & Tex. 1 Mt...1990	92
4	Do. 2 do. 1990	65
4	Mobile & Birm. Mt. Inc....1945	38
5	Do. P. Lien 1945	88
4	Mohawk & Mal. 1 Mt......1991	108
5	Montana Cent. 1 Mt.......1937	111½
5	Nashv., Chattan., & S. L. 1 Cons. Mt................1928	104½
5	Nash., Flor., & Shff. Mt...1937	97
4	N. Y. & Putnam 1 Cons. Mt. 1993	110
5	N. Y., Brooklyn, & Man. B. 1 Cons. Mt..............1935	110
4	N. Y. Cent. & Hud. R. Deb. Certs. 1890 1905	107
4	Do. Ext. Debt. Certs....1905	107
7	N. Y., L. Erie, & W. 1 Cons. Mt. (Erie) 1920	146
7	Do. 1 Con. Mt. Fd. Coup. 1920	143
5	N. Y., Onto., & W. Cons. 1 Mt.......................1939	110
4	Do. 4 p.c. Refund. Mt...1992	102
5	N. Y. & Rockaway B. 1 Mt. 1927	102½
6	Norfolk & West. Gn. Mt....1931	128
6	Do. Imp. & Ext.........1934	120
4	Do. 1 Cons. Mt......... —	85
6	N. Pacific Gn. 1 Mt. Ld. Gt. 1921	122
4	Do. P. Ln. Rl. & Ld. Gt. —	99
3	Do. Gn. Ln. Rl. & Ld. Gt. —	64
5	Oregon & Calif. 1 Mt.......1927	82
5	Oregon Rl. & Nav. Col. Tst. —	—
—	Oreg. Sh. Line & Utah Col. Trst. 5 p.c. G. Bonds 1919	50
6	Panama Skg. Fd. Subsidy..1910	106½
4½	Pennsylvania Rlrd. 1913	115½
4	Do. Equip. Tst. Ser. A..1914	104
4	Do. Cons. Mt...........1943	115
4½	Penna. Company 1st Mort. 1921	116½
5	Perkiomen 1 Mrt., 2nd ser..1918	91½
4½	{ Pitts., C., C., & St. Ls. Con. Mt. G.B., Ser. A } 1940-2	115
4	Do. Cons. Mort., Ser. D..1945	105
6	Pittsbgh., Cle., & Toledo ..1922	107½
4	Reading, Phil., & R. Genl. 1997	88
5	Richmond & Dan. Equip. ..1909	99½
5	Rio Grande Junc. 1st Mort. 1939	94
4	Rio Grande West 1st Tst. Mt. 1939	86
6	St. Joseph & Gd. Island ..1925	—
7	S. Louis Bridge 1st Mort ..1925	137½

American Railroad Bonds (*continued*) :

Last Div.	Name.	Price
5	S. Louis Mchts. Bdge. Term. 1st Mort....................1930	104½
4	S. Louis S. West 1st Mort..1989	77½
—	Do. 4 p.c. 2nd Mort. Inc. 1989	30
—	S. Louis Term. Cupples Sta. & Prop. 1st. Mrt. 4½ p.c. 1902-17	102
4½	St. Paul, Minn., & Manit. 1933	110½
6	Do. do. 1933	132½
6	Shamokin, Sunbury, &c. 2 Mt. 1925	109
5	S. & N. Alabama Cons. Mt. 1936	93½
5	Southern 1 Cons. Coup. 1994	96
4	Do. E. Tennes Reorg. Lien ..1938	98½
6	S. Pacific of Cal. 1 Mt....1905-12	114
4½	Trml. Assn. of S. Louis 1 Mt. 1939	113½
5	Do. 1 Cons. Mt. 1944	109
5	Texas & Pac. 1 Mt. 2000	103½
—	Do. 5 p.c. 2 Mt. Income 2000	35½
5	Toledo & Ohio Cent. 1 Mt. West. Div. 1935	105½
4½	Toledo., Walhon., Val., & Ohio 1 Mt. 1931-3	111½
6	Union Pacific 1 Mt. 1896-9	102½
5	Do. Coll. Trust.	—
—	Union Pac., Linc., & Color. 1 Mt. 1918	—
4	United N. Jersey Gen. Mt...1944	119½
6	Vicksbrg., Shrevept., & Pac. Pr. Ln. Mt. 1915	102½
5	Wabash 1 Mt. 1939	112
4	Wn. Pennsylvania Mt. 1928	109½
5	W. Virga. & Pittsbg. 1 Mt. 1990	88
5	Wheeling & L. Erie 1 Mt. (Wheelg. Div.) 5 p.c. 1928	90½
5	Do. Extd. Imp. Mt 1930	—
—	Do. do. Brown Shipley's Cts...	—
5	Willmar & Sioux Falls 1 Mt. 1938	111

STERLING.

Last Div.	Name.	Price
6	Alabama Gt. Sthn. Deb.....1906	104½
5	Do. Gen. Mort. ..1927-8	100
5	Alabama, N. Orl., Tex. & Pac. 5 p.c. "A" Dbs...1910-40	99
55/	Do. do. "B" do. 1910-40	51
—	Do. do. "C" do.	19
—	Allegheny Valley 1910	136
4	Atlantic 1st Leased Line Perp...	98
6	Baltimore and Ohio 1902	109
6	Do. do. 1910	118
5	Do. do. 1877........	97½
—	Do. Morgan's Certs. ..	97½
4½	Do. do. 1933	86
6	Chicago & Alton Cons. Mt. 1903	111
5	Chic, St. Paul & Kan. City Priority	108
6	Eastn. of Massachusetts 1906	117½
5	Illinois Cent. Skg. Fd.	106
5	Do. 1905	108
3½	Do. 1950	100½
4	Do. 1 Mt. 1951	114
3	Do. 1 Mt. 1951	94
6	Louisville & Nash., M. C. & L. Div., 1 Mt. 1902	104½
7	Do. 1 Mt. (Memphis & O.) 1901	111
47/4	Mexican Nat. "A" Certs. 5 p.c. Non. cum.	47
—	Do. "B" Certs.....	10
6	N.Y. & Canada 1 Mt.......1904	111
6	N. York Cent. & H.R. Mort. 1903	112
4½	N. York, Penns., & Ohio Pr. Ln. Extd. 1935	—
5	Do. Equip. Tst.	103½
5	Do. 5 p.c. Equip. Tst. (1890)	103½
6	Nrthn. Cent. Cons. Gen. Mt. ..	106
6	Pennsylvania Gen. Mt. 1910	129
6	Do. Cons. Skg. Fd. Mt. 1905	117
3½	Do. Cons. Mt. 1945	106
6	Phil. & Erie Cons. Mort ..1920	134½
6	Phil. & Reading Gen. Cons. Mort. 1911	127
6	Pittsbg. & Connells. Cons. 1926	114
—	Do. Morgan's Certs.....	114
4	St. Paul., Min., & Manitoba (Pac. Extn.) 1940	98
6	S. & N. Alabama 1903	107½
6	Union Pacific, Omaha Bridge 1896	—
6	Un. N. Jersey & C. Gen. Mt. 1901	112½

FOREIGN RAILWAYS.

Last Div.	Name.	Paid.	Price.
4/	Alagoas, Ltd., Shs.	20	6
5	Do. Deb. Stk., Red. ..	100	54½
6	Antofagasta, Ltd., Stk. ..	100	78
4	Do. Perp. Deb. Stk. ..	100	94
—	Arauco, Ld., Ord. Shs. ..	10	½
—	Do. 10 p.c. Cum. Pref.	10	1½
20/	Argentine Gt. W., Ld.,	20	15
20/	Do. 5 p.c. Cum. Pref. Shs.	20	20½
4	Do. 1 Deb. Stk.	100	104½
1/0/0	Argentine N.E., Ltd., 6 p.c. Cum. Pref. Stk. ..	100	11½
—	Do. 5 p.c. Deb. Stk., Red.	100	34½
2/	Arica and Tacna Shs. ..	20	1½
10/	Bahia & San Fcisco., Ld.,	20	11½
6/	Do. Timbo. Bch. Shs.	20	5
12/	Bahia, Blanca, & N.W. Ln. Prf. Cum. 6 p.c. ..	100	59
4	Do. 4 p.c. 1 Deb. Stk., Red.	100	96
6	Barranquilla R. & P., Ld., 6 p.c. 1 Deb. Stk., Red.	100	96

Foreign Railways (*continued*):—

Last Div.	Name.	Paid.	Price.
3/	Bilbao Riv. & Cantabn., Ltd., Ord.	3	6
—	Bolivar, Ltd., Shs.	10	1½
6	Do. 6 p.c. Deb. Stk.	100	96¼
—	Brazil Gt. Southn. Ltd., 7 p.c. Cum. Pref.	20	1½
6	Do. Perm. Deb. Stk	100	47½
6½	B. Ayres Gt. Southn., Ld., Ord. Stk.	100	155
5	Do. Pref. Stk.	100	140
4	Do. Deb. Stk.	100	117
30/	B. Ayres & Ensen. Port., Ltd., Ord. Stk.	100	62½
5	Do. Cum. 1 Pref. Stk.	100	119½
6/0/0	Do. 6p.c. Con. Pref. Stk.	100	104
4	Do. Deb. Stk., Irred.	100	112
10⅜	B. Ayres Northern, Ltd., Ord. Stk.	100	265
12½	Do. Pref. Stk.	100	320
5	Do. 5 p.c. Mt. Deb. Stk., Red.	100	113
3/15/0	B. Ayres & Pac., Ld., 7 p.c. 1 Pref. Stk. (Cum.)	100	103
4	Do. 1 Deb. Stk.	100	104
5/5/0	Do. 4½ p.c. 2 Deb. Stk.,	100	93
1	B Ayres & Rosario, Ltd., Ord. Stk.	100	75½
—	Do. New, £20 Shs.	20	22½
7/	Do. 7 p.c. Pref. Shs.	10	17½
7/	Do. Sunchales Ext.	10	15½
4	Do. Deb. Stk., Red.	100	109
12/	B. Ayres & Val. Trans., Ltd., 7 p.c. Cum. Pref.	20	7
4	Do. 4 p.c. "A" Deb. Stk., Red.	100	72
—	Do. 6 p.c. "B" Deb. Stk., Red.	100	48
6/	B. Ayres Westn. Ld. Ord.	10	11½
3/	Do. Def. Shs.	10	7½
5	Do. 5 p.c. Pref.	10	13½
4	Do. Deb. Stk	100	111
6	Cent. Arg. Deb. Sk. Rd.	100	160½
4	Do. Deb. Stk. Rd	100	112
6	Cent. Bahia L. Ord. Stk.	100	49½
6	Do. Deb. Stk., 1934	100	74½
5	Do. Deb. Stk., 1937	100	58
4/6	Cent. Uguy. East. Ext. L. Shs	10	6½
5	Do. Perm. Stk.	100	110
3/	Do. Nthn. Ext. L. Sh.	10	4½
5	Do. Perm. Deb. Stk.	100	106
3	Do. of Montev. Ltd., Ord. Stk	100	86
6	Do. Perm. Deb. Stk.	100	143
10/	Conde d'Eu, Ltd. Ord.	20	7½
—	Cordba & Rosar., Ltd., 6 p.c. Pref. Shs.	100	49
4	Do. 1 Deb. Stk	100	97½
75/	Do. 6 p.c. Deb. Stk	100	91
—	Cordba Cent., Ltd., 5 p.c. Cu. 1 Pref. Stk	100	90
—	Do. 5 p.c. Non-Cum. 2 Pref. Stk	100	53
5	Do. Deb. Stk	100	122
—	Costa Rica, Ltd., Shs	10	4½
8/	Dna. Thrsa. Chris., Ltd., 7 p.c. Pref. Shs.	20	4½
20/	E. Argentine, Ltd	100	45
6	Do. Deb. Stk	100	108
1/1	Egyptn. Dlta. Lgt. Rys., Ltd., £10 Pref. Shs.	8	8½
—	Entre Rios, L., Ord. Shs.	5	1
—	Do. Cu. 5 p.c. Pref.	5	3½
6/	Gt. Westn. Brazil, Ltd.,	20	11½
6	Do. Perm. Deb. Stk.	100	90½
6	Do. Extn. Deb. Stk.	100	76½
—	Int.-Oceanic Mex., Ltd., 7 p.c. Pref.	10	1½
4	Do. Deb. Stk	100	88
42/6	Do. 7 p.c. "A" Deb. Sk.	100	68
—	Do. 7 p.c. "B" Deb. Sk.	100	35
5/	La Guaira & Carac	10	7
5	Do. 5 p.c. Deb. Sk. Red.	100	102
8/4	Lembg.-Czern.-Jassy	30	25
1/	Lima, Ltd.	20	2½
—	Manila Ltd. 7 p.c. Cu. Pf.	10	½
20/6½	Mexican 2nd Pref. 6 p.c.	100	37
6	Do. Perp. Deb. Stk.	100	145
1/0/0	Mexican Sthrn., Ld., Ord.	100	26
—	Do. 4 p.c. 1 Db. Stk. Rd.	100	85
—	Do. 4 p.c. 2 do.	100	63
—	Mid. Urgy., Ltd.	100	20
5	Do. Deb. Stk.	100	63
12/	Minas & Rio, Ltd.	20	12½
5/2	Namur & Liege	20	12½
11/6	Do. Pref.	20	29
5/	Natal & Na. Cruz, Ld., 7 p.c. Cum Pref.	20	8½
—	Nitrate Ltd., Ord.	10	5½
—	Do. 7 p.c. Pr. Con. Or.	10	3½
—	Do. Def. Conv. Ord.	10	½
7/	N.-E. Urgy., Ltd., Ord.	10	15
7/	Do. 7 p.c. Pref.	10	15½
—	N.-W. Argentine Ld., 7 p.c. Pref.	10	3½
6	Do. 6 p.c. 1 Deb. Stk.	100	114
—	Do. 2 Deb. Stk.	100	94
—	N.W. Uruguay 6 p.c. 1 Pref. Stk.	100	17
—	Do. 5 p.c. 2 Pref. Stk.	100	7½
6	Do. 6 p.c. Deb. Stk.	100	80½
26/	Ottoman (Sm. Aid.)	20	16½
—	Paraguay Cntl., Ld., 5 p.c. Perm. Deb. Stk.	100	11
—	Piræus, Ath., & Pelo.	275	1½
5/	Pto. Alegre & N. Hambg. Ld., 7 p.c. Pref. Shs.	20	4½
6	Do. Mt. Deb. Stk. Red.	100	77½
—	Puerto Cabello & Val. Ld.	10	1½
5	Recife & S. Francisco	100	78
24/	R Claro S. Paulo, Ld., Sh.	10	22½
5	Do. Deb. Stk.	100	131
	Royal Sardinian Ord.	10	11½

Foreign Railways (*continued*):—

Last Div.	Name.	Paid.	Price.
5/	Royal Sardinian Pref.	10	12½
5/	Sambre & Meuse	20	18
5/6	Do. Pref.	10	12½
28/	San Paulo Ld.	20	35½
2/9½	Do. New Ord. £10 sh.	4	8½
2/	Do. 5 p.c. Non. Cm. Pref.	10	12½
5½	Do. Deb. Stk.	100	137
5	Do. 5 p.c. Deb. Stk.	100	128
—	S. Fé & Cordova, Gt. Sthn., Ld., Shares	100	55
6	Do. Perp. Deb. Stk.	100	124
3/2½	S. Austrian	20	7½
10/	Sthn. Braz. R. Gde. do Sul, Ld.	20	8½
6	Do. 6 p.c. Deb. Stk.	100	78
4	Swedish Centl., Ld., 4 p.c. Deb. Stk.	100	108
5	Do. Pref.	100	100
1/9	Taltal, Ld.	5	2½
—	Uruguay Nthn., Ld. 7 p.c. Pfd. Stk.	100	8
3½	Do. 5 p.c. Deb. Stk.	100	30
—	Villa Maria & Rufino, Ld., 6 p.c. Pref. Shs.	100	20
4	Do. 4 p.c. 1 Deb. Stk.	100	75
6/0/0	Do. 6 p.c. 2 Deb. Stk.	100	47
5/9	West Flanders	8½	21
5/6	Do. 5½ p.c. Pref.	10	18
3/	Wstn. of Havana, Ld.	10	4½

FOREIGN RAILWAY OBLIGATIONS

Per Cent.	Name.	Price.
6	Alagoas Ld., 6 p.c. Deb., Rd.	88½
—	Alcoy & Gandia, Ld., 5 p.c. Debs., Red.	25
5	Arauco., Ld., 5 p.c. 1st Mt., Rd.	67½
—	Do. 6 p.c. Mt. Deb., Rd.	47½
6	Brazil G. Sthn., L., Mt. Dbs., Rd.	89½
6	Do. Mt. Dbs. 1893, Rd.	48½
5½	Campos & Caran. Dbs., Rd.	77
6	Central Bahia, L., Dbs., Rd.	90½
5½	Conde d'Eu, L., Dbs., Rd.	78
6	Costa Rica, L., 1st Mt. Dbs., Rd.	109
6	Do. 2nd Dbs., Rd.	95
5	Do. Prior Mt. Db., Rd.	107
6	Cucuta Mt. Dbs., Rd.	106
5½	Donna Thrsa. Cris., L., Dbs., Rd.	75
3	Eastn. of France, £20 Dbs., Rd.	19½
4	Egyptn. Delta Light, L., Db., Rd.	100
—	Espito. Santo & Cara. 5 p.c. Stl. Dbs., Rd.	38
4	Gd. Russian Nic., Rd.	102
5	Inter-Oceanic Mex., L., 5 p.c. Pr. Ln. Dbs., Rd.	104
3	Ital. 3 p.c. Bds. A & B, Rd.	57½
—	Ituana 6 p.c. Debs., 1918	74
—	Leopoldina, 6 p.c. Dbs. £50 Bds.,	25
—	Do. do. Comms. Cert.	25
—	Do. 5 p.c. Stg. Dbs. (1888), Rd.	34
—	Do. do. Comm. Certs.	34
—	Do. 5 p.c. Stg. Dbs. (1890), Rd.	25
—	Do. do. Comms. Certs.	25
—	Macahé & Cam. 5 p.c. Dbs., Rd.	35
—	Do. do. Comms. Certs.	35
—	Do. (Cantagallo), 5 p.c., Red.	35
—	Do. do. Comm. Certs.	35
—	Manila Ltd., 6 p.c. Deb., Red.	24
6	Do. Prior Lien Mt., Rd.	105
6	Do. Series "B," Rd.	79
7	Matanzas & Sab., Rd.	101½
6	Minas & Rio, L., 6 p.c. Dbs., Rd.	101
5	Mogyana 5 p.c. Deb. Bds., Rd.	103
5	Moscow-Jaros., Rd.	106½
5½	Natal & Na. Cruz Ltd., 5½ p.c. Debs., Red.	88½
5	Nitrate, Ltd. Mt. Bds., Red.	83½
3	Nthn. France, Red.	19½
4	N. of S. Af. Rep. (Trnsvl.) Gu. Bds. Red.	98
3	Nthn. of Spain £20 Pri. Obs. Red.	9
6	Ottmn. (Smy to A.)(Kujk) Asst. Debs., Red.	109
6	Ottmn. (Seraik.) Asg. Debs. Red.	109
6	Ottmn. (Seraik.) Non-Asg. D., Rd	109
5	Ottmn. Kuyjk. Ext. Red.	109
5	Ottmn. Serkeuy. Ext. Red.	104
5	Ottmn. Tireh Ext. 1910	99
5	Ottmn. Debs, 1886, Red.	98
5	Do. 1888, Red. 1935	99
5	Do. 1893, Red. 1935	99
5	Ottmn. of Anlia. Debs., Rd.	93
5	Do. Ser. II.	89
4	Ottomn. Smyr. & Cas. Ext. Bds., Red.	83½
3	Paris, Lyon & Medit. (old sys., £20), Red.	19
3	Paris, Lyon & Medit. (new sys., £20), Red.	19½
30/	Piræus, At. & Pelp., 6 p.c. 1st Mt. Bds., Red.	88½
3	Do. 5 p.c. Mt. Bds., Red.	61½
4	Pretoria-Pietbg., Ltd., Red.	93
7	Puerto Cab. & Val., Ltd., 1st Mt. Debs., Red.	96
—	Rio de Jano. & Nthn., Ltd., 6 p.c. £100 Deb., Red.	25
—	Rio de Jano. (Gr. Para.), 5 p.c. 1st Mt. St. £100 Debs., Red.	25
3	Royal Sardinian, A, Rd. £20	12
3	Royal Sardinian, B., Rd. £20	12

Foreign Rly. Obligations (*continued*):—

Per Cent.	Name.	Price.
5	Ryl. Trns.-Afric. 5 p.c. 1st Mt. £100 Bds., Red.	61
7	Sagua La Grande, B pRd.	98
4	Sa. Fe & Cor. G.S., Ld. Pr. Ln. Bds.	103
5	Sa. Fe, 5 p.c. and Reg. Dbs.	81
3	South Austrian, £20 Red.	15½
3	South Austrian, (Ser. X.)	15½
3	South Italian £20 Obs. (Ser. A to G), Red.	12½
3½	S.W. of Venez. (Barq.), Ltd., 7 p.c. 1st Mt. £100 Debs.	57½
5	Taltal, Ltd., 5 p.c. 1st Ch. Debs., Red.	99
5	Utd. Rwys. Havana, Red.	94
3	Wtrn. of France, £20 Red.	19
6	Wrn. B. Ayres St. Mt. Debs., 1902	111
6	Wrn. B. Ayres, Reg. Cert.	109
5	Do. Mt. Bds.	122
6	Wtrn. of Havna., Ld, Mt. Dbs., Rd.	103
7	Wrn. Ry. San Paulo Red.	101
—	Wrn. Santa Fé, 7 p.c. Red.	43
4/7	Zafra & Huelva, 3 p.c. Red.	3

BANKS.

Div.	Name.	Paid.	Price.
1/9½	Agra, Ltd.	6	3½
4/2½	Anglo-Argentine, Ltd., £9	7	5½
8½ fls.	Anglo-Austrian	120 f	14
6/	Anglo-Californian, Ltd., £20 Shares	10	11½
4/	Anglo-Egyptian, Ltd., £15	5	6
3/6	Anglo-Foreign Bkg., Ltd.	7	8
2/	Anglo-Italian, Ltd.	5	7½
7/6	Bk. of Africa, Ltd., £18¾	6¼	10½
20/	Bk. of Australasia	40	55
10/	Bk. of Brit. Columbia	20	22
25/	Bk. of Brit. N. America	50	66
7/6	Bk. of Egypt, Ltd., £25	12½	19
5/	Bk. of Mauritius, Ltd.	10	10
18/	Bk. of N. S. Wales	20	38½
4 p.c.	Bk. of N. Zland. Gua. Stk.	100	103
6/	Bk. of Roumania, £20 Shs.	6	7½
2/6	Tarapaca & Ldn., Ltd., £10	5	3½
—	Bque. Fse. de l'Afri. du S.	100 f.	3½
f. 12.50	Bque. Internatle. de Paris	20	24
6/	Brit. Bk. of S. America, Ltd., £20 Shares	10	11
15/	Capital & Ctics., L., £50	10	39
16/	Chart. of India, &c.	20	31½
10/	City, Ltd., £40 Shares	10	20
18/	Colonial, £100 Shares	30	23
20/	Delhi and London, Ltd.	25	—
5/	German of London, Ltd.	10	10½
25/	Hong-Kong & Shanghai	28½	45
4/	Imperl. of Persia	6½	3½
10/	Imperl. Ottoman, £20 Shs	10	12½
9/	Intrnatl. of Ldn., Ld., £20	15	12
10/	Ionian, Ltd.	25	15
12/	Lloyds, Ltd., £50 Shs.	8	30½
10/	Ldn. & Braziln. Ltd., £20	10	18
44/	Ldn. & County, Ltd., £50	20	101
5/	Ldn. & Hanseatic, L., £20	10	11
22/6	Ldn. & Midland, L., £60	12½	53½
8/9	Ldn. & Provin., Ltd., £10	5	22½
39/	Ldn. & Riv. Plate, L., £25	15	53
2/1½	Ldn. & San Fcisco, Ltd.	7	4½
28/	Ldn. & Sth. West., L., £50	20	69
26/	Ldn. & Westmins., L., £100	20	55
3/	Ldn. of Mex. & S. Amer., Ltd., £10 Shs.	6	5½
15/	Ldn. Joint Stk., L., £100	15	34
9/7	Ldn., Paris & Amer., L. £20	16	26
2/4½	Merchant Bkg., L., £9	4	2½
6/3	Metropn, Ltd., £50 Shs.	5	14½
9/	National, Ltd., £50 Shs.	10	19½
4/5	Natl. of Mexico, $100 Shs.	$40	13
1/3	National of N. Z., L., £7½	2½	2½
3/	National S. Afric. Rep.	10	14½
18/10½	National Provcl. of Eng., Ltd., £75 Shs.	10½	51
21/7½	Do. do. £60 Shs.	12	58½
6/6	NorthEastn., Ltd., £20 Shs	6	14½
19/	Parr's, Ld., £100 Shs.	20	92
12/6	Prov. of Ireland, L., £100	12½	28½
40/	Stan'd. of S. Afric., L., £100	25	68
12/6	Union of Australia, L., £75	25	29
4 p.c.	Do. do. Ins. Stk. Dep. 1900	100	103
15/6	Union of Ldn., Ltd., £100	15½	35½

BREWERIES AND DISTILLERIES.

Div.	Name.	Paid.	Price.
4½	Albion Prp. 1 Mt. Db. Sk.	100	115
4	All Saints', L., Db. Sk. Rd.	100	99
6	Allsopp, Ltd	100	163
6	Do. Cum. Pref	100	160
4½	Do. Deb. Stk., Red.	100	118
3½	Do. Deb. Stk., Red.	100	102
4½	Alton & Co., L., Db., Rd	100	106
4½	Do. Mt. Bds., 1896	100	105
—	Arnold, Perrett, Ltd.	10	6
6	Do. Cum. Pref.	10	10½
4½	Do. 1 Mt. Db. Stk., Rd.	100	106

Breweries, &c. (*continued*):—

Div.	Name.	Paid.	Price.
5½	Arrol, A., & Sons, L., Cum. Pref. Shs.	10	10½
4½	Do. 1 Mt. Db. Stk., Rd.	100	106
6	Backus, 1 Mt. Db., Red.	100	50½
4	Barclay, Perk., L., Cu. Pf.	10	11½
3½	Do. Mt. Db. Stk., Red.	100	111
—	Barnsley, Ltd.	10	11
6	Do. Cum. Pref.	10	13
1/	Barrett's, Ltd	2½	1½
1/3	Do. 5 p.c. Pref.	2½	2½
3/	Bartholomay, Ltd.	10	4
8	Do. Cum. Pref.	10	9
6	Do. Deb.	100	102½
5	Bass, Ratcliff, Ltd., Cum. Pref. Stk.	100	146½
4½	Do. Mt. Db. Stk., Rd.	100	126
4	Bell, John, Ltd., 1 Mt. Deb. Stk., Red.	100	102
2/6	Benskin's, L., Cum. Pref.	5	—
4½	Do. 1 Mt. Db. Stk Red.	100	—
4½	Do. "B" Deb. Sk, Rd.	100	—
7/	Bentley's Yorks., Ltd.	10	17
6	Do. Cum. Pref.	10	12½
4½	Do. Mt. Debs., Red	100	109
4½	Do. do. 1 92, Red.	100	109
—	Bieckert's, Ltd.	20	2
5	Do. Debs., Red.	100	57
—	Birmingham., Ltd., 6 p.c. Cum. Pref	5	2½
4½	Do. Mt. Debs., Red.	50	40½
5½	Boardman's, Ld., Cm. Pf.	10	8½
4½	Do., Perp. 1 Mt. Db. Sk.	100	104½
4½	Brakspear, L., 1 D. Stk. Rd	100	109
4	Brandon's, L., 1 D. Stk. R.	100	103½
17/	Bristol (Georges) Ltd.	10	47
6	Do. Cum. Pref.	10	18
5	Do. Mt. Db. Sk. 1888 Rd.	100	115½
—	Bristol United, Ltd.	10	36½
6	Do. Cum. Pref.	10	16½
4½	Do. Db. Sk. Rd.	100	126
5½	Buckley's, L., C. Pre-prf.	10	11
4½	Do. 1 Mt. Db. Stk. Rd.	100	106½
4	Bullard & Sns, L., D. Sk. R.	100	106
6	Bushell, Watk., L., C. Pf.	10	14½
4½	Do. 1 Mt. Db. Sk. Rd.	100	112
5	Camden, Ltd., Cum. Pref.	10	11½
4½	Do. 1 Mt. Db. Sk. Rd.	100	110
5½	Cameron, Ltd., Cm. Prf.	10	13½
4½	Do. Mort Deb. Stk.	100	108
3½	Do. Perp Mt. Db. Sk.	100	100½
5	Cam'bell, J'stone, L., C. Pf.	5	5
4½	Do. 4½ p.c. 1 Mt. Db. Sk.	100	106
4	Campbell, Praed, L., Per. 1 Mort. Deb. Stk.	100	108
4	Cannon, L., Mt. Db. Stk.	100	109
4	Do. "B" Deb. Stk.	100	105
5	Castlemaine, L., 1 Mt. Db.	100	94
3½	Charrington, Ltd., Mort. Deb. Stk. Red.	100	107
2/	Cheltnhm. Orig., Ltd.	5	7
6	Do. Cum. Pref.	5	7½
4	Do. Debs. Red.	100	107
—	Chicago, Ltd.	10	3½
6	Do. Debs.	100	87½
—	Cincinnati, Ltd.	10	½
8	Do. Cum. Pref.	10	1½
10/	City of Baltimore	10	4
16/	Do. 8 p.c. Cum. Pref	10	8
24/	City of Chicago, Ltd.	10	1½
8	Do. Cum. Pref.	10	6
13	City of London, Ltd.	100	205½
5	Do. Cum. Pref.	100	138
4	Do. Mt. Deb. Stk., Rd.	100	112½
2/6	Colchester, Ltd.	5	5
7	Do. Pref.	5	7
4½	Do. Deb. Stk., Red.	100	120
5	Combe, Ltd., Cum. Pref.	10	14½
4	Do. Mt. Db. Stk, Rd.	100	112
3½	Do. Perp. Deb. Stk.	100	107
5	Comm'cial, L., D. Sk., Rd.	100	108½
5	Courage, L., Cm. Pref. Shs.	100	139½
4	Do. Irr. Mt. Deb. Stk.	100	130
3½	Do. Irr. "B" Mt. Db. Sk.	100	106
8	Daniell & Sons, Ltd.	10	6½
7	Do. Cum. Pref.	10	12
4½	Do. 1 Mt. Perp. Db. Sk.	100	108½
4½	Do. "B" Deb. Stk.	100	100
10d.	Dartford, Ltd.	5	4½
10d.	Do. Cum. Pref.	5	5½
4	Do. 1 Mt. Db. Sk. Rd.	100	101
4	Davenport, Ld., 1 D. Stk.	100	202½
10/	Denver United, Ltd.	10	½
8	Do. Cum. Pref.	10	5½
6	Do. Debs.	100	95½
4½	Deuchar, L., 1 D. Sk., Rd.	100	106
8/	Distillers, Ltd.	10	24
4½	Do. Mt. Db. Stk., Rd.	100	115½
—	Dublin Distillers, Ltd.	5	1½
6/	Do. Cum. Pref.	5	4½
4½	Do. Irr. Deb. Stk.	100	—
5	Eadie, Ltd., Cum. Pref.	10	11½
4	Do. Irr. 1 Mt. Db. Sk.	100	108
10/	Edinbgh. Utd., Ltd.	10	13
6	Do. Cum. Prf.	10	13½
5	Do. 1 Mt. Dbs.	100	110½
4	Eldridge, Pope, L. D. St. R.	100	109
3/	Emerald & Phœnix, Ltd.	10	1½
8	Do. Cum. Pref.	10	7
6	Empress Ltd., C. Pf.	10	11½
4½	Do. Mt. Deb. Stk.	100	105
10/	Farnham, Ltd.	10	15½
6	Do. Cum. Pref.	10	15
4	Fenwick, L., 1 D. Sk., Rd.	100	108
4	Flower & Sons, Irr. D. Sk.	100	111
4	Friary, L., 1 Db. Stk., Rd.	100	105½
4	Do. 1 "A" Db. Sk., Rd	100	102
4½	Groves, L., 1 Db. Sk., Rd	100	110
24	Guinness, Ltd.	100	600
6	Do. Cum. Prf. Stk.	100	188½
5	Do. Deb. Stk., Red.	100	123
6	Hall's Oxford L., Cm. Pf.	5	6½
6/	Hancock, Ld., Cm. Pf. Ord.	10	14
	Do. Def. Ord.	10	17½

Breweries, &c. (*continued*):—

Div.	Name.	Paid.	Price.
6	Hancock, Ld., Cum. Pref.	10	14
4	Do. 1 Deb. Stk., Rd.	100	112
5	Hoare, Ltd. Cum. Pref.	10	13½
5	Do. "A" Cum. Pref.	10	12½
4	Do. Mt. Deb. Stk., Rd.	100	111
3½	Do. do. do. Rd.	100	104
4/6	Hodgson's, Ltd.	5	9½
5	Do. 1 Mt. Db., Red.	—	120½
4	Do. 2 Mt. Db., 1906	—	102
4½	Hopcraft & N., Ltd., 1 Mt. Deb. Stk., Red.	100	103
5	Huggins, Ltd., Cm. Prf.	10	12½
4½	Do. 1st D. Stk. Rd.	100	113
4½	Do. "B" Db. Stk. Rd.	100	111
8/	Hull, Ltd.	10	17
7	Do. Cum. Pref.	10	15
4½	Ind, Coope, L., D. Sk., Rd.	100	119
4	Do. "B" Mt. Db. Stk. Rd.	100	115
8/	Indianapolis, Ltd.	10	3½
8	Do. Cm. Prf.	10	9
5/	Jones, Frank, Ltd.	10	3½
7½	Do. Cum. Pref.	10	8
5	Do. 1st Mort. Debs.	100	93½
4/	J. Kenward & Ct., Ltd.	5	5¾
4½	Kingsbury, L., 1 D. Sk., Rd	100	—
4	Lacon, L., D. Stk., Red.	100	110
4	Do. Irrd. "B" D. Sk.	100	107
4/	Lascelles, Ltd.	5	10½
6	Do. Cum. Pref.	5	7½
5	Leney, Ltd., Cum. Pref.	10	11½
4	Do. 1 Mt. Db. Stk. Rd.	100	104
17/	Lion, Ltd., £25 shares	17	50½
6/	Do. New £10 shares	6	17½
6	Do. Perp. Pref.	20	32
4	Do. B. Mt. Db. Sk. Rd.	100	110
4½	Lloyd & Y., Ltd., 1 Mt. Deb. Stk., Rd.	100	98½
4½	Locke & S., Ltd., Irr. 1st Mt. Deb. Stk.	100	100
4½	Lovibond, Ltd., 1st Mt. Deb. Stk., Rd.	100	102½
30/4	Lucas & Co., Ld., Deb. Stk.	100	107
8/	Manchester, Ltd.	10	18½
7	Do. Cum. Pref.	10	17½
5	Marston, J., L., Cm. Prf.	10	10½
4	Do. 1 Mt. Db. Sk., Rd.	100	101½
9/	Massey's Burnley, Ltd.	10	16½
6	Do. Cum. Pref.	10	14½
4½	McCracken, Ltd., 1 Mt. Deb., 1908	100	62½
5	McEwan, Ltd., Cm. Pref.	10	15
5	Meux, Ltd., Cum. Pref.	10	14½
4	Do. Mt. Db. Stk. Red.	100	111
4½	Michell & A., Ltd., 1 Mt. Deb. Stk. Red.	100	105
4½	MileEndDist. Db. Sk. Rd.	100	108
—	Milwaukee & Chic., Ltd.	10	1½
4/	Do. Cum. Pref.	10	6½
4½	Michell, Toms, L., Db.	50	55
6	Morgan, Ltd., Cum. Pref.	10	14½
10/	Nalder & Coll., Ltd.	10	32
6	Do. Cum. Pref.	10	16
4½	Do. Deb. Red.	100	113
3/	New Beeston, Ltd.	5	5
2/9	Do. Cum. Pref.	5	5
4	Do. Mt. Deb. Stk. Red.	100	97½
12/	Newcastle, Ltd.	10	20
6	Do. Cum. Pref.	10	15½
5	Do. 1 Mt. Deb., 1911	100	110½
4	Do. "A" Deb. Stk. Red.	100	105
6/	New England, Ltd	10	5
8	Do. Cum. Pref.	10	9¾
6	Do. Debs. Red	100	104½
4	New London, L., 1 D. Sk.	100	105
7/2	New Westminster, Ltd.	4	10½
2/4½	Do. Pref.	4	6½
—	New York, Ltd.	10	1
—	Do. 8 p.c. Cum. Pref.	10	4
6	Do. 1 Mt. Deb. Red.	100	80½
5	Noakes, Ld., Cum. Pref.	10	12
4	Do. 1 Mt. Db. Stk., Rd.	100	106
4½	Norfolk, L., "A" D. Sk. Rd.	100	106
10/	Northampton, Ld.	10	16½
7	Do. Cum. Pref.	10	15½
6	Do. Cum. Pref.	10	13
5	Do. 1 Mt. Per. Db. Sk.	100	127
4	Nth. East., L., 1 D. Sk. Rd.	100	102
4½	N. Worcesters., L. Per. 1 Mort. Deb. Stock	100	98½
6	Nottingham, L., Cm. Prf.	10	12
5	Do. 1 Mt. Deb. Stk., Red.	100	114
17/4	Do. "B" do. Red.	50	112
6/	Ohlsson' Cape, Ld.	5	16½
7	Do. Cum. Pref.	5	8½
4½	Do. 2nd Cum. Pref.	5	5½
5	Do. Deb. Stk., Red.	100	114
4½	Oldfield, L., 1 Mt. Db. Stk.	100	105
6	Page & Overt., L., Cm. Prf.	10	13½
4½	Do. 1 Mt. Dbs, Red.	100	108
10/	Parker's Burslem, Ltd.	10	25
6	Do. Cum. Pref.	10	15
4	Do. 1 Mt. Db. Stk., Red.	100	113
4	Persse, Ld., 1 Mt. Db. Rd.	100	96½
4	Phipps, L., Irr. 1 Db. Stk.	100	115
5	Plymouth, L., Min. Cu. Pf.	10	14
4½	Do. Mt. Deb. Stk., Red.	100	104½
4½	Pryor, Reid, L., 1 D.S., R.	100	105½
5	Reid's, Ld., Cm. Pref. Stk.	100	137½
4	Do. Mt. Deb. Stk., Red.	100	112
3½	Do. "B" Mt. Db. Stk., Rd	100	103
5	Rhondda Val., L., Cu. Pf	10	11
4½	Do. 1 Mt. Deb. Stk., Rd.	100	109
5	Robinson, Ld., Cum. Pref.	10	11½
4½	Do. 1 Mt. Perp. Db. Stk.	100	112
4/	Rochdale, Ltd.	10	5½
4½	Do. 1 Mt. Deb. Stk.	100	96½
7	Royal, Brentford, Ltd.	10	19½
	Do. Cum. Pref.	10	14½
4½	Do. 1 Mt. Dbs. Red	100	110
6/	St. Louis, Ltd.	10	4
8	Do. Cum. Pref.	10	8½
24/	St. Paull, Ltd.	10	10
7	Do. Cum. Pref.	10	12½
4½	Salt (T.), L., 1 Db. Sk. Rd.	100	111

Breweries, &c. (*continued*):—

Div.	Name.	Paid.	Price.
4½	Salt (T.), "B" Db. Stk. Red	100	108
—	San Francisco, Ltd.	10	⅛
—	Do. 8 p.c. Cum. Pref.	10	½
4½	Savill Brs., L., D. Sk. Rd.	100	117
4½	Scarboro., Ltd., 1 Db. Stk.	100	103
4	Shaw (Hy.), Ltd., 1 Mt. Db. Stk., Red.	100	104
22/	Showell's, Ltd.	10	32½
7	Do. Cum. Pref.	10	17½
3/	Do. Gua. Shs.	5	7½
4½	Do. Mt. Db. Stk., Red.	100	—
4	Simonds, L., 1 D. Sk., Rd.	100	111
5½	Simson & McP., L., Cu. Pf.	10	9
4½	Do. 1 Mt. Deb. Stk.	100	99
5/	Smith, Garrett, L., £20 Shs	10	15½
5	Do. Cum. Pref.	20	26
4½	Do. Mt. Db. Stk., Red.	100	—
5	Smith's, Tadcster, L., CPf	10	11½
4½	Do. Deb. Stk., Red.	100	112
4	Do. Deb. Stk., Red.	100	108
4½	Star, L., 1 M. Db. Stk., Rd.	100	104
4	Steward & P., L., 1 D. Sk.	100	113
9/	Strettons Derby, Ltd.	10	13
6	Do. Cum. Pref.	10	13
4	Do. Irr. 1 Mt. Db. Stk.	100	104½
4½	Strong, Romsey, L., 1 D.S.	100	115
5	Stroud, L., Db. Sk., Rd.	100	111½
4½	Tadcaster To'er, L., D. Sk.	100	113
8/	Tamplin, Ltd	10	21½
6	Do. Cum. Pref.	100	15
4	Do. "A" Db. Sk., Rd.	10	107
6	Thorne, Ltd., Cum. Pref.	10	14½
4	Do. Deb. Stk., Red.	100	104½
15/	Threlfall, Ltd.	10	47
6	Do. Cum. Pref.	10	16½
5	Do. 1 Mt. Dbs., Red.	100	116
4	Tollemache, L., D. Sk. Rd.	100	105
4	Truman, Hanb., D. Sk., R.	100	110
3	Do. "B" Mt. Db. Sk., Rd.	100	95
10/	United States, Ltd.	10	10
8	Do. Cum. Pref.	10	12
6	Do. 1 Mt. Deb.	100	107½
6/	Walker & H., Ld., Cm. Prf.	10	11½
4½	Do. 1 Mt. Deb. Stk., Red.	100	107
5	Walker, Peter, Ld. Cm. Prf.	10	14½
4	Do. 1 Mt. Dbs. Red.	100	111
4	Wallingford, L., D. Sk. Rd.	100	107
6	Watney, Ld., Cm. Prf. Sk.	100	170
5	Do. Mt. Db. Sk., Rd.	100	117½
4½	Do. "B" Mt. Db. Sk., Rd.	100	111
3½	Do. Mt. Db. Stk.	100	101
5	Watney, D., Ld., Cm. Prf.	10	12½
4½	Do. 1 Mt. Db. Stk.	100	108
5	Wenlock Ltd., Pref.	10	12½
4	Do. 1 Mt. Db. Sk., Rd.	100	108
5	West Cheshire, L., Cu. Pf.	10	10½
4	Do. Irred. 1 Mt. Db. Sk.	100	100
4½	Whitbread, L., Cu. Pf. Sh.	100	124½
4	Do. Db. Stk., Red.	100	112
3½	Do. "B" Db. Stk., Rd.	100	101
9/	Wolverhmpton & D. Ld.	10	16½
6	Do. Cum. Pref.	10	13½
4½	Do. 1 Mt. Dbs., Red.	100	108
5½	Worthington, Ld., Cm. Prf.	10	15½
5½	Do. Cum. "B" Pref.	10	13½
4½	Do. Mt. Db. Sk., Rd.	100	113
3½	Do. Irr. "B" Db. Stk.	100	104
10/	Yates's Castle, Ltd.	10	13½
5	Do. Cum. Pref.	10	11
5	Younger W., L., Cu. Pf. Sh.	100	137½

CANALS AND DOCKS.

Last Div.	Name.	Paid.	Price.
4	Birmingham Canal	100	145½
—	E. & W. India Dock	100	21½
4	Do. Deb. Stk.	100	111
50/	Do. Def. Deb. Stk.	100	89
3½	Do. 1st Mt. Certs.	100	110
4	Do. Mt. Bds. (1885)	—	100
40/	G. Junction Ord. Shs.	100	151½
6/	Do. do. Pref.	10	19
4½	King's Lynn Per. Db. Stk.	100	117½
2½	Leeds & Lpool Canal	100	72
2½	Lndn & St. Kath. Dks.	100	57
4½	Do. Pref.	100	136½
4½	Do. Pref., 1878	100	132½
4½	Do. Pref., 1882	100	128
4	Do. Deb. Stk.	100	135
—	Mchester Ship C. 5 p.c. Pf.	10	1½
3½	Do. 1st Perp. Mt. Deb.	100	98
—	Milford Dks. Db. Stk. "A"	100	20
2	Millwall Dk.	100	61
5	Do. Perp. Pref.	100	144½
4½	Do. Pref.	100	108½
5	Do. New Per. Prf., 1887	100	128½
5	Do. Per. Deb. Stk.	100	152½
4/	Newhaven Har.	10	14½
2	N. Metropolitan	100	65
5	Sharpness Nw. Pf. "A" Sk.	100	144½
4	Do. Deb. Stk.	100	120½
4	Sheffield & S. Yorks Nav. 4½ p.c. Pref. Stk.	100	117½
36.432	Suez Canal	20	135½
5	Surrey Comcl. Dok., Ord.	100	150½
5	Do. Min. 4 p.c. Pref. "A"	110	152½
5	Do. Pref. "B"	100	150½
5	Do. do. "C"	100	150
5	Do. do. "D"	100	145½
4½	Do. Deb. Stk.	100	154½

COMMERCIAL, INDUSTRIAL, &c.

Last Div.	Name.	Paid.	Price.
5	Accles, L., 1 Mt. Db., Red.	100	84½
5/	Aërated Bread, Ltd.	1	12½
—	African Gold Recovery, L.	1	½
2/	Aluminium, L., "A" Shs.	1	2½
4½	Do. 1 Mt. Db. Stk., Red.	100	99
5½	Amelia Nitr., L., 1 Mort. Deb., Red.	100	84½
7/	Anglo-Chil. Nitrate, Ltd., Cum. Pref.	10	7½
4½	Do. Cons. Mt. Bds., Red.	100	82½
4½	Anglo-Russian Cotton, Ld., 1 Charge Debs., Red.	100	97
11/3	Angus (G., & Co., L.), £10	7½	17
6/	Apollinaris, Ltd.	10	12½
5/	Do. 5 p.c. Cum. Pref.	10	11
4	Do. Irred. Deb. Stock	100	107
6/	Appleton, French, & S., L.	5	½
3/	Argentine Meat Pres., L., 7 p.c. Pref.	10	2½
5	Argentine Refinry, Db. Rd.	100	98
2/2	Armstrong, Whitw., Ltd.	1	3½
4	Do. Cum. Pref.	5	6½
5	Artisans', Labr. Dwllgs., L.	100	131½
4½	Do. Non-Cm. Prf., 1879	100	132½
4½	Do. do. 1884	100	132½
—	Asbestos & Asbestic, Ltd.	10	8½
2/7½	Ashley-grdns., L., C. Prf.	5	6½
4½	Do. 1 Mt. Deb. Stk.	100	115½
5/	Assam Rly. & Trdng., L., 8 p.c. Cum. Pref. "A"	10	15½
—	Do. Deferrd. "B" Shs.	1	4½
—	Do. do. (iss. f. pd)	1	3½
8/	Do. Cum. Pre-Prf. "A"	10	15
6/	Do. New Pref.	10	11½
5	Do. Debs., Red.	100	107
5	Do. Red. Mort. Debs.	100	110
6	Aust'lian Pastrl, L., Cu. Pf.	10	7½
6d.	Aylesbury Dairy, Ltd.	1	1½
4	Do. 4 p.c. Mt. Dbs.	100	104½
10/	Babcock & Wilcox, Ltd.	10	31
6	Do. 6 p.c. Cm. Prf.	10	16½
8	Baker (Chs.), L., Cm. Pf.	5	9
8	Do. "B," Cm. Pref.	5	8½
8d.	Barker (John), Ltd.	1	2½
5½	Do. Cum. Pref.	5	7½
4½	Do. Irred. 1 Mt. Db. Stk.	100	132
—	Barnagore Jute, Ltd.	5	3
5	Do. Cum. Pref.	5	4½
7½d.	Belgravia Dairy, Ltd.	1	1½
5/	Bell (R.) & Co., Ltd.	5	3½
1/	Bell's Asbestos, Ltd.	1	½
5	Do. Mt. Db. Bds., Rd.	100	103
10/	Bengal Mills, Ltd.	10	11½
6/	Do. 5 p.c. Cum. Prf.	10	10½
2/5	Benson (J.W.) L., Cm. Pf.	10	10½
12/4	Do. Perp. Mt. Db. Stk.	100	103½
6	Bergvik, L., 6 p.c. Cm. Pf.	10	12½
10/	Do. Dfd.	10	9½
4½	Do. 1 Dbs., Red.	100	103½
5/	Birm'ham Vinegar, Ltd.	5	10
5	Do. Cum. Pref.	5	5½
4½	Do. 1 Mt. Db. Stk., Rd.	100	108½
5	Boake (A.) L., 5 p.c. Cu. Pf.	10	10½
2/6	Bodega, Ltd.	5	8½
4½	Do. Mt. Deb. Stk., Rd.	100	111
8/	Bottomley & Brs., Ltd.	10	6½
6/	Do. 6 p.c. Pt.	10	9½
8½d.	Bovril, Ltd.	1	1½
1/0½	Do. Def.	1	1½
6½d	Do. Cum. Pref.	1	1
4½	Do. Deb. Stk.	100	103
5/	Bradbury, Gretrex., Ltd., £10 share	8	14
5/	Do. 5 p.c. Cum. Pref.	10	13½
5/	Brewers' Sugar, L., 5 p.c. Cum. Pref.	10	10½
2/6	Brighton Grd. Hotel, Ld.	5	3½
4	Do. Mt. Db. Stk., Red.	100	102½
5	Bristol Hotel & Palm. Co., Ltd. 1st Mt. Red. Deb.	100	107½
9½d.	British & Bengton's. Tea Tr. Asc., Ltd.	1	1½
5	Do. Cum. Prf.	5	5½
—	British Deli & Lgkat. Tobacco, Ltd.	1	1½
—	Do. Cum. Prf.	1	½
—	British Tea Table, Ltd.	1	2½
5½	Do. Cum. Pref.	1	1½
2/6	Brooke, Ben., & Co., Ltd., Cum. Pref.	5	5½
7/6	Brooke, Bond & Co., Ltd.	5	20½
6	Brown Brs., L., Cum. Pref.	5	6
6/	Browne & Eagle, Ltd.	10	14
5	Do. Cum. Pref.	10	13
4	Do. Mrt. Db. Sk., Red.	100	109
20/	Brunner, Mond, & Co., Lt.	10	42
7/	Do. £10 shares	3½	17
7	Do. Cum. Pref.	10	18
7	Do. £10 shares	5	8½
10/	Bryant & May, Ltd.	5	19½
2/	Bucknall, H., & Sons, Lt.	5	8
6	Do. Cum Pref.	5	8½
4/	Burke, E. & J., Ltd.	5	7½
6	Do. Cum. Pref.	5	7½
6	Do. Irred. Deb. Stk.	100	155
1/	Burlington Htls. Co., Ltd	1	1½
5	Do. Cum. Pref.	1	1½
4	Do. Perp. Deb. Stk.	100	106½
2/4	Bush, W. J., & Co., Ltd., Cum. Pref.	5	5½
36/8	Do. 1 Deb. Stk., Red.	100	104
5½	Callard, Stewart, & Watt, Ltd., Cum. Pref.	1	1½
4/	Callender's Cable L., Shs.	5	9½
4½	Do. 1 Deb. Stk., Red.	100	111½
—	Campbell, R., & Sons, Lt.	3	2½
6	Cantareira Water, Bd., Rd	100	99½
5	Do. (2nd issue)	100	92
4	Cartavio Sugar, Ltd., 6 p.c. 1st Debs., Red.	90	80
4/6	Cassell & Co., Ltd., £10	9	18½
5	Causton, Sir J., & Sons, Ltd., Cum. Pref.	10	13½

Commercial, &c. (*continued*):—

Last Div.	Name.	Paid.	Price.
4	Cent. Prod. Mkt. of B.A. 1st Mt. Str. Debs.	100	81
4	Chappell & Co., Ltd., Mt. Deb. Stk. Red.	100	102
6/	Chicago & N.W. Gran. 8 p.c. Cum. Pref.	10	2½
—	Chicago Packing & Prov.	10	6
8	Do. Cum. Pref.	10	10½
6/	City Offices, Ltd	36½	13
3½	Do. Mt. Deb. Stk.	100	108½
7/2½	Cy. London Real Prop., Ltd., £25 shs.	12	19
4/6	Do. £12½ shs.	7½	13½
3½	Do. Deb. Stk. Red.	100	108½
3½	Do. Deb. Stk. Red.	100	106½
3	Do.	100	101½
4/	Cy. of Santos Imprvts., Ltd., 7 p.c. Pref.	10	8½
20/	Clay, Bock, & Co., Ltd.	10	8
8	Do. Cum. Pref.	10	11
6	Do. Mort. Deb.	100	107½
20/	Coats, J. & P., Ltd.	10	62
6	Do. Cum. Pref.	10	18
4½	Do. Deb. Stk. Red.	100	111½
9½d.	Coburg Hotel, Ltd.	1	1½
4	Do. Deb. Stk. Red.	100	102
6	Colonial Consign & Dis., Ltd., Cum. Pref.	5	4½
4½	Do. 1st Mort. Debs.	100	97½
—	Colorado Nitrate, Ltd.	5	½
4/	Co. Gén. des Asphtes. de F., Ltd.	6	6½
5	Do. Non-Cm. Prf.	—	5½
5	Cook, J. W., & Co., Ltd., Cum. Pref.	5	5½
5	Cook, T., & Son, Egypt, Ltd., 1st Mt. Deb. Red.	100	110½
—	Cork Co., Ltd., 6 p.c. Cum. Pref.	5	2½
5	Cory, W., & Sn, L., Cu. Pf.	5	6½
4	Do. 1st Deb. Stk. Red.	100	109
8½d.	Crisp & Co., Ltd	1	1½
5½	Dc. Cum. Pref.	1	1½
—	Crompton & Co., Ltd., 7 p.c. Cum. Pref.	5	2½
5	Do. 1st Mt. Reg. Deb.	—	88½
4/6	Crossley, J., & Sons, Ltd.	5	8½
5	Do. Cum. Pref.	5	6½
—	Crystal Pal. Ord. "A" Stk.	100	8½
—	Do. "B" Red. Stk	100	1½
6	Do. 6 p.c. 1st 1887 Deb. Stk. Red.	100	117½
—	Do. 6 p.c. 2nd 1887 Deb. Stk. Red.	100	47½
—	Do. 6 p.c. 3rd 1887 Deb. Stk. Red.	100	19½
3	Do. 3 p.c. 1st 1895 Deb. Stk.	100	96½
—	Daimler Motor, Ltd	10	5
4/	Dalgety & Co., £20 Shs.	5	5½
4½	Do. Deb. Stk	100	123
4	Do.	100	114
7/	De Keyser's Ryl. Htl., L.	10	14
5	Do. Cum. Pref.	10	11½
4	Do. Deb. Stk., Red.	100	110
6	Denny, H., & Sons, Ltd., Cum. Pref.	10	15
5/3	Devas, Routledge & Co., L.	7	8½
5	Dickinson, J., & Co., L., Cum. Pref. Stk.	100	123
4½	Domin. Cottn. Mls., Ltd. Mt. Stg. Dbs.	100	97
6/	Dorman, Long & Co., L.	5	4½
—	Eastmans, Ltd.	10	3½
12/	Do. 8 p.c. Cum. Pref.	10	10½
2/6	E. C. Powder, Ltd.	3	5½
1/6	Edison & Swn Utd. Elec. Ltd., "A" £5 Shs.	3	2½
2/6	Do. fully-paid	5	4½
4½	Ekman Pulp & Ppr. Co., Ltd., Mt. Deb., Red.	100	95
1/1½	Electric Construc., Ltd.	2	2½
7	Do. Cum. Pref.	2	3½
25/	Eley Bros., Ltd.	10	39
—	Elmore's Cop. Deptg., L.	1	½
—	Elmore's Wire Mnfg., L.	2	½
—	Elysée Pal. Hotel Co., L.	5/	½
5 p.c.	Do. 5 p.c. £100 Db., Rd.	70	70
8½d.	Evans, Ben., & Co., Ltd.	1	1
5	Do. 1 Mt. Db. Sk., Rd.	100	104
8½d.	Evans., D. H., & Co., L.	1	2
6	Do. Cum. Pref.	1	1½
4½	Do. 1 Mt. Db. Sk., Rd.	100	111
2/1	*Evening News*, L., 5 p.c. Cum. Pref.	5	5½
5/3	Evered & Co., L., £10 Sh.	7	13
7/6	Do.	10	19½
4	Fairbairn Pastoral Co. Aust., L., 1 Mt. Db., Rd.	100	102
6	Fairfield Shipbldg., Ltd., Cum. Pref.	10	10
4½	Do. Mort. Deb. Stk.	100	107½
6/	Farmer & Co., Ld., 6 p.c. Cum. Pref.	10	13½
10	Field, J. C. & J., Ltd.	10	10
14/	Do. 7 p.c. Cum. Pref.	10	14
9d.	Fordham, W.B., & Sns, Ld.	1	2
5/6	Fore-st. Warehouse, Ltd.	11	9½
4	Do. Regd. Debs., Rd	100	103½
2/6	Foster, M. B. & Sons, Ltd.	4	6½
5	Do. Pref.	10	1½
9/	Foster, Porter, & Co., L.	10½	1½
4	Fowler, J., & Co. (Leeds) Ltd., 1 Mt. Deb., Red.	100	103½
3/	Fraser & Chalmers, Ltd.	3	1½
4½	Free, Rodwell & Co., Ltd. Deb Stk.	100	105½
6½d.	Furness, T., & Co., Ltd., 5½ p.c. Cum. Pref.	1	1
4½	Gartside & Co. (of Manchstr), L., 1 Mt. Db. Sk	100	110
5	Genl. Hydraul. Power, L.	100	200

Commercial, &c. (*continued*):—

Last Div.	Name.	Paid.	Price.
8/	Gillman & Spencer, Ltd.	5	2½
6	Do. Pref.	5	5
5	Do. Mort. Debs	50	51
4	Goldsbro., Mort & Co., L., "A" Deb. Stk., Red.	100	72½
—	Do. 3 p.c. "B" Inc. Deb. Stk., Red.	100	17
8/	Gordon Hotels, Ltd.	10	20½
5½	Do. Cum. Pref.	10	14½
4½	Do. Perp. Deb. Stk.	100	137½
4	Do. do.	100	124½
—	Greenwich Inld. Linoleum Co., Ltd.	1	¼
7	Greenwood & Batley, Ltd., Cum. Pref.	10	10
7½d.	Hagemann & Co., Ltd., 6 p.c. Cum. Pref.	1	1½
—	Hammond, Ltd.	10	½
—	Do. 8 p.c. Cum. Pref.	10	2
—	Do. 6 p.c. Cum. Inc. Stk. Red.	100	52½
4	Hampton & Sons, Ltd., 4 p.c. 1 Mt. Db. St. Red.	100	105
	Hans Crescent Htl., L., 6 p.c. Cum. Pref.	5	3
4	Do. 1 Mt. Deb. Stk.	100	85
5	Harmsworth, Ld., Cm. Pf.	1	1⅛
4/	Harrison, Barber, Ltd.	5	4½
3/	Harrod's Stores, Ltd.	1	4½
2/6	Do. Cum. Pref.	5	7½
5½	Hawaiian Comcl. & Sug. 1 Mt. Debs.	100	94½
5	Harell, Watson, Ld., Cm. Pref.	10	12
6/	Henley's Teleg., Ltd.	10	23
7	Do. Pref. Shs.	10	19½
4½	Do. Mt. Db. Stk., Rd.	100	114½
6	Henry, Ltd.	10	12½
5	Do. Cum. Pref.	10	13½
4½	Do. Mt. Debs., Red.	50	53
6	Hepworth, Ld., Cm. Prf.	10	11½
—	Herrmann, Ltd.	1	½
—	Hildesheimer, Ltd.	3	1½
9½d.	Holbrn. & Frasca, Ltd.	1	2½
5	Do. Cum. Pref.	10	12½
4	Do. Deb. Stk.	100	113
6	Home & Col. Stres, Ltd., Cum. Pref.	5	7½
6	Hood & M.'s Stres., Ltd., Cum. Pref.	1	½
—	Hook, C. T Ltd.	10	6
7/2	Hornsby, Ltd., £10 Shs.	8	3½
5/6	Do. 6 p.c. Cm. Pf. Sk.	100	90
—	Hotchks. Ordn., Ltd.	10	½
—	Do. 7 p.c. Cm. Prf.	10	4
5	Do. 1 Mt. Dbs., Rd.	100	95½
6	Htl. Cecil, Ld., Cm. Prf.	5	4½
4	Do. 1 Mt. D. Sk., R.	100	107½
8/	Howard & Bulgh, Ltd.	10	35
6	Do. Pref.	10	16
4	Do. Deb. Stk., Red.	100	107
5/	Howell, J., Ltd., £5 Shs.	4	9½
—	Howell & Js., Ld., £3½ Shs.	3	½
1/6	Humber, Ltd.	1	¾
6	Do. Cum. Pref.	1	¾
2/6	Hunter, Wilts., Ltd.	5	7½
2/7	Hyam Clthg., Ltd., 5 p.c. Cum. Pref.	5	5½
10/	Impl. Russn. Cotton, L.	5	6
5	Impd. Industl. Dwgs., Ld.	100	123½
6d.	Do. Defrd.	1	1½
25/	Impd. Wood Pave., Ltd.	10	15
5/	Ind. Rubber, Gutta Per. Telegraph Works, Ltd.	10	22½
4	Do. 1 Mt. Debs., Red.	100	105
6	Intern. Tea, Cum. Pref.	5	6½
7½d.	Jays, Ltd.	1	1⅛
5½	Do. Cum. Pref.	5	6½
8½d.	Jones & Higgins, Ltd.	1	2½
4½	Do. 1 Mt. Db. Sk., Rd.	100	113
5/	Kelly's Directory, Ltd., 5 p.c. Cum. Pref.	10	12½
4	Do. Mort. Db. Sk., Rd.	100	106
—	Kent Coal Expirtn. Ltd.	1	¼
9½d.	King, Howmann, Ltd.	1	1½
4/	Kinloch & Co., Ltd.	5	8½
6	Do. Pref.	5	7
5	Lady's Pictorial Pub., Ltd., Cum. Pref.	5	5
—	La Guaira Harb., Ltd., 7 p.c. Deb. Stk.	100	—
—	Do. 2 Mt. 7 p.c. Deb. Bds., Red.	100	—
4/	Lagunas Nitrate, Ltd.	5	2
2/	Lagunas Syn., Ltd.	5	1⅛
5	Do. 1 Mt. Debs., Red.	100	80
—	L. Copais Ld., 1 Mt. 6 p.c. Debs., Red.	100	35½
3/	Lautaro Nitrate, Ltd.	5	4
5	Do. 1 Mt. Debs., Red.	—	100
9/	Lawes Chem. L., £10 shs.	9	5½
14/	Do. N. Cm. Min. Pref.	10	13
—	Leeds Forge, 7 p.c. Cm. Pf.	5	3½
5	Do. 1 Mt. Debs., Red.	50	47½
5	Lever Bros., L., Cm. Pf.	10	13
6	Liberty, L., 6 p.c. Cm. Pf.	10	14½
20/	Liebig's, Ltd.	20	75
5	Lilley & Sk., L., Cm. Pf.	5	5½
3/	Linoleum Manftg., Ltd.	5	21
3/	Linotype, Ltd., Pref.	5	6
4/	Do. Def.	5	8
4/	Lister & Co., Ltd.	10	4
5	Do. Cum. Pref.	10	8½
5/	Liverpool. Nitrate	5	6½
—	Liverpool. Warehsg., Ltd.	10	3½
5½	Do. Cum. Pref.	10	8½
4	Do. 1 Mt. Db. Stk., Rd.	100	105½
5½	Lockharts, Ltd., Cm. Pf.	1	1½
4/6	Ldn. & Til. Lightrage £10	9	5½
6/	Ldn. Comcl. Sale Rms., Ltd.	10	18
—	Do. 1 Mt. Deb. Stk., Red.	100	104
3	London Nitrate, Ltd.	5	2

Commercial, &c. (*continued*):—

Last Div.	Name.	Paid.	Price.
4/	London Nitrate, Ld. 8 p.c. Cm. Min. Pf.	5	3½
8/	London Pavilion, Ltd.	5	7
2/6	London Produce Clg. Ho., Ltd., £10 Shares	2½	3½
4/	London Stereos., Ltd.	5	3
6d.	Ldn. Un. Laun. L. Cm. Pf.	1	½
8½d.	Louise, Ltd.	1	½
5½	Do. Cum. Pref.	1	½
5/	Lovell & Christmas, Ltd.	5	12
6	Do. Cum. Pref.	5	7½
4	Do. Mt. Deb. Stk., Red.	100	107
1/3	Lyons, Ltd.	1	3½
4½	Do. 1 Mt. Deb. Stk., Rd.	100	108½
10/	Machinery Trust, Ltd.	5	15
4½	Do. 4½ Deb. Stk.	100	106
6	MacLellan, L., Min. C. Pf.	10	8
5	Do. 1 Mt. Debs., 1900	100	101½
—	McEwan, J. & Co., Ltd.	10	1½
6	Do. Mt. Debs., Red.	100	80½
8	McNamara, L., Cm. Pref.	10	9
7½d.	Maison Virot, Ltd.	1	1½
2/7	Do. 6 p.c. Cum. Pref.	5	4½
5/	Manbré Sacc., L., Cm. Pf.	10	12
10/	Mangan Brze., L., £10 Shs.	6	15½
2/	Mason & Mason, Ltd.	5	3½
6	Do. Cum. Pref.	5	5½
—	Maynards, Ltd.	1	½
6	Do. Cum. Pref.	1	½
9½d.	Mazawattee Tea, Ltd.	1	1½
5	Do. Cum. Pref.	5	5½
6	Mellin's Food Cum. Pref.	5	7
4½	Met. Ascn. Imp. Dwlgs. L.	100	110
3½	Do. 1 Mt. Deb. Stk.	100	97
5	Metro. Indus. Dwlgs., Ltd.	5	5
4	Do. do. Cum. Pref.	5	5½
5	Metro. Prop., L., Cm. Pf.	5	6½
4½	Do. 1st Mt. Debs. Stk.	100	110½
6	Mexican Cotton 1 Mt. Db.	100	97½
4½	Mid. Class Dwlgs., L., Db.	100	120½
1/	Millars' Karri, Ltd.	1	2½
6	Do. Cum. Pref.	1	1½
5/	Milner's Safe, Ltd.	10	20½
10/	Moir & Son, Ltd., Pref.	5	9
6	Morgan Cruc., L., Cm. Pf.	10	15
2/	Morris, B., Ltd.	3½	3½
—	Murray L. 5½ p.c. C. Pf.	5	5½
—	Do. 4½ 1 Mt. Db. Sk. Rd.	100	103
2/6	Natnl. Dwlgs., L., 5 p.c. Pf.	5	1
1/7½	Nat. Safe Dep., Ltd.	4	3½
6	Do. Cum. Pref.	1	1½
—	Native Guano, Ltd.	5	½
5/	Nelson Bros., Ltd.	10	2½
5	Do. Deb. Stk., Red.	100	80½
4/	Neuchtel Asph., Ltd.	10	11
—	New Central Borneo, Ld.	1	—
10d.	New Darvel Tob., Ltd.	18/	1½
2/4½	New Explosives, Ltd.	3	2
5/3½	New Gd. Htl., Bham, L.	5	4
5½	Do. Pref.	5	4½
4	Do. 1 Mt. Db. Stk., Rd.	100	95½
—	New Julia Nitrate, Ltd.	10/	1/16
—	New Ldn. Borneo Tob., L.	16/	¼
1/6	New Premier Cycle, Ltd.	1	½
6	Do. 6 p.c. Cum. Pref.	1	¾
4½	Do. 4½ p.c. 1 Mt. Db. Rd	100	—
—	New Tamargl. Nitr., Ltd	1	1/16
—	Do. 8 p.c. Cum. Pref.	1	⅜
6	Do. 6 p.c. 1 Mt. Dbs. Rd.	100	65½
3/7¾d.	Newnes, G., L., Cm. Prf.	1	1⅛
1/3	Nitr. Provision, Ltd.	2½	½
24/	Nobel-Dynam., Ltd.	10	17½
—	North Brazn. Sugar, Ltd.	1	¼
10/	Oakey, Ltd.	10	31
6	Do. Cum. Pref.	10	16
4/	Paccha Jazp. Nitr., Ltd.	5	1
5	Pac. Borax, L., 1 Db. Rd.	100	110
—	Palace Hotel, Ltd.	10	6½
5½	Do. Cum. Pref.	10	9
4	Do. 1 Mt. Deb. Stk.	100	105
2/6	Palmer, Ltd.	5	1½
6	Do. Cum. Pref.	5	3½
9½d.	Paquin, Ltd.	1	½
6	Do. Cum. Pref.	5	4½
5½	Parnall, Ltd., Cum. Pref.	1	½
4/6	Pawsons, Ltd., £10 Shs.	6	6½
4	Do. Mt. Debs., Red.	100	107
6	Pearks, G. & T., Ltd., 6 p.c. Cum. Pref.	1	⅞
1/2½	Pears, Ltd.	1	1½
6	Do. Cum. Pref.	10	14½
5	Do. Deb. Stk.	100	129
5½	Pearson, C. A., L., Cu. Pf.	5	5½
4/3	Peebles, Ltd.	5	8
5	Do. Cum. Pref.	5	6½
4½	Do. Mt. Deb. Stk. Red.	100	110
5½	Peek Bros., Ltd., 1 Cum. Pref., Nos. 1-60,000	5	6½
3½	Do. 3½ p.c. 1 Db. Stk.	100	103½
7½d.	Pegamoid, Ltd.	1	½
—	Phospho-Guano, Ltd.	5	2½
—	Pillsbury-W. Fl. Mills, L.	10	2
16/	Do. 8 p.c. Cum. Pref.	10	6½
6	Do. 1 Mort. Debs.	100	96½
7½d.	Plummer, Ltd.	1	1½
5	Do. Cum. Pref.	5	5½
13/	Price's Candle, Ltd.	16	40
6	Priest Marians, L., Cm. Pf.	1	1½
6	Pryce Jones, Ld., Cm. Pf.	5	7½
5	Do. Deb. Stk.	100	120½
10.8d.	Pullman, Ltd.	1	1½
6d.	Do. Cum. Pref.	1	1½
[illegible]	Raleigh Cycle, Ltd.	1	½
6	Do. Cum. Pref.	1	¼
—	Recife Drnge. Ld. 1 Mt. Debs., R	100	19
6	Redfern, Ltd. Cum. Prf.	10	14½
5	Ridgways, Ltd., Cu. Pf.	5	5½
—	R. Janeiro Cy. Imps., Ld.	25	9½
5	Do. Debs.	100	89½
5	Do. 1880-1893	100	89½
11/	R. Jan Fl. Mills, Ltd.	7	6½
5	Do. 1 Mt. Debs., Rd.	100	94

Commercial, &c. (*continued*):—

Last Div.	Name.	Paid.	Price.
—	Riv. Plate Meat, Ltd.	5	3½
—	Do. Pref.	5	5
8½d.	Roberts, J. R., Ltd.	1	1½
5	Do. 1 Mt. Db. Sk., Rd.	100	112
8½d.	Roberts, T. R., Ltd.	1	2½
5	Do. Cum. Pref.	1	1½
3/	Rosario Nit., Ltd.	5	3½
5	Do. Debs., Red.	100	105
5	Do. Huara, Debs.	—	104
1/	Rover Cycle, Ltd.	1	½
6/	Ryl. Aquarium, Ltd.	5	4½
6	Do. Pref.	5	6
5	Ryl. Htl., Edin., Cm. Pf.	1	1½
1/9½	Ryl. Niger, Ltd., £10 Sh.	2	2½
6/	Do.	10	14½
3/	Ruston, Proctor, Ltd.	10	11
4½	Do. 1 Mort. Debs.	100	104
6/	Sadler, Ltd.	12	7
—	Sal. Carmen Nit., Ltd.	5	4½
9d.	Salmon & Gluck., Ltd.	1	1½
2/	Salt Union, Ltd.	10	1½
14/	Do. 7 p.c. Pref.	10	5½
4½	Do. Deb. Stk.	100	99½
4½	Do. "B" Deb. Sk., Rd.	100	97½
—	San Donato Nit., Ltd.	5	½
2/6	San Jorge Nit., Ltd.	5	3½
—	San Pablo Nit., Ltd.	5	½
—	San Sebastn. Nit., Ltd.	5	½
1/	Sanitas, Ltd	1	2½
—	Sa. Elena Nit., Ltd.	5	½
—	Sa. Rita Nit., Ltd.	5	2
10/	Savoy Hotel, Ltd.	10	19
7	Do. Pref.	10	16
4	Do. 1 Mt. Deb. Stk.	100	112½
5	Do. Debs., Red	100	102½
5	Do. & Ldn. For. Htl., Ltd., 5 p.c. Debs. Red.	100	99
1½d.	Schweppes, Ltd.	1	1⅛
—	Do. Def.	1	½
5	Do. Cum. Pref.	1	1½
4	Do. Deb. Stk.	100	108
1/	Singer Cyc., Ltd.	1	½
5½	Do Cum. Pref.	1	½
—	Smokeless Pwdr., Ltd.	1	½
5½d.	S. Eng. Dairies, Ltd., 6 p.c. Cum. Pref.	1	1½
—	Sowler Thos. L.	1	1½
—	Do. 5½ Cm. Pf.	5	5½
3/6	Spencer, Turner, & Co. Ltd	5	9
5	Do. Cum. Pref.	5	6½
5	Spicer, Ld., 5 p.c. Dbs. Rd.	100	65
4/	Spiers & Pond, Ltd.	10	20½
5	Do. 1 Mt. Debs., Red.	100	116½
5	Do. "A" Db. Stk., Rd.	100	110
5	Do. "B" 1 Db. Stk., Rd.	100	110
4	Do. Fd. "C" 1 Db. S., R.	100	103
5/	Spratt's, Ltd	5	13½
4	Do. Debs., 1914	—	105
5	Steiner Ld., Cm. Pf.	10	11
4	Do. 1 Mt. Db. Sk. Rd.	100	106
7/	Stewart & Clydesdale, L.	10	14½
6	Do. Cum. Pref.	10	15½
—	Swan & Edgar, L.	1	1½
1/3	Sweetmeat Automatic, L.	1	4
2/9	Teetgen, Ltd., Cum. Pref.	5	6
12/	Teleg. Construction., Ld.	12	40½
5	Do. Db. Bds., Rd., 1899	100	103½
3/0½	Tilling, Ld. 5½ p.c. Cm. Prf.	5	6½
4	Do. 4 p.c. 1 Dbs., Rd.	—	104
8½d.	Tower Tea, Ltd.	1	1½
5	Do. Cum. Pref.	5	5½
5	Travers, Ltd., Cum. Pref.	10	12½
4	Do. 1 Mt. Dbs., Rd.	100	106
6	Tucuman Sug., 1 Dbs., Rd.	100	100
4/	United Alkali, Ltd.	10	2
7	Do. Cum. Pref.	10	9
5	Do. Mt. Db. Stk., Rd.	100	110½
2½d.	United Horse Shoe, Ltd., Non-Cum. 8 p.c. Pref.	1	½
5	Un. Kingm. Tea, Cm. Prf.	5	5
2/	Un. Lankat Plant., Ltd.	1	2½
2/	Un. Limmer Asphlte., Ld.	3	4½
5/	Val de Travers Asph., L.	10	15
3/	V. den Bergh's, Ltd., Cm. Pref.	5	6½
6	Walkers, Park., L., C. Pf.	10	4
4½	Do. 1 Mt. Debs., Red.	100	90½
6/	Wallis, Thos. & Co., Ltd.	5	14
6	Do. Cum. Pref.	5	8½
5½	Waring, Ltd., Cum. Pref.	5	5½
4½	Do. 1 Mt. Db. Sk., Red.	100	111½
4½	Do. Irred. "B" Db. Stk.	100	104
12/	Waterlow, Dfd. Ord.	10	15½
12/	Do. Pref.	10	15
—	Do. Cum. Pref.	10	10½
10/	Waterlow Bros. & L., Ld.	10	9
1/2½	Welford, Ltd.	1	2½
4½	Do. Debs., Red.	100	107
4½d.	Welford's Surrey Dairies, Ltd.	1	1½
7½d.	West London Dairy, Ltd.	1	1
4½	Wharncliffe Dwllgs., L., Pf.	10	12
18/10	Do. 3 p.c. Irr. Mt. Db. Sk.	100	96
6d.	White, A. J., Ltd.	1	½
6	Do. 6 p.c. Cum. Pref.	1	⅞
4	White, J. Bazley, Ltd., 1 Mort. Debs., Red.	100	96½
5	White, R., Ltd., 1 Mort. Deb. Stock, Red.	100	104½
8/	White, Tomkins, Ltd	10	12½
5	Do. Cum. Pref.	10	12½
6	White, W. N., L., Cm. Pf.	1	1
2/6	Wickens, Pease & Co., L.	5	2
6	Wilkie, Ltd., Cum. Pref.	10	16
3/6	Willans & Robinson, Ltd.	5	8½
6	Do. Cum. Pref.	5	7
4½	Do. 1 Mt. Db. Stk., Red.	100	107
7½d.	Williamsons, L., Cm. Prf.	1	1½
6	Winterbottm. Book Cloth, Ltd., Cum. Prf.	10	15
3/	Yates, Ltd.	5	6½
6	Do. Cum. Pref.	5	6½
	Young's Paraffin, Ltd.	4	1½

CORPORATION STOCKS—COLONIAL AND FOREIGN.

Per Cent.	Name.	Paid.	Price.
6	Auckland City, '72 1904-24	100	118
6	Do. Cons., '79, Red. 1930	100	128½
5	Do. Deb. Ln., '83. 1934-8	100	117
6	Auckland Harb. Debs.	100	111½
5	Do. 1917	100	112
5	Do. 1936	100	116
5½	Balmain Boro' 1914	—	117
5	Boston City (U.S.)	100	102½
5	Do. 1900	100	107½
5	Brunswick Town 5 c. Debs. 1916-20	100	111
15/	B. Ayres City 6 p.c.	100	61
4½	Do. 4½ p.c.	100	77
5	Cape Town, City of	100	113
4	Do. 1943	100	114
4	Chicago, City of, Gold 1915	—	110
6	Christchurch 1926	100	130½
—	Cordoba City	100	17½
5	Duluth (U.S.) Gold 1926	—	110
6	Dunedin (Otago) 1925	100	127½
6	Do. 1906	100	113
5	Do. Consols 1908	100	113
4	Durban Insc. Stk. 1944	100	111
4	Essex Cnty., N. Jersey 1926	100	114½
5	Fitzroy, Melbrne. 1916-19	100	110
5	Gisborne Harbour 1915	100	110½
4	Greymouth Harbour 1925	100	111
4	Hamilton 1934	100	109
5	Hobart Town 1918-30	100	116
4	Do. 1940	100	107
4½	Invercargill Boro. Dbs. 1936	100	113
6	Kimberley Boro., S.A. Dbs.	—	104
4	Launceston Twn. Dbs. 1916	100	107
6	Lyttleton, N.Z., Harb. 1929	100	125
4	Melbourne Bd. of Wks. 1921	100	109
5	Melb. City Debs. 1897-1907	100	107½
4½	Do. Debs. 1908-27	100	113½
4	Do. Debs. 1915-20-22	100	105
5	Melbne. Harb. Bds., 1908-9	100	112
4½	Do. do. 1915	100	110
4	Do. do. 1918-21	100	106
4½	Melbrne. Tms. Dbs. 1914-16	100	113
4½	Do. Fire Brig. Db. 1921	100	109
5	Mexico City Stg.	100	92
4	Moncton N. Bruns. City	100	104
4½	Montevideo	100	59
5	Montreal Stg.	100	104
5	Do. 1874	100	104
5	Do. 1879	100	106
3½	Do. 1933	100	104
3	Do. Perm. Deb. Stk.	100	98
4	Do. Cons. Deb. Stk. 1932	100	113
6	Napier Boro. Consolid. 1914	100	119
5	Napier Harb. Debs. 1920	100	115
5	Do. Debs. 1928	100	107
6	New Plymouth Harb. Debs. 1909	100	106
6	New York City 1901	—	107½
3½	Do. 1910-26	—	106½
4½	Nth. Melbourne Debs. 1-600 1921	100	105
5	Oamaru Boro. Cons. 1920	100	101
6	Do. Harb. Bds. (Reg.)	100	74
25/	Do. 6 p.c. (Bearer) 1919	100	35
6	Otago Harb. Deb. Reg.	100	103
6	Do. 1877	100	107
6	Do. 1881 1921	100	115
5	Do. Debs. 1921	100	107
5	Do. Cons. 1934	100	105
6	Ottawa City	100	111
6	Do. 1904	100	115½
4½	Do. Debs. 1913	100	112
6	Port Elizabeth Waterworks	100	113½
5	Port Louis	100	111
5	Prahran Debs. 1917	100	111
4	Do. Debs. 1919	100	103
6	Quebec C. Coupon. 1875 1905	100	112
6	Do. do. 1876 1908	100	116
4½	Do. Debs. 1914-18	100	108
4	Do. Debs. 1923	100	108
3½	Do. Cns. Rg. Stk., Red.	100	101
5	Richmond (Melb.) Dbs. 1917	100	113
4	Rio Janeiro City	100	59
4	Rome City	100	—
4	Do. 2nd to 8th Iss.	100	94
—	Rosario C.	100	26½
—	Do.	100	26½
4	St. Catherine (Ont.) 1926	100	103
4	St. John, N.B., Debs. 1934	—	104
4½	St. Kilda (Melb) Dbs. 1918-21	100	104
4	St. Louis C. (Miss.) 1911	100	105
4	Do. 1917	100	106
3'65	Do. 1915	—	110
—	Santa Fé City Debs.	100	21
6	Santos City	100	95
6	Sofia City	100	86
5	Sth. Melbourne Debs. 1915	100	111
4½	Do. Debs. 1919	100	107
5	Sydney City 1904	100	109
4	Do. Debs. 1912-13	100	107
4	Do. do. (1894) 1919	100	109
7	Timaru Boro. 7 p.c. 1910	100	126½
5	Timaru Harb. Debs 1914	100	106
5	Do. Debs. 1916	100	106
6	Toronto City Wtrwks 1904-6	100	110
6	Do. Cons. Debs. 1898	100	101
5	Do. G. Cns. Dbs. 1919-20	100	118
4	Do. Stlg. 1922-8	100	107
4	Do. Local Improv.	100	102
3½	Do. 1929	100	105
5½	Valparaiso	100	101
4	Vancouver 1931	100	109
4	Do. 1932	100	108
6	Wanganui Harb. Dbs. 1905	100	110
6	Wellington Con. Deb. 1907	100	117
6	Do. Improv., 1879	100	126
6	Do. Wtrwks. Dbs., 1880	100	126
4½	Do. Debs., 1893 1933	100	116
4½	Wellington Harb. 1907	100	106
4	Westport Harb. Dbs. 1925	100	111
6	Winnipeg City Deb. 1907	—	118
5	Do. 1914	100	118

FINANCIAL, LAND, AND INVESTMENT.

Last Div.	Name.	Paid.	Price.
5	Agncy, Ld. & Fin. Aust., Ltd., Mt. Db. Stk., Rd.	100	90½
6	Amer. Frehld. Mt. of Lon., Ld., Cum. Pref. Stk.	100	82½
4½	Do. Deb. Stk., Red.	100	96
1/	Anglo-Amer. Db. Cor., L.	2	1
4	Do. Deb. Stk., Red	100	106½
5½	Ang.-Ceylon & Gen. Est., Ltd., Cons. Stk.	100	68
6	Do. Reg. Debs., Red.	100	106½
—	Ang.-Fch. Explorn., Ltd.	1	2¾
6	Do. Cum. Pref.	1	1½
—	Argent. Ld. & Inv., Ltd. £1 Shares	10/	nil
—	Do. Cum. Pref.	4	2
1/	Assets Fnders.' Sh., Ltd.,	4	1⅝
6/	Assets Realis., Ltd., Ord.,	5	9
5	Do. Cum. Pref.	5	6½
21/	Austrln. Agricl. £25 Shs.	21½	65½
—	Aust. N. Z. Mort., Ltd., £10 Shs.	1	1⅜d.
4½	Do. Deb. Stk., Red.	100	90½
4	Do. Deb. Stk., Red.	100	82½
4½	Australian Est. & Mt., L., 1 Mt. Deb. Stk., Red.	100	106
5	Do. "A" Mort. Deb. Stk., Red.	100	97
2/6	Australian Mort., Ld., & Fin., Ltd. £25 Shs.	5	4½
1/6	Do. New, £25 Shs.	3	2½
4	Do. Deb. Stk.	100	112
3	Do. Do.	100	85
5	Baring Est. 2 Mt. Debs., Red.	100	105
5	Bengal Presidy. 1 Mort. Deb., Red.	100	106
25/	British Amer. Ld. "A"	1	20
—	Do. "B"	24	6½
1/2½	Brit. & Amer. Mt., Ltd. £10 Shs.	2	¾
5/	Do. Pref.	10	10
4	Do. Deb. Stk., Red.	100	101
1/3	Brit. & Austrlsn Tst Ln., Ltd. £25 Shs.	2½	⅝
4½	Do. Perm. Debs., Red.	100	103
1½d.	Brit. N. Borneo. £1 Shs.	15/	1⅛
2½d.	Do.	1	1
—	Brit. S. Africa	1	2½
5	Do. Mt. Deb., Red.	—	97½
6	B. Aires Harb. Tst., Red.	100	100
12/6	Canada Co.	1	26
—	Canada N. W. Ld., Ltd.	$25	85½
—	Do. Pref.	$100	$54
4	Canada Perm. Loan & Sav. Perp. Deb. Stk.	100	99½
—	Curamalan Ld., 1 Mt. 7 p.c. Bds., Red.	—	92½
3/7½	Deb Corp., Ld., £10 Shs	4	3½
5	Do. Cum. Pref.	10	11½
4	Do. Perp. Deb. Stk.	100	116
9d.	Deb. Corp. Fders' Sh., Ld.	3	¾
4/5⅖	Eastn. Mt. & Agncy, Ld., "A"	10	6½
4½	Do. Deb. Stk., Red.	100	100
5	Equitable Revers. In. Ltd.	100	—
2/	Exploration, Ltd.	1	1½
1	Freehold Trst. of Austrln. Ltd. £10 Shs.	1	¾
4	Do. Perp. Deb. Stk.	100	102
—	Genl. Assets Purchase, Ltd., 5 p.c. Cum. Pref.	10	—
50/	Genl. Reversionary, Ltd.	100	—
4½	Holborn Vi. Land	100	105
4½	House Prop. & Inv.	100	86½
13/	Hudson's Bay	13	22½
4	Impl. Col. Fin. & Agcy. Corp.	100	94½
4½	Impl. Prop. Inv., Ltd., Deb. Stk., Red.	100	91½
2/6	Internatl. Fincial. Soc., Ltd. £7½ Shs.	2½	1½
4	Do. Deb. Stk., Red.	100	97½
1/9½	Ld. & Mtge. Egypt, Ltd. £18 Shs.	3	2½
5	Do. Debs., Red.	100	103
4½	Do. Debs., Red.	100	101
—	Ld. Corp. of Canada, Ltd.	1	⅛
4½	Ld. Mtge. Bk. of Texas Deb. Stk.	100	—
3½	Ld. Mtge. Bk. Victoria 4½ p.c. Deb. Stk.	100	78
2/9½	Law Debent. Corp., Ltd., £10 Shs.	2	2
4½	Do. Cum. Pref.,	10	12
4	Do. Deb. Stk.	100	119
1/	Ldn. & Australasian Deb. Corp., Ltd., £4 Shs.	2	½
4½	Do. 4½ p.c. Mt. Deb. Stk., Red.	100	101
—	Ldn. & Middx. Frhld. Est. £2 Shs.	35/	3½
2/6	Lndn. & N. Y. Inv. Corp., Ltd.	5	2
5	Do. 5 p.c. Cum. Pref.	10	9
1/6	Ldn. & Nth. Assets Corp., Ltd., £2 Shs.	1½	⅞
2/	Ldn. & N. Deb. Corp., L.	2	1½
4/	Ldn. & S. Afric. Explrn. Ltd.	½	14
2/	Mtge. Co. of R. Plate, Ltd. £10 Shs.	2	3½
4½	Do. Deb. Stk., Red.	100	112
4½	Morton, Rose Est., Ltd., 1st Mort. Debs.	—	101
6/	Natal Land Col. Ltd.	10	6½
4/	Do. 8 p.c. Pref., 1870	5	8½
5/6	Natl. Disct. L., £25 Shs.	5	10¾
4½	New Impl. Invest., Ltd. Pref. Stk.	100	61½
—	New Impl. Invest., Ltd. Def. Stk.	100	9
4	N. Zld. Ln. & Mer. Agcy., Ltd. Prf. Ln. Deb. Stk	100	97

Financial, Land, &c. (*continued*):—

Last Div.	Name.	Paid.	Price.
16/	N. Zld. Ln. & Mer. Agcy., Ltd. 5 p.c. "A" Db. Sk.	100	42½
—	N. Zld. Ln. & Mer. Agcy., Ltd., 5 p.c. "B" Db. Stk.	100	4
2/6	N. Zld. Tst. & Ln. Ltd., £25 Shs.	5	1½
12/6	N. Zld. Tst. & Ln. Ltd., 5 p.c. Cum. Pref.	25	19
—	N. Brit. Australsn. Ltd.	100	6½
—	Do. Irred. Guar.	100	32½
5	Do. Mort. Debs.	100	82½
4½	N. Queensld. Mort. & Inv., Ltd., Deb. Stk.	100	95
—	Oceana Co., Ltd.	—	—
6	Peel Riv., Ld. & Min. Ltd.	100	89
—	Peruvian Corp., Ltd.	100	2¾
—	Do. 4 p.c. Pref.	100	10
3	Do. 6 p.c. 1 Mt. Debs., Red.	100	42½
—	Queensld. Invest. & Ld. Mort. Pref. Ord. Stk.	100	20
3/7	Queensld. Invest. & Ld. Mort. Ord. Shs.	4	4
4	Queensld. Invest. & Ld. Mort. Perp. Debs.	100	90
3½	Rally. Roll Stk. Tst. Deb., 1903-6	100	100½
50/	Reversiony. Int. Soc., Ltd.	100	—
2/8½	Riv. Plate Trst., Loan & Agcy., L., "A" £10 Shs.	2	4⅝
1/6	Riv. Plate Trst., Loan & Agcy., Ltd., Def. "B"	5	4
	Riv. Plate Trst., Loan & Agy., L., Db. Stk., Red.	100	109
—	Santa Fé & Cord. Gt. South Land, Ltd.	20	5
—	Santa Fé Land	10	2½
2/	Scot. Amer. Invest., Ltd. £10 Shs.	2	2¾
2½	Scot. Australian Invest., Ltd., Cons.	100	32½
6	Scot. Australian Invest., Ltd., Guar. Pref.	100	135½
5	Scot. Australian Invest., Ltd., Guar. Pref.	100	106½
4	Scot. Australian Invest., Ltd., 4 p.c. Perp. Dbs.	100	105½
5	Sivagunga Zemdy., 1st Mort., Red.	100	101
20/	Sth. Australian	20	54½
3½	Stock Exchange Deb., Rd.	—	101½
—	Strait Develt., Ltd.	1	1/16
2/6	Texas Land & Mt., Ltd. £10 Shs.	2½	3
4½	Texas Land & Mt., Ltd., Deb. Stk., Red.	100	105
—	Transvaal Est. & Dev., L.	1	1/16
—	Transvaal Lands, Ltd., £1 Shs.	15/	⅜
—	Do. F. P.	1	½
—	Transvaal Mort., Loan, & Fin., Ltd., £10 Shs.	2	¼
2/	Tst & Agcy. of Austrlsa., Ltd., £10 Shs.	1	2
7/5	Do. Old, fully paid	10	15½
5/7	Do. New, fully paid	10	12½
5	Do. Cum. Pref.	10	12¾
3/	Trust & Loan of Canada, £20 Shs.	5	4½
1/9½	Do. New £20 Shs	3	2½
—	Tst. & Mort. of Iowa, Ltd., £10 Shs.	2½	¾
4½	Do. Deb. Stk. Red.	100	92½
—	Tst., Loan, & Agency of Mexico, Ltd., £10 Shs.	2	¼
—	Trsts., Exors, & Sec. Ins. Corp., Ltd., £10 Shs.	7	1⅝
5/	Union Dsc., Ld., £10 Shs.	5	11
—	Union Mort. & Agcy. of Aust., Ltd., £6 Shs.	2	—
6	Do. Pref. Stk.	100	35
—	Do. 6 p. Pref. £6 Shs.	2	½
4½	Do. Deb. Stk.	100	92½
4	Do. Deb. Stk.	100	85½
5	Do. Deb. Stk. Red.	100	96½
1/0	U.S. Deb. Cor. Ltd., £8 Shs.	1	⅛
5½	Do. Cum. Pref. Stk.	100	102½
4½	Do. Irred. Deb. Stk.	100	108½
5	U.S. Tst. & Guar. Cor., Ltd., Pref. Stk.	100	71½
6/	Van Dieman's	25	16
4	Walker's Prop. Cor., Ltd., Guar. 1 Mt. Deb. Stk.	100	109
4½	Wstr. Mort. & Inv., Ltd., Deb. Stk.	100	92½

FINANCIAL—TRUSTS.

Last Div.	Name.	Paid.	Price.
1/	Afric. City Prop., Ltd.	1	1½
6	Do. Cum. Pref.	1	1
4	Alliance Invt., Ltd., Cm. 4½ p.c. Prefd.	100	80½
—	Do. Defd.	100	13½
4	Do. Deb. Stk. Red.	100	106½
5	Amrcn. Invt., Ltd., Prfd.	100	124½
5	Do. Defd.	100	94½
4	Do. Deb. Stk. Red.	100	117½
4	Army & Navy Invt., Ltd., 5 p.c. Prefd.	100	80½
—	Do. Defd. Stk.	100	17½
4	Do. Deb. Stk.	100	105½
4	Atlas Investment, Ltd., Prefd. Stk.	100	70½
4½	Bankers' Invest., Ltd., Cum. Prefd.	100	106
1/0/0	Do. Defd.	100	28½
4	Do. Deb. Stk.	100	113

Financial—Trusts (*continued*):—

Last Div.	Name.	Paid.	Price.
3/	Brewery & Comml. Inv., Ltd., £10 Shs.	5	6
4	British Investment, Ltd., Cum. Prefd.	100	109½
5	Do. Defd.	100	104½
4	Do. Deb. Stk.	100	109½
6	Brit. Steam. Invst., Ltd., Prefd.	100	116½
8/0/0	Do. Defd.	100	70½
4½	Do. Perp. Deb. Stk.	100	120½
2/3	Car Trust Invst., Ltd., £10 Shs.	2½	2
5	Do. Pref.	100	105½
4	Do. Deb. Stk., 1915	100	105
4	Clnl. Sec., Ltd., Prefd.	100	108½
2	Do. Defd.	100	50
4	Consolidated, Ltd., Cum. 1st Pref.	100	94½
4	Do. 5 p.c. Cm. and do.	100	74½
—	Do. Defd.	100	14½
4½	Do. Deb. Stk.	100	111½
4½	Edinburgh Invest., Ltd., Cum. Prefd. Stk.	100	110½
4	Do. Deb. Stk. Red.	100	106½
5	Foreign, Amer. & Gen. Invt., Ltd., Prefd.	100	119½
2	Do. Defd.	100	56½
4	Do. Deb. Stk.	100	117½
5	Foreign & Colonial Invt., Ltd., Prefd.	100	135½
5½	Do. Defd.	100	97½
4½	Gas, Water & Gen. Invt., Cum. Prefd. Stk.	100	95
2	Do. Defd. Stk.	100	34½
4	Do. Deb. Stk.	100	106
5	Gen. & Com. Invt., Ltd., Prefd. Stk.	100	107½
2	Do. Defd. Stk.	100	37½
4	Do. Deb. Stk.	100	111½
1/9	Globe Telegph. & Tst., Ltd.	10	12½
6	Do. do. Pref.	10	18
4	Govt. & Genl. Invt., Ld., Prefd.	100	84½
3½	Do. Defd.	100	42½
4½	Govts. Stk. & other Secs. Invt., Ltd., Prefd.	100	91½
1	Do. Defd.	100	27
4½	Do. Deb. Stk.	100	110
4	Do. do.	100	104
4½	Guardian Invt., Ltd., Pfd.	100	92½
—	Do. Defd.	100	21½
4	Do. Deb. Stk.	100	105
5	Indian & Gen. Inv., Ltd., Cum. Prefd.	100	107½
2½	Do. Defd.	100	56
4½	Do. Deb. Stk.	100	121½
5	Indust. & Gen. Tst., Ltd., Unified	100	102½
3½	Do. Deb. Stk. Red.	100	102½
4½	Internat. Invt., Ltd., Cm. Prefd.	100	74½
—	Do. Defd.	100	11
4	Do. Deb. Stk.	100	104
4	Invest. Tst. Cor. Ltd. Pfd.	100	103
4	Do. Defd.	100	89
4	Do. Deb. Stk. Red.	100	107
25/	Ldn. Gen. Invest. Ltd., 5 p.c. Cum. Prefd.	100	111½
37/6	Do. Defd.	100	120
4½	Ldn. Scot. Amer. Ltd. Pfd.	100	104½
£3	Do. Defd.	100	59½
4	Do. Deb. Stk.	100	112
4	Ldn. Tst., Ltd., Cum. Prfd. Stk.	100	104
4	Do. Defd. Stk.	100	76½
4	Do. Deb. Stk., Red.	100	107
3½	Do. Mt. Deb. Stk., Red.	100	104
5	Mercantile Invt. & Gen., Ltd., Prefd.	100	115
2	Do. Defd.	100	54
4	Do. Deb. Stk.	100	117½
4	Merchants, Ltd., Pref. Stk.	100	105½
4	Do. Ord.	100	82
4	Do. Deb. Stk.	100	117
6	Municipal, Ltd., Prefd.	100	56½
—	Do. Defd.	100	18½
4½	Do. Debs.	100	113
4½	Do. Debs. "B"	100	99½
4½	Do. "C" Deb. Stk.	100	88½
5	New Investment, Ltd. Ord.	100	95½
5	Omnium Invest., Ltd., Pfd.	100	91½
1	Do. Defd.	100	26½
4	Do. Deb. Stk.	100	104
5/	Railway Deb. Tst. Ld., £10 Shs.	10	7½
5	Do. Debs., Red.	100	107½
4½	Do. Deb. Stk., 1911	100	105½
4	Do. do. 1927	100	107½
4	Railway Invst. Ltd., Prefd.	100	117
13/6	Do. Defd.	100	23
8/	Railway Share Trust & Agency "A"	8	6½
7½	Do. "B" Pref. Stk.	100	144½
4½	River Plate & Gen. Invt., Ltd., Prefd.	100	105
£8	Do. Defd.	100	50½
5	Scot. Invst., Ltd., Pfd. Stk.	100	96½
7½	Do. Defd.	100	26½
4	Do. Deb. Stk.	100	108
4½	Sec. Scottish Invst., Ltd., Cum. Prefd.	100	90½
£2	Do. Defd. Stk.	100	32
4	Do. Deb. Stk.	100	107½
7/6	Sth. Africa Gold Tst., Ltd.	1	4⅝
6	Do. Cum. Pref.	1	1
5½	Do. 1st Debs., Red.	100	102
1/9	Stock Conv. & Invest., Ltd., £5 Shs.	1	1⅝
4½	Do. do. 4½ p.c. Cm. Prf.	100	113½
3½	Do. Ldn. & N. W. 1st. Charge Prefd.	100	116½
4	Do do. 2nd Chge Prfd.	100	113
32/6	Do. do. Defd. Charge	100	31
3	Do. N. East. 1 Chge Pfd.	100	95

Financial—Trusts (*continued*):—

Last Div.	Name.	Paid.	Price.
37/6	Stock N. East Defd. Chge	100	40
6	Submarine Cables	100	141½
5	U.S. & S. Amer. Invest., Ltd., Prefd.	100	99½
2	Do. Defd.	100	29½
4	Do. Deb. Stk.	100	105½

GAS AND ELECTRIC LIGHTING.

Last Div.	Name.	Paid.	Price.
10/6	Alliance & Dublin Con. 10 p.c. Stand.	10	25½
7/6	Do. 7 p.c. Stand.	10	17
5	Austln. Gas Lght. (Syd.) Debs. 1902	100	106
5	Bay State of N. Jrsy. Sk. Fd. Tst. Bd., Red.	—	92½
3/	Bombay, Ltd.	5	6½
2/4½	Do. New	4	5½
12	Brentford Cons.	100	302½
9	Do. New	100	232½
5	Do. Pref.	100	147½
4	Do. Deb. Stk.	100	136
11½	Brighton & Hove Gen. Cons. Stk.	100	277½
8½	Do. "A" Cons. Stk.	100	202½
5	Bristol 5 p.c. Max.	100	132½
22/6	British Gas Light, Ltd.	20	57
11/6	Bromley Gas Consumrs.' 10 p.c. Stand.	10	26
8/6	Do. 7 p.c. Stand.	10	21
	Brush Electl. Enging., L.	—	2½
6	Do. 6 p.c. Pref.	—	2¾
4½	Do. Deb. Stk.	100	111
4½	Do. 2 Deb. Stk., Red.	100	103½
5/	B. Ayres (New), Ltd.	10	10
4	Do. Deb. Stk., Rd.	—	98
12/	Cagliari Gas & Wtr., Ltd.	20	31
8/	Cape Town & Dist. Gas Light & Coke, Ltd.	10	17½
4½	Do. Pref.	10	12½
6	Do. 1 Mt. Debs. 1910	50	60
3/	Charing Cross & Strand Elec. Sup., Ltd.	5	14½
4½	Do. Cum. Pref.	5	6½
2/6	Chelsea Elec. Sup., Ltd.	5	11½
4½	Do. Deb. Stk., Red.	100	116
5	Chic. Edison Co. 1 Mt., Red.	$1000	108
14/	City of Ldn. Elec. Lht., L.	10	29
—	Do. New	10	28½
6/	Do. Cum. Pref.	10	18
5	Do. Deb. Stk., Red.	100	131½
13½	Commercial, Cons.	100	342½
10½	Do. New	100	257½
4½	Do. Deb. Stk.	100	155½
14	Continental Union, Ltd.	100	249½
11	Do. Pref. Stk.	100	216½
—	County of Lon. & Brush Prov. Elec. Lg., Ltd.	10	15½
6	Do. Cum. Pref.	10	16
14	Croydon Comcl. Gas, Ld., "A" Stk., 10 p.c.	100	319½
11	Do. "B" Stk., 7 p.c.	100	265
5½	Crystal Pal. Dist. Ord. 5 p.c. Stk.	100	137½
5	Do. Pref. Stk.	100	141½
8/	European, Ltd.	10	26
6/	Do.	7½	18½
12½	Gas Light & Ck Cons. Stk., "A" Ord.	100	299½
4	Do. "B" (4 p.c. Max.)	100	122½
10	Do. "C," "D," & "E." (Pref.)	100	319½
5	Do. "F" (Pref.)	100	152½
7½	Do. "G" (Pref.)	100	222½
7	Do. "H" (7 p.c. Max.)	100	203½
10	Do. "J" (Pref.)	100	318½
6	Do. "K"	100	187½
4	Do. Deb. Stk.	100	139½
4½	Do. do.	100	157½
6	Do. do.	100	207½
8/	Hong Kong & China, Ld.	10	14½
—	House to House Elec. Light Sup., Ltd.	5	11
7	Do. Cum. Pref.	5	11½
10	Imperial Continental	100	217½
3½	Do. Deb. Stk., Red	100	104½
2/	Malta & Medit., Ltd.	5	5½
5/	Metrop. Elec. Sup., Ltd.	10	20½
3/8	Do. New	10	20
4½	Do. 1 Mt. Deb. Stk.	100	119
5	Metro. of Melbrne. Dbs. 1908-12	100	113
4½	Do. Debs. 1918-22-4	100	110
10/	Monte Video, Ltd.	20	16
8/	Notting Hill Elec. Ltg., Ltd.	10	17½
4/6	Oriental, Ltd.	5	8½
4/0½	Do. New	4½	7½
10d.	Do. do. 1879	1	1½
3/6	Ottoman, Ltd.	5	5
—	Para, Ltd.	—	—
6	People's Gas Lt. & C. of Chic. 2 Mt. 1904	100	105½
5	River Plate Elec. Lgt. & Trac., Ltd., 1 Deb. Stk.	—	92½
8½	Royal Elec. of Montreal	—	146
4½	Do. 1 Mt. Deb.	100	106
11/	St. James' & Pall Mall Elec. Light, Ltd.	5	19
7	Do. Pref.	5	10½
4	Do. Deb. Stk., Red.	100	108½
10/	San Paulo, Ltd.	10	16½

Gas and Electric (*continued*):—

Last Div.	Name.	Paid.	Price.
10	Sheffield Unit. Gas Lt. "A"	100	251½
10	Do. "B"	100	251½
10	Do. "C"	100	251½
—	Sth. Ldn. Elec. Sup., Ld.	2	3
5½	South Metropolitan	100	147½
3	Do. 3 p.c. Deb. Stk.	100	106½
12	Tottenham & Edmonton Gas Lt. & C., "A"	100	290
9	Do. "B"	100	210
7/	Tuscan, Ltd.	10	14
5	Do. Debs., Red.	100	101½
4/9	West Ham 10 p.c. Stan.	5	12
4/	Wstmnstr. Elec. Sup., Ld.	5	18½

INSURANCE

Last Div.	Name.	Paid.	Price.
4/	Alliance, £20 Shs.	44/	11½
10/	Alliance, Mar., & Gen., Ld., £100 Shs.	25	53
8/	Atlas, £50 Shs.	6	32
8/	British & For. Marine, Ld., £20 Shs.	4	25½
7½d.	British Law Fire, Ltd., £10 Shs.	1	1½
7/6	Clerical, Med., & Gen. Life, £25 Shs.	50/	16½
10/	Commercial Union, Ltd., £50 Shs.	5	45½
4	Do. "W. of Eng." Ter. Deb. Stk.	100	110½
60/	County Fire, £100 Shs.	80	195
5/	Eagle, £50 Shs.	5	½
4/	Employrs' Liability, Ltd., £10 Shs.	2	4½
—	Empress, Ltd., £5 Shs.	1	—
21/	Equity & Law, £100 Shs.	6	22
7/6	General Life, £100 Shs.	5	15
4½d.	Gresham Life, £5 Shs.	15/	2½
2/6	Guardian, Ld., £10 Shs.	5	11½
10/	Imperial, Ltd., £20 Shs.	5	30½
5/6	Imperial Life, £20 Shs.	4	6½
6/	Indemnity Mutual Mar., Ltd., £15 Shs.	3	12½
1/	Lancashire, £20 Shs.	2	5
7½d.	Law Acc. & Contin., Ltd., £5 Shs.	10/	1
5/	Law Fire, £100 Shs.	2½	18
4½d.	Law Guar. & Trust, Ltd., £10 Shs.	1	1½
9/	Law Life, £20 Shs.	2	25
2/9	Law Un. & Crown £10 Shs.	12/	7
4	Do. Deb. Stk., 1942	100	110½
14/6	Legal & General, £50 Shs.	8	15½
9d.	Lion Fire, Ltd., £8½ Shs.	1½	½
14/	Liverpool & London & Globe, Stk.	2	55
10/	Do. Globe £1 Ann.	—	36
15/	London, £25 Shs.	12½	63½
4/	Lond. & Lanc. Fire, £25 Shs.	2½	19½
2/	Lond. & Lanc. Life, £25 Shs.	2	5
10	Lond. & Prov. Mar., Ld., £10 Shs.	1	1½
2/	Lond. Guar. & Accident, Ltd., £5 Shs.	2	12
10/	Marine, Ltd., £25 Shs.	4½	44
2/	Maritime, Ltd., £10 Shs.	2	4½
1/6	Merc. Mar., Ld., £10 Shs.	2½	2½
1/	National Marine, Ltd., £9 Shs.	1	½
10/	N. Brit. & Merc., £25 Shs.	6½	43
20/	Northern, £100 Shs.	10	82
40/	Norwich Union Fire, £100 Shs.	12	127½
5/	Ocean Acc. & Guar., fy. pd.	5	21
1/	Do. £5 Shs.	1	4
7/6	Ocean, Marine, Ltd.	2½	9½
1/	Palatine, £10 Shs.	2	3½
2/6	Pelican, £10 Shs.	1	3½
12/	Phœnix, £50 Shs.	5	44
25/	Provident, £100 Shs.	10	36
3/	Railway Pasngrs., £10 Shs.	2	8½
2/6	Rock Life, £5 Shs.	10/	4½
8	Royal Exchange	100	360
18/	Royal, £20 Shs.	3	55½
4/	Sun, £10 Shs.	10/	11½
3/9	Sun Life, £10 Shs.	7½	15
6/	Thames & Mrsey. Marine, Ltd., £20 Shs.	2	10½
9/	Union, £10 Shs.	4	24½
4/	Union Marine, £20 Shs.	2½	9
12/	Universal Life, £100 Shs.	12	42
2/	World Marine, £5 Shs.	2	1½

IRON, COAL, AND STEEL.

Last Div.	Name.	Paid.	Price.
3/9	Barrow Hæm. Steel, Ltd.	7½	2½
9/	Do. 6 p.c. and Pref.	7½	7½
10/	Bolck., Vaugh. & C., Ld.	20	18
6/	Do. £8 liab.	12	10
7/6	Brown, J. & Co., Ltd., £20 Shs.	15	20½
7/6	Consett Iron, Ld., £10 Shs.	7½	29½
4/	Do. 8 p.c. Cum. Pref.	5	11
7/6	Ebbw Vale Steel, Iron & Coal, Ltd., £23 Shs.	20	7½
15/	General Mining Assn., Ld.	5½	7½
8/	Harvey Steel Co. of Gt. Britain, Ltd.	10	29
5	Lehigh V. Coal 1 Mt. 5 p.c. Guar. Gd. Cp. Bds.	—	98
42/6	Nantyglo & Blaina Iron, Ltd., Pref.	$60	97½
1/	Nerbudda Coal & Iron, Ltd., £3 Shs.	56/	1/16
—	Newport Abrcrn. Bk. Vein Steam Coal, Ltd.	10	4½
6/	New Sharlston Coll., Ltd. Pref.	20	10½
4½d.	Nw. Vancvr. Coal & Ld., L.	1	½
3/6	North's Navigation Coll. (1889) Ltd.	5	2½
10/	Do. 10 p.c. Cum. Pref.	5	7½
—	Rhymney Iron, Ltd.	5	1½
	Do. New, £5 Shs.	4½	½
5	Do. Mt. Debs., Red.	100	98½
5	Shelton Irn., Stl. & Cl. Co., Ltd., 1 Chg. Debs., Red.	100	99½
10	Sth. Hetton Coal, Ltd.	100	180½
	Vickers & Maxim, Ltd.	10	3
	Do. 5 p.c. Prfd. Stk.	100	132½

SHIPPING.

Last Div.	Name.	Paid.	Price.
4/	African Stm. Ship, £20 Shs.	16	9½
5/	Do. Fully-paid	20	13½
5/	Amazon Steam Nav., Ltd.	12½	9
8/	Castle Mail Pakts., Ltd., £20 Shs.	14	15½
3½	Do. 1st Deb. Stk., Red.	100	101
6/	China Mutual Steam, Ltd.	5	3
6	Do. Cum. Pref.	10	9½
10/	Cunard, Ltd.	20	10
5/	Do. £20 Shs.	10	4
4½	Furness, Withy, & Co., Ltd., 1 Mt. Dbs., Red.	100	105
6/	General Steam	15	8½
5/	Do. 5 p.c. Pref., 1874	10	9
5/	Do. 5 p.c. Pref., 1877	10	9
5/	Leyland & Co., Ltd.	10	15½
7/	Do. 7 p.c. Cum. Pref.	10	14½
2/11	Do. 4½ p.c. Cum. Pre-Pf.	3	10½
4	Do. 1st Mt. Dbs., Red.	100	106½
7/6	Mercantile Steam, Ltd.	5	7½
6/4½	New Zealand Ship., Ltd.,	6	5
4	Do. Deb. Stk., Red.	100	104
5/	Orient Steam, Ltd.	10	4½
5	P. & O. Steam, Cum. Prefd.	100	156½
19	Do. Defd.	100	232½
3½	Do. Deb. Stk.	100	121
5	Richelieu & Ont., 1st Mt. Debs., Red.	100	101
30/	Royal Mail, £100 Shs.	60	51
2/6	Shaw, Sav., & Alb., Ltd., "A" Pref.	5	5½
5/	Do. "B" Ord.	5	3½
8/	Union Steam, Ltd.	20	19½
4/	Do. New £20 Shs.	10	8½
4	Do. Deb. Stk., Red.	100	107
7/	Union of N.Z., Ltd.	10	10
5½	Wilson's & Fur.-Ley., 5½ p.c. Cum. Pref.	10	10½
4½	Do. 1 Mt. Db. Sk., Rd.	100	106½

TELEGRAPHS AND TELEPHONES.

Last Div.	Name.	Paid.	Price.
4	African Direct, Ltd., Mort. Debs., Red.	100	102
—	Amazon Telegraph, Ltd.	10	6½
19/6	Anglo-American, Ltd.	100	60
39/	Do. 6 p.c. Prefd. Ord.	100	108
—	Do. Defd. Ord.	100	12
3/	Brazilian Submarine, Ltd.	10	17
5	Do. Debs, 2 Series	100	114

Telegraphs and Telephones (*continued*):—

Last Div.	Name.	Paid.	Price.
4/	Chili Telephone, Ltd.	5	3½
$2½	Comcial. Cable, $100 Shs.	—	189½
4	Do. Stg. 500-yr. Deb. Stk. Red.	100	107
2½d.	Consd. Telpehone Constr., &c., Ltd.	10/	¼
8/	Cuba Submarine, Ltd.	10	8
10/	Do. 10 p.c. Pref.	10	16
2/	Direct Spanish, Ltd.	5	4½
5/	Do. 10 p.c. Cum. Pref.	5	10½
4½	Do. Debs.	50	104½
3/	Direct U.S. Cable, Ltd.	20	11
2/6	Eastern, Ltd.	10	18½
3/	Do. 6 p.c. Cum. Pref.	10	19½
4	Do. Mt. Deb. Stk., Red.	100	132½
2/6	Eastern Exten., Aus., & China, Ltd.	10	19
5	Do. (Aus. Gov. Sub.) Deb., Red.	100	101
5	Do. do. Bearer	100	101½
4	Do. Mort. Deb. Stk.	100	131½
5	Eastn. & S. Afric., Ltd., Mort. Deb. 1900	100	101
5	Do. Bearer	100	101½
4	Do. Mort. Debs. 1909	100	103½
4	Do. Mort. Debs. (Maur. Subsidy)	25	109½
5/	Grt. Nthn. Copenhagen	10	28
5	Do. Debs., Ser. B., Red.	100	102½
12/6	Indo-European, Ltd.	25	53½
6	London Platino-Brazilian, Ltd., Debs. 1904	100	109½
4/	Montevideo Telph., Ltd., 6 p.c. Pref.	5	2½
3/	National Telephone, Ltd.	5	7
6/	Do. Cum. 1 Pref.	10	17
6/	Do. Cum. 2 Pref.	10	16
5	Do. Non-Cum. 3 Pref.	5	6½
3½	Do. Deb. Stk., Red.	100	106½
4d.	Oriental Telephone, Ltd.	1	½
4	Pac. & Euro. Tlg. Dbs., Rd.	100	106½
4/	Reuter's, Ltd.	8	8½
5/	Un. Riv. Plate Telph., Ltd.	5	4½
5	Do. Deb. Stk., Red.	100	103½
6/	West African Telg., Ltd.	10	4½
5	Do. 5 p.c. Mt. Debs., Red.	100	104½
—	W. Coast of America, Ltd.	10	—
3/	Western & Brazilian, Ltd.	15	10½
3/	Do. 5 p.c. Pref. Ord.	7½	7½
—	Do. Defd. Ord.	7½	3½
4	Do. Deb. Stk., Red.	100	106
1/	W. India & Panama, Ltd.	10	½
6/	Do. Cum. 1 Pref.	10	8½
6/	Do. Cum. 2 Pref.	10	6
5	Do. Debs., Red.	100	106½
7	West. Union, 1 Mt. 1902 $	1000	107½
6	Do. 6 p.c. Stg. Bds., Rd.	100	102½

TRAMWAYS AND OMNIBUS.

Last Div.	Name.	Paid.	Price.
1/6	Anglo-Argentine, Ltd.	5	4
6	Do. Deb. Stk.	100	132½
4	Barcelona, Ltd.	10	12½
5	Do. Deb., Red.	100	102½
6/6	Belfast Street Trams.	10	17
—	Blackpl. & Fltwd. Tram., £10 Shs.	8	11½
4/	Bordeaux Tram. & O., Ltd.	10	13½
5	Do. Cum. Pref.	10	11½
—	Brazilian Street Ry., Ltd.	2	½
—	British Elec. Trac., Ltd.	10	17½
—	B. Ayres & Belg. Tram., Ltd., 6 p.c. Cum. Pref.	5	4½
6	Do. 1 Deb. Stk.	100	106½
—	B. Ayres. Gd. Nat., Ltd., 6 p.c 1 Deb. Bds., Red.	100	60
5½	Do. Pref. Debs., Red.	100	95½
1/	Calais, Ltd.	5	1
—	Calcutta, Ltd.	10	3½
—	Carthagena & Herr., Ltd.	10	3
5	Do. Deb., Red.	100	90
5	City of B'ham. Trams., Ltd., 5 p.c. Cum. Pref.	5	6
4	Do. 1 Mort. Debs., Rd.	100	106½
3/9	City of B. Ayres, Ltd.	5	7½
2/3	Do. Ext. £5 Shs.	3	4½
6	Do. Deb. Stk.	100	150
3/4	Edinburgh Street Tram.	4	3½
1/	Glasgow Tram. & Omni. Ltd., £9 Shs.	8	3½
3/7½	Imperial, Ltd.	6	15
2/	Lond., Depfd, & Greenwich, Prefd.	5	3½
nil	Do. Defd.	5	1
10½	Lond. Gen. Omni., Ltd.	100	206
4	Do. Deb., Red.	100	117½

Tramways and Omnibus (*continued*):—

Last Div.	Name.	Paid.	Price.
6/	London Road Car	6	11
28/6	Do. Red. 1 Mt. Deb. Stk.	100	108½
5	London St. Rly. (Prov., Ont.), Mt. Debs.	100	112
4/9	London St. Trams.	—	2½
12/9	London Trams., Ltd.	10	10
6/	Do. Non-Cum. Pref.	10	10½
5	Do. Mt. Db. Stk., Rd.	100	100½
5	Lynn & Boston 1 Mt. 1924 $	1000	107
5	Milwaukee Elec. Cons. Mt. $	1000	100½
5	Minneapolis St. 1 Cons. Mt. $	1000	96
5	Montreal St. Dbs., 1908	100	110
4½	Do. Debs., 1922	100	107
6/	Nth. Metropolitan	10	13½
1/9½	Nth. Staffords., Ltd.	6	4½
5/6	Provincial, Ltd.	10	7½
6/	Do. Cum. Pref.	10	13½
5	St. Paul City, 1937 $	1000	96
5	Do. Guar. Twin City Rap. Trans. $	1000	96
5/	Southampton	10	7
3/	South London	10	6
7/6	Sunderland, Ltd.	10	6½
4½	Toronto 1 Mt., Red.	100	107
2/6	Tramways Union, Ltd.	5	7½
4½	Do. Deb., Red.	100	109
5/	Vienna General Omnibus	5	6½
5	Do. 5 p.c. Mt. Deb., Red.	100	105
4/	Wolverhampton, Ltd.	10	6½

WATER WORKS.

Last Div.	Name.	Paid.	Price.
8/	Antwerp, Ltd.	20	22
6/	Cape Town District, Ltd.	5	6½
10½	Chelsea	100	337½
5	Do. Pref. Stk.	100	178½
4½	Do. Pref. Stk., 1875	100	158½
4½	Do. Deb. Stk.	100	162½
5/	City St. Petersburg, Ltd.	13	11
4/6	Colne Valley	10	15½
4	Do. Deb. Stock	100	137½
£4	Consol. of Rosar., Ltd., 4 p.c. 1 Deb. Stk., Red.	100	90
7½	East London	100	232½
4½	Do. Deb. Stk.	100	162½
3	Do. Deb. Stk., Red.	100	106
37/6	Grand Junction (Max. 10 p.c.) "A"	50	124½
18/9	Do. "B"	25	
18/9	Do. "C" (Max. 7½ p.c.)	25	57½
35/	Do. "D" (Max. 7 p.c.)	50	102½
4	Do. Deb. Stock	100	148½
13	Kent	100	360½
7	Do. New (Max. 7 p.c.)	100	215½
5/7½	Kimberley, Ltd.	7	5
6	Do. Debs., Red.	100	102½
6	Do. Deb. Stk., Red.	100	106½
10	Lambeth (Max. 10 p.c.)	100	307½
7½	Do. (Max. 7½ p.c.), 50 & 25	—	232½
4	Do. Deb. Stock	100	148½
3	Do. Red. Deb. Stock	100	105
10/	Montevideo, Ltd.	20	16½
5	Do. 1 Deb. Stk.	100	108½
5	Do. 2 Deb. Stk.	100	103½
132/9	New River New	100	449½
4	Do. Deb. Stk.	100	150½
4	Do. Deb. Stk. "B"	100	150½
—	Odessa, Ltd., "A" 6 p.c. Prefd.	20	—
nil	Do. "B" Deferred	20	—
4	Portland Con. Mt. "B," 1927	—	102½
8/	Seville, Ltd.	20	12½
5/6	Southend "Addl." Ord.	10	17½
6	Southwark and Vauxhall	100	167½
6	Do. "D" Shares (7½ p.c. max.)	100	164½
5	Do. Pref. Stock	100	177½
4	Do. "A" Deb. Stock	100	147½
3	Staines Resvirs. Jt. Com. Gua. Deb. Stk., Red.	100	106
7/	Tarapaca, Ltd.	10	9½
10	West Middlesex	100	321½
4½	Do. Deb. Stk.	100	163½
3	Do. Deb. Stk.	100	107

Prices Quoted on the Leading Provincial Exchanges.

ENGLISH.

In quoting the markets, B stands for Birmingham; Bl for Bristol; M for Manchester; L for Liverpool; and S for Sheffield.

CORPORATION STOCKS.

Chief Market.	Int or Div.	Name.	Amount paid.	Price.
M	3½	Bolton, Red. 1935 ..	100	116
M	3½	Burnley, Red. 1933..	100	116
M	3½	Bury, Red. 1946	100	118
L	2¾	Liverpool, Red. 1925	100	102½
B	3½	Longton, 1932	100	106
M	4	Oldham Prp. Db. Sk.	100	145
M	£1	Do. Gas&W.Ann.		34½
S	4	Rotherham 4 p.c., Red. 1927...... £6	1 an	114
S	3	Do. Red. 1920..	100	105
M	3½	Runcorn Red. 1923..	100	105
S	2¾	Sheffield Water Ann.	100	117½
S	3	Do.	3 an	90
L	3½	SouthportRed.1936 {	5 an 100	110
L	3	Do. Red.1914..	100	102½
M	3	Todmorden,Red.1914	100	104

RAILWAYS.

Chief Market.	Int or Div.	Name.	Amount paid.	Price.
Bl	4½	Bridgewater Pref. ..	100	137½
M	4	Cleator & Workton.	100	78
M	4	Do. 1883 Pref. ..	100	111
L	4	Cockermth. K. & P.	100	116
L	4	Isle of Man	5	6¾
L	5	Do. Pref.	5	6½
L	3	Liverpool Overhead	10	10¾
L	4	Do. Deb. Stk. ..	100	109
L	5	Do. Pref.	10	16
L	6	Maryport & Carlisle	100	170
S	6	Mid.Shef.& Roth.Pf.	100	231
Bl	35/	Neath & Brecon "A"	100	67½
M	4½	Oldham, Ashton, &c.	10	17
Bl	5½	Penarth Harbour ..	100	182½
Bl	4	Do. Deb. Stk. ..	100	145
Bl	3½	Do. Deb. Stk. ..	100	127
Bl	1½	Ross & Monmouth..	20	5¾
Bl	6	Do. Pref.	20	42½
M	3	Southport & Cheshire Deb. Stk.	100	104½
M	nil.	Do. Pref.	100	26
Bl	2½	West Somerset Gu...	100	96½
Bl	5	Wye Val. Deb. Stk.	100	164

BANKS.

Chief Market.	Int or Div.	Name.	Amount paid.	Price.
L	8/	Adelphi, L., £20 Shs.	10	16
L	12/6	Bk of L'ool, L., £100Sh	12½	39
B	5/6	Brmnghm. Dis. & C., Ltd., £20 Shs.....	4	10¾
B	6/3	Co. of Staffs., L., £40	5	13¾
S	17½	Crompton & Evans, Ltd., £20 Shs	4	14¾
M	14/	Lancs. & Yorks, Ltd., £20 Shs.....	10	31⅛
L	18/	Livrpl. Union, Ltd., £100 Shs.	20	60½
M	24/	Manchester & Co., Ltd., £100 Shs. ..	16	61½
M	20/	Mnchstr. & Livrpool. Dis., Ltd., £60 Shs.	10	51½
M	1/6	Mer. of Lancashire, Ltd., £20 Shs.....	3	6 1/16
L	16/	Nth. & Sth. Wales, Ltd., £40 Shs.....	10	35⅜
	5/	Notts Joint St., Ltd., £50 Shs..........	10	23
	4/	Oldham Joint Stk., Ltd., £20 Shs.....	4	11
S	10	Sheffield Banking, Ltd., £50 Shs.....	17½	51½
S	10	Do. & Rotherham, Ltd., £50 Shs...	8	26
S	15	Do. & Hallamsh., Ltd., £100 Shs..	25	62½
S	10	Do. Union, Ltd., £40 Shs.........	10	25
M	12/	Union of Manchester, Ltd., £25 Shs.. ..	11	27¾
M	10/	Williams, Deacon, &c. Ltd., £50 Shs.....	8	25¾
Bl	20	Wilts & Dorset, Ltd., £50 Shs..........	10	49
S	10/	York City & Co., Ltd., £10 Shs.....	3	13¾

BREWERIES.

Chief Market.	Int or Div.	Name.	Amount paid.	Price.
B	6	Ansell & Sons Pref.	10	15¾
B	5	Do. Debs.	100	110
L	7/	Bent's.............	10	19½
L	6	Do. Cum. Pref...	10	14⅜
L	4½	Do. Deb. Stk. ..	100	111
L	13/6	Birkenhead, £5 paid	5	22
L	13/6	Do. £10 paid....	10	25
M	9/	Boddington's	9	20⅜
M	5	Do. Cum. Pref...	10	13½
M	4	Do. Deb. Stk. ..	100	109
B	4½	Butler & Co. Db. Stk	100	110½
M	6	Chesters' Cum. Pref.	10	13¾
M	4½	Do. Debs.	100	112½
S	17/	Clarkson's Ord.	10	24½
S	6	Do. Cum. Prf. Stk.	10	14¾
M	4	Dutton & Co. Db.Sk.	100	104
M	4½	Hardy's Crown Debs.	100	111
B	6/	Holt	10	18½
B	5	Do. Cum. Pref...	10	12¾
B	4	Do. Debs.	100	108½
B	12/6	Lichfield	10	24
B	5	Do. Cum. Pref...	10	11¾
M	5½	Manchester Deb. Stk.	100	141
B	14	Mitchell, H., & Co.	10	38
B	6	Do. Cum. Pref...	10	15½
Bl	6	Oakhill Pref........	10	16½

Breweries (*continued*):—

Chief Market.	Int. or Div.	Name.	Amount paid.	Price.
M	5/	Springwell	10	10¾
M	7	Do. Pref.	10	13½
Bl	9	Stroud	10	17
Bl	6	Do. Pref	10	14½
M	6/	Taylor's Eagle......	10	11
M	7	Do. Cum. Pref ..	10	13½
M	5½	Do. Deb. Stk. ..	100	120½
S	10	Tennant Bros £20 shs	15	34½
S	10	Wheatley & Bates ..	10	14½
S	6	Do. Cum. Pref.	10	12¾

CANALS AND DOCKS.

Chief Market.	Int. or Div.	Name.	Amount paid.	Price.
Bl	5	Hill's Dry Dk. &c. £20	18	9
M	4	Manc. Ship Canal 1st Mt. Deb. Stk.	100	104
M	4	Do. 2nd do.	100	103
L	36/3	Mersey Dck. & Harb.	an.	118½
L	35/	Do.	an.	116
M	10/	Rochdale Canal	100	37½
B	35/	Staff. & Worc. Canal	100	76½
B	4½	Do. Deb. Stk....	100	137
Bl	4	Swansea Harb.......	100	114
B	27/6	Warwick & Birm. Cnl	100	66½
B	12/6	Do. & Napton do.	100	23

COMMERCIAL & INDUSTRIAL.

Chief Market.	Int. or Div.	Name.	Amount paid.	Price.
L	5	Agua Santa Mt. Debs	100	100
M	8/	Armitage, Sir E. & Sns Ltd...............	10	19
M	4	Do. Deb. 1910 ..	100	103
L	6	Ang. Chil. Nit. 1 Mt. Debs., 1919 ..	100	109½
Bl	8½	Bath Stone Firms ..	10	20
M	4/9½	Barlow & Jones, Ltd., £10 Shs.	8	10⅜
B	7/6	Birmgham. Ry. Car.	10	17½
B	6	Do. Pref.	10	16
B	16/8	Do. Small Arms	5	16½
M	£12	Blackpool Pier......	100	277½
M	5	Do. Tower Debs.	50	54½
M	3/	Do. Wi. Gar. & P.	5	4⅜
Bl	10	Bristl. & S.W.R.Wag. £20 Shs..........	3	6
Bl	8	Do. Wag. & Carri. £10 Shs..........	10	14¾
M	7/	Crosses & Winkwth. Ltd..............	5	12½
L	5	G. Angus & Co. Pref.	10	13⅜
Bl	5	Gloster. Carri. & W.		10½
Bl	5	Gt. Wstn. Cttn., Ltd.	20	15½
M	6	Hetherington, L. Prf.	10	8¾
M	4½	Do. Debs., 1910	100	99½
B	7½d.	Hinks (J. & Son), Ltd.	1	27/6
S	10/	Jessop & Sons, £50 Sh	30	28
S	10	Kayser, Ellsn. & Co. L.	5	10½
S	6	Do. Pref.	5	7⅜
M	7/6	Kellner-Partgton., L.	5	14½
M	4½	Do. Debs., 1914..	100	105½
M	5	Kerr Thread, Ltd., Debs.	100	101
B	17/	King's Norton Metal, £10 Shs..........	8½	18½
M	5/	Lancashire & Yorks. Wagon, Ltd.	10	9¾
L	10/	Liverpool Exch., Ltd.	20	27⅜
L	45/	Do. Grain Stge, Ltd.	50	108
L	2/6	Do. Rubber, Ltd...	5	7
M	9d.	Manchester Bond. Whse., L., £10 Shs.	4½	2¾
M	3/9	Do. Comcial. Bldgs., Ltd., £10 Shs.	5	10⅜
M	3/9	Do. No. 2, £10 Shs.	5	10⅜
M	2/3	Do. No. 3, £10 Shs.	5	7½
M	4/	Do. Corn, &c., Exchange, Ltd.	10	16¾
M	4	Do. Debs.	100	125
M	8	Do. Ryl. Exchge, L.	100	246½
B	5/	Midland Rlwy. Car. Wgn., Ld., £20 Sh.	10	14¾
Bl	5	Millers & Corys Dbs.	100	100½
B	12/6	Mint, Brgham., Ltd.	5	8
B	5	Do. Debs.	25	108
B	10/	Nettlefolds, Ltd.....	10	48
B	5	Do. Pref.	10	15½
S	9	Nth. Centrl. Wgn., L.	5	8⅜
B	15/	Patnt. Nut & Bolt, L.	10	35½
B	5	Do. Pref.	10	14½
B	1/	Perry & Co., Ltd. ..	1	31/
B	6d.	Do. Pref.	1	27/6
S	10	Round, J., & Co., L., £10 Shs.	6	12⅜
S	10	Rodgers, J., & Sons, L.	100	218
M	18/9	Rylands & Sons, Ltd., £20	15	39½
M	2/6	Do. paid up	20	45
M	4	Do. Debs. ..1909	100	106
S	5	Sanderson Brs. & Co., Ltd., Debs.	100	102
M	4½	Schwabe, S., & Co., Ltd., 1 Debs. 1914	100	104
S	7½	Sheffield Forge & Rolling, Ltd.	10	11½
L	—	Southport Pier, Ltd.	100	88½
L	2½	Do. W. Gdns., Ltd.	5	3½
Bl	5	Spillers & Bakers, Ltd, £10 Shs.	9	14¾
Bl	6	Do. Pref.	10	14½
B	5/	Union Rolling Stock, Ltd., £20 Shs....	5	7½
M	6/	Victoria Pr., S'port, L.	5	4⅜
Bl	8	Western Wagon & Property, Ltd.....	6	9¾
S	10	Westenholm, G., & Son, Ltd., £25 Shs.	20	24½
S	6¼	Yorksh. Wagon, Ltd.	2	2¾

FINANCIAL, TRUSTS, &c.

Chief Market.	Int. or Div.	Name.	Amount paid.	Price.
M	1/	Manchstr. Trst. £10 Shs.............	2	13/9
M	1/3	N. of Eng. T. Deb. & A., Ltd. £10 Shs.	2½	23/
M	3½	Do. 1 Mt. Debs...	100	96
L	—	Pacific Ln. & Inv., L.	2½	3
L	4	Do. Deb. Stk.....	100	102
L	—	United Trst., L. Prfd.	100	72½
L	—	Do. Deferred....	100	62½

GAS.

Chief Market.	Int. or Div.	Name.	Amount paid.	Price.
Bl	5	Bristol Gas (5 p.c.mx.)	100	128¾
Bl	4	Do. 1st Deb.	100	137
S	10	Gt. Grimsby "C" ..	10	202
L	10	Liverpool Utd. "A"	100	258
L	7	Do. "B"......	100	192
L	4	Do. Deb.	100	137
S	10	Sheffield Gas "A," "B," "C"	100	253
B	10½	Wolverhampton	100	225
B	3	Do. 6 p.c. Pref...	100	170½

INSURANCE.

Chief Market.	Int. or Div.	Name.	Amount paid.	Price.
M	6	Equitable F. & Acc. £5 Shs.	1	39/6
L	—	Liverpool Mortgage £10 Shs.	2	1 9/16
M	2/	Mchester. Fire £20 Shs	2	8
M	5/	National Boiler & G., Ltd., £10 Shs.	3	13¾
L	2/	Reliance Mar., Ltd., £10 Shs.	2	4 11/16
L	4/	Sea, Ltd., £10 Shs...	2	10 1/16
L	—	Stnd. Mar., L., £20 Sh.	4	8⅜
L	—	State Fire, L., £20 Sh.	1	2 5/16

COAL, IRON, AND STEEL.

Chief Market.	Int. or Div.	Name.	Amount paid.	Price.
Bl.	7/6	Albion Stm. Coal ..	10	11½
M	15/9	And. Knowles & S., Ltd., £37½ Shs. ..	23½	13½
M	5	Do. Mt. Debs. 1908	100	105½
Bl.	1/1½	Ashton V. Iron	100	26
S		Bessemer, Ltd.	10	20½
S	5	Do. Pref.	10	12¾
S	7	Briggs, H., & Co., "A" £15 Shs.....	12½	15⅜
S	7	Do. "B" £15 Shs.	8½	9⅜
S	20	Brown Baley's. Stl., L.	10	29¾
S	5	Brown, J., & Co., Cum. Pref.	10	13⅛
S	5	Cammell, C. & Co., Ltd.	85	12½
S	5	Do. Pref.	5	6⅝
M	5	Chatterley Whitfield. Col., Debs., 1905..	100	100½
Bl	4	Davis, D., & Sons, Ld.	10	9½
M	5	Evans, R., & Co., Ltd., Deb., 1910 ..	100	100½
S	12½	Fox, S., & Co., Ltd., £100 Shs.	80	176½
Bl	10	Gt. Wstn. Col., L., "A"	5	10
Bl	5	Do. "B"	5	4⅜
Bl	8	Main Colliery, Ltd.	10	7¾
B	2/6	Muntz's Metal, Ltd.	5	7¾
B	5	Do. Pref......	5	6½
M	2/6½	Nth. Lonsd. Iron and Steel, Ltd., £10 Sh.	8½	2½
Bl	6	North's Nav. Coll., Ltd., Debs.	100	105
S	60/	Parkgate Irn. & Stl., Ltd., £100 Shs. ..	75	71
M	6	Pearson & Knls., Ld., "A" Cum. Pref...	50	46
B	10/	Sandwell Pk. Col., L.	10	17½
M	6/3	Sheepbridge Coal and Iron, Ltd., "A"	25	17½
M	2/6	Do. "B"	10	7
M	5	Do. "C" Gua. Pf.	25	28½
Bl	4	South Wales Coll., Ltd., "A"	17	7½
S	55/	Staveley Coal & Iron, Ltd., "A" £100 Sh.	60	81½
S	55/	Do. "C"	60	82
M	1/10½	Tredegar Iron & Cl., Ld., "A" £10 Sh.	7½	2¾
M	1½	Do. "B" Stk. ..	100	34
M	2/	Wigan Cl. & Irn., Ld.	10	6½
M	1/6	Do. £10 Shs.	7½	3½

SHIPPING.

Chief Market.	Int. or Div.	Name.	Amount paid.	Price.
Bl		Bristol St. Nav. Pref.	10	11½
L	5/	Brit. & Af. St. Nav..	10	14
L	3/10½	British & Estn, Ltd.	6½	2⅜
L	10/	Pacific Stm. Nav., L.	25	24½
	10/	Wst. Ind. & Pac. St. Ltd., £25 Shs.....	20	29½

TRAMWAYS, &c.

Chief Market.	Int. or Div.	Name.	Amount paid.	Price.
B	5/	Brmngh. & Aston, L.	5	11⅜
B	5/	Do. Mid., Ltd. ..	10	7⅜
Bl	6/	Bristol Tr. & Car., Ltd..............	10	21
Bl	4/	Do. Debs.	100	121
L	6	I. of Man Elec., L., Pref.	1	1½
M	15/	Manchester C. & T, L., "A" £20 Shs.	15	27¾
M	10/	Do. "B"	10	19⅜

WATER WORKS.

Chief Market.	Int. or Div.	Name.	Amount paid.	Price.
Bl	7	Bristol	25	62
Bl	7	Do................	20	46½
Bl	58/	Do. 7 p.c. max. ..	100	159
Bl	4½	Do. Pref.	20	32½
Bl	5	Do. Pref.	10	18⅜
Bl	3½	Do. Deb.	100	129½
M	10	Fylde "A"........	100	335
M	7	Do. "B"	100	224
B	6	S. Staffs. Ord. "A"	100	168
B	—	Do. "B"	100	167
B	4	Do. Deb. Stk.	100	140
B	5	Do. Pf."A""B""C"	100	170
M	£3⅜	Stockport District ..	100	187½
B	2/	Wolverhampton New	5	6¾

SCOTTISH.

In quoting the markets, E stands for Edinburgh, and G for Glasgow.

RAILWAYS.

Chief Market.	Int. or Div.	Name.	Nom. Amount	Price.
E	6½	Arbroath and Forfar	25	51
G	2	Callander and Oban .	10	7½
G	4	Do. Deb. Stock	100	148
G	4½	Do. Pref.......	10	14½
G	4	Cathct. Dist. Deb. Stk.	100	148
E	5	Edin. and Bathgate .	100	179½
E	7	Forth & Clyde Junc.	100	226
G	4	Lanarks. and Ayrsh.	10	14
G	4	Do. & Dumbartons.	10	14¾
G	4	Do. Deb. Stk.	100	149

BANKS.

Chief Market.	Int. or Div.	Name.	Nom. Amount	Price.
G	12	Bank of Scotland ..	100	357½
G	16	British Linen	100	480
G	8	Caledonian, Ltd.....	2½	95/6
G	10	Clydesdale, Ltd.	10	23½
G	16	Commercl. of Scot., L.	20	88½
G	16	National of Scot. Ld.	100	422
G	8	Royal of Scotland ..	100	233
G	11	Union of Scotland, L.	10	26½

BREWERIES.

Chief Market.	Int. or Div.	Name.	Nom. Amount	Price.
E	5	Bernard, Thos. Pref.	10	10¾
E	5	Bernard, T. & J., Cum. Pref........	10	13
G	20	Highland Distilleries	3½	10⅜

CANALS AND DOCKS.

Chief Market.	Int. or Div.	Name.	Nom. Amount	Price.
G	4	Clyde Nav. 4 p.c....	100	125½
G	3½	Do. 3½ p.c.......	100	105
G	3½	Greenock Harb. "A"	100	100
G	2	Do. "B"	100	40

MISCELLANEOUS.

Chief Market.	Int. or Div.	Name.	Nom. Amount	Price.
G	4½	Alexander & Co. Debs.	100	110½
G	5	Baird, H., & Sns. C.P.	10	12½
E	10	Barry, Ostlere, & Co.	7½	12½
E	6	Do. Cum. Pref...	10	15 1/16
G	5	Brown, Stewart, Deb.	100	84
E	7½	Broxburn Oil	8½	8⅜
E	6	Do. Cum. Pref...	10	11 5/16
E	7	Edinburgh & Dist. Tram. Cum. Pref.	5	9
E	5	Gilroy, Sons, & Co. Debs.	100	99
G	3/	Glasgow Cot. Spin...	6	5¾
G	55/	Do. Royal Exchg.	46	111½
G	—	Pumpherston Oil Pf.	10	8¾
E	7	Scottish Assam Tea	10	11½
E	5	Scottish Waggon....	10	12½
G	5	Stoddard & Co. Pref.	10	12 1/16

FINANCIAL, LAND, AND INVESTMENT.

Chief Market.	Int. or Div.	Name.	Nom. Amount	Price.
G	1/	Assets Co...........	1	47/
E	4½	Investors' Mort. Pref.	100	99½
E	4	Do. Deb. Stk....	100	103½
E	4	Nthn. Inv. N. Zeal. Deb. Stk.	100	107
E	4	N. of Scot. Canadian Deb. Stk.	100	106
E	4½	Real & Deb. Corp. Deb. Stk.	100	107½

INSURANCE.

Chief Market.	Int. or Div.	Name.	Amount paid.	Price.
G	12/	Caledonian F. & Life	5	36
G	4/6	City of Glasgow Life	2½	13
E	19/	Edinburgh Life	20	55
G	13/1	Life Ass. of Scotland	8½	34½
E	8	Nat. Guar. & Surety	2	51/
G	17½	Scottish Union and National "A"	1	97/
G	17½	Do. "B"	3½	18

IRON, COAL, AND STEEL.

Chief Market.	Int. or Div.	Name.	Amount paid.	Price.
E	Nil.	Addie, Coll. Cm. Pref.	10	8
E	8/	Arniston Coal	8	14
E	9¼	Cairntable Gas Coal	8	86/
E	7½	Fife Coal	10	21
E	5	Do. Cum. Pref.	10	13½
G	7	Merry & Cunghame. Cum. Pref.	10	15½
G	5	Do. Debentures	100	106½
E	1/9	Niddrie & Benhar Cl.	1½	40/
G	5	Steel Com. of Scotlnd	—	
	—	"A" Deb. Stk.	100	113
G	6	Do. and Mt. "B"	100	105
E	—	Watson, John	8½	10½
E	6	Do. Cum. Pref.	7½	8½
E	12½	Wilson's & Cly. Coal	3	8½

IRISH.

In quoting the markets, B stands for Belfast, and D for Dublin.

CORPORATION STOCKS.

Chief Market.	Int. or Div.	Name.	Amount paid.	Price.
B	3½	Belfast, 1921	100	112
B	3½	Do. 1912	100	108½
B	3½	Do. 1924	100	109½
B	3	Do. 1955	100	106
B	3½	Do. Water Com.	100	117½
B	3	Do. do.	100	106
B	3½	Do. Harbour Com.	100	114
D	3½	Rathmines & Rathgar	100	110½
D	3½	Waterford Deb.	100	—

RAILWAYS.

Chief Market.	Int. or Div.	Name.	Amount Paid.	Price.
D	30/	Cork, Bandon, & S.C.	100	—
D	4	Do. Deb.	100	139½
D	4	Do. W. Cork Pref.	100	—
B	5½	Belfast & Northern	100	163½
B	4	Do. Deb.	100	145
B	4	Do. Pref.	100	141
B	6½	Belfast & C. Down	100	166
B	4	Do. Deb.	100	147
B	3	Do.	100	107½
B	4½	Do. 4½ Pref. B.	100	153½
B	5	Do. Guar.	100	172½
D	Nil.	Dublin, Wick. & Wex.	100	30½
D	4	Do. Deb.	100	125
D	4½	Do. Deb.	100	130
D	6	Do. Guar.	100	163
D	4	Do. C. of Dub. Junc.	100	—
D	5	Do. 1860 Pref.	100	117½
D	—	Do. 1864 Pref.	100	105
D	—	Do. 1865 Pref.	100	85
B	6½	Great Northern	100	182
B	4	Do. Deb.	100	147
B	4	Do. Pref. B.	100	145½
B	5½	Gt. South & Western	100	147
B	4	Do. Deb.	100	146½
B	4	Do. Guar.	100	145
D	45/	Midland Gt. Western	100	113
D	4	Do. Deb.	100	146½
D	4½	Do. Deb.	100	151½
D	4½	Do. Deb.	100	—
D	5	Do. Pref.	100	—
D	4	Do. Pref.	100	—
D	—	Waterford & Central	100	15½
D	3	Do. Deb.	100	105
D	3½	Do. Pref.	100	—
D	4	Waterfd. L., & W. Db.	100	128
D	4½	Do. Deb.	100	—
D	4	Do. Pref.	100	120
D	3½	Do. Pref.	100	95

BANKS.

Chief Market.	Int. or Div.	Name.	Amount paid.	Price.
B	50/	Belfast, Old, £125 Shs.	25	125
B	20/	Do. New, £125 Shs.	25	50½
D	2/	Hibernian, £20 Shs.	5	6½
D	2/	Munster & Leinster £5 Shs.	2	5½
B	11/	Northern, £50 Shs.		27½
D	13/	Royal, £50 Shs.	10	29½
B	5/	Ulster, £15 Shs.	2½	12½

BREWERIES AND DISTILLERIES.

Chief Market.	Int. or Div.	Name.	Amount paid.	Price.
D	10/	Castlebellingham & Drog	10	16½
D	6	Do. Pref.	10	16
D	4½	Do. Deb.	100	116
B	17/	Dunville & Co.	10	29½
B	6	Irish Distillery, Pref.	10	13
B	5	Do. Deb.	100	110
B	6	J. & J. M'Connell, Pf.	10	15½
B	13/6	Mitchell & Co.	9	20
B	5	Do. Deb.	10	11½
D	4½	Phœnix Brew. Deb.	100	—
B	6/	Wm. Cowan	10	13½
B	6	Do. Pref.	10	13½
B	8/	Young, King, & Co.	8	14

STEAM AND CANAL.

Chief Market.	Int. or Div.	Name.	Amount paid.	Price.
B	Nil	Belfast Steamship	50	35½
D	10/	British and Irish	50	—
D	15/	City of Dublin	100	63½
D	3½	Do. Deb.	100	105
D	30/	Dublin & L'pool. Bldg.	50	76
D	2/6	Dundalk & Newry	10	4½
D	3/6	Grand Canal	10	12
D	3	Do. Pref.	10	9½
D	3	Do. Deb.	100	99
B	30/	Irish Shipowners	100	63
B	3/	Ulster Steamship	5	5½

MISCELLANEOUS.

Chief Market.	Int. or Div.	Name.	Amount paid.	Price.
D	3/1	Arnott & Co.	4	7½
D	6	Do. Pref.	4	[illegible]
B	8/	Belfast Com. Bldgs.	10	11
B	37/6	Do. Ropework Co.	75	90
B	5	Do. do. Pref.	10	13½
B	2/	Do. Discount Co.	3	43/
B	5	Do. do. Pref.	5	4½
B	10/	Brookfield Linen	25	17½
B	Nil	Coey & Co.	25	4
B	5	Do. Deb.	50	49
B	4½	David Allen & S's Deb.	100†	108½
D	4/	Dublin Trams	10	21
D	6	Do. Pref.	10	18½
D	4	Do. Deb.	100	—
B	6/	Edenderry Spinning	10	9
B	25/	Falls Flax Spinning	25	35
B	17/	Forster, Green, & Co.	10	23
B	9/	Island Spinning	7½	7½
B	8/	Jas. Lindsay & Co.	8	16½
B	1/7½	John Arnott & Co.	4	4½
B	4½	Do. Deb.	50	56
D	5/	Kinahan & Co.	10	11½
D	5½	Do. Pref.	10	11½
D	4½	Do. Deb.	100	108½
B	12/	Kirker & Co.	10	10
B	5/	Leahy, Kelly, & Leahy	5	[illegible]
B	6	Do. Pref.	5	7½
B	2/4½	Lindsay Bros. Ltd.	8	7½
B	4½	Do. Deb.	50	56½
D	1/	National Assurance	2½	38/6
B	10/	Olley & Co.	5	7½
D	1/1½	Patriotic Assurance	2½	30/3
B	3/7½	P. Johnston & Son, L.	6	6½
B	10/	Robertson, F., & Co.	8	23½
B	10	Ulster Marine Insur.	5/	6/6
B	15/	York-street Flax	25	53½
B	6	Do. Pref.	10	15½
B	4½	Do. Deb.	100	120½

INDIAN AND CEYLON TEA COMPANIES.

Acres Planted.	Crop, 1897.	Paid up Capital.	Share.	Paid up.	Name.	Dividends. 1894.	1895.	1896.	Int. 1897.	Price.	Yield.	Reserve.	Balance Forward.	Working Capital.	Mortgages, Debs. or Pref. Capital not otherwise stated.
	lb.	£	£	£	INDIAN COMPANIES.							£	£	£	£
11,240	3,128,000	120,000	10	3	Amalgamated Estates	—	*	10	5	3⅞	8½	10,000	16,500	D52,950	—
		400,000	10	10	Do. Pref.	—	*	5	‡5	10½	4¾				
10,223	3,360,000	187,160	20	20	Assam	20	20	20	5	61	6½	55,000	1,730	D11,350	—
6,150	3,278,000	142,500	10	10	Assam Frontier	3	6	6	—	9	6¾	—	286	20,000	82,500
		142,500	10	10	Do. Pref.	6	6	6	3	11¼	5⅓				
2,087	830,000	66,745	5	5	Attaree Khat	12	12	8	3	7½	5¼	3,790	4,820	7,770	—
1,633	583,000	78,170	10	10	Borelli	4	4	5	—	8¾	5¾	—	3,256	D270	6,500 Pref.
1,720	812,000	60,825	5	5	British Indian	6	5	5	—	4¼	6	—	2,920	12,300	16,500 Pref.
3,223	2,247,000	114,500	5	5	Brahmapootra	20	18	20	6	14	7	—	28,440	41,600	.
3,754	1,617,000	76,500	10	10	Cachar and Dooars	*	8	7	—	10	7½	—	1,645	21,240	.
		76,500	10	10	Do. Pref.	*	6	6	3	12½	4¾				
3,946	2,083,000	72,010	1	1	Chargola	8	7	10	2½	1⅞	10½	3,000	3,300	—	—
		81,000	1	1	Do. Pref.	7	7	7	3½	1⅜	5				
1,971	942,000	33,000	5	5	Chubwa	10	8	10	3½	6¾	7½	10,000	2,043	D5,400	—
		33,000	5	5	Do. Pref.	7	7	7	3½	7	5				
32,250	11,500,000	120,000	10	3	Cons. Tea and Lands	—		10	5	3¾	7¾	65,000	14,240	D191,674	—
		1,000,000	10	10	Do. 1st Pref.	—	*	5	‡5	11½	4¾				
		400,000	10	10	Do. 2nd Pref.	—	*	7	‡7	12	5¾				
2,230	617,000	135,420	20	20	Darjeeling	5½	5½	6	—	23	5	5,552	1,565	1,700	—
2,114	445,000	60,000	10	10	Darjeeling Cons.	—		4/2	—	7	—	—	1,820	—	—
		60,000	10	10	Do. Pref.	—	*	5	2½	9½	5¼				
6,660	3,518,000	150,000	10	10	Dooars	12½	12½	12½	2½	21	6½	45,000	300	D32,000	—
		75,000	10	10	Do. Pref.	7	7	7	3½	17	4¼				
3,367	1,811,000	165,000	10	10	Doom Dooma	11¼	10	12½	5	22	5¾	30,000	4,032	—	10,000
1,377	582,000	61,120	5	5	Eastern Assam	¾	nil.	4	—	3	6⅔	—	1,790	—	10,000
4,038	1,675,000	85,000	10	10	East India and Ceylon		nil.	7	—	9	7¾	—	1,710	—	—
		85,000	10	10	Do. Pref.	*	6	6	3	13	4¾				
7,300	3,363,000	219,000	10	10	Empire of India	—	*	6/10	2	13	—	15,000	—	27,000	—
		219,000	10	10	Do. Pref.	—	*	5	2½	11½	4½				
1,180	540,000	94,060	10	10	Indian of Cachar	7	3½	3	—	5	6	6,070	—	7,120	—
3,050	824,000	83,500	5	5	Jhanzie	10	10	10	4	8¾	5¾	14,500	1,070	2,700	—
7,980	3,680,000	250,000	10	10	Jokai	10	10	10	5	18	5½	45,000	990	D9,000	—
		100,000	10	10	Do. Pref.	*	6	6	3	15½	3⅞				
5,224	1,563,000	100,000	20	20	Jorehant	20	20	20	—	60	6⅔	26,220	2,955	3,000	—
1,547	304,000	65,660	10	8	Lebong	15	15	15	5	17	6½	9,000	2,150	8,650	—
5,082	1,709,000	100,000	10	10	Lungla		10	6	3	9½	6½	—	1,543	D21,000	—
		100,000	10	10	Do. Pref.	*	6	6	3	12	5				
2,684	885,000	95,970	10	10	Majuli	7	5	5	—	7	7	—	2,606	560	—
1,375	380,000	91,840	1	1	Makum	—	—	2	—	1⅛	1¾	—	—	1,200	25,000
2,990	770,000	100,000	1	1	Moabund	—	—	*	—	1	—	—	—	-	—
		50,000	1	1	Do. Pref.	—	—	*	2½	1	5				
2,080	482,000	79,590	10	10	Scottish Assam	7	7	7	—	11¼	6¼	6,500	800	9,590	—
4,150	1,456,000	100,000	10	10	Singlo	6	8	5	1	9½	4¾	—	300	D5,200	—
		80,000	10	10	Do. Pref.	*	6½	6½	3½	13	5				
	Crop, 1896.				CEYLON COMPANIES.										
7,970	1,743,824	250,000	100	100	Anglo-Ceylon, & Gen.	—	*	5½	—	68	7¾	10,992	1,405	D72,844	166,520
1,836	685,741	50,000	10	10	Associated Tea	—	*	5	—	8¾	5¾	—	164	2,478	—
		60,000	10	10	Do. Pref.	—	*	6	—	10¾	5¾				
10,390	4,000,000§	167,380	10	10	Ceylon Tea Plantations	15	15	15	7	27¾	5¾	84,500	1,516	D30,819	—
		81,080	10	10	Do. Pref.	7	7	7	‡7	17¼	4¼				
5,722	1,542,700§	55,960	5	3	Ceylon & Oriental Est.	5	8	7	—	2¾	7¾	—	230	D2,047	71,000
		46,000	5	5	Do. Pref.	6	6	6	3	5¾	5¾				
2,157	801,629	111,330	5	5	Dimbula Valley	—	*	10	5	6¾	7	—	—	1,733	6,250
		62,607	5	5	Do. Pref.	—	*	6	3	6¾	4¾				
11,496	3,715,000	298,250	5	5	Eastern Prod. & Est.	3	5	6½	2½	6¾	4¾	20,000	11,740	D17,797	102,500
3,118	701,100	150,000	10	10	Lanka Plantations	4	5	5	‡5	7	6¾	—	495	D11,300	14,700 Pref.
2,193	1,050,000§	22,080	10	10	New Dimbula "A"	10	16	16	—	25	6	11,000	2,024	1,150	—
		55,710	10	10	Do. "B"	18	16	16	—	23	6¾				
		8,400	10	10	Do. "C"	nil.	8	14	—	15	8¾				
2,572	570,360	100,000	10	10	Ouvah	6	8	6	2	9¾	6½	4,000	1,151	D1,255	—
2,630	535,675	200,000	10	10	Nuwara Eliya	—	*	6	3	11¾	5¾	—	—	—	30,000
1,720	220,200	41,000	10	10	Scottish Ceylon	15	15	15	5	23	6¾	7,000	1,252	D3,970	—
		9,000	10	10	Do. Pref.	7	7	7	3½	17	3¾				
2,450	750,000§	56,000	10	6	Standard	12½	15	15	5	24	6¾	9,000	800	D14,012	4,000

* Company formed this year. Working-Capital Column.—In working-capital column, D stands for *debit*. † Interim dividends are given as actual distribution made. ‡ *Total* div. § Crop 1897.

Printed for the Proprietor by LOVE & WYMAN, LTD., Great Queen Street, London, W.C.; and Published by CLEMENT WILSON, at Norfolk House, Norfolk Street, Strand, London, W.C.

The Investors' Review

EDITED BY A. J. WILSON.

Vol. I.—No. 9. New Series. | FRIDAY, MARCH 4, 1898. | [Registered as a Newspaper.] | Price 6d. By post, 6½d

CONTENTS

The Investors' Review.

A Cloudy Outlook in the Money Market.

Doubts begin to be hinted at in the City regarding the future course of the Money Market. Had we only domestic affairs to deal with, the position would be simple enough. At the present time money is comparatively dear in the City, merely because the Government has a larger amount at its credit with the Bank of England than usual—a much larger amount than the average of departmental balances at the same date in any former year. This excessive total must soon be reduced in the ordinary course of affairs. By the third week of this month, at latest, heavy payments will have to be made, so as to prevent the Government from having to re-vote a number of credits unspent at the end of the financial year. This being so, a simple deduction would be to say that the present dearness cannot last more than another three weeks, and it may not last another fortnight. Within one month from now it is reasonable to assume that quite ten millions now held on Government account will be disbursed, and once more available for market purposes. Half that sum of money would be sufficient to change the present stringency to ease and comfortableness. Call loans would again be 1 per cent. or less, and the discount rate on its way downwards below 2 per cent.

Our Money market, however, cannot be summed up in this rough-and-ready fashion. It is subjected to world-wide influences, being still the great exchange centre for the financial and mercantile transactions of all nations, and it is now threatened from several quarters. There is first of all the new loan to China, one half of which, at least, or eight millions nominal, will have to be found within the next two months by the London market. In all probability very little of this eight millions will leave the country in the shape of bullion, but in the ordinary course it will be paid over to the Japanese Government and lodged by it in the Bank of England, where, until that Government pays it out again, it will be just as inaccessible to the outside borrower as the Home Treasury balances are at this moment. By and by, of course, Japan will pay this money away here, and not only our portion of it, but the eight millions to be provided by Germany as well. It will all come here in time, and all get disbursed, helping to ease our market. Still, for a time, the subscription of this loan may have the effect of prolonging the scarcity of floating credits in London.

Then the position of India has to be looked at. Extremely little information is allowed to filter through from Bombay or Calcutta with regard to the monetary situation in that dependency; but we do know that the bank rate in Calcutta is 12 per cent., and in Bombay 13 per cent. Further, we know that the Indian Government treasuries are not flush of cash, even if they were disposed to lend their balances to these banks so as to ease the money market. The revenue has been expended over frontier wars, and in meeting famine expenditure. A position of stringency in India therefore exists such as has never at any previous time in her history as a British possession been seen without being followed by dangerous convulsions in her mercantile credit. We believe some such convulsion to be not now far off, and that the Secretary of State for India in Council will be obliged to take most energetic measures to prevent a credit catastrophe in India, which might throw the whole finances of the Government there into the utmost confusion. Again and again this danger has been insisted upon in these columns, only to be pooh-poohed by the financial Dr. Panglosses of Simla and Downing-street. Let them say, then, why money should be 12 per cent. and 13 per cent. in the principal business centres of India, with commerce backward and industry more or less paralysed, if a crisis be not impending. We know one to be inevitable if existing conditions are not soon changed, and believe that the London market will have to find soon a very large sum of money if it is to be averted. India has a floating debt here now of six millions, and will require another ten at the very least to give ease to the commerce of the peninsula, and breathing space to its Government, borne to the earth now with obligations it cannot meet. Suppose an Indian loan floated between now and next May, that also will be detrimental to the expectation of cheap money this half-year. Money must soon be sent out to India to ease the tension there, either in gold, if the bureaucratic dementia about a "gold standard" is still to be encouraged, or in silver if the mints are to be reopened so as to allow banks and traders to obtain in the natural way sufficient currency for daily use. All money taken out of this market, in whatever form, reduces the supply of banking credit available for it, and as we have no spare supply of cash, it will require only moderate withdrawals to keep rates high.

Finally, coming westward still, we turn to the United States. Lately these have revived their demand for gold. Whether it is to be a formidable demand or not we cannot yet say; but the trade position, as exhibited in the *Commercial Chronicle* last to hand, is significant of an unusual power at present possessed by the States, to draw gold from Europe. The figures bring out favourable trade balance fully ten millions sterling above that at the end of January last year, and twenty-five millions larger than at the same date the year before. We must not lay too much stress upon these figures, because they are obscured in various ways, such as by transactions in stocks and shares, by remittances to American citizens in Europe, and by the payment of the interest due in Europe on American debts. Still, allowing for these, the fact that at the present time the trade statistics of the American Union show a balance of about fifty millions sterling in its favour, warn us to look for some shipments of gold to New York. If these shipments extend to only two or three millions sterling they will be of no consequence, because that and more can be provided by the fresh supplies of metal steadily pouring into London from the mines of Africa, Australia, and India. But should anything like ten millions be withdrawn, either from the London market alone, or from London, Paris, and Berlin, we should not be able to escape a 4 per cent. bank rate here, with a concurrent advance in rates in all principal Continental centres of credit.

We by no me[illegible] wish readers to infer that this upward movemen[illegible] money is going to occur, for we do not yet see a p[illegible]bility of it. All that we desire to emphasise is that such facts as are in sight ought to make dealers in money cautious in expecting cheapness to at once ensue when the Home Government has distributed its present excessive balances. So far is it from being probable that money will be cheaper for more than a week or two in consequence of this distribution, that we may even hold the view that it would be dearer but for the already mentioned constant inflow of new gold from the mines. Every one knows that the new supply is large and increasing, and that it has protected us against high discount rates during the past two years. We think it will protect us again, and perhaps avert an advance in discount rates beyond their present point before the autumn, unless something quite unforeseen occurs. It will not, however, be sufficient to enable the London market to work on much finer quotations than are now current. Any idea, in short, of extremely cheap money this year, seems to be out of the question, and there are weak spots enough around us—in Europe, in India, and we may say in Japan—to inculcate a wholesome watchfulness, lest we should be surprised by a quite unforeseeable advance in money and discount charges, just when we count on them to decline.

A Cold-Blooded Valuation of Rand Outcrop Shares.

The advice which it is attempted to offer in this article is intended for the numerous class of unfortunate speculators who have been stranded with South African mine shares at high prices, and are anxious to know whether they should continue to hold on the off chance of one day retrieving at least a portion of their losses, or whether they should sell and be done with it. It must be strictly understood that where an opinion expressed that it would be wiser to wait for a time, it is not to be implied that we consider any of these shares good speculative purchases. One of the first truisms which a "dabbler" in the mining market has to learn is that the public is invariably stuck with mine shares at high prices. For instance, it may be taken for granted that if certain shares have fluctuated between £2 and £6, any "outsiders" who have bought have done so at an average of nearer £5 than £3. That there are twenty chances to one against such a deal proving profitable should be apparent to the least unsuspecting mind. Anyone who backs a horse does so with some probability of having a fair run for his money. But the same cannot be said in mining speculation.

To commence with, some firm buys a piece of likely gold-bearing ground, very probably for a quite insignificant sum of money. Upon this foundation a company is organised, with a more or less bloated capital, according to the temper of the public at the moment, and all the shares are probably taken by the promoters. The property is then developed, but its true value is kept absolutely secret; and a market is made in the Stock Exchange for the shares by buying through one broker and selling through another. The engineers and managers write one set of reports for publication, and another for the private information of the promoters; the merits of the mine are advertised by means of newspaper puffs, editorial notices, and otherwise, and when the shares have reached a figure sufficiently high to satisfy the greed of the promoters they are sold to the public as rapidly as possible. If the "outsider" makes any money under these conditions by a further accidental rise, it can only be by the miscalculation of the promoter, who, in his own estimation, has sold too soon. This is how most "honest" mining concerns are managed in these days. There are various other stages, where the company owns no mine at all, or the ground is known to be unpayable, or where the mine is picked and the profits "faked," and so on. In face of this historical summary it will be understood that any sane person who buys mining shares at the bidding of interested people, or newspapers, deserves to lose money, and does mostly lose it anyway, whether he deserves to or not.

As, however, our object is to assist rather than to revile those who have unfortunately fallen into such traps, we shall now examine the position of those who purchased "Kaffir" shares in the boom of 1895.

In previous articles it has been pointed out that, so far, very few deep-level mine shares have yet been "planted" with the poor victimised public. The big financial corporations still hold fully 85 per cent. of the entire share capital of these concerns. With the outcrop mines, however, it is different; and it may be safely assumed that in this case 85 per cent. of the shares are owned by the public. The great year of the "off-loading" of outcrop shares was 1895, when the Gold Fields Company, by selling its immense holdings, was able to pay two dividends of 125 per cent. each on its ordinary capital, and to present besides a very handsome balance to its managing directors. The prices then reached have not since been touched; and consequently the question arises, should those who purchased then sell at a loss now, or continue to exercise their souls in patience and hold?

What are known as "Kaffir Outcrops" shares may be divided into two classes: (1) the genuine dividend payers; and (2) the doubtful or rubbish concerns. The Trust Companies mixed up with them must be placed in a third category. Dealing, first of all, with the dividend payers, we had prepared a table showing the prices ruling in January and September, 1895, when the majority of these shares were disposed of by the promoters; the prices in April, 1897, when a low level was reached, in consequence of political and other complications; and the prices to-day. But this table need not be printed. It is, indeed, too sad to bear looking at and every one knows that the majority of the public hold these shares to-day at a great loss.

We advise those who are wise to effect a gradual liquidation as favourable opportunities occur, and shall state the reasons for this as succinctly as possible. At the present level of prices the interest return, after making allowance for amortisation of capital, is, for this class of security, extremely small, being not more than 5 or 6 per cent., and this only after estimating for increased dividends in the future. The majority of the Rand outcrop mines still have "lives" of from ten to twelve years; some perhaps will last longer, and others expire sooner, but that is about the average. To allow sufficient margin for amortisation of the original capital invested, and to obtain a clear 10 per cent. interest, the yield on the shares of a mine with ten years' life should be 18 or 19 per cent., and with twelve years' life 17 or 18 per cent. If an 8 per cent. return is considered enough, then the yield for ten years should be 17 per cent., and for twelve years 15½ per cent. These figures are, of course, approximate. A merely casual examination of Rand "outcrops" will show that, at the prices now ruling, they are a long way off fulfilling these conditions.

Another reason why we think a gradual liquidation the best policy to pursue is that outcrop shares have been worked up in sympathy with the deep-level "rig," which for the time being has utterly failed. Then comes the question of intrinsic merit. When any class of securities becomes unduly inflated, it is sure, sooner or later, to find its natural bottom again, and we cannot help thinking that the time is not far distant when "Kaffir" shares will experience another great reaction as the result of a true understanding of their limited dividend-paying capabilities. Some of the mines have exhausted large parts of their property in gold reefs, and the actual proportion worked out has been found by careful calculations and actual survey. As the dividends yielded by the portions worked out are known, it is a comparatively easy task to ascertain what the remaining portions of the mines will give in dividends on the same basis. We have done this and the result appended is somewhat startling, for it shows that the present market valuations of some of the mines are even higher than their total prospective dividend-earning capacities. That is to say, a speculator in some cases is paying twenty-five shillings for a sovereign, reckoning nothing at all for interest. Of course, the "bull" will argue that future profits and dividends will be larger than those earned in the past, and this may be true enough; but, on the other hand, it must not be forgotten that the portions of the mines remaining unworked to-day contain less gold-bearing reef, claim for claim, than those worked out, owing to the flattening of the reefs in depth. Add 20, 30, or even 40 per cent. to the figures given to represent the probable increased profits resulting from lower working costs and other favourable factors, and the result is not materially altered. The comparison still shows that prices are standing at far too high a level.

There remains to be considered the position of those

who purchased the second class of Kaffir outcrop shares—the doubtful or rubbish concerns. It may be safely asserted that there is not the remotest chance of people ever getting their money back on these things. Any comparison of past and present share lists shows what an enormous depreciation has taken place in the prices of some of them. Of the Barnato group, Buffelsdoorn is a remarkable instance. That company's shares were sold out at from £3 to £9; they are now practically unsaleable at 12s. 6d. The only advice that can be given to unfortunate holders of these shares is to sell on any good news, rumours of reconstructions, or reported "rich strikes." Of the best of them, it might be judicious to continue to hold for a little longer Glencairns, Auroras, Crœsus, Gochs, Knights, Nigels, and Van Ryns. The others are more or less rubbish, and should be realised on a favourable market. Even the best are things to be held with little faith and less assurance.

Company.	Percentage of surface area of property exhausted.	Dividends paid to date on percentage worked out.	Percentage of surface area of property remaining.	Dividends obtainable from unworked portion in same ratio.	Market valuation of shares, with allowance made for dip claims.
		£		£	£
City and Suburban	14	477,000	86	3,000,000	2,955,000
Crown Reef	36	701,900	64	1,250,000	1,210,000a
Ferreira	23	861,700	77	2,800,000	2,495,000
Geldenhuis Estate	28	315,750	72	812,000	925,000
Jubilee	45	245,475	55	300,000	242,500b
Jumpers	56	206,500	44	163,000	275,000c
Langlaagte Estate	30	1,200,000	70	2,800,000	1,703,750
Meyer and Charlton	42	269,000	58	362,000	262,500d
New Primrose	27	542,444	73	1,467,000	1,900,000
Robinson	17	2,190,916	83	10,700,000	4,675,000
Wemmer	37	260,440	63	440,000	550,000e

a Owns fifty deep level claims and water rights not being worked, valued at £250,000.
b Owns seventeen deep level claims, valued at £170,000.
c Interest held in Jumpers Deep valued at £275,000.
d Owns eight deep level claims, valued at £180,000.
e Owns twenty-two deep level claims, valued at £110,000.

The Progress of Russia.

(FROM A RUSSIAN CORRESPONDENT.)

For the solution of the problem as to why particular investments are popular at certain times and unpopular at others, the consideration of physiological peculiarities are requisite as an exact appreciation of material facts. The motives which determine people in placing their capital in any particular groove cannot altogether escape the influence of their surrounding moral atmosphere; and it requires more perspicacity and independence of judgment than one might believe to avoid the contagion of the example or the influence of articles published in the Press. Writers themselves, even when their motives are pure and disinterested, are frequently swayed by consideration of expediency in estimating the economic situation and matters connected with the budget of a foreign country. They regulate their views by the fashion of the moment much more than by methodical scientific knowledge of the subject of which they speak.

These somewhat lugubrious reflections have been suggested to me by the attitude frequently adopted in regard to Russia in the English market. Englishmen were among the first to trade with Russia, and since the time when communication between the two countries was carried on principally by way of Archangel the English have derived much advantage from their relations with Muscovy. Until the middle of the present century the greatest firms of St. Petersburg bore English names, just as the finest of the monumental quays on the Neva is called "le Quai Anglais," or as the most luxurious and most of frequented business establishments is the "Magazin Anglais." The Crimean War did not stop this investment of English capital in Russia. It was reserved for the complications of 1876-77 to beget a serious coolness. In 1876, thanks to the efforts of Count Rentem, who was Minister of France for more than seventeen years, and who succeeded in introducing publicity for the Russian Budget, and to furnish the country with resources necessary for the construction of great lines of railways, the Russian Five per Cents rose above par. The attitude taken by Russia against Turkey was displeasing to the English Government, and to that large portion of the public which was carried away by an excess of the Jingoism which Lord Beaconsfield stimulated with his customary cleverness. The moment was seized by a party in the English Press to attack the finances of Russia, which had become a political enemy; and the writer of these lines can very well recall the controversies he had on the subject with Mr. Labouchere in the *World* and *Truth* at the time. Speculators on the Stock Exchange sold a commodity which they did not possess—Russian Five per Cent. Bonds; and every month at the settlement they had to pay heavy backwardations to the great benefit of the holders. The same thing happened when Anglo-Russian relations were strained by affairs in Afghanistan. German capitalists then reaped the benefit of London sales, and after this the interest of British capitalists in Russian stocks diminished, while it increased in Argentine and other adventures.

I do not wish to trace the history of European investments in Russia; it would be rather a curious story, and would show that the French did less for Russia than they imagine. The French bought Russian bonds on excellent terms at the time of the newspaper war, instigated by Prince Bismarck in his "reptile press" against Russian credit abroad. As often happens, Bismarck acted out of spite, without caring about the real situation. And just at this juncture, in 1887, came the turning point in the financial and economic history of Russia. Thanks to the straightforward and pacific policy of Alexander III., to the efforts of M. Burge in reforming taxation, the chronic deficiency was about to disappear, and the Russian Budget felt the effect of the European repugnance to supplementary credits beyond those accorded at the beginning of the year. The Russian funds, sold at a loss by Germans who heedlessly played the political game of their Chancellor, were taken by Frenchmen, Belgians, and Hollanders at a price 15 or 20 per cent. below those of to-day. It has been estimated that the French buyers realised a profit of 100 to 500 million of francs by the transaction. With the support of the French market, M. Wischnegradsky went on with the conversions of the exterior debts—conversions which brought no cash to Russia but which were useful for her credit. The co-operation of France is fully recognised in Russia, but some surprise is felt when French diplomatic agents state in official publications that it was French capital which re-established Russian finance. This is not true. The re-establishment of Russian finance, like monetary reform, is an eminently national work, the merit of which is divided between the sovereigns and statesmen who, during the last twenty years, have directed the finances of the Empire. Their restoration is a reality, not a fiction, as it is the fashion of certain London editors to allege many times a year.

English capitalists were formerly pioneers in the development of Russia's natural riches, notably of its commerce and its great metallurgical enterprises; but during the last twenty years Belgians have, in these respects, taken the leading part. This is owing to various circumstances—to the excellent results obtained by an enterprise founded by the great firm of Seraing, the Société Cockerill, under the name of La Dniéprovienne; to the old relations which exist between Russia and Belgium—where there is no customs duty on Russian cereals—and finally to the success of the tramways. The freedom which exists in Belgium for the organisation of enterprises, the comparative absence of fiscal imports as contrasted with the exorbitant charges in France, have helped in giving a Belgian form to many industrial enterprises. The Bourse lists of Lyons and Paris naturally include many shares in Russian companies, some of which are old and very prosperous.

In England, the tendency up to the present time has not been the same. Nevertheless, from certain indications, it would seem that attention is being again directed towards Russia as a field of activity for British capital and intelligence. This is sincerely to be desired. Russia still offers openings for capital, and the guarantees existing there for the protection of property and capital are at least equivalent to those of other countries. One of the present English Ministers (Lord George Hamilton) has recently rendered homage to the correctness and loyalty of Russia, especially in respect of her engagements in Central Asia.

It must not be forgotten that commercial relations between Russia and England are still active and important. Here are, in millions of roubles, the figures showing the extent of the foreign commerce of Russia :—

—	France.		Great Britain.		Germany.	
	Import.	Export.	Import.	Export.	Import.	Export.
Average 1872-80...	21	44	129	149	187	139
" 1881-85...	19	43	116	176	184	165
" 1886-90...	14	38	93	210	121	163
" 1891	16	43	76	172	103	191
" 1892	17	29	94	109	101	136
" 1893	27	62	111	143	100	131
" 1894	27	49	128	161	142	146

England, therefore, occupies, it will be seen, a very important place in the movement of Russian trade; and certainly the participation of English capital in Russian business might easily enlarge her present share in it.

One fact of real importance in this connection is the completion of the great monetary reforms, due to the young Emperor Nicolas II., and his Minister of Finance, M. Witte. This reform, which has been under consideration since 1887, has been carried out on lines that would do honour to a theoretical economist while yet in full conformity with the teachings of practical experience. The Russian monetary reform, in virtue of which the gold rouble becomes the monetary unit of the Empire, is not a fiction, nor a reform on paper; it is an unmistakable tangible reality. The Government has not only accumulated great quantities of gold; it has put this gold in circulation, withdrawn paper money, diminished its amount, and reduced the floating debt. The most determined partisans of a wise handling of the money market as an instrument for the metallic circulation of a country must have been able to read with satisfaction the passages which M. Witte has devoted to this grave question in his report on the Budget of 1898. I believe people in England scarcely understand our public finances. This must be my justification for placing before your readers some statistics on the subject.

During the decade 1887-1896 the extraordinary expenses of Russia increased to the sum of 1,466 million roubles, of which 409 millions were for the construction of railways, 161 millions for the assistance of the peasants suffering from bad harvests, and 21 millions to pay off the shareholders in railways bought up by the State, 135 millions to railway companies on whose account the State has issued bonds, and 42 millions to augment the capital of the Bank of Russia or in payment to the Banque Foncière de la Noblesse. In addition, 697 millions have been devoted to extraordinary redemptions, either of loans to be extinguished or of the debt of the State for paper money emitted. It may be added that by the action of the regular Sinking Fund 420 million roubles of the debt have been paid off during the last ten years. What have been the resources from which the Russian Government has been able to meet this extraordinary expenditure, of which a good fourth has been devoted to public works and nearly a half to debt redemption? New loans have provided 831 millions of the money, reimbursements by the railway companies 107 millions, various resources 57 millions, and the balance has come from ordinary Budget surpluses.

Railways play a great part in the Russian Budget, though less than in the Prussian. The State possesses 27,375 versts, say, 66 per cent. of the network of the empire, estimated at a cost of about £280,127,000. The net income of the system worked by the State amounted in 1896 to £4,750,000, or an average of about 4½ per cent. on the capital emitted.

The Russian statistical bulletin has published a very interesting work on the Budget, distinguishing between the resources accruing from taxation and those furnished by what is called the State industrial domain (railways, forests, &c.). In the Budget of 1889 the total receipts were put at 1,364½ million of roubles, and the total expenditure at 1,350 millions. Of this income the total of imports, taxes, customs dues, and contributions from taxation of every nature, provided no more than 735 millions. The difference—say 620 millions—came from the gross produce of the State railway system, sales of State forests, and other sources. It is essential to note this very important distinction if we are to appreciate properly the position of the taxpayers in Russia. It makes all the difference if we divide 1,364 millions of roubles by ninety-five millions of inhabitants, or merely 735 millions.

These figures and reflections, made by a conscientious observer, whose optimism is justified by the facts of the last twenty years, perhaps merit the attention of the English public, and may be useful as an equitable appreciation of the position of a great State in full development.

A Little Light on the Northern Territories' Gold Fields of Australia, Ltd.

To see the price of "Northern Terrors," as the market endearingly terms these shares, gyrating around 4½ for the £1 share, must give an outsider the idea that the properties owned by the company have already proved to be most valuable. As a fact, so far as the market and the public are concerned, very little is known about the company at all. Formed in July, 1896, its nineteen months of existence has produced little in the way of results from a mining point of view. From a market point of view, however, everything has happened to gratify desires; for the shares, by bold engineering, have been raised to their present giddy height, and doubtless the foolish public is beginning to think "there must be something in the thing after all if the price keeps up at this figure."

All we venture to say is, that before any faith is placed in the future of this concern, it should be clearly understood that some mining results ought to be recorded by this company, for the Northern Territories gold-helds were not discovered the day before yesterday, as Mr. Bottomley and his friends might make the public believe. In their prospectus of this company no reference is made to an earlier date than 1893, yet we have the record of one of the most important properties taken over by the Northern Territories Goldfields Company as far back as 1886. It may be as well to state that the "Terrors" Company, for the price of £225,000, acquired six properties, comprising nearly seven hundred acres, locally known as the Howley Group, Brock's Creek, Woolwonga, Eveleen (including the Eureka mine), Yam Creek and Lady Alice Union. Greatest stress was laid upon the Howley group, as in its case the result of no less than six crushings were recorded (the dates of these, however, were not given), whilst only one crushing was mentioned in the case of each of the five other properties.

It is precisely to the record of the Howley property that we should like to draw attention. As far back as November 15, 1886, a company was formed, called the Port Darwin Gold Mining Company, for purchasing and working the Howley Mine, situate near a tributary of the River Adelaide, and adjacent to the Howley township in the Northern territory of South Australia. The property was then said to have been worked for some years by private enterprise; but, perhaps prudently, nothing was said about the results obtained. From the start this Port Darwin Company appears to have had difficulties, and by December, 1887, the board had entirely changed. Mr. Hugh Watt, M.P., the far-famed ruler of the Chile—New Chile—Yuruari Mining Company, had apparently obtained control, and put himself into the position of chairman, with Colonel Gourley, M.P., and Mr. Henry George Slade as subordinate directors. More property was acquired, but complaint was made of the heavy expenditure, and no definite results seem to have been obtained. About this time Mr. Hugh Watt, M.P., figured as holder of 34,997 of the shares out of a total issue of 62,787. By 1889, however, his holding had sunk to 4,092, and it is not surprising that he then disappeared from the Board, Mr. H. G. Slade becomiug chairman, with F. H. Cheesewright and Mr. Leonard Welstead (formerly the secretary of the company) as the other directors. The secretaryship was taken over by Mr. J. M. Pates. The company was then in low water, for the two years of working had added to the debit balance. So in December, 1889, a reconstruction was proposed, and the Northern Territory Exploration Company, Limited, was registered for this purpose. No better luck, however, attended this effort, and the following letter had finally to be sent to the Registrar of Joint-Stock Companies by Mr. Pates:—

January 23, 1890.

Sir,—I am directed to inform you that this company (the Port Darwin Gold Mining Company) do not intend taking up the name of the Northern Territory Exploration Company, Limited, as the capital necessary to purchase the proposed new properties has not been subscribed, and the mortgagee has intimated foreclosure under his mortgage and bill of sale, and that the company has practically ceased to exist, possessing as it does no property or assets of any kind."

Altogether there could not have been a more hopeless wreck; but the company promoter had not done with the property, and in May, 1890, the Australian Development Company was formed, with Mr. H. G. Slade and Lord F. G. Godolphin Osborne as directors. This company purchased, or was to purchase, a property in the Northern Territories of South Australia for £50,000, which extended over 160 acres and covered the Howley Mine, formerly possessed by the Port Darwin Gold Mining Company. The shareholders in this new company included Mr. Leonard Welstead and Mr. J. M. Pates, so that there was no absence of the old connections. This new company would seem to have done little or nothing, and after an inglorious existence was dissolved by order of the Registrar of Joint-Stock Companies, under date Febru ry 22, 1895.

Public interest in the goldfields of the Northern Territories of South Australia was apparently smothered by these fiascos, and nothing more was heard of them for a little while. The whole thing might have slept in oblivion for ever had not that cloud-compelling financial Jove, Mr. H. Bottomley, one fine morning in 1896, stumbled across the neglected remains of these (on paper) particularly fine properties. The great man saw his opportunity, and at the touch of his magic wand the Northern Territories Syndicate, with a capital of £50,000 rose upon the paper-rubbish heaps of the previous failures.

After what has just been narrated, it will come as a kind of surprise to the reader that the venerated and more than half-forgotten Mr. Hugh Watt should turn up as "vendor" of the "Port Darwin" properties to this Syndicate. The contract in regard to the purchase runs as follows:—

Whereas Hugh Watt is absolutely entitled to certain valuable mines and mineral properties situated in the Northern Territories of South Australia, subject only to the payment of twenty thousand pounds, being the amount then required for completing the purchase of some of such properties.

For these properties Mr. Hugh Watt was to receive the said £20,000 in cash, and one-fourth of the nominal share capital of the company intended to be formed by the Syndicate. The Syndicate then sold these properties to the Northern Territories Gold Fields Company for £225,000, out of a total capital of £300,000, the balance of £75,000 being left for working capital. Then, in December, 1896, £295,000 of the capital was offered to the public at the modest price of £3 per £1 share, and we believe the reception given to the issue was very poor. One cannot be sure of this, for the Company has not filed a list of shareholders since it made the issue. Upon the new Company, however, Mr. H. G. Slade figures as a director, so that ties with the past are well maintained.

By dint of market operations the price of the shares has now been worked up to 4½, or a capitalisation of £1,350,000, for the 700 acres of doubtful, and, so far as is known, still unproved property. None the less is it a fact that, as we have shown, the framework of the concern is of the flimsiest character. Mr. Hugh Watt, who had the handling of a good section of the properties years ago, possibly by the payment of a moderate sum for options, and the promise of £20,000 in hard cash if the contracts were carried through, obtained the rights to the whole estate—rights forthwith, by a little manipulation, capitalised at £300,000. Notwithstanding a record of, we presume, twelve years' work, on and off, upon one of the properties, representing perhaps 160 acres of the 700 acres, all the prospectus contained about this particular property is that six crushings had taken place, with an average treatment of 55 tons in each crushing. Could a more abject tale of failure be recorded? yet an "Arabian Nights" sort of price was put upon the properties to start with. And now it is eclipsed by a still more gorgeous total on the market, although in the nineteen months of the new company's existence no regular returns of crushings appear to have been established. It is a mad time in the markets just now, and Mr. Bottomley has done his best with a will—the wonderful man!

Some More "Drew" Companies.

In accordance with our promise of last week we intend to deal shortly with a few of the concerns of Mr. Richard Collins Drew. First, as to Cowell, Craft, & Co. Since the verdict in the Grosvenor case, Drew has retired from the board of this company as managing director, and has given an undertaking in the Court of Chancery not to vote at the meeting of the company as a shareholder. The four businesses of Drew that this company was promoted to take over were purchased by a syndicate for £80,000, who agreed to sell them to the newly-formed company for £130,000 in cash or shares. We are glad to say that the prospectus issued to the public fell flat, and the syndicate only received £52,963 in cash and the balance in shares and debentures. Drew's share was £10,000 in cash with the rest of his consideration, £80,000, in shares and debentures. Out of the present capital of £150,000, this gentleman holds, or held when he was cross-examined in the Grosvenor case, £60,000 in shares and £30,000 in debentures, besides being managing director at £600 a year. That no information is forthcoming from this company is not surprising, and this seems to be the chronic state of companies that have got into the clutches of the Drew ring.

Drew, again, is (we wish we could write was) a director in Long's Hotel, Limited. Success seems hardly to have been the outcome of this adventure. In 1888 it was formed with £65,000 capital. In 1893 £2 10s. per share was written off as lost. The vendor guaranteed 10 per cent. for three years, which was paid, but for 1889-1890 and 1890-91 the distribution was only 5 per cent. For the next three years the loss on trading was £512, £71, and £110 respectively, but with what seems to have been a dying effort in 1894-1895 this was turned into a credit of £186. Since that date there have been no reports and no distribution. Though now a matter of ancient history, owing to the shareholders having swept away the old board and taken the affairs into their own hands, the connection of the Drew clique with the Alexandra Hotel is interesting. The directors for many years were three—namely, Lord Saye and Sele, G. A. Bolton, and George Bolton, managing director. Without the privity of the shareholders, in 1896, one T. E. Polden—who acquired twenty-five shares in January of that year from J. Jervis, one of the promoters of the company of Cowell, Drew, & Co. —was appointed managing director in succession to George Bolton. The remuneration of that gentleman was fixed at £300, rising to £500, in addition to his fees as a director. He was also at this time chairman of the board of Cowell, Craft, & Co. In their report on the affairs of this hotel the committee of investigation characterise Drew's connection with the affairs of the hotel as "most baneful." To say the least of it, that appears to us to be a term of the mildest description, considering the facts which are set forth in that report.

Since the verdict, the shareholders of the Grosvenor have held a meeting, and we cannot leave this sordid subject without one short reference to that proceeding. For colossal impudence the conduct of Newitt would be hard to beat. On ordering the Press to withdraw, a movement which was promptly checkmated by the shareholders, his statement, "we cannot allow you to stay here; there is enough publicity without that," is delightful for a man who has, with his co-directors, been found guilty of fraudulent conspiracy. Truly the motto of this ring all along has been "avoid publicity," but we trust that now light has been thrown on their dealings, the matter will be seriously taken in hand by a certain public official.

Economic and Financial Notes and Correspondence.

"SECOND THOUGHTS ABOUT RHODESIA."

The *National Review* for March contains another interesting article on this vast territory, by Mr. J. Y. F. Blake, in which he reviews some criticisms based upon his previous papers, and maintains his former conclusions. Amongst these conclusions the most important is an assertion that neither Mashona nor Matabeleland possess reefs containing payable gold. Even Mr. Blake's most determined critics admit that if gold does not turn up in quantities sufficient to establish a grand mining industry in the country, Rhodesia will, in the words of Mr. Selous, soon be "deserted by the home-born British." We are not able to pronounce judgment upon this view, never having been in the country, but, as we have said more than once before, Mr. Blake's writings bear a stamp of ingenuousness which helps to carry conviction to unprejudiced minds. Grant, however, that he is right, and still we imagine he is too sanguine altogether in shortening the original five years he gave for Rhodesia to be found out to one year. Although never an ounce of payable gold should be found in all that territory, it will take more than twelve months to convince the British public of the worthlessness of this vaunted acquisition. It has been deceived and intoxicated by the boastful words always employed in describing it, and, carried away by the Imperialist folly, sticks, against all evidence, to the faith that something magnificent will one of these days turn up.

For years before Mr. Blake came forward, with his plain narrative of facts and unimpassioned deductions, we have been striving to exhibit to the British public the hollowness of the financial side of the Chartered Company's fabric. Again and again it has been demonstrated, on irrefragable evidence, in the INVESTORS' REVIEW, that the Chartered Company was a financial bubble of the very worst description, blown out by a handful of individuals whose sole object, when put to the test of facts, was the filling of their own pockets at the expense of the simple British investor, or still more simple gambler. Facts and figures did not prevent "Chartered" shares from running up to £9, any more than they saved us from the unmeasured abuse always ready for those who seek to tell the truth without prejudice. It is invariably thus with popular crazes, and it will take a good deal more than twelve months to satisfy the public that in this portion of South Africa England has acquired a territory more useless to her than Sahara would be. Just look what is going on at the present time in the newspapers mostly under the control of the financiers who have more or less stripped the British public of its money. As we write even, laudatory messages and letters about Rhodesia are appearing in print, and will be believed far more readily than anything that can be said by an unprejudiced observer who never touched a share in the Chartered Company, or had anything whatever to do with any enterprise the founders of Rhodesia persuaded the British public to place money in. Let but one "paying lode" be found in all the plateau the company owns, and if that lode hold out for only six months, it will cost the nation untold millions.

MR. DAVID YULE ON INDIAN CURRENCY.

As usual, the chairman of the Bank of Calcutta had something worth hearing to say at the half-yearly meeting of its shareholders, held in that city on January 29 last. Had we space, we should be glad to print the whole speech; as it is, a few sentences from it must serve. The speaker winds up with what might have been his text: "India's great currency problem can be solved by her fields and by her looms, and by these alone"—but the whole speech enforces this dictum. It points out that trade has been half paralysed by the vagaries of exchange—vagaries the direct outcome of Government efforts to force up the value of the rupee in the vain quest of a fixed gold standard. "The life-blood of the currency policy of 1893 depends wholly on the scarcity of rupees, and as surely as December comes round once a year will the period of dear money return. If money this year gets cheaper before the end of June, the fact may be safely taken as a sign of a falling off in the trade activity of the country."

Just so: but where will the Government find itself with its enormous and growing yearly obligations, due in London, if Indian trade falls off? In its really insane efforts to make the remittance to London of money due by it easy through an artificially high rupee, it is destroying the sources whence the money can be drawn, and inflicting fearful losses upon the Indian business community, Indian bankers and investors, and the Indian people. Take the rest in Mr. Yule's own words:—

It is this desperate ambition to have 1s. 4d. exchange at any sacrifice that has wrought the failure of the currency legislation of 1893, and brought the people to the verge of ruin and discontent. What confidence can there be in a policy that buys rupees for 1s. 4$\frac{1}{16}$d. and sells them a few days after at 1s. 3$\frac{1}{16}$d., or declares that a limited amount of Telegraphic Transfer will be sold out of the 40 lakhs Councils offered and two weeks after sells the whole amount in that form? Can any business man have the patience to anticipate such vagaries, or to believe that they are working for the common good of the country? I think not. It is evident, too, that the Government have lost confidence in their ability to prevent fluctuations in exchange, and to maintain the rate at 1s. 4d. without utterly upsetting their revenues. The condition into which India has fallen may be gathered from a few words which fell from the Finance Minister's lips on 14th instant. He said: "It must be understood that we are not rolling in wealth while we are refusing aid to others, and our inability to advance money is due, not to any wilful obstinacy, but to want of adequate means. The Secretary of State cannot draw on us for more than we are able to pay. The fear is, therefore, that the market may reach a point where money will become actually unavailable, and merchants will find it impossible to sell their bills."

Is it possible that the Government of India see no danger to their revenues if such a state of things be allowed to continue? Do they still persist in holding that this country, as a whole, makes no loss in its international trade by an appreciation of its standard, since the lower price received for its exports is balanced by the lower price paid for its imports? The fallacy of this theory in its application to India needs no better illustration than what is happening in our markets for export produce.

How long can growers go on accepting fewer rupees for their produce while they have to pay the same rent, the same wages, and taxes with an increasing burden of debt at an increasing rate of interest? How long will the money-lenders suffer repayment of their advances to fall into arrear? The agricultural population of this country display great, even dogged patience at their toil, but the money-lenders have the doggedness without the patience. The village grogshop harbours the result—a dissolute and heart-broken peasant, once a thriving ryot. His loss to the land is the loss of revenue to Government, for the people cannot continue to cultivate land which gives no return. As a practical illustration of the effect of stringent money and depressed prices, I am informed by some of the largest indigo producers in the North-West that they will not sow next season. The land thus released may not be cultivated, for other products are about as profitless as indigo.

It is not in agricultural pursuits alone that the stringency of money is felt. Manufacturing industries are hampered in their operations by the inability or unwillingness of bankers to advance funds either for further extensions or for the purchase of raw material. The manufacturer, to get money, has, therefore, to dispose of his goods as he makes them, at the best prices the market will pay for them. Importers, too, have cause for complaint, for buyers take delivery of goods only under compulsion, owing to the absence of demand in retail. The fact is, the masses are unable to buy to the same extent as when money was cheap and plentiful. They have barely sufficient to purchase the food required to keep body and soul together. Comforts, such as new clothes, are out of the question. Some amelioration of the lot of the people is required, for nothing is so disposed to make a man discontented and rebellious as the stoppage of the wherewithal to buy these little comforts, which give some colour to the dull grey monotony of an Indian workman's existence.

Not many weeks ago the Government deprived a Rajah of the privileges of his rank for alleged harsh treatment of his ryots. I wonder whether there is any prospect of similar punishment being accorded to the authors of the 1893 policy. The only sensible remedy to the present unfortunate position of India and of her traders is to gradually reopen the mints to the coinage of silver. As London thinks in gold, let India think in silver. Instead of borrowing or purchasing gold, let rupees be sold in Calcutta, Bombay, and Madras by weekly tender, the tenderer of the greatest weight in silver bullion for each lot, say of one lakh of rupees, becoming the purchaser. The Government could fix a limit from time to time under which rupees would not be sold, thereby establishing an automatic silver currency regulated by the trade demand for money. This, with the application of the knife to certain of the home charges, would give to India the fullest measure of prosperity.

"FREE" AND "OPEN" PORTS IN CHINA.

Though the debate in the House of Commons on Tuesday was raised in the interests of Jingoism, and failed in its immediate purpose, it was made the means of giving us a tolerably clear indication of what Russia has promised in connection with the occupation of Port

Arthur. Before the discussion, Sir William Harcourt asked for the production of the communication in which Russia had stated her intention to make Port Arthur an open port. This, said Mr. Curzon, was impossible, as the negotiations with both Russia and Germany were still in progress; but the papers would be published soon, and would include the despatch referred to. During the subsequent discussion, however, Mr. Curzon clearly defined Russia's present position. She is to make Port Arthur an "open" port in any case, and there was nothing to preclude her from making it a "free" port. The difference between the two seems very well defined. A "free" port is one like Hong Kong, at which no tariff whatever is imposed on commerce. An "open" port is practically equivalent to a treaty port, where all trading communities are placed on an equality. Well, then, Russia is now bound to make Port Arthur an open port at least, and she may yet make it a free one, though that seems improbable. As an open port, however, neither Great Britain nor any other trading nation is placed at a disadvantage. The somewhat alarming insinuations made as to Russia's intentions would seem to be ill-founded. And we may conclude that the position of Germany in Kiao-Chau will be much the same as that of Russia at Port Arthur.

FRANCE AND WEST AFRICA.

Nothing could be more admirable than the tone and substance of M. Hanotaux's reply to the somewhat fire-eating interpellation of Prince d'Arenberg in the French Chamber of Deputies. The Prince, in his reference to the assassination of a French officer in Nigeria, meant to give the occasion a Jingo turn; but M. Hanotaux declined to be drawn in that direction. Indeed, from what he said, it seems clear that neither the British Government nor the Niger Company can in any sense be held responsible for the unfortunate death of M. de Bernis. On the general situation in West Africa M. Hanotaux declined to enter while the Anglo-French Commission was sitting; but he had confidence in the friendly dispositions of the two Governments; and the labours of the Commission had already "favourably prepared the ground." French interests had been "energetically and perseveringly defended," without, however, "excluding the desire to seek, if necessary, an equitable settlement by reciprocal concessions." Here lies the kernel of the whole business. There is plenty of room for concessions on both sides, and really none for quarrelling now that the French Minister has spoken so openly and so explicitly. We take it that a peaceable settlement of this question is near at hand. There never need have been any doubt of its possibility. To have acted otherwise would have been the veriest perversity of reckless folly.

THE OPERATIONS OF TRUSTS.

When mere business transactions are taken into account, one must not, it would seem, clamour for a high standard either of morals or prudence. Yet we confess to have expected rather better things from some of the trusts, whose wonderful story we told just seven years ago. The experience of the years that followed 1890 ought to have brought home to the directors of these concerns that much of the bad business they had done just prior to that date was a direct consequence of their greedy seeking after underwriting commissions, and their premium hunting. For a while this kind of speculation succeeds, but it usually ends by leading the trust or individual that indulges in a play with credit of this kind to possess more or less unmanageable heaps of paper, called "securities" by courtesy, whose destiny often is to become absolutely valueless; or the stuff has to be locked up and "nursed" for a great many years, at a cost that takes away all hope of profit, even should the nursing in the end give back some of the money sunk.

The period that has elapsed since 1890 has been long enough to allow many of the originally weak holdings of the Salomons and other trusts to become stronger, accordingly their own securities have again attained to a fair market value. A proportion of them also have cut down their capital by an application to the courts, so that their boards have been freed from a certain amount of responsibility. The consequence is that, aided by the recent advance in prices, these trusts find themselves in a position to satisfactorily realise a greater proportion of their assets than has been possible at any time since 1890. A great deal more shifting about of their investments has consequently been going on of late, and much of the changing has been admirably conducted. The experience of the past has not been without its lessons.

An unsatisfactory element, however, is found in the manner in which even the better sort of trusts tend to follow in the train of some harmful fashion in finance. Probably there is not a more distressful symptom, if the future is considered, than the process of Hooleyising prosperous companies. One has only to turn to the market in which this kind of finance was first freely indulged in—that for cycles and their accessories—to see what a palsying effect financial charlatanism of this kind brings upon an otherwise energetic and expansive industry. The evils are only too apparent even now, and yet a glance at the recently issued report of the Mercantile Investment and General Trust shows that powerful corporation to have lent its assistance to several of these wretched operations. In this report it is shown that during the past year the trust purchased 2,350 shares of the Austrian Incandescent Share Company, 9,225 Preference shares of Bovril, 2,650 shares of the English Incandescent Share Company, 2,000 Preference shares and £2,000 Debenture stock of Schweppes, 1,550 shares of the Second Austrian Incandescent Share Company, 6,000 Preference shares and 10,000 Ordinary shares of the Welsbach Incandescent Company, and 500 Preference shares of the Apollinaris and Johannis Company. Quite £40,000 of its spare cash must have been used in supporting the operations of latter-day financiers, and it stands to reason that if other trusts have followed the same policy the operations of the said financiers have been greatly assisted. The Mercantile and General Trust has certainly realised some of its holdings of these dangerous securities, but the initial objection to the character of this whole class of business is not removed by that.

THE COUNCIL OF FOREIGN BONDHOLDERS—A CORRECTION AND A PLAIN TALE.

By a slip we stated last week that this body had agreed to "accept 50 per cent. on the 'B' and 60 per cent. on the 'A' Costa Rica bonds, with interest cut down by one half as well." This should have been, "by cutting the interest down to one half." We apologise for the blunder, which was the more unpardonable because, as every one understands, this is the Council's own exclusive patent plan for releasing debtors from their obligations. We had no business to hint at any improvement on that patent.

At the present stage of the fight which independent certificate-holders in the Corporation of Foreign Bondholders are making to prevent the complete confiscation of their property, the following brief narration of facts drawn up by one of them should be valuable, although it goes over ground already in great part covered by articles which have from time to time appeared in this Review :—

The Corporation of Foreign Bondholders consists of 545 certificate-holders, who originally contributed £100 each, which has been the substratum upon which the funds of over £100,000 have been earned and accumulated and at present vested in the Corporation, after repaying all the certificate-holders £100 plus interest. These elect, under rules, the twenty-one members of Council who manage the affairs, but owing to the advantages of the Council who control the organisation and staff, the endeavours to put forward independent candidates by the body of certificate-holders has been frustrated, and elections and re-elections have for years past been practically a matter of co-option by the members of the Council. The Council have now formulated a Bill in Parliament which totally extinguishes the certificate-holders, and vests the funds and the whole Corporation in themselves.

The two requisite meetings have been held, and by majorities secured through the Council's advantageous position to obtain proxies (and including their own twenty-one votes which, being those of interested parties, are of more than questionable validity) the Bill has been allowed to proceed.

The Bill was prepared secretly, and notice of the first meeting was sprung upon the certificate-holders with only five days' notice, proxies to be in the hands of the secretary forty-eight hours previous to meeting, no copy of the Bill was sent, though to be had on application, hence any invitation of opposition proxies was simply impossible. It is true that five days' notice only for special meetings is provided by the articles of association, but it is obvious that this was intended for use in case the Council should be confronted in the course of business by some sudden emergency which required certificate-holders' immediate decision, and not for such a purpose as the present, which, although infinitely further reaching, and involving the existence of the Corporation, could have been dealt with leisurely after mature consideration.

A petition against this monstrous proposal has been very largely signed by certificate-holders, and has no doubt been lodged before now. It is inconceivable, notwithstanding the powerful interests of the promoters, that Parliament will establish a precedent striking at the very root of rights, property, and common sense.

Mr. McKinley and the "Maine" Ferment.

President McKinley deserves high commendation for the prudence and dignity with which he has met the efforts of the Jingos and Cuba annexationists of the United States to involve his administration in a war with Spain over the unhappy catastrophe in Havana harbour. "I will not be pigged into war," he has said, and his calmness and prudent firmness have placed him far higher in the esteem of his sensible countrymen, and in that of people on this side the Atlantic, than he ever stood before. How different his position is to-day from that of the President of the French Republic, who now appears before the world as the humble, if not cowering, slave of a Jesuit-governed military faction, "which has the horse, and only wants the man to mount him, in order to re-establish the empire" and destroy liberty in France—liberty already more than half strangled.

The Canadian Railway Rate War.

This appears to be little better than an infamy. Putting on one side the question as to how far such conflicts, always breaking out at unexpected moments, and when stock markets are "well in on the bull tack," originate in motives kindred to those actuating the basest of card-sharpers, it is surely a scandal that presidents and managers should be free to indulge in these conflicts in utter disregard of stockholders' interests and in the mere wantonness of their absolutism. This week the Grand Trunk Company has published its version of the origin of the latest of these fights, throwing back, in doing so, the guilt upon the Canadian Pacific. Which is telling the truth we have not the means to judge, but it may once more be pointed out that the Canadian Pacific Company was admittedly the first to indulge in extensive "cuts" of rates, and that its managers sought to screen themselves from condemnation by the usual sickening cant about the "all Canadian" and "Imperialist" character of their road. But a few weeks before these same managers had been boasting through the Press at their command of the complete harmony of interests that had been established between the Canadian Pacific and Great Northern and Northern Pacific Companies, both of which are United States lines pure and simple. The Vanderbilt roads, too, still supply the Canadian Pacific with its chief eastern outlet. So the British public will draw its own conclusions. It is at least sure upon one point. By such conflicts as that now in progress investors and speculators alike in the old country are from time to time stripped of large sums of money. Grand Trunk stockholders in particular have time and again been almost ruined by the unscrupulous tactics of the Canadian Pacific.

Midland Railway of W. Australia.

The following letter will interest debenture-holders in this railway :—

To the Editor.

Sir,—Before the Debenture-holders meet again it would be as well they should know that the directors of the company made an application to the Court of Chancery some time ago to get the ordinary shares of the company reduced from £5 shares to £1 shares, with the intention of relieving the shareholders who are credited with £1 a share paid, from all further liability, on the pretence that they had given up something to which they had no claim. This my solicitors, Messrs. Lyne & Holman, of 5 and 6, Great Winchester-street, E.C., opposed successfully, thus saving for the company a valuable asset of £800,000, for which, according to my counsel's opinion, the directors are liable. If the directors had succeeded in their application, they (the directors) would have been relieved from all liability for neglect in not calling up the share capital, or for any misstatement with regard to it in the prospectus.

A Debenture-holder.

Imperial Continental Waterworks, Limited.

We publish at the request of the directors of the imperial Continental Waterworks, Limited, the following reply, prepared by their engineer, to the letter from Mr. Brown appearin in The Investors' Review of January 28. This correspondence must now end :—

Gentlemen,—At the request of your secretary, I reply to so much as concerns me of the letter from Mr. Frederick A. G. Brown, of Genoa, published in The Investors' Review of January 28.

1. Mr. Brown states that "the population lying next to the company's reservoir" is contained in the small villages on the line of aqueduct. I should think these words were meant to describe the eastern part of the city and suburbs of Genoa, which the intended aqueduct first reaches; but it is immaterial, for in dry seasons, which are properly held to determine the question, there is at present "no adequate public supply" to the greater part of the city and suburbs of Genoa.

2. My statement with respect to the resources of the Gorzente Company was accurate. As an old director of that company, which depends for its supply upon the enormously fluctuating rainfall of Northern Italy, Mr. Brown must know that his statement of the quantity drawn from the reservoirs in 1897 is no measure whatever of what would follow after a dry winter. The *fill dyke* months of Northern Italy are October, November, December, January, and February. Now the rainfall of the five *fill dyke* months contributing to the supply of 1897 was so greatly in excess of the average of the last twenty-four years that the flow to the existing reservoirs in those months exceeded 70 per cent. above what they would receive during corresponding months of average rainfall, and was two and a half times as great as it would have been in corresponding months of occasional dry seasons.

What, after such a flow to the reservoirs, is the value of Mr. Brown's statement that an average of 424·24 litres per second passed from the reservoirs during 1897? They are quite incapable of yielding any such quantity after ordinary seasons, and the measure of the surplus, which the consumers enjoyed in 1897, is the measure of the deficiency which they will experience after correspondingly dry winters.

Mr. Brown's assumption that because the Gorzente Company own the "chief part of the 4,200 acres of barren hill-side which constitutes their gathering ground" they can, "independently of their concession, dispose of the water that falls on their land," is not a fact. These 4,200 acres form the catchment area from which the Gorzente Company are authorised to take 250 litres per second; and even if the Company own the whole 4,200 acres they would still be prohibited by law from taking more than 250 litres. It may be that the Company have infringed the terms of their concession, and taken more than the law gives them, but no volume in excess of the chartered limit is really secure. Granting even that the Gorzente Company could with impunity exceed their statutory limit, as Mr. Brown states it to have been exceeded in 1897, his case would scarcely be assisted, for in ordinarily dry seasons that company would not have the surplus water to dispose of.

3. Mr. Brown attempts to veil a statement in my last letter by proceeding to paragraph 3 of his letter, which is a reply to my No. 4. All I stated there is correct.

4. Paragraph 4 of Mr. Brown's letter purports to be a reply to my No. 6, which is correct in every particular, and does not state, as implied by Mr. Brown, that the Bisagno is necessary, in addition to the Concasca, for the supply of about 240,000 persons. The Concasca, I have consistently said, is alone sufficient, if the intended reservoir is constructed to its full size. The Bisagno is a still larger supply, available if ever required.

Mr. Brown further states that "the Bisagno, besides being polluted, is completely controlled by the intakes of the municipal aqueduct." If polluted, that pollution is now supplied direct to Genoa without storage or purification of any kind. The causes of pollution ought no doubt to have been remedied, and if I am responsible for the matter when the Concasca has to be supplemented, they will be remedied at comparatively small cost. On the second point Mr. Brown is singularly misinformed. Only a small portion of the available supply of the Bisagno is controlled by the municipal aqueduct.

5. Mr. Brown leaves untouched paragraphs 7 and 8 of my letter.

6. Concerning the Concasca and Bisagno Mr. Brown writes, "these sources have become insufficient and objectionable." In the matter of sufficiency, they yield an average flow, more than twice as great as that from all the supplies controlled by the Gorzente Company. That they have become "objectionable" to that company, I can well believe.

The issue between Mr. Brown and myself is shortly this. I assert and he denies that there is, except after wet winters, a great and crying demand for an adequate supply of pure water to the city and suburbs of Genoa. Of these facts I have satisfied myself by careful personal investigation and inquiry on the ground. That the residents of Genoa and the Government are of the same mind is shown by the requisition you have received from residents, and by the fact that the Government, recognising the inadequacy of the present supply, have granted, and from time to time renewed, a concession held by your company which, if Mr. Brown's contentions were true, would be a mere mischievous interference with existing interests, and would serve no useful purpose at all.

I am, Gentlemen, your obedient servant,

GEORGE F. DEACON.

THE SOUTH METROPOLITAN GAS COMPANY.

Mr. George Livesey's speeches at the meetings of this company are usually worth reading, and on February 16 he waxed eloquent about tar, its by-products, their uses, and the best means of obtaining the best price for this residual. At present, tar realises only 1d. per gallon, which is not its value as fuel, and Mr. Livesey argued that gas companies ought to combine and regulate supplies so that 4d. per gallon ought to be realised Although we do not profess to have any inside knowledge of the gas business, in which, of course, Mr. Livesey is *facile princeps*, we fail to see how the companies could gain very largely if such a combination were possible. The difficulty in the residual market is that the out-turn of the gas companies increases so largely that consumption cannot absorb the supply of by-products. After all, gas-making is the first consideration of these companies, and, if that goes on successfully, the directors and shareholders ought hardly to complain that this very success has knocked to pieces the market for residuals.

THE SCOTTISH AMERICAN INVESTMENT COMPANY.

We fully share Mr. Menzies' objection to criticism that is illegitimate, but his complaints are rather strained in the subjoined letter. Last week, in dealing with the annual report of his company, we wrote :—"Of the net revenue of £50,609, no less than £50,000 is absorbed in paying the dividend of 10 per cent., leaving only the odd £609 to be carried forward," which was strictly correct, as we were dealing with the way in which the company divided its profits up to the hilt, and, therefore, only took the revenue of the year into account, and paid no heed to the £6,000 brought forward from the preceding year, which allowed £6,609 to be carried forward. With regard to the matter of the interest charge, the difference comes to a splitting of hairs. Interest upon calls paid in advance only amounted to £1,012, out of a total of £74,191, and after Mr. Menzies has deducted this item he makes the charge 57½ per cent. of the interest on investments, whereas our general statement made it no mo e than 60 per cent. :—

To the Editor.

Edinburgh, March 1, 1898.

DEAR SIR,—Our attention has been called to an article in your issue of February 25 in regard to this company.

Your article is misleading, as one would naturally infer that £609 is the only sum carried forward, whereas, if you will turn to the report you will see that the sum carried forward was £6,609.

Again, you will see that the sum required for interest last year was £73,179; you have added interest on uncalled capital, which is, of course, postponed to the interest on the Debentures and Debenture stock; so that the charge for interest is only 57½ per cent. of the interest on investments, and only 54 per cent. of the total income of the company, exclusive of the sum brought from last year.

We do not object to any legitimate criticism, and, as the original shareholders of the company have in twenty-five years received in dividends three times the amount of their capital, they have confidence in the management, and are quite content; but it is only right that we should be fairly treated, and we ask you, therefore, to have the goodness to correct your statement in your next issue.—

We are, dear sir, yours truly, WM. JOHN MENZIES,
Managing Director.

A CURIOSITY.

The Economic Bank is a curiosity in a City where all kinds of novelties are tried. Although a bank, its directors are specially forbidden by the articles of association from engaging in discount operations, making any loans, or permitting overdrafts. Furthermore, the investments of the bank must be in Trustee stocks or Colonial Government securities, but money must not be used in mortgages. Its income thus depends entirely upon revenue from investments, and as it grants interest upon deposits, the question naturally arises whether the margin betwixt the two will bear the expenses of such banking. At present it does not, for 1896 closed with a debit of £835, and 1897 with a debit of £1,402. We should not, however, like to say that the institution will not grow—it has now £52,488 of current and deposit accounts—as, after all, people who deposit their money like to see what is done with it, which they can do in this case, for the list of investments is published and hung up in the offices of the bank. There is one great merit about a scheme like this, which is that the depositors can lose little or nothing.

Critical Index to New Investments

GARTSIDE'S (BROOKSIDE BREWERY), LIMITED.

Brewery at Ashton-under-Lyne was founded by the late John Cartside in 1830, and was in 1892, for family reasons, converted into a private limited company, with a nominal capital of £120,000. This has now been sold to the Conversion Guarantee Company, who bring it forward as a public company with a share capital of £350,000 in £10 shares, equally divided into ordinary and 5 per cent. cumulative preference shares. An issue is also made of £300,000 first mortgage 4½ per cent. debenture stock, which is offered at 103 per cent., while all the share capital is offered at par, except 2,500 ordinary shares reserved for future issue. William Wilson & Son, of Manchester, value the brewery, public-houses, and plant at £445,002, while book debts, loans, &c., with £25,000 working capital provided from this issue, make up a total valuation of £539,431. Profits are distinctly stated for four and a half years, those for year ended June, 1894, being £25,796, and for year ended June, 1897, £35,474, while for the last six months of 1897 they were £19,549. The average for the four and a half years is, therefore, at the rate of £30,650 per annum, whereas debenture stock interest and preference dividend will require as much as £21,500. The aggregate purchase price is fixed by the Conversion Company, who are the promoters, at £600,000, payable in cash, in addition to the premium on the debenture stock, and of this total, £550,000 will be paid to the original vendors. The chairman of the old company will subscribe for one-third of the ordinary and preference shares and debenture stock now offered—he could hardly do less if the former partners have any confidence left in the undertaking. It is no doubt a very good brewery business, but we do not think profits justify the capital being blown out from £120,000 to £650,000. Even taking the profits for the year ended June, 1897, the price represents over seventeen years' purchase, and considering the present tendency to curtail licences, we think investors are asked to buy at a very high price.

READ BROTHERS, LIMITED.

This business of export bottlers of Kentish Town was founded in 1877, by W. T. Read and J. W. Read, both of whom are dead; and the recent sale of the business by executors is the reason for the formation of this company. Capital £200,000 in £10 shares, half Ordinary and half 5 per cent. cumulative preference, with a 4 per cent. irredeemable first mortgage debenture stock issue for £65,000, the whole offered at par. Interest due March and September. The purchase price is £265,000 in cash, which, in spite of £75,000 being provided as working capital, seems ample, for only £41,000 is considered by Field & Blades to be the value of the freehold land, buildings, and fixed plant. This leaves a large sum represented by goodwill, brands, and trade-marks. Net profits for past six years average £18,946, and for last year they were £18,731, which is not an indication of progress—rather the other way. We believe, however, the business is sound, and the margin between debenture and preference interest and profits is over £11,000, so the debenture stock and preference shares should be good speculative investments.

HUDSON HOTELS, LIMITED.

Share capital, £125,000 in £1 shares, 75,000 being 5½ per cent. cumulative preference, 50,000 ordinary, and 500 "management" shares, the latter being subscribed by directors and entitled to one-tenth of profits remaining after paying preference dividend. There is also an issue of £125,000 four per cent. first mortgage debentures, repayable at par September 29, 1912, Interest due March and September. Debentures and preference shares offered for subscription at par. Company buys three hotels at Scarborough, one at Filey, and one near Robin Hood's Bay, all being fully licensed freehold properties, and the unlicensed freehold property at Filey. Charles Appleton, of Leeds, reports that in his opinion the value of the properties and furnishings, exclusive of consumable stock and goodwill, is £204,000. Bradley, Davis, & Co., chartered accountants, Scarborough, give a certificate about profits, but it amounts to nothing. After saying they have investigated the books of four of the hotels for four years 1893-6, they tell us that the books have not been kept in the case of each hotel on such a basis as to enable proper trading accounts to be prepared. But they have ascertained the gross receipts, and have had submitted to them a statement as to the estimated receipts likely to be derived from the hotel and the unlicensed house at Filey, from the new shops and café adjoining the Royal Hotel, Scarborough, and the additional income expected from advertisements and extensions. They are then careful to express the opinion that if these properties are thoroughly equipped and capably managed, the carrying on in them of a first-class business ought, under ordinary circumstances and good seasons, to result in a gross income of £40,000 per annum; and, taking into consideration the saving which should be effected by the amalgamation, a profit available of £13,000. What with the estimated, the likely, the if, the under, the taking, and the should be, as a certificate regarding profits it is not worth the paper it is written on. Mr. Bertini, described as an hotel expert, goes one better, and says the profits may be reasonably expected to considerably exceed the estimate of £13,000. For the properties, goodwill, &c., the vendor, Mr. W. J. Hudson, asks £240,500, including the ordinary shares and £190,500 in cash, which we think a lot too much, with due respect to the chartered accountants and the hotel expert. The product of their tillage will be nil in our opinion.

BIRT, POTTER, & HUGHES, LIMITED.

Company is formed to take over the business of shipowners, freight contractors, and merchants of this name from January 1. The firm of Allport & Hughes was founded prior to 1845; that of John Potter & Co. in 1868, and J. Gavin, Birt, & Co. in 1877. An amalgamation of these three firms took place in 1889, and the business has since 1894 been extended by the acquisition of interests in works in Australia connected with the refrigerated meat trade and in refrigerated steam ships. The capital is £200,000 in £5 shares, one half in ordinary shares taken by the vendors in full payment of the purchase money, and the other half in 5½ per cent. cumulative preference shares to provide additional working capital. Interest due April and October. After paying preference dividend, 20 per cent. of remaining profits of each year will be carried to a reserve until it amounts to £25,000. Profits for eight and three quarter years to December, 1897, averaged £14,176; for the past four years they averaged £19,558; and for last year they were £22,565. The prospectus is a very plausible document all through, and Spain Bros. & Co. draw up a little balance-sheet showing a total of £175,824, and including amongst the assets sundry debit balances, £66,286; trade investments, which are mainly interests in refrigerated steamers and meat-freezing works and wharves in Australia, £60,000; and goodwill, £32,500. This firm of accountants seem to go out of their way to point out that the sum at which these trade investments stand they have ascertained to be under the par value of the investments and below their cost, and, from information acquired during their investigation, they consider it to be also below their actual value. The accountants seem to be here stepping beyond their province. Is their zeal stimulated by an actual knowledge of the state of the Australian refrigerated meat trade? If so, it is an uncommon knowledge. In our opinion, a third of the amount would be a liberal valuation for these trade investments. What, too, is the real value of the sundry debit balances, or of "goodwill?" Leave the thing alone till more light comes.

SALVIATI, JESURUM, & CO., LIMITED.

With a total capital of £330,000 in £1 shares, of which 180,000 are cumulative 6 per cent. preference shares and the rest ordinary shares this undertaking is brought out to amalgamate various businesses in London and Vienna and thus stop existing competition. Business specialities of these firms comprise Venetian glass and art mosaics, fabrics and laces, carved wood and ornamental marbles, and bronzes and works of art. For various periods averaging five years Kemp, Ford certify average profits of five firms as being equal to £25,908 per annum; for last year they were £29,068, and an additional £2,000 is to be derived from another firm taken over. Freehold properties in Vienna are valued at £25,692, and in addition there are numerous leaseholds, while the stock-in-trade of the various firms on January 1, 1897, at cost price amounted to £101,686, and book debts, guaranteed to £8,699. For the businesses, goodwill, &c., the price asked is £300,000, of which £160,000 in cash, and £140,000 in ordinary shares. The public are invited to subscribe at par for the preference shares, which, besides their fixed interest, stand the off-chance of getting 25 per cent. of surplus profits after 8 per cent. has been paid on the ordinary, and 10 per cent. of the balance has been set aside for reserve. An undertaking difficult to judge. The stock-in-trade has had plenty of time to run down since January, 1890, and we see no valuation of the London freehold premises. Probably they are not important, in which case the goodwill would work out on a liberal scale. On the other hand the board has some good names on it, and, assuming that last year's profits are maintained, there would be a surplus of about £20,000 after paying the preference dividend.

SALSADELLA LITHOGRAPHIC STONE QUARRIES, LIMITED.

The company is to buy the stone quarry of Clotazos at Salsadella, in the Province of Castellon de la Plana, Spain, and the concession of the Consuelo Mine on the same property. Capital £120,000 in £1 shares, of which 71,667 are offered at par, while 28,333 shares go to the vendor with £61,667 in cash. Quarry is acquired as a going concern, but there are no figures as to output or of any profits having been made. The prospectus is rich in favourable remarks about Salsadella stone, which is said to be of the very finest quality and, when of large dimensions, commands, from £20 to £30 for each stone at an average cost of obtaining and preparing of only 3s. 7d. to 4s. Plenty of this stuff and the company would be in clover if the vendor did not care to keep it. We think it a very questionable thing to invest in.

BRIGG HORSE HAULAGE APPLIANCE COMPANY, LIMITED.

Company acquires British, American, foreign, and Colonial patents relating to Mr. T. E. Brigg's invention for minimising draught in connection with horse haulage for £50,000, half cash and half shares. The capital is £75,000 in £1 shares, of which 50,000 are offered for subscription. The appliance has been fitted to many vehicles belonging to large firms in and out of London, and it is an excellent thing, but whether it can be made a commercial success is more than we can say.

KNIGHT'S DEEP, LIMITED.

Issue at par of first debentures to the amount of £400,000, bearing interest at the rate of 5½ per cent. per annum, payable January and July. They are redeemable at par by fifteen annual drawings, commencing July, 1902, but can be paid off at 103 two years previously, on six months' notice, and holders can, before the end of June, 1900, convert into shares to be taken at the price of £4 per share of £1 nominal amount. The security is a floating charge on the assets of the company, and includes a fixed hypothecation of all the mining claims (other than prospectors' claims), plant, machinery, and other immovable assets in South Africa, and the debentures are issued on the terms that the company shall create no further issue to rank before, or *pari passu* with, these debentures. The payment of the principal and interest is guaranteed by the Consolidated Gold Fields of South Africa, Limited. The Knight's Deep Company was only registered in 1895, and is, compared with other deep levels, quite a youngster. Little is known about it over here outside the offices of the guarantor company, about which we have not a good opinion.

SOUTHDOWN AND EAST GRINSTEAD BREWERIES, LIMITED.

A company was formed in 1895 to buy the Southdown Brewery, Lewes, and the East Grinstead Brewery, and to lease the Dolphin Brewery at Cuckfield. The purchase price was £161,640, including £61,640 in cash. The share capital was £95,000, of which £50,000 was in 5 per cent. preference shares, with an issue of £50,000 4 per cent. perpetual debenture stock. The lease of the Dolphin Brewery and accompanying houses was at a rent of £836, with an option of purchase which the company is now going to exercise. It has also bought the Bear Brewery at Lewes, with 45 public and beer houses, and it is to pay for these that the company offers 2,500 more ordinary shares of £10 each at par; 4,500 preference at 10s. premium, and £96,000 4 per cent. debenture stock at 3 premium. Interest due January and July. Debenture capital is therefore nearly as much as the share capital; but Collins, Tootell, & Co. value the properties, book debts, and other assets, at £316,396, thus exceeding the debenture debt by £146,396. Profits for 1897 of the three breweries first secured were £11,400, while by the purchase of the freehold of the Dolphin a saving in rent and sinking fund of £936 will be effected, which will give a surplus after paying debenture and preference interest of £786, apart from profits from the Bear Brewery, and the rent of £1,918 receivable from the properties attached to this brewery. Upon this basis the debenture interest and preference dividend should be forthcoming while "pubs." abound, though the undertaking is certainly not one of the best class. The company has been spreading itself out too fast for our slow mind.

UNION STEAMSHIP COMPANY OF NEW ZEALAND.

Company offers £220,000 4 per cent. debenture stock at par repayable at par May 1, 1928, but can be redeemed in 1908 on six months' notice at 105. The object of the issue is the conversion of existing terminable debentures amounting to £218,757, holders of which will receive preferential allotment in exchange for present holdings. Security is a floating charge on the property and undertaking, exclusive of uncalled capital; and debenture stock outstanding is not to exceed one-half the paid up capital, the present limit being £298,460. Last report showed assets standing in the books on September 30, 1897, amounting to £1,128,792, of which shipping represented £813,600; coals, stores, &c., £57,770; wharf properties, &c., £120,564; sundry debtors, £66,223; and cash, £70,634, whilst the liabilities, including £227,690 terminable debentures, then amounted to £329,853. Company has been doing very well lately, and although the policy of turning terminable debentures into fixed debt is not to be admired, there seems to be margin enough after paying interest. So the stock will doubtless be taken up by holders of the terminable debentures.

DOMINION ATLANTIC RAILWAY COMPANY.

This undertaking is the result of union of the old Windsor and Annapolis and Yarmouth and Annapolis lines. It has been a pretty free borrower of late, and now wants another £150,000 which it raises in 4 per cent. second debenture stock offered at 99 per cent. It ranks equally with the existing issue of £100,000 like stock, and is repayable at par in July, 1956, or can be redeemed at 105 on six months' notice after July, 1916. Interest is due January and July. Money is required to provide additional traffic facilities to cope with growing through business between Halifax, Boston and St. Johns, and otherwise improve company's position. Profits for 1897 were £39,038, whereas to pay debenture stock interest, including this issue, and preference dividend will require £43,500. It is a slenderly-secured issue, and not very cheap.

ALLDAYS & ONION'S PNEUMATIC ENGINEERING COMPANY, LIMITED.

This company is issuing £80,000 4½ per cent. mortgage debenture bonds at 105 per cent.; redeemable on six months' notice at 108 per cent., and interest is due January and July. Of the total, £50,000 is reserved for conversion of existing debentures. Present company was formed in 1885, and has assets, apart from goodwill and patents, to the amount of £179,546, of which £43,000 is freehold and leasehold property; £37,000 plant and machinery; £40,672 stock-in-trade; £15,755 investments, and £41,618 sundry debtors, besides £2 per share uncalled capital. Profits for thirteen months to July, 1896, were £16,966, and for the next twelve months £18,301; while debenture interest will require only £3,600. Debenture bonds, therefore, appear to be secure enough.

S. HIGGINBOTHAM & CO., LIMITED.

Capital, £100,000 in £10 shares, 6,000 being 5 per cent. cumulative preference and 4,000 ordinary, all of which are offered for subscription at par. Business, which was founded about the beginning of the century, is that of merchants and calico printers, of Glasgow, London, and Manchester. The late company was incorporated in 1890, but from the outset was heavily burdened with mortgage and other debts and the Indian famine, plagues, and other foreign troubles; and lack of working capital rendered liquidation necessary, so that since August, 1897, the business has been carried on by the liquidator. Land, buildings, and fixed machinery were valued at £88,736 in 1896, and are now acquired for £30,000, while the movable assets fixed at a going valuation of £69,025, are acquired for £55,000. For the six and a half years to May last the average profits were £9,032 per annum, and for the last three and a-half years they were £11,012, so that if profits are maintained at this figure there should be a balance, after paying preference interest, of £6,500. Business is transferred from August 1 last, and since then working results are said to show progressive improvement; the available profits for the half-year ending January 31, 1898, being more than sufficient to pay 5 per cent. on the whole capital for the period. To buy shares in an undertaking which has suffered in the past is not particularly inviting, but the new company takes over assets at nearly a third of their former valuation, and if the capital is subscribed the new concern will start free from debt and with a working capital of £60,000 of which £15,000 will be cash and £45,000 stocks and book debts. Assuming that the latter are recoverable there [illegible] offic[illegible] be a chance, of successful working in the future.

about a sche.

EDISON-BELL CONSOLIDATED PHO.can lose littPANY LIMITED.

For £160,000, of which only £40,000 is taken in shares and debenture stock, company acquires letters patent for the United Kingdom and the Isle of Man, Australia, South Africa, South America and India, and the trade-marks for China and Japan granted to various people in relation to phonographs, graphophones, and similar appliances. Share capital is £110,000 in 10,000 £1 ordinary shares taken by vendors, and 10,000 6 per cent. cumulative preference shares of £10 each. There is also an issue of £85,000 5 per cent. first mortgage debenture stock (part of a total of £100,000), which, with 8,500 preference shares, is offered at par. Although the first patent is dated 1886, there is no reference to any profits having been made, only a series of estimates, which may or may not be realised, and, therefore, the concern can hardly, as yet, be recommended as an investment, however tempting as a "spec."

R. H. & S. ROGERS, LIMITED.

The object of this company is to acquire and extend the business of R. H. & S. Rogers, founded 50 years ago, shirt and collar warehousemen and manufacturers, of Addle-street, London, with factories at Rotherhithe, and at Coleraine, Ireland. Capital, £165,000 in £1 shares, 90,000 being ordinary and 75,000 5 per cent. cumulative preference. Properties, mainly leasehold, are valued at £34,455 and certificates says net profits for last ten years have steadily increased year by year, those for 1895 being £10,246; for 1896, £11,401, and for 1897, £12,440. Assets also include stock in trade, £29,243; and book debts, guaranteed, £21,839. Purchase price is £160,000, of which £25,000 is taken in preference shares, £29,998 in ordinary and the rest in cash. 'Tis an old business, and profits for last year show 7½ per cent. on ordinary shares which is nothing to go into ecstacies over.

A. GOERZ & COMPANY, LIMITED.

To begin with this is a Transvaal and not a British limited company. Then it is to be saddled with founders' shares taking 20 per cent. of all profits after the ordinary have received 10 per cent. non-cumulative. In addition these founders shares have the right to subscribe for half of any future issue of ordinary shares at the price of 30s.—or less than that price up to 250,000 shares. The total capital is to be £1,015,000 in £1 shares, 15,000 of which will be founders' shares, and the vendor company: Goerz & Company, Limited, limited under German Law, and the subscribers to the working capital of the new company take the whole of them. Out of the 1,000,000 ordinary shares, subscriptions are asked for 200,000 at £1 12s. 6d. per share, on what grounds we cannot for the life of us discern in this astounding prospectus. A list of the company's investments is given, but it is a list of names alone of South African ventures—many of them poor enough. So this does not help us, nor yet the information that—

In the opening balance-sheet of the new Company of August 1, 1897, the shares constituting part of the vendor company's assets were taken at the value of £387,499 instead of £524,303 which represented their then market value as appears in the closing balance-sheet of the old company of July 30, 1897. Likewise the claims, forming another part of the said assets and acquired in former years, which have been taken over at £120,000, were valued by Dr. F. H. Hatch at £167,400. Since the early part of August the market value of the shares taken over is practically unchanged.

This hardly justifies the purchase price of £640,000 paid by the new company for the old in fully-paid ordinary shares, part of which are now offered at 12s. 6d. premium. But what follows is more wonderful still.

"A Syndicate subscribed at the price of 25s. per share for the 360,000 ordinary shares (of which 160,000 shares are fully paid and 200,000 shares at present have 5s. paid) which were issued by the new company, outside of the 640,000 ordinary shares, which passed to the vendors. The premium of £90,000 paid on these 360,000 shares goes to a reserve account."

Decidedly this company should be given a wide berth, even by mere gamblers.

Company Reports and Balance-Sheets.

⁂ *The Editor will be much obliged to the Secretaries of Joint Stock Companies if they would kindly forward copies of Reports and Balance-Sheets direct to the Office of* THE INVESTORS' REVIEW, *Norfolk House, Norfolk-street, W.C., so as to insure prompt notice in these columns.*

COUNTY OF LONDON AND BRUSH PROVINCIAL ELECTRIC LIGHTING COMPANY.—Apparently this company has only begun to grapple with its business. Two of its London stations, supplying the Wandsworth, and Clerkenwell and St. Luke's divisions, have been completed in the year; but in the huge parish of Camberwell and a few small parishes adjacent to it the laying of cables has only just been started upon by the company. Furthermore, the confirmation of a provisional order has been obtained from Parliament, covering the Mile End, Old Town, St. George's-in-the-East, and Limehouse districts, and the consent of the local bodies has been obtained towards a provisional order covering the parishes of St. Giles', St. George's, Bloomsbury, and St. George the Martyr, with the western portion of Holborn. All this means much capital outlay for the company in districts where the demand for the light must be moderate at first, and where the price charged for energy must be moderate if consumption is to be encouraged. The law, we believe, compels the company to separate the capital expenditure and working account of each division, so that shareholders in the future will be able to gather how each venture fares. At present nothing can be said about this matter, for in neither of the two London divisions was energy generated during the whole year. The company also controls two provincial concerns, the Dover Electricity Supply Company and the Richmond (Surrey) Electric Light and Power Company, and both these returned a fair profit in the year. The company's interest in a third company of this class, the Bournemouth and Poole Electricity Supply Company, were disposed of to a new company, in which a fair interest was taken, but by the operation a substantial profit was obtained, which must have been about £13,000. With this sum the revenue received from the provincial companies and small balances from the London undertakings, the gross profit of £25,371 was produced for the year. After administrative charges and interest on temporary loans had been met, the net balance of £20,875 remained, and out of this the 6 per cent. interest upon the Preference capital was paid, leaving £10,090 to be carried forward. The sum of £5,643, received as premium upon new shares, has been applied as follows:—£3,253 in reduction of general preliminary expenses, £889 to writing off costs in connection with provisional orders, and £1,500 to reserve, raising its total to £5,000. Needless to say, the balance-sheet is in a state of flux, and shows large sums owing by and due to the company.

BARRETT'S BREWERY AND BOTTLING COMPANY.—This company struggles against great competition, which apparently forces down profits. Thus, £148,387 from sales last year, or practically the same as in 1896, produced only a net revenue of £16,118, as against a net profit of £17,553 in the preceding twelve months. The balance allowed of a dividend of 4½ per cent. upon the Ordinary shares, but to do this the amount forward had to be reduced, by £1,131, to the beggarly total of £96. The allowances for repairs, renewals, and depreciation appear to be good, and £2,000 of debentures were redeemed in the year, bringing down the outstanding total to £13,330. There is a reserve fund of £18,500, and a leasehold redemption fund of 3,641, but the £85,000 of goodwill, hung round the neck of the company by the promoters years ago, mars an otherwise favourable balance-sheet.

CAMPBELL, JOHNSTONE, & CO., LIMITED. — This London company, although new, issues a fair profit and loss account. Including £734 brought in, the net profits last year amounted to £18,210, of which £1,953 was set aside to reserve, raising its total to £4,000. Debenture and preference interest was met, a dividend of 10 per cent. paid upon the ordinary shares, and £1,998 carried forward. The allowance of £3,803 for depreciation seems fair, but £1,609 for repairs is rather low.

ARTISANS', LABOURERS', AND GENERAL DWELLINGS. — In the thirty-one years of this company's existence its issued capital has risen from £18,580 to £2,407,280, and its gross revenue last year amounted to no less than £170,927. Started with a philanthropic aim, it has developed into a thoroughly substantial form of undertaking, with a tendency to slip off into business a little above the original intention. The properties held are mostly freehold, leases belonging to them having been steadily repurchased year by year. Consequently allowances for leasehold redemption are slight except in the case of the "Block Buildings," which figure in the balance-sheet for £526,886, and necessitate about £1,000 being set aside each year for this purpose, which is not a large sum. There is a reserve of £171,323, but most of this, we believe, has come from premiums upon new issues, and the revenue is divided pretty closely each year. Thus the net revenue last year was £114,744, or £2,029 more than in 1896, and of this all but £1,361 was absorbed in the preference interest and dividend of 5 per cent. on the ordinary shares, the balance being used in placing £1,000 to revenue reserve and carrying £361 forward. The 5 per cent. dividend has been paid for nineteen years, and the regularity with which revenue fits in with the 5 per cent dividend makes one presume that any considerable balance above is used in improving the estates.

NEW LONDON BREWERY COMPANY.—Formed in March, 1897, only the prior charges of this company are, we believe, held by the public. The first report does not tell much, both the balance-sheet and profit and loss account being meagre; but apparently this does not matter much, for the profit last year amounted to £40,943, and the full fixed charges are only £18,000 per annum. In such cases the holders of ordinary shares can afford to be independent, and they announce that the directors will continue in office until 1900, as set forth in the articles of association. After meeting fixed charges, and paying £10,000 in interest to the vendors for the quarter of the year prior to the company being formed, a dividend of 12½ per cent. is declared, and £3,406 carried forward.

BARCELONA TRAMWAYS COMPANY.—This company earned a profit last year of £6,510, or about the same as in 1896. The sum of £5,610 was brought forward, and, after payment of preference interest and a dividend of 4 per cent. upon the ordinary shares, the balance of £4,165 is left. The company is transforming its system into one using electric traction, and proposes to do the same with a smaller company it controls. To provide funds for these purposes £100,000 of 4½ per cent. debenture stock has been issued.

O. C. HAWKES, LIMITED.—A small company founded a year cr so ago which has done very well. The net profit is returned as £13,593, and after meeting preference interest and placing £3,060 to reserve, the ordinary shares received 8 per cent. in dividends. The reserve will then stand at £10,000, which is not bad for a company with a total share capital of £150,000. There are no debentures or loans, while trading balances are well in favour of the company.

BORDEAUX TRAMWAYS AND OMNIBUS COMPANY.—This well-managed undertaking jogs along in a satisfactory manner. Gross receipts last year showed a substantial increase, while working expenses were lower, with the result that the net profit of £30,802 was £5,409 more than in 1896. The usual sum of £3,320 was set aside for depreciation, and, after adding £3,654 brought forward, the divisible balance of £31,136 was shown. This permitted of a dividend of 7 per cent. for the year on the ordinary shares, the carrying of £2,000 to the reserve fund, and an additional sum of £5,000 to the depreciation fund, leaving £2,891 to be carried forward. The extra addition to the depreciation fund is something unusual, and was decided upon after a careful examination of that fund by the board. It will now amount to £80,227, and is invested in high-class securities, interest from which is added above the allocations from revenue. Thus the real addition in the year has been £10,606. The reserve fund stands at £10,500, and is employed in the business. One can understand that a company worked in this manner is prosperous; and doubtless it will face the running out of its contract in a very different manner to the London Street Company. An attempt to supersede horse by electric traction has failed, as upon the committee appointed by the Municipal Council reporting in favour of the scheme, the Council rejected the report.

LONDON STREET TRAMWAYS COMPANY.—This is a mere wreck of its former self, and the working of the company from July 1 to October 14, 1897, produced enough to allow of a distribution of 12s. 6d. per share, with £3,819 left to carry forward. The balance in hand is said to be needed in view of the fact that several actions for compensation have still to be disposed of. On October 14 last, the undertaking was taken over by the North Metropolitan Company, which guarantees 5 per cent. per annum on a sum of about £118,153, and a further sum of £1,800 per annum until June 24, 1910. After returning £6 per share the capital remains at £124,000, and there is about £43,909 of unrealised assets. The prospect, therefore, is not very brilliant for a return of the remaining £4 per share, unless the annuity of the North Metropolitan Company is treated as a return of capital.

ABBEY ROAD AND ST. JOHN'S WOOD PERMANENT BUILDING SOCIETY.—This small building society seems to be very well managed. With £174,595 invested in mortgages, £152,048 is in mortgages under £1,000 apiece, and not one mortgage exceeds £5,000. There are no properties in possession at all, and the reserve amounts to £3,300. The society holds no deposit, yet has £8,000 invested in high-class securities, beside a fair amount of cash. A dividend of 5 per cent. was declared on the subscribing shares.

ALLIANCE ASSURANCE COMPANY.—For the year 1897 this company added £1,002,068 net to the total of its insurance policies, obtaining by the business net new premiums amounting to £56,706, about £215,000 of its gross commitments having been re-insured at a cost of little more than £7,300 of its gross new premiums. Adding the renewal premiums, the capital paid for annuities sold, the interest on the life fund, &c., this part of the business gave a total income of £472,601; expenses of management, including commission, absorbed £31,567, or 10 per cent. of the net life premiums; and claims, surrender values, annuities, cash bonuses, &c., took £224,514; altogether, £256,081. In the fire department the premium income was £536,651, and £54 4s. 6d. per cent. of this went to pay claims. In addition, £34 5s. 10d. of the premium income was absorbed by expenses of management and commissions. These payments will leave a surplus of £113,694, including £30,672 net received as interest and dividends on the fire funds. Out of this balance £5,000 was used to write down cost of premises, £3,217 went to pay income-tax, and £100,000 to pay a dividend of 8s. per share, or rather more than 18½ per cent. on the paid-up capital of £550,000. This left £5,478 to be added to the fire fund. The company's life funds amounted to £2,730,062 at the beginning of the year, and to £2,946,583 at the end, an increase of £216,521. This large sum is in great part invested in Home securities of the best class.

THE COMMERCIAL BANK OF AUSTRALIA, LIMITED.—In the December half-year this reorganised institution made a net profit of £53,222. Adding £4,299 brought forward, the total available balance was £57,521, out of which a dividend at the rate of 2 per cent. was paid on the preference shares, and £30,000 carried to special Assets Trust reserve account, leaving £6,350 to go forward. The balance-sheet shows unpaid calls amounting to £310,397, and calls paid in advance £106,233. Bank premises, at cost to new bank, stand at £454,453, which is a very large sum. A commencement has been made in laying by something against the bank's interest in the special Assets Trust Company, formed to take over its dead, or dormant, assets, which stand in the books at £993,356. One good feature about the business is, that it is not, apparently, being forced, but the future does not strike us as being very hopeful.

THE BROKEN HILL PROPRIETARY COMPANY, LIMITED.—This is fairly entitled to be called one of the greatest mines in the world. Since it started in 1885, it has paid no less than 116 dividends, aggregating £6,472,000, and in cash and shares received from subsidiary companies, the total return to its shareholders has been £8,880,000. For years back its directors and managers have had to contend with various difficulties, and not least with the fall in the price of silver. In 1885, the first year of working, the highest price of silver was 4s. 2d. per ounce and lowest 3s. 11½d., as against 2s. 6d. and 1s. 11¾d. in the year just closed. Sulphide ores again have given the company great trouble, but many difficulties have been surmounted and the mine remains a great property, with apparently a considerable period of life still before it. In the half-year ended November 30 last, operations were much interfered with by a fire at the mine which, for one thing, withdrew a large portion of the water supply from mining operations. Silver was also low in price, but some compensation for this was found in the increased price secured for lead. As a result of the six months' working the net profit was £111,128, which was not enough to pay the usual bi-monthly dividends. These, however, the directors continued to distribute, and drew the difference of £32,872 from the balance standing at the credit of profit and loss. They were quite justified in doing this, because the said balance even now amounts to £597,520, made up principally of liquid assets in cash, bullion, coke, and convertible stocks. In future, however, dividends will be paid quarterly, and the first one, at the same rate as the previous bi-monthly distributions, was paid on January 26 last. The company's works at Port Perry are described as being in excellent order, and a promising business has been started to deal with gold ores from Western Australian mines. It is not improbable that the dividends in the future may not be uniformly as good as they are now, but there seems little doubt that the company will long continue to give fair returns to its proprietors.

THE STAR LIFE ASSURANCE SOCIETY.—The directors report a prosperous business for 1897, 5,385 new policies having been issued, insuring £1,719,931; and yielding £70,145 in annual premiums. The total amount of insurances now in force is £16,620,612. Last year the total income was £709,229, and, after payment of claims amounting to £268,506, including bonus additions of £34,369, and meeting all expenses, a balance of £301,022 was left to be added to the assurance and annuity fund, which now amounts to £4,375,761, about £1,400,000 of it invested outside the United Kingdom. Commission and expenses of management came to about £92,000 for the year, or rather less than 17 per cent. of the premium income.

LONDON, PARIS, AND AMERICAN BANK, LIMITED.—For the year 1897, the directors of this bank report a net profit of £29,117, exclusive of £6,586 brought forward. Two dividends, making seven per cent. in all for the year, have been declared and paid, taking £16,000; this leaves £7,703 to be carried to the new year. The bank has a reserve fund of £170,000.

THE GREAT WESTERN COLLIERY COMPANY, LIMITED.—The accounts of this company made up to December last show net profits amounting to £18,964. After applying £5,000 to reserve, and adding the £805 brought forward, the available balance is £19,769, out of which the ordinary "B" shares receive dividends amounting to 5¼ per cent. for the whole year. This leaves £1,019 to be carried forward. The cost of rebuilding a fresh batch of coke ovens, £4,049, has been taken out of the special fund reserved for such purposes.

COMMERCIAL BANKING COMPANY OF SYDNEY.—The report for the second half of last year shows considerable improvement, both in respect of larger business and increased strength. Deposits are up £209,000; the note circulation, £76,000; and bills in circulation, £218,000. On the other side, cash balances and securities have risen £417,000, and bills discounted £87,000. The chief feature is the increase in Government securities, from £305,000 to £1,009,000, which is practically the amount of the reserve fund. The half-year's profit came to £45,996, or £900 more than in 1896, from which a dividend at the rate of 8 per cent. is paid. At the half-yearly meeting the chairman mentioned that the prospect of an abundant harvest has not been realised, but it was estimated that sufficient wheat will have been harvested to render foreign importations unnecessary for the present year. The deficient wool clip and reduction in flocks and herds by the drought make up a poor prospect for the immediate future.

TOWN AND COUNTY BANK.—Almost the same amount of profit was made last year by this little Scotch bank as in the previous twelve months—£36,973 against £36,439. The substantial dividend of 12½ per cent. is again paid, buildings account reduced by £1,500, Guarantee Fund increased by £4,000, and £1,000 added to Officers' Superannuation Fund. Deposits have increased £28,000 and the note circulation by £27,000, and together amount to £2,850,136, while the assets total up to £3,265,339. Amongst the latter "debentures, stocks and shares, loans on security of stocks, and other loans" is an item which might be very well sub-divided.

Bank of Mauritius.—The bank has hardly done so well as in 1896, the profit for last year being £16,320, against £17,421. A dividend of 5 per cent. for the year is again paid and £10,043 carried forward. Last year £10,000 was added to reserve, making it £15,000, only £1,144 being carried forward, and it was expected to have again carried £10,000 to this fund, but since the close of the year's accounts in Mauritius information has been received that failures of certain native firms have occurred, which will involve some loss to the bank, and, therefore, the whole balance is carried forward. This is unfortunate, as the bank had been making quiet progress during the three years it has been established, and a young institution like this will feel its first losses rather severely.

Surrey Commercial Dock Company. — The statement of tonnage shows that there has been much greater activity in the wood department during the past year, the increase in tonnage of wood-laden vessels being 84,940 tons. This has been offset, however, by a decrease of 81,452 tons in grain-laden vessels, owing to diminished import from Baltic ports, and consequently stocks in warehouse have been materially reduced. The revenue account shows hardly any variation in the net outcome, the profit for the year being £105,712, as compared with £105,001 for 1896. The usual 6 per cent. distribution is made, which absorbs a little more money than last year, owing to the recent issue of ordinary stock, but the balance carried forward is increased from £262,162 to £321,120, because the latter amount includes £48,087 premium on issue of new stock.

The Produce Markets.

GRAIN.

Wheat markets generally have been dull, with a tendency downward in price. English wheat was offered on Tuesday at Mark-lane at 6d. decline, but buyers were unwilling to respond, and there seems to have been no sales at even that figure. On Wednesday the attendance and trade were alike poor. English and foreign wheat held at Monday's rates, but buyers difficult to meet with. Flour, with a large arrival, was very dull. Maize was firm at recent currencies; buyers of mixed American, ex ship, at 16s., and sellers at 16s. 3d.; old corn held at 17s., ex quay, and Galatz-Bessarabian at 17s. 6d. to 17s. 9d. Barley was rather easier—Odessa-Nikolaieff, ex ship, 16s. to 16s. 3d.,; and Danubian 16s. to 16s. 3d. Oats were rather firmer, with an improved demand. Mixed clipped, ex ship, 15s. 6d. to 15s. 9d. Arrivals:—Wheat, 10,210 qr.; maize, 14,040 qr.; flour, 87,340 sacks; barley, 27,690 qr., and oats, 61,410 qr. The cargo market has been equally inactive, and on Wednesday sellers asked an advance of 3d., but buyers refused, and the close was dull at nominal rates. An advance of 3d. asked in maize checked business. Wheat options: June, ½ up; October, ½ down, with business for June. Barley firm, but quiet. Oats irregular. Spot parcels at Liverpool steady, but with a quiet demand. Prices unchanged. Red American futures opened ½d. to ¾d. higher, in sympathy with American advices, and moved in an upward direction during the morning on good buying, but when the demand had been satisfied the market fell off a trifle, the close being steady and ½d. to ¾d. per cental dearer than previous evening.

Official Closing Values (100 lb. deliveries—March 2).

	March.	May.	July.	Sept.	Dec.
Red American Wheat	7·10¼	7·3¾	7·2	6·6¾	6·3⅞

New York market has also ruled dull, with a tendency to decline, but recovered somewhat on Wednesday under the influences of steadier toned fore cable news. The market started with a steady tone, and May ⅛c. higher, and foreign buying orders, together with some "bears" covering, caused a further improvement, which was helped by a report that the Chicago clique was buying through a prominent commission house. During the middle of the day the market ruled dull; but later became again more active, fluctuating nervously in new positions, while distant months were sold off by "bears" on generally good crop prospects. The close was easy, with near months ⅛c. dearer; July unchanged, and September ⅛c. lower.

COTTON.

The spot market was fairly active throughout the week at hardening rates, though with periods of easiness. In American a good business has been done and quotations recovered Monday's reduction of 1/16 (middling, 3 11/16d.). Brazilian was quietly steady. A good demand continues in Egyptian at firm prices. Surats remain dull, but, in sympathy with other descriptions, quotations are advanced 1/16d. Futures on Wednesday opened at 1 to 1½ points dearer, and, with a good demand from "bears," improved slightly during the morning, especially for near months. The afternoon fully confirmed the improvement, but in the absence of sellers business was small. The market closed steady at a rise of 3 points or near and of 1 to 1½ points for distant positions. There has been a more buoyant spirit in New York, and on Wednesday the market closed steady 5 points up. The Southern markets are firm, with a general advance of 1/16c. to ⅛c. Futures opened steady and 2 points dearer on favourable Liverpool cables, continued to improve under the influence of "bears" covering and good buying orders from Europe, the South, and from outside speculators, and closed steady with near positions 5 to 3 points and distant 1 point better than Tuesday. It is anticipated that there will be a much larger area planted with cotton in America according to Messrs. Neill Bros., though this is regarded as of doubtful benefit. Messrs. Hubbard Brothers & Co., of New York, think it more in the nature of a disaster to the interests of the country.

New York Closing Values.

	Spot.	Mar.	April.	May.	June.	July.	Aug.	Sept.	Oct.	Nov.	Dec.	Jan.
Mar. 2 ..	6⅛	6·14	6.17	6.20	6·22	6·25	6·28	6·22	6·19	6·18	6·19	6·22

WOOL.

In wool there has been a sort of hand-to-mouth business. In some districts there has been a fair turn-over, but spinners only buy enough for immediate requirements. Though English wool is dull, mohair is firm, and merino is in considerable request at an advance. Holders are disinclined to sell. At the London Wool, Exchange on Tuesday, Messrs. H. Schwartze & Co. offered 3,055 bales of damaged China sheep's wool salved ex-Cromarty, China. The attendance was good, biddings were keen, and the bulk sold at from 2d. to 2¾d. per lb. A few lots realised 4d. to 4½d., while grays sold at 1½d. to 3½d. per lb. Continental and home representatives purchased about equal quantities.

METALS AND COAL.

Copper has been very active during the week, and has been advancing in price by "leaps and bounds," though one day there was a fall of 1s. 6d., which was recovered before the close of the market. The visible supply of the metal at the end of February shows a slight increase, Messrs. Henry R. Merton & Co.'s statistics giving the total stocks as 29,262 tons, compared with 29,076 tons on the 15th—a difference of 186 tons. The total deliveries of the month, however, having again exceeded the supplies—18,136 tons against 17,672 tons—the stock is smaller by 484 tons than at the end of January, and is 1,597 tons less than a year ago, 14,219 tons less than at the end of February, 1896, and as much as 25,928 tons less than at the same date in 1895.

Settlement Prices.

	Mar. 2. £ s. d.	Feb. 23. £ s. d.	Feb. 16. £ s. d.	Feb. 9. £ s. d.	Feb. 2. £ s. d.	Jan. 26. £ s. d.
Copper ..	50 7 6	49 17 6	49 10 0	49 5 0	49 2 6	48 17 6

The Glasgow pig iron market has also been strong, with a slight increase in rates. A fair business was done on Wednesday, 40,000 tons changing hands. Prices were very firm throughout, and at the last Scotch showed a further gain of 2½d. and Cleveland 1½d. A good deal of "short" covering was engaged in.

Settlement Prices.

	Mar. 2. s. d.	Feb. 23. s. d.	Feb. 16. s. d.	Feb. 9. s. d.	Feb. 2. s. d.	Jan. 26. s. d.
Scotch	46 6	46 3	45 7½	45 7¾	45 7½	46 0
Cleveland ..	40 10½	40 10¼	40 7½	40 4½	40 6	40 10½
Hematite ..	49 6	49 1½	48 9	48 7½	48 6	47 0

There has been a slight improvement in tone in the coal market, but the attendance at the Exchange on Wednesday was small. Sellers were predominant. In the seaborne department there was nothing offering, the cargoes unsold on Monday having been in the interim disposed of. The prices accepted were unsatisfactory, but on Wednesday, with the continuance of colder weather, the feeling was possibly a little brighter Official quotations remain at 16s. and 15s., usual terms in the Pool, for Hetton Wallsend and Lyons respectively. The better classes of steam coal were steady, and Welsh was firm, owing to the liberal exports, though common descriptions are very cheap. Best West Yorkshire, 9s. 9d. to 10s.; Barnsley selected, 8s.; soft nuts, 6s. 6d.; Sheffield Silkstones, 7s. 6d. to 8s.; best Derby blackshale, 9s. to 9s. 3d.; North Derby Tupton, 7s. to 7s. 3d.; Erewash brights, 6s. 9d. to 7s. 9d; and nuts, 6s. 6d. to 7s. 6d.

SUGAR.

The market has generally been firm, with a fair business, but no change in rates. Cane kinds quiet but firm. In beet futures little doing, though rates are steady. Refined British cubes have been in fairly good demand at steady prices. Crystals.—Yellows active at the recent decline; white, quiet but steady. Foreign.—Granulated steady, but very slow. Ready J H, Groningen, Glauzic and E C H sold at 11s.; March, E C H, 11s.; April, first marks, 11s. 0¾d.; May-August, 11s. 3d., buyers 11s. 3¾d., sellers f.o.b. Hamburg; April, P P Z, sold at 11s. 0¾d., f.o.b. Stettin.—Cubes—F M S, prompt, sold at 12s., and Meyer 12s. 7½d.; Hansa 12s., sellers f.o.b. Hamburg; W S R, prompt, 13s., sellers; S and T, 12s. 9d.; A S R and cut loaf, 12s. 9d., f.o.b. Amsterdam. Beet futures—March, 9s. 3½d. v.; April. 9s. 4½d. s.; May, 9s. 5½d. s.; June, 9s. 6½d. s.; July, 9s. 7½d. s.; August, 9s. 8d. v.; October-November-December, 9s. 6¾d.

TEA AND COFFEE.

Very little change, according to Messrs. Gow, Wilson, & Stanton has taken place in the Indian tea market, except that medium Pekoes and broken Pekoes occasionally show fractionally lower quotations. The official telegram gives exports to the United Kingdom for the second half of February as 930,000 lb. against 550,000 lb. for the same time last year, making the total from April 10 to the end of February as 133,350,000 lb. against 131,010,000 lb. during the same period last season. With heavy offerings, totalling 32,343 packages, the Ceylon market showed a further slight falling off in prices. The exceptionally good value now obtainable should have the effect of stimulating consumption in both home and foreign markets. The official wire gives exports to the United Kingdom for February as 6,750,000 lb. against 6,500,000 lb. same time last year, making the total from January 1 to the end of February 14,750,000 lb. against 15,000,000 lb. last year; it also estimates the quantity available for

March as 8½ to 9 million lb. Java was not represented, but catalogues are issued for 2,633 packages to be sold during the next fortnight.

Coffee has been quiet with a downward tendency. About twelve thousand packages have been sold by auction during the week, but the competition cannot be described as keen: Ceylon—middling to good bold bright gray, 109s. to 115s.; smalls, 99s.; peaberry, 121s. East India—bold common rough dull green to good coated pale bluish, 84s. 6d. to 108s.; low middling to middling, 67s. 6d. to 80s.; smalls 55s. to 63s. 6d.; peaberry, 84s. to 108s. Costa Rica—good bold dull coloury mixed, 104s. 6d. to 105s. 6d.; good middling, 89s.; peaberry, 109s. Salvador—middling to good bold dull green, 75s. to 81s. 6d.; low middling to middling pale greenish, 66s. to 68s.; peaberry, 84s. 6d. to 91s. Colombian—middling to good bold dull green, 74s. to 91s. 6d.; fine ordinary bold brownish, 46s.; smalls, 37s. to 46s.; peaberry, 89s. to 91s. 6d.

THE PROPERTY MARKET.

The activity and big sales of last week have been succeeded by dulness and somewhat trifling business this. Tuesday's sales at the Mart only realised a total of £6,643. The principal lot, the freehold of No. 12, Laurence Pountney-lane, City, submitted by Messrs. Debenham, Tewson, & Co., failed to find a purchaser, and was withdrawn at £7,000. A freehold residence, known as Edensor, in Finchley-road, Hampstead, put up by the same firm, met with a like fate, and was taken back at £3,500. Mr. C. W. Davies succeeded in disposing of all his lots for a total of £5,030, the chief item being a freehold residence, No. 6, Marlborough-place, Brighton, for which £1,795 was obtained. Things were also dull at Masons' Hall Tavern, where the only one of fourteen properties offered that changed hands was the free lease, with possession, of the "Duke of Wellington," in Haggerston-road. This realised £10,980. The premises are held for thirty-eight years at an annual rental of £100. Messrs. Thornton, Lumsden, & Newman were the auctioneers. A freehold residence, called Springfield, Moorgate, was sold by auction, at Rotherham, by Messrs. W. H. & J. A. Eadon, of Sheffield, for £1,560.

There was a considerable improvement at the Mart on Wednesday. Only two lots were returned "not sold," and the total sales for the day realised £18,170. Messrs. Rutley, Son, & Vine made the principal show, and commanded remarkable prices for some lots of freehold property. This firm disposed of about £12,000 of the day's results. It was altogether a day of "bricks and mortar."

Next Week's Meetings.

MONDAY, MARCH 7.

Civil Service Co-operative Society ...	The Criterion, 5 p.m.
Harrow and Stanmore Gas	Albion Tavern, 1 p.m.
International Investment Trust ...	Winchester House, noon.
Mersey Railway Debentures (Spec.)	Worcester House, 2 p.m.
North Provident and Guarantee ...	Edinburgh, 3.30 p.m.
State Fire Insurance	Liverpool, noon.

TUESDAY, MARCH 8.

Anglo Californian Bank	18, Austin Friars, 2 p.m.
Buenos Ayres Northern Ry. (Ex. Gen.)	Winchester House, noon.
Commercial Bank of Scotland ...	Edinburgh, 1 p.m.
Hageman & Co.	Cannon-street Hotel, noon.
Lea Bridge District Gas	3, Jeffreys-square, 2 p.m.
North Cornwall Ry.	57, Moorgate-street, noon.

WEDNESDAY, MARCH 9.

Alliance Assurance	Bartholomew-lane, noon.
Artisans' and General Dwellings (Gen. and Ex. Gen.)	Westminster Palace Hotel, noon.
Bordeaux Tramways & Omnibus ...	Winchester House, 2 p.m.
Cassell & Co	Memorial House, 2 p.m.
O. C. Hawkes	Birmingham, noon.
Railway Passengers' Assurance ...	64, Cornhill, noon.
San Salvador Spanish Iron Ore ...	Great Eastern Hotel, 12.30 p.m.
Star Life Insurance	32, Moorgate-street, noon.
Waterford & Tranmore Railway ...	Waterford, 1 p.m.

THURSDAY, MARCH 10.

Lever Brothers	Cannon-street Hotel, noon
London, Paris, and American Bank	Ditto, ditto.
Reversionary Interest Society ...	17, King's Arms-yard, noon.
Sheffield Tramway	23, Queen Victoria-street, 2 p.m.
Surrey Commercial Dock	106, Fenchurch-street, 1 p.m.

FRIDAY, MARCH 11.

Brighton and Hove General Gas ...	5, Great Winchester-street, 2 p.m.
Dominion Atlantic Railway... ...	6, Great Winchester-street, 1½ p.m.

MINING RETURNS.

MYALL UNITED GOLD MINING COMPANY.—Crushed, 2,100 tons, yielding 354 oz. of gold. Cyanide, 1,100 tons; yield, 407 oz. of gold.

MOUNT YAGAHONG.—1,000 tons of ore crushed from Star of East mine for yield of 540 oz. retorted gold, and 201 tons from Mount Yagahong for yield of 175 oz. retorted gold.

WELD HERCULES.—Tons crushed, 163; gold produced, 86 oz.; tailings, 4 dwt.

TOKATEA CONSOLS.—30 tons of ore crushed; yield, 90 oz. of retorted gold.

OTTO'S KOPJE.—7,223 loads washed, 197 carats won.

ALASKA TREADWELL.—Return for February, bullion shipment, $34,515; ore milled, 23,883 tons; sulpherets treated, 300 tons; bullion from sulphurets, $11,065.

NATAL COLLIERIES AND DURBAN COALING STATION.—Output of coal, January, 2,594 tons.

NEW QUEEN GOLD.—Result for fortnight ended February 26, 100 tons, yielding 80 oz.; Queencross, 168 tons, yielding 24 oz.

GREAT EASTERN COLLIERIES.—Output of coal for last month, 14,400 tons.

CUDDINGWARA.—Crushed 335 tons in 31 days; yield, 335 oz. of gold.

GOLDEN ARROW.—98 tons of ore crushed yielding 101 oz. gold.

CROWN UNITED.—For fortnight ended January 21; 40 tons crushed; yielded 19 oz. 5 dwt., including tailings.

PESTERENA UNITED.—For February, 445 tons of ore produced 521 oz. gold.

AUSTRALIAN CHAMPION REEF.—Battery ran eight days; crushed 270 tons for a yield of 75 oz. retorted gold from the old stopes and workings.

GREAT BOULDER PROPRIETARY.—Returns for fortnight ended February 28, 1,413 tons crushed, yield 2,220 oz. gold.

ALADDIN'S LAMP.—530 tons of ore crushed, yielding 550 oz. gold and one ton rich ore shipped, containing 36 oz.

INVERELL DIAMOND FIELDS.—668 carats from 64 loads washed by hand.

VICTORIA (CHARTERS TOWERS).—320 tons crushed yielded 461 oz. gold.

LADY ISABELLE.—Cleaned up 98 tons for 86 oz. gold.

BREMNAES.—Crushed, 100 tons of quartz; result, 21 oz. gold; assay of tailings, 6 dwts. per ton.

CHAMPION EXTENDED AND HOME RULE.—785 tons of ore crushed yielded 396 oz. of retorted gold.

FRANK SMITH DIAMOND.—3,300 loads washed produced 130 carats.

LEICESTER CONSOLIDATED DIAMOND.—From the mine, 3,200. Floors, lumps, and hopperings, 3,600 loads washed, producing 177 carats, including good stone 20 carats.

ST. AGNES GOLD REEFS.—Clean up to February 25 after crushing 370 tons of quartz, yield being 162 oz.

MYSORE WEST AND WYNAAD.—Crushings for February, 1,400 tons, yield 477 oz.

NORSEMAN GOLD MINES.—Return for February:—697 tons crushed, yielded 515 oz. of gold.

BAYLEY'S UNITED GOLD MINES.—February return:—679 tons, treated by cyanide, yielded 842 oz. of gold.

COROMANDEL GOLD MINING COMPANY OF INDIA.—During February crushed 1,200 tons of stone, producing 903 oz. of gold; 1,100 tons of tailings (cyanide process), 109 oz. Total, 1,012 oz. of gold.

OOREGUM GOLD MINING COMPANY OF INDIA.—Crushed during February, 4,698 tons of quartz, produced 3,548 oz. of gold; 4,300 tons of tailings produced 498 oz. Total, 4,046 oz. of gold.

Answers to Correspondents.

Questions about public securities, and on all points in company law, will be answered week by week, in the REVIEW, on the following terms and conditions:—

A fee of FIVE shillings must be remitted for each question put, provided they are questions about separate securities. Should a private letter be required, then an extra fee of FIVE shillings must be sent to cover the cost of such letter, the fee then being TEN shillings for one query only, and FIVE shillings for every subsequent one in the same letter. While making this concession the EDITOR will feel obliged if private replies are as much as possible dispensed with. It is wholly impossible to answer letters sent merely "with a stamped envelope enclosed for reply."

Correspondents will further greatly oblige by so framing their questions as to obviate the necessity to name securities in the replies. They should *number* the questions, keeping a copy for reference, thus:—"(1) Please inform me about the present position of the Rowenzori Development Co. (2) Is a dividend likely to be paid soon on the capital stock of the Congo-Sudan Railway?"

Answers to be given to all such questions by simply quoting the numbers 1, 2, 3, and so on. The EDITOR has a rooted objection to such forms of reply as—"I think your Timbuctoo Consols will go up," or "Sell your Slowcoach and Draggem Bonds," because this kind of thing is open to all sorts of abuses. By the plan suggested, and by using a fancy name to be replied to, each query can be kept absolutely private to the inquirer, and no scope whatever be given to market manipulations. Avoid, as names to be replied to, common words, like "investor," "inquirer," and so on, as also "bear" or "bull." Detached syllables of the inquirer's name, or initials reversed, will frequently do as well as anything, so long as the answer can be identified by the inquirer.

The EDITOR further respectfully requests that merely speculative questions should as far as possible be avoided. He by no means sets himself up as a market prophet, and can only undertake to provide the latest information regarding the securities asked about. This he will do faithfully and without bias.

Replies cannot be guaranteed in the same week if the letters demanding them reach the office of the INVESTORS' REVIEW, Norfolk House, Norfolk-street, W.C., later than the first post on Wednesday mornings.

TOUJOURS PRET.—I believe the management is honest and, so far, the record of the company has bee a fair one. Its ore is said to vary considerably in quality, and, as no information is published between the reports, it is impossible to say how far it has benefited by the rise in price. One point against it is an unsettled dispute with the Government. Though the shares have not improved so much as others of the same class, they are higher now than at any time last year. I should be disposed to wait until the report in May.

ORIGINAL READER.—The stock you mention is not quote officially, hence its omission from the list.

Established in the Reign of Queen Anne, A.D. 1714.

UNION Assurance Society.

Established in the Reign of Queen Anne, A.D. 1714.

FIRE AND LIFE.

Head Office—81, CORNHILL, E.C.
West End Branches—55, CHARING CROSS, S.W., & 70, BAKER STREET, W. } LONDON.

DIRECTORS, TRUSTEES, &c.

STEPHEN SOAMES, Esq., *Chairman.* CHARLES MORTIMER, Esq., *Deputy-Chairman.*

SIR JOHN WHITTAKER ELLIS, Bart., Ald.	WALTER R. HOARE, Esq.	J. TRUEMAN MILLS, Esq.	JOHN EDWARD WOODROFFE, Esq.
J. T. FIRBANK, Esq., M.P.	WILLIAM LATHAM, Esq., Q.C.	JAMES THOMPSON, Esq.	J. THORNTON ROGERS, Esq., *Hon. Director.*
	EARL OF LICHFIELD.	SIR FREDERICK WIGAN, Bart.	
Fire Manager—W. G. WILKINS.	*Sub-Fire Manager*—A. F. BAILEY.	*Actuary*—L. K. PAGDEN.	*Secretary*—CHARLES DARRELL.

Invested Funds, £3,000,000. Annual Income, £850,000. Subscribed Capital, £450,000.

FIRE DEPARTMENT.—The Directors are ready to receive Proposals for insuring Property generally at home and abroad, at equitable rates, and according to the risk to be protected.

LIFE DEPARTMENT.—The Bonus for the last 40 years has averaged £1 10s. per cent. per annum on the sum assured.

All Claims paid at the expiration of one month from the date of their being admitted by the Board, or in ordinary cases on proof of title.

The published Accounts give the fullest details as to the position of the Society.

CHARLES DARRELL, *Secretary.*

"INVESTORS' REVIEW."

SUBSCRIPTION PRICE, POST FREE :—

INVESTORS' REVIEW alone—

	Three Months.	Six Months.	One Year.
United Kingdom.	7s.	14s.	28s.
All Foreign Countries.	7s. 6d.	15s.	30s.

INVESTORS' REVIEW and INVESTMENT INDEX together—

	Three Months.	Six Months.	One Year.
United Kingdom.	9s. 6d.	18s. 6d.	36s.
All Foreign Countries.	9s. 10d.	19s. 6d.	38s. 6d.

Payable in Advance.

The INVESTMENT INDEX will continue for the present to be issued Quarterly, price 2s. net, and may be subscribed for separately, at 8s. 6d. per annum, or with the INVESTORS' REVIEW, as above.

Cheques and Postal Orders should be made payable to CLEMENT WILSON.

The INVESTORS' REVIEW can be obtained in Paris of Messrs. BOYVEAU ET CHEVILLET, 22, Rue de la Banque.

Of all Newsagents and at all Railway Bookstalls in the United Kingdom, or remit to The PUBLISHER, Norfolk House, Norfolk-street, Strand, W.C.

ALUMINIUM COOKING UTENSILS.

STEW PANS.

PRICES.

4"	5"	6"	7"	8"	9"	10"
4/3	5/3	6/9	8/3	10/-	12/-	15/3

EACH.

Delivered Free.

BOWEN & CO.,
6, Mount Pleasant,
Clerkenwell,
LONDON.

Absolutely Free from Poison.

LIGHT. HEALTHY. DURABLE.

THE PERFECTION OF COOKING UTENSILS.

CENTRAL PACIFIC RAILROAD.

A MEETING of Shareholders in the Central Pacific Railroad Co. favourable to the Lubbock as opposed to the Banbury Plan was held at Anderton's Hotel, Fleet Street, London, E.C., on Thursday, the 24th of February, 1898, at 2.30 p.m.

The Meeting was, with the approbation of a large body of other Shareholders, convened by Mr. Walter Morshead, on the requisition of thirty-five investors in Central Pacific Stock, asking him "to take such steps as he might deem expedient by advertising, convening meetings, or otherwise, for explaining the present position to our fellow Shareholders, and securing, as far as may be found practicable, a re-organisation on the basis of the Fairchild-Lubbock Plan."

The following RESOLUTIONS were submitted to the Meeting and carried unanimously :—

1. That a Committee of Shareholders and Banbury Certificate Holders be formed to support the Fairchild-Lubbock as against the Banbury Plan, and with the object of securing, as far as may be found practicable, a re-organisation on the basis of the Fairchild-Lubbock Plan, to take such steps as may be deemed expedient to represent and protect the interests of the Shareholders in the Central Pacific Railroad.

2. That such Committee should consist of the following Shareholders :—Mr. Aubrey Stanhope, Arthur's Club, London ; Mr. M. J. Horgan, 50, South Mall, Cork ; Mr. T. Stewart Jones, 43, Park Lane, London ; Mr. F. J. Longton, Woolton Hill, Liverpool ; Mr. Walter Morshead, Albany, Piccadilly, London ; and Mr. Edward Fox White, 59, Lexham Gardens, London, with power to add to their number.

Steps have been taken for the protection of the Stock, and further announcements will be made shortly. Meantime communications are invited, and papers will be forwarded to all Shareholders on application to W. C. GUNNER, Secretary, Shareholders' Protection Committee,

124, Chancery Lane, London, Room No. 12.

25th February, 1898.

CLEMENT WILSON'S PUBLICATIONS.

BOOKS BY A. J. WILSON,

Editor of the "Investors' Review" and "Investment Index."

Price in cloth, 1s. 6d. net (post free, 1s. 8d.) ; paper cover, 1s. net (post free, 1s. 2d.)

No. I.

PRACTICAL HINTS TO INVESTORS.

"The perusal of Mr. Wilson's handy book will repay those concerned in the matters treated of ; and as an example in terse and incisive English it may be read by the student and admirer of style."—*Manchester City News.*

No. II.

NOW READY. NEW EDITION, ENTIRELY REWRITTEN.

PLAIN ADVICE ABOUT LIFE INSURANCE.

"Pregnant with plain meaning, and hits hard, straight from the shoulder, as a work by Mr. Wilson usually does."—*Westminster Gazette.*

"Frank and out-spoken, and affords much useful information and guidance."—*Glasgow Herald.*

A GLOSSARY OF COLLOQUIAL, SLANG, AND TECHNICAL TERMS, in use on the Stock Exchange and in the Money Market. Edited by A. J. WILSON. Price 3s.

"A good deal of useful information is here presented in a very handy form."—*Times.*

"The work is a most useful one, and admirable in many respects."—*Pall Mall Gazette.*

"The book fills a gap among works of reference."—*Morning Post.*

"A book that will be found useful in the offices of a large class of business houses."—*Scotsman.*

"The explanations will be found helpful to all who wish to have a clear understanding of the language of the money and stock markets."—*Dundee Advertiser.*

CLEMENT WILSON, Norfolk House, Norfolk Street, W.C.

Notice to Subscribers.

Complaints are continually reaching us that the INVESTORS' REVIEW cannot be obtained at this and the other railway bookstall, that it does not reach Scotch and Irish cities till Monday, and that it is not delivered in the City till Saturday morning.

We publish on Friday in time for the REVIEW to be at all Metropolitan bookstalls by at latest 4 p.m., and we believe that it is there then, having no doubt that Messrs. W. H. Smith & Son do their best, but they have such a mass of papers to handle every day that a fresh one may well look almost like a personal enemy and be kept in short supply unless the reading public shows unmistakably that it is wanted. A little perseverance, therefore, in asking for the INVESTORS' REVIEW is all that should be required to remedy this defect.

All London newsagents can be in a position to distribute the paper on Friday afternoon if they please, and here also the only remedy is for subscribers to insist upon having it as soon as published. Arrangements have been made that all our direct City subscribers shall have their copies before 4 p.m. on Friday. As for the provinces, we can only say that the paper is delivered to the forwarding agents in ample time to be in every English and Scotch town, and in Dublin and Belfast, likewise, early on Saturday morning. Those despatched by post from this office can be delivered by the first London mail on Saturday in every part of the United Kingdom.

Cheques and Postal Orders should be made payable to CLEMENT WILSON.

The INVESTORS' REVIEW can be obtained in Paris of Messrs. BOYVEAU ET CHEVILLET, 22, Rue de la Banque.

ADVERTISEMENTS.

All Advertisements are received subject to approval, and should be sent in not later than 5 p.m. on Thursdays.

For tariff and particulars of positions open apply to the Advertisement Manager, Norfolk House, Norfolk-street, W.C.

To Correspondents.

The EDITOR cannot undertake to return rejected communications. Letters from correspondents must, in every case, be authenticated by the name and address of the writer.

The Investors' Review.

The Week's Money Market.

Short money has been in strong demand throughout the past seven days, and, as will be seen below, the market has had to reborrow more than the whole of its loans falling due at the Bank of England. The rate for day to day loans, therefore, moved up to 2¾ to 3 per cent., and seven day market loans have not been quoted under 2¾ per cent.

Discount rates hardened in sympathy and 2⅞ per cent. has become the general rate for three months' choice bills, 2¾ per cent. being charged, as a rule, upon longer-dated paper. Whatever inclination there was towards a slightly easier tone a week ago was quite dissipated by the appearance of a demand for gold on New York account. Offspring this of the "war-scare" and stock jobbing operations, at one time it ruled so strong as to lead to the purchase of all the gold in the open market, buyers having to bid 77s. 10½d. per ounce, before they obtained it all. The shippers also withdrew £500,000 from the Bank of France, and when that institution raised its premium for the metal they completed their order by buying £23,000 in eagles from the Bank of England on Tuesday. Since then the political ferment in the States has considerably subsided, prices of stocks have recovered, and the New York exchange has distinctly risen. The price of gold, however, hovers about 77s. 9⅞d. per ounce, and until the fast steamer has left to-morrow it would be premature to assume that the demand is over. Foreign exchanges continue to move in our favour, especially the German rate, which supports the view that a fair proportion of that country's share of the Chinese Loan will be sent over here, an operation encouraged by the fact that the outside market rate in Berlin is only 2½ per cent. So far there has been no release of Government money, but the rate of accumulation has diminished, and disbursements cannot now be long prevented. The withdrawal of £200,000 in sovereigns, for shipment to Buenos Ayres yesterday, was of no importance by itself, and if the United States demand comes to nothing, the Bank may even gather up a little bullion which it would be all the stronger for.

The £1,500,000 of Treasury Bills offered last Friday were applied for about eight and a half times over, the whole amount being allotted in twelve months' bills at an average rate of 2¼ per cent. Government departments and banks took the bulk of the issue, and so the payment for them on Wednesday did not have much effect upon the market. The Consols settlement did not influence rates, and it is probable that the market gained rather than lost by the adjustment of accounts, as the Government bought stock last month.

Not much more than £216,000 has been added to the "public" deposits or Government balances, the week's Bank return tells us. The Treasury disbursements, however, at the end of February might have been expected to reduce the total somewhat. They have not done so, and therefore, with the slight addition named, it stands at £18,811,093. And the open market has had to find nearly as much money for taxes as usual as the decrease in the "other" deposits, which are down by £847,653 to £35,914,840, proves. The money has been paid over to the Government, and by it dispersed in salaries, &c., at the end of the month. Hence the decline of £878,101 in the banking reserve, which is now £23,605,649. Notes and coin to more than that amount have gone into circulation, since £78,000 in gold came in from abroad. As the open market was already poor it has had to increase its borrowings at the Bank by £533,109 during the week, and the total of the "other" securities is now up to £35,579,185. The figures of the "Rest" in this week's return indicate that the Bank will be able to pay its stockholders a 5 per cent. dividend for the past six months. This is the same as it paid both in September and March last.

SILVER.

The weakness in this market has made further progress and the price for bars, both for immediate delivery and two months forward, is 25d. per ounce, as against 25 1/16d. per oz. a week ago. As we have said, the market is inherently weak, but a reason for this sharp decline was furnished by the revival of the rumour that the Indian Government will raise the duty upon silver. It is an old tale that serves to influence the market about every two months, but there is more inclination to lend an ear to the suggestion just now in view of the near approach of the Indian Budget statement. The "Bazaars" in India, whence this rumour emanated, usually know beforehand any important change that may be proposed in that Budget, and there is, therefore, a fair possibility that the rumour may only anticipate Sir J. Westland's statement. Such a policy has been strongly urged in certain quarters, but if it is carried out, will the Indian Government provide any plan for an increase of the currency? Silver still goes in large quantity to India in spite of the Government boycott, and must, therefore, serve as a medium for settling debts, although, perhaps, a cumbrous one; but if its employment is further penalised, will the Government provide the trader with an alternative instrument of payment? Meantime, the monetary stringency in the Peninsula enabled the India Council to sell about 88 lacs of bills and transfers, chiefly the latter, in the week ended Tuesday last, and the applications on Wednesday were again on a large scale, with fair sales of "specials" since. The amount to be offered next time has, therefore, been raised to 50 lacs. Indian exchanges have risen to 1s. 4 1/32d., but Chinese rates are weak on the decline in silver.

BANK OF ENGLAND.

AN ACCOUNT pursuant to the Act 7 and 8 Vict., cap. 32, for the Week ending on Wednesday, March 2, 1898.

ISSUE DEPARTMENT.

	£		£
Notes Issued	48,237,010	Government Debt	11,015,100
		Other Securities	5,784,900
		Gold Coin and Bullion	31,437,010
		Silver Bullion	—
	£48,237,010		£48,237,010

BANKING DEPARTMENT.

	£		£
Proprietors' Capital	14,553,000	Government Securities	13,987,565
Rest	3,745,749	Other Securities	35,579,185
Public Deposits (including Exchequer, Savings Banks, Commissioners of National Debt, and Dividend Accounts)	18,811,093	Notes	21,200,205
Other Deposits	35,914,840	Gold and Silver Coin	2,405,444
Seven Day and other Bills	147,987		
	£73,172,399		£73,172,399

Dated March 2, 1898.

H. G. BOWEN, *Chief Cashier.*

In the following table will be found the movements compared with the previous week, and also the totals for that week and the corresponding return last year:—

Banking Department.

Last Year. March 3.		Feb. 23, 1898.	March 2, 1898.	Increase.	Decrease.
£	Liabilities.	£	£	£	£
3,745,976	Rest	3,482,523	3,745,479	262,956	—
16,209,159	Pub. Deposits	18,594,790	18,811,093	216,303	—
39,789,829	Other do.	36,762,493	35,914,840	—	847,653
185,969	7 Day Bills	131,585	147,987	16,402	—
	Assets.			Decrease.	Increase.
14,410,858	Gov. Securities	13,994,565	13,987,565	7,000	—
30,318,084	Other do.	35,046,076	35,579,185	—	533,109
29,754,991	Total Reserve	24,483,750	23,605,649	878,101	—
				1,380,762	1,380,762
				Increase.	Decrease.
£		£	£	£	£
26,074,585	Note Circulation	26,353,465	27,036,805	683,340	—
53 p.c.	Proportion	44⅛ p.c.	43 p.c.	—	—
3 ,,	Bank Rate	3 ,,	3 ,,	—	—

Foreign Bullion movement for week £78,000 in.

LONDON BANKERS' CLEARING.

Week ending	1898.	1897.	Increase.	Decrease.
	£	£	£	£
Jan. 5	222,654,000	174,376,000	48,278,000	—
,, 12	144,603,000	127,315,000	17,288,000	—
,, 19	171,777,000	156,200,000	15,577,000	—
,, 26	134,247,000	118,667,000	15,560,000	—
Feb. 2	194,544,000	174,498,000	20,056,000	—
,, 9	137,804,000	129,809,000	8,995,000	—
,, 16	184,403,000	162,168,000	22,235,000	—
,, 23	132,450,000	131,777,000	673,000	—
March 2	190,157,000	177,852,000	12,305,000	—

BANK AND DISCOUNT RATES ABROAD.

	Bank Rate.	Altered.	Open Market.
Paris	2	March 14, 1895	1⅞
Berlin	3	February 20, 1898	2⅝
Hamburg	3	February 20, 1898	2⅝
Frankfort	3	February 20, 1898	2⅝
Amsterdam	3	April 13, 1897	2⅜
Brussels	3	April 28, 1896	2
Vienna	4	January 22, 1896	3⅝
Rome	5	August 27, 1895	3
St. Petersburg	5½	January 23, 1898	4½
Madrid	5	June 17, 1896	4
Lisbon	6	January 25, 1891	6
Stockholm	5	October 27, 1897	5
Copenhagen	4	January 20, 1898	4
Calcutta	12	February 24, 1898	—
Bombay	13	February 24, 1898	—
New York call money	1½ to 2	—	—

NEW YORK ASSOCIATED BANKS (dollar at 4s.).

	Feb. 26, 1898.	Feb. 19, 1898.	Feb. 12, 1898.	Feb. 27, 1897.
	£	£	£	£
Specie	23,838,000	23,366,000	22,904,000	16,788,000
Legal tenders	17,216,000	16,698,000	20,428,000	23,404,000
Loans and discounts	128,376,000	129,384,000	127,568,000	99,592,000
Circulation	2,745,400	2,755,600	2,783,000	3,098,000
Net deposits	145,542,000	147,719,000	147,716,000	114,754,000

Legal reserve is 25 per cent. of net deposits; therefore the total reserve (specie and legal tenders) exceeds this sum by £4,593,500, against an excess last week of £5,136,000.

BANK OF FRANCE (25 francs to the £).

	Mar. 3, 1898.	Feb. 24, 1898.	Feb. 17, 1898.	Mar. 4, 1897.
	£	£	£	£
Gold in hand	76,831,240	77,303,760	77,186,520	76,589,000
Silver in hand	48,565,440	48,512,260	48,319,680	49,225,000
Bills discounted	31,773,800	29,853,200	29,891,080	*43,600,000
Advances	14,730,240	14,562,600	14,626,160	—
Note circulation	152,206,720	148,445,560	149,163,880	147,337,000
Public deposits	6,241,720	7,965,080	8,140,720	7,701,000
Private deposits	18,736,040	21,682,240	19,704,960	19,683,000

Proportion between bullion and circulation 82⅛ per cent. against 84⅞ per cent. a week ago.

* Includes advances.

FOREIGN RATES OF EXCHANGE ON LONDON.

Place.	Usance.	Last week's.	Latest.	Place.	Usance.	Last week's.	Latest.
Paris	chqs.	25'28	25'28½	Italy	sight	26'61	26'60
Brussels	chqs.	25'31¼	25'33¾	Do. gold prem.	..	105'20	105'20
Amsterdam	short	12'07½	12'06½	Constantinople	3 mths	109'15	109'20
Berlin	short	20'44	20'45½	B. Ayres gd. pm.	..	167'30	171'20
Do.	3 mths	20'31	20'31½	Rio de Janeiro	90 dys	6⅜	6⅜
Hamburg	3 mths	20.30	20'30½	Valparaiso	90 dys	17⅝	17⅝
Frankfort	short	20'44	20'46	Calcutta	T. T.	1/4	1/4 1/32
Vienna	short	12.01½	12'02½	Bombay	T. T.	1/3 31/32	1/4 1/32
St. Petersburg	3 mths	93.95	93'95	Hong Kong	T. T.	1/10⅛	1/10
New York	60 dys	4'83½	4'84	Shanghai	T. T.	2/5⅞	2/5⅝
Lisbon	sight	35⅝	35⅝	Singapore	T. T.	1/10 5/16	1/10 3/16
Madrid	sight	33'80	33'93				

IMPERIAL BANK OF GERMANY (20 marks to the £).

	Feb. 23, 1898.	Feb. 15, 1898.	Feb. 7, 1898.	Feb. 23, 1897.
	£	£	£	£
Cash in hand	49,178,700	47,570,800	46,313,100	46,889,000
Bills discounted	25,905,600	25,612,000	26,750,000	*30,055,000
Advances on stocks	3,690,850	4,158,600	4,129,450	—
Note circulation	49,498,100	50,645,450	52,827,050	47,492,000
Public deposits	25,905,600	23,319,200	21,535,500	25,261,000

* Includes advances.

AUSTRIAN-HUNGARIAN BANK (1s. 8d. to the florin).

	Feb. 23, 1898.	Feb. 15, 1898.	Feb. 7, 1898.	Feb. 23, 1897.
	£	£	£	£
Gold reserve	30,615,083	30,324,417	30,347,666	30,774,000
Silver reserve	10,411,500	10,371,500	10,345,417	12,679,000
Foreign bills	1,254,740	1,318,917	1,382,333	—
Advances	1,832,166	1,859,333	1,887,250	—
Note circulation	50,579,333	51,074,417	52,209,333	57,733,000
Bills discounted	10,132,000	10,502,250	11,763,416	*1[illegible],642,000

* Includes advances.

NATIONAL BANK OF BELGIUM (25 francs to the £).

	Feb. 24, 1898.	Feb. 17, 1898.	Feb. 10, 1898.	Feb. 25, 1897.
	£	£	£	£
Coin and bullion	4,198,480	4,311,040	4,234,880	4,125,000
Other securities	17,290,680	17,011,600	17,204,400	16,356,000
Note circulation	19,255,680	19,145,960	19,348,560	18,669,000
Deposits	3,670,720	3,405,440	3,396,560	3,220,000

BANK OF SPAIN (25 pesetas to the £).

	Feb. 26, 1898.	Feb. 19, 1898.	Feb. 12, 1898.	Feb. 27, 1897.
	£	£	£	£
Gold	9,542,840	9,517,560	9,500,920	8,528,360
Silver	10,875,280	10,712,600	10,651,800	10,818,560
Bills discounted	21,491,840	21,763,160	21,855,320	8,108,880
Advances and loans	4,924,360	4,805,800	4,869,680	9,343,440
Notes in circulation	49,959,440	49,856,480	50,062,440	42,422,480
Treasury advances, coupon account	330,560	236,240	310,400	544,160
Treasury balances	988,500	887,400	547,840	2,912,280

LONDON COURSE OF EXCHANGE.

Place.	Usance.	Feb. 22.	Feb. 24.	March 1.	March 3.
Amsterdam and Rotterdam	short	12·1¾	12·1¾	12·2	12·2
Do. do.	3 months	12·3⅜	12·3½	12·3⅜	12·3½
Antwerp and Brussels	3 months	25·45	25·46¼	25·46¼	25·48¾
Hamburg	3 months	20·62	20·63	20·64	20·64
Berlin and German B. Places	3 months	20·62	20·63	20·64	20·64
Paris	cheques	25·28¾	25·30	25·30	25·31
Do.	3 months	25·43¾	25·42½	25·43¾	25·45
Marseilles	3 months	25·43¾	25·43¾	25·45	25·45
Switzerland	3 months	25·60	25·62½	25·62½	25·62½
Austria	3 months	12·16½	12·15	12·17½	12·15
St. Petersburg	3 months	25 1/16	25 1/16	25 1/16	25 1/16
Moscow	3 months	25	25	25	25
Italian Bank Places	3 months	26·87½	26·91¼	26·90	26·88¾
New York	60 days	49	49	49 11/16	49 11/16
Madrid and Spanish B. P.	3 months	35⅛	35	34 11/16	34¾
Lisbon	3 months	35	35	34 13/16	34¾
Oporto	3 months	35	35	34 13/16	34⅝
Copenhagen	3 months	18·38	18·38	18·38	18·38
Christiania	—	18·38	18·38	18·39	18·39
Stockholm	—	18·38	18·38	18·39	18·39

OPEN MARKET DISCOUNT.

	Per cent.
Thirty and sixty day remitted bills	2⅛
Three months "	2⅛
Four months "	2¼
Six months "	2⅜—2½
Three months fine inland bills	3
Four months "	3
Six months "	3—3¼

BANK AND DEPOSIT RATES.

	Per cent.
Bank of England minimum discount rate	3
" " short loan rates	3
Banker's rate on deposits	1½
Bill brokers' deposit rate (call)	2
" 7 and 14 days' notice	2¼
Current rates for 7 day loans	2½
" " for call loans	2¼—3

Stock Market Notes and Comments.

Our markets have been in the hands of the sensation-monger during the greater part of the past week. Nothing illustrates more strikingly the cosmopolitan character of the London Stock Exchange than the rapidity with which it responds to influences acting upon it from all the ends of the earth. Last week it was affected principally by the United States, where a political scare came upon the top of that caused by the railway rate conflict, and further depressed prices. There never was any sense in the Jingo outcry of certain American newspapers about the *Maine* disaster. No sensible person on either side of the Atlantic believed for one moment that the Spanish Government had anything to do with the destruction of the ship. Spain is not governed by assassins. Nor could it have been the work of the insurgent party in Cuba; they had no motive to do such a thing. All the probabilities point to an internal explosion, due either to spontaneous combustion in the coal bunkers of the vessel, or to the presence of some dangerous explosive in its magazines. Nothing, however, would serve American Jingos but a war with Spain, and their organs in the Press industriously circulated and caused to be transmitted to London the most unblushing lies about this lamentable accident, which had the effect of depressing not only American railroad securities, but Spanish bonds, and even, to a minor extent, our own Home Railway stocks. The Stock Exchange, in other words, is so sensitive that all departments suffer when one is attacked.

Appearances now indicate a calmer frame of mind, and prices have momentarily resumed their upward course, but we are not yet delivered from the railway rate conflict. The slight recovery of the last two days is due to the re-purchases of speculators for the fall, and cynics here do not scruple to say that it has been allowed to take place because Jingo Senators at Washington, and their supporters among the speculative American public, "have got all the stock they want." This is, and is not, a slander. Beyond question a very large amount of money has been won from British speculators through the "bear" operations of Americans in Wall-street and in London during the past fortnight. When the selling began here nothing was known publicly about the war of rates, and it went on merrily through the earlier stages of that war, down almost to the close of the hubbub made about the loss of the *Maine*. We are sorry to say that a great many people here have recently been selling "bears" also, and pretty near the bottom of the market. As usual, however, the shrewd wire-pullers who manage these things in America probably again stand to make money at our expense on a rising market. How often is it necessary to repeat that there is only one way to handle these American railroad securities with any degree of safety? It is to buy when prices are down no more than can be lifted and stowed away, and to pay no attention to episodes like that to which markets have been subjected in the last ten days, but quietly wait and sell when a favourable opportunity comes. This advice, of course, applies only to speculative securities. The best American investment stocks are as little affected by passing market ragings and plungings as are our English railway preference stocks.

A certain amount of depression has also been produced by the condition of our own money market, dealt with elsewhere. The decline in prices arising from the stringency of money has not been great, because credit has not been really very dear; but it has been sufficient to let observers see how great the trouble might be were money to advance to twice its present price, and stay at that rate for three months. Even with loans at 3½ per cent. to 4 per cent., numbers of speculative holders are being obliged to sell. This selling is, perhaps, specially noticeable in Argentine Government stocks, which are still sufficiently smudged to be more difficult to borrow upon than most securities of a better grade. For many months back money in the Stock Exchange has been 4 per cent. to 5 per cent. if lent on these bonds, when the current rate was little better than 3 per cent. Very little more is charged now than then on these bonds, yet speculative holders are being forced to let them go, and prices have been going backward, with only occasional small rebounds. The fall should not, in our opinion, tempt new buyers to come forward. Argentine stocks are in no sense investment securities. They have been skilfully worked up to high prices, and the deficits of the Government have been adroitly concealed; but there is no stability as yet in Argentine finance, and the promise of full payment of interest on the various loans was merely a piece of bounce indulged in "to inspire investors with confidence."

In all departments of the Stock Exchange business has been quiet and often difficult to transact. Had Paris not continued to support a few of its special favourites the fall in South African mine shares, and in some of the foreign government bonds, would have been greater than it is; and even with Home securities there has been no particular display of strength. The market is not now having money poured into it freely at any point, and, therefore, all sections of it stagnate and become dull, or flat, after each little spurt of activity. How long the Bourse will be able to maintain even its present appearance of strength no one can tell. We must not, however, forget that the agitation has again sprung up in Paris against the outside dealers forming the *Coulisse*. Two French papers in particular—*La Réforme Economique* and *l'Economiste Européen*—have begun to bitterly denounce the "foreigners," as they call them, who deal on the Paris Bourse, and popular sentiment is running so bitterly against all houses of Jewish origin that we should not be in the least surprised to see these houses begin to move their funds, and their business, to other centres, where race and creed hatreds are not fanned into activity by fanatical malice. We may be quite sure that such a transfer of capital could not take place without very serious consequences to quotations on the Paris market. In short, the situation is ticklish at many points, and requires to be watched with vigilance, for trouble may arise when least expected. The position of Spain, for instance, is extremely precarious in a financial sense, and the doubts beginning to prevail about the payment of the next coupon on the public debt are by no means ill founded. Spanish paper money is steadily depreciating, and the Government is not only spending a great deal more than its available revenue, but is also in such feeble credit as to be unable to raise a fresh loan. Default and reorganisation of Spanish debts cannot be very far off. A spasm of dearish money in Paris would bring it about at once.

We have dealt so fully with South African shares in other parts of this number, and during the past few weeks, that it is not necessary to enlarge upon this subject here, beyond noting the fact that the disposition to sell predominates, and that it appears to be beyond the power of the trusts and financial combinations to keep the market up. The way it sank, in places, on Wednesday is by no means pleasant to contemplate. As for the Western Australian market it seems to be still "Bottomley & Company," with empty pockets outside. The career of this man is a wonder and a mystery to us, but he certainly manages to "keep his corner" with wonderful resource and activity, and if the public contents itself with merely watching his performances it will be all right.

The Week's Stock Markets.

Stock markets have shown a slightly stronger tendency this week, but political uneasiness and monetary uncertainty have tended to restrict speculative business, and beyond a little reinvesting of dividends there has not been much inclination on the part of the public to join in. Apart from a large business in United States Railroad shares there has been no particular activity displayed in any department.

Consols are now quoted ex. the quarterly dividend, and the price shows hardly any change, but the hardening tendency of the discount market has caused a slight set back in some of the leading gilt-edged securities.

Highest and Lowest this Year.		Last Carrying over Price.	BRITISH FUNDS, &c.	Closing Price.	Rise or Fall.
113½	111½	—	Consols 2¾ p.c. (Money)...	112x.d.	—
113 7/16	112 3/16	112¾	Do. Account (Apl. 1)	112 5/16 x.d.	—
106¼	105¼	106	2½ p.c. Stock red. 1905 ...	105½x.d.	+ ⅛
363	347½	—	Bank of England Stock...	355½	+ ½
117	114¼	116	India 3½ p.c. Stk. red. 1931	115⅝x.d.	—
109½	107¼	108	Do. 3 p.c. Stk. red. 1948	107½x.d.	—
96¾	94	94½	Do. 2½ p.c. Stk. red. 1926	94x.d.	+ ½

The Home Railway market has been an idle one, and speculative business remains on a small scale, while the only items of interest have been the declaration of two of the Scotch companies' dividends. The distribution of 5 per cent. by the Caledonian Company was quite up to the most sanguine expectations, and this gave a rather firmer tone to the whole market, and Caledonian issues all advanced. Glasgow and South-Western deferred however, declined a point or so, the dividend of 5 per cent. being ¼ per cent. lower than a year ago. Unusual activity is now being displayed in the Clyde shipbuilding trade, and the large amount of arrears of work which has to be made up will, it is argued help the traffic on these lines considerably. Brighton deferred fell sharply, the traffic return being looked upon as unsatisfactory, but there is a certain amount of mystery about this week's figures, as possibly some of the season ticket payments do not fall in the same week in both year's returns. All other traffics were good, when due allowance is made for the big increases with which comparison is made. Central London shares have again been inquired for, but Metropolitan and Districts are weaker, and the stocks of the heavy lines have met with little or no support.

Highest and Lowest this Year.		Last Carrying over Price.	HOME RAILWAYS.	Closing Price.	Rise or Fall.
186	174	175¼	Brighton Def.	175¾	− ½
59½	55½	56¾	Caledonian Def.	57¼	+ ¼
20¾	19	19¾	Chatham Ordinary	20¼	—
77½	66	70	Great Central Pref.	70½	+ ¼
24¾	21¾	22	Do. Def.	22¼	+ ¼
124½	119¾	121	Great Eastern	121¼	+ ¼
61¾	53½	54¾	Great Northern Def.	53½	+ ½
179½	173½	176¾	Great Western	173½	− ¼
49½	45½	46	Hull and Barnsley	46½	+ ¼
149½	146½	147¼	Lanc. and Yorkshire	147¼	− ¼
136½	130¾	131	Metropolitan	131½	− 1
31	28¼	28¾	Metropolitan District	28¾	− ¼
88¾	85½	86¾	Midland Pref.	85½	− ¼
95½	90½	92	Do. Def.	90	− ½
93½	90½	91¼	North British Pref.	91¾	+ ¼
47½	43½	44¾	Do. Def.	44½	− ¼
181½	175½	179½	North Eastern	175¾	− ¼
205½	199¾	203½	North Western	200	− ¼
117½	110	110¾	South Eastern Def.	111½	− ¼
98¾	93½	97	South Western Def.	93¾	− ¼

A large amount of attention has naturally been devoted to United States Railroad shares. Towards the end of last week prices hardened up slightly in spite of a large amount of arbitrage selling, this being more than balanced by home buying, and the market has begun to ignore the daily batches of conflicting telegrams all purporting to explain the origin of the *Maine* disaster. After the process of weeding out weak operators had been concluded in Wall-street a healthier tone was apparent, and advices from Washington stating that there would be no difficulty in settling the *Maine* matter by diplomacy also helped to raise prices. Wall-street on the whole, however, has exhibited a feverish tendency, and the absence of the decision in the Nebraska maximum rate case, coupled with the uncertain political outlook, all tended to discourage operators. The shipments of gold from Europe to the United States had very little effect on prices, and after losing one day about as much as had been gained the day before, the net result is to leave quotations very much as they were. The Pennsylvania Company has issued a very favourable annual report, and the monthly statements of the Louisville and Nashville, and the Northern Pacific Companies were also up to expectations. Chicago and Milwaukee stock has fluctuated considerably on dividend rumours, a distribution of 5 per cent. being now looked for. It is stated that $6,000,000 out of a total of $8,600,000 guarantee notes of the Atchison Company have been converted into 4 per cent. general mortgage bonds. Last week's *Financial Chronicle* gave some interesting particulars of the earnings of 190 roads during the year 1897, the net earnings amounting to $349,166,347, or an increase of nearly $36,000,000. The changes in Canadian Railway issues were confined within narrow limits during the greater part of the week, but on Tuesday a rapid advance occurred on rumours, as yet unconfirmed, that the question of rates was about to be settled on the intervention of the Canadian Government. At any rate, large buying orders were received from Montreal, which were interpreted as meaning much about the same thing, and this was quite enough in itself to put prices up several points. A good Trunk statement for January was also published, and helped to harden prices.

Among foreign railway stocks a feature was the strength of Buenos Ayres and Ensenada issues, the rises ranging from 4 to 6. Several other South American stocks advanced moderately, but, on the other hand, Cordoba Central (Central Northern) income debentures have been pressed for sale, the traffic return again showing a big decrease, and it is now thought that the dividend will, at an outside estimate, not be above 2½ per cent. instead of the full 5 per cent. paid a year ago.

Highest and Lowest this Year.		Last Carrying over Price.	CANADIAN AND U.S. RAILWAYS.	Closing Prices.	Rise or Fall.
14 1/16	11¼	12½	Atchison Shares	12⅜	+ ⅜
34	27¾	29¾	Do. Pref.	29	+ ¾
15⅝	11⅛	13⅜	Central Pacific	13¼	+ ¼
99¾	94⅝	97¼	Chic. Mil. & St. Paul	97	+1⅜
14¼	11½	12¾	Denver Shares	12½	+ ⅛
54⅞	46⅝	50	Do. Prefd.	49½	+ 1
16⅜	14	14¾	Erie Shares	14⅝	+ ⅛
44⅛	37⅞	40½	Do. Prefd.	39⅝	− ⅜
62½	55¼	57¼	Louisville & Nashville	56⅞	+ ¾
14½	11 11/16	12½	Missouri & Texas	12¼	+ ¼
122⅜	108⅞	118	New York Central	117⅞	+2¼
57¼	47¾	51	Norfolk & West. Prefd.	50⅞	+ ⅞
70⅛	59⅝	64½	Northern Pacific Prefd.	65½	+3
19½	15 3/16	16½	Ontario Shares	16⅝	+ ¼
62½	58½	59¾	Pennsylvania	60	+ ⅛
12½	9⅝	10¼	Reading Shares	10	− ⅛
34⅛	28½	30½	Southern Prefd.	29⅝	+ ½
37⅛	26⅛	31½	Union Pacific	31¼	+1
20¼	16	17¼	Wabash Prefd.	17	—
30¼	26¼	27½	Do. Income Debs.	27	—
92¼	82¾	84½	Canadian Pacific	86½	+1¾
78⅛	69⅝	73	Grand Trunk Guar.	74⅜	+1¼
69⅛	57⅛	64½	Do. 1st Pref.	66¾	+1½
50⅛	37¼	44¼	Do. 2nd Pref.	46¼	+2
25⅛	19¼	21¾	Do. 3rd Pref.	22¾	+ ⅞
105¾	101⅝	103¼	Do. 4 p.c. Deb.	103	−1

The foreign market has been quiet, and prices have drooped but not to any appreciable extent, although the Paris Bourse was for several days thoroughly under the influence of the heavy fall in Spanish "Fours," caused by the tension between America and Spain, and the monthly settlement on the Bourse which began on Tuesday disclosed a very weak account in this stock. The price has since recovered part of the fall, but still leaves off well below last Thursday's quotation. Greek bonds advanced on the statement that the new indemnity loan had been arranged for by a syndicate, and a slight improvement is apparent in Hungarian and Russian bonds. As regards South American descriptions, Argentine Government and the Cedula issues have been depressed by the rising gold premium at Buenos Ayres, but a slight drop in the premium yesterday was promptly followed by a sharp rally in prices. Brazilian bonds have hardly moved, in spite of rumours to the effect that Brazil is likely to default in the payment of the next coupon of the external debt. A little more support came from Paris just at the last, when it was found that the account there was being settled rather more easily than had been anticipated.

Highest and Lowest this Year.		Last Carrying over Price.	FOREIGN BONDS.	Closing Price.	Rise or Fall.
94½	89	90¾	Argentine 5 p.c. 1886	91	+ ¼
92⅝	88½	90	Do. 6 p.c. Funding	89⅜	− ¼
76¾	71	73¾	Do. 5 p.c. B. Ay. Water	73¾	—
61⅜	59½	60¼	Brazilian 4 p.c. 1889	60¾	+ ½
69⅝	64¾	65¼	Do. 5 p.c. 1895	65½	+ ¼
65	60⅛	64	Do. 5 p.c. West Minas Ry.	61½xd.	—
108¾	106¼	108¼	Egyptian 4 p.c. Unified	108¼	—
104¾	102	104¼	Do. 3½ p.c. Pref.	104½	—
103	102	102¼	French 3 p.c. Rente	102½	—
41½	34½	40¾	Greek 4 p.c. Monopoly	41	+ ½
93 1/16	92¼	92⅝	Italian 5 p.c. Rente	93⅛	—
100	95¾	98	Mexican 6 p.c. 1888	98¼	− ¼
20⅞	19¾	20⅜	Portuguese 1 p.c.	20	+ ⅛
62¼	59	61	Spanish 4 p.c.	59⅜	− 1/16
45¼	43	44	Turkish 1 p.c. "B"	44⅝	+ ⅛
26 7/16	24 1/16	25¾	Do. 1 p.c. "C"	25 11/16	+ 1/16
22 1/16	21 13/16	22	Do. 1 p.c. "D"	22¼	+ ⅛
44⅞	40	43	Uruguay 3½ p.c. Bonds	44¼	+1½

Business has been slightly on the increase in Miscellaneous securities, and members have been deserting to this section from the now almost lifeless "Kaffir" market, turning their attention to Russian petroleum shares and the like. The price of the latter company's ordinary shares has been forced up from 18 to 25, and a "splitting" scheme is already being discussed. Another feature has been a sharp rise in Millar's Karri ordinary, a first dividend of 25 per cent. being talked of. Salt Union ordinary and preference issues have recovered part of the recent fall. Eastmans and Hammond Meat Company's shares have

Highest and Lowest this Year.		Last Carrying over Price.	FOREIGN RAILWAYS.	Closing Price.	Rise or Fall.
20¾	20	20¼	Argentine Gt. West. 5 p.c. Pref.	20¼	− ¼
158½	149	153	B. Ay. Gt. Southern Ord.	153	−1
78½	73	74½	B. Ay. and Rosario Ord.	75	—
12¼	11¼	11⅜	B. Ay. Western Ord.	11½	—
87¼	80½	81½	Central Argentine Ord.	83	—
92	88	90½	Cordoba and Rosario 6 p.c. Deb.	88	
95½	92½	92½	Cord. Cent. 4 p.c. Deb. (Cent. Nth. Sec.)	93	—
61⅜	50	54	Do. Income Deb. Stk.	52	−3
25¼	18	22¼	Mexican Ord. Stk.	22½	− ¾
83½	72	80	Do. 8 p.c. 1st Pref.	81½	− ¾

been enquired for, after a long retirement from the active list. The dividend of 7½ per cent. announced by the directors of Cassell's put the price of the shares down 30s., the distribution being 1½ per cent. lower than last year. Sulphide Corporation debentures have fallen 10, and Welsbach Gas stocks have shed still more of their premium. Electric lighting concerns continue in favour, a rise of 4 in Brush debentures being noticeable. Among Breweries, Guinness, ordinary is 10 lower, and Allsopp ordinary and preference have both been marked down about 3. South Hetton coal stock is higher, a dividend of 10 per cent. having been announced, and it is also proposed to split the stock into ordinary and preference shares of £10 each. A steady rise in Western and Brazilian Telegraph issues was attributed to some sort of an arrangement with the Direct West India Cable Company; Peebles debentures rose 2 on the satisfactory position of affairs disclosed at the meeting; and D. H. Evans ordinary and debentures are firmer on dividend rumours. The Lipton prospectus is expected in a day or two, and a premium of ¾ on the ordinary has already been set up to stimulate the zeal of the speculative investor.

There are few fresh features of interest noticeable at the close of the week. Grand Trunk stocks finished off with a smart rally, the weekly traffic return, in spite of rate-cutting and snow-storms, being again excellent, and the strength of Union Pacific and Northern Pacific issues, points rather to a belief that the rate question has taken a favourable turn. United States Railroad shares close rather below the best points, but still well above last week's level, the solitary exception being Reading ordinary. Mexican Railway and other silver securities have been adversely affected by the decline in the price of the metal, and South African and West Australian ventures show a further fall.

MINING AND FINANCE COMPANIES.

The South African market has been dull and neglected and little or no support has been received from Paris; on the contrary, operators on the Bourse here have sold freely everything from De Beers downwards, and the Cape has also been sending selling orders, the recent speech by the President of the Orange Free State not being at all well received over there. To make matters worse there are also some queer rumours about, and among other reports one to the effect that the Transvaal Government intends imposing a tax of 15 per cent. on the production of the mines. Little or nothing has been going on in the West Australian section, but copper shares have again attracted a good deal of attention. Rio Tinto is nearly 1 higher on the week, owing to a rise of 17s. 6d. in the price of the metal during the past fortnight, but the last returns show a slight increase in the visible supply of copper. Among Indian companies, Nundydroog is firmer, a cablegram from the mine stating that the flood is now under control.

Dividends Announced.

MISCELLANEOUS.

East London Water Works.—Dividend for the past half-year at the rate of 8 per cent. per annum. Balance forward, £19,627.

Surrey Commercial Dock Company.—£2 10s. per cent. on the ordinary stock and on preference stock "A," making, with the interim dividend paid in October, £5 per cent. for the year, and an additional bonus of £1 per cent.

Rockhampton Gas and Coke Company, Queensland.—Dividend at the rate of £8 per cent. per annum on the ordinary shares, and 9 per cent. per annum on the preference shares, for the six months ended December 31.

Aspinall's Enamel, Limited.—Usual balan[illegible]vidend of 6s. per share for the half-year ended December 3[illegible]

British Moss Litter Company, Limite[illegible]ividends at the rate of 6 per cent. per annum on th[illegible]res, and of 10 per cent. per annum on the ordinar[illegible] half-year ended December 31.

Goole Moss Litter Company, Limited[illegible]nd on the preference shares at the rate of 6 per c[illegible] the half-year ended December 31.

Gas, Water, and General Investment, Li[illegible]nds at the rate of 4½ per cent. per annum on the preferred s[illegible]lf-year ended January 28, and 1½ per cent. on the deferre[illegible]

Charles Kinloch & Co., Limited.—Further dividen[illegible] on the preference shares, and 4s. on the ordinary shares, making, with the interim paid in September, 6 per cent. for the year. £5,000 to be placed to reserve fund, and £1,875 carried forward.

Jeyes' Sanitary Compounds Company, Limited.—Dividend at the rate of 10 per cent. per annum, together with a bonus of 5 per cent. £4,000 placed to reserve, and £681 carried forward.

British and Colonial Steam Navigation Company, Limited.—6 per cent. declared on the ordinary shares.

Langlaagte Estate and Gold Mining Company.—Dividend at the rate of 30 per cent. per annum for the half-year ended December 31.

Nundydroog Company, Limited.—Balance dividend for 1897 of 3s. per share, payable March 26.

Brighton and Hove Co-operative Supply Association, Limited.—Interim dividend at the rate of 5 per cent. per annum.

Mount Morgan Gold Mining Company, Limited.—Dividend of 6d. a share for the month of February.

Ruth Mines, Limited.—Interim of 3s. per £1 share. £7,000 carried forward.

Brazilian Submarine Telegraph Company, Limited.—Interim dividend at the rate of 6 per cent. per annum for the quarter ended December 31 last, payable on the 25th inst.

Val de Travers Asphalte Paving Company, Limited.—Further dividend of 11s. per share, making, with that paid in September last, 16s. per share for 1897, together with a bonus of 2s. per share. £4,773 carried forward.

Vickers, Sons, & Maxim, Limited.—2s. per share on the ordinary shares, making 15 per cent. for 1897.

Railway Investment Company, Limited.—17s. 7d. per cent. on the deferred stock for the year ended January 31.

Junior Army and Navy Stores, Limited.—5 per cent. per annum, free of income tax, for 1897.

General and Commercial Investment Trust.—Dividends for the six months ended the 28th ult. at the rate of 5 per cent. per annum on the preferred stock, and at the rate of 2½ per cent. per annum on the deferred stock.

Commercial Cable Company.—A quarterly dividend of 1¾ per cent. on the capital stock.

BREWERIES.

New England Company, Limited.—Further dividend on the ordinary shares of 6s. per share, making 6 per cent. for the year ended December 31.

INSURANCE.

British Law Fire, Limited.—Payment of 3 per cent., as in 1896. £4,000 to reserve.

BANKS.

Dresdner Bank, Berlin.—Dividend for the past year of 9 per cent., as against 8 per cent. in 1896.

Bank of Australasia.—Dividend at the rate of 5 per cent. per annum, carrying forward £18,275 to next account.

RAILWAYS.

Glasgow and South-Western.—Dividend for the half-year to January 31 at the rate of 5 per cent. per annum, £7,364 carried forward. At the corresponding period of 1896-7 the dividend was at the rate of 5¼ per cent., with £5,562 forward.

Caledonian.—Dividend for the half-year to January 31 at the rate of 5 per cent. per annum, £9,500 being carried forward. For the same period of 1896-7 the distribution was the same, with £17,419 carried forward.

San Paulo (Brazilian) Railway Company.—Interim dividend for the half-year ended December 31 last on both ordinary and new ordinary shares at the rate of 11 per cent. per annum, carrying forward £105,000.

TRAMWAY AND OMNIBUS RECEIPTS.

For past week :—Belfast, −£104 ; Calais, +£31 ; Croydon, +£37 ; Glasgow, −£224 ; Lea Bridge, +£23 ; London & Deptford, −£26 ; London Southern, +£9 ; London General Omnibus, −£1,434 ; London Road Car, −£482 ; Metropolitan, −£498 ; North Staffordshire, −£20 ; South London, −£132 ; Woolwich & S. E. London, −£47 ; Bordeaux, +£24 ; Provincial, −£205 ; Southampton, −£51 ; Wolverhampton, −£13.

Anglo-Argentine, week ending January 31, £409 increase ; Vienna Omnibus, week ending February 19, £279 increase.

City of Buenos Ayres, week ending January 31, £644 increase.

Prices of Mine and Mining Finance Companies' Shares.

Shares £1 each, except where otherwise stated.

Australian.

Making-Up Price, Feb. 21.	Name.	Closing Price.	Rise or Fall.	Making-Up Price, Feb. 21.	Name	Closing Price.	Rise or Fall.
[illegible]	Aladdin	[illegible]	−[illegible]	[illegible]	Hampton Plains	[illegible]	−[illegible]
[illegible]	Associated	4		[illegible]	Hannan's Brownhill	[illegible]	+[illegible]
[illegible]	Do. Southern	1	−[illegible]	[illegible]	Hannan's Oroya	[illegible]	
14/	Brilliant, £2	14/[illegible]		13/3	Do. Proprietary	18/	−2/
[illegible]	Do. St. George's	[illegible]	−[illegible]	[illegible]	Do. Star	[illegible]	
12/	British Broken Hill	11/6	−/6	—	Ivanhoe, New	[illegible]	
[illegible]	Broken Hill Proprietary [illegible]	[illegible]		[illegible]	Kalgurli Mt. & Iron King, 18/	[illegible]	
—	Do. Junction	[illegible]		[illegible]	Kalgurli	[illegible]	+[illegible]
—	Do. Block 10	[illegible]		[illegible]	Lady Shenton	[illegible]	−[illegible]
[illegible]	Brownhill Extended	[illegible]	+[illegible]	[illegible]	Lake View Cons.	[illegible]	−[illegible]
[illegible]	Burbank's Birthday	[illegible]	−[illegible]	1	Do. Extended	[illegible]	−[illegible]
[illegible]	Central Boulder	1	−[illegible]	[illegible]	Do. South	1	−
5/6	Chaffers, 4/	5/6		[illegible]	London & Globe Finance	[illegible]	−
[illegible]	Colonial Finance, 15/	[illegible] pm	−[illegible]	[illegible]	London & W. A. Exploration	1	+
—	Crœsus S. United	[illegible]	−[illegible]	[illegible]	Do. Investment	[illegible]	+[illegible]
16/	Day Dawn Block	15/9		[illegible]	Mainland Consols	[illegible]	
1	E. Murchison	1	−[illegible]	[illegible]	North Boulder, 10/	[illegible]	
[illegible]	Gold Estates	[illegible]	−[illegible]	[illegible]	North Kalgurli	[illegible]	
4/3	Golden Arrow 19/	4/	−/6	[illegible]	Northern Territories	[illegible]	+[illegible]
[illegible]	Golden Horseshoe	[illegible]	−[illegible]	[illegible]	Peak Hill	[illegible]	−[illegible]
[illegible]	Golden Link	1		[illegible]	South Kalgurli	[illegible]	
1	Great Boulder, 2/	22/	−/9	[illegible]	W. A. Goldfields	2	
[illegible]	Do. Main Reef, 10/	[illegible]		[illegible]	W. A. Joint Stock	[illegible]	−[illegible]
[illegible]	Do. Perseverance	[illegible]		[illegible]	W. A. Market Trust	[illegible]	
[illegible]	Do. South	1		2	W. A. Loan & General Fin.	[illegible]	−[illegible]
[illegible]	Hainault	[illegible]	+[illegible]	[illegible]	White Feather	[illegible]	

South African.

Making-Up Price, Feb. 21.	Name.	Closing Price.	Rise or Fall.	Making-Up Price, Feb. 21.	Name	Closing Price.	Rise or Fall.
[illegible]	Angelo	[illegible]	−[illegible]	[illegible]	Langlaagte Estate	[illegible]	
[illegible]	Aurora West	[illegible]	−[illegible]	2/6	Lisbon-Berlyn	2/6	−/3
[illegible]	Bantjes	[illegible]	−[illegible]	[illegible]	May Consolidated	[illegible]	−[illegible]
10/	Barrett, 10/	9/	−1/6	[illegible]	Meyer and Charlton	[illegible]	−[illegible]
[illegible]	Bonanza	[illegible]	−[illegible]	[illegible]	Modderfontein	[illegible]	+[illegible]
[illegible]	Buffelsdoorn	[illegible]	−[illegible]	[illegible]	New Bultfontein	[illegible]	
[illegible]	Champ d'Or	[illegible]		[illegible]	New Primrose	[illegible]	−[illegible]
[illegible]	City and Suburban, £4	[illegible]	−[illegible]	[illegible]	Nigel	[illegible]	
[illegible]	Comet (New)	[illegible]		—	Nigel Deep	[illegible]	
[illegible]	Con. Deep Level	[illegible]	−[illegible]	[illegible]	North Randfontein	—	
13	Crown Deep	[illegible]	−[illegible]	6	Nourse Deep	6	−[illegible]
[illegible]	Crown Reef	[illegible]		[illegible]	Porges-Randfontein	[illegible]	
[illegible]	De Beers, £5	[illegible]	−[illegible]	[illegible]	Rand Mines	[illegible]	−2
[illegible]	Driefontein	[illegible]	−[illegible]	[illegible]	Randfontein	[illegible]	−[illegible]
[illegible]	Durban Roodepoort	[illegible]		[illegible]	Rietfontein	[illegible]	
[illegible]	Do. Deep	4		10	Robinson Deep	[illegible]	−[illegible]
[illegible]	East Rand	[illegible]	−[illegible]	[illegible]	Do. Gold, £5	[illegible]	−[illegible]
[illegible]	Ferreira	[illegible]	−[illegible]	[illegible]	Do. Randfontein	[illegible]	
[illegible]	Geldenhuis Deep	[illegible]	−[illegible]	[illegible]	Roodepoort Central Deep	[illegible]	−[illegible]
[illegible]	Do. Estate	[illegible]	−[illegible]	[illegible]	Rose Deep	[illegible]	−[illegible]
[illegible]	George Goch	[illegible]		3	Salisbury	[illegible]	−[illegible]
[illegible]	Ginsberg	[illegible]x	−[illegible]	[illegible]	Sheba	[illegible]	−[illegible]
2	Glencairn	2	−[illegible]	[illegible]	Simmer and Jack, £5	[illegible]	−[illegible]
[illegible]	Glen Deep	[illegible]	−[illegible]	[illegible]	Transvaal Gold	[illegible]	−[illegible]
[illegible]	Goldfields Deep	[illegible]	−[illegible]	3	Treasury	[illegible]	
[illegible]	Griqualand West	[illegible]		4	United Roodepoort	[illegible]	−[illegible]
[illegible]	Henry Nourse	[illegible]		[illegible]	Van Ryn	[illegible]	−[illegible]
[illegible]	Heriot	[illegible]	−[illegible]	[illegible]	Village Main Reef	[illegible]	−[illegible]
8	Jagersfontein	[illegible]	−[illegible]	[illegible]	Vogelstruis	[illegible]	+[illegible]
[illegible]	Jubilee	8	−[illegible]	[illegible]	Do. Deep	[illegible]	−[illegible]
[illegible]	Jumpers	5	−[illegible]	[illegible]	Wemmer	[illegible]	+[illegible]
[illegible]	Jumpers Deep	[illegible]	−[illegible]	[illegible]	West Rand	[illegible]	
[illegible]	Kleinfontein	[illegible]	−[illegible]	[illegible]	Wolhuter, £4	6	−[illegible]
[illegible]	Knight's	[illegible]	−[illegible]	[illegible]	Worcester	[illegible]	
[illegible]	Lancaster	[illegible]					

Land Exploration and Rhodesian.

Making-Up Price, Feb. 21.	Name.	Closing Price.	Rise or Fall.	Making-Up Price, Feb. 21.	Name	Closing Price.	Rise or Fall.
[illegible]	Anglo-French Ex.	[illegible]	−[illegible]	[illegible]	Mashonaland Central	[illegible]	
2	Barnato Consolidated	[illegible]	−[illegible]	[illegible]	Matabele Gold Reefs	[illegible]	
[illegible]	Bechuanaland Ex.	[illegible]	−[illegible]	[illegible]	Mozambique	2	−[illegible]
[illegible]	Chartered B.S.A.	[illegible]	−[illegible]	[illegible]	New African	[illegible]	−[illegible]
[illegible]	Clark's Cons.	[illegible]		[illegible]	Oceana Consolidated	[illegible]	−[illegible]
[illegible]	Colenbrander	[illegible]	−[illegible]	[illegible]	Rhodesia, Ltd.	[illegible]	−[illegible]
[illegible]	Cons. Goldfields	[illegible]	−[illegible]	[illegible]	Do. Exploration	[illegible]	−[illegible]
[illegible]	Do. Pref.	21/6		1	Do. Goldfields	1	−[illegible]
[illegible]	Exploration	[illegible]		[illegible]	S. A. Gold Trust	[illegible]	−
[illegible]	Geelong	[illegible]	−[illegible]	[illegible]	Tati Concessions	[illegible]	−
[illegible]	Henderson's Est.	[illegible]	−[illegible]	[illegible]	Transvaal Development	[illegible]	−[illegible]
[illegible]	Johannesburg Con. In.	[illegible]	−[illegible]	[illegible]	United Rhodesia	[illegible]	
[illegible]	Do. Water	1	−[illegible]	[illegible]	Willoughby	1	
[illegible]	Mashonaland Agency	[illegible]	−[illegible]	[illegible]	Zambesia Explor.		

Miscellaneous.

Making-Up Price, Feb. 21.	Name.	Closing Price.	Rise or Fall.	Making-Up Price, Feb. 21.	Name	Closing Price.	Rise or Fall.
[illegible]	Alamillos, £2	[illegible]		14/	Mysore Goldfields	12/6	
[illegible]	Anaconda, $25	[illegible]	−[illegible]	10/	Do. Reefs, 17/	9/	
10/	Balaghát, 18/	10/		15/	Do. West	14/6	−
[illegible]	Cape Copper, £2	[illegible]	+[illegible]	12/3	Do. Wynaad	12/	
[illegible]	Champion Reef, 10s.	[illegible]		[illegible]	Namaqua, £2	[illegible]	+[illegible]
[illegible]	Copiapo, £2	[illegible]		[illegible]	Nundydroog	[illegible]	+[illegible]
[illegible]	Coromandel	[illegible]		[illegible]	Ooregum	[illegible]	
[illegible]	Frontino & Bolivia	[illegible]		[illegible]	Do. Pref.	[illegible]	
[illegible]	Hall Mines	[illegible]		[illegible]	Rio Tinto Def., £5	[illegible]	+[illegible]
[illegible]	Libiola, £5	[illegible]		[illegible]	Do. Pref. £5	[illegible]	
[illegible]	Linares, £3	8		18/6	St. John del Rey	18/6	−/3
[illegible]	Mason & Barry, £3	[illegible]		18/9	Taitipu	[illegible]	+[illegible]
[illegible]	Mountain Copper, £5	[illegible]	−[illegible]	[illegible]	Tharsis, £2	[illegible]	
[illegible]	Mount Lyell, £3	14		[illegible]	Tolima "A," £5	[illegible]	+
[illegible]	Mount Lyell, North	[illegible]	−[illegible]	[illegible]	Waihi	[illegible]	−[illegible]
[illegible]	Mount Lyell, South	17/6		[illegible]	Waitekauri	[illegible]	−[illegible]
[illegible]	Mount Morgan, 17s. 6d.	[illegible]		[illegible]	Woodstock (N.Z.)	[illegible]	
[illegible]	Mysore, 10s.	[illegible]					

Railway Traffic Returns.

ALGECIRAS (GIBRALTAR) RAILWAY.—Traffic for week ended February 19, Ps. 20,860; increase, Ps. 2,920. Aggregate from July 1, Ps. 682,269; increase, Ps. 14,623.

BENGAL CENTRAL RAILWAY.—Traffic for week ending February 5, Rs. 19,159; increase, Rs. 1,610. Total from January 1, Rs. 105,826; increase, Rs. 13,071.

BURMA RAILWAYS.—Receipts for week ending January 29, Rs. 2,22,778; decrease, Rs. 33,916. Aggregate from January 1, Rs. 8,20,997; decrease, Rs. 1,61,116.

CLEATOR AND WORKINGTON.—Gross receipts for the week ending February 19 amounted to £998, a decrease of £180. Total receipts from January 1, £7,120, a decrease of £503.

COCKERMOUTH, KESWICK, AND PENRITH.—Gross receipts for the week ending February 12 amounted to £830, an increase of £42. Total receipts for six weeks £5,156, an increase of £598.

GREAT WESTERN OF BRAZIL RAILWAY.—Traffic for week ending January 15, $51,912; increase, $4,446. Aggregate receipts to date $128,172; increase, $11,952.

MOBILE AND BIRMINGHAM RAILROAD.—Traffic for first week of February, $7,290; increase, $1,255. Aggregate from July 1, $227,859; decrease, $13,080.

MANILA RAILWAY.—Traffic receipts for week ended February 26, $19,894; increase, $4,587. Aggregate from January 1, $150,178; increase, $37,721.

QUEBEC CENTRAL RAILWAY.—Receipts for fourth week of January, $5,334; decrease $1,200. Aggregate from July 1, $29,207; decrease $799.

ROHILKUND AND KUMAON RAILWAY.—Traffic for week ending January 29, Rs. 4,858; increase, Rs. 590. Aggregate from January 1, Rs. 22,044; decrease, Rs. 217.

VILLA MARIA AND RUFINO RAILWAY.—Traffic for week ending February 26, $6,901; increase, $37. Aggregate from January 1, $34,042; decrease, $5,521.

WEST FLANDERS RAILWAY.—Gross receipts for week ending February 27, £1,967; decrease, £201. Total from January 1, £16,764; increase, £389.

WEST OF INDIA PORTUGUESE RAILWAY.—Week ending February 5, Rs. 4,933; increase, Rs. 2,124.

ASSAM-BENGAL RAILWAY.—Traffic for week ended January 15, Rs. 24,224; increase, Rs. 1,631. Aggregate from January 1, Rs. 50,447; increase, Rs. 3,625.

PUERTO CABELLO AND VALENCIA RAILWAY.—Traffic receipts for week ending January 28, £878; decrease, £681. Aggregate from January 1, £3,049; decrease, £1,614.

CINCINNATI SOUTHERN RAILWAY. — Receipts for month of January, $332,000; increase, $69,000.

WESTERN RAILWAY OF SANTA FE.—Traffic receipts for week ending February 19, $46,214; increase, $8,494.

ALABAMA GREAT SOUTHERN RAILWAY.—Traffic for month of January, $165,000, increase $30,000.

DELHI, UMBALLA, AND KALKA RAILWAY.—Traffic for week ending February 26, Rs. 36,100; increase Rs. 6,500. Aggregate to date, Rs. 314,700; increase Rs. 1,28,000.

ALCOY AND GANDIA RAILWAY AND HARBOUR COMPANY.—Traffic fo[illegible] February 26 :—Ps. 8,100, increase ps. 100. Aggregate f[illegible] 1, ps. 86,700, increase ps. 8,650.

U[illegible]THERN RAILWAY.—Gross receipts for December, £9[illegible] £134. Aggregate for six months to December, [illegible]ease £208.

[illegible]OR AND WORKINGTON.—Gross receipts for the week ending February 26 amounted to £954, a decrease of £56. Total receipts from January 1, £8,074, a decrease of £559.

COCKERMOUTH, KESWICK, AND PENRITH.—Gross receipts for the week ending February 27 amounted to £786, an increase of £46. Aggregate receipts to date, £6,705, an increase of £640.

GREAT WESTERN OF BRAZIL RAILWAY.—Traffic for week ending January 22, $49,468; increase, $5,768. Aggregate receipts to date $177,640; increase, $17,721.

WESTERN OF SANTA FE RAILWAYS.—Gross receipts for week ending February 26, $44,690; increase, $14,690.

ENGLISH RAILWAYS.

Div. for half years. 1896	1896	1897	1897	Last Balance forward.	Amt. to pay 1 p.c. on Ord. for ½ yr.	NAME.	Date.	Gross Traffic for week: Amt.	Inc. or dec. on 1897.	Inc. or dec. on 1896.	No. of weeks	Gross Traffic for half-year to date: Amt.	Inc. or dec. on 1897.	Inc. or dec. on 1896.	Mileage.	Inc. on 1897.	Working	Prior Charges last ½ year.	Prop. add Cap. Exp. this ½ year.
				£	£												%	£	£
10	10	10	10	2,707	5,094	Barry	Feb 26	10,267	+1,676	+2,999	9	80,840	+2,325	+11,215	31	—	8·89	60,665	316,853
nil	nil	nil	nil	—	—	Brecon and Merthyr	Feb 27	1,410	+19	−102	9	13,722	+294	−129	61	—	—	—	—
nil	nil	nil	nil	3,979	4,749	Cambrian	Feb 27	4,914	+51	+537	*	34,489	+107	—	250	—	60·96	63,148	40,000
1½	1½	2	1¾	1,510	3,150	City and South London ..	Feb 27	1,065	+69	+119	9	9,630	−83	+770	3½	—	56·67	5,552	124,000
1	2	1½	2	7,895	13,210	Furness	Feb 27	9,104	+55	+864	*	70,875	+1,585	—	139	—	49·83	97,423	20,910
1	1½	½	1	2,207	27,470	Great Central (late M., S., & L.)	Feb 27	42,360	+545	+3,803	8	333,894	+5,899	+22,297	352½	—	57·17	607,386	1,200,000
2½	4¾	2	5	51,283	62,865	Great Eastern	Feb 27	78,590	+1,665	+8,304	8	612,919	+20,929	+59,577	1,156	7	55·35	860,138	250,000
3	5¼	3	5	15,094	102,496	Great Northern	Feb 27	93,730	+1,722	+9,236	9	827,149	+22,425	+64,489	1,071	8	61·36	641,485	750,000
4¼	7¾	4¾	7½	31,350	121,981	Great Western	Feb 27	166880	+3,960	+8,550	8	1,348,430	+36,500	+79,790	2,582	21	51·44	1,486,272	800,000
nil	2	nil	1¼	8,951	16,487	Hull and Barnsley	Feb 27	5,903	−380	+417	8	50,152	−2,641	+3,381	73	—	58·21	70,290	52,920
5	5¾	5	5½	21,495	83,704	Lancashire and Yorkshire ..	Feb 27	91,335	+2,377	+6,931	8	711,078	+25,206	+46,991	555½	25	56·70	674,745	451,976
4¾	8	4¾	8½	26,243	43,049	London, Brighton, & S. Coast	Feb 26	43,072	−1,544	+924	9	406,687	+24,458	+24,752	476½	—	50·20	407,042	240,735
nil	nil	nil	nil	72,294	56,296	London, Chatham, & Dover ..	Feb 27	25,322	−482	+1,504	8	205,572	+7,814	+15,144	185½	—	50·65	367,873	nil
6¼	8	6¼	7¾	89,535	204,068	London and North Western ..	Feb 27	225396	−1,192	+12,720	8	1,766,338	+41,457	+111707	1,911½	—	56·92	1,404,334	600,000
5	8½	8½	8½	23,038	59,367	London and South Western ..	Feb 27	64,331	−1,594	+2,595	8	511,014	+23,575	+38,523	941	6½	51·75	513,740	389,000
2¾	6	2¾	6½	14,592	6,691	London, Tilbury, & Southend	Feb 27	4,741	+173	+1,138	9	42,333	+3,168	+9,058	81	—	52·57	39,590	15,000
3¼	3¾	3¾	3¾	17,133	26,409	Metropolitan	Feb 27	15,962	+543	+1,637	*	133,532	+3,289	—	64	12	43·63	148,047	254,000
nil	nil	nil	nil	4,006	11,250	Metropolitan District	Feb 27	8,316	+407	+497	8	69,734	+2,807	+3,584	13	—	48·70	119,663	38,450
5	7	5½	6½	38,143	174,582	Midland	Feb 27	182916	+1,138	+18,087	9	1,596,026	+11,075	+104026	1,354¾	15¼	57·59	1,216,582	650,000
5¼	7½	5¾	7	22,374	138,189	North Eastern	Feb 26	139307	+3,512	+3,744	8	1,100,158	+29,294	+56,006	1,597¾	—	58·82	795,077	436,004
7½	7½	7½	7½	7,061	10,102	North London	Feb 27			Not recd			not	recvd.	12	—	50·90	49,973	7,600
4	5	4	4½	4,745	16,150	North Staffordshire	Feb 27	15,098	−819	+487	9	140,207	+7,833	+9,149	312	—	55·27	118,142	19,605
10	10	11		1,642	3,004	Rhymney	Feb 26	5,268	−362	+432	9	45,514	+939	+5,047	71	—	49·68	29,049	16,700
3	6¾	3½	6¾	4,054	50,215	South Eastern	Feb 26	38,691	+543	+2,419	*	322,034	+19,568	—	448	—	51·88	380,763	250,000
3½	3½	3½	3½	2,315	25,961	Taff Vale	Feb 26	15,974	+76	+589	9	137,497	−2,475	+3,634	121	—	54·90	94,800	92,000

* From January 1.

SCOTCH RAILWAYS.

5	5	5½	—	15,350	77,570	Caledonian	Feb 27	71,53	− 586	+ 4,633	4	271,003	+ 93	+ 16,778	851½	5	50·50	566,914	375,966
5	5½	5	—	5,886	24,639	Glasgow and South-Western	" 26	26,83	+ 200	+ 3,108	4	105,260	+ 1,754	+ 11,327	393½	—	55·12	221,120	180,556
3½	3½	3½	—	1,291	4,600	Great North of Scotland	" 26	7,31	− 1,238	+ 642	4	29,699	− 214	+ 2,548	331	15½	52·03	92,178	60,000
3	nil	2	—	10,477	12,820	Highland	" 27	8,602	+ 687	+ 1,158	26	236,028	+ 10,525	+ 12,927	479½	27½	55·63	78,976	,000
1	1¼	1	—	3,763	45,819	North British	" 27	66,441	+ 191	+ 1,868	4	261,647	+ 5,935	+ 6,207	1,230	23	44·65	821,766	426,009

IRISH RAILWAYS.

6½	6½	6½	—	5,466	1,700	Belfast and County Down ..	Feb. 18	2,046	+ 13	+ 206	*	13,940	+ 446	—	76½	—	55·58	17,690	10,000
5½	6½	5½	—	—	4,284	Belfast and Northern Counties	" 18	4,748	+ 271	− 361	*	33,319	+ 1,164	—	249	—	—	—	—
2	3	2	—	1,418	1,200	Cork, Bandon, and S. Coast ..	" 26	1,111	− 95	− 25	*	9,031	− 817	—	103	—	54·82	14,436	5,430
6½	6¾	6½	—	21,537	17,709	Great Northern	" 25	14,397	+ 759	+ 860	8	107,061	+ 5,840	+ 6,697	528	36	54·03	87,068	16,000
5½	5½	5½	5½	30,339	24,855	Great Southern and Western ..	" 25	—	—	—	not	received	—	—	603	13	51·45	72,800	46,582
4	4	4	4½	11,372	11,850	Midland Great Western ..	" 23	8,657	− 1,328	− 1,320	8	71,148	+ 3,782	+ 4,983	538	—	50·31	83,129	1,800
nil	nil	nil	nil	229	2,822	Waterford and Central ..	" 18	767	+ 47	—	*	6,923	+ 921	—	50½	—	53·24	6,858	1,500
nil	nil	nil	nil	1,936	2,987	Waterford, Limerick & W. ..	" 18	4,273	+ 68	+ 129	*	50,780	+ 2,914	—	350½	—	57·83	42,617	7,075

* From January 1.

FOREIGN RAILWAYS.

Mileage. Total.	Increase on 1897.	Increase on 1896.	Name.	Gross Traffic for Week. Week ending	Amount.	In. or Dec. upon 1897.	In. or Dec. upon 1896.	Gross Traffic to Date. No. of Weeks.	Amount.	In. or Dec. upon 1897.	In. or Dec. upon 1896.
					£	£	£		£	£	£
319	—	—	Argentine Great Western ..	Feb. 20	6,394	+ 575	+ 1,391	33	177,433	− 9,730	− 39,998
76½	—	—	Bahia and San Francisco	Feb. 5	2,718	+ 903	− 14	5	13,700	+ 4,227	+ 3,399
234	48	84	Bahia Blanca and North West ..	Jan. 30	902	− 88	− 51	31	24,287	+ 603	—
74	—	—	Buenos Ayres and Ensenada ..	Feb. 27	3,395	− 1,143	− 1,272	8	28,706	− 6,074	− 7,633
426	—	—	Buenos Ayres and Pacific ..	Feb. 26	6,977	− 2,150	− 1,275	34	214,203	− 51,942	+ 6,218
914	1	3	Buenos Ayres and Rosario ..	Feb. 26	17,568	+ 3,549	+ 1,363	8	143,350	+ 29,278	+ 19,739
1,409	30	68	Buenos Ayres Great Southern ..	Feb. 27	34,876	− 5,797	− 1,954	34	985,603	+ 62,727	+ 119,103
600	107	177	Buenos Ayres Western	Feb. 27	13,287	− 978	− 3,111	34	407,597	− 76,372	− 69,170
845	55	77	Central Argentine..	Feb. 26	22,649	+ 3,438	− 2,416	8	176,690	+ 34,810	− 87
297	—	—	Central Bahia	Dec. 31*	$114,389	− 84,668	+ $22,144	12 mos.	$1,307,205	+ $141,334	+ $196,199
271	—	—	Central Uruguay of Monte Video	Feb. 26	5,888	+ 861	− 767	34	203,177	− 646	− 16,392
128	—	—	Do. Eastern Extension	Feb. 26	1,188	− 247	− 394	34	41,274	+ 2,461	− 2,704
182	—	—	Do. Northern Extension	Feb. 26	486	− 60	− 607	34	21,586	− 1,958	− 6,025
280	—	—	Cordoba and Rosario	Feb. 20	3,025	+ 945	+ 653	34	71,520	− 18,365	− 1,545
228	—	—	Cordoba Central	Feb. 20	$18,500	− $5,290	− $3,300	7	$161,700	− $21,390	− $32,070
549	—	—	Do. Northern Extension	Feb. 20	$41,500	− $23,300	− $3,050	7	$320,290	− $116,970	− $68,980
237	—	—	Costa Rica..	Feb. 12	6,623	− 1,944	− 275	—	—	—	—
99	—	—	East Argentine	Jan. 16	737	− 77	+ 119	2	1,466	− 205	− 374
386	—	6	Entre Rios..	Feb. 26	2,840	+ 1,295	+ 895	34	48,547	+ 9,335	+ 8,717
555	—	24	Inter Oceanic of Mexico.. ..	Feb.	$67,600	+ $11,280	+ $20,920	34	$1,902,280	+ $277,040	+ $469,080
23	—	—	La Guaira and Caracas	Jan.	2,016	− 646	− 304	3	5,633	− 7,125	− 1,096
321	—	—	Mexican	Feb. 26	[illegible]	+ $600	—	8	$655,400	+ $58,550	—
1,846	—	—	Mexican Central	Feb. 21	$252,278	+ $6,909	+ $78,160	7	$1,835,471	+ $17,547	+ $453,356
1,217	—	—	Mexican National	Feb. 21	$115,407	+ $2,634	+ $40,697	7	$809,516	+ $92,343	+ $135,011
228	—	—	Mexican Southern	Feb. 28	$14,058	− $1,252	+ $2,398	48	$608,364	+ $86,675	+ $139,648
205	—	—	Minas and Rio	Dec. 31*	$177,973	+ $6,511	—	6 mos.	$1,174,610	+ $207,798	—
94	—	17	N. W. Argentine	Feb. 26	836	− 510	− 271	8	7,144	− 3,643	− 1,874
242	3	—	Nitrate	Feb. 28†	13,398	+ 3,536	− 3,756	7	54,493	− 1,349	− 28,233
300	—	—	Ottoman	Feb. 19	3,437	− 1,396	− 865	7	39,308	− 10,137	+ 4,470
77½	—	—	Recife and San Francisco ..	Jan. 1	5,144	+ 1,411	+ 138	—	—	—	—
86½	—	—	San Paulo	Jan. 30†	20,140	− 9,077	—	4	50,130	− 16,143	—
186	—	—	Santa Fe and Cordova	Feb. 19	4,315	+ 1,731	+ 1,588	—	41,813	− 19,954	− 2,318
110	—	—	Western of Havana	Feb. 26	1,740	− 90	+ 1,345	34	60,655	+ 5,587	− 1,805

* For month ended. † For fortnight ended.

INDIAN RAILWAYS.

Mileage. Total.	Increase on 1897.	Increase on 1896.	Name.	Gross Traffic for Week. Week ending	Amount.	In. or Dec. on 1897.	In. or Dec. on 1896	Gross Traffic to Date. No. of Weeks.	Amount.	In. or Dec. on 1897.	In. or Dec. on 1896.
862	—	—	Bengal Nagpur	Feb. 19	Rs.1.47.000	+ Rs. 8.825	− Rs.12.368	7	Rs.9.73.000	− Rs.69.000	− R.2.79.328
827	8	63	Bengal and North-Western ..	Jan. 29	Rs.1.41.490	+ Rs.27.447	+ Rs. 9.753	4	Rs.5.35.330	+ Rs.68.371	− Rs.1783
461	—	—	Bombay and Baroda	Feb. 26	£22,917	− £6,406	− £12,313	7	£181,775	− £31,431	− £95,670
1,884	2	13	East Indian	Feb. 26	Rs.11.72.000	− R.81.000	+ Rs.13.000	8	Rs.1.01.00.000	+ Rs.3.76.000	+ Rs24.16.000
1,491	—	—	Great Indian Penin.	Feb. 26	£72,151	+ £12,873	− £10,853	8	£511,958	+ £11,774	− £176,484
736	—	—	Indian Midland	Feb. 26	Rs.1.24.930	− Rs.5.991	+ Rs.34.645	8	Rs.11.07.233	+ Rs.17.188	+ Rs1.39.426
840	—	—	Madras	Feb. 12	£18,700	− £1,833	− £733	6	£116,037	− £1873	− £8,000
1,043	—	—	South Indian	Jan. 22	Rs.1.35.294	− Rs.20.384	− Rs.36.178	3	Rs.4.32.736	− Rs.33.708	− R.1.24.936

UNITED STATES AND CANADIAN RAILWAYS.

Mileage Total.	Increase on 1897.	Increase on 1896.	Name.	Gross Traffic for Week. Period Ending.	Amount.	In. or Dec. on 1897.	Gross Traffic to Date. No. of Weeks.	Amount.	In. or Dec. on 1897.
					dols.	dols.		dols.	dols.
917	—	—	Baltimore & Ohio S. Western ..	Feb. 21	129,461	+12,215	33	4,354,144	+412,364
6,568	92	156	Canadian Pacific	Feb. 21	351,000	+41,000	7	2,784,000	+506,000
922	—	—	Chicago Great Western	Feb. 21	102,390	−156	33	3,489,328	+478,397
6,169	—	469	Chicago, Mil., & St. Paul ..	Feb. 28	658,000	+103,000	6	4,755,801	+544,226
1,685	—	—	Denver & Rio Grande	Feb. 21	135,000	+35,600	33	5,371,700	+894,500
3,512	—	—	Grand Trunk, Main Line ..	Feb. 28	£73,048	+£5,294	8	£591,536	+£67,949
335	—	—	Do. Chic. & Grand Trunk	Feb. 28	£16,150	+£4,244	8	£119,069	+£22,942
189	—	—	Do. Det., G. H. & Mil...	Feb. 28	£3,594	−£74	8	£27,227	−£2,756
2,938	—	—	Louisville & Nashville	Feb. 21	435,270	+37,140	7	3,067,270	+795,140
2,197	137	137	Miss., K., & Texas	Feb. 21	210,966	13,126	33	8,603,546	+512,128
477	—	—	N. Y., Ontario, & W.	Feb. 21	58,901	−4,613	33	2,562,076	+86,269
1,570	—	—	Norfolk & Western	Feb. 21	210,000	+29,000	32	7,031,000	+749,000
3,499	336	—	Northern Pacific	Feb. 21	341,000	+84,000	7	2,436,000	+764,000
1,223	—	—	St. Louis S. Western	Feb. 21	113,000	+24,000	7	801,700	+141,100
4,654	—	—	Southern	Feb. 21	430,000	+29,000	33	1,647,812	+1,123,448
1,979	—	—	Wabash	Feb. 21	231,000	+17,000	7	1,752,406	+389,000

MONTHLY STATEMENTS.

Mileage. Total.	Increase on 1896.	Increase on 1895.	Name.	Net Earnings for Month. Month.	Amount.	In. or Dec. on 1896.	In. or Dec. on 1895.	Net Earnings to Date. No. of Months.	Amount.	In. or Dec. on 1896.	In. or Dec. on 1895.
					dols.	dols.	dols.		dols.	dols.	dols.
6,935	44	444	Atchison	December	986,000	+52,000	—	12	8,966,480	+176,951	—
6,547	103	106	Canadian Pacific	January	516,000	+142,000	—	—	—	—	—
6,169	—	469	Chicago, Mil., & St. Paul ..	January	757,000	+52,000	−30,713	—	—	—	—
1,685	—	—	Denver & Rio Grande	December	273,000	+57,121	−8,253	6	1,786,320	+249,850	−[illegible]
1,970	—	—	Erie..	January	371,000	+33,000	−107,852	—	—	—	—
3,512	—	—	Grand Trunk, Main Line ..	January	£87,400	+£34,284	+£37,725	—	—	—	—
335	—	—	Do. Chic. & Grand Trunk	January	£13,100	+£8,933	+£9,901	—	—	—	—
189	—	—	Do. Det. G. H. & Mil. ..	January	£1,800	+£692	+£1,939	—	—	—	—
3,127	—	239	Illinois Central*	December	2,555,303	+458,872	+349,241	12	24,723,399	+2,940,108	+[illegible]
2,396	—	—	New York Central*	January	3,505,000	+365,000	+27,034	—	—	—	—
477	—	—	New York Ontario, & W. ..	December	87,176	+14,635	+10,602	6	701,475	+4,958	+[illegible]
3,407	—	—	Pennsylvania	December	1,664,297	+26,100	−35,400	12	20,532,068	+2,328,900	+[illegible]
1,055	—	—	Phil. & Reading*	December	1,947,585	+208,345	—	6	11,886,164	+666,603	—

Prices Quoted on the London Stock Exchange.

Throughout the INVESTORS' REVIEW middle prices alone are quoted, the object being to give the public the approximate current quotations of every security of any consequence in existence. On the markets the buying and selling prices are both given, and are often wide apart where stocks are seldom dealt in. Other particulars will be found in the INVESTMENT INDEX published quarterly—January, April, July, and October—in connection with this REVIEW, price 2s., by post 2s. 2d. Where dividends are paid only once a year, an *italic* type is used to distinguish them. The London Stock Exchange Official List is quoted in the REVIEW almost entire, only very insignificant issues, or bonds falling due within the next two or three years, being omitted. But the list is subdivided into the leading, or active, stocks, and those less frequently dealt in. The former will be found under the head of "Stock Markets," and with more details than it is possible to give for the bulk of securities. By retaining the file of the INVESTORS' REVIEW any subscriber can follow for himself the movements of securities from week to week, and the INVESTMENT INDEX will from time to time help to fill up deficiencies in the information.

Tea Companies and Mines and Mining Finance Stocks are placed in special lists.

Among the abbreviations used are the following :—S. F. Snk. Fd. *sinking fund*; Certs., *certificates*; Debs. or Dbs., *debentures*; Db. or D.Stk., *debenture stock*; Pf., Prf., or Pref., *preference*; Prefd. or Pfd., *preferred*; Dfd., *deferred*; L. or Ltd., *limited*; Sh., *share*; Ans., *annuities*; Cu. or Cm., *cumulative*; Gu or Guar., *guaranteed*; Bds., *bonds*; S., Sr., or Ser., *series*; In., Ins., Insc., *inscribed*; Dr., Drgs., Drwgs., *drawings*; Stg., Strlg., *sterling*; Lia., *liable to*; Sp., Surp., *surplus*; Per., Perp., *perpetual*; Ln. *lien*; Lo. *loan*.

The dates following the names of securities are the years of issue or of redemption. Where shares are not fully paid up, their nominal amount is given with the name so that investors may know the liability upon them.

BRITISH FUNDS, &c.

Rate.	Name.	Price.
2¾	2¾ p.c.'s (Childers') Red.. 1905	105½
3	Local Loans Stk. 1912	112½
8	Metro. Police Deb. Stk. 1920	105½
—	Red Sea Ind. Tel. Ann. 1908	8½
4	Canada Gv. "Intcl. Rly." 1903	109½
4	Do. do. .. 1908	113
4	Do. Bonds 1910	117
4	Do. Bonds 1913	119½
3	Egyptian Gov. Gar.	106½
3	Mauritius Ins. Stk. 1940	115
4	Turkish Guar. 1855	109
[illegible]	Bank of Ireland Stk.	392½
3½	India Rupee Paper	62½
3½	Do. 1854-5	63½
3	Do. 1896-7 1916	57½
3½	Isle of Man Deb.	104
3	Do. Deb. Stk... 1919-29	103

CORPORATION AND COUNTY STOCKS.

FREE OF STAMP DUTY.

Rate.	Name.	Price.
3½	Metropolitan Con. 1929	119
3	Do. 1941	113
2½	Do. 1920-49	101
2½	L.C.C. Con. Stock 1920	100
3½	Comm. of Sewers, Scp., S.F. 1905	105
3½	Corp. of Lond. Bds...1897-1902	100½
3	Do. 1897-1912	103
3½	Do, Debs. Scp. .... S.F. 1916	106
2½	Do., Deb. Stk. Scrip .. 1927-57	100
3	Barnsley 1916-46	105
3	Barry 1914-46	101
3	Bath 1909-34	104
3	Batley 1914-44	101½
3½	Birmingham 1945	124
3	Do. 1947	112
2½	Do. 1926	99
3	Blackburn 1930	107
3	Bournemouth 1913-33	104
3½	Bradford 1945	118
3	Do. Deb. Stock .. 1954	112
3	Brighouse 1916-46	100
3½	Brighton 1946	118½
2½	Do. 1957	98
3	Burton-on-Trent 1913-43	102½
3	Cambridge 1913-43	104
3½	Cardiff 1935	119
3	Do. 1914-54	105
3	Cheltenham 1971	110
3	Chichester 1916-46	101
3½	Croydon	135½
3	Do. 1940	111½
3	Derby 1920-50	107
3	Devon C.C. 1917-33	104½
3½	Dewsbury 1930	111
3	Do. 1930	105
3	Dorset County 1922-32	107
3	Douglas (I. of Man) 1926	101
3	Dover 1913-43	102½
3½	Dublin 1944	113½
3	Eastbourne 1920-40	105
3	Edinburgh 1924	108
2½	Do. 1927	98
2½	Exeter 1917-57	96
3	Glamorgan County 1914-34	104
3½	Glasgow 1914	110½
3	Do. 1921	106½
2½	Do. 1925-40	99
3	Gloster 1915-55	103
3	Grimsby 1913-45	103½
3	Hampshire County 1914-34	105½
3	Hanley 1913-43	105
3	Harrogate 1914-34	103
3	Hastings 1915-54	105
2½	Hertfordshire C.C. 1916-36	99
3	Heston & Isleworth U.D.C. 1915-35	101
3	Huddersfield 1934	107
3½	Hull (1st iss.)	131½
3	Inverness 1914-44	102
3	Ipswich 1952	111
3	Lancaster 1919-55	104
2½	Leeds 1927	98
3½	Leicester 1934	115½
3	Lincoln 1919	104
3½	Liverpool	134

Corporation, &c. (*continued*) :—

Rate.	Name.	Price.
3	Manchester 1941	110
3	Mansfield 1915-45	100
3½	Middlesbro' 1909	105½
3½	Do. 1911-13	105
3	Do. 1915	104
3	Middlesex C.C. 1913-35	106
3½	Newcastle 1936	118½
3½	Do. Irred.	129½
2½	Do. 1915-36	101
3	Newcastle-under-Lyme.. 1909-44	101
3	Newport (Mon.) 1915-53	104½
3	Norwich 1952	112½
3	Nottingham	116
3	Oxford 1951	111
3	Penzance 1916-46	102½
3	Plymouth 1942	110
3	Pontypridd U.D.C. 1916-46	99
3	Poole 1915-45	102½
3½	Portsmouth........1916 24 & 27	112
3	Do. 1913-33	106½
3	Ramsey 1920-40	100
3	Ramsgate 1915-55	102
3	Reading	133
3	Do. 1962	109
3½	Rhyl U.D.C. 1953	110
3	Richmond (Surrey) 1942	106½
3	River Wear Debt Certs.	101
3	St. Helen's 1915-55	103
3	Scarbro' 1915-50	103
2½	Sheffield 1925-57	96
3	Shipley U.D.C. 1915-35	101
3	Somerset Co. 1923-33	107
3	South Shields 1915-45	104
2½	Southampton 1915-45	102
3	Southend-on-Sea 1916-46	102
3	Staffs C.C. 1915-35	105
3	Stockport 1914-54	104
3	Stockton 1932	104
3	Do. 1915-35	103
3	Surrey Co. 1922-32	106½
3½	Swansea	132
3	Do. 1955	106
3	Taunton 1918-3-9-43	102
3	Tees Conserv. Deb. Stk. 1947	101
3	Thames Conserv. "A" Deb. Stk. 1954	103½
3	Do. "B" Deb. Stk. 1954	103½
3	Torquay 1913-43	102½
3	Tunbridge Wells 1931	105
3	Tynemouth 1913	101
3	Wakefield 1929	103
3	Walsall 1932	108
3	West Bromwich 1930	108½
3½	West Ham 1929	112
3	Do. 1915	107
3	West Sussex C.C. 1913-35	106
3	Weston-s.-Mare Lcl Bd. 1914-44	101
3	Weymouth & Melc. Regis 1918	101
3	Widnes 1915-55	102
3	Wigan 1921	108
3	Windsor 1918-55	102½
3½	Wisbech 1947	113½
3½	Wolverhampton 1932	118½
3	Do. 1924-54	107
3	York 1916-41	107

SUBJECT TO STAMP DUTY.

Rate.	Name.	Price.
3½	Belfast City & Dis. Watr. 1938	116
3	Do. Red Stk. 1953-6	106
3½	Belfast 1924	104
4	Blackburn Con. Deb. Irred.	141½
3½	Do. do. Irred.	131
3½	Bristol	128½
3½	Burnley 1933	114
2½	Chesterfield Gas & Wtr. 1916-46	98
3½	Douglas Town 1921	105
3	Dover Harb. 1st Deb... 1956	104½
3½	Hull (2nd iss.)	129½
4	Leeds Deb. 1927	124
3½	Do.	115½
3	Do. 1927	107½
3	Leicester 1919-44	105
4	Manchester	149
3	Do. 1928	105
4½	Middlesboro' Mrts. 1908	111
3½	Newark on-Trent .. 1901-41	96
3½	Sheffield 1898-1916	105½
3½	Do. 1925-36	114
3	Do. 1925	104½
3½	Southampton S.F.	106
4½	Stockton Morts. 1908	112
3½	Worcester 1950	111

COLONIAL AND PROVINCIAL GOVERNMENT SECURITIES.

Rate.	Name.	Price.
6	British Columbia 1907	119½
4½	Do. Debs... 1917	111½
3	British Guiana Imgtn. Bds.	99½
5	Canada, "Intercol. Rail," 1903	111½
4	Do. (Bonds) 1904-5-6-8	107
4	Do. Reduced 1910	109
3½	Do. Bnds. 1909-34	105½
4	Do. Loan 1910-35	110
3	Do. Loan 1938	105
6	Cape of G. Hope 1900	—
5	Do. 1900	—
4½	Do. red. by an. draw.	111
4½	Do. 1879	111
4	Do. 1881	109
4	Do. 1917-23	118
4½	Ceylon	110
4	Do.	106½
4½	Fiji Gov. Deb. Sink. Fd.	102½
4	Jamaica Sink. Fd. 1923	103
5	Manitoba Debs 1910	113
5	Do. Ster. Bds. 1888	122
4	Do. Ster. Debs.	106
4	Mauritius, Cons. Debs. 1880	103½
4½	Natal, Sink. Fd. 1919	120
4	Do. do. 1926	116
3	Newfoundland Stg. Bds. 1941	100
3½	Do. do. .. 1947	100
3	Do. do.	88
5	New South Wales 1897-1902	104½
4	Do. 1903-5-8-9-12	105½
5	New Zealand 1914	118
5	Do. Cnsls. 1 p.c. per an. Sink. Fd.	104
3½	Nova Scotia Debs.	104
5	Quebec Prov. 1904-6	110
4½	Do. (drgs.)	104
5	Do. Strlg. Bds. 1912	115
4	Do. Strlg. Bds. 1928	110
4	Do. Strlg. Bds. 1934	108
4	Queensland 1913-15	107
4½	St. Lucia Debs.	100
6	South Australia 1897-1900	103½
6	Do. 1901-1918	118
5	Do. 1911-1920	115½
4	Do. 1899-1916	105
4	Do. 1929	110½
4	Do. 1916	109½
4	Do. 1917-18-24	113
6	Tasmania 1897-1901	104
4	Do. 1908-11, 1913-14-20	108
5	Trinidad Debs., an. drw. 1 p.c.	108
4	Victoria 1899-1901	101½
4½	Do. 1904	105
4	Do. Rail. Loan 1907	105
4	Do. Loans 1908-13	107
4½	West. Austr. 1 p.c. ac. Sink. Fd.	108
4	Do. do.	106

REGISTERED AND INSCRIBED STOCKS.

No stamp duty except for Canada 4 p.c. Reduced (½ per cent.).

Rate.	Name.	Price.
4	Antigua Insc. Stk. Red. 1919-44	109
3½	Barbados Insc. Stk. 1925-42	108
3	British Colum. Insc. Stk. 1941	104
4	British Guiana Insc. 1935	120
4	Canada Stk. Regd. ..1904-5-6-8	107
4	Do. 4 p.c. (late 5 p.c.) Regd. 1910	109
3½	Do. 3½ p.c. Stock Regd. 1909-34	105½
4	Do. Ln. for 4 milln. stg. 1910-35	110
3	Do. Stk. Regd. 1938	105
2½	Do. Insc. 1947	93
4	Cape G. Hope Regd. .. 1917-23	118
4	Do. (Ln. of '83) Insc. .. 1923	119
4	Do. Cons. Stk. Insc. 1916-36	116
3½	Do. Consol. Insc. Stock 1929-49	115
4	Ceylon Insc. Stock 1934	124
3	Do. 1940	107
4	Grenada Insc. Stock.... 1917-42	112
3½	Hong Kong Insc. Stock 1918-43	105½
4	Jamaica Insc. Stock.... 1934	121
—	Do. 1922-44	99
4	Mauritius Inscribed 1937	119
4	Natal Consd. Stk. Insc. 1927	116
4	Do. 1937	120
3½	Do. Inscribed Stock.. 1914-39	107
4	Newfoundland Inscribed 1913-38	108
4	Do. 1935	114
4	Do. Consd. Stk. Ins. 1936	114
4	N. S Wales Stock Insc. 1933	120
3½	Do. 1924	107
3½	Do. 1918	106
[illegible]	D 1935	99

Colonial, &c. (*continued*) :—

Rate.	Name.	Price.
4	N. Zealnd. Con. Stk. Ins. 1929	116
3½	Do. 1940	108
3	Do. Inscribed.... 1945	99
3	Quebec (Prov.) Ins. Stk. 1937	95
4	Queensland Stock Insc. 1915-24	111
3½	Do. 1921-4-30	105
3½	Do. 1945	109
3	Do. 1922-47	99
4	St. Lucia Insc. Stock .. 1919-44	112
4	S. Austrln. (1882-7) Reg. 1916-36	113
3½	Do. In. Stk. Reg. 1939	110
3	Do. 1916-26	100
3/	Do. 1916	100
3½	Tasmanian Insc. Stock.. 1920-40	109
4	Do. 1920-40	116
4	Trinidad Insc. Stock.... 1917-42	110
3	Do. 1922-44	98½
4	Victoria Rly. Loan '81, Inscribed Stock 1907	105
4	Victoria Insc. Stock 1908-13-19	107
4	Victoria (1883) Ins. Stk. 1920	111
3½	Do. Inscribed Stock 1921-3-6	105
4	Do. do. 1911-26	107
4	W. Austral. Insc. Stock 1934	120
4	Do. 1911-31	112
3½	Do. 1915-35	107
3	Do. 1915-35	98
3	Do. 1916-36	98

FOREIGN STOCKS, BONDS, &c.

COUPONS PAYABLE IN LONDON.

Last Div.	Name.	Price.
36/	Argentine Ry. Loan 6 p.c. 1881	90½
15/	Do. 5 p.c. 1884	71
30/	Do. N. Cent. Ry. Ext. 5 p.c. 1887-8-9	69½
30/	Do. 5 p.c. Trsy. Convs. 1887	71
5/4½	Do. 4½ p.c. Interl. Gld. 1888	66
27/	Do. 4½ p.c. Stlg. Extrl. 1888	67
10/6	Do. 3½ p.c. External .. 1889	50
4	Do. 4 p.c. Ry. Guar. Res....	60½
4½	Brazilian 1883	61
4½	Do. Gold 1879	68½
4½	Do. 1888	62
36/	Buenos Ayres 1884	90
6	Do. 1882-3-6	48
6	Bulgarian 1888	95
6	Do. Mort. Bonds 1892	95
4½	Chilian 1883	78
4½	Do. 1886	79
4½	Do. 1887	78
4½	Do. 1889	82½
5	Do. 1892	87
4½	Do. 1893	78
4½	Do. 1895	79
5	Do. 1896	86
7	Chinese Silver 1894	101
6	Do. Gold 1895	106
6	Do. Apl. '95 by dwgs. 1901-15	110½
5	Do. Red. dwgs. in 36 yr. 1896	101½
5	Do. Do. Regis. 1896	100
1½	Colmbn. 1½ to 3 p.c. Ext. Bds. 1896	17½
6	Cordova, Prov. 1886	26
—	Do. Eng. Ass. Certs.	25
—	Do. 6 p.c. 1887-8	26
—	Do. Eng. Ass. Certs.	25
3	Costa Rica "A"	32
2½	Do. "B"	27
3	Danish Gold 1914	98
10/	Ecuador N. Ext. Bds. 4½ p.c. ascn. to 5 p.c.	20
3½	Egypt'n Ins. Stk. lia. Stp. Dty. 1800	102
4½	Do. State Domain 1876	105½
4	Do. D. Sanieh, Red. .. 1905	106½
6	Entre Rios 1886-8	36
6	Do. Fndg. Ln. Bds. 1894-1921	32
6	Do. do. Parana City	27½
15/	Greek 1881	38
15/	Do. 1884	38
12/	Do. Rentes	31
15/	Do. (Piræus-Larissa Ry.)	36
7/6	Do. Fundg. Loan 1893	46
4	Guatemala Extl. Debt	34
6	Hawaiian	102½
4	Hungarian Gold Rentes	102½
3	Do. 1895	91½
6	Italian Irriga. Guar.	112½
	Do. Maremmana	94½
5	Japan 5 p.c.	102
	Mexican (Nat. R. Tehuantp c.)..	96½
	Do. Extrl. 1890	98½

Foreign Stocks, &c. (*continued*):—

Last Div.	Name.	Price.
6	Mexican Extrl. 1893	97
5	Do. Intrnl. Cons. Slvr.	39
5	Do. Intern. Rd. Bds. 2d. Ser.	39
4	Nicaragua 1886	80
3½	Norwegian, red. 1937, or earlier	100
3	Do. do. 1965, do.	99
3½	Do. 3½ p.c. Bnds.	103
1	Paraguay 1p.c. ris. 3p.c. 1886-96	16
5	Russian, 1822, £ Strlg.	149
3	Do. 1859	93
4	Do. (Nicolas Ry.) 1867-9	104
3	Do. Transcauc. Ry. 1882	94
4	Do. Con. R. R. Bd. Ser. I., 1889	104
4	Do. Do. II., 1889	104
4	Do. Do. III., 1891	103½
3½	Do. Bonds	101½
4	Do. Ln. (Dvinsk and Vitbsk)	103
6	Salvador 1889	65½
—	S. Domingo 4s. Unified: 1980	65½
6	San Luis Potosi Stg. 1889	94½
5	San Paulo (Brzl.), Stg. 1888	91½
6	Santa Fé 1883-4	37
—	Do. Eng. Ass. Certs. Dep.	35½
5	Do. 1888	47
—	Do. Eng. Ass. Certs. Dpsit.	46
5	Do. (W. Cnt. Col. Rly.) Mrt.	27
5	Do. & Reconq. Rly. Mort.	27
5	Spanish Quicksilvr Mort. 1870	103
3½	Swedish 1880	103
3	Do. 1888	99
53	Do. Conversion Loan 1894	101
45	Trans. Gov. Loan Red. 1903-40	105
30/	Tucuman (Prov.) 1888	69
	Turkish, Secd. on Egypt. Trib.	104½
3½	Turkish, Egpt. Trib., Ott. Bd., '94	100½
4	Do. Priority 1890	93
1	Do. Convted Series, "A"	65½
5	Do. Customs Ln. 1886	97½
5	Uruguay Bonds 1896	55
3	Venzula New Con. Debt 1881	36

COUPONS PAYABLE ABROAD.

Last Div.	Name.	Price.
7	Argent. Nat. Cedla. Sries, "B"	36
5	Austrian Ster. Rnts., ex 10fl., 1870	85
5	Do. do. do.	86
5	Do. Paper do. 1870	84
5	Do. do. do.	86
4	Do. Gld Rentes 1876	103
2½	Belgian exchange 25 fr.	92
3	Do. do.	101
3½	Danish Int., 1887, Rd. 1896	97½
3½	Do. '87, Red. by pur. or draw. fr. Dec., 1900	98½
2½	Dutch Certs. ex 12 gldrs.	87
3	Do. Bonds	99
3	Do. Insc. Stk.	98
3½	French Rentes	105½
3	Do. 1878, '81-4., Red.	101
3	German Imp. Ln. 1891	97
3	Do. do. 1892-3	97
3	Do. do. 1890-4	96
5	Japan Cons. Ln., '92, 3, & 5, Red.	47
36/9	Prussian Consols	102
3	" Cons. Stg. Ln. 1891	97
4	Rumanian Bds. 1890	—
4	Do. do. 1891	—
4	Utd. States, 1877, Red. 1907	116
4	Do. 1895, 30 yrs.	129
3½	Do. Maschsetts Gl. 1935	113½
3½	Do. Gold Bonds 1923	110½
2	Virginia Cpn. Bds., 3 p.c. from July, 1901	72

BRITISH RAILWAYS.

ORD. SHARES AND STOCKS.

Last Div.	Name.	Price.
10	Barry, Ord.	280½
4	Do. Prefd.	127
6	Do. Defd.	152½
5½	Caledonian, Ord.	158
3	Do. Prefd.	101
.	Do. Defd. Ord., No. 1	5
	Cambrian, Ord	6½
—	Do. Coast Cons.	6½
32/	Cardiff Ry. Pref. Ord.	117
3/	Central Lond. £10 Ord. Sh.	10½
2/9½	Do. do. £6 paid	6½
3½d.	Do. Pref. Half-Shares	1½
1/6	Do. Def. do.	5
1½	City and S. London	68
—	East London, Cons.	7
2½	Furness	66½
—	Glasgow and S. West. Pfd.	85
—	Do. do. Dfd.	66
—	Great Central, Ord. 1894	41
32/6	Do. London Exten.	77
3½	Great N. of Scotland	124
4	Great Northern, Prefd.	119
—	Do. Consolidated "A"	51
—	Do. do. "B"	191½
2	Highland	85½
4	Isle of Wight, Prefd.	120½
3	Do. Defd.	84½
—	Lancs. Derbys. and E. Cst.	
8½	L. Brighton and S. C. Ord.	186
37/11½	Do. New all pd.	186
6	Do. Prefd. Ord.	196½
20/	Do. Contgt. Rights Certs.	20½
5½	Lond. and S. Western Ord.	227½
4	Do. Preferred	135
6½	Lond., Tilb., and Southend	132½
—	Mersey, £20 shares	1
—	Metropolitan, New Ord.	129
2½	Do. Surplus Lands	96
4	North Cornwall, 4 p.c. Pref.	106½
7/6	Do. Deferred	27½
7½	North London	227½
4½	North Staffordshire	131

British Railways (*continued*):—

Last Div.	Name.	Price.
1/6	Plymouth, Devenport, and S. W. Junc. £10	9
3/	Port Talbot £10 Shares	8½
9d.	Rhondda Swns. B. £10 Sh.	5
10	Rhymney, Cons.	270½
4	Do. Prefd.	125
—	Do. Defd.	148½
6½	Scarboro', Bridlington Junc.	47½
6½	South Eastern, Ord	152
6	Do. Pref.	193
3½	Taff Vale	83
25/	Vale of Glamorgan	129½
2/2½	Waterloo & City £10 shares	14

LEASED AT FIXED RENTALS.

Last Div.	Name.	Price.
4	Birkenhead	149
5.10.0	East Lincnshire	215
5½	Hamsmith. & City Ord.	192½
4½	Lond. and Blackwll.	163½
4½	Do. £10 4½ p. c. Pref.	163½
56/6	Lond. & Green. Ord.	102
5	Do. 5 p. c. Pref.	180½
5	Nor. and Eastn. £50 Ord.	90
6	Do.	107
3½	N. Cornwall 3½ p. c. Stk.	128½
4⅗	Nott. & Granthm. R. & C.	148
3½	Portptk. & Wigtn. Guar. Stk.	126
9	Vict. Stn. & Pimlico Ord.	317½
4½	Do. 4½ p. c. Pref.	164
4/	West Lond. £20 Ord. Shs.	14½
4⅘	Weymouth & Portld.	160½

DEBENTURE STOCKS.

Last Div.	Name.	Price.
4	Alexandra Dks. & Ry.	132½
3	Barry, Cons.	109
4	Brecon & Mrthyr, New A	127½
4	Do. New B	107
4	Caledonian	153
4	Cambrian "A"	132½
4	Do. "B"	130½
4	Do. "C"	126½
4	Do. "D"	107½
3	Cardiff Rly.	105
4	City and S. Lond.	139
3½	Cleator & Working Junc.	118½
3	Devon & Som. "A"	105½
26/8	Do. "B" 4 p. c.	36
—	Do. "C" 4 p. c.	10
4	E. Lond. and Ch. 4 p. c. A	137
6/	Do. 2nd B	67½
—	Do. 3rd Ch. 4 p. c.	19½
—	Do. 4th do.	9½
3½	Do. 1st (3½ p. c.)	128½
2½	Do. 2½ p.c. (Whitech. Exn)	88
4	Forth Bridge	146
4	Furness	143
4	Glasgow and S. Western	151
5	Gt. Central	—
4½	Do.	159½
4	Gt. Eastern	148½
4	Gt. N. of Scotland	148½
3	Gt. Northern	115
4	Gt. Western	153½
4½	Do.	161½
4½	Do.	170½
5	Do.	190
2½	Do.	100
4	Highland	143½
3	Hull and Barnsley	106
3	Do. 2nd (3-4 p. c)	124
4	Isle of Wight	144½
3	Do. Cent. "A"	92½
4½	Do. "B"	115½
4	Do. "C"	82½
3	Lancs. & Yorkshire	115
4	Lancs. Derbys. & E. Cst.	123½
4	Lpool St. Hlen's & S. Lancs.	126
4½	Ldn. and Blackwall	159
4	Ldn. and Greenwich	148½
4	Lond., Brighton, &c.	151
4½	Do.	169
4½	Lond., Chath., &c., Arb.	159
4½	Do. "B"	158½
4	Do.	140
4	Do. 1883	139
3	Do.	107
3	Lond. & N. Western	117
3	Lond. & S. Westn. "A"	116
3	Do. Consld.	116
4	Lond., Til., & Southend	149½
—	Mersey, 5 p. c. (Act, 1866)	65
4	Metropolitan	148½
4½	Do.	164½
3½	Do.	129½
6	Met. District	209½
4	Do.	139
3	Midland	116½
4½	Mid-Wales "A"	137½
4	Neath & Brecon 1st	129
4	Do. "A 1"	119½
3	North British	112½
3	Do. 1893	111½
3½	N. Cornwall, Launcstn., &c.	128½

Debenture Stocks (*continued*):—

Last Div.	Name.	Price.
4	North Eastern	115
4½	North London	167
3	N. Staffordshire	114
4	Plym. Devpt. & S. W. Jn.	141½
4	Rhondda and Swan. Bay	130½
4	Rhymney	147½
4	South-Eastern	151½
5	Do.	188½
3½	Do.	130
3	Do.	116
3	Taff Vale	111
4	Tottenham & For. Gate	146
3	Vale of Glamorgan	105½
3	West Highld. (Gtd. by N. B.)	110½
4	Wrexham, Mold, &c. "A"	115½
4	Do. "B"	102½
4	Do. "C"	97½

GUARANTEED SHARES AND STOCKS.

Last Div.	Name.	Price.
4	Caledonian	150½
4	Do.	149
4	Forth Bridge	146
4	Furness 1881	137½
4	Glasgow & S. Western	148
4	Do. St. Enoch, Rent	148
6	Gt. Central	202
4½	Do. 1st Pref.	153½
3½	Do. Pref.	106
5	Do. Irred. S. Y. Rent	166½
4½	Do. do.	140½
4	Gt. Eastern, Rent	147
5	Do. Metropolitan	182½
4	Do.	147
4	Gt. N. of Scotland	141
4	Gt. Northern	148
5	Gt. Western, Rent	185½
5	Do. Cons.	184½
4	Lancs. & Yorkshire	148
5	L., Brighton & S. C.	183½
3½	L., Chat. & D. (Shrtlds.)	110½
4	L. & North Western	150
4	L. & South Western 1881	149
4½	Met. District, Ealing Rent	152
4½	Do. Fulham Rent	152
4	Do. Midland Rent	143½
4	Do. Mid. & Dist. Guar.	133½
4	Midland, Rent	149½
4	Do. Cons.	149½
3	Mid. & G. N. Jt., "A" Rnt.	109½
3	N. British, Lien	108
4	Do. Cons. Pref. No. 1	144
3	N. Cornwall, Wadebrge. Gu.	107
4	N. Eastern	148
5	N. Staff. Trent & M. £20 Shs.	36½
3½	Nott. Suburban Ord.	126½
20/6	S. E. Perp. Ann.	36½
4½	Do. 4½ p.c.	165½
3½	S. Yorks. Junc. Ord.	118½
4½	W. Cornwall (G. W., Br., Ex., & S. Dev. Joint Rent	163½
3	W. Highl. Ord. Stk. (Gua., N. B.)	106½

PREFERENCE SHARES AND STOCKS.

DIVIDENDS CONTINGENT ON PROFIT OF YEAR.

Last Div.	Name	Price.
4½	Alexandra Dks. & Ry. "A"	128½
5	Barry (First)	169½
4	Do. Consolidated	139½
4	Caledonian Cons., No. 1	147½
4	Do. do. No. 2	147
5	Do. do. 1878	181½
4	Do. Pref. 1884	146
4	Do. do. 1887 (Conv.)	155
—	Cambrian, No. 1 4 p. c. Pref.	74½
—	Do. No. 2 do.	39½
—	Do. No. 3 do.	19
—	Do. No. 4 do.	10
5	City & S. Lond. £10 shares	15½
—	Do. New	14
4	Furness, Cons. 1881	134½
4	Do. "A" 1881	131½
4	Do. "B" 1883	129½
4	Glasgow & S. Western	147
4	Do. No. 2	146
4	Do. 1888	144½
4	Do. 1891	143½
5	Gt. Central	166
4	Do.	134½
5	Do. Conv. 1872	155½
5	Do. do. 1874	154½
5	Do. do. 1876	154½
5	Do. do. 1879	153½
5	Do. do. 1881	152½
4	Do. 1889	115½
4	Do. 1891	109½
5	Do. 1894	113½
4	Gt. Eastern, Cons.	144
4	Do. 1886	143
4	Do. 1881	143
4	Do. 1884	143

Preference Shares, &c. (*continued*):—

Last Div.	Name.	Price.
4	Gt. Eastern, Cons. 1887	[illegible]
4	Do. 1888	[illegible]
3½	Do. 1890	[illegible]
3½	Do. 1893	[illegible]
—	Do. (Int. fr. Jan '99) 1893	[illegible]
4	Gt. North Scotland "A"	[illegible]
4	Do. "B"	[illegible]
4	Gt. Northern, Cons.	[illegible]
3	Do. 1896	[illegible]
5	Gt. Western Cons.	[illegible]
36/11	Hull & Barnsley Red. at 115	[illegible]
4	Isle of Wight	[illegible]
3	Lancs. & Yorkshire, Cons.	[illegible]
2/2½	Lanc. Drby & E. C. 5 p.c. £10	[illegible]
—	Do. 5 p.c. and £10	
5	Lond., Bright., &c., Cons.	[illegible]
5	Do. and Cons.	[illegible]
4½	Lond., Chat. & Dov. Arbitr.	[illegible]
20/	Do. 2nd Pref. 4½ p.c.	[illegible]
4	Lond. & N. Western	[illegible]
4	Lond. & S. Western 1881	[illegible]
4	Do. 1884	[illegible]
3½	Do.	[illegible]
4	Lond., Tilbury & Southend	[illegible]
4	Do. Cons., 1887	[illegible]
4	Do 1891	[illegible]
—	Mersey, 5 p.c. Perp.	—
4	Metropolitan, Perp.	[illegible]
4	Do. 1889	[illegible]
4	Do. Irred.	[illegible]
4	Do. 1887	[illegible]
4	Do. New	[illegible]
4½	Do.	[illegible]
3½	Do.	[illegible]
3	Do. Guar.	[illegible]
2½	Metrop. Dist. Extn 5 p.c.	[illegible]
4	Midland, Cons. Perpetual	[illegible]
4	N. British Cons., No. 2	[illegible]
4½	Do. Edin. & Glasgow	[illegible]
5	Do. 1865	[illegible]
5	Do. Conv. 1874	[illegible]
4½	Do. 1875	[illegible]
4½	Do. Conv. 1875	[illegible]
5	Do. do. 1879	[illegible]
4	Do. do. 1884	[illegible]
4	Do. do. 1888	[illegible]
4	Do. do. 1890	[illegible]
4	Do. do. 1892	[illegible]
4	N. Eastern	[illegible]
4½	N. Lond., Cons. 1866	[illegible]
4½	Do. 2nd Cons. 1875	[illegible]
3	N. Staffordshire	[illegible]
4½	Plym. Devpt. & S. W. Junc.	[illegible]
1/5	Port Talbot, &c., 4 p.c. £10 Shares, 4 paid	
5/	Rhondda & Swansea Bay, 5 p.c. £10 Shares	[illegible]
4	Rhymney, Cons.	[illegible]
4½	S. Eastern, Cons.	[illegible]
5	Do. do.	[illegible]
4	Do. Vested Cos'.	[illegible]
4	Do. 1891	[illegible]
3½	Do. 1893	[illegible]
2	Do. 3 p.c. after July 1900	[illegible]
4	Taff Vale	[illegible]

INDIAN RAILWAYS.

Last Div.	Name.	Paid.
3½	Assam Bengal, Ld., (3½ p.c. till June 30, then 3 p.c.)	100
4/	Barsi Light, Ld., £10 Shs.	10
6	Bengal and N. West., Ld.	100
4/	Do. £10 Shares	10
3/6	Do. 3½ p.c. Cum. Pf. Shs.	10
6½d.	Do.	4
2/3½	Bengal Central, Ld., £10 (3½ p.c. + ½th net earn)	5
3	Bengal Dooars, Ld.	100
4	Bengal Nagpr., Lim. (gua. 4 p.c. + 4th sp. pfts.)	100
7½	Bombay, Baroda, and C. I. (gua. 5 p.c.)	100
36/1	Burma, Ld. (gua. 2½ p.c. and ½ p.c. add. till 1901)	100
1/7	Do. £10 Shares	[illegible]
4	Delhi Umb. Kalka, Ld., Gua. 3½ p.c. + net earn.	100
4	Do. Deb. Stk., 1890 (1916)	100
9/10	Eastn. Bengal, "A" An. 1957	—
9/	Do. "B" 1957	—
4	Do. Gua. Deb. Stock	100
9/7½	East Ind. Ann. "A" (1953)	—
8/4½	Do. "C"	—
8/11½	Do. "B"	—
6⅟₁₆	Do. Def. Ann. Cap. (gua. 4 p.c. + ½th sp. pfts.)	—
115/9	East Ind. Def. Ann. "D"	—
4½	East Ind. Irred. Stock	100
5	Gt. Indian Penin., Gua. 5 p.c. + ½ surplus profits	100
4	Do. Irred. 4 p.c. Deb. St.	100
4	Indian Mid., Ld. (gua. 4 p.c. + ½th surplus pfts.)	100
51/	Madras Guar. + ½ sp. pfts.	100
48/6	Do. do.	[illegible]
46/	Do. do.	[illegible]
4	Nilgiri, Ld., 1st Deb. Stk.	100
4	Oude & Rohil. Db. Stk. Rd.	100
5⅞	Rohil. and Kumaon, Ld.	100
9/11	Scinde, Punj., and Delhi, "A" Ann., 1958	—
9/1	Do. "B" do.	—

Indian Railways (*continued*):—

Last Div.	NAME.	Paid.	Price.
4	South Behar, Ld., £10 shs.	100	100
3½	Do. Deb. Stk. Red.	100	103
4½	South Ind., Gu. Deb. Stk.	100	166½
5	South Indian, Ld. (gua. 3 p.c., and ½ spls. profits)	100	122½
5	Sthn. Mahratta, Ld. (3½ p.c. & ¼th net earnings)	100	118
4	Do. Deb. Stk. Red.	100	124
3½	Southern Punjab, Ld....	100	112
3½	Do. Deb. Stk. Red.	—	107
5	Nizam's Gua. State, Ld. [†	100	114½
4	Do. Mort. Deb., 1936	100	110
4	Do. do. Reg.	100	108
17/3½	Nizam's Gua. State, Ld., 3½ p.c. Mt. Deb. bearer....	—	95½
17/3½	Do. Reg. do. ..	—	94½
5	W. of India Portgese., Ld.	100	68½
5	Do. Deb. Stk., Red	100	98

RAILWAYS.—BRITISH POSSESSIONS.

Last Div.	NAME.	Paid.	Price.
5	Atlantic & N.W. Gua. 1 Mt. Bds., 1937	100	127
5/3	Buff. & L. Huron Ord. Sh.	10	13½
5½	Do. 1st Mt. Perp. Bds. 1879	100	141½
5½	Do. 2nd Mt. Perp. Bds.	100	141½
—	Calgary & Edmon. 6 p.c. 1st Mt. Stg. Bds. Red..	100	74½
5	Canada Cent. 1st Mt. Bds. Red.	100	105
4	Can. Pacific Pref. Stk.....	100	101
5	Do. Strl. 1st Mt. Deb. Bds. 1915	100	118
3½	Do. Ld. Grnt. Bds., 1938..	100	103
3½	Do. Ld. Grnt. Ins. Stk. ..	100	103
4	Do. Perp. Cons. Deb. Stk.	100	115
5	Do. Algoma Bch. 1st Mt. Bds., 1937	100	122
2	Demerara, Original Stock	100	49
7	Do. Perp. Pref. Stk.....	100	157½
9½d.	Do. 4 p.c. Cum. Ext. Pref. £10 Shs.	4	6½
—	Dominion Atlntc. Ord. Stk.	100	35½
25/	Do. 5 p.c. Pref. Stk.....	100	101
4	Do. 1st. Deb. Stk.......	100	110
4	Do. 2nd do. Red.	100	100
—	EmuBay&Mt. Bischoff, Ld.	5	4½
4½	Do. Irred. Deb. Stk....	100	93
nil.	Gd. Trunk of Canada, Stk.	100	8
6	Do. 2nd. Equip. Mt. Bds.	100	131½
5	Do. Perp. Deb. Stk... ...	100	138½
5	Do. Gt. Westn. Deb. Stk.	100	129½
5	Do. Nthn. of Can. 1st Mt. Bds., 1902	100	105
4	Do. do. Deb. Stk	100	103
5	Do. G. T. Geor. Bay & L. Erie 1 Mt., 1903	100	104
5	Do. Mid. of Can. Stl. 1st Mt. (Mid. Sec.) 1908....	100	108
5	Do. do. Cons. 1 Mt. Bds. 1912	100	108
5	Do. Mont. & Champ. 1 Mt. Bds., 1902	100	104
	Do. Welln., Grey & Brce. 7 p.c. Bds. 1 Mt.	100	111
4	Jamaica 1st Mtg. Bds. Red.	—	104
—	Manitoba & N. W., 6 p.c. 1st Mt. Bds., Red......	100	—
—	Do. Ldn. Bdhldrs. Certs.	—	—
5	Manitoba S. W. Col. 1 Mt. Bd., 1934 $1,000 price %	—	120
	Mid. of W. Aust. Ld. 6 p.c. 1 Mt. Dbs., Red.	100	25
4	Do. Deb. Bds., Red.	100	103
4	Nakusp & Slocan Bds., 1918	100	106
3	Natal Zululand Ld. Debs.,	100	79½
5	N. Brunswick 1st Mt. Stg. Bds., 1934	100	122
4	Do. Perp. Cons. Deb. Stk.	100	114
—	N. Zealand Mid., Ld., 5 p.c 1st Mt. Debs...........	100	35
6	Ontario & Queb. Cap. Stk.	$100	157½
5	Do. Perm. Deb. Stk......	100	145½
—	Qu'Appelle, L. Lake & Sask. 6 p.c. 1 Mt. Bds. Red.	100	43½
	Queb. & L. S. John, 1st Mt. Bds., 1909	100	25½
	Quebec Cent., Prior Ln. Bds., 1908	100	107
1½	Do. 5 p.c. Inc. Bds.	100	40
4	St. Lawr. & Ott. Stl. 1st Mt.	100	113
4	Shuswap & Okan., 1st Mt. Deb. Bds., 1915	100	76
5	Temiscouata, 5 p.c. Stl. 1st Deb. Bds., Red.........	100	9½
5	Do. (S. Franc. Brch.) 5 p.c. Stl. 1 Mt. Db. Bds., 1910	100	10
4	Toronto, Grey & B. 1st Mt.	100	113
1/2½	Well. & Mana. £5 Shs. ..	1	1
5	Do. Debs., 1908........	100	110
5	Do. 2nd Debs., 1908....	100	109
5	Do. 3rd do., 1908	100	108
6	Atlan. & St. Law. Shs., 6 p.c.	100	167
5	Gd. Trunk Mt. Bds., 1934	100	116½
5	Michigan Air Line, 5 p.c. 1st Mt. Bds., 1902......	100	104
4	Minneap., S. P. & Slt. Ste. Mar, 1st M. Bds., 1938	$1000	97

AMERICAN RAILROAD STOCKS AND SHARES.

Last Div.	NAME.	Paid.	Price.
6/	Alab. Gt. Sthn. A 6 p.c. Pref.	10/.	9
—	Do. do "B" Ord. ..	10/.	2
—	Alabma. N. Orl.-Tex. &c., "A" Pref.	10/.	⅜
—	Do. "B" Def.	10/.	⅛
5½	Atlant. First Lsd. Ls. Rtl. Trust..................	Stk.	98½
$2	Baltimore & Ohio Com. ..	$100	17
—	Baltimore Ohio S.W. Pref.	$100	7
—	Chesap. & Ohio Com.	$100	22¾
—	Chic. Gt. West. 5 p.c. Pref. Stock "A"............	$100	32½
—	Do. do. Scrip. In.......	—	30½
8/3	Do. 4 p.c. Deb. Stk.......	$100	70
4	Do. Interest in Scrip	$100	67½
$4	Chic. Junc. Rl. & Un. Stk. Yds. Com.	$100	116½
$1½	Do. 6 p.c. Cum. Pref.	$100	117½
$3½	Chic. Mil. & St. P. Pref...	$100	150
7	Cleve. & Pittsburgh......	$10	86½
$1½	Clev., Cincin., Chic., & St. Louis Com.	$100	—
—	Erie 4 p.c. Non-Cum. 1st Pf.	—	40¾
—	Do. 4 p.c. do. 2nd Pf.	—	20
—	Gt. Northern Pref.	$100	155
$2½	Illinois Cen. Lsd. Lines ..	$100	99
—	Kansas City, Pitts & G. ..	$100	24
$3	L. Shore & Mich. Sth. C.	$100	197½
—	Mex. Cen. Ltd. Com.	$100	6
—	Miss. Kan. & Tex. Pref...	$100	37½
2½	N.Y., Pen. & O. 1st Mt. Tst. Ltd., Ord.	—	50
4	Do. 1st Mort. Deb. Stk...	$100	93½
2	North Pennsylvania	$50	—
—	Northn. Pacific, Com.....	$100	25½
1¾	Pitts. F. Wayne & Chic...	$100	176
—	Reading 1st Pref.	$50	23½
—	Do. 2nd Pref.	$50	12½
—	S. Louis & S. Fran. Com.	$100	7
—	Do. 2nd Pref.	$100	26½
6	St. Louis Bridge 1st Pref..	$100	107
3	Do. 2nd Pref.	$100	50
6	Tunnel Rail. of St. Louis	$100	107
$1½	St. Paul, Min. and Man...	$100	137
—	Southern, Com.	$100	9
—	Wabash, Common........	$100	7

AMERICAN RAILROAD BONDS. CURRENCY.

Last Div.	NAME.	Price.
7	Albany & Susq. 1 Con. Mrt. 1906	122½
7	Allegheny Val. 1 Mt....... 1910	127½
5	Burling., Cedar Rap. & N. 1 Mt. 1906	109½
5	Canada Southern 1 Mt..... 1908	111
5	Chic. & N. West. Sk. Fd. Db. 1933	120½
5	Do. Deb. Coupon 1921	115½
6	Chicago & Tomah 1905	112½
5	Chic. Burl. & Q. Skg. Fd. 1901	102½
4	Do. Nebraska Ext....... —	102
6	Chic., Mil., & S. Pl., 1 Mt. S.W. Div.............. 1909	117½
7	Do. (S. Paul Div.) 1 Mt. 1902	132½
5	Do. (La Cross & D. 1919	112½
7	Do. 1 Mt. (Hast. & Dak.) 1910	132
5	Do. Chic. & Mis. Riv. 1 Mt. 1926	112½
5	Chic., Rock Is. and Pac. 1 Mt. Ext. 1934	108
6	Det., G. Haven & Mil. Equip 1918	110
6	Do. do. Cons. Mt. 1918	104½
6	Ill. Cent., 1 Mt., Chic. & S. 1898	—
7	Indianap. & Vin., 1 Mt. .. 1908	125
6	Do. do. 2 Mt. .. 1900	104½
6	Lehigh Val., Cons. Mt..... 1923	112½
—	Mexic. Cent., Ln. 2 Cons. Inc. —	6
7	N.Y. Cent. & H.R. Mt. Bonds 1903	119½
5	Do. Deb. 1904	109½
6	Penns. Cons. S. F M. 1905	119½
4	West Shore, 1 Mt. 2361	110

DITTO—GOLD.

Last Div.	NAME.	Price.
6	Alabama Gt. Sthn. 1 Mt. .. 1908	112
5	Do. Mid. 1 1928	96
4	Allegheny Val. Gen. Mt. .. 1942	108
4	Atch., Top., & S. Fé Gn. Mt. 1995	95
3	Do. Adj. Mt............. 1995	63½
5	Do. Equipt. Tmst. ...... —	104½
5	Atlantic & Dan. 1 Mt...... 1950	—
5	Baltimore & Ohio.......... 1925	100
5	Do. Speyer's Tst. Recpts. 1925	100
5	Do. Cons. Mt. 1988	104
4½	Do. 4½ p.c. 1 Mt. Term. 1934	86
4½	Do. Brown Shipley's Dep. Cts. —	86
5	Balt. Belt 5 p.c. 1 Mort..... 1990	90
4½	Balt. & Ohio S.W. 1 Mt. .. 1990	105
4½	Do. 4½ p.c. 1 Cons. Mt. 1893 1993	80
—	Do. Inc. Mt. 5 p.c. Cl. A —	31
—	Do. do. Cl. B —	11
5	Balt. & Ohio S.W. Term 5 p.c. 1942	99½
6	Balt. & Ptmac (Mn. L.) 1 Mt. 1911	127½
6	Do. do. (Tunnel) 1 Mt. 1911	126
4	Beech Creek 1 Mt. 1936	109
5	Do 2 Mort. 1936	116
4	Carthage & Adiron 1 Mt... 1981	109

American Railroad Bonds—Gold (*continued*):—

Last Div.	NAME.	Price.
5	Cent. of Georgia 1 Mort. .. 1945	117½
5	Do. Cons. Mt. 1945	92½
5	Cent. of N. Jrsy. Gn. Mt... 1987	118
6	Central Pacific, 1 Mort. 1898	102½
6	Do. Speyer's Certs....... —	106
5	Do. Land Grant 1900	102
5	Chesap. & Ohio 1st Cons. Mt. 1939	119
4½	Do. Gen. Mt............. 1992	83
6	Chic. & W. Ind. Gen. Mt. Skg. Fd. 1932	120
5	Chic. Mil. & St. Pl. (Chic. & L. Sup.) 1 Mt. 1921	114½
5	Do. Chic. & Pac. W. 1921	119½
5	Do. Wisc. & Minn. 1 Mt. 1921	114½
5	Do. Terminal Mt. 1914	114½
4	Do. General Mt. 1989	108
5	Chic. St. L. & N. Orleans.. 1951	122½
4	Do. 1 Mort. (Memphis) .. 1951	105½
4	Clevel., Cin., Chic. & St. L., 1 Mt. (Cairo)........... 1939	90
4	Do. 1 Mt. (Cinc., Wab., & Mich.) 1991	90
4	Do. 1 Col. Tst. Mt. (S. Louis) 1990	98½
4	Do. General Mt. 1993	84
4½	Clevel. & Mar. Mt. 1935	112
4½	Clevel. & Pittsburgh 1942	122½
4½	Do. Series B. 1942	124½
—	Colorado Mid. 1 Mt. 1936	68
—	Do. Bdhrs.' Comm. Certs. —	68
4	Dnvr. & R. Gde. 1 Cons. Mt. 1936	96
5	Do. Imp. Mort........... 1928	93
4	Detroit & Mack. 1 Lien 1995	92½
5	E. Tennes., Virg., & Grgia. Cons. Mt. 1956	114½
5	Elmira, Cort., & Nthn. Mt. 1914	102½
4	Erie 1 Cons. Mt. Pr. Ln. .. 1996	94
3	Do. Gen. Lien 1996	75
6	Galvest., Harrisb., &c., 1 Mt.....	107½
5	Georgia, Car. & N. 1 Mt. .. 1929	96
4½	Gd. Rpds. & Inda. Ex. 1 Mt. 1941	112½
5	Do. 1 Mt. (Muskegon) .. 1926	39½
3½	Illinois Cent. 1 Mt. 1951	104½
4	Do. 1952	107
4	Do. Cairo Bdge. .. 1950	103
4	Do. 1953	105
4	Do. General Mort. .. 1904	102½
—	Kans. City, Pitts. & G. 1 M. 1923	83
3½	L. Shore & Mich. Southern 1997	109
4½	Lehigh Val. N.Y. 1 Mt.... 1940	106
5	Lehigh Val. Term. 1 Mt. .. 1941	112½
5	Long Island 1931	122½
5	Do. Deb.......... 1934	102
5	Do. (N. Shore Bch.) 1 Cons. Mt. 1932	96
6	Louisville & Nash. G. Mt.. 1930	122
6	Do. 2 Mt. Sk. Fd. (S. & N. Alabama.......... 1910	108
6	Do. 1 Mt. N. Orl. & Mb. 1930	122½
5	Do. 1 Mt. Coll. Tst. ... 1931	109
4	Do. Unified 1940	91
4½	Do. Mobile & Montgy. 1 Mt. 1945	105½
4	Manhattan Cons. Mt. 1990	98
4	Mexican Cent. Cons. Mt. .. 1911	67
—	Do. 1 Cons. Inc, ...	16
6	Mexican Nat. 1 Mt......... 1927	108
3	Do. 2 Mt. 6 p.c. Inc. A 1917	58
—	Do. do. B.. 1917	10
3	Do. Matheson's Certs....	—
3	Michig. Cnt. (Battle Ck. & S.) 1 Mt. 1989	88
6	Minneap. & S. L. 1 Mt. Pacific Ext. 1921	120½
5	Do. 1 Consold. 1934	110
4	Minne., Slt. S. M. & A. 1 Mt. 1926	99
5	Minneapolis Westn. 1 Mt... 1911	105½
4	Miss. Kans. & Tex. 1 Mt... 1990	92
4	Do. 2 do. 1990	64
4	Mobile & Birm. Mt. Inc.... 1945	38
5	Do. P. Lien 1945	88
4	Mohawk & Mal. 1 Mt....... 1991	108
5	Montana Cent. 1 Mt....... 1937	111½
5	Nashv., Chattan., & S. L. 1 Cons. Mt................ 1928	104½
5	Nash., Flor., & Shff. Mt... 1937	97
4	N. Y. & Putnam 1 Cons. Mt. 1993	110
5	N. Y., Brooklyn, & Man. B. 1 Cons. Mt.............. 1935	110
4	N. Y. Cent. & Hud. R. Deb. Certs. 1890 1905	107
4	Do. Ext. Debt. Certs.... 1905	107
7	N. Y., L. Erie, & W. 1 Cons. Mt. (Erie) 1920	146
7	Do. 1 Con. Mt. Fd. Coup. 1920	143
5	N. Y., Onto., & W. Cons. 1 Mt........................ 1939	110
4	Do. 4 p.c. Refund. Mt.. 1992	102
5	N. Y. & Rockaway B. 1 Mt. 1927	102½
6	Norfolk & West. Gn. Mt.... 1931	128
6	Do. Imp. & Ext......... 1934	120
4	Do. 1 Cons. Mt........ —	84
6	N. Pacific Gn. 1 Mt. Ld. Gt. 1921	122
4	Do. P. Ln. Rl. & Ld. Gt. —	99
3	Do. Gn. Ln. Rl. & Ld. Gt. —	63
5	Oregon & Calif. 1 Mt....... 1927	82
5	Oregon Rl. & Nav. Col. Tst. —	—
6	Panama Skg. Fd. Subsidy.. 1910	105½
4½	Pennsylvania Rlrd. 1913	115½
4	Do. Equip. Tst. Ser. A.. 1914	104
4	Do. Cons. Mt.......... 1943	115
4½	Penna. Company 1st Mort. 1921	116½
5	Perkiomen 1 Mrt., 2nd ser.. 1918	91½
4½	{ Pitts., C., C., & St. Ls. Con. Mt. G.B., Ser. A } 1940-2	115
4	Do. Cons. Mort., Ser. D.. 1945	105
6	Pittsbgh., Cle., & Toledo .. 1922	107½
4	Reading, Phil., & R. Genl. 1997	86
5	Richmond & Dan. Equip. .. 1909	97½
5	Rio Grande Junc. 1st Mort. 1939	94
4	Rio Grande West 1st Tst. Mt. 1939	86
6	St. Joseph & Gd. Island .. 1925	—
7	S. Louis Bridge 1st Mort .. 1925	137½
5	S. Louis Mchts. Bdge. Term. 1st Mort................ 1930	104½

American Railroad Bonds (*continued*):

Last Div.	NAME.	Price.
4	S. Louis S. West 1st Mort.. 1989	77½
—	Do. 4 p.c. 2nd Mort. Inc. 1989	30
—	S. Louis Term. Cupplus Sta. & Prop. 1st. Mrt. 4½ p.c. 1902-17	102
4½	St. Paul, Minn., & Manit. 1933	110½
6	Do. do. 1933	132½
6	Shamokin, Sunbury, &c. 2 Mt. 1925	109
5	S. & N. Alabama Cons. Mt. 1936	98½
5	Southern 1 Cons. Coup. 1994	94
4	Do. E. Tennes Reorg. Lien .. 1938	98½
6	S. Pacific of Cal. 1 Mt... 1205-12	114
4½	Trml. Assn. of S. Louis 1 Mt. 1939	113½
5	Do. 1 Cons. Mt........... 1944	109
5	Texas & Pac. 1 Mt. 2000	103½
—	Do. 5 p.c. 2 Mt. Income 2000	35½
5	Toledo & Ohio Cent. 1 Mt. West. Div. 1935	105½
4½	Toledo., Walhon., Val., & Ohio 1 Mt. 1931-3	111½
6	Union Pacific 1 Mt. 1896-9	102½
5	Do. Coll. Trust.	—
—	Union Pac., Linc., & Color. 1 Mt. 1918	—
4	United N. Jersey Gen. Mt... 1944	115½
6	Vicksbrg., Shrevept., & Pac. Pr. Ln. Mt. 1915	102½
5	Wabash 1 Mt. 1939	112
4	Wn. Pennsylvania Mt. 1928	109½
5	W. Virga. & Pittsbg. 1 Mt. 1990	88
5	Wheeling & L. Erie 1 Mt. (Wheelg. Div.) 5 p.c. 1928	90½
5	Do. Extd. Imp. Mt 1930	—
—	Do. do. Brown Shipley's Cts..	—
5	Willmar & Sioux Falls 1 Mt. 1938	111

STERLING.

Last Div.	NAME.	Price.
6	Alabama Gt. Sthn. Deb..... 1906	104½
5	Do. Gen. Mort. .. 1927-8	100
5	Alabama, N. Orl., Tex. & Pac. 5 p.c. "A" Dbs... 1910-40	99
55/	Do. do. "B" do. 1910-40	51
—	Do. do. "C" do.	19
—	Allegheny Valley 1910	136
4	Atlantic 1st Leased Line Perp...	98
6	Baltimore and Ohio 1902	108
6	Do. do. 1910	118
5	Do. do. 1877........	97½
—	Do. Morgan's Certs. ..	97½
4½	Do. do. 1933	87½
6	Chicago & Alton Cons. Mt. 1903	111
5	Chic. St. Paul & Kan. City Priority	105
6	Eastn. of Massachusetts.... 1906	117½
5	Illinois Cent. Skg. Fd.	105
5	Do. 1905	108
3½	Do. 1950	100½
4	Do. 1 Mt. 1951	114
3	Do. 1 Mt. 1951	92½
6	Louisville & Nash., M. C. & L. Div., 1 Mt. 1902	104½
7	Do. 1 Mt. (Memphis & O.) 1901	111
47/4	Mexican Nat. "A" Certs. 5 p.c. Non. cum.	47
—	Do. "B" Certs....	10
6	N.Y. & Canada 1 Mt....... 1904	111½
6	N. York Cent. & H.R. Mort. 1903	112
4½	N. York, Penns., & Ohio Pr. Ln. Extd. 1935	—
5	Do. Equip. Tst.	103½
5	Do. 5 p.c. Equip. Tst. (1890)	103½
6	Nrthn. Cent. Cons. Gen. Mt. ..	106
6	Pennsylvania Gen. Mt. 1910	128
6	Do. Cons. Skg. Fd. Mt. 1905	116
3½	Do. Cons. Mt......... 1945	106
6	Phil. & Erie Cons. Mort .. 1920	134½
6	Phil. & Reading Gen. Cons. Mort. 1911	127
6	Pittsbg. & Connells. Cons. 1926	114
—	Do. Morgan's Certs....	114
4	St. Paul., Min., & Manitoba (Pac. Extn.) 1940	98
6	S. & N. Alabama 1903	107½
6	Union Pacific, Omaha Bridge 1896	—
6	Un. N. Jersey & C. Gen. Mt. 1901	108½

FOREIGN RAILWAYS.

Last Div.	NAME.	Paid.	Price.
4/	Alagoas, Ltd., Shs.......	20	6
5	Do. Deb. Stk., Red. ..	100	54½
6	Antofagasta, Ltd., Stk. ..	100	75
4	Do. Perp. Deb. Stk. ..	100	94
—	Arauco, Ld., Ord. Shs. ..	10	¼
—	Do. 10 p.c. Cum. Pref.	10	1½
20/	Argentine Gt. W., Ld.,	20	15
20/	Do. 5 p.c. Cum. Pref. Shs.	20	20½
4	Do. 1 Deb. Stk.	100	104
1/0/0	Argentine N.E., Ltd., 6 p.c. Cum. Pref. Stk. ..	100	11½
—	Do. 5 p.c. Deb. Stk., Red.	100	33½
2/	Arica and Tacna Shs. ..	20	1½
10/	Bahia & San Fcisco., Ld.,	20	11½
6/	Do. Timbo. Bch. Shs.	20	5
12/	Bahia, Blanca, & N.W. Ln. Prf. Cum. 6 p.c. ..	100	58
4	Do. 4 p.c. 1 Deb. Stk., Red.	100	95
6	Barranquilla R. & P., Ld., 6 p.c. 1 Deb. Stk., Red.	100	96

Foreign Railways (*continued*):—

Last Div.	Name.	Paid.	Price.
3/	Bilbao Riv. & Cantabn., Ltd., Ord.	3	6
—	Bolivar, Ltd., Shs.	10	1½
6	Do. 6 p.c. Deb. Stk.	100	96½
—	Brazil Gt. Southn. Ltd., 7 p.c. Cum. Pref.	20	1½
6	Do. Perm. Deb. Stk	100	47½
6½	B. Ayres Gt. Southn., Ld., Ord. Stk.	100	153
5	Do. Pref. Stk.	100	139
4	Do. Deb. Stk.	100	117
30/	B. Ayres & Ensen. Port., Ltd., Ord. Stk.	100	68
5	Do. Cum. 1 Pref. Stk.	100	125
6/0/0	Do. 6p.c.Con. Pref.Stk.	100	109
4	Do. Deb. Stk., Irred.	100	113
10⅘	B. Ayres Northern, Ltd., Ord. Stk.	100	265
12½	Do. Pref. Stk.	100	320
5	Do. 5 p.c. Mt. Deb.Stk., Red.	100	113
3/15/0	B. Ayres & Pac., Ld., 7 p.c. 1 Pref. Stk. (Cum.)	100	101
4	Do. 1 Deb. Stk.	100	103
5/5/0	Do. 4½ p.c. 2 Deb. Stk.	100	91
1	B. Ayres & Rosario, Ltd., Ord. Stk.	100	75
—	Do. New, £20 Shs.	20	22½
7/	Do. 7 p.c. Pref. Shs.	10	17½
7/	Do. Sunchales Ext.	10	15½
4	Do. Deb. Stk., Red.	100	109½
12/	B. Ayres & Val. Trans., Ltd., 7 p.c. Cum. Pref.	20	7
4	Do. 4 p.c. "A" Deb. Stk., Red.	100	72
—	Do. 6 p.c. "B" Deb. Stk., Red.	100	45
6/	B. Ayres Westn. Ld. Ord.	10	11½
3/	Do. Def. Shs.	10	7½
5	Do. 5 p.c. Pref.	10	13½
4	Do. Deb. Stk.	100	111
6	Cent. Arg. Deb. Sk. Rd.	100	160½
4	Do. Deb. Stk. Rd.	100	112
6	Cent. Bahia L. Ord. Stk.	100	45½
6	Do. Deb. Stk., 1934	100	74½
5	Do. Deb. Stk., 1937	100	58
1/6	Cent. Uguy. East. Ext. L. Shs.	10	6
5	Do. Perm. Stk.	100	110
3/	Do. Nthn. Ext. L. Sh.	10	4½
5	Do. Perm. Deb. Stk.	100	106
3	Do. of Montev. Ltd., Ord. Stk.	100	86
6	Do. Perm. Deb. Stk.	100	143
10/	Conde d'Eu, Ltd. Ord.	20	7½
—	Cordba & Rosar., Ltd., 6 p.c. Pref. Shs.	100	48
4	Do. 1 Deb. Stk.	100	95
45/	Do. 6 p.c. Deb. Stk.	100	88
—	Cordba Cent., Ltd., 5 p.c. Cu. 1 Pref. Stk.	100	86
—	Do. 5 p.c. Non-Cum. 2 Pref. Stk.	100	46
5	Do. Deb. Stk.	100	121
—	Costa Rica, Ltd., Shs.	10	4½
8/	Dna. Thrsa. Chris., Ltd., 7 p.c. Pref. Shs.	20	4½
20/	E. Argentine, Ltd.	100	45
6	Do. Deb. Stk.	100	108
2/1	Egyptn. Dlta. Lgt. Rys., Ltd., £10 Pref. Shs.	8	8½
—	Entre Rios, L., Ord. Shs.	5	½
—	Do. Cu. 5 p.c. Pref.	5	3½
6/	Gt. Westn. Brazil, Ltd.,	20	11
6	Do. Perm. Deb. Stk.	100	90½
6	Do. Extn. Deb. Stk.	100	76½
—	Int.-Oceanic Mex., Ltd., 7 p.c. Pref.	10	1½
4	Do. Deb. Stk.	100	88
42/6	Do. 7 p.c. "A" Deb. Sk.	100	69
—	Do. 7 p.c. "B" Deb. Sk.	100	35
5/	La Guaira & Carac.	10	7½
5	Do. 5 p.c. Deb. Sk. Red.	100	100
8/4	Lembg.-Czern.-Jassy	20	25
1/	Lima, Ltd.	20	2½
—	Manila Ltd. 7 p.c. Cu. Pf.	10	½
20/6½	Mexican and Pref. 6 p.c.	100	37
6	Do. Perp. Deb. Stk.	100	145
1/0/0	Mexican Sthrn., Ld., Ord.	100	26
—	Do. 4 p.c. 1 Db. Stk. Rd.	100	85
—	Do. 4 p.c. 2 do.	100	62
—	Mid. Urgy., Ltd.	100	20
5	Do. Deb. Stk.	100	63
12/	Minas & Rio, Ltd.	20	12½
5/2	Namur & Liege	20	12½
11/6	Do. Pref.	20	29
5/	Natal & Na. Cruz, Ld., 7 p.c. Cum Pref.	20	8
—	Nitrate Ltd., Ord.	10	5
—	Do. 7 p.c. Pr. Con. Or.	10	3½
—	Do. Def. Conv. Ord.	10	½
7/	N.-E. Urgy., Ltd., Ord.	10	15
7/	Do. 7 p.c. Pref.	10	15½
—	N.-W. Argentine Ld., 7 p.c. Pref.	10	2½
6	Do. 6 p.c. 1 Deb. Stk.	100	114
—	Do. 2 Deb. Stk.	100	94
—	N.W. Uruguay 6 p.c. 1 Pref. Stk.	100	17
—	Do. 5 p.c. 2 Pref. Stk.	100	7½
6	Do. 6 p.c. Deb. Stk.	100	80½
16/	Ottoman (Sm. Aid.)	20	16
—	Paraguay Cntl., Ld., 5 p.c. Perm. Deb. Stk.	100	11
—	Piræus, Ath., & Pelo.	2.75	1½
5/	Pto. Alegre & N. Hambg. Ld., 7 p.c. Pref. Shs.	20	4½
6	Do. Mt. Deb. Stk. Red.	100	77½
—	Puerto Cabello & Val. Ld.	10	1½
5	Recife & S. Francisco	100	77
14/	R Claro S. Paulo, Ld., Sh.	10	22½
5	Do. Deb. Stk.	100	131
	Royal Sardinian Ord	10	12

Foreign Railways (*continued*):—

Last Div.	Name.	Paid.	Price.
5/	Royal Sardinian Pref.	10	12½
5/	Sambre & Meuse	20	18
3/6	Do. Pref.	10	12½
28/	San Paulo Ld.	20	35
2/9½	Do. New Ord. £10 sh.	6	10½
2/	Do. 5 p.c. Non. Cm. Pref.	10	12½
5½	Do. Deb. Stk.	100	137
5	Do. 5 p.c. Deb. Stk.	100	128
—	S. Fé & Cordova, Gt. Sthn., Ld., Shares	100	55
6	Do. Perp. Deb. Stk.	100	124
3/2½	S. Austrian	20	7½
10/	Sthn. Braz. R. Gde. do Sul, Ld.	20	8½
6	Do. 6 p.c. Deb. Stk.	100	78
4	Swedish Centl., Ld., 4 p.c. Deb. Stk.	100	107
5	Do. Pref.	100	100
1/9	Taltal, Ld.	5	2½
—	Uruguay Nthn., Ld. 7 p.c. Pfd. Stk.	100	8
3½	Do. 5 p.c. Deb. Stk.	100	30
—	Villa Maria & Rufino, Ld., 6 p.c. Pref. Shs.	100	20
4	Do. 4 p.c. 1 Deb. Stk.	100	74
6/0/0	Do. 6 p.c. 2 Deb. Stk.	100	47
5/9	West Flanders	8½	21
5/6	Do. 5½ p.c. Pref.	10	18
3/	Wstn. of Havana, Ld.	10	4½

FOREIGN RAILWAY OBLIGATIONS

Per Cent.	Name.	Price.
6	Alagoas Ld., 6 p.c. Deb., Rd.	80½
—	Alcoy & Gandia, Ld., 5 p.c. Debs., Red.	25
5	Arauco., Ld., 5 p.c. 1st Mt., Rd.	66½
—	Do. 6 p.c. Mt. Deb., Rd.	45½
6	Brazil G. Sthn., L., Mt. Dbs., Rd.	80½
6	Do. Mt. Dbs. 1893, Rd.	48½
5½	Campos & Caran. Dbs., Rd.	77
6	Central Bahia, L., Dbs., Rd.	90½
5½	Conde d'Eu, L., Dbs., Rd.	78
6	Costa Rica, L., 1st Mt. Dbs., Rd.	110
6	Do. 2nd Dbs., Rd.	93
5	Do. Prior Mt. Db., Rd.	104
6	Cucuta Mt. Dbs., Rd.	106
5½	Donna Thrsa. Cris., L., Dbs., Rd.	75
3	Eastn. of France, £20 Dbs., Rd.	19½
4	Egyptn. Delta Light, L., Db., Rd.	100
—	Espito. Santo & Cara. 5 p.c. Stl. Dbs., Rd.	38
4	Gd. Russian Nic., Rd.	102
5	Inter-Oceanic Mex., L., 5 p.c. Pr. Ln. Dbs., Rd.	104
3	Ital. 3 p.c. Bds. A & B, Rd.	57½
—	Ituana 6 p.c. Debs., 1918	74
—	Leopoldina, 6 p.c. Dbs. £50 Bds.,	25
—	Do. do. Comms. Cert.	25
—	Do. 5 p.c. Stg. Dbs. (1888), Rd.	34
—	Do. do. Comm. Certs.	34
—	Do. 5 p.c. Stg. Dbs. (1890), Rd.	25
—	Do. do. Comms. Certs.	25
—	Macahé & Cam. 5 p.c. Dbs., Rd.	35
—	Do. do. Comms. Certs.	35
—	Do. (Cantagallo), 5 p.c., Red.	35
—	Do. do. Comm. Certs.	35
—	Manila Ltd., 6 p.c. Deb., Red.	24
6	Do. Prior Lien Mt., Rd.	106
6	Do. Series "B," Rd.	81
7	Matanzas & Sab., Rd.	101½
6	Minas & Rio, L., 6 p.c. Dbs., Rd.	101
5	Mogyana 5 p.c. Deb. Bds., Rd.	104
5	Moscow-Jaros., Rd.	106½
5½	Natal & Na. Cruz Ltd., 5½ p.c. Debs., Red.	87½
5	Nitrate, Ltd. Mt. Bds., Red.	82½
3	Nthn. France, Red.	19½
4	N. of S. Af. Rep. (Trnsvl.) Gu. Bds. Red.	98
3	Nthn. of Spain £20 Pri. Obs. Red.	9
6	Ottmn. (Smy to A.)(Kujk) Asnt. Debs., Red.	109
6	Ottmn. (Seraik.) Asg. Debs. Red.	109
6	Ottmn. (Seraik.) Non-Asg. D., Rd	109
5	Ottmn. Kuyjk. Ext. Red.	106
5	Ottmn. Serkeuy. Ext. Red.	101½
5	Ottmn. Tireh Ext. 1910	97
5	Ottmn. Debs, 1886, Red.	98
5	Do. 1888, Red. 1935	99
5	Do. 1893, Red. 1935	99
5	Ottmn. of Anlia. Debs., Rd.	93
5	Do. Ser. II.	89
4	Ottomn. Smyr. & Cas. Ext. Bds., Red.	83½
3	Paris, Lyon & Medit. (old sys., £20), Red.	19
3	Paris, Lyon & Medit. (new sys., £20), Red.	19½
50/	Piræus, At. & Pelp., 6 p.c. 1st Mt. Bds., Red.	88½
3	Do. 5 p.c. Mt. Bds., Red.	61½
4	Pretoria-Pietbg., Ltd., Red.	93
7	Puerto Cab. & Val., Ltd., 1st Mt. Debs., Red.	96
—	Rio de Jano. & Nthn., Ltd., 6 p.c. £100 Deb., Red.	25
—	Rio de Jano. (Gr. Para.), 5 p.c. 1st Mt. St. £100 Debs., Red.	25
3	Royal Sardinian, A, Rd. £20	12
3	Royal Sardinian, B., Rd. £20	12

Foreign Rly. Obligations (*continued*):—

Per Cent.	Name.	Price.
5	Ryl. Trns.-Afric. 5 p.c. 1st Mt. £100 Bds., Red.	61
7	Sagua La Grande, B p Rd.	98
4	Sa. Fe & Cor. G.S., Ld. Pr Ln. Bds.	104
5	Sa. Fe, 5 p.c. 2nd Reg. Dbs.	81
3	South Austrian, £20 Red.	15½
3	South Austrian, (Ser. X.)	15½
3	South Italian £20 Obs. (Ser. A to G), Red.	12½
3½	S. W. of Venez. (Barq.), Ltd., 7 p.c. 1st Mt. £100 Debs.	57½
5	Taltal, Ltd., 5 p.c. 1st Ch. Debs., Red.	99
5	Utd. Rwys. Havana, Red.	92½
3	Wtrn. of France, £20 Red.	19
6	Wrn. B. Ayres St. Mt. Debs., 1902	112
6	Wrn. B. Ayres, Reg. Cert.	109
5	Do. Mt. Bds.	122
6	Wtrn. of Havna., Ld. Mt. Dbs., Rd.	100
7	Wrn. Ry. San Paulo Red.	101
—	Wrn. Santa Fé, 7 p.c. Red.	42
4/7	Zafra & Huelva, 3 p.c. Red.	3

BANKS.

Div.	Name.	Paid.	Price.
1/9½	Agra, Ltd.	6	3½
4/2½	Anglo-Argentine, Ltd., £9	7	5½
8½ fls.	Anglo-Austrian	120 f	14
6/	Anglo-Californian, Ltd., £20 Shares	10	11½
4/	Anglo-Egyptian, Ltd., £15	3	6
5/	Anglo-Foreign Bkg., Ltd.	7	8
2/	Anglo-Italian, Ltd.	5	7½
7/6	Bk. of Africa, Ltd., £18¾	6¼	10½
20/	Bk. of Australasia	40	55
10/	Bk. of Brit. Columbia	20	22
25/	Bk. of Brit. N. America	50	66
20/	Bk. of Egypt, Ltd., £25	12½	18
5/	Bk. of Mauritius, Ltd.	10	9½
18/	Bk. of N. S. Wales	20	38½
4 p.c.	Bk. of N. Zland. Gua. Stk.	100	103
6/	Bk. of Roumania, £20 Shs.	6	7½
2/6	Tarapaca & Ldn., Ltd., £10	5	3½
—	Bque. Fse. de l'Afri. du S.	100f	3½
f. 12.50	Bque. Internatle. de Paris	20	24
6/	Brit. Bk. of S. America, Ltd., £20 Shares	10	11
16/	Capital & Cties., L., £50	10	39
16/	Chart. of India, &c.	20	32
10/	City, Ltd., £40 Shares	10	20
18/	Colonial, £100 Shares	30	22
10/	Delhi and London, Ltd.	25	—
5/	German of London, Ltd.	10	10½
25/	Hong-Kong & Shanghai	28½	45
4/	Imperl. of Persia	6½	3½
10/	Imperl. Ottoman, £20 Shs	10	12½
9/	Intrnatl. of Ldn., Ld., £20	15	12
10/	Ionian, Ltd.	25	15
16/	Lloyds, Ltd., £50 Shs.	8	29½
10/	Ldn. & Brazil. Ltd., £20	10	18
44/	Ldn. & County, Ltd., £80	20	100½
9/	Ldn. & Hanseatic, L., £20	10	10½
22/6	Ldn. & Midland, L., £60	12½	53½
8/9	Ldn. & Provin., Ltd., £10	5	22½
39/	Ldn. & Riv. Plate, L., £25	15	53
2/1½	Ldn. & San Fcisco, Ltd.	7	4½
28/	Ldn. & Sth. West., L., £50	20	69
26/	Ldn. & Westmins., L., £100	20	57
3/	Ldn. of Mex. & S. Amer., Ltd., £10 Shs.	6	5½
15/	Ldn. Joint Stk., L., £100	15	34
9/7	Ldn., Paris & Amer., L. £20	16	26
2/4½	Merchant Bkg., L., £9	4	2½
6/3	Metropn, Ltd., £50 Shs.	5	14½
9/	National, Ltd., £30 Shs.	10	19½
4/5	Natl. of Mexico, $100 Shs.	$40	13
1/3	National of N. Z., L., £7½	2½	2½
8/	National S. Afric. Rep.	10	14½
18/10½	National Provcl. of Eng., Ltd., £75 Shs.	10½	51½
21/7½	Do. do. £60 Shs.	12	58
6/6	North Eastn., Ltd., £20 Shs	6	14½
19/	Parr's, Ld., £100 Shs.	20	92
12/6	Prov. of Ireland, L., £100	12½	28½
40/	Stand. of S. Afric., L., £100	25	68
12/6	Union of Australia, L., £75	25	29
4 p.c.	Do. do. Ins. Stk. Dep. 1900	100	103
15/6	Union of Ldn., Ltd., £100	15½	36

BREWERIES AND DISTILLERIES.

Div.	Name.	Paid.	Price.
4½	Albion Prp. 1 Mt. Db. Sk.	100	115
4	All Saints', L., Db. Sk. Rd.	100	99
7	Allsopp, Ltd	100	156
6	Do. Cum. Pref	100	157
4½	Do. Deb. Stk., Red.	100	118
3½	Do. Deb. Stk., Red.	100	102
4½	Alton & Co., L., Db., Rd	100	106
4½	Do. Mt. Bds., 1896	100	105
—	Arnold, Perrett, Ltd.	10	6
6	Do. Cum. Pref.	10	10½
4½	Do. 1 Mt. Db. Stk., Rd.	100	106

Breweries &c. (*continued*):—

Div.	Name.	Paid.	Price.
5½	Arrol, A., & Sons, L., Cum. Pref. Shs.	10	[illegible]
4½	Do. 1 Mt. Db. Stk., Rd.	100	[illegible]
6	Backus, 1 Mt. Db., Red.	100	[illegible]
4	Barclay, Perk., L., Cu. Pf.	10	11½
3½	Do. Mt. Db. Stk., Red.	100	11[illegible]
—	Barnsley, Ltd.	10	11
6	Do. Cum. Pref.	10	13
1/	Barrett's, Ltd	2½	[illegible]
1/3	Do. 5 p.c. Pref.	2½	[illegible]
2/	Bartholomay, Ltd.	10	[illegible]
8	Do. Cum. Pref.	10	9
6	Do. Deb.	100	102½
5	Bass, Ratcliff, Ltd., Cum. Pref. Stk.	100	146½
4½	Do. Mt. Db. Stk., Rd.	100	126
4	Bell, J., L., 1 Mt. D. Stk., R	100	109
2/6	Benskin's, L., Cum. Pref.	5	—
4½	Do. 1 Mt. Db. Stk Red.	100	—
4½	Do. "B" Deb. Sk, Rd.	100	—
7/	Bentley's Yorks., Ltd.	10	11
6	Do. Cum. Pref.	10	13½
4½	Do. Mt. Debs., Red.	100	110
4½	Do. do. 1892, Red.	100	110
—	Bieckert's, Ltd.	20	2
5	Do. Debs., Red.	100	87
—	Birmingham., Ltd., 6 p.c. Cum. Pref.	5	[illegible]
4½	Do. Mt. Debs., Red.	50	40½
5½	Boardman's, Ld., Cm. Pf.	10	[illegible]
4½	Do., Perp. 1 Mt. Db. Sk.	100	104½
15/2	Brain & Co., Ltd.	100	101
4½	Brakspear, L., 1 D. Stk. Rd	100	108
4	Brandon's, L., 1 D. Stk. R.	100	108½
21/	Bristol (Georges) Ltd.	10	46
6	Do. Cum. Pref.	10	18
5	Do. Mt. Db. Sk. 1888 Rd.	100	115½
17/6	Bristol United, Ltd.	10	[illegible]
6	Do. Cum. Pref.	10	[illegible]
4½	Do. Db. Sk. Rd.	100	[illegible]
5½	Buckley's, L., C. Pre-prf.	10	11
4½	Do. 1 Mt. Db. Stk. Rd.	100	108½
4	Bullard & Sns, L., D. Sk. R.	100	108
6	Bushell, Watk., L., C. Pf.	10	14½
4½	Do. 1 Mt. Db. Sk. Rd.	100	112
5	Camden, Ltd., Cum. Pref.	10	11½
4½	Do. 1 Mt. Db. Sk. Rd.	100	108
5½	Cameron, Ltd., Cm. Pf.	10	13½
4½	Do. Mort Deb. Stk.	100	109
3½	Do. Perp Mt. Db. Sk.	100	100½
5	Cam'bell, J'stone, L., C. Pf.	5	6
4½	Do. 4½ p.c. 1 Mt. Db. Sk.	100	105
4	Campbell, Praed, L., Per. 1 Mort. Deb. Stk.	100	109
4	Cannon, L., Mt. Db. Stk.	100	109
4	Do. "B" Deb. Stk.	100	105
5	Castlemaine, L., 1 Mt. Db.	100	94
3½	Charrington, Ltd., Mort. Deb. Stk. Red.	100	107
2/	Cheltnhm. Orig., Ltd.	5	7
6	Do. Cum. Pref.	5	7½
4	Do. Debs. Red.	100	107
—	Chicago, Ltd.	10	3½
6	Do. Debs.	100	87½
—	Cincinnati, Ltd.	10	[illegible]
8	Do. Cum. Pref.	10	1½
10/	City of Baltimore	10	4
16/	Do. 8 p.c. Cum. Pref	10	8
14/	City of Chicago, Ltd.	10	1
8	Do. Cum. Pref.	10	6
13	City of London, Ltd.	100	205
5	Do. Cum. Pref.	100	138
4	Do. Mt. Deb. Stk., Rd.	100	112
2/	Colchester, Ltd.	5	5
7	Do. Pref.	5	7
4½	Do. Deb. Stk., Red.	100	110
5	Combe, Ltd., Cum. Pref.	10	14
4	Do. Mt. Db. Stk, Rd.	100	112
3½	Do. Perp. Deb. Stk.	100	107
5	Comm'cial, L., D. Sk., Rd.	100	106
5	Courage, L., Cm. Pref. Shs.	100	136
4	Do. Irr. Mt. Deb. Stk.	100	129
3½	Do. Irr. "B" Mt. Db. Sk.	100	106
8	Daniell & Sons, Ltd.	10	6
7	Do. Cum. Pref.	10	12
4½	Do. 1 Mt. Perp. Db. Sk.	100	106
4½	Do. "B" Deb. Stk.	100	100
10d.	Dartford, Ltd.	5	5
10d.	Do. Cum. Pref.	5	5
4	Do. 1 Mt. Db. Sk. Rd.	100	102
4	Davenport, Ld., 1 D. Stk.	100	[illegible]
10/	Denver United, Ltd.	10	3
8	Do. Cum. Pref.	10	[illegible]
6	Do. Debs.	100	96
4½	Deuchar, L., 1 D. Sk., Rd.	100	[illegible]
8/	Distillers, Ltd.	10	24
4½	Do. Mt. Db. Stk., Rd.	100	115
—	Dublin Distillers, Ltd.	5	1
6/	Do. Cum. Pref.	5	4
4½	Do. Irr. Deb. Stk.	100	—
5	Eadie, Ltd., Cum. Pref.	10	11
4	Do. Irr. 1 Mt. Db. Sk.	100	[illegible]
10/	Edinbgh. Utd., Ltd.	10	13
6	Do. Cum. Pf.	10	13
5	Do. 1 Mt. Dbs.	100	[illegible]
4	Eldridge, Pope, L. D. Sk. R.	100	[illegible]
2/	Emerald & Phoenix, Ltd.	10	1
8	Do. Cum. Pref.	10	6
6	Empress Ltd., C. Pf.	10	11
4½	Do. Mt. Deb. Stk.	100	105
10/	Farnham, Ltd.	10	[illegible]
6	Do. Cum. Pref.	10	[illegible]
4	Fenwick, L., 1 D. Sk., Rd.	100	103
4	Flower & Sons, Irr. D. Sk.	100	111
4	Friary, L., 1 Db. Stk., Rd.	100	[illegible]
4	Do. 1 "A" Db. Sk., Rd	100	[illegible]
4½	Groves, L., 1 Db. Sk., Rd	100	110
14	Guinness, Ltd.	100	[illegible]
6	Do. Cum. Prf. Stk.	100	[illegible]
5	Do. Deb. Stk., Red.	100	[illegible]
5	Hall's Oxford L., Cm. Pf.	5	[illegible]
6/	Hancock, Ld., Cm. Pf. Ord.	10	[illegible]
	Do. Def. Ord.	10	[illegible]

Breweries, &c. (*continued*) :—

Div.	Name.	Paid.	Price.
6	Hancock, Ld., Cum. Pref.	10	15½
4	Do. 1 Deb. Stk., Rd.	100	112
5	Hoare, Ltd. Cum. Pref.	10	13½
5	Do. "A" Cum. Pref.	10	12½
4	Do. Mt. Deb. Stk., Rd.	100	111
3½	Do. do. do. Rd.	100	104
4/6	Hodgson's, Ltd.	5	9½
5	Do. 1 Mt. Db., Red.	—	120½
4	Do. 2 Mt. Db., 1906	—	102
4½	Hopcraft & N., Ltd., 1 Mt. Deb. Stk., Red.	100	103
5	Huggins, Ltd., Cm. Prf.	10	12½
4½	Do. 1st D. Stk. Rd.	100	113
4½	Do. "B" Db. Stk. Rd.	100	111
8/	Hull, Ltd.	10	17
7	Do. Cum. Pref.	10	15
4½	Ind, Coope, L., D.Sk., Rd.	100	119
4	Do. "B" Mt. Db. Stk. Rd.	100	114
8/	Indiannapolis, Ltd.	10	3½
8	Do. Cm. Prf.	10	9½
5/	Jones, Frank, Ltd.	10	3½
7½	Do. Cum. Pref.	10	7½
5	Do. 1st Mort. Debs.	100	91½
4/	J. Kenward & Ct., Ltd.	5	5¾
4½	Kingsbury, L., 1 D.Sk., Rd	100	—
4	Lacon, L., D. Stk., Red.	100	110
4	Do. Irrd. "B" D. Sk.	100	107
4/	Lascelles, Ltd.	5	11
6	Do. Cum. Pref.	5	7½
5	Leney, Ltd., Cum. Pref.	10	11½
4	Do. 1 Mt. Db. Stk. Rd.	100	104
30/7½	Lion, Ltd., £25 shares	17	49½
10/9½	Do. New £10 shares	6	17
6	Do. Perp. Pref.	20	31
4	Do. B. Mt. Db. Sk. Rd.	100	110
4½	Lloyd & Y., Ltd., 1 Mt. Deb. Stk., Rd.	100	100½
4½	Locke & S., Ltd., Irr. 1st Mt. Deb. Stk.	100	100
4½	Lovibond, Ltd., 1st Mt. Deb. Stk., Rd.	100	102½
30/4	Lucas & Co., Ld., Deb. Stk.	100	107
8/	Manchester, Ltd.	10	18½
7	Do. Cum. Pref.	10	17½
5	Marston, J., L., Cm. Prf.	10	11
4	Do. 1 Mt. Db. Sk., Rd.	100	101½
9/	Massey's Burnley, Ltd.	10	16½
6	Do. Cum. Pref.	10	14½
4½	McCracken, Ltd., 1 Mt. Deb., 1908	100	61½
5	McEwan, Ltd., Cm. Pref.	10	15
5	Meux, Ltd., Cum. Pref.	10	14½
4	Do. Mt. Db. Stk. Red.	100	111
4½	Michell & A., Ltd., 1 Mt. Deb. Stk. Red	100	105
4½	Mile End Dist. Db. Sk. Rd.	100	109
—	Milwaukee & Chic., Ltd.	10	1½
4/	Do. Cum. Pref.	10	6¾
4½	Michell, Toms, L., Db.	50	55
6	Morgan, Ltd., Cum. Pref.	10	14½
10/	Nalder & Coll., Ltd.	10	34
6	Do. Cum. Pref.	10	16
4½	Do. Deb. Red.	100	113
3/	New Beeston, Ltd.	5	5
2/9	Do. Cum. Pref	5	5
4	Do. Mt. Deb. Stk. Red.	100	97½
12/	Newcastle, Ltd.	10	20
6	Do. Cum. Pref.	10	15½
5	Do. 1 Mt. Deb., 1911	100	110½
4	Do. "A" Deb. Stk. Red.	100	105
6/	New England, Ltd	10	5
8	Do. Cum. Pref.	10	9¾
6	Do. Debs. Red	100	104½
4	New London, L., 1 D.Sk.	100	105
7/2	New Westminster, Ltd.	4	10½
2/4½	Do. Pref.	4	6½
—	New York, Ltd.	10	1
—	Do. 8 p.c. Cum. Pref.	10	4½
6	Do. 1 Mt. Deb. Red.	100	80½
5	Noakes, Ld., Cum. Pref.	10	12½
4	Do. 1 Mt. Db. Stk., Rd.	100	106
4½	Norfolk, L., "A" D.Sk. Rd.	100	106
10/	Northampton, Ld.	10	16½
7	Do. Cum. Pref	10	15½
6	Do. Cum. Pref	10	13
5	Do. 1 Mt. Per. Db. Sk.	100	127
4	Nth. East., L., 1 D.Sk. Rd.	100	102
4½	N. Worcesters., L. Per. 1 Mort. Deb. Stock	100	98½
6	Nottingham, L., Cm. Prf.	10	12½
5	Do. 1 Mt. Deb. Stk., Red.	100	114
17/4	Do. "B" do. Red.	50	112
6/	Ohlsson' Cape, Ld.	5	16½
7	Do. Cum. Pref.	5	8½
4½	Do. 2nd Cum. Pref.	5	5½
5	Do. Deb. Stk., Red.	100	114
4½	Oldfield, L., 1 Mt. Db. Stk.	100	105
6	Page & Overt., L., Cm. Prf.	10	13½
4½	Do. 1 Mt. Dbs, Red.	100	108
10/	Parker's Burslem, Ltd.	10	25
6	Do. Cum. Pref.	10	15
4	Do. 1 Mt. Db. Stk., Red.	100	113
4	Persse, Ld., 1 Mt. Db. Rd.	100	95½
4	Phipps, L., Irr. 1 Db. Stk.	100	115
5	Plymouth, L., Min. Cu. Pf.	10	14
4½	Do. Mt. Deb. Stk., Red.	100	104½
4½	Pryor, Reid, L., 1 D.S., R.[†	100	105½
5	Reid's, Ld., Cm. Pref. Stk.	100	137½
4	Do. Mt. Deb. Stk., Red.	100	112
3½	Do. "B" Mt. Db. Stk., Rd	100	102
5	Rhondda Val., L., Cu. Pf	10	11
4½	Do. 1 Mt. Deb. Stk., Rd.	100	109
5	Robinson, Ld., Cum. Pref.	10	11½
4½	Do. 1 Mt. Perp. Db. Stk.	100	112
4/	Rochdale, Ltd.	10	5½
4½	Do. 1 Mt. Deb. Stk.	100	96½
7	Royal, Brentford, Ltd.	10	19½
	Do. Cum. Pref.	10	14½
4½	Do. 1 Mt. Dbs. Red	100	109
6/	St. Louis, Ltd.	10	4
8	Do. Cum. Pref.	10	8¾
14/	St. Pauli, Ltd.	10	10
7	Do. Cum. Pref.	10	12
4½	Salt (T.), L., 1 Db. Sk. Rd.	100	111

Breweries, &c. (*continued*) :—

Div.	Name.	Paid.	Price.
4½	Salt (T.), "B" Db. Stk. Red	100	108
—	San Francisco, Ltd.	10	¼
—	Do. 8 p.c. Cum. Pref.	10	¼
4½	Savill Brs., L., D. Sk. Rd.	100	117
4½	Scarboro., Ltd., 1 Db. Stk.	100	101
4	Shaw (Hy.), Ltd., 1 Mt. Db. Stk., Red.	100	104
22/	Showell's, Ltd.	10	32½
7	Do. Cum. Pref.	10	17½
3/	Do. Gua. Shs.	5	7½
4½	Do. Mt. Db. Stk., Red.	100	—
4	Simonds, L., 1 D. Sk., Rd.	100	109
5½	Simson & McP., L., Cu. Pf.	10	9½
4½	Do. 1 Mt. Deb. Stk.	100	100
5/	Smith, Garrett, L., £20 Shs	10	15½
5	Do. Cum. Pref.	20	26
—	Do. 3½ p.c. Mt. Db. Stk.	100	108½
5	Smith's, Tadcster, L., C Pf	10	12
4½	Do. Deb. Stk., Red.	100	112
4	Do. Deb. Stk. Red.	100	108
4½	Star, L., 1 M. Db. Stk., Rd.	100	105
4	Steward & P., L., 1 D. Sk.	100	113
9/	Strettons Derby, Ltd.	10	13
6	Do. Cum. Pref.	10	13
4	Do. Irr. 1 Mt. Db. Stk.	100	104½
4½	Strong, Romsey, L., 1 D.S.	100	115
5	Stroud, L., Db. Sk., Rd.	100	111½
4½	Tadcaster To'er, L., D.Sk.	100	113
8/	Tamplin, Ltd	10	21½
6	Do. Cum. Pref.	100	15
4	Do. "A" Db. Sk., Rd.	10	107
6	Thorne, Ltd., Cum. Pref.	10	14½
4	Do. Deb. Stk., Red.	100	105½
15/	Threlfall, Ltd.	10	47
6	Do. Cum. Pref.	10	16½
5	Do. 1 Mt. Dbs., Red.	100	116
4	Tollemache, L., D. Sk. Rd.	100	105
4	Truman, Hanb., D. Sk., R.	100	110
3	Do. "B" Mt. Db. Sk., Rd.	100	95
10/	United States, Ltd.	10	10
8	Do. Cum. Pref.	10	12
6	Do. 1 Mt. Deb	100	107½
6/	Walker & H., Ld., Cm. Prf.	10	11½
4½	Do. 1 Mt. Deb. Stk., Red.	100	107
5	Walker, Peter, Ld. Cm. Prf.	10	14½
4	Do. 1 Mt. Dbs. Red.	100	111
4	Wallingford, L., D.Sk. Rd.	100	107
6	Watney, Ld., Cm. Prf. Sk.	100	170
5	Do. Mt. Db. Sk., Rd.	100	117½
4½	Do. "B" Mt. Db. Sk., Rd.	100	111
3½	Do. Mt. Db. Stk.	100	101
5	Watney, D., Ld., Cm. Prf.	10	12½
4½	Do. 1 Mt. Db. Stk.	100	108
10/	Webster & Sons, Ltd.	10	16½
6	Do. Cum. Pref.	10	14
5	Wenlock Ltd., Pref.	10	12½
4	Do. 1 Mt. Db. Sk., Rd.	100	108
5	West Cheshire, L., Cu. Pf.	10	10½
4	Do. Irred. 1 Mt. Db. Sk.	100	100
4½	Whitbread, L., Cu. Pf. Sh.	100	124½
4	Do. Db. Stk., Red.	100	112
3½	Do. "B" Db. Stk., Rd.	100	101
9/	Wolverhmpton & D. Ld.	10	16½
6	Do. Cum. Pref.	10	13½
4½	Do. 1 Mt. Dbs., Red.	100	108
5½	Worthington, Ld., Cm. Prf.	10	15½
5½	Do. Cum. "B" Pref.	10	13½
4½	Do. Mt. Db. Sk., Rd.	100	113
3½	Do. Irr. "B" Db. Stk.	100	104
10/	Yates's Castle, Ltd.	10	13½
5	Do. Cum. Pref.	10	11
5	Younger W., L., Cu. Pf. Sh.	100	137½

CANALS AND DOCKS.

Last Div.	Name.	Paid.	Price.
4	Birmingham Canal	100	145½
—	E. & W. India Dock	100	21½
4	Do. Deb. Stk.	100	111
50/	Do. Def. Deb. Stk.	100	89
3½	Do. 1st Mt. Certs.	100	110
4	Do. Mt. Bds. (1885)	—	100
40/	G. Junction Ord. Shs.	100	151½
6/	Do. do. Pref.	10	19
4½	King's Lynn Per. Db. Stk.	100	117½
2½	Leeds & Lpool Canal	100	72
2½	Lndn & St. Kath. Dks.	100	57
4½	Do. Pref.	100	136½
4½	Do. Pref., 1878	100	132½
4½	Do. Pref., 1882	100	130
4	Do. Deb. Stk.	100	135
—	Mchester Ship C. 5 p.c. Pf.	10	1½
3½	Do. 1st Perp. Mt. Deb.	100	98
—	Milford Dks. Db. Stk. "A"	100	20
3½	Millwall Dk.	100	59
5	Do. Perp. Pref.	100	142½
4½	Do. Pref.	100	106½
5	Do. New Per. Prf., 1887	100	126½
5	Do. Per. Deb. Stk.	100	153½
4/	Newhaven Har.	10	14½
2½	N. Metropolitan	100	64
5	Sharpness Nw. Pf. "A" Sk.	100	144½
4	Do. Deb. Stk.	100	120½
4	Sheffield & S. Yorks Nav. 4½ p.c. Pref Stk.	100	117½
36.432	Suez Canal	20	137
5	Surrey Comcl. Dok., Ord.	100	150½
5	Do. Min. 4 p.c. Pref. "A"	100	152½
5	Do. Pref. "B"	100	150½
5	Do. 4½ "C"	100	150
5	Do. 1½ "D"	100	145½
4½	Do. Deb. Stk.	100	152½

COMMERCIAL, INDUSTRIAL, &c.

Last Div.	Name.	Paid.	Price.
5	Accles, L., 1 Mt. Db., Red.	100	84½
5/	Aërated Bread, Ltd.	1	12½
—	African Gold Recovery, L.	1	¼
2/	Aluminium, L., "A" Shs.	1	2¼
4½	Do. 1 Mt. Db. Stk., Red.	100	99
5½	Amelia Nitr., L., 1 Mort. Deb., Red.	100	82½
7/	Anglo-Chil. Nitrate, Ltd., Cum. Pref.	10	7½
4½	Do. Cons. Mt. Bds., Red.	100	82½
4½	Anglo-Russian Cotton, Ld., 1 Charge Debs., Red.	100	99
11/3	Angus (G., & Co., L.), £10	7½	17
6/	Apollinaris, Ltd.	10	12½
5/	Do. 5 p.c. Cum. Pref.	10	11
4	Do. Irred. Deb. Stock	100	107
5/	Appleton, French, & S., L.	5	½
3/	Argentine Meat Pres., L., 7 p.c. Pref.	10	2½
5	Argentine Refinry, Db. Rd.	100	98
2/2	Armstrong, Whitw., Ltd.	1	3½
4	Do. Cum. Pref.	5	6½
5	Artisans', Labr. Dwllgs., L.	100	131½
4½	Do. Non-Cm. Prf., 1879	100	132½
4½	Do. do. 1884	100	132½
—	Asbestos & Asbestic, Ltd.	10	8
2/7½	Ashley-grdns., L., C. Prf.	5	6
4½	Do. 1 Mt. Deb. Stk.	100	113½
5/	Assam Rly. & Trdng., L., 8 p.c. Cum. Pref. "A"	10	15½
—	Do. Deferrd. "B" Shs.	1	4½
—	Do. do. (iss. f. pd)	1	3½
8/	Do. Cum. Pre-Prf. "A"	10	15
6/	Do. New Pref.	10	11½
5	Do. Debs., Red.	100	107
5	Do. Red. Mort. Debs.	100	110
6	Aust'lian Pastrl, L., Cu. Pf.	10	7½
6d.	Aylesbury Dairy, Ltd.	1	1½
4	Do. 4 p.c. Mt. Dbs.	100	104½
10/	Babcock & Wilcox, Ltd.	10	31
6	Do. 6 p.c. Cm. Prf.	10	16½
8	Baker (Chs.), L., Cm. Pf.	5	9
8	Do. "B" Cm. Pref.	5	8½
8d.	Barker (John), Ltd.	1	2½
5½	Do. Cum. Pref.	5	7½
4½	Do. Irred. 1 Mt. Db. Stk.	100	132
—	Barnagore Jute, Ltd.	5	3
5	Do. Cum. Pref.	5	4½
7½d.	Belgravia Dairy, Ltd.	1	1½
5/	Bell (R.) & Co., Ltd.	5	3½
1/	Bell's Asbestos, Ltd.	1	¾
5	Do. Mt. Db. Bds., Rd.	100	103
10/	Bengal Mills, Ltd.	10	11½
6/	Do. 5 p.c. Cum. Prf.	10	10½
2/5	Benson (J.W.) L., Cm. Pf.	10	10½
12/4	Do. Perp. Mt. Db. Stk.	100	103½
6	Bergvik, L., 6 p.c. Cm. Pf.	10	12½
10/	Do. Dfd.	10	9½
4½	Do. 1 Dbs., Red.	100	103½
5/	Birm'ham Vinegar, Ltd.	5	10
5	Do. Cum. Pref.	5	5½
4½	Do. 1 Mt. Db. Stk., Rd.	100	108½
5	Boake (A.) L., 5 p.c. Cu. Pf.	10	10½
2/6	Bodega, Ltd.	5	8½
4½	Do. Mt. Deb. Stk., Rd.	100	111
6/	Bottomley & Brs., Ltd.	10	6½
6/	Do. 6 p.c. Pt.	10	9½
8½d.	Bovril, Ltd.	1	1
1/0½	Do. Def.	1	1½
6¼d	Do. Cum. Pref.	1	1
4½	Do. Deb. Stk.	100	103
5/	Bradbury, Gretrex., Ltd., £10 share	8	14
5/	Do. 5 p.c. Cum. Pref.	10	13½
5/	Brewers' Sugar, L., 5 p.c. Cum. Pref.	10	10¾
2/6	Brighton Grd. Hotel, Ld.	5	3½
4	Do. Mt. Db. Stk., Red.	100	102½
5	Bristol Hotel & Palm. Co., Ltd. 1st Mt. Red. Deb.	100	107
9½d.	British & Bengton's Tea Tr. Asc., Ltd.	1	1½
5	Do. Cum. Prf.	5	5½
—	British Deli & Lgkat. Tobacco, Ltd.	1	¾
—	Do. Cum. Prf.	1	¾
—	British Tea Table, Ltd.	1	2½
5½	Do. Cum. Pref.	1	1½
2/6	Brooke, Ben., & Co., Ltd., Cum. Pref.	5	5½
7/6	Brooke, Bond & Co., Ltd.	5	20½
6/	Brown Brs., L., Cum. Pref.	5	6
10	Browne & Eagle, Ltd.	10	13½
5	Do. Cum. Pref.	10	13
4	Do. Mrt. Db. Sk., Red.	100	109
20/	Brunner, Mond, & Co., Lt.	10	42
7/	Do. £10 shares	3½	17
7	Do. Cum. Pref.	10	18
7	Do. £10 shares	5	8½
10/	Bryant & May, Ltd.	5	19½
2/	Bucknall, H., & Sons, Lt.	5	8
6	Do. Cum Pref.	5	8½
4/	Burke, E. & J., Ltd.	5	7½
6	Do. Cum. Pref.	5	7½
6	Do. Irred. Deb. Stk.	100	155
1/	Burlington Htls. Co., Ld.	1	1½
5	Do. Cum. Pref.	1	1½
4	Do. Perp. Deb. Stk.	100	105½
2/4	Bush, W. J., & Co., Ltd., Cum. Pref.	5	5½
36/3	Do. 1 Deb. Stk., Red.	100	104
5½	Callard, Stewart, & Watt, Ltd., Cum. Pref.	1	1½
4/	Callender's Cable L., Shs.	5	5½
4½	Do. 1 Deb. Stk., Red.	100	111½
—	Campbell, R., & Sons, Lt.	3	2½
6	Cantareira Water, Bd., Rd	100	99½
5	Do. (2nd issue)	100	92
4	Cartavio Sugar, Ltd., 6 p.c. 1st Debs., Red.	20	80
4/6	Cassell & Co., Ltd., £10	9	17
5	Causton, Sir J., & Sons, Ltd., Cum. Pref.	10	13½

Commercial, &c. (*continued*) :—

Last Div.	Name.	Paid.	Price.
4	Cent. Prod. Mkt. of B.A. 1st Mt. Str. Debs.	100	81
4	Chappell & Co., Ltd., Mt. Deb. Stk. Red	100	102
6/	Chicago & N.W. Gran. 8 p.c. Cum. Pref.	10	3
—	Chicago Packing & Prov.	10	6
8	Do. Cum. Pref.	10	10½
6/	City Offices, Ltd	36½	13
3½	Do. Mt. Deb. Stk.	100	108½
7/2½	Cy. London Real Prop., Ltd., £25 shs.	12	19
4/6	Do. £12½ shs.	7½	13½
3½	Do. Deb. Stk. Red.	100	106½
3½	Do. Deb. Stk. Red.	100	106½
3	Do.	100	101½
4/	Cy. of Santos Imprvts., Ltd., 7 p.c. Pref.	10	8½
20/	Clay, Bock, & Co., Ltd.	10	7½
8	Do. Cum. Pref.	10	11
6	Do. Mort. Deb.	100	107½
20/	Coats, J. & P., Ltd.	10	61½
6	Do. Cum. Pref.	10	18
4½	Do. Deb. Stk. Red.	100	112½
9½d.	Coburg Hotel, Ltd	1	1½
4	Do. Deb. Stk. Red.	100	102
6	Colonial Consign & Dis., Ltd., Cum. Pref.	5	4½
4½	Do. 1st Mort. Debs.	100	97½
—	Colorado Nitrate, Ltd.	5	½
4/	Co. Gén des Asphtes. de F., Ltd	6	6½
5	Do. Non-Cm. Prf.	—	5¼
5	Cook, J. W., & Co., Ltd., Cum. Pref.	5	5½
5	Cook, T., & Son, Egypt, Ltd., 1st Mt. Deb. Red.	100	110½
—	Cork Co., Ltd., 6 p.c. Cum. Pref.	5	2½
5	Cory, W., & Sn, L., Cu. Pf.	5	6½
4	Do. 1st Deb. Stk. Red.	100	109
8½d.	Crisp & Co., Ltd	1	1½
5½	Do. Cum. Pref.	1	1½
—	Crompton & Co., Ltd., 7 p.c. Cum. Pref.	5	2½
5	Do. 1st Mt. Reg. Deb.	—	88½
4/6	Crossley, J., & Sons, Ltd.	5	8½
5	Do. Cum. Pref	5	6½
—	Crystal Pal. Ord. "A" Stk.	100	8½
—	Do. "B" Red. Stk	100	1½
6	Do. 6 p.c. 1st 1887 Deb. Stk. Red.	100	117½
—	Do. 6 p.c. 2nd 1887 Deb. Stk. Red.	100	45½
—	Do. 6 p.c. 3rd 1887 Deb. Stk. Red.	100	17½
3	Do. 3 p.c. 1st 1895 Deb. Stk.	100	95½
—	Daimler Motor, Ltd	10	6
4/	Dalgety & Co., £20 Shs.	5	5½
4½	Do. Deb. Stk	100	123
4	Do.	100	115
7/	De Keyser's Ryl. Htl., L.	10	14
5	Do. Cum. Pref	10	11½
4	Do. Deb. Stk., Red	100	110
6	Denny, H., & Sons, Ltd., Cum. Pref.	10	14½
5/3	Devas, Routledge & Co., L.	7	8½
5	Dickinson, J., & Co., L., Cum. Pref. Stk.	100	123
4½	Domin. Coltn. Mls., Ltd. Mt. Stg. Dbs.	100	97
6/	Dorman, Long & Co., L.	5	4½
—	Eastmans, Ltd	10	3½
12/	Do. 8 p.c. Cum. Pref.	10	10½
2/6	E. C. Powder, Ltd	3	5½
1/6	Edison & Swn Utd. Elec. Ltd., "A" £5 Shs.	3	2½
2/6	Do. fully-paid	5	4½
4½	Ekman Pulp & Ppr. Co., Ltd., Mt. Deb., Red	100	95
1/1½	Electric Construc., Ltd	2	2½
7	Do. Cum. Pref.	2	3½
25/	Eley Bros., Ltd.	10	39
—	Elmore's Cop. Deptg., L.	1	½
—	Elmore's Wire Mnfg., L.	2	¼
—	Elysée Pal. Hotel Co., L.	5/	¼
5 p.c.	Do. 5 p.c. £100 Db., Rd.	70	70
8½d.	Evans, Ben., & Co., Ltd.	1	1
5	Do. 1 Mt. Db. Sk., Rd.	100	104
8½d.	Evans., D. H., & Co., L.	1	2
6	Do. Cum. Pref.	1	1½
4½	Do. 1 Mt. Db. Sk., Rd.	100	113
2/1	*Evening News*, L., 5 p.c. Cum. Pref.	5	5½
5/3	Evered & Co., L., £10 Sh.	7	13
7/6	Do.	10	19
4	Fairbairn Pastoral Co., Aust., L., 1 Mt. Db., Rd.	100	102
6	Fairfield Shipbldg., Ltd., Cum. Pref.	10	10
	Do. Mort. Deb. Stk.	100	107½
6½	Farmer & Co., Ld., 6 p.c. Cum. Pref.	10	13½
10	Field, J. C. & J., Ltd.	10	10
14/	Do. 7 p.c. Cum. Pref.	10	14
9d.	Fordham, W.B., & Sns, Ld.	1	2
5/6	Fore-st. Warehouse, Ltd.	11	9½
4	Do. Regd. Debs., Rd.	100	103½
2/6	Foster, M. B. & Sons, Ltd.	4	6½
5	Do. Pref.	10	11½
9/	Foster, Porter, & Co., L.	10½	16½
4	Fowler, J., & Co. (Leeds), Ltd., 1 Mt. Deb., Red.	100	103½
3/	Fraser & Chalmers, Ltd.	3	1½
4½	Free, Rodwell & Co., Ltd., Deb Stk.	100	1
6½d.	Furness, T., & Co., Ltd., 5½ p.c. Cum. Pref.	1	
4½	Gartside & Co. (of Manchstr), L., 1 Mt. Db. Sk.	100	110
11	Genl. Hydraul. Power, L.	100	25[illegible]

Commercial, &c. (continued):—

Last Div.	Name.	Paid.	Price.
8/	Gillman & Spencer, Ltd.	5	2¼
6	Do. Pref.	5	5
4	Do. Mort. Debs.	50	51
4	Goldsbro., Mort & Co., L., "A" Deb. Stk., Red.	100	74½
—	Do. 3 p.c. "B" Inc. Deb. Stk., Red	100	17
8/	Gordon Hotels, Ltd.	10	20½
5½	Do. Cum. Pref.	10	14½
4½	Do. Perp. Deb. Stk.	100	137½
4	Do. do.	100	123½
—	Greenwich Inld. Linoleum Co., Ltd.	1	⅜
7	Greenwood & Batley, Ltd., Cum. Pref.	10	10
7½d.	Hagemann & Co., Ltd., 6 p.c. Cum. Pref.	1	1¼
—	Hammond, Ltd.	10	¾
—	Do. 8 p.c. Cum. Pref.	10	2½
—	Do. 6 p.c. Cum. Inc. Stk. Red.	100	52½
4	Hampton & Sons, Ltd., 4 p.c. 1 Mt. Db. St. Red.	100	106
	Hans Crescent Htl., L., 6 p.c. Cum. Pref.	5	3
4	Do. 1 Mt. Deb. Stk.	100	85
5	Harmsworth, Ld., Cm. Pf.	1	1⅛
4/	Harrison, Barber, Ltd.	5	4½
3/	Harrod's Stores, Ltd.	1	4½
2/6	Do. Cum. Pref.	5	7½
5½	Hawaiian Comcl. & Sug. 1 Mt. Debs.	100	94½
5	Hazell, Watson, L., C. P.	10	12
6/	Henley's Teleg., Ltd.	10	23½
7	Do. Pref. Shs.	10	19½
4½	Do. Mt. Db. Stk., Rd.	100	112½
6	Henry, Ltd.	10	12½
5	Do. Cum. Pref.	10	13½
4½	Do. Mt. Debs., Red.	50	53
6	Hepworth, Ld., Cm. Prf.	10	11½
—	Herrmann, Ltd.	1	¼
—	Hildesheimer, Ltd.	3	1½
9½d	Holbrn. & Frasca, Ltd.	1	2½
5	Do. Cum. Pref.	10	12½
4	Do. Deb. Stk.	100	113
6	Home & Col. Stres, L., C. P	5	7½
6	Hood & M.'s Stres., Ltd., Cum. Pref.	1	½
—	Hook, C. T. Ltd.	10	6
7/2	Hornsby, Ltd., £10 Shs.	8	3½
3/6	Do. 6 p.c. Cm. Pf. Sk.	100	90
—	Hotchks. Ordn., Ltd.	10	1
—	Do. 7 p.c. Cm. Prf.	10	4
5	Do. 1 Mt. Dbs., Rd.	100	93½
6	Htl. Cecil, Ld., Cm. Prf.	5	4½
4	Do. 1 Mt. D. Sk., R.	100	107½
8/	Howard & Bulgh, Ltd.	10	33
6	Do. Pref.	10	15
4	Do. Deb. Stk., Red.	100	107
5/	Howell, J., Ltd., £5 Shs.	4	9½
—	Howell & Js., Ld., £3½ Shs.	3	¾
1/6	Humber, Ltd.	1	1½
6	Do. Cum. Pref.	1	1⅛
2/6	Hunter, Wilts., Ltd.	5	7½
2/7	Hyam Clthg., Ltd., 5 p.c. Cum. Pref.	5	5½
10/	Impl. Russn. Cotton, L.	5	6
5	Impd. Industl. Dwgs., Ld.	100	130
6d.	Do. Defrd.	1	1½
23/	Impd. Wood Pave., Ltd.	10	15
13/	Ind. Rubber, Gutta Per. Telegraph Works, Ltd.	10	22
4	Do. 1 Mt. Debs., Red.	100	106
6	Intern. Tea, Cum. Pref.	5	6½
7½d.	Jays, Ltd.	1	1½
5½	Do. Cum. Pref.	5	6½
8½d.	Jones & Higgins, Ltd.	1	2½
4½	Do. 1 Mt. Db. Sk., Rd.	100	113
5/	Kelly's Directory, Ltd., 5 p.c. Cum. Pref.	10	12½
4	Do. Mort. Db. Sk., Rd.	100	105
—	Kent Coal Explrtn. Ltd.	1	⅞
9½d.	King, Howmann, Ltd.	1	1½
4/	Kinloch & Co., Ltd.	5	8½
6	Do. Pref.	5	7
5	Lady's Pictorial Pub., Ltd., Cum. Pref.	5	5
—	La Guaira Harb., Ltd., 7 p.c. Deb. Stk.	100	—
—	Do. 2 Mt. 7 p.c. Deb. Bds., Red.	100	—
4/	Lagunas Nitrate, Ltd.	5	2
2/	Lagunas Syn., Ltd.	5	1½
5	Do. 1 Mt. Debs., Red.	100	80
—	L. Copais Ld., 1 Mt. 6 p.c. Debs., Red.	100	35½
3/	Lautaro Nitrate, Ltd.	5	4½
5	Do. 1 Mt. Debs., Red.	—	100
9/	Lawes Chem. L., £10 shs.	9	5½
14/	Do. N. Cm. Min. Pref.	10	13
—	Leeds Forge, 7 p.c. Cm. Pf.	5	3½
5	Do. 1 Mt. Debs., Red.	50	47½
5	Lever Bros., L., Cm. Pf.	10	13
6	Liberty, L., 6 p.c. Cm. Pf.	10	15
20/	Liebig's, Ltd.	20	75
5	Lilley & Sk., L., Cm. Pf.	5	5½
39/4	Linoleum Manfctg., Ltd.	5	16
3/	Linotype, Ltd., Pref.	5	6
4/	Do. Def.	5	7½
4/	Lister & Co., Ltd.	10	4
5	Do. Cum. Pref.	10	8½
5/	Liverpool. Nitrate	5	5½
—	Liverpool. Warehsg., Ltd	10	3½
5½	Do. Cum. Pref.	10	8½
4	Do. 1 Mt. Db. Stk., Rd.	100	107
5½	Lockharts, Ltd., Cm. Pf.	1	1½
4/6	Ldn. & Til. Lightrage £10	9	6½
6/	Ldn. Comcl. Sale Rms., L.	10	7½
—	Do. 1 Mt. Deb. Stk., Red.	100	104
3	London Nitrate, Ltd.	5	2
4/	London Nitrate, Ld. 8 p.c. Cm. Min. Pf.	5	3½
8/	London [illegible], Ltd.	5	7

Commercial, &c. (continued):—

Last Div.	Name.	Paid.	Price.
2/6	London Produce Clg. Ho., Ltd., £10 Shares	2½	3½
4/	London Stereos., Ltd.	5	3
6d.	Ldn. Un. Laun. L. Cm. Pf.	1	¾
8½d.	Louise, Ltd.	1	⅜
5½	Do. Cum. Pref.	1	¾
5/	Lovell & Christmas, Ltd.	5	11½
6	Do. Cum. Pref.	5	7½
4	Do. Mt. Deb. Stk., Red.	100	107
1/3	Lyons, Ltd.	1	3½
4½	Do. 1 Mt. Deb. Stk., Rd.	100	110½
10/	Machinery Trust, Ltd.	5	15
4½	Do. 4½ Deb. Stk.	100	105
6	MacLellan, L., Min. C. Pf.	10	8
5	Do. 1 Mt. Debs., 1900	100	101½
—	McEwan, J. & Co., Ltd.	10	1½
6	Do. Mt. Debs., Red.	100	89½
8	McNamara, L., Cm. Pref.	10	9
7½d.	Maison Virot, Ltd.	1	1½
2/7	Do. 6 p.c. Cum. Pref.	5	4½
2/	Manbré Sacc., L., Cm. Pf.	10	12
10/	Mangan Brze., L., £10 Shs.	6	15½
2/	Mason & Mason, Ltd.	5	3
6	Do. Cum. Pref.	5	5½
—	Maynards, Ltd.	1	½
6	Do. Cum. Pref.	1	¾
9½d.	Mazawattee Tea, Ltd.	1	1½
5	Do. Cum. Pref.	5	5½
6	Mellin's Food Cum. Pref.	5	7
4½	Met. Ascn. Imp. Dwlgs. L.	100	110
3½	Do. 1 Mt. Deb. Stk.	100	97
5	Metro. In[illegible] Dwlgs., Ltd.	5	5
4	Do. do. Cum. Pref.	5	5½
5	Metro. Prop., L., Cm. Pf.	5	6½
4½	Do. 1st Mt. Debs. Stk.	100	108½
6	Mexican Cotton 1 Mt. Db.	100	97½
4½	Mid. Class Dwlgs., L., Db.	100	120½
1/	Millars' Karri, Ltd.	1	3
6	Do. Cum. Pref.	1	1½
5/	Milner's Safe, Ltd.	10	20½
[illegible]	Moir & Son, Ltd., Pref.	5	8½
6	Morgan Cruc., L., Cm. Pf.	10	15
2/	Morris, B., Ltd.	3½	3½
—	Murray L. 5½ p.c. C. Pf.	[illegible]	5½
—	Do. 4½ 1 Mt. Db. Sk. Rd.	100	108
—	Natnl. Dwlgs., L., 5 p.c. Pf.	5	½
1/7½	Nat. Safe Dep., Ltd.	4	3½
6	Do. Cum. Pref.	1	1½
—	Native Guano, Ltd.	5	¾
—	Nelson Bros., Ltd.	10	2½
5	Do. Deb. Stk., Red.	100	80½
4/	Neuchtel Asph., Ltd.	10	11
—	New Central Borneo, Ld.	1	—
10d.	New Darvel Tob., Ltd.	18/	1½
—	New Explosives, Ltd.	3	2
5/3½	New Gd. Htl., Bham, L.	5	4
5½	Do. Pref.	5	4½
4	Do. 1 Mt. Db. Stk., Rd.	100	96½
—	New Julia Nitrate, Ltd.	10/	½
—	New Ldn. Borneo Tob., L.	16/	¼
1/6	New Premier Cycle, Ltd.	1	½
6	Do. 6 p.c. Cum. Pref.	1	⅜
4½	Do. 4½ p.c. 1 Mt. Db. Rd	100	—
—	New Tamargl. Nitr., Ltd	1	½
—	Do. 8 p.c. Cum. Pref.	1	½
6	Do. 6 p.c. 1 Mt. Dbs. Rd.	100	65½
3/7½d.	Newnes, G., L., Cm. Prf.	1	1½
1/3	Nitr. Provision, Ltd.	2½	¾
24/	Nobel-Dynam., Ltd.	10	17½
—	North Brazn. Sugar, Ltd.	1	½
10/	Oakey, Ltd.	10	31
6	Do. Cum. Pref.	10	16
—	Paccha Jarp. Nitr., Ltd.	5	½
5	Pac. Borax, L., 1 Db. Rd.	100	110
—	Palace Hotel, Ltd.	10	5½
5½	Do. Cum. Pref.	10	8½
4	Do. 1 Mt. Deb. Stk.	100	104
2/6	Palmer, Ltd.	5	1½
6	Do. Cum. Pref.	5	3
9¾d.	Paquin, Ltd.	1	¾
6	Do. Cum. Pref.	5	4½
5½	Parnall, Ltd., Cum. Pref.	1	¾
4/6	Pawsons, Ltd., £10 Shs.	6	6½
4	Do. Mt. Debs., Red.	100	107
6	Pearks, G. & T., Ltd., 6 p.c. Cum. Pref.	1	¾
1/2½	Pears, Ltd.	1	1½
6	Do. Cum. Pref.	10	14
5	Do. Deb. Stk.	100	129
5½	Pearson, C. A., L., Cu. Pf.	5	5½
4/3	Peebles, Ltd.	5	8
5	Do. Cum. Pref.	5	6½
4½	Do. Mt. Deb. Stk. Red.	100	112½
5½	Peek Bros., Ltd., 1 Cum. Pref., Nos. 1-60,000	5	6½
3½	Do. 3½ p.c. 1 Db. Stk.	100	103½
7½d.	Pegamoid, Ltd.	1	¾
—	Phospho-Guano, Ltd.	5	2½
—	Pillsbury-W. Fl. Mills, L.	10	2
16/	Do. 8 p.c. Cum. Pref.	10	6½
6	Do. 1 Mort. Debs.	100	96½
7½d.	Plummer, Ltd.	1	1½
5	Do. Cum. Pref.	5	5
15/	Price's Candle, Ltd.	16	40
6	Priest Marians, L., Cm. Pf.	1	1½
6	Pryce Jones, Ld., Cm. Pf.	5	7½
5	Do. Deb. Stk.	100	120½
10.8d.	Pullman, Ltd.	1	1½
6d.	Do. Cum. Pref.	1	1½
1½d.	Raleigh Cycle, Ltd.	1	⅝
6	Do. Cum. Pref.	1	¾
—	Recife Drnge. Ld. 1 Mt. Debs., R	100	19
6	Redfern, Ltd. Cum. Prf.	10	14
5	Ridgways, Ltd., Cu. Pf.	5	5½
—	R. Janeiro Cy. Imps., Ld.	25	9½
5	Do. Debs.	100	89½
5	Do. 1889-1893	100	89½
11/	R. Jan Fl. Mills, Ltd.	7	6½
5	Do. 1 Mt. Debs., Rd.	100	94
—	Riv. Plate Meat, Ltd.	5	3½
—	Do. Pref.	5	5
8½d.	Roberts, J. R., Ltd.	1	1½

Commercial, &c. (continued):—

Last Div.	Name.	Paid.	Price.
5	Roberts 1 Mt. D. Sk., Rd.	100	112
8½d.	Roberts, T. R., Ltd.	1	2½
5	Do. Cum. Pref.	1	1½
3/	Rosario Nit., Ltd.	5	3½
5	Do. Debs., Red.	100	105
5	Do. Huara, Debs.	—	104
1/	Rover Cycle, Ltd.	1	¾
6/	Ryl. Aquarium, Ltd.	5	4½
6	Do. Pref.	5	6
5	Ryl. Htl., Edin., Cm. Pf.	1	1½
1/2½	Ryl. Niger, Ltd., £10 Sh.	2	2½
6/	Do.	10	14½
—	Russian Petroleum	10	24½
—	Do. 6½ p.c. Cm. Prf.	10	11½
3/	Ruston, Proctor, Ltd.	10	11
4½	Do. 1 Mort. Debs.	100	104
6/	Sadler, Ltd.	12	7
—	Sal. Carmen Nit., Ltd.	5	4½
9d.	Salmon & Gluck., Ltd.	1	1⅛
2/	Salt Union, Ltd.	10	1½
14/	[illegible]n. Sh. 7 p.c. Pref.	10	6
4½	[illegible]ra & Hud[illegible] Deb. Stk.	100	99½
4½	[illegible] Sk., Rd.	100	97½
—	[illegible], Ltd.	5	½
2/6	San Jorge Nit., Ltd.	5	3½
—	San Pablo Nit., Ltd.	5	¾
—	San Sebastn. Nit., Ltd.	5	¾
1/9	Sanitas, Ltd	1	2½
—	Sa. Elena Nit., Ltd.	5	¾
—	Sa. Rita Nit., Ltd.	5	2
10/	Savoy Hotel, Ltd.	10	19
7	Do. Pref.	10	16
4	Do. 1 Mt. Deb. Stk.	100	112½
5	Do. Debs., Red	100	102½
5	Do. & Ldn. For. Htl., Ltd., 5 p.c. Debs. Red.	100	99
1½d	Schweppes, Ltd.	1	1⅛
—	Do. Def.	1	⅞
5	Do. Cum. Pref.	1	1½
4	Do. Deb. Stk.	100	109
1/	Singer Cyc., Ltd.	1	⅞
5½	Do. Cum. Pref.	1	¾
—	Smokeless Pwdr., Ltd.	1	⅜
5½d.	S. Eng. Dairies, Ltd., 6 p.c. Cum. Pref.	1	1½
—	Sowler Thos. L.	1	1½
—	Do. 5½ Cm. Pf.	5	5½
3/6	Spencer, Turner, & Co. Ltd	5	9
5	Do. Cum. Pref.	5	6½
5	Spicer, Ld., 5 p.c. Dbs. Rd.	100	65
4/	Spiers & Pond, Ltd.	10	20
5	Do. 1 Mt. Debs., Red.	100	116½
5	Do. "A" Db. Stk., Rd.	100	[illegible]
5	Do. "B" 1 Db. Stk., Rd.	100	[illegible]
4	Do. Fd. "C" 1 Db. S., R.	100	[illegible]
5/	Spratt's, Ltd	5	[illegible]
4	Do. Debs., 1914	—	[illegible]
5	Steiner Ld., Cm. Pf.	10	[illegible]
4	Do. 1 Mt. Db. Sk. Rd.	100	[illegible]
7/	Stewart & Clydesdale, L.	10	14½
6	Do. Cum. Pref.	10	15½
35/5	Sulphide Corp.	100	80
—	Swan & Edgar, L.	1	1½
1/	Sweetmeat Automatic, L.	1	4
2/9	Teetgen, Ltd., Cum. Pref.	5	6
12/	Teleg. Construction., Ld	12	39
5	Do. Db. Bds., Rd., 1899	100	103½
3/0½	Tilling, Ld. 5½ p.c. Cm. Prf.	5	6½
4	Do. 4 p.c. 1 Dbs., Rd.	—	104
8½d.	Tower Tea, Ltd.	1	1½
5	Do. Cum. Pref.	5	5½
5	Travers, Ltd., Cum. Pref.	10	12½
4	Do. 1 Mt. Dbs., Rd.	100	106
6	Tucuman Sug., 1 Dbs., Rd.	100	100
4/	United Alkali, Ltd.	10	1½
7	Do. Cum. Pref.	10	9
5	Do. Mt. Db. Stk., Rd.	100	110½
2½d.	United Horse Shoe, Ltd., Non-Cum. 8 p.c. Pref.	1	⅛
5	Un. Kingm. Tea, Cm. Prf.	5	5
2/	Un. Lankat Plant., Ltd.	1	2½
2/	Un. Limmer Asphlte., Ld.	3	5
5/	Val de Travers Asph., L.	10	15
3/	V. den Bergh's, L., Cm. P.	5	6½
6	Walkers, Park., L., C. Pf.	10	4
4½	Do. 1 Mt. Debs., Red.	100	90½
6/	Wallis, Thos. & Co., Ltd.	5	14
6	Do. Cum. Pref.	5	8½
5½	Waring, Ltd., Cum. Pref.	5	5½
4½	Do. 1 Mt. Db. Sk., Red.	100	111½
4½	Do. Irred. "B" Db. Stk.	100	104
12/	Waterlow, Dfd. Ord.	10	15½
12/	Do. Pref.	10	15
—	Do. Cum. Pref.	10	10½
10/	Waterlow Bros. & L., Ld.	10	9
5	Do. Pref.	10	12
1/2½	Welford, Ltd.	1	2
4½	Do. Debs., Red.	100	107
1/	Welford's Surrey Dairies, Ltd.	1	1½
7½d.	West London Dairy, Ltd.	1	1
4½	Wharncliffe Dwllgs, L., Pf.	10	11½
18/10	Do. 3 p.c. Irr. Mt. Db. Sk.	100	96
6d.	White, A. J., Ltd.	1	¾
6	Do. 6 p.c. Cum. Pref.	1	¾
4	White, J. Bazley, Ltd., 1 Mort. Debs., Red	100	[illegible]
5	White, R., Ltd., 1 Mort. Deb. Stock, Red.	100	2½
5/	White, Tomkins, Ltd	10	12
5	Do. Cum. Pref.		1
6	White, W. N., L., Cm. Pf.		2½
2/6	Wickens, Pease & Co., L.		16
6	Wilkie, Ltd., Cum. Pref.		8½
3/6	Willans & Robinson, Ltd.		7½
6	Do. Cum. Pref.		107
4½	Do. 1 Mt. Db. Stk., Red.		1½
7½d.	Williamsons, L., Cm. Pr.		
6	Winterbottm. Book Cloth	10	15
	Ltd., Cum. Prf.	5	6½
3/	Yates, Ltd.	5	6½
6	Do. Cum.	4	1½
	Young's Paraffin, L.		

CORPORATION STOCKS—COLONIAL AND FOREIGN.

Per Cent.	Name.	Paid.	Price.
6	Auckland City, '72 1904-24	100	118
6	Do. Cons., '79, Red. 1930	100	138½
5	Do. Deb. Ln., '83..1934-8	100	117
6	Auckland Harb. Debs.	100	111½
5	Do. 1917	100	112
5	Do. 1936	100	116
5½	Balmain Boro' 1914	—	117
5	Boston City (U.S.)	100	102½
5	Do. 1909	100	107½
5	Brunswick Town 5 c. Debs. 1916-20	100	111
15/	B. Ayres City 6 p.c.	100	61
4½	Do. 4½ p.c.	100	77
5	Cape Town, City of	100	113
4	Do. 1943	100	115
4	Chicago, City of, Gold 1915	—	110
6	Christchurch 1926	100	130½
—	Cordoba City	100	17½
5	Duluth (U.S.) Gold 1926	—	110
6	Dunedin (Otago) 1925	100	127½
6	Do. 1906	100	113
5	Do. Consols 1908	100	113
4	Durban Insc. Stk. 1944	100	111
4	Essex Cnty., N. Jersey 1926	$100	114½
5	Fitzroy, Melbrne. 1916-19	100	110
5	Gisborne Harbour 1915	100	110½
4	Greymouth Harbour 1925	100	110
4	Hamilton 1934	100	109
5	Hobart Town 1918-30	100	116
4	Do. 1940	100	107
4½	Invercargill Boro. Dbs. 1936	100	113
6	Kimberley Boro., S.A. Dbs.	—	104
4	Launceston Twn. Dbs. 1916	100	107
6	Lyttleton, N.Z., Harb. 1929	100	125
4	Melbourne Bd. of Wks. 1921	100	109
5	Melb. City Debs. 1897-1907	100	107½
4½	Do. Debs. 1908-27	100	113½
4	Do. Debs. 1915-20-22	100	108
5	Melbne. Harb. Bds., 1908-9	100	112
4½	Do. do. 1915	100	110
4	Do. do. 1918-21	100	106
4½	Melbrne. Tms. Dbs. 1914-16	100	113
4½	Do. Fire Brig. Db. 1921	100	109
5	Mexico City Stg.	100	92
4	Moncton N. Bruns. City	100	104
4½	Montevideo	100	59
5	Montreal Stg.	100	104
5	Do. 1874	100	104
5	Do. 1879	100	106
3½	Do. 1932	100	104
3	Do. Perm. Deb. Stk.	100	98½
4	Camp[illegible] Deb. Stk. 1932	100	113
	1 Mort. De[illegible]solid. 1914	100	119
4	Cannon, L., Mt. [illegible] 1920	100	115
4	Do. "B" Deb. 1928	100	107
5	Castlemaine, L., 1 M[illegible]	—	108
3½	Charrington, Ltd., Mort. Deb. Stk. Red.	100	107½
2/	Cheltnhm. Orig., Ltd.	5	7½
6	Do. Cum. Pref.	5	[illegible]
4	Do. Debs. Red.	100	105
—	Chicago, Ltd.	100	101
6	Do. Debs.	100	74
—	Cincinnati, Ltd.	100	35
8	Do. Cum. Pref.	100	103
5/	City of Baltimore	100	107
6/	Do. 8 p.c. C[illegible] 1921	100	115
5	City of Chicago, 1921	100	107
5	Do. Cum. 1934	100	105
6	City of London,	100	111
6	Do. Cum. R[illegible] 1904	100	115½
4½	Do. Mt. [illegible]ebs. 1913	100	112
6	Colchester [illegible]h Waterworks	100	113½
5	Do.	100	111
5	Do. [illegible] 1917	100	111
4	[illegible]mb[illegible] Do. [illegible]ebs. 1919	100	103
6	Qu[illegible] Do. Coupon. 1875 1905	100	112
6	Do. 1878 1908	100	116
4½	D[illegible]m[illegible]bs. 1914-18	100	108
4	Do[illegible]bs. 1923	200	108
3½	Do[illegible] Rg. Stk., Red.	100	101
5	Richn. [illegible](Melb.) Dbs. 1917	100	113
4	Rio Ja[illegible]ro City	100	59
4	Rome [illegible]	100	—
4	Do. [illegible]d to 8th Iss.	100	94
—	Rosario	100	26½
—	Do.	100	26½
4	St. Cath[illegible]ne (Ont.) 1926	100	101
4	St. John, N.B., Debs. 1934	—	103
4½	St. Kild[illegible]elb) Dbs. 1918-21	100	104
4	St. Lou[illegible] (Miss.) 1911	100	106
4	Do. 1913	100	106
3·65	Do. 1915	—	110
—	Santa Fé [illegible]ty Debs.	00	21
6	Santos C[illegible]	100	96
6	Sofia Cit[illegible]	100	86
5	Sth. Me[illegible]urne Debs. 1915	100	111
4½	Do. Debs. 1929	100	107
5	Syd[illegible] City 1904	100	109
4	Do. Debs. 1912-13	100	107
4	Do. do. (1894) 1919	100	109
7	[illegible]maru Boro. 7 p.c. 1910	100	126½
	[illegible]imaru Harb. Debs 1914	100	106
	Do. Debs. 1916	100	106
	Toronto City Wtwks 1904-6	100	110
6	Do. Cons. Debs. 1898	100	101
5	Do. G. Cns. Dbs. 1919-20	100	118
4	Do. Strlg. 1922-8	100	107
4	Do. Local Improv.	100	102
3½	Do. 1929	100	105
5½	Valparaiso	100	102
4	Vancouver 1931	100	109
4	Do. 1932	100	108
6	Wanganui Harb. Dbs. 1905	100	110
6	Wellington Con. Deb. 1907	100	117
6	Do. Improv., 1879	100	123
6	Do. Wtrwks. Dbs., 1880	100	123
4½	Do. Debs., 1893 1933	100	116
4½	Wellington Harb. 1907	100	104
4	Westport Harb. Dbs. 1925	100	110
6	Winnipeg City Deb. 1907	—	118
5	Do. 1914	100	119

FINANCIAL, LAND, AND INVESTMENT.

Last Div.	Name.	Paid.	Price.
5	Agncy, Ld. & Fin. Aust., Ltd., Mt. Db. Stk., Rd.	100	90½
6	Amer. Frehld. Mt. of Lon., Ld., Cum. Pref. Stk. ..	100	82½
4½	Do. Deb. Stk., Red. ..	100	96
1/	Anglo-Amer. Db. Cor., L.	2	1
4	Do. Deb. Stk., Red ..	100	106½
5½	Ang.-Ceylon & Gen. Est., Ltd., Cons. Stk.	100	68
6	Do. Reg. Debs., Red.	100	106½
—	Ang.-Fch. Explorn., Ltd.	1	2 5/16
6	Do. Cum. Pref.	1	11/16
—	Argent. Ld. & Inv., Ltd. £1 Shares	10/	nil
—	Do. Cum. Pref.	4	2
1/	Assets Fnders.' Sh., Ltd.,	4	1¾
6/	Assets Realiz., Ltd., Ord.,	5	9
5	Do. Cum. Pref.	5	6½
26/	Austrln. Agricl £25 Shs.	21½	63½
—	Aust. N. Z. Mort., Ltd., £10 Shs.	1	1½d.
4½	Do. Deb. Stk., Red. ..	100	90½
4	Do. Deb. Stk., Red. ..	100	82½
4½	Australian Est. & Mt., L., 1 Mt. Deb. Stk., Red.	100	106
5	Do. "A" Mort. Deb. Stk., Red.	100	97
2/6	Australian Mort., Ld., & Fin., Ltd. £25 Shs. ..	5	4½
1/6	Do. New, £25 Shs. ..	3	2½
4	Do. Deb. Stk.	100	112
3	Do. Do.	100	85
5	Baring Est. 2 Mt. Debs., Red.	100	105
5	Bengal Presidy. 1 Mort. Deb., Red.	100	106
25/	British Amer. Ld. "A"	1	20
—	Do. "B"	24	6½
1/2½	Brit. & Amer. Mt., Ltd. £10 Shs.	2	¾
5/	Do. Pref.	10	10
4	Do. Deb. Stk., Red. ..	100	101
1/3	Brit. & Austrlsn Tst Ln., Ltd. £25 Shs.	2½	¾
4½	Do. Perm. Debs., Red.	100	103
1½d.	Brit. N. Borneo. £1 Shs.	15/	1/16
2½d.	Do.	1	1
—	Brit. S. Africa	1	2 3/16
5	Do. Mt. Deb., Red.	—	97
6	B. Aires Harb. Tst., Red.	100	100
12/6	Canada Co.	1	26
—	Canada N. W. Ld., Ltd.	$25	85½
—	Do. Pref.	$100	254
4	Canada Perm. Loan & Sav. Perp. Deb. Stk. ..	100	99½
—	Curamalan Ld., 1 Mt. 7 p.c. Bds., Red.	—	92½
3/7½	Deb Corp., Ld., £10 Shs	4	3½
5	Do. Cum. Pref.	10	11½
4	Do. Perp. Deb. Stk.	100	116
9d.	Deb. Corp. Fders' Sh., Ld.	3	⅞
4/5 1/10	Eastn. Mt. & Agncy, Ld., "A"	10	6½
4½	Do. Deb. Stk., Red.	100	100
5	Equitable Revers. In. Ltd.	100	—
8/	Exploration, Ltd.	1	1¾
1	Freehold Trst. of Austrln. Ltd. £10 Shs.	1	¾
4	Do. Perp. Deb. Stk.	100	102
—	Genl. Assets Purchase, Ltd., 5 p.c. Cum. Pref.	10	—
50/	Genl. Reversionary, Ltd.	100	—
3½	Holborn Vi. Land	100	105
3½	House Prop. & Inv.	100	86½
13/	Hudson's Bay	13	22½
4	Impl. Col. Fin. & Agcy. Corp.	100	95½
4½	Impl. Prop. Inv., Ltd., Deb. Stk., Red.	100	91½
2/6	Internatl. Fincial. Soc., Ltd. £7½ Shs.	2½	1½
4	Do. Deb. Stk., Red.	100	99½
1/9½	Ld. & Mtge. Egypt, Ltd. £18 Shs.	3	2½
5	Do. Debs., Red.	100	103
4½	Do. Debs., Red.	100	101
—	Ld. Corp. of Canada. Ltd.	1	⅞
4½	Ld. Mtge. Bk. of Texas Deb. Stk.	100	—
3½	Ld. Mtge. Bk. Victoria 4½ p.c. Deb. Stk.	100	78
2/9½	Law Debent. Corp., Ltd., £10 Shs.	2	2
4½	Do. Cum. Pref.,	10	12
4	Do. Deb. Stk.	100	119
1/	Ldn. & Australasian Deb. Corp., Ltd., £4 Shs. ..	2	½
4½	Do. 4½ p.c. Mt. Deb. Stk., Red.	100	101
1/9	Ldn. & Middx. Frhld. Est. £2 Shs.	35/	3½
2/6	Lndn. & N. Y. Inv. Corp., Ltd.	5	2
5	Do. 5 p.c. Cum. Pref.	10	9
1/6	Ldn. & Nth. Assets Corp., Ltd., £2 Shs.	1½	¾
2/	Ldn. & N. Deb. Corp., L.	2	1¼
4/	Ldn. & S. Afric. Explrn. Ltd.	½	14
2/	Mtge. Co. of R. Plate, Ltd. £10 Shs.	2	3½
4½	Do. Deb. Stk., Red.	100	112
4½	Morton, Rose Est., Ltd., 1st Mort. Debs.	—	101
6/	Natal Land Col. Ltd. ..	10	6¾
4/	Do. 8 p.c. Pref., 1870 ..	5	8½
5/6	Natl. Disct. L., £25 Shs.	5	10¾
4½	New Impl. Invest., Ltd. Pref. Stk.	100	61½
—	New Impl. Invest., Ltd. Def. Stk.	100	9
4	N. Zld. Ln. & Mer. Agcy., Ltd. Prf. Ln. Deb. Stk	100	98

Financial, Land, &c. (*continued*):—

Last Div.	Name.	Paid.	Price.
16/	N. Zld. Ln. & Mer. Agcy., Ltd. 5 p.c. "A" Db. Sk.	100	43½
—	N. Zld. Ln. & Mer. Agcy., Ltd., 5 p.c. "B" Db. Stk.	100	4
2/6	N. Zld. Tst. & Ln. Ltd., £25 Shs.	5	1½
12/6	N. Zld. Tst. & Ln. Ltd., 5 p.c. Cum. Pref.	25	19
—	N. Brit. Australsn. Ltd.	100	6½
—	Do. Irred. Guar.	100	32½
5	Do. Mort. Debs.	100	82½
4½	N. Queensld. Mort. & Inv., Ltd., Deb. Stk.	100	95
—	Oceana Co., Ltd.	—	—
6	Peel Riv., Ld. & Min. Ltd.	100	89
—	Peruvian Corp., Ltd.	100	2¾
—	Do. 4 p.c. Pref.	100	10
3	Do. 6 p.c. 1 Mt. Debs., Red.	100	42
—	Queensld. Invest. & Ld. Mort. Pref. Ord. Stk.	100	20
3/7	Queensld. Invest. & Ld. Mort. Ord. Shs.	4	4
4	Queensld. Invest. & Ld. Mort. Perp. Debs.	100	90
3½	Raily. Roll Stk. Tst. Deb., 1903-6	100	100½
50/	Reversiony. Int. Soc., Ltd.	100	—
2/8½	Riv. Plate Trst., Loan & Agcy., L., "A" £10 Shs.	2	4½
1/6	Riv. Plate Trst., Loan & Agcy., Ltd., Def. "B"	5	4
	Riv. Plate Trst., Loan & Agy., L., Db. Stk., Red.	100	109
—	Santa Fé & Cord. Gt. South Land, Ltd.	20	5
—	Santa Fé Land	10	2½
2/	Scot. Amer. Invest., Ltd. £10 Shs.	2	2¾
2½	Scot. Australian Invest., Ltd., Cons.	100	76½
6	Scot. Australian Invest., Ltd., Guar. Pref.	100	135½
5	Scot. Australian Invest., Ltd., Guar. Pref.	100	106½
4	Scot. Australian Invest., Ltd., 4 p.c. Perp. Dbs.	100	105½
5	Sivagunga Zemdy., 1st Mort., Red.	100	101
20/	Sth. Australian	20	52½
3½	Stock Exchange Deb., Rd.	—	101½
—	Strait Develt., Ltd.	1	5/16
2/6	Texas Land & Mt., Ltd. £10 Shs.	2½	3
4½	Texas Land & Mt., Ltd., Deb. Stk., Red.	100	105
—	Transvaal Est. & Dev., L.	1	½
—	Transvaal Lands, Ltd., £1 Shs.	15/	½
—	Do. F. P.	1	5/16
—	Transvaal Mort., Loan, & Fin., Ltd., £10 Shs. ..	2	½
2/	Tst & Agcy. of Austrlsa., Ltd., £10 Shs.	1	2½
7/5	Do. Old, fully paid ..	10	15½
5/7	Do. New, fully paid ..	10	12½
5	Do. Cum. Pref.	10	12½
3/	Trust & Loan of Canada, £20 Shs.	5	4½
1/9½	Do. New £20 Shs.	3	2½
—	Tst. & Mort. of Iowa, Ltd., £10 Shs.	2½	¾
4½	Do. Deb. Stk. Red.	100	92½
—	Tst., Loan, & Agency of Mexico, Ltd., £10 Shs.	2	½
—	Trsts., Exors, & Sec. Ins. Corp., Ltd., £10 Shs. ..	7	1½
5/	Union Dsc., Ld., £10 Shs.	5	11
—	Union Mort. & Agcy. of Aust., Ltd., £6 Shs. ..	2	—
6	Do. Pref. Stk.	100	35
—	Do. 6 p. Pref. £6 Shs.	2	½
4½	Do. Deb. Stk.	100	92½
4	Do. Deb. Stk.	100	85½
5	Do. Deb. Stk. Red. ..	100	96½
1/6	U.S. Deb. Cor. Ltd., £8 Shs.	1	⅛
5½	Do. Cum. Pref. Stk.	100	102½
4½	Do. Irred. Deb. Stk. ..	100	108½
5	U.S. Tst. & Guar. Cor., Ltd., Pref. Stk.	100	74½
6/	Van Dieman's	25	16
4	Walker's Prop. Cor., Ltd., Guar. 1 Mt. Deb. Stk. ..	100	109
4½	Wstr. Mort. & Inv., Ltd., Deb. Stk.	100	92½

FINANCIAL—TRUSTS.

Last Div.	Name.	Paid.	Price.
1/	Afric. City Prop., Ltd	1	1⅛
6	Do. Cum. Pref.	1	1
4	Alliance Invt., Ltd., Cm. 4½ p. c. Prefd.	100	80½
—	Do. Defd	100	13½
4	Do. Deb. Stk. Red. ..	100	105½
5	Amrcn. Invt., Ltd., Prfd.	100	124½
5	Do. Defd.	100	94½
4	Do. Deb. Stk. Red. ..	100	117½
4	Army & Navy Invt., Ltd., 5 p.c. Prefd.	100	82½
—	Do. Defd. Stk.	100	17½
4	Do. Deb. Stk.	100	107½
4	Atlas Investment, Ltd., Prefd. Stk.	100	70½
4½	Bankers' Invest., Ltd., Cum. Prefd.	100	107
1/0/0	Do. Defd	100	28½
4	Do. Deb. Stk	100	113
	Brewery & Comml. Inv., Ltd., £10 Shs.	5	6

Financial—Trusts (*continued*):—

Last Div.	Name.	Paid.	Price.
4	British Investment, Ltd., Cum. Prefd.	100	107
5	Do. Defd.	100	102½
4	Do. Deb. Stk.	100	109½
6	Brit. Steam. Invst., Ltd., Prefd.	100	116½
6/0/0	Do. Defd	100	70½
4½	Do. Perp. Deb. Stk ..	100	120½
1/9	Car Trust Invst., Ltd., £10 Shs.	2½	2
5	Do. Pref.	100	104½
4	Do. Deb. Stk., 1915 ..	100	105
4	Clnl. Sec., Ltd., Prefd. ..	100	108½
2	Do. Defd.	100	50
4	Consolidated, Ltd., Cum. 1st Pref.	100	94½
4	Do. 5 p.c. Cm. 2nd do.	100	74½
—	Do. Defd.	100	14½
4½	Do. Deb. Stk.	100	111½
—	Deb. Secs. Invst.	100	106½
—	Do. 4 p.c. Cm. Pf. Sk.	100	106½
4½	Edinburgh Invest., Ltd., Cum. Prefd. Stk.	100	109½
4	Do. Deb. Stk. Red.	100	106½
5	Foreign, Amer. & Gen. Invt., Ltd., Prefd.	100	117½
2	Do. Defd.	100	56½
4	Do. Deb. Stk.	100	117½
5	Foreign & Colonial Invt., Ltd., Prefd.	100	135½
5½	Do. Defd.	100	97½
4½	Gas, Water & Gen. Invt., Cum. Prefd. Stk.	100	95
3	Do. Defd. Stk.	100	38½
4	Do. Deb. Stk.	100	106
5	Gen. & Com. Invt., Ltd., Prefd. Stk.	100	108½
2	Do. Defd. Stk.	100	37½
4	Do. Deb. Stk.	100	111½
1/9	Globe Telegph. & Tst., Ltd.	10	12½
6	Do. do. Pref.	10	18
4	Govt. & Genl. Invt., Ld., Prefd.	100	84½
3½	Do. Defd.	100	42½
4½	Govts. Stk. & other Secs. Invt., Ltd., Prefd.	100	92½
1	Do. Defd.	100	27
4½	Do. Deb. Stk.	100	111
4	Do. do.	100	104
4½	Guardian Invt., Ltd., Pfd.	100	90½
—	Do. Defd.	100	21½
4	Do. Deb. Stk.	100	105
5	Indian & Gen. Inv., Ltd., Cum. Prefd.	100	107½
2½	Do. Defd.	100	56
4½	Do. Deb. Stk.	100	121½
5	Indust. & Gen. Tst., Ltd., Unified	100	102½
3½	Do. Deb. Stk. Red.	100	102½
4½	Internat. Invt., Ltd., Cm. Prefd.	100	75½
—	Do. Defd.	100	10
4	Do. Deb. Stk.	100	104
4	Invest. Tst. Cor. Ltd. Pfd.	100	103
4	Do. Defd.	100	89
4	Do. Deb. Stk. Red.	100	107
5	Ldn. Gen. Invest. Ltd., 5 p.c. Cum. Prefd.	100	110½
7½	Do. Defd.	100	118
4½	Ldn. Scot. Amer. Ltd. Pfd.	100	104½
£3	Do. Defd.	100	59½
4	Do. Deb. Stk.	100	112
4	Ldn. Tst., Ltd., Cum. Prfd. Stk.	100	104
4	Do. Defd. Stk.	100	76½
4	Do. Deb. Stk., Red.	100	107
3½	Do. Mt. Deb. Stk., Red.	100	104
5	Mercantile Invt. & Gen., Ltd., Prefd.	100	115
2	Do. Defd.	100	54
4	Do. Deb. Stk.	100	117½
4	Merchants, Ltd., Pref. Stk.	100	106½
4	Do. Ord.	100	82
4	Do. Deb. Stk.	100	117½
5	Municipal, Ltd., Prefd. ..	100	56½
—	Do. Defd.	100	18½
4½	Do. Debs.	100	113
4½	Do. Debs. "B"	100	99½
4½	Do. "C" Deb. Stk.	100	88½
5	New Investment, Ltd. Ord.	100	95½
5	Omnium Invest., Ltd., Pfd.	100	91½
1	Do. Defd.	100	26½
4	Do. Deb. Stk.	100	104
5/	Railway Deb. Tst. Ld., £20 Shs.	10	7
5	Do. Debs., Red. ..	100	107½
4½	Do. Deb. Stk., 1911	100	106½
4	Do. do. 1927	100	107½
4	Railway Invst. Ltd., Prefd.	100	117
18/6	Do. Defd.	100	23
8/	Railway Share Trust & Agency "A"	8	6½
7½	Do. "B" Pref. Stk.	100	145½
4½	River Plate & Gen. Invt., Ltd., Prefd.	100	105
£3	Do. Defd.	100	50½
5	Scot. Invst., Ltd., Pfd. Stk.	100	95½
3½	Do. Defd.	100	26½
4	Do. Deb. Stk.	100	108
4½	Sec. Scottish Invst., Ltd., Cum. Prefd.	100	89½
£2	Do. Defd. Stk.	100	32
4	Do. Deb. Stk.	100	107½
5/	Sth. Africa Gold Tst., Ltd.	1	4 3/8
6	Do. Cum. Pref	1	1
5½	Do. 1st Debs., Red.	100	102
1/9	Stock Conv. & Invest., Ltd., £5 Shs.	1	1½
4½	Do. do. 4½ p.c. Cm. Prf.	100	114½
3½	Do. Ldn. & N. W. 1st. Charge Prefd.	100	114½
4	Do do. 2nd Chge Prfd.	100	111
82/6	Do. do. Defd. Charge	100	31
3	Do. N. East. 1 Chge Pfd.	100	93

Financial—Trusts (*continued*):—

Last Div.	Name.	Paid.	Price.
87/6	Stock N. East Defd. Chge	100	40
6	Submarine Cables	100	141½
5	U.S. & S. Amer. Invest., Ltd., Prefd.	100	100½
2	Do. Defd.	100	29½
4	Do. Deb. Stk.	100	105½

GAS AND ELECTRIC LIGHTING.

Last Div.	Name.	Paid.	Price.
10/6	Alliance & Dublin Con. 10 p.c. Stand.	10	25½
7/6	Do. 7 p.c. Stand.	10	17
5	Austln. Gas Lght. (Syd.) Debs. 1902	100	106
5	Bay State of N. Jrsy. Sk. Fd. Tst. Bd., Red. ..	—	92½
3/	Bombay, Ltd.	5	6½
2/4½	Do. New	4	5½
12	Brentford Cons.	100	297½
9	Do. New	100	230½
5	Do. Pref.	100	147½
4	Do. Deb. Stk. ..	100	136
11½	Brighton & Hove Gen. Cons. Stk.	100	277½
8½	Do. "A" Cons. Stk.	100	202½
5	Bristol 5 p.c. Max.	100	132½
22/6	British Gas Light, Ltd.	20	56½
11/6	Bromley Gas Consumrs.' 10 p.c. Stand.	10	26
8/6	Do. 7 p.c. Stand.	10	21
—	Brush Electl. Enging., L.	—	2½
6	Do. 6 p.c. Pref.	—	2¾
4½	Do. Deb. Stk.	100	112
4½	Do. 2 Deb. Stk., Red.	100	103½
5/	B. Ayres (New), Ltd. ..	10	10
4	Do. Deb. Stk., Rd. ..	—	98
12/	Cagliari Gas & Wtr., Ltd.	20	31
8/	Cape Town & Dist. Gas Light & Coke, Ltd.	10	17½
4½	Do. Pref.	10	12½
6	Do. 1 Mt. Debs. 1910	50	60
4/	Charing Cross & Strand Elec. Sup., Ltd.	5	14½
4½	Do. Cum. Pref.	5	6½
2/6	Chelsea Elec. Sup., Ltd.	5	11½
4½	Do. Deb. Stk., Red.	100	116
5	Chic. Edis'n Co. 1 Mt., Rd.	$1000	108
14/	City of Ldn. Elec. Lht., L.	10	29
—	Do. New	10	28½
6/	Do. Cum. Pref.	10	18
5	Do. Deb. Stk., Red.	100	131½
13½	Commercial, Cons.	100	342½
10½	Do. New	100	257½
4½	Do. Deb. Stk.	100	155½
14	Continental Union, Ltd.	100	247½
11	Do. Pref. Stk.	100	216½
—	County of Lon. & Brush Prov. Elec. Lg., Ltd.	10	15¾
6	Do. Cum. Pref.	10	16
14	Croydon Comcl. Gas, Ld., "A" Stk., 10 p.c.	100	312½
11	Do. "B" Stk., 7 p.c.	100	260
5½	Crystal Pal. Dist. Ord. 5 p.c. Stk.	100	135½
5	Do. Pref. Stk.	100	141½
8/	European, Ltd.	10	26
6/	Do.	7½	18½
12½	Gas Light & Ck Cons. Stk., "A" Ord.	100	298
4	Do. "B" (4 p.c. Max.)	100	122½
10	Do. "C," "D," & "E" (Pref.)	100	319½
5	Do. "F" (Pref.)	100	152½
7½	Do. "G" (Pref.)	100	222½
7	Do. "H" (7 p.c. Max.)	100	202
10	Do. "J" (Pref.)	100	318½
6	Do. "K"	100	187½
4	Do. Deb. Stk.	100	132½
4½	Do. do.	100	157½
6	Do. do.	100	207½
8/	Hong Kong & China, Ld.	10	14½
—	House to House Elec. Light Sup., Ltd. ..	5	11½
7	Do. Cum. Pref.	5	11½
10	Imperial Continental ..	100	218
3½	Do. Deb. Stk., Red ..	100	104½
2/	Malta & Medit., Ltd. ..	5	5½
5/	Metrop. Elec. Sup., Ltd.	10	20½
3/8	Do. New	10	20
4½	Do. 1 Mt. Deb. Stk.	100	129
5	Metro. of Melbrne. Dbs. 1908-12	100	113
4½	Do. Debs. 1918-22-4	100	110
10/	Monte Video, Ltd.	20	16
9½	Newcastle-upon-Tyne ..	100	237½
—	Do. 3½ p.c. Deb. Stk.	100	117½
8/	Notting Hill Elec. Ltg., Ltd.	10	19½
4/6	Oriental, Ltd.	5	8½
4/0½	Do. New	4½	7½
10d½.	Do. do. 1879	1	1½
3/6	Ottoman, Ltd.	5	5
—	Para, Ltd.	—	—
6	People's Gas Lt. & C. of Chic. 2 Mt. 1904	100	105½
5	River Plate Elec. Lgt. & Trac., Ltd., 1 Deb. Stk.	—	92½
8o	Royal Elec. of Montreal	—	146
4½	Do. 1 Mt. Deb. ..	100	106
11/	St. James' & Pall Mall Elec. Light, Ltd. ..	5	19
7	Do. Pref.	5	10½
4	Do. Deb. Stk., Red.	100	108½

Gas and Electric (*continued*):—

Last Div.	Name.	Paid.	Price.
10/	San Paulo, Ltd.	10	16¼
10	Sheffield Unit. Gas Lt. "A"	100	251½
10	Do. "B"	100	251½
10	Do. "C"	100	251½
—	Sth. Ldn. Elec. Sup., Ld.	2	3
5½	South Metropolitan	100	145½
3	Do. 3 p.c. Deb. Stk.	100	106½
12	Tottenham & Edmonton Gas Lt. & C., "A"	100	290
9	Do. "B"	100	210
7/	Tuscan, Ltd.	10	14
5	Do. Debs., Red.	100	101½
4/9	West Ham 10 p.c. Stan.	5	12
8/	Wstmnstr. Elec. Sup., Ld.	5	19

INSURANCE.

Last Div.	Name.	Paid.	Price.
4/	Alliance, £20 Shs.	44/	11½
10/	Alliance, Mar., & Gen., Ld., £100 Shs.	25	53
5/	Atlas, £50 Shs.	6	32
12/	British & For. Marine, Ld., £20 Shs.	4	24½
7½d.	British Law Fire, Ltd., £10 Shs.	1	1½
7/6	Clerical, Med., & Gen. Life, £25 Shs.	50/	16½
10/	Commercial Union, Ltd., £50 Shs.	5	45
4	Do. "W. of Eng." Ter. Deb. Stk.	100	110½
£3	County Fire, £100 Shs.	80	190
3/	Eagle, £50 Shs.	5	½
4/	Employers' Liability, Ltd., £10 Shs.	2	4½
—	Empress, Ltd., £5 Shs.	1	—
21/	Equity & Law, £100 Shs.	6	22
7/6	General Life, £100 Shs.	5	15
4½d.	Gresham Life, £5 Shs.	15/	2½
2/6	Guardian, Ld., £10 Shs.	5	11¾
10/	Imperial, Ltd., £20 Shs.	5	30½
3/6	Imperial Life, £20 Shs.	4	6¾
6/	Indemnity Mutual Mar., Ltd., £15 Shs.	3	12½
1/	Lancashire, £20 Shs.	2	5
7½d.	Law Acc. & Contin., Ltd., £5 Shs.	10/	1
5/	Law Fire, £100 Shs.	2½	18
9½d.	Law Guar. & Trust, Ltd., £10 Shs.	1	1½
9/	Law Life, £20 Shs.	2	25
2/9	Law Un. & Crown £10 Shs.	12/	7
4	Do. Deb. Stk., 1942	100	110½
14/6	Legal & General, £50 Shs.	8	15½
9d.	Lion Fire, Ltd., £8½ Shs.	1½	¾
14/	Liverpool & London & Globe, Stk.	2	55
10/	Do. Globe £1 Ann.	—	36
25/	London, £25 Shs.	12½	63½
4/	Lond. & Lanc. Fire, £25 Shs	2½	19½
2/	Lond. & Lanc. Life, £25 Shs	2	5
1/	Lond. & Prov. Mar., Ld., £10 Shs.	1	1
2/	Lond. Guar. & Accident, Ltd., £5 Shs.	2	12
10/	Marine, Ltd., £25 Shs.	4½	44½
2/	Maritime, Ltd., £10 Shs.	2	4½
1/6	Merc. Mar., Ld., £10 Shs.	2½	2¾
—	National Marine, Ltd., £9 Shs.	1	½
10/	N. Brit. & Merc., £25 Shs.	6¼	43
20/	Northern, £100 Shs.	10	82
40/	Norwich Union Fire, £100 Shs.	12	126½
10/	Ocean Acc. & Guar., fy. pd.	5	21
2/	Do. £5 Shs.	1	4
7/6	Ocean, Marine, Ltd.	2½	9½
1/	Palatine, £10 Shs.	2	3½
2/6	Pelican, £10 Shs.	1	3¾
12/	Phoenix, £50 Shs.	5	44
—	Provident, £100 Shs.	10	36
3/	Railway Passngrs., £10 Shs.	2	8½
2/6	Rock Life, £5 Shs.	10/	4½
8	Royal Exchange	100	360
18/	Royal, £20 Shs.	3	55½
4/	Sun, £10 Shs.	10/	11¾
3/9	Sun Life, £10 Shs.	7½	15
6/	Thames & Mrsey. Marine, Ltd., £20 Shs.	2	10½
9/	Union, £10 Shs.	4	24½
4/	Union Marine, £20 Shs.	2½	9
12/	Universal Life, £100 Shs.	12	42
2/	World Marine, £5 Shs.	2	1½

IRON, COAL, AND STEEL.

Last Div.	Name.	Paid.	Price.
—	Barrow Hæm. Steel, Ltd.	7½	2
9/	Do. 6 p.c. and Pref.	7½	7½
10/	Bolck., Vaugh. & C., Ld.	20	18
6/	Do. £8 liab.	12	9½
7/6	Brown, J. & Co., Ltd., £20 Shs.	15	20
7/6	Consett Iron, Ld., £10 Shs.	7½	29½
4/	Do. 8 p.c. Cum. Pref.	5	11
7/9	Ebbw Vale Steel, Iron & Coal, Ltd., £23 Shs.	20	7
11/	General Mining Assn., Ld.	5½	7½
8/	Harvey Steel Co. of Gt. Britain, Ltd.	10	32
5	Lehigh V. Coal 1 Mt. 5 p.c. Guar. Gd. Cp. Bds.	—	98
42/6	Nantyglo & Blaina Iron, Ltd., Pref.	862	97½
1/	Nerbudda Coal & Iron, Ltd., £3 Shs.	56/	1/16
—	Newport Abercrn. Bk. Vein Steam Coal, Ltd.	10	4¾
—	New Sharlston Coll., Ltd. Pref.	20	10
4½d.	Nw. Vancvr. Coal & Ld., L.	1	⅛
—	North's Navigation Coll. (1889) Ltd.	5	2½
10/	Do. 10 p.c. Cum. Pref.	5	7½
—	Rhymney Iron, Ltd.	5	1½
	Do. New, £5 Shs.	4½	½
5	Do. Mt. Debs., Red.	100	98½
5	Shelton Irn., Stl. & Cl. Co., Ltd., 1 Chg. Debs., Red.	100	99½
10	Sth. Hetton Coal, Ltd.	100	194½
	Vickers & Maxim, Ltd.	10	3
	Do. 5 p.c. Prfd. Stk.	100	131½

SHIPPING.

Last Div.	Name.	Paid.	Price.
4/	African Stm. Ship, £20 Shs.	16	9½
5/	Do. Fully-paid	20	13½
5/	Amazon Steam Nav., Ltd.	12½	9
8/	Castle Mail Pakts., Ltd., £20 Shs.	14	15½
3½	Do. 1st Deb. Stk., Red.	100	101
0/	China Mutual Steam, Ltd.	5	3
6	Do. Cum. Pref.	10	9½
10/	Cunard, Ltd.	20	10
5/	Do. £20 Shs.	10	4
4½	Furness, Withy, & Co., Ltd., 1 Mt. Dbs., Red.	100	105
6/	General Steam	15	8½
5/	Do. 5 p.c. Pref., 1874	10	9
5/	Do. 5 p.c. Pref., 1877	10	9
5/	Leyland & Co., Ltd.	10	15¾
7/	Do. 7 p.c. Cum. Pref.	10	14½
2/11	Do. 4½ p.c. Cum. Pre-Pf.	3	10½
4	Do. 1st Mt. Dbs., Red.	100	106½
7/6	Mercantile Steam, Ltd.	5	7½
6/4½	New Zealand Ship., Ltd.,	6	5
4	Do. Deb. Stk., Red.	100	104
5/	Orient Steam, Ltd.	10	4½
5	P. & O. Steam, Cum. Prefd.	100	156½
19	Do. Defd.	100	234½
3½	Do. Deb. Stk.	100	119
5	Richelieu & Ont., 1st Mt. Debs., Red.	100	100
30/	Royal Mail, £100 Shs.	60	51
2/6	Shaw, Sav., & Alb., Ltd., "A" Pref.	5	5½
5/	Do. "B" Ord.	5	3½
8/	Union Steam, Ltd.	20	19½
4/	Do. New £20 Shs.	10	8½
4	Do. Deb. Stk., Red.	100	107
7/	Union of N.Z., Ltd.	10	10
5½	Wilson's & Fur.-Ley., 5½ p.c. Cum. Pref.	10	10½
4½	Do. 1 Mt. Db. Sk., Rd.	100	106½

TELEGRAPHS AND TELEPHONES.

Last Div.	Name.	Paid.	Price.
4	African Direct, Ltd., Mort. Debs., Red.	100	102
—	Amazon Telegraph, Ltd.	10	7
19/6	Anglo-American, Ltd.	100	60
39/	Do. 6 p.c. Prefd. Ord.	100	108
—	Do. Defd. Ord.	100	12
3/	Brazilian Submarine, Ltd.	10	17
5	Do. Debs., 2 Series	100	114

Telegraphs and Telephones (*continued*):—

Last Div.	Name.	Paid.	Price.
4/	Chili Telephone, Ltd.	5	3½
$2½	Comicial. Cable, $100 Shs.	—	189½
4	Do. Stg. 500-yr. Deb. Stk. Red.	100	107
2½d.	Consd. Telephone Constr., &c., Ltd.	10/	½
6/	Cuba Submarine, Ltd.	10	7
10/	Do. 10 p.c. Pref.	10	15
2/	Direct Spanish, Ltd.	5	4½
5/	Do. 10 p.c. Cum. Pref.	5	10½
4½	Do. Debs.	50	104½
3/	Direct U.S. Cable, Ltd.	20	11
2/6	Eastern, Ltd.	10	18½
3/	Do. 6 p.c. Cum. Pref.	10	19½
4	Do. Mt. Deb. Stk., Red.	100	132½
2/6	Eastern Exten., Aus., & China, Ltd.	10	19
5	Do. (Aus. Gov. Sub.) Deb., Red.	100	101
5	Do. do. Bearer	100	101½
4	Do. Mort. Deb. Stk.	100	131½
5	Eastn. & S. Afric., Ltd., Mort. Deb. 1900	100	101
5	Do. Bearer	100	101½
4	Do. Mort. Debs. 1909	100	103½
4	Do. Mort. Debs. (Maur. Subsidy)	25	109½
3/	Grt. Nthn. Copenhagen	10	29
5	Do. Debs., Ser. B., Red.	100	101½
12/6	Indo-European, Ltd.	25	53½
6	London Platino-Brazilian, Ltd., Debs. 1904	100	107½
4/	Montevideo Telph., Ltd., 6 p.c. Pref.	5	2½
3/	National Telephone, Ltd.	5	6¾
6/	Do. Cum. 1 Pref.	10	17
6/	Do. Cum. 2 Pref.	10	16
5	Do. Non-Cum. 3 Pref.	5	6
3½	Do. Deb. Stk., Red.	100	106½
4d.	Oriental Telephone, Ltd.	1	½
4	Pac. & Euro. Tlg. Dbs., Rd.	100	106½
4/	Reuter's, Ltd.	8	8½
5/	Un. Riv. Plate Telph., Ltd.	5	4½
5	Do. Deb. Stk., Red.	100	102½
—	West African Telg., Ltd.	10	4½
5	Do. 5 p.c. Mt. Debs., Red.	100	102½
—	W. Coast of America, Ltd.	10	—
3/	Western & Brazilian, Ltd.	15	11¾
3/	Do. 5 p.c. Pref. Ord.	7½	7¾
—	Do. Defd. Ord.	7½	4½
4	Do. Deb. Stk., Red.	100	107
1/	W. India & Panama, Ltd.	10	¾
6/	Do. Cum. 1 Pref.	10	8½
6/	Do. Cum. 2 Pref.	10	6
5	Do. Debs., Red.	100	106½
7	West. Union, 1 Mt. 1902 $	1000	107½
6	Do. 6 p.c. Stg. Bds., Rd.	100	102½

TRAMWAYS AND OMNIBUS.

Last Div.	Name.	Paid.	Price.
1/6	Anglo-Argentine, Ltd.	5	3½
6	Do. Deb. Stk.	100	132½
4	Barcelona, Ltd.	10	12½
5	Do. Deb., Red.	100	104½
7/6	Belfast Street Trams.	10	16½
—	Blackpl. & Fltwd. Tram., £10 Shs.	8	11½
4/	Bordeaux Tram. & O., Ltd.	10	12½
5	Do. Cum. Pref.	10	11½
—	Brazilian Street Ry., Ltd.	2	½
—	British Elec. Trac., Ltd.	10	16½
—	B. Ayres & Belg. Tram., Ltd., 6 p.c. Cum. Pref.	5	4½
6	Do. 1 Deb. Stk.	100	—
—	B. Ayres. Gd. Nat., Ltd., 6 p.c. 1 Deb. Bds., Red.	100	60
5½	Do. Pref. Debs., Red.	100	96½
1/	Calais, Ltd.	5	1
—	Calcutta, Ltd.	10	3½
—	Carthagena & Herr., Ltd.	10	3
5	Do. Deb., Red.	100	90
5	City of B'ham. Trams., Ltd., 5 p.c. Cum. Pref.	5	6
4	Do. 1 Mort. Debs., Rd.	100	106½
3/9	City of B. Ayres, Ltd.	5	7½
2/3	Do. Ext. £5 Shs.	3	4½
6	Do. Deb. Stk.	100	150
1/4	Edinburgh Street Tram.	4	3½
1/	Glasgow Tram. & Omni. Ltd., £10 Shs.	8	3½
3/7½	Imperial, Ltd.	6	15
3/	Lond., Deptfd, & Greenwich, Prefd.	5	5½
nil	Do. Defd.	5	1
10½	Lond. Gen. Omni., Ltd.	100	210
4	Do. Deb., Red.	100	117½

Tramways and Omnibus (*continued*):—

Last Div.	Name.	Paid.	Price.
4/9½	London Road Car	6	10½
28/6	Do. Red. 1 Mt. Deb. Stk.	100	106½
5	London St. Rly. (Prov., Ont.), Mt. Debs.	100	110
4/9	London St. Trams.	—	2½
12/9	London Trams., Ltd.	10	10
6/	Do. Non-Cum. Pref.	10	10½
5	Do. Mt. Db. Stk., Rd.	100	100½
5	Lynn & Boston 1 Mt. 1924 $	1000	107
5	Milwaukee Elec. Cons. Mt. $	1000	100½
5	Minneapolis St. 1 Cons. Mt. $	1000	96
5	Montreal St. Dbs., 1908	100	109
4½	Do. Debs., 1922	100	107
6/	Nth. Metropolitan	10	13½
1/9½	Nth. Staffords., Ltd.	6	4½
5/6	Provincial, Ltd.	10	7
6/	Do. Cum. Pref.	10	13
5	St. Paul City, 1937 $	1000	96
5	Do. Guar. Twin City Rap. Trans. $	1000	96
5/	Southampton	10	6½
2/	South London	10	8½
7/6	Sunderland, Ltd.	10	6½
4½	Toronto 1 Mt., Red.	100	107
2/6	Tramways Union, Ltd.	5	7½
4½	Do. Deb., Red.	100	109
5/	Vienna General Omnibus.	5	6½
5	Do. 5 p.c. Mt. Deb., Red.	100	103½
4/	Wolverhampton, Ltd.	10	6½

WATER WORKS.

Last Div.	Name.	Paid.	Price.
8/	Antwerp, Ltd.	20	22
6/	Cape Town District, Ltd.	5	6½
10½	Chelsea	100	337½
5	Do. Pref. Stk.	100	178½
4½	Do. Pref. Stk., 1875	100	158½
4½	Do. Deb. Stk.	100	162½
5/	City St. Petersburg, Ltd.	13	11
5/	Colne Valley	10	15½
4	Do. Deb. Stock	100	137½
£4	Consol. of Rosar., Ltd., 4 p.c. 1 Deb. Stk., Red.	100	90
7½	East London	100	234½
4½	Do. Deb. Stk.	100	162½
3	Do. Deb. Stk., Red.	100	106
37/6	Grand Junction (Max. 10 p.c.) "A"	50	124½
18/9	Do. "B"	25	
18/9	Do. "C" (Max. 7½ p.c.)	25	57½
35/	Do. "D" (Max. 7 p.c.)	50	102½
4	Do. Deb. Stock	100	149½
13	Kent	100	360½
7	Do. New (Max. 7 p.c.)	100	215½
5/7½	Kimberley, Ltd.	7	5
6	Do. Debs., Red.	100	102½
6	Do. Deb. Stk., Red.	100	105½
10	Lambeth (Max. 10 p.c.)	100	307½
7½	Do. (Max. 7½ p.c.), 50 & 25	—	232½
4	Do. Deb. Stock	100	148½
3	Do. Red. Deb. Stock	100	105
10/	Montevideo, Ltd.	20	16½
5	Do. 1 Deb. Stk.	100	108½
5	Do. 2 Deb. Stk.	100	103½
130/9	New River New	100	440½
4	Do. Deb. Stk.	100	150½
4	Do. Deb. Stk. "B"	100	150½
—	Odessa, Ltd., "A" 6 p.c. Prefd.	20	—
nil	Do. "B" Deferred	20	—
4	Portland Con. Mt. "B," 1927	—	102½
8/	Seville, Ltd.	20	12½
5/6	Southend "Addl." Ord.	10	17½
6	Southwark and Vauxhall	100	167½
6	Do. "D" Shares (7½ p.c. max.)	100	164½
5	Do. Pref. Stock	100	177½
4	Do. "A" Deb. Stock	100	147½
3	Staines Resrvirs. Jt. Com. Gua. Deb. Stk., Red.	100	106
7/	Tarapaca, Ltd.	20	9½
10	West Middlesex	100	321
4½	Do. Deb. Stk.	100	163½
3	Do. Deb. Stk.	100	107

Prices Quoted on the Leading Provincial Exchanges.

ENGLISH.

In quoting the markets, B stands for Birmingham; Bl for Bristol; M for Manchester; L for Liverpool; and S for Sheffield.

CORPORATION STOCKS.

Chief Market.	Int or Div.	Name.	Amount paid.	Price.
M	3½	Bolton, Red. 1935 ..	100	116
M	3½	Burnley, Red. 1933..	100	114
M	3½	Bury, Red. 1946	100	118
L	2½	Liverpool, Red. 1925	100	102½
B	3½	Longton, 1932	100	106
M	4	Oldham Prp. Db. Sk.	100	145
M	£1	Do. Gas & W. Ann.		34½
S	4	Rotherham 4 p.c., Red. 1927...... [£	1 an	114
S	3	Do. Red. 1920..	100	105
M	3½	Runcorn Red. 1923..	100	105
S	2½	Sheffield Water Ann.	100	117½
S	3	Do.	3 an	90
L	3½	Southport Red. 1936 {	5 an 100	112
L	3	Do. Red. 1914..	100	102½
M	3	Todmorden, Red. 1914	100	102

RAILWAYS.

Chief Market.	Int or Div.	Name.	Amount paid.	Price.
Bl	4½	Bridgewater Pref. ..	100	137½
M	4	Cleator & Workton.	100	78
M	4	Do. 1883 Pref. ..	100	111
L	4	Cockermth. K. & P.	100	116
L	4	Isle of Man	5	6⅜
L	5	Do. Pref.	5	6⅜
L	3	Liverpool Overhead	10	10½
L	4	Do. Deb. Stk. ..	100	109
L	5	Do. Pref.	10	16
L	6½	Maryport & Carlisle	100	167
S	6	Mid. Shef. & Roth. Pf.	100	231
Bl	55/	Neath & Brecon "A"	100	67½
M	4½	Oldham, Ashton, &c.	10	17
Bl	5½	Penarth Harbour ..	100	182½
Bl	4	Do. Deb. Stk. ..	100	145
Bl	3½	Do. Deb. Stk. ..	100	127
Bl	1½	Ross & Monmouth..	20	5½
Bl	6	Do. Pref.	20	42½
M	3	Southport & Cheshire Deb. Stk.	100	104½
M	nil.	Do. Pref.	100	26
Bl	2½	West Somerset Gu...	100	96½
Bl	5	Wye Val. Deb. Stk.	100	164

BANKS.

Chief Market.	Int or Div.	Name.	Amount paid.	Price.
L	8/	Adelphi, L., £20 Shs.	10	16
L	12/6	Bk of L'pool, L., £100 Sh	12½	39½
B	5/6	Brmnghm. Dis. & C., Ltd., £20 Shs.....	4	10¾
B	6/3	Co. of Staffs., L., £40	5	13¾
S	17½	Crompton & Evans, Ltd., £20 Shs	4	15
M	14/	Lancs. & Yorks, Ltd., £20 Shs.....	10	31⅝
L	30/	Livrpl. Union, Ltd., £100 Shs.	20	60½
M	24/	Manchester & Co., Ltd., £100 Shs. ..	16	62
M	20/	Mnchstr. & Livrpool. Dis., Ltd., £60 Shs.	10	51½
M	1/6	Mer. of Lancashire, Ltd., £20 Shs.....	3	6⅜
L	16/	Nth. & Sth. Wales, Ltd., £40 Shs.....	10	35⅝
B	5/	Notts Joint St., Ltd., £50 Shs..........	10	23
M	4/	Oldham Joint Stk., Ltd., £20 Shs.....	4	11
S	10	Sheffield Banking, Ltd., £50 Shs.....	17½	51½
S	10	Do. & Rotherham, Ltd., £50 Shs..	8	26½
S	15	Do. & Hallamsh., Ltd., £100 Shs..	25	63½
S	10	Do. Union, Ltd., £40 Shs.........	10	25
M	12/	Union of Manchester, Ltd., £25 Shs.. ..	11	27½
M	10/	Williams, Deacon, &c. Ltd., £50 Shs.....	8	26½
Bl	20	Wilts & Dorset, Ltd., £50 Shs..........	10	49
S	10/	York City & Co., Ltd., £10 Shs.....	3	13¾

BREWERIES.

Chief Market.	Int or Div.	Name.	Amount paid.	Price.
B	6	Ansell & Sons Pref.	10	15½
B	5	Do. Debs.	100	110
L	9/	Bent's	10	17½
L	6	Do. Cum. Pref...	10	14½
L	4½	Do. Deb. Stk. ..	100	111
L	13/6	Birkenhead, £5 paid	5	22
L	13/6	Do. £10 paid....	10	25
M	9/	Boddington's	9	20½
M	5	Do. Cum. Pref...	10	13½
M	4	Do. Deb. Stk. ..	100	109
B	4½	Butler & Co. Db. Stk	100	110½
M	6	Chesters' Cum. Pref.	10	13½
M	4½	Do. Debs.	100	112
S	17/	Clarkson's Ord.	10	24½
S	6	Do. Cum. Prf. Stk.	10	14½
M	4	Dutton & Co. Db. Sk.	100	104
M	4½	Hardy's Crown Debs.	100	111
B	10/	Holt	10	18½
B	5	Do. Cum. Pref...	10	12½
B	4	Do. Debs.	100	108½
B	12/6	Lichfield	10	24
B	5	Do. Cum. Pref...	10	11½
M	3½	Manchester Deb. Stk.	100	141
B	6/	Mitchell, H., & Co.	10	38
B	6	Do. Cum. Pref...	10	15½
Bl	6	Oakhill Pref........	10	16½

Breweries (*continued*) :—

Chief Market.	Int. or Div.	Name.	Amount paid.	Price.
M	5/	Springwell	10	10⅝
M	7	Do. Pref.	10	13¾
Bl	9	Stroud	10	17
Bl	6	Do. Pref	10	14½
M	6/	Taylor's Eagle......	10	11½
M	7	Do. Cum. Pref ..	10	13½
M	5½	Do. Deb. Stk. ..	100	117½
S	10	Tennant Bros £20 shs	15	34½
S	10	Wheatley & Bates ..	10	14½
S	6	Do. Cum. Pref.	10	12¾

CANALS AND DOCKS.

Chief Market.	Int. or Div.	Name.	Amount paid.	Price.
Bl	5	Hill's Dry Dk. &c. £20	18	9
M	4	Manc. Ship Canal 1st Mt. Deb. Stk.	100	104
M	4	Do. 2nd do.	100	103½
L	36/3	Mersey Dck. & Harb.	an.	118½
L	35/	Do.	an.	116
M	10/	Rochdale Canal	100	37½
B	35/	Staff. & Worc. Canal	100	76½
B	4½	Do. Deb. Stk....	100	137
Bl	4	Swansea Harb......	100	114½
B	27/6	Warwick & Birm. Cnl	100	66½
B	12/6	Do. & Napton do.	100	23

COMMERCIAL & INDUSTRIAL.

Chief Market.	Int. or Div.	Name.	Amount paid.	Price.
L	5	Agua Santa Mt. Debs	100	100
M	8/	Armitage, Sir E. & Sns Ltd..............	10	19
M	4	Do. Deb. 1910 ..	100	103
L	6	Ang. Chil. Nit. 1 Mt. Debs., 1919 ..	100	109½
Bl	8½	Bath Stone Firms ..	10	20
M	4/9½	Barlow & Jones, Ltd., £10 Shs.	8	10⅜
B	12/6	Birmgham. Ry. Car.	10	17½
B	6	Do. Pref.	10	16
B	16/8	Do. Small Arms	5	16½
M	£12	Blackpool Pier......	100	277½
M	5	Do. Tower Debs.	50	54½
M	3/	Do. Wi. Gar. & P.	5	4⅜
Bl	10	Bristl. & S. W. R. Wag. £20 Shs..........	3	6
Bl	8	Do. Wag. & Carri. £10 Shs..........	10	14½
M	7/	Crosses & Winkwth. Ltd..............	5	12½
L	5	G. Angus & Co. Pref.	10	13½
Bl	5	Gloster. Carri. & W.		10⅝
Bl	5	Gt. Wstn. Cttn., Ltd.	20	15½
M	6	Hetherington, L. Prf.	10	8½
M	4½	Do. Debs., 1910	100	99½
B	7½d.	Hinks (J. & Son), Ltd.	1	27/6
S	10/	Jessop & Sons, £50 Sh	30	28½
S	10	Kayser, Ellsn. & Co. L.	5	10⅝
S	6	Do. Pref.	5	7½
M	7/6	Kellner-Partgton., L.	5	14½
M	4½	Do. Debs., 1914..	100	105½
M	5	Kerr Thread, Ltd., Debs.	100	101
B	17/	King's Norton Metal, £10 Shs..........	8½	18½
M	5/	Lancashire & Yorks. Wagon, Ltd.	10	9½
L	10/	Liverpool Exch., Ltd.	20	27⅝
L	45/	Do. Grain Stge, Ltd.	50	108
L	5/	Do. Rubber, Ltd...	5	6½
M	9d.	Manchester Bond. Whse., L., £10 Shs.	4½	2½
M	3/9	Do. Comcial. Bldgs., Ltd., £10 Shs.	5	10⅝
M	3/9	Do. No. 2, £10 Shs.	5	10⅝
M	2/3	Do. No. 3, £10 Shs.	5	7½
M	4/	Do. Corn, &c., Exchange, Ltd.	10	16½
M	4	Do. Debs.	100	125
M	8	Do. Ryl. Exchge, L.	100	246½
B	5/	Midland Rlwy. Car. Wgn., Ld., £20 Sh.	10	14½
Bl	5	Millers & Corys Dbs.	100	100½
B	12/6	Mint, Brgham., Ltd.	5	8
B	5	Do. Debs.	25	108
B	10/	Nettlefolds, Ltd.....	10	48
B	5	Do. Pref.	10	15½
S	9	Nth. Centrl. Wgn., L.	5	8⅜
B	15/	Patnt. Nut & Bolt, L.	10	35½
B	5	Do. Pref.	10	14⅜
B	1/	Perry & Co., Ltd. ..	1	31/
B	6d.	Do. Pref.	1	27/6
S	10	Round, J., & Co., L., £10 Shs.	6	12⅜
S	10	Rodgers, J., & Sons, L.	100	211
M	18/9	Rylands & Sons, Ltd., £20	15	39½
M	2/6	Do. paid up	20	44½
M	4	Do. Debs. ..1909	100	106
S	5	Sanderson Brs. & Co., Ltd. Debs.	100	102
M	4½	Schwabe, S., & Co., Ltd., 1 Debs. 1914	100	104
S	7½	Sheffield Forge & Rolling, Ltd.	10	11½
L	80/	Southport Pier, Ltd.	100	88½
L	2½	Do. W. Gdns., Ltd.	5	3½
Bl	5	Spillers & Bakers, Ltd, £10 Shs.	9	14½
Bl	6	Do. Pref.	10	14½
B	5/	Union Rolling Stock, Ltd., £20 Shs.....	5	7½
M	6/	Victoria Pr., S'port, L.	5	4⅜
Bl	8	Western Wagon & Property, Ltd.....	6	9½
S	10	Westenholm, G., & Son, Ltd., £25 Shs.	20	24
S	6½	Yorksh. Wagon, Ltd.	2	2⅜

FINANCIAL, TRUSTS, &c.

Chief Market.	Int. or Div.	Name.	Amount paid.	Price.
M	1/	Manchstr. Trst. £10 Shs...............	2	13/9
M	1/3	N. of Eng. T. Deb. & A., Ltd. £10 Shs.	2½	26/
M	3½	Do. 1 Mt. Debs...	100	96
L	—	Pacific Ln. & Inv., L.	2½	3
L	4	Do. Deb. Stk.....	100	102
L	—	United Trst., L. Prfd.	100	72½
L	—	Do. Deferred....	100	62½

GAS.

Chief Market.	Int. or Div.	Name.	Amount paid.	Price.
Bl	5	Bristol Gas (5 p.c. mx.)	100	129½
Bl	4	Do. 1st Deb.	100	137
S	10	Gt. Grimsby "C" ..	10	201
L	10	Liverpool Utd. "A"	100	253
L	7	Do. "B"......	100	188½
L	4	Do. Deb.	100	137
S	10	Sheffield Gas "A," "B," "C"	100	253
B	10½	Wolverhampton	100	225
B	3	Do. 6 p.c. Pref...	100	170½

INSURANCE.

Chief Market.	Int. or Div.	Name.	Amount paid.	Price.
M	6	Equitable F. & Acc. £5 Shs.	1	40/
L	—	Liverpool Mortgage £10 Shs.	2	1 5/12
M	2/	Mchester. Fire £20 Shs	2	7½
M	5/	National Boiler & G., Ltd., £10 Shs.	3	13⅜
L	2/	Reliance Mar., Ltd., £10 Shs.	2	4 5/12
L	4/	Sea, Ltd., £10 Shs...	2	10 1/12
L	8/	Stnd. Mar., L., £20 Sh.	4	8⅜
L	—	State Fire, L., £20 Sh.	1	2½

COAL, IRON, AND STEEL.

Chief Market.	Int. or Div.	Name.	Amount paid.	Price.
Bl.	7/6	Albion Stm. Coal ..	10	11½
M	15/9	And. Knowles & S., Ltd., £37½ Shs. ..	23½	12½
M	5	Do. Mt. Debs. 1908	100	105½
Bl.	1/½	Ashton V. Iron	100	26
S		Bessemer, Ltd.	10	20½
S	5	Do. Pref.	10	12½
S	7	Briggs, H., & Co., "A" £15 Shs.....	12½	15⅜
S	7	Do. "B" £15 Shs.	8½	9⅜
S	20	Brown Baley's. Stl., L.	10	32½
S	5	Brown, J., & Co., Cum. Pref.	10	13 5/16
S	5	Cammell, C. & Co., Ltd.	85	12½
S	5	Do. Pref.	5	6⅜
M	5	Chatterley Whitfield. Col., Debs., 1905..	100	100½
Bl	4	Davis, D., & Sons, Ld.	10	9½
M	5	Evans, R., & Co., Ltd., Deb., 1910 ..	100	100½
S	12½	Fox, S., & Co., Ltd., £100 Shs.	80	178
Bl	10	Gt. Wstn. Col., L., "A"	5	10
Bl	5	Do. "B"	5	4⅜
Bl	8	Main Colliery, Ltd.	10	8
B	2/6	Muntz's Metal, Ltd.	5	7½
B	5	Do. Pref.......	5	6⅜
M	2/6½	Nth. Lonsd. Iron and Steel, Ltd., £10 Sh.	8½	2½
Bl	6	North's Nav. Coll., Ltd., Debs.	100	105
S	60/	Parkgate Irn. & Stl., Ltd., £100 Shs. ..	75	70½
M	6	Pearson & Knls., Ld., "A" Cum. Pref...	50	46
B	10/	Sandwell Pk. Col., L.	10	17½
M	6/3	Sheepbridge Coal and Iron, Ltd., "A"	25	17½
M	2/6	Do. "B"	10	6⅜
M	5	Do. "C" Gua. Pf.	25	28½
Bl	4	South Wales Coll., Ltd., "A"	17	7½
S	55/	Staveley Coal & Iron, Ltd., "A" £100 Sh.	60	81½
S	55/	Do. "C"	60	82
M	1/10½	Tredegar Iron & Cl., Ld., "A" £10 Sh.	7½	2½
M	1½	Do. "B" Stk. ..	100	37
M	2/	Wigan Cl. & Irn., Ld.	10	7
M	1/6	Do. £10 Shs.	7½	3½

SHIPPING.

Chief Market.	Int. or Div.	Name.	Amount paid.	Price.
Bl	6	Bristol St. Nav. Pref.	10	11½
L	15/	Brit. & Af. St. Nav..	10	13½
L	3/10½	British & Estn, Ltd.	6½	2 5/12
L	10/	Pacific Stm. Nav., L.	25	24½
L	10/	Wst. Ind. & Pac. St. Ltd., £25 Shs....	20	29½

TRAMWAYS, &c.

Chief Market.	Int. or Div.	Name.	Amount paid.	Price.
B	5/	Brmngh. & Aston, L.	5	11⅜
B	5/	Do. Mid., Ltd. ..	10	7⅜
Bl	6/	Bristol Tr. & Car., Ltd..............	10	21
B	4/	Do. Debs.	100	121
L	6	I. of Man Elec., L., Pref.	1	1½
M	15/	Manchester C. & T., L., "A" £20 Shs.	15	27⅜
M	10/	Do. "B"	10	19⅜

WATER WORKS.

Chief Market.	Int. or Div.	Name.	Amount paid.	Price.
Bl	7	Bristol	25	64
Bl	7	Do...............	20	46½
Bl	58/	Do. 7 p.c. max. ..	100	159
Bl	4½	Do. Pref.	20	32½
Bl	5	Do. Pref.	10	18⅜
Bl	3½	Do. Deb.	100	129½
M	10	Fylde "A"........	100	335
M	7	Do. "B"	100	224
B	6	S. Staffs. Ord. "A"	100	168
B	—	Do. "B"	100	167
B	4	Do. Deb. Stk.	100	140
B	5	Do. Pf "A" "B" "C"	100	170
M	£3⅜	Stockport District ..	100	187½
B	2/	Wolverhampton New	5	6½

SCOTTISH.

In quoting the markets, E stands for Edinburgh, and G for Glasgow.

RAILWAYS.

Chief Market.	Int. or Div.	Name.	Nom. Amount	Price.
E	5½	Arbroath and Forfar	25	51
G	2	Callander and Oban .	10	7½
G	4	Do. Deb. Stock	100	148
G	4½	Do. Pref.......	10	14½
G	4	Cathct. Dist. Deb. Stk.	100	148
E	5	Edin. and Bathgate .	100	179½
E	7	Forth & Clyde Junc.	100	226
G	4	Lanarks. and Ayrsh.	10	14
G	4	Do. & Dumbartons.	10	14½
G	4	Do. Deb. Stk.	100	149

BANKS.

Chief Market.	Int. or Div.	Name.	Nom. Amount	Price.
G	12	Bank of Scotland ..	100	357½
G	16	British Linen	100	490
G	8	Caledonian, Ltd.....	2½	95/6
G	10	Clydesdale, Ltd.	10	23½
G	16	Commercl. of Scot., L.	20	88½
G	16	National of Scot. Ld.	100	430
G	8	Royal of Scotland ..	100	233
G	11	Union of Scotland, L.	10	26½

BREWERIES.

Chief Market.	Int. or Div.	Name.	Nom. Amount	Price.
E	5	Bernard, Thos. Pref.	10	10½
E	5	Bernard, T. & J., Cum. Pref.........	10	13
G	20	Highland Distilleries	3½	10½

CANALS AND DOCKS.

Chief Market.	Int. or Div.	Name.	Nom. Amount	Price.
G	4	Clyde Nav. 4 p.c....	100	125½
G	3½	Do. 3½ p.c.......	100	105
G	3½	Greenock Harb. "A"	100	100
G	2	Do. "B"	100	40

MISCELLANEOUS.

Chief Market.	Int. or Div.	Name.	Nom. Amount	Price.
G	4½	Alexander & Co. Debs.	100	110½
G	5	Baird, H., & Sns. C. P.	10	12½
E	10	Barry, Ostlere, & Co.	7½	12½
E	6	Do. Cum. Pref...	10	15 1/16
G	5	Brown, Stewart, Deb.	100	84
E	7½	Broxburn Oil	8½	9
E	6	Do. Cum. Pref...	10	11 1/16
E	7	Edinburgh & Dist. Tram. Cum. Pref.	5	9
E	5	Gilroy, Sons, & Co. Debs.	100	99
G	9	Glasgow Cot. Spin...	6	5½
G	30/	Do. Royal Exchg.	46	110
G	—	Pumpherston Oil Pf.	10	8
E	7	Scottish Assam Tea	10	11 1/16
E	5	Scottish Waggon....	10	12¼
G	5	Stoddard & Co. Pref.	10	12 1/12

FINANCIAL, LAND, AND INVESTMENT.

Chief Market.	Int. or Div.	Name.	Nom. Amount	Price.
G	1/	Assets Co..........	1	47/
E	4½	Investors' Mort. Pref.	100	99½
E	4	Do. Deb. Stk....	100	103½
E	4	Nthn. Inv. N. Zeal. Deb. Stk.	100	107
E	4	N. of Scot. Canadian Deb. Stk.	100	106
E	4½	Real & Deb. Corp. Deb. Stk.	100	107½

INSURANCE.

Chief Market.	Int. or Div.	Name.	Amount paid.	Price.
G	12/	Caledonian F. & Life	5	36
G	4/6	City of Glasgow Life	2½	13
E	19/	Edinburgh Life	20	55
G	13/1	Life Ass. of Scotland	8½	34½
E	8	Nat. Guar. & Surety	2	52/
G	17½	Scottish Union and National "A"....	1	97/6
G	17½	Do. "B"	3½	18¼

IRON, COAL, AND STEEL.

Chief Market.	Int. or Div.	Name.	Amount paid.	Price.
E	Nil.	Addie, Coll. Cm. Pref.	10	8
E	8/	Arniston Coal	8	14
E	8½	Cairntable Gas Coal	8	86/
E	12	Fife Coal	10	20¾
E	5	Do. Cum. Pref..	10	13
G	7	Merry & Cunghame. Cum. Pref........	10	15½
G	5	Do. Debentures ..	100	106¼
E	1/9	Niddrie & Benhar Cl.	1½	41/
G	5	Steel Com. of Scotlnd	—	
	—	"A" Deb. Stk. ..	100	113
G	6	Do. and Mt. "B"	100	105
E	—	Watson, John	8½	10½
E	6	Do. Cum. Pref..	7½	8½
E	12½	Wilson's & Cly. C[illegible]l	3	8⅝

IRISH.

In quoting the markets [illegible] stands for Belfast, and D for Dublin.

CORPORATIO[illegible]KS.

Chief Market.	Int. or Div.	Name.	Amount paid.	Price.
B	3½	Belfast, 1921 [illegible]	100	112
B	3½	Do. 191[illegible]	100	108½
B	3½	Do. 1924........	100	109½
B	3	Do. 1955........	100	106
B	3½	Do. Water Com...	100	117½
B	3	Do. do.	100	106
B	3½	Do. Harbour Com.	100	114½
D	3½	Rathmines & Rathgar	100	110½
D	3½	Waterford Deb.	100	—

RAILWAYS.

Chief Market.	Int. or Div.	Name.	Amount Paid.	Price.
D	30/	Cork, Bandon, & S.C.	100	—
D	4	Do. Deb.........	100	130½
D	4	Do. W. Cork Pref.	100	—
B	5½	Belfast & Northern..	100	159¾
B	4	Do. Deb.........	100	146
B	4	Do. Pref.	100	141½
B	6½	Belfast & C. Down..	100	166
B	4	Do. Deb.........	100	147
B	3	Do.	100	107½
B	4½	Do. 4½ Pref. B...	100	153¾
B	5	Do. Guar.	100	172½
D	Nil.	Dublin, Wick. & Wex.	100	32
D	4	Do. Deb.........	100	126½
D	4½	Do. Deb.........	100	130
D	6	Do. Guar.	100	—
D	4	Do. C. of Dub. Junc.	100	—
D	5	Do. 1860 Pref. ..	100	—
D	—	Do. 1864 Pref. ..	100	—
D	—	Do. 1865 Pref. ..	100	90
B	6½	Great Northern	100	179½
B	4	Do. Deb.........	100	147
B	4	Do. Pref. B.	100	143½
B	5½	Gt. South & Western	100	142½
B	4	Do. Deb.	100	147½
B	4	Do. Guar.........	100	143
D	45/	Midland Gt. Western	100	116
D	4	Do. Deb.	100	146½
D	4½	Do. Deb.	100	151½
D	4½	Do. Deb.	100	—
D	5	Do. Pref.	100	173½
D	4	Do. Pref.	100	141
D	—	Waterford & Central	100	15½
D	3	Do. Deb.	100	105½
D	3½	Do. Pref.	100	134
D	4	Waterfd. L., & W. Db.	100	129½
D	4½	Do. Deb.	100	—
D	4	Do. Pref.	100	125
D	3½	Do. Pref.	100	100

BANKS.

Chief Market.	Int. or Div.	Name.	Amount paid.	Price.
B	50/	Belfast, Old, £125 Shs.	25	125½
B	20/	Do. New, £125 Shs.	25	50½
D	2/6	Hibernian, £20 Shs.	5	6⅝
D	2/	Munster & Leinster £5 Shs.	2	5⅛
B	11/	Northern, £50 Shs...		27½
D	13/	Royal, £50 Shs.	10	28½
B	5/	Ulster, £15 Shs.	2½	12½

BREWERIES AND DISTILLERIES.

Chief Market.	Int. or Div.	Name.	Amount paid.	Price.
D	10/	Castlebellingham & Drog............	10	16½
D	6	Do. Pref.	10	16
D	4½	Do. Deb.	100	116
B	17/	Dunville & Co.......	10	28½
B	6	Irish Distillery, Pref.	10	13½
B	5	Do. Deb.	100	110
B	6	J. & J. M'Connell, Pf.	10	15⅛
B	13/6	Mitchell & Co.......	9	20
B	5	Do. Deb.	10	11¼
D	4½	Phœnix Brew. Deb.	100	—
B	6/	Wm. Cowan........	10	13½
B	6	Do. Pref. ..	10	13½
B	8/	Young, King, & Co.	8	14

STEAM AND CANAL.

Chief Market.	Int. or Div.	Name.	Amount paid.	Price.
B	Nil	Belfast Steamship ..	50	35½
D	10/	British and Irish	50	—
D	15/	City of Dublin.......	100	63½
D	3½	Do. Deb.	100	105
D	30/	Dublin & L'pool. Bldg.	50	75
D	2/6	Dundalk & Newry..	10	4½
D	4/	Grand Canal.......	10	12½
D	3	Do. Pref. ..	10	9½
D	3	Do. Deb. ..	100	99
B	30/	Irish Shipowners....	100	63
B	3/	Ulster Steamship....	5	5½

MISCELLANEOUS.

Chief Market.	Int. or Div.	Name.	Amount paid.	Price.
D	3/1	Arnott & Co.	4	7½
D	6	Do. Pref. ..	4	5
B	8/	Belfast Com. Bldgs.	10	11
B	37/6	Do. Ropework Co.	75	90
B	5	Do. do. Pref.	10	13½
B	2/	Do. Discount Co..	3	45/
B	5	Do. do. Pref.	5	4½
B	10/	Brookfield Linen....	25	17½
B	Nil	Coey & Co.	25	4
B	5	Do. Deb.	90	49½
B	4½	David Allen&S's Deb.	100†	107½
D	4/	Dublin Trams	10	21
D	6	Do. Pref....	10	18½
D	4	Do. Deb....	100	—
B	6/	Edenderry Spinning.	10	9
B	25/	Falls Flax Spinning.	25	15
B	17/	Forster, Green, & Co.	10	22
B	9/	Island Spinning	7½	7½
B	8/	Jas. Lindsay & Co..	8	16½
B	1/7½	John Arnott & Co...	4	4½
B	4½	Do. Deb........	50	56
D	5/	Kinahan & Co.......	20	11½
D	5½	Do. Pref........	20	11½
D	4½	Do. Deb........	100	108½
B	12/	Kirker & Co.	10	10
B	5/	Leahy, Kelly, & Leahy	5	8
B	6	Do. Pref........	5	7½
B	2/4½	Lindsay Bros. Ltd...	8	7½
B	4½	Do. Deb........	50	56½
D	1/	National Assurance.	2½	38/
B	10/	Olley & Co.	5	7½
D	1/1½	Patriotic Assurance..	2½	30/3
B	3/7½	P. Johnston & Son, L.	6	6½
B	10/	Robertson, F., & Co.	8	23½
B	10	Ulster Marine Insur.	5/	6/6
B	15/	York-street Flax	25	35½
B	6	Do. Pref........	10	15½
B	4½	Do. Deb........	100	120½

INDIAN AND CEYLON TEA COMPANIES.

Acres Planted.	Crop, 1897.	Paid up Capital.	Share.	Paid up.	Name.	Dividends. 1894.	1895.	1896.	Int. 1897.	Price.	Yield.	Reserve.	Balance Forward.	Working Capital.	Mortgages, Debs. or Pref. Capital not otherwise stated.
	lb.	£	£	£	INDIAN COMPANIES.							£	£	£	£
11,240	3,128,000	120,000	10	3	Amalgamated Estates	—	*	10	5	3¼	8½	10,000	16,500	D52,050	—
		400,000	10	10	Do. Pref.	—	*	5	†5	10½	4¾				
10,223	3,960,000	187,160	20	20	Assam	20	20	20	5	60½	6½	55,000	1,730	D11,350	—
6,150	3,278,000	142,500	10	10	Assam Frontier........	¾	6	6	—	9	6½	—	286	20,000	82,500
		142,500	10	10	Do. Pref.	6	6	6	3	11¾	5¼				
2,087	839,000	66,745	5	5	Attaree Khat	12	12	8	3	7½	5½	3,790	4,820	7,770	—
1,633	583,000	78,170	10	10	Borelli	4	4	5	—	8	6¼	—	3,256	D270	6,500 Pref.
1,720	812,000	60,825	5	5	British Indian	6	5	5	—	4½	6	—	2,920	12,300	16,500 Pref.
3,223	2,247,000	114,500	5	5	Brahmapootra	20	18	20	6	13½	7	—	28,440	41,600	·
3,754	1,617,000	76,500	10	10	Cachar and Dooars	*	8	7	—	10½	6½	—	1,645	21,240	·
		76,500	10	10	Do. Pref.	*	6	6	3	12½	4¾				
3,946	2,083,000	72,010	1	1	Chargola	8	7	10	2½	1	10½	3,000	3,300	—	—
		81,000	1	1	Do. Pref.	7	7	7	3½	1¼	5				
1,971	942,000	33,000	5	5	Chubwa	10	8	10	3½	6½	7½	10,000	2,043	D5,400	—
		33,000	5	5	Do. Pref.	7	7	7	3½	7	5				
32,250	11,500,000	120,000	10	3	Cons. Tea and Lands	—	—	10	5	3½	7½	65,000	14,240	D191,674	—
		1,000,000	10	10	Do. 1st Pref.	—	*	5	†5	11½	4½				
		400,000	10	10	Do. 2nd Pref.	—	*	7	†7	12	5¾				
2,230	617,000	135,420	20	20	Darjeeling............	5½	5½	6	—	23	5	5,552	1,565	1,700	—
2,114	445,000	60,000	10	10	Darjeeling Cons........	—	—	4/2	—	7	—	—	1,320	—	—
		60,000	10	10	Do. Pref.	—	*	5	2½	9¼	5¼				
6,660	3,518,000	150,000	10	10	Dooars	12½	12½	12½	2½	20½	6¼	45,000	300	D32,000	—
		75,000	10	10	Do. Pref.	7	7	7	3½	17	4¼				
3,367	1,811,000	165,000	10	10	Doom Dooma	11¼	10	12½	5	22	5¾	30,000	4,032	—	10,000
1,377	582,000	61,120	5	5	Eastern Assam	½	nil.	4	—	3½	6¼	—	1,790	—	10,000
4,038	1,675,000	85,000	10	10	East India and Ceylon		nil.	7	—	9	7½	—	1,710	—	—
		85,000	10	10	Do. Pref.	*	6	6	3	13	4½				
7,500	3,363,000	219,000	10	10	Empire of India	—	*	6/10	2	12½	—	15,000	—	27,000	—
		219,000	10	10	Do. Pref.	—	*	5	2½	11¼	4½				
1,180	540,000	94,060	10	10	Indian of Cachar	7	3½	3	—	5	6	6,070	—	7,120	—
3,050	824,000	83,500	5	5	Jhanzie	10	10	10	4	8½	6	14,500	1,070	2,700	—
7,980	3,680,000	250,000	10	10	Jokai	10	10	10	5	18	5½	45,000	990	D9,000	—
		100,000	10	10	Do. Pref.	*	6	6	3	15½	3¾				
5,224	1,563,000	100,000	20	20	Jorehant	20	20	20	—	60	6½	26,220	2,955	3,000	—
1,547	504,000	65,660	10	8	Lebong	15	15	15	5	17	6½	9,000	2,150	8,650	—
5,082	1,709,000	100,000	10	10	Lungla	½	10	6	3	9½	6¼	—	1,543	D21,000	—
		100,000	10	10	Do. Pref.	*	6	6	3	12	5				
2,684	885,000	95,970	10	10	Majuli	7	5	5	—	7	7	—	2,606	560	—
1,375	380,000	91,840	1	1	Makum	—	—	2	—	1⅛	1½	—	—	1,800	25,000
2,990	770,000	100,000	1	1	Moabund	—	—	*	—	1	—	—	—	-	—
		50,000	1	1	Do. Pref.	—	—	*	2½	1	5				
1,080	482,000	79,590	10	10	Scottish Assam	½	7	7	—	11½	6¼	6,500	800	9,590	—
4,150	1,456,000	100,000	10	10	Singlo................	½	8	5	2	9½	4½	—	300	D5,200	—
		80,000	10	10	Do. Pref.	*	6½	6½	3½	13	5				
	Crop, 1896.				CEYLON COMPANIES.										
7,970	1,743,824	250,000	100	100	Anglo-Ceylon, & Gen.	—	*	5½	—	68	7½	10,992	1,405	D72,844	166,400
1,836	685,741	50,000	10	10	Associated Tea	—	*	5	—	8½	5½	—	164	2,478	—
		60,000	10	10	Do. Pref.	—	*	6	—	10½	5¾				
10,390	4,000,000§	167,380	10	10	Ceylon Tea Plantations ..	15	15	15	7	27½	5½	84,500	1,516	D30,819	—
		81,080	10	10	Do. Pref.	7	7	7	†7	17½	4¼				
5,722	1,542,700§	55,260	5	3	Ceylon & Oriental Est....	½	8	7	—	2	7½	—	230	D2,047	71,000
		46,000	5	5	Do. Pref.	6	6	6	3	5½	5½				
2,157	801,629	111,330	5	5	Dimbula Valley	—	*	10	5	6½	8	—	—	1,733	6,230
		62,607	5	5	Do. Pref.	—	*	6	3	6½	4¾				
11,496	3,715,000	298,250	5	5	Eastern Prod. & Est.	3	5	6½	2½	6½	4¾	20,000	11,740	D17,797	100,000
3,118	701,100	130,000	10	10	Lanka Plantations.......	4	5	5	†5	6½	6½	—	495	D11,300	14,700 Pref.
2,193	1,050,000§	22,080	10	10	New Dimbula "A"	10	16	16	—	25	6	11,000	2,004	1,150	—
		55,710	10	10	Do. "B"	18	16	16	—	23	6½				
		5,400	10	10	Do. "C"	nil.	8	14	—	15	8½				
2,572	570,360	100,000	10	10	Ouvah	6	8	6	2	9½	6½	4,000	1,151	D1,255	—
2,030	535,675	200,000	10	10	Nuwara Eliya	—	*	6	3	11½	5½	—	—	—	30,000
1,720	720,200	41,000	10	10	Scottish Ceylon	15	15	15	5	23	6½	7,000	1,252	D3,970	—
		9,000	10	10	Do. Pref.	7	7	7	3½	16½	4½				
2,450	750,000§	56,000	10	6	Standard	12½	15	15	5	13½	6½	9,000	800	D14,022	4,000

* Company formed this year. Working-Capital Column.—In working-capital column, D stands for *debit*. † Interim dividends are given as actual distribution made. ‡ *Total* div. § Crop 1897.

Printed for the Proprietor by LOVE & WYMAN, LTD., Great Queen Street, London, W.C.; and Published by CLEMENT WILSON at Norfolk House, Norfolk Street, Strand, London, W.C.

The Investors' Review

EDITED BY A. J. WILSON.

Vol. I.—No. 10. New Series. | FRIDAY, MARCH 11, 1898. | [Registered as a Newspaper.] | Price 6d. By post, 6½d

The Investment Index,

A Quarterly Supplement to the "Investors' Review."

Price 2s. net. 8s. 6d. per annum, post free.

THE INVESTMENT INDEX is an indispensable supplement to the Investors' Review. A file of it enables investors to follow the ups and downs of markets, and each number gives the return obtainable on all classes of securities at recent prices, arranged in a most convenient form for reference. Appended to its tables of figures are criticisms on company balance sheets, State Budgets, &c., similar to those in the Investors' Review.

Regarding it, the *Speaker* says: "The Quarterly 'Investment Index' is probably the handiest and fullest, as it is certainly the safest, of guides to the investor."

"The compilation of securities is particularly valuable."—*Pall Mall Gazette.*

"Its carefully classified list of securities will be found very valuable."—*Globe.*

"At no time has such a list of securities been more valuable than at the present."—*Star.*

"The invaluable 'Investors' Index.'"—*Sketch.*

"A most valuable compilation."—*Glasgow Herald.*

Subscription to the "Investors' Review" and "Investment Index," 36s. per annum, post free.

CLEMENT WILSON,
NORFOLK HOUSE NORFOLK STREET, LONDON, W.C.

THE

LAW GUARANTEE AND TRUST SOCIETY, LIMITED.

Capital Subscribed	£1,000,000
do. Paid-up	£100,000
do. Uncalled	£900,000
Reserve Fund	£70,000

FIDELITY GUARANTEES,
On behalf of Managers, Secretaries, Clerks, Cashiers, Collectors, &c.

DEBENTURE INSURANCE.
The advantages of such Insurance are as follows:—
1. The Debentures being guaranteed by the Society can be placed at not less than par, thus saving discount.
2. A lower rate of interest is willingly accepted.
3. The Society acting as Trustee for Debenture Holders also adds to the Security.

MORTGAGE INSURANCE.

CONTINGENCY INSURANCE,
In respect of Defects in Title, Lost Documents, Missing Beneficiaries, Re-Marriage, Issue and Name and Arms Risks, &c.

LICENSE INSURANCE.
Mortgagees of Licensed Property should always insure in a substantial Insurance Society against loss they may sustain by depreciation in consequence of the license being lost.

TRUSTEESHIPS for Debenture
Holders, and under Wills, Marriage Settlements, &c.

HEAD OFFICE:
49, CHANCERY LANE, LONDON.
CITY OFFICE:
56, MOORGATE STREET, E.C.

CONTENTS

The Investors' Review.

Russia and China.

We earnestly hope that the British public is not going to lose its head over the latest display of Russia's purpose towards Manchuria. To talk of going to war about that territory, or anything else, with a great Power like Russia is sheer madness—madness of a kind which is becoming traditional with certain sections of people in this country, whose utter want of a capacity for reflection was strikingly exemplified in the harangue of Lord Roberts in the House of Lords on Monday last. His speech, which the Service and Jingo papers have lauded to the skies as the words of a wise statesman, seemed to us little better than a prolonged howl of apprehension. At the very best it was devoted to the advocacy of a policy towards Russia which experience has taught us to be the most disastrous to our interests that the country has ever followed in modern times. The greatest fool living hardly now contends that the Crimean war was a wise episode in our history. Most people recognise that it was a terrible blunder, but we have never abandoned the policy which dictated that blunder; and one consequence of adhering to it has been that to-day India is brought almost to ruin as a British dependency. There never was any good reason why we should seek to block Russia's outlet southwards, or to an open ocean, as we have done. It was folly to support Turkey against Russian aggression, but we have toiled and schemed and done evil at an enormous cost to ourselves in order to checkmate Russia; and the net result is that we are, as an Imperial power, immensely weaker to-day, far more isolated also, than we should have been had we cordially admitted our blunder in making war on Russia in 1854, and as cordially helped her to spread the benefits of orderly government over regions of the earth now full of bloodshed and every conceivable infamy.

Doubtless, Russia herself has lost a great deal by our hostility, and not least in the direction of an enlargement of the civil liberties of her people. Had Englishmen been welcomed in Russia—in helping the Government to develop the country, to build its railways, to establish its industries, to improve its agriculture—the personal qualities of the Englishman, his profound love of individual liberty, his manliness and honesty, must have had a powerful influence in shaping the domestic policy of the Russian Government and in educating the people towards a conception of self-respect now scarcely to be found there, except amongst the aristocracy. But if Russia has lost something we have lost much more, and we are destined to be still the losers if we assume an attitude in China detrimentally hostile to Russian designs upon Manchuria. Instead of doing that, we ought to endeavour to placate Japan so as to prevent war between her and Russia, because, should war break out, it might become almost impossible for us, in our own interests, not to side with the Japanese. At all costs war ought to be prevented. It is in nobody's interest, least of all in that of China. Readers, we hope, noticed the interview with Sir William Des Vœux in Wednesday's newspapers. It was well worth reading and pondering over. We have room for only one extract of it, but it is enough to show the wisdom of the whole :

> It is the integrity of the real China which we have to guard, and to which all our strongest efforts should be directed. Militating much more against this object than the occupation of Manchuria is the control which Russia is reported to have acquired over Chinese armies. Her immediate object in obtaining it has unquestionably been to provide additional defence against possible attack by Japan. She would very probably relinquish it in exchange for assurance against such attack, and our acquiescence in respect of Manchuria. For many reasons I hold that Russia has no interest in being our enemy, and is only such because we force her to be so. Indeed, I am not without good reason for believing that she would gladly hold out her hand to us if we met her half way. If, however, on the above condition she was to refuse to give up her hold on China proper, it would then become clear that I am wrong, and that she intends hostility to us.

Sir William knows the East. He was Governor of Hong Kong, and has great Oriental experience, both Japanese and Chinese. His statement that Manchuria is not part of China proper, but only a conquered territory is perfectly accurate, and his advice to us to limit our efforts to the maintenance of the integrity of the eighteen provinces composing the ancient Empire of China is the best possible to follow. As he truly points out, Russia has long had designs upon Manchuria and the Leao-Tong Peninsula, and, from her point of view, such designs are perfectly reasonable. She wishes to utilise the resources of Siberia through ports ice-free all the year round. According to the ethics of modern empires—ethics strikingly exemplified by our conduct in every part of the world, Russia is perfectly justified in annexing this territory if she has the power, and power to do so she undoubtedly does possess. We could no more permanently prevent Russia from annexing this region than we could conquer her as an empire and hold her immense dominions as we hold India. The Japanese alone might be able to destroy her fleet next spring ; with our help it certainly could be destroyed, but what would either Japan or ourselves gain thereby ? Absolutely nothing. Neither they nor we could land and maintain armies to be marched into the interior to drive the Russians back. Steadily and surely her battalions would spread themselves over the country, without let or hindrance from us or any one. As steadily and surely a new fleet would be provided, and before many years were over, either by another war or through the persistence of a powerful race steadily marching onward in the fulfilment of its destiny, Russia would have all that she now desires and probably more. It is not by resistance we can stop Russia, but by friendliness and co-operation much might be done to open the regions which she annexes to our commerce. As Sir William Des Vœux says, if we draw off Japanese hostility, and effect an arrangement between the Japs and the Russians, whereby the former may be ensured room for expansion, it may be then in our power to get Russia to withdraw her demand for the control of the Chinese army—a demand obviously dictated by motives of self-defence. Russia wishes to train Chinese troops so that if Japan does recklessly plunge into war, her armies may receive a very different reception from what they got in the last fight. Look at it how we may, there is no ground for us to quarrel with Russia about China's northern dependency ; and we beseech the public to exercise prudence, to avoid indulgence in wild braggadocio language which can do no good, and, above all, to try to shake the mind clear of the absurd terrors about Russian designs and Russian machinations, to which Lord Roberts gave expression last Monday evening. To nourish this sentiment is to court our own undoing.

The Trade Returns for February.

Perhaps it is owing to the disturbed state of politics in all parts of the world that the figures of our foreign trade so far this year are proving to be so disappointing. The return for February shows a decrease of nearly 4 per cent. in the imports and rather more than 1 per cent. in the exports. This is not much in money, about £1,700,000 altogether on the two sides of the account, but the exports represent a decrease upon a decrease, since the figures for February last year were fully 9 per cent. below those for February, 1896. The outcome is, therefore, discouraging, and so far this year our imports are nearly 2 per cent. under those of 1897, and our exports quite 2 per cent. under. Only in the re-exports of foreign and colonial merchandise is there any enlargement, and these on the two months have risen over 6¼ per cent. When, however, we look into the details of the accounts we find less to be alarmed at than this summary way of speaking might lead people to suppose. Apparently we are less dependent on foreign supplies of grain this year than last, for there is a heavy decrease in our imports of wheat, which in spite of a rise in price amounting to about 1s. 3d. per cwt. has cost us nearly £700,000 less so far this year than in the first two months of 1897. All descriptions of cereals, in fact, except oats, have cost us less than last year, up to date. The decrease is slight, but considering the higher price ruling in some cases, it is satisfactory. The slight expansion in our imports of wheatmeal and flour do not offset the decrease in the imports of wheat itself.

Against this consolation, however, must be set the pronounced tendency to increase shown by our imports of dead meat of all descriptions. It is a progressive increase, the figures for 1898 being much larger than those for either of the two preceding years, with the result that the country has had to pay about £440,000 more under this head than in 1897, and about £100,000 more than in 1896, up to the end of February. Much the same testimony is afforded by such articles as eggs, for the supply of which we are becoming increasingly dependent on the Continent. Eggs are even coming to us from Russia, so unable are we to provide them at home. The import of articles of consumption which cannot be produced in this country is steady, and, on the whole, tending to increase—a proof, at least, that the consuming power of the nation has not been impaired. True, our imports of sugar, refined and unrefined, have been less this year than in the first two months of 1896, but they are distinctly larger than last year's. Our imports of tea are also distinctly progressive, although the return for February alone was less than that for the same month last year. Home consumption, however, does not seem to be expanding in this article at present, nor yet in foreign spirits; but the consumption of wines is on the increase, and so is that of tobacco. There is nothing important to be said of our imports of metals, except to note a decrease in the supply of copper ore and of regulus and precipitate. Our import of iron ore is also less, but that is probably merely a temporary drop in the figures, as we certainly require more iron every year, were it for nothing but to supply the demands of the Navy. Raw materials used for textile manufacturers show better on the whole in quantities than in values—a proof that we are buying on advantageous terms. In cotton, for example, the decrease in quantity for the two months is only 72,000 cwt. on a total of 4,420,366 cwt., but the decrease in value is nearly £2,000,000. For the month of February alone there is an increase of nearly 262,000 cwt. in the quantity, at the same time that the value has fallen off about £320,000. Flax is also cheaper, as well as hemp and silk, while the price of wool remains pretty much where it was a year ago. This cheapness is certainly favourable, and the decrease of more than £4,000,000 in the total value of the raw materials required for textile manufactures is not a thing to lament over, but represents in some measure a gain to manufacturers.

For when we turn to the exports we find that, although prices for these likewise are lower, they have not, on the average, gone down so far as the cost of raw materials. We are, therefore, now in a better position to compete in foreign markets than we should have been if prices for raw materials had remained where they were a year ago. In other respects, however, the exports of textiles are not in a very satisfactory position. Our trade appears to be on the decrease with a good many countries, not only in cotton and woollen fabrics, but in jute and linen as well. As regards cotton, in the first two months of this year, there has been a decline, more or less important, in our shipments to Germany, France, Italy, Turkey, Egypt, Dutch India, China, Central America, West Africa, South Africa, and Australasia. No doubt the loss in these instances is more than made g od by larger exports to Foreign West Africa, Austria, B azil, t e Argentine Republic, and, above all, to Indi ; but the fact remains that trade is languishing with many of our most important customers. This holds true also of exports of linen yarn, although not of linen piece goods. These last have lately been, one may say, stationary; but the figures show a notable decline compared with those for 1896, especially with the United States, British North America, Columbia, and France. As regards woollen goods, there is an increase in woollen and worsted yarn for the two months of this year over the same period of 1897, but a decrease on 1896, especially in the value; and woollen tissues have also fallen off very materially both in quantity and in value, the principal loss being attributable to the United States, to which we have this year so far sent only 425,600 yards, as against 1,376,400 in 1897, and 3,375,400 in 1896. China also is showing the disorganisation of its trade by taking less, and so are our Australasian possessions.

The testimony of the figures relating to worsted tissues is to the same effect, exports to the United States having fallen from upwards of 12,000,000 yards in the first two months of 1896, to less than 4,000,000 in the same period of the present year. It is notable here, also, that countries like France, China, and Japan are rapidly-declining customers; for the present, at all events. Neither is our trade in metals flourishing as we should like to see it, although in this instance we may still, perhaps, attribute the stagnation to the effects of the prolonged struggle in the engineering trade last year. Broadly, however, it may be said that the customers who are not in a position to borrow from us with a free hand are poor buyers of our iron, whether crude or manufactured. Fresh capital, for example, is obviously required to stimulate exports of mining machinery, which have fallen off this year £643,000, against which decrease there is a slight gain in the total exports of iron and steel, whose value, in spite of their paltry-looking totals in quantity, aggregated £1,696,421 for February, and £3,724,406 for the two months. There is a decrease in the month's figures compared with both the preceding Februarys, but on the two months there is a slight gain.

On the whole, the impression obtained by studying these returns is that business drags and is in places difficult to conduct with a reasonable prospect of profit. Our smaller exports even are suffering, or are at least non-progressive, such as those of soap, skins and furs, paper of most descriptions, and earthenware. To sum up, the total value of our imports for February amounted to £35,770,874, a decrease of £1,474,290, and of our exports to £17,641,849, a decrease of £222,873. For the two months to date, the value of the imports has amounted to £75,700,165 and the exports to £36,873,253, a decrease in the one case of £1,320,667, and in the other of £777,665. Re-exports, however, show a total of £9,994,318, an increase of £615,195, or 6·3 per cent. on the first two months of last year. Adding exports and re-exports together, and deducting their total from the value of the imports, there is a difference against the country, so to say, of about £29,000,000 on the trade of January and February, and this is set off by a million only of net exports of gold and silver in the same time, the country having lost £531,050 of its stock of gold since January 1, and £488,443 of its stock of silver. The position is, therefore, not altogether comfortable, with so many insolvent or half-insolvent debtor states, and such heavy war clouds around us.

An Example in American Life Office Methods.

The subjoined correspondence between the Mutual Life Society of New York and one of its policy-holders would be highly amusing, were it not for the manner in which the policy-holder has lost the use of his money. It seems that some six years ago he was induced to take out a twenty-year Endowment policy. Having some money by him, he was led by the agent to pay £200 down in a single premium for policies covering £325. The agent, he informs us, with whom the business was contracted, highly approved of this mode of payment, and told him that he would be able to get his money back if necessary, or else to borrow on the policy; not only so, but that the policy would always be saleable for what had been paid for it, since any bank would advance up to the £200 on such a very valuable piece of paper. This was nice, but the correspondence we print exhibits the other side of the picture.

About eighteen months ago, the policy holder desired to raise money on his investment, and applied to two banks where he was known with this object. Both told him that they certainly could not advance on a policy in an American office. Had it been in an English office the result would have been different. He then tried the Mutual of New York Office itself, and it refused also to lend on its own paper. Still gaining experience, the holder next tried a leading firm of auctioneers to see whether the policy was saleable, and was told by them that American life policies could only be sold with difficulty. Going back to the issuing society he tried again to secure the return of his money, and only received very vague letters on the subject—letters which kept begging the question. Finally he succeeded in reaching the General Manager, who told him that the policy had no surrender value, but that it might be changed for another kind of policy, for which they would give about £130. The offer was refused, and the Manager graciously intimated that he would never advise such a policy to be taken out, but did not repudiate the action of his agent, who, to all intents, had obviously practised a form of the "confidence trick" upon an unsuspecting victim. The correspondence speaks for itself. Readers, however, may note in it a description of the surrender values mentioned by three of the British offices to whom this client of the Mutual Life Office applied for information. The original letters on which each of these estimates are based lie before us, and fully bear out the writer of the letters, and are, in their straightforwardness, a suggestive contrast :—

February 10, 1898.

Sir,—Policies —— and ——, maturing ——, twenty year distribution.

I should be greatly obliged if you would let me know how much the Society would allow me if I surrendered the policies? Also please let me know what amount of cash I should have received for these policies in 1896, had they been taken out under the five year distribution scheme, but maturing in 1911 and surrendered at the end of the first five years.—I remain, yours faithfully,

X.

The Manager, Mutual Life Assurance of New York.

This letter was not acknowledged, so the policy-holder wrote again on February 15, and was answered the following day in the letter here subjoined :—

17 and 18, Cornhill, London, E.C.,
February 16, 1898.

Dear Sir,—I have to acknowledge receipt of your letters of the 10th and 15th inst., and, in reply to your inquiry, I may say that the Company are not prepared at the present time to make an offer for the purchase of Policies ——— and ———.—Yours truly,

D. C. Haldeman, General Manager.

February 17, 1898.

Dear Sir,—I am surprised to hear these policies have no surrender value. In an English office I should have had a valuable policy by now. I have made inquiry of three offices, and I find that for the same kind of policy as the one issued by you to me, in one case the surrender value at the end of the first year would have been 100 per cent. of the premium paid, in the two others 90 per cent., and in each the surrender value would increase with the age of the policy. The British offices act more justly than you do. I have also been informed that some of the American offices do grant surrender values. It is strange you do not. It appears that one who pays for his policy, as I did, is in a worse position than one paying for it by annual premiums. I shall certainly endeavour to point out to my friends the inadvisability of insuring in an office which does not grant surrender values. I observe you have ignored the last paragraph of my letter of the 10th.—I remain, &c.,

The Manager, &c. X.

17 and 18, Cornhill, E.C.,
February 18, 1898.

Dear Sir,—I have to acknowledge receipt of your letter of the 17th inst. I am very sorry you have seen fit to write in the strain you do. It was not our wish that you paid a single premium, nor was it our wish that you selected this kind of policy. You could not get the benefits of the Life option without the Endowment and the Distribution period being coterminous. In making comparisons you must compare things that are equal, which you are not doing. I venture to say that none of the companies you have referred to would duplicate the policy that you have taken with us.—Yours truly,

D. C. Haldeman, General Manager.

February 19, 1898.

Dear Sir,—I have to acknowledge the receipt of your letter of the 18th inst.

The reason I selected this class of policy and mode of payment was that I wished to have a policy easily negotiable, should at any time I require money, and your representative assured me that the policy I had selected would always fulfil my requirements. I also was told that though the bonus on the policy at its maturity would not be so great as on policies paid for by annual premiums, yet this would be compensated for by the extra negotiability. Knowing the English offices always gave some surrender values, I never thought at the time that you would not do the same. I asked one of your agents the other day whether my policy could be surrendered for a reasonable sum; his first answer was that he thought so, but would look the matter up; he then found he was wrong. I quite understand that the life option would be different if the distribution period was not conterminous with the maturity of the policy.

I am afraid I did not make my meaning clear. I wished to find out what options would have been given me at the expiration of the first five years had I chosen the same policy with a five years' distribution, and if one of the options was a cash payment what would have been the amount of the cash? I know the life option would have been different. British offices offer similar policies to yours, but with this advantage, viz., in the office I am thinking of, the surrender value at the end of the first year would be 100 per cent. of the premium paid, and this would increase with the age of the policy.

The policy is as follows :—Twenty year endowment annual payments for twenty years, or a single payment at maturity, cash for policy and bonus, or an annuity of 5 per cent. or sum assured, and bonus for life, and the sum assured and bonus to representatives at death, or the sum assured and bonus at maturity, could be sunk in an annuity. This is practically on the same lines, only in your case the bonus is not distributed until the end of the twenty years, and in theirs it is every five years, but the principle is the same.—Yours, &c.,

X.

The Manager, &c.

17 and 18, Cornhill, E.C.,
February 22, 1898.

Dear Sir,—I have to acknowledge receipt of your favour of the 19th inst., and as it seems useless to prolong our correspondence on the subject, I think it would be in every way more satisfactory if you would give me a call at your convenience. I shall be very pleased to explain fully to you our own policies, and to indicate where they are more advantageous than the other policies to which you refer.—Yours truly,

D. C. HALDEMAN, General Manager.

February 23, 1898.

DEAR SIR,—In reply to yours of February 22, 1898, I have to inform you I shall be unable to call on you at your office. You have not answered my questions yet.

If you do not grant surrender values and if you do not make loans on your policies, no policies issued by you can be so advantageous to Englishmen as policies issued by English companies. If you alter your rules, then possibly you may be able to boast of offering better terms, and the result may prove you are right.—Yours truly, X.

This fellow was getting troublesome, causing pre-eminent respectability within-the-law and the bond, some shade of annoyance. It therefore became necessary to speak plainly, and this Mr. Haldeman does in the following letter, which we conscientiously recommend as a model of its kind, objurgatory, persuasive, hortatory, unctuousy severe, and overlaid with an assumption of injured innocence which is "just lovely," as a young lady would say :—

17 and 18, Cornhill, E.C.,
February 24, 1898.

DEAR SIR,—I am surprised that you should write to me in the way you have in your letter of the 23rd inst., to hand this morning. If you did not know your own mind when you took out the policy, you must forgive my saying that you have no right to turn round now and censure the company; or because your policy does not contain options which you were at perfect liberty to have had you taken a different class of policy at the time, you surely cannot blame us ; the fault rests entirely with you.

It is not a question of changing our rules : it is a question of your having chosen one thing, and now, after a lapse of time, being sorry you did not choose another.

I am not aware, either, that you have the power to speak on behalf of Englishmen at large.

I must say that I do not think your letter is written sincerely. You know full well that we do give surrender values; all you have to do to know this is to read your own policy. Why you should make this statement now, when you know it is not true, I am at a loss to understand.

As I have already said, you chose certain ways of dealing with your policy. I have a case before me now, where a gentleman took the same class of policy as yours, but chose a different mode of settlement. He had to give up certain options that you have at the end of twenty years, but he preferred other advantages at the end of ten years, and he had the option of surrendering the policy at the end of the tenth year, receiving back no less than ninety-five per cent. of the premiums he has paid as a cash surrender value, although only half the endowment period has run, and, in addition, had he died before completion of the ten-year distribution period, the company guaranteed an addition to his policy, no less £5 1s. 2d. per cent. per annum. This is an actual result of a twenty-year endowment policy, with a ten-year distribution period, taken out at this office ten years ago.

It is our practice to be as courteous as possible to our policy-holders, and to give them every information that lies in our power; and you must forgive my saying now, that in face of your letter of the 23rd inst., I see no useful purpose in carrying on the correspondence any further.—Yours truly,

D. C. HALDEMAN, General Manager.

February 25, 1898.

DEAR SIR,—Seeing that in your answer to my first letter you stated that the society would not purchase my policies, I naturally concluded they had no surrender values. You now state you do grant surrender values. If so, what is the surrender value of my policies?—Yours faithfully, X.

17 and 18, Cornhill, E.C.,
March 3, 1898.

DEAR SIR,—I have to acknowledge receipt of your letter of the 25th ult. It seems futile to continue the correspondence, as you persistently ignore the fact that when you made your application to the company, you, in order to secure the full benefits of the survivorship principle, entered into an agreement with the company that no cash surrender value should be payable to you until the completion of the twenty-year distribution period which you selected. You were at perfect liberty when you insured to select a five, ten, fifteen, or twenty year distribution period, and having taken the last-mentioned you are not at liberty now to change the contract, as this would be tantamount to your making a selection against other policy-holders who had insured at the same time as yourself, and under the same conditions.—Yours truly,

D. C. HALDEMAN, General Manager.

March 4, 1898.

DEAR SIR,—Your letter of the 3rd is the first intimation I have had that policies in your company can only be surrendered for cash at the expiration of the distribution period selected. Had I known this I certainly should not have insured in your society. If you will refer to my previous letters you will find that the reason I took out the policies in question was that I might have a policy easily negotiable, and I am confident that when discussing the matter with your representative he never even hinted that I was under a wrong impression. I am now more convinced than ever that though your results may prove better than the results in English offices—but of this I have grave doubts—yet the permanent advantages are with the English offices.—Yours, &c., X.

17 and 18, Cornhill, E.C.,
March 5, 1898.

DEAR SIR,—I am utterly at a loss to understand your letter of the 4th inst. Surely as a business man, or a man with an ordinary amount of common sense, you cannot expect me to believe that you would send a written application to us applying for a particular kind of policy, and for a distribution period that must be coterminous with the endowment in order to obtain certain results, and in exchange for this application receive from us a contract setting forth the conditions on which the policy is issued, and that you never read through the application which you signed, or even read the policy which you received in exchange. If so, then it seems to me utterly incomprehensible, and all I can say is that, if it is so—and it must be if your contentions are right—then you have no one to blame but yourself, and you must not cast any reflections upon our representative, nor must you say that the company does not give surrender value.

I do not like to think that you are writing these letters to annoy us, but that is the only interpretation I can put upon them, seeing that you have refused to call here in response to my invitation, when I should perhaps have been able to explain everything to your satisfaction.

D. C. HALDEMAN, General Manager.

Is not this correspondence curious? There can be no question, either, that Mr. Haldeman is quite within his rights in leaving this unhappy fly in the net, who chose to be victimised by an "agent." Said fly is seeking to alter his "contract." Behold the "endorsement" on one of the policies in proof of his folly :

[Endorsement on Policy.] *Life Option.*

At the maturity of the endowment term of this policy, instead of accepting the cash settlement then provided for, the insured may continue this insurance for the full amount without medical examination, and without further payment of premium, by exchanging it within thirty days after such maturity for a paid-up policy of life insurance payable at death, participating annually in dividends, and in addition thereto the insured shall be entitled to a paid-up annuity of £8 for life, payments thereon to commence one year after said maturity. This policy is issued on the twenty year distribution plan ; it will be credited with its distributive share of surplus apportioned at the expiration of twenty years from date of such issue. Only twenty-year distribution policies in force at the end of such term and entitled thereto by year of issue, shall share in such distribution of surplus, and no other distribution to such policies shall be made at any previous time. All surplus so apportioned may be applied at the end of such period to increase the amounts under the life option and paid-up annuity *pro rata*, if previously requested in writing, or may then be drawn in cash.

In the language of Mr. Haldeman, no "business man or a man with an ordinary amount of common sense" would ever dream of signing such a contract as this, had the nature of it, and the fact that he was bound to part with all claim to any portion of his money for a term of twenty years, been made known to him beforehand. It is a contract so one-sided, so contrary to the usages in

English life insurance offices, that not one of them would, we believe, have taken this man's money on such terms. He has plainly been "hocussed" by the "agent," who probably netted £80 or £100 by the transaction, and upright men ought to be ashamed to be associated in any capacity with such "insurance." None the less is it true that, powerless as the victim of enterprise of this kind always is to legally prove fraud and misrepresentation against their "agents," the Mutual Life Office of New York is quite within the contract in sticking to the £200. The insurant's only consolation is that, if he lives, he may some fourteen years hence get it back with interest and some slender "bonus."

"Lipton's."

Undoubtedly Sir Thomas J. Lipton's business is at present a good one. He trades in things that people require as necessaries in their lives. By splendid organisation, command of unlimited banking capital, and a careful study of the wants of the common people, one of the most extensive provision businesses in the world has been built up in a comparatively short space of time. As the prospectus of the company to which Sir Thomas proposes to transfer this business observes: "There is practically no limit to the development of the business in goods which are required for daily consumption, and the company having hundreds of thousands of customers, has a ready market for any new article it may introduce from time to time." Not only so, but new commodities can be put before customers with a facility, and to an extent, no other organisation of the kind that we know of can hope just yet to rival. For example, a "fluid beef" has lately been put upon the market by Sir Thomas and very extensively advertised n competition with "Bovril" and other articles of the kind, and no doubt his servants will be able almost to pour it down customers' throats. Again, a few years ago—for the business altogether does not date more than fifteen years back, so far as we can recollect—Sir Thomas went extensively into Ceylon tea production, and amongst the estates taken over by the company are no less than twelve tea estates in Ceylon.

The profits of all this business have recently, it seems, been very large, and, according to the certificate ot Messrs. Turquand, Youngs, & Co., amounted to £176,984 in 1897, as against £68,046 in 1890. This is an increase of £108,938, or upwards of 160 per cent. in seven years. But these profits are, in a sense, gross profits, inasmuch as they have borne no deduction for interest on capital and loans, or for Sir Thomas Lipton's management. Nor, for that matter, does it seem to be the case that the cost of recent advertising has been deducted from them. This has been stupendous during the last few months.

Splendid as this business may be, we cannot say that we see value for two and a half millions of capital in it. On many essential points information is not produced in the prospectus, but we are told that the assets, consisting of tea, coffee, and cocoa estates in Ceylon, all freehold; of freehold and leasehold properties, factories, warehouses, and branch establishments throughout the United Kingdom and in Calcutta and Colombo; of plant, machinery, fixtures, and fittings, carts, vans, horses, &c., stock-in-trade, cash in hand, bills receivable, and book debts are valued by the vendor himself at merely £976,785. Add the £200,000 which is to be handed back to the company out of the purchase price of £2,466,666, deduct the total from the said purchase, and we find that the amount paid for goodwill, trade marks, and brands,' &c., is £1,289,821, or more than 50 per cent. of the entire amount given for the business. Besides this, interest at 4 per cent. per annum is to be paid on the purchase price from November 20 last to completion of purchase. We have no means whatever of testing the valuation, since the prospectus gives us no information. But we can see from the accountants' abstract of past profits that the business is a highly speculative one, and twice in the eight years shown it did not yield enough to pay the debenture interest and preference dividend on the proposed capital. Yet so eager is the temper of the Stock Exchange and the speculative public to get hold of such a seemingly splendid concern, that quite a week before the prospectus appeared, before even the nominal value of the shares was known in the market, dealings were entered into in the ordinary shares at ¾ premium. When it became public that these ordinary shares were to be £1 shares offered to the public at 5s. premium, the market price fell a little, but only for a day, and as we write the quotation is still ¾ premium on the ordinary, and 5s. premium on the preference. As a friend puts it: "The fact is that speculative eagerness is doing its best to throw a slur upon Sir Thomas Lipton's intelligence by offering him three-quarters of a million to a million more for his business than he himself thought it was worth."

There is no curing this feverish lust to gamble in anything presentable, or which can be made to appear so: nothing will cure it short of a bank smash. For many years we have held the view that the custom of floating companies with shares of £1 nominal value, fully-paid, would in the end cost the British public far more than it ever could lose by shares of a higher denomination only partly paid up. The £1 share is so handy for the small gambler. To have paid a £75 premium on a £100 share, or even a £7 10s. premium on a £10 share would have been more than nine-tenths of the habitual market gamblers would have cared to do, but 15s. on a £1 share looks nothing, therefore the multitude rushes to "deal" and get stripped. We know quite well that it is hopeless to contend against this spirit. If it cannot be gratified at one point, it will at another. No sooner have mine shares palled upon the public taste than something else must be laid hold of, to be played with and to lose money by; for money must ultimately be lost and in large amounts by companies such as this. Lipton's business is, let us grant, a good one now; ten years hence, five years hence, it may not be half so good. In buying it for nearly two and a half millions the public is capitalising a fluctuating profit, and paying in "goodwill" alone nearly ten times the amount of the average profits for the past three years.

Sir Thomas Lipton has no monopoly in any of the articles in which he deals. Some of his possessions to be taken over imply very serious risks to their owners, such as the Ceylon Tea estates. Nobody at all acquainted with the history of Ceylon could put trust in the durability of any industry carried on there. For a few years still the production of tea may yield large profits to all well-conducted Ceylon companies, but the day is sure to come when competition will reduce these profits; and a day might even arrive when they would disappear altogether, as the profits of coffee-growing did, not so many years back. In other directions the business must encounter fierce competition. How, for instance, can the directors be assured of "large additional profits" from the manufacture of beef extract and fluid beef? Not to speak of "Bovril," there are dozens of manufactures of this sort of article on the market, and the demand is not unlimited. To obtain a large sale, prices will have to be cut, and in proportion as they go down profits must tend to sink. The public, however, do not care a straw for this calculating view of the matter. The accountants tell them that the profits have mounted with astounding rapidity, and shares are bought on the assumption that they must continue to expand in the future as they have done in the brief past during which the business has been in existence. And for a few years all may go according to their wishes. The danger from over capitalisation seldom comes just at once; very frequently a fillip is given to a business through the sensation caused by its conversion into a public company. Sooner or later, however, over-capitalisation cripples the power to compete. New firms, less weighed down by capital charges, enter the field, and are able to undersell the overburdened corporations. What the public is here buying, then, is the chance, the speculative chance, of large future profits on a globular capitalisation represented by no solid assets whatever. Looking on such hints at a valuation as is vouchsafed about Sir Thomas Lipton's multifarious undertaking, we doubt whether there is really security of a first-class kind for the half million of debentures which are put with the property as a floating charge. Certainly there is no real security for one million of the capital, and there must be very heavy liabilities on leases, for it is not presumable that many of the establishments which the Company will have to carry on and maintain throughout the three kingdoms, are freehold property. Great numbers of them, we suspect, are held on leases of very short tenure. On this point also, however, there is no information, and it is more by what is not said than by what we see in print, that we are disposed to doubt exceedingly the future prosperity of this huge tea, fluid beef, cocoa, jam, sauce coffee, cake, and pork business.

Economic and Financial Notes and Correspondence.

THE NAVY ESTIMATES.

All we can now say about these is that they are inevitable in the present temper of the nation. Their amount however, is sufficiently large to cause us to ask how long and how far this kind of thing is to go on? The total estimate for the coming official year is £23,778,000, or nearly £2,000,000 more than the estimate put forth a year ago, and almost £1,500,000 more than the expenditure voted for this present year, including supplementary estimates. We learn that another 6,300 men are to be added to the officers and men of the navy, and ship building of course is to go on as furiously as ever. Three battle ships, four armoured cruisers and four sloops are to be laid down. Including the new orders there will be no less than ninety-five vessels of various descriptions under construction for the navy in the coming year, twelve of them being battle ships, the cost of which amounts to £1,000,000 or more a piece, and the utility of which grows more and more doubtful the more we have experience of them.

Going back to the past for a moment it is worth while taking note of the fact that twenty years ago the expenditure on the navy was less than £11,000,000. In fact, between 1855 and 1880 it never once reached a total of £12,000,000, and was for four years out of the period under £10,000,000. The foreign trade of the country was then not much smaller than it is now, but the fever of empire had not risen to its present height, nor had the farce of keeping the peace by over-arming come to be the prevailing fashion. Unquestionably this enormous expenditure, amounting for the Army and Navy together to some £44,000,000 of money, this coming financial year, is being provided for, to a considerable extent, out of the capital of the nation. It does not realise this fact yet; well for us will it be when the day of realisation arrives if we find ourselves in a position to build any more ships of war at all.

AND RUSSIA ALSO!

Yes, if England must have a huge unmaimable Navy, and Germany, France, and the United States ditto ditto, Russia cannot linger behind, especially now that she is to have at least one open port on the mid-ocean —Port Arthur. So the news comes that 90 million roubles will be devoted to new ships out of the current income of the Empire. We can only hope that the ships will be ordered or built here. It would be well for our ship-yards to have the United States, Russia, and Spain bidding against each other for the ships they have on hand for China, Japan, Brazil and other countries, whose zeal to have a big navy outruns the capacity of their treasuries to pay for the luxury. The ships must be bought ready made or nearly so, for there is no time to build them. Russia in particular, should hurry up, since not only will the North Pacific thaw soon, but the Turkish question will be upon us again in all its acuteness before the spring is well open. The Turk will not leave Thessaly we may be sure until forced. Russia will force him and the Dardanelles too. Then won't brand new ships of war come in useful. Ah! what a sad world it is, and how far from the peace it dreams of.

THE WAR FEVER IN THE UNITED STATES.

So, at last, the fashion just spoken of has spread to America, and the United States legislature has voted upwards of $50,000,000 to be devoted to an increase in the Navy. Mr. McKinley, in giving reasons for this step has fallen quite into the European, not to say British manner, and carefully points out that the money is to be laid out in the interests of peace. It is not for us, however, to criticise such a departure, much as we may lament that a peace-loving nation like the United States should fall into an imitation of us, where imitation is undesirable. We do not believe that this increase in the American Navy was necessary, but if the people think so and feel that they can spend the money, well, they must just do as they please. Some day, we suppose, a better temper will come to prevail among the great civilizing powers of the world, and the outcry for more armies and more fighting men stand a chance of being treated with the ridicule and contempt it essentially deserves. Modern armaments are a mockery when placed side by side with modern progress in the arts of peace. But they serve excellently well to dissipate a people's substance, and American iron masters and engineers now stand a chance of faring as richly as our own. They are quite right to get their innings when they see the chance, and democracies love, above all things, to be fooled out of their money.

The Bombay Riots.

Already have events in Bombay given the lie to Lord Sandhurst's officious optimism and in the most unpleasant way possible. A dissatisfied population in that city, the most Europeanised in the Peninsular, ridden down by troops, Mahommedans making common cause against Europeans with the Hindoos whom it is their wont to despise. Something must be wrong with the system of Government which rouses such passions. Why was no heed given to the representations of leading natives that the methods of inspection adopted by the Government in hunting down the plague were offensive to deep-rooted native prejudices, and calculated to induce riots—the very thing which has happened? Is it because the British civilian official is no longer in touch, still less in sympathy, with the natives? If so, and we fear much it is, our rule in India is indeed on a precarious basis. Much is plainly wrong out there. Is our incurable optimism to lead us to go blindly and trustingly on until the wrong produces mischief past remedy?

Finance and "Glory."

It is not surprising that Lord Roberts, in the grand manner of military critics, refused to discuss the financial aspects of the Indian Forward policy, in support of which he showed so much enthusiasm in the House of Lords on Monday night. Great as well as little military commanders only think of spending; and if their heedless squandering operations are promptly followed by bankruptcy or national ruin, they content themselves with the protest that "it is not their business" to consider how the money is obtained for their costly expeditions. The more need, therefore, for Ministers and civil officials who must consider carefully the question of ways and means, to keep a tight rein on military enthusiasts. Lord Salisbury has already shown his appreciation of this necessity. Even Lord George Hamilton admitted that there was some need of caution in the future, and Lord Onslow, the India Office spokesman in the House of Lords, was only following in the wake of the Premier when he reminded Lord Roberts that the Forward policy must be tempered by some consideration for the pockets of the Indian taxpayers. But what did Lord Lansdowne mean by unceremoniously "rounding" upon his Ministerial colleague, and telling him that he had misunderstood Lord Roberts's meaning? Is it no business of the Secretary pro War to think of financial matters? Or did he know, tea, cu throwing Lord Onslow overboard, that he was freehold ing the same unceremonious operation on Lord and bran. Lord Roberts made his meaning plain Kingdom ar the Forward policy had failed, he said, it machinery, fi cause it had not been carried far enough. stock-in-trade, cas downe's view? Was it he or Lord debts are valued sed the Ministerial opinion? Lord £976,785. Add the lain. It is not a point on which there should be divided counsels in the Government at least of all in the present condition of India.

A Warning to Bankers.

This day week a case was reported in *The Times*, which bankers should make a note of. A firm of engineers, Marshall, Sons, & Co., sued Brown, Janson & Co., bankers, for damages caused by fraudulent misrepresentation. The firm asked the bankers whether the National Skating Palace, Limited, was good in the way of business for £100, and received the following reply:—

"Confidential. For your private use, and without responsibility on our part."

"Dear Sirs,—We are in receipt of your letter of yesterday's date, and in reply thereto beg to inform you that the company mentioned is very respectable, and in our opinion may be considered quite good for your figures in the way of business.—We are, Dear Sirs, yours truly, Brown, Janson & Co."

On this opinion goods are supplied and never paid for. At that time the business with the Skating Palace Company was really in Brown, Janson & Co.'s hands, they holding a bond for £20,000, subsequently increased to £25,000, over the whole of its assets. The company had been placed in the hands of a receiver by Brown, Janson, & Co., who took possession of the assets. It was utterly bankrupt at the date when the goods were ordered. Failing to get their debt paid, and barred by the action of the company from excuting a judgment for it, Marshall, Sons, & Co., brought an action against the bankers for the amount of their bill, £104 odd; and as there was really no defence, the Lord Chief Justice mercifully allowed a juror to be withdrawn, on the understanding that the bankers would pay the claim, so as to avoid, as he remarked, casting on them "the slur of a verdict." The story was altogether an ugly one as told in court, and we trust it does not in any way represent average banking customs. Any way bankers will now know that the words "without responsibility" do not protect them against having to suffer for the consequences of opinion given about customers.

The Bill of the Council of Foreign Bondholders.

It was, we suppose, the clever tactics of Sir John Lubbock, which prevented any discussion of this Bill at the recent meeting of the Corporation. If so, he was again victorious. The measure, however, must not be left out of sight, and we again point out that it contains a principle which should not be conceded. It is beyond the power of Parliament to take the property of a Corporation and extinguish its proprietors, who are "permanent" members. No government has power to confiscate people's possessions in this fashion, nor yet to hand over what is confiscated to a section of the owners in the way the Bill proposes to hand over all the property of the Corporation to the Council. It is true, of course, that two legally held meetings of certificate-holders authorised this transfer, but we have already more than once indicated the questionable way in which these meetings were summoned and handled. The Bill has been treated in a hole-and-corner manner throughout—in a manner, we say deliberately, honourable men should not have allowed themselves to be associated with. Therefore, this part of the plot must be carefully examined into by a Parliamentary committee, and also the question how far executors dealing with deceased estates have been induced to sell certificates, found among the property in their charge, under the impression that such certificates possessed only a sentimental value. unquestionably those certificates have frequently been picked up through the agency of the Council's staff at less than one quarter of their real value, and that fact alone stamps the dealing as something eminently deserving investigation. We keep hammering at this subject, but not, it must be confessed, with great hope of doing good. Foreign bondholders are almost more apathetic than shareholders in joint stock companies. They will not help themselves—never have done. Had they been diligent in looking after their interests in the past the many scandalous debt compositions to which the Council of Foreign Bondholders has been a party in the course of its history, could never possibly have been brought about.

THE LONDON AND GLOBE AMALGAMATIONS.

Mr. Whitaker Wright has sent out another circular to the shareholders of half-a-dozen of its companies or groups of companies—Mainland Consols, Golden Crown, Wealth of Nations, Paddington Consols, Hannan's Golden Group and Hannan's Golden Treasure companies, which is really a beautiful production. Some of these shares "for a year or two commanded premiums of from 50 to 300 per cent." so he, in effect, says, you fellows have had "a good run for your money." That some of the mines are now in debt, that few, except the Wealth of Nations, have any working capital left, that sufficient water is not to be had, that "rich ore" no longer appears, that dividends never did come in sight, these are all nothing to the purpose. All that is now necessary to secure another market, "run" is fusion, and confusion, of interests within the wide-mouthed sack of the Standard Exploration Company, Limited, a thing whose very name should be worth 50 per cent. premum right off. We have more than once expressed a frank enough opinion on this new kind of bait, and shall not again labour the point. After all, Mr. Whitaker Wright is a very smart American, and if he can by this means or another draw a few more fortunes out of the public, who is to say him nay. Of substance in these properties we see none, capitalised as they have been and are to be. Some of them may originally have been wine and water, but in the new distillation the wine will disappear. Really though, this circular should be kept as a curiosity, and because one of these days the London and Globe and its dependencies might get into the Law Courts.

A KLONDIKE INVESTMENT!

A fortnight ago we called attention to the Central Klondike Gold Mining and Trading Company, Limited, which had been shown to be a swindle of the worst description. We refrained from any comment at that time, owing to the matter still being *sub-judice*. The company was promoted by one E. G. Savigny, and registered in November, 1897, without articles of association, so that the signatories became the first directors. The address of the company was that of the London and South Eastern Bank, an alias of Savigny, who acted as the bankers of the company. The nominal capital was £100,000, but in response to the prospectus the public only came forward with £16,454, which included £2,000 applied for by Savigny himself, which he never paid, and an application for 6,600 shares by "Chas. M Hosali," which was apparently in the writing of the *deus ex machinâ* Savigny, and in respect of which the company never received a penny. On December 29 it was found that this gentleman had drawn a cheque for £5,000 on the "bankers," which he had signed as director. This and other amounts were drawn without the knowledge of the board except one Aitken, who has just received, as a further share of the plunder, fifteen months' hard labour at the Old Bailey. Savigny has since been adjudged bankrupt, and like a prudent man has sought foreign air. It is to be hoped that he also will be allotted as soon as possible a temporary retirement in one of Her Majesty's prisons.

THE NORTHERN TERRITORIES COMPANY.

This week the Northern Territories Gold Fields of Australia has issued its report, and the document is quite in the usual Bottomley vein. The accounts are drawn up to September 30, and after working fourteen months the company appears to have spent £52,351 upon development and mining expenditure, and obtained £1,629 from rents and tributing, and £609 from gold won. Administrative charges had also to be met, so that the company has spent all but £1,023 of the £54,015 subscribed for working capital. On September 30, it had yet to receive £20,000 in calls on the shares of the insiders who supported the concern, and doubtless a good deal of this, if not all, has been called up and spent in the interim.

The gem of the report, however, is the announcement that the Howley property has been sold to a subsidiary company with a capital of £150,000, from which sale the Northern Territories Company is to receive £100,000 in shares. A large body of ore is stated to exist on this property, but the same thing was stated in 1886—only twelve years ago—when the Port Darwin Gold Mining Company opened a career that led to such disastrous results. The Northern Territories Co. is going to deal with the shares obtained from this transaction, and, doubtless, will distribute them to its own shareholders, who must then gloat over the fine company they are in. All this makes us think of the old Hansard Union days, and we fear wicked financiers may be doing Mr. Bottomley a mischief later on.

TUNIS TRANSFORMED BY FRANCE.

In his report on the "Regency of Tunis during the French Protectorate," Sir H. H. Johnston gives us a very attractive account of this country as it is after seventeen years of French rule and guidance. Formerly a lawless, ungovernable, bankrupt land, where neither life nor property was secure, the poor oppressed and the rich plundered; where to travel from one town to another was almost an impossibility on account of the danger and expense, it is now a peaceful and prosperous community, in which each individual has the protection of just laws for himself and his possessions, and where travelling is easy, cheap, and as safe as in England or France, nay safer, for Sir Henry tells us that an "enterprising missionary bicycles alone, or accompanied only by his wife, anywhere he pleases, and no one has ever said a disagreeable word to him or thrown a stone"!

The products of the country, agricultural, mineral, and manufacturing, have all been fostered and encouraged. It is solvent, and its commerce has increased in value over £2,000,000 per annum. Our own trade with it is nearly £700,000, and according to Sir H. J., might, with a little pushing, and less of the "take-it-or-leave-it and pay-on-delivery" manner of doing business, be greatly extended, in spite of the new differential tariff duties. These duties came into force at the beginning of the year, and though the differences at present are unimportant, it is the thin end of the wedge, and before long, to quote my authority again, "we must be prepared to see French goods enter Tunis free of duty." From a Frenchman's point of view, no doubt this is admirable policy, as tending to increase the trade of his own nation; but it is short-sighted, for other nations resent such selfish protection, and prefer the extension of rule on the part of a country like our own, where equal commercial advantages are granted to all alike.

The Shipping Garrotte and Foreign Competition.

Colonel Foss has written, and published at the office of the *Mercantile Guardian*, a sixpenny pamphlet on this subject, which is worth reading, although the writer swipes about him rather wildly. There are many facts scattered throughout his pages which the manufacturers and shippers of this country might weigh and ponder over. Most of them are extracted from official publications, and are highly suggestive. What, for example, are we to think of this? Conference steamers—that is to say, steamers in the ring—"carry American cotton goods from New York to Shanghai at 25s. to 26s. 6d., and out of this they pay the Atlantic steamer about 7s. 6d., leaving only 17s. 6d. to 19s. for the steamer from Liverpool to Shanghai. This is the same class of goods competing with the goods shipped from Liverpool, and paying the Conference steamer from Liverpool 47s. 6d." We presume the figures refer to tonnage rates, and the word "conference" means, of course shipping ring. On another page we are told that, in the last decade, eighteen new foreign lines have been established at Antwerp, and the increase at Hamburg has been equally marked. With two exceptions, these lines are unsubsidised, yet the tonnage of Hamburg has increased by 43 per cent., that of Bremen by 40 per cent., and that of Rotterdam by 52 per cent., while the tonnages of Glasgow and Liverpool have only increased 3½ per cent. and 3 per cent. respectively, and that of London no more than 13 per cent.

We presume these figures cover the same period of time, but what that period is the Colonel does not make clear. In fact, he has not marshalled his statements very well, and his pamphlet, therefore, fails to produce the effect it might do. For all that, it is well worth reading, not that we believe much good will come of this or any other effort to bring about a better state of affairs: the P. & O. Company is too well entrenched behind its great subsidy and its low standard of speed. It can, therefore, afford to coerce any line that enters into competition with it. Merchants and shippers, when they condescend to act together, might bring about reform, but this action requires a degree of loyalty and good comradeship not to be found yet amongst traders in any part of the world. Given combination and a resolute purpose to stand together, there would be nothing to hinder British manufacturers and merchants from putting on a line of steamers running, say, to India, China, and Japan, which, in the course of a twelvemonth might effect a revolution in rates and bring even the mighty P. & O. Company to its knees.

But money would have to be provided in order to stand the loss sure to arise from running these steamers, because the first thing that the P. & O. Company and the members of the "ring" would do would be to put down freights to a non-remunerative point. They would cut and cut until they might come to carry some things even for nothing, as Colonel Foss asserts the P. & O. Company once offered to carry cotton to Japan, But with money and combination even this form of coercion could be overcome, and a better state of things brought about. To expect that the British Parliament, or the authorities at the Post Office, or, we fear it must be added, the Board of Trade, will do anything to help British industry by cutting down or abolishing the disgraceful bounties now lavished upon certain lines of mail steamers, is as vain as to look for the millennium. Shippers, however, are so cowed that there is no probability of any stable combination of them being formed. nor can we hope much from the efforts Colonel Foss and his friends are making, through the issue of this pamphlet and in other ways, to establish an "Imperial trade co-operation." Sentimentalists alone will join them: the hard-fisted and suspicious merchant will submit to the tyranny of the rings, or escape from them by way of foreign ports. Nevertheless, we hope the public will read and think over this suggestive, if jumbled, essay.

"Maple's" Board in Elysium.

The Elysée Palace Hotel Company's prospectus was issued on January 20, 1897, and it was stated that the £200,000 of £1 ordinary shares proposed to be issued had been underwritten by subscribers for the £2,000 of deferred shares, the remaining £1,000 of such shares going to the vending company — the Compagnie Internationale des Grand Hotels. This latter concern also received £10,000 in cash, although the hotel has yet to be built. The share list on May 26, 1897, showed the following as the principal shareholders of this peculiar company :—

	No. of Shares. Ordinary.	Deferred
H. Adams	4,000	—
A. Bird	5,000	—
R. C. Blundell...	4,070	—
H. A. Campbell	5,000	—
G. Cooke	4,000	300
Cie Internationale des Grand Hotels	20,000	1,700
F. A. Dinham	3,000	125
M. de Fos	2,500	—
Sir F. H. Evans	5,000	125
E. Herbert	1,000	125
F. Lunniss	6,000	—
J. L. Lucas	500	—
Sir J. B. Maple...	14,700	—
T. Marisot	5,000	25
J. C. Merryweather	600	—
G. C. L. Nagelmackers	10,000	—
C. Neef	3,000	—
F. Peake	5,000	—
R. Peake	5,000	—
H. Requart	6,000	350
Vicomte de Segur	5,000	—
G. W. Wolff	1,009	—
C. H. Requart	6,950	350
H. M. Snow	—	25
	122,320	3,000

Monsieur G. C. L. Nagelmackers is Directeur-General of the Cie. Internationale des Wagon-lits and Director of the Cie. Internationale des Grand Hotels, both of which companies had an interest in the promotion of the new hotel. Sir Francis Evans is also a director, and the Vicomte de Segur is Vice-President, of these two companies. Sir John B. Maple is Governor of Maple & Co., Limited, who furnish the new hotel, Mr. A. Bird is Chairman of Maple & Co., and Messrs. H. A. Adams, R. C. Blundell, F. A. Denham, J. L. Lucas, F. Lunniss, C. H. Requart, and H. G. Requart, are all members of the Board of that company. The Messrs. Peake, we presume, are members of the firm of Peake, Bird, Collins, & Peake, solicitors, who are closely connected with Henry Frederick & Co., the hotel-building syndicate that works under the auspices of Maple & Co. Mr. G. Cooke is a director of the same company, and Mr. G. W. Woolf is a co-director with Sir F. H. Evans on the Board of the Union Steamship Company, which is, we believe, interested in the Cie. Internationale des Wagons-lit. One or two others appear to hold shares from collateral motives, so that the ordinary public, who, presumably, have subscribed the remaining £70,000 of capital, cannot have much to say about the management of affairs.

THE CITY OF LONDON ELECTRIC LIGHT COMPANY.

Evidently this company could pay a higher dividend than 10 per cent. before reducing its price of energy. We are glad, however, to see that it has not attempted to stand upon this right, but will lower its price from 8d. to 7d. per Board of Trade unit, the reduction dating from January 1 last. The chairman also stated at the meeting that if the business permitted, the board hoped to further reduce the price. This is a sensible policy, and removes the stain from this concern of charging the highest price for energy in London by virtue of a monopoly. We do not believe the company will lose by its move, for it has a splendid district to work upon; and other companies have found that a reduced price meant increased revenue. And yet the Gas Light and Coke Company is going to raise its price for gas!

RIVER PLATE TRUST AND AGENCY COMPANY.

In our "Reports and Balance Sheets" we point out that the excellent condition of this company, and its record of dividends in the past, through good and ill report, bear out the result of good management. Unfortuately, however, the share capital seems to have been arranged in the most objectionable fashion, as if to induce cautious people to abstain altogether from touching the shares. The "A" shares, of course, with their high dividend, yield very well, if revenue only is considered; but then they are only £2 paid, and have therefore a liability of £8 per share upon them. This is no light matter for the Debentures and Debenture stock total £1,095,896, as against a paid-up share capital of £686,512. The percentage of the latter to the former is certainly better than in other companies of this class, but that liability of £8 per share must be a "spectre at the feast" to any prudent holder, when he remembers the chances and vicissitudes of Argentine affairs.

But the company has £375,000 of "B" £5 shares, which are fully paid, and which one would think would be a favourite medium of investment. There again, however, the utmost care has been taken to make them a poor security for investment. The terms upon which these unfortunate shares receive dividend are that the "A" shares shall first have 6 per cent. cumulative, and after that surplus profits are divided equally between the "A" and "B" shares, without reference to the amount paid on each. Under this system the £300,000 of "A" shares last year received £40,500 in dividend, and the £375,000 of "B" shares £11,250. Net profits have risen by nearly 50 per cent. since 1892, and these "B" shares receive a 3 per cent dividend, and the prior charges in front of them are so great that the prospect of increase would be at once dissipated if profits suffered any, the most moderate reaction. Could a more unfortunate scheme of capitalisation be devised?

EAST RAND PROPRIETARY, LIMITED.

The history of this concern is a useful illustration of the curious methods of finance adopted by some South African promoters and directors. When the company was originally formed, it acquired a number of properties from a syndicate known as the "H. F."—the initials of Hanan & Farrar—with, however, the important proviso attached that the syndicate should receive 25 per cent. of the profits after £600,000 in dividends had been returned to the shareholders. It cannot be stated that a knowledge of this "lien" was intentionally concealed from the shareholders, but it is certain that very few of them were aware of its existence, and in the well-known text-book, "South African Mining and Finance," compiled by one of the directors, all mention of it was excluded. The shares at one time were run up to over £12, and a terrible awakening came when last year it was suggested that the H. F. Syndicate should be given 200,000 shares, or a capital of £950,000, for its rights. Investigation proved that the directors of the East Rand Proprietary, Limited, were also directors and proprietors of the H. F. Syndicate, a dual position which they still occupy. Moreover, Messrs. G. and F. Farrar, who practically control the company, are also members of a firm of machinery agents, and in this capacity supply the various mines of the group with their own machinery. The French shareholders combined, and, with a pertinacity which unfortunately is generally absent in English shareholders, refused to be thus despoiled, and the scheme, whereby the H. F. Syndicate, alias the East Rand directors, would have netted some £700,000 or £800,000, was rejected. But the H. F. Syndicate was not yet done with. It would not suit the gentlemen comprising it to wait until the parent concern returned £650,000 in dividends before they would be able to put their finger in the pie.

With a brilliant ingenuity, the East Rand directors have just carried by acclamation a remarkable scheme that secures to the syndicate the option to call upon the company to deliver to it 75,000 shares at £5 during one year, or a rather less number of shares at £5 10s. during a period of two years. Furthermore, it has obtained a first mortgage bond, to the extent of £375,000, on the whole of the assets. That is to say, if the company can be made a success, the market in the shares will be rigged and a very handsome profit made on the options; if it is a comparative failure, the syndicate holds a first mortgage on the property, and is, from its point of view, amply secured—a double-headed arrangement with a vengeance. What do the East Rand shareholders receive in return? If the H. F. Syndicate exercises its option to call the 75,000 shares, and only then, it has agreed to forego its right to participate in 25 per cent. of the profits until £800,000 instead of £650,000 has been returned to the shareholders "in specie or cash." How magnanimous! What value the H. F. Syndicate places on this lien may be gathered from the fact that it is shortly to be floated into a company with the ultimate intention, no doubt, of selling the shares to the public, as soon as all possible profit has been made out of the before-mentioned options. And the generosity of the directors of the East Rand Proprietary towards themselves in the form of the syndicate does not cease even here. After the original Company was formed, further property was acquired from an independent source, for 100,000 shares, worth to-day £450,000. The H. F. Syndicate not being the vendor, naturally had no right to participate in the profits. Under the scheme recently sanctioned, the Company has ceded to the Syndicate similar rights in respect to these additional assets, to those already held over the original mine. Perhaps it will be interesting to the reader to relate how the directors were able to obtain the consent of their shareholders to such an extraordinary course, especially after the opposition evinced towards their proposals a year ago.

It will be remembered that the entire financial Press—gutter and otherwise—was then unanimous in condemning the conduct of the board. The first step at reconciliation—we merely state a fact without drawing any conclusions—was an entire change of opinion on the part of the Press. The confidence of the French shareholders was gained by forming a Paris and London Committee, and placing several of their number on it. The subsidiary mines were loaded with huge machinery — the Comet owns one hundred stamps, of which to-day it is only working 40—thus necessitating the East Rand Proprietary being plunged heavily into debt. To raise the funds required for this policy, a bond of £375,000 was passed on the property, and shortly before it matured the amended scheme was placed before the shareholders to accept, or find the money as best they could. No wonder they chose the least harmful alternative. As to the value of the shares, it has been shown that, taking the most optimistic estimates the annual cash dividends for the next two or three years cannot amount to more than 16 or 18 per cent.; and, of course, if scrip is distributed it will be merely paying away some of the assets and weakening the company. Yet simpletons can be found to give £4 10s. for the £1 shares. As with many other mines on the Rand, only the richer reefs are being extracted; while profits, "lives," and other estimates are calculated on the assumption that all the ore bodies will be mined.

Critical Index to New Investments.

DOVER CORPORATION.

A further issue of £93,000 3 per cent. stock was offered for tender yesterday by the London and County Banking Company, the minimum price being 102 per cent. which is pretty lofty for a garrison town. It ranks in all respects similar to the existing stock which is quoted 102—5. £82,000 of this was offered two years ago at the same minimum, and was taken at an average price of £105 0s. 4d., the tenders amounting to £442,230. Of the present issue £70,000 is for purchases and works said to be remunerative. Estimated population of Dover 37,000; outstanding debt of Corporation £252,000. The desire to lend money to Dover on this occasion was much less strong, the applications reaching only £94,900. The largest tenders were at the minimum, but an average price was secured of £102 1s. 8d.

W. T. GLOVER & CO., LIMITED.

Company acquires business of Walter T. Glover & Co., manufacturers of insulated wire and cables for electric lighting, telephonic, telegraphic, and other purposes, now carried on at Salford, Westminster, and elsewhere. Capital is £200,000 in £1 shares, half ordinary and half 5 per cent. cumulative preference, and 67,000 of the latter are offered for subscription at par, the rest of the capital, with only £17,000 in cash, being taken by the vendors. Business is twenty years old, and profits for last four years have averaged £14,155, those for the past six months being £16,548, and for the previous twelve months £16,678. Assets amount to £135,425, including land works and plant £43,733; stock £49,436; and book debts guaranteed £41,049, and further assets will be acquired with the £50,000 of working capital provided by the present issue, while the amount required to discharge liabilities of the firm on 31st December las was £76,514. The position looks sound, and in view of the growing activity in this class of business, the preference shares should prove an investment.

PATENT DOUBLE PICK LOOM COMPANY, LIMITED.

This is described as a sound Home Industrial investment, and it may be for aught we know. The prospectus is headed "Revolution in Weaving; Double Pick Loom; 90 per cent. quicker, 50 per cent. cheaper, and can be applied to existing looms at a small cost." We are not authorities either in double or single pick looms, but can appreciate such a revolution if it is a fact. Just above this is printed in red ink the announcement that a contract has been made for the sale of the patents for Germany, France, and Belgium, for the sum of £80,000, the benefits of which will accrue to this company. If this means that the company will get the £80,000, we must admit being dazed by such generosity. Why did not the vendors net this for themselves? However, they know their own business best, and we leave them to it. But there is more to come, for not only does the company acquire the valuable inventions of Messrs. Slicer & d'Andria for the "Patent Double Pick Loom" which have been secured for the United Kingdom, France, Germany, Italy, Belgium, Portugal and Austria-Hungary, but likewise the benefit of an application which has been made for letters patent in Russia, as well as the right to apply for and take out patents in all other countries except the United States. There is much more of similar stuff, but space is running short. It is all calculated to make investors sell their Consols to come in. A slight reference is made in passing to revenue to b expected, and it takes the form of a rule-of-three sum. The idea is that if no more than 2½ per cent. of the 1,000,000 looms in Great Britain and Ireland are fitted at the small minimum royalty of £2 per loom per annum, this would afford an annual revenue from this source alone of £50,000. One other point consequently gets over us, and that is why, with such a prospect, the vendors take the £100,000 of purchase consideration in cash and not in shares. Being thus self-denying, the whole of the capital of £150,000, in £1 shares, which is offered by the Monarch Syndicate, can be secured by the public. Of the four directors who make up the board, the first two are north-country men, and we know nothing about them, but Samuel Jennings is chairman of such gems as the Monarch Syndicate, Limited, and of its offspring the Lucky Guss Gold Mine, and also of the Dunderberg Gold Mines, Limited, while the fourth director, Charles H. Tyndall, is connected with such successes as the Dixie Gold Mining Company, the Gem of Cue, the Great Mount Phœnix, the Lucky Guss, the Mid-Kent Coal Syndicate, the Monarch Syndicate, National Cycle and Motor-Car Insurance Company, Vehicular Insurance Company, and Walkers, Parker & Co., Limited. Confidence, under these circumstances, needs no stimulant.

"SHIP AND TURTLE" (PAINTER'S), LIMITED.

This Leadenhall-street hostelry, which dates from the reign of King Richard II., is held on a lease having another 64 years to run, at a ground rent of £1,700. Owing to failing health and retirement into private life, the sole proprietor seems to have sold the business to a Mr. Fox, who in turn offers it to the public for £100,000, o which only £20,000 is to be in shares. The capital is £60,000 in £1 shares, in equal moieties of ordinary and 5 per cent. cumulative preference shares; and there is an issue of £50,000 four per cent. first mortgage debenture stock, redeemable at 105 from July, 1918, or at par on July 1, 1961, and now offered for subscription at par. Interest due January and July. The value of the lease, goodwill, furniture, &c., is given in one lump sum of £80,000, so it is not possible to learn how much of it represents goodwill, while the takings for nine years are also given in the lump sum of £214,263, so that we cannot tell whether they have increased or diminished of late years. Upon the far more important point as to what profits have been, we are told nothing, except that it is hoped to work them up to £12,000. To invest in a thing of this sort upon such flimsy particulars is simply blind hookey.

ALBERT BAKER & CO., LIMITED.

These are described as the "up-to-date" tobacconists, and they offer their business, chief offices, and 22 branches, 3 of which are not yet opened, for £75,000 in cash, and £50,000 in shares. The capital is £200,000 in £1 shares, and the public is asked to subscribe for 100,000 of them, the remaining 50,000 being held in reserve. Not a figure is given as to any profits having been made in the past, and no mention is made as to any valuation of the stock to be taken over. It is true Salmon & Gluckstein, Limited, was successfully floated without these particulars being given, but we much doubt if the public will subscribe capital for Baker & Co., on such terms, and we think it will be very foolish if it does. When Albert Baker & Co., Limited, bought the business of A. Baker & Co., Limited, there were only 7 branches and £20,100 was accepted for it. The present vendors seem to think it has grown very much in value since them.

THE BRITISH DRYING CO., LIMITED.

This does not refer to clothes only, but to materials and refuse of every description. The company buys the British patent rights of Mr. Heinrich Hencke for the drying of distillers' dregs and other products, and similar rights granted to Mr. Richard Cunliffe, o Manchester, for drying machines; also two machines ready for immediate use. The capital is £85,000 in £1 shares, of which the vendors take 30,000 with £35,000 in cash. The prospectus contains full reference to the success of a drying company on the Continent, but this company, apart from the two machines, seems to buy nothing but patent rights, the value of which may possibly prove to have been over-estimated.

LAKE BENNETT AND KLONDIKE STEAM NAVIGATION COMPANY.

Capital £150,000, in £1 shares, 100,000 offered for subscription; remainder with £50,000 in cash go to vendor company, the Klondike Gold Reefs Exploration Company, Limited. The new company is to establish a line of steamers to run from the head of Lake Bennett to Dawson City, the monopoly for which route during the ensuing season is said to have been practically secured by this company, which acquires a contract whereby the Albion Ironworks Company, of Victoria, B.C., undertakes to build the machinery complete for three steamers, the parts to be delivered at Lake Bennett by May 24. So that shareholders should feel they are getting something tangible for their money, a complete sawmill is thrown in. Are we to learn from this that the "practically" secured monopoly will only last for one season, and that the steamers have yet to be built at Lake Bennett, and there fitted with machinery to come from Victoria, B.C.? Suppose there is any delay in getting the boats ready, and the rush is over, or may be even returning. Then what will the vessels do during the long winter? Oh, Klondike, Klondike! you will have much to answer for.

LIPTON, LIMITED.

Share capital £2,000,000, half in 5 per cent. cumulative preference shares and half in ordinary shares of £1 each. Debenture capital, £500,000 in 4 per cent. debenture stock, the said stock redeemable at 115 after September 30, 1920, on six months notice. It will also be redeemed at the same price in the event of the reconstructicn or amalgamation of the company. One third of each class of capital is taken by the vendor at par in part payment of the £2,466,666 given for the business. The employes, directors and friends subscribe for £83,333 debenture stock, 166,000 preference shares and the same number of ordinary shares, the two former at par and the latter at 5s. premium. This leaves £251,001 debenture stock, 500,067 preference shares and the same number of ordinary shares to be subscribed by the public; 5s. premium being asked on the ordinary shares. This concern is dealt with in a leader, and we need only add here that the rush of the public to secure allotments has been tremendous. Eighteen thousand letters of application came in one day to the National Bank of Scotland which has the account, and its office was crowded with eager applicants who came in person to tender their money. The preference shares, you see, are quoted at 5s. premium and the ordinary at 15s. to 17s. 6d. Sir. T. J. Lipton has consented to act as chairman for at least five years, and has wisely put his own managers on the board.

THE DEBENTURE CORPORATION, LIMITED.

Subscriptions are asked at the price of 115 per cent. for an issue of £200,000 4 per cent. Perpetual Debenture Stock, ranking *pari passu* with £1,000,000 stock already existing. Share capital subscribed, £3,000,000; paid-up, £1,800,000; reserve fund, £218,000. Interest due, January and July. Out of presen issue £376,900 Terminable Mortgage Debentures will be paid off March 31 next. General assets of Company at end of 1897 amounted to £3,714,000, apart from uncalled capital. Dividends for seven years ended 1892 were 10 per cent., the following year 8 per cent.; and the two next 5 per cent.; while for 1896 and 1897 7½ per cen was paid. Perhaps a good enough security, but very high priced, the yield being less than 3½ per cent.

BARNSLEY BREWERY CO., LIMITED.

Issue of £150,000 4 per cent. first mortgage debenture stock at 102 per cent. Interest due January and July, and stock is redeemable at 10 premium after 1923 on six months' notice. Share capital £210,000, and there now exists £140,000 first mortgage 4 per cent. debenture stock and £11,300 mortgage 5 per cent. debentures. Present issue, of which £50,000 has been already subscribed, with a reserve of £34,000, will be used in paying off the existing debenture stock and debentures, as well as sundry mortgages and other iabilities, amounting in all to £187,000. Security is a specific first mortgage on freehold, copyhold, and long leasehold properties, and a floating charge on fifteen licensed houses, stock and book debts, the whole of which figured in the books last July at £414,933, less trade liabilities, unpaid dividends, &c., amounting to £17,933. Profits for 1895 are certified at £18,496; for 1896 at £22,018 and for 1897 at £22,710. As interest on this new debenture stock will need only £6,000, the issue seems a good enough investment.

NEWFOUNDLAND COPPER COMPANY.

Capital, £250,000 in £1 shares, of which 125,000 are now offered. Company buys contracts for the purchase of certain leases, claims, licenses, and mining properties, with power to test them by working them for twelve months. Purchase price is £75,000, and in order to obtain complete titles to all the properties from the vendors and the Government, further sums of cash, not exceeding £11,500, and fully-paid shares, not exceeding £10,000, will have to be provided by the company. We do not think much of the arrangement, although a vague sort of estimate is drawn up, showing that under certain conditions a profit of £42,100 may possibly be made. Granting there is a moderate amount of copper in the properties, it is an easy matter to anticipate much profit with copper standing at over £50 per ton. We should not care to take a hand in the venture. Both the chairman, John Peters, and the vendor, Joseph Henry Collins, are connected with the California Milling and Mining Company, the New Colorado Silver Mining Company, and the Rocky Mountain Milling Company.

Company Reports and Balance-Sheets.

⁂ *The Editor will be much obliged to the Secretaries of Joint Stock Companies if they would kindly forward copies of Reports and Balance-Sheets direct to the Office of* THE INVESTORS' REVIEW, *Norfolk House, Norfolk-street, W.C., so as to insure prompt notice in these columns.*

PRUDENTIAL ASSURANCE COMPANY, LIMITED.—A week or two ago we gave some outline of the figures of this great company for 1897. The balance-sheet and report are now before us, and details can be filled up. Unquestionably this is a magnificent business, quite the greatest in the United Kingdom, and when we compare the methods by which it is conducted with those of the American life offices, against whose conduct we have had and shall have so much to say, we cannot but speak well of the Prudential. Last year in its ordinary branch it issued 65,893 new policies insuring £6,698,755, and producing £365,996 in new annual premiums. The total premiums in this department last year reached £2,774,264, an increase of £231,002 on 1896, and claims took only £707,643. This branch of the business is conducted at a cost of 10 per cent. of the premium income. In former years it was our regular habit to pitch into this company for its conduct of "Industrial" insurance. We did so on the ground of the wasteful expenditure involved in conducting it and also on the ground of the smallness of the benefits the working class insurers received in return for their money. A good deal has been reformed since those days, and, granting that it is a business which has to be carried on, there is no organisation in existence which conducts it with anything like the fairness and liberality now shown by the Prudential. This is proved by the fact that there is no longer any wholesale forfeiture of lapsed policies, such as once was the fashion. If the holder of a policy of five years standing is unable to continue the payments necessary to maintain it, what has been paid is no longer cancelled, but a fresh policy is granted for a smaller sum in place of the original one, this policy involving no further liability to its holder. Of these policies, 60,848 were granted last year, and the total number in force is now 549,889. This is fair treatment as far as it goes, and since the company is now so rich that it can well afford to deal handsomely with its clients, we hope to see such liberal treatment further developed. Expenses ratio is also improving in this department. An income, which amounted last year to no less than £4,793,591, was collected, at a cost of rather less than 40 per cent., including £461,525 charged against new business. There are now 12,546,132 policies in force in this branch, but how much they insure is not stated. As we mentioned on a previous occasion, however, the total funds of the Industrial branch exceed £15,200,000, and the total assets of the company altogether come to £30,438,337, showing an increase of £3,379,226 in one year. As the claims and surrenders in the ordinary branch came to less than £800,000, and those in the Industrial branch to only £1,833,404, or together about £2,600,000, it follows that the funds of the company must continue to increase with an even greater speed, since the interest income of the whole funds comes to nearly £915,000. Being thus rich, with the prospect of growing increasingly rich, and having its funds so far as the summary allows us to judge, very carefully invested, the directors have done well to deal liberally with their staff. In 1896 they set aside £50,000 to be divided amongst its members, and the same amount is now to be given out of last year's surplus. A provident fund has also been established on an equitable basis, to which members of the staff may subscribe voluntarily, the company undertaking to add 50 per cent. from its own funds to the amounts provided by the subscribers. The actuarial surplus of the two branches amounted to £1,631,825 at the end of the year, and after carrying forward £641,736, besides adding £100,000 to reserve, there remains £890,089 for distribution among participating policy holders and shareholders. Out of this the shareholders are to receive £363,750 in dividends and bonus.

PROVIDENT LIFE OFFICE.—Last year was the quinquennial valuation year of this very old life office, and the valuation report is appended to the ordinary statement of the year's business. We heartily wish these quinquennial valuations were done away with and that every insurance company followed the custom of valuing at the end of each year. No other reform would tend in our opinion to have a greater effect in popularising insurance business with the public, whose mind is befogged by these periodical estimates and calculations of profits at comparatively long dates. Taking the report for the year, we find that this office issued 931 insurance policies, insuring £376,005, and yielding £15,012 in premiums. Total premium income was £230,239, and the receipts from interest and dividends £124,463. Expenses of manangement and commissions absorbed rather less than 14½ per cent. of the premium income. The interest on the company's funds, whose total is now £3,213,446, averaged £3 18s. 10d. for the year, or 4d. more than in the previous year. As regards the quinquennial valuation, it shows a surplus of assets over liabilities amounting to £621,192. One half of this sum has been carried forward till the next quinquennial investigation, and the other half has been divided—£9,008 of it to shareholders and £301,588 of it to policy-holders. Shareholders thus receive but a very small proportion of the profits realised by the business, which is just as it should be.

CASSELL & COMPANY, LIMITED.—Profits in the past year fell off, being only £28,101 as against £35,673 in 1896. The dividend was therefore reduced to 7½ per cent. as against 9 per cent. a year ago, and dividends ranging between 8 and 10 per cent. for many years previous. A further £5,000 of 6 per cent. debentures were paid off, but the liquid assets are materially reduced. Stocks of volumes, publications, &c., tend to grow and now amount to £192,767, and the machinery and plant stands at a higher total. The reduction in profit is, therefore, particularly disappointing, and a little examination into the stock might not be amiss.

DAIRY SUPPLY COMPANY.—After placing £2,000 to reserve the net profit last year was £10,399, as compared with a net profit of £6,795 for 1896. This allows of a dividend of 7 per cent. and the carrying forward of £10,942, or £2,778 more than was brought in. The reserve fund now amounts to £12,000, and trading balances are well in favour of company. A small sum has been added to the debentures, but these only amount to £13,050, as against a share capital of £100,000. Including the balance forward, the reserves represent about 20 per cent. of the capital.

PRICE'S PATENT CANDLE COMPANY.—This old-established company has to announce that profits last year were distinctly below those of the two preceding years owing to the competition in business, which has necessitated a cutting down of prices both in the candle and soap departments. The board, too, are not very sanguine about an improvement in the immediate future. Fortunately, this company has never divided up to the hilt, and so can pay very good dividends in spite of reduced profits. Out of the net revenue of £77,531, the usual sum of £12,500 is written off for depreciation, £5,000 is placed to reserve, a dividend of £1 12s. 6d. per £16 share, or just over 10 per cent., is declared, and £6,013, or about the same sum as a year ago, is carried forward. The dividend for 1896 was £1 13s. 6d. per share, and for 1895 £1 12s. 6d. per share, but in those years more was carried to reserve. The balance-sheet is a very strong one, no less than £245,771 being invested in securities, although the reserves and provident funds only amount to £150,208. Trading balances are strongly in favour of company.

UNITED STATES DEBENTURE CORPORATION.—The revenue of this company last year was satisfactory, and after meeting charges and debenture interest the balance of £24,130 was left. Preference interest required £9,520, and a dividend of 7½ per cent. on the ordinary took £11,250. The sum of £3,500 was placed to general reserve, and £3,241 carried forward. A profit of £10,721 was realised in respect of investments, and this sum was added to capital reserve, raising its total to £35,243. The investments and loans are stated to be worth more than their book value, if the total reserves of £42,743 are deducted. The weak point of the concern is the small amount of paid up share capital, £323,090 to the £1,000,000 of 4½ per cent. debenture stock. Consequently, although such a good dividend was paid, debenture interest took £45,000 out of £69,130 of revenue left after administrative charges had been met. The uncertainties about the concern are heightened by the fact that the board does not publish a list of investments.

LEVER BROTHERS, LIMITED.—The report of this concern still consists of a mere skeleton balance-sheet, and a notification of how profits are divided. Of course, if preference shareholders, who have found about 60 per cent. of the capital, are satisfied with this form of statement no one else need grumble. Such bald accounts, however, render it impossible to give an opinion as to the worth of the assets or the reality of the profits which are set out. Last year it is claimed that these latter amounted to £222,026. The preference interest took £50,000, the 12½ per cent. dividend on the ordinary shares required £96,875, bonuses to customers absorbed £49,392, and £35,000 was carried to reserve. The latter fund will now amount to £150,000, which is not a large sum in a balance-sheet running over £2,300,000.

BILBAO RIVER AND CANTABRIAN RAILWAY COMPANY.—This company, in addition to the trials of the past, has now to meet the increased loss arising from the depreciation in the Spanish currency. Out of a net revenue of £61,115, no less than £13,272 had to be deducted for this reason, so that the available balance was reduced to £46,168. The sum of £30,000 was set aside for depreciation, and after including £1,725 brought in, dividends equivalent to 10 per cent. upon both ordinary and preference shares were declared, leaving £1,491 to be carried forward. By the deduction of the sum for depreciation, the balance sheet value of the undertaking is reduced to £112,184, as against £164,025 of share capital, and the difference is provided by £45,039 of securities in which the company has invested in order to replace its capital. The trading balances are level, and the only other item is £6,000 for stores. It is a remarkable record of what foresight can do for a company even in face of considerable difficulty.

UNITED STATES TRUST AND GUARANTEE CORPORATION.—This Trust seems to have shaken off the Lombard interest completely, and its revenue for the last few years appears to have allowed, after payment of preferred interest, a fair margin for additions to reserve. Last year, for instance, the income was £10,407, which permitted of £2,250 being placed to reserve, the 5 per cent. interest upon the preferred stock being met, and the amount forward being increased by £230. It look almost as if a new departure had been taken in the past year, for £47,628 was raised in the time by a loan from bankers, and the proceeds invested in securities. It is, therefore, a pity that a list of investments is not published. Such a list was published in 1892, and the securities shown in it must have prepared common-sense people for the trouble that followed. Now that a new departure has been effected, could not the board publish the list once again? Holders, and would-be holders, of the preferred stock would then be in a position to judge whether the present board is superior in judgment to the old one. Presumably its work of late years has been to nurse the legacies of an unfortunate past, but one would like to judge the ability to invest on one's own opinion.

RIVER PLATE TRUST LOAN AND AGENCY.—The affairs of this company show further improvement, and, after meeting charges and debenture interest, the net profit last year was £75,067. This allowed of a distribution of 13½ per cent. on the "A" shares, 3 per cent. on the "B" shares, the placing of £20,000 to reserve, and the carrying forward of £15,813, or £1,364 more than a year ago. The dividends distributed last year were the same, but only £10,000 was added to reserve. The board has ceased to write off the cost of properties and investments, presumably because depreciation no longer exists, but adds quite as much to reserve, which now stands at £180,000. The stability of the company, of course, depends upon the value of land in the Argentine Republic, for £1,349,449 of its money is, in first mortgages of freeholds there. It has, however, considerable liquid assets, chief among which is £100,000 of consols, valued at 95. General investments come to £281,874, bills receivable to £74,290, and cash to £53,396, of which about £25,000 would be required for the dividends. The company has completed a large block of buildings in Buenos Ayres at a cost of £81,885. About four-fifths of the offices in this building will be let out, and should form a fair addition to revenue.

The Bank of Victoria made a profit of £22,729 in the half-year ended December 31 last, and devoted £10,419 of it to paying a dividend at the rate of 5 per cent. on the preferred shares. The rest is added to the balance forward, which now amounts to £58,689. One-fifth of the remaining deferred deposits will be released on the 15th of next month. If the board could get the item, "advances £4,691,188," down to reasonable proportions, we should have hope. As it is, we cannot say much, but should like to know whether £257,000 is the amount creditors have lost by forfeited shares, and what the prospect is of the payment of £62,489 due on calls in arrear.

CALEDONIAN RAILWAY COMPANY.—Gross income for half-year ended January 1 last, including £58,004 from canal, £1,870,220, an increase of £44,002; working expenses, also railway and canal, £962,862, or £62,150 more. The railway cost £52 4s. 11d. per cent. of gross receipts to work, as against £49 19s. per cent. in the corresponding half-year, but the cost of working the canal was only £27 12s. 10d. per cent., against £29 7s. per cent. It follows that the net income on the whole business was less by about £20,000, but the same dividend, at the rate of 5 per cent. per annum, is paid as in 1897, only £9,545 is left to be carried forward against £17,418. The principal increases in expenditure were due to maintenance of way and works, &c., and to working the traffic. Rates and taxes have risen no less than £11,000 during the year to £52,851. The capital expenditure of the half-year was £243,411, much less than the estimate. For the current half-year this outlay is put at £441,447. The report is a lean one, and might give more details, percentages, and such like. Dividends become payable on April 1.

GLASGOW AND SOUTH-WESTERN RAILWAY COMPANY.—Gross income for half-year ended January 31 last, £754,039; expenses, £407,700; ratio of expenses to income, 54·1 per cent. Compared with twelve months ago, the revenue is £15,991 up and the expenses £17,859 up, so that the figures disclose the same tendency as those of the other railways, though not to the average extent. Net revenue is accordingly down £1,268. This should not have affected the dividend, but the directors have had to come down to a distribution at the rate of 5 per cent. on the old undivided stock, being at the rate of 2½ per cent. each on the preferred and deferred duplicates of that stock, instead of at the rate of 5¼ per cent., as a year ago, because the preferential charges have risen £3,873 within the year. Nothing at all is paid this time on the deferred contingent stock, and in the result £7,364 is carried forward, against £5,562 brought in. Capital expenditure last half-year came to £61,351, about £21,000 of it on working stock, and the estimated expenditure for the current half-year is £196,146. As there is a debit of £190,548 against capital now, a further issue of stock must be made soon, and the shareholders are to be asked to grant fresh capital powers for the more distant future. Dividends will be payable on the 25th inst.

CALLANDER AND OBAN RAILWAY COMPANY.—Earnings rose £1,375 and expenses £1,073 in the six months to January 31 last. A dividend at the rate of 1¾ per cent. on the ordinary shares absorbs £2,421 of the net balance of £2,652 and leaves £231 to be carried forward. The company spent £21,500 on capital account in the half-year and calculates on spending another £23,000 in the current half-year. Its gross revenue was £30,932, and its expenses £18,465, or almost 60 per cent. of the receipts. Dividends will be payable on April 15.

ATLAS ASSURANCE COMPANY.—In the life department 534 policies were issued last year, the ninetieth of the company's existence, insuring £354,486, and giving £15,010 in annual premiums, but £26,500 of this was re-insured at a cost of £1,227 in premiums, so that the net addition to the revenue was £11,783. Claims took £97,313, £89,812 of which fell on the company. The gross premium income was £143,724, an increase of £4,063, and the life funds were augmented by £86,485, so that they now amount to £1,584,195, mostly invested at home, but none of it in Ireland. Ratio of expenses to premium income 15·7 per cent. In the fire department the premium income was £357,521, and the losses £205,018, or 57·3 per cent. of the income. Expenses and commissions took another £123,652, so that the final balance to the good was only £28,850. This is carried to profit and loss, and £15,000 of it added to the fire fund, which will now stand at £385,000. Including income from interest the total surplus in this department for the year is £45,870, and £28,800 of it has been devoted to the payment of a dividend of 24s. per share, being 24 per cent. on the original paid-up capital. A balance of £2,070 is then left to be added to the reserve fund, raising it to £52,665.

AFRICAN CITY PROPERTIES TRUST.—With £366,162 invested in real estate, and shares in real estate companies in the Transvaal, this company earned a net revenue of £30,245. This included profit on sales of properties, so that one cannot say what the income from rents and dividends amounted to. Dividends equivalent to 12½ per cent. were declared upon the shares, £5,800 was added to reserve, and the balance was increased by £1,328 to £6,896. The reserve will then stand at £42,000, and so far £25,410 has been invested in high-class securities. The company is well in funds as it has recently issued £100,000 of debentures. Shareholders, however ought to remember that real-estate in the Transvaal is not of such a permanent character as in Great Britain, and should rather consider themselves as owners of leaseholds of short duration. Therefore a sinking fund ought to be established, specially to wipe off the capital expenditure, or else holders of the shares must do this for themselves.

VAL DE TRAVERS ASPHALTE COMPANY.—The weather was better for this company last year, and so the net profit of £13,773 was £3,572 more than that of the preceding year. Consequently, the ordinary shares receive 9 per cent. in dividend, as against 7 per cent. for 1896, and the balance forward is increased by £1,572 to £4,773. Before bringing out the net profit, the board set aside £2,000 to reserve, £1,000 to concessions redemption account, £2,628 for depreciation and maintenance of plant, and £863 off buildings. By prudent accumulations in this manner, the board has built up a balance sheet which is peculiarly liquid. With £100,000 of share capital and no debentures or loans, all but £19,867 is represented by assets, which would probably realise more than their book value. The only item which may be taken to represent the "business" is £19,867 for the concessions purchase account. This has been written down from a total of £61,170, and the time seems approaching when interest from investments will provide the amounts necessary to finally wipe it out.

GREAT NORTHERN RAILWAY COMPANY (IRELAND).—Gross receipts for the previous half-year, £448,105; working expenses, £224,846; ratio of expenses to income, 50·2 per cent.; increase in receipts, £24,382; ditto in expenses, £22,393, compared with corresponding half of 1896; therefore, the net profit on the six months' working was only £2,259 larger, including a gain of £270 in miscellaneous receipts. After meeting fixed charges, and placing £5,000 to reserve, the balance-sheet allows the payment of a dividend at the rate of 6¾ per cent. per annum on the rolling stock, or the same as a year ago, leaving £38,777 to be carried forward against £38,102. The capital expenditure in the half-year was £39,837, and another £22,000 is expected to be spent in the current half-year. Dividend warrants will be posted on the 28th inst.

The Lancashire and Yorkshire Accident Insurance Company, Limited, received £47,987 in premiums in the year ended January 31 last, and paid £26,902 in claims, besides £1,962 in bonuses. After paying commissions and expenses, £18,252, or 37½ per cent. of the premium income, a balance of £2,893 was left to be added to the reserve, making it £37,452. Out of this the directors propose to take £3,000 to pay a dividend of 1s. 6d. per share on the paid-up capital of £30,000. This dividend is payable on September 1 next.

JOHN BAZLEY WHITE & BROTHERS, LIMITED.—The report for last year is the best we have seen, and shareholders are to be congratulated upon the fact that the concern has at length been worked into something like shape. The company dates from 1883, when a cement manufacturer's business of the same name was absorbed at an enormous price, and ten years later three limited companies in the same line of business were absorbed, in order to moderate the competition which has ruled rampant during the greater part of the company's life, and is the original reason for the adoption of limited liability. The undertaking is saturated with capital, there being £630,000 of ordinary and £388,500 preference shares, with £393,900 first mortgage debentures, and now there appears in the balance-sheet £17,000, being mortgages on Bridge and Globe Works. Improvements and extensions, we are told, have been effected during the year, and two additional manufactories have been purchased, with the result that freehold and leasehold property, plant, &c., have been written up in the balance sheet from £550,255 to £604,949, while good-will, trade marks, &c., figure for the enormous total of £731,151. The company has, of course, got a very poor history. The reserve has had to be called upon to pay the preference dividend, but for 1896 a distribution of 1 per cent. was paid on the ordinary capital, and £1,072 was carried forward. Last year the company did very much better, the total revenue being £89,057, compared with £58,710, so that, besides increasing the dividend to 4 per cent. on the ordinary shares, the directors are able to add £10,000 to reserve. Reference is made to the improvement in the cement trade, both as to prices and demand, and the make and delivery of the finished products were the largest in the history of the concern. The company is said to have become the largest producer of Portland cement in the world, and from the fact that fees and fixed salaries to directors absorb £8,750, the managing director's special remuneration is only £1,121, we should think it ought to do a pretty big business.

JAY'S, LIMITED, fully maintains the promise of its prospectus. Profits for the year ended January 31 were £39,397, compared with £39,307 in the previous year, and £38,207 two years back. The dividend on the ordinary shares is again 7½ per cent., while £1,000 is placed to leasehold reserve, raising it to £2,000, and £9,000 is added to general reserve, making it £18,000, but this latter fund is not invested outside the business. Nothing is written off goodwill; on the contrary, the item freehold and leasehold buildings and goodwill has had £10,464 added to it, raising it to £301,936, and £5,525 has been spent on alterations and extension to premises. Stock-in-trade figures for £55,534, and there are sundry debtors for £52,906, which is somewhat heavy.

HAGEMANN & CO., LIMITED.—This company was formed two years back to buy a Dutch margarine business, but only the 6 per cent. preference shares were issued over here. Report for 1897 shows total profits of £51,582, of which expenses absob £32,365, leaving £19,216, and from this London expenses, and £2,500 written off machinery, plant, &c., take another £5,690, so that with £1,794 brought forward, the year's balance is £15,320. A dividend of 10 per cent. is paid on the ordinary capital; £2,500 added to reserve, and £820 carried forward. This will make the reserve £5,000, invested in securities outside the business. Sundry creditors, £27,082, and sundry debtors, £40,382, seem rather heavy. Position is satisfactory so far as can be judged from the meagre accounts submitted, and there is a good margin at present, after paying preference interest.

THE NATIONAL EXPLOSIVES COMPANY has again had a very good year. This is a reconstruction of the old company, which never paid a dividend, and the way profits are now distributed is that after the 6 per cent. has been paid on the preference shares the ordinary shares take 8 per cent., and of any balance half goes to holders of deferred shares and half to the preference and ordinary shares. The profits for the past year came to £26,204, which allows of dividends of 11 per cent. being paid on the ordinary shares and £4 4s. 6d. on the deferred shares. For 1896, the ordinary also received 11 per cent., but the deferred only got £3 17s. 6d. It is further proposed to write £5,000 off property account and to place £2,500 to reserve. No profit and loss account is supplied.

CHELSEA ELECTRICITY SUPPLY COMPANY.—The number of lamps connected by this company increased last year by 16,178 to a total of 96,638. Revenue went up still more rapidly, for gross receipts were £27,382, as against £21,355 in 1896. Working expenses certainly were larger, but they did not grow in proportion, and the net revenue of £14,554, compared with £10,361 in 1896. Thus, the number of lamps connected rose by 20 per cent., gross receipts by 28 per cent., and net revenue by 40 per cent., which shows that the company is benefiting from the effects of expansion in previous years. Including £1,526 brought in, and deducting £2,000 set aside for renewals and depreciation, the sum of £14,044 remains. After meeting debenture and preference interest, the balance permits of dividends equal to 6 per cent. on the ordinary shares, as compared with 5 per cent. for the preceding year. The moderate addition to the dividend is explained by the fact that a good deal more capital has been raised in the interval. Altogether £6,840 has been set aside out of revenue for renewals and depreciation, which is small compared with other compaoies, but there is a reserve fund of £36,177, composed of premiums received upon new shares. The two funds together have enabled about £32,000 more to be spent upon the undertaking than has been raised in share or debenture capital. A weak point of this company is that the founders claim one-third of the surplus profits above a dividend of 6 per cent. upon the ordinary shares.

HONG-KONG AND SHANGHAI BANKING CORPORATION.—The report for the second half of last year is most satisfactory, the net profit being $2,429,736, compared with $1,761,136 in 1896. The customary dividend of 25s. per share is paid, and $1,000,000 is transferred to reserve, being double the amount added a year ago. The directors also write $100,000 off dead stock, or in other words stores, which is the amount standing at debit of this account, and carry forward $298,863. The difference in exchange to be provided for is $571,428, against $501,368 a year ago, the exchange being now only 1s. 11⅝d., compared with 2s. 1⅝d. at the corresponding period, the exchange at which the dividend is declared being 4s. 6d. Comparing the balance-sheet figures would serve no good purpose, because several of the items a year ago were swollen by payments of loan instalments. With the new Chinese loan in hand there ought to be a good time in store for the bank, and to look for an early increase in dividend seems reasonable.

BRITISH BANK OF SOUTH AMERICA.—The report of the year's operations is unsatisfactory, and shareholders have to submit to a further reduction in dividend. Gross profits for 1897 were as good as £130,764 compared with £77,024 for 1896, but a smaller balance is brought forward, and a year ago £50,000 was taken from reserve to keep up the dividend. Consequently 16s. per share or 8 oz. was distributed. Nothing is now taken from reserve and the bank will be all the stronger for it, so the available balance is only £41,186, or £4,400 less than in 1896, in spite of the large gross profit, and the dividend is put down to 12s. per share or 6 per cent., a balance of £11,186 being carried forward. The balance sheet shows a material shrinkage in business, deposits being down fully £600,000 at £2,028,000, and bills payable £1,285,000 at £3,376,874, while on the other side cash has fallen from £1,489,000 to £935,000; bills receivable from £4,388,880 to £3,210,780, and other assets from £2,134,323 to £1,970,572. Bank premises have been written up £10,000 to £126,426, which rather surprises us. With the continued drop in the exchange and the consequent unsettlement of financial affairs in Brazil the Bank will, doubtless, have its business further curtailed and will need careful guidance.

WEST AUSTRALIAN BANK.—The profit last half year amounted to £18,251, or much the best showing yet made by this bank. It is the custom to treat this half-year as the end of the year, and so the large balance of £23,360 was brought forward from the first half of the year, making the available total £41,611 From this £25,000 is placed to reserve, and £8,750 is absorbed in the payment of a dividend at the customary rate of 17½ per cent. per annum, leaving £7,861 to be carried forward. The reserve will then staud at £175,000, as against a paid-up capital of £100,000. Deposits amount to £1,475,450, of which £429,921 bear interest. A year ago they totalled £1,750,602, of which £346,273 bore interest. The interest-bearing account, however, was much larger in 1895. The chief assets are £1,172,365 for bills receivable and other advances, and £594,377 specie and bullion.

The Produce Markets.

GRAIN.

The wheat trade has been dull throughout the week, with prices mostly in buyer's favour. At Mark-lane there has been a poor attendance and slow trade. On Wednesday there were scarcely any buyers. Flour, with continued large arrivals, did not attract attention. Maize steady at 16s. 1½d. to 16s. 3d., ex ship, for American mixed, 17s. ex quay for old corn, and 17s. 9d. for Galatz-Bessarabian. Barley quiet at 16s. 6d. to 18s. 9d. Odessa-Nikolaieff, and Danubian at 16s. 3d. to 16s. 6d. Oats steady, but business restricted. Mixed American, ex ship, 15s. 9d. The cargo market, which had been dull during the week, opened on Wednesday with an improved tone, but buyers were cautious, and, though disposed to deal, refused any advance. Late on Tuesday the *Strathgryfe*, 15,955 qr., Walla Walla, arrived, made 37s. 6d. for the Continent; the *Verbena*, 12,168 qr., January 5, changed hands at 35s. 10½d. To-day the *Macmillan*, 10,194 qr., January 25, has also been sold at 35s. 10½d. net; and the *Creswell*, 2,700 tons La Plata, on passage, at 35s. 3d. For the *Willkommen*, 11,279qr., Walla Walla, arrived, 37s. 3d. is bid; and for the *H. F. Glade*, 12,603 Californian, arrived, 38s. 4½d. was paid. Californian, near at hand, held at 38s. 3d. Spot parcels at Liverpool were firmly held at ½d. per cental advance, but the demand was quiet. Red American futures gained ½d. to ⅝d. per cental at opening on Wednesday, and further advanced owing to good buying orders, combined with light offerings. Some moderate fluctuations took place afterwards, and the market became dull and inactive. Just before the end the market fell rather sharply on pressure to sell, and the close was dull and irregular, ½d. per cental lower to ½d. advance on last night's rates.

OFFICIAL CLOSING VALUES (100 lb. deliveries—March 9).

	March.	May.	July.	Sept.	Dec.
Red American Wheat	7'10¼	7'5⅜	7'2	6'7⅞	6'1⅜

In New York, wheat has been steady on the whole, but on Tuesday dulness was produced by the action of the "bears." In the afternoon the market rallied with "bears" covering, owing to the fair decrease in "Bradstreets'" visible supply exhibit, and as regards distant positions on continued unfavourable crop reports from some leading winter wheat States. The close was steady at an advance of ¼c. to 1c. On Wednesday some foreign buying orders and cable advices of higher European markets caused the market to open ⅝c. dearer for May with a steady tone. Sentiment was generally inclined to favour the "bull" side, but when the foreign orders were filled the market relapsed into dulness, and sagged under some realisations, "bulls" being disappointed at the absence of an expected cold wave over the wheat belt. Early in the afternoon a rally followed on covering by the "bears," owing to unfavourable crop reports and an increased export business, but the tone again weakened somewhat towards the close on freer offerings. The session ended steady, with near months ⅛c. and September ¼c. higher, July being unchanged. Sales, 2,000,000 bushels.

COTTON.

The spot market in Liverpool was steady, with rather a firm tone, until Tuesday, when, with large offerings, quotations fell $\frac{1}{16}$d. (middling $\frac{1}{32}$d.). The decline was continued on Wednesday, but with a steadier undertone. Fair business in American. Brazilian and Egyptian quiet and steady. Surats continue idle and unchanged. Futures opened ½ point dearer, but with realisation receded the point in the forenoon. Dullness followed the reaction until the arrival of American cables, which were steadier than expected, and induced re-purchases by "bears" at a recovery of 1½ point, the close being steady at 1½ to two points net improvement. The New York Market fluctuated considerably during the week, with the general tendency lower, but on Wednesday there was a slight turn to one point higher, becoming firmer later on favourable late cables. Near the close, however, there was again a decline under a moderate accumulation of selling orders, and closed barely steady unchanged to two points down. Spot dull during the week.

NEW YORK CLOSING VALUES.

	Spot.	Mar.	April.	May.	June.	July.	Aug.	Sept.	Oct.	Nov.	Dec.	Jan.
Mar. 9 ..	6¼	6'05	6'07	6'10	6'10	6'13	6'15	6'14	6'12	6'10	6'12	6'13

WOOL.

Shortness of stocks and better reports from manufacturing centres point to higher prices in wool, especially in the case of merino staple. In some cases holders have declined to sale even at the enhanced rates. The list for the second series of the Colonial wool sales was closed on Saturday, and shows that the quantities available for the auctions, which commence on Tuesday, amount to about 222,000 bales, as against 358,000 bales for the corresponding series last year, or a decrease of 136,000 bales. Reduced arrivals are on this occasion noted from South Africa as well as Australia, the former contributing 5,400 bales and the latter 149,000 bales less than at this time last year. The diminution of the supply seems to point to higher prices; but it is hardly likely, in view of the heavy import duties, that America will be as keen in their biddings as they were in the early sales of last year.

METALS AND COAL.

Though there has been a very fair business doing in copper, the market fluctuated greatly. A rise in one day of 6s. 3d. was followed the next by a fall of 3s. 6d. On Wednesday there was a decided improvement in tone and greater steadiness. The market opened about 1s. 3d. dearer, and in spite of a restricted business, prices continued to improve steadily during the morning session, and by the close were fully 3s. 9d. to the good. Sales 300 tons, in cash, at £50 5s; Mid. March, £50 6s. 3d.; early May, £50 7s. 6d. and £50 10s., the last price being also accepted early for three months. The afternoon rates further improved 1s. 3d., the close being firm at an advance of 5s. on the day.

SETTLEMENT PRICES.

	Mar. 9.	Mar. 2.	Feb. 23.	Feb. 16.	Feb. 9.	Feb. 2.
	£ s. d.	£ s. d.	£ s. d.	£ s. d.	£ s. d.	£ s. d.
Copper ..	50 7 6	50 7 6	49 17 6	49 10 0	49 5 0	49 2 6

The Glasgow pig-iron market fluctuated somewhat, but a good business has been done, and large quantities have changed hands. Prices went up in the early part of the week, but declined later. On Monday the market was flat, apparently in sympathy with the depression in the stock markets. Scotch declined to 46s. 0½d., but recovered somewhat, and the loss at the close was only 1d. Cleveland fell 2d. On Wednesday buyers operated cautiously, and Scotch at the close was 1d. dearer, Cleveland being 1½d. higher.

SETTLEMENT PRICES.

	Mar. 9.	Mar. 2.	Feb. 23.	Feb. 16.	Feb. 9.	Feb. 2.
	s. d.	s. d.	s. d.	s. d.	s. d.	s. d.
Scotch	46 1½	46 6	46 3	45 7½	45 7½	45 7½
Cleveland ..	40 4½	40 10¼	40 10¼	40 7½	40 4½	40 6
Hematite ..	49 1½	49 6	49 1½	48 9	48 7½	48 6

The improved tone in the coal market has scarcely been maintained. A fair business has, however, been done, and the reports of the retail trade are satisfactory. In the seaborne department there is a better business, with a good demand for seconds, and prices show a partial improvement of fully 3d. Four cargoes were sold, the rates paid being somewhat higher than those recently accepted. The official quotations stand at 16s. and 15s., usual terms in the pool, for Hetton Wallsend and Lyons respectively. Since Monday seventeen cargoes have arrived in the Thames. The rail-trade cannot be called active, but the hardening in tone has made further progress, and for medium qualities there is a satisfactory inquiry. Steams of good quality are very firm at full prices, but inferior sorts are in a less favourable position and sellers are open to reasonable offers. Prices:—Best West Yorkshire, 9s. 9d. to 10s.; Barnsley selected, 8s.; soft nuts, 6s. 6d.; Sheffield Silkstones, 7s. 6d. to 8s.; best Derby blackshale, 9s. to 9s. 3d.; North Derby Tupton, 7s. to 7s. 3d.; Erewash brights, 6s. 9d. to 7s. 9d; and nuts, 6s. 6d. to 7s. 6d.

TEA AND COFFEE.

Coffee Auctions have been rather dull, and only good qualities maintained later rates, while other grades, especially common, were dull at 1s. to 2s. decline. The smaller supply of 1,555 packages at Auction on Wednesday met with a moderate demand and nearly all sold without quotable change. Guatemala—middling to good bold dull coloury, 75s. to 82s.; smalls, 40s. to 46s.; peaberry, 93s. Salvador, middling to bold dull greenish coloury, 68s. 6d. to 73s.; smalls, 38s. to 42s.; peaberry, 86s. Colombian—bold mottled pale grayish, 61s. 6d. to 65s. 6d.; low middling pale greenish, 63s. to 63s. 6d; good to fine ordinary greenish, 41s. to 54s. 6d. Ecuador—mixed dull greenish, 31s. Jamaica—low middling brownish coloury mixed, 59s. to 59s. 6d.; small mixed, 26s. 6d.; peaberry, 75s. Futures opened dull and declined 3d. to 6d., but recovered somewhat, closing steady. There is little to remark on in the tea market during the week. For some time there was a tendency to dulness, but the tone has on the whole been firm. Both Ceylon and Indian have sold well at the auctions, but broken Pekoes have declined.

Next Week's Meetings.

MONDAY, MARCH 14.

African City Properties Trust ...	Cannon-street Hotel, noon.
County of London and Brush Provincial Electric	Winchester House, 2 p.m.
Dairy Supply Company	28, Museum-street, 11.30 a.m.
Sheffield United Gas	Sheffield, 3 p.m.
United States Debenture Corporation	Winchester House, 12.30 p.m.

TUESDAY, MARCH 15.

Caledonian Railway (Gen. and Ex. Gen.)	Glasgow, 1.30 p.m.
Callander and Oban Railway (Gen.)	Glasgow, 3 p.m.
Equity and Law Life	15, Lincoln's-Inn-Fields, 1 p.m.
Gateshead and District Tramways...	Gateshead, 12.30 p.m.
Glasgow and South-Western Railway (Gen.)	Glasgow, noon.
Montreal Water and Power Company	40, Chancery-lane, 2.45 p.m.

WEDNESDAY, MARCH 16.

Anglo Romano Gas	4, St. Dunstan's-alley, 2 p.m.
Eastern Mortgage and Agency Company	Cannon-street Hotel, 3 p.m.
John Bazley White & Brothers ...	2, Lime-street-square, noon.
Val de Travers Asphalte Paving ...	Winchester House, 1 p.m.

THURSDAY, MARCH 17.

Bilbao River and Contabrian Railway	9, Bridge-street, S.W., 2 p.m.

FRIDAY, MARCH 18.

Insurances Corporation	Winchester House, 2.30 p.m.
Leeds and Liverpool Canal	Leeds, 11 a.m.
National Explosives Company ...	Winchester House, 2.30 p.m.
Price's Patent Candles	Cannon-street Hotel, noon.

Dividends Announced.

MISCELLANEOUS.

Maypole Company, Limited.—5 per cent. on the ordinary shares.

Lenares Lead Mining Company, Limited.—14s. per share, payable on the 19th inst.

Alamillos Company, Limited.—1s. 9d. per share, payable on the 19th inst.

London and British Columbia Gold Fields, Limited.—Interim dividend of 1s. per share on the ordinary shares.

Fortuna Company, Limited.—1s. per share.

Canterbury and Paragon.—Interim dividend at the rate of 6 per cent. for the six months ended January 31.

Lake View Consols.—Interim dividend of 50 per cent., being 10s. per share.

J. & C. H. Evans & Co.—Interim dividend of 6 per cent. per annum on the preference shares, and 10 per cent. per annum on the ordinary shares.

D. H. Evans & Co., Limited.—Final dividend of 8½ per cent. on the ordinary shares, making, with the interim dividend, 12 per cent. per annum, and £3 per share on the founders' shares, carrying forward £6,300.

North American Trust Company of London and New York.—Half-yearly dividend of 2½ per cent. $200,000 carried to surplus.

British Gas Light Company, Limited.—Dividend at the rate of 10 per cent. per annum for the half-year ended December 31 last, with a bonus of 2s. 6d. per share. Payable April 7.

Frontino and Bolivia Gold Mining Company, Limited.—Interim dividend of 2s. per share.

Johannesburg City and Suburban Tramway Company, Limited.—7½ per cent. has been declared.

Jones & Higgins, Limited.—Final dividend at the rate of 12 per cent. per annum for the six months ended 20th ult. upon the ordinary shares, making with interim dividend, 9½ per cent. for the year, as against 9 per cent. for the previous year."

Day Dawn Block and Wyndham Gold Mining Company, Limited.—Interim dividend of 9d. per share.

Yorkshire Engine Company.—Dividend at the rate of 12½ per cent., carrying forward £1,611.

Eastern Mortgage and Agency, Limited.—Four per cent. for the year to be paid, £2,500 added to reserve, and £273 carried forward.

Abingdon Works, Limited.—Interim dividend for the six months ended February 28, at the rates of 6 per cent. per annum on the preference shares, and 10 per cent. per annum on the ordinary shares.

G. W. Bacon & Co.—9 per cent. for the half-year ended December 31 last. £2,000 carried forward.

BANKS.

Standard of South Africa.—Dividend for the half-year ended December 31, at the rate of 10 per cent. per annum, with a bonus at the rate of 6 per cent. £20,000 added to reserve, £5,000 to pension fund, and about £20,500 carried forward.

Anglo-Austrian.—6¾ per cent., equal to 8 florins per share for 1897. £8,300 placed to reserve and £22,900 carried forward.

BREWERIES.

Hull Company.—12 per cent. per annum for the half-year ended December 31, making 10 per cent. for the year. £7,000 to reserve, and £1,072 carried forward.

Hudson's Cambridge and Pampisford.—7½ per cent. on the ordinary shares for the half-year ended December 31, making with interim of 5 per cent, 12½ per cent for the year. £1,128 carried forward.

RAILWAYS.

Callandar and Oban.—Dividend on the ordinary shares at the rate of 1⅞ per cent. per annnm for the half-year to January 31.

North British Railway.—Dividend is declared at the rate of 1¼ per cent. on the Ordinary stock, carrying forward £800. Last ear the dividend was at the same rate, £1,400 being carried forward.

THE PROPERTY MARKET.

The close of last week came out better than the beginning, the total sales of yesterday week mounting up to no less a sum than £61,395. Messrs. H. E. Foster & Crawfield were responsible for £42,450 of this amount, the principal item being the reversion to freehold ground rents and other securities of the estimated value of about £50,000; lives aged fifty-two and sixty-five. This lot realised £23,000. An insurance policy for £7,500 and profits, life aged seventy-two, realised £5,600. Another policy for £5,000 and profits, life aged seventy-two, realised £4,500; and a reversion to moiety of trust fund, estimated value £16,124, life aged fifty-seven, brought £4,525. On the same day Messrs. Stimson & Sons' sales amounted to a total of £10,960. Friday's total dropped to £18,375; but the total for the week was £91,825, as against £65,000 odd in the same week of 1897.

Sales at the Mart on Monday resulted in a total of £30,000, and of this amount £29,264 went to Mr. Alfred Richards, for gas stocks and shares. £10,000 ordinary stock of Plymouth and Stonehouse Gas Company fetched £15,220; Watford Gas, £1,760 "E" capital stock went for £4,361; ditto £10 additional shares of Haywards' Heath Gas brought £7,463; and £1,500 5 per cent. debenture stock of the Epsom and Ewell Gas Company went for £2,220.

A total of £55,970 at the Mart on Tuesday showed good business and tolerably keen competition for the property offered. But £37,500 of the total went for one lot, a parcel of freehold ground-rents, offered by Mr. F. H. B. Biddle, amounting to £1,282 13s. 3d., on properties in Nightingale-lane, &c., Wandsworth Common, with reversion in eighty-three years. They were bought by "Queen Anne's Bounty." Messrs. Holcomb, Betts, & Co. secured £5,400—a good figure—for the thirty and a half years' lease of No. 434, Oxford-street, and they also disposed of several other properties. Messrs. Rogers, Chapman, & Thomas, and G. E. Clarke were successful with most of their lots. At the Masons' Hall Tavern on Tuesday, Messrs. Godfrey, Ellis, & Co. disposed of the Daisy public-house, 33, Brompton-road, with the shop adjoining, held for terms of seventy-five and fifty-five years at a rental of £550, for the handsome sum of £36,000. A block of freehold property at Clifton, Bristol, comprising four shops and business, was bought some days ago for £3,510, after a very keen competition.

The sales at the Mart on Wednesday only reached a total of £14,465. The property offered was for the most part ordinary bricks and mortar, but the attendance was good, and the bidding fairly keen. Messrs. Edwin Fox & Bousfield offered a number of stocks and shares of different undertakings, for which the following prices were realised:—North Middlesex Gas Company, Limited, £10 original shares, fully paid, £25; £10 ordinary shares, fully paid, £17 10s. and £17 15s.; Cobham Gas Light and Coke Company, Limited, £5 shares, fully paid, £5 2s. 6d.; Sandown Park, Limited, £10 shares, fully paid, £12; Folkestone Racecourse Company, Limited, £1 shares, fully paid, £1; Gillmann & Spencer, Limited, £5 6 per cent. preference shares, fully paid, £5 2s. 6d.; Freehold and Leasehold Investment Company, Limited, £10 shares, £5 paid, £3 15s.; International Trustee, Assets, and Debenture Corporation, Limited, £1 ordinary shares, fully paid, £1 1s. Mr. Alfred Richards announces a sale of shares in the Lea Bridge District Gas Company for the 10th inst.

The estate of Drumkilbo, at Eassie, in Forfarshire, containing about 1,368 acres, with an annual rental of £1,427, sold at Edinburgh last week for £36,600, or about twenty-nine years' purchase.

Answers to Correspondents.

Questions about public securities, and on all points in company law, will be answered week by week, in the Review, on the following terms and conditions:—

A fee of FIVE shillings must be remitted for each question put, provided they are questions about separate securities. Should a private letter be required, then an extra fee of FIVE shillings must be sent to cover the cost of such letter, the fee then being TEN shillings for one query only, and FIVE shillings for every subsequent one in the same letter. While making this concession the Editor will feel obliged if private replies are as much as possible dispensed with. It is wholly impossible to answer letters sent merely "with a stamped envelope enclosed for reply."

Correspondents will further greatly oblige by so framing their questions as to obviate the necessity to name securities in the replies. They should *number* the questions, keeping a copy for reference, thus:—"(1) Please inform me about the present position of the Rowenzori Development Co. (2) Is a dividend likely to be paid soon on the capital stock of the Congo-Sudan Railway?"

Answers to be given to all such questions by simply quoting the numbers 1, 2, 3, and so on. The Editor has a rooted objection to such forms of reply as—"I think your Timbuctoo Consols will go up," or "Sell your Slowcoach and Draggem Bonds," because this kind of thing is open to all sorts of abuses. By the plan suggested, and by using a fancy name to be replied to, each query can be kept absolutely private to the inquirer, and no scope whatever be given to market manipulations. Avoid, as names to be replied to, common words, like "investor," "inquirer," and so on, as also "bear" or "bull." Detached syllables of the inquirer's name, or initials reversed, will frequently do as well as anything, so long as the answer can be identified by the inquirer.

The Editor further respectfully requests that merely speculative questions should as far as possible be avoided. He by no means sets himself up as a market prophet, and can only undertake to provide the latest information regarding the securities asked about. This he will do faithfully and without bias.

Replies cannot be guaranteed in the same week if the letters demanding them reach the office of the Investors' Review, Norfolk House, Norfolk-street, W.C., later than the first post on Wednesday mornings.

Y. F.—The effect of payment in full seems to be discounted, but I do not think there is any likelihood of a serious relapse. There is no haste to sell, but you might do so gradually on any improvement in the market, as it is only being sustained in order to float a fresh loan.

H. K.—Thanks, have made the alteration you suggest, but for your guidance would point out that the official quotation is only ex div. to-day.

W. G. R.—It is a fair security, and, unless political disturbances upset the investments held, might easily rise a little. The scheme for cancelling the uncalled capital has been dropped, so you have this to look to as well as the investments.

Express.—If you can buy about par it seems a reasonable investment. The line is an important one for the guarantor, and is therefore likely to be kept up properly, and not neglected as some of the other subsidiary lines have been.

S. J.—I see no reason why you should not, there is sufficient margin for the loan. Politics may, however, interfere with its success.

S. E.—Neither of the shares you mention seems to me tempting. Your other question I will answer by letter.

R. D.—I think you can make a more satisfactory exchange; will write you in a day or two.

Notice to Subscribers.

Complaints are continually reaching us that the INVESTORS' REVIEW cannot be obtained at this and the other railway bookstall, that it does not reach Scotch and Irish cities till Monday, and that it is not delivered in the City till Saturday morning.

We publish on Friday in time for the REVIEW to be at all Metropolitan bookstalls by at latest 4 p.m., and we believe that it is there then, having no doubt that Messrs. W. H. Smith & Son do their best, but they have such a mass of papers to handle every day that a fresh one may well look almost like a personal enemy and be kept in short supply unless the reading public shows unmistakably that it is wanted. A little perseverance, therefore, in asking for the INVESTORS' REVIEW is all that should be required to remedy this defect.

All London newsagents can be in a position to distribute the paper on Friday afternoon if they please, and here also the only remedy is for subscribers to insist upon having it as soon as published. Arrangements have been made that all our direct City subscribers shall have their copies before 4 p.m. on Friday. As for the provinces, we can only say that the paper is delivered to the forwarding agents in ample time to be in every English and Scotch town, and in Dublin and Belfast, likewise, early on Saturday morning. Those despatched by post from this office can be delivered by the first London mail on Saturday in every part of the United Kingdom.

Cheques and Postal Orders should be made payable to CLEMENT WILSON.

The INVESTORS' REVIEW can be obtained in Paris of Messrs. BOYVEAU ET CHEVILLET, 22, Rue de la Banque.

ADVERTISEMENTS.

All Advertisements are received subject to approval, and should be sent in not later than 5 p.m. on Thursdays.

For tariff and particulars of positions open apply to the Advertisement Manager, Norfolk House, Norfolk-street, W.C.

To Correspondents.

The EDITOR cannot undertake to return rejected communications. Letters from correspondents must, in every case, be authenticated by the name and address of the writer.

The Investors' Review.

The Week's Money Market.

A little less pressure for short loans was experienced at the end of last week, but since Monday the demand has been very keen, and business has been transacted throughout at 2¾ to 3 per cent. for both day-to-day and seven-day loans. All amounts falling due at the Bank have been renewed, and increased borrowings had to take place, so that in the week ended Wednesday last the market has been able to pay off very little of its debt. The India Council also lent as much as it wished at 3 per cent. With the Chinese Loan due next week, and other financial operations to follow, there is not likely to be much relief to the short loan market for some time yet.

The political tremor of the week naturally tightened up an already poverty-stricken Money Market, and since Monday the discount rate for two or three month's choice bills has been well maintained at 2 15/16 to 3 per cent. One affrighted establishment went so far on Monday as to quote discounts "subject to a change in the Bank Rate," but short of a disturbance of peace, there does not seem to be much room to fear an advance in the official minimum. The American demand for gold has certainly proved stronger than was expected, but it has both Paris and London to draw upon, while its influence here is counterbalanced, in a measure, by the unusually large arrivals of gold from abroad. Not only have the African shipments kept up, but a large amount of Japanese yen, to the extent of about £500,000, arrived in the week, and quite as much more of this coin is on the way here. The Bank of England appears to be desirous of obtaining their coins, and therefore on Monday raised its buying price for them again to 76s. 5d. per ounce, and at this price was able to secure the unsold portion of the shipment. This advanced price also applied to French and German coin, which are of the same fineness, and therefore a small amount of Napoleons likewise reached the Bank. The quotation for bar gold in the market has only risen to 77s. 10d¼. per ounce, which does not point to a very urgent demand from the States. Foreign exchanges have all moved still further in our favour, and with 25·31 quoted for the Paris cheque, more gold would have come from that quarter, had it not been that the Bank of France has raised its premium on gold to fully 5½ per mille. Apart from foreign demands upon the Bank's stock of gold, the coming Loans already cast their shadow over the market. The Chinese issue is just upon us, and Greece and the Transvaal cannot remain long out of the market, to say nothing of the possible demands of the Indian Government. No doubt the financial houses will arrange these matters so as to disturb the market as little as possible, but the knowledge that they lie in the future must tend to keep rates for both loans and discounts well up to the Bank's minimum.

The Stock Exchange Settlement showed heavy differences to be met in certain departments, but the volume of the account was sensibly reduced. Bankers, therefore, did not obtain much advance on the rates for loans current on the previous occasion, as, although 3¾ to 4 per cent. was quoted for account to account money, the majority of the business was done at the lower rate.

The Bank return issued yesterday indicated nothing but the prolongation of the dead-lock caused by the heaped-up balances of the Treasury. They fell off only £119,000 within the week, and still stand at £18,692,165. So the market has daily had to borrow and borrow from the Bank as its loans fell due, and the total of the "other" securities in the Bank's possession is still

£35,579,185, or only £320,000 less than a week ago. In the second week of December last these "other" securities amounted to less than £27,000,000. We may, therefore, infer that the market now owes the Bank at least £8,000,000 of the moneys held by the Exchequer; and that it will not be sensibly more at ease when all the Government disbursements, including the April dividends, have been made. Those who depend on banking credit should take note of this fact. Coupled with the drafts upon our market resources, known to be impending through projected loan operations, it warns us to look for no "cheap money" this spring or summer. Other items in the Bank return may be traced in our balance-sheet table compiled from it, and require no explanation here.

SILVER.

Bar silver recovered at one time to 25⅜d. per ounce upon purchases chiefly by those who had sold the metal previously. When these "bear" operations were rounded off the quotation sank slowly to its present level of 25⅝d. per ounce. At this figure there is no great desire to buy, as the market is awaiting the Indian Budget statement, which is due about the 20th inst. If the Indian Government means to make a fresh attempt to bolster up the exchange, the scheme will, doubtless, be touched upon by Sir J. Westland; and opinion seems to favour the view that such a scheme would involve further obstacles being placed in the way of sales of silver to India. With the Budget date so close upon us, it is useless discussing the matter further, until the actual proposals are known.

BANK OF ENGLAND.

AN ACCOUNT pursuant to the Act 7 and 8 Vict., cap. 32, for the Week ending on Wednesday, March 9, 1898.

ISSUE DEPARTMENT.

	£		£
Notes Issued	47,965,995	Government Debt	11,015,100
		Other Securities	5,784,900
		Gold Coin and Bullion	31,165,995
		Silver Bullion	—
	£47,965,995		£47,965,995

BANKING DEPARTMENT.

	£		£
Proprietors' Capital	14,553,000	Government Securities	13,987,565
Rest	3,750,565	Other Securities	35,259,306
Public Deposits (including Exchequer, Savings Banks, Commissioners of National Debt, and Dividend Accounts)	18,692,165	Notes	21,219,515
Other Deposits	35,789,100	Gold and Silver Coin	2,450,999
Seven Day and other Bills	141,555		
	£72,926,385		£72,926,385

Dated March 9, 1898.

H. G. BOWEN, *Chief Cashier.*

In the following table will be found the movements compared with the previous week, and also the totals for that week and the corresponding return last year:—

Banking Department.

Last Year. March 10.		March 2, 1898.	March 9, 1898.	Increase.	Decrease.
£	Liabilities.	£	£	£	£
3,751,564	Rest	3,745,479	3,750,565	5,086	—
16,977,495	Pub. Deposits	18,811,093	18,692,165	—	118,928
38,131,311	Other do.	35,914,840	35,789,100	—	125,740
204,615	7 Day Bills	147,987	141,555	—	6,432
	Assets.			Decrease.	Increase.
14,521,983	Gov. Securities	13,987,565	13,987,565	—	—
28,755,648	Other do.	35,579,185	35,259,306	319,879	—
30,340,354	Total Reserve	23,605,649	23,679,514	—	73,865
				324,965	324,965
				Increase.	Decrease.
£		£	£	£	£
25,857,700	Note Circulation.	27,036,805	26,746,480	—	290,325
54⅛ p.c.	Proportion	43 p.c.	43⅜ p.c.	—	—
3 "	Bank Rate	3 "	3 "	—	—

Foreign Bullion movement for week £49,000 out.

LONDON BANKERS' CLEARING.

Week ending	1898.	1897.	Increase.	Decrease.
	£	£	£	£
Jan. 5	222,654,000	174,376,000	48,278,000	—
" 12	144,603,000	127,315,000	17,288,000	—
" 19	171,777,000	156,200,000	15,577,000	—
" 26	134,247,000	118,667,000	15,580,000	—
Feb. 2	194,544,000	174,498,000	20,056,000	—
" 9	137,204,000	129,209,000	8,995,000	—
" 16	184,403,000	162,168,000	22,235,000	—
" 23	132,450,000	131,777,000	673,000	—
March 2	190,157,000	177,852,000	12,305,000	—
" 9	134,490,000	126,182,000	8,308,000	—

BANK AND DISCOUNT RATES ABROAD.

	Bank Rate.	Altered.	Open Market.
Paris	2	March 14, 1895	1⅞
Berlin	3	February 20, 1898	2⅞
Hamburg	3	February 20, 1898	2⅞
Frankfort	3	February 20, 1898	2¾
Amsterdam	3	April 13, 1897	2½
Brussels	3	April 28, 1896	2
Vienna	4	January 22, 1896	3½
Rome	5	August 27, 1895	3
St. Petersburg	5½	January 23, 1898	4½
Madrid	5	June 17, 1896	4
Lisbon	6	January 25, 1891	6
Stockholm	4	March 3, 1898	3½
Copenhagen	4	January 20, 1898	4
Calcutta	12	February 24, 1898	—
Bombay	13	February 24, 1898	—
New York call money	1½ to 2	—	—

NEW YORK ASSOCIATED BANKS (dollar at 4s.).

	Mar. 5, 1898.	Feb. 26, 1898.	Feb. 19, 1898.	Mar. 6, 1897.
	£	£	£	£
Specie	24,026,000	23,838,000	23,366,000	17,012,000
Legal tenders	15,440,000	17,216,000	18,698,000	22,972,000
Loans and discounts	125,632,000	128,376,000	129,384,000	100,412,000
Circulation	2,755,000	2,745,400	2,755,600	3,281,000
Net deposits	141,204,000	145,842,000	147,712,000	115,492,000

Legal reserve is 25 per cent. of net deposits; therefore the total reserve (specie and legal tenders) exceeds this sum by £4,165,000, against an excess last week of £4,593,500.

BANK OF FRANCE (25 francs to the £).

	Mar. 10, 1898.	Mar. 3, 1898.	Feb. 24, 1898.	Mar. 11, 1897.
	£	£	£	£
Gold in hand	75,721,080	76,831,040	77,303,760	76,556,000
Silver in hand	48,484,480	48,565,440	48,512,280	49,085,000
Bills discounted	27,240,040	31,773,800	29,853,200	*41,987,000
Advances	14,761,680	14,730,240	14,562,600	—
Note circulation	149,737,360	152,206,720	148,445,560	146,964,000
Public oeposits	5,430,600	6,041,720	7,965,080	7,655,000
Private deposits	19,888,680	18,758,040	21,089,240	17,904,000

Proportion between bullion and circulation 82⅜ per cent. against 82⅝ per cent. a week ago.

* Includes advances.

FOREIGN RATES OF EXCHANGE ON LONDON.

Place.	Usance.	Last week's.	Latest.	Place.	Usance.	Last week's.	Latest.
Paris	chqs.	25·28½	25·31¼	Italy	sight	26·60	26·66
Brussels	chqs.	25·33¾	25·36¼	Do. gold prem.	..	105·22	105·35
Amsterdam	short	12·05½	12·08½	Constantinople	3 mths	109·20	109·25
Berlin	short	20·45½	20·47	B. Ayres gd. pm.	..	171·20	168·80
Do.	3 mths	20·31½	20·32	Rio de Janeiro	90 dys	6⅝	6⅝
Hamburg	3 mths	20·30½	20·31	Valparaiso	90 dys	17⅞	17⅞
Frankfort	short	20·46	20·47	Calcutta	T. T.	1/4 1/32	1/4 1/16
Vienna	short	12·02½	12·03	Bombay	T. T.	1/4 1/32	1/4 1/32
St. Petersburg	3 mths	93·95	93·90	Hong Kong	T. T.	1/10	1/10⅛
New York	60 dys	4·82	4·81½	Shanghai	T. T.	2/5⅜	2/5⅜
Lisbon	sight	35⅞	35 1/16	Singapore	T. T.	1/10 3/16	1/10
Madrid	sight	34·65	34·05				

IMPERIAL BANK OF GERMANY (20 marks to the £).

	Mar. 3, 1898.	Feb. 23, 1898.	Feb. 15, 1898.	Feb. 27, 1897.
	£	£	£	£
Cash in hand	48,155,800	49,178,700	47,570,800	45,794,000
Bills discounted	27,442,600	25,905,600	25,612,000	*31,482,000
Advances on stocks	4,282,200	3,090,850	4,118,600	—
Note circulation	51,002,750	49,498,100	50,645,450	49,126,000
Public deposits	24,705,300	25,905,600	23,319,200	23,867,000

* Includes advances.

AUSTRIAN-HUNGARIAN BANK (1s. 8d. to the florin).

	Feb. 28, 1898.	Feb. 23, 1898.	Feb. 15, 1898.	Feb. 27, 1897.
	£	£	£	£
Gold reserve	30,715,583	30,615,083	30,324,417	30,950,000
Silver reserve	10,407,333	10,411,500	10,771,500	12,004,000
Foreign bills	1,214,333	1,254,740	1,318,917	—
Advances	1,863,833	1,832,106	1,250,333	—
Note circulation	51,068,416	50,579,333	51,674,417	55,823,000
Bills discounted	10,871,016	10,131,000	10,802,250	*11,407,000

* Includes advances.

NATIONAL BANK OF BELGIUM (25 francs to the £).

	Mar. 3, 1898.	Feb. 24, 1898.	Feb. 17, 1898.	Mar. 4, 1897.
	£	£	£	£
Coin and bullion	4,330,520	4,198,480	4,311,040	[illegible]
Other securities	17,024,440	17,090,650	17,011,000	[illegible]
Note circulation	18,900,040	19,255,050	19,145,000	[illegible]
Deposits	3,978,120	3,675,720	3,405,440	[illegible]

BANK OF SPAIN (25 pesetas to the £).

	Mar. 5, 1898.	Feb. 26, 1898.	Feb. 19, 1898.	Mar. 6, 1897.
	£	£	£	£
Gold	9,559,640	9,542,840	9,517,560	8,528,360
Silver	10,874,560	10,875,280	10,712,600	10,652,500
Bills discounted	23,260,360	21,491,840	21,763,160	7,894,840
Advances and loans	5,459,120	4,924,360	4,805,800	9,577,400
Notes in circulation	50,195,240	49,959,440	49,856,480	42,634,120
Treasury advances, coupon account	386,760	330,560	236,240	574,600
Treasury balances	1,483,160	988,500	887,400	2,914,040

LONDON COURSE OF EXCHANGE.

Place.	Usance.	March 1.	March 3.	March 8.	March 10.
Amsterdam and Rotterdam	short	12·2	12·2	12·2	12·2½
Do. do.	3 months	12·3¾	12·3¾	12·3¾	12·3⅞
Antwerp and Brussels	3 months	25·46¼	25·48¾	25·50	25·51¼
Hamburg	3 months	20·64	20·64	20·65	20·67
Berlin and German B. Places	3 months	20·64	20·64	20·65	20·67
Paris	cheques	25·30	25·31	25·32½	25·32½
Do.	3 months	25·43¾	25·45	25·46¼	25·46¼
Marseilles	3 months	25·45	25·45	25·46¼	25·47½
Switzerland	3 months	25·62½	25·62½	25·63	25·67½
Austria	3 months	12·17½	12·15	12·17½	12·17½
St. Petersburg	3 months	25 1/16	25 1/16	25 1/16	25
Moscow	3 months	25	25	25	24 15/16
Italian Bank Places	3 months	26·90	26·88¾	26·95	27·00
New York	60 days	49 1/16	49 1/16	49 1/16	49 1/16
Madrid and Spanish B. P.	3 months	34 5/16	34⅜	34 1/16	33 15/16
Lisbon	3 months	34 5/16	34⅜	34⅜	34 7/16
Oporto	3 months	34 5/16	34⅜	34⅜	34 5/16
Copenhagen	3 months	18·38	18·38	18·39	18·40
Christiania	—	18·39	18·39	18·40	18·40
Stockholm	—	18·39	18·39	18·40	18·40

OPEN MARKET DISCOUNT.

	Per cent.
Thirty and sixty day remitted bills	2 15/16—3
Three months "	2 15/16—3
Four months "	2⅞
Six months "	2⅞
Three months fine inland bills	3—3¼
Four months "	3—3¼
Six months "	3¼

BANK AND DEPOSIT RATES.

	Per cent.
Bank of England minimum discount rate	3
" " short loan rates	3
Banker's rate on deposits	1½
Bill brokers' deposit rate (call)	2
" 7 and 14 days' notice	2¼
Current rates for 7 day loans	2½—3
" " for call loans	2½—3

Stock Market Notes and Comments

THE chronicle of the week's scares will be found in the next article. Here we propose to press home some of the lessons they inculcate. Why is it that the Stock Exchange should be so prone to flurries, the product of every rumour no matter how silly in itself? Supposing the worst had happened in the beginning of the week and that the United States and Spain had gone to war, would that have been any reason for depressing the price of British railway debenture stocks several pounds per cent? Grant that Russia and Japan may fall out and come to blows as soon as the ice melts to let Russian ships of war out of the port of Vladivostock, should we for this reason all rush and sell Consols? Were Mr. Chamberlain to send an expedition into the Transvaal for the purpose of once more destroying the liberty granted to the Boers, is there any reason to expect that the commerce of the United Kingdom would there and then fall to pieces? If fire-eating Colonel Lugard, who is now on his way to West Africa, were to carry fire and sword into the territories we are disputing for there with the French, would that imply a blockade of French ports by the British Fleet, and a state of war between two countries which ought to be the best of friends? And if it did imply war, is the country so helpless that immediate ruin must be looked for? Why should the aged Queen's health be used to depress markets, as if she were merely a Mr. Cecil Rhodes?

We leave these questions to be answered by every man for himself, only remarking that none of the contingencies mentioned, not even the gravest, could be deemed probable on the reports flying about in the City during the past and present weeks. Nor do we think that sensible people there or elsewhere really believed in war of a serious character at any point. They shook their heads at each fearsome tale and said it was grave, but they did not in their hearts believe in an outbreak of hostilities. Yet prices went down and in many large groups of securities there was frequently no market at all, that is to say, a man with a few hundred pounds worth of stock to sell of a particular security might dispose of his little lot, but the man with thousands could not.

Does not this statement disclose to us something of the cause of the market's weakness? The Stock Exchange is like a quagmire thawing in times like these. While the frost was hard the bog gives firm foothold, but the thaw reveals it to be only a bottomless swamp. Fear has taken possession of men's minds, because the operations of the past few years, whereby prices of public securities have been lifted to unheard of heights, are now threatening to bear their natural fruit. All over the kingdom people are loaded up with pawned securities held by them on banking credits. So long as they got their money at low rates they were able to carry these stocks and live, but money has lately been dearer, and does not promise soon to become cheap again. Therefore, in all directions speculative holders of stocks are being obliged to throw off part of the obligations they had assumed in pledging these stocks to their bankers. The real reason of the proneness of our Stock Markets to take fright on the slightest provocation, is to be found in the moderate stiffness of the Money Market, acting on inflated quotations.

We quake because of the way we have gone on and on, heedlessly buying all sorts of stocks and shares at ridiculously high prices, without giving the slightest thought to the possibility of being able to sell them again, and banks have taken their full share in producing this inflation.

With their experience of the evil consequences of free lending when money is very cheap, they ought to have put a curb upon the market by demanding larger margins on their loans, the further prices went up. It is not the same thing to lend on London and North-Western Railway stock at £200 with a 10 per cent. margin as to carry out the same transaction when the price is £170. Every pound rise increases the risk of the lender, and ought to be provided for if business is to be conducted under ordinary considerations of prudence. There has been no prudence in bank lending these several years back. Not only have high class securities, such as the one named, been advanced upon lavishly at high and even excessive prices, and often with less than 10 per cent. of margin between the lender and loss—but questionable financial undertakings of every description have been treated as good banker's securities. Should any crisis arise, as it one day must, in consequence of this careless finance, we are confident that it will disclose a startling disregard of prudence on the part of some of our apparently strongest and most wealthy banks.

There is evidence before our eyes in last week's market fluctuations that this must be so. Why should Apollinaris shares, for example, dip as they have done, or Welsbach Incandescent stock, or Argentine Government and railway securities, or the shares of some favourite companies in the mining market? Is is not because this class of paper has been pawned in the happy times of cheap money, and is now being forced out, either by the inability of the pledger to pay the higher interest asked for, or by the banker insisting upon calling in such loans because his money is wanted elsewhere. Readers may depend upon it that, if anything, a war scare or a commercial crisis, or the failure of some foreign State to pay interest on its national debt, should force the open market rate of interest up to 6 per cent., there would be such a collapse in all these speculative classes of securities as cannot fail to bring some of our credit institutions into serious trouble.

We have often insisted on this view of markets before, but it was never more necessary to press it than now, because the London Money Market is slowly and surely working towards such a crisis, and by and by it will become so imminent that prudence will forbid us to talk about it. At present it is safe to insist upon the dangers lying ahead, because there is yet time for sensible people to guard against them by limiting their commitments and avoiding speculation as much as possible. The day is coming when it will be too late for them to do this. Understanding the motive for speaking thus bluntly, we hope our words will be taken as a hint to be careful. Hasty readers have been only too ready, when we have uttered words of warning such as these, to jump to the conclusion that we were looking for "a panic" or something of that sort next week. This is folly. They may depend upon it that if we saw any such disaster as a panic at hand we should use language calculated to sooth apprehensions rather than endeavour to excite them. We can mention the word "panic" now because the symptoms of one are only discernible in the distance, and by warning people against the treacherous character of market prices, against rushes after fancy market premiums, like those on Lipton's shares, we hope to avert the danger, not to bring it nearer. Seeing what one has seen repeatedly in the last two years, would it be fair or reasonable to advise the public, for instance, to buy Colonial securities at the present moment, when we know perfectly well that directly a pinch arises in money these securities are unsaleable? It is not a question of price at all; at such times, the market simply will not buy, and the reason why it will not is just as plain. These securities lie in banks, pawned in immense masses, carried on margins which have to be kept up as quotations go down. The nominal holders, underwriters, members of syndicates, and so on, in the majority of cases do not possess the means to keep up these margins long; their only resource, therefore, is to sustain quotations nominally as high as they possibly can by stopping business. The truth of this statement could be very easily tested by any man who likes to send his broker into the Exchange to sell 10,000 of almost any Colonial security on a bad day. In a lull of the apprehensions scouring over markets day by day the stock might be disposed of, if pressed, but it would be at a price well below the published quotation, and in all probability such price would not be marked so as to become public property. This is only one section of the quagmire of which we have spoken that the heat of dearer money is thawing. Of the others, such as the Mining and Miscellaneous markets, it is not necessary to enlarge.

We have dwelt upon the symptoms in one or other of them almost every week. All we now desire plainly to do is to inculcate caution, circumspection, and the drawing in of commitments that a man may feel beyond his strength to hold out under should the worst come. The fever of speculation has been great and unrestrained in the City for quite three years now, and it is going to produce its usual consequences, not immediately, not at a date to be fixed beforehand, but as surely as water finds its level. And to think that many of those whose ruin is certain should a serious war break out, should be among the people who clamour for a fight with France, with Russia, with any power they imagine to be standing in the way of that expansion of empire which is wasting our best strength.

The Week's Stock Markets.

On the Stock Exchange there was practically nothing doing the latter part of last week, as far as the general public was concerned, and prices gave way simply for want of support. The weakness of the Paris Bourse, caused by the action of the French Government in introducing legislation affecting the *coulisse*, was also reflected on markets here, and the continued stringency of the money market had a depressing effect on Consols and all other leading securities. The present week opened in a truly startling fashion, the news from Peking and New York causing a mild sort of panic, and the forced closing of weak "Bull" accounts help to make matters worse. On Tuesday a calmer view of the political situation was taken, and a partial rally occurred, later news regarding Spain and the United States being more satisfactory; but the move in the upward direction was destined to be short lived, an unfavourable impression being created by the report that the Queen's journey to the South of France had been delayed. Alarmist rumours spread like wild-fire, and the delay was at once put down to complications in foreign politics, nobody believing the story of Her Majesty's indisposition. The result was that for a time markets were reduced to a state of blind "funk," and a general stampede occurred. But a few buying orders from Paris and Wall-street, where a recovery soon set in, caused a smart reaction, although the volume of actual business was small, owing to the fortnightly settlement having begun.

Highest and Lowest this Year.		Last Carrying over Price.	BRITISH FUNDS, &c.	Closing Price.	Rise or Fall.
113⅛	111	—	Consols 2¾ p.c. (Money)...	111⅛	− ⅛
113$\frac{5}{16}$	111¼	112¾	Do. Account (Apl. 1)	111¼	−$\frac{9}{16}$
106⅛	105	106	2½ p.c. Stock red. 1905 ...	105¼	− ¼
363	347½	—	Bank of England Stock...	355½	—
117	114	116	India 3½ p.c. Stk. red. 1931	114¼	− ⅞
109½	106⅛	108	Do. 3 p.c. Stk. red. 1948	106¼	−1¼
96⅞	92½	94½	Do. 2½ p.c. Stk. red. 1926	93	−1

Consols declined steadily all the week, and after starting at about 112$\frac{1}{16}$ "marked" 111 on Tuesday, recovering since then to nearly last Thursday's level again. A heavy fall has taken place in the whole list of "gilt-edged" securities, the premier stocks of the leading Home railways suffering severely, while Indian railways and Colonial Government issues have fared but little better.

The Home Railway Market, in addition to all the other evils, has had one more to combat with in the shape of disappointing Board of Trade returns, but on the whole the market has come through the ordeal fairly well, and prices do not show any very serious losses on balance. Good traffics are again to hand, but little or no support has been forthcoming from the outside public. South Eastern Deferred was pressed for sale when the news of the rather sudden death of the chairman of the line was announced; but the price has since recovered, in common with the partial rally in the rest of the list. The North British dividend is about due, and the deferred stock has, as generally happens, "wobbled" rather wildly in anticipation of the event. Among the heavy stocks, Midland Deferred marks a big decline, this being principally due to the announcement recently made by the directors in reference to the question of wages. The settlement disclosed the usual "back" on Great Eastern, and the price recovered sharply. Rates generally were easy, although rather higher than a fortnight ago; North Western at ⅜ to ½, and Great Western at $\frac{5}{16}$ to $\frac{9}{16}$ being about ⅛ above last time.

Highest and Lowest this Year.		Last Carrying over Price.	HOME RAILWAYS.	Closing Price.	Rise or Fall.
186	172¾	174	Brighton Def.	174¼	−1⅜
59¼	55½	56⅛	Caledonian Def.	56	−1½
20⅝	19	19⅝	Chatham Ordinary	19½	− ⅜
77¼	66	70	Great Central Pref.	70	− ½
24⅜	21¾	22	Do. Def.	21⅞	− ⅜
124½	119⅝	121	Great Eastern	121	− ¼
61½	52	52⅝	Great Northern Def.	52⅞	−1
179⅛	171	171¼	Great Western	171	−2½
49¼	45¼	45¾	Hull and Barnsley	45¾	− ¾
149¼	146¼	146¾	Lanc. and Yorkshire	147	− ¼
136⅛	129½	130¼	Metropolitan	129½	−2
31	26¾	27¾	Metropolitan District	27¾	−1¼
88¾	83⅝	84	Midland Pref.	83⅞	−1¼
95⅜	86¾	87½	Do. Def.	86⅛	−3¼
93¼	90⅛	90¾	North British Pref.	91	− ¾
47½	42¾	43¼	Do. Def.	43⅜	−1½
181½	173⅜	174¼	North Eastern	174¼	−1
205⅛	197¾	198½	North Western	198⅜	−1⅜
117⅛	107¾	109½	South Eastern Def.	106¼	−2¼
98¾	91	91½	South Western Def.	91½	−2¼

United States Railroad shares were inclined to harden up when we last wrote, but the steadiness was only of short duration, although there was rather a lull, operators standing off pending the publication of the United States Commissioners' report on the *Maine* disaster. There was a sharp break in prices on Monday, caused by the demand on the part of Spain for the removal of the United States Consul-General at Havana, and other political complications induced a still deeper feeling of easiness. The Nebraska rate decision coming at any other time would have caused a jump in prices, as it has been given in favour of the railroads; but it was almost overlooked for the time being. When it was found that the Queen's journey was only to be delayed for a day or so, prices recovered quickly, and a few buying orders came to hand from New York, and further helped to put a little more backbone into the market. Wall-street nervousness seems, however, to have been considerably increased by the preparations for meeting trouble by the War and Navy departments, and some further passenger rate-cutting to the North-West by the Union Pacific Company is also responsible for part of the fall in that and kindred companies' stocks. The general rate for money at the settlement was 5½ to 6 per cent., easing off slightly towards the close, whereas last time 4½ to 5½ per cent. only was paid. A considerable reduction was apparent in the account, which seems to have been smaller than for several months past.

Helped by a good traffic return, Canadian Pacific Railway shares were on the up grade for several days, but it was hardly to be expected that they would fail to be affected by the general weakness. After dropping sharply, the price as quickly recovered and almost to last week's level, it being now confidently expected that the end of the rate war is in sight, as the President of the Canadian Pacific line is about to start for New York to attend the Railway Conference there. Grand Trunk stocks have followed in the steps of United States shares, but the recovery has been rather more pronounced, although all the lost ground has not been made up, the "bull" account in them being very weak.

Highest and Lowest this Year.		Last Carrying over Price.	CANADIAN AND U.S. RAILWAYS.	Closing Prices.	Rise or Fall.
14 5/16	11¼	12	Atchison Shares	12	− ⅜
34	25¾	27¼	Do. Pref.	26⅛	−2⅛
15⅝	11⅛	12¼	Central Pacific	12⅝	− ⅜
99¾	92¼	94½	Chic. Mil. & St. Paul	94⅝	−2⅜
14¼	11½	12	Denver Shares	12	− ½
54¼	45	47	Do. Prefd.	46¾	−2¾
16⅞	12½	13¼	Erie Shares	13¼	−1⅝
44⅞	35¼	36½	Do. Prefd.	36½	−3⅜
62½	51¼	52¾	Louisville & Nashville ...	52⅛	−4¾
14½	10¾	11¼	Missouri & Texas	11⅛	− ⅜
22¾	108⅛	116	New York Central	115½	−2
57¼	44½	47	Norfolk & West. Prefd....	47	−3⅛
70¼	59⅝	63	Northern Pacific Prefd....	62⅝	−2⅝
19½	14½	15¼	Ontario Shares	15¼	− ⅛
62½	58⅜	59	Pennsylvania	59	−1
12½	9	9¼	Reading Shares	9⅜	− ⅜
34¼	26⅞	28	Southern Prefd.	27¾	−1½
137⅜	26⅛	28	Union Pacific	27⅜	−3¼
20¼	14½	15½	Wabash Prefd.	15¾	−1¼
30¼	22	24	Do. Income Debs....	24½	−2¼
92¾	82⅝	86¼	Canadian Pacific	86	− ½
78¼	69⅛	72½	Grand Trunk Guar.	73⅜	−1½
69¼	57⅛	63¼	Do. 1st Pref.	65	−1¾
50¼	37¼	43½	Do. 2nd Pref.	44⅞	−1⅛
25¼	19¾	21¼	Do. 3rd Pref.	21¾	−1
105½	101½	102	Do. 4 p.c. Deb.	102½	− ½

In spite of the unsatisfactory state of politics abroad, the Foreign market has not been very much depressed, and apart from the heavy fall in Spanish "Fours" the changes in inter-Bourse securities are unimportant. Greek bonds have shown the firmest front in the whole list, but other changes have been in the downward direction. Chinese issues drooped on rumours that the new loan might possibly be delayed, but the tale was not, and did not deserve to be credited, and a recovery has since taken place. In South American stocks Uruguay 3½ per cent. mark a rise on the week, but Brazilian issues have been very depressed, owing to a steadily declining exchange at Rio, and Paris operators sold large blocks on Wednesday, as it was rumoured there that the payment of the coupons was going to be suspended. All the Continental bourses have been in a nervous state and entirely under the influence of alarmist rumours, and, in addition, the Paris Bourse, as mentioned above, has been very much upset by the course taken by the French Government to further strengthen the monopoly of the official brokers. Continuation rates were slightly firmer, ranging from 2 per cent. on Russian to 4 per cent. on Greek and Turkish. The rate on Spanish and Italian was about 4 per cent. as compared with 3½ per cent. last time.

Highest and Lowest this Year.		Last Carrying over Price.	FOREIGN BONDS.	Closing Price.	Rise or Fall.
94½	88	88¾	Argentine 5 p.c. 1886......	89	−2
92⅝	87½	87¾	Do. 6 p.c. Funding	88	−1¾
76¾	70¼	71¼	Do. 5 p.c. B. Ay. Water	71	−2⅝
61¾	54½	59	Brazilian 4 p.c. 1889	54½	−6¼
69⅞	58½	64	Do. 5 p.c. 1895	58½	−7
65	54⅛	60	Do. 5 p.c. West Minas Ry.	54½	−7
108¾	106¼	107¾	Egyptian 4 p.c. Unified...	107¼	− ½
104¾	102	104¼	Do. 3½ p.c. Pref. ...	104	− ¼
103	102	102½	French 3 p.c. Rente	102½	—
41⅞	34½	41	Greek 4 p.c. Monopoly ...	41¼	+ ¼
93 5/16	92¼	92⅝	Italian 5 p.c. Rente	92⅝	− ¼
100	95¼	98	Mexican 6 p.c. 1888	98	− ¼
20¾	19⅛	19¾	Portuguese 1 p.c.	19⅝	− ⅛
62½	55⅛	57½	Spanish 4 p.c.	56⅛	−3⅛
45¼	42¼	43	Turkish 1 p.c. "B"	42¼	−2⅝
26 7/16	24 1/16	25⅛	Do. 1 p.c. "C"	24⅛	−1 1/16
22 7/16	21 1/16	22	Do. 1 p.c. "D"	21⅛	− ⅛
46	40	44½	Uruguay 3½ p.c. Bonds...	45¼	+1

Foreign Railway stocks have been almost unsaleable, the falls registered from day to day extending to almost the whole list. About the only stocks unaffected were those of the leading Uruguayan companies, which have been remarkably steady, in sympathy with the rise in Uruguayan Government bonds. A partial rally is apparent in several cases towards the close, and good traffic returns have helped to impart a slightly firmer tone to this section. The old Mexican companies' stocks leave off considerably under last week's closing prices, the weakness of the Silver market helping to depress quotations; and a good traffic return, showing an increase of $5,700, only just helped to steady prices at the fall.

Highest and Lowest this Year.		Last Carrying over Price.	FOREIGN RAILWAYS.	Closing Price.	Rise or Fall.
20¾	19¾	19¾	Argentine Gt. West. 5 p.c. Pref.	—	—
158¼	149	150	B. Ay. Gt. Southern Ord..	151	−2
78½	69	71	B. Ay. and Rosario Ord...	72	−3
12¼	10¾	11⅛	B. Ay. Western Ord.	11¼	− ¼
87¼	79¼	80	Central Argentine Ord....	81	−2
92	85	85	Cordoba and Rosario 6 p.c. Deb.	85½	−2½
95½	89½	89½	Cord. Cent. 4 p.c. Deb. (Cent. Nth. Sec.)	90	−3
61¾	47½	48¼	Do. Income Deb. Stk. ...	50	−2
25¼	18	19½	Mexican Ord. Stk.	20	−2¼
83½	72	78	Do. 8 p.c. 1st Pref.	78	−3¼

In miscellaneous securities, the stocks of the leading Gas and Water Companies have been freely offered, owing partly to the result of the London County Council election, coupled with the general all round decline in other departments; and shrinkages are apparent in Banks, Insurance, and Electric Lighting Company's shares. Brewery properties, judging by the result of recent sales at the Mart and elsewhere, are not commanding anything like such high prices as those ruling of late, and a set back is noticeable in many of the leading brewery stocks. Russian Oil ordinary shares came down with a run, owing to the approach of the account, but the price rallied, in spite of a stiff rate of something like 3s. being charged for carrying over. Savoy Hotel shares are a very weak market, and several circulars have been issued lately by the directors, which seems to indicate a screw loose somewhere; at Any rate a serious dwindling away of profits is talked of aerated Bread, and the shares of the various other catering concerns have met with support; and a 12 per cent.

dividend on D. H. Evans ordinary has caused a further advance in that company's shares.

Just when markets looked like recovering a little, there came the news that the Russian Government proposed to spend ninety million roubles on their navy, and the interpretation put upon this was soon seen is the all round break away that followed. Consols fell sharply, and Home Railway stocks, especially the heavy lines, followed suit. The Foreign Market closed very weak, heavy selling orders of Brazilian bonds from Paris causing a further big drop, reaching to about seven points on the week, and Spanish 4 per cents. were also pressed for sale from the same quarter. The fall in the latter security also affected United States Railroad shares, and about the only firm market in the Stock Exchange was for Grand Trunk Railway stocks, which were favourably influenced by another remarkably good traffic return.

MINING AND FINANCE COMPANIES.

It was hardly to be expected that the South African market would be anything else but flat under the present circumstances, and a decline in prices has been steadily going on all the week. The conclusion of the settlement is being looked forward to with considerable apprehension, especially as regards the accounts of those who had to be helped over last time. De Beers fell heavily on large selling orders from Paris, but have since partly recovered on repurchases from that quarter. Continuation rates were not much heavier, except in a few instances, 6 to 8 per cent. being about the general charge. Western Australian ventures have been very depressed, and it was not until quite the last thing that a slightly firmer tendency set in. Copper shares also wind up the week with a rather better tone, after being a weak market. Indian shares have been comparatively steady, with little or nothing doing.

STOCK EXCHANGE "BOLSTERING."

There has been a good deal of forced liquidation in the "House" recently, and some failures are expected. It is to be hoped members will set their faces against any bolstering of those with large accounts open who cannot meet their engagements. Such methods are dangerous in the extreme, and do no permanent good. For the small man who is heavily hit, through no direct fault of his own, we have every sympathy, but it is not often he can find friends to assist him. On the other hand, the man who in good times makes money fast, only to spend it extravagently, and continues to run a large speculative account, we contend deserves neither help nor pity. If his account is such as to threaten the market, let it be taken off his hands, but only on condition that he leaves the Stock Exchange. Allowed to remain, with his difficulties hushed up, he continues to be a weak spot, and a source of danger to his fellow members. Surely, it is not in prudent policy for Stock Exchange men to foster such individuals in their midst. A man who, when times are good, makes money, lives in extravagant style, lays by no reserve, but continues to deal largely in speculative ventures, in not acting honestly. If markets move in his favour, well and good, but if the contrary happens he is simply speculating at other people's expense. He deserves no mercy and should receive none.

Agricultural land in Lincolnshire seems to have gone down very much during the last quarter of a century. A freehold farm of 87 acres at Leverton, was put up for sale the other day, and the highest bid for it was £2,100, at which it was withdrawn. In 1873 the property realised £6,200. Two freehold hotels in Scarborough were put up for sale a few days ago, but only one went off, public-house business having apparently become rather dull. For the Albert Hotel the bidding was spirited, and it was knocked down for £7,025. The highest bid for the Castle Hotel was only £6,000, and this lot was withdrawn. The freehold tavern known as the King's Arms, Kingsdown, Bristol, with dwelling-house and shop adjoining, was sold lately for £6,450.

It may seem a comparatively easy, if dignified, thing to preside over a public meeting; but that vision of ease only lasts until you have tried it. There is a great deal of law on the subject. The chairman's authority is carefully hedged in, and nobody should venture to undertake the duties of a president without knowing some of the law that should guide him. On this they will find clear explanations in a little volume entitled "The Law of Meetings," by George Blackwell (Butterworth & Co., London). It is very full and lucid.

MINING RETURNS.

QUEEN CROSS REEF.—Crushed 270 tons for 498 oz.; approximate value, £1,590.

ST. AUGUSTINE.—2,389 loads washed yielded 66 carats.

AUSTRALIA UNITED.—210 tons for 439 oz.

COROMANDEL.—1,200 tons of stone produced 903 oz. gold; 1,100 tons of tailings, cyanide process, produced 109 oz. gold.

BELLEVUE PROPRIETARY.—186 tons for 210 oz.

HALL MINES (B.C.).—5,436 tons of ore smelted, yielding 321 tons of matte containing approximately 125 tons copper, 77,020 oz. silver, 402 oz. gold.

BRILLIANT.—2,400 tons of stone crushed producing 3,000 oz. of gold.

BROKEN HILL PROPRIETARY.—19,450 tons of ore treated for the four weeks ended March 3; output from refinery, 1,061 oz. gold (estimated), 453,613 oz. silver, 2,437 tons lead, and 47 tons antimonial lead (estimated), the copper matte containing 16 tons copper (estimated) and 30,106 oz. silver (estimated).

CHAMPION REEF OF INDIA.—Last month's return:—7,050 tons of stone produced 9,094 oz.; 2,370 tons of tailings produced 606 oz.; and 4,620 tons of tailings (cyanide process) produced 1,294 oz.; total, 10,994 oz.

GIBRALTAR CONSOLIDATED.—Result for February:—1,267 tons, inclusive 400 tons low grade, 1,486 oz.; concentrates, 405 oz.; tailings, 140 oz.; total, 2,031 oz.

GOLD FIELDS OF MYSORE.—Last month's return:—42 oz. obtained from 700 tons sand, cyanide process; 234 oz. obtained from amalgamation.

IVANHOE.—Clean up for fortnight, 1,497 oz. of gold from 929 tons crushed. Total return for month of February, 2,851 oz. of gold from 1,722 tons crushed.

MYSORE.—6,875 tons of quartz produced 11,336 oz.; 2,580 tons of tailings produced 700 oz.; 1,545 tons of tailings (cyanide process) produced 254 oz.

MYSORE REEFS (KANGUNDY).—February return.—1,250 tons of ore crushed yielded 483 oz. of retorted gold.

NINE REEFS.—Last month's return.—1,000 tons milled amalgamation on plates, 103 oz.; cyanide 30 oz.

NUNDYDROOG.—Return for February.—2,900 tons of quartz produced 2,940 oz. of gold; 700 tons of tailings produced 84 oz.; 2,668 tons of tailings (cyanide process) produced 325 oz.—total, 3,349 oz.

OTTOS KOPJE.—8,380 loads washed, 231 carats won, including two stones each of 16 carats.

STANHOPE GOLD.—Last month's crushing yielded 1,654 oz.

UNITED IVY REEF.—Last month's output was 550 oz.; crushed, 964 tons.

KOFFYFONTEIN.—Return for February, 2,130 carats.

PIGG'S PEAK DEVELOPMENT.—For February.—Crushed, 1,700 tons for 202 oz. gold; cyanided, 2,200 tons for 380 oz. gold.

WORCESTER EXPLORATION AND GOLD.—Last month's crushing yielded 2,888 oz. of gold.

HIGHLAND CHIEF.—Crushed 287 tons; yield, 138 oz. retorted gold.

QUEENSLAND MENZIES.—Crushed 270 tons for 670 oz.

TOLIMA.—February estimated returns, £3,555.

PREMIER.—715 tons for 345 oz.

SALISBURY.—Last month's crushing yielded 2,450 oz.

WHITE FEATHER "REWARD."—Last clean-up, 527 tons crushed: yield, 252 oz. 5 dwts. gold.

VICTORIA AND QUEEN.—Partial clean up. Crushed 391 tons for 540 oz.

EASTLEIGH.—February, total output, 2,100 oz.

INVERELL DIAMOND FIELDS.—383 carats from thirty-eight loads washed by hand.

JUBILEE.—5,374 tons crushed for 1,959 oz. gold. Tailings 841 oz.

KIMBERLEY WATERWORKS.—Consumption of water for February, 12,000,000 gallons.

MOUNT DAVID (NEW SOUTH WALES).—400 tons crushed during month for 313 oz. of gold.

CASSEL COAL COMPANY.—Output for February, 19,600 tons.

CROWN DEEP.—Tons crushed, 19,000; yield in smelted gold from mill, 5,242 oz.; tons of sands and concentrates treated by cyanide works, 16,670; yield in smelted gold from sands and concentrates, 4,827 oz.; tons of slimes treated, 3,500; yield in smelted gold from slimes works, 179 oz.

DAY DAWN BLOCK AND WYNDHAM GOLD.—For fortnight ended the 5th inst.:—Tons crushed, 1,310; yield of gold, 1,470 oz., including tailings.

DURBAN-ROODEPOORT.—Results for February: Quartz milled, 9,990 tons for 5,007 oz.; tailings treated, 5,810 tons for 1,172 oz.

EAST MURCHISON UNITED.—Great Eastern: 760 tons of ore crushed, 950 oz. gold obtained. Donegal Leases: 530 tons of ore crushed, 445 oz. gold obtained.

FERREIRA.—Results for February: Crushed, 9,695 tons; bar gold extracted, 7,925 oz.; concentrates caught, 230 tons; assay value of concentrates, 5 oz. fine gold per ton, equal to, say, 1,150 oz. Cyanide works: Bullion produced from tailings, 3,002 oz.; total gold from all sources, 12,077 oz.

GELDENHUIS MAIN REEF.—Crushed, 2,100 tons; obtained 424 oz. of gold. No clean up cyanide works.

MIKADO (LAKE OF THE WOODS), ONTARIO.—February return:—Mill crushed 1,071 tons of ore, yielding 550 oz. of gold.

MOUNT USHER.—115 tons of ore crushed have yielded 88 oz. of gold.

NEW GUADALCAZAR QUICKSILVER MINES.—Production for the past month amounts to 8,100 lb., equal 108 flasks.

NEW KLEINFONTEIN.—Crushing for last month:—Tons crushed, 10,290; ounces recovered from mill, 3,680; tons treated by cyanide, 7,000; ounces recovered from cyanide, 2,312.

PREMIER TATI MONARCH REEF.—February return:—Crushed, 1,825 tons, including a considerable quantity of poor-grade ore on the dump; yield of retorted gold, 550 oz.

PRINCESS ESTATE AND GOLD.—Result for February:—Crushed, 4,960 tons, producing 1,805 oz.; extracted 920 oz. from tailings.

ROBINSON (WESTERN AUSTRALIA).—292 oz. of gold from 415 tons of ore, exclusive of concentrates and tailings.

TREASURY.—Output for February, 5,300 tons; yielded 3,844 oz.

WEMMER.—During February crushed 6,066 tons, yielding 4,208 oz.; cyanide plant—4,000 tons treated, yielding 825 oz.; and from concentrates 134 tons caught, assaying 115 dwt. per ton.

ANGELO.—Crushing for last month, 6,572 tons; ounces recovered from mill, 3,160; tons treated by cyanide, 5,043; ounces recovered from cyanide, 2,280; ounces recovered from slags, 428; total number of ounces recovered, 5,868.

BARRETT.—Yield for February, 800 oz.

BEACON.—Ounces of gold, 600; approximate value, £2,100, being an average yield of 1 oz. 3 dwt. 7 gr. per ton from 515 tons of ore crushed.

BURMA RUBY MINES.—The result of the mining for February was 71,000 loads washed, producing rubies valued at Rs. 96,000.

GLYNN'S LYDENBURG.—Results for February: from mill, crushed, 1,225 tons, obtained 419 oz. of fine gold; from cyanide works, treated, 800 tons, yield, 263 oz.; total, 682 oz.

GRAND CENTRAL.—Return for February: crushed, 4,230 tons of ore, yielding bullion estimated to realise $45,600, and concentrates to value estimated $18,000.

HANNAN'S BROWNHILL.—540 tons sands, 454 tons slimes treated, realised 1,840 oz. of gold.

HANNAN'S REWARD.—February returns: Cement crushed, 513 tons, yielding 85 oz. 17 dwt.

HENRY NOURSE.—Result of Febuary: Mill crushed 7,850 tons, producing 4,857 oz.; treated 6,130 tons cyanide, producing 2,866 oz.: total, 7,723 oz.

MONTANA.—Output for February was: Gold 2,150 oz., silver 5,960 oz., obtained from 5,925 tons of ore crushed in the mills.

NEW COMET.—Tons crushed, 4,683; ounces recovered from mill, 1,735: tons treated by cyanide, 3,631; ounces recovered, 1,010; ounces recovered from slags, 223; total number of ounces recovered, 2,968.

ROODEPOORT UNITED MAIN REEF.—Result for February: Crushed 6,645 tons, producing 3,130 oz.; cyanide, 927 oz.; total, 4,057 oz.

SHEBA.—Return for February: 6,800 tons of ore, 3,450 oz.; 3,480 tons tailings, 1,350 oz.; 138 tons of concentrates, 1,130 oz.; total, 5,930 oz.

TRANSVAAL.—Results for February: From mill—crushed 3,800 tons, obtained 3,553 oz. of fine gold; from cyanide works—treated 1,445 tons, yield 592 oz.: total, 4,145 oz.

MOUNT MORGAN (QUEENSLAND).—Tons chlorinated, 9,574; gold returned, 14,207 oz.

LISBON-BERLYN.—For February: Ore mined, 2,000 tons; ore crushed, 1 82 tons; treated by cyanide, 1,750 tons; fine gold recovered, 707 oz.; estimated value £3,000; estimated expenses, £2,375.

Consolidated Main Reef.—February production, 1,909 oz.

Crown Reef.—Output for February: Yield in smelted gold from stamp mill, 6,998 oz.; cyanide, 3,233 oz.; and from slimes, 101 oz.

De Lamar.—Return for February: Crushed, 900 tons; bullion produced in the mill (including clean-up), $18,845.

Frank Smith Diamond.—4,100 loads washed, producing 149 cts.

Geldenhuis Deep.—Results for February: Tons crushed by stamps, 20,700; yield in smelted gold from mill, 7,098 oz.; tons of sands and concentrates treated by cyanide works, 14,920; yield in smelted gold, 3,796 oz.; tons of slimes treated, 5,723; yield in smelted gold, 481 oz.

Ginsberg G. M.—February production, 2,754 oz.

Glencairn Main Reef.—February production, 6,512 oz.

Great Boulder Perseverance.—Amount of ore smelted for Febuary, 259 tons, returning 769 oz; 760 tons of ore milled for 807 oz.

Hannan's Virgina.—Crushed 400 tons, yielding 102 oz. gold.

Jumpers.—Results for February: crushed, 10,800 tons; obtained from mill, 3,788 oz.; from concentrates by cyanide, 570 oz.; and from tailings by cyanide, 981 oz.—total, 5,319 oz.

Klerksdorp Gold and Diamond.—From July to January the returns show that 25,132 tons of ore have been treated, yielding 5,623 oz. 6 dwt. of gold. Results of crushing for February, 707 oz.

Lancaster.—Result for February:—Crushed 7,020 tons, yielding 2,917 oz. over the plates; 2,457 tons of tailings were treated, having an average assay of 3¼ dwt. per ton.

Meyer and Charlton.—Result for February:—Crushed 8,334 tons, producing 2,528 oz., extracted 1,407 oz. from tailings; total, 3,935 oz.

New Australian Broken Hill Consols.—Two tons, containing 5,600 oz. of silver.

New Modderfontein.—Output for February, 4,874 tons yielded 2,434 oz.; cyanide, 401 oz.

New Primrose.—February production, 8,824 oz.

New Spes Bona.—February production, 2,986 oz.

Nourse Deep.—Results for February:—Tons crushed, 6,596; yield in smelted gold from mill, 2,375 oz.; tons of sands and concentrates treated by cyanide works, 4,991; yield in smelted gold from cyanide works, 2,267 oz.; total, 4,642 oz.

Rietfontein A.—Production for February, 5,049 oz.

Robinson Gold.—Production for February: Mill crushed 14,180 tons of ore; yielded in smelting gold, 9,543 oz.; from concentrates (by chlorination), 1,489 oz.; from tailings (cyanide process), 3,243 oz.; from slimes, 928 oz.; from own ore 15,203 oz.; from concentrates bought (by chlorination), 1,390 oz.; total gold recovered, 16,593 oz.

Roodepoort.—February production, 950 oz.

St. John Del Rey.—Gold produced for February: £10,100; yield per ton '44 of an ounce troy.

Van Ryn.—Production for February: Mill.—Tons milled, 9,561; number of ounces recovered, 2,474. Cyanide works.—Tons treated, 7,140; ounces recovered, 1,264. Total, 3,738 oz.

Village Main Reef.—Result for February: Crushed, 6,675 tons, yielding 3,576 oz.; cyanide treated, 6,750 tons, producing 1,782 oz.; total, 5,358 oz.

Wealth of Nations.—Crushed during the last twelve days, 270 tons, the gross yield being 236 oz. of gold.

Rose Deep.—Result for February: 100 stamps working 28 days crushed 13,118 tons yielding 5,655 oz. of gold; 10,031 tons treated by cyanide produced 3,005 oz. Total, 8,660 oz. of gold.

Henry Nourse Gold Mining Company.—Profit for month of February, £16,482.

Windsor Gold Mining Company.—Crushed 3,737 tons, yielding 1,191 oz. o gold; obtained by cyanide, 554 oz.

Wolhuter Gold Mines.—Result for February:—Crushed 12,380 tons, producing 3,918 oz.; obtained by cyanide, 2,757 oz. Total, 6,675 oz. of gold.

George Goch Amalgamated Gold Mining Company.—During February crushed 7,406 , yielding 1,638 oz. of gold, and 1,312 oz. of gold from tailings.

TRAMWAY AND OMNIBUS RECEIPTS.

For past week:—Belfast, + £83; Calais, − £7; Croydon, + £43; Glasgow, − £63; Lea Bridge, + £93; London & Deptford, + £18; London Southern, + £46; London General Omnibus, + £652; London Road Car, + £10; Metropolitan, + £238; North Staffordshire, + £10; South London, − £3; Woolwich & S. E. London, − £1; Provincial, − £70; Southampton, − £24; Wolverhampton, − £0.

Calcutta, + £127.

Anglo-Argentine, week ending February 7, £470 increase; City of Buenos Ayres, week ending January 31, £881 increase.

Italy's imports during 1897 amounted in value to 1,300,841,368 lires, and her exports to 1,115,815,841 lires, the latter the highest figure reached since 1883.

The death-rate in Birmingham has been so low during last year that the Birmingham Church of England Cemetery Company are only able to declare a dividend of 2s. 6d. per share instead of 5s., which has been the usual amount.

New Zealand last month exported 20,088 oz. of gold, of the value of £78,372. In the same month last year the weight exported was 26,039 oz.; the value being £104,457.

The adhesion of England to the Sugar Bounties Conference is said to have been virtually obtained, though under what conditions is not stated, and the first meeting is expected to be held about the end of April.

The output of the Indian Gold Mines for February amounted to 33,060 ozs., a decrease of 1,516 ozs., as compared with January, but an increase of 2,640 ozs. compared with February, 1897.

The scheme for organising a huge combination of fine cotton spinners and doublers has been approved and accepted by 32 firms, the contracts have been sent out to the amalgamating firms, and as soon as these are signed a provisional board will be called together to direct the issue of the prospectus, which, it is stated, will invite the subscription by the public of two-thirds of the capital, which is given as £5,000,000. The firms who have already entered the combination control over 2,250,000 spindles.

The exports of gold from Cape Colony for February amounted in value to £1,079,591.

The seven Australasian Colonies produced in 1897 is 521,544 oz. of gold more in 1897 than in 1896, the figures for the two years being 2,899,650 oz. and 2,378,126 oz. respectively.

The space allotted to England in the Paris Exhibition of 1900 is 60,000 ft. As this includes our Colonies and Canada asks for 60,000 ft. for herself, and New Zealand 100,000 ft., it seems pretty clear that Great Britain will be very indifferently represented at this advertising show.

Prices of Mine and Mining Finance Companies' Shares.

Shares £1 each, except where otherwise stated.

Australian.

Making-Up Price, Feb. 21.	Name.	Closing Price.	Rise or Fall.	Making-Up Price, Feb. 21.	Name	Closing Price.	Rise or Fall.
1[illegible]	Aladdin	1[illegible]		[illegible]	Hampton Plains	[illegible]	
3[illegible]	Associated	3[illegible]	−[illegible]	7[illegible]	Hannan's Brownhill	7[illegible]	−[illegible]
[illegible]	Do. Southern	1		[illegible]	Hannan's Oroya	[illegible]	−[illegible]
14/6	Brilliant, £2	14/6		15/	Do. Proprietary	16/6	−1/6
2[illegible]	Do. St. George's	2[illegible]	−[illegible]	[illegible]	Do. Star	[illegible]	−[illegible]
11/9	British Broken Hill	11/6		—	Ivanhoe, New	5[illegible]	−[illegible]
2[illegible]	Broken Hill Proprietary	2[illegible]	+[illegible]	[illegible]	Kalgurli Mt. & Iron King, 18/	[illegible]	−[illegible]
—	Do. Junction	1[illegible]		[illegible]	Kalgurli	5[illegible]	−[illegible]
—	Do. Block 10	3[illegible]		5[illegible]	Lady Shenton	[illegible]	−[illegible]
1[illegible]	Brownhill Extended	1[illegible]	−[illegible]	2[illegible]	Lake View Cons.	9[illegible]	−[illegible]
1[illegible]	Burbank's Birthday	1[illegible]		9[illegible]	Do. Extended	[illegible]	
[illegible]	Central Boulder	[illegible]	−[illegible]	[illegible]	Do. South	1[illegible]	+[illegible]
5/6	Chaffers, 4/	5/	−/6	1[illegible]	London & Globe Finance	1[illegible]	−[illegible]
1	Colonial Finance, 15/	[illegible] pm	−[illegible]	1[illegible]	London & W. A. Exploration	[illegible]	−[illegible]
—	Crœsus S. United	[illegible]		[illegible]	Do. Investment	[illegible]	−[illegible]
15/6	Day Dawn Block	15/	−/9	[illegible]	Mainland Consols	[illegible]	−[illegible]
1	E. Murchison	1		[illegible]	North Boulder, 10/	[illegible]	−[illegible]
[illegible]	Gold Estates	[illegible]		1[illegible]	North Kalgurli	1[illegible]	−[illegible]
4/	Golden Arrow 19/	3/6	−/6	4[illegible]	Northern Territories	4[illegible]	+[illegible]
7[illegible]	Golden Horseshoe	7	−[illegible]	2[illegible]	Peak Hill	2[illegible]	−[illegible]
[illegible]	Golden Link	[illegible]	−[illegible]	2[illegible]	South Kalgurli	2[illegible]	−[illegible]
[illegible]	Great Boulder, 2/	20/6	−1/6	1[illegible]	W. A. Goldfields	1[illegible]	−[illegible]
1[illegible]	Do. Main Reef, 10/	1[illegible]	−[illegible]	2[illegible]	W. A. Joint Stock	2[illegible]	
3[illegible]	Do. Perseverance	3[illegible]	−[illegible]	1[illegible]	W. A. Market Trust	1[illegible]	−[illegible]
1	Do. South	1		2	W. A. Loan & General Fin.	2	−[illegible]
2[illegible]	Hainault	2[illegible]	−[illegible]	[illegible]	White Feather	[illegible]	−[illegible]

South African.

Making-Up Price, Feb. 21.	Name.	Closing Price.	Rise or Fall.	Making-Up Price, Feb. 21.	Name	Closing Price.	Rise or Fall.
5[illegible]	Angelo	5	−[illegible]	3[illegible]	Langlaagte Estate	3[illegible]	−[illegible]
1[illegible]	Aurora West	1[illegible]		2/6	Lisbon-Berlyn	2/6	
[illegible]	Bantjes	[illegible]	−[illegible]	2[illegible]	May Consolidated	2[illegible]	+[illegible]
9/6	Barrett [illegible]/			4[illegible]	Meyer and Charlton	4[illegible]	
3[illegible]	Bona[illegible]	3[illegible]	−[illegible]	3[illegible]	Modderfontein	3[illegible]	−[illegible]
[illegible]	Buf[illegible]doorn	[illegible]	−[illegible]	[illegible]	New Bultfontein	[illegible]	
1[illegible]	Champ d'Or	1[illegible]	−[illegible]	3[illegible]	New Primrose	3[illegible]	−[illegible]
5[illegible]	City and Suburban, £4	5[illegible]	−[illegible]	1[illegible]	Nigel	1[illegible]	
2[illegible]	Comet (New)	2[illegible]	−[illegible]	—	Nigel Deep	1[illegible]	
4[illegible]	Con. Deep Level	4[illegible]	−[illegible]	[illegible]	North Randfontein	—	
11[illegible]	Crown Deep	11[illegible]	−[illegible]	5[illegible]	Nourse Deep	5[illegible]	−[illegible]
12	Crown Reef	11[illegible]	−[illegible]	1[illegible]	Porges-Randfontein	1[illegible]	−[illegible]
27[illegible]	De Beers, £5	28[illegible]	−1[illegible]	28[illegible]	Rand Mines	27[illegible]	−[illegible]
3[illegible]	Driefontein	3[illegible]	−[illegible]	1[illegible]	Randfontein	1[illegible]	−[illegible]
5[illegible]	Durban Roodepoort	5[illegible]	−[illegible]	2[illegible]	Rietfontein	2[illegible]	−[illegible]
3[illegible]	Do. Deep	3[illegible]	−[illegible]	10	Robinson Deep	9[illegible]	
4	East Rand	4	−[illegible]	8	Do. Gold, £5	8[illegible]	−[illegible]
24[illegible]	Ferreira	24[illegible]		[illegible]	Do. Randfontein	1	−[illegible]
6[illegible]	Geldenhuis Deep	6[illegible]		1[illegible]	Roodepoort Central Deep	1[illegible]	
4[illegible]	Do. Estate	4[illegible]		6[illegible]	Rose Deep	6[illegible]	−[illegible]
[illegible]	George Goch	[illegible]	−[illegible]	2[illegible]	Salisbury	2[illegible]	−[illegible]
2[illegible]	Ginsberg	2[illegible]	−[illegible]	2[illegible]	Sheba	2[illegible]	
1[illegible]	Glencairn	2		3[illegible]	Simmer and Jack, £5	3[illegible]	
2[illegible]	Glen Deep	2[illegible]	−[illegible]	3	Transvaal Gold	3[illegible]	−[illegible]
8[illegible]	Goldfields Deep	7[illegible]	−[illegible]	3	Treasury	3	−[illegible]
8[illegible]	Griqualand West	8[illegible]	−[illegible]	3[illegible]	United Roodepoort	3[illegible]	−[illegible]
8[illegible]	Henry Nourse	8[illegible]	−[illegible]	1[illegible]	Van Ryn	1[illegible]	
7[illegible]	Heriot	7[illegible]		5[illegible]	Village Main Reef	5[illegible]	−[illegible]
7[illegible]	Jagersfontein	7[illegible]	−[illegible]	1[illegible]	Vogelstruis	1[illegible]	
7[illegible]	Jubilee	7[illegible]	−[illegible]	[illegible]	Do. Deep	[illegible]	
4[illegible]	Jumpers	4[illegible]	−[illegible]	8[illegible]	Wemmer	8[illegible]	−[illegible]
5	Jumpers Deep	4[illegible]		[illegible]	West Rand	[illegible]	
2[illegible]	Kleinfontein	2[illegible]	−[illegible]	5[illegible]	Wolhuter, £4	5[illegible]	−[illegible]
2[illegible]	Knight's	3	−[illegible]	2	Worcester	2[illegible]	−[illegible]
2[illegible]	Lancaster	2[illegible]	−[illegible]				

Land Exploration and Rhodesian.

Making-Up Price, Feb. 21.	Name.	Closing Price.	Rise or Fall.	Making-Up Price, Feb. 21.	Name	Closing Price.	Rise or Fall.
2[illegible]	Anglo-French Ex.	2[illegible]	−[illegible]	[illegible]	Mashonaland Central	[illegible]	
1[illegible]	Barnato Consolidated	1[illegible]	−[illegible]	6	Matabele Gold Reefs	6[illegible]	−[illegible]
[illegible]	Bechuanaland Ex.	[illegible]		1[illegible]	Mozambique	1[illegible]	−[illegible]
2[illegible]	Chartered B.S.A.	2[illegible]	−[illegible]	1[illegible]	New African	1[illegible]	
[illegible]	Clark's Cons.	[illegible]		[illegible]	Oceana Consolidated	[illegible]	
[illegible]	Colenbrander	[illegible]		1[illegible]	Rhodesia, Ltd.	1[illegible]	−[illegible]
4[illegible]	Cons. Goldfields	4[illegible]	−[illegible]	4	Do. Exploration	4[illegible]	−[illegible]
1[illegible]	Do. Pref.	21/0	−/6	1	Do. Goldfields	[illegible]	−[illegible]
1[illegible]	Exploration	1[illegible]	−[illegible]	3[illegible]	S. A. Gold Trust	3[illegible]	−[illegible]
2[illegible]	Geelong	2[illegible]		[illegible]	Tati Concessions	[illegible]	
[illegible]	Henderson's Est.	[illegible]	−[illegible]	[illegible]	Transvaal Development	[illegible]	
1[illegible]	Johannesburg Con. In.	1[illegible]	−[illegible]	[illegible]	United Rhodesia	[illegible]	−[illegible]
1	Do. Water	1		1[illegible]	Willoughby	1	
1[illegible]	Mashonaland Agency	1[illegible]	−[illegible]	[illegible]	Zambesia Explor.	2[illegible]	

Miscellaneous.

Making-Up Price, Feb. 21.	Name.	Closing Price.	Rise or Fall.	Making-Up Price, Feb. 21.	Name	Closing Price.	Rise or Fall.
1[illegible]	Alamillos, £2	1[illegible]		13/	Mysore Goldfields	13/6	+1/
5	Anaconda, $25	5	−[illegible]	9/	Do. Reefs, 17/	9/	
9/6	Balaghât, 18/	10/		14/9	Do. West	14/[illegible]	−[illegible]
4[illegible]	Cape Copper, £2	4[illegible]	−[illegible]	12/	Do. Wynaad	12/	
4[illegible]	Champion Reef, 10s.	4[illegible]		2[illegible]	Namaqua, £2	2[illegible]	
2[illegible]	Copiapo, £2	2[illegible]		3[illegible]	Nundydroog	3[illegible]	−[illegible]
3[illegible]	Coromandel	3[illegible]		2[illegible]	Ooregum	2[illegible]	+[illegible]
2[illegible]	Frontino & Bolivia	2[illegible]		3[illegible]	Do. Pref.	3[illegible]	−[illegible]
1[illegible]	Hall Mines	1[illegible]	+[illegible]	28	Rio Tinto Def., £5	27[illegible]	−[illegible]
2[illegible]	Libiola, £5	2[illegible]		6	Do. Pref. £5	6[illegible]	−[illegible]
7[illegible]	Linares, £3	8		18/	St. John del Rey	18/	−[illegible]
3[illegible]	Mason & Barry, £3	3[illegible]	−[illegible]	17/	Taitapu	[illegible]	−[illegible]
5[illegible]	Mountain Copper, £5	5[illegible]	−[illegible]	7[illegible]	Tharsis, £2	7[illegible]	−[illegible]
13[illegible]	Mount Lyell, £3	13[illegible]	−[illegible]	3[illegible]	Tolima "A," £5	3[illegible]	−[illegible]
3[illegible]	Mount Lyell, North	3[illegible]	−[illegible]	4[illegible]	Waihi	4[illegible]	
16/3	Mount Lyell, South	[illegible]	−[illegible]	1[illegible]	Waitekauri	1[illegible]	
4[illegible]	Mount Morgan, 17s. 6d.	4[illegible]		1[illegible]	Woodstock (N.Z.)	1[illegible]	−[illegible]
5[illegible]	Mysore, 10s.	5[illegible]					

Railway Traffic Returns.

ALGECIRAS (GIBRALTAR) RAILWAY.—Traffic for week ended February 26, Ps. 16,445; decrease, Ps. 820. Aggregate from July 1, Ps. 698,714; increase, Ps. 13,803.

BENGAL CENTRAL RAILWAY.—Traffic for week ending February 12, Rs. 17,577; decrease, Rs. 358. Total from January 1, Rs. 123,403; increase, Rs. 12,713.

BURMA RAILWAYS.—Receipts for week ending February 5, Rs. 20,9,549; decrease, Rs. 41,614. Aggregate from January 1, Rs. 10,30,546; decrease, Rs. 2,02,730.

COCKERMOUTH, KESWICK, AND PENRITH.—Gross receipts for the week ending March 6 amounted to £770, an increase of £23. Total receipts to date £6,811, an increase of £663.

GREAT WESTERN OF BRAZIL RAILWAY.—Traffic for week ending January 29, $51,068; increase, $5,931. Aggregate receipts to date $228,709; increase, $23,652.

WESTERN OF SANTA FE RAILWAYS.—Gross receipts for week ending February 26, $44,690; increase, $14,690.

ALCOY AND GANDIA RAILWAY AND HARBOUR COMPANY.—Traffic for week, March 5:—Ps. 9,100, increase ps. 2,100. Aggregate from January 1, ps. 95.800, increase ps. 10,750.

MOBILE AND BIRMINGHAM RAILROAD.—Traffic for second week of February, $8,787; increase, $3,536. Aggregate from July 1, $236,647; decrease, $9,544.

VILLA MARIA AND RUFINO RAILWAY.—Traffic for week ending March 5, $4,358; decrease, $1,413 Aggregate from January 1, $38,436; decrease, $6,898.

WEST FLANDERS RAILWAY.—Gross receipts for week ending March 6, £2,012; increase, £109. Total from January 1, £18,976; increase, £500.

WEST OF INDIA PORTUGUESE RAILWAY.—Week ending February 12, Rs. 4,930; increase, Rs. 2,151.

ASSAM-BENGAL RAILWAY.—Traffic for week ended January 29, Rs. 24,556; increase, Rs. 724. Aggregate from January 1, Rs. 1,00,972; increase, Rs. 8,766.

PUERTO CABELLO AND VALENCIA RAILWAY.—Traffic receipts for week ending February 4, £1,080; increase, £111. Aggregate from January 1, £4,128; decrease, £1,604.

WESTERN RAILWAY OF SANTA FE.—Traffic receipts for week ending March 5, $51,255; increase, $25,605.

QUEBEC CENTRAL RAILWAY.—Receipts for second week of February, $5,514; decrease $1,154. Aggregate from July 1, $34,721; decrease $3,154.

CLEATOR AND WORKINGTON.—Gross receipts for the week ending March 5 amounted to £997, a decrease of £78. Total receipts from January 1, £9,071, a decrease of £637.

BILBAO RIVER AND CANTALERIAN RAILWAY.—Receipts for month of February, £8,470; decrease, £355.

GREAT NORTHERN RAILWAY OF MINNESOTA.—Traffic receipts for month of February, $1,274,000; increase, $252,000.

BENGAL DOOARS RAILWAY.—Traffic receipts from January 1 to February 5, Rs. 17,930; decrease, Rs. 4981.

H. H. THE NIZAM'S GUARANTEED STATE RAILWAYS.—Traffic receipts from January 1 to February 12. Rs. 400,636; increase, Rs. 1,553.

SOUTHERN PACIFIC RAILWAY.—The net earnings for the month of January, $1,390, 213; increase, $392,372.

ATLANTIC AND DANVILLE RAILWAY.—Traffic receipts for month of February, $40,913; increase, $3,840.

DOMINION ATLANTIC RAILWAY.—Receipts for month of February $29,710, decrease $760.

MIDLAND URUGUAY RAILWAY.—Receipts for month of February, £3,617, increase £1,381.

ENGLISH RAILWAYS.

Div. for half years. 1896	1896	1897	1897	Last Balance forward.	Amt. to pay 1 p.c. on Ord. for ½ yr.	NAME.	Date.	Gross Traffic for week: Amt.	Inc. or dec. on 1897.	Inc. or dec. on 1896.	No. of weeks	Gross Traffic for half-year to date: Amt.	Inc. or dec. on 1897.	Inc. or dec. on 1896.	Mileage.	Inc. on 1897.	Working	Prior Charges last ½ year.	Prop. add Cap. Exp. this ½ year.
				£	£												%	£	£
10	10	10	10	2,707	5,094	Barry	Mar. 5	9,783	+2,204	+4,922	10	90,623	+4,539	+16,137	31	—	8·89	60,665	316,853
nil	nil	nil	nil	—	—	Brecon and Merthyr	,, 6	1,311	+83	—	10	15,023	+377	—	61	—	—	—	—
nil	nil	nil	nil	3,979	4,749	Cambrian..	,, 6	4,365	−5	—	*	38,854	+102	—	250	—	60·96	63,148	40,000
1½	1¾	2	1¾	1,510	3,150	City and South London ..	,, 6	1,089	+27	—	10	10,719	−56	—	3½	—	56·67	5,552	124,000
1	2	1½	2	7,895	13,210	Furness	,, 6	8,823	+629	+1,210	*	79,698	+2,214	—	139	—	49·88	97,423	20,910
1	1½	½	1	2,207	27,470	Great Central (late M.,S.,& L.)	,, 6	42,188	+634	+2,846	9	376,082	+6,533	+19,784	352½	—	57·17	627,386	1,200,000
2½	4¾	2	5	51,283	62,865	Great Eastern	,, 6	79,936	+2,238	+7,030	9	692,855	+23,167	+54,413	1,156	—	55·35	860,138	250,000
3	5¾	3	5	15,094	102,496	Great Northern	,, 6	92,845	+6,662	+8,614	10	919,994	+29,078	—	1,071	8	61·36	641,485	750,000
4¾	7½	4¾	7½	31,350	121,981	Great Western	,, 6	171060	+6,580	+14,430	9	1,519,490	+43,080	+85,560	2,582	21	51·44	1,486,272	800,000
nil	2	nil	1¾	8,951	16,487	Hull and Barnsley	,, 6	6,129	+17	+840	9	56,281	−2,624	+1,083	73	—	58·21	70,290	52,920
5	5¾	5	5½	21,495	83,704	Lancashire and Yorkshire ..	,, 6	91,654	+2,182	+7,254	9	803,362	+27,388	+31,543	555½	25	56·70	674,745	451,976
4¾	8	4¾	8½	26,243	43,049	London, Brighton, & S. Coast	,, 5	47,764	+3,475	+6,790	10	454,451	+27,933	+33,697	476¾	—	50·20	407,042	240,735
nil	nil	nil	nil	72,294	56,296	London, Chatham, & Dover ..	,, 6	25,821	+1,373	+2,578	9	231,393	+9,187	+17,722	185½	—	50·65	367,873	nil
6½	8	6½	7¾	89,535	204,068	London and North Western ..	,, 6	226464	+10,588	+8,925	9	1,992,802	+52,045	+98,418	1,911½	—	56·92	1,404,534	600,000
5	8½	8½	8½	23,038	59,367	London and South Western ..	,, 6	64,100	+5,032	+7,421	9	575,114	+28,607	+45,619	941	6¼	51·73	513,740	389,000
2½	6	2½	6½	14,592	6,691	London, Tilbury, & Southend	,, 6	4,574	+471	+1,085	10	46,907	+3,657	+8,394	81	—	52·57	39,590	15,000
3½	3¾	3¾	3¾	17,133	26,409	Metropolitan	,, 6	16,075	+399	+1,329	*	149,607	+3,688	—	64	12	43·63	148,047	254,000
nil	nil	nil	nil	4,006	71,250	Metropolitan District	,, 6	8,600	+443	+565	9	78,334	+3,250	+3,574	13	—	48·70	119,663	38,450
5	7	5½	6½	38,143	174,582	Midland	,, 6	185468	+2,509	+9,409	10	1,781,494	+13,584	+96,453	1,354¾	15½	57·59	1,216,582	650,000
5½	7½	5¾	7	22,374	138,189	North Eastern	,, 5	145848	+2,467	+12,234	9	1,246,006	+31,761	+59,418	1,597¾	—	58·82	795,077	436,004
7¾	7¾	7¾	7½	7,061	10,102	North London	,, 6			Not recd			not	recvd.	12	—	50·90	49,973	7,600
4	5	4	4¾	4,745	16,150	North Staffordshire	,, 6	15,358	−1,439	−97	10	155,565	+6,394	+9,145	312	—	55·27	118,142	19,605
10	10	11		1,642	3,004	Rhymney..	,, 5	5,429	+698	+1,192	10	50,943	+1,637	+6,240	71	—	49·68	29,049	16,700
3	6¾	3½	6¾	4,054	50,215	South Eastern	,, 5	44,145	+2,618	+6,717	*	366,179	+22,668	—	448	—	51·88	380,763	250,000
3½	3½	3½	3½	2,315	25,961	Taff Vale..	,, 5	14,763	+499	+2,016	10	152,260	−1,976	+5,650	121	—	54·90	94,800	97,000

* From January 1.

SCOTCH RAILWAYS.

1896	1896	1897	1897	Last Balance forward.	Amt. to pay 1 p.c. on Ord. for ½ yr.	NAME.	Date.	Week Amt.	Inc. or dec. on 1897.	Inc. or dec. on 1896.	No. of weeks	Half-year Amt.	Inc. or dec. on 1897.	Inc. or dec. on 1896.	Mileage.	Inc. on 1897.	Working	Prior Charges last ½ year.	Prop. add Cap. Exp. this ½ year.
5	5	5½	5	9,544	78,066	Caledonian	Mar. 6	69,561	+ 4,738	+ 7,816	5	340,564	+ 4,831	+20,038	851½	5	50·38	588,248	141,477
5	5½	5	5	7,364	24,639	Glasgow and South-Western	,, 5	25,357	+ 1,227	+ 1,833	5	130,617	+ 2,981	+ 6,496	393½	—	54·69	221,663	106,145
3½	3¾	3½	—	1,291	4,600	Great North of Scotland	,, 5	7,226	− 101	+ 64	5	36,925	− 315	+ 824	331	15½	52·03	92,178	60,000
3	nil	2	—	10,477	12,820	Highland	,, 6	8,465	+ 685	+ 1,021	1	8,465	+ 685	1	479¾	27½	38·63	73,976	,000
1	1½	1	—	3,763	45,819	North British	,, 6	68,635	+ 2,859	+ 4,308	5	330,282	+ 8,794	+ 7,714	1,230	23	44·65	821,766	426,009

IRISH RAILWAYS.

1896	1896	1897	1897	Last Balance forward.	Amt. to pay 1 p.c. on Ord. for ½ yr.	NAME.	Date.	Week Amt.	Inc. or dec. on 1897.	Inc. or dec. on 1896.	No. of weeks	Half-year Amt.	Inc. or dec. on 1897.	Inc. or dec. on 1896.	Mileage.	Inc. on 1897.	Working	Prior Charges last ½ year.	Prop. add Cap. Exp. this ½ year.
6½	6½	6½	—	5,466	1,790	Belfast and County Down ..	Mar. 4	2,006	+ 88	+ 43	*	17,955	+ 441	—	76½	—	55·58	17,690	10,000
5½	6½	5½	—	—	4,284	Belfast and Northern Counties	,, 4	5,049	+ 287	+ 426	*	43,595	+ 1,807	—	249	—	—	—	—
2	3	2	—	1,418	1,200	Cork, Bandon, and S. Coast ..	,, 5	1,267	− 89	+ 131	*	10,299	− 907	—	103	—	54·82	14,436	5,450
6½	6¾	6½	6¾	38,776	17,816	Great Northern	,, 4	14,346	+ 602	+ 1,174	9	177,309	+ 6,442	+ 7,871	528	36	50·15	88,068	27,000
5½	5½	5½	5½	30,339	24,855	Great Southern and Western ..	,, 4	—	—	—	not	received	—	—	603	13	51·45	72,800	46,552
4	4	4	4½	11,372	11,850	Midland Great Western ..	,, 4	10,558	+ 635	+ 581	9	81,706	+ 4,417	+ 5,579	538	—	50·31	83,129	1,800
nil	nil	nil	nil	229	2,822	Waterford and Central ..	,, 4	812	+ 116	—	*	7,735	+ 1,037	—	50½	—	53·24	6,858	1,500
nil	nil	nil	nil	1,936	2,987	Waterford, Limerick & W. ..	,, 4	3,790	+ 207	− 354	*	54,570	+ 3,121	—	350½	—	57·83	42,617	7,075

* From January 1.

FOREIGN RAILWAYS.

Mileage: Total.	Increase on 1897.	Increase on 1896.	Name.	Gross Traffic for Week: Week ending	Amount.	In. or Dec. upon 1897.	In. or Dec. upon 1896.	Gross Traffic to Date: No. of Weeks.	Amount.	In. or Dec. upon 1897.	In. or Dec. upon 1896.
					£	£	£		£	£	£
319	—	—	Argentine Great Western	Feb. 20	6,394	+ 575	+ 1,391	33	177,433	− 9,730	− 39,998
76½	—	—	Bahia and San Francisco	Feb. 5	2,718	+ 903	− 14	5	13,700	+ 4,227	+ 3,599
234	48	84	Bahia Blanca and North West	Feb. 6	788	− 294	—	32	25,075	+ 309	—
74	—	—	Buenos Ayres and Ensenada	Mar. 6	2,977	− 779	− 1,360	9	31,683	− 6,853	− 8,973
426	—	—	Buenos Ayres and Pacific	Mar. 5	6,591	− 1,060	− 1,992	35	220,794	− 53,602	+ 4,226
914	1	3	Buenos Ayres and Rosario	Mar. 5	17,103	+ 5,981	+ 2,549	9	160,453	+ 35,259	+ 22,288
2,499	30	68	Buenos Ayres Great Southern	Mar. 6	34,185	+ 5,727	+ 3,130	35	1,019,788	+ 68,454	+ 149,233
602	107	177	Buenos Ayres Western	Mar. 6	12,035	− 927	− 4,269	35	419,632	− 77,299	− 74,039
845	55	77	Central Argentine	Mar. 5	23,178	+ 6,754	− 1,862	9	199,868	+ 41,564	− 1,949
197	—	—	Central Bahia	Dec. 31*	$114,389	− $4,658	+ $22,144	12 mos.	$1,307,205	+ $141,334	+ $196,150
271	—	—	Central Uruguay of Monte Video	Mar. 5	6,361	+ 885	− 983	35	209,538	+ 239	− 17,574
228	—	—	Do. Eastern Extension	Mar. 5	1,534	+ 481	− 36	35	42,808	+ 2,942	− 2,740
182	—	—	Do. Northern Extension	Mar. 5	637	+ 163	− 138	35	22,223	− 1,795	− 6,263
180	—	—	Cordoba and Rosario	Feb. 27	3,000	+ 960	− 75	35	74,520	− 17,405	− 1,620
228	—	—	Cordoba Central	Feb. 27	$18,000	− $7,000	− $9,280	8	$179,700	− $28,390	− $40,960
549	—	—	Do. Northern Extension	Feb. 27	$36,500	− $24,370	− $15,020	8	$356,790	− $141,390	− $83,940
137	—	—	Costa Rica	Feb. 19	7,058	− 2,548	− 235	7	34,636	− 12,321	− 809
99	—	—	East Argentine	Jan. 23	672	− 351	+ 36	3	2,138	− 556	− 338
386	—	6	Entre Rios	Mar. 5	2,342	+ 1,220	+ 436	35	50,839	+ 10,505	+ 9,123
555	—	24	Inter Oceanic of Mexico	Mar. 5	$65,500	+ $3,000	+ $23,254	35	$1,967,780	+ $280,040	+ $402,340
23	—	—	La Guaira and Caracas	Feb. 11	1,759	− 1,027	—	6	11,023	− 4,003	—
321	—	—	Mexican	Mar. 5	$76,700	+ $5,700	—	9	$732,100	+ $64,250	—
1,846	—	—	Mexican Central	Feb. 28	$271,697	+ $12,972	+ $57,430	8	$2,107,168	+ $30,319	+ $510,786
1,217	—	—	Mexican National	Feb. 28	$117,752	+ $9,279	+ $9,577	8	$927,268	+ $101,692	+ $164,388
228	—	—	Mexican Southern	Mar. 7	$14,475	+ $262	+ $1,759	40	$622,839	+ $46,937	+ $164,407
105	—	—	Minas and Rio	Jan. 31*	$133,941	− $20,733	—	7 mos.	$1,308,551	+ $187,065	—
94	—	17	N. W. Argentine	Feb. 26	836	− 510	− 271	8	7,144	− 3,643	− 1,874
242	3	—	Nitrate	Feb. 28†	13,598	+ 3,536	− 3,756	7	54,493	− 1,349	− 28,233
320	—	—	Ottoman	Feb. 26	3,095	− 2,430	− 358	8	40,403	− 12,594	+ 4,112
77½	—	—	Recife and San Francisco	Jan. 8	4,014	− 800	− 2,013	2	9,158	+ 611	− 1,875
86½	—	—	San Paulo	Jan. 30†	20,140	− 9,077	—	4	50,130	− 16,143	—
186	—	—	Santa Fe and Cordova	Feb. 19	4,315	+ 1,731	+ 1,075	—	41,813	− 19,954	− 2,318
110	—	—	Western of Havana	Mar. 5	1,625	− 207	+ 1,345	35	62,280	+ 5,380	− 750

* For month ended. † For fortnight ended.

INDIAN RAILWAYS.

Mileage: Total.	Increase on 1897.	Increase on 1896.	Name.	Gross Traffic for Week: Week ending	Amount.	In. or Dec. on 1897.	In. or Dec. on 1896	Gross Traffic to Date: No. of Weeks.	Amount.	In. or Dec. on 1897.	In. or Dec. on 1896.
862	—	—	Bengal Nagpur	Feb. 26	Rs.1.56.000	+ Rs.13.891	+ Rs.29.000	8	Rs.11.29.000	− Rs.1.49.770	− R.2.83.917
827	8	63	Bengal and North-Western	Feb. 5	Rs.1.37.880	+ Rs.20.886	− Rs.219	5	Rs.6.73.210	+ Rs.89.257	− Rs.1.942
461	—	—	Bombay and Baroda	Mar. 5	£24,198	− £457	− £7,677	8	£205,919	− £31,851	− £103,312
1,885	2	13	East Indian	Mar. 5	Rs.12.35.000	− Rs.16.000	− Rs.16.000	9	Rs.1.13.35.000	+ Rs.3.60.000	+ Rs.24.44.000
1,491	—	—	Great Indian Penin.	Mar.	£73,278	+ £17,637	+ £7,111	9	£587,756	+ £31,950	− £166,853
736	—	—	Indian Midland	Mar. 5	Rs.1.40.440	+ Rs.24.740	+ Rs.56.347	9	Rs.12.47.671	+ Rs.41.923	+ Rs.2.15.948
840	—	—	Madras	Feb. 26	£17,416	− £3,575	− £2,017	8	£152,428	− £6,731	− £29,634
1,043	—	—	South Indian	Feb. 5	Rs.1.47.087	− Rs.4.080	− Rs.26.879	5	Rs.7.27.030	− Rs.46.740	− Rs.1.78.661

UNITED STATES AND CANADIAN RAILWAYS.

Mileage: Total.	Increase on 1897.	Increase on 1896.	Name.	Gross Traffic for Week: Period Ending.	Amount.	In. or Dec. on 1897.	Gross Traffic to Date: No. of Weeks.	Amount.	In. or Dec. on 1897.
					dols.	dols.		dols.	dols.
917	—	—	Baltimore & Ohio S. Western	Feb. 28	143,757	+ 27,454	34	4,497,901	+ 439,818
6,568	92	156	Canadian Pacific	Feb. 28	377,000	+ 71,000	8	3,150,000	+ 575,000
902	—	—	Chicago Great Western	Feb. 28	107,131	− 14,109	34	3,596,459	+ 492,716
6,169	—	469	Chicago, Mil., & St. Paul	Mar. 7	639,000	+ 114,000	7	5,394,801	+ 658,220
1,685	—	—	Denver & Rio Grande	Feb. 28	138,600	+ 31,600	34	5,510,300	+ 926,100
3,512	—	—	Grand Trunk, Main Line	Mar. 5	£70,765	+ £4,150	9	£662,300	+ £72,099
335	—	—	Do. Chic. & Grand Trunk	Mar. 5	£15,933	+ £4,401	9	£135,002	+ £27,342
189	—	—	Do. Det., G. H. & Mil.	Mar. 5	£4,730	+ £1,201	9	£31,977	− £1,555
2,938	—	—	Louisville & Nashville	Feb. 28	436,000	+ 35,000	8	3,413,270	+ 830,140
2,197	137	137	Miss., K., & Texas	Feb. 28	221,881	+ 17,021	34	8,915,427	+ 529,149
477	—	—	N. Y., Ontario, & W.	Feb. 28	72,964	+ 2,712	34	2,635,040	+ 88,981
1,570	—	—	Norfolk & Western	Feb. 28	213,000	+ 58,000	33	7,154,000	+ 807,000
3,499	336	—	Northern Pacific	Feb. 28	449,000	+ 164,000	8	2,825,000	+ 928,000
1,223	—	—	St. Louis S. Western	Feb. 28	133,000	+ 31,000	8	934,700	+ 172,200
4,654	—	—	Southern	Feb. 28	436,000	+ 42,000	34	2,083,812	+ 1,165,448
1,979	—	—	Wabash	Feb. 28	243,000	+ 18,000	8	1,995,406	+ 407,000

Prices Quoted on the London Stock Exchange.

Throughout the INVESTORS' REVIEW middle prices alone are quoted, the object being to give the public the approximate current quotations of every security of any consequence in existence. On the markets the buying and selling prices are both given, and are often wide apart where stocks are seldom dealt in. Other particulars will be found in the INVESTMENT INDEX published quarterly—January, April, July, and October—in connection with this REVIEW, price 2s., by post 2s. 2d. Where dividends are paid only once a year, an *italic* type is used to distinguish them. The London Stock Exchange Official List is quoted in the REVIEW almost entire, only very insignificant issues, or bonds falling due within the next two or three years, being omitted. But the list is subdivided into the leading, or active, stocks, and those less frequently dealt in. The former will be found under the head of "Stock Markets," and with more details than it is possible to give for the bulk of securities. By retaining the file of the INVESTORS' REVIEW any subscriber can follow for himself the movements of securities from week to week, and the INVESTMENT INDEX will from time to time help to fill up deficiencies in the information.

Tea Companies and Mines and Mining Finance Stocks are placed in special lists.

Among the abbreviations used are the following:—S.F. Snk.Fd. *sinking fund*; Certs., *certificates*; Debs. or Dbs., *debentures*; Db. or D.Stk., *debenture stock*; Pf., Prf., or Pref., *preference*; Prefd. or Pfd., *preferred*; Dfd., *deferred*; L. or Ltd., *limited*; Sh., *share*; Ans., *annuities*; Cu. or Cm., *cumulative*; Gu or Guar., *guaranteed*; Bds., *bonds*; S., Sr., or Ser., *series*; In., Ins., Insc., *inscribed*; Dr., Drgs., Drwgs., *drawings*; Stg., Strlg., *sterling*; Lia., *liable to*; Sp., Surp., *surplus*; Per., Perp., *perpetual*; Ln. *lien*; Lo. *loan*.

The dates following the names of securities are the years of issue or of redemption. Where shares are not fully paid up, their nominal amount is given with the name so that investors may know the liability upon them.

BRITISH FUNDS, &c.

Rate.	Name.	Price.
2¾	2¾ p.c.'s (Childers') Red. .. 1905	105½
3	Local Loans Stk. 1912	112½
3	Metro. Police Deb. Stk. 1920	105½
—	Red Sea Ind. Tel. Ann. 1908	8½
4	Canada Gv. "Intcl. Rly." 1903	106
4	Do. do. .. 1908	113
4	Do. Bonds 1910	114
4	Do. Bonds 1913	113½
3	Egyptian Gov. Gar.	106½
3	Mauritius Ins. Stk. 1940	114
4	Turkish Guar. 1855	109
11½	Bank of Ireland Stk.	392½
3½	India Rupee Paper	62½
3½	Do. 1854-5	63½
3	Do. 1896-7 1916	55
3½	Isle of Man Deb.	104
3	Do. Deb. Stk... 1919-29	103

CORPORATION AND COUNTY STOCKS.

FREE OF STAMP DUTY.

Rate.	Name.	Price.
3½	Metropolitan Con. 1929	118½
3	Do. 1941	113
2½	Do. 1920-49	100
2½	L.C.C. Con. Stock 1920	100
3½	Comm. of Sewers, Scp, S.F. 1905	105
3½	Corp. of Lond. Bds... 1897-1902	100½
3	Do. 1897-1919	103
3½	Do, Debs. Scp. ...... S.F. 1916	106
2½	Do., Deb. Stk. Scrip .. 1927-57	100
3	Barnsley 1916-46	105
3	Barry 1914-46	101
3	Bath 1909-34	104
3	Batley 1914-44	101½
3½	Birmingham 1945	123
3	Do. 1947	112
2½	Do. 1926	93
3	Blackburn 1930	107
3	Bournemouth 1913-33	103
3½	Bradford 1945	118
3	Do. Deb. Stock .. 1954	112
3	Brighouse.............. 1916-46	100
3½	Brighton 1946	118½
2½	Do. 1937	98
3	Burton-on-Trent........ 1913-43	102½
3	Cambridge 1913-43	102
3½	Cardiff 1935	119
3	Do. 1914-54	105
3	Cheltenham............ 1971	110
3	Chichester 1916-46	101
3½	Croydon	135½
3	Do. 1940	111½
3	Derby 1920-50	107
3	Devon C.C.............. 1917-33	104½
3½	Dewsbury 1930	111
3	Do. 1930	105
3	Dorset County 1922-32	105
3	Douglas (I. of Man) 1926	101
3	Dover 1913-43	101½
3½	Dublin 1944	113½
3	Eastbourne 1920-40	105
3	Edinburgh 1924	108
2½	Do. 1927	93
2½	Exeter 1917-57	96
3	Glamorgan County 1914-34	104
3½	Glasgow 1914	110½
3	Do. 1921	106½
2½	Do. 1925-40	99
3	Gloster 1915-55	101
3	Grimsby 1913-45	103½
3	Hampshire County 1914-34	105½
3	Hanley 1913-43	105
3	Harrogate 1914-34	103
3	Hastings 1915-54	105
2½	Hertfordshire C.C. 1916-36	99
3	Heston & Isleworth U.D.C. 1915-35	101
3	Huddersfield 1934	107
3½	Hull (1st iss.)	131½
3	Inverness.............. 1914-44	102
3	Ipswich 1952	110½
3	Lancaster.............. 1919-55	104
2½	Leeds 1927	98
3½	Leicester 1934	115½
3	Lincoln.............. 1919	104
3½	Liverpool............	133½

Corporation, &c. (*continued*):—

Rate.	Name.	Price.
3	Manchester 1941	110
3	Mansfield.............. 1915-45	100
3½	Middlesbro' 1909	105½
3½	Do. 1911-13	105
3	Do. 1915	104
3	Middlesex C.C.......... 1915-35	106
3½	Newcastle 1936	118½
3½	Do. Irred.	129½
2½	Do. 1915-36	101
3	Newcastle-under-Lyme.. 1909-44	101
3	Newport (Mon.) 1915-55	104½
3	Norwich 1952	111½
3	Nottingham	116
3	Oxford 1951	109½
3	Penzance.............. 1916-46	101½
3	Plymouth 1949	110
3	Pontypridd U.D.C. 1916-46	99
3	Poole.............. 1915-45	102½
3½	Portsmouth........1916 24 & 97	112
3	Do. 1913-33	106½
3	Ramsey 1920-40	100
3	Ramsgate.............. 1915-35	102
3½	Reading	133
3	Do. 1962	103
3½	Rhyl U.D.C. 1953	110
3	Richmond (Surrey) 1942	106½
3	River Wear Debt Certs.	101
3	St. Helen's 1915-55	103
3	Scarbro' 1915-50	103
2½	Sheffield 1925-57	96
3	Shipley U.D.C. 1915-35	101
3	Somerset Co. 1923-33	107
3	South Shields.......... 1915-45	104
2½	Southampton 1915-45	101½
3	Southend-on-Sea 1916-46	102
3	Staffs C.C. 1915-35	105
3	Stockport.............. 1914-54	104
3	Stockton 1932	104
3	Do. 1915-35	103
3	Surrey Co. 1922-32	106½
3½	Swansea	132
3	Do. 1955	106
3	Taunton 1918 3-9-43	102
3	Tees Conserv. Deb. Stk. 1947	101
3	Thames Conserv. "A" Deb. Stk. 1954	103½
3	Do. "B" Deb. Stk. 1954	103½
3	Torquay 1913-43	102½
3	Tunbridge Wells 1931	105
3	Tynemouth 1913	101
3	Wakefield.............. 1929	103
3	Walsall.............. 1932	108
3	West Bromwich.......... 1930	108½
3½	West Ham 1929	110
3	Do. 1945	105
3	West Sussex C.C. 1915-35	106
3	Weston-s.-Mare Lcl Bd. 1914-44	101½
3	Weymouth & Melc. Regis 1918	101
3	Widnes.............. 1915-55	101
3	Wigan 1921	108
3	Windsor 1918-55	102½
3½	Wisbech 1947	113½
3½	Wolverhampton 1932	118½
3	Do. 1924-54	107
3	York 1916-41	107

SUBJECT TO STAMP DUTY.

Rate.	Name.	Price.
3½	Belfast City & Dis. Watr. 1938	116
3	Do. Red Stk. 1933-6	106
3½	Belfast 1924	104
4	Blackburn Con. Deb. Irred.	141½
3½	Do. do. Irred..............	131
3½	Bristol	128½
3½	Burnley.............. 1933	114
2½	Chesterfield Gas & Wtr. 1916-46	98
3½	Douglas Town 1921	105
3	Dover Harb. 1st Deb... 1956	104½
3½	Hull (2nd iss.)	129½
4	Leeds Deb.............. 1927	124
3½	Do.	115½
3	Do. 1927	107½
3	Leicester 1919-44	105
4	Manchester..............	150
3	Do. 1928	105
4½	Middlesboro' Mrts. 1908	111
3½	Newark on-Trent .. 1901-41	96
3½	Sheffield 1898-1916	105½
3½	Do. 1925-36	114
3	Do. 1925	104½
3½	Southampton .... S.F.	106
4½	Stockton Morts......... 1908	112
3½	Worcester.............. 1950	111

COLONIAL AND PROVINCIAL GOVERNMENT SECURITIES.

Rate.	Name.	Price.
6	British Columbia........ 1907	119½
4½	Do. Debs... 1917	111½
3	British Guiana Imgtn. Bds.	99½
5	Canada, "Intercol. Rail," 1903	111½
4	Do. (Bonds) 1904-5-6-8	107
4	Do. Reduced........ 1910	108
3½	Do. Bnds. 1909-34	104½
4	Do. Loan 1910-35	109
3	Do. Loan 1938	103
6	Cape of G. Hope 1900	—
5	Do. 1900	—
4½	Do. red. by an. draw.	111
4½	Do. 1879	111
4	Do. 1881	109
4	Do. 1917-23	118
4½	Ceylon	110
4	Do.	106½
4½	Fiji Gov. Deb. Sink. Fd.	102½
4	Jamaica Sink. Fd. 1923	103
5	Manitoba Debs.......... 1910	113
5	Do. Ster. Bds. 1888	122
4	Do. Ster. Debs.	106
4	Mauritius, Cons. Debs. 1880....	103½
4½	Natal, Sink. Fd........ 1919	120
4	Do. do. 1926	115
3½	Newfoundland Stg. Bds. 1941	100
3½	Do. do. .. 1947	100
3	Do. do.	88
5	New South Wales 1897-1902	104½
4	Do. 1903-5-8-9-10	105½
5	New Zealand 1914	118
5	Do. Cnsls. 1 p.c. per an. Sink. Fd.	104
3½	Nova Scotia Debs.	104
5	Quebec Prov. 1904-6	110
4½	Do. (drgs.)	104
5	Do. Strlg. Bds. 1912	115
4	Do. Strlg. Bds. 1928	110
4	Do. Strlg. Bds. 1934	108
4	Queensland 1913-15	107
4½	St. Lucia Debs..............	100
6	South Australia 1897-1900	103½
6	Do. 1901-1918	119
5	Do. 1911-1920	115½
4	Do. 1899-1916	105
4	Do. 1929	110½
4	Do. 1916	109½
4	Do. 1917-18-24	113
6	Tasmania 1897-1901	104
4	Do. 1908-11, 1913-14-20	108
5	Trinidad Debs., an. drw. 1 p c...	108
4	Victoria 1899-1901	101½
4½	Do. 1904	105
4	Do. Rail. Loan 1907	105
4	Do. Loans 1908-13	107
4½	West. Austr. 1 p.c. ac. Sink. Fd.	108
4	Do. do.	106

REGISTERED AND INSCRIBED STOCKS.

No stamp duty except for Canada 4 p.c. Reduced (½ per cent.).

Rate.	Name.	Price.
4	Antigua Insc. Stk. Red. 1919-44	109
3½	Barbados Insc. Stk. 1925-42	108
3	British Colum. Insc. Stk. 1941	103
4	British Guiana Insc..... 1935	120
4	Canada Stk. Regd. ..1904-5-6-8	107
4	Do. 4 p.c. (late 5 p.c.) Regd. 1910	108
3½	Do. 3½ p.c. Stock Regd. 1909-34	104½
4	Do. Ln. for 4 milln. stg. 1910-35	109
3	Do. Stk. Regd. 1938	103
2½	Do. Insc.............. 1947	92
4	Cape G. Hope Regd. .. 1917-23	118
4	Do. (Ln. of '83) Insc. .. 1923	119
4	Do. Cons. Stk. Insc..... 1916-36	115
3½	Do. Consol. Insc. Stock 1929-49	113
4	Ceylon Insc. Stock 1934	122
3	Do. 1940	104
4	Grenada Insc. Stock.... 1917-42	112
3½	Hong Kong Insc. Stock 1918-43	105½
4	Jamaica Insc. Stock.... 1934	121
—	Do. 1922-44	99
4	Mauritius Inscribed 1937	119
4	Natal Consd. Stk. Insc. 1927	115
4	Do. 1937	120
3½	Do. Inscribed Stock.. 1914-39	107
4	Newfoundland Inscribed 1913-38	108
4	Do. 1935	114
4	Do. Consd. Stk. Ins. 1936	114
4	N. S Wales Stock Insc. 1933	118
3½	Do. 1924	107
3½	Do. 1918	105
3	D 1935	98

Colonial, &c. (*continued*):—

Rate.	Name.	Price.
4	N. Zealnd. Con. Stk. Ins. 1929	115
3½	Do. 1940	107
3	Do. Inscribed.... 1945	99
3	Quebec (Prov.) Ins. Stk. 1937	95
4	Queensland Stock Insc. 1915-24	110½
3½	Do. 1921-4-30	105
3½	Do. 1945	109
3	Do. 1922-47	99
4	St. Lucia Insc. Stock .. 1919-44	112
4	S. Austrla. (1882-7) Reg. 1916-36	113
3½	Do. In. Stk. Reg. 1939	110
3	Do. 1916-26	99
3/	Do. 1916	99
3½	Tasmanian Insc. Stock.. 1920-40	106
4	Do. 1920-40	115
4	Trinidad Insc. Stock.... 1917-42	110
3	Do. 1922-44	98½
4	Victoria Rly. Loan '81, Inscribed Stock 1907	104
4	Victoria Insc. Stock 1908-13-19	107
4	Victoria (1883) Ins. Stk. 1920	110
3½	Do. Inscribed Stock 1921-3-6	104
4	Do. do. 1911-26	107
4	W. Austral. Insc. Stock 1934	120
4	Do. 1911-31	112
3½	Do. 1915-35	107
3	Do. 1915-35	98
3	Do. 1916-36	97

FOREIGN STOCKS, BONDS, &c.

COUPONS PAYABLE IN LONDON.

Last Div.	Name.	Price.
36/	Argentine Ry. Loan 6 p.c. 1881	90½
15/	Do. 5 p.c. 1884	69
30/	Do. N. Cent. Ry. Ext. 5 p.c. 1887-8-9	68½
30/	Do. 5 p.c. Trsy. Convs. 1887	69
5/4½	Do. 4½ p.c. Interl. Gld. 1888	66
27/	Do. 4½ p.c. Stlg. Extrl. 1888	67
10/6	Do. 3½ p.c. External .. 1889	48
4	Do. 4 p.c. Ry. Guar. Res....	58½
4½	Brazilian 1883	59
4½	Do. Gold.......... 1879	68½
4½	Do. 1888	60
36/	Buenos Ayres 1824	90
6	Do. 1882-3-6	48
6	Bulgarian.............. 1888	94
6	Do. Mort. Bonds 1892	94
4½	Chilian 1885	77
4½	Do. 1886	78
4½	Do. 1887	77
4½	Do. 1889	82½
5	Do. 1892	87
4½	Do. 1893	77
4½	Do. 1895	77
5	Do. 1896	85
7	Chinese Silver 1894	101
6	Do. Gold 1895	106
6	Do. Apl. '95 by dwgs. 1901-15	110½
5	Do. Red. dwgs. in 36 yr. 1896	100½
5	Do. Do. Regis. 1896	99
1½	Colmbn. 1½ to 3 p.c. Ext. Bds. 1896	17
6	Cordova, Prov. 1886	26
—	Do. Eng. Ass. Certs.	25
—	Do. 6 p.c. 1887-8	26
—	Do. Eng. Ass. Certs.	25
3	Costa Rica "A"	32
2½	Do. "B"	27
3	Danish Gold 1914	98
10/	Ecuador N. Ext. Bds. 4½ p.c. ascn. to 5 p.c..............	20
3½	Egypt'n Ins. Stk. lia. Stp. Dty. 1890	102
4	Do. State Domain 1878	105
4	Do. D. Sanieh, Red. .. 1905	105
6	Entre Rios.............. 1880-8	36
6	Do. Fndg. Ln. Bds. 1894-1921	32
6	Do. do. Parana City......	27½
15/	Greek 1881	38
15/	Do. 1884	35
12/	Do. Rentes..............	32
15/	Do. (Piræus-Larissa Ry.)	36
7/6	Do. Fundg. Loan 1893	46½
4	Guatemala Extl. Debt..........	34
6	Hawaiian	102½
4	Hungarian Gold Rentes........	102
3	Do. 1895	91½
6	Italian Irriga. Guar.	111½
5	Do. Maremmana	94½
5	Japan 5 p.c.	101
5	Mexican (Nat. R. Tehuantp c.)..	96½
6	Do. Extrl. 1893	

Foreign Stocks, &c. (*continued*):—

Last Div.	Name.	Price.
6	Mexican Extrl. 1893	96
5	Do. Intrnl. Cons. Slvr.	37½
5	Do Intern. Rd. Bds. 2d. Ser.	37¾
4	Nicaragua 1886	50
3½	Norwegian, red. 1937, or earlier	100
3	Do. do. 1965, do.	98
3½	Do. 3½ p.c. Bnds.	103
1	Paraguay 1p.c. ris. 3p.c. 1886-96	16
5	Russian, 1822, £ Strlg.	149
3	Do. 1859	94
4	Do. (Nicolas Ry.) 1867-9	104
3	Do. Transcauc. Ry. 1882	94
4	Do. Con. R. R. Bd. Ser. I., 1889	104
4	Do. Do. II., 1889	104
4	Do. Do. III., 1891	103½
3½	Do. Bonds	101
4	Do. Ln. (Dvinsk and Vitbsk)	103
6	Salvador 1889	65½
—	S. Domingo 4s. Unified: .. 1980	65¾
6	San Luis Potosi Stg. 1889	92
5	San Paulo (Brzl.), Stg. 1888	91½
6	Santa Fé 1883-4	35
—	Do. Eng. Ass. Certs. Dep.	34
5	Do. 1888	45
—	Do. Eng. Ass. Certs. Dpsit.	44
5	Do. (W. Cnt. Col. Rly.) Mrt.	26
5	Do. & Reconq. Rly. Mort.	26
5	Spanish Quickslvr Mort. 1870	103
3½	Swedish 1880	103
3	Do. 1888	98
53	Do. Conversion Loan 1894	100
45	Trans. Gov. Loan Red...1903-42	106
59/	Tucuman (Prov.) 1888	69
	Turkish, Secd. on Egypt. Trib.	104
3½	Turkish, Egpt. Trib., Ott. Bd., '94	99½
4	Do. Priority 1890	93
1	Do. Convted Series, "A"	65½
5	Do. Customs Ln. 1886	97½
5	Uruguay Bonds 1896	56½
3	Venzula New Con. Debt 1881	34½

COUPONS PAYABLE ABROAD.

Last Div.	Name.	Price.
7	Argent. Nat. Cedla. Srins, "B".	35
5	Austrian Ster. Rnts., ex 10fl., 1870	85
5	Do. do. do.	86
5	Do. Paper do. 1870	84
5	Do. do. do.	86
4	Do. Gld Rentes 1876	103
2½	Belgian exchange 25 fr.	92
3	Do. do.	101
3½	Danish Int., 1887, Rd. 1896	97½
3½	Do. '87, Red. by pur. or draw. fr. Dec., 1900	98½
2½	Dutch Certs. ex 12 gldrs.	87
3	Do. Bonds	99
3	Do. Insc. Stk.	98
3½	French Rentes	105½
3	Do. 1878, '81-4., Red.	101
3	German Imp. Ln. 1891	97
3	Do. do. 1892-3	97
3	Do. do. 1890-4	96
5	Japan Cons. Ln., '92, 3, & 5, Red.	47
36/9	Prussian Consols	102
3	" Cons. Stg. Ln. 1892	97
4	Rumanian Bds. 1890	—
4	Do. do. 1891	—
4	Utd. States, 1877, Red. 1907	116
4	Do. 1895, 30 yrs.	129
3½	Do. Maschsetts Gl. 1935	113½
3½	Do. Gold Bonds 1923	110½
2	Virginia Cpn. Bds., 3 p.c. from July, 1901	72

BRITISH RAILWAYS.

ORD. SHARES AND STOCKS.

Last Div.	Name.	Price.
10	Barry, Ord.	280½
4	Do. Prefd.	127
6	Do. Defd.	150½
5½	Caledonian, Ord.	156
3	Do. Prefd.	101
-	Do. Defd. Ord., No. 1	4½
	Cambrian, Ord	6½
—	Do. Coast Cons.	6½
32/	Cardiff Ry. Pref. Ord.	117
3/	Central Lond. £10 Ord. Sh.	10¾
1/9½	Do. do. £6 paid	6¾
3½d.	Do. Pref. Half-Shares	1¾
1/6	Do. Def. do.	4¾
1½	City and S. London	68
—	East London, Cons.	7
1½	Furness	65½
—	Glasgow and S. West. Pfd.	83
—	Do. do. Dfd.	66
—	Great Central, Ord....1894	40
32/0	Do. London Exten.	77
3½	Great N. of Scotland	125
4	Great Northern, Prefd.	118½
—	Do. Consolidated "A"	49
—	Do. do. "B"	191½
2	Highland	85½
4	Isle of Wight, Prefd.	120½
3	Do. Defd.	83½
—	Lancs. Derbys. and E. Cst.	
7½	L. Brighton and S. C. Ord.	185
37/11½	Do. New all pd.	186
6	Do. Prefd. Ord.	197
30/	Do. Contgt. Rights Certs.	20½
5½	Lond. and S. Western Ord.	222½
4	Do. Preferred	132
6½	Lond., Tilb., and Southend	133½
—	Mersey, £20 shares	1
—	Metropolitan, New Ord.	128
2½	Do. Surplus Lands	95
4	North Cornwall, 4 p.c. Pref.	106½
7½	Do. Deferred	27¾
7½	North London	225½
4½	North Staffordshire	131

British Railways (*continued*):—

Last Div.	Name.	Price.
1/6	Plymouth, Devenport, and S. W. Junc. £10	9
3/	Port Talbot £10 Shares	8½
9d.	Rhondda Swns. B. £10 Sh.	5
10	Rhymney, Cons.	270½
4	Do. Prefd.	125
—	Do. Defd.	149½
6½	Scarboro', Bridlington Junc.	47½
6½	South Eastern, Ord	151
6	Do. Pref.	193
3½	Taff Vale	82
25/	Vale of Glamorgan	129½
3	Waterloo & City	137½

LEASED AT FIXED RENTALS.

Last Div.	Name.	Price.
4	Birkenhead	148
5.19.0	East Lincnshire	215
5½	Hamsmith. & City Ord.	192½
4½	Lond. and Blackwll.	163½
4½	Do. £10 4½ p. c. Pref.	163½
56/6	Lond. & Green. Ord.	102
5	Do. 5 p. c. Pref.	180½
5	Nor. and Eastn. £50 Ord.	90
6	Do.	107
3½	N. Cornwall 3½ p. c. Stk.	122½
4$\frac{9}{16}$	Nott. & Granthm. R.&C.	147
3½	Portptk. & Wigtn. Guar. Stk.	126
9	Vict. Stn. & Pimlico Ord.	317½
4½	Do. 4½ p. c. Pref.	164
4/	West Lond. £20 Ord. Shs.	14½
4$\frac{9}{16}$	Weymouth & Portld.	160½

DEBENTURE STOCKS.

Last Div.	Name.	Price.
4	Alexandra Dks. & Ry.	132½
3	Barry, Cons.	109
4	Brecon & Mrthyr, New A	127½
4	Do. New B	107
4	Caledonian	152
4	Cambrian "A"	132½
4	Do. "B"	130½
4	Do. "C"	126½
4	Do. "D"	107½
3	Cardiff Rly.	104
4	City and S. Lond.	139
3½	Cleator & Working Junc.	118½
3	Devon & Som. "A"	105½
16/3	Do. "B" 4 p. c.	36
—	Do. "C" 4 p. c.	10
4	E. Lond. 2nd Ch. 4 p. c. A	137
5/	Do. 2nd B	67½
—	Do. 3rd Ch. 4 p. c.	19½
—	Do. 4th do.	9½
3½	Do. 1st (3½ p. c.)	128½
2½	Do. 2½ p.c.(Whitech. Exn).	88
4	Forth Bridge	144½
4	Furness	143
4	Glasgow and S. Western	150
5	Gt. Central	—
4½	Do.	158½
4	Gt. Eastern	147½
4	Gt. N. of Scotland	147½
3	Gt. Northern	114
4	Gt. Western	151½
4½	Do.	160½
4½	Do.	170½
5	Do.	187½
2½	Do.	100
4	Highland	143½
3	Hull and Barnsley	106
3	Do. 2nd (3-4 p. c).	124
4	Isle of Wight	144½
3	Do. Cent. "A"	92½
4½	Do. "B"	115½
4	Do. "C"	82½
3	Lancs. & Yorkshire	114
4	Lancs. Derbys. & E. Cst.	123½
4	Lpool St. Hlen's & S. Lancs.	126
4½	Ldn. and Blackwall	158
4	Ldn. and Greenwich	148½
4	Lond., Brighton, &c.	150
4½	Do.	168
4½	Lond., Chath., &c., Arb.	158½
4½	Do. "B"	157½
4	Do.	140
4	Do. 1883	139
3	Do.	107
3	Lond. & N. Western	116
3	Lond. & S. Westn. "A"	116
3	Do. Consld.	116
4	Lond., Til., & Southend	147½
—	Mersey, 5 p. c. (Act, 1866)	65
4	Metropolitan	147½
4½	Do.	164½
3½	Do.	129½
6	Met. District	208½
4	Do.	139
3	Midland	116
4½	Mid-Wales "A"	137½
4	Neath & Brecon 1st	129
4	Do. "A 1"	119½
3	North British	111½
3	Do. 1893	111½
3½	N. Cornwall, Launcstn., &c.	128½

Debenture Stocks (*continued*):—

Last Div.	Name.	Price.
3	North Eastern	115
4½	North London	167
3	N. Staffordshire	114
4	Plym. Devpt. & S.W. Jn.	141½
4	Rhondda and Swan. Bay	130½
4	Rhymney	146½
4	South-Eastern	150
5	Do.	186½
3½	Do.	127½
3	Do.	114½
3	Taff Vale	111
4	Tottenham & For. Gate	146
3	Vale of Glamorgan	105½
3	West Highld.(Gtd.by N.B.)	109
4	Wrexham, Mold, &c. "A"	115½
4	Do. "B"	102½
4	Do. "C"	97½

GUARANTEED SHARES AND STOCKS.

Last Div.	Name.	Price.
4	Caledonian	150½
4	Do.	149
4	Forth Bridge	142½
4	Furness 1881	137½
4	Glasgow & S. Western	146
4	Do. St. Enoch. Rent	146
6	Gt. Central	202
4½	Do. 1st Pref.	152½
3½	Do. Pref.	106
5	Do. Irred. S.Y. Rent	165½
4½	Do. do.	140½
4	Gt. Eastern, Rent	145
5	Do. Metropolitan	182½
4	Do.	144½
4	Gt. N. of Scotland	141
4	Gt. Northern	147
5	Gt. Western, Rent	182½
5	Do. Cons.	182½
4	Lancs. & Yorkshire	147
5	L., Brighton & S. C.	181½
3½	L., Chat. & D. (Shrtlds.)	110½
4	L. & North Western	148½
4	L. & South Western.. 1881	149
4½	Met. District, Ealing Rent	152
4½	Do. Fulham Rent	152
4	Do. Midland Rent	143½
4	Do. Mid. & Dist. Guar.	131½
4	Midland, Rent	148½
4	Do. Cons.	148½
3	Mid.&G.N. Jt., "A" Rnt.	109½
3	N. British, Lien	108
4	Do. Cons. Pref. No. 1	142
3	N. Cornwall. Wadebrge. Gu.	107
4	N. Eastern	147
5	N. Staff. Trent & M. £20 Shs.	36½
3½	Nott. Suburban Ord.	126½
20.6	S. E. Perp. Ann.	36
4½	Do. 4½ p.c.	164½
3½	S. Yorks. Junc. Ord.	118½
4½	W. Cornwall (G. W., Br., Ex., & S. Dev. Joint Rent	163½
3	W. Highl. Ord. Stk. (Gua., N.B.)	105½

PREFERENCE SHARES AND STOCKS.

DIVIDENDS CONTINGENT ON PROFIT OF YEAR.

Last Div.	Name	Price.
4½	Alexandra Dks. & Ry. "A"	128½
5	Barry (First)	169½
4	Do. Consolidated	139½
4	Caledonian Cons., No. 1	147
4	Do. do. No. 2	145½
5	Do. do. 1878	181½
4	Do. Pref. 1884	146
4	Do. do. 1887(Conv.)	155
—	Cambrian, No. 1 4 p.c. Pref.	72½
—	Do. No. 2 do.	39½
—	Do. No. 3 do.	19
—	Do. No. 4 do.	10
5	City & S. Lond. £10 shares	15½
—	Do. New	14
4	Furness, Cons. 1881	134½
4	Do. "A" 1881	131½
4	Do. "B" 1883	129½
4	Glasgow & S. Western	144½
4	Do. No. 2	144½
4	Do. 1888	143½
4	Do. 1891	143½
5	Gt. Central	165
4	Do.	132½
5	Do. Conv..... 1872	156½
5	Do. do. 1874	154½
5	Do. do. 1876	153½
5	Do. do. 1879	155½
5	Do. do. 1881	158½
4	Do. 1889	114½
4	Do. 1891	108½
5	Do. 1894	113½
4	Gt. Eastern, Cons.	142½
4	Do. 1886	142
4	Do. 1881	142
4	Do. 1884	142

Preference Shares, &c. (*continued*):—

Last Div.	Name.	Price.
4	Gt. Eastern, Cons..... 1887	142
4	Do. 1888	142
3½	Do. 1890	122½
3½	Do. 1893	121½
—	Do. (Int. fr. Jan '99)1893	117½
4	Gt. North Scotland "A"	136½
4	Do. "B"	135½
4	Gt. Northern, Cons.	143½
3	Do. 1896	107
5	Gt. Western Cons.	181½
36/11	Hull & Barnsley Red. at 115	108
4	Isle of Wight	133½
3	Lancs. & Yorkshire, Cons.	108
2/2½	Lanc. Drby & E.C. 5 p.c. £10	10½
—	Do. 5 p.c. 2nd £10	8½
5	Lond., Bright., &c., Cons.	181½
5	Do. 2nd Cons.	178½
4½	Lond., Chat. & Dov. Arbitr.	135
25/	Do. 2nd Pref. 4½ p.c.	93
4	Lond. & N. Western	144½
4	Lond. & S. Western..1881	145½
4	Do. 1884	144½
3½	Do.	128½
4	Lond., Tilbury & Southend	143½
4	Do. Cons., 1887	143½
4	Do 1891	143½
—	Mersey, 5 p.c. Perp.	—
4	Metropolitan, Perp.	143½
4	Do. 1882	143½
4	Do. Irred.	143½
4	Do. 1887	143½
4	Do. New	143½
4½	Do.	146½
3½	Do.	128½
3	Do. Guar.	101½
2½	Metrop. Dist. Exten 5 p.c.	111
4	Midland, Cons. Perpetual	146½
4	N. British Cons., No. 2	138½
4½	Do. Edin. & Glasgow	156½
5	Do. 1865	172½
5	Do. Conv. 1874	172½
4½	Do. 1873	156
4½	Do. Conv. 1875	156½
5	Do. do. 1879	172½
4	Do. do. 1884	140
4	Do. do. 1888	140
4	Do. do. 1890	140
4	Do. do. 1892	139
4	N. Eastern	144½
4½	N. Lond., Cons. 1866	176½
4½	Do. 2nd Cons. .. 1875	162½
3	N. Staffordshire	108½
4½	Plym. Devpt. & S. W. Junc.	159½
1/5	Port Talbot, &c., 4 p.c. £10 Shares, 4 paid	5
5/	Rhondda & Swansea Bay, 5 p.c. £10 Shares	13
4	Rhymney, Cons.	142
4½	S. Eastern, Cons.	162½
5	Do. do.	179½
4	Do. Vested Cos'.	143
4	Do. 1891	143
3½	Do. 1893	125½
2	Do. 3 p.c. after July 1900	105
4	Taff Vale	143

INDIAN RAILWAYS.

Last Div.	Name.	Paid.	Price.
3½	Assam Bengal, Ld., (3½ p.c. till June 30, then 3 p.c.)	100	102
4/	Barsi Light, Ld., £10 Shs.	10	10¾
6	Bengal and N. West., Ld.	100	149½
4/	Do. £10 Shares	10	14½
3/6	Do. 3½ p.c. Cum. Pf. Shs.	10	10½
8½d.	Do.	4	4½
2/3½	Bengal Central, Ld., £10 (3½ p.c. + ½th net earn)	5	5½
3	Bengal Dooars, Ld.	100	118
4	Bengal Nagpr., Lim. (gua. 4 p.c. + 4th sp. pfts.)	100	118
7½	Bombay, Baroda, and C. I. (gua. 5 p.c.)	100	213
36/1	Burma, Ld. (gua. 2½ p.c. and ½ p.c. add. till 1901)	100	108½
1/7	Do. £10 Shares	2½	3½
4	Delhi Umb. Kalka, Ld., Gua. 3½ p.c. + net earn.	100	132
4	Do. Deb. Stk., 1890 (1916)	100	113
9/10	Eastn. Bengal, "A" An. 1957	—	25
9/	Do. "B" 1957	—	31
4	Do. Gua. Deb. Stock	100	143½
9/7½	East Ind. Ann. "A" (1953)	—	[illegible]
8/4½	Do. "C"	—	[illegible]
8/11½	Do. "B"	—	[illegible]
6½	Do. Def. Ann. Cap. (gua. 4 p.c. + ½th sp. pfts.)	—	134
115/9	East Ind. Def. Ann. "D"	—	[illegible]
4½	East Ind. Irred. Stock	100	[illegible]
5	Gt. Indian Penin., Gua. 5 p.c. + ½ surplus profits.	100	170
4	Do. Irred. 4 p.c. Deb. St.	100	[illegible]
4	Indian Mid., Ld. (gua. 4 p.c. + ¼th surplus pfts.)	100	118
51/	Madras Guar. + ½ sp. pfts.	100	[illegible]
48/6	Do. do.	100	[illegible]
46/	Do. do.	100	[illegible]
4	Nilgiri, Ld., 1st Deb. Stk.	100	97
4	Oude & Robil. Db. Stk. Rd.	100	—
5½	Robil. and Kumaon, Ld.	100	132
9/11	Scinde, Punj., and Delhi, "A" Ann., 1958	—	25
9/1	Do. "B" do.	—	22

Indian Railways (*continued*):—

Last Div.	NAME.	Paid.	Price.
4	South Behar, Ld., £10 shs.	100	100
3½	Do. Deb. Stk. Red.	100	103
4½	South Ind., Gu. Deb. Stk.	100	166½
5	South Indian, Ld. (gua. 3 p.c., and ½ spls. profits)	100	122½
5	Sthn. Mahratta, Ld. (3½ p.c. & ¼th net earnings)	100	117
4	Do. Deb. Stk. Red.	100	123
3½	Southern Punjab, Ld....	100	112
3½	Do. Deb. Stk. Red.	—	107
5	Nizam's Gua. State, Ld. (†	100	114½
4	Do. Mort. Deb., 1936	100	110
4	Do. do. Reg.	100	109
«7/3½	Nizam's Gua. State, Ld., 3½ p.c. Mt. Deb. bearer	—	95½
«7/3½	Do. Reg. do. ..	—	94½
5	W. of India Portgese., Ld.	100	68½
5	Do. Deb. Stk., Red	100	99

RAILWAYS.—BRITISH POSSESSIONS.

Last Div.	NAME.	Paid.	Price.
5	Atlantic & N.W. Gua. 1 Mt. Bds., 1937	100	126
5/3	Buff. & L. Huron Ord. Sh.	10	13½
5½	Do. 1st Mt. Perp. Bds. 1879	100	141½
5½	Do. 2nd Mt. Perp. Bds.	100	141½
—	Calgary & Edmon. 6 p.c. 1st Mt. Stg. Bds. Red..	100	74½
5	Canada Cent. 1st Mt. Bds. Red.	100	106
4	Can. Pacific Pref. Stk....	100	101
5	Do. Strl. 1st Mt. Deb. Bds. 1915	100	118
3½	Do. Ld. Grnt. Bds., 1938..	100	108
3½	Do. Ld. Grnt. Ins. Stk. ..	100	108
4	Do. Perp. Cons. Deb. Stk.	100	113½
5	Do. Algoma Bch. 1st Mt. Bds., 1937	100	122
2	Demerara, Original Stock	100	49
7	Do. Perp. Pref. Stk.....	100	157½
9½d.	Do. 4 p.c. Cum. Ext. Pref. £10 Shs.	4	6½
—	Dominion Atlntc. Ord. Stk.	100	33½
—	Do. 5 p.c. Pref. Stk.....	100	101
4	Do. 1st. Deb. Stk.......	100	109
4	Do. 2nd do. Red.	100	100
—	Emu Bay & Mt. Bischoff, Ld.	5	4½
4½	Do. Irred. Deb. Stk....	100	98
nil.	Gd. Trunk of Canada, Stk.	100	7½
6	Do. 2nd. Equip. Mt. Bds.	100	131½
5	Do. Perp. Deb. Stk.....	100	136½
5	Do. Gt. Westn. Deb. Stk.	100	127½
5	Do. Nthn. of Can. 1st Mt. Bds, 1902	100	103½
4	Do. do. Deb. Stk	100	102
5	Do. G. T. Geor. Bay & L. Erie 1 Mt., 1903	100	104
5	Do. Mid. of Can. Stl. 1st Mt. (Mid. Sec.) 1908	100	108
5	Do. do. Cons. 1 Mt. Bds. 1912	100	108
5	Do. Mont. & Champ. 1 Mt. Bds., 1902	100	104
	Do. Welln., Grey & Brce. 7 p.c. Bds. 1 Mt.	100	111
—	Jamaica 1st Mtg. Bds. Red.	—	103
—	Manitoba & N. W., 6 p.c. 1st Mt. Bds., Red	100	—
—	Do. Ldn. Bdhldrs. Certs.	—	—
5	Manitoba S. W. Col. 1 Mt. Bd., 1934 $1,000 price %	—	120
—	Mid. of W. Aust. Ld. 6 p.c. 1 Mt. Dbs., Red.	100	25
4	Do. Deb. Bds., Red.	100	103
4	Nakusp & Slocan Bds., 1918	100	106
3	Natal Zululand Ld. Debs.,	100	79½
5	N. Brunswick 1st Mt. Stg. Bds., 1934	100	122
4	Do. Perp. Cons. Deb. Stk.	100	114
—	N. Zealand Mid., Ld., 5 p.c 1st Mt. Debs..........	100	35
6	Ontario & Queb. Cap. Stk.	$100	157½
5	Do. Perm. Deb. Stk......	100	144½
—	Qu'Appelle, L. Lake & Sask. 6 p.c. 1 Mt. Bds. Red.	100	43½
	Queb. & L. S. John, 1st Mt. Bds., 1909	100	25½
	Quebec Cent., Prior Ln. Bds., 1908	100	107
1½	Do. 5 p.c. Inc. Bds.	100	40
4	St. Lawr. & Ott. Stl. 1st Mt.	100	113
4	Shuswap & Okan., 1st Mt. Deb. Bds., 1915	100	76
5	Temiscouata, 5 p.c. Stl. 1st Deb. Bds., Red.........	100	9½
5	Do. (S. Franc. Brch.) 5 p.c. Stl. 1 Mt. Db. Bds., 1910	100	10
4	Toronto, Grey & B. 1st Mt.	100	113
1/2½	Well. & Mana. £5 Shs. ..	1	1
5	Do. Debs., 1908........	100	110
5	Do. 2nd Debs., 1908....	100	109
5	Do. 3rd do., 1908	100	108
6	Atlan. & St. Law. Shs., 6 p.c.	100	167
5	Gd. Trunk Mt. Bds., 1934	100	116½
5	Michigan Air Line, 5 p.c. 1st Mt. Bds., 1902......	100	104
4	Minneap., S. P. & Slt. Ste. Mar, 1st M Bds., 1938	$1000	97

AMERICAN RAILROAD STOCKS AND SHARES.

Last Div.	NAME.	Paid.	Price.
6/	Alab. Gt. Sthn. A 6 p.c. Pref.	10l.	9
—	Do. do "B" Ord. ..	10l.	2
—	Alabma. N. Orl.-Tex. &c., "A" Pref.	10l.	¾
—	Do. "B" Def.	10l.	¼
5½	Atlant. First Lsd. La. Rtl. Trust..............	Stk.	98½
—	Baltimore & Ohio Com. ..	$100	18
—	Baltimore Ohio S.W. Pref.	$100	7
—	Chesap. & Ohio Com.	$100	20
—	Chic. Gt. West. 5 p.c. Pref. Stock "A"	$100	30½
—	Do. do. Scrip. In.......	—	29½
8/3	Do. 4 p.c. Deb. Stk.......	$100	70
4	Do. Interest in Scrip	$100	65½
$4	Chic. Junc. Rl. & Un. Stk. Yds. Com.	$100	114½
$1½	Do. 6 p.c. Cum. Pref.	$100	117½
$3½	Chic. Mil. & St. P. Pref...	$100	150
7	Cleve. & Pittsburgh......	$50	86½
$1½	Clev., Cincin., Chic., & St. Louis Com.	$100	—
—	Erie 4 p.c. Non-Cum. 1st Pf.	—	37
—	Do. 4 p.c. do. 2nd Pf.	—	18
—	Gt. Northern Pref.	$100	155
$2½	Illinois Cen. Lsd. Lines ..	$100	99
—	Kansas City, Pitts & G. ..	$100	21
$3	L. Shore & Mich. Sth. C.	$100	195½
—	Mex. Cen. Ltd. Com.	$100	6
—	Miss. Kan. & Tex. Pref...	$100	37½
2½	N.Y., Pen. & O. 1st Mt. Tst. Ltd., Ord.	—	50
4	Do. 1st Mort. Deb. Stk. ..	$100	93½
2	North Pennsylvania	$50	—
—	Northn. Pacific, Com.	$100	23½
1½	Pitts. F. Wayne & Chic...	$100	176
—	Reading 1st Pref.	$50	21
—	Do. 2nd Pref.	$50	11½
—	S. Louis & S. Fran. Com.	$100	6½
—	Do. 2nd Pref.	$100	25
6	St. Louis Bridge 1st Pref..	$100	107
3	Do. 2nd Pref.	$100	50
6	Tunnel Rail. of St. Louis	$100	107
$1½	St. Paul, Min. and Man...	$100	137
—	Southern, Com.	$100	8½
—	Wabash, Common.......	$100	7

AMERICAN RAILROAD BONDS. CURRENCY.

Last Div.	NAME.		Price.
7	Albany & Susq. 1 Con. Mrt.	1906	122½
7	Allegheny Val. 1 Mt.......	1910	129½
5	Burling., Cedar Rap. & N. 1 Mt.	1906	109½
5	Canada Southern 1 Mt....	1908	111
5	Chic. & N. West. Sk. Fd. Db.	1933	120½
5	Do. Deb. Coupon	1921	115½
6	Chicago & Tomah	1905	112½
5	Chic. Burl. & Q. Skg. Fd.	1901	102½
4	Do. Nebraska Ext.......	—	102
6	Chic., Mil., & S. Pl., 1 Mt. S.W. Div..............	1909	117½
7	Do. (S. Paul Div.) 1 Mt.	1902	132½
5	Do. (La Cross & D.	1919	112½
7	Do. 1 Mt. (Hast. & Dak.)	1910	132
5	Do. Chic. & Mis. Riv. 1 Mt.	1926	112½
5	Chic., Rock Is. and Pac. 1 Mt. Ext.	1934	108
6	Det., G. Haven & Mil. Equip	1918	110
6	Do. do. Cons. Mt.	1918	104½
6	Ill. Cent., 1 Mt., Chic. & S.	1898	—
7	Indianap. & Vin., 1 Mt. ..	1908	125
6	Do. do. 2 Mt. ..	1900	104½
6	Lehigh Val., Cons. Mt....	1923	112½
—	Mexic. Cent., Ln. 2 Cons. Inc.	—	6
7	N.Y. Cent. & H.R. Mt. Bonds	1903	119½
5	Do. Deb.	1904	111
6	Penna. Cons. S. F M.	1905	119½
4	West Shore, 1 Mt.	2361	110

DITTO—GOLD.

Last Div.	NAME.	Price.
6	Alabama Gt. Sthn. 1 Mt. ..1908	112
5	Do. Mid. 1 1928	96
4	Allegheny Val. Gen. Mt. ..1942	108
4	Atch., Top., & S. Fé Gn. Mt. 1995	92½
3	Do. Adj. Mt. 1995	60½
5	Do. Equipt. Tmst. ...... —	104½
5	Atlantic & Dan. 1 Mt.......1950	—
5	Baltimore & Ohio...........1925	100
5	Do. Speyer's Tst. Recpts. 1925	100
5	Do. Cons. Mt. 1988	104
4½	Do. 4½ p.c. 1 Mt. Term. 1934	86
4½	Do. Brown Shipley's Dep. Cts. —	86
5	Balt. Belt 5 p.c. 1 Mort.....1990	90
4½	Balt. & Ohio S.W. 1 Mt. ..1990	105
4½	Do. 4½ p.c. 1 Cons. Mt. 1893 1993	80
—	Do. Inc. Mt. 5 p.c. Cl. A —	30
—	Do. do. Cl. B —	11
5	Balt. & Ohio S.W. Term 5 p.c. 1942	99½
6	Balt. & Ptmac (Mn. L.) 1 Mt. 1911	127½
6	Do. do. (Tunnel) 1 Mt. 1911	126
4	Beech Creek 1 Mt. 1936	109
5	Do 2 Mort. 1936	116
4	Carthage & Adiron 1 Mt...1981	100

American Railroad Bonds—Gold (*continued*):—

Last Div.	NAME.	Price.
5	Cent. of Georgia 1 Mort. ..1945	117½
5	Do. Cons. Mt. 1945	92½
5	Cent. of N. Jrsy. Gn. Mt...1987	118
6	Central Pacific, 1 Mort. 1898	102½
6	Do. Speyer's Certs. ...... —	106
5	Do. Land Grant 1900	102
5	Chesap. & Ohio 1st Cons. Mt. 1939	119
4½	Do. Gen. Mt.............1992	82
6	Chic. & W. Ind. Gen. Mt. Skg. Fd. 1932	120
5	Chic. Mil. & St. Pl. (Chic. & L. Sup.) 1 Mt. 1921	114½
5	Do. Chic. & Pac. W. 1921	119½
5	Do. Wisc. & Minn. 1 Mt. 1921	114½
5	Do. Terminal Mt. 1914	114½
4	Do. General Mt. 1989	108
5	Chic. St. L. & N. Orleans..1951	122½
4	Do. 1 Mort. (Memphis) ..1951	105½
4	Clevel., Cin., Chic. & St. L., 1 Mt. (Cairo) 1939	90
4	Do. 1 Mt. (Cinc., Wab., & Mich.) 1991	98
4	Do. 1 Col. Tst. Mt. (S. Louis) 1990	98½
4	Do. General Mt. 1993	82½
4½	Clevel. & Mar. Mt. 1935	114
4½	Clevel. & Pittsburgh 1942	122½
4½	Do. Series B. 1942	124½
—	Colorado Mid. 1 Mt. 1936	63½
—	Do. Bdhrs.' Comm. Certs. —	63½
4	Dnvr. & R. Gde. 1 Cons. Mt. 1936	93
5	Do. Imp. Mort...........1928	91
4	Detroit & Mack. 1 Lien 1995	92½
5	E. Tennes., Virg., & Grgia. Cons. Mt. 1956	114½
5	Elmira, Cort., & Nthn. Mt. 1914	102½
4	Erie 1 Cons. Mt. Pr. Ln. ..1996	92
3	Do. Gen. Lien 1996	72½
6	Galvest., Harrisb., &c., 1 Mt.	107½
5	Georgia, Car. & N. 1 Mt. ..1929	96
4½	Gd. Rpds. & Inda. Ex. 1 Mt. 1941	112½
5	Do. 1 Mt. (Muskegon) ..1926	39½
3½	Illinois Cent. 1 Mt. 1951	104½
4	Do. 1952	107
4	Do. Cairo Bdge. ..1950	103
4	Do. 1953	105
4	Do. General Mort. ..1904	102½
—	Kans. City, Pitts. & G. 1 M. 1923	82
3½	L. Shore & Mich. Southern 1997	109
4½	Lehigh Val. N.Y. 1 Mt.....1940	106
5	Lehigh Val. Term. 1 Mt. ..1941	112½
5	Long Island 1931	122½
5	Do. Deb. 1934	102
5	Do. (N. Shore Bch.) 1 Cons. Mt. 1932	96
6	Louisville & Nash. G. Mt. ..1930	122
6	Do. 2 Mt. Sk. Fd. (S. & N. Alabama........1910	108
6	Do. 1 Mt. N. Orl. & Mb. 1930	122½
5	Do. 1 Mt. Coll. Tst. ...1931	108
4	Do. Unified 1940	89
4½	Do. Mobile & Montgy. 1 Mt. 1945	105½
4	Manhattan Cons. Mt. 1990	98
4	Mexican Cent. Cons. Mt. ..1911	66
—	Do. 1 Cons. Inc, ...	16
6	Mexican Nat. 1 Mt..........1927	107
3	Do. 2 Mt. 6 p.c. Inc. A 1917	58
—	Do. do. B..1917	10
3	Do. Matheson's Certs.....	—
3	Michig. Cnt. (Battle Ck. & S.) 1 Mt. 1989	88
6	Minneap. & S. L. 1 Mt. Pacific Ext. 1921	120½
5	Do. 1 Consold. 1934	110
4	Minne., Slt. S. M. & A. 1 Mt. 1926	98
5	Minneapolis Westn. 1 Mt...1911	105½
4	Miss. Kans. & Tex. 1 Mt...1990	91
4	Do. 2 do. 1990	63
4	Mobile & Birm. Mt. Inc....1945	38
5	Do. P. Lien 1945	88
4	Mohawk & Mal. 1 Mt......1991	108
5	Montana Cent. 1 Mt........1937	111½
5	Nashv., Chattan., & S. L. 1 Cons. Mt...............1928	104½
5	Nash., Flor., & Shff. Mt...1937	97
4	N. Y. & Putnam 1 Cons. Mt. 1993	110
5	N. Y., Brooklyn, & Man. B. 1 Cons. Mt..............1935	110
4	N. Y. Cent. & Hud. R. Deb. Certs. 1890 1905	107
4	Do. Ext. Debt. Certs....1905	107
7	N. Y., L. Erie, & W. 1 Cons. Mt. (Erie) 1920	146
7	Do. 1 Con. Mt. Fd. Coup. 1920	143
5	N. Y., Onto., & W. Cons. 1 Mt.....................1939	110
4	Do. 4 p.c. Refund. Mt...1992	102
5	N. Y. & Rockaway B. 1 Mt. 1927	102½
6	Norfolk & West. Gn. Mt....1931	128
6	Do. Imp. & Ext.........1934	120
4	Do. 1 Cons. Mt........ —	83
6	N. Pacific Gn. 1 Mt. Ld. Gt. 1921	122
4	Do. P. Ln. Rl. & Ld. Gt. —	98
3	Do. Gn. Ln. Rl. & Ld. Gt. —	62
5	Oregon & Calif. 1 Mt.......1927	78½
5	Oregon Rl. & Nav. Col. Tst. —	—
6	Panama Skg. Fd. Subsidy..1910	105½
4½	Pennsylvania Rlrd. 1913	115½
4	Do. Equip. Tst. Ser. A..1914	104
4	Do. Cons. Mt............1943	115
4½	Penna. Company 1st Mort. 1921	116½
5	Perkiomen 1 Mrt., 2nd ser..1918	91½
4½	{ Pitts., C., C., & St. Ls. Con. Mt. G. B., Ser. A } 1940-2	115
4	Do. Cons. Mort., Ser. D..1945	104½
6	Pittsbgh., Cle., & Toledo ..1922	107½
4	Reading, Phil., & R. Genl. 1997	84
5	Richmond & Dan. Equip. ..1909	97½
5	Rio Grande Junc. 1st Mort. 1939	94
4	Rio Grande West 1st Tst. Mt. 1930	82½
6	St. Joseph & Gd. Island ..1925	—
7	S. Louis Bridge 1st Mort ..1925	137½
5	S. Louis Mchts. Bdge. Term. 1st Mort....................1930	104½

American Railroad Bonds (*continued*):

Last Div.	NAME.	Price.
4	S. Louis S. West 1st Mort...1989	77½
—	Do. 4 p.c. 2nd Mort. Inc. 1989	30
—	S. Louis Term. Cupples Sta. & Prop. 1st. Mrt. 4½ p.c. 1902-17	102
4½	St. Paul, Minn., & Manit. 1933	110½
6	Do. do. 1933	132½
6	Shamokin, Sunbury, &c. 2 Mt. 1925	109
5	S. & N. Alabama Cons. Mt. 1936	100
5	Southern 1 Cons. Coup. 1994	94
4	Do. E. Tennes Reorg. Lien ..1938	98½
6	S. Pacific of Cal. 1 Mt...1905-12	114
4½	Trml. Assn. of S. Louis 1 Mt. 1939	113½
5	Do. 1 Cons. Mt..........1944	109
5	Texas & Pac. 1 Mt. 2000	102½
—	Do. 5 p.c. 2 Mt. Income 2000	34½
5	Toledo & Ohio Cent. 1 Mt. West. Div. 1935	105½
4½	Toledo., Walhon., Val., & Ohio 1 Mt. 1931-3	111½
6	Union Pacific 1 Mt. 1896-9	102½
5	Do. Coll. Trust.	—
—	Union Pac., Linc., & Color. 1 Mt. 1918	—
4	United N. Jersey Gen. Mt...1944	115½
6	Vicksbrg., Shrevept., & Pac. Pr. Ln. Mt. 1915	102½
5	Wabash 1 Mt. 1939	112
4	Wn. Pennsylvania Mt. 1928	109½
5	W. Virga. & Pittsbg. 1 Mt. 1990	88
5	Wheeling & L. Erie 1 Mt. (Wheelg. Div.) 5 p.c. 1928	90½
5	Do. Extd. Imp. Mt 1930	—
—	Do. do. Brown Shipley's Cts...	—
5	Willmar & Sioux Falls 1 Mt. 1938	111

STERLING.

Last Div.	NAME.	Price.
6	Alabama Gt. Sthn. Deb.....1906	104½
5	Do. Gen. Mort. ..1927-8	100
5	Alabama, N. Orl., Tex. & Pac. 5 p.c. "A" Dbs. ..1910-40	99
55/	Do. do. "B" do. 1910-40	51
—	Do. do. "C" do.	19
—	Allegheny Valley 1910	136
4	Atlantic 1st Leased Line Perp...	98
6	Baltimore and Ohio 1902	107½
6	Do. do. 1910	118
5	Do. do. 1877........	97½
—	Do. Morgan's Certs. ..	97½
4½	Do. do. 1933	90
6	Chicago & Alton Cons. Mt. 1903	111
5	Chic. St. Paul & Kan. City Priority	106
6	Eastn. of Massachusetts....1906	117½
5	Illinois Cent. Skg Fd.	105
5	Do. 1905	108
3½	Do. 1950	99½
4	Do. 1 Mt. 1951	112
3	Do. 1 Mt. 1951	92½
6	Louisville & Nash., M. C. & L. Div., 1 Mt. 1902	104½
7	Do. 1 Mt. (Memphis & O.) 1901	111
47/4	Mexican Nat. "A" Certs. 5 p.c. Non. cum.	47
—	Do. "B" Certs.....	10
6	N.Y. & Canada 1 Mt........1904	111½
6	N. York Cent. & H.R. Mort. 1903	112
4½	N. York, Penns., & Ohio Pr. Ln. Extd. 1935	—
5	Do. Equip. Tst.	103½
5	Do. 5 p.c. Equip. Tst. (1890)	103½
6	Nrthn. Cent. Cons. Gen. Mt. ..	106
6	Pennsylvania Gen. Mt. 1910	128
6	Do. Cons. Skg. Fd. Mt. 1905	115½
3½	Do. Cons. Mt. 1945	106
6	Phil. & Erie Cons. Mort ..1920	134½
6	Phil. & Reading Gen. Cons. Mort. 1911	127
6	Pittsbg. & Connells. Cons. 1926	115
—	Do. Morgan's Certs....	115
4	St. Paul., Min., & Manitoba (Pac. Extn.) 1940	98
6	S. & N. Alabama 1903	107½
6	Union Pacific, Omaha Bridge 1896	—
6	Un. N. Jersey & C. Gen. Mt. 1901	109½

FOREIGN RAILWAYS.

Last Div.	NAME.	Paid.	Price.
4/	Alagoas Ld., Shs.......	20	6
5	Do. Deb. Stk., Red. ..	100	54½
6	Antofagasta Ltd., Stk. ..	100	73
4	Do. Perp. Deb. Stk. ..	100	91
—	Arauco, Ld., Ord. Shs. ..	10	½
—	Do. 7 p.c. Cum. Pref.	10	1½
5	Argentine Gt. W., Ld.,	100	75
5	Do. 5 p.c. Cum. Pref. Shs.	100	100
4	Do. 4 Deb. Stk.	100	103½
1/0/0	Argentine N.E., Ltd., 6 p.c. Cum. Pref. Stk. ..	100	11½
—	Do. 4 p.c. Deb. Stk., Red.	100	31
2/	Arica and Tacna Shs. ..	20	1½
10/	Bahia & San Fcisco., Ld.,	20	11
6/	Do. Timbo Bch. Shs.	20	5
12/	Bahia, Blanca, & N.W. Ln. Pf. Cum. 6 p.c. ..	100	55
4	Do. 4 p.c. Deb. Stk., Red.	100	95
6	Barranquilla R. & P., Ld., 6 p.c. 1 Deb. Stk., Red.	100	96

Foreign Railways (continued):—

Last Div.	Name.	Paid.	Price.
3/	Bilbao Riv. & Cantabn., Ltd., Ord.	3	6
—	Bolivar, Ltd., Shs.	10	1½
6	Do. 6 p.c. Deb. Stk.	100	96½
—	Brazil Gt. Southn. Ltd., 7 p.c. Cum. Pref.	20	1½
6	Do. Perm. Deb. Stk	100	47½
6½	B. Ayres Gt. Southn., Ld., Ord. Stk.	100	151
5	Do. Pref. Stk.	100	137
4	Do. Deb. Stk.	100	116¼
30/	B. Ayres & Ensen. Port., Ltd., Ord. Stk.	100	67
5	Do. Cum. 1 Pref. Stk.	100	124
6/0/0	Do. 6p.c.Con. Pref.Stk.	100	108
4	Do. Deb. Stk., Irred.	100	112
10⅜	B. Ayres Northern, Ltd., Ord. Stk.	100	265
12½	Do. Pref. Stk.	100	320
5	Do. 5 p.c. Mt. Deb. Stk., Red.	100	113
3/15/0	B. Ayres & Pac., Ld., 7 p.c. 1 Pref. Stk. (Cum.)	100	94
4	Do. 1 Deb. Stk.	100	103
5/5/0	Do. 4½ p.c. 2 Deb. Stk.	100	90
1	B Ayres & Rosario, Ltd., Ord. Stk.	100	72
—	Do. New, £20 Shs.	20	22½
7/	Do. 7 p.c. Pref. Shs.	10	17½
7/	Do. Sunchales Ext.	10	15½
4	Do. Deb. Stk., Red.	100	108½
12/	B. Ayres & Val. Trans., Ltd., 7 p.c. Cum. Pref.	20	7
4	Do. 4 p.c. "A" Deb. Stk., Red.	100	71
—	Do. 6 p.c. "B" Deb. Stk., Red.	100	44
6/	B. Ayres Westn. Ld. Ord.	10	11½
3/	Do. Def. Shs.	10	6½
5	Do. 5 p.c. Pref.	10	13½
4	Do. Deb. Stk	100	110½
6	Cent. Arg. Deb. Sk. Rd.	100	160½
4	Do. Deb. Stk. Rd.	100	112
6	Cent. Bahia L. Ord. Stk.	100	44½
	Do. Deb. Stk., 1934	100	74½
5	Do. Deb. Stk., 1937	100	58
1/6	Cent. Uguy. East. Ext. L. Shs	10	6
5	Do. Perm. Stk.	100	110
3/	Do. Nthn. Ext. L. Sh.	10	4½
5	Do. Perm. Deb. Stk.	100	106
3	Do. of Montev. Ltd., Ord. Stk	100	86
6	Do. Perm. Deb. Stk	100	143
10/	Conde d'Eu, Ltd. Ord.	20	7½
—	Cordba & Rosar., Ltd., 6 p.c. Pref. Shs.	100	42
4	Do. 1 Deb. Stk	100	94
75/	Do. 6 p.c. Deb. Stk	100	85½
—	Cordba Cent., Ltd., 5 p.c. Cu. 1 Pref. Stk	100	83½
—	Do. 5 p.c. Non-Cum. 2 Pref. Stk	100	46
5	Do. Deb. Stk.	100	120
—	Costa Rica, Ltd., Shs.	10	4½
8/	Dna. Thrsa. Chris., Ltd., 7 p.c. Pref. Shs.	20	4½
20/	E. Argentine, Ltd	100	40
6	Do. Deb. Stk	100	105
1/1	Egypcn. Dlta. Lgt. Rys., Ltd., £10 Pref. Shs.	8	8½
—	Entre Rios, L., Ord. Shs.	5	½
—	Do. Cu. 5 p.c. Pref.	5	2½
6/	Gt. Westn. Brazil, Ltd.	20	11
6	Do. Perm. Deb. Stk.	100	90½
6	Do. Extn. Deb. Stk.	100	76½
—	Int.-Oceanic Mex., Ltd., 7 p.c. Pref	10	1½
4	Do. Deb. Stk	100	86
42/6	Do. 7 p.c. "A" Deb. Sk.	100	66
—	Do. 7 p.c. "B" Deb. Sk.	100	33
5/	La Guaira & Carac.	20	7½
5	Do. 5 p.c. Deb. Sk. Red.	100	100
8/4	Lembg.-Czern.-Jassy	30	25
1/	Lima, Ltd.	20	2½
—	Manila Ltd. 7 p.c. Cu. Pf.	10	½
20/6½	Mexican and Pref. 6 p.c.	100	35
6	Do. Perp. Deb. Stk.	100	144½
1/0/0	Mexican Sthrn., Ld., Ord.	100	26
—	Do. 4 p.c. 1 Db. Stk. Rd.	100	85
—	Do. 4 p.c. 2 do.	100	62
—	Mid. Urgy., Ltd.	100	19
5	Do. Deb. Stk.	100	63
12/	Minas & Rio, Ltd.	20	12½
5/2	Namur & Liege	20	12½
11/6	Do. Pref.	20	29
5/	Natal & Na. Cruz, Ld., 7 p.c. Cum Pref.	20	8
—	Nitrate Ltd., Ord.	10	5
—	Do. 7 p.c. Pr. Con. Or.	10	3½
—	Do. Def. Conv. Ord.	10	½
7/	N.-E. Urgy., Ltd., Ord.	10	15
7/	Do. 7 p.c. Pref.	10	15½
—	N.-W. Argentine Ld., 7 p.c. Pref.	10	2½
6	Do. 6 p.c. 1 Deb. Stk.	100	113
—	Do. 2 Deb. Stk.	100	94
—	N.W. Uruguay 6 p.c. 1 Pref. Stk.	100	17
—	Do. 5 p.c. 2 Pref. Stk.	100	7½
6	Do. 6 p.c. Deb. Stk.	100	80½
16/	Ottoman (Sm. Aid.)	20	15½
—	Paraguay Cntl., Ld., 5 p.c. Perm. Deb. Stk.	100	11
—	Piræus, Ath., & Pelo.	275	1½
5/	Pto. Alegre & N. Hambg. Ld., 7 p.c. Pref. Shs.	20	4½
6	Do. Mt. Deb. Stk. Red.	100	77½
—	Puerto Cabello & Val. Ld.	10	1½
5	Recife & S. Francisco	100	75
24/	R Claro S. Paulo, Ld., Sh.	10	22½
5	Do. Deb. Stk.	100	129
	Royal Sardinian Ord.	10	11½

Foreign Railways (continued):—

Last Div.	Name.	Paid.	Price.
5/	Royal Sardinian Pref.	10	12
5/	Sambre & Meuse	20	18
5/6	Do. Pref.	10	12½
28/	San Paulo Ld.	20	35½
2/9½	Do. New Ord. £10 sh.	6	10½
2/	Do. 5 p.c. Non.Cm.Pref.	10	12½
5½	Do. Deb. Stk.	100	137
5	Do. 5 p.c. Deb. Stk	100	128
—	S. Fé & Cordova, Gt. Sthn., Ld., Shares	100	54
6	Do. Perp. Deb. Stk.	100	124
3/2½	S. Austrian	20	7½
10/	Sthn. Braz. R. Gde. do Sul, Ld.	20	8
6	Do. 6 p.c. Deb. Stk.	100	78
4	Swedish Centl., Ld., 4 p.c. Deb. Stk.	100	107
5	Do. Pref.	100	100
1/9	Taltal, Ld.	5	2½
—	Uruguay Nthn., Ld. 7 p.c. Pfd. Stk.	100	8
3½	Do. 5 p.c. Deb. Stk.	100	30
—	Villa Maria & Rufino, Ld., 6 p.c. Pref. Shs.	100	20
4	Do. 4 p.c. 1 Deb. Stk.	100	74
6/0/0	Do. 6 p.c. 2 Deb. Stk.	100	47
5/9	West Flanders	8½	21
5/6	Do. 5½ p.c. Pref.	10	18
3/	Wstn. of Havana, Ld.	10	4½

FOREIGN RAILWAY OBLIGATIONS

Per Cent.	Name.	Price.
6	Alagoas Ld., 6 p.c. Deb., Rd.	88½
—	Alcoy & Gandia, Ld., 5 p.c. Debs., Red.	25
5	Arauco., Ld., 5 p.c. 1st Mt., Rd.	66½
—	Do. 6 p.c. Mt. Deb., Rd.	45½
6	Brazil G. Sthn., L., Mt. Dbs., Rd.	89½
6	Do. Mt. Dbs. 1893, Rd.	48½
5½	Campos & Caran. Dbs., Rd.	76
6	Central Bahia, L., Dbs., Rd.	90½
5½	Conde d'Eu, L., Dbs., Rd.	78
6	Costa Rica, L., 1st Mt. Dbs., Rd.	110
6	Do. 2nd Dbs., Rd.	93
5	Do. Prior Mt. Db., Rd.	104
6	Cucuta Mt. Dbs., Rd.	106
5½	Donna Thrsa. Cris., L., Dbs., Rd.	75
3	Eastn. of France, £20 Dbs., Rd.	19½
4	Egyptn. Delta Light, L., Db., Rd.	100
—	Espito. Santo & Cara. 5 p.c. Stl. Dbs., Rd.	38
4	Gd. Russian Nic., Rd.	102
5	Inter-Oceanic Mex., L., 5 p.c. Pr. Ln. Dbs., Rd.	104
3	Ital. 3 p.c. Bds. A & B, Rd	57½
—	Ituana 6 p.c. Debs., 1918	74
—	Leopoldina, 6 p.c. Dbs. £50 Bds.	28
—	Do. do. Comms. Cert.	24
—	Do. 5 p.c. Stg. Dbs. (1888), Rd.	34
—	Do. do. Comm. Certs.	34
—	Do. 5 p.c. Stg. Dbs. (1890), Rd.	28
—	Do. do. Comms. Certs.	28
—	Macahé & Cam. 5 p.c. Dbs., Rd.	34
—	Do. do. Comms. Certs.	34
—	Do. (Cantagallo), 5 p.c., Red.	34
—	Do. do. Comm. Certs.	34
—	Manila Ltd., 6 p.c. Deb., Red.	28
6	Do. Prior Lien Mt., Rd.	105
6	Do. Series "B," Rd.	82
7	Matanzas & Sab., Rd.	101½
6	Minas & Rio, L., 6 p.c. Dbs., Rd.	100
5	Mogyana 5 p.c. Deb. Bds., Rd.	104
5	Moscow-Jaros., Rd.	106½
5½	Natal & Na. Cruz Ltd., 5½ p.c. Debs., Red.	87½
5	Nitrate, Ltd. Mt. Bds., Red.	82
3	Nthn. France, Red.	19½
4	N. of S. Af. Rep. (Trnsvl.) Gu. Bds. Red.	97
3	Nthn. of Spain £20 Pri. Obs. Red.	9
6	Ottmn. (Smy to A.)(Kujk) Asnt. Debs., Red.	109
6	Ottmn. (Seraik.) Asg. Debs. Red.	109
6	Ottmn. (Seraik) Non-Asg. D., Rd	109
5	Ottmn. Kuyjk. Ext. Red.	106
5	Ottmn. Serkeuy. Ext. Red.	101½
5	Ottmn. Tireh Ext. 1910	97
5	Ottmn. Debs, 1886, Red.	98
5	Do. 1888, Red. 1935	97½
5	Do. 1893, Red. 1935	99
5	Ottmn. of Anlia. Debs., Rd.	93
5	Do. Ser. II.	89
4	Ottomn. Smyr. & Cas. Ext Bds., Red.	83½
3	Paris, Lyon & Medit. (old sys., £20), Red.	19
3	Paris, Lyon & Medit. (new sys., £20), Red.	19½
50/	Piræus, At. & Pelp., 6 p.c. 1st Mt. Bds., Red.	88½
3	Do. 5 p.c. Mt. Bds., Red.	61½
4	Pretoria-Pietbg., Ltd., Red.	93
7	Puerto Cab. & Val., Ltd., 1st Mt. Debs., Red.	94
—	Rio de Jano. & Nthn., Ltd., 6 p.c. £100 Deb., Red.	24
—	Rio de Jano. (Gr. Para.), 5 p.c. 1st Mt. St. £100 Debs., Red.	24
3	Royal Sardinian, A, Rd. £20	12
3	Royal Sardinian, B., Rd. £20	12

Foreign Rly. Obligations (continued):—

Per Cent.	Name.	Price.
5	Ryl. Trns.-Afric. 5 p.c. 1st Mt. £100 Bds., Red.	61
7	Sagua La Grande, B pRd.	98
4	Sa. Fe & Cor. G.S., Ld. Pr. Ln. Bds.	104
5	Sa. Fe, 5 p.c 2nd Reg. Dbs.	81
3	South Austrian, £20 Red.	15½
3	South Austrian, (Ser X.)	15½
3	South Italian £20 Obs. (Ser. A to G), Red.	12½
3½	S.W. of Venez. (Barq.), Ltd., 7 p.c. 1st Mt. £100 Debs.	57½
5	Taltal, Ltd., 5 p.c. 1st Ch. Debs., Red.	99
5	Utd. Rwys. Havana, Red.	91½
3	Wtrn. of France, £20 Red.	19
6	Wrn. B. Ayres St. Mt. Debs., 1900	111
6	Wrn. B. Ayres, Reg. Cert.	109
5	Do. Mt. Bds.	122
6	Wtrn. of Havna., Ld. Mt. Dbs., Rd.	100
7	Wrn. Ry. San Paulo Red.	101
—	Wrn. Santa Fé 7 p.c. Red.	41
4/7	Zafra & Huelva, 3 p.c. Red.	3

BANKS.

Div.	Name.	Paid.	Price.
1/9½	Agra, Ltd.	6	3½
4/7½	Anglo-Argentine, Ltd., £9	7	5½
8½ fls.	Anglo-Austrian	120f.	14
6/	Anglo-Californian, Ltd., £20 Shares	10	11½
4/	Anglo-Egyptian, Ltd. £15	5	6
5/	Anglo-Foreign Bkg., Ltd.	7	8
2/	Anglo-Italian, Ltd.	5	7½
7/6	Bk. of Africa, Ltd., £18¾	6¼	10½
20/	Bk. of Australasia	40	54
10/	Bk. of Brit. Columbia	20	21½
25/	Bk. of Brit. N. America	50	66
20/	Bk. of Egypt, Ltd., £25	12½	18
5/	Bk. of Mauritius, Ltd.	10	9½
18/	Bk. of N. S. Wales	20	38½
4 p.c.	Bk. of N. Zland. Gua. Stk.	100	103
6/	Bk. of Roumania, £20 Shs.	6	7½
2/6	Tarapaca & Ldn., Ltd., £10	5	3½
—	Bque. Fse. de l'Afri. du S.	100f.	3½
f.12.50	Bque. Internatle. de Paris	20	24
6/	Brit. Bk. of S. America, Ltd., £20 Shares	10	10½
15/	Capital & Ctics., L., £50	10	39
16/	Chart. of India, &c.	20	32
10/	City, Ltd., £40 Shares	10	20
18/	Colonial, £100 Shares	30	22
10/	Delhi and London, Ltd.	25	—
5/	German of London, Ltd.	10	10½
25/	Hong-Kong & Shanghai	28½	45
4/	Imperl. of Persia	6½	3½
10/	Imperl. Ottoman, £20 Shs	10	12
9/	Intrnatl. of Ldn., Ld., £20	15	12
10/	Ionian, Ltd.	25	15
16/	Lloyds, Ltd., £50 Shs.	8	29½
10/	Ldn. & Braziln. Ltd., £20	10	18
44/	Ldn. & County, Ltd., £80	20	100½
9/	Ldn. & Hanseatic, L., £20	10	10½
22/6	Ldn. & Midland, L., £60	12½	53½
8/9	Ldn. & Provin., Ltd., £10	5	22½
39/	Ldn. & Riv. Plate, L., £25	15	53
2/1½	Ldn. & San Fcisco, Ltd.	7	4½
28/	Ldn. & Sth. West., L., £50	20	69
26/	Ldn. & Westmins., L., £100	20	56
3/	Ldn. of Mex. & S. Amer., Ltd., £10 Shs.	6	5½
15/	Ldn. Joint Stk., L., £100	15	33½
9/7	Ldn., Paris & Amer., L. £20	16	26
2/4½	Merchant Bkg., L., £9	4	2½
6/3	Metropn., Ltd., £50 Shs.	5	14½
9/	National, Ltd., £50 Shs.	10	19½
4/3	Natl. of Mexico, $100 Shs.	$40	13
1/3	National of N. Z., L., £7½	2½	2½
8/	National S. Afric. Rep.	10	15
18/10½	National Provcl. of Eng., Ltd., £75 Shs.	10½	51
21/7½	Do. do. £60 Shs.	12	56½
6/6	North Eastn., Ltd., £20 Shs	6	14½
19/	Parr's, Ld., £100 Shs.	20	91½
12/6	Prov. of Ireland, L., £100	12½	28½
40/	Stand. of S. Afric., L., £100	25	68
12/6	Union of Australia, L., £75	25	28
4 p.c.	Do. do. Ins. Stk. Dep. 1900	100	105
15/6	Union of Ldn., Ltd., £100	15½	36½

BREWERIES AND DISTILLERIES.

Div.	Name.	Paid.	Price.
4½	Albion Prp. 1 Mt. Db. Sk.	100	115
4	All Saints', L., Db. Sk. Rd.	100	99
7	Allsopp, Ltd	100	152
6	Do. Cum. Pref	100	157
4½	Do. Deb. Stk., Red.	100	118
3½	Do. Deb. Stk., Red.	100	102
4½	Alton & Co., L., Db., Rd	100	106
4½	Do. Mt. Bds., 1896	100	106
—	Arnold, Perrett, Ltd.	10	6
6	Do. Cum. Pref.	10	10½
4½	Do. 1 Mt. Db. Stk., Rd.	100	106

Breweries &c. (continued):—

Div.	Name.	Paid.	Price.
5½	Arrol, A., & Sons, L., Cum. Pref. Shs.	10	10½
4½	Do. 1 Mt. Db. Stk., Rd.	100	106
5	Backus, 1 Mt. Db., Red.	100	60
4	Barclay, Perk., L., Cu. Pf.	10	11½
3½	Do. Mt. Db. Stk., Red.	100	111
—	Barnsley, Ltd.	10	11
6	Do. Cum. Pref.	10	18½
1/	Barrett's, Ltd	2½	1½
1/3	Do. 5 p.c. Pref.	2½	[illegible]
3/	Bartholomay, Ltd.	10	4
8	Do. Cum. Pref.	10	9
6	Do. Deb.	100	102½
5	Bass, Ratcliff, Ltd., Cum. Pref. Stk.	100	145½
4½	Do. Mt. Db. Stk., Rd.	100	129
4	Bell, J., L., 1 Mt. D. Stk., R	100	100
2/6	Benskin's, L., Cum. Pref.	5	—
4½	Do. 1 Mt. Db. Stk Red.	100	—
4½	Do. "B" Deb. Sk, Rd.	100	—
7/	Bentley's Yorks., Ltd.	10	11
6/	Do. Cum. Pref.	10	12½
4½	Do. Mt. Debs., Red.	100	110
4½	Do. do. 1 92, Red.	100	110
—	Bleckert's, Ltd.	20	2
5	Do. Debs., Red.	100	57
—	Birmingham., Ltd., 6 p.c. Cum. Pref.	5	[illegible]
4½	Do. Mt. Debs., Red.	50	40½
5½	Boardman's, Ld., Cm. Pf.	10	[illegible]
4½	Do., Perp. 1 Mt. Db. Sk.	100	106½
15/2	Brain & Co., Ltd.	100	101
4½	Brakspear, L., 1 D. Stk. Rd	100	109
4	Brandon's, L., 1 D. Sek. R.	100	103½
21/	Bristol (Georges) Ltd.	10	46
6	Do. Cum. Pref.	10	18
5	Do. Mt. Db. Sk. 1888 Rd.	100	115½
17/6	Bristol United, Ltd.	10	[illegible]
6	Do. Cum. Pref.	10	16½
4½	Do. Db. Sk. Rd.	100	126
5½	Buckley's, L., C. Pre-pref.	10	11
4½	Do. 1 Mt. Db. Stk. Rd.	100	105½
4	Bullard & Sns, L., D. Sk. R.	100	107
6	Bushell, Watk., L., C. Pf.	10	14½
4½	Do. 1 Mt. Db. Sk. Rd.	100	112
5	Camden, Ltd., Cum. Pref.	10	11½
4½	Do. 1 Mt. Db. Sk. Rd.	100	108
5½	Cameron, Ltd., Cm. Pf.	10	13½
4½	Do. Mort Deb. Stk.	100	109
3½	Do. Perp Mt. Db. Sk.	100	100½
5	Cam'bell, J'stone, L., C. Pf.	5	5½
4½	Do. 4½ p.c. 1 Mt. Db. Sk.	100	105
4	Campbell, Praed, L., Per. 1 Mort. Deb. Stk.	100	109
4	Cannon, L., Mt. Db. Stk.	100	109
4	Do. "B" Deb. Stk.	100	105
5	Castlemaine, L., 1 Mt. Db.	100	94
3½	Charrington, Ltd., Mort. Deb. Stk. Red.	100	105
2/	Cheltnhm. Orig., Ltd.	5	7
6	Do. Cum. Pref.	5	7½
4	Do. Debs. Red.	100	107
10/	Chicago, Ltd.	10	3½
6	Do. Debs.	100	87½
—	Cincinnati, Ltd.	10	[illegible]
—	Do. Cum. Pref.	10	1½
10/	City of Baltimore	10	4
16/	Do. 8 p.c. Cum. Pref	10	8
14/	City of Chicago, Ltd.	10	1½
8	Do. Cum. Pref.	10	6
13	City of London, Ltd.	100	200½
5	Do. Cum. Pref.	100	137
4	Do. Mt. Deb. Stk., Rd.	100	112½
2/	Colchester, Ltd.	5	5
7	Do. Pref.	5	7
4½	Do. Deb. Stk., Red.	100	110
5	Combe, Ltd., Cum. Pref.	10	14½
4	Do. Mt. Db. Stk, Rd.	100	112
3½	Do. Perp. Deb. Stk.	100	107
5	Comm'cial, L., D. Sk., Rd.	100	108½
5	Courage, L., Cm. Pref. Shs.	100	[illegible]
4	Do. Irr. Mt. Deb. Stk.	100	129
3½	Do. Irr. "B" Mt. Db. Sk.	100	106
8	Daniell & Sons, Ltd.	10	7
7	Do. Cum. Pref.	10	12
4½	Do. 1 Mt. Perp. Db. Sk.	100	108½
4½	Do. "B" Deb. Stk.	100	100
10d.	Dartford, Ltd.	5	5
10d.	Do. Cum. Pref.	5	5½
4	Do. 1 Mt. Db. Sk. Rd.	100	106
4	Davenport, Ld., 1 D. Stk.	100	103½
10/	Denver United, Ltd.	10	3½
8	Do. Cum. Pref.	10	[illegible]
6	Do. Debs.	100	[illegible]
4½	Deuchar, L., 1 D. Sk., Rd.	100	108
8/	Distillers, Ltd.	10	28
4½	Do. Mt. Db. Stk., Rd.	100	115½
—	Dublin Distillers, Ltd.	5	1½
3/	Do. Cum. Pref.	5	4½
4½	Do. Irr. Deb. Stk.	100	—
5	Eadie, Ltd., Cum. Pref.	10	11½
4	Do. Irr. 1 Mt. Db. Sk.	100	108
10/	Edinbgh. Utd., Ltd.	10	13
6	Do. Cum. Pf.	10	13½
5	Do. 1 Mt. Dbs.	100	110½
4	Eldridge, Pope, L. D. St. R.	100	109
—	Emerald & Phœnix, Ltd.	10	1½
8	Do. Cum. Pref.	10	[illegible]
6	Empress Ltd., C. Pf.	10	11½
4½	Do. Mt. Deb. Stk.	100	106
10/	Farnham, Ltd.	10	14
6	Do. Cum. Pref.	10	15
4	Fenwick, L., 1 D. Sk., Rd.	100	105
4	Flower & Sons, Irr. D. Sk.	100	111
4	Friary, L., 1 Db. Stk., Rd.	100	105½
4	Do. 1 "A" Db. Sk., Rd	100	102
4½	Groves, L., 1 Db. Sk., Rd.	100	110
14	Guinness, Ltd.	100	[illegible]
6	Do. Cum. Prf. Stk.	100	[illegible]
5	Do. Deb. Stk., Red.	100	132
5	Hall's Oxford L., Cm. Pf.	5	5½
6/	Hancock, Ld., Cm. Pf. Ord.	10	14
7/	Do. Def. Ord.	10	17½

Breweries, &c. (*continued*) :—

Div.	Name.	Paid.	Price.
6	Hancock, Ld., Cum. Pref.	10	15½
4	Do. 1 Deb. Stk., Rd.	100	112
5	Hoare, Ltd. Cum. Pref.	10	13½
5	Do. "A" Cum. Pref.	10	12½
4	Do. Mt. Deb. Stk., Rd.	100	111
3½	Do. do. do. Rd.	100	104
4/6	Hodgson's, Ltd.	5	9½
5	Do. 1 Mt. Db., Red.	—	120½
4	Do. 2 Mt. Db., 1906	—	102
4½	Hopcraft & N., Ltd., 1 Mt. Deb. Stk., Red.	100	103
5	Huggins, Ltd., Cm. Prf.	10	12½
4½	Do. 1st D. Stk. Rd.	100	113
4½	Do. "B" Db. Stk. Rd.	100	111
8/	Hull, Ltd.	10	17
7	Do. Cum. Pref.	10	15
4½	Ind, Coope, L., D.Sk., Rd.	100	119
4	Do. "B" Mt. Db. Stk. Rd.	100	114
8/	Indianapolis, Ltd.	10	3½
8	Do. Cm. Prf.	10	9½
5/	Jones, Frank, Ltd	10	3½
7½	Do. Cum. Pref.	10	7½
5	Do. 1st Mort. Debs.	100	91½
4/	J. Kenward & Ct., Ltd.	5	5¾
4½	Kingsbury, L., 1 D.Sk., Rd	100	—
4	Lacon, L., D. Stk., Red.	100	110
4	Do. Irrd. "B" D. Sk.	100	107
4/	Lascelles, Ltd.	5	11
6	Do. Cum. Pref.	5	7½
5	Leney, Ltd., Cum. Pref.	10	11½
4	Do. 1 Mt. Db. Stk. Rd.	100	104
30/7½	Lion, Ltd., £25 shares	17	49½
10/9½	Do. New £10 shares	6	17
6	Do. Perp. Pref.	20	32
4	Do. B. Mt. Db. Sk. Rd.	100	110
4½	Lloyd & Y., Ltd., 1 Mt. Deb. Stk., Rd.	100	100½
4½	Locke & S., Ltd., Irr. 1st Mt. Deb. Stk.	100	100
4½	Lovibond, Ltd., 1st Mt. Deb. Stk., Rd.	100	102½
30/4	Lucas & Co., Ld., Deb. Stk.	100	107
8/	Manchester, Ltd.	10	18½
7	Do. Cum. Pref.	10	17½
5	Marston, J., L., Cm. Prf.	10	11
4	Do. 1 Mt. Db. Sk., Rd.	100	101½
9/	Massey's Burnley, Ltd.	10	17
6	Do. Cum. Pref.	10	14½
4½	McCracken, Ltd., 1 Mt. Deb., 1908	100	61½
5	McEwan, Ltd., Cm. Pref.	10	15
5	Meux, Ltd., Cum. Pref.	10	14½
4	Do. Mt. Db. Stk. Red.	100	111
4½	Michell & A., Ltd., 1 Mt. Deb. Stk. Red	100	105
4½	MileEndDist. Db. Sk. Rd.	100	109
—	Milwaukee & Chic., Ltd.	10	1½
4/	Do. Cum. Pref.	10	6½
4½	Michell, Toms, L., Db.	50	55
6	Morgan, Ltd., Cum. Pref.	10	14½
10/	Nalder & Coll., Ltd.	10	34
5	Do. Cum. Pref.	10	16
4½	Do. Deb. Red.	100	113
3/	New Beeston, Ltd.	5	5
2/9	Do. Cum. Pref.	5	5
4	Do. Mt. Deb. Stk. Red.	100	97½
12/	Newcastle, Ltd.	10	20
6	Do. Cum. Pref.	10	15½
5	Do. 1 Mt. Deb., 1911	100	110½
4	Do. "A" Deb. Stk. Red.	100	105
6	New England, Ltd	10	5
8	Do. Cum. Pref.	10	9½
6	Do. Debs. Red	100	104½
4	New London, L., 1 D.Sk.	100	104
7/2	New Westminster, Ltd.	4	10½
2/4½	Do. Pref.	4	6½
—	New York, Ltd.	10	1
—	Do. 8 p.c. Cum. Pref.	10	4½
6	Do. 1 Mt. Deb. Red.	100	80½
5	Noakes, Ld., Cum. Pref.	10	12½
4	Do 1 Mt. Db. Stk., Rd.	100	106
4½	Norfolk, L., "A" D.Sk. Rd.	100	106
10/	Northampton, Ld.	10	16½
7	Do. Cum. Pref.	10	15½
6	Do. Cum. Pref.	10	13
5	Do. 1 Mt. Per. Db. Sk.	100	127
4	Nth. East., L., 1 D.Sk. Rd.	100	102
4½	N. Worcesters., L. Per. 1 Mort. Deb. Stock	100	33½
6	Nottingham, L., Cm. Prf.	10	12½
5	Do. 1 Mt. Deb. Stk., Red.	100	114
17/4	Do. "B" do. Red.	50	112
6/	Ohlsson' Cape, Ld.	5	17
7	Do. Cum. Pref.	5	8½
4½	Do. 2nd Cum. Pref.	5	5½
5	Do. Deb. Stk., Red.	100	114
4½	Oldfield, L., 1 Mt. Db. Stk.	100	106
6	Page & Overt., L., Cm. Prf.	10	13½
4½	Do. 1 Mt. Dbs., Red.	100	108
10/	Parker's Burslem, Ltd.	10	24½
6	Do. Cum. Pref.	10	15
4	Do. 1 Mt. Db. Stk., Red.	100	113
4	Persse, Ld., 1 Mt. Db. Rd.	100	95½
4	Phipps, L., Irr. 1 Db. Stk.	100	115
5	Plymouth, L., Min. Cu. Pf.	10	14
4½	Do. Mt. Deb. Stk., Red.	100	104½
4½	Pryor, Reid, L., 1 D.S., R.	100	105½
5	Reid's, Ld., Cm. Pref. Stk.	100	137½
4	Do. Mt. Deb. Stk., Red.	100	112
3½	Do. "B" Mt. Db. Stk., Rd	100	102
5	Rhondda Val., L., Cu. Pf	10	11
4½	Do. 1 Mt. Deb. Stk., Rd.	100	109
5	Robinson, Ld., Cum. Pref.	10	11½
4½	Do. 1 Mt. Perp. Db. Stk.	100	112
4/	Rochdale, Ltd.	10	5½
4½	Do. 1 Mt. Deb. Stk.	100	91½
7	Royal, Brentford, Ltd.	10	21½
	Do. Cum. Pref.	10	15
4½	Do. 1 Mt. Dbs. Red	100	109
6/	St. Louis, Ltd	10	3½
8	Do. Cum. Pref.	10	8½
14/	St. Pauli, Ltd.	10	10
7	Do. Cum. Pref.	10	12
4½	Salt (T.), L., 1 Db. Sk. Rd.	100	111

Breweries, &c. (*continued*) :—

Div.	Name.	Paid.	Price.
4½	Salt (T.), "B" Db. Stk. Red	100	108
—	San Francisco, Ltd	10	½
—	Do. 8 p.c. Cum. Pref.	10	¾
4½	Savill Brs., L., D. Sk. Rd.	100	117
4½	Scarboro., Ltd., 1 Db. Stk.	100	101
4	Shaw (Hy.), Ltd., 1 Mt. Db. Stk., Red.	100	104
22/	Showell's, Ltd	10	33
7	Do. Cum. Pref.	10	17½
3/	Do. Gua. Shs.	5	7½
4½	Do. Mt. Db. Stk., Red.	100	—
4	Simonds, L., 1 D. Sk., Rd.	100	109
5½	Simson & McP., L., Cu. Pf.	10	9½
4½	Do. 1 Mt. Deb. Stk.	100	100
5/	Smith, Garrett, L., £20 Shs	10	16½
5	Do. Cum. Pref.	20	26
—	Do. 3½ p.c. Mt. Db. Stk.	100	109
5	Smith's, Tadcster, L., CPf	10	12
4½	Do. Deb. Stk., Red.	100	112
4	Do. Deb. Stk. Red.	100	108
4½	Star, L., 1 M. Db. Stk., Rd.	100	105
4	Steward & P., L., 1 D. Sk.	100	113
9/	Strettons Derby, Ltd.	10	13
6	Do. Cum. Pref.	10	13
4	Do. Irr. 1 Mt. Db. Stk.	100	103½
4½	Strong, Romsey, L., 1 D.S.	100	115
5	Stroud, L., Db. Sk., Rd.	100	111½
4½	Tadcaster To'er, L., D.Sk.	100	113
8/	Tamplin, Ltd	10	21½
6	Do. Cum. Pref.	100	15
4	Do. "A" Db. Sk., Rd.	10	107
6	Thorne, Ltd., Cum. Pref.	10	14½
4	Do. Deb. Stk., Red.	100	106½
15/	Threlfall, Ltd.	10	47
6	Do. Cum. Pref.	10	16½
5	Do. 1 Mt. Dbs., Red.	100	116
4	Tollemache, L., D. Sk. Rd.	100	105
4	Truman, Hanb., D. Sk., R.	100	110
3	Do. "B" Mt. Db. Sk., Rd.	100	95
10/	United States, Ltd.	10	10
8	Do. Cum. Pref.	10	12
6	Do. 1 Mt. Deb	100	107½
6/	Walker & H., Ld., Cm. Prf.	10	11½
4½	Do. 1 Mt. Deb. Stk., Red.	100	107
5	Walker, Peter, Ld. Cm. Prf.	10	14
4	Do. 1 Mt. Dbs. Red.	100	111
4	Wallingford, L., D.Sk. Rd.	100	107
6	Watney, Ld., Cm. Prf. Sk.	100	170
5	Do. Mt. Db. Sk., Rd.	100	117½
4½	Do. "B" Mt. Db. Sk., Rd.	100	111
3½	Do. Mt. Db. Stk.	100	101
5	Watney, D., Ld., Cm. Prf.	10	12½
4½	Do. 1 Mt. Db. Stk.	100	108
10/	Webster & Sons, Ltd.	10	16½
6	Do. Cum. Pref.	10	14
5	Wenlock Ltd., Pref.	10	12½
4	Do. 1 Mt. Db. Sk., Rd.	100	108
5	West Cheshire, L., Cu. Pf.	10	10½
4	Do. Irred. 1 Mt. Db. Sk.	100	100
4½	Whitbread, L., Cu. Pf. Sh.	100	124½
4	Do. Db. Stk., Red.	100	112
3½	Do. "B" Db. Stk., Rd.	100	100
9/	Wolverhmpton & D. Ld.	10	16½
6	Do. Cum. Pref.	10	13½
4½	Do. 1 Mt. Dbs., Red.	100	108
5½	Worthington, Ld., Cm. Prf.	10	15½
5½	Do. Cum. "B" Pref.	10	13½
4½	Do. Mt. Db. Sk., Rd.	100	113
3½	Do. Irr. "B" Db. Stk.	100	104
10/	Yates's Castle, Ltd	10	13½
5	Do. Cum. Pref.	10	11
5	Younger W., L., Cu. Pf. Sh.	100	135

CANALS AND DOCKS.

Last Div.	Name.	Paid.	Price.
4	Birmingham Canal	100	145½
—	E. & W. India Dock	100	21½
4	Do. Deb. Stk.	100	—
50/	Do. Def. Deb. Stk.	100	—
3½	Do. 1st Mt. Certs.	100	—
4	Do. Mt. Bds. (1885)	—	—
40/	G. Junction Ord. Shs.	100	151½
6/	Do. do. Pref.	10	19
4½	King's Lynn Per. Db. Stk.	100	117½
2½	Leeds & Lpool Canal	100	72
2½	Lndn & St. Kath. Dks.	100	57
4½	Do. Pref.	100	136½
4½	Do. Pref., 1878	100	132½
4½	Do. Pref., 1882	100	130
4	Do. Deb. Stk.	100	135
—	Mchester Ship C. 5 p.c. Pf.	10	1½
3½	Do. 1st Perp. Mt. Deb.	100	98
—	Milford Dks. Db. Stk. "A"	100	20
3½	Millwall Dk.	100	59
5	Do. Perp. Pref.	100	140½
4½	Do. Pref.	100	106½
5	Do. New Per. Prf., 1887	100	126½
5	Do. Per. Deb. Stk.	100	153½
4/	Newhaven Har.	10	14½
2½	N. Metropolitan	100	65
5	Sharpness Nw. Pf. "A" Sk.	100	144½
4	Do. Deb. Stk.	100	120½
4	Sheffield & S. Yorks Nav. 4½ p.c. Pref Stk.	100	117½
36.432	Suez Canal	20	137
5	Surrey Comcl. Dok., Ord.	100	143½
5	Do. Min. 4 p.c. Pref. "A"	100	152½
5	Do. Pref. "B"	100	150½
5	Do. do. "C"	100	130
5	Do. do. "D"	100	145½
4½	Do. Deb. Stk.	100	152½

COMMERCIAL, INDUSTRIAL, &c.

Last Div.	Name.	Paid.	Price.
5	Accles, L., 1 Mt. Db., Red.	100	84½
5/	Aërated Bread, Ltd.	1	12½
—	African Gold Recovery, L.	1	½
2/	Aluminium, L., "A" Shs.	1	2½
4½	Do. 1 Mt. Db. Stk., Red.	100	99
5½	Amelia Nitr., L., 1 Mort. Deb., Red.	100	82½
7/	Anglo-Chil. Nitrate, Ltd., Cum. Pref.	10	7½
4½	Do. Cons. Mt. Dbs., Red.	100	82½
4½	Anglo-Russian Cotton Ld., 1 Charge Debs., Red.	100	99
11/3	Angus (G., & Co., L.), £10	7½	17
6/	Apollinaris, Ltd.	10	11½
5/	Do. 5 p.c. Cum. Pref.	10	10½
4	Do. Irred. Deb. Stock	100	106
6/	Appleton, French, & S., L.	5	½
3/	Argentine Meat Pres., L., 7 p.c. Pref.	10	2½
5	Argentine Refinry, Db. Rd.	100	98
2/2	Armstrong, Whitw., Ltd.	1	3½
4	Do. Cum. Pref.	5	6½
5	Artisans', Labr. Dwllgs., L.	100	131½
4½	Do. Non-Cm. Prf., 1876	100	132½
4½	Do. do. 1884	100	132½
—	Asbestos & Asbestic, Ltd.	10	8
2/7½	Ashley-grdns., L., C. Prf.	5	6
4½	Do. 1 Mt. Deb. Stk.	100	112½
5/	Assam Rly. & Trdng., L., 8 p.c. Cum. Pref. "A"	10	15½
—	Do. Deferrd. "B" Shs.	1	4½
—	Do. do. (iss.f.pd)	1	3½
8/	Do. Cum. Pre-Prf. "A"	10	15
6/	Do. New Pref.	10	11½
5	Do. Debs., Red.	100	107
5	Do. Red. Mort. Debs.	100	111
6	Aust'lan Pastrl, L., Cu. Pf.	10	7½
6d.	Aylesbury Dairy, Ltd.	1	1½
4	Do. 4 p.c. Mt. Dbs.	100	104½
10/	Babcock & Wilcox, Ltd.	10	31
6	Do. 6 p.c. Cm. Prf.	10	16½
8	Baker (Chs.), L., Cm. Pf.	5	9
8	Do. "B" Cm. Pref.	5	8½
8d.	Barker (John), Ltd.	1	2½
5½	Do. Cum. Pref.	5	7½
4½	Do. Irred. 1 Mt. Db. Stk.	100	123
—	Barnagore Jute, Ltd.	5	3
5	Do. Cum. Pref.	5	4½
7½d.	Belgravia Dairy, Ltd.	1	1½
5/	Bell (R.) & Co., Ltd.	5	3½
1/	Bell's Asbestos, Ltd.	1	½
5	Do. Mt. Db. Bds., Rd.	100	103
10/	Bengal Mills, Ltd.	10	11½
6/	Do. 5 p.c. Cum. Prf.	10	10½
2/5	Benson (J. W.) L., Cm. Pf.	10	10½
12/4	Do. Perp. Mt. Db. Stk.	100	102½
6	Bergvik, L., 6 p.c. Cm. Pf.	10	12½
10/	Do. Dfd.	10	10
4½	Do. 1 Dbs., Red.	100	103½
5/	Birm'ham Vinegar, Ltd.	5	10
5	Do. Cum. Pref.	5	5½
4½	Do. 1 Mt. Db. Stk., Rd.	100	108½
5	Boake (A.) L., 5 p.c. Cu. Pf.	10	10½
2/6	Bodega, Ltd.	5	8½
4½	Do. Mt. Deb. Stk., Rd.	100	111
8/	Bottomley & Brs., Ltd.	10	6½
6/	Do. 6 p.c. Pf.	10	9½
8½d.	Bovril, Ltd.	1	1
1/0½	Do. Def.	1	1½
6½d	Do. Cum. Pref.	1	1
4½	Do. Deb. Stk.	100	103
5/	Bradbury, Gretrex., Ltd., £10 share	8	14
5/	Do. 5 p.c. Cum. Pref.	10	13½
5/	Brewers' Sugar, L., 5 p.c. Cum. Pref.	10	10½
—	Brighton Grd. Hotel, Ld.	5	3½
4	Do. Mt. Db. Stk., Red.	100	102½
5	Bristol Hotel & Palm. Co., Ltd. 1st Mt. Red. Deb.	100	106
9½d.	British & Bengton's Tea Tr. Asc., Ltd.	1	1½
5	Do. Cum. Prf.	5	5½
—	British Deli & Lgkat. Tobacco, Ltd.	1	½
—	Do. Cum. Prf.	1	½
—	British Tea Table, Ltd.	1	2½
5½	Do. Cum. Pref.	1	1½
2/6	Brooke, Ben., & Co., Ltd., Cum. Pref.	5	5½
7/6	Brooke, Bond & Co., Ltd.	5	20½
6/	Brown Brs., L., Cum. Pref.	5	6
10	Browne & Eagle, Ltd.	10	13½
5	Do. Cum. Pref.	10	13
4	Do. Mrt. Db. Sk., Red.	100	109
20/	Brunner, Mond, & Co., Lt.	10	42
7/	Do. £10 shares	3½	17
7	Do. Cum. Pref.	10	18
7	Do. £10 shares	5	8½
10/	Bryant & May, Ltd.	5	19½
2/	Bucknall, H., & Sons, Lt.	5	8
6	Do. Cum Pref.	5	8½
4/	Burke, E. & J., Ltd.	5	7½
6	Do. Cum. Pref.	5	7½
6	Do. Irred. Deb. Stk.	100	155
1/	Burlington Htls. Co., Ld.	1	1½
5	Do. Cum. Pref.	1	1½
4	Do. Perp. Deb. Stk.	100	105½
2/4	Bush, W. J., & Co., Ltd Cum. Pref.	5	5½
36/3	Do. 1 Deb. Stk., Red.	100	104
5½	Callard, Stewart, & Watt Ltd., Cum. Pref.	1	1½
4/	Callender's Cable L., Shs.	5	9½
4½	Do. 1 Deb. Stk., Red.	100	111½
—	Campbell, R., & Sons, Lt.	3	2½
6	Cantareira Water, Bd., Rd	100	99½
5	Do. (2nd issue)	100	92
4	Cartavio Sugar, Ltd., 6 p.c. 1st Debs., Red.	20	83½
4/6	Cassell & Co., Ltd., £10	9	17
5	Causton, Sir J., & Sons Ltd., Cum. Pref.	10	13½

Commercial, &c. (*continued*) :—

Last Div.	Name.	Paid.	Price.
4	Cent. Prod. Mkt. of B.A. 1st Mt. Str. Debs.	100	81
4	Chappell & Co., Ltd., Mt. Deb. Stk. Red	100	103
6/	Chicago & N.W. Gran. 8 p.c. Cum. Pref.	10	3
—	Chicago Packing & Prov.	10	6
8	Do. Cum. Pref.	10	10½
6/	City Offices, Ltd	36½	13
3½	Do. Mt. Deb. Stk.	100	108½
7/2½	Cy. London Real Prop., Ltd., £25 shs.	12	19
4/6	Do. £12½ shs.	7½	13½
3½	Do. Deb. Stk. Red.	100	108½
3½	Do. Deb. Stk. Red.	100	106½
3	Do.	100	101½
4/	Cy. of Santos Imprvts., Ltd., 7 p.c. Pref.	10	8½
20/	Clay, Bock, & Co., Ltd.	10	6
8	Do. Cum. Pref.	10	10
6	Do. Mort. Deb.	100	105½
20/	Coats, J. & P., Ltd.	10	61
6	Do. Cum. Pref.	10	18
4½	Do. Deb. Stk. Red.	100	112½
9½d.	Coburg Hotel, Ltd	1	1½
4	Do. Deb. Stk. Red.	100	102
6	Colonial Consign & Dis., Ltd., Cum. Pref.	5	4½
4½	Do. 1st Mort. Debs.	100	97½
—	Colorado Nitrate, Ltd.	5	½
4/	Co. Gén. des Asphtes. de F., Ltd	6	6½
5	Do, Non-Cm. Prf.	—	5½
5	Cook, J. W., & Co., Ltd., Cum. Pref	5	5½
5	Cook, T., & Son, Egypt, Ltd., 1st Mt. Deb. Red.	100	110½
—	Cork Co., Ltd., 6 p.c. Cum. Pref.	5	2½
5	Cory, W., & Sn, L., Cu. Pf.	5	6½
4	Do. 1st Deb. Stk. Red.	100	109
8½d.	Crisp & Co., Ltd	1	1½
5½	Do. Cum. Pref.	1	1½
—	Crompton & Co., Ltd., 7 p.c. Cum. Pref.	5	2½
5	Do. 1st Mt. Reg. Deb.	—	88½
4/6	Crossley, J., & Sons, Ltd.	5	8½
5	Do. Cum. Pref.	5	6½
—	Crystal Pal. Ord. "A" Stk.	100	8½
—	Do. "B" Red. Stk	100	1½
6	Do. 6 p.c. 1st 1887 Deb. Stk. Red.	100	117½
—	Do. 6 p.c. 2nd 1887 Deb. Stk. Red.	100	46½
—	Do. 6 p.c. 3rd 1887 Deb. Stk. Red.	100	17½
3	Do. 3 p.c. 1st 1895 Deb. Stk.	100	94½
—	Daimler Motor, Ltd.	10	6
4/	Dalgety & Co., £20 Shs.	5	5½
4½	Do. Deb. Stk.	100	123
4	Do.	100	115
7/	De Keyser's Ryl. Htl., L.	10	14
5	Do. Cum. Pref.	10	11½
4	Do. Deb. Stk., Red.	100	110
6	Denny, H., & Sons, Ltd., Cum. Pref.	10	14½
5/3	Devas, Routledge & Co., L.	7	6½
5	Dickinson, J., & Co., L., Cum. Pref. Stk.	100	123
4½	Domin. Cottn. Mls., Ltd. Mt. Stg. Dbs.	100	97
6/	Dorman, Long & Co., L.	5	4½
—	Eastmans, Ltd	10	3
12/	Do. 8 p.c. Cum. Pref.	10	10½
2/6	E. C. Powder, Ltd	3	5½
1/6	Edison & Swn Utd. Elec. Ltd., "A" £5 Shs.	3	2½
2/6	Do. fully-paid	5	4½
4½	Ekman Pulp & Ppr. Co., Ltd., Mt. Deb., Red.	100	95
1/1½	Electric Construc., Ltd.	2	2½
7	Do. Cum. Pref.	2	3½
2½/	Eley Bros., Ltd.	10	39
—	Elmore's Cop. Deptg., L.	1	½
—	Elmore's Wire Mnfg., L.	2	½
—	Elysée Pal. Hotel Co., L.	5/	½
5 p.c.	Do. 5 p.c. £100 Db., Rd.	70	70
8½d.	Evans, Ben., & Co., Ltd.	1	1
5	Do. 1 Mt. Db. Sk., Rd.	100	105
8½d.	Evans, D. H., & Co., L.	1	2½
6	Do. Cum. Pref.	1	1½
4½	Do. 1 Mt. Db. Sk., Rd.	100	113
2/1	*Evening News*, L., 5 p.c. Cum. Pref.	5	5½
5/3	Evered & Co., L., £10 Sh.	7	13
7/6	Do.	10	19
4	Fairbairn Pastoral Co., Aust., L., 1 Mt. Db., Rd.	100	102
6	Fairfield Shipbldg., Ltd., Cum. Pref.	10	10
4½	Do. Mort. Deb. Stk.	100	107½
6/	Farmer & Co., Ld., 6 p.c. Cum. Pref.	10	13½
10	Field, J. C. & J., Ltd.	10	10
14/	Do. 7 p.c. Cum. Pref.	10	14
9d.	Fordham, W. B., & Sns, Ld.	1	2
5/6	Fore-st. Warehouse, Ltd.	11	9½
4	Do. Regd. Debs., Rd.	100	103½
2/6	Foster, M. B. & Sons, Ltd.	4	6½
5	Do. Pref.	10	11½
9/	Foster, Porter, & Co., L.	10½	16½
4	Fowler, J., & Co. (Leeds), Ltd., 1 Mt. Deb., Red.	100	103½
3/	Fraser & Chalmers, Ltd.	3	1½
4½	Free, Rodwell & Co., Ltd., Deb Stk.	100	105½
6½d.	Furness, T., & Co., Ltd., 5½ p.c. Cum. Pref.	1	1
4½	Garside & Co. (of Manchstr), L., 1 Mt. Db. Sk.	100	110
11	Genl. Hydraul Power, L.	100	275

Commercial, &c. (*continued*):—

Last Div.	Name.	Paid.	Price.
8/	Gillman & Spencer, Ltd.	5	2½
6	Do. Pref.	5	5
5	Do. Mort. Debs.	50	51
4	Goldahren, Mort & Co., L., "A" Deb. Stk., Red.	100	74½
—	Do. 3 p.c. "B" Inc. Deb. Stk., Red.	100	17
8/	Gordon Hotels, Ltd.	10	20½
5½	Do. Cum. Pref.	10	14½
4½	Do. Perp. Deb. Stk.	100	137½
4	Do. do.	100	122½
—	Greenwich Inld. Linoleum Co., Ltd.	1	¾
7	Greenwood & Batley, Ltd., Cum. Pref.	10	10
7½d.	Hagemann & Co., Ltd., 6 p.c. Cum. Pref.	1	1½
—	Hammond, Ltd.	10	¾
—	Do. 8 p.c. Cum. Pref.	10	2¾
—	Do. 6 p.c. Cum. Inc. Stk. Red.	100	52½
4	Hampton & Sons, Ltd., 4 p.c. 1 Mt. Db. St. Red.	100	105
	Hans Crescent Htl., L., 6 p.c. Cum. Pref.	5	3
4	Do. 1 Mt. Deb. Stk.	100	85
5	Harmsworth, Ld., Cm. Pf.	1	1⅛
4/	Harrison, Barber, Ltd.	5	4½
3/	Harrod's Stores, Ltd.	1	4¾
2/6	Do. Cum. Pref.	5	7
5½	Hawaiian Comcl. & Sug.		
5	1 Mt. Debs.	100	94½
	Hazell, Watson, L., C. P.	10	12
6/	Henley's Teleg., Ltd.	10	23½
7	Do. Pref. Shs.	10	19½
4½	Do. Mt. Db. Stk., Rd.	100	112½
6	Henry, Ltd.	10	12½
5	Do. Cum. Pref.	10	13½
4½	Do. Mt. Debs., Red.	50	53
6	Hepworth, Ld., Cm. Prf.	10	11½
—	Herrmann, Ltd.	1	¾
—	Hildesheimer, Ltd.	3	1½
9½d	Holborn. & Frasca, Ltd.	1	2½
5	Do. Cum. Pref.	10	12½
4	Do. Deb. Stk.	100	113
6	Home & Col. Stres, L., C. P	5	7½
6	Hood & M.'s Stres., Ltd., Cum. Pref.	1	¼
—	Hook, C. T. Ltd.	10	6
7/2	Hornsby, Ltd., £10 Shs.	8	3½
3/6	Do. 6 p.c. Cm. Pf. Sk.	100	90
—	Horchks. Ordn., Ltd.	10	1
—	Do. 7 p.c. Cm. Prf.	10	4
5	Do. 1 Mt. Dbs., Rd.	100	95½
6	Htl. Cecil, Ld., Cm. Prf.	5	4½
4	Do. 1 Mt. D. Sk., R.	100	107½
8/	Howard & Bulgh, Ltd.	10	40
6	Do. Pref.	10	16
4	Do. Deb. Stk., Red.	100	107
5/	Howell, J., Ltd., £5 Shs.	4	9½
—	Howell & Js., Ld., £3½ Shs.	3	¾
1/6	Humber, Ltd.	1	[illegible]
6	Do. Cum. Pref.	1	[illegible]
2/6	Hunter, Wilts., Ltd.	5	7½
2/7	Hyam Clthg., Ltd., 5 p.c. Cum. Pref.	5	5½
10/	Impl. Russn. Cotton, L.	5	6
5	Impd. Industl. Dwgs., Ld.	100	130½
6d.	Do. Defrd.	1	1½
25/	Impd. Wood Pave., Ltd.	10	15
15/	Ind. Rubber, Gutta Per. Telegraph Works, Ltd.	10	22
4	Do. 1 Mt. Debs., Red.	100	105
6	Intern. Tea, Cum. Pref.	5	6½
7½d.	Jays, Ltd.	1	1½
5½	Do. Cum. Pref.	5	6½
8½d.	Jones & Higgins, Ltd.	1	2½
4½	Do. 1 Mt. Db. Sk., Rd.	100	113
5/	Kelly's Directory, Ltd., 5 p.c. Cum. Pref.	10	12½
4	Do. Mort. Db. Sk., Rd.	100	105
—	Kent Coal Explrtn. Ltd.	1	¾
9½d.	King, Howmann, Ltd.	1	1½
4/	Kinloch & Co., Ltd.	5	8½
6	Do. Pref.	5	7
5	Lady's Pictorial Pub., Ltd., Cum. Pref.	5	5
—	La Guaira Harb., Ltd., 7 p.c. Deb. Stk.	100	—
—	Do. 2 Mt. 7 p.c. Deb. Bds., Red.	100	—
4/	Lagunas Nitrate, Ltd.	5	2
2/	Lagunas Syn., Ltd.	5	1⅛
5	Do. 1 Mt. Debs., Red.	100	80
—	L. Copais Ld., 1 Mt. 6 p.c. Debs., Red.	100	35½
3/	Lautaro Nitrate, Ltd.	5	4½
5	Do. 1 Mt. Debs., Red.	—	100
9/	Lawes Chem. L., £10 shs.	9	5½
14/	Do. N. Cm. Min. Pref.	10	13
—	Leeds Forge, 7 p.c. Cm. Pf.	5	3½
5	Do. 1 Mt. Debs., Red.	50	47½
5	Lever Bros., L., Cm. Pf.	10	13½
6	Liberty, L., 6 p.c. Cm. Pf.	10	15
20/	Liebig's, Ltd.	20	75
5	Lilley & Sk., L., Cm. Pf.	5	5½
39/4	Linoleum Manftg., Ltd.	5	16
3/	Linotype, Ltd., Pref.	5	6
4/	Do. Def.	5	7½
4/	Lister & Co., Ltd.	10	4
5	Do. Cum. Pref.	10	8½
5/	Liverpool Nitrate	5	5½
—	Liverpool Warehsg., Ltd	10	3½
5½	Do. Cum. Pref.	10	8½
4	Do. 1 Mt. Db. Stk., Rd.	100	107
5½	Lockharts, Ltd., Cm. Pf.	1	1½
4/6	Ldn. & Til. Lightrage £10	9	6½
6/	Ldn. Comcl. Sale Rms., L.	10	17½
—	Do. 1 Mt. Deb. Stk., Red.	100	104
3	London Nitrate, Ltd.	5	2
4/	London Nitrate, Ld. 8 p.c. Cm. Min. Pf.	5	3½
8/	London Pavilion, Ltd.	5	7

Commercial, &c. (*continued*):—

Last Div.	Name.	Paid.	Price.
2/6	London Produce Clg. Ho., Ltd., £10 Shares	2½	3½
4/	London Stereos., Ltd.	5	3
6d.	Ldn. Un. Laun. L. Cm. Pf.	1	¾
8½d.	Louise, Ltd.	1	¾
5½	Do. Cum. Pref.	1	¾
5/	Lovell & Christmas, Ltd.	5	11½
6	Do. Cum. Pref.	5	7½
4	Do. Mt. Deb. Stk., Red.	100	107
1/3	Lyons, Ltd.	1	3½
4½	Do. 1 Mt. Deb., Stk., Rd.	100	110½
10/	Machinery Trust, Ltd.	5	15
4½	Do. 4½ Deb. Stk.	100	106
6	MacLellan, L., Min. C. Pf.	10	8
5	Do. 1 Mt. Debs., 1900	100	101½
—	McEwan, J. & Co., Ltd.	10	1½
6	Do. Mt. Debs., Red.	100	89½
8	McNamara, L., Cm. Pref.	10	9
7½d.	Maison Virot, Ltd.	1	1½
2/7	Do. 6 p.c. Cum. Pref.	5	4½
4/	Manbré Sacc., L., Cm. Pf.	10	12
10/	Mangan Brze., L., £10 Shs.	6	15½
2/	Mason & Mason, Ltd.	5	3
6	Do. Cum. Pref.	5	5½
—	Maynards, Ltd.	1	¾
6	Do. Cum. Pref.	1	¾
9½d.	Mazawattee Tea, Ltd.	1	1½
5	Do. Cum. Pref.	5	5½
6	Mellin's Food Cum. Pref.	5	7
4½	Met. Ascn. Imp. Dwlgs. L.	100	110
3½	Do. 1 Mt. Deb. Stk.	100	97
5	Metro. Indus. Dwlgs., Ltd.	5	5
4	Do. do. Cum. Pref.	5	5½
5	Metro. Prop., L., Cm. Pf.	5	6½
4½	Do. 1st Mt. Debs. Stk.	100	100½
6	Mexican Cotton 1 Mt Db.	100	96½
4½	Mid. Class Dwlgs., L., Db.	100	120½
1/	Millars' Karri, Ltd.	1	2½
6	Do. Cum. Pref.	1	1½
5/	Milner's Safe, Ltd.	10	20½
20/	Moir & Son, Ltd., Pref.	5	8½
6	Morgan Cruc., L., Cm. Pf.	10	15
2/	Morris, B., Ltd.	3½	3½
—	Murray L. 5½ p.c. C. Pf.	5	6½
—	Do. 4½ 1 Mt. Db. Sk. Rd.	100	108
—	Natnl. Dwlgs., L., 5 p.c. Pf.	5	1
1/7½	Nat. Safe Dep., Ltd.	4	3½
6	Do. Cum. Pref.	1	1½
—	Native Guano, Ltd.	5	¾
—	Nelson Bros., Ltd.	10	2½
5	Do. Deb. Stk., Red.	100	80½
4/	Neuchtel Asph., Ltd.	10	11
—	New Central Borneo, Ld.	1	—
10d.	New Darvel Tob., Ltd.	18/	1½
—	New Explosives, Ltd.	3	2½
5/7½	New Gd. Htl., Bham, L.	5	4
5½	Do. Pref.	5	4½
4	Do. 1 Mt. Db. Stk., Rd.	100	96½
—	New Julia Nitrate, Ltd.	10/	¼
—	New Ldn. Borneo Tob., L.	16/	¾
1/6	New Premier Cycle, Ltd.	1	¾
6	Do. 6 p.c. Cum. Pref.	1	¾
4½	Do. 4½ p.c. 1 Mt. Db. Rd	100	—
—	New Tamargl. Nitr., Ltd	1	⅛
—	Do. 8 p.c. Cum. Pref.	1	⅜
6	Do. 6 p.c. 1 Mt. Dbs. Rd.	100	65½
3·78d.	Newnes, G., L., Cm. Prf.	1	1½
1/3	Nitr. Provision, Ltd.	2½	¾
24/	Nobel-Dynam., Ltd.	10	17½
—	North Brazn. Sugar, Ltd.	1	¾
10/	Oakey, Ltd.	10	32
6	Do. Cum. Pref.	10	17
—	Paccha Jarp. Nitr., Ltd.	5	¾
5	Pac. Borax, L., 1 Db. Rd.	100	110
—	Palace Hotel, Ltd.	10	5½
5½	Do. Cum. Pref.	10	8½
4	Do. 1 Mt. Deb. Stk.	100	104
2/6	Palmer, Ltd.	5	1½
6	Do. Cum. Pref.	5	3
9½d.	Paquin, Ltd.	1	1
6	Do. Cum. Pref.	5	4½
5½	Parnall, Ltd., Cum. Pref.	1	¾
4/6	Pawsons, Ltd., £10 Shs.	6	6½
4	Do. Mt. Debs., Red.	100	107
6	Pearks, G. & T., Ltd., 6 p.c. Cum. Pref.	1	¾
1/2½	Pears, Ltd.	1	1½
6	Do. Cum. Pref.	10	14
5	Do. Deb. Stk.	100	129
5½	Pearson, C. A., L., Cu. Pf.	5	5½
4/3	Peebles, Ltd.	5	8
5	Do. Cum. Pref.	5	6½
4½	Do. Mt. Deb. Stk. Red.	100	113½
5½	Peek Bros., Ltd., 1 Cum. Pref., Nos. 1-60,000	5	6½
3½	Do. 3½ p.c. 1 Db. Stk.	100	103½
7½d.	Pegamoid, Ltd.	1	¾
—	Phospho-Guano, Ltd.	5	2½
—	Pillsbury-W. Fl. Mills, L.	10	2
16/	Do. 8 p.c. Cum. Pref.	10	6½
6	Do. 1 Mort. Debs.	100	95½
7½d.	Plummer, Ltd.	1	1½
5	Do. Cum. Pref.	5	5
15/	Price's Candle, Ltd.	16	39
6	Priest Marians, L., Cm. Pf.	1	1½
6	Pryce Jones, Ld., Cm. Pf.	5	7½
5	Do. Deb. Stk.	100	120½
10.8d.	Pullman, Ltd.	1	1½
6d.	Do. Cum. Pref.	1	1½
1 1/10	Raleigh Cycle, Ltd.	1	¾
6	Do. Cum. Pref.	1	¾
—	Recife Drnge. Ld. 1 Mt. Debs., R	100	19
6	Redfern, Ltd. Cum. Prf.	10	14
5	Ridgways, Ltd., Cu. Pf.	5	5½
—	R. Janeiro Cy. Imps., Ld.	25	10½
5	Do. Debs.	100	89½
5	Do. 1882-1893	100	88½
11/	R. Jan Fl. Mills, Ltd.	7	6½
5	Do. 1 Mt. Debs., Rd.	100	94
—	Riv. Plate Meat, Ltd.	5	3½
—	Do. Pref.	5	5
8½d.	Roberts, J. R., Ltd.	1	1½

Commercial, &c. (*continued*):—

Last Div.	Name.	Paid.	Price.
5	Roberts 1 Mt. D. Sk., Rd.	100	112
8½d.	Roberts, T. R., Ltd.	1	2½
5	Do. Cum. Pref.	1	1½
3/	Rosario Nit., Ltd.	5	3½
5	Do. Debs., Red.	100	105
5	Do. Huara, Debs.	—	104
1/	Rover Cycle, Ltd.	1	¾
6/	Ryl. Aquarium, Ltd.	5	4½
6	Do. Pref.	5	6
5	Ryl. Htl., Edin., Cm. Pf.	1	1½
1/2½	Ryl. Niger, Ltd., £10 Sh.	2	2½
6/	Do.	10	14½
—	Russian Petroleum	10	22½
—	Do. 6½ p.c. Cm. Prf.	10	11½
3/	Ruston, Proctor, Ltd.	10	11
4½	Do. 1 Mort. Debs.	100	104
6/	Sadler, Ltd.	12	7
—	Sal. Carmen Nit., Ltd.	5	4½
9d.	Salmon & Gluck., Ltd.	1	1½
	Salt Union, Ltd.	10	1½
1½	Do. 7 p.c. Pref.	10	6
4½	Do. Deb. Stk.	100	99½
4½	Do. "B" Deb. Sk., Rd.	100	97½
—	San Donato Nit., Ltd.	5	¾
2/6	San Jorge Nit., Ltd.	5	3½
—	San Pablo Nit., Ltd.	5	¾
—	San Sebastn. Nit., Ltd.	5	¾
1/9	Sanitas, Ltd	1	2½
—	Sa. Elena Nit., Ltd.	5	¾
—	Sa. Rita Nit., Ltd.	5	2
10/	Savoy Hotel, Ltd.	10	16
7	Do. Pref.	10	15
4	Do. 1 Mt. Deb. Stk.	100	112½
5	Do. Debs., Red	100	102½
5	Do. & Ldn. For. Htl., Ltd., 5 p.c. Debs. Red.	100	99
1½d.	Schweppes, Ltd.	1	1⅛
—	Do. Def.	1	¾
5	Do. Cum. Pref.	1	1½
4	Do. Deb. Stk.	100	109
1/	Singer Cyc., Ltd.	1	¾
5½	Do. Cum. Pref.	1	¾
—	Smokeless Pwdr., Ltd.	1	¼
5½d.	S. Eng. Dairies, Ltd., 6 p.c. Cum. Pref.	1	1½
—	Sowler Thos. L.	1	1½
—	Do. 5½ Cm. Pf.	5	5½
3/6	Spencer, Turner, & Co. Ltd	5	9
5	Do. Cum. Pref.	5	6½
5	Spicer, Ld., 5 p.c. Dbs. Rd.	100	65
4/	Spiers & Pond, Ltd.	10	20
5	Do. 1 Mt. Debs., Red.	100	116½
5	Do. "A" Db. Stk., Rd.	100	110
5	Do. "B" 1 Db. Stk., Rd.	100	110
4	Do. Fd. "C" 1 Db. S., R.	100	103
5/	Spratt's, Ltd	5	13½
4	Do. Debs., 1914	—	105
5	Steiner Ld., Cm. Pf.	10	11½
4	Do. 1 Mt. Db. Sk. Rd.	100	106
7/	Stewart & Clydesdale, L.	10	14½
6	Do. Cum. Pref.	10	15½
35/5	Sulphide Corp.	100	80
—	Swan & Edgar, L.	1	1½
1/	Sweetmeat Automatic, L.	1	4
2/9	Teetgen, Ltd., Cum. Pref.	5	6
12/	Teleg. Construction., Ld.	12	38½
5	Do. Db. Bds., Rd., 1899	100	103½
3/0½	Tilling, Ld. 5½ p.c. Cm. Prf.	5	6½
4	Do. 4 p.c. 1 Dbs., Rd.	—	104
8½d.	Tower Tea, Ltd.	1	1½
5	Do. Cum. Pref.	5	5½
5	Travers, Ltd., Cum. Pref.	10	12½
4	Do. 1 Mt. Dbs., Rd.	100	106
6	Tucuman Sug., 1 Dbs., Rd.	100	100
4/	United Alkali, Ltd.	10	1½
7	Do. Cum. Pref.	10	9
5	Do. Mt. Db. Stk., Rd.	100	109½
2½d.	United Horse Shoe, Ltd., Non-Cum. 8 p.c. Pref.	1	¼
5	Un. Kingm. Tea, Cm. Prf.	5	4½
2/	Un. Lankat Plant., Ltd.	1	2½
2/	Un. Limmer Asphlte., Ld.	3	5
5/	Val de Travers Asph., L.	10	15
3/	V. den Bergh's, L., Cm. P.	5	6½
6	Walkers, Park., L., C. Pf.	10	4
4½	Do. 1 Mt. Debs., Red.	100	90½
6/	Wallis, Thos. & Co., Ltd.	5	14
6	Do. Cum. Pref.	5	8½
5½	Waring, Ltd., Cum. Pref.	5	5½
4½	Do. 1 Mt. Db. Sk., Red.	100	111½
4½	Do. Irred. "B" Db. Stk.	100	104
12/	Waterlow, Dfd. Ord.	10	15½
12/	Do. Pref.	10	15
—	Do. Cum. Pref.	10	10½
10/	Waterlow Bros. & L., Ld.	10	9
5	Do. Pref.	10	12
1/2½	Welford, Ltd.	1	2
4½	Do. Debs., Red.	100	108
1/	Welford's Surrey Dairies, Ltd.	1	1½
7½d.	West London Dairy, Ltd.	1	1
4½	Wharncliffe Dwllgs., L., Pf.	10	11½
18/10	Do. 3 p.c. Irr. Mt. Db. Sk.	100	96
6d.	White, A. J., Ltd.	1	¾
6	Do. 6 p.c. Cum. Pref.	1	¾
4	White, J. Bazley, Ltd., 1 Mort. Debs., Red.	100	96½
5	White, R., Ltd., 1 Mort. Deb. Stock, Red.	100	104½
5/	White, Tomkins, Ltd.	10	12½
5	Do. Cum. Pref.	10	12
6	White, W. N., L., Cm. Pf.	1	1
2/6	Wickens, Pease & Co., L.	5	2½
6	Wilkie, Ltd., Cum. Pref.	10	16
3/6	Willans & Robinson, Ltd	5	8½
6	Do. Cum. Pref.	5	7½
4½	Do. 1 Mt. Db. Stk., Red.	100	107
7½d.	Williamsons, L., Cm. Prf.	1	1½
6	Winterbottm. Book Cloth Ltd., Cum. Prf.	10	15
3/	Yates, Ltd.	5	¾
6	Do. Cum. Pref.	5	5½
	Young's Paraffin, Ltd	4	1½

CORPORATION STOCKS—COLONIAL AND FOREIGN.

Per Cent.	Name.	Paid.	Price.
6	Auckland City, '72 1904-24	100	118
6	Do. Cons., '79, Red. 1930	100	138½
5	Do. Deb. Ln., '83..1934-8	100	117
6	Auckland Harb. Debs.	100	111½
5	Do. 1917	100	112
5	Do. 1936	100	116
5½	Balmain Boro' 1914	—	117
5	Boston City (U.S.)	100	102½
5	Do. 1902	100	107½
5	Brunswick Town 5. c. Debs. 1916-20	100	111
15/	B. Ayres City 6 p.c.	100	61
4½	Do. 4½ p.c.	100	77
5	Cape Town, City of	100	113
4	Do. 1943	100	116
4	Chicago, City of, Gold 1915	—	110
6	Christchurch 1926	100	130½
—	Cordoba City	100	17½
5	Duluth (U.S.) Gold 1926	—	110
6	Dunedin (Otago) 1925	100	127½
6	Do. 1906	100	113
5	Do. Consols 1908	100	113
4	Durban Insc. Stk. 1944	100	111
4	Essex Cnty., N. Jersey 1926	$100	114½
5	Fitzroy, Melbrne. 1916-19	100	110
5	Gisborne Harbour 1915	100	110½
4	Greymouth Harbour 1925	100	110
4	Hamilton 1934	100	110
5	Hobart Town 1918-30	100	116
4	Do. 1940	100	107
4½	Invercargill Boro. Dbs. 1936	100	113
6	Kimberley Boro., S.A. Dbs.	—	104
4	Launceston Twn. Dbs. 1916	100	107
6	Lyttleton, N.Z., Harb. 1929	100	125
4	Melbourne Bd. of Wks. 1921	100	109
5	Melb. City Debs. 1897-1907	100	107½
4½	Do. Debs. 1908-27	100	113½
4	Do. Debs. 1915-20-22	100	108
5	Melbne. Harb. Bds., 1908-9	100	112
4½	Do. do. 1915	100	110
4	Do. do. 1918-21	100	106
4½	Melbrne. Tms. Dbs. 1914-16	100	113
4½	Do. Fire Brig. Db. 1921	100	109
5	Mexico City Stg.	100	91½
4	Moncton N. Bruns. City	100	104
4½	Montevideo	100	58
5	Montreal Stg.	100	104
5	Do. 1874	100	104
5	Do. 1879	100	106
3½	Do. 1933	100	104
3	Do. Perm. Deb. Stk	100	98½
4	Do. Cons. Deb. Stk. 1932	100	113
6	Napier Boro. Consolid. 1914	100	119
5	Napier Harb. Debs. 1920	100	115
5	Do. Debs. 1928	100	107
6	New Plymouth Harb. Debs. 1909	100	108
6	New York City 1901	—	107½
3½	Do. 1910-26	—	105½
4½	Nth. Melbourne Debs. 1-600 1921	100	105
5	Oamaru Boro. Cons. 1920	100	101
6	Do. Harb. Bds. (Reg.)	100	74
25/	Do. 6 p.c. (Bearer) 1919	100	35
6	Otago Harb. Deb. Reg.	100	103
6	Do. 1877	100	107
6	Do. 1881 1921	100	115
5	Do. Debs. 1921	100	107
5	Do. Cons. 1934	100	105
6	Ottawa City	100	111
6	Do. 1904	100	115½
4½	Do. Debs. 1913	100	112
6	Port Elizabeth Waterworks	100	113½
5	Port Louis	100	111
5	Prahran Debs. 1917	100	111
4	Do. Debs. 1919	100	103
6	Quebec C. Coupon. 1875 1905	100	112
6	Do. do. 1878 1908	100	116
4½	Do. Debs. 1914-18	100	108
4	Do. Debs. 1923	100	108
3½	Do. Cns. Rg. Stk., Red.	100	101
5	Richmond (Melb.) Dbs. 1917	100	113
4	Rio Janeiro City	100	59
4	Rome City	100	—
4	Do. and to 8th Iss.	100	94
—	Rosario C.	100	26½
—	Do.	100	26½
4	St. Catherine (Ont.) 1926	100	101
4	St. John, N.B., Debs. 1934	—	103
4½	St. Kilda (Melb) Dbs. 1918-21	100	105
4	St. Louis C. (Miss.) 1911	100	106
4	Do. 1913	100	106
3·65	Do. 1915	—	110
—	Santa Fé City Debs.	100	21
6	Santos City	100	96
6	Sofia City	100	86
5	Sth. Melbourne Debs. 1915	100	111
4½	Do. Debs. 1919	100	107
5	Sydney City 1904	100	109
4	Do. Debs. 1912-13	100	107
4	Do. do. (1894) 1919	100	109
7	Timaru Boro. 7 p.c. 1910	100	126½
5	Timaru Harb. Debs 1914	100	106
5	Do. Debs. 1916	100	106
6	Toronto City Wtwks 1904-6	100	110
6	Do. Cons. Debs. 1898	100	101
5	Do. G. Cns. Dbs. 1919-20	100	118
4	Do. Stlg. 1922-8	100	107
4	Do. Local Improv.	100	102
3½	Do. 1929	100	105
5½	Valparaiso	100	101
4	Vancouver 1931	100	109
4	Do. 1932	100	108
6	Wanganui Harb. Dbs. 1905	100	110
6	Wellington Con. Deb. 1907	100	117
6	Do. Improv., 1879	100	123
6	Do. Wtrwks. Dbs., 1880	100	125
5	Do. Debs., 1893 1933	100	116
4	Wellington Harb. 1907	100	104
4½	Westport Harb. Dbs. 1925	100	110
5	Winnipeg City Deb. 1907	—	118
5	Do. 1914	100	118

FINANCIAL, LAND, AND INVESTMENT.

Last Div.	Name.	Paid.	Price.
5	Agency, Ld. & Fin. Aust., Ltd., Mt. Db. Stk., Rd.	100	90½
	Amer. Frehld. Mt. of Lon., Ld., Cum. Pref. Stk.	100	82½
4½	Do. Deb. Stk., Red.	100	93½
1/	Anglo-Amer. Db. Cor., L.	2	1
4	Do. Deb. Stk., Red	100	106½
5½	Ang.-Ceylon & Gen. Est., Ltd., Cons. Stk.	100	65
6	Do. Reg. Debs., Red.	100	106½
—	Ang.-Fch. Explorn., Ltd.	1	2¼
6	Do. Cum. Pref.	1	1½
—	Argent. Ld. & Inv., Ltd. £1 Shares	10/	nil
—	Do. Cum. Pref.	4	1¼
2/	Assets Fnders.' Sh., Ltd.	4	1½
6/	Assets Realiz., Ltd., Ord.	5	8¾
5	Do. Cum. Pref.	5	6¼
26/	Austrln. Agricl £25 Shs.	21½	63½
—	Aust. N. Z. Mort., Ltd., £10 Shs.	1	1½d.
4½	Do. Deb. Stk., Red.	100	90½
4	Do. Deb. Stk., Red.	100	82½
4½	Australian Est. & Mt., L., 1 Mt. Deb. Stk., Red.	100	106
5	Do. "A" Mort. Deb. Stk., Red.	100	97
2/6	Australian Mort., Ld., & Fin., Ltd. £25 Shs.	5	4½
1/6	Do. New, £25 Shs.	3	2½
4	Do. Deb. Stk	100	112
3	Do. Do.	100	85
5	Baring Est. 2 Mt. Debs., Red.	100	105
5	Bengal Presidy. 1 Mort. Deb., Red.	100	106
25/	British Amer. Ld. "A"	1	20
—	Do. "B"	24	6½
1/2½	Brit. & Amer. Mt., Ltd. £10 Shs.	2	¾
5/	Do. Pref.	10	10
4	Do. Deb. Stk., Red.	100	101
1/3	Brit. & Austrlsn Tst Ln., Ltd. £25 Shs.	2½	⅜
4½	Do. Perm. Debs., Red.	100	103
1½d.	Brit. N. Borneo. £1 Shs.	15/	1½
2½d.	Do.	1	1
—	Brit. S. Africa	1	2 11/16
5	Do. Mt. Deb., Red.	—	95
6	B. Aires Harb. Tst., Red.	100	100
12/6	Canada Co.	1	26
—	Canada N. W. Ld., Ltd.	$25	85½
—	Do. Pref.	$100	$54
4	Canada Perm. Loan & Sav. Perp. Deb. Stk.	100	99½
—	Curamalan Ld., 1 Mt. 7 p.c. Bds., Red.	—	92½
3/7½	Deb Corp. Ld., £10 Shs	4	3½
5	Do. Cum. Pref.	10	11½
4	Do. Perp. Deb. Stk.	100	116
9d.	Deb. Corp. Fders' Sh., Ld.	3	⅜
4/5 1/10	Eastn. Mt. & Agcy, Ld., "A"	10	6½
4½	Do. Deb. Stk., Red.	100	100
5	Equitable Revers. In. Ltd.	100	—
3/	Exploration, Ltd.	1	1⅝
1	Freehold Trst. of Austrla. Ltd. £10 Shs.	1	⅜
4	Do. Perp. Deb. Stk.	100	102
—	Genl. Assets Purchase, Ltd., 5 p.c. Cum. Pref.	10	—
50/	Genl. Reversionary, Ltd.	100	—
3½	Holborn Vi. Land	100	105
3½	House Prop. & Inv.	100	86½
13/	Hudson's Bay	13	21
4	Impl. Col. Fin. & Agcy. Corp.	100	95½
4½	Impl. Prop. Inv., Ltd., Deb. Stk., Red.	100	91½
2/6	Internatl. Fincial. Soc., Ltd. £7½ Shs.	2½	1¼
4	Do. Deb. Stk., Red.	100	99½
1/9½	Ld. & Mtge. Egypt, Ltd. £18 Shs.	3	2½
5	Do. Debs., Red.	100	103
4½	Do. Debs., Red.	100	101
—	Ld. Corp. of Canada, Ltd.	1	⅛
4½	Ld. Mtge. Bk. of Texas Deb. Stk.	100	—
3½	Ld. Mtge. Bk. Victoria 4½ p.c. Deb. Stk.	100	78
2/9½	Law Debent. Corp., Ltd., £10 Shs.	2	1½
4½	Do. Cum. Pref.,	10	12
4	Do. Deb. Stk.	100	119
1/	Ldn. & Australasian Deb. Corp., Ltd., £4 Shs.	2	½
4½	Do. 4½ p.c. Mt. Deb. Stk., Red.	100	101
1/9	Ldn. & Middx. Frhld. Est. £2 Shs.	35/	3½
2/6	Lndn. & N. Y. Inv. Corp., Ltd.	5	2
5	Do. 5 p.c. Cum. Pref.	10	9
1/6	Ldn. & Nth. Assets Corp., Ltd., £2 Shs.	1½	¾
2/	Ldn. & N. Deb. Corp., L.	2	1¼
4/	Ldn. & S. Afric. Explrn. Ltd.	½	13¾
2/	Mtge. Co. of R. Plate, Ltd. £10 Shs.	2	3½
4½	Do. Deb. Stk., Red.	100	112
4½	Morton, Rose Est., Ltd., 1st Mort. Debs.	—	101
6/	Natal Land Col. Ltd.	10	6½
4/	Do. 8 p.c. Pref., 1870	5	8½
5/6	Natl. Disct. L., £25 Shs.	5	10¾
4½	New Impl. Invest., Ltd. Pref. Stk.	100	60½
—	New Impl. Invest., Ltd. Def. Stk.	100	9
4	N. Zld. Ln. & Mer. Agcy., Ltd. Prf. I n Deb. Stk	100	98

Financial, Land, &c. (*continued*):—

Last Div.	Name.	Paid.	Price.
16/	N. Zld. Ln. & Mer. Agcy., Ltd. 5 p.c. "A" Db. Sk.	100	43½
—	N. Zld. Ln. & Mer. Agcy., Ltd., 5 p.c. "B" Db. Stk.	100	4
2/6	N. Zld. Tst. & Ln. Ltd., £25 Shs.	5	1½
12/6	N. Zld. Tst. & Ln. Ltd., 5 p.c. Cum. Pref.	25	19
—	N. Brit. Australsn. Ltd.	100	6½
—	Do. Irred. Guar.	100	32½
5	Do. Mort. Debs.	100	82½
4½	N. Queensld. Mort. & Inv., Ltd., Deb. Stk.	100	95
—	Oceana Co., Ltd.	—	—
6	Peel Riv., Ld. & Min. Ltd.	100	88½
—	Peruvian Corp., Ltd.	100	2¼
—	Do. 4 p.c. Pref.	100	9½
3	Do. 6 p.c. 1 Mt. Debs., Red.	100	41½
—	Queenld. Invest. & Ld. Mort. Pref. Ord. Stk.	100	20
3/7	Queenld. Invest. & Ld. Mort. Ord. Shs.	4	4
4	Queenld. Invest. & Ld. Mort. Perp. Debs.	100	90
3½	Raily. Roll Stk. Tst. Deb., 1903-6	100	100½
50/	Reversiony. Int. Soc., Ltd.	100	—
2/8½	Riv. Plate Trst., Loan & Agcy., L., "A" £10 Shs.	2	4½
1/6	Riv. Plate Trst., Loan & Agcy., Ltd., Def. "B"	5	3½
	Riv. Plate Trst., Loan & Agy., L., Db. Stk., Red.	100	109
—	Santa Fé & Cord. Gt. South Land, Ltd.	20	5
—	Santa Fé Land	10	2½
2/	Scot. Amer. Invest., Ltd. £10 Shs.	2	2¾
2½	Scot. Australian Invest., Ltd., Cons.	100	77½
6	Scot. Australian Invest., Ltd., Guar. Pref.	100	135½
5	Scot. Australian Invest., Ltd., Guar. Pref.	100	106½
4	Scot. Australian Invest., Ltd., 4 p.c. Perp. Dbs.	100	105½
5	Sivagunga Zemdy., 1st Mort., Red.	100	101
20/	Sth. Australian	20	52½
3½	Stock Exchange Deb., Rd.	—	101½
—	Strait Develt., Ltd.	1	1/10
2/6	Texas Land & Mt., Ltd. £10 Shs.	2½	3
4½	Texas Land & Mt., Ltd., Deb. Stk., Red.	100	105
—	Transvaal Est. & Dev., L.	1	½
—	Transvaal Lands, Ltd., £1 Shs.	15/	½
—	Do. F. P.	1	1/10
—	Transvaal Mort., Loan, & Fin., Ltd., £10 Shs.	2	½
2/	Tst & Agcy. of Austrlsa., Ltd., £10 Shs.	1	2
7/5	Do. Old, fully paid	10	15½
5/7	Do. New, fully paid	10	12½
5	Do. Cum. Pref.	10	12¾
3/	Trust & Loan of Canada, £20 Shs.	5	4½
1/9½	Do. New £20 Shs.	3	2¼
—	Tst. & Mort. of Iowa, Ltd., £10 Shs.	2½	⅜
4½	Do. Deb. Stk. Red.	100	92½
—	Tst., Loan, & Agency of Mexico, Ltd., £10 Shs.	2	½
—	Trsts., Exors, & Sec. Ins. Corp., Ltd., £10 Shs.	7	1⅝
5/	Union Dsc., Ld., £10 Shs.	5	10½
—	Union Mort. & Agcy. of Aust., Ltd., £6 Shs.	2	—
6	Do. Pref. Stk	100	35
—	Do. 6 p. Pref. £6 Shs.	2	¼
4½	Do. Deb. Stk	100	92½
4	Do. Deb. Stk	100	85½
5	Do. Deb. Stk. Red.	100	96½
1/0	U.S. Deb. Cor. Ltd., £8 Shs.	1	⅜
5½	Do. Cum. Pref. Stk	100	102½
4½	Do. Irred. Deb. Stk	100	109
5	U.S. Tst. & Guar. Cor., Ltd., Pref. Stk	100	77½
6/	Van Dieman's	25	16
4	Walker's Prop. Cor., Ltd., Guar. 1 Mt. Deb. Stk.	100	109
4½	Wstr. Mort. & Inv., Ltd., Deb. Stk.	100	92½

FINANCIAL—TRUSTS.

Last Div.	Name.	Paid.	Price.
1/	Afric. City Prop., Ltd	1	1⅜
6	Do. Cum. Pref.	1	1
4	Alliance Invt., Ltd., Cm. 4½ p. c. Prefd.	100	77½
—	Do. Defd	100	13½
4	Do. Deb. Stk. Red.	100	105½
5	Amrcn. Invt., Ltd., Prfd.	100	124½
5	Do. Defd.	100	94½
4	Do. Deb. Stk. Red.	100	117½
4	Army & Navy Invt., Ltd., 5 p.c. Prefd.	100	82½
—	Do. Defd. Stk.	100	17½
4	Do. Deb. Stk.	100	107½
4	Atlas Investment, Ltd., Prefd. Stk.	100	70½
4½	Bankers' Invest., Ltd., Cum. Prefd.	100	106
1/0/0	Do. Defd	100	28½
4	Do. Deb. Stk	100	113
:	Brewery & Comml. Inv., Ltd., £10 Shs.	5	5¾

Financial—Trusts (*continued*):—

Last Div.	Name.	Paid.	Price.
4	British Investment, Ltd., Cum. Prefd.	100	107
5	Do. Defd.	100	102½
4	Do. Deb. Stk.	100	109½
6	Brit. Steam. Invst., Ltd., Prefd.	100	116½
3/0/0	Do. Defd	100	70½
4½	Do. Perp. Deb. Stk	100	121½
1/9	Car Trust Invst., Ltd., £10 Shs.	2½	2
5	Do. Pref	100	103½
4	Do. Deb. Stk., 1915	100	105
4	Clnl. Sec., Ltd., Prefd.	100	109½
2	Do. Defd.	100	50
4	Consolidated, Ltd., Cum. 1st Pref.	100	92½
4	Do. 5 p.c. Cm. 2nd do.	100	74½
—	Do. Defd.	100	14½
4½	Do. Deb. Stk.	100	111½
—	Deb. Secs. Invst.	100	107½
—	Do. 4 p.c. Cm. Pf. Sk.	100	106½
4½	Edinburgh Invest., Ltd., Cum. Prefd. Stk.	100	109½
4	Do. Deb. Stk. Red.	100	106½
5	Foreign, Amer. & Gen. Invt., Ltd., Prefd.	100	116½
2	Do. Defd.	100	56½
4	Do. Deb. Stk.	100	116½
5	Foreign & Colonial Invt., Ltd., Prefd.	100	132½
5½	Do. Defd.	100	97½
4½	Gas, Water & Gen. Invt., Cum. Prefd. Stk.	100	95
3	Do. Defd. Stk.	100	38½
4	Do. Deb. Stk.	100	106
5	Gen. & Com. Invt., Ltd., Prefd. Stk.	100	108½
2	Do. Defd. Stk.	100	39½
4	Do. Deb. Stk.	100	112½
1/9	Globe Telegph. & Tst. Ltd.	10	12
6	Do. do. Pref.	10	18
4	Govt. & Genl. Invt., Ld., Prefd.	100	84½
3½	Do. Defd.	100	42½
4½	Govts. Stk. & other Secs. Invt., Ltd., Prefd.	100	91½
1	Do. Defd.	100	27
4½	Do. Deb. Stk.	100	111
4	Do. do.	100	104
4½	Guardian Invt., Ltd., Pfd.	100	88½
—	Do. Defd.	100	21½
4	Do. Deb. Stk.	100	104
5	Indian & Gen. Inv., Ltd., Cum. Prefd.	100	107½
2½	Do. Defd.	100	56
4½	Do. Deb. Stk.	100	121½
5	Indust. & Gen. Tst., Ltd., Unified	100	102½
3½	Do. Deb. Stk. Red.	100	101½
4½	Internat. Invt., Ltd., Cm. Prefd.	100	75½
—	Do. Defd.	100	10
4	Do. Deb. Stk.	100	103
4	Invest. Tst. Cor. Ltd. Pfd.	100	102
4	Do. Defd.	100	90
4	Do. Deb. Stk. Red.	100	106
5	Ldn. Gen. Invest. Ltd., 5 p.c. Cum. Prefd.	100	110½
7½	Do. Defd.	100	118
4½	Ldn. Scot. Amer. Ltd. Pfd.	100	104½
£3	Do. Defd.	100	59½
4	Do. Deb. Stk.	100	112
4	Ldn. Tst., Ltd., Cum. Prfd. Stk.	100	104
4	Do. Defd. Stk.	100	75½
4	Do. Deb. Stk., Red.	100	107
3½	Do. Mt. Deb. Stk., Red.	100	104
5	Mercantile Invt. & Gen., Ltd., Prefd.	100	115
2	Do. Defd.	100	51
4	Do. Deb. Stk.	100	116½
4	Merchants, Ltd., Pref. Stk.	100	106½
4	Do. Ord.	100	83
4	Do. Deb. Stk.	100	117½
5	Municipal, Ltd., Prefd.	100	55½
—	Do. Defd.	100	17½
4½	Do. Debs.	100	113
4½	Do. Debs. "B"	100	99½
4½	Do. "C" Deb. Stk.	100	88½
5	New Investment, Ltd. Ord.	100	93½
5	Omnium Invest., Ltd., Pfd.	100	91½
1	Do. Defd.	100	26½
4	Do. Deb. Stk.	100	104
5/	Railway Deb. Tst. Ld., £10 Shs.	10	7
5	Do. Debs., Red.	100	107½
4½	Do. Deb. Stk., 1911	100	107½
4	Do. do. 1927	100	107½
4	Railway Invst. Ltd., Prefd.	100	117
18/6	Do. Defd.	100	22
8/	Railway Share Trust & Agency "A"	8	6½
7½	Do. "B" Pref. Stk.	100	145½
4½	River Plate & Gen. Invt., Ltd., Prefd.	100	105
£3	Do. Defd.	100	50½
5	Scot. Invst., Ltd., Pfd. Stk.	100	94½
1½	Do. Defd.	100	26½
4	Do. Deb. Stk.	100	108
4½	Sec. Scottish Invst., Ltd., Cum. Prefd.	100	89½
£2	Do. Defd. Stk.	100	32
4	Do. Deb. Stk.	100	107½
5/	Sth. Africa Gold Tst., Ltd.	1	4
6	Do. Cum. Pref	1	1
5½	Do. 1st Debs., Red.	100	102
1/9	Stock Conv. & Invest., Ltd., £5 Shs.	1	1½
4½	Do. do. 4½ p.c. Cm. Prf.	100	114½
2½	Do. Ldn. & N. W. 1st. Charge Prefd.	100	114½
4	Do do. 2nd Chge Prfd.	100	111
32/6	Do. do. Defd. Charge	100	29½
3	Do. N. East. 1 Chge Pfd.	100	93

Financial—Trusts (*continued*):—

Last Div.	Name.	Paid.	Price.
37/6	Stock N. East Defd. Chge	100	39
6	Submarine Cables	100	141½
5	U.S. & S. Amer. Invest., Ltd., Prefd.	100	100½
2	Do. Defd.	100	29½
4	Do. Deb. Stk.	100	105½

GAS AND ELECTRIC LIGHTING.

Last Div.	Name.	Paid.	Price.
10/6	Alliance & Dublin Con. 10 p.c. Stand.	10	25½
7/6	Do. 7 p.c. Stand.	10	17
5	Austin. Gas Lght. (Syd.) Debs. 1902	100	106
5	Bay State of N. Jrsy. Sk. Fd. Tst. Bd., Red.	—	92½
3/	Bombay, Ltd.	5	6
2/4½	Do. New	4	5
12	Brentford Cons.	100	297½
9	Do. New	100	230½
5	Do. Pref.	100	147½
4	Do. Deb. Stk.	100	136
11½	Brighton & Hove Gen. Cons. Stk.	100	277½
8½	Do. "A" Cons. Stk.	100	202½
5	Bristol 5 p.c. Max.	100	132½
22/6	British Gas Light, Ltd.	20	56½
11/6	Bromley Gas Consumrs.' 10 p.c. Stand.	10	26
8/6	Do. 7 p.c. Stand.	10	21
—	Brush Electl. Enging., L.	—	2
6	Do. 6 p.c. Pref.	—	2½
4½	Do. Deb. Stk.	100	112
4½	Do. 2 Deb. Stk., Red.	100	103½
5/	B. Ayres (New), Ltd.	10	10
4	Do. Deb. Stk., Rd.	—	99
12/	Cagliari Gas & Wtr., Ltd.	20	31
8/	Cape Town & Dist. Gas Light & Coke, Ltd.	10	17½
4½	Do. Pref.	10	12½
6	Do. 1 Mt. Debs. 1910	50	60
4/	Charing Cross & Strand Elec. Sup., Ltd.	5	14
4½	Do. Cum. Pref.	5	6½
2/6	Chelsea Elec. Sup., Ltd.	5	11½
4½	Do. Deb. Stk., Red.	100	116
5	Chic. Edis'n Co. 1 Mt., Rd.	$1000	108
14/	City of Ldn. Elec. Lht., L.	10	28½
—	Do. New	10	28
6/	Do. Cum. Pref.	10	18
5	Do. Deb. Stk., Red.	100	131½
13½	Commercial, Cons.	100	342½
10½	Do. New	100	257½
4½	Do. Deb. Stk.	100	155½
14	Continental Union, Ltd.	100	230
11	Do. Pref. Stk.	100	210½
—	County of Lon. & Brush Prov. Elec. Lg., Ltd.	10	15
6	Do. Cum. Pref.	10	16
14	Croydon Comcl. Gas, Ld., "A" Stk., 10 p.c.	100	312½
11	Do. "B" Stk., 7 p.c.	100	260
5½	Crystal Pal. Dist. Ord. 5 p.c. Stk.	100	135½
5	Do. Pref. Stk.	100	141½
8/	European, Ltd.	10	26
6/	Do.	7½	18½
12½	Gas Light & Ck Cons. Stk., "A" Ord.	100	284½
4	Do. "B" (4 p.c. Max.)	100	122½
10	Do. "C," "D," & "E" (Pref.)	100	317½
5	Do. "F" (Pref.)	100	152½
7½	Do. "G" (Pref.)	100	222½
7	Do. "H" (7 p.c. Max.)	100	202
10	Do. "J" (Pref.)	100	315½
6	Do. "K"	100	187½
4	Do. Deb. Stk.	100	136½
4½	Do. do.	100	155½
6	Do. do.	100	207½
8/	Hong Kong & China, Ld.	10	14½
—	House to House Elec. Light Sup., Ltd.	5	11½
7	Do. Cum. Pref.	5	12
10	Imperial Continental	100	212½
3½	Do. Deb. Stk., Red	100	104½
2/	Malta & Medit., Ltd.	5	5½
5/	Metrop. Elec. Sup., Ltd.	10	21
3/8	Do. New	10	20½
4½	Do. 1 Mt. Deb. Stk.	100	119
5	Metro. of Melbrne. Dbs. 1908-12	100	113
4½	Do. Debs. 1918-22-4	100	110
10/	Monte Video, Ltd.	20	16
9½	Newcastle-upon-Tyne	100	237½
—	Do. 3½ p.c. Deb. Stk.	100	117½
8/	Notting Hill Elec. Ltg., Ltd.	10	20½
4/6	Oriental, Ltd.	5	8½
4/0½	Do. New	4½	7½
10½d.	Do. do. 1879	1	1½
3/6	Ottoman, Ltd.	5	5
—	Para, Ltd.	—	—
6	People's Gas Lt. & C. of Chic. 2 Mt. 1904	100	105½
5	River Plate Elec. Lgt. & Trac., Ltd., 1 Deb. Stk.	—	100
$2	Royal Elec. of Montreal	—	146
4½	Do. 1 Mt. Deb.	100	108
11/	St. James' & Pall Mall Elec. Light, Ltd.	5	19
7	Do. Pref.	5	10½
4	Do. Deb. Stk., Red.	100	108½

Gas and Electric (*continued*):—

Last Div.	Name.	Paid.	Price.
10/	San Paulo, Ltd.	10	16½
10	Sheffield Unit. Gas Lt. "A"	100	251½
10	Do. "B"	100	251½
10	Do. "C"	100	251½
—	Sth. Ldn. Elec. Sup., Ld.	2	3
5½	South Metropolitan	100	142½
3	Do. 3 p.c. Deb. Stk.	100	105½
12	Tottenham & Edmonton Gas Lt. & C., "A"	100	297
9	Do. "B"	100	210
7/	Tuscan, Ltd.	10	14
5	Do. Debs., Red.	100	101½
4/9	West Ham 10 p.c. Stan.	5	12
8/	Watmnstr. Elec. Sup., Ld.	5	19

INSURANCE.

Last Div.	Name.	Paid.	Price.
4/	Alliance, £20 Shs.	44/	11½
20/	Alliance, Mar., & Gen., Ld., £100 Shs.	25	53
5/	Atlas, £50 Shs.	6	32
12/	British & For. Marine, Ld., £20 Shs.	4	24½
7½d.	British Law Fire, Ltd., £10 Shs.	1	1½
7/6	Clerical, Med., & Gen. Life, £25 Shs.	50/	16½
10/	Commercial Union, Ltd., £50 Shs.	5	44
4	Do. "W. of Eng." Ter. Deb. Stk.	100	110½
£3	County Fire, £100 Shs.	80	190
2/	Eagle, £50 Shs.	5	4
4/	Employrs' Liability, Ltd., £10 Shs.	2	4½
—	Empress, Ltd., £5 Shs.	1	—
21/	Equity & Law, £100 Shs.	6	22
7/6	General Life, £100 Shs.	5	15
4½d.	Gresham Life, £5 Shs.	15/	2½
2/6	Guardian, Ld., £10 Shs.	5	11½
10/	Imperial, Ltd., £20 Shs.	5	30
5/6	Imperial Life, £20 Shs.	4	6½
6/	Indemnity Mutual Mar., Ltd., £15 Shs.	3	13½
1/	Lancashire, £20 Shs.	2	5
7½d.	Law Acc. & Contin., Ltd., £5 Shs.	10/	1
5/	Law Fire, £100 Shs.	2½	13
9½d.	Law Guar. & Trust, Ltd., £10 Shs.	1	1½
9/	Law Life, £20 Shs.	2	25
2/9	Law Un. & Crown £10 Shs.	12/	7
4	Do. Deb. Stk., 1942	100	110½
14/6	Legal & General, £50 Shs.	8	15½
9d.	Lion Fire, Ltd., £8½ Shs.	1¼	[illegible]
14/	Liverpool & London & Globe, Stk.	2	51½
10/	Do. Globe £1 Ann.	—	36
15/	London, £25 Shs.	12½	63½
4/	Lond. & Lanc. Fire, £25 Shs	2½	19
2/	Lond. & Lanc. Life, £25 Shs	2	5
1/	Lond. & Prov. Mar., Ld., £10 Shs.	1	1
2/	Lond. Guar. & Accident, Ltd., £5 Shs.	2	12
10/	Marine, Ltd., £25 Shs.	4½	44
2/	Maritime, Ltd., £10 Shs.	2	4½
1/6	Merc. Mar., Ld., £10 Shs.	2½	2½
—	National Marine, Ltd., £9 Shs.	1	¼
20/	N. Brit. & Merc., £25 Shs.	6¼	43
20/	Northern, £100 Shs.	10	82
40/	Norwich Union Fire, £100 Shs.	12	126½
10/	Ocean Acc. & Guar., fy. pd.	5	21
2/	Do. £5 Shs.	1	4
7/6	Ocean, Marine, Ltd.	2½	9½
1/	Palatine, £10 Shs.	2	3½
2/6	Pelican, £10 Shs.	1	3½
12/	Phœnix, £50 Shs.	5	44
—	Provident, £100 Shs.	10	36
3/	Railway Psangrs., £10 Shs.	2	8½
2/6	Rock Life, £5 Shs.	10/	4½
8	Royal Exchange	100	360
18/	Royal, £20 Shs.	3	55½
4/	Sun, £10 Shs.	10/	12
3/9	Sun Life, £10 Shs.	7½	15
6/	Thames & Mrsey. Marine, Ltd., £20 Shs.	2	10½
9/	Union, £10 Shs.	4	24½
4/	Union Marine, £20 Shs.	2½	9
12/	Universal Life, £100 Shs.	12	42
2/	World Marine, £5 Shs.	2	1½

IRON, COAL, AND STEEL.

Last Div.	Name.	Paid.	Price.
—	Barrow Hæm. Steel, Ltd.	7½	2
6/	Do. 6 p.c. 2nd Pref.	7½	7½
10/	Bolck., Vaugh. & C., Ld.	20	17½
6/	Do. £8 liab.	12	9½
7/6	Brown, J. & Co., Ltd., £20 Shs.	15	20
7/6	Consett Iron, Ld., £10 Shs.	7½	29½
4/	Do. 8 p.c. Cum. Pref.	5	11
7/7	Ebbw Vale Steel, Iron & Coal, Ltd., £25 Shs.	20	7
17/	General Mining Assn., Ld.	5½	7½
8/	Harvey Steel Co. of Gt. Britain, Ltd.	10	30
5	Lehigh V. Coal 1 Mt. 5 p.c. Guar. Gd. Cp. Bds.	—	98
42/6	Nantyglo & Blaina Iron, Ltd., Pref.	86a	97½
1/	Nerbudda Coal & Iron, Ltd., £3 Shs.	56/	1/16
—	Newport Abercrn. Bk. Vein Steam Coal, Ltd.	10	4½
—	New Shariston Coll., Ltd. Pref.	20	10
4½d.	Nw. Vancvr. Coal & Ld., L.	1	½
—	North's Navigation Coll. (1889) Ltd.	5	2½
10/	Do. 10 p.c. Cum. Pref.	5	7½
—	Rhymney Iron, Ltd.	5	1½
	Do. New, £5 Shs.	4½	2
5	Do. Mt. Debs., Red.	100	98½
5	Shelton Irn., Stl. & Cl. Co., Ltd., 1 Chg. Debs., Red.	100	99½
10	Sth. Hetton Coal, Ltd.	100	197½
	Vickers & Maxim, Ltd.	10	3
	Do. 5 p.c. Prfd. Stk.	100	132½

SHIPPING.

Last Div.	Name.	Paid.	Price.
4/	African Stm. Ship, £20 Shs.	16	9½
5/	Do. Fully-paid	20	13½
5/	Amazon Steam Nav., Ltd.	12½	9
8/	Castle Mail Pakts., Ltd., £20 Shs.	14	15½
3½	Do. 1st Deb. Stk., Red.	100	101
6/	China Mutual Steam, Ltd.	5	3
6	Do. Cum. Pref.	10	9½
10/	Cunard, Ltd.	20	10
5/	Do. £20 Shs.	10	4
4½	Furness, Withy, & Co., Ltd., 1 Mt. Dbs., Red.	100	105
6/	General Steam	15	8
5/	Do. 5 p.c. Pref., 1874	10	9
5/	Do. 5 p.c. Pref., 1877	10	9
3/	Leyland & Co., Ltd.	10	15½
7/	Do. 7 p.c. Cum. Pref.	10	14½
2/11	Do. 4½ p.c. Cum. Pre-Pf.	3	10½
4	Do. 1st Mt. Dbs., Red.	100	106½
7/6	Mercantile Steam, Ltd.	5	7½
6/4½	New Zealand Ship., Ltd.	6	8
4	Do. Deb. Stk., Red.	100	104
3/	Orient Steam, Ltd.	10	8½
5	P. & O. Steam, Cum. Prefd.	100	156½
17	Do. Defd.	100	235½
3½	Do. Deb. Stk.	100	120
5	Richelieu & Ont., 1st Mt. Debs., Red.	100	100
30/	Royal Mail, £100 Shs.	60	51
2/6	Shaw, Sav., & Alb., Ltd., "A" Pref.	5	5½
5/	Do. "B" Ord.	5	3½
8/	Union Steam, Ltd.	20	19½
4/	Do. New £20 Shs.	10	8½
4	Do. Deb. Stk., Red.	100	107
7/	Union of N.Z., Ltd.	10	10
5½	Wilson's & Fur.-Ley., 5½ p.c. Cum. Pref.	10	10½
4½	Do. 1 Mt. Db. Sk., Rd.	100	106½

TELEGRAPHS AND TELEPHONES.

Last Div.	Name.	Paid.	Price.
4	African Direct, Ltd., Mort. Debs., Red.	100	102
—	Amazon Telegraph, Ltd.	10	7
19/6	Anglo-American, Ltd.	100	60
39/	Do. 6 p.c. Prefd. Ord.	100	109
—	Do. Defd. Ord.	100	12
3/	Brazilian Submarine, Ltd.	10	17
5	Do. Debs., 2 Series	100	114

Telegraphs and Telephones (*continued*):—

Last Div.	Name.	Paid.	Price.
4/	Chili Telephone, Ltd.	5	3½
82½	Comcial. Cable, $100 Shs.	—	139½
4	Do. Stg. 500-yr. Deb. Stk. Red.	100	107
2½d.	Consd. Telpehone Constr., &c., Ltd.	10/	¼
6/	Cuba Submarine, Ltd.	10	7
10/	Do. 10 p.c. Pref.	10	15
2/	Direct Spanish, Ltd.	5	4½
5/	Do. 10 p.c. Cum. Pref.	5	10½
4½	Do. Debs.	90	104½
3/	Direct U.S. Cable, Ltd.	20	11
2/6	Eastern, Ltd.	10	18
3/	Do. 6 p.c. Cum. Pref.	10	19
4	Do. Mt. Deb. Stk., Red.	100	130½
2/6	Eastern Exten., Aus., & China, Ltd.	10	19
5	Do. (Aus. Gov. Sub.) Deb., Red.	100	101
5	Do. do. Bearer	100	101½
4	Do. Mort. Deb. Stk.	100	131½
5	Eastn. & S. Afric., Ltd., Mort. Deb. 1900	100	101
5	Do. Bearer	100	101½
4	Do. Mort. Debs. 1909	100	103½
4	Do. Mort. Debs. (Maur. Subsidy)	25	109½
5/	Grt. Nthn. Copenhagen	10	29½
5	Do. Debs., Ser. B., Red.	100	101½
12/6	Indo-European, Ltd.	25	53½
6	London Platino-Brazilian, Ltd., Debs. 1904	100	107½
4/	Montevideo Telph., Ltd., 6 p.c. Pref.	5	2½
3/	National Telephone, Ltd.	5	6½
6/	Do. Cum. 1 Pref.	10	17
6/	Do. Cum. 2 Pref.	10	16
5	Do. Non-Cum. 3 Pref.	5	6
3½	Do. Deb. Stk., Red.	100	106½
4d.	Oriental Telephone, Ltd.	1	½
4	Pac. & Euro. Tlg. Dbs., Rd.	100	106½
4/	Reuter's, Ltd.	8	8½
5/	Un. Riv. Plate Telph., Ltd.	5	4½
5	Do. Deb. Stk., Red.	100	108½
—	West African Telg., Ltd.	10	4½
5	Do. 5 p.c. Mt. Debs., Red.	100	102½
—	W. Coast of America, Ltd.	10	—
3/	Western & Brazilian, Ltd.	15	11½
3/	Do. 5 p.c. Pref. Ord.	7½	7½
—	Do. Defd. Ord.	7½	4
4	Do. Deb. Stk., Red.	100	107½
1/	W. India & Panama, Ltd.	10	½
6/	Do. Cum. 1 Pref.	10	8½
6/	Do. Cum. 2 Pref.	10	6
5	Do. Debs., Red.	100	106½
7	West. Union, 1 Mt. 1902 ($	1000	107½
6	Do. 6 p.c. Stg. Bds., Rd.	100	102½

TRAMWAYS AND OMNIBUS.

Last Div.	Name.	Paid.	Price.
1/5	Anglo-Argentine, Ltd.	5	3½
6	Do. Deb. Stk.	100	127½
4	Barcelona, Ltd.	10	12½
5	Do. Deb., Red.	100	104½
7/6	Belfast Street Trams.	10	16½
—	Blackpl. & Fltwd. Tram., £10 Shs.	8	13½
4/	Bordeaux Tram. & O., Ltd.	10	12½
5	Do. Cum. Pref.	10	11½
—	Brazilian Street Ry., Ltd.	2	½
—	British Elec. Trac., Ltd.	10	17
—	B. Ayres & Belg. Tram., Ltd., 6 p.c. Cum. Pref.	5	4½
6	Do. 1 Deb. Stk.	100	—
—	B. Ayres. Gd. Nat., Ltd., 6 p.c. 1 Deb. Bds., Red.	100	60
5½	Do. Pref. Debs., Red.	100	95½
1/	Calais, Ltd.	5	1
—	Calcutta, Ltd.	10	3½
—	Carthagena & Herr., Ltd.	10	3
5	Do. Deb., Red.	100	90
5	City of B'ham. Trams., Ltd., 5 p.c. Cum. Pref.	5	6
4	Do. 1 Mort. Debs., Rd.	100	106½
3/9	City of B. Ayres, Ltd.	5	7½
2/3	Do. Ext. £5 Shs.	3	4½
6	Do. Deb. Stk.	100	145
1/4	Edinburgh Street Tram.	4	3½
1/	Glasgow Tram. & Omni. Ltd., £9 Shs.	8	3
3/7½	Imperial, Ltd.	6	15
3/	Lond., Deptfd, & Greenwich, Prefd.	5	3½
nil	Do. Defd.	5	1
10½	Lond. Gen. Omni., Ltd.	100	210
4	Do. Deb., Red.	100	117½

Tramways and Omnibus (*continued*):—

Last Div.	Name.	Paid.	Price.
4/9½	London Road Car	6	10½
18/6	Do. Red. 1 Mt. Deb. Stk.	100	108½
5	London St. Rly. (Prov., Ont.), Mt. Debs.	100	110
4/9	London St. Trams.	—	2½
12/9	London Trams., Ltd.	10	10
6/	Do. Non-Cum. Pref.	10	10½
5	Do. Mt. Db. Stk., Rd.	100	100½
5	Lynn & Boston 1 Mt. 1924 $	1000	107
5	Milwaukee Elec. Cons. Mt. $	1000	100½
5	Minneapolis St. 1 Cons. Mt. $	1000	96
5	Montreal St. Dbs., 1908	100	109
4½	Do. Debs., 1922	100	107
6/	Nth. Metropolitan	10	13
1/9½	Nth. Staffords., Ltd.	6	4½
5/6	Provincial, Ltd.	10	7
6/	Do. Cum. Pref.	10	13
5	St. Paul City, 1937 $	1000	96
5	Do. Guar. Twin City Rap. Trans. $	1000	96
5/	Southampton	10	6½
4/	South London	10	5½
7/6	Sunderland, Ltd.	10	6½
4½	Toronto 1 Mt., Red.	100	107
2/6	Tramways Union, Ltd.	5	7½
4½	Do. Deb., Red.	100	109
3/	Vienna General Omnibus.	5	6½
5	Do. 5 p.c. Mt. Deb., Red.	100	103½
4/	Wolverhampton, Ltd.	10	6½

WATER WORKS.

Last Div.	Name.	Paid.	Price.
8/	Antwerp, Ltd.	20	22
6/	Cape Town District, Ltd.	5	6½
10½	Chelsea	100	337½
5	Do. Pref. Stk.	100	178½
4½	Do. Pref. Stk., 1875	100	158½
4½	Do. Deb. Stk.	100	162½
5/	City St. Petersburg, Ltd.	13	11
5/	Colne Valley	10	15½
4	Do. Deb. Stock	100	137½
£4	Consol. of Rosar., Ltd., 4 p.c. 1 Deb. Stk., Red.	100	91
7½	East London	100	230½
4½	Do. Deb. Stk.	100	162½
3	Do. Deb. Stk., Red.	100	106
37/6	Grand Junction (Max. 10 p.c.) "A"	50	122½
18/9	Do. "B"	25	122½
18/9	Do. "C" (Max. 7½ p.c.)	25	57½
35/	Do. "D" (Max. 7 p.c.)	50	104½
4	Do. Deb. Stock	100	149½
13	Kent	100	360½
7	Do. New (Max. 7 p.c.)	100	215½
5/7½	Kimberley, Ltd.	7	5
6	Do. Debs., Red.	100	102½
6	Do. Deb. Stk., Red.	100	105½
10	Lambeth (Max. 10 p.c.)	100	300½
7½	Do. (Max. 7½ p.c.), 50 & 25	—	232½
4	Do. Deb. Stock	100	148½
3	Do. Red. Deb. Stock	100	105
10/	Montevideo, Ltd.	20	16½
5	Do. 1 Deb. Stk.	100	108½
5	Do. 2 Deb. Stk.	100	103½
132/9	New River New	100	447½
4	Do. Deb. Stk.	100	149½
4	Do. Deb. Stk. "B"	100	149½
—	Odessa, Ltd., "A" 6 p.c. Prefd.	20	—
nil	Do. "B" Deferred	20	—
4	Portland Con. Mt. "B," 1927	—	102½
8/	Seville, Ltd.	20	12½
5/6	Southend "Addl." Ord.	10	17½
6	Southwark and Vauxhall	100	164
6	Do. "D" Shares (7½ p.c. max.)	100	162½
5	Do. Pref. Stock	100	176½
4	Do. "A" Deb. Stock	100	147½
3	Staines Resvirs. Jt. Com. Gua. Deb. Stk., Red.	100	105
7/	Tarapaca, Ltd.	10	9½
10	West Middlesex	100	315½
4½	Do. Deb. Stk.	100	163½
3	Do. Deb. Stk.	100	107

Prices Quoted on the Leading Provincial Exchanges.

ENGLISH.

In quoting the markets, B stands for Birmingham; Bl for Bristol; M for Manchester; L for Liverpool; and S for Sheffield.

CORPORATION STOCKS.

Chief Market.	Int or Div.	NAME.	Amount paid.	Price.
M	3½	Bolton, Red. 1935 ..	100	116
M	3½	Burnley, Red. 1933..	100	114
M	3½	Bury, Red. 1946	100	118
L	2¾	Liverpool, Red. 1925	100	102½
B	3½	Longton, 1932	100	106
M	4	Oldham Prp. Db. Sk.	100	145
M	£1	Do. Gas&W.Ann.		34½
S	4	Rotherham 4 p.c., Red. 1927...... [£	1 an	114
M	3½	Runcorn Red. 1923..	100	105
S	2¾	Sheffield Water Ann.	100	119
S	3	Do.	3 an	90
L	3½	Southport Red. 1936 {	5 an / 100	112
L	3	Do. Red. 1914..	100	102½
M	3	Todmorden, Red. 1914	100	102

RAILWAYS.

Chief Market.	Int or Div.	NAME.	Amount paid.	Price.
Bl	4½	Bridgewater Pref. ..	100	137½
M	4	Cleator & Workton.	100	78
M	4	Do. 1883 Pref. ..	100	111
L	4	Cockermth. K. & P.	100	116
L	4	Isle of Man	5	6¾
L	5	Do. Pref.	5	6⅝
L	3	Liverpool Overhead	10	10¼
L	4	Do. Deb. Stk. ..	100	109
L	5	Do. Pref.	10	16
L	6½	Maryport & Carlisle	100	167
S	6	Mid.Shef.& Roth.Pf.	100	231
Bl	35/	Neath & Brecon "A"	100	67½
M	4½	Oldham, Ashton, &c.	10	17
Bl	5½	Penarth Harbour ..	100	182½
Bl	4	Do. Deb. Stk. ..	100	145
Bl	3½	Do. Deb. Stk. ..	100	127
Bl	1½	Ross & Monmouth..	20	5½
Bl	6	Do. Pref.	20	42½
M	3	Southport & Cheshire Deb. Stk.	100	104½
M	nil.	Do. Pref.	100	22
Bl	2½	West Somerset Gu...	100	96½
Bl	5	Wye Val. Deb. Stk.	100	164

BANKS.

Chief Market.	Int or Div.	NAME.	Amount paid.	Price.
L	8/	Adelphi, L., £20 Shs.	10	16
L	12/6	Bk of L'ool, L., £100Sh	12½	39½
B	5/6	Brmnghm. Dis. & C., Ltd., £20 Shs.....	4	10¾
B	6/3	Co. of Staffs., L., £40	5	13¾
S	17½	Crompton & Evans, Ltd., £20 Shs	4	15
M	14/	Lancs. & Yorks, Ltd., £20 Shs....	10	31⅝
L	30/	Livrpl. Union, Ltd., £100 Shs.	20	60½
M	24/	Manchester & Co., Ltd., £100 Shs. ..	16	62
M	20/	Mnchstr. & Livrpool. Dis., Ltd., £60 Shs.	10	51½
M	1/6	Mer. of Lancashire, Ltd., £20 Shs.....	3	6¾
L	16/	Nth. & Sth. Wales, Ltd., £40 Shs.....	10	35⅝
B	20/	Notts Joint St., Ltd., £50 Shs..........	10	26¾
M	4/	Oldham Joint Stk., Ltd., £20 Shs.....	4	12½
S	15	Sheffield Banking, Ltd., £50 Shs.....	17½	51½
S	20	Do. & Rotherham, Ltd., £50 Shs...	8	26½
S	10	Do. & Hallamsh., Ltd., £100 Shs..	25	64
S	10	Do. Union, Ltd., £40 Shs........	10	25
M	12/	Union of Manchester, Ltd., £25 Shs.. ..	11	27¾
M	10/	Williams, Deacon, &c. Ltd., £50 Shs....	8	26½
Bl	20	Wilts & Dorset, Ltd., £50 Shs..........	10	49
S	5/6	York City & Co., Ltd., £10 Shs.....	3	13½

BREWERIES.

Chief Market.	Int or Div.	NAME.	Amount paid.	Price.
B	6	Ansell & Sons Pref.	10	15⅜
B	5	Do. Debs.	100	110
L	9/	Bent's..............	10	18
L	6	Do. Cum. Pref...	10	14½
L	4½	Do. Deb. Stk. ..	100	111
L	13/6	Birkenhead, £5 paid	5	22½
L	13/6	Do. £10 paid....	10	25
M	9/	Boddington's	9	20½
M	5	Do. Cum. Pref...	10	13¼
M	4	Do. Deb. Stk. ..	100	109
B	4½	Butler & Co. Db. Stk	100	110½
M	6	Chesters' Cum. Pref.	10	13½
M	4½	Do. Debs.	100	112
S	10/	Clarkson's Ord.	10	24
S	6	Do. Cum. Prf. Stk.	10	15
M	4	Dutton & Co. Db.Sk.	100	104
M	4½	Hardy's Crown Debs.	100	111
B	10/½	Holt	10	17⅜
B	5	Do. Cum. Pref. ..	10	12⅝
B	4	Do. Debs.	100	109
B	12/6	Lichfield	10	24
B	5	Do. Cum. Pref...	10	11¾
M	5½	Manchester Deb. Stk.	100	142
B	6/	Mitchell, H., & Co.	10	38
B	6	Do. Cum. Pref...	10	15⅜
Bl	6	Oakhill Pref........	10	16½

Breweries (*continued*):—

Chief Market.	Int. or Div.	NAME.	Amount paid.	Price.
M	5/	Springwell	10	10¾
M	7	Do. Pref.	10	13¼
Bl	9	Stroud	10	17
Bl	6	Do. Pref	10	14½
M	6/	Taylor's Eagle......	10	11½
M	7	Do. Cum. Pref ..	10	13½
M	3½	Do. Deb. Stk. ..	100	117½
S	10	Tennant Bros £20 shs	15	34
S	10	Wheatley & Bates ..	10	14
S	6	Do. Cum. Pref.	10	13

CANALS AND DOCKS.

Chief Market.	Int. or Div.	NAME.	Amount paid.	Price.
Bl	8	Hill's Dry Dk. &c. £20	18	9
M	4	Manc. Ship Canal 1st Mt. Deb. Stk.	100	104
M	4	Do. 2nd do.	100	103½
L	36/3	Mersey Dck. & Harb.	an.	118½
L	35/	Do.	an.	116
M	10/	Rochdale Canal	100	37½
B	37/6	Staff. & Worc. Canal	100	76½
B	4½	Do. Deb. Stk....	100	137
Bl	4	Swansea Harb......	100	114½
B	27/6	Warwick & Birm. Cnl	100	66½
B	12/6	Do. & Napton do.	100	23

COMMERCIAL & INDUSTRIAL.

Chief Market.	Int. or Div.	NAME.	Amount paid.	Price.
L	5	Agua Santa Mt. Debs	100	100
M	8/	Armitage, Sir E. & Sns Ltd.............	10	19
M	4	Do. Deb. 1910 ..	100	103
L	6	Ang. Chil. Nit. 1 Mt. Debs., 1919 ..	100	109½
Bl	8½	Bath Stone Firms ..	10	20
M	4/9½	Barlow & Jones, Ltd., £10 Shs.	8	10¾
B	12/6	Birmgham. Ry. Car.	10	17½
B	6	Do. Pref.	10	15¼
B	16/8	Do. Small Arms	5	16½
M	£12	Blackpool Pier......	100	277½
M	5	Do. Tower Debs.	50	54½
M	3/	Do. Wi. Gar. & P.	5	4¾
Bl	10	Bristl.&S.W.R.Wag. £20 Shs..........	3	6
Bl	8	Do. Wag. & Carri. £10 Shs..........	10	14¾
M	7/	Crosses & Winkwth. Ltd..............	5	12½
L	5	G. Angus & Co. Pref.	10	13¾
Bl	5	Gloster. Carri. & W.		10¼
Bl	5	Gt. Wstn. Cttn., Ltd.	20	15½
M	6	Hetherington, L. Prf.	10	8½
M	4½	Do. Debs., 1910	100	99
B	7½d.	Hinks (J. & Son), Ltd.	1	27/6
S	26/	Jessop & Sons, £50 Sh	30	28
S	10	Kayser, Ellsn. & Co. L.	5	11
S	6	Do. Pref.	5	7¾
M	7/6	Kellner-Partgton., L.	5	14½
M	4½	Do. Debs., 1914..	100	106½
M	5	Kerr Thread, Ltd., Debs.	100	101
B	17/	King's Norton Metal, £10 Shs..........	8½	18½
M	5/	Lancashire & Yorks. Wagon, Ltd.	10	9¾
L	10/	Liverpool Exch., Ltd.	20	27⅝
L	45/	Do. Grain Stge, Ltd.	50	108
L	5/	Do. Rubber, Ltd...	5	6¾
M	9d.	Manchester Bond. Whse., L., £10 Shs.	4½	2¾
M	3/9	Do. Comcial. Bldgs., Ltd., £10 Shs.	5	10⅝
M	4/	Do. No. 2, £10 Shs.	5	10¾
M	2/6	Do. No. 3, £10 Shs.	5	7½
M	5/	Do. Corn, &c., Exchange, Ltd.	10	16½
M	4	Do. Debs.	100	125
M	8	Do. Ryl. Exchge, L.	100	246½
B	5/	Midland Rlwy. Car. Wgn., Ld., £20 Sh.	10	14½
Bl	5	Millers & Corys Dbs.	100	100½
B	12/6	Mint, Brgham., Ltd.	5	7½
B	5	Do. Debs.	25	109
B	10/	Nettlefolds, Ltd.....	10	49
B	5	Do. Pref.	10	15½
S	9	Nth. Centrl. Wgn., L.	5	8½
B	15/	Patnt. Nut & Bolt, L.	10	33
B	5	Do. Pref.	10	14⅝
B	1/	Perry & Co., Ltd. ..	1	31/
B	6d.	Do. Pref.	1	29/3
S	10	Round, J., & Co., L., £10 Shs.	6	12½
S	15	Rodgers, J., & Sons, L.	100	212
M	18/9	Rylands & Sons, Ltd., £20	15	38¾
M	2/6	Do. paid up	20	44½
M	4	Do. Debs. ..1909	100	106
S	5	Sanderson Brs. & Co., Ltd. Debs.	100	102
M	4½	Schwabe, S., & Co., Ltd., 1 Debs. 1914	100	104
S	7½	Sheffield Forge & Rolling, Ltd.	10	11
L	80/	Southport Pier, Ltd.	100	88½
L	2½	Do. W. Gdns., Ltd.	5	3½
Bl	5	Spillers & Bakers, Ltd, £10 Shs.	9	14¾
Bl	6	Do. Pref.	10	14½
B	5/	Union Rolling Stock, Ltd., £20 Shs....	5	7½
M	5/	Victoria Pr., S'port, L.	5	4¾
Bl	8	Western Wagon & Property, Ltd....	6	9⅞
S	10	Wostenholm, G., & Son, Ltd., £25 Shs.	20	24
S	6½	Yorksh. Wagon, Ltd.	2	2¾

FINANCIAL, TRUSTS, &c.

Chief Market.	Int. or Div.	NAME.	Amount paid.	Price.
M	1/	Manchstr. Trst. £10 Shs..............	2	13/9
M	1/3	N. of Eng. T. Deb. & A., Ltd. £10 Shs.	2½	27/3
M	3½	Do. 1 Mt. Debs...	100	97
L	—	Pacific Ln. & Inv., L.	2½	2⅝
L	4	Do. Deb. Stk.....	100	102
L	—	United Trst., L. Prfd.	100	72½
L	—	Do. Deferred....	100	62½

GAS.

Chief Market.	Int. or Div.	NAME.	Amount paid.	Price.
Bl	5	Bristol Gas (5 p.c. mx.)	100	129½
Bl	4	Do. 1st Deb.	100	137
S	10	Gt. Grimsby "C" ..	10	200
L	10	Liverpool Utd. "A"	100	253
L	7	Do. "B"......	100	188½
L	4	Do. Deb.	100	137
S	10	Sheffield Gas "A," "B," "C"	100	253
B	10½	Wolverhampton	100	230
B	3	Do. 6 p.c. Pref...	100	168½

INSURANCE.

Chief Market.	Int. or Div.	NAME.	Amount paid.	Price.
M	6	Equitable F. & Acc. £5 Shs.	1	40/6
L	2/	Liverpool Mortgage £10 Shs.	2	1 5/16
M	2/	Mchester. Fire £20 Shs..............	2	7½
M	5/	National Boiler & G., Ltd., £10 Shs.	3	13⅜
L	2/	Reliance Mar., Ltd., £10 Shs.	2	4½
L	4/	Sea, Ltd., £10 Shs...	2	10 1/16
L	8/	Stnd. Mar., L., £20Sh.	4	8⅝
L	—	State Fire, L., £20Sh.	1	2 1/16

COAL, IRON, AND STEEL.

Chief Market.	Int. or Div.	NAME.	Amount paid.	Price.
Bl.	7/6	Albion Stm. Coal ..	10	11½
M	15/9	And. Knowles & S., Ltd., £37½ Shs...	23½	12½
M	5	Do. Mt. Debs. 1908	100	105½
Bl.	1/½	Ashton V. Iron	100	26
S	12½	Bessemer, Ltd.	10	20
S	5	Do. Pref.	10	12½
S	12/6	Briggs, H., & Co., "A" £15 Shs....	12½	15
S	8/6	Do. "B" £15 Shs.	8½	9½
S	20	Brown Baley's. Stl., L.	10	35
S	5	Brown, J., & Co., Cum. Pref.	10	13½
S	5	Cammell, C. & Co., Ltd.	85	12½
S	5	Do. Pref.	5	6⅝
M	5	Chatterley Whitfield. Col., Debs., 1905..	100	100½
Bl	4	Davis, D., & Sons, Ld.	10	10½
M	5	Evans, R., & Co., Ltd., Deb., 1910..	100	100½
S	12½	Fox, S., & Co., Ltd., £100 Shs.	80	178½
Bl	10	Gt. Wstn. Col., L., "A"	5	10
Bl	5	Do. "B"	5	4¾
Bl	8	Main Colliery, Ltd.	10	8
B	2/6	Muntz's Metal, Ltd.	5	8½
B	5	Do. Pref......	5	6½
M	2/6½	Nth. Lonsd. Iron and Steel, Ltd., £10 Sh.	8½	2½
Bl	6	North's Nav. Coll., Ltd., Debs.	100	105
S	30/	Parkgate Irn. & Stl., Ltd., £100 Shs. ..	75	71
M	6	Pearson & Knls., Ld., "A" Cum. Pref...	50	46
B	10/	Sandwell Pk. Col., L.	10	17½
M	6/3	Sheepbridge Coal and Iron, Ltd., "A"	25	16¾
M	2/6	Do. "B"	10	6¼
M	5	Do. "C" Gua. Pf.	25	28¼
Bl	4	South Wales Coll., Ltd., "A"	17	8¾
S	30/	Staveley Coal & Iron, Ltd., "A" £100 Sh.	60	81
S	30/	Do. "C"	60	82
M	1/10½	Tredegar Iron & Cl., Ld., "A" £10 Sh.	7½	2¾
M	1¼	Do. "B" Stk. ..	100	35
M	6/	Wigan Cl. & Irn., Ld.	10	7½
M	4/6	Do. £10 Shs.	7½	4

SHIPPING.

Chief Market.	Int. or Div.	NAME.	Amount paid.	Price.
Bl	6	Bristol St. Nav. Pref.	10	11¾
L	15/	Brit. & Af. St. Nav..	10	13½
L	5/10½	British & Estn, Ltd.	6½	2 11/16
L	10/	Pacific Stm. Nav., L.	25	24½
L	30/	Wst. Ind. & Pac. St. Ltd., £25 Shs....	20	27

TRAMWAYS, &c.

Chief Market.	Int. or Div.	NAME.	Amount paid.	Price.
B	5/	Brmngh. & Aston, L.	5	11⅜
B	5/	Do. Mid., Ltd. ..	10	7½
Bl	6/	Bristol Tr. & Car., Ltd..............	10	21
B	4/	Do. Debs.	100	121
L	6	I. of Man Elec., L., Pref.	1	1½
M	15/	Manchester C. & T, L., "A" £20 Shs.	15	27¾
M	10/	Do. "B"	10	19⅜

WATER WORKS.

Chief Market.	Int. or Div.	NAME.	Amount paid.	Price.
Bl	7	Bristol	25	63½
Bl	7	Do...............	20	48
Bl	58/	Do. 7 p.c. max. ..	100	159
Bl	4½	Do. Pref.	20	32½
Bl	5	Do. Pref.	10	18¾
Bl	3½	Do. Deb.	100	129½
M	10	Fylde "A"........	100	335
M	7	Do. "B"	100	224
B	6	S. Staffs. Ord. "A"	100	168
B	—	Do. "B"	100	167½
B	4	Do. Deb. Stk.	100	140
B	5	Do. Pf "A" "B" "C"	100	170
M	£3⅝	Stockport District ..	100	187½
B	2/	Wolverhampton New	5	6¾

SCOTTISH.

In quoting the markets, E stands for Edinburgh, and G for Glasgow.

RAILWAYS.

Chief Market.	Int. or Div.	NAME.	Nom. Amount	Price.
E	6½	Arbroath and Forfar	25	51
G	1½	Callander and Oban .	10	7½
G	4	Do. Deb. Stock	100	148
G	4½	Do. Pref.......	10	14½
G	4	Cathct. Dist. Deb. Stk.	100	148
E	5	Edin. and Bathgate .	100	179½
E	7	Forth & Clyde Junc.	100	226
G	4	Lanarks. and Ayrsh.	10	14
G	4	Do. & Dumbartons.	10	14¾
G	4	Do. Deb. Stk.	100	149

BANKS.

Chief Market.	Int. or Div.	NAME.	Nom. Amount	Price.
G	12	Bank of Scotland ..	100	357½
G	16	British Linen	100	490
G	8	Caledonian, Ltd.....	2½	95/6
G	10	Clydesdale, Ltd.	10	23½
G	16	Commercl. of Scot., L.	20	88½
G	16	National of Scot. Ld.	100	430
G	8	Royal of Scotland ..	100	233
G	11	Union of Scotland, L.	10	26½

BREWERIES.

Chief Market.	Int. or Div.	NAME.	Nom. Amount	Price.
E	5	Bernard, Thos. Pref.	10	10½
E	5	Bernard, T. & J., Cum. Pref.........	10	12 11/16
G	20	Highland Distilleries	3½	10½

CANALS AND DOCKS.

Chief Market.	Int. or Div.	NAME.	Nom. Amount	Price.
G	4	Clyde Nav. 4 p.c....	100	125½
G	3½	Do. 3½ p.c.......	100	105
G	3½	Greenock Harb. "A"	100	100
G	2	Do. "B"	100	40

MISCELLANEOUS.

Chief Market.	Int. or Div.	NAME.	Nom. Amount	Price.
G	4½	Alexander & Co. Debs.	100	110½
G	5	Baird, H., & Sns. C.P.	10	12½
E	10	Barry, Ostlere, & Co.	7½	12½
E	6	Do. Cum. Pref...	10	15 1/16
G	5	Brown, Stewart, Deb.	100	84
E	7½	Broxburn Oil	8½	9
E	6	Do. Cum. Pref...	10	11 1/16
E	7	Edinburgh & Dist. Tram. Cum. Pref.	5	9
E	5	Gilroy, Sons, & Co. Debs.	100	99
G	9	Glasgow Cot. Spin...	6	5½
G	30/	Do. Royal Exchg.	46	110
G	—	Pumpherston Oil Pf.	10	8¾
E	7	Scottish Assam Tea	10	11½
E	5	Scottish Waggon....	10	12 11/16
G	5	Stoddard & Co. Pref.	10	12⅜

FINANCIAL, LAND, AND INVESTMENT.

Chief Market.	Int. or Div.	NAME.	Nom. Amount	Price.
G	1/	Assets Co..........	1	47/
E	4½	Investors' Mort. Pref.	100	99½
E	4	Do. Deb. Stk....	100	103½
E	4	Nthn. Inv. N. Zeal. Deb. Stk.	100	107
E	4	N. of Scot. Canadian Deb. Stk.	100	106
E	4½	Real & Deb. Corp. Deb. Stk.	100	108½

INSURANCE.

Chief Market.	Int. or Div.	Name.	Amount paid.	Price.
G	12/	Caledonian F. & Life	5	36⅛
G	4/6	City of Glasgow Life	2½	12¾
E	19/	Edinburgh Life	20	55
G	13/1	Life Ass. of Scotland	8½	34½
E	8	Nat. Guar. & Surety	2	52/
G	17½	Scottish Union and National "A"....	1	97/6
G	17½	Do. "B"	3½	18¼

IRON, COAL, AND STEEL.

Chief Market.	Int. or Div.	Name.	Amount paid.	Price.
E	Nil.	Addie, Coll. Cm. Pref.	10	8
E	8/	Arniston Coal	2	14
E	2½	Cairntable Gas Coal	8	86/
E	12½	Fife Coal	10	20¾
E	5	Do. Cum. Pref..	10	13
G	7	Merry & Cunghame. Cum. Pref........	10	15⅞
G	5	Do. Debentures ..	100	105½
E	1/9	Niddrie & Benhar Cl.	1½	42/
G	5	Steel Com. of Scotlnd	—	
	—	"A" Deb. Stk. ..	100	113
G	6	Do. 2nd Mt. "B"	100	105
E	—	Watson, John	8½	10
E	6	Do. Cum. Pref..	7½	8½
E	12½	Wilson's & Cly. Coal	3	8½

IRISH.

In quoting the markets, B stands for Belfast, and D for Dublin.

CORPORATION STOCKS.

Chief Market.	Int. or Div.	Name.	Amount paid.	Price.
	3½	Belfast, 1921	100	112
	3½	Do. 1912........	100	108¾
	3½	Do. 1924........	100	109¼
B	3	Do. 1955........	100	106
B	3½	Do. Water Com...	100	117½
B	3	Do. do.	100	106
B	3½	Do. Harbour Com.	100	114¼
D	3½	Rathmines & Rathgar	100	110¼
D	3½	Waterford Deb.	100	—

RAILWAYS.

Chief Market.	Int. or Div.	Name.	Amount Paid.	Price.
D	30/	Cork, Bandon, & S.C.	100	—
D	4	Do. Deb........	100	139¼
D	4	Do. W. Cork Pref.	100	
B	5½	Belfast & Northern..	100	101
B	4	Do. Deb........	100	146
B	4	Do. Pref.	100	141½
B	6½	Belfast & C. Down..	100	166
B	4	Do. Deb........	100	147
B	3	Do.	100	107½
B	4½	Do. 4½ Pref. B...	100	153¾
B	5	Do. Guar.	100	172½
D	Nil.	Dublin, Wick. & Wex.	100	33
D	4	Do. Deb........	100	127½
D	4½	Do. Deb........	100	133
D	6	Do. Guar.	100	—
D	4	Do. C. of Dub. Junc.	100	—
D	5	Do. 1860 Pref. ..	100	116
D	50/	Do. 1864 Pref. ..	100	106
D	50/	Do. 1865 Pref. ..	100	94
B	6½	Great Northern	100	179
B	4	Do. Deb........	100	147
B	4	Do. Pref. B.	100	143¾
B	5½	Gt. South & Western	100	143
B	4	Do. Deb.	100	148½
B	4	Do. Guar........	100	144
D	45/	Midland Gt. Western	100	115
D	4	Do. Deb.	100	146½
D	4½	Do. Deb.	100	151½
D	4½	Do. Deb.	100	—
D	5	Do. Pref.	100	175
D	4	Do. Pref.	100	140½
D	—	Waterford & Central	100	15
D	3	Do. Deb.	100	105¼
D	3½	Do. Pref.	100	134
D	4	Waterfd. L., & W. Db.	100	129¼
D	4½	Do. Deb.	100	—
D	4	Do. Pref.	100	—
D	3½	Do. Pref.	100	—

BANKS.

Chief Market.	Int. or Div.	Name.	Amount paid.	Price.
B	50/	Belfast, Old, £125 Shs.	25	125½
B	20/	Do. New, £125 Shs.	25	50½
		Hibernian, £20 Shs.	5	6½
D	2/	Munster & Leinster £5 Shs.	2	5¼
B	11/	Northern, £50 Shs...		27
D	13/	Royal, £50 Shs.	10	29¾
B	5/	Ulster, £15 Shs.	2½	12½

BREWERIES AND DISTILLERIES.

Chief Market.	Int. or Div.	Name.	Amount paid.	Price.
D	10/	Castlebellingham & Drog.	10	16½
D	6	Do. Pref.	10	15½
D	4½	Do. Deb.	100	116
B	17/	Dunville & Co.......	10	28¼
B	6	Irish Distillery, Pref.	10	13½
B	5	Do. Deb.	100	110
B	6	J. & J. M'Connell, Pf.	10	15⅛
B	13/6	Mitchell & Co.......	9	19¼
B	5	Do. Deb.	10	11½
D	4½	Phœnix Brew. Deb.	100	—
B	6/	Wm. Cowan........	10	13½
B	6	Do. Pref. ..	10	13½
B	8/	Young, King, & Co.	8	14

STEAM AND CANAL.

Chief Market.	Int. or Div.	Name.	Amount paid.	Price.
B	Nil	Belfast Steamship ..	50	35½
D	10/	British and Irish	50	—
D	15/	City of Dublin......	100	60½
D	3½	Do. Deb.	100	105
D	30/	Dublin & L'pool. Bldg.	50	75
D	2/6	Dundalk & Newry..	10	4½
D	4/	Grand Canal........	10	12⅛
D	3	Do. Pref. ..	10	9½
D	3	Do. Deb. ..	100	99
B	30/	Irish Shipowners....	100	63
B	3/	Ulster Steamship....	5	5½

MISCELLANEOUS.

Chief Market.	Int. or Div.	Name.	Amount paid.	Price.
D	3/1	Arnott & Co.	4	7⅜
D	6	Do. Pref. ..	4	6¼
B	8/	Belfast Com. Bldgs.	10	11
B	37/6	Do. Ropework Co.	75	91
B	5	Do. do. Pref.	10	13½
B	2/	Do. Discount Co..	3	43/
B	5	Do. do. Pref.	5	6½
B	10/	Brookfield Linen....	25	17½
B	Nil	Coey & Co.	25	4
B	5	Do. Deb.	50	49½
B	4½	David Allen & S's Deb.	100	108
D	4/	Dublin Trams	10	20⅛
D	6	Do. Pref.....	10	18⅛
D	4	Do. Deb....	100	—
B	8/	Edenderry Spinning .	10	9
B	25/	Falls Flax Spinning .	25	15
B	17/	Forster, Green, & Co.	10	22
B	9/	Island Spinning	7½	7½
B	8/	Jas. Lindsay & Co..	8	16½
B	1/7½	John Arnott & Co...	4	4½
B	4½	Do. Deb........	50	56
D	5/	Kinahan & Co.......	10	11¾
D	5½	Do. Pref........	10	11½
D	4½	Do. Deb........	100	108½
B	12/	Kirker & Co.	10	10
B	5/	Leahy, Kelly, & Leahy	5	8¾
B	6	Do. Pref.......	5	7⅛
B	2/4½	Lindsay Bros. Ltd...	8	7½
B	4½	Do. Deb........	50	56½
D	1/	National Assurance .	2½	38/
B	10/	Olley & Co.	5	7⅛
D	1/1½	Patriotic Assurance..	2½	30/3
B	3/7½	P. Johnston & Son, L.	6	6½
B	10/	Robertson, F., & Co.	8	23½
B	10	Ulster Marine Insur.	5/	7/6
B	15/	York-street Flax	25	33½
B	6	Do. Pref.......	10	15½
B	4½	Do. Deb.......	100	120½

INDIAN AND CEYLON TEA COMPANIES.

Acres Planted.	Crop, 1897.	Paid up Capital.	Share.	Paid up.	Name.	Dividends. 1894.	1895.	1896.	Int. 1897.	Price.	Yield.	Reserve.	Balance Forward.	Working Capital.	Mortgages, Debs. or Pref. Capital not otherwise stated.
	lb.	£	£	£	**INDIAN COMPANIES.**							£	£	£	£
11,240	3,128,000	120,000	10	3	Amalgamated Estates	—	*	10	5	3⅞	8½	10,000	16,500	D52,950	—
		400,000	10	10	Do. Pref.	—	*	5	15	10⅞	4¾				
10,223	3,360,000	187,160	20	20	Assam	20	20	20	5	60½	6½	55,000	1,730	D11,350	—
6,150	3,278,000	142,500	10	10	Assam Frontier..........	3	6	6	—	8½	6½	—	286	20,000	82,500
		142,500	10	10	Do. Pref.	6	6	6	3	11¾	5¼				
2,087	839,000	66,745	5	5	Attaree Khat	12	12	8	3	7¾	5½	3,790	4,820	7,770	—
1,633	583,000	78,170	10	10	Borelli	4	4	5	—	8	6¼	—	3,256	D270	6,500 Pref.
1,770	812,000	60,825	5	5	British Indian	6	5	5	—	4½	6	—	2,920	12,300	16,500 Pref.
3,223	2,247,000	114,500	5	5	Brahmapootra	20	18	20	6	13½	7	—	28,440	41,600	
3,754	1,617,000	76,500	10	10	Cachar and Dooars	*	8	7	—	10	6¾	—	1,645	21,240	
		76,500	10	10	Do. Pref.	*	6	6	3	12½	4¾				
3,946	2,083,000	72,010	1	1	Chargola	8	7	10	2½	1¼	10½	3,000	3,300	—	—
		81,000	1	1	Do. Pref.	7	7	7	3½	1⅛	5				
1,971	942,000	33,000	5	5	Chubwa	10	8	10	3½	6½	7½	10,000	2,043	D5,400	—
		33,000	5	5	Do. Pref.	7	7	7	3½	7	5				
32,250	11,500,000	120,000	10	3	Cons. Tea and Lands	—	*	10	5	3¼	7½	65,000	14,240	D191,674	—
		1,000,000	10	10	Do. 1st Pref.	—	*	5	15	11¼	4½				
		400,000	10	10	Do. 2nd Pref.	—	*	7	17	12	5¾				
2,230	617,000	135,420	20	20	Darjeeling..............	5½	5½	6	—	23	5	5,552	1,565	1,700	—
2,114	445,000	60,000	10	10	Darjeeling Cons..........	—	—	4/2	—	7	—	—	1,820	—	—
		60,000	10	10	Do. Pref.	—	*	5	2½	9¾	5¼				
6,660	3,518,000	150,000	10	10	Dooars	12½	12½	12½	2½	20½	6¼	45,000	300	D32,000	—
		75,000	10	10	Do. Pref.	7	7	7	3½	17	4½				
3,367	1,811,000	165,000	10	10	Doom Dooma	11¼	10	12½	5	22	5½	30,000	4,032	—	10,000
1,377	582,000	61,120	5	5	Eastern Assam	5	nil.	4	—	3¼	6¼	—	1,790	—	10,000
4,038	1,675,000	85,000	10	10	East India and Ceylon	*	nil.	7	—	9	7¾	—	1,710	—	—
		85,000	10	10	Do. Pref.	*	6	6	3	12½	4¾				
7,500	3,363,000	219,000	10	10	Empire of India	—	*	6/10	2½	12¾	—	15,000	—	27,000	—
		219,000	10	10	Do. Pref.	—	*	5	2½	11	4¾				
1,180	540,000	94,060	10	10	Indian of Cachar	7	3½	3	—	5	6	6,070	—	7,120	—
3,050	824,000	83,500	5	5	Jhanzie	10	10	10	4	8½	6	14,500	1,070	2,700	—
7,980	3,680,000	250,000	10	10	Jokai	10	10	10	5	18	5½	45,000	990	D9,000	—
		100,000	10	10	Do. Pref.	*	6	6	3	14¾	4				
5,224	1,563,000	100,000	20	20	Jorehaut	20	20	20	—	60	6¾	76,220	2,955	3,000	—
1,547	504,000	65,660	10	8	Lebong	15	15	15	5	17	6¼	9,000	2,150	8,650	—
5,082	1,709,000	100,000	10	10	Lungla		10	6	3	9½	6¼	—	1,543	D21,000	—
		100,000	10	10	Do. Pref.	*	6	6	3	11¾	5½				
2,684	885,000	95,970	10	10	Majuli	7	5	5	—	7	7	—	2,606	560	—
1,375	380,000	91,840	1	1	Makum	—	—	2	—	1 1/12	1½	—	—	1,200	25,000
2,990	770,000	100,000	1	1	Moabund	—	—	*	—	1	—	—	—	-	—
		50,000	1	1	Do. Pref.	—	—	*	2½	1	5				
1,080	482,000	79,590	10	10	Scottish Assam	7	7	7	—	11½	6¼	6,500	800	9,590	—
4,150	1,456,000	100,000	10	10	Singlo..................	*	8	5	1	9¾	4½	—	300	D5,200	—
		80,000	10	10	Do. Pref.	*	6½	6½	3½	13	5				
	Crop, 1896.				**CEYLON COMPANIES.**										
7,970	1,743,824	250,000	100	100	Anglo-Ceylon, & Gen.	—	*	5½	—	61	7¾	10,992	1,405	D72,844	166,620
1,836	685,741	50,000	10	10	Associated Tea	—	*	5	—	8¾	5¾	—	164	2,478	—
		60,000	10	10	Do. Pref.	—	*	6	—	10¾	5¾				
20,390	4,000,000§	167,380	10	10	Ceylon Tea Plantations ..	15	15	15	7	27¾	5½	84,500	1,516	D30,819	—
		81,080	10	10	Do. Pref.	7	7	7	17	17	4¾				
5,722	1,542,700§	55,260	5	3	Ceylon & Oriental Est.....	5	8	7	—	2¾	7¾	—	230	D2,047	71,000
		46,000	5	5	Do. Pref.	6	6	6	3	5¾	5¼				
2,157	801,629	111,330	5	5	Dimbula Valley	—	*	10	5	6¼	8	—	—	1,733	6,250
		62,607	5	5	Do. Pref.	—	*	6	3	6¼	4¾				
11,496	3,715,000	298,250	5	5	Eastern Prod. & Est.	3	5	6½	2½	6¼	5	20,000	11,740	D17,797	100,900
3,118	701,100	150,000	10	10	Lanka Plantations........	4	5	5	15	6¾	6¾	—	495	D11,300	14,700 Pref.
2,193	1,050,000§	22,080	10	10	New Dimbula "A"	10	16	16	—	25	6	11,000	2,024	1,150	8,400
		55,710	10	10	Do. "B"	18	16	16	—	22½	6¼				
2,572	570,360	100,000	10	10	Ouvah	6	8	6	2	9¾	6¼	4,000	1,151	D1,255	—
2,630	535,675	200,000	10	10	Nuwara Eliya	—	*	6	3	11½	5¼	—	—	—	30,000
1,720	720,200	41,000	10	10	Scottish Ceylon	15	15	15	5	23	6¾	7,000	1,252	D3,970	—
		9,000	10	10	Do. Pref.	7	7	7	3½	16¼	4½				
2,450	750,000§	56,000	10	6	Standard	12½	15	15	5	13½	6¾	9,000	800	D14,012	4,000

* Company formed this year. Working-Capital Column.—In working-capital column, D stands for *debit*. † Interim dividends are given as actual distribution made. ‡ *Total* div. § Crop 1897.

Printed for the Proprietor by Love & Wyman, Ltd., Great Queen Street, London, W.C.; and Published by Clement Wilson at Norfolk House, Norfolk Street, Strand, London, W.C.

The Investors' Review

EDITED BY A. J. WILSON.

Vol. I.—No. 11. New Series. | FRIDAY, MARCH 18, 1898. | [Registered as a Newspaper.] | Price 6d. By post, 6½d

Notice to Subscribers.

Complaints are continually reaching us that the INVESTORS' REVIEW cannot be obtained at this and the other railway bookstall, that it does not reach Scotch and Irish cities till Monday, and that it is not delivered in the City till Saturday morning.

We publish on Friday in time for the REVIEW to be at all Metropolitan bookstalls by at latest 4 p.m., and we believe that it is there then, having no doubt that Messrs. W. H. Smith & Son do their best, but they have such a mass of papers to handle every day that a fresh one may well look almost like a personal enemy and be kept in short supply unless the reading public shows unmistakably that it is wanted. A little perseverance, therefore, in asking for the INVESTORS' REVIEW is all that should be required to remedy this defect.

All London newsagents can be in a position to distribute the paper on Friday afternoon if they please, and here also the only remedy is for subscribers to insist upon having it as soon as published. Arrangements have been made that all our direct City subscribers shall have their copies before 4 p.m. on Friday. As for the provinces, we can only say that the paper is delivered to the forwarding agents in ample time to be in every English and Scotch town, and in Dublin and Belfast, likewise, early on Saturday morning. Those despatched by post from this office can be delivered by the first London mail on Saturday in every part of the United Kingdom.

Cheques and Postal Orders should be made payable to CLEMENT WILSON.

The INVESTORS' REVIEW can be obtained in Paris of Messrs. BOYVEAU ET CHEVILLET, 22, Rue de la Banque.

ADVERTISEMENTS.

All Advertisements are received subject to approval, and should be sent in not later than 5 p.m. on Thursdays.

The advertisements of American Life Insurance Offices are vigorously excluded from the INVESTORS' REVIEW, and have been so since it commenced as a Quarterly Magazine in 1892.

For tariff and particulars of positions open apply to the Advertisement Manager, Norfolk House, Norfolk-street, W.C.

CONTENTS

The Investors' Review.

The Bank of England, and the Gold demand.

In the early days of the week there was a pretty general disposition among dealers in banking credits to look for an advance in the Bank rate yesterday. We could never quite fall in with this view, because the necessity for the step did not seem apparent. A demand for gold on account of New York had arisen, and, if they wished it, the American people seem to have the power to take away a great deal of the metal from Europe this spring. But they do not possess this power in any special way over us; the Continent is their debtor for foods much more than we are, and continental markets felt the effects of their weaker position the moment the gold demand arose. Paris became the point upon which the orders converged, and if the Bank of France had not put up the premium on the metal to 6 per mille and followed this step up by refusing to sell bar gold at all, the entire amount New York wanted would have gone from Paris. By, in a sense quite real up to a point, suspending specie payments, the Bank of France threw the buyers of gold back on London, and considerable amounts in American eagles have been withdrawn from the Bank for New York, at the same time that all the bar gold offering outside has likewise been snapped up.

We have faced this demand, a factitious one, created by political exigencies in the States much more than by commerce, and it has up to the present cost the Bank of England so little—less than £500,000 within the past fortnight—that no adequate pretext is afforded to put up the rate. A step of this grave kind now, moreover, would probably tend to have the effect of depressing rather than maintaining rates of discount a little later on, when a moderately firm market would be beneficial. And the fact that Continental Exchange rates are strongly in our favour now, that of Paris most unusually so, offers another cogent reason against hasty changes. It would be almost unheard of to force up the price of money here under such conditions, and a rate established on so feeble a basis could not be stable. In fact, if the directors of the Bank of England had raised their rate yesterday to 4 per cent. they would have driven the market to conclude that some formidable political danger lay ahead which compelled precautions to be taken. In a business sense there is no visible necessity for the step and up to the present never has been.

The market is right enough as it is. For some time to come the Bank will retain control of it and force it to work so as to keep pretty near the 3 per cent. official rate. We shall thus have no cheap money this spring, but neither is it going to be very dear, as far as we can see. At the existing range of rates we shall not collect much gold, nor will we lose much—always barring some currency cantrip played upon India. The mere sale of the Chinese loan will tend to collect money in London, and to keep the German Exchange, at least, in our favour. On the whole, then, we are glad that the Bank Court allowed no passing market fears to sway them yesterday. In keeping the official discount rate at 3 per cent., the directors are retaining an effectual hold upon the market, and with that the power to make the market follow them should the necessity for an advance arise later on. We are not out of the wood because the bank rate remains at 3 per cent., but dealers in credit will be happier in their minds than they would have been had a perplexing change taken place.

Some Dangers Inherent in Dependence upon Mercenary Troops.

Many people seem to think that we are of those who believe that the British Empire should give up arms altogether, and depend for its existence on "the brotherhood of nations." It is always hard to get the average reader to draw distinctions. What we have said on this head, and shall continue to say, is that we do not get value for our money either in army or navy, and that, as regards the army, it is nearly useless to make provisions for larger numbers of men while the administration of the War Office is unreformed, surcharged with prejudice, and traditionally corrupt. Further, we have insisted often that the modern system of expansion, in virtue of which great tropical wastes, where Anglo-Saxons cannot settle or thrive, are becoming more and more a charge upon the home tax-payer without prospect of compensation, for money thus sunk through enlarged trade is forcing the country toward recruitment by some form or other of compulsory service. On the old lines we can neither fill the ranks of our regiments nor man our navy. So weak are we that were the country to enter now upon a great war, it is probable that we should begin with a complete breakdown in all our fighting organisation; and assuredly a great war would involve the abandonment of expeditions like those of the Soudan, or into the back lands of the West Coast of Africa, to say nothing of the Uganda protectorate with its East African Railway, or of Rhodesia.

Try to look at the position with an unprejudiced mind. Surely it is unwise to rage and foam at the mouth with the passion of an over-heated patriotism, when a suggestion is made that we might be stronger if we had not so many small jobs in the fighting and conquering line always on hand, in places of the earth more or less distant from any safe base of operations. Look how weak this kind of thing tends to make the country when any great emergency arises, such as the struggle which has begun at Pekin over the partition of China. Do not our numerous commitments in other parts of the world help to cripple us in the Far East? We talk in bragging tones about "fighting Russia," "giving the French a jolly good hiding," "putting the Germans in their place," and so on, and only make ourselves ridiculous, because, as a plain matter of fact, we are not in a position to do any one of these things, owing to our involvements elsewhere—involvements that not only draw off ships of war and our troops, but absorb likewise, year after year, enormous sums of money, money it will soon be increasingly difficult to find. The consequence of our restless expansiveness in savage and tropical regions, where there is little scope for commerce, has been to draw the country into a war-standard of expenditure in time of peace. A great conflict would, therefore, find us without either the men or the means to carry it on. We are already reduced in China to the humble rôle of money-lender. Our wealth is about the only agent we have left with which to checkmate Russia and Germany, and it cannot long be effective. It is, moreover, all out on mortgage, so that we have no reserves to draw upon when the supreme hour of danger does come. Suppose Japan, whose fury is almost uncontrollable against Russia, refuses to hand over Wei-hai-Wei in May next, when the last instalment of the war indemnity is paid to her by China, and announces that she will hold the place until Russia comes to terms with her about Port Arthur, Manchuria and the Corean Peninsula. And suppose, further, that Russia, with a haughty contempt for the sea power of Japan, decides to go to war to assert her "right" to carve out of China whatever territory she pleases, where shall we come in? Dare we back the Japanese? Where are the ships and men, where is the money with which we could do this? "Russia has no fleet there which could stand up against Japan alone," many allege, and the allegation is probably true. But an army is wanted as well as a fleet, and a large army, too. We have not got it. All our available troops are engaged elsewhere, and most of the available officers as well—warring among the mountains beyond the North-West frontier of India; garrisoning South Africa; conducting campaigns in the Nile Valley; quelling mutinies in Uganda; leading armies of mercenaries into the uplands of the Niger basin; holding down Egypt with the "mailed fist"; and as regards the nearer East, where our fleet is assisting to maintain anarchy in Crete, trembling lest the flames of war should fill the Balkan Peninsular or Asia Minor in the spring, and lead to the seizure of Constantinople by Russia. Could we move 10,000 men to try to prevent this seizure? No, not one thousand without raising acute dangers elsewhere.

We have mentioned mercenaries, and is it not by the aid of mercenary troops that all our wars are now carried on? And have not these troops again and again proved a source of danger to the Empire? To say nothing of the Indian Mutiny, is it not the fact that the Soudan was lost to Egypt through the weakness of British-led mercenaries? Does not the present trouble in Uganda spring from the same source? What but weakness and liability to sudden disaster can come to the Empire through its daily increasing dependence on this class of fighting men? We are continually asked to admire the "loyalty" of our Native army in India; but let a disaster befall us at any point in our widely-scattered dominions, and could we trust to that loyalty? Did not British officers talk in the same way down to the very day when the Mutiny broke out in 1857? After the struggle had actually begun, did not officers frequently lose their lives by refusing to believe that the soldiers they commanded could be other than loyal? It is not the fashion nowadays to read such books as Gibbon's "Decline and Fall of the Roman Empire." We therefore hold it useless to appeal to the experience that history affords of the danger to liberty inherent in an extensive dependence upon alien mercenaries; and it is possible that our own freedom may never be directly menaced thereby. But the solidarity and maintaining power of our Empire as a whole undoubtedly is menaced more and more by this very habit, and our brand-new policy of expansion, no matter where, is putting the country in this dilemma: either it must coerce Englishmen, Scotchmen, and Irishmen to serve as soldiers and sailors, thereby weakening the kingdom in the capacity to maintain its industrial supremacy, or we must trust the controlling, discipline, and the fighting expeditions our Empire and our conquests demand more and more to alien soldiers.

That such dependence must be a source of weakness should be evident to the meanest comprehension, but let us help such by an illustration. If war broke out in the further East, as it may do this spring, between Japan and Russia, and if our paramount commercial interest in China obliged us to take part in this war, could we place an amount of confidence in our native army sufficient to allow us confidently to withdraw, say, 20,000 of the British garrison in India for the Chinese war? We could not: the most fanatical believer in the loyalty of the Indian native army would not dare to maintain that we could. What is much more likely to be necessary is an increase of the British garrison of India; for Russia has but to make a demonstration Afghanistan way to put India, from one end to the other, in a ferment of expectation essentially unloyal. And as we cannot spare British troops in sufficient numbers both to augment the Indian garrison and to fight a war in China, the outcome would be more British troops to India and Sepoys to China. We should have to fight there with an army mainly composed of mercenaries saturated with discontent at being removed from their native land. It would be in Asia as in Africa, and no sensible man can deny that an empire functioning and ruling under such conditions is on its way to trouble. Will the reader turn these things over in his mind and decide for himself how far it is wise to go on spreading out dominions which have already far outgrown our capacity to rule them with the aid of home-bred soldiers? And alongside this actual empire, disjointed, full of incongruities, covering many regions where existence to races from a temperate climate is difficult or dangerous, where settlement and multiplication by such races are impossible, place the fairer picture of an Anglo-Saxon brotherhood of nations in America, in Australia, in South Africa working together with the grand old mother land for the good of mankind and the progress of the world. How far away such a dream appears now when the earth is full of wars and threats of war, when the clatter of armed men drowns the hum of the loom in all men's ears; when men's faculties are bent unceasingly towards the production of instruments of death! It is as if an Armageddon were at hand.

A New Irish Muddle.

(From a Correspondent.)

Whoever knows anything about the Irish Land Question and the certainty it involves of large drafts on the purse and patience of the British and Irish taxpayer to solve it, must dread addition to the perennial trouble it causes. Yet in the new Local Government measure we have such an addition, and it would be well the taxpayer should realise that the land muddle is to be made straight by his cash and credit. This order might be thought big enough without having added to it a Local Taxation muddle, also evidently meant to be solved at his expense.

The facts lie in a nutshell. The rateable valuation of Ireland was (1891) £14,027,858, in which total agricultural holdings accounted for £9,971,987. The actual rates levied (1896) on the whole country came to £3,095,517, of which £752,056 was town taxation, exclusive however of the poor rate on towns. Under the measure now proposed, the landowner becomes entirely exempt from local taxation, while the agricultural occupier, now paying the whole of the cess and half the poor-rate, becomes exempt from half the former, calculated on a standard year. In the agricultural districts, almost the entire area of the island, this strikes out of the valuation book half the fund liable for rates. The small class thus becoming exempt in whole or part is far the richest section of the ratepayers; and of the £750,000 a year to be given out of the general taxpayer's money, £600,000 at least goes to this class. But the mischief does not end with this. The ratepayers are divided into two classes, one a propertied and privileged class paying no rates or half rates, the other a non-propertied, non-privileged class, paying in full. The last, in many districts the most numerous, in all the poorest, will henceforth become exposed to exorbitant exactions on a small fraction of the valuation. It is already oppressively, though unequally, taxed, and will now become more uniformly exposed to weightier burdens. It gets no share of the grant, but, under the great contraction of the taxable fund, it becomes liable in extreme degree to impossible and violently fluctuating rates, as the result of any, even the smallest, increase of expenditure falling on the narrow area of incidence. And a large increase of expenditure is inevitable under the new system. Whatever may be urged against the present local administration it is extremely cheap, so much so as to be inefficient. The present cost of administration in the counties is only 6·6 per cent., and in the unions for poor relief 10·58 per cent., greatly below what it is in England.

The mass of the privileged class of ratepayers will be disappointed; what it gets will not compensate it for the consequences flowing from the conjunction of a narrowed taxable fund with increase of expenditure. Of the 486,865 agricultural holdings in Ireland 68·3 per cent. have a valuation below £15, and 88·9 per cent. of the whole are below £40. Under the existing system this mass is exposed to exorbitant rates owing to its poverty and to estate-rating. Its share of the £750,000, about £150,000, would be at the best an inappreciable boon, but the benefit of it is certain to disappear entirely as a consequence of any increase in expenditure.

The larger occupiers over £50 valuation, whose holdings number 40,783, collectively get an appreciable boon, but in respect of a large number of them, what is given with one hand is taken away by the other, under the enactment of union rating. Union rating, the abolition of 3,444 areas of rating in which the rate arbitrarily varies from 4d. to 5s. 10d. in the £, is in itself a highly desirable reform, but as it is now proposed to be done, the discontent of those who, expecting a favour, will have their burden increased, is sure to greatly outweigh the gratitude of those who are doubly benefited by the agricultural grant and by union rating. The proposed re-adjustment is in very many cases not only violent, but, as effected, unjust and uncalled for.

The landowners of course come in for the plum. They not only get a large part of the £750,000, but become practically altogether exempt from local taxation in respect of a rental of £10,000,000. Mr. Chamberlain not long ago told his constituents at Birmingham that the Irish landlords pay the bulk of the local rates, and others of Her Majesty's ministers have been pathetic in urging the necessity of protecting them from confiscation under the title of taxation. But they are protected already up to the hilt: it would be strange were it otherwise in the country they so long governed despotically. They pay virtually none of the county cess, and only a part of the poor-rate—nominally a half, really, under the system of electoral or estate rating, less than a quarter. This is at once apparent from the fact that of the £750,000 to be now drawn from the general taxpayer, £250,000 to £300,000 will amply suffice to entirely exempt landlords from local taxation. Surely this shows that they pay less than a tenth of the rates assessed on real property rates whose total amounts to £3,000,000. Further, it is notorious in Ireland that subsequent to 1838, when the poor-rate was imposed, rents were raised, as they were again in 1852 when Mr. Gladstone extended the Income Tax to Ireland. In point of fact, the rental of Irish land, at present paying nothing like its fair share of local rates, throws the burden unjustly and inequitably on a mass of small occupiers, thus contributing in no small degree to the discontent and unrest of the country. Such inequality is now, instead of being remedied, about to be made worse; £750,000 of the British taxpayer's money is to be not merely wasted, but really so applied as to aggravate a gross existing abuse. Who can doubt that this proposed rate will soon produce a state of things which must call for, and is, perhaps, meant in the end to call for, larger demands on the general revenue of the United Kingdom. The exemption of rental from local taxation, the odious and invidious creation of a privileged class of ratepayers, the intolerably heavy burden which a narrowed area of incidence must place on a large body of non-privileged ratepayers, will be made the grounds for placing local burdens entirely on the general taxpayer.

It may be said that the Irish people want a system of democratic local government, and are willing to pay for it. But the question is one not of will alone but of ability as well. The people want, in the cant of politics, taxation according to representation, and they get it with the whole rental of the country and half the interest of the agricultural occupier struck out of the taxable fund. The deception inherent in this proposal would, in working, be intensely irritating, even if practicable, which it is not. A taxable fund curtailed to the extent proposed would not yield enough to support local administration without entailing insufferable burdens on the poorest class of ratepayers. So the logical consequence of the exemption of the wealthy ratepayers must be, in the end, the exemption of the poorer too, at the cost of the general taxpayer, whose representative, the State, would nevertheless have no effective control over elected local bodies. The helpless supreme Government would assuredly be denounced as tyrannical if it dared to interfere with the vagaries of these bodies. This is the new muddle, political and financial, which our legislators are, apparently with unanimity, preparing for us in Ireland and in Great Britain.

If our "democratic" Parliament votes away the taxpayer's money to exempt the Irish landed interest from liability to local rates, already unfairly light, not to relieve or re-adjust local taxation but to enhance the liability of the mass of ratepayers, can we expect that "democratic" local bodies will act in any better spirit? In Ireland from end to end, untempered elements of class and party tyranny abound, and we cannot hope to find in its local councils the qualities so conspicuously wanting in the action of Parliament.

The Accountant's Certificate in a Prospectus.

When a limited liability company is formed to take over a "going concern" the amount of its capital is presumably adjusted in order to provide the following:—1. The sum required to buy the tangible assets of the old firm. 2. The sum required to buy the goodwill of the old firm. 3. The sum required by the new company for "working" capital. The first of these items is, or should be, clearly defined in the reports of expert valuators; the third depends entirely upon the individual character of the business to be transferred; the value of the second is supposed to be ascertainable from the accountant's report certifying the past profits. To the curious outsider who has his funds snugly invested, the post-prandial perusal of the documents which pass for "certificates of past profits" contained in his daily budget of prospectuses must be a pleasing and amusing excitement, but to investors the fact that anything but a perfectly straightforward certificate should be granted by an accountant is no joke, and it is now, very properly, beginning to emerge as a serious matter for the profession of accountancy also.

It is no difficult task to determine what represents "a perfectly straightforward certificate." An accountant's duty is to examine the books of the old firm, and declare to the public what he finds there as the result of its trading. His certificate, therefore, should state the actual amount of profit earned in each of a certain number of past years, and at the same time should narrate how these amounts have been arrived at. This may seem obvious enough, but it is a lamentable truth that promoters too often see reasons for departing from this course. What is even more culpable is the fact that accountants are often prevailed upon to conceal or juggle inconvenient facts, presumably in order to curry favour with the promoters and obtain the position of auditor to the company.

One of the favourite methods of hoodwinking the public is that of averaging the profits earned during a certain number of past years, and certifying the sum arrived at as the "average profits" for the last three, five, or seven years, as the case may be. The objection to this is, of course, that, for all the public knows, it may be purchasing a business which has been steadily declining in late years; indeed, it is almost safe to assume when this method is adopted that such is the case. A curious example was seen lately in the flotation of a small aërated water company. In this prospectus the average profit for three years was certified in the manner described, but on looking further into the prospectus one found that the estimated value of the assets, exclusive of goodwill, was over £15,000, while the purchase price of the business was £14,000. As the vendor also agreed to pay all the flotation expenses he evidently considered that the goodwill of his business was best represented by a minus quantity. Thus the value of the accountant's certificate was, to say the least of it, considerably discounted.

A method which is often adopted is that of certifying a statement of profits which only covers the trading of a few months, and estimating therefrom the probable profits for a whole year. This, of course, is a palpable "juggle," and it is extraordinary that investors should be considered capable of being contented with averages deduced in this way from the results of a period selected by the vendors to suit their own interests.

In one flotation of a recent date a sort of combination of these two unsatisfactory methods was adopted, which was even more unsatisfactory than either taken singly. In the certificate given by the accountants in this instance, the profits for three years were jumbled up together, and the average taken; then a period of thirteen months was taken by itself!

A third method is that of making a pure estimate of future profits. As we are considering only the case of a "going concern" flotation, some good reason must be adduced for asking the public to be satisfied with an estimate. Frequently this is recognised and a reason given; sometimes, owing to stupendous improvements in machinery or methods of production, past profits are declared to be no criterion of future ones; or, perhaps, the influx of new business which is to result from the introduction of new capital is put forward by way of justification. Whatever the excuse is, however, one point should be duly noted. An estimate given by an expert member of the trade which the company is formed to carry on, may have a certain value, but the estimate of one who is presumably skilled in accountancy alone is rarely worth the paper on which it is written. A glaring example of this was furnished recently in the prospectus of a distillery company. The capital of this company was £200,000; the amount of the valuation £150,000, and the profits, as estimated by two practical distillers, exceeded £56,000.

A certificate was granted by a firm of chartered accountants saying that they had had submitted to them, "in order to save publication in detail," the statements prepared by the two practical distillers, and that they found "the estimate of profit fully borne out by these statements, which together show an estimated profit of £65,422 per annum." Surely one may assume that the word of the "two practical distillers" would have been as satisfactory to the investing public as that of the accountants, and one is therefore almost forced to the suspicion that the matter was cast in the shape of an accountant's report in order to catch ignorant or unwary capitalists.

A class of certificate which at first sight appears perfectly satisfactory is that which declares that past profits have been sufficient to pay a certain percentage on the capital of the new company. But, in spite of its apparent straightforwardness, this method is also open to objection. In such cases the public is rarely informed what depreciation has been written off or what allowances have been made for bad debts or other contingencies. In the recent flotation of an hotel company where this method was adopted in the prospectus, a fixed annual sum was charged for ordinary repairs and renewals, "which sum the manager certified as being amply sufficient." As the accountant had evidently been compelled to resort to the manager for assistance, one could hardly consider this remark to be "amply sufficient" information of how the results contained in his certificate were brought out.

Then there are many certificates granted by accountants which cannot be placed in any of these classes, some apparently straightforward, others conveniently vague. One of the most impudent of these was that given by a chartered accountant in the flotation of a soap company in October last. This stated that for the five years to March, 1896, the profits had been equivalent to twelve per cent. on the capital employed. What the "capital employed" was or had been, what ratio it bore to the issued capital of the new company, why the certificate of profits stopped at a date over eighteen months previous to the issue of the prospectus, are mysteries upon which the vendors did not deign to shed light. As the *Economist* remarked at the time, the certificate was "an utter burlesque of what such a document should be," and "such a certificate from a chartered accountant is calculated to bring the business of accountancy into contempt."

When such certificates are given by accountants, and remarks regarding accountancy are made by leading financial papers such as those quoted from the *Economist*, it is surely time for the profession to recognise its position in this matter. There can be no doubt that, whether the public puts the accountant's certificate to its chief use—the valuation of the goodwill—or not, the statement of profits does possess great weight. A frank statement of past results is undoubtedly a most potent factor in a successful flotation. There is, however, a section of the investing public which is lamentably gullible, and which, on reading such a certificate as the one last noticed, remembers only the words "12 per cent. on the capital employed." To these investors much loss, which is directly traceable to such misleading statements, must accrue. There is reason to hope, however, that the ranks of this division of the public are being gradually thinned by experience, and there is now considerable danger that the injury done to the public will, in the near future, rebound upon the reputation of the accountants. Were accountants to take a firm stand in this matter, refusing to sign certificates that could be misconstrued in any detail, they could lessen considerably the chances which unscrupulous promoters possess of deceiving the public. On the other hand, by acquiescing in the concealment of misrepresentation of material facts, they do incalculable harm both to the public and to themselves.

Economic and Financial Notes and Correspondence.

The Marquis of Salisbury.

Men of all political parties, we feel sure, will regret that the Prime Minister and Foreign Secretary should be laid aside from work by ill health at the present critical state of foreign affairs. Partisans may gibe at his lordship and accuse him of vacillation, and make fun of his capacity to retreat from difficult situations by way of "graceful concessions." We have ourselves differed strongly from his line of policy in regard to Turkish affairs, whether in Armenia, in Crete, or in Greece. We felt that it was due, both to the moral responsibilities and the power of England, that he should have assumed a more masterful attitude all through the recent troubles of the moribund Turkish Empire. None the less is it true that Lord Salisbury has exercised on many occasions a wise discretion, that he is a man of peace, anxious above all things to prevent the entanglement of this country in a disastrous war; that his long experience and strong common sense have frequently enabled him to steer us out of troubles a rasher man would have brought down upon the nation's head. And the worst of it is there is no man visible at present at all able to replace this statesman, whose patriotism is undoubted, whose ability is great beyond that of any of his colleagues, and whose knowledge of diplomacy is more extensive than that of any Englishman now living. All parties in the State may, therefore, be trusted to join cordially in the hope that his lordship may soon be restored to health and vigour, so as to be able to resume the anxious, incessant, and too often thankless labours of his office.

Mr. Cecil Rhodes and the Transvaal.

A Reuter's telegram from Capetown published yesterday, announces that Mr. Rhodes in a speech at Salt River used the following language: "You must decide whether you will go on patting the back of the Transvaal Government or whether you will take up a Constitutional position, and say 'We remonstrate with you, and hope you will change, because you are embarrassing the union of South Africa.' There are now eighty thousand people in the Transvaal, a number which will soon be raised to five hundred thousand, and if we do right we shall constitutionally support their claims for just rights rather than support the Government which just happens to be successful on the basis of the vote of fifteen thousand."

This is very specious, but not true so far as the position of the Transvaal Government is concerned. It is not a "constitutional" attitude to allege that this Government is in the wrong in defending the liberties handed back to it by the Government of England. No doubt it is [illegible] way clever, and certainly cunning, to endeavour to represent the South African question as a question of equal rights for all, and to hold up the foreigners within the South African Republic as a body of people denied their just liberties, but there is no getting away from the fact that this kind of thing is not merely contrary to fact but directly provocative of a fresh outbreak of race hostilities in South Africa. There should be no mistake in the minds of the British public on this question. If we follow the lead set by Mr. Cecil Rhodes, in harangues like that from which we quote, we shall be landed once more in a South African conflict where we shall be almost completely in the wrong. Grant that the Boers are obstructive when they exclude aliens from the franchise, have they not the right so to do, and have they not good excuse for thus acting in the treatment they have received from us again and again during the period when we have been supreme in South Africa? Mr. Rhodes's policy is still the policy of the Jameson raid; is it likewise that of Mr. Chamberlain?

The United States and Cuba.

We have not abandoned the hope that the difficulties between these two Powers may yet be settled without war. For one thing, as an American correspondent shows in a letter which we print below, the American people as a whole are actuated by excellent motives in desiring to see an end put to the anarchy prevailing in Cuba. They are not moved by a desire for annexing it, but by a humane impulse to remove from their doors an open sore full of danger to their own people. Another source of hope is the fact that Spain is too exhausted to maintain a fight. As the able special correspondent of the *Times* in Havana pointed out in a very interesting letter published by that paper on Monday last, the Cuban rebellion has cost Spain already some £60,000,000, if the £12,000,000 of unpaid arrears of Cuban taxes are counted in, the occupation of the island entails on Spain an expenditure of £1,600,000 per month at the present time. Were the cost of a naval war with the United States to be added to this frightful burden upon Spain's resources her bankruptcy must ensue within a very few weeks. It is perilously near now. The Madrid Exchange is going up steadily, so that the piastre is now depreciated quite 40 per cent., and the Bank of Spain is so over-weighted by the task of sustaining the credit of the State that very little more would force it to suspend.

Under these circumstances, with an empty Treasury, with an unready fleet, and without means to augment the revenue at any point, the Spanish Government must in a little time be forced by circumstances to put its pride in its pockets, and accept the inevitable. The knowledge that this is so helps to account for the recrudescence of an old proposal on the part of the American people to buy the freedom of Cuba from Spain outright, for money down. Some two years ago indirect negotiations were entered into for effecting this purchase, and we believe the American Government was willing to hand Spain a hundred million sterling in order to liberate Cuba. Spanish pride scorned to entertain any such proposal; but pride does not fill the Treasury, nor cause surpluses to arise in place of yawning deficits; therefore, we are inclined to think that if a money transaction could be arranged under some guise which would cover Spain's humiliation it would afford a solution acceptable to all parties. One thing is certain, Spain cannot go on much longer on the present lines without re-awakening revolutionary movements at home. Then Cuba and all might be lost in one upheaval. Señor Sagasta's Ministry appears to be beginning to show some perception of this danger, and the faster the United States prepares for war, the greater may be the certainty that war will not break out.

DEAR MR. WILSON,—Practically speaking, we know no more about prospects of war with Spain than you do. If it was most any other country I would say there would be no war, for we certainly don't want one, but you know Spain, her characteristics, and embarrassments, and that she may be expected to do the wrong thing, unless by accident. Cuba has been a constant worry for a half century, and especially for the past two or three years, a large bill of expense to us, of which we are heartily tired; and when you add the barbarities carried on under our noses, and that owing to the miserable sanitary conditions at Havana, it is likely to send us yellow fever any year, always causing many deaths, and a tremendous loss to several States, you will readily understand our great desire for a finish.

Evidently preparations are being pushed forward rapidly, but the Administration says little, and allows but little to leak out. It is not running this thing with a "brass band." I imagine, however, that when the time comes, the position assumed will be unequivocal, and will be a pretty clean bill of health. The general impression is that after war is actually under way, business will not be greatly affected, and that Cuba will be worth the war's cost, either as our own, or independent, and bonded for enough to repay our outlays. The contest, if it comes, will be very interesting from a scientific standpoint, as it will be the first opportunity for fairly testing the practicability of the various new armoured warships, torpedo boats, &c., and it will be especially interesting to us in testing our coast defences.

There is a steadily growing conviction that our true policy is, the best possible coast defences, a very small Army, and comparatively small Navy; but while feeling pretty confident in regard to the sufficiency of our coast defences, a fight with Spain will, no doubt, develop important defects, and it will cost us much less to gain experience through a war with that country, than with a stronger Power, and, no doubt, Spain has enough good ships to test our defences. As an instance, showing the deep-rooted prejudice against increasing the Army or Navy, absolute necessity is demanded to be shown before Congress will grant an increase of two artillery regiments for use on the coast defences.

SIR WILLIAM ROBINSON'S VIEWS ON CHINA.

This gentleman, who has just returned to England after having been Governor of Hong Kong for six years, has been giving his views about the affairs in the far East, and in particular about the defence of Hong Kong. They are so apposite and interesting that we venture to extract some portions of the interview with him, so that they may be available for future reference. It is pleasant to see that a more sensible and right-minded view regarding our position in the far East seems beginning to prevail. We hope, though, that the "partition" policy will not be the one we shall have to follow in China in order to keep the door open for our trade.

I must say I do not share the alarm felt by some regarding the political situation in China, neither do I believe that Russia's policy in that part of the world should be regarded as necessarily inimical to us. I approve entirely of Germany's action in taking Kiao-Chau. She did exactly what we might have done, and what we shall probably ultimately have to do if friendly concessions are not made to us. In pursuing her present course Russia is simply carrying out a definite policy which she has been steadily and with determination pursuing for years—a policy which, as I have said, is not unfriendly to us, but which in any case it is now too late for us to attempt to stop. I do not believe that the acquisition by the Czar's Government of Port Arthur will do any harm to England, if that and other ports are kept open. So long as we have Free Trade, Russia's action will not only not hamper us, but will even be in some ways helpful. She intends to come as far as Port Arthur, and I do not believe she will come further. Already she practically possesses the whole of Manchuria. We must recognise that Russia means to have an open port, and under the conditions I have mentioned I am in favour of an *entente* with Russia, the result of which would be of mutual advantage. Our own policy is, above all things, to insist upon Free Trade and an open door. That is all we want; and as the policy of Germany and the United States is in this respect identical with our own, we should work with those countries in the accomplishment of our aim. We ought undoubtedly to keep a firm hold of the whole of the Yangtse Valley. Beyond all this, we must insist on the fulfilment of all the Clauses of the famous Tientsin Treaty, and if the Imperial Government of China object, coercion, in my humble opinion, should follow. Although I do not believe that the partition of China has yet commenced, there is a feeling in Hong Kong and Shanghai that the provinces cannot long hold together. Already they are to a certain extent independent, not only of each other, but also of the Imperial Government.

THE FIRST OF THE WEST INDIAN "DOLES."

Mr. Chamberlain has obtained the sanction of the House of Commons, by very considerable majorities, to the first of his proposed doles to the West Indies. The amount thus voted is £120,000. A large proportion of this sum—£90,000 in all—is to be applied in wiping off certain deficits, which have accumulated in eight of the islands, and which those colonies are declared to be entirely unable to discharge. Now, this method of meeting what Mr. Chamberlain calls the "cost of decent administration," is, to say the least of it, a very questionable proceeding; for, from all that the Colonial Secretary stated, this will not be a mere occasional dole to help a temporarily crippled colony over a temporarily difficult stile, but must become practically an annual charge upon the mother country. Mr. Chamberlain made no note of the charges of extravagant administration brought against these colonies. A few economies had been introduced, but these would not enable the spendthrift islands to pay their administrative way. The limit of taxation had been reached there. England must make good the deficit. Nay, from his complimentary reference to the "wise expenditure" of France and Germany on their colonies, Mr. Chamberlain seems to have lost faith in the good old English policy, that the first and chief lesson given the colonies, is that they must learn to pay their way. Of course we are assured that in every case where a grant is made in those islands, the Government mean to see that "we have full and ample control over taxation and expenditure." A pleasing assurance truly, considering the admirable way in which the House of Commons exercises its "full and ample control over taxation and expenditure" at home! It looks as if one distinguishing feature of Mr. Chamberlain's tenure of power at the Colonial Office will be that he has taken the first step towards the financial demoralisation of our colonies.

Something may perhaps be said for the scheme for the disposal of the remaining portion of the supplementary vote, amounting to £30,000. It is to be applied in making roads, in helping the negroes to settle on the land as peasant proprietors, and in encouraging new industries. We do owe these negroes something. In a moment of somewhat reckless generosity, we paid the West Indian planters £20,000,000 to buy the freedom of their slaves. They were shrewd gentlemen these planters; and, while grumbling loudly, they pocketed the money, and left the island much poorer than it was before. They got fortunes, the slaves were left in a position considerably nearer starvation than they had been. This was the real beginning of the trouble which has ever since oppressed the island. It may be an excellent thing to buy out some or all of the landlords, but it may be made the very reverse. It all depends on how the scheme is carried out. Mr. Chamberlain pledged himself that, so far as he personally could, nothing like exorbitant prices should be given for land or buildings. If he succeeds in that the proposal may do well. It is worth a trial, but it will have to be very jealously watched, lest it ends in doing more harm than good—in being a mere scheme for putting money in the pockets of the landowners in place of benefitting the colony at large.

But this, it seems, is only a small part of the great project for the advantage of the West Indies which the Government are understood to have elaborated. Mr. Chamberlain could not explain the general proposals on Monday night because he is at present engaged in preliminary negotiations for "reciprocity arrangements" between the United States and Canada and the West Indies in regard to the reception by the former countries of West Indian products. It is a question of how far Protective duties may be modified on either side. Mr. Chamberlain spoke as if the West Indies were being asked to make too great a "sacrifice"—a sacrifice, be it remembered, of import duties which bear with undue weight upon the poorer inhabitants of the colony, and have undoubtedly greatly retarded its prosperity and industrial development. But Mr. Chamberlain is hopeful. If these reciprocity arrangements are concluded, it will, in his opinion, be equivalent to a "bounty" for the sugar growers. If this is all the Colonial Secretary hopes for, he will have done little indeed for the general prosperity of the West Indies. The colony cannot be improved by Protection, whether in the shape of "reciprocity arrangements" or bounties. But we must wait for the unfolding of the Government proposals. Meantime, we note that Mr Chamberlain objects to his grants being called "doles." He prefers to call them the "necessary expenses of empire"—the specious pretext under which we have been called upon to nearly triple our naval expenditure within twenty years.

Antofagasta (Chili) and Bolivia Railway Company, Limited.

Mr. Ottomar Haupt is a very clever fellow and writes with great intelligence. We always peruse his letters in the *Financial Times* with much interest and instruction. But he has some failings, and when he gets upon a gold standard for India we cannot follow him, still less when he falls foul of this railway company. Perhaps it is because his interests lie with the Huanchaca Mining Company, whose shares he some two years ago praised as the finest investment a man could have, that he becomes so savage when he thinks of this railway, interest at 6 per cent. on whose capital stock has been guaranteed by the mining company down to 1903. He really should moderate his wrath, for it would appear that neither the mine nor the railway are deserving of either pity or anger because of their connection with each other.

A very interesting report is before us drawn up by Mr. George Stielow, one of the directors of the Antofagasta Railway, as the result of a visit made by him to the property. From this report we not only learn that the mining company suffered no loss by working the railway last year, but, on the contrary, made a profit of £2,800; and we learned from last year's Huanchaca report that part of the debt incurred to that company by the railway for advances on account of interest was in 1896 repaid out of earnings. This is healthy enough, but what is still better is the fact that the general traffic of the line is becoming larger every month, we may say, and that it, therefore, is growing more independent of the traffic brought to it by the Huanchaca Company. People must not be led away by the notion that if the Huanchaca mine has had to shut down because of the water in its deeper levels—a most merciful flood by the way for those who work in it—the railway company would there and then fall into an impecunious position. It would do nothing of the kind. As the director whose report we deal with points out, although this current year will show a falling off in the gross receipts, just as the latter part of 1897 did, through a reduction in the Huanchaca traffic, the earnings from the general business are likely to continue to be sufficient to cover the Huanchaca company's guarantee.

In other words the Antofagasta line might be able by its Bolivian traffic alone to meet its engagements and, were it freed from all connection with the Huanchaca Company at once, its common stock would be in no danger of falling into default. Apparently in spite of drawbacks, such as we describe, the property is well maintained, and in good condition. Assume therefore, that it will require further capital expenditure within the next few years, and that either the port of Antofagasta itself must have a large sum spent upon it; or that another port will have to be found towards which the main line must be diverted, and at the very worst the company might still be able to pay 4 per cent. on its common stock. The traffic of Bolivia is increasing, and must increase, quite apart from the mineral devolpment going on.

We have no interest whatever in this property, and therefore can speak impartially enough when we say that it does not appear to us that holders of either the debenture stock or the common stock should sell on the present depressed market. They have been doing so through a mistake, and also through the clamour raised by Mr. Haupt, who, in what he deems to be the interests of his pet mine, desires to have the guaranteed annuity on the stock reduced at once to 4 per cent. We see no reason why this reduction should take place. In all probability the line will be able to clear off its debt to the Huanchaca Company by the time that Company is freed from its present guarantee. At all events the railway stock holders must not let themselves be bullied into a release of the Huanchaca Company, still less of the Chilian Government, until its position becomes very different from what it now is.

Sir George Lewis and Sir Henry Hawkins on Usurers.

Some remarkable evidence was laid before the Committee of the House of Commons on money lending by this gentleman last week. He, for one thing, emphatically defended the Jews from the accusation of being the only usurers in the country, and declared that Jews who did follow this loathsome occupation were despised and loathed by the Jewish community, and were not allowed to hold any public position therein. Further, the Jewish clergy, he stated, preach against them and their usages. His testimony was all the more valuable because he himself is a Jew, and we have no hesitation in saying that he spoke the truth. It is the bad Jew who gives the whole race a character with the public that it does not deserve. In regard to remedies Sir George thinks that a clause in the proposed Act running as follows, would do something to check the mischief :—

That whosoever, being a professional money-lender or manager, clerk, or agent, shall circulate or concur in circulating or publishing any statement knowing it to be false with intent to deceive injure or defraud any person by entering into contract for the loan of money shall be guilty of misdemeanour.

We are not sure whether this enactment would attain the end sought, because it appears to us the evils of usury lie much deeper down than any law can reach. Public opinion, frequently enlightened by such testimony as this distinguished lawyer gave, and the cultivation of simpler habits of living, might do more in the long run to destroy this canker than any law could be trusted to accomplish. As helping towards this illumination of the public mind, we quote the following from Sir George Lewis's evidence :—

There was a notorious case the other day, and he ventured to think that if it had not been for the facilities money-lenders gave, and the way in which a debtor became entangled, and the way in which he got into the hands of money-lenders, the crime for which that young nobleman was suffering would not have been committed. The first thing the money-lender did was to see who was the father and who were the relations, and what was the chance of screwing money out of them. He had heard of another case where a man had borrowed hundreds of thousands of pounds at the rate of 40 per cent. What possibility was there of that man being otherwise than ruined? He for one would be glad to see a heavy blow struck at West End usurers. He never knew a borrower gain advantage. A case was known of one money-lender who came over without a shilling who was now lending money to the extent of £40,000. Where did that come from?

After noticing action taken by Mr. Labouchere, Sir George Lewis said, in reply to members of the Committee, that he did not think any objection would be raised by legitimate bankers to legislation. Questioned by Mr. Ascroft, he believed it would benefit both poor and rich if these money-lenders were swept off the face of the earth. At the present moment the laws were all in favour of the money-lenders, and none were in favour of their victims. In Germany the usury laws worked well, and in America he was told there was no usury at all. He would not go so far as to say that money should be irrecoverable if lent to post-office clerks and others, who in borrowing of money-lenders were disobeying the rules of their offices. The difference between a banker and a professional money-lender was quite clear to everybody.

On Tuesday last Mr. Justice Hawkins also gave most valuable evidence, and it is interesting to note that he inclined to the opinion that the usury laws should be re-enacted in some form. In the United States, if money is lent above a certain rate of interest, it seems that the lender forfeits both interest and principal. Sir Henry Hawkins thinks that a good system, and we are disposed to agree with him. These debts to harpy money-lenders ought to be irrecoverable. Even this, however, would not eradicate the evil, and the danger of a strict usury law is that it drives the crime against society underneath the surface. As it is, very few cases of extortion come before the Courts out of all those that daily occur. None at all might come if the law were made stringent against the wretches who prey upon the needy and simple. Both Sir George Lewis and Sir Henry Hawkins emphasised the manner in which the trade of the usurer and the habit of gambling on the turf formed interdependent halves, as it were, of a system by which young men are ruined. Would it not be advisable to see whether some more stringent regulations could not be drawn up with a view to check if not to put an end to betting on horse races, especially in the young? The staid respectable citizen has very little conception how widely this pernicious habit prevails in the community. It affects all classes and does more to destroy the youth of the present generation than anything else we can point to. In the meantime to register usurers like pawnbrokers, to compel them to keep accounts of their transactions, open to inspection, and to strictly hold them at ransom for any unscrupulous practice, might do something to mitigate the evil.

THE URUGUAYAN COUP D'ETAT.

Uruguay seems to be rejoicing greatly over its recent coup d'état. It is regarded as a relief from an intolerable burden borne not very patiently for a good many years. The banished Assembly is denounced as having been an agglomeration of corrupt jobbers and bribers, while Senor Cuesta, the new dictator, is lauded as a strong man, and an upright. He may be so. Thus far he has, to all appearance, acted with firmness, judgment, and decision. He has been perfectly straightforward; and if we may trust in his manifesto—an able document—he means to behave like another George Washington or Cincinnatus. As soon as the Council of State has reformed the electoral law, and has convoked a new Assembly, Senor Cuesto intimates that he will retire from the Presidency as well as from politics, into private life. If so, Uruguay will doubtless be grateful. Occasionally dictators may even be desirable. They are not necessarily bad. "By their fruits ye shall know them." England has had her dictator, and on the whole it is acknowledged that his reign was beneficial. But it depends upon the individual; and in South America the rule of dictators has not always been beneficial. It may, generally does, require a revolution to displace one; and, on the whole, they cannot be regarded as desirable rulers unless in extreme and exceptional circumstances. Senor Cuesta, however, has undoubtedly, for the present, tranquilised Uruguay. The finances, he declares, have been managed with honesty and economy. There is cash in hand for all demands, and if his policy is continued he thinks there need be no dread of future deficits. He has not undertaken any public works—he was too busy putting the administration into order for that—but the way is prepared for them. The harvest is good, and trade is brisk. If Senor Cuesta purges the electoral laws, and secures a freely elected Assembly, he may retire with the goodwill and respect of all. But even with Senor Cuesta, worthy though he may be of the praise bestowed on him, a permanent dictatorship is neither desirable nor commendable.

AGITATION IN AUSTRIA.

Austria is in a peculiarly unfortunate position. It has been celebrating, in quiet and orderly demonstrations, the revolution of 1848, without apparently realizing that right in front of it hovers what may prove another revolution. One of lesser magnitude, perhaps, but still of serious dimensions. The Constitution is at present suspended; and the Emperor Francis Joseph is practically as absolute as ever was Maria Theresa. The Reichsrath reassembles shortly, and an attempt is being made to secure some sort of working Ministerial majority; but there is little hope of real success. It may be that such a majority may be secured for the passing of the Budget and the Ausgleich with Hungary; but after these chaos must come again. The rival linguistic parties cannot breath the same air without fighting. The Germans insist on dominating the Legislature, or stopping legislation if they cannot. The Czechs are equally determined not to submit to the Germans; and so the obstruction in the Reichsrath is sure to be resumed after the adoption of the Budget and the Ausgleich—possibly before. Count Thun is credited with a good deal of vigour and firmness. What will he do if confronted with German obstruction? The expectation is that he will dissolve, but to dissolve on the existing franchise would be but to return a body of delegates similar to the present. The Emperor may, if he chooses, revert to the old electoral law, and have a Reichsrath elected by the various Diets. But the probability is that the burden of responsibility will continue to rest on the Imperial shoulders as it does now. The Emperor is forced to be a dictator in spite of himself. The future is very uncertain. The uncertainty is seriously affecting trade; it checks and weakens Austrian international policy. This is the Emperor's Jubilee year; but he is afraid to encourage festivity lest it degenerate into riot. Yet he is the sole tie that binds the somewhat heterogeneous Empire together. His death would release the warring atoms; and the dissolution of the ancient Empire is not at all an improbable contingency. Indeed, there is a rumour that the first incentive to the Russo-French *entente* was a desire to be prepared for the partition of Austria when the time came. We do not believe the rumour; but the mere fact that it could be set afloat is significant of a great deal.

Mr. Woolf Joel.

No one could avoid being shocked at the tragic death of this young man. We are sorry for his fate and for the distress which it has brought upon his relatives and friends. Sympathy of this kind, however, is no justification for the manner in which some of the newspapers have been prostrating themselves before the shrine of Barnato Brothers, and lauding in a most fulsome manner "the business enterprise," the "great success" and "the marvellous aptitude at combinations to make money" and so on, which have distinguished the career of this firm. Surely journalists, if no longer endowed with self-respect, might at least remember that the British public, whether as investor or speculator, has nothing whatever to thank Messrs. Barnato Bros. for except the sorrowful and chastening experience of huge and irretrievable losses. From first to last the dealings of this firm with markets and the public have been of a description about which the less said the better. Where can the finger be pointed to one of their enterprises which has turned out well? Is there a single company floated by them in which British shareholders have any power of control, or to command information valuable to themselves? There is not one. But there are many whose operations, judged by their consequences, have been shaped wholly with an eye to plunder. It is necessary to protest against the indiscriminate praise which is nowadays so readily showered down upon any notorious individual, or group of individuals, merely because it is supposed that he or it is enormously rich. To the sad-eyed thousands whose vanished savings have gone to swell the millions of these Barnatos, the shocking deaths of one and another of them will seem as a judgment of Heaven on crimes human laws cannot apparently be framed to reach.

The Grosvenor Hotel.

We wonder what can have induced the board of this noted or notorious hotel to change its ground within the small space of fifteen days. At the meeting of the company after the verdict, the directors would accept nothing, and would do nothing. Now, when an application is made to the Court of Appeal to appoint receivers and managers, they are ready to submit to any order the Court might see fit to make. It would have been interesting from a legal standpoint had they resisted such an order. There is only one authority on the subject, and it is to be found in two decisions of Vice-Chancellor Malins in 1873, where, owing to internal disputes in a Company, a receiver was granted until a proper governing body could be appointed. The gravest doubts, however, have been thrown on those cases by the present Master of the Rolls, in his book on Company Law. As matters now stand, Mr. Kimber, M.P., Mr. Russell Spokes, and Sir William Fitzwigram will act for six months without remuneration as managers, and it is sincerely to be hoped that this undertaking will have a new lease of life, having thrown off the weight which was crushing the life out of it.

One of Mr. Whitaker-Wright's "Successes."

By this time every one knows about the "mines that failed" of the London and Globe group. The meetings, adjourned meetings, confirmatory meetings, and non-confirmatory meetings, of those unfortunate concerns have proved quite a golden harvest to the financial Press in an otherwise quiet time. It appears now to be the turn of the "successes" of the group to attract a little attention. The Ivanhoe is peculiarly a child after the kind of Mr. Wright's desires. Formed originally with a capital of £20,000, by the aid of the financier's air-pump the capital has been blown out to £1,000,000, very little in the way of fresh cash being added. Last October the great crowning operation took place, the £50,000 of capital then existing being converted by a registration at Somerset House into £960,000. In this swell-out the London and Globe Corporation obtained £210,000 of the capital as a perquisite for performing the feat, and the inflated capital was offered to the public at par—£5 per share.

We should imagine the response by investors was less than half-hearted, but the London and Globe Corporation nothing daunted, boldly ran the price of the new shares up to £7 each. Then, doubtless, with the desire to let outsiders in at a "cheap" price, the quotation was dropped to 6½, and remained between this and 6$\frac{5}{16}$ from November to the end of February. Although five months had elapsed by this time, no dividend was declared, and the special settlement in the new shares—that discoverer of things unseen—was due on March 15. Accordingly, the price of the shares began to sink, and since the commencement of the month they have fallen from 6 5/16 to 5. Weak "bulls" are said to be realising, but we should fancy that professional operators could not have been attracted towards this particularly fragile specimen of the financial wind-flower.

The record of crushings by the concern forms a charming commentary upon the prescience of its controllers in capitalising at the present high figure. In the following table we give these results together with the prices of the shares at the different dates :—

Monthly Periods 1897.	Tons crushed.	Ounces obtained.	Yield per ton.	Price.	Price per old share.
		oz.	oz.	£	£
August 10	1,335	2,319	1·7	12	—
Sept. 6	1,274	2,258	1·7	12⅞	—
Oct. 30..............	2,438	4,623	1·8	{ 14⅝ { 7	—
Nov. 30	669	1,323	1·9	6½	26
Dec. 31	2,695	4,891	1·9	6 5/16	25¼
Jan. 31..............	1,556	2,759	1·8	6½	26
Feb. 28	1,722	2,851	1·7	6⅜	25½
Present price..........	—	—	—	5	20

Please pay special attention to the "price per old share" in the table. This is the equivalent of the price quoted then for the old shares in the company with a capital of £50,000 that were dealt in before October last. In that month the new shares became the sole medium of dealing, and at that time we pointed out the extravagant quotations at which they had been started. Just then, though, the crushings seemed to come very much to the assistance of the market, but since the present year opened they have been disappointing, and the inevitable special settlement has brought a collapse in the price, bringing it down to the point at which the London and Globe is the proud, and perhaps, directly or indirectly, nearly the only holder.

Swift as the decline has been of late, the present quotation is still very high, for it represents about £20 for the old £1 share. The property only consists of twenty-four acres with a twenty-stamp mill at work, and the yield of gold is diminishing, for the average for the first six months of 1897 was 2·2 oz. per ton, as against the 1·7 oz. per ton obtained in the last return. We doubt whether the mad time in the undeveloped days of the Rand ever saw such a high capitalisation on as slender a foundation, and even in the West Australian market there is nothing to set quite in a position with it. All this will be fully understood later on, but experience is often dearly bought. We can only trust that our warnings, oft repeated, have in this instance helped to keep most folk from paying the price.

LIPTON'S, LIMITED.

An eminent accountant writes to us to point out that we have understated the amount paid for goodwill, &c., by the shareholders of this new company. He says: "The £200,000 is not to be deducted from the purchase price, but is to be supplied by the public subscriptions for the capital, partly by the 5s. premium on the ordinary shares reserved for public subscription." Probably our correspondent is right in this matter, but it did not seem to us to be clearly stated in the prospectus, and therefore we gave the vendor the benefit of the doubt. Assuming that we were wrong and our correspondent right, the total amount paid for goodwill, trade marks, &c., is £1,489,821, or more than 60 per cent. of the entire price given for the business, instead of 50 per cent. as we stated. It was bad enough on our showing, and this view only emphasises the madness of the public, which has wept and prayed in thousands for "just one little allotment" in the shares.

THE NORTHERN TERRITORIES MEETING.

Quite an Arabian Nights entertainment was provided by the organisers of this concern. The Chairman, Mr. Robert Smith, J.P., who has had a sadly wide and, we fear, woefully unfortunate experience of mining companies of recent years, was comparatively prosaic in his analysis of the wonderful balance-sheet, and in his account of the work done upon the properties. When it is remembered that it represents eighteen months' labour, very little seems to have been done, and tangible results seem entirely wanting. In his explanation of the accounts, as might have been expected, he made no reference to the sale of shares to the public at £3. How many were sold at this figure we don't know, but presumably some were, and the £2 per share have apparently been pocketed by the adventurous spirits who control the company. Actually the accounts show a little over a thousand pounds in cash ; add calls in arrear "since paid" £2,800, and the cash to be refunded by the Howley mine, say £9,000, we get a total of less than £13,000, a small sum, truly, to develop such wonderful properties. Mr. Bottomley, however, changed the whole character of the meeting when he spoke, and, throwing prosaic language, and something else, to the winds, launched into brilliant estimates as to the wealth of the properties. One little gem in his speech will suffice to convince those who know anything about mining either that Mr. Bottomley for vivid imagination cannot be beaten, or that he has some one at his beck and call possessed of a truly oriental cast of mind. He does not profess to make the statement upon his own knowledge, which is highly prudent on his part.

He said, "My own advices are to the effect that in one of your properties alone—I refer to the Eureka group of mines—you have upwards of £3,000,000 in value of ore in sight and ready to be crushed." Now, the Chairman had just previously stated that upon this Eureka property the shaft had been sunk 114 feet, and apparently 386 feet of driving had been carried out. Is it possible that ore to this value could have been disclosed in a mere scratching of the ground such a statement implies? But Mr. Bottomley knew his audience and was just tickling the ears of those who are as ignorant about mining as he himself appears to be. Doubtless he relies for pocket results more upon the announcement that he and his friends have created a shortage of shares upon the market than on mere prophesy of this kind. That is a good deal more in the line of an operator like Mr. Bottomley, and market men will give his hopefulness as to the future its true meaning and value.

THE CEYLON AND ORIENTAL ESTATES COMPANY.

It is a nice thing for a financial gentleman to come along and offer a better price to a company for the right to buy it up lock, stock, and barrel, than can be obtained by resort to the market. This is what

Mr. Ford has offered to do to the Ceylon and Oriental Estates Company, and he has agreed to forfeit £3,000 if he does not carry his bargain through before June 30. It is a small sum to pay for an option of this kind, and we are not surprised that the old chairman of the company, Mr. H. C. Smith, objected strongly to the scheme *in toto*. Surely the board which has overlooked a company's affairs for ten years or more knows its capabilities better than an outsider, who offers a high price for it upon the understanding that he is going to sell it again. It is not like one undertaking amalgamating with another, for there economies are often brought into play, but it is the case of a dealer in securities buying up the concern by staking a small sum as forfeit money in the hope of making a large profit by selling to the public at an extravagant figure. If the scheme does not go through he loses £3,000, if it succeeds he possibly gambles himself into a fortune. Meantime, this concern, which by hard labour has been brought out of the sloughs of an unfortunate past into the position of paying substantial dividends, will be once again at the mercy of the company-promoting financier. Of course he may make a substantial company of it yet, for the old concern suffered from the liability upon its shares, but he also may not.

With a Hooley, Hooley Ho!

And is it really so? The renowned Ernest Terah Hooley is going to limit himself, and merely to a million. His generosity overwhelms us, and we should have given the statement no credence had it appeared anywhere else than in the *Financial News*. But there it is in black and white—Hooley, Limited, and capitalised at a trumpery million, with his contracts, his flotations, his ten years' managing directorial life, and all. Had the figures been ten millions, now, we should have felt that the grandeur of the man had been adequately cyphered up. Is there not a mistake somewhere? Hooley, going, going at a million! Never! At this rate he will be gone in no time. His friends should really see to it that he does not thus throw himself away.

The British Insulated Wire Company.

The re-organised company of this title did very well in the eight months of its existence last year, but its claim that "the rate of profits actually realised has been in excess of the estimate inserted in the company's prospectus" is hardly supported by facts. In the prospectus the profits for the first four months of 1887 were stated at £16,890, *being at the rate of £52,692 per annum* and for the last eight months of that year they amounted to £33,281, or, at the rate of £44,374 per annum. In the matter of gross profits the anticipations of the prospectus were therefore not fulfilled, but if we turn to the item of net profits the result is somewhat better. In the prospectus it was stated that after paying debenture and preference interest, the net surplus ought to be £27,725 available for depreciation, reserve fund, and dividend on ordinary shares. Adding the £2,222 set aside for depreciation, the net profits of the eight months as returned in the report were £19,976, or at the rate of £26,632 per annum. This is below the estimate, but less so than in the case of gross profits and the improvement in this respect is due to the fact that the prospectus allowed for full interest on the preference capital or £6,000 per annum, whereas only £1,740 was paid, or at the rate of £2,320 per annum.

Pushful Japan.

Japan has just made a new advance in civilisation. It has issued a guide-book all about itself. But the book is a novelty in its way. It is an official publication. Perhaps there are no independent publishers in Japan. It is written in English, and the language is sometimes quaint, often peculiar, but generally wonderfully accurate. This little volume is uncompromisingly commercial. It is described as being "mainly for the use of foreign visitors to Japan." So we must suppose that the principal visitors to Japan are commercial men. Here we have nothing—or almost nothing—but statistics of imports and exports. There is a little about the geography of this wonderful Empire; nothing about its history. That is a pity. We should have liked to have been officially informed that it possesses a written history extending over 2,000 years; that its sovereigns have formed an unbroken dynasty since 660 B.C.; and that the present Emperor is the 121st of his race.

But of all this we hear nothing. We get but a "general view of commerce and industry in the Empire of Japan." The most ancient date we have observed in the volume is 1858. Since then 2,117 miles of railways have been constructed—580 miles by the Government, and 1,537 by private companies; 1,572 miles are now in course of construction. Japan has risen from an insignificant Eastern Power, with no commerce to speak of, to be the leading Power of the Far East, and the only one whose commerce is worth special mention. She is going ahead in manufactures, and in some respects has advanced so far as to be an adept in the manufacture of shoddy goods—one of those signs of nineteenth century civilisation which we may hope Japan may soon see the folly of. There is no need to go into detail as to the figures packed in this little volume. They, of course, leave us in no doubt as to the immense progress made by Japan; and they make it plain, also, how great is the business Great Britain—not to mention our colonies—is doing with Japan. We take a large quantity of her manufactured cotton goods—so does America — a notable quantity of her lacquered wares, bronze wares, ingot and slab copper. America and Canada, however, seem to take the chief portion of her tea—largely green tea. Of the goods which Great Britain sends to Japan, we may note cotton yarn, grey shirtings, white shirtings, T cloth, Turkey reds, cotton velvets, and cotton satins. In neither of these does any other country come near us—not even Germany. The latter does take the lead, however, in woollen yarns and flannels, while Britain again comes to the front in blankets. It is also worth noting that Britain takes an unmistakable lead in iron goods, especially in iron pipes and tubes, and in steel; while in various sorts of machinery, railway carriages, and steam boilers and engines, neither the United States nor Germany come anywhere near Great Britain. This seems rather surprising, for we should have expected America to have been well up to us in these articles.

Another official publication gives us a somewhat closer glimpse of industrial Japan. It is the report of an investigation conducted at the instance of the Department of Agriculture and Commerce into the working of industrial companies throughout the country. There are only 172 of these; the company promoter does not therefore seem to have been much abroad on the islands. Taking the companies altogether, their total paid-up capital and loans amounted to 34,424,364 yen, and the profit realised upon that was 2,272,647 yen, or an average rate of 6·6 per annum. Not a bad average; but then it seems that out of the 172 there were sixty-one that not only earned no profit, but lost to the tune of 251,803 yen on a working capital of 5,720,075 yen. What the real cause of the losses may have been no indication is given, but the amount of capital possessed to start with is not to be called overpowering, and probably over-sanguine or reckless trading did the rest. But eighty-nine of the companies earned an average dividend of 13·5 per cent., with an aggregate capital of 28,698,287 yen. Japan may not yet have many millionaires, but apparently she is not without a fair proportion of shrewd and sound business men.

SOUTH AFRICAN MINING NOTES.

THE FALL IN DEEP LEVELS.

Since the series of articles on the Rand deep levels appeared in these columns a depreciation has taken place in deep level shares of fully 20 or 30 per cent., and, although a reaction has been witnessed from the lowest points touched, the public still wisely refrain from coming into the market to any great extent. Deep levels, whatever may be the immediate course of prices, have not yet fallen to their true speculative value. It is interesting to notice that no sooner is the attempt to maintain an artificial level of prices partly abandoned than down come tumbling both the outputs and profits of the mines. This only confirms our previously expressed view that the mines are manipulated to meet the necessities of the market. The set-back in values occurred first; the fall in outputs and profits followed afterwards. The result of all this is that the simpletons, who a few months ago indulged in fantastic predictions as to the dividend-paying capabilites of deep levels, based on the earnings then being announced, have now to entirely revise their calculations.

How large the set-back in the profits has been may be seen by comparing the December and February figures of some of the Companies. The Crown Deep in December, with 160 stamps, earned £21,000; in February, with 180 stamps, only £9,000. The Crown Reef (the outcrop mine), with 120 stamps, working under the same conditions, earned £17,000 during the same month. So if it were not for the limited length of its life, the comparison would be all in favour of the outcrop. In December, the Rose Deep profit was £16,939; in February, £13,000. The Nourse Deep declared a profit of £7,710 in January; last month it only earned £5,600. Other examples might be multiplied, but it is unnecessary.

THE RAND MINES MEETING.

The fact that the annual meeting of the Rand Mines, Limited—the great parent trust of the deep levels—is to be held in Johannesburg on the 24th inst. has installed hope into the sinking heart of many a weary Kaffir "bull." It is rumoured, with a certain amount of authority, that the shareholders are to be consulted as to the advisability of splitting the shares, this, of course, with the object of bringing them more within the reach of the small speculator. Consider for a moment what this signifies. Mr. Beit, in his evidence before the South African Committee, stated that his firm held two-thirds of the entire capital of the Rand Mines Corporation. As vendors, they, with others, also possess the right to 25 per cent. of the profits after the shareholders have received dividends totalling 100 per cent. No doubt what will happen is that dividends of 100 per cent, will be first paid to enable the vendors to rank for their portion of the profits. Their lien will then be capitalised in some form or another, and the shares afterwards "split." Why should the shares be so sub-divided unless it is that Messrs. Wernher, Beit & Co. wish to create a freer market to enable them the more easily to unload their holdings on the public? The intention is perfectly obvious. When Rand mines are split, then it is that the market proppers and privileged holders will wish to sell their shares.

DIVIDENDS BY TRUST COMPANIES.

And this leads to another interesting question in connection with deep level trust companies. Concerns of this class have no goodwill, their profits are not made by trading or manufacturing, and the only possible manner in which they can earn dividends is by the disposal of their assets. Even profits accruing from dividends paid by their subsidiary mines are in reality obtained by the exhaustion of assets, for the mines will one day be worked out and valueless. If these South African trust companies confined themselves to distributing profits received from the legitimate working of their mines there would be nothing to object to; but they do not. The invariable practice is to declare large dividends, resulting from the actual sale of shares and ground, the proceeds of which, in reality, should be regarded partly as a return of capital. With this course pursued, a trust company has a "life" limited in length in much the same manner as an ordinary mine. This point is nearly always overlooked. Speculators who pay £27 or £28 for Rand mines should remember that the only way in which the company can at present distribute large sums to its shareholders is by parting with assets which it has to depend upon for future profits. The question is, in how many years can the directors sell sufficient of their shares and mining properties at the required profit to return £28 to each shareholder, and what assets will the company possess at the end of that period?

A CASE OF OVER-CAPITALISATION.

The Simmer and Jack Proprietary Company is a typical example of the gross over-capitalisation of some of the Rand mines. Its issued capital is £4,700,000, besides which there are £200,000 or £300,000 unredeemed debentures in existence. Floated originally with a capital of £85,000, for some years it continued to pay annual dividends of 40 per cent. The Goldfields of South Africa, Limited, then took the company in band, and by selling it additional mining ground gradually increased the capital up to its present figure. A very elaborate programme of work was then drawn up, including the erection of a 280-stamp mill; but while the capital has increased, the yield of gold has as steadily decreased. The recovery of gold for every ton crushed in 1890 was £3 1s. 4d., falling by stages until, in 1895, it was £1 18s. 6d. Portions of the new mill have now been crushing for some four months, during which the yield has only averaged £1 4s. 6d. per ton. The costs are declared to be very low—about 18s. 6d. per ton—but as other mines, fully as well equipped and probably better managed, cannot work under 25s. or 26s., this figure cannot be relied upon. What is certain, therefore, is, that if any profit is being made, it is exceedingly small; while it is noteworthy that the company has abandoned the usual custom of announcing monthly the result of its operations. There is very little chance that the company can earn any but the smallest dividends on its huge capital, while there are those who do not hesitate to predict its complete ultimate collapse. Over £1,000,000 sterling has been spent in the development of the ground, and the shares in its sub-flotations have had to be sold to pay off a portion of a large debt contracted. As the Gold Fields has a very large stake in this mine, its prospects are in no way improved by this state of affairs.

Critical Index to New Investments.

CHINESE IMPERIAL GOVERNMENT FOUR-AND-A-HALF PER CENT. GOLD LOAN OF 1898.

This loan, amounting to £16,000,000, will be offered to the public on Monday at 90 per cent., a price which gives just 5 per cent. to the buyer, by the Hong-Kong and Shanghai Banking Corporation here, and by the Deutsch-Asiatische Bank, Berlin. The last instalment of the price will be payable on the 3rd of May next. It will be a forty-five years' loan, redeemable at 100 by annual drawings through an accumulative sinking fund, and it is secured on the balance of the Imperial Maritime Customs left over from the service of previous loans, and as a first charge free from all encumbrances on the general and salt Likin of certain ports and districts in the Yangtse Valley, and adjoining province of Chekiang, viz., the ports of Soochow and Kiu Kiang, and the districts of Sunghu & Eastern Chekiang, Hupeh and Anhui, the last two for salt tax. All these duties are placed in the control of the Inspector General of the Chinese Imperial Maritime Customs. As the available balance of these customs is about three million Haikwan taels, and as these Likin revenues are valued at five million taels, making eight millions in all, or at 2s. 9d. per tael, £1,100,000 there appears to be ample security for a loan, whose service requires only £835,232, and we think the investment a good one. Yet so fickle is the temper of the City at present, that we should not be in the least surprised were the underwriters to have a considerable portion of it left on their hands.

UNITED BREWERIES OF WESTERN AUSTRALIA, LIMITED.

Two breweries are to be bought, the Stanley and Perth and the Port Brewery of Freemantle, whose united profits for two years are said to have averaged £10,435 per annum. A valuer in Perth, says his estimate of value of the Stanley Brewery is £60,200, which bald statement will, no doubt, bring in a lot of investors, and the same man cabled his valuation of the Port Brewery as £22,300; but apparently a barrel or two more has been found, and therefore subsequent advices increase the total to about £24,200. The capital is £150,000 in £1 shares, of which 75,000 are ordinary, and 75,000 6 per cent. cumulative preference, while the purchase price is £105,000 including £76,667 in cash. The promoters, who sell at a profit, are Westralia Industries, Limited, and it strikes us the undertaking has not been brought forward entirely to benefit the London Market. Still, Western Australia one way and another has got so much out of investors on this side that there is nothing like having one more try.

JOHN SUMMERS & CO., LIMITED.

Company is formed to buy business of ironmasters, iron and steel manufacturers, &c., established in 1850, and carried on at the Stalybridge and latterly at Connah's Quay. Reason for sale is to facilitate dealing with partners' interests and to provide more working capital for extension of works. Share capital £200,000 in 10,000 £10 ordinary and 10,000 £10 cumulative five per cent. preference shares. All ordinary and half preference go to vendors in satisfaction of purchase money; remaining preference shares held in reserve. Manchester, Liverpool, and District Bank invite applications for an issue of £100,000 four and a quarter first mortgage debenture stock at par; it can be redeemed at 105 after 1912 on six months' notice. Interest due January and July. Assets forming security amount to £261,419, including freehold land, works, and plant valued at £182,750; stock £46,205, and the remainder book debts and cash, guaranteed. Accountants certify that average yearly profits for last three years have been sufficient to pay debenture interest four times over. According to this the debentures should be a fair investment.

YEATMAN & CO., LIMITED.

For the purpose of buying the business of the private firm of Yeatman & Co., manufacturers of yeast powder, soups, jam and other delicacies, the company is formed with a capital of £200,000, half in ordinary £1 shares, and half in five and a-half per cent. cumulative preference £5 shares. Subscriptions invited for 13,334 preference, and 66,667 ordinary shares. Freehold properties valued at £41,035; plant, &c., at £8,287; stock, cash, bills receivable and debts estimated at £23,379; making a total of £72,601. Purchase price £155,000, so the value of the goodwill is about £80,000. Profits for last three years are given at £13,430; £13,614 and £13,601, which certainly shows lack of growth, but this may be supplied by the recent opening of a marmalade department, from which much seems to be expected.

STANLEY GIBBONS, LIMITED.

Capital £75,000 in £1 shares, and £45,000 in 5 per cent. first debentures of £50 each. Subscriptions at par invited for 50,000 shares and 640 debentures, remainder of shares and debentures with £64,000 in cash, taken by vendors. Debentures redeemable by annual drawings commencing June, 1901, at 5 per cent. premium business, foreign stamp dealers and publishers, established in 1856. A good deal is printed about increase in cash receipts, but all we are told about profits is that for three years ended June 30 last they averaged £11,399 per annum. Lease, fittings, stock-in-trade are valued at £90,638. A peculiar business for investment, capitalised at a high figure.

JOHN, SON & WATT'S, LIMITED.

Formed with a share capital of £85,000 in £1 shares, the public are asked to subscribe for 29,500 6 per cent. cumulative preference shares. There have been issued £35,000 in 5 per cent. debentures of £50 each, and these are redeemable after March 1905, at £52 10s. each. The company buys a fancy box, chromo-lithographic, letter-press printers, &c., business, established in 1842, for a purchase price of £100,000. The shares do not seem inviting, as there is little to judge the concern by. No valuation is supplied as to the properties; the amount of the trade liabilities to be taken over by the company is not stated, and the accountant's certificate regarding profits is confined to an average annual for last three years of £9,713. More light is needed.

CROWBOROUGH DISTRICT WATER CO.

The little Sussex town of Crowborough needs £30,000 to finish construction of high and low service reservoirs and pumping station, and to lay mains. It therefore offers through Barclay & Co. 2,364 ordinary shares of £10 each, 636 having been privately subscribed, and the issue price is par. No particulars are supplied as to the population of Crowborough, or of its capabilities to pay for a water supply, and therefore the shares appear a suitable investment for Crowborough alone.

GRAND THEATRE (CROYDON), LIMITED.

Capital, £50,000 in £1 shares, half ordinary and half 6 per cent. cumulative preference. Board consists of directors of Grand Theatre, Islington, and the latter has acquired from George Edwardes a ninety-nine years' lease of the Croydon house which has recently been rebuilt on a somewhat sumptuous scale. Gross profits for the year of the latter are approximately £9,605, and the net profit £5,020, but this we take it will be considerably lowered by directors' fees, ground rent, and depreciation. The property to be acquired is valued at £35,350, and the purchase price is £35,000, so that in taking it all in cash the lessors display prudence.

Company Reports and Balance-Sheets.

*** *The Editor will be much obliged to the Secretaries of Joint Stock Companies if they would kindly forward copies of Reports and Balance-Sheets direct to the Office of* THE INVESTORS' REVIEW, *Norfolk House, Norfolk-street, W.C., so as to insure prompt notice in these columns.*

THE COMMERCIAL CABLE COMPANY.—The Report of the Directors of this company for the past year discloses a highly flourishing position. After reserving $11,750 to meet depreciation of spare cable, the net revenue was $1,200,155, an increase of $76,502 on the previous year. This was from the cables alone, and the company's land lines gave in addition a revenue of $645,185, after setting aside $60,000 to meet depreciation. Altogether, therefore, the Company had $1,845,341 to divide, out of which it paid the interest on its bonds and debenture stock, and dividends and a bonus aggregating 8 per cent. on the capital stock of $10,000,000. These two payments absorbed $1,440,000, leaving $405,431 to be carried forward. The balance to the credit of revenue at the end of 1896, after adding $250,000 invested in United States Government bonds to the reserve fund, amounted to $596,678, and the directors have set aside a further $250,000 out of the balance of $1,002,089, which last year's balance added to that of 1896 gives, to still further strengthen the reserve fund, which now stands at $2,608,329. Also the directors set aside $275,000 as a reserve "for the insurance of stations, apparatus, and repairing steamer," and for any special expenditure necessary to the maintenance of the company's property. After providing all this, $477,019 is still left to be carried forward. The fixed charges of the company absorbed only 34½ of the total of the net revenue of the combined cable and land-systems. During the year 3,966 miles of additional wire have been put up on the company's land lines system. The balance-sheet shows current liabilities of $524,084, and current assets amounting to $1,158,469. Altogether the exhibit is one of remarkable strength and prosperity. No wonder the Canadians desire their "all Imperial" Pacific cable project to be tacked on to such a corporation.

BURY, ROCHDALE, AND OLDHAM TRAMWAY COMPANY.—This is a mechanically-worked tramway, and in the half-year ended January 31 last, the company, with receipts amounting to £21,709, earned a net profit of £2,984. Out of this £500 was placed to reserve against depreciation, the debenture bonds received interest at the rate of £2s 8d. 4d. per annum, and the shares a dividend at the rate of 6 per cent. per annum. The debenture bonds, strangely enough, receive only a fixed rate of interest of 2 per cent., but receive half the surplus profits after 5 per cent. has been paid upon the shares.

LAW LAND COMPANY, LIMITED.—By acquisition of neighbouring properties this concern is growing into one of importance. The gross rental last year amounted to £27,599, or an increase of £3,269 over that of the preceding year. After meeting charges the net revenue came to £7,482, as compared with £4,708 in 1896. More share capital had been raised in the time so that, in order to pay the 6 per cent. upon the ordinary shares, the addition to reserve was only £2,000, as against £3,500 a year ago. Leasehold redemption, however, received £758 instead of £500, and £812 was devoted towards writing off expenses of issuing capital. The record is therefore good, and the reserve fund now amounts to £12,000, and the leaseholds redemption fund to £4,872. It would be a sound policy to invest these funds outside the business. Temporary loans have certainly been granted to the extent of £27,000, but if these are to the leaseholders and tenants, it is little different to having the money in the business.

GENERAL AND COMMERCIAL INVESTMENT TRUST.—The revenue of this trust improved to the extent of £1,281 in the year, and amounted to £39,169. After meeting debenture interest and charges, a net balance of £21,689 was left, which permitted of the payment of the preferred interest and a dividend of 2½ per cent. on the deferred stock, or ½ per cent. more than in the preceding year. Nothing was added to reserve from revenue, but the trustees, as in previous years, handed over £2,500 from their remuneration to this fund, which had to bear £1,302 from loss on securities realised, and its total now amounts to £32,154. The liability upon securities held has been reduced by £2,600 in the year to £44,455, and, apart from a moderate sum upon 500 Bank of New Zealand shares, this item does not seem a matter of importance. A study of the investments brings out the fact that the trust is peculiarly free from thoroughly hopeless lock-ups, although, of course, the price paid for some of the securities must have been high. Many investments have appreciated considerably, and, so far as we can gather, the sums obtained from realisations have been carefully and judiciously employed.

BRITISH INSULATED WIRE COMPANY.—The company is evidently doing a large business, but there appears to be a great desire to pay high dividends. For the eight months ended December 31 the profits were £33,304, and after meeting administrative charges, setting aside £2,222 for depreciation, and writing £1,770 off preliminary expenses, there is a net balance of £19,494. Of this £1,740 is taken for preference interest, and a dividend at the rate of 15 per cent. per annum is declared upon the ordinary shares, leaving £1,629, of which £1,500 is written off patents and goodwill, and £129 carried forward. The patents and goodwill account stand in the balance-sheet for £117,119, out of total assets amounting to £322,652, and, with such a large percentage assigned to this doubtful form of asset, we should have preferred to see a start made with a reserve fund before such a high dividend was paid.

NORTH BRITISH RAILWAY COMPANY.—Gross receipts for half-year to January 31 last, £1,924,485; expenses, £935,594; increase in receipts, £66,659; ditto in expenses, £41,894. Little of the gross gain thus remained, the small net increase being £25,000 in fact, and it was nearly all absorbed in additional preference dividend charges. These amount to £491,433 in the past half-year as against £471,476 in the corresponding half-year, or £20,000 more. Consequently the company is able to pay no additional dividend on its ordinary stocks. The "ordinary preference" receives its 3 per cent. per annum, and the other ordinary, known as "North British Deferred," gets 1¼ per cent. per annum, or 12s. 6d. per cent. for the six months. Not a fat return this by any means, but then the company is much overborne by its disproportionate preference capital, and by its continuously heavy capital outlay. Last half-year it spent £324,407 on capital account, and the estimated expenditure in the current six months is £540,800. The Waverley works at Edinburgh are proving very costly, but may ultimately repay the company.

LONDON GUARANTEE AND ACCIDENT COMPANY, LIMITED.—Premium income for the year 1897 £201,763, claims due and accrued £98,657. Expenses, commission and income tax £85,400, or altogether £184,000. The company received £11,093 in interest on its invested funds amounting to £323,398. After placing £3,000 to reserve, raising it to £100,000, and paying the preference share dividend, a dividend of 6s. per share is declared on the ordinary capital, making, with the interim dividend of 2s. per share, 8s. or 20 per cent. for the whole year. What this leaves the directors do not state, and there is no use guessing.

ACCIDENT INSURANCE COMPANY, LIMITED.—Total income for 1897, including £3,275 from interest, &c., £65,077. Claims took £29,489 and bonuses to policy-holders £3,792. Out of the balance of £37,935 left after paying everything, this balance being about £3,500 larger than that brought in, a "bonus" of 5 per cent. is declared on the paid-up capital, making with the dividend 10 per cent. for the year. This would, we calculate, leave about £33,000 to go forward as reserve. Why are the reports and accounts of these accident companies so imperfect?

THE SCOTTISH LIFE ASSURANCE COMPANY, LIMITED, issued 578 new policies last year, insuring £251,275 and yielding £15,571 in new premiums. The total premium income of the year was £66,815, or deducting re-insurances, £61,314, of which £6,538 represented single premiums. The company also received £15,031 for annuities sold. Claims took £11,721, and expenses and commissions £10,791, or 17·6 per cent. of the premium income. The total life funds of the company at the year's end amounted to £400,784, an increase of £60,900 within the year. The company has an accident branch, the funds of which amounted to £16,796 at the year's end, or about £1,800 more than at the beginning. The expenses of this branch came to nearly 48 per cent. of the premium income. A sum of £1,900 was absorbed out of the income of this branch, of which £2,717 came from interest and dividends, in paying a part of the pividend to the shareholders, which was at the rate of 6½ per cent. der annum.

AGRA BANK.—A good improvement is shown in the annual report, the net profit for 1897, including £2,326 brought forward, being £26,260, as compared with £20,326 in 1896, when £138 was brought in. The dividend is consequently put up from 3 to 3½ per cent. for the year, and the considerably increased balance of £5,260 is carried forward. The bank's capital of £600,000 is now held entirely in sterling, which is a great improvement on the half gold and half silver of former days, but the reserve of £20,000 might with advantage be increased at an early date. Deposits are rather less, but still exceed a million sterling, current accounts being up £43,000, while fixed deposits are £66,000 less, which to some extent explains the increased profits, the reduction in interest being £6,000. The division of bills payable and loans payable gives the balance-sheet a better appearance, and owing to the change adopted regarding the accounts, both bills and loans payable, and bills receivable show a reduction of something like a million sterling each, while investments have risen from £93,316 to £272,178, against which has to be set a reduction of £82,000 in cash in hand. Deposits now stand at £1,013,837, while cash and investments figure for £394,000, or nearly 39 per cent.

SPRATT'S PATENT, LIMITED.—The past year's working has not turned out so well as the previous year, and that was bad compared with 1895. In the latter year the profit was £25,462, and in 1896 £20,529, but it has now further declined to £18,714. The usual £2,000 is written off trade debtors, and £3,000 is this time written off premises, goodwill, &c., as compared with £2,000 in previous years, so that after paying the customary dividend of 12½ per cent., only £4,333 is carried forward, or £3,000 less than a year ago. Last year's tale is reprinted of continuous increase of sales, more than offset by increased cost of materials and freights, while the advance in the price of flour is said to more than account for the variation in the trade profit, although many expenses were economised. The reserves used in the business stand as before, but premises, plant &c., owing to annual additions, have further increased to £230,268. Unless a change comes soon, a reduction in dividend seems to be drawing near.

CHINA MUTUAL STEAM NAVIGATION COMPANY.—The company did better last year, but it is a long way off being a typical success. Profits realised came to £66,314, or £7,650 more than in the preceding year, and after deducting expenses and interest, there remains a balance of £53,368 against £44,552. The directors add £37,000 to the depreciation, boiler, and reserve fund, which is thus raised to £123,769, while the fleet stands in the balance-sheet for as much as £646,159, or £522,390 net, which represents rather more than £11 per ton. The ordinary shareholders have £5,020 divided amongst them by way of a dividend of 6 per cent. For 1892, which was a time of trouble for the company, only the preference dividend was paid, but for 1893-4 the ordinary shares received 5 per cent., and since then the dividend has been 6 per cent. Possibly the developments now going on in the Far East may prove beneficial to the undertaking.

LIMMER ASPHALTE PAVING COMPANY.—This successful undertaking, with its modest capital of £22,500, continues to make good progress. Last year the gross profits on works executed and asphalte sold came to £11,360, compared with £9,225 in 1896. Expenses were not more than £3,719, and after adding £1,250 to reserve, writing £400 off for depreciation and £1,250 off preliminary expenses, being the balance of mines account, there remains £5,039, out of which shareholders get a dividend of 10 per cent., with a bonus of 1s. per share, or 15 per cent. for the year. At the corresponding period no bonus was paid, but for the three previous years the return was 15 per cent. The reserve for maintenance of contracts and for equalisation of dividends stands at £3,500, and there are sundry creditors and bills payable amounting to £4,139. Sundry debtors figure for the comparatively large sum of £16,084, but stock, plant and machinery, and the mines and factory in France represent together only £13,835, and the freehold premises have been written down to £400. This shows what can be done by a well-managed company with only a light capital.

THE MOUNTAIN COPPER COMPANY was brought out over here in 1896 with a capital of £1,250,000 in £5 shares, the purchase price being £416,630 in shares and £733,370 in cash. The properties are situated at Iron Mountain, State of California, and when acquired were said to be largely opened up. The first report shows that £39,043 has been spent during the year on the mines, buildings, and plant in California, and £2,465 in New Jersey. The net profits for the first year come to £63,144, which just allows of 5 per cent. being paid on the share capital. Nothing is allowed for depreciation, which is to be dealt with in future years. With the present high price of copper, this is not a very brilliant result, and there will have to be a good improvement in the future to justify the purchase price.

The Produce Markets.

GRAIN.

Until Wednesday, the tone of the wheat market may be described as quiet, but firm, with indifferent business doing, but on that day buyers were few at Mark-lane, and these few were utterly indifferent. The consequence was that English wheat declined 3d., while foreign was neglected, and a decline of 6d. failed to attract buyers. Spot parcels at Liverpool were also slow, with ½d. per cental decline. Futures were also quiet, with indifferent business, and a decline in Red American of ½d. to ¾d. per cental. In the Cargo Market there has been scarcely any movement, and on Wednesday the market was dull and featureless. There was, however, no quotable change in price. Late on Tuesday, 14,000 qr. Walla-Wall, March, changed hands at 34s. For the Salvatore Ciampa, 11,455 qr. Californian, arrived, 38s. 9d. is wanted; for the Sierra Estrella, 9,655 qr., 38s. 3d. is asked on sample, and for the Anaurius, 10,876 qr., 38s. 6d. Californian, December, is obtainable at about 37s. 9d., and early March at 35s. 6d. Walla-Walla, January, can be had at 36s. 3d., February at 35s. 9d., and prompt at 34s. 3d. Parcels inactive. No. 2 Calcutta, April-May, sold at 34s. for Hamburg. The surplus for shipment in the four months ending with June, is believed to be about 30,000,000 bushels, and, though the Indian wheat harvest promises well, any great decline in prices need hardly be expected. Wheat options, 2d. down to ½d. up. Maize ½d. down for early months.

OFFICIAL CLOSING VALUES (100 lb. deliveries—March 16).

	March.	May.	July.	Sept.	Dec.
Red American Wheat	7'9½	7'4½	7'0¼	6'6¾	6'4¼

New York reports have, on the whole, shown improvement. There has been a better political feeling, and greater confidence in the maintenance of peace. On Wednesday "bearish" influences were at work, and after sharp fluctuations, a decline set in, and there was no further rally. The export demand was fair.

COTTON.

In their last circular, Messrs. Neill Bros. say :—"The phenomenal deliveries of the past two months are doubtless the outcome of the rich yield on the lands fertilised by the floods of last spring ; but they may also point to a more extensive planting than was generally supposed, upon land bordering the flooded region, at the period when it was feared that the waters would not run off in time to plant cotton. Notwithstanding its previous enormous takings, the Continent of Europe has continued to absorb the lion's share of the exports, having taken for the five weeks 496,000 bales, against 301,000 last year and 299,000 in 1895. Liverpool, though still behind, has somewhat improved her comparison with the ten million year, having taken 387,000 bales against 308,000 in 1895. American spinners continue to add to their already large stock." The Liverpool spot market rather dull to begin with, but became more active towards the close of the week. Futures on Wednesday were ½ to 1 point higher. Manchester sales on a small scale, New York fluctuating, but spot was rather dull, and with little change. Futures on Wednesday quiet at opening, and declined a point, but rallied later, and closed 1 point dearer on the day.

NEW YORK CLOSING VALUES.

	Spot.	Mar.	April.	May.	June.	July.	Aug.	Sept.	Oct.	Nov.	Dec.	Jan.
Mar. 16 ..	6¼	5·95	5·95	6·00	6·01	6·04	6·06	6·03	6·03	6·03	6·05	6·08

WOOL.

Messrs. Jacomb, Son, & Co., state that the second series of wool sales began on the 15th with a total available quantity of 218,000 bales against 357,000 at this time last year. Competition was extremely animated from a large concourse of buyers. Of Australasian merino wools scoured descriptions may be quoted, on the average, 5 to 7½ per cent., and greasy 5 per cent. dearer than at the close of last sales. Fine cross-breds, with keen demand from the Home districts, ruled firm, but coarser sorts were occasionally easier. Competition was not very animated at the Liverpool sales, which commenced on the 14th. Prices showed a slight decline. As to subsequent London sales, Messrs. H. Schwartze & Co. write :—"The sale passed off with animated competition, opening rates being fully maintained, and for scoured merino often exceeded" ; and Messrs. Du Croz, Doxat and Co. say :—"The sale passed off with keen competition, all marines showing a hardening tendency. Cross-breds show no improvement."

METALS AND COAL.

Copper has been active throughout the week, with a considerable advance in price. The opening on Wednesday was firm, and 2s. 6d. higher, with cash at £50 10s., June 3, £50 15s. ; and three months £50 16s. 3d., which advanced to £50 11s. 3d., £50 16s. 3d., and £50 17s. 6d. respectively by the close of the first 'Change. Other dates operated in were April 7 and 12 at £50 12s. 6d., and the 30th at £50 13s. 9d., some 1,100 tons changing hands. Although 200 tons covered the afternoon's business, the tone continued strong, and was helped by the publication of the mid-monthly statistics, which revealed a reduction in the visible supply of no less than 1,259 tons on the fortnight. End of March sold at £50 13s. 9d., and April 25 and 20 at 1s. 3d. more.

SETTLEMENT PRICES.

	Mar. 16.	Mar. 9.	Mar. 2.	Feb. 23.	Feb. 16.	Feb. 9.
	£ s. d.	£ s. d.	£ s. d.	£ s. d.	£ s. d.	£ s. d.
Copper ..	50 12 6	50 7 6	50 7 6	49 17 6	49 10 0	49 5 0

The Glasgow pig-iron market inactive for the most part, but improved on Wednesday, when operations amounted to 50,000 tons. The tone was very firm until near the close, but Scotch closed under the best, selling being considered as better than buying, but on the day the price made 1d. Cleveland was supported by one of the big houses and rose 3d. Cumberland hematite gained 2d.

SETTLEMENT PRICES.

	Mar. 16	Mar. 9.	Mar. 2.	Feb. 23.	Feb. 16.	Feb. 9.
	s. d.	s. d.	s. d.	s. d.	s. d.	s. d.
Scotch ..	48 4½	46 1½	46 6	46 3	45 7½	45 7½
Cleveland ..	40 9	40 4½	40 10½	40 10½	40 7½	40 4½
Hematite ..	48 6	49 1½	49 6	49 1½	48 9	48 7½

Warmer weather has checked business on the London Coal Exchange. In the seaborne department, however, advantage was apparently taken of the material reduction in merchants' stocks which has recently taken place, and with a good demand two or three cargoes have changed hands at fully late rates, some of the coal being sold ahead. The official quotations remain at 16s. and 15s. for Hetton Wallsend and Lyons respectively. Since Monday twenty coal-laden vessels have arrived in the Thames. The inland trade is not quotably worse, but the market, owing to the scarcity of orders, is in a less satisfactory position and quieter all round. Steams are decidedly dull, with inland descriptions weak. North country coals are steady, owing to the diversion of tonnage in that direction ; but so far as Welsh descriptions are concerned the situation is unchanged.

SUGAR.

Cane sugars have been tolerably steady, even firm, though they got rather easier towards end of week. Beet futures dull. No quotable change in prices. Imports of sugar into United Kingdom, all ports, week ended March 12, raw and refined, 29,458 tons, against 25,510 tons for the corresponding week last year ; total since January 1, 266,826 tons, against 216,190 tons last year.

TEA AND COFFEE.

Coffee has been irregular throughout, with a tendency to lower prices. At the auctions, good qualities brought steady prices, but no increase. Ceylon—good bold to fine extra bold coloury, 108s. to 118s. ; good middling, 106s. ; small, 77s. ; peaberry, 116s. East India—bold common greenish foxy to fine bold blue, 67s. to 107s. ; low to good middling, 64s. to 90s. 6d. ; smalls, 43s. to 69s. 6d. ; peaberry, 73s. 6d. to 111s.

Tea dull, and the tone at the auctions was very depressed. Still a good deal was sold without reduction in price. Wednesday's auctions comprised 3,000 packages Indian, and autumnal flavoured were eagerly competed for at very full rates. 1,400 Java were also disposed of, previous rates being about maintained.

THE PROPERTY MARKET.

Last week's business at the Auction Mart ran up to the remarkable total of £165,364—the total for the same week in 1897 having been £96,654. Among lots unnoticed in last week's REVIEW was one of Messrs. Farebrother, Ellis & Co., a freehold building estate of four acres in London-road, Croydon, which sold for £6,000, or £1,500 an acre, a figure which local men acquainted with the ground seemed to consider highly satisfactory. Three freehold shops in High-road, Kilburn, the combined rental being £170 a year, were sold by the same firm at £6,150, a figure which must be regarded as fairly satisfactory. Messrs. Stimson & Sons disposed of houses Nos. 13 to 27 (odd), Aldridge-road villas, Westbourne Park, leasehold for a term of 58½ years, at £80 ground rent, and having an annual rental value of £480, at £4,190. On Friday Messrs. Moss & Jameson obtained £18,000 for a freehold building estate at Bexhill-on-Sea, containing an area of about 15½ acres. Four freehold houses, Nos. 150 to 156 (even), Weston-street, Bermondsey, producing a yearly rental of £150 16s., put up by the same firm, made £1,850. Messrs. E. and S. Smith disposed of two villa residences called Park View and Shirley, in Muswell-road, Muswell-hill, rental £83 per annum, for £1,335.

Monday was rather an "off" day at the Mart, and the total sales amounted to only £18,950. Much of the property offered was building land, two plots in Ilford-lane, Ilford, containing nearly 21 acres, offered by Mr. J. W. Kemsley, realising £9,300, rather over £440 per acre. Another notable sale was a freehold ground-rent of £65 per annum, secured on 166, High Holborn, with reversion in 83 years, which, offered by Mr. T. Woods, fetched £2,000.

Tuesday's sales at the Mart realised the fine total of £65,838, of which £25,000 fell to the lot of Messrs. Debenham, Tewson, & Co., for the freehold business premises, Nos. 27, 29, and 29½, Gracechurch-street. The same firm disposed of the freehold of No. 62, St. James's-street, for £8,100. It was a day of freeholds. Messrs. Chinnock, Galsworthy, & Co. put together an aggregate of £16,360, freehold ground rents at Shepherd's Bush being responsible for a large proportion of that sum. Messrs. Bignolds & Eason sold the freehold premises at 8, Old Compton-street, Soho, for £2,000. Is there a slump in licensed properties? Several of these were put up at Masons' Hall Tavern on Tuesday, but not one of them changed hands.

Some sales by private treaty effected by Messrs. Grant, Whieldon & Co. are worth noting. No. 39, Kensington-square, freehold residence, with possession, area 6,825 square feet, £5,000 ; Nos. 21 and 23, Ball-street, Kensington, freehold, with possession, £3,000 ; No. 54, Clifton-hill, St. John's-wood, lease 38 years at £8 10s., with possession, £800 ; and a parcel of freehold ground-rents amounting to £60 per annum, five times secured on houses let on agreements, reversion in seventy-four years, £1,920 (thirty-two years' purchase).

Wednesday showed a total of sales at the Mart of £17,975, of which amount Mr. Alfred Richards was responsible for £13,045, derived from £10 shares in the Lea Bridge District Gas Company, which realised £19 15s. to £20 5s. each. The other lots consisted of leasehold properties in London, for which there was some keen competition.

In last week's INVESTORS' REVIEW the name of Mr. F. H. B. Riddle was, by mistake, printed as Biddle.

The somewhat famous historical seat of "Rawdon," Hoddesdon, Herts., has just been sold by Messrs. Millar, Son & Co. It is built in the Elizabethan style, of date 1622. The previous owner expended £50,000 in restoring it. The interior is decorated with the armorial bearings of former owners, and there is some fine statuary as well as excellently carved oak panelling. The price at which the property changed hands is not stated.

Several lots of freehold ground rents at Birmingham Heath were sold by Messrs. Frank Smith & Wilson at the high average of 33½ years' purchase. A fully licensed house in Bradford, put up for auction last week, was withdrawn at £12,000. A freehold farm of twenty acres at Hebden Bridge, Yorkshire, was recently disposed of for £1,375.

TRAMWAY AND OMNIBUS RECEIPTS.

For past week :—Belfast, + £36 ; Calais, + £3 ; Croydon, + £10 ; Glasgow, – £61 ; Lea Bridge, + £72 ; London & Deptford, + £14 ; London Southern, + £50 ; London General Omnibus, – £50 ; London Road Car, – £130 ; Metropolitan, – £36 ; North Staffordshire, + £10 ; South London, – £46 ; Woolwich & S. E. London, – £7 ; Provincial, – £222 ; Southampton, – £58 ; Wolverhampton, – £1.

Barcelona, – £179 ; Bordeaux, – £216.

Anglo-Argentine, week ending February 7, £470 increase ;

City of Buenos Ayres, week ending February 14, £751 increase

Dividends Announced.

MISCELLANEOUS.

BROKEN HILL WATER SUPPLY, LIMITED.—6d. per share.

BURY, ROCHDALE, AND OLDHAM TRAMWAY COMPANY, LIMITED.—6 per cent. per annum.

G. W. BACON & CO., LIMITED.—9 per cent. for the half-year ended December 31 last; £2,000 carried forward.

GRAND HOTEL, MONTE CARLO, LIMITED.—Interim dividend of 5 per cent. on the Ordinary shares.

DURBAN ROODEPOORT GOLD MINING COMPANY, LIMITED.—Interim dividend of 4s. per share on account of the year 1898 ending December 31.

FRENCH HARVEY STEEL COMPANY.—Dividend of 12.71 fr. per part de fondateur (vendor shares) upon presentation of Coupon No. 3. Also 187.25 fr. per share upon the social shares, of which 18 fr. will be placed towards amortisément of these shares, and the balance—namely, 6.25 fr. paid in cash in Paris.

LAKE VIEW CONSOLS, LIMITED.—Further dividend for the current year of 10s. per share.

GRAND THEATRE, ISLINGTON, LIMITED.—Interim dividend at the rate of 10 per cent. per annum for the six months ended 31st inst.

JOINTLESS RIM, LIMITED.—Interim dividend at the rate of 9d. per share.

HENRY BUCKNALL & SONS, LIMITED.—Interim dividend for the half-year ended February 28 at the rate of 6 per cent. per annum on the Ordinary shares.

BRITISH AND AMERICAN MORTGAGE COMPANY, LIMITED.—4 per cent. on the ordinary shares, making 7 per cent. for 1897.

SAVOY HOTEL, LIMITED.—5s. per share dividend is proposed, making 7½ for year; £4,000 placed to reserve and £1,751 carried forward.

DIRECT SPANISH TELEGRAPH COMPANY, LIMITED.—Divideed at the rate of 4 per cent. per annum on the ordinary shares, and of 10 per cent. per annum on the preference shares, for the half-year ended December 31.

BRILLIANT AND ST. GEORGE UNITED GOLD MINING COMPANY, LIMITED.—1s. per share is announced.

NEW HERIOT GOLD MINING COMPANY, LIMITED.—25 per cent. The warrants may be expected to arrive in Europe about the end of May next.

IMPERIAL TRAMWAYS COMPANY.—Dividend at the rate of 6 per cent. per annum, leaving £68 to be carried forward.

IVANHOE GOLD MINING COMPANY.—Further cash distribution at the rate of 10s. per share has been declared.

SHEBA GOLD MINING COMPANY, LIMITED.—9d. per share, payable on April 2.

CROWN REEF GOLD MINING COMPANY.—100 per cent for the second half of last year.

SCHULTZE GUNPOWDER COMPANY, LIMITED.—£20 per cent. has been declared.

PARKE'S DRUG STORES.—Dividend on the ordinary shares for the half-year ended December 31, at the rate of 6 per cent. per annum.

BIRMINGHAM SMALL ARMS.—Interim dividend at the rate of 5 per cent. per annum on the preference shares, and of 5s. per share on the ordinary shares.

SEPTIMUS PARSONAGE & CO.—Further dividend of 4 per cent. on the ordinary shares, making 8 per cent. for 1897. £4,000 to reserve, and £2,557 carried forward.

EBENEZER ROBERTS & SONS, LIMITED.—Dividend at the rate of 6 per cent. per annum on the preference and ordinary shares for 1897.

DUNDEE COAL & ESTATES COMPANY, LIMITED.—Quarterly dividend at the rate of 10 per cent.

GELDENHUIS ESTATE & GOLD MINING COMPANY, LIMITED.—Fifty per cent. has been declared.

ASSOCIATED TEA ESTATES OF CEYLON.—Interim dividends for the period ending December, 1897, at the rate of 6 per cent. per annum on the preference shares, and 5 per cent. per annum on the ordinary shares have been declared.

EASTERN TELEGRAPH COMPANY.—Interim dividend of 2s. 6d. per share on the ordinary shares.

AFRICAN STEAM SHIP.—A dividend of 12s. per share for the six months ended December, 1897, making with the interim dividend, a total distribution of 16s. per share for the year.

BANKS.

ROBINSON SOUTH AFRICAN.—Interim dividend of 2s. per share on the ordinary shares.

AGRA.—Further dividend for 1897 at the rate of 4 per cent. per annum will be payable on April 1.

ANGLO-ITALIAN, LIMITED.—Dividend for the second of 1897 at the rate of 10 per cent. per annum, making, with the interim already paid, 7 per cent. for the year.

INSURANCE.

MANCHESTER FIRE.—Dividend and bonus making total for the year of 15 per cent.

RAILWAYS.

BUENOS AYRES WESTERN, LIMITED.—Interim dividend of 3s. 6d. per share, equal to a dividend at the rate of 3½ per cent. per annum on the ordinary share capital. Balance forward, £5,531.

HORNCASTLE (LINCOLNSHIRE).—Dividend at the rate of 9 per cent. Balance forward, £237.

WELLINGTON AND MANAWATU RAILWAY COMPANY.—Five per cent. for the year ended February 28.

Answers to Correspondents.

Questions about public securities, and on all points in company law, will be answered week by week, in the REVIEW, on the following terms and conditions:—

A fee of FIVE shillings must be remitted for each question put, provided they are questions about separate securities. Should a private letter be required, then an extra fee of FIVE shillings must be sent to cover the cost of such letter, the fee then being TEN shillings for one query only, and FIVE shillings for every subsequent one in the same letter. While making this concession the EDITOR will feel obliged if private replies are as much as possible dispensed with. It is wholly impossible to answer letters sent merely "with a stamped envelope enclosed for reply."

Correspondents will further greatly oblige by so framing their questions as to obviate the necessity to name securities in the replies. They should *number* the questions, keeping a copy for reference, thus:—"(1) Please inform me about the present position of the Rowenzori Development Co. (2) Is a dividend likely to be paid soon on the capital stock of the Congo-Sudan Railway?"

Answers to be given to all such questions by simply quoting the numbers 1, 2, 3, and so on. The EDITOR has a rooted objection to such forms of reply as—"I think your Timbuctoo Consols will go up," or "Sell your Slowcoach and Draggem Bonds," because this kind of thing is open to all sorts of abuses. By the plan suggested, and by using a fancy name to be replied to, each query can be kept absolutely private to the inquirer, and no scope whatever be given to market manipulations. Avoid, as names to be replied to, common words, like "investor," "inquirer," and so on, as also "bear" or "bull." Detached syllables of the inquirer's name, or initials reversed, will frequently do as well as anything, so long as the answer can be identified by the inquirer.

The EDITOR further respectfully requests that merely speculative questions should as far as possible be avoided. He by no means sets himself up as a market prophet, and can only undertake to provide the latest information regarding the securities asked about. This he will do faithfully and without bias.

Replies cannot be guaranteed in the same week if the letters demanding them reach the office of the INVESTORS' REVIEW, Norfolk House, Norfolk-street, W.C., later than the first post on Wednesday mornings.

M.B.L. I think you might hold for the present, as there seems to be some chance of a recovery. Financially the position is exceedingly weak, but it seems probable that those interested will give support, if so you ought to have a more favourable opportunity of selling.

Next Week's Meetings.

SATURDAY, MARCH 19.

Central London Ry. (spec.)	16, Great George-street, S.W., noon
Co-operative Insurance	Manchester, 3.30 p.m.

MONDAY, MARCH 21.

Bodega	Winchester House, noon.
British Linen Co. Bank	Edinburgh, 1 p.m.
Crescens, Robinson & Co. ...	26-28, Newington Causeway, 1 p.m.
Jays	Swallow-place, W., 3 p.m.
Plate Steamship	14, Billiter-street, 11.30 a.m.
Scottish Alliance Insurance... ...	Glasgow, noon.
South London Electric Supply ...	Winchester House, noon.

TUESDAY, MARCH 22.

J. Mandleberg & Co.	Manchester, noon.
London & Northern Assets	Cannon-street Hotel, 1 p.m.

WEDNESDAY, MARCH 23.

British Gas Light	11, George-yard, 12.30 p.m.
Indemnity Mutual Marine	Winchester House, noon.
Law Union and Crown Fire and Life	126, Chancery-lane, 1 p.m.

THURSDAY, MARCH 24.

Agra Bank	Cannon-street Hotel, 12.30 p.m.
Antofagasta and Bolivia Railway ...	Winchester House, 3 p.m.
British American Land	40, Old Broad-street, 12.30 p.m.
British Bank of South America ...	2A, Moorgate-street, 12.30 p.m.
General and Commercial Investment Trust	Cannon-street Hotel, 12 noon.
Mauritius Land, Credit, and Agency Company	16, Rood-lane, 3.15 p.m.
North British Railway	Edinburgh, 12.30 p.m.
Priest, Marians, Bethell, Moss & Co.	56, St. Mary-Axe, 3 p.m.

FRIDAY, MARCH 25.

Atlas Assurance	Cheapside, noon.
Bolckow, Vaughan & Co.	Manchester, noon.
Clacton-on-Sea Pier	33, Walbrook, noon.

What is New Zealand afraid of? The Government has decided on greatly strengthening the military resources of the Colony. A field battery, of the most modern pattern, is to be established, and the volunteer force is to be greatly increased.

To Correspondents.

The Editor cannot undertake to return rejected communications. Letters from correspondents must, in every case, be authenticated by the name and address of the writer.

The Investors' Review.

The Week's Money Market.

Although the Money Market has been more agitated in the past few days than for a long time past, rates for day-to-day money and short loans have ruled easier than of late. At times no more than 2¼ per cent. could be obtained for day-to-day money, and since Monday the general charge has been 2¼ to 2¾ per cent., with the higher figure demanded for loans for a week. The very anxieties of the time have produced a moderation in rates, as the large discount operations undertaken at the Bank of England, part of which may have been prompted by precautionary motives, left the market with more money on its hands than it needed at the moment.

Discount rates at one time were very firm, and 3⅜ to 3½ per cent. was by no means an exceptional quotation, for the melting of two and three months' bank bills. To bid so high above the official minimum was clear evidence that the market, or a section of it, feared an advance in the Bank-rate, and, no doubt, if the political uncertainties lead to an outbreak of hostilities this feared movement will take place. Short of this extreme contingency the prospects of a rise are not very assured, and directly the political turmoil calmed down, the market fine discount rate subsided to about the official minimum. The decline was aided by the knowledge that the £3,325,000 of Treasury Bills maturing on April 4 will not be immediately renewed. Although of late maturing paper of this class has been found to be mainly held by Government departments, out of such a large repayment the market ought to obtain a fair amount of relief. Then, although Government disbursements have not yet commenced in earnest, the distribution of the Consol dividends is now near at hand. There is, therefore, prospect that the recent intolerable shortness of cash will be mitigated to a marked extent, but the gradual liquidation of indebtedness to the Bank of England will draw much of the money away again, unless supplies of gold and credits come in from abroad. Therefore, the tension is not likely to be slackened until the United States demand for gold has diminished. Nearly half a million was taken for that quarter in the week, and such a drain cannot be long ignored. There are signs that it may moderate, but being based upon political anxieties nothing is sure. Continental exchanges have moved still further in our favour, and there is little doubt that if they are maintained at their present level for any time, gold will drift to us from that quarter.

Nothing in the Bank return published yesterday supported an advance in the Bank rate. The large business the Bank did during the week has made little change in its totals. Borrowings by the market have increased £556,904, making the total of "other" securities £35,816,210, so of this money £483,456 has been added to "other" deposits. Government deposits are also larger by £257,188 at £18,979,353, which is about the largest total ever attained, so that the looked-for dispersal of treasury balances has not yet begun. Part of the £435,000 in gold withdrawn for export has been replaced by coin returned from circulation, so that the net decrease in the Bank's stock of bullion is only £279,425. The balance of the loss has been more than compensated for by the return of notes likewise, and the net result is an increase of £37,585 in the Banking reserve, which now stands at £23,717,099. A small amount, £165,555, has been added to Government securities. Adding this to the increase in the "other" securities, the Bank has paid out £702,000 in all against security, and the market has, as we have said, retained £483,000 of it—a poor sum for its necessities, but this should be the last week of extreme poverty.

SILVER.

A sharp recovery has been experienced in this market during the week, and the price for bars on the spot has advanced 1/16d. to 25⅝d. per ounce. The "forward" quotation, however, has not moved so briskly, being only 1/16d. higher, at 25⅜d. per ounce. A recovery on the Indian price of the metal to 67½ per 100 tolas, was the reason for the movement, and the increased demand in India is ascribed to anticipations as to the Budget statement by Sir J. Westland. It may, however, be due to mere closing of "bear" operations entered upon when the increased duty upon silver was first mooted. Even at the time we write the date of the Budget statement is not absolutely fixed, but the 21st still remains the most probable day, and it is further added that it will be "discussed" on the 28th, which means that some change in taxation will be proposed. The applications for Council drafts on Wednesday were on a moderate scale, and only 36 lacs were sold, the Council refusing about 12 lacs at low quotations. Great complaint is made about the state of trade at Bombay owing to the disturbed condition of the city from plague and other causes, and although this ought to be the busy season there the Bank of Bombay reported a considerble addition to its balances. Indian exchanges have therefore weakened materially, but Chinese rates have risen ⅛d. to ⅜d. upon the improved price of silver.

BANK OF ENGLAND.

AN ACCOUNT pursuant to the Act 7 and 8 Vict., cap. 32, for the Week ending on Wednesday, March 16, 1898.

ISSUE DEPARTMENT.

	£		£
Notes Issued	47,573,390	Government Debt	11,015,100
		Other Securities	5,784,900
		Gold Coin and Bullion	30,773,390
		Silver Bullion	—
	£47,573,390		£47,573,390

BANKING DEPARTMENT.

	£		£
Proprietors' Capital	14,553,000	Government Securities	14,153,120
Rest	3,777,599	Other Securities	35,816,210
Public Deposits (including Exchequer, Savings Banks, Commissioners of National Debt, and Dividend Accounts)	18,979,353	Notes	21,143,920
Other Deposits	36,272,556	Gold and Silver Coin	2,573,179
Seven Day and other Bills	103,921		
	£73,686,429		£73,686,429

Dated March 17, 1898.

H. G. BOWEN, *Chief Cashier.*

In the following table will be found the movements compared with the previous week, and also the totals for that week and the corresponding return last year:—

Banking Department.

Last Year. March 17.		March 9, 1898.	March 16, 1898.	Increase.	Decrease.
£	Liabilities.	£	£	£	£
3,758,608	Rest	3,730,565	3,777,599	47,034	—
16,835,294	Pub. Deposits	18,692,165	18,979,353	287,188	—
38,540,872	Other do.	35,789,100	36,272,556	483,456	—
193,059	7 Day Bills	141,555	103,921	—	37,634
	Assets.			Decrease.	Increase.
14,387,883	Gov. Securities	13,987,565	14,153,120	—	165,555
28,911,575	Other do.	35,259,306	35,816,210	—	556,904
30,581,375	Total Reserve	23,679,514	23,717,099	—	37,585
				797,678	797,678
				Increase.	Decrease.
£		£	£	£	£
25,899,170	Note Circulation	26,746,480	26,429,470	—	317,010
55 p.c.	Proportion	43⅜ p.c.	42⅞ p.c.	—	—
3 "	Bank Rate	3 "	3 "	—	—

Foreign Bullion movement for week £435,000 out.

LONDON BANKERS' CLEARING.

Week ending	1898.	1897.	Increase.	Decrease.
	£	£	£	£
Jan. 5	222,654,000	174,376,000	48,278,000	—
" 12	144,603,000	127,315,000	17,288,000	—
" 19	171,777,000	156,200,000	15,577,000	—
" 26	134,247,000	118,667,000	15,580,000	—
Feb. 2	194,544,000	174,498,000	20,056,000	—
" 9	137,204,000	129,209,000	8,995,000	—
" 16	184,403,000	162,168,000	22,235,000	—
" 23	132,450,000	131,777,000	673,000	—
March 2	190,157,000	177,852,000	12,305,000	—
" 9	134,490,000	126,182,000	8,308,000	—
" 16	174,377,000	148,937,000	25,440,000	—

BANK AND DISCOUNT RATES ABROAD.

	Bank Rate.	Altered.	Open Market.
Paris	2	March 14, 1895	1¾
Berlin	3	February 20, 1898	2⅝
Hamburg	3	February 20, 1898	2⅝
Frankfort	3	February 20, 1898	3
Amsterdam	3	April 13, 1897	2¼
Brussels	3	April 28, 1896	2
Vienna	4	January 22, 1896	3⅜
Rome	5	August 27, 1895	3
St. Petersburg	5½	January 23, 1898	5
Madrid	5	June 17, 1896	4
Lisbon	6	January 25, 1891	6
Stockholm	4	March 3, 1898	3½
Copenhagen	4	January 20, 1898	4
Calcutta	12	February 24, 1898	—
Bombay	13	February 24, 1898	—
New York call money	1½ to 2	—	—

NEW YORK ASSOCIATED BANKS (dollar at 4s.).

	Mar. 12, 1898.	Mar. 5, 1898.	Feb. 26, 1898.	Mar. 13, 1897.
	£	£	£	£
Specie	24,812,000	24,026,000	23,838,000	17,054,000
Legal tenders	14,506,000	15,440,000	17,216,000	22,452,000
Loans and discounts	123,572,000	125,652,000	128,376,000	101,182,000
Circulation	2,759,200	2,755,000	2,745,400	3,242,000
Net deposits	139,096,000	141,204,000	145,842,000	115,738,000

Legal reserve is 25 per cent. of net deposits; therefore the total reserve (specie and legal tenders) exceeds this sum by £4,544,000, against an excess last week of £4,165,000.

BANK OF FRANCE (25 francs to the £).

	Mar. 17, 1898.	Mar. 10, 1898.	Mar. 3, 1898.	Mar. 18, 1897.
	£	£	£	£
Gold in hand	74,905,080	75,721,080	76,831,240	76,674,000
Silver in hand	48,521,880	48,484,480	48,565,440	49,088,000
Bills discounted	27,375,280	27,240,040	31,773,800	*42,782,000
Advances	14,665,520	14,761,680	14,730,240	—
Note circulation	149,170,880	149,757,360	152,206,720	146,676,000
Public deposits	5,788,240	5,430,600	6,041,720	7,613,000
Private deposits	16,764,240	17,888,680	18,756,040	19,120,000

Proportion between bullion and circulation 82¼ per cent. against 82⅜ per cent. a week ago.

* Includes advances.

FOREIGN RATES OF EXCHANGE ON LONDON.

Place.	Usance.	Last week's.	Latest.	Place.	Usance.	Last week's.	Latest.
Paris	chqs.	25·31½	25·30½	Italy	sight	26·66	26·78
Brussels	chqs.	25·36¼	25·37	Do. gold prem.	..	105·35	105·67½
Amsterdam	short	12·08¼	12·09¾	Constantinople	3 mths	109·25	110
Berlin	short	20·47	20·48	B. Ayres gd. pm.	..	168·80	164·70
Do.	3 mths	20·32	20·31½	Rio de Janeiro	90 dys	6$\frac{1}{16}$	6$\frac{3}{32}$
Hamburg	3 mths	20·31	20.31½	Valparaiso	90 dys	17⅝	17⅝
Frankfort	short	20·47	20·48	Calcutta	T. T.	1/4$\frac{1}{32}$	1/3$\frac{31}{32}$
Vienna	short	12·03	12.04½	Bombay	T. T.	1/4$\frac{1}{32}$	1/3$\frac{31}{32}$
St. Petersburg	3 mths	93·90	94.00	Hong Kong	T. T.	1/10⅜	1/10⅜
New York	60 dys	4·81½	4·80⅝	Shanghai	T. T.	2/5⅜	2/5½
Lisbon	sight	35$\frac{1}{16}$	34⅞	Singapore	T. T.	1/10	1/10½
Madrid	sight	34·65	35·47½				

IMPERIAL BANK OF GERMANY (20 marks to the £).

	Mar. 7, 1898.	Mar. 1, 1898.	Feb. 23, 1898.	Mar. 6, 1897.
	£	£	£	£
Cash in hand	47,989,250	48,155,800	49,178,700	45,738,000
Bills discounted	28,107,950	27,442,600	25,905,600	*30,407,000
Advances on stocks	3,746,650	4,282,200	3,690,850	—
Note circulation	51,058,500	51,092,750	49,498,100	48,602,000
Public deposits	24,558,350	24,705,300	25,905,600	23,341,000

* Includes advances.

AUSTRIAN-HUNGARIAN BANK (1s. 8d. to the florin).

	Mar. 7, 1898.	Feb. 28, 1898.	Feb. 23, 1898.	Mar. 7, 1897.
	£	£	£	£
Gold reserve	30,754,925	30,715,583	30,615,083	30,972,000
Silver reserve	10,402,500	10,407,333	10,411,500	12,665,000
Foreign bills	1,114,750	1,214,333	1,254,740	—
Advances	1,862,000	1,885,833	1,832,166	—
Note circulation	51,904,250	51,908,416	50,579,333	58,692,000
Bills discounted	11,312,583	10,871,916	10,132,000	*16,007,000

* Includes advances.

NATIONAL BANK OF BELGIUM (25 francs to the £).

	Mar. 10, 1898.	Mar. 3, 1898.	Feb. 24, 1898.	Mar. 11, 1897.
	£	£	£	£
Coin and bullion	4,186,040	4,339,520	4,198,480	4,198,000
Other securities	16,691,720	17,024,440	17,290,680	15,843,000
Note circulation	19,023,080	18,900,040	19,255,680	18,301,000
Deposits	3,342,400	3,978,120	3,670,720	3,104,000

BANK OF SPAIN (25 pesetas to the £).

	Mar. 12, 1898.	Mar. 5, 1898.	Feb. 26, 1898.	Mar. 13, 1897.
	£	£	£	£
Gold	9,577,760	9,559,640	9,542,840	8,528,760
Silver	10,860,040	10,874,560	10,875,280	10,746,680
Bills discounted	23,381,120	23,260,360	21,491,840	7,911,120
Advances and loans	5,501,320	5,459,120	4,924,360	9,688,040
Notes in circulation	50,385,600	50,195,240	49,959,440	42,670,400
Treasury advances, coupon account	313,960	386,760	330,560	314,880
Treasury balances	1,526,080	1,483,160	988,500	2,689,560

OPEN MARKET DISCOUNT.

	Per cent.
Thirty and sixty day remitted bills	2¾—3
Three months "	2⅞—3
Four months "	2¾
Six months "	2¾
Three months fine inland bills	3—3¼
Four months "	3—3¼
Six months "	3½

BANK AND DEPOSIT RATES.

	Per cent.
Bank of England minimum discount rate	3
" " short loan rates	3
Banker's rate on deposits	1½
Bill brokers' deposit rate (call)	2
" 7 and 14 days' notice	2¼
Current rates for 7 day loans	2½—2¾
" " for call loans	2¼—2½

Stock Market Notes and Comments.

Since we last wrote a calmer feeling has come to prevail on the Stock Exchange, but it would be too much to hope that it is an enduring feeling. Markets are just as ready to be scared again to-morrow as they were last week. Nothing essential is altered in their position, and the recovery in prices which took place in the first half of this week represents little more than the effect of repurchases by operators for the fall, who rush to buy back directly acute spasms of alarm are over.

Over and above all political causes of disturbance we have to reckon with the position of the Money Market. As has been frequently pointed out in these columns this is uncertain enough and ticklish enough to wither up many kinds of speculation, and to put the values of many securities to a test they have not been subjected to for years. Were the minds of the public delivered from fears about Spain and the United States, about Turkey and Bulgaria, or Turkey and Armenia, or Russia and Armenia, or Russia and China, or Japan and Russia, or the Boers and Mr. Chamberlain, or Mr. Chamberlain and France, they would still be disturbed and rendered fearful by the probability that we shall have no cheap money this summer. It is not necessary to go over again the effects dearer money are sure to produce on the prices of public securities, but one point may again be emphasised. It is that buying of a kind will be stopped, should money grow, or keep, dear. We do not mean the small investment buying, that goes on more or less at all times and in all circumstances, but the large speculative buying. This is sure to be narrowed down to small dimensions, if money remains anything near 4 per cent. on Stock Exchange loans this summer. The prospect, then, is one rather of markets frequently unsettled, and only occasionally calm, than of active dealings at advancing quotations. Many things will be put to the test should money not fall again below 3 per cent. in the next six months, and we do not think it will fall much, if at all, below that.

One considerable disturbing influence which must not be lost sight of is the practical extinction of the outside broker, or *coulissier*, in Paris. The Government of France seems to be determined upon this step, and has at its call a majority of the Chambers sufficient to allow it to effect its purpose. Therefore, a large displacement of capital will, in all probability, occur in the course of the present year, and a group of houses which has been instrumental in transacting nearly three-fourths of the business in stocks and shares done in Paris will be broken up and dispersed to other centres, carrying their capital with them. What effect this great upheaval may have on prices we cannot predict. It may be, almost certainly will be, a much smaller effect in the first instance than people would naturally suppose, because capital in its modern form is nearly as imponderable as electricity. It is not necessary for a stockbroker to have a "clearance sale" before he removes his business to fresh premises. The ejected *coulissier* can transfer his affairs and effects to Brussels, to Frankfort, to Antwerp, to Amsterdam, or to London, without being under any necessity to disturb markets by unloading his stock. With the prospect of ejectment before them it is not at all unlikely many Parisian firms have already placed their funds, and perhaps some of their securities, in other cities without causing any flutter on any stock exchange. But although no immediate effect is to be looked for, the more remote consequences of such a change as the French Ministry is now forcing through the Chambers must, we think, be of a hurtful kind.

It will be a bad thing for international stock dealings of all descriptions when the great market of Paris becomes in a manner a closed market. The volume of business done on it must be less as the result of this change, and it would not surprise us if the effect upon the dealings in French funds of all descriptions proved in the course of time to be disastrous enough to sensibly lower their prices. Often since the present French Republic was founded the outside brokers in Paris have rendered most valuable service to the established order of government, by sustaining the price of rentes in ticklish times, so that public confidence in the stability of republican institutions might not be impaired. Whether the Government will be able to do this when it has destroyed the great unlicensed market remains to be seen ; but we should doubt it.

Quite a flurry upwards took place in Transvaal shares on Tuesday, and a smaller one in Rhodesian ones on Wednesday. No rational explanation of this has been forthcoming, and probably it requires none ; for reason has long forsaken these sections of the Exchange. But the market, as we have always insisted, is held up by certain finance houses, trusts, and so on, who play with it as a tiger cub might with a kid. They can move quotations up when they please, and let them down equally when it suits them. This week's demonstration, therefore, was probably meant to show the public that nothing adverse was likely to arise from the murder of Mr. Woolf Joel, or that Cecil Rhodes is still a name to conjure with. Or it may have been the result of repurchases of "bears" put out some time ago with the purpose of raking in a little more money from the public, for said public still deals fatuously and infatuatedly to a small extent in South African shares. It is not, however, speculative buying on the part of the public which helps these large market operators so much at present as the selling of real holders, brought to agony point by the prolonged downward tendency of the market. Such unfortunate people keep throwing out their tens and twenties and fifties and hundreds of shares, always at dwindling prices, and the policy of the great operators is as far as possible to sell ahead of such. They put out extensive "bears" at any favourable chance, and then wait until the continual droppings of small sales have brought prices down sufficiently to enable them to repurchase at a great profit to themselves what they had sold at higher quotations.

From past experience we should not be at all surprised to learn that the upward spurt of this week was nothing more than a preparation for a fresh "bear raid" of this very description. The moral still is, that this is a most dangerous market for any one of a speculative turn to touch on any terms. When prices are strong, holders of all South African shares, even the very best among them, should make it a point to be always selling out a little so as to escape in time. This counsel is the more suited to present circumstances, because politics in South Africa are getting to a fermenting stage, a stage which may afford Mr. Chamberlain great scope for the exercise of his unrivalled talents in provocation.

We need not dwell on the position of other markets. That for American railroad securities must now continue feverish until the Cuban question is settled one way or another. Here, however, we should on the whole be disposed to buy on any fall, and assuredly no man who can hold what he has bought ought to sell while the intermittent fever prevails. But the effect, supposing war does come between Spain and the United States, would at worst be transitory, in an adverse sense, and might be stimulating. Railways most certainly would not suffer by war in traffic or earnings, and they might gain ; for, as a correspondent has pointed out, were the worst to come to the worst, and the Atlantic ports of the United States to be all blockaded by Spain, the trade of the country could still find ample outlet through the ports of Mexico and the Canadian Dominion. Moreover, the large additional expenditure now to be entered upon in strengthening the United States Navy must have a great effect in stimulating railway receipts. Therefore, the public ought not to be disheartened or alarmed by the most gruesome rumours regarding the dispute between America and Spain, nor yet by downward plungings in markets. If people keep their heads cool, and buy when the scaremonger is howling in his most lugubrious tones, they will gain by their coolness and decision in the long run.

The Week's Stock Markets.

After the excitement of last week, markets present quite a humdrum appearance, and the fortnightly settlement having been got through with only two small casualties, members have now settled down to face a nineteen-day account. The unsettled condition of the Paris Bourse tended to retard any very decided improvement here and it was not until Wednesday that a more cheerful tone, both at home and abroad, caused a general all-round recovery, which has since been maintained.

Home Government securities have kept remarkably steady, the movements in Consols being confined within narrow limits, but Indian Government stocks show a further decline. The hardening tendency of the money market has had the usual effect on Colonial Government issues, and all the senior securities of the leading Home railway companies have also shared in the fall.

Highest and Lowest this Year.	Last Carrying over Price.	BRITISH FUNDS, &c.	Closing Price.	Rise or Fall.
113½ 111	—	Consols 2¾ p.c. (Money)...	111⅞	+ ⅜
113 1/16 111¼	112¾	Do. Account (Apl. 1)	112	+ ¼
106¼ 104¾	106	2½ p.c. Stock red. 1905 ...	105¼	—
363 347½	—	Bank of England Stock...	356	+ ½
117 113⅛	116	India 3½ p.c. Stk. red. 1931	114	— ¼
109¼ 105⅝	108	Do. 3 p.c. Stk. red. 1948	106	— ¼
96⅜ 92½	94⅝	Do. 2½ p.c. Stk. red. 1926	93	—

In the Home Railway Market, business has been very quiet, with but few speculative transactions, the net result of the week's operations being that quotations in most instances show little change on balance. Midland deferred was very depressed on rumours of trouble among the employés, but a sharp rise on Wednesday wiped out the greater part of previous losses. North-Eastern and North-Western stocks were also pressed for sale, but have since recovered, the traffic returns showing substantial gains, especially in goods traffic. The Southern lines were adversely affected by what at first sight appeared to be poor traffics, but made up the lost ground before the close.

Highest and Lowest this Year.	Last Carrying over Price.	HOME RAILWAYS.	Closing Price.	Rise or Fall.
186 172¾	174	Brighton Def.	175	+ ¾
59¼ 55⅝	56⅛	Caledonian Def.	57⅛	+ 1⅛
20⅛ 19	19⅜	Chatham Ordinary	19⅜	+ ⅛
77¼ 66	70	Great Central Pref.	69	— 1
24⅞ 21¾	22	Do. Def.	22	+ ⅛
124½ 119⅝	121	Great Eastern	121⅝	+ ⅝
61¾ 52	52⅝	Great Northern Def.	53¼	+ ⅝
179⅝ 170⅝	171¼	Great Western	172¼	+ 1¼
49¼ 45¼	45¾	Hull and Barnsley.........	46⅞	+ 1
149¼ 146¼	146¾	Lanc. and Yorkshire	147½	+ ½
136⅛ 128⅝	130¼	Metropolitan	129½	—
31 26¾	27¾	Metropolitan District......	28¼	+ ½
88¾ 83¼	84	Midland Pref.	84	+ ¼
95⅝ 85⅛	87¼	Do. Def.	87½	+ ⅜
93¼ 90⅛	90¾	North British Pref.	91¼	+ ¼
47½ 42¾	43¼	Do. Def.	43⅝	+ ½
181½ 173¾	174⅛	North Eastern...............	174⅞	—
205⅝ 197¾	198½	North Western	199⅞	+ 1⅜
117½ 107¾	109½	South Eastern Def.	109¾	+ ⅝
98⅝ 91	91½	South Western Def.	92	+ ⅝

United States Railroad shares had a short period of firmness towards the close of last week, which gave place to a ridiculous panic in Wall-street on Saturday. Prices fell all of a heap for no particular reason, and as a specimen of the absurd rumours current in New York, one, to the effect that the German Emperor was going to help Spain retain Cuba, may be mentioned as a sample. Prices on this side did not entirely respond, but kept well above parity, and the tone soon became steadier on a renewal of Home purchases. Wall-street having once calmed down, soon began to send higher prices, the prospects of further arrivals of gold from Europe, and the absence of any additional war-like rumours, being quite sufficient to induce rapid "bear" coverings. The latest solution of the Cuban difficulty, viz., that America should raise a loan and buy Cuba outright, is hardly yet taken seriously, but the Government of Washington in taking this line would only follow its traditions, for it bought the State of Louisiana from France. Although not quite back to last week's level, there is no very serious shrinkage noticeable in the whole list, and the latest advices to hand, pointing to an early settlement of the North-Western rate war, caused a firm tone to prevail all through the list.

Canadian Pacific Railway shares were helped by a good traffic return, showing an increase of $129,000, but the bogey of more rate-cutting trouble again being raised caused a sharp reaction. Later advices, however, state that at the conference of the trans-continental roads, a sub-committee was appointed, which hopes to be able to report an agreement upon a basis of settlement by the end of the week. A recovery followed, and the price finally shows hardly any change on balance.

Grand Trunk stocks, after several ups and downs, also wind up about where they stood last Thursday.

Highest and Lowest this Year.	Last Carrying over Price.	CANADIAN AND U.S. RAILWAYS.	Closing Prices.	Rise or Fall.
14 5/16 11	12	Atchison Shares	11½	— ½
34 23¾	27¼	Do. Pref.	26½	— ¾
15⅝ 11⅝	12¼	Central Pacific..............	12¾	+ ⅛
99¾ 89	94½	Chic. Mil. & St. Paul......	92⅜	— 2¼
14¼ 11	12	Denver Shares	11⅞	— ⅛
54⅛ 44½	47	Do. Prefd.	46½	— ⅜
16⅝ 12½	13⅛	Erie Shares	13¼	— ¾
44⅛ 33¼	36½	Do. Prefd.	36	— ½
62½ 47¾	52¾	Louisville & Nashville ...	50⅝	— 1½
14½ 10¾	11¼	Missouri & Texas	11½	—
22¾ 108½	116	New York Central	114¼	— ¾
57¼ 44¼	47	Norfolk & West. Prefd....	46⅞	— ⅜
70⅛ 59½	63	Northern Pacific Prefd....	62⅞	+ ¼
19½ 14¼	15½	Ontario Shares	15¼	—
62½ 57⅛	59	Pennsylvania	59½	+ ½
12½ 8¼	9¼	Reading Shares	9	— ⅜
34½ 25⅝	28	Southern Prefd.	27	— ¾
37⅛ 24½	28	Union Pacific	27	— ⅞
20¼ 14½	15½	Wabash Prefd.	16	+ ¼
130¼ 22	24	Do. Income Debs....	24¼	— ¼
92¾ 81½	86¼	Canadian Pacific............	85xd	+ 1½
78⅛ 69⅝	72½	Grand Trunk Guar.	74½	+ 1⅛
69½ 57⅛	63¾	Do. 1st Pref.	66½	+ 1½
50⅛ 37¼	43½	Do. 2nd Pref.	46⅝	+ 1¾
25¼ 19¼	21¼	Do. 3rd Pref.	22½	+ ¾
105¾ 101½	102	Do. 4 p.c. Deb.	103	+ ½

The market for Foreign Government securities has to a certain extent got the better of its fit of nervousness, and apart from the violent fluctuations in Spanish "Fours," prices have not moved to any appreciable extent in either direction. A favourable impression was created on the Continental Bourses by the speech made by Mr. Goschen on Friday last, but this soon wore off, and Paris operators did very little else but sell heavily for several days on end. The *coulisse*, being threatened with extinction, gave not the slightest support, although it is now hoped that the Senate may not ratify the decision of the Chamber on the Bourse reorganisation scheme. Certain rather heavy sales on Monday were attributed to a big failure at Lyons, and this was partly the cause of the extreme weakness of Spanish Four per Cents. The official announcement of the Delegate of the Government of Spain that the coupons will be paid as usual having removed that doubt, a sharp rally in the price soon followed, and the healthier tone apparent on the Continental Bourses has imparted quite a cheerful tone to the markets here. Italian Rente dropped earlier in the week in sympathy with other stocks, but buying orders have since come to hand from Berlin. Greek bonds keep very steady, and it is believed that Great Britain, France, and Russia will guarantee the whole of the new loan. The news of the postponement of the New Chinese issue tended to depress the price of existing loans for a time, but as it is now expected that

Highest and Lowest this Year.	Last Carrying over Price.	FOREIGN BONDS.	Closing Price.	Rise or Fall.
94½ 88	88¾	Argentine 5 p.c. 1886......	90¼	+ 1¼
92⅝ 87¼	87¾	Do. 6 p.c. Funding	89½	+ 1½
76¾ 70	71¼	Do. 5 p.c. B. Ay. Water	72	+ 1
61¾ 51⅞	59	Brazilian 4 p.c. 1889	56¼	+ 1¾
69⅞ 57	64	Do. 5 p.c. 1895	60	+ 1½
65 53	60	Do. 5 p.c. West Minas Ry.....................	56	+ 1½
108¾ 106¼	107¾	Egyptian 4 p.c. Unified...	107½	— ¼
104¾ 102	104¼	Do. 3½ p.c. Pref. ...	104¼	+ ¼
103 102	102½	French 3 p.c. Rente	102½	—
43⅛ 34½	41	Greek 4 p.c. Monopoly...	43	+ 1½
93 5/16 91½	92⅝	Italian 5 p.c. Rente	92½	+ ⅛
100 95¾	98	Mexican 6 p.c. 1888	98¼	+ ¼
20⅞ 19	19¾	Portuguese 1 p.c.	19½	+ ¼
62¾ 52	57½	Spanish 4 p.c.	54⅛	— 1¼
45½ 41	43	Turkish 1 p.c. "B"	42¾xd	+ 1
26 7/16 23½	25⅛	Do. 1 p.c. "C"	24½xd	— ⅛
22 1/16 20¾	22	Do. 1 p.c. "D"	21⅜xd	—
46⅞ 40	44½	Uruguay 3½ p.c. Bonds...	45¾	+ ½

the prospectus will certainly appear on Saturday or Monday, there has been a recovery to last week's level again. As regards South American descriptions the principal activity has been in the Brazilian bonds, which show a partial recovery, although not yet amounting to half of the recent serious fall. The Rio exchange is slightly better, and the advertisements announcing the payment of the coupons as usual have duly appeared, while the rumour that the Brazilian Government contemplated a further issue of paper has not been credited. Argentine issues are a little firmer, the gold premium at Buenos Ayres being 5 or 6 points lower.

Highest and Lowest this Year.		Last Carrying over Price.	FOREIGN RAILWAYS.	Closing Price.	Rise or Fall.
100	100		Argentine Gt. West. 5 p.c. Pref. Stock..................	100	—
158½	149	150	B. Ay. Gt. Southern Ord..	151	—
78½	69	71	B. Ay. and Rosario Ord...	72	—
12¼	10¾	11⅛	B. Ay. Western Ord.......	11	−¼
87¼	79½	80	Central Argentine Ord....	80½	−⅛
92	83½	85	Cordoba and Rosario 6 p.c. Deb.	84	−1½
95½	88	89½	Cord. Cent. 4 p.c. Deb. (Cent. Nth. Sec.)	89	−1
61¾	47½	48½	Do. Income Deb. Stk. ...	49	−1
25¼	18	19½	Mexican Ord. Stk.	20½	+½
83½	72	78	Do. 8 p.c. 1st Pref.........	77½	−½

Foreign Railway stocks still continue on the down grade, and no support whatever seems forthcoming to give even the slightest semblance of steadiness to this section of the Stock Exchange. Traffic returns were fairly good, but the dividend announcement by the Buenos Ayres Western Company was decidedly disappointing. Mexican issues picked up a little owing to a rise in the price of silver, but changes are all in the adverse direction as compared with a week ago.

Among Miscellaneous securities, Gas Light "A" marks a big advance, on the passing through its first stage of the company's Bill for consolidating their various stocks. In Brewery issues Guinness has risen sharply, Allsopp is also higher after moving up and down on alternate days, and a steady rise has been going on in Daniell ordinary shares. Armstrong, Bolckow Vaughan, Vickers and Maxim shares have attracted attention; Hudson's Bay, Spiers & Pond debentures, and Russian Petroleum ordinary also register rises, but, on the other hand, South Metropolitan Gas, East London Water, Savoy Hotel, Clay Bockd ebentures, and several electric lighting companies' issues are lower.

Markets close the week with a firm tendency, with the exception of that for United States Railroad shares, which was weakened by the expected publication to-day (Friday) of the report on the *Maine* disaster, and Spanish four per cent. were also slightly weaker at the last for the same reason. Consols and Indian Government stocks left off with a firmer tone owing to the Bank rate being unaltered, and a demand for Home Railway Preference stocks for investment purposes was soon apparent after the decision of the Bank directors was known. A sharp rally also occurred in all Home Railway Ordinary stocks, and the list finally shows mostly rises on the week. Large buying orders from Montreal put up the prices of Canadian Pacific and Grand Trunk issues, and a demand also sprang up just at the last for Argentine and Mexican Railway stocks. West Australian mines close firm, and South African with an irregular tendency.

Mining and Finance Companies.

Realisations, chiefly on Continental account, caused a still further decline in the whole list of South African ventures, and the news of the murder of Mr. Woolf Joel, of course, tended to increase the general weakness. The poor Rand output was also a disappointment, although the falling off was attributed to the scarcity of native labour, and the fact that it was a short month. President Kruger's outspoken remarks in the Volksraad, especially his reference to troublesome times ahead, were followed by selling orders from the Cape, and prices slipped back a little further. On Tuesday there was a slight rally, which has since grown rather more pronounced, professional support being forthcoming, which was the means of putting up the price of Rand Mines, and one or two of the leading favourites. Satisfactory dividend announcements by the Crown Reefs, Heriot, and Geldenhuis companies, also encouraged operators for the rise. West Australian shares gave way under the influence of steady sales, but towards the close a partial recovery is apparent, and a little activity on the Adelaide Market is reported, after about three weeks' inanition. Among Indian shares the chief feature was the steady rise in Ooregum, otherwise there has been no disposition to enter on fresh commitments. Rio Tinto copper shares fell sharply during the earlier part of the week on heavy sales from Paris, where there has been an extensive reduction of accounts owing to the action against the *coulisse*, but, as in the case of all other mines, a firmer tone set in towards the close, and a further reduction in the visible supply of copper is again reported.

WATER TRUST, MINING, AND PUBLIC CRUSHING COMPANY OF WESTERN AUSTRALIA, LIMITED.

A correspondent writes to complain of having only just received a copy of the directors' report. Being a fairly large shareholder it certainly seems a matter requiring explanation, for the report is dated November 10, 1897, and was presented at a meeting of shareholders held ten days after. We can only suggest that our correspondent's name was missed in November, and that shareholders are now being whipped up again. After looking through the report it is easy to understand the diffidence of the directors in bringing it forward, for it contains the fateful word "reconstruction." Knowing little or nothing about the company's obscure history we have taken the trouble to look into it now, and curiosity was rewarded by finding it fairly interesting.

The company was formed in the autumn of 1895 to acquire water rights near the town of Northam, half a mile from the Government railway, and 295 miles from Coolgardie, together with sufficient freehold land for the erection of crushing and reduction works, also various mining properties, including the Golden Pig mine, comprising about sixty acres. The capital was £250,000 in £1 shares, of which 120,000 shares were taken by the vendor, and 80,000 were offered for subscription at par. The glories set forth in the prospectus were sufficiently brilliant to attract speculators on this side, for were they not told that the lagoon constituted the only permanent supply of fresh water within a radius of 200 miles from Southern Cross, and that the mining properties had been proved to contain payable reefs carrying from 8 dwt. to 2½ oz. per ton? It was proposed to erect a large crushing plant to crush ore partly from the Golden Pig mines and partly for the public, and it was pointed out that the charges then made at Southern Cross and Coolgardie for crushing ore ranged from £3 to £5 per ton, whereas it was estimated the company could treat the ore, carriage included, for 5s. only, and make a substantial profit. Moreover, the Government offered the right of running private rolling stock on their railways for the transport of ore from Southern Cross to the company's proposed crushing mills, the Government supplying locomotives, fuel, and working staff, at 7s. per ton, and also the right of carrying back fresh water to the goldfields as a return loading at only 5s. per ton, the company guaranteeing a minimum traffic of 60,000 tons of ore and 30,000 tons of water per annum. Mr. J. R. Chaffey, reporting on the Golden Pig lease, estimated the average yield of the ore by battery treatment at 10 dwt. of gold per ton, which with "the enormous body of stone at hand, would give a steady and handsome profit." Finally, the working capital provided was considered ample to cover the cost of the installation of the company on a "sound and satisfactory basis."

Nothing seemed wanting, therefore, but to rush for the shares and wait for dividends. After a lapse of a couple of years, during which time shareholders, no doubt, built many castles in the air as to how the dividend money was accumulating, the directors brought forward their report for two years ended August 31 last, the profit and loss account showing that the expenditure had run away with £21,167 in earning £4,439. According to the balance-sheet, in addition to the £120,000 in shares given for the property, railway sidings had cost £2,733 net; land and buildings, £1,710;

and plant and machinery, £53,013. On the wonderful Golden Pig mine £8,826 had been spent, and the very remunerative amount of £11 9s. 8d. gold recovered. On another property, the New Victoria South, £7,399 had been spent, and £2,288 gold recovered, and on the Enterprise mine, £1,641 had been spent and £330 gold recovered. Various other items made up the total of £212,712. This meant that all the capital of £200,000, less £267 calls in arrear, had been used up, and hat a mortgage, sundry creditors, and a bank over-draft had come between expectant shareholders and profits. Therefore, an issue of debentures was offered the shareholders early last year, but it was not taken up. This sulky and ungenerous attitude of the shareholders in keeping the rest of their money for their own use or to help Bottomley, put the board in a bit of a fix, for they were unable to add plant to treat the tailings, without which mine-owners would not send their ore to the company's mill; the title-deeds of the property had to be lodged as security for the bank's over-draft, and a bill of sale had to be given on some new trucks ordered. Then the general manager at Northam found he had had enough of it, and took £500 to terminate his engagement, and the board in Western Australia was asked to resign, one member of it being allowed to join the London board, viz., Mr. Eugene Vanzetti, the original vendor of the mine to come. There never was a board of directors so plagued before. Nothing seemed to go right. Even the Government made their Menzies Railway terminus at Kalgoorlie, instead of Coolgardie, where it should have passed through the company's property; and, when asked to make a branch line, pleaded want of funds. Thus there was nothing left to do but to bring forward the inevitable reconstruction scheme, and to sell the undertaking to a company to be called the Northam Mills and Mining Company, Limited, with a nominal capital of £250,000 in £1 shares, upon which 16s. 6d. was credited as paid, leaving 3s. 6d. a share to be called up. This, if obtained, would have produced £35,000, of which £10,000 was required to satisfy existing liabilities. With the rest the necessary plant was to be purchased, as well as ores, so that by this time probably the company's treasury has again experience of a vacuum. Even if well supplied with money, we see small hope, for during the five months it was crushing last year the yield was only 14 dwt. to the ton, which would never mean anything for the shareholders in such a distant region and without cheap transport facilities. Our correspondent will not join the reconstruction, and thereby shows wisdom, for if there is a clear case of throwing good money after bad this seems one. In the circumstances, therefore, the grumbling about not receiving the report ought to be changed to a feeling of thankfulness. The misfortune lay in ever having seen the prospectus and believed in it.

A VIGOROUS RIVAL OF FRENCH RAILWAYS.

The great water highways, being owned by the State, are used by the public at very small cost in France. The sea and rivers are free to everybody, and the canals, although they, too, belong to the State, can be used with almost as little expense. Water transport in France is, in fact, a serious rival to the railways. During the past twenty years, owing to the increased adoption of machinery, and to the abolition of taxes on navigation, there has been a steady and constant improvement in water traffic, the only drawbacks being occasioned by unfavourable climatic conditions, and in that period the growth of internal navigation has been incomparably greater than that of the railways, showing an increase of 27 per cent. in the average distance of the merchandise carried by boats. The number of tons advanced by 80 per cent., whilst the increase for the railways was only 18 per cent. The canals of the north and east furnished the greater part of this increase, the prosperity of the iron and coal industries occasioning a traffic beyond all precedent. That between Paris on the one hand, and the North and Belgium on the other, represents a traffic which averages more than 3 million tons. The exchanges by water between the East and the North gave last year 1½ millions, so that the canal of Saint Quentin, which forms the common trunk of those two great systems, was the medium of transport for a mean of 4½ millions of tons of merchandise, and its locks have just been doubled. The Seine is the great medium by which the wheat from America and the wines from Spain and Italy reach Paris. The canals of the centre, whose improvement is much less than those in the North seem now to have taken an upward tendency.

This navigation or system is used mainly for importation, the goods carried by rivers and canals amounting to 41 per cent. of the general total received in France, whilst those sent from France in the same manner only reach 28 per cent. It plays a very important part, not only in the importation of wheat and wines landed at Rouen or at Hâvre, but even of coal, most of that sent from England and Belgium finding its way to the interior by water. Whilst the railways are compelled to conform to their fixed tariff, and are obliged to meet any demands which may be made upon them without overstepping the delay allowed by law, the tariff for transport by water is not fixed, and the navigation companies have no time limit as regards delivery.

The improvement in internal water transport is not a mere flash in the pan, and there seems no valid reason for believing that it will not be further developed. The introduction of electricity as motive power, the improvement in the boats, the end of the unfortunate engineers' strike in England, and, finally, the inability of the railways to cope with a larger traffic, are all very important elements which will lend powerful aid to the development of water carriage in the near future. The Paris Exhibition of 1900 will, temporarily at least, increase the transport to Paris of building material of all kinds. To take full advantage of this special demand, the railways will have to construct additional rolling stock and workshops, increase their staff and their depôts, and even make new lines in order to relieve those already overburdened with traffic. All this could not be done under a cost to each of the railway companies of from 130 to 150 million francs. This is a remarkable illustration of the exceptional position the river and canal traffic enjoys in its competition with the railways. The question of the extension of the canal system excites much interest in France. That country, which expended 15,000 million francs on its railways, and now complains that its system is inferior to that of other countries, is becoming tired of debates concerning the improvement of its water arteries, which form the second part of the great plan of public works. Several municipalities and Chambers of Commerce have offered the State to contribute a part of the necessary cost, and to lend the other part at very little interest, or even none at all. The Government has accepted several hundred millions. The Ministry has deposited some bills sanctioning this understanding, and Parliament, which has already voted the re-purchase of the "Canal du Midi," and another, is about to begin the solution of the problem. The construction of the canal "Paris Port de mer," from Rouen to Paris, which will cost six millions, the alteration of the bed of "La Loire," which will cost three-and-a-half millions, and the completion of other works referred to above, would greatly benefit the water interest; but it would be almost wholly at the expense of the railways, and would particularly injure the systems owned by the State and by the Ouest, Midi, and Orléans Companies. The merchant is, as a general rule, indifferent whether his goods are carried by train or by water, so long as they arrive safely; and the railways, unable to engage in a battle of tariffs with their adversary, look with dread on the dangerous position in which they will soon be placed by their powerful opponent, who will menace their receipts at the very moment when their expenses must be considerably increased.

The shares of the French railways have sensibly risen during the past year, and are still in great demand. In order to justify this rise it has been announced that an increase in the dividends of the companies will shortly take place. This announcement is not meant seriously, however, and English holders would act prudently in selling without hesitation at the present prices.

According to the British consular report upon Milan, the chief inspector there notifies that tuberculosis exists among the cows on the irrigated plains near Milan, to the extent of 26·30 per cent. No doubt, as our Consul says, the sanitary conditions of that district "leaves much to be desired." But how much of the milk of these diseased cows goes to make up Gorgonzola and Parmesan cheese? This is a question in which a good many of us are interested.

Will the Turks move? It is understood, so says a Paris telegram, that as soon as the British and French Governments have laid before their respective Parliaments the conditions for guaranteeing the Greek loan, a note will be presented to the Sultan, informing him that, on payment of the first instalment of the debt, he will be expected to carry out at once his share of the understanding to which he appended his signature. The succeeding instalments will be paid only after it has been ascertained that the evacuation of Greek territory proceeds. The Sultan, however, is ingenious in framing excuses for delay. Then will Russia join in the warning?

The strike movement in Bombay seems to have made an impression on the Governor. He has announced that search parties are to be abolished experimentally, and all suspicion cases of plague are to be reported by the head men of the various communities. There is to be no inspection of corpses or measures entailing delay in the performance of funeral rites.

Prices of Mine and Mining Finance Companies' Shares.

Shares £1 each, except where otherwise stated.

AUSTRALIAN.

Making-Up Price, Feb. 21.	Name.	Closing Price.	Rise or Fall.	Making-Up Price, Feb. 21.	Name	Closing Price.	Rise or Fall.
1 1/16	Aladdin	1 1/16		7 3/4	Hannan' Brownhill	7 3/4	+ 1/16
3 13/16	Associated	3 11/16	− 1/16	[illegible]	Hannan's Oroya	[illegible]	− 1/16
[illegible]	Do. Southern	[illegible]	− 1/16	16/	Do. Proprietary	16/6	
14/6	Brilliant, £2	14/		[illegible]	Do. Star	[illegible]	
2 1/4	Do. St. George's	2 1/4		—	Ivanhoe, New	5 [illegible]	− [illegible]
11/9	British Broken Hill	12/	+ /6	[illegible]	Kalgurli Mt. & Iron King, 18/	[illegible]	− 1/16
2 3/8	Broken Hill Proprietary	2 1/16	− 1/16	5 1/16	Kalgurli	5 1/16	+ 1/16
—	Do. Block 10	3 1/4		9 [illegible]	Lady Shenton	9 1/16	+ 1/16
1 1/16	Brownhill Extended	1 1/16		9 1/2	Lake View Cons.	9 1/2	+ [illegible]
1 1/16	Burbank's Birthday	1 1/16		[illegible]	Do. Extended	1	+ 1/16
[illegible]	Central Boulder	[illegible]		1 1/16	Do. South	1 1/16	− 1/16
5/6	Chaffers, 4/	5/6	+ /6	1 1/16	London & Globe Finance	1 1/16	− 1/16
1	Colonial Finance, 15/	par	− [illegible]	[illegible]	London & W. A. Exploration	[illegible]	− 1/16
—	Crœsus S. United	1/16		[illegible]	Do. Investment	[illegible]	
15/6	Day Dawn Block	15/6	+ /6	[illegible]	Mainland Consols	[illegible]	+ [illegible]
1	E. Murchison	1		[illegible]	North Boulder, 10/	[illegible]	+ 1/16
[illegible]	Gold Estates	[illegible]		1 1/4	North Kalgurli	1 1/4	
4/	Golden Arrow 19/	4/	+ /6	4 [illegible]	Northern Territories	4 [illegible]	+ 1/16
7 [illegible]	Golden Horseshoe	7		2 1/2	Peak Hill	2 1/2	+ [illegible]
[illegible]	Golden Link	1	+ [illegible]	2 1/16	South Kalgurli	2 1/16	
[illegible]	Great Boulder, 2/	21/	+ /6	1 [illegible]	W. A. Goldfields	1 [illegible]	
1 [illegible]	Do. Main Reef, 10/	1 1/16	+ 1/16	2 [illegible]	W. A. Joint Stock	2 [illegible]	+ 1/16
3 [illegible]	Do. Perseverance	3	− [illegible]	1 [illegible]	W. A. Market Trust	1 1/16	− 1/16
1	Do. South	1		2	W. A. Loan & General Fin.	1 [illegible]	− 1/16
2 [illegible]	Hainault	2 [illegible]	+ 1/16	[illegible]	White Feather	[illegible]	
[illegible]	Hampton Plains	[illegible]	− 1/16				

LAND EXPLORATION AND RHODESIAN.

Making-Up Price, Feb. 21.	Name.	Closing Price.	Rise or Fall.	Making-Up Price, Feb. 21.	Name	Closing Price.	Rise or Fall.
2 [illegible]	Anglo-French Ex.	2 [illegible]	− 1/16	[illegible]	Mashonaland Central	[illegible]	
1 [illegible]	Barnato Consolidated	1 [illegible]		6	Matabele Gold Reefs	6 [illegible]	+ [illegible]
[illegible]	Bechuanaland Ex.	[illegible]		1 [illegible]	Mozambique	2 1/16	+ [illegible]
2 [illegible]	Chartered B.S.A.	2 [illegible]	+ 1/16	1 1/16	New African	1 1/16	+ 1/16
[illegible]	Clark's Cons.	[illegible]		[illegible]	Oceana Consolidated	[illegible]	
[illegible]	Colenbrander	[illegible]		1 [illegible]	Rhodesia, Ltd.	1 1/16	
4 [illegible]	Cons. Goldfields	4	− [illegible]	4	Do. Exploration	4 [illegible]	
1 1/16	Do. Pref.	21/0		1	Do. Goldfields	[illegible]	
1 [illegible]	Exploration	1 [illegible]		3 [illegible]	S. A. Gold Trust	3 [illegible]	+ 1/16
2 1/16	Geelong	2 [illegible]	− [illegible]	[illegible]	Tati Concessions	1	+ 1/16
[illegible]	Henderson's Est.	[illegible]	− 1/16	[illegible]	Transvaal Development	[illegible]	
1 1/16	Johannesburg Con. In.	1 [illegible]	− 1/16	[illegible]	United Rhodesia	[illegible]	+ 1/16
1	Do. Water	1		1 1/16	Willoughby	1 [illegible]	+ [illegible]
1 [illegible]	Mashonaland Agency	1 [illegible]		[illegible]	Zambesia Explor.	[illegible]	− [illegible]

MISCELLANEOUS.

Making-Up Price, Feb. 21.	Name.	Closing Price.	Rise or Fall.	Making-Up Price, Feb. 21.	Name	Closing Price.	Rise or Fall.
1 1/4	Alamillos, £2	1 1/4		13/	Mysore Goldfields	13/6	
5	Anaconda, $25	5		9/	Do. Reefs, 17/	8/6	− /6
9/6	Balaghât, 18/	10/		14/9	Do. West	15/	+ /6
4 [illegible]	Cape Copper, £2	4 [illegible]	+ 1/16	12/	Do. Wynaad	11/6	− /6
4 [illegible]	Champion Reef, 10s.	5	+ 1/16	2 1/16	Namaqua, £2	2 1/16	+ 1/16
2 [illegible]	Copiapo, £2	2 [illegible]		3 [illegible]	Nundydroog	3 [illegible]	
3 [illegible]	Coromandel	3 [illegible]		2 [illegible]	Ooregum	3 1/16	+ 1/16
2 [illegible]	Frontino & Bolivia	2 1/16		3 1/16	Do. Pref.	3 [illegible]	+ [illegible]
1 [illegible]	Hall Mines	1 [illegible]		28	Rio Tinto Def., £5	28 1/16	+ [illegible]
2 [illegible]	Libiola, £5	2 [illegible]		6	Do. Pref. £5	6 1/16	
7 [illegible]	Linares, £3	8		18/	St. John del Rey	17/6	− /6
3 [illegible]	Mason & Barry, £3	3 [illegible]		17/	Taitipu	[illegible]	
5 [illegible]	Mountain Copper, £5	5	− 1/16	7 [illegible]	Tharsis, £2	7 [illegible]	+ [illegible]
13 [illegible]	Mount Lyell, £3	13 [illegible]		3 [illegible]	Tolima "A," £5	3 [illegible]	
2 [illegible]	Mount Lyell, North	3 [illegible]		4 [illegible]	Waihi	4 [illegible] x	
16/3	Mount Lyell, South	[illegible]		1 [illegible]	Waitekauri	1 [illegible]	
4 [illegible]	Mount Morgan, 17s. 6d.	4 [illegible] x		1 1/16	Woodstock (N.Z.)	1 1/16	− [illegible]
5 [illegible]	Mysore, 10s.	5 [illegible] x					

SOUTH AFRICAN.

Making-Up Price, Feb. 21.	Name.	Closing Price.	Rise or Fall.	Making-Up Price, Feb. 21.	Name	Closing Price.	Rise or Fall.
5 [illegible]	Angelo	4 [illegible]	− [illegible]	3 [illegible]	Langlaagte Estate	3 [illegible] x	
1 [illegible]	Aurora West	1 [illegible]	+ 1/16	2/6	Lisbon-Berlyn	2/3	− /3
[illegible]	Bantjes	[illegible]		2 [illegible]	May Consolidated	2 [illegible]	+ [illegible]
9/6	Barrett, 10/	9/6	+ /6	4 [illegible]	Meyer and Charlton	4 [illegible]	− [illegible]
3 [illegible]	Bonanza	3 [illegible]	+ [illegible]	3 [illegible]	Modderfontein	3 [illegible]	+ 1/16
[illegible]	Buffelsdoorn	1/16		[illegible]	New Bultfontein	[illegible]	
1 [illegible]	Champ d'Or	1 [illegible]	− [illegible]	3 [illegible]	New Primrose	3 [illegible]	
5 [illegible]	City and Suburban, £4	5 1/16 x		1 1/16	Nigel	1 [illegible]	− [illegible]
2 [illegible]	Comet (New)	2 [illegible]	− 1/16	—	Nigel Deep	1 [illegible]	
4 [illegible]	Con. Deep Level	4 [illegible]		[illegible]	North Randfontein	[illegible]	
11 [illegible]	Crown Deep	11 [illegible]		5 [illegible]	Nourse Deep	5	− [illegible]
12	Crown Reef	11 [illegible]		1 [illegible]	Porges-Randfontein	1 [illegible]	
27 [illegible]	De Beers, £5	27 [illegible]	− 1 [illegible]	28 [illegible]	Rand Mines	27 [illegible]	
3 [illegible]	Driefontein	3 [illegible]	+ [illegible]	1 1/16	Randfontein	1 1/16	− 1/16
5 [illegible]	Durban Roodepoort	5 [illegible]	+ [illegible]	2 [illegible]	Rietfontein	2 1/16	− 1/16
3 [illegible]	Do. Deep	3 [illegible]	+ [illegible]	10	Robinson Deep	9 [illegible]	− [illegible]
4	East Rand	4		8	Do. Gold, £5	8 [illegible]	+ [illegible]
24 [illegible]	Ferreira	24 [illegible]	− [illegible]	[illegible]	Do. Randfontein	1	
6 [illegible]	Geldenhuis Deep	6 [illegible]	− [illegible]	1 [illegible]	Roodepoort Central Deep	1 [illegible]	− [illegible]
4 [illegible]	Do. Estate	4 1/16	+ 1/16	6 [illegible]	Rose Deep	6	− [illegible]
[illegible]	George Goch	[illegible]	− 1/16	2 [illegible]	Salisbury	2 [illegible]	
2 [illegible]	Ginsberg	2 1/16		2 1/16	Sheba	2	− 1/16
1 [illegible]	Glencairn	2		3 [illegible]	Simmer and Jack, £5	3 1/16	− 1/16
8 [illegible]	Goldfields Deep	7 [illegible]	− 1/16	3	Transvaal Gold	3 [illegible]	
8 [illegible]	Griqualand West	8 [illegible] x		3	Treasury	3	
8 [illegible]	Henry Nourse	8 [illegible]	+ [illegible]	3 [illegible]	United Roodepoort	3 [illegible]	
7 [illegible]	Heriot	7 [illegible]	+ [illegible]	1 [illegible]	Van Ryn	1 [illegible]	
7 [illegible]	Jagersfontein	7 [illegible]	− [illegible]	5 1/16	Village Main Reef	5 [illegible]	− [illegible]
7 [illegible]	Jubilee	7 [illegible] x		1 [illegible]	Vogelstruis	1 [illegible]	− [illegible]
4 [illegible]	Jumpers	4 [illegible]	− [illegible]	[illegible]	Do. Deep	[illegible]	+ [illegible]
2 [illegible]	Kleinfontein	2 1/16	− [illegible]	8 1/16	Wemmer	8 [illegible]	
2 [illegible]	Knight's	3 [illegible]	+ [illegible]	[illegible]	West Rand	[illegible]	
2 [illegible]	Lancaster	2 [illegible]	− 1/16	5 [illegible]	Wolhuter, £4	5 [illegible]	− [illegible]
				2	Worcester	2 [illegible]	

American Customs' officers have received orders from the Treasury at Washington to assess countervailing duties on sugars imported from France.

MINING RETURNS.

BALMORAL MAIN REEF.—For February, 2,015 oz.

NATAL COLLERIES AND DURBAN COALING STATION.—Output of coal in February, 3,100 tons.

NEW ZEALAND CROWN.—Tons mined 1,300, tons crushed 1,511.

SONS OF GWALIA.—For February: Crushed 960 tons, yield 1,139 oz. Tailings 23 dwts.

REGINA (CANADA).—For February: 510 tons milled, yielding 165 oz. gold.

WAITEKAURI.—£5,486 from 1,730 tons.

NEW HERIOT.—Last month's crushing yielded 5,737 oz., profit £9,642.

NIGEL.—Last month's crushing yielded: Battery 1,296 oz., cyanide 1,477 oz.

MOUNT MALCOLM.—Cleaned up on March 5: 529 tons, crushed for 474 oz.

CITY AND SUBURBAN.—Last month's crushing yielded 9,678 oz., profit £15,451.

BLOCK B LANGLAAGTE ESTATE.—Mill: Ore crushed, 11,704 tons of 2,000 lb.; gold retorted, 2,982 oz. Tailings (cyanide process).—Tons treated, 6,300; gold recovered, 1,434 oz. Concentrates (cyanide process).—Tons treated, 156; gold recovered, 350 oz.

BONANZA.—From mill: crushed, 5,184 tons, obtained 4,629 oz. of gold. From cyanide and slimes works—treated 5,036 tons, yielding 3,112 oz. Total, 7,741 oz.

CONSOLIDATED MAIN REEF.—Mill: 3,630 tons crushed, producing 1,386 oz. gold; cyanide: 2,880 tons treated, producing 323 oz. gold.

CONSOLIDATED MURCHISON.—Crushed 308 tons, obtained 320 oz. of gold.

CROWN REEF.—Results for February: Crushed by mill, 13,192 tons; yield in smelted gold, 6,998 oz., from cyanide works 3,232 oz., and from slimes works 101 oz.

GOLD REEFS OF WEST AFRICA, LIMITED.—Crushed during February, 190 tons of ore, which have yielded about 314 oz. of gold.

LAKE VIEW CONSOLS.—Clean up for February: Crushed, 4,583 tons; yield, 4,485 oz. 9 dwts. of gold; tailings assay 12 dwts. per ton. Cyanide returns: 4,037 tons treated yielded 2,690 oz. 17 dwt. of gold; tailings assay 2 dwt. 4 gr. per ton. Concentrates: 100 tons value 220 oz. of gold.

LANGLAAGTE ESTATE.—Ore crushed, 15,388 tons of 2,000 lb.: gold retorted, 5,497 oz. Tailings (cyanide process): Tons treated, 11,700; gold recovered, 2,207 oz. Concentrates (Cyanide process): Tons treated, 536; gold recovered, 1,436 oz.

LANGLAAGTE STAR.—February: Ore crushed, 4,724 tons of 2,000 lb.; gold retorted, 2,468 oz. Tailings (cyanide process): Tons treated, 4,321; gold recovered, 956 oz.

NORTH RANDFONTEIN.—For February: Ore crushed, 5,321 tons of 2,000 lb.; gold retorted, 1,341 oz. Tailings (cyanide process): Tons treated, 3,120; gold recovered, 463 oz. Concentrates (cyanide process): Tons treated, 70; gold recovered, 168 oz.

OTTOS KOPJE DIAMOND MINES.—8,410 loads washed during week ended March 10; 219 carats of diamonds won.

PORGES RANDFONTEIN.—Ore crushed, 6,620 tons of 2,000 lb.; gold retorted, 2,399 oz. Tailings (cyanide process): Tons treated, 4,875; gold recovered, 743 oz. Concentrates (cyanide process): Tons treated, 110; gold recovered, 390 oz.

ROBINSON RANDFONTEIN.—Ore crushed, 4,014 tons of 2,000 lb.; gold retorted, 1,871 oz. Tailings (cyanide process): Tons treated, 3,300; gold recovered, 598 oz. Concentrates (cyanide process): Tons treated, 630; gold recovered, 167 oz.

SIMMER AND JACK.—During February—Crushed 24,550 tons, obtained 5,881 oz. of gold from mill; 203 oz. of gold by chlorination; and 3,000 oz. of gold from tailings by cyanide.

WELD HERCULES.—Tons crushed, 216; produced, 123 oz. of gold.

WEST RAND, LIMITED.—Crushed, 3,407 tons; yielded, 1,061 oz.; cyanide treated, 2,668 tons; yielded, 723 oz.

WINTER'S GOLD.—100 tons yielded 129 oz.

WITWATERSRANDT (KNIGHT'S).—Crushed, 14,700 tons; yielding, 4,038 oz.; 9,860 tons cyanide tailings treated, yielding 1,427 oz. gold.

GELDENHUIS.—Results for February: Crushed, 15,840 tons; obtained from mill, 7,394 oz.; from concentrates by cyanide, 989 oz.; from tailings by cyanide, 2,144 oz.; from slimes by cyanide, 492 oz.; total, 10,019 oz.

HIGHLAND CHIEF.—Crushed, 225 tons; yield of retorted gold, 108 oz.

PAHANG CORPORATION, LIMITED.—February returns: Jeram Lumpong mill, 1,113 tons of stone crushed, producing 70 tons of black tin. Jeram Batang mill: 625 tons of stone crushed, producing 10 tons of black tin.

PAARL CENTRAL.—Results for February: From mill—Crushed, 6,088 tons, yielding 1,617 oz. of gold. From cyanide works—treated, 4,530 tons, yielding 923 oz.

YORK.—4,356 tons were crushed in February, yielding 1,245 oz., while 3,915 tons of tailings gave 956 oz.

VICTORIA (CHARTERS TOWERS).—275 tons crushed yielded 425 oz. gold.

INVERELL DIAMOND FIELDS.—421 carats of diamonds from 43 loads washed by hand.

BRITISH BROKEN HILL PROPRIETARY.—For fortnight ended March 10: 3,205 tons crude ore produced 483 tons concentrates, which contain 309 tons lead and 13,732 oz. silver.

BRILLIANT AND ST. GEORGE.—Crushed during the month: 2,240 tons for 3,313 oz. of gold.

CROWN DEEP.—Results for February: tons crushed by 160 stamps, 19,000; yield in smelted gold, 5,242 oz.; tons of sands and concentrates treated by cyanide, 16,670; yield, 4,827 oz.; tons of slimes treated, 3,500; yield, 179 oz.

GELDENHUIS DEEP.—Results for February: tons crushed by 180 stamps, 20,700; yield in smelted gold, 7,089 oz.; tons of sands and concentrates treated by cyanide, 14,020; yield, 3,796 oz.; tons of slime treated, 5,723; yield, 481 oz. Total, 11,366 oz.

NOURSE DEEP.—Results for February: tons crushed, 6,596; yield, 2,377 oz.; tons of sands and concentrates treated by cyanide, 4,991; yield, 2,267 oz. Total, 4,642 oz.

ROSE DEEP.—Results for February: tons crushed, 13,118; yield, 5,655 oz.; tons of sands and concentrates treated by cyanide, 10,031; yield in smelted gold, 3,005 oz. Total, 8,660 oz.

ST. AGNES GOLD REEFS.—Clean-up after crushing, 180 tons of quartz; gross yield, 149 oz.

SALISBURY GOLD MINING COMPANY.—During January the mill crushed 5,440 tons of ore, which yielded 1,028 oz. 6 dwt. of gold; the cyanide works treated 3,066 tons of tailings, yielding 498 oz. 19 dwt. of gold.

ALASKA MEXICAN.—February return; bullion shipment, $23,372; ore milled, 10,486 tons; sulphurets treated, 223 tons; bullion from sulphurets, $5,951.

CAYLLOMA SILVER.—February production: 9,250 oz. ores, 11,750 oz. bullion.

MENZIES LADY SHENTON.—Crushed: 48 tons for 140 oz. from the 115-ft. level, 45 tons for 69 oz. from the 50-ft. level.

NEW QUEEN.—Result of crushing for past fortnight: No. 4 formation, 100 tons, yielding 40 oz. of gold; 1,220 ft. formation, 115 tons, yielding 101 oz. gold.

WAIHI, LIMITED.—Bullion return for 25 days, £11,000 from 2,900 tons.

WENTWORTH PROPRIETARY.—Four weeks' return: 610 tons of ore crushed, yielding 809 oz., and 2 tons rich crude ore have been shipped containing 131 oz.

MOODIE'S.—Tons crushed, 960; ounces obtained, 750.

BURBANK'S BIRTHDAY GIFT.—Crushed, 460 tons; yield, 621 oz. free gold, exclusive of tailings.

FRANK SMITH DIAMOND.—5,700 loads washed, producing 200 cts. (value £375).

TRANSVAAL COAL TRUST.—Output for February 14,000 tons.

CUE 1 GOLD MINE.—Crushed 790 tons, yielding 590 oz.; cleaned up plates, 615 oz.

New Zealand frozen meat is certainly not losing in popularity. Official statistics show that, while in the first half of last year, the total shipments were 43,593,102 lbs. of mutton and 2,129,140 lbs. of beef, in the second half of the year the amounts were 50,030,521 lbs. of mutton and 6,111,184 lbs.—increase of 16,437,419 lbs. in mutton and 6,111,184 lbs. in beef. There are enormous advances; but the company seem to expect a better trade still, for they have just ordered, it is said, four new steamers expressly designed for the transit of frozen meat.

Railway Traffic Returns.

ALGECIRAS (GIBRALTAR) RAILWAY.—Traffic for week ended March 5, Ps. 20,570; increase Ps. 3,710. Aggregate from July 1, Ps. 719,284; increase, Ps. 17,513.

BENGAL CENTRAL RAILWAY.—Traffic for week ending February 19, Rs. 18,424; decrease, Rs. 350. Total from January 1, Rs. 141,827; increase, Rs. 12,363.

BURMA RAILWAYS.—Receipts for week ending February 12, Rs. 2,09,931; decrease, Rs. 54,355. Aggregate from January 1, Rs. 12,40,477; decrease, Rs. 2,57,085.

GREAT WESTERN OF BRAZIL RAILWAY.—Traffic for week ending February 5, $36,643; increase, $8,848. Aggregate receipts to date $265,370; increase, $32,519.

WESTERN OF SANTA FE RAILWAYS.—Gross receipts for week ending March 5, $44,069; increase, $27,397.

ALCOY AND GANDIA RAILWAY AND HARBOUR COMPANY.—Traffic for week, March 12:—Ps. 13,100, increase Ps. 100. Aggregate from January 1, Ps. 108,900, increase Ps. 10,850.

MOBILE AND BIRMINGHAM RAILROAD.—Traffic for third week of February, $9,302; increase, $3,427. Aggregate from July 1, $245,949; decrease, $6,116.

VILLA MARIA AND RUFINO RAILWAY.—Traffic for week ending March 12; $5,595; increase, $480 Aggregate from January 1, $44,031, decrease $6,418.

WEST FLANDERS RAILWAY.—Gross receipts for week ending March 13, £1,976; decrease, £73. Total from January 1, £22,040; increase, £612.

WEST OF INDIA PORTUGUESE RAILWAY.—Week ending February 19, Rs. 4,997; increase, Rs. 1,065.

ASSAM-BENGAL RAILWAY.—Traffic for week ended February 5, Rs. 20,929; decrease, Rs. 1,709. Aggregate from January 1, Rs. 1,21,901; increase, Rs. 7,057.

QUEBEC CENTRAL RAILWAY.—Receipts for third week of February, $4,683; decrease $3,273. Aggregate from July 1, $39,404; decrease $6,428.

BENGAL DOOARS RAILWAY.—Traffic receipts from January 1 to February 12, Rs. 20,280; decrease, Rs. 5,832.

H. H. THE NIZAM'S GUARANTEED STATE RAILWAYS.—Traffic receipts from January 1 to February 19. Rs. 538,968; increase, Rs. 6,172.

ROHILKUND AND KUMAON RAILWAY.—Traffic receipts for week ending February 12, Rs. 4,532; decrease, Rs. 636. Aggregate from January 1, Rs. 31,524; decrease, Rs. 1,216.

SOUTHERN MAHRATTA RAILWAY.—Receipts for week ended February 19, Rs. 1,03,513; decrease, Rs. 14,751.

MANILA RAILWAY.—Receipts for week ending March 12, $20,410; increase, $5,185. Aggregate from January 1, $192,287; increase, $48,585.

CLEATOR AND WORKINGTON.—Gross receipts for the week ending March 12 amounted to £1,015, a decrease of £61. Total receipts from January 1, £10,086, a decrease of £698.

COCKERMOUTH AND KESWICK RAILWAY.—Receipts for week ending March 12, £798; increase, £78. Aggregate from January 1, £8,273; increase, £742.

ENGLISH RAILWAYS.

Div. for half years. 1896	1896	1897	1897	Last Balance forward.	Amt. to pay 1 p.c. on Ord. for ½ yr.	NAME.	Date.	Gross Traffic for week: Amt.	Inc. or dec. on 1897.	Inc. or dec. on 1896.	No. of weeks	Gross Traffic for half-year to date: Amt.	Inc. or dec. on 1897.	Inc. or dec. on 1896.	Mileage.	Inc. on 1897.	Working	Prior Charges last ½ year.	Prop. add Cap. Exp. this ½ year
				£	£												%	£	£
10	10	10	10	2,707	5,094	Barry	Mar 12	9,151	+171	+1,741	11	99,774	+4,700	+17,878	31	—	8·89	60,665	316,853
nil	nil	nil	nil	—	—	Brecon and Merthyr	" 13	1,422	+21	−227	11	16,455	+398	+457	61	—	—	—	—
nil	nil	nil	nil	3,979	4,749	Cambrian	" 13	4,914	+457	+1,048	*	43,768	+559	—	250	—	60·96	63,148	40,000
1½	1¼	2	1¾	1,510	3,130	City and South London	" 13	1,077	+46	+128	11	11,796	−10	+1,010	3½	—	56·67	5,552	124,000
1	2	1½	2	7,895	13,210	Furness	" 13	8,947	+349	+724	*	83,645	+2,563	—	139	—	49·88	97,423	20,910
1	1½	½	1	2,207	27,470	Great Central (late M., S., & L.)	" 13	42,580	−95	+2,768	10	418,662	+6,438	+22,552	352½	—	57.17	627,386	1,200,000
1½	4½	2	5	51,283	62,865	Great Eastern	" 13	78,795	+4,409	+9,833	10	771,650	+27,576	+64,246	1,156	—	55·35	860,138	250,000
3	5½	3	5	15,094	102,496	Great Northern	" 13	93,447	+2,593	+7,836	11	1,013,441	+31,680	+70,902	1,071	8	61·36	641,485	750,000
4½	7½	4½	7½	31,350	121,981	Great Western	" 13	170440	−1,070	+4,670	10	1,689,930	+42,010	+90,230	2,582	21	51·44	1,486,272	800,000
nil	2	nil	1½	8,951	16,487	Hull and Barnsley	" 13	6,644	+254	+1,223	10	62,025	−2,370	+3,206	73	—	58·21	70,290	52,920
5	5½	5	5½	21,495	83,704	Lancashire and Yorkshire	" 13	91,752	+2,348	+5,723	10	895,114	+29,736	+37,266	555½	25	56·70	674,745	451,976
4½	8	4½	8½	26,243	43,040	London, Brighton, & S. Coast	" 12	43,996	+9	+2,238	11	498,447	+27,042	+35,930	476½	—	50·20	407,042	240,735
nil	nil	nil	nil	72,294	56,896	London, Chatham, & Dover	" 13	25,520	+412	+1,365	10	256,913	+9,599	+10,057	185½	—	50·65	367,873	nil
6¼	8	6½	7½	89,535	204,068	London and North Western	" 13	223635	+2,132	+14,454	10	2,216,437	+54,177	+112872	1,911½	—	56·92	1,404,534	600,000
5	8½	5	8½	23,038	59,367	London and South Western	" 13	63,287	+1,087	+3,855	10	638,401	+29,694	+49,474	941	6½	51·75	513,740	389,000
2½	6	2½	6½	14,590	6,691	London, Tilbury, & Southend	" 13	4,604	+248	+644	11	51,511	+3,905	+9,038	81	—	52·57	39,590	15,000
3½	3¾	3¾	3¾	17,133	26,409	Metropolitan	" 13	16,082	+381	+1,214	*	165,689	+4,069	—	64	—	43·63	148,047	254,000
nil	nil	nil	nil	4,006	11,250	Metropolitan District	" 13	3,451	+359	+416	10	86,785	+3,609	+3,990	13	—	48·70	119,663	38,450
5	7	5½	6½	38,143	174,582	Midland	" 13	188531	+11,239	+21,608	11	1,970,025	+24,283	+118061	1,354¾	15½	57·59	1,216,582	650,000
5½	7½	5¾	7	22,374	138,189	North Eastern	" 12	140301	−4,331	+10,895	10	1,386,307	+27,430	+70,313	1,597¾	—	58·82	795,077	436,004
7½	7½	7½	7½	7,061	10,102	North London	" 13			Not recd			not	recvd.	12	—	50·90	49,973	7,600
4	5	4	4½	4,745	16,150	North Staffordshire	" 13	15,394	+392	+1,484	11	170,959	+6,786	+10,629	312	—	55·27	118,142	19,605
10	10	11		1,642	3,004	Rhymney	" 12	4,503	−836	−231	11	55,446	+800	+6,009	71	—	49·68	29,049	16,700
3	6⅝	3½	6⅝	4,054	50,215	South Eastern	" 12	39,051	+256	+3,281	*	405,230	+22,534	—	448	—	51·88	380,763	250,000
3½	3½	3½	3½	2,315	25,961	Taff Vale	" 12	14,657	−2,053	−604	11	266,917	−4,029	+5,046	121	—	54·90	94,800	92,000

* From January 1.

SCOTCH RAILWAYS.

Div. 1896	1896	1897	1897	Last Balance forward	Amt. to pay 1 p.c. on Ord. for ½ yr.	Name	Date	Week Amt.	Inc. or dec. on 1897	Inc. or dec. on 1896	No. of weeks	Half-year Amt.	Inc. or dec. on 1897	Inc. or dec. on 1896	Mileage	Inc. on 1897	Working	Prior Charges	Prop. add Cap. Exp.
5	5	5½	5	9,544	78,066	Caledonian	Mar. 13	71,606	+ 3,600	+ 4,376	6	412,170	+ 8,431	+24,414	851½	5	50·38	588,248	441,477
5	5½	5	5	7,364	24,639	Glasgow and South-Western	" 12	26,488	+ 1,183	+ 1,802	6	157,105	+ 4,164	+ 8,208	393½	—	54·69	221,663	196,145
3½	3½	3½	—	1,291	4,600	Great North of Scotland	" 12	7,455	+ 111	− 8	6	44,370	− 204	+ 706	331	15½	52·03	92,178	60,000
3	nil	2	—	10,477	12,820	Highland	" 13	7,959	+ 99	+ 702	2	16,424	+ 784	+ 1,723	479¾	27¾	58·63	78,976	,000
1	1½	1	1½	819	45,819	North British	" 13	68,687	+ 1,623	+ 3,253	6	398,969	+ 10,417	+ 10,967	1,230	23	48·62	944,809	540,800

IRISH RAILWAYS.

Div. 1896	1896	1897	1897	Last Balance forward	Amt. to pay 1 p.c. on Ord. for ½ yr.	Name	Date	Week Amt.	Inc. or dec. on 1897	Inc. or dec. on 1896	No. of weeks	Half-year Amt.	Inc. or dec. on 1897	Inc. or dec. on 1896	Mileage	Inc. on 1897	Working	Prior Charges	Prop. add Cap. Exp.
6½	6½	6½	—	5,466	1,790	Belfast and County Down	Mar. 11	2,563	+ 510	+ 661	*	20,519	+ 952	—	76½	—	55·58	17,690	10,000
5½	6½	5½	—	—	4,264	Belfast and Northern Counties	" 11	4,979	+ 393	+ 356	*	48,574	+ 2,200	—	249	—	—	—	—
2	3	2	—	1,418	1,200	Cork, Bandon, and S. Coast†	" 12	1,135	− 71	− 208	*	11,434	− 978	—	103	—	54·82	14,436	5,430
6½	6¾	6½	6¾	38,776	17,816	Great Northern	" 11	14,607	+ 708	+ 1,084	10	136,916	+ 7,150	+ 8,955	528	36	50·15	88,068	22,000
5½	5½	5½	5½	30,329	24,855	Great Southern and Western	" 11	—	—	—	not	received	—	—	603	13	51·45	72,802	46,580
4	4	4	4½	11,372	11,850	Midland Great Western	" 11	9,320	− 31	− 526	10	91,026	+ 4,386	+ 5,053	538	—	50·31	83,129	1,800
nil	nil	nil	nil	229	2,822	Waterford and Central	" 11	932	+ 136	—	*	8,667	+ 1,173	—	59½	—	53·24	6,858	1,500
nil	nil	nil	nil	1,936	2,987	Waterford, Limerick & W.	" 11	4,761	+ 83	+ 1,466	*	59,331	+ 3,204	—	350½	—	57·83	42,627	7,075

* From January 1 † Eight weeks' strike

FOREIGN RAILWAYS.

Mileage. Total.	Increase on 1897.	Increase on 1896.	Name.	Gross Traffic for Week. Week ending	Amount.	In. or Dec. upon 1897.	In. or Dec. upon 1896.	Gross Traffic to Date. No. of Weeks.	Amount.	In. or Dec. upon 1897.	In. or Dec. upon 1896.
					£	£	£		£	£	£
319	—	—	Argentine Great Western	Mar. 11	7,014	+ 612	+ 1,469	34	197,532	− 9,237	+ 43,934
76½	—	—	Bahia and San Francisco	Feb. 19	3,581	+ 1,388	+ 2,516	7	20,523	+ 6,685	+ 6,206
234	48	84	Bahia Blanca and North West	Feb. 13	904	+ 188	+ 235	33	25,980	+ 409	—
74	—	—	Buenos Ayres and Ensenada	Mar. 13	3,884	− 97	− 870	10	35,567	− 6,950	− 9,843
426	—	—	Buenos Ayres and Pacific	Mar. 12	8,929	+ 486	+ 618	36	229,723	− 52,516	+ 4,843
914	1	3	Buenos Ayres and Rosario	Mar. 12	17,282	+ 6,703	+ 2,424	10	177,735	+ 41,960	+ 24,730
1,499	30	68	Buenos Ayres Great Southern	Mar. 13	39,520	+ 4,628	+ 8,310	36	1,059,308	+ 73,082	+ 157,743
602	107	177	Buenos Ayres Western	Mar. 13	13,999	− 346	− 2,129	36	433,631	− 77,645	− 76,168
845	55	77	Central Argentine	Mar. 12	21,376	+ 5,726	+ 470	10	221,944	+ 47,290	− 1,479
197	—	—	Central Bahia	Dec. 31*	$114,389	− $4,668	+ $22,144	12 mos.	$1,307,205	+ $141,334	+ $196,139
271	—	—	Central Uruguay of Monte Video	Mar. 12	5,676	+ 1,239	+ 238	36	215,214	+ 1,478	− 17,336
228	—	—	Do. Eastern Extension	Mar. 12	1,825	+ 750	+ 449	36	44,633	+ 3,692	− 2,301
182	—	—	Do. Northern Extension	Mar. 12	543	+ 88	− 202	36	22,766	− 1,707	− 6,365
180	—	—	Cordoba and Rosario	Mar. 6	2,350	+ 905	− 355	36	76,870	− 16,500	− 1,975
128	—	—	Cordoba Central	Mar. 6	$19,000	− $3,810	− $5,600	9	$198,700	− $32,200	− $45,060
549	—	—	Do. Northern Extension	Mar. 6	$37,500	− $7,000	− $11,750	9	$204,290	− $148,340	− $95,690
137	—	—	Costa Rica	Feb. 26	6,955	− 2,202	− 8	8	41,591	− 14,623	− 837
99	—	—	East Argentine	Jan. 30	687	− 80	− 353	4	2,825	− 636	− 692
386	—	6	Entre Rios	Mar. 12	2,482	+ 823	+ 1,001	36	53,321	+ 11,328	+ 10,124
555	—	24	Inter Oceanic of Mexico	Mar. 12	$67,100	+ $17,250	+ $19,500	36	$2,034,880	+ $297,290	+ $511,820
23	—	—	La Guaira and Caracas	Feb. 11	1,759	− 1,027	—	6	11,023	− 4,003	—
321	—	—	Mexican	Mar. 12	$83,100	+ $11,600	—	10	$815,200	+ $75,850	—
1,846	—	—	Mexican Central	Mar. 7	$240,202	+ $31,525	+ $33,986	10	$2,347,370	+ $32,044	+ $544,772
1,217	—	—	Mexican National	Mar. 7	$103,829	− $5,094	+ $19,142	9	$1,031,097	+ $96,528	+ $183,730
228	—	—	Mexican Southern	Mar. 14	$13,089	− $3,261	+ $4,759	50	$635,778	+ $83,526	+ $164,407
106	—	—	Minas and Rio	Jan. 31*	$133,941	− $20,733	—	7 mos.	$1,308,551	+ $187,065	—
94	—	17	N. W. Argentine	Mar. 11	658	− 363	− 540	10	8,689	− 5,985	− 3,675
242	3	—	Nitrate	Mar. 15	18,010	+ 2,625	− 2,333	9	72,503	+ 1,349	− 31,915
320	—	—	Ottoman	Mar. 5	3,800	− 2,241	+ 170	9	46,203	− 18,117	+ 5,280
77½	—	—	Recife and San Francisco	Jan. 15	5,771	− 526	− 1,013	3	14,929	+ 84	− 2,888
86½	—	—	San Paulo	Feb. 13†	20,974	− 4,502	—	6	71,004	− 9,017	—
286	—	—	Santa Fe and Cordova	Mar. 12	3,676	+ 1,625	+ 348	37	52,676	− 14,965	− 2,924
110	—	—	Western of Havana	Mar. 12	1,900	+ 17	+ 1,340	36	64,180	+ 5,397	+ 580

* For month ended. † For fortnight ended.

INDIAN RAILWAYS.

Mileage. Total.	Increase on 1897.	Increase on 1896.	Name.	Gross Traffic for Week. Week ending	Amount.	In. or Dec. on 1897.	In. or Dec. on 1896	Gross Traffic to Date. No. of Weeks.	Amount.	In. or Dec. on 1897.	In. or Dec. on 1896.
862	—	—	Bengal Nagpur	Mar. 5	Rs.1.62.000	+ Rs.17.452	+ Rs.26.000	9	Rs.12.91.000	− Rs.1.32.319	− Rs.2.59.017
827	8	63	Bengal and North-Western	Feb. 12	Rs.1.32.210	+ Rs.20.105	+ Rs.9.123	6	Rs.8.05.490	+ Rs.1.09.362	+ Rs.7.181
461	—	—	Bombay and Baroda	Mar. 5	£24,108	− £457	− £7,677	8	£205,919	− £31,851	− £103,312
1,885	2	13	East Indian	Mar. 12	Rs.11.52.000	− Rs.1.63.000	+ Rs.22.000	10	Rs.1.24.87.000	+ Rs.1.97.000	+ Rs.4.66.000
1,491	—	—	Great Indian Penin.	Mar. 12	£58,988	− £597	− £11,521	10	£648,871	+ £33,481	− £176,247
736	—	—	Indian Midland	Mar. 12	Rs.1.15.290	− Rs.12.186	+ Rs.11.510	10	Rs.13.64.261	+ Rs.31.035	+ Rs.2.28.767
840	—	—	Madras	Mar. 5	£18,700	+ £2,017	− £733	9	£171,128	− £8,748	− £10,934
1,043	—	—	South Indian	Feb. 12	Rs.1.52.756	− Rs.26.035	− Rs.7.618	6	Rs.9.03.806	− Rs.66.077	− Rs.1.86.279

UNITED STATES AND CANADIAN RAILWAYS.

Mileage Total.	Increase on 1897.	Increase on 1896.	Name.	Gross Traffic for Week. Period Ending.	Amount.	In. or Dec. on 1897.	Gross Traffic to Date. No. of Weeks.	Amount.	In. or Dec. on 1897.
					dols.	dols.		dols.	dols.
917	—	—	Baltimore & Ohio S. Western	Mar. 7	139,000	+8,000	35	4,636,901	+447,818
6,568	92	156	Canadian Pacific	Mar. 7	454,000	+129,000	9	3,614,000	+704,000
922	—	—	Chicago Great Western	Mar. 7	111,029	+15,442	35	3,707,488	+508,158
6,169	—	469	Chicago, Mil., & St. Paul	Mar. 14	664,000	+149,000	10	6,058,801	+807,220
1,685	—	—	Denver & Rio Grande	Mar. 7	137,000	+29,000	35	5,647,300	+955,100
3,512	—	—	Grand Trunk, Main Line	Mar. 12	£74,710	+£7,616	10	£737,017	+£79,715
335	—	—	Do. Chic. & Grand Trunk	Mar. 12	£19,574	+£7,371	10	£154,576	+£34,713
189	—	—	Do. Det., G. H. & Mil.	Mar. 12	£3,607	−£19	10	£35,584	−£1,574
2,938	—	—	Louisville & Nashville	Mar. 7	421,000	+40,000	9	3,834,270	+870,140
2,197	137	137	Miss., K., & Texas	Mar. 7	212,000	+31,000	35	9,127,427	+560,149
477	—	—	N. Y., Ontario, & W.	Mar. 7	59,000	+5,000	35	2,694,040	+93,981
1,570	—	—	Norfolk & Western	Mar. 7	241,000	+10,000	35	7,395,000	+817,000
3,499	336	—	Northern Pacific	Mar. 7	408,000	+151,000	9	3,293,000	+1,079,000
1,223	—	—	St. Louis S. Western	Mar. 7	100,000	+13,000	9	1,034,700	+185,100
4,654	—	—	Southern	Mar. 7	432,000	+39,000	35	2,515,812	+1,204,448
1,979	—	—	Wabash	Mar. 7	271,000	+58,000	9	2,256,406	+465,000

MONTHLY STATEMENTS.

Mileage. Total.	Increase on 1896.	Increase on 1895.	Name.	Net Earnings for Month. Month.	Amount.	In. or Dec. on 1896.	In. or Dec. on 1895.	Net Earnings to Date. No. of Months.	Amount.	In. or Dec. on 1896.	In. or Dec. on 1895.
					dols	dols.	dols.		dols.	dols.	dols.
6,935	44	444	Atchison	December	986,000	+52,000	—	12	8,966,480	+176,951	—
6,547	103	106	Canadian Pacific	January	516,000	+142,000	—	—	—	—	—
6,169	—	469	Chicago, Mil., & St. Paul	January	757,000	+52,000	−30,773	—	—	—	—
1,685	—	—	Denver & Rio Grande	January	239,000	+65,802	+19,198	7	2,025,645	+314,978	−31,082
1,970	—	—	Erie	January	371,000	+33,000	−107,852	—	—	—	—
3,512	—	—	Grand Trunk, Main Line	January	£87,400	+£34,284	+£37,725	—	—	—	—
335	—	—	Do. Chic. & Grand Trunk	January	£13,100	+£8,933	+£9,901	—	—	—	—
189	—	—	Do. Det. G. H. & Mil.	January	£1,800	+£692	+£1,939	—	—	—	—
3,127	—	239	Illinois Central*	January	2,303,898	+405,636	+383,269	—	—	—	—
2,396	—	—	New York Central*	February	3,429,000	+128,000	+222,359	2	6,934,000	+492,597	+49,397
477	—	—	New York Ontario, & W.	January	74,400	+32,100	+11,504	7	775,900	+37,200	+55,958
1,570	—	—	Norfolk & Western	January	283,000	+14,000	+48,326	—	—	—	—
3,407	—	—	Pennsylvania	January	1,159,797	+26,600	+109,000	—	—	—	—
1,055	—	—	Phil. & Reading*	January	1,724,479	+214,601	—	—	—	—	—

* Statements of gross traffic.

Prices Quoted on the London Stock Exchange.

Throughout the INVESTORS' REVIEW middle prices alone are quoted, the object being to give the public the approximate current quotations of every security of any consequence in existence. On the markets the buying and selling prices are both given, and are often wide apart where stocks are seldom dealt in. Other particulars will be found in the INVESTMENT INDEX published quarterly—January, April, July, and October—in connection with this REVIEW, price 2s., by post 2s. 2d. Where dividends are paid only once a year, an *italic* type is used to distinguish them. The London Stock Exchange Official List is quoted in the REVIEW almost entire, only very insignificant issues, or bonds falling due within the next two or three years, being omitted. But the list is subdivided into the leading, or active, stocks, and those less frequently dealt in. The former will be found under the head of "Stock Markets," and with more details than it is possible to give for the bulk of securities. By retaining the file of the INVESTORS' REVIEW any subscriber can follow for himself the movements of securities from week to week, and the INVESTMENT INDEX will from time to time help to fill up deficiencies in the information.

Tea Companies and Mines and Mining Finance Stocks are placed in special lists.

Among the abbreviations used are the following:—S.F. Snk.Fd. *sinking fund*; Certs., *certificates*; Debs. or Dbs., *debentures*; Db. or D.Stk., *debenture stock*; Pf., Prf., or Pref., *preference*; Prefd. or Pfd., *preferred*; Dfd., *deferred*; L. or Ltd., *limited*; Sh., *share*; Ans., *annuities*; Cu. or Cm., *cumulative*; Gu or Guar., *guaranteed*; Bds., *bonds*; S., Sr., or Ser., *series*; In., Ins., Insc., *inscribed*; Dr., Drgs., Drwgs., *drawings*; Stg., Strlg., *sterling*; Lia., *liable to*; Sp., Surp., *surplus*; Per., Perp., *perpetual*; Ln. *lien*; Lo. *loan*.

The dates following the names of securities are the years of issue or of redemption. Where shares are not fully paid up, their nominal amount is given with the name so that investors may know the liability upon them.

BRITISH FUNDS, &c.

Rate.	Name.	Price.
2¾	2¾ p.c.'s(Childers')Red.. 1905	105½
3	Local Loans Stk. 1912	112
3	Metro. Police Deb. Stk. 1920	105½
—	Red Sea Ind. Tel. Ann. 1908	8½
4	Canada Gv. "Intcl. Rly." 1903	106
4	Do. do. .. 1908	113
4	Do. Bonds 1910	114
4	Do. Bonds 1913	119½
3	Egyptian Gov. Gar.	106½
3	Mauritius Ins. Stk. 1940	114
4	Turkish Guar. 1855	109
11½	Bank of Ireland Stk.	392½
3½	India Rupee Paper	62½
3½	Do. 1854-5	63½
3	Do. 1896-7 1916	55
3½	Isle of Man Deb.	104
3	Do. Deb. Stk... 1919-29	103

CORPORATION AND COUNTY STOCKS.

FREE OF STAMP DUTY.

Rate.	Name.	Price.
3½	Metropolitan Con. 1929	117½
3	Do. 1941	113
2½	Do. 1920-49	100
2½	L.C.C. Con. Stock 1920	99½
3½	Comm. of Sewers, Scp., S.F. 1905	105
3½	Corp. of Lond. Bds...1897-1902	100½
3	Do. 1897-1919	103
3½	Do, Debs. Scp. ...... S.F. 1916	106
2½	Do., Deb. Stk. Scrip .. 1927-57	100
3	Barnsley 1916-46	105
3	Barry 1914-46	101
3	Bath 1909-34	101½
3	Batley 1914-44	101½
3½	Birmingham 1945	123
3	Do. 1947	112
2½	Do. 1926	98
3	Blackburn 1930	107
3	Bournemouth 1913-33	104
3½	Bradford 1945	118
3	Do. Deb. Stock .. 1954	110
3	Brighouse.............. 1916-46	100
3½	Brighton 1946	117½
2½	Do. 1957	98
3	Burton-on-Trent........ 1913-43	102½
3	Cambridge 1913-43	102
3½	Cardiff 1935	119
3	Do. 1914-54	105
3	Cheltenham.............. 1971	110
3	Chichester 1916-46	101
3½	Croydon	134
3	Do. 1940	111½
3	Derby 1920-50	107
3	Devon C.C.............. 1917-33	104½
3½	Dewsbury 1930	111
3	Do. 1930	105
3	Dorset County 1922-32	105
3	Douglas (I. of Man) 1926	101
3	Dover 1913-43	102
3½	Dublin 1944	113½
3	Eastbourne 1920-40	105
3	Edinburgh 1924	108
2½	Do. 1927	98
2½	Exeter 1917-57	96
3	Glamorgan County 1914-34	104
3½	Glasgow 1914	110½
3	Do. 1921	106½
2½	Do. 1925-40	99
3	Gloster 1915-55	101
3	Grimsby 1913-45	103½
3	Hampshire County 1914-34	105½
3	Hanley 1913-43	105
3	Harrogate 1914-34	103
3	Hastings 1915-54	105
2½	Hertfordshire C.C. 1916-36	98
3	Heston & Isleworth U.D.C. 1915-35	101
3	Huddersfield 1934	107
3½	Hull (1st iss.)	131½
3	Inverness.............. 1914-44	102
3	Ipswich 1952	110½
3	Lancaster.............. 1919-55	103
2½	Leeds 1927	98
3½	Leicester 1934	115½
3	Lincoln.............. 1919	104
3½	Liverpool..............	133½

Corporation, &c. (*continued*):—

Rate.	Name.	Price.
3	Manchester 1941	110
3	Mansfield.............. 1915-45	100
3½	Middlesbro'.............. 1909	105½
3½	Do. 1911-13	105
3	Do. 1915	104
3	Middlesex C.C.......... 1915-35	106
3½	Newcastle 1936	118½
3½	Do. Irred.	129½
2½	Do. 1915-36	101
3	Newcastle-under-Lyme.. 1909-44	101
3	Newport (Mon.) 1915-53	104½
3	Norwich 1952	111½
3	Nottingham	116
3	Oxford 1951	109½
3	Penzance.............. 1916-46	100½
3	Plymouth 1942	110
3	Pontypridd U.D.C. 1916-46	99
3	Poole.............. 1915-45	102½
3½	Portsmouth........1916 24 & 27	112
3	Do. 1913-33	106½
3	Ramsey 1920-40	100
3	Ramsgate.............. 1915-55	102
3½	Reading	131½
3	Do. 1962	109
3½	Rhyl U.D.C. 1953	110
3	Richmond (Surrey) 1942	106½
3	River Wear Debt Certs.	101
3	St. Helen's 1915-55	103
3	Scarbro' 1915-50	103
2½	Sheffield 1925-57	96
3	Shipley U.D.C.......... 1915-35	101
3	Somerset Co. 1923-33	107
3	South Shields.......... 1915-45	104
2½	Southampton 1915-45	102
3	Southend-on-Sea 1916-46	102
3	Staffs C.C. 1915-35	105
3	Stockport.............. 1914-54	104
3	Stockton 1932	104
3	Do. 1915-35	103
3	Surrey Co. 1922-32	106½
3½	Swansea	131
3	Do. 1955	106
3	Taunton 1918 3-9-43	102
3	Tees Conserv. Deb. Stk. 1947	101
3	Thames Conserv. "A" Deb. Stk.............. 1954	103½
3	Do. "B" Deb. Stk. 1954	103½
3	Torquay 1913-43	102½
3	Tunbridge Wells 1931	103
3	Tynemouth 1913	101
3	Wakefield.............. 1929	103
3	Walsall.............. 1932	108
3	West Bromwich........ 1930	108½
3½	West Ham 1929	110
3	Do. 1945	105
3	West Sussex C.C. 1915-35	106
3	Weston-s.-Mare Lcl Bd. 1914-44	101½
3	Weymouth&Melc. Regis 1918	101
3	Widnes.............. 1915-55	101
3	Wigan 1921	108
3	Windsor 1918-55	102½
3½	Wisbech 1947	113½
3½	Wolverhampton 1932	118½
3	Do. 1924-54	107
3	York 1916-41	107

SUBJECT TO STAMP DUTY.

Rate.	Name.	Price.
3½	Belfast City & Dis. Watr. 1938	116
3	Do. Red Stk. 1953-6	106
3½	Belfast 1924	104
4	Blackburn Con. Deb. Irred.	141½
3½	Do. do. Irred..............	131
3½	Bristol	128½
3½	Burnley.............. 1933	114
2½	Chesterfield Gas & Wtr. 1916-46	98
3½	Douglas Town 1921	105
3	Dover Harb. 1st Deb... 1956	104½
3½	Hull (2nd iss.)	129½
4	Leeds Deb.............. 1927	124
3½	Do.	115½
3	Do. 1927	106
3	Leicester 1919-44	105
4	Manchester..............	150
3	Do. 1928	104½
4½	Middlesboro' Mrts. 1908	111
3½	Newark on-Trent .. 1901-41	96
3½	Sheffield 1898-1916	105½
3½	Do. 1925-36	114
3	Do. 1925	104½
3½	Southampton .... S.F.	106
4½	Stockton Morts.......... 1908	112
3½	Worcester.............. 1950	109

COLONIAL AND PROVINCIAL GOVERNMENT SECURITIES.

Rate.	Name.	Price.
6	British Columbia........ 1907	119½
4½	Do. Debs... 1917	111½
3	British Guiana Imgtn. Bds.	99½
5	Canada, "Intercol. Rail," 1903	111½
4	Do. (Bonds) 1904-5-6-8	106
4	Do. Reduced 1910	107½
3½	Do. Bnds. 1909-34	103½
4	Do. Loan 1910-35	107½
3	Do. Loan 1938	102
6	Cape of G. Hope 1900	—
5	Do. 1900	—
4½	Do. red. by an. draw.	110
4½	Do. 1879	110
4	Do. 1881	109
4	Do. 1917-23	118
4½	Ceylon	110
4	Do.	106½
4½	Fiji Gov. Deb. Sink. Fd.	101½
4	Jamaica Sink. Fd. 1923	103
5	Manitoba Debs.......... 1910	113
5	Do. Ster. Bds. 1888	122
4	Do. Ster. Debs.	106
4	Mauritius, Cons. Debs. 1880...	103½
4½	Natal, Sink. Fd.......... 1919	118
4	Do. do. 1926	115
3½	Newfoundland Stg. Bds. 1941	99
3½	Do. do. .. 1947	99
3	Do. do.	88
5	New South Wales 1897-1902	104½
4	Do. 1903-5-8-9-12	105
5	New Zealand 1914	118
5	Do. Cnsls. 1 p.c. per an. Sink. Fd.	104
3½	Nova Scotia Debs.	104
5	Quebec Prov. 1904-6	110
4½	Do. (drgs.)	104
5	Do. Strlg. Bds. 1912	115
4	Do. Strlg. Bds. 1928	110
4	Do. Strlg. Bds. 1934	108
4	Queensland 1913-15	106½
4½	St. Lucia Debs..............	100
6	South Australia 1897-1900	103½
6	Do. 1901-1918	119
5	Do. 1911-1920	115½
4	Do. 1899-1916	105
4	Do. 1929	110½
4	Do. 1916	108½
4	Do. 1917-18-24	112½
6	Tasmania 1897-1901	104
4	Do. 1908-11, 1913-14-20	107½
5	Trinidad Debs., an. drw. 1 p c...	106
4	Victoria 1899-1901	101½
4½	Do. 1904	105
4	Do. Rail. Loan 1907	104
4	Do. Loans 1908-13	106
4½	West. Austr. 1 p.c. ar. Sink. Fd.	108
4	Do. do.	106

REGISTERED AND INSCRIBED STOCKS.

No stamp duty except for Canada 4 p.c. Reduced (½ per cent.).

Rate.	Name.	Price.
4	Antigua Insc. Stk. Red. 1919-44	109
3½	Barbados Insc. Stk. 1925-42	108
3	British Colum. Insc. Stk. 1941	103
4	British Guiana Insc..... 1935	120
4	Canada Stk. Regd. ..1904-5-6-8	106
4	Do. 4 p.c. (late 5 p.c.) Regd. 1910	107½
3½	Do. 3½ p.c. Stock Regd. 1909-34	103½
4	Do. Ln. for 4 milln. stg. 1910-35	107½
3	Do. Stk. Regd. 1938	102
2½	Do. Insc.............. 1947	92
4	Cape G. Hope Regd. .. 1917-23	118
4	Do. (Ln. of '83) Insc. .. 1923	119
4	Do. Cons. Stk. Insc..... 1916-36	112
3½	Do. Consol. Insc. Stock 1929-49	112
4	Ceylon Insc. Stock 1934	121
3	Do. 1940	104
4	Grenada Insc. Stock.... 1917-42	112
3½	Hong Kong Insc. Stock 1918-43	103½
4	Jamaica Insc. Stock.... 1934	121
—	Do. 1922-44	99
4	Mauritius Inscribed 1937	119
4	Natal Consd. Stk. Insc. 1927	115
4	Do. 1937	120
3½	Do. Inscribed Stock.. 1914-39	107
4	Newfoundland Inscribed 1913-38	107
4	Do. 1935	114
4	Do. Consd. Stk. Ins. 1936	114
4	N. S Wales Stock Insc. 1933	118
3½	Do. 1924	106
3½	Do. 1918	105
3	D 1935	98

Colonial, &c. (*continued*):—

Rate.	Name.	Price.
4	N. Zealnd. Con. Stk. Ins. 1929	115
3½	Do. 1940	107
3	Do. Inscribed.... 1945	98
3	Quebec (Prov.) Ins. Stk. 1937	96
4	Queensland Stock Insc. 1915-24	110½
3½	Do. 1921-4-30	105
3½	Do. 1945	108
3	Do. 1922-47	99
4	St. Lucia Insc. Stock .. 1919-44	112
4	S. Austrln. (1882-7) Reg. 1916-36	111
3½	Do. In. Stk. Reg. 1939	110
3	Do. 1916-26	99
3/	Do. 1916	99
3½	Tasmanian Insc. Stock.. 1920-40	106
4	Do. 1920-40	115
4	Trinidad Insc. Stock.... 1917-42	119
3	Do. 1922-44	98½
4	Victoria Rly. Loan '81, Inscribed Stock 1907	104
4	Victoria Insc. Stock 1908-13-19	107
4	Victoria (1885) Ins. Stk. 1920	110
3½	Do. Inscribed Stock 1921-3-6	104
4	Do. do. 1911-26	107
4	W. Austral. Insc. Stock 1934	120
4	Do. 1911-31	110
3½	Do. 1915-35	107
3	Do. 1915-35	97½
3	Do. 1916-36	96½

FOREIGN STOCKS, BONDS, &c.

COUPONS PAYABLE IN LONDON.

Last Div.	Name.	Price.
36/	Argentine Ry. Loan 6 p.c. 1881	90½
15/	Do. 5 p.c. 1884	68
30/	Do. N. Cent. Ry. Ext. 5 p.c. 1887-8-9	68
30/	Do. 5 p.c. Trsy. Convs. 1887	68
5/4½	Do. 4½ p.c. Interl. Gld. 1888	66
27/	Do. 4½ p.c. Stlg. Extrl. 1888	67
10/6	Do. 3½ p.c. External .. 1889	49
4	Do. 4 p.c. Ry. Guar. Res....	57½
4½	Brazilian 1883	56
4½	Do. Gold.......... 1879	68½
4½	Do. 1888	57
36/	Buenos Ayres 1824	90
6	Do. 1882-3-6	47
6	Bulgarian 1888	93
6	Do. Mort. Bonds 1892	93
4½	Chilian 1885	77
4½	Do. 1886	78
4½	Do. 1887	77
4½	Do. 1889	82½
5	Do. 1892	86
4½	Do. 1893	77
4½	Do. 1895	77
5	Do. 1896	85
7	Chinese Silver 1894	101
6	Do. Gold 1895	105
6	Do. Apl. '95 by dwgs. 1901-15	110½
5	Do. Red. dwgs. in 36 yr. 1896	100½
5	Do. Do. Regis. 1896	99
1½	Colmbn. 1½ to 3 p.c. Ext. Bds. 1896	17
6	Cordova, Prov. 1886	26
—	Do. Eng. Ass. Certs.	25
—	Do. 6 p.c. 1887-8	26
—	Do. Eng. Ass. Certs.	25
3	Costa Rica "A"	32
2½	Do. "B"	27
3	Danish Gold 1914	98
10/	Ecuador N. Ext. Bds. 4½ p.c. ascn. to 5 p.c..............	20
3½	Egypt'n Ins. Stk. lia. Stp. Dty. 1890	101½
4	Do. State Domain 1878	104½
4	Do. D. Sanieh, Red. .. 1905	105
6	Entre Rios.............. 1886-8	36
6	Do. Fndg. Ln. Bds. 1894-1921	32
6	Do. do. Parana City......	27½
15/	Greek 1881	39
15/	Do. 1884	39
12/	Do. Rentes..............	33½
15/	Do. (Piræus-Larissa Ry.)	37
7/6	Do. Fundg. Loan 1893	42
4	Guatemala Extl. Debt..........	34
6	Hawaiian	102½
4	Hungarian Gold Rentes........	101½
3	Do. 1895	91½
6	Italian Irriga. Guar.	111½
5	Do. Maremmana	94½
5	Japan 5 p.c.	100
5	Mexican (Nat. R. Tehuantp c.) ..	96½
6	Do. Extrl. 1893	

Foreign Stocks, &c. (*continued*):—

Last Div.	Name.	Price.
6	Mexican Extrl. 1893	96
5	Do. Intrnl. Cons. Slvr.	37½
5	Do. Intern. Rd. Bds. 2d. Ser.	37½
4	Nicaragua 1886	50
3½	Norwegian, red. 1937, or earlier	—
3	Do. do. 1965, do.	98
3½	Do. 3½ p.c. Bnds.	103
1	Paraguay 1p.c. ris. 3p.c. 1886-96	16
5	Russian, 1822, £ Strlg.	149
3	Do. 1859	94
4	Do. (Nicolas Ry.) 1867-9	104
3	Do. Transcauc. Ry. 1882	94
4	Do. Con. R. R. Bd. Ser. I., 1889	104
4	Do. Do. II., 1889	104
4	Do. Do. III., 1891	103½
3½	Do. Bonds	100½
4	Do. Ln. (Dvinsk and Vitbsk)	103
6	Salvador 1889	67½
—	S Domingo 4s. Unified ... 1930	65½
6	San Luis Potosi Stg. 1889	93
5	San Paulo (Brzl.), Stg. 1888	91½
6	Santa Fé 1883-4	35
—	Do. Eng. Ass. Certs. Dep.	34
5	Do. 1888	45
—	Do. Eng. Ass. Certs. Dpsit.	44
5	Do. (W. Cnt. Col. Rly.) Mrt.	25
5	Do. & Reconq. Rly. Mort.	25
5	Spanish Quicksilvr Mort. 1870	103
3½	Swedish 1880	103
3	Do. 1888	98
3	Do. Conversion Loan 1894	100
45	Trans. Gov. Loan Red. ... 1903-42	104
59/	Tucuman (Prov.) 1888	69
	Turkish, Secd. on Egypt. Trib.	103½
3½	Turkish, Egpt. Trib., Ott. Bd., '94	99
4	Do. Priority 1890	90½
1	Do. Convted Series, "A"	65½
5	Do. Customs Ln. 1886	97½
5	Uruguay Bonds 1896	57
3	Venzula New Con. Debt 1881	34½

COUPONS PAYABLE ABROAD.

Last Div.	Name.	Price.
7	Argent. Nat. Cedla. Sries. "B".	35
5	Austrian Ster. Rnts., ex 10fl., 1870	85
5	Do. do. do.	86
5	Do. Paper do. 1870	84
5	Do. do. do.	86
4	Do. Gld Rentes 1876	104
2½	Belgian exchange 25 fr.	92
3	Do. do.	101
3½	Danish Int., 1887, Rd. 1896	97½
3½	Do. '87, Red. by pur. or draw. fr. Dec., 1900	98½
2½	Dutch Certs. ex 12 gldrs.	87
3	Do. Bonds	98
3	Do. Insc. Stk.	97
3½	French Rentes	105½
3	Do. 1878, '81-4., Red.	101
3	German Imp. Ln. 1891	96½
3	Do. do. 1892-3	96½
3	Do. do. 1890-4	96
5	Japan Cons. Ln., '99, 3' & 5, Red.	46
30/9	Prussian Consols	102
3	" Cons. Stg. Ln. 1891	97
4	Rumanian Bds. 1890	—
4	Do. do. 1891	—
4	Utd. States, 1877, Red. ... 1907	114
4	Do. 1895, 30 yrs.	128
3½	Do. Maschsetts Gl. 1935	113½
3½	Do. Gold Bonds ... 1923	110½
2	Virginia Cpn. Bds., 3 p.c. from July, 1901	70

BRITISH RAILWAYS.

ORD. SHARES AND STOCKS.

Last Div.	Name.	Price.
10	Barry, Ord.	280½
4	Do. Prefd.	126
6	Do. Defd.	150½
5½	Caledonian, Ord.	157
3	Do. Prefd.	100
	Do. Defd. Ord., No. 1	4½
	Cambrian, Ord	6½
—	Do. Coast Cons.	6½
32/	Cardiff Ry. Pref. Ord.	117
3/	Central Lond. £10 Ord. Sh.	10½
1/9½	Do. do. £6 paid	6½
3½d.	Do. Pref. Half-Shares	1½
1/6	Do. Def. do.	4½
1½	City and S. London	67
—	East London, Cons.	6½
2	Furness	64½
—	Glasgow and S. West. Pfd.	83
—	Do. do. Dfd.	66
—	Great Central, Ord ... 1894	40
32/0	Do. London Exten.	76
3½	Great N. of Scotland	124
4	Great Northern, Prefd.	118
—	Do. Consolidated "A"	49
—	Do. do. "B"	191½
2	Highland	84½
4	Isle of Wight, Prefd.	120½
3	Do. Defd.	83½
—	Lancs. Derbys. and E. Cst.	4
8½	L. Brighton and S. C. Ord.	186
27/11½	Do. New all pd.	186
6	Do. Prefd. Ord.	197
10/	Do. Contgt. Rights Certs.	20½
5½	Lond. and S. Western Ord.	223½
4	Do. Preferred	132
6½	Lond., Tilb., and Southend	133½
—	Mersey, £20 shares	½
—	Metropolitan, New Ord.	129
2½	Do. Surplus Lands	95
4	North Cornwall, 4 p.c. Pref.	104½
12/6	Do. Deferred	22½
7½	North London	225½
4½	North Staffordshire	131

British Railways (*continued*):—

Last Div.	Name.	Price.
1/6	Plymouth, Devenport, and S. W. Junc. £10	9
3/	Port Talbot £10 Shares	8½
9d.	Rhondda Swns. B. £10 Sh.	5
10	Rhymney, Cons.	266½
4	Do. Prefd.	123
6½	Do. Defd.	147½
—	Scarboro', Bridlington Junc.	47½
6½	South Eastern, Ord	151
6	Do. Pref.	193
3½	Taff Vale	81
25/	Vale of Glamorgan	129½
3	Waterloo & City	137½

LEASED AT FIXED RENTALS.

Last Div.	Name.	Price.
4	Birkenhead	146
5.19.0	East Lincnshire	209½
5½	Hamsmith. & City Ord.	192½
4½	Lond. and Blackwll.	163½
4½	Do. £10 4½ p. c. Pref.	163½
56/6	Lond. & Green. Ord.	102
5	Do. 5 p. c. Pref.	180½
5	Nor. and Eastn. £50 Ord.	90
6	Do.	107
3½	N. Cornwall 3½ p. c. Stk.	128½
4½	Nott. & Granthm. R. & C.	147
3½	Portptk. & Wigtn. Guar. Stk.	126
9	Vict. Stn. & Pimlico Ord.	317½
4½	Do. 4½ p. c. Pref.	164
4/	West Lond. £20 Ord. Shs.	14½
4½	Weymouth & Portld.	160½

DEBENTURE STOCKS.

Last Div.	Name.	Price.
4	Alexandra Dks. & Ry.	132½
3	Barry, Cons.	109
4	Brecon & Mrthyr, New A	127½
4	Do. New B	107
4	Caledonian	150½
4	Cambrian "A"	132½
4	Do. "B"	130½
4	Do. "C"	126½
4	Do. "D"	107½
3	Cardiff Rly.	104
4	City and S. Lond.	139
3½	Cleator & Working Junc.	118½
3	Devon & Som. "A"	105½
10/3	Do. "B" 4 p. c.	36
—	Do. "C" 4 p. c.	10
4	E. Lond. and Ch. 4 p. c. A	137
5/	Do. and B	67½
—	Do. 3rd Ch. 4 p. c.	19½
—	Do. 4th do.	9½
3½	Do. 1st (3½ p. c.)	128½
2½	Do. 2½ p.c. (Whitech. Exn).	88
4	Forth Bridge	144½
4	Furness	143
4	Glasgow and S. Western	150
5	Gt. Central	—
4½	Do.	157½
4	Gt. Eastern	147½
4	Gt. N. of Scotland	147½
3	Gt. Northern	113½
4	Gt. Western	151½
4½	Do.	160½
4½	Do.	169
5	Do.	187½
2½	Do.	100
4	Highland	143½
3	Hull and Barnsley	105½
3	Do. and (3-4 p. c).	124
4	Isle of Wight	144½
3	Do. Cent. "A"	92½
4½	Do. "B"	115½
4	Do. "C"	82½
3	Lancs. & Yorkshire	113½
4	Lancs. Derbys. & E. Cst.	123½
4	Lpool St. Hlen's & S. Lancs.	126
4½	Ldn. and Blackwall	158
4	Ldn. and Greenwich	148½
4	Lond., Brighton, &c.	150
4½	Do.	169
4½	Lond., Chath., &c., Arb.	157½
4½	Do. "B"	156½
4	Do.	140
4	Do. 1883	139
3	Do.	107
3	Lond. & N. Western	116
3	Lond. & S. Westn. "A"	115
3	Do. Consld.	115
4	Lond., Til., & Southend	147½
—	Mersey, 5 p. c. (Act, 1866)	65
4	Metropolitan	147½
4½	Do.	164½
3½	Do.	129½
6	Met. District	208½
4	Do.	139
3	Midland	115
4½	Mid-Wales "A"	137½
4	Neath & Brecon 1st	129
4	Do. "A 1"	119½
3	North British	109½
3	Do. 1893	106½
3½	N. Cornwall, Launcstn., &c.	126½

Debenture Stocks (*continued*):—

Last Div.	Name.	Price.
3	North Eastern	113
4½	North London	167
3	N. Staffordshire	113½
4	Plym. Devpt. & S.W. Jn.	141½
4	Rhondda and Swan. Bay	130½
4	Rhymney	146½
4	South-Eastern	150
5	Do.	166½
3½	Do.	127½
3	Do.	113½
3	Taff Vale	111
4	Tottenham & For. Gate	146
3	Vale of Glamorgan	105½
3	West Highld. (Gtd. by N.B.)	108½
4	Wrexham, Mold, &c. "A"	115½
4	Do. "B"	102½
4	Do. "C"	97½

GUARANTEED SHARES AND STOCKS.

Last Div.	Name.	Price.
4	Caledonian	150½
4	Do.	148
4	Forth Bridge	142½
4	Furness ... 1881	137½
4	Glasgow & S. Western	146
4	Do. St. Enoch. Rent	146
6	Gt. Central	200½
4½	Do. 1st Pref.	152½
3½	Do. Pref.	104½
5	Do. Irred. S.Y. Rent	161½
4½	Do. do.	139½
4	Gt. Eastern, Rent	145
5	Do. Metropolitan	182½
4	Do.	144½
4	Gt. N. of Scotland	141
4	Gt. Northern	146½
5	Gt. Western, Rent	180½
5	Do. Cons.	180½
4	Lancs. & Yorkshire	146½
5	L., Brighton & S. C.	181½
3½	L., Chat. & D. (Shrtlds.)	110½
4	L. & North Western	147½
4	L. & South Western ... 1881	147½
4½	Met. District, Ealing Rent	152
4½	Do. Fulham Rent	152
4	Do. Midland Rent	143½
4	Do. Mid. & Dist. Guar.	128½
4	Midland, Rent	147½
4	Do. Cons.	147½
3	Mid. & G. N. Jt., "A" Rnt.	109½
3	N. British, Lien	107
4	Do. Cons. Pref. No. 1	142
3	N. Cornwall, Wadebrge. Gu.	107
4	N. Eastern	146½
5	N. Staff. Trent & M. £20 Shs.	36
3½	Notl. Suburban Ord.	126½
20/6	S. E. Perp. Ann.	36
4½	Do. 4½ p.c.	163½
3½	S. Yorks. Junc. Ord.	118½
4½	W. Cornwall (G. W., Br., Ex., & S. Dev. Joint Rent	160
3	W. Highl. Ord. Stk. (Gua., N.B.)	105½

PREFERENCE SHARES AND STOCKS.

DIVIDENDS CONTINGENT ON PROFIT OF YEAR.

Last Div.	Name	Price.
4½	Alexandra Dks. & Ry. "A"	128½
5	Barry (First)	160½
4	Do. Consolidated	138½
4	Caledonian Cons., No. 1	147
4	Do. do. No. 2	145½
5	Do. do. ... 1878	180
4	Do. Pref. ... 1884	144½
4	Do. do. 1887 (Conv.)	155
—	Cambrian, No. 1 4 p.c. Pref.	72½
—	Do. No. 2 do.	39½
—	Do. No. 3 do.	19
—	Do. No. 4 do.	10
5	City & S. Lond. £10 shares	15½
—	Do. New	14
4	Furness, Cons. ... 1881	134½
4	Do. "A" 1881	131½
4	Do. "B" 1883	129½
4	Glasgow & S. Western	144½
4	Do. No. 2	144½
4	Do. 1888	143½
4	Do. 1891	143½
5	Gt. Central	162½
4	Do.	132½
5	Do. Conv. ... 1872	155½
5	Do. do. ... 1874	154½
5	Do. do. ... 1876	153½
5	Do. do. ... 1879	153½
5	Do. do. ... 1881	152½
4	Do. ... 1889	114½
4	Do. ... 1891	106½
5	Do. ... 1894	111½
4	Gt. Eastern, Cons.	142½
4	Do. ... 1886	141½
4	Do. ... 1881	141½
4	Do. ... 1884	141½

Preference Shares, &c. (*continued*):—

Last Div.	Name.	Price.
4	Gt. Eastern, Cons. ... 1887	141½
4	Do. ... 1888	141½
3½	Do. ... 1890	121½
3½	Do. ... 1893	121½
—	Do. (Int. fr. Jan '99) 1893	117½
4	Gt. North Scotland "A"	136½
4	Do. "B"	135½
4	Gt. Northern, Cons.	142½
3	Do. ... 1896	107
5	Gt. Western Cons.	180½
36/11	Hull & Barnsley Red. at 115	107
4	Isle of Wight	135½
3	Lancs. & Yorkshire, Cons.	108
2/2½	Lanc. Drby & E.C. 5 p.c. £10	10½
—	Do. 5 p.c. and £10	9½
5	Lond., Bright., &c., Cons.	181½
5	Do. and Cons.	180½
4½	Lond., Chat. & Dov. Arbitr.	136½
2/1	Do. 2nd Pref. 4½ p.c.	93
4	Lond. & N. Western	146½
4	Lond. & S. Western ... 1881	145½
4	Do. ... 1884	144½
3½	Do.	127½
4	Lond., Tilbury & Southend	142½
4	Do. Cons., 1887	142½
4	Do ... 1891	142½
—	Mersey, 5 p.c. Perp.	—
4	Metropolitan, Perp.	149½
4	Do. ... 1882	142½
4	Do. Irred.	142½
4	Do. ... 1887	142½
4	Do. New	142½
4½	Do.	166½
3½	Do.	134½
3	Do. Guar.	101½
2½	Metrop. Dist. Exten 5 p.c.	111
4	Midland, Cons. Perpetual	146½
4	N. British Cons., No. 2	138½
4½	Do. Edin. & Glasgow	156½
5	Do. ... 1865	172½
5	Do. Conv. ... 1874	172½
4½	Do. ... 1875	156½
4½	Do. Conv. ... 1875	156½
5	Do. do. ... 1879	172½
4	Do. do. ... 1884	140
4	Do. do. ... 1888	140
4	Do. do. ... 1890	140
4	Do. do. ... 1890	139
4	N. Eastern	144½
4½	N. Lond., Cons. ... 1866	174½
4½	Do. and Cons. ... 1875	160
3	N. Staffordshire	107
4½	Plym. Devpt. & S. W. Junc.	152½
1/3	Port Talbot, &c., 4 p.c. £10 Shares, 4 paid	5
5/	Rhondda & Swansea Bay, 5 p.c. £10 Shares	13
4	Rhymney, Cons.	180
4½	S. Eastern, Cons.	162½
5	Do. do.	178½
4	Do. Vested Cos'.	143
4	Do. ... 1891	143
3½	Do. ... 1893	125½
2	Do. 3 p.c. after July 1900	104½
4	Taff Vale	143

INDIAN RAILWAYS.

Last Div.	Name.	Paid.	Price.
3½	Assam Bengal, Ld., (3½ p.c. till June 30, then 3 p.c.)	100	102
4/	Barsi Light, Ld., £10 Shs.	10	10½
6	Bengal and N. West., Ld.	100	149½
4/	Do. £10 Shares	10	14½
3/6	Do. 3½ p.c. Cum. Pf. Shs.	10	10½
8½d.	Do.	4	4½
2/3½	Bengal Central, Ld., £10 (3½ p.c. + ¼th net earn)	5	5½
3	Bengal Dooars, Ld.	100	118
4	Bengal Nagpr., Lim. (gua. 4 p.c. + 4th sp. pfts.)	100	115
7½	Bombay, Baroda, and C. I. (gua. 5 p.c.)	100	213
36/1	Burma, Ld. (gua. 2½ p.c. and ½ p.c. add. till 1901)	100	108½
1/7	Do. £10 Shares	2½	3½
4	Delhi Umb. Kalka, Ld., Gua. 3½ p.c. + net earn.	100	122
4	Do. Deb. Stk., 1890 (1926)	100	113
9/10	Eatn. Bengal, "A" An. 1957	—	25
9/	Do. "B" 1957	—	23
4	Do. Gua. Deb. Stock	100	145½
9/7½	East Ind. Ann. "A" (1953)	—	25
8/4½	Do. "C"	—	22
8/11½	Do. "B"	—	22
6½	Do. Def. Ann. Cap. (gua. 4 p.c. + ½th sp. pfts.)	—	154
115/9	East Ind. Def. Ann. "D"	—	150
4½	East Ind. Irred. Stock	100	164½
5	Gt. Indian Penin., Gua. 5 p.c. + ½ surplus profits	100	170
4	Do. Irred. 4 p.c. Deb. St.	100	144½
4	Indian Mid., Ld. (gua. 4 p.c. + ¼th surplus pfts.)	100	115
51/	Madras Guar. + ½ sp. pfts.	100	166
48/6	Do. do.	100	156
46/	Do. do.	100	146
4	Nilgiri, Ld., 1st Deb. Stk.	100	97
4	Oude & Rohil. Db. Stk. Rd.	100	—
5⅛	Rohil. and Kumaon, Ld.	100	132
9/11	Scinde, Punj., and Delhi, "A" Ann., 1958	—	25
9/1	Do. "B" do.	—	22

Indian Railways (*continued*):—

Last Div.	Name.	Paid.	Price.
4	South Behar, Ld., £10 shs.	100	100
3½	Do. Deb. Stk. Red.	100	103
4½	South Ind., Gu. Deb. Stk.	100	164½
5	South Indian, Ld. (gua. 3 p.c., and ¼ spls. profits)	100	122½
5	Sthn. Mahratta, Ld. (3½ p.c. & ¼th net earnings)	100	117
4	Do. Deb. Stk. Red.	100	122
3½	Southern Punjab, Ld.	100	112
3½	Do. Deb. Stk. Red.	—	107
5	Nizam's Gua. State, Ld. (†	100	114½
4	Do. Mort. Deb., 1936	100	109
4	Do. do. Reg.	100	108
17/3½	Nizam's Gua. State, Ld., 3½ p.c. Mt. Deb. bearer	—	95½
17/3½	Do. Reg. do. ..	—	94½
5	W. of India Portgese., Ld.	100	68½
5	Do. Deb. Stk., Red	100	99

RAILWAYS.—BRITISH POSSESSIONS.

Last Div.	Name.	Paid.	Price.
5	Atlantic & N.W. Gua. 1 Mt. Bds., 1937	100	126
5/3	Buff. & L. Huron Ord. Sh.	10	13½
5½	Do. 1st Mt. Perp. Bds. 1879	100	141½
5½	Do. 2nd Mt. Perp. Bds.	100	141½
—	Calgary & Edmon. 6 p.c. 1st Mt. Stg. Bds. Red..	100	74½
5	Canada Cent. 1st Mt. Bds. Red.	100	105
4	Can. Pacific Pref. Stk.....	100	99
5	Do. Strl. 1st Mt. Deb. Bds. 1915	100	118
3½	Do. Ld. Grnt. Bds., 1938..	100	108
3½	Do. Ld. Grnt. Ins. Stk. ..	100	108
4	Do. Perp. Cons. Deb. Stk.	100	113½
5	Do. Algoma Bch. 1st Mt. Bds., 1937	100	122
2	Demerara, Original Stock	100	49
7	Do. Perp. Pref. Stk......	100	157½
9½d.	Do. 4 p.c. Cum. Ext. Pref. £10 Shs.	4	6½
—	Dominion Atlntc. Ord. Stk.	100	33½
—	Do. 5 p.c. Pref. Stk.....	100	101
4	Do. 1st. Deb. Stk.......	100	109
4	Do. 2nd do. Red.	100	100
—	EmuBay&Mt.Bischoff, Ld.	5	4½
4½	Do. Irred. Deb. Stk....	100	98
nil.	Gd. Trunk of Canada, Stk.	100	8
6	Do. 2nd. Equip. Mt. Bds.	100	131½
5	Do. Perp. Deb. Stk......	100	136½
5	Do. Gt. Westn. Deb. Stk.	100	127½
5	Do. Nthn. of Can. 1st Mt. Bds., 1902	100	103½
4	Do. do. Deb. Stk	100	102
5	Do. G. T. Geor. Bay & L. Erie 1 Mt., 1903	100	104
5	Do. Mid. of Can. Stl. 1st Mt. (Mid. Sec.) 1908	100	107
5	Do. do. Cons. 1 Mt. Bds. 1912	100	107
5	Do. Mont. & Champ. 1 Mt. Bds., 1902	100	104
	Do. Welln., Grey & Brce. 7 p.c. Bds. 1 Mt.	100	111
—	Jamaica 1st Mtg. Bds. Red.	—	103
—	Manitoba & N. W., 6 p.c. 1st Mt. Bds., Red	100	—
—	Do. Ldn. Bdhldrs. Certs.	—	—
5	Manitoba S. W. Col. 1 Mt. Bd., 1934 $1,000 price %	—	120
—	Mid. of W. Aust. Ld. 6 p.c. 1 Mt. Dbs., Red.	100	25
4	Do. Deb. Bds., Red.	100	103
4	Nakusp & Slocan Bds., 1918	100	106
3	Natal Zululand Ld. Debs.,	100	79½
5	N. Brunswick 1st Mt. Stg. Bds., 1934	100	122
4	Do. Perp. Cons. Deb. Stk.	100	114
—	N. Zealand Mid., Ld., 5 p.c 1st Mt. Debs..........	100	35
6	Ontario & Queb. Cap. Stk.	$100	157½
5	Do. Perm. Deb. Stk......	100	144½
—	Qu'Appelle, L. Lake & Sask. 6p.c. 1 Mt. Bds. Red.	100	43½
	Queb. & L. S. John, 1st Mt. Bds., 1909	100	25½
	Quebec Cent., Prior Ln. Bds., 1908	100	107
1½	Do. 5 p.c. Inc. Bds.	100	40
4	St. Lawr. & Ott. Stl. 1st Mt.	100	113
4	Shuswap & Okan., 1st Mt. Deb. Bds., 1915	100	76
5	Temiscouata, 5 p.c. Stl. 1st Deb. Bds., Red.........	100	9½
5	Do. (S. Franc. Brch.) 5 p.c. Stl. 1 Mt. Db. Bds., 1910	100	10
4	Toronto, Grey & B. 1st Mt.	100	113
1/2½	Well. & Mana. £5 Shs. ..	1	1
5	Do. Debs., 1908........	100	110
5	Do. 2nd Debs., 1908....	100	109
5	Do. 3rd do., 1908	100	108
6	Atlan. & St. Law. Shs., 6 p.c.	100	164
5	Gd. Trunk Mt. Bds., 1934	100	116½
5	Michigan Air Line, 5 p.c. 1st Mt. Bds., 1902......	100	104
4	Minneap., S. P. & Slt. Ste. Mar, 1st M Bds., 1938	$1000	97

AMERICAN RAILROAD STOCKS AND SHARES.

Last Div.	Name.	Paid.	Price.
6/	Alab. Gt. Sthn. A 6 p.c. Pref.	10*l.*	9
—	Do. do "B" Ord. ..	10*l.*	2
—	Alabma. N. Orl.-Tex. &c., "A" Pref.	10*l.*	½
—	Do. "B" Def.	10*l.*	¼
5½	Atlant. First Lsd. Ls. Rtl. Trust..................	Stk.	98½
—	Baltimore & Ohio Com. ..	$100	17
—	Baltimore Ohio S.W. Pref.	$100	7
—	Chesap. & Ohio Com.	$100	19½
—	Chic. Gt. West. 5 p.c. Pref. Stock "A"	$100	30½
—	Do. do. Scrip. In.......	—	29½
8/3	Do. 4 p.c. Deb. Stk.......	$100	70
4	Do. Interest in Scrip	$100	65½
$4	Chic. Junc. Rl. & Un. Stk. Yds. Com.	$100	110½
$1½	Do. 6 p.c. Cum. Pref.	$100	110½
$3½	Chic. Mil. & St. P. Pref...	$100	150
7	Cleve. & Pittsburgh	$10	86½
$1½	Clev., Cincin., Chic., & St. Louis Com.	$100	—
—	Erie 4 p.c. Non-Cum. 1st Pf.	—	36
—	Do. 4 p.c. do. 2nd Pf.	—	18
—	Gt. Northern Pref.	$100	155
$2½	Illinois Cen. Lsd. Lines ..	$100	99
—	Kansas City, Pitts & G. ..	$100	21
$3	L. Shore & Mich. Sth. C.	$100	192
—	Mex. Cen. Ltd. Com.	$100	6
—	Miss. Kan. & Tex. Pref...	$100	37½
2½	N.Y., Pen. & O. 1st Mt. Tst. Ltd., Ord.	—	50
4	Do. 1st Mort. Deb. Stk. ..	$100	93½
8	North Pennsylvania	$50	—
—	Northn. Pacific, Com......	$100	22½
1½	Pitts. F. Wayne & Chic...	$100	174
—	Reading 1st Pref.	$50	20
—	Do. 2nd Pref.	$50	10½
—	S. Louis & S. Fran. Com.	$100	6½
—	Do. 2nd Pref.	$100	25
6	St. Louis Bridge 1st Pref..	$100	107
3	Do. 2nd Pref.	$100	50
6	Tunnel Rail. of St. Louis	$100	107
$1½	St. Paul, Min. and Man...	$100	137
—	Southern, Com.	$100	8
—	Wabash, Common........	$100	7

AMERICAN RAILROAD BONDS. CURRENCY.

Last Div.	Name.	Price.
7	Albany & Susq. 1 Con. Mrt. 1906	118
7	Allegheny Val. 1 Mt....... 1910	125½
5	Burling., Cedar Rap. & N. 1 Mt. 1906	109½
5	Canada Southern 1 Mt..... 1908	111
5	Chic. & N. West. Sk. Fd. Db. 1933	120½
5	Do. Deb. Coupon 1921	115½
6	Chicago & Tomah 1905	112½
5	Chic. Burl. & Q. Skg. Fd. 1901	102½
4	Do. Nebraska Ext....... —	102
6	Chic., Mil., & S. Pl., 1 Mt. S.W. Div.............. 1909	117½
7	Do. (S. Paul Div.) 1 Mt. 1902	132½
5	Do. (La Cross & D. 1919	112½
7	Do. 1 Mt. (Hast. & Dak.) 1910	132
5	Do. Chic. & Mis. Riv. 1 Mt. 1926	112½
5	Chic., Rock Is. and Pac. 1 Mt. Ext. 1934	108
6	Det., G. Haven & Mil. Equip 1918	105
6	Do. do. Cons. Mt. 1918	102½
6	Ill. Cent., 1 Mt., Chic. & S. 1898	—
7	Indianap. & Vin., 1 Mt. .. 1908	125
6	Do. do. 2 Mt. .. 1900	104½
6	Lehigh Val., Cons. Mt..... 1923	112½
—	Mexic. Cent., Ln. 2 Cons. Inc. . —	6
7	N.Y. Cent. & H.R. Mt. Bonds 1903	119½
5	Do. Deb. 1904	111
6	Penns. Cons. S. F M. 1905	119½
4	West Shore, 1 Mt. 2361	110

DITTO—GOLD.

Last Div.	Name.	Price.
6	Alabama Gt. Sthn. 1 Mt. .. 1908	112
5	Do. Mid. 1 1928	96
4	Allegheny Val. Gen. Mt. .. 1942	107
4	Atch., Top., & S. Fé Gn. Mt. 1995	89½
3	Do. Adj. Mt............. 1995	59½
5	Do. Equipt. Tmst. ...... —	102½
5	Atlantic & Dan. 1 Mt....... 1950	—
5	Baltimore & Onio.......... 1925	100
5	Do. Speyer's Tst. Recpts. 1925	100
5	Do. Cons. Mt. 1988	104
4½	Do. 4½ p.c. 1 Mt. Term. 1934	86
4½	Do. Brown Shipley's Dep. Cts. —	86
5	Balt. Belt 5 p.c. 1 Mort..... 1990	90
4½	Balt. & Ohio S.W. 1 Mt. .. 1990	105
4½	Do. 4½ p.c. 1 Cons. Mt. 1893 1993	78
—	Do. Inc. Mt. 5 p.c. Cl. A —	29½
—	Do. do. Cl. B —	11
5	Balt. & Ohio S.W. Term 5 p.c. 1942	99½
6	Balt. & Ptmac (Mn. L.) 1 Mt. 1911	124
6	Do. do. (Tunnel) 1 Mt. 1911	126
4	Beech Creek 1 Mt. 1936	109
5	Do 2 Mort. 1936	116
4	Carthage & Adiron 1 Mt... 19[illegible]	10[illegible]

American Railroad Bonds—Gold (*continued*):—

Last Div.	Name.	Price.
5	Cent. of Georgia 1 Mort. .. 1945	117½
5	Do. Cons. Mt. 1945	92½
5	Cent. of N. Jrsy. Gn. Mt... 1987	116
6	Central Pacific, 1 Mort. 1898	102½
6	Do. Speyer's Certs....... —	106
5	Do. Land Grant 1900	100
5	Chesap. & Ohio 1st Cons. Mt. 1939	117½
4½	Do. Gen. Mt............ 1992	81
6	Chic. & W. Ind. Gen. Mt. Skg. Fd. 1932	120
5	Chic. Mil. & St. Pl. (Chic. & L. Sup.) 1 Mt. 1921	114½
5	Do. Chic. & Pac. W. 1921	119½
5	Do. Wisc. & Minn. 1 Mt. 1921	114½
5	Do. Terminal Mt. 1914	114½
4	Do. General Mt. 1989	108
5	Chic. St. L. & N. Orleans.. 1951	122½
4	Do. 1 Mort. (Memphis) .. 1951	105½
4	Clevel., Cin., Chic. & St. L., 1 Mt. (Cairo)............ 1939	90
4	Do. 1 Mt. (Cinc., Wab., & Mich.) 1991	90
4	Do. 1 Col. Tst. Mt. (S. Louis) 1990	98½
4	Do. General Mt. 1993	82½
4½	Clevel. & Mar. Mt. 1935	114
4½	Clevel. & Pittsburgh 1942	122½
4½	Do. Series B. 1942	122½
—	Colorado Mid. 1 Mt. 1936	63½
—	Do. Bdhrs.' Comm. Certs. —	63½
4	Dnvr. & R. Gde. 1 Cons. Mt. 1936	93
5	Do Imp. Mort........... 1928	91
4	Detroit & Mack. 1 Lien 1995	92½
5	E. Tennes., Virg., & Grgia. Cons. Mt. 1956	114½
5	Elmira, Cort., & Nthn. Mt. 1914	—
4	Erie 1 Cons. Mt. Pr. Ln. .. 1996	91
3	Do. Gen. Lien 1996	71
6	Galvest., Harrisb., &c., 1 Mt.....	107½
5	Georgia, Car. & N. 1 Mt. .. 1929	96
4½	Gd. Rpds & Inda. Ex. 1 Mt. 1941	112½
5	Do. 1 Mt. (Muskegon) .. 1926	39½
3½	Illinois Cent. 1 Mt. 1951	104½
4	Do. 1952	105
4	Do. Cairo Bdge. .. 1950	102
4	Do. 1953	104
4	Do. General Mort. .. 1904	102½
5	Kans. City, Pitts. & G. 1 M. 1923	80
3½	L. Shore & Mich. Southern 1997	109
4½	Lehigh Val. N.Y. 1 Mt..... 1940	106
5	Lehigh Val. Term. 1 Mt. .. 1941	109½
5	Long Island 1931	120½
5	Do. Deb............ 1934	102
5	Do. (N. Shore Bch.) 1 Cons. Mt. 1932	94
6	Louisville & Nash. G. Mt.. 1930	122
6	Do. 2 Mt. Sk. Fd. (S. & N. Alabama....... 1910	104½
6	Do. 1 Mt. N. Orl. & Mb. 1930	122½
5	Do. 1 Mt. Coll. Tst. ... 1931	108
4	Do. Unified 1940	89
4½	Do. Mobile & Montgy. 1 Mt. 1945	105½
4	Manhattan Cons. Mt....... 1990	96
4	Mexican Cent. Cons. Mt. .. 1911	66
—	Do. 1 Cons. Inc, ...	15
6	Mexican Nat. 1 Mt......... 1927	107
3	Do. 2 Mt. 6 p.c. Inc. A 1917	58
—	Do. do. B.. 1917	10
3	Do. Matheson's Certs.....	—
3	Michig. Cnt. (Battle Ck. & S.) 1 Mt. 1989	88
6	Minneap. & S. L. 1 Mt. Pacific Ext. 1921	117½
5	Do. 1 Consold. 1934	107½
4	Minne., Slt. S. M. & A. 1 Mt. 1926	98
5	Minneapolis Westn. 1 Mt... 1911	105½
4	Miss. Kans. & Tex. 1 Mt... 1990	89
4	Do. 2 do. 1990	62
4	Mobile & Birm. Mt. Inc.... 1945	38
5	Do. P. Lien 1945	88
4	Mohawk & Mal. 1 Mt...... 1991	108
5	Montana Cent. 1 Mt. 1937	111½
5	Nashv., Chattan., & S. L. 1 Cons. Mt............... 1928	102½
5	Nash., Flor., & Shff. Mt... 1937	95½
4	N. Y. & Putnam 1 Cons. Mt. 1993	108
5	N. Y., Brooklyn, & Man. B. 1 Cons. Mt............. 1935	107½
4	N. Y. Cent. & Hud. R. Deb. Certs. 1890 1905	107
4	Do. Ext. Debt. Certs.... 1905	107
7	N. Y., L. Erie, & W. 1 Cons. Mt. (Erie) 1920	142½
7	Do. 1 Con. Mt. Fd. Coup. 1920	140
5	N. Y., Onto., & W. Cons. 1 Mt.................... 1939	110
4	Do. 4 p.c. Refund. Mt.. 1992	102
5	N. Y. & Rockaway B. 1 Mt. 1927	102½
6	Norfolk & West. Gn. Mt.... 1931	128
6	Do. Imp. & Ext........ 1934	120
4	Do. 1 Cons. Mt........ —	78
6	N. Pacific Gn. 1 Mt. Ld. Gt. 1921	—
4	Do. P. Ln. Rl. & Ld. Gt. —	97
3	Do. Gn. Ln. Rl. & Ld. Gt. —	61½
5	Oregon & Calif. 1 Mt....... 1927	78½
5	Oregon Rl. & Nav. Col. Tst. —	—
6	Panama Skg. Fd. Subsidy.. 1910	105½
4½	Pennsylvania Rlrd. 1913	115½
4	Do. Equip. Tst. Ser. A.. 1914	104
4	Do. Cons. Mt........... 1943	115
4½	Penna. Company 1st Mort. 1921	116½
5	Perkiomen 1 Mrt., 2nd ser.. 1918	91½
4½	{ Pitts., C., C., & St. Ls. Con. Mt. G. B., Ser. A } 1940-2	113
4	Do. Cons. Mort., Ser. D.. 1945	105
6	Pittsbgh., Cle., & Toledo .. 1922	107½
4	Reading, Phil., & R. Genl. 1997	83
5	Richmond & Dan. Equip. .. 1909	97½
5	Rio Grande Junc. 1st Mort. 1939	94
4	Rio Grande West 1st Tst. Mt. 1939	82½
6	St. Joseph & Gd. Island .. 1925	—
7	S. Louis Bridge 1st Mort 1928	134½
5	S. Louis Mchts. Bdge. Term. 1st Mort................. 1930	102½

American Railroad Bonds (*continued*):

Last Div.	Name	Price.
4	S. Louis S. West 1st Mort.. 1989	77½
—	Do. 4 p.c. 2nd Mort. Inc. 1989	30
—	S. Louis Term. Cupples Sta. & Prop. 1st. Mrt. 4½ p.c. 1902-17	102
4½	St. Paul, Minn., & Manit. 1933	110½
6	Do. do. 1933	132½
6	Shamokin, Sunbury, &c. 2 Mt. 1925	109
5	S. & N. Alabama Cons. Mt. 1936	97½
5	Southern 1 Cons. Coup. 1994	93
4	Do. E. Tennes Reorg. Lien .. 1938	100
6	S. Pacific of Cal. 1 Mt... 1905-12	111
4½	Trml. Assn. of S. Louis 1 Mt. 1939	111½
5	Do. 1 Cons. Mt.......... 1944	109
5	Texas & Pac. 1 Mt......... 2000	102½
—	Do. 5 p.c. 2 Mt. Income 2000	34½
5	Toledo & Ohio Cent. 1 Mt. West. Div. 1935	102½
4½	Toledo., Walhon., Val., & Ohio 1 Mt. 1931-3	111½
6	Union Pacific 1 Mt. 1896-9	102½
5	Do. Coll. Trust.	—
—	Union Pac., Linc., & Color. 1 Mt. 1918	—
4	United N. Jersey Gen. Mt... 1944	115½
6	Vicksbrg., Shrevept., & Pac. Pr. Ln. Mt. 1915	102½
5	Wabash 1 Mt. 1939	112
4	Wn. Pennsylvania Mt. 1928	109½
5	W. Virga. & Pittsbg. 1 Mt. 1990	88
5	Wheeling & L. Erie 1 Mt. (Wheelg. Div.) 5 p.c. 1928	90½
5	Do. Extn. Imp. Mt. 1930	90
—	Do. do. Brown Shipley's Cts...	—
5	Willmar & Sioux Falls 1 Mt. 1938	111

STERLING.

Last Div.	Name	Price.
6	Alabama Gt. Sthn. Deb..... 1906	104½
5	Do. Gen. Mort. .. 1927-8	100
5	Alabama, N. Orl., Tex. & Pac. 5 p.c. "A" Dbs... 1910-40	99
55/	Do. do. "B" do. 1910-40	51
—	Do. do. "C" do.	19
—	Allegheny Valley 1910	136
4	Atlantic 1st Leased Line Perp...	98
6	Baltimore and Ohio 1902	107½
6	Do. do. 1910	118
5	Do. do. 1877........	97½
—	Do. Morgan's Certs. ..	97½
4½	Do. do. 1933	89
6	Chicago & Alton Cons. Mt. 1903	111
5	Chic. St. Paul & Kan. City Priority	106
6	Eastn. of Massachusetts.... 1906	117½
5	Illinois Cent. Skg. Fd.	106
5	Do. 1905	108
3½	Do. 1950	99½
4	Do. 1 Mt. 1951	112
3	Do. 1 Mt. 1951	92½
6	Louisville & Nash., M. C. & L. Div., 1 Mt. 1902	104½
7	Do. 1 Mt. (Memphis & O.)..................... 1901	111
47/4	Mexican Nat. "A" Certs. 5 p.c. Non. cum.	47
—	Do. "B" Certs....	10
6	N.Y. & Canada 1 Mt....... 1904	111½
6	N. York Cent. & H.R. Mort. 1903	112
4½	N. York, Penns., & Ohio Pr. Ln. Extd. 1935	—
5	Do. Equip. Tst.	103½
5	Do. 5 p.c. Equip. Tst. (1890)	103½
6	Nrthn. Cent. Cons. Gen. Mt. ..	106
6	Pennsylvania Gen. Mt. 1910	126
6	Do. Cons. Skg. Fd. Mt. 1905	114½
3½	Do. Cons. Mt.......... 1945	106
6	Phil. & Erie Cons. Mort .. 1920	134½
6	Phil. & Reading Gen. Cons. Mort. 1911	126
6	Pittsbg. & Connells. Cons. 1926	115
—	Do. Morgan's Certs....	115
4	St. Paul., Min., & Manitoba (Pac. Extn.) 1940	98
6	S. & N. Alabama.......... 1903	107½
6	Union Pacific, Omaha Bridge 1896	—
6	Un. N. Jersey & C. Gen. Mt. 1901	109½

FOREIGN RAILWAYS.

Last Div.	Name.	Paid.	Price.
4/	Alagoas, Ltd., Shs.......	20	6
5	Do. Deb. Stk., Red. ..	100	50
6	Antofagasta, Ltd., Stk. ..	100	72
4	Do. Perp. Deb. Stk. ..	100	90
—	Arauco, Ld., Ord. Shs. ..	10	½
—	Do. 10 p.c. Cum. Pref.	10	1½
5	Argentine Gt. W., Ld.,	100	73
5	Do. 5 p.c. Cum. Pref. Shs.	100	100
4	Do. 1 Deb. Stk.	100	104
1/0/0	Argentine N.E., Ltd., 6 p.c. Cum. Pref. Stk. ..	100	10
—	Do. 5 p.c. Deb. Stk., Red.	100	31
2/	Arica and Tacna Shs. ..	20	1½
10/	Bahia & San Fcisco., Ld.,	20	11
6/	Do. Timbo. Bch. Shs.	20	5
12/	Bahia, Blanca, & N.W. Ln. Prf. Cum. 6 p.c. ..	100	55
4	Do. 4 p.c. 1 Deb. Stk., Red.	100	86
6	Barranquilla R. & P., Ld., 6 p.c. 1 Deb. Stk., Red.	100	96

Foreign Railways (*continued*):—

Last Div.	Name.	Paid.	Price.
3/	Bilbao Riv. & Cantabn., Ltd., Ord.	3	6
—	Bolivar, Ltd., Shs.	10	1½
6	Do. 6 p.c. Deb. Stk.	100	96½
—	Brazil Gt. Southn. Ltd., 7 p.c. Cum. Pref.	20	1½
6	Do. Perm. Deb. Stk	100	47½
6½	B. Ayres Gt. Southn., Ld., Ord. Stk.	100	150
5	Do. Pref. Stk.	100	137
4	Do. Deb. Stk.	100	117
30/	B. Ayres & Ensen. Port., Ltd., Ord. Stk.	100	67
5	Do. Cum. 1 Pref. Stk.	100	123
6/0/0	Do. 6p.c.Con. Pref.Stk.	100	107
4	Do. Deb. Stk., Irred.	100	112
10⅜	B. Ayres Northern, Ltd., Ord. Stk.	100	265
12½	Do. Pref. Stk.	100	320
5	Do. 5 p.c. Mt. Deb. Stk., Red.	100	113
3/15/0	B. Ayres & Pac., Ld., 7 p.c. 1 Pref. Stk. (Cum.)	100	90
4	Do. 1 Deb. Stk.	100	102
5/5/0	Do. 4½ p.c. 2 Deb. Stk.	100	90
2	B Ayres & Rosario, Ltd., Ord. Stk.	100	71½
—	Do. New, £20 Shs.	20	22½
7/	Do. 7 p.c. Pref. Shs.	10	17½
7/	Do. Sunchales Ext.	10	15½
4	Do. Deb. Stk., Red.	100	108½
12/	B. Ayres & Val. Trans., Ltd., 7 p.c. Cum. Pref.	20	7
4	Do. 4 p.c. "A" Deb. Stk., Red.	100	71
—	Do. 6 p.c. "B" Deb. Stk., Red.	100	44
6/	B. Ayres Westn. Ld. Ord.	10	10½
3/	Do. Def. Shs.	10	6½
5	Do. 5 p.c. Pref.	10	12½
4	Do. Deb. Stk.	100	109½
6	Cent. Arg. Deb. Sk. Rd.	100	160½
4	Do. Deb. Stk. Rd.	100	112
6	Cent. Bahia L. Ord. Stk.	100	44½
	Do. Deb. Stk., 1934	100	72½
5	Do. Deb. Stk., 1937	100	58
1/6	Cent. Uguy. East. Ext. L. Shs.	10	6
5	Do. Perm. Stk.	100	111
3/	Do. Nthn. Ext. L. Sh.	10	4½
5	Do. Perm. Deb. Stk.	100	106
3	Do. of Montev. Ltd., Ord. Stk.	100	85
6	Do. Perm. Deb. Stk.	100	143
10/	Conde d'Eu, Ltd. Ord.	20	7
—	Cordba & Rosar., Ltd., 6 p.c. Pref. Shs.	100	42½
4	Do. 1 Deb. Stk.	100	94
5/	Do. 6 p.c. Deb. Stk.	100	84
—	Cordba Cent., Ltd., 5 p.c. Cu. 1 Pref. Stk.	100	83½
—	Do. 5 p.c. Non-Cum. 2 Pref. Stk.	100	46
5	Do. Deb. Stk.	100	120
—	Costa Rica, Ltd., Shs.	10	4½
8/	Dna. Thrsa. Chris., Ltd., 7 p.c. Pref. Shs.	20	4½
20/	E. Argentine, Ltd	100	40
6	Do. Deb. Stk.	100	105
1/1	Egyptn. Dlta. Lgt. Rys., Ltd., £10 Pref. Shs.	8	8½
—	Entre Rios, L., Ord. Shs.	5	½
—	Do. Cu. 5 p.c. Pref.	5	2½
6/	Gt. Westn. Brazil, Ltd.,	20	11
6	Do. Perm. Deb. Stk.	100	90½
6	Do. Extn. Deb. Stk.	100	76½
—	Int.-Oceanic Mex., Ltd., 7 p.c. Pref.	10	1½
4	Do. Deb. Stk.	100	84
42/6	Do. 7 p.c. "A" Deb. Sk.	100	65
—	Do. 7 p.c. "B" Deb. Sk.	100	32
5/	La Guaira & Carac.	10	7½
5	Do. 5 p.c. Deb. Sk. Red.	100	100
8/4	Lembg.-Czern.-Jassy	30	25
1/	Lima, Ltd.	20	2½
—	Manila Ltd. 7 p.c. Cu. Pf.	10	½
20/6½	Mexican 2nd Pref. 6 p.c.	100	34
6	Do. Perp. Deb. Stk.	100	143
1/0/0	Mexican Sthrn., Ld., Ord.	100	26
—	Do. 4 p.c. 1 Db. Stk. Rd.	100	85
—	Do. 4 p.c. 2 do.	100	62
—	Mid. Urgy., Ltd.	100	19
5	Do. Deb. Stk.	100	63
12/	Minas & Rio, Ltd.	20	12½
5/2	Namur & Liege	20	12½
11/6	Do. Pref.	20	29
5/	Natal & Na. Cruz, Ld., 7 p.c. Cum Pref.	20	8
—	Nitrate Ltd., Ord.	10	5
—	Do. 7 p.c. Pr. Con. Or.	10	3½
—	Do. Def. Conv. Ord.	10	½
7/	N.-E. Urgy., Ltd., Ord.	10	15
7/	Do. 7 p.c. Pref.	10	15½
—	N.-W. Argentine Ld., 7 p.c. Pref.	10	2½
6	Do. 6 p.c. 1 Deb. Stk.	100	113
—	Do. 2 Deb. Stk.	100	94
—	N.W. Uruguay 6 p.c. 1 Pref. Stk.	100	17
—	Do. 5 p.c. 2 Pref. Stk.	100	7½
6	Do. 6 p.c. Deb. Stk.	100	80½
16/	Ottoman (Sm. Aid.)	20	15½
—	Paraguay Cntl., Ld., 5 p.c. Perm. Deb. Stk.	100	11
—	Piræus, Ath., & Pelo.	275	1½
5/	Pto. Alegre & N. Hambg. Ld., 7 p.c. Pref. Shs.	20	4½
6	Do. Mt. Deb. Stk. Red.	100	77½
—	Puerto Cabello & Val. Ld.	10	1½
5	Recife & S. Francisco	100	74
14/	R. Claro S. Paulo, Ld., Sh.	10	22½
5	Do. Deb. Stk.	100	129
	Royal Sardinian Ord.	10	11½

Foreign Railways (*continued*):—

Last Div.	Name.	Paid.	Price.
5/	Royal Sardinian Pref.	10	12½
5/	Sambre & Meuse	20	18
5/6	Do. Pref.	10	12½
28/	San Paulo Ld.	20	35½
2/9½	Do. New Ord. £10 sh.	6	10½
2/	Do. 5 p.c. Non. Cm. Pref.	10	12½
5½	Do. Deb. Stk.	100	135
5	Do. 5 p.c. Deb. Stk.	100	128
—	S. Fé & Cordova, Gt. Sthn., Ld., Shares	100	51½
6	Do. Perp. Deb. Stk.	100	123
3/2½	S. Austrian	20	7½
10/	Sthn. Braz. R. Gde. do Sul, Ld.	20	8
6	Do. 6 p.c. Deb. Stk.	100	75
4	Swedish Centl., Ld., 4 p.c. Deb. Stk.	100	107
5	Do. Pref.	100	100
1/9	Taltal, Ld.	5	2½
—	Uruguay Nthn., Ld. 7 p.c. Pfd. Stk.	100	8
3½	Do. 5 p.c. Deb. Stk.	100	30
—	Villa Maria & Rufino, Ld., 6 p.c. Pref. Shs.	100	20
4	Do. 4 p.c. 1 Deb. Stk.	100	74
6/0/0	Do. 6 p.c. 2 Deb. Stk.	100	47
5/9	West Flanders	8½	21
5/6	Do. 5½ p.c. Pref.	10	18
3/	Wstn. of Havana, Ld.	10	4½

FOREIGN RAILWAY OBLIGATIONS

Per Cent.	Name.	Price.
6	Alagoas Ld., 6 p.c. Deb., Rd.	88½
—	Alcoy & Gandia, Ld., 5 p.c. Debs., Red.	25
5	Arauco., Ld., 5 p.c. 1st Mt., Rd.	64½
—	Do. 6 p.c. Mt. Deb., Rd.	44
6	Brazil G. Sthn., L., Mt. Dbs., Rd.	80½
6	Do. Mt. Dbs. 1893, Rd.	48½
5½	Campos & Caran. Dbs., Rd.	76
6	Central Bahia, L., Dbs., Rd.	90½
5½	Conde d'Eu, L., Dbs., Rd.	78
6	Costa Rica, L., 1st Mt. Dbs., Rd.	110
6	Do. 2nd Dbs., Rd.	93
5	Do. Prior Mt. Db., Rd.	104
6	Cucuta Mt. Dbs., Rd.	106
5½	Donna Thrsa. Cris., L., Dbs., Rd.	75
3	Eastn. of France, £20 Dbs., Rd.	19½
4	Egyptn. Delta Light, L., Db., Rd.	100
—	Espito. Santo & Cara. 5 p.c. Stl. Dbs., Rd.	38
4	Gd. Russian Nic., Rd.	102
5	Inter-Oceanic Mex., L., 5 p.c. Pr. Ln. Dbs., Rd.	104
3	Ital. 3 p.c. Bds. A & B, Rd.	57½
—	Ituana 6 p.c. Debs., 1918	74
—	Leopoldina, 6 p.c. Dbs. £50 Bds.,	23
—	Do. do. Comms. Cert.	23
—	Do. 5 p.c. Stg. Dbs. (1888), Rd.	33
—	Do. do. Comm. Certs.	33
—	Do. 5 p.c. Stg. Dbs. (1890), Rd.	23
—	Do. do. Comms. Certs.	23
—	Macahé & Cam. 5 p.c. Dbs., Rd.	33
—	Do. do. Comms. Certs.	33
—	Do. (Cantagallo), 5 p.c., Red.	33
—	Do. do. Comm. Certs.	33
—	Manila Ltd., 6 p.c. Deb., Red.	23
6	Do. Prior Lien Mt., Rd.	105
6	Do. Series "B," Rd.	81
7	Matanzas & Sab., Rd.	101½
6	Minas & Rio, L., 6 p.c. Dbs., Rd.	97
5	Mogyana 5 p.c. Deb. Bds., Rd.	104
5	Moscow-Jaros., Rd.	106½
5½	Natal & Na. Cruz Ltd., 5½ p.c. Debs., Red.	86
5	Nitrate, Ltd. Mt. Bds., Red.	80
3	Nthn. France, Red.	19½
4	N. of S. Af. Rep. (Trnsvl.) Gu. Bds. Red.	96
3	Nthn. of Spain £20 Pri. Obs. Red.	9
6	Ottmn. (Smy to A.) (Kujk) Asnt. Debs., Red.	109
6	Ottmn. (Seraik.) Asg. Debs. Red.	109
6	Ottmn. (Seraik) Non-Asg. D., Rd	109
5	Ottmn. Kuyjk. Ext. Red.	106
5	Ottmn. Serkeuy. Ext. Red.	101½
5	Ottmn. Tireh Ext. 1910	97
5	Ottmn. Debs, 1886, Red.	98
5	Do. 1888, Red. 1935	97½
5	Do. 1893, Red. 1935	99
5	Ottmn. of Anlia. Debs., Rd.	93
5	Do. Ser. II.	89
4	Ottomn. Smyr. & Cas. Ext. Bds., Red.	83½
3	Paris, Lyon & Medit. (old sys., £20), Red.	19
3	Paris, Lyon & Medit. (new sys., £20), Red.	19½
50/	Piræus, At. & Pelp., 6 p.c. 1st Mt. Bds., Red.	88½
3	Do. 5 p.c. Mt. Bds., Red.	61½
4	Pretoria-Pietbg., Ltd., Red.	93
7	Puerto Cab. & Val., Ltd., 1st Mt. Debs., Red.	94
—	Rio de Jano. & Nthn., Ltd., 6 p.c. £100 Deb., Red.	23
—	Rio de Jano. (Gr. Para.), 5 p.c. 1st Mt. St. £100 Debs., Red.	23
3	Royal Sardinian, A, Rd. £20	12
3	Royal Sardinian, B., Rd. £20	12

Foreign Rly. Obligations (*continued*):—

Per Cent.	Name.	Price.
5	Ryl. Trns.-Afric. 5 p.c. 1st Mt. £100 Bds., Red.	61
7	Sagua La Grande, B pRd.	98
4	Sa. Fe & Cor. G.S., Ld. Pr Ln. Bds.	104
5	Sa. Fe, 5 p.c. and Reg. Dbs.	81
3	South Austrian, £20 Red.	15½
3	South Austrian, (Ser X.)	16½
3	South Italian £20 Obs. (Ser. A to G), Red.	12½
3½	S. W. of Venez. (Barq.), Ltd., 7 p.c. 1st Mt. £100 Debs.	57½
5	Taltal, Ltd., 5 p.c. 1st Ch. Debs., Red.	99
5	Utd. Rwys. Havana, Red.	91½
3	Wtrn. of France, £20 Red.	19
6	Wrn. B. Ayres St. Mt. Debs., 1900	111
6	Wrn. B. Ayres, Reg. Cert.	109
5	Do. Mt. Bds.	122
6	Wtrn. of Havna., Ld, Mt. Dbs., Rd.	98
7	Wrn. Ry. San Paulo Red.	101
—	Wrn. Santa Fé, 7 p.c. Red.	40
4/7	Zafra & Huelva, 3 p.c. Red.	3

BANKS.

Div.	Name.	Paid.	Price.
1/9½	Agra, Ltd.	6	3½
4/2½	Anglo-Argentine, Ltd., £9	7	5½
8½ fls.	Anglo-Austrian	120f	14
6/	Anglo-Californian, Ltd., £20 Shares	10	11
4/	Anglo-Egyptian, Ltd., £15	5	6
5/	Anglo-Foreign Bkg., Ltd.	7	8
2/	Anglo-Italian, Ltd.	5	7½
7/6	Bk. of Africa, Ltd., £18¾	6¼	10½
20/	Bk. of Australasia	40	53
10/	Bk. of Brit. Columbia	20	21
25/	Bk. of Brit. N. America	50	66
20/	Bk. of Egypt, Ltd., £25	12½	18
5/	Bk. of Mauritius, Ltd.	10	9½
18/	Bk. of N. S. Wales	20	38
4 p.c.	Bk. of N. Zland. Gua. Stk.	100	103
6/	Bk. of Roumania, £20 Shs.	6	7½
2/6	Tarapaca & Ldn., Ltd., £10	5	3½
—	Bque. Fse. de l'Afri. du S.	100f	3½
f. 12.50	Bque. Internatle. de Paris	20	24
6/	Brit. Bk. of S. America, Ltd., £20 Shares	10	10½
16/	Capital & Cties., L., £50	10	39
16/	Chart. of India, &c.	20	32
10/	City, Ltd., £40 Shares	10	20
18/	Colonial, £100 Shares	30	21
10/	Delhi and London, Ltd.	25	—
5/	German of London, Ltd.	10	10½
25/	Hong-Kong & Shanghai	28½	44
4/	Imperl. of Persia	6½	3½
10/	Imperl. Ottoman, £20 Shs	10	11½
12/	Intrnatl. of Ldn., Ld., £20	15	11½
10/	Ionian, Ltd.	25	15
16/	Lloyds, Ltd., £50 Shs.	8	29½
10/	Ldn. & Brazil. Ltd., £20	10	18
44/	Ldn. & County, Ltd., £80	20	101
9/	Ldn. & Hanseatic, L., £20	10	10½
22/6	Ldn. & Midland, L., £60	12½	53½
8/9	Ldn. & Provin., Ltd., £10	5	22½
30/	Ldn. & Riv. Plate, L., £25	15	50
2/1½	Ldn. & San Fcisco, Ltd.	7	4½
28/	Ldn. & Sth. West., L., £50	20	70
26/	Ldn. & Westmins., L., £100	20	56½
3/	Ldn. of Mex. & S. Amer., Ltd., £10 Shs.	6	5½
15/	Ldn. Joint Stk., L., £100	15	33½
12/9½	Ldn., Paris & Amer., L. £20	16	25
2/4½	Merchant Bkg., L., £9	4	2½
6/3	Metropn, Ltd., £50 Shs.	5	14½
9/	National, Ltd., £50 Shs.	10	19½
4/5	Natl. of Mexico, $100 Shs.	$40	13
1/3	National of N. Z., L., £7½	2½	2
3/	National S. Afric. Rep.	10	15
18/10½	National Provcl. of Eng., Ltd., £75 Shs.	10½	50½
21/7½	Do. do. £60 Shs.	12	57
6/6	North Eastn., Ltd., £20 Shs	6	14½
19/	Parr's, Ld., £100 Shs.	20	91½
12/6	Prov. of Ireland, L., £100	12½	28½
40/	Stand. of S. Afric., L., £100	25	67
12/6	Union of Australia, L., £75	25	28
4 p.c.	Do. do. Ins. Stk. Dep. 1900	100	103
15/6	Union of Ldn., Ltd., £100	15½	35½

BREWERIES AND DISTILLERIES.

Div.	Name.	Paid.	Price.
4½	Albion Prp. 1 Mt. Db. Sk.	100	115
4	All Saints, L., Db. Sk. Rd.	100	99
7	Allsopp, Ltd.	100	154
6	Do. Cum. Pref	100	157
4½	Do. Deb. Stk., Red.	100	118
3½	Do. Deb. Stk., Red.	100	102
4½	Alton & Co., L., Db., Rd	100	106
4½	Do. Mt. Bds., 1896	100	105
—	Arnold, Perrett, Ltd.	10	6
6	Do. Cum. Pref.	10	10½
4½	Do. 1 Mt. Db. Stk., Rd.	100	106

Breweries &c. (*continued*):—

Div.	Name.	Paid.	Price.
5½	Arrol, A., & Sons, L., Cum. Pref. Shs.	10	10½
4½	Do. 1 Mt. Db. Stk., Rd.	100	106
5	Backus, 1 Mt. Db., Red.	100	60
4	Barclay, Perk., L., Cu. Pf.	10	11½
3½	Do. Mt. Db. Stk., Red.	100	111
—	Barnsley, Ltd.	10	11
6	Do. Cum. Pref.	10	13½
1/3	Barrett's, Ltd.	[illegible]	1½
1/3	Do. 5 p.c. Pref.	[illegible]	2½
3/	Bartholomay, Ltd.	20	4
8	Do. Cum. Pref.	20	9
6	Do. Deb.	100	102½
5	Bass, Ratcliff, Ltd., Cum. Pref. Stk.	100	144½
4½	Do. Mt. Db. Stk., Rd.	100	128
4	Bell, J., L., 1 Mt. D. Stk., R	100	100
2/6	Benskin's, L., Cum. Pref.	5	—
4½	Do. 1 Mt. Db. Stk Red.	100	—
4½	Do. "B" Deb. Sk. Rd.	100	—
7/	Bentley's Yorks., Ltd.	20	11
6/	Do. Cum. Pref.	10	12½
4½	Do. Mt. Debs., Red.	100	110
4½	Do. do. 1 92, Red.	100	110
—	Bieckert's, Ltd.	20	2
5	Do. Debs., Red.	100	57
—	Birmingham., Ltd., 6 p.c. Cum. Pref.	5	2½
4½	Do. Mt. Debs., Red.	50	40½
5½	Boardman's, Ld., Cm. Pf.	10	8½
4½	Do., Perp. 1 Mt. Db. Sk.	100	105½
15/2	Brain & Co., Ltd.	100	102
4½	Brakspear, L., 1 D. Stk. Rd	100	109
4	Brandon's, L., 1 D. Stk. R.	100	103½
21/	Bristol (Georges) Ltd.	10	46
6	Do. Cum. Pref.	10	18
5	Do. Mt. Db. Sk. 1888 Rd.	100	115½
17/6	Bristol United, Ltd.	10	35½
6	Do. Cum. Pref.	10	16½
4½	Do. Db. Sk. Rd.	100	128
5½	Buckley's, L., C. Pre-prf.	10	11
4½	Do. 1 Mt. Db. Stk. Rd.	100	105½
4	Bullard & Sns, L., D. Sk. R.	100	107
6	Bushell, Watk., L., C. Pf.	10	14
4½	Do. 1 Mt. Db. Sk. Rd.	100	112
5	Camden, Ltd., Cum. Pref.	10	11½
4½	Do. 1 Mt. Db. Sk. Rd.	100	108
5½	Cameron, Ltd., Cm. Prf.	10	13½
4½	Do. Mort Deb. Stk.	100	108
3½	Do. Perp Mt. Db. Sk.	100	100½
5	Cam'bell, J'stone, L., C. Pf.	5	6½
4½	Do. 4½ p.c. 1 Mt. Db. Sk.	100	106
4	Campbell, Praed, L., Per. 1 Mort. Deb. Stk.	100	109
4	Cannon, L., Mt. Db. Stk.	100	109
4	Do. "B" Deb. Stk.	100	105
5	Castlemaine, L., 1 Mt. Db.	100	94
3½	Charrington, Ltd., Mort. Deb. Stk. Red.	100	106
2/	Cheltnhm. Orig., Ltd.	5	7
6	Do. Cum. Pref.	5	7½
4	Do. Debs. Red.	100	107
10/	Chicago, Ltd.	10	3½
6	Do. Debs.	100	87½
—	Cincinnati, Ltd.	10	½
—	Do. Cum. Pref.	10	1½
10/	City of Baltimore	10	4
16/	Do. 8 p.c. Cum. Pref	10	8
14/	City of Chicago, Ltd.	10	1½
8	Do. Cum. Pref.	10	6
13	City of London, Ltd.	100	205½
5	Do. Cum. Pref.	100	137
4	Do. Mt. Deb. Stk., Rd.	100	113½
2/	Colchester, Ltd.	5	5
7	Do. Pref.	5	7
4½	Do. Deb. Stk., Red.	100	110
5	Combe, Ltd., Cum. Pref.	10	14½
4	Do. Mt. Db. Stk, Rd.	100	112
3½	Do. Perp. Deb. Stk.	100	107
5	Comm'cial, L., D. Sk., Rd.	100	108½
5	Courage, L., Cm. Pref. Shs.	100	139½
4	Do. Irr. Mt. Deb. Stk.	100	128
3½	Do. Irr. "B" Mt. Db. Sk.	100	106
8	Daniell & Sons, Ltd.	10	9
7	Do. Cum. Pref.	10	12½
4½	Do. 1 Mt. Perp. Db. Sk.	100	108½
4½	Do. "B" Deb. Stk.	100	102
10d.	Dartford, Ltd.	5	5
10d.	Do. Cum. Pref.	5	5½
4	Do. 1 Mt. Db. Sk. Rd.	100	102
4	Davenport, Ld., 1 D. Stk.	100	102½
10/	Denver United, Ltd.	10	3½
8	Do. Cum. Pref.	10	8½
6	Do. Debs.	100	95½
4½	Deuchar, L., 1 D. Sk., Rd.	100	106
8/	Distillers, Ltd.	10	24
4½	Do. Mt. Db. Stk., Rd.	100	115½
—	Dublin Distillers, Ltd.	5	1½
3/	Do. Cum. Pref.	5	4½
4½	Do. Irr. Deb. Stk.	100	—
5	Eadie, Ltd., Cum. Pref.	10	11½
4	Do. Irr. 1 Mt. Db. Sk.	100	108
10/	Edinbgh. Utd., Ltd.	10	13
6	Do. Cum. Prf.	10	13½
5	Do. 1 Mt. Dbs.	100	110½
4	Eldridge, Pope, L. D. St. R.	100	109
—	Emerald & Phoenix, Ltd.	10	1½
8	Do. Cum. Pref.	10	6½
6	Empress Ltd., C. Pf.	10	11½
4½	Do. Mt. Deb. Stk.	100	105
10/	Farnham, Ltd.	10	16
6	Do. Cum. Pref.	10	15
4	Fenwick, L., 1 D. Sk., Rd.	100	105
4	Flower & Sons, Irr. D. Sk.	100	111
4	Friary, L., 1 Db. Stk., Rd.	100	105½
4	Do. 1 "A" Db. Sk., Rd	100	108
4½	Groves, L., 1 Db. Sk., Rd.	100	110
14	Guinness, Ltd.	100	568
6	Do. Cum. Prf. Stk.	100	168½
5	Do. Deb. Stk., Red.	100	122
5	Hall's Oxford L., Cm. Pf.	5	5½
6/	Hancock, Ld., Cm. Pf. Ord.	10	14
7/	Do. Def. Ord.	10	17½

Breweries, &c. (*continued*) :—

Div.	Name.	Paid.	Price.
6	Hancock, Ld., Cum. Pref.	10	15½
4	Do. 1 Deb. Stk., Rd.	100	112
5	Hoare, Ltd. Cum. Pref..	10	13½
5	Do. "A" Cum. Pref..	10	12½
4	Do. Mt. Deb. Stk., Rd.	100	111
3½	Do. do. do. Rd.	100	104
4/6	Hodgson's, Ltd.	5	10
5	Do. 1 Mt. Db., Red..	—	120½
4	Do. 2 Mt. Db., 1906..	—	102
4½	Hopcraft & N., Ltd., 1 Mt. Deb. Stk., Red.	100	103
5	Huggins, Ltd., Cm. Prf..	10	12½
4½	Do. 1st D. Stk. Rd...	100	113
4½	Do. "B" Db. Stk. Rd.	100	111
8/	Hull, Ltd.	10	17
7	Do. Cum. Pref.	10	15
4½	Ind, Coope, L., D.Sk., Rd.	100	117
4	Do. "B" Mt. Db. Stk. Rd.	100	114
8/	Indiannpolis, Ltd.	10	3½
8	Do. Cm. Prf.	10	9½
5/	Jones, Frank, Ltd.	10	3½
7½	Do. Cum. Pref.	10	7½
5	Do. 1st Mort. Debs. ..	100	91½
4/	J. Kenward & Co., Ltd...	5	5½
4½	Kingsbury, L., 1 D.Sk., Rd	100	—
4	Lacon, L., D. Stk., Red.	100	110
4	Do. Irrd. "B" D. Sk.	100	106
4/	Lascelles, Ltd.	5	11
6	Do. Cum. Pref.	5	7½
5	Leney, Ltd., Cum. Pref.	10	11½
4	Do. 1 Mt. Db. Stk. Rd.	100	104
30/7½	Lion, Ltd., £25 shares..	17	49½
10/9½	Do. New £10 shares..	6	17
6	Do. Perp. Pref.	20	32
4	Do. B. Mt. Db. Sk. Rd.	100	110
4½	Lloyd & Y., Ltd., 1 Mt. Deb. Stk., Rd.	100	100½
4½	Locke & S., Ltd., Irr. 1st Mt. Deb. Stk.	100	101
4½	Lovibond, Ltd., 1st Mt. Deb. Stk., Rd.	100	102½
30/4	Lucas & Co., Ld., Deb. Stk.	100	107
8/	Manchester, Ltd.	10	18½
7	Do. Cum. Pref.	10	17½
5	Marston, J., L., Cm. Prf.	10	10½
4	Do. 1 Mt. Db. Sk., Rd.	100	101½
9/	Massey's Burnley, Ltd...	10	17
6	Do. Cum. Pref.	10	14½
4½	McCracken, Ltd., 1 Mt. Deb., 1908	100	61½
5	McEwan, Ltd., Cm. Pref.	10	15
5	Meux, Ltd., Cum. Pref..	10	14½
4	Do. Mt. Db. Stk. Red.	100	111
4½	Michell & A., Ltd., 1 Mt. Deb. Stk. Red.	100	105
4½	Mile End Dist. Db. Sk. Rd.	100	109
—	Milwaukee & Chic., Ltd.	10	1½
4/	Do. Cum. Pref.	10	6½
4½	Michell, Toms, L., Db...	50	57
6	Morgan, Ltd., Cum. Pref.	10	14½
10/	Nalder & Coll., Ltd.	10	34½
6	Do. Cum. Pref..	10	16
4½	Do. Deb. Red...	100	113
3/	New Beeston, Ltd.	5	5
2/9	Do. Cum. Pref.	5	5
4	Do. Mt. Deb. Stk. Red.	100	97½
12/	Newcastle, Ltd.	10	19½
6	Do. Cum. Pref.	10	15
5	Do. 1 Mt. Deb., 1911	100	110½
4	Do. "A" Deb. Stk. Red.	100	104
6	New England, Ltd	10	5
8	Do. Cum. Pref.	10	9½
6	Do. Debs. Red	100	104½
4	New London, L., 1 D.Sk.	100	103
7/2	New Westminster, Ltd..	4	10½
2/4½	Do. Pref.	4	6½
—	New York, Ltd.	10	1
—	Do. 8 p.c. Cum. Pref.	10	4½
6	Do. 1 Mt. Deb. Red.	100	80½
5	Noakes, Ld., Cum. Pref.	10	12½
4	Do. 1 Mt. Db. Stk., Rd.	100	106
4½	Norfolk, L., "A" D.Sk. Rd.	100	106
20/	Northampton, Ld.	10	16½
7	Do. Cum. Pref.	10	15½
6	Do. Cum. Pref.	10	13
5	Do. 1 Mt. Per. Db. Sk.	100	128
4	Nth. East., L., 1 D.Sk. Rd.	100	102
4½	N. Worcesters., L. Per. 1 Mort. Deb. Stock	100	98½
6	Nottingham, L., Cm. Prf.	10	12
5	Do. 1 Mt. Deb. Stk., Red.	100	114
17/4	Do. "B" do. Red.	50	112
6/	Ohlsson' Cape, Ld.	5	17
7	Do. Cum. Pref.	5	8½
4½	Do. 2nd Cum. Pref.	5	5½
5	Do. Deb. Stk., Red.	100	114
4½	Oldfield, L., 1 Mt. Db. Stk.	100	106
6	Page & Overt., L., Cm. Prf.	10	13½
4½	Do. 1 Mt. Dbs., Red.	100	109
10/	Parker's Burslem, Ltd. ..	10	24½
6	Do. Cum. Pref.	10	15
4	Do. 1 Mt. Db. Stk., Red.	100	113
4	Persse, Ld., 1 Mt. Db. Rd.	100	95½
4	Phipps, L., Irr. 1 Db. Stk.	100	115
5	Plymouth, L., Min. Cu. Pf.	10	13½
4½	Do. Mt. Deb. Stk., Red.	100	104½
4½	Pryor, Reid, L., 1 D.S., R.	100	105½
5	Reid's, Ld., Cm. Pref. Stk.	100	137½
4	Do. Mt. Deb. Stk., Red.	100	112
3½	Do. "B" Mt. Db. Stk., Rd	100	102
5	Rhondda Val., L., Cu. Pf	10	11
4½	Do. 1 Mt. Deb. Stk., Rd.	100	109
5	Robinson, Ld., Cum. Pref.	10	11½
4½	Do. 1 Mt. Perp. Db. Stk.	100	112
4/	Rochdale, Ltd.	10	5½
4½	Do. 1 Mt. Deb. Stk. ..	100	98½
7	Royal, Brentford, Ltd. ..	10	20½
	Do. Cum. Pref. ..	10	15
4½	Do. 1 Mt. Db. Red	100	109
6/	St. Louis, Ltd.	10	4
8	Do. Cum. Pref.	10	8½
14/	St. Pauli, Ltd.	10	10
7	Do. Cum. Pref.	10	12
4½	Salt (T.), L., 1 Db. Sk. Rd.	100	111

Breweries, &c. (*continued*) :—

Div.	Name.	Paid.	Price.
4½	Salt (T.), "B" Db. Stk. Red	100	108
—	San Francisco, Ltd.	10	½
—	Do. 8 p.c. Cum. Pref...	10	½
4½	Savill Brs., L., D. Sk. Rd.	100	117
4½	Scarboro., Ltd., 1 Db. Stk.	100	101
4	Shaw (Hy.), Ltd., 1 Mt. Db. Stk., Red.	100	104
22/	Showell's, Ltd.	10	33½
7	Do. Cum. Pref.	10	17½
3/	Do. Gua. Shs.	5	7½
4½	Do. Mt. Db. Stk., Red.	100	—
4	Simonds, L., 1 D. Sk., Rd.	100	109
5½	Simson & McP., L., Cu. Pf.	10	9½
4½	Do. 1 Mt. Deb. Stk. ..	100	100
5/	Smith, Garrett, L., £20 Shs	10	16½
5	Do. Cum. Pref.	20	26
—	Do. 3½ p.c. Mt. Db. Stk.	100	109
5	Smith's, Tadcster, L., CPf	10	12½
4½	Do. Deb. Stk., Red. ..	100	112
4	Do. Deb. Stk. Red. ..	100	108
4½	Star, L., 1 M. Db. Stk., Rd.	100	105
4	Steward & P., L., 1 D. Sk.	100	113
9/	Strettons Derby, Ltd.	10	13
6	Do. Cum. Pref.	10	13
4	Do. Irr. 1 Mt. Db. Stk.	100	103½
4½	Strong, Romsey, L., 1 D.S.	100	115
5	Stroud, L., Db. Sk., Rd.	100	111½
4½	Tadcaster To'er, L., D.Sk.	100	113
8/	Tamplin, Ltd.	10	21½
6	Do. Cum. Pref.	100	15
4	Do. "A" Db. Sk., Rd.	10	107
6	Thorne, Ltd., Cum. Pref.	10	14½
4	Do. Deb. Stk., Red...	100	105½
15/	Threlfall, Ltd.	10	47
6	Do. Cum. Pref.	10	16½
5	Do. 1 Mt. Dbs., Red.	100	116
4	Tollemache, L., D. Sk. Rd.	100	105
4	Truman, Hanb., D. Sk., R.	100	110
3	Do. "B" Mt. Db. Sk., Rd.	100	95
10/	United States, Ltd.	10	10
8	Do. Cum. Pref.	10	12
6	Do. 1 Mt. Deb.	100	107½
6/	Walker & H., Ld., Cm. Prf.	10	11½
4½	Do. 1 Mt. Deb. Stk., Red.	100	107
5	Walker, Peter, Ld. Cm. Prf.	10	14
4	Do. 1 Mt. Dbs. Red. ..	100	111
4	Wallingford, L., D. Sk. Rd.	100	107
6	Watney, Ld., Cm. Prf. Sk.	100	170
5	Do. Mt. Db. Sk., Rd.	100	117½
4½	Do. "B" Mt. Db. Sk., Rd.	100	112
3½	Do. Mt. Db. Stk.	100	101
5	Watney, D., Ld., Cm. Prf.	10	12½
4½	Do. 1 Mt. Db. Stk. ..	100	108
10/	Webster & Sons, Ltd. ..	10	16½
6	Do. Cum. Pref. ..	10	14
5	Wenlock Ltd., Pref.	10	12½
4	Do. 1 Mt. Db. Sk., Rd.	100	108
5	West Cheshire, L., Cu. Pf.	10	10½
4	Do. Irred. 1 Mt. Db. Sk.	100	100
4½	Whitbread, L., Cu. Pf. Sh.	100	124½
4	Do. Db. Stk., Red.	100	112
3½	Do. "B" Db. Stk., Rd.	100	100
9/	Wolverhmpton & D. Ld..	10	16½
6	Do. Cum. Pref.	10	13½
4½	Do. 1 Mt. Dbs., Red.	100	108
5½	Worthington, Ld., Cm. Prf.	10	15½
5½	Do. Cum. "B" Pref.	10	13½
4½	Do. Mt. Db. Sk., Rd.	100	114
3½	Do. Irr. "B" Db. Stk.	100	104½
10/	Yates's Castle, Ltd.	10	13½
5	Do. Cum. Pref.	10	11
5	Younger W., L., Cu. Pf. Sh.	100	135

CANALS AND DOCKS.

Last Div.	Name.	Paid.	Price.
4	Birmingham Canal	100	142½
—	E. & W. India Dock	100	21½
4	Do. Deb. Stk.	100	—
50/	Do. Def. Deb. Stk.	100	—
3½	Do. 1st Mt. Certs.	100	—
4	Do. Mt. Bds. (1885) ..	—	—
40/	G. Junction Ord. Shs...	100	151½
6/	Do. do. Pref.	10	19
4½	King's Lynn Per. Db. Stk.	100	117½
2½	Leeds & Lpool Canal	100	72
2½	Lndn & St. Kath. Dks. ..	100	57
4½	Do. Pref.	100	136½
4½	Do. Pref., 1878	100	132½
4½	Do. Pref., 1882	100	130
4	Do. Deb. Stk.	100	135
—	Mchester Ship C. 5 p.c. Pf.	10	1½
3½	Do. 1st Perp. Mt. Deb.	100	98
—	Milford Dks. Db. Stk. "A"	100	20
3½	Millwall Dk.	100	59
5	Do. Perp. Pref.	100	140½
4½	Do. Pref.	100	105½
5	Do. New Per. Prf., 1887	100	126½
5	Do. Per. Deb. Stk.	100	152½
4/	Newhaven Har.	10	14½
2½	N. Metropolitan	100	65
5	Sharpness Nw. Pf. "A" Sk.	100	144½
4	Do. Deb. Stk.	100	120½
4	Sheffield & S. Yorks Nav. 4½ p.c. Pref Stk.	100	117½
36.432	Suez Canal	20	136
7	Surrey Comcl. Dok., Ord.	100	147½
7	Do. Min. 4 p.c. Pref. "A"	110	150
5	Do. Pref. "B"	100	148½
5	Do. do. "C"	100	148½
5	Do. do. "D"	100	144½
4½	Do. Deb. Stk.	100	152½

COMMERCIAL, INDUSTRIAL, &c.

Last Div.	Name.	Paid.	Price.
5	Accles, L., 1 Mt. Db., Red.	100	84½
5/	Aërated Bread, Ltd.	1	12½
—	African Gold Recovery, L.	1	½
2/	Aluminium, L., "A" Shs.	1	2
4½	Do. 1 Mt. Db. Stk., Red.	100	99
5½	Amelia Nitr., L., 1 Mort. Deb., Red.	100	82½
7/	Anglo-Chil. Nitrate, Ltd., Cum. Pref.	10	7½
4½	Do. Cons. Mt. Bds., Red.	100	82½
4½	Anglo-Russian Cotton, Ld., 1 Charge Debs., Red.	100	99
11/3	Angus (G., & Co., L.), £10	7½	17
6/	Apollinaris, Ltd.	10	11½
5/	Do. 5 p.c. Cum. Pref.	10	10½
4	Do. Irred. Deb. Stock	100	106
6/	Appleton, French, & S., L.	5	½
3/	Argentine Meat Pres., L., 7 p.c. Pref.	10	2½
5	Argentine Refinry, Db. Rd.	100	98
2/2	Armstrong, Whitw., Ltd.	1	3½
4	Do. Cum. Pref.	5	6½
5	Artisans', Labr. Dwllgs., L.	100	131½
4½	Do. Non-Cm. Prf., 1879	100	132½
4½	Do. do. 1884	100	132½
—	Asbestos & Asbestic, Ltd.	10	8
2/7½	Ashley-grdns., L., C. Prf.	5	6
4½	Do. 1 Mt. Deb. Stk.	100	112½
5/	Assam Rly. & Trdng., L., 8 p.c. Cum. Pref. "A"	10	15½
—	Do. Deferrd. "B" Shs.	1	4½
—	Do. do. (iss. f. pd)	1	3½
8/	Do. Cum. Pre-Prf. "A"	10	15
6/	Do. New Pref.	10	11½
5	Do. Debs., Red.	100	107
5	Do. Red. Mort. Debs.	100	111
6	Aust'lian Pastrl, L., Cu. Pf.	10	7½
8d.	Aylesbury Dairy, Ltd. ..	1	1½
4	Do. 4 p.c. Mt. Dbs.	100	104½
10/	Babcock & Wilcox, Ltd.	10	30
6	Do. 6 p.c. Cm. Prf.	10	16½
8	Baker (Chs.), L., Cm. Pf.	5	9
8	Do. "B," Cm. Pref.	5	8½
8d.	Barker (John), Ltd.	1	2½
5½	Do. Cum. Pref.	5	7½
4½	Do. Irred. 1 Mt. Db. Stk.	100	131
—	Barnagore Jute, Ltd.	5	3
5	Do. Cum. Pref.	5	4½
7½d.	Belgravia Dairy, Ltd. ..	1	1½
5/	Bell (R.) & Co., Ltd.	5	3½
1/	Bell's Asbestos, Ltd.	1	½
5	Do. Mt. Db. Bds., Rd.	100	103
10/	Bengal Mills, Ltd.	10	11½
6/	Do. 5 p.c. Cum. Prf.	10	10½
2/5	Benson (J.W.) L., Cm. Pf.	10	10½
12/4	Do. Perp. Mt. Db. Stk.	100	102½
6	Bergvik, L., 6 p.c. Cm. Pf.	10	12
12/	Do. Dfd.	10	9½
4½	Do. 1 Dbs., Red. ..	100	103½
5/	Birm'ham Vinegar, Ltd.	5	10
5	Do. Cum. Pref.	5	5½
4½	Do. 1 Mt. Db. Stk., Rd.	100	108½
5	Boake (A.) L., 5 p.c. Cu. Pf.	10	10½
2/6	Bodega, Ltd.	5	8½
4½	Do. Mt. Deb. Stk., Rd.	100	111
8/	Bottomley & Brs., Ltd..	10	6½
6/	Do. 6 p.c. Pt.	10	9½
8½d.	Bovril, Ltd.	1	1
1/0½	Do. Def.	1	½
6½d.	Do. Cum. Pref...	1	1
4½	Do. Deb. Stk. ..	100	102
5/	Bradbury, Gretrex., Ltd., £10 share	8	14
5/	Do. 5 p.c. Cum. Pref.	10	13½
5/	Brewers' Sugar, L., 5 p.c. Cum. Pref.	10	10½
3/6	Brighton Grd. Hotel, Ld.	5	3½
4	Do Mt. Db. Stk., Red.	100	102½
5	Bristol Hotel & Palm. Co., Ltd. 1st Mt. Red. Deb.	100	106
9½d.	British & Bengton's. Tea Tr. Asc., Ltd.	1	1½
5	Do. Cum. Prf.	5	5½
—	British Deli & Lgkat. Tobacco, Ltd.	1	½
—	Do. Cum. Prf.	1	½
—	British Tea Table, Ltd...	1	2½
5½	Do. Cum. Pref.	1	1½
2/6	Brooke, Ben., & Co., Ltd., Cum. Pref.	5	5½
7/6	Brooke, Bond & Co., Ltd.	5	20½
6/	Brown Brs., L., Cum. Pref.	5	6
10/	Browne & Eagle, Ltd. ..	10	13½
5	Do. Cum. Pref.	10	13
4	Do. Mrt. Db. Sk., Red.	100	109
20/	Brunner, Mond, & Co., Lt.	10	41
7/	Do. £10 shares	3½	17
7	Do. Cum. Pref.	10	18
7	Do. £10 shares	5	8½
10/	Bryant & May, Ltd.	5	19½
2/	Bucknall, H., & Sons, Lt.	5	8
6	Do. Cum Pref.	5	8½
4/	Burke, E. & J., Ltd.	5	7½
6	Do. Cum. Pref.	5	7½
6	Do. Irred. Deb. Stk...	100	155
1/	Burlington Htls. Co., Ltd	1	1½
5	Do. Cum. Pref.	1	1½
4	Do. Perp. Deb. Stk. ..	100	105½
2/4	Bush, W. J., & Co., Ltd., Cum. Pref.	5	5½
36/8	Do. 1 Deb. Stk., Red.	100	104
5½	Callard, Stewart, & Watt, Ltd., Cum. Pref.	1	1½
4/	Callender's Cable L., Shs.	5	9½
4½	Do. 1 Deb. Stk., Red.	100	111½
—	Campbell, R., & Sons, Lt.	3	2½
6	Cantareira Water, Bd., Rd	100	99½
5	Do. (2nd issue)	100	92
4	Cartavio Sugar, Ltd., 6 p.c. 1st Debs., Red. ..	20	82½
9/	Cassell & Co., Ltd., £10	9	16
5	Causton, Sir J., & Sons, Ltd., Cum. Pref.	10	13½

Commercial, &c. (*continued*) :—

Last Div.	Name.	Paid.	Price.
4	Cent. Prod. Mkt. of B.A. 1st Mt. Str. Debs.	100	81
4	Chappell & Co., Ltd., Mt. Deb. Stk. Red	100	103
6/	Chicago & N.W. Gran. 8 p.c. Cum. Pref.	10	3
—	Chicago Packing & Prov.	10	6
8	Do. Cum. Pref.	10	10½
6/	City Offices, Ltd	36½	13
3½	Do. Mt. Deb. Stk...	100	108½
7/2½	Cy. London Real Prop., Ltd., £25 shs.	12	19
4/6	Do. £12½ shs.	7½	13½
3½	Do. Deb. Stk. Red...	100	108½
3½	Do. Deb. Stk. Red...	100	106½
3	Do.	100	101½
4/	Cy. of Santos Imprvts., Ltd., 7 p.c. Pref.	10	8½
20/	Clay, Bock, & Co., Ltd...	10	6
8	Do. Cum. Pref.	10	10
6	Do. Mort. Deb.	100	103½
20/	Coats, J. & P., Ltd.	10	60
6	Do. Cum. Pref.	10	18
4½	Do. Deb. Stk. Red.	100	112½
9½d.	Coburg Hotel, Ltd	1	1½
4	Do. Deb. Stk. Red.	100	102
6	Colonial Consign & Dis., Ltd., Cum. Pref.	5	4½
4½	Do. 1st Mort. Debs..	100	96½
—	Colorado Nitrate, Ltd. ..	5	½
4/	Co. Gén. des Asphtes. de F., Ltd.	6	6½
5	Do, Non-Cm. Prf. ..	—	5½
5	Cook, J. W., & Co., Ltd., Cum. Pref.	5	5½
5	Cook, T., & Son, Egypt, Ltd., 1st Mt. Deb. Red.	100	110½
—	Cork Co., Ltd., 6 p.c. Cum. Pref.	5	2½
5	Cory, W., & Sn, L., Cu. Pf.	5	6½
4	Do. 1st Deb. Stk. Red.	100	109
8½d.	Crisp & Co., Ltd	1	1½
5½	Do. Cum. Pref.	1	1½
—	Crompton & Co., Ltd., 7 p.c. Cum. Pref.	5	2½
5	Do. 1st Mt. Reg. Deb.	—	88½
4/6	Crossley, J., & Sons, Ltd.	5	8½
5	Do. Cum. Pref.	5	6½
—	Crystal Pal. Ord. "A" Stk.	100	8½
—	Do. "B" Red. Stk	100	1½
6	Do. 6 p.c. 1st 1887 Deb. Stk. Red. ..	100	117½
—	Do. 6 p.c. 2nd 1887 Deb. Stk. Red. ..	100	43½
—	Do. 6 p.c. 3rd 1887 Deb. Stk. Red. ..	100	17½
3	Do. 3 p.c. 1st 1895 Deb. Stk.	100	94½
—	Daimler Motor, Ltd	10	6
4/	Dalgety & Co., £20 Shs.	5	5½
4½	Do. Deb. Stk	100	123
4	Do.	100	115
7/	De Keyser's Ryl. Htl., L.	10	14
5	Do. Cum. Pref.	10	11½
4	Do. Deb. Stk., Red..	100	110
6	Denny, H., & Sons, Ltd., Cum. Pref.	10	14½
5/3	Devas, Routledge & Co., L.	7	8½
5	Dickinson, J., & Co., L., Cum. Pref. Stk.	100	123
4½	Domin. Cottn. Mls., Ltd. Mt. Stg. Dbs.	100	97
6/	Dorman, Long & Co., L.	5	4½
—	Eastmans, Ltd	10	3
12/	Do. 8 p.c. Cum. Pref.	10	10½
2/6	E. C. Powder, Ltd	3	5½
1/6	Edison & Swn Utd. Elec. Ltd., "A" £5 Shs.	3	2½
2/6	Do. fully-paid	5	4½
4½	Ekman Pulp & Ppr. Co., Ltd., Mt. Deb., Red..	100	95
1/1½	Electric Construc., Ltd..	2	2½
7	Do. Cum. Pref.	2	3½
25/	Eley Bros., Ltd.	10	38
—	Elmore's Cop. Deptg., L.	1	½
—	Elmore's Wire Mnfg., L.	2	½
—	Elysée Pal. Hotel Co., L.	5/	½
5 p.c.	Do. 5 p.c. £100 Db., Rd.	70	70
8½d.	Evans, Ben., & Co., Ltd.	1	1
5	Do. 1 Mt. Db. Sk., Rd.	100	105
8½d.	Evans., D. H., & Co., L.	1	2½
6	Do. Cum. Pref.	1	1½
4½	Do. 1 Mt. Db. Sk., Rd.	100	112
2/1	*Evening News*, L., 5 p.c. Cum. Pref.	5	5½
5/3	Evered & Co., L., £10 Sh.	7	13
7/6	Do.	10	19
4	Fairbairn Pastoral Co., Aust., L., 1 Mt. Db., Rd.	100	102
6	Fairfield Shipbldg., Ltd., Cum. Pref.	10	10
4½	Do. Mort. Deb. Stk..	100	107½
6/	Farmer & Co., Ld., 6 p.c. Cum. Pref.	10	13½
10	Field, J. C. & J., Ltd. ..	10	10
14/	Do. 7 p.c. Cum. Pref.	10	14
1/3	Fordham, W.B., & Sns, Ld.	1	2
5/6	Fore-st. Warehouse, Ltd.	11	9½
4	Do. Regd. Debs., Rd.	100	103½
3/6	Foster, M. B. & Sons, Ltd.	4	6½
5	Do. Pref.	10	11½
20/	Foster, Porter, & Co., L.	10½	16½
4	Fowler, J., & Co. (Leeds), Ltd., 1 Mt. Deb., Red.	100	103½
3/	Fraser & Chalmers, Ltd..	3	1½
4½	Free, Rodwell & Co., Ltd., Deb Stk.	100	105½
6½d.	Furness, T., & Co., Ltd., 5½ p.c. Cum. Pref.	1	½
4½	Gartside & Co. (of Manchstr), L., 1 Mt. Db. Sk.	100	110
11	Genl. Hydraul Power, L.	100	275

Commercial, &c. (continued):—

Last Div.	Name.	Paid.	Price.
8/	Gillman & Spencer, Ltd.	5	2¼
6	Do. Pref.	5	5
5	Do. Mort. Debs.	50	51
4	Goldsbro., Mort & Co., L., "A" Deb. Stk., Red.	100	74½
—	Do. 3 p.c. "B" Inc. Deb. Stk., Red.	100	17
8/	Gordon Hotels, Ltd.	10	20¼
5½	Do. Cum. Pref.	10	14¼
4½	Do. Perp. Deb. Stk.	100	137½
4	Do. do.	100	122½
—	Greenwich Inld. Linoleum Co., Ltd.	1	½
7	Greenwood & Batley, Ltd., Cum. Pref.	10	10
7½d.	Hagemann & Co., Ltd., 6 p.c. Cum. Pref.	1	1¼
—	Hammond, Ltd.	10	½
—	Do. 8 p.c. Cum. Pref.	10	2½
—	Do. 6 p.c. Cum. Inc. Stk. Red.	100	52½
4	Hampton & Sons, Ltd., 4 p.c. 1 Mt. Db. St. Red.	100	106
	Hans Crescent Htl., L., 6 p.c. Cum. Pref.	5	3
4	Do. 1 Mt. Deb. Stk.	100	90
5	Harmsworth, Ld., Cm. Pf.	1	1⅛
4/	Harrison, Barber, Ltd.	5	4½
3/	Harrod's Stores, Ltd.	1	4¾
2/6	Do. Cum. Pref.	5	7½
5½	Hawaiian Comcl. & Sug. 1 Mt. Debs.	100	94½
5	Hazell, Watson, L., C. P.	10	12
6/	Henley's Teleg., Ltd.	10	23
7	Do. Pref. Shs.	10	19
4½	Do. Mt. Db. Stk., Rd.	100	112½
6	Henry, Ltd.	10	12½
5	Do. Cum. Pref.	10	13¾
4½	Do. Mt. Debs., Red.	50	53
6	Hepworth, Ld., Cm. Prf.	10	11
—	Herrmann, Ltd.	1	⅛
—	Hildesheimer, Ltd.	3	1
1/2½	Holbrn. & Frasca, Ltd.	1	2
5	Do. Cum. Pref.	10	12
4	Do. Deb. Stk.	100	113
6	Home & Col. Stres, L., C. P	5	7½
6	Hood & M.'s Stres., Ltd., Cum. Pref.	1	½
—	Hook, C. T Ltd.	10	6
7/2	Hornby, Ltd., £10 Shs.	8	3½
5/6	Do. 6 p.c. Cm. Pf. Sk.	100	90
—	Hotchks. Ordn., Ltd.	10	1
—	Do. 7 p.c. Cm. Prf.	10	4
5	Do. 1 Mt. Dbs., Rd.	100	96½
6	Htl. Cecil, Ld., Cm. Prf.	5	4½
4	Do. 1 Mt. D. Sk., R.	100	107½
8/	Howard & Bulgh, Ltd.	10	40
6	Do. Pref.	10	16
4	Do. Deb. Stk., Red.	100	107
5/	Howell, J., Ltd., £5 Shs.	4	9½
—	Howell & Js., Ld., £3½ Shs.	3	½
1/6	Humber, Ltd.	1	½
6	Do. Cum. Pref.	1	½
5/6	Hunter, Wilts., Ltd.	5	7
2/7	Hyam Clthg., Ltd., 5 p.c. Cum. Pref.	5	5½
10/	Impl. Rusn. Cotton, L.	5	6
5	Impd. Industl. Dwgs., Ld.	100	130½
6d.	Do. Defrd.	1	1¼
25/	Impd. Wood Pave., Ltd.	10	15
15/	Ind. Rubber, Gutta Per. Telegraph Works, Ltd.	10	22
4	Do. 1 Mt. Debs., Red.	100	106
6	Intern. Tea, Cum. Pref.	5	6¾
7½d.	Jays, Ltd.	1	1¼
5½	Do. Cum. Pref.	5	6¾
8½d.	Jones & Higgins, Ltd.	1	2¼
4½	Do. 1 Mt. Db. Sk., Rd.	100	113
5/	Kelly's Directory, Ltd., 5 p.c. Cum. Pref.	10	12½
4	Do. Mort. Db. Sk., Rd.	100	106
—	Kent Coal Explrtn. Ltd.	1	½
9½d.	King, Howmann, Ltd.	1	1⅛
4/	Kinloch & Co., Ltd.	5	8½
6	Do. Pref.	5	7
5	Lady's Pictorial Pub., Ltd., Cum. Pref.	5	6
—	La Guaira Harb., Ltd., 7 p.c. Deb. Stk.	100	—
—	Do. 2 Mt. 7 p.c. Deb. Bds., Red.	100	—
4/	Lagunas Nitrate, Ltd.	5	2
2/	Lagunas Syn., Ltd.	5	1½
5	Do. 1 Mt. Debs., Red.	100	80½
—	L. Copais Ld., 1 Mt. 6 p.c. Debs., Red.	100	35½
3/	Lautaro Nitrate, Ltd.	5	4
5	Do. 1 Mt. Debs., Red.	—	100
9/	Lawes Chem. L., £10 shs	9	5½
14/	Do. N. Cm. Min. Pref.	10	13
—	Leeds Forge, 7 p.c. Cm. Pf	5	3¼
5	Do. 1 Mt. Debs., Red	50	47½
5	Lever Bros., L., Cm. Pf	10	13½
6	Liberty, L., 6 p.c. Cm. Pf	10	15
20/	Liebig's, Ltd.	20	75
5	Lilley & Sk., L., Cm. Pf	5	5½
30/4	Linoleum Mnftg., Ltd	5	16
3/	Linotype, Ltd., Pref.	5	6
4/	Do. Def.	5	8
4/	Lister & Co., Ltd.	10	4
5	Do. Cum. Pref.	10	8½
5/	Liverpool Nitrate	5	5
—	Liverpool Warehsg., Ltd	10	3½
5½	Do. Cum. Pref.	10	8½
4	Do. 1 Mt. Db. Stk., Rd	100	107
5½	Lockharts, Ltd., Cm. Pf	1	1½
4/6	Ldn. & Til. Lightrage £10	6	6½
6/	Ldn. Comcl. Sale Rms., L.	10	17½
3	Do. 1 Mt. Deb. Stk., Red.	100	103
3	London Nitrate, Ltd.	5	1½
4/	London Nitrate, Ld. 1 p.c. Cm. Min. Pf.	5	3½
8/	London Pavilion, Ltd.	5	7

Commercial, &c. (continued):—

Last Div.	Name.	Paid.	Price.
2/6	London Produce Clg. Ho., Ltd., £10 Shares	2½	3½
4/	London Stereos., Ltd.	5	3
6d.	Ldn. Un. Laun. L. Cm. Pf.	1	½
8½d.	Louise, Ltd.	1	½
5½	Do. Cum. Pref.	1	½
5/	Lovell & Christmas, Ltd.	5	11½
6	Do. Cum. Pref.	5	7½
4	Do. Mt. Deb. Stk., Red.	100	107
1/3	Lyons, Ltd.	1	3½
4½	Do. 1 Mt. Deb., Stk., Rd.	100	111½
10/	Machinery Trust, Ltd.	5	15
4½	Do. 4½ Deb. Stk.	100	106
6	MacLellan, L., Min. C. Pf.	10	8
5	Do. 1 Mt. Debs., 1900	100	101½
—	McEwan, J. & Co., Ltd.	10	1½
6	Do. Mt. Debs., Red.	100	89½
8	McNamara, L., Cm. Pref.	10	9
7½d.	Maison Virot, Ltd.	1	1½
2/7	Do. 6 p.c. Cum. Pref.	5	4½
8/	Manbré Sacc., L., Cm. Pf.	10	12
10/	Mangan Brze., L., £10 Shs.	6	15½
2/	Mason & Mason, Ltd.	5	3
6	Do. Cum. Pref.	5	5½
—	Maynards, Ltd.	1	½
6	Do. Cum. Pref.	1	½
9½d.	Mazawattee Tea, Ltd.	1	1½
5	Do. Cum. Pref.	5	5½
6	Mellin's Food Cum. Pref.	5	7
4½	Met. Ascn. Imp. Dwlgs. L.	100	110
3½	Do. 1 Mt. Deb. Stk.	100	97
5	Metro. Indus. Dwlgs., Ltd.	5	5
4	Do. do. Cum. Pref.	5	5½
5	Metro. Prop., L., Cm. Pf.	5	6½
4½	Do. 1st Mt. Debs. Stk.	100	108½
6	Mexican Cotton 1 Mt. Db.	100	96½
4½	Mid. Class Dwlgs., L., Db.	100	120½
1/	Millars' Karri, Ltd.	1	3½
6	Do. Cum. Pref.	1	1½
2/	Milner's Safe, Ltd.	10	20½
2½/	Moir & Son, Ltd., Pref.	5	8½
6	Morgan Cruc., L., Cm. Pf.	10	15
9/	Morris, B., Ltd.	3½	3½
—	Murray L. 5½ p.c. C. Pf.	5	5½
—	Do. 4½ 1 Mt. Db. Sk. Rd.	100	108
—	Natnl. Dwlgs., L., 5 p.c. Pf.	5	1
1/7½	Nat. Safe Dep., Ltd.	4	3½
6	Do. Cum. Pref.	1	1½
—	Native Guano, Ltd.	5	½
—	Nelson Bros., Ltd.	10	2½
5	Do. Deb. Stk., Red.	100	80½
4/	Neuchtel Asph., Ltd.	10	11
—	New Central Borneo, Ld.	1	—
10d.	New Darvel Tob., Ltd.	18/	1½
—	New Explosives, Ltd.	3	2½
5/7½	New Gd. Htl., Bham, L.	5	4
5½	Do. Pref.	5	4½
4	Do. 1 Mt. Db. Stk., Rd.	100	95½
—	New Julia Nitrate, Ltd.	10/	½
—	New Ldn. Borneo Tob., L.	16/	½
1/6	New Premier Cycle, Ltd.	1	½
6	Do. 6 p.c. Cum. Pref.	1	½
4½	Do. 4½ p.c. 1 Mt. Db. Rd	100	—
—	New Tamargl. Nitr., Ltd	1	½
—	Do. 8 p.c. Cum. Pref.	1	½
6	Do. 6 p.c. 1 Mt. Dbs. Rd.	100	62½
3/7½d.	Newnes, G., L., Cm. Prf.	1	1½
1/3	Nitr. Provision, Ltd.	2½	½
24/	Nobel-Dynam., Ltd.	10	17½
—	North Brazn. Sugar, Ltd.	1	½
15/	Oakey, Ltd.	10	31
6	Do. Cum. Pref.	10	17
—	Paccha Jazp. Nitr., Ltd.	5	½
5	Pac. Borax, L., 1 Db. Rd.	100	110
—	Palace Hotel, Ltd.	10	5½
5½	Do. Cum. Pref.	10	8½
4	Do. 1 Mt. Deb. Stk.	100	104
2/6	Palmer, Ltd.	5	1½
6	Do. Cum. Pref.	5	3
9½d.	Paquin, Ltd.	1	1½
6	Do. Cum. Pref.	5	4½
5½	Parnall, Ltd., Cum. Pref.	1	½
4/6	Pawsons, Ltd., £10 Shs.	6	6½
4	Do. Mt. Debs., Red.	100	107
6	Pearks, G. & T., Ltd., 6 p.c. Cum. Pref.	1	½
1/2½	Pears, Ltd.	1	1⅛
6	Do. Cum. Pref.	10	14
5	Do. Deb. Stk.	100	128
5½	Pearson, C. A., L., Cu. Pf.	5	5¼
4/3	Peebles, Ltd.	5	8
5	Do. Cum. Pref.	5	6½
4½	Do. Mt. Deb. Stk. Red.	100	113½
5½	Peek Bros., Ltd., 1 Cum. Pref., Nos. 1-60,000	5	6½
3½	Do. 3½ p.c. 1 Db. Stk.	100	103½
7½d.	Pegamoid, Ltd.	1	½
—	Phospho-Guano, Ltd.	5	2½
—	Pillsbury-W. Fl. Mills, L.	10	2
16/	Do. 8 p.c. Cum. Pref.	10	6½
6	Do. 1 Mort. Debs.	100	96½
7½d.	Plummer, Ltd.	1	1½
5	Do. Cum. Pref.	5	5
15/	Price's Candle, Ltd.	16	38
6	Priest Marians, L., Cm. Pf.	1	1½
6	Pryce Jones, Ld., Cm. Pf.	5	7½
5	Do. Deb. Stk.	100	122½
10.6d.	Pullman, Ltd.	1	1½
6d.	Do. Cum. Pref.	1	1½
11½d.	Raleigh Cycle, Ltd.	1	½
6	Do. Cum. Pref.	1	½
—	Recife Drnge. Ld. 1 Mt. Debs., R.	100	19
6	Redfern, Ltd. Cum. Prf.	10	14
5	Ridgways, Ltd., Cu. Pf.	5	5½
—	R. Janeiro Cy. Imps., Ld.	25	10½
5	Do. Debs.	100	89½
5	Do. 1880-1899	100	88½
21/	R. Jan Fl. Mills, Ltd.	7	6½
5	Do. 1 Mt. Debs., Rd.	100	94
—	Riv. Plate Meat, Ltd.	5	3½
—	Do. Pref.	5	5
8½d.	Roberts, J. R., Ltd.	1	1½

Commercial, &c. (continued):—

Last Div.	Name.	Paid.	Price.
5	Roberts 1 Mt. D. Sk., Rd.	100	112
8½d.	Roberts, T. R., Ltd.	1	2½
5	Do. Cum. Pref.	1	1½
3/	Rosario Nit., Ltd.	5	3½
5	Do. Debs., Red.	100	106
5	Do. Huara, Debs.	—	104
1/	Rover Cycle, Ltd.	1	½
6/	Ryl. Aquarium, Ltd.	5	4½
6	Do. Pref.	5	6
5	Ryl. Htl., Edin., Cm. Pf.	1	1½
1/2½	Ryl. Niger, Ltd., £10 Sh.	2	2½
6/	Do.	10	14½
—	Russian Petroleum	10	22
—	Do. 6½ p.c. Cm. Prf.	10	11½
3/	Ruston, Proctor, Ltd.	10	11
4½	Do. 1 Mort. Debs.	100	104
6/	Sadler, Ltd.	10	7
—	Sal. Carmen Nit., Ltd.	5	4½
9d.	Salmon & Gluck., Ltd.	1	1⅛
	Salt Union, Ltd.	10	1½
1½	Do. 7 p.c. Pref.	10	6
4½	Do. Deb. Stk.	100	100½
4½	Do. "B" Deb. Sk., Rd.	100	97½
—	San Donato Nit., Ltd.	5	½
2/6	San Jorge Nit., Ltd.	5	3½
—	San Pablo Nit., Ltd.	5	½
—	San Sebastn. Nit., Ltd.	5	½
1/9	Sanitas, Ltd	1	2½
—	Sa. Elena Nit., Ltd.	5	½
—	Sa. Rita Nit., Ltd.	5	2
10/	Savoy Hotel, Ltd.	10	15
7	Do. Pref.	10	15
4	Do. 1 Mt. Deb. Stk.	100	111½
5	Do. Debs., Red	100	102½
5	Do. & Ldn. For. Htl., Ltd., 5 p.c. Debs. Red.	100	99
1½d.	Schweppes, Ltd.	1	1⅛
—	Do. Def.	1	½
5	Do. Cum. Pref.	1	1½
4	Do. Deb. Stk.	100	108
1/	Singer Cyc., Ltd.	1	½
5½	Do Cum. Pref.	1	½
—	Smokeless Pwdr., Ltd.	1	½
5½d.	S. Eng. Dairies, Ltd., 6 p.c. Cum. Pref.	1	1½
—	Sowler Thos. L.	1	1½
—	Do. 5½ Cm. Pf.	5	5½
4/6	Spencer, Turner, & Co. Ltd	5	8½
5	Do. Cum. Pref.	5	6½
5	Spicer, Ld., 5 p.c. Dbs. Rd.	100	65
4/	Spiers & Pond, Ltd.	10	20
5	Do. 1 Mt. Debs., Red.	100	117½
5	Do. "A" Db. Stk., Rd.	100	111
5	Do. "B" 1 Db. Stk., Rd.	100	111
4	Do. Fd. "C" 1 Db. S., R.	100	104
5/	Spratt's, Ltd	5	13½
4	Do. Debs., 1914	—	105
5	Steiner Ld., Cm. Pf.	10	11½
4	Do. 1 Mt. Db. Sk. Rd.	100	106
7/	Stewart & Clydesdale, L.	10	14½
6	Do. Cum. Pref.	10	15½
33/3	Sulphide Corp.	100	80
—	Swan & Edgar, L.	1	1½
1/	Sweetmeat Automatic, L.	1	½
2/9	Teetgen, Ltd., Cum. Pref.	5	6
24/	Teleg. Construction., Ld.	12	37½
5	Do. Db. Bds., Rd., 1899	100	103½
3/0½	Tilling, Ld. 5½ p.c. Cm. Prf.	5	6½
4	Do. 4 p.c. 1 Dbs., Rd.	—	104
8½d.	Tower Tea, Ltd.	1	1½
5	Do. Cum. Pref.	5	5½
5	Travers, Ltd., Cum. Pref.	10	12½
4	Do. 1 Mt. Dbs., Rd.	100	106
6	Tucuman Sug., 1 Dbs., Rd.	100	100
4/	United Alkali, Ltd.	10	1½
7	Do. Cum. Pref.	10	9
5	Do. Mt. Db. Stk., Rd.	100	108½
9½d.	United Horse Shoe, Ltd., Non-Cum. 8 p.c. Pref.	1	½
5	Un. Kingm. Tea, Cm. Prf.	5	4½
2/	Un. Lankat Plant., Ltd.	1	2½
4/	Un. Limmer Asphlte., Ld.	3	4½
5/	Val de Travers Asph., L.	10	15½
3/	V. den Bergh's, L., Cm. P.	5	6½
6	Walkers, Park., L., C. Pf.	10	4
4½	Do. 1 Mt. Debs., Red.	100	90½
6/	Wallis, Thos. & Co., Ltd.	5	14
6	Do. Cum. Pref.	5	8½
5½	Waring, Ltd., Cum. Pref.	5	5½
4½	Do. 1 Mt. Db. Sk., Red.	100	115
4½	Do. Irred. "B" Db. Stk.	100	105
12/	Waterlow, Dfd. Ord.	10	15½
12/	Do. Pref.	10	15
—	Do. Cum. Pref.	10	10½
10/	Waterlow Bros. & L., Ld.	10	9
5	Do. Pref.	10	12
1/2½	Welford, Ltd.	1	2
4½	Do. Debs., Red.	100	108
1/	Welford's Surrey Dairies, Ltd.	1	1½
7½d.	West London Dairy, Ltd.	1	1
4½	Wharncliffe Dwllgs., L., Pf.	10	11½
18/10	Do. 3 p.c. Irr. Mt. Db. Sk.	100	96
6d.	White, A. J., Ltd.	1	½
6	Do. 6 p.c. Cum. Pref.	1	½
4	White, J. Bazley, Ltd., 1 Mort. Debs., Red	100	98½
5	White, R., Ltd., 1 Mort. Deb. Stock, Red.	100	104½
5/	White, Tomkins, Ltd	10	12½
5	Do. Cum. Pref.	10	12
6	White, W. N., L., Cm. Pf.	1	1
2/6	Wickens, Pease & Co., L.	5	2½
6	Wilkie, Ltd., Cum. Pref.	10	16
3/6	Willans & Robinson, Ltd.	5	8½
6	Do. Cum. Pref.	5	7½
4½	Do. 1 Mt. Db. Stk., Red.	100	107
7½d.	Williamsons, L., Cm. Prf.	1	1½
6	Winterbottm. Book Cloth, Ltd., Cum. Prf.	10	15
3/	Yates, Ltd.	5	6½
6	Do. Cum. Pref.	5	6½
	Young's Paraffin, Ltd.	4	3½

CORPORATION STOCKS—COLONIAL AND FOREIGN.

Per Cent.	Name.	Paid.	Price.
6	Auckland City, '72 1904-24	100	118
6	Do. Cons., '79, Red. 1930	100	136½
5	Do. Deb. Ln., '83..1934-8	100	117
6	Auckland Harb. Debs.	100	111½
5	Do. 1917	100	115
5	Do. 1936	100	116
3½	Balmain Boro' 1914	—	117
5	Boston City (U.S.)	100	102½
5	Do. 1909	100	107½
5	Brunswick Town 5 c. Debs. 1916-20	100	111
7½/	B. Ayres City 6 p.c.	100	57
4½	Do. 4½ p.c.	100	78
5	Cape Town, City of	100	113
4	Do. 1943	100	116
4	Chicago, City of, Gold 1915	—	110
6	Christchurch 1926	100	131½
—	Cordoba City	100	17½
5	Duluth (U.S.) Gold 1926	—	110
6	Dunedin (Otago) 1925	100	127½
6	Do. 1926	100	113
5	Do. Consols 1908	100	113
4	Durban Insc. Stk. 1944	100	111
4	Essex Cnty., N. Jersey 1926	100	114½
5	Fitzroy, Melbrne. 1916-19	100	110
5	Gisborne Harbour 1915	100	110½
4	Greymouth Harbour 1925	100	110
4	Hamilton 1934	100	110
5	Hobart Town 1918-30	100	116
4	Do. 1940	100	107
4½	Invercargill Boro. Dbs. 1936	100	113
6	Kimberley Boro., S.A. Dbs.	—	104
4	Launceston Twn. Dbs. 1916	100	107
6	Lyttleton, N.Z., Harb. 1929	100	125
4	Melbourne Bd. of Wks. 1921	100	108
5	Melb. City Debs. 1897-1907	100	107½
4½	Do. Debs. 1908-27	100	112½
4	Do. Debs. 1915-20-22	100	108
5	Melbne. Harb. Bds., 1908-9	100	112
4½	Do. do. 1915	100	110
4	Do. do. 1918-21	100	105
4½	Melbrne. Tms. Dbs. 1914-16	100	113
4½	Do. Fire Brig. Db. 1921	100	110
5	Mexico City Stg.	100	91
4	Moncton N. Bruns. City	100	103
4½	Montevideo	100	58
5	Montreal Stg.	100	104
5	Do. 1874	100	104
5	Do. 1879	100	106
3½	Do. 1933	100	106
3	Do. Perm. Deb. Stk.	100	98½
4	Do. Cons. Deb. Stk. 1932	100	113
6	Napier Boro. Consolid. 1914	100	119
5	Napier Harb. Debs. 1920	100	115
5	Do. Debs. 1928	100	107
6	New Plymouth Harb. Debs. 1909	100	108
6	New York City 1901	—	107½
3½	Do. 1910-26	—	105½
4½	Nth. Melbourne Debs. 1-600 1921	100	105
5	Oamaru Boro. Cons. 1920	100	101
6	Do. Harb. Bds. (Reg.)	100	74
25/	Do. 6 p.c. (Bearer) 1919	100	35
6	Otago Harb. Deb. Reg.	100	108
6	Do. 1877	100	107
6	Do. 1881 1921	100	115
5	Do. Debs. 1921	100	107
5	Do. Cons. 1934	100	105
6	Ottawa City	100	111
6	Do. 1904	100	113½
4½	Do. Debs. 1915	100	112
6	Port Elizabeth Waterworks	100	113½
5	Port Louis	100	111
5	Prahran Debs. 1917	100	111
4	Do. Debs. 1919	100	105
6	Quebec C. Coupon. 1875 1905	100	112
6	Do. do. 1878 1908	100	116
4½	Do. Debs. 1914-18	100	108
4	Do. Debs. 1923	100	108
3½	Do. Cns. Rg. Stk., Red.	100	101
5	Richmond (Melb.) Dbs. 1917	100	115
4	Rio Janeiro City	100	59
4	Rome City	100	[illegible]
4	Do. 2nd to 8th Iss.	100	85
—	Rosario C.	100	[illegible]
—	Do.	100	[illegible]
4	St. Catherine (Ont.) 1926	100	103
4	St. John, N.B., Debs. 1934	—	103
4½	St. Kilda (Melb.) Dbs. 1918-21	100	105
4	St. Louis C. (Miss.) 1911	100	[illegible]
4	Do. 1913	100	[illegible]
3·65	Do. 1925	—	110
—	Santa Fé City Debs.	100	[illegible]
6	Santos City	100	[illegible]
6	Sofia City	100	[illegible]
5	Sth. Melbourne Debs. 1915	100	111
4½	Do. Debs. 1919	100	107
5	Sydney City 1904	100	109
4	Do. Debs. 1912-13	100	107
4	Do. do. (1894) 1919	100	109
7	Timaru Boro. 7 p.c. 1920	100	138½
5	Timaru Harb. Debs 1914	100	108
5	Do. Debs. 1916	100	108
6	Toronto City Wtrwks. 1904-6	100	110
6	Do. Cons. Debs. 1898	100	102
5	Do. G. Cns. Dbs. 1919-20	100	113
4	Do. Strlg. 1922-8	100	107
4	Do. Local Improv.	100	102
3½	Do. 1929	100	102
5½	Valparaiso	100	[illegible]
4	Vancouver 1931	100	[illegible]
4	Do. 1932	100	[illegible]
6	Wanganui Harb. Dbs. 1905	100	[illegible]
6	Wellington Con. Deb. 1907	100	[illegible]
6	Do. Improv., 1879	100	[illegible]
6	Do. Wtrwks. Dbs., 1880	100	[illegible]
4½	Do. Debs., 1893 1933	100	[illegible]
4½	Wellington Harb. 1907	100	[illegible]
4	Westport Harb. Dbs. 1925	100	[illegible]
6	Winnipeg City Debs. 1907	—	[illegible]
5	Do. 1914	100	[illegible]

FINANCIAL, LAND, AND INVESTMENT.

Last Div.	Name.	Paid.	Price.
5	Agency, Ld. & Fin. Aust., Ltd., Mt. Db. Stk., Rd.	100	90½
	Amer. Frehld. Mt. of Lon., Ld., Cum. Pref. Stk.	100	87½
4½	Do. Deb. Stk., Red.	100	93
1/	Anglo-Amer. Db. Cor., L.	2	1
4	Do. Deb. Stk., Red	100	106½
5½	Ang.-Ceylon & Gen. Est., Ltd., Cons. Stk.	100	65
6	Do. Reg. Debs., Red.	100	106¼
—	Ang.-Fch. Explorn., Ltd.	1	2½
6	Do. Cum. Pref.	1	11/16
—	Argent. Ld. & Inv., Ltd. £1 Shares	10/	nil
—	Do. Cum. Pref.	4	1½
1/	Assets Fnders.' Sh., Ltd.,	4	1⅝
6/	Assets Realis., Ltd., Ord.,	5	9
5	Do. Cum. Pref.	5	6½
26/	Austrln. Agricl £25 Shs.	21½	63½
—	Aust. N. Z. Mort., Ltd., £10 Shs.	1	1½d.
4½	Do. Deb. Stk., Red.	100	90½
4	Do. Deb. Stk., Red.	100	82½
4½	Australian Est. & Mt., L., 1 Mt. Deb. Stk., Red.	100	106
5	Do. "A" Mort. Deb. Stk., Red.	100	97
2/6	Australian Mort., Ld., & Fin., Ltd. £25 Shs.	5	4
1/6	Do. New, £25 Shs.	3	2½
4	Do. Deb. Stk.	100	110½
3	Do. Do.	100	85
5	Baring Est. 2 Mt. Debs., Red.	100	105
5	Bengal Presidy. 1 Mort. Deb., Red.	100	106
25/	British Amer. Ld. "A"	1	20
—	Do. "B"	24	7
1/2½	Brit. & Amer. Mt., Ltd. £10 Shs.	2	¾
5/	Do. Pref.	10	10
4	Do. Deb. Stk., Red.	100	100
1/3	Brit. & Austrlsn Tst Ln., Ltd. £25 Shs.	2½	¾
4½	Do. Perm. Debs., Red.	100	103
1½d.	Brit. N. Borneo. £1 Shs.	15/	½
2½d.	Do.	1	1
—	Brit. S. Africa	1	2¾
5	Do. Mt. Deb., Red.	—	96
6	B. Aires Harb. Tst., Red.	100	100
12/6	Canada Co.	1	26
—	Canada N. W. Ld., Ltd.	$25	35½
—	Do. Pref.	$100	$54
4	Canada Perm. Loan & Sav. Perp. Deb. Stk.	100	99½
—	Curamalan Ld., 1 Mt. 7 p.c. Bds., Red.	—	92½
3/7½	Deb Corp., Ld., £10 Shs	4	3½
5	Do. Cum. Pref.	10	11½
4	Do. Perp. Deb. Stk.	100	116
9d.	Deb. Corp. Fders' Sh., Ld.	3	¾
4/5⅞	Eastn. Mt. & Agncy, Ld., "A"	10	6
4½	Do. Deb. Stk., Red.	100	100
5	Equitable Revers. In. Ltd.	100	—
2/	Exploration, Ltd.	1	1 5/16
1	Freehold Trst. of Austrla. Ltd. £10 Shs.	1	¾
4	Do. Perp. Deb. Stk.	100	102
—	Genl. Assets Purchase, Ltd., 5 p.c. Cum. Pref.	10	—
70/	Genl. Reversionary, Ltd.	100	—
3½	Holborn Vi. Land	100	105
3½	House Prop. & Inv.	100	86½
13/	Hudson's Bay	13	21
4	Impl. Col. Fin. & Agcy. Corp.	100	95½
4½	Impl. Prop. Inv., Ltd., Deb. Stk., Red.	100	91½
2/6	Internatl. Fincial. Soc., Ltd. £7½ Shs.	2½	1½
4	Do. Deb. Stk., Red.	100	99½
1/9½	Ld. & Mtge. Egypt, Ltd. £18 Shs.	3	2½
5	Do. Debs., Red.	100	103
4½	Do. Debs., Red.	100	101
—	Ld. Corp. of Canada, Ltd.	1	½
4½	Ld. Mtge. Bk. of Texas Deb. Stk.	100	—
3½	Ld. Mtge. Bk. Victoria 4½ p.c. Deb. Stk.	100	78
2/9½	Law Debent. Corp., Ltd., £10 Shs.	2	1½
4½	Do. Cum. Pref.,	10	12
4	Do. Deb. Stk.	100	119
1/	Ldn. & Australasian Deb. Corp., Ltd., £4 Shs.	2	½
4½	Do. 4½ p.c. Mt. Deb. Stk., Red.	100	101
1/9	Ldn. & Middx. Frhld. Est. £2 Shs.	35/	3
2/6	Lndn. & N. Y. Inv. Corp., Ltd.	5	1¾
5	Do. 5 p.c. Cum. Pref.	10	9
1/6	Ldn. & Nth. Assets Corp., Ltd., £2 Shs.	1½	¾
2	Ldn. & N. Deb. Corp., L.	2	1½
4	Ldn. & S. Afric. Explrn. Ltd.	½	13½
2/	Mtge. Co. of R. Plate, Ltd. £10 Shs.	2	3½
4½	Do. Deb. Stk., Red.	100	112
4½	Morton, Rose Est., Ltd., 1st Mort. Debs.	—	101
6/	Natal Land Col. Ltd.	10	7
4/	Do. 8 p.c. Pref., 1870	5	8½
5/6	Natl. Disct. L., £25 Shs	5	10¾
4½	New Impl. Invest., Ltd. Pref. Stk.	100	60½
—	New Impl. Invest., Ltd Def. Stk.	100	9
4	N. Zld. Ln. & Mer. Agcy. Ltd. Prf. Ln Deb. Stk	100	98

Financial, Land, &c. (*continued*):—

Last Div.	Name.	Paid.	Price.
16/	N. Zld. Ln. & Mer. Agcy., Ltd. 5 p.c. "A" Db. Sk.	100	43½
—	N. Zld. Ln. & Mer. Agcy., Ltd., 5 p.c. "B" Db. Stk.	100	4
2/6	N. Zld. Tst. & Ln. Ltd., £25 Shs.	5	1½
12/6	N. Zld. Tst. & Ln. Ltd., 5 p.c. Cum. Pref.	25	19
—	N. Brit. Australsn. Ltd.	100	6½
—	Do. Irred. Guar.	100	32½
5	Do. Mort. Debs.	100	82½
4½	N. Queensld. Mort. & Inv., Ltd., Deb. Stk.	100	95
—	Oceana Co., Ltd.	—	—
6	Peel Riv., Ld. & Min. Ltd.	100	88½
—	Peruvian Corp., Ltd.	100	2½
—	Do. 4 p.c. Pref.	100	9½
3	Do. 6 p.c. 1 Mt. Debs., Red.	100	40½
—	Queensld. Invest. & Ld. Mort. Pref. Ord. Stk.	100	20
3/7	Queensld. Invest. & Ld. Mort. Ord. Shs.	4	4
4	Queensld. Invest. & Ld. Mort. Perp. Debs.	100	90
3½	Raily. Roll Stk. Tst. Deb., 1903-6	100	100½
50/	Reversiony. Int. Soc., Ltd.	100	—
2/8½	Riv. Plate Trst., Loan & Agcy., L., "A" £10 Shs.	2	4½
1/6	Riv. Plate Trst., Loan & Agcy., Ltd., Def. "B"	5	3½
	Riv. Plate Trst., Loan & Agy., L., Db. Stk., Red.	100	109
—	Santa Fé & Cord. Gt. South Land, Ltd.	20	5
—	Santa Fé Land	10	2½
2/	Scot. Amer. Invest., Ltd. £10 Shs.	2	2¾
2½	Scot. Australian Invest., Ltd., Cons.	100	79½
6	Scot. Australian Invest., Ltd., Guar. Pref.	100	135½
5	Scot. Australian Invest., Ltd., Guar. Pref.	100	106½
4	Scot. Australian Invest., Ltd., 4 p.c. Perp. Dbs.	100	105½
5	Sivagunga Zemdy., 1st Mort., Red.	100	101
20/	Sth. Australian	20	52½
3½	Stock Exchange Deb., Rd.	—	101½
—	Strait Develt., Ltd.	1	1/16
2/6	Texas Land & Mt., Ltd. £10 Shs.	2½	3
4½	Texas Land & Mt., Ltd., Deb. Stk., Red.	100	105
—	Transvaal Est. & Dev., L.	1	½
—	Transvaal Lands, Ltd., £1 Shs.	15/	½
—	Do. F. P.	1	5/16
—	Transvaal Mort., Loan, & Fin., Ltd., £10 Shs.	2	½
2/	Tst & Agcy. of Austrlsa., Ltd., £10 Shs.	1	2
7/5	Do. Old, fully paid	10	15½
5/7	Do. New, fully paid	10	12½
5	Do. Cum. Pref.	10	12½
3/	Trust & Loan of Canada, £20 Shs.	5	4½
1/9½	Do. New £20 Shs.	3	2½
—	Tst. & Mort. of Iowa, Ltd., £10 Shs.	2½	¾
4½	Do. Deb. Stk. Red.	100	92½
—	Tst., Loan, & Agency of Mexico, Ltd., £10 Shs.	2	½
—	Trsts., Exors, & Sec. Ins. Corp., Ltd., £10 Shs.	7	1¾
5/	Union Dsc., Ld., £10 Shs.	5	10½
—	Union Mort. & Agcy. of Aust., Ltd., £6 Shs.	2	—
6	Do. Pref. Stk.	100	35
—	Do. 6 p. Pref. £6 Shs.	2	½
4½	Do. Deb. Stk.	100	52½
4	Do. Deb. Stk.	100	85½
5	Do. Deb. Stk. Red.	100	96½
1/6	U.S. Deb. Cor. Ltd., £1 Shs.	1	⅛
5½	Do. Cum. Pref. Stk.	100	102½
4½	Do. Irred. Deb. Stk.	100	109
5	U.S. Tst. & Gunr. Cor. Ltd., Pref. Stk.	100	77½
6/	Van Dieman's	25	16
4	Walker's Prop. Cor., Ltd. Gunr. 1 Mt. Deb. Stk.	100	109
4½	Wstr. Mort. & Inv., Ltd. Deb. Stk.	100	92½

FINANCIAL—TRUSTS.

Last Div.	Name.	Paid.	Price.
1/	Afric. City Prop., Ltd	1	1½
6	Do. Cum. Pref.	1	1 1/16
4	Alliance Invt., Ltd., Cm. 4½ p. c. Prefd.	100	74½
—	Do. Defd	100	13½
4	Do. Deb. Stk. Red.	100	105½
5	Amrcn. Invt., Ltd., Prfd.	100	124½
5	Do. Defd.	100	94½
4	Do. Deb. Stk. Red.	100	117½
4	Army & Navy Invt., Ltd., 5 p.c. Prefd.	100	82½
—	Do. Dfd. Stk.	100	17½
4	Do. Deb. Stk.	100	107½
4	Atlas Investment, Ltd., Prefd. Stk.	100	70½
4½	Bankers' Invest., Ltd., Cum. Prefd.	100	106
1/0/0	Do. Defd	100	28½
4	Do. Deb. Stk	100	114
	Brewery & Comml. Inv., Ltd., £10 Shs.	5	5½

Financial—Trusts (*continued*):—

Last Div.	Name.	Paid.	Price.
4	British Investment, Ltd., Cum. Prefd.	100	108
5	Do. Defd.	100	102½
4	Do. Deb. Stk.	100	108½
6	Brit. Steam. Invst., Ltd., Prefd.	100	116½
3/0/0	Do. Defd	100	70½
4½	Do. Perp. Deb. Stk	100	121½
1/9	Car Trust Invst., Ltd., £10 Shs.	2½	2
5	Do. Pref.	100	102½
4	Do. Deb. Stk., 1915	100	105
4	Cinl. Sec., Ltd., Prefd.	100	107½
2½	Do. Defd.	100	47½
4	Consolidated, Ltd., Cum. 1st Pref.	100	92½
4	Do. 5 p.c. Cm. 2nd do.	100	74½
—	Do. Defd.	100	14½
4½	Do. Deb. Stk.	100	111½
—	Deb. Secs. Invst.	100	107½
—	Do. 4 p.c. Cm. Pf. Sk.	100	106½
4½	Edinburgh Invest., Ltd., Cum. Prefd. Stk.	100	109½
4	Do. Deb. Stk. Red.	100	106½
5	Foreign, Amer. & Gen. Invt., Ltd., Prefd.	100	117½
2	Do. Defd.	100	56½
4	Do. Deb. Stk.	100	115½
5	Foreign & Colonial Invt., Ltd., Prefd.	100	132½
5½	Do. Defd.	100	97½
4½	Gas, Water & Gen. Invt., Cum. Prefd. Stk.	100	92½
3	Do. Defd. Stk.	100	38½
4	Do. Deb. Stk.	100	106
5	Gen. & Com. Invt., Ltd., Prefd. Stk.	100	108½
2	Do. Defd. Stk.	100	39½
4	Do. Deb. Stk.	100	112½
1/9	Globe Telegph. & Tst., Ltd.	10	12
6	Do. do. Pref.	10	17¾
4	Govt. & Genl. Invt., Ld., Prefd.	100	84½
3½	Do. Defd.	100	42½
4½	Govts. Stk. & other Secs. Invt., Ltd., Prefd.	100	90½
1	Do. Defd.	100	27
4½	Do. Deb. Stk.	100	111
4	Do. do.	100	104
4½	Guardian Invt., Ltd., Pfd.	100	88½
—	Do. Defd.	100	20½
4	Do. Deb. Stk.	100	104
5	Indian & Gen. Inv., Ltd., Cum. Prefd.	100	107½
2½	Do. Defd.	100	56
4½	Do. Deb. Stk.	100	121½
5	Indust. & Gen. Tst., Ltd., Unified	100	102½
3½	Do. Deb. Stk. Red.	100	101½
4½	Internat. Invt., Ltd., Cm. Prefd.	100	71½
—	Do. Defd.	100	9
4	Do. Deb. Stk.	100	102
4	Invest. Tst. Cor. Ltd. Pfd.	100	102
4	Do. Defd.	100	92
4	Do. Deb. Stk. Red.	100	106
5	Ldn. Gen. Invest. Ltd., 5 p.c. Cum. Prefd.	100	110½
7½	Do. Defd.	100	118
4½	Ldn. Scot. Amer. Ltd. Pfd.	100	104½
£3	Do. Defd.	100	59½
4	Do. Deb. Stk.	100	112
4	Ldn. Tst., Ltd., Cum. Prfd. Stk.	100	105
4	Do. Defd. Stk.	100	75½
4	Do. Deb. Stk., Red.	100	107
3½	Do. Mt. Deb. Stk., Red.	100	104
5	Mercantile Invt. & Gen., Ltd., Prefd.	100	112½
3	Do. Defd.	100	48½
4	Do. Deb. Stk.	100	116½
4	Merchants, Ltd., Pref. Stk.	100	104½
4	Do. Ord.	100	81
4	Do. Deb. Stk.	100	117½
6	Municipal, Ltd., Prefd.	100	55½
—	Do. Defd.	100	17½
4½	Do. Debs.	100	113
4½	Do. Debs. "B"	100	99½
4½	Do. "C" Deb. Stk.	100	88½
6	New Investment, Ltd. Ord.	100	92½
5	Omnium Invest., Ltd., Pfd.	100	91½
4	Do. Defd.	100	26½
4	Do. Deb. Stk.	100	104
5/	Railway Deb. Tst. Ld. £10 Shs.	10	7
5	Do. Debs., Red.	100	107½
4½	Do. Deb Stk., 1911	100	107½
4	Do. do. 1922	100	107½
4	Railway Invst. Ltd., Prefd	100	117
15/6	Do. Defd	100	22
8/	Railway Share Trust & Agency "A"	8	6½
7½	Do. "B" Pref. Stk.	100	145½
4½	River Plate & Gen. Invt., Ltd., Prefd.	100	105
£3	Do. Defd.	100	50½
5	Scot. Invst., Ltd., Pfd. Stk.	100	94½
3½	Do. Defd.	100	[illegible]
4	Do. Deb. Stk	100	108
4½	Sec. Scottish Invst., Ltd. Cum. Prefd.	100	89½
£2	Do. Defd. Stk.	100	2
4	Do. Deb. Stk.	100	107½
5/	Sth. Africa Gold Tst., Ltd	1	4
6	Do. Cum. Pref	1	1
5½	Do. 1st Debs., Red	100	102
1/9	Stock Conv. & Invest. Ltd., £5 Shs.	1	1½
4½	Do. do. 4½ p.c. Cm. Prf	100	141
3½	Do. Ldn. & N. W. 1st. Charge Prefd.	100	141½
4	Do do. 2nd Chge Prfd.	100	1
32/6	Do. do. Defd. Charge	100	30
3	Do. N. East. 1 Chge Pfd.	100	[illegible]

Financial—Trusts (*continued*):—

Last Div.	Name.	Paid.	Price.
37/6	Stock N. East Defd. Chge	100	39
6	Submarine Cables	100	141½
5	U.S. & S. Amer. Invest., Ltd., Prefd.	100	100½
2	Do. Defd.	100	29½
4	Do. Deb. Stk.	100	105½

GAS AND ELECTRIC LIGHTING.

Last Div.	Name.	Paid.	Price.
10/6	Alliance & Dublin Con. 10 p.c. Stand.	10	25½
7/6	Do. 7 p.c. Stand.	10	17
5	Austln. Gas Lght. (Syd.) Debs. 1902	100	106
5	Bay State of N. Jrsy. Sk. Fd. Tst. Bd., Red.	—	92½
3/	Bombay, Ltd.	5	6
2/4½	Do. New	4	5
12	Brentford Cons.	100	297½
9	Do. New	100	230½
5	Do. Pref.	100	144½
4	Do. Deb. Stk.	100	136
11½	Brighton & Hove Gen. Cons. Stk.	100	277½
8½	Do. "A" Cons. Stk.	100	202½
5	Bristol 5 p.c. Max.	100	132½
22/6	British Gas Light, Ltd.	20	56½
11/6	Bromley Gas Consumrs.' 10 p.c. Stand.	10	26
8/6	Do. 7 p.c. Stand.	10	21
—	Brush Electl. Enging., L.	—	2
6	Do. 6 p.c. Pref.	—	2½
4½	Do. Deb. Stk.	100	112
4½	Do. 2 Deb. Stk., Red.	100	103½
5/	B. Ayres (New), Ltd.	10	10
4	Do. Deb. Stk., Rd.	—	99
12/6	Cagliari Gas & Wtr., Ltd.	20	30½
8/	Cape Town & Dist. Gas Light & Coke, Ltd.	10	17½
4½	Do. Pref.	10	12½
6	Do. 1 Mt. Debs. 1910	50	60
4/	Charing Cross & Strand Elec. Sup., Ltd.	5	14
4½	Do. Cum. Pref.	5	6½
2/6	Chelsea Elec. Sup., Ltd.	5	11½
4½	Do. Deb. Stk., Red.	100	116
5	Chic. Edis'n Co. 1 Mt., Rd.	$1000	106
20/	City of Ldn. Elec. Lht., L.	10	26½
19/7	Do. New	10	26½
6	Do. Cum. Pref.	10	18
5	Do. Deb. Stk., Red.	100	131½
13½	Commercial, Cons.	100	342½
10½	Do. New	100	257½
4½	Do. Deb. Stk.	100	155½
14	Continental Union, Ltd.	100	230
11	Do. Pref. Stk.	100	210½
—	County of Lon. & Brush Prov. Elec. Lg., Ltd.	10	15
6	Do. Cum. Pref.	10	16
14	Croydon Comcl. Gas, Ld., "A" Stk., 10 p.c.	100	312½
11	Do. "B" Stk., 7 p.c.	100	260
5½	Crystal Pal. Dist. Ord. 5 p.c. Stk.	100	133½
5	Do. Pref. Stk.	100	141½
8/	European, Ltd.	10	25½
6/	Do.	7½	18
12½	Gas Light & Ck Cons. Stk., "A" Ord.	100	295½
4	Do. "B" (4 p.c. Max.)	100	122½
10	Do. "C," "D," & "E" (Pref.)	100	317½
5	Do. "F" (Pref.)	100	152½
7½	Do. "G" (Pref.)	100	222½
7	Do. "H" (7 p.c. Max.)	100	199½
10	Do. "J" (Pref.)	100	315½
6	Do. "K"	100	187½
4	Do. Deb. Stk.	100	136½
4½	Do. do.	100	155½
6	Do. do.	100	207½
8/	Hong Kong & China, Ld.	10	14½
—	House to House Elec. Light Sup., Ltd.	5	11½
7	Do. Cum. Pref.	5	12
10	Imperial Continental	100	214½
3½	Do. Deb. Stk., Red	100	104½
2/	Malta & Medit., Ltd.	5	5½
5/	Metrop Elec. Sup., Ltd.	10	21
3/8	Do. New	10	21
4½	Do. 1 Mt. Deb. Stk.	100	119
5	Metro. of Melbrne. Dbs. 1908-12	100	113
4½	Do. Debs. 1918-22-4	100	110
10/	Monte Video, Ltd.	20	16
9½	Newcastle-upon-Tyne	100	237½
	Do. 3½ p.c. Deb. Stk.	100	117½
12/	Notting Hill Elec. Ltg., Ltd.	10	20
4/6	Oriental, Ltd.	5	8½
[illegible]	Do. New	4½	7½
[illegible]	Do. do. 1870	1	1½
3/6	Ottoman, Ltd.	5	4½
—	Para, Ltd.	—	—
6	People's Gas Lt. & C. of Chic. 2 Mt. 1904	100	105½
5	River Plate Elec. Lgt. & Trac., Ltd., 1 Deb. Stk.	—	92½
8½	Royal Elec. of Montreal	—	146
4½	Do. 1 Mt. Deb.	100	106
11/	St. James' & Pall Mall Elec. Light, Ltd.	5	19
7	Do. Pref.	5	10½
4	Do. Deb. Stk., Red.	100	108½

Gas and Electric (*continued*):—

Last Div.	Name.	Paid.	Price.
20/	San Paulo, Ltd.	10	16½
20	Sheffield Unit. Gas Lt. "A"	100	251½
20	Do. "B"	100	251½
20	Do. "C"	100	251½
—	Sth. Ldn. Elec. Sup., Ld.	2	2½
5¼	South Metropolitan	100	138½
3	Do. 3 p.c. Deb. Stk.	100	106½
12	Tottenham & Edmonton Gas Lt. & C., "A"	100	290
9	Do. "B"	100	210
7/	Tuscan, Ltd.	10	14
5	Do. Debs., Red.	100	101½
5/	West Ham 10 p.c. Stan.	5	12
8/	Wstmnstr. Elec. Sup., Ld.	5	18

INSURANCE.

Last Div.	Name.	Paid.	Price.
4/	Alliance, £20 Shs.	44/	11½
20/	Alliance, Mar., & Gen., Ld., £100 Shs.	25	53
8/	Atlas, £50 Shs.	6	32
12/	British & For. Marine, Ld., £20 Shs.	4	24
7½d.	British Law Fire, Ltd., £10 Shs.	1	1½
7/6	Clerical, Med., & Gen. Life, £25 Shs.	50/	16½
20/	Commercial Union, Ltd., £50 Shs.	5	43½
4	Do. "W. of Eng." Ter. Deb. Stk.	100	110½
£9	County Fire, £100 Shs.	80	190
5/	Eagle, £50 Shs.	5	½
4/	Employers' Liability, Ltd., £10 Shs.	2	4½
.	Empress, Ltd., £5 Shs.	1	—
21/	Equity & Law, £100 Shs.	6	23
7/6	General Life, £100 Shs.	5	15
4½d.	Gresham Life, £5 Shs.	15/	2½
2/6	Guardian, Ld., £10 Shs.	5	11½
20/	Imperial, Ltd., £20 Shs.	5	29½
5/6	Imperial Life, £20 Shs.	4	6½
6/	Indemnity Mutual Mar., Ltd., £15 Shs.	3	12½
1/	Lancashire, £20 Shs.	2	5
7½d.	Law Acc. & Contin., Ltd., £5 Shs.	10/	1
5/	Law Fire, £100 Shs.	2½	18
9½d.	Law Guar. & Trust, Ltd., £10 Shs.	1	1½
9/	Law Life, £20 Shs.	2	25
2/9	Law Un. & Crown £10 Shs.	12/	7
4	Do. Deb. Stk., 1942	100	110½
14/6	Legal & General, £50 Shs.	8	15½
9d.	Lion Fire, Ltd., £8½ Shs.	1½	½
14/	Liverpool & London & Globe, Stk.	2	54½
10/	Do. Globe £1 Ann.	—	36
25/	London, £25 Shs.	12½	63½
4/	Lond. & Lanc. Fire, £25 Shs	2½	19
2/	Lond. & Lanc. Life, £25 Shs	2	5
1/	Lond. & Prov. Mar., Ld., £10 Shs.	1	1
2/	Lond. Guar. & Accident, Ltd., £5 Shs.	2	12
10/	Marine, Ltd., £25 Shs.	4½	43½
2/	Maritime, Ltd., £10 Shs.	2	4½
1/6	Merc. Mar., Ld., £10 Shs.	2½	2½
—	National Marine, Ltd., £9 Shs.	1	½
10/	N. Brit. & Merc., £25 Shs.	6½	43
20/	Northern, £100 Shs.	10	82
40/	Norwich Union Fire, £100 Shs.	12	126½
10/	Ocean Acc. & Guar., fy. pd.	5	21½
2/	Do. £5 Shs.	1	4
7/6	Ocean, Marine, Ltd.	2½	9½
1/	Palatine, £10 Shs.	2	3½
2/6	Pelican, £10 Shs.	1	3½
12/	Phœnix, £50 Shs.	5	44
£6	Provident, £100 Shs.	10	31
5/	Railway Pasngrs., £10 Shs.	2	8½
2/6	Rock Life, £5 Shs.	10/	4½
8	Royal Exchange	100	360
18/	Royal, £20 Shs.	3	54½
4/	Sun, £10 Shs.	10/	12
3/9	Sun Life, £10 Shs.	7½	15
6/	Thames & Mrsey. Marine, Ltd., £20 Shs.	2	10½
9/	Union, £10 Shs.	4	24½
	Union Marine, £20 Shs.	2½	9
	Universal Life, £100 Shs.	12	42
	World Marine, £5 Shs.	2	1½

IRON, COAL, AND STEEL.

Last Div.	Name.	Paid.	Price.
—	Barrow Hæm. Steel, Ltd.	7½	2
9/	Do. 6 p.c. 2nd Pref.	7½	7
10/	Bolck., Vaugh. & C., Ld.	20	18
6/	Do. £8 liab.	12	9½
7/6	Brown, J. & Co., Ltd., £20 Shs.	15	20
7/6	Consett Iron, Ld., £10 Shs.	7½	29½
4/	Do. 8 p.c. Cum. Pref.	5	11
7/6	Ebbw Vale Steel, Iron & Coal, Ltd., £23 Shs.	20	6½
15/	General Mining Assn., Ld.	5½	7½
8/	Harvey Steel Co. of Gt. Britain, Ltd.	10	30
5	Lehigh V. Coal 1 Mt. 5 p.c. Guar. Gd. Cp. Bds.	—	98
42/6	Nantyglo & Blaina Iron, Ltd., Pref.	862	97½
1/	Nerbudda Coal & Iron, Ltd., £3 Shs.	56/	$\frac{1}{16}$
—	Newport Abrcrn. Bk. Vein Steam Coal, Ltd.	10	4½
5/	New Sharlston Coll., Ltd. Pref.	20	10
4½d.	Nw. Vancvr. Coal & Ld., L.	1	½
—	North's Navigation Coll. (1889) Ltd.	5	3
10/	Do. 10 p.c. Cum. Pref.	5	7½
—	Rhymney Iron, Ltd.	5	1½
	Do. New, £5 Shs.	4½	½
5	Do. Mt. Debs., Red.	100	98½
5	Shelton Irn., Stl. & Cl. Co., Ltd., 1 Chg. Debs., Red.	100	99½
10	Sth. Hetton Coal, Ltd.	100	—
	Vickers & Maxim, Ltd.	1	3½
	Do. 5 p.c. Prfd. Stk.	100	132½

SHIPPING.

Last Div.	Name.	Paid.	Price.
4/	African Stm. Ship, £20 Shs.	16	10
5/	Do. Fully-paid	20	14
2/	Amazon Steam Nav., Ltd.	19½	9
8/	Castle Mail Pakts., Ltd., £20 Shs.	14	15½
3½	Do. 1st Deb. Stk., Red.	100	102
6/	China Mutual Steam, Ltd.	5	3
6	Do. Cum. Pref.	10	9½
10/	Cunard, Ltd.	20	9½
5/	Do. £20 Shs.	10	3½
4½	Furness, Withy, & Co., Ltd., 1 Mt. Dbs., Red.	100	106
6/	General Steam	15	8
5/	Do. 5 p.c. Pref., 1874	10	9
5/	Do. 5 p.c. Pref., 1877	10	8½
5/	Leyland & Co., Ltd.	10	17½
7/	Do. 7 p.c. Cum. Pref.	10	14½
2/11	Do. 4½ p.c. Cum. Pre-Pf.	3	10½
4	Do. 1st Mt. Dbs., Red.	100	106½
7/6	Mercantile Steam, Ltd.	5	7½
6/4½	New Zealand Ship., Ltd.,	6	5
4	Do. Deb. Stk., Red.	100	104
5/	Orient Steam, Ltd.	10	5½
5	P. & O. Steam, Cum. Prefd.	100	156½
19	Do. Defd.	100	235½
3½	Do. Deb. Stk.	100	120
5	Richelieu & Ont., 1st Mt. Debs., Red.	100	100
30/	Royal Mail, £100 Shs.	60	51
2/6	Shaw, Sav., & Alb., Ltd., "A" Pref.	5	5½
5/	Do. "B" Ord.	5	4
8/	Union Steam, Ltd.	20	20
4/	Do. New £20 Shs.	10	8½
4	Do. Deb. Stk., Red.	100	100
7/	Union of N.Z., Ltd.	10	10
5½	Wilson's & Fur.-Ley., 5½ p.c. Cum. Pref.	10	10½
4½	Do. 1 Mt. Db. Sk., Rd.	100	106½

TELEGRAPHS AND TELEPHONES.

Last Div.	Name.	Paid.	Price.
4	African Direct, Ltd., Mort. Debs., Red.	100	102
—	Amazon Telegraph, Ltd.	10	7½
19/6	Anglo-American, Ltd.	100	60
39/	Do. 6 p.c. Prefd. Ord.	100	109
—	Do. Defd. Ord.	100	11½
3/	Brazilian Submarine, Ltd.	10	17
5	Do. Debs., 2 Series	100	114

Telegraphs and Telephones (*continued*):—

Last Div.	Name.	Paid.	Price.
4/	Chili Telephone, Ltd.	5	3½
$2	Comcial. Cable, $100 Shs.	—	189½
4	Do. Stg. 500-yr. Deb. Stk. Red.	100	107
2½d.	Consd. Telpehone Constr., &c., Ltd.	10/	½
6/	Cuba Submarine, Ltd.	10	7
10/	Do. 10 p.c. Pref.	10	15
2/	Direct Spanish, Ltd.	5	4½
5/	Do. 10 p.c. Cum. Pref.	5	10½
4½	Do. Debs.	50	104½
3/	Direct U.S. Cable, Ltd.	20	11
2/6	Eastern, Ltd.	10	18
3/	Do. 6 p.c. Cum. Pref.	10	19
4	Do. Mt. Deb. Stk., Red.	100	130½
2/6	Eastern Exten., Aus., & China, Ltd.	10	19
5	Do. (Aus. Gov. Sub.) Deb., Red.	100	101
5	Do. do. Bearer	100	101½
4	Do. Mort. Deb. Stk.	100	129½
5	Eastn. & S. Afric., Ltd., Mort. Deb. 1900	100	101
5	Do. Bearer	100	101½
4	Do. Mort. Debs. 1909	100	103½
4	Do. Mort. Debs. (Maur. Subsidy)	25	108½
5/	Grt. Nthn. Copenhagen	10	29½
5	Do. Debs., Ser. B., Red.	100	101½
12/6	Indo-European, Ltd.	25	53½
6	London Platino-Brazilian, Ltd., Debs. 1904	100	107½
4/	Montevideo Telph., Ltd., 6 p.c. Pref.	5	2½
3/	National Telephone, Ltd.	5	6½
6/	Do. Cum. 1 Pref.	10	17
6/	Do. Cum. 2 Pref.	10	16
5	Do. Non-Cum. 3 Pref.	5	6
3½	Do. Deb. Stk., Red.	100	104½
4d.	Oriental Telephone, Ltd.	1	½
4	Pac. & Euro. Tlg. Dbs., Rd.	100	106½
4/	Reuter's, Ltd.	8	8½
5/	Un. Riv. Plate Telph., Ltd.	5	4½
5	Do. Deb. Stk., Red.	100	107½
—	West African Telg., Ltd.	10	4½
5	Do. 5 p.c. Mt. Debs., Red.	100	102½
—	W. Coast of America, Ltd.	10	—
3/	Western & Brazilian, Ltd.	15	11½
3/	Do. 5 p.c. Pref. Ord.	7½	7
—	Do. Defd. Ord.	7½	4½
4	Do. Deb. Stk., Red.	100	107½
1/	W. India & Panama, Ltd.	10	½
6/	Do. Cum. 1 Pref.	10	8½
6/	Do. Cum. 2 Pref.	10	6
5	Do. Debs., Red.	100	106½
7	West. Union, 1 Mt. 1900 ($	1000	107½
6	Do. 6 p.c. Stg. Bds., Rd.	100	102½

TRAMWAYS AND OMNIBUS.

Last Div.	Name.	Paid.	Price.
1/6	Anglo-Argentine, Ltd.	5	4
6	Do. Deb. Stk.	100	127½
4/	Barcelona, Ltd.	10	12½
5	Do. Deb., Red.	100	104½
7/6	Belfast Street Trams.	10	16½
—	Blackpl. & Fltwd. Tram., £10 Shs.	8	13½
10/	Bordeaux Tram. & O., Ltd.	10	12
5	Do. Cum. Pref.	10	11½
—	Brazilian Street Ry., Ltd.	2	½
—	British Elec. Trac., Ltd.	10	17
—	B. Ayres & Belg. Tram., Ltd., 6 p.c. Cum. Pref.	5	—
6	Do. 1 Deb. Stk.	100	—
—	B. Ayres. Gd. Nat., Ltd., 6 p.c 1 Deb. Bds., Red.	100	60
5½	Do. Pref. Debs., Red.	100	96½
1/	Calais, Ltd.	5	1
—	Calcutta, Ltd.	10	3½
—	Carthagena & Herr., Ltd.	10	3
5	Do. Deb., Red.	100	90
5	City of B'ham. Trams., Ltd., 5 p.c. Cum. Pref.	5	6
4	Do. 1 Mort. Debs., Rd.	100	107½
3/9	City of B. Ayres, Ltd.	5	7½
2/3	Do. Ext. £5 Shs.	3	4½
6	Do. Deb. Stk.	100	145
1/4	Edinburgh Street Tram.	4	3½
1/	Glasgow Tram. & Omni. Ltd., £9 Shs.	8	3
3/7½	Imperial, Ltd.	6	15
3/	Lond., Deptfd, & Greenwich, Prefd.	5	3½
nil	Do. Defd.	5	1
10½	Lond. Gen. Omni., Ltd.	100	205
4	Do. Deb., Red.	100	117½

Tramways and Omnibus (*continued*):—

Last Div.	Name.	Paid.	Price.
4/9½	London Road Car	6	10½
28/6	Do. Red. 1 Mt. Deb. Stk.	100	108½
5	London St. Rly. (Prov., Ont.), Mt. Debs.	100	110
12/6	London St. Trams.	—	2
12/9	London Trams., Ltd.	10	10
6/	Do. Non-Cum. Pref.	10	10½
5	Do. Mt. Db. Stk., Rd.	100	100½
5	Lynn & Boston 1 Mt. 1924 $	1000	107
5	Milwaukee Elec. Cons. Mt. $	1000	100½
5	Minneapolis St. 1 Cons. Mt. $	1000	98
5	Montreal St. Dbs., 1908	100	109
4½	Do. Debs., 1922	100	107
6/	Nth. Metropolitan	10	13
1/9½	Nth. Staffords., Ltd.	6	4½
5/6	Provincial, Ltd.	10	7
6/	Do. Cum. Pref.	10	13
5	St. Paul City, 1937 $	1000	96
5	Do. Guar. Twin City Rap. Trans. $	1000	96
5/	Southampton	10	6½
5/	South London	10	5½
7/6	Sunderland, Ltd.	10	6½
4½	Toronto 1 Mt., Red.	100	107
2/6	Tramways Union, Ltd.	5	7½
4½	Do. Deb., Red.	100	109
5/	Vienna General Omnibus.	5	6½
5	Do. 5 p.c. Mt. Deb., Red.	100	108½
4/	Wolverhampton, Ltd.	10	6½

WATER WORKS.

Last Div.	Name.	Paid.	Price.
8/	Antwerp, Ltd.	20	22
6/	Cape Town District, Ltd.	5	6½
10½	Chelsea	100	337½
5	Do. Pref. Stk.	100	178½
4½	Do. Pref. Stk., 1875	100	158½
4½	Do. Deb. Stk.	100	152½
5/	City St. Petersburg, Ltd.	13	11
5/	Colne Valley	10	15½
4	Do. Deb. Stock	100	137½
£4	Consol. of Rosar., Ltd., 4 p.c. 1 Deb. Stk., Red.	100	92
7½	East London	100	226½
4½	Do. Deb. Stk.	100	160½
3	Do. Deb. Stk., Red.	100	106
37/6	Grand Junction (Max. 10 p.c.) "A"	50	122½
18/9	Do. "B"	25	
18/9	Do. "C" (Max. 7½ p.c.)	25	56½
35/	Do. "D" (Max. 7 p.c.)	50	104½
4	Do. Deb. Stock	100	160½
13	Kent	100	360½
7	Do. New (Max. 7 p.c.)	100	215½
6/7½	Kimberley, Ltd.	7	6
6	Do. Debs., Red.	100	108½
6	Do. Deb. Stk., Red.	100	105½
10	Lambeth (Max. 10 p.c.)	100	300½
7½	Do. (Max. 7½ p.c.), 50 & 25	—	[illegible]
4	Do. Deb. Stock	100	148½
3	Do. Red. Deb. Stock	100	105
10/	Montevideo, Ltd.	20	16½
5	Do. 1 Deb. Stk.	100	108½
5	Do. 2 Deb. Stk.	100	108½
132/9	New River New	100	447½
4	Do. Deb. Stk.	100	140½
4	Do. Deb. Stk. "B"	100	140½
—	Odessa, Ltd., "A" 6 p.c. Prefd.	20	—
nil	Do. "B" Deferred	20	—
4	Portland Con. Mt. "B," 1927	—	102½
8/	Seville, Ltd.	20	12½
5/6	Southend "Addl." Ord.	10	17½
6	Southwark and Vauxhall	100	157½
6	Do. "D" Shares (7½ p.c. max.)	100	168½
5	Do. Pref. Stock	100	176½
4	Do. "A" Deb. Stock	100	147½
3	Staines Resvirs. Jt. Com. Gua. Deb. Stk., Red.	100	105
7/	Tarapaca, Ltd.	10	10
10	West Middlesex	100	314½
4½	Do. Deb. Stk.	100	163½
3	Do Deb. Stk.	100	106

Prices Quoted on the Leading Provincial Exchanges.

ENGLISH.

In quoting the markets, B stands for Birmingham; Bl for Bristol; M for Manchester; L for Liverpool; and S for Sheffield.

CORPORATION STOCKS.

Chief Market.	Int or Div.	NAME.	Amount paid.	Price.
M	3½	Bolton, Red. 1935 ..	100	116
M	3½	Burnley, Red. 1933 ..	100	114
M	3½	Bury, Red. 1946	100	118
L	2½	Liverpool, Red. 1925	100	102¼
B	3½	Longton, 1932	100	106
M	4	Oldham Prp. Db. Sk.	100	146
M	£1	Do. Gas & W. Ann.		34½
S	4	Rotherham 4 p.c., Red. 1927 ..... (£	1 an	114
M	3½	Runcorn Red. 1923 ..	100	105
S	2½	Sheffield Water Ann.	100	118¼
S	3	Do.	3 an	90
L	3½	Southport Red. 1936 {	5 an 100	112
L	3	Do. Red. 1914 ..	100	102½
M	3	Todmorden, Red. 1914	100	102

RAILWAYS.

Chief Market.	Int or Div.	NAME.	Amount paid.	Price.
Bl	4½	Bridgewater Pref. ..	100	135½
M	1½	Cleator & Workton.	100	76
M	4	Do. 1883 Pref. ..	100	109
L	4	Cockermth. K. & P.	100	113½
L	4	Isle of Man	5	6½
L	5	Do. Pref.	5	6½
L	3	Liverpool Overhead	10	10¾
L	4	Do. Deb. Stk. ..	100	109
L	5	Do. Pref.	10	16
L	6½	Maryport & Carlisle	100	167
S	6	Mid. Shef. & Roth. Pf.	100	231
Bl	35/	Neath & Brecon "A"	100	67½
M	4½	Oldham, Ashton, &c.	10	16¼
Bl	5½	Penarth Harbour ..	100	182½
Bl	4	Do. Deb. Stk. ..	100	145
Bl	3½	Do. Deb. Stk. ..	100	127
Bl	1½	Ross & Monmouth ..	20	5½
Bl	6	Do. Pref.	20	42½
M	3	Southport & Cheshire Deb. Stk.	100	104½
M	nil.	Do Pref.	100	22
Bl	2½	West Somerset Gu. ..	100	96½
Bl	5	Wye Val. Deb. Stk.	100	164

BANKS.

Chief Market.	Int or Div.	NAME.	Amount paid.	Price.
L	8/	Adelphi, L., £20 Shs.	10	16½
L	12/6	Bk of L'pool, L., £100 Sh	12½	39½
B	5/6	Brmnghm. Dis. & C., Ltd., £20 Shs.	4	10½
B	6/3	Co. of Staffs., L., £40	5	13½
S	17½	Crompton & Evans, Ltd., £20 Shs	4	15
M	14/	Lancs. & Yorks, Ltd., £20 Shs.	10	31¼
L	30/	Livrpl. Union, Ltd., £100 Shs.	20	60¼
M	24/	Manchester & Co., Ltd., £100 Shs. ..	16	62
M	20/	Mnchstr. & Livrpool. Dis., Ltd., £60 Shs.	10	51½
M	1/6	Mer. of Lancashire, Ltd., £20 Shs.	3	6⅜
L	16/	Nth. & Sth. Wales, Ltd., £40 Shs.	10	35⅜
B	20/	Notts Joint St., Ltd., £50 Shs.	10	26¾
M	4/	Oldham Joint Stk., Ltd., £20 Shs.	4	12½
S	15	Sheffield Banking, Ltd., £50 Shs.	17½	51½
S	20	Do. & Rotherham, Ltd., £50 Shs. ..	8	26⅜
S	10	Do. & Hallamsh., Ltd., £100 Shs. ..	25	64½
S	10	Do. Union, Ltd., £40 Shs.	10	25
M	12/	Union of Manchester, Ltd., £25 Shs.	11	27½
M	10/	Williams, Deacon, &c. Ltd., £50 Shs.	8	26⅛
Bl	20	Wilts & Dorset, Ltd., £50 Shs.	10	49
S	5/6	York City & Co., Ltd., £10 Shs.	3	13

BREWERIES.

Chief Market.	Int or Div.	NAME.	Amount paid.	Price.
B	6	Ansell & Sons Pref.	10	15⅜
B	5	Do. Debs.	100	110
L	9/	Bent's	10	18½
L	6	Do. Cum. Pref. ..	10	14½
L	4½	Do. Deb. Stk. ..	100	111
L	13/6	Birkenhead, £5 paid	5	22⅛
L	13/6	Do. £10 paid	10	25
M	9/	Boddington's	9	20½
M	5	Do. Cum. Pref. ..	10	13½
M	4	Do. Deb. Stk. ..	100	109
B	4½	Butler & Co. Db. Stk	100	110½
M	6	Chesters' Cum. Pref.	10	13½
M	4½	Do. Debs.	100	112
S	10/	Clarkson's Ord.	10	23
S	6	Do. Cum. Prf. Stk.	10	14⅜
M	4	Dutton & Co. Db. Sk.	100	104
M	4½	Hardy's Crown Debs.	100	111
B	10/	Holt	10	17½
B	5	Do. Cum. Pref. ..	10	12½
B	4	Do. Debs.	100	109½
B	12/6	Lichfield	10	24
B	5	Do. Cum. Pref. ..	10	11¾
M	5½	Manchester Deb. Stk.	100	142
B	6/	Mitchell, H., & Co.	10	38
B	6	Do. Cum. Pref. ..	10	15¾
B	6	Oakhill Pref.	10	16½

Breweries (continued):—

Chief Market.	Int. or Div.	NAME.	Amount paid.	Price.
M	5/	Springwell	10	10¾
M	7	Do. Pref.	10	13½
Bl	9	Stroud	10	17
Bl	6	Do. Pref	10	14½
M	6/	Taylor's Eagle	10	11½
M	7	Do. Cum. Pref ..	10	13½
M	5½	Do. Deb. Stk. ..	100	117½
S	10	Tennant Bros £20 shs	15	34½
S	10	Wheatley & Bates ..	10	14½
S	6	Do. Cum. Pref.	10	12⅝

CANALS AND DOCKS.

Chief Market.	Int. or Div.	NAME.	Amount paid.	Price.
Bl	3	Hill's Dry Dk. &c. £20	18	9
M	4	Manc. Ship Canal 1st Mt. Deb. Stk.	100	104
M	4	Do. 2nd do.	100	103½
L	36/3	Mersey Dck. & Harb.	an.	118½
L	35/	Do.	an.	117
M	10/	Rochdale Canal	100	37½
B	37/6	Staff. & Worc. Canal	100	76½
B	4½	Do. Deb. Stk	100	137
Bl	4	Swansea Harb	100	114½
B	27/6	Warwick & Birm. Cnl	100	66½
B	12/6	Do. & Napton do.	100	23

COMMERCIAL & INDUSTRIAL.

Chief Market.	Int. or Div.	NAME.	Amount paid.	Price.
L	5	Agua Santa Mt. Debs	100	100
M	8/	Armitage, Sir E. & Sns Ltd.	10	19
M	4	Do. Deb. 1910 ..	100	103
L	6	Ang. Chil. Nit. 1 Mt. Debs., 1919 ..	100	109½
Bl	8½	Bath Stone Firms ..	10	20
M	4/9½	Barlow & Jones, Ltd., £10 Shs.	8	10⅜
B	12/6	Birmgham. Ry. Car.	10	17½
B	6	Do. Pref.	10	15½
B	16/8	Do. Small Arms	5	15½
M	£12	Blackpool Pier	100	277½
M	5	Do. Tower Debs.	50	54½
M	3/	Do. Wi. Gar. & P.	5	4⅝
Bl	10	Bristl. & S. W. R. Wag. £20 Shs.	3	5⅜
Bl	8	Do. Wag. & Carri. £10 Shs.	10	14⅜
M	7/	Crosses & Winkwth. Ltd.	5	12½
L	5	G. Angus & Co. Pref.	10	13½
Bl	5	Gloster. Carri. & W.		10½
Bl	5	Gt. Wstn. Cttn., Ltd.	20	15½
M	6	Hetherington, L. Prf.	10	8½
M	4½	Do. Debs., 1910	100	98½
B	7½d.	Hinks (J. & Son), Ltd.	1	27/6
S	26/	Jessop & Sons, £50 Sh	30	26⅜
S	10	Kayser, Ellsn. & Co. L.	5	11½
S	6	Do. Pref.	5	7¾
M	7/6	Kellner-Partgton., L.	5	14½
M	4½	Do. Debs., 1914	100	105½
M	5	Kerr Thread, Ltd., Debs.	100	101
B	17/	King's Norton Metal, £10 Shs.	8½	18½
M	5/	Lancashire & Yorks. Wagon, Ltd.	10	9⅜
L	10/	Liverpool Exch., Ltd.	20	27¾
L	45/	Do. Grain Stge, Ltd.	50	108
L	5/	Do. Rubber, Ltd. ..	5	6⅝
M	9d.	Manchester Bond. Whse., L., £10 Shs.	4½	2⅜
M	3/9	Do. Comcial. Bldgs., Ltd., £10 Shs.	5	10⅜
M	4/	Do. No. 2, £10 Shs.	5	10⅜
M	2/6	Do. No. 3, £10 Shs.	5	7½
M	5/	Do. Corn, &c., Exchange, Ltd.	10	16½
M	4	Do. Debs.	100	126
M	8	Do. Ryl. Exchge, L.	100	246½
B	5/	Midland Rlwy. Car. Wgn., Ld., £20 Sh.	10	14½
Bl	5	Millers & Corys Dbs.	100	100½
B	12/6	Mint, Brgham., Ltd.	5	7⅜
B	5	Do. Debs.	25	107
B	10/	Nettlefolds, Ltd.	10	50
B	5	Do. Pref.	10	15½
S	9	Nth. Centrl. Wgn., L.	5	8½
B	15/	Patnt. Nut & Bolt, L.	10	34
B	5	Do. Pref.	10	14⅜
B	1/	Perry & Co., Ltd. ..	1	28/9
B	6d.	Do. Pref.	1	27/
S	10	Round, J., & Co., L., £10 Shs.	6	12⅜
S	15	Rodgers, J., & Sons, L.	100	213
M	18/9	Rylands & Sons, Ltd., £20	15	38¾
M	2/6	Do. paid up	20	43½
M	4	Do. Debs. .. 1909	100	106
S	5	Sanderson Brs. & Co., Ltd. Debs.	100	102
M	4½	Schwabe, S., & Co., Ltd., 1 Debs. 1914	100	104
S	7½	Sheffield Forge & Rolling, Ltd.	10	11½
L	80/	Southport Pier, Ltd.	100	88½
L	2½	Do. W. Gdns., Ltd.	5	3½
Bl	5	Spillers & Bakers, Ltd, £10 Shs.	9	14⅜
Bl	6	Do. Pref.	10	14½
B	5/	Union Rolling Stock, Ltd., £20 Shs.	5	7½
M	6/	Victoria Pr., S'port, L.	5	4⅜
Bl	8	Western Wagon & Property, Ltd.	6	9⅜
S	10	Wostenholm, G., & Son, Ltd., £25 Shs.	20	22¾
S	6½	Yorksh. Wagon, Ltd.	2	2¾

FINANCIAL, TRUSTS, &c.

Chief Market.	Int. or Div.	NAME.	Amount paid.	Price.
M	1/	Manchstr. Trst. £10 Shs.	2	13/9
M	1/3	N. of Eng. T. Deb. & A., Ltd. £10 Shs.	2½	27/3
M	3½	Do. 1 Mt. Debs. ..	100	97
L	—	Pacific Ln. & Inv., L.	2½	2⅝
L	4	Do. Deb. Stk.	100	102
L	—	United Trst., L. Prfd.	100	72½
L	—	Do. Deferred	100	62½

GAS.

Chief Market.	Int. or Div.	NAME.	Amount paid.	Price.
Bl	5	Bristol Gas (5 p.c. mx.)	100	128½
Bl	4	Do. 1st Deb.	100	137
S	10	Gt. Grimsby "C" ..	10	201
L	10	Liverpool Utd. "A"	100	253
L	7	Do. "B"	100	188
L	4	Do. Deb.	100	137
S	10	Sheffield Gas "A," "B," "C"	100	253
B	10½	Wolverhampton	100	230
B	3	Do. 6 p.c. Pref. ..	100	172

INSURANCE.

Chief Market.	Int. or Div.	NAME.	Amount paid.	Price.
M	6	Equitable F. & Acc. £5 Shs.	1	40/6
L	2/	Liverpool Mortgage £10 Shs.	2	1 5/12
M	2/	Mchester. Fire £20 Shs	2	7⅜
M	5/	National Boiler & G., Ltd., £10 Shs.	3	13⅜
L	2/	Reliance Mar., Ltd., £10 Shs.	2	4½
L	4/	Sea, Ltd., £10 Shs. ..	2	10 1/16
L	8/	Stnd. Mar., L., £20 Sh.	4	8
L	1/	State Fire, L., £20 Sh.	1	2

COAL, IRON, AND STEEL.

Chief Market.	Int. or Div.	NAME.	Amount paid.	Price.
Bl.	17	Albion Stm. Coal ..	10	11½
M	15/0	And. Knowles & S., Ltd., £37½ Shs. ..	23½	12½
M	5	Do. Mt. Debs. 1908	100	105½
Bl.	1/½	Ashton V. Iron	100	26
S	12½	Bessemer, Ltd.	10	20½
S	5	Do. Pref.	10	12¾
S	12/6	Briggs, H., & Co., "A" £15 Shs.	12½	15⅜
S	8/6	Do. "B" £15 Shs.	8½	9⅜
S	20	Brown Baley's. Stl., L.	10	33½
S	5	Brown, J., & Co., Cum. Pref.	10	13½
S	5	Cammell, C. & Co., Ltd.	85	12½
S	5	Do. Pref.	5	6⅝
M	5	Chatterley Whitfield. Col., Debs., 1905 ..	100	100½
Bl	—	Davis, D., & Sons, Ld.	10	10½
M	5	Evans, R., & Co., Ltd., Deb., 1910 ..	100	100½
S	12½	Fox, S., & Co., Ltd., £100 Shs.	80	178
Bl	10	Gt. Wstn. Col., L., "A"	5	10
Bl	6	Do. "B"	5	4½
Bl	8	Main Colliery, Ltd.	10	8
B	2/6	Muntz's Metal, Ltd.	5	8
B	5	Do. Pref.	5	6½
M	2/6½	Nth. Lonsd. Iron and Steel, Ltd., £10 Sh.	8½	2½
Bl	6	North's Nav. Coll., Ltd., Debs.	100	105
S	30/	Parkgate Irn. & Stl., Ltd., £100 Shs. ..	75	70¾
M	6	Pearson & Knls., Ld., "A" Cum. Pref. ..	50	46
B	10/	Sandwell Pk. Col., L.	10	17
M	6/3	Sheepbridge Coal and Iron, Ltd., "A"	25	17½
M	2/6	Do. "B"	10	6⅜
M	5	Do. "C" Gua. Pf.	25	28½
Bl	4	South Wales Coll., Ltd., "A"	17	8¾
S	30/	Staveley Coal & Iron, Ltd., "A" £100 Sh.	60	81
S	30/	Do. "C"	60	82
M	1/10½	Tredegar Iron & Cl., Ld., "A" £10 Sh.	7½	2⅜
M	1½	Do. "B" Stk. ..	100	35
M	6/	Wigan Cl. & Irn., Ld.	10	7½
M	4/6	Do. £10 Shs.	7½	4

SHIPPING.

Chief Market.	Int. or Div.	NAME.	Amount paid.	Price.
Bl	6	Bristol St. Nav. Pref.	10	11¾
L	15/	Brit. & Af. St. Nav. .	10	13½
L	8/10½	British & Estn, Ltd.	6½	2½
L	10/	Pacific Stm. Nav., L.	25	24⅜
L	30/	Wst. Ind. & Pac. St. Ltd., £25 Shs.	20	27

TRAMWAYS, &c.

Chief Market.	Int. or Div.	NAME.	Amount paid.	Price.
B	5/	Brmngh. & Aston, L.	5	11½
B	5/	Do. Mid., Ltd. ..	10	7⅜
Bl	6/	Bristol Tr. & Car., Ltd.	10	21
B	4/	Do. Debs.	100	121
L	6	I. of Man Elec., L., Pref.	1	1½
M	15/	Manchester C. & T., L., "A" £20 Shs.	15	27½
M	10/	Do. "B"	10	19½

WATER WORKS.

Chief Market.	Int. or Div.	NAME.	Amount paid.	Price.
Bl	7	Bristol	25	63½
Bl	7	Do.	20	48
Bl	5⅞/	Do. 7 p.c. max. ..	100	159
Bl	4½	Do. Pref.	20	32½
Bl	5	Do. Pref.	10	18⅜
Bl	3½	Do. Deb.	100	129½
M	10	Fylde "A"	100	335
M	7	Do. "B"	100	224
B	6	S. Staffs. Ord. "A"	100	165
B	—	Do. "B"	100	164
B	4	Do. Deb. Stk.	100	140
B	5	Do. Pf "A" "B" "C"	100	170
M	£3¾	Stockport District ..	100	184½
B	2/	Wolverhampton New	5	6⅝

SCOTTISH.

In quoting the markets, E stands for Edinburgh, and G for Glasgow.

RAILWAYS.

Chief Market.	Int. or Div.	NAME.	Num. Amount	Price.
E	5½	Arbroath and Forfar	25	51
G	2	Callander and Oban .	10	7½
G	4	Do. Deb. Stock	100	148
G	4½	Do. Pref.	10	14½
G	4	Cathct. Dist. Deb. Stk.	100	148
E	5	Edin. and Bathgate .	100	179½
E	7	Forth & Clyde Junc.	100	222½
G	4	Lanarks. and Ayrsh.	10	14
G	4	Do. & Dumbartons.	10	14½
G	4	Do. Deb. Stk.	100	149

BANKS.

Chief Market.	Int. or Div.	NAME.	Num. Amount	Price.
	12	Bank of Scotland ..	100	361
	16	British Linen	100	500
	8	Caledonian, Ltd.	2½	95/6
	10	Clydesdale, Ltd.	10	23½
	16	Commercl. of Scot., L.	20	88½
	16	National of Scot. Ld.	100	428½
G	8	Royal of Scotland ..	100	224
G	11	Union of Scotland, L.	10	26½

BREWERIES.

Chief Market.	Int. or Div.	NAME.	Num. Amount	Price.
E	5	Bernard, Thos. Pref.	10	10¾
E	5	Bernard, T. & J., Cum. Pref.	10	12½
G	20	Highland Distilleries	3½	10¾

CANALS AND DOCKS.

Chief Market.	Int. or Div.	NAME.	Num. Amount	Price.
G	4	Clyde Nav. 4 p.c.	100	125½
G	3½	Do. 3½ p.c.	100	105
G	3½	Greenock Harb. "A"	100	100
G	2	Do. "B"	100	40

MISCELLANEOUS.

Chief Market.	Int. or Div.	NAME.	Num. Amount	Price.
G	4½	Alexander & Co. Debs.	100	110½
G	5	Baird, H., & Sns. C. P.	10	12½
E	10	Barry, Ostlere, & Co.	7½	12½
E	6	Do. Cum. Pref. ..	10	15 1/16
G	5	Brown, Stewart, Deb.	100	84
E	7½	Broxburn Oil	8½	8½
E	6	Do. Cum. Pref. ..	10	11 1/16
E	7	Edinburgh & Dist. Tram. Cum. Pref.	5	9
E	5	Gilroy, Sons, & Co. Debs.	100	99
G	9	Glasgow Cot. Spin. ..	6	5½
G	30/	Do. Royal Exchg.	46	110
G	—	Pumpherston Oil Pf.	10	8⅜
E	7	Scottish Assam Tea	10	11½
E	5	Scottish Waggon	10	12½
G	5	Stoddard & Co. Pref.	10	12½

FINANCIAL, LAND, AND INVESTMENT.

Chief Market.	Int. or Div.	NAME.	Num. Amount	Price.
G	1/	Assets Co.	1	47/
E	4½	Investors' Mort. Pref.	100	99½
E	4	Do. Deb. Stk.	100	103½
E	4	Nthn. Inv. N. Zeal. Deb. Stk.	100	107
E	4	N. of Scot. Canadian Deb. Stk.	100	106
E	4½	Real & Deb. Corp. Deb. Stk.	100	108½

INSURANCE.

Chief Market.	Int. or Div.	Name.	Amount paid.	Price.
G	19/	Caledonian F. & Life	5	36⅛
G	4/6	City of Glasgow Life	2½	12¾
E	19/	Edinburgh Life	20	55
G	13/1	Life Ass. of Scotland	8⅓	34½
E	8	Nat. Guar. & Surety	2	52/
G	17½	Scottish Union and National "A"	1	97/6
G	17½	Do. "B"	3¾	18¼

IRON, COAL, AND STEEL.

Chief Market.	Int. or Div.	Name.	Amount paid.	Price.
E	Nil.	Addie, Coll. Cm. Pref.	10	8
E	8/	Arniston Coal	8	14
E	2½	Cairntable Gas Coal	8	86/
E	12½	Fife Coal	10	20½
E	5	Do. Cum. Pref.	10	13
G	7	Merry & Cunghame. Cum. Pref.	10	15¾
G	5	Do. Debentures	100	105½
E	1/9	Niddrie & Benhar Cl.	1½	42/
G	5	Steel Com. of Scotland	—	
	—	"A" Deb. Stk.	100	113
G	6	Do. and Mt. "B"	100	105
E	—	Watson, John	8½	10
E	6	Do. Cum. Pref.	7½	8½
E	12½	Wilson's & Cly. Coal	3	8⅛

IRISH.

In quoting the markets, B stands for Belfast, and D for Dublin.

CORPORATION STOCKS.

Chief Market.	Int. or Div.	Name.	Amount paid.	Price.
B	3½	Belfast, 1921	100	112
B	3½	Do. 1912	100	108½
B	3½	Do. 1924	100	109½
B	3	Do. 1955	100	106
B	3½	Do. Water Com.	100	117½
B	3	Do. do.	100	106
B	3½	Do. Harbour Com.	100	114½
D	3½	Rathmines & Rathgar	100	110½
D	3½	Waterford Deb.	100	—

RAILWAYS.

Chief Market.	Int. or Div.	Name.	Amount Paid.	Price.
D	30/	Cork, Bandon, & S.C.	100	—
D	4	Do. Deb.	100	139½
D	4	Do. W. Cork Pref.	100	
B	5½	Belfast & Northern	100	161
B	4	Do. Deb.	100	146
B	4	Do. Pref.	100	141½
B	6½	Belfast & C. Down	100	166
B	4	Do. Deb.	100	147
B	3	Do.	100	107½
B	4½	Do. 4½ Pref. B.	100	153½
B	5	Do. Guar.	100	172½
D	Nil.	Dublin, Wick. & Wex.	100	34
D	4	Do. Deb.	100	127½
D	4½	Do. Deb.	100	133½
D	6	Do. Guar.	100	166
D	4	Do. C. of Dub. Junc.	100	—
D	5	Do. 1860 Pref.	100	116
D	50/	Do. 1864 Pref.	100	106
D	50/	Do. 1865 Pref.	100	94
B	6½	Great Northern	100	179
B	4	Do. Deb.	100	147
B	4	Do. Pref. B.	100	143½
B	5½	Gt. South & Western	100	143
B	4	Do. Deb.	100	148½
B	4	Do. Guar.	100	144
D	45/	Midland Gt. Western	100	114
D	4	Do. Deb.	100	146½
D	4½	Do. Deb.	100	151½
D	4½	Do. Deb.	100	—
D	5	Do. Pref.	100	175
D	4	Do. Pref.	100	140½
D	—	Waterford & Central	100	15
D	3	Do. Deb.	100	—
D	3½	Do. Pref.	100	—
D	4	Waterfd. L., & W. Db.	100	129½
D	4½	Do. Deb.	100	—
D	4	Do. Pref.	100	126½
D	3½	Do. Pref.	100	—

BANKS.

Chief Market.	Int. or Div.	Name.	Amount paid.	Price.
B	50/	Belfast, Old, £125 Shs.	25	125½
P	20/	Do. New, £125 Shs.	25	50½
D		Hibernian, £20 Shs.	5	6½
D	2/	Munster & Leinster £5 Shs.	2	5½
B	11/	Northern, £50 Shs.		27
D	12/	Royal, £50 Shs.	10	—
B	5/	Ulster, £15 Shs.	2½	12½

BREWERIES AND DISTILLERIES.

Chief Market.	Int. or Div.	Name.	Amount paid.	Price.
D	10/	Castlebellingham & Drog	10	16½
D	6	Do. Pref.	10	15½
D	4½	Do. Deb.	100	—
B	17/	Dunville & Co.	10	28½
B	6	Irish Distillery, Pref.	10	13½
B	5	Do. Deb.	100	110
B	6	J. & J. M'Connell, Pf.	10	15⅛
B	13/6	Mitchell & Co.	9	19½
B	5	Do. Deb.	10	11½
D	4½	Phœnix Brew. Deb.	100	—
B	6/	Wm. Cowan	10	13½
B	6	Do. Pref.	10	13½
B	8/	Young, King, & Co.	8	14

STEAM AND CANAL.

Chief Market.	Int. or Div.	Name.	Amount paid.	Price.
B	Nil	Belfast Steamship	50	35½
D	10/	British and Irish	50	—
D	15/	City of Dublin	100	60½
D	3½	Do. Deb.	100	105
D	30/	Dublin & Lpool. Bldg.	50	75
D	2/6	Dundalk & Newry	10	4½
D	4/	Grand Canal	10	11½
D	3	Do. Pref.	10	9½
D	3	Do. Deb.	100	99
B	30/	Irish Shipowners	100	63
B	3/	Ulster Steamship	5	5½

MISCELLANEOUS.

Chief Market.	Int. or Div.	Name.	Amount paid.	Price.
D	3/1	Arnott & Co.	4	—
D	6	Do. Pref.	4	—
B	8/	Belfast Com. Bldgs.	10	11
B	37/6	Do. Ropework Co.	75	91
B	5	Do. do. Pref.	10	13½
B	2/	Do. Discount Co.	3	43/
B	5	Do. do. Pref.	5	4½
B	10/	Brookfield Linen	25	17½
B	Nil	Coey & Co.	25	4
B	5	Do. Deb.	50	40½
B	4½	David Allen & S's Deb.	100	108
D	4/	Dublin Trams	10	20
D	6	Do. Pref.	10	18⅛
D	4	Do. Deb.	100	—
B	5/	Edenderry Spinning	10	9
B	25/	Falls Flax Spinning	25	15
B	17/	Forster, Green, & Co.	10	22
B	9/	Island Spinning	7½	7½
B	8/	Jas. Lindsay & Co.	8	16½
B	1/7½	John Arnott & Co.	4	4½
B	4½	Do. Deb.	50	56
D	5/	Kinahan & Co.	10	11½
D	5½	Do. Pref.	10	11½
D	4½	Do. Deb.	100	109½
B	12/	Kirker & Co.	10	10
B	5/	Leahy, Kelly, & Leahy	5	5½
B	6	Do. Pref.	5	7⅛
B	2/4½	Lindsay Bros. Ltd.	8	7½
B	4½	Do. Deb.	50	56½
D	1/	National Assurance	2½	32/
B	10/	Olley & Co.	5	7⅛
D	1/1½	Patriotic Assurance	2½	30/6
B	3/7½	P. Johnston & Son, L.	6	6½
B	10/	Robertson, F., & Co.	8	23½
B	10	Ulster Marine Insur.	5/	7/6
B	15/	York-street Flax	25	33½
B	6	Do. Pref.	10	15½
B	4½	Do. Deb.	100	120½

INDIAN AND CEYLON TEA COMPANIES.

Acres Planted.	Crop, 1897.	Paid up Capital.	Share.	Paid up.	Name.	Dividends. 1894.	1895.	1896.	Int. 1897.	Price.	Yield.	Reserve.	Balance Forward.	Working Capital.	Mortgages, Debs. or Pref. Capital not otherwise stated.
	lb.	£	£	£	INDIAN COMPANIES.							£	£	£	£
11,240	3,128,000	120,000	10	3	Amalgamated Estates	—	*	10	5	3½	8¼	10,000	16,500	D52,950	—
		400,000	10	10	Do. Pref.	—	*	5	‡5	10½	4¾				
10,223	3,560,000	187,160	20	20	Assam	20	20	20	5	60½	6½	55,000	1,730	D11,350	—
6,150	3,278,000	142,500	10	10	Assam Frontier	3	6	6	—	8¼	6¾	—	286	20,000	82,500
		142,500	10	10	Do. Pref.	6	6	6	3	11½	5¼				
2,087	839,000	66,745	5	5	Attaree Khat	12	12	8	3	7½	5½	3,790	4,820	7,770	—
1,633	383,000	78,170	10	10	Borelli	4	4	5	—	8	6¼	—	3,256	D270	6,900 Pref.
1,720	812,000	60,825	5	5	British Indian	6	5	5	—	4¼	6	—	2,920	12,300	16,500 Pref.
3,223	2,247,000	114,500	5	5	Brahmapootra	20	18	20	6	13½	7	—	28,440	41,600	.
3,734	1,617,000	76,500	10	10	Cachar and Dooars	*	8	7	—	10	6¾	—	1,645	21,240	.
		76,500	10	10	Do. Pref.	*	6	6	3	12½	4¾				
3,946	2,083,000	72,010	1	1	Chargola	8	7	10	2½	[illegible]	10½	3,000	3,300	—	—
		81,000	1	1	Do. Pref.	7	7	7	3½	1½	5				
1,971	942,000	33,000	5	5	Chubwa	10	8	10	3½	6½	7½	10,000	2,043	D5,400	—
		33,000	5	5	Do. Pref.	7	7	7	3½	7	5				
32,250	11,300,000	120,000	10	3	Cons. Tea and Lands	—		10	5	4	7½	65,000	14,240	D191,674	—
		1,000,000	10	10	Do. 1st Pref.	—	*	5	‡5	11½	4¼				
		400,000	10	10	Do. 2nd Pref.	—	*	7	‡7	12	5¾				
2,230	617,000	135,420	20	20	Darjeeling	5½	5½	6	—	23	5	5,552	1,565	1,700	—
2,114	445,000	60,000	10	10	Darjeeling Cons.	—	*	4/2	—	7	—	—	1,820	—	—
		60,000	10	10	Do. Pref.	—	*	5	2½	9¼	5¼				
6,660	3,518,000	150,000	10	10	Dooars	12½	12½	12½	2½	20	6¼	45,000	300	D32,000	—
		75,000	10	10	Do. Pref.	7	7	7	3½	17	4¼				
3,367	1,811,000	165,000	10	10	Doom Dooma	11¾	10	12½	5	22	5¾	30,000	4,032	—	10,000
1,377	582,000	61,120	5	5	Eastern Assam	5	nil.	4	—	3½	6¼	—	1,790	—	10,000
4,038	1,675,000	85,000	10	10	East India and Ceylon	5	nil.	7	—	9	7½	—	1,710	—	—
		85,000	10	10	Do. Pref.	*	6	6	3	12½	4¾				
7,500	3,363,000	219,000	10	10	Empire of India	—	*	6/10	2½	12	—	15,000	—	27,000	—
		219,000	10	10	Do. Pref.	—	*	5	2½	11	4½				
1,180	540,000	94,060	10	10	Indian of Cachar	7	3½	3	—	4½	6¾	6,070	—	7,120	—
3,050	824,000	83,500	5	5	Jhanzie	10	10	10	4	8¼	6	14,500	1,070	2,700	—
7,980	3,680,000	250,000	10	10	Jokai	10	10	10	5	18	5½	45,000	990	D9,000	—
		100,000	10	10	Do. Pref.	*	6	6	3	15	4				
5,224	1,563,000	100,000	20	20	Jorehaut	20	20	20	—	59	6¾	36,220	2,955	3,000	—
1,547	504,000	65,660	10	8	Lebong	15	15	15	5	16½	7½	9,000	2,150	8,650	—
5,082	1,709,000	100,000	10	10	Lungla	5	10	6	3	9½	6¼	—	1,543	D21,000	—
		100,000	10	10	Do. Pref.	*	6	6	3	11½	5¼				
2,684	885,000	95,970	10	10	Majuli	7	5	5	—	6½	7½	—	2,606	560	—
1,375	380,000	91,840	1	1	Makum	—	—	2	—	1⅛	1½	—	—	1,900	25,000
2,990	770,000	100,000	1	1	Moabund	—	—	*	—	1	—	—	—	—	—
		50,000	1	1	Do. Pref.	—	—	*	2½	1	5				
1,080	482,000	79,590	10	10	Scottish Assam	7	7	7	—	11	6½	6,500	800	9,590	—
4,150	1,456,000	100,000	10	10	Singlo		8	5	1	9½	4¾	—	300	D5,200	—
		80,000	10	10	Do. Pref.	*	6½	6½	3½	13	5				
	Crop, 1896.				CEYLON COMPANIES.										
7,970	1,743,824	250,000	100	100	Anglo-Ceylon, & Gen.	—	*	5½	—	65	7¾	10,998	1,405	D72,844	166,620
1,836	685,741	50,000	10	10	Associated Tea	—	*	5	—	8¼	6	—	164	2,478	—
		60,000	10	10	Do. Pref.	—	*	6	—	10½	5¾				
10,390	4,000,000§	167,380	10	10	Ceylon Tea Plantations	15	15	15	7	27½	5½	84,500	1,516	D30,819	—
		81,080	10	10	Do. Pref.	7	7	7	‡7	17	4¼				
5,722	1,542,700§	55,260	5	3	Ceylon & Oriental Est.	5	8	7	—	2½	7½	—	230	D2,047	71,000
		46,000	5	5	Do. Pref.	6	6	6	3	5	5¾				
2,157	801,629	111,330	5	5	Dimbula Valley	—	*	10	5	6½	8	—	—	1,733	6,250
		62,607	5	5	Do. Pref.	—	*	6	3	6¼	4¾				
11,496	3,715,000	298,250	5	5	Eastern Prod. & Est.	3	5	6½	2½	6½	5	20,000	11,740	D17,797	108,500
3,118	701,100	150,000	10	10	Lanka Plantations	4	5	5	‡5	6½	6¾	—	495	D11,300	14,700 Pref.
2,193	1,050,000§	22,080	10	10	New Dimbula "A"	10	16	16	4	25xd	6	11,000	2,024	1,150	8,400
		55,710	10	10	Do. "B"	18	16	16	4	22½xd	6½				
2,572	570,360	100,000	10	10	Ouvah	6	8	6	2	9½	6¼	4,000	1,151	D1,255	—
2,630	535,675	200,000	10	10	Nuwara Eliya	—	*	6	3	11¾	5¼	—	—	—	30,000
1,720	720,200	41,000	10	10	Scottish Ceylon	15	15	15	5	22	6¾	7,000	1,252	D3,970	9,000 Pref.
2,450	750,000§	39,000	10	6	Standard	12½	15	15	5	13½	6¼	9,000	800	D14,012	4,000
		17,000	10	10	Do.	12½	15	15	5	22½	6¾				

Working-Capital Column.—In working-capital column, D stands for *debit*.

* Company formed this year. † Interim dividends are given as actual distribution made. ‡ *Total* div. § Crop 1897.

Printed for the Proprietor by LOVE & WYMAN, LTD., Great Queen Street, London, W.C.; and Published by CLEMENT WILSON at Norfolk House, Norfolk Street, Strand, London, W.C.

The Investors' Review

EDITED BY A. J. WILSON.

Vol. I.—No. 12. New Series. | FRIDAY, MARCH 25, 1898. | [Registered as a Newspaper.] | Price 6d. By post, 6½d

CONTENTS

The Investors' Review.

A Romantic Indian Budget.

Telegraphic advices for some time back have been preparing the British public for an optimistic Budget statement. It has now made its appearance, and deserves to be carefully studied by the public-spirited citizens of the United Kingdom. In the Viceroy's summary of it we are informed that the deficit for the year closing on the 31st inst. will be 52,800,000 rupees, or about 30,000,000 more than the estimate put forward a year ago. This deficiency is accounted for by the cost of famine relief, which is put at almost 54,000,000 rupees, and the war expenditure of 36,400,000 rupees, not estimated at all in the Budget of March last. The famine expenditure is about 18,000,000 rupees larger than the first estimate, but the final general result will apparently be about 7,000,000 rupees better than the estimate of December last, owing to savings by a propped-up exchange, and the postponement of railway expenditure. Several sources of revenue are better than the estimates to the amount of 7,600,000 rupees, but the opium revenue fell off 5,700,000 rupees. It is impossible to say how far the figures may have been "adjusted" to produce this result. Even when we receive the full budget minute this may not be possible, so we may leave this statement as it stands, and turn to the Budget for the coming year, merely with the remark that if the famine has cost so little and involved so little loss of income, as Sir James Westland says, it is the cheapest calamity of the kind India has ever known. And the same statement applies to the cost of the Frontier war.

We believe neither. According to the telegram, the surplus estimated in the new Budget to accrue at the end of March, 1899, will be 8,900,000 rupees. We shall be delighted to congratulate the Government of India should that hope be realised, and it may be if India continues to borrow well. Only 105,700,000 rupees was spent from capital account by the State and company railways during the year now at its close, but the expenditure for the coming year is to be raised to 132,000,000 rupees, making about 238,000,000 rupees for the two years. As all this money will have in some way or other to be borrowed, it is easy to see that considerable stimulus will thus be given to the resources of the Government. In the meantime, a loan of £6,000,000 sterling, £2,640,000 of which represents new money, is to be raised in this country, and in addition a rupee loan for 30,000,000 is to be emitted in India, making together, say, £4,500,000 net to be added to the debt of the Indian Government during the coming year. Over and above this, we presume that the moneys to be raised by the various railway companies in pursuance of their policy of extension will also afford relief. The floating debt of £6,000,000 now outstanding in London is to be renewed, but no mention appears to be made of the six or seven millions sterling shortage on this year's Council drawings.

It will be noticed that, apart from the application of the blind eye to inconvenient unliquidated accounts, the whole question of the outcome of the Budget turns upon the rate of exchange. It appears that the rate realised on remittances made during the present year has been about 1s. 3⅜d. per rupee, and the Budget estimates are based upon the same average for the coming year. But, as has just been mentioned, about £7,000,000 of the Simla Government's English obligations were not drawn for this year at all. In the coming year they are to be drawn for to the full, or the admitted full. At least, so we gather from the announcement that the total of the drawings is to be £16,000,000. This, we presume, does not cover "stores," but represents merely the net obligations of the Government of India on its public debt, railway annuities, army charges, and so on. We are not, indeed, certain that £16,000,000 anything like covers all these, but for the present accept the statement as it stands, merely remarking that the Home charges on account of the army of India amounted in 1895-96 to fully £3,000,000, whereas the effective army charges set down in the Budget of March last as payable in England was little more than £1,000,000. As these charges steadily expand, we do not see how the money required to pay them can be a diminishing amount.

The important question, however, which is to be now discussed is the capacity of the Indian trade to bear the full £16,000,000, which will mean a payment out of the Indian treasuries of about 280,000,000 of rupees on the Government's own adopted exchange. Now, as we pointed out some weeks ago, the margin in the value of Indian exports over imports is frequently below this total, and tends to fall further below it the more Indian trade becomes hampered by an artificial exchange. In 1896-97 it fell to rather less than 240,000,000 of rupees, but take it at 370,000,000, which was the margin shown in favour of India by the trade of 1894-95, and still the full weight of the Indian Government Home charges is more than this trade can bear. For we must never forget that there are a variety of other remittances from India which must be taken into account in any estimate of its true economic position. A few weeks ago we summarised these, and, for the twentieth time or so, repeated the estimate that the aggregate of all charges, private and State, to be met every year in England out of the surplus exports of Indian produce could not be less than £30,000,000, or between 450,000,000 and 500,000,000 rupees, according as the exchange value of the rupee fluctuates. The foreign trade of India has not borne half this charge for any three years running this generation back. In that of the ten years between 1887-8 and 1896-7 inclusive, the excess of exports over imports fell nearly 25,000,000 rupees short of covering acknowledged Government drawings alone, if we include Government imports in the total. Leaving out these imports, which we know to be substantially always paid for with borrowed money, and dealing with the trading figures alone, the excess of the exports for the whole of these ten years only overtopped the total amount of the Indian Council's drafts upon Indian Treasuries by about 3,000,000 rupees. That is to say, in reality, India has had to give the entire value of her exports over imports to cover the Home obligations of her Government.

It is clearly hopeless under such an economic condition for the Government of India to hope to maintain an average rate of exchange of 1s. 3⅜d. per rupee, now when the trade of the country has been disorganised by the currency bounties; and the consequence of its attempt to draw up to £16,000,000 in the coming year must be a fall in the exchange, unless the borrowings of the State, or of its guaranteed railway companies, are largely augmented in order to create an artificial credit for India in London. This is the actual position, and in face of it it is worse than folly for Indian officials to persist in imagining that they can control the rate of exchange in spite of economic laws, common sense, and past experience. India has one source, and one alone, out of which to meet the enormous obligations laid upon her in England by her British rulers, and that source is the excess value of her exports over that of her imports. Unless this excess could be increased beyond any precedent, India must continue to live by loans, and when loans are no longer possible cannot fail to suspend payment. This is as plain as that two and two make four.

At the end of the Viceroy's telegram we have a jubilant paragraph, setting forth how wonderfully India has prospered during the past twenty years. We quote it here, as it may be interesting to refer back to one of these days when the dreams of the romancer are over:

> "So far as revenue goes we have, even after charging off Rx.13,660,000 spent from revenue account on construction of rail ways, more than paid our way, including all expenditure on war, special defence works, and famine. So far as capital transactions go, we have raised under various conditions, and spent upon railway and irrigation works, harbour works and docks, municipal projects, and agricultural improvements, a sum equal, at 1s. 4d. per rupee, to Rx.198,820,000, and we are, after all this expenditure, better off by Rx.500,000 per annum than before we undertook it. Moreover, it must be remembered, this view is concerned with direct financial returns only, and omits any consideration of the effect of all this expenditure on development of revenue and of its economic and administrative aspects." These results and the signs of early recovery from the disasters of famine, plague, and war are used to repeat and enforce Sir J. Strachey's deprecation of assistance from the English Exchequer.

It is impossible to test in detail such figures as are here quoted. They are, indeed, purely fanciful, but some facts contained in the statistics of India deserve to be considered against them, and among the most striking of these, as bearing upon the prosperity of the natives under our rule, are the figures relating to what we may call, in Irish language, the "evictions" of the Indian agricultural population from their holdings. These figures are both startling and melancholy. Between 1882 and 1887 the total number of "compulsory transfers of real property" in British India never amounted in any one year to 1,000,000. The total was 756,780 in 1882, and 948,513 in 1887, according to one "Statistical Abstract"; according to another and later, the total in 1887-8 was 1,230,089. This had risen to 1,469,936 in 1890-91, to 1,729,850 in 1891-92, to 1,793,406 in 1893-94, to 1,817,767 in 1895-96, the latest year for which we have the returns. In the year just preceding, it had been a few thousands higher still. Voluntary transfers of the same kind of property also increased during the same period, but not at the same ratio. Assuming the figures for 1882 to be correct, the increase shown in 1895-96 over that year was fully 140 per cent. Surely this is a most important testimony to the increasing poverty of the people of the country under our rule. Grant that the revenues have been maintained, and that the State has done everything claimed in the passage just quoted, the fact remains that the evidence of distress among the people as the result of this success steadily accumulates. It could not be otherwise.

The people of India have been subjected for more than a generation to a forcing process nourished by liberal appeals to the money-lender. Had the great works of which the British administration boasts been created by economy, and paid for out of husbanded income, then, indeed, the Indian people would have had cause to rejoice in our rule. The reverse of this, however, has been the course pursued. Every description of extravagance has been committed without let or hindrance from home. On needless frontier wars alone, as Colonel Hanna has pointed out in his admirable little book entitled "Backwards or Forwards?"—wars on the north-west frontier, including those of Afghanistan, including the permanent increase they have necessitated in the British Army of occupation, and the cost of the wasteful railway lines they have caused us to build—have been spent at India's charges between 1878 and 1896 no less than 714,850,480 rupees. In the same period the home charges of the Simla Government have increased by £8,000,000 per annum. The cost of the police in India has nearly doubled, the cost of the army has risen more than one-third, and the cost of the political departments has more than doubled—all within the same period. Through none of this frightful waste have the Indian people benefited to the extent of one single rupee, outside the wages paid to the additional troops and to the swarms of workmen who have secured employment in strategic railway and useless fortification building at the expense of the cultivators—mainly at the expense of the patient and industrious population of the Ganges Valley. Why will not the civil officials in India look at the matter from this common-sense point of view instead of trudging around in a vicious circle, dreaming of imaginary rates of exchange, cooking up fancy statements to show how "prosperous" the country is, with their eyes wholly shut to the bottomless abyss towards which they are hurrying the empire, themselves and England?

American Life Office Investments.—1.

We are now going to deal with a branch of this subject which is of the highest importance to those who invest in American Life policies. If the securities invested in by such of these concerns as do business in this country are of a first-class description, then, whatever objection we may take to their methods, one danger of the future would be mitigated, if not removed: the danger of their some day ceasing to meet their engagements. On their more current business it must not be forgotten that they still have, thanks to their high charges, considerable margin, and were the reduced bonuses they now promise to pay to disappear altogether this margin would be somewhat enlarged. The "bonus" is not of the essence of the contract. Deduct what is occasionally paid in this way, and these American offices could still flourish in waste and continue to bring out their balance-sheets every year so as to display large surpluses.

But all and every device would fail if these offices placed their funds in poor or bad securities. Now, they are obliged to publish each year in the State of New York a detailed list of their holdings in all kinds of securities, and we have this statement for the year 1896 before us. It may at once be stated that they do not strike us altogether favourably, but there is a difference in the position of the three concerns with which we are dealing which ought to be first of all emphasised. The best office of the three is undoubtedly the New York Life. To begin with this appears to be the only one of the three which grants advances on its own policies, assigned to it as security. Out of its total invested assets of $107,570,593, nearly $6,000,000 are represented by such loans. Then the New York Life also holds more United States Government bonds than either of the other two, and the rest of its money is, on the whole, well placed amongst the highest or better class of United States railroad bonds. Also, this company is an extensive holder of foreign government securities, and, speaking broadly, has distributed the bulk of the money thus invested in those which may be regarded as of the best class. The small amount placed by it in such securities as Argentine, Brazilian, or Cuban bonds would not affect its stability in the slightest were the entire amount to turn out a dead loss. So far as we have been able to judge from the list this company has avoided speculative stocks to an extent which deserves to be emphasised and commended. But it must also be pointed out that a considerable proportion of its investments are of a description which would be difficult to realise, on any call upon the company for an immediate large sum in cash. The securities may be good to hold, but they are not particularly marketable. A large amount of money, for example, has been placed by the company in the divisional and main line bonds of Chicago, Milwaukee, and St. Paul Railroad, the Chicago and North-Western Railroad, and in the Missouri Pacific, the New York, Lake Erie and Western first and improvement mortgages, the Northern Pacific terminal bonds, and in the Sanitary District of Chicago bonds. Also this company holds a good deal of preferred and common stocks, not only of railways, but in banks and trust companies. On the whole, however, there is little to object to in its investment list, for policy-holders in the United States at any rate, and if we had nothing else against it we should let it alone.

Turning to the other two companies, we come into a decidedly more speculative atmosphere. Both the Equitable of the United States and the Mutual of New York concerns, for example, are large lenders upon the Wall-street Stock Exchange, and possibly on other American Stock Exchanges. The one had lent out in this way $11,723,700 at the date of the last return, and the other $11,091,525, or considerably over £2,000,000 in each case. Of course, they have security for these advances, but it does not strike us that the security is in all cases first class. The Equitable, for instance, had lent $250,000 upon $125,000 stock of the National Bank of Denver. To be sure, its statistical compiler placed the market value of this stock at $312,500 when the return was drawn up, but the security was not first-class even so. Another $800,000 was lent on the security of Western Union Telegraph stock, Baltimore and Ohio railroad stock, and Baltimore and Ohio South-Western 4½ per cent. bonds, with other smaller items. The large amount of $3,258,000 had been advanced against deposits of Louisville, Cincinnati, and Lexington 4½ per cent.—the principal item—together with Great Northern Collateral Trust "fours" and preferred stock, Northern Pacific General Lien 3 per cents., Southern Railway of Georgia guaranteed stock, Cairo, Arkansas, and Texas 7 per cent. bonds, Guaranty Trust stock, Atchison, Topeka and Santa Fé notes.

The list of pledges held by the Mutual Company is even more diversified, not to say ragged, and comprises a great number of securities of which we never heard in this country. They may not be the worse on that account, but we may notice that $350,000 has been advanced against debentures of the Frank Jones Brewing Company, whose par value is $824,985, and whose market value at the time of the return was $494,991. Another $900,000 has been lent against a deposit of $1,080,000 in 5 per cent. first bonds of the Broadway Realty Company. Most of the other loans were in much smaller amounts, which is following a wise principle, and the security held against them was of all kinds, good and perhaps not good. Thus $600,000 was lent on Louisville and Nashville 4 per cent. unified bonds, par value $990,000, market value $773,000; $775,000 on Western Union Telegraph stock and Fairmont, Morganstown, and Pittsburgh Railroad 4½ per cent. bonds, this latter being a dependency of the at present bankrupt Baltimore and Ohio Railroad; $400,000 on South and North Alabama Railroad consolidated 5 per cents. and Pensacola and Atlantic Railroad 6 per cent. guaranteed "firsts" (the former a poor concern, the latter a small limb of the Louisville and Nashville); and $500,000 on New Jersey Central stock and Delaware and Lackawanna "half stock." At the date of the list the market value of the portions of these two stocks held by the company was $5,000 below the amount of the loan.

We cannot proceed further with this analysis this week for want of space, but shall resume it in a proximate number. In the meantime, we should like to know what the Equitable of the United States office means by advertising its British Branch as a separate and, as it were, self-contained concern? We cannot find that its British provided funds are invested here. They certainly are not in anybody's control here as trustees.

The Moods of the City and their Danger.

How changing they are! One day, all feathers displayed, we are ruffling it like heroes, and the next creeping about with gloomy faces. Just at present the inclination is to be out of temper with everything and everybody; so much so that the hottest of fire-eating—at a safe distance—Jingoes is comparatively quiet, and the opinion can be heard tentatively expressed in unexpected quarters that after all it may not be such good fun to play conquering hero among savages, wherever any such are left and to be got at. Nay, the heresy has been broached that it might be foolish to go slaying our neighbours the French for the sake of a strip, or strips, of African soil which may never be of the slightest use to us. These, though, are extreme views and based on the stomach. You see all these wars and rumours of war are "spoiling business"—not merely the business of the company promoter and the stock and share jobber, important though these may as affording the means of livelihood, let alone fortune, to thousands in their tens—but all mercantile business as well. Trade is "slow" with many places, because of these agitations in favour of war now prevalent East, West, North, and South. Merchants are, therefore, growing impatient, bankers, in some cases, prudent, and commission agents and brokers hungry. Everybody wishes these disputes might have speedy end; curses delays with his whole heart.

Are we to conclude, then, that the end desired is universal peace? By no manner of means. The dissatisfaction and impatience now felt and expressed is far more likely to end in a clamour for war with some "Power" or other than in an earnest appeal for peace. What men are chafing over is doubt and uncertainty. If diplomacy, with its slow and labouring march, cannot solve doubt and clear the atmosphere, so that men may "see their way" to this, and the other undertaking, then the cry will arise for a solution by arbitrament of arms. This is our City mood at present, and it constitutes a real danger. So much warlike talk has been indulged in that the public mind is becoming habituated to the notion that by war alone can certain disputes be satisfactorily brought to an end. We see the effect of this same kind of instruction in the present temper of the United States people over Cuba. They do not want war with Spain, and never as a mass did want it. But their "Yellow" press, contractor and monopolist suborned, has so dinned the idea of war into their minds that they are now prepared, not merely to risk war, but to rate in their impatience those slow coaches like Mr. McKinley who are not prepared at once to declare it. A little more delay and such a mood may force war.

It is the same with us, and the pressure exercised by this heated, crude form of public opinion on the proceedings of Ministers of State and diplomatists becomes at times irresistable. However much men may in their hearts think that the Gold Coast Uplands are not worth fighting for, that the gift of them to France *en bloc* would be a snare and a curse to her, their exasperation has been excited to so great a degree by the haggling, the accusations of bad faith, the seeming obstinacy, and, above all, the prevarications, as they appear to us, of the French Government, that most of them—we speak of the City only—would shout with joy were war to be declared within a week. Stagnation breeds recklessness of mind, and recklessness, stimulated by the truculent writings of the stay-at-home scribes, is almost ready to assume a blood-spilling and destructive turn. So many impending bankruptcies, too, so many financial rascalities of all degrees, could be buried away safely beneath the *débris* of a crisis produced by a big war, that the multitude of the conscienceless is on the side of strife, and it is a great multitude. Unquestionably the hour is anxious, the prospects dark. Yet we hope still, and shall go on hoping that counsels of peace will prevail, not in Africa only, but in China, where France is acting very foolishly for her own best interests, playing a game supposed to be Russia's, without resources of her own to profit by it even if it succeeded. It cannot succeed. Were France friendly and a free trader we might let her officials swagger and "claim" and clamour to their heart's content, jogging on our way in calmness. Protectionist, hostile in business and jealously exclusive as France is under her present *régime*, we dare not allow her even the semblance of success. That is our temper over the Chinese question, and Frenchmen cannot too soon know it. One step too far and our blood will up, beyond statesman's or anybody's power to still it again until torrents of it have dyed the earth. In favour of peace because we are sulky, "humpish," and out of temper? Not a bit of it.

The London and Westminster Contract Corporation, Limited.

Probably most of our readers have given but slight attention to the extraordinary story about this company which has been in part unfolded before Mr. Registrar Hood at the London Bankruptcy Court. It is worth more than passing attention, because it gives us an example of the purely highway robbery kind of finance, such as has not often been surpassed. Two American gentleman, it would appear, came over to this country some time ago, and, by some means or other, managed to connect themselves with one or two respectable people, perfectly innocent of business. Among others they laid hold of Sir James Linton, the well-known artist, and President of the Royal Institute of Painters in Water-Colours, a man of high respectability, and also, we should judge, of extreme simplicity of mind. By making skilful use of this gentleman's name, the pair succeeded in hatching a series of companies, the sole object of which is now seen to have been to abstract money from the British investor.

A leading spirit in the adventure was a Mr. Brotherton, and it was expected that he would appear and give evidence before the Registrar. He even engaged counsel to represent him, but at the last moment thought better of it, and is now said to have retired to his native country, following, in this respect, the example of his co-conspirator, Mr. Van Ee. The Official Receiver, therefore, Mr. Wheeler, had, as Mr. Spokes, one of the counsel, put it, to proceed to play Hamlet with the part of the Prince left out. Sir James Linton was called and made a very sad exhibition of himself. We do not wish to blame him for anything except excessive folly and trustfulness, but to a man in his position the reflections caused by the consequences produced by his guileless and fatuous trustfulness must be as poignantly bitter as if he had committed some crime. The particular company whose affairs were being investigated was by no means the first that the gentlemen from America had produced during their busy visit. Around it, supporting it, clothing it, giving it a serious look, was grouped quite a number of others, all perfectly shadowy in character. There was the British Exploration Company, and the Debenture and Share Trust Syndicate, both of which were simply *noms de guerre* for the said American gentlemen. Under these names they hatched, among other eggs, the London and Westminster Contract Corporation, which has a nice mouth-filling, respectable sort of name, with, ultimately, a nominal capital of £250,000, which was not an excessive capital if the ostensible business—to promote mining and industrial undertakings and to buy shares in such or generally to finance concerns in need of money—had been adhered to; but there was never anything to finance, any mine to handle, nor any real company to promote. It was mummery all through.

The various companies, or names of companies rather, under which Brotherton and Van Ee operated were pure creations of their exuberant faculty of inventiveness. From the first the nominal share capital was merely a few cyphers written down against each name. The mock companies bought each others' "shares," and played the game of finance and investment for a little time very prettily with nothing at all behind, until the British public had been drawn in to part with a considerable amount of its cash. This successfully accomplished, the whole thing collapsed like the pricked bubble it was.

Sir James Linton told the Registrar that he received £250 a year as chairman of the Contract Corporation, and had altogether obtained £435 in the shape of fees. Poor fellow, he sold his name and his respectable standing at a very low figure; but that he did it in ignorance we have not a doubt, and we can only hope that the punishment he has received for his silliness will act as a warning to others similarly tempted, and prevent many an honest man from besmirching himself for life by touching finance in any shape. Just see what this worthy artist lent himself to. Of the share capital of the "Debenture Share Trust"—another "B. & Van Ee" canvass shall we call it?—£15,000 out of £21,000, the total amount issued, was "held," to use the ordinary language, by the two worthies. The first prospectus of the L. & W. Contract Corporation, offered £50,000 shares to the public, and that simple public subscribed £36,000. Sir James Linton and the other directors of the "British Pioneers"—still another show thing—received an "option" to take up 2,000 shares of this corporation issue just for nothing at all. The success of this first flight whetted the appetites of the two Americans, and they proceeded to conduct various other curious enterprises, which it is not necessary for us to detail, all with the object of scooping up some of our money. In fact, the reader would get as bewildered as we do among numerous pretty names cropping up, all utilised for the purpose of extracting plunder. There was the "City of London Joint Stock Trust," among others, and the "British Exploration Company." The latter sold two "mining leases" to the Corporation, we gather, and the said Corporation, a few weeks later, parted with "half its interest" to the "City of London Joint Stock Trust," at an apparent profit. In this way, the Corporation was "making money." The whole dealing was fictitious, of course, but on the strength of this purely "confidence trick" bargain, a dividend of 40 per cent. was paid on its then "capital." The said capital at that time actually, or presumedly, paid-up being only about £2,000 on which this 40 per cent. dividend meant an outlay of but £900. On the strength of this notable feat a second prospectus was issued in October, 1896, offering £100,000 worth of fresh £1 shares at 50 per cent. premium, and, of course, the 40 per cent. dividend was meant to do splendid duty in making this body attractive. So the game went on, the Corporation "buying" rubbishy shares from the Debenture and Share Trust, "contracting" to purchase patents relating to the Lee-Metford rifle—which patents somehow could not be quite got hold of—for what were, in the circumstances, enormous sums of money.

While this was going on Mr. Brotherton was busy "making a market" in the Corporation shares, which constituted the main "draw," through the board of the "British Pioneers," one of the many aliases. Having in a small way "made" this market, the additional shares were launched and a great effort made to trade them off. Happily, it never was particularly successful, although we believe the two merry fellows at the bottom of the illusion did succeed in extracting some £60,000 to £70,000 from the gullible investor. Behind the various concerns or labels there never was any genuine business of any description. It was hocus-pocus from first to last, and the company names used were simply Brotherton & Van Ee, disguised as "limited liability" companies. Thus the "City of London Joint Stock Trust," one of their names, was entitled to a "commission" on shares in the London and Westminster Contract Corporation, sold through its means, these shares being, of course, really Brotherton and Van Ee's bits of paper. And, on the strength of this kind of business, the "Trust" was made to show a profit, and a dividend of 20 per cent. was declared on its "capital," for the purpose of being utilised in the prospectus of the "Corporation." It only took £120 it seems to pay this dividend—the pair probably took it from one pocket and put it into the other—but the public did not know the hollowness of the entire affair, and could hardly be blamed for being taken in.

When shareholders discovered the character of the tricks by which they had been ensnared, it is to their credit that they combined together in order to bring the two perpetrators of the frauds to justice. We are afraid they will not succeed in doing this, and understand that a considerable portion, if not the whole, of the plunder the two men succeeded in laying hold of has been conveyed out of the country, so that neither the men nor the money they have stolen can be got at—unless they could be charged with some crime which would secure their extradition. Whether they get back their money or not, or whether they succeed in punishing these two scamps or not, they certainly deserve the thanks of the public for affording it an object-lesson in fraudulent company promotion, which ought to be exceedingly valuable if people would only take note of it and lay it to heart. These men from America only made a perfectly unscrupulous use of methods of business which are every day employed to palm off upon the public undertakings of all descriptions, from the most worthless even to the best. Company promotion has sunk to a state of degradation and uncleanness in the City of London such as was never paralleled before, and it makes the establishment of a genuine joint stock undertaking in any line of business almost impossible. Every support should be given to the official receiver to lay bare the uttermost depths of this particular piece of roguery were it only to help to bring about reforms.

Brightening Trade Prospects.

With all that there is to disturb the public mind and frighten the timid in China, in West Africa, in the United States and Spain, in India, not to speak of Crete, the mutterings of revolt in the Balkans, or the deadlock continued in Austria by the irreconcilable racial warriors, it would not have been surprising if trade at home and abroad had shown symptoms of decline rather than prosperity. It is not easy to account for it, but the fact is that trade is just now advancing by "leaps and bounds." There is scarcely a single complaint of too few orders; but a good many announcements that further contracts cannot be undertaken for early delivery. Traders and manufacturers seem alike to have made up their minds that, whatever may be the diplomatic troubles in the far East or the near East, in Cuba or West Africa, there will be no war, and so they devote themselves quietly to the development of their business. In Birmingham, indeed, such bellicose preparations as have been making in the United States have been utilised to bring "grist to the mill" there. Various Birmingham firms have busied themselves in "looking up" orders at Washington, and there is a confident anticipation of good business in that direction. Perhaps the most unexpected proof of rising prosperity is the extraordinary strength displayed at the March wool sales in London. Nothing exceptional was hoped for in that trade previous to the opening of these sales. In iron and steel, in shipbuilding, and other trades, even greater activity is shown. It seems probable that we are only now realising the full advantage derivable from the termination of the unfortunate engineers' strike.

It is, perhaps, in the iron and steel trade that the greatest activity is manifest. This is the case alike in Scotland, England, and America. The Scotch railway traffics have been going steadily up, and from the daily reports received from trade centres there, it seems reasonable to anticipate that the increase in traffics will continue for months to come. The pressure on the Scotch iron and steel trades has not for ten years been so great as it is now. Producers are working at their utmost stretch, and, of course, insist on full prices. Ironmasters can hardly deliver fast enough. A similar condition of affairs exists in America. Miners have received an advance in wages, and the output of pig-iron does not keep pace with the demand. Waterworks extensions are proving quite as serviceable in Birmingham as the war preparations in other countries. The local tube and pipe makers are extremely busy, and a contract for 6,000 tons of riveted steel pipes has just been placed with a local firm for the Birmingham Waterworks extensions. Larger contracts are under negotiation. Then the Nile railway extension adds to the demand for railway material and locomotives; and Birmingham has at present some big contracts in hand for the Midland and other home railways as well as for India. Engineers are also having a busy time with machine tools and drilling and lifting appliances. Sheffield is equally busy. There seems to have been some anxiety as to the future of the armour-plate industry, though not on the part of those most deeply interested. The fact is that the manufacturers have been entirely remodelling their plant for the adoption of the Krupp system, and the full work of production will not be resumed until the new plant has been tested. Then the manufacturers declare they will be able to produce as much armour as is likely to be required by the English and foreign governments combined. Iron and steel makers in Sheffield are fully booked, and similar reports come from the other iron districts.

Shipbuilders on the Clyde and on the Tyne are rejoicing as well as iron and steel manufacturers. Since the first of this month, Clyde shipbuilders have booked orders for fully 50,000 tons gross of shipping. These include three new American liners—the Allan Line taking two steamers of 10,000 tons each, the Dominion Line one twin screw steamer, and the Cunard a couple of cargo boats 550 feet long. Of course, with all this trade activity, the coal business is beginning to look up, after rather a long period of indifferent dulness. But in this connection, difficulties have arisen in regard to the Welsh sliding scale. The workmen demanded better terms, and after a good deal of negotiation, the colliery proprietors have served notices upon 130,000 miners to terminate contracts at the end of the month. This, however, is described as a merely precautionary measure, and is not likely to be followed by suspension of work. Indeed, even without the sliding scale, the workmen do not seem to contemplate a strike, for at present prices, they appear to think they might almost be better without than with the scale. But with steam coal steadily rising, and the general demand as steadily increasing, we cannot imagine that either side can be willing to carry the dispute to extremities. In Barnsley 2,000 men have been on strike for six months; but other disputes are now being amicably arranged. This is no time for quarrelling in the coal or any trade.

The Corporation of Foreign Bondholders.

We have been engaged in a thankless task. It has been repeatedly stated by us that 545 members of the Corporation of Foreign Bondholders exist, and that their Council of twenty-one has by a surprise movement made ready to turn out all the rest of their co-proprietors. A careful investigation of the reports of the meetings held by the Corporation since 1880, reports collated from several different newspapers, make it clear to our mind that the permanent members have had the best of the encounter, and that the Council does not show to advantage. It has been more or less of a "pious fraud" from the first, and often a tool of the worst class of loan-monger or jobber in discredited bonds. One of the earliest discoveries made by members taking an intelligent interest in the Corporation's affairs has been that the money subscribed by them was applied in a different way from what they had proposed. Further the melancholy fact has to be recorded, that in proportion as the £100 subscribed by each member was paid back, with interest at 5 per cent. those who received the money, or a certain number of them, ceased thenceforth to take any interest in the Council's proceedings. Those alone who still were bondholders, as all had been at the beginning, discussed at each meeting how the interest of members could be kept alive so as to make sure that the Council should be controlled and bondholders consulted.

This study has made it completely evident that the purpose of those members, whose claims have been represented subsequently in a wholly different light, was an excellent one and thoroughly in the interests of their fellow bondholders. Mr. Jackson, Mr. Marriott, Mr. Staples, Mr. Costello and many others raised at successive meetings the question of the assets. Mr. Henderson was one of the first to do this, and Mr. Cohen and Mr. Bishop, each in turn, discussed the question, from the double point of view of the right of the permanent members to the estate of the Corporation and the means of assuring to the whole body an effectual control of the Council, inclusive of its dealings with the accounts in accordance with the articles of association. One or two individuals have, on occasion, referred to the assets on the basis of distribution by them among the members. Apart from this the one and only motive expressed has been to assure to the whole body an adequate representation of the holders of foreign bonds on the Council and on the committees more or less originated and guided, or played upon, by it.

Now we come to this precious Bill of Sir John Lubbock's. From time to time the suggestion has been made at meetings that a Bill should be drafted with a view to give to permanent members the possession of rights which the Council has ruled to be denied to them, by registration of the Corporation under limited liability. This, however, was an entirely different object from that sought under the Bill now before Parliament. The object of this is to evict the permanent members, and it is an object completely subversive of justice and fair play.

What has the Council ever done that it should serve itself heir to the entire property of the members of the Corporation? After having undertaken formally to render gratuitous services it has procured votes giving to itself the sum of £3,200 a year out of the income of the Corporation. It has ignored, and neglected or put off from time to time, every suggestion made by members for the satisfactory settlement of those questions which affect the position of the whole body. Not only so, but, instead of consulting their fellow members as proposed at several open meetings devoted to the subject of this Bill, the twenty-one men forming the Council, or an inner clique of them, have held secret conferences on the subject and systematically prevented the truth from leaking out. In fact, secrecy was a condition preliminary to being allowed to take any share in these conferences, which we are therefore justified in describing as hole and corner cabals for upright business men to be ashamed of.

Having gone about the matter in this furtive way, the men in the plot proceeded to spring their matured confiscation scheme upon the Corporation without even condescending to communicate the details of it, asking for proxies merely on the faith of their own assurance. By such proceedings the concoctors of the scheme of confiscation succeeded in obtaining the statutory majority, and carried their Bill by twelve votes. To this hour the great bulk of the members, we believe, have not seen this Bill.

Already attention has been directed by us, on more

than one occasion to the contemptible way in which the dealings in certificates of permanent membership have been carried on, and it is interesting to note, in connection therewith, that between February, 1896, when Mr. John Flemming proposed the committee to consider and report upon a plan of reorganisation, and the date when the Bill was finally brought to the vote, votes given to the Council at meetings of the Corporation have increased very nearly in proportion to the number of transfers passed. Does not this tend to prove that certificates have only been allowed to pass into the hands of Sir John Lubbock's friends and partisans? We think it does, and the question ought to be raised whether a searching examination should not now be made as to how these favourable votes were acquired; whether, for instance, the secretary of the Council has been occupied in canvassing executors and others to procure the sale of certificates from sources of which the Council has exclusive knowledge, and in preventing other independent purchasers from obtaining such certificates as were in the market. Should an inquiry demonstrate that this is what has been going on, the Council ought to be called to account for employing such very questionable means of securing votes. In any case, this body has secretly prepared a scheme of confiscation the reverse of the one Mr. John Flemming openly propounded in 1896, and it will be a public scandal if the Bill embodying it is allowed to pass through Parliament and become law. We do not believe for a moment that it can pass, if the light of publicity is kept shining upon it.

Economic and Financial Notes and Correspondence.

VIVE L'EMPEREUR!

Really the Colonial Secretary seems to be a little hard on those worthy gentlemen who have retired from active service as Colonial governors, and on the Press. Two such men have recently come home from abroad, namely Sir William des Vœux and Sir William Robinson, and both have been "interviewed" by enterprising journalists, to whom they have expressed frankly their opinions on the far Eastern question. In doing this they, we humbly think, performed a valuable public service, because we drudging, tax-distilling citizens have very little means of knowing anything about such a question—about any foreign or colonial question, in fact—unless men in authority communicate their opinions to us. It is useless to look for light to the Colonial Office, and even Blue Books, when they tardily appear, are often more calculated to darken knowledge than to increase it. But this kind of frankness, indulged in by men of knowledge and ripe experience, does not suit our high and mighty Colonial Secretary at all, and he has issued a circular warning, these gentlemen, his humble satraps, against a continuance of the—to his high imperial mind—most obnoxious practice. Surely the country will not endorse this hand-handed proceeding, or is it prepared to endorse anything, if so be that a big and costly war could be got up somewhere, for the benefit of the iron and brimstone trades, of the thousand and ten selfish interests that scent pelf in slaughter?

THE CHINESE FOUR-AND-A-HALF PER. CENT. LOAN.

It has been a failure so far as a public subscription goes, and the underwriters have had to stick to the larger part of it. The failure arose wholly from the changed conditions prevailing in the money market. Had the issue been made a month earlier in all probability there would have been a full public subscription, for the loan is a very fair security of the more speculative class. It no doubt stands behind the other loans China has had to emit, but as long as the present order of things prevaiis within that empire, the revenues assigned to this loan will be collected, after a little time, just as readily as those assigned for the service of the other loans now are. And if China is to be broken up none of the loans will be worth much. In one sense, though, this new loan is better fenced against damage than some of the others since Germans are interested in it to the extent of one half. They, at least, will not sit down tamely under the efforts of rivals to undermine the security.

In connection with the underwriting of this loan one bit of sharp dealing is the object of considerable animadversion. It appears, according to the story, that one firm which had underwritten a very large amount of it ignored the clause in the contract which forbade the sale, "direct or indirect," of any portion of it before allotment, so far as to sell to others the underwriting rights for a profit of one half of one per cent. By so doing operators were able to sell "bears" of the loan on the Stock Exchange, and then go and cover these sales by taking as much as they wanted of the amount the accommodating underwriters had to dispose of. Suppose a speculator sold £20,000 of the bonds at par, and went and subscribed for the same amount of the loan with the underwriters at 1½ discount. The result was a sure profit obtained at absolutely no risk. Of course, such a mode of doing business implied an absolute disregard of fairplay and honour, but we fear the thing happened just thus to the gain of the unscrupulous few. Those underwriters, on the other hand, who have honourably kept their bargain see all chance of immediate profit disappearing, as the scrip closed last night at 1¾ to 1½ discount and the market is spiritless and without support.

INDIAN BORROWINGS.

Sometimes a little light is afforded by a question in the House of Commons. Here is one put by the member for Cardiff and Lord George Hamilton's answer to it. We are sorry his lordship did not go further, but perhaps Mr. Maclean will push him on to tell the country what amount of foreign capital has been embarked in India, between 1860, say, and the present year, by (1) the State, (2) the guaranteed and other railways, and (3) private enterprise. The return might afford half-a-dozen India Office clerks a week's healthy employment and would be most useful in giving the public a means of knowing what the Indian people have to pay out to us every year. The quality of the "progress" they have made under our rule would also then become more apparent than it is now:—

MR. MACLEAN asked the Secretary of State for India whether the deficit for the year 1897-98 announced in the Indian Budget, Rx. 5,280,000, includes or excludes the £4,000,000 sterling equivalent say to Rx. 6,000,000, borrowed in England, and applied in part payment of the Home charges for the year; and what are the total net amounts of the actual additions to the Debt of India in 1897-98, and estimated to be added in 1898-99, without reckoning capital raised for expenditure on reproductive public works.

LORD G. HAMILTON.—The deficit of Rx. 5,280,000 in 1897-98 is the excess of expenditure chargeable against revenue over the revenue of the year. It includes the interest charged in the year in respect of sterling debt incurred; but, in arriving at the amount of the deficit, the money raised by borrowing in the year is not reckoned as part of the revenue of the year. It is, however, included in the ways and means, out of which the deficit and capital expenditure have been met. 2. The total additions of the debt of India in 1897-98 and 1898-99 are estimated as follows:—In England, £11,112,600; in India, Rx. 5,424,900; but I am at present unable to say how much of this has been or will be applied to expenditure on reproductive public works until I get the full detailed accounts. The railway capital expenditure in both years was large.

OUR TRADE WITH THE FAR EAST.

Sir. Robert Giffen, in a letter to yesterday's *Times*, supplies a valuable correction to the exaggerated language used about this portion of our business by that enthusiastic Empire-stretcher, Mr. Colquhoun. He begins by quoting the figures in the latest "Statistical Abstract," to prove that the entire value of this trade, including that with the Dutch East Indies was, in 1896, £31,675,000. Of this total £11,721,000 represented our imports from, and £19,854,000 our exports to the Far East. Instead, therefore, of being "one-sixth" of our entire foreign trade, this total represents only about one twenty-fourth of it. Even this is not to be despised. It is, indeed, too valuable a portion of our business to lose, and what we keep insisting upon is that the great population of China alone ought to stimulate us to bring about a considerable increase in the volume of the business, both ways. Some further comparative statistics, compiled by Sir Robert Giffen, are interesting enough to be quoted entire:—

Comparing these figures, again, with our trade with British India, we find that our imports from India in 1896 amounted to £25,285,467, and our exports thereto to £30,841,551, making a total of £56,000,000, or nearly double our whole trade with the Far East. If we included Ceylon with India, these imports and exports would be increased by about £6,000,000, giving a total almost exactly double our trade with the Far East.

To give a further idea of the scale of our Far East trade with reference to our imports and exports generally, we may notice that our imports and exports with Russia amount to £34,000,000 or more than the whole of this Far East trade; with Germany to £61,000,000, or about double; with France to 70,000,000, or more than double; with the United States to £138,000,000, or more than four times; and with Australasia to £54,000,000, or one-and-a-half times the Far East trade. The Far East trade is thus important in its own place, but it has not the importance for us of other parts of our foreign trade.

Of course, there is a movement of bullion and specie to be reckoned as well as an import and export of merchandise, but the proportions of our trade with the Far East to our total trade would not be varied by including the bullion and specie.

It is also quite true that the Far East trades with other parts of the British Empire, especially with India, the exports of opium from India to China being a well-known fact. Our shipping interests in China and the Far East are also considerable, more in proportion to our total shipping, I should say, than the imports and exports are to our total trade. But recognising all this we must also recognise that for our import and export trade, as it is commonly understood, China and the Far East are not so very important. The most important countries for us are in truth those very rivals of whose tariffs and protectionist proceedings we have reason to complain, but with whom our trade nevertheless goes on, owing, I believe, to natural causes, and to our own free trade policy, which the protectionist policy of other nations is wholly unable to overcome.

In the concluding sentences of this extract we, needless to say, thoroughly agree, and it is because we do so that we believe it possible for a greater expansion in our trade with the Far East to be attainable than Sir Robert Giffen seems willing to allow. Our free trade policy ought to stand us in as good stead there as everywhere else, provided that we do not allow rivals to plant themselves down in the richest parts of the Chinese Empire and start "exclusive dealings" there for the benefit of their own, more or less, State-sustained manufacturers.

WESTERN AUSTRALIAN BOASTING.

Listen to Sir John Forrest, the Premier of the Colony, upon them. He had been "banqueting" at Menzies on the occasion of the opening of the new railway, plentifully borrowed for, and thus delivered himself:—

During the last two years railway connection had been established with Kalgurli, Kanowna, Boulder, and Menzies, and would be carried further if the prosperity of the mining industry warranted it. There was now, continued the Premier, a continuous line of 1,000 miles from Albany, and another for fifty miles to the goldfields at Coolgardie. The water scheme, which had been started, would, although costing £2,250,000 and £300,000 yearly to keep up, pay for itself within twenty years. The mines which were now worked at a loss would, with an increased water supply, yield profits. The gold production of the colony during January last had been greater than that of Victoria and Queensland combined. The annual trade amounted in value to £10,000,000. Seven years ago there was a population of 50,000, with a revenue of £400,000; at present the population was 160,000, with a revenue of £3,000,000 The colony was, however, capable of holding millions instead of this 160,000, inasmuch as it comprised one-third of Australia.

This is most enthralling progress in more senses than one. But what if Coolgardie should fail or "give out" soon? Then the water scheme and other fine public works might grow just a trifle burdensome. Gold is at its best a poor thing to rely on for permanent prosperity. It cannot be sown and reaped you see, and therefore Sir John's glowing anticipations should be well "salted" before swallowing.

"A NEW IRISH MUDDLE."

The writer of the subjoined letter is perfectly justified in saying that the taxation muddle now to be created in Ireland is only a replica of the one already existing in England. Unquestionably, the tendency of recent Imperial finance has been to produce inextricable confusion in the relations between the State and local authorities, and, in producing this, to stimulate wasteful expenditure all over the country at the expense, in the long run, of those least able to meet it. And, as regards Ireland, we cannot do better than quote the words of Mr. Morley in the debate on the second reading of the New Local Government (Ireland) Bill:—

The end of this will be that the Land Commissioners will come round to adjudicate upon the rents of an estate which has been improved by county expenditure, which has come out of the pockets of the tenants, broadly speaking, and the landlord, who has contributed nothing to that expenditure, will himself reap the benefit by having his rents increased. This, in my judgment, unless I misread the Bill altogether, goes to the very root of the policy of the Bill and justifies me in saying boldly what I only hinted at on the occasion of the first reading, that the Bill does give the landlord much more—both in the shape of rent and exemption from contributions to local burdens—than we understood was to be given when we first had the Bill before us. The hon. member for South Tyrone, I recollect, once wrote that he would vote for a Bill for expropriating Lord Clanricarde. But the hon. member is now the partner in a Bill which, so far from expropriating gentlemen like Lord Clanricarde who so absolve themselves from all their social responsibilities, will in effect give a great boon to men of that stamp, and the more absentee they are and the more ready to relieve themselves from their social responsibilities, the greater will be the boon which will be conferred upon them.

While recognising the truth of a statement of this kind, and noting the tendency of all these contributions in aid to entangle the Imperial Treasury in obligations which must one day seriously embarrass it, at the same time that they afford no permanent or substantial relief whatever to either the ratepayer or the taxpayer, it must be frankly acknowledged that protest of any kind is absolutely useless. The nation is either unaware of the dangers lying ahead for it, and created by this dole and bribe system of finance, or it has become so apathetic through its prosperity that it does not care to what lengths in extravagance and in pledging its future resources its chosen representatives may go. In regard to this Irish Bill, nothing is really more amusing to a student of political movements than the readiness with which the Irish landlords accept its provisions for granting local self-government in exchange for the £730,000 to be put in their pockets, unless it be the eagerness with which "patriots" like Mr. Timothy Healy cry, "Take all the money ye want, yer honours! We make you most entirely welcome to it!" Probably such men see the prospect of a nice political cock-pit to be opened for themselves in the future, where they may crow their loudest, and quarrel their hardest, once the landlords have received their bribe and gone.

To the Editor.

SIR,—Is not what your correspondent calls "a new Irish muddle" merely an extension to Ireland of the English finance muddle? If the principle of the Agricultural Rates Act is good for England, why not for Ireland? The present Government have extended what Lord Farrer called in 1891 "the easy and cowardly plan of subsidising local bodies by doles from Imperial funds, ill selected, ill applied, and ill distributed—doles demoralising at once to the giver and to the receivers." I agree with your correspondent that the proposed dole will go to the people who want it least: a very large part will go to absentee landlords who never spend a penny, or do a day's duty in the districts from which they draw large and excessive rentals. The rest will ultimately find its way into the pockets of the landlords also, for the value of their land for rent or sale must depend on the amount of taxation to which it is subject.

If such a grant was needed in England in aid of distressed agriculture, it is far more needed in Ireland where rural taxation has been increasing year by year. There are some districts where the local taxation is equal to from 1s. 3d. to 1s. 2d. of the rental now obtainable. Another objection to the distribution of the grant is that it will go into the pockets of the classes who are always supporting increased Imperial expenditure, who clamour for ironclads, forward policies, and extension of the Empire. If England gets any benefit from the expenditure on these things, Ireland certainly does not, yet over £10,000,000 are collected in Ireland by the Imperial authorities.

The most immoral feature of all in this measure is the coupling the grant with the local government scheme, a most barefaced bribe to the landlords for accepting a measure, which they otherwise would oppose to the death: and making the people buy the privilege of local self-government, so long promised, and so long denied to them. This exemption of rental in Ireland from taxation is a curious contrast with the attempts made by the London County Council to make rentals, that now escape, liable for their fair proportion of the local rates, a reasonable principle that seems to receive the approval of the Moderates, as well as the Progressives.
—Your obedient servant, AN IRISHMAN.

WEST INDIAN DEFICITS.

Appended are some figures abstracted from the accounts of our West Indian possessions for the past two years. They reveal a net deficit for the whole period of £179,458, but the shortcoming for 1897 was less than half that of the previous year. This shows that the position is not so desperate as West Indians and Mr. Chamberlain would have us believe, and afford a strong argument against making grants, like the one just voted, a permanent charge on the home taxpayer. If they had any manliness or sense of shame, most Indian planters would never dream of asking for an annual alms, but they appear to have neither the one nor the other, still less any commercial enterprise. But if they are too lazy or careless to help themselves, what claim can they possibly have to slip their hands every year into our pockets?

	1896 Decrease.	1896 Increase.	1897. Decrease	1897. Increase.
	£	£	£	£
Jamaica	22,142	—	46,969	—
Leeward I. (5)	46,292	—	10,577	—
Bahamas	—	1,122	—	4,992
Grenada	5,207	—	3,978	—
St. Lucia	9,014	—	729	—
St. Vincent	3,452	—	1,104	—
Barbados	5,724	—	—	1,562
Trinidad	6,630	—	—	23,870
Tobago	—	373	—	52
British Guiana	28,744	—	34,841	—
British Honduras	7,257	—	—	7,364
Bermuda	—	4,824	461	—
Turks & Caicos Islands	—	2,540	—	6,864
	£134,462	£8,859	£98,659	£44,704
	8,859		44,704	
Net deficit	£125,603		£53,855	

THE WATERWAYS OF IRELAND.

The following extract from the speech made by Mr. James McCann, the chairman, at the last half-yearly meeting of the Grand Canal (Ireland) Company, raises a question of far greater importance to the future well-being of Ireland than many of those with which Parliament spends its time. Inland navigation has been too much neglected in all the three kingdoms, but nowhere is that neglect more glaring than in the sister island. Yet in a perfected and extended system of canals its need for cheap transit for heavy goods might be met over a wide area of the country, provided the waterways are created and maintained in complete independence of the railway companies, whose competitor and freight corrective they ought to be:—

Ireland seems to me to be the one great agricultural country in the world in which at the present day no attempt is made to utilise or improve the waterways which, rightly understood, could be made to benefit largely every interest in the country, particularly agricultural, which may be said to be our sole interest, and having studied the question closely, Ireland seems to me to be the country amongst all those I have named most suitable for development in this respect.

The unfailing supply of water possessed by our navigable rivers and canals; the absence of interruption to traffic by frost (the Grand Canal has not been closed by frost more than an average of a week in the year during the past 100 years; the number of ports we possess all round the coast, particularly on the eastern side; and the comparative proximity of the furthest navigable waterway to the nearest port appears to me to give by nature a position of superiority to this country for the development of canal traffic not possessed by any other country I know of. Moreover, horse traction and the labour in connection with it, should be cheap in Ireland. It may be said, however, that the country could be benefited in this way only in the immediate vicinity of these waterways.

Such is not the case, as under a properly arranged system canal traffic could be through booked at so many points with the railways, that the entire country could be made to feel the full benefit.

I will not weary you further with the general observations which do not strictly appertain to the business of our meeting. Having given a good deal of attention over a number of years to this question of the Irish carrying trade (I am a railway director as well as a member of this Canal Board), I hold strong views in the direction indicated, and I wish to state these views on the off chance that they might, now or hereafter, lead to some action being taken in the interests of the country.

I am not sanguine, however, of any practical results; the great railway companies, directly and indirectly, dominate the commercial life of Ireland, and they are not favourable to canals and navigable rivers. It will also be found that the views of those who govern us are formed and directed by the opinions of the Boards of these great railway corporations, and there is no counteracting influence exercised by the public, who seem to be interested in other subjects which must certainly be more absorbing, but in my opinion not more practical, than this great question of the Irish carrying trade.

ALLSOPP DEFERRED ORDINARY STOCK.

We should not be surprised if it proves to be very much "deferred," and the Stock Exchange does well, perhaps, to be angry about the issue of it. Yet what could the directors do? To live, let alone to prosper, they had to buy "pubs" right and left as outlets for their fluids, and they could not for ever go on issuing debentures or debenture stocks to pay for these, because the paper could not be disposed of. Besides, to take this course would have meant slow suicide for the company, whose future is not too well assured at any time. Hence the device of creating a duplicate amount of ordinary stock (£1,100,000) to be issued in bits as the "pub" buying line in the business demanded. It is an ingenious device, and well calculated to bring the company more discredit than cash, but needs must. And should affairs prosper, under cash stimulants of this sort, until the old ordinary stock—henceforth to be the "preferred" ordinary, entitled to a maximum 7 per cent. dividend—becomes a stable investment security what scope for gambling might not lie in the new stuff! But will the money be forthcoming? That we cannot say. We should be sorry to find any of it, but then we never were among Allsopp stockholders, and cannot understand their enthusiasm.

COMPANY PROMOTIONS AND LIBEL ACTIONS.

Scarcely a week passes without some incident which clearly shows the necessity for the interference of the Legislature with the promotion of companies. Libel actions, proceedings in the courts of bankruptcy and winding up, and prosecutions at the Old Bailey, all bear eloquent testimony for some legislative control. Some interesting facts relating to several concerns floated to secure a portion of the public's spare cash came to light in the libel action brought by that mighty hunter and explorer, Martin Thomas Kays against Mr. Hess of the *Critic*. That astute gentleman, knowing that the British investor preferred concessions to the skin of the lion, proceeded to acquire a small freehold estate of some 325 square miles in the wilds of Bechuanaland.

No less than five companies were promoted to take over from Kays and his partner the Khama Concession, namely the African Exploration Gold Mining and Estates Company, The Mines Contract Company, the African Landed Estates Company, the Setlagoli Gold and Demaraland Company, and last but not least Hutton's (Bechuanaland) Gold Reefs Development Company. There is no doubt, according to the first map which was issued with the prospectus, that this peculiar estate should have been brought to the public notice for show and exhibition purposes. Rivers ran up the mountains, and during the time that the various companies were being formed to take it over, it changed its position by some three degrees of longitude. Truly a wondrous property!

THE BOTTOMLEY TRUSTS.

One gets rather tired of Mr. Bottomley, but we cannot help remarking that his two "gilt-edged" trusts—the West Australian Joint Stock Trust and the West Australian Loan and General—only pay their final dividends for last year in scrip. This is a very simple process which many must wish they were in a position to copy. How nice it would be if the grocer, the butcher, and the bootmaker could be paid by everybody in paper after the same style. Merely print upon a little piece of paper some fancy design, and there you have an instrument wherewith dividends and other pressing debts can be paid! If the world could be run upon this principle, what a fine time it would be for all those who do not produce; perhaps not so good, though, for those who do. Unfortunately, our matter of fact mind has never fallen in with these views, and the only commentary we can make upon the matter is that if this is the best attainable result for the two "gilt-edged"—should we not rather say gilded?—Bottomley beauties, the future of the poor West Australian Market Trust can only be described as something "painful and lingering."

BANKING HOURS.

The money article of the *Daily News* is well qualified to speak the inner mind of the banking clerk, but we are afraid that its half-thrown-out suggestion that the banks should open at 9.30 in the morning, instead of 9 o'clock, will fall upon barren ground. It might be all very well if the rule could be applied to the public offices of the City pure and simple, for there in the first hour of the day is, perhaps, one of comparative leisure—although much work even there must be done early; but a very different tale has to be reported from the suburbs. There the offices have a busy time between 9 and 9.30 in the morning, as their customers often call in on their way to business. The London and South-Western Bank a short time back, in opening an office at Richmond, followed its usual course as to the hour of opening, and upset the other banks in that "Sleepy Hollow," which had been accustomed to open at 10 in the morning. All kinds of dreadful prophecies have been uttered in regard to its boldness in the matter, but we venture to affirm that a few years hence all the banks at Richmond will open at 9 o'clock. The clerks can make it up, as Charles Lamb did at the India House, by going away the earlier.

A STRANGE SHARE.

In 1894 the British American Land Company obtained an Act whereby its 5,597 of £25 shares were divided into 5,597 "A" shares of £1 each, and 5,597 "B" of £24 each, the "A" shares to receive 25s. per annum as interest, and the "B" shares to receive no interest at all, but to be redeemed by purchases out of surplus revenue. In this way the shareholders were first to receive 5 per cent. upon their investment and the remainder of the net revenue was to go in redemption of capital. So far this arrangement has worked out satisfactorily, for since the Act has been put into force

1,088 "B" shares have been redeemed, at prices ranging from £6½ per share downwards, and, in this way, £26,112 nominal of capital has been wiped out. The balance left over this year after paying the 25s. dividend is £4,000, which will permit of the redemption of about £13,000 nominal of "B" shares, at their present prices of £7 per share, bringing their total down to £95,000, valued at about £30,000 in the market.

As they bear no interest there will not be much inducement for outsiders to pay high prices for these shares, but if Canadian affairs continue hopeful, the holders will be inclined to refrain from surrendering them when the company comes in to bid, and so the price must gradually rise. To hold them is a strange sort of speculation in which the individual backs his own opinion as to the future of Canadian land. If all goes well, the most tenacious holders may obtain £24 per share for their "B" shares—above that figure the price cannot go as drawings would then take the place of bidding—but the loss of interest upon the money might easily take away much of the seeming profit, while, of course, a turn in the Canadian real estate market might indefinitely postpone re-payment.

THE DIVISION OF DRAPERY PROFITS.

In our reports and balance-sheets we deal with three drapery companies, all working in London, and it is interesting to note the manner in which they have divided their profits. They draw up their accounts differently, so that it is impossible to say that "net profit" means exactly the same thing in each case, but we have endeavoured to make it as uniform as possible in the following table :—

	D. H. Evans & Co.	Jones & Higgins.	T. R. Roberts.
	£	£	£
Net profit	32,800	22,407	17,908
To Reserve	1,834	5,490	700
Debenture Redemption	835	—	—
Preference Dividend	4,800	—	1,740
Ordinary Dividend	14,400	12,350	7,980
Founders or Managers	6,000	3,250	2,812
Dividend	12 p.c.	9½ p.c.	10½ p.c.

A glance at the figures ought to satisfy anyone who understands business that the 9½ per cent. dividend of Jones & Higgins is far better secured than the higher distributions of the two other concerns, and a look into the balance-sheets shows that that concern is distinctly superior in every respect, although it pays a lower rate of dividend.

MORE ABOUT AMERICAN LIFE OFFICE METHODS.

Subjoined is a plain-spoken note from the provinces on this subject, and plain-speaking is emphatically required. Within the last day or two we have ascertained that at least one agent of these alien institutions has been going about declaring that the hostility shown to them by the INVESTORS' REVIEW is due to the fact that they "have refused to give it their advertisements." The exact contrary is the truth, and we shall take care to make this plain in future. When this REVIEW was started as a quarterly magazine in February, 1892, we decided to absolutely refuse the advertisements of all these concerns, and this decision has been adhered to throughout.

To the Editor.

March, 1898.

SIR,—I see the strong remarks you make in your INVESTORS' REVIEW of February 4 and March 11 about the Mutual of New York. This company nearly got me to insure with them, and did get a friend of mine for £1,300. I proposed a policy with them for £500, for which I was to pay an annual premium for twenty years of £20 14s. 7d., and upon this annual premium I was told I should get 3½ per cent. compound interest at the end of twenty years. They estimated the sum I should get at £571 7s. 1d. I worked out £20 14s. 7d. paid yearly at 3½ per cent. compound, and found it came to £606 14s. 8d., also at 3 per cent., which came out at £573 14s. 2d. The manager here and the agent were actually fools enough to assure me that £20 14s. 7d. paid yearly at 3½ per cent. compound came to £571 7s. 1d., and even when I proved it came to more, they said anyway it was over 3½ per cent. They are getting a quantity of people to insure on the strength of leading men who have insured with them for large sums, and they told several friends and myself that they had one of our leading statesmen in for £50,000. It turns out that this statement is true to the extent of £20,000 only, *i.e.*, it is 60 per cent. lie. I am now sorry that I did not take note of more of the leading men they had upon their paper, so that I could write them. It looks to me as if they are working the country for all it is worth, and when they can drain it no more they will clear out.—Yours faithfully, H. O.

Critical Index to New Investments.

JOHNSON, MATTHEY & CO., LIMITED.

This company, which was formed in 1894 to carry on the business of assayers, refiners, and metallurgical chemists, of Hatton-garden, established upwards of a century ago, has a share capital of £900,000, which is all held by the late firm. There is now offered an issue of £250,000 4 per cent. mortgage debenture stock at 102 per cent.; it forms part of a total of £400,000, and is repayable by March, 1948, at par, but is redeemable at any time on six months' notice at 112 per cent. Interest due January and July. Imports of the precious metals into England are largely increasing, and it has become desirable to have command of an increased amount of money. Extra capital has hitherto been furnished by the directors, but for family reasons it is now considered preferable to provide it on a more permanent basis. The amount at present so under advance is £152,000. Assets are large and good, the total being £542,000, of which freehold properties represent £123,000; stock of gold, silver, platinum, &c., £263,843; cash, £70,000; and besides this there will be £98,000 net from the present issue, and there is £150,000 uncalled share capital. Figures of profits are not supplied, but Jarvis & Co., the accountants, say that average profits for past five years have been sufficient to pay the interest upon the debenture stock now to be issued, more than six times over, or, in other words, they may be said to have exceeded £60,000. It is a first-class business, evidently very profitable, and the large assets should make the debentures a good investment. Yet we cannot help wishing the information more complete. Why put a premium of 12 per cent. on the debentures if redeemed before the due date?

APLIN & BARRETT AND THE WESTERN COUNTIES CREAMERIES, LIMITED.

With this neat title a Company is formed, having Robarts, Lubbock & Co., Stuckey's, and the Wilts and Dorset as its bankers, to buy the old established business of Aplin & Barrett, cheddar cheese and butter merchants, of Yeovil, Somerset, with which is to be amalgamated the businesses of the Western Counties Creamery and of a sausage manufactory now carried on by Maynard's Pure Food Company. It seems a pity the sausage business is not included in the title. The capital is £100,000 in £1 shares, half ordinary and half 6 per cent. cumulative preference, of which 34,000 ordinary shares, with £28,000 in cash, are taken by the vendors. The cheese business is about half a century old, and the sausage business rather older, but the creamery only dates from 1888. Profits for 1896 are certified at £5,218, and for 1897 at £7,791, whereas the dividend on the preference shares will want only £3,000. Upon this showing, they would appear to be pretty safe, but it is quite a local affair, and Yeovil people will know more about it than the London market.

"FINANCIAL NEWS," LIMITED.

The company was originally registered early in 1885, and was reconstructed at the end of 1888 with a capital of £100,000, in £1 shares, half being ordinary and half 6 per cent. preference, and 48,358 shares of each class were issued as purchase money. Profits having increased, the undertaking is to be again reconstructed with a capital of £200,000, in £1 shares, 50,000 being ordinary and £150,000 5 per cent. cumulative preference. Purchase price this time is £200,000, including £100,000 in cash and all the ordinary shares, while the public have offered them 100,000 preference shares. Company acquires leasehold premises in Abchurch-lane, goodwill of paper and stock and book debts of vendor, together with a cash reserve fund of £30,000. The net profits for three years are certified to show an average of over £31,000 a year. How long will that continue when the present company-hatching fashion is at an end ?

OMNIBUS AND TRAMCAR CIGARETTE AUTOMATIC SUPPLY COMPANY, LIMITED.

If this company is floated, Louis Coen, the vendor, will be in luck. In the first place, he appoints himself managing director of the company ; he then sells to it the rights granted to him for seven years to supply cigarettes from boxes placed on the vehicles of the London General Omnibus, the Road Car, the North Metropolitan Tramways, and Tilling & Co., and also the patent rights of L. Coen's Improved Automatic Delivery Machines, 2,000 of which machines he contracts to supply. He also reserves an option to supply the cigarettes, and having made the future pretty comfortable for himself, he takes £85,000, including £55,000 in cash, for his contracts, his rights, and his 2,000 machines. From prince to peasant has apparently been studied, for the cigarettes will be supplied at prices of from one to four a penny, and the prospectus says it is anticipated that the two-a-penny and four-a-penny cigarettes will be sold by millions. Everyone is, in short, expected to smoke cigarettes, and it is added that the rent of 1s. per week per machine may even be provided by the 'bus companies' servants' purchases alone. Naturally, the success of the Sweetmeat Automatic Supply Company is brought forward, but this is not due to selling cigarettes. We see no greater prospect of this company earning much in the way of dividends on its capital of £100,000 in £1 shares than other similar companies had before they passed away.

COPPER ESTATES OF WESTERN AUSTRALIA, LIMITED.

For £60,000 in shares and £15,000 in cash, out of a capital of £100,000 in £1 shares, the company acquires the Wanerenooka Copper Mine, and an option to purchase other copper estates in the same neighbourhood situate near the township of Northampton, Western Australia, 34 miles north of the Port of Geraldton, the line from which runs to within half-a-mile of the properties. As far back as 1842, copper and lead lodes are said to have been opened up on the property, but the high cost of cartage, the gold discoveries offering greater inducements, and the low price of copper, suspended further development. Plant capable of raising 100 tons of ore per day is being erected, and on the basis of each ton containing 15 per cent. of copper, an output of 300 tons per week would result in a profit of £52,500 per annum. That such would prove the actual result may well be doubted, and it is an easy matter to build up a fine estimate with copper standing at over £50 per ton.

ATKINSONS' BREWERY, LIMITED.

Company takes over as a going concern Atkinsons', Limited, of the Ashton Park Brewery, Birmingham, to which is to be added 80 licensed houses. The business was started in 1878, and was sold to the old company in 1890. The capital subscribed and paid up was then only £60,000, and there was an issue of 5 per cent. debentures to the amount of £70,000. Farebrother, Ellis, & Co. now give an unsatisfactory certificate, as they often do, merely stating their opinion of the value of the brewery, licensed houses, and other properties to be acquired at the lump sum of £505,000, while other assets make up another £30,549. The share capital of the new company is £350,000, in 20,000 5 per cent. cumulative preference of £10 each, and 30,000 ordinary shares of £5 each. The former are offered at par, with an issue of £275,000 4 per cent. irredeemable first mortgage debenture stock, offered at 103. The preference and debenture stock interest will require £21,000, whereas the last three year's profits have been only £12,655, £15,736, and £19,150, without deduction for interest on debentures and loans, income-tax, or directors' fees. The purchase price for this choice gem is £625,000, in addition to the premium on the debenture issue, and the vendor, Thomas Edkins, would like to take £483,250 in cash. Of course much profit is expected from the new houses, much more in fact than from the old business itself, but the prospectus is rather an impudent production, and the concern should certainly be left alone.

THE SMELTING CORPORATION, LIMITED.

Applications are invited for 250,000 shares of £1 each, out of a total capital of £600,000, the vendors, the Burnham Syndicate, Limited, taking 350,000 shares, out of a total purchase price of £430,000 which is a promising sign. Company is formed to acquire from the Burnham Syndicate their business and patent rights for the treatment of refractory ores of silver, lead, zinc, gold, &c. A smelting plant has been at work at Swansea for nearly two years, but continuous operations did not commence until after January 31, 1897. A lease of a site on the Manchester Ship Canal is to be taken and plant erected at a cost of £90,000, and additions are to be made to the Swansea Works costing £10,000, so that the working capital left will be £60,000. The purchase price seems a very high figure to give mainly for patents, for there is nothing more to go upon than just a statement that during the eleven months ended December last, 10,872 tons of ore were treated at a smelting profit of £9,521, exclusive of profit to be obtained from the desilverising of the lead. It is true that a dividend of 20 per cent. is spoken of, and that the Right Hon. William Lidderdale is chairman of the board, but an investment in the shares seems, nevertheless, attended with a certain amount of risk.

COSTA RICA ELECTRIC LIGHT AND TRACTION COMPANY, LIMITED.

The object of this company is to supply electric light and electric traction in San José, the capital of Costa Rica, population 35,000 ; and to supply electric light in Cartago, population 18,000. The company takes over from vendor fully paid all the shares of the local company (capital £60,000) owning the existing electric light system in each of the two cities, the net income from the existing installations being £4,800. The share capital is £130,000, in £1 shares, and there is an issue of £130,000 5 per cent. first debentures in bonds at 90 per cent., interest on which is payable January and July. They are repayable at par in 1948, but can be redeemed at any time on six months' notice at 105 per cent. The vendor takes £107,000 in cash and the whole of the share capital. This leaves only £10,000 for working capital, which seems small enough. To meet the interest on the debentures, the revenue is not yet sufficient, and the share capital being of the same amount as the debenture issue, and wholly in the hands of the vendor, makes the security very thin.

ELECTRIC INSTALLATION COMPANY, LIMITED.

The object of this undertaking is to make installations of electric plant for lighting or other purposes in public institutions, hotels, factories, &c., on the hire-purchase system or on rental. Capital, £100,000 in £1 shares, all of which is offered for subscription. The initial outlay will thus be avoided, and the company proposes to supply customers finding their own power with a complete installation at a rental approximating the average yearly gas bill. The idea is not at all a bad one, and will no doubt be readily adopted by large firms, but we take it that some time will elapse before the company becomes a good dividend-payer.

Company Reports and Balance-Sheets.

*** *The Editor will be much obliged to the Secretaries of Joint Stock Companies if they would kindly forward copies of Reports and Balance-Sheets direct to the Office of* THE INVESTORS' REVIEW, *Norfolk House, Norfolk-street, W.C., so as to insure prompt notice in these columns.*

RIO DE JANEIRO CITY IMPROVEMENTS COMPANY.—It is useless to criticise the results of last year, as this company has just effected an arrangement with the Government whereby the accounts will be settled at a fair rate of exchange. The necessary measure passed both Chambers last December, but the Ministry of Public Works has not yet arranged the details of this important change. As it is the accounts for last year reflect the effect of an average working exchange of 7⅜d. as against a nominal exchange of 27d. After allowing for doubtful debts and loss in exchange the revenue was £127,611, and working expenses, debenture interest, and sinking fund charges, came to £128,866, leaving a loss of £1,155 on this account. In addition, £13,600 of debentures had to be redeemed, so that the company was £14,854 to the bad on the year. As £8,812 was brought in, the debit balance was only £6,041. This was written off the reserve, which will now stand at £68,958. Up to date

£187,200 of the debentures have been redeemed, and the amount outstanding is only £597,800. The company appears also to have substantial resources outside its reserve fund, so that if once the revenue was placed upon a fair basis, a change for the better ought to supervene. But, unfortunately, the revenue comes to a great extent directly from the Central Government, and, however, willing that institution may be to play the honest citizen, we are rather doubtful wheth er it has the power.

CITY OFFICES COMPANY.—The revenue of this company improved last year, and, after meeting working charges, the net profit was £10,411 as against £9,504 in 1896. This allowed of a dividend of 12s. per £36 10s. paid share, as against 11s. per share for 1896, and 10s. per share for 1895. There has thus been a fair improvement in the dividends of this company, and further evidence that it has done well is set forth in the schedule of portions of properties unlet, which amounted at the end of last year to £505, as against £995 in 1896, and £1,125 in 1895. At the same time the interest charges have been reduced by dint of rearrangements, so that they practically rest upon a 3½ per cent. basis. It may therefore be assumed that the profits of last year are pretty well the best that can be looked for, and it will be a wise step if the board cuts off some of the redundant capital. The present dividend, well as it compares with former years, represents about 1⅝ per cent. upon the paid-up capital, and this paltry return, combined with the £3 10s. per share of uncalled capital, renders the shares a poor investment. To recover the old capital is well-nigh beyond the range of hope, and to recognise this fact would lead to a healthier balance-sheet. As it is this account has improved of late years, but the properties must stand far above their intrinsic value.

WILLANS & ROBINSON, LIMITED.—After setting aside £5,277 for depreciation, the profits last half year, including £1,859 brought forward, were £10,053. A dividend at the rate of 8 per cent. per annum is proposed as against 7 per cent. in previous half-years. The sum of £2,000 is carried to Debenture Redemption Fund, and £1,500 to the reserve fund, leaving £2,012 to be carried forward. The reserve fund will then amount to £13,646, and the Debenture Redemption Fund to £6,000, all of which is separately invested. The properties appear to be carefully written down, and the trading balances are well in favour of the company.

EXPRESS DAIRY COMPANY.—This prosperous company made further progress last year, and without further addition to capital the net profit was £2,400 higher at £11,375. This enabled £1,316 to be written off expenditure on new branches, reducing that item in the balance-sheet to £1,593. The sum of £2,000 is placed to reserve, as against £1,000 last year, and the dividend is increased ½ per cent. to 6 per cent. The balance forward is then raised £465 to the substantial total of £3,936, and with the reserve of £8,000 forms a substantial backing to the company. Four more refreshment depôts have been opened in the year, all in the City, and the company has now more of these depôts than dairy branches. As the expenditure upon their foundation is practically taken out of revenue, the profits ought to further improve.

DIRECT SPANISH TELEGRAPH COMPANY.—In the past year the revenue amounted to £27,575, or a decrease of £2,878 on 1896, but in that latter year the increase was nearly £5,000, so that progress on the whole continues. A part of the decline, too, is accounted for by the reductions of rates and the mode of counting the words in telegrams adopted at the Budapesth Conference, which came into force on July 1 last. Such improvements in the tariff are bound to lead to better business later on, although the present year, which will have the reductions in force for the whole twelve months, can hardly be expected to see the lost ground recovered. Ordinary working expenses were £223 higher, but there were no repairs to cable; while in the previous year the reserve fund had been repaid the amounts previously taken from it for revenue purposes in earlier years. Consequently after meeting all charges the net balance was £12,975, as against £10,818 in 1896. The usual sum of £5,000 was placed to reserve, and the dividends of 10 per cent. on the preference and 4 per cent. on the ordinary shares declared, leaving a balance of £2,489. It appears that in 1894, the construction of a new breakwater at Bilbao had caused the company to expend £3,514 in removing the shore-end of the Falmouth Bilbao Cable to a point outside the new breakwater. This sum has since been carried as an asset in the balance-sheet, but the Spanish courts having refused to make the Harbour authorities responsible for the amount, the board has decided to write it off. Accordingly the balance of £2,489 is used for this purpose, and the remaining £1,025 is taken from reserve, and will be repaid to it out of the revenue of future years. The reserve amounts now to £44,769, and is wholly invested in high class securities, the interest upon which goes directly to this fund. As the cost of cables, land lines and stations only comes to £141,847, this is a good percentage, especially as a Debenture Redemption Fund of £4,062 has already been accumulated towards the extinction of the £30,000 of 4½ per cent. debentures.

SUNNYGAMA (CEYLON) TEA ESTATES COMPANY.—Although this company had forty-three more acres of old tea than in 1896, the out-turn fell off 41,000 lb., owing to an unfavourable season. A rather better average was obtained for the portion sold in London, but the gross revenue was £735 lower at £19,825, and expenditure was considerably higher owing to the advance in the value of the rupee, and so the net revenue was only £3,951 as against £6,213 in 1896. As this company has established no reserves, the only course was to reduce the dividend, and the ordinary shares, therefore, receive 6 per cent. as against 12 per cent. for 1896. To make matters worse the directors continue their old policy of adding the cost of new extensions and permanent buildings to capital, and, consequently, have issued £10,000 more of six per cent. preference shares, which with the £10,000 of 6 per cent. debentures, makes £25,000 of prior capital with a charge of £1,500 per annum. The outlook for the £50,000 of ordinary capital is, therefore, exceedingly black, unless the board alters its policy post-haste.

OTTOMAN RAILWAY FROM SMYRNA TO AIDIN.—In the past half-year this company earned £221,680, or £2,951 more than in the second half of 1896. Working expenses, however, rose still more rapidly, and the net profit of £131,455 was £2,905 less. Owing to a better result in the previous half-year a dividend of 22s. per share, or 5½ per cent., was declared, as against 16s. per share, or 4 per cent. for 1896, and £10,903 was carried forward, as against £12,502 a year ago. This reduction in the balance is rather rash, as the board states that receipts in the current half-year show a considerable decrease owing to the winter being exceptionally severe, and the Anatolian Railway is reported to be making great exertions to divert merchandise coming to the head of the company's line to its own system. Unfortunately the application of the company for an extension of the line has not yet been acceded to, although it is being vigorously pressed at Constantinople.

BRITISH AMERICAN LAND COMPANY.—The boom which has been going on in Canada has had its influence upon the receipts of this company, and the net revenue for last year came to £12,473, or £2,619 above that of 1896. The "A" shares, therefore, received their maximum dividend of 25s. per share, and £4,000 was set aside to purchase "B" shares. The revenue of the year benefited from the disposal of 2¼ acres in Sherbrooke for the large sum of £3,393, mainly due to a sale of water-power to the Local Street Railway Company, and the company has also been fortunate in getting rid of some of its uncultivated land. As the "B" shares stand about £7 for the £24 share, the £4,000 of capital to purchase them should cancel about £13,000, and the share capital will then be reduced to about £100,000, against which assets to the amount of £138,000 will be held. Of this, £32,851 is represented by 105,606 acres of uncultivated land, £29,991 by land, buildings, &c. at Sherbrooke City, £49,361 by instalments due for land sold, and the balance is made up of investments, cash, and a saw mill. It is a very satisfactory statement, and the "B" shares may possibly rise in value, but as they bear no interest the inclination to buy them should not be carried to an extreme point.

THE NEW ZEALAND JOINT STOCK AND LAND CORPORATION, LIMITED.—In their report for the year 1897, the directors state that the company had a prosperous year, and earned net profits amounting to £73,518 by their finance business, of which £53,013 has been realised in cash, the remainder being represented by profits on shares not yet sold, which seems to be rather an imprudent mode of reckoning things. However, out of the profits, interim dividends at the rate of 30 per cent. per annum have been paid between December 31, 1896, and June 30, 1897, and a final dividend at the same rate is now declared, making 30 per cent. for the year on the ordinary shares. Such a splendid return enables the founders' shares, amounting to £5,000, to receive £13,752 as their little slice, or a dividend of £2 15s. per £1 share, that is 275 per cent. We can guess pretty well what this brilliant finance will end in, and it is noticeable that the balance-sheet at the end of the year showed cash in hand amounting to only £1,906, while amongst the assets were advances upon security from account to account 31,000 shares valued at £60,500, and uncompleted ventures at cost £16,000. We need not criticise.

THE CANADIAN PACIFIC RAILWAY COMPANY.—This company does not yet see fit to forward its annual report to the office of the *Investors' Review*, and therefore we are a week late in noticing it. It is a good report, and the company did an excellent and profitable business especially for the last eight months of the year. Gross earnings were $24,049,535, working expenses $13,745,759, and net earnings from the operation of the roads $10,303,776. To this various items of receipts from interest, wholly or partly received from subsidiary lines have to be added, making the entire net income $10,644,482. From this fixed charges to the amount of $6,783,367 have to be deducted, and after paying these and the preference stock dividend for the year, the ordinary stock has received an aggregate of 4 per cent. for the whole year, namely 1½ per cent. in October last and 2½ per cent. payable next week. After all these distributions have been met $897,088 is left to carry forward. Working expenses took 57·16 per cent of the gross earnings as compared with 60·80 per cent. in 1896. The report states that the company has already benefited, and expects still further to benefit, from the discovery of extraordinary deposits of gold in the Canadian Yukon territory. We fear this will be but a transitory source of prosperity, and the prospect opened up by the construction of a line of railway through the Crows' Nest Pass is much more encouraging to the hope of permanent benefit. In making this railway the Dominion Government is interested to the extent of $11,000 per mile, which is to be its contribution, apparently without compensation from the company, or return of any kind. In every direction the company is launching out with large capital expenditure, buying up little bits of line, acquiring charters of roads nobody but it could build or make good use of, and so on. Considerable prospective increases in the capital account are therefore to be expected, but if it be true that the coal deposits to be made accessible by the Crows' Nest Railway are of such an extraordinary character that the aggregate thickness of the beds in the immediate vicinity of the line exceeds 125 ft. in coal of excellent quality, and capable of furnishing superior coke, then the heaviest portion of its immediate fresh capital expenditure should amply justify itself in the course of time. Besides extending its land lines the company has bought steamers for some of the inland lakes, and to carry on traffic in the Pacific between Vancouver and Victoria and Yukon. All this kind of outlay for traffic has required capital outlay on rolling stock, besides the building of a great grain elevator at Owen Sound, and another at Fort-William. On the whole, however, the immediate prospects of the company are better than we have known them to be for a long time back.

BRITISH LAW FIRE INSURANCE COMPANY.—For the year 1897 this company received a net premium income of £57,256, being an increase of £2,126 on 1895. The net losses came to £29,768, being at the rate of 51·9 per cent. of the premium income. Expenses and commissions amounted to about £25,000, or almost 45 per cent. of the premium income, so that there was very little margin on the year's business. The company, however, received £3,670 from dividends and interest, and £834 as profit on the sale of investments. Adding these amounts to the small balance left on the current business, there was a sum of £5,101 available for distribution, and £4,000 of this has been placed to reserve raising it to £27,000. A dividend at the rate of 3 per cent. for the year is paid out of the balance, and £1,101 is left to carry forward. It is stated in the revenue account that a substantial amount of the management expenses, consisting mainly of directors' fees, has been given up, so that nothing is apparently wanting on the part of the management to make the business prosperous.

THE EXPLORATION COMPANY.—The reports of this company are always of a meagre character, but this time there is a chastened spirit about the document that is well in consonance with the facts. For the whole year ended December 31 last, the gross profits amounted to £180,733, as against £147,924 for the six months and eleven days dealt with in the previous report. General expenses, directors' fees and percentages, and investigation expenses come to £36,941, and there is that first cloud, "the size of a man's hand," in the shape of £1,204 written off for depreciation. We wonder what this item will grow to when stock is taken later on. The balance of £158,754 is left, which permits of a dividend of 12½ per cent. as against 20 per cent. at the corresponding period last year. The sum of £20,754 is then carried forward, as compared with £14,744 at the end of 1895. The board speaks with confidence about their investments in the Central London Railway and two Electric Traction companies, and, no doubt, they will, with time, do well by those investments; but if the mining ventures of the concern account largely for the £1,353,197 of sundry investments in the balance-sheet, we rather pity shareholders their future prospects. It is, however, essentially a marketing company, and perhaps the unhealthy mines it created have only a sentimental interest to its board. Needless to say no lists of investment is furnished, so that there are no means of ascertaining how matters stand. We note premises have been written up a bit, but loans against security and both credit and debit balances are materially lower. After the dividend is paid the investments will represent about 80 per cent. of the assets, and the company is therefore more and more dependent upon their successful realisation.

NATAL LAND AND COLONIZATION COMPANY.—Owing to a reduction in the land sales, as a consequence of the rinderpest plague, the revenue of this company was £779 less at £22,350. Interest charges were rather lower and so the net profit of £14,341 was only £387 below that of 1896. After paying preference dividend the ordinary shares received 3¼ per cent. or 4 per cent. more than for 1896, and £944 is carried forward. The reserve fund remains at £7,000, while the debenture and loan debt is a little lower at £43,150. The assets appear to be of a good character, the only item needing reduction being £2,559 for "fencing expenditure." The 385,728 acres of land, house and town properties, &c., valued at £422,063, ought to be well worth the book estimate if it is even only moderately well situated.

BANDARAPALA CEYLON COMPANY.—This small tea company had 416 acres of tea in full bearing in 1897, as against 286 acres in 1896, or an increase of about 45 per cent. Yet owing to a lower price for tea and heavier working expenses, chiefly through the rise in the rupee, the net profit of £3,037 was £394 less than in 1896. The dividend of 10 per cent. is maintained, but only £295 is written off for depreciation, as against £500 a year ago, and the balance forward of £66, is £374 less. Considerable extensions are in progress, but the cost is all placed to capital, and consequently there is a considerable increase in the shares and debentures issued. The tiny reserve of £1,512 is invested outside.

THE IMPERIAL (FIRE) INSURANCE COMPANY.—The board of this company does not publish an annual report, and only circulates an abstract of its balance-sheet privately. This is an old habit and a pity, as the company has by no means anything to be ashamed of, although it did not do so well last year as in the two immediately preceding. Its 1897 premium income was £611,279, and of this £356,046 or 58·25 per cent. went to pay losses. Expenses of management, commissions, &c., took about £226,000 more, or almost 37 per cent. of the premiums, so that altogether 95·21 per cent. of the income of the year disappeared in losses and current working charges. Out of £611,279 received only £29,250 remained as profit at the year's end. To this has to be added nearly £56,000 received as interest, &c., making the entire available balance some £85,000. Of this, £10,000 odd is added to the general reserve, raising it to £675,110. The remainder is apparently absorbed in dividends on the paid-up capital of £300,000, amounting to 25 per cent. per annum, but these dividends will only be declared at the meeting of proprietors. Besides the general reserve there is a varying special reserve against unexpired notes amounting this time to £203,592. In 1896 the percentage of losses and expenses to premiums was 90·75, and in 1895, 90·49. Last year was therefore poor, but the company is rich and powerful.

MANCHESTER FIRE ASSURANCE COMPANY.—The net premiums received by this company in 1897, including those from the "America" Company of New York amounted to £850,600, or £3,120 more than in 1896. The combined losses, including full provision for all unsettled claims, came to £491,755, or say 57·8 per cent. of the net premium income. Expenses of all kinds, including home, foreign, and colonial taxes and agents' commissions, amounted to £297,000, or almost 35 per cent. of the premium income, so that altogether about 92 per cent. of that income was absorbed by the current outgoings of the year. Nevertheless, nearly £62,000 remained as net receipts to be added to the £24,159 received from interest, &c., on investments. Adding a balance of £17,102 from the "American" of New York account, the amount available for allocation is £103,215, out of which the directors paid an interim dividend of 2 per cent. per share last September, and they declare a further dividend at the same rate now, together with a bonus of 2s. per share, making in all 15 per cent. for the year. After making various other provisions and payments a balance of £47,609 is left to be added to the funds for the year. The capital and reserve funds now amount to £801,391, and have increased to this figure from £463,699 at December 31, 1892. The company's funds appear to be well invested.

CANADA NORTH-WEST LAND COMPANY, LIMITED.—The year 1897 has been more satisfactory for this company than the previous one, as it has sold nearly 39,000 acres, an increase of 18,000 acres over 1896. The average price received per acre was a little less, \$5·40 against \$5·69; expenses per acre, \$0·15, a decrease of \$0·06. Profit and loss shows a balance of \$5,535 to the debit, compared with \$21,300 in 1896. The directors speak hopefully of the present year, and may have reason to do so, but the thing is not fat at best.

THE BANK OF AFRICA did very well during the second half of last year all things considered. It made a profit of £43,466, compared with £39,571 in the corresponding half, of which £31,500 is used in paying a dividend of 6s. 3d. per share and a bonus of 1s. 3d. per share, being together at the rate of 12 per cent. per annum, as in 1896. The amount added to reserve is increased from £7,500 to £10,000, and the contribution to Pension Fund from £1,000 to £1,500, and there is still the larger balance of £9,325 to be carried forward. Reserve now stands at £325,000, or 65 per cent. of the paid-up capital, and the bank's securities have been increased by £23,000 to £424,326. Deposits at £3,905,000 are down £473,000, and on the assets side there is a corresponding reduction of £319,000 in loans and advances, but bills discounted show the satisfactory increase of £40,000 to £935,000. The steady progress of the bank's business has continued, though the announcement that the branches at Klerksdorp, Newcastle, and Roodepoort have been closed is not very cheering.

THE LONDON BANK OF MEXICO AND SOUTH AMERICA did much better last year than in 1896, the profits reaching £64,404, including £10,907 brought forward, whereas in the preceding year the profits with a similar amount brought in were only £42,908. The dividend, however, is kept at 8s. per share for the year, or 8 per cent., £20,000 of the increased profit being added to reserve, which is raised to £170,000, against which investments in London amount to £192,000, being, somewhat strangely, nearly £30,000 less than a year ago. The directors have been able to sell at a satisfactory profit some of the bank's holding of shares in the Banco de Londres y Mexico, and this item now stands in the balance-sheet at £239,583. On the other hand, the amalgamation effected last June between the Lima branch and the Banco del Callao, has saddled the bank with £75,000 worth of shares in the new bank, the Banco del Peru y Londres, at least that is the figure they stand in the balance-sheet, as investments, at. Current accounts amount to £139,000, and bills payable to £232,000, while a year ago these items together amounted to £896,000. Cash has declined from £300,000 to £52,000, and loans and advances from £219,000 to £187,000. These movements do not denote expansion of business and the shares of the bank hardly seem of the best investment class. Sir Francis Evans has retired from the board after an association with the bank of seventeen years.

CENTRAL URUGUAY RAILWAY COMPANY OF MONTE VIDEO.—The interim report for the second half of last year is not as satisfactory as could be wished. Gross receipts were £18,444 less than in 1896, and the saving in expenses was only £6,753. The result of the working is a disposable balance of £30,138, of which £30,000 is used in paying an interim dividend at the rate of 3 per cent. per annum, or the same as was paid a year ago. Although the decrease in gross receipts was 11·65 per cent., the working expenses amounted to 51·71 per cent., against 49·95 per cent. In explanation of the poor result, it appears that passenger traffic suffered very severely during the first three months of the half-year from the revolution, while the maize harvest last season was almost completely destroyed by locusts, 3,714 tons only having been transported, as against 54,187 tons in the corresponding half-year. In giving 88 for the ordinary stock, the buyer at present gets a return of less than 1¾ per cent., which is far from attractive, but prospects of better times for Uruguay are much more hopeful—though, for how long? Much is hoped from Senor Cuestas, while as regards this company it appears that large areas have again been planted with maize, and the wheat harvest and wool clip have both been good, so that the outlook is considered to have materially improved.

METROPOLITAN ELECTRIC SUPPLY COMPANY.—The revenue of this company in the past year amounted to £138,267 as against £116,459 in 1896, and after meeting all expenses the net balance is £43,721, as compared with £34,191 a year ago. The sum of £15,000 was set aside for depreciation as against £12,000 in each of the two preceding years. Dividends amounting to 6 per cent. for the year or 1 per cent. more than for 1896 are proposed, and £1,774 is carried forward. The number of 8-candle power lamps supplied by the company increased from 308,000 to 360,000, and since the close of the year the number connected has risen to 374,000. After deducting £3,375, the depreciation account stands at £42,895, and the company has also had the benefit of £35,429 received as premiums upon new capital. Therefore, with £845,000 of capital it has spent £850,831 upon the undertaking, has £31,198 invested in high class securities, and has an additional £30,000 to its credit after settling all its trading liabilities. Truly the benefit of accumulations is very apparent in these electric lighting concerns. Unfortunately the company has not settled with its founders shares, a matter of considerable importance now as these shares are entitled to half the surplus profits after 7 per cent. has been paid on the ordinary shares.

D. H. EVANS & CO.—Each year sees the capital of this concern rise, but we are not too sure that the balance-sheet improves with age. The properties, stocks, and fixtures all continue to advance in value at a pace that does not make one feel too comfortable, and when we think of the £371,000 of share, debenture, and mortgage capital, the future must be feared. Last year, however, the company claimed to do well, although it was not generally a good year for bnsiness in this class of trade. Gross profit came to £89,569, and the board could not refrain from bringing into this account £2,452 received as premium upon new shares. After paying expenses and debenture interest, setting aside £3,488 for repairs, renewals, and depreciation, writing £487 off preliminary expenses, and putting £835 to debenture redemption, the balance of £31,975 remains. This allows of 12 per cent. being paid upon the ordinary shares, and £3 per share upon the founders' shares, £1,834 being placed to reserve, and £6,182 being carried forward. The reserve will then amount to £5,531, and the debenture redemption fund to £2,219.

T. R. ROBERTS, LIMITED.—Profits last year amounted to £16,209, after setting aside £1,844 for repairs, and £500 for depreciation. The ordinary shares receive 10½ per cent. in dividends, the management shares £2,627, and the sum of £1,001 is set aside towards redemption of leases, general reserve, and doubtful debts. The general reserve will then amount to £2,000, and the leasehold redemption fund to £1,701. The purchase of the freehold of a part of the property has been effected at a cost of £22,000, and preference shares will be issued to pay this amount.

JONES & HIGGINS, LIMITED.—The profits of this firm of general providers last year were £29,297, as against £28,954 in the preceding year. This allowed of £5,490 being carried to reserve, the declaration of dividends equal to 9½ per cent. upon the ordinary shares, the allotment of £3,250 to the directors and managers, and the carrying forward of £2,616. The reserve will now amount to £19,318 which is a large amount to have accumulated in the short time of this company's existence, and the prosperous state of the finances is shown by the fact that the whole of this is invested in securities. Trading liabilities, in fact, are a mere shadow. At the same time we should like to see a few more details in the profit and loss account, such as allowance for depreciation, repairs, and renewals. No trade secret would be divulged with the information, and as leasehold properties and fixtures, and loose plant form a considerable proportion of the assets, the matter is not of trifling importance. The dividend is ½ per cent. higher than last year, but shareholders should not look for any important increase, as profits have to be divided by three after 7 per cent. is paid in dividend, one-third going to the shareholders, one-third to the directors and managers, and one-third to reserve.

THE NUNDYDROOG COMPANY, LIMITED.—In 1897 this Indian gold mine produced £211,397 worth of gold at a gross cost of £78,532, plus a royalty of £10,570 paid to the Mysore Government. Minor adjustments brought the net income to £123,551. This meant an increase of £43,772 in the receipts, and of £29,364 in the profits. From this depreciation, income-tax, &c., took £29,955, and out of the balances of £93,994 then left, three dividends, 2s. 6d. in July, 3s. in November, and 3s. in the present month, have been or will be paid, making in all 42½ per cent. for year, as against 32½ per cent. in 1896. Out of £25,795 spent on capital account during the year, no less than £23,579 was charged against the year's profit. A slight reduction of 22 grs. per ton in the yield of gold marked the operations of the year, but the proportion is still 1 oz. 1 dwt. per ton, and the condition of the company is altogether a satisfactory one, in spite of the trouble which arose in October last from water in the Deep Levels, a trouble overcome in January—increased pumping power.

THE BUENOS AYRES WESTERN RAILWAY COMPANY has had a very bad time, the falling off in gross receipts for the second half of last year being no less than £64,232, or 18·12 per cent. A very trifling amount was saved in expenses, so the reduction in net profit was £60,881, or 31·54 per cent. This poor showing is due entirely to injury by locusts to the maize crop, as is shown by the fact that the decrease of 235,000 tons in the quantity of maize carried represents a loss in receipts of £64,136, which is almost exactly the difference in gross receipts. In spite of this the cost of working was 54·47 per cent., against 45·55 per cent. in 1896, although everything possible, it is said, was done to keep expenses down. The result is that the available balance is only £66,780, and the dividend has to be lowered from 6s. per share to 3s. 6d. per share, a balance of £5,530 being carried forward.

FRENCH HARVEY STEEL COMPANY.—During 1897 this company received 308,007 francs from licensees an increase of 146,393 francs, the net profit amounted to 289,275. After payment of 5 per cent. to the legal reserve, 5 per cent. interest on the "social" shares, directors' fees, &c., there remained 254,094 francs, out of which 190,050 francs has been set aside for the amortisation of the "social" shares, and 63,350 francs distributed among the 4,950 founders' shares. According to the constitution of this company, its social shares will rank equally with the founders' when all their uncalled capital has been provided for out of profits and the cash paid on them returned. The directors state that they have still to collect a balance of 730,000 francs as royalties on orders received, but not complete during 1897. Further orders are expected this year, so this little company ought to do well.

The Produce Markets.

GRAIN.

The Wheat Market has been weak throughout the week. English buyers were especially reserved. Little or nothing was done at Mark-lane; but there is now a good Continental demand, which resulted on Wednesday in 3d. advance on white sorts. The following sales are reported;—The Alice A. Leigh, 20,320 qr., Walla-Walla, February 17, at 35s. 7½d.; the Howard D. Troop, 15,524 qr., November 13, at 37s.; the Bandeneira, 13,123 qr., November 12, at 37s.; and the Zinita, 11,000 qr., shipping or shipped, at 34s. For the arrived Californian, Olivebank, 38s. is asked, and for the Inveresk 38s. is bid. For November 38s. is offered and this price will buy December. A steamer of 13,000 qr., No. 1 Northern Spring, March-April 15, sold at 38s. Manitoba, April-May, is offered at 39s. Maize steady as a rule. Barley dull in early part of the week, and there was a decline of 3d. per bin. On Wednesday, however, the market showed more steadiness. Oats quiet with rather a downward tendency. Wheat options ⅛d. to ⅜d. up. At Liverpool, spot parcels in quiet demand, but steady. On Wednesday Red American futures on American advices gained ¼d. per cautel at the opening, but soon after lost half the advance. Market inactive at first, but strengthened later on a renewed Continental demand for cargoes. The market further improved on higher opening cables, but later advices being disappointing a quiet tone prevailed at the close, with values ¼d. to ⅜d. per cental dearer.

OFFICIAL CLOSING VALUES (100lb. deliveries—March 23).

	March.	May.	July.	Sept.	Dec.
Red American Wheat	7·8¾	7·3½	7·1¼	6·7	6·6⅞

COTTON.

There has been no particular movement in cotton during the week. The spot market has been quiet, with occasional spurts of activity, and an easy undertone. In American, at Liverpool, on Wednesday a fair business was done, but at slight concessions. Brazilian was quiet, and Surat neglected without change in values. Egyptians were in better demand at the recent reduction in prices. Futures opened 1 point lower owing to discouraging cable advices, and varied but little in the forenoon, business being dull until the last hour, when America again appeared as a seller, and caused a further slight recession, the close being quiet at 1 to 1½ point decline on the day. Reports from Manchester are all of almost unmitigated dulness. There has been a small trade for Calcutta, but no improvement for Bombay, while for China staples some orders are reported. Cloth prices, as a rule, are unchanged, and holders are confident. In New York there has been constant fluctuation, but on Wednesday the fall was considerable under "bear" hammering war rumours, and selling by both "bulls" and "bears." Towards the end a partial recovery took place. The Southern markets were weaker, with declines of 1/16d. at Galveston, Norfolk, and Memfliss.

NEW YORK CLOSING VALUES.

	Spot.	Mar.	April.	May.	June.	July.	Aug.	Sept.	Oct.	Nov.	Dec.	Jan.
Mar. 23 ..	6 5/32	5·81	5·81	5·85	5·86	5·89	5·90	5·51	5·91	5·91	5·92	5·94

WOOL.

The second series of colonial wool sale will close on April 1. The attendance of buyers continues large, and competition is strong and widespread. Messrs. Jacomb, Son & Co., in their yesterday's circular say:—"As regards merino wools, scoureds are in exceptional demand and show a rise of nearly 10 per cent. upon January rates, the advance being more particulary marked in the case of medium qualities. In greasy descriptions, notwithstanding the lack of support from representatives of the U.S.A., who were much in evidence for these last sales, the better classes rule now fully up to prices then current, with occasionally a fractional advance, medium and inferior sorts are 7½ per cent. dearer. Pieces and broken are most keenly competed for at the full advance. Cross-bred wools, which opened in not such strong demand as of late, have since somewhat improved; fine descriptions share in the advance noted for merinos to the extent of fully 5 per cent., medium sorts sell steadily at late rates, but coarse and lower qualities are about 5 per cent. under last auction currency. Lamb's wool, when free, meets slightly enhanced values, but burry and faulty such are sensibly in buyers' favour. Slipped parcels of cross-breds character are not in large supply and show but little change. Merinos reflect the better tone noticeable above. Cape and Natal wools have also shared in the improvement noticed in Australasian; better descriptions of grease are about 5 per cent. dearer, and medium to good scoureds are fully as dear as late sales with an occasional advantage to the seller."

METALS AND COAL.

Copper has continued strong throughout the week, several advances in price having taken place. On Wednesday, however, the improvement received a check, and a decline of 1s. 3d. took place early in the day. Some 750 tons sold, cash and end March, £51, the latter date and April 14, £51 1s. 3d., while three months was bought at £51 7s. 6d. and £51 6s. 3d. The tone became weaker in the afternoon, when another 200 tons changed hands in three months at £51 3s. 9d. and £51 5s., the market closing steady, with further sellers at the higher figure, which is a decline of 3s. 9d. on the day.

SETTLEMENT PRICES.

	Mar. 23.	Mar. 16.	Mar. 9.	Mar. 2.	Feb. 23.	Feb. 16.
	£ s. d.	£ s. d.	£ s. d.	£ s. d.	£ s. d.	£ s. d.
Copper ..	50 17 6	50 12 6	50 7 6	50 7 6	49 17 6	49 10 0

The activity in the Glasgow pig-iron market has been less during the last few days. Still, a good business has been done, and the outlook is excellent. On Wednesday not more than 10,000 tons changed hands. Prices remained steady. Rather a small business at Middlesbrough, but Birmingham cheerful, and the demand at Wolverhampton is well supported, new orders to hand equalling those near completion.

SETTLEMENT PRICES.

	Mar. 23		Mar. 16		Mar. 9.		Mar. 2.		Feb. 23.		Feb. 16.	
	s.	d.	s.	d.	s.	d.	s.	d.	s.	d.	s.	d.
Scotch	46	0	48	4½	46	1½	46	6	46	3	45	7½
Cleveland ..	40	1½	40	9	40	4½	40	10½	40	10½	40	7½
Hematite ..	49	0	48	6	49	1½	49	6	49	1½	43	9

Small business in coal done in the London Exchange, but in the North and in Wales the business is large and extending. The trouble about the Welsh sliding scale looks somewhat gloomy, a deadlock having been produced by the refusal of the men to grant plenary powers for the settlement of the quarrel to their representatives, and the employers refusing to renew negociation unless the men's representatives had those powers. Official quotations in London are 15s. and 14s., usual terms in the pool, for Hetton Wallsend and Lyons respectively. Since Monday, 23 coal-laden vessels have been reported as arrived in the Thames. Inland trade was more or less unsatisfactory, some classes of coal being rather pressed for sale, while other descriptions remain steady. The business in steam coal does not present any new phase. Best West Yorkshire, 9s. 9d. to 10s.; Barnsley selected, 8s.; soft nuts, 6s. 6d.; Sheffield silkstones, 7s. 6d. to 8s.; best Derby black shale, 9s. to 9s. 3d.; North Derby Tupton, 7s. to 7s. 3d.; Erewash brights, 6s. 9d. to 7s. 9d.; nuts, 6s. 6d. to 7s. 6d.

SUGAR.

Little can be said about sugar. The dulness continues, especially in beet. Futures dull, and prices still in buyers' favour. Cane kinds quiet and unchanged.

Mr. Czarnikôw, in his yesterday's circular, thinks "there is no doubt that certain outside influences have had the effect of inducing greater caution, notwithstanding that statistically the position is not unfavourable, and is likely to improve as the year proceeds."

TEA AND COFFEE.

Spot market for coffee more active in the beginning than towards end of week. Sales at auction not so steady, except for finer qualities. Rates unchanged. Futures weak and inactive. Jamaica, 1s. to 2s. lower. Colombian chiefly bought in. East India, bold common greenish foxy to fine blue, 77s. to 108s.; low to good middling, 75s. to 91s. 6d.; smalls, 44s. 6d. to 69s. 6d.; peaberry, 94s. to 111s. Colombian, good small green mixed, 40s.; peaberry, 80s. 6d. Jamaica, fine ordinary green, 44s.; good to fine greenish, 30s. to 35s. September Santos sold at 28s. 9d.

There was brisker competition at the tea auctions both on Tuesday and Wednesday. On the latter day 4,000 packages Indian, and 500 Java were sold, and previous prices fully maintained. Terminal market for China and for Indian quiet and unchanged. Good common black Congou: March, $4\frac{3}{8}$d.; April, $4\frac{3}{8}$d.; May, $4\frac{3}{8}$d.; June, $4\frac{3}{8}$d. Indian—Type 1: March, 7d.; April $7\frac{1}{16}$d.; May, $7\frac{1}{16}$d. Indian—Type 2: March. $6\frac{1}{8}$d.; April, $6\frac{1}{8}$d.; May, $6\frac{1}{8}$d. Ceylon, March, $7\frac{5}{8}$d.

Next Week's Meetings.

MONDAY, MARCH 28.

American Investment Trust ...	Cannon-street Hotel, noon.
Anglo-Austrian Bank	Vienna.
Bank of China and Japan	Cannon-street Hotel, noon.
Bournemouth and Poole Electric ...	Winchester House, 2 p.m.
Foreign, American, and General Investment	Cannon-street Hotel, 1 p.m.
London Chamber of Commerce ...	Botolph House, 2.30 p.m.
Mersey Railway	Worcester House, 2 p.m.
Metropolitan Railway of Constantinople	1, Walbrook, noon.
United States Trust and Guarantee Corporation	Winchester House, 2 p.m.

TUESDAY, MARCH 29.

Alexander Thom & Co.	Dublin.
City Offices	34, Old Broad-street, 1 p.m.
Crédit Foncier of Mauritius... ...	Cannon-street Hotel, noon.
Direct Spanish Telegraph	Winchester House, 2 p.m.
Law Reversionary Interest... ...	24, Lincoln's Inn Fields, noon.
Leopoldina Railway	Winchester House, noon.
Metropolitan Electric Supply ...	Winchester House, noon.
Ottoman Railway (Smyrna to Aidin)	Winchester House, noon.
Rio de Janeiro City Improvements	Winchester House, 11.30 a.m.
Southend Waterworks	4. Great George-street, S.W., noon.
Tynemouth Gas	North Shields, 3 p.m.

WEDNESDAY, MARCH 30.

Bank of Africa	Cannon-street Hotel, 1 p.m.
Banque Internationale de Paris ...	Paris, 3.30 p.m.
British Shipowners Company ...	Liverpool, noon.
Canada Company	1, East India Avenue, 1.30 p.m.
Eagle Insurance	79, Pall Mall, 1 p.m.
English and Scottish Law Life ...	12, Waterloo Place, 3 p.m.
Exploration Company	Cannon-street Hotel, 2.30 p.m.
Lanarkshire and Ayrshire Railway...	Glasgow, 1 p.m.
London Assurance	7, Royal Exchange, noon.
London Bank of Mexico and South America	Cannon-street Hotel, 12.30 p.m.
Lynton and Barnstaple Railway ...	Guildhall, noon.
Southern Punjaub	70, Cornhill, 1 p.m.
Willans & Robinson	Cannon-street Hotel, 3 p.m.

THURSDAY, MARCH 31.

Bank of Australasia	4, Threadneedle-street, 1 p.m.
International Sleeping Car	Brussels, 2 p.m.
Jones & Higgins	19, Rye-lane, noon.
London Southern Tramways ...	7, Poultry, 1 p.m.
T. R. Roberts	Winchester House, noon.

FRIDAY, APRIL 1.

Bahia and San Francisco (Timbo Branch)	Winchester House, noon.
Nundydroog Gold Mining Company	Cannon-street Hotel, noon.

Dividends Announced.

MISCELLANEOUS.

ANGLO SICILIAN SULPHUR COMPANY, LIMITED.—Interim dividend on the preference shares at the rate of 6 per cent. per annum for the half-year ended January 31st.

AMERICAN INVESTMENT TRUST, LIMITED.—Dividend at the rate of 5 per cent. per annum on both the preferred and deferred stocks for the half-year ended 15th inst. £2'154 carried forward.

DELTA METAL COMPANY, LIMITED.—8 per cent. declared.

ÆRATED BREAD COMPANY, LIMITED.—Interim dividend of 2s. 6d. per share.

LONDON AND SOUTH AFRICAN EXPLORATION COMPANY, LIMITED.—3s. 6d. per share for the quarter ending 31st inst.

VICTORIA AND QUEEN GOLD—6d per share.

T. & R. ROBERTS, LIMITED.—2½ per cent. on the preference shares, making 5 per cent. for the year; and 7 per cent. on the ordinary shares, making 10½ per cent. for the year.

EXPRESS DAIRY COMPANY, LIMITED.—Final dividend of 3s. 6d. per share, making 6 per cent. for the year. £2,000 transferred to reserve, and £3,936 carried forward.

FOREIGN, AMERICAN AND GENERAL INVESTMENTS TRUST COMPANY, LIMITED.—Dividends for the half-year ended March 15, at the rate of 5 per cent. per annum on the preferred stock, and at the rate of 4 per cent. per annum on the deferred. £3,032 carried forward.

HOME AND COLONIAL STORES, LIMITED.—Interim dividend of 3s. per share on the ordinary shares.

ROBEY & CO., LIMITED.—10s. per share dividend, £4,000 added to reserve, and £770 carried forward.

ANGLO-ARGENTINE TRAMWAYS COMPANY, LIMITED.—1s. 6d. per share, which, with the interim paid in October last, makes 3s. per share for the year. £5,000 to be added to reserve and £1,634 carried forward.

R. BELL & COMPANY, LIMITED.—5½ per cent. for the year ending December 31, 1897.

FREEHOLD TRUST COMPANY OF AUSTRALIA, LIMITED.—Interim dividend at the rate of 5 per cent. per annum for the half-year ended December 31.

EXPLORATION COMPANY, LIMITED.—Dividend at the rate of 12½ per cent., 2s. 6d. per share, for the year, leaving £20,754 to be carried forward.

PETER ROBINSON.—Dividend on the ordinary shares at the rate of 12 per cent. per annum; £8,930 added to sinking fund, £10,000 to general reserve, and balance forward of £9,677.

LONDON AND VANCOUVER FINANCE AND DEVELOPMENT.—2s. per share for the year ended January 11.

UNION FINANCIAL SYNDICATE.—Interim dividend of 12s. per share upon the ordinary shares, and of £18 3s. 7d. per share upon the deferred shares.

LONDON AND ORANGE FREE STATE EXPLORATION.—12½ per cent.

DANE'S DISCOUNT COMPANY, LIMITED.—Interim dividend at the rate of 10 per cent. per annum for the three months ended March 31.

PALMER'S STORES, LIMITED.—Interim dividend will shortly be declared at the rate of 10 per cent. per annum on the ordinary shares.

ALLDAYS AND ONIONS' PNEUMATIC ENGINEERING COMPANY, LIMITED.—Interim dividend for the half-year ended january, at the rate of 6 per cent. per annum upon the preference, and 5 per cent. on the ordinary share.

BOOTS, LIMITED.—Quarterly dividend at the rate of 6 per cent. per annum on the preference shares, and 10 per cent. per annum on the ordinary shares.

EASTMAN'S, LIMITED.—Dividend of 8 per cent. in the preference shares. £4,489 carried forward.

DAY DAWN BLOCK AND WYNDHAM GOLD MINING COMPANY, LIMITED.—Interim dividend of 9d. per share.

BREWERIES.

PAGE & OVERTON'S.—Interim dividend on the ordinary share capital at the rate of £10 per cent. per annum for the six months ended February 28.

RAILWAYS.

NORTH-EASTERN OF URUGUAY, LIMITED.—Interim dividend at the rate of 7 per cent. per annum on both the preference and ordinary shares for the half-year ended December 31.

CENTRAL URUGUAY NORTHERN EXTENSION, LIMITED.—Interim dividend of 3s. 6d. per share on the share capital of the company; balance forward of £1,788.

CENTRAL URUAUAY EASTERN EXTENSION, LIMITED.—Interim dividend of 3s. 6d. per share on the share capital of the company (at the rate of 3½ per cent. per annum). £1,768 carried forward.

MEXICAN NATIONAL.—Dividend of 3½ per cent. on second mortgage A bonds.

BUENOS AYRES AND ROSARIO, LIMITED.—Balance dividend at the rate of 3 per cent. per annum on the ordinary stock, making with the interim dividend 2 per cent. for the year.

TRAMWAY AND OMNIBUS RECEIPTS.

For past week:—Belfast, + £214; Calais, − £6; Croydon, − £53; Glasgow, + £327; Lea Bridge, + £109; London & Deptford, − £28; London Southern, + £93; London General Omnibus, + £1,500; London Road Car, + £336; Metropolitan, + £040; North Staffordshire, + £10; South London, + £25; Woolwich & S. E. London, + £26; Provincial, − £8; Southampton, − £15; Wolverhampton, − £12; Sunderland, + £1; Swansea, − £9.

Barcelona, − £179; Bordeaux, − £201; Calcutta, + £237.

Anglo-Argentine, week ending February 21, £230 increase; City of Buenos Ayres, week ending February 21, £508 increase.

Notice to Subscribers.

Complaints are continually reaching us that the INVESTORS' REVIEW cannot be obtained at this and the other railway bookstall, that it does not reach Scotch and Irish cities till Monday, and that it is not delivered in the City till Saturday morning.

We publish on Friday in time for the REVIEW to be at all Metropolitan bookstalls by at latest 4 p.m., and we believe that it is there then, having no doubt that Messrs. W. H. Smith & Son do their best, but they have such a mass of papers to handle every day that a fresh one may well look almost like a personal enemy and be kept in short supply unless the reading public shows unmistakably that it is wanted. A little perseverance, therefore, in asking for the INVESTORS' REVIEW is all that should be required to remedy this defect.

All London newsagents can be in a position to distribute the paper on Friday afternoon if they please, and here also the only remedy is for subscribers to insist upon having it as soon as published. Arrangements have been made that all our direct City subscribers shall have their copies before 4 p.m. on Friday. As for the provinces, we can only say that the paper is delivered to the forwarding agents in ample time to be in every English and Scotch town, and in Dublin and Belfast, likewise, early on Saturday morning. Those despatched by post from this office can be delivered by the first London mail on Saturday in every part of the United Kingdom.

Cheques and Postal Orders should be made payable to CLEMENT WILSON.

The INVESTORS' REVIEW can be obtained in Paris of Messrs. BOYVEAU ET CHEVILLET, 22, Rue de la Banque.

ADVERTISEMENTS.

All Advertisements are received subject to approval, and should be sent in not later than 5 p.m. on Thursdays.

The advertisements of American Life Insurance Offices are rigorously excluded from the INVESTORS' REVIEW, and have been so since it commenced as a Quarterly Magazine in 1892.

For tariff and particulars of positions open apply to the Advertisement Manager, Norfolk House, Norfolk-street, W.C.

To Correspondents.

The EDITOR cannot undertake to return rejected communications. Letters from correspondents must, in every case, be authenticated by the name and address of the writer.

The Investors' Review.

The Week's Money Market.

The market has been better supplied with funds during the past seven days, partly because a little Japanese money has been released, and also because demands have been less. All loans falling due at the Bank of England were at first repaid, and only trifling sums have been borrowed from it within the last day or two, and from the India Council. The rate for day-to-day money has gradually weakened until 2 per cent. is about the general charge, while seven day market loans are quoted $2\frac{1}{4}$ to $2\frac{3}{4}$ per cent., a little harder latterly than earlier in the week.

Discount charges have also naturally eased to a slight extent, but the political uncertainties prevent any important movement. The outbreak once again of the warlike feeling in the United States has caused a relapse in the New York exchange, and the demand for gold on American account is therefore increased with the price of gold quoted 77s. $10\frac{3}{4}$d. to 77s. 11d. per ounce. The market, too, although less immediately dependent upon the Bank of England, is still poorly supplied with funds. End of the month requirements and the Stock Exchange settlement will probably cause the market to renew its borrowings on a considerable scale, and although the first week in April should see it receive a good deal of cash from the Government dividends, and the payment of maturing treasury Bills, the money cannot be called its own, as its debt to the Bank is so large. In any case, discount rates are likely to be maintained at about $2\frac{13}{16}$ to $2\frac{7}{8}$ per cent., and if New York renews its demands upon the stock of gold at the Bank, a revival of the former pressure may easily be experienced. Continental exchanges have fallen back a little during the week, but Paris continues to meet a proportion of the American demand. No important sums have come to our assistance from other quarters, but a few sovereigns have been shipped here from Vienna.

The Treasury Bills for £1,719,700 offered for tender on Wednesday were keenly competed for, the applications amounting to £13,681,000. The whole amount was allotted in twelve months' bills at an average rate of just $2\frac{5}{16}$ per cent. Such a rate should point to an easier market later on, but Treasury Bills and Consols are things by themselves, and each year they become less representative of the tendency in the Money and Stock Markets.

Yesterday's Bank return disclosed how illusory the superficial indications of ease in the Money Market really are. Instead of possessing a greater command over funds, the open market is really poorer, as is shown by the decrease of £1,270,291 in the "other" deposits now down to £35,002,265. The money thus lost to general use as banking credit has gone to pay off debt on "other" securities to the extent of £448,818, and to swell the Government balances by £638,871. These last are now at the altogether excessive total of £19,618,224 and cannot now long remain undepleted. "Other" securities stand at £35,367,392, a good £7,000,000 of which may be taken to represent the moneys the market, one way or another, has obtained from the Bank. The reserve of the Banking Department is lower by £201,811, at £23,515,288, although £141,000 in sovereigns came in from abroad in the course of the week. About £100,000 of this gold, however, went into circulation, together with £246,000 in notes, and this coming week the movement in the same direction will still further temporarily reduce the reserve.

SILVER.

Once again we have a repetition of familiar conditions in this market. The "bear," although perhaps he may be right in his premises, has been too eager to grasp his profit, and so he finds himself an unwilling buyer in a market that is waiting for him to come and fulfil his contracts. The Indian Budget contained no reference to the currency problem at all, and although it has since transpired that a scheme is on foot to push the gold standard on a bit, the news is not definite enough to help the seller of silver who is short. Accordingly, the price of the metal has been put up against him, and the quotation for bars on the spot has risen 3/16d. to 27 7/16d. per ounce, but the forward quotation is only 1/16d. higher, at 25 15/16d. per ounce. At the same time, the Indian demand is better, as the fears about an increased duty have been in a measure allayed, and the price there has risen to 68 for both spot and forward, as against 66½ and 65½ respectively, a week ago. No steadiness, however, can be expected in the market until the intentions of the Indian Government are disclosed. The Budget was disappointing in one respect for the sum proposed to be drawn is £16,000,000, or £3,000,000 above the sum budgeted for a year ago. It had been hoped by the exchange market, that the whole of the borrowings would have been made on this side, and the news has caused the exchange to decline 1/32d. to 1s. 3⅞d. Chinese rates have improved slightly in sympathy with silver, but buying is not possible at present prices.

BANK OF ENGLAND.

AN ACCOUNT pursuant to the Act 7 and 8 Vict., cap. 32, for the Week ending on Wednesday, March 23, 1898.

ISSUE DEPARTMENT.

	£		£
Notes Issued	47,671,610	Government Debt	11,015,100
		Other Securities	5,784,900
		Gold Coin and Bullion	30,871,610
		Silver Bullion	—
	£47,671,610		£47,671,610

BANKING DEPARTMENT.

	£		£
Proprietors' Capital	14,553,000	Government Securities	14,208,979
Rest	3,818,597	Other Securities	35,367,392
Public Deposits (including Exchequer, Savings Banks, Commissioners of National Debt, and Dividend Accounts)	19,618,224	Notes	20,996,155
Other Deposits	35,002,265	Gold and Silver Coin	2,519,133
Seven Day and other Bills	99,573		
	£73,091,659		£73,091,659

Dated March 24, 1898.

H. G. BOWEN, *Chief Cashier.*

In the following table will be found the movements compared with the previous week, and also the totals for that week and the corresponding return last year:—

Banking Department.

Last Year. March 24.		March 16, 1898.	March 23, 1898.	Increase.	Decrease.
£	Liabilities.	£	£	£	£
3,798,722	Rest	3,777,599	3,818,597	40,998	—
17,139,415	Pub. Deposits	18,979,353	19,618,224	638,871	—
38,079,697	Other do.	36,272,556	35,002,265	—	1,270,291
173,841	7 Day Bills	103,921	99,573	—	4,348
	Assets.			Decrease.	Increase.
14,387,883	Gov. Securities	14,153,120	14,208,979	—	55,859
28,710,862	Other do.	35,816,210	35,367,392	448,818	—
28,150,415	Total Reserve	23,717,099	23,515,288	201,811	—
				1,330,498	1,330,498
				Increase.	Decrease.
£		£	£	£	£
26,199,805	Note Circulation.	26,429,470	26,675,455	245,985	—
55⅜ p.c.	Proportion	42⅞ p.c.	43 p.c.	—	—
3 "	Bank Rate	3 "	3 "	—	—

Foreign Bullion movement for week £141,000 in.

LONDON BANKERS' CLEARING.

Week ending	1898.	1897.	Increase.	Decrease.
	£	£	£	£
Jan. 5	222,654,000	174,376,000	48,278,000	—
" 12	144,603,000	127,315,000	17,288,000	—
" 19	171,777,000	156,200,000	15,577,000	—
" 26	134,247,000	118,667,000	15,580,000	—
Feb. 2	194,544,000	174,498,000	20,056,000	—
" 9	137,204,000	129,209,000	8,995,000	—
" 16	184,403,000	162,168,000	22,215,000	—
" 23	132,450,000	131,777,000	673,000	—
March 2	190,157,000	177,852,000	12,305,000	—
" 9	134,490,000	126,182,000	8,308,000	—
" 16	174,377,000	148,937,000	25,440,000	—
" 23	129,828,000	118,578,000	11,250,000	—

BANK AND DISCOUNT RATES ABROAD.

	Bank Rate.	Altered.	Open Market.
Paris	2	March 14, 1895	1⅞
Berlin	3	February 20, 1898	2⅞
Hamburg	3	February 20, 1898	2⅞
Frankfort	3	February 20, 1898	2⅞
Amsterdam	3	April 13, 1897	2⅞
Brussels	3	April 28, 1896	2
Vienna	4	January 22, 1896	3¾
Rome	5	August 27, 1895	3
St. Petersburg	5½	January 23, 1898	5
Madrid	5	June 17, 1896	4
Lisbon	6	January 25, 1891	6
Stockholm	4	March 3, 1898	3½
Copenhagen	4	January 20, 1898	4
Calcutta	12	February 24, 1898	—
Bombay	11	February 24, 1898	—
New York call money	1½ to 2	—	—

NEW YORK ASSOCIATED BANKS (dollar at 4s.).

	Mar. 19, 1898.	Mar. 12, 1898.	Mar. 5, 1898.	Mar. 20, 1897.
	£	£	£	£
Specie	25,856,000	24,812,000	24,026,000	17,106,000
Legal tenders	14,166,000	14,506,000	15,440,000	21,244,000
Loans and discounts	121,456,000	123,572,000	125,652,000	105,274,000
Circulation	2,773,000	2,759,200	2,755,000	3,190,600
Net deposits	137,636,000	139,096,000	141,204,000	114,866,000

Legal reserve is 25 per cent. of net deposits; therefore the total reserve (specie and legal tenders) exceeds this sum by £5,613,000, against an excess last week of £4,544,000.

BANK OF FRANCE (25 francs to the £).

	Mar. 24, 1898.	Mar. 17, 1898.	Mar. 10, 1898.	Mar. 25, 1897.
	£	£	£	£
Gold in hand	74,711,760	74,905,080	75,721,080	76,787,000
Silver in hand	48,672,000	48,521,880	48,484,480	49,086,000
Bills discounted	26,606,760	27,375,280	27,240,040	*40,483,000
Advances	14,663,560	14,665,520	14,761,680	—
Note circulation	147,950,560	149,170,880	149,757,360	144,906,000
Public deposits	6,329,680	5,788,240	5,430,600	8,020,000
Private deposits	17,484,960	16,764,240	17,888,680	18,909,000

Proportion between bullion and circulation 83⅜ per cent. against 82⅜ per cent. a week ago.

* Includes advances.

FOREIGN RATES OF EXCHANGE ON LONDON.

Place.	Usance.	Last week's.	Latest.	Place.	Usance.	Last week's.	Latest.
Paris	chqs.	25'30½	25'30	Italy	sight	26'78	26'73
Brussels	chqs.	25'37	25'35	Do. gold prem.	..	105'67½	105'70
Amsterdam	short	12'09¾	12'10¼	Constantinople	3 mths	110	109'30
Berlin	short	20'48	20'48½	B. Ayres gd. pm.	..	164'70	167'20
Do.	3 mths	20'31½	20'32½	Rio de Janeiro	90 dys.	6 5/16	6 1/16
Hamburg	3 mths	20.31½	20'32½	Valparaiso	90 dys.	17⅝	17 9/16
Frankfort	short	20'48	20'47	Calcutta	T. T.	1/3 15/16	1/3⅞
Vienna	short	12.04½	12'03	Bombay	T. T.	1/3 15/16	1/3⅞
St. Petersburg	3 mths	94.00	94'05	Hong Kong	T. T.	1/10⅜	1/10½
New York	60 dys	4'80⅝	4'81¼	Shanghai	T. T.	2/5⅝	2/5¾
Lisbon	sight	34⅜	34 13/32	Singapore	T. T.	1/10½	1/10 9/16
Madrid	sight	35'47½	35'15				

IMPERIAL BANK OF GERMANY (20 marks to the £).

	Mar. 15, 1898.	Mar. 7, 1898.	Mar. 1, 1898.	Mar. 13, 1897.
	£	£	£	£
Cash in hand	48,690,500	47,989,250	48,155,800	46,335,000
Bills discounted	29,026,650	28,107,950	27,442,600	*30,403,000
Advances on stocks	3,889,800	3,746,650	4,282,200	—
Note circulation	51,392,700	51,058,500	51,092,750	48,347,000
Public deposits	26,679,700	24,558,350	24,705,300	24,706,000

* Includes advances.

AUSTRIAN-HUNGARIAN BANK (1s. 8d. to the florin).

	Mar. 15, 1898.	Mar. 7, 1898.	Feb. 28, 1898.	Mar. 14, 1897.
	£	£	£	£
Gold reserve	30,706,833	30,754,925	30,715,583	30,929,000
Silver reserve	10,426,666	10,402,500	10,407,333	12,619,000
Foreign bills	1,001,833	1,114,750	1,214,333	—
Advances	1,828,416	1,802,000	1,885,833	—
Note circulation	51,250,166	51,004,250	51,008,416	57,754,000
Bills discounted	10,709,000	11,312,583	10,671,916	*14,642,000

* Includes advances.

NATIONAL BANK OF BELGIUM (25 francs to the £).

	Mar. 17, 1898.	Mar. 10, 1898.	Mar. 3, 1898.	Mar. 18, 1897.
	£	£	£	£
Coin and bullion	4,307,600	4,156,040	4,339,520	4,805,020
Other securities	16,629,400	16,601,720	17,024,440	15,561,480
Note circulation	18,015,400	19,023,080	18,000,040	18,178,600
Deposits	3,511,000	3,747,400	3,078,120	3,364,440

BANK OF SPAIN (25 pesetas to the £).

	Mar. 18, 1898.	Mar. 12, 1898.	Mar. 5, 1898.	Mar. 20, 1897.
	£	£	£	£
Gold	9,595,360	9,577,760	9,539,640	8,528,360
Silver	10,864,540	10,860,040	10,874,550	10,863,280
Bills discounted	23,365,280	23,381,120	23,262,360	7,878,840
Advances and loans	5,561,000	5,501,320	5,459,120	9,570,280
Notes in circulation	50,206,280	50,385,600	50,195,240	42,304,240
Treasury advances, coupon account	329,880	313,960	386,760	425,000
Treasury balances	1,971,680	1,526,080	1,483,160	1,186,600

LONDON COURSE OF EXCHANGE.

Place.	Usance.	March 15.	March 17.	March 22.	March 24.
Amsterdam and Rotterdam	short	12·2¼	12·2½	12·2¾	12·2¾
Do. do.	3 months	12·4	12·4½	12·4½	12·4½
Antwerp and Brussels	3 months	25·52½	25·52½	25·50	25·48¾
Hamburg	3 months	20·68	20·68	20·65	20·65
Berlin and German B. Places	3 months	20·69	20·69	20·66	20·66
Paris	cheques	25·35	25·32½	25·30	25·31¼
Do.	3 months	25·48¾	25·47½	25·45	25·45
Marseilles	3 months	25·50	25·47½	25·45	25·47½
Switzerland	3 months	25·72½	25·70	25·65	25·67½
Austria	3 months	12·20	12·18¾	12·16¼	12·16¼
St. Petersburg	3 months	25	25	25	25
Moscow	3 months	24 11/16	24 21/32	24 21/32	24 21/32
Italian Bank Places	3 months	27·10	27·07½	27·02½	27·00
New York	60 days	49 1/16	49 1/16	49 1/16	49 1/16
Madrid and Spanish B. P.	3 months	33	33 1/16	33⅜	33¼
Lisbon	3 months	34 1/16	34⅛	34 1/16	34 1/16
Oporto	3 months	34 1/16	34⅛	34 1/16	34 1/16
Copenhagen	3 months	18·41	18·41	18·41	18·41
Christiania	3 months	18·42	18·42	18·42	18·42
Stockholm	3 months	18·42	18·42	18·42	18·42

OPEN MARKET DISCOUNT.

	Per cent.
Thirty and sixty day remitted bills	2¾
Three months "	2¾
Four months "	2¾
Six months "	2¾
Three months fine inland bills	3
Four months "	3
Six months "	3

BANK AND DEPOSIT RATES.

	Per cent.
Bank of England minimum discount rate	3
" " short loan rates	3
Banker's rate on deposits	1½
Bill brokers' deposit rate (call)	2
" 7 and 14 days' notice	2¼
Current rates for 7 day loans	2½—2¾
" " for call loans	2 —2½

Stock Market Notes and Comments.

These had better be brief this week, as there is really nothing fresh to say, and it is useless to labour again over the old story. The Stock Exchange is passing through a trying period of perplexity and lassitude. For investors this is not altogether an adverse condition. If they will select the securities they purchase carefully and buy moderately they may do well, although trying times appear to lie ahead for some considerable period. Still, this is a better time to buy than to sell, and unless where there are heavy commitments, sustained on credit, which have to be liquidated, and ought to be, we can advise no one to be a seller of proved securities in present circumstances.

One point which may again be referred to is the approaching destruction of the great open market in Paris. After a time this should have the effect of bringing a larger volume of business to the London Stock Exchange, but until the *coulisse* has liquidated its commitments, and transferred its business to Brussels or some other Continental centre, there will be a great want of activity in most of its favoured securities. We must be prepared for this and for a further decline in South African shares as a consequence. The public should pay no attention whatever to the puffs and prophesies of a coming "boom" in this department. The only shares in which a rising market may be still looked for are the few dealt in by the official brokers in Paris, the *agents de change*. Recruited as these will be by, perhaps, twenty of the strongest firms among the outside brokers, they may be powerful enough to raise the prices of Rand Mines, De Beers and Rio Tinto shares in particular, even above their present perilous elevation; but we should not advise people here to take any share in this operation. It will require to be liquidated one day, and we have seen the proud *parquet* of the Bourse humiliated by such a liquidation before now.

Another quarter in which activity, with expanding market and higher prices, may be looked for is that occupied by the shares of the iron, steel, and coal companies at home, which must benefit by the prodigious expenditure on ships of war which is now the fashion with us and with every great Power claiming to be civilised. Essentially this shipbuilding mania is a contractors' affair, and enormous sums of money will flow to mine owners and ironmasters as the consequence of it. Already the excitement has broken out in Sheffield, where the great armoured plate manufacturing firms are situated, and the shares in such companies as Cammell & Co., John Brown & Co., or Vickers' are on the ascendant. Those of many other related concerns ought also to go up in the natural order of things, and the wave of speculation may extend again to Home railway stocks, stagnant though these now are. If prudent people will take note of this movement, and keep their heads, they might be able, in some cases, to get enough out of the movement to pay their increased taxation for a year or two. To ask anybody seriously and deliberately to invest in such shares on the strength of a fashion which must pass away, if civilisation is to retain its foothold on this planet, and mankind to make progress towards something better than the art of mutual destruction, would be to give very irresponsible advice.

The settlement, which begins to-morrow with mining contangos, will again be a ticklish one, and we should not be at all surprised to behold trouble both in the "Kaffir Circus" and in the Australasian section. The latter is, in fact, liquidating, as we write, some weak account or another, in the shares of the London and Globe group principally, and there are a few tissue-paper "fortunes" to crumble around it before long. Stand clear, therefore; and, above all, no "averaging." That is fatal in such markets.

The Week's Stock Markets.

There is very little to be said about markets this week, and the tendency on the whole has been deadly dull, with few features of interest and little or no business. The strained condition of affairs between Spain and the United States has been the principal factor in bringing about the present state of affairs, added, of course, to the fact that the nineteen-day account is still dragging on. Consols have hardly moved all the week, Indian Government securities also remaining fairly steady; but rupee paper declined in sympathy with a weaker exchange, and several Indian railway stocks have also depreciated. The altered condition of the money market has caused a slight recovery in Colonial Government and Home Corporation issues. Bank of England stock is 3½ lower than a week ago.

Highest and Lowest this Year.		Last Carrying over Price.	BRITISH FUNDS, &c.	Closing Price.	Rise or Fall.
113⅜	111	—	Consols 2¾ p.c. (Money)...	111⅝	−⅛
113 7/16	111¼	112⅜	Do. Account (Apl. 1)	111¾	−⅛
106¼	104¾	106	2½ p.c. Stock red. 1905 ...	105⅛	−⅛
363	346	—	Bank of England Stock...	347 x.	−3½
117	113½	116	India 3½ p.c. Stk. red. 1931	114	—
109½	105½	108	Do. 3 p.c. Stk. red. 1948	106	—
96¾	92½	94½	Do. 2½ p.c. Stk. red. 1925	93	—

Almost the only feature in the Home Railway market was a sudden jump of nearly 5 in Hull and Barnsley, due to a statement to the effect that a new arrangement had been made with the North-Eastern Company for the joint working of the Dock at Hull. This scheme apparently is not quite so favourable a one as was at first anticipated, and Hull and Barnsley stock promptly lost about half the previous rise. North-Eastern Consols were not much affected by the news, showing only a slight rise, but other changes in the list are in the downward direction, the Scottish stocks being especially weak in spite of good traffic returns. The disastrous collision on the South-Eastern line at Lewisham caused a slight decline in the deferred stock of that company, but a satisfactory weekly return helped to restore the price to about the old level. Central London shares have again met with a fair amount of support, this being no doubt partly due to the news that Sir Henry Oakley is to be the new chairman. Midland stocks were depressed by sales, caused by the further trouble among the employés, and the other heavy lines were dull in sympathy.

Highest and Lowest this Year.	Last Carrying over Price.	HOME RAILWAYS.	Closing Price.	Rise or Fall.
186 172¾	174	Brighton Def.	174⅜	−⅝
59½ 55½	56⅛	Caledonian Def.	56⅜	−⅜
20⅝ 19	19⅝	Chatham Ordinary	19½	−⅛
77¼ 66	70	Great Central Pref.	69	—
24⅝ 21¾	22	Do. Def.	22	—
124½ 119⅝	121	Great Eastern	121⅛	−½
61¾ 52	52⅜	Great Northern Def.	52¾	−⅜
179⅝ 170⅞	171¼	Great Western	171⅞	−⅜
51¾ 45¼	45¾	Hull and Barnsley	48¾	+2
149¼ 146¼	146¾	Lanc. and Yorkshire	147	−⅛
136⅛ 128¾	130¼	Metropolitan	129	−⅜
31 26¾	27¾	Metropolitan District	27⅞	−⅜
88¾ 83¼	84	Midland Pref.	84	—
95⅝ 85⅛	87¼	Do. Def.	86	−1½
93¼ 90⅛	90¾	North British Pref.	90¾	−⅛
47½ 42¾	43¼	Do. Def.	43⅛	−¾
181½ 173¾	174½	North Eastern	174¼	−½
205⅛ 197¾	198½	North Western	199	−¼
117⅛ 107¾	109½	South Eastern Def.	108⅝	−1⅛
98¾ 91	91⅝	South Western Def.	91½	−⅛

As regards United States Railroad shares, the growing feeling of uneasiness owing to the delay in the appearance of the report of the Committee on the *Maine* disaster, has had a depressing effect, and prices, after advancing moderately for a time, eventually fell away upon the renewal of Home selling. A semi-official announcement states that the *Maine* report will now probably be published on Monday next, and pending the appearance of this momentous document, business has been confined within very narrow limits, and the final quotations are about the worst of the week. Canadian issues have declined in sympathy, and in the absence of fresh particulars regarding the rate war, prices have been marked down steadily day by day. A sub-committee of the Grand Trunk and the American roads interested in the rate-cutting war, is going to Montreal next week to meet the Canadian Pacific officials.

Highest and Lowest this Year.	Last Carrying over Price.	CANADIAN AND U.S. RAILWAYS.	Closing Prices.	Rise or Fall.
14 5/16 11	12	Atchison Shares	11⅜	−⅞
34 23¾	27¼	Do. Pref.	25	−1⅛
15⅝ 11⅛	12¼	Central Pacific	11⅞	−⅜
99⅝ 89	94½	Chic. Mil. & St. Paul	90	−2⅜
14¼ 11	12	Denver Shares	11½	−⅜
54⅛ 43⅞	47	Do. Prefd.	43⅝	−2¼
16⅝ 12½	13⅛	Erie Shares	12⅞	−⅜
44⅛ 33¼	36½	Do. Prefd.	34⅝	−1⅝
62½ 47¾	52¾	Louisville & Nashville	48	−2⅝
14½ 10¾	11¼	Missouri & Texas	11	−½
122¾ 108½	116	New York Central	112½	−2¼
57¾ 44¼	47	Norfolk & West. Prefd.	45⅛	−1⅜
70⅛ 59½	63	Northern Pacific Prefd.	61½	−1⅝
19½ 14¼	15¼	Ontario Shares	14⅝	−⅝
62⅛ 57½	59	Pennsylvania	58¼	−⅝
12½ 8⅛	9¼	Reading Shares	8⅝	−⅝
34⅛ 25⅝	28	Southern Prefd.	25¾	−1¼
37⅛ 24½	28	Union Pacific	25⅝	−1⅜
20¼ 14⅝	15½	Wabash Prefd.	15	−1
30⅛ 22	24	Do. Income Debs.	23½	−⅜
92¾ 81½	86¼	Canadian Pacific	83½	−1½
78⅛ 69⅞	72½	Grand Trunk Guar.	73¼	−1¼
69⅛ 57⅛	63¾	Do. 1st Pref.	65⅜	−1¼
50⅛ 37¼	43½	Do. 2nd Pref.	45⅝	−1
25⅛ 19¼	21¼	Do. 3rd Pref.	21¾	−⅝
105¼ 101½	102	Do. 4 p.c. Deb.	103	—

Business in the Foreign market was almost at a standstill for several days, and prices hardly moved. On Tuesday the tone hardened, but for a very brief period, and the next day saw a sharp break in Spanish "Fours" on heavy French selling, and a consequent relapse in most other leading counters. The Paris Bourse has been dull and uninteresting, although there was a slight increase in business quite at the beginning of the week, on rumours that the stocks not quoted in the *parquet* were going to be exempt from the yearly stamp duties, and that these duties were only to be paid on new issues. In the event of the re-organisation scheme being passed by the French Senate, it is thought that a considerable number of the *coulisse* firms will transfer their seat of operations to Brussels. Apart from the further serious fall in Spanish "Fours," there is no special feature in inter-Bourse stocks. Chinese issues were dull owing to the very poor applications for the new loan, but Greek bonds again show a slight improvement, and Egyptian Unified and Preference are higher. Turning to the South American section, Uruguay 3½ per cent. mark a rise, after being very depressed, and the ministerial crisis in Chile, where the members of the Cabinet have been dismissed, is responsible for the drop of several points in the various Chilian loans. Brazilian bonds weakened still more, owing to the unsettled financial outlook at Rio, and a rise in the gold premium at Buenos Ayres has caused a set-back in the Argentine group.

Highest and Lowest this Year.	Last Carrying over Price.	FOREIGN BONDS.	Closing Price.	Rise or Fall.
94½ 88	88¾	Argentine 5 p.c. 1886	88	−2
92⅝ 87¼	87¾	Do. 6 p.c. Funding	87¾	−1¾
76¾ 69½	71¼	Do. 5 p.c. B. Ay. Water	69¾	−2¼
61¾ 51⅞	59	Brazilian 4 p.c. 1889	54½	−1¾
69⅝ 57½	64	Do. 5 p.c. 1895	58	−2
65 53	60	Do. 5 p.c. West Minas Ry.	54½	−1⅛
108¾ 106½	107¾	Egyptian 4 p.c. Unified	108	+⅛
104¾ 102	104¼	Do. 3½ p.c. Pref.	104¼	—
103 102	102½	French 3 p.c. Rente	102½	—
44 34½	41	Greek 4 p.c. Monopoly	44	+1
93 9/16 91¾	92⅝	Italian 5 p.c. Rente	92¼	−⅜
100 95¾	98	Mexican 6 p.c. 1888	98¼	—
20⅞ 19	19¾	Portuguese 1 p.c.	19⅝	−⅛
64⅛ 52	57½	Spanish 4 p.c.	55¼	−1⅝
45⅛ 41	43	Turkish 1 p.c. "B"	42¼	−⅜
26 1/16 23½	25⅛	Do. 1 p.c. "C"	24⅛	−⅜
22 7/16 20¾	22	Do. 1 p.c. "D"	21 3/16	−3/16
46⅝ 40	44½	Uruguay 3½ p.c. Bonds	45¾	—

Changes in Foreign Railway stocks have again been in an adverse direction, the good traffic returns published by the Argentine lines having very little effect. Uruguayan Company's are again the exception, and show a further advance, but the rise in the price of silver made no impression on any of the Mexican Company's emissions.

Highest and Lowest this Year.	Last Carrying over Price.	FOREIGN RAILWAYS.	Closing Price.	Rise or Fall.
100 99½		Argentine Gt. West. 5 p.c. Pref. Stock	100	—
158¼ 149	150	B. Ay. Gt. Southern Ord.	150	−1
78½ 69	71	B. Ay. and Rosario Ord.	70½	−1½
12¼ 10¾	11⅛	B. Ay. Western Ord.	11	—
87¼ 77¾	80	Central Argentine Ord.	78	−2⅛
92 83	85	Cordoba and Rosario 6 p.c. Deb.	84	—
95½ 88	89½	Cord. Cent. 4 p.c. Deb. (Cent. Nth. Sec.)	88½	−¾
61¾ 47½	48½	Do. Income Deb. Stk.	48½	−⅛
25¾ 18	19½	Mexican Ord. Stk.	19½	−1
83½ 72	78	Do. 8 p.c. 1st Pref.	76	−1½

Dealings have not been very numerous in the Miscellaneous market, apart from those in the few leading favourites, but there has been a slight increase in the volume of small investment business, and changes on the whole have been in favour of holders. The circular issued by the Allsopp board met with a good deal of adverse criticism, the proposal to issue an additional £1,100,000 in the shape of deferred shares for the purpose of purchasing more licensed houses, not meeting with approval. Allsopp Ordinary stock moved up several points, only to lose the advantage gained, and other brewery issues have remained inactive. The various firms of the Vickers & Maxim and Armstrong type have been getting big orders of late, and a considerable appreciation in the value of their shares is apparent; but judging from the dismal report just issued by the Hotchkiss Company, misfortune still dogs the footsteps of that ill-fated concern. Satisfactory-looking reports by T. R. Roberts and several other kindred concerns has led to an inquiry for their shares, and there has also been active dealings at higher prices in Anglo-Argentine Tramways, Birmingham Vinegar, and William Cory Preference. On the other hand, Clay, Bock issues declined on the passing of the dividend; Indian tea companies have been pressed for sale; Hammond Meat Income stock marks a big decline, and a heavy fall has taken place in cycle companies' shares, Dunlop deferred being almost unsaleable. Welsbach issues are considerably lower, in spite of the satisfactory meeting.

The week closed amid depressing surroundings, and from Consols downwards there was an all-round decline in prices just at the last. Home Corporation issues were especially weak, and Home Railway stocks were also pressed for sale. A little support was forthcoming at one time for United States Railroad shares, but this soon died away, and Canadian Pacific and Grand Trunk issues closed almost at the worst points. Among Foreign Government bonds, Spanish "Fours" rallied a little towards the close on re-purchases from Paris, but the rest of the list shows nothing but falls, and the new Chinese loan was called 1⅝ discount. Rio Tinto Copper shares also left off below the highest price.

Mining and Finance Companies.

The South African market has presented the same dreary appearance this week as last, and falls again preponderate. De Beers diamond shares rallied sharply towards the last, and a few others followed to a lesser extent, but business has been on a very small scale, and purely professional. Western Australian shares have met with a little more support, but the few rises registered earlier in the week have been mostly lost again. Copper shares continue to find favour, and Rio Tinto is again considerably higher, a dividend of 25s. being looked for; but the Mount Lyell group was adversely affected by a poor return made by the parent company. Indian shares remain very firm, a number of satisfactory reports coming to hand, and the Nundydroog directors now state that the water in their mine is being gradually got under.

MINING RETURNS.

Londonderry.—320 tons crushed for yield of 477 oz. gold.

Wassau (Gold Coast).—587 tons of ore crushed yielded 745 ozs. bar gold.

Anglo Mexican for February):—Crushed 1,000 tons. $36,270 (U.S. gold).

Westralia and East Extension.—Crushed 1,675 tons: yield of smelted gold 1,104 ozs.

Great Boulder Proprietary.—For fortnight ended March 14: tons crushed 1,435, yield of gold 3,273 oz.

Ottos Kopje Diamond.—During week ended March 17, 8,357 loads washed for 942 carats of diamonds.

Bellevue Proprietary.—Clean up for fortnight ended March 12, 167 tons yielding 333 oz.

St. Augustin.—For week ended March 12, 3,418 loads yielded 93 carats.

Cuddingwarra.—Crushed 175 tons for 150 oz.

Anglo-Mexican.—Result from treatment of tailings by cyanide during February, $12,878 (United States gold); tons treated, 820.

Brilliant Block.—Crushed during the month, 1,214 tons of quartz for 534 oz. of gold.

Ivanhoe Gold Corporation.—Clean up March 15, 1,394 oz. of gold from 830 tons crushed.

Mount Lyell.—From February 10 to March 9 inclusive, a total quantity of 9,248 tons of ore has been treated, 8,427 tons from open cuts assaying before treatment—copper, 3·24 per cent.; silver, 4·24 oz. per ton; gold, ·239 oz. per ton; 821 tons from No. 4 Tunnel assaying before treatment—copper, 6·12 per cent.; silver, 6·51 oz. per ton; gold, ·059 oz. per ton. The converters have produced during the same period 313 tons blister copper, containing—copper, 309 tons; silver, 35,588 oz.; gold, 2,001 oz.

St. John del Rey.—Gold produce, March 1 to 11, £5,182; yield per ton, ·57 of an oz. troy.

Wealth of Nations.—Crushed during the last 14 days, 260 tons, the gross yield being 140 oz. of gold.

Hyderabad (Deccan).—The output of coal from the Singareni Collieries for the four weeks ended February 26, was 31,040 tons.

Hauraki.—Crushed, 150 tons for 518 oz.

St. Augustin Diamond.—1,134 loads of mine ground washed, and 2,156 loads surface lumps: Yield, 118 carats.

Victory (Charters Towers).—Crushing for fortnight from No. 3 shaft: 114 tons for 538 oz. of gold.

Lady Shenton.—Crushed, 630 tons; yield, 1,630 oz.; tailings, 19 dwts.

Consolidated Murchison.—Crushed 372 tons, obtained 391 oz.

Day Dawn Block and Wyndham.—Result of crushing for fortnight ending 19 inst.:—Tons crushed, 1,330; yielded, 1,272 oz.

Ouro Preto.—February return:—5,558 tons of ore produced 1,449 oz.

Palmarejo.—Return for February:—Crushed, 1,900 tons; panned, 1,150 tons; producing $29,000.

Queensland Menzies.—Crushed for fortnight, 100 tons for 641 oz.

Frank Smith Diamond.—5,900 loads washed producing 159 carats.

Leicester Consolidated Diamond.—Three week's return:—Loads washed from the mine, 10,750; from the floors, 12,025; carats produced, 503.

Melbourne Democrat.—Crushed 350 tons of ore for 240 oz. of gold.

New Australian Broken Hill Consols.—Fortnight's output:—2 tons 8 cwt. containing 9,300 oz. of silver.

Answers to Correspondents.

Questions about public securities, and on all points in company law, will be answered week by week, in the Review, on the following terms and conditions:—

A fee of five shillings must be remitted for each question put, provided they are questions about separate securities. Should a private letter be required, then an extra fee of five shillings must be sent to cover the cost of such letter, the fee then being ten shillings for one query only, and five shillings for every subsequent one in the same letter. While making this concession the Editor will feel obliged if private replies are as much as possible dispensed with. It is wholly impossible to answer letters sent merely "with a stamped envelope enclosed for reply."

Correspondents will further greatly oblige by so framing their questions as to obviate the necessity to name securities in the replies. They should *number* the questions, keeping a copy for reference, thus:—"(1) Please inform me about the present position of the Rowenzori Development Co. (2) Is a dividend likely to be paid soon on the capital stock of the Congo-Sudan Railway?"

Answers to be given to all such questions by simply quoting the numbers 1, 2, 3, and so on. The Editor has a rooted objection to such forms of reply as—"I think your Timbuctoo Consols will go up," or "Sell your Slowcoach and Draggem Bonds," because this kind of thing is open to all sorts of abuses. By the plan suggested, and by using a fancy name to be replied to, each query can be kept absolutely private to the inquirer, and no scope whatever be given to market manipulations. Avoid, as names to be replied to, common words, like "investor," "inquirer," and so on, as also "bear" or "bull." Detached syllables of the inquirer's name, or initials reversed, will frequently do as well as anything, so long as the answer can be identified by the inquirer.

The Editor further respectfully requests that merely speculative questions should as far as possible be avoided. He by no means sets himself up as a market prophet, and can only undertake to provide the latest information regarding the securities asked about. This he will do faithfully and without bias.

Replies cannot be guaranteed in the same week if the letters demanding them reach the office of the Investors' Review, Norfolk House, Norfolk-street, W.C., later than the first post on Wednesday mornings.

W. K.—I do not think you should sell. Traffics are very satisfactory, and the road has always earned its fixed charges. Its association with the Eastern system is as much to blame for the fall as anything. Better times are expected after the reorganisation of its neighbour. Given honest management, the system as a whole should do well, for it passes through important trade centres.

N. P. Y.—They have fallen in sympathy with the rest of the market. At their present price they seem high enough as they only return 10 per cent., without any allowance made for the life of the properties. In addition to the capital, which is a fair amount, there are debentures of about £100,000, to be repaid within five years. A great number of claims are owned and they are, it is true, not capitalised at a high figure, but many of them may prove utterly worthless. If the shares fall further they might be worth picking up as a speculative venture, but I do not think they are very tempting just now.

Y. F.—It is very difficult to say if it is right to average now or not. At the moment it would seem prudent to hold off. Traffics are not expanding to any extent, and working expenses are increasing. I think you will find the directors gave warning of this probable increase at the last meeting. I am inclined to think there is no hurry to buy, as there promises to be little activity in markets just yet. Should there be signs of quieter politics, and a more stable money market, you might purchase a little stock to assist in reducing the cost, but it will be a long time, I am afraid, before you will see a rise to the price you have paid.

THE PROPERTY MARKET.

An aggregate of £207,783 in the sales for last week, as contrasted with £66,578 for the corresponding week of last year, is certainly a very remarkable—almost unique—experience at the Mart. Yet it resulted from what may be called the ordinary run of business. No very exceptional lots were offered during the week, but there was a good and steady demand. The principal feature in the business on Friday was Messrs. Montagu & Robinson's sale of the freehold of 17, Finsbury-pavement, City, for £9,200—£10 per foot. A satisfactory price for the vendor, though a much better was obtained for a freehold in Gracechurch-street, with an area of 21,000 ft., for which £12 per foot was paid. Messrs. Baker & Sons dealt successfully with some copyhold and leasehold properties at Lambeth and Fulham, and other firms also contributed to the day's returns, which amounted to £16,370. Turning to yesterday week, the leading event was the sale by Messrs. H. E. Foster & Cranfield of a perpetual rent-charge of £1,600 per annum, arising from the estates of Castlehill and Ashgrove, Ayrshire, for which they obtained thirty years' purchase, or £48,000. Their periodical sale also comprised several important reversions, &c., the chief lots being:—The reversions to four one-sevenths of a trust fund of the estimated value of £41,000, life aged eighty-two, £18,400; the reversion to one-third of a trust estate, estimated value, £13,715, life aged seventy, £2,460; the reversion to one-third of a trust fund, estimated value £9,200, life aged fifty-four; also the contingent reversion to one-third of a trust estate, estimated value £3,500, lives aged fifty-four and twenty-four,

£1,275; freehold rent-charges of £44 7s. 4d. at Bradfield St. George, Suffolk, £1,050. Fifteen £10 shares (£7 paid) in the *Graphic* and *Daily Graphic* fetched £795, the total of the sale being £74,315.

Business at the Mart on Monday was only middling—the total of the day's sales amounting to £19,360. Messrs. Wriford & Dixons sold some freehold houses in Horn-terrace, St. Margaret's, for £3,000. The same auctioneers bought in a freehold residence in Gloucester-road, Teddington, enclosed in half an acre of ground, for which only £1,350 was offered. Another freehold residence, 45, Linden-gardens, Bayswater, offered by Messrs. E. and A. Swain, went for £2,250, and a third freehold, 233, East India Dock-road, changed hands at £1,400. There were various other freehold properties set up for sale on Monday, and were all disposed of at fair prices—one at Enfield, Lynton-Dene, by Mr. Alfred Richards, at £1,000; five freehold houses at Catford, offered by Messrs. S. Walker & Son, fetched £1,625; and another lot in Jutland-road, by the same firm, brought £2,235.

The principal event at the Mart on Tuesday—when the day's sales realised £33,162, was the sale by Messrs. Debenham, Tewson & Co., of a block of freehold property at Highbury Corner, covering an area of 22,356 ft., and including three shops and other buildings in Holloway-road, which realised the satisfactory price of £14,000. Messrs. Bean, Burnett & Eldridge sold, among other lots, freeholds in Dawson-place, Bayswater, and High-street, Ilford, and building plots at Sydenham. Messrs. Field & Sons disposed of some free- and leasehold properties in the south of London at good figures, and bricks and mortar were freely dealt in by other firms. At the Mason's Hall Tavern on Tuesday, the licensed house known as "The Princess of Wales," in John-road, Wandsworth, held for fifty-nine years at an annual rent of £109, was sold by Messrs. Adams & Glover for £17,520.

Wednesday's total at the Mart amounted to £63,810, and contained some important lots. Messrs. Douglas Young & Co. sold a freehold building estate of about 17¼ acres in Fortis Green-road, Muswell Hill, for £17,600, and the freehold of the Bell public-house in Old Bailey, City, for £13,300. Messrs. Thurgood & Martin were also very successful with several lots of freehold building land at Wimbledon, a block in Trinity-road, &c., a little over eleven acres in extent, changing hands at £13,500, and another block in Queen's-road, &c., covering an area of 4 acres 2 roods 4 poles, making £6,200. Messrs. Edwin Fox & Bousfield offered for sale a freehold property known as St. John's House, Clerkenwell-road, having a superficial area of about 11,300 feet, let on lease for a term, of which four and a half years are unexpired, at an annual rent of £1,058. The property went at the very satisfactory price of £15,700. The remaining lots were of minor importance, but the competition was on the whole considerable.

A conference was held on Wednesday at the Mansion House, when a resolution was unanimously passed urging upon Government the purchase of the Crystal Palace. It was urged that the Commissioners of the International Exhibition of 1851 had in their possession £200,000, which might be appropriated for the purchase of the Palace. It was mentioned that if £750,000 were forthcoming there would be no difficulty about the acquisition of the property.

CANADA'S MINERAL OUTPUT.

The advance summary showing the mineral production of Canada in 1897 bears out our recent remarks on the mining activity, and the potentialities of the country. The value of all minerals obtained is given as $28,789,173 compared with $22,609,825 in 1896, being an increase of $6,179,348. Nearly the whole of this net increase occurs under the head of metals, which total $13,996,234 against $8,055,945 in 1896, or an increase of $5,940,289. And among metals, gold is an easy first with $6,190,000 against $2,780,086, increase 122·6 per cent., being followed by silver with $3,322,905 against $2,149,503, increase 54·6 per cent.; copper, $1,501,660, against $1,021,960, increase 46·9 per cent.; nickel, $1,399,176, against $1,188,990, increase 17·7 per cent.; and lead, $1,396,853, against $721,159, increase 93·7 per cent. These percentage increases are estimated on the basis of value only; in quantity, silver rose by 73·4 per cent., lead by 61·2 per cent., and copper by 41·6 per cent. Iron is the only metal which has fallen away, the production being 71,451 tons, worth $178,716, against 91,906 tons, worth $191,557—that is to say, a decrease of 22·3 per cent. in quantity, and 6·7 per cent. in value. The increase in gold is attributed to the progress of mining in the Klondyke region and in the Trail Creek, and other districts of British Columbia; in silver and lead to British Columbia alone; and in copper partly to this province and partly to the development of the copper-nickel mattes of Sudbury, Ontario. Among non-metals there has been no particular change; the output of coal has increased slightly, and the output of petroleum has diminished slightly. It is to be noted that coal accounted for 25·31 per cent. of last year's total production, against 31·94 per cent. in 1896; gold for 21·50 per cent., against 12·30 per cent.; and silver for 11·54 per cent., against 9·50 per cent.

NOTICES.

Messrs. Campion & Co. announce that they have taken into partnership Mr. Horace Quare. The style and title of the firm will remain as heretofore.

Messrs. W. I. Carr, Sons & Todd announce that they are taking into partnership Mr. Harold Denison Arbuthnot, who has been with them for some years. The style of the firm will remain unchanged.

The Hon. Mr. Justice Grantham has been elected a director of the Equity and Law Life Assurance Society, in the room of the Rt. Hon. Sir Edward Kay, deceased.

Prices of Mine and Mining Finance Companies' Shares.

Shares £1 each, except where otherwise stated.

AUSTRALIAN.

Making-Up Price, Feb. 21.	Name.	Closing Price.	Rise or Fall.	Making-Up Price, Feb. 21.	Name	Closing Price.	Rise or Fall.
1 1/16	Aladdin	1⅜	−1/16	7⅞	Hannan's Brownhill	7½	−⅜
3 1/16	Associated	3½	−1/16	⅞	Hannan's Oroya	⅞	
15/16	Do. Southern	⅞	−1/16	16/	Do. Proprietary	16/	−/6
14/6	Brilliant, £2	14/		⅞	Do. Star	⅞	
2⅛	Do. St. George's	2½	+⅜	—	Ivanhoe, New	5⅛	−⅛
11/9	British Broken Hill	12/		⅞	Kalgurli Mt. & Iron King, 18/	⅞	
2⅜	Broken Hill Proprietary	2½	+1/16	5 1/16	Kalgurli	4⅞	−5/16
—	Do. Block 10	3¼		2⅜	Lady Shenton	2 1/16	−⅛
1 3/16	Brownhill Extended	1 3/16		9½	Lake View Cons.	9	−½
1 1/16	Burbank's Birthday	1 1/16		11/16	Do. Extended	⅝	−⅛
15/16	Central Boulder	⅞	−1/16	1 1/16	Do. South	1 1/16	
5/0	Chaffers, 4/	5/6		1 1/16	London & Globe Finance	1 1/16	−⅛
1	Colonial Finance, 15/	1/16 pm	+1/16	15/16	London & W. A. Exploration	⅞	
—	Crœsus S. United	⅝	+1/16	15/16	Do. Investment	11/16	
15/6	Day Dawn Block	15/	−/6	⅝	Mainland Consols	7/16	−1/16
1	E. Murchison	1		11/16	North Boulder, 10/	¾	−1/16
⅜	Gold Estates	⅜		1⅜	North Kalgurli	1⅜	−
4/	Golden Arrow 19/	4/		4⅞	Northern Territories	4 1/16	−
7½	Golden Horseshoe	7 1/16	+3/16	2⅛	Peak Hill	2⅜	+¼
⅞	Golden Link	15/16	−1/16	2 1/16	South Kalgurli	2 1/16	
11/16	Great Boulder, 2/	20/6	−/6	1⅞	W. A. Goldfields	1⅞	−⅛
1½	Do. Main Reef, 10/	1⅜	−1/16	2⅛	W. A. Joint Stock	2⅛	−⅛
3⅜	Do. Perseverance	2⅞	−⅛	1½	W. A. Market Trust	1 1/16	
1	Do. South	15/16	−1/16	2	W. A. Loan & General Fin.	1½	−1/16
2⅜	Hainault	2 1/16	−1/16	⅝	White Feather	1/16	
⅜	Hampton Plains	¾	−⅛				

SOUTH AFRICAN.

Making-Up Price, Feb. 21.	Name.	Closing Price.	Rise or Fall.	Making-Up Price, Feb. 21.	Name	Closing Price.	Rise or Fall.
5½	Angelo	4⅞		2/6	Lisbon-Berlyn	2/3	
1 3/16	Aurora West	1	−⅛	2¼	May Consolidated	2¼	
⅞	Bantjes	13/16	−1/16	4⅞	Meyer and Charlton	4⅞	
9/6	Barrett, 10/	10/	+/6	3⅞	Modderfontein	3⅞	−⅛
3⅞	Bonanza	3⅞		15/16	New Bultfontein	1	+⅛
⅞	Buffelsdoorn	8/3	−/6	3¼	New Primrose	3 1/16	−1/16
5¾	City and Suburban, £4	5½	−1/16	1 1/16	Nigel	1⅞	
2⅜	Comet (New)	2 1/16	−¼	—	Nigel Deep	1⅞	
4⅞	Con. Deep Level	4 1/16	−1/16	⅞	North Randfontein	⅞	
11½	Crown Deep	11½		5⅜	Nourse Deep	4⅞	−⅛
12	Crown Reef	12	+½	1⅛	Porges-Randfontein	1 1/16	−1/16
27½	De Beers, £5	26 11/16 x		28¼	Rand Mines	27⅞	−¼
3¼	Driefontein	3⅞		1 3/16	Randfontein	1⅞	−1/16
5½	Durban Roodepoort	5⅞	−⅛	2⅜	Rietfontein	2 1/16	
3⅜	Do. Deep	3⅜		10	Robinson Deep	9⅞	
4	East Rand	3 11/16	−3/16	8	Do. Gold, £5	8	−½
24½	Ferreira	24½	−½	⅞	Do. Randfontein	13/16	−1/16
6⅜	Geldenhuis Deep	6⅜	+½	1⅞	Roodepoort Central Deep	1⅞	
4⅞	Do. Estate	4 5/16	−⅜	6¼	Rose Deep	6½	+⅛
11/16	George Goch	13/16	−1/16	2⅜	Salisbury	2⅜	
2⅛	Ginsberg	2	−1/16	2 1/16	Sheba	1 13/16	−1/16
1 11/16	Glencairn	1 11/16	−1/16	3⅜	Simmer and Jack, £5	3	−1/16
8½	Goldfields Deep	7 13/16		3	Transvaal Gold	3	−¼
8⅛	Griqualand West	8⅜	+⅛	3	Treasury	3	
8¾	Henry Nourse	8⅜	−⅜	3 11/16	United Roodepoort	3⅞	
7½	Heriot	7⅞	+⅛	1 11/16	Van Ryn	1⅞	
7¾	Jagersfontein	7⅞		5 7/16	Village Main Reef	5⅜	−⅛
7⅜	Jubilee	7⅜	−⅛	1⅞	Vogelstruis	1⅞	+⅛
4⅜	Jumpers	4¾		11/16	Do. Deep	11/16	−1/16
2⅜	Kleinfontein	2	−1/16	8 3/16	Wemmer	8½	−⅛
2 11/16	Knight's	3	−⅛	⅞	West Rand	⅞	
2⅜	Lancaster	2½		5 15/16	Wolhuter, £4	5½ x	
3½	Langlaagte Estate	3⅜	−⅛	2	Worcester	2⅝	

LAND EXPLORATION AND RHODESIAN.

Making-Up Price, Feb. 21.	Name.	Closing Price.	Rise or Fall.	Making-Up Price, Feb. 21.	Name	Closing Price.	Rise or Fall.
2⅜	Anglo-French Ex.	2¼	−⅛	9/16	Mashonaland Central	⅝	
1 11/16	Barnato Consolidated	1½	−1/16	6	Matabele Gold Reefs	6½	−¼
⅞	Bechuanaland Ex.	⅞		1 11/16	Mozambique	2 1/16	
2 11/16	Chartered B.S.A.	2 11/16	−1/16	1 5/16	New African	1 1/16	
⅜	Clark's Cons.	5/16		⅞	Oceana Consolidated	⅞	
⅞	Colenbrander	⅞		1¼	Rhodesia, Ltd.	1⅛	−1/16
4⅜	Cons. Goldfields	3 11/16	−1/16	4	Do. Exploration	4	−¼
1 1/16	Do. Pref.	20/	−1/	1	Do. Goldfields	11/16	
1⅜	Exploration	1 11/16	+1/16	3⅞	S. A. Gold Trust	3⅞	−1/16
2 1/16	Geelong	2 1/16	+1/16	11/16	Tati Concessions	⅝	−⅛
¾	Henderson's Est.	11/16		⅞	Transvaal Development	⅞	
1 3/16	Johannesburg Con. In.	1 1/16	−1/16	⅞	United Rhodesia	⅞	−1/16
1	Do. Water	1		1 1/16	Willoughby	1 1/16	
1 13/16	Mashonaland Agency	1 3/16	−1/16	⅜	Zambesia Explor.	¾	

MISCELLANEOUS.

Making-Up Price, Feb. 21.	Name.	Closing Price.	Rise or Fall.	Making-Up Price, Feb. 21.	Name	Closing Price.	Rise or Fall.
1¼	Alamillos, £2	1¼		13/	Mysore Goldfields	13/	−/6
5	Anaconda, $25	5 1/16	+1/16	9/	Do. Reefs, 17/	7/6	−1/
9/6	Balaghât, 18/	10/		14/9	Do. West	14/6	−/6
4⅛	Cape Copper, £2	4 13/16	+3/16	12/	Do. Wynaad	11/6	
4 15/16	Champion Reef, 10s.	4 13/16	−1/16	2 1/16	Namaqua, £2	2 1/16	
2⅜	Copiapo, £2	2⅜		3⅞	Nundydroog	3⅛	
3⅜	Coromandel	3 1/16	−1/16	2⅞	Ooregum	3 1/16	
2⅜	Frontino & Bolivia	2 1/16	−⅛	3 1/16	Do. Pref.	3⅞	
1 11/16	Hall Mines	1⅞		28	Rio Tinto Def., £5	20½	+11/16
2 11/16	Libiola, £5	2⅞		6	Do. Pref. £5	6¼	+1/16
7⅞	Linares, £3	8⅜	+⅛	18/	St. John del Rey	17/6	
3⅞	Mason & Barry, £3	3 11/16	+1/16	17/	Taitapu	11/16	
5½	Mountain Copper, £5	5 1/16	+1/16	7⅞	Tharsis, £2	7 1/16	+3/16
13⅞	Mount Lyell, £3	13⅞	−⅛	3⅞	Tolima "A," £5	3	−¼
2⅞	Mount Lyell, North	2⅜	−1/16	4⅞	Wajhi	4 1/16	−1/16
16/3	Mount Lyell, South	15/16	−⅛	1⅞	Waitekauri	1⅛	−1/16
4⅞	Mount Morgan, 17s. 6d.	4 1/16	−1/16	1 1/16	Woodstock (N.Z.)	1 1/16	
5⅞	Mysore, 10s.	5⅞ x					

A Sydney telegram states that the Premier of New Zealand is favourable to the issue of a loan of £2,000,000 to be expended in railways and irrigation. Of course he does. How possibly could New Zealand live if it did not borrow for one object or another?

AFRICAN MINING RETURNS.

Dividends Declared in 1896	1897	1898	Capital Issued.	Nominal Amount of Share.	Name of Company.	Monthly Crushings. December. Tons.	Oz.	Dwt. per ton	January. Tons.	Oz	Dwt. per ton.	February. Tons.	Oz.	Dwt. per ton.	Totals. Months.	Ozs.	Profits Declared. Dec.	Jan.	Feb.	Totals. Months.	—	Stamps now Working.
p.c.	p.c.	p.c.	£	£													£	£	£		£	
—	—	25	225,000	1	Angelo	12,340	5,844	9.4	12,657	5,863	9.3	11,615	5,868	11.0	2	11,731	12,591	12,636	13,803	2	26,439	60
—	—	—	130,000	1	Balmoral	7,340	1,596	4.3	12,770	2,318	3.7	—	2,015	—	2	4,333	—	1,456	1,000	2	2,456	60
—	75	—	200,000	1	Bonanza	12,265	7,886	12.8	11,627	8,036	13.8	10,220	7,741	15.1	2	15,777	18,272	18,430	18,545	2	37,975	40
—	—	—	550,000	1	Buffelsdoorn ..	31,635	3,750	2.3	33,118	3,607	2.2	—	3,034	—	2	6,641	—	—	—	—	—	75
—	—	—	133,000	1	Champ d'Or ..	7,315	3,368	9.2	8,989	3,193	7.0	—	2,998	—	2	6,191	—	—	—	—	—	50
5	15	—	1,360,000	4	City and Suburban	33,409	11,792	7.0	32,345	11,032	6.8	—	9,678	—	2	20,710	21,658	18,553	15,451	2	34,004	160
—	—	—	224,635	1	Comet	9,427	3,229	6.8	9,707	3,231	6.6	8,314	2,968	7.1	2	6,199	5,838	4,814	4,812	2	9,626	40
—	—	—	300,000	1	Crown Deep ..	38,030	14,034	7.4	42,262	13,429	6.3	39,170	10,248	5.2	2	23,675	21,000	17,000	9,086	2	26,086	160
110	170	100	120,000	1	Crown Reef.. ..	26,730	12,298	9.2	34,787	12,110	7.0	—	10,332	—	2	22,442	22,764	22,379	19,537	2	41,916	120
55	80	20	125,000	1	Durban Roodepoort	17,700	6,080	6.9	16,635	6,105	7.2	15,800	6,179	7.1	2	13,284	—	—	—	—	—	80
275	300	—	90,000	1	Ferreira	18,453	13,196	14.3	18,480	12,213	13.2	—	12,097	—	2	24,310	30,870	27,775	27,320	2	55,095	80
12½	45	50	200,000	1	Geldenhuis Estate..	29,450	9,461	6.4	34,857	10,088	5.8	—	10,019	—	2	20,107	15,900	17,475	18,825	2	36,300	120
—	30	—	280,000	1	Geldenhuis Deep ..	30,724	10,008	6.5	35,890	11,493	6.3	41,343	11,366	5.5	2	22,859	14,980	17,686	18,414	2	36,100	180
—	10	—	150,000	1	Gelden. Main Reef	5,766	1,055	3.6	5,734	1,310	4.6	2,100	424	4.0	2	1,734	3	566	c2,050	2	c1,484	30
—	—	—	325,000	1	George Goch ..	17,731	3,179	3.6	13,691	3,068	4.5	—	2,950	—	2	6,018	—	—	—	—	—	120
—	25	—	160,000	1	Ginsberg	8,789	2,476	5.6	8,795	2,383	5.4	—	2,154	—	2	4,537	3,705	4,385	3,191	2	7,576	40
—	—	—	500,000	1	Glencairn	27,980	6,699	4.8	27,584	6,749	4.9	—	6,512	—	2	13,261	10,645	11,107	10,239	2	21,346	110
30	125	—	125,000	1	Henry Nourse ..	15,150	7,334	9.7	15,200	7,608	10.0	13,980	7,723	11.0	2	15,331	16,150	14,571	16,482	2	31,053	60
85	100	25	111,864	1	Heriot	15,950	6,010	7.5	15,622	5,832	7.4	—	5,737	—	2	11,569	10,467	10,030	9,642	2	19,672	70
350	500	125	81,000	1	Johan. Pioneer ..	5,278	4,337	16.4	4,637	3,723	16.0	—	3,865	—	2	7,588	—	—	—	—	—	30
60	90	—	50,000	1	Jubilee	8,745	3,073	7.0	9,038	3,092	6.8	—	2,800	—	2	5,890	—	—	—	—	—	50
30	60	—	100,000	1	Jumpers	12,300	5,646	9.2	19,246	5,407	5.6	—	5,319	—	2	10,726	7,150	6,160	7,150	2	14,310	100
—	—	—	231,250	1	Kleinfontein ..	18,543	5,133	5.5	18,212	5,163	5.6	17,290	4,942	5.7	2	10,105	5,676	5,441	4,905	2	10,346	95
—	—	—	311,980	1	Knight's	23,210	4,983	4.3	24,290	5,215	4.3	24,560	5,485	4.4	2	10,700	—	3,076	—	1	3,076	120
30	30	—	470,000	1	Langlaagte Estate..	44,278	9,029	4.3	37,695	8,692	5.1	27,624	7,840	5.6	2	16,632	—	—	—	—	—	175
—	—	—	550,000	1	Lang. Block B. ..	19,118	4,484	4.7	19,129	4,709	4.9	18,160	4,760	5.2	2	9,475	—	—	—	—	—	75
—	—	—	250,000	1	Langlaagte Star ..	9,623	4,020	8.3	9,673	4,031	8.3	9,045	3,424	7.5	2	7,455	—	—	—	—	—	30
20	—	—	275,000	1	May Consolidated	22,354	6,086	5.4	22,399	6,509	5.8	20,292	7,371	7.2	2	13,880	6,002	8,217	—	1	8,217	90
20	50	—	85,000	1	Meyer and Charlton	15,264	3,871	5.7	14,400	3,910	5.4	—	3,935	—	2	7,845	5,345	5,348	5,893	2	11,241	80
—	—	—	949,620	4	Modderfontein ..	—	—	—	—	—	—	—	2,835	—	1	2,835	—	—	—	—	—	60
—	—	—	200,000	1	Nigel	6,570	2,803	8.5	6,970	2,831	8.1	—	2,773	—	2	5,604	—	—	—	—	—	25
—	—	—	300,000	1	Nth. Randfontein..	10,007	2,354	4.7	9,801	1,944	3.9	8,514	1,972	4.6	2	3,916	—	—	—	—	—	40
—	—	—	374,934	1	Nourse Deep ..	—	6,099	—	13,023	5,410	8.3	11,587	4,642	8.0	2	10,042	3,215	7,710	5,604	2	13,314	60
—	—	—	400,000	1	Paarl Central ..	11,343	3,285	5.8	9,604	2,535	5.3	10,618	2,540	4.8	2	5,075	—	—	—	—	—	60
—	10	—	487,500	1	Porges Randfontein	13,318	4,502	6.7	11,692	3,981	6.8	11,605	3,532	6.1	2	7,513	—	—	—	—	—	60
—	50	—	300,000	1	Primrose	37,581	9,704	5.1	37,789	9,137	4.8	—	8,824	—	2	17,961	14,161	12,463	11,664	2	24,127	160
—	10	—	165,000	1	Princess Estate ..	8,611	2,979	6.8	8,688	2,837	6.5	—	2,725	—	2	5,562	2,614	2,002	1,850	2	3,852	40
—	—	—	270,000	1	Rietfontein	a	—	—	4,265	769	3.6	—	3,004	—	2	3,773	—	—	3,115	1	3,115	50
—	—	—	300,000	1	Rietfontein "A" ..	13,202	5,235	7.9	13,255	5,545	8.4	—	5,049	—	2	10,594	11,767	11,145	9,682	2	20,827	50
12	15	—	2,750,000	5	Robinson	31,792	16,847	10.6	31,440	b15,574	9.9	—	15,203	—	2	30,777	42,000	36,530	35,000	2	71,530	120
—	—	—	600,000	1	Robinson R'dfontein	9,184	3,373	7.3	9,700	3,341	6.9	7,944	2,566	6.5	2	5,907	—	—	—	—	—	35
—	—	—	175,000	1	Roodepoort Gold ..	5,405	1,182	4.4	5,805	1,266	4.4	—	950	—	2	2,216	—	52	—	—	—	40
25	40	—	150,000	1	Roodepoort United	12,321	4,414	7.1	11,760	4,423	7.5	—	4,057	—	2	8,480	7,455	7,240	6,680	2	13,912	70
—	—	—	400,000	1	Rose Deep	26,345	9,491	7.2	27,058	9,666	7.1	23,149	8,660	7.5	2	18,326	16,900	15,900	12,932	2	28,832	100
—	—	—	100,000	1	Salisbury	8,366	2,150	5.1	8,506	2,427	5.7	—	2,450	—	2	4,877	—	—	—	—	—	50
20	20	3¾	1,075,000	1	Sheba	9,500	9,005	18.9	11,760	6,400	10.9	10,418	5,930	11.4	2	12,330	—	—	—	—	—	120
—	—	—	4,700,000	5	Simmer and Jack ..	35,080	8,120	4.6	44,760	10,163	4.5	—	9,081	—	2	19,244	—	—	—	—	—	100
—	—	—	235,000	1	Spes Bona	9,259	2,091	4.5	9,100	2,037	4.5	—	2,286	—	2	4,323	771	451	—	1	451	40
—	15	—	35,000	1	Stanhope	4,585	1,089	4.7	4,428	1,058	4.7	—	1,054	—	2	2,112	—	—	—	—	—	20
—	—	—	604,225	1	Trans. G. M. Est...	14,322	4,581	6.4	14,032	6,600	9.4	5,344	4,145	15.5	2	10,745	12,305	10,138	10,400	2	20,538	75
—	—	—	540,000	4	Treasury	11,664	3,770	6.5	9,574	3,585	7.5	—	3,844	—	2	7,429	6,124	5,876	6,436	2	12,312	40
—	—	—	177,000	1	Van Ryn	19,290	4,002	4.1	19,942	4,189	4.2	16,701	3,738	4.5	2	7,927	—	—	1,440	1	1,440	80
—	—	—	170,000	1	Van Ryn West ..	14,260	3,938	5.5	15,430	4,463	5.8	—	d	—	—	—	3,000	9,018		1	9,018	80
—	—	—	260,000	1	Village Main Reef..	—	—	—	6,510	3,499	5.4	13,425	5,356	7.9	2	8,857	—	—	8,621	1	8,621	60
75	100	—	80,000	1	Wemmer	11,161	5,987	10.7	10,998	6,072	11.0	10,200	5,803	11.3	2	11,875	12,215	13,190	12,561	2	25,751	50
—	—	—	400,000	1	West Rand	6,853	1,732	5.0	6,879	1,889	5.5	6,075	1,784	5.9	2	3,673	—	—	—	—	—	30
—	10	—	860,000	4	Wolhuter	22,718	7,670	6.7	22,265	7,559	6.8	—	6,675	—	2	14,234	10,621	10,823	9,027	2	19,850	100
55	30	15	95,722	1	Worcester	5,140	2,615	7.8	5,204	2,023	7.8	—	2,888	—	2	4,911	—	5,033	—	1	5,033	40
—	—	—	90,000	1	York	6,545	1,849	5.6	9,483	2,302	4.9	8,271	2,201	5.3	—	—	—	—	—	—	—	40

a Mill restarted January 7. b Exclusive of yield from Concentrates bought—3,835 oz. in December, 1,396 oz. in January, and 1,320 oz. in February. c Loss. d Absorbed by Van Ryn Estate Company.

SOUTH AFRICAN CRUSHINGS.

The February crushings are a little disappointing, and for the first time since July show a falling off compared with the preceding month. Excluding outside returns the Rand output for the month was 297,975 oz. against 313,526 oz. for January. This is a reduction of 5 per cent., but February contained three days less than January, representing about 9 per cent. of the output so that the result is not so bad as it looks. Complaint is again made of shortness of native labour, the Robinson group reporting that their mines were worked with only half their necessary complement, while other company's put forward various reasons. The Transvaal Gold Mining and Estates Company had no clean up from its central cyanide works; the Balmoral Company had a delay owing to break-down of the pump; the new Primrose Company said delay was caused by compressor breakdown; and the Enisberg Company reported delay through repairs to engine. On the other hand the New Rietfontein had its first full result since the resumption of crushing, and the Village Main Reef Company did much better. On the question of profits, however, the result was less satisfactory. The Henry Nourse Jumpers and Treasury Companies made bette profits, more in accordance with their December earnings, but the Geldenhuis Main Reef made a loss of £2,050; and there was a considerable reduction in the profits of the City and Suburban, Crown Deep, Crown Reef, Glencairn, Primrose, Nourse Deep, Rietfontein "A," Robinson, Rose Deep, Wolhuter, and Worcester Companies, besides small reductions in many other cases. In connection with the continued decrease in profits in face of reduced working expenses, it is interesting to call attention to the remarks of Mr. George Albu when presiding over the annual meeting last month of the Meyer and Charlton Company. This gentleman stated that the profit made in 1897 was £18,000 more than in 1896, although the actual yield of the mine had been less. Working expenses had been kept down to the exceptional low figure of 16s. 4d., compared with 23s. 7d. in 1896, 24s. 9d. in 1895, and 27s. 8d. in 1894. This is, we fear, a somewhat exceptional case, otherwise it would be a hard nut for President Kruger and his supporters to crack in connection with their present policy of refusing to lessen the load borne by the gold-mining industry. If other companies have been able to lower their cost of working in anything like the same proportion, it only shows up their reduced profits in a worse light.

Railway Traffic Returns.

ALGECIRAS (GIBRALTAR) RAILWAY.—Traffic for week ended March 12, Ps. 19,740; increase Ps. 2,300. Aggregate from July 1, Ps. 739,024; increase, Ps. 19,813.

BENGAL CENTRAL RAILWAY.—Traffic for week ending February 26, Rs. 25,947; increase, Rs. 9,183. Total from January 1, Rs. 167,774; increase, Rs. 21,546.

BURMA RAILWAYS.—Receipts for week ending February 19, Rs. 2,08,764; decrease, Rs. 16,376. Aggregate from January 1, Rs. 14,49,241; decrease, Rs. 2,73,461.

GREAT WESTERN OF BRAZIL RAILWAY.—Traffic for week ending February 12, $39,146; decrease, $1,265. Aggregate receipts to date $304,516; increase, $31,253.

ALCOY AND GANDIA RAILWAY AND HARBOUR COMPANY.—Traffic for week, March 19:—Ps. 9,500, decrease Ps. 500. Aggregate from January 1, Ps. 118,400, increase Ps. 10,350.

MOBILE AND BIRMINGHAM RAILROAD.—Traffic for first week of March, $7,146; increase, $10. Aggregate from July 1, $261,695; decrease, $5,068.

VILLA MARIA AND RUFINO RAILWAY.—Traffic for week ending March 19, $4,816; decrease, $644. Aggregate from January 1, $48,847, decrease $7,062.

WEST FLANDERS RAILWAY.—Gross receipts for week ending March 20, £2,029; decrease, £16. Total from January 1, £24,149; increase, £597.

WEST OF INDIA PORTUGUESE RAILWAY.—Week ending February 26, Rs. 3,741; increase, Rs. 52.

ASSAM-BENGAL RAILWAY.—Traffic for week ended February 12, Rs. 25,004; increase, Rs. 6,339. Aggregate from January 1, Rs. 1,44,811; increase, Rs. 11,302.

QUEBEC CENTRAL RAILWAY.—Receipts for first week of March $5,024; decrease $1,260. Aggregate from July 1, $51,305; decrease $9,515.

BENGAL DOOARS RAILWAY.—Traffic receipts from January 1 to February 19, Rs. 23,180; decrease, Rs. 6,828.

H. H. THE NIZAM'S GUARANTEED STATE RAILWAYS.—Traffic receipts from January 1 to February 26. Rs. 629,384; increase, Rs. 12,984.

ROHILKUND AND KUMAON RAILWAY.—Traffic receipts for week ending February 19, Rs. 5,637; decrease, Rs. 55. Aggregate from January 1, Rs. 37,161; decrease, Rs. 1,271.

SOUTHERN MAHRATTA RAILWAY.—Receipts for week ended February 26, Rs. 99,276; decrease, Rs. 39,430.

MANILA RAILWAY.—Receipts for week ending March 19, $19,793; increase, $3,175. Aggregate from January 1, $212,080; increase, $51,760.

CLEATOR AND WORKINGTON.—Gross receipts for the week ending March 12 amounted to £1,015, a decrease of £61. Total receipts from January 1, £10,086, a decrease of £698.

COCKERMOUTH AND KESWICK RAILWAY.—Receipts for week ending March 12, £798; increase, £78. Aggregate from January 1, £8,273; increase, £742.

DELHI UMBALLA KALKA RAILWAY.—Traffic receipts for week ending March 12, Rs. 27,300; decrease, Rs. 400. Total from commencement of half-year, Rs. 3,76,300; increase, Rs. 1,37,900.

ANTOFAGASTA AND BOLIVIA RAILWAY.—Traffic receipts for month of February, $353,000; decrease, $67,000. Total from January 1, $657,000; decrease, $178,000.

PUERTO CABELLO AND VALENCIA RAILWAY.—Traffic return for week ended February 11, £958; decrease, £745. Aggregate from January 1, £5,087: decrease, £2,348.

COCKERMOUTH AND KESWICK RAILWAY.—Traffic receipts for week ending March 19, £840; increase, £61. Aggregate from January 1, £8,309; increase, £804.

CLEATOR AND WORKINGTON JUNCTION RAILWAY.—Receipts for week ending March 19, £1,161; increase, £149. Aggregate from January 1, £11,247; decrease, £549.

WESTERN OF SANTA FE RAILWAY.—Traffic receipts for week ending March 19, $50,920; increase, $26,360.

ENGLISH RAILWAYS.

Div. for half years. 1896	1896	1897	1897	Last Balance forward.	Amt. to pay 1 p.c. on Ord. for ½ yr.	NAME.	Date.	Gross Traffic for week: Amt.	Inc. or dec. on 1897.	Inc. or dec. on 1896.	No. of weeks	Gross Traffic for half-year to date: Amt.	Inc. or dec. on 1897.	Inc. or dec. on 1896.	Mileage.	Inc. on 1897.	Working	Prior Charges last ½ year.	Prop. add Cap. Exp. this ½ year
				£	£												%	£	£
10	10	10	10	2,707	5,094	Barry	Mar. 19	10,033	+810	+3,301	12	109,807	+5,510	+20,889	31	—	8·89	60,665	316,853
nil	nil	nil	nil	—	—	Brecon and Merthyr	,, 20	1,383	+45	−211	12	17,838	+444	−672	61	—	—	—	—
nil	nil	nil	nil	3,979	4,749	Cambrian	,, 20	5,050	+321	+920	*	48,818	+880	—	250	—	60·96	63,146	40,000
2½	1¾	2	1¾	1,510	3,150	City and South London	,, 20	1,030	+18	+78	12	12,826	+8	+1,088	3½	—	56·67	5,552	124,000
1	2	1½	2	7,895	13,210	Furness	,, 20	8,709	+55	+571	*	97,354	+2,618	—	139	—	49·88	97,423	20,910
2	1½	½	1	2,207	27,470	Great Central (late M., S., & L.)	,, 20	43,152	−115	+2,275	11	461,814	+6,323	+26,721	352½	—	57·17	627,386	1,200,000
2½	4¾	2	5	51,283	62,865	Great Eastern	,, 20	79,847	+2,091	+8,910	11	851,497	+29,667	+73,156	1,158½	2	55·35	860,138	250,000
3	5½	3	5	15,094	102,496	Great Northern	,, 20	94,389	+3,207	+10,147	12	1,107,830	+34,887	+81,049	1,071	8	61·36	641,485	750,000
4¾	7¼	4¾	7½	31,350	121,981	Great Western	,, 20	174800	+3,720	+9,800	11	1,864,730	+45,730	+100030	2,582	21	51·44	1,486,272	800,000
nil	2	nil	1¾	8,951	16,487	Hull and Barnsley	,, 20	6,888	+122	+1,267	11	69,813	−2,248	+4,473	73	—	58·21	70,290	52,9[illegible]
5	5¾	5	5½	21,495	83,704	Lancashire and Yorkshire	,, 20	90,828	+1,915	+3,911	11	985,942	+31,651	+41,177	555½	25	56·70	674,745	451,976
4¾	8	4¾	8½	26,243	43,049	London, Brighton, & S. Coast	,, 19	45,739	+1,049	+3,723	12	544,186	+28,991	+39,653	476½	—	50·20	407,042	240,735
nil	nil	nil	nil	72,294	56,296	London, Chatham, & Dover	,, 20	26,335	+447	+1,382	11	283,248	+10,046	+20,469	185¼	—	50·65	367,873	nil
6½	8	6½	7¾	89,535	204,068	London and North Western	,, 20	226747	+5,916	+13,962	11	2,443,184	+60,093	+126834	1,911½	—	56·92	1,404,534	600,000
5	8½	8½	8½	23,038	59,367	London and South Western	,, 20	67,274	+1,374	+4,726	11	705,675	+31,068	+54,200	941	6½	51·75	513,740	389,000
2½	6	2½	6½	14,592	6,691	London, Tilbury, & Southend	,, 20	4,789	+365	+1,097	12	56,300	+4,270	+10,137	81	—	52·57	39,590	15,000
3½	3⅞	3¾	3¾	17,133	26,409	Metropolitan	,, 20	16,215	+406	+1,367	*	181,904	+4,475	—	64	—	43·63	148,047	254,000
nil	nil	nil	nil	4,006	11,250	Metropolitan District	,, 20	8,457	+307	+467	11	95,242	+3,916	+4,457	13	—	48·70	119,663	38,450
5	7	5½	6½	38,143	174,582	Midland	,, 20	188206	+4,902	+20,578	12	2,158,231	+29,725	+138639	1,354¾	15½	57·59	1,216,582	650,000
5½	7½	5¾	7	22,374	138,189	North Eastern	,, 19	142876	−1,979	+7,210	11	1,529,183	+25,451	+77,573	1,597¾	—	58·82	795,077	436,004
7½	7½	7½	7½	7,061	10,102	North London	,, 20			Not recd			not	recvd.	12	—	50·90	49,973	7,600
4	5	4	4½	4,745	16,150	North Staffordshire	,, 20	15,337	−813	+1,215	12	186,296	+5,973	+11,844	312	—	55·27	118,142	19,605
10	10	11		1,642	3,004	Rhymney	,, 19	5,379	+398	+596	12	60,826	+1,198	+6,606	71	—	49·68	29,049	16,700
3	6⅝	3½	6⅝	4,054	50,215	South Eastern	,, 19	39,614	+2,339	+4,081	*	414,845	+24,656	—	448	—	51·88	380,763	230,000
3½	3½	3½	3½	2,315	25,961	Taff Vale	,, 19	15,429	−640	+849	12	182,346	−4,669	+5,895	121	—	54·90	94,800	92,000

* From January 1.

SCOTCH RAILWAYS.

5	5	5½	5	9,544	78,066	Caledonian	Mar. 20	70,562	+ 2,583	+ 3,708	7	482,732	+ 11,014	+ 28,122	851½	5	50·38	588,248	441,477
5	5½	5	5	7,364	24,639	Glasgow and South-Western	,, 19	26,531	+ 862	+ 1,320	7	183,636	+ 5,033	+ 9,818	393½	—	54·69	221,663	106,145
3½	3½	3½	—	1,291	4,600	Great North of Scotland	,, 19	7,601	+ 190	+ 412	7	51,971	− 14	+ 1,118	331	15½	52·03	92,178	60,000
3	nil	2	—	10,477	12,820	Highland	,, 20	8,226	+ 173	+ 540	3	24,650	+ 957	+ 2,263	479¾	27½	58·63	78,976	,000
1	1¼	1	1¼	819	45,819	North British	,, 20	69,976	+ 1,804	+ 4,860	7	463,945	+ 12,221	+ 15,827	1,230	23	48·62	944,809	540,800

IRISH RAILWAYS.

6½	6½	6½	—	5,466	1,790	Belfast and County Down	Mar. 18	2,121	+ 229	+ 297	*	22,640	+ 1,182	—	76½	—	55·58	17,690	10,000
5½	6½	5½	—	—	4,284	Belfast and Northern Counties	,, 18	5,480	+ 664	+ 508	*	54,054	+ 2,864	—	249	—	—	—	—
2	3	2	—	1,418	1,200	Cork, Bandon, and S. Coast†	,, 19	1,403	− 87	− 35	*	12,838	− 1,060	—	103	—	54·82	14,436	5,450
6½	6¾	6½	6¾	38,776	17,816	Great Northern	,, 18	15,289	+ 767	+ 962	11	152,205	+ 7,917	+ 9,917	528	36	50·15	88,068	22,000
5½	5½	5½	5½	30,339	24,855	Great Southern and Western	,, 18	—	—	—	not	received	—	—	603	13	51·45	72,802	46,582
4	4	4	4½	11,372	11,850	Midland Great Western	,, 18	10,166	+ 738	+ 999	11	101,192	+ 5,124	+ 6,052	538	—	50·31	83,129	1,800
nil	nil	nil	nil	229	2,822	Waterford and Central	,, 18	798	+ 154	—	*	9,465	+ 1,327	—	59½	—	53·24	6,858	1,500
nil	nil	nil	nil	1,936	2,987	Waterford, Limerick & W.	,, 18	4,391	+ 209	+ 580	*	63,722	+ 3,413	—	350½	—	57·83	42,017	7,075

* From January 1. † Eight weeks' strike

FOREIGN RAILWAYS.

Mileage. Total.	Increase on 1897.	Increase on 1896.	Name.	Gross Traffic for Week. Week ending	Amount.	In. or Dec. upon 1897.	In. or Dec. upon 1896.	Gross Traffic to Date. No. of Weeks.	Amount.	In. or Dec. upon 1897.	In. or Dec. upon 1896.
					£	£	£		£	£	£
319	—	—	Argentine Great Western ..	Mar. 18	8,422	+ 1,205	+ 1,655	35	205,954	− 8,032	+ 45,589
76½	—	—	Bahia and San Francisco ..	Feb. 19	3,581	+ 1,388	+ 1,516	7	20,523	+ 6,685	+ 6,206
234	48	84	Bahia Blanca and North West ..	Feb. 20	992	+ 113	+ 331	34	26,972	+ 610	—
74	—	—	Buenos Ayres and Ensenada ..	Mar. 20	3,610	− 214	− 657	11	30,177	− 7,164	− 10,500
426	—	—	Buenos Ayres and Pacific ..	Mar. 19	8,129	− 139	+ 416	37	237,852	− 52,655	+ 5,262
914	1	3	Buenos Ayres and Rosario ..	Mar. 19	17,121	+ 6,586	+ 2,683	11	194,856	+ 48,548	+ 27,395
2,499	30	68	Buenos Ayres Great Southern ..	Mar. 20	39,695	+ 6,376	+ 9,125	37	1,099,003	+ 79,458	+ 166,869
602	107	177	Buenos Ayres Western	Mar. 20	13,743	+ 424	− 1,771	37	447,374	− 77,221	+ 77,939
845	55	77	Central Argentine	Mar. 19	23,570	+ 8,607	+ 4,595	11	244,814	+ 55,897	+ 3,726
197	—	—	Central Bahia	Dec. 31*	$114,389	− $4,688	+ $22,144	12 mos.	$1,307,205	+ $141,334	+ $196,150
271	—	—	Central Uruguay of Monte Video	Mar. 19	6,766	+ 2,734	+ 1,309	37	221,980	+ 4,212	− 16,027
128	—	—	Do. Eastern Extension	Mar. 19	1,566	+ 520	+ 107	37	46,199	+ 4,212	− 2,194
182	—	—	Do. Northern Extension	Mar. 19	620	+ 328	− 290	37	23,386	− 1,379	− 6,555
180	—	—	Cordoba and Rosario	Mar. 13	2,045	+ 560	− 455	37	78,915	− 15,940	− 3,150
128	—	—	Cordoba Central	Mar. 13	$21,000	− $3,200	− $3,000	10	$219,700	− $35,400	− $48,960
549	—	—	Do. Northern Extension	Mar. 13	$41,000	− $17,660	− $10,240	10	$435,290	− $166,000	− $105,930
237	—	—	Costa Rica	Mar. 5	7,251	− 52	+ 1,542	9	48,842	− 14,675	+ 705
99	—	—	East Argentine	Feb. 6	562	− 310	− 17	5	3,387	− 946	− 708
386	—	6	Entre Rios	Mar. 19	2,890	+ 1,814	− 1,474	37	56,211	+ 13,142	− 11,598
555	—	24	Inter Oceanic of Mexico	Mar. 19	$66,100	+ $16,250	+ $23,950	37	$2,100,980	+ $313,540	+ $535,770
23	—	—	La Guaira and Caracas	Feb. 25	1,779	− 779	− 1,138	8	15,641	− 5,235	− 3,528
322	—	—	Mexican	Mar. 19	$88,000	+ $13,800	—	11	$903,200	+ $88,850	—
1,846	—	—	Mexican Central	Mar. 14	$267,222	+ $28,888	+ $64,615	11	$2,614,592	+ $240,932	+ $609,387
1,217	—	—	Mexican National	Mar. 14	$119,626	+ $2,789	+ $34,222	11	$1,150,723	+ $200,317	+ $217,952
228	—	—	Mexican Southern	Mar. 21	$13,660	+ $670	+ $376	51	$649,438	+ $84,196	+ $167,638
205	—	—	Minas and Rio	Jan. 31*	$133,941	− $20,733	—	7 mos.	$1,308,551	+ $187,065	—
94	—	17	N. W. Argentine	Mar. 19	850	− 706	− 531	11	9,539	− 6,621	− 4,210
242	3	—	Nitrate	Mar. 15†	18,010	+ 2,625	− 2,333	9	72,503	+ 1,349	− 31,915
320	—	—	Ottoman	Mar. 12	4,807	+ 393	+ 635	10	51,010	− 13,542	+ 4,017
77½	—	—	Recife and San Francisco ..	Jan. 22	5,698	− 176	− 1,136	4	20,698	− 82	− 4,027
86½	—	—	San Paulo	Feb. 13†	20,974	− 4,508	—	6	71,004	− 9,017	—
186	—	—	Santa Fe and Cordova	Mar. 19	3,366	+ 1,426	− 181	38	56,042	− 13,539	− 3,105
110	—	—	Western of Havana	Mar. 19	1,835	+ 116	+ 1,430	37	66,015	+ 5,503	+ 2,000

* For month ended. † For fortnight ended.

INDIAN RAILWAYS.

Mileage. Total.	Increase on 1897.	Increase on 1896.	Name.	Gross Traffic for Week. Week ending	Amount.	In. or Dec. on 1897.	In. or Dec. on 1896	Gross Traffic to Date. No. of Weeks.	Amount.	In. or Dec. on 1897.	In. or Dec. on 1896.
862	—	—	Bengal Nagpur	Mar. 5	Rs.1.62.000	+Rs.17.452	+Rs.26.000	9	Rs.12.91.000	−Rs.1.32.319	−Rs2.59.917
827	8	63	Bengal and North-Western ..	Feb. 19	Rs.1.41.700	+Rs.12.756	+Rs.16.046	7	Rs.9.47.120	+Rs.1.22.118	+Rs2.23.027
461	—	—	Bombay and Baroda	Mar. 5	£24,108	− £457	− £7,677	8	£205,919	−£31,851	−£103,312
1,885	2	13	East Indian	Mar. 19	Rs.13.06.000	+Rs.12.000	+R.2.32.000	11	Rs.1.37.93.000	+Rs.2.09.000	+Rs6.98.000
1,491	—	—	Great Indian Penin.	Mar. 12	£58,988	−£597	−£11,521	10	£648,871	+£33,481	−£176,247
736	—	—	Indian Midland	Mar. 19	Rs.1.20.490	−Rs.14.111	+Rs.15.055	11	Rs.14.95.759	+Rs.27.930	+Rs2.54.830
840	—	—	Madras	Mar. 12	£19,617	−£1,925	−£182	10	£190,745	−£10,673	−£11,117
1,043	—	—	South Indian	Feb. 12	Rs.1.52.756	−Rs.26.035	−Rs.7.618	6	Rs.9.03.806	−Rs.66.977	−Rs1.86.279

UNITED STATES AND CANADIAN RAILWAYS.

Mileage Total.	Increase on 1897.	Increase on 1896.	Name.	Gross Traffic for Week. Period Ending.	Amount.	In. or Dec. on 1897.	Gross Traffic to Date. No. of Weeks.	Amount.	In. or Dec. on 1897.
					dols.	dols.		dols.	dols.
917	—	—	Baltimore & Ohio S. Western ..	Mar. 14	143,171	+46,145	36	4,779,948	+493,821
6,568	92	136	Canadian Pacific	Mar. 14	492,000	+169,000	10	4,106,000	+873,000
922	—	—	Chicago Great Western	Mar. 14	101,937	+24,255	36	3,818,425	+532,413
6,169	—	469	Chicago, Mil., & St. Paul ..	Mar. 21	666,000	+138,000	11	6,724,801	+965,000
1,685	—	—	Denver & Rio Grande	Mar. 14	135,600	+26,900	36	5,782,400	+981,700
3,512	—	—	Grand Trunk, Main Line ..	Mar. 21	£7,438	+£6,488	11	£811,396	+£86,202
335	—	—	Do. Chic. & Grand Trunk	Mar. 21	£14,856	+£2,382	11	£169,432	+£37,095
189	—	—	Do. Det., G. H. & Mil. ..	Mar. 21	£3,938	−£50	11	£39,522	−£1,624
2,938	—	—	Louisville & Nashville	Mar. 14	421,905	+28,480	10	4,256,175	+898,620
2,197	137	137	Miss., K., & Texas	Mar. 14	188,146	+14,094	36	9,315,137	+574,332
477	—	—	N. Y., Ontario, & W.	Mar. 14	68,466	+7,228	36	2,762,555	+100,986
1,570	—	—	Norfolk & Western	Mar. 14	256,000	+32,000	36	7,651,000	+849,000
3,499	336	—	Northern Pacific	Mar. 14	395,000	+128,000	10	3,688,000	+1,111,000
1,223	—	—	St. Louis S. Western	Mar. 14	94,000	+26,000	10	1,128,700	+211,100
4,654	—	—	Southern	Mar. 14	430,000	+50,000	36	1,945,812	+1,254,448
1,979	—	—	Wabash	Mar. 14	256,000	+52,000	10	2,522,406	+517,000

Prices Quoted on the London Stock Exchange.

Throughout the INVESTORS' REVIEW middle prices alone are quoted, the object being to give the public the approximate current quotations of every security of any consequence in existence. On the markets the buying and selling prices are both given, and are often wide apart where stocks are seldom dealt in. Other particulars will be found in the INVESTMENT INDEX published quarterly—January, April, July, and October—in connection with this REVIEW, price 2s., by post 2s. 2d. Where dividends are paid only once a year, an *italic* type is used to distinguish them. The London Stock Exchange Official List is quoted in the REVIEW almost entire, only very insignificant issues, or bonds falling due within the next two or three years, being omitted. But the list is subdivided into the leading, or active, stocks, and those less frequently dealt in. The former will be found under the head of "Stock Markets," and with more details than it is possible to give for the bulk of securities. By retaining the file of the INVESTORS' REVIEW any subscriber can follow for himself the movements of securities from week to week, and the INVESTMENT INDEX will from time to time help to fill up deficiencies in the information.

Tea Companies and Mines and Mining Finance Stocks are placed in special lists.

Among the abbreviations used are the following:—S. F. Snk. Fd. *sinking fund*; Certs., *certificates*; Debs. or Dbs., *debentures*; Db. or D.Stk., *debenture stock*; Pf., Prf., or Pref., *preference*; Prefd. or Pfd., *preferred*; Dfd., *deferred*; L. or Ltd., *limited*; Sh., *share*; Ans., *annuities*; Cu. or Cm., *cumulative*; Gu or Guar., *guaranteed*; Bds., *bonds*; S., Sr., or Ser., *series*; In., Ins., Insc., *inscribed*; Dr., Drgs., Drwgs., *drawings*; Sig., Strlg., *sterling*; Lia., *liable to*; Sp., Surp., *surplus*; Per., Perp., *perpetual*; Ln. *lien*; Lo. *loan*.

The dates following the names of securities are the years of issue or of redemption. Where shares are not fully paid up, their nominal amount is given with the name so that investors may know the liability upon them.

BRITISH FUNDS, &c.

Rate.	Name.	Price.
2¾	2¾ p.c.'s (Childers') Red.. 1905	105½
3	Local Loans Stk. 1912	112
3	Metro. Police Deb. Stk. 1920	105½
—	Red Sea Ind. Tel. Ann. 1908	8½
4	Canada Gv. "Intcl. Rly." 1903	106
4	Do. do. .. 1908	113
4	Do. Bonds 1910	114
4	Do. Bonds 1913	119½
3	Egyptian Gov. Gar.	106½
3	Mauritius Ins. Stk. 1940	114
4	Turkish Guar. 1855	109
11½	Bank of Ireland Stk.	392½
3½	India Rupee Paper	62½
3½	Do. 1854-5	63
3	Do. 1896-7 1916	55
3½	Isle of Man Deb.	104
3	Do. Deb. Stk... 1919-29	103

CORPORATION AND COUNTY STOCKS.

FREE OF STAMP DUTY.

Rate.	Name.	Price.
3½	Metropolitan Con. 1929	117½
3	Do. 1941	113
2½	Do. 1920-49	100
2½	L.C.C. Con. Stock 1920	99
3½	Comm. of Sewers, Scp, S.F. 1905	105
3½	Corp. of Lond. Bds...1897-1902	100½
3	Do. 1897-1912	103
3½	Do, Debs. Scp. .... S.F. 1916	105
2½	Do., Deb. Stk. Scrip .. 1927-57	100
3	Barnsley 1916-46	105
3	Barry 1914-46	101
3	Bath 1909-34	102
3	Batley 1914-44	101½
3½	Birmingham 1945	123
3	Do. 1947	112
2½	Do. 1926	98
3	Blackburn 1930	107
3	Bournemouth 1913-33	103
3½	Bradford 1945	118
3	Do. Deb. Stock .. 1954	110
3	Brighouse.............. 1916-46	100
3½	Brighton 1946	118½
2½	Do. 1957	98
3	Burton-on-Trent........ 1913-43	102½
3	Cambridge 1913-43	103
3½	Cardiff 1935	112
3	Do. 1914-54	104½
3	Cheltenham............ 1971	108
3	Chichester 1916-46	101
3½	Croydon	134
3	Do. 1940	111½
3	Derby 1920-50	107
3	Devon C.C. 1917-33	104½
3½	Dewsbury 1930	109
3	Do. 1930	103
3	Dorset County 1922-32	105
3	Douglas (I. of Man) 1926	101
3	Dover 1913-43	102
3½	Dublin 1944	113½
3	Eastbourne 1920-40	105
3	Edinburgh 1924	108
2½	Do. 1927	98
2½	Exeter 1917-57	96
3	Glamorgan County 1914-34	104
3½	Glasgow 1914	110½
3	Do. 1921	106½
2½	Do. 1925-40	99
3	Gloster 1915-55	101
3	Grimsby 1913-45	103½
3	Hampshire County 1914-34	105½
3	Hanley 1913-43	105
3	Harrogate 1914-34	103
3	Hastings 1915-54	104½
2½	Hertfordshire C.C. 1916-36	98
3	Heston & Isleworth U.D.C. 1915-35	101
3	Huddersfield 1934	107
3½	Hull (1st iss.)	131½
3	Inverness............. 1914-44	102
3	Ipswich 1952	110½
3	Lancaster............. 1919-55	103
2½	Leeds 1927	98
3½	Leicester 1934	114½
3	Lincoln.............. 1919	104
3½	Liverpool............	133½

Corporation, &c. (*continued*):—

Rate.	Name.	Price.
3	Manchester 1941	109½
3	Mansfield............. 1915-45	100
3½	Middlesbro'........... 1909	105½
3½	Do. 1911-13	105
3	Do. 1915	104
3	Middlesex C.C.......... 1915-35	106
3½	Newcastle 1936	118½
3½	Do. Irred.	129½
2½	Do. 1915-36	101
3	Newcastle-under-Lyme.. 1909-44	101
3	Newport (Mon.) 1915-55	104½
3	Norwich 1952	111½
3	Nottingham	116
3	Oxford 1951	109½
3	Penzance 1916-46	100½
3	Plymouth 1942	110
3	Pontypridd U.D.C. 1916-46	99
3	Poole.................. 1915-45	102½
3½	Portsmouth.......1916 24 & 27	112
3	Do. 1913-33	106½
3	Ramsey 1920-40	100
3	Ramsgate.............. 1915-55	102
3½	Reading	131½
3	Do. 1962	109
3½	Rhyl U.D.C. 1953	110
3	Richmond (Surrey) 1942	104½
3	River Wear Debt Certs.	101
3	St. Helen's 1915-55	103
3	Scarbro' 1915-50	103
2½	Sheffield 1925-57	96
3	Shipley U.D.C.......... 1915-35	101
3	Somerset Co. 1923-33	107
3	South Shields.......... 1915-45	104
2½	Southampton 1915-45	102
3	Southend-on-Sea 1916-46	102
3	Staffs C.C. 1915-35	104½
3	Stockport............. 1914-54	104
3	Stockton 1932	104
3	Do. 1915-35	103
3	Surrey Co. 1922-32	105½
3½	Swansea	130
3	Do. 1955	106
3	Taunton 1918 3-9-43	102
3	Tees Conserv. Deb. Stk. 1947	101
3	Thames Conserv. "A" Deb. Stk. 1954	103½
3	Do. "B" Deb. Stk. 1954	103½
3	Torquay 1913-43	102½
3	Tunbridge Wells 1931	103
3	Tynemouth............. 1913	101
3	Wakefield............. 1929	102
3	Walsall............... 1932	108
3	West Bromwich........ 1930	106½
3½	West Ham 1929	110
3	Do. 1945	105
3	West Sussex C.C. 1915-35	106
3	Weston-s.-Mare Lcl Bd. 1914-44	101½
3	Weymouth&Melc. Regis 1918	101
3	Widnes............... 1915-55	101
3	Wigan 1921	106
3	Windsor 1918-55	102½
3½	Wisbech 1947	113½
3½	Wolverhampton 1932	118
3	Do. 1924-54	107
3	York 1916-41	106½

SUBJECT TO STAMP DUTY.

Rate.	Name.	Price.
3½	Belfast City & Dis. Watr. 1938	114
3	Do. Red Stk. 1953-6	106
3½	Belfast 1924	103
4	Blackburn Con. Deb. Irred.	141½
3½	Do. do. Irred.	131
3½	Bristol	130½
3½	Burnley............. 1933	114
2½	Chesterfield Gas & Wtr. 1916-46	98
3½	Douglas Town 1921	105
3	Dover Harb. 1st Deb... 1956	104½
3½	Hull (2nd iss.)	129½
4	Leeds Deb............. 1927	124
3½	Do.	115½
3	Do. 1927	106
3	Leicester 1919-44	105
4	Manchester	150
3	Do. 1928	104½
4½	Middlesboro' Mrts. 1908	111
3½	Newark on-Trent .. 1901-41	96
3½	Sheffield 1898-1916	105½
3½	Do. 1925-36	114
3	Do. 1925	104½
3½	Southampton .... S.F.	106
4½	Stockton Mrts......... 1908	112
3½	Worcester............ 1950	109

COLONIAL AND PROVINCIAL GOVERNMENT SECURITIES.

Rate.	Name.	Price.
6	British Columbia........ 1907	119½
4½	Do. Debs... 1917	111½
3	British Guiana Imgtn. Bds.	99½
5	Canada, "Intercol. Rail," 1903	111½
4	Do. (Bonds) 1904-5-6-8	106
4	Do. Reduced 1910	107½
3½	Do. Bnds. 1909-34	104½
4	Do. Loan 1910-35	107½
3	Do. Loan 1938	103
6	Cape of G. Hope 1900	—
5	Do. 1900	—
4½	Do. red. by an. draw.	110
4½	Do. 1879	110
4	Do. 1881	109
4	Do. 1917-23	118
4½	Ceylon	110
4	Do.	106½
4½	Fiji Gov. Deb. Sink. Fd.	101½
4	Jamaica Sink. Fd. 1923	103
5	Manitoba Debs.......... 1910	113
5	Do. Ster. Bds. 1888	122
4	Do. Ster. Debs.	106
4	Mauritius, Cons. Debs. 1880....	103½
4½	Natal, Sink. Fd......... 1919	118
4	Do. do. 1926	115
3½	Newfoundland Stg. Bds. 1941	99
3½	Do. do. .. 1947	99
3	Do. do.	88
5	New South Wales 1897-1902	104½
4	Do. 1903-5-8-9-17	105
5	New Zealand 1914	118
5	Do. Cnsls. 1 p.c. per an. Sink. Fd.	104
3½	Nova Scotia Debs.	104
5	Quebec Prov. 1904-6	110
4½	Do. (drgs.)	104
5	Do. Strlg. Bds. 1912	115
4	Do. Strlg. Bds. 1928	110
4	Do. Strlg. Bds. 1934	108
4	Queensland 1913-15	106½
4½	St. Lucia Debs................	102½
6	South Australia 1897-1900	103½
6	Do. 1901-1918	120
5	Do. 1911-1920	115½
4	Do. 1899-1916	105
4	Do. 1929	108½
4	Do. 1916	108½
4	Do. 1917-18-24	112½
6	Tasmania 1897-1901	104
4	Do. 1908-11, 1913-14-20	107½
5	Trinidad Debs., an. drw. 1 p c...	106
4	Victoria 1899-1901	101½
4½	Do. 1904	105
4	Do. Rail. Loan 1907	104
4	Do. Loans 1908-13	107
4½	West. Austr. 1 p.c. ac. Sink. Fd.	109
4	Do. do.	106

REGISTERED AND INSCRIBED STOCKS.

No stamp duty except for Canada 4 p.c. Reduced (½ per cent.).

Rate.	Name.	Price.
4	Antigua Insc. Stk. Red. 1919-44	109
3½	Barbados Insc. Stk. 1925-42	108
3	British Colum. Insc. Stk. 1941	103
4	British Guiana Insc..... 1935	120
4	Canada Stk. Regd. ..1904-5-6-8	107
4	Do. 4 p.c. (late 5 p.c.) Regd. 1910	107½
3½	Do. 3½ p.c. Stock Regd. 1909-34	103½
4	Do. Ln. for 4 milln. stg. 1910-35	107½
3	Do. Stk. Regd. 1938	103
2½	Do. Insc. 1947	90
4	Cape G. Hope Regd. .. 1917-23	118
4	Do. (Ln. of '83) Insc. .. 1923	119
4	Do. Cons. Stk. Insc..... 1916-36	112
3½	Do. Consol. Insc. Stock 1929-49	112
4	Ceylon Insc. Stock 1934	121
3	Do. 1940	104
4	Grenada Insc. Stock.... 1917-42	112
3½	Hong Kong Insc. Stock 1918-43	103½
4	Jamaica Insc. Stock.... 1934	121
—	Do. 1922-44	99
4	Mauritius Inscribed 1937	119
4	Natal Consd. Stk. Insc. 1927	115
4	Do. 1937	120
3½	Do. Inscribed Stock.. 1914-39	107
4	Newfoundland Inscribed 1913-38	107
4	Do. 1935	114
4	Do. Consd. Stk. Ins. 1936	114
4	N. S Wales Stock Insc. 1933	119
3½	Do. 1924	106
3½	Do. 1918	105
3	D 1935	98

Colonial, &c. (*continued*):—

Rate.	Name.	Price.
4	N. Zealnd. Con. Stk. Ins. 1929	115
3½	Do. 1940	107
3	Do. Inscribed.... 1945	99
3	Quebec (Prov.) Ins. Stk. 1937	93
4	Queensland Stock Insc. 1915-24	110½
3½	Do. 1921-4-30	104
3½	Do. 1945	103
3	Do. 1922-47	98½
4	St. Lucia Insc. Stock .. 1919-44	112
4	S. Austrln. (1882-7) Reg. 1916-36	110
3½	Do. In. Stk. Reg. 1939	110
3	Do. 1916-26	100
3/	Do. 1916	100
3½	Tasmanian Insc. Stock.. 1920-40	106
4	Do. 1920-40	116
4	Trinidad Insc. Stock.... 1917-42	110
3	Do. 1922-44	98½
4	Victoria Rly. Loan '81, Inscribed Stock 1907	104
4	Victoria Insc. Stock 1908-13-19	107
4	Victoria (1885) Ins. Stk. 1920	111
3½	Do. Inscribed Stock 1921-3-6	104
4	Do. do. 1911-26	108
4	W. Austral. Insc. Stock 1934	119
4	Do. 1911-31	110
3½	Do. 1915-35	107
3	Do. 1915-35	98
3	Do. 1916-36	97½

FOREIGN STOCKS, BONDS, &c.

COUPONS PAYABLE IN LONDON.

Last Div.	Name.	Price.
36/	Argentine Ry. Loan 6 p.c. 1881	89½
15/	Do. 5 p.c. 1884	68
30/	Do. N. Cent. Ry. Ext. 5 p.c. 1887-8-9	67½
30/	Do. 5 p.c. Trsy. Convs. 1887	68
5/4½	Do. 4½ p.c. Interl. Gld. 1888	65
27/	Do. 4½ p.c. Stlg. Extrl. 1888	66
10/6	Do. 3½ p.c. External .. 1889	48
4	Do. 4 p.c. Ry. Guar. Res....	57½
4½	Brazilian 1883	56
4½	Do. Gold........ 1879	68½
4½	Do. 1888	58
36/	Buenos Ayres 1824	82½
6	Do. 1882-3-6	47
6	Bulgarian 1888	94
6	Do. Mort. Bonds 1892	94
4½	Chilian 1885	75
4½	Do. 1886	75
4½	Do. 1887	75
4½	Do. 1889	81½
5	Do. 1892	84
4½	Do. 1893	75
4½	Do. 1895	75
5	Do. 1896	82
7	Chinese Silver 1894	101
6	Do. Gold 1895	105
6	Do. Apl. '95 by dwgs. 1901-15	110½
5	Do. Red. dwgs. in 36 yr. 1896	100½
5	Do. Do. Regis. 1896	99
1½	Colmbn. 1½ to 3 p.c. Ext. Bds. 1896	17
6	Cordova, Prov. 1886	27
—	Do. Eng. Ass. Certs.	26
—	Do. 6 p.c. 1887-8	27
—	Do. Eng. Ass. Certs.	26
3	Costa Rica "A"	32
2½	Do. "B"	27
3	Danish Gold 1914	98
10/	Ecuador N. Ext. Bds. 4½ p.c. ascn. to 5 p.c.	21
3½	Egypt'n Ins. Stk. lia. Sip. Dty. 1800	100½
4	Do. State Domain 1878	104½
4	Do. D. Sanieh, Red. .. 1905	105
6	Entre Rios.............. 1886-8	37
6	Do. Fndg. Ln. Bds. 1894-1921	32
6	Do. do. Parana City......	27½
15/	Greek 1881	40
15/	Do. 1884	40
12/	Do. Rentes................	33½
15/	Do. (Piræus-Larissa Ry.)	38
7/6	Do. Fundg. Loan 1893	47
4	Guatemala Extl. Debt..........	33
6	Hawaiian	102½
4	Hungarian Gold Rentes........	102
3	Do. 1895	91½
6	Italian Irriga. Guar.	111½
5	Do. Maremmana	94½
5	Japan 5 p.c.	100½
5	Mexican (Nat. R. Tehuantp c.)..	96½
6	Do. Extrl. 1893	

Foreign Stocks, &c. (*continued*):—

Last Div.	Name.	Price.
6	Mexican Extrl. 1893	96½
5	Do. Intrnl. Cons. Slvr.	37½
5	Do Intern. Rd. Bds. 2d. Ser.	37½
4	Nicaragua 1886	50
3½	Norwegian, red. 1937, or earlier	98
3	Do. do. 1965, do.	98
3½	Do. 3½ p.c. Bnds.	104
1	Paraguay 1p.c. ris. 3p.c. 1886-96	16
5	Russian, 1822, £ Strlg.	149
3	Do. 1859	94
4	Do. (Nicolas Ry.) 1867-9	104
3	Do. Transcauc. Ry. 1882	94
4	Do. Con. R. R. Bd. Ser. I., 1889	104
4	Do. Do. II., 1889	104
4	Do. Do. III., 1891	103½
3½	Do. Bonds	101
4	Do. Ln. (Dvinsk and Vitbsk)	103
6	Salvador 1889	64
—	S Domingo 4s. Unified: 1980	65½
6	San Luis Potosi Stg. 1889	93
5	San Paulo (Brzl.), Stg. 1888	91½
6	Santa Fé 1883-4	36
—	Do. Eng. Ass. Certs. Dep.	35
5	Do. 1888	47
—	Do. Eng. Ass. Certs. Dpsit.	46
5	Do. (W. Cnt. Col. Rly.) Mrt.	25
5	Do. & Reconq. Rly. Mort.	25
5	Spanish Quickslvr Mort. 1870	103
3½	Swedish 1880	103
3	Do. 1888	98
53	Do. Conversion Loan 1894	100
45	Trans. Gov. Loan Red. 1903-42	104
59/	Tucuman (Prov.) 1888	69
	Turkish, Secd. on Egypt. Trib.	103¼
3½	Turkish, Egpt. Trib., Ott. Bd., '94	99½
4	Do. Priority 1890	90½
1	Do. Convted Series, "A"	65½
5	Do. Customs Ln. 1886	95½
5	Uruguay Bonds 1896	56
3	Venzula New Con. Debt 1881	34½

COUPONS PAYABLE ABROAD.

Last Div.	Name.	Price.
7	Argent. Nat. Cedla. Sries, "B"	35½
5	Austrian Ster. Rnts., ex 10fl., 1870	85
5	Do. do. do.	87
5	Do. Paper do. 1870	84
5	Do. do. do.	86
4	Do. Gld Rentes 1876	104
2½	Belgian exchange 25 fr.	92
3	Do. do.	101
3½	Danish Int., 1887, Rd. 1896	97½
3½	Do. '87, Red. by pur. or draw. fr. Dec., 1900	98½
2½	Dutch Certs. ex 12 gldrs.	87
3	Do. Bonds	98
3	Do. Insc. Stk.	97
3½	French Rentes	105½
3	Do. 1878, '81-4., Red.	101
3	German Imp. Ln. 1891	96½
3	Do. do. 1892-3	96½
3	Do. do. 1890-4	96
5	Japan Cons. Ln., '92, 3, & 5, Red.	46
36/9	Prussian Consols	102
3	" Cons. Stg. Ln. 1892	97
4	Rumanian Bds. 1890	—
4	Do. do. 1891	—
4	Utd. States, 1877, Red. 1907	114
4	Do. 1895, 30 yrs.	128
3½	Do. Maschsetts Gl. 1935	113½
3½	Do. Gold Bonds 1923	110½
2	Virginia Cpn. Bds., 3 p.c. from July, 1902	70

BRITISH RAILWAYS.

ORD. SHARES AND STOCKS.

Last Div.	Name.	Price.
10	Barry, Ord.	280½
4	Do. Prefd.	126
6	Do. Defd.	150½
5½	Caledonian, Ord.	157
3	Do. Prefd.	100½
.	Do. Defd. Ord., No. 1	4½
	Cambrian, Ord.	6½
—	Do. Coast Cons.	6½
32/	Cardiff Ry. Pref. Ord.	117
3/	Central Lond. £10 Ord. Sh.	10½
1/9½	Do. do. £6 paid	6½
3½d.	Do. Pref. Half-Shares.	1½
1/6	Do. Def. do.	4½
1½	City and S. London	67
—	East London, Cons.	6⅝
2	Furness	64½
—	Glasgow and S. West. Pfd.	83
—	Do. do. Dfd.	66
—	Great Central, Ord. 1894	39½
32/6	Do. London Exten.	75
3½	Great N. of Scotland	124
4	Great Northern, Prefd.	118
—	Do. Consolidated "A"	50
—	Do. do. "B"	191½
2	Highland	84½
4	Isle of Wight, Prefd.	120½
3	Do. Defd.	83½
—	Lancs. Derbys. and E. Cst.	4
8½	L. Brighton and S. C. Ord.	186
37/11½	Do. New all pd.	186
6	Do. Prefd. Ord.	198
30/	Do. Contgt. Rights Certs.	16½
5½	Lond. and S. Western Ord.	222½
4	Do. Preferred	132
6½	Lond., Tilb., and Southend	133½
—	Mersey, £20 shares	½
—	Metropolitan, New Ord.	129
2½	Do. Surplus Lands	95
4	North Cornwall, 4 p.c. Pref.	104½
12/6	Do. Deferred	22½
7½	North London	225½
4½	North Staffordshire	131

British Railways (*continued*):—

Last Div.	Name.	Price.
1/6	Plymouth, Devenport, and S. W. Junc. £10	9
3/	Port Talbot £10 Shares	8½
9d.	Rhondda Swns. B. £10 Sh.	5
10	Rhymney, Cons.	268½
4	Do. Prefd.	123
6½	Do. Defd.	147½
—	Scarboro', Bridlington Junc.	47½
6½	South Eastern, Ord	151
6	Do. Pref.	193
3½	Taff Vale	81
25/	Vale of Glamorgan	129½
3	Waterloo & City	137½

LEASED AT FIXED RENTALS.

Last Div.	Name.	Price.
4	Birkenhead	146
5.19.0	East Lincnshire	209½
5½	Hammsmith. & City Ord.	192½
4½	Lond. and Blackwll.	162½
4½	Do. £10 4½ p. c. Pref.	162½
56/6	Lond. & Green. Ord.	102
5	Do. 5 p. c. Pref.	180½
5	Nor. and Eastn. £50 Ord.	89
6	Do.	106
3½	N. Cornwall 3½ p. c. Stk.	128½
4⅞	Nott. & Granthm. R. & C.	147
3½	Portptk. & Wigtn. Guar. Stk.	126
9	Vict. Stn. & Pimlico Ord.	317½
4½	Do. 4½ p. c. Pref.	164
4/	West Lond. £20 Ord. Shs.	14½
4½	Weymouth & Portld.	160½

DEBENTURE STOCKS.

Last Div.	Name.	Price.
4	Alexandra Dks. & Ry.	132½
3	Barry, Cons.	109
4	Brecon & Mrthyr, New A	127½
4	Do. New B	107
4	Caledonian	150½
4	Cambrian "A"	132½
4	Do. "B"	130½
4	Do. "C"	126½
4	Do. "D"	107½
3	Cardiff Rly.	102½
4	City and S. Lond.	139
3½	Cleator & Working Junc.	118½
3	Devon & Som. "A"	105½
16/3	Do. "B" 4 p. c.	36
—	Do. "C" 4 p. c.	10
4	E. Lond. 2nd Ch. 4 p. c. A	137
6/	Do. 2nd B	67½
—	Do. 3rd Ch. 4 p. c.	19½
—	Do. 4th do.	9½
3½	Do. 1st (3½ p. c.)	122½
2½	Do. 2½ p.c. (Whitech. Exn)	88
4	Forth Bridge	143½
4	Furness	143
4	Glasgow and S. Western	150
5	Gt. Central	—
4½	Do.	157½
4	Gt. Eastern	147½
4	Gt. N. of Scotland	147½
3	Gt. Northern	113½
4	Gt. Western	151½
4½	Do.	160½
4½	Do.	168½
5	Do.	186½
2½	Do.	100
4	Highland	143½
3	Hull and Barnsley	105½
3	Do. 2nd (3-4 p. c)	124
4	Isle of Wight	144½
3	Do. Cent. "A"	92½
4½	Do. "B"	115½
4	Do. "C"	82½
3	Lancs. & Yorkshire	113½
4	Lancs. Derbys. & E. Cst.	123½
4	Lpool St. Hlen's & S. Lancs.	126
4½	Ldn. and Blackwall	158
4	Ldn. and Greenwich	148½
4	Lond., Brighton, &c.	150
4½	Do.	169
4½	Lond., Chath., &c., Arb.	157½
4½	Do. "B"	155½
4	Do.	138½
4	Do. 1883	138½
3	Do.	107
3	Lond. & N. Western	116
3	Lond. & S. Westn. "A"	114
3	Do. Consld.	114
4	Lond., Til., & Southend	147½
—	Mersey, 5 p. c. (Act, 1866)	65
4	Metropolitan	147½
4½	Do.	164½
3½	Do.	129½
6	Met. District	208½
4	Do.	139
3	Midland	115
4½	Mid-Wales "A"	137½
4	Neath & Brecon 1st	129
4	Do. "A 1"	119½
3	North British	109½
3	Do. 1893	108½
3½	N. Cornwall, Launcstn., &c.	128½

Debenture Stocks (*continued*):—

Last Div.	Name.	Price.
4	North Eastern	114
4½	North London	167
3	N. Staffordshire	111½
4	Plym. Devpt. & S.W. Jn.	141½
4	Rhondda and Swan. Bay	130½
4	Rhymney	146½
4	South-Eastern	149
5	Do.	186½
3½	Do.	127½
3	Do.	113½
3	Taff Vale	110
4	Tottenham & For. Gate	146
3	Vale of Glamorgan	106½
3	West Highld. (Gtd. by N.B.)	108½
4	Wrexham, Mold, &c. "A"	115½
4	Do. "B"	102½
4	Do. "C"	97½

GUARANTEED SHARES AND STOCKS.

Last Div.	Name.	Price.
4	Caledonian	150½
4	Do.	148
4	Forth Bridge	142½
4	Furness 1881	137½
4	Glasgow & S. Western	146
4	Do. St. Enoch, Rent	146
6	Gt. Central	200
4½	Do. 1st Pref.	152½
2½	Do. Pref.	104½
5	Do. Irred. S.Y. Rent	161½
4½	Do. do.	139½
4	Gt. Eastern, Rent	144½
5	Do. Metropolitan	182½
4	Do.	144½
4	Gt. N. of Scotland	141
4	Gt. Northern	146½
5	Gt. Western, Rent	181½
5	Do. Cons.	182½
4	Lancs. & Yorkshire	146½
5	L., Brighton & S. C.	180½
3½	L., Chat. & D. (Shrtlds.)	110½
4	L. & North Western	147½
4	L. & South Western 1881	147½
4½	Met. District, Ealing Rent	151
4½	Do. Fulham Rent	152
4	Do. Midland Rent	143½
4	Do. Mid. & Dist. Guar.	128½
4	Midland, Rent	147½
4	Do. Cons.	147½
3	Mid. & G.N. Jt., "A" Rnt.	107½
3	N. British, Lien	107
4	Do. Cons. Pref. No. 1	142
3	N. Cornwall, Wadebrge. Gu.	107
4	N. Eastern	145½
5	N. Staff. Trent & M. £20 Shs.	36
3½	Nott. Suburban Ord.	125½
20/6	S. E. Perp. Ann.	36
4½	Do. 4½ p.c.	163½
3½	S. Yorks. Junc. Ord.	118½
4½	W. Cornwall (G. W., Br., Ex., & S. Dev. Joint Rent	160
3	W. Highl. Ord. Stk. (Gua., N.B.)	105½

PREFERENCE SHARES AND STOCKS.

DIVIDENDS CONTINGENT ON PROFIT OF YEAR.

Last Div.	Name	Price.
4½	Alexandra Dks. & Ry. "A"	128½
5	Barry (First)	169½
4	Do. Consolidated	138½
4	Caledonian Cons., No. 1	147
4	Do. do. No. 2	145½
5	Do. do. 1878	180
4	Do. Pref. 1884	144½
4	Do. do. 1887 (Conv.)	155
—	Cambrian, No. 1 4 p.c. Pref.	72½
—	Do. No. 2 do.	39½
—	Do. No. 3 do.	19
—	Do. No. 4 do.	10
5	City & S. Lond. £10 shares	15½
—	Do. New	14
4	Furness, Cons. 1881	134½
4	Do. "A" 1881	131½
4	Do. "B" 1883	129½
4	Glasgow & S. Western	143½
4	Do. No. 2	143½
4	Do. 1888	143½
4	Do. 1891	143½
5	Gt. Central	162½
4	Do.	132½
5	Do. Conv. 1872	156½
5	Do. do. 1874	154½
5	Do. do. 1876	153½
5	Do. do. 1879	153½
5	Do. do. 1881	152½
4	Do. 1889	113½
4	Do. 1891	107½
5	Do. 1894	108½
4	Gt. Eastern, Cons.	142
4	Do. 1886	141½
4	Do. 1881	141½
4	Do. 1884	141½

Preference Shares, &c. (*continued*):—

Last Div.	Name.	Price.
4	Gt. Eastern, Cons. 1887	141½
4	Do. 1888	141½
3½	Do. 1890	121½
3½	Do. 1893	121½
—	Do. (Int. fr. Jan '99) 1893	117½
4	Gt. North Scotland "A"	136½
4	Do. "B"	136½
4	Gt. Northern, Cons.	142½
3	Do. 1896	107
5	Gt. Western Cons.	180½
36/11	Hull & Barnsley Red. at 115	108
4	Isle of Wight	133½
3	Lancs. & Yorkshire, Cons.	108
2/2½	Lanc. Drby & E.C. 5 p.c. £10	10½
—	Do. 5 p.c. 2nd £10	9½
5	Lond., Brighn., &c., Cons.	178½
5	Do. 2nd Cons.	178½
4½	Lond., Chat. & Dov. Arbitr.	136½
25/	Do. 2nd Pref. 4½ p.c.	93
4	Lond. & N. Western	146½
4	Lond. & S. Western 1881	145½
4	Do. 1884	144½
3½	Do.	127½
4	Lond., Tilbury & Southend	142½
4	Do. Cons., 1887	142½
4	Do 1891	142½
—	Mersey, 5 p.c. Perp.	—
4	Metropolitan, Perp.	141½
4	Do. 1882	141½
4	Do. Irred.	141½
4	Do. 1887	141½
4	Do. New	141½
4½	Do.	146½
3½	Do.	124½
3	Do. Guar.	101½
2½	Metrop. Dist. Exten 5 p.c.	111
4	Midland, Cons. Perpetual	146½
4	N. British Cons., No. 2	138½
4½	Do. Edin. & Glasgow	156½
5	Do. 1865	172½
5	Do. Conv. 1874	172½
4½	Do. 1875	156½
4½	Do. Conv. 1875	156½
5	Do. do. 1879	172½
4	Do. do. 1884	140
4	Do. do. 1888	140
4	Do. do. 1890	140
4	Do. do. 1892	139
4	N. Eastern	144½
4½	N. Lond., Cons. 1866	174½
4½	Do. 2nd Cons. 1875	160
3	N. Staffordshire	107
4½	Plym. Devpt. & S. W. Junc.	151½
7/5	Port Talbot, &c., 4 p.c. £20 Shares, 4 paid	5
5/	Rhondda & Swansea Bay, 5 p.c. £10 Shares	13
4	Rhymney, Cons.	142
4½	S. Eastern, Cons.	162½
5	Do. do.	178½
4	Do. Vested Cos'.	143
4	Do. 1891	143
3½	Do. 1893	126½
2	Do. 3 p.c. after July 1900	103½
4	Taff Vale	143

INDIAN RAILWAYS.

Last Div.	Name.	Paid.	Price.
3½	Assam Bengal, Ld., (3½ p.c. till June 30, then 3 p.c.)	100	102
4/	Barsi Light, Ld., £10 Shs.	10	109
6	Bengal and N. West., Ld.	100	149
4/	Do. £10 Shares	10	14
3/6	Do. 3½ p.c. Cum. Pf. Shs.	10	10
8½d.	Do.	4	4
2/3½	Bengal Central, Ld., £10 (3½ p.c. + ¼th net earn)	5	50
3	Bengal Dooars, Ld.	100	[illegible]
4	Bengal Nagpr., Lim. (gua. 4 p.c. + 4th sp. pfts.)	100	118
7½	Bombay, Baroda, and C. I. (gua. 5 p.c.)	100	203
36/2	Burma, Ld. (gua. 2½ p.c. and ½ p.c. add. till 1901)	100	[illegible]
1/7	Do. £10 Shares	4½	[illegible]
4	Delhi Umb. Kalka, Ld., Gua. 3½ p.c. + net earn.	100	[illegible]
4	Do. Deb. Stk., 1890 (1916)	100	113
9/10	Estn. Bengal, "A" An. 1957	—	[illegible]
9/	Do. "B" 1957	—	[illegible]
4	Do. Gua. Deb. Stock	100	[illegible]
9/7½	East Ind. Ann. "A" (1953)	—	[illegible]
8/4½	Do. "C"	—	[illegible]
8/11½	Do. "B"	—	31
6½	Do. Def. Ann. Cap. (gua. 4 p.c. + ¼th sp. pfts.)	—	[illegible]
115/9	East Ind. Def. Ann. "D"	—	[illegible]
4½	East Ind. Irred. Stock	100	[illegible]
5	Gt. Indian Penin., Gua. 5 p.c. + ½ surplus profits	100	[illegible]
4	Do. Irred. 4 p.c. Deb. St.	100	[illegible]
4	Indian Mid., Ld. (gua. 4 p.c. + ¼th surplus pfts.)	100	118
51/	Madras Guar. + ½ sp. pfts.	100	[illegible]
48/6	Do. do.	100	[illegible]
46/	Do. do.	100	[illegible]
4	Nilgiri, Ld., 1st Deb. Stk.	100	97
4	Oude & Rohil. Db. Stk. Rd.	100	—
5⅞	Rohil. and Kumaon, Ld.	100	[illegible]
9/11	Scinde, Punj., and Delhi, "A" Ann., 1958	—	[illegible]
9/1	Do. "B" do.	—	[illegible]

Indian Railways (*continued*):—

Last Div.	Name.	Paid.	Price.
4	South Behar, Ld., £10 shs.	100	100
3½	Do. Deb. Stk. Red.	100	103
4½	South Ind., Gu. Deb. Stk.	100	162½
5	South Indian, Ld. (gua. 3 p.c., and ½ spls. profits)	100	122½
5	Sthn. Mahratta, Ld. (3½ p.c. & ¼th net earnings)	100	116
4	Do. Deb. Stk. Red.	100	122
3½	Southern Punjab, Ld.	100	112
3½	Do. Deb. Stk. Red.	—	107
5	Nizam's Gua. State, Ld. (†	100	114½
4	Do. Mort. Deb., 1936	100	109
4	Do. do. Reg.	100	108
€7/3½	Nizam's Gua. State, Ld., 3½ p.c. Mt. Deb. bearer	—	95½
€7/3½	Do. Reg. do. ..	—	94½
5	W. of India Portgese., Ld.	100	68½
5	Do. Deb. Stk., Red	100	99

RAILWAYS.—BRITISH POSSESSIONS.

Last Div.	Name.	Paid.	Price.
5	Atlantic & N.W. Gua. 1 Mt. Bds., 1937	100	126
5/3	Buff. & L. Huron Ord. Sh.	10	13½
5½	Do. 1st Mt. Perp. Bds. 1879	100	141½
5½	Do. 2nd Mt. Perp. Bds.	100	141½
—	Calgary & Edmon. 6 p.c. 1st Mt. Stg. Bds. Red..	100	75½
5	Canada Cent. 1st Mt. Bds. Red.	100	105
4	Can. Pacific Pref. Stk.....	100	100
5	Do. Strl. 1st Mt. Deb. Bds. 1915	100	118
3½	Do. Ld. Grnt. Bds., 1938..	100	108
3½	Do. Ld. Grnt. Ins. Stk. ..	100	108
4	Do. Perp. Cons. Deb. Stk.	100	114
5	Do. Algoma Bch. 1st Mt. Bds., 1937	100	122
2	Demerara, Original Stock	100	49
7	Do. Perp. Pref. Stk.....	100	157½
9½d.	Do. 4 p.c. Cum. Ext. Pref. £10 Shs.	4	6½
—	Dominion Atlntc. Ord. Stk.	100	33½
—	Do. 5 p.c. Pref. Stk.....	100	101
4	Do. 1st. Deb. Stk.......	100	109
4	Do. 2nd do. Red.	100	100
—	Emu Bay & Mt. Bischoff, Ld.	5	4½
4½	Do. Irred. Deb. Stk....	100	98
nil.	Gd. Trunk of Canada, Stk.	100	8
6	Do. 2nd. Equip. Mt. Bds.	100	131½
5	Do. Perp. Deb. Stk	100	137½
5	Do. Gt. Westn. Deb. Stk.	100	128½
5	Do. Nthn. of Can. 1st Mt. Bds, 1902	100	103½
4	Do. do. Deb. Stk	100	102
5	Do. G. T. Geor. Bay & L. Erie 1 Mt., 1903	100	104
5	Do. Mid. of Can. Stl. 1st Mt. (Mid. Sec.) 1908	100	107
5	Do. do. Cons. 1 Mt. Bds. 1912	100	107
5	Do. Mont. & Champ. 1 Mt. Bds., 1902	100	104
	Do. Welln., Grey & Brce. 7 p.c. Bds. 1 Mt.	100	110
—	Jamaica 1st Mtg. Bds. Red.	—	103
—	Manitoba & N. W., 6 p.c. 1st Mt. Bds., Red	100	—
—	Do. Ldn. Bdhldrs. Certs.	—	—
5	Manitoba S. W. Col. 1 Mt. Bd., 1934 $1,000 price %	—	120
—	Mid. of W. Aust. Ld. 6 p.c. 1 Mt. Dbs., Red.	100	25
4	Do. Deb. Bds., Red.	100	103
4	Nakusp & Slocan Bds., 1918	100	106
3	Natal Zululand Ld. Debs.,	100	79½
5	N. Brunswick 1st Mt. Stg. Bds., 1934	100	122
4	Do. Perp. Cons. Deb. Stk.	100	114
—	N. Zealand Mid., Ld., 5 p.c. 1st Mt. Debs............	100	35
6	Ontario & Queb. Cap. Stk.	$100	156½
5	Do. Perm. Deb. Stk......	100	144½
—	Qu'Appelle, L. Lake & Sask. 6 p.c. 1 Mt. Bds. Red.	100	43½
	Queb. & L. S. John, 1st Mt. Bds., 1909	100	25½
	Quebec Cent., Prior Ln. Bds., 1908	100	107
2½	Do. 5 p.c. Inc. Bds.	100	40
4	St. Lawr. & Ott. Stl. 1st Mt.	100	113
4	Shuswap & Okan., 1st Mt. Deb. Bds., 1915	100	76
5	Temiscouata, 5 p.c. Stl. 1st Deb. Bds., Red.........	100	9½
5	Do. (S. Franc. Brch.) 5 p.c. Stl. 1 Mt. Db. Bds., 1910	100	10
4	Toronto, Grey & B. 1st Mt.	100	112
£/2½	Well. & Mana. £5 Shs. ..	1	1
5	Do. Debs., 1908	100	110
5	Do. 2nd Debs., 1908....	100	109
5	Do. 3rd do., 1908	100	108
6	Atlan. & St. Law. Shs., 6 p.c.	100	163½
5	Gd. Trunk Mt. Bds., 1934	100	116½
5	Michigan Air Line, 5 p.c. 1st Mt. Bds., 1902	100	104
4	Minneap., S. P. & Slt. Ste. Mar, 1st M Bds., 1938	$1000	97

AMERICAN RAILROAD STOCKS AND SHARES.

Last Div.	Name.	Paid.	Price.
6/	Alab. Gt. Sthn. A 6 p.c. Pref.	10l.	9
—	Do. do "B" Ord. ..	10l.	2
—	Alabma. N. Orl.-Tex. &c., "A" Pref.	10l.	½
—	Do. "B" Def.	10l.	½
5½	Atlant. First Lsd. Ls. Rtl. Trust..................	Stk.	98½
—	Baltimore & Ohio Com. ..	$100	17
—	Baltimore Ohio S.W. Pref.	$100	7
—	Chesap. & Ohio Com.	$100	18½
—	Chic. Gt. West. 5 p.c. Pref. Stock "A"	$100	30½
—	Do. do. Scrip. In.......	—	29½
8/3	Do. 4 p.c. Deb. Stk.......	$100	70
4	Do. Interest in Scrip	$100	65½
$4	Chic. Junc. Rl. & Un. Stk. Yds. Com.	$100	108½
$1½	Do. 6 p.c. Cum. Pref.	$100	112½
$3½	Chic. Mil. & St. P. Pref...	$100	150
7	Cleve. & Pittsburgh	$10	86½
$1½	Clev., Cincin., Chic., & St. Louis Com.	$100	—
—	Erie 4 p.c. Non-Cum. 1st Pf.	—	34½
—	Do. 4 p.c. do. 2nd Pf.	—	18
—	Gt. Northern Pref.	$100	155
$2½	Illinois Cen. Lsd. Lines ..	$100	99
—	Kansas City, Pitts & G. ..	$100	20
$3	L. Shore & Mich. Sth. C.	$100	192½
—	Mex. Cen. Ltd. Com.	$100	6
—	Miss. Kan. & Tex. Pref...	$100	32½
2½	N.Y., Pen. & O. 1st Mt. Tst. Ltd., Ord.	—	48½
4	Do. 1st Mort. Deb. Stk. ..	$100	93½
8	North Pennsylvania	$50	—
—	Northn. Pacific, Com.....	$100	21½
1½	Pitts. F. Wayne & Chic...	$100	174
—	Reading 1st Pref.	$50	19
—	Do. 2nd Pref.	$50	10
—	S. Louis & S. Fran. Com.	$100	6½
—	Do. 2nd Pref.	$100	25
6	St. Louis Bridge 1st Pref..	$100	107
3	Do. 2nd Pref.	$100	50
6	Tunnel Rail. of St. Louis	$100	107
$1½	St. Paul, Min. and Man...	$100	137
—	Southern, Com.	$100	8
—	Wabash, Common	$100	7

AMERICAN RAILROAD BONDS. CURRENCY.

Last Div.	Name.	Price.
7	Albany & Susq. 1 Con. Mrt. 1906	118
7	Allegheny Val. 1 Mt. 1910	125½
5	Burling., Cedar Rap. & N. 1 Mt. 1906	109½
5	Canada Southern 1 Mt. 1908	111
5	Chic. & N. West. Sk. Fd. Db. 1933	120½
5	Do. Deb. Coupon 1921	115½
6	Chicago & Tomah 1905	112½
5	Chic. Burl. & Q. Skg. Fd. 1901	102½
4	Do. Nebraska Ext. ...... —	102
6	Chic., Mil., & S. Pl., 1 Mt. S.W. Div............... 1909	117½
7	Do. (S. Paul Div.) 1 Mt. 1902	132½
5	Do. (La Cross & D. 1919	112½
7	Do. 1 Mt. (Hast. & Dak.) 1910	132
5	Do. Chic. & Mis. Riv. 1 Mt. 1926	112½
5	Chic., Rock Is. and Pac. 1 Mt. Ext. 1934	108
6	Det., G. Haven & Mil. Equip 1918	105
6	Do. do. Cons. Mt. 1918	102½
6	Ill. Cent., 1 Mt., Chic. & S. 1898	—
7	Indianap. & Vin., 1 Mt. .. 1908	125
6	Do. do. 2 Mt. .. 1900	104½
6	Lehigh Val., Cons. Mt..... 1923	112½
—	Mexic. Cent., Ln. 2 Cons. Inc. ..	5
7	N.Y. Cent. & H.R. Mt. Bonds 1903	119½
5	Do. Deb. 1904	111
6	Penns. Cons. S. F M. 1905	119½
4	West Shore, 1 Mt. 2361	110

DITTO—GOLD.

Last Div.	Name.	Price.
6	Alabama Gt. Sthn. 1 Mt. .. 1908	112
5	Do. Mid. 1 1928	96
4	Allegheny Val. Gen. Mt. .. 1942	107
4	Atch., Top., & S. Fé Gn. Mt. 1995	90
3	Do. Adj. Mt. 1995	58
5	Do. Equipt. Tmst. ...... —	102½
5	Atlantic & Dan 1 Mt. 1950	—
5	Baltimore & Ohio 1925	97½
5	Do. Speyer's Tst. Recpts. 1925	96
5	Do. Cons. Mt. 1988	104
4½	Do. 4½ p.c. 1 Mt. Term. 1934	84
4½	Do. Brown Shipley's Dep. Cts. —	84
5	Balt. Belt 5 p.c. 1 Mort..... 1990	90
4½	Balt. & Ohio S.W. 1 Mt. .. 1990	103
4½	Do. 4½ p.c. 1 Cons. Mt. 1893 1993	78
—	Do. Inc. Mt. 5 p.c. Cl. A —	29½
—	Do. do. Cl. B —	11
5	Balt. & Ohio S.W. Term 5 p.c. 1942	99½
6	Balt. & Ptmac (Mn. L.) 1 Mt. 1911	124
6	Do. do. (Tunnel) 1 Mt. 1911	126
4	Beech Creek 1 Mt. 1936	109
5	Do 2 Mort. 1936	116
4	Carthage & Adiron 1 Mt... 1981	109

American Railroad Bonds—Gold (*continued*):—

Last Div.	Name.	Price.
5	Cent. of Georgia 1 Mort. .. 1945	117½
5	Do. Cons. Mt. 1945	92½
5	Cent. of N. Jrsy. Gn. Mt... 1987	114½
6	Central Pacific, 1 Mort. 1898	102½
6	Do. Speyer's Certs. ...... —	106
5	Do. Land Grant 1900	100
5	Chesap. & Ohio 1st Cons. Mt. 1939	117½
4½	Do. Gen. Mt. 1992	81
6	Chic. & W. Ind. Gen. Mt. Skg. Fd. 1932	120
5	Chic. Mil. & St. Pl. (Chic. & L. Sup.) 1 Mt. 1921	114½
5	Do. Chic. & Pac. W. 1921	119½
5	Do. Wisc. & Minn. 1 Mt. 1921	114½
5	Do. Terminal Mt. 1914	114½
4	Do. General Mt. 1989	108
5	Chic. St. L. & N. Orleans.. 1951	122½
4	Do. 1 Mort. (Memphis) .. 1951	105½
4	Clevel, Cin., Chic. & St. L. 1 Mt. (Cairo) 1939	90
4	Do. 1 Mt. (Cinc., Wab., & Mich.) 1991	90
4	Do. 1 Col. Tst. Mt. (S. Louis) 1990	98½
4	Do. General Mt. 1993	82½
4½	Clevel. & Mar. Mt. 1935	114
4½	Clevel. & Pittsburgh 1942	122½
4½	Do. Series B. 1942	122½
—	Colorado Mid. 1 Mt. 1936	63½
—	Do. Bdhrs.' Comm. Certs. —	63½
4	Dnvr. & R. Gde. 1 Cons. Mt. 1936	93
5	Do Imp. Mort. 1928	92
4	Detroit & Mack. 1 Lien 1995	92½
5	E. Tennes., Virg., & Grgia. Cons. Mt. 1956	114½
5	Elmira, Cort., & Nthn. Mt. 1914	100
4	Erie 1 Cons. Mt. Pr. Ln. .. 1996	90
3	Do. Gen. Lien 1996	71
6	Galvest., Harrisb., &c., 1 Mt.	107½
5	Georgia, Car. & N. 1 Mt. .. 1929	96
4½	Gd. Rpds & Inda. Ex. 1 Mt. 1941	112½
5	Do. 1 Mt. (Muskegon) .. 1926	39½
3½	Illinois Cent. 1 Mt. 1951	104½
4	Do. 1952	105
4	Do. Cairo Bdge. .. 1950	102
4	Do. 1953	104
4	Do. General Mort. .. 1904	102½
5	Kans. City, Pitts. & G. 1 M. 1923	80
3½	L. Shore & Mich. Southern 1997	109
4½	Lehigh Val. N.Y. 1 Mt..... 1940	106
5	Lehigh Val. Term. 1 Mt. .. 1941	109½
5	Long Island 1931	120½
5	Do. Deb. 1934	102
5	Do. (N. Shore Bch.) 1 Cons. Mt. 1932	94
6	Louisville & Nash. G. Mt.. 1930	121
6	Do. 2 Mt. Sk. Fd. (S. & N. Alabama 1910	104½
6	Do. 1 Mt. N Orl. & Mb. 1930	122½
5	Do. 1 Mt. Coll. Tst. ... 1931	106
4	Do. Unified 1940	88
4½	Do. Mobile & Montgy. 1 Mt. 1945	105½
4	Manhattan Cons. Mt. 1990	96
4	Mexican Cent. Cons. Mt. .. 1911	66
—	Do. 1 Cons. Inc, ...	15
6	Mexican Nat. 1 Mt. 1927	107
3	Do. 2 Mt. 6 p.c. Inc. A 1917	58
—	Do. do. B.. 1917	10
3	Do. Matheson's Certs.....	—
3	Michig. Cnt. (Battle Ck. & S.) 1 Mt. 1989	88
6	Minneap. & S. L. 1 Mt. Pacific Ext. 1921	117½
5	Do. 1 Consold. 1934	107½
4	Minne., Slt. S. M. & A. 1 Mt. 1926	98
5	Minneapolis Westn. 1 Mt... 1911	105½
4	Miss. Kans. & Tex. 1 Mt... 1990	89
4	Do. 2 do. 1990	61
4	Mobile & Birm. Mt. Inc.... 1945	38
5	Do. P. Lien 1945	88
4	Mohawk & Mal. 1 Mt. 1991	108
5	Montana Cent. 1 Mt. 1937	111½
5	Nashv., Chattan., & S. L. 1 Cons. Mt. 1928	102½
5	Nash., Flor., & Shff. Mt... 1937	95½
4	N. Y. & Putnam 1 Cons. Mt. 1993	108
5	N. Y., Brooklyn, & Man. B. 1 Cons. Mt. 1935	107½
4	N. Y. Cent. & Hud. R. Deb. Certs. 1890 1905	107
4	Do. Ext. Debt. Certs.... 1905	107
7	N. Y., L. Erie, & W. 1 Cons. Mt. (Erie) 1920	142½
7	Do. 1 Con. Mt. Fd. Coup. 1920	140
5	N. Y., Onto., & W. Cons. 1 Mt. 1939	110
4	Do. 4 p.c. Refund. Mt.. 1992	99
5	N. Y. & Rockaway B. 1 Mt. 1927	102½
6	Norfolk & West. Gn. Mt.... 1931	128
6	Do. Imp. & Ext 1934	118½
4	Do. 1 Cons. Mt. .... —	79
6	N. Pacific Gn. 1 Mt. Ld. Gt. 1921	
4	Do. P. Ln. Rl. & Ld. Gt. —	97
3	Do. Gn. Ln. Rl. & Ld. Gt. —	61½
5	Oregon & Calif. 1 Mt. 1927	78½
5	Oregon Rl. & Nav. Col. Tst. —	—
6	Panama Skg. Fd. Subsidy.. 1910	106½
4½	Pennsylvania Rlrd. 1913	115
4	Do. Equip. Tst. Ser. A.. 1914	104
4	Do. Cons. Mt. 1941	115
4½	Penna. Company 1st Mort. 1921	114
5	Perkiomen 1 Mrt., 2nd ser.. 1918	91½
4½	Pitts., C., C., & St. Ls. Con. Mt. G.B., Ser. A 1940-2	113
4	Do. Cons. Mort., Ser. D.. 1945	106
6	Pittsbgh., Cle., & Toledo .. 1922	107½
4	Reading, Phil., & R. Genl. 1997	83
5	Richmond & Dan. Equip. .. 1909	97½
5	Rio Grande Junc. 1st Mort. 1939	94
4	Rio Grande West 1st Tst. Mt. 1939	82½
6	St. Joseph & Gd. Island .. 1925	—
7	S. Louis Bridge 1st Mort 1928	134½
5	S. Louis Mchts. Bdge. Term. 1st Mort. 1930	102½

American Railroad Bonds (*continued*):

Last Div.	Name.	Price.
4	S. Louis S. West 1st Mort.. 1989	77½
—	Do. 4 p.c. 2nd Mort. Inc. 1989	30
—	S. Louis Term. Cupples Sta. & Prop. 1st. Mrt. 4½ p.c. 1902-17	102
4½	St. Paul, Minn., & Manit. 1933	110½
6	Do. do. 1933	132½
6	Shamokin, Sunbury, &c. 2 Mt. 1925	109
5	S. & N. Alabama Cons. Mt. 1936	97½
5	Southern 1 Cons. Coup. 1994	93
4	Do. E. Tennes Reorg. Lien .. 1938	100
6	S. Pacific of Cal. 1 Mt... 1905-12	111
4½	Trml. Assn. of S. Louis 1 Mt. 1939	111½
5	Do. 1 Cons. Mt. 1944	109
5	Texas & Pac. 1 Mt. 2000	100½
—	Do. 5 p.c. 2 Mt. Income 2000	30
5	Toledo & Ohio Cent. 1 Mt. West. Div. 1935	102½
4½	Toledo., Walhon., Val., & Ohio 1 Mt. 1931-3	111½
6	Union Pacific 1 Mt. 1896-9	102½
5	Do. Coll. Trust.	—
—	Union Pac., Linc., & Color. 1 Mt. 1918	—
4	United N. Jersey Gen. Mt... 1944	115½
6	Vicksbrg., Shrevept., & Pac. Pr. Ln. Mt. 1915	102½
5	Wabash 1 Mt. 1939	112
4	Wn. Pennsylvania Mt. 1928	109½
5	W. Virga. & Pittsbg. 1 Mt. 1990	88
5	Wheeling & L. Erie 1 Mt. (Wheelg. Div.) 5 p.c. 1928	90½
5	Do. Extn. Imp. Mt. 1930	90
—	Do. do. Brown Shipley's Cts...	—
5	Willmar & Sioux Falls 1 Mt. 1938	111

STERLING.

Last Div.	Name.	Price.
6	Alabama Gt. Sthn. Deb..... 1906	104½
5	Do. Gen. Mort. .. 1927-8	100
5	Alabama, N. Orl., Tex. & Pac. 5 p.c. "A" Dbs... 1910-40	99
55/	Do. do. "B" do. 1910-40	50
—	Do. do. "C" do.	19
—	Allegheny Valley 1910	136
4	Atlantic 1st Leased Line Perp...	98
6	Baltimore and Ohio 1902	107½
6	Do. do. 1910	118
5	Do. do. 1877.........	97½
—	Do. Morgan's Certs. ..	97½
4½	Do. do. 1933	89
6	Chicago & Alton Cons. Mt. 1903	112
5	Chic. St. Paul & Kan. City Priority	105
6	Eastn. of Massachusetts.... 1906	117½
5	Illinois Cent. Skg Fd.	105
5	Do. 1905	108
3½	Do. 1950	99½
4	Do. 1 Mt. 1951	112
3	Do. 1 Mt. 1951	92½
6	Louisville & Nash., M. C. & L. Div., 1 Mt. 1902	104½
7	Do. 1 Mt. (Memphis & O.) 1901	111
47/4	Mexican Nat. "A" Certs. 5 p.c. Non. cum.	47
—	Do. "B" Certs....	10
6	N.Y. & Canada 1 Mt. 1904	111½
6	N. York Cent. & H.R. Mort. 1903	112
4½	N. York, Penns., & Ohio Pr. Ln. Extd. 1935	—
5	Do. Equip. Tst.	103½
5	Do. 5 p.c. Equip. Tst. (1890)	103½
6	Nthn. Cent. Cons. Gen. Mt. ..	106
6	Pennsylvania Gen. Mt. 1910	126
6	Do. Cons. Skg. Fd. Mt. 1905	115½
3½	Do. Cons. Mt. 1945	106
6	Phil. & Erie Cons. Mort .. 1920	134½
6	Phil. & Reading Gen. Cons. Mort. 1911	126
6	Pittsbg. & Connells. Cons. 1926	116
—	Do. Morgan's Certs....	116
4	St. Paul., Min., & Manitoba (Pac. Extn.) 1940	97
6	S. & N. Alabama 1903	107½
6	Union Pacific, Omaha Bridge 1896	—
6	Un. N. Jersey & C. Gen. Mt. 1901	109½

FOREIGN RAILWAYS.

Last Div.	Name.	Paid.	Price.
4/	Ala[illegible]as, Ld., Shs.	20	6
5	[illegible] Deb. Stk., Red. ..	100	50
6	An[illegible]fagasta, Ltd., Stk. ..	100	71
4	[illegible] Perp. Deb. Stk. ..	100	90
—	Ara[illegible] Ld., Ord. Shs. ..	10	½
—	[illegible] 10 p.c. Cum. Pref.	10	1½
5	Arg[illegible]ne Gt. W., Ld.,	100	72
5	[illegible] 5 p.c. Cum. Pref. Shs.	100	100
4	[illegible] Deb. Stk.	100	103½
[illegible]	Ar[illegible]ne N.E., Ltd., 6 p.c. Cum. Pref. Stk. ..	100	10½
-	[illegible] 5 p.c. Deb. Stk., Red.	100	31
2/	[illegible]nd Tacna Shs. ..	20	1½
[illegible]	[illegible] & San Fcisco., Ld.,	20	11
[illegible]	[illegible] mbo. Bch. Shs.	20	5
[illegible]	[illegible] Blanca, & N.W. [illegible] Pref. Cum. 6 p.c. ..	100	54
[illegible]	[illegible] eb. Stk., Red.	100	96
6	[illegible]villa R. & P., Ld.,		96
	[illegible] Deb. Stk., Red.	100	

Foreign Railways (*continued*):—

Last Div.	Name.	Paid.	Price.
3/	Bilbao Riv. & Cantabn., Ltd., Ord.	3	6
—	Bolivar, Ltd., Shs.	10	1¾
6	Do. 6 p.c. Deb. Stk.	100	96½
—	Brazil Gt. Southn. Ltd., 7 p.c. Cum. Pref.	20	1¼
6	Do. Perm. Deb. Stk	100	47½
6½	B. Ayres Gt. Southn., Ld., Ord. Stk.	100	150
5	Do. Pref. Stk.	100	136
4	Do. Deb. Stk.	100	117
30/	B. Ayres & Ensen. Port., Ltd., Ord. Stk.	100	65
5	Do. Cum. 1 Pref. Stk.	100	123
6/0/0	Do. 6p.c.Con. Pref.Stk.	100	108
4	Do. Deb. Stk., Irred.	100	110
10⅝	B. Ayres Northern, Ltd., Ord. Stk.	100	265
12½	Do. Pref. Stk.	100	320
5	Do. 5 p.c. Mt. Deb. Stk., Red.	100	113
3/15/0	B. Ayres & Pac., Ld., 7 p.c. 1 Pref. Stk. (Cum.)	100	90
4	Do. 1 Deb. Stk.	100	101
5/5/0	Do. 4½ p.c. 2 Deb. Stk.	100	90
1	B Ayres & Rosario, Ltd., Ord. Stk.	100	72½
—	Do. New, £20 Shs.	20	22
7/	Do. 7 p.c. Pref. Shs.	10	17½
7/	Do. Sunchales Ext.	10	15½
4	Do. Deb. Stk., Red.	100	108
12/	B. Ayres & Val. Trans., Ltd., 7 p.c. Cum. Pref.	20	6½
4	Do. 4 p.c. "A" Deb. Stk., Red.	100	71
—	Do. 6 p.c. "B" Deb. Stk., Red.	100	44
6/	B. Ayres Westn. Ld. Ord.	10	11
3/	Do. Def. Shs.	10	6½
5	Do. 5 p.c. Pref.	10	12¾
4	Do. Deb. Stk.	100	108½
6	Cent. Arg. Deb. Sk. Rd.	100	160½
4	Do. Deb. Stk. Rd.	100	111
6	Cent. Bahia L. Ord. Stk.	100	44½
	Do. Deb. Stk., 1934	100	72½
5	Do. Deb. Stk., 1937	100	58
1/6	Cent. Uguy. East. Ext. L. Shs.	10	6
5	Do. Perm. Stk.	100	111
3/	Do. Nthn. Ext. L. Sh.	10	4½
5	Do. Perm. Deb. Stk	100	106
3	Do. of Montev. Ltd., Ord. Stk	100	87
6	Do. Perm. Deb. Stk	100	143
10/	Conde d'Eu, Ltd. Ord.	20	7
—	Cordba & Rosar., Ltd., 6 p.c. Pref. Shs.	100	42½
4	Do. 1 Deb. Stk	100	92
5/	Do. 6 p.c. Deb. Stk	100	84
—	Cordba Cent., Ltd., 5 p.c. Cu. 1 Pref. Stk.	100	83½
—	Do. 5 p.c. Non-Cum. 2 Pref. Stk	100	46
5	Do. Deb. Stk	100	120
—	Costa Rica, Ltd., Shs.	10	4¾
8/	Dna. Thrsa. Chris., Ltd., 7 p.c. Pref. Shs.	20	4½
20/	E. Argentine, Ltd	100	40
6	Do. Deb. Stk	100	105
1/1	Egypen. Dlta. Lgt. Rys., Ltd., £10 Pref. Shs.	8	8½
—	Entre Rios, L., Ord. Shs.	5	¾
—	Do. Cu. 5 p.c. Pref.	5	2¼
6/	Gt. Westn. Brazil, Ltd.,	20	10
6	Do. Perm. Deb. Stk	100	90½
6	Do. Extn. Deb. Stk	100	76½
—	Int.-Oceanic Mex., Ltd., 7 p.c. Pref.	10	1¾
4	Do. Deb. Stk	100	84
42/6	Do. 7 p.c. "A" Deb. Sk.	100	67
—	Do. 7 p.c. "B" Deb. Sk.	100	31
5/	La Guaira & Carac.	10	7½
5	Do. 5 p.c. Deb. Sk. Red.	100	100
8/4	Lembg.-Czern.-Jassy	30	25
1/	Lima, Ltd.	20	2½
—	Manila Ltd. 7 p.c. Cu. Pf.	10	¾
20/6½	Mexican 2nd Pref. 6 p.c.	100	34
6	Do. Perp. Deb. Stk.	100	142
1/0/0	Mexican Sthrn., Ld., Ord.	100	24
—	Do. 4 p.c. 1 Db. Stk. Rd.	100	84
—	Do. 4 p.c. 2 do.	100	61
—	Mid. Urgy., Ltd.	100	19
5	Do. Deb. Stk	100	63
12/	Minas & Rio, Ltd	20	11
5/2	Namur & Liege	20	12½
11/6	Do. Pref.	20	29
5/	Natal & Na. Cruz, Ld., 7 p.c. Cum Pref.	20	7½
—	Nitrate Ltd., Ord.	10	5
—	Do. 7 p.c. Pr. Con. Or.	10	3½
—	Do. Def. Conv. Ord.	10	¾
7/	N.-E. Urgy., Ltd., Ord	10	15
7/	Do. 7 p.c. Pref.	10	15½
—	N.-W. Argentine Ld., 7 p.c. Pref.	10	2½
6	Do. 6 p.c. 1 Deb. Stk.	100	113
—	Do. 2 Deb. Stk.	100	94
—	N.W. Uruguay 6 p.c. 1 Pref. Stk.	100	17
—	Do. 5 p.c. 2 Pref. Stk.	100	7¾
6	Do. 6 p.c. Deb. Stk	100	80½
16/	Ottoman (Sm. Aid.)	20	15¼
—	Paraguay Cntl., Ld., 5 p.c. Perm. Deb. Stk.	100	11
—	Piræus, Ath., & Pelo.	275	1½
5/	Pto. Alegre & N. Hambg. Ld., 7 p.c. Pref. Shs.	20	4
6	Do. Mt. Deb. Stk. Red.	100	77½
—	Puerto Cabello & Val. Ld.	10	1¾
5	Recife & S. Francisco	00	74
14/	R. Claro S. Paulo, Ld., Sh.	10	22½
5	Do. Deb. Stk.	100	127
	Royal Sardinian Ord	10	11¾

Foreign Railways (*continued*):—

Last Div.	Name.	Paid.	Price.
5/	Royal Sardinian Pref.	10	12½
5/	Sambre & Meuse	20	18
5/6	Do. Pref.	10	12½
28/	San Paulo Ld.	20	35½
2/9½	Do. New Ord. £10 sh.	6	10½
2/	Do. 5 p.c. Non. Cm. Pref.	10	12½
5½	Do. Deb. Stk.	100	135
5	Do. 5 p.c. Deb. Stk	100	128
—	S. Fé & Cordova, Gt. Sthn., Ld., Shares	100	51½
6	Do. Perp. Deb. Stk.	100	123
3/2½	S. Austrian	20	7½
10/	Sthn. Braz. R. Gde. do Sul, Ld.	20	8
6	Do. 6 p.c. Deb. Stk.	100	75
4	Swedish Centl., Ld., 4 p.c. Deb. Stk.	100	107
5	Do. Pref.	100	100
1/9	Taltal, Ld.	5	2½
—	Uruguay Nthn., Ld. 7 p.c. Pfd. Stk.	100	8
3½	Do. 5 p.c. Deb. Stk.	100	30
—	Villa Maria & Rufino, Ld., 6 p.c. Pref. Shs.	100	20
4	Do. 4 p.c. 1 Deb. Stk.	100	74
6/0/0	Do. 6 p.c. 2 Deb. Stk.	100	47
5/9	West Flanders	8½	21
5/6	Do. 5½ p.c. Pref.	10	18
3/	Wstn. of Havana, Ld.	10	4½

FOREIGN RAILWAY OBLIGATIONS

Per Cent.	Name.	Price.
6	Alagoas Ld., 6 p.c. Deb., Rd.	88½
—	Alcoy & Gandia, Ld., 5 p.c. Debs., Red.	25
5	Arauco., Ld., 5 p.c. 1st Mt., Rd.	64½
—	Do. 6 p.c. Mt. Deb., Rd.	44
6	Brazil G. Sthn., L., Mt. Dbs., Rd.	80½
6	Do. Mt. Dbs. 1893, Rd.	48½
5½	Campos & Caran. Dbs., Rd.	76
6	Central Bahia, L., Dbs., Rd.	90½
5½	Conde d'Eu, L., Dbs., Rd.	76
6	Costa Rica, L., 1st Mt. Dbs., Rd.	111
6	Do. 2nd Dbs., Rd.	93
5	Do. Prior Mt. Db., Rd.	104
6	Cucuta Mt. Dbs., Rd.	106
5½	Donna Thrsa. Cris., L., Dbs., Rd.	73
3	Eastn. of France, £20 Dbs., Rd.	19½
4	Egyptn. Delta Light, L., Db., Rd.	100
—	Espito. Santo & Cara. 5 p.c. Stl. Dbs., Rd.	38
4	Gd. Russian Nic., Rd.	102
5	Inter-Oceanic Mex., L., 5 p.c. Pr. Ln. Dbs., Rd.	103
3	Ital. 3 p.c. Bds. A & B, Rd.	57½
—	Ituana 6 p.c. Debs., 1918	74
—	Leopoldina, 6 p.c. Dbs. £50 Bds.,	22
—	Do. do. Comms. Cert.	22
—	Do. 5 p.c. Stg. Dbs. (1888), Rd.	31
—	Do. do. Comm. Certs.	31
—	Do. 5 p.c. Stg. Dbs. (1890), Rd.	22
—	Do. do. Comms. Certs.	22
—	Macahé & Cam. 5 p.c. Dbs., Rd.	31
—	Do. do. Comms. Certs.	31
—	Do. (Cantagallo), 5 p.c., Red.	31
—	Do. do. Comm. Certs.	31
—	Manila Ltd., 6 p.c. Deb., Red.	23
6	Do. Prior Lien Mt., Rd.	105
6	Do. Series "B," Rd.	80
7	Matanzas & Sab., Rd.	101½
6	Minas & Rio, L., 6 p.c. Dbs., Rd.	96
5	Mogyana 5 p.c. Deb. Bds., Rd.	104
5	Moscow-Jaros., Rd.	106½
5½	Natal & Na. Cruz Ltd., 5½ p.c. Debs., Red.	86
5	Nitrate, Ltd. Mt. Bds., Red.	80
3	Nthn. France, Red.	19½
4	N. of S. Af. Rep. (Trnsvl.) Gu. Bds. Red.	96
3	Nthn. of Spain £20 Pri. Obs. Red.	9
6	Ottmn. (Smy to A.)(Kujk) Asnt. Debs., Red.	109
6	Ottmn. (Seraik.) Asg. Debs. Red.	109
6	Ottmn. (Seraik.) Non-Asg. D., Rd	109
5	Ottmn. Kuyjk. Ext. Red.	106
5	Ottmn. Serkeuy. Ext. Red.	101½
5	Ottmn. Tireh Ext. 1910	98
5	Ottmn. Debs, 1886, Red.	98
5	Do. 1888, Red. 1935	97½
5	Do. 1893, Red. 1935	99
5	Ottmn. of Anlia. Debs., Rd.	93
5	Do. Ser. II.	89
4	Ottomn. Smyr. & Cas. Ext. Bds., Red.	83½
3	Paris, Lyon & Medit. (old sys., £20), Red.	19
3	Paris, Lyon & Medit. (new sys., £20), Red.	19½
50/	Piræus, At. & Pelp., 6 p.c. 1st Mt. Bds., Red.	88½
3	Do 5 p.c. Mt. Bds., Red.	61½
4	Pretoria-Pietbg., Ltd., Red.	93
7	Puerto Cab. & Val., Ltd., 1st Mt. Debs., Red.	94
—	Rio de Jano. & Nthn., Ltd., 6 p.c. £100 Deb., Red.	22
—	Rio de Jano. (Gr. Para.), 5 p.c. 1st Mt. St. £100 Debs., Red.	22
7	Royal Sardinian, A, Rd. £20	12
	Royal Sardinian, B., Rd. £20	12

Foreign Rly. Obligations (*continued*):—

Per Cent.	Name.	Price.
5	Ryl. Trns.-Afric. 5 p.c. 1st Mt. £100 Bds., Red.	61
7	Sagua La Grande, B pRd.	98
4	Sa. Fe & Cor. G.S., Ld. Pr. Ln. Bds.	104
5	Sa. Fe, 5 p.c. 2nd Reg. Dbs.	80
3	South Austrian, £20 Red.	15½
3	South Austrian, (Ser X.)	15½
3	South Italian £20 Obs. (Ser. A to G), Red.	12½
3½	S.W. of Venez. (Barq.), Ltd., 7 p.c. 1st Mt. £100 Debs.	55½
5	Taltal, Ltd., 5 p.c. 1st Ch. Debs., Red.	99
5	Utd. Rwys. Havana, Red.	91½
3	Wtrn. of France, £20 Red.	19
6	Wrn. B. Ayres St. Mt. Debs., 1900	111
6	Wrn. B. Ayres, Reg. Cert.	109
5	Do. Mt. Bds.	122
6	Wtrn. of Havna., Ld. Mt. Dbs., Rd.	98
7	Wrn. Ry. San Paulo Red.	101
—	Wrn. Santa Fé 7 p.c. Red.	38
4/7	Zafra & Huelva, 3 p.c. Red.	3

BANKS.

Div.	Name.	Paid.	Price.
1/9½	Agra, Ltd.	6	3½
4/2½	Anglo-Argentine, Ltd., £9	7	5½
8½ fls.	Anglo-Austrian	120 fl.	14
6/	Anglo-Californian, Ltd., £20 Shares	10	11
4/	Anglo-Egyptian, Ltd., £15	5	6
5/	Anglo-Foreign Bkg., Ltd.	7	8
2/	Anglo-Italian, Ltd.	5	7½
7/6	Bk. of Africa, Ltd., £18¾	6¼	10½
20/	Bk. of Australasia	40	53
10/	Bk. of Brit. Columbia	20	21
25/	Bk. of Brit. N. America	50	66
20/	Bk. of Egypt, Ltd., £25	12½	18
5/	Bk. of Mauritius, Ltd.	10	9½
18/	Bk. of N. S. Wales	20	36½
4 p.c.	Bk. of N. Zland. Gua. Stk.	100	103
6/	Bk. of Roumania, £20 Shs.	6	7½
2/6	Tarapaca & Ldn., Ltd., £10	5	3½
—	Bque. Fse. de l'Afri. du S.	100 f.	3½
f. 12.50	Bque. Internatle. de Paris	20	24
6/	Brit. Bk. of S. America, Ltd., £20 Shares	10	10
16/	Capital & Cties., L., £50	10	39
16/	Chart. of India, &c.	20	32
10/	City, Ltd., £40 Shares	10	19½
18/	Colonial, £100 Shares	30	21
10/	Delhi and London, Ltd.	25	—
5/	German of London, Ltd.	10	10½
25/	Hong-Kong & Shanghai	28½	44
4/	Imperl. of Persia	6½	3½
10/	Imperl. Ottoman, £20 Shs	10	11½
12/	Intrnatl. of Ldn., Ld., £20	15	11½
10/	Ionian, Ltd.	25	15
16/	Lloyds, Ltd., £50 Shs.	8	29½
10/	Ldn. & Braziln. Ltd., £20	10	18
44/	Ldn. & County, Ltd., £80	20	101
9/	Ldn. & Hanseatic, L., £20	10	10½
22/6	Ldn. & Midland, L., £60	12½	53½
8/9	Ldn. & Provin., Ltd., £10	5	22½
39/	Ldn. & Riv. Plate, L., £25	15	50½
2/1½	Ldn. & San Fcisco, Ltd.	7	4½
28/	Ldn. & Sth. West., L., £50	20	69
26/	Ldn. & Westmins., L., £100	20	56
3/	Ldn. of Mex. & S. Amer., Ltd., £10 Shs.	6	5½
15/	Ldn. Joint Stk., L., £100	15	33½
12/9½	Ldn., Paris & Amer., L. £20	16	25
2/4½	Merchant Bkg., L., £9	4	2¾
6/3	Metropn, Ltd., £50 Shs.	5	14½
9/	National, Ltd., £50 Shs.	10	19½
4/5	Natl. of Mexico, $100 Shs.	$40	13
1/3	National of N. Z., L., £7½	2½	2
3/	National S. Afric. Rep.	10	15
18/10½	National Provcl. of Eng., Ltd., £75 Shs.	10½	50½
21/7½	Do. do. £60 Shs.	12	57
6/6	North Eastn., Ltd., £20 Shs	6	14½
19/	Parr's, Ld., £100 Shs.	20	91½
12/6	Prov. of Ireland, L., £100	12½	28½
40/	Stand. of S. Afric., L., £100	25	67
19/6	Union of Australia, L., £75	25	28
4 p.c.	Do. do. Ins. Stk. Dep. 1900	100	102
15/6	Union of Ldn., Ltd., £100	15½	35½

BREWERIES AND DISTILLERIES

Div.	Name.	Paid.	Price.
4½	Albion Prp. 1 Mt. Db. Sk.	100	115
4	All Saints', L., Db. Sk. Rd.	100	99
7	Allsopp, Ltd	100	154
6	Do. Cum. Pref	100	159
4½	Do. Deb. Stk., Red.	100	118
3½	Do. Deb. Stk., Red.	100	102
4½	Alton & Co., L., Db., Rd	100	106
4½	Do. Mt. Bds., 1896	100	105
—	Arnold, Perrett, Ltd.	20	6
6	Do. Cum. Pref.	10	10½
4½	Do. 1 Mt. Db. Stk., Rd.	100	106

Breweries &c. (*continued*):—

Div.	Name.	Paid.	Price.
5½	Arrol, A., & Sons, L. Cum. Pref. Shs.	10	10½
4½	Do. 1 Mt. Db. Stk., Rd.	100	106
5	Backus, 1 Mt. Db., Red.	100	61
4	Barclay, Perk., L., Cu. Pf.	10	11½
3½	Do. Mt. Db. Stk., Red.	100	111
—	Barnsley, Ltd.	10	12
6	Do. Cum. Pref.	10	14
1/3	Barrett's, Ltd	2½	1½
1/3	Do. 5 p.c. Pref.	2½	2¼
3/	Bartholomay, Ltd.	10	4
8	Do. Cum. Pref.	10	9
6	Do. Deb.	100	102½
5	Bass, Ratcliff, Ltd., Cum. Pref. Stk.	100	144½
4½	Do. Mt. Db. Stk., Rd.	100	126
4	Bell, J., L., 1 Mt. D. Stk., R	100	100
2/6	Benskin's, L., Cum. Pref.	5	—
4½	Do. 1 Mt. Db. Stk Red.	100	—
4½	Do. "B" Deb. Sk, Rd.	100	—
7/	Bentley's Yorks., Ltd.	10	11½
6/	Do. Cum. Pref.	10	12½
4½	Do. Mt. Debs., Red	100	110
4½	Do. do. 1892, Red.	100	110
—	Bieckert's, Ltd.	20	2
5	Do. Debs., Red.	100	57
—	Birmingham., Ltd., 6 p.c. Cum. Pref.	5	2½
4½	Do. Mt. Debs., Red.	50	40½
5½	Boardman's, Ld., Cm. Pf.	10	8½
4½	Do., Perp. 1 Mt. Db. Sk.	100	105½
15/2	Brain & Co., Ltd.	100	102
4½	Brakspear, L., 1 D. Stk. Rd	100	109
4	Brandon's, L., 1 D. Stk. R.	100	105½
21/	Bristol (Georges) Ltd.	10	46
6	Do. Cum. Pref.	10	18
5	Do. Mt. Db. Sk. 1888 Rd.	100	115½
17/6	Bristol United, Ltd.	10	35½
6	Do. Cum. Pref.	10	16½
4½	Do. Db. Sk. Rd.	100	126
5½	Buckley's, L., C. Pre-pf.	10	11
4½	Do. 1 Mt. Db. Stk. Rd.	100	105½
4	Bullard & Sns, L., D. Sk. R.	100	107
6	Bushell, Watk., L., C. Pf.	10	14
4½	Do. 1 Mt. Db. Sk. Rd.	100	112
5	Camden, Ltd., Cum. Pref.	10	11½
4½	Do. 1 Mt. Db. Sk. Rd.	100	108
5½	Cameron, Ltd., Cm. Prf.	10	13½
4½	Do. Mort Deb. Stk.	100	108
3½	Do. Perp Mt. Db. Sk.	100	100½
5	Cam'bell, J'stone, L., C. Pf.	5	6½
4½	Do. 4½ p.c. 1 Mt. Db. Sk.	100	105
4	Campbell, Praed, L., Per. 1 Mort. Deb. Stk.	100	108
4	Cannon, L., Mt. Db. Stk.	100	109
4	Do. "B" Deb. Stk.	100	104
5	Castlemaine, L., 1 Mt. Db.	100	94
3½	Charrington, Ltd., Mort. Deb. Stk. Red.	100	106
2/	Cheltnhm. Orig., Ltd.	5	7
6	Do. Cum. Pref.	5	7½
4	Do. Debs. Red.	100	107
10/	Chicago, Ltd.	10	3½
6	Do. Debs.	100	87½
—	Cincinnati, Ltd.	10	[illegible]
—	Do. Cum. Pref.	10	1½
10/	City of Baltimore	10	4
16/	Do. 8 p.c. Cum. Pref	10	8
14/	City of Chicago, Ltd.	10	1½
8	Do. Cum. Pref.	10	6
13	City of London, Ltd.	100	205½
5	Do. Cum. Pref.	100	137
4	Do. Mt. Deb. Stk., Rd.	100	112½
2/	Colchester, Ltd.	5	5
7	Do. Pref.	5	7
4½	Do. Deb. Stk., Red.	100	110
5	Combe, Ltd., Cum. Pref.	10	14½
4	Do. Mt. Db. Stk, Rd.	100	112
3½	Do. Perp. Deb. Stk.	100	107
5	Comm'cial, L., D. Sk., Rd.	100	108½
5	Courage, L., Cm. Pref. Shs.	100	130½
4	Do. Irr. Mt. Deb. Stk.	100	128
3½	Do. Irr. "B" Mt. Db. Sk.	100	106
8	Daniell & Sons, Ltd.	10	8½
7	Do. Cum. Pref.	10	12½
4½	Do. 1 Mt. Perp. Db. Sk.	100	108½
4½	Do. "B" Deb. Stk.	100	102
10d.	Dartford, Ltd.	5	5
10d.	Do. Cum. Pref.	5	5½
4	Do. 1 Mt. Db. Sk. Rd	100	108
4	Davenport, Ld., 1 D. Stk.	100	108½
10/	Denver United, Ltd.	10	3½
8	Do. Cum. Pref.	10	8½
6	Do. Debs.	100	90½
4½	Deuchar, L., 1 D. Sk., Rd.	100	108
6/	Distillers, Ltd.	10	24
4½	Do. Mt. Db. Stk., Rd.	100	115½
—	Dublin Distillers, Ltd.	5	1½
3/	Do. Cum. Pref.	5	4½
4½	Do. Irr. Deb. Stk.	100	—
5	Eadie, Ltd., Cum. Pref.	10	11½
4	Do. Irr. 1 Mt. Db. Sk.	100	108
10/	Edinbgh. Utd., Ltd.	10	13
6	Do. Cum. Prf.	10	13½
5	Do. 1 Mt. Dbs.	100	110½
4	Eldridge, Pope, L. D. St. R.	100	109
—	Emerald & Phœnix, Ltd.	10	1½
8	Do. Cum. Pref.	10	6½
6	Empress Ltd., C. Pf.	10	11½
4½	Do. Mt. Deb. Stk.	100	105
10/	Farnham, Ltd.	10	14
6	Do. Cum. Pref.	10	15
4	Fenwick, L., 1 D. Sk., Rd.	100	105
4	Flower & Sons, Irr. D. Sk.	100	111
4	Friary, L., 1 Db. Stk., Rd.	100	105½
4	Do. 1 "A" Db. Sk., Rd	100	102
4½	Groves, L., 1 Db. Sk., Rd.	100	110
14	Guinness, Ltd.	100	565
6	Do. Cum. Prf. Stk.	100	168½
5	Do. Deb. Stk., Red.	100	122
5	Hall's Oxford L., Cm. Pf.	5	5½
6/	Hancock, Ld., Cm. Pf. Ord.	10	14
7/	Do. Def. Ord.	10	17½

Breweries, &c. (*continued*) :—

Div.	Name.	Paid.	Price.
6	Hancock, Ld., Cum. Pref.	10	15½
4	Do. 1 Deb. Stk., Rd.	100	112
5	Hoare, Ltd. Cum. Pref.	10	13½
5	Do. "A" Cum. Pref.	10	12½
4	Do. Mt. Deb. Stk., Rd.	100	111
3½	Do. do. do. Rd.	100	104
4/6	Hodgson's, Ltd.	5	10
5	Do. 1 Mt. Db., Red.	—	120½
4	Do. 2 Mt. Db., 1906	—	102
4½	Hopcraft & N., Ltd., 1 Mt. Deb. Stk., Red.	100	103
5	Huggins, Ltd., Cm. Prf.	10	12½
4½	Do. 1st D. Stk. Rd.	100	113
4½	Do. "B" Db. Stk. Rd.	100	111
8/	Hull, Ltd.	10	18
7	Do. Cum. Pref.	10	15
4½	Ind, Coope, L., D. Sk., Rd.	100	118
4	Do. "B" Mt. Db. Stk. Rd.	100	114
8/	Indianapolis, Ltd.	10	3½
8	Do. Cm. Prf.	10	9½
5/	Jones, Frank, Ltd.	10	3½
7½	Do. Cum. Pref.	10	7½
5	Do. 1st Mort. Debs.	100	91½
4/	J. Kenward & Ct., Ltd.	5	5½
4½	Kingsbury, L., 1 D. Sk., Rd	100	—
4	Lacon, L., D. Stk., Red.	100	110
4	Do. Irrd. "B" D. Sk.	100	106
4/	Lascelles, Ltd.	5	11
6	Do. Cum. Pref.	5	7½
5	Leney, Ltd., Cum. Pref.	10	11½
4	Do. 1 Mt. Db. Stk. Rd.	100	104
30/7½	Lion, Ltd., £25 shares	17	49½
10/9½	Do. New £10 shares	6	17
6	Do. Perp. Pref.	20	33
4	Do. B. Mt. Db. Sk. Rd.	100	109
4½	Lloyd & Y., Ltd., 1 Mt. Deb. Stk., Rd.	100	100½
4½	Locke & S., Ltd., Irr. 1st Mt. Deb. Stk.	100	101
4½	Lovibond, Ltd., 1st Mt. Deb. Stk., Rd.	100	102½
30/4	Lucas & Co., Ld., Deb. Stk.	100	107
8/	Manchester, Ltd.	10	19
7	Do. Cum. Pref.	10	17
5	Marston, J., L., Cm. Prf.	10	10½
4	Do. 1 Mt. Db. Sk., Rd.	100	101½
9/	Massey's Burnley, Ltd.	10	17
6	Do. Cum. Pref.	10	14½
4½	McCracken, Ltd., 1 Mt. Deb., 1908	100	61½
5	McEwan, Ltd., Cm. Pref.	10	15
5	Meux, Ltd., Cum. Pref.	10	14½
4	Do. Mt. Db. Stk. Red.	100	111
4½	Michell & A., Ltd., 1 Mt. Deb. Stk. Red.	100	106
4½	Mile End Dist. Db. Sk. Rd.	100	109
—	Milwaukee & Chic., Ltd.	10	1½
4/	Do. Cum. Pref.	10	6½
4½	Michell, Toms, L., Db.	50	57
6	Morgan, Ltd., Cum. Pref.	10	14½
10/	Nalder & Coll., Ltd.	10	35
6	Do. Cum. Pref.	10	16
4½	Do. Deb. Red.	100	113
3/	New Beeston, Ltd.	5	4½
2/9	Do. Cum. Pref.	5	5
4	Do. Mt. Deb. Stk. Red.	100	97½
12/	Newcastle, Ltd.	10	19½
6	Do. Cum. Pref.	10	15
5	Do. 1 Mt. Deb., 1911	100	110½
4	Do. "A" Deb. Stk. Red.	100	104
6	New England, Ltd.	10	5
8	Do. Cum. Pref.	10	9½
6	Do. Debs. Red.	100	104½
4	New London, L., 1 D. Sk.	100	103
7/2	New Westminster, Ltd.	4	10½
2/4½	Do. Pref.	4	6½
—	New York, Ltd.	10	1
—	Do. 8 p.c. Cum. Pref.	10	4½
6	Do. 1 Mt. Deb. Red.	100	80½
5	Noakes, Ld., Cum. Pref.	10	12½
4	Do 1 Mt. Db. Stk., Rd.	100	106
4½	Norfolk, L., "A" D. Sk. Rd.	100	106
10/	Northampton, Ld.	10	16½
7	Do. Cum. Pref.	10	15½
6	Do. Cum. Pref.	10	13
5	Do. 1 Mt. Per. Db. Sk.	100	128
4	Nth. East., L., 1 D. Sk. Rd.	100	102
4½	N. Worcesters., L. Per. 1 Mort. Deb. Stock	100	88½
6	Nottingham, L., Cm. Prf.	10	12
5	Do. 1 Mt. Deb. Stk., Red.	100	114
17/4	Do. "B" do. Red.	50	112
6/	Ohlsson' Cape, Ld.	5	17
7	Do. Cum. Pref.	5	8½
4½	Do. 2nd Cum. Pref.	5	5½
5	Do. Deb. Stk., Red.	100	114
4½	Oldfield, L., 1 Mt. Db. Stk.	100	106
6	Page & Overt., L., Cm. Prf.	10	13½
4½	Do. 1 Mt. Dbs., Red.	100	109
10/	Parker's Burslem, Ltd.	10	24½
6	Do. Cum. Pref.	10	15
4	Do. 1 Mt. Db. Stk., Red.	100	113
4	Persse, Ld., 1 Mt. Db. Rd.	100	95½
4	Phipps, L., Irr. 1 Db. Stk.	100	115
8	Plymouth, L., Min. Cu. Pf.	10	13½
4½	Do. Mt. Deb. Stk., Red.	100	104½
4½	Pryor, Reid, L., 1 D.S., R.(†	100	105½
5	Reid's, Ld., Cm. Pref. Stk.	100	137½
4	Do. Mt. Deb. Stk., Red.	100	112
3½	Do. "B" Mt. Db. Stk., Rd	100	102
5	Rhondda Val., L., Cu. Pf	10	11
4½	Do. 1 Mt. Deb. Stk., Rd.	100	109
5	Robinson, Ld., Cum. Pref.	10	11½
4½	Do. 1 Mt. Perp. Db. Stk.	100	112
4/	Rochdale, Ltd.	10	5½
4½	Do. 1 Mt. Deb. Stk.	100	98½
7	Royal, Brentford, Ltd.	10	20½
	Do. Cum. Pref.	10	15
4½	Do. 1 Mt. Dbs. Red	100	109
6/	St. Louis, Ltd.	10	4
8	Do. Cum. Pref.	10	8½
14/	St. Pauli, Ltd.	10	10
7	Do. Cum. Pref.	10	12
4½	Salt (T.), L., 1 Db. Sk. Rd.	100	110

Breweries, &c. (*continued*) :—

Div.	Name.	Paid.	Price.
4½	Salt (T.), "B" Db. Stk. Red	100	108
—	San Francisco, Ltd.	10	½
—	Do. 8 p.c. Cum. Pref.	10	½
4½	Savill Brs., L., D. Sk. Rd.	100	118
4½	Scarboro., Ltd., 1 Db. Stk.	100	101
4	Shaw (Hy.), Ltd., 1 Mt. Db. Stk., Red.	100	104
22/	Showell's, Ltd.	10	33½
7	Do. Cum. Pref.	10	17½
3/	Do. Gua. Shs.	5	7½
4½	Do. Mt. Db. Stk., Red.	100	—
4	Simonds, L., 1 D. Sk., Rd.	100	109
5½	Simson & McP., L., Cu. Pf.	10	9½
4½	Do. 1 Mt. Deb. Stk.	100	100
5/	Smith, Garrett, L., £20 Shs	10	16½
5	Do. Cum. Pref.	20	26
—	Do. 3½ p.c. Mt. Db. Stk.	100	109
5	Smith's, Tadcster, L., C Pf	10	12½
4½	Do. Deb. Stk., Red.	100	112
4	Do. Deb. Stk. Red.	100	108
4½	Star, L., 1 M. Db. Stk., Rd.	100	105
4	Steward & P., L., 1 D. Sk.	100	113
9/	Strettons Derby, Ltd.	10	13
6	Do. Cum. Pref.	10	13
4	Do. Irr. 1 Mt. Db. Stk.	100	103½
4½	Strong, Romsey, L., 1 D. S.	100	115
5	Stroud, L., Db. Sk., Rd.	100	111½
4½	Tadcaster To'er, L., D. Sk.	100	113
8/	Tamplin, Ltd.	10	21½
6	Do. Cum. Pref.	100	15
4	Do. "A" Db. Sk., Rd.	10	107
6	Thorne, Ltd., Cum. Pref.	10	14½
4	Do. Deb. Stk., Red.	100	105½
15/	Threlfall, Ltd.	10	47
6	Do. Cum. Pref.	10	16½
5	Do. 1 Mt. Dbs., Red.	100	116
4	Tollemache, L., D. Sk. Rd.	100	105
4	Truman, Hanb., D. Sk., R.	100	110
3	Do. "B" Mt. Db. Sk., Rd.	100	95
10/	United States, Ltd.	10	10
8	Do. Cum. Pref.	10	12
6	Do. 1 Mt. Deb.	100	107½
6/	Walker & H., Ld., Cm. Prf.	10	11½
4½	Do. 1 Mt. Deb. Stk., Red.	100	107
5	Walker, Peter, Ld. Cm. Prf.	10	14
4	Do. 1 Mt. Dbs. Red.	100	111
4	Wallingford, L., D. Sk. Rd.	100	107
6	Watney, Ld., Cm. Prf. Sk.	100	170
5	Do. Mt. Db. Sk., Rd.	100	117½
4½	Do. "B" Mt. Db. Sk., Rd.	100	112
3½	Do. Mt. Db. Stk.	100	101
5	Watney, D., Ld., Cm. Prf.	10	12½
4½	Do. 1 Mt. Db. Stk.	100	108
10/	Webster & Sons, Ltd.	10	16½
6	Do. Cum. Pref.	10	14
5	Wenlock Ltd., Pref.	10	12½
4	Do. 1 Mt. Db. Sk., Rd.	100	108
5	West Cheshire, L., Cu. Pf.	10	10½
4	Do. Irred. 1 Mt. Db. Sk.	100	99
4½	Whitbread, L., Cu. Pf. Sh.	100	124½
4	Do. Db. Stk., Red.	100	112
3½	Do. "B" Db. Stk., Rd.	100	100
9/	Wolverhmpton & D. Ld.	10	16½
6	Do. Cum. Pref.	10	13½
4½	Do. 1 Mt. Dbs., Red.	100	108
5½	Worthington, Ld., Cm. Prf.	10	15½
5½	Do. Cum. "B" Pref.	10	13½
4½	Do. Mt. Db. Sk., Rd.	100	114
3½	Do. Irr. "B" Db. Stk.	100	104½
10/	Yates's Castle, Ltd.	10	13½
5	Do. Cum. Pref.	10	11
5	Younger W., L., Cu. Pf. Sh.	100	135

CANALS AND DOCKS.

Last Div.	Name.	Paid.	Price.
4	Birmingham Canal	100	142½
—	E. & W. India Dock	100	21
4	Do. Deb. Stk.	100	—
50/	Do. Def. Deb. Stk.	100	—
3½	Do. 1st Mt. Certs.	100	—
4	Do. Mt. Bds. (1885)	—	—
40/	G. Junction Ord. Shs.	100	151½
6/	Do. do. Pref.	10	19
4½	King's Lynn Per. Db. Stk.	100	117½
2½	Leeds & Lpool Canal	100	72
2½	Lndn & St. Kath. Dks.	100	57
4½	Do. Pref.	100	136½
4½	Do. Pref., 1878	100	132½
4½	Do. Pref., 1882	100	130
4	Do. Deb. Stk.	100	134½
—	Mchester Ship C. 5 p.c. Pf.	10	1½
3½	Do. 1st Perp. Mt. Deb.	100	98
—	Milford Dks. Db. Stk. "A"	100	18½
3½	Millwall Dk.	100	59
5	Do. Perp. Pref.	100	140½
4½	Do. Pref.	100	106½
5	Do. New Per. Prf., 1887	100	126½
5	Do. Per. Deb. Stk.	100	152½
4/	Newhaven Hbr.	10	14½
2½	N. Metropolitan	100	65
5	Sharpness Nw. Pf. "A" Sk.	100	144½
4	Do. Deb. Stk.	100	120½
4	Sheffield & S. Yorks Nav. 4½ p.c. Pref Stk.	100	117½
36.432	Suez Canal	20	137
7	Surrey Comcl. Dok., Ord.	100	147½
7	Do. Min. 4 p.c. Pref. "A"	110	150
5	Do. Pref. "B"	100	148½
5	Do do. "C"	100	148½
5	Do. do. "D"	100	144½
4½	Do. Deb. Stk.	100	152½

COMMERCIAL, INDUSTRIAL, &c.

Last Div.	Name.	Paid.	Price.
5	Accles, L., 1 Mt. Db., Red.	100	84½
5/	Aërated Bread, Ltd.	1	13
—	African Gold Recovery, L.	1	½
2/	Aluminium, L., "A" Shs.	1	2
4½	Do. 1 Mt. Db. Stk., Red.	100	99
5½	Amelia Nitr., L., 1 Mort. Deb., Red.	100	82½
7/	Anglo-Chil. Nitrate, Ltd., Cum. Pref.	10	6½
4½	Do. Cons. Mt. Bds., Red.	100	71½
4½	Anglo-Russian Cotton, Ld., 1 Charge Debs., Red.	100	99
11/3	Angus (G., & Co., L.), £10	7½	17
6/	Apollinaris, Ltd.	10	11½
5/	Do. 5 p.c. Cum. Pref.	10	10½
4	Do. Irred. Deb. Stock	100	106
8/	Appleton, French, & S., L.	5	½
3/	Argentine Meat Pres., L., 7 p.c. Pref.	10	2½
5	Argentine Refinry, Db. Rd.	100	98
2/2	Armstrong, Whitw., Ltd.	1	3½
4	Do. Cum. Pref.	5	6½
5	Artisans', Labr. Dwllgs., L.	100	131½
4½	Do. Non-Cm. Prf., 1879	100	132½
4½	Do. do. 1884	100	132½
—	Asbestos & Asbestic, Ltd.	10	8
2/7½	Ashley-grdns., L., C. Prf.	5	6½
4½	Do. 1 Mt. Deb. Stk.	100	112½
5/	Assam Rly. & Trdng., L., 8 p.c. Cum. Pref. "A"	10	15½
—	Do. Deferrd. "B" Shs.	1	4½
—	Do. do. (iss. f. pd)	1	3½
8/	Do. Cum. Pre-Prf. "A"	10	15
6/	Do. New Pref.	10	11½
5	Do. Debs., Red.	100	107
5	Do. Red. Mort. Debs.	100	111
6	Aust'lian Pastrl, L., Cu. Pf.	10	7½
8d.	Aylesbury Dairy, Ltd.	1	1½
4	Do. 4 p.c. Mt. Dbs.	100	104½
10/	Babcock & Wilcox, Ltd.	10	30
6	Do. 6 p.c. Cm. Prf.	10	16
8	Baker (Chs.), L., Cm. Pf.	5	9
8	Do. "B" Cm. Pref.	5	8½
8d.	Barker (John), Ltd.	1	2½
5½	Do. Cum. Pref.	5	7½
4½	Do. Irred. 1 Mt. Db. Stk.	100	131
—	Barnagore Jute, Ltd.	5	3
5	Do. Cum. Pref.	5	4½
7½d.	Belgravia Dairy, Ltd.	1	1½
5/	Bell (R.) & Co., Ltd.	5	4½
1/	Bell's Asbestos, Ltd.	1	½
5	Do. Mt. Db. Bds., Rd.	100	103
10/	Bengal Mills, Ltd.	10	11½
6/	Do. 5 p.c. Cum. Prf.	10	10½
2/5	Benson (J. W.) L., Cm. Pf.	10	10½
12/4	Do. Perp. Mt. Db. Stk.	100	102½
6	Bergvik, L., 6 p.c. Cm. Pf.	10	12
12/	Do. Dfd.	10	9½
4½	Do. 1 Dbs., Red.	100	103½
5/	Birm'ham Vinegar, Ltd.	5	11
5	Do. Cum. Pref.	5	5½
4½	Do. 1 Mt. Db. Stk., Rd.	100	108½
5	Boake (A.) L., 5 p.c. Cu. Pf.	10	10½
2/6	Bodega, Ltd.	5	8½
4½	Do. Mt. Deb. Stk., Rd.	100	111
8/	Bottomley & Brs., Ltd.	10	6½
6/	Do. 6 p.c. Pt.	10	9½
8½d.	Bovril, Ltd.	1	1½
1/0½	Do. Def.	1	½
6½d.	Do. Cum. Pref.	1	1
4½	Do. Deb. Stk.	100	101
5/	Bradbury, Gretrex., Ltd., £10 share	8	14
5/	Do. 5 p.c. Cum. Pref.	10	13½
5/	Brewers' Sugar, L., 5 p.c. Cum. Pref.	10	10½
3/6	Brighton Grd. Hotel, Ld.	5	3½
4	Do Mt. Db. Stk., Red.	100	102½
5	Bristol Hotel & Palm. Co., Ltd. 1st Mt. Red. Deb.	100	106
9½d.	British & Bengton's Tea Tr. Asc., Ltd.	1	1½
5	Do. Cum. Prf.	5	5½
—	British Deli & Lgkat. Tobacco, Ltd.	1	½
—	Do. Cum. Prf.	1	½
—	British Tea Table, Ltd.	1	2½
5½	Do. Cum. Pref.	1	1½
2/6	Brooke, Ben., & Co., Ltd., Cum. Pref.	5	5½
7/6	Brooke, Bond & Co., Ltd.	5	20½
6/	Brown Brs., L., Cum. Pref.	5	6
10/	Browne & Eagle, Ltd.	10	13½
5	Do. Cum. Pref.	10	13
4	Do. Mrt. Db. Sk., Red.	100	110
20/	Brunner, Mond, & Co., Lt.	10	41
7/	Do. £10 shares	3½	17
7	Do. Cum. Pref.	10	18
7	Do. £10 shares	5	8½
10/	Bryant & May, Ltd.	5	19½
2/	Bucknall, H., & Sons, Lt.	5	8
6	Do. Cum Pref.	5	8½
4/	Burke, E. & J., Ltd.	5	7½
6	Do. Cum. Pref.	5	7½
6	Do. Irred. Deb. Stk.	100	155
1/	Burlington Htls. Co., Ld.	1	1½
5	Do. Cum. Pref.	1	1
4	Do. Perp. Deb. Stk.	100	106½
2/4	Bush, W. J., & Co., Ltd., Cum. Pref.	5	5½
36/8	Do. 1 Deb. Stk., Red.	100	104
5½	Callard, Stewart, & Watt, Ltd., Cum. Pref.	1	1½
4/	Callender's Cable L., Shs.	5	9½
4½	Do. 1 Deb. Stk., Red.	100	111½
—	Campbell, R., & Sons, Lt.	3	2½
6	Cantareira Water, Bd., Rd	100	99½
5	Do. (2nd issue)	100	92
4	Cartavio Sugar, Ltd., 6 p.c. 1st Debs., Red.	90	82½
9/	Cassell & Co., Ltd., £10	9	16
5	Causton, Sir J., & Sons, Ltd., Cum. Pref.	10	13½

Commercial, &c. (*continued*) :—

Last Div.	Name.	Paid.	Price
4	Cent. Prod. Mkt. of B.A 1st Mt. Str. Debs.	100	81
4	Chappell & Co., Ltd. Mt. Deb. Stk. Red.	100	103
6/	Chicago & N.W. Gran. 8 p.c. Cum. Pref.	10	3
—	Chicago Packing & Prov.	10	6
8	Do. Cum. Pref.	10	10½
6/	City Offices, Ltd.	36½	13½
3½	Do. Mt. Deb. Stk.	100	106½
7/2½	Cy. London Real Prop. Ltd., £25 shs.	12	19
4/6	Do. £12½ shs.	7½	13½
3½	Do. Deb. Stk. Red.	100	108½
3½	Do. Deb. Stk. Red.	100	106½
3	Do.	100	101½
4/	Cy. of Santos Imprvts, Ltd., 7 p.c. Pref.	10	8½
20/	Clay, Bock, & Co., Ltd.	10	5
8	Do. Cum. Pref.	10	9½
6	Do. Mort. Deb.	100	102½
20/	Coats, J. & P., Ltd.	10	60½
6	Do. Cum. Pref.	10	18
4½	Do. Deb. Stk. Red.	100	111½
9½d.	Coburg Hotel, Ltd.	1	1½
4	Do. Deb. Stk. Red.	100	102
6	Colonial Consign & Dis. Ltd., Cum. Pref.	5	4½
4½	Do. 1st Mort. Debs.	100	96½
—	Colorado Nitrate, Ltd.	5	½
4/	Co. Gén. des Asphtes. de F., Ltd.	6	6½
5	Do. Non-Cm. Prf.	—	5½
5	Cook, J. W., & Co., Ltd. Cum. Pref.	5	5½
5	Cook, T., & Son, Egypt Ltd., 1st Mt. Deb. Red	100	110½
—	Cork Co., Ltd., 6 p.c. Cum. Pref.	5	2½
5	Cory, W., & Sn, L., Cu. Pf.	5	6½
4	Do. 1st Deb. Stk. Red.	100	109
8½d.	Crisp & Co., Ltd.	1	1½
5½	Do. Cum. Pref.	1	1½
—	Crompton & Co., Ltd., 7 p.c. Cum. Pref.	5	2½
5	Do. 1st Mt. Reg. Deb.	—	88½
4/6	Crossley, J., & Sons, Ltd.	5	8½
5	Do. Cum. Pref.	5	6½
—	Crystal Pal. Ord. "A" Stk.	100	8½
—	Do. "B" Red. Stk	100	1½
6	Do. 6 p.c. 1st 1887 Deb. Stk. Red.	100	117½
—	Do. 6 p.c. 2nd 1887 Deb. Stk. Red.	100	43½
—	Do. 6 p.c. 3rd 1887 Deb. Stk. Red.	100	17½
3	Do. 3 p.c. 1st 1895 Deb. Stk.	100	94½
—	Daimler Motor, Ltd.	10	6
4/	Dalgety & Co., £20 Shs.	5	5½
4½	Do. Deb. Stk.	100	123
4	Do.	100	115
7/	De Keyser's Ryl. Htl., L.	10	14
5	Do. Cum. Pref.	10	11½
4	Do. Deb. Stk., Red.	100	110
6	Denny, H., & Sons, Ltd., Cum. Pref.	10	14½
5/3	Devas, Routledge & Co., L.	7	8½
5	Dickinson, J., & Co., L., Cum. Pref. Stk.	100	123
4½	Domin. Cottn. Mls., Ltd. Mt. Stg. Dbs.	100	97
6/	Dorman, Long & Co., L.	5	4½
—	Eastmans, Ltd.	10	2½
12/	Do. 8 p.c. Cum. Pref.	10	10½
2/6	E. C. Powder, Ltd.	3	5
1/6	Edison & Swn Utd. Elec. Ltd., "A" £5 Shs.	3	2½
2/6	Do. fully-paid	5	4½
4½	Ekman Pulp & Ppr. Co., Ltd., Mt. Deb., Red.	100	96
1/1½	Electric Construc., Ltd.	4	2½
7	Do. Cum. Pref.	2	3½
25/	Eley Bros., Ltd.	10	38
—	Elmore's Cop. Deptg., L.	1	½
—	Elmore's Wire Mnfg., L.	2	½
—	Elysée Pal. Hotel Co., L.	5/	½
5 p.c.	Do. 5 p.c. £100 Db., Rd.	70	70
8½d.	Evans, Ben., & Co., Ltd.	1	1
5	Do. 1 Mt. Db. Sk., Rd.	100	107½
8½d.	Evans, D. H., & Co., L.	1	2½
6	Do. Cum. Pref.	1	1½
4½	Do. 1 Mt. Db. Sk., Rd.	100	112
2/1	*Evening News*, L., 5 p.c. Cum. Pref.	5	5½
5/3	Evered & Co., L., £10 Sh.	7	13
7/6	Do.	10	19
4	Fairbairn Pastoral Co., Aust., L., 1 Mt. Db., Rd.	100	102
6	Fairfield Shipbldg., Ltd., Cum. Pref.	10	10
4½	Do. Mort. Deb. Stk.	100	107½
6/	Farmer & Co., Ld., 6 p.c. Cum. Pref.	10	13½
10	Field, J. C. & J., Ltd.	10	10
14/	Do. 7 p.c. Cum. Pref.	10	14
1/3	Fordham, W.B., & Sns, Ld.	1	2
5/6	Fore-st. Warehouse, Ltd.	11	9½
4	Do. Regd. Debs., Rd.	100	103½
3/6	Foster, M. B. & Sons, Ltd.	4	6½
5	Do. Pref.	10	11½
9/	Foster, Porter, & Co., L.	10½	16
4	Fowler, J., & Co. (Leeds), Ltd., 1 Mt. Deb., Red.	100	103½
3/	Fraser & Chalmers, Ltd.	3	2
4½	Free, Rodwell & Co., Ltd., Deb Stk.	100	106½
6½d.	Furness, T., & Co., Ltd., 5½ p.c. Cum. Pref.	1	½
4½	Garside & Co. (of Manchstr), L., 1 Mt. Db. Sk.	100	111
11	Genl. Hydraul Power, L.	100	275

Commercial, &c. (continued):—

Last Div.	Name.	Paid.	Price.
8/	Gillman & Spencer, Ltd.	5	2¼
6	Do. Pref.	5	4½
5	Do. Mort. Debs.	50	51
4	Goldsbro., Mort & Co., L., "A" Deb. Stk., Red.	100	74½
—	Do. 3 p.c. "B" Inc. Deb. Stk., Red	100	15
8/	Gordon Hotels, Ltd.	10	20
5½	Do. Cum. Pref.	10	14½
4½	Do. Perp. Deb. Stk.	100	137½
4	Do. do.	100	122½
—	Greenwich Inld. Linoleum Co., Ltd.	1	¾
7	Greenwood & Batley, Ltd., Cum. Pref.	10	10
7½d.	Hagemann & Co., Ltd., 6 p.c. Cum. Pref.	1	1
—	Hammond, Ltd.	10	¼
—	Do. 8 p.c. Cum. Pref.	10	2½
—	Do. 6 p.c. Cum. Inc. Stk. Red.	100	45
4	Hampton & Sons, Ltd., 4 p.c. 1 Mt. Db. St. Red.	100	105
	Hans Crescent Htl., L., 6 p.c. Cum. Pref.	5	3
4	Do. 1 Mt. Deb. Stk.	100	90
5	Harmsworth, Ld., Cm. Pf.	1	1⅛
4/	Harrison, Barber, Ltd.	5	4½
3/	Harrod's Stores, Ltd.	1	4½
2/6	Do. Cum. Pref.	5	7½
5½	Hawaiian Comcl. & Sug. 1 Mt. Debs.	100	94½
5	Hazell, Watson, L., C. P.	10	12
18/	Henley's Teleg., Ltd.	10	23
7	Do. Pref. Shs.	10	19
4½	Do. Mt. Db. Stk., Rd.	100	112½
6	Henry, Ltd.	10	12½
5	Do. Cum. Pref.	10	13½
4½	Do. Mt. Debs., Red.	50	53
6	Hepworth, Ld., Cm. Prf.	10	11
—	Herrmann, Ltd.	1	⅛
—	Hildesheimer, Ltd.	3	1
1/2½	Holbrn. & Frasca, Ltd.	1	2
5	Do. Cum. Pref.	10	11½
4	Do. Deb. Stk.	100	113
6	Home & Col. Stres, L., C.P	5	7½
6	Hoorl & M.'s Stres., Ltd., Cum. Pref.	1	½
—	Hook, C. T Ltd.	10	6
7/2	Hornsby, Ltd., £10 Shs.	8	3½
5/6	Do. 6 p.c. Cm. Pf. Sk.	100	90
—	Hotchks. Ordn., Ltd.	10	1
—	Do. 7 p.c. Cm. Prf.	10	4
5	Do. 1 Mt. Dbs., Rd.	100	95½
6	Htl. Cecil, Ld., Cm. Prf.	5	4½
4	Do. 1 Mt. D. Sk., R.	100	107½
8/	Howard & Bulgh, Ltd.	10	40
6	Do. Pref.	10	16
4	Do. Deb. Stk., Red.	100	107
5/	Howell, J., Ltd., £5 Shs.	4	9
—	Howell & Js., Ld., £3½ Shs.	3	¼
1/6	Humber, Ltd.	1	⅜
6	Do. Cum. Pref.	1	½
5/6	Hunter, Wilts., Ltd.	5	7
2/7	Hyam Clthg., Ltd., 5 p.c. Cum. Pref.	5	5½
10/	Impl. Russn. Cotton, L.	5	6
4	Imp'vd. Industl. Dwgs., Ld.	100	130½
6d.	Do. Defrd.	1	1½
2½/	Impd. Wood Pave., Ltd.	10	15
15/	Ind. Rubber, Gutta Per. Telegraph Works, Ltd.	10	22
4	Do. 1 Mt. Debs., Red.	100	106
6	Intern. Tea, Cum. Pref.	5	6½
7½d.	Jays, Ltd.	1	1½
5½	Do. Cum. Pref.	5	6½
2½d.	Jones & Higgins, Ltd.	1	2½
4½	Do. 1 Mt. Db. Sk., Rd.	100	113
5/	Kelly's Directory, Ltd., 5 p.c. Cum. Pref.	10	12½
4	Do. Mort. Db. Sk., Rd.	100	106
—	Kent Coal Explrtn. Ltd.	1	¼
9½d.	King, Howmann, Ltd.	1	1½
4/	Kinloch & Co., Ltd.	5	8½
6	Do. Pref.	5	7
5	Lady's Pictorial Pub., Ltd., Cum. Pref.	5	5
—	La Guaira Harb., Ltd., 7 p.c. Deb. Stk.	100	—
—	Do. 2 Mt. 7 p.c. Deb. Bds., Red.	100	—
4/	Lagunas Nitrate, Ltd.	5	2
2/	Lagunas Syn., Ltd.	5	1
5	Do. 2 Mt. Debs., Red.	100	80
—	L. Copais Ld., 1 Mt. 6 p.c. Debs., Red.	100	35½
3/	Lautaro Nitrate, Ltd.	5	4
7	Do. 1 Mt. Debs., Red.	—	100
9/	Lawes Chem. L., £10 shs.	9	5½
22/	Do. N. Cm. Min. Pref.	10	12½
—	Leeds Forge, 7 p.c. Cm. Pf.	5	3½
5	Do. 2 Mt. Debs., Red.	50	50
5	Lever Bros., L., Cm. Pf.	10	13½
6	Liberty, L., 6 p.c. Cm. Pf.	10	15
20/	Liebig's, Ltd.	20	75
5	Lilley & Sk., L., Cm. Pf.	5	5½
22/4	Linoleum Manftg., Ltd.	5	16
3/	Linotype, Ltd., Pref.	5	6
4/	Do. Def.	5	8
4/	Lister & Co., Ltd.	10	4
5	Do. Cum. Pref.	10	8½
3/	Liverpool Nitrate	5	5
—	Liverpool Warehsg., Ltd	10	3½
3½	Do. Cum. Pref.	10	8½
4	Do. 1 Mt. Db. Stk., Rd.	100	107
5½	Lockharts, Ltd., Cm. Pf.	1	1½
4/6	Ldn. & Til. Lightrage £10	9	6½
6/	Ldn. Comcl. Sale Rms., L.	10	17½
3	Do. 1 Mt. Deb. Stk., Red.	100	103
3	London Nitrate, Ltd.	5	1½
4/	London Nitrate, Ld. 8 p.c. Cm. Min. Pf.	5	3½
8/	London Pavilion, Ltd.	5	7

Commercial, &c. (continued):—

Last Div.	Name.	Paid.	Price.
2/6	London Produce Clg. Ho., Ltd., £10 Shares	2½	3½
4/	London Stereos., Ltd.	5	3
6d.	Ldn. Un. Laun. L. Cm. Pf.	1	¼
8½d.	Louise, Ltd.	1	¼
5½	Do. Cum. Pref.	1	¾
5/	Lovell & Christmas, Ltd.	5	11½
6	Do. Cum. Pref.	5	7½
4	Do. Mt. Deb. Stk., Red.	100	107
1/3	Lyons, Ltd.	1	3½
4½	Do. 1 Mt. Deb. Stk., Rd.	100	111½
10/	Machinery Trust, Ltd.	5	15
4½	Do. 4½ Deb. Stk.	100	108
6	MacLellan, L., Min. C. Pf.	10	8
5	Do. 1 Mt. Debs., 1900	100	101½
—	McEwan, J. & Co., Ltd.	10	1½
6	Do. Mt. Debs., Red.	100	89½
8	McNamara, L., Cm. Pref.	10	9
7½d.	Maison Virot, Ltd.	1	1½
2/7	Do. 6 p.c. Cum. Pref.	5	4½
5/	Manbré Sacc., L., Cm. Pf.	10	12
10/	Maugan Brze., L., £10 Shs.	6	15½
2/	Mason & Mason, Ltd.	5	3
6	Do. Cum. Pref.	5	5½
—	Maynards, Ltd.	1	¼
6	Do. Cum. Pref.	1	⅞
9½d.	Mazawattee Tea, Ltd.	1	1½
5	Do. Cum. Pref.	5	5½
6	Mellin's Food Cum. Pref.	5	6½
4½	Met. Ascn. Imp. Dwlgs. L.	100	110
3½	Do. 1 Mt. Deb. Stk.	100	97
5	Metro. Indus. Dwlgs., Ltd.	5	5
4	Do. do. Cum. Pref.	5	5½
5	Metro. Prop., L., Cm. Pf.	5	5½
4½	Do. 1st Mt. Debs. Stk.	100	108½
6	Mexican Cotton 1 Mt Db.	100	96½
4½	Mid. Class Dwlgs., L., Db.	100	120½
1/	Millars' Karri, Ltd.	1	3½
6	Do. Cum. Pref.	1	1½
5/	Milner's Safe, Ltd.	10	20½
10/	Moir & Son, Ltd., Pref.	5	8½
6	Morgan Cruc., L., Cm. Pf.	10	15
2/	Morris, B., Ltd.	3½	3½
—	Murray L. 5½ p.c. C. Pf.	5	5½
—	Do. 4½ 1 Mt. Db. Sk. Rd.	100	108
—	Natnl. Dwlgs., L., 5 p.c. Pf.	5	1
1/7½	Nat. Safe Dep., Ltd.	4	3½
6	Do. Cum. Pref.	1	1½
—	Native Guano, Ltd.	5	¾
—	Nelson Bros., Ltd.	10	2½
5	Do. Deb. Stk., Red.	100	80½
4/	Neuchtel Asph., Ltd.	10	11
—	New Central Borneo, Ld.	1	—
10d.	New Darvel Tob., Ltd.	18/	1½
1/6	New Explosives, Ltd.	3	2½
5/3½	New Gd. Htl., Bham, L.	5	4
5½	Do. Pref.	5	4½
4	Do. 1 Mt. Db. Stk., Rd.	100	96½
—	New Julia Nitrate, Ltd.	10/	½
—	New Ldn. Borneo Tob., L.	16/	¾
1/6	New Premier Cycle, Ltd.	1	½
6	Do. 6 p.c. Cum. Pref.	1	¾
4½	Do. 4½ p.c. 1 Mt. Db. Rd	100	—
—	New Tamargl. Nitr., Ltd	1	½
—	Do. 8 p.c. Cum. Pref.	1	¾
6	Do. 6 p.c. 1 Mt. Dbs. Rd.	100	62½
3/7½d.	Newnes, G., L., Cm. Prf.	1	1½
1/3	Nitr. Provision, Ltd.	2½	¼
24/	Nobel-Dynam., Ltd.	10	18
—	North Brazn. Sugar, Ltd.	1	¼
15/	Oakey, Ltd.	10	31
6	Do. Cum. Pref.	10	17
—	Paccha Jazp. Nitr., Ltd.	5	½
5	Pne. Borax, L., 1 Db. Rd.	100	110
—	Palace Hotel, Ltd.	10	5½
5½	Do. Cum. Pref.	10	8½
4	Do. 1 Mt. Deb. Stk.	100	104
2/6	Palmer, Ltd	5	1½
6	Do. Cum. Pref.	5	3
9½d.	Paquin, Ltd.	1	1
6	Do. Cum. Pref.	5	4½
5½	Parnall, Ltd., Cum. Pref.	1	¾
4/6	Pawsons, Ltd., £10 Shs.	6	6½
4	Do. Mt. Debs., Red.	100	106
6	Pearks, G. & T., Ltd., 6 p.c. Cum. Pref.	1	¾
1/2½	Pears, Ltd.	1	1½
6	Do. Cum. Pref.	10	14½
5	Do. Deb. Stk.	100	129
5½	Pearson, C. A., L., Cu. Pf.	5	5½
4/3	Peebles, Ltd.	5	8
5	Do. Cum. Pref.	5	6½
4½	Do. Mt. Deb. Stk. Red.	100	113½
5½	Peek Bros., Ltd., 1 Cum. Pref., Nos. 1-60,000	5	6½
3½	Do. 3½ p.c. 1 Db. Stk.	100	103½
7½d.	Pegamoid, Ltd.	1	¾
—	Phospho-Guano, Ltd.	5	2½
—	Pillsbury-W. Fl. Mills, L.	10	2
16/	Do. 8 p.c. Cum. Pref.	10	6½
6	Do. 1 Mort. Debs.	100	95½
7½d.	Plummer, Ltd.	1	1½
5	Do. Cum. Pref.	5	5
15/	Price's Candle, Ltd.	16	37
6	Priest Marians, L., Cm. Pf.	1	1½
6	Pryce Jones, Ld., Cm. Pf.	5	7½
5	Do. Deb. Stk.	100	124½
10.8d.	Pullman, Ltd.	1	1½
6d.	Do. Cum. Pref.	1	1½
11½d.	Raleigh Cycle, Ltd.	1	⅞
6	Do. Cum. Pref.	1	1
—	Recife Drnge. Ld. 1 Mt. Dbs., R	100	19
6	Redfern, Ltd. Cum. Prf.	10	14
5	Ridgways, Ltd., Cu. Pf.	5	5½
—	R. Janeiro Cy. Imps., Ld.	25	9½
5	Do. Debs.	100	11½
5	Do. 1880-1893	100	8½
11/	R. Jan Fl. Mills, Ltd.	7	6½
5	Do. 1 Mt. Debs., Rd.	100	94
—	Riv. Plate Meat, Ltd.	5	3½
—	Do. Pref.	5	5
8½d.	Roberts, J. R., Ltd.	1	1½

Commercial, &c. (continued):—

Last Div.	Name.	Paid.	Price.
5	Roberts 1 Mt. D. Sk., Rd.	100	112
8½d.	Roberts, T. R., Ltd.	1	2½
5	Do. Cum. Pref.	1	1½
3/	Rosario Nit., Ltd.	5	3½
5	Do. Debs., Red.	100	105
5	Do. Huara, Debs.	—	104
1/	Rover Cycle, Ltd.	1	¾
6/	Ryl. Aquarium, Ltd.	5	4½
6	Do. Pref.	5	6
5	Ryl. Htl., Edin., Cm. Pf.	1	1½
1/2½	Ryl. Niger, Ltd., £10 Sh.	2	2½
6/	Do.	10	14½
—	Russian Petroleum	10	21½
—	Do. 6½ p.c. Cm. Prf.	10	11
3/	Ruston, Proctor, Ltd.	10	11
4½	Do. 1 Mort. Debs.	100	104
6/	Sadler, Ltd.	12	7
—	Sal. Carmen Nit., Ltd.	5	4½
9d.	Salmon & Gluck., Ltd.	1	1½
—	Salt Union, Ltd.	10	1½
1½	Do. 7 p.c. Pref.	10	6
4½	Do. Deb. Stk.	100	100½
4½	Do. "B" Deb. Sk., Rd.	100	97½
—	San Donato Nit., Ltd.	5	¾
2/6	San Jorge Nit., Ltd.	5	3½
—	San Pablo Nit., Ltd.	5	¾
—	San Sebastn. Nit., Ltd.	5	¾
1/9	Sanitas, Ltd	1	2½
—	Sa. Elena Nit., Ltd.	5	¾
—	Sa. Rita Nit., Ltd.	5	2
10/	Savoy Hotel, Ltd.	10	17
7	Do. Pref.	10	15
4	Do. 1 Mt. Deb. Stk.	100	111½
5	Do. Debs., Red	100	102½
5	Do. & Ldn. For. Htl., Ltd., 5 p.c. Debs. Red.	100	99
1½d.	Schweppes, Ltd.	1	1⅛
—	Do. Def.	1	⅞
5	Do. Cum. Pref.	1	1½
4	Do. Deb. Stk.	100	108
1/	Singer Cyc., Ltd.	1	½
5½	Do Cum. Pref.	1	¾
—	Smokeless Pwdr., Ltd.	1	¼
5½d.	S. Eng. Dairies, Ltd., 6 p.c. Cum. Pref.	1	1½
—	Sowler Thos. L.	1	1½
—	Do. 5½ Cm. Pf.	5	5½
4/6	Spencer, Turner, & Co. Ltd	5	8½
5	Do. Cum. Pref.	5	6½
5	Spicer, Ld., 5 p.c. Dbs. Rd.	100	65
4/	Spiers & Pond, Ltd.	10	20½
5	Do. 1 Mt. Debs., Red.	100	117½
5	Do. "A" Db. Stk., Rd.	100	111
5	Do. "B" 1 Db. Stk., Rd.	100	111
4	Do. Fd. "C" 1 Db. S., R.	100	104
5/	Spratt's, Ltd	5	13½
4	Do. Debs., 1914	—	105
5	Steiner Ld., Cm. Pf.	10	11½
4	Do. 1 Mt. Db. Sk. Rd.	100	106
7/	Stewart & Clydesdale, L.	10	14½
6	Do. Cum. Pref.	10	15½
35/3	Sulphide Corp.	100	80
—	Swan & Edgar, L.	1	1½
1/	Sweetmeat Automatic, L.	1	4
2/9	Teetgen, Ltd., Cum. Pref.	5	6
24/	Teleg. Construction., Ltd.	12	37½
5	Do. Db. Bds., Rd., 1899	100	103½
3/0½	Tilling, Ld. 5½ p.c. Cm. Prf.	5	6½
4	Do. 4 p.c. 1 Dbs., Rd.	—	104
8½d.	Tower Tea, Ltd.	1	1½
5	Do. Cum. Pref.	5	5½
5	Travers, Ltd., Cum. Pref.	10	12½
4	Do. 1 Mt. Dbs., Rd.	100	105
6	Tucuman Sug., 1 Dbs., Rd.	100	100
4/	United Alkali, Ltd.	10	1½
7	Do. Cum. Pref.	10	9
5	Do. Mt. Db. Stk., Rd.	100	109½
2½d.	United Horse Shoe, Ltd., Non-Cum. 8 p.c. Pref.	1	⅜
5	Un. Kingm. Tea, Cm. Prf.	5	4½
2/	Un. Lankat Plant., Ltd.	1	2½
4/	Un. Limmer Asphlte., Ld.	3	4½
5/	Val de Travers Asph., L.	10	16
3/	V. den Bergh's, L., Cm. P.	5	6½
6	Walkers, Park., L., C. Pf.	10	3
4½	Do. 1 Mt. Debs., Red.	100	90½
6/	Wallis, Thos. & Co., Ltd.	5	14
6	Do. Cum. Pref.	5	8½
5½	Waring, Ltd., Cum. Pref.	5	5½
4½	Do. 1 Mt. Db. Sk., Red.	100	113
4½	Do. Irred. "B" Db. Stk.	100	105
12/	Waterlow, Dfd. Ord.	10	15½
12/	Do. Pref.	10	15
—	Do. Cum. Pref.	10	10½
10/	Waterlow Bros. & L., Ld.	10	9
5	Do. Pref.	10	12
1/2½	Welford, Ltd.	1	2
4½	Do. Debs., Red.	100	108
1/	Welford's Surrey Dairies, Ltd.	1	1½
7½d.	West London Dairy, Ltd.	1	1
4½	Wharncliffe Dwlgs., L., Pf.	10	11½
18/10	Do. 3 p.c. Irr. Mt. Db. Sk.	100	96
6d.	White, A. J., Ltd.	1	¾
6	Do. 6 p.c. Cum. Pref.	1	⅞
4	White, J. Bazley, Ltd., 1 Mort. Debs., Red	100	100½
5	White, R., Ltd., 1 Mort. Deb. Stock, Red.	100	104½
5/	White, Tomkins, Ltd	10	12½
5	Do. Cum. Pref.	10	12
6	White, W. N., L., Cm. Pf.	1	1
2/6	Wickens, Pease & Co., L.	5	3½
6	Wilkie, Ltd., Cum. Pref.	10	16
3/6	Willans & Robinson, Ltd.	5	8½
6	Do. Cum. Pref.	5	7½
4½	Do. 1 Mt. Db. Stk., Red.	100	107
7½d.	Williamsons, L., Cm. Prf.	1	1½
6	Winterbottm. Book Cloth, Ltd., Cum. Prf.	10	15
3/	Yates, Ltd.	5	6½
6	Do. Cum. Pref.	5	6½
	Young's Paraffin, Ltd.	4	1½

CORPORATION STOCKS—COLONIAL AND FOREIGN.

Per Cent.	Name.	Paid.	Price.
6	Auckland City, '72 1904-24	100	118
6	Do. Cons., '79, Red. 1930	100	138½
5	Do. Deb. Ln., '83..1934-8	100	117
6	Auckland Harb. Debs.	100	111½
5	Do. 1917	100	113
5	Do. 1936	100	116
5½	Balmain Boro' 1914	—	117
5	Boston City (U.S.)	100	102½
5	Do. 1909	100	107½
5	Brunswick Town 5 c. Debs. 1916-20	100	111
15/	B. Ayres City 6 p.c.	100	57
4½	Do. 4½ p.c.	100	78
5	Cape Town, City of	100	113
4	Do. 1943	100	116
4	Chicago, City of, Gold 1915	—	110
6	Christchurch 1926	100	131½
—	Cordoba City	100	17½
5	Duluth (U.S.) Gold 1926	—	110
6	Dunedin (Otago) 1925	100	127½
6	Do. 1906	100	113
5	Do. Consols 1908	100	113
4	Durban Insc. Stk. 1944	100	111
4	Essex Cnty., N. Jersey 1926	$100	114½
5	Fitzroy, Melbrne. 1916-19	100	110
5	Gisborne Harbour 1915	100	110½
4	Greymouth Harbour 1925	100	110
4	Hamilton 1934	100	110
5	Hobart Town 1918-30	100	116
4	Do. 1940	100	107
4½	Invercargill Boro. Dbs. 1936	100	113
6	Kimberley Boro., S.A. Dbs.	—	104
4	Launceston Twn. Dbs. 1916	100	107
6	Lyttleton, N.Z., Harb. 1929	100	125
4	Melbourne Bd. of Wks. 1921	100	109
5	Melb. City Debs. 1897-1907	100	107½
4½	Do. Debs. 1908-27	100	113½
4	Do. Debs. 1915-20-22	100	108
5	Melbne. Harb. Bds., 1908-9	100	112
4½	Do. do. 1915	100	110
4	Do. do. 1918-21	100	106
4½	Melbrne. Tms. Dbs. 1914-16	100	113
4½	Do. Fire Brig. Db. 1901	100	110
5	Mexico City Stg.	100	91
4	Moncton N. Bruns. City	100	103
4½	Montevideo	100	58
5	Montreal Stg.	100	104
5	Do. 1874	100	104
5	Do. 1879	100	106
3½	Do. 1933	100	104
3	Do. Perm. Deb. Stk.	100	98½
4	Do. Cons. Deb. Stk. 1932	100	113
6	Napier Boro. Consolid. 1914	100	119
5	Napier Harb. Debs. 1920	100	115
5	Do. Debs. 1928	100	107
6	New Plymouth Harb. Debs. 1909	100	108
6	New York City 1901	—	107½
3½	Do. 1910-26	—	106½
4½	Nth. Melbourne Debs. 1-600 1921	100	105
5	Oamaru Boro. Cons. 1920	100	101
6	Do. Harb. Bds. (Reg.)	100	74
25/	Do. 6 p.c. (Bearer) 1919	100	35
6	Otago Harb. Deb. Reg.	100	103
6	Do. 1877	100	107
6	Do. 1881 1921	100	115
5	Do. Debs. 1921	100	107
5	Do. Cons. 1934	100	105
6	Ottawa City	100	111
6	Do. 1904	100	115½
4½	Do. Debs. 1913	100	112
6	Port Elizabeth Waterworks	100	113½
5	Port Louis	100	111
5	Prahran Debs. 1917	100	111
4	Do. Debs. 1919	100	103
6	Quebec C. Coupon. 1875 1905	100	112
6	Do. do. 1878 1908	100	116
4½	Do. Debs. 1914-18	100	108
4	Do. Debs. 1923	100	108
3½	Do. Cns. Rg. Stk., Red.	100	101
5	Richmond (Melb.) Dbs. 1917	100	113
4	Rio Janeiro City	100	57
4	Rome City	100	—
4	Do. and to 8th Iss.	100	94
—	Rosario C.	100	26½
—	Do.	100	26½
4	St. Catherine (Ont.) 1926	100	101
4	St. John, N.B., Debs. 1934	—	103
4½	St. Kilda (Melb) Dbs. 1918-21	100	105
4	St. Louis C. (Miss.) 1911	100	106
4	Do. 1913	100	106
3·65	Do. 1915	—	110
—	Santa Fé City Debs.	00	21
6	Santos City	100	95
6	Sofia City	100	83
5	Sth. Melbourne Debs. 1915	100	111
4½	Do. Debs. 1919	100	107
5	Sydney City 1904	100	109
4	Do. Debs. 1912-13	100	107
4	Do. do. (1894) 1919	100	109
7	Timaru Boro. 7 p.c. 1910	100	126½
5	Timaru Harb. Debs 1914	100	106
5	Do. Debs. 1916	100	106
6	Toronto City Wtwks 1904-6	100	115
6	Do. Cons. Debs. 1898	100	101
5	Do. G. Cns. Dbs. 1919-20	100	118
4	Do. Stelg. 1922-8	100	107
4	Do. Local Improv.	100	102
3½	Do. 1929	100	105
5½	Valparaiso	100	100
4	Vancouver 1931	100	109
4	Do. 1932	100	108
6	Wanganui Harb. Dbs. 1905	100	110
6	Wellington Con. Deb. 1907	100	117
6	Do. Improv., 1879	100	123
6	Do. Wtrwks. Dbs., 1880	100	123
4½	Do. Debs., 1893 1933	100	116
4½	Wellington Harb. 1907	100	104
4	Westport Harb. Dbs. 1925	100	110
6	Winnipeg City Deb. 1907	—	118
5	Do. 1914	100	119

FINANCIAL, LAND, AND INVESTMENT.

Last Div.	Name.	Paid.	Price.
5	Agency, Ld. & Fin. Aust., Ltd., Mt. Db. Stk., Rd.	100	90½
	Amer. Frehld. Mt. of Lon., Ld., Cum. Pref. Stk.	100	87½
4½	Do. Deb. Stk., Red.	100	93
1/	Anglo-Amer. Db. Cor., L.	2	1
4	Do. Deb. Stk., Red	100	106½
5½	Ang.-Ceylon & Gen. Est., Ltd., Cons. Stk.	100	65
6	Do. Reg. Debs., Red.	100	106½
—	Ang.-Fch. Explorn., Ltd.	1	2½
6	Do. Cum. Pref.	1	1½
—	Argent. Ld. & Inv., Ltd. £1 Shares	10/	nil
—	Do. Cum. Pref.	4	1½
1/	Assets Fnders.' Sh., Ltd.,	4	1½
6/	Assets Realiz., Ltd., Ord.,	5	9
5	Do. Cum. Pref.	5	6½
26/	Austrln. Agricl £25 Shs.	21½	63½
—	Aust. N. Z. Mort., Ltd., £10 Shs.	1	1½d.
4½	Do. Deb. Stk., Red.	100	90½
4	Do. Deb. Stk., Red.	100	82½
4½	Australian Est. & Mt., L., 1 Mt. Deb. Stk., Red.	100	106
5	Do. "A" Mort. Deb. Stk., Red.	100	97
2/6	Australian Mort., Ld., & Fin., Ltd. £25 Shs.	5	4
1/6	Do. New, £25 Shs.	3	2½
4	Do. Deb. Stk.	100	110½
3	Do. Do.	100	85
5	Baring Est. 2 Mt. Debs., Red.	100	105
5	Bengal Presidy. 1 Mort. Deb., Red.	100	106
25/	British Amer. Ld. "A"	1	20
—	Do. "B"	24	7
1/2½	Brit. & Amer. Mt., Ltd. £10 Shs.	2	½
5/	Do. Pref.	10	10
4	Do. Deb. Stk., Red.	100	101
1/3	Brit. & Austrlsn Tst Ln., Ltd. £25 Shs.	2½	⅝
4½	Do. Perm. Debs., Red.	100	103
1½d.	Brit. N. Borneo. £1 Shs.	15/	11/16
2½d.	Do.	1	1
—	Brit. S. Africa	1	2 11/16
5	Do. Mt. Deb., Red.	—	97
6	B. Aires Harb. Tst., Red.	100	100
12/6	Canada Co.	1	26
—	Canada N. W. Ld., Ltd.	$25	$3½
—	Do. Pref.	$100	$50½
4	Canada Perm. Loan & Sav. Perp. Deb. Stk.	100	99½
—	Curamalan Ld., 1 Mt. 7 p.c. Bds., Red.	—	92½
3/7½	Deb Corp., Ld., £10 Shs	4	3½
5	Do. Cum. Pref.	10	11½
4	Do. Perp. Deb. Stk.	100	115
9d.	Deb. Corp. Fders' Sh., Ld.	3	⅜
4/5[illegible]	Eastn. Mt. & Agncy, Ld., "A"	10	6
4½	Do. Deb. Stk., Red.	100	100
5	Equitable Revers. In. Ltd.	100	—
2/	Exploration, Ltd.	1	1 11/16
1	Freehold Trst. of Austrln. Ltd. £10 Shs.	1	¾
4	Do. Perp. Deb. Stk.	100	102
—	Genl. Assets Purchase, Ltd., 5 p.c. Cum. Pref.	10	—
70/	Genl. Reversionary, Ltd.	100	—
4½	Holborn Vi. Land	100	105
4½	House Prop. & Inv.	100	85½
13/	Hudson's Bay	13	22
4	Impl. Col. Fin. & Agcy. Corp.	100	94½
4½	Impl. Prop. Inv., Ltd., Deb. Stk., Red.	100	91½
2/6	Internatl. Fincial. Soc., Ltd. £7½ Shs.	2½	1½
4	Do. Deb. Stk., Red.	100	99½
1/9½	Ld. & Mtge. Egypt, Ltd. £18 Shs.	3	2½
5	Do. Debs., Red.	100	103
4½	Do. Debs., Red.	100	101
—	Ld. Corp. of Canada, Ltd.	1	⅜
4½	Ld. Mtge. Bk. of Texas Deb. Stk.	100	—
3½	Ld. Mtge. Bk. Victoria 4½ p.c. Deb. Stk.	100	78
2/9½	Law Debent. Corp., Ltd., £10 Shs.	2	1¾
4½	Do. Cum. Pref.,	10	12
4	Do. Deb. Stk.	100	119
1/	Ldn. & Australasian Deb. Corp., Ltd., £4 Shs.	2	½
4½	Do. 4½ p.c. Mt. Deb. Stk., Red.	100	101
1/9	Ldn. & Middx. Frhld. Est. £2 Shs.	35/	3
2/6	Lndn. & N. Y. Inv. Corp., Ltd.	5	1¾
5	Do. 5 p.c. Cum. Pref.	10	9
1/6	Ldn. & Nth. Assets Corp., Ltd., £2 Shs.	1½	⅞
[illegible]	Ldn. & N. Deb. Corp., L.	2	1¼
4	Ldn. & S. Afric. Explrn. Ltd.	½	13½
2/	Mtge. Co. of R. Plate, Ltd. £10 Shs.	2	3½
4½	Do. Deb. Stk., Red.	100	113
4½	Morton, Rose Est., Ltd., 1st Mort. Debs.	—	101
6/	Natal Land Col. Ltd.	10	7½
4/	Do. 8 p.c. Pref., 1870	5	8½
5/6	Natl. Disct. L., £25 Shs.	5	10½
4½	New Impl. Invest., Ltd. Pref. Stk.	100	60½
—	New Impl. Invest., Ltd. Def. Stk.	100	9
4	N. Zld. Ln. & Mer. Agcy., L. d. Prf. ... Deb. Stk	100	97

Financial, Land, &c. (*continued*):—

Last Div.	Name.	Paid.	Price.
16/	N. Zld. Ln. & Mer. Agcy., Ltd. 5 p.c. "A" Db. Sk.	100	43½
—	N. Zld. Ln. & Mer. Agcy., Ltd., 5 p.c. "B" Db. Stk.	100	4
2/6	N. Zld. Tst. & Ln. Ltd., £25 Shs.	5	1¼
12/6	N. Zld. Tst. & Ln. Ltd., 5 p.c. Cum. Pref.	25	19
—	N. Brit. Australsn. Ltd.	100	6½
—	Do. Irred. Guar.	100	32½
5	Do. Mort. Debs.	100	82½
4½	N. Queensld. Mort. & Inv., Ltd., Deb. Stk.	100	95
—	Oceana Co., Ltd.	—	—
6	Peel Riv., Ld. & Min. Ltd.	100	88½
—	Peruvian Corp., Ltd.	100	2¼
—	Do. 4 p.c. Pref.	100	10
3	Do. 6 p.c. 1 Mt. Debs., Red.	100	41½
—	Queenld. Invest. & Ld. Mort. Pref. Ord. Stk.	100	20
3/7	Queenld. Invest. & Ld. Mort. Ord. Shs.	4	4
4	Queenld. Invest. & Ld. Mort. Perp. Debs.	100	90
3½	Raily. Roll Stk. Tst. Deb., 1903-6	100	100½
50/	Reversiony. Int. Soc., Ltd.	100	—
2/8½	Riv. Plate Trst., Loan & Agcy., L., "A" £10 Shs.	2	4⅝
1/6	Riv. Plate Trst., Loan & Agcy., Ltd., Def. "B"	5	3⅝
	Riv. Plate Trst., Loan & Agy., L., Db. Stk., Red.	100	109
—	Santa Fé & Cord. Gt. South Land, Ltd.	20	5
—	Santa Fé Land	10	2½
2/	Scot. Amer. Invest., Ltd. £10 Shs.	2	2¾
2½	Scot. Australian Invest., Ltd., Cons.	100	79½
6	Scot. Australian Invest., Ltd., Guar. Pref.	100	135½
5	Scot. Australian Invest., Ltd., Guar. Pref.	100	106½
4	Scot. Australian Invest., Ltd., 4 p.c. Perp. Dbs.	100	105½
5	Sivagunga Zemdy., 1st Mort., Red.	100	101
20/	Sth. Australian	20	52½
3½	Stock Exchange Deb., Rd.	—	101½
—	Strait Develt., Ltd.	1	5/16
2/6	Texas Land & Mt., Ltd. £10 Shs.	2½	3
4½	Texas Land & Mt., Ltd., Deb. Stk., Red.	100	105
—	Transvaal Est. & Dev., L.	1	½
—	Transvaal Lands, Ltd., £1 Shs.	15/	⅜
—	Do. F. P.	1	5/16
—	Transvaal Mort., Loan, & Fin., Ltd., £10 Shs.	2	½
2/	Tst & Agcy. of Austrlsa., Ltd., £10 Shs.	1	2
7/5	Do. Old, fully paid	10	15½
5/7	Do. New, fully paid	10	12½
5	Do. Cum. Pref.	10	12½
3/	Trust & Loan of Canada, £20 Shs.	5	4½
1/9½	Do. New £20 Shs	3	2½
—	Tst. & Mort. of Iowa, Ltd., £10 Shs.	2½	¾
4½	Do. Deb. Stk. Red.	100	92½
—	Tst., Loan, & Agency of Mexico, Ltd., £10 Shs.	2	½
—	Trsts., Exors, & Sec. Ins. Corp., Ltd., £10 Shs.	7	1¾
5/	Union Dsc., Ld., £10 Shs.	5	10½
—	Union Mort. & Agcy. of Aust., Ltd., £6 Shs.	2	—
6	Do. Pref. Stk	100	35
—	Do. 6 p. Pref. £6 Shs.	2	¾
4½	Do. Deb. Stk	100	92½
4	Do. Deb. Stk	100	85½
5	Do. Deb. Stk. Red.	100	96½
1/6	U.S. Deb. Cor. Ltd., £8 Shs.	1	⅜
5½	Do. Cum. Pref. Stk.	100	102½
4½	Do. Irred. Deb. Stk.	100	107½
5	U.S. Tst. & Guar. Cor., Ltd., Pref. Stk.	100	77½
6/	Van Dieman's	25	16
4	Walker's Prop. Cor., Ltd., Guar. 1 Mt. Deb. Stk.	100	109
4½	Wstr. Mort. & Inv., Ltd., Deb. Stk.	100	92½

FINANCIAL—TRUSTS.

Last Div.	Name.	Paid.	Price.
1/	Afric City Prop., Ltd	1	1½
6	Do. Cum. Pref.	1	1 1/16
4	Alliance Invt., Ltd., Cm. 4½ p.c. Prefd.	100	74½
—	Do. Defd	100	13½
4	Do. Deb. Stk. Red.	100	105½
5	Amrcn. Invt., Ltd., Prfd.	100	124½
5	Do. Defd.	100	94½
4	Do. Deb. Stk. Red.	100	117½
4	Army & Navy Invt., Ltd., 5 p.c. Prefd.	100	82½
—	Do. Defd. Stk.	100	17½
4	Do. Deb. Stk.	100	107½
4	Atlas Investment, Ltd., Prefd. Stk.	100	70½
4½	Bankers' Invest., Ltd., Cum. Prefd.	100	106
1/0/0	Do. Defd	100	28½
4	Do. Deb. Stk	100	113
	Brewery & Comml. Inv., Ltd., £10 Shs.	4	5½

Financial—Trusts (*continued*):—

Last Div.	Name.	Paid.	Price.
4	British Investment, Ltd., Cum. Prefd.	100	102
5	Do. Defd.	100	102½
4	Do. Deb. Stk.	100	108½
6	Brit. Steam. Invst., Ltd., Prefd.	100	116½
3/0/0	Do. Defd	100	70½
4½	Do. Perp. Deb. Stk	100	121½
1/9	Car Trust Invst., Ltd., £10 Shs.	2½	2
5	Do. Pref.	100	102½
4	Do. Deb. Stk., 1915	100	105
4	Clnl. Sec., Ltd., Prefd.	100	107½
2½	Do. Defd.	100	47½
4	Consolidated, Ltd., Cum. 1st Pref.	100	92½
4	Do. 5 p.c. Cm. 2nd do.	100	73½
—	Do. Defd.	100	14½
4½	Do. Deb. Stk.	100	111½
—	Deb. Secs. Invst.	100	105½
—	Do. 4 p.c. Cm. Pf. Sk.	100	105½
4½	Edinburgh Invest., Ltd., Cum. Prefd. Stk.	100	109½
4	Do. Deb. Stk. Red.	100	106½
5	Foreign, Amer. & Gen. Invt., Ltd., Prefd.	100	117½
2	Do. Defd.	100	54½
4	Do. Deb. Stk.	100	115½
5	Foreign & Colonial Invt., Ltd., Prefd.	100	133½
5½	Do. Defd.	100	97½
4½	Gas, Water & Gen. Invt., Cum. Prefd. Stk.	100	90½
3	Do. Defd. Stk.	100	38½
4	Do. Deb. Stk.	100	106
5	Gen. & Com. Invt., Ltd., Prefd. Stk.	100	108½
2	Do. Defd. Stk.	100	39½
4	Do. Deb. Stk.	100	113½
1/9	Globe Telegph. & Tst., Ltd.	10	12
6	Do. do. Pref.	10	17½
4	Govt. & Genl. Invt., Ld., Prefd.	100	84½
3½	Do. Defd.	100	42½
4½	Govts. Stk. & other Secs. Invt., Ltd., Prefd.	100	90½
1	Do. Defd.	100	27
4½	Do. Deb. Stk.	100	111
4	Do. do.	100	104
4½	Guardian Invt., Ltd., Pfd.	100	88½
—	Do. Defd.	100	20½
4	Do. Deb. Stk.	100	104
5	Indian & Gen. Inv., Ltd., Cum. Prefd.	100	107½
2½	Do. Defd.	100	56
4½	Do. Deb. Stk.	100	121½
5	Indust. & Gen. Tst., Ltd., Unified	100	102½
3½	Do. Deb. Stk. Red.	100	101½
4½	Internat. Invt., Ltd., Cm. Prefd.	100	71½
—	Do. Defd.	100	9
4	Do. Deb. Stk.	100	102
4	Invest. Tst. Cor. Ltd. Pfd.	100	102
4	Do. Defd.	100	93
4	Do. Deb. Stk. Red.	100	106
5	Ldn. Gen. Invest. Ltd., 5 p.c. Cum. Prefd.	100	109½
7½	Do. Defd.	100	118
4½	Ldn. Scot. Amer. Ltd. Pfd.	100	104½
£3	Do. Defd.	100	59½
4	Do. Deb. Stk.	100	112
4	Ldn. Tst., Ltd., Cum. Prfd. Stk.	100	105
4	Do. Defd. Stk.	100	75½
4	Do. Deb. Stk., Red.	100	107
3½	Do. Mt. Deb. Stk., Red.	100	104
5	Mercantile Invt. & Gen., Ltd., Prefd.	100	112½
3	Do. Defd.	100	48½
4	Do. Deb. Stk.	100	115½
4	Merchants, Ltd., Pref. Stk.	100	104½
4	Do. Ord.	100	81
4	Do. Deb. Stk.	100	116½
5	Municipal, Ltd., Prefd.	100	55½
—	Do. Defd.	100	17½
4½	Do. Debs.	100	113
4½	Do. Debs. "B"	100	99½
4½	Do. "C" Deb. Stk.	100	88½
5	New Investment. Ltd. Ord.	100	92½
5	Omnium Invest., Ltd., Pfd.	100	91½
1	Do. Defd.	100	26½
4	Do. Deb. Stk.	100	104
5/	Railway Deb. Tst. Ld., £10 Shs.	10	6¾
5	Do. Debs., Red.	100	107½
4½	Do. Deb. Stk., 1911	100	107½
4	Do. do. 1927	100	107½
4	Railway Invst. Ltd., Prefd.	100	114
18/6	Do. Defd.	100	21½
8/	Railway Share Trust & Agency "A"	8	6½
7½	Do. "B" Pref. Stk.	100	145½
4½	River Plate & Gen. Invt., Ltd., Prefd.	100	105
£3	Do. Defd.	100	50½
5	Scot. Invst., Ltd., Pfd. Stk.	100	94½
1½	Do. Defd.	100	26½
4	Do. Deb. Stk.	100	108
4½	Sec. Scottish Invst., Ltd., Cum. Prefd.	100	89½
£2	Do. Defd. Stk.	100	32
4	Do. Deb. Stk.	100	107½
5/	Sth. Africa Gold Tst., Ltd.	1	3½
6	Do. Cum. Pref	1	1
5½	Do. 1st Debs., Red.	100	102
1/9	Stock Conv. & Invest., Ltd., £5 Shs.	1	1½
4½	Do. do. 4½ p.c. Cm. Prf.	100	114½
3½	Do. Ldn. & N. W. 1st Charge Prefd.	100	114½
4	Do do. 2nd Chge Prfd.	100	111
32/6	Do. do. Defd. Charge	100	30
3	Do. N. East. 1 Chge Pfd.	100	93

Financial—Trusts (*continued*):—

Last Div.	Name.	Paid.	Price.
32/6	Stock N. East Defd. Chge	100	39
6	Submarine Cables	100	141½
5	U.S. & S. Amer. Invest., Ltd., Prefd.	100	100½
2	Do. Defd.	100	29½
4	Do. Deb. Stk.	100	105½

GAS AND ELECTRIC LIGHTING.

Last Div.	Name.	Paid.	Price.
10/6	Alliance & Dublin Con. 10 p.c. Stand.	10	24½
7/6	Do. 7 p.c. Stand.	10	17
5	Austln. Gas Lght. (Syd.) Debs. 1902	100	106
5	Bay State of N. Jrsy. Sk. Fd. Tst. Bd., Red.	—	92½
3/	Bombay, Ltd.	5	6
2/4½	Do. New	4	5
12	Brentford Cons.	100	297½
9	Do. New	100	230½
5	Do. Pref.	100	142½
4	Do. Deb. Stk.	100	136
11½	Brighton & Hove Gen. Cons. Stk.	100	277½
8½	Do. "A" Cons. Stk.	100	202½
5	Bristol 5 p.c. Max.	100	129½
22/6	British Gas Light, Ltd.	20	56½
11/6	Bromley Gas Consumrs.' 10 p.c. Stand.	10	26
8/6	Do. 7 p.c. Stand.	10	21
—	Brush Electl. Enging., L.	—	1½
6	Do. 6 p.c. Pref.	—	2½
4½	Do. Deb. Stk.	100	112
4½	Do. 2 Deb. Stk., Red.	100	103½
5/	B. Ayres (New), Ltd.	10	9½
4	Do. Deb. Stk., Rd.	—	94
18/6	Cagliari Gas & Wtr., Ltd.	20	30½
8/	Cape Town & Dist. Gas Light & Coke, Ltd.	10	17½
4½	Do. Pref.	10	12½
6	Do. 1 Mt. Debs. 1910	50	60
4/	Charing Cross & Strand Elec. Sup., Ltd.	5	14
4½	Do. Cum. Pref.	5	6½
2/6	Chelsea Elec. Sup., Ltd.	5	11½
4½	Do. Deb. Stk., Red.	100	116
5	Chic. Edis'n Co. 1 Mt., Rd.	$1000	106
20/	City of Ldn. Elec. Lht., L.	10	24½
—	Do. New	10	13
6	Do. Cum. Pref.	10	18
5	Do. Deb. Stk., Red.	100	131½
13½	Commercial, Cons.	100	342½
10½	Do. New	100	257½
4½	Do. Deb. Stk.	100	155½
14	Continental Union, Ltd.	100	230
11	Do. Pref. Stk.	100	210½
—	County of Lon. & Brush Prov. Elec. Lg., Ltd.	10	15
6	Do. Cum. Pref.	10	16
14	Croydon Comcl. Gas, Ld., "A" Stk., 10 p.c.	100	312½
11	Do. "B" Stk., 7 p.c.	100	250
5½	Crystal Pal. Dist. Ord. 5 p.c. Stk.	100	132½
5	Do. Pref. Stk.	100	141½
8/	European, Ltd.	10	25½
6/	Do.	7½	18
12½	Gas Light & Ck Cons. Stk., "A" Ord.	100	292½
4	Do. "B" (4 p.c. Max.)	100	122½
10	Do. "C," "D," & "E" (Pref.)	100	312½
5	Do. "F" (Pref.)	100	152½
7½	Do. "G" (Pref.)	100	222½
7	Do. "H" (7 p.c. Max.)	100	197½
10	Do. "J" (Pref.)	100	312½
6	Do. "K"	100	185½
4	Do. Deb. Stk.	100	134½
4½	Do. do.	100	152½
6	Do. do.	100	204½
8/	Hong Kong & China, Ld.	10	14½
—	House to House Elec. Light Sup., Ltd.	5	11½
7	Do. Cum. Pref.	5	12
10	Imperial Continental	100	214½
3½	Do. Deb. Stk., Red	100	104½
2/	Malta & Medit., Ltd.	5	5½
5/	Metrop. Elec. Sup., Ltd.	10	21½
3/8	Do. New	10	21
4½	Do. 1 Mt. Deb. Stk.	100	119
5	Metro. of Melbrne. Dbs. 1908-12	100	113
4½	Do. Debs. 1918-22-4	100	110
10/	Monte Video, Ltd.	20	16
9½	Newcastle-upon-Tyne	100	237½
—	Do. 3½ p.c. Deb. Stk.	100	117½
12/	Notting Hill Elec. Ltg., Ltd.	10	20
4/6	Oriental, Ltd.	5	8½
4/0½	Do. New	4½	7½
10d½.	Do. do. 1879	1	1½
3/6	Ottoman, Ltd.	5	4½
—	Para, Ltd.	—	—
6	People's Gas Lt. & C. of Chic. 2 Mt. 1904	100	105½
5	River Plate Elec. Lgt. & Trac., Ltd., 1 Deb. Stk.	—	92½
8½	Royal Elec. of Montreal	—	146
4½	Do. 1 Mt. Deb.	100	106
11/	St. James' & Pall Mall Elec. Light, Ltd.	5	18½
7	Do. Pref.	5	10½
4	Do. Deb. Stk., Red.	100	108½

Gas and Electric (*continued*) :—

Last Div.	Name.	Paid.	Price.
10/	San Paulo, Ltd.	10	16¼
10	Sheffield Unit. Gas Lt. "A"	100	251½
10	Do. "B"	100	251½
10	Do. "C"	100	251½
—	Sth. Ldn. Elec. Sup., Ld.	2	2½
5¼	South Metropolitan	100	137½
3	Do. 3 p.c. Deb. Stk.	100	106½
12	Tottenham & Edmonton Gas Lt. & C., "A"	100	290
9	Do. "B"	100	210
7/	Tuscan, Ltd.	10	14
5	Do. Debs., Red.	100	101½
5/	West Ham 10 p.c. Stan.	5	12
8/	Wstmnstr. Elec. Sup., Ld.	5	17½

INSURANCE

Last Div.	Name.	Paid.	Price.
4/	Alliance, £20 Shs.	44/	11¼
10/	Alliance, Mar., & Gen., Ld., £100 Shs.	25	53
5/	Atlas, £50 Shs.	6	32
12/	British & For. Marine, Ld., £20 Shs.	4	24
7½d.	British Law Fire, Ltd., £10 Shs.	1	1½
7/6	Clerical, Med., & Gen. Life, £25 Shs.	50/	16½
10/	Commercial Union, Ltd., £50 Shs.	5	43½
4	Do. "W. of Eng." Ter. Deb. Stk.	100	110½
£9	County Fire, £100 Shs.	80	190
2/	Eagle, £50 Shs.	5	½
4/	Employrs' Liability, Ltd., £10 Shs.	2	4¾
.	Empress, Ltd., £5 Shs.	1	—
21/	Equity & Law, £100 Shs.	6	23
7/6	General Life, £100 Shs.	5	15
4½d.	Gresham Life, £5 Shs.	15/	2½
2/6	Guardian, Ld., £10 Shs.	5	11½
20/	Imperial, Ltd., £20 Shs.	5	29½
3/6	Imperial Life, £20 Shs.	4	6¾
6/	Indemnity Mutual Mar., Ltd., £15 Shs.	3	12¼
1/	Lancashire, £20 Shs.	2	5
7½d.	Law Acc. & Contin., Ltd., £5 Shs.	10/	1
5/	Law Fire, £100 Shs.	2½	18
7½d.	Law Guar. & Trust, Ltd., £10 Shs.	1	1½
9/	Law Life, £20 Shs.	2	25
2/9	Law Un. & Crown £10Shs	12/	7
4	Do. Deb. Stk., 1942	100	110½
24/6	Legal & General, £50Shs.	8	15½
9d.	Lion Fire, Ltd., £8½ Shs.	1½	½
24/	Liverpool & London & Globe, Stk	2	54
20/	Do. Globe £1 Ann	—	36
25/	London, £25 Shs.	12½	63½
4/	Lond. & Lanc. Fire, £25Shs	2½	19
2/	Lond. & Lanc. Life, £25Shs	2	5½
1/	Lond. & Prov. Mar., Ld., £10 Shs.	1	1
2/	Lond. Guar. & Accident, Ltd., £5 Shs.	2	12
10/	Marine, Ltd., £25 Shs.	4½	43
2/	Maritime, Ltd., £10 Shs.	2	4½
1/6	Merc. Mar., Ld., £10 Shs.	2½	2¾
—	National Marine, Ltd., £9 Shs.	1	½
10/	N. Brit. & Merc., £25 Shs.	6¼	42
20/	Northern, £100 Shs.	10	82
40/	Norwich Union Fire, £100 Shs.	12	126½
10/	Ocean Acc. & Guar., fy. pd.	5	21½
2/	Do. £5 Shs.	1	4
7/6	Ocean, Marine, Ltd.	2½	9½
1/	Palatine, £10 Shs.	2	3½
2/6	Pelican, £10 Shs.	1	3¼
22/	Phœnix, £50 Shs.	5	44
£6	Provident, £100 Shs.	10	31
5/	Railway Psngrs., £10Shs.	2	8½
2/6	Rock Life, £5 Shs.	10/	4½
8	Royal Exchange	100	360
18/	Royal, £20 Shs.	3	54½
4/	Sun, £10Shs.	10/	12
3/9	Sun Life, £10 Shs.	7½	14½
6/	Thames & Mrsey. Marine, Ltd., £20 Shs.	2	10½
9/	Union, £10 Shs.	4	24½
4/	Union Marine, £20 Shs.	2½	9
12/	Universal Life, £100 Shs.	12	42
8/	World Marine, £5 Shs.	2	1½

IRON, COAL, AND STEEL.

Last Div.	Name.	Paid.	Price.
—	Barrow Hæm. Steel, Ltd.	7½	2
9/	Do. 6 p.c. 2nd Pref.	7½	7
10/	Bolck., Vaugh. & C., Ld.	20	18
6/	Do. £8 liab.	12	9½
7/6	Brown, J. & Co., Ltd., £20 Shs.	15	21
7/6	Consett Iron, Ld., £10 Shs.	7½	29½
4/	Do. 8 p.c. Cum. Pref.	5	11
7/6	Ebbw Vale Steel, Iron & Coal, Ltd., £23 Shs.	20	6½
15/	General Mining Assn., Ld.	5½	7½
8/	Harvey Steel Co. of Gt. Britain, Ltd.	10	30
5	Lehigh V. Coal 1 Mt. 5 p.c. Guar. Gd. Cp. Bds.	—	98
42/6	Nantyglo & Blaina Iron, Ltd., Pref.	$62	97½
1/	Nerbudda Coal & Iron, Ltd., £3 Shs.	56/	1/16
—	Newport Abrcrn. Bk. Vein Steam Coal, Ltd.	10	4½
5/	New Sharlston Coll., Ltd. Pref	20	10
4½d.	Nw. Vancvr. Coal & Ld., L.	1	½
—	North's Navigation Coll. (1889) Ltd.	5	3
10/	Do. 10 p.c. Cum. Pref.	5	7½
—	Rhymney Iron, Ltd.	5	1½
	Do. New, £5 Shs.	4½	½
5	Do. Mt. Debs., Red.	100	98½
5	Shelton Irn., Stl. & Cl. Co., Ltd., 1 Chg. Debs., Red.	100	99½
10	Sth. Hetton Coal, Ltd.	100	—
	Vickers & Maxim, Ltd.	1	3½
	Do. 5 p.c. Prfd. Stk.	100	133½

SHIPPING.

Last Div.	Name.	Paid.	Price.
4/	African Stm. Ship, £20 Shs.	16	10½
5/	Do. Fully-paid	20	15
5/	Amazon Steam Nav., Ltd.	12½	9
8/	Castle Mail Pakts., Ltd., £20 Shs.	14	15½
3½	Do. 1st Deb. Stk., Red.	100	102
6/	China Mutual Steam, Ltd.	5	3
6	Do. Cum. Pref.	10	10
10/	Cunard, Ltd.	20	9½
5/	Do. £20 Shs.	10	3½
4½	Furness, Withy, & Co., Ltd., 1 Mt. Dbs., Red.	100	106
6/	General Steam	15	8
5/	Do. 5 p.c. Pref., 1874	10	9
5/	Do. 5 p.c. Pref., 1877	10	8½
5/	Leyland & Co., Ltd.	10	17½
7/	Do. 7 p.c. Cum. Pref.	10	14½
2/11	Do. 4½ p.c. Cum. Pre-Pf.	3	10½
4	Do. 1st Mt. Dbs., Red.	100	106½
7/6	Mercantile Steam, Ltd.	5	7½
6/4½	New Zealand Ship., Ltd.,	6	5
4	Do. Deb. Stk., Red.	100	104
5/	Orient Steam, Ltd.	10	5½
5	P. & O. Steam, Cum. Prefd.	100	156½
19	Do. Defd.	100	237½
3½	Do. Deb. Stk.	100	120
5	Richelieu & Ont., 1st Mt. Debs., Red.	100	100
30/	Royal Mail, £100 Shs.	60	51
2/6	Shaw, Sav., & Alb., Ltd., "A" Pref.	5	5½
5/	Do. "B" Ord.	5	4
8/	Union Steam, Ltd.	20	20
4/	Do. New £20 Shs.	10	8¾
4	Do. Deb. Stk., Red.	100	106
7/	Union of N.Z., Ltd.	10	10
5½	Wilson's & Fur.-Ley., 5½ p.c. Cum. Pref.	10	10½
4½	Do. 1 Mt. Db. Sk., Rd.	100	106½

TELEGRAPHS AND TELEPHONES.

Last Div.	Name.	Paid.	Price.
4	African Direct, Ltd., Mort. Debs., Red.	100	102
—	Amazon Telegraph, Ltd.	10	7½
19/6	Anglo-American, Ltd.	100	60½
39/	Do. 6 p.c. Prefd. Ord.	100	110
—	Do. Defd. Ord.	100	12
3/	Brazilian Submarine, Ltd.	10	17
5	Do. Debs., 2 Series	100	114

Telegraphs and Telephones (*continued*) :—

Last Div.	Name.	Paid.	Price.
4/	Chili Telephone, Ltd.	5	3½
$2½	Comicial. Cable, $100 Shs.	—	189½
4	Do. Stg. 500-yr. Deb. Stk. Red.	100	107
2½d.	Consd. Telpehone Constr., &c., Ltd.	10/	½
6/	Cuba Submarine, Ltd.	10	7
10/	Do. 10 p.c. Pref.	10	15
2/	Direct Spanish, Ltd.	5	4½
5/	Do. 10 p.c. Cum. Pref.	5	10½
4½	Do. Debs.	50	104½
3/	Direct U.S. Cable, Ltd.	20	11
2/6	Eastern, Ltd.	10	18
3/	Do. 6 p.c. Cum. Pref.	10	19
4	Do. Mt. Deb. Stk., Red.	100	129½
2/6	Eastern Exten., Aus., & China, Ltd.	10	19
5	Do. (Aus. Gov. Sub.) Deb., Red.	100	101
5	Do. do. Bearer	100	101½
4	Do. Mort. Deb. Stk.	100	129½
5	Eastn. & S. Afric., Ltd., Mort. Deb. 1900	100	101
5	Do. Bearer	100	101½
4	Do. Mort. Debs. 1909	100	103½
4	Do. Mort. Debs. (Maur. Subsidy)	25	108½
5/	Grt. Nthn. Copenhagen	10	30
5	Do. Debs., Ser. B., Red.	100	101½
12/6	Indo-European, Ltd.	25	53½
6	London Platino-Brazilian, Ltd., Debs. 1904	100	107½
4/	Montevideo Telph., Ltd., 6 p.c. Pref.	5	2½
3/	National Telephone, Ltd.	5	6¾
6/	Do. Cum. 1 Pref.	10	17
6/	Do. Cum. 2 Pref.	10	16
5	Do. Non-Cum. 3 Pref.	5	6
3½	Do. Deb. Stk., Red.	100	104½
4d.	Oriental Telephone, Ltd.	1	1/16
4	Pac. & Euro. Tlg. Dbs., Rd.	100	106½
4/	Reuter's, Ltd.	8	8½
5/	Un. Riv. Plate Telph., Ltd.	5	4½
5	Do. Deb. Stk., Red.	100	106½
—	West African Telg., Ltd.	10	4
5	Do. 5 p.c. Mt. Debs., Red.	100	102½
—	W. Coast of America, Ltd.	10	½
3/	Western & Brazilian, Ltd.	15	12
3/	Do. 5 p.c. Pref. Ord.	7½	7½
—	Do. Defd. Ord.	7½	4½
4	Do. Deb. Stk., Red.	100	107½
1/	W. India & Panama, Ltd.	10	½
6/	Do. Cum. 1 Pref.	10	7½
6/	Do. Cum. 2 Pref.	10	6
5	Do. Debs., Red.	100	106½
7	West. Union, 1 Mt. 1902 ($	1000	107½
6	Do. 6 p.c. Stg. Bds., Rd.	100	102½

TRAMWAYS AND OMNIBUS.

Last Div.	Name.	Paid.	Price.
1/6	Anglo-Argentine, Ltd	5	3½
6	Do. Deb. Stk.	100	127½
4/	Barcelona, Ltd	10	12½
5	Do. Deb., Red.	100	104½
7/6	Belfast Street Trams.	10	16½
—	Blackpl. & Fltwd. Tram., £10 Shs.	8	13
10/	Bordeaux Tram. & O. Ltd.	10	12
5	Do. Cum. Pref.	10	11½
—	Brazilian Street Ry., Ltd.	2	½
—	British Elec. Trac., Ltd.	10	16½
—	B. Ayres & Belg. Tram., Ltd., 6 p.c. Cum. Pref.	5	—
6	Do. 1 Deb. Stk.	100	—
—	B. Ayres. Gd. Nat., Ltd., 6 p.c 1 Deb. Bds., Red.	100	57½
5½	Do. Pref. Debs., Red.	100	95½
1/	Calais, Ltd.	5	1
—	Calcutta, Ltd.	10	3½
—	Carthagena & Herr., Ltd.	10	3
5	Do. Deb., Red.	100	90
5	City of B'ham. Trams., Ltd., 5 p.c. Cum. Pref.	5	6
4	Do. 1 Mort. Debs., Rd.	100	107½
3/9	City of B. Ayres, Ltd	5	7½
2/3	Do. Ext. £5 Shs.	3	4½
6	Do. Deb. Stk.	100	145
1/4	Edinburgh Street Tram	4	4
1/	Glasgow Tram. & Omni. Ltd., £9 Shs.	8	
3/7½	Imperial, Ltd.	6	15
3/	Lond., Deptfd, & Greenwich, Prefd.	5	3½
nil	Do. Defd.	5	1
10½	Lond. Gen. Omni., Ltd.	100	205
4	Do. Deb., Red.	100	17½

Tramways and Omnibus (*continued*) :—

Last Div.	Name.	Paid.	Price.
4/9½	London Road Car	6	10½
28/6	Do. Red. 1 Mt. Deb. Stk.	100	108½
5	London St. Rly. (Prov., Ont.), Mt. Debs.	100	110
12/6	London St. Trams.	—	2
12/9	London Trams., Ltd.	10	10
6/	Do. Non-Cum. Pref.	10	10½
5	Do. Mt. Db. Stk., Rd.	100	101½
5	Lynn & Boston 1 Mt. 1924 $	1000	107
5	Milwaukee Elec. Cons. Mt. $	1000	100½
5	Minneapolis St. 1 Cons. Mt $	1000	96
5	Montreal St. Dbs., 1908	100	109
4½	Do. Debs., 1922	100	107
6/	Nth. Metropolitan	10	13
1/9½	Nth. Staffords., Ltd.	6	4½
5/6	Provincial, Ltd	10	7
6/	Do. Cum. Pref.	10	13
5	St. Paul City, 1937 $	1000	96
5	Do. Guar. Twin City Rap. Trans. $	1000	96
5/	Southampton	10	6½
5/	South London	10	5½
7/6	Sunderland, Ltd.	10	6½
4½	Toronto 1 Mt., Red.	100	107
2/6	Tramways Union, Ltd.	5	7½
4½	Do. Deb., Red.	100	109
5/	Vienna General Omnibus.	5	6½
5	Do. 5 p.c. Mt. Deb., Red.	100	103½
4/	Wolverhampton, Ltd	10	6½

WATER WORKS.

Last Div.	Name.	Paid.	Price.
8/	Antwerp, Ltd.	20	22
6/	Cape Town District, Ltd.	5	7
10½	Chelsea	100	335½
5	Do. Pref. Stk.	100	178½
4½	Do. Pref. Stk., 1875	100	158½
4½	Do. Deb. Stk.	100	162½
3/6	City St. Petersburg, Ltd.	13	11
5/	Colne Valley	10	15½
4	Do. Deb. Stock	100	137½
£4	Consol. of Rosar., Ltd., 4 p.c. 1 Deb. Stk., Red.	100	92
7½	East London	100	226½
4½	Do. Deb. Stk.	100	162½
3	Do. Deb. Stk., Red.	100	106
37/6	Grand Junction (Max. 10 p.c.) "A"	50	122½
18/9	Do. "B"	25	
18/9	Do. "C" (Max. 7½ p.c.)	25	55½
35/	Do. "D" (Max. 7 p.c.)	50	104½
4	Do. Deb. Stock	100	149½
13	Kent	100	360½
7	Do. New (Max. 7 p.c.)	100	215½
6/7½	Kimberley, Ltd.	7	5
6	Do. Debs., Red.	100	102½
6	Do. Deb. Stk., Red.	100	105½
10	Lambeth (Max. 10 p.c.)	100	300½
7½	Do. (Max. 7½ p.c.), 50 & 25	—	232½
4	Do. Deb. Stock	100	148½
3	Do. Red. Deb. Stock	100	105
10/	Montevideo, Ltd.	20	16½
5	Do. 1 Deb. Stk.	100	108½
5	Do. 2 Deb. Stk.	100	103½
132/9	New River New	100	447½
4	Do. Deb. Stk.	100	149½
4	Do. Deb. Stk. "B"	100	149½
—	Odessa, Ltd., "A" 6 p.c. Prefd.	20	—
nil	Do. "B" Deferred	20	—
4	Portland Con. Mt. "B," 1927	—	102½
8/	Seville, Ltd.	20	12½
5/6	Southend "Addl." Ord.	10	17½
6	Southwark and Vauxhall	100	157½
6	Do. "D" Shares (7½ p.c. max.)	100	162½
5	Do. Pref. Stock	100	176½
4	Do. "A" Deb. Stock	100	147½
3	Staines Resvirs. Jt. Com. Gua. Deb. Stk., Red.	100	105
7/	Tarapaca, Ltd.	10	10
10	West Middlesex	100	308½
4½	Do. Deb. Stk.	100	163½
3	Do Deb. Stk.	100	106

Prices Quoted on the Leading Provincial Exchanges.

ENGLISH.

In quoting the markets, B stands for Birmingham; Bl for Bristol; M for Manchester; L for Liverpool; and S for Sheffield.

CORPORATION STOCKS.

Chief Market.	Int or Div.	Name.	Amount paid.	Price.
M	3½	Bolton, Red. 1935 ..	100	115½
M	3½	Burnley, Red. 1933..	100	114
M	3½	Bury, Red. 1946	100	116½
L	2¾	Liverpool, Red. 1925	100	102¾
B	3½	Longton, 1932	100	106
M	4	Oldham Prp. Db. Sk.	100	146
M	£1	Do. Gas & W. Ann.		34½
S	4	Rotherham 4 p.c., Red. 1927...... [£	1 an	114
M	3½	Runcorn Red. 1923..	100	105
S	2¾	Sheffield Water Ann.	100	118¼
S	3	Do.	3 an	90
L	3½	Southport Red. 1936	5 an / 100	112
L	3	Do. Red. 1914..	100	102½
M	3	Todmorden, Red. 1914	100	102

RAILWAYS.

Chief Market.	Int or Div.	Name.	Amount paid.	Price.
Bl	4½	Bridgewater Pref. ..	100	135½
M	1¾	Cleator & Workton.	100	76
M	4	Do. 1883 Pref. ..	100	109
L	4	Cockermth. K. & P.	100	113½
L	4	Isle of Man	5	6¾
L	5	Do. Pref.	5	6¾
L	3	Liverpool Overhead	10	10¾
L	4	Do. Deb. Stk. ..	100	110
L	5	Do. Pref.	10	16
L	6½	Maryport & Carlisle	100	167
S	6	Mid. Shef. & Roth. Pf.	100	231
Bl	35/	Neath & Brecon "A"	100	67½
M	4¾	Oldham, Ashton, &c.	10	16¾
Bl	5½	Penarth Harbour ..	100	182½
Bl	4	Do. Deb. Stk. ..	100	145
Bl	3½	Do. Deb. Stk. ..	100	127
Bl	1¾	Ross & Monmouth..	20	5¾
Bl	6	Do. Pref.	20	42½
M	3	Southport & Cheshire Deb. Stk.	100	104½
M	nil.	Do. Pref.	100	22
Bl	2¾	West Somerset Gu...	100	96½
Bl	5	Wye Val. Deb. Stk.	100	164

BANKS.

Chief Market.	Int or Div.	Name.	Amount paid.	Price.
L	8/	Adelphi, L., £20 Shs.	10	16½
L	12/6	Bk of L'pool, L., £100 Sh	12½	39⅝
B	5/6	Brmnghm. Dis. & C., Ltd., £20 Shs.....	4	10½
B	6/3	Co. of Staffs., L., £40	5	13¾
S	17½	Crompton & Evans, Ltd., £20 Shs	4	15
M	14/	Lancs. & Yorks, Ltd., £20 Shs.....	10	31⅝
L	30/	Livrpl. Union, Ltd., £100 Shs.	20	60¾
M	24/	Manchester & Co., Ltd., £100 Shs. ..	16	61½
M	20/	Mnchstr. & Livrpool. Dis., Ltd., £60 Shs.	10	51½
M	1/6	Mer. of Lancashire, Ltd., £20 Shs.....	3	6⅝
L	16/	Nth. & Sth. Wales, Ltd., £40 Shs.....	10	35¾
B	20/	Notts Joint St., Ltd., £50 Shs..........	10	26¾
M	4/	Oldham Joint Stk., Ltd., £20 Shs.....	4	12⅝
S	15	Sheffield Banking, Ltd., £50 Shs.....	17½	51½
S	20	Do. & Rotherham, Ltd., £50 Shs...	8	26⅝
S	10	Do. & Hallamsh., Ltd., £100 Shs..	25	65
S	10	Do. Union, Ltd., £40 Shs.........	10	25½
M	12/	Union of Manchester, Ltd., £25 Shs.. ..	11	27½
M	10/	Williams, Deacon, &c. Ltd., £50 Shs.....	8	26¼
Bl	20	Wilts & Dorset, Ltd., £50 Shs..........	10	49
S	5/6	York City & Co., Ltd., £10 Shs.....	3	13

BREWERIES.

Chief Market.	Int or Div.	Name.	Amount paid.	Price.
B	6	Ansell & Sons Pref.	10	15⅜
B	5	Do. Debs.	100	110
L	9/	Bent's..............	10	18⅜
L	6	Do. Cum. Pref...	10	14 1/16
L	4½	Do. Deb. Stk. ..	100	111
L	13/6	Birkenhead, £5 paid	5	22¼
L	13/6	Do. £10 paid...,	10	25
M	9/	Boddington's	9	19½
M	5	Do. Cum. Pref...	10	13
M	4	Do. Deb. Stk. ..	100	109½
B	4½	Butler & Co. Db. Stk	100	110½
M	6	Chesters' Cum. Pref.	10	13½
M	4½	Do. Debs.	100	112
S	10/	Clarkson's Ord.	10	23
S	6	Do. Cum. Prf. Stk.	10	14⅜
M	4	Dutton & Co. Db. Sk.	100	104
M	4½	Hardy's Crown Debs.	100	111
B	10/	Holt	10	17⅜
B	5	Do. Cum. Pref...	10	12½
B	4	Do. Debs.	100	109½
B	12/6	Lichfield	10	24
B	5	Do. Cum. Pref...	10	11½
M	5½	Manchester Deb. Stk.	100	142
B	6/	Mitchell, H., & Co.	10	38
B	6	Do. Cum. Pref...	10	15⅜
B	6	Oakhill Pref........	10	16½

Breweries (continued):—

Chief Market.	Int. or Div.	Name.	Amount paid.	Price.
M	5/	Springwell	10	10¾
M	7	Do. Pref.	10	13½
Bl	9	Stroud	10	16½
Bl	6	Do. Pref......	10	14¼
M	6/	Taylor's Eagle......	10	11½
M	7	Do. Cum. Pref ..	10	13½
M	3½	Do. Deb. Stk. ..	100	117½
S	10	Tennant Bros £20 shs	15	34½
S	10	Wheatley & Bates ..	10	14¾
S	6	Do. Cum. Pref.	10	12⅜

CANALS AND DOCKS.

Chief Market.	Int. or Div.	Name.	Amount paid.	Price.
Bl	8	Hill's Dry Dk. &c. £20	18	9
M	4	Manc. Ship Canal 1st Mt. Deb. Stk.	100	104
M	4	Do. 2nd do.	100	103½
L	36/3	Mersey Dck. & Harb.	an.	118¼
L	35/	Do.	an.	117
M	10/	Rochdale Canal	100	37
B	37/6	Staff. & Worc. Canal	100	76½
B	4½	Do. Deb. Stk....	100	137
Bl	4	Swansea Harb.......	100	114
B	27/6	Warwick & Birm. Cnl	100	66½
B	12/6	Do. & Napton do.	100	23

COMMERCIAL & INDUSTRIAL.

Chief Market.	Int. or Div.	Name.	Amount paid.	Price.
L	5	Agua Santa Mt. Debs	100	100
M	8/	Armitage, Sir E. & Sns Ltd.............	10	19
M	4	Do. Deb. 1910 ..	100	103
L	6	Ang. Chil. Nit. 1 Mt. Debs., 1919 ..	100	109½
Bl	8½	Bath Stone Firms ..	10	20
M	4/9¾	Barlow & Jones, Ltd., £10 Shs.	8	10⅜
B	12/6	Birmghm. Ry. Car.	10	17½
B	6	Do. Pref.	10	15½
B	16/8	Do. Small Arms	5	15½
M	£12	Blackpool Pier......	100	277½
M	5	Do. Tower Debs.	50	54½
M	2/	Do. Wi. Gar. & P.	5	4⅝
Bl	10	Bristl. & S. W. R. Wag. £20 Shs...........	3	5¾
Bl	8	Do. Wag. & Carri. £10 Shs..........	10	14½
M	7/	Crosses & Winkwth. Ltd.............	5	12½
L	5	G. Angus & Co. Pref.	10	13⅝
Bl	5	Gloster. Carri. & W.		10⅛
Bl	5	Gt. Wstn. Cttn., Ltd.	20	15½
M	6	Hetherington, L. Prf.	10	8½
M	4½	Do. Debs., 1910	100	98½
B	7½d.	Hinks (J. & Son), Ltd.	1	27/6
S	20/	Jessop & Sons, £50 Sh	30	27
S	10	Kayser, Ellsn. & Co. L.	5	11⅝
S	6	Do. Pref.	5	7½
M	7/6	Kellner-Partgton., L.	5	14½
M	4½	Do. Debs., 1914..	100	105½
M	5	Kerr Thread, Ltd., Debs.	100	101
B	17/	King's Norton Metal, £10 Shs..........	8½	18½
M	5/	Lancashire & Yorks. Wagon, Ltd.	10	9¾
L	10/	Liverpool Exch., Ltd.	20	27½
L	45/	Do. Grain Stge, Ltd.	50	108
L	5/	Do. Rubber, Ltd...	5	6⅛
M	9d.	Manchester Bond. Whse., L., £10 Shs.	4½	2½
M	3/9	Do. Comcial. Bldgs., Ltd., £10 Shs.	5	10½
M	4/	Do. No. 2, £10 Shs.	5	10½
M	2/6	Do. No. 3, £10 Shs.	5	7½
M	5/	Do. Corn, &c., Exchange, Ltd.	10	16½
M	4	Do. Debs.	100	126
M	8	Do. Ryl. Exchge, L.	100	246½
B	5/	Midland Rlwy. Car. Wgn., Ld., £20 Sh.	10	14½
Bl	5	Millers & Corys Dbs.	100	100½
B	12/6	Mint, Brgham., Ltd.	5	7⅝
B	5	Do. Debs.	25	107
B	10/	Nettlefolds, Ltd.....	10	50
B	5	Do. Pref.	10	15½
S	9	Nth. Centrl. Wgn., L.	5	8⅝
B	15/	Patnt. Nut & Bolt, L.	10	34
B	5	Do. Pref.	10	14½
B	1/	Perry & Co., Ltd. ..	1	28/9
B	6d.	Do. Pref.	1	27/
S	10	Round, J., & Co., L., £10 Shs.	6	12⅝
S	15	Rodgers, J., & Sons, L.	100	213
M	18/9	Rylands & Sons, Ltd., £20	15	38¾
M	2/6	Do. paid up	20	43½
M	4	Do. Debs. ..1909	100	106
S	5	Sanderson Brs. & Co., Ltd, Debs.	100	102
M	4½	Schwabe, S., & Co., Ltd., 1 Debs. 1914	100	104
S	7½	Sheffield Forge & Rolling, Ltd.	10	11½
L	80/	Southport Pier, Ltd.	100	88¼
L	2½	Do. W. Gdns., Ltd.	5	3½
Bl	5	Spillers & Bakers, Ltd, £10 Shs.	9	14½
Bl	6	Do. Pref.	10	14½
B	5/	Union Rolling Stock, Ltd., £20 Shs.....	5	7½
M	6/	Victoria Pr., S'port, L.	5	4⅝
Bl	8	Western Wagon & Property, Ltd.....	6	9⅜
S	10	Wostenholm, G., & Son, Ltd., £25 Shs.	20	22⅜
S	6½	Yorksh. Wagon, Ltd.	2	2⅜

FINANCIAL, TRUSTS, &c.

Chief Market.	Int. or Div.	Name.	Amount paid.	Price.
M	1/	Manchstr. Trst. £10 Shs...............	2	13/9
M	1/3	N. of Eng. T. Deb. & A., Ltd. £10 Shs.	2½	27/3
M	3½	Do. 1 Mt. Debs...	100	97
L	—	Pacific Ln. & Inv., L.	2½	2⅝
L	4	Do. Deb. Stk.....	100	102
L	—	United Trst., L. Prfd.	100	72½
L	—	Do. Deferred....	100	62½

GAS.

Chief Market.	Int. or Div.	Name.	Amount paid.	Price.
Bl	5	Bristol Gas (5 p.c. mx.)	100	126½
Bl	4	Do. 1st Deb.	100	137
S	10	Gt. Grimsby "C" ..	10	201
L	10	Liverpool Utd. "A"	100	245
L	7	Do. "B"......	100	178
L	4	Do. Deb.	100	137
S	10	Sheffield Gas "A," "B," "C"	100	248
B	10½	Wolverhampton	100	230
B	3	Do. 6 p.c. Pref...	100	172

INSURANCE.

Chief Market.	Int. or Div.	Name.	Amount paid.	Price.
M	6	Equitable F. & Acc. £5 Shs.	1	39/
L	2/	Liverpool Mortgage £10 Shs.	2	1 1/16
M	2/	Mchester. Fire £20 Shs	2	7¾
M	5/	National Boiler & G., Ltd., £10 Shs.	3	13⅜
L	2/	Reliance Mar., Ltd., £10 Shs.	2	4⅝
L	4/	Sea, Ltd., £10 Shs...	2	10 1/16
L	8/	Stnd. Mar., L., £20 Sh.	4	8 1/16
L	1/	State Fire, L., £20 Sh.	1	2 1/16

COAL, IRON, AND STEEL.

Chief Market.	Int. or Div.	Name.	Amount paid.	Price.
Bl.	12	Albion Stm. Coal ..	10	11½
M	15/9	And. Knowles & S., Ltd., £37½ Shs. ..	23½	12½
M	5	Do. Mt. Debs. 1908	100	105½
Bl.	1/½	Ashton V. Iron	100	26
S	12½	Bessemer, Ltd.	10	20½
S	5	Do. Pref.	10	12¼
S	12/6	Briggs, H., & Co., "A" £15 Shs.....	12½	15⅝
S	8/6	Do. "B" £15 Shs.	8½	9⅜
S	20	Brown Baley's Stl., L.	10	33
S	5	Brown, J., & Co., Cum. Pref.	10	13½
S	5	Cammell, C. & Co., Ltd.	85	12½
S	5	Do. Pref.	5	6⅝
M	5	Chatterley Whitfield. Col., Debs., 1905..	100	100½
Bl	—	Davis, D., & Sons, Ld.	10	10½
M	5	Evans, R., & Co., Ltd., Deb., 1910 ..	100	100½
S	12½	Fox, S., & Co., Ltd., £100 Shs.	80	178
Bl	10	Gt. Wstn. Col., L., "A"	5	10½
Bl	6	Do. "B"	5	4½
Bl	8	Main Colliery, Ltd.	10	8
B	2/6	Muntz's Metal, Ltd.	5	8
B	5	Do. Pref.......	5	6½
M	2/6¾	Nth. Lonsd. Iron and Steel, Ltd., £10 Sh.	8½	2½
Bl	6	North's Nav. Coll., Ltd., Debs.	100	105
S	30/	Parkgate Irn. & Stl., Ltd., £100 Shs. ..	75	70½
M	6	Pearson & Knls., Ld., "A" Cum. Pref...	50	46
B	10/	Sandwell Pk. Col., L.	10	17
M	6/3	Sheepbridge Coal and Iron, Ltd., "A"	25	17¾
M	2/6	Do. "B"	10	6½
M	5	Do. "C" Gua. Pf.	25	28½
Bl	4	South Wales Coll., Ltd., "A"	17	8½
S	30/	Staveley Coal & Iron, Ltd., "A" £100 Sh.	60	81
S	30/	Do. "C"	60	82
M	1/10½	Tredegar Iron & Cl., Ld., "A" £10 Sh.	7½	2⅜
M	1½	Do. "B" Stk. ..	100	35
M	6/	Wigan Cl. & Irn., Ld.	10	7
M	4/6	Do. £10 Shs.	7½	4

SHIPPING.

Chief Market.	Int. or Div.	Name.	Amount paid.	Price.
Bl	6	Bristol St. Nav. Pref.	10	11¾
L	15/	Brit. & Af. St. Nav..	10	13½
L	5/10½	British & Estn, Ltd.	6½	2 11/16
L	10/	Pacific Stm. Nav., L.	25	24½
L	30/	Wst. Ind. & Pac. St. Ltd., £25 Shs.....	20	27

TRAMWAYS, &c.

Chief Market.	Int. or Div.	Name.	Amount paid.	Price.
B	5/	Brmngh. & Aston, L.	5	11½
B	5/	Do. Mid., Ltd...	10	7⅜
Bl	6/	Bristol Tr. & Car., Ltd.............	10	20½
B	4/	Do. Debs.	100	121
L	6	I. of Man Elec., L., Pref.	1	1½
M	15/	Manchester C. & T., L., "A" £20 Shs.	15	27¾
M	10/	Do. "B"	10	18¾

WATER WORKS.

Chief Market.	Int. or Div.	Name.	Amount paid.	Price.
Bl	7	Bristol	25	63½
Bl	7	Do.............	20	48
Bl	58/	Do. 7 p.c. max. ..	100	161
Bl	4½	Do. Pref.	20	32½
Bl	5	Do. Pref.	10	18½
Bl	3½	Do. Deb.	100	129½
M	10	Fylde "A".......	100	335
M	7	Do. "B"	100	224
B	6	S. Staffs. Ord. "A"	100	165
B	—	Do. "B"	100	164
B	4	Do. Deb. Stk. ...	100	140
B	5	Do. Pf "A" "B" "C"	100	170
M	£3½	Stockport District ..	100	184½
B	2/	Wolverhampton New	5	6½

SCOTTISH.

In quoting the markets, E stands for Edinburgh, and G for Glasgow.

RAILWAYS.

Chief Market.	Int. or Div.	Name.	Nom. Amount	Price.
E	5½	Arbroath and Forfar	25	51
G	2	Callander and Oban.	10	7½
G	4	Do. Deb. Stock	100	148
G	4½	Do. Pref.......	10	14½
G	4	Cathct. Dist. Deb. Stk.	100	148
E	5	Edin. and Bathgate .	100	179½
E	7	Forth & Clyde Junc.	100	222½
G	4	Lanarks. and Ayrsh.	10	14
G	4	Do. & Dumbartons.	10	14½
G	4	Do. Deb. Stk.	100	149

BANKS.

Chief Market.	Int. or Div.	Name.	Nom. Amount	Price.
G	12	Bank of Scotland ..	100	361
G	16	British Linen	100	500
G	8	Caledonian, Ltd.....	2½	97/
G	10	Clydesdale, Ltd.	10	23½
G	16	Commercl. of Scot., L.	20	88½
G	16	National of Scot. Ld.	100	426
G	8	Royal of Scotland ..	100	234
G	11	Union of Scotland, L.	10	26 11/16

BREWERIES.

Chief Market.	Int. or Div.	Name.	Nom. Amount	Price.
E	5	Bernard, Thos. Pref.	10	10½
E	5	Bernard, T. & J., Cum. Pref........	10	12½
G	20	Highland Distilleries	3½	10½

CANALS AND DOCKS.

Chief Market.	Int. or Div.	Name.	Nom. Amount	Price.
G	4	Clyde Nav. 4 p.c....	100	125½
G	3½	Do. 3½ p.c.......	100	105
G	3½	Greenock Harb. "A"	100	100
G	2	Do. "B"	100	40

MISCELLANEOUS.

Chief Market.	Int. or Div.	Name.	Nom. Amount	Price.
G	4½	Alexander & Co. Debs.	100	110½
G	5	Baird, H., & Sns. C.P.	10	12½
E	10	Barry, Ostlere, & Co.	7½	12½
E	6	Do. Cum. Pref...	10	15 1/16
G	5	Brown, Stewart, Deb.	100	84
E	7½	Broxburn Oil	8½	8½
E	6	Do. Cum. Pref...	10	11 1/16
E	7	Edinburgh & Dist. Tram. Cum. Pref.	5	9
E	5	Gilroy, Sons, & Co. Debs.	100	99
G	9	Glasgow Cot. Spin...	6	5½
G	30/	Do. Royal Exchg.	46	110
G	—	Pumpherston Oil Pf.	10	8¾
E	7	Scottish Assam Tea	10	11½
E	5	Scottish Waggon....	10	12½
G	5	Stoddard & Co. Pref.	10	12½

FINANCIAL, LAND, AND INVESTMENT.

Chief Market.	Int. or Div.	Name.	Nom. Amount	Price.
G	1/	Assets Co..........	1	47/
E	4½	Investors' Mort. Pref.	100	99½
E	4	Do. Deb. Stk....	100	103½
E	4	Nthn. Inv. N. Zeal. Deb. Stk.	100	107
E	4	N. of Scot. Canadian Deb. Stk.	100	106
E	4½	Real & Deb. Corp. Deb. Stk.	100	108

INSURANCE.

Chief Market.	Int. or Div.	Name.	Amount paid.	Price.
G	12/	Caledonian F. & Life	5	35½
G	4/6	City of Glasgow Life	2½	12½
E	19/	Edinburgh Life	20	55
G	13/1	Life Ass. of Scotland	8½	34½
E	8	Nat. Guar. & Surety	2	52/
G	17½	Scottish Union and National "A"....	1	97/
G	17½	Do. "B"	3½	18¼

IRON, COAL, AND STEEL.

Chief Market.	Int. or Div.	Name.	Amount paid.	Price.
E	Nil.	Addie, Coll. Cm. Pref.	10	7½
E	8/	Arniston Coal	8	14
E	2½	Cairntable Gas Coal	8	86/
E	12½	Fife Coal	10	20½
E	5	Do. Cum. Pref..	10	13
G	7	Merry & Cunghame. Cum. Pref........	10	15⅞
G	5	Do. Debentures ..	100	105¼
E	1/9	Niddrie & Benhar Cl.	1½	41/3
G	5	Steel Com. of Scotlnd	—	
	—	"A" Deb. Stk. ..	100	113
G	6	Do. and Mt. "B"	100	110
E	—	Watson, John	8½	10½
E	6	Do. Cum. Pref..	7½	8½
E	12½	Wilson's & Cly. Coal	3	8⁷⁄₁₆

IRISH.

In quoting the markets, B stands for Belfast, and D for Dublin.

CORPORATION STOCKS.

Chief Market.	Int. or Div.	Name.	Amount paid.	Price.
B	3½	Belfast, 1921	100	112
B	3½	Do. 1912	100	107½
B	3½	Do. 1924	100	109½
B	3	Do. 1955	100	106
B	3½	Do. Water Com...	100	117
B	3	Do. do.	100	106
B	3½	Do. Harbour Com.	100	114½
D	3½	Rathmines & Rathgar	100	110½
D	3½	Waterford Deb.	100	—

RAILWAYS.

Chief Market.	Int. or Div.	Name.	Amount Paid.	Price.
D	30/	Cork, Bandon, & S.C.	100	78
D	4	Do. Deb........	100	139½
D	4	Do. W. Cork Pref.	100	—
B	5½	Belfast & Northern..	100	160
B	4	Do. Deb........	100	146
B	4	Do. Pref.	100	141½
B	6½	Belfast & C. Down..	100	167
B	4	Do. Deb........	100	147
B	3	Do.	100	107½
B	4½	Do. 4½ Pref. B...	100	153½
B	5	Do. Guar.	100	173
D	Nil.	Dublin, Wick. & Wex.	100	36
D	4	Do. Deb........	100	127½
D	4½	Do. Deb........	100	134
D	6	Do. Guar.	100	170
D	4	Do. C. of Dub. Junc.	100	—
D	5	Do. 1860 Pref. ..	100	121
D	50/	Do. 1864 Pref. ..	100	106
D	50/	Do. 1865 Pref. ..	100	94½
B	6½	Great Northern	100	178½
B	4	Do. Deb........	100	148
B	4	Do. Pref. B.	100	143½
B	5½	Gt. South & Western	100	144
B	4	Do. Deb.	100	148½
B	4	Do. Guar........	100	144
D	45/	Midland Gt. Western	100	114
D	4	Do. Deb.	100	146½
D	4½	Do. Deb.	100	151½
D	4½	Do. Deb.	100	—
D	5	Do. Pref.	100	175
D	4	Do. Pref.	100	—
D	—	Waterford & Central	100	15
D	3	Do. Deb.	100	—
D	3½	Do. Pref.	100	134
D	4	Waterfd. L., & W. Db.	100	129½
D	4½	Do. Deb.	100	—
D	4	Do. Pref.	100	125½
D	3½	Do. Pref.	100	—

BANKS.

Chief Market.	Int. or Div.	Name.	Amount paid.	Price.
B	50/	Belfast, Old, £125 Shs.	25	126½
B	20/	Do. New, £125 Shs.	25	50½
D		Hibernian, £20 Shs.	5	6½
D	2/	Munster & Leinster £5 Shs.	2	5½
B	11/	Northern, £50 Shs...	10	26½
D	12/	Royal, £50 Shs.	10	28½
B	5/	Ulster, £15 Shs.	2½	12⅛

BREWERIES AND DISTILLERIES.

Chief Market.	Int. or Div.	Name.	Amount paid.	Price.
D	10/	Castlebellingham & Drog	10	16½
D	6	Do. Pref.	10	15½
D	4½	Do. Deb.	100	115
B	17/	Dunville & Co.......	10	28½
B	6	Irish Distillery, Pref.	10	13½
B	5	Do. Deb.	100	110
B	6	J. & J. M'Connell, Pf.	10	15⅛
B	13/6	Mitchell & Co.......	9	19½
B	5	Do. Deb.	10	11½
D	4½	Phœnix Brew. Deb.	100	95
B	6/	Wm. Cowan........	10	13½
B	6	Do. Pref. ..	10	13½
B	8/	Young, King, & Co.	8	14

STEAM AND CANAL.

Chief Market.	Int. or Div.	Name.	Amount paid.	Price.
B	Nil	Belfast Steamship ..	50	35½
D	10/	British and Irish	50	—
D	15/	City of Dublin......	100	61
D	3½	Do. Deb.	100	105
D	30/	Dublin & Lpool. Bldg.	50	75
D	2/6	Dundalk & Newry..	10	4½
D	4/	Grand Canal........	10	11½
D	3	Do. Pref. ..	10	9½
D	3	Do. Deb. ..	100	99
B	30/	Irish Shipowners....	100	65
B	3/	Ulster Steamship....	5	6

MISCELLANEOUS.

Chief Market.	Int. or Div.	Name.	Amount paid.	Price.
D	3/1	Arnott & Co.	4	—
D	6	Do. Pref. ..	4	6½
B	8/	Belfast Com. Bldgs.	10	17
B	37/6	Do. Ropework Co.	75	92
B	5	Do. do. Pref.	10	13½
B	2/	Do. Discount Co..	3	43/
B	5	Do. do. Pref.	5	4½
B	10/	Brookfield Linen....	25	17½
B	Nil	Coey & Co.	25	4
B	5	Do. Deb.	50	49½
B	4½	David Allen&S's Deb.	100	107½
D	4/	Dublin Trams	10	19½
D	6	Do. Pref.....	10	18⅛
D	4	Do. Deb.....	100	—
B	5/	Edenderry Spinning.	10	9
B	25/	Falls Flax Spinning.	25	15
B	17/	Forster, Green, & Co.	10	22½
B	9/	Island Spinning	7½	7½
B	8/	Jas. Lindsay & Co..	8	16½
B	1/7½	John Arnott & Co...	4	4⅛
B	4½	Do. Deb........	50	56
D	5/	Kinahan & Co.......	10	11½
D	5½	Do. Pref........	10	11½
D	4½	Do. Deb........	100	108½
B	12/	Kirker & Co.	10	10
B	5/	Leahy, Kelly, & Leahy	5	8½
B	6	Do. Pref........	5	7⅛
B	4/	Lindsay Bros. Ltd...	8	7½
B	4½	Do. Deb........	50	56½
D	1/	National Assurance.	2½	39/
B	10/	Olley & Co.	5	7⅛
D	1/1½	Patriotic Assurance..	2½	29/6
B	3/7½	P. Johnston & Son, L.	6	6½
B	10/	Robertson, F., & Co.	8	23½
B	10	Ulster Marine Insur.	5/	7/
B	15/	York-street Flax	25	33½
B	6	Do. Pref........	10	15½
B	4½	Do. Deb........	100	120½

INDIAN AND CEYLON TEA COMPANIES.

Acres Planted.	Crop, 1897.	Paid up Capital.	Share.	Paid up.	Name.	Dividends. 1894.	1895.	1896.	Int. 1897.	Price.	Yield.	Reserve.	Balance Forward.	Working Capital.	Mortgages, Debs. or Pref. Capital not otherwise stated.
	lb.	£	£	£	INDIAN COMPANIES.							£	£	£	£
11,240	3,128,000	120,000	10	3	Amalgamated Estates	—	*	10	5	3½	8½	10,000	16,500	D52,950	—
		400,000	10	10	Do. Pref.	—	*	5	15	10½	4¾				
10,223	3,560,000	187,160	20	20	Assam	20	20	20	5	60½	6½	55,000	1,730	D11,350	—
6,150	3,278,000	142,500	10	10	Assam Frontier........	3	6	6	—	8¾	6¾	—	286	20,000	82,500
		142,500	10	10	Do. Pref.	6	6	6	3	11½	5¼				
2,087	839,000	66,745	5	5	Attaree Khat	12	12	8	3	7½	5½	3,790	4,820	7,770	—
1,633	583,000	78,170	10	10	Borelli	4	4	5	—	8	6¼	—	3,256	D970	6,500 Pref.
1,720	812,000	60,825	5	5	British Indian	6	5	5	—	4	6	—	2,920	12,300	16,500 Pref.
3,223	2,247,000	114,500	5	5	Brahmapootra	20	18	20	6	13	7½	—	28,440	41,600	
3,754	1,617,000	76,500	10	10	Cachar and Dooars	*	8	7	—	10	6½	—	1,645	21,240	
		76,500	10	10	Do. Pref.	*	6	6	3	12½	4½				
3,946	2,083,000	72,010	1	1	Chargola	8	7	10	2½	1	10½	3,000	3,300	—	—
		81,000	1	1	Do. Pref.	7	7	7	3½	1½	5				
2,971	942,000	33,000	5	5	Chubwa	10	8	10	3½	6½	7½	10,000	2,043	D5,400	—
		33,000	5	5	Do. Pref.	7	7	7	3½	7	5				
32,250	11,500,000	120,000	10	3	Cons. Tea and Lands	—	*	10	5	3½	7½	65,000	14,240	D191,674	—
		1,000,000	10	10	Do. 1st Pref.	—	*	5	‡5	11½	4½				
		400,000	10	10	Do. 2nd Pref.	—	*	7	‡7	12	5½				
2,230	617,000	135,420	20	20	Darjeeling............	5½	5½	6	—	22½	5	5,352	1,565	1,700	—
2,114	445,000	60,000	10	10	Darjeeling Cons.........	—	*	4/2	—	7	—	—	1,820	—	—
		60,000	10	10	Do. Pref.	—	*	5	2½	9½	5½				
6,660	3,518,000	150,000	10	10	Dooars	12½	12½	12½	2½	18½	6½	45,000	300	D32,000	—
		75,000	10	10	Do. Pref.	7	7	7	3½	16½	4½				
3,367	1,811,000	165,000	10	10	Doom Dooma	11¼	10	12½	5	22	5½	30,000	4,032	—	10,000
1,377	582,000	61,120	5	5	Eastern Assam	5	nil.	4	—	3½	6½	—	1,790	—	10,000
4,038	1,675,000	85,000	10	10	East India and Ceylon	*	nil.	7	—	9	7½	—	1,710	—	—
		85,000	10	10	Do. Pref.	*	6	6	3	12	5				
7,500	3,363,000	219,000	10	10	Empire of India	—	*	6/10	2½	12	—	15,000	—	27,000	—
		219,000	10	10	Do. Pref.	—	*	5	2½	11	4½				
1,180	540,000	94,060	10	10	Indian of Cachar	7	3½	3	—	4½	6½	6,070	—	7,120	—
3,050	824,000	83,500	5	5	Jhanzie	10	10	10	4	8½	6	14,500	1,070	2,700	—
7,980	3,680,000	250,000	10	10	Jokai	10	10	10	5	18	5½	45,000	990	D9,000	—
		100,000	10	10	Do. Pref.	*	6	6	3	14½	4				
5,224	1,563,000	100,000	20	20	Jorehaut	20	20	20	—	60	6½	36,220	2,955	3,000	—
1,547	504,000	65,660	10	8	Lebong	15	15	15	5	16½	7½	9,000	2,150	8,650	—
5,082	1,709,000	100,000	10	10	Lungla	*	10	6	3	9	6½	—	1,543	D21,000	—
		100,000	10	10	Do. Pref.	*	6	6	3	11½	5½				
2,684	885,000	95,970	10	10	Majuli	7	5	5	—	6½	7½	—	2,606	560	—
1,375	380,000	91,840	1	¼	Makum	—	—	2	—	1⅛	1½	—	—	1,200	25,000
2,990	770,000	100,000	1	1	Moabund	—	—	*	—	1	—	—	—	—	—
		50,000	1	1	Do. Pref.	—	—	*	2½	1	5				
1,080	482,000	79,590	10	10	Scottish Assam	7	7	7	—	11	6½	6,500	800	9,590	—
4,150	1,456,000	100,000	10	10	Singlo................	*	8	5	1	9	5½	—	300	D5,200	—
		80,000	10	10	Do. Pref.	*	6½	6½	3½	13	5				
	Crop, 1896.				CEYLON COMPANIES.										
7,970	1,743,824	250,000	100	100	Anglo-Ceylon, & Gen.	—	*	5½	—	65	7½	10,992	1,405	D72,844	166,620
1,836	685,741	50,000	10	10	Associated Tea	—	*	5	2½	8	6½	—	164	2,478	—
		60,000	10	10	Do. Pref.	—	*	6	3	10½	5½				
10,390	4,000,000§	167,380	10	10	Ceylon Tea Plantations ..	15	15	15	7	27½	5½	84,500	1,516	D30,819	—
		81,080	10	10	Do. Pref.	7	7	7	‡7	17	4½				
5,722	1,542,700§	55,960	5	3	Ceylon & Oriental Est....	5	8	7	—	9½	7½	—	230	D2,047	71,000
		46,000	5	5	Do. Pref.	6	6	6	3	5	5½				
2,157	801,629	111,330	5	5	Dimbula Valley	—	*	10	5	6½	8	—	—	1,733	6,250
		62,607	5	5	Do. Pref.	—	*	6	3	6½	4½				
11,496	3,715,000	298,250	5	5	Eastern Prod. & Est.	3	5	6½	2½	6½	5½	20,000	11,740	D17,797	108,500
3,118	701,100	150,000	10	10	Lanka Plantations.......	4	5	5	‡5	6½	6½	—	495	D11,300	14,700 Pref.
2,193	1,050,000§	22,080	10	10	New Dimbula "A"	10	16	16	4	24xd	6	11,000	2,024	1,150	8,400
		55,710	10	10	Do. "B"	18	16	16	4	21½xd	6½				
2,572	570,360	100,000	10	10	Ouvah	6	8	6	2	9	6½	4,000	1,151	D1,255	—
2,630	535,675	200,000	10	10	Nuwara Eliya	—	*	6	3	11	5½	—	—	—	30,000
1,720	720,200	41,000	10	10	Scottish Ceylon	15	15	15	5	22½	6½	7,000	1,252	D3,970	9,000 Pref.
2,450	750,000§	39,000	10	6	Standard	12½	15	15	5	14	6½	9,000	800	D24,018	4,000
		17,000	10	10	Do..................	12½	15	15	5	22	6½				

* Company formed this year.

Working-Capital Column.—In working-capital column, D stands for *debit*.
† Interim dividends are given as actual distribution made. ‡ *Total* div. § Crop 1897.

Printed for the Proprietor by Love & Wyman, Ltd., Great Queen Street, London, W.C.; and Published by Clement Wilson at Norfolk House, Norfolk Street, Strand, London, W.C.

The Investors' Review

EDITED BY A. J. WILSON.

Vol. I.—No. 13. New Series. | FRIDAY, APRIL 1, 1898. | [Registered as a Newspaper.] | Price 6d. By post, 6½d

NOTICE.—Owing to the Holidays the INVESTORS' REVIEW *will next week be published on Thursday in place of Friday afternoon.*

Notice to Subscribers.

Complaints are continually reaching us that the INVESTORS' REVIEW cannot be obtained at this and the other railway bookstall, that it does not reach Scotch and Irish cities till Monday, and that it is not delivered in the City till Saturday morning.

We publish on Friday in time for the REVIEW to be at all Metropolitan bookstalls by at latest 4 p.m., and we believe that it is there then, having no doubt that Messrs. W. H. Smith & Son do their best, but they have such a mass of papers to handle every day that a fresh one may well look almost like a personal enemy and be kept in short supply unless the reading public shows unmistakably that it is wanted. A little perseverance, therefore, in asking for the INVESTORS' REVIEW is all that should be required to remedy this defect.

All London newsagents can be in a position to distribute the paper on Friday afternoon if they please, and here also the only remedy is for subscribers to insist upon having it as soon as published. Arrangements have been made that all our direct City subscribers shall have their copies before 4 p.m. on Friday. As for the provinces, we can only say that the paper is delivered to the forwarding agents in ample time to be in every English and Scotch town, and in Dublin and Belfast, likewise, early on Saturday morning. Those despatched by post from this office can be delivered by the first London mail on Saturday in every part of the United Kingdom.

ADVERTISEMENTS.

All Advertisements are received subject to approval, and should be sent in not later than 5 p.m. on Thursdays.

The advertisements of American Life Insurance Offices are rigorously excluded from the INVESTORS' REVIEW, and have been so since it commenced as a Quarterly Magazine in 1892.

For tariff and particulars of positions open apply to the Advertisement Manager, Norfolk House, Norfolk-street, W.C.

CONTENTS

The Investors' Review.

The National Expenditure.

Few people realise the speed at which the resources of the country are being absorbed by the extravagant expenditure of the present government. What the exact amount disbursed in the year now closed has been cannot be accurately stated until the Budget is produced. There have been so many supplementary estimates, some of which fall only in part upon the income of the year, and there is so much money, voted a year ago, which Mr. Goschen in particular has been unable to get rid of in time, that the exact figures cannot be stated. He did, indeed, say that £1,400,000 could not be paid away within the year because the lock-out of the engineers in the last six months of 1897 had prevented contractors from delivering the materials on order. This estimate might, perhaps, be modified a little by now, as these contractors have been working under tremendous pressure since their men returned from their enforced *chômage*.

Broad facts, however, can be laid before the public and they deserve study. We find, looking back a little, that the average expenditure upon the army and navy for the five years ended yesterday, is at least £9,000,000 more per annum than for the five years ended March 31, 1887. This is a tidy addition to the burden of the people, but it is nothing like the whole truth. In all probability the total expenditure for the year on which we have now entered will be nearer £107,000,000 than £105,000,000. Take it, however, at £105,000,000 and it is £19,000,000 more than the total for 1890. We have attained to these high figures, be it recollected, in time of peace, and there is no doubt whatever that in reaching them we are doing our utmost to provoke war. There has not been a time, within this generation at least, when the itching for war, somewhere, with some power, has been anything like so violent as it is to-day.

The attitude of a large section of the nation reminds one of a story about a magic sword which recently appeared in one of the lighter magazines. According to this, the man who grasped the handle of that sword became possessed of a passionate desire to commit murder, a desire which could only be quenched in blood; and the horror of the feeling was deepened by the sense of being fiend-driven which the man had. It seemed utterly impossible for him, once he had grasped this magic handle, to let it go again; the spirit in it, as it were, took possession of him and drove him forward to commit murders by an irresistible impulse. And we, as a nation, are getting into much this state, thanks to the constant talking of "preparation for war," and to the constant demand upon our resources for more and more money to be devoted to the providing of unprecedented accumulations of warlike furniture as a means of "preserving peace." Should this fashion go on unchecked much longer, we fear bloodthirsty passions will become irresistible, and a quarrel one day break out between us and some powerful neighbour, with results we shall doubtless live bitterly to mourn.

At present, attention should be concentrated on the ways by which the money for this excessive outlay is found. It is a subject of great interest to the taxpayer, but he has been singularly apathetic about it in recent years, and the source of his apathy lies probably in the fact that comparatively little fresh taxation has been resorted to in order to find ways and means. What has been going on has been the dissipation of immense resources which, in former years, and under guidance of a more enlightened and pacific spirit among rulers and ruled alike, were employed to lighten the burdens of taxation. Two sources have mainly furnished the additional moneys required by the present system of lavish outlay, apart from the natural growth of what we may describe as permanent sources of revenue. These have been the new Death Duties and the Income Tax; and somewhat more than half of the new money has come from the former. That is to say, the income-tax has not been raised since 1895. It was 6d. in the pound from 1889 to 1893 inclusive; in 1894 it was raised to 7d., and 1895 to 8d., where it has stood ever since. We have to go back to 1884 to find it as low as 5d. In that year it yielded £10,718,000. In the last four years it has yielded from £15,600,000 up to nearly £17,000,000. We may consequently say that an average of £6,000,000 per annum in excess of the fivepenny standard yield has been drawn from this source in recent years to assist the Government in its expenditure upon the fighting forces of the country. The sum is large, but it is principally extracted from the pockets of classes in the community which are saturated with the new Imperialism, or collected from profits made by the greatly increased numbers of joint stock companies now in existence, or, yet again, from people of large realised wealth, so that the weight of it has not excited that amount of general discontent which might have been expected. It does not touch the artisan; and thanks to exemption from income tax up to £160 per annum, the great bulk of clerks and minor functionaries in the employment of companies and private firms are either wholly or partially delivered from the impost. In fact, incomes up to £500 a year have the load lightened to them more or less, and therefore the great majority of those who pay the tax do not feel its full weight, and the small minority that do are either powerless to agitate against it, or, from their wealth, indifferent to it.

Equally safe from the efforts of the agitator to produce reform in the direction of economies are the death duties, especially as recognised by Sir William Harcourt. His duties, in fact, constitute a tax upon capital pure and simple. They have been enormously prolific beyond prevision, but they fall on the capital value of estates, and whatever suffering they may cause to inheritors of small properties they, for this very reason, have produced nothing like general discontent. And these duties also have given in the last four years £5,000,000 to £7,000,000 towards meeting the enlarged expenditure of the country, over and above the portion of them assigned to local bodies to encourage their extravagance. It follows from this that the old sources of revenue whose incidence falls upon the community at large have not been disturbed. There have been no additions to the Customs duties nor to Excise, and the yield from these has only increased in a normal way, through the increase in population, or in the well-being of the community. Customs, for example are only about £1,000,000 more now than they have been on the average any time during the last ten or twelve years, and Excise yields very little more now than it did from 1882 to 1885, and rather less than in the years 1876 to 1879. These considerations explain to a large extent the indifference of the country to the way in which the overflowing public revenue is spent, and afford ground for the belief that this indifference is destined to continue, until such time as all the excess resources of Income Tax and Death Duties have been exhausted, and the Government has to fall back upon the indirect duties levied upon the whole population. How long it will be before this critical turning point arrives we dare not prophesy; but the pace we are going at is undoubtedly fast now, and is increasing in celerity, after a fashion which may well excite apprehension in reflecting minds. For it is quite possible that already the revenue from both Income Tax and Death Duties has reached high water mark and that the next few years may see some decline in it. Should expenditure continue to expand as it has been doing, while revenue at the same time contracts a little, we shall very soon be brought to book, and obliged to consider whether a new Customs tariff shall not be set up once more, or whether we shall not quadruple, say, the duty on beer. At no distant day, we may be reasonably certain, the present system of dispersing the bounteous national income, in great prepartions for war, in doles and *largesse* here, there, and in the West Indies, in excessive subventions to this and that, this enterprise or the other, must bring the nation face to face with a revision of its fiscal system. It may do something worse than this, but we need not go further now. Enough has surely been said to set people thinking.

The Triumph of Russia in China.

In one sense it is perhaps fortunate that the minds of the people of this country have to be occupied with the affairs of Empire in so many parts of the globe at one and the same time. Were it otherwise, and had we been able to concentrate our whole attention upon the far East, the probability is by no means small that we should have so much excited ourselves about the encroachments of Russia in that quarter as to have clamoured for war. Certainly, from some points of view, the position out there is a grave one, and the latest news seems to justify the opinion that our diplomacy has been completely over-matched by that of the Cabinet of St. Petersburg. Not only has Russia obtained Port Arthur but also the neighbouring port of Ta-lien-wan, to both of which places she is now free to build the terminal section of her Trans-Siberian railway.

Nor is this the worst of it. Until the other day Russian officials were displaying an aggressive attitude in Corea. Not so long ago this attitude was pronounced enough to threaten a rupture with Great Britain over the question of the control of Corean finances, at present in the hands of an Englishman. Now all this is suddenly changed. Russia withdraws from Corea, and, rumour has it, allows Japan to have a free hand there. Should this be the truth, and it seems at least probable, the Japanese hostility to Russian aggression in China may now be to some extent abated. Japan could hardly have allowed Russia to obtain the possession of a territory lying at her very doors, and from whose ports the sea of Japan could have been dominated. Holding Corea, therefore, Russia was bound to come into collision with the Japanese, and if war had broken out between these two powers this Spring, Russian prestige in China might have been imperilled, if not for some time destroyed, as the Japanese are splendid fighters and possessed of a more powerful navy than the Russians could send into those waters. By allowing Japan to replace her in Corea, if she likes, Russia has played a master stroke of policy, which may not only remove danger from her path but which also might tend, in time, to wean the Japanese from any desire for other European alliances.

Thus the tendency of Russian diplomacy is to isolate Great Britain in the Far East, and the question our statesmen have to solve is, what attitude we shall assume towards her under the new circumstances. We think it can, at present, be no other than a pacific and friendly attitude. It is not easy, as we have said before, to attempt to fight Russia there, and not much more easy to attempt to checkmate her in diplomacy. She will have her Manchurian railway whether we like it or not, and therefore a sensible course for us to take is to behave with the utmost friendliness to the great northern Power, so as to secure for our commerce plenty of elbow room all over China; and, if spheres of influence are going to develop, we must again repeat the advice that the portions of China which we should commercially keep hold on are the Yang-tze valley and the provinces adjacent. There lie the richest parts of China, the parts most accessible to us, the parts most densely populated also, and therefore those affording the greatest scope to the extension of our trade. We need not go to war about this, all that we have to insist upon, is the opening up of the country at every point where we desire access. Whether we should have an arsenal and fortified posts on various points near the mouths of the river, and commanding the Yellow Sea from the south, such as the principal Chusan islands, is a matter which circumstances must determine, but we are clearly bound to be vigilant in the highest degree to prevent other claimants from coming forward and setting up exclusive "rights" of any sort in the Middle Kingdom. Were France wisely guided, she would join us in demanding and maintaining this liberty. Germany, we take it, must do so.

In the circumstances it is, perhaps, well that our fleet should have been ordered to fit out and to go north; but it is not well that our Secretary of State for Foreign Affairs should be an invalid, and living in the South of France. We have great respect and sympathy for Lord Salisbury and a genuine desire to see him well again and back at the Foreign Office. Yet it is impossible not to agree with the *Times* that he cannot continue both Prime Minister and Foreign Secretary; and, least of all, that he can remain Foreign Secretary when disabled by illness. We stand at what appears to be a most critical juncture in Eastern affairs. Upon the wise, firm, and manly guidance of our policy at the present time towards China, and towards Russian aggressions in China, depend not merely the future of our home trade with that vast empire but the future of India's trade and of the trade of all our Eastern possessions. Can we trust a commission of ministers, presided over by Mr. Balfour, to supply this firmness and wisdom? We cannot, because such an arrangement destroys individual responsibility and promotes rashness, hasty advances, and precipitate retreats. We do not regard Mr. Balfour as a strong man, and he has never given proof of possessing a quarter of the industry of his uncle; yet we had much rather see Mr. Balfour at the Foreign Office, or even Mr. Curzon, than that he and the Duke of Devonshire, Sir Michael Hicks-Beach and Mr. Chamberlain should frame its decisions as a committee with Lord Salisbury as a far away referee. The Duke is easy-going and phlegmatic; both Mr. Chamberlain and Sir Michael Hicks-Beach are quick-tempered and rash in speech and deed. In any division of opinion they are but too certain to prevail over their colleagues of calmer mind, and, being irresponsible as individuals, to decide to meet aggression by agression. What is the fleet moving for if some step of the kind be not in the wind?

Assuming that we must in self-defence at some time or other "lease" a place or places of arms in China, is it expedient that this should be done now, just when the Pekin Government is humiliated in its own eyes and in the sight of the world? We have the gravest doubts about it, because to begin with it is not for our ultimate advantage that the Chinese Government should continue in a state of humiliation. Can it be doubted that were we to forcibly lay hold of any part of China now we should be really playing Russia's game instead of our own, by still further weakening the prestige of an authority it is plainly Russia's object to dominate if not to overthrow? We think not, and therefore conceive that our wisest policy is to commit no act of agression against the Chinese, but rather to lead them to look upon us as supporters of the Imperial power. They should see our strength undoubtedly, but this strength should not be used except to give weight to our requests for the opening up of those parts of the country we desire to trade in. The Chinese might be told that if they furthered British commercial interests in this way, and in allowing railways to be constructed in districts and provinces duly indicated, they would so link their own interests with ours that we should be compelled to aid them in repelling aggression from other quarters. This is an obligation which would be ours in any case ; doubly ours if we "grab" land from the Chinese without leave. We therefore assume no dangerous obligation ; or, if dangerous, none which could be avoided if we are to hold the position we do in Chinese trade and keep it open to Indian trade. And for assuming this attitude we might, were it necessary, receive voluntarily the *points d'appui* we require without recourse to threats or demonstrations in arms.

Japan, it is said, means to enter into no embarrassing alliances with any European Power. She will be friendly with all, but make nowhere any sacrifice of her freedom of action. In this she is wise, and her policy is one we should imitate. It is none of our business to quarrel with any European Power or with China, but to hold vigilantly by our own interests in all friendliness to others, setting up no exclusive pretensions, but, at the same time, letting all know that we do not mean to allow our liberty to be interfered with at any point. Holding calmly and firmly to this attitude and promising to stand by the Chinese if they are further put upon, we can afford to wait events. Waiting is less costly to us than to any other power ; or at least we can afford better to wait. Any rash step now might precipitate a conflict without defining the position, and we confess we fear this rashness, and that a war may break out which would wind up in a scramble to appropriate the fragments of China, a scramble infinitely disturbing to our interests there, and, in the result, sure to be unprofitable to us.

The Danger of War over Cuba.

People in this country are now beginning to understand why the United States have worked themselves up into such a heat of passion over the Cuban question. We have in great measure been without information as to what went on in the island ever since the last rebellion broke out, except such as came to us from Havanna. What the insurgents were doing, how they lived, what treatment they received when they fell into the hands of the Spaniards—of all these things and many others we have been entirely ignorant. But the people of the United States have known all along what was going on, and from the first a large body of the more humane and intelligent among them have been horrified by stories of cruelty and famine, especially while the garrisoned portions of the island were under the Draconian rule of General Weyler. This rule lasted so long, and did such mischief, that the autonomous policy to be pursued under the new Captain-General has no chance of success. Spain's remedial measures, in short, have come too late. The people of Cuba, although weakened by disease and starvation, will never again submit to Spanish rule in any form. Those of them who have been massed, "concentrated" the official term is, in cities, under the eye of Spanish troops, are dying every week in thousands of hunger and disease, and the people of the United States can no longer stand by indifferent to their miseries.

Before these miseries the *Maine* question falls into the background. Whether the ship was destroyed by a mine in the harbour as the American commission, in a very moderately worded report, have decided, or by the blowing up of one of its own magazines, is not now a matter of such supreme interest in the United States as it was at first. All other sentiments have become absorbed in the passionate determination at all costs to drive Spain out of Cuba.

When a people reaches this heat of sympathy it will go all lengths, and, therefore, we may make up our minds that, although they have long held back from any overt act of hostility, the American people will now compel Mr. McKinley's Cabinet to energetically intervene for the relief of the sufferings of Cubans cooped up in Spanish garrisoned towns, and in all probability this interference will be regarded as an act of hostility by Spain. A declaration of war may follow and the two powers come into collision. This seems inevitable in the present temper of both nations, in spite of the highly praiseworthy endeavour of Mr. McKinley and his Cabinet to reach the desired end—Cuban freedom—by pacific means. Spanish pride will not give way, even when the Spanish conscience knows that it may be doing wrong. Cuba, the last great possession of Spain beyond sea, we sadly fear will not be parted with until it has been once more fought for. There may be temporising and delay for a few days, or even weeks, but the tension is too great to be endured long, and war may break out now at any moment. It is just as well to recognise this fact. In this war, should it come, the people of the Union may, we feel sure, rely upon the sympathies of England. The more we get to know of what has gone on in Cuba during the last three years the more readily will we support the determination to put an end to a state of things which is a disgrace to the end of the nineteenth century, to any modern age.

These last two or three days the telegrams from New York have been less warlike, and we have not the slightest doubt but what the Cabinet in Washington will leave no means untried to preserve peace—no means except one. They dare not now leave Cuba alone. Intervention to mitigate the sufferings of its inhabitants must take place, and the point to be considered is—will Spain submit to this intervention without going to war? We doubt it much. Indeed, our only trust in the maintenance of peace lies in Spain's pecuniary difficulties. Were war to break out between her and the American Union, default upon her debt and the suspension of payment by the National Bank must at once ensue, and create extreme hardship throughout the Kingdom, for the Spanish people and the Bank of Spain together hold, perhaps, three-fourths of the whole country's indebtedness as well as that of Cuba. French bankers have been trying to escape from their commitments in Spain for a long time back, and with considerable success. But a bankrupt National Government would mean early defeat at sea and revolution, or bankruptcy alone might mean revolution without waiting for defeat to come, as come it surely will. Spain can no more hope to beat the United States than it can reconquer Cuba.

Possibly the knowledge of this impotence, a knowledge the Government of the Queen Regent doubtless fully possesses, might prompt Senor Sagasta to accept the United States' terms—freedom to Cuba, plus an annual tribute sufficient to guarantee at least a portion of the Cuban debt. It is assuredly prompting him to temporise with Mr McKinley. Here again, however, it appears to us that he runs great danger of inviting rebellion at home against the Queen Regent's authority. The Carlists have been intriguing for many years against her, republicanism is by no means dead within the country, and to all political parties, and every variety of discontent, such as hard living engenders—and life has been hard in Spain for a long time, is excessively hard now —a patriotic sentiment against the surrender of Cuba, and against dictation in any shape powerfully appeals. The Spanish Government is thus between the Devil and the deep sea, and in its desperation may resort to desperate measures. Here, we imagine, far more than in the jingo outburst of the least responsible classes among the American people, lies the true risk that the present crisis may end in bloodshed. If Cuba is delivered by Mr. McKinley's intervention the present *régime* in Spain is probably doomed to be short-lived. Should it elect to fight the United States rather than to tamely await destruction from within it, may perish more gloriously, but perish it will. And we fear war.

The Money Market.

Nervousness is always to be deprecated among dealers in banking credit, and we regret to see so much of it at the present time. Prospects, we quite admit, are not so unclouded as we should like to see them ; at the same time it does not strike us that there is anything to be particularly afraid of, unless the market has commitments beyond its strength of whose existence we know nothing. Let us look at what is known. To begin with, the existing pinch, which every few days drives the discount market nearly off its head with flurry and fear, is in the main artificial. The Government holds larger balances at the Bank of England than it ever did before in the whole course of the nation's history. This is a misfortune, but the causes being well known it ought not to fright people, because some of the money thus held up must soon be released. In less than another week the dividends will be distributed, and that alone will afford considerable relief. We should say that it would release the market altogether from tension, were it not for either one of the two following considerations. One is the heavy indebtedness of the market to the Bank of England on loans and bills discounted, an indebtedness which may amount to £8,000,000, and might be considerably more ; and the other is the large unspent and, for the moment, unspendable balances, which the Government will have in hand when the dividends have been paid, and cannot distribute because the bills it is held to meet have not yet come in. The indebtedness of the market is in any case probably greater than all the money it can receive, directly or indirectly from the payment of the Home and Indian Government dividends, and these locked-up balances afford an additional reason why it will remain more or less subject to the Bank during the current quarter. It must be this because it has no spare means to begin with, and because the Government will for some time have larger balances in its possession than usual.

All this may be true enough, but why should we be alarmed at it? In a little time the position must right itself, and, apart from politics, there is nothing ahead of a very dangerous kind to upset credit. The heaviest demand to be immediately met is the new Chinese loan, which will require about £7,000,000 from us within the next month, assuming the Germans able to find all their half of the money. But surely that can be financed without difficulty and, unless India and several of our Colonies come upon us suddenly for large sums before we have digested the Chinese loan, there should be no cause to disturb ourselves. Money will be moderately dear this summer and that seems about all. Commerce is not at present exacting in its credit requirements, and we have, as is insisted on elsewhere, no large volume of speculation carried on in the Stock Exchange. Why then is the market so frightened that a little parcel of gold withdrawn from the Bank for export to New York causes it at once to talk about a 4 per cent. Bank rate, as if that meant chaos? The feeling, we imagine, comes to a large extent from the unfamiliarity of dealers in money with moderately high rates. They have been demoralised by a long course of money at 10s. to 20s. per cent. per annum, and a 4 per cent. Bank rate in prospect has therefore now quite as startling an effect upon their minds as a 6 or 7 per cent. rate would have had ten years ago. Perhaps also, as we have often pointed out, the hidden commitments of private speculators, based upon a continuance of very low rates for money, are excessive, and bankers may be apprehensive of very severe depression in securities should money go higher. We have no doubt this is the case with many of them, and because it is we have frequently insisted that these unwieldy accounts should be liquidated as much as possible while there is time.

There should be time enough gradually to do this before the autumn, and if it is done judiciously and systematically, not only private investors, but insurance companies, banks themselves, and other institutions with large funds to invest, have quite enough resources at their disposal to be able to relieve the market, and prevent anything like serious trouble when real dearness in money does arrive, as it might six months hence. We shall have that dearness without doubt, sooner or later; everything is making in that direction. In all probability, if the Bank rate is not to be further raised now, or during the summer, through some sudden war-created demand upon the stock of gold, we shall see sensibly higher rates before next winter. Why wait until then before attempting to adjust speculative accounts? It is better to liquidate slowly and without flurry now, when the disposition to invest is still powerful with the community. For no sooner does the Bank rate reach 4 per cent. than the market will become at once haunted with visions of a 5 per cent. rate ahead, and investment business will grow more and more difficult. The wish to buy has moderated considerably already.

Short of a war-produced demand, we do not see any reason why the Bank rate should go up further during this summer. It may not go down; indeed, we do not think it could very well go down in presence of so many dangerous complications abroad, but it need not go higher. The steady inflow of new bullion from our Colonial possessions should alone be sufficient to guarantee us against any further advance. This being so we trust the money market will calm itself down, and not work under so much nervous tension as has lately prevailed. These excitements are wearing and might become dangerous ; or else, if after a time they prove to be without grounds, they may give place to reckless indifference of consequences more alarming still. After this week the worst should be over for some time to come, and all that the Bank of England will then be able to do is to exercise a sustaining and steadying influence upon rates, a function necessary on its part at the present time, and one we think sure to be judiciously and carefully exercised by it. The skill and discretion with which it has been managed all through the more acute stages of the present scarcity of banking credit in the open market cannot be too highly praised.

Mr. Lindsay's Patent Currency Plan for India and Administrative Futility.

There is nothing particularly new in it. It has been agitating the British community in India for some time, and has now received the imprimatur of no less a person than Mr. Ottomar Haupt, a gentleman who has boxed the compass in currency theories within the last twenty years. Worse than that, and more serious, there is a belief that the present Chancellor of the Exchequer leans towards the adoption of some such absurdity. What is this scheme? It is nothing less than to establish a gold standard for India, not only without a gold currency, which even lunatics on this question seem now to understand to be impossible, but without a gold coinage of any sort. A patent regulator, to be called a "sterling conversion fund," is, it seems, to be located in London. How this fund is to be raised we do not know, not having seen Mr. Lindsay's pamphlet but only discussions upon it, and Mr. Haupt's letter in Tuesday's *Financial Times*. The only way we can think of in which the money could be found here is by raising a loan of, say, twenty-five millions sterling, with the help of which it might be quite easy to keep up the Indian Exchange to 1s 4d. by simply drawing on the fund to meet Indian indebtedness here until it was exhausted. Then the process could be repeated. This is simplicity itself, but we really do not see how it could help India, nor do we even think anybody else can see it, if in full possession of their seven senses.

Why cannot these nostrum mongers recognise the initial fact that India is overburdened with debt to England and that she has no means to meet it? You cannot establish a suitable currency on a basis of the inability of a nation to fairly and squarely meet its current obligations. Of course, when any discussion arises about this matter in connection with India the bimetallists are to the fore, and Sir William Houldsworth must intervene in the present one with a letter to the *Times*. His effusion is more comic this time than the average, and he confesses himself anxious to fix a minimum point below which the exchange could not go. He should study the evidence taken before the Usury Committee, because he would find there some slight clue to the difficulty of accomplishing this ardent desire of his. When a debtor is hopelessly insolvent he is not in a position to dictate terms to his creditors. It is just thus with India. The people of India have to find about twice as much as they are able to do, one year with another, out of their surplus resources. The bills drawn upon them for this intolerable amount of money are consequently in redundant supply upon the market, and they fall in price accordingly. Vary the simile, and the position is just the same. Would Sir William Houldsworth fix a minimum price for wheat no matter what the harvest was? If he could not, how is he going to fix a minimum price for any other commodity, such as the Council drafts upon India, when the amount of these drafts, which would have to be sold to meet all requirements, often exceeds the entire excess value of India's exports over her imports? Clearly there is a continuous over-supply of paper here, and that state of things could never be remedied by any currency device imaginable by man. Only you never can get a bimetallist or an Indian official to look at this part of the subject. The latter demands 1s. 4d. for his rupee as a minimum, and does not apparently care a hang, so long as he gets it, whether India should go bankrupt or not.

Just look at the hopelessness of securing any statesmanlike handling of this, the most momentous aspect of the subject. Not one single speech delivered in the House of Commons on Tuesday night dwelt upon the real difficulty of India. Mr. Vicary Gibbs became very eloquent in regard to the colossal blunder of closing the Mints in 1893. Lord George Hamilton confessed himself a bimetallist of a quarter of a century's standing. Sir William Harcourt upheld the closing of the Mints, and supported the determination of the Simla Government to establish a gold standard, in defiance of the impossibility to create a gold currency of the slightest utility to the small wants of the poor Indian population; and Mr. Maclean, who knows more about India than any man who took a share in the discussion, alone to some decree lifted the debate above the level of a mere academic currency wrangle. And even Mr. Maclean did not press home the truth as it ought to be pressed, although he was quite right in his opinion that the old system of keeping the Mints open to the unlimited coinage of rupees, without fixing any ratio whatever, and leaving money to find its own level was the best. Indeed, this is the only method by which British India can hope to prolong its existence as an Empire capable in some degree of meeting the excessive burdens laid upon it.

But what hope can we have that the Departmental Committee now to be set to work to investigate and theorise over this question will throw the slightest real light upon it? No Indian official will admit that the borrow and waste policy pursued by the Simla Government, and backed by every Government at home since the Mutiny, is one which is leading India, as represented by the Imperial *Raj*, directly to national insolvency. We should be utterly sick of the whole subject were it not for the appalling consequences certain to flow from the refusal of authorities here and in India to recognise the gravity of the position. As it is, a feeling akin to despair comes over the mind as one beholds this great possession of ours being hurried forward towards a crisis which must involve the continuance of our dominion there. We know quite well that as long as India can continue to raise loans on one pretext or another at the present pace—and altogether she raised nearly £8,000,000 last year without counting what money the railways procured, the amount of which we do not yet know—bankruptcy will be staved off. But let our money market reach a position of great stringency, lasting over many months, and India will not be able to borrow. Then shall we see what all this jabber about a "gold standard," and fixing a "minimum value for the rupee," and whether the mints should be opened or closed, really comes to. One fact which the British public must have driven into its mind is the fact that, one year with another, India is not able out of its own resources to meet charges laid upon it by its extravagant alien Government. As Mr. Maclean reminded the House, Lord Herschel's Commission pointed out that "under the old system the expansion in the revenue had largely provided for the additional calls which the falling exchange had made on the Government of India," but under the present system this must give way to stagnation and decline. Decline is seen now, and a most serious decline, in the revenue from opium; shrinkage, at least temporary, is to be seen in the land revenue; and if the policy of hoisting the price of the rupee, regardless of consequences and of economic circumstances is persisted in, this land revenue must permanently fall off. Here we have another danger threatening the stability of Indian finance, and nobody in power, nor any responsible politician out of power, seems to have the slightest inkling of the true position. "Fix the exchange value of the rupee" they one and all say, and appear to be destined to say till the trumpet of Doom summons them and their fatuities to judgment.

Electric Lighting Companies.

Further progress in the way of higher dividends is shown by the reports of the leading London companies. Excepting the House to House, all the solvent companies declared substantial dividends that were higher than any announced in preceding years, as the following table shows :—

Companies.	Works Started.	Dividends last Five Years. 1893.	1894.	1895.	1896.	1897.
Charing Cross and Strand	1891	4½	4½	5	6	7
Chelsea	1889	5	5	5	5	6
City of London ...	1891	—	2½	5	7	10
House to House ...	1889	—	—	—	—	4
Kensington and Knightsbridge...	1887	5	5	5	7	10
Metropolitan ...	1888	2½	3	4	5	6
Notting Hill ...	1891	—	1	2	4	6
St. James and Pall Mall ...	1889	4½	6½	7¼*	10½*	14½*
Westminster ...	1891	4	5	7	9*	12

* In addition, there were dividends on Founders' shares.

Prior to 1893 few of the companies paid dividends, and those distributed were seldom important. The House to House Electric has not only commenced paying dividends on the ordinary shares, but, having received £11,926 from premiums upon new shares, it has, by its aid and sums from revenue, wiped out the £15,642 of unsatisfactory assets shown in the balance-sheet under the head of Preliminary Expenses and Construction Business Account. It is now in a position to dispose of its profits in the future as it wishes. The County of London and Brush certainly shows a substantial profit for the past year, but it is so mixed up with the realisation of an important holding in a provincial company that we do not treat the money as an ordinary profit. The London Electric Supply Corporation still remains in a comatose condition as a corporation, but we believe that an effort will be made this summer to put its affairs in order. The Westminster Company in the year abolished its founders' shares in a most satisfactory manner, and the St. James' and Pall Mall has just carried through the same operation. Its arrangement is very similar to that of the Westminster, the founders subscribing for £60,000 of ordinary shares as a set off against the extinction of their rights. If profits only keep up to their present level the ordinary shareholders ought to benefit by the arrangement.

Reasons for the satisfactory statements of the companies are abundantly plain when their revenue accounts are examined. In every case a substantial advance is shown in the income, and clearly the companies are reaping benefits from the outlays of previous years. Their record in this respect for the last two years is shown in the following table :—

Companies.	1896. Total Revenue.	1896. Profit.	1896. Sums put to Depreciation or Reserve out of Revenue.	1897. Total Revenue.	1897. Profit.	1897. Sums put to Depreciation or Reserve out of Revenue.
	£	£	£	£	£	£
Charing Cross and Strand ...	39,118	15,288	5,476	48,914	18,907	5,247
Chelsea	21,355	8,361	2,000	27,382	12,554	2,000
City of London	148,510	64,567	2,612	186,836	88,151	6,529
House to House	17,442	6,431	4,704	20,810	9,033	4,391
Kensington and Knightsbridge	36,332	12,937	7,127	43,910	14,639	8,061
Metropolitan ...	116,459	34,191	13,000	138,267	43,721	15,000
Notting Hill......	8,552	3,736	1,080	11,625	5,804	1,050
St. james' and Pall Mall	55,939	25,339	10,125	68,269	30,534	9,270
Westminster ...	86,632	40,431	16,100	107,366	49,585	15,371

While the increase in gross revenue is good that in net is better, notwithstanding the fact that there is usually a diminution in the amount received for energy. At the same time the deductions out of revenue on account of depreciation, reserve, &c., have not as a rule grown in proportion, and, indeed, in one or two cases they are even less. This is usually due to the fact that the deduction of amounts requisite to clear off doubtful assets, such as preliminary expenses, &c., have been finished. Now that this has been accomplished, we should like to see a little more inclination to accumulate reserves. The Westminster is the only one that sets aside an amount each year for sinking fund, and yet all these companies are leasehold undertakings. When the time comes to settle with the local authorities, it is better to have some accumulations to lean upon, than to meet the crisis empty-handed, as the tramway companies did some years back. To establish a fund of this kind at the present time would only entail a small annual allocation, which could be treated as reserve, and would be a handy nest-egg at the end. The report of the City of London claims that £21,866 has been put to depreciation and reserve out of revenue, but as £15,437 of the working expenses were provided either out of capital or premium reserves, we have only credited it with the net amount after deducting this sum. Needless to say the substantial sums put to depreciation each year have had a most favourable effect upon the balance sheets of the companies, which show in most cases more spent upon the undertaking than has been raised in capital, in addition to investments outside the business and a steadily growing balance of debts owing for energy from consumers.

The growing profits of the companies may have aroused anxieties as to the likelihood of pressure being brought to bear from outside which may lead to reductions in dividend. The local authorities certainly have the power, after a company has been seven years at work, to appeal to the Board of Trade for a reduction in the price of energy, but of course in such a case a grievance arising from a monopoly would have to be demonstrated. At present such a grievance cannot be said to exist in regard to electric lighting, for the companies have first to fight the gas companies, and then to fight each other, since it is almost the rule that more than one company supplies a district. The consequence of such competition is seen in charges that are much below those laid down by statute, and in the following we set this matter out more clearly :—

Companies.	Board of Trade Units sold. 1896.	1897.	Statutory price per unit.	Actual charge per unit. 1896.	1897.	Lamps connected, 8 c.p.
Charing Cross and Strand...	1,944,402	2,615,508	8d.	4·70d.	4·40d.	107,542
Chelsea	813,764	1,061,970	10d.	5·88d.	5·77d.	96,638
City of London	5,488,500	6,634,486*	8d.	6·50d.	6·50d.*	296,012
House to House	643,693	811,255	8d.	6·05d.	5·74d.	66,364
Kensington and Knightsbridge	1,514,729	1,898,362	8d.	5·45d.	5·27d.	137,953
London Electric	2,000,000	2,500,000	6d.	—	—	—
Metropolitan ...	4,075,000	5,282,784*	8d.	6·35d.	6·35d.*	360,000
Notting Hill ...	230,787	354,969	8d.	7·65d.	6·91d.	33,000
St. James' and Pall Mall......	2,404,431	3,028,242	8d.	5·39d.	5·26d.	126,827
Westminster ...	3,503,054	4,355,781	8d.	5·56d.	5·55d.	290,561
	22,608,360	28,543,354				

* Estimated.

We include the London Electric Supply in the foregoing table in order to give the total amount of energy supplied by the companies in London, and we believe its charges are very similar to those of the St. James' and Westminster companies. From the table it will be seen that excepting the City of London and Notting Hill companies, which we believe are in the position of monopolists, the actual charge is well below 6d. per Board of Trade unit, save in the case of the Metropolitan Electric Company. Why the latter should keep to its present antiquated charge is a mystery, for it must invite encroachments upon its area such as it suffered a short time back, and, of course, the Notting Hill openly invites such procedure by its oppressive rate. The City of London is relieved from such vulgar considerations by the protecting shield thrown over its operations by the action of the City Corporation and of Parliament. It has, however, announced a reduction of 1d. per unit in its price, making the nominal figure 7d., but we believe this reduction will not apply to all customers. The majority, however, of the companies can look with indifference to any possible action on the part of local authorities under present conditions, but in their own interest a further reduction may be advisable. The Charing Cross and Strand is the pioneer in this matter, and although it has to meet keener competition than any other company of the group, its sale increased proportionately the most last year. Therefore, reduced prices point to increased consumption, and consequently the companies have a considerable reserve in this direction. We had intended to deal in detail with the operations of the newer companies such as the South London and County of London and Brush, but space will not permit of this in the present article.

Economic and Financial Notes and Correspondence.

The Duke of Fife and Earl Grey on the "Chartered" Company.

Both these noblemen delivered interesting speeches at the annual dinner of the Royal Colonial Institute last Wednesday. The Duke made the confession that he thought the days of Chartered Companies were over—that he thought them an anachronism, in fact—and one regrets that he had not reached this conclusion long ago; for if he has retained a holding in the British South Africa Company's shares, he stands to lose money by them, which would be a pity indeed. But he had parted with a substantial bundle of his once large number of shares in the good "booming" days, and after all he may be able to express his matured convictions in comfort and serenity of mind. Being no longer a director, he naturally had nothing to tell us about the company's finances, over which complete darkness has brooded since April, 1895. But Earl Grey, who was lately Administrator of Rhodesia, and is still an ardent believer in the company and an expansionist of the most enthusiastic kind, by company or otherwise, supplied the omission at one point. He spoke in glowing words about the company's lavishness in developing its territories. "The Chartered Company," said he, "has found £10,000,000 and upwards for developing Rhodesia and making it into what the noble Duke had described from the report."

This is news indeed, and must mean a tremendous bill to be presented by the directors in their forthcoming report. For, as all men know, there has only been £3,500,000 nominal of share capital so far issued, and about £2,000,000 of this went straight into the pockets of the promoters or their associates. They, not the company, or the territory of Rhodesia, grew fat and flourishing on the magical premiums to which these shares went up in response to the buying of imperial enthusiasts. The other million and a half of £1 shares were, true enough, sold at various prices, which brought the company, in the aggregate, £3,750,000, but out of this £750,000 of 6 per cent. debentures were paid off at a first-class "bonus" to such subscribers as had held on to them, or to those who bought them when the market was flat. Another £1,250,000 in debentures was subsequently created and issued at 97½ per cent. and this is all the money we know of that Rhodesia can have had from its company. That is to say, the entire sum available after allowing for the debentures paid off, and for the discounts and premiums on such debenture issues repayment, cannot have much exceeded £4,500,000. Revenue, as we know, down to March 31, 1893, had given nothing for development or any other capitalised purposes in the early years of the company's life, and cannot have done so since, with Matabele rebellions and what not to pay for. Consequently the company must now be in want of about £6,000,000 to pay its accumulated debts, and to go on with, if Lord Grey's figures are correct.

The Dangerous Position of Mauritius.

It is not alone India which suffers from the wonderful currency experiments of the Government. Mauritius has apparently been brought to the verge of universal bankruptcy by it, owing to the disorganisation of business in India, to the dearness of cereals, the low prices for sugar, and the scarcity of money. The banks in the island lately raised their rate of interest to 15 per cent., and their rate for advances on dock warrants to 12 per cent. Not only so, but the oldest and most respected bank the island possesses, namely, the Commercial Bank, established sixty years ago and always the friend of planters and traders, was obliged to petition the Government for an advance of a million of rupees in order to enable it to tide over a temporary difficulty. The bank was not insolvent ; on the contrary it possessed 400,000 rupees in excess of the one-third value of the notes as stipulated by law, and it had large sums of money due to it in Bombay, which it could not get home. Nevertheless it was driven to ask assistance. Apparently, also, one of its neighbours, instead of helping it, did the best it could to throw trouble in its way by collecting its notes and sending them in for payment, locking up the proceeds so as to restrict circulation. Apart from all this, however, the island is unquestionably in a very depressed condition, and its sugar planters are looking anxiously forward to the time when the abolition of bounties by European beet sugar producers may once more give it a chance to live. We are inclined to think that if a more intelligent currency policy prevailed in India, Mauritius might have outlets for her produce in that direction sufficient to enable her to live even were European countries to cling still to their errors. But who can hope for enlightenment in the Indian Government, red taped and routined as it is out of all individuality, a mere slave of the latest word-juggle of which it becomes the captive.

THE GREEK LOAN AND NEAR EAST TROUBLES.

Of course the House of Commons made no difficulty about sanctioning the resolution authorising the Government to join with France and Russia in guaranteeing the raising of a new Greek loan. If Greece was to continue in existence at all, this guarantee was essential ; but now that it has been granted, the trouble is, not about getting the money—that will be an easy matter—but whether the Turk, when the money is offered him, will agree to begin the evacuation of Thessaly within the time stipulated by the treaty with Greece. We may take it for granted that he will only move on compulsion. He is, no doubt, in a very impecunious condition, has already mortgaged a considerable portion of the war indemnity, and must be anxious to have the whole sum as soon as possible. But Thessaly is to him an exceptionally tempting morsel. It is a fertile territory and was once his own. It will certainly need all the "persuasion" of all the Powers to induce him to leave. The Sultan is fertile in excuses and slippery in action. He may baffle the Concert as he has done before ; and, looking to the extraordinary mess the Powers have made of affairs in Crete, there can be no great confidence in their ability to prevent a serious muddle in connection with Thessaly. Sir Michael Hicks-Beach told the House of Commons that the Powers were aware of the risk, and were at one in their determination to compel the Turks to depart. But how long will this harmony and determination last? There's the rub.

Meantime, the muddle in Crete is neither ended, nor are the Powers apparently giving themselves any trouble about it. Germany and Austria have both withdrawn their ships from the island. Whether they have withdrawn from further interference in Cretan affairs seems uncertain. They make no sign. There is even a doubt if the Concert still exists, though Mr. Curzon says it does. The Sultan is using all his arts to induce the Powers to agree to appoint a Turkish subject as Governor. He has suggested several, but so far they have all been rejected, and up to the present Prince George of Greece holds the held—as candidate. Neither Austria nor Germany seems to raise any further objections to his appointment, yet he is not appointed. Perhaps the Powers are too interested in developments in the Far East to care about the miseries of Crete in the Near East ; but disturbance in the Near East would be a very troublesome business, and a serious additional complication in a very complicated situation.

And complications may arise elsewhere than in Crete. There is seething unrest in the Balkans. Prince Ferdinand has returned to Bulgaria after a sojourn of three weeks in Vienna. He has seen the Emperor Francis Joseph and has made his peace with him, and no doubt his Majesty has used all his influence to induce the Prince to follow a policy of peace. In some measure evidently he succeeded. No sooner had he returned to Sofia than Prince Ferdinand took means to assure the Sultan that nothing was further from his wish or intention than any disturbance of the peace. The Sultan immediately reciprocated the Prince's good wishes, adding that he, too, was passionately desirous of the continuance of peace. True, he had sent some troops into Macedonia, but that was merely for defensive purposes, to cope with the insurgent bands that so persistently make their appearance in Macedonia during the spring. This pleasing exchange of compliments and assurances is pretty, but it does not change the aspect of affairs in the Balkans. Neither Sultan nor Prince has the decision of war or peace there in his hands. That depends upon their big neighbours, and more particularly Russia. It is quite conceivable that it may also depend in some measure on the course of events in the Far East. What is certain, however, is that there is not a single province in the Balkans that is not eager to spring to arms on receiving the hint "from above."

INDIAN VICEROY ON HIS DEFENCE.

Lord Elgin seems to have felt the necessity of making some defence of the policy he has recently been carrying out in India. It was but natural. That policy has been so strongly assailed that we can quite understand even an Indian Viceroy feeling it to be incumbent upon him to notice, in some way, the comments of his critics. Yet Lord Elgin really takes us no further than we were before. He regards the forward policy as the only possible one. He denies that the late expedition was a failure. On the contrary, it has thoroughly cowed the tribes, who have, he says, confessed their defeat, and paid every rupee, and every rifle, demanded of them. About the paying up there is probably no mistake. The tribes have been beaten for the present. They could not help themselves. But that the hillmen have ceased to look forward to a possibility of revenge we do not believe. As will be seen from the subjoined extract Lord Elgin hardly believes it himself :—

The task of the Government is not easy in the near future. However cautious and sympathetic our policy, outbreaks must be expected from time to time, and they must be promptly and vigorously suppressed and punished. But I think that in this policy lies the best hope of peace, because it is founded on reason and justice, inasmuch as, on the one hand, while abstaining from arrogant assertion of authority, it does not shut out from hopes of improvement and progress men whose chief fault is that they have never come under civilising influences which established peace and order bring with them, and, on the other hand, it recognises that it is one of the first duties of the Government to adapt the measures it undertakes to the resources of the country.

Just so. Lord Elgin admits that there must be trouble in the future. The tribes did not ask for our interference; they resented it, and fought in defence of their independence. We have advanced our frontier far over the hills—made it almost conterminous with Afghanistan. We shall have to keep numerous strongly guarded military posts for the observation of the Afridis. There will be constant skirmishes; there may even be complications with the Ameer of Afghanistan, who cannot be expected to relish our breaking down the barriers which have hitherto separated us from his dominions. All this has been done by the Imperial Government in the name of India; but the only result for her is the accumulation of taxes and debts which she can never pay. Nor is even that the worst; for her trade and industry are embarrassed and crippled in every direction by these mad expeditions in search of a "scientific frontier" which can be defended only at a cost which would mean ruin to the country.

The Mines Contract Company.

We regret that by an inadvertence in our last week's comments on the case of Kays *v.* Hess we included the name of the Mines Contract Company in the list of companies promoted to take over the Khana Concession. The real fact of the case was that this concession was offered to the Mines Contract Company, but owing to the title the directors refused to have anything to do with it. This company has been in existence since 1888, and stands in an entirely different category from the others included in the list, into which, by mistake its name had crept.

"Another Irish Muddle."

The subjoined corrects a blunder which should not have escaped us last week:—

arch 29, 1898.

SIR,—In a letter of mine in your issue of the 25th inst. by an error of the printer, or of mine, I am made to say that the local taxation is from :s. 3d. to 1s. 2d. of the rental. It should have been from one third to one half of the rental. There are places where the local taxation on agricultural holdings is from six to over twenty shillings per statute acre. Local taxation has been steadily increasing in Ireland, while in England it appears that rural rates have been continually decreasing.—Your obedient servant,

An Irishman.

Uruguayan Debt and Trade.

It is not perhaps a bad sign for Uruguay that even now in the first flush of his great success Senor Cuestas finds the number of his critics—captious and otherwise—increasing rather than diminishing. It is also to his credit that, virtual dictator though he be, he seems in no way to interfere with the freedom of these critics. They are allowed to speak openly, and they seem to avail themselves of this liberty with the utmost frankness, to say the least. If, however, the statements made by his friends as to the condition of the Republic be anything like correct, he and his council do quite right in devoting their energies to the promotion of economy in the public service, while disregarding the accusations levelled at them of having been actuated by selfish ambition, and so forth. There is ample scope for the exercise of their zeal in economic savings; and they must have already enormously diminished the current public expenditure by the reduction of extravagant salaries and the dismissal of officials whose only duty seems to have been to draw their handsome pay monthly. But there are extravagances which cannot be removed or mitigated so easily. There is the public debt, for example, the official statement of which up to December 31, 1897, has been issued. At that date the total debt was $120,765,097, or close upon £25,000,000 sterling. Taking the population of the Republic at 843,000 odd—though that is only an estimate, officials having had no time or inclination in recent years for the taking of a census—this gives us a public debt of about $143, or almost £31 per head of the population, an amount that gives Uruguay a very respectable position indeed among debt-loving Governments.

Then it must be remembered that this debt has all been accumulated in about 40 years—the larger portion of it within the last 24 years. In 1860 it amounted to the modest sum of $2,726,000; in 1874 it had grown to the very respectable total of $42,000,000 odd, leaving $79,400,000 as the accumulation of the last 24 years, the time during which what is called the "Collectivist" faction was in power. Now, judging by the trade returns, this enormous increase in the public debt was not induced by any falling off in business. Last year the exports exceeded the imports by about $10,000,000. During the previous eight or ten years, at least, the "balance of trade" was favourable to the Republic and from 1891 to 1897 is said to have amounted to about $56,000,000. Yet all this time the powers that were went on steadily adding to the public debt until it has reached the dimensions we have stated. The task before Senor Cuestas and his Council of State is a very onerous one. Their particular Augean stable is peculiarly dirty, and until they have made their progress in cleansing operations sufficiently manifest the credit of Uruguay cannot be looked upon as safe or secure.

British and German Trade.

A careful comparison of the foreign commerce of Great Britain and Germany could not fail to be both interesting and instructive. In most things the Germans have become our most notable rivals, though in some articles, especially certain sorts of machinery, steel rails, and pig-iron, America is cutting in upon both. It is, therefore, most desirable to know with some approach to accuracy how far Germany is making up to us in the commercial struggle. The task has been essayed by Mr. H. Gastrell, our Commercial Attaché at Berlin, in a recent report to the Foreign Office; but, unfortunately, Mr. Gastrell has to confess at the outset that an exact comparison is impossible, in consequence of a somewhat arbitrary division of its foreign trade introduced by Germany, so that its exports of domestic produce and imports for home consumption—that is, what has been known as "special" trade—might be presented distinct and separate. But the official record of Germany's trade for 1897, showing these variations, has not yet been completed. Mr. Gastrell has had, therefore, to estimate what is "special" or distinct from the re-export or "improvement" trade—the trade in dutiable raw materials and partly finished articles worked up into the finished shape, and sent out of the country again without payment of duty.

As we have said, however, Mr. Gastrell admits that this change of method in arraying their statistics has made an accurate comparison of values practically impossible. Some broad results, however, are deduced with a sufficient approach to accuracy to be useful. For one thing, it seems to be shown that generally, as we have before seen exemplified in reports on particular countries, British trade has been diminishing, while German trade has been advancing. The diminution is not to be called serious, or such as to excite alarm, nor can it be yet regarded as a permanent feature in our trade comparison with Germany. But last year our exports decreased about 2·4 per cent., while those of Germany increased rather over 1.3 per cent. The total value of British domestic exports is still nearly one-third greater than those of Germany. The net difference in value of these exports has always been largely in favour of Great Britain, but this preponderance would appear to be diminishing, though not with what may be called decisive movement. In 1895 the difference was £59,995,016; in 1896 it went up to £63,889,051; but by 1897 it had fallen to £55,702,553.

Although the comparison may not yet be quite exact, there seems no reason to doubt that German traders are advancing upon us. There is still a considerable gap between the two rivals; but so far, it has been diminishing. Whether this diminution will continue at the same rate it is impossible to say. We think it doubtful. It may be that it will yet take a turn the other way. The matter is, of course, in the hands of our traders and manufacturers. We do not see that they need be beaten in the contest—a friendly one, let us always remember, and likely to continue so. If the German chemical and linen trades flourish exceedingly, our iron and steel trade is still far superior to theirs, while our exports of cottons and cotton yarns certainly have not lost their old lead. We have the immense advantage of perfect freedom of trade, though we may now begin to hope that Germany's commercial experience is sufficiently extensive to teach her the folly of protective tariffs; and that we may yet see the fruits of this chastened experience embodied in the new commercial treaty now being negotiated between the two countries.

BRAZILIAN RAILWAYS.

We have on several occasions drawn attention to the miserable condition of the finances of most of the Brazilian guaranteed railways. Started originally on a bad basis, the depreciation in the currency has so affected their revenues that the position of most of these is now piteous in the extreme. Three fairly important companies of this class issued their reports during the week, and in the following table we roughly analyse the results :—

	Bahia & San Francisco. £	Natal & Nova Cruz. £	Recife & São Francisco. £
Revenue	132,105	5,046	201,573
Working expenses	168,932	12,427	191,451
Debit balance	36,827	7,381	*10,122
Guarantee	126,900	43,281	83,305
Debenture interest	—	11,651	5,437
Debenture redemption	—	13,175	14,000
Dividend	90,000	10,874	60,000
Rate per cent.	5 p. c.	4½ p. c.	5 p. c.

* Credit Balance.

Thus only one of the trio was able to meet even its working expenses without dipping into the Government guarantee, and any dividend would have been out of the question if this resource had not been at hand. The Natal and Nova Cruz, in fact, would have been bankrupt without this assistance, for after meeting the debit balance on working and debenture interest little more than half the guarantee was left. The position is all the worse when it is borne in mind that the Bahia and San Francisco and the Recife and Sao Francisco have both raised their tariffs in order to meet the fall in exchange. The right to do this had long been looked for as a means of relief from the strain imposed by a falling currency, but apparently it has not sufficed to bring about an improvement, for the Recife enjoyed the higher tariff for the whole of the year, and the Bahia and San Francisco for nine months. The question naturally arises, What will become of these unhappy lines if the Brazilian Government breaks down in its guarantee? It is going to break down somewhere ere long we may be sure.

THE CHARTERED BANK OF INDIA.

It is quite an achievement for this bank to be able to distribute 9 per cent. in dividend for the past year, as its board does not follow the easy-going course adopted by most London banks of paying what they can out of profits and building up the reserve out of premiums upon new issues. The policy adopted, of late years at least—for the history of the bank runs back to 1853—has been to raise the dividend by 1 per cent. when the reserve has been increased by £100,000. Thus in 1880 the reserve rose to £200,000, and the dividend was increased from 6 to 7 per cent. after the lower rate had been paid for five years. By 1889 the reserve had been further raised to £300,000, and accordingly 8 per cent. was distributed for two years, only to drop back to 7 per cent. again for three years, as the reserve had to be dipped into to meet exceptional losses. The sums then taken were replaced, and 8 per cent. was paid for 1894, 1895, and 1896.

The placing of £75,000 to reserve now will raise that fund to £450,000, and so the higher distribution of 9 per cent. is made, with the knowledge that half the distance to another advance is covered. The statement is exceptionally favourable, as last half-year must have been peculiarly trying to Eastern banks, and the Chartered had the additional misfortune of losing the services of its manager, Mr. Forrest, for some part of the time, owing to ill-health. The policy of building up the reserve out of profits has been deliberately adopted, for the bank has the power to issue more capital, despite the fact that it is constituted by Charter.

OUR COPPER SUPPLIES.

Messrs. Henry R. Merton & Co. send us an admirable table showing the principal sources of our copper supply, with the quantities delivered every year from 1881 to 1897. The figures are in many ways interesting. In 1888, the year of the great boom in copper, when the average price of G.M.B.'s mounted up from £42 3s. in 1887 to £76, the total quantity imported was 258,026 tons, as compared with 223,798 tons in 1887. From 1888 the quantities imported steadily increased. In 1892, for example, it had reached 310,472 tons, and though there was a drop in the following year to 303,530 tons, in 1894 it again bounded up to 324,505 tons. In 1895 it went on to 334,565 tons; in 1896 to 373,863 tons; and last year it reached the formidable total of 396,728 tons. It is equally interesting to note the sources of our supply; and perhaps one of the most noteworthy in the lot is Japan, which, in 1881, sent us only 3,000 tons, and went on almost uninterruptedly increasing its output until, in 1897, it sent us 23,000 tons. Australia also is becoming a rising competitor in the copper field. In 1881, it sent us 10,000 tons, and after, in the succeeding three years, going up to 14,000 tons, it dwindled year by year until, in 1892, its supply fell as low as 6,500 tons. But then the turn came, and the imports gradually increased until, in 1897, they reached the respectable total of 17,000 tons. But the most remarkable of all is the increase in the supply from the United States. In 1881 they sent us 30,882 tons; but this has been improved upon every year, until, in 1897 it had reached the magnificent total of 216,108 tons. There have been great fluctuations in the average price of G.M.B.'s. From the extreme price of £76 in 1888, it fell in 1889 to £49 10s. 6d.; rose to £54 1s. in 1890; fell to £51 3s. in 1891; to £45 9s. 6d. in 1892; to £43 6s. 9d. in 1893, and reached £40 2s. 6d. in 1894. In the following year it improved to £42 17s. 6d.; went to £47 4s. 8d. in 1896; and last year it reached an average of £49 10s.

In Praise of the Canadian North-West.

A correspondent sends us the following letter in reply to our remarks of last week in reference to the position of the Canadian North-West Land Company. His glorious anticipations will, we trust, be realised, but we should not advise people to "lock up" more than spare cash :—

To the Editor.

Sir,—A few weeks ago an eminent financial contemporary in an interesting article described Canada as the next promising field for investment. Canada certainly has made rapid strides during the past twelve months, politically, commercially, and agriculturally. Politically she has set the mother country a good example in denouncing those absurd German and Belgian treaties, and has shown her independent thought and Imperial aspirations in granting preferential rates to Great Britain.

Commercially she is progressing, as the returns of her banks show, and her agricultural progress is evidenced by the prosperous condition of her farmers.

It is in regard to the last-named part of the subject that I wish to make a few remarks. The English public like a lock-up security, one that, though remaining unproductive for a brief period, is likely soon to double in value.

Such a security, I think, is to be found in the shares of the landed companies of Canada, notably the Hudson's Bay, and the Canada North-West Land Company. The former has a virtual monopoly of the fur trade, has an excellent business (very well managed) as stone dealers, paying a fair dividend from these sources alone. But the great future value of its shares lies in its landed estate, comprising over seven millions of acres, mainly situated in the great fertile belt of the North-West Territories of Canada. The company is pursuing a Conservative policy in regard to its lands, and does not seek to force sales unduly, while every year that passes is adding to their value.

The Canada North-West Land Company possesses about two millions of acres of specially selected land in the most fertile part of Manitoba and Assiniboia, well placed for railway communication with Winnipeg and Montreal on the one hand, and the great grain centres of St. Paul and Minneapolis on the other.

Now it is well known that Uncle Sam has parted with his vast domain, and has not now practically speaking a single homestead of good land fit for settlement. It is true some of the railroads have portions of their land grants still to sell, but two or three years' emigration such as we have seen would swallow up these lands as well, and then there remains only the wheat lands of the Canadian North West for farming emigrants to settle upon.

Already the tide of emigration, which has so long been intercepted by the United States, is now overflowing into Manitoba and neighbouring provinces, with the result that land is now selling at fair prices, where, a few years ago, buyers could not be had at almost any price.

The Canadian North-West Land Company's sales have been doubling themselves in a geometrical ratio for the last three or four years, and it only needs this to be continued for a similar further period for the whole of its lands to be disposed of. Every acre sold increases the value of those unsold; and as the Government homesteads are nearly all taken up, and the railway lands largely sold in the districts where the company's estate lies, the company has almost a monopoly of the good lands in that favoured part of the fertile belt, the South West of Manitoba and Assiniboia. And yet the company's shares sell only about half price. Surely the public has overlooked the great future value—I should say the great immediate future value—of these shares.

The Canadian Land Company is a case in point. It paid much higher prices for its lands, and for many years paid no dividends, but when its lands did come into demand it soon repaid to its shareholders all their capital, with the exception of £1, and for years that £1 share was selling in the market at £90 and over; and even now, when most of the company's estate has been realised, it is quoted at £25 to £27. Why may not history repeat itself—if not fully, yet approximately? *Verbum sap.*

Yours, &c., A—— C——.

THE YEAR'S REVENUE.

Another record broken. The final Revenue accounts for the year ended yesterday show a net increase in receipts by the Exchequer of £2,664,119. During the first quarter the increase was £944,413, the second gave £195,100, the third £260,535, and the last £1,264,071. Truly, these are wonderful results, when we remember that in his last Budget Sir Michael Hicks-Beach estimated that there would be a decrease of £906,000 in the year's revenues. Customs, he considered, would produce an increase of £246,000 and Excise £290,000. The actual receipts give him increases of £544,000 and £840,000 respectively. Stamps are up £300,000 instead of down £350,000. Post-Office receipts give £310,000 more, and Telegraphs £100,000, in place of estimated increases of £34,000 and £50,000. Property and income tax show £600,000 additional, or £350,000 over the Chancellor's estimates. This item gives the large total of £17,250,000 for the year. The most remarkable difference is, however, in the estimate of Estate Duties. A decrease of £1,130,000 was expected, but the receipts give an increase of £270,000. Under this head the total receipts were £15,327,882, of which £11,100,000 went into the Exchequer, and the balance to Local Taxation account.

In short, a grand total of £106,614,004 has been gathered into the Exchequer, and in addition, £9,402,310 have been handed over to local bodies. For the year the nation's income has been £116,016,344, or a total net increase of £3,817,767.

What consolation is there for the taxpayer in all this array of figures? Precious little, we fear. Judging from the estimates of expenditure for the coming year the Chancellor will be able to promise nothing in the way of reduction in taxation. Our Army and Navy want about £43,000,000, other services about £37,000,000, and Debt Charges £26,000,000. Items such as the promised grant to Ireland will make a total estimated expenditure of about £107,000,000. With such a sum to be extracted from the taxpayers, how can any relief be given them? They must be content with visions of glory, and congratulate themselves that they help in producing the largest revenue account in the world.

Minerva Works, Tunbridge, Huddersfield, with four houses adjoining, were sold on Tuesday by Messrs. Eddison, Taylor & Booth, for £13,000. The property is held for a term of 999 years, at a ground rent of £59 2s. 6d. per annum.

The plague has broken out at Jeddah, and several deaths are already reported. There seems little doubt that the epidemic will get to Mecca as pilgrims arrive, and no doubt whatever that some of the returning pilgrims will bring it with them to Europe. Cairo is greatly alarmed at the prospect.

SOUTH AFRICAN MINING NOTES.

Rand Mines.

The annual meeting of this deep level Trust Company has been held in Johannesburg, but it has apparently not supplied the tonic to the Kaffir market which some people expected. A profit of £350,000, equal to 100 per cent., is not so very grand after all on shares standing at 2,800 per cent. premium, and especially when nearly the whole of that profit has had to be reinvested either to assist in financing the subsidiary mines or to support the market by purchases of shares. How this sum has been earned, the cable reports received leave us somewhat in doubt; but from the fact that 68,000 shares in different mines have been disposed of, it must be assumed that the greater portion of the profit is the result of share realisations. And even this is probably not the full extent to which the share holdings have been sacrificed, for it must be remembered that during the past year the company has had to subscribe for its proportion of new capital issued by several of its "baby" concerns, and had not large sales been effected the holdings of shares would have shown large increases from this cause. Take one case as an example. In July 1897, the Crown Deep offered for subscription a certain number of its reserve shares which were allotted to the shareholders at the rate of one share for five. The Rand Mines Corporation possessed, according to its 1896 report, 194,050 Crown Deeps, and would, therefore, by right of these have to take up 38,810 additional shares. But as the holding in this mine, presuming the *Standard and Diggers' News'* cabled report of the meeting is correct, has only increased by 22,800 shares, it is obvious that the balance of 16,010 shares has been sold. No blame, of course, attaches to the directors for unloading portions of their share assets as favourable opportunities occur; but it is plain that the assumption frequently put forward in this journal that the "deep level" market is manipulated to enable these sales to be made, is an accurate one. And as a dividend of 100 per cent. is promised during the present year, it is evident that this process of liquidation must continue, and if anything at even a greater speed than before.

In face of all this it is amusing to find the chairman posing as an injured martyr, and trying to convince the shareholders that the directors "aim at making the corporation a producing one, and not a mere speculation." How do they expect to pay sufficiently large dividends to justify the present quotation for the shares, unless the subsidiary shares are sold at big figures? Certainly the profits earned by the mines will not enable them to do so. Another point which should not be lost sight of is the method by which the profits are arrived at. These South African Mining Trusts are very fond of asserting that all the profits they declare are "realised profits." In a way, no doubt, this is partly true; but these self-same concerns have a convenient knack of valuing their assets at cost, no matter how much they may depreciate on the market.

We are aware that the majority of the Rand Mines' share and claim assets are worth more than they stand in the balance-sheet at; still there are exceptions. Towards the end of last year, if we are not mistaken, the Corporation subscribed for 50,000 or 60,000 Nourse Deep shares, part of a new issue, at the price of £6 10s. These shares are now quoted about £2 per share lower, so that there is a loss of £100,000 on this transaction alone. Has this been taken into consideration in declaring the profit of £350,000? Again a very large loss must have been incurred in connection with the Paarl Central property, a mine which is now working at a loss, and is, we believe, recognised to be unpayable. How has this been dealt with? Reviewing the progress of the actual mining work accomplished by the Corporation in the past year, the directors and managers are entitled to considerable praise. Five of the mines are now producing gold, while several others are nearing the same stage, and the enterprise which has effected this is to be commended. All the greater pity then, that with such excellent properties at command, the directors cannot think more of the mines and less of the market.

The Debts of Deep Levels.

Some time ago, in referring to the financial positions of the deep level mines, we commented upon the very heavy debts which the majority of these concerns have contracted. It may, perhaps, be advisable to now give a few further details. Of the mines now crushing and announcing monthly profits the Geldenhuis Deep has a debenture charge of £150,000; the Rose Deep is mortgaged to the tune of £150,000; the Jumpers Deep is pawned in a similar manner for £350,000; and the Crown Deep owes £80,000. The Simmer & Jack East carries £500,000 debentures; the Robinson Deep, £300,000; the Durban Deep, Vogelstruis Deep, and Witwatersrand Deep, each £200,000; while Rand Mines have £1,000,000 debentures issued with power to create a further £250,000. The Rose Deep has been crushing for five or six months, and the Crown Deep for seven or eight months, and both mines have regularly declared large profits. How comes it then, that they are still so heavily in debt? The profits announced each month by several South African Mining Companies, as we have already pointed out, are more or less illusory, because, instead of the revenue being debited with all expenditure, much of it is being carried to "capital account." This explains why these mines have not yet been able to place themselves in a sound financial condition.

Critical Index to New Investments.

JARRAH TIMBER AND WOOD PAVING CORPORATION, LIMITED.

The Corporation buys various mills in Western Australia, timber yards in the city of Perth, and the West Australian timber business of Palfreman, Foster & Co., of New Broad-street, London, who have carried out contracts for street paving with sundry corporations and vestries in London and the provinces. Various statements—satisfactory and otherwise—are made about profits, but the main idea seems to be that the net profit realisable from an output of 600 loads per week works out at £40,500 per annum, though whether this will be obtainable for any length of time with all these Jarrah wood companies in the field the future alone can tell us. The capital is £250,000 in £1 shares, 150,000 being ordinary and the remainder 7 per cent. cumulative preference, and excepting £35,000 for working capital, the whole of this goes in payment for the property. We see nothing whatever to justify such a price. The board is a weak one, the chairman being connected with four cycle undertakings, including the Automatic Cycle Rack Company, while three other directors are on the board of the Zoroastrian Mining Company. When little is known about a new company it is always as well to study the names on the board. But apart from this our impression of the affair is not favourable.

NEW SCHULTZE GUNPOWDER COMPANY, LIMITED.

This is a conversion of an old company, which is quite the fashionable thing to do nowadays. The original company dates from 1868, and was re-registered in 1892, the capital being £100,000 in £10 shares, of which £60,000 has been issued and paid up; but half of this was only issued last year and paid for out of the reserve fund. Dividends for seven years ended 1888 were 5 per cent.; for 1889, 7½ per cent., for 1890, 15 per cent., and for the last six years 20 per cent. This successful little company is now to expand itself into an undertaking with a capital of £325,000 in £5 shares, in equal parts of ordinary and 5 per cent. cumulative preference shares; and Robert Austen, the vendor, acting between the two companies, has fixed the purchase price at £317,000—all but £100,000 to be cash. Profits for six years are clearly stated, those for 1892 being only £7,380, while for 1895 they were £13,859; for 1896, £19,409, and for 1897, £28,921. Such a sharp increase naturally suggests something very exceptional in the demand and possibly doubts about its continuing have prompted a sale before they run back. Investors can learn from the prospectus what notable triumphs have been obtained by using the powder in that manly sport of pigeon shooting, but they cannot learn anything about the valuation of the properties for which this immense purchase price is to be given; nor, indeed, do we find any reference to assets. However small they may be, they ought to have been given. An increase in the paid-up capital from £60,000 to £325,000 is a little pyrotechnic display not unworthy of the powder.

THOMAS PHILLIPS & CO., LIMITED.

Thomas Phillips, it appears, buys the Diamond Brewery, Dover and the Park Brewery, Camberwell, on what terms is not stated and sells them with his own brewery, known as the Abbey Brewery West Malling, Kent, with seventy licensed properties, of which eighteen are freehold, for £210,000 including £70,000 in ordinary shares. The valuation furnished by Bromley, Son, & Kelday is £215,105, but it is given in one lump sum, and is therefore unsatisfactory, while the same firm report that the net average annual profits for the past two years have amounted to upwards of £12,730, which is no use at all as indicating progress, or otherwise, made by the business. Thomas Phillips appoints himself managing director for three years, and the company has to pay him for stock-in-trade, loans, and book debts, in addition to the purchase price. The share capital is £160,000 in 16,000 5½ per cent. cumulative preference shares of £5 each, and 80,000 ordinary shares of £1 each. There is also an issue of £100,000 first mortgage debenture stock offered at par, and redeemable on six months' notice after June, 1908, at 105. Sir Edward Sullivan is chairman of the company, which seems to be brought out to benefit Thomas Phillips very much first.

ELECTRIC SUPPLY COMPANY OF WESTERN AUSTRALIA, LIMITED.

This company is formed to take over an established undertaking, already earning profits. The undertaking is no less important than the Westralian Electric Lighting and Supply Company, which works the town of Coolgardie, claiming a population of 20,000 people, of whom very few, we should say, could afford to pay for electric lighting. As to the earning of profits, Chalmers, Wade, & Co., chartered accountants, find that the gross receipts derived from July 10 to December 31, 1897, from the supply of current were at the rate of £6,790 per annum. Allowing 50 per cent. for expenses we get the substantial net profit of £3,395, and this remunerative concern is to be acquired for £70,000 in cash, out of a total capital of £100,000 in £1 shares. The prospectus contains many references in the usual laudatory style adopted when speaking of Coolgardie, and we can only express our disappointment that the gold there is not sufficiently brilliant to light up the town without using electricity.

DR. TIBBLES' VI-COCOA (1898), LIMITED.

This concern is brought out to buy up Dr. Tibbles' Vi-Cocoa, Limited, for £300,000 including £100,000 in cash. It seems to buy nothing very tangible, but it gets leasehold premises, plant and machinery, fixtures, fittings, stock-in-trade, book debts, trade marks, formulæ, and all other assets, including goodwill and £21,801 of liabilities. In the first year, ended November, 1896, the vending company seems to have made a loss of £6,832, but from December 1, 1896, to November 25, 1897, one firm of accountants certifies that the net profits were £72,832, and that for the three months ended February 28, 1898 (the best quarter of the year for this business) they exceeded £25,000, in which certificate another firm of accountants, like the parrot, concurs. Now the original syndicate of two years back had a paid-up capital of £10,000, while the capital of the new creation is £400,000 in £1 shares, half ordinary and half 6 per cent. cumulative preference Such a swelling out almost requires a Harness' Electric Belt to keep it from bursting.

CHADBURN'S (SHIP) TELEGRAPH COMPANY, LIMITED.

The businesses offered for sale are said to have been established over half a century. A Liverpool valuer certifies the total valuation for building, machinery, and stock belonging to Chadburn & Son, Limited, and Thomas Bassnett, Limited, at £33,000, and a statement of profits is produced which has to our thinking an unsatisfactory look about it. The capital is £120,000 in £1 shares, half ordinary and half 6 per cent. cumulative preference, and the purchase price is £105,000, including £20,000 in shares; but the company does not buy direct but through the Victoria Syndicate, Limited. The company apparently starts well, as the contracts now on hand include orders for a complete installation of Chadburn's telegraphs upon thirty-two of her Majesty's ships. But after that—and how much longer have the patents to run?

TRANTOM'S, LIMITED.

This shade of Lipton's is a Liverpool affair, and is formed to buy the business of food preparer, fruit preserver, tea-dealer, and grocer and provision merchant, carried on by Joseph Trantom, together with the business recently acquired by him of W. E. Harper, carried on under the style of Harper's Stores. Share capital £50,000 in £1 shares, 32,500 being 6 per cent. cumulative preference and the remainder ordinary. The latter, with £15,000 in cash, is the purchase price. Only 17,500 preference shares are offered now, while the profits for the three years ended February, 1898, were £2,816, £2,975, and £2,917. If the shares are worth having, Liverpool would, no doubt, take them without overstraining itself.

MUTUAL TELEPHONE COMPANY, LIMITED.

Capital, £250,000 in £5 shares of which 30,000 are ordinary and 20,000 5 per cent. cumulative preference. Board is very numerous, consisting of 13 members—all Manchester and Salford men, who think Manchester and district might be supplied with an improved system at less rates. There can be little doubt about this, but is this company going to do it? The National Telephone Company has issued a circular pointing out that a company under the same name was formed eight years ago, which in 1894 went into liquidation, and the working capital of £60,870 was therefore lost. But this company may stand a better chance, though, under the circumstances, the shares might be left to Manchester capitalists. Any competitor to the National Company is deserving of support, for the system constituting its monopoly is a burden grievous to be borne.

HUGGINS & CO., LIMITED.

This brewery company was formed in 1894, and has a share capital of £200,000, all but £60,000 of preference being held by the directors and their families. There is also £360,000 of 4½ per cent. debenture stock. The purchase price in 1894 was £340,000, including £217,000 in cash. A new company is now brought out to acquire the old company, and the purchase price is now put at £1,100,000, of which £329,900 is to be cash. The entire capital of the new company is £1,400,000, in 35,000 ordinary and 50,000 4½ per cent. cumulative preference shares of £10 each, and £550,000 in 3½ per cent. first mortgage irredeemable debenture stock, but only a portion of each class is offered, the price being par. On September 30, 1893, brewery premises, properties, and other assets were valued at £310,606, and on September 30 last the corresponding items stood at £812,801, of which £490,844 was loans to customers on mortgage, while during the four years ended September last net profits have steadily mounted from £27,761 to £65,532. It is stated that the business has very largely increased, and it is essential further capital should be raised for the purchase of new properties, for which purpose £300,000 will be reserved out of the present issue on which it is estimated an additional profit of £20,000 per annum will be earned. As debenture stock, interest, and preference share dividend will require only £41,750, there is still a good margin of profit left, so, in spite of the heavy increase in capital, the shares and debenture stock still seem a good brewery investment.

LLOYD & YORATH, LIMITED.

This Monmouthshire company offers an issue of £70,000 4½ per cent. first mortgage debenture stock, and £50,000 5 per cent "A" debenture stock at par. Former is redeemable after 1906, at 110, and the latter, at 110, by means of a sinking fund, within 54 years. This will make the debenture capital £220,000 against a share capital of only £150,000. The money is wanted to pay for the recently acquired business of Searle & Herring, Limited, of Newport, Mon., costing £137,145, and for the acquisition of further properties. So the old game of absorption goes on. Profits of Lloyd & Yorath for year ended November 30, 1897, are certified at £11,140, and of Searle & Herring for year ended March 31, 1897, at £7,558, and for nine months, to end of last year, at £6,036, while increased profits are expected from the consolidation. Against the £18,698 of profits, debenture interest and sinking fund will require £10,400. So the stocks now offered may be considered moderately good second-class investments.

PACIFIC BORAX AND REDWOOD'S CHEMICAL WORKS LIMITED.

The share capital amounts to £545,000, and there is also issued £97,500 first mortgage 5 per cent. debentures. The company now offers through the Indian and General Investment Trust an issue of £150,000 second mortgage 5 per cent. debentures at 102 per cent. redeemable, at three months' notice, at 104. Money is wanted to pay for additional property. Net profits for year ended March 31, 1897, were £57,235, while the interest on the two issues, sinking fund, &c., will require £15,690 per annum. This is an American enterprise, and when issued, all the £310,000 of ordinary shares were taken by the vendors, so its second debentures are not an investment we should care to risk much in, notwithstanding the large surplus shown by profits over interest charge.

SHELTON IRON, STEEL, AND COAL COMPANY, LIMITED.

Issue of £100,000 6 per cent. second mortgage debentures at par. They are redeemable at par by sinking fund of 2 per cent. per cent. per annum, commencing in 1903, and will rank after the first charge 5 per cent. debentures, of which there are outstanding £83,600. Share capital amounts to £500,000. Company was formed in 1889 to take over properties at Stoke-on-Trent. Money is wanted to take advantage of new lease of minerals, and to meet certain expenditure on the steel works. As the profits for 1896 were £23,040, and for 1897, £30,636, the debentures seem a fair second-rate investment, especially looking at the 6 per cent. interest.

BRITISH & FOREIGN DU BOIS COMPANY, LIMITED.

The capital of this reconstructed concern is £150,000 in £1 shares, of which 90,000 are 7 per cent. preference and the remainder ordinary. This company has been brought out to acquire the British Du Bois Manufacturing Company, Limited, which was only formed last year to take over the English business of the parent company, with a capital of £100,000, and to amalgamate with it a similar business now being carried on in Germany. Business consists chiefly of manufacturing and selling a lead trap and other appliances for sanitary purposes. There is a full statement of the English company's profits which have grown from £7,107 in 1892 to £11,110 in 1897, but although the German business has been established 12 years, all we are told is that its net profit for 1897 amounted to £3,002. There is no statement about the valuation of any assets, but £140,000 is asked for the business, payable £60,000 in ordinary shares and £80,000 in cash. Whatever strength the English company had, we should say, will be considerably diminished by tacking on to it the German business, which, after twelve years' working, can show only £3,000 profit. This continued shuffling of the cards benefits others than the shareholders.

"HOLBROOK'S WORCESTERSHIRE SAUCE," LIMITED.

Object is to buy trading rights in the sale of the sauce in the United States and Canada from the Birmingham Vinegar Brewery Company. For twenty years the sauce is claimed to have been "a staple article of food," the sales of which are now at the rate of upwards of 5,500,000 bottles annually, no size mentioned. The capital is £100,000, in £1 shares, half ordinary and half 6 per cent. preference, all of which are now issued. The Vinegar Company is to manufacture the sauce and supply it to this company upon terms which are not disclosed, and £60,000 is to be paid as purchase price to a middleman, which altogether seems a saucy arrangement.

BENGAL DOOARS RAILWAY COMPANY, LIMITED.

The National Bank of India, Limited, is receiving subscriptions for £250,000 in £10 shares of this company, at a premium of 10s. per share. The total share capital of the company is £400,000, and £150,000 of it has already been issued and converted into stock. This completing issue will be merged into the other when fully paid up. According to the prospectus three extensions of the existing lines will be constructed, and a map is given with the prospectus, showing that they will run through excellent tea-growing districts. The Indian Government has the usual option to buy the company out at the end of 25 years, and the Government may be asked to work the lines for 40 per cent. of the gross receipts in certain contingencies, but the capital has no direct guarantee. It ought not to require one with lines placed as they are.

Company Reports and Balance-Sheets.

THE GRAND TRUNK RAILWAY COMPANY OF CANADA.—Gross receipts for the half-year ended December 31, £2,247,151, working expenses, £1,434,804, increase in gross receipts, £135,617, decrease in working expenses, £67,986. The percentage of expenses to income was thus reduced from 69·32 in the second half of 1896 to 62·11 in the past half-year, and the net income was increased by £196,235. This is the result on the main line and its immediate dependents. On the two controlled lines, the Chicago and Grand Trunk and the Detroit, Grand Haven and Milwaukee, the recovery was also considerable. The former did not exhibit much increase in the gross receipts, only £6,045 in fact, but the working expenses were brought down £11,208, so that the profit was £38,325, or £17,253 more than in the corresponding half-year. The net revenue charges of this company payable by the Grand Trunk Company amounted to £87,792, being slightly smaller than in December, 1896. The deficiency was therefore £49,467 as against £67,417 in 1896, an improvement of £17,950. This deficiency has to be made good by the parent company, as also that of the Detroit Company. This latter also picked up considerably, its traffic receipts showing an increase of £6,102, and its expenses a decrease of £15,271, so that the net balance was £35,235 against £13,862, an improvement of £21,373, and a sum sufficient within £2,174 of that required to cover fixed charges. The year before the deficiency was £24,917. Both these lines have been a tremendous burden upon the company for many years back, and their aggregate indebtedness to the Grand Trunk now amounts to £927,680 for interest advanced by it on their behalf. Of course, it is not out of pocket altogether to this extent, because a good deal of the interest, on the Chicago line at all events, is due to itself. Still, it has had to find a great deal of money, and this is the balance-sheet position. We hope the improvement now shown is the beginning of better things in the future. Adding various small items of revenue to the net income from traffic the grand total of the net income of the company for the half-year was £920,236, an improvement of £212,629 on December 1896. Of this sum £644,972 went to meet the interest charges, rents and advances to subsidiary lines, leaving a surplus of £275,263, which wiped out the whole of the deficiency shown at the end of the June half-year leaving £10,289 to be carried forward to the current half-year. For the whole year the improvement in net income was £321,000. The Grand Trunk is thus well lifted out of the slough into which it had been allowed to tumble by lax management and, we fear, corruption. Every credit ought to be given to the present board, and above all to the present General Manager, Mr. Hays, for the immense change that has taken place. It always seemed to us that the working expenses of the company were excessive, and the savings which have been effected under the new control fully justify this view. They appear to be legitimate savings moreover, and we see no indication that the lines are being starved. Less seems to have been spent on some items, such as renewals of ties, repairs and renewals of bridges, of buildings, of fences, of passenger and freight cars, and of docks and wharves. Superintendence, again, has cost rather less, general expenses also somewhat less, and repairs to roadway rather more, and the directors state that in the half-year 514 new modern freight cars were provided from revenue. On the other hand it has to be pointed out that the capital expenditure of the company continues to be on a pretty liberal scale. It amounted to £215,149 in the six months under review, but £130,242 of this was on account of reconstruction of the Victoria Jubilee Bridge at Montreal, a work that ought not to have been necessary at the present time had it originally been properly gone about. How far the management is justified in charging £35,357 to capital account for new rolling stock and in debiting the same account with the cost of increased weight of rails and with part cost of the substitution of stone and iron bridges for wooden ones we cannot judge, but have doubts upon the point. Nevertheless, making allowance for all items of this kind, it appears to us that the company has entered upon a period of greater prosperity than it has known for many years back, and we trust that the dispute which has unfortunately broken out between it and the Canadian Pacific Company will not last long enough, or produce changes important enough, to alter the prospect for the worse.

THE ENGLISH ASSOCIATION OF AMERICAN BOND AND SHAREHOLDERS, LIMITED.—This little company earned £4,127 gross in 1897, and spent £2,866 in doing so. The net revenue therefore was £1,261, which, added to £1,082 brought forward, gave a balance of £2,343 to be dealt with. Out of this the maximum dividend of 7½ per cent. is paid, taking £775 and leaving £1,568 to be carried forward. During the first part of the year there was very little doing in American railroad securities here, so that the business was restricted, but the company fulfils a very useful function and might well be taken more advantage of than it is by English holders of such securities, who are often at a loss for a rallying point in times of difficulty.

BAHIA AND SAN FRANCISCO RAILWAY COMPANY.—The permission to advance the tariff appears to have affected the revenue of this company favourably, for it amounted in the half-year ended December 31 last to £68,114, as compared with £48,820 in the corresponding half of 1896. Expenses were only £1,056 higher, but even then the debit balance on working the line was £19,101. The Brazilian Government came to the rescue with its guarantee of £63,000, and a net balance of £44,172 was produced, which permitted of a dividend at the usual rate of 5 per cent. per annum, with the help of a mere £827 from the reserves, which still amount to £96,358. The revolution in the state of Bahia is said to have collapsed, but apparently the company gained very largely in the half-year from the transport of Government troops and stores on that account. The Timbo branch fared more miserably than the main undertaking, for with £7,588 of receipts the debit balance on working was £5,113. After reserving the Government guarantee of £8,943, and drawing £752 from suspense account, only 3 per cent. in dividend could be paid.

RECIPE AND SAO FRANCISCO (PERNAMBUCO) RAILWAY COMPANY.—For the second year this company has been able to charge a higher tariff to meet the fall in exchange, and the result is apparently a great decline in traffic. The number of passengers carried fell off 25 per cent., and the decrease in goods was quite as great. The revenue of the half-year now being dealt with declined £50,410 to a total of £197,292, and the working expenses only fell off £12,495 to a total of £190,443. These totals are in sterling, at the fanciful exchange of 27d., but taking currency figures the net balance was 52,578 milreis, or, roughly speaking, £1,500. For a Brazilian guaranteed railway this was affluence, and the balance was handed over to the Government, which paid its guarantee in gold. The company, therefore, received £40,141 on this account, which permitted it to redeem £7,000 of debentures and pay 5 per cent. in dividend upon the shares.

NATAL AND NOVA CRUZ (BRAZILIAN) RAILWAY COMPANY.—With a gross revenue of £5,046, the expenses of this company amounted to £12,427, so that the loss on working the line was £7,381. The Brazilian Government paid over its guaranteed interest, amounting to £43,281, and this enabled debenture interest to be met, £13,175 to be placed to debenture redemption, and the payment of a dividend of 4½ per cent. upon the shares. One third of the cost of a bridge, or £483, is to be written off out of revenue.

ALLIANCE AND DUBLIN CONSUMERS' GAS COMPANY.—The revenue of this undertaking in the second half of 1897 was £797 less than in the corresponding half of 1896, the reduction being wholly due to the depreciation in the value of residuals, as gas revenue was £2,400 more. Expenditure was larger and the net revenue of £36,473 was £2,030 below that of the second half of 1896. To pay the usual dividend of 10½ per cent. per annum, and 7½ per cent. per annum upon the two classes of shares, £2,502 had to be taken from the reserve fund, which now stands at £43,514. There is also a contingency fund of £7,370, an insurance fund of £2,901, and a leasehold renewal fund of £902.

MONTE VIDEO WATERWORKS COMPANY.—This is an important undertaking with £350,000 of debenture stock and £400,000 of share capital. The company must have done well in the past, for it has accumulated a reserve of £60,000, and a depreciation fund o £15,000, but this does not apply to the last six years, during which nothing has been added to the reserve, and only £2,742 to the depreciation fund. Last year was a bad one in Uruguay, so it is not surprising that the gross revenue diminished by £2,905, and the net by £3,992. Its total of £47,364 just permitted of the payment of debenture and other interest, the setting aside of £2,000 against possible bad debts, and the payment of a 5 per cent. dividend upon the ordinary shares. The position is not a satisfactory one, but, of course, allowance must be made for a bad year. Should revenue improve the amount set aside in the future for depreciation should be sufficient to make up for the lack of any addition this year.

LONDON SOUTHERN TRAMWAYS COMPANY.—The receipts of last year increased £2,056, and the net revenue of £5,067 was £609 larger. The sum of £2,000 was placed to the credit of Permanent Way Suspense account, and £800 to a Horse Renewal account, and out of the balance a dividend of 3s. per share, or 1½ per cent., is proposed. The same distribution was made for 1896, but in previous years the record was much worse.

THOMAS TILLING, LIMITED.—With the large revenue of £225,224 for last year, the profit on working was £34,388. Horse renewals, and depreciation of rolling stock and harness are mentioned in the accounts, but the sums so devoted are not stated separately, and only depreciation of machinery and leaseholds is accounted for clearly. The preliminary expenses of £130 were paid off, and £11,776 went to the vendors as their share of profits previous to incorporation of the company. The balance of £20,787 permits of the payment of the preference dividend, the setting aside of £1,500 to reserve, a dividend of 10 per cent. upon the ordinary shares, and the carrying forward of £4,247. We should not have thought much of this statement if the ordinary shares had been held by the public, but they are entirely in the hands of the old partners, and only the preference and debenture capital is held outside. As the annual charge on this capital is only £11,750, the profits appear to cover it about three times, so that it ought to be thoroughly well secured, and of course the rest of the matter is purely a private concern for the ordinary shareholders.

ANGLO-ARGENTINE TRAMWAYS COMPANY.—This company seems to be in a poor way. With an increase of £6,493 in receipts during 1897 expenses were £14,133, so that the profit of £56,833 was £7,640 below that of 1896. The sum of £5,000 is placed to reserve and dividends equal to 3 per cent. declared, as against 3½ per cent. for the previous year. The reserve fund will then amount to £23,672, but we note that the sum of £8,804 towards municipal paving was added to capital, and out of £6,028 spent upon permanent way renewals only £5,000 was paid for out of revenue. This policy has been carried on for some years past, with the result that £15,791 is credited to this very unrealisable account. Altogether, we do not like the report.

EAGLE INSURANCE COMPANY.—For the past year this company's income from premiums was £170,363 net, and it also received £100,220 for annuities sold on 82 lives. Life policy claims paid amounted to £255,883 and expenses of management, exclusive of that on the annuity business, which was small, came to £28,264, or about 16·3 per cent, of the premium income. It will be seen that the claims were high, probably because this company represents a considerable number of small offices, absorbed by it in past years, whose lives were "matured," and therefore fall in with greater rapidity than is usual. In these circumstances the directors have done wisely in allowing their actuary, Mr. Colenso, to value their accumulations on a 3 per cent. interest basis, notwithstanding the fact that the net rate of interest received on their investments last year averaged £4 2s. per cent. As Mr. Colenso points out in an interesting special report, this strict method of valuation has the effect of sweeping away the whole actuarial surplus which would have been available as bonuses upon the company's policies during the next five years, and this will be a disappointment, without doubt, to the holders of such policies. At the same time, as the directors also say in their report, this present disadvantage is fitly counterbalanced by the very strong and satisfactory condition in which such a valuation leaves the company. In other words the future position is strengthened, and very materially strengthened, at the expense of a little present privation; for, had the valuation been made 3½ per cent, the amount available for the policy holders would only have been £87,000. The ratio of expenses to income is, as will be noted, somewhat high, but not sufficiently so to sensibly weaken the company's position, and we have no doubt that efforts will be made to reduce it. As it is the company's accumulated funds now amount to £2,594,867, the greater part of which is invested at home, and, as far as we can judge, very well invested.

FREDERICK LEYLAND & CO., LIMITED.—The report of this company for the past year appears to be quite satisfactory. The gross profit came to £203,604, and 9 per cent. has been paid on the ordinary shares for the year, after writing off £42,000 for depreciation, transferring £75,000 to the reserve fund for equalisation of dividends, making it £125,000, adding £15,000 to the insurance reserve fund, raising it to £65,000, and writing off the bonus on the conversion of debentures, and the cost of issue of the 4½ per cent. pre-preference shares, amounting to £9,676. During the year £150,000, in 4½ per cent. accumulative pre-preference shares was issued, leaving £50,000 still to be disposed of, and the company's bonds were converted into 4 per cent. debentures, and extended to 1921. All this is very good, but we are sorry to see the announcement that in future no profit and loss account will be issued, because the reserves for the equalisation of dividends and insurance amount together to a sum equal to the outstanding ordinary capital. It seems the Articles of Association give the directors power to take this step when this condition is fulfilled, but we do not see the wisdom of it, and deprecate secrecy of any kind in regard to a shipping company in which the public has large interests. The balance-sheet shows investments at cost to the amount of £156,453, including investments in the company's own debentures. Would it not have been expedient to state what proportion of the money lies in these debentures? In other respects the balance-sheet appears to us a clean one, but we are not sure that £42,000 was enough to write off for depreciation, especially when an unknown amount figures in the capital account for goodwill.

THE CRÉDIT FONCIER OF MAURITIUS.—In the past year the directors in this company claim to have done a very good business, and the claim seems to be justified. Certainly the company's money ought to be well secured, since it has only advanced £641,603 against properties the "reported value" of which is £1,474,037. After charging £12,300 for loss by exchange on £20,000 remitted home, the directors are able to pay a 5 per cent. dividend on the ordinary capital, to place £6,000 to general reserve, increasing it to £65,000, and £6,000 to the exchange reserve, making it a similar amount, and still to leave £1,040 to be carried forward. The debenture debt was reduced during the year by £25,320, and the profit and loss account does not indicate any interest in arrear. Altogether this company manages to do wonderfully well, whatever the condition of the island may be, and it has now weathered the ups and downs of thirty-four years.

THE OOREGUM GOLD MINING COMPANY OF INDIA, LIMITED.—In 1897 this company won 55,819 oz. of gold which was less by 9,756 oz. than the total for the preceding year, a result due to deterioration in the quality of the stone treated. Nevertheless, the net profit was £60,318 out of which dividends aggregating 2s. 6d. per share have been paid on the ordinary shares and 4s. 6d. on the preference, or 12½ and 22½ per cent. respectively, the final shilling now. Since the year closed, prospects have decidedly improved because the board has followed the wise policy of going down after the ore, and success has followed. "A large reserve of first-class ore" has been opened at various depths in the Southern extension from Taylor's shaft.

EVERED & CO., LIMITED.—The net profit for the year 1897 was £25,147. Adding the £7,288 brought forward the available balance was £32,453, and out of this the ordinary shares get 7½ per cent. for the twelve months in two equal instalments, together with a bonus of 2½ per cent., making the entire return 10 per cent. for the year. This is very good, and equally so is the manner in which cost of goodwill, leases, patents, &c., are being written down. In all, £9,018 is thus applied and £6,361 is left still to be carried forward. The directors say that an increased amount of business was done in the past year. This year the full amount of paid-up capital ranks for dividend.

THE EAST LONDON WATERWORKS COMPANY issues a satisfactory report, showing an increase in revenue for the past half-year of £10,912, accompanied by a reduction of £3,592 in expenses. The available balance is £88,433, of which £68,822 is absorbed in paying a dividend on the ordinary stock at the rate of 8 per cent. per annum. This compares with only 7 per cent. a year ago, and the increased balance of £19,610 is now carried forward. The company has eleven subsidiary and storage reservoirs, covering an area of 316 acres, and having a capacity of 1,215,000,000 gallons. This sounds as if the company ought to be able to prevent a recurrence of the water famine.

BANK OF AUSTRALASIA.—The business keeps in a somewhat stationary position. During the half-year to October 11 a net profit of £40,278 was made, which compares with £40,400 for the same period in 1896, and the dividend is again £1 per share, or at the rate of 5 per cent. per annum. According to the balance-sheet deposits are down £835,000 to £12,860,000, while bills payable are down £35,000 at £2,000,873. The feature on the assets side is a reduction of £849,000 in loans, the total of which is now only £486,000, so that in spite of the smaller deposits another £100,000 has had to be put into securities, which amount to £812,668. The expected improvement referred to in the last report was not fulfilled owing to renewal of drought, which has resulted in a reduction in shipments of wool, partly offset by improvement in the price. This is ancient history, however, as the report is nearly six months old before shareholders get it.

MERCANTILE BANK OF INDIA.—The operations during the past year show results very similar to those obtained in 1896. Net profits, including £10,563 brought forward, were £31,673, compared with £31,188 in the previous year, when £8,047 was brought in, so that the bank has hardly done so well. After paying the full 5 per cent. on the "A" shares and 3 per cent for the year on the "B," £11,048 is left to carry forward. Fixed deposits show a small reduction, while bills payable have increased to a greater extent. The bank has been moving its investments, the total of which is now only £232,360, compared with £314,478 last year. The holding of rupee paper has been reduced from £271,348 to £75,577, and part of the money has been put into Indian Guaranteed Railway debentures.

THE ANGLO-AUSTRIAN BANK made less profit last year, £168,915 against £181,030 in 1896, and therefore the dividend is lowered from 8½ fls. or $7\frac{1}{12}$ per cent. to 8 fls. or 6⅔ per cent., while the balance carried forward is £3,200 less. The capital of the bank is £2,000,000, and it has a reserve of £333,473, stocks and shares held representing £257,969; Falkenau Coal mines £26,276; house property £90,140, and the Vienna office, £143,611. Compared with 1896, deposit notes in circulation have just doubled, while bills payable are up £102,000, and sundry creditors £462,000. On the other side there is an increase of £300,000 in bills receivable, £185,000 in advances against securities and warrants, and £232,000 in sundry debtors. Syndicates, on the other hand, are down £124,000 at £203,130, this being apparently an underwriting account. The bank has not done so well, and the balance sheet is hardly so strong as its predecessor.

BUENOS AYRES AND ROSARIO RAILWAY COMPANY.—Compared with 1896, the outcome of last year's business makes as bad a showing as any we have come across of the Argentine railway reports so far issued. Gross receipts fell off to the extent of £56,089, although 24,188 more passengers were carried, and the carriage of the company's own material yielded £7,419 more. The gross weight carried was 110,224 tons less than in 1896, but 84,074 more train miles were run, and the expenses increased by £13,481, there being, consequently, a reduction of £69,571 in net receipts, or over 19 per cent. The percentage of working expenses to receipts rose from 50·22 to 56·4 per cent., which is higher than for several years past. For 1897 the dividend on the ordinary stock is only 2 per cent., which compares with 3 per cent. for the previous year, and 2 per cent. for 1895. The reduced revenue is ascribed to the almost total failure of the cereal crops through frost and locusts, while the increase in expenses was due to extra cost of coal and minor influences. Prospects for the current year, however, are much better owing to the good wheat harvest and the appreciation of the paper currency.

THE PROPERTY MARKET.

Last week showed no slackening in the almost abnormal activity at Tokenhouse Yard. The total returns amounted to £165,987, or £63,270 over the corresponding week of last year. There was a brisk business for investment purposes in the brick and mortar class of property. The keen competition for building land in or near the metropolis, was also noticeable. Several properties with speculative building values likewise sold well. One at Wimbledon, of 4½ acres, went for about £1,380 per acre; another of 11 acres brought £1,133 per acre; while a third of 17½ acres at Muswell-hill, realised £1,020 an acre. Another notable feature of the week was the falling-off in the demand for licensed properties. This may be regarded as a reaction against the undue inflation which has been observed in this class of property during the past few years. It is coming down to something nearer to what may be called its natural value. The total sales for yesterday week amounted to £30,000 odd, mostly in freehold properties. One freehold ground rent of £300 per annum, secured on 50, Nicholas-lane, City, with reversion in 46½ years, was withdrawn at £12,000. Freehold ground rents, amounting to £48 per annum, secured on Nos. 1 to 15 (odd), Brunswick-road, Upper Holloway, reversion in 46 years, £1,435; a freehold residence, Durnford House, Balham-high-road, let on lease at £110 a year, £1,700; two blocks of freehold building land in The Crescent and The Avenue, Barnes, were disposed of by Messrs. Chesterton & Sons for £1,470 and £1,600 respectively, a price approaching £5 a foot. A freehold residence called Mascot, in Love-lane, Pinner, let at £70 per annum, realised, under the hammer of Messrs. Farebrother, Ellis & Co., £1,250. Messrs. Newbon, Edwards & Shephard sold the freehold of No. 3, Newcastle-place, Clerkenwell, comprising a dwelling house, two workshops, and yard in rear, for £1,000; a leasehold residence, No. 265, Camden-road, Holloway, held for a term of 59½ years at £13 12s. 6d. ground rent, for £2,000; two freehold houses and shops, Nos. 134 and 136, Albion-road, Stoke Newington, let at an annual rental of £130, for £2,400, and several smaller lots. Among the more important properties disposed of by Messrs. Stimson & Sons, was a freehold shop and dwelling-house, 145, Newington-butts, with six cottages in the rear, the whole producing a rental of £166 a year, which changed hands at £3,000.

This week began at the Mart on Monday with sales amounting to the respectable total of £33,465, only five of the lots offered remaining unsold. The Riviera Hotel at Maidenhead, offered by Mr. J. C, Platt, of Hammersmith, with an unexpired term of 65 years, brodght, with the furniture, £6,000. Mr. Platt also disposed of two copyhold houses in Hammersmith, of an estimated rental of £85, at £1,380. A leasehold house, No. 6, Henrietta-street, Cavendish-square, having the short term of 28 years to run, was disposed of by Messrs. Elliott, Son and Boyton for £2,320. Amongst the lots placed by other firms were a parcel of freehold ground rents at Wandsworth which sold at £3,300; a freehold residential property at Theydon Bois, Essex, which brought £2,375; freehold and copyhold properties at Woodford and Chigwell, and two small freeholds in Soho. A policy of insurance for £10,000, with profits, on a life aged 67, was sold by Messrs. G. A. Wilkinson & Son for £6,860. The Crown lease of 6, St. Martin's-mews, Trafalgar-square, returned as unsold last Friday, was actually disposed of by Messrs. Hampton & Sons before leaving the Mart, at the price of £1,350. Mr. Alfred Richards announces a sale of gas and water debenture and ordinary stocks and shares at the Mart on Monday next. These include stocks and shares in the Maidstone Gas Company, Hornsey Gas Company, Romford Gas Company, Romford Gas and Coke Company, Limited, Ascot District Gas Company, Bournemouth Gas and Water Company, and Walton-on-Thames and Weybridge Gas Company.

Answers to Correspondents.

Questions about public securities, and on all points in company law, will be answered week by week, in the REVIEW, on the following terms and conditions:—

A fee of FIVE shillings must be remitted for each question put, provided they are questions about separate securities. Should a private letter be required, then an extra fee of FIVE shillings must be sent to cover the cost of such letter, the fee then being TEN shillings for one query only, and FIVE shillings for every subsequent one in the same letter. While making this concession the EDITOR will feel obliged if private replies are as much as possible dispensed with. It is wholly impossible to answer letters sent merely "with a stamped envelope enclosed for reply."

Correspondents will further greatly oblige by so framing their questions as to obviate the necessity to name securities in the replies. They should *number* the questions, keeping a copy for reference, thus:—"(1) Please inform me about the present position of the Rowenzori Development Co. (2) Is a dividend likely to be paid soon on the capital stock of the Congo-Sudan Railway?"

Answers to be given to all such questions by simply quoting the numbers 1, 2, 3, and so on. The EDITOR has a rooted objection to such forms of reply as—"I think your Timbuctoo Consols will go up," or "Sell your Slowcoach and Draggem Bonds," because this kind of thing is open to all sorts of abuses. By the plan suggested, and by using a fancy name to be replied to, each query can be kept absolutely private to the inquirer, and no scope whatever be given to market manipulations. Avoid, as names to be replied to, common words, like "investor," "inquirer," and so on, as also "bear" or "bull." Detached syllables of the inquirer's name, or initials reversed, will frequently do as well as anything, so long as the answer can be identified by the inquirer.

The EDITOR further respectfully requests that merely speculative questions should as far as possible be avoided. He by no means sets himself up as a market prophet, and can only undertake to provide the latest information regarding the securities asked about. This he will do faithfully and without bias.

Replies cannot be guaranteed in the same week if the letters demanding them reach the office of the INVESTORS' REVIEW, Norfolk House, Norfolk-street, W.C., later than the first post on Wednesday mornings.

J. B.—I think you should send your bonds in now. The firm is, perhaps, wanting in brains, but it is largely interested on its own account. A scheme of reorganisation is expected very soon, which will be managed here by another and stronger firm. It is to be hoped the scheme will be a thorough one, as this company has a favourable position geographically, and with proper management ought to gather a profitable business.

C. H. S.—So far as I can discover there is good reason to hope that your company will be able to pull round. The unfortunate failure of the first property acquired was quite unexpected, but the directors are, I am still assured, honest and capable, and they hope to improve the company's position before long.

Next Week's Meetings.

MONDAY, APRIL 4.	
Anglo-Argentine Tramways	Cannon-street Hotel, noon.
Charles Baker & Co.	Inns of Courts Hotel, 4 p.m.
English Association of American Bond and Shareholders	5, Great Winchester-street, noon.
Espuela Land and Cattle	Suffolk House, 11 a.m.
D. H. Evans & Co.	Oxford-street, 3.30 p.m.
Hannan's, Sir John Forrest Gold Mines	Winchester House, 2 p.m.
Kelani Valley Tea	16, Philpot-lane, noon.
Monte Video Waterworks	52, Moorgate-street, 3 p.m.
TUESDAY, APRIL 5.	
Australian Shale Syndicate	34, Old Broad-street, 11 a.m.
Bank of Scotland	Edinburgh, 12.30 p.m.
British Empire Mutual Life ...	Cannon-street Hotel, noon.
Grand Trunk Railway of Canada ...	Cannon-street Hotel, 2 p.m.
Manchester Fire Assurance ...	Manchester, noon.
Natal & Nova Cruz Railway ...	Winchester House, 2.30 p.m.
Natal Land and Colonization ...	Winchester House, noon.
Paquin	Cannon-street Hotel, noon.
Pacific and San Francisco Pernambuco	Cannon-street Hotel, 1 p.m.
Septimus Parsonage & Co.	Cannon-street Hotel, 2.30 p.m.
Standard Bank of South Africa ...	Cannon-street Hotel, 1 p.m.
WEDNESDAY, APRIL 6.	
Canadian Pacific	Montreal, noon.
Delhi and London Bank	123, Bishopsgate-street Within noon.
Joint Stock Assets Company ...	18, Austin-Friars, 2 p.m.
Kimberley Waterworks	Cannon-street Hotel, 1 p.m.
Lanarkshire and Dumbartonshire Railway	Glasgow, 3 p.m.
Newhaven Harbour	London Bridge Terminus, 1 p.m.
Ooregum Gold Mining of India ...	Cannon-street Hotel, noon.
Phœnix Assurance	19, Lombard-street, 1.30 p.m.
Swedish Assurance	3, Lothbury, 1.30 p.m.
Thomas Tilling	Cannon-street Hotel, 3.30 p.m.
THURSDAY, APRIL 7.	
Commercial Gas Company	Cannon-street Hotel, noon.
East London Waterworks	St. Helen's-place, noon.
Scottish Widows' Fund and Life Assurance	Edinburgh, 2 p.m.

CLEMENT WILSON'S PUBLICATIONS.

LEGAL EPITOMES FOR GENERAL USE.

Price 2s. 6d. Fcap. 8vo, cloth.

No. I.

LAW OF SALES OF STOCKS AND SHARES. By Charles Frampton Stallard, M.A. (Oxon.), of Gray's Inn, late Holt Scholar, Barrister-at-Law.

"The law is clearly and concisely given, and the book should certainly assist those who are concerned in dealings with stocks and shares."—*Law Times*.

"Cannot fail to be of service to many who have dealings in stocks and shares."—*Bankers' Magazine*.

No. II.

LAW OF BANKS AND BANKERS. By W. de Bracy Herbert, M.A., LL.M., of the Inner Temple, Barrister-at-Law.

"A clear and readable exposition of the English law of Banker and Customer."—*Scotsman*.

"Clear and simple in its style . . . and appears to be absolutely accurate."—*Law Times*.

No. III.

LAW OF DIRECTORS' AND PROMOTERS' LIABILITIES. By R. Storry Deans, LL.B. (London), of Gray's Inn, Barrister-at-Law, sometime Holder of Inns of Court Studentship, Arden Scholar of Gray's Inn, &c.

"A clearly written and useful book upon a subject of general interest."—*Manchester Guardian*.

"It is well fitted to be of assistance to directors, promoters, and shareholders."—*Dundee Advertiser*.

No. IV.

Now Ready.

THE LAW OF FIXTURES AND REPAIRS AS BETWEEN LANDLORD AND TENANT. By W. de Bracy Herbert, M.A., LL.M., of the Inner Temple, Barrister-at-Law.

"Explains the law on the question plainly and concisely, but, at the same time, with accuracy, and will prove serviceable to property-owners, agents, and tenants."—*Manchester Guardian*.

"An excellent handbook."—*Yorkshire Post*.

In Preparation.

No. V.

THE LAW RELATING TO COMMISSION AGENTS, and more particularly Auctioneers, Estate and House Agents, and Public-House Brokers. By H. M. Giveen, B.A., of Lincoln's Inn and the Oxford Circuit, Barrister-at-Law; sometime Holder of the Inns of Court Studentship and of the Vinerian Scholarship.

"INVESTORS' REVIEW."

SUBSCRIPTION PRICE, POST FREE:—

Investors' Review alone—

United Kingdom.

Three Months.	Six Months.	One Year.
7s.	14s.	28s.

All Foreign Countries.

Three Months.	Six Months.	One Year.
7s. 6d.	15s.	30s.

Investors' Review and Investment Index together—

United Kingdom.

Three Months.	Six Months.	One Year.
9s. 6d.	18s. 6d.	36s.

All Foreign Countries.

Three Months.	Six Months.	One Year.
9s. 10d.	19s. 6d.	38s. 6d.

Payable in Advance.

Cheques and Postal Orders should be made payable to Clement Wilson.

The Investors' Review can be obtained in Paris of Messrs. Boyveau et Chevillet, 22, Rue de la Banque.

Of all Newsagents and at all Railway Bookstalls in the United Kingdom, or remit to The PUBLISHER, Norfolk House, Norfolk-street, Strand, W.C.

BACK NUMBERS.

Less than a dozen complete sets now remain of the first four Quarterly Numbers of the "Investors' Review," so that the first Number of all can only be supplied in volume form, price **21s.** net. The Volume for 1893 is also composed of Quarterly Parts, and its price is the same. The seven Quarterly Parts from Number II. onwards can still be had separately, price 5s. net. For the succeeding four years down to December, 1897, the "Review" is in Monthly Numbers.

All Monthly Numbers more than six months old will now be charged 1s. 6d. net, and all Half-yearly Volumes 10s. 6d. net (by post, 2d. and 10d. extra for the Number or Volume).

Cloth Cases for binding the "Review" and the "Index" are charged for as follows:—For Annual Volumes of the "Review," 1s. 6d.; for Semi-annual Volumes, 1s. 3d.; and for Yearly Volumes of the "Index," also 1s. 3d. Postage, in all instances, 2d. extra.

Volume I. (July, 1895—April, 1896) and Volume II. (July, 1896—April, 1897) of the "Investment Index" now ready, price 9s. 6d. each, net (post free, 10s.).

The Investment Index,

A Quarterly Supplement to the "Investors' Review."

Price 2s. net. 8s. 6d. per annum, post free.

THE INVESTMENT INDEX is an indispensable supplement to the Investors' Review. A file of it enables investors to follow the ups and downs of markets, and each number gives the return obtainable on all classes of securities at recent prices, arranged in a most convenient form for reference. Appended to its tables of figures are criticisms on company balance sheets, State Budgets, &c., similar to those in the Investors' Review.

Regarding it, the *Speaker* says: "The Quarterly 'Investment Index' is probably the handiest and fullest, as it is certainly the safest, of guides to the investor."

"The compilation of securities is particularly valuable."—*Pall Mall Gazette.*

"Its carefully classified list of securities will be found very valuable."—*Globe.*

"At no time has such a list of securities been more valuable than the present."—*Star.*

"The invaluable 'Investors' Index.'"—*Sketch.*

"A most valuable compilation."—*Glasgow Herald.*

Subscription to the "Investors' Review" and "Investment Index," 36s. per annum, post free.

CLEMENT WILSON,
NORFOLK HOUSE NORFOLK STREET, LONDON, W.C.

ESTABLISHED 1824.

CLERICAL, MEDICAL AND GENERAL

LIFE ASSURANCE SOCIETY.

Chief Office:

15, ST. JAMES'S SQUARE, LONDON, S.W.

CHAIRMAN, RIGHT HON. SIR JOHN ROBERT MOWBRAY, BART., D.C.L., M.P.

Assets nearly 3½ MILLIONS Sterling.

VALUATION RATE OF INTEREST 2½ PER CENT. ONLY.

The Results of the 1897 Valuation showed—

1. INCREASED RESERVES.
2. INCREASED PROFITS.

THE TOTAL SURPLUS DIVIDED WAS

£515,346.

Which was larger by £86,896 than any previously distributed, and represented the

HIGHEST RATE OF PROFIT EVER DECLARED

by the Society.

The Bonus Report, (1897), Prospectus, Forms of Proposal, and every information on application.

15, ST. JAMES'S SQUARE, LONDON, S.W.

W. J. H. WHITTALL, Actuary and Secretary.

To Correspondents.

The EDITOR cannot undertake to return rejected communications.

Letters from correspondents must, in every case, be authenticated by the name and address of the writer.

Telegraphic Address: "Unveiling, London."

The Investors' Review.

The Week's Money Market.

With the Stock Exchange settlement, end of the month requirements, and Treasury Bill payments in the week, the floating resources of the Money Market have been amply employed. A spice of nervousness was added by the current political uncertainties, so that rates for short loans and day to day money gradually hardened until 2¾ to 3 per cent. are quoted for both, as against 2¼ to 2¾ per cent. a week ago. Recourse had to be had to the Bank pretty freely, as is shown by the addition of £3,671,000 to the "other securities" in the Bank return. A good deal of this money, however, went to the credit of the private deposits, and will not be needed now that the end of the month is passed.

Political uneasiness was strong enough at one time to cause 3⅛ to 3¼ per cent. to be quoted for the discount of three months' choice bills, and a good deal of business was done "subject to the action of the Bank." Anxiety, of course, was principally aroused by the increased demand for gold on American account. This is looked upon entirely as arising out of political considerations. Since the opening of the year the States have received fully eight millions sterling, a sum that should quite represent any favourable trading balance that required to be liquidated in gold. To moderate the drafts upon its stock of the metal, the Bank of England raised its price for eagles on Wednesday to 76s. 8d. per ounce, which is the highest price that can be demanded, as it virtually represents bar gold at 77s. 11¾d. per ounce outside, and to advance the price by another halfpenny would cause sovereigns to be taken as the cheaper form of remittance. If, therefore, the drain does not moderate, the only protective move left will be to advance the Bank Rate; but that step was not adopted yesterday, and the directors are evidently indisposed to make the change while hope remains that the urgency of the demand will lessen. Home requirements, which have been so prominent in the past quarter, ought now to be less pressing, for next week the Government dividends and the repayment of Treasury bills will take place; and further Government disbursements must lead to the market for a time becoming less dependent upon the Bank. The Chinese Loan, however, must not be forgotten, as 50 per cent. of the loan is to be called up in April—25 per cent. on the 7th, and 25 per cent. on the 21st—and the remaining 25 per cent. will have to be provided on May 3. With the underwriters—that is, the market so largely interested in these payments—there is likely to be some pressure at these dates, unless the political horizon improves very much in the meantime. Short of this much-desired change, there does not seem to be any prospect of ease returning immediately to the market, although conditions must improve as time goes on. Meantime the discount houses quote the rate for three months' choice bills at 2¹⁵⁄₁₆ per cent., with rather more tendency to take paper.

The Stock Exchange Settlement came this time in a busy week, and so bankers were able to charge 3¾ to 4 per cent. for loans to the "House," especially as a little uneasiness prevailed as to the condition of the Account. No difficulties of importance came to the surface, and the reduction of speculative commitments has made such progress that rates are bound to be easier on the next occasion, even if the Money Market itself does not fall away much in the interval.

Yesterday's Bank return showed, as we have just mentioned, an increase of £3,671,745 in the "other" securities, chiefly three-day loans, and the momentary indebtedness of the market to the Bank must be over £10,000,000. Of this money £1,810,463 went on to the "other" deposits, raising them to £36,812,728, and £1,852,925 of it passed into the active circulation or out of the country in the shape of gold. The "public" deposits, or Government balances stand within £3,000, of where they did a week ago and, short of that amount, are still at the highest total ever seen. But the money will now begin to be dispersed and part of the increase in the note circulation will also soon return. Deducting the £316,000 net in gold exported, the increase of the active circulation in notes and gold on the week is £1,537,000, and the Banking Reserve has fallen to £21,662,363.

SILVER.

The price of the white metal has remained steady during the past seven days, and the quotation of 25 11/16d. for bars on the spot is but little different from that current a week ago. The market has become more settled, owing to the knowledge that the currency scheme of the Indian Government is to be relegated to a Departmental Committee, which will mean that some time must elapse before any action is taken in the matter. Evidently "bear" operations have not yet been unlocked, for the price "two months forward" is below that for immediate delivery, and until this divergence is removed it will be impossible to judge the real tone of the market. The India Council sold freely throughout, and in the week ended Tuesday last, disposed of about 93 lacs in bills and transfers. Since then it has sold 52 lacs or about £325,000, which will bring up the total sales of the Council in its financial year to about £9,420,000, or only £580,000 short of the amount looked for last December. It is a better record than many expected in December, but there is a great gulf betwixt the amount and the total of £16,000,000 proposed to be drawn in the year just opened. Indian exchanges have been remarkably steady, but Chinese rates have fallen to a moderate extent.

BANK OF ENGLAND.

AN ACCOUNT pursuant to the Act 7 and 8 Vict., cap. 32, for the Week ending on Wednesday, March 30, 1898.

ISSUE DEPARTMENT.

	£		£
Notes Issued	46,626,580	Government Debt	11,015,100
		Other Securities	5,784,900
		Gold Coin and Bullion	29,826,580
		Silver Bullion	—
	£46,626,580		£46,626,580

BANKING DEPARTMENT.

	£		£
Proprietors' Capital	14,553,000	Government Securities	14,208,979
Rest	3,819,072	Other Securities	39,039,137
Public Deposits (including Exchequer, Savings Banks, Commissioners of National Debt, and Dividend Accounts)	19,615,529	Notes	19,024,895
Other Deposits	36,812,728	Gold and Silver Coin	2,637,468
Seven Day and other Bills	109,150		
	£74,909,479		£74,909,479

Dated March 31, 1898.

H. G. BOWEN, *Chief Cashier.*

In the following table will be found the movements compared with the previous week, and also the totals for that week and the corresponding return last year:—

Banking Department.

Last Year. March 31.		March 23, 1898.	March 30, 1898.	Increase.	Decrease.
£	Liabilities.	£	£	£	£
3,790,185	Rest	3,818,597	3,819,072	1,475	—
16,150,425	Pub. Deposits	19,618,224	19,615,529	—	2,695
38,550,156	Other do.	35,002,265	36,812,728	1,810,463	—
157,726	7 Day Bills	99,573	109,150	9,577	—
	Assets.			Decrease.	Increase.
14,372,883	Gov. Securities	14,208,979	14,208,979	—	—
29,942,459	Other do.	35,367,392	39,039,137	—	3,671,745
28,856,150	Total Reserve	23,515,288	21,662,363	1,852,925	—
				3,674,440	3,674,440
				Increase.	Decrease.
£		£	£	£	£
27,256,305	Note Circulation.	26,675,455	27,601,685	926,230	—
52⅝ p.c.	Proportion	43 p.c.	38¼ p.c.	—	—
3 ,,	Bank Rate	3 ,,	3 ,,	—	—

Foreign Bullion movement for week £316,000 out.

LONDON BANKERS' CLEARING.

Week ending	1898.	1897.	Increase.	Decrease.
	£	£	£	£
Jan. 5	222,654,000	174,376,000	48,278,000	—
,, 12	144,603,000	127,315,000	17,288,000	—
,, 19	171,777,000	156,200,000	15,577,000	—
,, 26	134,247,000	118,667,000	15,580,000	—
Feb. 2	194,544,000	174,498,000	20,056,000	—
,, 9	137,204,000	129,209,000	8,9,5,000	—
,, 16	184,403,000	162,168,000	22,235,000	—
,, 23	132,450,000	131,777,000	673,000	—
March 2	190,157,000	177,852,000	12,305,000	—
,, 9	134,490,000	126,182,000	8,308,000	—
,, 16	174,377,000	148,937,000	25,440,000	—
,, 23	129,828,000	118,578,000	11,250,000	—
,, 30	170,668,000	158,421,000	12,247,000	—

BANK AND DISCOUNT RATES ABROAD.

	Bank Rate.	Altered.	Open Market.
Paris	2	March 14, 1895	1¾
Berlin	3	February 20, 1898	2¾
Hamburg	3	February 20, 1898	2¾
Frankfort	3	February 20, 1898	3
Amsterdam	3	April 13, 1897	2⅝
Brussels	3	April 28, 1896	2
Vienna	4	January 22, 1896	3½
Rome	5	August 27, 1895	3
St. Petersburg	5½	January 23, 1898	4½
Madrid	5	June 17, 1896	4
Lisbon	6	January 25, 1891	6
Stockholm	4	March 3, 1898	3½
Copenhagen	4	January 20, 1898	4
Calcutta	12	February 24, 1898	—
Bombay	13	February 24, 1898	—
New York call money	1½ to 2	—	—

NEW YORK ASSOCIATED BANKS (dollar at 4s.).

	Mar. 26, 1898.	Mar. 19, 1898.	Mar. 12, 1898.	Mar. 27, 1897.
	£	£	£	£
Specie	27,258,000	25,856,000	24,812,000	17,200,000
Legal tenders	13,794,000	14,166,000	14,506,000	21,166,000
Loans and discounts	120,034,000	121,456,000	123,572,000	100,896,000
Circulation	2,772,000	2,773,000	2,759,200	3,166,000
Net deposits	137,130,000	137,636,000	139,096,000	114,344,000

Legal reserve is 25 per cent. of net deposits; therefore the total reserve (specie and legal tenders) exceeds this sum by £6,769,500, against an excess last week of £5,613,000.

BANK OF FRANCE (25 francs to the £).

	Mar. 31, 1898.	Mar. 24, 1898.	Mar. 17, 1898.	April 1, 1897.
	£	£	£	£
Gold in hand	74,495,040	74,711,760	74,905,080	76,736,000
Silver in hand	48,723,600	48,672,000	48,521,880	49,073,000
Bills discounted	35,452,400	26,606,760	27,375,280	*45,553,000
Advances	14,796,120	14,663,560	14,665,520	—
Note circulation	153,313,920	147,930,560	149,170,880	148,082,000
Public deposits	7,006,640	6,329,680	5,758,240	8,641,000
Private deposits	22,984,800	17,484,960	16,764,240	19,491,000

Proportion between bullion and circulation 80⅜ per cent. against 83⅜ per cent. a week ago.

* Includes advances.

FOREIGN RATES OF EXCHANGE ON LONDON.

Place.	Usance.	Last week's.	Latest.	Place.	Usance.	Last week's.	Latest.
Paris	chqs.	25·30	25·31¼	Italy	sight	26·73	26·80
Brussels	chqs.	25·35	25·38¾	Do. gold prem.	..	105·70	105·90
Amsterdam	short	12·10¼	12·10¾	Constantinople	3 mths	109·30	109·35
Berlin	short	20·48½	20·48½	B. Ayres gd. pm.	..	167·20	163·20
Do.	3 mths	20·32½	20·30½	Rio de Janeiro	90 dys	6 1/32	6
Hamburg	3 mths	20·32½	20.32½	Valparaiso	90 dys	17 5/16	17⅜
Frankfort	short	20·47	20·48	Calcutta	T. T.	1/3 15/16	1/3 31/32
Vienna	short	12·03	12.05	Bombay	T. T.	1/3 15/16	1/3 31/32
St. Petersburg	3 mths	94·05	94.05	Hong Kong	T. T.	1/10½	1/10¼
New York	60 dys	4·81½	4·80¾	Shanghai	T. T.	2/5⅜	2/5⅜
Lisbon	sight	34 11/16	34 11/16	Singapore	T. T.	1/10 5/16	1/10 5/16
Madrid	sight	35·15	35·75				

IMPERIAL BANK OF GERMANY (20 marks to the £).

	Mar. 23, 1898.	Mar. 15, 1898.	Mar. 7, 1898.	Mar. 23, 1897.
	£	£	£	£
Cash in hand	48,746,650	48,699,500	47,989,250	46,814,000
Bills discounted	40,330,600	29,026,650	28,107,950	*30,636,000
Advances on stocks	3,842,700	3,889,800	3,746,650	—
Note circulation	52,066,650	51,392,700	51,058,500	49,365,000
Public deposits	27,515,400	26,679,700	24,558,350	24,459,000

* Includes advances

AUSTRIAN-HUNGARIAN BANK (1s. 8d. to the florin).

	Mar. 23, 1898.	Mar. 15, 1898.	Mar. 7, 1898.	Mar. 23, 1897.
	£	£	£	£
Gold reserve	30,535,665	30,706,833	30,754,925	25,842,000
Silver reserve	10,449,666	10,426,666	10,402,500	10,522,000
Foreign bills	1,004,000	1,001,833	1,114,750	—
Advances	1,846,416	1,828,416	1,862,000	—
Note circulation	50,790,000	51,250,166	51,904,250	47,864,000
Bills discounted	10,643,416	10,709,000	11,312,583	*11,973,000

* Includes advances.

NATIONAL BANK OF BELGIUM (25 francs to the £).

	Mar. 24, 1898.	Mar. 17, 1898.	Mar. 10, 1898.	Mar. 18, 1897
	£	£	£	£
Coin and bullion	4,168,920	4,307,600	4,186,040	4,175,000
Other securities	16,939,440	16,629,400	16,691,720	16,846,000
Note circulation	19,009,400	18,915,400	19,023,080	18,505,000
Deposits	3,558,400	3,531,000	3,342,400	3,108,000

BANK OF SPAIN (25 pesetas to the £).

	Mar. 26, 1898.	Mar. 18, 1898.	Mar. 12, 1898.	Mar. 27, 1897.
	£	£	£	£
Gold	9,624,960	9,595,360	9,577,760	8,528,360
Silver	10,862,440	10,864,540	10,860,040	10,774,680
Bills discounted	24,274,280	23,365,280	23,381,120	7,869,240
Advances and loans	5,122,960	5,561,000	5,501,320	9,914,800
Notes in circulation	50,255,280	50,206,280	50,385,600	42,233,560
Treasury advances, coupon account	364,080	329,880	313,960	437,400
Treasury balances	2,169,200	1,971,680	1,526,080	3,524,280

LONDON COURSE OF EXCHANGE.

Place.	Usance.	March 22.	March 24.	March 29.	March 31.
Amsterdam and Rotterdam	short	12·2¼	12·2¼	12·2½	12·2½
Do. do.	3 months	12·4⅜	12·4⅜	12·4½	12·4½
Antwerp and Brussels	3 months	25·50	25·48¾	25·52½	25·51¼
Hamburg	3 months	20·65	20·65	20·68	20·68
Berlin and German B. Places	3 months	20·66	20·66	20·68	20·68
Paris	cheques	25·30	25·31¼	25·33¾	25·33¾
Do.	3 months	25·45	25·45	25·48¾	25·47½
Marseilles	3 months	25·45	25·47½	25·48¾	25·48¾
Switzerland	3 months	25·65	25·67½	25·67½	25·67½
Austria	3 months	12·16¼	12·16¼	12·18¾	12·16¼
St. Petersburg	3 months	25	25	25	25
Moscow	3 months	24 15/16	24 15/16	24 15/16	24 15/16
Italian Bank Places	3 months	27·02½	27·00	27·15	27·10
New York	60 days	49 1/16	49 1/16	49 1/16	49 1/16
Madrid and Spanish B. P.	3 months	33¾	33⅜	32 15/16	33 1/16
Lisbon	3 months	34 3/16	34 1/16	34¼	34¼
Oporto	3 months	34 3/16	34 1/16	34¼	34¼
Copenhagen	3 months	18·41	18·41	18·41	18·41
Christiania	3 months	18·42	18·42	18·42	18·42
Stockholm	3 months	18·42	18·42	18·42	18·42

OPEN MARKET DISCOUNT.

	Per cent.
Thirty and sixty day remitted bills	2⅞—3
Three months "	2⅞—3
Four months "	2⅞
Six months "	2¾—2⅞
Three months fine inland bills	3
Four months "	3
Six months "	3

BANK AND DEPOSIT RATES.

	Per cent.
Bank of England minimum discount rate	3
" " short loan rates	3
Banker's rate on deposits	1½
Bill brokers' deposit rate (call)	2
" 7 and 14 days' notice	2¼
Current rates for 7 day loans	2½—2¾
" " for call loans	2¾

Stock Market Notes and Comments.

We have had a very worrying week indeed upon the Stock Exchange, and the anxiety prevailing there is quite as great as that which has oppressed the money market. It is not that there is anything particularly wrong inside the Stock Exchange itself; weak accounts there are in plenty within it, but, so far as has yet been revealed, no excessive masses of speculation exist. On the contrary, the members have for some time been reducing their commitments, paying off loans, and generally refraining from entering upon business involving great risks. Outside the House, however, there are abundant sources of trouble, and the worry these cause only find their counterpart within it—the most sensitive business organisation which exists. Again and again attention has been drawn in these columns to the practice of banks in lending to private customers to excessive amounts in the aggregate on a mere margin of value, amounting to 5 per cent. or 10 per cent. more than the market price of securities pawned with them. This margin business is already being put to the test by the slight increase in the current value of loanable capital, and some banks at least have begun to try to retrieve their position by forcing their customers to realise. A great fountain of really unplaced stocks is thus being opened up, which may well cause the Stock Exchange much perturbation of mind. We see the effects of the process in the steady decline which goes on in Colonial securities and in the best secured class of our own railways.

The class of people, who may be described as quasi-investors, holding these stocks for the sake of the income they get from them over and above the interest they pay to their bankers for the money advanced, are day by day beholding the little capital they furnish to provide these margins disappearing. Also they now have to pay more for money in many instances than the investment yields to them, and these two influences together are compelling realisations. Against these the volume of new buying is comparatively small, so that the Stock Exchange stands in danger of having quantities of stock "dumped" upon it, for which there is no immediate demand. To protect itself against such a troublesome inflow of securities, for the time being unmarketable, its members naturally quote prices lower and lower even when no business of any moment is doing. These tactics, however, are only effective up to a point. Should money go higher, and loans on securities command 5 per cent., then the resulting fall in prices, induced by the jobbers to try and protect themselves, must have the effect of increasing the rush of sellers.

This is one aspect of Stock Exchange business. Another is the effect of the syndicating system, which has extended to quite unprecedented dimensions during the long years of abnormally cheap money. All round the City groups of adventurous speculators have joined in underwriting all descriptions of stocks, shares of industrial companies, and such like. No outsider can have the slightest idea of the strength of the force originating in a mere 3 per cent. bank rate, which is already driving out the individual speculative investor and pressing upon the *syndicataires* who hold shares by the ten thousand, Colonial loans by the hundred thousand, and industrial debentures in excessive amounts, the public has never had time, or means, to relieve them of. No other cause of depression appears to exist outside the Stock Exchange, or in, to account for the anxieties prevailing there, yet we do not remember a time, not even the time preceding the collapse of speculation in November 1890, when doubt, perplexity, and anxiety held greater sway over the minds of brokers and jobbers.

In such circumstances it would be unwise to counsel the public to buy with any freedom securities in any department, not even the best securities. We believe the day is not distant when prices will be still more favourable to them than they are at present. The rumours of wars, the agitation about Chinese affairs, about Cuban affairs, about West Africa, and such like—to which we shall presently have to add tremors about Thessaly, and the Turkish dominions generally—must cause frequent sharp fluctuations in prices, quite irrespective of the general pressure downwards coming from the sources just indicated; and when quotations are very low in consequence of some wave of fear there is a strong temptation to buy. Probably, too, buying would pay at such moments, because every violent fall is followed by an nearly equally violent rebound. Still, this kind of business is only for the speculator on the spot. Those at a distance ought not to enter into it; those who have other business to attend to should fly from it; and the investor, even the speculative investor, could find no sure profit in it, one account with another. We say this because the trend of prices, as we may call it, is, on the average, downwards, and the best that a man could hope for as the result of any purchases made on flat markets is a snatch profit. The risk, therefore, of securing even this much is too great to be encountered by prudent folk, because no one could be sure that upon the top of the political scare of to-day a still worse scare to-morrow may not come. To-day it is "peace" in the newspapers between Spain and the United States, to-morrow it may be war. There is no knowing from moment to moment when the next alarm will be sprung upon the market. Never in modern days did politics all over the world seeth and ferment as they are now doing. Everyone, therefore, who is in any way over-committed in public securities ought to imitate the policy of the shrewd members of the Stock Exchange, and relieve himself of whatever appears likely to cause anxiety or embarrassment while yet there is time. But, equally emphatically, we insist that this is not a time for the investment holder of good securities of any kind to sell.

Within the last day or two it will have been noted that some upward movements have taken place in South African and Western Australian mining and mine finance shares. We are glad to see this movement, and hope it will continue long enough to enable those of the public—and their number is multitude—who have been sitting upon these shares to sell at better advantage than they have lately been able to do. We can assure such that it is not through buying of individuals among the public that this advance is being brought about. It is all the product of "inside" influences, as the market phrase goes. Nobody should buy on any such "lead"; the wise policy is to sell and be done with every share of the kind whose price appears at all inflated. Holders may do this without any fear as to the ultimate result; even if they are disposed to invest again in such shares they may be quite sure that by waiting they will have opportunities of doing so far more advantageous than any they ever saw in the days of inflation.

The Week's Stock Markets.

There was no increase in activity on the Stock Exchange until the week was far advanced, little or no interest being taken by the outside public, and the bad weather and the partial interruption of telegraphic communication all tended to restrict business. The account which began on Monday was easily arranged, but it was a pleasant surprise to all concerned to find that no failures were announced, in spite of the heavy differences that had to be met. With the account out of the way and more satisfactory news from abroad, prices have rallied in a surprising manner, and the bear squeeze which has been going on for the last day or two in Wall-street has sent prices of United States shares up with a run, and this has spread to all departments.

Highest and Lowest this Year.	Last Carrying over Price.	BRITISH FUNDS, &c.	Closing Price.	Rise or Fall.
113⅛ 110⅞	—	Consols 2¾ p.c. (Money)...	111⅛	−⅛
113 1/16 111⅛	111¼	Do. Account (May 5)	111¼	−¼
106¼ 104⅛	104¾	2½ p.c. Stock red. 1905 ...	104⅜	−⅜
363 345	—	Bank of England Stock...	347½	—
117 112⅝	113	India 3½ p.c. Stk. red. 1931	113¼	−¼
109½ 105	105¼	Do. 3 p.c. Stk. red. 1948	105½	−¼
96⅝ 92	92½	Do. 2½ p.c. Stk. red. 1926	93	—

Consols have exhibited a drooping tendency, the latest development of the Chinese question and the news that the British fleet was preparing for a move, sending the price down to 110⅞, being the lowest of the year. The weakness was also partly due to the harder tendency of the money market, and the heavy gold withdrawals for the United States. A slight recovery from the lower level has taken place just at the last, and the upward movement was helped by the moderate contango rate of 2½ to 3, which, considering the value of money just now, was not excessive. Indian and Colonial Government issues are weaker, and Home Corporation stocks mark declines in many cases.

In the Home Railway market a general decline in prices occurred during the concluding days of last week, and there was very little business, and absolutely nothing in the shape of outside support. The present week also started with a still further shrinkage, but a recovery set in when the account disclosed a scarcity of stock, and prices quickly rose in sympathy with the improvements n all other departments, and the earlier losses were soon more than wiped out. Continuation rates were light at the settlement, and eased off still more before the conclusion of the account. Great Eastern stock was again very scarce, and ½ to ¼ "back" was quoted; North-Western went off to "even" after being ¼ contango, and the rate on Great Western, Midland, and North-Eastern ranged from ⅛ to ¼. Brighton "A" finished about ¼ backwardation after opening at quite ⅜ contango, and the price rose sharply. Considering the bad weather last week the traffic returns were satisfactory, most of them comparing with big "takes" last year. Underground stocks have been a dull market, the miserable weather causing a heavy falling off in the Boat Race traffic last Saturday.

Highest and Lowest this Year.	Last Carrying over Price.	HOME RAILWAYS.	Closing Price.	Rise or Fall.
186 172½	173¼	Brighton Def.	175½	+1⅛
59¼ 55½	56¼	Caledonian Def.	56⅝x.d.	+1
20⅜ 18⅝	19¼	Chatham Ordinary	19⅛	−⅛
77¼ 66	69	Great Central Pref.	69	—
24⅝ 21⅞	21¾	Do. Def.	22¼	+¼
124½ 119⅝	120½	Great Eastern	121⅜	+¼
61½ 51¼	52	Great Northern Def.	53¼	+½
179⅛ 170⅞	171¼	Great Western	172¾	+⅜
51¾ 45¼	48	Hull and Barnsley	48¼	−½
149¼ 146¼	146½	Lanc. and Yorkshire	147	—
136¼ 127¼	129	Metropolitan	129	—
31 26¾	27½	Metropolitan District	27¾	−⅛
88¾ 83¼	84	Midland Pref.	84½	+⅛
95⅝ 84⅞	85¼	Do. Def.	87	+1
93¼ 89	90	North British Pref.	89¼x.d.	—
47½ 42⅜	42¾	Do. Def.	43⅜	+⅞
181½ 172¾	173¼	North Eastern	174¼	—
205½ 197¾	198¼	North Western	199¼	+¼
117⅛ 107	107¼	South Eastern Def.	109¼	+⅝
98¾ 91	91	South Western Def.	92	+½

The market for United States Railroad shares had one short interval of firmness prior to the collapse on Saturday last, the temporary hardening up being due to the statement made by M. Hanotaux regarding the relations between France and England. Heavy sales then became the order of the day, and rumours of war were thick in the air; but there was quite a bear scare in Wall-street on Monday, followed by a rush to cover outstanding short contracts, on the report that Spain was prepared to accept President McKinley's plan of intervention as regards Cuban affairs. The big advance in Wall-street was followed on this side, and a good deal of realising on the part of home operators did not do much towards checking the upward move. The rally did not take place until after the making-up prices had been fixed, so that some tolerably heavy differences were disclosed. Money was not much wanted, and the account proved to be a very light one. Canadian Pacific shares, after a temporary decline, leave off the week with a substantial gain, although the February statement was a poor one, exhibiting only a small net increase; but it is again asserted that the rate war is all but over, and on the strength of this, the price rose several points. Grand Trunk stocks also followed more or less on the same lines, and the latest prices are the best of the week, and higher than those ruling when we last wrote.

Highest and Lowest this Year.	Last Carrying over Price.	CANADIAN AND U.S. RAILWAYS.	Closing Prices.	Rise or Fall.
14 1/16 10⅞	11¼	Atchison Shares	12	+⅝
34 23¾	24½	Do. Pref.	27⅛	+2⅛
15⅝ 11⅛	11½	Central Pacific	12⅝	+¾
99¾ 88⅝	90¼	Chic. Mil. & St. Paul	94½x.d.	+7
14¼ 10⅞	11¼	Denver Shares	11½	+¼
54¼ 42½	43	Do. Prefd.	46	+2⅛
16⅝ 12⅛	12¼	Erie Shares	13¼	+⅝
44⅞ 32	33	Do. Prefd.	36	+1⅝
62½ 46⅛	47½	Louisville & Nashville ...	52⅞	+4⅞
14½ 10½	11	Missouri & Texas	12	+1
122¾ 108⅛	110½	New York Central	115¾xd	+4¼
57¼ 43	44¾	Norfolk & West. Prefd.	48¼	+3⅜
70⅛ 59¼	60½	Northern Pacific Prefd.	65⅛	+4⅝
19½ 13¾	14	Ontario Shares	15⅛	+⅛
62⅛ 57¼	57¾	Pennsylvania	59¼	+1
12½ 8	8⅛	Reading Shares	8⅛	+⅛
34¼ 24½	25¼	Southern Prefd.	27¾	+2
37⅛ 19⅜*	17*	Union Pacific	21⅛*	+3⅞
20¼ 14½	15	Wabash Prefd.	16¼	+1¼
30¼ 22	22½	Do. Income Debs.	24¾	+1¼
92¾ 81⅝	82¾	Canadian Pacific	84⅛	+1
78⅛ 69⅞	72	Grand Trunk Guar.	74½	+1¼
69⅛ 57⅛	64½	Do. 1st Pref.	67	+1⅜
50⅛ 37¼	44¾	Do. 2nd Pref.	48	+2⅝
25⅛ 19¼	21¼	Do. 3rd Pref.	22⅞	+1⅛
105¾ 101½	103	Do. 4 p.c. Deb.	102⅜xd	+1⅜

* E.x. $7½ new Pfd. stock.

Needless to say the Foreign market has been very unsettled, the principal amount of interest again being centred in Spanish "Fours," which were at one time forced down to 48½, and dragging the whole list with them. Alarmist reports were also industriously circulated regarding the position in the Far East, while the announcement that China had acceded to Russia's demands helped to further depress prices. Saturday witnessed a panic among holders of Spanish 4 per cent. on the Paris Bourse, a *canard* to the effect that Spain had declared war against the United States being the principal reason for the fright. A calmer feeling prevailed on all the Continental bourses on Tuesday, and prices, once on the up-grade, soon boomed away merrily, while the news that Spain was ready to meet the United States Government in the matter of Cuba caused a big jump in Spanish stock, more than sufficient to wipe out the previous loss. Chinese issues advanced on influential buying, and the new loan is now only about 1 discount. Greek bonds have maintained their recent advance, and the news that the indemnity loan convention has been signed by the ambassadors of the leading Powers has tended still more to harden the prices of the existing loans. The position of affairs between the Argentine Republic and Chile with regard to the boundary question has once more threatened to assume a serious aspect, and rumours were current that a new Argentine loan was on the *tapis*. The general improvement, however, has since extended to South American descriptions, and with the exception of Brazilian bonds, which have again been under a cloud owing to a further decline in the Rio exchange, there is a more healthy look about the whole list. Continuation rates in this market generally ruled round about 4 per cent., that being the charge on Spanish, while Uruguay 3½ per cent. were carried over at 3 per cent., and Chilian at about 5 per cent. The making-up price of Spanish 4 per cent. was 8½ lower than at the last account.

Highest and Lowest this Year.	Last Carrying over Price.	FOREIGN BONDS.	Closing Price.	Rise or Fall.
94½ 86½	86½	Argentine 5 p.c. 1886......	89¼	+1¼
92⅜ 85¾	86	Do. 6 p.c. Funding	89¼	+1⅛
76¾ 67⅛	68	Do. 5 p.c. B. Ay. Water	70	+ ¼
61⅜ 51⅞	53	Brazilian 4 p.c. 1889	53¼	−1¼
69⅝ 56	56½	Do. 5 p.c. 1895	55½	−2½
65 52½	53	Do. 5 p.c. West Minas Ry..................	53½	−1
108¾ 106¼	107¾	Egyptian 4 p.c. Unified...	108	—
104¾ 102	104¼	Do. 3½ p.c. Pref. ...	104¼	—
103 102	102½	French 3 p.c. Rente	102½	—
44⅝ 34½	43½	Greek 4 p.c. Monopoly...	44⅝	+1⅜
93 9/16 91¾	91½	Italian 5 p.c. Rente	92½	+ ¼
100 95¾	98	Mexican 6 p.c. 1888	98¾	+ ½
20⅞ 19	19¼	Portuguese 1 p.c.	19½	+ ⅛
62¼ 48½	49	Spanish 4 p.c.	53	− ½
45⅛ 41	41	Turkish 1 p.c. "B"	43	+ ¾
26 7/16 23½	23¾	Do. 1 p.c. "C"	24½	+ ⅜
22 7/16 20¾	20¾	Do. 1 p.c. "D"	21 7/16	+ ¼
46⅝ 40	45	Uruguay 3½ p.c. Bonds...	45¾	—

Foreign railway emissions close rather above the worst, the serious decline which took place at the beginning of the week having brought out a few buyers, who were further encouraged by the very satisfactory traffics. The proposal of the Buenos Ayres Great Southern directors to absorb the Ensenada Company was also responsible for some of the later buying of the stocks of these companies.

Highest and Lowest this Year.	Last Carrying over Price.	FOREIGN RAILWAYS.	Closing Price.	Rise or Fall.
100 99⅛	99½	Argentine Gt. West. 5 p.c. Pref. Stock..................	100	—
158¼ 144	145	B. Ay. Gt. Southern Ord..	150	—
78½ 68	68½	B. Ay. and Rosario Ord...	71½	+1
12¼ 10⅜	10⅞	B. Ay. Western Ord.......	10⅜x.d.	—
87¼ 74	74½	Central Argentine Ord....	78½	+ ½
92 83	83½	Cordoba and Rosario 6 p.c. Deb.	84	—
95½ 86½	87½	Cord. Cent. 4 p.c. Deb. (Cent. Nth. Sec.)	87½	−1
61⅜ 47	46½	Do. Income Deb. Stk. ...	47½	−1
25¼ 18	19	Mexican Ord. Stk.	19¾	+ ¼
83½ 72	75	Do. 8 p.c. 1st Pref.........	70½	+ ½

The Miscellaneous Market has again been invaded by dealers from the South African section, but there has not been very much business to encourage the new contingent. A sharp recovery is apparent in Welsbach Gas issues, on various glowing reports about new patents, &c. Birmingham Vinegar ordinary again marks an advance, and rises have also taken place in New Explosives, J. and P. Coats, and several electric lighting concerns. On the other side, a further decline has occurred in Tea companies, and among other industrial ventures, Pryce Jones debentures, Savoy Hotel, and Spiers & Pond shares all show losses. Southwark and Vauxhall Water "D" shares have fallen 8. At the Allsopp meeting, the proposals of the directors for increasing the capital, after being rejected by the shareholders, were declared carried by a majority of proxies, and a little selling by holders has caused a slight set-back in the ordinary stock. Cycle companies' shares have been again thrown on the market, and buyers are still few and far between. A satisfactory dividend was responsible for a rise of 1½ in Chartered Bank of India, but P. & O. deferred fell 2 on the loss of the *China*. The premium on Lipton ordinary has slipped back to ⅞ on sales by allottees.

Markets on the whole close with rather a dull tendency, due, more than anything else, to a break in Spanish 4 per cent. on heavy selling orders from Paris. The sales, apparently, were made more on financial than political grounds, but they had the effect of depressing prices in other departments, more particularly that for United States Railroad shares. Spanish 4 per cent. left off finally at about last week's level, but Brazilian bonds marked a serious loss. Home Railway stocks closed fairly steady, at rather below the best points of the week, but still considerably higher than last Thursday. United States Railroad shares present an unbroken list of rises, headed by Milwaukee, which is $7 up, but some heavy sales of Grand Trunk issues, just at the last, rather spoiled the look of the week's previous sharp advance. Consols closed firm, and almost at the best points, and there has also been a further recovery in Foreign Railway stocks.

MINING AND FINANCE COMPANIES.

The South African market has been comparatively steady, but business continues on the smallest possible scale, and Paris operators have entirely neglected "Kaffirs" of late. Prices hardened a little more on a rumour which was circulated on Wednesday that President Kruger was dead, and the latest quotations are the best of the week. Rates of continuation were just the same as last time, and the account was a very small one. In Western Australian ventures Golden Horse Shoe and Hannan's Brown Hill have met with support, and the tone on the whole has been steady to firm. Indian shares remain quiet at about last week's level, and copper securities close firm after being a rather dull market.

MINING RETURNS.

ALASKA TREADWELL.—March return.—Bullion shipment, $33,270. Ore milled 21,493 tons. Sulphurets treated, 348 tons. Bullion from sulphurets, $12,520.

WELD-HERCULES.—Crushed 191 tons, producing 101 oz. gold; tailings, 2 dwt.

GOLCONDA.—605 tons crushed, yielding 449 oz; tailings, 2 dwt.

OTTO'S KOPJE.—7,968 loads washed during week ended March 24; 196 carats of diamonds won, including one stone of 11½ carats.

HIGHLAND CHIEF.—Crushed, 270 tons; yield of retorted gold, 88 oz. 135 ton Dorothy shaft, 62 oz.

MYALL'S UNITED.—Crushed 2,000 tons for a yield of 260 oz. gold. 1,200 tons tailings treated by cyanide, yield 437 oz. gold.

LAKE GEORGE.—During January 2,633 tons crude ore crushed. Production of concentrated matte was 149 tons, containing 260 oz. gold 11,366 oz. silver, and 4,843 units of copper.

MENZIES ALPHA LEASES.—46 tons crushed, yielding 292 oz.

BRITISH BROKEN HILL PROPRIETARY.—Returns for fortnight ended March 24, 3,564 tons; crude ore produced 543 tons concentrates which contain 349 tons lead and 14,378 oz. silver.

ALADDIN'S LAMP.—Four weeks' return:—372 tons of ore crushed, yielding 430 oz., and one ton of rich crude ore has been shipped, containing 30 oz.

AUSTRALIAN CHAMPION REEF.—Crushed, 180 tons, yielding 195 oz.

NEW QUEEN.—1,270 ft. formation, crushed, 335 tons, yielding 202 oz. (gold).

ST. JOHN DEL REY.—Gold produce March 12 to 21, £5,812; yield per ton, 73 of an oz. troy.

SULPHIDE CORPORATION.—Have shipped India 132 tons of bullion, containing 20,900 oz. silver; Warrigal, 110 tons, containing 9,400 oz.

VICTORIA (CHARTERS TOWERS).—300 tons crushed, yielded 417 oz. gold.

LABUAN AND BORNEO.—For week ended March 27.—Output.—First quality, 850 tons; second quality, 125 tons. Sold locally.—First quality, 700 tons; second quality, 25 tons.

GREAT BOULDER PROPRIETARY.—For fortnight ended March 28: 1432 tons crushed, yielded 3,161 oz.

QUEENSLAND MENZIES.—Crushed 90 tons for 312 oz.

QUEEN CROSS REEF.—Partial clean up of 270 tons for 704 oz. gold.

Dividends Announced.

MISCELLANEOUS.

HAURAKI GOLD MINING COMPANY, LIMITED.—6d. per share has been declared.

J. & P. COATS, LIMITED.—Interim dividend at the rate of 20s. per share, being the same as that a year ago.

ZEEHAN-MONTANA MINE, LIMITED.—Further interim dividend of 9d. per share.

EAST LONDON WATERWORKS COMPANY.—Dividends at the rate of 8 per cent. per annum for the past half-year.

DIMBULA VALLEY (CEYLON) TEA COMPANY, LIMITED.—Final dividend of 3 per cent. on the preference shares for the year ending March 31.

SPIERS & POND, LIMITED.—4s. per share, making 12s. per share paid on account of the dividend for the year ended March 31.

NEW JAGERSFONTEIN MINING AND EXPLORATION, LIMITED.—Dividend of 6 per cent. (equal to 6s. per share) for the half-year ending March 31.

BROKEN HILL PROPRIETARY, LIMITED.—1s. 6d. per share for the quarter ending April.

EVERED & CO., LIMITED.—Dividend at the rate of 7½ per cent. per annum for the past half-year, making, with the interim dividend, 7½ per cent. for the year, and a bonus of 2½ per cent.

BRILLIANT GOLD MINING COMPANY, LIMITED.—6d. per share.

MASON & BARRY, LIMITED.—4s. per share for the year ended December 31, 1897.

CALLARD, STEWART, & WATT, LIMITED.—Interim dividend at the rate of 5½ per cent. per annum on the preference shares.

WACKRILL & CO.—5 per cent. per annum on the ordinary and preference shares.

DIRECT UNITED STATES CABLE COMPANY, LIMITED.—Interim dividend of 3s. per share for the quarter ending March 31.

CARLISLE CONSOLIDATED GOLD MINES, LIMITED.—First quarterly dividend at the rate of 2½ per cent. per annum.

GLOBE TELEGRAPH AND TRUST COMPANY, LIMITED.—Interim dividend of 2s. 6d. per share on the ordinary shares.

MOUNT MORGAN GOLD MINING COMPANY, LIMITED.—6d. a share for the month of March.

HODGSON'S KINGSTON BREWERY COMPANY.—Interim dividend at the rate of 3s. 6d. per share, for the six months ended March 31, 1898.

RIO TINTO COMPANY.—Dividend announced of £1 per share, making a total distribution of £2 for the year. The sum of £40,000 is placed to reserve fund, and £21,700 carried forward.

THARSIS SULPHUR AND COPPER.—Dividend for past half-year announced at 25 per cent. (equal to 10s. per share), writing off £48,047 and carrying forward £14,165. Last year the dividend was 17½ per cent., with £38,395 written off, and £15,708 carried forward.

COLUMBIAN HYDRAULIC MINING COMPANY, LIMITED.—Dividend of 6d. per share.

QUEENSLAND—MENZIES' GOLD.—Dividend of 6d per share.

CHAMPION REEF GOLD MINING COMPANY OF INDIA.—Interim dividend of 3s. 6d. per share.

JUBILEE GOLD COMPANY, LIMITED.—5s. per share.

LOUISE & CO.—Further dividend of 3½ per cent. on the ordinary shares, making, with dividend paid in September last, 7 per cent. for the year ended February 22. £1,368 carried forward.

NORTH GERMAN LLOYD COMPANY announce 5 per cent. for the past year.

A. & F. PEARS, LIMITED.—Interim dividend for the six months ended December 31, on the ordinary shares at the rate of 8 per cent. per annum.

BAYLISS, THOMAS & CO., LIMITED.—Interim dividend at the rate of 10 per cent per annum for the half-year ended March 31.

BREWERIES.

BRANDON'S, PUTNEY, LIMITED.—Dividend on the ordinary shares at the rate of 10 per cent. per annum for the six months ended December 31, making, with the interim already paid, 7½ per cent. for 1897.

RAILWAYS.

OTTOMAN RAILWAY FROM SMYRNA TO AIDAN.—A dividend of 22s. per share, payable on the 6th inst.

WESTERN OF FRANCE COMPANY.—The dividend for 1897 is at the rate of £7 14s. per cent. per annum as in 1896.

TOURNAY TO JURBISE.—Dividend for the second half of 1897 has been fixed at 9s. 7d. per share on the dividend share, 6s. per share on the preference share, and £24 19s. 11½d. per share on the Jouissance shares.

CENTRAL ARGENTINE RAILWAY.—The directors recommend payment of a balance dividend of 1 per cent. for the year 1897 on the paid-up capital of the company, making, with the interim dividend, a total dividend of 1¾ per cent. for the year.

BANKS.

TARAPACA AND LONDON.—Interim dividend of 2s. 6d. per share, being at the rate of 5 per cent. per annum.

CHARTERED OF INDIA, AUSTRALIA, AND CHINA.—Dividend to be declared for the past half-year at the rate of 10 per cent. per annum, making, with the interim dividend, 9 per cent. for the year; £75,000 to be added to reserve, £5,000 to the officers' superannuation fund and £12,403 carried forward.

On and after April 1 the London Bank of Australia, Limited, 2, Old Broad-street, will pay the coupons then due of the City of Newcastle, New South Wales, five and four per cent. debentures.

Messrs. Glyn, Mills, Currie & Co. notify that they are prepared to pay the drawn bonds and coupons of the Mexican five per cent. internal redeemable debt, due April 1 next at the exchange of 22½d. per dollar.

The Comptoir National d'Escompte de Paris, 52, Threadneedle-street, E.C., has been instructed to receive for payment coupons due April 1, 1898, on the Imperial Russian Government Three per Cent. Gold Loan, 1894 (Series 2).

Prices of Mine and Mining Finance Companies' Shares.

Shares £1 each, except where otherwise stated.

AUSTRALIAN.

Making-Up Price, Mar. 26.	Name.	Closing Price.	Rise or Fall.	Making-Up Price, Mar. 26.	Name.	Closing Price.	Rise or Fall.
1⅞	Aladdin	1⅞		7¼	Hannan's Brownhill	7 11/16	+ 1/16
3 5/16	Associated	3⅜	+ 1/16	⅞	Hannan's Oroya	¾	
⅜	Do. Southern	⅜		15/	Do. Proprietary	15/6	− /6
13/9	Brilliant, £2	14/		¾	Do. Star	¾	
2⅛	Do. St. George's	2⅛	− ⅛	4 15/16	Ivanhoe, New	5⅛	
11/6	British Broken Hill	11/3	− /9	½	Kalgurli Mt. & Iron King, 18/	¾	− ⅛
2 3/16	Broken Hill Proprietary	2 1/16	− ⅛	4 15/16	Kalgurli	5 3/16	+ 3/16
—	Do. Block 10	3½		2 5/16	Lady Shenton	2 5/16	+ ⅛
1 5/16	Brownhill Extended	1¼	− 1/16	8¾	Lake View Cons.	9⅝	+ ⅞
1 5/16	Burbank's Birthday	1 5/16		⅞	Do. Extended	13/16	− 1/16
¾	Central Boulder	¾		1	Do. South	1 1/16	
5/6	Chaffers, 4/	5/6		1¼	London & Globe Finance	1¼	+ 3/16
¼	Colonial Finance, 15/	¼ pm		¾	London & W.A. Exploration	¾	
—	Crœsus S. United	¾	− ⅛	11/16	Do. Investment	11/16	
15/	Day Dawn Block	15/		⅞	Mainland Consols	5/16	
1	E. Murchison	1		¾	North Boulder, 10/	¾	
⅝	Gold Estates	⅝		1 5/16	North Kalgurli	1⅜	
4/3	Golden Arrow 19/	4/		4¾	Northern Territories	4⅝	− 1/16
7 5/16	Golden Horseshoe	7 5/16	+ ⅛	2¾	Peak Hill	2 5/16	− 1/16
⅞	Golden Link	1	+ 1/16	2	South Kalgurli	2 1/16	− ⅛
1	Great Boulder, 2/	20/6x	+ /6	1 11/16	W. A. Goldfields	1 11/16	− 1/16
1 5/16	Do. Main Reef, 10/	1 5/16	+ 1/16	2 5/16	W. A. Joint Stock	2 3/16	− 1/16
2⅞	Do. Perseverance	3	+ ⅛	1 1/16	W. A. Market Trust	15/16x	− 1/16
15/16	Do. South	1	+ 1/16	1⅛	W. A. Loan & General Fin.	1 1/16	− 1/16
2	Hainault	2 1/16		¾	White Feather	5/16	
¾	Hampton Plains	¾					

SOUTH AFRICAN.

Making-Up Price, Mar. 26.	Name.	Closing Price.	Rise or Fall.	Making-Up Price, Mar. 26.	Name.	Closing Price.	Rise or Fall.
4 15/16	Angelo	5⅛	+ ⅛	2/3	Lisbon-Berlyn	2/6	+ /3
1¼	Aurora West	1		2¼	May Consolidated	2¼	
¾	Bantjes	13/16		4⅝	Meyer and Charlton	4⅝	
9/6	Barrett, 10/	10/		3 5/16	Modderfontein	3 7/16	+ 1/16
3¼	Bonanza	3 5/16	+ 1/16	1	New Bultfontein	1	
¾	Buffelsdoorn	8/9	+ /6	3 5/16	New Primrose	3⅜	+ ⅛
5¼	City and Suburban, £4	5⅜	+ ⅛	1⅜	Nigel	1⅜	
9 5/16	Comet (New)	9⅜	+ 1/16	—	Nigel Deep	1 1/16	− 1/16
4 5/16	Con. Deep Level	4⅜	+ 1/16	¾	North Randfontein	¾	
11	Crown Deep	11½		4¾	Nourse Deep	5¼	+ ⅜
12	Crown Reef	12⅛	+ ⅛	1 7/16	Porges-Randfontein	1⅜	+ 1/16
26½	De Beers, £5	26¾	+ 1/16	27 11/16	Rand Mines	28¼	+ 1/16
3⅜	Driefontein	3½	+ 1/16	1⅝	Randfontein	1 5/16	+ 1/16
5¼	Durban Roodepoort	5⅜	+ ⅛	2	Rietfontein	2 1/16	
3 5/16	Do. Deep	3⅛	− ⅛	9¼	Robinson Deep	9⅝	+ ⅜
3 13/16	East Rand	4 3/16	+ ⅜	8	Do. Gold, £5	8	
24¼	Ferreira	23½x		15/16	Do. Randfontein	15/16	
6¼	Geldenhuis Deep	6¼x		1⅝	Roodepoort Central Deep	1⅝	
4⅜	Do. Estate	4⅜	+ 1/16	6	Rose Deep	6⅛	+ ⅛
⅞	George Goch	⅞	+ 1/16	2⅜	Salisbury	2¼	
2	Ginsberg	2⅛	+ ⅛	1 5/16	Sheba	1 5/16	
1 15/16	Glencairn	2	+ 1/16	2⅝	Simmer and Jack, £5	3	
7 15/16	Goldfields Deep	8⅜	+ 5/16	3	Transvaal Gold	3⅛	+ ⅛
8¾	Griqualand West	8½	− ⅛	3	Treasury	3	
8¼	Henry Nourse	8¼x		3 11/16	United Roodepoort	3¾x	+ ⅛
7 5/16	Heriot	7⅝	+ ⅛	1 5/16	Van Ryn	1⅜	+ 1/16
7⅝	Jagersfontein	7⅝		5¼	Village Main Reef	5⅜	+ ⅛
7⅞	Jubilee	8	+ ⅜	1¼	Vogelstruis	1⅜	
4⅝	Jumpers	4⅝		¾	Do. Deep	13/16	+ ⅛
2 5/16	Kleinfontein	2 5/16	+ 1/16	8¼	Wemmer	9⅛	+ ⅜
3 5/16	Knight's	3⅜	+ ⅛	¾	West Rand	¾	
2 5/16	Lancaster	2 5/16	+ 1/16	5¼	Wolhuter, £4	5⅜	+ ⅛
3⅜	Langlaagte Estate	3 5/16	+ 1/16	2 5/16	Worcester	2⅜	

LAND EXPLORATION AND RHODESIAN.

Making-Up Price, Mar. 26.	Name.	Closing Price.	Rise or Fall.	Making-Up Price, Mar. 26.	Name.	Closing Price.	Rise or Fall.
2¼	Anglo-French Ex.	2⅜	+ ⅛	5/16	Mashonaland Central	5/16	+ 1/16
1 11/16	Barnato Consolidated	1 13/16	+ 1/16	6⅛	Matabele Gold Reefs	6⅜	+ ⅛
⅝	Bechuanaland Ex.	⅝		2	Mozambique	2 1/16	
2 1/16	Chartered B.S.A.	2⅛	+ 1/16	1⅜	New African	1 7/16	+ ⅛
⅝	Clark's Cons.	9/16		11/16	Oceana Consolidated	⅝	
⅞	Colenbrander	⅞		1⅛	Rhodesia, Ltd.	1 3/16	+ 1/16
3 11/16	Cons. Goldfields	4⅛	+ 5/16	4	Do. Exploration	4	
1	Do. Pref.	20/		1	Do. Goldfields	1	+ 1/16
1 11/16	Exploration	1 11/16		3⅞	S. A. Gold Trust	4	+ ⅛
2⅜	Geelong	2 7/16	+ ⅛	¾	Tati Concessions	15/16	+ 1/16
11/16	Henderson's Est.	11/16		⅝	Transvaal Development	⅝	+ ⅛
1 5/16	Johannesburg Con. In.	1⅜	+ 1/16	½	United Rhodesia	½	
1	Do. Water	1		1 1/16	Willoughby	1 1/16	
1 5/16	Mashonaland Agency	1 5/16		¾	Zambesia Explor.	¾	

MISCELLANEOUS.

Making-Up Price, Mar. 26.	Name.	Closing Price.	Rise or Fall.	Making-Up Price, Mar. 26.	Name.	Closing Price.	Rise or Fall.
1½	Alamillos, £2	1⅜	− ⅛	13/6	Mysore Goldfields	12/	− 1/
4⅞	Anaconda, $25	5¼	+ 1/16	7/6	Do. Reefs, 17/	6/6	− 1/
9/6	Balaghât, 18/	9/	− 1/	14/6	Do. West	14/	− /6
4⅝	Cape Copper, £2	4½	− 1/16	11/	Do. Wynaad	11/6	
4 13/16	Champion Reef, 10s.	5	+ 1/16	2 5/16	Namaqua, £2	2¼	− 1/16
2¼	Copiapo, £2	2 3/16	− 1/16	3 5/16	Nundydroog	3⅜	
3 5/16	Coromandel	3 5/16		3 5/16	Ooregum	3⅜	+ 1/16
2 5/16	Frontino & Bolivia	2 5/16x		3⅜	Do. Pref.	3 7/16	+ 1/16
1¼	Hall Mines	1 3/16	− 1/16	28	Rio Tinto Def., £5	28 11/16	− 1/16
2⅞	Libiola, £5	2⅞		6⅛	Do. Pref. £5	6⅛	
7⅞	Linares, £3	8⅛		17/6	St. John del Rey	17/x	
3⅞	Mason & Barry, £3	3 15/16	+ ⅛	13/9	Taitipu	13/16	−
5	Mountain Copper, £5	5 5/16		7⅞	Tharsis, £2	7 5/16	
13½	Mount Lyell, £3	13⅝	+ ⅛	2⅞	Tolima "A," £5	3	
2⅞	Mount Lyell, North	3	+ ⅛	4½	Waihi	4 5/16	
14/	Mount Lyell, South	11/16		1⅝	Waitekauri	1 11/16	+ 1/16
4½	Mount Morgan, 17s. 6d.	4 5/16		1 5/16	Woodstock (N.Z.)	1 5/16	
5⅜	Mysore, 10s.	5⅜					

Mr. Francis Villiers Hornby has been appointed secretary of the Union Bank of London, Limited, in succession to Mr. C. H. R. Wollaston, who has retired from that post and has been elected a director of the bank.

Railway Traffic Returns.

ALGECIRAS (GIBRALTAR) RAILWAY.—Traffic for week ended March 19, Ps. 19,690; increase Ps. 1,597. Aggregate from July 1, Ps. 758,714; increase, Ps. 21,410.

BENGAL CENTRAL RAILWAY.—Traffic for week ending March 5, Rs. 19,291; increase, Rs. 2,365. Total from January 1, Rs. 186,497; increase, Rs. 23,343.

BURMA RAILWAYS.—Receipts for week ending February 26, Rs. 2,05,965; decrease, Rs. 20,074. Aggregate from January 1, Rs. 16,55,206; decrease, Rs. 2,93,535.

GREAT WESTERN OF BRAZIL RAILWAY.—Traffic for week ending February 12, $39,146; decrease, $1,265. Aggregate receipts to date $304,516; increase, $31,253.

ALCOY AND GANDIA RAILWAY AND HARBOUR COMPANY.—Traffic for week, March 26 :—Ps. 4,900, decrease Ps. 7,100. Aggregate from January 1, Ps. 123,300, increase Ps. 3,250.

VILLA MARIA AND RUFINO RAILWAY.—Traffic for week ending March 26, $6,269; increase, $2,201. Aggregate from January 1, $55,116, decrease $4,861.

WEST FLANDERS RAILWAY.—Gross receipts for week ending March 27, £1,944; increase, £47. Total from January 1, £26,093; increase, £644.

WEST OF INDIA PORTUGUESE RAILWAY.—Week ending March 5, Rs. 5,270; increase, Rs. 1,722.

ASSAM-BENGAL RAILWAY.—Traffic for week ended February 19, Rs. 27,506; increase, Rs. 7,760. Aggregate from January 1, Rs. 1,72,349; increase, Rs. 19,095.

BENGAL DOOARS RAILWAY.—Traffic receipts from January 1 to February 19, Rs. 23,180; decrease, Rs. 6,828.

H. H. THE NIZAM'S GUARANTEED STATE RAILWAYS.—Traffic receipts from January 1 to February 26. Rs. 629,384; increase, Rs. 12,984.

ROHILKUND AND KUMAON RAILWAY.—Traffic receipts for week ending February 26, Rs. 6,217; decrease, Rs. 116. Aggregate from January 1, Rs. 43,378; decrease, Rs. 1,387.

SOUTHERN MAHRATTA RAILWAY.—Receipts for week ended March 5, Rs. 104,121; decrease, Rs. 16,569.

MANILA RAILWAY.—Receipts for week ending March 26, $21,009; increase, $5,292. Aggregate from January 1, $233,089; increase, $57,052.

SOUTHERN PACIFIC RAILWAY.—The net earnings for the month of February, $1,470,137; increase, $622,711.

DELHI UMBALLA KALKA RAILWAY.—Traffic receipts for week ending March 26, Rs. 35,800; increase, Rs. 300. Total from commencement of half-year, Rs. 4,46,600; increase, Rs. 1,43,000.

ANTOFAGASTA AND BOLIVIA RAILWAY.—Traffic receipts for month of February, $353,000; decrease, $67,000. Total from January 1, $657,000; decrease, $178,000.

PUERTO CABELLO AND VALENCIA RAILWAY.—Traffic return for week ended February 11, £958; decrease, £745. Aggregate from January 1, £5,087: decrease, £2,348.

WESTERN OF SANTA FE RAILWAYS.—Gross receipts for week ending March 26, $52,890; increase, $26,580.

MOBILE AND BIRMINGHAM RAILROTD.—Traffic for second week of March, $6,706; increase, $220. Aggregate from July 1, $268,401; decrease, $4,847.

CLEATOR AND WORKINGTON.—Gross receipts for the week ending March 26 amounted to £1,027, a decrease of £60. Total receipts from January 1, £12,274, a decrease of £609.

COCKERMOUTH AND KESWICK RAILWAY.—Receipts for the week ending March 26, £817; increase, £147. Aggregate from January 1, £9,931; increase, £952.

QUEBEC CENTRAL RAILWAY.—Receipts for second week of March, $8,559; increase, $621. Aggregate from July 1, $59,865; decrease, $8,893.

BOLIVAR RAILWAY.—Traffic receipts for February, £3,351; decrease £1,691. Total for eight months to date, £13,445; decrease, £7,494.

TRAMWAY AND OMNIBUS RECEIPTS.

For past week :—Belfast, −£75; Calais, +£20; Croydon, −£15; Glasgow, −£166; Lea Bridge, +£9; London & Deptford, −£43; London Southern, −£39; London General Omnibus, −£2,389; London Road Car, −£924; Metropolitan, −£1,327; North Staffordshire, +£1; South London, −£265; Woolwich & S. E. London, −£48; Provincial, −£210; Southampton, −£27; Wolverhampton, −£29; Sunderland, −£2; Swansea, −£11.

Barcelona, +£7; Bordeaux, −£82.

Anglo-Argentine, week ending February 28, £302 increase; City of Buenos Ayres, week ending February 21, £508 increase.

ENGLISH RAILWAYS.

Div. for half years. 1896	1896	1897	1897	Last Balance forward.	Amt. to pay 1 p.c. on Ord. for ½ yr.	NAME.	Date.	Gross Traffic for week: Amt.	Inc. or dec. on 1897.	Inc. or dec. on 1896.	No. of weeks	Gross Traffic for half-year to date: Amt.	Inc. or dec. on 1897.	Inc. or dec. on 1896.	Mileage.	Inc. on 1897.	Working	Prior Charges last ½ year.	Prop. add Cap. Exp. this ½ year
				£	£												%	£	£
10	10	10	10	2,707	5,094	Barry	Mar 26	8,228	−807	+61	13	118,035	+4,703	+20,950	31	—	8·89	60,665	316,853
nil	nil	nil	nil	—	—	Brecon and Merthyr	,, 27	1,389	+91	−197	13	19,227	+535	−863	61	—	—	—	—
nil	nil	nil	nil	3,979	4,749	Cambrian	,, 27	4,711	+61	+592	*	53,529	+941	—	250	—	60·96	63,148	40,000
2¾	1¾	2	1¾	1,510	3,150	City and South London	,, 27	1,066	+92	+148	13	13,891	+100	+1,235	3¼	—	56·67	5,552	124,000
2	2	1½	2	7,895	13,210	Furness	,, 27	9,017	+386	+553	*	106,371	+3,004	—	139	—	49·88	97,423	20,910
1	1½	½	1	2,207	27,470	Great Central (late M., S., & L.)	,, 27	44,366	−1,295	+3,489	12	506,180	+5,028	+30,210	352½	—	57·17	627,386	1,200,000
1½	4¾	2	5	51,283	62,865	Great Eastern	,, 27	75,735	−542	+5,942	12	927,232	+29,125	+79,098	1,158¼	2	55·35	860,138	250,000
3	5½	3	5	15,094	102,496	Great Northern	,, 27	92,534	−407	+3,799	13	1,200,364	+34,480	+84,848	1,071	8	61·16	641,485	750,000
4½	7¼	4¾	7¼	31,350	121,981	Great Western	,, 27	175100	−683	+6,480	12	2,039,830	+45,050	+106510	2,582	21	51·44	1,486,272	800,000
nil	2	nil	1¾	8,951	16,487	Hull and Barnsley	,, 27	6,316	+244	+782	12	76,129	−2,004	+5,355	73	—	58·21	70,290	52,54[illegible]
5	5¾	5	5¾	21,495	83,704	Lancashire and Yorkshire	,, 27	93,153	+1,080	+3,561	12	1,079,095	+32,731	+44,738	555½	25	56·70	674,745	451,976
4¾	8	4¾	8¾	26,243	43,049	London, Brighton, & S. Coast	,, 26	43,196	−1,434	+748	13	587,382	+27,557	+40,401	476¾	—	50·20	407,042	240,735
nil	nil	nil	nil	72,294	56,296	London, Chatham, & Dover	,, 27	25,241	−724	−234	12	308,489	+9,322	+20,235	185¼	—	50·65	367,873	nil
6½	8	6½	7¾	89,535	204,068	London and North Western	,, 27	225962	−2,417	+10,064	12	2,669,146	+57,676	+136898	1,911½	—	56·92	1,404,534	600,000
5	8½	8½	8½	23,038	59,367	London and South Western	,, 27	66,916	+577	+2,365	12	772,591	+31,645	+56,565	941	6½	51·75	513,740	389,000
2¾	6	2½	6¼	14,592	6,691	London, Tilbury, & Southend	,, 27	4,472	−473	+392	13	60,772	+3,797	+10,529	81	—	52·57	39,590	15,000
3¼	3¾	3¾	3¾	17,133	26,409	Metropolitan	,, 27	16,013	+309	+1,165	*	197,917	+4,784	—	64	—	43·63	148,047	254,000
nil	nil	nil	nil	4,006	11,250	Metropolitan District	,, 27	†8,670	+771	+602	12	103,912	+4,687	+5,059	13	—	48·70	110,663	38,450
5	7	5½	6½	38,143	174,582	Midland	,, 27	183576	−1,554	+14,411	13	2,341,807	+28,171	+153050	1,354¾	15½	57·59	1,216,582	650,000
5½	7½	5¾	7	22,374	138,189	North Eastern	,, 26	139677	−2,278	+2,110	12	1,668,860	+23,173	+79,633	1,597¾	—	58·82	795,077	436,004
7½	7½	7½	7½	7,061	10,102	North London	,, 27			Not recd.			not	recvd.	12	—	50·90	49,971	7,600
4	5	4	4½	4,745	16,150	North Staffordshire	,, 27	15,179	−204	+529	13	201,475	+5,769	+12,373	312	—	53·27	118,142	19,605
10	10	11		1,642	3,004	Rhymney	,, 26	5,151	+512	+700	13	65,977	+1,710	+7,305	71	—	49·68	29,049	16,700
3	6¾	3½	6¾	4,054	50,215	South Eastern	,, 26	37,461	−1,500	+742	*	482,306	+23,397	—	448	—	51·88	380,763	250,000
3½	3½	3½	3½	2,315	25,961	Taff Vale	,, 26	15,011	−514	+443	13	197,357	−5,183	+6,338	121	—	54·90	94,800	92,000

* From January 1. † Includes Universities Boat Race Traffics.

SCOTCH RAILWAYS.

5	5	5¼	5	9,544	78,066	Caledonian	Mar. 27	72,671	+ 1,289	+ 3,269	8	555,403	+ 12,303	+ 31,391	851¼	5	50·38	588,248	441,477
5	5½	5	5	7,364	24,639	Glasgow and South-Western	,, 26	26,755	+ 1,171	+ 1,469	8	210,391	+ 6,204	+ 11,287	393½	—	54·69	221,663	106,145
3½	3½	3½	—	1,291	4,600	Great North of Scotland	,, 26	7,543	− 63	− 15	8	59,514	− 77	+ 1,103	331	15½	52·03	92,178	60,000
3	nil	2	—	10,477	12,820	Highland	,, 27	8,062	− 116	+ 146	4	32,712	+ 841	+ 2,409	479½	27½	58·63	78,976	,000
1	1¼	1	1¼	819	45,819	North British	,, 27	68,507	+ 1,138	+ 2,278	8	537,452	+ 13,359	+ 18,105	1,230	23	48·62	944,809	540,800

IRISH RAILWAYS.

6½	6½	6½	—	5,466	1,790	Belfast and County Down	Mar. 25	1,996	+ 86	+ 297	*	24,636	+ 1,268	—	76½	—	55·38	17,690	10,000
5½	6½	5½	—	—	4,284	Belfast and Northern Counties	,, 25	3,453	+ 323	+ 508	*	50,507	+ 3,187	—	249	—	—	—	—
2	3	2	—	1,418	1,200	Cork, Bandon, and S. Coast†	,, 26	1,234	− 98	− 35	*	14,072	− 1,165	—	103	—	54·82	14,436	5,450
6½	6¾	6½	6¾	38,776	17,816	Great Northern	,, 25	14,705	+ 664	+ 899	12	166,910	+ 8,581	+ 10,816	528	36	50·15	83,068	22,000
5½	5½	5½	5½	30,339	24,855	Great Southern and Western	,, 25	—	—	—	not	received	—	—	603	13	51·45	72,804	40,562
4	4	4	4½	11,372	11,850	Midland Great Western	,, 25	10,143	+ 235	+ 742	12	111,335	+ 5,359	+ 6,794	538	—	50·31	83,129	1,800
nil	nil	nil	nil	229	2,822	Waterford and Central	,, 25	813	+ 3	—	*	10,278	+ 1,310	—	59½	—	53·24	6,858	1,500
nil	nil	nil	nil	1,936	2,987	Waterford, Limerick & W.	,, 25	4,415	+ 3	+ 580	*	68,137	+ 3,410	—	350½	—	57·83	42,017	7,075

* From January 1. † Eight weeks' strike

FOREIGN RAILWAYS.

Mileage. Total.	Increase on 1897.	Increase on 1896.	Name.	Gross Traffic for Week. Week ending	Amount.	In. or Dec. upon 1897.	In. or Dec. upon 1896.	Gross Traffic to Date. No. of Weeks.	Amount.	In. or Dec. upon 1897.	In. or Dec. upon 1896.
					£	£	£		£	£	£
319	—	—	Argentine Great Western ..	Mar. 25	8,295	+ 570	+ 1,692	38	214,249	− 7,433	+ 42,282
76½	—	—	Bahia and San Francisco ..	Mar. 5	4,752	+ 2,104	+ 2,594	8	28,428	+ 9,854	+ 10,193
234	48	84	Bahia Blanca and North West ..	Feb. 27	736	− 26	—	35	27,707	+ 513	—
74	—	—	Buenos Ayres and Ensenada ..	Mar. 27	3,112	− 459	− 829	12	42,289	− 7,623	− 11,329
426	—	—	Buenos Ayres and Pacific ..	Mar. 26	8,537	− 279	− 19	38	246,339	− 32,933	− 5,293
914	1	3	Buenos Ayres and Rosario ..	Mar. 26	17,074	+ 5,353	+ 4,234	12	211,930	+ 53,911	+ 31,629
2,499	30	68	Buenos Ayres Great Southern ..	Mar. 27	34,043	+ 2,386	+ 1,759	38	1,133,046	+ 81,844	+ 168,627
602	107	177	Buenos Ayres Western ..	Mar. 27	11,706	− 2,832	− 3,309	38	459,080	− 80,053	− 81,338
245	55	77	Central Argentine ..	Mar. 26	23,791	+ 9,448	+ 5,290	12	268,605	+ 65,345	+ 8,406
297	—	—	Central Bahia ..	Jan. 31*	$133,559	− $3,944	+ $12,753	—	—	—	—
271	—	—	Central Uruguay of Monte Video	Mar. 26	5,711	+ 2,436	− 79	38	227,691	+ 6,658	− 16,106
228	—	—	Do. Eastern Extension	Mar. 26	1,626	+ 802	+ 265	38	47,825	+ 5,014	− 1,929
182	—	—	Do. Northern Extension	Mar. 26	673	+ 396	− 168	38	24,059	− 953	− 6,723
180	—	—	Cordoba and Rosario ..	Mar. 20	2,065	− 230	+ 145	38	80,975	− 16,170	− 2,292
128	—	—	Cordoba Central ..	Mar. 20	$21,000	− $3,500	− $3,750	11	$240,700	− $38,900	− $52,710
549	—	—	Do. Northern Extension	Mar. 20	$49,000	− $18,149	− $3,730	11	$484,290	− $184,110	− $109,660
237	—	—	Costa Rica ..	Mar. 12	7,892	− 97	+ 441	10	56,734	− 14,722	+ 1,146
99	—	—	East Argentine ..	Feb. 6	562	− 310	− 17	5	3,387	− 946	− 708
386	—	6	Entre Rios ..	Mar. 26	2,982	+ 1,945	+ 1,487	38	59,193	+ 15,087	+ 13,085
355	—	24	Inter Oceanic of Mexico ..	Mar. 26	$68,300	+ $12,700	+ $24,200	38	$2,269,280	+ $325,210	+ $559,970
23	—	—	La Guaira and Caracas ..	Feb. 25	1,779	− 779	− 1,138	8	15,641	− 5,235	− 3,525
321	—	—	Mexican ..	Mar. 26	$77,000	+ $4,000	—	12	$980,200	+ $92,830	—
1,846	—	—	Mexican Central ..	Mar. 21	$246,326	+ $699	+ $70,255	12	$2,260,918	+ $41,631	+ $679,642
3,217	—	—	Mexican National ..	Mar. 21	$115,745	+ $705	+ $32,584	12	$1,260,468	+ $100,422	+ $250,538
228	—	—	Mexican Southern ..	Mar. 21	$13,660	+ $670	+ $376	51	$649,438	+ $84,196	+ $167,638
206	—	—	Minas and Rio ..	Jan. 31*	$133,941	− $20,733	—	7 mos.	$1,308,551	+ $187,035	—
94	—		N. W. Argentine ..	Mar. 26	1,001	− 527	− 436	12	10,540	− 7,144	− 4,642
242	3	—	Nitrate ..	Mar. 15†	18,010	+ 2,625	− 2,333	9	72,503	+ 1,349	− 31,925
320	—	—	Ottoman ..	Mar. 19	4,613	− 1,011	+ 685	11	55,623	− 14,553	+ 5,661
77½	—	—	Recife and San Francisco ..	Jan. 29	6,419	− 368	− 932	5	27,047	− 651	− 4,955
86½	—	—	San Paulo ..	Feb. 27†	17,481	− 7,056	—	8	88,485	− 16,073	—
186	—	—	Santa Fe and Cordova ..	Mar. 26	4,484	+ 2,890	+ 999	39	60,526	− 10,649	− 2,108
110	—	—	Western of Havana ..	Mar. 26	1,845	+ 108	+ 1,225	38	67,860	+ 5,621	+ 3,245

* For month ended. † For fortnight ended.

INDIAN RAILWAYS.

Mileage. Total.	Increase on 1897.	Increase on 1896.	Name.	Gross Traffic for Week. Week ending	Amount.	In. or Dec. on 1897.	In. or Dec. on 1896	Gross Traffic to Date. No. of Weeks.	Amount.	In. or Dec. on 1897.	In. or Dec. on 1896.
862	—	—	Bengal Nagpur ..	Mar. 26	Rs.1.69.000	+ Rs.35.962	—	12	Rs.17.69.000	− Rs.77.668	—
827	8	63	Bengal and North-Western ..	Feb. 26	Rs.1.34.850	+ Rs.13.660	+ Rs.7.303	8	Rs.10.81.970	+ Rs.1.34.778	+ Rs.30.530
461	—	—	Bombay and Baroda ..	Mar. 26	£30,525	+ £4,966	—	12	£279,469	− £33,506	—
1,885	2	13	East Indian ..	Mar. 26	Rs.12.87.000	+ Rs.56.000	+ R.1.60.000	12	Rs.1.50.80.000	+ Rs.2.65.000	+ Rs8.58.000
1,491	—	—	Great Indian Penin. ..	Mar. 26	£78,742	+ £16,555	− £4,572	12	£787,105	+ £66,376	− £198,701
736	—	—	Indian Midland ..	Mar. 26	Rs.1.27.600	+ Rs.17.635	+ Rs.19.461	12	Rs.16.23.359	+ Rs.2.61.975	+ Rs2.74.290
840	—	—	Madras ..	Mar. 12	£19,617	− £1,925	− £182	10	£190,745	− £10,673	− £11,127
1,043	—	—	South Indian ..	Feb. [illegible]	Rs.1.5[illegible]	− Rs.26.035	− Rs.7.618	6	Rs.9.03.806	− Rs.66.997	− Rs1.86.279

UNITED STATES AND CANADIAN RAILWAYS.

Mileage Total.	Increase on 1897.	Increase on 1896.	Name.	Gross Traffic for Week. Period Ending.	Amount.	In. or Dec. on 1897.	Gross Traffic to Date. No. of Weeks.	Amount.	In. or Dec. on 1897.
					dols.	dols.		dols.	dols.
917	—	—	Baltimore & Ohio S. Western ..	Mar. 21	145,428	+29,964	37	4,925,376	+523,785
6,518	92	156	Canadian Pacific ..	Mar. 21	463,000	+138,000	11	4,569,000	+1,011,000
922	—	—	Chicago Great Western ..	Mar. 21	110,545	+14,180	37	3,908,810	+525,663
6,109	—	469	Chicago, Mil., & St. Paul ..	Mar. 21	666,000	+158,000	11	6,724,801	+965,000
1,685	—	—	Denver & Rio Grande ..	Mar. 21	137,500	+14,800	37	5,919,900	+996,909
3,512	—	—	Grand Trunk, Main Line ..	Mar. 21	£7,438	+£6,488	11	£817,396	+£86,202
335	—	—	Do. Chic. & Grand Trunk	Mar. 21	£14,856	+£2,322	11	£169,432	+£37,095
189	—	—	Do. Det., G. H. & Mil...	Mar. 21	£3,938	−£50	11	£39,522	−£1,624
2,938	—	—	Louisville & Nashville ..	Mar. 21	411,000	+34,000	11	4,667,175	+932,621
2,197	137	137	Miss., K., & Texas ..	Mar. 21	159,358	−12,183	37	9,474,495	+562,147
477	—	—	N. Y., Ontario, & W. ..	Mar. 21	65,540	+250	37	2,828,095	+101,235
1,570	—	—	Norfolk & Western ..	Mar. 21	239,000	+19,000	37	7,890,000	+868,000
3,499	336	—	Northern Pacific ..	Mar. 21	390,000	+105,000	11	4,070,000	+1,216,000
1,223	—	—	St. Louis S. Western ..	Mar. 21	89,000	+25,000	11	1,217,700	+236,100
4,654	—	—	Southern ..	Mar. 21	388,000	+17,000	37	3,333,812	+1,271,448
1,979	—	—	Wabash ..	Mar. 21	253,000	+41,000	11	2,775,406	+558,000

MONTHLY STATEMENTS.

Mileage. Total.	Increase on 1896.	Increase on 1895.	Name.	Net Earnings for Month. Month.	Amount.	In. or Dec. on 1897.	In. or Dec. on 1896.	Net Earnings to Date. No. of Months.	Amount.	In. or Dec. on 1897.	In. or Dec. on 1896.
					dols	dols.	dols.		dols.	dols.	dols.
6,935	44	444	Atchison ..	February	746,000	+191,000	+129,318	2	1,240,434	+313,670	−139,884
6,547	103	106	Canadian Pacific ..	February	424,000	+39,000	+19,268	2	940,000	+182,000	+110,328
6,169	—	469	Chicago, Mil., & St. Paul ..	January	757,000	+32,000	−30,713	—	—	—	—
1,685	—	—	Denver & Rio Grande ..	January	239,000	+65,802	+19,198	7	2,025,645	+314,978	−31,082
1,970	—	—	Erie ..	January	371,000	+33,000	−107,852	—	—	—	—
3,512	—	—	Grand Trunk, Main Line	January	£87,400	+£34,284	+£37,725	—	—	—	—
335	—	—	Do. Chic. & Grand Trunk	January	£13,100	+£8,933	+£9,901	—	—	—	—
189	—	—	Do. Det. G. H. & Mil. .	January	£1,800	+£692	+£1,939	—	—	—	—
3,127	—	239	Illinois Central* ..	February	2,177,767	+413,527	+422,489	2	4,481,665	+819,013	+805,758
2,396	—	—	New York Central* ..	February	3,429,000	+128,000	+222,339	2	6,934,000	+492,597	249,393
477	—	—	New York Ontario, & W. ..	February	57,800	−3,800	+19,504	9	831,700	+33,400	+75,462
1,570	—	—	Norfolk & Western ..	January	283,000	+14,000	+48,326	—	—	—	—
3,407	—	—	Pennsylvania ..	January	1,152,797	+26,600	+109,000	—	—	—	—
1,0[illegible]	—	—	Phil. & Reading* ..	January	1,724,472	+214,601	—	—	—	—	—

* Statements of gross traffic

Prices Quoted on the London Stock Exchange.

Throughout the INVESTORS' REVIEW middle prices alone are quoted, the object being to give the public the approximate current quotations of every security of any consequence in existence. On the markets the buying and selling prices are both given, and are often wide apart where stocks are seldom dealt in. Other particulars will be found in the INVESTMENT INDEX published quarterly—January, April, July, and October—in connection with this REVIEW, price 2s., by post 2s. 2d. Where dividends are paid only once a year, an *italic* type is used to distinguish them. The London Stock Exchange Official List is quoted in the REVIEW almost entire, only very insignificant issues, or bonds falling due within the next two or three years, being omitted. But the list is subdivided into the leading, or active, stocks, and those less frequently dealt in. The former will be found under the head of "Stock Markets," and with more details than it is possible to give for the bulk of securities. By retaining the file of the INVESTORS' REVIEW any subscriber can follow for himself the movements of securities from week to week, and the INVESTMENT INDEX will from time to time help to fill up deficiencies in the information.

Tea Companies and Mines and Mining Finance Stocks are placed in special lists.

Among the abbreviations used are the following:—S.F. Snk. Fd. *sinking fund*; Certs., *certificates*; Debs. or Dbs., *debentures*; Db. or D.Stk., *debenture stock*; Pf., Prf., or Pref., *preference*; Prefd. or Pfd., *preferred*; Dfd., *deferred*; L. or Ltd., *limited*; Sh., *share*; Ans., *annuities*; Cu. or Cm., *cumulative*; Gu or Guar., *guaranteed*; Bds., *bonds*; S., Sr., or Ser., *series*; In., Ins., Insc., *inscribed*; Dr., Drgs., Drwgs., *drawings*; Stg., Strlg., *sterling*; Lia., *liable to*; Sp., Surp., *surplus*; Per., Perp., *perpetual*; Ln. *lien*; Lo. *loan*.

The dates following the names of securities are the years of issue or of redemption. Where shares are not fully paid up, their nominal amount is given with the name so that investors may know the liability upon them.

BRITISH FUNDS, &c.

Rate.	Name.	Price.
2¾	2¾ p.c.'s (Childers') Red.. 1905	105½
3	Local Loans Stk. 1912	111
3	Metro. Police Deb. Stk. 1920	105½
—	Red Sea Ind. Tel. Ann. 1908	8½
4	Canada Gv. "Intcl. Rly." 1903	105
4	Do. do. .. 1908	113
4	Do. Bonds 1910	114
4	Do. Bonds 1913	119½
3	Egyptian Gov. Gar.	106½
3	Mauritius Ins. Stk. 1940	114
4	Turkish Guar. 1855	109
[illegible]	Bank of Ireland Stk.	392½
3½	India Rupee Paper	62½
3½	Do. 1854-5	62
3	Do. 1896-7 1916	55
3½	Isle of Man Deb.	104
3	Do. Deb. Stk... 1919-29	103

CORPORATION AND COUNTY STOCKS.

FREE OF STAMP DUTY.

Rate.	Name.	Price.
3½	Metropolitan Con. 1929	117½
3	Do. 1941	112½
2½	Do. 1920-49	100
2½	L.C.C. Con. Stock 1920	99
3½	Comm. of Sewers, Scp., S.F. 1905	105
3½	Corp. of Lond. Bds...1897-1902	100½
3	Do. 1897-1912	103
3½	Do, Debs. Scp. ...... S.F. 1916	105
2½	Do., Deb. Stk. Scrip .. 1927-57	99
3	Barnsley 1916-46	105
3	Barry 1914-46	101
3	Bath 1909-34	102
3	Batley 1914-44	101½
3½	Birmingham 1945	121
3	Do. 1947	111
2½	Do. 1926	98
3	Blackburn 1930	106½
3	Bournemouth 1913-33	103
3½	Bradford 1945	116½
3	Do. Deb. Stock .. 1954	108
3	Brighouse.............. 1916-46	100
3½	Brighton 1946	118½
2½	Do. 1957	98
3	Burton-on-Trent........ 1913-43	102½
3	Cambridge 1913-43	102
3½	Cardiff 1935	116½
3	Do. 1914-54	102
3	Cheltenham............ 1971	108
3	Chichester 1916-46	101
3½	Croydon	134
3	Do. 1940	102½
3	Derby 1920-50	107
3	Devon C.C.............. 1917-33	104½
3½	Dewsbury 1930	109
3	Do. 1930	103
3	Dorset County 1922-32	105
3	Douglas (I. of Man) 1926	101
3	Dover 1913-43	101
3½	Dublin 1944	113½
3	Eastbourne 1920-40	104
3	Edinburgh 1924	108
2½	Do. 1927	98
2½	Exeter 1917-57	96
3	Glamorgan County 1914-34	104
3½	Glasgow 1914	110½
3	Do. 1921	106½
2½	Do. 1925-40	99
3	Gloster 1915-55	101
3	Grimsby 1913-45	103
3	Hampshire County 1914-34	105½
3	Hanley 1913-43	105
3	Harrogate 1914-34	103
3	Hastings 1915-54	103½
2½	Hertfordshire C.C. 1916-36	98
3	Heston & Isleworth U.D.C. 1915-35	101
3	Huddersfield 1934	107
3½	Hull (1st iss.)	131½
3	Inverness 1914-44	101
3	Ipswich 1952	108½
3	Lancaster.............. 1919-55	103
2½	Leeds 1927	98
3½	Leicester 1934	114½
3	Lincoln................ 1919	103
3½	Liverpool..............	133½

Corporation, &c. (*continued*):—

Rate.	Name.	Price.
3	Manchester 1941	103½
3	Mansfield.............. 1915-45	100
3½	Middlesbro' 1909	105½
3½	Do. 1911-13	105
3	Do. 1915	104
3	Middlesex C.C.......... 1915-35	106
3½	Newcastle 1936	118½
3½	Do. Irred.	129½
2½	Do. 1915-36	101
3	Newcastle-under-Lyme.. 1909-44	101
3	Newport (Mon.) 1915-55	101½
3	Norwich 1952	111½
3	Nottingham	115
3	Oxford 1951	109½
3	Penzance 1916-46	100½
3	Plymouth 1942	110
3	Pontypridd U.D.C. 1916-46	98
3	Poole.................. 1915-45	101
3½	Portsmouth........1916 24 & 27	112
3	Do. 1913-33	106½
3	Ramsey 1920-40	100
3	Ramsgate.............. 1915-55	101
3½	Reading	130½
3	Do. 1962	109
3½	Rhyl U.D.C. 1953	110
3	Richmond (Surrey) 1942	104½
3	River Wear Debt Certs.	100
3	St. Helen's 1915-55	102
3	Scarbro' 1915-50	102
2½	Sheffield 1925-57	96
3	Shipley U.D.C.......... 1915-35	100
3	Somerset Co. 1923-33	105
3	South Shields 1915-45	102
2¾	Southampton 1915-45	102
3	Southend-on-Sea 1916-46	102
3	Staffs C.C. 1915-35	102
3	Stockport.............. 1914-54	103
3	Stockton 1932	104
3	Do. 1915-35	103
3	Surrey Co. 1922-32	105½
3½	Swansea	130
3	Do. 1955	106
3	Taunton 19183-9-43	101
3	Tees Conserv. Deb. Stk. 1947	101
3	Thames Conserv. "A" Deb. Stk............ 1954	103½
3	Do. "B" Deb. Stk. 1954	103½
3	Torquay 1913-43	101½
3	Tunbridge Wells 1931	102
3	Tynemouth 1913	101
3	Wakefield.............. 1929	101
3	Walsall................ 1932	108
3	West Bromwich........ 1930	106½
3½	West Ham 1929	110
3	Do. 1945	105
3	West Sussex C.C. 1915-35	106
3	Weston-s.-Mare Lcl Bd. 1914-44	101½
3	Weymouth & Melc. Regis 1918	101
3	Widnes................ 1915-55	101
3	Wigan 1921	106
3	Windsor 1918-55	102
3½	Wisbech 1947	113½
3½	Wolverhampton 1932	118
3	Do. 1924-54	107
3	York 1916-41	106½

SUBJECT TO STAMP DUTY.

Rate.	Name.	Price.
3½	Belfast City & Dis. Watr. 1938	114
3	Do. Red Stk. 1953-6	106
3½	Belfast 1924	103
4	Blackburn Con. Deb. Irred.	141½
3½	Do. do. Irred..............	130
3½	Bristol	130½
3½	Burnley.............. 1933	114
2½	Chesterfield Gas & Wtr. 1916-46	98
3½	Douglas Town 1921	105
3	Dover Harb. 1st Deb... 1956	104½
3½	Hull (2nd iss.)	129½
4	Leeds Deb............. 1927	124
3½	Do.	115½
3	Do. 1927	106
3	Leicester 1919-44	105
4	Manchester..................	148
3	Do. 1928	104½
4½	Middlesboro' Mrts. 1908	111
3½	Newark on-Trent .. 1901-41	96
3½	Sheffield 1898-1916	105½
3½	Do. 1925-36	114
3	Do. 1925	104½
3½	Southampton .... S.F.	106
4½	Stockton Morts.......... 1906	112
3½	Worcester.............. 1950	119

COLONIAL AND PROVINCIAL GOVERNMENT SECURITIES.

Rate.	Name.	Price.
6	British Columbia........ 1907	119½
4½	Do. Debs... 1917	111½
3	British Guiana Imgtn. Bds.	99½
5	Canada, "Intercol. Rail," 1903	111½
4	Do. (Bonds) 1904-5-6-8	106
4	Do. Reduced........ 1910	107½
3½	Do. Bnds. 1909-34	103½
4	Do. Loan 1910-35	107½
3	Do. Loan 1938	101
6	Cape of G. Hope 1900	—
5	Do. 1900	—
4½	Do. red. by an. draw.	110
4½	Do. 1879	110
4	Do. 1881	109
4	Do. 1917-23	118
4½	Ceylon	110
4	Do.	106½
4½	Fiji Gov. Deb. Sink. Fd.	101½
4	Jamaica Sink. Fd. 1923	103
5	Manitoba Debs.......... 1910	113
5	Do. Ster. Bds. 1888	122
4	Do. Ster. Debs.	106
4	Mauritius, Cons. Debs. 1880...	103½
4½	Natal, Sink. Fd......... 1919	118
4	Do. do. 1926	115
3½	Newfoundland Stg. Bds. 1941	98
3½	Do. do. .. 1947	98
3	Do. do.	86½
5	New South Wales 1897-1902	104½
4	Do. 1903-5-8-9-10	105
5	New Zealand 1914	118
5	Do. Cnsls. 1 p.c. per an. Sink. Fd.	104
3½	Nova Scotia Debs.	104
5	Quebec Prov. 1904-6	110
4½	Do. (drgs.)	104
5	Do. Strlg. Bds. 1912	115
4	Do. Strlg. Bds. 1928	110
4	Do. Strlg. Bds. 1934	108
4	Queensland 1913-15	106½
4½	St. Lucia Debs................	102½
6	South Australia 1897-1900	103½
6	Do. 1901-1918	119
5	Do. 1911-1920	116
4	Do. 1899-1916	105
4	Do. 1929	108½
4	Do. 1916	108½
4	Do. 1917-18-24	112½
6	Tasmania 1897-1901	104
4	Do. 1908-11, 1913-14-20	107½
5	Trinidad Debs., an. drw. 1 p c...	106
4	Victoria 1899-1901	101½
4½	Do. 1904	105
4	Do. Rail. Loan 1907	104
4	Do. Loans 1908-13	107
4½	West. Austr. 1 p.c. ac. Sink. Fd.	109
4	Do. do.	106

REGISTERED AND INSCRIBED STOCKS.

No stamp duty except for Canada 4 p.c. Reduced (½ per cent.).

Rate.	Name.	Price.
4	Antigua Insc. Stk. Red. 1919-44	109
3½	Barbados Insc. Stk. 1925-42	108
3	British Colum. Insc. Stk. 1941	101½
4	British Guiana Insc..... 1935	118½
4	Canada Stk. Regd. ..1904-5-6-8	107
4	Do. 4 p.c. (late 5 p.c.) Regd. 1910	107½
3½	Do. 3½ p.c. Stock Regd. 1909-34	103½
4	Do. Ln. for 4 milln. stg. 1910-35	107½
3	Do. Stk. Regd. 1938	101
2½	Do. Insc.............. 1947	90
4	Cape G. Hope Regd. .. 1917-23	117
4	Do. (Ln. of '83) Insc. .. 1923	119
4	Do. Cons. Stk. Insc.... 1916-36	112
3½	Do. Consol. Insc. Stock 1929-49	110
4	Ceylon Insc. Stock 1934	118½
3	Do. 1940	104
4	Grenada Insc. Stock.... 1917-42	112
3½	Hong Kong Insc. Stock 1918-43	103½
4	Jamaica Insc. Stock.... 1934	121
—	Do. 1922-44	99
4	Mauritius Inscribed 1937	118½
4	Natal Consd. Stk. Insc. 1927	115
4	Do. 1937	119
3½	Do. Inscribed Stock.. 1914-39	107
4	Newfoundland Inscribed 1913-38	107
4	Do. 1935	113
4	Do. Consd. Stk. Ins. 1936	113
4	N. S Wales Stock Insc. 1933	117
3½	Do. 1924	105
3½	Do. 1918	104
3	Do. 1935	97

Colonial, &c. (*continued*):—

Rate.	Name.	Price.
4	N. Zealnd. Con. Stk. Ins. 1929	114
3½	Do. 1940	107
3	Do. Inscribed.... 1945	99
3	Quebec (Prov.) Ins. Stk. 1937	93
4	Queensland Stock Insc. 1915-24	110½
3½	Do. 1921-4-30	104
3½	Do. 1945	103
3	Do. 1922-47	98
4	St. Lucia Insc. Stock .. 1919-44	112
4	S. Austrln. (1882-7) Reg. 1916-36	110
3½	Do. In. Stk. Reg. 1939	108
3	Do. 1916-26	99
3/	Do. 1916	99
3½	Tasmanian Insc. Stock.. 1920-40	106
4	Do. 1920-40	116
4	Trinidad Insc. Stock.... 1917-42	110
3	Do. 1922-44	98½
4	Victoria Rly. Loan '81, Inscribed Stock 1907	104
4	Victoria Insc. Stock 1908-13-19	107
4	Victoria (1883) Ins. Stk. 1920	110
3½	Do. Inscribed Stock 1921-3-6	103
4	Do. do. 1911-26	108
4	W. Austral. Insc. Stock 1934	116½
4	Do. 1911-31	109
3½	Do. 1915-35	106
3	Do. 1915-35	98
3	Do. 1916-36	97

FOREIGN STOCKS, BONDS, &c.

COUPONS PAYABLE IN LONDON.

Last Div.	Name.	Price.
36/	Argentine Ry. Loan 6 p.c. 1881	87½
15/	Do. 5 p.c. 1884	67
30/	Do. N. Cent. Ry. Ext. 5 p.c. 1887-8-9	66½
30/	Do. 5 p.c. Trsy. Convs. 1887	68
5/4½	Do. 4½ p.c. Interl. Gld. 1888	65
27/	Do. 4½ p.c. Stlg. Extrl. 1888	67
10/6	Do. 3½ p.c. External .. 1889	48
4	Do. 4 p.c. Ry. Guar. Res....	57½
4½	Brazilian 1883	55
4½	Do. Gold.......... 1879	65
4½	Do. 1888	57
36/	Buenos Ayres 1824	82½
6	Do. 1882-3-6	47
6	Bulgarian 1888	94
6	Do. Mort. Bonds 1892	93
4½	Chilian 1885	73
4½	Do. 1886	74
4½	Do. 1887	73
4½	Do. 1889	81½
5	Do. 1892	83
4½	Do. 1893	73
4½	Do. 1895	74
5	Do. 1896	82
7	Chinese Silver 1894	101
6	Do. Gold 1895	106
6	Do. Apl. '95 by dwgs. 1901-15	108½
5	Do. Red. dwgs. in 36 yr. 1896	101
5	Do. Do. Regis. 1896	99
1½	Colmbn. 1½ to 3 p.c. Ext. Bds. 1896	17
6	Cordova, Prov. 1886	25
—	Do. Eng. Ass. Certs.	24
—	Do. 6 p.c. 1887-8	25
—	Do. Eng. Ass. Certs.	24
3	Costa Rica "A"	31
2½	Do. "B"	26
3	Danish Gold 1914	98
10/	Ecuador N. Ext. Bds. 4½ p.c. ascn. to 5 p.c.	22
3½	Egypt'n Ins. Stk. lia. Stp. Dty. 1890	100
4	Do. State Domain 1878	104½
4	Do. D. Sanieh, Red. .. 1905	104½
6	Entre Rios.............. 1886-8	35
6	Do. Fndg. Ln. Bds. 1894-1921	32
6	Do. do. Parana City......	27½
15/	Greek 1881	40
15/	Do. 1884	40
12/	Do. Rentes..................	34
15/	Do. (Piræus-Larissa Ry.)	35
7/6	Do. Fundg. Loan 1893	46
4	Guatemala Extl. Debt..........	33
6	Hawaiian	102½
4	Hungarian Gold Rentes........	101½
3	Do. 1895	91½
6	Italian Irriga. Guar.	111½
5	Do. Maremmana	94½
5	Japan 5 p.c.	100½
5	Mexican (Nat. R. Tehuantpec.)..	96½
6	Do. Extrl. 1890	98

Foreign Stocks, &c. (*continued*):—

Last Div.	Name.	Price.
6	Mexican Extrl. 1893	96½
5	Do. Intrnl. Cons. Slvr.	37¾
5	Do Intern. Rd. Bds. 2d. Ser.	37½
4	Nicaragua 1886	50
3½	Norwegian, red. 1937, or earlier	98
3	Do. do. 1965, do.	98
3½	Do. 3½ p.c. Bnds.	104
1	Paraguay 1p.c. ris. 3p.c. 1886-96	16
5	Russian, 1822, £ Strlg.	149
3	Do. 1859	94
4	Do. (Nicolas Ry.) 1867-9	103
3	Do. Transcauc. Ry. 1882	94
4	Do. Con. R. R. Bd. Ser. I., 1889	103
4	Do. Do. II., 1889	103
4	Do. Do. III., 1891	103½
3½	Do. Bonds	101
4	Do. Ln. (Dvinsk and Vitbsk)	103
6	Salvador 1889	64
—	S Domingo 4s. Unified: 1980	65½
6	San Luis Potosi Stg. 1889	93
5	San Paulo (Brzl.), Stg. 1888	91½
6	Santa Fé 1883-4	35
—	Do. Eng. Ass. Certs. Dep.	34
5	Do. 1888	45
—	Do. Eng. Ass. Certs. Dpsit.	44
5	Do. (W. Cnt. Col. Rly.) Mrt.	25
5	Do. & Reconq. Rly. Mort.	25
5	Spanish Quickslvr Mort. 1870	103
½	Swedish 1880	103
3	Do. 1888	98
53	Do. Conversion Loan 1894	100
45	Trans. Gov. Loan Red. 1903-42	103
59/	Tucuman (Prov.) 1888	69
	Turkish, Secd. on Egypt. Trib.	103½
3½	Turkish, Egpt. Trib., Ott. Bd., '94	99¼
4	Do. Priority 1890	90½
1	Do. Convted Series, "A"	65½
5	Do. Customs Ln. 1886	95½
5	Uruguay Bonds 1896	57½
3	Venzula New Con. Debt 1881	35

COUPONS PAYABLE ABROAD.

Last Div.	Name.	Price.
7	Argent. Nat. Cedla. Sries. "B".	34½
5	Austrian Ster. Rnts., ex 10fl., 1870	85
5	Do. do. do.	87
5	Do. Paper do. 1870	84
5	Do. do. do.	86
4	Do. Gld Rentes 1876	104
2½	Belgian exchange 25 fr.	92
3	Do. do.	101
3½	Danish Int., 1887, Rd. 1896	98½
3½	Do. '87, Red. by pur. or draw. fr. Dec., 1900	99
2½	Dutch Certs. ex 12 gldrs.	87
3	Do. Bonds	98
3	Do. Insc. Stk.	97
3½	French Rentes	105½
3	Do. 1878, '81-4., Red.	101
3	German Imp. Ln. 1891	96½
3	Do. do. 1892-3	96½
3	Do. do. 1890-4	96
5	Japan Cons. Ln., '92, 3, & 5, Red.	46
30/9	Prussian Consols	102
3	" Cons. Stg. Ln. 1891	97
4	Rumanian Bds. 1890	—
4	Do. do. 1891	—
4	Utd. States, 1877, Red. 1907	114
4	Do. 1895, 30 yrs.	128
3½	Do. Maschsetts Gl. 1935	113½
3½	Do. Gold Bonds 1923	110½
2	Virginia Cpn. Bds., 3 p.c. from July, 1901	70

BRITISH RAILWAYS.

ORD. SHARES AND STOCKS.

Last Div.	Name.	Price.
10	Barry, Ord.	280½
4	Do. Prefd.	126
6	Do. Defd.	150½
5	Caledonian, Ord.	155
3	Do. Prefd.	99
—	Do. Defd. Ord., No. 2	4½
	Cambrian, Ord	6½
—	Do. Coast Cons.	6½
32/	Cardiff Ry. Pref. Ord.	117
3/	Central Lond. £10 Ord. Sh.	10½
1/9½	Do. do. £6 paid	6¼
3½d.	Do. Pref. Half-Shares	1½
1/6	Do. Def. do.	4½
1½	City and S. London	67
—	East London, Cons.	6½
2	Furness	63½
2½	Glasgow and S. West. Pfd.	81
2½	Do. do. Dfd.	64
3	Great Central, Ord. 1894	40
32/0	Do. London Exten.	75
3½	Great N. of Scotland	122
4	Great Northern, Prefd.	118¼
—	Do. Consolidated "A"	50
—	Do. do. "B"	191½
2	Highland	82½
4	Isle of Wight, Prefd.	120½
3	Do. Defd.	83½
—	Lancs. Derbys. and E. Cst.	4
8½	L. Brighton and S. C. Ord.	186
37/11½	Do. New all pd.	186
6	Do. Prefd. Ord.	198
30/	Do. Contgt. Rights Certs.	16½
5½	Lond. and S. Western Ord.	222½
4	Do. Preferred	132
6½	Lond., Tilb., and Southend	133½
—	Mersey, £20 shares	½
—	Metropolitan, New Ord.	129
2½	Do. Surplus Lands	95
4	North Cornwall, 4 p.c. Pref.	104½
38/6	Do. Deferred	22½
7½	North London	224½
5	North Staffordshire	131

British Railways (*continued*):—

Last Div.	Name.	Price.
3/3	Plymouth, Devenport, and S. W. Junc. £10	8½
3/	Port Talbot £10 Shares	9
9d.	Rhondda Swns. B. £10 Sh.	5
10	Rhymney, Cons.	267½
4	Do. Prefd.	123
6⅘	Do. Defd.	147½
1½	Scarboro', Bridlington Junc.	47½
6½	South Eastern, Ord.	150
6	Do. Pref.	193
3½	Taff Vale	81
25/	Vale of Glamorgan	129½
3	Waterloo & City	136½

LEASED AT FIXED RENTALS.

Last Div.	Name.	Price.
4	Birkenhead	146
5.19.0	East Lincnshire	207½
5½	Hamsmith. & City Ord.	192½
4½	Lond. and Blackwll.	162½
4½	Do. £10 4½ p. c. Pref.	162½
56/6	Lond. & Green. Ord.	102
5	Do. 5 p. c. Pref.	178½
5	Nor. and Eastn. £50 Ord.	89¼
6	Do.	106
3½	N. Cornwall 3½ p. c. Stk.	126
4⅓	Nott. & Granthm. R. & C.	144½
3½	Portptk. & Wigtn. Guar. Stk.	123½
9	Vict. Stn. & Pimlico Ord.	317½
4½	Do. 4½ p. c. Pref.	162½
4/	West Lond. £20 Ord. Shs.	14
4⅓	Weymouth & Portld.	160½

DEBENTURE STOCKS.

Last Div.	Name.	Price.
4	Alexandra Dks. & Ry.	132½
3	Barry, Cons.	108½
4	Brecon & Mrthyr, New A	127½
4	Do. New B	107
4	Caledonian	150½
4	Cambrian "A"	132½
4	Do. "B"	130½
4	Do. "C"	126½
4	Do. "D"	107½
3	Cardiff Rly.	102½
4	City and S. Lond.	139
3½	Cleator & Working Junc.	118½
3	Devon & Som. "A"	103½
26/8	Do. "B" 4 p. c.	36
—	Do. "C" 4 p. c.	10
4	E. Lond. and Ch. 4 p. c. A	137
6/	Do. 2nd B	67½
—	Do. 3rd Ch. 4 p. c.	18½
—	Do. 4th do.	9½
3½	Do. 1st (3½ p. c.)	128½
2½	Do. 2½ p.c. (Whitech. Exn).	88
4	Forth Bridge	143½
4	Furness	143
4	Glasgow and S. Western	150
5	Gt. Central	—
4½	Do.	155½
4	Gt. Eastern	147
4	Gt. N. of Scotland	147½
3	Gt. Northern	113½
4	Gt. Western	150½
4½	Do.	160½
4½	Do.	167½
5	Do.	186½
2½	Do.	100
4	Highland	143½
3	Hull and Barnsley	105½
3	Do. 2nd (3-4 p. c).	123
4	Isle of Wight	144½
3	Do. Cent. "A"	92½
4½	Do. "B"	115½
4	Do. "C"	82½
3	Lancs. & Yorkshire	113½
4	Lancs. Derbys. & E. Cst.	123½
4	Lpool St. Hlen's & S. Lancs.	126
4½	Ldn. and Blackwall	158
4	Ldn. and Greenwich	148½
4	Lond., Brighton, &c.	149
4½	Do.	166½
4½	Lond., Chath., &c., Arb.	156½
4½	Do. "B"	155½
4	Do.	138½
4	Do. 1883	138½
3	Do.	107
3	Lond. & N. Western	116
3	Lond. & S. Westn. "A"	114½
3	Do. Consld.	114½
4	Lond., Til., & Southend	147½
—	Mersey, 5 p. c. (Act, 1866)	65
4	Metropolitan	147½
4½	Do.	164½
3½	Do.	129½
6	Met District	206½
4	Do.	139
3	Midland	115
4½	Mid-Wales "A"	137½
4	Neath & Brecon 1st	129
4	Do. "A 1"	118½
3	North British	110
3	Do. 1893	108½
3½	N. Cornwall, Launcstn., &c.	128½

Debenture Stocks (*continued*):—

Last Div.	Name.	Price.
3	North Eastern	114
4½	North London	167
3	N. Staffordshire	111½
4	Plym. Devpt. & S.W. Jn.	141½
4	Rhondda and Swan. Bay	130½
4	Rhymney	146½
4	South-Eastern	147½
5	Do.	184½
3½	Do.	127½
3	Do.	113½
3	Taff Vale	110
4	Tottenham & For. Gate	146
3	Vale of Glamorgan	105½
3	West Highld. (Gtd. by N.B.)	108
4	Wrexham, Mold, &c. "A"	115½
4	Do. "B"	102½
4	Do. "C"	97½

GUARANTEED SHARES AND STOCKS.

Last Div.	Name.	Price.
4	Caledonian	149½
4	Do.	145
4	Forth Bridge	142½
4	Furness 1881	137½
4	Glasgow & S. Western	143
4	Do. St. Enoch, Rent	143
6	Gt. Central	199½
4½	Do. 1st Pref.	152½
3½	Do. Pref.	104½
5	Do. Irred. S.Y. Rent	161½
4½	Do. do.	139½
4	Gt. Eastern, Rent	144½
5	Do. Metropolitan	180
4	Do.	144½
4	Gt. N. of Scotland	138½
4	Gt. Northern	146½
5	Gt. Western, Rent	181½
5	Do. Cons.	180½
4	Lancs. & Yorkshire	146½
5	L., Brighton & S. C.	180½
3½	L., Chat. & D. (Shrtlds.)	110½
4	L. & North Western	148
4	L. & South Western 1881	147½
4½	Met. District, Ealing Rent	151
4½	Do. Fulham Rent	152
4	Do. Midland Rent	143½
4	Do. Mid. & Dist. Guar.	128½
4	Midland, Rent	147½
4	Do. Cons.	147½
3	Mid. & G.N. Jt., "A" Rnt.	107½
3	N. British, Lien	106½
4	Do. Cons. Pref. No. 1	140½
3	N. Cornwall, Wadebrge. Gu.	107
4	N. Eastern	146½
5	N. Staff. Trent & M. £20 Shs.	36
3½	Nott. Suburban Ord.	123½
20/6	S. E. Perp. Ann.	36
4½	Do. 4½ p.c.	163½
3½	S. Yorks. Junc. Ord.	118½
4½	W. Cornwall (G. W., Br., Ex., & S. Dev. Joint Rent	158½
3	W. Highl. Ord. Stk. (Gua., N.B.)	105½

PREFERENCE SHARES AND STOCKS.

DIVIDENDS CONTINGENT ON PROFIT OF YEAR.

Last Div.	Name	Price.
4½	Alexandra Dks. & Ry. "A"	125½
5	Barry (First)	169½
4	Do. Consolidated	138½
4	Caledonian Cons., No. 1	144½
4	Do. do. No. 2	143½
5	Do. do. 1878	177½
4	Do. Pref. 1884	142
4	Do. do. 1887 (Conv.)	151
—	Cambrian, No. 1 4 p.c. Pref.	72½
—	Do. No. 2 do.	39½
—	Do. No. 3 do.	19
—	Do. No. 4 do.	10
5	City & S. Lond. £10 shares	15½
—	Do. New	14
4	Furness, Cons. 1881	134½
4	Do. "A" 1881	131½
4	Do. "B" 1883	129½
4	Glasgow & S. Western	141
4	Do. No. 2	141
4	Do. 1888	139
4	Do. 1891	139
5	Gt. Central	162½
4	Do.	132½
5	Do. Conv. 1872	155½
5	Do. do. 1874	154½
5	Do. do. 1876	153½
5	Do. do. 1879	153½
5	Do. do. 1881	148½
4	Do. 1889	113½
4	Do. 1891	107
5	Do. 1894	108½
4	Gt. Eastern, Cons.	142
4	Do. 1886	141½
4	Do. 1881	141½
4	Do. 1884	141½

Preference Shares, &c. (*continued*):—

Last Div.	Name.	Price.
4	Gt. Eastern, Cons. 1887	140½
4	Do. 1888	140½
3½	Do. 1890	121½
3½	Do. 1893	121½
—	Do. (Int. fr. Jan '99) 1893	117½
4	Gt. North Scotland "A"	134½
4	Do. "B"	133½
4	Gt. Northern, Cons.	142½
3	Do. 1896	107
5	Gt. Western Cons.	180
36/11	Hull & Barnsley Red. at 115	107
4	Isle of Wight	133½
3	Lancs. & Yorkshire, Cons.	108
2/2½	Lanc. Drby & E.C. 5 p.c. £10	10½
—	Do. 5 p.c. 2nd £10	9½
5	Lond., Bright., &c., Cons.	178½
5	Do. 2nd Cons.	177½
4½	Lond., Chat. & Dov. Arbitr.	136½
25/	Do. 2nd Pref. 4½ p.c.	93
4	Lond. & N. Western	146½
4	Lond. & S. Western 1881	145
4	Do. 1884	143½
3½	Do.	127½
4	Lond., Tilbury & Southend	142½
4	Do. Cons., 1887	141½
4	Do 1891	141½
—	Mersey, 5 p.c. Perp.	—
4	Metropolitan, Perp.	141½
4	Do. 1882	141½
4	Do. Irred.	141½
4	Do. 1887	141½
4	Do. New	141½
4½	Do.	146½
3½	Do.	124½
3	Do. Guar.	101½
2½	Metrop. Dist. Exten 5 p.c.	110
4	Midland, Cons. Perpetual	146
4	N. British Cons., No. 2	137
4½	Do. Edin. & Glasgow	153½
5	Do. 1865	169½
5	Do. Conv. 1874	169½
4½	Do. 1875	152½
4½	Do. Conv. 1875	153½
5	Do. do. 1879	169½
4	Do. do. 1884	138
4	Do. do. 1888	138
4	Do. do. 1890	138
4	Do. do. 1892	137
4	N. Eastern	143½
4½	N. Lond., Cons. 1866	174½
4½	Do. 2nd Cons. 1875	160
3	N. Staffordshire	107
4½	Plym. Devpt. & S. W. Junc.	149½
1/5	Port Talbot, &c., 4 p.c. £10 Shares, 4 paid	5
5/	Rhondda & Swansea Bay, 5 p.c. £10 Shares	13
4	Rhymney, Cons.	142
4½	S. Eastern, Cons.	162½
5	Do. do.	178½
4	Do. Vested Cos'.	143
4	Do. 1891	143
3½	Do. 1893	125½
2	Do. 3 p.c. after July 1900	103½
4	Taff Vale	143

INDIAN RAILWAYS.

Last Div.	Name.	Paid.	Price.
3½	Assam Bengal, Ld., (3½ p.c. till June 30, then 3 p.c.)	100	102
4/	Barsi Light, Ld., £10 Shs.	10	10½
6	Bengal and N. West., Ld.	100	149½
4/	Do. £10 Shares	10	14½
3/6	Do. 3½ p.c. Cum. Pf. Shs.	10	10½
8½d.	Do.	4	4½
2/3½	Bengal Central, Ld., £10 (3½ p.c. + ¼th net earn)	5	5½
3	Bengal Dooars, Ld.	100	118
4	Bengal Nagpr., Lim. (gua. 4 p.c. + 4th sp. pfts.)	100	115
7½	Bombay, Baroda, and C. I. (gua. 5 p.c.)	100	213
36/1	Burma, Ld. (gua. 2½ p.c. and ½ p.c. add. till 1901)	100	108½
1/7	Do. £10 Shares		3½
4	Delhi Umb. Kalka, Ld., Gua. 3½ p.c. + net earn.	100	123
4	Do. Deb. Stk., 1890 (1916)	100	111
9/10	Estn. Bengal, "A" An. 1957	—	25
9/	Do. "B" 1957	—	30
4	Do. Gua. Deb. Stock	100	140½
9/7½	East Ind. Ann. "A" (1953)	—	27
8/4½	Do. "C"	—	28
8/11½	Do. "B"	—	30
6⅛	Do. Def. Ann. Cap. (gua. 4 p.c. + ½th sp. pfts.)	—	152
115/9	East Ind. Def. Ann. "D"	—	158
4½	East Ind. Irred. Stock	100	160½
5	Gt. Indian Penin., Gua. 5 p.c. + ½ surplus profits	100	167½
4	Do. Irred. 4 p.c. Deb. St.	100	140½
4	Indian Mid., Ld. (gua. 4 p.c. + ¼th surplus pfts.)	100	115
51/	Madras Guar. + ½ sp. pfts.	100	166
48/6	Do. do.	100	156
46/	Do. do.	100	146
4	Nilgiri, Ld., 1st Deb. Stk.	100	97
4	Oude & Rohil. Db. Stk. Rd.	100	—
5⅛	Rohil. and Kumaon, Ld.	100	132
9/11	Scinde, Punj., and Delhi, "A" Ann., 1958	—	25
9/1	Do. "B" do.	—	30

Indian Railways (*continued*):—

Last Div.	Name.	Paid.	Price.
4	South Behar, Ld., £10 shs.	100	100
3½	Do. Deb. Stk. Red.	100	103
4½	South Ind., Gu. Deb. Stk.	100	162½
5	South Indian, Ld. (gua. 3 p.c., and ½ spls. profits)	100	122½
5	Sthn. Mahratta, Ld. (3½ p.c. & ¼th net earnings)	100	116
4	Do. Deb. Stk. Red.	100	120
3½	Southern Punjab, Ld.	100	110
3½	Do. Deb. Stk. Red.	—	105
5	Nizam's Gun. State, Ld. [†	100	114½
4	Do. Mort. Deb., 1936	100	109
4	Do. do. Reg.	100	108
*7/3½	Nizam's Gua. State, Ld., 3½ p.c. Mt. Deb. bearer	—	94½
*7/3½	Do. Reg. do. ..	—	93½
5	W. of India Portgese., Ld.	100	68½
5	Do. Deb. Stk., Red	100	99

RAILWAYS.—BRITISH POSSESSIONS.

Last Div.	Name.	Paid.	Price.
5	Atlantic & N.W. Gua. 1 Mt. Bds., 1937	100	125½
5/3	Buff. & L. Huron Ord. Sh.	10	13½
5½	Do. 1st Mt. Perp. Bds. 1879	100	141½
5½	Do. 2nd Mt. Perp. Bds.	100	141½
—	Calgary & Edmon. 6 p.c. 1st Mt. Stg. Bds. Red..	100	75½
5	Canadn Cent. 1st Mt. Bds. Red.	100	106
4	Can. Pacific Pref. Stk.	100	100
5	Do. Strl. 1st Mt. Deb. Bds. 1915	100	118
3½	Do. Ld. Grnt. Bds., 1938..	100	107
3½	Do. Ld. Grnt. Ins. Stk. ..	100	108
4	Do. Perp. Cons. Deb. Stk.	100	114
5	Do. Algoma Bch. 1st Mt. Bds., 1937	100	122
2	Demerara, Original Stock	100	47
7	Do. Perp. Pref. Stk......	100	155½
9½d.	Do. 4 p.c. Cum. Ext. Pref. £10 Shs.	4	6½
—	Dominion Atlntc. Ord. Stk.	100	33½
5	Do. 5 p.c. Pref. Stk.....	100	100
4	Do. 1st. Deb. Stk.......	100	106
4	Do. 2nd do. Red.	100	100
—	EmuBay&Mt.Bischoff, Ld.	5	4½
4½	Do. Irred. Deb. Stk....	100	98
nil.	Gd. Trunk of Canada, Stk.	100	8½
6	Do. 2nd. Equip. Mt. Bds.	100	130½
5	Do. Perp. Deb. Stk.......	100	136½
5	Do. Gt. Westn. Deb. Stk.	100	128½
5	Do. Nthn. of Can. 1st Mt. Bds., 1902	100	102½
4	Do. do. Deb. Stk	100	102
5	Do. G. T. Geor. Bay & L. Erie 1 Mt., 1903	100	104
5	Do. Mid. of Can. Stl. 1st Mt. (Mid. Sec.) 1908	100	106
5	Do.do.Cons.1 Mt.Bds. 1912	100	107
5	Do. Mont. & Champ. 1 Mt. Bds., 1902	100	104
	Do. Welln., Grey & Brce. 7 p.c. Bds. 1 Mt.	100	110
—	Jamaica 1st Mtg. Bds. Red.	—	103
—	Manitoba & N. W., 6 p.c. 1st Mt. Bds., Red	100	—
—	Do. Ldn. Bdhldrs. Certs.	—	—
5	Manitoba S. W. Col. 1 Mt. Bd., 1934 $1,000 price %	—	120
—	Mid. of W. Aust. Ld. 6 p.c. 1 Mt. Dbs., Red.	100	25
4	Do. Deb. Bds., Red.	100	103
4	Nakusp & Slocan Bds., 1918	100	106
3	Natal Zululand Ld. Debs.,	100	79½
5	N. Brunswick 1st Mt. Stg. Bds., 1934	100	121
4	Do. Perp. Cons. Deb. Stk.	100	114
—	N. Zealand Mid., Ld., 5 p.c 1st Mt. Debs...........	100	35
6	Ontario & Queb. Cap. Stk.	$100	155½
5	Do. Perm. Deb. Stk......	100	142½
—	Qu'Appelle, L. Lake & Sask.6p.c.1 Mt.Bds.Red.	100	41½
	Queb. & L. S. John, 1st Mt. Bds., 1909	100	25½
	Quebec Cent., Prior Ln. Bds., 1908	100	107
4½	Do. 5 p.c. Inc. Bds.	100	39
4	St. Lawr. & Ott. Stl. 1st Mt.	100	113
4	Shuswap & Okan., 1st Mt. Deb. Bds., 1915	100	76
5	Temiscouata, 5 p.c. Stl. 1st Deb. Bds., Red.........	100	9½
5	Do. (S. Franc. Brch.) 5 p.c. Stl. 1 Mt. Db. Bds., 1910	100	10
4	Toronto, Grey & B. 1st Mt.	100	112
1/2½	Well. & Mana. £5 Shs. ..	1	1
5	Do. Debs., 1908	100	110
5	Do. 2nd Debs., 1908	100	109
5	Do. 3rd do., 1908	100	108
6	Atlan. & St.Law.Shs.,6 p.c.	100	162½
5	Gd. Trunk Mt. Bds., 1934	100	116½
5	Michigan Air Line, 5 p.c. 1st Mt. Bds., 1902......	100	104
4	Minneap., S. P. & Slt. Ste. Mar, 1st M Bds., 1938	$1000	97

AMERICAN RAILROAD STOCKS AND SHARES.

Last Div.	Name.	Paid.	Price.
6/	Alab. Gt. Sthn. A 6 p.c. Pref.	10*l*.	9
—	Do. do "B" Ord. ..	10*l*.	2
—	Alabma. N. Orl.-Tex. &c., "A" Pref.	10*l*.	½
—	Do. "B" Def.	10*l*.	½
5½	Atlant. First Lsd. Ls. Rtl. Trust..................	Stk.	98½
—	Baltimore & Ohio Com. ..	$100	17
—	Baltimore Ohio S.W. Pref.	$100	5
—	Chesap. & Ohio Com.	$100	20
—	Chic. Gt. West. 5 p.c. Pref. Stock "A"	$100	30½
—	Do. do. Scrip. In.......	—	28
8/3	Do. 4 p.c. Deb. Stk.......	$100	70
4	Do. Interest in Scrip	$100	65½
$4	Chic. Junc. Rl. & Un. Stk. Yds. Com.	$100	111½
$1½	Do. 6 p.c. Cum. Pref.	$100	111
$3½	Chic. Mil. & St. P. Pref...	$100	146
7	Cleve. & Pittsburgh......	$10	86½
$1½	Clev., Cincin., Chic., & St. Louis Com.............	$100	—
—	Erie 4 p.c. Non-Cum. 1st Pf.	—	35½
—	Do. 4 p.c. do. 2nd Pf.	—	17
—	Gt. Northern Pref.	$100	155
$2½	Illinois Cen. Lsd. Lines ..	$100	95½
—	Kansas City, Pitts & G. ..	$100	20
$3	L. Shore & Mich. Sth. C.	$100	190
—	Mex. Cen. Ltd. Com.	$100	6
—	Miss. Kan. & Tex. Pref...	$100	32½
2½	N.Y., Pen. & O. 1st Mt. Tst. Ltd., Ord.	—	48½
4	Do. 1st Mort. Deb. Stk. ..	$100	93½
8	North Pennsylvania	$50	—
—	Northn. Pacific, Com......	$100	24½
1½	Pitts. F. Wayne & Chic...	$100	174
—	Reading 1st Pref.	$50	20½
—	Do. 2nd Pref.	$50	10½
—	S. Louis & S. Fran. Com.	$100	6½
—	Do. 2nd Pref.	$100	25
6	St. Louis Bridge 1st Pref..	$100	107
3	Do. 2nd Pref.	$100	50
6	Tunnel Rail. of St. Louis	$100	107
$1½	St. Paul, Min. and Man...	$100	130
—	Southern, Com.	$100	8½
—	Wabash, Common........	$100	7

AMERICAN RAILROAD BONDS. CURRENCY.

Last Div.	Name.		Price.
7	Albany & Susq. 1 Con. Mrt.	1906	118
7	Allegheny Val. 1 Mt.......	1910	125½
5	Burling., Cedar Rap. & N. 1 Mt.	1906	109½
5	Canada Southern 1 Mt.....	1908	111
5	Chic. & N. West. Sk. Fd. Db.	1933	120½
5	Do. Deb. Coupon	1921	115½
6	Chicago & Tomah	1905	112½
5	Chic. Burl. & Q. Skg. Fd.	1901	102½
4	Do. Nebraska Ext.......	—	102
6	Chic., Mil., & S. Pl., 1 Mt. S.W. Div...............	1909	117½
7	Do. (S. Paul Div.) 1 Mt.	1902	132½
5	Do. (La Cross & D.	1919	112½
7	Do. 1 Mt. (Hast. & Dak.)	1910	132
5	Do. Chic. & Mis. Riv. 1 Mt.	1926	112½
5	Chic., Rock Is. and Pac. 1 Mt. Ext.	1934	108
6	Det., G. Haven & Mil. Equip	1918	105
6	Do. do. Cons. Mt.	1918	102½
6	Ill. Cent., 1 Mt., Chic. & S.	1898	—
7	Indianap. & Vin., 1 Mt. ..	1908	125
6	Do. do. 2 Mt. ..	1900	104½
6	Lehigh Val., Cons. Mt.	1923	112½
—	Mexic. Cent., Ln. 2 Cons. Inc.	—	5
7	N.Y. Cent. & H.R. Mt. Bonds	1903	119½
5	Do. Deb.	1904	111
6	Penns. Cons. S. F M.	1905	118
4	West Shore, 1 Mt.	2361	110

DITTO–GOLD.

Last Div.	Name.	Price.
6	Alabama Gt. Sthn. 1 Mt. ..1908	114
5	Do. Mid. 1 1928	96
4	Allegheny Val. Gen. Mt. ..1942	107
4	Atch., Top., & S. Fé Gn. Mt. 1995	91
3	Do. Adj. Mt..............1995	61
5	Do. Equipt. Tmst. ...... —	102½
5	Atlantic & Dan. 1 Mt.......1950	—
5	Baltimore & Ohio...........1925	97½
5	Do. Speyer's Tst. Recpts. 1925	96
5	Do. Cons. Mt. 1988	102½
4½	Do. 4½ p.c. 1 Mt. Term. 1934	84
4½	Do. Brown Shipley's Dep. Cts. —	84
5	Balt. Belt 5 p.c. 1 Mort.....1990	90
4½	Balt. & Ohio S.W. 1 Mt. ..1990	102½
4½	Do. 4½ p.c. 1 Cons. Mt. 1893 1993	78
—	Do. Inc. Mt. 5 p.c. Cl. A —	29½
—	Do. do. Cl. B —	11
5	Balt. & Ohio S.W. Term 5 p.c. 1942	99½
6	Balt. & Ptmac (Mn. L.) 1 Mt. 1911	124
6	Do. do. (Tunnel) 1 Mt. 1911	126
4	Beech Creek 1 Mt. 1936	109
5	Do 2 Mort. 1936	116
4	Carthage & Adiron 1 Mt...1981	109

American Railroad Bonds—Gold (*continued*):—

Last Div.	Name.	Price.
5	Cent. of Georgia 1 Mort. ..1945	117½
5	Do. Cons. Mt. 1945	92½
5	Cent. of N. Jrsy. Gn. Mt...1987	113½
6	Central Pacific, 1 Mort. 1898	102½
6	Do. Speyer's Certs. ...... —	106
5	Do. Land Grant 1900	100½
5	Chesap. & Ohio 1st Cons. Mt. 1939	116½
4½	Do. Gen. Mt. 1992	80
6	Chic. & W. Ind. Gen. Mt. Skg. Fd. 1932	120
5	Chic. Mil. & St. Pl. (Chic. & L. Sup.) 1 Mt. 1921	114½
5	Do. Chic. & Pac. W. 1921	117½
5	Do. Wisc. & Minn. 1 Mt. 1921	114½
5	Do. Terminal Mt. 1914	114½
4	Do. General Mt. 1989	108
5	Chic. St. L. & N. Orleans..1951	122½
4	Do. 1 Mort. (Memphis) ..1951	105½
4	Clevel., Cin., Chic. & St. L. 1 Mt. (Cairo)............1939	90
4	Do. 1 Mt. (Cinc., Wab., & Mich.) 1991	90
4	Do. 1 Col. Tst. Mt. (S. Louis) 1990	98½
4	Do. General Mt. 1993	82½
4½	Clevel. & Mar. Mt. 1935	114
4½	Clevel. & Pittsburgh 1942	119½
4½	Do. Series B. 1942	119½
—	Colorado Mid. 1 Mt. 1936	63½
—	Do. Bdhrs.' Comm. Certs. —	63½
4	Dnvr. & R. Gde. 1 Cons. Mt. 1936	93
5	Do. Imp. Mort............1928	91
4	Detroit & Mack. 1 Lien 1995	92½
5	E. Tennes., Virg., & Grgia. Cons. Mt. 1956	114½
5	Elmira, Cort., & Nthn. Mt. 1914	100
4	Erie 1 Cons. Mt. Pr. Ln. ..1996	91
3	Do. Gen. Lien 1996	72
6	Galvest., Harrisb., &c., 1 Mt.....	107½
5	Georgia, Car. & N. 1 Mt. ..1929	96
4½	d Rpds & Inda. Ex. 1 Mt. 1941	112½
5	G Do. 1 Mt. (Muskegon) ..1926	39½
3½	Illinois Cent. 1 Mt. 1951	104½
4	Do. 1952	105
4	Do. Cairo Bdge. ..1950	102
4	Do. 1953	104
4	Do. General Mort. ..1904	102½
5	Kans. City, Pitts. & G. 1 M. 1923	80
3½	L. Shore & Mich. Southern 1997	109
4½	Lehigh Val. N.Y. 1 Mt.....1940	105
5	Lehigh Val. Term. 1 Mt. ..1941	109½
5	Long Island 1931	120½
5	Do. Deb...........1934	102
5	Do. (N. Shore Bch.) 1 Cons. Mt. 1932	94
6	Louisville & Nash. G. Mt..1930	121
6	Do. 2 Mt. Sk. Fd. (S. & N. Alabama........1910	104½
6	Do. 1 Mt. N. Orl. & Mb. 1930	122½
5	Do. 1 Mt. Coll. Tst. ...1931	106
4	Do. Unified 1940	87½
4½	Do. Mobile & Montgy. 1 Mt. 1945	105½
4	Manhattan Cons. Mt. 1990	96
4	Mexican Cent. Cons. Mt. ..1911	66
—	Do. 1 Cons. Inc, ...	15
6	Mexican Nat. 1 Mt.........1927	105½
3	Do. 2 Mt. 6 p.c. Inc. A 1917	58
—	Do. do. B..1917	10
3	Do. Matheson's Certs.....	—
3	Michig. Cnt. (Battle Ck. & S.) 1 Mt. 1989	88
6	Minneap. & S. L. 1 Mt. Pacific Ext. 1921	117½
5	Do. 1 Consold. 1934	107½
4	Minne., Slt. S. M. & A. 1 Mt. 1926	97
5	Minneapolis Westn. 1 Mt...1911	105½
4	Miss. Kans. & Tex. 1 Mt...1990	89
4	Do. 2 do. 1990	63
4	Mobile & Birm. Mt. Inc....1945	38
5	Do. P. Lien 1945	88
4	Mohawk & Mal. 1 Mt......1991	108
5	Montana Cent. 1 Mt. 1937	111½
5	Nashv., Chattan., & S. L. 1 Cons. Mt................1928	102½
5	Nash., Flor., & Shff. Mt...1937	95½
4	N. Y. & Putnam 1 Cons. Mt. 1993	108
5	N. Y., Brooklyn, & Man. B. 1 Cons. Mt...............1935	107½
4	N. Y. Cent. & Hud. R. Deb. Certs. 1890 1905	106
4	Do. Ext. Debt. Certs....1905	106
7	N. Y., L. Erie, & W. 1 Cons. Mt. (Erie) 1920	142½
7	Do. 1 Con. Mt. Fd. Coup. 1920	140
5	N. Y., Onto., & W. Cons. 1 Mt.........................1939	110
4	Do. 4 p.c. Refund. Mt..1992	99
5	N. Y. & Rockaway B. 1 Mt. 1927	102½
6	Norfolk & West. Gn. Mt....1931	128
6	Do. Imp. & Ext..........1934	118½
4	Do. 1 Cons. Mt........ —	81
6	N. Pacific Gn. 1 Mt. Ld. Gt. 1921	—
4	Do. P. Ln. Rl. & Ld. Gt. —	96
3	Do. Gn. Ln. Rl. & Ld. Gt. —	62
5	Oregon & Calif. 1 Mt.......1927	78½
5	Oregon Rl. & Nav. Col. Tst. —	—
6	Panama Skg. Fd. Subsidy..1910	105½
4½	Pennsylvania Rlrd. 1913	115
4	Do. Equip. Tst. Ser. A..1914	104
4	Do. Cons. Mt............1943	115
4½	Penna. Company 1st Mort. 1921	114
5	Perkiomen 1 Mrt., 2nd ser..1918	91½
4½	{ Pitts., C., C., & St. Ls. Con. Mt. G.B., Ser. A } 1940-2	113
4	Do. Cons. Mort., Ser. D..1945	106
6	Pittsbgh., Cle., & Toledo ..1922	107½
4	Reading, Phil., & R. Genl. 1997	84
5	Richmond & Dan. Equip. ..1909	97½
5	Rio Grande Junc. 1st Mort. 1939	94
4	Rio Grande West 1st Tst. Mt. 1939	82½
6	St. Joseph & Gd. Island ..1925	—
7	S. Louis Bridge 1st Mort ..1925	134½
5	S. Louis Mchts. Bdge. Term. 1st Mort.................1930	102½

American Railroad Bonds (*continued*):

Last Div.	Name.	Price.
4	S. Louis S. West 1st Mort..1989	77½
—	Do. 4 p.c. 2nd Mort. Inc. 1989	30
—	S. Louis Term. Cupples Sta. & Prop. 1st. Mrt. 4½ p.c. 1902-17	102
4½	St. Paul, Minn., & Manit. 1933	110½
6	Do. do. 1933	132½
6	Shamokin, Sunbury, &c. 2 Mt. 1925	109
5	S. & N. Alabama Cons. Mt. 1936	97½
5	Southern 1 Cons. Coup. 1994	91½
4	Do. E. Tennes Reorg. Lien ..1938	100
6	S. Pacific of Cal. 1 Mt...1905-12	111
4½	Trml. Assn. of S. Louis 1 Mt. 1939	111½
5	Do. 1 Cons. Mt..........1944	109
5	Texas & Pac. 1 Mt..........2000	100½
—	Do. 5 p.c. 2 Mt. Income 2000	30
5	Toledo & Ohio Cent. 1 Mt. West. Div. 1935	102½
4½	Toledo., Walhon., Val., & Ohio 1 Mt. 1931-3	111½
6	Union Pacific 1 Mt. 1896-9	95
5	Do. Coll. Trust.	—
—	Union Pac., Linc., & Color. 1 Mt. 1918	—
4	United N. Jersey Gen. Mt...1944	115½
6	Vicksbrg., Shrevept., & Pac. Pr. Ln. Mt. 1915	102½
5	Wabash 1 Mt. 1939	112
4	Wn. Pennsylvania Mt. 1928	109½
5	W. Virga. & Pittsbg. 1 Mt. 1990	88
5	Wheeling & L. Erie 1 Mt. (Wheelg. Div.) 5 p.c. 1928	90½
5	Do. Extn. Imp. Mt. 1930	90
—	Do. do. Brown Shipley's Cts...	—
5	Willmar & Sioux Falls 1 Mt. 1938	111

STERLING.

Last Div.	Name.	Price.
6	Alabama Gt. Sthn. Deb.....1906	104½
5	Do. Gen. Mort. ..1927-8	100
5	Alabama, N. Orl., Tex. & Pac. 5 p.c. "A" Dbs...1910-40	99
55/	Do. do. "B" do. 1910-40	50
—	Do. do. "C" do.	19
—	Allegheny Valley 1910	135
4	Atlantic 1st Leased Line Perp...	98
6	Baltimore and Ohio 1902	107½
6	Do. do. 1910	118
5	Do. do. 1877.........	97½
—	Do. Morgan's Certs. ..	97½
4½	Do. do. 1933	89
6	Chicago & Alton Cons. Mt. 1903	112
5	Chic. St. Paul & Kan. City Priority	106
6	Eastn. of Massachusetts....1906	117½
5	Illinois Cent. Skg. Fd.	106
5	Do. 1905	108
3½	Do. 1950	99½
4	Do. 1 Mt. 1951	112
3	Do. 1 Mt. 1951	92½
6	Louisville & Nash., M. C. & L. Div., 1 Mt. 1902	104½
7	Do. 1 Mt. (Memphis & O.) 1901	111
47/4	Mexican Nat. "A" Certs. 5 p.c. Non. cum.	47
—	Do. "B" Certs.....	10
6	N.Y. & Canada 1 Mt........1904	111½
6	N. York Cent. & H.R. Mort. 1903	112
4½	N. York, Penns., & Ohio Pr. Ln. Extd. 1935	—
5	Do. Equip. Tst.	103½
5	Do. 5 p.c. Equip. Tst. (1890)	103½
	Nthn. Cent. Cons. Gen. Mt. ..	106
6	Pennsylvania Gen. Mt. 1910	126
6	Do. Cons. Skg. Fd. Mt. 1905	114½
½	Do. Cons. Mt. 1945	106
	Phil. & Erie Cons. Mort ..1920	134½
½ 6	Phil. & Reading Gen. Cons. Mort. 1911	126
6	Pittsbg. & Connells. Cons. 1926	115
—	Do. Morgan's Certs.....	116
4	St. Paul., Min., & Manitoba (Pac. Extn.) 1940	96½
6	S. & N. Alabama 1903	107½
6	Union Pacific, Omaha Bridge 1896	—
6	Un. N. Jersey & C. Gen. Mt. 1901	109½

FOREIGN RAILWAYS.

Last Div.	Name.	Paid.	Price.
4/	Alagoas, Ltd., Shs.......	20	6
5	Do. Deb. Stk., Red. ..	100	50
6	Antofagasta, Ltd., Stk. ..	100	68
4	Do. Perp. Deb. Stk. ..	100	90
—	Arauco, Ld., Ord. Shs. ..	10	½
—	Do. 10 p.c. Cum. Pref.	10	1½
5	Argentine Gt. W., Ld.,	100	72
5	Do. 5 p.c. Cum. Pref. Shs.	100	100
4	Do. 1 Deb. Stk.	100	103½
1/0/0	Argentine N.E., Ltd., 6 p.c. Cum. Pref. Stk. ..	100	10½
—	Do. 5 p.c. Deb. Stk., Red.	100	31
2/	Arica and Tacna Shs. ..	20	1½
10/	Bahia & San Fcisco., Ld.,	20	10½
6/	Do. Timbo. Bch. Shs.	20	5
12/	Bahia, Blanca, & N.W. Ln. Prf. Cum. 6 p.c. ..	100	53½
4	Do. 4 p.c. 1 Deb. Stk., Red.	100	93
6	Barranquilla R. & P., Ld., 6 p.c. 1 Deb. Stk., Red.	100	96

Foreign Railways (*continued*):—

Last Div	Name.	Paid.	Price.
3/	Bilbao Riv. & Cantabn., Ltd., Ord.	3	6
—	Bolivar, Ltd., Shs.	10	1¾
6	Do. 6 p.c. Deb. Stk.	100	96½
—	Brazil Gt. Southn. Ltd., 7 p.c. Cum. Pref.	20	1½
6	Do. Perm. Deb. Stk	100	47½
6½	B. Ayres Gt. Southn. Ld., Ord. Stk.	100	150
5	Do. Pref. Stk.	100	136
4	Do. Deb. Stk.	100	116
30/	B. Ayres & Ensen. Port., Ltd., Ord. Stk.	100	67
5	Do. Cum. 1 Pref. Stk.	100	122
6/0/0	Do. 6p.c.Con. Pref.Stk.	100	106
4	Do. Deb. Stk., Irred.	100	110
10⅛	B. Ayres Northern, Ltd., Ord. Stk.	100	265
12½	Do. Pref. Stk.	100	320
5	Do. 5 p.c. Mt. Deb. Stk., Red.	100	113
3/15/0	B. Ayres & Pac., Ld., 7 p.c. 1 Pref. Stk. (Cum.)	100	87
4	Do. 1 Deb. Stk.	100	100
5/5/0	Do. 4½ p.c. 2 Deb. Stk.	100	90
1	B Ayres & Rosario, Ltd., Ord. Stk.	100	71½
—	Do. New, £20 Shs.	20	—
7/	Do. 7 p.c. Pref. Shs.	10	17
7/	Do. Sunchales Ext.	10	14½
4	Do. Deb. Stk., Red.	100	108
12	B. Ayres & Val. Trans., Ltd., 7 p.c. Cum. Pref.	20	6½
	Do. 4 p.c. "A" Deb. Stk., Red.	100	71
—	Do. 6 p.c. "B" Deb. Stk., Red.	100	44
3/6	B. Ayres Westn. Ld. Ord.	10	10½
3/	Do. Def. Shs.	10	6½
5	Do. 5 p.c. Pref.	10	12½
4	Do. Deb. Stk.	100	107½
6	Cent. Arg. Deb. Sk. Rd.	100	160½
4	Do. Deb. Stk. Rd.	100	111
6	Cent. Bahia L. Ord. Stk.	100	42
	Do. Deb. Stk., 1934	100	72½
5	Do. Deb. Stk., 1937	100	58
3/6	Cent. Uguy. East. Ext. L. Shs.	10	5½
5	Do. Perm. Stk.	100	111
3/6	Do. Nthn. Ext. L. Sh.	10	4½
5	Do. Perm. Deb. Stk.	100	106
3	Do. of Montev. Ltd., Ord. Stk.	100	86
6	Do. Perm. Deb. Stk.	100	140
10/	Conde d'Eu, Ltd. Ord.	20	7
—	Cordba & Rosar., Ltd., 6 p.c. Pref. Shs.	100	42½
4	Do. 1 Deb. Stk.	100	91
15/	Do. 6 p.c. Deb. Stk.	100	84
—	Cordba Cent., Ltd., 5 p.c. Cu. 1 Pref. Stk.	100	83½
—	Do. 5 p.c. Non-Cum. 2 Pref. Stk.	100	46
5	Do. Deb. Stk.	100	120
—	Costa Rica, Ltd., Shs.	10	4½
8/	Dna. Thrsa. Chris., Ltd., 7 p.c. Pref. Shs.	20	4
20/	E. Argentine, Ltd.	100	40
6	Do. Deb. Stk.	100	104
1/1	Egyptn. Dlta. Lgt. Rys., Ltd., £10 Pref. Shs.	8	8½
—	Entre Rios, L., Ord. Shs.	5	½
—	Do. Cu. 5 p.c. Pref.	5	3
6/	Gt. Westn. Brazil, Ltd.,	20	10
6	Do. Perm. Deb. Stk.	100	90½
6	Do. Extn. Deb. Stk.	100	76½
—	Int.-Oceanic Mex., Ltd., 7 p.c. Pref.	10	1½
4	Do. Deb. Stk.	100	84
42/6	Do. 7 p.c. "A" Deb. Sk.	100	67
—	Do. 7 p.c. "B" Deb. Sk.	100	31
5/	La Guaira & Carac.	10	7½
5	Do. 5 p.c. Deb. Sk. Red.	100	100
8/4	Lembg.-Czern.-Jassy	30	25
1/	Lima, Ltd.	20	2½
—	Manila Ltd. 7 p.c. Cu. Pf.	10	½
20/6½	Mexican 2nd Pref. 6 p.c.	100	34
6	Do. Perp. Deb. Stk.	100	140
1/0/0	Mexican Sthrn., Ld., Ord.	100	23
—	Do. 4 p.c. 1 Db. Stk. Rd.	100	84
—	Do. 4 p.c. 2 do.	100	61
—	Mid. Urgy., Ltd.	100	18½
5	Do. Deb. Stk.	100	64
12/	Minas & Rio, Ltd.	20	9½
5/2	Namur & Liege	20	12½
11/6	Do. Pref.	20	29
/	Natal & Na. Cruz, Ld., 7 p.c. Cum Pref.	20	7½
—	Nitrate Ltd., Ord.	10	5
—	Do. 7 p.c. Pr. Con. Or.	10	3½
—	Do. Def. Conv. Ord.	10	½
7/	N.-E. Urgy., Ltd., Ord.	10	14½
7/	Do. 7 p.c. Pref.	10	15
—	N.-W. Argentine Ld., 7 p.c. Pref.	10	2½
6	Do. 6 p.c. 1 Deb. Stk.	100	113
—	Do. 2 Deb. Stk.	100	94
—	N.W. Uruguay 6 p.c. 1 Pref. Stk.	100	17
—	Do. 5 p.c. 2 Pref. Stk.	100	7½
6	Do. 6 p.c. Deb. Stk.	100	80½
22/	Ottoman (Sm. Aid.)	20	14½
—	Paraguay Cntl., Ld., 5 p.c. Perm. Deb. Stk.	100	11
—	Piræus, Ath., & Pelo.	275	1½
	Pto. Alegre & N. Hambg. Ld., 7 p.c. Pref. Shs.	20	4
6	Do. Mt. Deb. Stk. Red.	100	77½
—	Puerto Cabello & Val. Ld.	10	1½
5	Recife & S. Francisco	100	73
2	R Ciaro S. Paulo, Ld., Sh.	10	22½
	Do. Deb. Stk.	100	127
	Royal Sardinian Ord.	10	11½

Foreign Railways (*continued*):—

Last Div.	Name.	Paid.	Price.
5/	Royal Sardinian Pref.	10	12½
5/	Sambre & Meuse	20	18
5/6	Do. Pref.	10	12½
28/	San Paulo Ld.	20	35
2/9½	Do. New Ord. £10 sh.	6	10
2/	Do. 5 p.c. Non. Cm. Pref.	10	12
5½	Do. Deb. Stk.	100	134
5	Do. 5 p.c. Deb. Stk.	100	127
—	S. Fé & Cordova, Gt. Sthn., Ld., Shares	100	51½
6	Do. Perp. Deb. Stk.	100	123
3/2½	S. Austrian	20	7½
10/	Sthn. Braz. R. Gde. do Sul, Ld.	20	8
6	Do. 6 p.c. Deb. Stk.	100	71½
4	Swedish Centl., Ld., 4 p.c. Deb. Stk.	100	107
5	Do. Pref.	100	100
1/9	Taltal, Ld.	5	2½
—	Uruguay Nthn., Ld. 7 p.c. Pfd. Stk.	100	8
3½	Do. 5 p.c. Deb. Stk.	100	30
—	Villa Maria & Rufino, Ld., 6 p.c. Pref. Shs.	100	20
4	Do. 4 p.c. 1 Deb. Stk.	100	74
6/0/0	Do. 6 p.c. 2 Deb. Stk.	100	47
5/9	West Flanders	8½	21
5/6	Do. 5½ p.c. Pref.	10	18
3/	Wstn. of Havana, Ld.	10	4½

FOREIGN RAILWAY OBLIGATIONS

Per Cent.	Name.	Price.
6	Alagoas Ld., 6 p.c. Deb., Rd.	83½
—	Alcoy & Gandia, Ld., 5 p.c. Debs., Red.	25
5	Arauco., Ld., 5 p.c. 1st Mt., Rd.	64½
—	Do. 6 p.c. Mt. Deb., Rd.	44
6	Brazil G. Sthn., L., Mt. Dbs., Rd.	80½
6	Do. Mt. Dbs. 1893, Rd.	43½
5½	Campos & Caran. Dbs., Rd.	76
6	Central Bahia, L., Dbs., Rd.	90½
5½	Conde d'Eu, L., Dbs., Rd.	76
6	Costa Rica, L., 1st Mt. Dbs., Rd.	111
6	Do. 2nd Dbs., Rd.	92
5	Do. Prior Mt. Db., Rd.	104
6	Cucuta Mt. Dbs., Rd.	106
5½	Donna Thrsa. Cris., L., Dbs., Rd.	71½
3	Eastn. of France, £20 Dbs., Rd.	19
4	Egyptn. Delta Light, L., Db., Rd.	100
—	Espito. Santo & Cara. 5 p.c. Stl. Dbs., Rd.	38
4	Gd. Russian Nic., Rd.	102
5	Inter-Oceanic Mex., L., 5 p.c. Pr. Ln. Dbs., Rd.	103
3	Ital. 3 p.c. Bds. A & B, Rd.	57½
—	Ituana 6 p.c. Debs., 1918	74
—	Leopoldina, 6 p.c. Dbs. £50 Bds.,	21
—	Do. do. Comms. Cert.	21
—	Do. 5 p.c. Stg. Dbs. (1888), Rd.	30
—	Do. do. Comm. Certs.	30
—	Do. 5 p.c. Stg. Dbs. (1890), Rd.	21
—	Do. do. Comms. Certs.	21
—	Macahé & Cam. 5 p.c. Dbs., Rd.	30
—	Do. do. Comms. Certs.	30
—	Do. (Cantagallo), 5 p.c., Red.	30
—	Do. do. Comm. Certs.	30
—	Manila Ltd., 6 p.c. Deb., Red.	23
6	Do. Prior Lien Mt., Rd.	104
6	Do. Series "B," Rd.	80
7	Matanzas & Sab., Rd.	101½
6	Minas & Rio, L., 6 p.c. Dbs., Rd.	96
5	Mogyana 5 p.c. Deb. Bds., Rd.	104
5	Moscow-Jaros., Rd.	106½
5½	Natal & Na. Cruz Ltd., 5½ p.c. Debs., Red.	86
5	Nitrate, Ltd. Mt. Bds., Red.	80
3	Nthn. France, Red.	19
4	N. of S. Af. Rep. (Trnsvl.) Gu. Bds. Red.	95
3	Nthn. of Spain £20 Pri. Obs. Red.	8½
6	Ottmn. (Smy to A.) (Kujk) Asnt. Debs., Red.	109
6	Ottmn. (Seraik.) Asg. Debs. Red.	109
6	Ottmn. (Seraik.) Non-Asg. D., Rd	109
5	Ottmn. Kuyjk. Ext. Red.	106
5	Ottmn. Serkeuy. Ext. Red.	101½
5	Ottmn. Tireh Ext. 1910	98
5	Ottmn. Debs, 1886, Red.	98½
5	Do. 1888, Red. 1935	97½
5	Do. 1893, Red. 1935	99
5	Ottmn. of Anlia. Debs., Rd.	93
5	Do. Ser. II	89
4	Ottomn. Smyr. & Cas. Ext. Bds., Red.	83½
3	Paris, Lyon & Medit. (old sys., £20), Red.	19
3	Paris, Lyon & Medit. (new sys., £20), Red.	19
50/	Piræus, At. & Pelp., 6 p.c. 1st Mt. Bds., Red.	88½
3	Do. 5 p.c. Mt. Bds., Red.	66½
4	Pretoria-Pietbg., Ltd., Red.	93
7	Puerto Cab. & Val., Ltd., 1st Mt. Debs., Red.	94
—	Rio de Jano. & Nthn., Ltd., 6 p.c. £100 Deb., Red.	21
—	Rio de Jano. (Gr. Para.), 5 p.c. 1st Mt. St. £100 Debs., Red.	21
2	Royal Sardinian, A, Rd. £20	12
	Royal Sardinian, B., Rd. £20	12

Foreign Rly. Obligations (*continued*):—

Per Cent.	Name.	Price.
5	Ryl. Trns.-Afric. 5 p.c. 1st Mt. £100 Bds., Red.	61
7	Sagua La Grande, B pRd.	98
4	Sa. Fe & Cor. G.S., Ld. Pr Ln. Bds.	104
5	Sa. Fe, 5 p.c. 2nd Reg. Dbs.	80
3	South Austrian, £20 Red.	15½
3	South Austrian, (Ser. X.)	15½
3	South Italian £20 Obs. (Ser. A to G), Red.	12½
3½	S.W. of Venez. (Barq.), Ltd., 7 p.c. 1st Mt. £100 Debs.	55½
5	Taltal, Ltd., 5 p.c. 1st Ch. Debs., Red.	98
5	Utd. Rwys. Havana, Red.	88
3	Wtrn. of France, £20 Red.	19
6	Wrn. B. Ayres St. Mt. Debs., 1902	111
6	Wrn. B. Ayres, Reg. Cert.	109
5	Do. Mt. Bds.	122
6	Wtrn. of Havna., Ld, Mt. Dbs., Rd.	98
7	Wrn. Ry. San Paulo Red.	102
—	Wrn. Santa Fé, 7 p.c. Red.	38
4/7	Zafra & Huelva, 3 p.c. Red.	3

BANKS.

Div.	Name.	Paid.	Price.
2/4½	Agra, Ltd.	6	3½
4/2½	Anglo-Argentine, Ltd., £9	7	5½
8 fls.	Anglo-Austrian	120f	13½
6/	Anglo-Californian, Ltd., £20 Shares	10	11
4/	Anglo-Egyptian, Ltd., £15	5	6
5/	Anglo-Foreign Bkg., Ltd.	7	8
7/	Anglo-Italian, Ltd.	5	7
7/6	Bk. of Africa, Ltd., £18¾	6¼	10½
20/	Bk. of Australasia	40	51
10/	Bk. of Brit. Columbia	20	20½
25/	Bk. of Brit. N. America	50	65
20/	Bk. of Egypt, Ltd., £25	12½	18
5/	Bk. of Mauritius, Ltd.	10	9½
18/	Bk. of N. S. Wales	20	38½
4 p.c.	Bk. of N. Zland. Gua. Stk.	100	103
6/	Bk. of Roumania, £20 Shs.	6	7½
2/6	Tarapaca & Ldn., Ltd., £10	5	3½
—	Bque. Fse. de l'Afri. du S.	100f	3½
f.12.50	Bque. Internatle. de Paris	20	24
6/	Brit. Bk. of S. America, Ltd., £20 Shares	10	10
16/	Capital & Cties., L., £50	10	39
16/	Chart. of India, &c.	20	32½
10/	City, Ltd., £40 Shares	10	19½
18/	Colonial, £100 Shares	30	21
10/	Delhi and London, Ltd.	25	—
5/	German of London, Ltd.	10	10½
25/	Hong-Kong & Shanghai	28½	43½
4/	Imperl. of Persia	6½	3½
10/	Imperl. Ottoman, £20 Shs	10	11½
12/	Intrnatl. of Ldn., Ld., £20	15	11½
10/	Ionian, Ltd.	25	15
16/	Lloyds, Ltd., £50 Shs.	8	30
10/	Ldn. & Braziln. Ltd., £20	10	18
44/	Ldn. & County, Ltd., £80	20	101
9/	Ldn. & Hanseatic, L., £20	10	10½
22/6	Ldn. & Midland, L., £60	12½	53½
8/9	Ldn. & Provin., Ltd., £10	5	22½
39/	Ldn. & Riv. Plate, L., £25	15	50
2/1½	Ldn. & San Fcisco, Ltd.	7	4½
28/	Ldn. & Sth. West., L., £50	20	69
26/	Ldn. & Westmins., L., £100	20	55½
3/	Ldn. of Mex. & S. Amer., Ltd., £10 Shs.	6	5½
15/	Ldn. Joint Stk., L., £100	15	33½
12/9½	Ldn., Paris & Amer., L. £20	16	25
2/4½	Merchant Bkg., L., £9	4	2½
6/3	Metropn, Ltd., £50 Shs.	5	14½
9/	National, Ltd., £50 Shs.	10	19½
4/5	Natl. of Mexico, $100 Shs.	$40	13
1/3	National of N. Z., L., £7½	2½	2
3/	National S. Afric. Rep.	10	15
18/10½	National Provcl. of Eng., Ltd., £75 Shs.	10½	49½
21/7½	Do. do. £60 Shs.	12	56½
6/6	NorthEastn., Ltd., £20 Shs	6	14½
19/	Parr's, Ld., £100 Shs.	20	92
12/6	Prov. of Ireland, L., £100	12½	28½
40/	Stand. of S. Afric., L., £100	25	67
12/6	Union of Australia L., £75	25	28
4 p.c.	Do. do. Ins. Stk. Dep. 1900	100	102
15/6	Union of Ldn., Ltd., £100	15½	35½

BREWERIES AND DISTILLERIES.

Div.	Name.	Paid.	Price.
4½	Albion Prp. 1 Mt. Db. Sk.	100	112
4	All Saints', L., Db. Sk. Rd.	100	97
7	Allsopp, Ltd.	100	153
6	Do. Cum. Pref	100	158
4½	Do. Deb. Stk., Red.	100	118
3½	Do. Deb. Stk., Red.	100	101
4½	Alton & Co., L., Db., Rd	100	106
4½	Do. Mt. Bds., 1896	100	105
—	Arnold, Perrett, Ltd.	10	6
6	Do. Cum. Pref.	10	10
4½	Do. 1 Mt. Db. Stk., Rd.	100	106

Breweries &c. (*continued*):—

Div.	Name.	Paid.	Price.
5½	Arrol, A., & Sons, L., Cum. Pref. Shs.	10	10
4½	Do. 1 Mt. Db. Stk., Rd.	100	104
5	Backus, 1 Mt. Db., Red.	100	61
4	Barclay, Perk., L., Cu. Pf.	10	11½
3½	Do. Mt. Db. Stk., Red.	100	110
—	Barnsley, Ltd.	10	12
6	Do. Cum. Pref.	10	14
1/3	Barrett's, Ltd	2½	1½
1/3	Do. 5 p.c. Pref.	2½	2½
3/	Bartholomay, Ltd.	10	3½
8	Do. Cum. Pref.	10	9
6	Do. Deb.	100	100½
5	Bass, Ratcliff, Ltd., Cum. Pref. Stk.	100	144½
4½	Do. Mt. Db. Stk., Rd.	100	126
4	Bell, J., L., 1 Mt. D. Stk., R	100	100
2/6	Benskin's, L., Cum. Pref.	5	—
4½	Do. 1 Mt. Db. Stk Red.	100	—
4½	Do. "B" Deb. Sk, Rd.	100	—
7/	Bentley's Yorks., Ltd.	10	11½
6/	Do. Cum. Pref.	10	12½
4½	Do. Mt. Debs., Red.	100	110
4½	Do. do. 1892, Red.	100	110
—	Bieckert's, Ltd.	20	2
5	Do. Debs., Red.	100	57
—	Birmingham., Ltd., 6 p.c. Cum. Pref.	5	2½
4½	Do. Mt. Debs., Red.	50	40½
5½	Boardman's, Ld., Cm. Pf.	10	8½
4½	Do., Perp. 1 Mt. Db. Sk.	100	105½
30/9	Brain & Co., Ltd.	100	100
4½	Brakspear, L., 1 D. Stk. Rd	100	109
4	Brandon's, L., 1 D. Stk. R.	100	105½
21/	Bristol (Georges) Ltd.	10	46
6	Do. Cum. Pref.	10	18
5	Do. Mt. Db. Sk. 1888 Rd.	100	115½
17/6	Bristol United, Ltd.	10	35
6	Do. Cum. Pref.	10	16½
4½	Do. Db. Sk. Rd.	100	126
5½	Buckley's, L., C. Pre-prf.	10	10½
4½	Do. 1 Mt. Db. Stk. Rd.	100	105½
4	Bullard & Sns, L., D. Sk. R.	100	105
6	Bushell, Watk., L., C. Pf.	10	14
4½	Do. 1 Mt. Db. Sk. Rd.	100	112
5	Camden, Ltd., Cum. Pref.	10	11½
4½	Do. 1 Mt. Db. Sk. Rd.	100	108
5½	Cameron, Ltd., Cm. Prf.	10	13½
4½	Do. Mort Deb. Stk.	100	108
3½	Do. Perp Mt. Db. Sk.	100	100½
5	Cam'bell, J'stone, L., C. Pf.	5	5½
4½	Do. 4½ p.c. 1 Mt. Db. Sk.	100	105
4	Campbell, Praed, L., Per. 1 Mort. Deb. Stk.	100	106
4	Cannon, L., Mt. Db. Stk.	100	109
4	Do. "B" Deb. Stk.	100	104
5	Castlemaine, L., 1 Mt. Db.	100	94
3½	Charrington, Ltd., Mort. Deb. Stk. Red.	100	106
2/	Cheltnhm. Orig., Ltd.	5	7
6	Do. Cum. Pref.	5	7½
4	Do. Debs. Red.	100	107
10/	Chicago, Ltd.	10	3½
6	Do. Debs.	100	87½
—	Cincinnati, Ltd.	10	½
—	Do. Cum. Pref.	10	1½
10/	City of Baltimore	10	4
16/	Do. 8 p.c. Cum. Pref	10	8
14/	City of Chicago, Ltd.	10	1½
8	Do. Cum. Pref.	10	6
13	City of London, Ltd.	100	205½
5	Do. Cum. Pref.	100	137
4	Do. Mt. Deb. Stk., Rd.	100	112½
2/	Colchester, Ltd.	5	5
7	Do. Pref.	5	7
4½	Do. Deb. Stk., Red.	100	109
5	Combe, Ltd., Cum. Pref.	10	14½
4	Do. Mt. Db. Stk, Rd.	100	112
3½	Do. Perp. Deb. Stk.	100	107
5	Comm'cial, L., D. Sk., Rd.	100	106½
5	Courage, L., Cm. Pref. Shs.	100	137½
4	Do. Irr. Mt. Deb. Stk.	100	126
3½	Do. Irr. "B" Mt. Db. Sk.	100	104
8	Daniell & Sons, Ltd.	10	
7	Do. Cum. Pref.	10	12½
4½	Do. 1 Mt. Perp. Db. Sk.	100	108½
4½	Do. "B" Deb. Stk.	100	102
10d.	Dartford, Ltd.	5	5
2/9	Do. Cum. Pref.	5	5½
4	Do. 1 Mt. Db. Sk. Rd.	100	100
4	Davenport, Ld., 1 D. Stk.	100	102½
10/	Denver United, Ltd.	10	3½
8	Do. Cum. Pref.	10	8½
6	Do. Debs.	100	98½
4½	Deuchar, L., 1 D. Sk., Rd.	100	108
8/	Distillers, Ltd.	10	24
4½	Do. Mt. Db. Stk., Rd.	100	115½
—	Dublin Distillers, Ltd.	5	1½
3/	Do. Cum. Pref.	5	4½
4½	Do. Irr. Deb. Stk.	100	—
5	Eadie, Ltd., Cum. Pref.	10	11
4	Do. Irr. 1 Mt. Db. Sk.	100	106
10/	Edinbgh. Utd., Ltd.	10	13
6	Do. Cum. Prf.	10	13½
5	Do. 1 Mt. Dbs.	100	110½
4	Eldridge, Pope, L. D. St. R.	100	107
—	Emerald & Phœnix, Ltd.	10	1½
8	Do. Cum. Pref.	10	6½
6	Empress Ltd., C. Pf.	10	11½
4½	Do. Mt. Deb. Stk.	100	106
10/	Farnham, Ltd.	10	16½
6	Do. Cum. Pref.	10	14½
4	Fenwick, L., 1 D. Sk., Rd.	100	103
4	Flower & Sons, Irr. D. Sk.	100	111
4	Friary, L., 1 Db. Stk., Rd.	100	103½
4	Do. 1 "A" Db. Sk., Rd	100	100
4½	Groves, L., 1 Db. Sk., Rd.	100	110
14	Guinness, Ltd.	100	593
6	Do. Cum. Prf. Stk.	100	189½
5	Do. Deb. Stk., Red.	100	122
5	Hall's Oxford L., Cm. Pf.	5	5½
6/	Hancock, Ld., Cm. Pf. Ord.	10	14
7/	Do. Def. Ord.	10	17½

Breweries, &c. (*continued*) :—

Div.	Name.	Paid.	Price.
6	Hancock, Ld., Cum. Pref.	10	15½
4	Do. 1 Deb. Stk., Rd.	100	112
5	Hoare, Ltd. Cum. Pref.	10	12¾
5	Do. "A" Cum. Pref.	10	12
4	Do. Mt. Deb. Stk., Rd.	100	111
3½	Do. do. do. Rd.	100	104
4/6	Hodgson's, Ltd.	5	10
5	Do. 1 Mt. Db., Red.	—	120½
4	Do. 2 Mt. Db., 1906	—	102
4½	Hopcraft & N., Ltd., 1 Mt. Deb. Stk., Red.	100	103
5	Huggins, Ltd., Cm. Prf.	10	12¾
4½	Do. 1st D. Stk. Rd.	100	113
4½	Do. "B" Db. Stk. Rd.	100	111
22/	Hull, Ltd.	10	17
7	Do. Cum. Pref.	10	14½
4½	Ind, Coope, L., D.Sk., Rd.	100	118
4	Do. "B" Mt. Db. Stk. Rd.	100	111
8/	Indianapolis, Ltd.	10	3½
8	Do. Cm. Prf.	10	9¾
5/	Jones, Frank, Ltd.	10	3½
7½	Do. Cum. Pref.	10	7½
5	Do. 1st Mort. Debs.	100	90½
4/	J. Kenward & Ct., Ltd.	5	5½
4½	Kingsbury, L., 1 D.Sk., Rd	100	—
4	Lacon, L., D. Stk., Red.	100	110
4	Do. Irrd. "B" D. Sk.	100	106
4/	Lascelles, Ltd.	5	11
6	Do. Cum. Pref.	5	7¾
5	Leney, Ltd., Cum. Pref.	10	11½
4	Do. 1 Mt. Db. Stk. Rd.	100	102
30/7½	Lion, Ltd., £25 shares	17	49½
10/9¼	Do. New £10 shares	6	17
6	Do. Perp. Pref.	20	33
4	Do. B. Mt. Db. Sk. Rd.	100	107
4½	Lloyd & Y., Ltd., 1 Mt. Deb. Stk., Rd.	100	100½
4½	Locke & S., Ltd., Irr. 1st Mt. Deb. Stk.	100	101
4½	Lovibond, Ltd., 1st Mt. Deb. Stk., Rd.	100	102½
30/4	Lucas & Co., Ld., Deb. Stk.	100	107
8/	Manchester, Ltd.	10	19
7	Do. Cum. Pref.	10	16½
5	Marston, J., L., Cm. Prf.	10	10¾
4	Do. 1 Mt. Db. Sk., Rd.	100	101½
9/	Massey's Burnley, Ltd.	10	17
6	Do. Cum. Pref.	10	14½
4½	McCracken, Ltd., 1 Mt. Deb., 1908	100	61½
5	McEwan, Ltd., Cm. Pref.	10	15
5	Meux, Ltd., Cum. Pref.	10	14
4	Do. Mt. Db. Stk. Red.	100	111
4½	Michell & A., Ltd., 1 Mt. Deb. Stk. Red.	100	106
4½	MileEndDist.Db.Sk.Rd.	100	109
—	Milwaukee & Chic., Ltd.	10	1½
4/	Do. Cum. Pref.	10	6½
4½	Michell, Toms, L., Db.	50	57
6	Morgan, Ltd., Cum. Pref.	10	14½
20/	Nalder & Coll., Ltd.	10	35
6	Do. Cum. Pref.	10	15¾
4½	Do. Deb. Red.	100	113
3/	New Beeston, Ltd.	5	4½
2/9	Do. Cum. Pref.	5	5
4	Do. Mt. Deb. Stk. Red.	100	95½
12/	Newcastle, Ltd.	10	19½
6	Do. Cum. Pref.	10	15
5	Do. 1 Mt. Deb., 1911	100	110½
4	Do. "A" Deb. Stk. Red.	100	104
6	New England, Ltd	10	5
8	Do. Cum. Pref.	10	9¾
6	Do. Debs. Red.	100	104½
4	New London, L., 1 D.Sk.	100	103
7/2	New Westminster, Ltd.	4	10½
2/4½	Do. Pref.	4	6½
—	New York, Ltd.	10	1
—	Do. 8 p.c. Cum. Pref.	10	4½
6	Do. 1 Mt. Deb. Red.	100	80½
5	Noakes, Ld., Cum. Pref.	10	12
4	Do 1 Mt. Db. Stk., Rd.	100	104
4½	Norfolk, L., "A" D.Sk.Rd.	100	106
10/	Northampton, Ld.	10	16
7	Do. Cum. Pref.	10	16
6	Do. Cum. Pref.	10	12½
5	Do. 1 Mt. Per. Db.Sk.	100	126
4	Nth. East., L., 1 D.Sk.Rd.	100	102
4½	N. Worcesters., L. Per. 1 Mort. Deb. Stock	100	98½
6	Nottingham, L., Cm. Prf.	10	12
5	Do. 1 Mt. Deb. Stk., Red.	100	114
17/4	Do. "B" do. Red.	50	112
6/	Ohlsson' Cape, Ld.	5	17
7	Do. Cum. Pref.	5	8¾
4½	Do. 2nd Cum. Pref.	5	5½
5	Do. Deb. Stk., Red.	100	113
4½	Oldfield, L., 1 Mt. Db. Stk.	100	106
6	Page & Overt., L., Cm. Prf.	10	13¾
4½	Do. 1 Mt. Dbs., Red.	100	109
10/	Parker's Burslem, Ltd.	10	24½
6	Do. Cum. Pref.	10	15
4	Do. 1 Mt. Db. Stk., Red.	100	111
4	Persse, Ld., 1 Mt. Db. Rd.	100	96½
4	Phipps, L., Irr. 1 Db. Stk.	100	113
8	Plymouth, L., Min. Cu. Pf.	10	13½
4½	Do. Mt. Deb. Stk., Red.	100	104½
4½	Pryor, Reid, L., 1 D.S., R.(†	100	103½
5	Reid's, Ld., Cm. Pref. Stk.	100	137½
4	Do. Mt. Deb. Stk., Red.	100	112
3½	Do. "B" Mt. Db. Stk., Rd	100	102
5	Rhondda Val., L., Cu. Pf	10	11
4½	Do. 1 Mt. Deb. Stk., Rd.	100	109
5	Robinson, Ld., Cum. Pref.	10	11½
4½	Do. 1 Mt. Perp. Db. Stk.	100	112
4/	Rochdale, Ltd.	10	6
4½	Do. 1 Mt. Deb. Stk.	100	98½
7	Royal, Brentford, Ltd.	10	21
	Do. Cum. Pref.	10	15
4½	Do. 1 Mt. Dbs. Red	100	109
6/	St. Louis, Ltd.	10	4
8	Do. Cum. Pref.	10	8¾
24/	St. Pauli, Ltd.	10	10
7	Do. Cum. Pref.	10	12
4½	Salt (T.), L., 1 Db. Sk. Rd.	100	110

Breweries, &c. (*continued*) :—

Div.	Name.	Paid.	Price.
4½	Salt (T.), "B" Db. Stk. Red	100	108
—	San Francisco, Ltd.	10	¼
—	Do. 8 p.c. Cum. Pref.	10	½
4½	Savill Brs., L., D. Sk. Rd.	100	118
4½	Scarboro., Ltd., 1 Db. Stk.	100	101
4	Shaw (Hy.), Ltd., 1 Mt. Db. Stk., Red.	100	104
22/	Showell's, Ltd.	10	33
7	Do. Cum. Pref.	10	17½
3/	Do. Gua. Shs.	5	7½
4½	Do. Mt. Db. Stk., Red.	100	—
4	Simonds, L., 1 D. Sk., Rd.	100	109
5½	Simson & McP., L., Cu. Pf.	10	9½
4½	Do. 1 Mt. Deb. Stk.	100	100
5/	Smith, Garrett, L., £20 Shs	10	16½
5	Do. Cum. Pref.	20	26
3½	Do. 3½ p.c. Mt. Db. Stk.	100	107
5	Smith's, Tadcster, L., CPf	10	12
4½	Do. Deb. Stk., Red.	100	112
4	Do. Deb. Stk. Red.	100	108
4½	Star, L., 1 M. Db. Stk., Rd.	100	106
4	Steward & P., L., 1 D. Sk.	100	111
9/	Strettons Derby, Ltd.	10	13
6	Do. Cum. Pref.	10	13½
4	Do. Irr. 1 Mt. Db. Stk.	100	103½
4½	Strong, Romsey, L., 1 D. S.	100	115
5	Stroud, L., Db. Sk., Rd.	100	111½
4½	Tadcaster To'er, L., D.Sk.	100	113
8/	Tamplin, Ltd	10	21
6	Do. Cum. Pref.	100	15
4	Do. "A" Db. Sk., Rd.	10	107
6	Thorne, Ltd., Cum. Pref.	10	14½
4	Do. Deb. Stk., Red.	100	105½
15/	Threlfall, Ltd.	10	47
6	Do. Cum. Pref.	10	16½
5	Do. 1 Mt. Dbs., Red.	100	116
4	Tollemache, L., D. Sk. Rd.	100	105
4	Truman, Hanb., D. Sk., R.	100	110
3	Do. "B" Mt. Db. Sk., Rd.	100	95
10/	United States, Ltd.	10	10
8	Do. Cum. Pref.	10	12
6	Do. 1 Mt. Deb	100	107½
6/	Walker & H., Ld., Cm. Prf.	10	11½
4½	Do. 1 Mt. Deb. Stk., Red.	100	107
5	Walker, Peter, Ld. Cm. Prf.	10	14
4	Do. 1 Mt. Dbs. Red.	100	111
4	Wallingford, L., D.Sk.Rd.	100	107
6	Watney, Ld., Cm. Prf. Sk.	100	167½
5	Do. Mt. Db. Sk., Rd.	100	115½
4½	Do. "B" Mt. Db. Sk., Rd.	100	112
3½	Do. Mt. Db. Stk.	100	101
5	Watney, D., Ld., Cm. Prf.	10	12½
4½	Do. 1 Mt. Db. Stk.	100	106
10/	Webster & Sons, Ltd.	10	16½
6	Do. Cum. Pref.	10	14
5	Wenlock Ltd., Pref.	10	12½
4	Do. 1 Mt. Db. Sk., Rd.	100	108
5	West Cheshire, L., Cu. Pf.	10	10½
4	Do. Irred. 1 Mt. Db. Sk.	100	99
4½	Whitbread, L., Cu. Pf. Sh.	100	124½
4	Do. Db. Stk., Red.	100	112
3½	Do. "B" Db. Stk., Rd.	100	100
9/	Wolverhmpton & D. Ld.	10	16½
6	Do. Cum. Pref.	10	13½
4½	Do. 1 Mt. Dbs., Red.	100	108
5½	Worthington, Ld., Cm. Prf.	10	15½
5½	Do. Cum. "B" Pref.	10	13¾
4½	Do. Mt. Db. Sk., Rd.	100	112
3½	Do. Irr. "B" Db. Stk.	100	102
10/	Yates's Castle, Ltd.	10	13½
5	Do. Cum. Pref.	10	11
5	Younger W., L., Cu. Pf. Sh.	100	135

CANALS AND DOCKS.

Last Div.	Name.	Paid.	Price.
4	Birmingham Canal	100	142½
—	E. & W. India Dock	100	21
4	Do. Deb. Stk.	100	—
50/	Do. Def. Deb. Stk.	100	—
3½	Do. 1st Mt. Certs.	100	—
4	Do. Mt. Bds. (1885)	—	—
40/	G. Junction Ord. Shs.	100	151½
6/	Do. do. Pref.	10	19
4½	King's Lynn Per. Db. Stk.	100	118½
2½	Leeds & Lpool Canal	100	71
2½	Lndn & St. Kath. Dks.	100	56
4½	Do. Pref.	100	136½
4½	Do. Pref., 1878	100	132½
4½	Do. Pref., 1882	100	130
4	Do. Deb. Stk.	100	134½
—	Mchester Ship C. 5 p.c. Pf.	10	1½
3½	Do. 1st Perp. Mt. Deb.	100	98
—	Milford Dks. Db. Stk. "A"	100	18½
3½	Millwall Dk.	100	59
5	Do. Perp. Pref.	100	140½
4½	Do. Pref.	100	106½
5	Do. New Per. Prf., 1887	100	126½
5	Do. Per. Deb. Stk.	100	152½
4/	Newhaven Har.	10	14½
2½	N. Metropolitan	100	65
5	Sharpness Nw. Pf. "A" Sk.	100	144½
4	Do. Deb. Stk.	100	118¼
4	Sheffield & S. Yorks Nav. 4½ p.c. Pref Stk.	100	117½
36.432	Suez Canal	20	137
7	Surrey Comcl. Dok., Ord.	100	148½
7	Do. Min. 4 p.c. Pref. "A"	110	150
5	Do. Pref. "B"	100	148½
5	Do do. "C"	100	148½
5	Do. do. "D"	100	144½
4½	Do. Deb. Stk.	100	152½

COMMERCIAL, INDUSTRIAL, &c.

Last Div.	Name.	Paid.	Price.
5	Accles, L., 1 Mt. Db., Red.	100	84½
2/6	Aërated Bread, Ltd.	1	12¾
—	African Gold Recovery, L.	1	¼
2/	Aluminium, L., "A" Shs.	1	2
4½	Do. 1 Mt. Db. Stk., Red.	100	97
5½	Amelia Nitr., L., 1 Mort. Deb., Red.	100	82½
7/	Anglo-Chil. Nitrate, Ltd., Cum. Pref.	10	6½
4½	Do. Cons. Mt. Bds., Red.	100	79½
4½	Anglo-Russian Cotton, Ld., 1 Charge Debs., Red.	100	99
11/3	Angus (G., & Co., L.), £10	7½	17
6/	Apollinaris, Ltd.	10	11½
5/	Do. 5 p.c. Cum. Pref.	10	10½
4	Do. Irred. Deb. Stock	100	104
6/	Appleton, French, & S., L.	5	½
3/	Argentine Meat Pres., L., 7 p.c. Pref.	10	2½
5	Argentine Refinry, Db. Rd.	100	98
6d.	Armstrong, Whitw., Ltd.	1	3¾
4	Do. Cum. Pref.	5	6½
5	Artisans', Labr. Dwllgs., L.	100	131½
4½	Do. Non-Cm. Prf., 1879	100	132½
4½	Do. do. 1884	100	132½
—	Asbestos & Asbestic, Ltd.	10	8
2/7½	Ashley-grdns., L., C. Prf.	5	6½
4½	Do. 1 Mt. Deb. Stk.	100	112½
5/	Assam Rly. & Trdng., L., 8 p.c. Cum. Pref. "A"	10	15½
—	Do. Deferrd. "B" Shs.	1	4½
—	Do. do. (iss.f.pd)	1	3½
8/	Do. Cum. Pre-Prf. "A"	10	15
6/	Do. New Pref.	10	11½
5	Do. Debs., Red.	100	107
5	Do. Red. Mort. Debs.	100	111
6	Aust'lian Pastrl, L., Cu. Pf.	10	7½
8d.	Aylesbury Dairy, Ltd.	1	1½
4	Do. 4 p.c. Mt. Dbs.	100	104½
10/	Babcock & Wilcox, Ltd.	10	30
6	Do. 6 p.c. Cm. Prf.	10	16
8	Baker (Chs.), L., Cm. Pf.	5	9
8	Do. "B," Cm. Pref.	5	8½
8d.	Barker (John), Ltd.	1	2¾
5½	Do. Cum. Pref.	5	7½
4½	Do. Irred. 1 Mt. Db. Stk.	100	130
—	Barnagore Jute, Ltd.	5	3
5	Do. Cum. Pref.	5	4¾
7½d.	Belgravia Dairy, Ltd.	1	1½
5/	Bell (R.) & Co., Ltd.	5	3½
1/	Bell's Asbestos, Ltd.	1	¾
5	Do. Mt. Db. Bds., Rd.	100	103
10/	Bengal Mills, Ltd.	10	11½
6/	Do. 5 p.c. Cum. Prf.	10	10½
2/5	Benson (J.W.) L., Cm. Pf.	10	10½
4	Do. Perp. Mt. Db. Stk.	100	101
6	Bergvik, L., 6 p.c. Cm. Pf.	10	12
12/	Do. Dfd.	10	9½
4½	Do. 1 Dbs., Red.	100	103½
5/	Birm'ham Vinegar, Ltd.	5	13
5	Do. Cum. Pref.	5	5½
4½	Do. 1 Mt. Db. Stk., Rd.	100	109½
5	Boake (A.) L., 5 p.c. Cu. Pf.	10	10¾
2/6	Bodega, Ltd.	5	8½
4½	Do. Mt. Deb. Stk., Rd.	100	111
8/	Bottomley & Brs., Ltd.	10	6½
6/	Do. 6 p.c. Pt.	10	9½
8½d.	Bovril, Ltd.	1	1½
1/0½	Do. Def.	1	[illegible]
6½d.	Do. Cum. Pref.	1	[illegible]
4½	Do. Deb. Stk.	100	101
5/	Bradbury, Gretrex., Ltd., £10 share	8	14
5/	Do. 5 p.c. Cum. Pref.	10	13½
5/	Brewers' Sugar, L., 5 p.c. Cum. Pref.	10	10½
3/6	Brighton Grd. Hotel, Ld.	5	3½
4	Do Mt. Db. Stk., Red.	100	100½
5	Bristol Hotel & Palm. Co., Ltd. 1st Mt. Red. Deb.	100	106
9½d.	British & Bengton's. Tea Tr. Asc., Ltd.	1	1½
5	Do. Cum. Prf.	5	5½
—	British Deli & Lgkat. Tobacco, Ltd.	1	½
—	Do. Cum. Prf.	1	½
—	British Tea Table, Ltd.	1	2½
5½	Do. Cum. Pref.	1	1½
2/6	Brooke, Ben., & Co., Ltd., Cum. Pref.	5	5¾
7/6	Brooke, Bond & Co., Ltd.	5	20½
3/	Brown Brs., L., Cum. Pref.	5	5½
10/	Browne & Eagle, Ltd.	10	13½
5	Do. Cum. Pref.	10	13
4	Do. Mrt. Db. Sk., Red.	100	110
20/	Brunner, Mond, & Co., Lt.	10	41
7/	Do. £10 shares	3½	17
7	Do. Cum. Pref.	10	18
7	Do. £10 shares	5	8½
10/	Bryant & May, Ltd.	5	19½
3/	Bucknall, H., & Sons, Lt.	5	7½
6	Do. Cum Pref.	5	8
4/	Burke, E. & J., Ltd.	5	7½
6	Do. Cum. Pref.	5	7½
6	Do. Irred. Deb. Stk.	100	155
1/	Burlington Htls. Co., Ltd	1	1½
5	Do. Cum. Pref.	1	1
4	Do. Perp. Deb. Stk.	100	106½
5	Bush, W. J., & Co., Ltd. Cum. Pref.	5	5½
4	Do. 1 Deb. Stk., Red.	100	102
5½	Callard, Stewart, & Watt, Ltd., Cum. Pref.	1	1½
4/	Callender's Cable L., Shs.	5	9½
4½	Do. 1 Deb. Stk., Red.	100	111½
—	Campbell, R., & Sons, Lt.	3	2½
6	Cantareira Water, Bd., Rd	100	99½
5	Do. (2nd issue)	100	92
4	Cartavio Sugar, Ltd., 6 p.c. 1st Debs., Red.	80	82½
9/	Cassell & Co., Ltd., £10	9	15½
5	Causton, Sir J., & Sons, Ltd., Cum. Pref.	10	13½

Commercial, &c. (*continued*) :—

Last Div.	Name.	Paid.	Price.
4	Cent. Prod. Mkt. of B.A 1st Mt. Str. Debs.	100	81
4	Chappell & Co., Ltd. Mt. Deb. Stk. Red.	100	103
6/	Chicago & N.W. Gran 8 p.c. Cum. Pref.	10	[illegible]
—	Chicago Packing & Prov.	10	6
8	Do. Cum. Pref.	10	10½
6/	City Offices, Ltd	36½	13½
3½	Do. Mt. Deb. Stk.	100	108½
7/2½	Cy. London Real Prop., Ltd., £25 shs.	12	19
4/6	Do. £12½ shs.	7½	13½
3½	Do. Deb. Stk. Red.	100	106½
3½	Do. Deb. Stk. Red.	100	105½
3	Do.	100	100½
4/	Cy. of Santos Imprvts., Ltd., 7 p.c. Pref.	10	8½
20/	Clay, Bock, & Co., Ltd.	10	5
8	Do. Cum. Pref.	10	10
6	Do. Mort. Deb.	100	102½
20/	Coats, J. & P., Ltd.	10	60½
6	Do. Cum. Pref.	10	19
4½	Do. Deb. Stk. Red.	100	111½
9½d.	Coburg Hotel, Ltd	1	1½
4	Do. Deb. Stk. Red.	100	102
6	Colonial Consign & Dis., Ltd., Cum. Pref.	5	4¾
4½	Do. 1st Mort. Debs.	100	96½
—	Colorado Nitrate, Ltd.	5	½
4/	Co. Gén. des Asphtes. de F., Ltd	6	6½
5	Do, Non-Cm. Prf.	—	5½
5	Cook, J. W., & Co., Ltd., Cum. Pref.	5	5¾
5	Cook, T., & Son, Egypt, Ltd., 1st Mt. Deb. Red.	100	110½
—	Cork Co., Ltd., 6 p.c. Cum. Pref.	5	2½
5	Cory, W., & Sn, L., Cu. Pf.	5	6¾
4	Do. 1st Deb. Stk. Red.	100	107
8½d.	Crisp & Co., Ltd	1	1¾
5½	Do. Cum. Pref.	1	1½
—	Crompton & Co., Ltd., 7 p.c. Cum. Pref.	5	2
5	Do. 1st Mt. Reg. Deb.	—	88½
4/6	Crossley, J., & Sons, Ltd.	5	8½
5	Do. Cum. Pref.	5	6½
—	Crystal Pal. Ord. "A" Stk.	100	8½
—	Do. "B" Red. Stk	100	1½
6	Do. 6 p.c. 1st 1887 Deb. Stk. Red.	100	117½
—	Do. 6 p.c. 2nd 1887 Deb. Stk. Red.	100	43½
—	Do. 6 p.c. 3rd 1887 Deb. Stk. Red.	100	17½
3	Do. 3 p.c. 1st 1895 Deb. Stk.	100	94½
—	Daimler Motor, Ltd	10	6
4/	Dalgety & Co., £20 Shs.	5	5½
4½	Do. Deb. Stk	100	123
4	Do.	100	115
7/	De Keyser's Ryl. Htl., L.	10	14
5	Do. Cum. Pref.	10	11½
4	Do. Deb. Stk., Red.	100	110
6	Denny, H., & Sons, Ltd., Cum. Pref.	10	14½
5/3	Devas, Routledge & Co. L.	7	8½
5	Dickinson, J., & Co., L., Cum. Pref. Stk.	100	12[illegible]
4½	Domin. Cottn. Mls., Ltd. Mt. Stg. Dbs.	100	97
6/	Dorman, Long & Co., L.	5	4½
—	Eastmans, Ltd	10	2¾
12/	Do. 8 p.c. Cum. Pref.	10	10½
2/6	E. C. Powder, Ltd	3	5½
1/6	Edison & Swn Utd. Elec. Ltd., "A" £5 Shs.	3	2½
2/6	Do. fully-paid	5	4½
4½	Ekman Pulp & Ppr. Co., Ltd., Mt. Deb., Red.	100	96
1/1½	Electric Construc., Ltd.	2	2¾
7	Do. Cum. Pref.	2	3½
2½/	Eley Bros., Ltd.	10	38
—	Elmore's Cop. Deptg., L.	1	¾
—	Elmore's Wire Mnfg., L.	2	½
—	Elysée Pal. Hotel Co., L.	5/	½
5 p.c.	Do. 5 p.c. £100 Db. Rd.	70	95
8½d.	Evans, Ben., & Co., Ltd.	1	1
5	Do. 1 Mt. Db. Sk., Rd.	100	107½
8½d.	Evans, D. H., & Co., L.	1	2½
6	Do. Cum. Pref.	1	1½
4½	Do. 1 Mt. Db. Sk., Rd.	100	112
2/1	*Evening News*, L., 5 p.c. Cum. Pref.	5	5½
5/3	Evered & Co., L., £10 Sh.	7	13
7/6	Do.	10	19
4	Fairbairn Pastoral Co., Aust., L., 1 Mt. Db., Rd.	100	102
6	Fairfield Shipbldg., Ltd., Cum. Pref.	10	10
4½	Do. Mort. Deb. Stk.	100	107½
6/	Farmer & Co., Ld., 6 p.c. Cum. Pref.	10	13½
10	Field, J. C. & J., Ltd.	10	10
14/	Do. 7 p.c. Cum. Pref.	10	14
1/3	Fordham, W.B., & Sns. Ld.	1	2
5/6	Fore-st. Warehouse, Ltd	11	5½
4	Do. Regd. Debs., Rd.	100	103½
3/6	Foster, M. R. & Sons, Ltd.	4	6
5	Do. Pref.	10	11½
9/	Foster, Porter, & Co., L.	10½	15½
4	Fowler, J., & Co. (Leeds) Ltd., 1 Mt. Deb., Red.	100	103½
3/	Fraser & Chalmers, Ltd.	3	2½
4½	Free, Rodwell & Co., Ltd., Deb Stk.	100	102½
6½d.	Furness, T., & Co., Ltd., 5½ p.c. Cum. Pref.	1	¾
4½	Garside & Co. (of Manchstr), L., 1 Mt. Db. Sk.	100	117
11	Genl. Hydraul Power, L.	...	275

Commercial, &c. (*continued*):—

Last Div.	Name.	Paid.	Price.
2/	Gillman & Spencer, Ltd.	5	2½
6	Do. Pref.	5	4½
5	Do. Mort. Debs.	50	51
4	Goldsbro., Mort & Co., L., "A" Deb. Stk., Red.	100	74½
—	Do. 3 p.c. "B" Inc. Deb. Stk., Red.	100	14
8/	Gordon Hotels, Ltd.	10	20
5½	Do. Cum. Pref.	10	14¾
4½	Do. Perp. Deb. Stk.	100	137½
4	Do. do.	100	122½
—	Greenwich Inld. Linoleum Co., Ltd.	1	¾
7	Greenwood & Batley, Ltd., Cum. Pref.	10	10
7½d.	Hagemann & Co., Ltd., 6 p.c. Cum. Pref.	1	1
—	Hammond, Ltd.	10	¾
—	Do. 8 p.c. Cum. Pref.	10	2½
—	Do. 6 p.c. Cum. Inc. Stk. Red.	100	45
4	Hampton & Sons, Ltd., 4 p.c. 1 Mt. Db. St. Red.	100	105
	Hans Crescent Htl., L., 6 p.c. Cum. Pref.	5	3
4	Do. 1 Mt. Deb. Stk.	100	90
5	Harmsworth, Ld., Cm. Pf.	1	1⅛
4/	Harrison, Barber, Ltd.	5	4½
3/	Harrod's Stores, Ltd.	1	4½
2/6	Do. Cum. Pref.	5	7½
5½	Hawaiian Comcl. & Sug. 1 Mt. Debs.	100	94½
5	Hazell, Watson, L., C. P.	10	12
18/	Henley's Teleg., Ltd.	10	22½
7	Do. Pref. Shs.	10	19
4½	Do. Mt. Db. Stk., Rd.	100	112½
6	Henry, Ltd.	10	12½
5	Do. Cum. Pref.	10	13½
4½	Do. Mt. Debs., Red.	50	53
6	Hepworth, Ld., Cm. Prf.	10	11
—	Herrmann, Ltd.	1	½
—	Hildesheimer, Ltd.	3	1½
1/2½	Holbrn. & Frasca, Ltd.	1	2
5	Do. Cum. Pref.	10	11½
4	Do. Deb. Stk.	100	113
6	Home & Col. Stres, L., C. P	5	7½
6	Hood & M.'s Stres., Ltd., Cum. Pref.	1	½
6	Hook, C. T Ltd.	10	6
7/2	Hornsby, Ltd., £10 Shs.	8	3½
5/6	Do. 6 p.c. Cm. Pf. Sk.	100	90
—	Hotchks. Ordn., Ltd.	10	1
—	Do. 7 p.c. Cm. Prf.	10	4
5	Do. 1 Mt. Dbs., Rd.	100	95½
6	Htl. Cecil, Ld., Cm. Prf.	5	4
4	Do. 1 Mt. D. Sk., R.	100	105½
8/	Heward & Bulgh, Ltd.	10	40
6	Do. Pref.	10	16
4	Do. Deb. Stk., Red.	100	107
5/	Howell, J., Ltd., £5 Shs.	4	9
—	Howell & Js., Ld., £3½ Shs.	3	½
1/6	Humber, Ltd.	1	¾
6	Do. Cum. Pref.	1	¾
5/6	Hunter, Wilts., Ltd.	5	7
2/7	Hyam Clthg., Ltd., 5 p.c. Cum. Pref.	5	5½
10/	Impl. Russn. Cotton, L.	5	6
5	Impd. Industl. Dwgs., Ld.	100	130½
6d.	Do. Defrd.	1	1½
25/	Impd. Wood Pave., Ltd.	10	15
15/	Ind. Rubber, Gutta Per. Telegraph Works, Ltd.	10	22
4	Do. 1 Mt. Debs., Red.	100	104
6	Intern. Tea, Cum. Pref.	5	6½
10½d.	Jays, Ltd.	1	1½
5½	Do. Cum. Pref.	5	6½
8½d.	Jones & Higgins, Ltd.	1	2½
4½	Do. 1 Mt. Db. Sk., Rd.	100	113
5/	Kelly's Directory, Ltd., 5 p.c. Cum. Pref.	10	12¾
4	Do. Mort. Db. Sk., Rd.	100	106
—	Kent Coal Explrtn. Ltd.	1	½
9½d.	King, Howmann, Ltd.	1	1½
4/	Kinloch & Co., Ltd.	5	8½
6	Do. Pref.	5	7
5	Lady's Pictorial Pub., Ltd., Cum. Pref.	5	5
—	La Guaira Harb., Ltd., 7 p.c. Deb. Stk.	100	—
—	Do. 2 Mt. 7 p.c. Deb. Bds., Red.	100	—
4/	Lagunas Nitrate, Ltd.	5	2
2/	Lagunas Syn., Ltd.	5	1
5	Do. 1 Mt. Debs., Red.	100	81½
—	L. Copais Ld., 1 Mt. 6 p.c. Debs., Red.	100	35½
3/	Lautaro Nitrate, Ltd.	5	4
5	Do. 1 Mt. Debs., Red.	—	100
9/	Lawes Chem. L., £10 shs.	9	5½
14/	Do. N. Cm. Min. Pref.	10	12½
—	Leeds Forge, 7 p.c. Cm. Pf.	5	3½
5	Do. 1 Mt. Debs., Red.	50	50
5	Lever Bros., L., Cm. Pf.	10	13½
6	Liberty, L., 6 p.c. Cm. Pf.	10	15
20/	Liebig's, Ltd.	20	73½
5	Lilley & Sk., L., Cm. Pf.	5	5½
39/4	Linoleum Manftg., Ltd.	5	16
3/	Linotype, Ltd., Pref.	5	5½
5/	Do. Def.	5	7½
4/	Lister & Co., Ltd.	10	4
5	Do. Cum. Pref.	10	8½
5/	Liverpool Nitrate	5	5
—	Liverpool Warehsg., Ltd	10	3½
5½	Do. Cum. Pref.	10	8½
4	Do. 1 Mt. Db. Stk., Rd.	100	105
5½	Lockharts, Ltd., Cm. Pf.	1	1½
4/6	Ldn. & Til. Lightrage £10	9	6½
6/	Ldn. Comcl. Sale Rms., L.	10	17½
3	Do. 1 Mt. Deb. Stk., Red.	100	103
3	London Nitrate, Ltd.	5	1½
4/	London Nitrate, Ld. 8 p.c. Cm. Min. Pf.	5	3½
8/	London Pavilion, Ltd.	5	7

Commercial, &c. (*continued*):—

Last Div.	Name.	Paid.	Price.
2/6	London Produce Clg. Ho., Ltd., £10 Shares	2½	3½
4/	London Stereos., Ltd.	5	3
6d.	Ldn. Un. Laun. L. Cm. Pf.	1	½
8½d.	Louise, Ltd.	1	½
5½	Do. Cum. Pref.	1	½
5/	Lovell & Christmas, Ltd.	5	11½
6	Do. Cum. Pref.	5	7½
4	Do. Mt. Deb. Stk., Red.	100	107
1/3	Lyons, Ltd.	1	3½
4½	Do. 1 Mt. Deb., Stk., Rd.	100	111½
10/	Machinery Trust, Ltd.	5	14½
4½	Do. 4½ Deb. Stk.	100	105
6	MacLellan, L., Min. C. Pf.	10	8
5	Do. 1 Mt. Debs., 1900	100	101½
—	McEwan, J. & Co., Ltd.	10	1½
6	Do. Mt. Debs., Red.	100	89½
8	McNamara, L., Cm. Pref.	10	9
7½d.	Maison Virot, Ltd.	1	1½
2/7	Do. 6 p.c. Cum. Pref.	5	4½
5/	Manbré Sacc., L., Cm. Pf.	10	12
10/	Mangan Brze., L., £10 Shs.	6	15½
2/	Mason & Mason, Ltd.	5	2½
6	Do. Cum. Pref.	5	5½
—	Maynards, Ltd.	1	½
6	Do. Cum. Pref.	1	½
9½d.	Mazawattee Tea, Ltd.	1	1½
5	Do. Cum. Pref.	5	5½
6	Mellin's Food Cum. Pref.	5	6½
4½	Met. Ascn. Imp. Dwlgs. L.	100	110
3½	Do. 1 Mt. Deb. Stk.	100	97
5	Metro. Indus. Dwlgs., Ltd.	5	5
4	Do. do. Cum. Pref.	5	5½
5	Metro. Prop., L., Cm. Pf.	5	5½
4½	Do. 1st Mt. Debs. Stk.	100	108½
6	Mexican Cotton 1 Mt. Db.	100	96½
4½	Mid. Class Dwlgs., L., Db.	100	120½
1/	Millars' Karri, Ltd.	1	3½
6	Do. Cum. Pref.	1	1½
5/	Milner's Safe, Ltd.	10	20½
10/	Moir & Son, Ltd., Pref.	5	8½
6	Morgan Cruc., L., Cm. Pf.	10	14¾
2/	Morris, B., Ltd.	3½	3½
—	Murray L. 5½ p.c. C. Pf.	5	5½
—	Do. 4½ 1 Mt. Db. Sk. Rd.	100	108
—	Natnl. Dwlgs., L., 5 p.c. Pf.	5	1
1/7½	Nat. Safe Dep., Ltd.	4	3½
6	Do. Cum. Pref.	1	1½
—	Native Guano, Ltd.	5	½
—	Nelson Bros., Ltd.	10	2½
5	Do. Deb. Stk., Red.	100	80½
4/	Neuchtel Asph., Ltd.	10	11
—	New Central Borneo, Ld.	1	—
10d.	New Darvel Tob., Ltd.	18/	1½
1/6	New Explosives, Ltd.	3	3
5/3½	New Gd. Htl., Bham, L.	5	4
5½	Do. Pref.	5	4½
4	Do. 1 Mt. Db. Stk., Rd.	100	96½
—	New Julia Nitrate, Ltd.	10/	⅛
—	New Ldn. Borneo Tob., L.	16/	½
1/6	New Premier Cycle, Ltd.	1	½
6	Do. 6 p.c. Cum. Pref.	1	½
4½	Do. 4½ p.c. 1 Mt. Db. Rd	100	—
—	New Tamargl. Nitr., Ltd	1	⅛
—	Do. 8 p.c. Cum. Pref.	1	½
6	Do. 6 p.c. 1 Mt. Dbs. Rd.	100	62½
3'78d.	Newnes, G., L., Cm. Prf.	1	1½
1/3	Nitr. Provision, Ltd.	2½	½
24/	Nobel-Dynam., Ltd.	10	18
—	North Brazn. Sugar, Ltd.	1	½
15/	Oakey, Ltd.	10	31
6	Do. Cum. Pref.	10	17
—	Paccha Jazp. Nitr., Ltd.	5	½
5	Pac. Borax, L., 1 Db. Rd.	100	110
—	Palace Hotel, Ltd.	10	5½
5½	Do. Cum. Pref.	10	8½
4	Do. 1 Mt. Deb. Stk.	100	104
2/6	Palmer, Ltd.	5	1½
6	Do. Cum. Pref.	5	3
9⅗d.	Paquin, Ltd.	1	1
6	Do. Cum. Pref.	5	4½
5½	Parnall, Ltd., Cum. Pref.	1	½
4/6	Pawsons, Ltd., £10 Shs.	6	6½
4	Do. Mt. Debs., Red.	100	106
6	Pearks, G. & T., Ltd., 6 p.c. Cum. Pref.	1	½
9½d.	Pears, Ltd.	1	1½
6	Do. Cum. Pref.	10	14
5	Do. Deb. Stk.	100	129
5½	Pearson, C. A., L., Cu. Pf.	5	5½
4/3	Peebles, Ltd.	5	8
5	Do. Cum. Pref.	5	6½
4½	Do. Mt. Deb. Stk. Red.	100	113½
5½	Peek Bros., Ltd., 1 Cum. Pref., Nos. 1-60,000	5	6
3½	Do. 3½ p.c. 1 Db. Stk.	100	103½
7½d.	Pegamoid, Ltd.	1	½
—	Phospho-Guano, Ltd.	5	2½
—	Pillsbury-W. Fl. Mills, L.	10	2
16/	Do. 8 p.c. Cum. Pref.	10	6½
6	Do. 1 Mort. Debs.	100	95½
29⅗d.	Plummer, Ltd.	1	1½
5	Do. Cum. Pref.	5	5½
7/6	Price's Candle, Ltd.	16	36
6	Priest Marians, L., Cm. Pf.	1	1½
6	Pryce Jones, Ld., Cm. Pf.	5	7½
5	Do. Deb. Stk.	100	122
10.8d.	Pullman, Ltd.	1	1½
6d.	Do. Cum. Pref.	1	1½
11⅛d.	Raleigh Cycle, Ltd.	1	½
6	Do. Cum. Pref.	1	½
—	Recife Drnge. Ld. 1 Mt. Debs., R	100	19
6	Redfern, Ltd. Cum. Prf.	10	14
5	Ridgways, Ltd., Cu. Pf.	5	5½
—	R. Janeiro Cy. Imps. Ld.	25	9½
5	Do. Debs.	100	89½
5	Do. 1882-1893	100	88½
11/	R. Jan Fl. Mills, Ltd.	7	6½
5	Do. 1 Mt. Debs., Rd.	100	94
—	Riv. Plate Meat, Ltd.	5	3½
—	Do. Pref.	5	5
8½d.	Roberts, J. R., Ltd.	1	1½

Commercial, &c. (*continued*):—

Last Div.	Name.	Paid.	Price.
5	Roberts 1 Mt. D. Sk., Rd.	100	112
8½d.	Roberts, T. R., Ltd.	1	2½
5	Do. Cum. Pref.	1	1½
3/	Rosario Nit., Ltd.	5	3½
5	Do. Debs., Red.	100	105
5	Do. Huara, Debs.	—	104
1/	Rover Cycle, Ltd.	1	½
6/	Ryl. Aquarium, Ltd.	5	4½
6	Do. Pref.	5	6
5	Ryl. Htl., Edin., Cm. Pf.	1	1½
1/2½	Ryl. Niger, Ltd., £10 Sh.	2	3
6/	Do.	10	16
—	Russian Petroleum	10	21
—	Do. 6½ p.c. Cm. Prf.	10	11
3/	Ruston, Proctor, Ltd.	10	11
4½	Do. 1 Mort. Debs.	100	104
6/	Sadler, Ltd.	12	7
—	Sal. Carmen Nit., Ltd.	5	4½
9d.	Salmon & Gluck., Ltd.	1	1⅛
—	Salt Union, Ltd.	10	1½
1½	Do. 7 p.c. Pref.	10	6
4½	Do. Deb. Stk.	100	100½
4½	Do. "B" Deb. Sk., Rd.	100	97½
—	San Donato Nit., Ltd.	5	½
2/6	San Jorge Nit., Ltd.	5	3½
—	San Pablo Nit., Ltd.	5	½
—	San Sebastn. Nit., Ltd.	5	½
1/9	Sanitas, Ltd	1	2½
—	Sa. Elena Nit., Ltd.	5	½
—	Sa. Rita Nit., Ltd.	5	2
5/	Savoy Hotel, Ltd.	10	16
7	Do. Pref.	10	13½
4	Do. 1 Mt. Deb. Stk.	100	111½
5	Do. Debs., Red	100	102½
5	Do. & Ldn. For. Htl., Ltd., 5 p.c. Debs. Red.	100	99
1½d.	Schweppes, Ltd.	1	1⅛
—	Do. Def.	1	⅛
5	Do. Cum. Pref.	1	1½
4	Do. Deb. Stk.	100	108
1/	Singer Cyc., Ltd.	1	½
5½	Do Cum. Pref.	1	½
—	Smokeless Pwdr., Ltd.	1	½
5½d.	S. Eng. Dairies, Ltd., 6 p.c. Cum. Pref.	1	1½
—	Sowler Thos. L.	1	1½
3/4½	Do. 5½ Cm. Pf.	5	5½
4/6	Spencer, Turner, & Co. Ltd	5	8½
5	Do. Cum. Pref.	5	6½
5	Spicer, Ld., 5 p.c. Dbs. Rd.	100	65
4/	Spiers & Pond, Ltd.	10	20½
5	Do. 1 Mt. Debs., Red.	100	117½
5	Do. "A" Db. Stk., Rd.	100	111
5	Do. "B" 1 Db. Stk., Rd.	100	111
4	Do. Fd. "C" 1 Db. S., R.	100	104
7/6	Spratt's, Ltd	5	13
4	Do. Debs., 1914	—	105
5	Steiner Ld., Cm. Pf.	10	11½
4	Do. 1 Mt. Db. Sk. Rd.	100	106
9/	Stewart & Clydesdale, L.	10	14
6	Do. Cum. Pref.	10	15
35/5	Sulphide Corp.	100	80
1/	Swan & Edgar, L.	1	1½
1/	Sweetmeat Automatic, L.	1	4
2/9	Teetgen, Ltd., Cum. Pref.	5	6
24/	Teleg. Construction., Ld.	12	36½
5	Do. Db. Bds., Rd., 1899	100	103½
3/0½	Tilling, Ld. 5½ p.c. Cm. Prf.	5	6½
4	Do. 4 p.c. 1 Dbs., Rd.	—	104
8½d.	Tower Tea, Ltd.	1	1½
5	Do. Cum. Pref.	5	5½
5	Travers, Ltd., Cum. Pref.	10	12½
4	Do. 1 Mt. Dbs., Rd.	100	105
6	Tucuman Sug., 1 Dbs., Rd.	100	100
4/	United Alkali, Ltd.	10	1½
7	Do. Cum. Pref.	10	8
5	Do. Mt. Db. Stk., Rd.	100	109½
2½d.	United Horse Shoe, Ltd., Non-Cum. 8 p.c. Pref.	1	⅛
5	Un. Kingm. Tea, Cm. Prf.	5	4½
2/	Un. Lankat Plant., Ltd.	1	2
4/	Un. Limmer Asphlte., Ld.	3	4½
13/	Val de Travers Asph., L.	10	15½
3/	V. den Bergh's, L., Cm. P.	5	6½
6	Walkers, Park., L., C. Pf.	10	3
4½	Do. 1 Mt. Debs., Red.	100	90½
6/	Wallis, Thos. & Co., Ltd.	5	14
6	Do. Cum. Pref.	5	8½
5½	Waring, Ltd., Cum. Pref.	5	5½
4½	Do. 1 Mt. Db. Sk., Red.	100	113
4½	Do. Irred. "B" Db. Stk.	100	105
12/	Waterlow, Dfd. Ord.	10	14½
4/	Do. Pref.	10	14½
3½	Do. Cum. Pref.	10	10½
10/	Waterlow Bros. & L., Ld.	10	9
5	Do. Pref.	10	12
1/2½	Welford, Ltd.	1	2
4½	Do. Debs., Red.	100	108
1/	Welford's Surrey Dairies, Ltd.	1	1½
7½d.	West London Dairy, Ltd.	1	1
4½	Wharncliffe Dwllgs., L., Pf.	10	11½
18/10	Do. 3 p.c. Irr. Mt. Db. Sk.	100	96
6d.	White, A. J., Ltd.	1	½
6	Do. 6 p.c. Cum. Pref.	1	½
4	White, J. Barley, Ltd., 1 Mort. Debs., Red.	100	100½
5	White, R., Ltd., 1 Mort. Deb. Stock, Red.	100	104½
5/	White, Tomkins, Ltd	10	12
5	Do. Cum. Pref.	10	11½
6	White, W. N., L., Cm. Pf.	1	1
2/6	Wickens, Pease & Co., L.	5	3½
6	Wilkie, Ltd., Cum. Pref.	10	15½
3/6	Willans & Robinson, Ltd.	5	8½
6	Do. Cum. Pref.	5	7½
4½	Do. 1 Mt. Db. Stk., Red.	100	108
7½d.	Williamsons, L., Cm. Prf.	1	1½
6	Winterbottm. Book Cloth, Ltd., Cum. Prf.	10	15
3/	Yates, Ltd.	5	6½
6	Do. Cum. Pref.	5	6½
	Young's Paraffin, Ltd.	4	1½

CORPORATION STOCKS—COLONIAL AND FOREIGN.

Per Cent.	Name.	Paid.	Price.
6	Auckland City, '72 1904-24	100	118
6	Do. Cons., '79, Red. 1930	100	138½
5	Do. Deb. Ln., '83..1934-8	100	117
6	Auckland Harb. Debs.	100	111½
5	Do. 1917	100	113
5	Do. 1936	100	116
5½	Balmain Boro' 1914	—	117
5	Boston City (U.S.)	100	102½
5	Do. 1902	100	107½
5	Brunswick Town 5. c. Debs. 1916-20	100	111
15/	B. Ayres City 6 p.c.	100	57
4½	Do. 4½ p.c.	100	75
5	Cape Town, City of	100	113
4	Do. 1943	100	116
4	Chicago, City of, Gold 1915	—	110
6	Christchurch 1926	100	131½
—	Cordoba City	100	17½
5	Duluth (U.S.) Gold 1926	—	110
6	Dunedin (Otago) 1925	100	127½
6	Do. 1906	100	113
5	Do. Consols 1908	100	113
4	Durban Insc. Stk. 1944	100	111
4	Essex Cnty., N. Jersey 1926	$100	114½
5	Fitzroy, Melbrne. 1916-19	100	110
5	Gisborne Harbour 1915	100	110½
4	Greymouth Harbour 1925	100	110
4	Hamilton 1934	100	110
5	Hobart Town 1918-30	100	116
4	Do. 1940	100	107
4½	Invercargill Boro. Dbs. 1936	100	113
6	Kimberley Boro., S.A. Dbs.	—	104
4	Launceston Twn. Dbs. 1916	100	107
6	Lyttleton, N.Z., Harb. 1929	100	125
4	Melbourne Bd. of Wks. 1921	100	109
5	Melb. City Debs. 1897-1907	100	107½
4½	Do. Debs. 1908-27	100	113½
4	Do. Debs. 1915-20-22	100	108
5	Melbne. Harb. Bds., 1908-9	100	112
4½	Do. do. 1915	100	110
4	Do. do. 1918-21	100	105
4½	Melbrne. Tms, Dbs. 1914-16	100	113
4½	Do. Fire Brig. Db. 1921	100	110
5	Mexico City Stg.	100	91½
4	Moncton N. Bruns. City	100	103
4½	Montevideo	100	59
5	Montreal Stg.	100	108
5	Do. 1874	100	104
5	Do. 1879	100	106
3½	Do. 1933	100	104
3	Do. Perm. Deb. Stk.	100	98½
4	Do. Cons. Deb. Stk. 1932	100	113
6	Napier Boro. Consolid. 1914	100	119
5	Napier Harb. Debs. 1920	100	115
5	Do. Debs. 1928	100	107
6	New Plymouth Harb. Debs. 1909	100	108
6	New York City 1901	—	107½
3½	Do. 1910-26	—	105½
4½	Nth. Melbourne Debs. 1-600 1921	100	105
5	Oamaru Boro. Cons. 1920	100	101
6	Do. Harb. Bds. (Reg.)	100	74
25/	Do. 6 p.c. (Bearer) 1919	100	35
6	Otago Harb. Deb. Reg.	100	105
6	Do. 1877	100	107
6	Do. 1881 1921	100	115
5	Do. Debs. 1921	100	107
5	Do. Cons. 1934	100	105
6	Ottawa City	100	111
6	Do. 1904	100	115½
4½	Do. Debs. 1913	100	112
6	Port Elizabeth Waterworks	100	113½
5	Port Louis	100	111
5	Prahran Debs. 1917	100	111
4	Do. Debs. 1919	100	103
6	Quebec C. Coupon. 1875 1905	100	112
6	Do. do. 1878 1908	100	116
4½	Do. Debs. 1914-18	100	108
4	Do. Debs. 1923	200	108
3½	Do. Cns. Rg. Stk., Red.	100	101
5	Richmond (Melb.) Dbs. 1917	100	113
4	Rio Janeiro City	100	57
4	Rome City	100	—
4	Do. 2nd to 8th Iss.	100	94
—	Rosario C.	100	26½
—	Do.	100	26½
4	St. Catherine (Ont.) 1926	100	101
4	St. John, N.B., Debs. 1934	—	103
4½	St. Kilda (Melb) Dbs. 1918-21	100	106
4	St. Louis C. (Miss.) 1911	100	106
4	Do. 1913	100	106
3'65	Do. 1915	—	110
—	Santa Fé City Debs.	00	21
6	Santos City	100	95
6	Sofia City	100	83
5	Sth. Melbourne Debs. 1915	100	111
4½	Do. Debs. 1919	100	107
5	Sydney City 1904	100	109
4	Do. Debs. 1912-13	100	107
4	Do. do. (1894) 1919	100	109
7	Timaru Boro. 7 p.c. 1910	100	126½
5	Timaru Harb. Debs 1914	100	106
5	Do. Debs. 1916	100	106
6	Toronto City Wtwks 1904-6	100	115
6	Do. Cons. Debs. 1898	100	101
5	Do. G. Cns. Dbs. 1919-20	100	118
4	Do. Strlg. 1922-8	100	107
4	Do. Local Improv.	100	102
3½	Do. 1929	100	105
5½	Valparaiso	100	100
4	Vancouver 1931	100	109
4	Do. 1932	100	106
6	Wanganui Harb. Dbs. 1905	100	110
6	Wellington Con. Deb. 1907	100	117
6	Do. Improv., 1879	100	123
6	Do. Wtrwks. Dbs., 1880	100	123
4½	Do. Debs., 1893 1933	100	116
4½	Wellington Harb. 1907	100	104
4	Westport Harb. Dbs. 1925	100	110
6	Winnipeg City Debs. 1907	—	118
5	Do. 1914	100	118

FINANCIAL, LAND, AND INVESTMENT.

Last Div.	Name.	Paid.	Price.
5	Agency, Ld. & Fin. Aust., Ltd., Mt. Db. Stk., Rd.	100	90½
	Amer. Frehld. Mt. of Lon., Ld., Cum. Pref. Stk.	100	87½
4½	Do. Deb. Stk., Red.	100	93
1/	Anglo-Amer. Db. Cor., L.	2	1
4	Do. Deb. Stk., Red	100	106½
5½	Ang.-Ceylon & Gen. Est., Ltd., Cons. Stk.	100	65
6	Do. Reg. Debs., Red.	100	105½
—	Ang.-Fch. Explorn., Ltd.	1	2 1/16
6	Do. Cum. Pref.	1	15/16
—	Argent. Ld. & Inv., Ltd. £1 Shares	10/	nil
—	Do. Cum. Pref.	4	1¼
1/	Assets Fnders.' Sh., Ltd.,	4	1⅝
6/	Assets Realis., Ltd., Ord.,	5	8¾
5	Do. Cum. Pref.	5	6½
26/	Austrln. Agricl. £25 Shs.	21½	63½
—	Aust. N. Z. Mort., Ltd., £10 Shs.	1	1½d.
4½	Do. Deb. Stk., Red.	100	90½
4	Do. Deb. Stk., Red.	100	82½
4½	Australian Est. & Mt., L., 1 Mt. Deb. Stk., Red.	100	104
5	Do. "A" Mort. Deb. Stk., Red.	100	96
2/6	Australian Mort., Ld., & Fin., Ltd. £25 Shs.	5	4
1/6	Do. New, £25 Shs.	3	2½
4	Do. Deb. Stk.	100	110½
3	Do. Do.	100	85
5	Baring Est. 2 Mt. Debs., Red.	100	105
5	Bengal Presidy. 1 Mort. Deb., Red.	100	106
25/	British Amer. Ld. "A"	1	19
—	Do. "B"	24	7
1/7½	Brit. & Amer. Mt., Ltd. £10 Shs.	2	½
5/	Do. Pref.	10	10
4	Do. Deb. Stk., Red.	100	102
1/3	Brit. & Austrlsn Tst Ln., Ltd. £25 Shs.	2½	⅝
4½	Do. Perm. Debs., Red.	100	103
1½d.	Brit. N. Borneo. £1 Shs.	15/	1½
2½d.	Do.	1	1
—	Brit. S. Africa	1	2 11/16
5	Do. Mt. Deb., Red.	—	97
6	B. Aires Harb. Tst., Red.	100	100
12/6	Canada Co.	1	26
—	Canada N. W. Ld., Ltd.	$25	$3½
—	Do. Pref.	$100	$50½
4	Canada Perm. Loan & Sav. Perp. Deb. Stk.	100	99½
—	Curamalan Ld., 1 Mt. 7 p.c. Bds., Red.	—	92½
3/7½	Deb Corp., Ld., £10 Shs	4	3½
5	Do. Cum. Pref.	10	11½
4	Do. Perp. Deb. Stk.	100	113
9d.	Deb. Corp. Fders' Sh., Ld.	3	⅜
4/5 1/16	Eastn. Mt. & Agncy, Ld., "A"	10	6
4½	Do. Deb. Stk., Red.	100	100
5	Equitable Revers. In. Ltd.	100	—
2/	Exploration, Ltd.	1	1 11/16
1	Freehold Trst. of Austrla. Ltd. £10 Shs.	1	¾
4	Do. Perp. Deb. Stk.	100	100
—	Genl. Assets Purchase, Ltd., 5 p.c. Cum. Pref.	10	—
70/	Genl. Reversionary, Ltd.	100	—
3½	Holborn Vi. Land	100	105
3½	House Prop. & Inv.	100	85½
13/	Hudson's Bay	13	21½
4	Impl. Col. Fin. & Agcy. Corp.	100	94½
4½	Impl. Prop. Inv., Ltd., Deb. Stk., Red.	100	91½
2/6	Internatl. Fincial. Soc., Ltd. £7½ Shs.	2½	1½
4	Do. Deb. Stk., Red.	100	99½
1/9½	Ld. & Mtge. Egypt, Ltd. £18 Shs.	3	2¾
5	Do. Debs., Red.	100	103
4½	Do. Debs., Red.	100	101
—	Ld. Corp. of Canada, Ltd.	1	⅝
4½	Ld. Mtge. Bk. of Texas Deb. Stk.	100	—
3½	Ld. Mtge. Bk. Victoria 4½ p.c. Deb. Stk.	100	78
2/9½	Law Debent. Corp., Ltd., £10 Shs.	2	1¾
4½	Do. Cum. Pref.,	10	12
4	Do. Deb. Stk.	100	118
1/	Ldn. & Australasian Deb. Corp., Ltd., £4 Shs.	2	½
4½	Do. 4½ p.c. Mt. Deb. Stk., Red.	100	99
1/9	Ldn. & Middx. Frhld. Est. £2 Shs.	35/	3
2/6	Lndn. & N. Y. Inv. Corp., Ltd.	5	1¾
5	Do. 5 p.c. Cum. Pref.	10	8½
1/6	Ldn. & Nth. Assets Corp., Ltd., £2 Shs.	1½	⅞
2	Ldn. & N. Deb. Corp., L.	2	1½
4	Ldn. & S. Afric. Explrn. Ltd.	½	13¾
2/	Mtge. Co. of R. Plate, Ltd. £10 Shs.	2	3½
4½	Do. Deb. Stk., Red.	100	113
4½	Morton, Rose Est., Ltd., 1st Mort. Debs.	—	101
6/	Natal Land Col. Ltd.	10	7½
4/	Do. 8 p.c. Pref., 1870	5	8½
5/6	Natl. Disct. L., £25 Shs.	5	10½
4½	New Impl. Invest., Ltd. Pref. Stk.	100	60½
—	New Impl. Invest., Ltd. Def. Stk.	100	9
4	N. Zld. Ln. & Mer. Agcy., Ltd. Prf. Ln, Deb. Stk	100	94

Financial, Land, &c. (*continued*):—

Last Div.	Name.	Paid.	Price.
2/6	N. Zld. Tst. & Ln. Ltd., £25 Shs.	5	1½
12/6	N. Zld. Tst. & Ln. Ltd., 5 p.c. Cum. Pref.	25	19
—	N. Brit. Australsn. Ltd.	100	6½
—	Do. Irred. Guar.	100	32½
5	Do. Mort. Debs.	100	82½
4½	N. Queensld. Mort. & Inv., Ltd., Deb. Stk.	100	94½
—	Oceana Co., Ltd.	—	—
6	Peel Riv., Ld. & Min. Ltd.	100	88½
—	Peruvian Corp., Ltd.	100	2½
—	Do. 4 p.c. Pref.	100	9½
3	Do. 6 p.c. 1 Mt. Debs., Red.	100	41½
—	Queenld. Invest. & Ld. Mort. Pref. Ord. Stk.	100	20
3/7	Queenld. Invest. & Ld. Mort. Ord. Shs.	4	4
4	Queenld. Invest. & Ld. Mort. Perp. Debs.	100	90
3½	Raily. Roll Stk. Tst. Deb., 1903-6	100	100½
50/	Reversiony. Int. Soc., Ltd.	100	—
2/8½	Riv. Plate Trst., Loan & Agcy., L., "A" £10 Shs.	2	4½
1/6	Riv. Plate Trst., Loan & Agcy., Ltd., Def. "B"	5	3½
	Riv. Plate Trst., Loan & Agy., L., Db. Stk., Red.	100	109
—	Santa Fé & Cord. Gt. South Land, Ltd.	20	5
—	Santa Fé Land	10	2½
2/	Scot. Amer. Invest., Ltd. £10 Shs.	2	2¾
2½	Scot. Australian Invest., Ltd., Cons.	100	79½
6	Scot. Australian Invest., Ltd., Guar. Pref.	100	135½
5	Scot. Australian Invest., Ltd., Guar. Pref.	100	106½
4	Scot. Australian Invest., Ltd., 4 p.c. Perp. Dbs.	100	105½
5	Sivagunga Zemdy., 1st Mort., Red.	100	101
20/	Sth. Australian	20	52½
3½	Stock Exchange Deb., Rd.	—	101½
—	Strait Develt., Ltd.	1	1/16
2/6	Texas Land & Mt., Ltd. £10 Shs.	2½	3
4½	Texas Land & Mt., Ltd., Deb. Stk., Red.	100	105
—	Transvaal Est. & Dev., L.	1	1/16
—	Transvaal Lands, Ltd., £1 Shs.	15/	½
—	Do. F. P.	1	1/16
—	Transvaal Mort., Loan, & Fin., Ltd., £10 Shs.	2	½
2/	Tst & Agcy. of Austrlsa., Ltd., £10 Shs.	1	2
7/5	Do. Old, fully paid	10	15½
5/7	Do. New, fully paid	10	12½
5	Do. Cum. Pref.	10	12½
3/	Trust & Loan of Canada, £20 Shs.	5	4½
1/9½	Do. New £20 Shs	3	2½
—	Tst. & Mort. of Iowa, Ltd., £10 Shs.	2½	¾
4½	Do. Deb. Stk. Red.	100	92½
—	Tst., Loan, & Agency of Mexico, Ltd., £10 Shs.	2	½
—	Trsts., Exors, & Sec. Ins. Corp., Ltd., £10 Shs.	7	1½
5/	Union Dsc., Ld., £10 Shs.	5	10½
—	Union Mort. & Agcy. of Aust., Ltd., £6 Shs.	2	—
6	Do. Pref. Stk	100	30
—	Do. 6 p. Pref. £6 Shs.	2	½
4½	Do. Deb. Stk	100	92½
4	Do. Deb. Stk	100	85½
5	Do. Deb. Stk. Red.	100	96½
1/6	U.S. Deb. Cor. Ltd., £8 Shs.	1	⅝
5½	Do. Cum. Pref. Stk.	100	100½
4½	Do. Irred. Deb. Stk.	100	106½
5	U.S. Tst. & Guar. Cor., Ltd., Pref. Stk.	100	75½
6/	Van Dieman's	25	16
4	Walker's Prop. Cor., Ltd., Guar. 1 Mt. Deb. Stk.	100	109
4½	Wstr. Mort. & Inv., Ltd., Deb. Stk.	100	92½

FINANCIAL—TRUSTS.

Last Div.	Name.	Paid.	Price.
1/6	Afric City Prop., Ltd	1	1⅝
6	Do. Cum. Pref.	1	1
4	Alliance Invt., Ltd., Cm. 4½ p. c. Prefd.	100	75½
—	Do. Defd	100	13½
4	Do. Deb. Stk. Red.	100	105½
5	Amrcn. Invt., Ltd., Prfd.	100	121½
5	Do. Defd.	100	90½
4	Do. Deb. Stk. Red.	100	117½
4	Army & Navy Invt., Ltd., 5 p.c. Prefd.	100	82½
—	Do. Defd. Stk.	100	16½
4	Do. Deb. Stk.	100	107½
4	Atlas Investment, Ltd., Prefd. Stk.	100	70½
4½	Bankers' Invest., Ltd., Cum. Prefd.	100	106
1/0/0	Do. Defd	100	27½
4	Do. Deb. Stk	100	113
	Brewery & Comml. Inv., Ltd., £10 Shs.	4	5½

Financial—Trusts (*continued*):—

Last Div.	Name.	Paid.	Price.
4	British Investment, Ltd., Cum. Prefd.	100	108
5	Do. Defd.	100	102½
4	Do. Deb. Stk.	100	108½
6	Brit. Steam. Invst., Ltd., Prefd.	100	116½
3/0/0	Do. Defd	100	70½
4½	Do. Perp. Deb. Stk	100	121½
1/9	Car Trust Invst., Ltd., £10 Shs.	9½	2
5	Do. Pref.	100	100
4	Do. Deb. Stk., 1915	100	105
4	Cml. Sec., Ltd., Prefd.	100	106½
2½	Do. Defd.	100	47½
4	Consolidated, Ltd., Cum. 1st Pref.	100	92
4	Do. 5 p.c. Cm. 2nd do.	100	73½
—	Do. Defd.	100	14½
4½	Do. Deb. Stk.	100	111½
—	Deb. Secs. Invst.	100	105½
—	Do. 4 p.c. Cm. Pf. Sk.	100	105½
4½	Edinburgh Invest., Ltd., Cum. Prefd. Stk.	100	109½
4	Do. Deb. Stk. Red.	100	106½
5	Foreign, Amer. & Gen. Invt., Ltd., Prefd.	100	115½
2	Do. Defd.	100	52½
4	Do. Deb. Stk.	100	115½
5	Foreign & Colonial Invt., Ltd., Prefd.	100	133½
5½	Do. Defd.	100	98½
4½	Gas, Water & Gen. Invt., Cum. Prefd. Stk.	100	87½
3	Do. Defd. Stk.	100	36½
4	Do. Deb. Stk.	100	106
5	Gen. & Com. Invt., Ltd., Prefd. Stk.	100	105½
2	Do. Defd. Stk.	100	36½
4	Do. Deb. Stk.	100	113½
1/9	Globe Telegph. & Tst., Ltd.	10	12
6	Do. do. Pref.	10	17½
4	Govt. & Genl. Invt., Ld., Prefd.	100	84½
3½	Do. Defd.	100	42½
4½	Govts. Stk. & other Secs. Invt., Ltd., Prefd.	100	89½
1	Do. Defd.	100	26
4½	Do. Deb. Stk.	100	111
4	Do. do.	100	104
4½	Guardian Invt., Ltd., Pfd.	100	87½
—	Do. Defd.	100	20½
4	Do. Deb. Stk.	100	104
5	Indian & Gen. Inv., Ltd., Cum. Prefd.	100	107½
2½	Do. Defd.	100	56
4½	Do. Deb. Stk.	100	121½
5	Indust. & Gen. Tst., Ltd., Unified	100	102½
3½	Do. Deb. Stk. Red.	100	101½
4½	Internat. Invt., Ltd., Cm. Prefd.	100	71½
—	Do. Defd.	100	9
4	Do. Deb. Stk.	100	101
4	Invest. Tst. Cor. Ltd. Pfd.	100	102
4	Do. Defd.	100	93
4	Do. Deb. Stk. Red.	100	106
5	Ldn. Gen. Invest. Ltd., 5 p.c. Cum. Prefd.	100	109½
7½	Do. Defd.	100	118
4½	Ldn. Scot. Amer. Ltd. Pfd.	100	105½
£3	Do. Defd.	100	59½
4	Do. Deb. Stk.	100	112
4	Ldn. Tst., Ltd., Cum. Prfd. Stk.	100	105
4	Do. Defd. Stk.	100	75½
4	Do. Deb. Stk., Red.	100	108
3½	Do. Mt. Deb. Stk., Red.	100	104
5	Mercantile Invt. & Gen., Ltd., Prefd.	100	111½
3	Do. Defd.	100	48½
4	Do. Deb. Stk.	100	112½
4	Merchants, Ltd., Pref. Stk.	100	104½
4	Do. Ord.	100	81
4	Do. Deb. Stk.	100	116½
6	Municipal, Ltd., Prefd.	100	55½
—	Do. Defd.	100	17½
4½	Do. Debs.	100	112
4½	Do. Debs. "B"	100	99½
4½	Do. "C" Deb. Stk.	100	88½
5	New Investment, Ltd. Ord.	100	92½
5	Omnium Invest., Ltd., Pfd.	100	91½
1	Do. Defd.	100	26½
4	Do. Deb. Stk.	100	104
5/	Railway Deb. Tst. Ld., £20 Shs.	10	6½
5	Do. Debs., Red.	100	107½
4½	Do. Deb. Stk., 1911	100	107½
4	Do. do. 1927	100	106½
4	Railway Invst. Ltd., Prefd.	100	111
17/7	Do. Defd.	100	20½
8/	Railway Share Trust & Agency "A"	8	6
7½	Do. "B" Pref. Stk.	100	146½
4½	River Plate & Gen. Invt., Ltd., Prefd.	100	105
£3	Do. Defd.	100	50½
5	Scot. Invst., Ltd., Pfd. Stk.	100	94½
1½	Do. Defd.	100	26½
4	Do. Deb. Stk.	100	108
4½	Sec. Scottish Invst., Ltd., Cum. Prefd.	100	86½
£3	Do. Defd. Stk.	100	32
4	Do. Deb. Stk.	100	107½
3/	Sth. Africa Gold Tst., Ltd.	1	4⅝
6	Do. Cum. Pref	1	1
5½	Do. 1st Debs., Red.	100	102
1/9	Stock Conv. & Invest., Ltd., £5 Shs.	1	1⅜
4½	Do. do. 4½ p.c. Cm. Prf.	100	114½
3½	Do. Ldn. & N. W. 1st. Charge Prefd.	100	114½
4	Do do. 2nd Chge Prfd.	100	111
32/6	Do. do. Defd. Charge	100	30
3	Do. N. East. 1 Chge Pfd.	100	93

Financial—Trusts (*continued*):—

Last Div.	Name.	Paid.	Price.
37/6	Stock N. East Defd. Chge	100	39
6	Submarine Cables	100	142½
5	U.S. & S. Amer. Invest., Ltd., Prefd.	100	100½
2	Do. Defd.	100	29½
4	Do. Deb. Stk.	100	106½

GAS AND ELECTRIC LIGHTING.

Last Div.	Name.	Paid.	Price.
10/6	Alliance & Dublin Con. 10 p.c. Stand.	10	24½
7/6	Do. 7 p.c. Stand.	10	17
5	Austln. Gas Lght. (Syd.) Debs. 1909	100	106
5	Bay State of N. Jrsy. Sk. Fd. Tst. Bd., Red.	—	92½
3/	Bombay, Ltd.	5	6
2/4½	Do. New	4	5
12	Brentford Cons.	100	297½
9	Do. New	100	227½
5	Do. Pref.	100	142½
4	Do. Deb. Stk.	100	136
11½	Brighton & Hove Gen. Cons. Stk.	100	272½
8½	Do. "A" Cons. Stk.	100	197½
5	Bristol 5 p.c. Max.	100	129½
22/6	British Gas Light, Ltd.	20	55½
11/6	Bromley Gas Consumrs.' 10 p.c. Stand.	10	25
8/6	Do. 7 p.c. Stand.	10	21
—	Brush Electl. Enging., L.	—	1⅞
6	Do. 6 p.c. Pref.	—	2½
4½	Do. Deb. Stk.	100	112
4½	Do. 2 Deb. Stk., Red.	100	103½
5/	B. Ayres (New), Ltd.	10	9½
4	Do. Deb. Stk., Rd.	—	99
18/6	Cagliari Gas & Wtr., Ltd.	20	30½
8/	Cape Town & Dist. Gas Light & Coke, Ltd.	10	17½
4½	Do. Pref.	10	12½
6	Do. 1 Mt. Debs. 1910	50	60
4/	Charing Cross & Strand Elec. Sup., Ltd.	5	14
4½	Do. Cum. Pref.	5	6½
3/	Chelsea Elec. Sup., Ltd.	5	10½
4½	Do. Deb. Stk., Red.	100	116
5	Chic. Edis'n Co. 1 Mt., Rd.	$1000	106
20/	City of Ldn. Elec. Lht., L.	10	26
—	Do. New	10	13
6	Do. Cum. Pref.	10	18
5	Do. Deb. Stk., Red.	100	131½
13½	Commercial, Cons.	100	342½
10½	Do. New	100	257½
4½	Do. Deb. Stk.	100	155½
14	Continental Union, Ltd.	100	230
11	Do. Pref. Stk.	100	210½
—	County of Lon. & Brush Prov. Elec. Lg., Ltd.	10	15
6	Do. Cum. Pref.	10	15½
14	Croydon Comcl. Gas, Ld., "A" Stk., 10 p.c.	100	312½
11	Do. "B" Stk., 7 p.c.	100	260
5½	Crystal Pal. Dist. Ord. 5 p.c. Stk.	100	130½
5	Do. Pref. Stk.	100	141½
8/	European, Ltd.	10	24½
6/	Do.	7½	17½
12¾	Gas Light & Ck Cons. Stk., "A" Ord.	100	289½
4	Do. "B" (4 p.c. Max.)	100	120½
10	Do. "C," "D," & "E" (Pref.)	100	310
5	Do. "F" (Pref.)	100	152½
7½	Do. "G" (Pref.)	100	222½
7	Do. "H" (7 p.c. Max.)	100	197½
10	Do. "J" (Pref.)	100	310
6	Do. "K"	100	185½
4	Do. Deb. Stk.	100	134½
4½	Do. do.	100	152½
6	Do. do.	100	204½
8/	Hong Kong & China, Ld.	10	14½
4/	House to House Elec. Light Sup., Ltd.	5	11
7	Do. Cum. Pref.	5	11½
10	Imperial Continental	100	215½
3½	Do. Deb. Stk., Red	100	104½
2/	Malta & Medit., Ltd.	5	5½
7/	Metrop. Elec. Sup., Ltd.	10	20½
6/	Do. New	10	20½
4½	Do. 1 Mt. Deb. Stk.	100	119
5	Metro. of Melbrne. Dbs. 1908-12	100	113
4½	Do. Debs. 1918-22-4	100	110
10/	Monte Video, Ltd.	20	18½
9½	Newcastle-upon-Tyne	100	237½
—	Do. 3½ p.c. Deb. Stk.	100	117½
12/	Notting Hill Elec. Ltg., Ltd.	10	20
4/6	Oriental, Ltd.	5	8½
4/0½	Do. New	4½	7½
10d½.	Do. do. 1870	1	1½
3/6	Ottoman, Ltd.	5	4⅝
—	Para, Ltd.	—	—
6	People's Gas Lt. & C. of Chic. 2 Mt. 1904	100	106½
5	River Plate Elec. Lgt. & Trac., Ltd., 1 Deb. Stk.	—	92½
$2	Royal Elec. of Montreal	—	146
4½	Do. 1 Mt. Deb.	100	106
11/	St. James' & Pall Mall Elec. Light, Ltd.	5	18½
7	Do. Pref.	5	10½
4	Do. Deb. Stk., Red.	100	108½

Gas and Electric (*continued*) :—

Last Div.	Name.	Paid.	Price.
10/	San Paulo, Ltd.	10	16½
10	Sheffield Unit. Gas Lt. "A"	100	251½
10	Do. "B"	100	251½
10	Do. "C"	100	251½
—	Sth. Ldn. Elec. Sup., Ld.	2	2½
5½	South Metropolitan	100	137½
3	Do. 3 p.c. Deb. Stk.	100	105½
12	Tottenham & Edmonton Gas Lt. & C., "A"	100	290
9	Do. "B"	100	210
7/	Tuscan, Ltd.	10	14
5	Do. Debs., Red.	100	101½
4/	West Ham 10 p.c. Stan.	5	12
8/	Westmnstr. Elec. Sup., Ld.	5	17½

INSURANCE.

Last Div.	Name.	Paid.	Price.
4/	Alliance, £20 Shs.	44/	10½
20/	Alliance, Mar., & Gen., Ld., £100 Shs.	25	53
19/	Atlas, £50 Shs.	6	31
12/	British & For. Marine, Ld., £20 Shs.	4	24
7½d.	British Law Fire, Ltd., £10 Shs.	1	1½
7/6	Clerical, Med., & Gen. Life, £25 Shs.	50/	16½
20/	Commercial Union, Ltd., £50 Shs.	5	43½
4	Do. "W. of Eng." Ter. Deb. Stk.	100	110½
£9	County Fire, £100 Shs. ..	80	190
2/	Eagle, £50 Shs.	5	½
4/	Employrs' Liability, Ltd., £10 Shs.	2	4½
.	Empress, Ltd., £5 Shs. ..	1	—
21/	Equity & Law, £100 Shs.	6	23
7/6	General Life, £100 Shs. ..	5	15
4½d.	Gresham Life, £5 Shs. ..	15/	2½
2/6	Guardian, Ld., £10 Shs.	5	11½
20/	Imperial, Ltd., £20 Shs. .	5	29½
5/6	Imperial Life, £20 Shs. ..	4	6½
6/	Indemnity Mutual Mar., Ltd., £15 Shs.	3	12
1/	Lancashire, £20 Shs.	2	5
7½d.	Law Acc. & Contin., Ltd., £5 Shs.	10/	1
5/	Law Fire, £100 Shs.	2½	18
9½d.	Law Guar. & Trust, Ltd., £10 Shs.	1	1½
9/	Law Life, £20 Shs.	2	25
2/9	Law Un. & Crown £10Shs	12/	7
4	Do. Deb. Stk., 1942 ..	100	110½
14/6	Legal & General, £50Shs.	8	15½
9d.	Lion Fire, Ltd., £8½ Shs.	1½	½
14/	Liverpool & London & Globe, Stk.	2	54
20/	Do. Globe £1 Ann ..	—	36
15/	London, £25 Shs.	12½	63½
4/	Lond. & Lanc. Fire, £25Shs	2½	19
2/	Lond. & Lanc. Life, £25Shs	2	5½
1/	Lond. & Prov. Mar., Ld., £10 Shs.	1	½
6/	Lond. Guar. & Accident, Ltd., £5 Shs.	2	11½
10/	Marine, Ltd., £25 Shs. ..	4½	43
2/	Maritime, Ltd., £10 Shs.	2	4½
1/6	Merc. Mar., Ld., £10 Shs.	2½	2½
—	National Marine, Ltd., £9 Shs.	1	½
20/	N. Brit. & Merc., £25Shs.	6½	41½
20/	Northern, £100 Shs.	10	81
40/	Norwich Union Fire, £100 Shs.	12	126½
10/	Ocean Acc. & Guar., fy. pd.	5	22
2/	Do. £5 Shs.	1	4
7/6	Ocean, Marine, Ltd.	2½	9½
1/	Palatine, £10 Shs.	2	3½
2/6	Pelican, £10 Shs.	1	3½
12/	Phœnix, £50 Shs.	5	44
£6	Provident, £100 Shs.	10	31
5/	Railway Pasngrs., £10Shs.	2	8½
2/6	Rock Life, £5 Shs.	10/	4½
8	Royal Exchange	100	360
18/	Royal, £20 Shs.	3	54
4/	Sun, £10 Shs.	10/	12
3/9	Sun Life, £10 Shs.	7½	14½
6/	Thames & Mrsey. Marine, Ltd., £20 Shs.	2	10½
9/	Union, £10 Shs.	4	24½
4/	Union Marine, £20 Shs. .	2½	9
12/	Universal Life, £100 Shs.	12	42
2/	World Marine, £5 Shs. ..	2	1½

IRON, COAL, AND STEEL.

Last Div.	Name.	Paid.	Price.
—	Barrow Hæm. Steel, Ltd.	7½	2
9/	Do. 6 p.c. 2nd Pref. ..	7½	7
30/	Bolck., Vaugh. & C., Ld.	20	17½
12/	Do. £8 liab.	12	9½
7/6	Brown, J. & Co., Ltd., £20 Shs.	15	21
7/6	Consett Iron, Ld., £10Shs.	7½	30
4/	Do. 8 p.c. Cum. Pref.	5	11
7/6	Ebbw Vale Steel, Iron & Coal, Ltd., £25 Shs. ..	20	6½
15/	General Mining Assn., Ld.	5½	7½
8/	Harvey Steel Co. of Gt. Britain, Ltd.	10	29
5	Lehigh V. Coal 1 Mt. 5 p.c. Guar. Gd. Cp. Bds.	—	95½
42/6	Nantyglo & Blaina Iron, Ltd., Pref.	862	97½
1/	Nerbudda Coal & Iron, Ltd., £3 Shs.	56/	1/16
—	Newport Abrcrn. Bk. Vein Steam Coal, Ltd.	10	4½
5/	New Sharlston Coll., Ltd. Pref.	20	10
4½d.	Nw. Vancvr. Coal & Ld., L.	1	½
2/6	North's Navigation Coll. (1889) Ltd.	5	2½
10/	Do. 10 p.c. Cum. Pref.	5	7½
—	Rhymney Iron, Ltd.	5	1½
	Do. New, £5 Shs. ..	4½	½
5	Do. Mt. Debs., Red.	100	98½
5	Shelton Irn., Stl. & Cl. Co., Ltd., 1 Chg. Debs., Red.	100	99½
50/	Sth. Hetton Coal, Ltd. ..	100	—
2/	Vickers & Maxim, Ltd. ..	1	3½
5	Do. 5 p.c. Prfd. Stk.	100	130½

SHIPPING.

Last Div.	Name.	Paid.	Price.
4/	African Stm. Ship, £20 Shs.	16	11
5/	Do. Fully-paid	20	15½
5/	Amazon Steam Nav., Ltd.	12½	9
8/	Castle Mail Pakts., Ltd., £20 Shs.	14	15½
3½	Do. 1st Deb. Stk., Red.	100	102
6/	China Mutual Steam, Ltd.	5	2½
6	Do. Cum. Pref.	10	9½
10/	Cunard, Ltd.	20	9½
5/	Do. £20 Shs.	10	3½
4½	Furness, Withy, & Co., Ltd., 1 Mt. Dbs., Red.	100	106
6/	General Steam	15	8
5/	Do. 5 p.c. Pref., 1874 ..	10	9
5/	Do. 5 p.c. Pref., 1877 ..	10	8½
5/	Leyland & Co., Ltd.	10	18½
7/	Do. 7 p.c. Cum. Pref. ..	10	14½
2/11	Do. 4½ p.c. Cum. Pre-Pf.	3	10½
4	Do. 1st Mt. Dbs., Red.	100	106½
7/6	Mercantile Steam, Ltd. ..	5	7½
6/4½	New Zealand Ship., Ltd.,	6	5
4	Do. Deb. Stk., Red. ..	100	104
5/	Orient Steam, Ltd.	10	5
5	P. & O. Steam, Cum. Prefd.	100	154½
19	Do. Defd.	100	235½
3½	Do. Deb. Stk.	100	120
5	Richelieu & Ont., 1st Mt. Debs., Red.	100	100
30/	Royal Mail, £100 Shs.	60	51
2/6	Shaw, Sav., & Alb., Ltd., "A" Pref.	5	5½
5/	Do. "B" Ord.	5	4
8/	Union Steam, Ltd.	20	20
4/	Do. New £20 Shs.	10	8½
4	Do. Deb. Stk., Red. ..	100	106
7/	Union of N.Z., Ltd.	10	10
5½	Wilson's & Fur.-Ley., 5½ p.c. Cum. Pref.	10	10½
4½	Do. 1 Mt. Db. Sk., Rd.	100	106½

TELEGRAPHS AND TELEPHONES.

Last Div.	Name.	Paid.	Price.
4	African Direct, Ltd., Mort. Debs., Red.	100	102
—	Amazon Telegraph, Ltd..	10	7½
19/6	Anglo-American, Ltd. ..	100	60½
39/	Do. 6 p.c. Prefd. Ord. ..	100	1[illegible]
—	Do. Defd. Ord.	100	12½
3/	Brazilian Submarine, Ltd.	10	16½
5	Do. Debs., 2 Series....	100	114

Telegraphs and Telephones (*continued*) :—

Last Div.	Name.	Paid.	Price.
4/	Chili Telephone, Ltd.	5	3½
$1½	Comcial. Cable, $100 Shs.	—	187½
4	Do. Stg. 500-yr. Deb. Stk. Red.	100	106
2½d.	Consd. Telpehone Constr., &c., Ltd.	10/	½
6/	Cuba Submarine, Ltd. ..	10	7
10/	Do. 10 p.c. Pref.	10	15
2/	Direct Spanish, Ltd.	5	4½
5/	Do. 10 p.c. Cum. Pref..	5	10½
4½	Do. Debs.	50	104½
3/	Direct U.S. Cable, Ltd. ..	20	11
2/6	Eastern, Ltd.	10	18
3/	Do. 6 p.c. Cum. Pref. ..	10	19
4	Do. Mt. Deb. Stk., Red.	100	129½
2/6	Eastern Exten., Aus., & China, Ltd.	10	19
5	Do. (Aus. Gov. Sub.) Deb., Red.	100	101
5	Do. do. Bearer ..	100	101½
4	Do. Mort. Deb. Stk. ..	100	129½
5	Eastn. & S. Afric., Ltd., Mort. Deb. 1900	100	101
5	Do. Bearer	100	101½
4	Do. Mort. Debs. ..1909	100	103½
4	Do. Mort. Debs. (Maur. Subsidy)	25	108½
5/	Grt. Nthn. Copenhagen. ..	10	30
5	Do. Debs., Ser. B., Red.	100	101½
12/6	Indo-European, Ltd.	25	53½
6	London Platino-Brazilian, Ltd., Debs. 1904	100	107½
4/	Montevideo Telph., Ltd., 6 p.c. Pref.	5	2½
3/	National Telephone, Ltd.	5	6½
6/	Do. Cum. 1 Pref.	10	17
6/	Do. Cum. 2 Pref.	10	16
5	Do. Non-Cum. 3 Pref..	5	5½
3½	Do. Deb. Stk., Red. ..	100	104½
4d.	Oriental Telephone, Ltd..	1	½
4	Pac. & Euro. Tlg. Dbs., Rd.	100	106½
4/	Reuter's, Ltd.	8	8½
5/	Un. Riv. Plate Telph., Ltd.	5	4½
5	Do. Deb. Stk., Red. ..	100	106½
—	West African Telg., Ltd..	10	4
5	Do. 5 p.c. Mt. Debs., Red.	100	100½
—	W. Coast of America, Ltd.	10	½
3/	Western & Brazilian, Ltd.	15	12½
3/	Do. 5 p.c. Pref. Ord. ..	7½	8
—	Do. Defd. Ord.	7½	4½
4	Do. Deb. Stk., Red. ..	100	107½
1/	W. India & Panama, Ltd..	10	½
6/	Do. Cum. 1 Pref.	10	7½
6/	Do. Cum. 2 Pref.	10	6
5	Do. Debs., Red.	100	106½
7	West. Union, 1 Mt. 1902($)	1000	107½
6	Do. 6 p.c. Stg. Bds., Rd.	100	102½

TRAMWAYS AND OMNIBUS.

Last Div.	Name.	Paid.	Price.
1/6	Anglo-Argentine, Ltd.	5	3½
6	Do. Deb. Stk.	100	127½
4/	Barcelona, Ltd.	10	12
5	Do. Deb., Red.	100	105½
7/6	Belfast Street Trams.	10	16½
—	Blackpl. & Fltwd. Tram., £10 Shs.	8	13
10/	Bordeaux Tram. & O., Ltd.	10	12
5	Do. Cum. Pref.	10	11
—	Brazilian Street Ry., Ltd.	2	½
—	British Elec. Trac., Ltd..	10	16½
—	B. Ayres & Belg. Tram., Ltd., 6 p.c. Cum. Pref.	5	—
6	Do. 1 Deb. Stk.	100	—
—	B. Ayres. Gd. Nat., Ltd., 6 p.c 1 Deb. Bds., Red.	100	57½
5½	Do. Pref. Debs., Red.	100	95½
1/	Calais, Ltd.	5	1
—	Calcutta, Ltd.	10	3½
—	Carthagena & Herr., Ltd.	10	3
5	Do. Deb., Red.	100	90
5	City of B'ham. Trams., Ltd., 5 p.c. Cum. Pref.	5	6
4	Do. 1 Mort. Debs., Rd.	100	107½
3/9	City of B. Ayres, Ltd.	5	7½
2/3	Do. Ext. £5 Shs.	3	4½
6	Do. Deb. Stk	100	145
1/4	Edinburgh Street Tram ..	4	4
1/	Glasgow Tram. & Omni. Ltd., £9 Shs.	8	
3/7½	Imperial, Ltd.	6	15
3/	Lond., Deptfd, & Greenwich, Prefd.	5	3½
nil	Do. Defd.	5	1
10½	Lond. Gen. Omni., Ltd. ..	100	205
4	Do. Deb., Red.	100	117½

Tramways and Omnibus (*continued*) :—

Last Div.	Name.	Paid.	Price.
4/9½	London Road Car	6	10½
28/6	Do. Red. 1 Mt. Deb. Stk.	100	108½
5	London St. Rly. (Prov., Ont.) Mt. Debs.	100	110
12/6	London St. Trams.	—	2
12/9	London Trams., Ltd.	10	10
6/	Do. Non-Cum. Pref. ..	10	10½
5	Do. Mt. Db. Stk., Rd.	100	100
5	Lynn & Boston 1 Mt. 1924 .... $	1000	107
5	Milwaukee Elec. Cons. Mt. .... $	1000	100½
5	Minneapolis St. 1 Cons. Mt. .... $	1000	96
5	Montreal St. Dbs., 1908 ..	100	109
4½	Do. Debs., 1922	100	107
6/	Nth. Metropolitan	10	13
1/9½	Nth. Staffords., Ltd.	6	4½
5/6	Provincial, Ltd	10	7
6/	Do. Cum. Pref.	10	13
5	St. Paul City, 1937 .... $	1000	96
5	Do. Guar. Twin City Rap. Trans. .... $	1000	96
5/	Southampton	10	6½
5/	South London	10	5½
7/6	Sunderland, Ltd.	10	6½
4½	Toronto 1 Mt., Red.	100	106
2/6	Tramways Union, Ltd. ..	5	7½
4½	Do. Deb., Red.	100	109
5/	Vienna General Omnibus.	5	6½
5	Do. 5 p.c. Mt. Deb., Red.	100	103½
4/	Wolverhampton, Ltd	10	6½

WATER WORKS.

Last Div.	Name.	Paid.	Price.
8/	Antwerp, Ltd.	20	22
6/	Cape Town District, Ltd.	5	7
10½	Chelsea	100	335½
5	Do. Pref. Stk.	100	178½
4½	Do. Pref. Stk., 1875 ..	100	158½
4½	Do. Deb. Stk.	100	160½
5/6	City St. Petersburg, Ltd.	13	11
5/	Colne Valley	10	15½
4	Do. Deb. Stock ..	100	137½
£4	Consol. of Rosar., Ltd., 4 p.c. 1 Deb. Stk., Red. ..	100	92
7½	East London	100	286½
4½	Do. Deb. Stk.	100	162½
3	Do. Deb. Stk., Red.	100	106
37/6	Grand Junction (Max. 10 p.c.) "A"	50	122½
18/9	Do. "B"	25	
18/9	Do. "C" (Max. 7½ p.c.)	25	55½
35/	Do. "D" (Max. 7 p.c.)	50	104½
4	Do. Deb. Stock	100	147½
13	Kent	100	360½
7	Do. New (Max. 7 p.c.) .	100	215½
5/7½	Kimberley, Ltd.	7	5½
6	Do. Debs., Red.	100	104½
6	Do. Deb. Stk., Red ..	100	107½
10	Lambeth (Max. 10 p.c.) ..	100	300½
7½	Do. (Max. 7½ p.c.), 50 & 25	—	233
4	Do. Deb. Stock	100	147½
3	Do. Red. Deb. Stock ..	100	103
10/	Montevideo, Ltd.	20	16½
5	Do. 1 Deb. Stk. ..	100	108½
5	Do. 2 Deb. Stk. ..	100	103½
132/9	New River New	100	447
4	Do. Deb. Stk.	100	147½
4	Do. Deb. Stk. "B"	100	147½
—	Odessa, Ltd., "A" 6 p.c. Prefd.	20	—
nil	Do. "B" Deferred	20	—
4	Portland Con. Mt. "B," 1937	—	102½
8/	Seville, Ltd.	20	12
5/6	Southend "Addl." Ord. ..	10	17½
6	Southwark and Vauxhall .	100	157½
6	Do. "D" Shares (7½ p.c. max.)	100	154½
5	Do. Pref. Stock	100	176½
4	Do. "A" Deb. Stock	100	147½
3	Staines Resvirs. Jt. Com. Gua. Deb. Stk., Red. ..	100	106
7/	Tarapaca, Ltd.	10	9½
10	West Middlesex	100	307½
4½	Do. Deb. Stk.	100	163½
3	Do Deb. Stk.	100	10[illegible]

Prices Quoted on the Leading Provincial Exchanges.

ENGLISH.

In quoting the markets, B stands for Birmingham; Bl for Bristol; M for Manchester; L for Liverpool; and S for Sheffield.

CORPORATION STOCKS.

Chief Market.	Int or Div.	Name.	Amount paid.	Price.
M	3½	Bolton, Red. 1935 ..	100	115½
M	3½	Burnley, Red. 1933 ..	100	114
M	3½	Bury, Red. 1946	100	116½
L	2¾	Liverpool, Red. 1925	100	102¼
B	3½	Longton, 1932	100	106
M	4	Oldham Prp. Db. Sk.	100	146
M	£1	Do. Gas & W. Ann.		34½
S	4	Rotherham 4 p.c., Red. 1927 ...... (£	1 an	112
M	3½	Runcorn Red. 1923 ..	100	105
S	2¾	Sheffield Water Ann.	100	118½
S	3	Do.	3 an	90
L	3½	Southport Red. 1936 {	5 an 100	112
L	3	Do. Red. 1914 ..	100	102½
M	3	Todmorden, Red. 1914	100	102

RAILWAYS.

Chief Market.	Int or Div.	Name.	Amount paid.	Price.
Bl	4½	Bridgewater Pref. ..	100	135½
M	1½	Cleator & Workton.	100	76
M	4	Do. 1883 Pref. ..	100	109
L	4	Cockermth. K. & P.	100	113½
L	4	Isle of Man	5	6¼
L	5	Do. Pref.	5	6½
L	3	Liverpool Overhead	10	10½
L	4	Do. Deb. Stk. ..	100	110
L	5	Do. Pref.	10	16
L	6½	Maryport & Carlisle	100	167
S	6	Mid. Shef. & Roth. Pf.	100	231
Bl	45/	Neath & Brecon "A"	100	65½
M	4½	Oldham, Ashton. &c.	10	16¾
Bl	5½	Penarth Harbour ..	100	182½
Bl	4	Do. Deb. Stk. ..	100	145
Bl	3½	Do. Deb. Stk. ..	100	127
Bl	1½	Ross & Monmouth ..	20	5½
Bl	6	Do. Pref.	20	42½
M	3	Southport & Cheshire Deb. Stk.	100	104½
M	nil.	Do. Pref.	100	22
Bl	2½	West Somerset Gu...	100	96½
Bl	5	Wye Val. Deb. Stk.	100	164

BANKS.

Chief Market.	Int or Div.	Name.	Amount paid.	Price.
L	8/	Adelphi, L., £20 Shs.	10	16⅛
L	12/6	Bk of L'pool, L., £100 Sh	12½	39½
B	5/6	Brmnghm. Dis. & C., Ltd., £20 Shs.	4	10½
B	6/3	Co. of Staffs., L., £40	5	13½
S	17½	Crompton & Evans, Ltd., £20 Shs	4	15
M	14/	Lancs. & Yorks, Ltd., £20 Shs.	10	31½
L	30/	Livrpl. Union, Ltd., £100 Shs.	20	60¾
M	24/	Manchester & Co., Ltd., £100 Shs. ..	16	61¾
M	20/	Mnchstr. & Livrpool. Dis., Ltd., £60 Shs.	10	51½
M	1/6	Mer. of Lancashire, Ltd., £20 Shs.	3	6½
L	16/	Nth. & Sth. Wales, Ltd., £40 Shs.	10	35¾
B	20/	Notts Joint St., Ltd., £50 Shs.	10	26¾
M	4/	Oldham Joint Stk., Ltd., £20 Shs.	4	12½
S	15	Sheffield Banking, Ltd., £50 Shs.	17½	51½
S	20	Do. & Rotherham, Ltd., £50 Shs. ..	8	26½
S	10	Do. & Hallamsh., Ltd., £100 Shs. .	25	65
S	10	Do. Union, Ltd., £40 Shs.	10	25½
M	12/	Union of Manchester, Ltd., £25 Shs. ..	11	27½
M	10/	Williams, Deacon, &c. Ltd., £50 Shs.	8	25¾
Bl	20	Wilts & Dorset, Ltd., £50 Shs.	10	49½
S	5/6	York City & Co., Ltd., £10 Shs.	3	13

BREWERIES.

Chief Market.	Int or Div.	Name.	Amount paid.	Price.
B	6	Ansell & Sons Pref.	10	15½
B	5	Do. Debs.	100	110
L	9/	Bent's	10	18½
L	6	Do. Cum. Pref...	10	14$\frac{5}{16}$
L	4½	Do. Deb. Stk. ..	100	111
L	13/6	Birkenhead, £5 paid	5	22¼
L	13/6	Do. £10 paid	10	25
M	9/	Boddington's	9	19½
M	5	Do. Cum. Pref...	10	12½
M	4	Do. Deb. Stk. ..	100	109½
B	4½	Butler & Co. Db. Stk	100	111
M	6	Chesters' Cum. Pref.	10	13½
M	4½	Do. Debs.	100	112
S	10/	Clarkson's Ord.	10	23
S	6	Do. Cum. Prf. Stk.	10	14½
M	4	Dutton & Co. Db. Sk.	100	104
M	4½	Hardy's Crown Debs.	100	111
B	10/	Holt	10	18½
B	5	Do. Cum. Pref...	10	12¾
B	4	Do. Debs.	100	109½
B	12/6	Lichfield	10	24
B	5	Do. Cum. Pref...	10	12
M	3½	Manchester Deb. Stk.	100	142
B	6/	Mitchell, H., & Co.	10	39
B	6	Do. Cum. Pref...	10	15¾
B	6	Oakhill Pref........	10	16¾

Breweries (*continued*):—

Chief Market.	Int. or Div.	Name.	Amount paid.	Price.
M	5/	Springwell	10	10¾
M	7	Do. Pref.	10	13½
Bl	9	Stroud	10	16½
Bl	6	Do. Pref	10	14½
M	6/	Taylor's Eagle......	10	12
M	7	Do. Cum. Pref ..	10	13½
M	5½	Do. Deb. Stk. ..	100	117½
S	10	Tennant Bros £20 shs	15	33½
S	10	Wheatley & Bates ..	10	14½
S	6	Do. Cum. Pref.	10	12¾

CANALS AND DOCKS.

Chief Market.	Int. or Div.	Name.	Amount paid.	Price.
Bl	5	Hill's Dry Dk. &c. £20	18	9
M	4	Manc. Ship Canal 1st Mt. Deb. Stk.	100	104
M	4	Do. 2nd do.	100	103½
L	36/3	Mersey Dck. & Harb.	an.	118½
L	35/	Do.	an.	117
M	10/	Rochdale Canal	100	36½
B	37/6	Staff. & Worc. Canal	100	75½
B	4½	Do. Deb. Stk....	100	137
Bl	4	Swansea Harb......	100	114
B	27/6	Warwick & Birm. Cnl	100	66½
B	12/6	Do. & Napton do.	100	23

COMMERCIAL & INDUSTRIAL.

Chief Market.	Int. or Div.	Name.	Amount paid.	Price.
L	5	Agua Santa Mt. Debs	100	100
M	8/	Armitage, Sir E. & Sns Ltd	10	19
M	4	Do. Deb. 1910 ..	100	103
L	6	Ang. Chil. Nit. 1 Mt. Debs., 1919 ..	100	109½
Bl	11	Bath Stone Firms ..	10	19
M	4/9½	Barlow & Jones, Ltd., £10 Shs.	8	10¾
B	12/6	Birmgham. Ry. Car.	10	17
B	6	Do. Pref.	10	15½
B	5/	Do. Small Arms	5	15½
M	£12	Blackpool Pier......	100	277½
M	5	Do. Tower Debs.	50	54½
M	3/	Do. Wi. Gar. & P.	5	4½
Bl	10	Bristl. & S. W. R. Wag. £20 Shs.	3	5½
Bl	8	Do. Wag. & Carri. £10 Shs.	10	14¼
M	7/	Crosses & Winkwth. Ltd.	5	12½
L	5	G. Angus & Co. Pref.	10	13½
Bl	5	Gloster. Carri. & W.		10½
Bl	5	Gt. Wstn. Cttn., Ltd.	20	15
M	6	Hetherington, L. Prf.	10	8½
M	4½	Do. Debs., 1910	100	98½
B	7½d.	Hinks (J. & Son), Ltd.	1	27/6
S	26/	Jessop & Sons, £50 Sh	30	27½
S	10	Kayser, Ellsn. & Co. L.	5	11½
S	6	Do. Pref.	5	7½
M	7/6	Kellner-Partgton., L.	5	14½
M	4½	Do. Debs., 1914 ..	100	105½
M	5	Kerr Thread, Ltd., Debs.	100	101
B	17/	King's Norton Metal, £10 Shs.	8½	19½
M	5/	Lancashire & Yorks. Wagon, Ltd.	10	9¾
L	10/	Liverpool Exch., Ltd.	20	28
L	45/	Do. Grain Stge, Ltd.	50	108
L	5/	Do. Rubber, Ltd...	5	5½
M	9d.	Manchester Bond. Whse., L., £10 Shs.	4½	2½
M	3/9	Do. Comcial. Bldgs., Ltd., £10 Shs.	5	10½
M	4/	Do. No. 2, £10 Shs.	5	10½
M	2/6	Do. No. 3, £10 Shs.	5	7½
M	5/	Do. Corn, &c., Exchange, Ltd.	10	16½
M	4	Do. Debs.	100	126
M	8	Do. Ryl. Exchge, L.	100	246½
B	5/	Midland Rlwy. Car. Wgn., Ld., £20 Sh.	10	14½
Bl	5	Millers & Corys Dbs.	100	100½
B	12/6	Mint, Brgham., Ltd.	5	7¾
B	5	Do. Debs.	25	107
B	10/	Nettlefolds, Ltd.....	10	50
B	5	Do. Pref.	10	15½
S	9	Nth. Centrl. Wgn., L.	5	8¾
B	15/	Patnt. Nut & Bolt, L.	10	34
B	5	Do. Pref.	10	14½
B	1/	Perry & Co., Ltd. ..	1	28/
B	6d.	Do. Pref.	1	27/
S	10	Round, J., & Co., L., £10 Shs.	6	12½
S	15	Rodgers, J., & Sons, L.	100	213
M	18/9	Rylands & Sons, Ltd., £20	15	38¾
M	2/6	Do. paid up	20	43¼
M	4	Do. Debs. .. 1909	100	106
S	5	Sanderson Brs. & Co., Ltd. Debs.	100	102
M	4½	Schwabe, S., & Co., Ltd., 1 Debs. 1914	100	104
S	7½	Sheffield Forge & Rolling, Ltd.	10	11½
L	80/	Southport Pier, Ltd.	100	88½
L	2½	Do. W. Gdns., Ltd.	5	3½
Bl	5	Spillers & Bakers, Ltd, £10 Shs.	9	14¾
Bl	6	Do. Pref.	10	14
B	5/	Union Rolling Stock, Ltd., £20 Shs.	5	7½
M	5/	Victoria Pr., S'port, L.	5	4½
Bl	8	Western Wagon & Property, Ltd.....	6	9½
S	10	Wostenholm, G., & Son, Ltd., £25 Shs.	20	22½
S	6½	Yorksh. Wagon, Ltd.	2	2½

FINANCIAL, TRUSTS, &c.

Chief Market.	Int. or Div.	Name.	Amount paid.	Price.
M	1/	Manchstr. Trst. £10 Shs.	2	13/9
M	1/3	N. of Eng. T. Deb. & A., Ltd. £10 Shs.	2½	27/
M	3½	Do. 1 Mt. Debs...	100	97
L	—	Pacific Ln. & Inv., L.	2½	2¾
L	4	Do. Deb. Stk.....	100	103
L	—	United Trst., L. Prfd.	100	72½
L	—	Do. Deferred....	100	62½

GAS.

Chief Market.	Int. or Div.	Name.	Amount paid.	Price.
Bl	5	Bristol Gas (5 p.c. mx.)	100	128
Bl	4	Do. 1st Deb.	100	137
S	10	Gt. Grimsby "C" ..	10	201
L	10	Liverpool Utd. "A"	100	245
L	7	Do. "B"......	100	178
L	4	Do. Deb.	100	137
S	10	Sheffield Gas "A," "B," "C"	100	248
B	10½	Wolverhampton	100	230
B	3	Do. 6 p.c. Pref...	100	172

INSURANCE.

Chief Market.	Int. or Div.	Name.	Amount paid.	Price.
M	6	Equitable F. & Acc. £5 Shs.	1	39/
L	2/	Liverpool Mortgage £10 Shs.	2	1$\frac{5}{16}$
M	2/	Mchester. Fire £20 Shs	2	7¾
M	5/	National Boiler & G., Ltd., £10 Shs.	3	13½
L	2/	Reliance Mar., Ltd., £10 Shs.	2	4½
L	4/	Sea, Ltd., £10 Shs...	2	10$\frac{5}{16}$
L	8/	Stnd. Mar., L., £20 Sh.	4	8$\frac{3}{16}$
L	1/	State Fire, L., £20 Sh.	1	2$\frac{1}{16}$

COAL, IRON, AND STEEL.

Chief Market.	Int. or Div.	Name.	Amount paid.	Price.
Bl.	12	Albion Stm. Coal ..	10	11½
M	15/9	And. Knowles & S., Ltd., £37½ Shs. ..	23½	12½
M	5	Do. Mt. Debs. 1908	100	105½
Bl.	1/½	Ashton V. Iron	100	26
S	12½	Bessemer, Ltd.	10	20$\frac{1}{16}$
S	5	Do. Pref.	10	12½
S	12/6	Briggs, H., & Co., "A" £15 Shs.	12½	15½
S	8/6	Do. "B" £15 Shs.	8½	9½
S	20	Brown Baley's Stl., L.	10	33
S	5	Brown, J., & Co., Cum. Pref.	10	13$\frac{1}{16}$
S	5	Cammell, C. & Co., Ltd.	85	13½
S	5	Do. Pref.	5	6⅛
M	5	Chatterley Whitfield. Col., Debs., 1905 ..	100	100½
Bl	—	Davis, D., & Sons, Ld.	10	10
M	5	Evans, R., & Co., Ltd., Deb., 1910 ..	100	100½
S	12½	Fox, S., & Co., Ltd., £100 Shs.	80	178
Bl	10	Gt. Wstn. Col., L., "A"	5	10½
Bl	6	Do. "B"	5	4½
Bl	8	Main Colliery, Ltd.	10	8
B	5/	Muntz's Metal, Ltd.	5	8½
B	5	Do. Pref......	5	6½
M	2/6½	Nth. Lonsd. Iron and Steel, Ltd., £10 Sh.	8½	2½
Bl	6	North's Nav. Coll., Ltd., Debs.	100	105
S	30/	Parkgate Irn. & Stl., Ltd., £100 Shs. ..	75	69
M	6	Pearson & Knls., Ld., "A" Cum. Pref...	50	46
B	10/	Sandwell Pk. Col., L.	10	17
M	6/3	Sheepbridge Coal and Iron, Ltd., "A"	25	17¾
M	2/6	Do. "B"	10	6¾
M	5	Do. "C" Gua. Pf.	25	28¾
Bl	4	South Wales Coll., Ltd., "A"	17	8½
S	30/	Staveley Coal & Iron, Ltd., "A" £100 Sh.	60	81
S	30/	Do. "C"	60	82
M	1/10½	Tredegar Iron & Cl., Ld., "A" £10 Sh.	7½	2½
M	1½	Do. "B" Stk. ..	100	35
M	6/	Wigan Cl. & Irn., Ld.	10	7
M	4/6	Do. £10 Shs.	7½	4

SHIPPING.

Chief Market.	Int. or Div.	Name.	Amount paid.	Price.
Bl	6	Bristol St. Nav. Pref.	10	11½
L	15/	Brit. & Af. St. Nav..	10	13½
L	8/10½	British & Estn, Ltd.	6½	2¾
L	10/	Pacific Stm. Nav., L.	25	24¾
L	30/	Wst. Ind. & Pac. St. Ltd., £25 Shs.	20	26¾

TRAMWAYS, &c.

Chief Market.	Int. or Div.	Name.	Amount paid.	Price.
B	5/	Brmngh. & Aston, L.	5	11
B	5/	Do. Mid., Ltd...	10	7¾
Bl	6/	Bristol Tr. & Car., Ltd..............	10	20½
Bl	4/	Do. Debs.	100	121
L	6	I. of Man Elec., L., Pref.	1	1½
M	15/	Manchester C. & T, L., "A" £20 Shs.	15	27¾
M	10/	Do. "B"	10	18¾

WATER WORKS.

Chief Market.	Int. or Div.	Name.	Amount paid.	Price.
Bl	7	Bristol	25	62½
Bl	7	Do...............	20	47½
Bl	58/	Do. 7 p.c. max. ..	100	158½
Bl	4½	Do. Pref.	20	32½
Bl	5	Do. Pref.	10	18
Bl	3½	Do. Deb.	100	129½
M	10	Fylde "A"........	100	335
M	7	Do. "B"	100	224
B	6	S. Staffs. Ord. "A"	100	165
B	—	Do. "B"	100	164
B	4	Do. Deb. Stk.	100	140
B	5	Do. Pf "A" "B" "C"	100	170
M	£3½	Stockport District ..	100	184½
B	2/	Wolverhampton New	5	6½

SCOTTISH.

In quoting the markets, E stands for Edinburgh, and G for Glasgow.

RAILWAYS.

Chief Market.	Int. or Div.	Name.	Nom. Amount	Price.
E	6½	Arbroath and Forfar	25	49½
G	1½	Callander and Oban .	10	7$\frac{1}{16}$
G	4	Do. Deb. Stock	100	148
G	4½	Do. Pref.......	10	14½
G	4	Cathct. Dist. Deb. Stk.	100	148
E	5	Edin. and Bathgate .	100	179½
E	7	Forth & Clyde Junc.	100	222½
G	4	Lanarks. and Ayrsh.	10	14
G	4	Do. & Dumbartons.	10	14½
G	4	Do. Deb. Stk.	100	149

BANKS.

Chief Market.	Int. or Div.	Name.	Nom. Amount	Price.
G	12	Bank of Scotland ..	100	361
G	16	British Linen	100	499½
G	8	Caledonian, Ltd.....	2½	97/
G	10	Clydesdale, Ltd.	10	23
G	16	Commercl. of Scot., L.	20	88½
G	16	National of Scot. Ld.	100	420
G	8	Royal of Scotland ..	100	234
G	11	Union of Scotland, L.	10	26$\frac{11}{16}$

BREWERIES.

Chief Market.	Int. or Div.	Name.	Nom. Amount	Price.
E	5	Bernard, Thos. Pref.	10	10½
E	5	Bernard, T. & J., Cum. Pref........	10	12½
G	20	Highland Distilleries	3½	10½

CANALS AND DOCKS.

Chief Market.	Int. or Div.	Name.	Nom. Amount	Price.
G	4	Clyde Nav. 4 p.c....	100	125½
G	3½	Do. 3½ p.c.......	100	105
G	3½	Greenock Harb. "A"	100	100
G	2	Do. "B"	100	33½

MISCELLANEOUS.

Chief Market.	Int. or Div.	Name.	Nom. Amount	Price.
G	4½	Alexander & Co. Debs.	100	110½
G	5	Baird, H., & Sns. C. P.	10	12½
E	12	Barry, Ostlere, & Co.	7½	12$\frac{5}{16}$
E	6	Do. Cum. Pref...	10	15$\frac{5}{16}$
G	5	Brown, Stewart, Deb.	100	84
E	7½	Broxburn Oil	8½	8½
E	6	Do. Cum. Pref...	10	11$\frac{1}{16}$
E	7	Edinburgh & Dist. Tram. Cum. Pref.	5	9
E	5	Gilroy, Sons, & Co. Debs.	100	99
G	9	Glasgow Cot. Spin...	6	5½
G	30/	Do. Royal Exchg.	46	110
G	—	Pumpherston Oil Pf.	10	8¾
E	7	Scottish Assam Tea	10	11½
E	5	Scottish Waggon....	10	12½
G	5	Stoddard & Co. Pref.	10	12½

FINANCIAL, LAND, AND INVESTMENT.

Chief Market.	Int. or Div.	Name.	Nom. Amount	Price.
G	1/	Assets Co............	1	47/
E	4½	Investors' Mort. Pref.	100	99½
E	4	Do. Deb. Stk....	100	103½
E	4	Nthn. Inv. N. Zeal. Deb. Stk.	100	107
E	4	N. of Scot. Canadian Deb. Stk.	100	106
E	4½	Real & Deb. Corp. Deb. Stk.	100	108½

INSURANCE.

Chief Market.	Int. or Div.	Name.	Amount paid.	Price.
G	12/	Caledonian F. & Life	5	36
G	4/6	City of Glasgow Life	2½	12¾
E	19/	Edinburgh Life	20	55
G	13/1	Life Ass. of Scotland	8¼	34½
E	8	Nat. Guar. & Surety	2	52/
G	17½	Scottish Union and National "A"....	1	94/6
G	17½	Do. "B"	3¾	18¼

IRON, COAL, AND STEEL.

Chief Market.	Int. or Div.	Name.	Amount paid.	Price.
E	Nil.	Addie, Coll. Cm. Pref.	10	7¾
E	8/	Arniston Coal	8	14
E	2½	Cairntable Gas Coal	8	86/
E	12½	Fife Coal	10	20¾
E	5	Do. Cum. Pref..	10	13
G	7	Merry & Cunghame. Cum. Pref........	10	15¾
G	5	Do. Debentures ..	100	105½
E	1/9	Niddrie & Benhar Cl.	1½	41/3
G	5	Steel Com. of Scotlnd	—	
	—	"A" Deb. Stk. ..	100	113
G	6	Do. and Mt. "B"	100	110
E	—	Watson, John	6¼	10¾
E	6	Do. Cum. Pref..	7½	8½
E	12½	Wilson's & Cly. Coal	3	8⅛

IRISH.

In quoting the markets, B stands for Belfast, and D for Dublin.

CORPORATION STOCKS.

Chief Market.	Int. or Div.	Name.	Amount paid.	Price.
B	3½	Belfast, 1921	100	112
B	3½	Do. 1919........	100	107½
B	3½	Do. 1924........	100	109½
B	3	Do. 1955........	100	106
B	3½	Do. Water Com...	100	117
B	3	Do. do.	100	106
B	3½	Do. Harbour Com.	100	114¼
D	3½	Rathmines & Rathgar	100	110½
D	3½	Waterford Deb.	100	—

RAILWAYS.

Chief Market.	Int. or Div.	Name.	Amount Paid.	Price.
D	30/	Cork, Bandon, & S.C.	100	78
D	4	Do. Deb.........	100	139¼
D	4	Do. W. Cork Pref.	100	—
B	5½	Belfast & Northern..	100	160
B	4	Do. Deb.........	100	146
B	4	Do. Pref.	100	141½
B	6½	Belfast & C. Down..	100	167
B	4	Do. Deb.........	100	147
B	3	Do.	100	107½
B	4½	Do. 4½ Pref. B...	100	153¾
B	5	Do. Guar.	100	173
D	Nil.	Dublin, Wick. & Wex.	100	82
D	4	Do. Deb.........	100	127½
D	4½	Do. Deb.........	100	134
D	6	Do. Guar.	100	170
D	4	Do. C. of Dub. Junc.	100	—
D	5	Do. 1860 Pref. ..	100	120½
D	50/	Do. 1864 Pref. ..	100	107½
D	50/	Do. 1865 Pref. ..	100	94½
B	67/6	Great Northern	100	179
B	4	Do. Deb.........	100	147
B	4	Do. Pref. B.	100	143½
B	5½	Gt. South & Western	100	144
B	4	Do. Deb.	100	148½
B	4	Do. Guar.........	100	144
D	45/	Midland Gt. Western	100	114
D	4	Do. Deb.	100	146½
D	4½	Do. Deb.	100	151½
D	4½	Do. Deb.	100	—
D	5	Do. Pref.	100	175
D	4	Do. Pref.	100	—
D	—	Waterford & Central	100	15
D	3	Do. Deb.	100	—
D	3½	Do. Pref.	100	134
D	4	Waterfd. L., & W. Db.	100	129½
D	4½	Do. Deb.	100	—
D	4	Do. Pref.	100	127
D	3½	Do. Pref.	100	101½

BANKS.

Chief Market.	Int. or Div.	Name.	Amount paid.	Price.
B	50/	Belfast, Old, £125 Shs.	25	126½
B	20/	Do. New, £125 Shs.	25	50½
D		Hibernian, £20 Shs.	5	6⅛
D	2/	Munster & Leinster £5 Shs.	2	5¼
B	11/	Northern, £50 Shs...	10	26½
D	12/	Royal, £30 Shs.	10	28¼
B	3/	Ulster, £15 Shs.	2½	12¾

BREWERIES AND DISTILLERIES.

Chief Market.	Int. or Div.	Name.	Amount paid.	Price.
D	10/	Castlebellingham & Drog	10	16½
D	6	Do. Pref.	10	15½
D	4½	Do. Deb.	100	115
B	17/	Dunville & Co.......	10	28¼
B	6	Irish Distillery, Pref.	10	13½
B	5	Do. Deb.	100	110
B	6	J. & J. M'Connell, Pf.	10	15⅛
B	13/6	Mitchell & Co.......	9	19½
B	5	Do. Deb.	10	11½
D	4½	Phœnix Brew. Deb.	100	95
B	6/	Wm. Cowan........	10	13½
B	6	Do. Pref. ..	10	13⅛
B	8/	Young, King, & Co.	8	14

STEAM AND CANAL.

Chief Market.	Int. or Div.	Name.	Amount paid.	Price.
B	Nil	Belfast Steamship ..	50	35½
D	20/	British and Irish	50	—
D	15/	City of Dublin......	100	60
D	3½	Do. Deb.	100	105
D	30/	Dublin & L'pool. Bldg.	50	75
D	2/6	Dundalk & Newry..	10	4½
D	4/	Grand Canal........	10	11⅛
D	3	Do. Pref. ..	10	9⅛
D	3	Do. Deb. ..	100	99
B	30/	Irish Shipowners....	100	65
B	3/	Ulster Steamship....	5	6

MISCELLANEOUS.

Chief Market.	Int. or Div.	Name.	Amount paid.	Price.
D	3/1	Arnott & Co.	4	7½
D	6	Do. Pref. ..	4	6¼
B	8/	Belfast Com. Bldgs.	10	11
B	37/6	Do. Ropework Co.	75	92
B	5	Do. do. Pref.	10	13½
B	2/	Do. Discount Co..	3	45/
B	5	Do. do. Pref.	5	4¾
B	10/	Brookfield Linen....	25	17¾
B	Nil	Coey & Co.	25	4
B	5	Do. Deb.	50	49¾
B	4½	David Allen & S's Deb.	100	107
D	4/	Dublin Trams	10	19⅛
D	6	Do. Pref.....	10	18½
D	4	Do. Deb.....	100	—
B	5/	Edenderry Spinning .	10	9
B	25/	Falls Flax Spinning .	25	15
B	17/	Forster, Green, & Co.	10	22½
B	9/	Island Spinning	7½	7¾
B	8/	Jas. Lindsay & Co..	8	16¾
B	1/7½	John Arnott & Co...	4	4⅛
B	4½	Do. Deb.........	50	56
D	5/	Kinahan & Co.......	10	11¾
D	5½	Do. Pref........	10	11¾
D	4½	Do. Deb........	100	109¾
B	12/	Kirker & Co.	10	10
B	5/	Leahy, Kelly, & Leahy	5	8¼
B	6	Do. Pref........	5	7⅛
B	4/	Lindsay Bros. Ltd...	8	7¾
B	4½	Do. Deb........	50	56½
D	1/	National Assurance .	2½	39/
B	10/	Olley & Co.	5	7⅛
D	1/1½	Patriotic Assurance..	2½	30/
B	3/7½	P. Johnston & Son, L.	6	6¼
B	10/	Robertson, F., & Co.	8	23½
B	10	Ulster Marine Insur.	5/	7/
B	15/	York-street Flax	25	33¾
B	6	Do. Pref........	10	15¾
B	4½	Do. Deb........	100	120

INDIAN AND CEYLON TEA COMPANIES.

Acres Planted.	Crop, 1897.	Paid up Capital.	Share.	Paid up.	Name.	Dividends. 1894.	1895.	1896.	Int. 1897.	Price.	Yield.	Reserve.	Balance Forward.	Working Capital.	Mortgages, Debs. or Pref. Capital not otherwise stated.
	lb.	£	£	£	INDIAN COMPANIES.							£	£	£	£
11,240	3,128,000	120,000	10	3	Amalgamated Estates	—	*	10	5	3½	8¼	10,000	16,500	D52,950	—
		400,000	10	10	Do. Pref.	—	*	5	‡5	10½	4¾				
10,223	3,360,000	187,160	20	20	Assam	20	20	20	5	60½	6½	55,000	1,730	D11,350	—
6,130	3,278,000	142,500	10	10	Assam Frontier..........	3	6	6	—	8¾	6¾	—	286	20,000	82,500
		142,500	10	10	Do. Pref.	6	6	6	3	11½	5¼				
2,087	839,000	66,745	5	5	Attaree Khat	12	12	8	3	7¾	5½	3,790	4,820	7,770	—
1,633	583,000	78,170	10	10	Borelli	4	4	5	—	8	6¼	—	3,256	D270	6,500 Pref.
1,720	812,000	60,825	5	5	British Indian	6	5	5	—	4	6	—	2,920	12,300	16,500 Pref.
3,223	2,247,000	114,500	5	5	Brahmapootra	20	18	20	6	13	7½	—	28,440	41,600	.
3,754	1,617,000	76,500	10	10	Cachar and Dooars	*	8	7	—	10	6½	—	1,645	21,240	.
		76,500	10	10	Do. Pref.	*	6	6	3	12	5				
3,946	2,083,000	72,010	1	1	Chargola	8	7	10	2½	[illegible]	10½	3,000	3,300	—	—
		81,000	1	1	Do. Pref.	7	7	7	3½	1¾	5				
1,971	942,000	33,000	5	5	Chubwa	10	8	10	3½	6¼	8	10,000	2,043	D5,400	—
		33,000	5	5	Do. Pref.	7	7	7	3½	7	5				
32,250	11,500,000	120,000	10	3	Cons. Tea and Lands	—	—	10	5	3⅞	7¼	65,000	14,240	D191,674	—
		1,000,000	10	10	Do. 1st Pref.	—	*	5	‡5	11	4½				
		400,000	10	10	Do. 2nd Pref.	—	*	7	‡7	11⅛	5½				
2,230	617,000	135,420	20	20	Darjeeling..............	5½	5½	6	—	22½	5	5,552	1,565	1,700	—
2,114	445,000	60,000	10	10	Darjeeling Cons..........	—	—	4/2	—	6	—	—	1,820	—	—
		60,000	10	10	Do. Pref.	—	*	5	2½	9¼	5½				
6,660	3,518,000	150,000	10	10	Dooars	12½	12½	12½	2½	18½	6¾	45,000	300	D32,000	—
		75,000	10	10	Do. Pref.	7	7	7	3½	16	4½				
3,367	1,811,000	165,000	10	10	Doom Dooma	11¼	10	12½	5	21½	5½	30,000	4,032	—	10,000
1,377	582,000	61,120	5	5	Eastern Assam	5	nil.	4	—	3½	6¾	—	1,790	—	10,000
4,038	1,675,000	85,000	10	10	East India and Ceylon	*	nil.	7	—	8¼	7¾	—	1,710	—	—
		85,000	10	10	Do. Pref.	*	6	6	3	11¾	5¼				
7,500	3,363,000	219,000	10	10	Empire of India	—	*	6/10	2½	11¾	—	15,000	—	27,000	—
		219,000	20	10	Do. Pref.	—	*	5	2½	11	4½				
1,180	540,000	94,060	10	10	Indian of Cachar	7	3½	3	—	4¼	6¾	6,070	—	7,120	—
3,050	824,000	83,500	5	5	Jhanzie	10	10	10	4	8⅜	6	14,500	1,070	2,700	—
7,980	3,680,000	250,000	10	10	Jokai	10	10	10	5	18	5½	45,000	990	D9,000	—
		100,000	10	10	Do. Pref.	*	6	6	3	14¼	4				
5,224	1,563,000	100,000	20	20	Jorehaut	20	20	20	—	58	6¾	36,220	2,955	3,000	—
1,547	504,000	65,660	10	8	Lebong	15	15	15	5	16½	7¼	9,000	2,150	8,650	—
5,082	1,709,000	100,000	10	10	Lungla	[illegible]	10	6	3	9	6½	—	1,543	D21,000	—
		100,000	10	10	Do. Pref.	*	6	6	3	11¼	5½				
2,684	885,000	95,970	10	10	Majuli	7	5	5	—	6¾	7¼	—	2,606	560	—
1,375	380,000	91,840	1	1	Makum	—	—	2	—	1½	1½	—	—	1,200	25,000
2,990	770,000	100,000	1	1	Moabund	—	—	*	—	1	—	—	—	—	—
		50,000	1	1	Do. Pref.	—	—	*	2½	1	5				
1,080	482,000	79,590	10	10	Scottish Assam	7	7	7	—	10¾	6½	6,500	800	9,590	—
4,150	1,456,000	100,000	10	10	Singlo..................	7	8	5	1	8¾	5¾	—	300	D5,200	—
		80,000	10	10	Do. Pref.	*	6½	6½	3½	13	5				
	Crop, 1896.				CEYLON COMPANIES.										
7,970	1,743,824	250,000	100	100	Anglo-Ceylon, & Gen.	—	*	5½	—	65	8½	10,992	1,405	D72,844	166,580
1,836	685,741	50,000	10	10	Associated Tea	—	*	5	2½	7¼xd	6¾	—	164	2,478	—
		60,000	10	10	Do. Pref.	—	*	6	3	10¾xd	5¾				
10,390	4,000,000§	167,380	10	10	Ceylon Tea Plantations ..	15	15	15	7	27	5½	84,500	1,516	D30,819	—
		81,080	10	10	Do. Pref.	7	7	7	‡7	16¾	4¼				
5,722	1,542,700§	55,260	5	3	Ceylon & Oriental Est.....	5	8	7	—	2¾	7¼	—	230	D2,047	71,000
		46,000	5	5	Do. Pref.	6	6	6	3	5	5¾				
2,157	801,609	111,330	5	5	Dimbula Valley	—	*	10	5	6	8¼	—	—	1,733	6,250
		62,607	5	5	Do. Pref.	—	*	6	3	6¾	4½				
11,496	3,715,000	298,250	5	5	Eastern Prod. & Est.	3	5	6½	2½	6½	5½	20,000	11,740	D17,797	100,500
3,118	701,100	150,000	10	10	Lanka Plantations........	4	5	5	‡5	6⅜	6¾	—	495	D11,300	14,700 Pref.
2,193	1,050,000§	22,080	10	10	New Dimbula "A"	20	16	16	4	24	6	11,000	2,024	1,150	8,400
		55,710	10	10	Do. "B"	18	16	16	4	22	7¼				
2,572	570,360	100,000	10	10	Ouvah	6	8	6	2	8½	7	4,000	1,151	D1,255	—
2,630	535,675	200,000	10	10	Nuwara Eliya	—	*	6	3	11	5½	—	—	—	30,000
1,720	720,200	41,000	10	10	Scottish Ceylon	15	15	15	5	21½	6¾	7,000	1,252	D3,970	9,000 Pref.
2,450	750,000§	39,000	10	6	Standard	19¼	15	15	5	14	6¾	9,000	800	D14,012	4,000
		17,000	10	10	Do....................	19½	15	15	5	22	6¾				

* Company formed this year.
Working-Capital Column.—In working-capital column, D stands for *debit*.
‡ Interim dividends are given as actual distribution made. † *Total* div. § Crop 1897.

Printed for the Proprietor by Love & Wyman, Ltd., Great Queen Street, London, W.C.; and Published by Clement Wilson at Norfolk House, Norfolk Street, Strand, London, W.C.

The Investors' Review

EDITED BY A. J. WILSON.

Vol. I.—No. 14. New Series. FRIDAY, APRIL 8, 1898. [Registered as a Newspaper.] Price 6d. By post, 6½d

Notice to Subscribers.

Complaints are continually reaching us that the INVESTORS' REVIEW cannot be obtained at this and the other railway bookstall, that it does not reach Scotch and Irish cities till Monday, and that it is not delivered in the City till Saturday morning.

We publish on Friday in time for the REVIEW to be at all Metropolitan bookstalls by at latest 4 p.m., and we believe that it is there then, having no doubt that Messrs. W. H. Smith & Son do their best, but they have such a mass of papers to handle every day that a fresh one may well look almost like a personal enemy and be kept in short supply unless the reading public shows unmistakably that it is wanted. A little perseverance, therefore, in asking for the INVESTORS' REVIEW is all that should be required to remedy this defect.

All London newsagents can be in a position to distribute the paper on Friday afternoon if they please, and here also the only remedy is for subscribers to insist upon having it as soon as published. Arrangements have been made that all our direct City subscribers shall have their copies before 4 p.m. on Friday. As for the provinces, we can only say that the paper is delivered to the forwarding agents in ample time to be in every English and Scotch town, and in Dublin and Belfast, likewise, early on Saturday morning. Those despatched by post from this office can be delivered by the first London mail on Saturday in every part of the United Kingdom.

ADVERTISEMENTS.

All Advertisements are received subject to approval, and should be sent in not later than 5 p.m. on Thursdays.

The advertisements of American Life Insurance Offices are rigorously excluded from the INVESTORS' REVIEW, and have been so since it commenced as a Quarterly Magazine in 1892.

For tariff and particulars of positions open apply to the Advertisement Manager, Norfolk House, Norfolk-street, W.C.

CONTENTS

The Investors' Review.

England's Latest Move in China.

Tuesday's discussion in the House of Commons contributed very little to the nation's enlightenment upon the subject of our appropriation of Wei-hai-wei. Mr. Balfour had nothing really to tell the House or the country which it did not know before through the enterprise of the *Times* correspondent in Pekin. He filled in the details of the story to some extent, and made the surprising admission that it was not until the 22nd of last month that the Marquis of Salisbury woke up to the necessity of remonstrating with Russia over her domineering attitude towards the beaten and dispirited Chinese and her absorption of Port Arthur. Sir William Harcourt naturally made great play of the apparent shilly-shallying of the Foreign Office, and other opponents of the Government had their say against the policy of counter aggression as it might be called, which the country has now plunged into, but the whole thing was rather tame and pointless. It is perfectly true that the policy of the "open door" has not been adhered to, but there ought to be no disposition to accuse the present Government of being the first to depart from it. The drifting has been inevitable, and we are very sure that the Liberal Party, had it been in power, would not have done much otherwise.

Last week the Press of this country was almost unanimous in its condemnation of Lord Salisbury and his Government for their bungling, as it was called, in China—for allowing themselves to be outwitted by

Russia. Now the clamour has died away before the news that our Ambassador in Pekin has obtained for us a "lease" of Wei-hai-wei, to endure as long as Russia's occupation of Port Arthur. The news pleased nearly everybody, barring the discontented by profession, and a few people like Sir Charles Dilke, who recognise that such a possession in China implies a new departure which may cost us dear. He thinks that twenty thousand men will be required to garrison the place unless we enter into a compact with the Japanese to do garrison duty for us, and wants to know this, that, and many things. Really we scarcely understand what these jingos would be at. They howl at the Government when it does not occupy territory and join in the policy of grab, and they grumble when it does. To us it appears that some step such as this has been inevitable ever since the Germans and Russians commenced their aggressive policy in the Chinese Empire, unless we could have made up our minds to cordially agree with Russia. It was simply impossible that we could stand still and allow our great commercial interests in the far East to be jeopardised while these powers were cowing the Chinaman, and, by their behaviour, leading him to suppose that the power of England was on the wane. All that we have contended for was that we should enter into no engagements having for object the partition of China among several Powers; but it was equally clear to us that steps would sooner or later have to be taken to put ourselves in a position to defend liberty for our commerce in China whenever that liberty should be threatened. To effectually do this a post much further north than Hong Kong was necessary, and on the whole Wei-hai-wai may do as well for the purpose in view as any other place. It lies rather too far north, perhaps, and we should have preferred Chusan if not too costly to hold; but it is at any rate a better place for the purpose of watching over the northern commerce of China than even Port Arthur itself.

What is to be feared, however, is not the consequence to our finances of this annexation, for such it is, but what may flow out from this policy to China. Evidently the "sphere of influence" policy is spreading. No sooner has one power taken a step in advance than the others are anxious to get in front of it. Initially, these difficulties may be said to have begun when we allowed Russia, Germany, and France to snatch the fruits of their victory out of the hands of the Japanese—All the rest has followed in natural sequence, through our "neutrality" as it was called at that time — Russian domination at Pekin, the German aggression in Shan-tung, and the French restlessness in the south. For the moment the *pas* is with France, not that we have much to fear from her, weak as she is and with no population to spare; still France, by making a noise, has got something down south, and the something may some day threaten our supremacy at Canton or elsewhere: then we should have to take another move. Already, indeed, many people are clamouring for a fortified post on the mainland opposite Hong Kong, and if this clamour is yielded to Germany will look about for something else, and the neck to neck race for the Chinese Empire will go on merrily, until the grabbers come into collision. Then there will be a fight. That, to cut a long story short, seems to be the ultimate consequences likely to flow from what is now going on, and it is a pity that we could not have managed to gain our ends, which are only commercial ends, in China, without entering upon this career; but the mistake which led to this is not one for which the Marquis of Salisbury should fairly be held responsible. It originated much earlier, and the step he has now taken is certainly one which has been forced upon him both by popular outcry and the moves made in the game by the other players.

Possibilities Surrounding a War between Spain and the United States.

In the City the rapid and sharp fluctuation in the prices of securities is a fit index of the agitation and doubt which have taken possession of the public mind over this question. It does not seem reasonable that every class of security, from Consols down to South African mines, should plunge downward in price when the political barometer points to war between the United States and Spain. Surely at the very worst that war could not damage our interests to any appreciable extent. It would not much interrupt our commerce with the American Union even were the Spanish fleet to blockade all its Atlantic ports. In that event, as we have already pointed out, American produce would find its way to Europe over the railways of the Canadian Dominion and Mexico. Even were privateering to be resorted to, as it may be—the United States having abstained from signing the Declaration of Paris—and that in consequence we were obliged to send a fleet to protect our merchant marine, the result should not be disastrous to us. The trade of Cuba, on the other hand, has already been so disorganised that its complete temporary extinction with ourselves and our West Indian possessions would not leave much trace on the great commerce of the United Kingdom.

And as for Spain; well, Spain undoubtedly runs the greatest risk of national bankruptcy through a war with such a power as the United States. National bankruptcy seems only a question of time in any event for Spain, and we do not suppose that the suspension of payment upon the enormous debt of that country would have any appreciable consequence here. The English public has long ceased to invest in Spanish bonds. They are dealt in on the London market because it is an international market into which Americans, Spaniards, and Frenchmen come to transact their business. Throughout the present scare American speculators have been systematic "bears" of Spanish bonds, and the impression is that they have won immense sums of money from the French speculators who have been equally systematic "bulls." Much buying and selling, the product of this antagonism, has taken place on the London Stock Exchange, but the English people have had scarcely any share in the play, and we doubt very much if a default by Spain would bring a hundred people in this country into the hands of their creditors. Nor need the trade of Spain be materially damaged unless revolution follows bankruptcy there, as is by no means improbable. Then, indeed, for a time we should see a diminution in Spanish imports from the United Kingdom, and dullness might arise in consequence in some branches of our export trade. In all this, however, there is nothing really to alarm us, and the puzzle is unsolved—why should war between powers, whose interests involve no danger for us through sharing in the fray, cause such perturbation and excitement, paralysing business and reducing the Stock Exchange day after day to a condition of helpless suspense?

One explanation of the apparent inadequacy of the causes adduced to produce such effects is no doubt to be found in the perilously inflated condition of our markets at most points. Prices are extremely high compared with the average range of former years, and what is really feared is such a strain upon our money market as might cause a further advance in the rate of discount. Such an advance could not take place without, as we have frequently demonstrated, compelling a great number of holders of stocks upon borrowed money to sell; and it is almost certain that, should war break out between Spain and the United States, further heavy drafts upon our small stock of gold would take place. Already the mere prospect of war has caused us to lose, not much of the Bank of England's stock certainly, but the whole fresh supply of the metal coming into the market. Let war break out and the probability is that some millions of gold would be taken from the Bank of England by the States within a very short space of time—enough of the metal probably to send our Bank rate to five per cent. This contingency alone is sufficient to account for the excessive nervousness and the feeling of dread now prevalent, and to make everybody indebted to bankers for capital anxious about the future.

It would be waste of time for us to dwell much on this aspect of the present political crisis; it has been harped on to weariness already in these columns. Passing then from it, we come to another question which is even of greater general importance, and on whose answer likewise the fate of our markets for securities to no small extent depends. This question is, whether the war would be short and sharp or a long drawn out struggle? If the war should turn out to be merely an episode of a few weeks' duration, at the end of which Cuba would have secured freedom and Spain be driven out of the West Indies for ever, crushed and beaten, then the effects of conflict would very soon be obliterated, and the United States might be trusted to recover without serious strain on their public credit. Spain, no doubt, would at once be bankrupt in such an event, and probably soon plunged into the chaos of revolution. Undoubtedly the hope in the States is that war, if it does occur, will be short and sharp, but we can have no assurance upon the point, and hardly share this view. Should the eminent Spaniard, whose opinions were set forth in Tuesday's *Times* by the Paris correspondent of the paper, adequately represent the views of his nation, and we have little doubt that they do, then war may by no means be a thing of a few weeks. Let us note what he says—

I repeat, it is not on Europe that we count, but on ourselves; on God and our right. There is still in Spain plenty of good gold and good blood. We shall spare neither. We shall send all the soldiers we can. The Americans, if they attempt it, will not vanquish 250,000 men, which is the number we shall shortly have in Cuba, and they will have to kill us one by one to the last man. We shall deal American trade more rapid and telling blows than America will ever deal us, for if we cannot [capture vessels we can wreck them.

Yes, I admit that we have blundered in Cuba; but for fifty years we have not been sufficiently masters of the island to govern in peace, reform abuses, and introduce a milder form of administration. If we now succumb, we shall not be the only ones. There are other possessions in the hands of Europeans which the Americans will seize as a logical consequence of their triumph over us. The Pope, I am told, is intervening. Leo XIII. still has in his mind the ironical triumph which Bismarck secured for him in the question of the Caroline Islands. But this time he will perceive that the Americans are more mad with pride and with scorn of others than all the nations of Europe. They will not heed him more than others. The only thing which will make them hesitate is the necessity of paying for their premeditated conquest by mountains of ruins and torrents of blood. Upon this alone do I count for arresting the strong arm raised by America against what she considers weak Spain. But, where God guides and strikes, men's plans frequently miscarry, and to judge of the victory we must wait for the last battle in the criminal conflict about to be waged in the name of force and of the pride of prosperity.

Here we have the utterances of a man who has made up his mind to sacrifice everything, and life itself, for what he deems the honour of his country. It is little use to put against passionate pride of this description calculations about Spain's inability to maintain a prolonged war, for we know that no country fights more desperately, or with greater determination, than one whose very existence as a coherent State hangs in the balance. Mere bankruptcy cannot always shorten wars entered upon in this spirit. Not only so, but the statement that Spain will soon have a quarter of a million soldiers in the island warns us that the United States could not hope to liberate Cuba by a mere naval demonstration. Their people must be prepared to land a large army in the eastern or central portions of the island, now in the hands of the provincial government, to join the insurgent forces in a determined land campaign whose object it will be to drive the Spanish troops into the sea. We need not say that this looks a most formidable undertaking, which may involve the expenditure of a great many millions and the loss of tens of thousands of human lives. Not only must this campaign be undertaken, but the insurgents will have to be fed as well as the non-combatant inhabitants of the island, and the feeding will have to be paid for by the United States as well as the provisions carried between the American ports and the landing places in Cuba under protection of a powerful fleet.

No doubt, should the Spanish Navy be destroyed at an early stage of the conflict, or so crippled as to become incapable of offence, this part of the undertaking would be rendered comparatively easy of accomplishment, and such a victory could not fail to disorganise and dispirit the Spanish forces in the island. This preliminary victory, however, is not nearly so assured as the advocates of war in the United States appear to think. The Spanish Navy is probably the stronger of the two at the present time. It is said to be badly manned and officered, especially officered, but men and officers may be trusted to fight with all the old Spanish resolution. The United States Navy, on the other hand, is notoriously defective in its personnel, so far as the command of fighting sailors is concerned, and it is smaller than that of Spain. It is not, therefore, inherently improbable that the struggle at sea might be of some duration, and should it be so the United States will at once be brought face to face with very considerable financial difficulties. We must not forget that their Government would enter upon this war, not only possessed of no money in hand, but with an empty treasury. The Dingley tariff has proved disastrous to the revenue already, and the true condition of the Federal Treasury has only been obscured for a little time by the flush of business created through the deficiency of the crops in Europe last year and the abundant one in the States. A check at the outset would stimulate the American people, whose resources are great, whose national credit is first-class, to raise whatever money might be necessary in order to provide vessels and men sufficient to overcome the Spaniards. But the debt in this way incurred could not fail to bring considerable trouble upon the nation's finances when the war was over, and to create acute difficulties in regard to the currency. Such consequences might be very far reaching indeed, not only on the commercial prosperity of the Union, but upon our trade therewith and our investment interests therein; and we see in such remote contingencies a deeper and more enduring reason for disquiet than any lying in the immediate effect of an outbreak of hostilities upon our money-market.

But will war break out? Really at the moment of writing no man can say. Passion is rising both in Spain and in the United States, and though, so far, President McKinley seems to have stood fast, calmly endeavouring to breast the swelling tide, we do not know the moment when he may be swept off his feet by the fury of those who are clamouring for strife. So far away as we are, we cannot estimate the strength of popular feeling, the combined strength of the varied nations impelling the nation towards war; but it is possible to recognise that the situation has now become almost a hopeless one from the point of view of the maintenance of peace. We have Spain determined and the Cubans equally determined—witness that remarkable letter in last Monday's *Daily Chronicle* from its correspondent, Mr. Musgrave, who succeeded in reaching the head quarters of the provisional government of Cuba before falling into the hands of the Spaniards, and by them being summarily ejected from the island. In that letter President Maso emphatically declared that the motto of the Cubans is "Independence or death." If the United States people, in their sympathy with this attitude of the Cubans, are equally determined to assist in liberating the island, then peace has become impossible, and such episodes as the offer of the Pope to mediate between the belligerents become almost pathetically laughable. Looking at all the circumstances, as far as we can get at the drift of them through the din of excited passions, we still fear that the end of the present suspense must be bloodshed, a war the ultimate fruits of which no man can foresee. Victory for the States will only bring to the front for them a new procession of troubles Victory for Spain—ah, that seems impossible. For centuries her lot has been defeat.

Two Great German Banks and Continental Banking Habits.

We have before us the reports for the year 1897 of the Deutsche Bank and the Dresdner Bank, both of which institutions have risen to a great position in international trade and bill discounting within a comparatively short number of years. The paid-up capital of the Deutsche Bank is now £7,500,000, and the reserve fund £2,263,781, showing an increase of £2,500,000 in the paid-up capital, and of £281,230 in the reserve fund within the year, the company having issued 50,000,000 marks of new capital last year to meet the expansion of its business. The Dresdner Bank has followed the same policy, and its capital fully paid-up has increased from £4,250,000 to £5,500,000 in 1897, the reserve fund being in the same time raised £400,000 by the addition to it of the premium of 36½ per cent. obtained on the new shares. No English banks, except the Bank of England, have such paid-up capitals, in proportion to their commitments, as these two great German institutions now possess. The total in the balance-sheet of the Deutsche Bank amounts to little more than £36,000,000, and that in the Dresdner Bank to less than £21,200,000, yet the capital and reserve fund in the one case amount to nearly £9,750,000, and, in the other, after the last call had been paid up, as it was on the 1st inst., to £6,875,000. We cannot help thinking that such a position as to capital places these banks on a much more satisfactory basis than that on which English banks so largely rest. Here we build up enormous liabilities on current and deposit accounts, not upon the paid up capital, but upon the illusive strength of the uncalled portion of that capital for which the shareholders remain liable. Thus we frequently find now-a-days British banks, with from £20,000,000 to £50,000,000 of liabilities to depositors, whose paid up capital rarely amounts to as much as £3,500,000, and whose capital and reserve together never equal the total even of the Dresdner Bank.

On the other hand German banking, and most Continental banking, follows lines which would be repudiated as unsafe by the banks of this country. In the United Kingdom we still cling, at all events, to the form of keeping the assets of banks in a more or less liquid condition, so as to conform to the imminent liability on deposits at call. But these two German banks enter into all sorts of commitments and engagements which are supposed to be relegated here to the finance houses, so called. They take their share in promoting companies, and place capital in other enterprises just as if they were Barings, or Rothschilds or Morgans, or even mere Hooleys. The Deutsche Bank, for instance, announces that it has placed shares of two banks of which it became owners in its balance sheet at cost price, and it has entered into more or less large commitments in the Anatolian railway, in the German Trust Company, and in the Company for Electric Elevated and Underground railways in Berlin. In like manner the Dresdner Bank directors announce that in conjunction with a firm in Berlin they have formed a Mexican Electric Works, Limited, for the purpose of lighting the City of Mexico with electricity; and they pride themselves upon the extension of their commission business, and in that for the purchase and sale of stocks. In short, while not excluding commercial affairs, these Continental institutions openly and frankly carry on the trade of loan monger and company promoter, as well as that of stock and share broker on the markets. They also, and in consequence, take a large share in the arbitrage business which goes on between Bourse and Bourse.

That there are risks of a grave description in this mixture of businesses, nominally held distinct under our banking habits, is strikingly shown by the last report of another of these conglomerate institutions, the Laenderbank of Vienna. This institution had a speculative origin, having been one of the creations of M. Bontoux, the founder of the French Union Générale of lamentable memory. It did not fail when that institution foundered, but on the contrary seems to have been occasionally very prosperous. Had it not been so it could not possibly have withstood the strain of the tremendous losses it has now been obliged to acknowledge—losses aggregating nearly 10,000,000 florins. It has had to withdraw 6,000,000 florins from the extraordinary reserve, 2,500,000 florins from the special reserve, and to write off 1,250,000 florins from the profits of 1897, making 9,750,000 florins swept away in one year. Not necessarily, however, losses in that year, because the business is of that financial kind which causes losses to emerge slowly. The Vienna correspondent of the *Financial News* said in that paper the other day—and we give it as an example of the kind of business done—that last year, when the affairs of the Austrian Enamel Company were made public, the Laenderbank was obliged to buy back all the shares in this company, which had originally been issued by its instrumentality at a very high premium; and, in another instance, it sold the shares of a calico manufactory in Prague at a nominal price in order to avoid a call. It has suffered, in short, the usual woes inseparable from the trade of an unsuccessful company promoter, and this kind of risk falls directly upon such banks as we are dealing with, without any intermediatory finance house, or group of houses, to intercept part of the force of the blow.

Viewing the affairs of these institutions from this standpoint, we may be inclined to plume ourselves upon our more conservative banking customs. To some extent this satisfaction is well grounded, but we are not at all sure that competition has not, in recent years, been secretly drawing British banks more and more into the same channels of business which these German banks follow in the open. What some of our banks, at any rate, have been doing is to promote the promoter of companies, if we may use the phrase. They stand directly behind the adventurous fellows who manufacture companies and launch into new enterprises of all descriptions, often with excessive capitals, and lend these men their credit to an extent which would never be allowed by the shareholders were the facts suspected. This is unquestionably true at the present time, and before passing judgment upon the Continental method of business we must wait for the results of some of this hidden sustenance of financiers in the case of banks at home.

Looking at the matter without prejudice we cannot say that there is anything radically unsound in the German methods as here disclosed, at least not for the creditors of these banks on current account. What both the Deutsche and the Dresdner Banks risk is their own capital and reserves, and as long as the commitments involve them in no risks exceeding the amount of these funds, the danger to public credit arising through their promotion of dangerous or doubtful enterprises seems small. One point, however, in connection with the large development of the commercial side, or apparently commercial side, of the business done by these banks deserves careful attention here, and that is the extent to which they sustain their financial operations by means of money obtained from the discount of their acceptances on the London market. The balance sheet of the Deutsche Bank does not specifically define the amount of acceptances it has afloat, but there is an item, "bills payable," which we may take to represent acceptances, in the main if not entirely, and that stands at £6,525,590. In the same manner the Dresdner Bank shows "acceptances against credits and securities" to the amount of £5,031,283. These two together come to more than £11,500,000, and a recent estimate put the amount of the acceptances of these two banks continually afloat in the London market at about £8,000,000. Here we have at once opened up a very serious question for London dealers in credit.—How far do these acceptances represent ordinary commercial transactions, how far credit created to sustain the company-promoting enterprise and industrial finance in which these banks are engaged? We cannot answer this question, but it points to a necessity for care in the selection of the bills tendered to the market by such foreign institutions, and we are not sure that the free circulation of so much of their paper in London is a thing to be joyful about. In former days and under old-fashioned arrangements, such paper could not have been melted here without the endorsement of an English merchant-banking house of known wealth and unlimited credit. Now these bills rank with the best. What do they really represent? Is there a holder who can say?

American Life Office Investments.—2.

Turning to the investment lists proper of the Equitable and Mutual of New York offices neither of which, let us emphasise, lend on their own policies, we find that neither the one nor the other is an extensive holder of United States Government Bonds, nor does either of them appear to have any money at all invested in Great Britain. The Equitable is a considerable holder in the Northern Pacific Railway Company, in the Pittsburg, C.C. and St. Louis, the Pittsburg, McKeesport, and Youghiogheny, the St. Louis and San Francisco, the St. Louis and Iron Mountain—all bonds apparently—the Union Pacific—whether bonds or shares is not stated, the New York, Lake Erie, and Western, Prior and General Lien Bonds, and in something else of the company's, it is not stated what. The Chicago, St. Paul, Minneapolis, and Manitoba—bonds we presume—the C. C. C. and St. Louis, the Pittsburg C. C. and St. Louis, the St. Louis and Iron Mountain, the Manhattan, the Metropolitan Elevated, the Missouri Pacific, the New York Elevated, the Old Colony, the Ohio and Mississippi, and many similar, all form depositories for large amounts of the company's funds. The Western Union Telegraph, and the Mercantile Trust Company stocks, The C. C. C. and St. Louis Preferred stock, Chicago and North-Western Common stock, Baltimore and Ohio Common stock, Western National Bank stock, and so on and so on, go to swell the list, and indicate a very mixed lot of investments indeed, to which we may add a certain amount of Prussian, Italian, Russian, German, Brazilian, Servian, Hungarian, and Cape of Good Hope and Australian government stocks, but the aggregate of these latter is small. The company has over $1,000,000 in "Wabash"— this is all the entry,—about $116,000 in "City of Woonsocket," about $1,400,000 in "Union Pacific," $2,170,000 in Albany and Susquehanna; $1,107,000 in "Central of Georgia Consolidated," about $7,760,000 in "North-West" consolidated debenture, Fremont, &c., &c.—presumably the various issues of the Chicago and North Western Railway Company. We mention these as mere samples of the medley; Toronto, Quebec, Montreal, "City of St. Lawrence," "City of Manchester"—not "Manchester, England"—City of

New York, "City of Lynn," "City of Somerville," and other municipal bonds all help to swell up the total of $109,595,489 at which the invested fund of this company stood on Dec. 31st last.

Varied, however, as the Equitable's list is, and diluted with a good many securities which we cannot think highly of, or about whose quality we can form no opinion of any sort, it appears to us to be excelled in odd miscellaneousness by that of the Mutual, although this latter concern has distributed its investments over a greater variety of securities, and is doubtless wisely guided in having so done. It has gone in very largely for small holdings in county bonds all over the United States. These small county debts may be quite good, and probably are all right in most instances; but they would, we fear, be of no use to British policyholders were any trouble to arise. The Mutual alone puts British Government consols in its investment list to the amount necessary to fulfil the stipulations of the Act of Parliament when it originally began business here. No doubt the others had made the same deposit, but it does not now figure in their investment list, so we may assume that they took the money home again as soon as they could. For the rest the Mutual is a considerable holder of Austrian and Italian rentes, Prussian consols, Canadian provincial Government bonds — New Brunswick and Nova Scotia—State of Virginia bonds, Montreal City bonds, Georgia City bonds, Toronto bonds, and so on. Among its other investments deserving of special mention we may give Erie Railway bonds, grade not stated, Sandusky and Cleveland bonds, Richmond and Danville bonds, South Carolina and Georgia bonds, Texas and New Orleans Railroad bonds, Wabash Railroad bonds ($2,042,650), Western Railroad of Alabama bonds, Brooklyn Union Gas and Brooklyn Wharf and Warehouse bonds, Philadelphia Bourse bonds, Sharon Estate Company bonds, United States Mortgage and Trust Company bonds, American Exchange National Bank stock, Central Trust stock, Guaranty Trust Company stock, National Bank of Commerce stock, National Union Bank stock, Pennsylvania Railroad stock, Title Guarantee and Trust Company stock, and United States Mortgage and Trust Company stock. All these names we have given represent individual investments of amounts exceeding $250,000, and the company holds what we should consider very large sums in some of them, presumably bought at high prices. For instance, the nominal value of the Guaranty Trust Company stock owned by it, is $1,200,181, and the market value is placed at $3,389,040. This is an unusually large increase, even in such an investment list, none of the other Trust companies securities held by the company showing anything like such a rise. It would be interesting to know at what price the Mutual Life bought, and how the market price is ascertained, seeing that it holds all but $800,000 of the company's capital. Where is the rest of the stock, this $800,000? Do the officers of the Mutual own it, and how is a market made for it so that the actual price can be proved?

Although the lists of the Equitable and the Mutual Offices are deficient in particulars, so that we are throughout very often unable to say what class of bond is held in such concerns as the Erie, the Equitable Gas Company, the Sharon and Estate Company, the Illinois Central Railroad, the Georgia Railroad and Banking Company, the Dakota Central Railroad Company, and so on, it is plain enough that a large proportion of the investments are by no means first class. This may be reasonably inferred from the return itself, and is to some extent proved by the fact that comparatively few of the securities stand much above their "book-value" to the companies, while a certain proportion of them are below it. For instance, such things as the Richmond, York River, &c., bonds—unspecified—the San Antonio and Aransas pass bonds, the Seaboard and Roanoke bonds, the South Carolina and Georgia bonds, the Indiana, Decatur &c., bonds, the Consolidated Gas stock, the Louisville and Terrehaut bonds in the Mutual list stand below cost price. In the same way the Equitable Company shows depreciation on some of its Chesapeake and Ohio, Chicago, Burlington and Quincey, Metropolitan Elevated, Michigan Central, Rome, Watertown and Ogdensburg, United States Government, and Brazilian Government bonds, and on its large holdings in St. Louis and Iron Mountain issues. Also, and this is true of all three concerns, many securities in themselves good enough, have obviously been purchased at what may be called "top of the market" figures, so that the margin between the companies and loss is both narrow and precarious.

What renders facts and inferences like these of great importance is the practice, common to all the companies, of adding the market value profits to the assets so as to swell out the totals of their resources. Thus the Equitable Company puts down $2,796,863 as "market value of stocks and bonds over book" value; the Mutual Company, $6,675,887; and the New York Life, $5,876,275. The practice appears to be universal among American life offices, and it is not a prudent one. Doubtless these unrealised, and possibly unrealisable "values" are used in the summaries prepared for European consumption, to help to show what splendid "surpluses" these life offices can attain to, their excessive and wholly indefensible extravagancies in current expenditure, notwithstanding. Surely enough has now been said to justify the warnings we have given to the British public to have nothing whatever to do with such concerns.

What we have said, furthermore, lends emphasis to the advice which we have also given, that British policy-holders in these offices should take steps to ascertain for themselves what their real position is. If these policy-holders united together they could easily, at a very minute individual cost, obtain competent men to go to America, with a mandate from them these companies dare not disregard, to thoroughly overhaul the securities the companies possess, and to examine into their methods of dealing with investments and of lending on the Stock Exchange. We have taken some trouble to try and compare the lists of 1893 with those of 1896, but owing to the vagueness with which the items are set forth there is not much to be gained by the comparison. However, we have picked out a few items, put together with what completeness was attainable, and tabulated them below to indicate how the investments vary. The table might have been made much longer, but we doubt whether it would have afforded much more light on what we regard as the speculative element entering into the investment habits of these companies. In the aggregate the three companies had upwards of £120,000,000 of money invested at the date of the latest return before us; and over their share in these investments British policy-holders have no more control than they have over the private affairs of the Emperor of Russia.

One of the ablest and keenest of our critics has informed us that we are wrong in anticipating anything like failure from these American life offices. Unquestionably we are. They may live long after many a British office has "gone under" through foolish straightforwardness. What with the free revenue accruing from lapses and surrenders and the absence of surrender values, a business conducted in the way we have revealed possesses an incalculable "reserve vitality," which nothing but a wholesale destruction among its invested funds could overcome. But what about its effect upon life insurance business in general? Do the managers of British life offices suppose that facts such as have been disclosed in the present series of articles do not get talked about, or that, among the ignorant who hear, the same kind of tactics fail to be attributed more or less to all life insurance offices? Why cannot our offices move in their own protection to have fuller accounts published of all life business, to have the British business of American offices separately stated in the Board of Trade Returns, and to help policy-holders in American offices to secure some hold over the money they provide, now invested, or lent to speculators, in the United States under the absolute control of men in no way responsible to them? If they hold back much longer they may depend upon it that "something will happen" some day to make them bitterly regret their apathy. The figures in the following tables represent "book" values alone :—

EQUITABLE LIFE OF THE UNITED STATES.

Name.	1893.	1896.
	$	$
St. Louis & Iron Mountain Railroad Bonds	2,286,000	2,899,000
Baltimore and Ohio Railroad Stock	705,000	1,171,000
Albany & Susquehanna	1,158,000	2,172,000
Chicago, Burlington, & Quincy	4,715,000	10,255,000
Wabash	—	1,035,000
Chicago & N. Western	7,626,000	8,437,000
Chicago, Milwaukee, & St. Paul	4,994,000	4,468,000
Cleveland, Cincinnati, Chicago, & St. Louis	2,774,000	4,254,000
Illinois Central Stock	1,034,000	1,131,000
Manhattan	1,048,000	1,515,000
Erie Railroad	2,563,000	3,216,000
Missouri Pacific	1,325,000	1,773,000
Western Union Telegraph	2,220,000	2,618,000
Union Pacific	—	1,138,000
Central of Georgia	—	1,657,000
Chicago, St. Paul, Minn., & Omaha Railroad	648,000	1,765,000
Chicago, Rock Island, and Pacific Stock	1,478,000	1,170,000
Atchison, Topeka, and Santa Fé Railroad	—	308,040
New York, Lackawanna, and Western	69,000	2,278,000
Australia and New Zealand Fixed Deposit	1,026,000	—
Pittsburg, Cinn., Chicago, and St. Louis	—	2,197,000
Pennsylvania	1,508,000	1,243,000
Great Northern	1,489,000	2,036,000
Lake Shore and Michigan Southern	871,000	1,371,000
Chesapeake and Ohio Railroad Bonds	1,400,000	1,975,000
Morris and Essex	1,629,000	1,925,000
Montreal City	420,000	674,000
Italian Government Bonds	382,000	537,000

MUTUAL OF NEW YORK.

	$	$
New York, New Haven, & Hartford	1,935,000	2,913,000
Chicago & North-Western	2,530,000	3,067,000
Chicago, Milwaukee, & St. Paul	3,375,000	3,233,000
Chicago, Burlington, & Quincy	447,000	1,933,000
Sharon Estate	—	1,200,000
Wabash Bonds	1,003,000	2,042,000
United States Mortgage & Trust	1,562,000	3,754,000
Erie Railroad Bonds	92,000	816,000
Province of New Brunswick	219,000	219,000
New York, Lackawanna, & Western Bonds	1,064,000	—
Newark, New Jersey Bonds	156,000	1,981,000
Western Union Telegraph	617,000	1,148,000
Rensslaer & Saratoga Railroad Stock	—	1,422,000
Toronto, Canada bonds	460,000	460,000
Guaranty Trust Company	—	1,200,000
Central of Georgia Railroad Bonds	—	3,310,000
Cleveland, Cincinnati, Chicago, & St. Louis	1,321,000	1,836,000
Morris & Essex	31,000	392,000
Michigan Central	1,320,000	667,000
Central Trust Company Stock	—	1,116,000
Title Guarantee & Trust Company Stock	—	1,157,000
Brooklyn Union Gas Company Bonds	—	1,093,000
Brooklyn Wharf & Warehouse	—	2,880,000
Equitable Gas Light Company of New York	529,000	1,034,000
Illinois Central Railroad Bonds	1,833,000	1,000,000
Prussian Government Consols	276,000	663,000
Italian Government Rentes	107,000	439,000
British Consols	99,000	99,000
Canadian Government Bonds	—	154,000
State of Georgia Bonds	1,032,000	185,000
Jersey City, New Jersey, Bonds	1,642,000	1,279,000

NEW YORK LIFE.

Chicago and North-Western Railroad	6,991,000	7,516,000
Great Northern Railroad	2,670,000	2,940,000
Chicago, Milwaukee, and St. Paul Railroad	729,000	1,255,000
Louisville and Nashville	—	1,035,000
Lehigh Valley Terminal Bonds	2,018,000	1,009,000
Missouri Pacific	1,035,000	1,034,000
Russian Government	1,688,000	3,038,000
Italian Government	515,000	808,000
Prussian Government	856,000	1,036,000
Cuba Loan of 1890	—	25,000
Chicago and West Indiana Railroad	1,006,000	1,142,000
Chicago, St. Paul, Minn., and Omaha	1,192,000	1,187,000
Central of Georgia	1,483,000	1,936,000
Fremont Elkhorn & Missouri Valley Bonds	1,057,000	1,174,000
Chicago, Burlington, & Quincy	591,000	1,709,000
Cleveland, Loraine, & Wheeling	—	574,000
Lake Shore & Michigan Southern	2,321,000	2,242,000
New York, Lake Erie, & Western Railroad	2,342,000	1,556,000
St. Paul, Minn. Gas Light Company Bonds	399,000	824,000
St. Paul, Minn., & Manitoba Railroad	2,192,000	2,422,000

The Prussian Budget for 1898—99.

At the first glance Prussia seems to contrive to spend nearly as much as we do; in fact the Budget for the new financial year balances at £109,376,369, which is more than we contrived last year to spend on Imperial purposes, even in our present mood of excessive extravagance, and it amounts to £7,000,000 more than the total for the year just closed. When, however, we look under the surface a very different state of things to ours is disclosed. First of all the share of taxation in producing this great revenue is only about £19,000,000, exclusive of say £13,500,000 handed over to Prussia out of the revenues collected by the Imperial authorities of Germany. Putting that contribution at £14,000,000, and the total taxation embraced in the gross £109,000,000 odd is only £33,000,000. More than half the entire gross receipts are derivable from the railways owned by the State, and of the balance about £4,500,000 gross comes from State domains and forests, over £4,000,000 from the lottery, and nearly £7,000,000 from mines and salines. With the exception of the lottery—which is a vicious thing in any State, and a most expensive one to the Prussian nation, since the gross receipts of £4,124,000 yield less than half a million net—the great bulk of the Prussian revenue consists of earnings from State property of one kind or another, and of services rendered to the community. The railways alone are estimated to yield nearly £21,000,000 net in the current year, and after allowing £10,500,000 for the interest on railway debt, and about £1,800,000 for its amortization, there is still nearly £8,750,000 of this left for general State purposes.

We often hear complaints in this country about the manner in which German State railways are worked so as to stimulate exports of German manufactures. There is no doubt much truth in these complaints, and such figures as we have given show how easy it is for the German Imperial authority, and for Prussia, which constitutes the great bulk of the Empire, to carry goods at moderate charges. Our British railways have cost more than twice as much per mile as the Prussian lines have done. British railway companies, further, never pay off any of their debts, but continually add to them, so that the burden of capital they have to carry has reached altogether gigantic proportions. Our 21,277 miles of railway in the three kingdoms stood at the end of 1896, at a capitalised cost of nearly £1,030,000,000, of which £650,000,000 represented the debenture and preference capital. Prussia has more than 17,000 miles of railway, the capitalised cost of which at the present time amounts to about £340,000,000. The gross receipts of these Prussian railways are estimated at £60,485,826 in the present year; those of our railways in 1896, the latest year for which we have complete returns, were little over £90,000,000. It costs our companies an average of 56 per cent. of the gross receipts to work their lines, in spite of their habit of charging so many things to capital account. In Prussia the estimated cost exceeds 65 per cent., but then in the Prussian expenditure there is, apparently, included for the present year £2,000,000, to be spent out of revenue on new works, and £1,800,000 devoted to reduction of railway debt. According to law, three-quarters of 1 per cent. of the total railway debt must be paid off every year out of revenue. In this manner £29,000,000 has already been paid off, and in addition £33,000,000 has either been paid off by ordinary and extraordinary amortization or met out of yearly surpluses, so that the debt outstanding at the end of the financial year, 1896-97, was only £250,000,000. Adding the reserve of £4,000,000, set aside to meet unforeseen expenses, to increase rolling stock and such like, the total amount devoted in fifteen years to the ordinary expenditure of the State out of the proceeds of the State railways has been £56,000,000. In the Budget of the present year, after meeting interest and amortization it is calculated that £15,500,000 will be left out of the railway income for the ordinary purposes of State. No wonder that the Germans are able to reduce railway freight charges to any amount necessary to enable them to command foreign markets.

From an economic and business point of view this is the most interesting feature in the Prussian Budget, because the Government of Prussia is the largest owner of railways in the world and has pursued an enlightened and consistent policy which not only England but the United States and France have already bitter reason to regret that they did not in some respect imitate. Assuredly our system of allowing private companies to expend capital on the public highways of the country, without check of any kind, and to charge for their services almost what they please, within very liberal limits, constitutes a danger to our commercial supremacy which it would be difficult to exaggerate. By keeping the railways in its own hands and managing them economically the kingdom of Prussia, acting in harmony with the Empire of Germany, of which it is the backbone and mainstay, is not only able to accommodate the public cheaply but to reduce systematically the capital account burdens, and to develop traffic in all directions. How well this policy has answered is seen, not only in the figures we have given, but in those relating to the expansion of railway business. In 1882 the surplus derived by the State from railway administration was less than £7,000,000, in the year just closed it exceeded £25,000,000. This, of course, is before deducting the interest upon railway capital spent. For the whole period, from 1882 to 1896-97, the aggregate surplus was £223,000,000, out of which £129,000,000 went to pay debt interest. In addition £6,600,000 for the same period of time was appropriated out of the railway net receipts to meet State expenditure which would otherwise have had to be borrowed for. Even then a very large sum was left to the State. Mr. Spring Rice, who has compiled this suggestive report, puts this sum at £92,000,000 in fifteen years. Of course, we do not say that the drill sergeant method of conducting business to which the German mind has acclimatized itself, would suit here, nor can we advocate the State ownership of railways so as to transform them in this country into a huge system of indirect taxation, but we decidedly think that a great mistake was made in giving British railway companies a freehold of their property, and we are now paying to some extent for this mistake in the excessive and arbitrary charges levied upon the internal and over-sea traffic of the kingdom. In the future we shall suffer still more severely on this account unless the managers of our railways recognise that they must close their capital accounts and devote their energies to the development of traffic by means of its better organisation and reduced freights.

Economic and Financial Notes and Correspondence.

The Directorate of the Chartered Company.

Now that Mr. Cecil Rhodes has come home we may expect to have some light thrown upon the affairs of this company, but in order to deal with it effectually the report must be in our hands. Meantime the interesting question of Mr. Rhodes's re-election to a seat upon the board has arisen. In some quarters this step is deprecated on account of his connection with the Jameson raid. We do not share the opinion that either he or Mr. Beit should be excluded from the directorate on this account. On the contrary it seems to us advisable that both these men should return to the posts from which they have been ejected. They more than any other men have made splendid fortunes out of their Chartered shares, and as the company will require a great deal of money in the near future it would be a seemly thing for them to come forward and provide it with, say, a couple of millions each, out of the many millions they have amassed. Mr. Rhodes is stated to have boasted many times of being worth ten millions, and probably Mr. Beit could even cap this splendid total. Neither then would be any the poorer in a wealth-enjoying sense were they to hand back a few of these millions to aid in the development of Rhodesia. For this reason alone we hope they will both be returned to seats on the new board, and that when they are there it will be for the shareholders to put pressure upon them to provide funds for the development of the great estate.

Suppose they were asked to find five millions as a beginning, receiving deferred shares in the company for the money, such shares to have no right to any dividend until the existing capital had been paid back 100 per cent. in dividends. That would be a perfectly reasonable arrangement, especially as all the first anticipations about the productiveness of Mashonaland and Matabeleland have been so lamentably falsified. Seeing also that Messrs. Beit and Rhodes took a leading share in instigating the Jamieson raid, out of which the Matabele rebellion arose, bringing in its train so many disasters, it would be a fitting reparation on the part of these men to hand over a considerable portion of the money they realized by the sale of the shares originally handed to them for nothing, so to say, out of the capital of the Chartered Company. They could have sold many of these shares at from £8 to £9 a piece, and doubtless did sell them for very handsome premiums in great numbers. Now, therefore, is the time for these gentlemen to exhibit themselves as genuine imperialists, making sacrifices for the good of the Empire they profess to love and ardently desire to extend. By all means put them back on the board of the Chartered Company, and let us see what their self-sacrificing capacity may be. Mr. Rhodes's patriotic words have been diluvial for so reticent a man. Now for the deeds to prove them true.

The End of the Zola Episode.

Is it really the end or only the close of the second act in a very miserable drama? We fear the latter is the case. Nothing has been settled by the judgment of the Court of Cassation, except the fact that the proceedings against M. Zola were illegal from the first. This is something to be thankful for, but the whole question raised by the arrogant assumption of dictatorial powers by the supreme Staff of the French army, with the Minister of War at their head, and the further question of the illegal condemnation of Captain Dreyfus remain where they were, except that the glaring scandals of both are now placed in higher relief. It is surely impossible for the French people to remain acquiescent in these scandals. We notice from the lists of the *Siècle* that the women of France are rallying nobly to the side of justice. Will the men of France take the same course and grapple with this military insolence, which is threatening to embroil the country once more in revolutionary outbreaks? No answer can be given to such questions until after the elections to be held next month; but in the meantime there is much cause for anxiety, because the civil government of France is plainly in the hands of weak, temporising, and timorous men—men afraid of standing by truth and justice, afraid to do anything except to bribe and pamper and create monopolies and cringe before the men of the sword. This kind of government is an evil augury for the French Republic, and we may well be anxious for its future. A peaceful and friendly France is the best neighbour that England could have at all times. With France on our side in European squabbles we should be strong beyond the power of any combination to break up. But France, as now governed, could not be the genuine friend of England, of anybody, and there is a danger in the near future that her strength may fall into the guiding hands of the Chauvinist class of men who are always England's bitterest foes, and traitors to the best interests of their native country. We must not, cannot interfere, but it is open to us to show unostentatious sympathy for all those who are striving in France at the present time to lift its politics and its Government out of the degraded condition into which they have fallen. The fight which men like MM. Clemenceau and Yves Guyot are leading in France is one in which free men and lovers of true freedom all the world over must join through sympathy, even when unable to take their share with hand and pen.

The Welsh Coal Crisis.

Just as trade, having recovered from the effects of the engineers' dispute, was beginning to advance with healthy vigour, another check has been administered to our prosperity by what seems a wantonly provoked quarrel in the South Wales coal trade. Already, it seems, 120,000 men are idle—not because they have been locked out by the employers, but because they had become impatient, and were not disposed to wait the outcome of the negotiations. It is quite probable that in the course of next week there may be a full-blown strike of 130,000 or 140,000 colliers on our hands. It is not now a case of a "tyrannical" lock-out. There is no hint of a wish on the part of the employers to "smash" the trade union, because there is, strictly speaking, no trade union in Wales. The dispute is the work of the men themselves. They refuse to listen to their leaders, most of whom have urged the men to return to work, and to abide the end of the negotiations, which are still open. The employers seem ready to receive the men back to work, appear perfectly willing to discuss the matters in dispute, and to do their utmost to arrive at a settlement.

But thus far the miners refuse to listen to their leaders or to heed their employers. The dispute centres in the sliding scale, which has been working for years in South Wales to the apparent satisfaction of all parties. Six months ago, however, the colliers gave notice to terminate the sliding scale. They denounced it as unfair to them. It was drawn up at a time when wages were abnormally low, and the lowest rate recognised, the men urge, works prejudically for them. But as by the sliding scale wages are regulated according to a certain ratio to the price of coal, it does not seem clear how it can have any prejudicial influence on the men's wages. The real aim of the colliers, however, appears to be to establish a "minimum wage" somewhat higher than the amount fixed according to the lowest price in the scale. They also wish to obtain control of the output, so that they may stop work whenever there seems to them a danger that larger stocks may accumulate than they altogether approve of. About a month ago the employers gave notice to terminate all contracts—a merely precautionary measure whose enforcement would depend on the progress of the negotiations for a settlement. In the course of these it was discovered by the employers that the men's representatives had no authority to conclude a settlement of the dispute; and they refused to continue the negotiations, unless the men's representatives received plenary powers for this purpose. It was then arranged that a ballot should be taken; and in order that this might be done, the employers postponed the term of their notice to terminate contracts until the 9th April. The sliding sale, however, came nominally to a termination on the 1st of April, and, ignoring the arrangement made by the employers, about 40,000 of the colliers ceased work on that date. Others have followed their example, until now, as we have said, about 120,000 men are idle. The ballot resulted in a refusal, by 44,872 to 14,500 votes, to grant the plenary powers asked for, and the business has now been further complicated by the formulation of a demand for an immediate advance of 20 per cent. in wages.

At present, then, there seems no hope of averting a disastrous strike, recklessly provoked by the men themselves, the result of which it is easy to foresee. The men must certainly be worsted in the struggle, and trade will suffer seriously. Some ironworks have indeed been already closed in Wales, and doubtless this unfortunate course will be forced upon others, though perhaps not all; for Welsh steam coal is not a monopoly. It is the best of the kind, but at a push like the present Newcastle coal will do. The Tyne has, therefore, benefited immensely by the folly of the Welsh colliers. Trade in general, however, must necessarily suffer, and the loss to the community will be very great. And all because this mob of colliers, disregarding the leaders they had elected, and taking their "humours for their warrant," put forward extravagant demands that it would be impossible, and indeed foolish, for the employers to entertain.

Competition in Electric Lighting.

Complaint is made in some quarters that the Board of Trade is being appealed to for powers to enter into competition with the Metropolitan Electric Light Company throughout almost the whole of its district. That, however, is only what could have been expected, for only last week in our article on electric light companies we pointed out the danger in which the Metropolitan Company stood of encouraging such competition owing to its high charge for energy. As it is the Marylebone Vestry asks for power to establish works of its own in that parish, and the Charing Cross and Strand and County of London and Brush companies are asking for powers to enter the other districts of the company except the parish of Paddington, which will be left a little longer as a preserve to the Metropolitan Company.

Very likely these powers will be granted, for the Metropolitan had to submit to the loss of a portion of its monopoly a year or two back, as it is the settled determination of the Board of Trade to encourage competition. Then we shall see the Charing Cross and Strand competing with its charge of 4·40d. per Board of Trade unit against the 6·35d. or so levied by the Metropolitan Company. We should not be surprised if the Metropolitan Company suffers somewhat from the comparison, and if so the shareholders will only have the directors to thank. A moderate rate of about 5½d. per Board of Trade unit would have acted as a protection against invasion for some time to come, and the longer a company has unfettered possession of a district the stronger does its hold become. The board of the Notting Hill Company ought to take warning from this example for their charge of about 7d. per Board of Trade unit is still more oppressive.

The Buenos Ayres and Ensenada Absorption.

The details of the long talked of absorption by the Buenos Ayres Great Southern Railway Company of the Buenos Ayres and Ensenada Port Railway Company have now been published. Under the scheme the 4 per cent. debenture stock of the merged line will be exchanged for 4 per cent. debenture stock of the Buenos Ayres Great Southern Company, and the following are the terms of exchange for the other securities:—£92 of Southern 5 per cent. preference for every £100 of Ensenada 5 per cent. preference stock; £70 of Southern ordinary stock for every £100 of Ensenada 6 per cent. non-cumulative preference stock, and £50 of Southern ordinary stock for every £100 of Ensenada ordinary stock. Considering the different character of the two undertakings the scheme appears to be a fair one, but we are afraid that the holders of the 6 per cent. non-cumulative preference stock will grumble. Although the Buenos Ayres Great Southern is a wonderful line its ordinary stock cannot yet be considered better than a 6 per cent. stock. By receiving 70 per cent. of this the holders of the 6 per cent. preference will agree to cutting down their income to about £4 4s. per cent., with certainly a prospect of a share in improved earnings, but also with the risk of receiving less if profits fall off.

But the Buenos Ayres Great Southern could not in fairness to itself offer a better price, because this 6 per cent. preference stock represents the watering of the old Ensenada 7 per cent. preference stock. In 1895 the £600,000 of that stock was converted into £900,000 of new capital, £600,000 of which was to bear cumulative interest at 5 per cent., and £300,000 at 6 per cent., non-cumulative. By this stupid arrangement, carried through, no doubt, with stock-jobbing views, the fixed charges of the line were increased £6,000 per annum, and it should be remembered that for several years previous the old preference stock had not received full interest. The Southern Company could not therefore treat this 6 per cent. preference stock as a real 6 per cent. stock. Meantime the price of this stock was started last year about 90 and has been up to 113 in its time. Purchasers high up may feel inclined to complain of the diminution of revenue, but then, of course, they ought not to have paid such an extravagant price for the stock. If the Southern Company had not come along and absorbed the undertaking, experience would probably have brought out the fact that the intrinsic value of the stock did not warrant such quotations.

LOW FLASH POINT AMERICAN PETROLEUM.

If the Select Committee of the House of Commons which for four years has been so patiently investigating the question of petroleum and its dangers, is to be guided by the Home Office evidence recently presented to it, its labour will have practically been in vain. Instead of promoting legislation it will have laid the seeds of an angry trade agitation and have postponed, perhaps made impossible, any effectual Parliamentary action. We cannot altogether comprehend Sir Vivian Majendie's objections to raising the flash point. The evidence that it is the low flash point oil that has been responsible for most of the enormous number of lamp fatalities reported within the last year or two seems to have been overpowering and indisputable. Sir V. Majendie himself hardly disputes it, but if, he suggests, you raise this flash point, you will make people imagine that all danger has been removed, and so induce carelessness on their part. Therefore, he urges, leave the flash point alone; make new regulations for the storage of oil; look sharply after the small shopkeepers especially; multiply trade restrictions, and all will come right. It is quite possible that more stringent regulations are required for the storage and sale of petroleum, but these are matters upon which the oil-dealers will have to be heard, and if the committee are to adopt Sir Vivian Majendie's recommendations legislation would be postponed to the Greek Kalends. But the first object of the Legislature ought to be the prevention of fatal accidents from lamp explosions. The raising of the flash point would be the immediate means of at least diminishing the number of these accidents; why not at once attain this end by passing a simple measure forbidding the sale of oil below a certain flash point for use as an illuminant in dwelling-houses? Why complicate the question and endanger legislation by insisting upon restrictions upon trade which would be sure to raise a storm of opposition? Such a prohibition already exists in the United States. The coarse and dangerous rubbish which the Standard Oil Trust pours into this country cannot be sold in America; why should we be more considerate with the Oil Trust than the Government of the United States? Let us first insist on taking obvious and simple measures for the protection of life; the restriction and regulation of traders may follow at a convenient season when deliberate consideration and discussion shall have satisfied us as to how far we can go in that direction.

THE TELEPHONE FAILURE.

The recent discussion in the House of Commons upon our wretched telephone service cannot be very pleasant reading to the National Telephone Company. Not that they are particularly sensitive to criticism; if they were they would long ago have applied themselves with such energy as they can command to remedying the defects of the system for whose administration they are responsible. They cannot be in ignorance as to what these defects are. The public complaints have been loud and constant. Indeed, the whole system is defective; there is hardly a sound point about it. The price to the customers, in London at all events, is all but prohibitive; the plant is old and out of date; and the working of the service is, as a rule, exasperating. All this the company have been told over and over again—until their customers have almost got tired of complaining. But the company gave no heed to remonstrance. They believed themselves in possession of a monopoly which they had carefully built up—to sell apparently to the State when the commercial world had become sufficiently exasperated to refuse to put up longer with what, in some sense, may be characterised as a gigantic nuisance. If, however, the corporation are careless of complaint and criticism, they will possibly be induced to give some thoughtful attention to the probable result of the inquiry to be held by the Select Committee which Mr. Hanbury, as representing the Treasury, induced the House of Commons to appoint. This Committee may make their monopoly worthless, or nearly so. The Post-office have not been able to do much in the way of competition with the monopoly. They refused to grant a licence to the Glasgow Town Council, which proposed to set up a telephone system of its own, so badly had the citizens been served by the existing system. It is doubtful whether a municipality can legally hold such a licence. Hence the inquiry by a Select Committee. It will at least set that doubt at rest; perhaps it will discover a way out of the difficulty, and so relieve the Post-office administration from further hesitation about granting the Glasgow licence. Anyhow, these corporate telephone monopolists have been plainly told that the State will not buy their doubtful stock and antiquated plant. They are, it seems, willing to sell their business "as a going concern," for £6,000,000. Mr. Hanbury thinks the Post-office might establish a better service for two millions and a half. But this could hardly be done until 1911, when the present monopoly expires. It is to be hoped, therefore, that the Select Committee will find a way to extend and improve the telephone service while leaving the company severely alone.

VALETUDINARIAN TRADERS.

A deputation of gentlemen interested in the milling industry of Austria waited the other day on the Government to give a lugubrious recital of their business woes, and to appeal against the inroads of the more pushful millers on the other side of the hedge—Hungary to wit. These Austrian millers seem to be, in one sense, the Edie Ochiltrees, the sturdy beggars of industry; in another, its weaklings. They beseeched the Minister to shut off Hungarian competition from them by the erection of a customs barrier wall, so that, without exertion, they might keep their Austrian customers to themselves, and charge them as they would without fear of the "millers over the way." It is not surprising. It is the bent of the protective mind. Such energy as natures of this sort exhibit is displayed in seeking shelter from the rough winds of the world. They would, if they could, introduce customs barriers between different streets, or between different sides of the same street. The Hungarians have shown energy and shrewdness in the conduct of business generally, and the consequence is that trade in the Transleithan province has been making great advances. On the Austrian side things seem different. Traders there appear to prefer the petite culture, to trim their own little patch of industrial allotment, to charge what they like and do as they like, undisturbed by pushing intruders of a more adventurous spirit. It is, of course, very hard upon the unfortunate consumers; but with so many governments lending a willing ear to the complaints of the nerveless and lazy, what wonder if we seem relapsing into the barbarism which secludes trade, and coddles it until it becomes a permanent invalid, unable to stand except with the help of State monopolies. The consumers might help themselves if they would but revolt against this system of protective coddling at their expense; but they seem slow to discover the costly frauds which their own Governments practise upon them under the pretence of "encouraging native industry." A direful and a demoralizing system!

Three Small Ceylon Tea Companies.

The vicissitudes of plantation operations are well set forth in the return of three small Ceylon tea-growing companies. We have dealt with the results of these companies in former years, and then pointed out the necessity of greater heed to reserves in the case of the Edarapolla and Panawal companies. Only too surely have our fears been vindicated by the reports they have just issued. The one company of the three—the Kelani Valley—which has shown some caution in the past is the very one that has come out best in the record of the year's work.

All three companies had a large acreage to deal with in the year, but in every case a decrease would have been seen had not the Edarapolla included six months' crop from a new estate in its returns. The weather undoubtedly was bad in Ceylon last year for tea growing, but this fact was not accompanied by a higher price for teas as might have been expected. The return of mature acreage, total crop, and price obtained was as follows:—

	Mature Acreage.		Crop.		Price per lb.	
	1896.	1897.	1896.	1897.	1896.	1897.
			lbs.	lbs.	d.	d.
Edarapolla	471	821*	358,324	401,105	6½	5
Kelani v.	1,013	1,200	638,145	632,023	6⅝	6½
Panawal	510	577	279,471	258,309	6¼	5⅝

* 251 acres of this only for six months.

In addition to the low price of tea, the companies had to contend with heavier working charges, owing to the rise in exchange and the higher price of rice in consequence of the famine in India. The net profits of two of them therefore shrank considerably as the following table shows:—

	Net Profits		Put to depreciation, &c.		Dividend Per cent.	
	1896.	1897.	1896.	1897.	1896.	1897.
	£	£	£	£		
Edarapolla..............	2,795	1,128	595	18	10	5
Kelani v.	3,017	3,178	708	721	10	10
Panawal	1,912	609	181	101*	8	2

* Taken away from balances.

The Panawal did very badly, as, after paying 2 per cent. as an interim dividend on the ordinary shares, in September, it was only able to meet the interest on the preference at the end of the year by swallowing up the whole balance forward and creating a small debit balance. With such variations in profits as set forth here, can we consider the Edarapolla and Panawal boards well advised in paying such high dividends in 1896? Of course it will be urged that they did not know the future, but they knew the past, and that should have told them that tea-growing was essentially a speculative industry subject to many variations. How the Kelina Valley produced such a good profit is rather a mystery, in view of the circumstances of the year and the reduced price obtained for the tea.

"Tape Prices."

The recent case of Rucker v. Calvert shows the amount of reliance which can be placed upon the "tape prices" of stocks and shares which appear in the daily press. The shares in question in that case appeared in several share lists as of the value of some £40 when in truth they were really worth nil. The wise action of the Stock Exchange in forbidding tape machines to be supplied to certain outside brokers becomes apparent, for, as one witness observed, there is no physical force to prevent a person sending a purely fictitious price on the tape. This being so it is clear that an easy door would be opened to all kinds of frauds which happily the committee of the Stock Exchange has promptly closed.

Another of Mr. Whitaker Wright's "Successes."

The policy of this Triton amongst the minnows of the West Australian market appears to be working towards its proper end very quickly. To over-capitalise a property seems the aim of all latter-day geniuses, but Mr. Wright may perhaps hold that his operations in regard to the Lake View Consols fell short of his best efforts. He found the predecessor of this company in the shape of the Lake View and Boulder East Company, a local company with £40,000 share capital, and no liability. This modest total he converted into £220,000 by registering a new company in May, 1896, and £30,000 more cash was to be put into the undertaking out of this, so that it was not all fluff and swelling.

To make up for this moderate addition of working capital, care was taken that, after the exchange, the shares should be started upon a higher platform altogether, as to price, in just the same manner as the same group of market engineers is endeavouring to elevate Ivanhoes. In the case of "Lake Views" the operation was probably more successful, and with talk about what "increased stamping power" would do for the company, the price was worked up to £12⅜ per £1 share, or about £70 apiece for the old shares. It was a matter of hope, for we believe no dividend was announced between May, 1896, and October, 1897, which is rather a long interval even for a mining company.

Soon after the larger number of stamps were brought into play, the returns from the mine, both in regard to quantity and quality, fell off to a shocking extent. This has had a depressing effect upon the prices of the share, as the following table sets forth :—

Months.	Stamps at work.	Yield of gold.	Per ton from mill.	Per ton from tailings.	Price per share.
		oz.	oz.	oz.	
June	20	4,754	2·3	1·2	7⅛
July	20	6,253	2·2	1·04	8 5/16
August	20	5,742	2·3	1·15	8⅜
September	40	6,007	2·1	1·2	9 5/16
October	60	9,564	1·9	1·08	12
November	60	8,551	1·4	·79	12⅜
December	60	8,615	1·1	·88	11 5/16
January	40	7,554	·9	·75	10⅜
February	40	7,396	·9	·84	9 11/16

Present price..................8¼

The last two months only forty stamps were run as the old mill broke down, which is quite a mercy, or the yield per ton might have suffered still more. Certainly two dividends of 10s. per share have been declared, one in October last and the other this month, but it is extremely doubtful whether distributions can be kept up at this or any regular pace. Meantime, people will wonder where all the favourable news came from regarding the future when the shares were hoisted up to 12⅝. If it came from insiders they were woefully deceived, but no one can beat a latter-day financier for innocence and simplicity of mind.

BRITISH TRADE IN HAVRE.

Until last year it seemed as if Havre was being gradually choked by the protective legislation of 1892. The decline in its trade had been steady year after year. But 1897 saw a considerable revival in commercial activity—though reduced prices did not correspondingly swell the profits of local commercial dealers—and the Customs receipts rose to more than £3,000,000. The revival may be but temporary. Much of it was owing to the large importation of grain made necessary by the deficiency of the French harvest, and some of it by the exceptional shipments of cotton, owing to the abundant American crop, and consequent diminution in prices. Our latest Consular report shows us that we are still largely interested in Havre. British shipping tops the list there : an easy lead by 976 steamers to 360 French and 240 German. This lead is steadily increasing—even more, apparently, in the tonnage of the ships than in the number. Our Consul throws out a useful hint to shipowners that they should leave their shipmasters some latitude as to the discharge of crews at Havre. It is often difficult to procure any but a French crew there, and the regulations to be observed as to French sailors under the age of forty render their engagement troublesome, and often costly. Goods of British manufacture continue for the most part to hold their own at Havre and district. Of English hats and caps 21,851 were imported into Havre direct, while at other ports the local houses were supplied by English firms having agencies in Paris. There is a good market for Australian hides ; and bicycles and stationery have to be added to the list of British goods which are much in demand in Havre and neighbourhood.

But there are lessons in detail which our manufacturers have yet to learn, and Sheffield cutlery, though its reputation is untarnished, is being excluded from Havre, because the manufacturers have not given attention to the quality of lightness enforced by the peculiarities of the French customs tariff. This tariff is based largely on the actual weight of the article imported. German manufacturers promptly appreciated the importance of this fact, and studied lightness in articles intended for the French market. Hence their ability to curtail the trade in Sheffield cutlery, not because German cutlery is better, but because it is lighter, and pays less duty than the Sheffield article. In one respect the slow-moving British manufacturer, however, has at last made an important advance. He has had his trade circulars drawn up in decent French, with prices given in local currency, and weights and measures in the decimal system. But in this respect they are far behind even the Americans, who have long had their trade circulars "done up" in French, English, and Spanish—of course also with prices in local currency and weights in the decimal system. The result has been that American machinery has largely superseded British in France. Now, however, that our manufacturers have seen the necessity of having trade circulars in French, they may condescend to adapt themselves to the languages and usages of other countries, and even try to check the invasion of trade rivals by the employment of a few energetic commercial travellers who know other tongues besides their own.

THE JAPANESE BUDGET.

The Japanese Budget Estimates for 1898–9, which have come to possess considerable interest for the western world, represent a slight decrease on the estimated totals of 1897–8. The expenditure is put at 229,000,000 yen, and the revenue at 212,000,000 yen, or a deficit of 17,000,000 yen, which is to be covered by a "financial programme." For 1897–8 the sum of ordinary and extraordinary revenue was put at 239,750,482 yen, and the sum of ordinary and extraordinary expenditure at 239,664,459 yen. The expectation of a surplus of 86,023 yen shown in these figures has not been fulfilled. Some of the new taxes have yielded considerably less than was anticipated, while some of the appropriations have proved to be inadequate, and the result is a deficit which is variously estimated at 30,000,000 yen and 45,000,000 yen, and which will bring the accumulated deficit to something like 130,000,000 yen. The diminution, slight though it is, in the revenue estimate for 1898–9 seems to show that the officials of the Japanese Finance Department are less sanguine than they were a year ago of the country's ability to stand increased taxation. Certainly some of the devices adopted for obtaining revenue were not very commendable, and we should not be surprised to hear that they have been abandoned as pettifogging, or at any rate that their burden has been lightened. The Government is about to take over the practical monopoly of tobacco ; and that, though vexatious enough to the people, should bring in considerable additional revenue. But the Finance Minister will probably find all his work cut out to keep the year's deficit from exceeding the 17,000,000 yen anticipated.

Speculation is busy as to the precise form which the "financial programme" will take. Will there be a foreign loan, or an increase of taxes ? Or, again, will the Treasury contrive to jog along for a time with the arrears of the war indemnity, of which they demand payment by May next, and which is to be provided by the forthcoming Chinese Loan ? The Finance Minister is averse to a foreign loan and the people have shown very plainly that they are averse to more taxation ; so that, in all probability, the last course will be adopted. But a considerable proportion of the money will be required to pay the bills for new warships and other similar luxuries, and will go out of the country almost as soon as it comes in ; and after the liquidation of the budget deficits of the past three years there will not be much left to ease that financial stringency which is causing so much havoc among commercial men in the land. When the gold standard law came into force we took the liberty of doubting whether the gentlemen responsible for it quite realised its bearings. It is a fact that, so far, the law has worked as much injury as benefit to Japan, and has crippled much of its trade with the silver-using countries of the East.

THE MEXICAN BUDGET.

Even the strongest republican must sometimes admit that Dictatorships do good. Certainly Don Porfirio Diaz, who has now been under the name of constitutional President, Dictator of Mexico for many years, is a ruler of whom his country may well be proud; and in nothing has the character of his administration been more conspicuously shown to be enlightened than in the management of the finances of the State. He found them in confusion, his country discredited abroad, unable to raise money for public works, and generally looked upon with suspicion as a debtor prone to break its engagements. Mexico is to-day in the enjoyment of as good repute on European money markets as any State of Spanish origin in all America. The Budget just issued in English for the year 1898-99 undertakes to show in some degree how the improvement has been brought about. It has been by the substitution of order in place of chaos. The accounts are fully and minutely given, every department of revenue and expenditure is passed under review and carefully weighed. Therefore, the Finance Minister and the Government, as well as the creditors of the State, are fairly able to estimate the position, and to put forward anticipations which have every probability of being realised. Mexico, as everyone knows, has suffered very severely from the depreciation of silver, but the Government has never made any attempt to play tricks with its currency, and has borne the increased burden imposed by the depreciated exchange out of the increased revenues which, as far as we can judge, have been carefully nursed into productiveness. There has also been, of course, a considerable increase in the debt of the country, but less on account of the Government, as far as the figures before us disclose, than on account of public enterprises undertaken with Government help and under Government sanction. Great developments, for example, have taken place in the mining industries of Mexico, and, in spite of the low price of silver, the yield of that metal from Mexican mines is well maintained.

The result of these and other improvements is that the public revenue for 1898-99 is estimated at M$.51,6559,500, which is M$.547,383 above the revenue from 1896-97, but expenses, including supplementary credits, amount to rather more than M$.52,000,000, so that there would be a deficit if the revenue could not be augmented. It is, however, apparently easy to increase the revenue, and Don José Yves Limantour, the able Finance Minister, proposes to get what money he requires to balance his Budget by means of a slight additional tax on the producers of drinks, more or less alcoholic. Should his anticipation on this head be realised, the budget for the coming year will just about balance with a mere M$.20,000 over. That a country like Mexico should be able to produce a revenue of M$.52,000,000 for its Federal Government, over and above the revenues to be found in addition for its State Governments, may seem a considerable strain upon a country whose population is so poor, and from some points of view it is so. At the same time, if the dictator lives long and keeps his power, and continues to devote his energies to the opening up of the enormous resources of his country, there ought to be no danger of anything like such defaults upon the Mexican public debts as we were familiar with in the past. The total amount of the public debt of Mexico, including a small floating debt, is nearly M$.202,290,798. This is not an excessive debt taken by itself, but the State is also under considerable obligations to the public on account of railway guarantees, and such like. Still, reckoning everything in the Budget, the presentment is a satisfactory one and affords good hope that the Government of the Republic is progressing towards better things, towards a day when it may really become a constitutional one.

Critical Index to New Investments.

THE LINOTYPE COMPANY, LIMITED.

The company is again a borrower, this time in the shape of an issue of £250,000 4 per cent. first mortgage debentures of £5 each. They form part of a total of £1,000,000, and £24,905 has been already subscribed, the balance being offered at 102. Interes quarterly from July 1. Debentures are repayable at 105 on March 31, 1923, but company reserves the right to redeem them at any time on six months' notice at 107. Company wants funds to acquire freehold land at Broadheath, near Manchester, for building new works, &c. Share capital, fully paid, is £2,000,000, and the debentures are secured by a first mortgage on freeholds and other permanent assets, and a floating charge on the whole undertaking, the assets standing in the balance-sheet at the end of last December at £2,429,952. Debenture interest will require £10,000, while the net profits for 1896 were £123,255; and for 1897 £162,882, of which £21,984 was premium on new issue of shares., There is, therefore, at present ample margin for this issue of debentures, but we hope the directors will exercise their remaining borrowing powers with great caution. The business now is good, and so far these machines hold their own, but the day might come when serious competition may have to be faced.

YOUNG & CO.'S BREWERY, LIMITED.

Company owns the Ram Brewery, Wandsworth, S.W. Business dates from 1834, and the present company took it over in 1890 owing to the death of Mr. Young, who was then sole partner. Capital, fully paid 1,500 5 per cent. preference and 2,300 ordinary shares, all of £100 each, the whole of which was subscribed by the family and by officials of brewery. Assets then amounted to £392,779 and liabilities to £62,901. Since 1890 trade has considerably increased through purchase of additional houses and by improvements, and the values of the properties stood in the books on December 31 last at £613,798, of which brewery premises represented £43,940; freehold public-houses, £244,471; leaseholds, £123,937; and loans and interest, £108,188. There are no debentures or mortgages; the only liabilities, other than share capital and £70,000 reserve invested in business, being sundry creditors, rents payable, customers' deposits, and advances to carry out recent purchases, amounting in all to £120,105. The company now offers for subscription at 103, through the London and Westminster Bank, an issue of £150,000 irredeemable 3½ per cent. mortgage debenture stock being part of an authorised issue of £300,000. Interest due January and July. As the profit rental from the several brewery properties for the year ended June 30 last was £10,221, and for the six months to December 31 last, £5,570, irrespective of trade profits, and the interest on the present issue will require only £5,250, the debenture stock appears to an excellent security, the only point to quibble at being the high price asked for it, which reduces the yield to £3 7s. 11d. per cent.

RUBBER ESTATES OF PARA, LIMITED.

Capital £350,000 in £1 shares, divided equally into ordinary and 7 per cent. cumulative preference shares. The object of this formation is to buy the rubber estates of the Visconde de S. Domingos, which are being sold owing to the advanced age of the Visconde. The estates have yielded large revenues for a number of years, the prospectus says, but no information is given of any net profits having been made. Apart from some unreliable estimates, not a figure is given about past profits, not even for one year. Yet the public are asked to pay £300,000 to the Anglo-African Gold Properties, Limited, who are the present vendors, though they do not seem to have bought the properties at first hand. In view of the heavy depreciation in the exchange, and what looks very like approaching national bankruptcy, we should imagine an investment in the shares of the Rubber Estates of Para would be attended with very considerable risk.

GEORGE INGHAM & CO., LIMITED.

Mr. George Ingham, worsted spinner, of the Prospect Mill, Greetland, near Halifax, York, has sold his business, commenced in 1863, to the Central Finance Corporation, who, as promoters, are reselling it to the company at a profit; the purchase price being £55,000, in addition to which the stock-in-trade has to be paid for. Capital, £100,000; present issue, £90,000, in £10 shares, half ordinary and half 5 per cent. cumulative preference. The purchase price is to be cash, but the directors, which include the founder of the business, have taken £23,000 of the present issue, in equal proportions of preference and ordinary shares. Freehold properties, plant, and goodwill (formed on the basis of two years average profits over the last five years) are valued by two valuers at £55,157. Statement about profits is not so full as it ought to be. For five years they are certified to have amounted to £45,747, giving an average of £9,149 per annum, but considering that in one year they were only £5,428, it is evident they are of a more fluctuating nature than we should have expected. Under these circumstances, we should leave it to Yorkshiremen, who will probably subscribe the money if the undertaking is as good as made out. And they ought to know.

G. & C. & E. NUTHALL & SONS, LIMITED.

The company buys and amalgamates two cook, confectioner wine and spirit, &c., businesses in Kingston-on-Thames. Share capital £100,000 in £1 shares, present issue being 50,000 shares, and there is also issued at par £40,000 4 per cent. mortgage debenture stock, power being reserved to redeem the stock by annual drawings of £2,000 a year at 110. The number of honoured patrons of the businesses is, in the words of the prospectus, large, and the block of freeholds is a combination "very unique." Sudlow Herrick & Sons certify present value of freeholds and leaseholds at £42,000, but to make up this amount they have to throw in the wine and spirit licence. Profits are not given year by year, but those of G. & C. Nuthall for three years ended September last are certified to have amounted to £15,598, and those of E. Nuthall & Sons for two years ended December last to £3,714, giving an average for the year of £7,056, but this is without charging for wear and tear of plant and for management. The purchase price of £81,100, of which £51,434 is to be cash, represents about twelve years' purchase, and appears to be a good deal beyond what the businesses justify. The security for the debentures is very slender, while as to the shares, the board is to take one-third the surplus profits beyond 8 per cent. dividend, in addition to their fees. There are plenty of wealthy people in Kingston who can afford to pay for such luxuries.

Company Reports and Balance-Sheets.

LONDON, EDINBURGH, AND GLASGOW ASSURANCE COMPANY, LIMITED.—It is an astonishing thing that a company of this character should continue to meet with large and even with increasing patronage. Originally one of the creations of the indefatigable Jabez Spencer Balfour, at his collapse it was taken over by a few men who saw their way to work it up into some kind of position, and contrary to our expectations they seem to have in a manner succeeded. Last year the gross premium income was £309,385 of which no less than £262,661 came from what is called the "non-participating" branch of the business. This is a new name for "industrial" insurance, one of the most expensive forms for provision of burial that can be imagined, at least as conducted by this company. What it actually does cost is not told in the figures, as expenses and commission are wrapped up so that it is impossible to say, how much is attributable to each branch of the business. We learn, however, from the Life Insurance Account that the expenses and commissions of the entire business came to more than 45·4 per cent. of the net premium income, the income, that is to say, less the amount paid for re-assurance. This is pretty stiff, and the effect is seen in the smallness of the accumulative funds. The directors claim that they have paid in claims and grants up to the end of last year, from the date when the company began business, no less than £1,198,890, and the total Life Assurance funds in hand at the end of last year amount to only £173,360. As there is an "ordinary" branch, with apparently a considerable business, and a "participating premium income" branch, which also, we presume, involves some future liability, it is fair to infer that the industrial or "non-particitating" business is conducted much as fire assurance is, with such a high scale of premiums that the conductors are able to count upon the payment of all current claims out of the current year's income, with an ample margin for right royal spending. So far, however, as we can judge, even this small accumulation cannot be said to belong to the privileged class of policyholders, if the term may be used, since the company has debenture debt of £99,650 in 4½ per cent. debenture stock. Presumably these debentures form the first charge upon all the Company's assets ranking even before the policy-holders. This is not a satisfactory position, look at it how one may, and should not the interest payable upon these debentures be included in the working expenses as well as the interest on the preference capital? In our opinion it ought to be, as well as the amounts written off investments, leasehold property, furniture, and fittings, agents, balances, and the cost of the quinquennial valuation. Were these outgoings added to the charges the revenue has to bear every year the cost of conducting the affairs of the Company would amount to over 49 per cent. of the net premium income. And this takes no account of the accident insurance branch, which enjoyed an income of £12,397 in the past year, the whole of which, together with about £340 of the small fund of £5,625 at the credit of this branch twelve months before, was absorbed in payment of claims and in commission and expenses. It seems to us idle to discuss the position of this concern from any point of view afforded by the experience of ordinary life assurance business. We can only regret that so many of the working classes should be found willing to contribute to such prosperity as it appears to enjoy. Is the rate of interest payable upon the preference capital 9 per cent. per annum or what?

THE SECOND SCOTTISH AMERICAN TRUST COMPANY, LIMITED.—For the year ended March 1, 1898, this company obtained a net revenue of £34,841, exclusive of £6,264, brought forward, or equal to £8 14s. 2d. on the paid-up capital of £400,000. Out of this £2,000 was added to reserve, raising it to £80,000, and £31,900 devoted to 8½ per cent. dividend on the shares for the year, 4 per cent. of which was paid in September last. A balance of £6,037 is after all left to be carried to the new year. The value of the securities held by the company is equal to £182 10s. 4d. per £100 share. This is thoroughly satisfactory, but these Dundee Trust companies have always been carefully organised and have accordingly done well.

THE SCOTTISH WIDOWS' FUND LIFE ASSURANCE SOCIETY.—In the year ended 31st December last this life office issued 2,162 policies, insuring £1,466,733. A small amount of this was re-insured, and the result was a net addition to the premium income of £56,318, but this included £4,181 in single premiums. Claims, death and survivance, took £720,630, and the broad result for the year was an increase of £642,237 in the accumulated fund, which now amounts to £14,142,983. The average rate of interest obtained on the funds in the year was £3 18s. 9d. per cent., without deducting income-tax, and expenses of management and commission absorbed £9 16s. 3d. per cent. of the premium income, or £6 4s. 5d. per cent. of the total income, the Society having received £544,011 in interest and rents. This is altogether a satisfactory exhibit. Bonus additions on the 579 claims, amounted to an average of 54 per cent. of the amount insured and the bonuses on 48 endowment policies which became claims amounted to an average of 34 per cent. The directors of the society are about to introduce an endowment and income insurance policy of the kind already issued by several offices. According to the balance-sheet the society has £1,810,604 invested in mortgages on property out of the United Kingdom, and its investments in Indian, Colonial, and Foreign Government and Municipal securities amount to £2,226,000, besides which there is £1,814,605 placed in American railway gold mortgage bonds, making nearly £6,000,000 placed abroad altogether out of £14,352,483. The proportion is large, but there is no indication whatever that any of the revenue on these properties is in arrear, and first-class American railroad bonds at any rate ought to be as good securities as can be got.

THE BRITISH EMPIRE MUTUAL LIFE ASSURANCE COMPANY.—Last year this society issued 1,185 new policies, insuring £711,940. After deducting reassurance, the net premium income resulting was £24,222. The total premium income was £278,231, and the revenue from interest was £101,730, or at the rate of £3 18s. per cent., after deducting income-tax on the average funds of the year invested and uninvested. Claims took £154,312, and expenses and commission about £49,000, or nearly 17·4 per cent. of the premium income. At the end of the year the total funds amounted to £2,671,413, having been increased by £121,471 during the year. This is not a large increase considering the business done, but £27,885 was paid to members as a cash bonus out of the profits during the year and, of course, the percentage of expenses is somewhat high, although this also is set off by the fact that they include the cost of periodical valuation and distribution of bonuses in the past year. Otherwise the directors say the percentage on the premium income shows a reduction. The bulk of the Company's money is invested at home, £367,659 in mortgages on property out of the United Kingdom and £328,013 in Indian Government securities. The company absorbed the Positive Life Office a short time ago and a note to the balance sheet says that the Indian business taken over from that company is still reckoned at 2s. to the rupee on both the debit and credit sides of the account. We can hardly tell what this means without a separate statement of that business, but the system seems open to objection.

COMMERCIAL GAS COMPANY.—Revenue from gas increased £7,633 in the second half of 1896, but residuals brought in £3,824 less. Working expenses, as a result of the larger amount of gas sold, increased £3,372, and net revenue was accordingly only £463 higher at £47,910. The balance of £1,582 brought in was £6,732 less than a year ago, and as more capital has been issued in the time, the company has to draw upon its reserve in order to pay the usual dividends at the rate of 13½ per cent. per annum upon the old stock and of 10½ per cent. per annum upon the new stock. The amount to be withdrawn is not stated, and in view of the increased capital it is difficult to say what will be required; but the sum cannot be large we should imagine. The reserve at present amounts to £44,267, and the insurance fund to £28,652.

SAN JORGE NITRATE COMPANY.—Last year was undoubtedly a poor year for nitrate companies, and this concern did well in earning a net profit of £26,510 in the time. As the company had in previous years a depreciation fund of 60,000, the Board considered itself perfectly justified in paying away the whole of the sum, and a little more in dividends equal to 7½ per cent. for the year, the balance forward being £1,615 less than the sum brought in. Owing to the combination, the company had been restricted to 4½ months' work, but this wretched arrangement broke down at the end of October, and the company has resumed work under normal conditions. Of course talk is on foot about another combination, but the Board do not seem inclined to go into this except on favourable terms to the company. If profits rise again it ought not to be forgotten that no sum was placed to depreciation account on this occasion, for the £60,000 to that account is the only sinking fund against the large sum of £351,589 paid for the property. Apparently the sum has been kept pretty clear of the undertaking, quite £45,000 being in cash and investments, and only some £15,000 locked up in nitrate and iodine.

ROBINSON GOLD MINE (W. A).—This modest West Australian mining company issues a business-like report. In the fifteen months dealt with, gold was obtained to the value of £31,981, and mining and milling cost £12,494 or £2 1s. 8d. per ton. Administrative and other charges in London and Australia appear to have been high for they came to £4,290, and after £1,698 had been written off for depreciation, the net balance of £12,058 was left. Three dividends amounting in all to 10 per cent. had already been paid requiring £7,905, and the Board determined to carry the balance of £4,153 forward in view of the expenditure incidental to the erection of the new 10 stamps, the cyanide plant and further proposed developments. The directors speak hopefully about the future, but the main shaft at the time the report was issued was only down 200ft., so that little yet can be known about the wealth or poverty of the gold bearing strata.

Bank of Scotland.—Apart from one untoward matter the report for the past year is satisfactory. After providing for bad and doubtful debts *in the general business*—the words in italics were not in the last report and are explained below—the net profits for the year ended February 28, 1897, were £175,215, or nearly £3,000 more than in 1896. The balance brought in, however, was only £15,904 compared with £33,562, so after paying the usual dividend of 12 per cent. for the year, the amount applied in reduction of the heritable property account is only £5,000 against £15,000 last year. The balance remaining is £36,120, making with the reserve fund £861,120. The figures in the balance-sheet are encouraging, there being a small increase in the note circulation, an addition of £400,000 to the deposits, the total of which is not far short of £15,000,000, and an increase of £110,000 in acceptances, the liabilities to the public being now raised to exactly 17¼ millions. On the assets side the stock of cash and investments is £730,000 larger at £8,133,000, and in this connection we think Government securities might in future be separated from money in London at call. Bills discounted and advances, on the other hand, show a reduction of £520,000 to £9,383,000, but taken altogether the display is a good one and the bank has strengthened its position during the year. The only blemish is the tardy acknowledgment that £150,000 has to be set aside to provide for loss anticipated in connection with the realisation of the property of a firm having estates in the West Indies which are said to have become depreciated through the operation of the Continental Sugar bounties. Fortunately the bank has a good reserve, and £125,000 of this amount is taken from it, the balance being taken from profits in hand. The reserve is thus reduced to £700,000, and only £11,120 is carried forward to the new account. It is a pity that when losses like this occur they are not met in the first instance, for by postponing them they only increase, and in this case there could have been little or no ground to expect the account to right itself however much the management might have hoped.

Royal Sardinian Railway Company.—The result of the past year's working shows that the line is not making progress. Total receipts were 5,007 lire more under their guarantee, and 5,000 lire more than in 1896, but the company received nearly 5,000 lire more from interest on capital invested, so that the receipts from traffic showed a small falling off. Outgoings, on the other hand, were larger by 5,000 lire, but the increase in working expenses proper was as much as 37,654 lire, offset by a saving of nearly 24,000 lire through the better exchange, and a reduction of 6,400 lire in taxes. It is fair to add, however, that expenses were swollen to the extent of 40,000 lire by the writing off of this sum as a result of the decision of an arbitration in a long pending law suit. The outcome of the working is a profit of 1,625,888 lire, which, while practically the same total as for the previous year, shows to what an extent the company has to depend upon the Government guarantee of 6,749,283 lire. Fortunately for the company this guarantee goes on until 1976, the terms being that the Government pays the company an annuity of 14,800 lire per kilometre and guarantees minimum gross receipts of 7,000 lire per kilometre per annum. Of the receipts in excess of this, 7,000 lire, 46 per cent., goes to the company and 54 per cent. is applied in reduction of the amounts paid by the Government under the guarantee. The available balance for the year is 1,625,888 lire, of which the company has to carry 5 per cent. to the reserve fund, raising it to 1,402,767 lire, and the rest is used in paying a dividend of 6 per cent. on the shares and in reimbursing 175 shares drawn last December. Excepting in 1893 when 5⅗ per cent. was paid this has been the regular dividend for the past seven years. Such a dividend is all right while it lasts, but the business of the line certainly shows no expansion, and what will occur to the company suppose the privilege of belonging to the Triple Alliance were to cause a breakdown of Italian credit?

Redfern, Limited.—The gross profits of this high-class tailoring company were maintained last year; the total of £96,225 comparing with £96,970 in 1896. Expenses, however, were higher, and the net profit of £28,630 was £4,196 less. The same dividend, 8 per cent., was paid on the ordinary shares as for 1896, but only £2,500 was added to reserve, as against £5,000 a year back. The amount carried forward is also slightly less. The reserve now amounts to £15,000, and as the public holds only the preference capital, the charge upon which is £6,000, the margin of security is very good. There is, moreover, a satisfactory clause in the articles of association, which prevents the ordinary shares receiving a higher dividend than 10 per cent. until the reserve amounts to £20,000. The balance-sheet does not appear to have improved, the stock being about £4,000 higher at £42,324, and "debts due to company" £16,000 higher at £88,722. In spite of the reserve these movements have necessitated a loan of £12,000 from the bankers of the company.

The Salt Union, Limited.—The committee of shareholders appointed at the annual meeting held on February 28, have lost no time in approaching the directors in a "friendly spirit," with the result that several members of the old board have given up their seats in view of the removal of the head office to Liverpool. The committee have since induced the following local gentlemen to consent to act as directors, if elected:—Mr. William Harvey Alexander (Messrs. John Rems & Co.), merchant, Liverpool; Mr. George Henry Cox, Liverpool, vice-president of the Liverpool Chamber of Commerce; Mr. John Holt, merchant, Liverpool, chairman of John Holt & Co. (Liverpool), Limited, and chairman of the Wirral Waterworks Company, and of the West Cheshire Water Company; Mr. Archibald Roxburgh (Messrs. Cockbain, Allardice & Co.), merchant, Liverpool; and Mr. Thomas Bland Royden, J.P., shipowner, Liverpool, director of the Union Marine Insurance Company, late M.P. for Liverpool; Mr. Herman John Falk and Mr. Thomas Ward, who have been associated with the company from its commencement, will retain their seats on the board. A meeting of the company will be held at Winchester House, Old Broad-street on 28th April, when the above gentlemen will be proposed for election. The names strike us as being good and belonging to Liverpool commercial men, which looks well for the future, but the financial position needs careful attention before anything can be done to work the Union into anything like a commercial success.

Kimberley Waterworks Company.—The business of this company has improved very much of late years, and its sale of 143 millions of gallons last year compares well with 115 millions in 1896, 82¾ millions in 1895, and only 65¾ millions in 1894. Income has not grown in the same proportion, for the gross receipts last year were £52,256, as against £49,370 in the previous twelve months. Working expenses, however, were actually less, so that the net revenue was £31,108, or £5,783 more than in 1896. This is the best statement for a number of years, and after raising the dividend by 1 per cent. to 5 per cent., the board added £5,099 to contingency fund, practically the reserve, as against £2,798, transferred a year ago. Depreciation upon plant and tools was allowed for at the usual rate, but £4,642 was written off the construction and property account, as against £3,291. The contingency fund now amounts to £12,500, and its importance is shown in the redemption last year of £3,500 of 6 per cent. mortgage debentures without the investments of the company, which amount to £25,065, having to be trenched upon. The balance-sheet in fact is a very good one, and probably the company was never in better financial condition.

TRADE OF GUAYAQUIL.

Guayaquil, the principal port of the Republic of Ecuador, has suffered considerably in recent years. There were serious fires in 1896; in 1897 great damage was done by the heavy rains to the cacao and coffee crops, from 25 to 50 per cent. of which were lost, while the rice crop in the coast provinces was destroyed. Then the Government authorised a new coinage of silver by one of the banks, and some months afterwards promulgated a law compelling the banks to hold half their metallic reserve in gold, which had to be imported from abroad. The strain on exchange transactions was very severe, and in December the banks suspended nearly all discount operations. Though the country is at peace, a large army is kept up, but the revenue has been increased and trade is fairly good. British commercial travellers, so our Consul informs us, do occasionally visit the country, and, as a rule, have expressed themselves satisfied with their share of the import trade. That is pleasant to hear. But there is more. The common kinds of cutlery, previously supplied by Germany, are being competed for by English manufacturers, who are regaining the trade in some measure. The Republic gets all her candles from Belgium. About 6,000 tons of sugar were produced in the Republic, some 2,000 of which were exported.

The Furness Railway Company in the construction of their new passenger brake vans are making them 34 feet in length, which will enable the company to provide a special platform, seven inches in height at one end, for half-a-dozen bicycles. Each bicycle fits into a separate leather-padded groove on this platform, and there is another groove at the end of the van for one of the wheels to fit in. Straps are also provided from side to side of the van, which fasten round the handle of each bicycle to prevent oscillation. The machines are thus made perfectly secure, and, further, are kept quite apart from the general luggage. The public will be glad to know of any movement for the safe carriage by railway of bicycles. Credit is due for this simple and effective arrangement to Mr. W. F. Pettigrew, the company's locomotive and carriage and wagon superintendent.

Is the Portuguese Government anxious to make a "corner" in corn? It has authorised, so Reuter tells us, the importation of sixty million kilogrammes of corn from abroad. What for? The Portuguese demand for cereals cannot be great. There has been no deficiency in the country; what, then, makes the Government so anxious for the importation of so large a quantity of corn? Is it in the hope that Spain, in the event of war with the United States, may be in sore straits for corn, and thus be ready to pay good prices to whomsoever can supply her? It is a queer policy for even a Portuguese Government to adopt.

Damage to the extent of $500,000,000 has been done by earthquake in the navy yard at Maine Island, in California. Severe shocks were felt in various parts of the same state, doing serious injury to buildings, and, of course, greatly alarming the inhabitants.

France demands 500,000,000 fr. from the Porte as an indemnity for the losses sustained by religious establishments in Anatolia, at the time of the massacres. Further demands may be made later for damage to commercial interests.

Hungary is chafing greatly under the Dingley Tariff. During a recent discussion in the Diet it was strongly urged that the Austrian and Hungarian Governments should take action in the matter, even if they went the length of adopting retaliatory measures. The Minister of Commerce admitted that the Hungarian sugar export trade in particular had suffered from the American duties; but the initiative could not be taken by Hungary alone. He suggested that it might be possible for the European States affected by the American tariff to agree upon a course of united action and proceed with vigour. Probably the Minister was thinking of the assembling of the Bounty Conference at Brussels.

THE PROPERTY MARKET.

The total of last week's sales at the Mart again exceeded £200,000, as compared with £115,013 in the same week of last year. Everything indicates that the investing public have turned with something like enthusiasm to property investments. The reason for this eagerness may not be quite apparent, but it is remarkable that in the week before Easter the total should run so high. Ground rents figured conspicuously at the sales, and the demand for them was constant and keen.

Bexhill-on-Sea seems rapidly developing as a watering place, and as an indication of the rising value of land there we may note that Messrs. Moss & Jameson recently sold 15¾ acres adjoining Station-road there at £18,000, or an average of £1,145 an acre. The same firm are shortly to offer at the Mart two freehold estates at Bexhill—Wakeham's Farm, containing about 18 acres, and Popp's Farm, comprising 21 acres. Messrs. Daniel Watney & Sons have sold by private treaty the freehold ground rent of £300 per annum, with reversion in 46 years, secured on premises in Nicholas-lane, City, which was recently offered at the Mart, and then withdrawn at £12,000. Sefton Lodge, Newmarket, the residence of the late Duchess of Montrose, has been sold by private contract by Messrs. Maple & Co.

The total sales at the Mart were not so high on Monday as we have recently become accustomed to, but they still reached the respectable amount of £29,793. A large part of this was supplied by Mr. Alfred Richards, who drew £10,361 for various gas and water shares and stocks. Brewery shares and debentures were also dealt in to a considerable extent by Messrs. Alfred Thomas, Peyer and Miles. But breweries themselves did not seem to be in request. The same firm offered two which were not sold. One was the Union Brewery, Wisbech, with ninety tied houses. It was withdrawn at £67,000. The other was Perrett's Brewery at Wandsworth, with four licensed houses. It was withdrawn at £9,500. Mr. T. B. Westacott was successful in disposing of some leasehold properties at Camden Town, &c., and Messrs. Wootton & Green sold six houses in Hillfield-avenue, Hornsey. Messrs. Fuller, Moon & Fuller, had a considerable sale of freehold properties at Croydon a few days ago. The bidding was spirited, and the lots went off at good prices.

There was little doing at the Mart on Tuesday. The attendance was restricted, and several of the lots had been withdrawn, while the total of the day's sales only amounted to £17,880. Some freehold ground-rents at South Tottenham were sold by Messrs. G. Gouldsmith, Son, & Co., at fair prices. They also disposed of some leasehold ground-rents at Crouch Hill for a very good return. Messrs. Willis & Crouch sold four freehold houses in Loraine-road, Holloway, for £2,990, and Messrs. Allen & Hoar disposed of two freehold houses in Mattison-road, Harringay, at £1,030, and four plots of freehold building land at Harlesden at £956.

A number of licensed houses were offered at Mason's Hall Tavern on Tuesday, though several failed to find purchasers. Messrs. J. J. Orgill, Marks, & Orgill, disposed of the freehold with possession, of the Duke of St. Albans, Highgate-road, at £14,000. The free lease and goodwill of the Lincoln Hotel, South-street, Manchester-square, offered by Mr. N. Rolfe, went for £7,800. Among those withdrawn were the Victoria, Holloway-road, bought in at £32,000, the Prince of Wales, Bishop's-road, Paddington, and the house No. 3, Bishop's-road, withdrawn at £50,000; and the Hertford-Arms, Park-street, Hyde Park, taken back at £20,000.

Fresh trouble has arisen between Russia and Turkey as to the payment of the arrears of the war indemnity. The Porte seemed inclined to pay away portions of the Greek indemnity in increasing its armaments. Russia dislikes this notion, and requires the payment of Russia's reduced demand of £T750,000 in cash. The Porte offers to pay £T150,000 annually until the arrears have been cleared off; but Russia insists on prompt cash payment. If she persists in this demand, it will take another big slice out of the Greek war indemnity.

Since the return of Sir John Forrest to Perth, the Westralian Cabinet has been considering the relations between the alluvial diggers and the holders of gold-mining leases. It has been decided to withdraw the amendment to Regulation 103, restricting the operations of alluvial diggers on any leasehold to a depth of 10 ft. from the surface. A new regulation will be issued under the authority of the Governor in Council protecting the necessary workings of the leaseholders against the encroachments of alluvial miners.

The West Australian Government are said to be considering the offer of a French syndicate to construct a water system for Coolgardie at a cost of £2,300,000.

According to the final gold returns for Queensland for 1897, the yield for the year was 807,928 oz., of the value of £2,553,141, an increase of 167,543 oz. The value of the Charters Towers yield was £1,030,671, Mount Morgan £710,040, and Gympie £335,033.

In his opening address to the Mexican Congress, the President of the Republic reports no change of importance in the economic situation nor in the condition of the treasury.

Things are beginning to look gloomy again on the Bulgarian frontier. The peaceful assurances exchanged between the Sultan and Prince Ferdinand seem to have been only diplomatic waste of breath. The Bulgarian journals are assuming a threatening tone towards Turkey. Bulgarian armed bands are making their way into Macedonia, where uneasy agitation has been renewed, and if it goes on simmering—as it probably will—there may be serious trouble there in a short time.

Answers to Correspondents.

Questions about public securities, and on all points in company law, will be answered week by week, in the REVIEW, on the following terms and conditions:—

A fee of FIVE shillings must be remitted for each question put, provided they are questions about separate securities. Should a private letter be required, then an extra fee of FIVE shillings must be sent to cover the cost of such letter, the fee then being TEN shillings for one query only, and FIVE shillings for every subsequent one in the same letter. While making this concession the EDITOR will feel obliged if private replies are as much as possible dispensed with. It is wholly impossible to answer letters sent merely "with a stamped envelope enclosed for reply."

Correspondents will further greatly oblige by so framing their questions as to obviate the necessity to name securities in the replies. They should *number* the questions, keeping a copy for reference, thus:—"(1) Please inform me about the present position of the Rowenzori Development Co. (2) Is a dividend likely to be paid soon on the capital stock of the Congo-Sudan Railway?"

Answers to be given to all such questions by simply quoting the numbers 1, 2, 3, and so on. The EDITOR has a rooted objection to such forms of reply as—"I think your Timbuctoo Consols will go up," or "Sell your Slowcoach and Draggem Bonds," because this kind of thing is open to all sorts of abuses. By the plan suggested, and by using a fancy name to be replied to, each query can be kept absolutely private to the inquirer, and no scope whatever be given to market manipulations. Avoid, as names to be replied to, common words, like "investor," "inquirer," and so on, as also "bear" or "bull." Detached syllables of the inquirer's name, or initials reversed, will frequently do as well as anything, so long as the answer can be identified by the inquirer.

The EDITOR further respectfully requests that merely speculative questions should as far as possible be avoided. He by no means sets himself up as a market prophet, and can only undertake to provide the latest information regarding the securities asked about. This he will do faithfully and without bias.

Replies cannot be guaranteed in the same week if the letters demanding them reach the office of the INVESTORS' REVIEW, Norfolk House, Norfolk-street, W.C., later than the first post on Wednesday mornings.

C. H. (Surrey).—Your best plan will be to get your bankers to introduce you to a respectable firm. No such restriction as you mention is made by members of the Stock Exchange. Very few brokers will refuse to carry through small transactions provided they are bona fide.

WHIST.—Your letter has reached me just before going to press, too late to enable me to reply in this number. The company has not sent me a copy of its report, but I am endeavouring to secure one; if I am successful in doing so before the holidays I will send you a note in answer to your query.

Next Week's Meetings.

TUESDAY, APRIL 12.

Cunard Steamship ... ... Liverpool, noon.

WEDNESDAY, APRIL 13

Crieff & Comrie Railway ... ... Comrie, 12.30 p.m.
Edinburgh Life Assurance ... ... Edinburgh, 2 p.m.
Great Laxey ... ... Cannon Street Hotel, noon.
New Trinidad Lake Asphalte ... 5, Newman's Court, 1.45 p.m.

THURSDAY, APRIL 14.

Anglo Continental Gas Syndicate ... Winchester House, 3.30 p.m.

FRIDAY, APRIL 15

Edinburgh North American Investment ... ... Edinburgh, 3 p.m.

SATURDAY, APRIL 16.

Eastern Mortgage and Agency ... Cannon-street Hotel, 3 p.m.

TRAMWAY AND OMNIBUS RECEIPTS.

For past week:—Croydon, + £52; Glasgow, + £222; Lea Bridge, + £9; London & Deptford, + £19; London Southern, + £106; Metropolitan, + £623; North Staffordshire—£24; South London – £44; Woolwich & S. E. London, + £4; Southampton, – £27; Wolverhampton, + £10; Swansea, – £22.

Bordeaux, – £313.

Anglo-Argentine, week ending March 28, £26 increase; City of Buenos Ayres, week ending February 21, £508 increase.

The Canadian Government has introduced a Bill for the reduction of postage on inland letters from 3c. to 2c. per oz. Newspapers, which are at present sent free, are henceforth to be charged ½c per lb.

It is significant to note that the Spanish floating debt has increased during the month of March by 1,254,602 pesetas.

To Correspondents.

The Editor cannot undertake to return rejected communications.
Letters from correspondents must, in every case, be authenticated by the name and address of the writer.
Telegraphic Address: "Unveiling, London."

The Investors' Review.

The Week's Money Market.

The past seven days have been exceptionally busy ones for the short loan market. During the greater part of the time the India Council called in money, vigorously, and as large sums were due to be repaid to the Bank of England, rates for short loans were kept up at 2½ to 2¾ per cent. The repayment of Treasury Bills on Monday, and the distribution of the British and Indian Government dividends on Tuesday, caused rates for day-to-day loans to drop to 2 to 2½ per cent., but it is significant that on the latter day the whole of the amount due to the Bank of England for maturing loans and bills could not be provided. Since then the uncertainty about the future has caused the rate for day-to-day money to rise to 2½ per cent., and loans for a week to be quoted 2½ to 2¾ per cent. Yesterday, indeed, the market became very firm, and 2¾ per cent. was frequently paid, the large withdrawal of gold, and the fears about Cuba inducing people to look for an advance in the Bank rate to-day to 3½ per cent. This advance is much more probable now than it was before the Bank had parted with the dividend money. Yet we scarcely see ground for an advance now, apart from politics. The Bank has only lost £298,000 in gold on the week. This is not enough by itself to support even a 3½ per cent. Bank rate.

Discount rates have been even more firmly maintained than charges for loans. Last Thursday the rate for three months' choice bills was $2\frac{15}{16}$ per cent., and since then it has not fallen below 2¾ per cent., to which it declined just after the dividends were out. The gravity of the news from the United States has, however, caused it to advance again, and the latest quotation yesterday was $2\frac{13}{16}$ per cent., with some disposition to deal subject to the Bank's decision. The demand for gold on American account is so strong that the Bank rate would have been raised before this, had it not been for the large arrivals of gold from various quarters. Not only does South Africa send a considerable amount each week, but fair sums in Japanese yen come in by every steamer, and, of course, the shipments of gold from Australia to San Francisco can be reckoned as an offset to the demand upon our market. At the present juncture it is impossible to speak with any degree of certainty about this matter, but the New York exchange has fallen rather sharply in the last few days, and the demand has, therefore, increased. Let this burdensome drain be removed and the arrivals of gold would at once cause the market to weaken, in spite of the large sums due to the Bank of England. Payments on account of the Chinese Loan may cause a little pressure at times in the month, but no doubt the Hong-Kong and Shanghai Bank will re-lend in the market the instalments it receives, and so the full effect of the payments will be staved off until May 8, when the £12,000,000 has to be handed over to the Japanese Government. Even then it should not be forgotten that the large payments by the latter country in the United Kingdom must quickly free the portion of the sum provided here, and perhaps also some part of the quota contributed by Germany, the payment of which is not unlikely to bring gold from Berlin to London. The Paris Exchange has fallen back, but the Berlin rate has risen, and preparations are evidently being made there for the transfer of cash to us. We publish too early this week to be able to give the usual analysis of the Bank returns.

SILVER.

There has been a steady demand for the metal on Indian account, and a little buying for the Continent, with the result that the price has moved up 1/16d. to 26d. per ounce. At this figure producers were quite prepared to sell, and so the market may be considered in a fairly normal condition. There is certainly a difference of ⅛d. between the "spot" and "forward" quotation, which implies a moderately over-sold market, but such a fact is not likely to have much influence early in the month. Indeed, the nervous symptoms so prominent a short time back have disappeared since it has transpired that the Indian currency matter has been referred to a Departmental Committee. The market feels that it may rest in peace for a while, and not until the deliberations of that committee approach an end is the ferment likely to recommence. The India Council has sold its drafts steadily during the week, and it has shown every desire to meet the market, the price not being raised for specials until 10 lakhs had been sold. The official statement for the year ended March 31st. shows that Rs.14,72,07,928 were sold, realising in sterling £9,450,165, or an average rate of 1s. 3·407d. per rupee. Indian transfers have risen 1/16d., and Chinese rates have moved up in the last day or so owing to the improvement in silver.

BANK AND DISCOUNT RATES ABROAD.

	Bank Rate.	Altered.	Open Market.
Paris	2	March 14, 1895	1⅞
Berlin	3	February 20, 1898	2⅝
Hamburg	3	February 20, 1898	2⅝
Frankfort	3	February 20, 1898	2⅝
Amsterdam	3	April 13, 1897	2¾
Brussels	3	April 28, 1896	2
Vienna	4	January 22, 1896	3⅝
Rome	5	August 27, 1895	3
St. Petersburg	5½	January 23, 1898	4½
Madrid	5	June 17, 1896	4
Lisbon	6	January 25, 1891	6
Stockholm	4	March 3, 1898	3½
Copenhagen	4	January 20, 1898	4
Calcutta	12	February 24, 1898	—
Bombay	13	February 24, 1898	—
New York call money	2 to 2½	—	—

NEW YORK ASSOCIATED BANKS (dollar at 4s.).

	April 2, 1898.	Mar. 26, 1898.	Mar. 19, 1898.	April 3, 1897.
	£	£	£	£
Specie	28,312,000	27,258,000	25,856,000	17,198,000
Legal tenders	12,944,000	13,794,000	14,166,000	20,796,000
Loans and discounts	119,170,000	120,034,000	121,456,000	100,546,000
Circulation	2,773,200	2,772,000	2,773,000	3,140,000
Net deposits	136,448,000	137,130,000	137,636,000	113,846,000

Legal reserve is 25 per cent. of net deposits; therefore the total reserve (specie and legal tenders) exceeds this sum by £7,144,000, against an excess last week of £6,769,500.

FOREIGN RATES OF EXCHANGE ON LONDON.

Place.	Usance.	Last week's.	Latest.	Place.	Usance.	Last week's.	Latest.
Paris	chqs.	25·31¼	25·30	Italy	sight	26·80	26·78
Brussels	chqs.	25·38¾	25·37	Do. gold prem.	..	105·90	105·90
Amsterdam	short	12·10½	12·08½	Constantinople	3 mths	109·35	109·35
Berlin	short	20·48½	20·49	B. Ayres gd. pm.	..	163·20	165·10
Do.	3 mths	20·32½	20·34	Rio de Janeiro	90 dys	6	6
Hamburg	3 mths	20,32½	20·33½	Valparaiso	90 dys	17⅞	17⅞
Frankfort	short	20·48	20·49	Calcutta	T. T.	1/3 11/16	1/3¾
Vienna	short	12.05	12·04½	Bombay	T. T.	1/3 11/16	1/3¾
St. Petersburg	3 mths	94.05	94·15	Hong Kong	T. T.	1/10⅜	1/10½
New York	60 dys	4·80⅛	4·80⅜	Shanghai	T. T.	2/5⅞	2/6
Lisbon	sight	34 11/16	34 11/16	Singapore	T. T.	1/10 5/16	1/10⅜
Madrid	sight	35·75	36·00				

IMPERIAL BANK OF GERMANY (20 marks to the £).

	Mar. 31, 1898.	Mar. 23, 1898.	Mar. 15, 1898.	Mar. 31, 1897.
	£	£	£	£
Cash in hand	44,141,650	48,746,650	48,699,500	43,048,000
Bills discounted	38,314,850	30,330,600	29,026,650	*41,309,000
Advances on stocks	6,210,700	3,842,700	3,889,800	—
Note circulation	64,060,850	52,066,650	51,392,700	60,064,000
Public deposits	22,647,900	27,515,400	26,679,700	20,552,000

* Includes advances.

AUSTRIAN-HUNGARIAN BANK (1s. 8d. to the florin).

	Mar. 31, 1898.	Mar. 23, 1898.	Mar. 15, 1898.	Mar. 31, 1897.
	£	£	£	£
Gold reserve	30,521,166	30,535,666	30,706,833	25,987,000
Silver reserve	10,453,250	10,449,666	10,426,666	10,516,000
Foreign bills	1,012,167	1,004,000	1,001,833	—
Advances	1,877,750	1,846,416	1,828,416	—
Note circulation	52,621,750	50,799,000	51,250,166	50,481,000
Bills discounted	12,437,416	10,643,416	10,709,000	*14,235,000

* Includes advances.

NATIONAL BANK OF BELGIUM (25 francs to the £).

	Mar. 31, 1898.	Mar. 24, 1898.	Mar. 17, 1898.	April 1, 1897
	£	£	£	£
Coin and bullion	4,153,480	4,168,920	4,307,600	4,347,000
Other securities	17,589,680	16,939,440	16,629,400	16,090,000
Note circulation	19,866,960	19,009,400	18,915,400	18,714,000
Deposits	3,412,680	3,558,400	3,531,000	3,081,000

BANK OF SPAIN (25 pesetas to the £).

	April 2, 1898.	Mar. 26, 1898.	Mar. 18, 1898.	April 3, 1897.
	£	£	£	£
Gold	9,631,120	9,624,960	9,595,360	8,528,360
Silver	10,614,600	10,862,440	10,864,540	10,797,320
Bills discounted	24,628,640	24,274,280	23,365,280	7,969,360
Advances and loans	5,287,440	5,122,960	5,561,000	10,101,880
Notes in circulation	51,074,480	50,255,280	50,206,280	42,905,480
Treasury advances, coupon account	79,600	364,080	329,880	265,400
Treasury balances	2,720	2,169,200	1,971,680	1,094,360

LONDON COURSE OF EXCHANGE.

Place.	Usance.	March 24.	March 29.	March 31.	April 5.
Amsterdam and Rotterdam	short	12·2½	12·2½	12·2½	12·2
Do. do.	3 months	12·4½	12·4½	12·4½	12·3⅞
Antwerp and Brussels	3 months	25·48¾	25·52½	25·51¼	25·51¼
Hamburg	3 months	20·65	20·68	20·63	20·65
Berlin and German B. Places	3 months	20·66	20·58	20·68	20·66
Paris	cheques	25·31¼	25·33¾	25·33¾	25·31¼
Do.	3 months	25·45	25·48¾	25·47½	25·45
Marseilles	3 months	25·47½	25·48¾	25·48¾	25·46¼
Switzerland	3 months	25·67½	25·67½	25·67½	25·65
Austria	3 months	12·16¼	12·18¾	12·16¼	12·16¼
St. Petersburg	3 months	25	25	25	24 15/16
Moscow	3 months	24 15/16	24 15/16	24 15/16	24⅞
Italian Bank Places	3 months	27·00	27·15	27·10	27·5
New York	60 days	49 1/16	49 1/16	49 1/16	49 1/16
Madrid and Spanish B. P.	3 months	33½	32 15/16	33 1/16	33
Lisbon	3 months	34 1/16	34⅛	34⅛	34⅛
Oporto	3 months	34 1/16	34⅛	34⅛	34⅛
Copenhagen	3 months	18·41	18·41	18·41	18·42
Christiania	3 months	18·42	18·42	18·42	18·42
Stockholm	3 months	18·42	18·42	18·42	18·42

OPEN MARKET DISCOUNT.

	Per cent.
Thirty and sixty day remitted bills	2⅞—3
Three months "	2⅞—3
Four months "	2⅞
Six months "	2¾—2⅞
Three months fine inland bills	3 —3¼
Four months "	3 —3¼
Six months "	3¼—3½

BANK AND DEPOSIT RATES.

	Per cent.
Bank of England minimum discount rate	3
" " short loan rates	3
Banker's rate on deposits	1½
Bill brokers' deposit rate (call)	2
" 7 and 14 days' notice	2¼
Current rates for 7 day loans	2½—2¾
" " for call loans	2½—2¾

Stock Market Notes and Comments.

These need be but brief this week. In one sense there are no markets. The allottees of Lipton's shares have kept a few brokers and jobbers busy in a small way, selling their five and ten share allotment letters, and there is of course the general routine of investment transactions going on. Here and there, also, speculative accounts are being closed by people who prefer to be out of the hands of dealers in credit at a time like the present. But all this kind of thing does not mean "business" in the sense of a steady inpour of new orders from people who buy £10,000 of a stock because they have money enough to pay for £1,000, or from those who tempt fate and forswear fortune with £50,000 when they could not pay for £500. It is this sort of speculative traffic which three-fourths of the members of the Stock Exchange feel the want of now, and whose absence they proclaim by bemoaning to all and sundry that "there is nothing doing; positively not a thing doing." Had the Stock Exchange investment business alone to live by, three-fourths of its members would be driven away to other spheres for a livelihood, and the shares of the building would be knocking about somewhere near par.

For the present it is just this speculative and half-speculative business which is about dead, so far as the private or individual operators on the market go. The Arbitrageurs and groups of financial "combines" have things all their own way, and a considerable amount of money has been lost and won by them over the "war" and "no war" flying rumours about Cuba alone. This kind of speculation in brigades and squadrons, however, is not conducive to a diffusion of wealth over the Stock Exchange as a whole. A man must be "in with the group" before he can hope to touch any of its winnings. Woe betide the fellow who thinks he knows what the game is to be, and takes to imitating what he esteems to be the tactics of this "bull" or that "bear" party. It is a hundred to one he gets knocked over in the *mêlée* and relieved of his purse. The numbers so treated have been so great in the last few months—if we embrace South African clique gambling we may say the last few years—that a serious-minded individual speculator is for the time being nearly as difficult to find as the honest man sought by Diogenes, and a wail over his absence rises daily from thousands of throats on the Stock Exchange.

He will come back again, do not fear, dear jobbers and brokers. All that he is doing now is to wait till he "sees his way," or thinks he does, which is quite as good for market purposes or better. No sooner is his own mind clear upon that point that he will rush forward, and be as ready as ever to put fortunes in your way by joyfully staking his own. Let the market then go and take its Easter recess in good spirits. Lively times are coming by-and-bye, when money grows dearer, and prices have been "shaken out a bit." In view of this "shaking out" would it not be prudent, though, for every one fond of peace of mind to reduce accounts carried in borrowed money at each opportunity given by beaten "bear" or triumphant "bull"? It is the craft whose sails are spread when the storm strikes it which founders. This is not a time to have any sail out on the treacherous ocean of international stock gambling. Absolute owners of good securities can afford to keep away from markets now and wait quietly for the better days to come. Owners in name and in pawn had better beware.

The Week's Stock Markets.

Business on the Stock Exchange was on a very limited scale during the closing hours of last week, no one caring to increase their commitments in view of the unsettled aspect of foreign affairs. Saturday witnessed a considerable shake out, without much actual business, and the week closed in a very depressed style, the relations between Spain and the United States then seeming to have reached a most critical stage. The present

Highest and Lowest this Year.		Last Carrying over Price.	BRITISH FUNDS, &c.	Closing Price.	Rise or Fall.
113⅛	110⅞	—	Consols 2¾ p.c. (Money)...	111	−½
113$\frac{1}{16}$	111⅛	111¼	Do. Account (May 5)	111½	−⅜
106¼	104½	104¾	2½ p.c. Stock red. 1905 ...	104¾	—
363	345	—	Bank of England Stock...	348	+½
117	112⅜	113	India 3½ p.c. Stk. red. 1931	113½	—
109½	105	105¼	Do. 3 p.c. Stk. red. 1948	106¼	+½
96⅜	92	92½	Do. 2½ p.c. Stk. red. 1926	93	—

week, however, opened brighter, markets once again recovering in a wonderful manner; but profit taking soon spoilt the look of things again, and the closing of accounts prior to the holidays, the prospects of peace between Spain and the United States being now regarded as less favourable, and the strained relations between Turkey and Bulgaria, all acted as pretty considerable dampers on markets generally.

Consols were very steady until just before the close of business on Saturday, when the price gave way sharply, since when a partial recovery has occurred, the demand on the part of Great Britain for a lease of Wei-Hai-Wei on the evacuation of that port by the Japanese being favourably received. Indian Government securities also gave way at one time, and then recovered, but Bank of Ireland stock is 2½ lower.

Highest and Lowest this Year.		Last Carrying over Price.	HOME RAILWAYS.	Closing Price.	Rise or Fall.
186	172½	173¼	Brighton Def.	175½	—
59½	55¾	56¼	Caledonian Def.	56⅝	—
20⅜	18¾	19¼	Chatham Ordinary	19⅝	+ ¼
77¼	66	69	Great Central Pref.	67	−2
24⅝	21⅞	21⅞	Do. Def.	22	− ⅛
124½	119⅝	120½	Great Eastern	121⅛	− ¼
61½	51½	52	Great Northern Def.	53¼	—
179⅛	170¾	171¼	Great Western	172	− ¾
51¼	45½	48	Hull and Barnsley	48½	+ ⅛
149¼	146½	146½	Lanc. and Yorkshire	147	—
136¼	127⅞	129	Metropolitan	129	—
31	26¾	27½	Metropolitan District	27½	− ¼
88⅝	83½	84	Midland Pref.	85¼	+ ¾
95⅝	84½	85¼	Do. Def.	87½	+ ⅛
93¼	88⅝	90	North British Pref.	88¾	− ⅛
47½	42¼	42¾	Do. Def.	43⅜	—
181½	172⅞	173¼	North Eastern	174½	—
205⅛	197¾	198¼	North Western	199	− ¼
117⅛	107	107¼	South Eastern Def.	109⅝	+ ⅛
98¾	91	91	South Western Def.	92	—

Home Railway stocks have been fairly well supported, and even on Saturday when all other markets were very depressed, prices did not give way to any appreciable extent. The general improvement which set in on Monday soon carried quotations up rather above last week's closing, and the prospects of good holiday traffics helped to strengthen the market, although the dispute in the South Wales coal trade has acted somewhat as a damper. This strike will, it is thought, benefit the Midland Company, as a certain amount of traffic is sure to be diverted, and a demand sprang up for Midland deferred on the strength of this theory.

Highest and Lowest this Year.		Last Carrying over Price.	CANADIAN AND U.S. RAILWAYS.	Closing Prices.	Rise or Fall.
14$\frac{5}{16}$	10⅞	11¼	Atchison Shares	11⅝	− ⅜
34	23¾	24½	Do. Pref.	26	−1⅜
15⅝	11⅛	11⅝	Central Pacific	12⅜	− ¼
99¾	88⅝	90¼	Chic. Mil. & St. Paul	91¼	−3¼
14¼	10⅞	11½	Denver Shares	11¾	—
54½	42½	43	Do. Prefd.	44¾	−1¼
16⅝	12⅜	12¼	Erie Shares	12⅜	− ⅜
44⅞	32	33	Do. Prefd.	33½	−2⅛
62½	46⅛	47½	Louisville & Nashville ...	50⅛	−2⅛
14½	10½	11	Missouri & Texas	11⅛	− ⅜
122¾	108½	110½	New York Central	113⅛	−2¼
57¼	43	44¾	Norfolk & West. Prefd.	46⅛	−1⅜
70⅛	59¼	60½	Northern Pacific Prefd.	63⅛	−2⅜
19½	13¾	14	Ontario Shares	14¾	− ⅜
62½	57¼	57¾	Pennsylvania	58¼	− ¾
12½	8	8½	Reading Shares	8⅜	− ¼
34½	24½	25½	Southern Prefd.	26½	−1¼
37⅛	18¾	17*	Union Pacific	20⅜	−1⅛
20¼	14⅛	15	Wabash Prefd.	16	− ¼
30¼	22	22½	Do. Income Debs.	23¾	−1
92¾	81⅜	82¼	Canadian Pacific	83	−1⅛
78½	69⅛	72	Grand Trunk Guar.	73¾	− ⅞
69½	57⅛	64½	Do. 1st Pref.	66½	− ⅛
50⅛	37¼	44¾	Do. 2nd Pref.	47	−1
25¼	19¾	21¼	Do. 3rd Pref.	22⅜	− ⅛
105¾	101½	103	Do. 4 p.c. Deb.	102¾	—

United States Railroad shares have simply followed the various ups and downs of Spanish stock, although the fall on Friday and Saturday last was accentuated by the rumour that President McKinley was about to issue his promised statement on the reply of the Spanish Government. When the recovery set in and a small "bear" panic was reported from Wall-street, the advance was largely helped by buyers who considered that the contingency of war was about discounted at the present level, and then the receipt of telegrams pointing to a probability of the Pope's mediation caused a jump amounting to something like $5 in some cases, and to a greater or less rise in the whole list. This sharp recovery was followed by the inevitable profit-taking, and a reaction was the natural result, while the news that the Wall-street market is to remain open on Good Friday, indicates that the latest turn events have taken is regarded as a very serious one by New York operators. The usual tables compiled by the *Financial Chronicle* show that the gross earnings of 78 roads for the third week in March increased by 16·46 per cent.

Highest and Lowest this Year.		Last Carrying over Price.	FOREIGN BONDS.	Closing Price.	Rise or Fall.
94½	86½	86½	Argentine 5 p.c. 1886......	88¼	−1
92⅝	85¾	86	Do. 6 p.c. Funding	86¼ x.d.	−1
76¾	67⅛	68	Do. 5 p.c. B. Ay. Water	69	−1
61⅞	47⅛	53	Brazilian 4 p.c. 1889	48½	−4¾
69⅝	51	56½	Do. 5 p.c. 1895	53½	−2
65	48¾	53	Do. 5 p.c. West Minas Ry....................	50	−3½
108¾	106¼	107¾	Egyptian 4 p.c. Unified...	108	—
104¾	102	104¼	Do. 3½ p.c. Pref. ...	104¼	—
103	101⅞	102½	French 3 p.c. Rente	102 x.d.	+ ¼
44⅞	34½	43½	Greek 4 p.c. Monopoly...	44	− ⅜
93 3/16	91¾	91¼	Italian 5 p.c. Rente	92	− ¼
100	95¾	98	Mexican 6 p.c. 1888	97 x.d.	− ¼
20⅞	19	19⅛	Portuguese 1 p.c.	19⅛	− ⅜
62¼	47⅛	49	Spanish 4 p.c.	48⅛ x.d.	−3⅞
45¼	41	41	Turkish 1 p.c. "B"	42¼	− ¾
26 1/16	23¼	23¾	Do. 1 p.c. "C"	24⅝	− ⅛
22 1/16	20¾	20¾	Do. 1 p.c. "D"	21¼	− 3/16
46⅞	40	45	Uruguay 3½ p.c. Bonds...	45⅞	− ¼

Canadian Pacific shares after dropping to 82¼, recovered to about last week's level, the traffic return for the last ten days of March being a very good one. Grand Trunk stocks were also helped by an excellent return, coupled with a satisfactory working statement for February. The conference, which assembled at Buffalo to try and adjust the rates of the North-Western traffic, has failed to come to any definite decision, and has adjourned for a fortnight. At the half-yearly meeting of the Grand Trunk Company Sir C. Rivers Wilson spoke hopefully of the prospects of a speedy settlement of the rate war.

The Foreign market has varied day by day, from steady to firm, and then back to the lowest depths of depression, according to the varying phases of the political outlook. Spanish 4 per cents. have, of course, been the barometer of the whole market, and, in fact, of all markets, the price going from 53 to 47⅛ and up again to 51½, and then once more slipping back. The whole list was very depressed on Saturday, but the more hopeful view taken of the political situation on Monday caused a smart rally, which has again been lost in the face of the latest intelligence from Washington and Madrid. Prices on this side have followed the lead of Paris, where the Bourse has been entirely under the influence of war rumours all the week. In spite of a vigorous effort on the part of several members of the French senate to get the Bourse reform amendment separated from the Budget, it was decided to retain the connection, and the amendment was eventually agreed to. The quashing of the sentence on M. Zola also produced an unfavourable impression, and the settlement which is in progress has caused a good deal of uneasiness, the contango on Spanish stock being considerably higher than at the previous account. Heavy sales of Russian bonds on Saturday by several of the big French houses helped still further to weaken a market which had already gone almost to pieces, but the rally on Monday was general, all the Continental bourses sending more cheerful reports, principally on the reported mediation of the Pope in the dispute between Spain and the United States. This rumour served its turn before being officially denied. Among South American descriptions, Brazilian bonds have steadily gone from bad to worse, on apprehensions of financial difficulties at Rio, and the exchange has come lower day by day. One of the causes of the present state of affairs is undoubtedly the fall of over 40 per cent. in the price of coffee. Argentine issues drooped on the news that arrangements for a new loan are now being made, but the latest prices are not the worst of the week. Uruguayan bonds keep very steady, and have been helped by the notification of a remittance for the debt service.

Highest and Lowest this Year.		Last Carrying over Price.	FOREIGN RAILWAYS.	Closing Price.	Rise or Fall.
100	99½	99½	Argentine Gt. West. 5 p.c. Pref. Stock..................	100	—
158¼	144	145	B. Ay. Gt. Southern Ord..	147	−3
78½	68	68½	B. Ay. and Rosario Ord...	70	−1½
12¼	10⅜	10⅝	B. Ay. Western Ord.......	10¾	—
87¼	74	74½	Central Argentine Ord....	76½	−2
92	83	83½	Cordoba and Rosario 6 p.c. Deb.	83	−1½
95½	86½	87½	Curd. Cent. 4 p.c. Deb. (Cent. Nth. Sec.)	87½	—
61¾	45	46½	Do. Income Deb. Stk. ...	42½	−2
25⅝	18	19	Mexican Ord. Stk.	19¼	− ½
83½	72	75	Do. 8 p.c. 1st Pref.	75½	− 1

Among foreign railway stocks there has been a partial recovery in some of the leading Argentine descriptions, notably Buenos Ayres and Ensenada, which was firmer in connection with the sale of the line to the Great Southern Company. Cordoba Central Income stock marks a further decline, last week's traffic showing a decrease of over $20,000, and Alagoas 5 per cents. fell 7½.

The Miscellaneous market was not affected much by political scares or rumours, but business has quieted down in view of the approaching holidays. Cycle companies' shares have met with a little more support, due, no doubt, to the approach of the cycling season. A large business has been transacted in Lipton's shares without causing much change in the price. Birmingham Vinegar ordinary again marks an advance, and several electric lighting concerns have met with support. Coal and iron companies' emissions gave way owing to the strike in the Welsh coal trade; London General Omnibus stock has fallen 5; Gas Light A is lower, and a heavy fall occurred in Water stocks, Chelsea marking a decline of 10½. National Telephone issues were pressed for sale on the decision of the Government to appoint a Select Committee to consider the whole question of telephonic communication. Fairfield Shipbuilding shares and debentures are higher, but Armstrong and Bolckow Vaughan relapsed after last week's rise. Anglo-American Telegraph stocks close firm on the announcement of the full dividend on the preferred stock.

Markets closed the week in a state of suspense, and business was reduced to practically a standstill, while the rumour that £750,000 was to leave the Bank to-morrow (Thursday) for the United States, was viewed as an adverse feature. United States Railroad shares left off at nearly the lowest level, and the list presents an all round decline on the week. Home Railway stocks were dull in sympathy, although the traffic returns were very good. Among foreign stocks Spanish four per cent. were finally quoted nearly 4 lower than last Thursday, but a partial rally occurred just at the last in Brazilian bonds owing to a recovery in the Rio Exchange. Consols were slightly easier on the news of the gold withdrawal.

MINING AND FINANCE COMPANIES.

The South African market, after several changes of tendency, finally closes without much of a move either way. Buying orders from Paris on Monday lifted the price of De Beers and one or two of the other leading counters, and Chartered shares were firmer on the arrival of Mr. Rhodes in England. Another falling-off is looked for in the results of the past month's working, owing to the scarcity of native labour. West Australian ventures remain dull and neglected, but copper shares have been active at higher prices. The Anaconda dividend was again on a 5 per cent. basis, although the rise in the price of the metal and the increase in the output during the past year, had led some operators to look for an increased distribution. Indian shares were in demand, on satisfactory crushing returns.

Notes on Books.

La Bourse Anglaise. Par Georges Boudon, Avocat de la Cour d'Appel de Paris. Paris: A. Pedone; London: Clement Wilson.

M. Boudon has produced an interesting and suggestive book, which may be read with profit even by members of the Stock Exchange. It comes out at an opportune moment, for the probability is that the coming disruption of the open market in Paris will bring a large addition to the international business already transacted here in stocks and shares. M. Boudon prefaces his analysis of the constitution and methods of the Stock Exchange with several interesting chapters on what may be called the trade policy of England, the first of which, forming the introduction to the whole, is entitled La Suprématie Anglaise. They are indicative of painstaking research into the commercial history of the United Kingdom, and show the author to be a man not only of culture but of enlightened ideas. The conclusion he comes to is that France would do well, not exactly to imitate us, but to adopt an enlightened national policy of her own. "The day," he says, "that France, without imitating anybody, is able to substitute a national policy for its present parochial one; when the State, instead of paralysing private initiative, will do its best to provoke it in becoming its auxiliary to draw French capital towards the development of French enterprise: on that day France will cease to have any necessity either to be jealous of, or to fear the omnipotence of England." This remark is made at the close of a survey in which the economic, colonial, and scholastic policy of England have been subjected to a brief, but on the whole careful and intelligent analysis. The description of the Stock Exchange is also well done, and wonderfully accurate, considering that it is the production of a man who is in a practical way unfamiliar with English habits of business. At the end a French translation of the rules of the Stock Exchange is printed. We can honestly commend the book to the attention of those of our readers interested in the subject. In the next edition M. Boudon would do well to have the proofs read by some Englishman. English plurals and possessives have considerably bothered him.

Some Suggestions in Regard to Life Office Accounting, including inter alia *an Arrangement of the American Card System suitable for the Requirements of British Offices.* A. D. Lindsay Turnbull.

This essay was read by Mr. Lindsay Turnbull before the Actuarial Society of Edinburgh. It is highly technical, and, therefore, quite above our criticism, but we have looked through it with interest, and can see that it is a very thoughtful production full of valuable suggestions for the improvement of book-keeping suitable to Life Offices. It must have cost a great deal of labour to prepare and should be welcome to the profession of which Mr. Turnbull is evidently a very able member.

The New Zealand Official Year Book, 1897.

Some facts from the interesting official year book for 1897, prepared under instructions from the Right Honourable R. J. Seddon, P.C., Premier, by E. J. von Dadelszen, Registrar-General, will be useful for investors at the present time. The estimated population of the Colony on December 31, 1896, was 754,016; of this number 714,162 was the white population, exclusive of the Maories. There seems to have been very little increase in the total during the year through arrivals from other countries. This population imported in 1896 £7,137,320, including specie, a total smaller than that of 1885, but larger than the figures for any intervening year by a trifling amount. The export trade for the same period amounted to £9,321,105, of which total £9,177,336 consisted of the produce of the Colony. In respect of this import and export trade it will thus be seen that the Colony is more favourably placed than some of its neighbours,' and it would need to be, for it has a public national debt of £44,353,686, which involves an annual burden upon the community of £1,738,622. This is exclusive of the local debts, which amounted at the same date, namely, March 31, 1897, to £6,806,656, the annual burden upon which is about £440,000. The compiler of the statistics institutes a comparison between the indebtedness of New Zealand and that of the other Australasian Colonies, in virtue of which New Zealand is shown to have a burden of only £60 13s. 9d. per head as against £69 4s. 2d. for Queensland, and £65 16s. 10d. for South Australia. This comparison is vitiated by the omission of the local debts. Add these and New Zealand stands at the top of the tree. It is certainly highest in the amount of taxation per head if we exclude Western Australia, whose present position is altogether abnormal. In the financial year 1896—1897, the Colony raised £2,521,911 by what may be described as national taxation, and in addition local-governing bodies of all descriptions raised £592,902 for the year 1895—1896, the latest apparently for which Mr. von Dadelszen had figures. How the unfortunate inhabitants stand up under such a burden has always been a mystery to us, and will continue to be one. In these various figures of indebtedness we do not see the guaranteed loan made to the Bank of New Zealand, but that loan, amounting to £2,000,000, is as much a burden upon the Colony as any other obligation. Its trade has to find the interest upon it, all of which comes to investors in this country. Of course there is a budget surplus; Mr. Seddon always has that. It comes to £354,286 for the year ended March 31, 1897. In the same year the "Gross public Debt" of the Colony increased by £1,315,838. A surplus obtained at such a price is not cheap by any means, but we know New Zealand must borrow to live.

Through South Africa: By Henry M. Stanley, M.P. London: Sampson Low, Marston & Company.

We cannot quite understand why Mr. Stanley should have published this book. It will not enhance his reputation, nor can it assist the Chartered Company, with whom the author's sympathies evidently run. Mr. Stanley was a guest at the festivities in connection with the opening of the railway to Bulawayo. His impressions were hurriedly received, and equally hurriedly committed to writing for the *South Africa* newspaper.

It is not, perhaps, to be wondered at that they are sometimes crude in themselves, as well as somewhat crudely expressed. But, if so, what was the necessity for publishing them in book form. He writes enthusiastically about Bulawayo—"a city that must, if all goes well, grow to great distinction." He shows more enthusiasm about the gold mines than Mr. Rhodes himself. Mr. Stanley is convinced that gold is to be had in paying quantities; Rhodesia is the "centre of auriferous fields." But it should have a railway to Beira. Rhodesia can never rival the Transvaal, perhaps, but "it is not much inferior," and were Bulawayo nearer to the sea and nearer to the best mines, its "great distinction" might not be so very far off. We hope so; but for the present its distinction and prosperity are alike postponed. Practical men are chary in expressing their views about the auriferous fields, the development of which has been sadly delayed. Were gold to be had in paying quantities, there would not be very serious trouble about the railway to Beira. But in paying quantities gold has not yet been found, and no one who knows seems greatly impressed with the hope that it will be. As to the agricultural capabilities of Rhodesia, Mr. Stanley is also more, much more, enthusiastic than Mr. Rhodes; but on this subject he finds serious fault with the Chartered Company, which has sold all the best land to big companies that will not sell again save at a big profit. So the smaller capitalist, who would become the industrious pioneer in opening up the country, is forbidden the land. With its gold mines yet undeveloped, and the working agriculturist kept at a distance by the big grabbing companies, the prosperity of Rhodesia, if it ever comes, must be very much in the future indeed. Mr. Stanley, however, did not confine his hurried observations to Rhodesia; and though he has much to say that is uncomplimentary about the Boers, he yet admits that they are not entirely to blame for the backwardness of Cape Colony. They "cling to old-fashioned ideas somewhat more tenaciously than they ought to do," but "they do not object to private companies or individuals making irrigation works, or planting groves, which thrive so wonderfully; and as Cape Colony has been British for over ninety years, it is rather hard that the Boer should have all the blame." That is very true; and if Mr. Stanley had borne this in mind during and after his conversation with President Kruger he might have drawn his picture of that astute though primitive Boer statesman with less coarseness, less spitefulness, and a greater admixture of "sweet reasonableness."

The Law of Fixtures and Repairs, as between Landlord and Tenant: By W. de Bracy Herbert, M.A., LL.M., of the Inner Temple. London: Clement Wilson.

This is a very lucid, very concise, and very comprehensive explanation and epitome of the law as to fixtures and repairs as between landlord and tenant. It is not an argument as to what the law is, or ought to be, upon certain points raised, but a clear statement of what the law has been shown to be in cases decided in the courts. To the tenant especially, the work must be valuable, for very few seem fully to comprehend the extent of the responsibilities they undertake when renting a house or shop. We continually hear of tenants being rushed into serious costs very much to their own surprise, because they had not made themselves acquainted with the eccentricities of the law of landlord and tenant. Very few occupiers of houses, we suppose, will imagine, what it seems is the fact, that "apart from any agreement to the contrary, the tenant must continue to pay his rent, although the premises are destroyed by fire, and he cannot compel his landlord to rebuild the premises, even where he (the landlord) has received the insurance money." That does seem a very erroneous and very unfair provision of the law, and a burnt-out tenant, who had probably lost most of his furniture, and had of course been compelled to remove to another house, would probably be very indignant if presented with a bill for the rent of a building that had nothing but the blackened walls standing; but he would nevertheless have to pay if the landlord chose to take the case into court. The law indeed is rich in surprises—disagreeable, most of them—for the tenant. A careful perusal of Mr. Herbert's little book would save many an unfortunate tenant from loss in pocket and in temper. If the state of the law as between tenant and landlord were more generally known, it is not unlikely that the demand for its reform in the direction of equity would attain such volume as to be heard at Westminster, and attended to. But in this work, Mr. Herbert does not pose as a reformer; he is simply an expositor, and a very lucid expositor of the law as it is.

We have received a copy of the "Mercantile Year Book and Directory of Exporters," edited by Mr. Lindley Jones, and published at the *Mercantile Guardian's* offices in London. The list of exporters and their addresses seems very exhaustive, and the volume, a handy one, must be of great use to the vast numbers of people interested in the export trade of this country, which last year amounted to £234,550,003. It is as a Directory that the book is useful; the flights of Customs philosophy in the brief preface are not of a particularly brilliant order.

Sir A. Milner is at present on a visit to the Orange Free State. He had a cordial reception at Bloemfontein, and, in reply to an address of welcome, made the sensible remark that if there were more personal intercourse between those who worked the complicated machinery of South Africa a better understanding would prevail. Of course there would. Sir Alfred might make the same remark at Pretoria. He was subsequently present at the opening of the Free State Volksraad, where the President declared that the tension was abating, and that the relations of the colonies were more friendly. There seems no valid reason why they should not become yet more so.

Arrangements are being made for raising a new Argentine loan. It is to be a "popular loan" of 30,000,000 pesos, and is to be applied to "the completion of armaments."

It is stated that "every facility is now being offered by the Transvaal Government, the Railway Commissioner, and the Netherlands Railway towards the completion of the Pretoria-Pietersburg Railroad."

The French Senate has at last disposed of the Budget. It has been sent back to the Chamber of Deputies with only slight amendment. It is about time. The Budget has never before been so long in arrear, and it has been necessary to grant four months' votes on account.

A great part of Shawneetown, Illinois, has been destroyed by the breaking of a levee on the Ohio River about a mile above the town. The levee had shown weakness for several days; but beyond placing a guard at it to give warning of danger, no steps seem to have been taken to strengthen it. Steamers laden with provisions have been sent for the relief of the inhabitants.

Consider the promptitude of the telegraphic service and its ways A correspondent of the *Times* tells us that one day recently he handed in a telegram at Fleet-street, at 2.2 p.m., asking a client to meet him at the Law Courts as soon as possible. The telegram was not received at the Grenville-street, W.C., post-office until 3.13., and was not delivered in a street off Brunwick-square until a good deal later. Moral: Make no appointments by telegraph unless, say, about a day ahead.

The *Times* Colombo correspondent reports that there is great alarm in Ceylon on the Indian currency question. Local business and the export interest are suffering terribly, and urgent memorials are being sent to Mr. Chamberlain.

Dividends Announced.

MISCELLANEOUS.

ALADDIN'S LAMP GOLD MINING COMPANY, LIMITED.—Interim dividend of 1s. per share.

NOAKES AND COMPANY, LIMITED.—Interim dividend for the half-year at the rate of 10 per cent. per annum.

CUNARD STEAMSHIP, LIMITED.—2½ per cent. for 1897.

JOHN BAYLEY, WHITE AND BROTHERS, LIMITED.—Final dividend of 3 per cent. in the preference shares, making, with the interim dividend already paid, 6 per cent. for 1897, also 4 per cent. on the ordinary shares.

WEST AUSTRALIAN JOINT STOCK TRUST AND FINANCE CORPORATION, LIMITED.—Interim dividend at the rate of 20 per cent. per annum for the quarter ended March 31.

WEST AUSTRALIAN LOAN AND GENERAL FINANCE, LTD.—Interim dividend at the rate of 20 per cent. per annum for the quarter ended March 31.

CRISP & CO., LTD.—Payment recommended on the ordinary shares of a dividend at the rate of 11 per cent. per annum for the year ended February 19, less 3½ per cent. interim paid in October last; and also payment of 13s. 6d. per share on the founders' shares.

DUNDEE COAL AND ESTATES.—Quarterly dividend of 2½ per cent. has been paid.

KETTNER'S LTD.—Interim dividend at the rate of 5 per cent. per annum for the six months ended March 27.

PROGRESS CYCLE COMPANY, LIMITED.—Dividends at the rate of 10 per cent. per annum on the ordinary shares, and 7 per cent. on the preference shares for the six months ended March 31.

CASSEL COAL COMPANY, LIMITED.—Interim dividend of 5 per cent. for the half year ended January 31.

EXPLORATION AND GOLD MINING ASSOCIATION, LIMITED.—Dividend for 1897 at the rate of 17 per cent. on the ordinary shares, and 13¾ per cent. on the deferred shares.

ANGLO AMERICAN TELEGRAPH COMPANY, LIMITED.—Interim dividend for the quarter ended March 31, of 15s. per cent. on the ordinary stock, and £1 10s. per cent. on the preferred.

ANACONDA COPPER MINING COMPANY.—Dividend at the rate of 5 per cent. for the six months ended March 31, being at the rate of 10 per cent. per annum, payable May 2.

AVONDALE HOTEL AND HATCHETT'S RESTAURANT, LIMITED.—Interim dividend on the preference shares at the rate of 6 per cent. per annum for the period from the date of payment of the respective instalments to March 31.

J. R. ROBERTS' STORES.—Final dividend upon the ordinary shares of 3½ per cent. for the year ended February 13, which, with the 3½ per cent. interim already paid, makes 7 per cent. for the year.

INDO-EUROPEAN TELEGRAPH COMPANY, LIMITED.—Dividend for the six months ended December 31 last of 17s. 6d. per share, making, with the interim already paid, 6 per cent. and a bonus of 20s. per share, making in all 10 per cent. for the year.

BENGAL MILLS COMPANY, LIMITED.—5 per cent. on the preference and 10 per cent. on the ordinary shares, and a balance of £10,235 carried forward.

BRITISH ASSAM TEA COMPANY, LIMITED.—6 per cent. on the ordinary shares.

STEPHEN SMITH & CO. (HALL'S WINE).—Payment of the dividend on the 6 per cent. preference shares.

MENZIES' WATERWORKS, LIMITED.—1s. per share, equal to 5 per cent. on the capital of the company.

CITY OF BUENOS AYRES TRAMWAYS COMPANY, LIMITED.—For 1897 a balance dividend of 3s. 9d. upon the fully-paid shares, and of 2s. 3d. upon those of the eighth issue; £5,000 to be placed to reserve and £2,614 carried forward.

IMPERIAL CONTINENTAL GAS ASSOCIATION.—Directors recommend a dvidend of 5 per cent. for the half-year ended December 31 last.

ROYAL MAIL STEAM PACKETS.—Dividend of £1 10s. per share for the half-year ended December 31, 1897.

JOHN BARKER & CO.—Dividend upon the ordinary shares of 2s. 1d. per share, making with the interim dividend already paid, 13¾ per cent. for the year.

SAN PAULO GAS COMPANY.—Directors recommend a dividend for the year 1897, at the rate of 10 per cent. per annum.

ORIENTAL TELEPHONE COMPANY.—Dividend of 8d. per share, making with the interim dividend 5 per cent. for 1897.

RAILWAYS.

BUENOS AYRES GREAT SOUTHERN LIMITED.—Interim dividend on the ordinary stock for the half-year ended December 31, at the rate of 5½ per cent. per annum, £9,971 to be carried forward.

RIO CLARO SAO PAULO COMPANY, LIMITED.—7 per cent. for the half-year, making, with interim, 14 per cent. for the year.

GREAT WESTERN OF BRAZIL RAILWAY.—Dividend of 2 per cent. on the share capital, making with the interim dividend, 3½ per cent. for the year ended December 31, 1897, carrying forward, £5,586.

HIGHLAND RAILWAY COMPANY.—Dividend for the past half-year at the rate of ½ per cent. per annum, carrying forward £1,806.

BANK

NATIONAL OF THE SOUTH AFRICAN REPUBLIC.—Dividend at the rate of 10 per cent. per annum for 1897.

BREWERY.

DARTFORD COMPANY LIMITED.—Dividend at the rate of 5½ per cent. per annum for the six months ended March 31.

Prices of Mine and Mining Finance Companies' Shares.

Shares £1 each, except where otherwise stated.

AUSTRALIAN.

Making-Up Price, Mar. 26.	Name.	Closing Price.	Rise or Fall.	Making-Up Price, Mar. 26.	Name.	Closing Price.	Rise or Fall.
1⅜	Aladdin	1⅜		7¼	Hannan's Brownhill	7 1/16	−¼
3 1/16	Associated	3 1/16		⅝	Hannan's Oroya	⅝	
⅜	Do. Southern	⅜	−⅛	15/	Do. Proprietary	14/6	−1/
13/9	Brilliant, £2	14/		⅜	Do. Star	11/16	−1/16
2⅜	Do. St. George's	2⅜		4 [illegible]	Ivanhoe, New	5 [illegible]	−[illegible]
11/6	British Broken Hill	10/3	−1/	[illegible]	Kalgurli Mt. & Iron King, 18/	⅜	
2 1/16	Broken Hill Proprietary	2¼	+[illegible]	4 [illegible]	Kalgurli	5	−1/16
—	Do. Block 10	3⅜		2 [illegible]	Lady Shenton	2⅜	−1/16
1 1/16	Brownhill Extended	1 1/16	+1/16	8¼	Lake View Cons.	9	−⅛
1 [illegible]	Burbank's Birthday	1⅜	−1/16	⅜	Do. Extended	⅜	−1/16
⅜	Central Boulder	⅜	−⅛	1	Do. South	1 1/16	
5/6	Chaffers, 4/	5/3	−3/	1⅜	London & Globe Finance	1 1/16	−1/16
⅜	Colonial Finance, 15/	½ pm		⅜	London & W.A. Exploration	⅜	
—	Crœsus S. United	1/16	−1/16	[illegible]	Do. Investment	[illegible]	
15/	Day Dawn Block	14/	−1/	⅜	Mainland Consols	1/16	
[illegible]	E. Murchison	1 1/16	+1/16	⅜	North Boulder, 10/	[illegible]	+1/16
⅜	Gold Estates	[illegible]	−1/16	1 [illegible]	North Kalgurli	1 [illegible]	+[illegible]
4/3	Golden Arrow 19/	5/	+1/	4¼	Northern Territories	4	−⅛
7 1/16	Golden Horseshoe	7¼	−1/16	2⅜	Peak Hill	2¼	−1/16
⅜	Golden Link	1		2	South Kalgurli	2 1/16	
1	Great Boulder, 2/	19/3	−1/16	1 [illegible]	W. A. Goldfields	1 [illegible]	
1 1/16	Do. Main Reef, 10/	1 1/16		2 1/16	W. A. Joint Stock	2 1/16	−⅛
2¼	Do. Perseverance	2¼	−⅛	1 [illegible]	W. A. Market Trust	[illegible]	
[illegible]	Do. South	[illegible]	−1/16	1⅜	W. A. Loan & General Fin.	1 [illegible]	
2	Hainault	1 [illegible]	−1/16	⅜	White Feather	[illegible]	
⅜	Hampton Plains	[illegible]	+1/16				

SOUTH AFRICAN.

Making-Up Price, Mar. 26.	Name.	Closing Price.	Rise or Fall.	Making-Up Price, Mar. 26.	Name.	Closing Price.	Rise or Fall.
4 [illegible]	Angelo	5⅜		2/3	Lisbon-Berlyn	2/6	
1⅜	Aurora West	1		2¼	May Consolidated	2 [illegible]	+[illegible]
⅜	Bantjes	[illegible]		4¼	Meyer and Charlton	4¼	−⅛
9/6	Barrett, 10/	9/6	−/6	3 1/16	Modderfontein	3 [illegible]	
3⅜	Bonanza	3 [illegible]		1	New Bultfontein	1	
⅜	Buffelsdoorn	8/9		3 1/16	New Primrose	3 [illegible]	
5¼	City and Suburban, £4	5 [illegible]	+[illegible]	1⅜	Nigel	1⅜	
2 1/16	Comet (New)	2 1/16	−1/16	—	Nigel Deep	1 [illegible]	
4 1/16	Con. Deep Level	5	+⅛	⅜	North Randfontein	⅜	
11	Crown Deep	11¼		4⅜	Nourse Deep	5¼	−⅛
12	Crown Reef	12¼	+¼	1 [illegible]	Porges-Randfontein	1¼	
26¼	De Beers, £5	26¼	−¼	27 [illegible]	Rand Mines	28¼	+⅛
3¼	Driefontein	3 [illegible]		1⅜	Randfontein	1 [illegible]	
5¼	Durban Roodepoort	5¼		2	Rietfontein	2¼	+[illegible]
3 [illegible]	Do. Deep	3⅜		9¼	Robinson Deep	9¼	
3 1/16	East Rand	4¼	+1/16	8	Do. Gold, £5	7¼	−⅛
24¼	Ferreira	2 [illegible]		[illegible]	Do. Randfontein	[illegible]	
6¼	Geldenhuis Deep	6⅜		1⅜	Roodepoort Central Deep	1⅜	
4⅜	Do. Estate	5	+⅛	6	Rose Deep	6¼	−⅛
⅜	George Goch	[illegible]	−1/16	2⅜	Salisbury	2⅜	
2	Ginsberg	2¼		1 [illegible]	Sheba	1 [illegible]	
1 [illegible]	Glencairn	1 [illegible]	−1/16	2⅜	Simmer and Jack, £5	3	
7 [illegible]	Goldfields Deep	8¼	+⅛	3	Transvaal Gold	3⅜	
8¼	Griqualand West	8½	−½	3	Treasury	3	
8¼	Henry Nourse	9	+¼	3 [illegible]	United Roodepoort	3⅜	
7 1/16	Heriot	8	+¼	1 [illegible]	Van Ryn	1 [illegible]	−⅛
7¼	Jagersfontein	7⅜	−⅜	5¼	Village Main Reef	5 [illegible]	+[illegible]
7¼	Jubilee	8		1⅜	Vogelstruis	1 1/16	−[illegible]
4¼	Jumpers	4 [illegible]	+1/16	⅜	Do. Deep	[illegible]	
2 1/16	Kleinfontein	2 1/16	+¼	8¼	Wemmer	9¼	+⅛
3 1/16	Knight's	3 1/16	−1/16	⅜	West Rand	⅜	
2 1/16	Lancaster	2 1/16	−⅛	5¼	Wolhuter, £4	5⅜	+⅛
3⅜	Langlaagte Estate	3 1/16		2 1/16	Worcester	2 1/16	+[illegible]

LAND EXPLORATION AND RHODESIAN.

Making-Up Price, Mar. 26.	Name.	Closing Price.	Rise or Fall.	Making-Up Price, Mar. 26.	Name.	Closing Price.	Rise or Fall.
2¼	Anglo-French Ex.	2¼	−⅛	[illegible]	Mashonaland Central	[illegible]	+[illegible]
1 [illegible]	Barnato Consolidated	1⅜	−1/16	6⅜	Matabele Gold Reefs	6¼	+⅛
⅜	Bechuanaland Ex.	⅜		2	Mozambique	2¼	+[illegible]
2 [illegible]	Chartered B.S.A.	2 [illegible]	+1/16	1⅜	New African	1 [illegible]	
⅜	Clark's Cons.	[illegible]		[illegible]	Oceana Consolidated	⅜	
⅜	Colenbrander	[illegible]	+1/16	1⅜	Rhodesia, Ltd.	1 [illegible]	+⅛
3 [illegible]	Cons. Goldfields	4 [illegible]	+[illegible]	4	Do. Exploration	4¼	+⅛
1	Do. Pref.	20/6	+/6	1	Do. Goldfields	1⅜	+⅛
1 [illegible]	Exploration	1 [illegible]		3⅜	S. A. Gold Trust	4	
2⅜	Geelong	2 [illegible]	+⅛	⅜	Tati Concessions	[illegible]	
[illegible]	Henderson's Est.	[illegible]		⅜	Transvaal Development	⅜	
1 [illegible]	Johannesburg Con. In.	1⅜		⅜	United Rhodesia	[illegible]	+[illegible]
1	Do. Water	1		1 [illegible]	Willoughby	1 [illegible]	+⅛
1 [illegible]	Mashonaland Agency	1 [illegible]	+⅛	⅜	Zambesia Explor.	⅜	

MISCELLANEOUS.

Making-Up Price, Mar. 26.	Name.	Closing Price.	Rise or Fall.	Making-Up Price, Mar. 26.	Name.	Closing Price.	Rise or Fall.
1⅜	Alamillos, £2	1⅜		13/6	Mysore Goldfields	12/6	+/6
4⅜	Anaconda, $25	5⅜	−⅛	7/6	Do. Reefs, 17/	7/	+/6
9/6	Balaghât, 18/	8/6	−/6	14/6	Do. West	12/6	−1/6
4⅜	Cape Copper, £2	4⅜		11/	Do. Wynaad	9/	−[illegible]
4 [illegible]	Champion Reef, 10s.	5 1/16	+1/16	2 1/16	Namaqua, £2	2¼	+⅛
2¼	Copiapo, £2	2 1/16		3 1/16	Nundydroog	3 [illegible]	−1/16
3 1/16	Coromandel	3 1/16		3 [illegible]	Ooregum	3¼	−⅛
2 [illegible]	Frontino & Bolivia	2¼	−1/16	3¼	Do. Pref.	3 [illegible]	−⅛
1¼	Hall Mines	1 1/16		28	Rio Tinto Def., £5	28 [illegible]	−⅛
2¼	Libiola, £5	2¼		6¼	Do. Pref. £5	6¼	
7¼	Linares, £3	8¼		17/6	St. John del Rey	17/	
3¼	Mason & Barry, £3	3 [illegible]		13/9	Taitipu	[illegible]	
5	Mountain Copper, £5	5	−1/16	7⅜	Tharsis, £2	7 [illegible]	
13¼	Mount Lyell, £3	13⅜	−½	2¼	Tolima "A," £5	2¼	−⅛
2⅜	Mount Lyell, North	2 [illegible]	−1/16	4¼	Waihi	4 1/16	
14/	Mount Lyell, South	[illegible]		1⅜	Waitekauri	1⅜	
4⅜	Mount Morgan, 17s. 6d.	4⅜	−1/16	1 1/16	Woodstock (N.Z.)	1 1/16	
5⅜	Mysore, 10s.	5⅜					

The Queensland gold returns for March show a total of 74,500 oz.

WEST AUSTRALIAN MINE CRUSHINGS.

Capital Issued.	Property.	Goldfields.	NAME OF COMPANY.	November.		December.		January.		February.		Total since Crushing Began.	
£	Acres.			Tons.	Oz.	Tons.	Oz.	Tons.	Oz.	Tons.	Oz.	Tons.	Oz.
61,426	108	Murchison	Agamemnon	255	202	380	270	600	350	—	—	8,957	5,037
97,007	129	Mount Margaret	Arrow Brownhill	156	159	162	134	—	—	—	—	378	339
425,000	156	Kalgoorlie	Associated G. M. of W. A.	2,498	4,499	1,750	2,355	3,246	6,741	1,800	1,500	12,415	37,721
155,000	100	Coolgardie	Bayley's United	613	912	772	872	869	1,015	679	842	13,936	63,486
150,000	41	East Murchison	Bellevue Proprietary	336	864	455	642	269	485	486	604	1,676	3,057
150,007	106	Coolgardie	Big Blow	57	28	125	65	150	70	—	—	763	327
150,000	39	Coolgardie	Burbank's Birthday Gift	750	1,325	630	1,108	961	1,558	833	1,126	9,749	23,622
250,000	51	Murchison	Champion Reef	1,100	443	730	175	560	101	373	168	10,216	4,956
64,660	132	Pilbarra	Consolidated G. M. of W. A.	60	68	—	—	69	112	—	—	1,733	2,858
113,000	112	Murchison	Consolidated Murchison	1,012	1,106	862	880	812	821	789	813	28,092	17,571
100,000	12	Murchison	Cue No. 1	422	371	740	545	820	565	790	1,205	10,342	8,365
92,197	42	Murchison	Cue Victory	250	151	—	—	494	325	—	—	2,364	2,647
122,830	77	Mount Margaret	Diorite King	68	95	60	82	64	58	—	—	397	981
130,000	117	East Murchison	East Murchison United	1,315	1,860	1,950	2,100	1,410	1,630	1,290	1,305	14,918	22,889
54,139	40	Yalgoo	Emerald Reward	—	—	230	218	—	—	—	—	2,104	3,512
85,000	84	Murchison	Golconda	345	845	370	850	—	—	605	449	4,785	10,776
182,380	60	N. E. Coolgardie	Golden Arrow	70	53	68	83	—	—	98	101	805	651
100,000	24	Kalgoorlie	Golden Horse Shoe	—	—	—	—	—	—	—	—	—	—
175,000	24	Kalgoorlie	Great Boulder Perseverance	894	1,676	1,022	1,417	1,040	933	1,019	1,666	15,658	30,365
160,000	85	Kalgoorlie	Great Boulder Proprietary	2,704	6,965	2,575	6,509	2,756	6,599	2,841	6,513	56,080	179,016
60,000	24	Coolgardie	Great Boulder Main Reef	520	970	648	1,634	730	1,200	—	863	4,293	11,282
105,000	48	Yalgoo	Gullewa	150	263	75	126	169	247	270	339	1,774	2,587
85,000	20	Kalgoorlie	Hannan's Brownhill	121	496	210	1,696	963	2,285	994	1,840	7,030	34,470
240,000	36	Kalgoorlie	Hannan's Oroya	639	288	776	275	832	374	—	—	3,273	1,607
75,000	27	Kalgoorlie	Hannan's Reward	473	159	452	165	472	146	513	85	4,249	2,686
1,000,000	24	Kalgoorlie	Ivanhoe	1,867	3,656	2,595	4,891	1,555	2,760	1,722	2,851	15,352	48,605
160,000	36	North Coolgardie	Lady Shenton	590	1,512	415	1,861	552	1,518	600	1,650	7,743	16,795
250,000	48	Kalgoorlie	Lake View Consols	6,445	8,552	7,988	8,615	8,573	7,554	7,850	7,396	45,035	111,172
150,000	20	Kalgoorlie	Lake View South	—	—	—	—	1,500	331	1,122	221	2,622	552
65,000	38	Murchison	Light of Asia	—	—	—	—	168	142	200	189	2,067	1,360
119,444	32	Coolgardie	Lindsay's Consolidated	205	140	418	216	682	182	—	—	3,162	1,763
699,999	67	Coolgardie	Londonderry	100	195	330	652	—	—	320	477	2,149	12,905
224,125	156	North Coolgardie	Menzies Consolidated	761	731	455	601	743	644	630	597	7,815	7,656
193,100	44	North Coolgardie	Menzies Crusoe	167	134	185	199	330	244	933	799	7,898	14,515
173,811	91	North Coolgardie	Menzies Gold Reefs Proprietary	125	130	—	—	50	154	60	102	4,840	7,623
200,000	102	Mount Margaret	Mount Malcolm Proprietary	270	318	202	362	470	444	529	474	2,213	2,522
85,000	84	Murchison	Mount Yagahong	385	471	575	612	—	—	1,201	715	4,941	4,133
200,000	164	Dundas	Norseman Gold	612	648	680	410	630	444	697	515	3,806	3,811
120,000	19	Kalgoorlie	North Boulder	507	324	577	738	1,241	575	699	671	8,262	13,678
215,000	143	Mount Margaret	North Star	424	356	352	564	408	386	95	166	3,938	4,045
25,799	36	Coolgardie	Premier Gold	380	354	378	253	710	484	715	345	8,040	10,340
65,003	12	Murchison	Princess Royal (Cue)	460	444	550	429	290	219	130	126	3,040	3,227
31,387	19½	N. Coolgardie	Queensland Menzies	312	827	330	913	304	1,144	220	670	4,579	17,873
78,984	51	N. E. Coolgardie	Robinson (W.A.)	495	470	660	610	650	439	415	292	6,957	9,149
—	168	Mount Margaret	Sons of Gwalia	800	993	840	1,213	1,260	1,577	960	1,139	6,907	9,607
200,000	98	Coolgardie	Westralia and East Extension	1,634	1,723	1,611	1,339	1,306	856	1,882	1,236	10,829	10,167
110,993	72	Murchison	Weld Hercules	—	—	—	—	—	—	579	346	2,171	1,410
75,000	66	N. E. Coolgardie	White Feather Reward Claim	638	305	516	225	611	280	527	282	11,381	10,915
240,300	48	N. E. Coolgardie	White Feather Main Reef	750	410	880	252	698	341	600	380	5,333	3,434

MINING RETURNS.

BAYLEY'S UNITED.—Four weeks ended March 25: 690 tons tailings treated by cyanide, yield 738 oz. gold.

BRILLIANT.—3,000 tons of stone crushed for a yield of 3,200 oz. gold.

GREAT EASTERN COLLIERIES.—Output for March 15,500 tons.

BELLEVUE PROPRIETARY.—Clean up for fortnight ended March 26: 159 tons, yields 392 oz.

GREAT BOULDER MAIN REEF.—830 tons crushed yielded 1,100 oz.

VICTORIA AND QUEEN.—Partial clean up of 432 tons for 735 oz. gold.

HAURAKI.—Crushed 230 tons, yield 556 oz.

HANNAN'S OROYA.—Crushed 902 tons, yield 545 oz. gold.

BURBANKS' BIRTHDAY GIFT.—Crushed 470 tons, yield 645 oz. free gold exclusive tailings.

CRESCENT.—14 days, 350 tons, 53 oz.

LAKE GEORGE.—During February 3,501·83 tons of crude ore were furnaced, giving 157·50 tons of matte and 1·12 tons of bullion containing 326 oz. of gold, 1,384 oz. of silver, and 5,817 units of copper, equal to a recovery of metals per ton of ore—1·86 dwt. gold, 3·73 oz. silver, and 1·66 per cent. copper. 125 tons of matte have been shipped per Australia.

NEW OPTIONS.—"Second-class ore, Monarch, total amount 300 tons, 129 oz."

SMELTING COMPANY OF AUSTRALIA.—From January 1 to February 17 3,506 tons of ore were treated containing 571 tons lead, 56 tons copper, 4,374 oz. gold, and 62,173 oz. silver.

BROKEN-HILL PROPRIETARY CO.—For four weeks ended March 31: 23,915 tons of ore treated, and output from the refinery was 1,513 oz. of gold, 331,026 oz. silver, 2,199 tons of lead, and 45 tons antimonial lead; the copper matter containing three tons of copper and 19,770 oz. silver (estimated). In the above refinery return is included the product from the treatment of purchased ores.

DUNDEE COAL AND ESTATES COMPANY.—Output for March: 17,000 tons.

OTTOS KOPJE.—5,008 loads washed, 125 carats of diamonds won.

PESTARENA UNITED.—Return for March: 521 tons of ore produced 593 oz.

AUSTRALIA UNITED.—Crushed 145 tons of ore, which yielded 297 oz. of gold.

CHAMPION REEF.—7,452 tons of stone produced 9,163 oz., 2,440 tons of tailings produced 610 oz., and 4,620 tons of tailings (cyanide process) produced 1,267 oz.

COROMANDEL.—1,300 tons of stone produced 901 oz. of gold, and 1,200 tons of tailings (cyanide process) 110 oz.

GOLD FIELDS OF MYSORE.—42 oz. of gold obtained from 700 tons sand (cyanide process), 218 oz. of gold obtained from amalgamation.

MYSORE.—7,150 tons of quartz produced 11,390 oz. of gold, 2,810 tons of tailings produced 751 oz., and 1,820 tons of tailings (cyanide process) produced 217 oz.

MYSORE WEST.—Mysore Wynaad—Result of crushings for March: 1,400 tons, 411 oz. of gold.

NINE REEFS.—1,100 tons of stone crushed yielded by amalgamation 93 oz. of gold, by cyanide process 63 oz. of gold.

NORSEMAN, BALL MILL.—Crushing return for March, 704 oz.; 803 tons of ore crushed.

NUNDYDROOG.—3,100 tons of quartz produced 2,595 oz. of gold; 800 tons of tailings produced 90 oz. of gold; 3,248 tons of tailings (cyanide process) produced 490 oz. of gold.

OOREGUM.—5,612 tons of quartz produced 3,577 oz. of gold; 4,876 tons of tailings produced 617 oz.

REGINA (CANADA).—Crushed 550 tons, obtained 190 oz. gold.

TOLIMA.—March estimated returns (75 tons), £2,086.

UNITED IVY REEF.—Last month's crushing yielded 530 oz.: crushed 991 tons.

WEALTH OF NATIONS.—Crushed during the last 16 days of the month 337 tons, the gross yield being 347 oz. Total return for March, 597 tons; gross yield, 487 oz.

IVANHOE.—Clean up for two weeks 1,681 oz., from 1,126 tons crushed. Tailings assay 15 dwts. per ton.

VICTORY (CHARTERS TOWERS).—Crushed 110 tons for 389 oz

NORTH BOULDER.—329 oz. gold from 373 tons crushed.

PREMIER, NEW ZEALAND.—Crushed in March 595 tons for 362 oz. gold. Tailings produced 124 oz.

DAY DAWN BLOCK AND WYNDHAM.—Result for past fortnight:—Tons crushed, 1,250; yield of gold, 1,023 oz., including tailings.

GLYNN'S LYNDENBURG.—Results for March:—From mill—crushed, 1,270 tons; obtained, 543 oz. of fine gold. From cyanide works—treated, 924 tons; yield, 345 oz. —total, 888 oz.

MOUNT USHER.—Clean up from 170 tons gave 36 oz. of gold.

MYSORE REEFS (KANGUNDY).—March return:—1,000 tons of ore crushed have yielded 381 oz. of gold.

NEW KLEINFONTEIN COMPANY.—Crushing for last month:—Tons crushed, 11,359 ounces recovered 3,524. Tons treated by cyanide, 7,702; oz. recovered, 1,131.

PADDINGTON CONSL.—Crushed during March, 1,900 tons, yielding 665 oz. of gold.

BURMA RUBY MINES.—Result for March was 68,000 loads washed, producing rubies valued at Rs. 80,000.

PIGG'S PEAK DEVELOPMENT.—Crushed 2,400 tons for 358 oz. of gold; cyanided, 2,550 tons for 530 oz. of gold.

FERREIRA GOLD MINING COMPANY.—Crushed during March, 11,314 tons, producing 7,917 oz.; value of concentrates caught, 1,375 oz.; yield by cyanide, 3,007 oz. Total, 12,299 oz. of gold.

WORCESTER EXPLORATION AND GOLD MINING COMPANY.—Last month's crushing yielded 2,674 oz. of gold.

HENRY NOURSE GOLD MINING COMPANY.—Result of operations for March; mill ran 26 days, crushed 8,680 tons, producing 5,179 oz. Cyanide, 6,450 tons treated 3,129 oz. Total, 8,308 oz. of gold.

EASTLEIGH MINES.—60 stamps ran 26 days. Total output 2,560 oz.

BEACON GOLD MINES.—Obtained 562 ozs. of gold from 557 tons of ore crushed, value £1,980. Profit, £970.

MONTANA MINING COMPANY.—Total output for March: 6,290 tons of ore produced. 2,133 ozs. of gold and 6,030 ozs. of silver. Estimated value $45,800. Net profit $3,300.

ENGLISH RAILWAYS.

Div. for half years. 1896	1896	1897	1897	Last Balance forward.	Amt. to pay 1 p.c. on Ord. for ½ yr.	NAME.	Date.	Gross Traffic for week: Amt.	Inc. or dec. on 1897.	Inc. or dec. on 1896.	No. of weeks.	Gross Traffic for half-year to date: Amt.	Inc. or dec. on 1897.	Inc. or dec. on 1896.	Mileage.	Inc. on 1897.	Working	Prior Charges last ½ year.	Prop. add Cap. Exp. this ½ year.
				£	£												%	£	£
10	10	10	10	2,707	5,094	Barry	Mar 26	8,298	−807	+61	13	118,035	+4,703	+20,950	31	—	6·89	60,665	316,853
nil	nil	nil	nil	—	—	Brecon and Merthyr	Apr. 3	1,409	+13	−186	14	20,635	+546	−1,055	61	—	—	—	—
nil	nil	nil	nil	3,979	4,749	Cambrian	,, 3	5,067	+37	+532	*	58,596	+978	—	250	—	60·56	63,148	40,000
1½	1½	2	1½	1,510	3,150	City and South London ..	,, 3	1,050	+24	+233	14	14,942	+124	+1,471	3½	—	56·07	5,552	124,000
1	2	1½	2	7,895	13,210	Furness	Mar 27	9,017	+386	+553	*	106,371	+3,004	—	139	—	49·88	97,423	20,910
1	1½	½	1	2,207	27,470	Great Central (late M.,S.,& L.)	,, 27	44,366	−1,295	+3,489	12	506,180	+5,025	+30,210	352½	—	57·17	627,386	1,200,000
1½	4½	2	5	51,283	82,805	Great Eastern	Apr. 3	76,076	+2,125	−3,715	13	1,005,308	+31,250	+75,203	1,158½	2	55·35	860,138	250,000
3	5½	3	5	15,094	102,496	Great Northern	Mar 27	92,534	−407	+3,799	13	1,200,364	+34,480	+84,848	1,071	8	61·36	641,485	750,000
4½	7½	4½	7½	31,350	121,981	Great Western	,, 27	175100	−680	+6,480	12	2,039,830	+45,050	+106316	2,582	21	51·44	1,486,272	800,000
nil	2	nil	1½	8,951	16,487	Hull and Barnsley	Apr. 3	6,981	+858	+1,897	13	83,110	−1,146	+7,081	73	—	58·21	70,290	52,5[illegible]
5	5¾	5	5½	27,495	83,704	Lancashire and Yorkshire ..	,, 3	89,374	−675	†−13682	13	1,168,469	+32,656	+29,058	555½	25	56·70	674,745	451,976
4½	8	4½	8½	26,243	41,049	London, Brighton, & S. Coast	,, 2	49,450	−590	†−14513	14	636,832	+27,037	+25,888	476½	—	50·26	407,042	249,735
nil	nil	nil	nil	72,294	55,296	London, Chatham, & Dover ..	,, 3	27,730	+14	†−5,465	13	336,219	+9,336	+14,830	185½	—	50·65	367,873	nil
6½	8	6½	7½	89,535	204,068	London and North Western ..	Mar 27	225962	−2,417	+10,064	12	2,669,146	+57,676	+136698	1,911½	—	56·92	1,404,534	600,000
5	8½	8½	8½	23,038	59,367	London and South Western ..	Apr. 3	68,278	+568	†−10452	13	840,869	+32,213	+46,473	941	6½	51·75	513,740	389,000
2½	6	2½	6½	14,592	6,691	London, Tilbury, & Southend	,, 3	4,990	+274	†+138	14	65,762	+4,071	+10,687	81	—	52·57	39,550	15,000
3½	3½	3½	3½	17,133	26,409	Metropolitan	,, 3	16,469	+252	‡+1,068	*	214,388	+5,036	—	64	—	43·63	148,047	254,000
nil	nil	nil	nil	4,006	11,250	Metropolitan District	,, 3	8,571	‡−181	+384	13	112,490	+4,530	+5,445	13	—	45·70	119,663	38,450
5	7	5½	6½	38,143	174,582	Midland	,, 3	185133	+10,238	+11,374	14	2,526,940	+36,405	+164424	1,354½	15½	57·59	1,216,582	650,000
5½	7½	5½	7	22,374	138,183	North Eastern	,, 2	142150	−2,639	−4,491	13	1,811,010	+20,534	+75,142	1,597½	—	58·82	795,077	436,004
7½	7½	7½	7½	7,001	10,104	North London	,, 3			Not recd.			not	recvd.	12	—	50·90	49,973	7,600
4	5	4	4½	4,745	16,150	North Staffordshire	,, 3	15,572	−27	+174	14	217,047	+5,742	+12,547	312	—	55·27	118,142	19,605
10	10	11		1,642	3,004	Rhymney	Mar 26	5,151	+512	+700	13	65,977	+1,716	+7,305	71	—	49·68	29,049	16,700
3	6½	3½	6½	4,054	50,215	South Eastern	Apr. 2	45,265	+944	†−7,441	*	527,575	+25,107	—	448	—	51·88	380,763	250,000
3½	3½	3½	3½	2,315	25,961	Taff Vale	,, 2	13,672	−2,500	+470	14	211,030	−7,692	+6,808	121	—	54·90	94,800	92,000

* From January 1. † Includes Good Friday Traffic. ‡ Includes Universities' Boat Race Traffic in 1897

SCOTCH RAILWAYS.

1896	1896	1897	1897	Last Balance forward.	Amt. to pay 1 p.c. on Ord. for ½ yr.	NAME.	Date.	Amt.	Inc. or dec. on 1897.	Inc. or dec. on 1896.	No. of weeks.	Amt.	Inc. or dec. on 1897.	Inc. or dec. on 1896.	Mileage.	Inc. on 1897.	Working	Prior Charges last ½ year.	Prop. add Cap. Exp. this ½ year.
5	5	5½	5	9,544	78,066	Caledonian	Mar. 27	72,671	+ 1,289	+ 3,269	8	555,403	+ 12,303	+ 31,391	851½	5	50·38	588,248	441,477
5	5½	5	5	7,364	24,679	Glasgow and South-Western	,, 26	26,755	+ 1,171	+ 1,469	8	210,391	+ 6,204	+ 11,287	393½	—	54·69	221,663	106,145
3½	3½	3½	—	1,291	4,600	Great North of Scotland	Apr. 2	7,895	+ 175	+ 224	9	67,409	+ 98	+ 1,327	331	15½	52·03	92,178	60,000
3	nil		—	10,477	12,820	Highland	,, 3	8,636	+ 377	+ 11	5	41,348	+ 1,218	+ 2,490	479½	27½	58·63	78,976	,000
1	1½	1	1½	819	45,819	North British	Mar. 27	68,507	+ 1,138	+ 2,278	8	537,452	+ 13,359	+ 18,105	1,230	23	48·62	944,809	40,800

IRISH RAILWAYS.

1896	1896	1897	1897	Last Balance forward.	Amt. to pay 1 p.c. on Ord. for ½ yr.	NAME.	Date.	Amt.	Inc. or dec. on 1897.	Inc. or dec. on 1896.	No. of weeks.	Amt.	Inc. or dec. on 1897.	Inc. or dec. on 1896.	Mileage.	Inc. on 1897.	Working	Prior Charges last ½ year.	Prop. add Cap. Exp. this ½ year.
6½	6½	6½	—	5,466	1,750	Belfast and County Down ..	Apr. 1	1,899	− 493	− 137	*	26,536	+ 775	—	76½	—	55·58	17,690	10,000
5½	6½	5½	—	—	4,284	Belfast and Northern Counties	,, 1	5,102	+ 57	+ 241	*	64,609	+ 3,238	—	249	—	—	—	—
2	3	2	—	1,418	1,200	Cork, Bandon, and S. Coast† ..	,, 2	1,143	+ 4	+ 292	*	15,216	− 1,161	—	103	—	54·82	14,436	5,450
6½	6½	6½	6½	38,776	17,516	Great Northern	,, 1	15,446	+ 816	+ 1,024	13	182,356	+ 9,397	+ 12,830	528	36	50·15	88,068	22,000
5½	5½	5½	5½	30,339	24,155	Great Southern and Western ..	,, 1	—	—	—	not	received	—	—	603	13	51·45	72,802	46,582
4	4	4	4½	11,372	11,850	Midland Great Western ..	,, 1	10,558	+ 9	+ 650	13	221,893	+ 5,368	+ 7,444	538	—	50·32	83,129	1,800
nil	nil	nil	nil	229	2,822	Waterford and Central ..	,, 3	873	+ 146	—	*	11,151	+ 1,476	—	59½	—	53·24	6,898	1,500
nil	nil	nil	nil	1,536	2,987	Waterford, Limerick & W. ..	,, 1	4,976	− 28	+ 686	*	73,111	+ 3,398	—	350½	—	57·83	42,617	7,075

* From January 1. † Eight weeks' strike

The Commission for the delimitation of the Burmo-Chinese frontier seems to have collapsed. The Chinese and English Commissioners have met and separated without doing anything There is a complete deadlock. Why?

A Chinese censor, said to be of the highest rank, has, it seems, in a memorial to the Emperor, accused the members of the Tsung-li-Yamen of being in the Russian pay. The sum paid them he fixes at 10,000,000 taels; but he adds that Li Hung Chang has received a million and a half of taels on his own account. This distinguished censor demands a full inquiry into his statements, offering as a condition that if Li Hung Chang be found guiltless in the matter, he himself (the censor) shall be decapitated; but if, on the other hand, the accusation should be proved, he prays for the execution of Li Hung Chang. The challenger has the courage of his convictions at all events.

The Chamber of Mines at Bulawayo expresses much regret at the retirement of the Duke of Fife from the directorate of the British South Africa Company, but the Chamber, it will no doubt be satisfactory to know, considers the proposed new form of government preferable in every respect to direct Imperial control.

The present right of full entry of British goods into Siberia from the Kara Sea, which Russia proposed to suspend, is to be continued on the recommendation of the Commission appointed to inquire into the matter, though several minor restrictions in the interests of Russian trade are to be introduced. Siberian traders themselves were the first to protest against the suspension.

Fierce indignation has been aroused in New Zealand by the presentation of a bill for £1,700 on account of the Prime Minister's expenses during the Jubilee tour. It was understood by the colonists that the expenses of the Colonial Premiers who came here for the Jubilee rejoicings were to be defrayed by England. Then why this bill for £1,700?

Newfoundland has a public debt of $17,000,000, upon which it pays an average interest of 4 per cent. If this interest were reduced to 2½ per cent., the colonists think it would be a great relief, which, of course, it would. They are to appeal to the mother country, therefore, to lend its guarantee, by which the interest might be reduced to the desired extent. If the Home Government are not too busy considering schemes for increasing the Navy, perhaps they will listen to the cry of the Newfoundlanders.

NOTICES.

Lieut.-Col. E. L. Marryat, R.E., secretary of the Rohilkund and Kumaon Railway Company, having joined the Board, has been appointed managing director.

At the meeting of the Court of Directors of the Royal Mail Steam Packet Company held yesterday, Admiral Ch[illegible], C.B., Deputy Chairman of the Company, was elected Chairman in place of Mr. T. R. Tufnell deceased, and Mr. Herbert Edemann, was elected Deputy Chairman.

Railway Traffic Returns.

BURMA RAILWAYS.—Receipts for week ending February 26, Rs. 2,05,965; decrease, Rs. 20,074. Aggregate from January 1, Rs. 16,55,206; decrease, Rs. 2,93,535.

GREAT WESTERN OF BRAZIL RAILWAY.—Traffic for week ending February 12, $39,146; decrease, $1,265. Aggregate receipts to date $304,516; increase, $31,253.

ALCOY AND GANDIA RAILWAY AND HARBOUR COMPANY.—Traffic for week, April 2:—Ps. 6,000, increase Ps. 2,400. Aggregate from January 1, Ps. 129,300, increase Ps. 3,650.

VILLA MARIA AND RUFINO RAILWAY.—Traffic for week ending March 26, $6,269; increase, $2,201. Aggregate from January 1, $55,116, decrease $4,861.

WEST FLANDERS RAILWAY.—Gross receipts for week ending March 27, £1,944; increase, £47. Total from January 1, £26,093; increase, £644.

WEST OF INDIA PORTUGUESE RAILWAY.—Week ending March 5, Rs. 5,270; increase, Rs. 1,722.

ROHILKUND AND KUMAON RAILWAY.—Traffic receipts for week ending February 26, Rs. 6,217; decrease, Rs. 116. Aggregate from January 1, Rs. 43,378; decrease, Rs. 1,387.

SOUTHERN MAHRATTA RAILWAY.—Receipts for week ended March 5, Rs. 104,121; decrease, Rs. 16,569.

MANILA RAILWAY.—Receipts for week ending April 2, $21,533; increase, $5,815. Aggregate from January 1, $254,622; increase, $62,867.

CLEATOR AND WORKINGTON.—Gross receipts for the week ending March 26 amounted to £1,027, a decrease of £60. Total receipts from January 1, £12,274, a decrease of £609.

COCKERMOUTH AND KESWICK RAILWAY.—Receipts for the week ending March 26, £817; increase, £147. Aggregate from January 1, £9,931; increase, £952.

QUEBEC CENTRAL RAILWAY.—Receipts for second week of March, $8,559; increase, $621. Aggregate from July 1, $59,865; decrease, $8,893.

PUERTO CABELLO AND VALENCIA RAILWAY.—Traffic return for week ended February 25, £1,063; decrease, £754. Aggregate from January 1, £7,426: decrease, £3,700.

WESTERN OF SANTA FE RAILWAYS.—Gross receipts for week ending March 26, $52,890; increase, $26,580.

MOBILE AND BIRMINGHAM RAILROAD.—Traffic for second week of March, $6,706; increase, $220. Aggregate from July 1, $268,401; decrease, $4,847.

ALGECIRAS (GIBRALTAR) RAILWAY.—Traffic for week ended March 26, Ps. 18,218; increase Ps. 2,378. Aggregate from July 1, Ps. 776,932; increase, Ps. 23,788.

BENGAL CENTRAL RAILWAY.—Traffic for week ending March 5, Rs. 19,291; increase, Rs. 2,365. Total from January 1, Rs. 186,497; increase, Rs. 23,343

ASSAM-BENGAL RAILWAY.—Traffic for week ended February 19, Rs. 27,506; increase, Rs. 7,760. Aggregate from January 1, Rs. 1,72,349; increase, Rs. 19,095.

BENGAL DOOARS RAILWAY.—Traffic receipts from January 1 to February 19, Rs. 23,180; decrease, Rs. 6,828.

H. H. THE NIZAM'S GUARANTEED STATE RAILWAYS.—Traffic receipts from January 1 to February 26. Rs. 629,384; increase, Rs. 12,984.

DELHI UMBALLA KALKA RAILWAY.—Traffic receipts for week ending March 26, Rs. 35,800; increase, Rs. 300. Total from commencement of half-year, Rs. 4,46,600; increase, Rs. 1,43,000.

SOUTHERN PACIFIC RAILWAY.—The net earnings for the month of February, $1,470,137; increase, $622,711.

VILLA MARIA AND RUFINO RAILWAY.—Traffic for week ending April 2, $8,806; increase, $4,173. Aggregate from January 1, $63,922; decrease, $688.

ROHILKUND AND KUMAON RAILWAY.—Traffic for week ending March 5, Rs. 8,951; decrease, Rs. 5,512. Aggregate from January 1, Rs. 50,062; decrease, Rs. 9,166.

WEST FLANDERS RAILWAY.—Gross receipts for week ending April 3, £1,927; increase, £5. Total from January 1, £29,149; increase, £670.

PERUVIAN CORPORATION RAILWAYS.—Receipts for month of March were $259,350; increase, $15,875.

WESTERN OF SANTA FE RAILWAY.—Traffic receipts for week ending April 2, $50,710; increase, $28,940.

DELHI UMBALLA KALKA RAILWAY.—Receipts for week ending April 7, Rs. 30,700; increase Rs. 3,600. Aggregate from January 1, Rs, 4,84,300; increase. 1,46,600.

INDIAN AND CEYLON TEA COMPANIES.

Acres Planted.	Crop, 1897.	Paid up Capital.	Share.	Paid up.	Name.	Dividends. 1894.	1895.	1896.	Int. 1897.	Price.	Yield.	Reserve.	Balance Forward.	Working Capital.	Mortgages, Debs. or Pref. Capital not otherwise stated.
	lb.	£	£	£	INDIAN COMPANIES.							£	£	£	£
11,240	3,128,000	120,000	10	3	Amalgamated Estates	—	*	10	5	3½	8½	10,000	16,500	D52,950	—
		400,000	10	10	Do. Pref.	—	*	5	†5	10¼	4¾				
10,223	3,560,000	187,160	20	20	Assam	20	20	20	5	60	6⅔	55,000	1,730	D11,350	—
6,150	3,278,000	142,500	10	10	Assam Frontier	3	6	6	—	8¾	6¾	—	285	20,000	82,500
		142,500	10	10	Do. Pref.	6	6	6	3	11¼	5¼				
2,087	839,000	66,745	5	5	Attaree Khat	12	12	8	3	7¼	5½	3,790	4,820	7,770	—
1,633	583,000	78,170	10	10	Borelli	4	4	5	—	8	6¼	—	3,296	D270	6,500 Pref.
1,720	812,000	60,825	5	5	British Indian	6	5	5	—	4	6	—	2,920	12,300	16,500 Pref.
3,223	2,247,000	114,500	5	5	Brahmapootra	20	18	20	6	13	7¾	—	28,440	41,600	*
3,754	1,617,000	76,500	10	10	Cachar and Dooars	*	8	7	—	10¼	6¾	—	1,645	21,240	*
		76,500	10	10	Do. Pref.	*	6	6	3	12	5				
3,946	2,083,000	72,010	1	1	Chargola	8	7	10	2½	⅞	10¼	3,000	3,300	—	—
		81,000	1	1	Do. Pref.	7	7	7	3½	1⅜	5				
1,971	942,000	33,000	5	5	Chubwa	10	8	10	3½	6¼	8	10,000	2,043	D5,400	—
		33,000	5	5	Do. Pref.	7	7	7	3½	7	5				
32,250	11,500,000	120,000	10	3	Cons. Tea and Lands	—	—	10	5	3⅜	7½	65,000	14,240	D191,674	—
		1,000,000	10	10	Do. 1st Pref.	—	*	5	†5	11 1/16	4½				
		400,000	10	10	Do. 2nd Pref.	—	*	7	†7	11⅞	5¾				
2,230	617,000	135,420	20	20	Darjeeling	5½	5½	6	—	22½	5	5,552	1,565	1,700	—
2,114	445,000	60,000	10	10	Darjeeling Cons.	—	*	4/2	—	6	—	—	1,820	—	—
		60,000	10	10	Do. Pref.	—	*	5	2½	9¾	5¼				
6,660	3,518,000	150,000	10	10	Dooars	12½	12½	12½	2½	18½	6⅔	45,000	300	D32,000	—
		75,000	10	10	Do. Pref.	7	7	7	3½	16	4¾				
3,367	1,811,000	165,000	10	10	Doom Dooma	11¾	10	12½	5	21½	5¾	30,000	4,032	—	10,000
1,377	582,000	61,120	5	5	Eastern Assam	5	nil.	4	—	3	6¾	—	1,790	—	10,000
4,038	1,675,000	85,000	10	10	East India and Ceylon	*	nil.	7	—	8¾	7¾	—	1,710	—	—
		85,000	10	10	Do. Pref.	*	6	6	3	11¾	5¼				
7,500	3,363,000	219,000	10	10	Empire of India	—	*	6/10	2½	11¼	—	15,000	—	27,000	—
		219,000	10	10	Do. Pref.	—	*	5	2½	10¼	4¾				
1,180	540,000	94,060	10	10	Indian of Cachar	7	3½	3	—	4¾	6¾	6,070	—	7,120	—
3,050	824,000	83,500	5	5	Jhanzie	10	10	10	4	8½	6	14,500	2,070	2,700	—
7,980	3,680,000	250,000	10	10	Jokai	10	10	10	5	17¾	5½	45,000	990	D9,000	—
		100,000	10	10	Do. Pref.	*	6	6	3	15	4				
5,224	1,563,000	100,000	20	20	Jorehaut	20	20	20	—	58	6¾	36,220	2,955	3,000	—
1,547	504,000	65,660	10	8	Lebong	15	15	15	5	16½	7¾	9,000	2,150	8,650	—
5,082	1,709,000	100,000	10	10	Lungla	*	10	6	3	9	6¾	—	1,543	D21,000	—
		100,000	10	10	Do. Pref.	*	6	6	3	11¼	5¼				
2,684	885,000	95,970	10	10	Majuli	7	5	5	—	6¾	7½	—	2,606	560	—
1,375	380,000	91,840	1	1	Makum	—	—	2	—	1⅛	1½	—	—	1,200	25,000
2,990	770,000	100,000	1	1	Mosburd	—	—	*	—	1	—	—	—	—	—
		50,000	1	1	Do. Pref.	—	—	*	2½	1	5				
1,080	482,000	79,590	10	10	Scottish Assam	7	7	7	—	10¾	6½	6,500	800	9,590	—
4,150	1,456,000	100,000	10	10	Singlo	7	8	5	1	8¾	5¾	—	300	D3,200	—
		80,000	10	10	Do. Pref.	*	6½	6½	3½	13⅛	5				
	Crop, 1896.				CEYLON COMPANIES.										
7,970	1,743,824	250,000	100	100	Anglo-Ceylon, & Gen.	—	*	5½	—	65	8½	10,992	1,405	D72,844	166,580
1,836	685,741	50,000	10	10	Associated Tea	—	*	5	2½	7¼xd	6¾	—	164	2,478	—
		60,000	10	10	Do. Pref.	—	*	6	3	10¼xd.	5¾				
10,390	4,000,000§	167,380	10	10	Ceylon Tea Plantations	15	15	15	7	27	5½	84,500	1,516	D90,849	—
		81,080	10	10	Do. Pref.	7	7	7	†7	17½	4¾				
5,722	1,542,700§	55,260	5	3	Ceylon & Oriental Est.	5	8	7	—	2½	7¾	—	230	D2,047	71,000
		46,000	5	5	Do. Pref.	6	6	6	3	5	5¾				
2,157	801,629	111,330	5	5	Dimbula Valley	—	*	10	5	6¼	8¼	—	—	1,733	6,250
		62,607	5	5	Do. Pref.	—	*	6	3	6¾	4¾				
11,496	3,715,000	298,250	5	5	Eastern Prod. & Est.	3	5	6½	2½	6¾	5¼	20,000	11,740	D17,797	108,900
3,118	701,100	150,000	10	10	Lanka Plantations	4	5	5	†5	6½	6¾	—	495	D11,300	14,700 Pref.
2,193	1,050,000§	22,080	10	10	New Dimbula "A"	13	16	16	4	24	6	11,000	2,024	1,150	8,400
		55,710	10	10	Do. "B"	18	16	16	4	22	7½				
2,572	570,360	100,000	10	10	Oovah	6	8	6	2	8½	7	4,000	1,151	D1,255	—
2,030	535,675	200,000	10	10	Nuwara Eliya	—	*	6	3	11	5¾	—	—	—	30,000
1,720	720,200	41,000	10	10	Scottish Ceylon	15	15	15	5	21½	6¾	7,000	1,253	D3,070	9,000 Pref.
2,450	750,000§	39,000	10	6	Standard	12½	15	15	5	14	6¾	9,000	800	D14,012	4,000
		17,000	10	10	Do.	12½	15	15	5	22	6½				

Working-Capital Column.—In working-capita column, D stands for *debit*.

* Company formed this year. † Interim dividends are given as actual distribution made. ‡ *Total* div. § Crop 1897.

FOREIGN RAILWAYS.

Mileage. Total.	Increase on 1897.	Increase on 1896.	Name.	Gross Traffic for Week. Week ending	Amount.	In. or Dec. upon 1897.	In. or Dec. upon 1896.	Gross Traffic to Date. No. of Weeks.	Amount.	In. or Dec. upon 1897.	In. or Dec. upon 1896.
					£	£	£		£	£	£
319	—	—	Argentine Great Western	Mar. 25	8,295	+ 570	+ 1,692	38	214,249	— 7,453	+ 46,281
76½	—	—	Bahia and San Francisco	Mar. 5	4,759	+ 2,104	+ 2,594	8	28,428	+ 9,854	+ 10,193
234	48	84	Bahia Blanca and North West	Mar. 6	656	— 212	—	36	28,364	+ 372	—
74	—	—	Buenos Ayres and Ensenada	Apr. 3	3,173	— 446	— 908	13	45,462	— 8,069	— 12,257
426	—	—	Buenos Ayres and Pacific	Apr. 2	9,034	+ 364	+ 794	39	255,423	— 52,569	+ 6,037
924	1	3	Buenos Ayres and Rosario	Mar. 26	17,074	+ 5,353	+ 4,234	12	211,930	+ 53,901	+ 31,629
2,499	30	68	Buenos Ayres Great Southern	Apr. 3	34,208	+ 5,414	+ 3,667	39	1,167,254	+ 67,258	+ 172,396
602	107	177	Buenos Ayres Western	Apr. 3	14,137	+ 2,846	+ 511	39	473,217	— 77,207	— 80,827
845	55	77	Central Argentine	Mar. 26	23,791	+ 9,448	+ 5,290	12	268,605	+ 65,345	+ 8,406
297	—	—	Central Bahia	Jan. 31*	$133,559	— $3,944	+ $12,758	—	—	—	—
271	—	—	Central Uruguay of Monte Video	Apr. 2	6,140	+ 2,958	— 79	39	233,831	+ 0,626	— 15,780
228	—	—	Do. Eastern Extension	Apr. 2	1,657	+ 644	+ 326	39	49,482	+ 5,658	— 1,417
182	—	—	Do. Northern Extension	Apr. 2	714	+ 434	+ 450	39	24,773	— 544	— 6,593
180	—	—	Cordoba and Rosario	Mar. 27	1,990	+ 110	+ 130	39	62,965	— 16,660	— 2,325
128	—	—	Cordoba Central	Mar. 27	$20,000	— $3,500	— $5,710	12	$260,700	— $42,400	— $58,420
549	—	—	Do. Northern Extension	Mar. 27	$48,500	— $20,450	— $7,270	12	$532,790	— $204,590	— $116,930
137	—	—	Costa Rica	Mar. 12	7,898	— 97	+ 441	10	56,734	— 14,722	+ 1,146
60	—	—	East Argentine	Feb. 20	970	+ 293	+ 243	7	5,286	— 411	— 321
366	—	6	Entre Rios	Mar. 26	2,982	+ 1,945	+ 1,487	38	59,193	+ 15,087	+ 13,085
555	—	24	Inter Oceanic of Mexico	Apr. 2	$72,200	+ $17,890	+ $30,630	39	$2,247,090	+ $349,740	+ $596,220
23	—	—	La Guaira and Caracas	Feb. 25	1,779	— 779	— 1,138	8	15,641	— 5,235	— 3,525
321	—	—	Mexican	Apr. 2	$85,000	+ $7,000	—	13	$1,065,200	+ $99,850	—
1,846	—	—	Mexican Central	Mar. 31‡	$399,300	+ $8,726	+ $116,391	13	$3,260,218	+ $30,370	+ $796,033
1,217	—	—	Mexican National	Mar. 31‡	$160,222	— $5,858	+ $14,070	13	$1,426,690	+ $94,566	+ $264,566
228	—	—	Mexican Southern	Mar. 31‡	$24,132	— $3,271	+ $5,811	52	$673,570	+ $80,925	+ $173,449
205	—	—	Minas and Rio	Feb. 31*	$128,262	+ $16,417	—	8 mos.	$1,436,813	+ $203,482	—
94	—		N. W. Argentine	Mar. 26	1,001	— 327	— 436	12	10,540	— 7,144	— 4,642
242	3	—	Nitrate	Mar. 31†	16,187	— 1,604	— 4,405	11	88,690	— 328	— 40,320
300	—	—	Ottoman	Mar. 26	4,651	— 764	+ 372	12	60,464	— 15,127	+ 6,164
77½	—	—	Recife and San Francisco	Feb. 5	5,675	+ 2,275	— 1,047	6	32,722	+ 624	— 6,002
86½	—	—	San Paulo	Feb. 27†	27,481	— 7,056	—	8	88,485	— 16,073	—
186	—	—	Santa Fe and Cordova	Mar. 26	4,484	+ 2,890	+ 999	39	60,526	— 10,649	— 2,106
110	—	—	Western of Havana	Apr. 2	1,930	+ 28	+ 1,370	39	69,790	+ 5,649	+ 4,615

* For month ended. † For fortnight ended. ‡ For ten days ended.

INDIAN RAILWAYS.

Mileage. Total.	Increase on 1897.	Increase on 1896.	Name.	Gross Traffic for Week. Week ending	Amount.	In. or Dec. on 1897.	In. or Dec. on 1896	Gross Traffic to Date. No. of Weeks.	Amount.	In. or Dec. on 1897.	In. or Dec. on 1896.
862	—	—	Bengal Nagpur	Mar. 26	Rs.1.60.000	+Rs.35.962	—	12	Rs.17.60.000	—Rs.77.668	—
827	8	63	Bengal and North-Western	Mar. 5	Rs.1.36.360	+Rs.28.545	+Rs.1.945	9	Rs.12.18.350	+Rs.1.64.303	+Rs.32.475
461	—	—	Bombay and Baroda	Mar. 26	£30,525	+£4,966	—	12	£279,469	—£33,506	—
1,885	2	13	East Indian	Apr. 2	Rs.13.23.000	+Rs.38.000	+R.1.93.000	13	Rs.1.64.03.000	+Rs.3.03.000	+R.10.57.000
2,491	—	—	Great Indian Penin.	Mar. 26	£78,742	+£16,555	—£4,572	12	£787,105	+£66,376	—£198,701
336	—	—	Indian Midland	Mar. 26	Rs.1.27.600	+Rs.17.635	+Rs.19.461	12	Rs.16.23.359	+Rs.2.61.975	+Rs.88.74.990
840	—	—	Madras	Mar. 26	£19,892	—£2,383	+£184	12	£230,620	—£14,431	—£9,650
1,043	—	—	South Indian	Feb. 12	Rs.1.52.756	—Rs.26.013	—Rs.7.618	6	Rs.9.03.806	—Rs.66.077	—Rs.1.86.079

UNITED STATES AND CANADIAN RAILWAYS.

Mileage Total.	Increase on 1897.	Increase on 1896.	Name.	Gross Traffic for Week. Period Ending.	Amount.	In. or Dec. on 1897.	Gross Traffic to Date. No. of Weeks.	Amount.	In. or Dec. on 1897.
					dols.	dols.		dols.	dols.
937	—	—	Baltimore & Ohio S. Western	Mar. 31‡	173,000	—1,000	38	5,108,376	+522,785
6,568	90	156	Canadian Pacific	Mar. 31‡	641,000	+105,000	12	5,217,000	+1,103,000
922	—	—	Chicago Great Western	Mar. 31‡	157,275	+8,357	38	4,066,085	+534,020
6,169	—	469	Chicago, Mil., & St. Paul	Mar. 31‡	947,300	+138,300	12	7,672,101	+1,123,300
1,685	—	—	Denver & Rio Grande	Mar. 31‡	205,000	+30,200	38	6,124,900	+1,026,700
3,512	—	—	Grand Trunk, Main Line	Mar. 31‡	£108,729	+£9,777	12	£920,125	+£95,980
335	—	—	Do. Chic. & Grand Trunk	Mar. 31‡	£24,702	+£7,784	12	£194,134	+£44,879
189	—	—	Do. Det., G. H. & Mil.	Mar. 31‡	£5,071	—£619	12	£44,593	—£2,243
2,938	—	—	Louisville & Nashville	Mar. 31‡	577,000	+33,000	12	5,244,175	+965,620
2,197	137	137	Miss., K., & Texas	Mar. 31‡	261,000	+1,000	38	9,735,495	+563,149
477	—	—	N. Y., Ontario, & W.	Mar. 31‡	110,102	+3,138	38	2,938,197	+104,374
1,570	—	—	Norfolk & Western	Mar. 31‡	200,000	+2,000	38	8,090,000	+870,000
3,499	336	—	Northern Pacific	Mar. 21	390,000	+105,000	11	4,070,000	+1,216,000
1,223	—	—	St. Louis S. Western	Mar. 21	89,000	+25,000	11	1,217,700	+236,100
4,654	—	—	Southern	Mar. 31‡	548,000	—14,000	38	3,881,812	+1,257,448
1,979	—	—	Wabash	Mar. 31‡	317,000	+71,000	12	3,092,406	+629,000

‡ For ten days ended.

MONTHLY STATEMENTS.

Mileage. Total.	Increase on 1896.	Increase on 1895.	Name.	Net Earnings for Month. Month.	Amount.	In. or Dec. on 1897.	In. or Dec. on 1896.	Net Earnings to Date. No. of Months.	Amount.	In. or Dec. on 1897.	In. or Dec. on 1896.
					dols	dols.	dols.		dols.	dols.	dols.
6,935	44	444	Atchison	February	746,000	+191,000	+129,318	2	1,240,434	+313,670	—139,884
6,547	103	106	Canadian Pacific	February	424,000	+39,000	+19,268	2	940,000	+182,000	+110,318
6,169	—	469	Chicago, Mil., & St. Paul	January	757,000	+52,000	—30,713	—	—	—	—
1,665	—	—	Denver & Rio Grande	February	219,000	+52,500	+22,731	8	2,244,907	+367,739	—8,088
1,970	—	—	Erie	January	371,000	+33,000	—107,852	—	—	—	—
3,512	—	—	Grand Trunk, Main Line	February	£56,453	+£13,757	+£25,860	2	£143,853	+£48,041	+64,910
335	—	—	Do. Chic. & Grand Trunk	February	£8,210	+£5,197	+5,595	2	£21,310	+£14,130	+15,582
189	—	—	Do. Det. G. H. & Mil.	February	£528	—£1,369	—207	2	£2,328	—£677	+1,459
3,127	—	239	Illinois Central*	February	2,177,767	+413,527	+422,489	2	4,481,665	+819,013	+805,758
2,396	—	—	New York Central*	February	3,429,000	+128,000	+222,359	2	6,934,000	+492,397	249,393
477	—	—	New York Ontario, & W.	February	57,800	—3,800	+19,504	9	835,700	+33,400	+75,462
1,570	—	—	Norfolk & Western	February	242,000	+69,000	+43,259	2	525,000	+83,247	+91,585
3,407	—	—	Pennsylvania	January	1,359,101	+65,700	+236,000	2	2,511,898	92,400	+345,000
1,055	—	—	Phil. & Reading	February	584,382	—44,678	—	8	6,865,202	+446,422	—

* Statements of gross traffic.

Prices Quoted on the London Stock Exchange.

Throughout the INVESTORS' REVIEW middle prices alone are quoted, the object being to give the public the approximate current quotations of every security of any consequence in existence. On the markets the buying and selling prices are both given, and are often wide apart where stocks are seldom dealt in. Other particulars will be found in the INVESTMENT INDEX published quarterly—January, April, July, and October—in connection with this REVIEW, price 2s., by post 2s. 2d. Where dividends are paid only once a year, an *italic* type is used to distinguish them. The London Stock Exchange Official List is quoted in the REVIEW almost entire, only very insignificant issues, or bonds falling due within the next two or three years, being omitted. But the list is subdivided into the leading, or active, stocks, and those less frequently dealt in. The former will be found under the head of "Stock Markets," and with more details than it is possible to give for the bulk of securities. By retaining the file of the INVESTORS' REVIEW any subscriber can follow for himself the movements of securities from week to week, and the INVESTMENT INDEX will from time to time help to fill up deficiencies in the information.

Tea Companies and Mines and Mining Finance Stocks are placed in special lists.

Among the abbreviations used are the following:—S.F. Snk.Fd. *sinking fund*; Certs., *certificates*; Debs. or Dbs., *debentures*; Db. or D.Stk., *debenture stock*; Pf., Prf., or Pref., *preference*; Prefd. or Pfd., *preferred*; Dfd., *deferred*; L. or Ltd., *limited*; Sh., *share*; Ans., *annuities*; Cu. or Cm., *cumulative*; Gu or Guar., *guaranteed*; Bds., *bonds*; S., Sr., or Ser., *series*; In., Ins., Insc., *inscribed*; Dr., Drgs., Drwgs., *drawings*; Stg., Strlg., *sterling*; Lia., *liable to*; Sp., Surp., *surplus*; Per., Perp., *perpetual*; Ln. *lien*; Lo. *loan*.

The dates following the names of securities are the years of issue or of redemption. Where shares are not fully paid up, their nominal amount is given with the name so that investors may know the liability upon them.

BRITISH FUNDS, &c.

Rate.	Name.	Price.
2¾	2¾ p.c.'s (Childers') Red.. 1905	105½
3	Local Loans Stk. 1912	110½
3	Metro. Police Deb. Stk. 1920	105½
—	Red Sea Ind. Tel. Ann. 1908	8½
4	Canada Gv. "Intcl. Rly." 1903	104
4	Do. do. .. 1908	111
4	Do. Bonds 1910	112
4	Do. Bonds 1913	117½
3	Egyptian Gov. Gar.	106½
3	Mauritius Ins. Stk. 1940	114
4	Turkish Guar. 1855	109
a 1½	Bank of Ireland Stk.	390
3½	India Rupee Paper	62½
3½	Do. 1854-5	62
3	Do. 1896-7 1916	55
3½	Isle of Man Deb.	104
3	Do. Deb. Stk... 1919-29	103

CORPORATION AND COUNTY STOCKS.

FREE OF STAMP DUTY.

Rate.	Name.	Price.
3½	Metropolitan Con. 1929	116½
3	Do. 1941	112
2½	Do. 1920-49	100
2½	L.C.C. Con. Stock 1920	99
3½	Comm. of Sewers, Scp, S.F. 1905	105
3½	Corp. of Lond. Bds...1897-1902	100½
3	Do. 1897-1912	101
3½	Do, Debs. Scp. ...... S.F. 1916	105
2½	Do., Deb. Stk. Scrip .. 1927-57	99
3	Barnsley 1916-46	105
3	Barry 1914-46	101
3	Bath 1909-34	102
3	Batley 1914-44	101½
3½	Birmingham 1945	121
3	Do. 1947	111
2½	Do. 1926	98
3	Blackburn 1930	106½
3	Bournemouth 1913-33	103
3½	Bradford 1945	116½
3	Do. Deb. Stock .. 1954	108
3	Brighouse.............. 1916-46	100
3½	Brighton 1946	117
2½	Do. 1957	97
3	Burton-on-Trent........ 1913-43	102½
3	Cambridge 1913-43	103
3½	Cardiff 1935	116½
3	Do. 1914-54	103
3	Cheltenham............ 1971	108
3	Chichester 1916-46	101
3½	Croydon	134
3	Do. 1940	107½
3	Derby 1920-50	107
3	Devon C.C............... 1917-33	104½
3½	Dewsbury 1930	109
3	Do. 1930	103
3	Dorset County 1922-32	105
3	Douglas (I. of Man) 1926	101
3	Dover 1913-43	101
3½	Dublin 1944	113½
3	Eastbourne 1920-40	104
3	Edinburgh 1924	108
2½	Do. 1927	98
2½	Exeter 1917-57	96
3	Glamorgan County 1914-34	104
3½	Glasgow 1914	110½
3	Do. 1921	106½
2½	Do. 1925-40	99
3	Gloster 1915-55	101
3	Grimsby 1913-43	103
3	Hampshire County 1914-34	105½
3	Hanley 1913-43	105
3	Harrogate 1914-34	103
3	Hastings 1915-54	103½
2½	Hertfordshire C.C. 1916-36	98
3	Heston & Isleworth U.D.C. 1915-35	101
3	Huddersfield 1934	107
3½	Hull (1st iss.)	131½
3	Inverness.............. 1914-44	101
3	Ipswich 1952	108½
3	Lancaster.............. 1919-55	103
2½	Leeds 1927	98
3½	Leicester 1934	115½
3	Lincoln.................. 1919	103
3½	Liverpool..............	133½

Corporation, &c. (*continued*):—

Rate.	Name.	Price.
3	Manchester 1941	108½
3	Mansfield.............. 1915-45	100
3½	Middlesbro'............ 1909	105½
3½	Do. 1911-13	105
3	Do. 1915	104
3	Middlesex C.C........ 1915-35	106
3½	Newcastle 1936	118½
3½	Do. Irred.	129½
2¾	Do. 1915-36	100
3	Newcastle-under-Lyme.. 1909-44	101
3	Newport (Mon.) 1915-55	101½
3	Norwich 1952	111½
3	Nottingham	114
3	Oxford 1951	109½
3	Penzance 1916-46	100½
3	Plymouth 1942	110
3	Pontypridd U.D.C. 1916-46	98
3	Poole.................. 1915-45	101
3½	Portsmouth........1916 24 & 27	112
3	Do. 1913-33	106½
3	Ramsey 1920-40	100
3	Ramsgate.............. 1915-55	102
3½	Reading	130½
3	Do. 1962	109
3½	Rhyl U.D.C. 1953	110
3	Richmond (Surrey) 1942	104½
3	River Wear Debt Certs.	100
3	St. Helen's 1915-55	182
3	Scarbro' 1915-50	102
2½	Sheffield 1925-57	96
3	Shipley U.D.C.......... 1915-35	100
3	Somerset Co. 1923-33	106
3	South Shields.......... 1915-45	102
2½	Southampton 1915-45	102
3	Southend-on-Sea 1916-46	102
3	Staffs C.C. 1915-35	102
3	Stockport.............. 1914-54	103
3	Stockton 1932	104
3	Do. 1915-35	103
3	Surrey Co. 1922-32	105½
3½	Swansea	130
3	Do. 1955	106
3	Taunton 1918-3-9-43	101
3	Tees Conserv. Deb. Stk. 1947	100
3	Thames Conserv. "A" Deb. Stk............ 1954	103½
3	Do. "B" Deb. Stk. 1954	103½
3	Torquay 1913-43	101½
3	Tunbridge Wells 1931	102
3	Tynemouth 1913	101
3	Wakefield.............. 1929	101
3	Walsall................ 1932	108
3	West Bromwich........ 1930	106½
3½	West Ham 1929	110
3	Do. 1945	105
3	West Sussex C.C. 1915-35	106
3	Weston-s.-Mare Lcl.Bd. 1914-44	101½
3	Weymouth&Melc. Regis 1918	101
3	Widnes................ 1915-55	101
3	Wigan 1921	106
3	Windsor 1918-55	102
3½	Wisbech 1947	113½
3½	Wolverhampton 1932	118
3	Do. 1924-54	107
3	York 1916-41	106½

SUBJECT TO STAMP DUTY.

Rate.	Name.	Price.
3½	Belfast City & Dis. Watr. 1938	114
3	Do. Red Stk. 1953-6	106
3½	Belfast 1924	103
4	Blackburn Con. Deb. Irred.	141½
3½	Do. do. Irred............	130
3½	Bristol	130½
3½	Burnley.................. 1933	114
2½	Chesterfield Gas & Wtr. 1916-46	98
3½	Douglas Town 1921	105
3	Dover Harb. 1st Deb... 1956	104½
3½	Hull (2nd iss.)	128½
4	Leeds Deb.............. 1927	124
3½	Do.	115½
3	Do. 1927	106
3	Leicester 1919-44	105
4	Manchester..................	148
3	Do. 1928	104½
4½	Middlesboro' Mrts. 1908	111
3½	Newark on-Trent .. 1901-41	96
3½	Sheffield 1898-1916	105½
3½	Do. 1925-36	114
3	Do. 1925	104½
3½	Southampton .... S.F.	106
4½	Stockton Morts.......... 1908	112
3½	Worcester.............. 1950	109

COLONIAL AND PROVINCIAL GOVERNMENT SECURITIES.

Rate.	Name.	Price.
6	British Columbia........ 1907	119½
4½	Do. Debs.. 1917	111½
3	British Guiana Imgtn. Bds.	99½
5	Canada, "Intercol. Rail," 1903	109
4	Do. (Bonds) 1904-5-6-8	105
4	Do. Reduced 1910	107½
3½	Do. Bnds. 1909-34	104
4	Do. Loan 1910-35	107½
3	Do. Loan 1938	101
6	Cape of G. Hope 1900	—
5	Do. 1900	—
4½	Do. red. by an. draw.	110
4½	Do. 1879	110
4	Do. 1881	108
4	Do. 1917-23	116
4½	Ceylon	110
4	Do.	106½
4½	Fiji Gov. Deb. Sink. Fd.	101½
4	Jamaica Sink. Fd. 1923	103
5	Manitoba Debs.......... 1910	113
5	Do. Ster. Bds. 1888	122
4	Do. Ster. Debs.	106
4	Mauritius, Cons. Debs. 1880...	103½
4½	Natal, Sink. Fd. 1919	118
4	Do. do. 1926	115
3½	Newfoundland Stg. Bds. 1941	97
3½	Do. do. .. 1947	97
3	Do. do.	86½
5	New South Wales 1897-1902	104½
4	Do. 1903-5-8-9-12	105
5	New Zealand 1914	118
5	Do. Cnsls. 1 p.c. per an. Sink. Fd.	104
3½	Nova Scotia Debs.	104
5	Quebec Prov. 1904-6	110
4½	Do. (drgs.)	104
5	Do. Strlg. Bds. 1912	115
4	Do. Strlg. Bds. 1928	110
4	Do. Strlg. Bds. 1934	108
4	Queensland 1913-15	106
4½	St. Lucia Debs..................	102½
6	South Australia 1897-1900	103½
6	Do. 1901-1918	119
5	Do. 1911-1920	116
4	Do. 1899-1916	105
4	Do. 1929	108½
4	Do. 1916	106½
4	Do. 1917-18-24	110
6	Tasmania 1897-1901	104
4	Do. 1908-11, 1913-14-20	107½
5	Trinidad Debs., an. drw. 1 p c...	106
4	Victoria 1899-1901	101½
4½	Do. 1904	105
4	Do. Rail. Loan 1907	104
4	Do. Loans 1908-13	105
4½	West. Austr. 1 p.c. ac. Sink. Fd.	107
4	Do. do.	106

REGISTERED AND INSCRIBED STOCKS.

No stamp duty except for Canada 4 p.c. Reduced (½ per cent.).

Rate.	Name.	Price.
4	Antigua Insc. Stk. Red. 1919-44	109
3½	Barbados Insc. Stk. 1925-42	108
3	British Colum. Insc. Stk. 1941	101½
4	British Guiana Insc..... 1935	118½
4	Canada Stk. Regd. ..1904-5-6-8	107
4	Do. 4 p.c. (late 5 p.c.) Regd. 1910	107½
3½	Do. 3½ p.c. Stock Regd. 1909-34	104
4	Do. Ln. for 4 milln. stg. 1910-35	107½
3	Do. Stk. Regd. 1938	101
2½	Do. Insc................ 1947	90
4	Cape G. Hope Regd. .. 1917-23	116
4	Do. (Ln. of '83) Insc. .. 1923	117
4	Do. Cons. Stk. Insc..... 1916-36	110
3½	Do. Consol. Insc. Stock 1929-49	109
4	Ceylon Insc. Stock 1934	118½
3	Do. 1940	102
4	Grenada Insc. Stock.... 1917-42	112
3½	Hong Kong Insc. Stock 1918-43	103½
4	Jamaica Insc. Stock.... 1934	121
—	Do. 1922-44	99
4	Mauritius Inscribed 1937	118½
4	Natal Consd. Stk. Insc. 1927	115
4	Do. 1937	119
3½	Do. Inscribed Stock.. 1914-39	106
4	Newfoundland Inscribed 1913-38	107
4	Do. 1935	113
4	Do. Consd. Stk. Ins. 1936	113
4	N. S Wales Stock Insc. 1933	117
3½	Do. 1924	105
3½	Do. 1918	104
3	D 1935	97

Colonial, &c. (*continued*):—

Rate.	Name.	Price.
4	N. Zealnd. Con. Stk. Ins. 1929	112
3½	Do 1940	107
3	Do. Inscribed.... 1945	99
3	Quebec (Prov.) Ins. Stk. 1937	93½
4	Queensland Stock Insc. 1915-24	109½
3½	Do. 1921-4-30	104
3½	Do. 1945	108
3	Do. 1922-47	98
4	St. Lucia Insc. Stock .. 1919-44	112
4	S. Austrln. (1882-7) Reg. 1916-36	108½
3½	Do. In. Stk. Reg. 1939	108
3	Do. 1916-26	99
3/	Do. 1916	99
3½	Tasmanian Insc. Stock.. 1920-40	106
4	Do. 1920-40	116
4	Trinidad Insc. Stock.... 1917-42	110
3	Do. 1922-44	98½
4	Victoria Rly. Loan '81, Inscribed Stock 1907	104
4	Victoria Insc. Stock 1908-13-19	107
4	Victoria (1883) Ins. Stk. 1920	110
3½	Do. Inscribed Stock 1921-3-6	103
4	Do. do. 1911-26	108
4	W. Austral. Insc. Stock 1934	116½
4	Do. 1911-31	109
3½	Do. 1915-35	104
3	Do. 1915-35	96½
3	Do. 1916-30	97

FOREIGN STOCKS, BONDS, &c.

COUPONS PAYABLE IN LONDON.

Last Div.	Name.	Price.
36/	Argentine Ry. Loan 6 p.c. 1881	87½
15/	Do. 5 p.c. 1884	67
30/	Do. N. Cent. Ry. Ext. 5 p.c. 1887-8-9	66
30/	Do. 5 p.c. Trsy. Convs. 1887	66
5/4½	Do. 4½ p.c. Interl. Gld.. 1888	65
27/	Do. 4½ p.c. Stlg. Extrl. 1888	65
10/6	Do. 3½ p.c. External .. 1889	43
4	Do. 4 p.c. Ry. Guar. Res....	57½
4½	Brazilian 1883	50
4½	Do. Gold.......... 1879	63
4½	Do. 1888	50
36/	Buenos Ayres 1824	82½
6	Do. 1882-3-6	47
6	Bulgarian 1888	93
6	Do. Mort. Bonds 1892	93
4½	Chilian 1885	73
4½	Do. 1886	75
4½	Do. 1887	73
4½	Do. 1889	81½
5	Do. 1892	84
4½	Do. 1893	73
4½	Do. 1895	73
5	Do. 1896	83
7	Chinese Silver 1894	101
6	Do. Gold 1895	105
6	Do. Apl. '95 by dwgs. 1901-15	108½
5	Do. Red. dwgs. in 36 yr. 1896	98½
5	Do. Do. Regis. 1896	99
1½	Colmbn. 1½ to 3 p.c. Ext. Bds. 1896	17½
6	Cordova, Prov. 1886	26
—	Do. Eng. Ass. Certs.	25
—	Do. 6 p.c. 1887-8	26
—	Do. Eng. Ass. Certs.	25
3	Costa Rica "A"	30
2½	Do. "B"	25
3	Danish Gold 1914	98
10/	Ecuador N. Ext. Bds. 4½ p.c. ascn. to 5 p.c....................	22
3½	Egypt'n Ins. Stk. lia. Sep. Dty. 1890	100
4	Do. State Domain 1878	104½
4	Do. D. Sanieh, Red. .. 1905	104½
6	Entre Rios................ 1886-8	35
6	Do. Fndg. Ln. Bds. 1894-1921	35
6	Do. do. Parana City......	27½
15/	Greek 1881	40
13/	Do. 1884	40
12/	Do. Rentes..................	33
15/	Do. (Piræus-Larissa Ry.)	38
3/6	Do. Fundg. Loan 1893	44½
4	Guatemala Extl. Debt..........	30
6	Hawaiian	102½
4	Hungarian Gold Rentes........	101½
3	Do. 1895	91½
6	Italian Irriga. Guar.	111½
5	Do. Maremmana	94½
5	Japan 5 p.c.	100½
5	Mexican (Nat. R. Tehuantp c.)..	96½
6	Do. Extrl. 1893	[illegible]

Foreign Stocks, &c. (*continued*):—

Last Div.	Name.	Price
6	Mexican Extrl. 1893	96½
5	Do. Intrnl Cons. Slvr.	35
5	Do. Intern. Rd. Bds. 2d. Ser.	36
4	Nicaragua 1886	50
3½	Norwegian, red. 1937, or earlier	98
3	Do. do. 1965, do.	98
3½	Do. 3½ p.c. Bnds.	104
1	Paraguay 1p.c. ris. 3p.c. 1886-96	16
5	Russian, 1822, £ Strlg.	149
3	Do. 1859	96
4	Do. (Nicolas Ry.) 1867-9	103
3	Do. Transcauc. Ry. 1882	94
4	Do. Con. R. R. Bd. Ser. I., 1889	102½
4	Do. Do. II., 1889	102½
4	Do. Do. III., 1891	102
3½	Do. Bonds	100½
4	Do. Ln. (Dvinsk and Vitbsk)	101
6	Salvador 1889	64
—	S Domingo 4s. Unified 1980	63½
6	San Luis Potosi Stg. 1889	89
5	San Paulo (Brzl.), Stg. 1888	90
6	Santa Fé 1883-4	35
—	Do. Eng. Ass. Certs. Dep.	34
5	Do. 1888	45
—	Do. Eng. Ass. Certs. Dpsit.	44
5	Do. (W. Cnt. Col. Rly.) Mrt.	25
5	Do. & Reconq. Rly. Mort.	25
5	Spanish Quicksilvr Mort. 1870	103
3½	Swedish 1880	102
3	Do. 1888	98
53	Do. Conversion Loan 1894	99
45	Trans. Gov. Loan Red. 1903-42	103
50/	Tucuman (Prov.) 1888	69
	Turkish, Secd. on Egypt. Trib.	103½
3½	Turkish, Egpt. Trib., Ott. Bd., '94	99¼
4	Do. Priority 1890	90½
1	Do. Convted Series, "A"	65½
5	Do. Customs Ln. 1886	95½
5	Uruguay Bonds 1896	55
3	Venzuela New Con. Debt 1881	35

COUPONS PAYABLE ABROAD.

Last Div.	Name.	Price
7	Argent. Nat. Cedla. Sries, "B"	35
5	Austrian Ster. Rnts., ex 10fl., 1870	85
5	Do. do. do.	85
5	Do. Paper do. 1870	84
5	Do. do. do.	86
4	Do. Gld Rentes 1876	102
2½	Belgian exchange 25 fr.	92
3	Do. do.	101
3½	Danish Int., 1887, Rd. 1896	98½
3½	Do. '87, Red. by pur. or draw. fr. Dec., 1900	99
2½	Dutch Certs. ex 12 gldrs.	87
3	Do. Bonds	98
3	Do. Insc. Stk.	97
3½	French Rentes	106½
3	Do. 1878, '81-4, Red.	102
3	German Imp. Ln. 1891	95
3	Do. do. 1892-3	95
3	Do. do. 1890-4	96
5	Japan Cons. Ln., '92, 3, & 5, Red.	46
36/9	Prussian Consols	102
3	" Cons. Stg. Ln. 1891	96
4	Rumanian Bds. 1890	—
4	Do. do. 1891	—
4	Utd. States, 1877, Red. 1907	114
4	Do. 1895, 30 yrs.	128
3½	Do. Maschsetts Gl. 1935	113½
3½	Do. Gold Bonds 1923	110½
2	Virginia Cpn. Bds., 3 p.c. from July, 1901	70

BRITISH RAILWAYS.

ORD. SHARES AND STOCKS.

Last Div.	Name.	Price.
10	Barry, Ord.	277½
4	Do. Prefd.	126
6	Do. Defd.	150½
5	Caledonian, Ord.	155
3	Do. Prefd.	88½
—	Do. Defd. Ord., No. 1	4½
	Cambrian, Ord.	6½
—	Do. Coast Cons.	6½
32/	Cardiff Ry. Pref. Ord.	117
3/	Central Lond. £10 Ord. Sh.	10½
3/9½	Do. do. £6 paid	6½
3½d.	Do. Pref. Half-Shares	1½
2/6	Do. Def. do.	4½
1½	City and S. London	68
—	East London, Cons.	6½
2	Furness	63½
2½	Glasgow and S. West. Pfd.	80
2½	Do. do. Dfd.	63
3	Great Central, Ord. 1894	40
32/0	Do. London Exten.	73
3½	Great N. of Scotland	122
4	Great Northern, Prefd.	119
—	Do. Consolidated "A"	50
—	Do. do. "B"	191½
2	Highland	82½
4	Isle of Wight, Prefd.	120½
3	Do. Defd.	83½
½	Lancs. Derbys. and E. Cst.	4
8½	L. Brighton and S. C. Ord.	186
27/11½	Do. New all pd.	186
6	Do. Prefd. Ord.	197
11/	Do. Contgt. Rights Certs.	16½
5½	Lond. and S. Western Ord.	222½
4	Do. Preferred	132
6½	Lond., Tilb., and Southend	133½
—	Mersey, £20 shares	
—	Metropolitan, New Ord.	129
2½	Do. Surplus Lands	95
4	North Cornwall, 4 p.c. Pref.	104½
22/6	Do. Deferred	22½
7½	North London	224½
4½	North Staffordshire	131

British Railways (*continued*):—

Last Div.	Name.	Price.
3/3	Plymouth, Devenport, and S. W. Junc. £10	8½
3/	Port Talbot £10 Shares	9
9d.	Rhondda Swns. B. £10 Sh.	5
10	Rhymney, Cons.	267½
4	Do. Prefd.	123
6½	Do. Defd.	147½
1½	Scarboro', Bridlington Junc.	47½
6½	South Eastern, Ord.	150
6	Do. Pref.	193
3½	Taff Vale	80
25/	Vale of Glamorgan	129½
3	Waterloo & City	136½

LEASED AT FIXED RENTALS.

Last Div.	Name.	Price.
4	Birkenhead	146
5.19.0	East Lincnshire	207½
5½	Hamsmith. & City Ord.	192½
4½	Lond. and Blackwll.	162½
4½	Do. £10 4½ p. c. Pref.	163½
56/6	Lond. & Green. Ord.	101
5	Do. 5 p. c. Pref.	178½
5	Nor. and Eastn. £50 Ord.	89
6	Do.	205
3½	N. Cornwall 3½ p. c. Stk.	125
4 9/16	Nott. & Granthm. R. & C.	144½
3½	Portptk. & Wigtn. Guar. Stk.	123½
9	Vict. Stn. & Pimlico Ord.	317½
4½	Do. 4½ p. c. Pref.	162½
4/	West Lond. £20 Ord. Shs.	14
4 7/8	Weymouth & Portld.	160½

DEBENTURE STOCKS.

Last Div.	Name.	Price.
4	Alexandra Dks. & Ry.	132½
3	Barry, Cons.	108
4	Brecon & Mrthyr, New A	127½
4	Do. New B	105
4	Caledonian	150½
4	Cambrian "A"	132½
4	Do. "B"	130½
4	Do. "C"	126½
4	Do. "D"	107½
3	Cardiff Rly.	102½
4	City and S. Lond.	139
3½	Cleator & Working Junc.	118½
3	Devon & Som. "A"	103½
16/3	Do. "B" 4 p. c.	36
—	Do. "C" 4 p. c.	10
4	E. Lond. 2nd Ch. 4 p. c. A	137
6/	Do. 2nd B	67½
—	Do. 3rd Ch. 4 p. c.	18½
—	Do. 4th do.	9½
3½	Do. 1st (3½ p. c.)	128½
2½	Do. 2½ p.c. (Whitech. Exn)	88
4	Forth Bridge	143½
4	Furness	143
4	Glasgow and S. Western	150
5	Gt. Central	—
4½	Do.	155½
4	Gt. Eastern	147
4	Gt. N. of Scotland	146½
3	Gt. Northern	113
4	Gt. Western	150½
4½	Do.	160½
4½	Do.	167½
5	Do.	186½
2½	Do.	100
4	Highland	143½
3	Hull and Barnsley	105½
3	Do. 2nd (3-4 p. c.)	123
4	Isle of Wight	144½
3	Do. Cent. "A"	92½
4½	Do. "B"	115½
4	Do. "C"	82½
3	Lancs. & Yorkshire	114
4	Lancs. Derbys. & E. Cst.	123½
4	Lpool St. Hlen's & S. Lancs.	126
4½	Ldn. and Blackwall	158
4	Ldn. and Greenwich	148½
4	Lond., Brighton, &c.	149
4½	Do.	166½
4½	Lond., Chath., &c., Arb.	156½
4½	Do. "B"	155½
4	Do.	138½
4	Do. 1883	138½
3	Do.	107
3	Lond. & N. Western	116
3	Lond. & S. Westn. "A"	114½
3	Do. Consld.	114½
4	Lond., Til., & Southend	147½
—	Mersey, 5 p. c. (Act, 1866)	65
4	Metropolitan	147½
4½	Do.	164½
3½	Do.	1[illegible]
6	Met. District	306½
4	Do.	139
2½	Midland	96
4½	Mid-Wales "A"	137½
4	Neath & Brecon 1st	129
4	Do. "A 1"	118½
3	North British	110
3	Do. 1897	108½
3½	N. Cornwall, Launcestn., &c	106½

Debenture Stocks (*continued*):—

Last Div.	Name.	Price.
3	North Eastern	114
4½	North London	167
3	N. Staffordshire	111
4	Plym. Devpt. & S. W. Jn.	141½
4	Rhondda and Swan. Bay	130½
4	Rhymney	146½
4	South-Eastern	147½
5	Do.	184½
3½	Do.	127½
3	Do.	113½
3	Taff Vale	109½
4	Tottenham & For. Gate	146
3	Vale of Glamorgan	105½
3	West Highld. (Gtd. by N. B.)	108
4	Wrexham, Mold, &c. "A"	115½
4	Do. "B"	102½
4	Do. "C"	97½

GUARANTEED SHARES AND STOCKS.

Last Div.	Name.	Price.
4	Caledonian	148½
4	Do.	145
4	Forth Bridge	142
4	Furness 1881	137½
4	Glasgow & S. Western	143
4	Do. St. Enoch. Rent	143
6	Gt. Central	199½
4½	Do. 1st Pref.	152½
3½	Do. Pref.	104½
5	Do. Irred. S Y. Rent	161½
4½	Do. do.	139½
4	Gt. Eastern, Rent	144½
5	Do. Metropolitan	180
4	Do.	144½
4	Gt. N. of Scotland	138½
4	Gt. Northern	146½
5	Gt. Western, Rent	182½
5	Do. Cons.	181½
4	Lancs. & Yorkshire	146½
5	L., Brighton & S. C.	180½
3½	L., Chat. & D. (Shrtlds.)	110½
4	L. & North Western	148
4	L. & South Western 1881	147½
4½	Met. District, Ealing Rent	151
4½	Do. Fulham Rent	152
4	Do. Midland Rent	143½
4	Do. Mid. & Dist. Guar.	128½
2½	Midland, Cons. Perp.	93
3	Mid. & G. N. Jt., "A" Rnt.	108½
3	N. British, Lien	106½
4	Do. Cons. Pref. No. 1	140½
3	N. Cornwall, Wadebrge. Gu.	107
4	N. Eastern	146½
5	N. Staff. Trent & M. £10 Shs.	36
3½	Nott. Suburban Ord.	123½
20/6	S. E. Perp. Ann.	36
4½	Do. 4½ p.c.	163½
3½	S. Yorks. Junc. Ord.	118½
4½	W. Cornwall (G. W., Br., Ex., & S. Dev. Joint Rent	152½
3	W. Highl. Ord. Stk. (Gua., N.B.)	105½

PREFERENCE SHARES AND STOCKS.

DIVIDENDS CONTINGENT ON PROFIT OF YEAR.

Last Div.	Name	Price.
4½	Alexandra Dks. & Ry. "A"	125½
5	Barry (First)	169½
4	Do. Consolidated	138½
4	Caledonian Cons., No. 1	144½
4	Do. do. No. 2	143½
5	Do. do. 1878	177½
4	Do. Pref. 1884	142
4	Do. do. 1887 (Conv.)	152½
—	Cambrian, No. 1 4 p.c. Pref.	72½
—	Do. No. 2 do.	39½
—	Do. No. 3 do.	19
—	Do. No. 4 do.	10
5	City & S. Lond. £10 shares	15½
—	Do. New	14
4	Furness, Cons. 1881	134½
4	Do. "A" 1881	131½
4	Do. "B" 1883	129½
4	Glasgow & S. Western	142½
4	Do. No. 2	141
4	Do. 1888	140
4	Do. 1891	140
5	Gt. Central	162½
4	Do.	132½
5	Do. Conv. 1872	155½
5	Do. do. 1874	154½
5	Do. do. 1876	153½
5	Do. do. 1879	153½
5	Do. do. 1881	148½
4	Do. 1889	112½
4	Do. 1891	106½
5	Do. 1894	105½
4	Gt. Eastern, Cons.	142
4	Do. 1886	141½
4	Do. 1881	141½
4	Do. 1884	141½

Preference Shares, &c. (*continued*):—

Last Div.	Name.	Price.
4	Gt. Eastern, Cons. 1887	140½
4	Do. 1888	140½
3½	Do. 1890	122½
3½	Do. 1893	121½
—	Do. (Int. fr. Jan '99) 1893	117½
4	Gt. North Scotland "A"	134½
4	Do. "B"	133½
4	Gt. Northern, Cons.	143
3	Do. 1896	107
5	Gt. Western Cons.	180
36/11	Hull & Barnsley Red. at 115	107
4	Isle of Wight	133½
3	Lancs. & Yorkshire, Cons.	107
9/2½	Lanc. Drby & E.C. 5 p.c. £10	10½
—	Do. 5 p.c. 2nd £10	9½
5	Lond., Bright., &c., Cons.	178½
5	Do. and Cons.	177½
4½	Lond., Chat. & Dov. Arbitr.	136½
25/	Do. 2nd Pref. 4½ p.c.	93
4	Lond. & N. Western	146
4	Lond. & S. Western 1881	145½
4	Do. 1884	143½
3½	Do.	127½
4	Lond., Tilbury & Southend	142½
4	Do. Cons., 1887	142½
4	Do. 1891	142½
—	Mersey, 5 p.c. Perp.	—
4	Metropolitan, Perp.	141½
4	Do. 1882	142½
4	Do. Irred.	147½
4	Do. 1887	142½
4	Do. New	142½
4½	Do.	146½
3½	Do.	124½
3	Do. Guar.	101½
2½	Metrop. Dist. Exten 5 p.c.	110
2½	Midland, Perp. Pref.	92
4	N. British Cons., No. 2	137
4½	Do. Edin. & Glasgow	153½
5	Do. 1865	169½
5	Do. Conv. 1874	169½
4½	Do. 1875	152½
4½	Do. Conv. 1875	153½
5	Do. do. 1879	169½
4	Do. do. 1884	138
4	Do. do. 1888	138
4	Do. do. 1890	137½
4	Do. do. 1892	137½
4	N. Eastern	144
4½	N. Lond., Cons. 1866	174½
4½	Do. and Cons. 1875	160
3	N. Staffordshire	107
4½	Plym. Devpt. & S. W. Junc.	149½
1/5	Port Talbot, &c., 4 p.c. £10 Shares, 4 paid	5
5/	Rhondda & Swansea Bay, 5 p.c. £10 Shares	13
4	Rhymney, Cons.	140½
4½	S. Eastern, Cons.	162½
5	Do. do.	178½
4	Do. Vested Cos'.	143
4	Do. 1891	143
3½	Do. 1893	125½
2	Do. 3 p.c. after July 1900	103½
4	Taff Vale	142½

INDIAN RAILWAYS.

Last Div.	Name.	Paid.	Price.
3½	Assam Bengal, Ld., (3½ p.c. till June 30, then 3 p.c.)	100	102
4/	Barsi Light, Ld., £10 Shs.	10	10½
6	Bengal and N. West., Ld.	100	149½
4/	Do. £10 Shares	10	14½
3/6	Do. 3½ p.c. Cum. Pf. Shs.	10	10½
8½d.	Do.	4	4½
2/3½	Bengal Central, Ld., £10 (3½ p.c. + ½th net earn)	5	5½
3	Bengal Dooars, Ld.	100	118
4	Bengal Nagpr., Lim. (gua. 4 p.c. + 4th sp. pfts.)	100	115
7½	Bombay, Baroda, and C. I. (gua. 5 p.c.)	100	213
36/1	Burma, Ld. (gua. 2½ p.c. and ½ p.c. add. till 1901)	100	108½
1/7	Do. £10 Shares		3½
4	Delhi Umb. Kalka, Ld., Gua. 3½ p.c. + net earn.	100	123
4	Do. Deb. Stk., 1890 (1916)	100	111
9/10	Estn. Bengal, "A" An. 1957	—	25
9/	Do. "B" 1957	—	30
4	Do. Gua. Deb. Stock	100	140½
9/7½	East Ind. Ann. "A" (1953)	—	27
8/4½	Do. "C"	—	28
8/11½	Do. "B"	—	30
6	Do. Def. Ann. Cap. (gua. 4 p.c. + ½th sp. pfts.)	—	182
115/9	East Ind. Def. Ann. "D"	—	166
4½	East Ind. Irred. Stock	100	160½
5	Gt. Indian Penin., Gua. 5 p.c. + ½ surplus profits	100	167½
4	Do. Irred. 4 p.c. Deb. St.	100	140½
4	Indian Mid., Ld. (gua. 4 p.c. + ½th surplus pfts.)	100	118
51/	Madras Guar. + ½ p. pfts.	100	166
48/6	Do. do.	100	156
46/	Do. do.	100	146
4	Nilgiri, Ld., 1st Deb. Stk.	100	97
4	Oude & Rohil. Db. Stk. Rd.	100	—
5 3/8	Rohil. and Kumaon, Ld.	100	132
9/11	Scinde, Punj., and Delhi, "A" Ann., 1958	—	25
9/1	Do. "B" do.	—	30

Indian Railways (*continued*):—

Last Div.	NAME.	Paid.	Price.
4	South Behar, Ld., £10 shs.	100	100
3½	Do. Deb. Stk. Red.	100	103
4½	South Ind., Gu. Deb. Stk.	100	160½
5	South Indian, Ld. (gua. 3 p.c., and ½ spls. profits)	100	122½
5	Sthn. Mahratta, Ld. (3½ p.c. & ¼th net earnings)	100	116
4	Do. Deb. Stk. Red.	100	120
3½	Southern Punjab, Ld.	100	108
3½	Do. Deb. Stk. Red.	—	105
5	Nizam's Gua. State, Ld. (†	100	114½
4	Do. Mort. Deb., 1936	100	109
4	Do. do. Reg.	100	108
17/3½	Nizam's Gua. State, Ld., 3½ p.c. Mt. Deb. bearer	—	94½
17/3½	Do. Reg. do. ..	—	93½
5	W. of India Portgese., Ld.	100	68½
5	Do. Deb. Stk., Red	100	99

RAILWAYS.—BRITISH POSSESSIONS.

Last Div.	NAME.	Paid.	Price.
5	Atlantic & N.W. Gua. 1 Mt. Bds., 1937	100	125½
5/3	Buff. & L. Huron Ord. Sh.	10	13½
5½	Do. 1st Mt. Perp. Bds. 1879	100	141½
5½	Do. 2nd Mt. Perp. Bds.	100	141½
—	Calgary & Edmon. 6 p.c. 1st Mt. Stg. Bds. Red..	100	75½
5	Canada Cent. 1st Mt. Bds. Red.	100	103
4	Can. Pacific Pref. Stk.....	100	100
5	Do. Strl. 1st Mt. Deb. Bds. 1915	100	118
3½	Do. Ld. Grnt. Bds., 1938..	100	107
3½	Do. Ld. Grnt. Ins. Stk. ..	100	107
4	Do. Perp. Cons. Deb. Stk.	100	114
5	Do. Algoma Bch. 1st Mt. Bds., 1937	100	122
2	Demerara, Original Stock	100	47
7	Do. Perp. Pref. Stk.....	100	155½
9½d.	Do. 4 p.c. Cum. Ext. Pref. £10 Shs.	4	6½
—	Dominion Atlntc. Ord. Stk.	100	33½
5	Do. 5 p.c. Pref. Stk.....	100	97½
4	Do. 1st. Deb. Stk......	100	106
4	Do. 2nd do. Red.	100	100
—	Emu Bay & Mt. Bischoff, Ld.	5	4½
4½	Do. Irred. Deb. Stk....	100	98
nil.	Gd. Trunk of Canada, Stk.	100	8½
6	Do. 2nd. Equip. Mt. Bds.	100	130½
5	Do. Perp. Deb. Stk.......	100	136½
5	Do. Gt. Westn. Deb. Stk.	100	128½
5	Do. Nthn. of Can. 1st Mt. Bds., 1902	100	102½
4	Do. do. Deb. Stk	100	102
5	Do. G. T. Geor. Bay & L. Erie 1 Mt., 1903	100	104
5	Do. Mid. of Can. Stl. 1st Mt. (Mid. Sec.) 1908	100	106
5	Do. do. Cons. 1 Mt. Bds. 1912	100	107
5	Do. Mont. & Champ. 1 Mt. Bds., 1902	100	103
	Do. Welln., Grey & Brce. 7 p.c. Bds. 1 Mt.	100	109
—	Jamaica 1st Mtg. Bds. Red.	—	103
—	Manitoba & N. W., 6 p.c. 1st Mt. Bds., Red......	100	—
—	Do. Ldn. Bdhldrs. Certs.	—	—
5	Manitoba S. W. Col. 1 Mt. Bd., 1934 $1,000 price %	—	120
—	Mid. of W. Aust. Ld. 6 p.c. 1 Mt. Dbs., Red.	100	25
4	Do. Deb. Bds., Red.	100	103
4	Nakusp & Slocan Bds., 1918	100	106
3	Natal Zululand Ld. Debs.,	100	77½
5	N. Brunswick 1st Mt. Stg. Bds., 1934	100	121
4	Do. Perp. Cons. Deb. Stk.	100	114
—	N. Zealand Mid., Ld., 5 p.c 1st Mt. Debs..........	100	35
6	Ontario & Queb. Cap. Stk.	$100	155½
5	Do. Perm. Deb. Stk......	100	142½
—	Qu'Appelle, L. Lake & Sask. 6 p.c. 1 Mt. Bds. Red.	100	41½
	Queb. & L. S. John, 1st Mt. Bds., 1909	100	25½
	Quebec Cent., Prior Ln. Bds., 1908	100	107
1½	Do. 5 p.c. Inc. Bds.	100	39
4	St. Lawr. & Ott. Stl. 1st Mt.	100	113
4	Shuswap & Okan., 1st Mt. Deb. Bds., 1915	100	76
5	Temiscouata, 5 p.c. Stl. 1st Deb. Bds., Red.........	100	9½
5	Do. (S. Franc. Brch.) 5 p.c. Stl. 1 Mt. Db. Bds., 1910	100	10
4	Toronto, Grey & B. 1st Mt.	100	112
1/2½	Well. & Mana. £5 Shs. ..	1	1
5	Do. Debs., 1908	100	110
5	Do. 2nd Debs., 1908	100	109
5	Do. 3rd do., 1908	100	108
6	Atlan. & St. Law. Shs., 6 p.c.	100	162½
5	Gd. Trunk Mt. Bds., 1934	100	116½
5	Michigan Air Line, 5 p.c. 1st Mt. Bds., 1902	100	104
4	Minneap., S. P. & Slt. Ste. Mar, 1st M Bds., 1938	$1000	98

AMERICAN RAILROAD STOCKS AND SHARES.

Last Div.	NAME.	Paid.	Price.
6/	Alab. Gt. Sthn. A 6 p.c. Pref.	10/.	9
—	Do. do "B" Ord. ..	10/.	2
—	Alabma. N. Orl.-Tex. &c. "A" Pref.	10/.	[illegible]
—	Do. "B" Def.	10/.	[illegible]
5½	Atlant. First Lsd. Ls. Rtl. Trust....................	Stk.	93½
—	Baltimore & Ohio Com. .	$100	17
—	Baltimore Ohio S.W. Pref	$100	6
—	Chesap. & Ohio Com. ...	$100	19½
—	Chic. Gt. West. 5 p.c. Pref. Stock "A"	$100	30½
—	Do. do. Scrip. In.......	—	27
8/3	Do. 4 p.c. Deb. Stk.......	$100	67½
4	Do. Interest in Scrip ...	$100	63½
$4	Chic. Junc. Rl. & Un. Stk. Yds. Com.	$100	110½
$1½	Do. 6 p.c. Cum. Pref.	$100	113½
$3½	Chic. Mil. & St. P. Pref...	$100	146
7	Cleve. & Pittsburgh......	$10	86½
$1½	Clev., Cincin., Chic., & St. Louis Com.	$100	—
—	Erie 4 p.c. Non-Cum. 1st Pf.	—	34½
—	Do. 4 p.c. do. 2nd Pf.	—	18
—	Gt. Northern Pref.	$100	155
$2½	Illinois Cen. Lsd. Lines ..	$100	95½
—	Kansas City, Pitts & G. ..	$100	20
$3	L. Shore & Mich. Sth. C.	$100	190
—	Mex. Cen. Ltd. Com.	$100	5
—	Miss. Kan. & Tex. Pref...	$100	32½
2½	N.Y., Pen. & O. 1st Mt. Tst. Ltd., Ord.	—	48½
4	Do. 1st Mort. Deb. Stk. ..	$100	93½
$	North Pennsylvania	$50	—
—	Northn. Pacific, Com.....	$100	24
1½	Pitts. F. Wayne & Chic...	$100	174
—	Reading 1st Pref.	$50	20½
—	Do. 2nd Pref.	$50	10½
—	S. Louis & S. Fran. Com.	$100	6½
—	Do. 2nd Pref.	$100	25
6	St. Louis Bridge 1st Pref..	$100	107
3	Do. 2nd Pref.	$100	50
6	Tunnel Rail. of St. Louis	$100	107
$1½	St. Paul, Min. and Man...	$100	130
—	Southern, Com.	$100	8½
—	Wabash, Common........	$100	7

AMERICAN RAILROAD BONDS. CURRENCY.

Last Div.	NAME.		Price.
7	Albany & Susq. 1 Con. Mrt.	1906	118
7	Allegheny Val. 1 Mt.......	1910	125½
5	Burling., Cedar Rap. & N. 1 Mt.	1906	109½
5	Canada Southern 1 Mt.....	1908	111
5	Chic. & N. West. Sk. Fd. Db.	1933	120½
5	Do. Deb. Coupon	1921	112½
6	Chicago & Tomah	1905	112½
5	Chic. Burl. & Q. Skg. Fd.	1901	102½
4	Do. Nebraska Ext.......	—	100½
6	Chic., Mil., & S. Pl., 1 Mt. S.W. Div...............	1909	117½
7	Do. (S. Paul Div.) 1 Mt.	1902	132½
5	Do. (La Cross & D.	1919	112½
7	Do. 1 Mt. (Hast. & Dak.)	1910	132
5	Do. Chic. & Mis. Riv. 1 Mt.	1926	112½
5	Chic., Rock Is. and Pac. 1 Mt. Ext.	1934	108
6	Det., G. Haven & Mil. Equip	1918	105
6	Do. do. Cons. Mt.	1918	102½
6	Ill. Cent., 1 Mt., Chic. & S.	1898	—
7	Indianap. & Vin., 1 Mt. ..	1908	125
6	Do. do. 2 Mt. ..	1900	104½
6	Lehigh Val., Cons. Mt....	1923	112½
—	Mexic. Cent., Ln. 2 Cons. Inc.	—	5
7	N.Y. Cent. & H. R. Mt. Bonds	1903	119½
5	Do. Deb.	1904	111
6	Penns. Cons. S. F M.	1905	118
4	West Shore, 1 Mt.	2361	110

DITTO—GOLD.

Last Div.	NAME.	Price.
6	Alabama Gt. Sthn. 1 Mt. ..1908	114
5	Do. Mid. 1 1928	96
4	Allegheny Val. Gen. Mt. ..1942	107
4	Atch., Top., & S. Fé Gn. Mt. 1995	90½
3	Do. Adj. Mt..............1995	61
5	Do. Equipt. Tmst. .... —	102½
5	Atlantic & Dan. 1 Mt.......1950	96½
5	Baltimore & Ohio..........1925	97½
5	Do. Speyer's Tst. Recpts. 1925	96
5	Do. Cons. Mt. 1988	102½
4½	Do. 4½ p.c. 1 Mt. Term. 1934	84
4½	Do. Brown Shipley's Dep. Cts. —	84
5	Balt. Belt 5 p.c. 1 Mort......1990	90
4½	Balt. & Ohio S.W. 1 Mt. ..1990	102½
4½	Do. 4½ p.c. 1 Cons. Mt. 1893 1993	78
—	Do. Inc. Mt. 5 p.c. Cl. A —	29½
—	Do. do. Cl. B —	11
5	Balt. & Ohio S.W. Term 5 p.c. 1942	99½
6	Balt. & Ptmac (Mn. L.) 1 Mt. 1911	124
6	Do. do. (Tunnel) 1 Mt. 1911	126
4	Beech Creek 1 Mt. 1936	109
5	Do 2 Mort. 1936	116
4	Carthage & Adiron 1 Mt...1981	109

American Railroad Bonds—Gold (*continued*):—

Last Div.	NAME.	Price.
5	Cent. of Georgia 1 Mort. ..194[illegible]	117½
5	Do. Cons. Mt. ......194[illegible]	92½
5	Cent. of N. Jrsy. Gn. Mt...198[illegible]	113½
6	Central Pacific, 1 Mort. ....189[illegible]	102½
6	Do. Speyer's Certs. ...... —	106
5	Do Land Grant ....190[illegible]	100½
5	Chesap. & Ohio 1st Cons. Mt. 193[illegible]	116½
4½	Do. Gen. Mt............199[illegible]	80
6	Chic. & W. Ind. Gen. Mt. Skg. Fd. 193	120
5	Chic. Mil. & St. Pl. (Chic. & L. Sup.) 1 Mt. 192	114½
5	Do. Chic. & Pac. W. 192	117½
5	Do. Wisc. & Minn. 1 Mt. 192	114½
5	Do. Terminal Mt. 1914	114½
4	Do. General Mt. ....198[illegible]	108
5	Chic. St. L. & N. Orleans..1951	122½
4	Do. 1 Mort. (Memphis) ..1951	105½
4	Clevel., Cin., Chic. & St. L., 1 Mt. (Cairo)............1939	90
4	Do. 1 Mt. (Cinc., Wab., & Mich.) 1991	98
4	Do. 1 Col. Tst. Mt. (S. Louis) 1990	98½
4	Do General Mt. 1993	82½
4½	Clevel. & Mar. Mt. 1935	114
4½	Clevel. & Pittsburgh 1942	116½
4½	Do. Series B. 1942	116½
—	Colorado Mid. 1 Mt. 1936	63½
—	Do. Bdhrs.' Comm. Certs. —	63½
4	Dnvr. & R. Gde. 1 Cons. Mt. 1936	93
5	Do Imp. Mort...........1928	92
4	Detroit & Mack. 1 Lien 1995	92½
5	E. Tennes., Virg., & Grgia. Cons. Mt. 1956	114½
5	Elmira, Cort., & Nthn. Mt. 1914	100
4	Erie 1 Cons. Mt. Pr. Ln. ..1996	90
3	Do. Gen. Lien 1996	72
6	Galvest., Harrisb., &c., 1 Mt.	107½
5	Georgia, Car. & N. 1 Mt. ..1929	96
4½	Gd Rpds & Inda. Ex. 1 Mt. 1941	112½
5	Do. 1 Mt. (Muskegon) ..1926	39½
3½	Illinois Cent. 1 Mt. 1951	104½
4	Do. 1952	105
4	Do. Cairo Bdge. ..1950	102
4	Do. 1953	104
4	Do. General Mort. ..1904	102½
5	Kans. City, Pitts. & G. 1 M. 1923	80
3½	L. Shore & Mich. Southern 1997	109
4½	Lehigh Val. N.Y. 1 Mt.....1940	105
5	Lehigh Val. Term. 1 Mt. ..1941	109½
5	Long Island 1931	120½
5	Do. Deb..........1934	102
5	Do. (N. Shore Bch.) 1 Cons. Mt. 1932	94
6	Louisville & Nash. G. Mt ..1930	121
6	Do. 2 Mt. Sk. Fd. (S. & N. Alabama.........1910	104½
6	Do. 1 Mt. N. Orl. & Mb. 1930	122½
5	Do. 1 Mt. Coll. Tst. ...1931	106
4	Do. Unified 1940	87½
4½	Do. Mobile & Montgy. 1 Mt. 1945	105½
4	Manhattan Cons. Mt. 1990	96
4	Mexican Cent. Cons. Mt. ..1911	66
—	Do. 1 Cons. Inc, ...	15
6	Mexican Nat. 1 Mt..........1927	106½
3½	Do. 2 Mt. 6 p.c. Inc. A 1917	54
—	Do. do. B..1917	10
3	Do. Matheson's Certs....	—
3	Michig. Cnt. (Battle Ck. & S.) 1 Mt. 1989	88
6	Minneap. & S. L. 1 Mt. Pacific Ext. 1921	117½
5	Do. 1 Consold. 1934	107½
4	Minne., Slt. S. M. & A. 1 Mt. 1926	98
5	Minneapolis Westn. 1 Mt...1911	105½
4	Miss. Kans. & Tex. 1 Mt...1990	89
4	Do. 2 do. 1990	62
4	Mobile & Birm. Mt. Inc....1945	38
5	Do. P. Lien 1945	88
4	Mohawk & Mal. 1 Mt.......1991	108
5	Montana Cent. 1 Mt. 1937	111½
5	Nashv., Chattan., & S. L. 1 Cons. Mt...................1928	102½
5	Nash., Flor., & Shff. Mt...1937	95½
4	N. Y. & Putnam 1 Cons. Mt. 1993	108
5	N. Y., Brooklyn, & Man. B. 1 Cons. Mt..............1935	107½
4	N. Y. Cent. & Hud. R. Deb. Certs. 1890 1905	106
4	Do. Ext. Debt. Certs....1905	106
7	N. Y., L. Erie, & W. 1 Cons. Mt. (Erie) 1920	142½
7	Do. 1 Con. Mt. Fd. Coup. 1920	140
5	N. Y., Onto., & W. Cons. 1 Mt.....................1939	110
4	Do. 4 p.c. Refund. Mt...1992	99
5	N. Y. & Rockaway B. 1 Mt. 1927	102½
6	Norfolk & West. Gn. Mt....1931	128
6	Do. Imp. & Ext..........1934	118½
4	Do. 1 Cons. Mt........ —	81
6	N. Pacific Gn. 1 Mt. Ld. Gt. 1921	—
4	Do. P. Ln. Rl. & Ld. Gt. —	96
3	Do. Gn. Ln. Rl. & Ld. Gt. —	62
5	Oregon & Calif. 1 Mt.......1927	78½
5	Oregon Rl. & Nav. Col. Tst. —	—
6	Panama Skg. Fd. Subsidy..1910	105½
4½	Pennsylvania Rlrd. 1913	115
4	Do. Equip. Tst. Ser. A..1914	104
4	Do. Cons. Mt...........1943	115
4½	Penna. Company 1st Mort. 1921	114
5	Perkiomen 1 Mrt., 2nd ser..1918	91½
4½	{ Pitts., C., C., & St. Ls. Con. Mt. G. B., Ser. A } 1940-2	112½
4	Do. Cons. Mort., Ser. D..1945	105
6	Pittsbgh., Cle., & Toledo ..1922	107½
4	Reading, Phil., & R. Genl. 1997	83
5	Richmond & Dan. Equip. ..1909	97½
5	Rio Grande Junc. 1st Mort. 1939	94
4	Rio Grande West 1st Tst. Mt. 1939	82½
6	St. Joseph & Gd. Island ..1925	—
7	S. Louis Bridge 1st Mort ..1925	134½
5	S. Louis Mchts. Bdge. Term. 1st Mort...............193[illegible]	108½

American Railroad Bonds (*continued*):

Last Div.	NAME.	Price.
4	S. Louis S. West 1st Mort..1989	77½
—	Do. 4 p.c. 2nd Mort. Inc. 1989	30
—	S. Louis Term. Cupples Sta. & Prop. 1st. Mrt. 4½ p.c. 1909-17	102
4½	St. Paul, Minn., & Manit. 1933	110½
6	Do. do. 1933	132½
6	Shamokin, Sunbury, &c. 2 Mt. 1925	109
5	S. & N. Alabama Cons. Mt. 1936	97½
5	Southern 1 Cons. Coup. 1994	91½
4	Do. E. Tennes Reorg. Lien ..1938	100
6	S. Pacific of Cal. 1 Mt...1905-12	111
4½	Trml. Assn. of S. Louis 1 Mt. 1939	111½
5	Do. 1 Cons. Mt...........1944	109
5	Texas & Pac. 1 Mt.........2000	100½
—	Do. 5 p.c. 2 Mt. Income 2000	30
5	Toledo & Ohio Cent. 1 Mt. West. Div. ....193[illegible]	102½
4½	Toledo., Walhon., Val., & Ohio 1 Mt. 1931-5	171½
—	Union Pacific 1 Mt. 4 p.c. ..1947	94
—	Union Pac., Linc., & Color. 1 Mt. 1918	—
4	United N. Jersey Gen. Mt...1944	115½
6	Vicksbrg., Shrevept., & Pac. Pr. Ln. Mt. 1915	102½
5	Wabash 1 Mt. 1939	112
4	Wn. Pennsylvania Mt. 1928	106½
5	W. Virga. & Pittsbg. 1 Mt. 1990	88
5	Wheeling & L. Erie 1 Mt. (Wheelg. Div.) 5 p.c. 1928	90½
5	Do. Extn. Imp. Mt. 1930	90
—	Do. do. Brown Shipley's Cts...	—
5	Willmar & Sioux Falls 1 Mt. 1938	111

STERLING.

Last Div.	NAME.	Price.
6	Alabama Gt. Sthn. Deb.....1906	104½
5	Do. Gen. Mort. ..1927-8	99
5	Alabama, N. Orl., Tex. & Pac. 5 p.c. "A" Dbs...1910-40	99
55/	Do. do. "B" do. 1910-40	52
—	Do. do. "C" do.	19
—	Allegheny Valley 1910	131½
4	Atlantic 1st Leased Line Perp...	98
6	Baltimore and Ohio 1902	107½
6	Do. do. 1910	118
5	Do. do. 1877.........	97½
—	Do. Morgan's Certs. ..	97½
4½	Do. do. 1933	89
6	Chicago & Alton Cons. Mt. 1903	112
5	Chic. St. Paul & Kan. City Priority	105
6	Eastn. of Massachusetts....1906	117½
5	Illinois Cent. Skg. Fd.	103
5	Do. 1905	108
3½	Do. 1950	99½
4	Do. 1 Mt. 1951	110
3	Do. 1 Mt. 1951	92½
6	Louisville & Nash., M. C. & L. Div., 1 Mt. 1902	104½
7	Do. 2 Mt. (Memphis & O.)..........................1901	111
47/4	Mexican Nat. "A" Certs. 5 p.c. Non. cum.	47
—	Do. "B" Certs....	10
6	N.Y. & Canada 1 Mt........1904	111½
6	N. York Cent. & H.R. Mort. 1903	112
4½	N. York, Penns., & Ohio Pr. Ln. Extd. 1935	—
5	Do. Equip. Tst.	103½
5	Do. 5 p.c. Equip. Tst. (1890)	103½
6	Nrthn. Cent. Cons. Gen. Mt. ..	106
6	Pennsylvania Gen. Mt. 1910	126
6	Do. Cons. Skg. Fd. Mt. 1905	114½
3½	Do. Cons. Mt..........1943	105½
6	Phil. & Erie Cons. Mort ..1920	134½
6	Phil. & Reading Gen. Cons. Mort. 1911	126
6	Pittsbg. & Connells. Cons. 1926	115
—	Do. Morgan's Certs.....	115
4	St. Paul., Min., & Manitoba (Pac. Extn.) 1940	96½
6	S. & N. Alabama...........1902	107½
6	Un. N. Jersey & C. Gen. Mt. 1901	109½

FOREIGN RAILWAYS

Last Div.	NAME.	Paid.	Price.
4/	Alagoas, Ltd., Shs.	20	6
5	Do. Deb. Stk., Red. ..	100	42½
6	Antofagasta, Ltd., Stk. ..	100	68
4	Do. Perp. Deb. Stk. ..	100	90
—	Arauco, Ld., Ord. Shs. ..	10	,
—	Do. 10 p.c. Cum. Pref.	10	1
5	Argentine Gt. W., Ld.,	100	72
5	Do. 5 p.c. Cum. Pref. Shs.	100	100
4	Do. 1 Deb. Stk.	100	103½
1/0/0	Argentine N.E., Ltd., 6 p.c. Cum. Pref. Stk. ..	100	10½
—	Do. 5 p.c. Deb. Stk., Red.	100	31
2/	Arica and Tacna Shs. ..	20	1½
10/	Bahia & San Fcisco., Ld.,	20	10½
6/	Do. Timbo. Bch. Shs.	20	5
12/	Bahia, Blanca, & N.W. Ln. Prf. Cum. 6 p.c. ..	100	53½
4	Do. 4 p.c. 1 Deb. Stk., Red.	100	93
6	Barranquilla R. & P., Ld., 6 p.c. 1 Deb. Stk., Red.	100	

Foreign Railways (*continued*):—

Last Div.	Name.	Paid.	Price.
3/	Bilbao Riv. & Cantabn., Ltd., Ord.	3	6
—	Bolivar, Ltd., Shs.	10	1½
6	Do. 6 p.c. Deb. Stk.	100	96½
—	Brazil Gt. Southn. Ltd., 7 p.c. Cum. Pref.	20	1½
6	Do. Perm. Deb. Stk	100	42½
6½	B. Ayres Gt. Southn. Ld., Ord. Stk.	100	147
5	Do. Pref. Stk.	100	136
4	Do. Deb. Stk.	100	115½
30/	B. Ayres & Ensen. Port., Ltd., Ord. Stk.	100	68
5	Do. Cum. 1 Pref. Stk.	100	122
6/0/0	Do. 6p.c.Con. Pref.Stk.	100	101
4	Do. Deb. Stk., Irred.	100	111
10⅞	B. Ayres Northern, Ltd., Ord. Stk.	100	265
12½	Do. Pref. Stk.	100	320
5	Do. 5 p.c. Mt. Deb. Stk., Red.	100	113
3/15/0	B. Ayres & Pac., Ld., 7 p.c. 1 Pref. Stk. (Cum.)	100	84
4	Do. 1 Deb. Stk.	100	100
5/5/0	Do. 4½ p.c. 2 Deb. Stk.	100	89
1	B Ayres & Rosario, Ltd., Ord. Stk.	100	70
—	Do. New, £10 Shs.	20	—
7/	Do. 7 p.c. Pref. Shs.	10	17
7/	Do. Sunchales Ext.	10	14½
4	Do. Deb. Stk., Red.	100	107½
—	B. Ayres & Val. Trans., Ltd., 7 p.c. Cum. Pref.	20	6½
4	Do. 4 p.c. "A" Deb. Stk., Red.	100	71
—	Do. 6 p.c. "B" Deb. Stk., Red.	100	44
3/6	B. Ayres Westn. Ld. Ord.	10	10½
3/	Do. Def. Shs	10	6½
5	Do. 5 p.c. Pref.	10	12½
4	Do. Deb. Stk	100	107½
6	Cent.Arg. Deb.Sk. Rd.	100	160½
4	Do. Deb. Stk. Rd.	100	111
6	Cent. Bahia L. Ord. Stk.	100	42
	Do. Deb. Stk., 1934	100	72½
5	Do. Deb. Stk., 1937	100	58
3/6	Cent. Uguy. East. Ext. L. Shs.	10	5½
5	Do. Perm. Stk.	100	111
3/6	Do. Nthn. Ext. L. Sh.	10	4½
5	Do. Perm. Deb. Stk.	100	106
3	Do. of Montev. Ltd., Ord. Stk.	100	86
6	Do. Perm. Deb. Stk.	100	140
10/	Conde d'Eu, Ltd. Ord.	20	7
—	Cordba & Rosar., Ltd., 6 p.c. Pref. Shs.	100	42½
4	Do. 1 Deb. Stk.	100	91
7½/	Do. 6 p.c. Deb. Stk.	100	93
—	Cordba Cent., Ltd., 5 p.c. Cu. 1 Pref. Stk	100	83½
—	Do. 5 p.c. Non-Cum. 2 Pref. Stk	100	46
5	Do. Deb. Stk.	100	119
—	Costa Rica, Ltd., Shs.	10	4½
8/	Dna. Thrsa. Chris., Ltd., 7 p.c. Pref. Shs.	20	4
20/	E. Argentine, Ltd	100	40
6	Do. Deb. Stk	100	104
1/1	Egyptn. Dlta. Lgt. Rys., Ltd., £10 Pref. Shs.	8	8½
—	Entre Rios, L., Ord. Shs.	5	½
—	Do. Cu. 5 p.c. Pref.	5	2½
6/	Gt. Westn. Brazil, Ltd.,	20	9½
6	Do. Perm. Deb. Stk.	100	90½
6	Do. Extn. Deb. Stk.	100	76½
—	Int.-Oceanic Mex., Ltd., 7 p.c. Pref.	10	1½
4	Do. Deb. Stk	100	84
42/6	Do. 7 p.c. "A" Deb. Sk.	100	67
—	Do. 7 p.c. "B" Deb. Sk.	100	31
5/	La Guaira & Carac	10	7½
5	Do. 5 p.c. Deb. Sk. Red.	100	100
8/4	Lembg.-Czern.-Jassy	30	25
1/	Lima, Ltd.	20	2½
—	Manila Ltd. 7 p.c. Cu. Pf.	10	½
20/6½	Mexican 2nd Pref. 6 p.c.	100	33
6	Do. Perp. Deb. Stk.	100	139
1/0/0	Mexican Sthrn., Ld., Ord.	100	23
—	Do. 4 p.c. 1 Db. Stk. Rd.	100	83
—	Do. 4 p.c. 2 do.	100	61
—	Mid. Urgy., Ltd.	100	18½
4	Do. Deb. Stk.	100	64
12/	Minas & Rio, Ltd.	20	9½
5/2	Namur & Liege	20	12½
11/6	Do. Pref	20	29
5/	Natal & Na. Cruz, Ld., 7 p.c. Cum Pref.	20	7
—	Nitrate Ltd., Ord.	10	5
—	Do. 7 p.c. Pr. Con. Or.	10	3½
—	Do. Def. Conv. Ord.	10	½
7/	N.-E. Urgy., Ltd., Ord	10	14½
7/	Do. 7 p.c. Pref.	10	15
—	N.-W. Argentine Ld., 7 p.c. Pref.	10	2½
6	Do. 6 p.c. 1 Deb. Stk.	100	113
—	Do. 2 Deb. Stk.	100	94
—	N.W. Uruguay 6 p.c. 1 Pref. Stk.	100	17
—	Do. 5 p.c. 2 Pref. Stk.	100	7½
6	Do. 6 p.c. Deb. Stk.	100	80½
22/	Ottoman (Sm. Aid.)	20	14
—	Paraguay Cntl., Ld., 5 p.c. Perm. Deb. Stk.	100	11
—	Piræus, Ath., & Pelo.	275	1¼
	Pto. Alegre & N. Hambg. Ld., 7 p.c. Pref. Shs.	20	4
6	Do. Mt. Deb. Stk. Red.	100	77½
—	Puerto Cabello & Val. Ld.	10	1½
5	Recife & S. Francisco	100	73
24	R Claro S. Paulo, Ld., Sh.	10	22½
5	Do. Deb. Stk.	100	127
5	Royal Sardinian Ord.	10	11½

Foreign Railways (*continued*):—

Last Div.	Name.	Paid.	Price.
5/	Royal Sardinian Pref.	10	12½
5/	Sambre & Meuse	20	18
5/6	Do. Pref.	10	12½
28/	San Paulo Ld.	20	35
2/9½	Do. New Ord. £10 sh.	6	9½
2/	Do. 5 p.c. Non.Cm.Pref.	10	12
5½	Do. Deb. Stk.	100	134
5	Do. 5 p.c. Deb. Stk	100	127
—	S. Fé & Cordova, Gt. Sthn., Ld., Shares	100	51½
6	Do. Perp. Deb. Stk.	100	123
3/2½	S. Austrian	20	7
10/	Sthn. Braz. R. Gde. do Sul, Ld.	20	8
6	Do. 6 p.c. Deb. Stk.	100	71½
4	Swedish Centl., Ld., 4 p.c. Deb. Stk.	100	107
5	Do. Pref.	100	100
1/9	Taltal, Ld.	5	2½
—	Uruguay Nthn., Ld. 7 p.c. Pfd. Stk.	100	8
3½	Do. 5 p.c. Deb. Stk.	100	30
—	Villa Maria & Rufino, Ld., 6 p.c. Pref. Shs.	100	20
4	Do. 4 p.c. 1 Deb. Stk.	100	74
6/0/0	Do. 6 p.c. 2 Deb. Stk.	100	47
5/9	West Flanders	8½	21
5/6	Do. 5½ p.c. Pref.	10	18
3/	Watn. of Havana, Ld.	10	4½

FOREIGN RAILWAY OBLIGATIONS

Per Cent.	Name.	Price.
6	Alagoas Ld., 6 p.c. Deb., Rd.	88½
—	Alcoy & Gandia, Ld., 5 p.c. Debs., Red.	25
5	Arauco., Ld., 5 p.c. 1st Mt., Rd.	62½
—	Do. 6 p.c. Mt. Deb., Rd.	42½
6	Brazil G. Sthn., L., Mt. Dbs., Rd.	89½
6	Do. Mt. Dbs. 1893, Rd.	48½
5½	Campos & Caran. Dbs., Rd.	76
6	Central Bahia, L., Dbs., Rd.	90½
5½	Conde d'Eu, L., Dbs., Rd.	76
6	Costa Rica, L., 1st Mt. Dbs., Rd.	111
6	Do. 2nd Dbs., Rd.	92
5	Do. Prior Mt. Db., Rd.	104
6	Cucuta Mt. Dbs., Rd.	106
5½	Donna Thrsa. Cris., L., Dbs., Rd.	71
3	Eastn. of France, £20 Dbs., Rd.	19
4	Egyptn. Delta Light, L., Db., Rd	98
—	Espito. Santo & Cara. 5 p.c. Stl. Dbs., Rd.	38
4	Gd. Russian Nic., Rd.	102
5	Inter-Oceanic Mex., L., 5 p.c. Pr. Ln. Dbs., Rd.	103
3	Ital. 3 p.c. Bds. A & B, Rd	57½
—	Ituana 6 p.c. Debs., 1918	74
—	Leopoldina, 6 p.c. Dbs. £50 Bds.,	21
—	Do. do. Comms. Cert.	21
—	Do. 5 p.c. Stg. Dbs. (1888), Rd.	30
—	Do. do. Comm. Certs.	30
—	Do. 5 p.c. Stg. Dbs. (1890), Rd.	21
—	Do. do. Comms. Certs.	21
—	Macahé & Cam. 5 p.c. Dbs., Rd.	29
—	Do. do. Comms. Certs.	29
—	Do. (Cantagallo), 5 p.c., Red.	30
—	Do. do. Comm. Certs.	30
—	Manila Ltd., 6 p.c. Deb., Red.	23
6	Do. Prior Lien Mt., Rd.	104
6	Do. Series "B," Rd.	80
7	Matanzas & Sab., Rd.	101½
6	Minas & Rio, L., 6 p.c. Dbs., Rd.	96
5	Mogyana 5 p.c. Deb. Bds., Rd.	104
5	Moscow-Jaros., Rd.	106½
5½	Natal & Na. Cruz Ltd., 5½ p.c. Debs., Red.	93
5	Nitrate, Ltd. Mt. Bds., Red.	79
3	Nthn. France, Red.	19
4	N. of S. Af. Rep. (Trnsvl.) Gu. Bds. Red.	95
3	Nthn. of Spain £20 Pri. Obs. Red.	8½
6	Ottmn. (Smy to A.)(Kujk) Asnt. Debs., Red.	109
6	Ottmn. (Seraik.) Asg. Debs. Red.	109
6	Ottmn. (Seraik.) Non-Asg. D., Rd	109
5	Ottmn. Kuyjk. Ext. Red.	106
5	Ottmn. Serkeuy. Ext. Red.	101½
5	Ottmn Tireh Ext. 1910	98
5	Ottmn. Debs, 1886, Red.	97
5	Do. 1888, Red. 1935	97½
5	Do. 1893, Red. 1935	99
5	Ottmn. of Anlia. Debs., Rd.	90½
5	Do. Ser. II.	87
4	Ottomn. Smyr. & Cas. Ext Bds., Red.	83½
3	Paris, Lyon & Medit. (old sys., £20), Red.	19
3	Paris, Lyon & Medit. (new sys., £20), Red.	18½
50/	Piræus, At. & Pelp., 6 p.c. 1st Mt. Bds., Red.	91½
3	Do. 5 p.c. Mt. Bds., Red.	71
4	Pretoria-Pietbg., Ltd., Red.	93
7	Puerto Cab. & Val., Ltd., 1st Mt. Debs., Red.	93
—	Rio de Jano. & Nthn., Ltd., 6p.c. £100 Deb., Red.	21
—	Rio de Jano. (Gr. Para.), 5 p.c. 1st Mt. St. £100 Debs., Red.	21
2	Royal Sardinian, A, Rd. £20	11½
3	Royal Sardinian, B., Rd. £20	12

Foreign Rly. Obligations (*continued*):—

Per Cent.	Name.	Price.
5	Ryl. Trns.-Afric. 5 p.c. 1st Mt. £100 Bds., Red.	61
7	Sagua La Grande, B pRd.	98
4	Sa. Fe&Cor. G.S., Ld. Pr Ln. Bds.	104
5	Sa. Fe, 5 p.c. 2nd Reg. Dbs.	80
3	South Austrian, £20 Red.	15½
3	South Austrian, (Ser. X.)	15½
3	South Italian £20 Obs. (Ser. A to G), Red.	12½
3½	S.W. of Venez. (Barq.), Ltd., 7 p.c. 1st Mt. £100 Debs.	55½
5	Taltal, Ltd., 5 p.c. 1st Ch. Debs., Red.	99
5	Utd. Rwys. Havana, Red.	88
3	Wtrn. of France, £20 Red.	19
6	Wrn. B. Ayres St. Mt. Debs., 1902	108
6	Wrn. B. Ayres, Reg. Cert.	106½
5	Do. Mt. Bds.	122
6	Wtrn. of Havna., Ld. Mt. Dbs., Rd.	98
7	Wrn. Ry. San Paulo Red.	99
—	Wrn. Santa Fé, 7 p.c. Red.	38
2/8	Zafra & Huelva, 3 p.c. Red.	2½

BANKS.

Div.	Name.	Paid.	Price.
2/4½	Agra, Ltd.	6	3½
4/2½	Anglo-Argentine, Ltd., £9	7	5½
8 fls.	Anglo-Austrian	120f.	13½
6/	Anglo-Californian, Ltd., £20 Shares	10	11
4/	Anglo-Egyptian, Ltd., £15	5	6
5/	Anglo-Foreign Bkg., Ltd.	7	8
7/	Anglo-Italian, Ltd.	5	7
7/6	Bk. of Africa, Ltd., £18¾	6½	10½
20/	Bk. of Australasia	40	50
10/	Bk. of Brit. Columbia	20	20½
25/	Bk. of Brit. N. America	50	64
20/	Bk. of Egypt, Ltd., £25	12½	18½
5/	Bk. of Mauritius, Ltd.	10	9½
18/	Bk. of N. S. Wales	20	38
4 p.c.	Bk. of N. Zland. Gua. Stk.	100	103
6/	Bk. of Roumania, £20 Shs.	6	7½
2/6	Tarapaca & Ldn., Ltd., £10	5	3½
—	Bque. Fse. de l'Afri. du S.	100f.	3½
f.22.50	Bque. Internatle. de Paris	20	23
6/	Brit. Bk. of S. America, Ltd., £20 Shares	10	10
15/	Capital & Cties., L., £50	10	39
16/	Chart. of India, &c.	20	32½
10/	City, Ltd., £40 Shares	10	19½
18/	Colonial, £100 Shares	30	22
10/	Delhi and London, Ltd.	25	—
5/	German of London, Ltd.	10	10½
25/	Hong-Kong & Shanghai	28½	44½
4/	Imperl. of Persia	6½	3½
10/	Imperl. Ottoman, £20 Shs	10	11½
12/	Intrnatl. of Ldn., Ld., £20	15	11½
10/	Ionian, Ltd.	25	15
16/	Lloyds, Ltd., £50 Shs.	8	30
10/	Ldn. & Braziln. Ltd., £20	10	18
44/	Ldn. & County, Ltd., £80	20	101½
9/	Ldn. & Hanseatic, L., £20	10	10½
22/6	Ldn. & Midland, L., £60	12½	53½
8/9	Ldn. & Provin., Ltd., £10	5	22½
39/	Ldn. & Riv. Plate, L., £25	15	50
2/1½	Ldn. & San Fcisco, Ltd.	7	4½
28/	Ldn. & Sth. West., Ld., £50	20	68
26/	Ldn. & Westmin., L., £100	20	55½
3/	Ldn. of Mex. & S. Amer., Ltd., £10 Shs.	6	5½
15/	Ldn. Joint Stk., L., £100	15	33½
12/9½	Ldn., Paris & Amer., L. £20	16	25
2/4½	Merchant Bkg., L., £9	4	2½
6/3	Metropn, Ltd., £50 Shs.	5	14½
9/	National, Ltd., £50 Shs.	10	19½
4/5	Natl. of Mexico, $100 Shs.	$40	13
1/3	National of N. Zl., L., £7½	2½	2
3/	National S. Afric. Rep.	10	15
18/10½	National Provcl. of Eng., Ltd., £75 Shs.	10½	49½
21/7½	Do. do. £60 Shs.	12	56½
6/6	NorthEastn., Ltd., £20 Shs	6	14½
19/	Parr's, Ld., £100 Shs.	20	91½
12/6	Prov. of Ireland, L., £100	12½	28½
40/	Stand. of S. Afric., L., £100	25	67
12/6	Union of Australia, L., £75	25	27½
4 p.c.	Do. do. Ins. Stk. Dep. 1900	100	102
15/6	Union of Ldn., Ltd., £100	15½	35½

BREWERIES AND DISTILLERIES

Div.	Name.	Paid.	Price.
4½	Albion Prp. 1 Mt. Db. Sk.	100	112
4	All Saints', L., Db. Sk. Rd.	100	97
7	Allsopp, Ltd.	100	152
6	Do. Cum. Pref	100	157
4½	Do. Deb. Stk., Red.	100	118
3½	Do. Deb. Stk., Red.	100	101
4½	Alton & Co., L., Db., Rd	100	104
4½	Do. Mt. Bds., 1896	100	103
—	Arnold, Perrett, Ltd.	10	6
6	Do. Cum. Pref.	10	10
4½	Do. 1 Mt. Db. Stk., Rd.	100	106

Breweries &c. (*continued*):—

Div.	Name.	Paid.	Price.
5½	Arrol, A., & Sons, L., Cum. Pref. Shs.	10	10
4½	Do. 1 Mt. Db. Stk., Rd.	100	104
5	Backus, 1 Mt. Db., Red.	100	61
4	Barclay, Perk., L., Cu. Pf.	10	11½
3½	Do. Mt. Db. Stk., Red.	100	110
—	Barnsley, Ltd.	10	12
6	Do. Cum. Pref.	10	14
1/3	Barrett's, Ltd	2½	1½
1/3	Do. 5 p.c. Pref.	2½	2½
3/	Bartholomay, Ltd.	10	3
8	Do. Cum. Pref.	10	9
6	Do. Deb.	100	100½
5	Bass, Ratcliff, Ltd., Cum. Pref. Stk.	100	144½
4½	Do. Mt. Db. Stk., Rd.	100	126
4	Bell, J., L., 1 Mt. D. Stk., R	100	100
2/6	Benskin's, L., Cum. Pref.	5	—
4½	Do. 1 Mt. Db. Stk Red.	100	—
4½	Do. "B" Deb. Sk, Rd.	100	—
7/	Bentley's Yorks., Ltd.	10	11½
6/	Do. Cum. Pref.	10	12½
4½	Do. Mt. Debs., Red.	100	110
4½	Do. do. 1892, Red.	100	110
—	Bieckert's, Ltd.	20	2
5	Do. Debs., Red.	100	57
—	Birmingham., Ltd., 6 p.c. Cum. Pref.	5	2½
4½	Do. Mt. Debs., Red.	50	40½
5½	Boardman's, Ld., Cm. Pf.	10	8½
4½	Do., Perp. 1 Mt. Db. Sk.	100	105½
3/1/9	Brain & Co., Ltd.	100	101
4½	Brakspear, L., 1 D. Stk. Rd	100	109
4	Brandon's, L., 1 D. Stk. R.	100	106½
21/	Bristol (Georges) Ltd.	10	46
6	Do. Cum. Pref.	10	18
5	Do. Mt. Db. Sk. 1888 Rd.	100	115½
17/6	Bristol United, Ltd.	10	35
6	Do. Cum. Pref.	10	16½
4½	Do. Db. Sk. Rd.	100	126
5½	Buckley's, L., C. Pre-prf.	10	10½
4½	Do. 1 Mt. Db. Stk. Rd.	100	105½
4	Bullard & Sns, L., D. Sk. R.	100	105
6	Bushell, Watk., L., C. Pf.	10	14
4½	Do. 1 Mt. Db. Sk. Rd.	100	112
5	Camden, Ltd., Cum. Pref.	10	11½
4½	Do. 1 Mt. Db. Sk. Rd.	100	108
5½	Cameron, Ltd., Cm. Prf.	10	13½
4½	Do. Mort Deb. Stk.	100	108
3½	Do. Perp Mt. Db. Sk.	100	100½
5	Cam'bell, J'stone, L., C. Pf.	5	5½
4½	Do. 4½ p.c. 1 Mt. Db. Sk.	100	105
4	Campbell, Praed, L., Per. 1 Mort. Deb. Stk.	100	106
4	Cannon, L., Mt. Db. Stk.	100	109
4	Do. "B" Deb. Stk.	100	104
5	Castlemaine, L., 1 Mt. Db.	100	94
3½	Charrington, Ltd., Mort. Deb. Stk. Red.	100	106
2/	Cheltnhm. Orig., Ltd.	5	7
6	Do. Cum. Pref.	5	7½
4	Do. Debs. Red.	100	107
10/	Chicago, Ltd.	10	3½
6	Do. Debs.	100	84½
—	Cincinnati, Ltd.	10	½
—	Do. Cum. Pref.	10	1½
10/	City of Baltimore	10	4
16/	Do. 8 p.c. Cum. Pref	10	8
14/	City of Chicago, Ltd.	10	1½
8	Do. Cum. Pref.	10	6
13	City of London, Ltd.	100	206½
5	Do. Cum. Pref.	100	137
4	Do. Mt. Deb. Stk., Rd.	100	112½
2/	Colchester, Ltd.	5	5
7	Do. Pref.	5	7
4½	Do. Deb. Stk., Red.	100	109
5	Combe, Ltd., Cum. Pref.	10	14½
4	Do. Mt. Db. Stk, Rd.	100	111
3½	Do. Perp. Deb. Stk.	100	107
5	Comm'cial, L., D. Sk., Rd.	100	107½
5	Courage, L., Cm. Pref. Shs.	100	137½
4	Do. Irr. Mt. Deb. Stk.	100	126
3½	Do. Irr. "B" Mt. Db. Sk.	100	104
8	Daniell & Sons, Ltd.	10	
7	Do. Cum. Pref.	10	12½
4½	Do. 1 Mt. Perp. Db. Sk.	100	108½
4½	Do. "B" Deb. Stk.	100	102
10d.	Dartford, Ltd.	5	5
2/9	Do. Cum. Pref.	5	5½
4	Do. 1 Mt. Db. Sk. Rd.	100	99
4	Davenport, Ld., 1 D. Stk.	100	102½
10/	Denver United, Ltd.	10	3½
8	Do. Cum. Pref.	10	8½
6	Do. Debs.	100	98½
4½	Deuchar, L., 1 D. Sk., Rd.	100	108
8/	Distillers, Ltd.	10	24
4½	Do. Mt. Db. Stk., Rd.	100	115½
—	Dublin Distillers, Ltd.	5	1½
3/	Do. Cum. Pref.	5	4½
4½	Do. Irr. Deb. Stk.	100	—
5	Eadie, Ltd., Cum. Pref.	10	11
4	Do. Irr. 1 Mt. Db. Sk.	100	106
10/	Edinbgh. Utd., Ltd.	10	13
6	Do. Cum. Prf.	10	13½
5	Do. 1 Mt. Dbs.	100	110½
4	Eldridge, Pope, L. D. St. R.	100	107
—	Emerald & Phœnix, Ltd.	10	1½
8	Do. Cum. Pref.	10	6½
6	Empress Ltd., C. Pf.	10	11½
4½	Do. Mt. Deb. Stk.	100	106
10/	Farnham, Ltd.	10	16½
6	Do. Cum. Pref.	10	14½
4	Fenwick, L., 1 D. Sk., Rd.	100	108
4	Flower & Sons, Irr. D. Sk.	100	111
4	Friary, L., 1 Db. Stk., Rd.	100	103½
4	Do. 1 "A" Db. Sk., Rd	100	100
4½	Groves, L., 1 Db. Sk., Rd.	100	110
14	Guinness, Ltd.	100	593
6	Do. Cum. Prf. Stk.	100	189½
5	Do. Deb. Stk., Red.	100	122
5	Hall's Oxford L., Cm. Pf.	5	5½
6/	Hancock, Ld., Cm. Pf. Ord.	10	14
7/	Do. Def. Ord.	10	17½

Breweries, &c. (*continued*) :—

Div.	Name.	Paid.	Price.
6	Hancock, Ld., Cum. Pref.	10	15½
4	Do. 1 Deb. Stk., Rd.	100	112
5	Hoare, Ltd. Cum. Pref.	10	12¾
5	Do. "A" Cum. Pref.	10	12½
4	Do. Mt. Deb. Stk., Rd.	100	111
3½	Do. do. do. Rd.	100	104
4/6	Hodgson's, Ltd.	5	10
5	Do. 1 Mt. Db., Red.	—	120½
4	Do. 2 Mt. Db., 1906	—	102
4½	Hopcraft & N., Ltd., 1 Mt. Deb. Stk., Red.	100	103
5	Huggins, Ltd., Cm. Prf.	10	12¾
4½	Do. 1st D. Stk. Rd.	100	113
4½	Do. "B" Db. Stk. Rd.	100	111
10/	Hull, Ltd.	10	17
7	Do. Cum. Pref.	10	14½
4½	Ind, Coope, L., D. Sk., Rd.	100	118
4	Do. "B" Mt. Db. Stk. Rd.	100	111
8/	Indianapolis, Ltd.	10	3½
8	Do. Cm. Prf.	10	9½
5/	Jones, Frank, Ltd.	10	3½
7½	Do. Cum. Pref.	10	7½
5	Do. 1st Mort. Debs.	100	90½
4/	J. Kenward & Ct., Ltd.	5	5½
4½	Kingsbury, L., 1 D. Sk., Rd	100	—
4	Lacon, L., D. Stk., Red.	100	110
4	Do. Irrd. "B" D. Sk	100	106
4/	Lascelles, Ltd.	5	11
6	Do. Cum. Pref.	5	7¾
5	Leney, Ltd., Cum. Pref.	10	11½
4	Do. 1 Mt. Db. Stk. Rd.	100	102
30/7½	Lion, Ltd., £25 shares	17	49½
10/9½	Do. New £10 shares	6	17
6	Do. Perp. Pref.	20	33
4	Do. B. Mt. Db. Sk. Rd.	100	107
4½	Lloyd & Y., Ltd., 1 Mt. Deb. Stk., Rd.	100	100½
4½	Locke & S., Ltd., Irr. 1st Mt. Deb. Stk.	100	101
4½	Lovibond, Ltd., 1st Mt. Deb. Stk., Rd.	100	102½
30/4	Lucas & Co., Ld., Deb. Stk.	100	107
8/	Manchester, Ltd.	10	19
7	Do. Cum. Pref.	10	17
5	Marston, J., L., Cm. Prf.	10	10¾
4	Do. 1 Mt. Db. Sk., Rd.	100	101½
9/	Massey's Burnley, Ltd.	10	17
6	Do. Cum. Pref.	10	14½
4½	McCracken, Ltd., 1 Mt. Deb., 1908	100	59½
5	McEwan, Ltd., Cm. Pref.	10	14
5	Meux, Ltd., Cum. Pref.	10	14
4	Do. Mt. Db. Stk. Red.	100	111
4½	Michell & A., Ltd., 1 Mt. Deb. Stk. Red.	100	105
4½	Mile End Dist. Db. Sk. Rd.	100	109
—	Milwaukee & Chic., Ltd.	10	1½
4/	Do. Cum. Pref.	10	6½
4½	Michell, Toms, L., Db.	50	57
6	Morgan, Ltd., Cum. Pref.	10	14½
20/	Nalder & Coll., Ltd.	10	35
5	Do. Cum. Pref.	10	15½
4½	Do. Deb. Red.	100	112
12/	Newcastle, Ltd.	10	19½
6	Do. Cum. Pref.	10	15
5	Do. 1 Mt. Deb., 1911	100	111½
4	Do. "A" Deb. Stk. Red.	100	104
6	New England, Ltd	10	5
8	Do. Cum. Pref.	10	9¾
6	Do. Debs. Red	100	101½
4	New London, L., 1 D. Sk.	100	103
7/2	New Westminster, Ltd.	4	10½
2/4½	Do. Pref.	4	6½
—	New York, Ltd.	10	1
—	Do. 8 p.c. Cum. Pref.	10	4½
6	Do. 1 Mt. Deb. Red.	100	77½
5	Noakes, Ld., Cum. Pref.	10	12
4	Do. 1 Mt. Db. Stk., Rd.	100	104
4½	Norfolk, L., "A" D. Sk. Rd.	100	106
10/	Northampton, Ld.	10	16½
7	Do. Cum. Pref.	10	16
6	Do. Cum. Pref.	10	12½
5	Do. 1 Mt. Per. Db. Sk.	100	126
4	Nth. East., L., 1 D. Sk. Rd.	100	102
4½	N. Worcesters., L. Per. 1 Mort. Deb. Stock	100	98½
6	Nottingham, L., Cm. Prf.	10	12
5	Do. 1 Mt. Deb. Stk., Red.	100	114
17/4	Do. "B" do. Red.	50	112
6/	Ohlsson' Cape, Ld.	5	17
7	Do. Cum. Pref.	5	8¾
4½	Do. 2nd Cum. Pref.	5	5½
5	Do. Deb. Stk., Red.	100	113
4½	Oldfield, L., 1 Mt. Db. Stk.	100	106
6	Page & Overt., L., Cm. Prf.	10	13½
4½	Do. 1 Mt. Dbs., Red.	100	109
10/	Parker's Burslem, Ltd.	10	24½
6	Do. Cum. Pref.	10	15
4	Do. 1 Mt. Db. Stk., Red.	100	111
4	Persse, Ld., 1 Mt. Db. Rd.	100	95½
4	Phipps, L., Irr. 1 Db. Stk.	100	113
8	Plymouth, L., Min. Cu. Pf.	10	13½
4½	Do. Mt. Deb. Stk., Red.	100	104½
4½	Pryor, Reid, L., 1 D. S., R.[†]	100	103½
5	Reid's, Ld., Cm. Pref. Stk.	100	137½
4	Do. Mt. Deb. Stk., Red.	100	112
3½	Do. "B" Mt. Db. Stk., Rd	100	102
5	Rhondda Val., L., Cu. Pf	10	11
4½	Do. 1 Mt. Deb. Stk., Rd.	100	109
5	Robinson, Ld., Cum. Pref.	10	11½
4½	Do. 1 Mt. Perp. Db. Stk.	100	112
4/	Rochdale, Ltd.	10	6
4½	Do. 1 Mt. Deb. Stk.	100	98½
7	Royal, Brentford, Ltd.	10	21
	Do. Cum. Pref.	10	15
4½	Do. 1 Mt. Dbs. Red	100	107
6/	St. Louis, Ltd.	10	4
8	Do. Cum. Pref.	10	8½
14/	St. Pauli, Ltd.	10	10
7	Do. Cum. Pref.	10	12
4½	Salt (T.), L., 1 Db. Sk. Rd.	100	110
4½	Do. "B" Db. Stk. Red	100	108
—	San Francisco, Ltd.	10	¾
—	Do. 8 p.c. Cum. Pref.	10	¾

Breweries, &c. (*continued*) :—

Div.	Name.	Paid.	Price.
4½	Savill Brs., L., D. Sk. Rd.	100	118
4½	Scarboro., Ltd., 1 Db. Stk.	100	101
4	Shaw (Hy.), Ltd., 1 Mt. Db. Stk., Red.	100	104
22/	Showell's, Ltd.	10	33
7	Do. Cum. Pref.	10	17½
3/	Do. Gun. Shs.	5	7½
4½	Do. Mt. Db. Stk., Red.	100	—
4	Simonds, L., 1 D. Sk., Rd.	100	109
5½	Simson & McP., L., Cu. Pf.	10	9½
4½	Do. 1 Mt. Deb. Stk.	100	100
5/	Smith, Garrett, L., £20 Shs	10	16½
5	Do. Cum. Pref.	20	26
3½	Do. 3½ p.c. Mt. Db. Stk.	100	107
5	Smith's, Tadcster, L., CPf	10	12
4½	Do. Deb. Stk., Red.	100	112
4	Do. Deb. Stk. Red.	100	108
4½	Star, L., 1 M. Db. Stk., Rd.	100	106
4	Steward & P., L., 1 D. Sk.	100	111
9/	Strettons Derby, Ltd.	10	13
6	Do. Cum. Pref.	10	13½
4	Do. Irr. 1 Mt. Db. Stk.	100	103½
4½	Strong, Romsey, L., 1 D. S.	100	115
5	Stroud, L., Db. Sk., Rd.	100	111½
4½	Tadcaster To'er, L., D. Sk.	100	113
8/	Tamplin, Ltd	10	21
6	Do. Cum. Pref.	100	15
4	Do. "A" Db. Sk., Rd.	10	107
6	Thorne, Ltd., Cum. Pref.	10	14½
4	Do. Deb. Stk., Red.	100	105½
15/	Threlfall, Ltd.	10	46
6	Do. Cum. Pref.	10	16½
5	Do. 1 Mt. Dbs., Red.	100	116
4	Tollemache, L., D. Sk. Rd.	100	105
4	Truman, Hanb., D. Sk., R.	100	110
3	Do. "B" Mt. Db. Sk., Rd.	100	95
10/	United States, Ltd.	10	10
8	Do. Cum. Pref.	10	12
6	Do. 1 Mt. Deb.	100	107½
6/	Walker & H., Ld., Cm. Prf.	10	11½
4½	Do. 1 Mt. Deb. Stk., Red.	100	107
5	Walker, Peter, Ld. Cm. Prf.	10	13½
4	Do. 1 Mt. Dbs. Red.	100	111
4	Wallingford, L., D. Sk. Rd.	100	107
6	Watney, Ld., Cm. Prf. Sk.	100	167½
5	Do. Mt. Db. Sk., Rd.	100	115½
4½	Do. "B" Mt. Db. Sk., Rd.	100	112
3½	Do. Mt. Db. Stk.	100	101
5	Watney, D., Ld., Cm. Prf.	10	12½
4½	Do. 1 Mt. Db. Stk.	100	106
10/	Webster & Sons, Ltd.	10	16½
6	Do. Cum. Pref.	10	14
5	Wenlock Ltd., Pref.	10	12½
4	Do. 1 Mt. Db. Sk., Rd.	100	108
5	West Cheshire, L., Cu. Pf.	10	10½
4	Do. Irred. 1 Mt. Db. Sk.	100	99
4½	Whitbread, L., Cu. Pf. Sh.	100	124½
4	Do. Db. Stk., Red.	100	111
3½	Do. "B" Db. Stk., Rd.	100	101
9/	Wolverhmpton & D. Ld.	10	16½
6	Do. Cum. Pref.	10	13½
4½	Do. 1 Mt. Dbs., Red.	100	108
5½	Worthington, Ld., Cm. Prf.	10	15½
5½	Do. Cum. "B" Pref.	10	13½
4½	Do. Mt. Db. Sk., Rd.	100	112
3½	Do. Irr. "B" Db. Stk.	100	102
10/	Yates's Castle, Ltd.	10	13½
5	Do. Cum. Pref.	10	11
5	Younger W., L., Cu. Pf. Sh.	100	135

CANALS AND DOCKS.

Last Div.	Name.	Paid.	Price.
4	Birmingham Canal	100	142½
—	E. & W. India Dock	100	21
4	Do. Deb. Stk.	100	—
50/	Do. Def. Deb. Stk.	100	—
3½	Do. 1st Mt. Certs.	100	—
4	Do. Mt. Bds. (1885)	—	—
40/	G. Junction Ord. Shs.	100	151½
6/	Do. do. Pref.	10	19
4½	King's Lynn Per. Db. Stk.	100	118½
2½	Leeds & Lpool Canal	100	71
2½	Lndn & St. Kath. Dks.	100	56
4½	Do. Pref.	100	136½
4½	Do. Pref., 1878	100	132½
4½	Do. Pref., 1882	100	130
4	Do. Deb. Stk.	100	134½
—	Mchester Ship C. 5 p.c. Pf.	10	1½
3½	Do. 1st Perp. Mt. Deb.	100	98
—	Milford Dks. Db. Stk. "A"	100	18½
3½	Millwall Dk.	100	59
5	Do. Perp. Pref.	100	140½
4½	Do. Pref.	100	106½
5	Do. New Per. Prf., 1887	100	126½
5	Do. Per. Deb. Stk.	100	152½
4/	Newhaven Har.	10	14½
2½	N. Metropolitan	100	66
5	Sharpness Nw. Pf. "A" Sk.	100	144½
4	Do. Deb. Stk.	100	118½
4	Sheffield & S. Yorks Nav. 4½ p.c. Pref Stk.	100	117½
36.432	Suez Canal	20	138
7	Surrey Comcl. Dok., Ord.	100	148½
7	Do. Min. 4 p.c. Pref. "A"	110	150
5	Do. Pref. "B"	100	148½
5	Do do. "C"	100	148½
5	Do. do. "D"	100	144½
4½	Do. Deb. Stk.	100	152½

COMMERCIAL, INDUSTRIAL, &c.

Last Div.	Name.	Paid.	Price.
5	Accles, L., 1 Mt. Db., Red.	100	84¾
2/6	Aërated Bread, Ltd.	1	12¾
—	African Gold Recovery, L.	1	¼
2/	Aluminium, L., "A" Shs.	1	2
4½	Do. 1 Mt. Db. Stk., Red.	100	97
5½	Amelia Nitr., L., 1 Mort. Deb., Red.	100	82½
7/	Anglo-Chil. Nitrate, Ltd., Cum. Pref.	10	6½
4½	Do. Cons. Mt. Bds., Red.	100	79½
4½	Anglo-Russian Cotton, Ld., 1 Charge Debs., Red.	100	99
11/3	Angus (G., & Co., L.), £10	7½	17
6/	Apollinaris, Ltd.	10	11½
5/	Do. 5 p.c. Cum. Pref.	10	10½
4	Do. Irred. Deb. Stock	100	104
6/	Appleton, French, & S., L.	5	[illegible]
3/	Argentine Meat Pres., L., 7 p.c. Pref.	10	2½
5	Argentine Refinry, Db. Rd.	100	98
6d.	Armstrong, Whitw., Ltd.	1	3½
4	Do. Cum. Pref.	5	6½
5	Artisans', Labr. Dwllgs., L.	100	131½
4½	Do. Non-Cm. Prf., 1870	100	132½
4½	Do. do. 1884	100	132½
—	Asbestos & Asbestic, Ltd.	10	7½
2/7½	Ashley-grdns., L., C. Prf.	5	6½
4½	Do. 1 Mt. Deb. Stk.	100	112½
5/	Assam Rly. & Trdng., L., 8 p.c. Cum. Pref. "A"	10	15½
—	Do. Deferrd. "B" Shs.	1	4½
—	Do. do. (iss. f. pd)	1	3½
8/	Do. Cum. Pre-Prf. "A"	10	15
6/	Do. New Pref.	10	11½
5	Do. Debs., Red.	100	107
5	Do. Red. Mort. Debs.	100	109
6	Aust'lian Pastrl, L., Cu. Pf.	10	7½
8d.	Aylesbury Dairy, Ltd.	1	1½
4	Do. 4 p.c. Mt. Dbs.	100	104½
10/	Babcock & Wilcox, Ltd.	10	30
6	Do. 6 p.c. Cm. Prf.	10	16
8	Baker (Chs.), L., Cm. Pf.	5	9
8	Do. "B" Cm. Pref.	5	8½
8d.	Barker (John), Ltd.	1	2½
5½	Do. Cum. Pref.	5	7½
4½	Do. Irred. 1 Mt. Db. Stk.	100	130
—	Barnagore Jute, Ltd.	5	3
5	Do. Cum. Pref.	5	4½
7½d.	Belgravia Dairy, Ltd.	1	1½
5/6	Bell (R.) & Co., Ltd.	5	3½
1/	Bell's Asbestos, Ltd.	1	¾
5	Do. Mt. Db. Bds., Rd.	100	103
10/	Bengal Mills, Ltd.	10	11½
6/	Do. 5 p.c. Cum. Prf.	10	10½
2/5	Benson (J. W.) L., Cm. Pf.	10	10½
4	Do. Perp. Mt. Db. Stk.	100	101
6	Bergvik, L., 6 p.c. Cm. Pf.	10	12
12/	Do. Dfd.	10	9½
4½	Do. 1 Dbs., Red.	100	103½
5/	Birm'ham Vinegar, Ltd.	5	15
5	Do. Cum. Pref.	5	5½
4½	Do. 1 Mt. Db. Stk., Rd.	100	108½
5	Boake (A.) L., 5 p.c. Cu. Pf.	10	10½
2/6	Bodega, Ltd.	5	8½
4½	Do. Mt. Deb. Stk., Rd.	100	111
8/	Bottomley & Brs., Ltd.	10	6½
6/	Do. 6 p.c. Pt.	10	9½
8½d.	Bovril, Ltd.	1	[illegible]
1/0½	Do. Def.	1	⅞
6½d.	Do. Cum. Pref.	1	1
4½	Do. Deb. Stk.	100	101
5/	Bradbury, Gretrex., Ltd., £10 share	8	14
5/	Do. 5 p.c. Cum. Pref.	10	13½
5/	Brewers' Sugar, L., 5 p.c. Cum. Pref.	10	10½
3/6	Brighton Grd. Hotel, Ld.	5	3½
4	Do Mt. Db. Stk., Red.	100	100½
5	Bristol Hotel & Palm. Co., Ltd. 1st Mt. Red. Deb.	100	105
9½d.	British & Bengton's. Tea Tr. Asc., Ltd.	1	1½
5	Do. Cum. Prf.	5	5½
—	British Deli & Lgkat. Tobacco, Ltd.	1	½
—	Do. Cum. Prf.	1	½
—	British Tea Table, Ltd.	1	2½
5½	Do. Cum. Pref.	1	1½
2/6	Brooke, Ben., & Co., Ltd., Cum. Pref.	5	5½
7/6	Brooke, Bond & Co., Ltd.	5	20
3/	Brown Brs., L., Cum. Pref.	5	5½
10/	Browne & Eagle, Ltd.	10	13½
5	Do. Cum. Pref.	10	13
4	Do. Mrt. Db. Sk., Red.	100	110
20/	Brunner, Mond, & Co., Lt.	[illegible]	41
7/	Do. £10 shares	3½	17
7	Do. Cum. Pref.	10	18
7	Do. £10 shares	5	8½
10/	Bryant & May, Ltd.	5	20
3/	Bucknall, H., & Sons, Lt.	5	7½
6	Do. Cum Pref.	5	8
4/	Burke, E. & J., Ltd.	5	7½
6	Do. Cum. Pref.	5	7½
6	Do. Irred. Deb. Stk.	100	155
1/	Burlington Htls. Co., Ltd.	1	1½
5	Do. Cum. Pref.	1	1
4	Do. Perp. Deb. Stk.	100	105½
5	Bush, W. J., & Co., Ltd. Cum. Pref.	5	5½
4	Do. 1 Deb. Stk., Red.	100	102
5½	Callard, Stewart, & Watt, Ltd., Cum. Pref.	1	1½
4/	Callender's Cable L., Shs.	5	9½
4½	Do. 1 Deb. Stk., Red.	100	111½
—	Campbell, R., & Sons, Lt.	3	2½
6	Cantareira Water, Bd., Rd	100	99½
5	Do. (2nd issue)	100	90
4	Cartavio Sugar, Ltd., 6 p.c. 1st Debs., Red.	20	82½
9/	Cassell & Co., Ltd., £10	9	15½
5	Causton, Sir J., & Sons, Ltd., Cum. Pref.	10	13½

Commercial, &c. (*continued*) :—

Last Div.	Name.	Paid.	Price.
4	Cent. Prod. Mkt. of B.A. 1st Mt. Str. Debs.	100	81
4	Chappell & Co., Ltd., Mt. Deb. Stk. Red	100	103
6/	Chicago & N.W. Gran. 8 p.c. Cum. Pref.	10	3
—	Chicago Packing & Prov.	10	6
8	Do. Cum. Pref.	10	10½
6/	City Offices, Ltd	36½	13½
3½	Do. Mt. Deb. Stk.	100	108½
7/2½	Cy. London Real Prop., Ltd., £25 shs.	12	19
4/6	Do. £12½ shs.	7½	13½
3½	Do. Deb. Stk. Red.	100	106½
3½	Do. Deb. Stk. Red.	100	106½
3	Do.	100	100½
4/	Cy. of Santos Imprvts.,		
20/	Ltd., 7 p.c. Pref.	10	8½
8	Clay, Bock, & Co., Ltd.	10	5
6	Do. Cum. Pref.	10	10
20/	Do. Mort. Deb.	100	102½
6	Coats, J. & P., Ltd.	10	60½
4½	Do. Cum. Pref.	10	18
	Do. Deb. Stk. Red.	100	112½
9½d	Coburg Hotel, Ltd	1	1½
4	Do. Deb. Stk. Red.	100	102
6	Colonial Consign & Dis., Ltd., Cum. Pref.	5	4½
4½	Do. 1st Mort. Debs.	100	96½
—	Colorado Nitrate, Ltd.	5	½
4/	Co. Gén. des Asphtes. de F., Ltd.	6	6½
5	Do, Non-Cm. Prf.	—	5½
5	Cook, J. W., & Co., Ltd., Cum. Pref.	5	5½
5	Cook, T., & Son, Egypt, Ltd., 1st Mt. Deb. Red.	100	110½
—	Cork Co., Ltd., 6 p.c. Cum. Pref.	5	2½
5	Cory, W., & Sn, L., Cu. Pf.	5	6½
4	Do. 1st Deb. Stk. Red.	100	107
8½d.	Crisp & Co., Ltd	1	1½
5½	De. Cum. Pref.	1	1½
—	Crompton & Co., Ltd., 7 p.c. Cum. Pref.	5	2
5	Do. 1st Mt. Reg. Deb.	—	88½
4/6	Crossley, J., & Sons, Ltd.	5	8½
5	Do. Cum. Pref.	5	6½
—	Crystal Pal. Ord. "A" Stk.	100	8½
—	Do. "B" Red. Stk	100	1½
6	Do. 6 p.c. 1st 1887 Deb. Stk. Red.	100	117½
—	Do. 6 p.c. 2nd 1887 Deb. Stk. Red.	100	42½
—	Do. 6 p.c. 3rd 1887 Deb. Stk. Red.	100	17½
3	Do. 3 p.c. 1st 1895 Deb. Stk.	100	94½
—	Daimler Motor, Ltd.	10	6
4/	Dalgety & Co., £20 Shs.	5	5½
4½	Do. Deb. Stk.	100	123
4	Do.	100	115
7/	De Keyser's Ryl. Htl., L.	10	14
5	Do. Cum. Pref.	10	11½
4	Do. Deb. Stk., Red.	100	110
6	Denny, H., & Sons, Ltd., Cum. Pref.	10	14½
5/3	Devas, Routledge & Co., L.	7	8½
5	Dickinson, J., & Co., L., Cum. Pref. Stk.	100	123
4½	Domin. Cottn. Mls., Ltd. Mt. Stg. Dbs.	100	97
6/	Dorman, Long & Co., L.	5	4½
—	Eastmans, Ltd	10	2½
12/	Do. 8 p.c. Cum. Pref.	10	10½
2/6	F. C. Powder, Ltd	3	5½
1/6	Edison & Swn Utd. Elec. Ltd., "A" £5 Shs.	3	2½
2/6	Do. fully-paid	5	4½
4½	Ekman Pulp & Ppr. Co., Ltd., Mt. Deb., Red.	100	96
1/1½	Electric Construc., Ltd.	2	2½
7	Do. Cum. Pref.	2	3½
25/	Eley Bros., Ltd.	10	38
—	Elmore's Cop. Deptg., L.	1	[illegible]
—	Elmore's Wire Mnfg., L.	2	[illegible]
—	Elysée Pal. Hotel Co., L.	5/	[illegible]
5 p.c.	Do. 5 p.c. £100 Db., Rd.	70	95
8½d.	Evans, Ben., & Co., Ltd.	1	1
5	Do. 1 Mt. Db. Sk., Rd.	100	106
8½d.	Evans, D. H., & Co., L.	1	2½
6	Do. Cum. Pref.	1	1½
4½	Do. 1 Mt. Db. Sk., Rd.	100	112
2/1	*Evening News*, L., 5 p.c. Cum. Pref.	5	5½
5/3	Evered & Co., L., £10 Sh.	7	13
7/6	Do.	10	19
4	Fairbairn Pastoral Co., Aust., L., 1 Mt. Db., Rd.	100	102
6	Fairfield Shipbldg., Ltd., Cum. Pref.	10	10½
4½	Do. Mort. Deb. Stk.	100	109½
6/	Farmer & Co., Ld., 6 p.c. Cum. Pref.	10	13½
10	Field, J. C. & J., Ltd.	10	10
14/	Do. 7 p.c. Cum. Pref.	10	14
1/3	Fordham, W. B., & Sns. Ld.	2	2
5/6	Fore-st. Warehouse, Ltd.	11	9½
4	Do. Regd. Debs., Rd.	100	103½
3/6	Foster, M. B. & Sons, Ltd.	4	6
5	Do. Pref.	10	11½
9/	Foster, Porter, & Co., L.	10½	15½
4	Fowler, J., & Co. (Leeds) Ltd., 1 Mt. Deb., Red.	100	103½
3/	Fraser & Chalmers, Ltd.	3	2½
4½	Free, Rodwell & Co., Ltd. Deb Stk.	100	104
6½d.	Furness, T., & Co., Ltd., 5½ p.c. Cum. Pref.	1	
4½	Gartside & Co. (of Manchstr), L., 1 Mt. Db. Sk.	100	[illegible]
11	Genl. Hydraul. Power, L.	100	27½

Commercial, &c. (*continued*):—

Last Div.	Name.	Paid.	Price.
8/	Gillman & Spencer, Ltd	5	2½
6	Do. Pref.	5	4¼
5	Do. Mort. Debs.	50	51
4	Goldsbro., Mort & Co., L., "A" Deb. Stk., Red.	100	74½
—	Do. 3 p.c. "B" Inc. Deb. Stk., Red	100	14
8/	Gordon Hotels, Ltd.	10	20
5½	Do. Cum. Pref.	10	14½
4½	Do. Perp. Deb. Stk.	100	137½
4	Do. do.	100	122½
—	Greenwich Inld. Linoleum Co., Ltd.	1	⅛
7	Greenwood & Batley, Ltd., Cum. Pref.	10	10
7½d.	Hagemann & Co., Ltd., 6 p.c. Cum. Pref.	1	1
—	Hammond, Ltd.	10	¼
—	Do. 8 p.c. Cum. Pref.	10	2½
—	Do. 6 p.c. Cum. Inc. Stk. Red.	100	45
4	Hampton & Sons, Ltd., 4 p.c. 1 Mt. Db. St. Red.	100	105
	Hans Crescent Htl., L., 6 p.c. Cum. Pref.	5	3
4	Do. 1 Mt. Deb. Stk.	100	90
5	Harmsworth, Ld., Cm. Pf.	1	1⅛
4/	Harrison, Barber, Ltd.	5	4½
3/	Harrod's Stores, Ltd.	1	4½
2/6	Do. Cum. Pref.	5	7½
5½	Hawaiian Comcl. & Sug. 1 Mt. Debs.	100	91½
5	Hazell, Watson, L., C. P.	10	12
18/	Henley's Teleg., Ltd.	10	22½
7	Do. Pref. Shs.	10	19
4½	Do. Mt. Db. Stk., Rd.	100	112½
6	Henry, Ltd.	10	12½
5	Do. Cum. Pref.	10	13½
4½	Do. Mt. Debs., Red.	50	53
6	Hepworth, Ld., Cm. Prf.	10	11
—	Herrmann, Ltd.	1	⅛
—	Hildesheimer, Ltd.	3	1½
1/2½	Holbrn. & Frasca, Ltd.	1	2
5	Do. Cum. Pref.	10	11½
4	Do. Deb. Stk.	100	113
6	Home & Col. Stres, L., C. P	5	7½
6	Hood & M.'s Stres., Ltd., Cum. Pref.	1	¼
6	Hook, C. T. Ltd.	10	6
7/2	Hornsby, Ltd., £10 Shs.	8	3
5/6	Do. 6 p.c. Cm. Pf. Sk.	100	90
—	Hotchks. Ordn., Ltd.	10	1
—	Do. 7 p.c. Cm. Prf.	10	4
5	Do. 1 Mt. Dbs., Rd.	100	95½
6	Htl. Cecil, Ld., Cm. Prf.	5	4
4	Do. 1 Mt. D. Sk., R.	100	105½
8/	Howard & Bulgh, Ltd.	10	38
6	Do. Pref.	10	16
4	Do. Deb. Stk., Red.	100	107
5/	Howell, J., Ltd., £5 Shs.	4	9
—	Howell & Js., Ld., £3½ Shs.	3	⅛
2/6	Humber, Ltd.	1	⅜
6	Do. Cum. Pref.	1	¾
5/6	Hunter, Wilts., Ltd.	5	7
2/7	Hyam Clthg., Ltd., 5 p.c. Cum. Pref.	5	5½
10/	Impl. Russn. Cotton, L.	5	6
5	Impd. Industl. Dwgs., Ld.	100	130½
6d.	Do. Defrd.	1	1½
25/	Impd. Wood Pave., Ltd.	10	15
15/	Ind. Rubber, Gutta Per. Telegraph Works, Ltd.	10	21½
4	Do. 1 Mt. Debs., Red.	100	104
6	Intern. Tea, Cum. Pref.	5	6½
10½d.	Jays, Ltd.	1	1½
5½	Do. Cum. Pref.	5	6½
8½d.	Jones & Higgins, Ltd.	1	2½
4½	Do. 1 Mt. Db. Sk., Rd.	100	113
5/	Kelly's Directory, Ltd., 5 p.c. Cum. Pref.	10	12½
4	Do. Mort. Db. Sk., Rd.	100	106
—	Kent Coal Explrtn. Ltd.	1	⅜
9½d.	King, Howmann, Ltd.	1	1½
4/	Kinloch & Co., Ltd.	5	8½
6	Do. Pref.	5	7
5	Lady's Pictorial Pub., Ltd., Cum. Pref.	5	5
—	La Guaira Harb., Ltd., 7 p.c. Deb. Stk.	100	—
—	Do. 2 Mt. 7 p.c. Deb. Bds., Red.	100	—
4/	Lagunas Nitrate, Ltd.	5	2
2/	Lagunas Syn., Ltd.	5	1
5	Do. 1 Mt. Debs., Red.	100	80
—	L. Copais Ld., 1 Mt. 6 p.c. Debs., Red.	100	35½
3/	Lautaro Nitrate, Ltd.	5	4
5	Do. 1 Mt. Debs., Red.	—	100
9/	Lawes Chem. L., £10 shs.	9	5½
24/	Do. N. Cm. Min. Pref.	10	12½
—	Leeds Forge, 7 p.c. Cm. Pf.	5	3½
5	Do. 1 Mt. Debs., Red.	50	48
5	Lever Bros., L., Cm. Pf.	10	13½
6	Liberty, L., 6 p.c. Cm. Pf.	10	15
20/	Liebig's, Ltd.	20	73½
5	Lilley & Sk., L., Cm. Pf.	5	5½
30/4	Linoleum Manfg. Ltd.	5	16
3/	Linotype, Ltd., Pre	5	5½
3/	Do. Def.	5	7½
4/	Lister & Co., Ltd.	10	4
5	Do. Cum. Pref.	10	8½
8/	Liverpool. Nitrate	5	5
—	Liverpool. Warehsg., Ltd	10	3½
5½	Do. Cum. Pref.	10	8½
4	Do. 1 Mt. Db. Stk., Rd.	100	105
5½	Lockharts, Ltd., Cm. Pf.	1	1½
4/6	Ldn. & Til. Lighterage £10	9	6½
6/	Ldn. Comcl. Sale Rms., L.	10	17½
3	Do. 1 Mt. Deb. Stk., Red.	100	103
3	London Nitrate, Ltd.	5	1½
4/	London Nitrate, Ld. 8 p.c. Cm. Min. Pf.	5	3½
8/	London Pavilion, Ltd.	5	7

Commercial, &c. (*continued*):—

Last Div.	Name.	Paid.	Price.
2/6	London Produce Clg. Ho., Ltd., £10 Shares	2½	3½
4/	London Stereos., Ltd.	5	3
6d.	Ldn. Un. Laun. L. Cm. Pf.	1	⅛
8½d.	Louise, Ltd.	1	⅛
5½	Do. Cum. Pref.	1	⅛
5/	Lovell & Christmas, Ltd.	5	11½
6	Do. Cum. Pref.	5	7½
4	Do. Mt. Deb. Stk., Red.	100	107
1/3	Lyons, Ltd.	1	3½
4½	Do. 1 Mt. Deb. Stk., Rd.	100	111½
10/	Machinery Trust, Ltd.	5	14½
4½	Do. 4½ Deb. Stk.	100	106
6	MacLellan, L., Min. C. Pf.	10	9½
5	Do. 1 Mt. Debs., 1900	100	101½
—	McEwan, J. & Co., Ltd.	10	1½
6	Do. Mt. Debs., Red.	100	89½
8	McNamara, L., Cm. Pref.	10	9
7½d.	Maison Virot, Ltd.	1	1½
2/7	Do. 6 p.c. Cum. Pref.	5	4½
5/	Manbré Sacc., L., Cm. Pf.	10	12
10/	Mangan Brze., L., £10 Shs.	6	15½
2/	Mason & Mason, Ltd.	5	2½
6	Do. Cum. Pref.	5	5½
—	Maynards, Ltd.	1	⅛
6	Do. Cum. Pref.	1	⅛
9½d.	Mazawattee Tea, Ltd.	1	1½
5	Do. Cum. Pref.	5	5½
6	Mellin's Food Cum. Pref.	5	6½
4½	Met. Ascn. Imp. Dwlgs. L.	100	110
3½	Do. 1 Mt. Deb. Stk.	100	97
5	Metro. Indus. Dwlgs., Ltd.	5	5
4	Do. do. Cum. Pref.	5	5½
5	Metro. Prop., L., Cm. Pf.	5	5½
4½	Do. 1st Mt. Debs. Stk.	100	108½
6	Mexican Cotton 1 Mt Db.	100	93½
4½	Mid. Class Dwlgs., L., Db.	100	120½
1/	Millars' Karri, Ltd.	1	3½
6	Do. Cum. Pref.	1	1½
5/	Milner's Safe, Ltd.	10	20½
10/	Moir & Son, Ltd., Pref.	5	8½
6	Morgan Cruc., L., Cm. Pf.	10	14½
2/	Morris, B., Ltd.	3½	3½
—	Murray L. 5½ p.c. C. Pf.	5	5½
—	Do. 4½ 1 Mt. Db. Sk. Rd.	100	108
—	Natnl. Dwlgs., L., 5 p.c. Pf.	5	1
1/7½	Nat. Safe Dep., Ltd.	4	3½
6	Do. Cum. Pref.	1	1½
—	Native Guano, Ltd.	5	⅛
—	Nelson Bros., Ltd.	10	2½
5	Do. Deb. Stk., Red.	100	80½
4/	Neuchtel Asph., Ltd.	10	10½
—	New Central Borneo, Ld.	1	—
10d.	New Darvel Tob., Ltd.	18/	1½
1/6	New Explosives, Ltd.	3	3
5/3½	New Gd. Htl., Bham, L.	5	4
5½	Do. Pref.	5	4½
4	Do. 1 Mt. Db. Stk., Rd.	100	96½
—	New Julia Nitrate, Ltd.	10/	½
—	New Ldn. Borneo Tob., L.	16/	⅛
1/6	New Premier Cycle, Ltd.	1	⅛
6	Do. 6 p.c. Cum. Pref.	1	⅛
4½	Do. 4½ p.c. 1 Mt. Db. Rd	100	—
—	New Tamargl. Nitr., Ltd	1	⅛
—	Do. 8 p.c. Cum. Pref.	1	⅛
6	Do. 6 p.c. 1 Mt. Dbs. Rd.	100	62½
3·78d.	Newnes, G., L., Cm. Prf.	1	1½
1/3	Nitr. Provision, Ltd.	2½	⅛
24/	Nobel-Dynam., Ltd.	10	18½
—	North Brazn. Sugar, Ltd.	1	⅛
15/	Oakey, Ltd.	10	31
6	Do. Cum. Pref.	10	17
—	Paccha Jazp. Nitr., Ltd.	5	½
5	Pac. Borax, L., 1 Db. Rd.	100	110
—	Palace Hotel, Ltd.	10	5½
5½	Do. Cum. Pref.	10	8½
4	Do. 1 Mt. Deb. Stk.	100	104
2/6	Palmer, Ltd.	5	1½
6	Do. Cum. Pref.	5	2½
9 1/10d.	Paquin, Ltd.	1	1
6	Do. Cum. Pref.	5	4½
5½	Parnall, Ltd., Cum. Pref.	1	⅛
4/6	Pawsons, Ltd., £10 Shs.	6	6½
4	Do. Mt. Debs., Red.	100	106
6	Pearks, G. & T., Ltd., 6 p.c. Cum. Pref.	1	⅛
9½d.	Pears, Ltd.	1	1½
6	Do. Cum. Pref.	10	14
5	Do. Deb. Stk.	100	129
5½	Pearson, C. A., L., Cu. Pf.	5	5½
4/3	Peebles, Ltd.	5	8
5	Do. Cum. Pref.	5	6½
4½	Do. Mt. Deb. Stk. Red.	100	113½
5½	Peek Bros., Ltd., 1 Cum. Pref., Nos. 1-60,000	5	6
3½	Do. 3½ p.c. 1 Db. Stk.	100	103½
7½d.	Pegamoid, Ltd.	1	⅛
—	Phospho-Guano, Ltd.	5	2½
—	Pillsbury-W. Fl. Mills, L.	10	2
16/	Do. 8 p.c. Cum. Pref.	10	6½
6	Do. 1 Mort. Debs.	100	95½
9½d.	Plummer, Ltd.	1	1½
5	Do. Cum. Pref.	5	5½
7/6	Price's Candle, Ltd.	16	36
6	Priest Marians, L., Cm. Pf.	1	1½
6	Pryce Jones, Ld., Cm. Pf.	5	7½
5	Do. Deb. Stk.	100	122
10½d.	Pullman, Ltd.	1	1½
6d.	Do. Cum. Pref.	1	1½
11 1/10	Raleigh Cycle, Ltd.	1	⅛
6	Do. Cum. Pref.	1	⅛
—	Recife Drnge. Ld. 1 Mt. Debs., R	100	19
6	Redfern, Ltd. Cum. Prf.	10	14
5	Ridgways, Ltd., Cu. Pf.	5	5½
—	R. Janeiro Cy. Imps. Ld.	25	9
5	Do. Debs.	100	86½
5	Do. 1882-1893	100	86½
11/	R. Jan Fl. Mills, Ltd.	7	6½
5	Do. 1 Mt. Debs., Rd.	100	94
—	Riv. Plate Meat, Ltd.	5	3½
—	Do. Pref.	5	5
8½d.	Roberts, J. R., Ltd.	1	1½

Commercial, &c. (*continued*):—

Last Div.	Name.	Paid.	Price.
5	Roberts 1 Mt. D. Sk., Rd.	100	112
8½d.	Roberts, T. R., Ltd.	1	2½
5	Do. Cum. Pref.	1	1½
3/	Rosario Nit., Ltd.	5	3½
5	Do. Debs., Red.	100	105
5	Do. Huara, Debs.	—	104
1/	Rover Cycle, Ltd.	1	⅛
6/	Ryl. Aquarium, Ltd.	5	4½
6	Do. Pref.	5	6
5	Ryl. Htl., Edin., Cm. Pf.	1	1½
1/2½	Ryl. Niger, Ltd., £10 Sh.	2	3
6/	Do.	10	16
—	Russian Petroleum	10	21
—	Do. 6½ p.c. Cm. Prf.	10	11
3/	Ruston, Proctor, Ltd.	10	11
4½	Do. 1 Mort. Debs.	100	104
6/	Sadler, Ltd.	12	7
—	Sal. Carmen Nit., Ltd.	5	4
9d.	Salmon & Gluck., Ltd.	1	1⅛
	Salt Union, Ltd.	10	1½
1½	Do. 7 p.c. Pref.	10	5½
4½	Do. Deb. Stk.	100	101½
4½	Do. "B" Deb. Sk., Rd.	100	97½
—	San Donato Nit., Ltd.	5	⅛
2/6	San Jorge Nit., Ltd.	5	3½
—	San Pablo Nit., Ltd.	5	⅛
—	San Sebastn. Nit., Ltd.	5	⅛
1/9	Sanitas, Ltd	1	2½
—	Sa. Elena Nit., Ltd.	5	⅛
—	Sa. Rita Nit., Ltd.	5	1½
5/	Savoy Hotel, Ltd.	10	16
7	Do. Pref.	10	13½
4	Do. 1 Mt. Deb. Stk.	100	111½
5	Do. Debs., Red	100	102½
5	Do. & Ldn. For. Htl., Ltd., 5 p.c. Debs. Red.	100	99
1½d.	Schweppes, Ltd.	1	1⅛
—	Do Def.	1	⅛
5	Do. Cum. Pref.	1	1½
4	Do. Deb. Stk.	100	108
1/	Singer Cyc., Ltd.	1	⅛
5½	Do Cum. Pref.	1	⅛
—	Smokeless Pwdr., Ltd.	1	⅛
5½d.	S. Eng. Dairies, Ltd., 6 p.c. Cum. Pref.	1	1½
—	Sowler Thos. L.	1	1½
3/4½	Do. 5½ Cm. Pf.	5	5½
4/6	Spencer, Turner, & Co. Ltd	5	8½
5	Do. Cum. Pref.	5	6½
5	Spicer, Ld., 5 p.c. Dbs. Rd.	100	65
4/	Spiers & Pond, Ltd.	10	21
5	Do. 1 Mt. Debs., Red.	100	117½
5	Do. "A" Db. Stk., Rd.	100	111
5	Do. "B" 1 Db. Stk., Rd.	100	111
4	Do. Fd. "C" 1 Db. S., R.	100	104
7/6	Spratt's, Ltd	5	13
4	Do. Debs., 1914	—	105
5	Steiner Ld., Cm. Pf.	10	11½
4	Do. 1 Mt. Db. Sk. Rd.	100	106
9/	Stewart & Clydesdale, L.	10	14
6	Do. Cum. Pref.	10	15
35/5	Sulphide Corp.	100	80
1/	Swan & Edgar, L.	1	1½
1/	Sweetmeat Automatic, L.	1	4
2/9	Teetgen, Ltd., Cum. Pref.	5	6
24/	Teleg. Construction., Ld.	12	36½
5	Do. Db. Bds., Rd., 1899	100	103½
3/0½	Tilling, Ld. 5½ p.c. Cm. Prf.	5	6½
4	Do. 4 p.c. 1 Dbs., Rd.	—	104
8½d.	Tower Tea, Ltd.	1	1½
5	Do. Cum. Pref.	5	5½
5	Travers, Ltd., Cum. Pref.	10	12½
4	Do. 1 Mt. Dbs., Rd.	100	105
6	Tucuman Sug., 1 Dbs., Rd.	100	100
4/	United Alkali, Ltd.	10	1½
7	Do. Cum. Pref.	10	7½
5	Do. Mt. Db. Stk., Rd.	100	109½
2½d.	United Horse Shoe, Ltd., Non-Cum. 8 p.c. Pref.	1	⅛
5	Un. Kingm. Tea, Cm. Prf.	5	4½
2/	Un. Lankat Plant., Ltd.	1	2
4/	Un. Limmer Asphlte., Ld.	3	4½
13/	Val de Travers Asph., L.	10	15½
3/	V. den Bergh's, L., Cm. P.	5	6½
6	Walkers, Park., L., C. Pf.	10	3
4½	Do. 1 Mt. Debs., Red.	100	90½
6/	Wallis, Thos. & Co., Ltd.	5	14
6	Do. Cum. Pref.	5	8½
5½	Waring, Ltd., Cum. Pref.	5	5½
4½	Do. 1 Mt. Db. Sk., Red.	100	113
4½	Do. Irred. "B" Db. Stk.	100	105
12/	Waterlow, Dfd. Ord.	10	14½
4/	Do. Pref.	10	14½
3½	Do. Cum. Pref.	10	10½
10/	Waterlow Bros. & L., Ld.	10	9
5	Do. Pref.	10	12½
1/2½	Welford, Ltd.	1	2
4½	Do. Debs., Red.	100	108
1/	Welford's Surrey Dairies, Ltd.	1	1½
7½d.	West London Dairy, Ltd.	1	1
4½	Wharncliffe Dwllgs, L., Pf.	10	11½
18/10	Do. 3 p.c. Irr. Mt. Db. Sk.	100	96
6d.	White, A. J., Ltd.	1	⅛
6	Do. 6 p.c. Cum. Pref.	1	⅛
4	White, J. Bazley, Ltd., 1 Mort. Debs., Red	100	100½
5	White, R., Ltd., 1 Mort. Deb. Stock, Red.	100	104½
5/	White, Tomkins, Ltd	10	12
5	Do. Cum. Pref.	10	11½
6	White, W. N., L., Cm. Pf.	1	1
2/6	Wickens, Pease & Co., L.	5	3½
6	Wilkie, Ltd., Cum. Pref.	10	15½
3/6	Willans & Robinson, Ltd.	5	9½
6	Do. Cum. Pref.	5	7½
4½	Do. 1 Mt. Db. Stk., Red.	100	108
7½d.	Williamsons, L., Cm. Prf.	1	1½
6	Winterbottm. Book Cloth, Ltd., Cum. Prf.	10	15
3/	Yates, Ltd.	5	6½
6	Do. Cum. Pref.	5	6½
	Young's Paraffin, Ltd.	4	1½

CORPORATION STOCKS—COLONIAL AND FOREIGN.

Per Cent.	Name.	Paid.	Price.
6	Auckland City, '72 1904-24	100	118
6	Do. Cons., '79, Red. 1930	100	138½
5	Do. Deb. Ln., '83 . . 1934-8	100	117
6	Auckland Harb. Debs.	100	111½
5	Do. 1917	100	115
5	Do. 1936	100	116
5½	Balmain Boro' 1914	—	116
5	Boston City (U.S.)	100	102½
5	Do. 1902	100	105
5	Brunswick Town 5. c. Debs. 1916-20	100	111
15/	B. Ayres City 6 p.c.	100	57
4½	Do. 4½ p.c.	100	75
5	Cape Town, City of	100	115
4	Do. 1943	100	116
4	Chicago, City of, Gold 1915	—	110
6	Christchurch 1926	100	131½
—	Cordoba City	100	17½
5	Duluth (U.S.) Gold 1926	—	110
6	Dunedin (Otago) 1925	100	127½
6	Do. 1906	100	115
5	Do. Consols 1908	100	111
4	Durban Insc. Stk. 1944	100	111
4	Essex Cnty., N. Jersey 1926	100	114½
5	Fitzroy, Melbrne. 1916-19	100	110
5	Gisborne Harbour 1915	100	110½
4	Greymouth Harbour 1925	100	110
4	Hamilton 1934	100	108
5	Hobart Town 1918-30	100	116
4	Do. 1940	100	107
4½	Invercargill Boro. Dbs. 1936	100	111
6	Kimberley Boro., S.A. Dbs.	—	102
4	Launceston Twn. Dbs. 1916	100	107
6	Lyttleton, N.Z., Harb. 1929	100	125
4	Melbourne Bd. of Wks. 1921	100	107
5	Melb. City Debs. 1897-1907	100	107½
4½	Do. Debs. 1908-27	100	113½
4	Do. Debs. 1915-20-22	100	106
5	Melbne. Harb. Bds., 1908-9	100	112
4½	Do. do. 1915	100	110
4	Do. do. 1918-21	100	105
4½	Melbrne. Tms, Dbs. 1914-16	100	113
4½	Do. Fire Brig. Db. 1921	100	108
5	Mexico City Stg.	100	90
4	Moncton N. Bruns. City	100	103
4½	Montevideo	100	59
5	Montreal Stg.	100	104
5	Do. 1874	100	104
5	Do. 1879	100	106
3½	Do. 1933	100	104
3	Do. Perm. Deb. Stk.	100	98½
4	Do. Cons. Deb. Stk. 1932	100	113
6	Napier Boro. Consolid. 1914	100	119
5	Napier Harb. Debs. 1920	100	115
5	Do. Debs. 1928	100	107
6	New Plymouth Harb. Debs. 1909	100	108
6	New York City 1901	—	107½
3½	Do. 1910-26	—	105½
4½	Nth. Melbourne Debs. 1-600 1921	100	105
5	Oamaru Boro. Cons. 1920	100	101
6	Do. Harb. Bds. (Reg.)	100	74
25/	Do. 6 p.c. (Bearer) 1919	100	35
6	Otago Harb. Deb. Reg.	100	103
6	Do. 1877	100	107
6	Do. 1881 1921	100	115
5	Do. Debs. 1921	100	107
5	Do. Cons. 1934	100	105
6	Ottawa City	100	111
6	Do. 1904	100	113½
4½	Do. Debs. 1913	100	112
6	Port Elizabeth Waterworks	100	111
5	Port Louis	100	111
5	Prahran Debs. 1917	100	109
4	Do. Debs. 1919	100	102
6	QuebecC. Coupon. 1875 1905	100	112
6	Do. do. 1878 1908	100	116
4½	Do. Debs. 1914-18	100	108
4	Do. Debs. 1923	200	108
3½	Do. Cns. Rg. Stk., Red.	100	101
5	Richmond (Melb.) Dbs. 1917	100	113
4	Rio Janeiro City	100	57
4	Rome City	100	—
4	Do. 2nd to 8th Iss.	100	92
—	Rosario C.	100	26½
—	Do.	100	26½
4	St. Catherine (Ont.) 1926	100	101
4	St. John, N.B., Debs. 1934	—	103
4½	St. Kilda (Melb) Dbs. 1918-21	100	105
4	St. Louis C. (Miss.) 1911	100	106
4	Do. 1913	100	103½
3·65	Do. 1915	—	110
—	Santa Fé City Debs.	100	21
6	Santos City	100	95
6	Sofia City	100	83
5	Sth. Melbourne Debs. 1915	100	111
4½	Do. Debs. 1919	100	107
5	Sydney City 1904	100	109
4	Do. Debs. 1912-13	100	107
4	Do. do. (1894) 1919	100	109
7	Timaru Boro. 7 p.c. 1910	100	126½
5	Timaru Harb. Debs 1914	100	107
5	Do. Debs. 1916	100	106
6	Toronto City Wtwks 1904-6	100	114
6	Do. Cons. Debs. 1898	100	101
5	Do. G. Cns. Dbs. 1919-20	100	118
4	Do. Strlg. 1922-8	100	107
4	Do. Local Improv.	100	102
3½	Do. 1929	100	105
5½	Valparaiso	100	100
4	Vancouver 1931	100	107
4	Do. 1932	100	108
6	Wanganui Harb. Dbs. 1905	100	110
6	Wellington Con. Deb. 1907	100	117
6	Do. Improv., 1879	100	125
6	Do. Wtrwks. Dbs., 1880	100	123
4½	Do. Debs., 1893 1933	100	116
4½	Wellington Harb. 1907	100	104
4	Westport Harb. Dbs. 1903	100	110
6	Winnipeg City Deb. 1907	—	118
5	Do. 1914	100	119

FINANCIAL, LAND, AND INVESTMENT.

Last Div.	Name.	Paid.	Price.
5	Agency, Ld. & Fin. Aust., Ltd., Mt. Db. Stk., Rd.	100	90½
	Amer. Frehld. Mt. of Lon., Ld., Cum. Pref. Stk.	100	87½
4½	Do. Deb. Stk., Red.	100	93
1/	Anglo-Amer. Db. Cor., L.	2	1
4	Do. Deb. Stk., Red	100	106½
5½	Ang.-Ceylon & Gen. Est., Ltd., Cons. Stk.	100	65
6	Do. Reg. Debs., Red.	100	102½
—	Ang.-Fch. Explorn., Ltd.	1	2 5/16
6	Do. Cum. Pref.	1	11/16
—	Argent. Ld. & Inv., Ltd. £1 Shares	10/	nil
—	Do. Cum. Pref.	4	1½
1/	Assets Fnders.' Sh., Ltd.,	4	1⅜
6/	Assets Realis., Ltd., Ord.,	5	8¼
5	Do. Cum. Pref.	5	6½
26/	Austrln. Agricl £25 Shs.	21½	63½
—	Aust. N. Z. Mort., Ltd., £10 Shs.	1	1½d.
4½	Do. Deb. Stk., Red.	100	90½
4	Do. Deb. Stk., Red.	100	82½
4½	Australian Est. & Mt., L., 1 Mt. Deb. Stk., Red.	100	104
5	Do. "A" Mort. Deb. Stk., Red.	100	96
2/6	Australian Mort., Ld., & Fin., Ltd. £25 Shs.	5	4
1/6	Do. New, £25 Shs.	3	2½
4	Do. Deb. Stk.	100	110½
3	Do. Do.	100	85
5	Baring Est. 2 Mt. Debs., Red.	100	105
5	Bengal Presidy. 1 Mort. Deb., Red.	100	106
25/	British Amer. Ld. "A"	1	19
—	Do. "B"	24	7
1/7½	Brit. & Amer. Mt., Ltd. £10 Shs.	2	½
5/	Do. Pref.	10	10
4	Do. Deb. Stk., Red.	100	102
1/3	Brit. & Austrian Tst Ln., Ltd. £25 Shs.	2½	¾
4½	Do. Perm. Debs., Red.	100	103
1½d.	Brit. N. Borneo. £1 Shs.	15/	½
2½d.	Do.	1	1
—	Brit. S. Africa	1	2 13/16
5	Do. Mt. Deb., Red.	—	97
6	B. Aires Harb. Tst., Red.	100	99
12/6	Canada Co.	1	26
—	Canada N. W. Ld., Ltd.	$25	83½
—	Do. Pref.	$100	$50½
4	Canada Perm. Loan & Sav. Perp. Deb. Stk.	100	99½
—	Curamalan Ld., 1 Mt. 7 p.c. Bds., Red.	—	94½
3/7½	Deb Corp., Ld., £10 Shs	4	3
5	Do. Cum. Pref.	10	11½
4	Do. Perp. Deb. Stk.	100	111
9d.	Deb. Corp. Fders' Sh., Ld.	3	⅜
4/5⅛	Eastn. Mt. & Agency, Ld., "A"	10	6
4½	Do. Deb. Stk., Red.	100	100
5	Equitable Revers. In. Ltd.	100	—
2/	Exploration, Ltd.	1	1 11/16
1	Freehold Trst. of Austria. Ltd. £10 Shs.	1	¾
4	Do. Perp. Deb. Stk.	100	100
—	Genl. Assets Purchase, Ltd., 5 p.c. Cum. Pref.	10	—
70/	Genl. Reversionary, Ltd.	100	—
3½	Holborn Vi. Land	100	105
3½	House Prop. & Inv.	100	85½
13/	Hudson's Bay	13	21
—	Hyderabad (Deccan)	5	3
4	Impl. Col. Fin. & Agcy. Corp.	100	94½
4½	Impl. Prop. Inv., Ltd., Deb. Stk., Red.	100	91½
2/6	Internatl. Fincial. Soc., Ltd. £7½ Shs.	2½	1¼
4	Do. Deb. Stk., Red.	100	99½
1/9½	Ld. & Mtge. Egypt, Ltd. £18 Shs.	3	2¾
5	Do. Debs., Red.	100	103
4½	Do. Debs., Red.	100	101
—	Ld. Corp. of Canada, Ltd.	1	⅝
4½	Ld. Mtge. Bk. of Texas Deb. Stk.	100	—
3½	Ld. Mtge. Bk. Victoria 4½ p.c. Deb. Stk.	100	78
2/9½	Law Debent. Corp., Ltd., £10 Shs.	2	1¾
4½	Do. Cum. Pref.,	10	12
4	Do. Deb. Stk.	100	116
—	Law Land, L., 4½ Cm. Prf.	5	5½
1/	Ldn. & Australasian Deb. Corp., Ltd., £4 Shs.	2	½
4½	Do. 4½ p.c. Mt. Deb. Stk., Red.	100	99
1/9	Ldn. & Middx. Frhld. Est. £2 Shs.	35/	3
2/6	Lndn. & N. Y. Inv. Corp., Ltd.	5	1¾
5	Do. 5 p.c. Cum. Pref.	10	8½
1/6	Ldn. & Nth. Assets Corp., Ltd., £2 Shs.	1½	¾
2	Ldn. & N. Deb. Corp., L.	2	1½
4	Ldn. & S. Afric. Explrn. Ltd.	½	13¾
2/	Mtge. Co. of R. Plate, Ltd. £10 Shs.	2	3½
4½	Do. Deb. Stk., Red.	100	113
4½	Morton, Rose Est., Ltd., 1st Mort. Debs.	—	101
6/	Natal Land Col. Ltd.	10	7½
4/	Do. 8 p.c. Pref., 1870	5	8½
5/6	Natl. Disct. L., £25 Shs.	5	10½
4½	New Impl. Invest., Ltd. Pref. Stk.	100	61½
—	New Impl. Invest., Ltd. Def. Stk.	100	9

Financial, Land, &c. (*continued*):—

Last Div.	Name.	Paid.	Price.
3½	N. Zld. Assets Real Deb.	100	99
4	N. Zld. Ln. & Mer. Agcy., Ltd Prf. Ln, Deb. Stk	100	94
2/6	N. Zld. Tst. & Ln. Ltd., £25 Shs.	5	1½
12/6	N. Zld. Tst. & Ln. Ltd., 5 p.c. Cum. Pref.	25	19
—	N. Brit. Australsn. Ltd.	100	6½
—	Do. Irred. Guar.	100	32½
5	Do. Mort. Debs.	100	82½
4½	N. Queensld. Mort. & Inv., Ltd., Deb. Stk.	100	92
—	Oceana Co., Ltd.	—	—
6	Peel Riv., Ld. & Min. Ltd.	100	88½
—	Peruvian Corp., Ltd.	100	2½
—	Do. 4 p.c. Pref.	100	9½
3	Do. 6 p.c. 1 Mt. Debs., Red.	100	40
—	Queenld. Invest. & Ld. Mort. Pref. Ord. Stk.	100	20
3/7	Queenld. Invest. & Ld. Mort. Ord. Shs.	4	4
4	Queenld. Invest. & Ld. Mort. Perp. Debs.	100	88
3½	Raily. Roll Stk. Tst. Deb., 1903-6	100	100½
50/	Reversiony. Int. Soc., Ltd.	100	—
2/8½	Riv. Plate Trst., Loan & Agcy., L., "A" £10 Shs.	2	4
1/6	Riv. Plate Trst., Loan & Agcy., Ltd., Def. "B"	5	3½
	Riv. Plate Trst., Loan & Agy., L., Db. Stk., Red.	100	109
—	Santa Fé & Cord. Gt. South Land, Ltd.	20	5
—	Santa Fé Land	10	2½
2/	Scot. Amer. Invest., Ltd. £10 Shs.	2	2¾
2½	Scot. Australian Invest., Ltd., Cons.	100	78½
6	Scot. Australian Invest., Ltd., Guar. Pref.	100	135½
5	Scot. Australian Invest., Ltd., Guar. Pref.	100	106½
4	Scot. Australian Invest., Ltd., 4 p.c. Perp. Dbs.	100	105½
5	Sivagunga Zemdy., 1st Mort., Red.	100	101
20/	Sth. Australian	20	52½
3½	Stock Exchange Deb., Rd.	—	101½
—	Strait Develt., Ltd.	1	5/16
2/6	Texas Land & Mt., Ltd. £10 Shs.	2½	3
4½	Texas Land & Mt., Ltd., Deb. Stk., Red.	100	105
—	Transvaal Est. & Dev., L.	1	11/16
—	Transvaal Lands, Ltd., £1 Shs.	15/	½
—	Do. F. P.	1	15/16
—	Transvaal Mort., Loan, & Fin., Ltd., £10 Shs.	2	½
2/	Tst & Agcy. of Austrlsa., Ltd., £10 Shs.	1	2
7/5	Do. Old, fully paid	10	15½
5/7	Do. New, fully paid	10	12½
5	Do. Cum. Pref.	10	12½
3/	Trust & Loan of Canada, £20 Shs.	5	4½
1/9½	Do. New £20 Shs.	3	2¼
—	Tst. & Mort. of Iowa, Ltd., £10 Shs.	2½	¾
4½	Do. Deb. Stk. Red.	100	92½
—	Tst., Loan, & Agency of Mexico, Ltd., £10 Shs.	2	½
—	Trsts., Exors, & Sec. Ins. Corp., Ltd., £10 Shs.	7	1⅜
4	Do. Irred. Deb. Stk.	100	106½
5/	Union Dsc., Ld., £10 Shs.	5	10½
—	Union Mort. & Agcy. of Aust., Ltd., £6 Shs.	2	—
6	Do. Pref. Stk.	100	30
—	Do. 6 p. Pref. £6 Shs.	2	½
4½	Do. Deb. Stk.	100	92½
4	Do. Deb. Stk.	100	85½
5	Do. Deb. Stk. Red.	100	96½
1/6	U.S. Deb. Cor. Ltd., £8 Shs.	1	⅝
5½	Do. Cum. Pref. Stk.	100	100½
4½	Do. Irred. Deb. Stk.	100	106½
5	U.S. Tst. & Guar. Cor., Ltd., Pref. Stk.	100	77½
6/	Van Dieman's	25	16
4	Walker's Prop. Cor., Ltd., Guar. 1 Mt. Deb. Stk.	100	109
4½	Wstr. Mort. & Inv., Ltd., Deb. Stk.	100	92½

FINANCIAL—TRUSTS.

Last Div.	Name.	Paid.	Price.
1/6	Afric City Prop., Ltd	1	1⅜
6	Do. Cum. Pref.	1	1
4	Alliance Invt., Ltd., Cm. 4½ p. c. Prefd.	100	75½
—	Do. Defd.	100	13½
4	Do. Deb. Stk. Red.	100	105½
5	Amrcn. Invt., Ltd., Prfd.	100	120½
5	Do. Defd.	100	90½
4	Do. Deb. Stk. Red.	100	117½
4	Army & Navy Invt., Ltd., 5 p.c. Prefd.	100	82½
—	Do. Defd. Stk.	100	16½
4	Do. Deb. Stk.	100	107½
4	Atlas Investment, Ltd., Prefd. Stk.	100	70½
4½	Bankers' Invest., Ltd., Cum. Prefd.	100	106
1/0/0	Do. Defd	100	27½
4	Do. Deb. Stk	100	113
	Brewery & Comml. Inv., Ltd., £10 Shs.	5	6

Financial—Trusts (*continued*):—

Last Div.	Name.	Paid.	Price.
4	British Investment, Ltd., Cum. Prefd.	100	108
5	Do. Defd.	100	102½
4	Do. Deb. Stk.	100	108½
6	Brit. Steam. Invst., Ltd., Prefd.	100	116½
3/0/0	Do. Defd	100	70½
4½	Do. Perp. Deb. Stk	100	121½
1/9	Car Trust Invst., Ltd., £10 Shs.	2½	2
5	Do. Pref.	100	101
4	Do. Deb. Stk., 1915	100	106
4	Cinl. Sec., Ltd., Prefd.	100	106½
2½	Do. Defd.	100	47½
4	Consolidated, Ltd., Cum. 1st Pref.	100	92
4	Do. 5 p.c. Cm. 2nd do.	100	73½
—	Do. Defd.	100	14½
4½	Do. Deb. Stk.	100	111½
—	Deb. Secs. Invst.	100	105½
—	Do. 4 p.c. Cm. Pf. Sk.	100	106½
4½	Edinburgh Invest., Ltd., Cum. Prefd. Stk.	100	109½
4	Do. Deb. Stk. Red.	100	106½
5	Foreign, Amer. & Gen. Invt., Ltd., Prefd.	100	115½
2	Do. Defd.	100	50½
4	Do. Deb. Stk.	100	115½
5	Foreign & Colonial Invt., Ltd., Prefd.	100	134½
5½	Do. Defd.	100	99
4½	Gas, Water & Gen. Invt., Cum. Prefd. Stk.	100	86½
3	Do. Defd. Stk.	100	36½
4	Do. Deb. Stk.	100	106
5	Gen. & Com. Invt., Ltd., Prefd. Stk.	100	106½
2	Do. Defd. Stk.	100	36½
4	Do. Deb. Stk.	100	113½
1/9	Globe Telegph. & Tst., Ltd.	10	12
6	Do. do. Pref.	10	17¾
4	Govt. & Genl. Invt., Ld., Prefd.	100	84½
3½	Do. Defd.	100	42½
4½	Govts. Stk. & other Secs. Invt., Ltd., Prefd.	100	89½
1	Do. Defd.	100	26
4½	Do. Deb. Stk.	100	111
4	Do. do.	100	104
4½	Guardian Invt., Ltd., Pfd.	100	87½
—	Do. Defd.	100	20½
4	Do. Deb. Stk.	100	104
5	Indian & Gen. Inv., Ltd., Cum. Prefd.	100	107½
2½	Do. Defd.	100	56
4½	Do. Deb. Stk.	100	121½
5	Indust. & Gen. Tst., Ltd., Unified	100	102½
3½	Do. Deb. Stk. Red.	100	101½
4½	Internat. Invt., Ltd., Cm. Prefd.	100	71½
—	Do. Defd.	100	7½
4	Do. Deb. Stk.	100	101
4	Invest. Tst. Cor. Ltd. Pfd.	100	102
4	Do. Defd.	100	93
4	Do. Deb. Stk. Red.	100	106
5	Ldn. Gen. Invest. Ltd., 5 p.c. Cum. Prefd.	100	109½
7½	Do. Defd.	100	118
4½	Ldn. Scot. Amer. Ltd. Pfd.	100	105½
£3	Do. Defd.	100	59½
4	Do. Deb. Stk.	100	112
4	Ldn. Tst., Ltd., Cum. Prfd. Stk.	100	106
4	Do. Defd. Stk.	100	74½
4	Do. Deb. Stk., Red.	100	108
3½	Do. Mt. Deb. Stk., Red.	100	104
5	Mercantile Invt. & Gen., Ltd., Prefd.	100	111
3	Do. Defd.	100	46½
4	Do. Deb. Stk.	100	112½
4	Merchants, Ltd., Pref. Stk.	100	104½
4	Do. Ord.	100	80
4	Do. Deb. Stk.	100	117½
6	Municipal, Ltd., Prefd.	100	55½
—	Do. Defd.	100	17½
4½	Do. Debs.	100	112
4½	Do. Debs. "B"	100	99½
4½	Do. "C" Deb. Stk.	100	88½
5	New Investment, Ltd. Ord.	100	92½
5	Omnium Invest., Ltd., Pfd.	100	91½
1	Do. Defd.	100	26½
4	Do. Deb. Stk.	100	104
5/	Railway Deb. Tst. Ld., £20 Shs.	10	6½
5	Do. Debs., Red.	100	107½
4½	Do. Deb. Stk., 1911	100	107½
4	Do. do. 1927	100	106½
4	Railway Invst. Ltd., Prefd.	100	112
17/7	Do. Defd.	100	21
8/	Railway Share Trust & Agency "A"	8	6
7½	Do. "B" Pref. Stk.	100	146½
4½	River Plate & Gen. Invt., Ltd., Prefd.	100	105
£8	Do. Defd.	100	50½
5	Scot. Invst., Ltd., Pfd. Stk.	100	94½
1½	Do. Defd.	100	26½
4	Do. Deb. Stk.	100	108
4½	Sec. Scottish Invst., Ltd., Cum. Prefd.	100	86½
£8	Do. Defd. Stk.	100	32
4	Do. Deb. Stk.	100	107½
5/	Sth. Africa Gold Tst., Ltd.	1	4
6	Do. Cum. Pref	1	1
5½	Do. 1st Debs., Red.	100	102
1/9	Stock Conv. & Invest., Ltd., £5 Shs.	1	1⅜
4½	Do. do. 4½ p.c. Cm. Prf.	100	114½
2½	Do. Ldn. & N. W. 1st. Charge Prefd.	100	114½
4	Do do. 2nd Chge Prfd.	100	111
32/6	Do. do. Defd. Charge	100	30
3	Do. N. East. 1 Chge Pfd.	100	91½

Financial—Trusts (*continued*):—

Last Div.	Name.	Paid.	Price.
37/6	Stock N. East Defd. Chge	100	39
6	Submarine Cables	100	142½
5	U.S. & S. Amer. Invest., Ltd., Prefd.	100	100½
2	Do. Defd.	100	22½
4	Do. Deb. Stk.	100	105½

GAS AND ELECTRIC LIGHTING.

Last Div.	Name.	Paid.	Price.
10/6	Alliance & Dublin Con. 10 p.c. Stand.	10	24½
7/6	Do. 7 p.c. Stand.	10	17
5	Austln. Gas Lght. (Syd.) Debs. 1902	100	106
5	Bay State of N. Jrsy. Sk. Fd. Tst. Bd., Red.	—	92½
3/	Bombay, Ltd.	5	6
2/4½	Do. New	4	5
12	Brentford Cons.	100	295½
9	Do. New	100	225½
5	Do. Pref.	100	142½
4	Do. Deb. Stk.	100	136
11½	Brighton & Hove Gen. Cons. Stk.	100	272½
8½	Do. "A" Cons. Stk.	100	197½
5	Bristol 5 p.c. Max.	100	129½
22/6	British Gas Light, Ltd.	20	55½
11/6	Bromley Gas Consumrs.' 10 p.c. Stand.	10	26
8/6	Do. 7 p.c. Stand.	10	21
—	Brush Electl. Enging., L.	—	1¾
6	Do. 6 p.c. Pref.	—	2¾
4½	Do. Deb. Stk.	100	112
4½	Do. 2 Deb. Stk., Red.	100	103½
5/	B. Ayres (New), Ltd.	10	9½
4	Do. Deb. Stk., Rd.	—	99
18/6	Cagliari Gas & Wtr., Ltd.	20	31
8/	Cape Town & Dist. Gas Light & Coke, Ltd.	10	17½
4½	Do. Pref.	10	12½
6	Do. 1 Mt. Debs. 1910	50	60
4/	Charing Cross & Strand Elec. Sup., Ltd.	5	14
4½	Do. Cum. Pref.	5	6½
3/	Chelsea Elec. Sup., Ltd.	5	10½
4½	Do. Deb. Stk., Red.	100	116
5	Chic. Edis'n Co. 1 Mt., Rd.	$1000	106
20/	City of Ldn. Elec. Lht., L.	10	26½
—	Do. New £10 Shs.	5	19½
6	Do. Cum. Pref.	10	18
5	Do. Deb. Stk., Red.	100	131½
13½	Commercial, Cons.	100	342½
10½	Do. New	100	257½
4½	Do. Deb. Stk.	100	155½
14	Continental Union, Ltd.	100	230
11	Do. Pref. Stk.	100	209½
—	County of Lon. & Brush Prov. Elec. Lg., Ltd.	10	15
6	Do. Cum. Pref.	10	15¾
14	Croydon Comcl. Gas, Ld., "A" Stk., 10 p.c.	100	312½
11	Do. "B" Stk., 7 p.c.	100	260
5½	Crystal Pal. Dist. Ord. 5 p.c. Stk.	100	130½
5	Do. Pref. Stk.	100	141½
8/	European, Ltd.	10	24½
6/	Do.	7½	17½
12½	Gas Light & Ck Cons. Stk., "A" Ord.	100	282½
4	Do. "B" (4 p.c. Max.)	100	120½
10	Do. "C," "D," & "E" (Pref.)	100	310
5	Do. "F" (Pref.)	100	152½
7½	Do. "G" (Pref.)	100	222½
7	Do. "H" (7 p.c. Max.)	100	197½
10	Do. "J" (Pref.)	100	310
6	Do. "K"	100	186½
4	Do. Deb. Stk.	100	134½
4½	Do. do.	100	152½
6	Do. do.	100	204½
8/	Hong Kong & China, Ld.	10	14½
4/	House to House Elec. Light Sup., Ltd.	5	11
7	Do. Cum. Pref.	5	11¾
10	Imperial Continental	100	215½
3½	Do. Deb. Stk., Red	100	104½
2/	Malta & Medit., Ltd.	5	5½
7/	Metrop. Elec. Sup., Ltd.	10	20½
6/	Do. New	10	20½
4½	Do. 1 Mt. Deb. Stk.	100	119
5	Metro. of Melbrne. Dbs. 1908-12	100	111
4½	Do. Debs. 1918-22-4	100	103
10/	Monte Video, Ltd.	20	15½
9½	Newcastle-upon-Tyne	100	237½
—	Do. 3½ p.c. Deb. Stk.	100	117½
12/	Notting Hill Elec. Ltg., Ltd.	10	20½
4/6	Oriental, Ltd.	5	8½
4/0½	Do. New	4½	7½
10½d.	Do. do. 1879	1	1½
3/6	Ottoman, Ltd.	5	4½
—	Para, Ltd.	—	—
6	People's Gas Lt. & C. of Chic. 2 Mt. 1904	100	105½
5	River Plate Elec. Lgt. & Trac., Ltd., 1 Deb. Stk.	—	92½
8½	Royal Elec. of Montreal	—	144
4½	Do. 1 Mt. Deb.	100	104
11/	St. James' & Pall Mall Elec. Light, Ltd.	5	18½
7	Do. Pref.	5	10½
4	Do. Deb. Stk., Red.	100	106½

Gas and Electric (*continued*):—

Last Div.	Name.	Paid.	Price.
10/	San Paulo, Ltd.	10	16¼
10	Sheffield Unit. Gas Lt. "A"	100	251½
10	Do. "B"	100	251½
10	Do. "C"	100	251½
—	Sth. Ldn. Elec. Sup., Ld.	2	2¾
5½	South Metropolitan	100	137½
3	Do. 3 p.c. Deb. Stk.	100	106½
12	Tottenham & Edmonton Gas Lt. & C., "A"	100	290
9	Do. "B"	100	210
7/	Tuscan, Ltd.	10	14
5	Do. Debs., Red.	100	101½
5/	West Ham 10 p.c. Stan.	5	12
8/	Wstmnstr. Elec. Sup., Ld.	5	17½

INSURANCE.

Last Div.	Name.	Paid.	Price.
4/	Alliance, £20 Shs.	44/	10¾
10/	Alliance, Mar., & Gen., Ld., £100 Shs.	25	53
19/	Atlas, £50 Shs.	6	31
12/	British & For. Marine, Ld., £20 Shs.	4	24
7½d.	British Law Fire, Ltd., £10 Shs.	1	1½
7/6	Clerical, Med., & Gen. Life, £25 Shs.	50/	16½
10/	Commercial Union, Ltd., £50 Shs.	5	44
4	Do. "W. of Eng." Ter. Deb. Stk.	100	110½
£9	County Fire, £100 Shs.	80	190
5/	Eagle, £50 Shs.	5	½
4/	Employers' Liability, Ltd., £10 Shs.	2	4½
.	Empress, Ltd., £5 Shs.	1	—
81/	Equity & Law, £100 Shs.	6	23
7/6	General Life, £100 Shs.	5	15
4½d.	Gresham Life, £5 Shs.	15/	2½
2/6	Guardian, Ld., £10 Shs.	5	11½
10/	Imperial, Ltd., £20 Shs.	5	29½
5/6	Imperial Life, £20 Shs.	4	6¾
6/	Indemnity Mutual Mar., Ltd., £15 Shs.	3	12
1/	Lancashire, £20 Shs.	2	5
7½d.	Law Acc. & Contin., Ltd., £5 Shs.	10/	1
5/	Law Fire, £100 Shs.	2½	18
9½d.	Law Guar. & Trust, Ltd., £10 Shs.	1	1⅜
9/	Law Life, £20 Shs.	2	25
2/9	Law Un. & Crown £10 Shs	12/	7
4	Do. Deb. Stk., 1942	100	110½
14/6	Legal & General, £50 Shs.	8	15½
9d.	Lion Fire, Ltd., £8½ Shs.	1½	⅜
14/	Liverpool & London & Globe, Stk.	2	54
10/	Do. Globe £1 Ann	—	36
15/	London, £25 Shs.	12½	63
4/	Lond. & Lanc. Fire, £25 Shs	2½	19½
2/	Lond. & Lanc. Life, £25 Shs	2	5¾
1/	Lond. & Prov. Mar., Ld., £10 Shs.	1	¾
6/	Lond. Guar. & Accident, Ltd., £5 Shs.	2	11½
40/	Marine, Ltd., £25 Shs.	4½	43
2/	Maritime, Ltd., £10 Shs.	2	4½
1/6	Merc. Mar., Ld., £10 Shs.	2½	2½
—	National Marine, Ltd., £9 Shs.	1	½
10/	N. Brit. & Merc., £25 Shs.	6¼	41½
20/	Northern, £100 Shs.	10	81
40/	Norwich Union Fire, £100 Shs.	12	126½
10/	Ocean Acc. & Guar., fy. pd.	5	22
2/	Do. £5 Shs.	1	4
7/6	Ocean, Marine, Ltd.	2½	9½
1/	Palatine, £10 Shs.	2	3½
2/6	Pelican, £10 Shs.	1	3¼
12/	Phœnix, £50 Shs.	5	44
£6	Provident, £100 Shs.	10	31
5/	Railway Passngrs., £10 Shs.	2	8½
2/6	Rock Life, £5 Shs.	10/	4½
8	Royal Exchange	100	360
18/	Royal, £20 Shs.	3	54½
4/	Sun, £10 Shs.	10/	12
3/9	Sun Life, £10 Shs.	7½	14½
6	Thames & Mrsey. Marine, Ltd., £20 Shs.	2	10½
9	Union, £10 Shs.	4	24½
4/	Union Marine, £20 Shs.	2½	9
12/	Universal Life, £100 Shs.	12	42
2/	World Marine, £5 Shs.	2	1½

IRON, COAL, AND STEEL.

Last Div.	Name.	Paid.	Price.
—	Barrow Hæm. Steel, Ltd.	7½	2
9/	Do. 6 p.c. 2nd Pref.	7½	7
10/	Bolck., Vaugh. & C., Ld.	20	17
6/	Do. £8 liab.	12	9
7/6	Brown, J. & Co., Ltd., £20 Shs.	15	20½
7/6	Consett Iron, Ld., £10 Shs.	7½	29½
4/	Do. 8 p.c. Cum. Pref.	5	11
7/6	Ebbw Vale Steel, Iron & Coal, Ltd., £23 Shs.	20	6¾
15/	General Mining Assn., Ld.	5½	7½
8/	Harvey Steel Co. of Gt. Britain, Ltd.	10	29
5	Lehigh V. Coal 1 Mt. 5 p.c. Guar. Gd. Cp. Bds.	—	95½
42/6	Nantyglo & Blaina Iron, Ltd., Pref.	$62	97½
1/	Nerbudda Coal & Iron, Ltd., £3 Shs.	56/	1/16
—	Newport Abrcrn. Bk. Vein Steam Coal, Ltd.	10	4½
5/	New Sharlston Coll., Ltd. Pref	20	10
4½d.	Nw. Vancvr. Coal & Ld., L.	1	½
2/6	North's Navigation Coll. (1889) Ltd.	5	2¾
10/	Do. 10 p.c. Cum. Pref.	5	7½
—	Rhymney Iron, Ltd.	5	1½
	Do. New, £5 Shs.	4½	¾
5	Do. Mt. Debs., Red.	100	98½
5	Shelton Irn., Stl. & Cl. Co., Ltd., 1 Chg. Debs., Red.	100	99½
50/	Sth. Hetton Coal, Ltd.	100	—
2/	Vickers & Maxim, Ltd.	1	3¾
5	Do. 5 p.c. Prfd. Stk.	100	130½

SHIPPING.

Last Div.	Name.	Paid.	Price.
4/	African Stm. Ship, £20 Shs.	16	11
5/	Do. Fully-paid	20	15½
5/	Amazon Steam Nav., Ltd.	12½	9
8/	Castle Mail Pakts., Ltd., £20 Shs.	14	16
3½	Do. 1st Deb. Stk., Red.	100	102
6/	China Mutual Steam, Ltd.	5	2½
6	Do. Cum. Pref.	10	9½
10/	Cunard, Ltd.	20	10
5/	Do. £20 Shs.	10	4
4½	Furness, Withy, & Co., Ltd., 1 Mt. Dbs., Red.	100	106
6/	General Steam	15	8
5/	Do. 5 p.c. Pref., 1874	10	9
5/	Do. 5 p.c. Pref., 1877	10	8½
5/	Leyland & Co., Ltd.	10	20
7/	Do. 7 p.c. Cum. Pref.	10	14½
2/11	Do. 4½ p.c. Cum. Pre-Pf.	3	10¾
4	Do. 1st Mt. Dbs., Red.	100	106½
7/6	Mercantile Steam, Ltd.	5	7½
6/4½	New Zealand Ship., Ltd.,	6	5
4	Do. Deb. Stk., Red.	100	104
5/	Orient Steam, Ltd.	10	5
5	P. & O. Steam, Cum. Prefd.	100	154½
19	Do. Defd.	100	235½
3½	Do. Deb. Stk.	100	118
5	Richelieu & Ont., 1st Mt. Debs., Red.	100	100
30/	Royal Mail, £100 Shs.	60	52
2/6	Shaw, Sav., & Alb., Ltd., "A" Pref.	5	5½
5/	Do. "B" Ord.	5	4
8/	Union Steam, Ltd.	20	20
4/	Do. New £20 Shs.	10	8½
4	Do. Deb. Stk., Red.	100	106
7/	Union of N.Z., Ltd.	10	10
5½	Wilson's & Fur.-Ley., 5½ p.c. Cum. Pref.	10	10½
4½	Do. 1 Mt. Db. Sk., Rd.	100	106½

TELEGRAPHS AND TELEPHONES.

Last Div.	Name.	Paid.	Price.
4	African Direct, Ltd., Mort. Debs., Red.	100	102
—	Amazon Telegraph, Ltd.	10	7½
19/6	Anglo-American, Ltd.	100	62¾
39/	Do. 6 p.c. Prefd. Ord.	100	112
—	Do. Defd. Ord.	100	13
3/	Brazilian Submarine, Ltd.	10	16¾
5	Do. Debs., 2 Series	100	114

Telegraphs and Telephones (*continued*):—

Last Div.	Name.	Paid.	Price.
4/	Chili Telephone, Ltd.	5	3½
$12	Comcial. Cable, $100 Shs.	—	187½
4	Do. Stg. 500-yr. Deb. Stk. Red.	100	106
2½d.	Consd. Telpehone Constr., &c., Ltd.	10/	⅛
6/	Cuba Submarine, Ltd.	10	7
10/	Do. 10 p.c. Pref.	10	15
2/	Direct Spanish, Ltd.	5	4½
5/	Do. 10 p.c. Cum. Pref.	5	10½
4½	Do. Debs.	50	104½
3/	Direct U.S. Cable, Ltd.	20	11
2/6	Eastern, Ltd.	10	18
3/	Do. 6 p.c. Cum. Pref.	10	19
4	Do. Mt. Deb. Stk., Red.	100	129½
2/6	Eastern Exten., Aus., & China, Ltd.	10	19
5	Do. (Aus. Gov. Sub.) Deb., Red.	100	101
5	Do. do. Bearer	100	101½
4	Do. Mort. Deb. Stk.	100	129½
5	Eastn. & S. Afric., Ltd., Mort. Deb. 1900	100	101
5	Do. Bearer	100	101½
4	Do. Mort. Debs. 1909	100	103½
4	Do. Mort. Debs. (Maur. Subsidy)	25	108½
5/	Grt. Nthn. Copenhagen	10	30
5	Do. Debs., Ser. B., Red.	100	101½
12/6	Indo-European, Ltd.	25	53½
6	London Platino-Brazilian, Ltd., Debs. 1904	100	107½
4/	Montevideo Telph., Ltd., 6 p.c. Pref.	5	2½
3/	National Telephone, Ltd.	5	5¾
6/	Do. Cum. 1 Pref.	10	17
6/	Do. Cum. 2 Pref.	10	16
5	Do. Non-Cum. 3 Pref.	5	5¾
3½	Do. Deb. Stk., Red.	100	102½
4d.	Oriental Telephone, Ltd.	1	¾
4	Pac. & Euro. Tlg. Dbs., Rd.	100	106½
4/	Reuter's, Ltd.	8	8½
5/	Un. Riv. Plate Telph., Ltd.	5	4½
5	Do. Deb. Stk., Red.	100	106½
—	West African Telg., Ltd.	10	4
5	Do. 5 p.c. Mt. Debs., Red.	100	100½
—	W. Coast of America, Ltd.	10	½
3/	Western & Brazilian, Ltd.	15	12½
3/	Do. 5 p.c. Pref. Ord.	7½	8
—	Do. Defd. Ord.	7½	4½
4	Do. Deb. Stk., Red.	100	107½
1/	W. India & Panama, Ltd.	10	½
6/	Do. Cum. 1 Pref.	10	7½
6/	Do. Cum. 2 Pref.	10	6
5	Do. Debs., Red.	100	106½
7	West. Union, 1 Mt. 1902 ($	1000	107½
6	Do. 6 p.c. Stg. Bds., Rd.	100	102½

TRAMWAYS AND OMNIBUS.

Last Div.	Name.	Paid.	Price.
1/6	Anglo-Argentine, Ltd.	5	3½
6	Do. Deb. Stk.	100	127½
4/	Barcelona, Ltd.	10	12
5	Do. Deb., Red.	100	105½
7/6	Belfast Street Trams.	10	16½
—	Blackpl. & Fltwd. Tram., £10 Shs.	8	13
10/	Bordeaux Tram. & O., Ltd.	10	11½
5	Do. Cum. Pref.	10	11
—	Brazilian Street Ry., Ltd.	2	½
—	British Elec. Trac., Ltd.	10	16½
—	B. Ayres & Belg. Tram., Ltd., 6 p.c. Cum. Pref.	5	—
6	Do. 1 Deb. Stk.	100	—
—	B. Ayres. Gd. Nat., Ltd., 6 p.c 1 Deb. Bds., Red.	100	54½
5½	Do. Pref. Debs., Red.	100	95½
1/	Calais, Ltd.	5	1
—	Calcutta, Ltd.	10	3½
—	Carthagena & Herr., Ltd.	10	3
5	Do. Deb., Red.	100	90
5	City of B'ham. Trams., Ltd., 5 p.c. Cum. Pref.	5	6
4	Do. 1 Mort. Debs., Rd.	100	107½
3/9	City of B. Ayres, Ltd.	5	7½
2/3	Do. Ext. £5 Shs.	3	4½
6	Do. Deb. Stk	100	145
1/4	Edinburgh Street Tram.	4	4
1/	Glasgow Tram. & Omni. Ltd., £9 Shs.	8	
3/7½	Imperial, Ltd.	6	15
3/	Lond., Deptfd, & Greenwich, Prefd.	5	3½
nil	Do. Defd.	5	1
10½	Lond. Gen. Omni., Ltd.	100	200
4	Do. Deb., Red.	100	115½

Tramways and Omnibus (*continued*):—

Last Div.	Name.	Paid.	Price.
4/9½	London Road Car	6	10¾
28/6	Do. Red. 1 Mt. Deb. Stk.	100	108½
5	London St. Rly. (Prov., Ont.), Mt. Debs.	100	110
12/6	London St. Trams.	—	2
12/9	London Trams., Ltd.	10	10
6/	Do. Non-Cum. Pref.	10	10½
5	Do. Mt. Db. Stk., Rd.	100	99½
5	Lynn & Boston 1 Mt. 1924 $	1000	107
5	Milwaukee Elec. Cons. Mt. $	1000	100½
5	Minneapolis St. 1 Cons. Mt $	1000	96
5	Montreal St. Dbs., 1908	100	109
4½	Do. Debs., 1922	100	107
6/	Nth. Metropolitan	10	13
1/9½	Nth. Staffords., Ltd.	6	4½
5/6	Provincial, Ltd.	10	7
6/	Do. Cum. Pref.	10	13½
5	St. Paul City, 1937 $	1000	96
5	Do. Guar. Twin City Rap. Trans. $	1000	96
5/	Southampton	10	6½
5/	South London	10	5½
7/6	Sunderland, Ltd.	10	6½
4½	Toronto 1 Mt., Red.	100	106
2/6	Tramways Union, Ltd.	5	7
4½	Do. Deb., Red.	100	109
5/	Vienna General Omnibus.	5	6½
5	Do. 5 p.c. Mt. Deb., Red.	100	103½
4/	Wolverhampton, Ltd.	10	6½

WATER WORKS.

Last Div.	Name.	Paid.	Price.
8/	Antwerp, Ltd.	20	22
6/	Cape Town District, Ltd.	5	7
10½	Chelsea	100	325
5	Do. Pref. Stk.	100	178½
4½	Do. Pref. Stk., 1875	100	158½
4½	Do. Deb. Stk.	100	160½
5/6	City St. Petersburg, Ltd.	13	11
5/	Colne Valley	10	15½
4	Do. Deb. Stock	100	137½
£4	Consol. of Rosar., Ltd., 4 p.c. 1 Deb. Stk., Red.	100	92
7½	East London	100	229½
4½	Do. Deb. Stk.	100	162
3	Do. Deb. Stk., Red.	100	106
37/6	Grand Junction (Max. 10 p.c.) "A"	50	122½
18/9	Do. "B"	25	
18/9	Do. "C" (Max. 7½ p.c.)	25	55½
35/	Do. "D" (Max. 7 p.c.)	50	104½
4	Do. Deb. Stock	100	145½
13	Kent	100	360½
7	Do. New (Max. 7 p.c.)	100	215½
5/7½	Kimberley, Ltd.	7	5½
6	Do. Debs., Red.	100	104½
6	Do. Deb. Stk., Red.	100	107½
10	Lambeth (Max. 10 p.c.)	100	300½
7½	Do. (Max. 7½ p.c.), 50 & 25	—	233
4	Do. Deb. Stock	100	142½
3	Do. Red. Deb. Stock	100	103
10/	Montevideo, Ltd.	20	16½
5	Do. 1 Deb. Stk.	100	108½
5	Do. 2 Deb. Stk.	100	103½
132/9	New River New	100	445½
4	Do. Deb. Stk.	100	144½
4	Do. Deb. Stk. "B"	100	144½
—	Odessa, Ltd., "A" 6 p.c. Prefd.	20	—
nil	Do. "B" Deferred	20	—
4	Portland Con. Mt. "B," 1927	—	102½
8/	Seville, Ltd.	20	12
5/6	Southend "Addl." Ord.	10	17½
6	Southwark and Vauxhall	100	157½
6	Do. "D" Shares (7½ p.c. max.)	100	154½
5	Do. Pref. Stock	100	176½
4	Do. "A" Deb. Stock	100	147½
3	Staines Resvirs. Jt. Com. Gua. Deb. Stk., Red.	100	106
7/	Tarapaca, Ltd.	10	9½
10	West Middlesex	100	305½
4½	Do. Deb. Stk.	100	162½
3	Do Deb. Stk.	100	106

Printed for the Proprietor by LOVE & WYMAN, LTD., Great Queen Street, London, W.C.; and Published by CLEMENT WILSON

The Investors' Review

EDITED BY A. J. WILSON.

Vol. I.—No. 15. New Series. FRIDAY, APRIL 15, 1898. [Registered as a Newspaper.] Price 6d. By post, 6½d

Notice to Subscribers.

Complaints are continually reaching us that the INVESTORS' REVIEW cannot be obtained at this and the other railway bookstall, that it does not reach Scotch and Irish cities till Monday, and that it is not delivered in the City till Saturday morning.

We publish on Friday in time for the REVIEW to be at all Metropolitan bookstalls by at latest 4 p.m., and we believe that it is there then, having no doubt that Messrs. W. H. Smith & Son do their best, but they have such a mass of papers to handle every day that a fresh one may well look almost like a personal enemy and be kept in short supply unless the reading public shows unmistakably that it is wanted. A little perseverance, therefore, in asking for the INVESTORS' REVIEW is all that should be required to remedy this defect.

All London newsagents can be in a position to distribute the paper on Friday afternoon if they please, and here also the only remedy is for subscribers to insist upon having it as soon as published. Arrangements have been made that all our direct City subscribers shall have their copies before 4 p.m. on Friday. As for the provinces, we can only say that the paper is delivered to the forwarding agents in ample time to be in every English and Scotch town, and in Dublin and Belfast, likewise, early on Saturday morning. Those despatched by post from this office can be delivered by the first London mail on Saturday in every part of the United Kingdom.

ADVERTISEMENTS.

All Advertisements are received subject to approval, and should be sent in not later than 5 p.m. on Thursdays.

The advertisements of American Life Insurance Offices are rigorously excluded from the INVESTORS' REVIEW, and have been so since it commenced as a Quarterly Magazine in 1892.

For tariff and particulars of positions open apply to the Advertisement Manager, Norfolk House, Norfolk-street, W.C.

CONTENTS

The Investors' Review.

A Hardening Money Market.

Last week we had to write too early to be able to publish the decision of the Bank directors to raise their rate of discount to 4 per cent. The step in one sense took the market by surprise, in another it did not. That is to say, feelings of self-interest to some extent prompted dealers in money to hope for no worse than a 3½ per cent. rate, and a sort of pained surprise pervaded financial circles when the rate announced was 4 per cent. Evidently, however, it would have been quite useless for the Bank to move only half a step, and it is already very doubtful whether this 4 per cent. will be sufficient to stop further drafts upon the stock of gold. To bring gold back to us we may be already quite certain that 4 per cent. is not enough. We shall have to have a 5 per cent. Bank rate before any substantial strengthening of the reserve can be hoped for. The market recognises this by the manner in which it is keeping discount rates close up to the Bank minimum.

One consolatory feature, however, remains, and that is the power possessed by the Bank to make its rate effective. All through the present quarter it will be in command of the open market, and if necessities arising from bullion movements, or through the absorption of floating capital in a war between Spain and the United States, make a 5 per cent. rate advisable, the directors of the Bank can compel the open market to work close up to this standard. In some respects this is the only redeeming feature now descernible. In nearly all other directions the prospect is far from satisfactory, and if it were not for the splendid output of new gold from the mines, we should look for a grave crisis in our credit system at no distant date. Happily, there is a large amount of gold coming in to satisfy the demands of foreign buyers. Still, even with this the year bids fair to be a troubled one for those much dependent on banking credit. We know nothing further about the intentions of the Indian Government with regard to a "gold standard," and whether that fantastic scheme, published last Sunday in a paper called the *Sunday Special*, be a forecast of Indian bureaucratic designs or not, is not of much consequence. What is plain enough is that India will require much assistance this year, and the dearer money becomes here the more urgent will be the necessity of India to have this assistance. Not only so, but our Australian Colonies will feel the need of more money directly credit becomes difficult here, and all State or corporate borrowers must come upon an open market which has no spare credit to dispose of. The worst of it is, too, that a good many sources of weakness are to be found at home. Credit has been far too much distended in recent years, as we have been continually insisting, and it will be very difficult to contract it under the conditions now prevailing in the money market. It must, however, be contracted if we are to regain a sound financial position, and the far-seeing banker and merchant is already drawing in his loans, or moderating his demand for loans. The process is a healthy one, and if carried out with caution will have most salutary effects upon the financial position in the City.

We ought to be strong there, for all around us there are abundant signs of approaching distress. We have noted elsewhere the positions of the money markets of France and Germany, and shall not advert further to that aspect of the subject. But the approaching collapse of Spain will not only accentuate the troubles of these markets, especially that of Paris, but cause some reflex disturbance here; and then Russia must not be left out of account. Russia will require more money this year for her great Siberian railway, and will probably find the Paris market unable to give it to her. Japan also is in necessities beyond what the last payment made to her by China can meet. A Greek loan is coming on the market immediately; it is borrow, borrow, everywhere. And the whole borrowing system of the world may be considered in a sense to rest upon the stability of the London market at the present time. If we keep financially strong here, and hold our resources, which are immense, well in hand, a profitable business may be open to us in supplying the immediate necessities of over-spending States all the world through. On the other hand, should our market become strained and incapable of affording relief to all who require it, the consequence to the international credit system of the world might be very serious. This, however, is not the immediately pressing question which we have to keep in view. It is, rather, How long will it be before the Bank rate has to be advanced to 5 per cent.? We cannot tell, except inferentially. Our Bank reserve wants strengthening. It ought to be ten millions larger than it is, and must be that if we are going to safely outride any severe credit storm. Now, a 4 per cent. rate is not endowed with attracting power sufficient to strengthen the reserve; therefore, an advance is certain to come, and should the directors of the Bank make up their minds to accumulate a larger reserve, it will come soon. They ought to take this course because, in their desire not to harass the market, they have let the reserve fall too low. It would not, for example, be sufficient to cover the demands any two out of twenty-five or more other banks in the country could pour in upon it in a day or two should a real crisis arise. Assume, then, that the banking reserve is to be strengthened, as the altered circumstances evoked by the Cuban dispute alone demand, and an advance in the Bank rate ought to take place within the next few weeks. Should war break out at once between Spain and the United States, as seems certain, a 5 per cent. Bank rate ought to be established with the least delay compatible with reasonable warning. This, briefly, is the position; and in our view, although there should be no haste, there ought to be no undue delay in putting the rate further up, especially now that the directors of the Bank are relieved from any imputation of taking advantage of the exhaustion, produced by the collection of the revenue, to make profit at the expense of the market. No help in creating a strong reserve can be looked for from any of the other joint stock banks. The Bank of England must accomplish the duty alone.

President M'Kinley's Cuban Message.

The variety of opinions expressed about this State paper are a striking testimony to its laboured weakness, and yet there seems to be a definite enough purpose behind the mass of verbosity. In another column we print a summary of it, because, in spite of its preachiness and long drawn-out fumbling in search of an argument, it promises to be a document of great historical importance. Nothing in it is more remarkable than the revelation it gives of the attitude of average American political sentiment towards European countries. A more undiplomatic State paper, in our sense of the word, could not be imagined. Mr. M'Kinley views the Cuban question purely from the standpoint of America, and the greatest weakness of his deliverances arises from his ignorance of Spain and Spanish ideals. That he should still be optimistic about peace and accord between his country and Spain over Cuba is a further striking proof of the isolation in which American statesmen exist. It is quite impossible for us to realise that attitude to the full, but there should be no mistake about the consequences it will in the present instance produce. The President of the American Union has emphatically declared it to be the clear duty of his Government to intervene in the Cuban dispute, to force itself upon Spain there, and to relieve the distress of the inhabitants who have been huddled into the towns by the sixteenth-century brutality of General Weyler, and still we are told the President believes in peace, apparently finding many of his countrymen to agree with him. There can be no peace based on such an attitude. Spain is kept from revolution at the present moment entirely by the belief of the people that the Government of the Queen-Regent will fight. Preparations for war, we are told, are going on with the utmost rapidity and regardless of expense, and war must ensue unless the American people are prepared to disown the policy enunciated by their

Chief Magistrate. Their representatives, at least, seem to be anything but that. In their passionate eagerness to drive the Spaniards from Cuba they abandoned all semblance of self-restraint on Wednesday, and, amid scenes of the wildest disorder, demanded instant war, heaping insults the while on Spain.

We are quite willing to believe that the American people are reluctant to draw the sword, but they have now been committed to a policy which, as it seems to us, must compel them to do so. Their Government cannot now draw back from the attempt to send relief to the starving inhabitants of the island, and this relief must be sent under guard of ships of war. The Spanish Navy is certain to oppose these ships, and thus war might even break cut suddenly without formal declaration.

The President has asked the Congress for liberty to act on the lines laid down in his Message, and that liberty is sure to be accorded. A war fever has begun to rage throughout the country. All parties in the State seem to be ready to support intervention, and the disappointment of the Jingo, or annexationist, faction rests upon the absence from the Message of any indication as to what the ultimate fate of Cuba is to be. This faction wishes to incorporate it in the American Union, but we are quite sure that the best class of American citizens have no share in this baneful ambition. Nor has Congress, if we may judge by the drafts of the resolutions laid before both houses by their Committees on Foreign Affairs. It is only fair to the United States to recognise that the sentiment of the general body of the people is in the main a noble one. They desire to free Cuba, not to conquer it; not to make it a field to be exploited by the unscrupulous financial element far too much in evidence in American affairs, and if this high purpose is adhered to, unquestionably the States will have the sympathy of the British public. We have no desire to injure Spain, nor any hostility towards Spain, but we cannot shut our eyes to the fact that Spain has failed completely and absolutely to govern any dependency it ever possessed, wisely and to good purpose. The effect of her cruel and selfish maladministration is still visible all over Central and South America. When the territories there, so long subjected to the ravages of her governors and officials, broke away and became independent they found themselves in a condition too imperfect to be able to organise freedom, and it is only in our day that a great country like the Argentine Republic is beginning, and only beginning, to recover from the lawless misrule to which it was a prey for half a century after the Spaniard was driven out. The small States of Central America are still existing in a condition more or less chaotic, and Mexico is prospering under veiled despotism. Spain has failed, then, and deserves no sympathy whatever at our hands for the loss of what remains of her once glorious empire in the new world. We quite understand that her people are incapable of recognising their failure, that their sentiments of pride, inherited from a splendid past, prompt them to cling with the utmost tenacity to what remains of their empire. But that does not alter the fact that they deserve to lose it. Their misrule and the rapacity and corruption of the governors they have sent to Cuba have turned that fair island into a place of devastation and the home of misery. The brutalities of General Weyler put the finishing touch to the sufferings of the people, and not 5 per cent. of the remaining inhabitants, native born Cubans, have any desire that their country should continue dependent on Spain. We may be sorry that this fate should overtake a mother of nations, but free Englishmen cannot for a moment sympathise with the Spanish Government, or support it in a struggle to regain the island. Sooner or later it must have been free. The attempt to hold it has exhausted Spanish resources and brought the Treasury to the verge of national bankruptcy. By intervening now the United States will hasten the deliverance of Cuba and consummate the bankruptcy of Old Spain.

Curiously enough, discussions in London about this momentous question more or less overlook the real issues behind it. They take very little cognisance of the attitude of Spain, and speak of the Queen-Regent's Government as if it were a stable institution, like that of the German Empire or of Russia. It is a Government born of revolution, and it is destined to perish by revolution, in our opinion. By fighting the United States in one last desperate struggle to retain the Pearl of the Antilles, Queen Christina may hold on to her throne for a little time longer, but the inevitable defeat which must come will hurl her from that throne and give Spain some other kind of government. What kind it is impossible to forecast. Were the Ministry presided over by Senor Sagasta to temporise with the United States now and refuse to take up M'Kinley's challenge, it and the Queen-Regent would be hurled from power in less than a week. The instability of the Spanish Government is thus, in some respects, the most certain factor in determining the course of events in the immediate future. Spain, beggared though she may be, will not enter into the financial transactions so often proposed to her whereby Cuban security might be purchased and her finances relieved. The passions of the people are such that her Government must fight, and the United States cannot take a step towards carrying out their benevolent policy towards Cuba without provoking immediate war. This seems to us to be, in the main, the outline of the existing situation. What will develop when the struggle actually breaks out we cannot attempt to forecast. War is an ugly thing always, and the evil passions it evokes often lay hold of good men and carry them far from the line of conduct their nobler impulses would prompt them to pursue. It may be that the lust of conquest will come to dominate the United States when victory crowns their efforts, and it will be all the more likely to do so should victory prove difficult, slow of attainment, and very costly. We hope this will not be the case, and are perfectly sure that, up to now, the great body of intelligent American citizens have no more idea of appropriating Cuba as an imperial possession than we have. A mere cry for annexation would by itself fail to arouse any enthusiasm. It is because the war party and the annexationist can appeal to the compassionate sentiments of men and women, outraged as such by the story of Spanish inhumanity, that war for the deliverance of Cuba has become a popular demand.

The Report of the Chartered Company.

At last the directors of this company have taken the shareholders and the public somewhat into their confidence. Three voluminous pamphlets have been issued dealing with the history of the company for the two years ended March 31, 1897. The information therefore is still twelve months behind date, and there seems no good ground for this slowness now that the Bechuanaland railway has been completed to Bulawayo, and that the telegraph is nearly all over Rhodesia. Would it not be better, then, if the directors were to delay the issue of their annual reports—for we suppose they will be annual in future—for another month. or so to enable them to bring their facts and figures something like up to date? As far as they go the information in these various reports—one of which gives the history of the Matabeleland rebellion, another the story of the company's administrative action, and the third the report proper, with the accounts—is full and up to a point not unsatisfactory. A good deal of work has been done, and the country is now quiet enough to admit of settlers spreading over it, as well as to allow mining enterprise to be prosecuted with zeal. Not only has the railway from Capetown been completed to Bulawayo, but the opposition line, as we may call it, from Beira has made considerable progress and should soon be open to Salisbury. Leaving out of account, for the moment, the cost of the struggle with the Matabele, the ordinary receipts and expenditure of the company resulted in a surplus of £59,651 for the year ended March 31, 1896, but for the succeeding year there was a deficiency of £180,950, so that the aggregate excess of expenditure over income up to March 31, 1897, amounts to £1,145,205. Adding in the cost of putting down the rebellion, which is returned in the accounts as amounting to £2,265,876, including compensation—the said compensation having been paid to the amount of £360,000—the total shortcoming would be £3,410,000. Put in another way, the rebellion has absorbed the whole of the money obtained by the company as premiums on its later issues of shares, together with about £200,000 of the last debenture issue.

In their report the directors say that although they have not yet received the completed accounts for the year ended March 31 last, the revenue, exclusive of land sales, in that period amounted to £196,653, being the highest figure since the incorporation of the company. What the expenditure has been they cannot tell, but intimate that it has been "abnormally high," owing to the high rate of transport, and to the fact that the Mashonaland rebellion was only finally subdued in September last. In addition to the amount brought into the accounts as to the cost of the disturbances, and of compensation and food distribution to natives, the company seems to have spent nearly three-quarters of a million more, which, we presume, will appear in the accounts for the past year, when they come along twelve months from now. They say in the report that the total outlay on this head has amounted to "about three millions," all of which has been paid, and a balance of half a million is left to meet the ordinary expenses of the company. We cannot quite find this balance in the accounts appended to the report. It is true that the balance-sheet for March 31, 1897, shows cash under various heads to the amount of £597,083, but from this we have to deduct £159,000, representing creditors in London on open account, and bank overdrafts and creditors in South Africa. Allow that only £90,000 of this should really be charged against the cash in hand, and the total of that cash would still be little over half a million, while the large expenditure of the past year, not yet ascertained, has subsequently had to be provided for. The directors, however, speak of this half-million in the present tense; "it now remains," they say, "to meet the ordinary expenses of the company." We do not understand this, but it is noticeable that between March 31, 1896, and the same date in 1897 a quarter of a million in Consols, and five thousand De Beers shares had been sold to eke out the company's resources, and now another million and a half of new £1 shares is to be created and 250,000 of them issued immediately at £1 per share premium in order to give the company another half million to go on with. But the directors say that this money is not really wanted for current expenses. Hitherto the company has abstained from entering directly into the mining business, but the truncated board, for there are only four directors left now, think that "it would be advisable for the company acting under competent expert advice to join, under due safeguards, in providing the capital necessary for the development of particular properties," so they are raising this money. This also we do not quite understand, seeing that there are such a number of Rhodesian mining companies already in existence whose capital ought to be available for this purpose. We can afford to wait for further illumination, but meanwhile must be forgiven for regarding this issue of capital as ample confirmation of our oft-repeated, and as often officially denied, statement that company was hard up and in need of fresh money. Before passing on to deal with the financial position and prospects of the shareholders we may note once more that the company is responsible for twenty years for the interest on the £2,000,000 spent on building the railway to Bulawayo, and for the interest until October 1, 1919, on the debenture capital issued and to be issued by the Mashonaland Railway Company. Up to the present £1,150,000 of this latter capital has been issued. For the first four months, however, of its existence the Bulawayo line not only paid its expenses but earned a net revenue of £56,688, and while the "mining industry" is being prosecuted with the zeal of fervid hope the line ought not to be a burden on the finances of the guaranteeing company. But if gold be not forthcoming? Well, let us see.

In most respects, gold or no gold, it does not seem to us that the prospects of Chartered shareholders are particularly brilliant, even on a sanguine view of the future. Everything depends on finding payable gold in quantity. Should this gold be found, population will flow into the territory and money will circulate, bringing considerable revenue to the Chartered Company. But even so its prospects of a large free revenue to pay away in dividends are very small, within a measurable number of years. The first duty before the directors will be to wipe off the accumulated deficit now visible on the revenue account. Then they ought clearly to write off the cost of the Matabele rebellion, or, as we have already suggested, and better still, get the money back, with compensation for indirect losses, from Messrs. Rhodes and Beit, or others of the De Beers group, by whom both the Chartered Company itself and the Jameson raid were planned and organised. We are very glad to see that Messrs. Cecil Rhodes, Alfred Beit, and Rochfort Maguire are coming back upon the board, and trust they re-appear on the understanding that the money they caused the Chartered shareholders to lose will be handsomely returned to them. Helped by such a restitution the outlook would be rather brighter, but at the best it does not seem to us to be very promising. With the quarter of a million of new shares, to be issued at once, the outstanding share capital of the company will amount to about 3,700,000 shares. A mere 10 per cent. dividend on this would require say £370,000, and that is the very smallest dividend which, one year with another, shareholders ought to expect, seeing that they are called upon to pay £2 even now for the £1 share, and notwithstanding the fact that a deficit of more than a million stares them in the face. But it will not be so easy in the future to float these shares as it has been in the past. To be sure, the directors hint delicately that the deficits on their administrative account, "the cost incurred in the settlement of the country," &c., not met by revenue, "will constitute a public debt whenever the inhabitants of Rhodesia are prepared to take over full responsibility for its administration." In this way the board hopes to see the company "reimbursed a considerable portion of its outlay." We hope it may be, for the unfortunate shareholders' sake. But how about the inhabitants themselves? They will have to find interest on this indefinite debt, plus, on the present capital basis, £200,000 a year for railway bond interest, £62,500 for Chartered Company's debentures interest, and, say, £500,000 as a 10 per cent. dividend on the £5,000,000 to which the share capital of the company will mount when all the newly-created shares are issued, as they soon will be. Their lot is not the most brilliant. But this is not all, by any means. Dozens of hungry shareholders in mining companies will be looking for returns. To meet the hopes of these, in addition to the modest requirements of the Chartered Company, as here outlined, a free revenue of at least £3,000,000 would be necessary. Need we add another word? Yes, what about Lord Grey's assertion that the Chartered Company has spent about £10,000,000 in developing Rhodesia? Does he stand by this assertion? We cannot make this amount even by including the 2,000,000 shares constituting promoters' swag and the £3,000,000 lost by the Jameson-raid-provoked Matabele rebellion.

British Foreign Trade in March.

Looking at the disturbed state of the world the returns of our over-sea business for the last month may be considered, if not cheerful, at least no worse than the circumstances would lead us to expect. In some respects, however, the large increase in imports, coming alongside a further decrease in exports, is to be lamented at the present time. The disparity between the two sides of our trading account in March was more marked than at the beginning of the year, imports having increased nearly 6¾ per cent., while exports have gone down 3¾ per cent. In other words, our imports were valued at £43,413,000, or £2,758,000 more than in March, 1897, while our exports were only £20,834,000, or £813,000 less. Taking the three months together, imports are only 1⅓ per cent. larger, and exports little more than 2½ per cent. less, than they were for the first quarter of last year. The figures for the month are thus decidedly worse than the average for the three months, and we received only a very small compensation in our increase of the exports of foreign and colonial produce. These amounted to £15,110,000 for the first three months of the present year, being an increase of £461,000, or about 3 per cent. on the same period of 1897.

Of course, as we have often explained, too much stress must not be laid upon sectional returns of this description, nor is it necessary to be alarmed at the steady expansion of our imports, because this might be due to the greater productiveness of our foreign investments, quite as much as to any tendency towards extravagance amongst the people. At the same time, and however well based our large import trade may be, its abounding excess can occasionally cause some inconvenience to us, and it is calculated to do so at the present time. We have more to pay for, and less goods exported to pay with, than is convenient at a moment when the demands upon the stock of gold in the country are persistent and formidable. Traders do not wait twelve months or more for the balance to adjust itself, either through the return of interest upon money invested abroad, or through the enlarged exports which, sooner or later, always arise out of enlarged imports. Wheat and dead meat and raw cotton and wool, with all the other raw products, which we buy either to consume or to turn into articles for sale, have got to be paid for promptly, and therefore our excessive importations just now add to the difficulties of the monetary position dealt with elsewhere in this number. We see traces of it, very distinct traces, in the statistics of bullion movements for the month and for the three months. A larger amount of new gold has come into this country during the present year up to date than in the same period of any previous year that we remember. No less than £4,442,000 in gold reached us during March, and in the three months we have received £9,259,000. The whole of this gold has been exported again since the first of January, and £914,000 of our existing stock as well. When we bethink ourselves how slender our stock is, and how necessary for our banking credit it is that it should be growing larger instead of growing smaller, and when, further, we consider that the enormously increased output of gold is not benefitting our reserve of the metal to the extent of a single sovereign, although it may indirectly benefit our commerce by enlarging our purchasing power, the seriousness of the position will be somewhat clearer. In a word, the manner in which our foreign trade is expanding on the import side alone is at present decidedly inconvenient.

Is there any hope, then, of an immediate expansion in our exports of commodities to counterbalance these heavy imports? We fear not; several powerful influences are against it. We should be disposed to put high customs tariff at the head of the list, were it not for the fact that these tariffs do not very sensibly hamper business if the people who have to submit to them possess the means to buy according to their tastes. If, however, the people who live under these tariffs are poor, and becoming poorer, the influence high duties exert in checking or destroying outlets for our products becomes powerful. At the present moment an examination of the detailed figures in these Board of Trade Returns demonstrates that, whether through poverty or through the effect of political unrest, tariffs are damaging our business at many points. Our trade is declining with most Continental nations in nearly all branches of textile industry, and almost in proportion to the height of the duties set up against us. France, for example, whose tariff and other fiscal restrictions are almost Napoleonic in their rigour, is gradually becoming a closed market to us for cotton and woollen manufactures and for yarns of all descriptions—if we except linen goods and silks, the trade in which is never more than insignificant with this country. Trade with Germany makes really very little progress; with Italy it tends to dwindle, and with Spain, where we can trace Spanish figures in the return, it is at the very best stagnant, with a tendency downwards. And the worst of it is that in very few places outside Europe are our manufacturers and merchants receiving present compensation for this weakness nearer home. Our own Colonies are nearly all buying less than they did, Canada alone is doing a little, not much, more business with us; but, obviously, it cannot be a flourishing business for any length of time, so long as the necessities of the Dominion, to put it gently, compel its rulers to exact enormous duties on many British productions. We really wish Canadians had a sense of humour, for it might prevent them from making such curious mistakes as that of first raising a rate of duty against the world, and then ostentatiously putting the mother country on a "favoured nation" footing towards said increased duty, which, in not a few instances, leaves her industrial products at a greater disadvantage than they would have been at had no change at all taken place in the tariff, nor any "privilege" been ostentatiously accorded to us. They surely cannot be aware, these Canadians, that we look upon this kind of thing here as being much like the action of the shopkeeper who marks goods in his window at "25 per cent. discount on the usual price," having first taken good care to put 30 per cent. on. This is by the way, however.

Most of our Colonies have been doing less with us lately than they used to do. Those in Australasia, in particular, are now buying smaller quantities of most of our staple products. South Africa also is by no means a lavish customer, and whatever the sentiment of unity may be in regard to the Empire, it certainly is not a sentiment which transforms itself into pounds, shillings, and pence through the medium of our Board of Trade Returns. We may, however, freely forgive these Colonies, and particularly Australasia, for the immediate slackness of their trade, since their great purchases in the past were paid for with money borrowed here, the load of which remains to cripple their present purchasing capacity. From this point of view the backwardness of our Colonial trade may be a healthy indication which ought to be welcomed as affording a hope that better economic conditions are arising among them through thrift and abstention from borrowing.

Strangely enough, the countries that have been doing most of late to sustain the volume of our commerce, in textiles at all events, are British India and the Republic of Brazil. The imports of British cotton goods to India have been very much larger this year than last, and during the month of March alone the increased value is nearly half a million pounds. This, we fear, indicates unhealthy trading, because the people of India are certainly less able to buy our goods now than they were even twelve months ago. Their poverty is greater over large areas of the peninsula, and such trade as there is has been materially interfered with both by famine and plague. We must consequently look upon this expansion in business more as a result of an artificial rate of exchange than as the natural growth of enlarged prosperity. By forcing up the exchange value of the rupee the British exporter to India has been able to exchange that rupee to a greater advantage for sovereigns, and has, in consequence, glutted the market with goods, a proportion of which may remain for some time in warehouses and be financed partly on the money markets of India, quite straitened enough without this. As regards Brazil, the cause of expansion is not so obvious. The Brazilian exchange has been falling and lies now in the neighbourhood of 6d. for the milreis, the par value of which not so many years ago was 2s. 3d. This decline assuredly gives no stimulus to the importer in Brazil to buy, nor to the exporter here to sell, and yet it is a fact that Brazil is conspicuous as an increasingly large buyer of cotton piece goods at the present time. It may be only a temporary movement and we must not pass judgment upon it in haste, but trade in that direction requires watching, especially if continued returns indicate that it is being forced against the stream.

Of other South American States Argentina alone gives indication of reviving business with us, although the figures are not yet up to the level of those of 1896. Doubtless, however, the enlarged exports now going on from Argentina to Europe will be counterbalanced presently by increased imports from us. All Central American States appear to be in a bad way at present, through causes we cannot off-hand define. Possibly they are suffering, as we are, from the dog-in-the-manger fiscal policy of the United States. It is from the United States at any rate that our commerce is suffering most of all at present. All branches of our exports to the Union are feeling the effects of the Dingley tariff, except perhaps the linen trade. That has not fallen off appreciably either in quantity or value, nor has our export of jute manufactures suffered much, but the quantity of unbleached cotton piece goods, and of woollen and worsted goods of all descriptions has fallen off more or less seriously, woollen most of all. Two years ago the value of woollen and worsted manufactures sent from this country to the United States in the first three months of the year was £458,000. In the first three months of the present year it was less than £82,000. In like manner the value of cotton manufactures of all kinds has fallen from £528,000 to £408,000, most of the fall taking place in the unbleached or undyed fabrics. Exports of lace to the United States have also fallen off in value, and their tariff, or else our clumsiness, has almost completely shut out every kind of British machinery. We shall survive all this and come out victorious, there is not the least doubt, but the lesson of these returns is emphatically one of increased industry and greater thrift. This is not a time for the wage earner to wrangle over his pay, but to set to work to see how much more he can produce. Still less is it a time to drain £20,000,000 a year more than was wont out of the earnings and savings of the nation to be spent in preparations for war.

The Irish Local Taxation Muddle.

(FROM A CORRESPONDENT).

I am afraid it is only too true that protest of any kind against the financial proposals of the Irish Local Government measure is, as the editor of the INVESTORS' REVIEW has stated, absolutely useless. But it is often expedient to place on record a protest which, useless at the moment, still remains to justify future action when occasion for such action arises. The Liberal party did make such a protest by voting against the English Agricultural Rating Act, and it can scarcely be doubted that this Rating Act is helping to give it an opportunity of acting on its protest.

That Act is not in the least doing anything in the way of relieving "agricultural depression." No one really thought it would. But it must not at all be taken as parallel to what is now proposed to be done in the case of Ireland. The population of England is 29,000,000, of which only 3,000,000 at the outside are engaged in agriculture, and of these last only 223,000 are farmers, and as such recipients with the few landlords of the Agricultural Grant. There are 759,000 agricultural labourers, who, of course, as consumers of dutiable articles, help to pay the grant. But, as is evident, the 26,000,000 or 27,000,000 of the English population, holding all but a fraction of the valuation, great cities, towns, manufacturing centres, bear the burden. It is a folly, but they are able to bear it, and much more. It is quite otherwise in the case of Ireland. Of its 4,700,000 inhabitants, 2,978,000 subsist on 486,000 agricultural holdings, leaving 1,722,000 for the towns and villages. The valuation of the agricultural holdings is just about £10,000,000; of the non-agricultural, £4,500,000. But the valuation of the agricultural holdings has to be considered with the remark that, while the population on the small holdings is to be entirely credited to them, that on the larger is mainly made up of labourers and farm servants. Now, of the 486,000 agricultural holdings, those under £15 valuation alone are 332,556 in number, have a total valuation of £2,029,616, and support a population of 1,631,528. This enables me to say at once that the whole agricultural population of Ireland is made up, all but an insignificant fraction, of small occupiers and labourers, and that the valuation of the holdings of the former is about £3,000,000 out of £10,000,000.

Now the assessed rates being £3,095,000 the non-agricultural valuation pays one-half of them already—that is, £4,500,000 pays £1,500,000, which will be allowed to be very heavy taxation, while the agricultural valuation, £10,000,000, pays only an equal amount—£1,500,000. But in reality this agricultural valuation includes £10,000,000 rental, which pays only one-fifth of the rates, or £300,000, leaving £1,200,000 to be borne by the occupiers' interest, whatever that is. I know no reason why the inhabitants of Irish country towns and villages, poorer even than the occupiers of rural areas, should pay double the rates of the latter. Nor do I see why the rental, by far the most valuable element in the agricultural valuation, should almost entirely escape local burdens, necessary in order that it should accrue at all.

What is proposed to be done now is to impose £730,000 new taxation on the Irish people, a mass of already heavily taxed townfolk, small occupiers, and labourers, to exempt a rental of £10,000,000 from rates. "But the occupiers get part, say, £400,000 of it." Yes the section of them the Irish call "land-grabbers," he section responsible for the depopulation, disaffection and agrarian crime of the country even more than the landlords. Of the 486,000 holdings there are 15,000 over £100 valuation; total valuation £2,140,000, and population only 299,000, mostly labourers and farm servants. These 15,000 large occupiers represent the class who, with the landowners, pocket the £730,000. The small occupiers, some 2,000,000, get less than nothing, a negative quantity. In Ireland general revenue comes mainly from dutiable articles, the consumption of which nearly follows numbers. If the two millions of small occupiers get £100,000 of the grant, as general taxpayers they will have to pay at least £300,000 for it. The "land-grabber" gets the money, and besides, under Irish social and political conditions, all local power, which enables him to carry out the traditional policy of his class with reinforced vigour.

It has to be said for the financial transaction that it is the common expression of historical experience, and finds perhaps its most striking modern illustration in the great democratic community on the other side of the Atlantic. But still there is an engaging *naïveté* all its own about this plan of ours for encouraging agriculture by taxing spades. It is assumed that the £730,000 is Irish money. Our Irish financial authorities would be angry if we hinted otherwise; they even claim that part of the English agricultural grant is Irish money. Be it so; having a good firm road under our feet we have no idea of venturing on a bog neither land nor water. If the Irish choose to exempt by far the most valuable part of their local taxable fund from rates for the sake of the landlords and "land grabbers," we believe the Irish taxpayer must be unable to meet the cost of local administration. It is their own argument that he is frightfully overtaxed, and it looks like it when, for rates alone, a valuation of £4,500,000 pays £1,500,000, and £10,000,000, less by a rental of the same amount, pays £1,200,000. But the only way to remedy this is to make rental and the "landgrabber's" interest, now to a great extent exempt under a differential rating system, pay its fair share. It is no remedy to put £730,000 on the Irish general taxpayers, who to a great extent are small agricultural occupiers. And if the Irish pay part of the English agricultural grant, it is because they are relatively heavier contributors to indirect revenue. The remedy for that is to get rid of the grant, not to extend its vicious principle in aggravated form to the much poorer country. It is certain that every addition to indirect taxation tells most heavily against the Irish people. But the Irish financial "reformers" go farther. I have seen it proposed that the landlords and "landgrabbers" should be relieved of the Income Tax and Death Duties, of course without condescending to tell us at whose expense. But with the command of the Irish representation and press and local government in future, these gentlemen may well count the poor helpless Irish people as nothing, and the man who, like Mr. Davitt, really thinks for them, as a mere crank.

The principle of the English Agricultural Rating Act and of the proposed Irish measure is certainly the same; but what is a folly which Englishmen can grin at and bear, is a crime in the case of Ireland. Propping up and strengthening landlords, "land grabbers," and absentees, is to aggravate the real causes of the depopulation, pauperism, and disaffection of the country. That would be bad enough in itself, but it is much worse when effected at the expense of the Irish taxpayer, already over-burdened, at the same time imposing the inevitable contingency of increased rates on the present real ratepayers, those who pay £1,500,000 in towns and villages on a valuation of £4,500,000, and those who pay £1,200,000 on £10,000,000, less a rental of £10,000,000.

Our Trade and War.—1.

Some years ago the late Lord Derby remarked that the greatest British interest was Peace, but people nowadays, while they acknowledge this to be true, seem to attach a great deal more importance to making themselves ready for battle. Lord Salisbury complains that a section of the public, including (it is alleged by outsiders) some intimate connection with his own Cabinet, appear to be desirous of fighting the world at large and simultaneously, notwithstanding the fair share of alarums and excursions that we have on hand in different quarters of the globe. Lord Selborne says that the nation is suffering from suppressed irritation, presumably because we are not at war with at least two, or perhaps three, of the great Powers, in addition to our other commitments of a warlike nature. Lord Rosebery, in attending the recent dinner of the Associated Chambers of Commerce, remarked that while he expected to be a guest at a function at which peaceful trade subjects were discussed, he found himself assisting in what was more like an amateur Council of War. Mr. Ritchie, the President of the Board of Trade, made remarks of a similar character. All this points to a very serious position indeed, especially as it is emphasised by votes for the navy and army so unprecedentedly heavy that, including the interest on the debt, our expenditure for past wars and preparing for future ones is over £70,000,000 this year, or £1 15s. per annum per head of our population, or £8 15s. per average family of five persons. As this expenditure is generally defended or explained by the necessities of our trade, it is of interest to look into the statistics of our business with the rest of the world.

The general argument is that our possessions outside these islands, known as the British Empire, are due to past wars, that inter-imperial trade is all important to us, and that we should continue to make our dominions expand, by force if necessary, with a view to pegging out claims for posterity. On this theory our territories, especially in Africa, have been increased to an enormous extent during the past few years, following on which policy and the fact that we are not the only nation that pursues it, we have had to immensely increase our land and sea forces. In this connection the following figures are worthy of consideration :—

Totals of British Trade.

Imports.

Year.	From Foreign Countries.		From the British Empire.	
	Amount.	Per Cent. of Whole.	Amount.	Per Cent. of Whole.
	£		£	
1882............	313,500,000	75·9	99,400,000	24·06
1896............	348,600,000	78·3	93,200,000	21·09

Exports.

Year.	To Foreign Countries.		To British Empire.	
	Amount.	Per Cent. of Whole.	Amount.	Per Cent. of Whole.
	£		£	
1882............	214,300,000	69·9	92,300,000	30·1
1896............	205,700,000	69·4	90,600,000	30·5

Total Trade.

Year.	From Foreign Countries.		From British Empire.		Grand Totals.
	Amount.	Per Cent. of Whole.	Amount.	Per Cent. of Whole.	
	£		£		
1882......	527,800,000	73·3	191,700,000	26·6	719,500,000
1896......	554,300,000	75·0	183,800,000	24·9	738,100,000

It follows from these figures that only one-fourth of our trade is done with the British Empire, and that three-fourths is done with foreigners, and that our business with our own people is decreasing, while what we do with others is increasing. We are all proud, as we may well be, of the magnificent heritage we have received from our forefathers, and are all absolutely determined that there shall be no diminution of those dominions on which the sun never sets. It is, however, on much nobler and loftier grounds than commercial ones that our glorious empire has been built up and is maintained. It certainly was not founded on the principle of the huckster desiring to extend his connection, for

> Trade's proud empire hastes to swift decay
> As ocean sweeps the laboured mole away.

Our ancestors never conquered a third of the globe on the principles now so often pressed upon us. Besides, if England determined to go a gunning, simply in order to annex fresh branches to her shop, where is she to do so? The whole of the temperate regions of the world are already occupied, mainly by ourselves or our children, and by the great powers of Europe, so that further conquests of territory in regions where the English race can thrive are absolutely impossible. There remain, therefore, only tropical or semi-civilised countries, and practically the whole of these, with the exception of China, are already annexed by some great Power—mainly, again, by ourselves. Further, it is with people inhabiting temperate and civilised countries that our trade is mainly done. The following table shows British trade with tropical or semi-tropical countries :—

—	Imports.	Exports.	Total.	Population.	Trade per head.
	£	£	£	£	s. d.
Haiti	92,000	295,000	387,000	?	—
China and Hong Kong	3,000,000	8,400,000	11,400,000	400,000,000	0 6¾
Japan	1,241,000	6,160,000	7,401,000	48,000,000	3 1
West Coast of Africa, British and Foreign	1,988,000	2,200,000	4,188,000	?	—
	6,321,000	17,055,000	23,376,000	460,000,000	—
India, &c.	32,200,000	33,900,000	56,100,000	312,000,000	4 2
Total	38,521,000	50,955,000	79,476,000	772,000,000	2 0¾

Here again is a table showing British trade with temperate countries :—

Imports and Exports.

Population	265,000,000
Trade	£658,700,000
Per head	£2 15s. 9d.

So far as such rough statistics can carry us, it would seem that 17 per cent. of our trade is done with the tropics, and 83 per cent. with the temperate zones or with civilised states. Per head the latter do about 27 times as much business with us as the tropics, and this is quite natural. A tropical denizen need take no thought wherewithal he shall be clothed, or how he shall be warmed and fed, and relatively little thought what he shall eat. A blazing sun diminishes or removes the necessity for clothing or fuel or houses, and a handful of rice or a few bananas are enough for food. The elder Mr. Weller waxed indignant on the exportation of "moral pocket 'andkerchers and flannel veskits" to negroes who cared for none of these things—but he was very wishful to apply straight "veskits" to erroneous philanthropists. Lord Salisbury is apparently of a similar opinion as regards certain unspecified war-mongers.

Economic and Financial Notes and Correspondence.

The Victory of Atbara—and After.

Whatever doubt we may have about the remoter consequences of the renewed effort to annex the Soudan to Egypt, it would be churlish to withhold hearty praise to the General and troops by whom this notable victory was won. Its completeness is the most gratifying thing of all since it renders further opposition of a formidable kind by the Khalifa and his Baggaras highly improbable. Further bloodshed of a wholesale kind has even become well nigh impossible, and surely this is a fact to be thankful for, especially in a country where blood has flowed in torrents these fifteen years past.

But what are we to do now? The troops will receive their medals, their officers and leader promotion and titles, all in the profuse fashion of the day. That goes without saying; but how is Egypt to bear the expenses of a reoccupation of a vast territory, now mostly desert, and of the re-establishment of a government at Khartoum? The reoccupied country is in no condition to furnish any part of the expense, stripped bare as it is and depopulated by the rapacious cruelty of the Mahdists. And what are we going to gain by this conquest? Employment for Englishmen, perhaps; but likewise the burden of supervising the new Government—nominally, that of the Khedive.

It is all very well to succeed in these wars. The glory may be great, and the conduct of British-led troops is nearly always something of which to be proud, as far as deeds of war of any sort can justifiably excite pride. But is it wise for us to scatter our energy in this manner over distant portions of the globe always difficult of access, and usually far from an inexpensive base? The imperialism which dictates these distant expeditions has from the first appeared to us a species of madness, and success in a fight cannot change our judgment in this instance. Sir Herbert Kitchener's victory is not the end, but the beginning of trouble. It opens up a great vista of conquest and of complications—with the French in the western Soudan, with Germany in the south, with Abyssinia in the east. We have entered upon the conquest and expansion of yet one more empire, whose responsibilities will weigh heavier and heavier upon us and tax our strength the more the further we go. And all the time we are overburdened with cares elsewhere—cares which might become dangers.

Let but a quarrel arise between us and Russia and where would our resources for holding the Soudan be found? We can obtain no compensation in that country for many years to come, its trade may never be worth to us one month's business with France, one week's business with the United States, a tenth part of the value of our trade with China. And we risk the loss of much of this good and sure trade with densely populated countries to gratify a restless itch for conquest. Who among us benefits by the gratification of this itch, except the "medals and ribbons" bands of the fighters? Why does the nation refuse to look at these deeds of arms from this common-sense standpoint? We are not usually a feather-pated people, and yet militarism has now apparently got complete hold of us, so that we shout ourselves hoarse, like a Roman crowd, in expressing our delight over a successful slaying match, and place feats of that sort far above the noblest achievements of the men who spend their lives in contributing to the happiness of their fellow-creatures through the expansion of industry and commerce. An abdication of manliness such as this is ominous of many things. Already we are weak before great Powers by reason of our many responsibilities.

The Paris Money Market.

Among the numerous indications that the French volcano is becoming hot to eruption point, the condition of the Paris money market is not the least significant. We do not see how the Bank of France can long adhere to its policy of refusing to sell gold without bringing the convertibility of its enormous mass of paper money into doubt. "Protection all round," which is the policy of the present ministry, is driving capital out of the country, and causing its foreign trade to contract or to become less profitable. The blow levelled at the open market in stocks and shares has given an immense impetus to this outflow of capital begun, perhaps, by the necessity for unusually large and expensive imports of food, and the crisis in Spanish affairs is doing much to put it out of the power of the French people to sell securities abroad to meet extraordinary calls thus arising upon the national funds. Here, indeed, the worst of the money difficulty lies. Apart from their Egyptian and Russian bonds the French have very little in the way of securities that they could sell abroad, and not much even of these could be sold at anything near the present quotations. With nothing particular to sell in the way of international securities France must export gold, and its departure will force the Bank of France to advance its rate. A 4 per cent. bank rate coming just before the general elections might evoke dangerous sentiments in the minds of a large body of the electorate, and would undoubtedly render M. Méline's administration very unpopular. This might not be by any means a misfortune were there something better ready to take its place. We can only trust that there is, although there are few indications of its existence in sight amid the storm of passions, all making for revolution, now agitating the French people. But common-sense, of which Frenchmen have far more than we give them credit for, may yet be victorious over revolutionary factions even though these should be reinforced by an untoward money market.

Dearer Money in Germany.

It would be curious were the eagerness of the Germans to stand beside the English as international money-lenders to bring about a banking or monetary crisis in Berlin. The probability that it will is not inconsiderable, since the Berlin money market, to use an expressive if rather vulgar Americanism, has obviously "bitten off a good deal more than it can chew," in contracting to take half the last Chinese loan. And the worst of it is that payment must be so prompt. China has to hand over some £12,000,000 of it to Japan in the beginning of next month, and in all probability

German banks will have to remit gold to London to cover their share of the money. Japan has a weakness for the Bank of England, and is comfortable in mind when its balances lie snugly in its keeping. Besides, most of the money is owing here by Japan, or will be as its naval programme gets filled in, and it is handiest to have the cash on the spot. In all probability, then, Berlin will have to remit gold to London in large amounts within the next three weeks. The export has already been pretty heavy, and we are nowise surprised to see "Bank rate" 4 per cent. in Germany. Soon it may be 5 per cent., and then difficulties will begin, especially as dearer money in London is already making it less easy for German banks to flood our market with their acceptances. By itself 5 per cent. would not hurt, it is the conjunction of circumstances which threaten mischief.

The Arauco Company, Limited.

It is much to be desired that this concern, which has now gone into liquidation, may not be allowed to pass out of sight without a very close examination into its origin and history. More than a million of capital is involved in it and we do not believe, from facts that are before us, that one half of this money was ever legitimately put into the company's affairs, or that the purchases of some of these properties at least were honestly made. It is rather a shameful story, but one very difficult to tell in the columns of a journal like this, or indeed to print at all except as the report of a public examination of the directors before a judge. We emphatically think that this examination ought to take place. It will be one more scandal if the people who were at the inception of this company, and who undoubtedly profited by it while it continued to exist, should not be called upon to give an account of their stewardship. One of the shareholders, Mr. Penfold, plainly stated at the recent meeting of the company that two of the directors, the late Colonel North and a Mr. Edmundson, applied for practically £90,000 worth out of a £100,000 worth of preference shares issued in December, 1886, and began disposing of their allotments in April, 1887. An examination of the Register of Shareholders proves this to be the case, and in fact the share issues appear to have been usually made to a great extent in this way.

North and the others sold their shares issued in February, 1897, steadily throughout the year, and in the same manner subsequent issues of shares passed into the hands of this man, his associates and "dummies," to be unloaded upon the public at more or less handsome profits. To facilitate this unloading the most sophisticated and misleading reports were manufactured and issued about the prospects and condition of the company, which were set forth as being of the most roseate description. Concessions were bought which turned out to be worth nothing, but for which large amounts of money were paid by the shareholders, or at least for which large amounts of share capital were created to be traded off upon an unsuspecting public. This kind of business involves very little risk to those conducting it from the inside. Long before the shares allotted to them are paid up they begin to sell, the "premium" being then probably at its highest, and long ere the liability for calls comes home they are clear of the affair, with all the small capital originally advanced back in their pockets, ten, twenty, fifty times over.

One thing that requires elucidation is the history of the coal concession which they bought with a lawsuit upon it. By the loss of this lawsuit this "concession" was rendered valueless, but the disaster was hidden up and another practically worthless property purchased about which the most outrageously extravagant and misleading language was used by the late Colonel North. "We have the refusal," said he, "of this property for fifteen days and another party wants to give £250,000 for it." All the time this mean imposture was unfolding itself the directors professed to be working for nothing; but one of their number had an agreement whereby he received 5 per cent. on the purchases and sales effected by him as sole agent of the Arauco Company, and 2½ per cent. commission on its freight business. This is only the briefest possible outline of a very disgraceful history, but we shall be quite prepared to supplement it and with greater emphasis, backed by extracts from the minutes of the board meetings and other documentary evidence, if the shareholders are willing and ready to bestir themselves to have the affairs of the company investigated to the bottom, with a view to obtaining restitution of some of the money of which they have been plundered. Colonel North is dead, but there are others alive who ought to be made to pay back what they have obtained out of financing this company. All that is wanted is pluck and unity of purpose among the aggrieved proprietors.

More Light on Northern "Terrors."

In spite of the fervid eloquence of Mr. Bottomley and the ready manner in which the "shareholders," dear simple folk, endorsed his views, we must again state distinctly that the constitution of this concern is of a most suspicious character. The more we examine its past history the more evident are the sordid nature of its surroundings and the utterly disappointing character of the results heretofore obtained. In our previous article of March 4, we stated that the Port Darwin Gold Mining Company, whose property now constitutes the backbone of the present Northern Territories Company, fell under the control of Mr. Hugh Watt, a man of unsavoury memory, more particularly in connection with the Chile-New Chile-Yuruari-Caratal reconstructions. Since then we have discovered that this man Watt was practically the founder of the company, arranging the Board to suit himself. He throughout its history took the leading share in its management, the first secretary having been Mr. Leonard Welstead, his brother-in-law, who subsequently became a director and went out in this capacity to the mine. We stated that the property was foreclosed upon by the mortgagee about 1890, but did not know until recently that the mortgagee was Mr. Hugh Watt himself! This we believe to be the fact, since Watt appeared as the vendor to Mr. Bottomley's "Terrors" company.

We have thus established that the Howley Mine, which forms the chief property of the Northern Territories Goldfields of South Australia, was twelve years ago promoted as a company by the said Watt, who worked it for about four years, sending out to the spot an expensive plant. At the end of this time it was foreclosed upon by this latter-day financier, and taken back by him for a mere bagatelle, shareholders in the unfortunate Port Darwin Company, we believe, never having had a chance to say "yea" or "nay" regarding the sacrifice of their property. After these revelations, and in view of information supplied to us, it seems only reasonable that we should call upon Mr. Bottomley to answer the following questions:—

(1) Is it a fact that the Howley Mine was offered in London and sold for £1,500 in cash?

(2) Is it a fact that the North and South Union Group of mines, which comprised more than the other properties making up the list of the Northern Territories Company's holding, were offered about in London for £3,000 in cash?

(3) Is it a fact that the ore is very refractory, and that the Port Darwin Company in its four years of existence —from 1886 to 1890—with complete machinery on the spot, never obtained any systematic returns?

(4) Does the Northern Territories Goldfields of South Australia hold any other property, outside those contained in the Howley Group and the North and South Union Group, mentioned above?

It may be inconvenient for Mr. Bottomley to answer these questions, but he will soon begin to discover that something more is required at his hands than the musty generalisations and soft sawder hitherto furnished by him about the property of this company. The public does not, even in its maddest times, capitalise properties of this character at £1,000,000, as is done by the present price of Northern "Terrors," and the sooner it understands the true character of the adventure the more likely it is to avoid touching the shares.

"Awakening" of Austria.

It is now Austria's turn. She, too, it seems, has been awakened by the recent hubbub in the Far East to a sense of danger from the weakness of her navy. Where, however, the danger lurks it would be difficult to tell; for even Austrian Jingoes admit that her present navy is perfectly sufficient to protect her commerce and to guard her coasts. She has, we are told, no ambition for the acquisition of colonies, even if there were any left for her to acquire. Then why this uneasy rush for the building of new warships? For no reason apparently but a feeling of annoyance that Austria has been unable to send a fleet to China to seize, like other great Powers, a port or a province, or both, from the submissive Chinese Government. Germany has got ahead of her, and is likely to continue so; for, by the time Austria's first new ironclad is built, there may be little room to spare for new-comers. Still Austria is bent on having a big or, at least, a bigger navy than she has. A grant of 55,000,000 florins for this purpose is to be asked from the Parliamentary Delegations when they meet next week. It will add heavily to the financial burdens of the taxpayers; and these are already much more onerous than most people are aware of. Austria has for more than a dozen years kept herself in a state of complete preparedness for a war with Russia. It would have taken place many years ago but for the intervention of Prince Bismarck. But Austria keeps up her preparations. Her army, the *Times* Vienna correspondent avers, is in a state bordering on perfection. This, of course, means enormous expense; yet there is now to be added to it the costly luxury of a great navy craze. In a country such as Austria it seems a great and foolish vanity. It has surely enough already on its hands. Its warring races cannot agree even on an official language. They can neither separate nor live together in amity. They compel the Emperor to rule despotically in spite of himself, and to the close of his reign sober-minded Austrians look with well-founded dread and anxiety. In such circumstances it is surely a mistaken policy to insist on a large addition to an already sufficient navy. Italy, in this respect, is more prudent; she is selling ships, not adding to their number.

Cowell, Craft, & Co.

A few weeks ago we dealt with some of the concerns in which Mr. Richard Collins Drew was the leading spirit. Last week we read that one of these had been wound up under an order of the Court. This was the business of Cowell, Craft, & Co., which was promoted by one J. Jervis, with Drew to take over the goodwills, premises, &c., of Cowell & Drew, Gummand & Co., Craft & Co., & Rush's Laundry. The public were unappreciative, and the undertaking has not been a success. Mr. Justice Wright in making the order said there would be the fullest investigation into the affairs of the company, and we shall await the result with interest.

Wanted, a Hercules!

There is no doubt that the company Augean stable is in a bad condition. Recent investigations of several of the most outrageous swindles and fraudulent promotions show that some strong action is imperatively necessary. The power of holders of "underwriting" and "commission" shares to outvote bonâ fide shareholders is little short of a scandal, as well as the difficulty of obtaining any impartial investigation of the affairs of a company. Piecemeal legislation is useless. Strong sweeping reforms giving the means of first finding abuses and then the power of crushing them are required. But who will bring them forward?

German Enterprise.

"How often of late years has the remark been made that British commercial men are not up to date." Thus writes Mr. T. R. Mulvany in his report on Trade in Germany, and we might quote the same remark from almost every trade report that reaches us. Englishmen, we are continually told, are too old-fashioned, too "upish," and not sufficiently adaptable to make way with foreigners in this competitive age. The Germans, on the other hand, are adaptability itself, and can learn the language and conform to the customs of any land in which they may find themselves, and, in fact, so well do they thrive in "furrin' parts," that frequently, in the words of the song, "The Fatherland, the happy Fatherland, never sees them any more," so glad do they seem to get away from it.

Mr. Mulvany's picture of commerce and enterprise is certainly very glowing and his figures prove that the nation has indeed made rapid strides during the past few years, and threatens to take the shine out of us all if we do not look to our laurels. The secret of this success our Consul puts down to the "military organisation applied to trade and industry to meet the requirements thereof," and to a moderate protective tariff. But it is rather soon to say that this "military discipline will always be a success. The people themselves do not like it, Germany as an empire is still in its infancy, and the old maxim of "train up a child," &c., in many cases proves a fallacy. Still that it has been successful so far is beyond doubt. Germany at the present day is a great military power, and promises to be a great naval one, and there are many of its institutions from which, if we would only pocket our pride, we might take a lesson. Their State-controlled railways carry freight at such moderate prices, in some cases below the cost of production, as to make it impossible for foreign traders to compete with them in their home markets. Their industrial companies are managed by men with a technical knowledge of the concern. Their mines are not governed by a number of unpractical directors, but by a manager over whom is placed a board of supervision; and last but not least the professional company promoter is an unknown quantity, and "hence the tremendous dead weight of promotion capital does not exist."

Farmers' Troubles.

Among the troubles that afflict the agriculturist, the most tantalising is the weather. It can never be depended upon; and the modern prophets, smart though they be, have not proved of much use to the farmer. For a considerable time he has been anxious about the long-continued drought. The winter was mild enough, but unusually dry. The spring corn has been sown, at least in England, though there is a good deal yet to do in Scotland; the potatoes have been planted, and the mangold crop has been laid in the ground under tolerably favourable conditions. In these operations the drought was serviceable; but a good downpour of rain would have been welcomed even if it had somewhat delayed sowing. Pastures were at a standstill for want of moisture. Dairy farmers and graziers were especially anxious on this score. Rain has fallen within the last week or so in many districts, but hardly in sufficient quantities to be satisfactory. Still it has done some good. It was in time to help the newly-sown mangold; and the young spring corn and pastures were greatly refreshed by it. But vegetation craves for more, and it is to be hoped it will not be long delayed. The cold and frost at the close of March and early in April have not done so much harm as might have been expected. Fruit trees look well. The recent sunny weather has forced forth the bloom of plum and other fruits in great abundance. On the whole, though more rain is wanted, it cannot be said that the prospect for the farmer is bad; it is at least fair.

Dairy farmers have at present a special grievance of their own. A Cherbourg company threatens to flood our markets with what is called fresh milk. They even propose floating a company in this country, into which they mean to entice as many milk-dealers as they can. A herb has been discovered—so our Consul at Cherbourg vouches—which has antiseptic properties, and will keep milk fresh for six days. The Cherbourg company have bought the secret of distilling from this herb a liquor one drop of which will preserve the sweetness of a gallon of milk for a week. The prospect is naturally not relished by our dairy-farmers. They insist that the milk so treated is really drugged, and ought to be subject to the same sanitary restrictions as our home supply. It is possible there may be something in this objection. Chemical analysis only affords us negative results; it has not discovered the antiseptic drug, or whatever it may be, in the milk. The only supposition is that it must evaporate; but if it evaporates, how can it continue to affect the milk, so as to keep it fresh? Our own farmers insist that there is danger to health in milk thus treated, and would prevent its importation. But that is surely a mistake. Are our farmers not guilty of using antiseptics in the milk with which they supply us? It would be valuable in a sanitary sense if our milk supply were sterilised, and the Cherbourg people say they can do this if antiseptics are forbidden. So, no doubt, could our own dairymen. It is a matter for inquiry and experiment. We must not prohibit the importation of this milk unless it can be showu that it is dangerous to the public health; and as yet this has not been proved.

Great Central Railway Finance.

The directors of this company are issuing Lloyds' Bonds to their contractors, and these contractors are selling them in the City for what they can get. It seems a pity that the company should be reduced to this. Not that we object to the creation of temporary debt on capital account in itself. It would have been better had the whole debt of our railways been in terminable bonds instead of a perpetual bond upon them. But what is serious is the issue of these Lloyds' bonds without intimation to the regular proprietors of the company. They ought to know the proposed amount of the bond and the nature of the security given. Formerly a bond of this description issued by a railway company was regarded as a prior lien, taking precedence even of debenture stocks. Is it so in the present instance, or will the preference stocks alone find a new security placed in front of them? Perhaps the directors will say what they are doing, and how much money they are likely still to want. The London Extension, upon which the old Manchester, Sheffield, and Lincolnshire Company embarked so confidently, is surely costing far more money than was ever estimated for.

The Buenos Ayres Great Southern's New Capital.

Excellently as this premier Argentine railway is managed, we must confess that we do not like the manner in which the board proposes to raise fresh capital. The proposition is to issue forthwith £2,250,000 in "Four per Cent. Extension Shares, 1902," at a premium of £1 10s. per £10 share, the premiums of £337,500 thus received to be devoted to paying the 4 per cent. interest upon the new shares until 1902, after which date they will be merged into the ordinary capital, and rank for dividends in the usual way. By this arrangement there will be no charge against revenue during the four years, and this to our mind must unduly benefit the net earnings of that period.

Thus, of the money raised £600,000 is to be lent to a dock company upon security of first mortgage debentures, which, we presume, will bear interest. Then 275 miles of railway will be built with part of the money. One-sixth of the distance has already the lines laid down, so that a year hence the bulk of this new mileage ought to be open, and we dare say two years hence will see it all completed. New rolling stock is also to be purchased, and improvements on the main line are to be effected. The rolling stock can be purchased as soon as the money is raised, and the improvements will doubtless be pushed on quickly, so that we should imagine the company would have the full benefit of this extra mileage, revenue from its dock debentures, new rolling stock, and general improvements, for at least two years without it costing revenue a fraction.

In many ways the company would gain from the expenditure of this money, and so during at least two of the years during which interest is to be paid out of capital quite an unnatural condition of the revenue account would prevail. In the ordinary course of events we should have expected the dividends of this line to improve, and under such a stimulus they might easily rise to 8 per cent., if the board were inclined to distribute freely. In 1902, however, a change would come over the scene, for then the £2,250,000 of extension capital would come in for full rights. It would not be a question of finding the difference between four and eight per cent. upon that amount of capital, but of providing the whole eight per cent., as the four per cent. will until then be paid out of capital, and £2,250,000 is not a slight percentage of the ordinary capital, for its present amount is only £9,000,000. Something of the kind happened previously with this company, for in the years 1884 to 1889 it issued £440,000 of capital bearing a fixed rate of interest until 1894. In the interval dividends of 10 per cent. were paid, but by the time the last amount of capital obtained the full power to share in profits the dividends had declined to 5 per cent. Of course this decline was not wholly due to the extra capital, but we venture to affirm that the 10 per cent. might not have been paid for so long had the capital issues been arranged otherwise.

The Welsh Coal Strike.

Except in the increased injury to trade, there is no real change in the position of affairs in South Wales. The representatives of the colliers and of the employers had another brief conference on Tuesday; but as the former had no power to conclude an arrangement, there was no practical outcome of the meeting. The men, however, formulated their demands more precisely than they have yet done, and the employers intimated that, while still open to negotiation on the general question, they would in no circumstances accept the proposals for a minimum wage, or for the appointment of an umpire. This narrows the matters in dispute considerably, and if the men decide to drop those two propositions, and consent to confer plenary powers on their representatives, there is reason to believe that an agreement may be arrived at. Both sides seem to prefer the sliding scale arrangement, only the men wish that wages should in no case go below a certain limit, however much the price of coal may be reduced. The demand is unreasonable. If persisted in, it must lead to a prolonged struggle; but it need not yet be taken for granted that it will be persisted in, and hopes of an early arrangement of the quarrel are still entertained. It rests, however, with the men themselves; and, as they have revolted against their old leaders, and are not very confident about their new, there is great uncertainty about the immediate result.

ARGENTINE TRADE IN 1897.

A very interesting report on this subject has been compiled for the Foreign Office, by Mr. E. A. M. Laing, acting British Consul at Buenos Ayres. Its main lesson is that if a country is given a government capable of maintaining some kind of order and peace,

it makes progress even under adverse conditions. And the conditions were adverse in the Argentine last year, for the harvest of 1896 was practically destroyed by locusts and unfavourable weather, so that the people started badly. Then, to add to the difficulties of the agricultural population, the premium on gold kept falling all through the year. This had the effect of reducing the return measured in gold, which the producer got for whatever he had to sell, and, at the same time, he had to pay his labour and general expenses on the same scale as before. That is to say, while he only received an average of 291.36 paper dollars in 1897 for 100 dollars gold, as compared with an average of 296.16 in 1896, and of 344.39 in 1895, he was not able to proportionately reduce his labour bill. This kind of pinch illustrates the evil of a depreciated currency. When a nation's money begins to recover from the effects of a great depreciation the recovery inflicts a positive hardship upon all those who have to sell at a gold valuation the goods they produce in order to live. Nevertheless, Argentina has been steadily advancing. Foreign capital, especially German capital—borrowed in London perhaps—has been flowing into the country, and the railway companies, still principally English, have been extending their lines and bringing new districts in the great territory of the Republic within reach of settlers and markets. A great tract of country, for example, is being opened towards the west and south by the extension which the Great Southern Railway is building from Bahia Blanca to the confluence of the rivers Limay and Nouquen. This line runs south-west from Bahia Blanca until it meets the Rio Colorado, along whose south bank it goes for 65 miles, and then across the Rio Negro. When completed, the line will be 348 miles long, and will run through a country where excellent grazing land lies, while in the valleys of the Colorado and Negro rivers there are large areas which may be irrigated at small cost. Already population and building materials are flowing south-westward with the line, and Mr. Laing thinks that at no distant date an extension may take place to the rich slopes of the Cordillera, an extension which will establish a connection with Southern Chili.

Although the country is slowly making way, its foreign commerce last year bore unmistakeable traces of the locust plague. Imports fell from upwards of $112,000,000 to about $98,300,000, and exports from $116,800,000 to $101,170,000. England still leads in supplying Argentina with goods, the total received from us being valued at about $36,400,000 last year, which was a long way ahead of any other country, Germany and France coming next with little more than $11,000,000 each. But we do not occupy anything like the same position as purchasers of Argentine goods. France takes the lead there, and last year received nearly $23,000,000 worth as against about $13,000,000 sent to this country. Germany, even, buys more Argentine products than we do, her purchases last year amounting to rather more than $14,000,000. This is explained by the fact that France and Germany are very much larger importers of Argentine wool than we are. France took 188,000 bales last year, Germany about 98,000 bales and Belgium over 80,000, as against 19,500 sent to the United Kingdom. Mr. Laing, however, seems to imply that our neighbours did not retain all the goods nominally consigned to them, and that our proportion in the Argentine exports may be larger than appears. Our position as a great meat-eating nation is signally illustrated by the fact that last year we imported upwards of 2,000,000 frozen wethers, no other country taking any share in this trade except France, whose purchases amounted to about 57,400.

So far as competition goes, although the Germans are extremely busy in starting new companies out in Argentina, especially electrical companies, it does not appear that we are really losing ground as traders. Where other nations, and the Germans in particular, are making headway against us is in the production of inferior goods, got up in imitation of high-quality English goods and sold as such, passed off upon the ignorant who imagine that they are getting for very low price the same article they used to pay a better price for. This is not very honourable trade competition, but it is one we must put up with until the consumers in the Republic have been educated by experience. What hinders our business more than anything else is the tariff, and the tariff is, of course, a direct product of the monstrous debt which the "boodlers" of the past have piled upon the unhappy Republic. This tariff, for instance, hits bar iron so severely that a local firm, taking advantage of the export duty placed on old iron by an unenlightened government, buys up scrap iron, at its own price almost, and manufactures it into new bars. But we hold our own in industrial machinery of all sorts, which Mr. Laing reports to have been in brisk demand, more especially the good qualities of English make. He, however, emphatically adjures British manufacturers to be more careful in the packing of their goods and to show greater willingness to meet their customers' wants. In both these respects the habits of Continental dealers and producers are in marked and favourable contrast with our own. Not only should goods be well packed, but each case should be marked on the outside in plain figures with both the net and gross weight in kilos, and the measurement in metres, and the said weights and measures should be noted on the invoices.

Mr. Laing gives the Argentine Government great credit for its success in fighting the locusts. We hope he has not been misled in this matter, for his opinion is not quite in accordance with what we are hearing from other quarters. Its intentions are, no doubt, excellent, but the performance is by no means always equal to the desires of the amiable law-makers. Allusion is made towards the end of the Report to the resumption of full payment of the interest upon the national debt, the total figures of which are put by Mr. Laing at $425,000,000 gold, or $535 per head. Of course, there is no revenue to meet this generous determination of the Government, and, as we have often pointed out, it has been in far too great a hurry to play the supra-honest debtor. It has been able to "realise" only deficits every year since the crisis of 1890, and the deficit for 1898 is apparently estimated at $9,000,000 paper. This is to be made good in a very characteristic, but extremely objectionable way by compelling foreign insurance companies working in the country to buy $7,000,000 paper in 5 per cent. bonds at 80 per cent. of their face value, and by transferring $2,000,000 paper, estimated to be the "profits" on the working of the insolvent National Bank, to the Treasury. That is to say, $2,000,000 notes, which should have been cancelled and burnt according to law, will be re-issued. Even this, we fear, will not fill the gap, and the latest news in the City of London is that the Government of the Republic is busy arranging for the issue of a new loan in Europe. We have been expecting this for a long time. It was not wholly generosity which dictated the resolution to resume debt payments in full, whether there was revenue to do it with or not, but an unquenchable desire to finger more of our money. We are disposed, though, to think that in their haste to do this, the Argentine politicians have over-reached themselves this time. English investors have not yet forgotten 1890 and what followed it, and it will be extremely difficult to get them to subscribe a new Argentine loan at the present time. A very good thing also will it be for political honesty, and for the progress of Argentine, if people here do button up their pockets and refuse to lend a penny. Argentine is not marvellously well governed now; its greatest weakness, indeed, is in the character of its administration, the wastefulness of its politicians, and the feebleness of the central authority. Slowly, however, the power of the Buenos Ayres Government is becoming consolidated, and the country has been making progress in spite of all drawbacks. It will therefore come out right end up if left to grow naturally without help on a large scale from such dangerous stimulants as borrowed money always is. The progress in the future should be equally great with what it has been in the past eight years, and far more solid. The country is capable of being a great nation and will become one in time, we have not the least doubt, unless its prospects are damaged, or wrecked, by the corrupt influences which so nearly brought it to destruction in November, 1890. And, loan or no loan, 1898 is destined to be more prosperous than its immediate predecessor so far as the commerce of the Republic is concerned for the harvest is much larger, and better prices are obtained for the exportable surplus.

THE LIFE INSURANCE BLUE BOOK FOR 1896.

It is a pity the officials responsible for the production of this valuable compilation cannot manage to get it out some time within the twelve months succeeding the date of the figures. It has only come out a week or two ago and the balance-sheets of many of the companies for another year have already, in many cases, been made public. This gives an out-of-date aspect to the Board of Trade volume. Still, when it does come it is a thing to treasure. At present we can find room for only a few figures from the summaries appended to the returns made by the various insurance offices. These summaries show that at the date of the balance-sheets embraced in the compilation, the funds possessed by the ninety-two life offices dealt with aggregated £263,830,000. The "ordinary" life companies had an income of £19,605,000 from premiums alone and the industrial companies, of which there are eleven altogether making returns—seven of them doing no other business—a premium income of £7,151,000. Altogether these companies received nearly £27,000,000 from premiums, £2,336,000 came to them as capital paid in against annuities purchased, and £8,445,000 was their income from interest and dividends. These figures give some idea of the magnitude of the business, and this idea is still further enhanced by the statement that the liabilities of these companies on insurance policies of all kinds aggregate £714,000,000, against which they have resources in life and annuity funds alone of £223,626,000. Their income increased last year by nearly £1,500,000, and the claims paid were £445,000 less than in the preceding year. On the whole, therefore, British companies are flourishing and growing in wealth. We may note that the average cost of conducting the industrial business exceeded 44 per cent. of the premium income. It should also, perhaps, be stated that the accounts here dealt with are by no means for a uniform period of time. Most of them are for the year ended December 31, 1896, but the return of the Friends' Provident comes down to November 20, 1897, and the Clerical, Medical, and General to June 30, 1897; the Life Association of Scotland to April 5, 1897; the National Guardian to June 30, 1897; the University to April 30, 1897, and so on. Consequently, it is possibly less the fault of the Board of Trade than of the insurance office officials that this return is so long in appearing after the date when the earlier balance-sheets, which form the great majority, have been made public.

IN THE DUTCH WEST INDIES.

Curaçoa seems to be in a rather depressed condition, what with its decreasing trade, financial deficits, and uncertain agriculture, and from Mr. Consul Jesurin's account of affairs there does not seem to be much present likelihood of matters improving. Prices in European and American markets are so low, tariffs so high, and competition so keen that profits in most cases are almost impossible to realise, and in one or two instances—the export of salt to the United States for example—the result is frequently a loss. The financial deficit for 1895 was over 108,000 fl.; for 1896 over 199,000 fl., and when the official statistics for 1897 are complete, the result, Mr. Jesurin tells us, will prove to be much worse. Pension disbursements, annually increasing, will amount to 14,766 fl. in 1898. The accounts of the Government schools show a deficit of 30,000 fl., which in 1898 will be much larger; and, in fact, the only institution which seems to have a balance on the right side is the Post-office. The island of Aruba, to be sure, possesses not unprofitable gold mines, but all that the Treasury receives from them is a paltry £200 a year, paid by the Mines company as rent. It is pleasant for us to know that under such distressing circumstances the importation of Wrexham Lager Beer is steadily on the increase, and whereas formerly it was unknown, at present the consumption is 25 per cent. of the total imports of this article. Our trade on the whole does not seem to have suffered much during the past few years, and in 1896 our exports to the country comprised about one-third of the entire merchandise brought there. But our shipping has fallen off greatly in the last year, due we are told to the fact that the Prince Line steamers have ceased calling at the port, and it might be well to consider the previous suggestion of establishing a British line of fast steamers to call there regularly as the American, French, Italian and Dutch lines do.

Critical Index to New Investments.

MANCHESTER AND LIVERPOOL TRANSPORT COMPANY, LIMITED.

The capital of this new creation is £300,000, in £1 shares, of which 200,000 are ordinary, and 100,000 deferred. No dividend can be paid on the latter in any year until 8 per cent. has been paid on the ordinary shares, in which case the deferred are entitled to the balance of profits available for distribution up to 8 per cent. and two-thirds of any surplus, the other third going to the ordinary shares. Subscriptions are invited for 150,000 ordinary shares while 65,000 deferred shares, with £6,000 in cash, go to the vendor, who appears to be Percy James Harmer, while E. H. Forwood, of the firm of Forwood Brothers & Co., who are the managers of the undertaking, is interested in the agreement and in the purchase consideration. The company will undertake the transport of merchandise by steamers between Manchester, Liverpool, and Birkenhead, through the Manchester Ship Canal. Steamers are to be constructed of varying capacity up to 1,000 tons, capable of performing the voyage between Manchester and Liverpool within six hours, and a dividend of at least 10 per cent. on the ordinary shares is spoken of. As a commercial undertaking we should rather doubt its chance of success, but the venture is so essentially local that investors here will no doubt leave the shares to Manchester and Liverpool.

BENT'S BREWERY COMPANY, LIMITED.

This Liverpool undertaking invites subscriptions for £50,000 in 5,000 6 per cent. cumulative preference shares of £10 each at 4 premium, which is a little under the market quotation of the existing shares, and at this price the yield is 4½ per cent. This additional capital is required to repay advances obtained to purchase licensed premises, and to pay for more properties. The premiums are to be added to the reserve, at present standing at £51,443. The company has done very well in the past, and the £10 ordinary shares, which stand at 17½, have received progressive dividends during the last three years of 6, 7, and 8 per cent. But existing share and debenture holders will naturally have preference in the allotment.

ROUMANIAN FOUR PER CENT. GOLD LOAN.

This loan, which is for 180 million francs, is being issued in Paris, the price being 93 per cent., and 105 million francs are for conversion purposes, the balance being for public works. The Société Générale de Paris, London Agency, will receive applications for the conversion of outstanding bonds of the Roumanian 5 per cent. 1875 loan and of the 5 per cent. Roumanian Rente Amortissable issued from 1881 to 1888, applications for the latter being only entertained to the extent of 36,320,000 francs. The issue price is decidedly high, and the terms offered should bring in outstanding bonds freely.

Company Reports and Balance-Sheets.

*** *The Editor will be much obliged to the Secretaries of Joint Stock Companies if they would kindly forward copies of Reports and Balance-Sheets direct to the Office of* The Investors' Review, *Norfolk House, Norfolk-street, W.C., so as to insure prompt notice in these columns.*

Buenos Ayres Great Southern Railway Company.—The half-yearly report of this company, just issued, is very much in the nature of an interim statement, but considerable information is furnished as to its current affairs. The half-year was not a good one for business in the Argentine Republic, but the receipts of the line increased by £43,416 to a total of £680,895. Working expenses were £33,567 higher at £288,947, and the net profit was therefore only £9,849 better at £391,948. The bad crops of the year 1897 were reflected in a heavy decrease in the carriage of cereals; but that is not an important section of the company's business, and other traffic more than made up for the loss. A little competition was experienced with the Buenos Ayres Western line, but the company is not troubled much in that way, and the increase of 2·38 per cent. to 42·44 per cent. in the percentage of working expenses was more the result of sixty-six additional miles of line being open, and a higher price for coal. The average gold premium of the six months was practically the same as in the corresponding half of 1896, and so it did not affect the figures. After meeting preference and debenture interest, the balance of £257,471 permits of a dividend at the rate of 5½ per cent. per annum, and the carrying forward of £9,971. This is ½ per cent. above the dividend declared a year ago, but the large increase of traffic in the current half-year has emboldened the Board to advance the rate. The company is extending its operations on all sides, and with a view to carry out its projects, the capital will be increased by £4,000,000. Of this £2,250,000 will be issued immediately as 4 per cent. extension shares 1902, bearing interest at that rate until the date mentioned, when they will rank with the ordinary stock. The new shares will be issued at a premium of £1 10s. per £10 share, and the premiums so received will be used to provide the interest upon the new capital until 1902. With the money an important section of 256 miles will be built from the station 25 de Mayo to Saavedra, forming an important loop on the most western part of the company's territory in the province of Buenos Ayres. Then £600,000 will be subscribed towards a new company that will build an important dock on the Riachuelo at Buenos Ayres, and several minor branches, and the improvement of the port at Bahia Blanca will be provided out of the funds thus found. None of the money, however, appears to be needed for the great extension to Nuequen, which was furnished out of the recent debenture issue. Progress on this extension is satisfactory and quite a half of the work appears to have been completed. The absorption of the Buenos Ayres and Ensenada Railway Company will hand over to the company the only line that works independently of it in the province of Buenos Ayres south of that city. It serves the coast towns just south of the city, including La Plata, the state capital and in exchange for it the Buenos Ayres Great Southern will issue £517,300 of 4 per cent. debenture stock, £552,000 5 per cent. preference stock, and £660,000 ordinary stock, all this being in addition to the £2,250,000 of Extension capital; but the preference and ordinary capital forms part of the £4,000,000 new capital to be created. The company has thus spread itself out on every side, but the policy pursued is a definite one, and it seems to be rendering competition impossible, by its energy and foresight. The only line that in any way draws upon its territory is the Buenos Ayres Western, and if the latter obtains control of the Bahia Blanca and North-Western Company this competition might become more pronounced, but it could only be rendered important by great developments in the future, which at present are hardly in the range of practical politics. Therefore, to the Buenos Ayres Great Southern is left the task of developing the southern portion of the Argentine Republic that centres round the Rio Negro, which in the opinion of many is one of the most hopeful regions of that vast Republic. We trust it will deal mercifully with the settlers in its strength.

RIO CLARO SÃO PAULO RAILWAY COMPANY.—The revenue of this company last year amounted to £137,237, and including sundry balances the available sum at its command was £141,291. After payment of debenture interest, the shares received 14 per cent. in dividend, and a balance of £3,530 was carried forward. As is well known the revenue is derived from bonds of the Companhia Paulista de Vias Ferreas & Fluviaes, a substantial Brazilian undertaking that has leased the line. Last year with the exchange at 7½d. per milreis, the latter concern earned a net profit equal to £390,625, while the full service of the bonds held by the Rio Claro Company, including redemption, was only £163,625, and there is, we believe, virtually no debt in front of those bonds. At the same time, it is doubtful whether the dividends on the Rio Claro Company will be maintained at their present rate. The Paulista Company commenced to redeem its bonds a year ago, and by this time has paid off £56,400. Each year the amount redeemed will increase as redemption is cumulative, and so the amount received for interest on bonds held by the Rio Claro Company must diminish. The latter company invests the money received for redeemed bonds to the best advantage, but of course the return from these investments cannot amount to 3½ per cent., whereas 5 per cent. was received upon the bonds redeemed. The process will be a slow one, but it will be sure, and as the revenue has been divided pretty well up to the hilt in the past, there is no margin to meet a decline, save by reduction of dividend.

H. HERRMANN, LIMITED.—This company, for manufacturing furniture, produced £12,017 profit last year, as against £14,134 in 1896. After adding £2,965, brought forward, the total permitted of the payment of the interest on the preference shares, a dividend of 7 per cent. on the ordinary shares, the placing of £1,498 to reserve, and the carrying forward of £3,124. The amount put to reserve commences that fund, but in the two previous years £3,198 was written off "Purchase of Business Account," virtually goodwill, and £4,244 was written off the stock, the balance forward being built up in the last three years. The balance-sheet ought, therefore, to have improved. The company has had to increase its loan from its bankers by £2,000 to £20,000, but by doing so it has cleared off the debt of £4,372 to the estate of the late vendor. In the past year the capital was divided into equal parts of 6 per cent. preference shares and ordinary shares, but no water was introduced, and the preference shares ought to be a fair investment to a moderate extent. We should like to see more details in the profit and loss account.

CITY OF BUENOS TRAMWAYS COMPANY.—Last year the gross receipts increased £19,438, to £222,128, and the working expenses £14,680 to £158,570. The net revenue of £63,557 was therefore £4,758 higher, and after placing £10,000 to reserve, 7½ per cent. in dividends is paid upon the shares, and slightly more is carried forward. The reserve fund now amounts to £87,231, and of this fair sum £23,677 is invested in high class securities, and the balance has been employed upon the undertaking. Of late the investments have not been increased, as considerable expenditure has been entailed by improvements and extensions. A Fodder Reserve Fund of £8,000, however, has been built up of late years, which, we presume, is available for a sudden rise in the prices of horse forage. The capital is well adjusted, for there is only £116,000 of debentures to £675,000 of share capital. Like all the Buenos Ayrean tramways, the company suffers from the action of the Municipality, having to pay 6 per cent. of its takings to that rapacious body, which does not fulfil its own engagements, and at the same time has to spend considerable sums on new paving.

SAN PAULO (BRAZILIAN) RAILWAY COMPANY.—In the half-year ended December 31 the gross revenue amounted to £405,188, and working expenses to £187,964, with a net revenue of £217,223, compared with £230,893 in the corresponding half of 1896. After adding £32,840 brought forward, a dividend at the rate of 11 per cent. per annum is proposed, and £105,448 is carried forward. The dividends upon the new preference and ordinary shares do not fall upon revenue, as they are provided out of a fund formed by the premiums received upon the new issues. No allusion is made to the attempt by the Mogyana Company to obtain capital to provide a competing line, but it is stated that the new works for doubling the line of the San Paulo Company are progressing satisfactorily. The dividend is 2 per cent. lower than that declared for the year ended June 30 last, and the decline must be considered as a result of the low exchange. This low exchange, however, ought to help the business of the country, and later on the company should benefit from the growth of general business. The Santos Harbour Works are being gradually finished, and this ought to help the company's traffic.

THE LONDON LIFE ASSOCIATION, LIMITED.—A justifiable pride is shown by the directors of this company over its results for the past year ended December 31, the ninety-first of its existence. Not only was the new business good, yielding new premiums amounting to £11,940, of which £9,264 represented renewal premiums, but the mortality was exceptionally favourable. There were only 92 deaths involving claims in 165 policies amounting to £186,100, whereas the life table used indicated a theoretical liability of £312,256. Fifteen policies for £17,882 were surrendered and their surrender values amounted to no less than £7,568, as against £6,128 received in premiums, so that the holders got back all they had paid and nearly a quarter as much again, which is very good investment indeed. Another 11 policies covering £16,750 lapsed, but we presume their existence had been but brief. The gross premium income was £346,616, and the interest income £174,549, or together £521,165. After meeting all out-goings, £126,437 was added to the life funds, raising their total to £4,508,100. This is a non-commission mutual office and the expenses of management took only £16,623, or about 4·7 per cent. of the premium income. The company has the bulk of its funds in home securities, but £571,377 is in Colonial Government securities, £248,700 in Indian and Colonial railway securities, and £184,619 in American railroad gold bonds. The directors have decided to take up endowment business and whole life insurance, with limited term premium payments.

THE SUN LIFE ASSURANCE SOCIETY.—Last year this society issued 2,329 new life policies, insuring £1,092,382, and yielding £43,939 in premiums; after deducting re-insurances against both these amounts. The total premium income was £419,986, and interest, dividends, and rents returned £135,026, making the total income of the life business £555,221. Claims, well within expectation, took £235,224, including bonuses. Policy-holders further received £91,534 by way of cash bonuses, surrenders absorbed £20,855, and commissions and expenses, including valuation expenses, £69,057. With sundry smaller expenses the total outgoings are brought up to £472,520. Adding £55,217 received in the twelve months for annuities over the balance left, enabled the total funds to be increased £284,443 to £3,957,198 at the end of the year. An accident and general department has been established for the transaction of personal accident, Employers' Liability, and Workmen's Compensation insurance. Expenses and commissions took fully 16·4 per cent of the premium income, but £5,000 was laid out on the valuation and the bonus distribution. Nearly the whole of the company's money is invested in domestic securities.

LINOTYPE COMPANY, LIMITED.—This company is a re-arrangement, effected in December, 1896, of an older concern of the same name. The report, issued last month, is therefore the second under the new régime. There is again an increase in the profits from the sale of machines, royalties, &c. In 1896 the balance of profit and loss account amounted to £123,255, and in 1897 to £140,898. By adding to this balance £21,984, premiums received on new issue of shares, the total is further increased to £162,882, a very respectable total. Dividends of 6 per cent. on the preferred and 9 per cent. on the deferred have been paid. £25,000 is added to reserve, making this fund £281,875. New works have been erected, and to pay for these a mortgage debt has been added to the Company's liabilities; the authorised issue is one million, of which £250,000 has been issued. In the present condition of the Company's business there is ample margin for this amount of debt, but we must confess our examination of the balance sheet does not impress us with a high opinion of the Company's financial strength. By the re-arrangement of the share capital £812,000 was added to liabilities as bonus to the old shareholders. True the founders' shares have been wiped out, but this is perhaps the only feature in favour of the writing up of the capital. Patents and goodwill stand at £1,906,592. They may be worth this value and no doubt are, at present, but we certainly think the directors would be acting as cautious men of business in using some of the handsome profits now being earned in writing down this asset. Further the reserve fund is employed in the business, a very fashionable custom, but one which does not add that strength to the financial position of a company which the name "reserve" would imply. We hope the directors will turn their efforts toward the strengthening their company instead of the distributing of big dividends; they will be able all the easier to meet competition if such should spring up.

THE HIGHLAND RAILWAY COMPANY.—Gross receipts for the half-year ended February 28, 1898, £235,063, expenditure £157,853, including a round £3,000 for Parliamentary expenses. Proportion of expenses to receipts 67·2 per cent. A balance of £10,477 was brought forward. Receipts rose nearly £11,000, and expenses about £9,000. The net revenue, balances forward included, was only £87,710, and after meeting all fixed and preference charges there was only £8,218 left, out of which a dividend at the rate of ½ per cent. per annum is declared. This leaves only £1,807 to be carried forward, so the company really did not earn a penny for its shareholders in the past half-year, and could not have paid more than ¼ per cent. per annum had its Parliamentary charges come out of revenue. Why is it that the figures in the directors' report of these in the appended balance-sheet do not always agree? Within the six months the company spent £121,232 on capital account, and looks to spending £131,250 in the current half-year. Dividends are payable on May 5.

THE NORTH BRITISH AND NEW ZEALAND INVESTMENT COMPANY, LIMITED.—In their eleventh Annual Report the directors of this company state that the net profit to December 31 was £2,063, out of which £400 was put to reserve, and £1,291 devoted to the payment of a dividend of 5 per cent. on the share capital. Directors receive £200 for their services, and £172 is left to carry forward, or about £100 less than was brought in. Lending at paying rates continues difficult in New Zealand, so further sums have been brought home during the year, and £8,900 of debentures were paid off. This is, on the whole, the best thing that could happen.

The Central Argentine Railway Company has a very sorry tale to tell about the past year's working, the falling off in the gross receipts being £196,130, and in the net £150,768. Goods traffic yielded £143,259 less, and passenger £30,245 less. There were 319,326 fewer passengers carried, and 670,635 tons less of goods, but the percentage of expenses to receipts rose from 52¾ to nearly 60 per cent. All this is due to the damage done by locusts to the maize crop and the consequent loss inflicted on the country at large. After paying interest, rent charge, and Western section annuity, there remains only £127,673, of which a dividend of 1¾ per cent. for the year absorbs all but £10,158, which is carried forward. The company has so far done much better this year, the receipts for the first quarter showing an improvement of £73,000, but the stock does not offer much inducement to a purchaser, for if the dividend were to rise this year to 3 per cent. the yield on the present price would be under 4 per cent.

Entre Rios Railway Company.—The results of the working during the second half of last year are more unfavourable even than those of a year ago, the working expenses exceeding the receipts by £3,068, while the loss for the corresponding period of 1896 was £2,246. A decrease of £617 in passenger receipts was largely offset by an increase of £581 in goods, the latter being a satisfactory feature considering there was no wheat or maize to carry. Expenses increased by £906, but as this is due to repairs to carriages and wagons and to the permanent way, it should bear fruit in the future. The company received its interest as usual on its Argentine Funding bonds, but, of course, got nothing from the Entre Rios Government, so that with £7,283 brought in, the net receipts come to only £10,982, and after deducting the loss on the half year's working, the balance carried forward is reduced to £7,913. This poor display is attributed solely to the impoverished condition to which the province was reduced by the locust plague in the early part of 1897. Prospects, however, are more encouraging, as with an abundant wheat crop—an estimated yield of 250,000 tons being looked for, against 34,000 tons produced last year—the gross receipts for the first two months of 1898 have been higher than at any period since the railway commenced running, and the net receipts have been sufficient to recoup the whole of the £3,069 lost during the past six months, and to leave a profit of £5,625 on the eight months' working. We can only hope the improvement will be maintained, but at best the company's existence is a miserable one.

Cunard Steamship Company.—This report is somewhat disappointing, the profits for the year, with £2,181 brought forward, amounting to £222,475, or £27,000 less than those for 1896, when the amount brought forward was only £1,465. The very moderate dividend of 2½ per cent. is again paid, but the amount reserved for depreciation is only £166,938 against £184,822, and for the Insurance fund £27,999 against £32,417, and to pay the dividend £15,000 has to be taken from the Insurance fund compared with £10,000 transferred a year ago. The company suffered from loss of passenger traffic between Europe and the United States and the report in this connection describes 1897 as the worst of recent years. As showing how considerably Atlantic lines have suffered, the report says that in the first cabin business the total falling off for British and continental lines compared with 1896 was about 14 per cent; in second cabin 5 per cent., and in steerage 18 per cent. And what, we wonder, will be the falling off when war breaks out between Spain and the United States?

The Rio Tinto Company.—The twenty-fifth annual report makes a capital exhibit owing to the better price obtained for copper, the average having been £49 2s. 6d., compared with £46 15s. 9d. per ton for 1896. There seems to have been no desire to take too great advantage of the higher price, or perhaps it was thought wise not to press the metal forward too freely for the pyrites extracted during the year, amounting to 1,388,026 tons, were 49,306 tons less than in the previous year, the average copper contents being 2·810 per cent., compared with 2·931 per cent., and the 20,826 tons of copper produced at the mines was only 9 tons more than in 1896. Yet the profit on the sale of produce which was £626,287 in 1895, and £828,103 in 1896, further increased sharply to £987,523, the total receipts for the year, including £21,532 brought forward, reaching £1,132,145, or £159,888 more than in the previous year, and as much as £403,464 above the total two years back. With this great improvement in profits it was an easy matter to add £40,000 to reserve, raising it to £140,000, but the amount written off plant, &c., is only increased from £23,667 last year to £24,180. Administration expenses, both here and in Spain, were somewhat heavier, and taxes and dues came to £49,332, or £10,263 more than in 1896. Of the increase of £113,131 in net profit, all but £735 is distributed amongst the shareholders, the dividend for the year on the ordinary shares being £2 or 40 per cent. This is equivalent to a distribution of 22½ per cent. on the former undivided capital compared with 19 per cent. for the previous year, and only 11 per cent. for 1895. Good as the dividend is, the market was looking for more because the interim dividend had been 20 per cent., which encouraged expectations of a higher payment at the end of the year. As the stamps on the old share warrants could not be transferred to the new, the full duty of treble the ordinary transfer stamp (30s. per cent.) had to be paid on all the new shares issued in the form of warrants to bearer, which, with other charges incidental to the transaction, resulted in an expenditure of £52,389, and this amount has been charged to the account which bears the expenses of issue of the 4 per cent. mortgage bonds. This item stands in the balance-sheet at £165,031, but £56,160 of this has been written off, being the amount of the sinking fund on the mortgage bonds, and the whole of this account will be extinguished in the next two years. The ore on hand and produce afloat at the end of the year was valued at £693,000 compared with £736,925 in 1896, and the extension and development works and overburden account stand at £181,112, as against £194,330.

Tarapaca Waterworks Company.—Although a dividend of 7½ per cent. is again to be paid, the company did not do so well last year as in 1896, the net profit being only £40,404, compared with £53,000, so that after placing £10,000 to the account for the redemption of the debentures, and £10,000 to General Reserve, the balance carried forward is reduced from £17,393 to £8,050. The amount set aside for the redemption of the £50,000 of debentures is now complete, but only £20,000 is to be paid off at once, the remaining £30,000 having been continued for three years, owing to large expenditure for additional springs. Considering the depression in the nitrate industry the company has done very well, and we should have thought the debentures might have been renewed at less than 5½ per cent, but the debenture interest for the next few years will require only £1,650. One little drawback is that as a result of a decision of the Chili Courts the company has got to pay during the current year £10,000 for premiums on the vendor's shares, and possibly more if his claim for back dividends is established. But this is a matter which will only temporarily affect the revenue account.

The Ionian Bank.—Continued steady progress is reported, the gross profits which in 1895 were £19,459, and in 1896, £20,197, showing a further improvement during the six months ending December 31 last, to £21,089. The dividend is kept at the usual rate of 4 per cent. per annum, but the rest or undivided profit carried forward is increased to £29,314. The note circulation amounting to £222,770 shows a small increase, and there is a trifling addition to current accounts which stand at £76,000, but deposits bearing interest have increased from £206,000 to £236,000. Bills discounted and loans and advances are not much changed, but the bank has put more of its money into investments, and the loan to the Greek Government under convention for forced currency of its note circulation and its holding of Greek Government Treasury Bills both show moderate additions.

Eastern Produce and Estates Company.—Like the bulk of Ceylon tea-growing concerns, this company earned less profit last year than in the preceding twelve months. Income was £10,011 less at £121,180, but the produce on hand was £3,678 more, and £1,557 more was brought in. Working expenses on the estates were £1,751 higher, and administrative charges were a little more, but debenture interest was less. The net balance therefore of £44,731 was only £4,614 below that for 1896. Out of this £7,875 was used to redeem debentures, and £5,000 was placed to reserve. Dividend amounting to 7 per cent. for the year was then declared, and £10,878 was left to be carried forward, or a little less than was brought in. In the preceding year £13,125 was used to redeem debentures, and £5,000 was also put to reserve, but the dividend was only 6½ per cent. The board, however, had every reason to allow a small increase in dividend for the extra ½ per cent. only represented £1,495, and working expenses were unnaturally high last year, owing to the extra cost of rice arising from the Indian famine. The reserve now amounts to £25,000 and is practically invested outside the business. The balance forward will permit of the debentures being reduced this year to £95,000 as against an original issue of £195,200, and in the meantime the share capital has not increased. The acreage under tea only increased 115 acres, and the bulk of it is mature. The crop last year was about 200,000 lbs. below the estimate, and the average price of 7·06d. per lb. was ·27d. under the average of 1896.

Russian Petroleum and Liquid Fuel Company.—Dividend on ordinary shares £1. Advices from Baku show estimated production of petroleum from date of taking over properties to March 12 last was over 40,000,000 poods, which included the output of two prolific fountains. The greater portion of this has been sold at favourable rates. The £10 shares are to be divided into £1 shares.

PRESIDENT M'KINLEY'S MESSAGE.

The long-delayed Message of President M'Kinley in reference to Cuban affairs was sent to the Congress on Monday last. This, he says, had become his duty by reason of the warfare that for more than three years had raged in Cuba. He did so "because of the intimate connection of the Cuban question with the States of our Union, and the grave relation that the course which it is now incumbent upon the nation to adopt must needs bear to the traditional policy of our Government, if it is to accord with the precepts laid down by the founders of the Republic and religiously observed by succeeding administrations." The present revolutionary movement in the island, the President points out, is but the successor of similar insurrections, each of which has subjected the United States to great effort and expense in enforcing neutrality laws, has caused enormous losses to American trade and commerce, and, by the exercise of cruel, barbarous, and uncivilised practices of warfare, has shocked the sensibilities and offended the humane sympathies of the American people. Referring to the exaggeration of all these evils which has attended the present struggle, and to the fruitless efforts of his predecessors to secure peace, the President describes the vain endeavours of Spain to suppress the insurrection by the "concentration" policy :—

The efforts of Spain to suppress the insurrection have been increased by the addition to the horrors of strife of a new and inhuman phase, happily unprecedented in the modern history of civilized Christian people. The peasantry, including all dwelling in the open agricultural interior, were driven into the garrison towns or isolated places held by troops. The raising and movement of provisions were interdicted, fields were laid waste, dwellings unroofed and fired, and mills destroyed—in short, everything that could desolate the land and render it unfit for human habitation and support was commanded and executed by one or other of the contesting parties. When the present Administration took office, the agricultural population of Cuba, to the estimated number of 300,000, was herded within the towns and their immediate vicinage, deprived of means of support, rendered destitute of shelter, left poorly clad, and exposed to most unsanitary conditions. As the scarcity of food increased with the devastation of the depopulated areas of production, destitution and want became misery and starvation. From month to month the death-rate increased to an alarming ratio; and by March, 1897, according to conservative estimates from official Spanish sources, the mortality among the Reconcentrados from starvation and the diseases thereto incident exceeded 50 per cent. of the total number.

Having referred to his previous efforts in connection with the situation in Cuba, to American relief measures, and the recognition by the Spanish Government of the necessity for a change in the condition of the Reconcentrados as well as the efforts for its amelioration, the President gives the conclusion at which he has arrived in the following sentences :—"The continuation of the strife means the extermination of one or both parties. Realising this, it appears my duty in a spirit of true friendliness no less to Spain than to the Cubans, to seek to bring about the immediate termination of the war."

He goes on to say that he does not think it expedient or wise, at present, to recognise the independence of the so-called Cuban Republic. There remains the alternative of intervention to end the war, either as an impartial neutral by imposing a rational compromise between the contestants, or as the active ally of one or other of the parties. The forcible intervention of the United States as a neutral to stop the war would be justifiable on rational grounds, which President M'Kinley thus summarises :—

First, in the cause of humanity, to put an end to the barbarities, bloodshed, starvation, and horrible miseries now existing there, and which the parties to the conflict are either unable or unwilling to stop or mitigate. It is no answer to say, "This is all in another country belonging to another nation, and is, therefore, none of our business." It is especially our duty, for it is right at our door. Secondly, we owe it to our citizens in Cuba to afford them that protection and indemnity for life and property which no Government there can or will afford, and, to that end, to terminate conditions which deprive them of legal protection. Thirdly, the right to intervene may be justified by the very serious injury to the commerce, trade, and business of the people, by the wanton destruction of property and the devastation of the island. Fourthly, the present condition of affairs in Cuba is a constant menace to our peace and entails upon this Government enormous expense. With such a conflict waged for years in an island so near, with which our people have such trade and business relations, where the lives and liberty of our citizens are in constant danger, their property destroyed, themselves ruined, where our trading vessels are liable to seizure and are seized at our very door by the warships of a foreign nation, the expeditions of filibusterers that we are powerless altogether to prevent, and the irritating questions and entanglements thus arising—all these and others that I need not mention, with the resulting strained relations, are a constant menace to our peace and compel us to keep on a semi-war footing with a nation with which we are at peace.

Coming to the destruction of the battleship *Maine*, President M'Kinley says :—

These elements of danger and disorder, already pointed out, have been strikingly illustrated by a tragic event which has deeply moved the American people. I have already transmitted to Congress the report of the Naval Court of inquiry on the destruction of the battleship *Maine* in the harbour of Havana. The destruction of that noble vessel has filled the national heart with inexpressible horror. Two hundred and fifty-eight brave sailors and marines and two officers of our Navy, reposing in the fancied security of a friendly harbour, have been hurled to death. Grief and want have been brought to their homes, and sorrow to the nation. The Naval Court of inquiry, which, needless to say, commands the unqualified confidence of the Government, was unanimous in its conclusion that the destruction of the *Maine* was caused by a submarine mine. It did not place the responsibility—that remains to be fixed. In any event, the destruction of the *Maine*, by whatever exterior cause, is a patent and impressive proof of a state of things in Cuba that is intolerable. That condition has been shown to be such that the Spanish Government cannot assure safety and security to a vessel of the American Navy in the harbour of Havana on a mission of peace and rightfully there.

Referring to the proposal made by Spain to refer to arbitration all differences which might arise on this matter, the President simply says, "To this I made no reply." The President finally enunciates his conviction that a long trial has proved that the object for which Spain has waged the war cannot be attained :—

The only hope of relief and repose from a condition which can no longer be endured is in the enforced pacification of Cuba. In the name of humanity, in the name of civilization, on behalf of the endangered American interests which give us the right and duty to speak and act, the war in Cuba must stop. In view of these facts and these considerations, I ask Congress to authorise and empower the President to take measures to secure the full and final termination of hostilities between the Government of Spain and the people of Cuba, and to secure in the island the establishment of a stable Government capable of maintaining order and observing its international obligations, ensuring the peace, tranquillity, and security of its citizens, as well as our own, and to use the military and naval forces of the United States as may be necessary for these purposes and the interest of humanity. And to aid in preserving the lives of the starving people of the island I recommend that the distribution of food supplies be continued, and that an appropriation be made out of the Public Treasury to supplement the charity of our citizens. The issue is now with Congress. It is a solemn responsibility. I have exhausted every effort to relieve the intolerable condition of affairs at our own doors. Prepared to execute every obligation imposed upon me by the Constitution and law, I await your action.

The Message closes with a reference to the decree of the Spanish Government, directing General Blanco to proclaim an armistice. The fact of this armistice, the President says, was not communicated to him until after the preparation of his Message. He is sure it will receive the attention of Congress. "If," he concludes, "this measure attains a successful result, then our aspirations as a Christian, peace-loving people will be realised. If it fails, it will be only another justification of our contemplated action." The Message was referred to the Foreign Committees of both Houses.

These Committees on Wednesday presented resolutions to the Senate and to the House of Representatives declaring for instant war with Spain. The Senate Committee also declared their belief that the "destruction of the *Maine* was compassed either by the official act of the Spanish authorities (and the ascertaining of the particular person is not material), or was made possible by negligence on their part, so willing and so gross as to be equivalent in culpability to positive criminal action." The Naval Committee of Inquiry reported that they had not obtained evidence "fixing the responsibility for the destruction of the *Maine* upon any person or persons." In the House of Representatives a suggestion for a discussion upon the resolution raised a tremendous row, during which men fought, called each other "liar" and "scoundrel," and rushed about like madmen. It was a scene such as has not been witnessed for years, even in the House of Representatives. A minority report was presented to the Senate, simply recommending the recognition of the Cuban Republic. The final decision may not be given for a few days yet.

THE PROPERTY MARKET.

The sales at Tokenhouse Yard last week dropped down to a total value of £63,528. Of course the holidays affected both the amount and the character of the property offered; but the returns contrast strongly with the total of the corresponding week of last year, which amounted to the handsome sum of £156,896. The returns for the month of March, however, are remarkably satisfactory, as may be seen from the following official summary :—

	March, 1897.	March, 1898.
At the Mart	£393,981	£817,000
Country and suburban	314,464	587,438
Private contract sales	65,495	53,510
	£773,940	£1,457,948
Amount of sales reported from January 1 to March 31		£2,550,798

The aggregate for yesterday week was £8,100, and to this total Messrs. H. E. Foster & Cranfield contributed £7,110. Their principal lot was a reversion to one-eleventh share of trust funds of the estimated value of £44,100, life aged 64, for which £2,130 was paid.

Some of the provincial sales are worth noting. A site abutting on Briggate and Trinity-street, Leeds, comprising 813 square yards, on which are licensed house and other properties, was disposed of for £28,700. The site of the Battle of the Standard (A.D. 1138), at Northallerton, Yorks, comprising 64 acres, was sold for £1,115. Private treaty sales include the ground lease of Savoy-mansions, a block of offices and flats in the liberty of the Savoy, at a price approaching £20,000. The Cardiff Tin Stamping and Enamel Works, leasehold for eighty-nine years, rental £330, changed hands at £15,000, while Lynn Farm, near Cardiff, 15½ acres, went for £1,510. Mr. E. D. Newman, at Uxbridge, among other freehold properties, disposed of Whittingham's Farm, with dwelling, buildings, and 23 acres of market garden land, for £3,000. A freehold farm, 79½ acres, at Harlton, Cambridgeshire, was sold by Messrs. Wright & Scruby for £1,000.

There was little or nothing doing at the Mart on Tuesday and Wednesday.

The *Estates Gazette* notices a new system of land purchase, which it considers likely to take hold—that of paying a small proportion of the purchase-money down, and the rest in instalments over a certain term of years, to cover interest and principal. Messrs. Lumleys, for instance, offer to sell a farm of 111 acres in Kent on the plan of taking 15 per cent. of the price on sale, and the balance in seventy half-yearly payments of 2½ per cent., the total amount being paid off in thirty-five years. The purchaser, however, has the option of paying off the balance at any time without notice.

Mr. Alfred Richards announces the sale of a large and valuable block of freehold property in Wood-green, at the Mart on the 18th inst.

Mr. A. Dowell recently sold at Edinburgh the estates of Harperfield and Greenstrands, Lesmahagow, Lanarkshire, comprising an area of 333 acres, for £10,000.

The German Emperor has made a "graceful concession" to British susceptibilities. On hearing of the victory of Atbara, he immediately telegraphed to the English Ambassador in Berlin, expressing the pleasure he felt, and asking that his congratulations might be conveyed to the Marquis of Salisbury and the Sirdar. The incident is not without its significance. It may not be intended to wipe out the famous telegram to President Kruger, but it may perhaps be taken as in some sort an acknowledgment—a cordial acknowledgment—of the nice things said by Mr. Balfour as to Anglo-German relations in the Far East.

Liverpool and Manchester merchants connected with Sierra Leone take a very serious view of the revolt out there. Mr. James D. Marcus, who has had factories in the colony for many years, and has only just arrived in England, says the disturbance has been caused by the hut tax, and will continue as long as an attempt is made to collect that obnoxious impost, which every trader in the Colony objected to the Government putting in force. At the Colonial Office, however, they say there is every reason for hoping that the rising was merely local and altogether unimportant. There has been nothing in the form of regular warfare.

To Correspondents.

The Editor cannot undertake to return rejected communications. Letters from correspondents must, in every case, be authenticated the name and address of the writer.

Telegraphic Address: "Unveiling, London."

The Investors' Review.

The Week's Money Market.

The advance in the Bank rate to 4 per cent. last week had little effect upon the market for short loans, which continues to be fairly supplied with balances left over from the Government disbursements. For a time 3 to $3\frac{1}{4}$ per cent. was quoted for day to day loans, but during the greater part of the week about $2\frac{3}{4}$ per cent. was the working figure. Loans for a week, however, ruled throughout at about 3 to $3\frac{1}{4}$ per cent. As the Bank of England sponges up loose cash this ease must diminish, if the political position does not improve, and a gradual approach towards the official minimum will be obligatory even for short advances. The discount houses upon the Bank's advance only raised their allowances on deposits by $\frac{1}{2}$ per cent. to $2\frac{1}{2}$ per cent. for "call" and $2\frac{3}{4}$ per cent. for "notice," but a further advance will be necessary on their part when the market hardens, as it soon must. The joint stock banks, of course, increased their rate of interest on deposits by 1 per cent. to $2\frac{1}{2}$ per cent. That is their automatic proportion.

Discount charges moved more closely in accord with the Bank rate than money rates, the political uncertainties having greater weight when the period to be reviewed runs over months instead of days. At first there was an inclination to quote $3\frac{1}{2}$ per cent. for three months' choice bills, but this quickly changed to $3\frac{5}{8}$ to $3\frac{3}{4}$ per cent, and for the last day or so $3\frac{7}{8}$ to $3\frac{7}{8}$ per cent. has been the ruling figure for choice bills of all dates running up to six months. The volume of bills on offer has also increased, especially long dated bills, so that the possibilities of a further hardening of the market are being anticipated. Now that the reserve of the Bank of England stands at only £18,433,000, the directors may be expected to take active steps to prevent any serious further depletion of its stock of gold. To attract the metal it has raised its buying price of German and French coin to 76s. 6d. per oz., but at present the open market is bidding higher for the coins, and, as matters stand, the Bank could not obtain gold from this quarter. Gold, however, ought to come from Berlin as, although the Bank of Germany has raised its minimum to 4 per cent., the value of money in Berlin has not responded, and 3 per cent. is the outside quotation. The Paris cheque has also risen to $25{\cdot}33\frac{1}{2}$, so that we should have considerable assistance from the Continent in meeting any further demands for gold on American account. If the political position grows worse, however, the United States will certainly press for gold more vigorously, and may easily cause our rate to rise to 5 per cent. The conditions, therefore, favour a hard market, even if the political position is not aggravated.

The Stock Exchange settlement was an easy one, but the rate for advances was raised by about $\frac{1}{2}$ per cent. to $4\frac{1}{4}$ to $4\frac{1}{2}$ per cent. The lower rate, however, was that mostly current for old money, and there was very little fresh borrowing done.

Yesterday's Bank return was nothing like so sensational as that for the previous week, which we print below for reference. One or two points, however, in the figures deserve attention. To begin with, the market has not been in the least enriched by the disbursement of Government moneys. "Public" deposits, which represent treasury and departmental balances, have fallen off £638,082 during the week, but the whole of the money, together with £556,4:6 from the "other" deposits, which contains the bankers' balances and other market moneys, has been absorbed in paying off loans due at the Bank, or in meeting matured bills of Exchange held by it. "Other" securities are accordingly down £1,324,090, but their total of £34,087,675 is still far above the normal amount, and indicates that the market must have, let us say, to be moderate, quite £6,000,000 of its pledged securities or bills to redeem, probably mostly the latter. And all the time the Bank is losing gold. No decrease took place in the reserve last week. On the contrary, it increased by £82,711 to £18,433,658; but this increase is altogether due to the return of notes from circulation. Gold has gone out—£183,000 of it for abroad—to the amount of £598,484 within the week. This and the previous week's domestic absorption is, no doubt, due in the main to the Easter holidays; but its withdrawal none the less weakens the Bank's stock of gold for the time being, and it is now down at £29,436,488. Some people have supposed that other banks are taking to hoarding gold. We wish they were, but the figures do not support this view, and, as a matter of fact, less gold has gone into circulation this April than last. It is not the domestic ebb and flow which bothers us, but the export of the metal to America and the market bareness. Both these point to an early further advance in the Bank rate.

Silver.

At one time the price of bar silver for immediate delivery declined to $25\frac{11}{16}$d. per oz., but there has been a fair amount of buying from India, and supplies have been small, so that the quotation recovered to 26d. per oz. At this figure the metal was offered freely and the price fell back to $25\frac{11}{16}$d. per oz. The two months' forward quotation has ruled at $\frac{1}{16}$d. below the spot price throughout the week. Monetary pressure has increased in the Indian cities, and the exchange has risen to 1s. $3\frac{13}{16}$d. For all that the "bazaar" quotation for silver has remained at about $67\frac{1}{4}$ for spot, and consequently the purchases on that account are easily explained. No heed was paid to the statement that the contents of the despatch sent by the Indian Government to the Home Government were known in Calcutta, as the information came through an untrustworthy source. At the same time, the raising of a loan of 20 millions sterling under Imperial guarantee, and the melting down of rupees, is a psuedo-heroic policy that the Indian Government in its present muddle might easily make a despairing grab at. A little talk was also indulged in as to the chance of the Hispano-American dispute affecting supplies of silver in the market, but the opinion seemed to prevail that the metal could easily come by indirect routes if Spanish cruisers proved troublesome. The India Council sold its drafts easily this week at a higher price, one lac of transfers actually going at 1s. $4\frac{1}{32}$d.

BANK OF ENGLAND.

AN ACCOUNT pursuant to the Act 7 and 8 Vict., cap. 32, for the Week ending on Wednesday, April 6, 1898.

ISSUE DEPARTMENT.

	£		£
Notes Issued	44,297,260	Government Debt	11,015,100
		Other Securities	5,784,900
		Gold Coin and Bullion	27,497,260
		Silver Bullion	—
	£44,297,260		£44,297,260

BANKING DEPARTMENT.

	£		£
Proprietors' Capital	14,553,000	Government Securities	13,197,953
Rest	3,105,758	Other Securities	35,411,765
Public Deposits (including Exchequer, Savings Banks, Commissioners of National Debt, and Dividend Accounts)	12,634,596	Notes	15,813,855
Other Deposits	36,462,596	Gold and Silver Coin	2,537,692
Seven Day and other Bills	144,715		
	£66,960,665		£66,960,665

Dated April 7, 1898.

H. G. BOWEN, *Chief Cashier.*

AN ACCOUNT pursuant to the Act 7 and 8 Vict., cap. 32, for the Week ending on Wednesday, April 13, 1898.

ISSUE DEPARTMENT.

	£		£
Notes Issued	43,759,275	Government Debt	11,015,100
		Other Securities	5,784,900
		Gold Coin and Bullion	26,959,275
		Silver Bullion	—
	£43,759,275		£43,759,275

BANKING DEPARTMENT.

	£		£
Proprietors' Capital	14,553,000	Government Securities	13,197,953
Rest	3,170,215	Other Securities	34,087,675
Public Deposits (including Exchequer, Savings Banks, Commissioners of National Debt, and Dividend Accounts)	11,996,514	Notes	15,956,465
Other Deposits	35,906,140	Gold and Silver Coin	2,477,193
Seven Day and other Bills	93,417		
	£65,719,286		£65,719,286

Dated April 14, 1898.

H. G. BOWEN, *Chief Cashier*.

In the following table will be found the movements compared with the previous week, and also the totals for that week and the corresponding return last year :—

Banking Department.

Last Year. April 14.		April 6, 1898.	April 13, 1898.	Increase.	Decrease.
£	Liabilities.	£	£	£	£
3,136,262	Rest	3,165,758	3,170,215	4,457	—
10,945,120	Pub. Deposits	12,634,596	11,996,514	—	638,082
38,817,957	Other do.	36,462,596	35,906,140	—	556,456
199,780	7 Day Bills	144,715	93,417	—	51,298
	Assets.			Decrease.	Increase.
13,842,586	Gov. Securities	13,197,953	13,197,953	—	—
28,451,585	Other do.	35,411,765	34,087,675	1,324,090	—
25,357,948	Total Reserve	18,350,947	18,433,658	—	82,711
				1,328,547	1,328,547
				Increase.	Decrease.
£		£	£	£	£
27,839,865	Note Circulation	28,484,005	27,802,810	—	681,195
50⅝ p.c.	Proportion	37¼ p.c.	38⅜ p.c.	—	—
2½ "	Bank Rate	4 "	4 "	—	—

Foreign Bullion movement for week £183,000 out.

LONDON BANKERS' CLEARING.

Month of	1898.	1897.	Increase.	Decrease.
	£	£	£	£
January	673,281,000	576,558,000	96,723,000	—
February	648,601,000	597,652,000	50,949,000	—
Week ending				
March 2	190,157,000	177,852,000	12,305,000	—
" 9	134,490,000	126,182,000	8,308,000	—
" 16	174,377,000	148,937,000	25,440,000	—
" 23	129,828,000	118,578,000	11,250,000	—
" 30	170,668,000	158,421,000	12,247,000	—
April 6	186,540,000	147,789,000	38,751,000	—
" 13	112,101,000	154,099,000	—	41,998,000
Total to date	2,330,975,000	2,138,973,000	192,002,000	—

BANK AND DISCOUNT RATES ABROAD.

	Bank Rate.	Altered.	Open Market.
Paris	2	March 14, 1895	1⅞
Berlin	4	April 9, 1898	3⅝
Hamburg	4	April 9, 1898	3⅝
Frankfort	4	April 9, 1898	3½
Amsterdam	3	April 13, 1897	2¾
Brussels	3	April 28, 1896	2
Vienna	4	January 22, 1896	3⅞
Rome	5	August 27, 1895	3
St. Petersburg	5½	January 23, 1898	4¾
Madrid	5	June 17, 1896	4
Lisbon	6	January 25, 1891	6
Stockholm	4	March 3, 1898	3½
Copenhagen	4	January 20, 1898	4
Calcutta	12	February 24, 1898	—
Bombay	13	February 24, 1898	—
New York call money	3½ to 4	—	—

NEW YORK ASSOCIATED BANKS (dollar at 4s.).

	April 9, 1898.	April 2, 1898.	Mar. 26, 1898.	April 10, 1897.
	£	£	£	£
Specie	28,416,000	28,312,000	27,258,000	17,174,000
Legal tenders	11,904,000	12,944,000	13,794,000	20,356,000
Loans and discounts	117,556,000	119,170,000	120,034,000	100,502,000
Circulation	2,776,800	2,773,200	2,772,000	3,118,000
Net deposits	133,968,000	136,448,000	137,130,000	113,184,000

Legal reserve is 25 per cent. of net deposits; therefore the total reserve (specie and legal tenders) exceeds this sum by £6,828,000, against an excess last week of £7,184,000.

BANK OF FRANCE (25 francs to the £).

	April 14, 1898.	April 7, 1898.	Mar. 31, 1898.	April 15, 1897.
	£	£	£	£
Gold in hand	74,178,120	74,319,320	74,495,040	76,572,000
Silver in hand	48,617,720	48,694,480	48,723,600	48,810,000
Bills discounted	33,449,840	30,617,960	35,452,400	*43,260,000
Advances	15,171,080	15,790,560	14,796,120	—
Note circulation	151,102,520	150,324,320	153,313,920	150,481,000
Public deposits	6,911,320	5,576,400	7,206,640	5,645,000
Private deposits	21,160,120	19,578,640	19,106,000	17,724,000

Proportion between bullion and circulation 81⅞ per cent. against 81⅞ per cent. a week ago.

* Includes advances.

FOREIGN RATES OF EXCHANGE ON LONDON.

Place.	Usance.	Last week's.	Latest.	Place.	Usance.	Last week's.	Latest.
Paris	chqs.	25·30	25·34½	Italy	sight	26·78	26·87½
Brussels	chqs.	25·37	25·40	Do. gold prem.	..	105·90	106·15
Amsterdam	short	12·08¼	12·10½	Constantinople	3 mths	109·35	109·30
Berlin	short	20·49	20·51½	B. Ayres gd. pm.	..	165·10	165·50
Do.	3 mths	20·34	20·32	Rio de Janeiro	90 dys	6	6
Hamburg	3 mths	20·33½	20.31	Valparaiso	90 dys	17¾	17⅞
Frankfort	short	20·49	20·52	Calcutta	T. T.	1/3¾	1/4
Vienna	short	12·01½	12.09	Bombay	T. T.	1/3¾	1/3½
St. Petersburg	3 mths	94·15	94.10	Hong Kong	T. T.	1/10½	1/10½
New York	60 dys	4·80¾	4·80½	Shanghai	T. T.	2/6	2/5⅞
Lisbon	sight	34 13/16	34⅞	Singapore	T. T.	1/10½	1/10⅞
Madrid	sight	36·60	36·32				

IMPERIAL BANK OF GERMANY (20 marks to the £).

	April 7, 1898.	Mar. 31, 1898.	Mar. 23, 1898.	April 7, 1897.
	£	£	£	£
Cash in hand	43,269,700	44,141,650	48,746,650	47,801,000
Bills discounted	37,171,950	38,514,850	30,330,600	*38,603,000
Advances on stocks	5,340,800	6,210,700	3,842,700	—
Note circulation	60,696,700	64,060,850	52,066,650	57,636,000
Public deposits	22,931,900	22,647,900	27,515,400	23,309,000

* Includes advances

AUSTRIAN-HUNGARIAN BANK (1s. 8d. to the florin).

	April 7, 1898.	Mar. 31, 1898.	Mar. 23, 1898.	April 7, 1897.
	£	£	£	£
Gold reserve	30,577,750	30,521,166	30,535,666	26,063,000
Silver reserve	10,448,660	10,453,250	10,449,666	10,503,000
Foreign bills	916,750	1,012,167	1,004,000	—
Advances	1,806,083	1,877,750	1,846,416	—
Note circulation	52,850,416	52,621,750	50,799,000	50,252,000
Bills discounted	12,442,333	12,437,416	10,643,416	*14,190,000

* Includes advances

NATIONAL BANK OF BELGIUM (25 francs to the £).

	April 7, 1898.	Mar. 31, 1898.	Mar. 24, 1898.	April 8, 1897.
	£	£	£	£
Coin and bullion	4,134,280	4,158,480	4,168,920	4,262,000
Other securities	16,916,360	17,589,680	16,939,440	15,785,000
Note circulation	19,274,720	19,866,960	19,009,400	18,652,000
Deposits	3,174,320	3,412,680	3,558,400	2,750,000

BANK OF SPAIN (25 pesetas to the £).

	April 9, 1898.	April 2, 1898.	Mar. 26, 1898.	April 10, 1897.
	£	£	£	£
Gold	9,643,800	9,631,120	9,624,960	8,528,400
Silver	10,472,880	10,614,600	10,862,440	10,527,960
Bills discounted	24,532,120	24,628,640	24,274,280	7,764,840
Advances and loans	5,226,040	5,287,440	5,122,960	9,982,360
Notes in circulation	51,614,320	51,074,480	50,255,280	43,242,760
Treasury advances, coupon account	97,640	79,600	364,080	200,240
Treasury balances	20,200	2,720	2,169,200	662,120

LONDON COURSE OF EXCHANGE.

Place.	Usance.	March 29.	March 31.	April 5.	April 14.
Amsterdam and Rotterdam	short	12·2½	12·2½	12·2	12·2½
Do. do.	3 months	12·4½	12·4½	12·3⅞	12·4⅞
Antwerp and Brussels	3 months	25·52½	25·51¼	25·51¼	25·58¾
Hamburg	3 months	20·68	20·63	20·65	20·74
Berlin and German B. Places	3 months	20·58	20·68	20·66	20·74
Paris	cheques	25·33¾	25·33¾	25·31¼	25·35
Do.	3 months	25·48¾	25·47½	25·45	25·50
Marseilles	3 months	25·48¾	25·48¾	25·46¼	25·51¼
Switzerland	3 months	25·67½	25·67½	25·65	25·67½
Austria	3 months	12·18¾	12·16¼	12·16¼	12·25
St. Petersburg	3 months	25	25	24 15/16	24 15/16
Moscow	3 months	24 15/16	24 15/16	24⅞	24⅞
Italian Bank Places	3 months	27·15	27·10	27·30	27·35
New York	60 days	49 1/16	49 1/16	49 1/16	49
Madrid and Spanish B. P.	3 months	32 1/16	33 1/16	33	31⅞
Lisbon	3 months	34⅛	34⅛	34⅛	34
Oporto	3 months	34⅛	34⅛	34⅛	34
Copenhagen	3 months	18·41	18·41	18·42	18·42
Christiania	3 months	18·42	18·42	18·42	18·42
Stockholm	3 months	18·42	18·42	18·42	18·43

OPEN MARKET DISCOUNT.

	Per cent.
Thirty and sixty day remitted bills	3¼
Three months "	3½
Four months "	3½
Six months "	3½
Three months fine inland bills	4 —4½
Four months "	4 —4½
Six months "	4½—4½

BANK AND DEPOSIT RATES.

	Per cent.
Bank of England minimum discount rate	4
" " short loan rates	4
Banker's rate on deposits	2½
Bill brokers' deposit rate (call)	2½
" 7 and 14 days' notice	2¾
Current rates for 7 day loans	3—3¼
" " for call loans	2¾—3

Stock Market Notes and Comments.

Most of the past week has been a holiday, and during the days that the market was open no business to speak of has been done. As we are writing the fortnightly account is in process of settlement, and so small is it that no difficulties are apprehended in connection therewith. We have therefore really very little to say about the past and there can be but slender temptation to launch out upon the future. All markets are in a state of suspended animation, pending the issue of the present dispute between Spain and America. It is no use for a man to have decided views on the course of prices, because there is so little scope for acting upon them that were he convinced of peace he could not be an extensive "bull," and were he certain of war he would find it equally difficult to sell a large "bear." This perhaps is fortunate, certainly for the Stock Exchange it is. Its commitments are small, and therein lies its strength. Were there enormous speculative accounts unliquidated within the markets at the present moment we should have serious trouble disclosed there at no distant day. But these dangerous speculative positions do not exist, so far as we can discover. There is no evidence of them in the account carried on from fortnight to fortnight. What, however, we do see is plenty of evidence that the public outside is pretty heavily loaded up, and dearer money is sure to bring a larger and larger supply of privately pawned stock into the market. It is dribbling in now and generally proving difficult of sale. The time is consequently drawing nearer when investors will have more favourable opportunities to buy than they have had for a long time back. Also it is to be noted that some *chateaux d' Espagne* of finance which have been constructed during the times of cheap money, with the rapidity of Aladdin's palace of delight, are beginning to shrivel up. Should we have money at 5 per cent. for a few months there will be some curious revelations in this direction from which the public may perhaps acquire a little transitory sense of prudence. The clover and honey days of living on the margins of interest are over and gone, for this year at any rate. We shall have much more to say in this column when the harvest of folly begins to be gathered. At present we can only note the drift of things and continue to advise people with money to invest to be in no hurry to buy. Prices will be more favourable ere long.

The Week's Stock Markets.

Stock markets opened very firm on Thursday last on the news of the postponement of Mr. M'Kinley's message, and Spanish stock and United States Railroad shares quickly rose several points, but the rise in the Bank rate and unfavourable political rumours soon had an adverse effect and the earlier advance was lost. By the time the Stock Exchange was re-opened after the Easter holidays Mr. M'Kinley's message was known; but it was not sufficiently definite in its expression to encourage speculators, while the arranging of the account, although a very light one, and the absence of many of the leading Jewish members, tended to restrict business to such an extent that it was practically at a standstill on Tuesday. Since then the decision of the Committee of the United States Senate has been received. Their report recommending Cuban independence had a depressing effect on prices, confirming the impression that war is inevitable unless the European Powers intervene. The Paris Bourse became very weak, and Wall-street operators, finding that London was selling heavily, threw large blocks of stock on the market, and the latest quotations are considerably below those ruling at the end of last week.

Highest and Lowest this Year.		Last Carrying over Price.	BRITISH FUNDS, &c.	Closing Price.	Rise or Fall.
113⅛	110	—	Consols 2¾ p.c. (Money)...	110 7/16	− 9/16
113 5/16	110½	111¼	Do. Account (May 5)	110 9/16	− 7/16
106¼	103⅛	104¾	2½ p.c. Stock red. 1905 ...	103½	−1¼
363	345	—	Bank of England Stock...	347½	− ½
117	112	113	India 3½ p.c. Stk. red. 1931	112½	− ¾
109½	105	105½	Do. 3 p.c. Stk. red. 1948	105	−1¼
96⅞	91	92½	Do. 2½ p.c. Stk. red. 1926	91	−2

Consols have given way under the influence of dearer money and the continued uncertainty of the political outlook, and the price touched 110⅛ at one time, that being the lowest point of the year. Other investment stocks have been depressed, Colonial Government securities being especially weak, while the premier stocks of the leading Home Railway companies show a further shrinkage.

As regards Home Railway stocks there is very little to be said. The Easter traffic returns were considered satisfactory and, despite the almost entire absence of business, prices were well maintained until Wednesday, when they gave way in sympathy with the sharp break in Spanish bonds. South-Eastern Deferred became especially weak, for no particular reason, and the whole list shows adverse changes. Continuation rates were much about the same as last time. Great Eastern was carried over at about 3/16 backwardation, but quite at the last there was a small contango. Great Western and North-Western rates were ¼ to ⅜, and Midland and North-Eastern 1/16 to ⅛ per cent. The settlement gave little trouble, the account open being very small.

Highest and Lowest this Year.		Last Carrying over Price.	HOME RAILWAYS.	Closing Price.	Rise or Fall.
186	172½	175⅝	Brighton Def.	174¾	− ¾
59¼	55⅜	56¼	Caledonian Def.	55⅜	−1
20⅞	18⅞	19¼	Chatham Ordinary	19	− ⅜
77¼	66	67	Great Central Pref.	66½	− ½
24⅜	21¾	22	Do. Def.	22	—
124½	119⅝	121⅜	Great Eastern	120⅝	− ⅝
61½	51¼	53	Great Northern Def.	52½	− ½
179⅝	170¾	172	Great Western	171½	− ½
51½	45¼	48¾	Hull and Barnsley.........	48¼	− ½
149¼	146¼	147½	Lanc. and Yorkshire	147¼	+ ¼
136⅛	127½	129	Metropolitan	129	—
31	26¾	27½	Metropolitan District......	27½	—
88⅜	83¼	85	Midland Pref.	84½	− ¾
95⅜	84⅛	87½	Do. Def.	86¾	− ⅝
93½	88	88¾	North British Pref.	88¼	− ½
47½	42⅝	43¼	Do. Def.	42⅝	− ⅜
181½	172¾	174¼	North Eastern...............	173⅜	− ⅜
205½	197¾	199	North Western	198¼	− ½
117⅛	107	109½	South Eastern Def.	108	−1⅜
98¾	90¼	91	South Western Def.	90¾	−1¼

Although the Wall Street market was kept open all through the Easter holidays it might as well have been closed for all the good it has done. Business was practically at a standstill, the time being almost entirely taken up in discussing the political situation. The delay in the appearance of the President's message was viewed favourably, and repurchases by bear operators on Monday, on the news of the Spanish armistice in Cuba, sent prices up a little, but when Mr. M'Kinley's

Message came out there was a relapse, although not much stock was forthcoming. New York naturally waited to see how the London Stock Exchange would receive the President's message, but it was considered much too vague to encourage speculation either for the rise or fall. The action of Congress was awaited with considerable interest, and when the committee of the Senate announced their decision, the liquidation which followed caused a big break in prices, and no support whatever was forthcoming. The *Financial Chronicle* tables show an increase of 10·13 per cent. in the gross takings of seventy roads for the fourth week in March. Canadian and Grand Trunk stocks had their one brief interval of firmness, the traffic returns being again good, but quotations have since followed the downward trend in all other departments, and are now well below those of last week. Nothing further has been heard of the rate-cutting question, beyond the announcement that the committe has still failed to arrive at any decision in the matter.

Highest and Lowest this Year.		Last Carrying over Price.	CANADIAN AND U.S. RAILWAYS.	Closing Prices.	Rise or Fall.
14 1/16	10⅞	11¾	Atchison Shares	11½	− ⅛
34	23¾	26½	Do. Pref.	26	—
15⅜	11⅛	12½	Central Pacific	12¼	− ⅛
99¾	88⅝	92½	Chic. Mil. & St. Paul	90⅝	− ⅝
14¼	10⅞	11½	Denver Shares	11⅛	− ⅜
54⅛	42½	44¾	Do. Prefd.	44	− ¾
16⅝	12⅜	12¾	Erie Shares	12½	− ¼
44⅞	32	34	Do. Prefd.	33	− 1
62½	46⅛	51½	Louisville & Nashville	50	− 1½
14½	10⅝	11	Missouri & Texas	11	− ⅛
122½	108½	115	New York Central	113	− ½
57¼	43	46¾	Norfolk & West. Prefd.	46	− ⅝
70⅛	59¼	64¼	Northern Pacific Prefd.	62½	− 1
19⅞	13⅜	14⅜	Ontario Shares	14¾	—
62½	57¼	58½	Pennsylvania	57⅞	− ⅝
12⅛	8	8¾	Reading Shares	8¼	− ⅜
34⅛	24½	27	Southern Prefd.	26⅝	+ ⅛
37⅛	18⅞	20⅛	Union Pacific	20	− ⅜
20¼	14⅝	16	Wabash Prefd.	15¾	− ¼
30⅛	22	23½	Do. Income Debs.	23	− ⅝
92⅞	81⅜	83	Canadian Pacific	82¼	−
78⅛	69⅞	73½	Grand Trunk Guar.	72¾	− 1
69½	57⅛	66½	Do. 1st Pref.	65½	− 1¾
50⅛	37¼	47½	Do. 2nd Pref.	46¼	− ¾
25¼	19¼	22½	Do. 3rd Pref.	21⅞	− ½
105¾	101½	102½	Do. 4 p.c. Deb.	103	+ ¾

Apart from the rapid ups and downs of Spanish four per cents. there has been little of interest happening in the Foreign market, and the tendency, after being fairly steady, finally became decidedly weak. Spanish bonds rushed up to 50¾ on Thursday on the postponement of Mr. M'Kinley's message, and then dropped to 44⅞, and after rallying to 45½ again slipped back. A sharp decline has also taken place in Italian Rente, and

Highest and Lowest this Year.		Last Carrying over Price.	FOREIGN BONDS.	Closing Price.	Rise or Fall.
94½	86½	88	Argentine 5 p.c. 1886	86⅜	−1½
92⅜	84¼	86½	Do. 6 p.c. Funding	84¼	−2
76¾	67⅛	68¾	Do. 5 p.c. B. Ay. Water	67¼	−1¾
61¾	45½	47½	Brazilian 4 p.c. 1889	45½	−3
69⅝	50	52	Do. 5 p.c. 1895	50½	−3
65	47	49	Do. 5 p.c. West Minas Ry.	47½	−2½
108¾	106½	107⅞	Egyptian 4 p.c. Unified	107¾	− ¼
104¾	102	104¼	Do. 3½ p.c. Pref.	103¾	− ½
103	101	101½	French 3 p.c. Rente	101	−1
44⅜	34½	44	Greek 4 p.c. Monopoly	43	−1
93 1/16	90¼	92	Italian 5 p.c. Rente	91	−1
100	95⅜	96⅜	Mexican 6 p.c. 1888	96	−1
20⅞	18¼	18⅞	Portuguese 1 p.c.	18¼	− ⅞
62¼	42¼	47¾	Spanish 4 p.c.	43¾	−4⅜
45⅛	40½	41¾	Turkish 1 p.c. "B"	41	−1¼
26 1/16	23¼	24⅜	Do. 1 p.c. "C"	23½	− ⅞
22 1/16	20¼	21	Do. 1 p.c. "D"	20½	− ¾
46⅝	40	45½	Uruguay 3½ p.c. Bonds	45¾	+ ¼

Russian, Turkish, and Portuguese stocks have all been pressed for sale. South American descriptions, apart from the steadiness of Uruguay 3½ per cent., also present a weaker appearance, the further fall in the Rio Exchange still seriously affecting Brazilian bonds, and Argentine and Chilian are lower in sympathy. All the Continental bourses have been in a very nervous state, and it did not take much selling to put prices down. The settlement in this department was a very simple matter, and continuation rates generally ruled about ½ per cent. higher than last time, Spanish and Italian being carried over at from 3 to 5 per cent.

Highest and Lowest this Year.		Last Carrying over Price.	FOREIGN RAILWAYS.	Closing Price.	Rise or Fall.
100	99½	99½	Argentine Gt. West. 5 p.c. Pref. Stock	100	—
158½	144	147	B. Ay. Gt. Southern Ord.	146	− 1
78½	68	70	B. Ay. and Rosario Ord.	70½	+ ½
12¼	10½	10⅜	B. Ay. Western Ord.	10¾	—
87¼	74	77	Central Argentine Ord.	77	+ ½
92	83	82½	Cordoba and Rosario 6 p.c. Deb.	83	—
95½	86½	87	Cord. Cent. 4 p.c. Deb. (Cent. Nth. Sec.)	87½	—
61¾	45	45½	Do. Income Deb. Stk.	46	+ ½
25½	18	19¼	Mexican Ord. Stk.	19	− ¼
83½	72	75	Do. 8 p.c. 1st Pref.	74½	− 1

Foreign railway stocks have been entirely neglected, almost the only changes noticeable being a fall of 2½ in Buenos Ayres and Ensenada, and a slight recovery in Cordoba Central (Central Northern) income stock.

About the only feature in the Miscellaneous Market was a sharp rise in Russian Petroleum ordinary, fresh rumours of "splitting" being again circulated. Changes in the upward direction are also noticeable in Liebigs, Spiers & Pond, Vickers and Maxim, Lyons, and Elysée Palace Hotel debentures, but on the other hand, Brewery issues have been pressed for sale, Guinness ordinary falling 10, Combe debentures 2, and several others were marked down a point. Electric lighting companies' shares are lower in several instances, and declines have also taken place in Birmingham Vinegar, Peebles, Spratts, and British Electric Traction. Lipton issues have been hardly mentioned.

The feature right up to the close of business was the activity in Spanish stock, which finally closed well above the lowest point of the week. The Paris Bourse was very weak, and the heavy fall in Italian, Spanish, Argentine, and Brazilian, as well as Rio Tinto and De Beers shares, which took place early to-day (Thursday), was entirely due to sales from Paris. The recovery in Spanish 4 per cent. helped to strengthen United States Railroad shares which closed fairly steady, a good deal of bear covering taking place. Consols were weaker, although not closing at the worst, and Home Railway stocks picked up a little when it was found that the Bank rate was not changed.

MINING AND FINANCE COMPANIES.

In the South African market there has been little or nothing doing, and prices have hardly moved, except Chartered shares, which fell to 2 9/16 on the proposal to issue 250,000 new shares at 2. The settlement was more than usually uninteresting, and one of the lightest known. Rates showed but little change in spite of the rise in the Bank rate, Rand mines being continued at about 6, and East Rand at 7 per cent., the general charge being 7 to 9 per cent. Western Australian ventures call for no special mention, copper shares remain fairly steady, and Indian shares close firm, the rise in Ooregum being due to the remarks made by the chairman at the meeting.

The Russian Embassy at Constantinople has again demanded the appointment of Prince George as Governor of Crete, and the King of Greece is said to have declared that the matter is practically settled. It is about time.

The voluntary opening of new treaty ports by the Chinese Government is said to have been done with a view to inducing England to agree to a revision of the tariff in accordance with Article XXVI. of the Treaty of Tientsin.

Dividends Announced.

MISCELLANEOUS.

MONTANA MINING COMPANY, LIMITED.—Dividend of 3d. per share.

BAYLISS, THOMAS & CO.—Interim dividend of 10 per cent. per annum for the six months ended March 31.

DOUGLAS SOUTHERN ELECTRIC TRAMWAY, LIMITED.—3 per cent. on the 7 per cent. preference shares. Balance forward, £205.

LONDON STOCK EXCHANGE.—Dividend of £4 10s. per share, making with the interim paid on November 2, £7 10s. per share for the year. £5,000 to be placed to reserve, leaving £34,939 to be carried forward.

R. & J. PULLMAN, LTD.—Interim dividend on the ordinary shares for the half-year at the rate of 7 per cent. per annum, also the half-year's dividend on the 5 per cent. preference shares.

BRILLIANT AND ST. GEORGE UNITED GOLD MINING COMPANY, LTD.—1s. per share is announced.

CRESCENS, ROBINSON, & CO., LIMITED.—7s. per share on the ordinary shares for the six months ended December 31.

EASTERN PRODUCE AND ESTATES COMPANY, LIMITED.—Final dividend on the ordinary shares of 4½ per cent., making 7 per cent. for the year.

UNION STEAMSHIP COMPANY, LIMITED.—Dividend for the half-year ended December 31 at the rate of 14s. per share on the fully-paid shares, and 7s. per share on the shares with £10 paid, which, with the interim paid in October last, will make a total dividend for the year of £5 10s. per cent.

BONANZA, LIMITED.—Interim dividend of 50 per cent., being at the rate of 100 per cent. per annum, for the half-year ending April 30.

GREAT EASTERN COLLIERIES, LIMITED.—Dividend of 5 per cent.

TRUST AND AGENCY OF AUSTRALASIA.—Dividend of 2s. per share, making a total distribution for the year 1897 of 20 per cent.

VAN DEN BERGH'S.—Dividend on the ordinary shares at the rate of 10 per cent. per annum.

BREWERIES.

BARTHOLOMAY CO. (ROCHESTER).—Interim dividend on the preference shares for the six months ended March 31 at the rate of 8 per cent. per annum.

INSURANCE.

COMMERCIAL UNION CO.—20s. per share, making with interim 30 per cent. for the year as compared with 25 per cent. for 1896.

RAILWAYS.

GREAT NORTHERN (UNITED STATES).—Quarterly dividend of 1¾ per cent. upon the preferred stock, and a quarterly dividend of 1¾ per cent. on the St. Paul, Minneapolis and Manitoba Railway Company's 6 per cent. guaranteed shares.

WELLINGTON AND MANAWATU COMPANY.—5 per cent. dividend declared.

TALTAL RAILWAY.—Interim dividend for the half-year ended December 31 of 1s. 3d. per share.

MINING RETURNS.

KOFFYFONTEIN.—Returns for March are 2,500 carats diamonds.

FRANK SMITH DIAMOND.—5,500 loads washed, producing 209 carats.

KIMBERLEY WATERWORKS.—Consumption of water for March, 13,250,000 gallons.

NIGEL.—Crushing for March.—Battery 1,295 oz.; cyanide 1,573 oz.

MALAYAN (PAHANG) EXPLORATION.—1,700 tons crushed, 593 oz. gold; value £2,100.

HENRY NOURSE.—Crushed 8,680 tons, producing 5,179 oz. Cyanide, 6,450 tons treated, yielding 3,129 oz.

LEICESTER CONSOLIDATED.—From mine, 3,725; from floors, lumps and hoppenings, 3,175 loads washed, producing 235 carats.

HALL MINES.—7,437 tons of ore smelted, yielding 357 tons matte containing (approximately) 156 tons copper, 111,490 oz. silver, 272 oz. gold.

NORTHERN TERRITORIES GOLD FIELDS OF AUSTRALIA.—1,200 tons treated 887 oz. troy.

SONS OF GWALIA.—Tons crushed 990; yield in oz. 1,241; tailings assay 28 dwt. per ton.

FERREIRA.—Crushed 11,314 tons, bar gold extracted 7,017 oz., concentrates caught 275 tons. Cyanide works—bullion produced from tailings, 3,007 oz.

CITY AND SUBURBAN.—Crushing for last month yielded 11,030 oz.; profit, £17,326.

WINDSOR.—From mill.—Crushed 3,482 tons; obtained 1,189 oz.; from cyanide works obtained 655 oz. Profit for month £3,027.

CHAMP D'OR.—Crushed during March 5,672 tons, yielding 2,190 oz.; cyanide, 3,685 tons treated, yielding 778 oz.

TRANSVAAL GOLD MINING ESTATES.—From mill—Crushed, 8,860 tons; obtained 3,350 oz. fine gold. From outside cyanide works, tons treated 2,497; yield 993 oz. gold. Central cyanide works, tons treated 6,920; yield 2,411 oz. gold.

JUMPERS DEEP.—Tons crushed by 75 stamps, 9,550; yield in fine gold, 3,119 oz. Sands and concentrates treated by cyanide, 4,000 tons; yield, 1,079 oz. fine gold.

GELDENHUIS MAIN REEF.—Gold from mill, 542 oz.; gold cyanide works, 410 oz. Ore milled, 1,634 tons; tailings treated, 2,640 tons.

GRAND CENTRAL.—Crushed, 4,500 tons, yielding bullion estimated at $55,000; concentrates estimated to realise $15,000; expenses for the month, $29,000.

GREAT BOULDER PERSEVERANCE.—Returns from smelting works, 247 tons for 894 oz.; 770 tons of ore milled for 807 oz.

JUBILEE.—Tons crushed, 5,595, obtained 2,065 oz. Tailings yielded 733 oz.; total, 2,798 oz.

NEW GUADALCAZAR QUICKSILVER.—The production of quicksilver for the past month amounts to 11,000 lb. = 146⅔ flasks.

SIAM COMPANY (LIMITED).—Kabin Mine, 58 tons ore crushed from Sydenham shaft, producing 32 oz. gold, and 395 tons ore crushed from Beresford shaft, producing 155 oz. gold.

SHEBA.—6,880 tons of ore, 2,680 oz.; 3,780 tons of tailings, 910 oz.; 130 tons of concentrates, 780 oz.; total, 4,370 oz.

ST. JOHN DEL REY.—Produce month of March, £17,962 yield per ton, ·66 of an ounce troy.

ALASKA MEXICAN.—Return for March:—Milled, 13 200 tons; sulphurets treated, 216 tons; bullion from sulphurets, $10,047.

BALMORAL MAIN REEF.—2,425 oz.

BLOCK B LANGLAAGTE ESTATE.—Mill.—Ore crushed, 12,490 tons of 2,000 lb.; gold retorted, 2,860 oz. Tailings (cyanide process).—Tons treated, 7,200; gold recovered, 1,563 oz. Concentrates (cyanide process).—Tons treated, 192; gold recovered, 504 oz. Total gold recovered, 4,927 oz.

BRILLIANT AND ST. GEORGE.—Crushed during the month, 1,768 tons of quartz for 2,322 oz. of gold.

CASSEL COAL.—Output for March, 15,350 tons.

CONSOLIDATED MAIN REEF.—March production.—2,015 oz. from 5,139 tons; 894 oz. from 4,584 tons cyanide; total, 2,909 oz.

CONSOLIDATED MURCHISON.—Crushed 384 tons, obtained 399 oz. of gold.

CROWN DEEP.—Tons crushed by stamps, 20,200; Yield in fine gold from mill, 4,566 oz.; tons of sand and concentrates treated by cyanide works, 17,330; yield in fine gold from sands and concentrates, 4,915 oz.; tons of slimes treated, 2,860; yield in fine gold from slimes, 237 oz.

CROWN REEF.—Crushed by mill.—13,911 tons; yield in smelted gold, 7,312 oz.; yield in smelted gold from cyanide works 3,882 oz.; Yield in smelted gold from slimes works (including balance for February and output for March), 886 oz.

DURBAN-ROODEPOORT.—Results for March:—Quartz milled, 10,120 tons for 5,060 oz.; tailings treated, 6,545 tons for 1,281 oz.; total, 6,341 oz.

GELDENHUIS DEEP.—Results for March:—Tons crushed by stamps, 24,100; Yield in fine gold 6,851 oz.; tons of sands and concentrates treated by cyanide works, 18,090; yield in fine gold, 3,703 oz.; tons of slimes treated, 6,038; yield in fine gold from slimes works, 290 oz.

GELDENHUIS ESTATE.—Results for March: Crushed 16,008 tons; obtained from mill, 6,394 oz.; obtained from concentrates by cyanide, 896 oz.; obtained from tailings by cyanide, 2,252 oz.; obtained from slimes by cyanide, 498 oz.; slags, &c. equal to 703 oz.—total, 10,743 oz.

GEORGE GOCH AMALGAMATED.—Result during March: 7,956 tons crushed, yielding 1,715 oz., and 1,292 oz. from tailings.

GINSBURG.—March production, 2,591 oz.

GLENCAIRN MAIN REEF.—March production, 6,958 oz.

HANNAN'S REWARD.—Results for March: Cement crushed 950 tons, yield 120 oz.

KALGURLI.—245 tons sent to South Australia for treatment have yielded a result of 2,100 oz. of gold.

LANCASTER.—Crushed, 7,980 tons, yielding 2,817 oz.; treated 7,580 tons by cyanide, yielding 1,399 oz.

LANGLAAGTE ESTATE.—Production for March:—Mill.—Ore crushed, 18,985 tons of 2,000 lb.; gold retorted, 6,657 oz. Tailings, cyanide process.—Tons treated, 11,700; gold recovered, 1,662 oz. Concentrates, cyanide process.—Tons treated, 434; gold recovered, 1,872 oz.

LANGLAAGTE STAR.—Production for March:—Mill.—Ore crushed, 5,302 tons of 2,000 lb.; gold retorted, 2,532 oz. Tailings, cyanide process.—Tons treated, 5,760; gold recovered, 966 oz.

MEYER AND CHARLTON.—Crushed, 9,348 tons; gold won, 2,720 oz.; extracted 1,175 oz. from tailings.

MIKADO (LAKE OF THE WOODS DISTRICT), ONTARIO.—Mill crushed 1,116 tons, yielding 530 oz.

NEW HERIOT.—Last month's crushing yielded 5,824 oz. Profit, £8,705.

NEW PRIMROSE.—March production, 9,484 oz.

NEW QUEEN.—Result of crushing for past fortnight:—1,220 ft. formation—335 tons, yielding 295 oz.; No. 4 formation—67 tons, yielding 42 oz. gold.

NEW RIETFONTEIN.—March production, 2,087 oz.

NEW SPES BONA.—March production, 2,122 oz.

NEW ZEALAND CROWN MINES.—Tons mined during month, 1,700; tons crushed, 1,764.

NORTH RANDFONTEIN.—Production for March:—Mill—ore crushed 6,447 tons of 2,000 lb., gold retorted 1,732 oz; tailings, cyanide process—tons treated 3,360, gold recovered 472 oz.; concentrates, cyanide process—tons treated 85, gold recovered 189 oz.

NOURSE DEEP.—Results for March; Tons crushed by stamps, 7,648; yield in fine gold from mill, 2,165 oz.; tons of sands and concentrates treated by cyanide works, 6,080; yield in fine gold, 1,902 oz.

OTTOS KOPJE.—7,030 loads washed during the week ended April 7; 240 carats of diamonds won, including one stone of 15 carats. March output, 900 carats, realised £1,115.

PORGES RANDFONTEIN.—Production for March: Mill—ore crushed, 7,220 tons of 2,000 lb.; gold retorted, 2,627 oz.; tailings, cyanide process—tons treated, 3,250; gold recovered, 548 oz.; concentrates, cyanide process—tons treated, 111; gold recovered, 366 oz.

PRINCESS ESTATE.—Result for March: Crushed, 5,150 tons; gold won, 1,894 oz.; extracted from tailings, 826 oz.; total, 2,720 oz.

RIETFONTEIN A.—March production, 4,737 oz.

ROBINSON.—Production for March:—Mill—crushed, 14,918 tons of ore; yielded in smelted gold, 10,640 oz.; from concentrates (by chlorination), 2,214 oz.; from tailings (cyanide process), 3,422 oz.; from slimes, 1,178 oz.; from own ore, 16,454 oz.; from concentrates bought (by chlorination), 2,913 oz.

ROBINSON RANDFONTEIN.—Production for March:—Mill.—Ore crushed, 4,593 tons of 2,000 lb.: gold retorted, 1,979 oz. Tailing (Cyanide process):—Tons treated, 3,520; gold recovered, 523 oz. Concentrates (Cyanide process):—Tons treated, 64: gold recovered, 194 oz.

ROODEPOORT.—March production, 986 oz.

ROODEPOORT UNITED MAIN REEF.—Result for March:—Crushed, 7,930 tons, producing 2,999 oz.; cyanide, 923 oz.; total, 3,922 oz.

ROSE DEEP.—Results for March:—Tons crushed by stamps, 16,651; Yield in fine gold, 5,465 oz.; tons of sands and concentrates treated by cyanide works, 19,773; yield in fine gold, 2,881 oz.

VAN RYN.—Crushed, 11,153 tons, yielding 3,011 oz. Cyanide, 7,560 tons treated, yielding 1,362 oz.

VILLAGE MAIN REEF.—Result for March:—Crushed, 7,978 tons, yielding 4,089 oz.; treated, 4,930 tons cyanide, producing 1,875 oz.

WAITEKAURI.—During the month ended March 26 the mill yielded £4,760 from 1,675 tons.

WEMMER.—Result during March:—Mill crushed 7,094 tons, yielding 4,392 oz. Cyanide plant—4,875 tons treated, yielding 916 oz., and from concentrates, 170 tons caught, assaying 110 dwt. per ton. Total, 6,243 oz.

WENTWORTH GOLD FIELDS.—Four weeks' return:—615 tons of ore have been crushed, containing 785 oz.; and one ton rich crude ore has been shipped, containing 77 oz.

WEST RAND.—Crushed 3,960 tons, yielded 967 oz. Cyanide treated 2,705 tons, yielded 803 oz.

WITWATERSRAND.—Result during March:—Mill crushed 15,150 tons, yielding 3,951 oz.; 10,530 tons cyanide tailings treated, yielding 1,525 oz.

ANGELO.—Crushing for last month:—Tons crushed, 6,569; ounces recovered, 3,162; tons treated by cyanide, 5,132; ounces recovered, 2,383; ounces recovered from slags, 167.

BUFFELSDOORN.—Production for March, 2,902 oz.

CAYLLOMA SILVER.—March production was 13,000 oz. fine silver in export ore and 12,500 oz. fine silver in bullion.

FRANK SMITH DIAMOND.—5,100 loads washed, producing 221 carats.

GREAT BOULDER PROPRIETARY.—For the fortnight ended April 12:—Tons crushed, 1,415; yield of gold in ounces, 3,146.

HANNAN'S BROWN HILL.—550 tons of sands, 453 tons of slimes treated; 1,830 oz. of gold recovered.

"JUMPERS."—Crushed, 17,500 tons; obtained from mill, 3,670 oz. of gold; from concentrates by cyanide, 503 oz. of gold; from tailings by cyanide, 900 oz. of gold.

NEW COMET.—Crushing for last month:—Tons crushed, 4,861; ounces recovered, 1,818; tons treated by cyanide, 3,765; ounces recovered, 1,060; ounces recovered from slags, 50.

PAARL CENTRAL.—From mill.—Crushed, 6,615 tons, yielding 1,556 oz. of gold. From cyanide works.—Treated 4,700 tons, yielding 1,055 oz.—total, 2,611 oz.

PREMIER TATI MONARCH REEF.—Returns for March: 1,500 tons crushed, including 275 tons surface low grade ore; yield of retorted gold, 503 oz.

ROBINSON (WESTERN AUSTRALIA).—During March, 570 tons were crushed, yielding 143 oz. gold, exclusive of tailings and concentrates.

RUTH MINES.—Output for March; 346 tons of ore, giving an estimated net profit of $7,850.

TREASURY.—Output for March: 5,600 tons yielded 3,813 oz.

WAIHI GOLD.—Bullion return from old mill only for 24 days, £11,350 from 3,200 tons.

WELD HERCULES.—Crushed 207 tons, produced 135 oz. of gold.

WOLHUTER.—Result for March: Crushed 13,431 tons, total ounces bullion and cyanide, 6,936.

BURBANK'S BIRTHDAY GIFT.—Total amount crushed for March, 2,400 tons, yielded 1,926 oz.

MOODIE'S.—Tons crushed 900, yield 494 oz.

MOUNT MORGAN.—Tons chlorinated, 11,324; gold returned, 14,094 oz.

Answers to Correspondents.

Questions about public securities, and on all points in company law, will be answered week by week, in the REVIEW, on the following terms and conditions :—

A fee of FIVE shillings must be remitted for each question put, provided they are questions about separate securities. Should a private letter be required, then an extra fee of FIVE shillings must be sent to cover the cost of such letter, the fee then being TEN shillings for one query only, and FIVE shillings for every subsequent one in the same letter. While making this concession the EDITOR will feel obliged if private replies are as much as possible dispensed with. It is wholly impossible to answer letters sent merely "with a stamped envelope enclosed for reply."

Correspondents will further greatly oblige by so framing their questions as to obviate the necessity to name securities in the replies. They should *number* the questions, keeping a copy for reference, thus :—"(1) Please inform me about the present position of the Rowenzori Development Co. (2) Is a dividend likely to be paid soon on the capital stock of the Congo-Sudan Railway ?

Answers to be given to all such questions by simply quoting the numbers 1, 2, 3, and so on. The EDITOR has a rooted objection to such forms of reply as—"I think your Timbuctoo Consols will go up," or "Sell your Slowcoach and Draggem Bonds," because this kind of thing is open to all sorts of abuses. By the plan suggested, and by using a fancy name to be replied to, each query can be kept absolutely private to the inquirer, and no scope whatever be given to market manipulations. Avoid, as names to be replied to, common words, like "investor," "inquirer," and so on, as also "bear" or "bull." Detached syllables of the inquirer's name, or initials reversed, will frequently do as well as anything, so long as the answer can be identified by the inquirer.

The EDITOR further respectfully requests that merely speculative questions should as far as possible be avoided. He by no means sets himself up as a market prophet, and can only undertake to provide the latest information regarding the securities asked about. This he will do faithfully and without bias.

Replies cannot be guaranteed in the same week if the letters demanding them reach the office of the INVESTORS' REVIEW, Norfolk House, Norfolk-street, W.C., later than the first post on Wednesday mornings.

L. E. H. (Kensington).—1. The company is, I believe, an honest one. 2. Only if considered a speculative investment. 3. I do not, neither for nor against. 4. Competition is hardly likely. 5. A decrease in population is the chief source of danger to the undertaking; from the nature of the industry it follows such might happen. It has been rumoured that the mines are being rapidly exhausted, but a new process of treating ores, which have hitherto been unworkable, it is hoped will assist in prolonging their life. Apart from the reasons you mention, this uncertainty helps to keep down the price. The company's reserve is not very large, and a buyer should certainly put aside part of his dividends as a private contingency fund. Dealings are carried out on the Stock Exchange, though the shares are not officially quoted. I am returning papers as requested.

B. H.—3 and 4, 1, 2. The two last have not, I think, much chance of improving in value, though both are honest and well managed.

NOTICES

Messrs. Blake, Boissevain, & Co. advise holders of Dutch Committee certificates issued against deposit of the Union Pacific, Lincoln, & Colorado Five per Cent. bonds that they are prepared to exchange the same against the securities of the Union Pacific Railroad Company. Each holder of a $1,000 certificate, in addition to his proportion of Union Pacific securities, will be entitled to receive a cash payment of £4 2s. 1d., being 2 per cent. of the face value of his bonds. Holders of original bonds who have not, so far, deposited are given the opportunity to do so at the office of Messrs. Blake, Boissevain, & Co. up to and including April 23 on payment of a fine of 2 per cent. of the face value of their bonds, and will, upon deposit, become entitled to the new securities and cash payment mentioned above, but bonds not deposited by that date will be irrevocably excluded from any participation in the agreement with the New York Union Pacific Reorganization Committee, under which the new securities are issued to holders.

The coupons due May 1 next on the Chinese Imperial Government seven per cent. silver loan of 1894 will be paid, on and after that date, at the offices of the Hong Kong and Shanghai Banking Corporation, 31, Lombard-street, E.C.

The numbers are published of the bonds of the Kingdom of Hungary three per cent. gold loan which were drawn on the 1st inst., for payment on and after July 1, 1898. The drawn bonds will cease to bear interest from the date of their maturity.

Lloyds Bank Limited notifies that in order to prepare the half-yearly dividends due May 1 on the Tynemouth Corporation three per cent. redeemable stock, and the South Shields Corporation three per cent. redeemable stock, the balance of the several accounts will be struck on the night of the 16th inst., and that on and after the 18th inst. the stocks will be transferable ex dividend.

With regard to the Guatemala External Debt the Council of Foreign Bondholders have received telegraphic advices from Guatemala stating that the Legislature has reduced the duty on coffee to $1 silver from July 1. This reduction is in violation of the agreement entered into with the bondholders, which fixes the duty at $1½ gold for ten years from August, 1895.

No trouble seems at present to be apprehended in connection with the Russian demand for the transit of warships and troops through the Dardanelles. The rumour that Austria contemplated raising objections is denied, and it is further explained that Russia has asked leave of the Porte for only one war vessel and two thousand troops to pass through the Bosphorus, not twenty thousand as has been reported. The Sultan granted the necessary permission of course. How could he refuse?

Prices of Mine and Mining Finance Companies' Shares.

Shares £1 each except where otherwise stated

AUSTRALIAN.

Making-Up Price, Apr. 12.	Name	Closing Price.	Rise or Fall.	Making-Up Price, Apr. 12.	Name	Closing Price.	Rise or Fall.
1½	Aladdin	1¼	−⅛	⅞	Hannan's Star	1⅛	
3½	Associated	3⅛	−⅛	4	Ivanhoe, New	4	−⅛
[illegible]	Do. Southern	½		[illegible]	Kalgurli Mt. & Iron King, 18/	[illegible]	+ [illegible]
1½	Brownhill Extended	1	−⅛	4	Kalgurli	4	− [illegible]
1½	Burbank's Birthday	1	− [illegible]	2	Lady Shenton	2	−⅛
[illegible]	Central Boulder	½		8¼	Lake View Cons.	8	− [illegible]
5/6	Chaffers, 4/	4/9	−/3	[illegible]	Do. Extended	[illegible]	+ [illegible]
[illegible]	Colonial Finance, 15/	[illegible] pm		1	Do. South	1	
—	Crœsus S. United	[illegible]		1⅛	London & Globe Finance	1	− [illegible]
1	E. Murchison	1	− [illegible]	[illegible]	London & W. A. Exploration	½	
5/	Golden Arrow 19/	4/6	−/6	[illegible]	Do. Investment	½	+ [illegible]
7½	Golden Horseshoe	7	−½	[illegible]	Mainland Consols	½	+ [illegible]
[illegible]	Golden Link	[illegible]	− [illegible]	[illegible]	North Boulder, 10/	½	− [illegible]
19/6	Great Boulder, 2/	18/3	−1/	1	North Kalgurli	1	−⅛
1½	Do. Main Reef, 10/	1	−⅛	—	Northern Territories	3½	−½
3	Do. Perseverance	2	− [illegible]	2½	Peak Hill	2½	
[illegible]	Do. South	[illegible]		2	South Kalgurli	1	− [illegible]
2	Hainault	1½	− [illegible]	1	W. A. Goldfields	1	− [illegible]
[illegible]	Hampton Plains	½	− [illegible]	2	W. A. Joint Stock	1	− [illegible]
7½	Hannan's Brownhill	7½	− [illegible]	1	W. A. Market Trust	[illegible]	−⅛
[illegible]	Hannan's Oroya	[illegible]	− [illegible]	1	W. A. Loan & General Fin.	1	−⅛
15/	Do. Proprietary	14/	−/6	½	White Feather	[illegible]	

SOUTH AFRICAN.

Making-Up Price, Apr. 12.	Name	Closing Price.	Rise or Fall.	Making-Up Price, Apr. 12.	Name	Closing Price.	Rise or Fall.
5½	Angelo	5	−⅛	2/6	Lisbon-Berlyn	2/6	
1	Aurora West	1		2½	May Consolidated	2	+⅛
[illegible]	Bantjes	[illegible]		4½	Meyer and Charlton	4½	
9/6	Barrett, 10/	9/0		4	Modderfontein	3½	− [illegible]
3½	Bonanza	3½	− [illegible]	1	New Bultfontein	1	+ [illegible]
7/	Buffelsdoorn	7/	−1/9	3	New Primrose	3½	− [illegible]
5½	City and Suburban, £4	5		1	Nigel	1½	+⅛
2	Comet (New)	2½	− [illegible]	—	Nigel Deep	1	+⅛
5½	Con. Deep Level	5		½	North Randfontein	½	
11	Crown Deep	11	−¼	5½	Nourse Deep	5	−⅛
12½	Crown Reef	12½		1½	Porges-Randfontein	1	− [illegible]
26½	De Beers, £5	25	−1	29½	Rand Mines	28½	−½
3	Driefontein	3½	− [illegible]	1½	Randfontein	1½	− [illegible]
5½	Durban Roodepoort	5½		2½	Rietfontein	2½	
3½	Do. Deep	3½	−½	9½	Robinson Deep	9½	−½
4	East Rand	4	+ [illegible]	7½	Do. Gold, £5	7½	
23½	Ferreira	22½	−½	[illegible]	Do. Randfontein	[illegible]	
6½	Geldenhuis Deep	6½		1	Roodepoort Central Deep	1	− [illegible]
5	Do. Estate	5		6½	Rose Deep	6½	−½
[illegible]	George Goch	½	− [illegible]	2	Salisbury	2	−½
2½	Ginsberg	2½		1	Sheba	1	− [illegible]
1	Glencairn	1½	− [illegible]	3	Simmer and Jack, £5	2½	−⅛
8½	Goldfields Deep	8½	−½	3½	Transvaal Gold	3½	
8½	Griqualand West	8½		3½	Treasury	3	
9	Henry Nourse	8½	−½	3	United Roodepoort	3½	
8	Heriot	7½	−⅛	1	Van Ryn	1	
7½	Jagersfontein	7½		5	Village Main Reef	5	
8	Jubilee	7½	−½	1½	Vogelstruis	1½	− [illegible]
4	Jumpers	4½	− [illegible]	[illegible]	Do. Deep	[illegible]	−⅛
2½	Kleinfontein	2	−½	9½	Wemmer	9½	
3	Knight's	3	−⅛	½	West Rand	½	
2	Lancaster	2		5	Wolhuter, £4	5½	−⅛
3	Langlaagte Estate	3		2½	Worcester	2	

LAND EXPLORATION AND RHODESIAN

Making-Up Price, Apr. 12.	Name	Closing Price.	Rise or Fall.	Making-Up Price, Apr. 12.	Name	Closing Price.	Rise or Fall.
2½	Anglo-French Ex.	2½	−⅛	[illegible]	Mashonaland Central	[illegible]	
1½	Barnato Consolidated	1½		6½	Matabele Gold Reefs	7	+⅛
[illegible]	Bechuanaland Ex.	½		2	Mozambique	2	− [illegible]
2	Chartered B.S.A.	2	−½	½	Ocean Consolidated	½	
[illegible]	Clark's Cons.	[illegible]		1	Rhodesia, Ltd.	1	− [illegible]
[illegible]	Colenbrander	[illegible]		4½	Do. Exploration	4½	−⅛
4	Cons. Goldfields	4	−½	1½	Do. Goldfields	1½	
1	Do. Pref.	20/	−/6	4	S. A. Gold Trust	3½	−⅛
1	Exploration	1		1	Tati Concessions	[illegible]	
2	Geelong	2½	− [illegible]	½	Transvaal Development	½	
[illegible]	Henderson's Est.	½	− [illegible]	[illegible]	United Rhodesia	[illegible]	
1½	Johannesburg Con. In.	1½		1½	Willoughby	1½	− [illegible]
1	Do. Water	1		½	Zambesia Explor.	½	
1½	Mashonaland Agency	1½	− [illegible]				

MISCELLANEOUS

Making-Up Price, Apr. 12.	Name	Closing Price.	Rise or Fall.	Making-Up Price, Apr. 12.	Name	Closing Price.	Rise or Fall.
1½	Alamillos, £2	1½		13/6	Mount Lyell, South	[illegible]	
5½	Anaconda, $25	5	− [illegible]	4½	Mount Morgan, 17s. 6d.	4½	
8/	Balaghât, 18/	8/	−/6	5½	Mysore, 10s.	5½	
13/9	Brilliant, £2	13/6	−/6	13/	Mysore Goldfields	12/6	
2½	Do. St. George's	2½		7/	Do. Reefs, 17/	7/	
9/6	British Broken Hill	9/6	−9	10/	Do. West	8/6	−4′
2	Broken Hill Proprietary	2½		8/	Do. Wynaad	6/0	−⅛
—	Do. Block 10	3½		2	Namaqua, £2	2	− [illegible]
4½	Cape Copper, £2	4½		3½	Nundydroog	3	
5	Champion Reef, 10s.	5	− [illegible]	3	Ooregum	3½	+⅛
2½	Copiapo, £2	2½	− [illegible]	3	Do. Pref.	4½	+ [illegible]
3	Coromandel	3	− [illegible]	28½	Rio Tinto Def., £5	27½	− [illegible]
14/	Day Dawn Block	14/		6½	Do. Pref. £5	6½	
2	Frontino & Bolivia	2½	+½	17/6	St. John del Rey	17/	
1½	Hall Mines	1	−½	8/9	Taitapu	[illegible]	−⅛
2	Libiola, £5	2½		7½	Tharsis, £2	7	
8	Linares, £3	8	−½	2½	Tolima "A," £5	2½	−⅛
4	Mason & Barry, £3	3½		4	Waihi	4½	− [illegible]
5	Mountain Copper, £5	5		1	Waitekauri	1	
13½	Mount Lyell, £3	13	−½	1	Woodstock (N.Z.)	1	
2½	Mount Lyell, North	2½	− [illegible]				

The German Asiatic Bank is to establish a branch at Kiao-Chau in a short time. Other banks are expected to follow its example.

Next Week's Meetings.

MONDAY, APRIL 18.

Crystal Palace	Cannon-street Hotel, noon.
Leland Stanford Gold Mining Co. ...	3, Clements-lane, noon.
Louise & Co.	Winchester House, noon.
Matabele Gold Reefs & Estate ...	Cannon-street Hotel, noon.
Redfern	Cannon-street Hotel, 11 a.m.
Rhodesia Goldfields	Cannon-street Hotel, 2.30 p.m.
Tarapaca Waterworks	Winchester House, noon.

TUESDAY, APRIL 19

British Shipowners	Liverpool, 1.30 p.m.
Calcutta Tramways	11, Abchurch-lane, 12.30 p.m.
Candelaria Waterworks and Milling	Winchester House, 11.30 a.m.
Croydon Tramways (Adj. Gen.) ...	Guildhall Tavern, 2 p.m.
London and Brazilian Bank ...	7, Tokenhouse-yard, noon.
Mercantile Bank of India	Winchester House, 1 p.m.
Rio Claro São Paulo	Cannon-street Hotel, 2.30 p.m.
San Jorge Nitrate	Winchester House, 2 p.m.
Scottish Metropolitan Life	Edinburgh, 3 p.m.
Standard Life Assurance	Edinburgh, 2 p.m.
Tottenham and Forest Gate Railway	28, Great George-st., S.W., 3.30 p.m

WEDNESDAY, APRIL 20.

Buenos Ayres Great Southern Railway	Cannon-street Hotel, noon.
Chartered Bank of India, Aust., and China	Cannon-street Hotel, 1 p.m.
Indo-European Telegraph	Winchester House, 12.30 p.m.
Tharsis Sulphur and Copper ..	Glasgow.

THURSDAY, APRIL 21.

British South Africa Company ...	Cannon Street Hotel, noon.
City of Buenos Ayres Tramways ...	Winchester House, 12.30 p.m.
Hall Mines	Winchester House, 2 p.m.
Sierra Buttes Gold Mines	Cannon-street Hotel, noon.

FRIDAY, APRIL 22.

Achilles Goldfields	Winchester House, noon.
Economic Life Assurance	6, New Bridge-street, 1 p.m.
San Paulo Brazilian Railway ...	Cannon-street Hotel, 1 p.m.

TRAMWAY AND OMNIBUS RECEIPTS.

For past week :—Aberdeen District, + £51 ; Belfast, + £276 ; Bury, Rochdale, and Oldham, + £240 ; Birmingham and Aston, + £47 ; Burnley and District, + £140 ; Calais, + £18 ; City of Birmingham, + £451 ; Dublin and Lucan Steam + £42 ; Lea Bridge, + £534 ; London & Deptford, + £98 ; London Southern, – £39 ; London General Omnibus, + £2,002 ; London Road Car, + £327 ; Metropolitan, + £2,314 ; North Staffordshire + £24 ; South London, + £254 ; Provincial, + £342 ; Southampton, + £63 ; Sunderland, + £80 ; Swansea, + £40.

Bordeaux, + £74 ; Calcutta, + £119.

Anglo-Argentine, week ending March 14, £586 increase ; City of Buenos Ayres, week ending February 21, £508 increase.

Milan cotton-spinners have made an urgent appeal to the Italian Foreign Minister to know how neutrals may be affected in the event of war between Spain and the United States. Their cotton supply comes almost entirely from the Southern States. The cargoes are always paid for at the port of embarkation, and are often shipped on Spanish or American vessels. If war broke out would the belligerents be held ultimately responsible for the capture or damage or loss which might be inflicted on the citizens of neutral Powers? The Foreign Minister's reply was exceedingly guarded. It amounted only to this, that, if war should break out, the Italian Government would associate itself with other Governments in all measures which appear "best calculated to render less serious for neutrals the war between the two States which did not adhere to the Declaration of Paris in 1856." That is rather cold comfort, but nothing more could have been said in the business. As neither the United States nor Spain is bound by the Paris Declaration, it is entirely in the discretion of the two countries named how they may treat neutrals in such circumstances.

A Parliamentary return just issued enlightens us as to the cost of our telegraph service since 1870. On the whole, it has resulted in considerable loss. In the twenty-eight years the total amount received has been £48,985,040, and the total expenditure, including interest on stock created on account of the telegraph service and redemption of debt, £49,999,827, an excess of expenditure over receipts of £1,014,787. Excluding interest the expenditure was £47,362,845, leaving a balance of receipts over expenditure of £1,622,195. In eleven out of the twenty-eight years there were deficiencies—the years being 1884 to 1888, and 1892 to 1897 inclusive, so that the profit on the business done is not growing apparently.

There has been some softening in the language of the Bulgarian Press towards Turkey, and Prince Ferdinand, confident that there will be no early breach of the peace, has gone back to Vienna, where his mother, the Princess Clementine, is now convalescent. A few weeks, however, may possibly alter the aspect of affairs. The time for active operations in Macedonia has not, so the Athen's correspondent of the *Times* assures us, yet arrived. But it may not be long delayed.

There would seem to be no present remedy for the deplorably unsatisfactory working of the mixed tribunal at Cairo. M. Bellet, President of the Court of Appeal at Alexandria, was asked to come to the rescue, but he declared it to be impossible for the Egyptian Government to provide a remedy, "because it is obliged to accept the nominees of the various European Governments, who are too often mere incapables," some of them without either legal or judicial training. Which are the Governments that thus make Cairo a dumping ground for their favourite noodles?

The gold exported from New Zealand during March amounted to 24,467 oz., of the value of £94,857, as against 18,644 oz., value £72,702 in the same month last year.

There has been a serious mistake somewhere as to the cost of the proposed foot tunnel under the Thames at Greenwich. The amount for which the London County Council obtained the sanction of Parliament was only £70,500, but the amended estimates now show that the total cost will not be less than £155,150. The acceptance of tenders is, therefore, postponed to enable the Council to obtain Parliamentary sanction for the additional cost.

There is further trouble for Spain—a rising in Celbu, one of the Philippine group. It may be serious, though it is said at present to be of "no importance." Of course no rising is officially admitted to be of importance until it is impossible to hush it up or hide it.

The gold output of Victoria amounted for the first quarter of the year to 174,754 oz., an increase of 13,968 oz.

Messrs. J. & R. Coats, the great Paisley thread firm, are said to have been making experiments with a thread which, after undergoing a particular process, gives an imitation of silk. What success has been obtained is not yet known. Similar experiments have been made by other firms, and a Bradford house did obtain a fair result, but actual success cannot be said to have been obtained yet by any of them.

After having been closed for nine years, the Alexandra Palace at Muswell Hill has been re-opened as a place of entertainment. It was well patronised during the holidays ; but whether it will prove popular enough to produce a dividend for the patient shareholders remains to be seen.

Francis Richard H. Jordan, the absconding director of the Brinsmead Company, who was arrested at Capetown on March 23, has been brought up at the Mansion House, charged with fraud in connection with the formation of the company, and remanded in custody. He was undefended and said little himself.

The Clyde Trustees recently made reductions in river dues calculated to amount to £17,370 ; but this amount has already been made up by increased trade, and if the present ratio of increase continues, the Trust will have a surplus of £50,000 for the year.

The American-Australian Line steamer, which left Sydney on the 10th inst., took 300,000 sovereigns for San Francisco.

Sir Frederick Abel has issued what is ostensibly a defence of the Imperial Institute, but is really only an excuse for its shortcomings, and in considerable measure a confession of failure. Sir Frederick admits it was "an unfortunate circumstance" that the Institute was placed so far from the commercial centre of London, that it has not practically realised the proposed system of commercial correspondence with the colonies, and that a lack of funds has prevented other work that was contemplated being accomplished. However ornamental, the Institute has certainly proved a useless establishment.

We are glad to hear that the plague mortality in Bombay is steadily decreasing, while the returns of the Port Trust show a substantial recovery in Bombay trade during the quarter.

Traveller's tales continue to come from Klondyke. The latest is that of three miners, who assert that about 20 tons of gold—worth about £2,000,000—will be sent out as soon as navigation opens. Of course, there are also the usual stories of the finding of big nuggets. We must wait for their confirmation, however, "until the navigation opens."

An Imperial Ukase has been issued in Russia decreeing that the total amount of fine silver roubles and small coins in circulation shall not amount to more than three times as many roubles as there are people in Russia. Fine silver roubles are to be lawful tender up to 25 roubles as between private individuals, and the Imperial treasury will accept payments in silver of any sum whatsoever, except in the case of Customs dues or other imports paid in gold, where only accounts not exceeding five roubles may be paid in silver.

The President of the Council at Athens has been assuring Thessalian deputies that the evacuation of Thessaly will certainly commence on April 15. The Turkish troops, we are further told, are ready to move to Volo, the port of debarkation, and the commandant has given orders for a complete abstention from excesses. We are glad to hear it, and shall be still more glad to see the evacuation successfully completed.

They seem to take things very leisurely at the Japanese Treasury. The final accounts of the expenditure and revenue in connection with the war were only presented to the throne a few weeks ago after verification by the Board of Auditors. The total expenditure is given as 200,915,508 yen.

Here is good news from New York. There seems some prospect of a comparatively early arrangement of the Alaskan sealing question being concluded. The United States proposed it, and Lord Salisbury assented, suggesting that other Canadian questions be submitted simultaneously to a joint commission. To this the American President agreed, and a Conference on the subject will shortly assemble at Washington.

Railway Traffic Returns.

Burma Railways. — Receipts for week ending March 5, Rs. 2,07,073; decrease, Rs. 6,096. Aggregate from January 1, Rs. 18,85,292; decrease, Rs. 2,76,018.

Great Western of Brazil Railway.—Traffic for week ending February 26, $32,551; increase, $2,282. Aggregate receipts to date $376,101; increase, $41,096.

Alcoy and Gandia Railway and Harbour Company.—Traffic for week, April 9:—Ps. 5,400, increase Ps. 150. Aggregate from January 1, Ps. 134,700, increase Ps. 3,800.

Villa Maria and Rufino Railway.—Traffic for week ending April 9, $2,976; decrease, $784. Aggregate from January 1, $66,898, decrease $1,472.

West Flanders Railway.—Gross receipts for week ending April 10, £2,045; increase, £171. Total from January 1, £31,246; increase, £840.

West of India Portuguese Railway.—Week ending March 19, Rs. 3,745; increase, Rs. 960.

Quebec Central Railway.—Receipts for third week of March, $8,362; decrease, $823. Aggregate from July 1, $68,227; decrease, $9,717.

Mobile and Birmingham Railroad.—Traffic for third week of March, $7,472; increase, $856. Aggregate from July 1, $275,874; decrease, $3,991.

Algeciras (Gibraltar) Railway.—Traffic for week ended April 2, Ps. 18,950; increase Ps. 540. Aggregate from July 1, Ps. 795,882; increase, Ps. 24,328.

Bengal Central Railway.—Traffic for week ending March 15, Rs. 19,300; increase, Rs. 550. Total from January 1, Rs. 2,05,797; increase, Rs. 23,893

Assam-Bengal Railway.—Traffic for week ended February 26, Rs. 27,005; increase, Rs. 2,645. Aggregate from January 1, Rs. 2,00,014; increase, Rs. 22,400.

Atlantic and Danville Railway.—Traffic receipts for month of March, $53,321; increase, $7,337.

Midland Uruguay Railway.—Receipts for month of March, £3,510; increase, £395.

Bengal Central Railway.—Traffic receipts for the week ended March 19, Rs. 20,256; increase, Rs. 3,158; aggregate from January, Rs. 228,087; increase, Rs. 29,085.

Burma Railways.—Traffic return for week ending March 19, Rs. 2,07,025; decrease, Rs. 5,409. Aggregate from January 1st, Rs. 21,08,173; decrease, Rs. 2,66,171.

Cockermouth and Keswick Railway.—Traffic return for week ending April 9, £803; increase, £64. Aggregate from January 1, £10,740; increase, £1,081.

Delhi Umballa Kalka Railway.—Receipts for week ended April 9, Rs. 34,000; increase Rs. 2,800. Aggregate from January 1, Rs, 5,18,300; increase, 1,49,400.

Cleator and Workington Junction Railway.—Traffic receipts for week ending April 9, £919; decrease, £145. Aggregate from January 1, £14,293; decrease, £754.

Rohilkund and Kumaon Railway.—Traffic receipts for week ending March 12, Rs. 6,525; decrease, Rs. 3,064. Aggregate from January 1, Rs. 57,034; decrease, Rs. 11,783.

Great Western of Brazil.—Traffic receipts for week ending March 5, $36,171; increase, $14,360. Aggregate from January 1, $412,273; increase, $55,456.

ENGLISH RAILWAYS.

Div. for half years. 1896	1896	1897	1897	Last Balance forward.	Amt. to pay 1 p.c. on Ord. for ½ yr.	Name.	Date.	Gross Traffic for week: Amt.	Inc. or dec. on 1897.	Inc. or dec. on 1896.	No. of weeks	Gross Traffic for half-year to date: Amt.	Inc. or dec. on 1897.	Inc. or dec. on 1896.	Mileage.	Inc. on 1897.	Working	Prior Charges last ½ year.	Prop. add Cap. Exp. this ½ year
				£	£												%	£	£
10	10	10	10	2,707	5,094	Barry	Apr. 9	4,432	−4,074	−3,306	15	130,308	+203	+18,319	31	—	8·29	60,665	316,853
nil	nil	nil	nil	—	—	Brecon and Merthyr	" 10	1,224	−179	−489	15	21,859	+369	−1,542	61	—	—	—	—
nil	nil	nil	nil	3,979	4,749	Cambrian	" 10	5,436	+294	+280	*	64,032	+1,272	—	250	—	60·96	63,148	40,000
1½	1½	2	1½	1,510	3,150	City and South London ..	" 10	884	−137	+16	15	15,826	−13	+1,487	3½	—	56·67	5,552	124,000
2	2	1½	2	7,895	13,210	Furness .. — ..	" 10	8,632	−287	−66	*	124,057	+2,974	—	139	—	49·88	97,423	20,910
1	1½	½	1	2,207	27,470	Great Cent. (late M., S., & L.)	" 10	43,686	+1,062	+3,795	14	593,757	+8,116	+34,084	352½	—	57.17	627,386	1,200,000
2½	4½	2	5	51,283	62,865	Great Eastern	" 10	†95,954	+15,499	‡+17293	14	1,101,262	+46,749	+92,676	1,158¼	2	55·35	860,138	250,000
3	5¼	3	5	15,094	102,496	Great Northern	" 10	†97,673	+4,325	‡+12311	15	1,394,784	+44,551	+105308	1,071	8	61·36	641,485	750,000
4½	7¼	4½	7¼	31,350	121,981	Great Western	" 10	†184,270	+3,090	‡+2,630	14	2,396,320	+45,300	+105060	2,582	21	51·44	1,486,272	800,000
nil	2	nil	1½	8,951	16,487	Hull and Barnsley	" 10	6,450	+231	+1,198	14	89,560	−915	+8,280	73	—	58·21	70,290	52,844
5	5¼	5	5¼	21,495	83,704	Lancashire and Yorkshire ..	" 10	†109,105	+19,421	‡+15725	14	1,277,574	+51,477	+44,783	555½	25	56·70	674,745	451,976
4¾	8	4½	8¼	26,243	43,049	Lon., Brighton, & S. Coast	" 9	†63,953	+14,865	‡+9,010	15	700,787	+41,902	+34,898	470½	—	50·20	407,042	240,735
nil	nil	nil	nil	72,294	56,296	London, Chatham, & Dover	" 10	†35,402	+7,525	‡+4,959	14	371,621	+16,861	+19,789	185½	—	50·65	367,873	nil
6½	8	6½	7½	89,535	204,068	London and North Western	" 10	†241,572	+10,467	+21,992	14	3,153,232	+76,714	+176177	1,911½	—	56·92	1,404,534	600,000
5	8½	8½	8½	23,038	59,367	London and South Western	" 10	†83,984	+17,670	‡+9,460	14	924,853	+49,883	+55,933	941	6½	51·75	513,740	389,000
2½	6	2½	6½	14,592	6,691	Lon., Tilbury, & Southend	" 10	†5,996	+1,019	‡+447	15	71,758	+5,090	+11,134	81	—	52·37	39,590	15,000
3½	3⅞	3¾	3⅞	17,133	26,409	Metropolitan	" 10	16,449	+164	+500	*	230,835	+5,200	—	64	—	43·63	148,047	254,000
nil	nil	nil	nil	4,006	11,250	Metropolitan District ..	" 10	†7,503	−794	—	14	119,993	+3,712	—	13	—	48·70	119,663	38,450
5	7	5½	6½	38,143	174,582	Midland	" 10	†198,601	+7,177	+18,713	15	2,725,541	+45,586	+183137	1,354¾	15½	57·39	1,216,582	650,000
5½	7¼	5¾	7	22,374	138,189	North Eastern	" 9	†153,744	+5,809	‡+12738	14	1,964,754	+26,343	+87,880	1,597¾	—	58·82	795,077	436,004
7¼	7½	7½	7½	7,061	10,102	North London	" 10			Not recd			not	recvd.	12	—	50·90	49,973	7,600
4	5	4	4½	4,745	16,150	North Staffordshire	" 10	17,082	+821	+901	15	234,129	+6,563	+13,448	312	—	55·27	118,142	19,605
10	10	11		1,642	3,004	Rhymney	" 9	2,912	−160	−1,514	15	73,569	−571	+6,590	71	—	49·68	29,049	16,700
3	6⅛	3½	6⅛	4,054	50,215	South Eastern	" 9	†58,238	+15,379	‡+10757	*	585,813	+40,277	—	448	—	51·88	380,763	250,000
3½	3½	3½	3½	2,315	25,961	Taff Vale	" 9	6,205	−8,299	−8,229	15	217,235	−15,991	−1,421	121	—	54·90	94,800	92,000

* From January 1. † Includes Good Friday Traffic. ‡ Includes Easter week.

SCOTCH RAILWAYS.

5	5	5¼	5	9,544	78,066	Caledonian	Apr. 10	76,188	+ 5,183	+ †1,896	10	706,165	+ 19,864	+ 38,787	851½	5	50·38	588,248	441,477
5	5½	5	5	7,364	24,639	Glasgow and South-Western	" 9	29,790	+ 1,569	+ †821	10	268,247	+ 8,960	+ 12,494	393½	—	54·69	221,663	196,145
3½	3½	3½	—	1,291	4,600	Great North of Scotland	" 9	8,070	− 419	− 63	10	75,479	− 321	+ 1,264	331	15½	52·03	92,178	60,000
	nil		—	10,477	12,820	Highland	" 10	9,601	+ 668	+ 976	6	50,949	+ 1,886	+ 3,396	479¾	27¾	58·63	78,976	,000
	1½	1	1¼	819	45,819	North British	" 10	76,800	+ 3,780	+ 2,899	10	685,863	+ 18,179	+ 22,197	1,230	23	48·62	944,809	40,500

† Glasgow Spring Holiday.

IRISH RAILWAYS.

6½	6½	6½	—	5,466	1,790	Belfast and County Down ..	Apr. 8	2,095	+ 112	− 1,512	*	28,631	+ 887	—	76½	—	55·58	17,690	10,000
5½	6½	5½	—	—	4,984	Belfast and Northern Counties	" 8	5,834	+ 1,040	− 313	*	70,443	+ 4,278	—	249	—	—	—	—
2	3	2	—	1,418	1,200	Cork, Bandon, and S. Coast† ..	" 9	1,327	− 37	− 36	*	16,543	− 1,198	—	103	—	54·82	14,436	5,452
6½	6¾	6½	6¾	38,776	17,816	Great Northern	" 8	15,153	+ 776	− 1,123	14	197,509	+ 10,273	+ 10,707	528	36	50·18	88,068	22,000
5½	5½	5½	5½	30,339	24,855	Great Southern and Western ..	" 8	—	—	—	not	received	—	—	603	13	51·45	72,8—	46,562
	4	4	4½	11,372	11,850	Midland Great Western ..	" 8	9,633	+ 204	− 108	14	131,526	+ 5,572	+ 7,336	538	—	50·31	83,129	1,800
nil	nil	nil	nil	229	2,822	Waterford and Central ..	" 8	765	− 99	—	*	11,926	+ 1,447	—	59½	—	53·24	6,858	1,500
nil	nil	nil	nil	1,936	2,987	Waterford, Limerick & W. ..	" 8	3,200	− 472	+ 31	*	70,311	+ 2,926	—	350½	—	57·83	42,617	7,075

* From January 1. † Eight weeks' strike.

FOREIGN RAILWAYS.

Mileage. Total.	Increase on 1897.	Increase on 1896.	Name	Gross Traffic for Week. Week ending	Amount.	In. or Dec. upon 1897.	In. or Dec. upon 1896.	Gross Traffic to Date. No. of Weeks.	Amount.	In. or Dec. upon 1897.	In. or Dec. upon 1896.
					£	£	£		£	£	£
319	—	—	Argentine Great Western	Apr. 8	6,311	+ 904	+ 2,133	39	222,560	− 13,738	− 44,141
76½	—	—	Bahia and San Francisco	Mar. 19	3,330	+ 881	+ 1,483	12	35,707	+ 10,130	+ 13,741
234	48	84	Bahia Blanca and North West	Mar. 13	762	− 160	—	37	29,126	+ 212	—
74	—	—	Buenos Ayres and Ensenada	Apr. 10	3,316	− 648	− 973	14	48,778	− 8,717	− 13,230
425	—	—	Buenos Ayres and Pacific	Apr. 9	8,126	− 1,628	+ 320	40	263,549	− 54,197	+ 6,357
914	1	3	Buenos Ayres and Rosario	Apr. 9	16,611	+ 5,016	+ 3,812	14	246,915	+ 66,330	+ 41,298
2,499	30	68	Buenos Ayres Great Southern	Apr. 10	31,597	− 1,142	+ 3,424	40	1,198,831	+ 86,116	+ 176,050
602	107	177	Buenos Ayres Western	Apr. 10	11,047	− 1,922	− 4,682	40	464,264	− 79,129	− 85,508
845	55	77	Central Argentine	Apr. 9	20,108	+ 4,484	+ 3,701	14	313,583	+ 77,808	+ 20,644
297	—	—	Central Bahia	Jan. 31*	$133,550	− $3,944	+ $12,758	—	—	—	—
271	—	—	Central Uruguay of Monte Video	Apr. 9	4,928	+ 1,781	− 772	40	238,759	+ 11,407	− 16,552
228	—	—	Do. Eastern Extension	Apr. 9	1,348	+ 665	− 258	40	50,830	+ 6,323	− 1,737
182	—	—	Do. Northern Extension	Apr. 9	465	+ 208	− 350	40	25,238	− 341	− 6,943
180	—	—	Cordoba and Rosario	Apr. 3	2,245	+ 430	+ 125	40	85,565	− 15,275	− 1,845
298	—	—	Cordoba Central	Apr. 3	$22,000	− $3,170	− $5,660	13	$282,700	− $45,570	− $64,021
549	—	—	Do. Northern Extension	Apr. 3	$51,000	− $11,340	− $16,650	13	$583,790	− $215,930	− $123,580
237	—	—	Costa Rica	Mar. 26	5,864	− 726	− 17	13	68,357	− 16,888	− 2,591
99	—	—	East Argentine	Feb. 20	970	+ 293	+ 243	7	5,286	− 411	− 321
386	—	6	Entre Rios	Apr. 9	2,062	+ 1,091	+ 495	40	64,021	+ 18,151	+ 15,247
555	—	24	Inter Oceanic of Mexico	Apr. 9	$63,700	+ $14,400	+ $22,650	40	$2,310,790	+ $364,140	+ $718,869
23	—	—	La Guaira and Caracas	Feb. 25	1,779	− 779	− 1,138	8	15,641	− 5,235	− 3,525
321	—	—	Mexican	Apr. 9	$77,200	+ $4,200	—	14	$1,142,400	+ $104,050	—
1,846	—	—	Mexican Central	Apr. 7	$278,789	+ $38,617	+ $92,710	14	$3,539,007	+ $888,987	+ $888,743
1,217	—	—	Mexican National	Apr. 7	$113,027	+ $7,651	+ $36,918	14	$1,539,717	+ $202,217	+ $301,484
228	—	—	Mexican Southern	Apr. 7	$14,660	− $119	+ $4,097	—	—	—	—
206	—	—	Minas and Rio	Feb. 31*	$128,262	+ $16,417	—	8 mos.	$1,436,813	+ $203,482	—
94	—		N. W. Argentine	Apr. 9	1,460	+ 9	—	14	—	—	—
242	3	—	Nitrate	Mar. 31†	16,187	− 1,604	− 4,405	11	88,690	− 328	− 40,320
300	—	—	Ottoman	Apr. 3	4,839	− 348	+ 862	13	65,303	− 15,565	+ 7,026
77½	—	—	Recife and San Francisco	Feb. 12	6,410	+ 267	− 508	7	39,133	+ 892	− 6,509
86½	—	—	San Paulo	Feb. 27†	17,481	− 7,056	—	8	88,485	− 16,073	—
186	—	—	Santa Fe and Cordova	Apr. 9†	2,394	+ 957	− 824	41	67,179	− 6,465	− 2,132
110	—	—	Western of Havana	Apr. 9	1,680	− 115	+ 680	40	71,470	+ 5,534	+ 5,295

* For month ended. † For fortnight ended.

INDIAN RAILWAYS.

Mileage. Total.	Increase on 1897.	Increase on 1896.	Name.	Gross Traffic for Week. Week ending	Amount.	In. or Dec. on 1897.	In. or Dec. on 1896.	Gross Traffic to Date. No. of Weeks.	Amount.	In. or Dec. on 1897.	In. or Dec. on 1896.
862	—	—	Bengal Nagpur	Apr. 9	Rs.1.80.000	+ Rs.43.846	+ Rs.25.696	13	Rs.21.38.651	+ Rs.16.865	− Rs.270.633
827	8	63	Bengal and North-Western	Mar. 12	Rs.1.22.840	+ Rs.9.800	+ Rs.1.933	11	Rs.13.41.190	+ Rs.1.74.123	− Rs.30.540
461	—	—	Bombay and Baroda	Apr. 9	£35,017	+ £8,941	− £5,937	15	£351,338	− £14,042	− £140,979
1,885	2	13	East Indian	Apr. 9	Rs.12.41.000	− Rs.30.000	+ Rs.87.000	14	Rs.1.76.44.000	+ Rs.2.73.000	+ Rs13.38.000
1,491	—	—	Great Indian Penin.	Apr. 9	£80,236	+ £27,454	− £4,747	14	£951,694	+ £119,268	− £200,402
736	—	—	Indian Midland	Apr. 9	Rs.1.48.990	+ Rs.31.453	+ Rs.24.270	14	Rs.19.13.385	+ Rs.91.074	+ Rs329.580
840	—	—	Madras	Apr. 2	£19,983	+ £642	+ £1,925	13	£250,602	− £14,073	− £7,726
1,043	—	—	South Indian	Mar. 19	Rs.1.45.240	− Rs.13.548	− Rs.14.384	11	Rs.1.503.668	− Rs.239.870	− Rs237.346

UNITED STATES AND CANADIAN RAILWAYS.

Mileage. Total.	Increase on 1897.	Increase on 1896.	Name.	Gross Traffic for Week. Period Ending.	Amount.	In. or Dec. on 1897.	Gross Traffic to Date. No. of Weeks.	Amount.	In. or Dec. on 1897.
					dols.	dols.		dols.	dols.
917	—	—	Baltimore & Ohio S. Western	Apr. 7	132,000	+ 18,000	39	5,240,376	+ 540,785
6,568	92	156	Canadian Pacific	Apr. 7	448,000	+ 69,000	13	5,665,000	+ 1,172,000
922	—	—	Chicago Great Western	Apr. 7	87,792	− 10,593	39	4,153,877	+ 523,427
6,169	—	469	Chicago, Mil., & St. Paul	Apr. 7	607,000	+ 113,000	13	8,279,101	+ 1,236,300
1,685	—	—	Denver & Rio Grande	Apr. 7	143,000	+ 21,000	39	6,267,900	+ 1,047,700
3,512	—	—	Grand Trunk, Main Line	Apr. 7	£77,638	+ £5,668	13	£997,763	+ £101,648
335	—	—	Do. Chic. & Grand Trunk	Apr. 7	£15,625	+ £3,550	13	£209,759	+ £48,429
189	—	—	Do. Det., G. H. & Mil.	Apr. 7	£3,527	− £562	13	£48,110	− £2,805
2,938	—	—	Louisville & Nashville	Apr. 7	383,000	+ 10,000	13	5,627,175	+ 975,600
2,197	137	137	Miss., K., & Texas	Apr. 7	200,601	− 27,036	39	9,936,536	+ 535,975
477	—	—	N. Y., Ontario, & W.	Apr. 7	58,510	− 8,018	39	2,996,707	+ 96,356
1,570	—	—	Norfolk & Western	Apr. 7	225,000	+ 16,000	39	8,315,000	+ 886,000
3,499	336	—	Northern Pacific	Mar. 21	390,000	+ 105,000	11	4,070,000	+ 1,216,000
1,223	—	—	St. Louis S. Western	Mar. 21	89,000	+ 25,000	11	1,217,790	+ 236,100
4,654	—	—	Southern	Apr. 7	381,000	+ 40,000	39	4,626,812	+ 1,297,448
1,979	—	—	Wabash	Apr. 7	236,000	+ 44,000	13	3,328,406	+ 673,000

MONTHLY STATEMENTS.

Mileage. Total.	Increase on 1896	Increase on 1895.	Name.	Net Earnings for Month. Month.	Amount.	In. or Dec. on 1897.	In. or Dec. on 1896.	Net Earnings to Date. No. of Months.	Amount.	In. or Dec. on 1897.	In. or Dec. on 1896.
					dols.	dols.	dols.		dols.	dols.	dols.
6,935	44	444	Atchison	February	746,000	+ 191,000	+ 129,318	2	1,240,434	+ 313,670	− 139,884
16,547	203	106	Canadian Pacific	February	424,000	+ 39,000	+ 19,268	2	940,000	+ 182,000	+ 110,328
6,169	—	469	Chicago, Mil., & St. Paul	January	757,000	+ 52,000	− 30,773	—	—	—	—
1,685	—	—	Denver & Rio Grande	February	219,000	+ 52,500	+ 22,731	8	2,244,907	+ 367,739	− 8,088
1,970	—	—	Erie	January	371,000	+ 33,000	− 107,852	—	—	—	—
3,512	—	—	Grand Trunk, Main Line	February	£56,453	+ £13,757	+ £25,860	2	£143,853	+ £48,041	+ 64,910
335	—	—	Do. Chic. & Grand Trunk	February	£8,210	+ £5,197	+ 5,595	2	£21,310	+ £14,130	+ 15,582
189	—	—	Do. Det. G. H. & Mil.	February	£528	− £1,369	− 207	2	£2,328	− £677	+ 1,459
3,127	—	239	Illinois Central*	February	2,177,767	+ 413,527	+ 422,489	2	4,481,665	+ 819,013	+ 805,758
2,396	—	—	New York Central*	February	3,429,000	+ 198,000	+ 222,359	2	6,934,000	+ 492,597	249,393
477	—	—	New York Ontario, & W.	February	57,800	− 3,800	+ 19,504	9	835,700	+ 33,400	+ 75,462
1,570	—	—	Norfolk & Western	February	242,000	+ 69,000	+ 43,259	2	525,000	+ 83,247	+ 91,585
3,407	—	—	Pennsylvania	January	1,359,102	+ 65,700	+ 230,000	2	2,511,898	92,400	+ 345,000
1,055	—	—	Phil. & Reading	February	[illegible]	[illegible]	—	8	[illegible]	+ 446,422	—

* [illegible] of gross traffic.

Prices Quoted on the London Stock Exchange.

Throughout the INVESTORS' REVIEW middle prices alone are quoted, the object being to give the public the approximate current quotations of every security of any consequence in existence. On the markets the buying and selling prices are both given, and are often wide apart where stocks are seldom dealt in. Other particulars will be found in the INVESTMENT INDEX published quarterly—January, April, July, and October—in connection with this REVIEW, price 2s., by post 2s. 2d. Where dividends are paid only once a year, an *italic* type is used to distinguish them. The London Stock Exchange Official List is quoted in the REVIEW almost entire, only very insignificant issues, or bonds falling due within the next two or three years, being omitted. But the list is subdivided into the leading, or active, stocks, and those less frequently dealt in. The former will be found under the head of "Stock Markets," and with more details than it is possible to give for the bulk of securities. By retaining the file of the INVESTORS' REVIEW any subscriber can follow for himself the movements of securities from week to week, and the INVESTMENT INDEX will from time to time help to fill up deficiencies in the information.

Tea Companies and Mines and Mining Finance Stocks are placed in special lists.

Among the abbreviations used are the following:—S.F. Snk. Fd. *sinking fund*; Certs., *certificates*; Debs. or Dbs., *debentures*; Db. or D.Stk., *debenture stock*; Pf., Prf., or Pref., *preference*; Prefd. or Pfd., *preferred*; Dfd., *deferred*; L. or Ltd., *limited*; Sh., *share*; Ans., *annuities*; Cu. or Cm., *cumulative*; Gu or Guar., *guaranteed*; Bds., *bonds*; S., Sr., or Ser., *series*; In., Ins., Insc., *inscribed*; Dr., Drgs., Drwgs., *drawings*; Stg., Strlg., *sterling*; Lia., *liable to*; Sp., Surp., *surplus*; Per., Perp., *perpetual*; Ln. *lien*; Lo. *loan*.

The dates following the names of securities are the years of issue or of redemption. Where shares are not fully paid up, their nominal amount is given with the name so that investors may know the liability upon them.

BRITISH FUNDS, &c.

Rate	Name.	Price.
2¾	2¾ p.c.'s (Childers') Red.. 1905	104
3	Local Loans Stk. 1912	110
3	Metro. Police Deb. Stk. 1920	105½
—	Red Sea Ind. Tel. Ann. 1908	8½
4	Canada Gv. "Intcl. Rly." 1903	104
4	Do. do. .. 1908	111
4	Do. Bonds 1910	112
4	Do. Bonds 1913	117½
3	Egyptian Gov. Gar.	106½
3	Mauritius Ins. Stk. 1940	114
4	Turkish Guar. 1855	109
11½	Bank of Ireland Stk.	390
3½	India Rupee Paper	61
3½	Do. 1854-5	62
3	Do. 1896-7 1916	55
3½	Isle of Man Deb.	104
3	Do. Deb. Stk... 1919-29	103

CORPORATION AND COUNTY STOCKS.

FREE OF STAMP DUTY.

Rate	Name.	Price.
3½	Metropolitan Con. 1929	116½
3	Do. 1941	109
2½	Do. 1920-40	99
2½	L.C.C. Con. Stock 1920	99
3½	Comm. of Sewers, Scp., S.F. 1905	106
3½	Corp. of Lond. Bds...1897-1902	100½
3	Do. 1897-1912	101
3½	Do, Debs. Scp. ...... S.F. 1916	105
2½	Do., Deb. Stk. Scrip .. 1927-57	99
3	Barnsley 1916-46	105
3	Barry 1914-46	101
3	Bath 1909-34	102
3	Batley 1914-44	101½
3½	Birmingham 1945	121
3	Do. 1947	111
2½	Do. 1926	98
3	Blackburn 1930	106½
3	Bournemouth 1913-33	103
3½	Bradford 1945	116½
3	Do. Deb. Stock .. 1954	108
3	Brighouse 1916-46	100
3½	Brighton 1946	117
2½	Do. 1957	97
3	Burton-on-Trent 1913-43	102½
3	Cambridge 1913-43	103
3½	Cardiff 1935	116½
3	Do. 1914-54	103
3	Cheltenham 1971	108
3	Chichester 1916-46	101
3½	Croydon	134
3	Do. 1940	102½
3	Derby 1920-50	107
3	Devon C.C. 1917-33	104½
3½	Dewsbury 1930	109
3	Do. 1930	103
3	Dorset County 1922-32	105
3	Douglas (I. of Man) 1926	101
3	Dover 1913-43	101
3½	Dublin 1944	113½
3	Eastbourne 1920-40	104
3	Edinburgh 1924	108
2½	Do. 1927	98
2½	Exeter 1917-57	96
3	Glamorgan County 1914-34	104
3½	Glasgow 1914	110½
3	Do. 1921	106½
2½	Do. 1925-40	99
3	Gloster 1915-55	101
3	Grimsby 1913-45	103
3	Hampshire County 1914-34	105½
3	Hanley 1913-43	105
3	Harrogate 1914-34	103
3	Hastings 1915-54	103½
2½	Hertfordshire C.C. 1916-36	98
3	Heston & Isleworth U.D.C. 1915-35	101
3	Huddersfield 1934	107
3½	Hull (1st iss.)	131½
3	Inverness 1914-44	101
3	Ipswich 1952	108½
3	Lancaster 1919-55	103
2½	Leeds 1927	98
3½	Leicester 1934	116
3	Lincoln 1910	102
3½	Liverpool	132½

Corporation, &c. (*continued*):—

Rate	Name.	Price.
3	Manchester 1941	108½
3	Mansfield 1915-45	100
3½	Middlesbro' 1909	105½
3½	Do. 1911-13	105
3	Do. 1915	104
3	Middlesex C.C. 1915-35	106
3½	Newcastle 1936	118½
3½	Do. Irred.	129½
2½	Do. 1915-36	100
3	Newcastle-under-Lyme.. 1909-44	101
3	Newport (Mon.) 1915-55	101½
3	Norwich 1952	111½
3	Nottingham	114
3	Oxford 1951	109½
3	Penzance 1916-46	100½
3	Plymouth 1942	110
3	Pontypridd U.D.C. 1916-46	98
3	Poole 1915-45	101
3½	Portsmouth ......1916 24 & 27	112
3	Do. 1913-33	106½
3	Ramsey 1920-40	100
3	Ramsgate 1915-55	102
3½	Reading	130½
3	Do. 1962	109
3½	Rhyl U.D.C. 1953	110
3	Richmond (Surrey) 1942	104½
3	River Wear Debt Certs.	100
3	St. Helen's 1915-55	102
3	Scarbro' 1915-50	102
2½	Sheffield 1925-57	96
3	Shipley U.D.C. 1915-35	100
3	Somerset Co. 1923-33	106
3	South Shields 1915-45	102
2½	Southampton 1915-45	102
3	Southend-on-Sea 1916-46	102
3	Staffs C.C. 1915-35	102
3	Stockport 1914-54	103
3-	Stockton 1932	104
3	Do. 1915-35	103
3	Surrey Co. 1922-32	105½
3½	Swansea	130
3	Do. 1955	106
3	Taunton 1918 3-9-43	101
3	Tees Conserv. Deb. Stk. 1947	100
3	Thames Conserv. "A" Deb. Stk. 1954	103½
3	Do. "B" Deb. Stk. 1954	103½
3	Torquay 1913-43	101½
3	Tunbridge Wells 1931	101½
3	Tynemouth 1913	101
3	Wakefield 1929	101½
3	Walsall 1932	108
3	West Bromwich 1930	106½
3½	West Ham 1929	110
3	Do. 1945	105
3	West Sussex C.C. 1915-35	106
3	Weston-s.-Mare Lcl Bd. 1914-44	101½
3	Weymouth&Melc. Regis 1918	101
3	Widnes 1915-55	101
3	Wigan 1921	106
3	Windsor 1918-55	102
3½	Wisbech 1947	113½
3½	Wolverhampton 1932	118
3	Do. 1924-54	107
3	York 1916-41	106½

SUBJECT TO STAMP DUTY.

Rate	Name.	Price.
3½	Belfast City & Dis. Watr. 1938	114
3	Do. Red Stk. 1953-6	106
3½	Belfast 1924	103
4	Blackburn Con. Deb. Irred.	141½
3½	Do. do. Irred.	130
3½	Bristol	130½
3½	Burnley 1933	114
2½	Chesterfield Gas & Wtr. 1916-46	98
3½	Douglas Town 1921	105
3	Dover Harb. 1st Deb... 1936	104½
3½	Hull (2nd iss.)	128½
4	Leeds Deb. 1927	124
3½	Do.	115½
3	Do. 1927	106
3	Leicester 1919-44	105
4	Manchester	148
3	Do. 1928	104½
4½	Middlesboro' Mrts. 1908	111
3½	Newark on-Trent — 1901-41	96
3½	Sheffield 1898-1916	105½
3½	Do. 1925-36	114
3	Do. 1925	104½
3½	Southampton .... S.F.	106
4½	Stockton Morts. 1908	110½
3½	Worcester 1950	109

COLONIAL AND PROVINCIAL GOVERNMENT SECURITIES.

Rate	Name.	Price.
6	British Columbia 1907	119½
4½	Do. Debs... 1917	111½
3	British Guiana Imgtn. Bds.	99½
5	Canada, "Intercol. Rail," 1903	109
4	Do. (Bonds) 1904-5-6-8	106
4	Do. Reduced 1910	107½
3½	Do. Bnds. 1909-34	104
4	Do. Loan 1910-35	107½
3	Do. Loan 1938	101
6	Cape of G. Hope 1900	—
5	Do. 1900	—
4½	Do. red. by an. draw.	109
4½	Do. 1879	109
4	Do. 1881	108
4	Do. 1917-23	113½
4½	Ceylon	110
4	Do.	106½
4½	Fiji Gov. Deb. Sink. Fd.	101½
4	Jamaica Sink. Fd. 1923	103
5	Manitoba Debs 1910	113
5	Do. Ster. Bds. 1888	119½
4	Do. Ster. Debs.	106
4	Mauritius, Cons. Debs. 1880....	103½
4½	Natal, Sink. Fd. 1919	118
4	Do. do. 1926	115
3½	Newfoundland Stg. Bds. 1941	97
3½	Do. do. .. 1947	97
3	Do. do.	86½
5	New South Wales 1897-1902	104½
4	Do. 1903-5-8-9-10	105
5	New Zealand 1914	118
5	Do. Cnsls. 1 p.c. per an. Sink. Fd.	104
3½	Nova Scotia Debs.	104
5	Quebec Prov. 1904-6	110
4½	Do. (drgs.)	104
5	Do. Strlg. Bds. 1912	115
4	Do. Strlg. Bds. 1928	110
4	Do. Strlg. Bds. 1934	108
4	Queensland 1913-15	105
4½	St. Lucia Debs.	102½
6	South Australia 1897-1900	103½
6	Do. 1901-1918	119
5	Do. 1911-1920	116
4	Do. 1899-1916	105
4	Do. 1929	108½
4	Do. 1916	106½
4	Do. 1917-18-24	109
6	Tasmania 1897-1901	104
4	Do. 1908-11, 1913-14-20	107½
5	Trinidad Debs., an. drw. 1 p c...	106
4	Victoria 1899-1901	101½
4½	Do. 1904	105
4	Do. Rail. Loan 1907	104
4	Do. Loans 1908-13	105
4½	West. Austr. 1 p.c. ar. Sink. Fd.	107
4	Do. do.	106

REGISTERED AND INSCRIBED STOCKS.

No stamp duty except for Canada 4 p.c. Reduced (½ per cent.).

Rate	Name.	Price.
4	Antigua Insc. Stk. Red. 1919-44	109
3½	Barbados Insc. Stk. 1925-42	108
3	British Colum. Insc. Stk. 1941	101½
4	British Guiana Insc. 1935	118½
4	Canada Stk. Regd. ..1904-5-6-8	106
4	Do. 4 p.c. (late 5 p.c.) Regd. 1910	106½
3½	Do. 3½ p.c. Stock Regd. 1909-34	104
4	Do. Ln. for 4 milln. stg. 1910-35	107½
3	Do. Stk. Regd. 1938	101
2½	Do. Insc. 1947	90
4	Cape G. Hope Regd. .. 1917-23	113½
4	Do. (Ln. of '83) Insc. .. 1923	116
4	Do. Cons. Stk. Insc. 1916-36	110
3½	Do. Consol. Insc. Stock 1929-49	108
4	Ceylon Insc. Stock 1934	118½
3	Do. 1940	102
4	Grenada Insc. Stock 1917-42	112
3½	Hong Kong Insc. Stock 1918-43	103½
4	Jamaica Insc. Stock 1934	119
—	Do. 1922-44	99
4	Mauritius Inscribed 1937	118½
4	Natal Consd. Stk. Insc. 1927	115
4	Do. 1937	119
3½	Do. Inscribed Stock.. 1914-39	106
4	Newfoundland Inscribed 1913-38	106
4	Do. 1935	113
4	Do. Consd. Stk. Ins. 1936	113
4	N. S. Wales Stock Insc. 1933	116
3½	Do. 1924	104
3½	Do. 1918	104
3	D 1935	96

Colonial, &c. (*continued*):—

Rate	Name.	Price.
4	N. Zealnd. Con. Stk. Ins. 1929	111
3½	Do 1940	106
3	Do. Inscribed 1945	99
3	Quebec (Prov.) Ins. Stk. 1937	93½
4	Queensland Stock Insc. 1915-24	[illegible]
3½	Do. 1921-4-30	103
3½	Do. 1945	106
3	Do. 1922-47	97
4	St. Lucia Insc. Stock .. 1919-44	112
4	S. Austrln. (1882-7) Reg. 1915-35	107½
3½	Do. In. Stk. Reg. 1939	107
3	Do. 1916-26	99
3/	Do. 1916	99
3½	Tasmanian Insc. Stock.. 1920-40	106
4	Do. 1920-40	116
4	Trinidad Insc. Stock 1917-42	110
3	Do. 1922-44	98
4	Victoria Rly. Loan '81 Inscribed Stock 1907	104
4	Victoria Insc. Stock 1908-13-15	107
4	Victoria (1883) Ins. Stk. 1920	110
3½	Do. Inscribed Stock 1921-34	103
4	Do. do. 1911-25	108
4	W. Austral. Insc. Stock 1931	116½
4	Do. 1911-31	109
3½	Do. 1913-35	104
3	Do. 1915-37	95½
3	Do. 1916-3	97

FOREIGN STOCKS, BONDS, &c.

COUPONS PAYABLE IN LONDON.

Last Div.	Name.	Price.
36/	Argentine Ry. Loan 6 p.c. 1881	87½
15/	Do. 5 p.c. 1884	67
30/	Do. N. Cent. Ry. Ext. 5 p.c. 1887-8-9	65½
30/	Do. 5 p.c. Trsy. Convs. 1887	66
5/4½	Do. 4½ p.c. Interl. Gld. 1888	65
27/	Do. 4½ p.c. Stlg. Extrl. 1888	65
10/6	Do. 3½ p.c. External .. 1889	48
4	Do. 4 p.c. Ry. Guar. Res	56
4½	Brazilian 1883	49
4½	Do. Gold 1879	60½
4½	Do. 1888	49
36/	Buenos Ayres 1824	62½
6	Do. 1882-3-6	46
6	Bulgarian 1888	93
6	Do. Mort. Bonds 1892	93
4½	Chilian 1885	73
4½	Do. 1886	75
4½	Do. 1887	73
4½	Do. 1889	81½
5	Do. 1892	84
4½	Do. 1893	73
4½	Do. 1895	73
5	Do. 1896	83
7	Chinese Silver 1894	101
6	Do. Gold 1895	105
6	Do. Apl. '95 by dwgs. 1901-15	108½
5	Do. Red. dwgs. in 36 yr. 1896	98
5	Do. Do. Regis. 1896	98
1½	Colmbn. 1½ to 3 p.c. Ext. Bds. 1896	17½
6	Cordova, Prov. 1886	25
—	Do. Eng. Ass. Certs.	24
—	Do. 6 p.c. 1887-8	25
—	Do. Eng. Ass. Certs.	24
3	Costa Rica "A"	30
2½	Do. "B"	23
3	Danish Gold 1914	93
10/	Ecuador N. Ext. Bds. 4½ p.c. ascn. to 5 p.c.	22
3½	Egypt'n Ins. Stk. lia. Sp. Dty. 1885	100
4	Do. State Domain 1878	104½
4	Do. D. Sanieh, Red. .. 1905	104½
6	Entre Rios 1886-8	35
6	Do. Falg. Ln. Bds. 1894-1921	35
6	Do. do. Parana City	27½
15/	Greek 1881	40
15/	Do. 1884	40
12/	Do. Rentes	33
15/	Do. (Piræus-Larissa Ry.)	38
3/6	Do. Fundg. Loan 1893	44½
4	Guatemala Extl. Debt	26½
6	Hawaiian	102½
4	Hungarian Gold Rentes	101½
3	Do. 1895	91½
6	Italian Irriga. Guar.	111½
5	Do. Maremmana	94½
5	Japan 5 p c.	101
5	Mexican (Nat. R. Tehuantp c.)..	99½
6	Do. Extrl. 1893	97

Foreign Stocks, &c. (*continued*):—

Last Div.	Name.	Price.
6	Mexican Extrl. 1893	96½
5	Do. Intrnl. Cons. Slvr.	36
5	Do. Intern. Rd. Bds. 2d. Ser.	36
4	Nicaragua 1886	50
3½	Norwegian, red. 1937, or earlier	98
3	Do. do. 1905, do.	98
3½	Do. 3½ p.c. Bnds.	104
1	Paraguay 1p.c. ris. 3p.c. 1886-96	16
5	Russian, 1822, £ Strlg.	149
3	Do. 1859	95
4	Do. (Nicolas Ry.) 1867-9	103
3	Do. Transcauc. Ry. 1882	94
4	Do. Con. R. R. Bd. Ser. I., 1889	102
4	Do. Do. II., 1889	102
4	Do. Do. III., 1891	102
3½	Do. Bonds	100½
4	Do. Ln. (Dvinsk and Vitbsk)	101
6	Salvador 1889	64
—	S Domingo 4s. Unified: .. 1980	63½
6	San Luis Potosi Stg. 1889	88
5	San Paulo (Brzl.), Stg. 1888	90
6	Santa Fé 1883-1	35
—	Do. Eng. Ass. Certs. Dep.	34
5	Do. 1888	45
—	Do. Eng. Ass. Certs. Dpsit.	44
5	Do. (W. Cnt. Col. Rly.) Mrt.	23
5	Do. & Reconq. Rly. Mort.	23
5	Spanish Quicksilvr Mort. 1870	103
3½	Swedish 1880	102
3	Do. 1888	98
53	Do. Conversion Loan 1891	99
45	Trans. Gov. Loan Red....1903-42	103
59/	Tucuman (Prov.) 1888	69
4	Turkish, Secd. on Egypt. Trib.	101
3½	Turkish, Egpt. Trib., Ott. Bd., '94	99¼
4	Do. Priority 1890	90½
1	Do. Convted Series, "A"	65½
5	Do. Customs Ln. 1886	95½
5	Uruguay Bonds 1896	56
3	Venezuela New Con. Debt 1881	35

COUPONS PAYABLE ABROAD.

Last Div.	Name.	Price.
7	Argent. Nat. Cedla. Sries. "B".	35
5	Austrian Ster. Rnts., ex 10fl., 1870	85
5	Do. do. do.	85
5	Do. Paper do. 1870	84
5	Do. do. do.	86
4	Do. Gld Rentes 1876	102
2½	Belgian exchange 25 fr.	92
3	Do. do.	101
3½	Danish Int., 1887, Rd. 1896	—
2½	Dutch Certs. ex 12 gldrs.	87
3	Do. Bonds	98
3	Do. Insc. Stk.	97
3½	French Rentes	105½
3	Do. 1878, '81-4., Red.	101
3	German Imp. Ln. 1891	95
3	Do. do. 1892-3	95
3	Do. do. 1890-4	96
5	Japan Cons. Ln., '92, 3, & 5, Red.	46
36/9	Prussian Consols	102
3	„ Cons. Stg. Ln. 1891	96
4	Rumanian Bds. 1890	—
4	Do. do. 1891	—
4	Utd. States, 1877, Red. 1907	114
4	Do. 1895, 30 yrs.	128
3½	Do. Maschsetts Gl. 1935	113½
3½	Do. Gold Bonds 1927	110½
2	Virginia Cpn. Bds., 3 p.c. from July, 1901	70

BRITISH RAILWAYS.

ORD. SHARES AND STOCKS.

Last Div.	Name.	Price.
10	Barry, Ord.	277½
4	Do. Prefd.	126
6	Do. Defd.	150½
5	Caledonian, Ord.	155
3	Do. Prefd.	98½
—	Do. Defd. Ord., No. 1	4½
	Cambrian, Ord	6½
—	Do. Coast Cons.	6½
32/	Cardiff Ry. Pref. Ord.	117
3/	Central Lond. £10 Ord. Sh.	10½
1/9½	Do. do. £6 paid	6½
3½d.	Do. Pref. Half-Shares	1½
1/6	Do. Def. do.	4½
1½	City and S. London	69
—	East London, Cons.	6½
2	Furness	63½
2½	Glasgow and S. West. Pfd.	80
2½	Do. do. Dfd.	63
3	Great Central, Ord....1894	40
32/0	Do. London Exten.	72
—	Great N. of Scotland, Pfd.	90
—	Do. Dfd.	32
4	Great Northern, Prefd.	119
—	Do. Consolidated "A"	50
—	Do. do. "B"	191½
2	Highland	81½
4	Isle of Wight, Prefd.	120½
3	Do. Defd.	83½
	Lancs. Derbys. and E. Cst.	4
8½	L. Brighton and S. C. Ord.	186
6	Do. Prefd. Ord.	197
30/	Do. Contgt. Rights Certs.	16½
5½	Lond. and S. Western Ord.	222½
4	Do. Preferred	132
6½	Lond., Tilb., and Southend	133½
—	Mersey, £20 shares	½
—	Metropolitan, New Ord.	129
2½	Do. Surplus Lands	95
4	North Cornwall, 4 p.c. Pref.	104½
18/6	Do. Deferred	22½
7½	North London	224½
4½	North Staffordshire	131

British Railways (*continued*):—

Last Div.	Name.	Price.
3/3	Plymouth, Devenport, and S. W. Junc. £10	9
3/	Port Talbot £10 Shares	9
9d.	Rhondda Swns. B. £10 Sh.	8
10	Rhymney, Cons.	267½
4	Do. Prefd.	123
6½	Do. Defd.	147½
7½	Scarboro', Bridlington Junc.	47½
6½	South Eastern, Ord	150
6	Do. Pref.	193
3½	Taff Vale	79
25/	Vale of Glamorgan	129½
3	Waterloo & City	136½

LEASED AT FIXED RENTALS.

Last Div.	Name.	Price.
4	Birkenhead	146
5.19.0	East Lincnshire	207½
5½	Hamsmith. & City Ord.	192½
4½	Lond. and Blackwll.	162½
4½	Do. £10 4½ p. c. Pref.	16½
56/6	Lond. & Green. Ord.	101
5	Do. 5 p. c. Pref.	178½
5	Nor. and Eastn. £50 Ord.	89
6	Do.	106
3½	N. Cornwall 3½ p. c. Stk.	126
4½	Nott. & Granthm. R. & C.	144½
3½	Portptk. & Wigtn. Guar. Stk.	123½
9	Vict. Stn. & Pimlico Ord.	317½
4½	Do. 4½ p. c. Pref.	162½
4/	West Lond. £20 Ord. Shs.	14
4½	Weymouth & Portld.	160½

DEBENTURE STOCKS.

Last Div.	Name.	Price.
4	Alexandra Dks. & Ry.	132½
3	Barry, Cons.	108
4	Brecon & Mrthyr, New A	127½
4	Do. New B	105
4	Caledonian	150½
4	Cambrian "A"	132½
4	Do. "B"	130½
4	Do. "C"	126½
4	Do. "D"	107½
3	Cardiff Rly.	102½
4	City and S. Lond.	139
3½	Cleator & Working Junc.	118½
3	Devon & Som. "A"	103½
16/8	Do. "B" 4 p. c.	36
—	Do. "C" 4 p. c.	10
4	E. Lond. and Ch. 4 p. c. A	137
8/	Do. and B	67½
—	Do. 3rd Ch. 4 p. c.	18½
—	Do. 4th do.	9½
3½	Do. 1st (3½ p. c.)	128½
2½	Do. 2½ p.c. (Whitech. Exn).	88
4	Forth Bridge	143½
4	Furness	143
4	Glasgow and S. Western	150
5	Gt. Central	—
4½	Do.	155½
4	Gt. Eastern	147
4	Gt. N. of Scotland	146½
3	Gt. Northern	113
4	Gt. Western	150½
4½	Do.	159½
4½	Do.	167½
5	Do.	186½
2½	Do.	99
4	Highland	143½
3	Hull and Barnsley	105½
3	Do. and (3-4 p. c)	122
4	Isle of Wight	144½
3	Do. Cent. "A"	92½
4½	Do. "B"	115½
4	Do. "C"	82½
3	Lancs. & Yorkshire	114
4	Lancs. Derbys. & E. Cst.	123½
4	Lpool St. Hlen's & S. Lancs.	126
4½	Ldn. and Blackwall	158
4	Ldn. and Greenwich	148½
4	Lond., Brighton, &c.	149
4½	Do.	166½
4½	Lond., Chath., &c., Arb.	155½
4½	Do. "B"	156½
4	Do.	132½
4	Do. 1883	132½
3	Do.	107
3	Lond. & N. Western	116
3	Lond. & S. Westn. "A"	114½
3	Do. Consld.	114½
4	Lond., Til., & Southend	147
—	Mersey, 5 p. c. (Act, 1866)	65
4	Metropolitan	147
4½	Do.	164½
3½	Do.	128½
6	Met. District	207½
4	Do.	139
2½	Midland	96
4½	Mid-Wales "A"	137½
4	Neath & Brecon 1st	129
4	Do. "A 2"	118½
3	North British	110
3	Do. 1893	108½
3½	N. Cornwall, Launcstn., &c.	126½

Debenture Stocks (*continued*):—

Last Div.	Name.	Price.
3	North Eastern	111
4½	North London	165½
3	N. Staffordshire	111
4	Plym. Devpt. & S.W. Jn.	141½
4	Rhondda and Swan. Bay	130½
4	Rhymney	146½
4	South-Eastern	147½
5	Do.	184½
3½	Do.	127½
3	Do.	113½
3	Taff Vale	109½
4	Tottenham & For. Gate	146
3	Vale of Glamorgan	105½
3	West Highld. (Gtd. by N.B.)	108
4	Wrexham, Mold, &c. "A"	115½
4	Do. "B"	102½
4	Do. "C"	97½

GUARANTEED SHARES AND STOCKS.

Last Div.	Name.	Price.
4	Caledonian	148½
4	Do.	145
4	Forth Bridge	142
4	Furness 1881	137½
4	Glasgow & S. Western	143
4	Do. St. Enoch. Rent	143
6	Gt. Central	199½
4½	Do. 1st Pref.	152½
3½	Do. Pref.	104½
5	Do. Irred. S.Y. Rent	161½
4½	Do. do.	139½
4	Gt. Eastern, Rent	144½
5	Do. Metropolitan	180
4	Do.	144½
4	Gt. N. of Scotland	138½
4	Gt. Northern	146½
5	Gt. Western, Rent	182½
5	Do. Cons.	181½
4	Lancs. & Yorkshire	146½
5	L., Brighton & S. C.	180½
3½	L., Chat. & D. (Shrtkls.)	110½
4	L. & North Western	147½
4	L. & South Western.. 1881	147½
4½	Met. District, Ealing Rent	151
4½	Do. Fulham Rent	152
4	Do. Midland Rent	143½
4	Do. Mid. & Dist. Guar.	128½
2½	Midland, Cons. Perp.	93
3	Mid. & G. N. Jt., "A" Rnt.	108½
3	N. British, Lien	106½
4	Do. Cons. Pref. No. 1	140½
3	N. Cornwall, Wadebrge. Gu.	107
4	N. Eastern	146½
5	N. Staff. Trent & M. £20Shs.	36
3½	Nott. Suburban Ord.	123½
20/6	S. E. Perp. Ann.	36
4½	Do. 4½ p.c.	163½
3½	S. Yorks. Junc. Ord.	118½
4½	W. Cornwall (G. W., Br., Ex., & S. Dev. Joint Rent	158½
3	W. Highl. Ord. Stk. (Gua., N.B.)	105½

PREFERENCE SHARES AND STOCKS.

DIVIDENDS CONTINGENT ON PROFIT OF YEAR.

Last Div.	Name	Price.
4½	Alexandra Dks. & Ry. "A"	125½
5	Barry (First)	169½
4	Do. Consolidated	138½
4	Caledonian Cons., No. 1	144½
4	Do. do. No. 2	143½
5	Do. do. 1878	177½
4	Do. Pref. 1884	142
4	Do. do. 1887 (Conv.)	152½
—	Cambrian, No. 1 4 p. c. Pref.	72½
—	Do. No. 2 do.	39½
—	Do. No. 3 do.	19
—	Do. No. 4 do.	10
5	City & S. Lond. £10 shares	15½
—	Do. New	14
4	Furness, Cons. 1881	134½
4	Do. "A" 1881	131½
4	Do. "B" 1883	129½
4	Glasgow & S. Western	142½
4	Do. No. 2	141
4	Do. 1888	140
4	Do. 1891	140
5	Gt. Central	162½
4	Do.	132½
5	Do. Conv. 1872	155½
5	Do. do. 1874	154½
5	Do. do. 1876	153½
5	Do. do. 1879	153½
5	Do. do. 1881	148½
4	Do. 1889	112½
4	Do. 1891	106½
5	Do. 1894	104½
4	Gt. Eastern, Cons.	142
4	Do. 1886	141½
4	Do. 1881	141½
4	Do. 1884	141½

Preference Shares, &c. (*continued*):—

Last Div.	Name.	Price.
4	Gt. Eastern, Cons. 1887	140½
4	Do. 1888	140½
3½	Do. 1890	122½
3½	Do. 1893	121½
—	Do. (Int. fr. Jan '99) 1893	117½
4	Gt. North Scotland "A"	134½
4	Do. "B"	133½
4	Gt. Northern, Cons.	143
3	Do. 1896	107
5	Gt. Western Cons.	180½
36/11	Hull & Barnsley Red. at 115	107
4	Isle of Wight	133½
3	Lancs. & Yorkshire, Cons.	108
2/2½	Lanc. Drby & E.C. 5 p.c. £10	10½
—	Do. 5 p.c. and £10	9½
5	Lond., Bright., &c., Cons.	178½
5	Do. 2nd Cons.	177½
4½	Lond., Chat. & Dov. Arbitr.	136
25/	Do. 2nd Pref. 4½ p.c.	92
4	Lond. & N. Western	146
4	Lond. & S. Western.. 1881	145½
4	Do. 1884	143½
3½	Do.	127½
4	Lond., Tilbury & Southend	142½
4	Do. Cons., 1887	142½
4	Do 1891	142½
—	Mersey, 5 p.c. Perp.	—
4	Metropolitan, Perp.	141½
4	Do. 1882	141½
4	Do. Irred.	141½
4	Do. 1887	141½
4	Do. New	141½
4½	Do.	146½
3½	Do.	124½
3	Do. Guar.	101½
2½	Metrop. Dist. Exten 5 p.c.	110
2½	Midland, Perp. Pref.	92
4	N. British Cons., No. 2	137
4½	Do. Edin. & Glasgow	152½
5	Do. 1865	169½
5	Do. Conv. 1874	169½
4½	Do. 1875	152½
4½	Do. Conv. 1875	153½
5	Do. do. 1879	169½
4	Do. do. 1884	137½
4	Do. do. 1888	138
4	Do. do. 1890	137½
4	Do. do. 1892	137½
4	N. Eastern	144
4½	N. Lond., Cons. 1866	174½
4½	Do. and Cons. .. 1875	160
3	N. Staffordshire	107
4½	Plym. Devpt. & S. W. Junc.	149½
1/5	Port Talbot, &c., 4 p.c. £10 Shares, 4 paid	5
5/	Rhondda & Swansea Bay, 5 p.c. £10 Shares	13
4	Rhymney, Cons.	140½
4½	S. Eastern, Cons.	162½
5	Do. do.	178½
4	Do. Vested Cos'.	143
4	Do. 1891	143
3½	Do. 1893	125½
2	Do. 3 p.c. after July 1900	103½
4	Taff Vale	142½

INDIAN RAILWAYS.

Last Div.	Name.	Paid.	Price.
3½	Assam Bengal, Ld., (3½ p.c. till June 30, then 3 p.c.)	100	102
4/	Barsi Light, Ld., £10 Shs.	10	10½
6	Bengal and N. West., Ld.	100	149½
4/	Do. £10 Shares	10	14½
3/6	Do. 3½ p.c. Cum. Pf. Shs.	10	10½
8½d.	Do.	4	4½
2/3½	Bengal Central, Ld., £10 (3½ p.c. + ½th net earn)	5	5½
3	Bengal Dooars, Ld.	100	118
4	Bengal Nagpr., Lim. (gua. 4 p.c. + 4th sp. pfts.)	100	114
7½	Bombay, Baroda, and C. I. (gua. 5 p.c.)	100	213
36/1	Burma, Ld. (gua. 2½ p.c. and ½ p.c. add. till 1901)	100	108½
1/7	Do. £10 Shares		3½
4	Delhi Umb. Kalka, Ld., Gua. 3½ p.c. + net earn.	100	123
4	Do. Deb. Stk., 1890 (1916)	100	111
9/10	Estn. Bengal, "A" An. 1957	—	25
9/	Do. "B" 1957	—	30
4	Do. Gua. Deb. Stock	100	140½
9/7½	East Ind. Ann. "A" (1953)	—	27
8/4½	Do. "C"	—	28
8/11½	Do. "B"	—	30
6½	Do. Def. Ann. Cap. (gua. 4 p.c. + ½th sp. pfts.)	—	152
115/9	East Ind. Def. Ann. "D"	—	158
4½	East Ind. Irred. Stock	100	160
5	Gt. Indian Penin., Gua 5 p.c. + ½ surplus profits	100	167½
4	Do. Irred. 4 p.c. Deb. St.	100	139½
4	Indian Mid., Ld. (gua. 4 p.c. + ½th surplus pfts.)	100	114
51/	Madras Guar. + ½ sp. pfts.	100	166
48/6	Do. do.	100	156
46/	Do. do.	100	146
4	Nilgiri, Ld., 1st Deb. Stk.	100	97
4	Oude & Rohil. Db. Stk. Rd.	100	—
3½	Rohil. and Kumaon, Ld.	100	132
9/11	Scinde, Punj., and Delhi, "A" Ann., 1958	—	25
9/1	Do. "B" do.	—	30

Indian Railways (*continued*):—

Last Div.	NAME.	Paid.	Price.
4	South Behar, Ld., £10 shs.	100	100
3½	Do. Deb. Stk. Red.	100	103
4½	South Ind., Gu. Deb. Stk.	100	160½
5	South Indian, Ld. (gua. 3 p.c., and ¼ spls. profits)	100	122½
5	Sthn. Mahratta, Ld. (3½ p.c. & ¼th net earnings)	100	116
4	Do. Deb. Stk. Red.	100	120
3½	Southern Punjab, Ld.	100	107
3½	Do. Deb. Stk. Red.	—	105
5	Nizam's Gua. State, Ld. (†	100	114½
4	Do. Mort. Deb., 1936	100	109
4	Do. do. Reg.	100	108
7/3½	Nizam's Gua. State, Ld., 3½ p.c. Mt. Deb. bearer	—	94½
7/3½	Do. Reg. do.	—	93½
5	W. of India Portgese., Ld.	100	68½
5	Do. Deb. Stk., Red	100	99

RAILWAYS.—BRITISH POSSESSIONS.

Last Div.	NAME.	Paid.	Price.
5	Atlantic & N.W. Gua. 1 Mt. Bds., 1937	100	125½
5/3	Buff. & L. Huron Ord. Sh.	10	13½
5½	Do. 1st Mt. Perp. Bds. 1879	100	141½
5½	Do. 2nd Mt. Perp. Bds	100	141½
—	Calgary & Edmon. 6 p.c. 1st Mt. Stg. Bds. Red	100	75½
5	Canada Cent. 1st Mt. Bds. Red.	100	103
4	Can. Pacific Pref. Stk.	100	100
5	Do. Strl. 1st Mt. Deb. Bds 1915	100	118
3½	Do. Ld. Grnt. Bds., 1938	100	107
3½	Do. Ld. Grnt. Ins. Stk.	100	107
4	Do. Perp. Cons. Deb. Stk.	100	114
5	Do. Algoma Bch. 1st Mt. Bds., 1937	100	121
2	Demerara, Original Stock	100	47
7	Do. Perp. Pref. Stk.	100	155½
9½d.	Do. 4 p.c. Cum. Ext. Pref. £10 Shs.	4	6½
—	Dominion Atlntc. Ord. Stk	100	33½
5	Do. 5 p.c. Pref. Stk.	100	97½
4	Do. 1st. Deb. Stk.	100	104½
4	Do. 2nd do. Red.	100	100
—	Emu Bay & Mt. Bischoff, Ld	5	4½
4½	Do. Irred. Deb. Stk	100	93
nil.	Gd. Trunk of Canada, Stk	100	8
6	Do. 2nd. Equip. Mt. Bds.	100	130½
5	Do. Perp Deb. Stk.	100	135½
5	Do. Gt. Westn. Deb. Stk.	100	123½
5	Do. Nthn. of Can. 1st Mt. Bds, 1902	100	102½
4	Do. do. Deb. Stk	100	102
5	Do. G. T. Geor. Bay & L Erie 1 Mt., 1903	100	104
5	Do. Mid. of Can. Stl. 1st Mt. (Mid. Sec.) 1908	100	106
5	Do. do. Cons. 1 Mt. Bds. 1912	100	107
5	Do. Mont. & Champ. 1 Mt. Bds., 1902	100	103
	Do. Welln., Grey & Brce. 7 p.c. Bds. 1 Mt.	100	109
—	Jamaica 1st Mtg. Bds. Red.	—	103
—	Manitoba & N. W., 6 p.c. 1st Mt. Bds., Red	100	—
—	Do. Ldn. Bdhldrs. Certs.	—	—
5	Manitoba S. W. Col. 1 Mt. Bd., 1934 $1,000 price %	—	120
—	Mid. of W. Aust. Ld. 6 p.c. 1 Mt. Dbs., Red.	100	25
4	Do. Deb. Bds., Red.	100	103
4	Nakusp & Slocan Bds., 1918	100	106
3	Natal Zululand Ld. Debs.,	100	77½
5	N. Brunswick 1st Mt. Stg. Bds., 1934	100	121
4	Do. Perp. Cons. Deb. Stk.	100	114
—	N. Zealand Mid., Ld., 5 p.c. 1st Mt. Debs.	100	35
6	Ontario & Queb. Cap. Stk.	$100	155½
5	Do. Perm. Deb. Stk.	100	142½
—	Qu'Appelle, L. Lake & Sask. 6 p.c. 1 Mt. Bds. Red.	100	41½
	Queb. & L. S. John, 1st Mt. Bds., 1909	100	25½
	Quebec Cent., Prior Ln. Bds., 1908	100	107
2)	Do. 5 p.c. Inc. Bds.	100	39
4	St. Lawr. & Ott. Stl. 1st Mt.	100	113
4	Shuswap & Okan., 1st Mt. Deb. Bds., 1915	100	76
5	Temiscouata, 5 p.c. Stl. 1st Deb. Bds., Red.	100	9½
5	Do. (S. Franc. Brch.) 5 p.c. Stl. 1 Mt. Db. Bds., 1910	100	10
4	Toronto, Grey & B. 1st Mt.	100	112
1/2½	Well. & Mana. £5 Shs.	1	1
5	Do. Debs., 1908	100	110
5	Do. 2nd Debs., 1908	100	109
5	Do. 3rd do., 1908	100	108
6	Atlan. & St. Law. Shs., 6 p.c.	100	162½
5	Gd. Trunk Mt. Bds., 1934	100	116½
5	Michigan Air Line, 5 p.c. 1st Mt. Bds., 1902	100	104
4	Minneap., S. P. & Slt. Ste. Mar, 1st M Bds., 1938	$1000	98

AMERICAN RAILROAD STOCKS AND SHARES.

Last Div.	NAME.	Paid.	Price.
6/	Alab. Gt. Sthn. A 6 p.c. Pref.	10/.	9
—	Do. do "B" Ord.	10/.	2
—	Alabma. N. Orl.-Tex. &c., "A" Pref.	10/.	⅜
—	Do. "B" Def.	10/.	¼
5½	Atlant. First Lsd. Ls. Rtl. Trust	Stk.	97½
—	Baltimore & Ohio Com.	$100	17
—	Baltimore Ohio S.W. Pref.	$100	6
—	Chesap. & Ohio Com.	$100	19½
—	Chic. Gt. West. 5 p.c. Pref. Stock "A"	$100	30½
—	Do. do. Scrip. In.	—	27
8/3	Do. 4 p.c. Deb. Stk.	$100	67½
4	Do. Interest in Scrip	$100	63½
$4	Chic. Junc. Rl. & Un. Stk. Yds. Com.	$100	112½
$1½	Do. 6 p.c. Cum. Pref.	$100	114½
$3½	Chic. Mil. & St. P. Pref.	$100	146
7	Cleve. & Pittsburgh	$10	86½
$1½	Clev., Cincin, Chic., & St. Louis Com.	$100	—
—	Erie 4 p.c. Non-Cum. 1st Pf.	—	34
—	Do. 4 p.c. do. 2nd Pf.	—	18
—	Gt. Northern Pref.	$100	155
$2½	Illinois Cen. Lsd. Lines	$100	95½
—	Kansas City, Pitts & G.	$100	20
$3	L. Shore & Mich. Sth. C.	$100	190
—	Mex. Cen. Ltd. Com.	$100	5
—	Miss. Kan. & Tex. Pref.	$100	32½
2½	N.Y., Pen. & O. 1st Mt. Tst. Ltd., Ord.	—	48½
4	Do. 1st Mort. Deb. Stk.	$100	93½
8	North Pennsylvania	$50	—
—	Northn. Pacific, Com.	$100	24
1½	Pitts. F. Wayne & Chic.	$100	174
—	Reading 1st Pref.	$50	20½
—	Do. 2nd Pref.	$50	10½
—	S. Louis & S. Fran. Com.	$100	6½
—	Do. 2nd Pref.	$100	25
6	St. Louis Bridge 1st Pref.	$100	107
3	Do. 2nd Pref.	$100	50
6	Tunnel Rail. of St. Louis	$100	107
$1½	St. Paul, Min. and Man.	$100	130
—	Southern, Com.	$100	8
—	Wabash, Common	$100	7

AMERICAN RAILROAD BONDS. CURRENCY.

Last Div.	NAME.		Price.
7	Albany & Susq. 1 Con. Mrt.	1906	118
7	Allegheny Val. 1 Mt.	1910	125½
5	Burling., Cedar Rap. & N. 1 Mt.	1906	109½
5	Canada Southern 1 Mt.	1908	111
5	Chic. & N. West. Sk. Fd. Db.	1933	120½
5	Do. Deb. Coupon	1921	112½
6	Chicago & Tomah	1905	112½
5	Chic. Burl. & Q. Skg. Fd.	1901	102½
4	Do. Nebraska Ext.	—	100½
6	Chic., Mil., & S. Pl., 1 Mt. S.W. Div.	1909	117½
7	Do. (S. Paul Div.) 1 Mt.	1902	132½
5	Do. (La Cross & D.	1919	112½
7	Do. 1 Mt. (Hast. & Dak.)	1910	132
5	Do. Chic. & Mis. Riv. 1 Mt.	1926	112½
5	Chic., Rock Is. and Pac. 1 Mt. Ext.	1934	108
6	Det., G. Haven & Mil. Equip	1918	105
6	Do. do. Cons. Mt.	1918	102½
6	Ill. Cent., 1 Mt., Chic. & S.	1898	—
7	Indianap. & Vin., 1 Mt.	1908	125
6	Do. do. 2 Mt.	1900	104½
6	Lehigh Val., Cons. Mt.	1923	112½
—	Mexic. Cent., Ln. 2 Cons. Inc.	—	5
7	N.Y. Cent. & H.R. Mt. Bonds	1903	119½
5	Do. Deb.	1904	111
6	Penns. Cons. S. F M.	1905	118
4	West Shore, 1 Mt.	2361	110

DITTO—GOLD.

Last Div.	NAME.		Price.
6	Alabama Gt. Sthn. 1 Mt.	1908	114
5	Do. Mid. 1	1928	95½
4	Allegheny Val. Gen. Mt.	1942	107
4	Atch., Top., & S. Fé Gn. Mt.	1995	90½
3	Do. Adj. Mt.	1995	60½
5	Do. Equipt. Tmst.	—	102½
5	Atlantic & Dan. 1 Mt.	1950	96½
5	Baltimore & Ohio	1925	97½
5	Do. Speyer's Tst. Recpts.	1925	96
5	Do. Cons. Mt.	1988	102½
4½	Do. 4½ p.c. 1 Mt. Term.	1934	84
4½	Do. Brown Shipley's Dep. Cts.	—	84
5	Balt. Belt 5 p.c. 1 Mort.	1990	90
4½	Balt. & Ohio S.W. 1 Mt.	1990	102½
4½	Do. 4½ p.c. 1 Cons. Mt. 1893	1993	78
—	Do. Inc. Mt. 5 p.c. Cl. A	—	29½
—	Do. do. Cl. B	—	11
5	Balt. & Ohio S.W. Term 5 p.c.	1942	99½
6	Balt. & Ptmac (Mn. L.) 1 Mt.	1911	124
6	Do. do. (Tunnel) 1 Mt.	1911	126
4	Beech Creek 1 Mt.	1936	109
5	Do 2 Mort.	1936	116
4	Carthage & Adiron 1 Mt.	1981	109

American Railroad Bonds—Gold (*continued*):—

Last Div.	NAME.		Price.
5	Cent. of Georgia 1 Mort.	1945	117½
5	Do. Cons. Mt.	1945	92½
5	Cent. of N. Jrsy. Gn. Mt.	1987	113½
6	Central Pacific, 1 Mort.	1898	102½
6	Do. Speyer's Certs.	—	106
5	Do Land Grant	1900	99
5	Chesap. & Ohio 1st Cons. Mt.	1939	115½
4½	Do. Gen. Mt.	1992	80
6	Chic. & W. Ind. Gen. Mt. Skg. Fd.	1932	120
5	Chic. Mil. & St. Pl. (Chic. & L. Sup.) 1 Mt.	1921	114½
5	Do. Chic. & Pac. W.	1921	117½
5	Do. Wisc. & Minn. 1 Mt.	1921	114½
5	Do. Terminal Mt.	1914	114½
4	Do. General Mt.	1989	106½
5	Chic. St. L. & N. Orleans	1951	122½
4	Do. 1 Mort. (Memphis)	1951	105½
4	Clevel, Cin., Chic. & St. L. 1 Mt. (Cairo)	1939	90
4	Do. 1 Mt. (Cinc., Wab., & Mich.)	1991	90
4	Do. 1 Col. Tst. Mt. (S. Louis)	1990	98½
4	Do General Mt.	1993	82½
4½	Clevel. & Mar. Mt.	1935	114
4½	Clevel. & Pittsburgh	1942	116½
4½	Do. Series B.	1942	116½
—	Colorado Mid 1 Mt.	1936	63½
—	Do. Bdhrs.' Comm. Certs.	—	63½
4	Dnvr. & R. Gde. 1 Cons. Mt.	1936	93
5	Do Imp. Mort.	1928	92
4	Detroit & Mack. 1 Lien	1995	92½
5	E. Tennes., Virg., & Grgia. Cons. Mt.	1956	114½
5	Elmira, Cort., & Nthn. Mt.	1914	100
4	Erie 1 Cons. Mt. Pr. Ln.	1996	90
3	Do. Gen. Lien	1996	72
6	Galvest, Harrisb., &c., 1 Mt.		107½
5	Georgia, Car. & N. 1 Mt.	1929	96
4½	Gd Rpds & Indn. Ex. 1 Mt.	1941	112½
5	Do. 1 Mt. (Muskegon)	1926	39½
3½	Illinois Cent. 1 Mt.	1951	104½
4	Do.	1952	105
4	Do. Cairo Bdge.	1950	102
4	Do.	1953	104
4	Do. General Mort.	1904	102½
5	Kans. City, Pitts. & G. 1 M.	1923	80
3½	L Shore & Mich. Southern	1997	109
4½	Lehigh Val. N.Y. 1 Mt.	1940	105
5	Lehigh Val. Term. 1 Mt.	1941	109½
5	Long Island	1931	117½
5	Do. Deb.	1934	102
5	Do. (N. Shore Bch.) 1 Cons. Mt.	1932	94
6	Louisville & Nash. G. Mt.	1930	121
6	Do. 2 Mt. Sk. Fd. (S. & N. Alabama	1910	194½
6	Do. 1 Mt. N Orl & Mb.	1930	122½
5	Do. 1 Mt. Coll. Tst.	1931	104½
4	Do. Unified	1940	88
4½	Do. Mobile & Montgy. 1 Mt.	1945	105½
4	Manhattan Cons. Mt.	1990	96
4	Mexican Cent. Cons. Mt.	1911	66
—	Do. 1 Cons. Inc,		15
6	Mexican Nat. 1 Mt.	1927	105½
3½	Do. 2 Mt. 6 p.c. Inc. A	1917	54
—	Do. do. B.	1917	10
3	Do. Matheson's Certs.		—
3	Michig. Cnt. (Battle Ck. & S.) 1 Mt.	1989	88
6	Minneap. & S. L. 1 Mt. Pacific Ext.	1921	117½
5	Do. 1 Consold.	1934	107½
4	Minne., Slt S. M. & A. 1 Mt.	1926	98
5	Minneapolis Westn. 1 Mt.	1911	105½
4	Miss. Kans. & Tex. 1 Mt.	1990	89
4	Do. 2 do.	1990	62
4	Mobile & Birm. Mt. Inc.	1945	38
5	Do. P. Lien	1945	88
4	Mohawk & Mal. 1 Mt.	1991	108
5	Montana Cent. 1 Mt.	1937	111½
5	Nashv., Chattan., & S. L. 1 Cons. Mt.	1928	102½
5	Nash., Flor., & Shff. Mt.	1937	95½
4	N. Y. & Putnam 1 Cons. Mt.	1993	108
5	N. Y., Brooklyn, & Man. B. 1 Cons. Mt.	1935	107½
4	N. Y. Cent. & Hud. R. Deb. Certs. 1890	1905	105
4	Do. Ext. Debt. Certs.	1905	105
7	N. Y., L. Erie, & W. 1 Cons. Mt. (Erie)	1920	139½
7	Do. 1 Con. Mt. Fd. Coup.	1920	137½
5	N. Y., Onto., & W. Cons. 1 Mt.	1939	110
4	Do. 4 p.c. Refund. Mt.	1992	99
5	N. Y. & Rockaway B. 1 Mt.	1927	102½
6	Norfolk & West. Gn. Mt.	1931	126½
6	Do. Imp. & Ext.	1934	118½
4	Do. 1 Cons. Mt.	—	81
6	N. Pacific Gn. 1 Mt. Ld. Gt.	1921	—
4	Do. P. Ln. Rl. & Ld. Gt.	—	96
3	Do. Gn. Ln. Rl. & Ld. Gt.	—	61½
5	Oregon & Calif. 1 Mt.	1927	78½
5	Oregon Rl. & Nav. Col. Tst.	—	—
6	Panama Skg. Fd. Subsidy	1910	106½
4½	Pennsylvania Rlnl.	1913	115
4	Do. Equip. Tst. Ser. A.	1914	104
4	Do. Cons. Mt.	1943	115
4½	Penna. Company 1st Mort.	1921	114
5	Perkiomen 1 Mrt., 2nd ser.	1918	91½
4½	Pitts., C., C., & St. Ls. Con. Mt. G. B., Ser. A	1940-2	112½
4	Do. Cons. Mort., Ser. D.	1945	105
6	Pittsbgh., Cle., & Toledo	1922	101½
4	Reading, Phil., & R. Genl.	1997	83
5	Richmond & Dan. Equip.	1909	97½
5	Rio Grande Junc. 1st Mort.	1939	94
4	Rio Grande West 1st Tst. Mt.	1939	82½
6	St. Joseph & Gd. Island	1925	—
7	S. Louis Bridge 1st Mort	1925	134½
5	S. Louis Mchts. Bdge. Term. 1st Mort.	1930	102½

American Railroad Bonds (*continued*):

Last Div.	NAME.		Price.
4	S. Louis S. West 1st Mort.	1989	77½
—	Do. 4 p.c. 2nd Mort. Inc.	1989	30
—	S. Louis Term. Cupples Sta. & Prop. 1st. Mt. 4½ p.c.	1909-17	102
4½	St. Paul Minn., & Manit.	1933	109
6	Do. do.	1933	132½
6	Shamokin, Sunbury, &c. 2 Mt.	1925	109
5	S. & N. Alabama Cons. Mt.	1936	97½
5	Southern 1 Cons. Coup.	1994	91½
4	Do. E. Tennes Reorg. Lien	1938	100
6	S. Pacific of Cal. 1 Mt.	1905-12	111
4½	Trml. Assn. of S. Louis 1 Mt.	1939	111½
5	Do. 1 Cons. Mt.	1944	109
5	Texas & Pac. 1 Mt.	2000	100½
—	Do. 5 p.c. 2 Mt. Income	2000	30
5	Toledo & Ohio Cent. 1 Mt. West. Div.	1935	102½
4½	Toledo., Walhon., Val., & Ohio 1 Mt.	1931-3	111½
—	Union Pacific 1 Mt. 4 p.c.	1947	94
—	Union Pac., Linc., & Color. 1 Mt.	1918	—
4	United N. Jersey Gen. Mt.	1944	115½
6	Vicksbrg., Shrevept., & Pac. Pr. Ln. Mt.	1915	102½
5	Wabash 1 Mt.	1939	109½
4	Wn. Pennsylvania Mt.	1928	109½
5	W. Virga. & Pittsbg. 1 Mt.	1990	83
5	Wheeling & L. Erie 1 Mt. (Wheelg. Div.) 5 p.c.	1928	90½
5	Do. Extn. Imp. Mt.	1930	90
—	Do. do. Brown Shipley's Cts.		—
5	Willmar & Sioux Falls 1 Mt.	1938	111

STERLING.

Last Div.	NAME.		Price.
6	Alabama Gt. Sthn. Deb.	1906	104½
5	Do. Gen. Mort.	1927-8	99
5	Alabama, N. Orl., Tex. & Pac. 5 p.c. "A" Dbs.	1910-40	99
55/	Do. do. "B" do.	1910-40	52
—	Do. do. "C" do.		19
—	Allegheny Valley	1910	120½
4	Atlantic 1st Leased Line Perp.		98
6	Baltimore and Ohio	1902	107
6	Do. do.	1910	118
5	Do. do. 1877		96½
—	Do. Morgan's Certs.		96½
4½	Do. do.	1933	89½
6	Chicago & Alton Cons. Mt.	1903	112
5	Chic. St. Paul & Kan. City Priority		105
6	Eastn. of Massachusetts	1906	117½
5	Illinois Cent. Skg. Fd.		103
5	Do.	1905	108
3½	Do.	1950	99½
4	Do. 1 Mt.	1951	110
3	Do. 1 Mt.	1951	92½
6	Louisville & Nash., M. C. & L. Div., 1 Mt.	1902	104½
7	Do. 1 Mt. (Memphis & O.)	1901	111
47/4	Mexican Nat. "A" Certs. 5 p.c. Non. cum.		45½
—	Do. "B" Certs.		10
6	N.Y. & Canada 1 Mt.	1904	111½
6	N. York Cent. & H.R. Mort.	1903	112
4½	N. York, Penns., & Ohio Pr. Ln. Extd.	1935	—
5	Do. Equip. Tst.		103½
5	Do. 5 p.c. Equip. Tst. (1890)		103½
6	Nrthn. Cent. Cons. Gen. Mt.		106
6	Pennsylvania Gen. Mt.	1910	126
6	Do. Cons. Skg. Fd. Mt.	1905	113½
3½	Do. Cons. Mt.	1945	105½
6	Phil. & Erie Cons. Mort	1920	134½
6	Phil. & Reading Gen. Cons. Mort.	1911	126
6	Pittsbg. & Connells. Cons.	1926	116
—	Do. Morgan's Certs.		116
4	St. Paul., Min., & Manitoba (Pac. Extn.)	1940	96½
6	S. & N. Alabama	1903	107½
6	Un. N. Jersey & C. Gen. Mt.	1901	109½

FOREIGN RAILWAYS

Last Div.	NAME.	Paid.	Price.
4/	Alagoas, Ld., Shs.	20	4½
5	Do. Deb. Stk., Red.	100	42½
6	Antofagasta, Ltd., Stk.	100	68
4	Do. Perp. Deb. Stk.	100	90
—	Arauco, Ld., Ord. Shs.	10	½
—	Do. 10 p.c. Cum. Pref.	10	½
5	Argentine Gt. W., Ld.,	100	72
5	Do. 5 p.c. Cum. Pref. Shs.	100	100
4	Do. 1 Deb. Stk.	100	103½
1/0/0	Argentine N. E., Ltd., 6 p.c. Cum. Pref. Stk.	100	10½
—	Do. 5 p.c. Deb. Stk., Red.	100	31
2/	Arica and Tacna Shs.	20	1½
10/	Bahia & San Fcisco., Ld.,	20	10½
6/	Do. Timbo. Bch. Shs.	20	5
12/	Bahia, Blanca, & N.W. Ln. Prf. Cum. 6 p.c.	100	53½
4	Do. 4 p.c. 1 Deb. Stk., Red.	100	83
6	Barranquilla R. & P., Ld., 6 p.c. 1 Deb. Stk., Red.	100	

Foreign Railways (*continued*):—

Last Div.	Name.	Paid.	Price.
3/	Bilbao Riv. & Cantabn., Ltd., Ord.	3	6
—	Bolivar, Ltd., Shs.	10	1⅜
6	Do. 6 p.c. Deb. Stk.	100	96½
—	Brazil Gt. Southn. Ltd., 7 p.c. Cum. Pref.	20	1¼
6	Do. Perm. Deb. Stk	100	39½
6½	B. Ayres Gt. Southn. Ld., Ord. Stk.	100	147
5	Do. Pref. Stk.	100	136
4	Do. Deb. Stk.	100	115½
30/	B. Ayres & Ensen. Port., Ltd., Ord. Stk.	100	64½
5	Do. Cum. 1 Pref. Stk.	100	121
6/0/0	Do. 6p.c.Con. Pref.Stk.	100	101
4	Do. Deb. Stk., Irred.	100	113
10⅛	B. Ayres Northern, Ltd., Ord. Stk.	100	265
12¾	Do. Pref. Stk.	100	320
5	Do. 5 p.c. Mt. Deb. Stk., Red.	100	113
3/15/0	B. Ayres & Pac., Ld., 7 p.c. 1 Pref. Stk. (Cum.)	100	86
4	Do. 1 Deb. Stk.	100	100
5/5/0	Do. 4½ p.c. 2 Deb. Stk.	100	89
1	B. Ayres & Rosario, Ltd., Ord. Stk.	100	70½
—	Do. New, £20 Shs.	20	—
7/	Do. 7 p.c. Pref. Shs.	10	17
7/	Do. Sunchales Ext.	10	14¾
4	Do. Deb. Stk., Red.	100	107½
—	B. Ayres & Val. Trans., Ltd., 7 p.c. Cum. Pref.	20	6½
4	Do. 4 p.c. "A" Deb. Stk., Red.	100	71
—	Do. 6 p.c. "B" Deb. Stk. Red.	100	44
3/6	B. Ayres Westn. Ld. Ord.	10	10¾
3/	Do. Def. Shs.	10	6¾
5	Do. 5 p.c. Pref.	10	12¾
4	Do. Deb. Stk	100	107
6	Cent. Arg. Deb. Sk. Rd.	100	160½
4	Do. Deb. Stk. Rd	100	111
6	Cent. Bahia L. Ord. Stk.	100	42
	Do. Deb. Stk., 1934	100	72½
5	Do. Deb. Stk., 1937	100	58
3/6	Cent. Uguy. East. Ext. L. Shs	10	5¾
5	Do. Perm. Stk.	100	111
3/6	Do. Nthn. Ext. L. Sh.	10	4½
5	Do. Perm. Deb. Stk	100	106
3	Do. of Montev. Ltd., Ord. Stk	100	86
6	Do. Perm. Deb. Stk	100	140
10/	Conde d'Eu, Ltd. Ord.	20	7
—	Cordba & Rosar., Ltd., 6 p.c. Pref. Shs.	100	42½
4	Do. 1 Deb. Stk	100	91
75/	Do. 6 p.c. Deb. Stk	100	93
—	Cordba Cent., Ltd., 5 p.c. Cu. 1 Pref. Stk	100	83½
—	Do. 5 p.c. Non-Cum. 2 Pref. Stk	100	46
5	Do. Deb. Stk	100	119
—	Costa Rica, Ltd., Shs	10	4⅜
8/	Dna. Thrsa. Chris., Ltd., 7 p.c. Pref. Shs.	20	4
20/	E. Argentine, Ltd	100	40
6	Do. Deb. Stk	100	104
1/1	Egyptn. Dlta. Lgt. Rys., Ltd., £10 Pref. Shs.	8	10½
—	Entre Rios, L., Ord. Shs.	5	¾
—	Do. Cu. 5 p.c. Pref.	5	2¾
6/	Gt. Westn. Brazil, Ltd.,	20	9¼
6	Do. Perm. Deb. Stk	100	90½
6	Do. Extn. Deb. Stk	100	76½
—	Int.-Oceanic Mex., Ltd., 7 p.c. Pref	10	1¾
4	Do. Deb. Stk	100	84
42/6	Do. 7 p.c. "A" Deb. Sk.	100	67
—	Do. 7 p.c. "B" Deb. Sk.	100	31
5/	La Guaira & Carac	10	7½
5	Do. 5 p.c. Deb. Sk. Red.	100	100
8/4	Lembg.-Czern.-Jassy	30	25
1/	Lima, Ltd.	20	2½
—	Manila Ltd. 7 p.c. Cu. Pf.	10	¾
20/6½	Mexican 2nd Pref. 6 p.c.	100	33
6	Do. Perp. Deb. Stk.	100	139
1/0/0	Mexican Sthrn., Ld., Ord.	100	23
—	Do. 4 p.c. 1 Db. Stk. Rd.	100	83
—	Do. 4 p.c. 2 do.	100	61
—	Mid. Urgy., Ltd.	100	18½
4	Do. Deb. Stk	100	64
12/	Minas & Rio, Ltd.	20	9½
5/2	Namur & Liege	20	12½
11/6	Do. Pref.	20	29
5/	Natal & Na. Cruz, Ld., 7 p.c. Cum Pref.	20	7
—	Nitrate Ltd., Ord.	10	5
—	Do. 7 p.c. Pr. Con. Or.	10	3½
—	Do. Def. Conv. Ord.	10	¾
7/	N.-E. Urgy., Ltd., Ord	10	14½
7/	Do. 7 p.c. Pref.	10	15
—	N.-W. Argentine Ld., 7 p.c. Pref.	10	2½
6	Do. 6 p.c. 1 Deb. Stk.	100	113
—	Do. 2 Deb. Stk.	100	94
—	N.W. Uruguay 6 p.c. 1 Pref. Stk.	100	17
—	Do. 5 p.c. 2 Pref. Stk.	100	7½
6	Do. 6 p.c. Deb. Stk	100	80½
22/	Ottoman (Sm. Ald.)	20	14
—	Paraguay Cntl., Ld., 5 p.c. Perm. Deb. Stk	100	11
—	Piræus, Ath., & Pelo.	275	1½
	Pto. Alegre & N. Hambg Ld., 7 p.c. Pref. Shs.	20	4
6	Do. Mt. Deb. Stk. Red.	100	77½
—	Puerto Cabello & Val. Ld.	10	1⅜
5	Recife & S. Francisco	100	71
14	R Claro S. Paulo, Ld., Sh.	10	22½
5	Do. Deb. Stk.	100	126
5	Royal Sardinian Ord	10	11¾

Foreign Railways (*continued*):—

Last Div.	Name.	Paid.	Price.
5/	Royal Sardinian Pref.	10	12½
5/	Sambre & Meuse	20	18
5/6	Do. Pref.	10	12½
28/	San Paulo Ld.	20	34½
2/9½	Do. New Ord. £10 sh.	6	9¾
2/	Do. 5 p.c. Non.Cm.Pref.	10	12
5½	Do. Deb. Stk.	100	133
5	Do. 5 p.c. Deb. Stk	100	127
—	S. Fé & Cordova, Gt. Sthn., Ld., Shares	100	50½
6	Do. Perp. Deb. Stk.	100	122
3/2½	S. Austrian	20	7
10/	Sthn. Braz. R. Gde. do Sul, Ld.	20	7½
6	Do. 6 p.c. Deb. Stk.	100	71½
4	Swedish Centl., Ld., 4 p.c. Deb. Stk.	100	107
5	Do. Pref.	100	100
1/9	Taltal, Ld.	5	2½
—	Uruguay Nthn., Ld. 7 p.c. Pfd. Stk.	100	8
3½	Do. 5 p.c. Deb. Stk.	100	30
—	Villa Maria & Rufino, Ld., 6 p.c. Pref. Shs.	100	20
4	Do. 4 p.c. 1 Deb. Stk.	100	74
6/0/0	Do. 6 p.c. 2 Deb. Stk.	100	47
5/9	West Flanders	8½	21
5/6	Do. 5½ p.c. Pref.	10	18
3/	Watn. of Havana, Ld.	10	4½

FOREIGN RAILWAY OBLIGATIONS

Per Cent.	Name.	Price.
6	Alagoas Ld., 6 p.c. Deb., Rd.	82½
—	Alcoy & Gandia, Ld., 5 p.c. Debs., Red.	25
5	Arauco., Ld., 5 p.c. 1st Mt., Rd.	62½
—	Do. 6 p.c. Mt. Deb., Rd.	42½
6	Brazil G. Sthn., L., Mt. Dbs., Rd.	83½
6	Do. Mt. Dbs. 1893, Rd.	49½
5½	Campos & Caran. Dbs., Rd.	76
6	Central Bahia, L., Dbs., Rd.	90½
5½	Conde d'Eu, L., Dbs., Rd.	76
6	Costa Rica, L., 1st Mt. Dbs., Rd.	111
6	Do. 2nd Dbs., Rd.	92
5	Do. Prior Mt. Db., Rd.	104
6	Cucuta Mt. Dbs., Rd.	102
5½	Donna Thrsa. Cris., L., Dbs., Rd.	70
3	Eastn. of France, £20 Dbs., Rd.	19
4	Egyptn. Delta Light, L., Db., Rd	90½
—	Espito. Santo & Cara. 5 p.c. Stl. Dbs., Rd.	38
4	Gd. Russian Nic., Rd.	102
5	Inter-Oceanic Mex., L., 5 p.c. Pr. Ln. Dbs., Rd.	103
3	Ital. 3 p.c. Bds. A & B, Rd	57½
—	Ituana 6 p.c. Debs., 1918	74
—	Leopoldina, 6 p.c. Dbs. £50 Bds.,	21
—	Do. do. Comms. Cert.	21
—	Do. 5 p.c. Stg. Dbs. (1888), Rd.	30
—	Do. do. Comm. Certs.	30
—	Do. 5 p.c. Stg. Dbs. (1890), Rd.	21
—	Do. do. Comms. Certs.	21
—	Macahé & Cam. 5 p.c. Dbs., Rd.	29
—	Do. do. Comms. Certs.	29
—	Do. (Cantagallo), 5 p.c., Red.	30
—	Do. do. Comm. Certs.	30
—	Manila Ltd., 6 p.c. Deb., Red.	23
6	Do. Prior Lien Mt., Rd.	104
6	Do. Series "B," Rd.	80
7	Matanzas & Sab., Rd.	101½
6	Minas & Rio, L., 6 p.c. Dbs., Rd.	96
5	Mogyana 5 p.c. Deb. Bds., Rd.	104
5	Moscow-Jaros., Rd.	106½
5½	Natal & Na. Cruz Ltd., 5½ p.c. Debs., Red.	93
5	Nitrate, Ltd. Mt. Bds., Red.	79
3	Nthn. France, Red.	19
4	N. of S. Af. Rep. (Trnsvl.) Gu. Bds. Red.	95
3	Nthn. of Spain £20 Pri. Obs. Red.	8½
6	Ottmn. (Smy to A.)(Kujk) Asnt. Debs., Red.	109
6	Ottmn. (Seraik.) Asg. Debs. Red.	109
6	Ottmn. (Seraik) Non-Asg. D., Rd	109
5	Ottmn. Kuyjk. Ext. Red.	106
5	Ottmn. Serkeuy. Ext. Red.	101½
5	Ottmn. Tireh Ext. 1910	98
5	Ottmn. Debs, 1886, Red.	97
5	Do. 1888, Red. 1935	97½
5	Do. 1893, Red. 1935	99
5	Ottmn. of Anlia. Debs., Rd.	90½
5	Do. Ser. II.	87
4	Ottomn. Smyr. & Cas. Ext Bds., Red.	83½
3	Paris, Lyon & Medit. (old sys., £20), Red.	19
3	Paris, Lyon & Medit. (new sys., £20), Red.	18¾
50/	Piræus, At. & Pelp., 6 p.c. 1st Mt. Dbs., Red.	91½
3	Do. 5 p.c. Mt. Bds., Red.	71
4	Pretoria-Pietbg., Ltd., Red.	93
7	Puerto Cab. & Val., Ltd., 1st Mt. Debs., Red.	91
—	Rio de Jano. & Nthn., Ltd., 6 p.c. £100 Deb., Red.	21
—	Rio de Jano. (Gr. Para.), 5 p.c. 1st Mt. St. £100 Debs., Red.	21
2	Royal Sardinian, A, Rd. £20	11½
3	Royal Sardinian, B., Rd. £20	12

Foreign Rly. Obligations (*continued*):—

Per Cent.	Name.	Price.
5	Ryl. Trns.-Afric. 5 p.c. 1st Mt. £100 Bds., Red.	61
7	Sagua La Grande, B pRd.	98
4	Sa. Fe & Cor. G.S., Ld. Pr. Ln. Bds.	104
5	Sa. Fe, 5 p.c. and Reg. Dbs.	80
3	South Austrian, £20 Red.	15½
3	South Austrian, (Ser X.)	15½
3	South Italian £20 Obs. (Ser. A to G), Red.	12½
3½	S.W. of Venez (Barq.), Ltd., 7 p.c. 1st Mt. £100 Debs.	55½
5	Taltal, Ltd., 5 p.c. 1st Ch. Debs., Red.	98
5	Utd. Rwys. Havana, Red.	87
3	Wtrn. of France, £20 Red.	19
6	Wrn. B. Ayres St. Mt. Debs., 1902	108
6	Wrn. B. Ayres, Reg. Cert.	106½
5	Do. Mt. Bds.	122
6	Wtrn. of Havna., Ld, Mt. Dbs., Rd.	97
7	Wrn. Ry. San Paulo Red.	99
—	Wrn. Santa Fé 7 p.c. Red.	38
2/8	Zafra & Huelva, 3 p.c. Red.	2¾

BANKS.

Div.	Name.	Paid.	Price.
2/4½	Agra, Ltd.	6	3½
4/2½	Anglo-Argentine, Ltd., £9	7	5½
8 fls.	Anglo-Austrian	120 fl	13½
6/	Anglo-Californian, Ltd., £20 Shares	10	11
4/	Anglo-Egyptian, Ltd., £15	5	6
5/	Anglo-Foreign Bkg., Ltd.	7	8
7/	Anglo-Italian, Ltd.	5	7
7/6	Bk. of Africa, Ltd., £18¾	6¼	10½
20/	Bk. of Australasia	40	50
10/	Bk. of Brit. Columbia	20	20½
25/	Bk. of Brit. N. America	50	64
20/	Bk. of Egypt, Ltd., £25	12½	19
5/	Bk. of Mauritius, Ltd.	10	9½
18/	Bk. of N. S. Wales	20	38
4 p.c.	Bk. of N. Zland. Gua. Stk.	100	102
6/	Bk. of Roumania, £20 Shs.	6	7½
2/6	Tarapaca & Ldn., Ltd., £10	5	3½
—	Bque. Fse. de l'Afri. du S.	100 f.	3½
f. 22.50	Bque. Internatle. de Paris	20	23
6/	Brit. Bk. of S. America, Ltd., £20 Shares	10	10
16/	Capital & Cties., L., £50	10	39
16/	Chart. of India, &c.	20	32½
10/	City, Ltd., £40 Shares	10	20
18/	Colonial, £100 Shares	30	22
10/	Delhi and London, Ltd.	25	—
5/	German of London, Ltd.	10	10½
25/	Hong-Kong & Shanghai	28½	44½
4/	Imperl. of Persia	6½	3½
10/	Imperl. Ottoman, £20 Shs	10	11½
12/	Intrnatl. of Ldn., Ld., £20	15	11½
10/	Ionian, Ltd.	25	15
16/	Lloyds, Ltd., £50 Shs.	8	30
10/	Ldn. & Braziln. Ltd., £20	10	17
44/	Ldn. & County, Ltd., £80	20	101½
9/	Ldn. & Hanseatic, L., £20	10	10½
22/6	Ldn. & Midland, L., £60	12½	53½
8/9	Ldn. & Provin., Ltd., £10	5	22½
39/	Ldn. & Riv. Plate, L., £25	15	50
2/1½	Ldn. & San Fcisco, Ltd.	7	4½
28/	Ldn. & Sth. West., L., £50	20	68
26/	Ldn. & Westmins., L., £100	20	55½
3/	Ldn. of Mex. & S. Amer., Ltd., £10 Shs.	6	5¾
15/	Ldn. Joint Stk., L., £100	15	33½
12/9½	Ldn., Paris & Amer., L. £20	16	25
2/4½	Merchant Bkg., L., £9	4	2¾
6/3	Metropn, Ltd., £50 Shs.	5	14½
9/	National, Ltd., £50 Shs.	10	19½
4/3	Natl. of Mexico, $100 Shs.	$40	13
1/3	National of N. Z., L., £7½	2½	2
3/	National S. Afric. Rep.	10	14½
18/10½	National Provcl. of Eng., Ltd., £75 Shs.	10½	50
21/7½	Do. do. £60 Shs.	12	57
6/6	North Eastn., Ltd., £20 Shs	6	15
19/	Parr's, Ld., £100 Shs.	20	91½
12/6	Prov. of Ireland, L., £100	12½	28½
40/	Stand. of S. Afric., L., £100	25	66
12/6	Union of Australia, L., £75	25	27
4 p.c.	Do. do. Ins. Stk. Dep. 1900	100	102
15/6	Union of Ldn., Ltd., £100	15½	35½

BREWERIES AND DISTILLERIES

Div.	Name.	Paid.	Price.
4½	Albion Prp. 1 Mt. Db. Sk.	100	111
4	All Saints', L., Db. Sk. Rd.	100	97
7	Allsopp, Ltd	100	152
6	Do. Cum. Pref	100	156
4½	Do. Deb. Stk., Red.	100	118
3½	Do. Deb. Stk., Red.	100	101
4½	Alton & Co., L., Db., Rd	100	104
4½	Do. Mt. Bds., 1896	100	103
—	Arnold, Perrett, Ltd.	10	6
6	Do. Cum. Pref.	10	10
4½	Do. 1 Mt. Db. Stk., Rd	100	106

Breweries &c. (*continued*):—

Div.	Name.	Paid.	Price.
5½	Arrol, A., & Sons, L., Cum. Pref. Shs.	10	10
4½	Do. 1 Mt. Db. Stk., Rd.	100	104
5	Backus, 1 Mt. Db., Red.	100	61
4	Barclay, Perk., L., Cu. Pf.	10	17½
3½	Do. Mt. Db. Stk., Red.	100	110
—	Barnsley, Ltd.	10	12
6	Do. Cum. Pref.	10	14
1/3	Barrett's, Ltd	2½	1½
1/3	Do. 5 p.c. Pref.	2½	2½
3/	Bartholomay, Ltd	10	3
8	Do. Cum. Pref.	10	8
6	Do. Deb.	100	100½
5	Bass, Ratcliff, Ltd., Cum. Pref. Stk.	100	144½
4½	Do. Mt. Db. Stk., Rd.	100	125
4	Bell, J., L., 1 Mt. D. Stk., R	100	100
2/6	Benskin's, L., Cum. Pref.	5	—
4½	Do. 1 Mt. Db. Stk Red.	100	—
4½	Do. "B" Deb. Sk, Rd.	100	—
7/	Bentley's Yorks., Ltd.	10	11½
6/	Do. Cum. Pref.	10	12½
4½	Do. Mt. Debs., Red.	100	110
4½	Do. do. 1892, Red.	100	110
—	Bieckert's, Ltd.	20	2
5	Do. Debs., Red.	100	57
—	Birmingham., Ltd., 6 p.c. Cum. Pref.	5	2½
4½	Do. Mt. Debs., Red.	50	40½
5½	Boardman's, Ld., Cm. Pf.	10	8½
4½	Do., Perp. 1 Mt. Db. Sk.	100	105½
30/9	Brain & Co., Ltd.	100	101
4½	Brakspear, L., 1 D. Stk. Rd	100	109
4	Brandon's, L., 1 D. Stk. R.	100	105½
21/	Bristol (Georges) Ltd.	10	46
6	Do. Cum. Pref.	10	18
5	Do. Mt. Db. Sk. 1888 Rd.	100	115½
17/6	Bristol United, Ltd.	10	35
6	Do. Cum. Pref.	10	16½
4½	Do. Db. Sk. Rd.	100	126
5½	Buckley's, L., C. Pre-prf.	10	10¾
4½	Do. 1 Mt. Db. Stk. Rd.	100	106½
4	Bullard & Sns, L., D. Sk. R.	100	105
6	Bushell, Watk., L., C. Pf.	10	14
4½	Do. 1 Mt. Db. Sk. Rd.	100	112
5	Camden, Ltd., Cum. Pref.	10	11½
4½	Do. 1 Mt. Db. Sk. Rd.	100	108
5½	Cameron, Ltd., Cm. Prf.	10	13½
4½	Do. Mort Deb. Stk.	100	108
3½	Do. Perp Mt. Db. Sk.	100	100½
5	Cam'bell, J'stone, L., C. Pf.	5	5
4½	Do. 4½ p.c. 1 Mt. Db. Sk.	100	105
4	Campbell, Praed, L., Per. 1 Mort. Deb. Stk.	100	106
4	Cannon, L., Mt. Db. Stk.	100	109
4	Do. "B" Deb. Stk.	100	104
5	Castlemaine, L., 1 Mt. Db.	100	94
3½	Charrington, Ltd., Mort. Deb. Stk. Red.	100	107
2/	Cheltnhm. Orig., Ltd.	5	7
6	Do. Cum. Pref.	5	7½
4	Do. Debs. Red.	100	107
10/	Chicago, Ltd.	10	3½
6	Do. Debs.	100	84½
—	Cincinnati, Ltd.	10	½
—	Do. Cum. Pref.	10	1½
10/	City of Baltimore	10	4
16/	Do. 8 p.c. Cum. Prf.	10	8
14/	City of Chicago, Ltd.	10	1¾
8	Do. Cum. Pref.	10	6
13	City of London, Ltd.	100	205½
5	Do. Cum. Pref.	100	137
4	Do. Mt. Deb. Stk., Rd.	100	112
2/	Colchester, Ltd.	5	5
7	Do. Pref.	5	7
4½	Do. Deb. Stk., Red.	100	109
5	Combe, Ltd., Cum. Pref.	10	14½
4	Do. Mt. Db. Stk, Rd.	100	108
3½	Do. Perp. Deb. Stk.	100	107
5	Comm'cial, L., D. Sk., Rd.	100	107½
5	Courage, L., Cm. Pref. Shs.	100	136½
4	Do. Irr. Mt. Deb. Stk.	100	126
3½	Do. Irr. "B" Mt. Db. Sk.	100	104
8	Daniell & Sons, Ltd.	10	
7	Do. Cum. Pref.	10	12½
4½	Do. 1 Mt. Perp. Db. Sk.	100	108½
4½	Do. "B" Deb. Stk.	100	102
10d.	Dartford, Ltd.	5	5½
2/9	Do. Cum. Pref.	5	5½
4	Do. 1 Mt. Db. Sk. Rd.	100	99
4	Davenport, Ld., 1 D. Stk.	100	102½
10/	Denver United, Ltd.	10	3½
8	Do. Cum. Pref.	10	8½
6	Do. Debs.	100	98½
4½	Deuchar, L., 1 D. Sk., Rd.	100	108
8/	Distillers, Ltd.	10	23½
4½	Do. Mt. Db. Stk., Rd.	100	115½
—	Dublin Distillers, Ltd.	5	1½
3/	Do. Cum. Pref.	5	4½
4½	Do. Irr. Deb. Stk.	100	—
5	Eadie, Ltd., Cum. Pref.	10	11
4	Do. Irr. 1 Mt. Db. Sk.	100	106
10/	Edinbgh. Utd., Ltd.	10	13
6	Do. Cum. Prf.	10	13½
5	Do. 1 Mt. Dbs.	100	110½
4	Eldridge, Pope, L. D. St. R.	100	107
—	Emerald & Phœnix, Ltd.	10	1½
8	Do. Cum. Pref.	10	6½
6	Empress Ltd., C. Pf.	10	11½
4½	Do. Mt. Deb. Stk.	100	105
10/	Farnham, Ltd.	10	16¾
6	Do. Cum. Pref.	10	14½
4	Fenwick, L., 1 D. Sk., Rd.	100	103
4	Flower & Sons, Irr. D. Sk.	100	111
4	Friary, L., 1 Db. Stk., Rd.	100	103½
4	Do. 1 "A" Db. Sk., Rd	100	100
4½	Groves, L., 1 Db. Sk., Rd.	100	110
14	Guinness, Ltd.	100	560
6	Do. Cum. Prf. Stk	100	189½
5	Do. Deb. Stk., Red.	100	122
5	Hall's Oxford L., Cm. Pf.	5	5½
6/	Hancock, Ld., Cm. Pf. Ord.	10	14
7/	Do. Def. Ord.	10	17½

Breweries, &c. (*continued*) :—

Div.	Name.	Paid.	Price.
6	Hancock, Ld., Cum. Pref.	10	15½
4	Do. 1 Deb. Stk., Rd.	100	112
5	Hoare, Ltd. Cum. Pref.	10	12¾
5	Do. "A" Cum. Pref.	10	12½
4	Do. Mt. Deb. Stk., Rd.	100	111
3½	Do. do. do. Rd.	100	104
4/6	Hodgson's, Ltd.	5	10
5	Do. 1 Mt. Db., Red.	—	120½
4	Do. 2 Mt. Db., 1906	—	102
4½	Hopcraft & N., Ltd., 1 Mt. Deb. Stk., Red.	100	103
5	Huggins, Ltd., Cm. Prf.	10	—
4½	Do. 1st D. Stk. Rd.	100	—
4½	Do. "B" Db. Stk. Rd.	100	—
12/	Hull, Ltd.	10	17
7	Do. Cum. Pref.	10	14½
4½	Ind, Coope, L., D.Sk., Rd.	100	118
4	Do. "B" Mt. Db. Stk. Rd.	100	111
3/	Indianapolis, Ltd.	10	3½
8	Do. Cm. Prf.	10	9½
5/	Jones, Frank, Ltd.	10	3½
7½	Do. Cum. Pref.	10	7½
5	Do. 1st Mort. Debs.	100	90½
4/	J. Kenward & Co., Ltd.	5	5½
4½	Kingsbury, L., 1 D.Sk., Rd	100	—
4	Lacon, L., D. Stk., Red.	100	110
4	Do. Irrd. "B" D. Sk.	100	106
4/	Lascelles, Ltd.	5	11
6	Do. Cum. Pref.	5	7¾
5	Leney, Ltd., Cum. Pref.	10	11½
4	Do. 1 Mt. Db. Stk. Rd.	100	102
30/7½	Lion, Ltd., £25 shares	17	49½
10/9	Do. New £10 shares	6	17
6	Do. Perp. Pref.	20	33
4	Do. B. Mt. Db. Sk. Rd.	100	107
4½	Lloyd & Y., Ltd., 1 Mt. Deb. Stk., Rd.	100	108½
4½	Locke & S., Ltd., Irr. 1st Mt. Deb. Stk.	100	101
4½	Lovibond, Ltd., 1st Mt. Deb. Stk., Rd.	100	102½
30/4	Lucas & Co., Ld., Deb. Stk.	100	107
8/	Manchester, Ltd.	10	19½
7	Do. Cum. Pref.	10	17
5	Marston, J., L., Cm. Prf.	10	10¾
4	Do. 1 Mt. Db. Sk., Rd.	100	101½
9/	Massey's Burnley, Ltd.	10	17
6	Do. Cum. Pref.	10	14½
4½	McCracken, Ltd., 1 Mt. Deb., 1908	100	59½
5	McEwan, Ltd., Cm. Pref.	10	14
5	Meux, Ltd., Cum. Pref.	10	14
4	Do. Mt. Db. Stk. Red.	100	111
4½	Michell & A., Ltd., 1 Mt. Deb. Stk. Red	100	105
4½	Mile End Dist. Db. Sk. Rd.	100	111
—	Milwaukee & Chic., Ltd.	10	1½
4/	Do. Cum. Pref.	10	6½
4½	Michell, Toms, L., Db.	50	57
6	Morgan, Ltd., Cum. Pref.	10	14½
10/	Nalder & Coll., Ltd.	10	35
6	Do. Cum. Pref.	10	15¾
4½	Do. Deb. Red.	100	112
12/	Newcastle, Ltd.	10	19½
6	Do. Cum. Pref.	10	14¾
5	Do. 1 Mt. Deb., 1911	100	111½
4	Do. "A" Deb. Stk. Red.	100	104
6	New England, Ltd	10	5
8	Do. Cum. Pref.	10	9¾
6	Do. Debs. Red	100	101½
4	New London, L., 1 D.Sk.	100	103
7/2	New Westminster, Ltd.	4	10½
2/4½	Do. Pref.	4	6½
—	New York, Ltd.	10	1
—	Do. 8 p.c. Cum. Pref.	10	4½
6	Do. 1 Mt. Deb. Red.	100	77½
5	Noakes, Ld., Cum. Pref.	10	12
4	Do 1 Mt. Db. Stk., Rd.	100	104
4½	Norfolk, L., "A" D.Sk. Rd	100	106
10/	Northampton, Ld.	10	16½
7	Do. Cum. Pref.	10	16
6	Do. Cum. Pref.	10	12½
5	Do. 1 Mt. Per. Db. Sk.	100	126
4	Nth. East., L., 1 D. Sk. Rd.	100	102
4½	N. Worcesters., L. Per. 1 Mort. Deb. Stock	100	97½
6	Nottingham, L., Cm. Prf.	10	11¼
5	Do. 1 Mt. Deb. Stk., Red.	100	114
27/4	Do. "B" do. Red.	50	112
6/	Ohlsson' Cape, Ld.	5	17
7	Do. Cum. Pref.	5	8¾
4½	Do. 2nd Cum. Pref.	5	5½
5	Do. Deb. Stk., Red.	100	113
4½	Oldfield, L., 1 Mt. Db. Stk.	100	106
6	Page & Overt., L., Cm. Prf.	10	13¾
4½	Do. 1 Mt. Dbs, Red.	100	109
10/	Parker's Burslem, Ltd.	10	24½
6	Do. Cum. Pref.	10	15
4	Do. 1 Mt. Dr. Stk., Red.	100	111
4	Persse, Ld., 1 Mt. Db. Rd.	100	95½
4	Phipps, L., Irr. 1 Db. Stk.	100	113
8	Plymouth, L., Min. Cu. Pf.	10	13½
4½	Do. Mt. Deb. Stk., Red.	100	104½
4½	Pryor, Reid, L., 1 D.S., R.	100	103½
5	Reid's, Ld., Cm. Pref. Stk.	100	137½
4	Do. Mt. Deb. Stk., Red	100	112
3½	Do. "B" Mt. Db. Stk., Rd	100	102
5	Rhondda Val., L., Cu. Pf	10	11
4½	Do. 1 Mt. Deb. Stk., Rd	100	109
5	Robinson, Ld., Cum. Pref.	10	11½
4½	Do. 1 Mt. Perp. Db. Stk.	100	112
4/	Rochdale, Ltd.	10	6
4½	Do. 1 Mt. Deb. Stk.	100	98½
7	Royal, Brentford, Ltd.	10	21
	Do. Cum. Pref.	10	15
4½	Do. 1 Mt. Dbs. Red	100	107
6/	St. Louis, Ltd.	10	4
8	Do. Cum. Pref.	10	8½
24/	St. Pauli, Ltd.	10	10
7	Do. Cum. Pref.	10	12
4½	Salt (T.), L., 1 Db. Sk. Rd.	100	110
4½	Do. "B" Db. Stk. Red	100	108
—	San Francisco, Ltd.	10	⅛
—	Do. 8 p.c. Cum. Pref.	10	¼

Breweries, &c. (*continued*) :—

Div.	Name.	Paid.	Price.
4½	Savill Brs., L., D. Sk. Rd.	100	118
4½	Scarboro., Ltd., 1 Db. Stk.	100	101
4	Shaw (Hy.), Ltd., 1 Mt. Db. Stk., Red.	100	104
22/	Showell's, Ltd	10	32½
7	Do. Cum. Pref.	10	17½
3/	Do. Gua. Shs.	5	7½
4½	Do. Mt. Db. Stk., Red.	100	—
4	Simonds, L., 1 D. Sk., Rd.	100	111
5½	Simson & McP., L., Cu. Pf.	10	9½
4½	Do. 1 Mt. Deb. Stk.	100	100
5/	Smith, Garrett, L., £20 Shs	10	16½
5	Do. Cum. Pref.	20	26
3½	Do. 3½ p.c. Mt. Db. Stk.	100	107
5	Smith's, Tadcaster, L., C Pf	10	12
4½	Do. Deb. Stk., Red.	100	112
4	Do. Deb. Stk. Red.	100	108
4½	Star, L., 1 M. Db. Stk., Rd.	100	105
4	Steward & P., L., 1 D. Sk.	100	111
9/	Strettons Derby, Ltd.	10	13
6	Do. Cum. Pref.	10	13½
4	Do. Irr. 1 Mt. Db. Stk.	100	103½
4½	Strong, Romsey, L., 1 D. S.	100	115
5	Stroud, L., Db. Sk., Rd.	100	111½
4½	Tadcaster To'er, L., D. Sk.	100	113
8/	Tamplin, Ltd	10	21
6	Do. Cum. Pref.	100	15
4	Do. "A" Db. Sk., Rd.	10	107
6	Thorne, Ltd., Cum. Pref.	10	14½
4	Do. Deb. Stk., Red.	100	105½
15/	Threlfall, Ltd.	10	46
6	Do. Cum. Pref.	10	16½
5	Do. 1 Mt. Dbs., Red.	100	116
4	Tollemache, L., D. Sk. Rd.	100	105
4	Truman, Hanb., D. Sk., R.	100	110
3	Do. "B" Mt. Db. Sk., Rd.	100	95
10/	United States, Ltd.	10	10
8	Do. Cum. Pref.	10	12
6	Do. 1 Mt. Deb	100	108½
6/	Walker & H., Ld., Cm. Prf.	10	11
4½	Do. 1 Mt. Deb. Stk., Red.	100	107
5	Walker, Peter, Ld. Cm. Prf.	10	13½
4	Do. 1 Mt. Dbs. Red.	100	111
4	Wallingford, L., D. Sk. Rd.	100	107
6	Watney, Ld., Cm. Prf. Sk.	100	167
5	Do. Mt. Db. Sk., Rd.	100	115½
4½	Do. "B" Mt. Db. Sk., Rd.	100	112
3½	Do. Mt. Db. Stk.	100	101
5	Watney, D., Ld., Cm. Prf.	10	12½
4½	Do. 1 Mt. Db. Stk.	100	106
10/	Webster & Sons, Ltd.	10	16¾
6	Do. Cum. Pref.	10	14
5	Wenlock Ltd Pref.	10	12½
4	Do. 1 Mt. Db. Sk., Rd.	100	108
5	West Cheshire, L., Cu. Pf.	10	10½
4	Do. Irred. 1 Mt. Db. Sk.	100	99
4½	Whitbread, L., Cu. Pf. Sh.	100	124½
4	Do. Db. Stk., Red.	100	110
3½	Do. "B" Db. Stk., Rd.	100	101
9/	Wolverhmpton & D. Ld.	10	16½
6	Do. Cum. Pref.	10	13½
4½	Do. 1 Mt. Dbs., Red.	100	108
5½	Worthington, Ld., Cm. Prf.	10	15½
5½	Do. Cum. "B" Pref.	10	13¾
4½	Do. Mt. Db. Sk., Rd.	100	112
3½	Do. Irr. "B" Db. Stk.	100	102
10/	Yates's Castle, Ltd.	10	13½
5	Do. Cum. Pref.	10	11
5	Younger W., L., Cu. Pf. Sh.	100	135

CANALS AND DOCKS.

Last Div.	Name.	Paid.	Price.
4	Birmingham Canal	100	142½
—	E. & W. India Dock	100	20½
—	Do. 4 p.c. Prf. Stk.	100	75
—	Do. P.L. Deb. Stk.	100	100
—	Do. Cons. Deb. Stk.	100	90
40/	G. Junction Ord. Shs.	100	151½
6/	Do. do. Pref.	10	19
4½	King's Lynn Per. Db. Stk.	100	118½
2½	Leeds & Lpool Canal	100	71
2½	Lndn & St. Kath. Dks.	100	56
4½	Do. Pref.	100	136½
4½	Do. Pref., 1878	100	132½
4½	Do. Pref., 1882	100	130
4	Do. Deb. Stk.	100	134½
—	Mchester Ship C. 5 p.c. Pf.	10	1½
3½	Do. 1st Perp. Mt. Deb.	100	98
—	Milford Dks. Db. Stk. "A"	100	18½
3¾	Millwall Dk.	100	59
5	Do. Perp. Prf.	100	140½
4½	Do. Prf.	100	106½
5	Do. New Per. Prf., 1887	100	126½
5	Do. Per. Deb. Stk.	100	152½
4/	Newhaven Har.	10	14½
2½	N. Metropolitan	100	66
5	Sharpness Nw. Pf. "A" Sk.	100	144½
4	Do. Deb. Stk.	100	118½
4	Sheffield & S. Yorks Nav. 4½ p.c. Pref Stk.	100	117½
36.432	Suez Canal	20	138
7	Surrey Co.nci. Dok., Ord.	100	148½
7	Do. Min. 4 p.c. Pref. "A"	110	150
5	Do. Pref. "B"	100	148½
5	Do do. "C"	100	148½
5	Do. do. "D"	100	144½
4½	Do. Deb. Stk.	100	152½

COMMERCIAL, INDUSTRIAL, &c.

Last Div.	Name.	Paid.	Price.
5	Accles, L., 1 Mt. Db., Red.	100	84½
2/6	Aërated Bread, Ltd.	1	12¾
—	African Gold Recovery, L.	1	¼
2/	Aluminium, L., "A" Shs.	1	2
4½	Do. 1 Mt. Db. Stk., Red.	100	97
5½	Amelia Nitr., L., 1 Murt. Deb., Red.	100	82½
7/	Anglo-Chil. Nitrate, Ltd., Cum. Pref.	10	6½
4½	Do. Cons. Mt. Bds., Red.	100	79½
4½	Anglo-Russian Cotton, Ld., 1 Charge Debs., Red.	100	99
11/3	Angus (G., & Co., L.), £10	7½	17
6/	Apollinaris, Ltd.	10	11¾
5/	Do. 5 p.c. Cum. Pref.	10	10¾
4	Do. Irred. Deb. Stock	100	104
6/	Appleton, French, & S., L.	5	½
3/	Argentine Meat Pres., L., 7 p.c. Pref.	10	2½
5	Argentine Refinry, Db. Rd.	100	98
6d.	Armstrong, Whitw., Ltd.	1	3½
4	Do. Cum. Pref.	5	6½
5	Artisans', Labr. Dwllgs., L.	100	131½
4½	Do. Non-Cm. Prf., 1879	100	132½
4½	Do. do. 1884	100	132½
—	Asbestos & Asbestic, Ltd.	10	7½
2/7½	Ashley-grdns., L., C. Prf.	5	6¼
4½	Do. 1 Mt. Deb. Stk.	100	112½
5/	Assam Rly. & Trdng., L., 8 p.c. Cum. Pref. "A"	10	15
—	Do. Deferrd. "B" Shs.	1	4
—	Do. do. (iss. f. pd)	1	3½
8/	Do. Cum. Pre-Prf. "A"	10	15
6/	Do. New Pref.	10	11½
5	Do. Debs., Red.	100	107
5	Do. Red. Mort. Debs.	100	109
6	Aust'lian Pastrl, L., Cu. Pf.	10	7
8d.	Aylesbury Dairy, Ltd.	1	1¼
4	Do. 4 p.c. Mt. Dbs.	100	104½
10/	Babcock & Wilcox, Ltd.	10	30
6	Do. 6 p.c. Cm. Prf.	10	16
8	Baker (Chs.), L., Cm. Pf.	5	9
8	Do. "B" Cm. Pref.	5	8½
8d.	Barker (John), Ltd.	1	2¼
5½	Do. Cum. Pref.	5	7¼
4½	Do. Irred. 1 Mt. Db. Stk.	100	130
—	Barnagore Jute, Ltd.	5	3
5	Do. Cum. Pref.	5	4¾
7½d.	Belgravia Dairy, Ltd.	1	1½
5/6	Bell (R.) & Co., Ltd.	5	3½
1/	Bell's Asbestos, Ltd.	1	½
5	Do. Mt. Db. Bds., Rd.	100	105
10/	Bengal Mills, Ltd.	10	11½
6/	Do. 5 p.c. Cum. Prf.	10	10½
2/5	Benson (J.W.) L., Cm. Pf.	10	10½
4	Do. Perp. Mt. Db. Stk.	100	101
6	Bergvik, L., 6 p.c. Cm. Pf.	10	12
12/	Do. Dfd.	10	9½
4½	Do. 1 Dbs., Red.	100	103½
3/	Birm'ham Vinegar, Ltd.	5	14½
5	Do. Cum. Pref.	5	5½
4½	Do. 1 Mt. Db. Stk., Rd.	100	109½
5	Boake (A.) L., 5 p.c. Cu. Pf.	10	10¾
2/6	Bodega, Ltd.	5	8½
4½	Do. Mt. Deb. Stk., Rd.	100	111
8/	Bottomley & Brs., Ltd.	10	6½
6/	Do. 6 p.c. Pt.	10	9½
8½d.	Bovril, Ltd.	1	⅞
1/0½	Do. Def.	1	⅝
6½d	Do. Cum. Pref.	1	1
4½	Do. Deb. Stk.	100	101
5/	Bradbury, Gretrex., Ltd., £10 share	8	14
5/	Do. 5 p.c. Cum. Pref.	10	13½
5/	Brewers' Sugar, L., 5 p.c. Cum. Pref.	10	10½
3/6	Brighton Grd. Hotel, Ld.	5	3½
4	Do Mt. Db. Stk., Red.	100	100½
5	Bristol Hotel & Palm. Co., Ltd. 1st Mt. Red. Deb.	100	105
9½d.	British & Bengton's. Tea Tr. Asc., Ltd.	1	1½
5	Do. Cum. Prf.	5	5½
—	British Deli & Lgkat. Tobacco, Ltd.	1	¼
—	Do. Cum. Prf.	1	½
—	British Tea Table, Ltd.	1	2¾
5½	Do. Cum. Pref.	1	1¼
2/6	Brooke, Ben., & Co., Ltd., Cum. Pref.	5	5¾
7/6	Brooke, Bond & Co., Ltd.	5	20
3/	Brown Brs., L., Cum. Pref.	5	5¾
10/	Browne & Eagle, Ltd.	10	13½
5	Do. Cum. Pref.	10	13
4	Do. Mrt. Db. Sk., Red.	100	110
20/	Brunner, Mond, & Co., Lt.	0	41
7/	Do. £10 shares	3½	17
7	Do. Cum. Pref.	10	18
7	Do. £10 shares	5	8½
10/	Bryant & May, Ltd.	5	20
3/	Bucknall, H., & Sons, Lt.	5	7½
6	Do. Cum Pref.	5	8
4/	Burke, E. & J., Ltd.	5	7¼
6	Do. Cum. Pref.	5	7½
6	Do. Irred. Deb. Stk.	100	155
1/	Burlington Htls. Co., Ltd.	1	1½
5	Do. Cum. Pref.	1	1
4	Do. Perp. Deb. Stk.	100	106½
5	Bush, W. J., & Co., Ltd. Cum. Pref.	5	5½
4	Do. 1 Deb. Stk., Red.	100	102
5½	Callard, Stewart, & Watt, Ltd., Cum. Pref.	1	1½
4/	Callender's Cable L., Shs.	5	9½
4½	Do. 1 Deb. Stk., Red.	100	111½
—	Campbell, R., & Sons, Lt.	3	2½
6	Cantareira Water, Bd., Rd	100	99½
5	Do. (2nd issue)	100	90
4	Cartavio Sugar, Ltd., 6 p.c. 1st Debs., Red.	80	82½
9/	Cassell & Co., Ltd., £10	9	15½
5	Causton, Sir J., & Sons, Ltd. Cum. Pref.	10	13½

Commercial, &c. (*continued*) :—

Div.	Name.	Paid.	Price.
4	Cent. Prod. Mkt. of B.A. 1st Mt. Str. Debs.	100	81
4	Chappell & Co., Ltd., Mt. Deb. Stk. Red.	100	103
6/	Chicago & N.W. Gran. 8 p.c. Cum. Pref.	10	3
—	Chicago Packing & Prov.	10	6
8	Do. Cum. Pref.	10	10½
6/	City Offices, Ltd	36½	13½
3½	Do. Mt. Deb. Stk.	100	108½
7/2½	Cy. London Real Prop., Ltd., £25 shs.	12	19
4/6	Do. £12½ shs.	7½	13½
3½	Do. Deb. Stk. Red.	100	106½
3½	Do. Deb. Stk. Red.	100	105½
3	Do.	100	100½
4/	Cy. of Santos Imprvts., Ltd., 7 p.c. Pref.	10	8½
20/	Clay, Bock, & Co., Ltd.	10	6
8	Do. Cum. Pref.	10	10
6	Do. Mort. Deb.	100	103½
20/	Coats, J. & P., Ltd.	10	60½
6	Do. Cum. Pref.	10	18
4½	Do. Deb. Stk. Red.	100	112½
9½d	Coburg Hotel, Ltd	1	1½
4	Do. Deb. Stk. Red.	100	102
6	Colonial Consign & Dis., Ltd., Cum. Pref.	5	4¾
4½	Do. 1st Mort. Debs.	100	96½
—	Colorado Nitrate, Ltd.	5	½
4/	Co. Gen des Asphtes. de F., Ltd.	6	6½
5	Do. Non-Cm. Prf.	—	5½
5	Cook, J. W., & Co., Ltd., Cum. Pref.	5	5¾
5	Cook, T., & Son, Egypt, Ltd., 1st Mt. Deb. Red.	100	110½
—	Cork Co., Ltd., 6 p.c. Cum. Pref.	5	2
5	Cory, W., & Sn, L., Cu. Pf.	5	6½
4	Do. 1st Deb. Stk. Red.	100	108
8½d.	Crisp & Co., Ltd	1	1¾
5½	Do. Cum. Pref.	1	1½
—	Crompton & Co., Ltd., 7 p.c. Cum. Pref.	5	2½
5	Do. 1st Mt. Reg. Deb.	—	89½
4/6	Crossley, J., & Sons, Ltd.	5	8½
5	Do. Cum. Pref.	5	6½
—	Crystal Pal. Ord. "A" Stk.	100	8½
—	Do. "B" Red. Stk	100	1½
6	Do. 6 p.c. 1st 1887 Deb. Stk. Red.	100	117½
—	Do. 6 p.c. 2nd 1887 Deb. Stk. Red.	100	42½
—	Do. 6 p.c. 3rd 1887 Deb. Stk. Red.	100	17½
3	Do. 3 p.c. 1st 1895 Deb. Stk.	100	94½
—	Daimler Motor, Ltd.	10	6
4/	Dalgety & Co., £20 Shs.	5	5½
4½	Do. Deb. Stk.	100	123
4	Do.	100	115
7/	De Keyser's Ryl. Htl., L.	10	14
5	Do. Cum. Pref.	10	11½
4	Do. Deb. Stk., Red.	100	110
6	Denny, H., & Sons, Ltd., Cum. Pref.	10	14½
5/3	Davas, Routledge & Co., L.	7	8¾
5	Dickinson, J., & Co., L., Cum. Pref. Stk.	100	123
4½	Domin. Cottn. Mls., Ltd. Mt. Stg. Dbs.	100	97
6/	Dorman, Long & Co., L.	5	4½
—	Eastmans, Ltd	10	2½
12/	Do. 8 p.c. Cum. Pref.	10	10
2/6	E. C. Powder, Ltd	3	
1/6	Edison & Swn Utd. Elec. Ltd., "A" £5 Shs.	3	
2/6	Do. fully-paid	5	
4½	Ekman Pulp & Ppr. Co., Ltd., Mt. Deb., Red.	100	96
1/1½	Electric Construc., Ltd.	2	2¾
7	Do. Cum. Pref.	2	3½
25/	Eley Bros., Ltd.	10	38
—	Elmore's Cop. Deptg., L.	1	⅜
—	Elmore's Wire Mnfg., L.	2	½
—	Elysée Pal. Hotel Co., L.	5/	½
5 p.c.	Do. 5 p.c. £100 Db., Rd.	70	97½
8½d.	Evans, Ben., & Co., Ltd.	1	1
5	Do. 1 Mt. Db. Sk., Rd.	100	108
8½d.	Evans, D. H., & Co., L.	1	2½
6	Do. Cum. Pref.	1	1½
4½	Do. 1 Mt. Db. Sk., Rd.	100	112
2/1	*Evening News*, L., 5 p.c. Cum. Pref.	5	5½
5/3	Evered & Co., L., £10 Sh.	7	13
7/6	Do.	10	19
4	Fairbairn Pastoral Co., Aust., L., 1 Mt. Db., Rd.	100	102
6	Fairfield Shipbldg., Ltd., Cum. Pref.	10	10½
4½	Do. Mort. Deb. Stk.	100	109½
6/	Farmer & Co., Ld., 6 p.c. Cum. Pref.	10	13½
10	Field, J. C. & J., Ltd.	10	10
14/	Do. 7 p.c. Cum. Pref.	10	14
1/3	Fordham, W. B., & Sns, Ld.	1	2
5/6	Fore-st. Warehouse, Ltd.	11	9½
4	Do. Regd. Debs., Rd.	100	103½
3/6	Foster, M. B. & Sons, Ltd.	4	6
5	Do. Pref.	10	11½
9/	Foster, Porter, & Co., L.	10	15½
4	Fowler, J., & Co. (Leeds), Ltd., 1 Mt. Deb., Red.	100	103½
3/	Fraser & Chalmers, Ltd.	3	2½
4½	Free, Rodwell & Co., Ltd., Deb Stk.	100	101½
6½d.	Furness, T., & Co., Ltd., 5½ p.c. Cum. Pref.	1	½
4½	Garside & Co. (of Manchstr), L., 1 Mt. Db. Sk.	100	102
11	Genl. Hydraul. Power, L.	10	275

Commercial, &c. (*continued*):—

Last Div.	Name.	Paid.	Price.
8/	Gillman & Spencer, Ltd.	5	2½
6	Do. Pref.	5	4¾
5	Do. Mort. Debs.	50	51
4	Goldsbro., Mort & Co., L., "A" Deb. Stk., Red.	100	73½
—	Do. 3 p.c. "B" Inc. Deb. Stk., Red.	100	14
8/	Gordon Hotels, Ltd.	10	20
5½	Do. Cum. Pref.	10	14½
4½	Do. Perp. Deb. Stk.	100	137½
4	Do. do.	100	122½
—	Greenwich Inld. Linoleum Co., Ltd.	1	¾
7	Greenwood & Batley, Ltd., Cum. Pref.	10	10
7½d.	Hagemann & Co., Ltd., 6 p.c. Cum. Pref.	1	1
—	Hammond, Ltd.	10	½
—	Do. 8 p.c. Cum. Pref.	10	2½
—	Do. 6 p.c. Cum. Inc. Stk. Red.	100	45
4	Hampton & Sons, Ltd., 4 p.c. 1 Mt. Db. St. Red.	100	106
—	Hans Crescent Htl., L., 6 p.c. Cum. Pref.	5	3
4	Do. 1 Mt. Deb. Stk.	100	90
5	Harmsworth, Ld., Cm. Pf.	1	1⅛
4/	Harrison, Barber, Ltd.	5	4½
3/	Harrod's Stores, Ltd.	1	4¼
2/6	Do. Cum. Pref.	5	7¼
5½	Hawaiian Comcl. & Sug. 1 Mt. Debs.	100	91½
5	Hazell, Watson, L., C. P.	10	12
18/	Henley's Teleg., Ltd.	10	22½
7	Do. Pref. Shs.	10	19
4½	Do. Mt. Db. Stk., Rd.	100	112½
6	Henry, Ltd.	10	12½
5	Do. Cum. Pref.	10	13½
4½	Do. Mt. Debs., Red.	50	53
6	Hepworth, Ld., Cm. Prf.	10	11
—	Herrmann, Ltd.	1	½
—	Hildesheimer, Ltd.	3	1½
1/2½	Holbrn. & Frasca, Ltd.	1	2
5	Do. Cum. Pref.	10	11½
4	Do. Deb. Stk.	100	113
6	Home & Col. Stres., L., C. P	5	7¾
6	Hood & M.'s Stres., Ltd., Cum. Pref.	1	½
6	Hook, C. T Ltd.	10	6
7/2	Hornsby, Ltd., £10 Shs.	8	3
5/6	Do. 6 p.c. Cm. Pf. Sk.	100	90
—	Hotchks. Ordn., Ltd.	10	1
—	Do. 7 p.c. Cm. Prf.	10	4
5	Do. 1 Mt. Dbs., Rd.	100	95½
6	Htl. Cecil, Ld., Cm. Prf.	5	4½
4	Do. 1 Mt. D. Sk., R.	100	105½
8/	Heward & Bulgh, Ltd.	10	38
6	Do. Pref.	10	16
4	Do. Deb. Stk., Red.	100	107
5/	Howell, J., Ltd., £5 Shs.	4	9
—	Howell & Js., Ld., £3½ Shs.	3	½
1/6	Humber, Ltd.	1	¾
6	Do. Cum. Pref.	1	½
5/6	Hunter, Wilts., Ltd.	5	7
2/7	Hyam Clthg., Ltd., 5 p.c. Cum. Pref.	5	5½
40/	Impl. Russn. Cotton, L.	5	6
5	Impd. Industl. Dwgs., Ld.	100	130½
6d.	Do. Defrd.	1	1½
25/	Impd. Wood Pave., Ltd.	10	15½
15/	Ind. Rubber, Gutta Per. Telegraph Works, Ltd.	10	21½
4	Do. 1 Mt. Debs., Red.	100	104
6	Intern. Tea, Cum. Pref.	5	6½
20½d.	Jays, Ltd.	1	1¾
5½	Do. Cum. Pref.	5	6¾
8½d.	Jones & Higgins, Ltd.	1	2½
4½	Do. 1 Mt. Db. Sk., Rd.	100	113
5/	Kelly's Directory, Ltd., 5 p.c. Cum. Pref.	10	12¾
4	Do. Mort. Db. Sk., Rd.	100	106
—	Kent Coal Explrtn. Ltd.	1	¾
9½d.	King, Howmann, Ltd.	1	1¼
4/	Kinloch & Co., Ltd.	5	8½
6	Do. Pref.	5	7
5	Lady's Pictorial Pub., Ltd., Cum. Pref.	5	5
—	La Guaira Harb., Ltd., 7 p.c. Deb. Stk.	100	—
—	Do. 2 Mt. 7 p.c. Deb. Bds., Red.	100	—
4/	Lagunas Nitrate, Ltd.	5	2
2/	Lagunas Syn., Ltd.	5	1
5	Do. 1 Mt. Debs., Red.	100	80
—	L. Copais Ld., 1 Mt. 6 p.c. Debs., Red.	100	35½
3/	Lautaro Nitrate, Ltd.	5	4
5	Do. 1 Mt. Debs., Red.	—	100
9/	Lawes Chem. L., £10 shs.	9	5½
14/	Do. N. Cm. Min. Pref.	10	12½
—	Leeds Forge, 7 p.c. Cm. Pf.	5	3½
5	Do. 1 Mt. Debs., Red.	90	47
5	Lever Bros., L., Cm. Pf.	10	13½
6	Liberty, L., 6 p.c. Cm. Pf.	10	15
20/	Liebig's, Ltd.	20	75
5	Lilley & Sk., L., Cm. Pf.	5	5½
39/4	Linoleum Manfg Ltd.	5	16
3/	Linotype, Ltd., Pre	5	5½
5/	Do. Def.	5	7½
4/	Lister & Co., Ltd.	10	4
5	Do. Cum. Pref.	10	8½
5/	Liverpool Nitrate	5	5
—	Liverpool Warehsg., Ltd	10	3½
5½	Do. Cum. Pref.	10	8½
4	Do. 1 Mt. Db. Stk., Rd.	100	105
5½	Lockharts, Ltd., Cm. Pf.	1	1½
4/6	Ldn. & Til. Lightrage £10	9	6½
6/	Ldn. Comcl. Sale Rms., L.	10	17½
3	Do. 1 Mt. Deb. Stk., Red.	100	103
3	London Nitrate, Ltd.	5	1½
4/	London Nitrate, Ld. 1 p.c. Cm. Min. Pf.	5	3½
8/	London Pavilion, Ltd.	5	7

Commercial, &c. (*continued*):—

Last Div.	Name.	Paid.	Price.
2/6	London Produce Clg. Ho., Ltd., £10 Shares	2½	3½
4/	London Stereos., Ltd.	5	3
6d.	Ldn. Un. Laun. L. Cm. Pf.	1	½
8½d.	Louise, Ltd.	1	½
5½	Do. Cum. Pref.	1	½
5/	Lovell & Christmas, Ltd.	5	11½
6	Do. Cum. Pref.	5	7½
4	Do. Mt. Deb. Stk., Red.	100	107
1/3	Lyons, Ltd.	1	4
4½	Do. 1 Mt. Deb., Stk., Rd.	100	111½
10/	Machinery Trust, Ltd.	5	14
4½	Do. 4½ Deb. Stk.	100	104
6	MacLellan, L., Min. C. Pf.	10	9½
5	Do. 1 Mt. Debs., 1900	100	101½
—	McEwan, J. & Co., Ltd.	10	1½
6	Do. Mt. Debs., Red.	100	89½
8	McNamara, L., Cm. Pref.	10	9
7½d.	Maison Virot, Ltd.	1	1½
2/7	Do. 6 p.c. Cum. Pref.	5	4½
5/	Manbré Sacc., L., Cm. Pf.	10	12
10/	Mangan Brze., L., £10 Shs.	6	15½
2/	Mason & Mason, Ltd.	5	2½
6	Do. Cum. Pref.	5	5½
—	Maynards, Ltd.	1	½
6	Do. Cum. Pref.	1	½
9½d.	Mazawattee Tea, Ltd.	1	1½
5	Do. Cum. Pref.	5	5½
6	Mellin's Food Cum. Pref.	5	6½
4½	Met. Ascn. Imp. Dwigs. L.	100	110
3½	Do. 1 Mt. Deb. Stk.	100	97
5	Metro. Indus. Dwigs., Ltd.	5	5
4	Do. do. Cum. Pref.	5	5½
5	Metro. Prop., L., Cm. Pf.	5	5½
4½	Do. 1st Mt. Debs. Stk.	100	103½
6	Mexican Cotton 1 Mt Db.	100	93½
4½	Mid. Class Dwigs., L., Db.	100	120½
1/	Millars' Karri, Ltd.	1	3½
6	Do. Cum. Pref.	1	1½
5/	Milner's Safe, Ltd.	10	20½
10/	Moir & Son, Ltd., Pref.	5	8½
6	Morgan Cruc., L., Cm. Pf.	10	14½
2/	Morris, B., Ltd.	3½	3½
—	Murray L. 5½ p.c. C. Pf.	5	5½
—	Do. 4½ 1 Mt. Db. Sk. Rd.	100	108
—	Natnl. Dwigs., L., 5 p.c. Pf.	5	1
1/7½	Nat. Safe Dep., Ltd.	4	3½
6	Do. Cum. Pref.	1	1½
—	Native Guano, Ltd.	5	½
—	Nelson Bros., Ltd.	10	2½
5	Do. Deb. Stk., Red.	100	80½
4/	Neuchtel Asph., Ltd.	10	10½
—	New Central Borneo, Ld.	1	—
10d.	New Darvel Tob., Ltd.	18/	1½
1/6	New Explosives, Ltd.	3	3½
5/3½	New Gd. Htl., Bham, L.	5	4
5½	Do. Pref.	5	4½
4	Do. 1 Mt. Db. Stk., Rd.	100	96½
—	New Julia Nitrate, Ltd.	10/	⅛
—	New Ldn. Borneo Tob., L.	16/	½
1/6	New Premier Cycle, Ltd.	1	½
6	Do. 6 p.c. Cum. Pref.	1	¼
4½	Do. 4½ p.c. 1 Mt. Db. Rd	100	—
—	New Tamargl. Nitr., Ltd	1	⅛
—	Do. 8 p.c. Cum. Pref.	1	⅜
6	Do. 6 p.c. 1 Mt. Dbs. Rd.	100	62½
3/7½d.	Newnes, G., L., Cm. Prf.	1	1½
1/3	Nitr. Provision, Ltd.	2½	½
24/	Nobel-Dynam., Ltd.	10	18½
—	North Brazn. Sugar, Ltd.	1	½
15/	Oakey, Ltd.	10	31
6	Do. Cum. Pref.	10	17
—	Paccha Jarp. Nitr., Ltd.	5	½
5	Pac. Borax, L., 1 Db. Rd.	100	110
—	Palace Hotel, Ltd.	10	5½
5½	Do. Cum. Pref.	10	8½
4	Do. 1 Mt. Deb. Stk.	100	104
2/6	Palmer, Ltd.	5	1½
6	Do. Cum. Pref.	5	2½
9⅞d.	Paquin, Ltd.	1	1
6	Do. Cum. Pref.	5	4½
5½	Parnall, Ltd., Cum. Pref.	1	½
4/6	Pawsons, Ltd., £10 Shs.	6	6½
4	Do. Mt. Debs., Red.	100	106
6	Pearks, G. & T., Ltd., 6 p.c. Cum. Pref.	1	¾
9½d.	Pears, Ltd.	1	1⅜
6	Do. Cum. Pref.	10	14
5	Do. Deb. Stk.	100	129
5½	Pearson, C. A., L., Cu. Pf.	5	5½
4/3	Peebles, Ltd.	5	7½
5	Do. Cum. Pref.	5	6½
4½	Do. Mt. Deb. Stk. Red.	100	113½
5½	Peek Bros., Ltd., 1 Cum. Pref., Nos. 1-60,000	5	6
3½	Do. 3½ p.c. 1 Db. Stk.	100	103½
7½d.	Pegamoid, Ltd.	1	½
—	Phospho-Guano, Ltd.	5	2½
—	Pillsbury-W. Fl. Mills, L.	10	2
16/	Do. 8 p.c. Cum. Pref.	10	6½
6	Do. 1 Mort. Debs.	100	95½
9½d.	Plummer, Ltd.	1	1½
5	Do. Cum. Pref.	5	5½
7/6	Price's Candle, Ltd.	16	36
6	Priest Marians, L., Cm. Pf.	1	1½
6	Pryce Jones, Ld., Cm. Pf.	5	7½
5	Do. Deb. Stk.	100	122
10½d.	Pullman, Ltd.	1	1½
6d.	Do. Cum. Pref.	1	1½
11½	Raleigh Cycle, Ltd.	1	½
6	Do. Cum. Pref.	1	½
—	Recife Drnge. Ld. 1 Mt. Debs., R	100	19
6	Redfern, Ltd. Cum. Prf.	10	14
5	Ridgways, Ltd., Cu. Pf.	5	5½
—	R. Janeiro Cy. Imps. Ld.	25	8½
5	Do. Debs.	100	86½
5	Do. 1882-1893	100	86½
11/	R. Jan Fl. Mills, Ltd.	7	6½
5	Do. 1 Mt. Debs., Rd.	100	94
—	Riv. Plate Meat, Ltd.	5	3½
—	Do. Pref.	5	5
8½d.	Roberts, J. R., Ltd.	1	1½

Commercial, &c. (*continued*):—

Last Div.	Name.	Paid.	Price.
5	Roberts 1 Mt. D. Sk., Rd.	100	112
8½d.	Roberts, T. R., Ltd.	1	2½
5	Do. Cum. Pref.	1	1½
3/	Rosario Nit., Ltd.	5	3½
5	Do. Debs., Red.	100	103
5	Do. Huara, Debs.	—	104
1/	Rover Cycle, Ltd.	1	½
6/	Ryl. Aquarium, Ltd.	5	4½
6	Do. Pref.	5	6
5	Ryl. Htl., Edin., Cm. Pf.	1	1½
1/2½	Ryl. Niger, Ltd., £10 Sh.	2	3
6/	Do.	10	15½
—	Russian Petroleum	10	24½
—	Do. 6½ p.c. Cm. Prf.	10	11
3/	Ruston, Proctor, Ltd.	10	11
4½	Do. 1 Mort. Debs.	100	104
6/	Sadler, Ltd.	11	7
—	Sal. Carmen Nit., Ltd.	5	4
9d.	Salmon & Gluck., Ltd.	1	1⅜
—	Salt Union, Ltd.	10	1½
1½	Do. 7 p.c. Pref.	10	5½
4½	Do. Deb. Stk.	100	101½
4½	Do. "B" Deb. Sk., Rd.	100	97½
—	San Donato Nit., Ltd.	5	½
2/6	San Jorge Nit., Ltd.	5	3½
—	San Pablo Nit., Ltd.	5	½
—	San Sebastn. Nit., Ltd.	5	½
1/9	Sanitas, Ltd	1	2½
—	Sa. Elena Nit., Ltd.	5	½
—	Sa. Rita Nit., Ltd.	5	1½
5/	Savoy Hotel, Ltd.	10	16
7	Do. Pref.	10	14
4	Do. 1 Mt. Deb. Stk.	100	111½
5	Do. Debs., Red	100	102½
5	Do. & Ldn. For. Htl., Ltd., 5 p.c. Debs. Red.	100	99
1½d.	Schweppes, Ltd.	1	1⅛
—	Do Def.	1	⅜
5	Do. Cum. Pref.	1	1¼
4	Do. Deb. Stk.	100	108
1/	Singer Cyc., Ltd.	1	⅜
5½	Do Cum. Pref.	1	½
—	Smokeless Pwdr., Ltd.	1	¼
5½d.	S. Eng. Dairies, Ltd., 6 p.c. Cum. Pref.	1	1½
—	Sowler Thos. L.	1	1½
3/4½	Do. 5½ Cm. Pf.	5	5½
4/6	Spencer, Turner, & Co. Ltd	5	8½
5	Do. Cum. Pref.	5	6½
5	Spicer, Ld., 5 p.c. Dbs. Rd.	100	65
4/	Spiers & Pond, Ltd.	10	22
5	Do. 1 Mt. Debs., Red.	100	117½
5	Do. "A" Db. Stk., Rd.	100	111
5	Do. "B" 1 Db. Stk., Rd.	100	111
4	Do. Fd. "C" 1 Db. S., R.	100	104
7/6	Spratt's, Ltd	5	12½
4	Do. Debs., 1914	—	105
5	Steiner Ld., Cm. Pf.	10	11½
4	Do. 1 Mt. Db. Sk. Rd.	100	106
9/	Stewart & Clydesdale, L.	10	14
6	Do. Cum. Pref.	10	15
35/3	Sulphide Corp.	100	80
1/	Swan & Edgar, L.	1	1½
1/	Sweetmeat Automatic, L.	1	4
2/9	Teetgen, Ltd., Cum. Pref.	5	6
24/	Teleg. Construction., Ld.	12	35½
5	Do. Db. Bds., Rd., 1899	100	103½
3/0½	Tilling, Ld. 5½ p.c. Cm. Prf.	5	6½
4	Do. 4 p.c. 1 Dbs., Rd.	—	104
8½d.	Tower Tea, Ltd.	1	1½
5	Do. Cum. Pref.	5	5½
5	Travers, Ltd., Cum. Pref.	10	12½
4	Do. 1 Mt. Dbs., Rd.	100	105
6	Tucuman Sug., 1 Dbs., Rd.	100	100
4/	United Alkali, Ltd.	10	1½
7	Do. Cum. Pref.	10	7½
5	Do. Mt. Db. Stk., Rd.	100	109½
2½d.	United Horse Shoe, Ltd., Non-Cum. 8 p.c. Pref.	1	⅛
5	Un. Kingm. Tea, Cm. Prf.	5	4½
2/	Un. Lankat Plant., Ltd.	1	2
4/	Un. Limmer Asphlte., Ld.	3	4½
13/	Val de Travers Asph., L.	10	15½
3/	V. den Bergh's, L., Cm. P.	5	6½
6	Walkers, Park., L., C. Pf.	10	3
4½	Do. 1 Mt. Debs., Red.	100	90½
6/	Wallis, Thos. & Co., Ltd.	5	14
6	Do. Cum. Pref.	5	8½
5½	Waring, Ltd., Cum. Pref.	5	5⅜
4½	Do. 1 Mt. Db. Sk., Red.	100	113
4½	Do. Irred. "B" Db. Stk.	100	105
12/	Waterlow, Dfd. Ord.	10	14½
4/	Do. Pref.	10	14½
3½	Do. Cum. Pref.	10	10½
10/	Waterlow Bros. & L., Ld.	10	9
5	Do. Pref.	10	12½
1/2½	Welford, Ltd.	1	2
4½	Do. Debs., Red.	100	108
1/	Welford's Surrey Dairies, Ltd.	1	1½
7½d.	West London Dairy, Ltd.	1	1
4½	Wharncliffe Dwllgs., L., Pf.	10	11½
18/10	Do. 3 p.c. Irr. Mt. Db. Sk.	100	96
6d.	White, A. J., Ltd.	1	½
6	Do. 6 p.c. Cum. Pref.	1	½
4	White, J. Bazley, Ltd., 1 Mort. Debs., Red	100	90½
5	White, R., Ltd., 1 Mort. Deb. Stock, Red.	100	104½
5/	White, Tomkins, Ltd	10	12
5	Do. Cum. Pref.	10	11½
6	White, W. N., L., Cm. Pf.	1	1
2/6	Wickens, Pease & Co., L.	5	3½
6	Wilkie, Ltd., Cum. Pref.	10	15½
3/6	Willans & Robinson, Ltd.	5	8½
6	Do. Cum. Pref.	5	7½
4½	Do. 1 Mt. Db. Stk., Red.	100	108
7½d.	Williamsons, L., Cm. Prf.	1	1½
6	Winterbottm. Book Cloth, Ltd., Cum. Prf.	10	15
3/	Yates, Ltd.	5	6½
6	Do. Cum. Pref.	5	6½
	Young's Paraffin. Ltd.	4	1½

CORPORATION STOCKS—COLONIAL AND FOREIGN.

Per Cent.	Name.	Paid.	Price.
6	Auckland City, '72 1904-24	100	118
6	Do. Cons., '79, Red. 1930	100	138½
5	Do. Deb. Ln., '83..1934-8	100	117
6	Auckland Harb. Debs.	100	111½
5	Do. 1917	100	111
5	Do. 1936	100	116
5½	Balmain Boro' 1914	—	115
5	Boston City (U.S.)	100	102½
5	Do. 1900	100	105
5	Brunswick Town 5 c. Debs. 1916-20	100	111
15/	B. Ayres City 6 p.c.	100	57
4½	Do. 4½ p.c.	100	75
5	Cape Town, City of	100	113
4	Do. 1943	100	116
4	Chicago, City of, Gold 1915	—	110
6	Christchurch 1926	100	131½
—	Cordoba City	100	17½
5	Duluth (U.S.) Gold 1926	—	110
6	Dunedin (Otago) 1925	100	127½
6	Do. 1906	100	113
5	Do. Consols 1908	100	111
4	Durban Insc. Stk. 1944	100	111
4	Essex Cnty., N. Jersey 1926	$100	114½
5	Fitzroy, Melbrne. 1916-19	100	110
5	Gisborne Harbour 1915	100	110½
4	Greymouth Harbour 192-	100	110
4	Hamilton 193-	100	108
5	Hobart Town 1918-3-	100	116
4	Do. 194-	100	107
4½	Invercargill Boro. Dbs. 193-	100	111
6	Kimberley Boro., S.A. Dbs	—	102
4	Launceston Twn. Dbs. 191-	100	107
6	Lyttleton, N.Z., Harb. 192-	100	125
4	Melbourne Bd. of Wks. 192-	100	107
5	Melb. City Debs. 1897-19-	100	107½
4½	Do. Debs. 1908-2-	100	113½
4	Do. Debs. 1915-20-2-	100	108
5	Melbne. Harb. Bds., 1908-	100	112
4½	Do. do. 191-	100	110
4	Do. do. 1918-2-	100	105
4½	Melbrne. Tms. Dbs. 1914-1-	100	113
4½	Do. Fire Brig. Db. 192-	100	108
5	Mexico City Stg.	100	90
4	Moncton N. Bruns. City	100	103
4½	Montevideo	100	59
5	Montreal Stg.	100	104
5	Do. 1874	100	104
5	Do. 1879	100	106
3½	Do. 193-	100	104
3	Do. Perm. Deb. Stk.	100	98½
4	Do. Cons. Deb. Stk. 193-	100	113
6	Napier Boro. Consolid. 191-	100	119
5	Napier Harb. Debs. 192-	100	115
5	Do. Debs. 192-	100	107
6	New Plymouth Harb. Debs. 190-	100	108
6	New York City 190-	—	107½
3½	Do. 1910-2-	—	105½
4½	Nth. Melbourne Debs. 1-600 192-	100	105
5	Oamaru Boro. Cons. 192-	100	101
6	Do. Harb. Bds. (Reg.	100	74
25/	Do. 6 p.c. (Bearer) 1919	100	35
6	Otago Harb. Deb. Reg.	100	103
6	Do. 1877	100	107
6	Do. 1881 192-	100	115
5	Do. Debs. 1921	100	107
5	Do. Cons. 1934	100	105
6	Ottawa City	100	111
6	Do. 1904	100	113½
4½	Do. Debs. 1915	100	110
6	Port Elizabeth Waterworks	100	111
5	Port Louis	100	111
5	Prahran Debs. 1917	100	108
4	Do. Debs. 1919	100	102
6	Quebec C. Coupon. 1875 1905	100	112
6	Do. do. 1878 1908	100	116
4½	Do. Debs. 1914-18	100	108
4	Do. Debs. 1923	100	108
3½	Do. Cns. Rg. Stk., Red.	100	101
5	Richmond (Melb.) Dbs. 1917	100	113
4	Rio Janeiro City	100	57
4	Rome City	100	—
4	Do. 2nd to 8th Iss.	100	92
—	Rosario C.	100	25½
—	Do.	100	25½
4	St. Catherine (Ont.) 1926	100	101
4	St. John, N.B., Debs. 1934	—	103
4½	St. Kilda (Melb) Dbs. 1918-21	100	105
4	St. Louis C. (Miss.) 1911	100	106
4	Do. 1913	100	103½
3·65	Do. 1915	—	110
—	Santa Fé City Debs.	100	21
6	Santos City	100	95
6	Sofia City	100	83
5	Sth. Melbourne Debs. 1915	100	111
4½	Do. Debs. 1919	100	107
5	Sydney City 1904	100	109
4	Do. Debs. 1912-13	100	107
4	Do. do. (1894) 1919	100	109
7	Timaru Boro. 7 p.c. 1910	100	126½
5	Timaru Harb. Debs 1914	100	107
5	Do. Debs. 1916	100	106
6	Toronto City Wtwks 1904-6	100	114
6	Do. Cons. Debs. 1898	100	101
5	Do. G. Cns. Dbs. 1919-20	100	118
4	Do. Strlg. 1922-8	100	107
4	Do. Local Improv.	100	102
3½	Do. 1929	100	105
5½	Valparaiso	100	100
4	Vancouver 1931	100	107
4	Do. 1932	100	108
6	Wanganui Harb. Dbs. 1905	100	110
6	Wellington Con. Deb. 1907	100	117
6	Do. Improv., 1879	100	123
6	Do. Wtrwks. Dbs., 1880	100	123
4½	Do. Debs., 1893 1933	100	116
4½	Wellington Harb. 1907	100	104
4	Westport Harb. Dbs. 1925	100	110
6	Winnipeg City Deb. 1907	—	118
5	Do. 1914	100	119

FINANCIAL, LAND, AND INVESTMENT.

Last Div.	Name.	Paid.	Price.
5	Agency, Ld. & Fin. Aust., Ltd., Mt. Db. Stk., Rd.	100	90½
	Amer. Frehld. Mt. of Lon., Ld., Cum. Pref. Stk. ..	100	87½
4½	Do. Deb. Stk., Red. ..	100	93
1/	Anglo-Amer. Db. Cor., L.	2	1
4	Do. Deb. Stk., Red ..	100	106½
5½	Ang.-Ceylon & Gen. Est., Ltd., Cons. Stk.	100	65
6	Do. Reg. Debs., Red.	100	102½
—	Ang.-Fch. Explorn., Ltd.	1	2 1/16
6	Do. Cum. Pref.	1	1 1/16
—	Argent. Ld. & Inv., Ltd. £1 Shares	10/	nil
—	Do. Cum. Pref.	4	1¾
1/	Assets Fnders.' Sh., Ltd.,	4	1⅜
6/	Assets Realiz., Ltd., Ord.,	5	8¾
5	Do. Cum. Pref.	5	6½
26/	Austrln. Agricl £25 Shs.	21½	63½
—	Aust. N. Z. Mort., Ltd., £10 Shs.	1	1½d.
4½	Do. Deb. Stk., Red. ..	100	90½
4	Do. Deb. Stk., Red. ..	100	82½
4½	Australian Est. & Mt., L., 1 Mt. Deb. Stk., Red.	100	104
5	Do. "A" Mort. Deb. Stk., Red.	100	96
2/6	Australian Mort., Ld., & Fin., Ltd. £25 Shs. ..	5	4
1/6	Do. New, £25 Shs...	3	3
4	Do. Deb. Stk........	100	110½
3	Do. Do.	100	85
5	Baring Est. 2 Mt. Debs., Red.	100	105
5	Bengal Presidy. 1 Mort. Deb., Red.	100	106
25/	British Amer. Ld. "A"	1	19
—	Do. "B"	24	7
1/7½	Brit. & Amer. Mt., Ltd. £10 Shs.	2	½
5/	Do. Pref.	10	10
4	Do. Deb. Stk., Red. ..	100	103
1/3	Brit. & Austrlsn Tst Ln., Ltd. £25 Shs.	2½	¾
4½	Do. Perm. Debs., Red.	100	103
1½d.	Brit. N. Borneo. £1 Shs.	15/	1½
2½d.	Do.	1	1
—	Brit. S. Africa	1	2⅞
5	Do. Mt. Deb., Red.	—	97
6	B. Aires Harb. Tst., Red.	100	99
12/6	Canada Co.	1	26
—	Canada N. W. Ld., Ltd.	$25	$3½
—	Do. Pref.	$100	$50½
4	Canada Perm. Loan & Sav. Perp. Deb. Stk...	100	99½
—	Curamalan Ld., 1 Mt. 7 p.c. Bds., Red.	—	94½
3/7½	Deb Corp., Ld., £10 Shs	4	3
5	Do. Cum. Pref.	10	11½
4	Do. Perp. Deb. Stk...	100	111
9d.	Deb. Corp. Fders' Sh., Ld.	3	⅜
4/5 3/20	Eastn. Mt. & Agncy, Ld., "A"	10	6
4½	Do. Deb. Stk., Red.	100	100
5	Equitable Revers. In. Ltd.	100	—
2/	Exploration, Ltd.	1	1 11/16
1	Freehold Trst. of Austria. Ltd. £10 Shs.	1	¾
4	Do. Perp. Deb. Stk...	100	100
—	Genl. Assets Purchase, Ltd., 5 p.c. Cum. Pref.	10	—
70/	Genl. Reversionary, Ltd.	100	—
3½	Holborn Vi. Land	100	105
3½	House Prop. & Inv.	100	85½
13/	Hudson's Bay	13	21½
—	Hyderabad (Deccan)	5	3
4	Impl. Col. Fin. & Agcy. Corp.	100	94½
4½	Impl. Prop. Inv., Ltd., Deb. Stk., Red.	100	91½
2/6	Internatl. Fincial. Soc., Ltd. £7½ Shs.	2½	1½
4	Do. Deb. Stk., Red...	100	99½
1/9½	Ld. & Mtge. Egypt, Ltd. £18 Shs.	3	2¾
5	Do. Debs., Red.	100	103
4½	Do. Debs., Red.	100	101
—	Ld. Corp. of Canada, Ltd.	1	⅛
4½	Ld. Mtge. Bk. of Texas Deb. Stk.	100	—
3½	Ld. Mtge. Bk. Victoria 4½ p.c. Deb. Stk.	100	78
2/9½	Law Debent. Corp., Ltd., £10 Shs.	2	1¾
4½	Do. Cum. Pref., ...	10	12
4	Do. Deb. Stk.	100	116
—	Law Land, L., 4½ Cm. Prf.	5	5½
1/	Ldn. & Australasian Deb. Corp., Ltd., £4 Shs. ..	2	½
4½	Do. 4½ p.c. Mt. Deb. Stk., Red.	100	99
1/9	Ldn. & Middx. Frhld. Est. £2 Shs.	35/	3
2/6	Lndn. & N. Y. Inv. Corp., Ltd.	5	1¾
5	Do. 5 p.c. Cum. Pref...	10	8½
1/6	Ldn. & Nth. Assets Corp., Ltd., £2 Shs.	1½	¾
2	Ldn. & N. Deb. Corp., L.	2	1½
4	Ldn. & S. Afric. Explrn. Ltd.	½	13½
2/	Mtge. Co. of R. Plate, Ltd. £10 Shs.	2	3½
4½	Do. Deb. Stk., Red...	100	113
4½	Morton, Rose Est., Ltd., 1st Mort. Debs.	—	101
6/	Natal Land Col. Ltd. ..	10	7½
4/	Do. 8 p.c. Pref., 1870..	5	8½
5/6	Natl. Disct. L., £25 Shs.	5	10½
4½	New Impl. Invest., Ltd. Pref. Stk.	100	62½
—	New Impl. Invest., Ltd. Def. Stk.	100	9

Financial, Land, &c. (*continued*):—

Last Div.	Name.	Paid.	Price.
3½	N. Zld. Assets Real Deb.	100	99
4	N. Zld. Ln. & Mer. Agcy., Ltd Prf. Ln, Deb. Stk	100	94
2/6	N. Zld. Tst. & Ln. Ltd., £25 Shs.	5	1½
12/6	N. Zld. Tst. & Ln. Ltd., 5 p.c. Cum. Pref.	25	19
—	N. Brit. Australsn. Ltd...	100	6½
—	Do. Irred. Guar.....	100	32½
5	Do. Mort. Debs.....	100	82½
4½	N. Queensld. Mort. & Inv., Ltd., Deb. Stk.	100	92
—	Oceana Co., Ltd.	—	—
6	Peel Riv., Ld. & Min. Ltd.	100	88½
—	Peruvian Corp., Ltd.	100	2½
—	Do. 4 p.c. Pref.	100	9½
3	Do. 6 p.c. 1 Mt. Debs., Red.	100	40
—	Queenld. Invest. & Ld... Mort. Pref. Ord. Stk...	100	20
3/7	Queenld. Invest. & Ld. Mort. Ord. Shs.	4	4
4	Queenld. Invest. & Ld. Mort. Perp. Debs.	100	88
3½	Raily. Roll Stk. Tst. Deb., 1903-6	100	100½
50/	Reversiony. Int. Soc., Ltd.	100	—
2/8½	Riv. Plate Trst., Loan & Agcy., L., "A" £10 Shs.	2	4
1/6	Riv. Plate Trst., Loan & Agcy., Ltd., Def. "B"	5	3½
	Riv. Plate Trst., Loan & Agy., L., Db. Stk., Red.	100	109
—	Santa Fé & Cord. Gt. South Land, Ltd.	20	5
—	Santa Fé Land	10	2½
2/	Scot. Amer. Invest., Ltd. £10 Shs.	2	2¾
2½	Scot. Australian Invest., Ltd., Cons.	100	78½
6	Scot. Australian Invest., Ltd., Guar. Pref.	100	135½
5	Scot. Australian Invest., Ltd., Guar. Pref......	100	106½
4	Scot. Australian Invest., Ltd., 4 p.c. Perp. Dbs.	100	106½
5	Sivagunga Zemdy., 1st Mort., Red.	100	101
20/	Sth. Australian..........	20	52½
3½	Stock Exchange Deb., Rd.	—	101½
—	Strait Develt., Ltd......	1	5/16
2/6	Texas Land & Mt., Ltd. £10 Shs.	2½	3
4½	Texas Land & Mt., Ltd., Deb. Stk., Red.	100	105
—	Transvaal Est. & Dev., L.	1	11/16
—	Transvaal Lands, Ltd., £1 Shs.	15/	½
—	Do. F. P..........	1	5/16
—	Transvaal Mort., Loan, & Fin., Ltd., £10 Shs. ..	2	½
2/	Tst & Agcy. of Austrlsa., Ltd., £10 Shs.	1	2
7/5	Do. Old, fully paid ..	10	15½
5/7	Do. New, fully paid ..	10	12½
5	Do. Cum. Pref.......	10	12½
3/	Trust & Loan of Canada, £20 Shs.	5	4½
1/9½	Do. New £20 Shs....	3	2½
—	Tst. & Mort. of Iowa, Ltd., £10 Shs.	2½	¾
4½	Do. Deb. Stk. Red...	100	92½
—	Tst., Loan, & Agency of Mexico, Ltd., £10 Shs.	2	½
—	Trsts., Exors, & Sec. Ins. Corp., Ltd., £10 Shs..	7	1¾
4	Do. Irred. Deb. Stk.	100	106½
5/	Union Dsc., Ld., £10 Shs.	5	10½
—	Union Mort. & Agcy. of Aust., Ltd., £6 Shs. ..	2	—
6	Do. Pref. Stk........	100	30
—	Do. 6 p. Pref. £6 Shs.	2	½
4½	Do. Deb. Stk........	100	92½
4	Do. Deb. Stk........	100	85½
5	Do. Deb. Stk. Red...	100	96½
1/6	U.S. Deb. Cor. Ltd., £8 Shs.	1	½
5½	Do. Cum. Pref. Stk .	100	100½
4½	Do. Irred. Deb. Stk..	100	106½
5	U.S. Tst. & Guar. Cor., Ltd., Pref. Stk........	100	77½
6/	Van Dieman's	25	16
4	Walker's Prop. Cor., Ltd., Gunr. 1 Mt. Deb. Stk..	100	109
4½	Wstr. Mort. & Inv., Ltd., Deb. Stk.	100	92½

FINANCIAL—TRUSTS.

Last Div.	Name.	Paid.	Price.
1/6	Afric City Prop., Ltd...	1	1½
6	Do. Cum. Pref.......	1	1 1/16
4	Alliance Invt., Ltd., Cm. 4½ p. c. Prefd.	100	74½
—	Do. Defd...........	100	13½
4	Do. Deb. Stk. Red...	100	106½
5	Amrcn. Invt., Ltd., Prfd.	100	120½
5	Do. Defd.	100	90½
4	Do. Deb. Stk. Red...	100	117½
4	Army & Navy Invt., Ltd., 5 p.c. Prefd.	100	83½
—	Do. Defd. Stk.	100	16½
4	Do. Deb. Stk.	100	107½
4	Atlas Investment, Ltd., Prefd. Stk.	100	70½
4½	Bankers' Invest., Ltd., Cum. Prefd.	100	106
1/0/0	Do. Defd...........	100	27½
4	Do. Deb. Stk.......	100	113
	Brewery & Comml. Inv., Ltd., £10 Shs.	5	6

Financial—Trusts (*continued*):—

Last Div.	Name.	Paid.	Price.
4	British Investment, Ltd., Cum. Prefd.	100	108
5	Do. Defd.	100	102½
4	Do. Deb. Stk.	100	108½
6	Brit. Steam. Invst., Ltd., Prefd.	100	116½
3/0/0	Do. Defd...........	100	70½
4½	Do. Perp. Deb. Stk ..	100	121½
1/9	Car Trust Invst., Ltd., £10 Shs.	2½	2
5	Do. Pref	100	101
4	Do. Deb. Stk., 1915..	100	106
4	Cinl. Sec., Ltd., Prefd. ..	100	106½
2½	Do. Defd.	100	47½
4	Consolidated, Ltd., Cum. 1st Pref.	100	92
4	Do. 5 p.c. Cm. 2nd do.	100	73½
—	Do. Defd.	100	14½
4½	Do. Deb. Stk.	100	112½
—	Deb. Secs. Invst........	100	105½
—	Do. 4 p.c. Cm. Pf. Sk.	100	106½
4½	Edinburgh Invest., Ltd., Cum. Prefd. Stk........	100	109½
4	Do. Deb. Stk. Red.	100	106½
5	Foreign, Amer. & Gen. Invt., Ltd., Prefd.	100	115½
2	Do. Defd.	100	50½
4	Do. Deb. Stk.	100	115½
5	Foreign & Colonial Invt., Ltd., Prefd.	100	135½
5½	Do. Defd.	100	99½
4½	Gas, Water & Gen. Invt., Cum. Prefd. Stk.......	100	86½
8	Do. Defd. Stk.	100	36½
4	Do. Deb. Stk.	100	106
5	Gen. & Com. Invt., Ltd., Prefd. Stk............	100	106½
2	Do. Defd. Stk.	100	36½
4	Do. Deb. Stk.	100	113½
1/9	Globe Telegph. & Tst., Ltd.	10	12
6	Do. do. Pref.	10	17½
4	Govt. & Genl. Invt., Ld., Prefd.	100	84½
3½	Do. Defd.	100	42½
4½	Govts. Stk. & other Secs. Invt., Ltd., Prefd.	100	89½
1	Do. Defd.	100	26
4½	Do. Deb. Stk.	100	111
4	Do. do.	100	104
4½	Guardian Invt., Ltd., Pfd.	100	87½
—	Do. Defd.	100	19½
4	Do. Deb. Stk.	100	104
5	Indian & Gen. Inv., Ltd., Cum. Prefd.	100	107½
2½	Do. Defd.	100	56
4½	Do. Deb. Stk.	100	121½
5	Indust. & Gen. Tst., Ltd., Unified	100	101½
3½	Do. Deb. Stk. Red.	100	101½
4½	Internat. Invt., Ltd., Cm. Prefd.	100	69½
—	Do. Defd.	100	7½
4	Do. Deb. Stk.	100	101
4	Invest. Tst. Cor. Ltd. Pfd.	100	102
4	Do. Defd.	100	93
4	Do. Deb. Stk. Red.	100	105
5	Ldn. Gen. Invest. Ltd., 5 p.c. Cum. Prefd.	100	109½
7½	Do. Defd.	100	118
4½	Ldn. Scot. Amer. Ltd. Pfd.	100	106½
£3	Do. Defd.	100	59½
4	Do. Deb. Stk.	100	112
4	Ldn. Tst., Ltd., Cum. Prfd. Stk.	100	106
4	Do. Defd. Stk.	100	74½
4	Do. Deb. Stk., Red.	100	108
3½	Do. Mt. Deb. Stk., Red.	100	104
5	Mercantile Invt. & Gen., Ltd., Prefd.	100	111
3	Do. Defd.	100	46½
4	Do. Deb. Stk.	100	112½
4	Merchants, Ltd., Pref. Stk.	100	105½
4	Do. Ord.	100	80
4	Do. Deb. Stk.	100	117½
5	Municipal, Ltd., Prefd...	100	55½
—	Do. Defd.	100	17½
4½	Do. Debs.	100	112
4½	Do. Debs. "B".....	100	99½
4½	Do. "C" Deb. Stk.	100	88½
5	New Investment, Ltd. Ord.	100	92½
5	Omnium Invest., Ltd., Pfd.	100	91½
1	Do. Defd....	100	26½
4	Do. Deb. Stk.	100	104
5/	Railway Deb. Tst. Ld., £10 Shs.	10	6½
5	Do. Debs., Red. ..	100	107½
4½	Do. Deb. Stk., 1911	100	107½
4	Do. do. 1927	100	106½
4	Railway Invst. Ltd., Prefd.	100	112
17/7	Do. Defd.	100	20½
8/	Railway Share Trust & Agency "A"	8	6
7½	Do. "B" Pref. Stk.	100	146½
4½	River Plate & Gen. Invt., Ltd., Prefd.	100	105
£3	Do. Defd.	100	50½
5	Scot. Invst., Ltd., Pfd. Stk.	100	94½
1½	Do. Defd...	100	26½
4	Do. Deb. Stk.	100	108
4½	Sec. Scottish Invst., Ltd., Cum. Prefd.	100	86½
£2	Do. Defd. Stk.	100	32
4	Do. Deb. Stk.	100	107½
5/	Sth. Africa Gold Tst., Ltd.	1	4
6	Do. Cum. Pref	1	1
5½	Do. 1st Debs., Red.	100	102
1/9	Stock Conv. & Invest., Ltd., £5 Shs.	1	1¾
4½	Do. do. 4½ p.c. Cm. Prf.	100	114½
2½	Do. Ldn. & N. W. 1st. Charge Prefd.	100	114½
4	Do do. 2nd Chge Prfd.	100	111
82/6	Do. do. Defd. Charge	100	30
3	Do. N. East. 1 Chge Pfd.	100	91½

Financial—Trusts (*continued*):—

Last Div.	Name.	Paid.	Price.
57/6	Stock N. East Defd. Chge	100	39
6	Submarine Cables	100	142½
5	U.S. & S. Amer. Invest., Ltd., Prefd.	100	100½
2	Do. Defd.	100	28½
4	Do. Deb. Stk.	100	105½

GAS AND ELECTRIC LIGHTING.

Last Div.	Name.	Paid.	Price.
10/6	Alliance & Dublin Con. 10 p.c. Stand.	10	24½
7/6	Do. 7 p.c. Stand...	10	17
5	Austln. Gas Lght. (Syd.) Debs. 1902	100	106
5	Bay State of N. Jrsy. Sk. Fd. Tst. Bd., Red. ..	—	92½
3/	Bombay, Ltd..........	5	6
2/4½	Do. New	4	5
12	Brentford Cons.	100	295½
9	Do. New	100	225½
5	Do. Pref.	100	142½
4	Do. Deb. Stk. ..	100	136
11½	Brighton & Hove Gen. Cons. Stk.	100	272½
8½	Do. "A" Cons. Stk.	100	197½
5	Bristol 5 p.c. Max.	100	129½
22/6	British Gas Light, Ltd.	20	55½
11/6	Bromley Gas Consumrs.' 10 p.c. Stand.	10	26
8/6	Do. 7 p.c. Stand...	10	21
—	Brush Electl. Enging., L.	—	1¾
6	Do. 6 p.c. Pref.	—	2½
4½	Do. Deb. Stk.	100	112
4½	Do. 2 Deb. Stk., Red.	100	103½
5/	B. Ayres (New), Ltd. ..	10	9½
4	Do. Deb. Stk., Rd. ..	—	99
18/6	Cagliari Gas & Wtr., Ltd.	20	31
8/	Cape Town & Dist. Gas Light & Coke, Ltd.	10	16½
4½	Do. Pref.	10	12½
6	Do. 1 Mt. Debs. 1910	50	60
4/	Charing Cross & Strand Elec. Sup., Ltd.....	5	14
4½	Do. Cum. Pref.	5	6½
3/	Chelsea Elec. Sup., Ltd.	5	10½
4½	Do. Deb. Stk., Red.	100	116
5	Chic. Edis'n Co. 1 Mt., Rd.	$1000	106
20/	City of Ldn. Elec. Lht., L.	10	26½
—	Do. New £10 Shs...	5	19½
6	Do. Cum. Pref.	10	18
5	Do. Deb. Stk., Red.	100	131½
13½	Commercial, Cons.	100	342½
10½	Do. New	100	257½
4½	Do. Deb. Stk.	100	155½
14	Continental Union, Ltd.	100	230
11	Do. Pref. Stk.	100	209½
—	County of Lon. & Brush Prov. Elec. Lg., Ltd.	10	15
6	Do. Cum. Pref.	10	15½
14	Croydon Comcl. Gas, Ld., "A" Stk., 10 p.c. ..	100	312½
11	Do. "B" Stk., 7 p.c.	100	260
5½	Crystal Pal. Dist. Ord. 5 p.c. Stk.	100	130½
5	Do. Pref. Stk.	100	141½
8/	European, Ltd.	10	24½
6/	Do.	7½	17½
12½	Gas Light & Ck Cons. Stk., "A" Ord....	100	285½
4	Do. "B" (4 p.c. Max.)	100	120½
10	Do. "C," "D," & "E" (Pref.)	100	310
5	Do. "F" (Pref.)	100	152½
7½	Do. "G" (Pref.)	100	222½
7	Do. "H" (7 p.c. Max.)	100	197½
10	Do. "J" (Pref.)......	100	310
6	Do. "K"	100	186½
4	Do. Deb. Stk.	100	134½
4½	Do. do.	100	152½
6	Do. do.	100	204½
8/	Hong Kong & China, Ld.	10	14½
4/	House to House Elec. Light Sup., Ltd. ..	5	11
7	Do. Cum. Pref.	5	11½
10	Imperial Continental ..	100	215½
3½	Do. Deb. Stk., Red ..	100	104½
2/	Malta & Medit., Ltd. ..	5	5½
7/	Metrop. Elec. Sup., Ltd.	10	20
6/	Do. New	10	20
4½	Do. 1 Mt. Deb. Stk.	100	119
5	Metro. of Melbrne. Dbs. 1908-12	100	111
4½	Do. Debs.. 1918-22-4	100	108
10/	Monte Video, Ltd.	20	15½
9½	Newcastle-upon-Tyne ..	100	237½
—	Do. 3½ p.c. Deb. Stk.	100	117½
12/	Notting Hill Elec. Ltg., Ltd.	10	20½
4/6	Oriental, Ltd.........	5	8
4/0½	Do. New	4½	7
10d.	Do. do. 1875	1	1
3/6	Ottoman, Ltd.	5	4½
—	Para, Ltd.	—	—
6	People's Gas Lt. & C. of Chic. 2 Mt..... 1904	100	105½
5	River Plate Elec. Lgt. & Trac., Ltd., 1 Deb. Stk.	—	92½
8	Royal Elec. of Montreal	—	144
4½	Do. 1 Mt. Deb. ..	100	104
11/	St. James' & Pall Mall Elec. Light, Ltd. ..	5	18
7	Do. Pref.	5	10½
4	Do. Deb. Stk., Red.	100	106½

Gas and Electric (*continued*) :—

Last Div.	Name.	Paid.	Price.
10/	San Paulo, Ltd.	10	16½
10	Sheffield Unit. Gas Lt. "A"	100	251½
10	Do. "B"	100	251½
10	Do. "C"	100	251½
—	Sth. Ldn. Elec. Sup., Ld.	2	2¾
5½	South Metropolitan	100	137½
3	Do. 3 p.c. Deb. Stk.	100	104½
12	Tottenham & Edmonton Gas Lt. & C., "A"	100	290
9	Do. "B"	100	210
7/	Tuscan, Ltd.	10	14
5	Do. Debs., Red.	100	101½
5/	West Ham 10 p.c. Stan.	5	12
8/	Wstmnstr. Elec. Sup., Ld.	5	17

INSURANCE.

Last Div.	Name.	Paid.	Price.
4/	Alliance, £20 Shs.	44/	10½
10/	Alliance, Mar., & Gen., Ld., £100 Shs.	25	53
19/	Atlas, £50 Shs.	6	31
12/	British & For. Marine, Ld., £20 Shs.	4	24
7½d.	British Law Fire, Ltd., £10 Shs.	1	1½
7/6	Clerical, Med., & Gen. Life, £25 Shs.	50/	16½
10/	Commercial Union, Ltd., £50 Shs.	5	45½
4	Do. "W. of Eng." Ter. Deb. Stk.	100	110½
£9	County Fire, £100 Shs.	80	190
3/	Eagle, £50 Shs.	5	½
4/	Employrs' Liability, Ltd., £10 Shs.	2	4½
.	Empress, Ltd., £5 Shs.	1	—
21/	Equity & Law, £100 Shs.	6	23
7/6	General Life, £100 Shs.	5	15
4½d.	Gresham Life, £5 Shs.	15/	2½
2/6	Guardian, Ld., £10 Shs.	5	11½
10/	Imperial, Ltd., £20 Shs.	5	29½
3/6	Imperial Life, £20 Shs.	4	6¾
6/	Indemnity Mutual Mar., Ltd., £15 Shs.	3	12
1/	Lancashire, £20 Shs.	2	5
7½d.	Law Acc. & Contin., Ltd., £5 Shs.	10/	1
5/	Law Fire, £100 Shs.	2½	18
9½d.	Law Guar. & Trust, Ltd., £10 Shs.	1	1⅞
9/	Law Life, £20 Shs.	2	25
2/9	Law Un. & Crown £10Shs	12/	7
4	Do. Deb. Stk., 1942	100	110½
14/6	Legal & General, £50Shs.	8	16½
9d.	Lion Fire, Ltd., £8½ Shs.	1½	¾
24/	Liverpool & London & Globe, Stk.	2	54
20/	Do. Globe £1 Ann	—	36
25/	London, £25 Shs.	12½	62½
4/	Lond. & Lanc. Fire, £25Shs	2½	19½
2/	Lond. & Lanc. Life, £25Shs	2	5¾
1/	Lond. & Prov. Mar., Ld., £10 Shs.	1	¾
6/	Lond. Guar. & Accident, Ltd., £5 Shs.	2	11½
40/	Marine, Ltd., £25 Shs.	4½	43
2/	Maritime, Ltd., £10 Shs.	2	4½
1/6	Merc. Mar., Ld., £10 Shs.	2½	2¾
—	National Marine, Ltd., £9 Shs.	1	¾
20/	N. Brit. & Merc., £25 Shs.	6¼	43
20/	Northern, £100 Shs.	10	81
40/	Norwich Union Fire, £100 Shs.	12	126½
20/	Ocean Acc. & Guar., fy. pd.	5	22
2/	Do. £5 Shs.	1	4
7/6	Ocean, Marine, Ltd.	2½	9
1/	Palatine, £10 Shs.	2	3½
2/6	Pelican, £10 Shs.	1	3¾
12/	Phœnix, £50 Shs.	5	44
£6	Provident, £100 Shs.	10	31
5/	Railway Pasngrs., £10Shs.	2	8½
2/6	Rock Life, £5 Shs.	10/	4½
8	Royal Exchange	100	360
28/	Royal, £20 Shs.	3	55
4/	Sun, £10 Shs.	10/	11½
3/9	Sun Life, £10 Shs.	7½	14½
6	Thames & Mrsey. Marine, Ltd., £20 Shs.	2	10½
9	Union, £10 Shs.	4	24½
4/	Union Marine, £20 Shs.	2½	8¾
12/	Universal Life, £100 Shs.	12	42
2/	World Marine, £5 Shs.	2	1½

IRON, COAL, AND STEEL.

Last Div.	Name.	Paid.	Price.
—	Barrow Hæm. Steel, Ltd.	7½	2
9/	Do. 6 p.c. 2nd Pref.	7½	7
10/	Bolck., Vaugh. & C., Ld.	20	17
6/	Do. £8 liab	12	9
7/6	Brown, J. & Co., Ltd., £20 Shs.	15	20½
7/6	Consett Iron, Ld., £10 Shs.	7½	29½
4/	Do. 8 p.c. Cum. Pref.	5	11
7/6	Ebbw Vale Steel, Iron & Coal, Ltd., £23 Shs.	20	6¾
15/	General Mining Assn., Ld.	5½	7½
8/	Harvey Steel Co. of Gt. Britain, Ltd.	10	29
5	Lehigh V. Coal 1 Mt. 5 p.c. Guar. Gd. Cp. Bds.	—	95½
42/6	Nantyglo & Blaina Iron, Ltd., Pref.	862	97½
1/	Nerbudda Coal & Iron, Ltd., £3 Shs.	56/	1/16
—	Newport Abercrn. Bk. Vein Steam Coal, Ltd.	10	4¾
5/	New Shariston Coll., Ltd. Pref.	20	10
4½d.	Nw. Vancvr. Coal & Ld., L.	1	½
2/6	North's Navigation Coll. (1889) Ltd.	5	2¾
10/	Do. 10 p.c. Cum. Pref.	5	6¾
—	Rhymney Iron, Ltd.	5	1½
	Do. New, £5 Shs.	4½	¾
5	Do. Mt. Debs., Red.	100	98½
5	Shelton Irn., Stl. & Cl. Co., Ltd., 1 Chg. Debs., Red.	100	99½
50/	Sth. Hetton Coal, Ltd.	100	—
2/	Vickers & Maxim, Ltd.	1	3½
5	Do. 5 p.c. Prfd. Stk.	100	130½

SHIPPING.

Last Div.	Name.	Paid.	Price.
4/	African Stm. Ship, £20 Shs.	16	11
5/	Do. Fully-paid	20	15½
5/	Amazon Steam Nav., Ltd.	12½	9
8/	Castle Mail Pakts., Ltd., £20 Shs.	14	16
3½	Do. 1st Deb. Stk., Red.	100	102
6/	China Mutual Steam, Ltd.	5	2½
6	Do. Cum. Pref.	10	9½
10/	Cunard, Ltd.	20	10
5/	Do. £20 Shs.	10	4
4½	Furness, Withy, & Co., Ltd., 1 Mt. Dbs., Red.	100	106
6/	General Steam	15	8
5/	Do. 5 p.c. Pref., 1874	10	9
5/	Do. 5 p.c. Pref., 1877	10	8½
5/	Leyland & Co., Ltd.	10	20
7/	Do. 7 p.c. Cum. Pref.	10	14½
2/11	Do. 4½ p.c. Cum. Pre-Pf.	3	10½
4	Do. 1st Mt. Dbs., Red.	100	106½
7/6	Mercantile Steam, Ltd.	5	7½
6/4½	New Zealand Ship., Ltd.,	6	5
4	Do. Deb. Stk., Red.	100	104
5/	Orient Steam, Ltd.	10	5
5	P. & O. Steam, Cum. Prefd.	100	154½
19	Do. Defd.	100	234½
3½	Do. Deb. Stk.	100	113
5	Richelieu & Ont., 1st Mt. Debs., Red.	100	100
30/	Royal Mail, £100 Shs.	60	52
2/6	Shaw, Sav., & Alb., Ltd., "A" Pref.	5	5½
5/	Do. "B" Ord.	5	3½
8/	Union Steam, Ltd.	20	20
4/	Do. New £20 Shs.	10	8½
4	Do. Deb. Stk., Red.	100	106
7/	Union of N.Z., Ltd.	10	10
5½	Wilson's & Fur.-Ley., 5½ p.c. Cum. Pref.	10	10½
4½	Do. 1 Mt. Db. Sk., Rd.	100	106½

TELEGRAPHS AND TELEPHONES.

Last Div.	Name.	Paid.	Price.
4	African Direct, Ltd., Mort. Debs., Red.	100	102
—	Amazon Telegraph, Ltd.	10	7½
19/6	Anglo-American, Ltd.	100	62½
39/	Do. 6 p.c. Prefd. Ord.	100	112
—	Do. Defd. Ord.	100	13
3/	Brazilian Submarine, Ltd.	10	16¾
5	Do. Debs., 2 Series	100	114

Telegraphs and Telephones (*continued*) :—

Last Div.	Name.	Paid.	Price.
4/	Chili Telephone, Ltd.	5	3½
$1½	Comcial. Cable, $100 Shs.	—	187½
4	Do. Stg. 500-yr. Deb. Stk. Red.	100	105
2½d.	Consd. Telpehone Constr., &c., Ltd.	10/	¼
6/	Cuba Submarine, Ltd.	10	7
10/	Do. 10 p.c. Pref.	10	15
2/	Direct Spanish, Ltd.	5	4½
5/	Do. 10 p.c. Cum. Pref.	5	10½
4½	Do. Debs.	50	104½
3/	Direct U.S. Cable, Ltd.	20	11
2/6	Eastern, Ltd.	10	18
3/	Do. 6 p.c. Cum. Pref.	10	19
4	Do. Mt. Deb. Stk., Red.	100	129½
2/6	Eastern Exten., Aus., & China, Ltd.	10	19
5	Do. (Aus. Gov. Sub.) Deb., Red.	100	101
5	Do. do. Bearer	100	101½
4	Do. Mort. Deb. Stk.	100	129½
5	Eastn. & S. Afric., Ltd., Mort. Deb. 1900	100	101
5	Do. Bearer	100	101½
4	Do. Mort. Debs. 1909	100	103½
4	Do. Mort. Debs. (Maur. Subsidy)	25	108½
5/	Grt. Nthn. Copenhagen	10	30
5	Do. Debs., Ser. B., Red.	100	101½
12/6	Indo-European, Ltd.	25	53½
6	London Platino-Brazilian, Ltd., Debs. 1904	100	107½
4/	Montevideo Telph., Ltd., 6 p.c. Pref.	5	2½
3/	National Telephone, Ltd.	5	5¾
6/	Do. Cum. 1 Pref.	10	17
6/	Do. Cum. 2 Pref.	10	16
5	Do. Non-Cum. 3 Pref.	5	5¾
3½	Do. Deb. Stk., Red.	100	102½
4d.	Oriental Telephone, Ltd.	1	½
4	Pac. & Euro. Tlg. Dbs., Rd.	100	106½
4/	Reuter's, Ltd.	8	8½
5/	Un. Riv. Plate Telph., Ltd.	5	4½
5	Do. Deb. Stk., Red.	100	106½
—	West African Telg., Ltd.	10	4
5	Do. 5 p.c. Mt. Debs., Red.	100	100½
—	W. Coast of America, Ltd.	10	¾
3/	Western & Brazilian, Ltd.	15	12½
3/	Do. 5 p.c. Pref. Ord.	7½	8
—	Do. Defd. Ord.	7½	4¾
4	Do. Deb. Stk., Red.	100	107½
1/	W. India & Panama, Ltd.	10	¾
6/	Do. Cum. 1 Pref.	10	7½
6/	Do. Cum. 2 Pref.	10	6
5	Do. Debs., Red.	100	106½
7	West. Union, 1 Mt. 1900 ($)	1000	107½
6	Do. 6 p.c. Stg. Bds., Rd.	100	102½

TRAMWAYS AND OMNIBUS.

Last Div.	Name.	Paid.	Price.
1/6	Anglo-Argentine, Ltd.	5	3½
6	Do. Deb. Stk.	100	127½
4/	Barcelona, Ltd.	10	12
5	Do. Deb., Red.	100	105½
7/6	Belfast Street Trams.	10	16½
—	Blackpl. & Fltwd. Tram., £10 Shs.	8	13
10/	Bordeaux Tram. & O., Ltd.	10	11½
5	Do. Cum. Pref.	10	11
—	Brazilian Street Ry., Ltd.	2	½
—	British Elec. Trac., Ltd.	10	16½
—	B. Ayres & Belg. Tram., Ltd., 6 p.c. Cum. Pref.	5	—
6	Do. 1 Deb. Stk.	100	—
—	B. Ayres. Gd. Nat., Ltd., 6 p.c 1 Deb. Bds., Red.	100	54½
5½	Do. Pref. Debs., Red.	100	95½
1/	Calais, Ltd.	5	1
—	Calcutta, Ltd.	10	3½
—	Carthagena & Herr., Ltd.	10	3
5	Do. Deb., Red.	100	90
5	City of B'ham. Trams., Ltd., 5 p.c. Cum. Pref.	5	6
4	Do. 1 Mort. Debs., Rd.	100	107½
3/9	City of B. Ayres, Ltd.	5	7½
2/3	Do. Ext. £5 Shs.	3	4½
6	Do. Deb. Stk	100	145
1/4	Edinburgh Street Tram.	4	4
1/	Glasgow Tram. & Omni. Ltd., £9 Shs.	8	
3/7½	Imperial, Ltd.	6	14½
3/	Lond., Deptfd, & Greenwich, Prefd.	5	3½
nil	Do. Defd.	5	1
10½	Lond. Gen. Omni., Ltd.	100	200
4	Do. Deb., Red.	100	15½

Tramways and Omnibus (*continued*) :—

Last Div.	Name.	Paid.	Price.
4/9½	London Road Car	6	10½
26/6	Do. Red. 1 Mt. Deb. Stk.	100	108½
5	London St. Rly. (Prov., Ont.), Mt. Debs.	100	110
12/6	London St. Trams.	—	2
12/9	London Trams., Ltd.	10	10
6/	Do. Non-Cum. Pref.	10	10½
5	Do. Mt. Db. Stk., Rd.	100	101
5	Lynn & Boston 1 Mt. 1924 $	1000	107
5	Milwaukee Elec. Cons. Mt. $	1000	100½
5	Minneapolis St. 1 Cons. Mt. $	1000	96
5	Montreal St. Dbs., 1908	100	109
4½	Do. Debs., 1922	100	107
6/	Nth. Metropolitan	10	13
1/9½	Nth. Staffords., Ltd.	6	5
5/6	Provincial, Ltd.	10	7
6/	Do. Cum. Pref.	10	13½
5	St. Paul City, 1937 $	1000	96
5	Do. Guar. Twin City Rap. Trans. $	1000	96
5/	Southampton	10	6½
5/	South London	10	5½
7/6	Sunderland, Ltd.	10	7½
4½	Toronto 1 Mt., Red.	100	106
2/6	Tramways Union, Ltd.	5	6½
4½	Do. Deb., Red.	100	109
5/	Vienna General Omnibus	5	5½
5	Do. 5 p.c. Mt. Deb., Red.	100	103½
4/	Wolverhampton, Ltd.	10	4½

WATER WORKS.

Last Div.	Name.	Paid.	Price.
8/	Antwerp, Ltd.	20	22
6/	Cape Town District, Ltd.	5	7
10½	Chelsea	100	325
5	Do. Pref. Stk.	100	178½
4½	Do. Pref. Stk., 1875	100	158½
4½	Do. Deb. Stk.	100	160½
3/6	City St. Petersburg, Ltd.	13	11
5/	Colne Valley	10	15½
4	Do. Deb. Stock	100	137½
£4	Consol. of Rosar., Ltd., 4 p.c. 1 Deb. Stk., Red.	100	92
7½	East London	100	229½
4½	Do. Deb. Stk.	100	162
3	Do. Deb. Stk., Red.	100	106
37/6	Grand Junction (Max. 10 p.c.) "A"	50	121
18/9	Do. "B"	25	
18/9	Do. "C" (Max. 7½ p.c.)	25	55½
35/	Do. "D" (Max. 7 p.c.)	50	104½
4	Do. Deb. Stock	100	145½
13	Kent	100	360½
7	Do. New (Max. 7 p.c.)	100	215½
5/7½	Kimberley, Ltd.	7	5½
6	Do. Debs., Red.	100	104½
6	Do. Deb. Stk., Red.	100	107½
10	Lambeth (Max. 10 p.c.)	100	300½
7½	Do. (Max. 7½ p.c.), 50 & 25	—	233
4	Do. Deb. Stock	100	142½
3	Do. Red. Deb. Stock	100	103
10/	Montevideo, Ltd.	20	16½
5	Do. 1 Deb. Stk.	100	108½
5	Do. 2 Deb. Stk.	100	103½
132/9	New River New	100	445½
4	Do. Deb. Stk.	100	144½
4	Do. Deb. Stk. "B"	100	144½
—	Odessa, Ltd., "A" 6 p.c. Prefd.	20	—
nil	Do. "B" Deferred	20	—
4	Portland Con. Mt. "B," 1927	—	102½
8/	Seville, Ltd.	20	12
5/6	Southend "Addl." Ord.	10	17½
6	Southwark and Vauxhall	100	157½
6	Do. "D" Shares (7½ p.c. max.)	100	154½
5	Do. Pref. Stock	100	176½
4	Do. "A" Deb. Stock	100	147½
3	Staines Resvirs. Jt. Com. Gua. Deb. Stk., Red.	100	106
7/	Tarapaca, Ltd.	10	9½
10	West Middlesex	100	305½
4½	Do. Deb. Stk.	100	162½
3	Do Deb. Stk.	100	106

Prices Quoted on the Leading Provincial Exchanges.

ENGLISH.

In quoting the markets, B stands for Birmingham; Bl for Bristol; M for Manchester; L for Liverpool; and S for Sheffield.

CORPORATION STOCKS.

Chief Market.	Int or Div.	NAME.	Amount paid.	Price.
M	3½	Bolton, Red. 1935 ..	100	114
M	3½	Burnley, Red. 1933..	100	114
M	3½	Bury, Red. 1946	100	116½
L	2½	Liverpool, Red. 1925	100	102½
B	3½	Longton, 1932	100	106
M	4	Oldham Prp. Db. Sk.	100	146
M	£1	Do. Gas & W. Ann.		34½
S	4	Rotherham 4 p.c., Red. 1927 ...... [£	1 an	112
M	3½	Runcorn Red. 1923..	100	104
S	2½	Sheffield Water Ann.	100	118½
S	3	Do.	3 an	90
L	3½	Southport Red. 1936 {	5 an / 100	112
L	3	Do. Red. 1914..	100	102½
M	3	Todmorden, Red. 1914	100	102

RAILWAYS.

Chief Market.	Int or Div.	NAME.	Amount paid.	Price.
B	4½	Bridgewater Pref. ..	100	135½
M	1½	Cleator & Workton.	100	76
M	4	Do. 1883 Pref. ..	100	109
L	4	Cockermth. K. & P.	100	113½
L	4	Isle of Man	5	6½
L	5	Do. Pref.	5	6½
L	3	Liverpool Overhead	10	10½
L	4	Do. Deb. Stk. ..	100	110
L	5	Do. Pref.	10	16
L	6½	Maryport & Carlisle	100	167
S	6	Mid. Shef. & Roth. Pf.	100	231
Bl	45/	Neath & Brecon "A"	100	65½
M	4½	Oldham, Ashton, &c.	10	16½
Bl	5½	Penarth Harbour ..	100	182½
Bl	4	Do. Deb. Stk. ..	100	145
Bl	3½	Do. Deb. Stk. ..	100	127
Bl	1½	Ross & Monmouth..	20	5½
Bl	6	Do. Pref.	20	42½
M	3	Southport & Cheshire Deb. Stk.	100	104½
M	nil.	Do. Pref.	100	22
Bl	2½	West Somerset Gu...	100	96½
Bl	5	Wye Val. Deb. Stk.	100	164

BANKS.

Chief Market.	Int or Div.	NAME.	Amount paid.	Price.
L	8/	Adelphi, L., £20 Shs.	10	16⅛
L	12/6	Bk of L'ool, L., £100 Sh	12½	39½
B	5/6	Brmnghm. Dis. & C., Ltd., £20 Shs.	4	10½
B	6/3	Co. of Staffs., L., £40	5	13½
S	17½	Crompton & Evans, Ltd., £20 Shs	4	15
M	14/	Lancs. & Yorks, Ltd., £20 Shs.	10	31½
L	30/	Livrpl. Union, Ltd., £100 Shs.	20	60½
M	24/	Manchester & Co., Ltd., £100 Shs. ..	16	61½
M	20/	Mnchstr. & Livrpool. Dis., Ltd., £60 Shs.	10	51½
M	1/6	Mer. of Lancashire, Ltd., £20 Shs.	3	6½
L	16/	Nth. & Sth. Wales, Ltd., £40 Shs.	10	35½
B	20/	Notts Joint St., Ltd., £50 Shs.	10	26½
M	4/	Oldham Joint Stk., Ltd., £20 Shs.	4	12½
S	15	Sheffield Banking, Ltd., £50 Shs.	17½	51½
S	20	Do. & Rotherham, Ltd., £50 Shs. ..	8	26½
S	10	Do. & Hallamsh., Ltd., £100 Shs. ..	25	65½
S	10	Do. Union, Ltd., £40 Shs.	10	25½
M	12/	Union of Manchester, Ltd., £25 Shs. ..	11	27½
M	10/	Williams, Deacon, &c. Ltd., £50 Shs.	8	25½
Bl	20	Wilts & Dorset, Ltd., £50 Shs.	10	49½
S	5/6	York City & Co., Ltd., £10 Shs.	3	13

BREWERIES.

Chief Market.	Int or Div.	NAME.	Amount paid.	Price.
B	6	Ansell & Sons' Pref.	10	15½
B	5	Do. Debs.	100	110
L	9/	Bent's	10	19
L	6	Do. Cum. Pref...	10	14½
L	4½	Do. Deb. Stk. ..	100	111
L	13/6	Birkenhead, £5 paid	5	22½
L	13/6	Do. £10 paid....	10	27½
M	9/	Boddington's	9	19½
M	5	Do. Cum. Pref...	10	12½
M	4	Do. Deb. Stk. ..	100	107½
B	4½	Butler & Co. Db. Stk	100	111
M	6	Chesters' Cum. Pref.	10	13½
M	4½	Do. Debs.	100	109
S	10/	Clarkson's Ord.	10	23
S	6	Do. Cum. Prf. Stk.	10	14
M	4	Dutton & Co. Db. Sk.	100	104
M	4½	Hardy's Crown Debs.	100	111
B	10/	Holt	10	18½
B	5	Do. Cum. Pref. ..	10	12½
B	4	Do. Debs.	100	109½
B	12/6	Lichfield	10	—
B	5	Do. Cum. Pref...	10	12
M	5½	Manchester Deb. Stk.	100	142
B	6/	Mitchell, H., & Co.	10	40
B	6	Do. Cum. Pref...	10	15½
Bl	6	Oakhill Pref.	10	16½

Breweries (continued):—

Chief Market.	Int. or Div.	NAME.	Amount paid.	Price.
M	5/	Springwell	10	10½
M	7	Do. Pref.	10	13½
Bl	9	Stroud	10	16½
Bl	6	Do. Pref	10	14½
M	6/	Taylor's Eagle	10	11½
M	7	Do. Cum. Pref ..	10	13½
M	4½	Do. Deb. Stk. ..	100	117½
S	10	Tennant Bros £20 shs	15	33½
S	10	Wheatley & Bates ..	10	14½
S	6	Do. Cum. Pref.	10	12½

CANALS AND DOCKS.

Chief Market.	Int. or Div.	NAME.	Amount paid.	Price.
Bl	5	Hill's Dry Dk. &c. £20	18	9
M	4	Manc. Ship Canal 1st Mt. Deb. Stk.	100	104
M	4	Do. 2nd do.	100	103½
L	36/3	Mersey Dck. & Harb.	an.	118½
L	35/	Do.	an.	117
M	10/	Rochdale Canal	100	36½
B	37/6	Staff. & Worc. Canal	100	75½
B	4½	Do. Deb. Stk....	100	137
Bl	4	Swansea Harb......	100	114
B	27/6	Warwick & Birm. Cnl	100	66½
B	12/6	Do. & Napton do.	100	23

COMMERCIAL & INDUSTRIAL.

Chief Market.	Int. or Div.	NAME.	Amount paid.	Price.
L	5	Agua Santa Mt. Debs	100	100
M	8/	Armitage, Sir E. & Sns Ltd.	10	19
M	4	Do. Deb. 1910 ..	100	101
L	6	Ang. Chil. Nit. 1 Mt. Debs., 1919 ..	100	109½
Bl	11	Bath Stone Firms ..	10	19
M	4/9½	Barlow & Jones, Ltd., £10 Shs.	8	10½
B	12/6	Birmgham. Ry. Car.	10	16½
B	6	Do. Pref.	10	15½
B	5/	Do. Small Arms	5	14½
M	£18	Blackpool Pier	100	277½
M	5	Do. Tower Debs.	50	54½
M	3/	Do. Wi. Gar. & P.	5	4½
Bl	10	Bristl. & S. W. R. Wag. £20 Shs.	3	5½
Bl	8	Do. Wag. & Carri. £10 Shs.	10	14½
M	7/	Crosses & Winkwth. Ltd.	5	12½
L	5	G. Angus & Co. Pref.	10	13½
Bl	5	Gloster. Carri. & W.		10½
Bl	5	Gt. Wstn. Cttn., Ltd.	20	15
M	6	Hetherington, L. Prf.	10	8½
M	4½	Do. Debs., 1910	100	98½
B	7½d.	Hinks (J. & Son), Ltd.	1	27/6
S	26/	Jessop & Sons, £50 Sh	30	27½
S	10	Kayser, Ellsn. & Co. L.	5	11½
S	6	Do. Pref.	5	7½
M	7/6	Kellner-Partgton., L.	5	14½
M	4½	Do. Debs., 1914..	100	106
M	5	Kerr Thread, Ltd., Debs.	100	101
B	17/	King's Norton Metal, £10 Shs.	8½	19½
M	5/	Lancashire & Yorks. Wagon, Ltd.	10	10½
L	10/	Liverpool Exch., Ltd.	20	28
L	45/	Do. Grain Stge, Ltd.	50	108
L	5/	Do. Rubber, Ltd...	5	5½
M	9d.	Manchester Bond. Whse., L., £10 Shs.	4½	2½
M	3/9	Do. Comcial. Bldgs., Ltd., £10 Shs.	5	10½
M	4/	Do. No. 2, £10 Shs.	5	10½
M	2/6	Do. No. 3, £10 Shs.	5	7½
M	5/	Do. Corn, &c., Exchange, Ltd.	10	16½
M	4	Do. Debs.	100	126
M	8	Do. Ryl. Exchge, L.	100	246½
B	5/	Midland Rlwy. Car. Wgn., Ld., £20 Sh.	10	14½
Bl	5	Millers & Corys Dbs.	100	100½
B	12/6	Mint, Brgham., Ltd.	5	7½
B	5	Do. Debs.	25	108
B	10/	Nettlefolds, Ltd.....	10	50
B	5	Do. Pref.	10	15½
S	9	Nth. Centrl. Wgn., L.	5	8½
B	15/	Patnt. Nut & Bolt, L.	10	34
B	5	Do. Pref.	10	14½
B	1/	Perry & Co., Ltd. ..	1	27/
B	6d.	Do. Pref.	1	27/
S	10	Round, J., & Co., L., £10 Shs.	6	12½
S	15	Rodgers, J., & Sons, L.	100	213
M	12/9	Rylands & Sons, Ltd., £20	15	38½
M	2/6	Do. paid up	20	43½
M	4	Do. Debs. .. 1909	100	106
S	5	Sanderson Brs. & Co., Ltd, Debs.	100	102
M	4½	Schwabe, S., & Co., Ltd., 1 Debs. 1914	100	102
S	7½	Sheffield Forge & Rolling, Ltd.	10	11½
L	80/	Southport Pier, Ltd.	100	88½
L	9½	Do. W. Gdns., Ltd.	5	3½
Bl	5	Spillers & Bakers, Ltd, £10 Shs.	9	14½
Bl	6	Do. Pref.	10	14
B	5/	Union Rolling Stock, Ltd., £20 Shs.	5	7½
M	5/	Victoria Pr., S'port, L.	5	4½
Bl	8	Western Wagon & Property, Ltd.	6	9½
S	10	Wostenholm, G., & Son, Ltd., £25 Shs.	20	22½
S	6½	Yorksh. Wagon, Ltd.	2	2½

FINANCIAL, TRUSTS, &c.

Chief Market.	Int. or Div.	NAME.	Amount paid.	Price.
M	1/	Manchstr. Trst. £10 Shs.	£2	13/9
M	1/3	N. of Eng. T. Deb. & A., Ltd. £10 Shs.	2½	27/6
M	3½	Do. 1 Mt. Debs...	100	97
L	—	Pacific Ln. & Inv., L.	2½	2½
L	4	Do. Deb. Stk.....	100	103
L	—	United Trst., L. Prfd.	100	72½
L	—	Do. Deferred....	100	62½

GAS.

Chief Market.	Int. or Div.	NAME.	Amount paid.	Price.
Bl	5	Bristol Gas (5 p.c. mx.)	100	128½
Bl	4	Do. 1st Deb.	100	137
S	10	Gt. Grimsby "C" ..	10	201
L	10	Liverpool Utd. "A"	100	235
L	7	Do. "B"......	100	176
L	4	Do. Deb.	100	137
S	10	Sheffield Gas "A," "B," "C"	100	248
B	10½	Wolverhampton	100	230
B	3	Do. 6 p.c. Pref...	100	172

INSURANCE.

Chief Market.	Int. or Div.	NAME.	Amount paid.	Price.
M	6	Equitable F. & Acc. £5 Shs.	1	38/9
L	2/	Liverpool Mortgage £10 Shs.	2	1⁵⁄₁₆
M	2/	Mchester. Fire £20 Shs	2	7⁵⁄₁₆
M	5/	National Boiler & G., Ltd., £10 Shs.	3	13½
L	2/	Reliance Mar., Ltd., £10 Shs.	2	4½
L	4/	Sea, Ltd., £10 Shs...	2	10½
L	8/	Stnd. Mar., L., £20 Sh.	4	8⅛
L	1/	State Fire, L., £20 Sh.	1	2⅛

COAL, IRON, AND STEEL.

Chief Market.	Int. or Div.	NAME.	Amount paid.	Price.
Bl.	12	Albion Stm. Coal ..	10	11½
M	15/9	And. Knowles & S., Ltd., £37½ Shs. ..	23½	14½
M	5	Do. Mt. Debs. 1908	100	105½
Bl.	1/½	Ashton V. Iron	100	25
S	12½	Bessemer, Ltd.	10	20⅛
S	5	Do. Pref.	10	12½
S	12/6	Briggs, H., & Co., "A" £15 Shs.	12½	15½
S	8/6	Do. "B" £15 Shs.	8½	9½
S	20	Brown Baley's. Stl., L.	10	33
S	5	Brown, J., & Co., Cum. Pref.	10	13½
S	5	Cammell, C. & Co., Ltd.	85	134
S	5	Do. Pref.	5	6½
M	5	Chatterley Whitfield. Col., Debs., 1905..	100	100½
Bl	—	Davis, D., & Sons, Ld.	10	10
M	5	Evans, R., & Co., Ltd., Deb., 1910 ..	100	101
S	12½	Fox, S., & Co., Ltd., £100 Shs.	80	178
Bl	10	Gt. Wstn. Col., L., "A"	5	10½
Bl	6	Do. "B"	5	4½
Bl	5	Main Colliery, Ltd.	10	7½
B	5/	Muntz's Metal, Ltd.	5	8½
B	5	Do. Pref.......	5	6½
M	2/6½	Nth. Lonsd. Iron and Steel, Ltd., £10 Sh.	8½	2½
Bl	6	North's Nav. Coll., Ltd., Debs.	100	105
S	30/	Parkgate Irn. & Stl., Ltd., £100 Shs. ..	75	69½
M	6	Pearson & Knls., Ld., "A" Cum. Pref...	50	46
B	10/	Sandwell Pk. Col., L.	10	17½
M	6/3	Sheepbridge Coal and Iron, Ltd., "A"	25	18½
M	2/6	Do. "B"	10	7½
M	5	Do. "C" Gua. Pf.	25	28½
Bl	4	South Wales Coll., Ltd., "A"	17	8½
S	30/	Staveley Coal & Iron, Ltd., "A" £100 Sh.	60	80½
S	30/	Do. "C"	60	82
M	1/10½	Tredegar Iron & Cl., Ld., "A" £10 Sh.	7½	2½
M	1½	Do. "B" Stk. ..	100	35
M	6/	Wigan Cl. & Irn., Ld.	10	7
M	4/6	Do. £10 Shs.	7½	4

SHIPPING.

Chief Market.	Int. or Div.	NAME.	Amount paid.	Price.
Bl	6	Bristol St. Nav. Pref.	10	11½
L	15/	Brit. & Af. St. Nav..	10	13½
L	3/10½	British & Estn, Ltd.	6½	2½
L	10/	Pacific Stm. Nav., L.	25	24½
L	30/	Wst. Ind. & Pac. St. Ltd., £25 Shs....	20	28

TRAMWAYS, &c.

Chief Market.	Int. or Div.	NAME.	Amount paid.	Price.
B	5/	Brmngh. & Aston, L.	5	11
B	5/	Do. Mid., Ltd...	10	7½
Bl	6/	Bristol Tr. & Car., Ltd.	10	20½
Bl	4/	Do. Debs.	100	122
L	6	I. of Man Elec., L., Pref.	1	1½
M	15/	Manchester C. & T., L., "A" £20 Shs.	15	27½
M	10/	Do. "B"	10	18½

WATER WORKS.

Chief Market.	Int. or Div.	NAME.	Amount paid.	Price.
Bl	7	Bristol	25	62½
Bl	7	Do.	20	47½
Bl	58/	Do. 7 p.c. max. ..	100	158½
Bl	4½	Do. Pref.	20	32½
Bl	5	Do. Pref.	10	17½
Bl	3½	Do. Deb.	100	129½
M	10	Fylde "A"	100	335
M	7	Do. "B"	100	224
B	6	S. Staffs. Ord. "A"	100	166
B	—	Do. "B"	100	164
B	4	Do. Deb. Stk.	100	140
B	5	Do. Pf. "A" "B" "C"	100	170
M	£3½	Stockport District ..	100	184½
B	2/	Wolverhampton New	5	6½

SCOTTISH.

In quoting the markets, E stands for Edinburgh, and G for Glasgow.

RAILWAYS.

Chief Market.	Int. or Div.	NAME.	Nom. Amount	Price.
E	6½	Arbroath and Forfar	25	49½
G	1½	Callander and Oban .	10	7⅛
G	4	Do. Deb. Stock	100	148
G	4½	Do. Pref.......	10	14½
G	4	Cathct. Dist. Deb. Stk.	100	148
E	5	Edin. and Bathgate .	100	179½
E	7	Forth & Clyde Junc.	100	222½
G	4	Lanarks. and Ayrsh.	10	14
G	4	Do. & Dumbartons.	10	14½
G	4	Do. Deb. Stk.	100	149

BANKS.

Chief Market.	Int. or Div.	NAME.	Nom. Amount	Price.
G	12	Bank of Scotland ..	100	361
G	16	British Linen	100	495
G	8	Caledonian, Ltd.....	2½	97/
G	10	Clydesdale, Ltd.	10	23⅛
G	16	Commercl. of Scot., L.	20	87½
G	16	National of Scot. Ld.	100	417
G	8	Royal of Scotland ..	100	234
G	11	Union of Scotland, L.	10	26⅛

BREWERIES.

Chief Market.	Int. or Div.	NAME.	Nom. Amount	Price.
E	5	Bernard, Thos. Pref.	10	10½
E	5	Bernard, T. & J., Cum. Pref........	10	12½
G	20	Highland Distilleries	3½	10½

CANALS AND DOCKS.

Chief Market.	Int. or Div.	NAME.	Nom. Amount	Price.
G	4	Clyde Nav. 4 p.c....	100	125
G	3½	Do. 3½ p.c.......	100	105
G	3½	Greenock Harb. "A"	100	101
G	2	Do. "B"	100	38½

MISCELLANEOUS.

Chief Market.	Int. or Div.	NAME.	Nom. Amount	Price.
G	4½	Alexander & Co. Debs.	100	110½
G	5	Alexander Ferguson & Co. Cum. Pref..	10	11½
G	5	Baird, H., & Sns. C.P.	10	12½
E	12	Barry, Ostlere, & Co.	7½	12½
E	6	Do. Cum. Pref...	10	15
G	5	Brown, Stewart, Deb.	100	84
E	7½	Broxburn Oil	8½	8½
E	6	Do. Cum. Pref...	10	11⅛
E	7	Edinburgh & Dist. Tram. Cum Pref.	5	9
E	5	Gilroy, Sns, & Co. Dbs.	100	99
G	9	Glasgow Cot. Spin...	6	5½
G	30/	Do. Royal Exchg.	46	110
G	—	Pumpherston Oil Pf.	10	8½
E	7	Scottish Assam Tea	10	11½
E	5	Scottish Waggon....	10	12½
G	5	Stoddard & Co. Pref.	10	12⅛

FINANCIAL, LAND, AND INVESTMENT.

Chief Market.	Int. or Div.	NAME.	Nom. Amount	Price.
G	2/	Assets Co...........	1	47/
E	4½	Investors' Mort. Pref.	100	99½
E	4	Do. Deb. Stk....	100	103
E	4	Nthn. Inv. N. Zeal. Deb. Stk.	100	107
E	4	N. of Scot. Canadian Deb. Stk.	100	106
E	4½	Real & Deb. Corp. Deb. Stk.	100	108½

INSURANCE.

Chief Market.	Int. or Div.	Name.	Amount paid.	Price.
G	12/	Caledonian F. & Life	5	36½
G	4/6	City of Glasgow Life	2½	12¼
E	19/	Edinburgh Life	20	55
G	13/1	Life Ass. of Scotland	8½	34½
E	8	Nat. Guar. & Surety	2	52/
G	17½	Scottish Union and National "A"....	1	94/
G	17½	Do. "B"	3½	18¼

IRON, COAL, AND STEEL.

Chief Market.	Int. or Div.	Name.	Amount paid.	Price.
E	Nil.	Addie, Coll. Cm. Pref.	10	7¾
E	8/	Arniston Coal	8	14
E	8½	Cairntable Gas Coal	8	86/
E	12½	Fife Coal	10	20¼
E	5	Do. Cum. Pref..	10	13
G	7	Merry & Cunghame. Cum. Pref........	10	16
G	5	Do. Debentures ..	100	106½
E	1/9	Niddrie & Benhar Cl.	1½	41/
G	5	Steel Com. of Scotlnd	—	
	—	"A" Deb. Stk. ..	100	113
G	6	Do. and Mt. "B"	100	110
E	—	Watson, John	8½	11
E	6	Do. Cum. Pref..	7½	8½
E	12½	Wilson's & Cly. Coal	3	8¾

IRISH.

In quoting the markets, B stands for Belfast, and D for Dublin.

CORPORATION STOCKS.

Chief Market.	Int. or Div.	Name.	Amount paid.	Price.
B	3½	Belfast, 1921	100	111½
B	3½	Do. 1912........	100	106¾
B	3½	Do. 1924........	100	108½
B	3	Do. 1955........	100	105½
B	3½	Do. Water Com...	100	114½
B	3	Do. do.	100	106
B	3½	Do. Harbour Com.	100	112¾
D	3½	Rathmines & Rathgar	100	110
D	3½	Waterford Deb.	100	—

RAILWAYS.

Chief Market.	Int. or Div.	Name.	Amount Paid.	Price.
D	30/	Cork, Bandon, & S.C.	100	77
D	4	Do. Deb.........	100	139½
D	4	Do. W. Cork Pref.	100	—
B	63/	Belfast & Northern..	100	159½
B	4	Do. Deb.........	100	146
B	4	Do. Pref.	100	141½
B	6½	Belfast & C. Down..	100	167½
B	4	Do. Deb.........	100	147
B	3	Do.	100	107½
B	4½	Do. 4½ Pref. B...	100	153½
B	5	Do. Guar.	100	173
D	Nil.	Dublin, Wick. & Wex.	100	32
D	4	Do. Deb.........	100	—
D	4½	Do. Deb.........	100	—
D	6	Do. Guar.	100	169½
D	4	Do. C. of Dub. Junc.	100	—
D	5	Do. 1860 Pref. ..	100	120½
D	50/	Do. 1864 Pref. ..	100	107
D	50/	Do. 1865 Pref. ..	100	94
B	67/6	Great Northern	100	178½
B	4	Do. Deb.........	100	147
B	4	Do. Pref. B.	100	143½
B	5½	Gt. South & Western	100	145½
B	4	Do. Deb.	100	148½
B	4	Do. Guar.........	100	142½
D	45/	Midland Gt. Western	100	115
D	4	Do. Deb.	100	140
D	4½	Do. Deb.	100	151½
D	4½	Do. Deb.	100	—
D	5	Do. Pref.	100	174
D	4	Do. Pref.	100	137
D	—	Waterford & Central	100	15
D	3	Do. Deb.	100	—
D	3½	Do. Pref.	100	134
D	4	Waterfd. L., & W. Db.	100	133
D	4½	Do. Deb.	100	—
D	4	Do. Pref.	100	130
D	3½	Do. Pref.	100	102

BANKS.

Chief Market.	Int. or Div.	Name.	Amount paid.	Price.
B	50/	Belfast, Old, £125 Shs.	25	126½
P	20/	Do. New, £125 Shs.	25	50½
D		Hibernian, £20 Shs.	5	6⅛
D	2/	Munster & Leinster £5 Shs.	2	5⅛
B	11/	Northern, £50 Shs...	10	26½
D	12/	Royal, £50 Shs.	10	28½
B	5/	Ulster, £15 Shs.	2½	12⅞

BREWERIES AND DISTILLERIES.

Chief Market.	Int. or Div.	Name.	Amount paid.	Price.
D	10/	Castlebellingham & Drog	10	16½
D	6	Do. Pref.	10	15½
D	4½	Do. Deb.	100	115
B	17/	Dunville & Co.......	10	28½
B	6	Irish Distillery, Pref.	10	13
B	5	Do. Deb.	100	110
B	6	J. & J. M'Connell, Pf.	10	15⅛
B	13/6	Mitchell & Co.......	9	19½
B	5	Do. Deb.	10	11½
D	4½	Phœnix Brew. Deb.	100	95
B	6/	Wm. Cowan.........	10	13½
B	6	Do. Pref. ..	10	13⅛
B	8/	Young, King, & Co.	8	14

STEAM AND CANAL.

Chief Market.	Int. or Div.	Name.	Amount paid.	Price.
B	Nil	Belfast Steamship ..	50	35½
D	10/	British and Irish	50	—
D	15/	City of Dublin......	100	60½
D	3½	Do. Deb.	100	105
D	30/	Dublin & Lpool. Bldg.	50	74
D	2/6	Dundalk & Newry..	10	4½
D	4/	Grand Canal........	10	112
D	3	Do. Pref. ..	10	9½
D	3	Do. Deb. ..	100	99½
B	30/	Irish Shipowners....	100	65
B	3/	Ulster Steamship....	5	6

MISCELLANEOUS.

Chief Market.	Int. or Div.	Name.	Amount paid.	Price.
D	3/1	Arnott & Co.	4	7½
D	6	Do. Pref. ..	4	6¾
B	8/	Belfast Com. Bldgs.	10	11
B	37/6	Do. Ropework Co.	75	93½
B	5	Do. do. Pref.	10	13
B	2/	Do. Discount Co.	3	43/
B	5	Do. do. Pref.	5	4½
B	10/	Brookfield Linen....	25	17½
B	Nil	Coey & Co.	25	4
B	5	Do. Deb.	50	48½
B	4½	David Allen & S's Deb.	100	107
D	4/	Dublin Trams	10	19½
D	6	Do. Pref.....	10	18½
D	4	Do. Deb....	100	—
B	8/	Edenderry Spinning.	10	9
B	25/	Falls Flax Spinning.	25	15
B	17/	Forster, Green, & Co.	10	21½
B	9/	Island Spinning	7½	7½
B	8/	Jas. Lindsay & Co..	8	16½
B	1/7½	John Arnott & Co...	4	4⅛
B	4½	Do. Deb.........	50	56
D	5/	Kinahan & Co.......	10	11½
D	5½	Do. Pref........	10	11½
D	4½	Do. Deb........	100	109½
B	12/	Kirker & Co.	10	10
B	5/	Leahy, Kelly, & Leahy	5	8½
B	6	Do. Pref........	5	7⅛
B	4/	Lindsay Bros. Ltd...	8	7½
B	4½	Do. Deb........	50	56½
D	1/	National Assurance.	2½	38/
B	10/	Olley & Co.	5	7⅛
D	1/1½	Patriotic Assurance..	2½	29/6
B	3/7½	P. Johnston & Son, L.	6	6½
B	10/	Robertson, F., & Co.	8	23½
B	10	Ulster Marine Insur.	5/	7/
B	15/	York-street Flax	25	33½
B	6	Do. Pref........	10	15½
B	4½	Do. Deb........	100	120

INDIAN AND CEYLON TEA COMPANIES.

Acres Planted.	Crop, 1897.	Paid up Capital.	Share.	Paid up.	Name.	Dividends. 1894.	1895.	1896.	Int. 1897.	Price.	Yield.	Reserve.	Balance Forward.	Working Capital.	Mortgages, Debs. or Pref. Capital not otherwise stated.
	lb.	£	£	£	INDIAN COMPANIES.							£	£	£	£
11,240	3,128,000	120,000	10	3	Amalgamated Estates	—	*	10	5	3¾	8½	10,000	16,500	D52,950	—
		400,000	10	10	Do. Pref.	—	*	5	‡5	10	5				
10,223	3,560,000	187,160	20	20	Assam	20	20	20	5	60	6¼	55,000	1,730	D11,350	—
6,150	3,278,000	142,500	10	10	Assam Frontier..........	3	6	6	—	8¾	6¾	—	286	20,000	82,500
		142,500	10	10	Do. Pref.	6	6	6	3	11½	5¼				
2,087	839,000	66,745	5	5	Attaree Khat	12	12	8	3	7½	5¾	3,790	4,820	7,770	—
1,633	583,000	78,170	10	10	Borelli	4	4	5	—	8	6¼	—	3,256	D270	6,500 Pref.
1,720	812,000	60,825	5	5	British Indian	6	5	5	—	4	6	—	2,920	12,300	16,500 Pref.
3,223	2,247,000	114,500	5	5	Brahmapootra	20	18	20	6	13	7½	—	28,440	41,600	*
3,754	1,617,000	76,500	10	10	Cachar and Dooars	*	8	7	—	10¾	6	—	1,645	21,240	*
		76,500	10	10	Do. Pref.	*	6	6	3	11¼	5¼				
3,946	2,083,000	72,010	1	1	Chargola	8	7	10	2½	[illegible]	10½	3,000	3,300	—	—
		81,000	1	1	Do. Pref.	7	7	7	3½	1¼	5¼				
1,971	942,000	33,000	5	5	Chubwa	10	8	10	3½	6	8½	10,000	2,043	D5,400	—
		33,000	5	5	Do. Pref.	7	7	7	3½	7	5				
32,250	11,500,000	120,000	10	3	Cons. Tea and Lands	—	*	10	5	3¾	7¼	65,000	14,240	D191,674	—
		1,000,000	10	10	Do. 1st Pref.	—	*	5	‡5	11¼	4¾				
		400,000	10	10	Do. 2nd Pref.	—	*	7	‡7	12	5¾				
2,230	617,000	135,420	20	20	Darjeeling..............	5½	5½	6	—	22½	5	5,552	1,565	1,700	—
2,114	445,000	60,000	10	10	Darjeeling Cons..........	—		4/2	—	6	—	—	1,820	—	—
		60,000	10	10	Do. Pref.	—	*	5	2½	9¼	5½				
6,660	3,518,000	150,000	10	10	Dooars	12½	12½	12½	2½	18½	6¾	45,000	300	D32,000	—
		75,000	10	10	Do. Pref.	7	7	7	3½	16	4¾				
3,367	1,811,000	165,000	10	10	Doom Dooma	11½	10	12½	5	22	5¾	30,000	4,032	—	10,000
1,377	582,000	61,120	5	5	Eastern Assam	5 *	nil.	4	—	3	6¾	—	1,790	—	10,000
4,038	1,675,000	85,000	10	10	East India and Ceylon	*	nil.	7	—	8¼	7¾	—	1,710	—	—
		85,000	10	10	Do. Pref.	*	6	6	3	11½	5¼				
7,500	3,363,000	219,000	10	10	Empire of India	—	*	6/10	2½	11¼	—	15,000	—	27,000	—
		219,000	10	10	Do. Pref.	—	*	5	2½	10¾	4¾				
1,180	540,000	94,060	10	10	Indian of Cachar	7	3½	3	—	4¾	6¾	6,070	—	7,120	—
3,050	824,000	83,500	5	5	Jhanzie	10	10	10	4	8¾	6	14,500	1,070	2,700	—
7,980	3,680,000	250,000	10	10	Jokai	10	10	10	5	17¾	5½	45,000	990	D9,000	—
		100,000	10	10	Do. Pref.	*	6	6	3	14¾	4¾				
5,224	1,563,000	100,000	20	20	Jorehaut	20	20	20	—	58	6¾	36,220	2,955	3,000	—
1,547	504,000	65,660	10	8	Lebong	15 *	15	15	5	16½	7¾	9,000	2,150	8,650	—
5,082	1,709,000	100,000	10	10	Lungla		10	6	3	8¼	6¾	—	1,543	D21,000	—
		100,000	10	10	Do. Pref.	*	6	6	3	11½	5¼				
2,684	883,000	95,970	10	10	Majuli	7	5	5	—	6¾	7¾	—	2,606	560	—
1,375	380,000	91,840	1	1	Makum	—	—	2	—	1½	1½	—	—	1,200	25,000
2,990	770,000	100,000	1	1	Moabund	—	—	*	—	1	—	—	—	—	—
		50,000	1	1	Do. Pref.	—	—	*	2½	1	5				
1,080	482,000	79,590	10	10	Scottish Assam	7 *	7	7	—	10¾	6¾	6,500	800	9,590	—
4,150	1,456,000	100,000	10	10	Singlo..................		8	5	1	8¾	5¾	—	300	D5,200	—
		80,000	10	10	Do. Pref.	*	6½	6½	3½	13¾	5				
	Crop, 1896.				CEYLON COMPANIES.										
7,970	1,743,824	250,000	100	100	Anglo-Ceylon, & Gen.	—	*	5½	—	65	8½	10,992	1,405	D72,844	166,520
1,836	685,741	50,000	10	10	Associated Tea	—	*	5	2½	7¾	6¾	—	164	2,478	—
		60,000	10	10	Do. Pref.	—	*	6	3	10¾	5¾				
10,390	4,000,000§	167,380	10	10	Ceylon Tea Plantations ..	15	15	15	7	27	5¾	84,500	1,516	D30,819	—
		81,080	10	10	Do. Pref.	7	7	7	‡7	16¾	4¾				
5,722	1,542,700§	55,960	5	3	Ceylon & Oriental Est.....	5	8	7	—	2¾	7¾	—	230	D2,047	71,000
		46,000	5	5	Do. Pref.	6	6	6	3	5	6				
2,157	801,629	111,330	5	5	Dimbula Valley	—	*	10	5	6	8	—	—	1,733	6,250
		62,607	5	5	Do. Pref.	—	*	6	3	6¾	4¾				
11,496	3,715,000	298,250	5	5	Eastern Prod. & Est.	3	5	6½	2½	6¾	5¾	20,000	11,740	D17,797	102,500
3,118	701,100	150,000	10	10	Lanka Plantations........	4	5	5	‡5	6¾	6¾	—	495	D11,300	14,700 Pref.
2,193	1,050,000§	22,080	10	10	New Dimbula "A"	10	16	16	4	24	6	11,000	2,024	1,150	8,400
		55,710	10	10	Do. "B"	18	16	16	4	22	7½				
2,572	570,360	100,000	10	10	Ouvah	6	8	6	2	8¾	7	4,000	1,151	D1,255	—
2,630	535,675	200,000	10	10	Nuwara Eliya	—	*	6	16	11¾	5¾	—	—	—	30,000
1,720	720,200	41,000	10	10	Scottish Ceylon	15	15	15	5	22	6¾	7,000	1,252	D3,970	9,000 Pref.
2,450	750,000§	39,000	10	6	Standard	12½	15	15	5	14	6¾	9,000	800	D14,012	4,000
		17,000	10	10	Do...................	12½	15	15	‡15	22	6¾				

* Company formed this year.

Working-Capital Column.—In working-capita column, D stands for *debit*.
† Interim dividends are given as actual distribution made.
‡ *Total* div.
§ Crop 1897

Printed for the Proprietor by Love & Wyman, Ltd., Great Queen Street, London, W.C.; and Published by Clement Wilson at Norfolk House, Norfolk Street, Strand, London, W.C

The Investors' Review

EDITED BY A. J. WILSON.

Vol. I.—No. 16. New Series. | FRIDAY, APRIL 22, 1898. | [Registered as a Newspaper.] | Price 6d. By post, 6½d

CONTENTS

The Investors' Review.

Shall We Soon Have a Five per Cent. Bank Rate?

It is not an off-hand matter to answer this question, but we are bound to say that 5 per cent. seems less immediately probable this week than it did last. Several favourable features have come to the surface in the meantime, and chief of all an increased import of gold. We knew, indeed, that Germany was likely to send large amounts here on account of the Chinese loan, but doubted whether it would be of much benefit to the open market, or that it would outweigh the increased exports of the metal to the United States, consequent on the outbreak of hostilities. At the time that we are writing the probability is that there will be enough gold arriving to enable the Bank of England to meet any immediate American demand without further advancing its rate for another week, at all events, and the directors were quite right not to move it up yesterday.

It is estimated that within the next four or five weeks some four millions in gold may reach this country, and we should not be surprised to see this amount exceeded, because in the month of March alone our imports of the metal exceeded four millions, as we pointed out last week. Then the spring currency demand for domestic purposes has already passed its worst and in a few weeks' time some coin will be returning from Scotland

and Ireland, as well as from the English provincial business centres. It is just possible, therefore, that the market may rub along in much its present condition for some weeks longer. All, however, is only conjecture, because we have an unknown quantity to deal with in the demands of the United States. If they choose, or if they want the money, there cannot be a question that they can take large sums in gold from us within a very few days. They might easily ship, for instance, a couple of millions within a week, for their banks hold large amounts in sterling-bills which could be poured in on us at any moment. Even were gold known to be on the way here, and proved to be on the way by the advances the Bank of England has undertaken to make without interest against shipments of it before arrival, the nervousness of the market would be too great in the event of such a draft on our resources, were no protective measure adopted in the shape of an advance in the Bank rate to 5 per cent. The sum of the matter, therefore, is that while we have good reason to hope that money will not become much dearer, an early advance in the rate to 5 per cent. is by no means improbable.

Our own market can, we think, stand a 5 per cent. Bank rate should it come. Certainly the business of the country ought to be able to stand it, and we do not think that the finance market, as we may call it, has yet attained to such a rickety condition as would cause it to topple over if subjected to the pressure 5 per cent. involves. It would, however, be altogether different with the French market, and we must keep an eye upon that throughout the coming months. Its present prospects do not please us at all. Not only has the enormous expenditure of the French Government told heavily upon the further resources of the French people, but its recent fiscal policy, and its determination to uproot the great band of open-market brokers and bankers, all tend to produce a serious dislocation of credit in France. It will be in vain for the Bank of France to keep down its rate at 2 per cent., should our official rate go to 5 per cent., and struggle against exports of gold by advancing its premium on the metal. Capital is leaving France too fast on many accounts to make this policy any longer practicable. The Bank of France may before long have to raise its rate to 4 per cent., and the consequences of an advance to 3 per cent. only might be serious just now. Hence, probably, the weak policy of its directors in doing nothing to protect their market. This is but another way of pointing out how exceedingly cosmopolitan the London money market now is. Thanks to its supreme position the action of the Bank of England tells with immense force on every money market in Europe. And the consequences to distant markets of an advance in its rate to 5 per cent. might be so serious as to bring back trouble to us from abroad. What will India do, to take another example, should money become stringent here, and 5 per cent. does mean stringency nowadays. The leading Presidency Banks have been striving for months to keep their doors open: will they be able to keep them open with money difficult to obtain and dear in London? We should like to hear the opinion of some thoughtful and experienced banker on this question. Meanwhile, the nearer our open market works to Bank rate the better will it be.

The Hispano-American War.

Before these words can reach the eyes of our readers the final step will certainly have been taken which must render war inevitable between the United States and Spain. On Wednesday morning, President McKinley signed the Resolutions finally passed by both Houses of Congress, after a brief struggle on the part of extremists in the Senate to embody in them a recognition of the independence of Cuba. These Resolutions, which we print below*, transmitted to Madrid in some more or less diplomatic form, must bring on a conflict, but who shall fire the first shot may remain for some little time a matter of conjecture. In obedience to the directions of Congress the United States Executive may send a fleet at once into Cuban waters, where it will immediately be attacked by the Spanish vessels of war there; and if any attempt at landing is made, we shall have a bitter strife on land as well as at sea in full career, perhaps before another week has passed. A bold enemy, as Spain once was, might take the initiative and send vessels of war, half privateers, to harass American commerce and disturb the repose of American ports along the Atlantic coast, but Spain is not, we fear, capable now of daring such as this. If her rulers are prudent, at any rate, they will act on the defensive, for in spite of the boasts of the Spaniard, their country is by no means in a position to sustain a prolonged struggle under modern conditions of warfare, and with a power like the States.

Wednesday's newspapers contained a very striking interview with a Spanish diplomatist, described as being of the highest standing, in which the leading characteristics of Spanish pride and notions of honour were exhibited in the highest degree. According to this gentleman, Spain will fight to the last to retain Cuba, although her misgovernment of Cuba has long made her a disgrace to civilisation. He does not fear division among the people. Carlist and anarchist, republican and socialist, men of every political colour, will stand together with their backs to the wall and fight to the last so that Cuba may not be lost to Spain. A long tirade in this strain is wound up with the following peroration, which we quote and commend to the study of our American readers. It will give them a better notion of the characteristics of the Spanish mind than any recent utterance we have seen:—

There is no question at present as regards money in Spain to carry on the war. Money can be had. The national subscription

* Whereas the abhorrent conditions which have existed for more than three years in the island of Cuba, so near our own borders, have shocked the moral sense of the people of the United States, and have been a disgrace to Christian civilisation, and culminating as they have in the destruction of a United States battleship with 266 of its officers and crew, while on a friendly visit to the harbour of Havana, cannot longer be endured, as has been set forth by the President of the United States in his Message to Congress on April 11, 1898, upon which the action of Congress was requested: It is therefore resolved:

1. That the people of the island of Cuba are, and of right ought to be, free and independent.

2. That it is the duty of the United States to demand, and the Government of the United States does hereby demand, that the Government of Spain shall at once relinquish its authority and government in the island of Cuba, and withdraw its land and naval forces from Cuba and Cuban waters.

3. That the President of the United States be, and hereby is, directed and empowered to use the entire land and naval forces of the United States, and to call into the actual service of the United States the militia of the States to such an extent as may be necessary to carry these Resolutions into effect.

4. That the United States hereby disclaims any disposition or intention to exercise sovereignty, jurisdiction, or control over the said island except for the pacification thereof, and asserts its determination, when that is accomplished, to leave the government and control of the island to its people.

for war is overwhelming—everybody is giving up something. The Queen has headed the list, and the people, to the very women in the fields, are giving even their small pieces of jewellery and their savings. Spain is not financially moribund as some would make believe, and our resources are enormous where national honour is at stake. The Bank of Spain is rich and is with the Government; and there is also the power to put back the payments on the debts of the country, which, of course, would be a last resource. A suspension of payments under this head would not go hard with any one. As to the payment of our soldiers, it is said that our men in Cuba have not been paid for twelve months. That is nothing: a Spanish soldier gets his food and his clothes while on service, and when he goes on leave the whole of his past earnings are given to him in a lump sum. So in this case. Payments may be backward, but the soldiers generally desire it to be so, in order that when they return to their homes they can have their money in bulk. Every man who now joins the army will be quite willing to forego his daily pay under the circumstances.

Spanish resources, discipline, and national honour are all on our side!

Notwithstanding this vaunting confidence we do not believe that Spain can sustain a prolonged conflict. She has not the means. So far is her Bank from being "strong," that at the present moment its resources are strained almost to breaking point. The paper money emitted by it amounts to some fifty-two millions sterling, against which the Bank holds less than ten millions sterling in gold. All through the Cuban rebellion the Bank has been drawn upon by the Government to make good the deficiences in the revenue. It has had to advance money on Cuban bonds which could not be emitted to the public, to provide money for the coupons due on the Spanish debt, and to find the interest on the Cuban debt which otherwise must have gone into default. The war, in short, begins for Spain with an empty Treasury and exhausted credit; and it is to be feared that not all the jewels that the Spanish women can contribute, nor all the subscriptions handed into the Treasury by citizens of every degree, from the Queen Regent downwards, will do much to fill the yawning cavity which must immediately open in the Budget. Modern wars are dependent upon finance to an immeasurably greater extent than wars of former generations. One might almost say that the country with the longest purse is sure to be the victor. In the present instance we have very little doubt that victory will lie ultimately with the United States, and we should not be in the least surprised if her triumph came quickly. In spite of his boasting the Spaniard must know that he cannot continue to devastate Cuba under pretence of ruling it. The hand of fate is upon him. His race he is so proud of has had its chance in the world, none a greater chance, and it has been flung away. Judgment has long ago gone forth against the Spaniard as a ruler and decreed his expulsion from dominions conquered by his sword and cursed by his sway. On the other hand, by avoiding a great battle and sticking to the forts which protect Havana harbour, the Spaniards might give the United States far more trouble than the war party there appears to count on. As we pointed out three weeks ago, when first we insisted that war must come, the American people appear to labour under many delusions in regard both to their own strength and to Spain's capacity for prolonged resistance. Strangest of all seems to be the delusion of President McKinley, if the New York correspondent of the *Daily News* correctly reports his ideas. The President, this gentleman telegraphed on Wednesday night, still holds the notion that the Spaniards may permit him to send food to the "interned" Cubans starving behind the Spanish lines. A chance of peace, he thinks, lies in this quiescence. He must, indeed, be a simple-minded and benevolent gentleman if he can adhere to this idea after reading the speech of the Queen Regent to the Cortes and the accounts of the enthusiasm of the Spanish people. But the truth is, the American people and their President have, as we have insisted more than once, completely misunderstood the Spaniards, and have been totally unable to measure the effects which their words and acts have on the Spanish mind. And they may have to pay dear for their mistake.

Should this latest war of deliverance end soon its effects will not be of an enduring description on European money markets, nor on the prosperity of the United States, but it is quite certain that Spain must default upon her public debt. This consummation, however, was on its way in any case and was merely a question of time. It is quite consistent with experience of Castilian notions of "honour," as one has remarked, for Spanish statesmen to repudiate public obligations while clinging to the remnants of a once magnificent dominion. Should the war last for any length of time there would, of course, have to be large creations of United States debt, and the money procured by these creations would have to come to some extent from this side. We notice with interest that the Washington Government proposes to open a domestic loan for subscription throughout the country by the people. The bonds will be on sale at post-offices and other public places throughout the Union. A good deal of money may be collected in this manner, but we are not sure that the nation will, even in its present enthusiasm, find as much as twenty-five millions sterling, because it cannot spare the money. A war of three years, which the Spanish diplomatist predicts, would absorb a good deal more than that, and the United States would have to come to London, the only market in Europe probably able to help her. We should be quite willing to lend whatever sum is required on terms; but it might be prudent on the part of our Government, should the opportunity arise through American necessities, to make some stipulation to the effect that the hostile commercial policy, pursued by the American people towards us in particular, should be to some degree modified if we are to assist them in their foreign war with our capital. This, however, is not an immediate question, and it is not necessary to speculate over what is to be. The one significant fact is, that war has practically commenced between two Powers, one great and the other wrapped up in the memory of past greatness. War of all kinds means destruction of capital, waste of life and money, and it will be time enough to deal with the causes and the effects of this struggle when it has made some progress.

The Disappearance of the Coulisse.

The question of the disappearance of the Coulisse is so grave, and touches so many and considerable interests, that it vitally concerns not only financiers but the general public also. Legally, the Paris Bourse is formed of sixty Agents de Change, who constitute the Parquet. Its organisation strikes an Englishman as somewhat strange, and he cannot fail to compare the Paris market with that of London. He wonders why it is not organised on the system of our Stock Exchange, which facilitates all business transactions to the owners of stocks. The French Government has not thought fit to alter the situation of the Parquet and of the free market (the Coulisse) by abolishing the monopoly of the Agents de Change, but in compliance with the demand of the official agents it has just condemned the Coulisse to extinction, and the sentence will be carried out at once. The number of the official Agents de Change was fixed by the code of commerce of the First Empire, their number in 1793 having been 138. The values quoted at that time were very limited, but although the conditions are now very different, and the number of stocks now on the market amount to many hundreds, the Agents de Change are still only sixty. It is permissible to ask if the old laws and the new measures to be decreed will really accomplish that which is desired, or whether they will bring about a totally different result? In striking at the liberty of transactions on securities it is not improbable that an extremely disastrous perturbation may be caused to the general prosperity, and occasion much injury to the business of the future. The industrial and financial movement has created a formidable quantity of certificates representing a large part of the national wealth, and the permanent circulation of these values is consequently of much general interest. Unfortunately, the restricted number of the Agents de Change, even though increased to eighty, and the prominent place which the public funds and the stocks of the great financial and industrial companies occupy in their operations, prevent them from giving due care and consideration to smaller affairs. The shares issued by companies and public loans other than those of the State are thus condemned to remain always in the same hands, which is contrary to their nature and to the conditions under which they were bought, or to suffer, through the lack of a public market, a constant depreciation which must very unfavourably influence public opinion on the principle of association. In consequence of the exercise of a monopoly which, though not satisfying the public needs, is compelled to transgress the very laws of its being, an immense portion of the national wealth is forced to remain unfruitful. The Corporation of the Agents de Change has never had a constitution so opposed to the general interest as that which it is about to acquire. It cannot be thought for a moment that the eighty Agents will suffice for the necessities of the circulation of the great personal fortune of France; and it is very doubtful if their organisation is sufficiently well ordered to give satisfaction to capitalists.

It is absolutely certain that public affairs will suffer from the manner in which they will be conducted, and that the insufficiency of the intermediaries will be so evident that their situation will soon become perilous; their limited number makes its impossible for them to transact the immense amount of business which will be expected of them. It cannot be doubted that to concentrate all the negotiations of a vast quantity of certificates of various kinds on a market restricted and without possible competition, is to render that market confused, disordered, and inaccessible to the public, whose interests will be sacrificed to private interests, and the final result will be that capital will cease to patronise it.

On the demand of the Company of the Agents de Change the Coulisse has been legally destroyed, as was the case about 1860, and the negotiation of all kinds of values except Rentes, the railways, and the great financial companies will be without intermediaries from July 1. The law gives to the Agents de Change *alone* the right of conducting negotiations, which makes them in fact official brokers, since they are forbidden under severe penalties to conduct any commercial or banking enterprise. The disappearance of the Coulisse will enlarge the scope of the operations of the Agents de Change, and they will establish correspondents and even representatives in the principal towns of France and abroad, as is done by bankers, and they will receive and transmit orders from place to place. These operations constitute what is called "arbitrages," and are settled by means of current accounts and commercial bills. These are really banking operations, and the Agents de Change will thus be brought to do the same thing as the suppressed *coulissiers*. It is clear that the destruction of the free market, which will raise the value of the firms of the Agents de Change, will result in completely altering the mission with which the law has invested them, and that in spite of themselves they will be obliged to become, at the same time, both ministerial officers and bankers, and this situation will expose them to great risks. Firms will soon change hands frequently, and disasters may happen which will remind one of what followed the *débâcle* of 1882. It seems to us that the official character of the Agents de Change would not suffer in the least were it decided that negotiations which must, or are desired to have an authentic character could not be conducted except through their medium; but that all operations involving risks should be denied them, as they are to the notaries. In that case the Agent would become a species of commercial notary recommended to the confidence of both Frenchmen and foreigners. We may mention here that the Coulisse brought considerable capital to the Paris market, as well as a prodigious activity and a large extension of business. It included several houses with a large capital, and conducted financial operations of a speculative nature for its clients. Whilst the Agents de Change met the needs of the capitalists and saving public, the Coulisse gave its services mainly to bankers, business men, and speculators. In 1872, M. Thiers, and, later on, M. Tirard, publicly acknowledged the useful rôle played by the Coulisse in the interest of the public credit, and it was in consideration of that that it has been permitted to continue its operations for forty years.

The monopoly and the free market could certainly be conciliated by making the *coulissiers* pay a tax in the form of a stamp to the Company of the Agents de Change in compensation for the presumed injury they may cause it; this arrangement would have the effect of uniting the interests of the Parquet to those of the Coulisse. To thus concentrate all the operations of the free market in the hands of the Syndicate of the Agents would be equivalent to giving to the latter a mission of public order which would considerably increase the importance of their functions. The existence of the free market, that is to say, the surveillance exercised, the solidity created, and the responsibilities offered by a large number of intermediaries, would give to the market a security that it cannot possess under the new regulation. Small capitalists, who will be henceforth sacrificed to the larger, will find neither aid nor counsel in the Agents de Change, who will naturally neglect affairs of little importance, and will on some occasion, perhaps not far distant, refuse to respond to a national loan; for that *clientèle* which has hitherto proved itself so useful will have taken its money elsewhere. By driving away the Coulisse the Parquet will create a state of inertia which will cause the country to doubt both its strength and its resources. In the midst of an apathy which will only be aroused by suspicion or fear, the slightest disturbance in the financial economy of France will inspire the greatest alarm. M. Cochery would show himself to be as expert in finance as he proved himself a good administrator of the Post Office fifteen years ago, if he would allow the tremendous wealth of France to circulate, to increase, and to expand by permitting it the liberty hitherto enjoyed. That country meets with little trouble a really formidable budget, and would continue to do so without excessive grumbling if the fortune of its citizens developed in the same proportion as the charges which are imposed on them; but to attain that result it is indispensable that individual activity should be encouraged instead of paralysed by the privileges of monopolists and by the restrictive measures which are to-day condemned by all farseeing men.

Our Trade and War.—II.

WEST AFRICA AND CHINA.

How little tropical man requires of England may be judged from our trade with our West African colonies, some of which we have held for centuries. The following returns are significant:—

—	Imports.	Exports.	Total.
	£	£	£
Niger	312,000	607,000	919,000
Lagos	1,256,000	562,000	1,818,000
Sierra Leone and Gambia	291,000	381,000	672,000
	1,859,000	1,550,000	3,409,000

With foreign West Africa, our trade is £779,000 all told, and though it would be much more, no doubt, were it not for the protective system of Germany and France, the trade with our own colonies, and with the great back country they serve, shows how trifling it would be at the best. The negro wants no clothes, and a few Birmingham or other beads content him as ornaments. The small arms of that enterprising centre are not allowed to be imported for fear of their becoming inconvenient for European rulers, nor are electro-plate and steel pens in much demand. For an immense distance inland man has to war with nature and malaria in such irresistible forms that even the negro cannot stand against them. Miss Kingsley, in her fascinating book on West Africa, shows that the population is only maintained by the arrival of fresh tribes from the far interior, who sooner or later die out. With the exception of Algeria, we hold, in South and Central Africa, the whole of that continent which possesses no value for commercial purposes, nor can ever possess any. Yet there are many people who would apparently welcome war in order that we might obtain still more fetid mangrove swamps in West Africa.

Another and much larger section would direct our warlike attention to China, and (without touching on political considerations at all, or discussing whether our Government has done well or ill in the urgent crisis in the Far East) it is quite possible to calmly examine the trade aspects of the question. The teeming population of China is supposed to number some 400,000,000. The Chinese are in their own way highly civilised, with a civilisation far older than our own, and in commercial matters their organisation is remarkably good, while they are as able as merchants as any people in the world. Since we opened China by force of arms, the import tariffs of the Empire have been reasonable, and although internal duties may add to them, there does not appear to be nearly the difficulty in introducing English goods that exists in protectionist countries. The system of inland navigation is wonderfully good, and an enormous population lives in the great river valleys where they can easily be reached by foreign traders. Nevertheless, with our practical monopoly of the China trade for something over half a century, our imports from and exports to China only amount to £11,400,000 a year, a trade of 6¾d. per head. With the British Empire as a whole the trade appears much more important, as of the Chinese imports in 1895 of 180,000,000 Haikwan taels (£29,400,000) no less than 143,000,000 taels were from the British Empire. Of this total, however, 88,000,000 taels, or about one-half of the whole, were from our colony of Hong Kong, and undoubtedly included an immense quantity of goods sent to that great free emporium from countries outside the British Empire. The British exports to Hong Kong in 1895 were under £10,000,000, while the exports from Hong Kong to China were over £14,000,000. In the same way about one-half of the Chinese exports appear from the returns to be to the British Empire, but again about two-thirds of this total were sent for distribution to Hong Kong. The figures for direct trade with our colonies are separately given, confirming the idea that much that goes to Hong Kong is from other countries than our possessions. A little over one-third of the total Chinese imports consists of cotton goods, machinery, metals, and manufactures which interest England more or less; and about one-sixth consists of opium, which is of great importance to India. So far as cotton goods are concerned, the English trade can only be a temporary one, as the Chinese have coal and cotton of their own, and are rapidly starting spinning factories. China, also, is rich in minerals, which only await development. The introduction of railways might work a great change, but as things are the small impression we have made on the Chinese is shown by our miserable export trade of 5d. a head. Our exports to protectionist Russia are 40 per cent. more in amount than to all China, and are four times as much per head of the population. The Metropolitan Press is full of invitations to action that might easily mean that we should have to fight Russia, Germany, and France combined on the subject of China. But our exports to those countries are eight times what we send to China, so that from a business point of view such an awful and world-wide war would be suicidal. Of course points of national honour might necessitate such an appalling conflict; but the point we are upon is the desirability or the reverse of such a war for trade purposes. Our Government is of course absolutely right in endeavouring to keep the doors of China open as wide as possible, but very different questions would arise if we defied half the civilized world, say, about 230,000,000 of Russians, French, and Germans, if they attempted to close some of the back entries, an intention which they altogether deny.

Four Important Ceylon Tea Companies.

Ceylon tea companies, as a rule, are small, but in the past week four of the large ones issued their reports. Each company complains of a lower price obtained for its tea, and naturally the higher exchange and enhanced cost of rice, through the Indian famine, adversely affected profits. It might be well to explain that the cost of rice affects the companies from the fact that they are bound to supply their coolies at a fixed price, and in times of high prices the companies have to pay a good deal more for the grain than the amount received back from the coolies. The exchange for the year 1897 averaged just about 1d. per rupee higher than in 1896, which meant an increased working charge of about ¼d. per lb., while the higher price of rice represented nearly another ¼d. per lb. So the companies had their charges increased by ½d. per lb., in addition to which a lower price was obtained for their tea. The increase in acreage, too, was very moderate, as the following table sets forth :—

	Mature area.		Crop.		Price per lb.	
	1896. acres.	1897. acres.	1896. lb.	1897. lb.	1896. d.	1897. d.
Ceylon Tea Plantations..................	7,998	8,067	3,763,167	4,000,516	8¼	7⅞
Eastern Prod. and Estates	9,490	9,565	3,715,000	3,635,000	7⅝	7 1/16
Nuwara Eliya	1,734*	2,302*	565,692	899,223	9⅜	9¼
Standard	1,519	1,680	602,773	749,680	9⅜	9¼

* Part of this worked for only some months in year.

The Eastern Produce Company actually obtained a smaller crop, but the Nuwara Eliya had an output exceeding the estimates. In its case, however, the increase is in a great measure due to the fact that it is a new company, and in 1896 it evidently did not gather the full crop upon its acreage. The Standard Company included another estate it had purchased, but even then the yield per acre is higher, while the Ceylon Tea Plantations had merely an ordinary increase. Under these circumstances the profits of the companies working under normal conditions were bound to be lower, and the following table gives the amount and the manner in which it was divided :—

	Net Profits.		Put to Reserve, &c.		Dividend.	
	1896.	1897.	1896.	1897.	1896.	1867.
	£	£	£	£	Per cent.	Per cent.
Ceylon Tea Plantations..................	48,896	43,713	18,392	11,600	15	15
Eastern Prod. and Estates	48,212	40,890	23,219	14,963	6½	7
Nuwara Eliya	9,910	13,584	953	1,023	6	6
Standard..................	10,991	10,920	2,500	2,000	15	15

The increased profit of the Nuwara Eliya was mostly due to its working the greater part of its estates for the whole year, but it must have done relatively better than the other three companies. Yet the margin set aside for reserve before paying the dividend compares badly with them. The fact that the older concerns have been so prudent in the past mainly accounts for their good exhibit at the present time. In spite of the decline in profit, the Eastern Produce is able to pay a higher dividend (this, however, only represents £1,500), and sets aside nearly 40 per cent. of its profits to reserve and depreciation, and the two others pay the same dividend, the Standard setting aside nearly 20 per cent., and the Ceylon Tea Plantations 25 per cent of their profits to reserves. Beside these statements, the deduction of £1,023 by the Nuwara Eliya, or about 7 per cent. of the profits, is poor, especially when it is remembered that £481 of the sum is represented by the writing off of the balance of preliminary expenses. Yet this company, of the quartette, needed most in the way of accumulation from revenue, for taking the generally accepted formula, its capital cost works out at £89 per mature acre, as against about £30 per mature acre for the Eastern Produce and Standard Companies, and £21 per acre for the Ceylon Tea Plantations. Of course, we know that an acre of the Nuwara Eliya must be more valuable than an acre of the other three, for on an average it obtained last year 518 lb. of tea per acre, worth 9¼d. per lb. Accordingly, in working out the formula we have treated every acre of immature Nuwara Eliya tea as being worth £40 an acre, as against £20 per acre for the immature tea of the other companies. Even allowing for these circumstances, we must assume that the company is highly capitalised, and it would have been more prudent to have paid less in dividend and studied reserves to a greater extent. It is, however, a high-grade company, and so far has not worked the whole of its properties for a year. Of course the shares of the Eastern Produce, Ceylon Tea Plantations, and Standard Companies stand at higher premiums in the market than those of the Nuwara Eliya, but even when this is taken into account the latter company compares badly. Treating debenture and loan capital as being worth par, the market valuation per mature acre works out as follows :—

	Market valuation.	Deduction for reserves and immature acreage.	Mature acreage.	Market value per acre.	Profit per acre.
	£	£		£	£
Ceylon Tea Plantations......	581,654	109,951	8,067	58	5¾
Eastern Prod. & Estates......	485,000	96,258	9,565	41	5½
Nuwara Eliya	250,000	25,517	2,302	97	8¼
Standard	136,100	20,055	1,680	69	7

Yet if we take the present price of £11 per £10 share for Nuwara Eliya, £27 per £10 share for Ceylon Tea Plantations, £6⅜ per £5 share for Eastern Produce, and £14 per £6 share for Standard, we find the yield to an investor works out at about 5½ per cent. in each case. It is not, perhaps, a high return for an industry subject to fluctuations of exceeding severity, but then the three older companies have never paid dividends up to the hilt, and last year their profits were reduced from every cause. Rice will certainly not be so dear this year, and in other respects these older concerns ought to be better fitted to meet the future than the weedy productions of the last few years. We are glad to learn that the increased cost of working last year has proved a blessing in disguise to prudently worked concerns, as the putting out of heavy extensions has been brought to a standstill. Many of the new companies were to do this upon borrowed money, but the money has not been forthcoming, and so the extensions have had to be postponed. A year or two back, when Sir James Muir, the Buchanans, and others of that enterprising *genus* were launching their ill-balanced productions, the older concerns were very much in the state of mind assigned to Wellington at Waterloo by French writers when they say, he prayed "for night or Blucher." In the tea-growing industry "night and Blucher" have come together in the shape of a high exchange and low prices, and the consequence is that crudely formed and wasteful schemes are feeling the pinch severely. It is yet too early to estimate the mischief such have given rise to, but of one thing we may be certain, the bad results achieved by a number of them will effectually prevent more capital being put into this industry for some time to come.

The Budget.

The Chancellor of the Exchequer delivered his Budget speech in the House of Commons yesterday afternoon, and, as we anticipated, he had small consolation to offer the taxpayer. Though the Imperial Revenue has been enormous, the expenditure has managed to keep pace with it fairly well. A surplus of £3,678,000 was realised in the year just closed. Out of this £2,550,000 have already been appropriated for public buildings, and the remainder stays in the Exchequer.

A year ago in his estimates Sir Michael was very modest, as he had to confess last night. No doubt the high death-rate among millionaires during the last twelve months has made his forecast more erroneous than it otherwise would have been, but still he was modest, and we cannot blame him for being so. We trust that his errors of past years, for 1897 was not the first, will not have drawn him into a snare, and that he may not have "o'erleaped himself" to fall on the other side in this Budget. He estimates the revenue at £108,615,000 and the expenditure at £106,829,000, giving a surplus of £1,786,000, and this is all there is for the taxpayer out of this vast sum. It is not enough to allow a penny off the income-tax: that would take £2,150,000, he tells us. As a sort of half-way measure incomes between £400 and £700 are to enjoy abatements on a sliding scale. We doubt the wisdom of this policy, as it seems to us to give relief to a class of people who have no real claim to such consideration. Further, the proposed change only involves a paltry amount, £100,000 a year, and looks unpleasantly like a vote-catching project, designed to tickle the ears of the minor *bourgeoisie*. The question arises, where is this principle going to stop? We observe that the House received the announcement that cigars were not to share in the relief granted to tobacco with protest and dissent, and Sir Michael will find that grievances against the tax gatherers are not confined to those with incomes below £700 a year.

It is satisfactory to note that the revenue authorities are waking up to the bad effects of the engaging habit known as "grogging," which consists, according to Sir Michael's description, of "getting hold of the emptied spirit casks, soaking them with water, and selling the spirits secured in that way free of duty." In one case, it appears, as much as 124,000 gallons of proof spirits had been thus obtained. The thought makes one's mouth water, but we agree with the Chancellor that the law dealing with this interesting industry should be strengthened.

Opinions will differ as to whether indirect taxation should have been reduced at all as long as direct imposts are at a height which is simply outrageous in time of peace. However, Sir Michael seems to have decided that such a reduction was necessary to round off the beauties of his Budget, and after hesitating between tea and tobacco—from both of which, as he told the Committee, he is a total abstainer—he has plumped for tobacco. It appears that the weed is consumed but moderately in these islands. The Frenchman smokes 2 lb. 5 oz. per head, the Austrian 2 lb. 13 oz., the meditative inhabitant of the Happy Fatherland 3 lb., and the Belgian comes in an easy winner with 4 lb. 12 oz.: yet the Briton, "though we are a richer country and are not averse to paying for our personal indulgences, and the working class is better off," consumes only 1 lb. 13 oz. Sir Michael believes that there is room for expansion here, and hopes, with his genial optimism, that the reduction of 6d. a lb. on unmanufactured tobacco will reach the consumer. We beg to doubt this, seeing that the fragrant weed is usually bought by the ounce, and 6d. in the pound works out at an inconsiderable fraction—from the point of view of the retailer—on the ounce. The percentage of moisture is also to be reduced, "and as drier tobacco is more quickly consumed," quoth the Chancellor, with his tongue in his cheek, "the seller will have the prospect of obtaining advantage." Quite so; but why claim this as a benefit to the consumer?

Altogether, the Chancellor's speech was well digested, clearly expressed, and business-like. It introduced no heroic alterations in our fiscal system, and if its novelties were of a rather peddling order, they are not likely to provoke much vehement criticism from any quarter. We must suggest, however, in conclusion, that the possible effects of the war that is now beginning were perhaps passed over a little hastily. It is easy enough to hope that "any disturbance in the western hemisphere will be more than compensated by the happy improvement in the condition of India, and by the result of events that have recently occurred in the Far East;" but is the improvement in India already so "happy"? We would fain believe it; but, on the other hand, the possibilities of disturbance to trade, owing to the Spanish-American war, are exceedingly serious.

Economic and Financial Notes and Correspondence.

THAT BLESSED "CHARTERED" COMPANY.

It is unfortunate for us that the long-delayed meeting of the shareholders in this company should be held on a day, and at an hour, which makes it impossible for us to deal adequately with it in this week's number. Perhaps, however, nothing will be revealed of any such tremendous importance that it cannot keep a week for criticism. If we may judge by the documents the directors have drawn up and made public the chairman's story will be a very simple one. Indeed, there is no story, only a good deal of vain boasting about what has been done, and of random prophecy as to what is going to happen in the future, when the gold is found on the mulberry trees. We have searched through the three books, as we may call them, issued a week ago, and cannot find in them any fact of a consolatory kind to Chartered shareholders. Some people have told us that we let the directors down too easily last week; but really there was nothing new to say about them or the company they are supposed to govern, and the time is past for any effective criticism calculated to protect the unsuspecting investor from loss through purchasing "Chartered" shares. The folly has played itself out for the present, and if there be gold in Rhodesia, a thing no man yet knows, it is only fair that those who have been victimised into buying these shares at ridiculous prices should have the chance a discovery of rich gold deposits will give them to pass their investment on to some others as trustful in mind as they were. For our part we are altogether suspicious about the alleged richness of reefs and what not, paraded in these reports. Not a single fact is found in any of them leading to the inference that a "mine" of any richness is known to exist. The directors of the company, his Grace the Duke of Abercorn, Earl Grey, Lord Gifford, and Mr. George Cawston, call attention to the statement made by two or three of the mining companies printed as an appendix to their report. We have looked at these, and there is nothing in them of the least value in guiding the judgment of the investor. In short, it is the absence of facts which excites our suspicion far more than the statements actually made, although these are wretched enough from every point of view. Vague talk about excellent land for settlement, if irrigation could be arranged for, a large scheme of railway extensions, a full-dress parade of officialdom, showing a tremendous machinery erected to conduct the affairs of less than five thousand whites, lamentation for the scarcity of labour—a scarcity it is proposed apparently to remedy by importing coolies from abroad—these and such like statements and communications, mixed up with abundant doses of prophecy, form the substance of the reports, and they at no point give the lie to the opinions expressed by the late Lord Randolph Churchill in those frank letters written by him during his memorable journey through Mashonaland. We recommend those who think of touching this speculation to go back to the book in which these letters are reprinted, and to read the chapters there on the agriculture and mining prospects of the territory he went through. When they have done that we hardly think they will invest even now in Chartered shares, although there is a chance of making 6d. to 8d. per share on the current market price out of the new allotment.

Mr. Rhodes, we may however say now, made a great speech, in which he condescended to correct the assertion made by Earl Grey that the company had spent £10,000,000 in "developing Rhodesia." "As a matter of fact," said the orator, "it was between five and six millions, and it was raised by debenture debt." This fogs us nearly as much as the "Earl's" assertion, but it at least seems to admit tacitly that all the share capital of the company, and all the premiums netted on the later issues of it, went in promoter's gratifications, and in paying the cost of the rebellion. For the rest, he spoke with more than his usual confidence about the presence of payable gold in the country, boasted of his Bulawayo railway, "which cost only about £3,000 per mile, and was now paying about £40,000 per annum," and told the audience—a cheering, vehemently enthusiastic crowd—that he had asked the Government to help him to find the £2,000,000 required to extend the railway from Bulawayo to Tanganyika, a distance of 800 miles. "When we get to Tanganyika," he rolled out, "we shall have Kitchener coming down from Khartoum," doubtless with cent. per cent. dividends in his pockets. The whole harangue was first-class jingo-finance of this description, with barely an ounce of sober fact to buoy it upon. And it was touched in with a dashing cynicism never quite absent from any utterance of Mr. Rhodes. "Don't gamble in shares," he cried, "I do not wish to see that,"—which is good of him, considering, and makes us think that he really does read the Investors' Review now and then for his chastening. But what has the taxpayer to say about the proposal that he should guarantee 3 per cent., or a subsidy, to the Tanganyika Railway?

The Expulsion of "The Times" Correspondent from Havana.

On many grounds this is to be regretted, and not least because it is a step which proclaims once more to the world the jealous and intolerant character of the Spaniard. No man could be less a cause of offence than Mr. Charles Akers, the *Times'* special correspondent, himself, except in one regard—he has a habit of telling the truth. But he never puts the truth forward offensively—witness his recent letter, quoted by us some weeks ago, on the evil case into which Spanish finance has fallen through having to bear the cost of this long-drawn-out struggle of the Cubans for independence. The figures therein massed ought to have been of the greatest value in the world to the Spaniards had they been a sensible people instead of proud moonists, dreaming of a past that was great and grandiose certainly, but never glorious with the glory of freedom and humanity. It would have been invaluable just now to have had a man of Mr. Akers's acumen and probity, clear-eyed and practical, on the island, ready to let the world know from time to time what was going on; and the natural result of his expulsion will be to dispose Englishmen to put no faith whatever in any news emanating from Spanish sources. But Spain was ever obscurantist and secretive.

Shall Coal be Contraband of War?

War being now practically declared between the United States and Spain, a question of great importance, both to the two belligerent parties and to neutral States, presses for immediate solution, viz., shall coal be considered as contraband of war? Since the Declaration of Paris in 1856 there has been no war between two naval powers, and therefore the question has never been decided in practice, but international lawyers are, generally speaking, agreed that coal should be declared contraband, as, owing to the advance made in steam navigation, it has become the most necessary of all stores in naval warfare. But though jurists recognise this fact, Governments do not; for Russia in 1884 declared that she would be no party to any article in any Treaty which declared coal to be contraband of war. In the approaching struggle, however, it would be in the interests of both belligerents, and especially in that of the United States, if the rule were laid down that all coal being carried to any port in the country of either of the belligerents should be contraband of war, no matter whether it was destined for re-coaling ships of war or for purely peaceful purposes. Owing to the fact that the war, in the beginning at any rate, will be carried on almost entirely round about Cuba, this rule would prove of immense benefit to the United States, for they could then stop and seize all cargoes of coal, covered by a neutral flag, going to Cuban or other Spanish ports in the West Indies. The Spanish Navy would then, after the stock in their bases on that side of the Atlantic had been exhausted, become absolutely helpless, incapable either of preventing the States from landing troops in Cuba, or of interfering with what American over-sea trade remains. British shipowners and coalmasters, therefore, must not be surprised if the United States Prize Courts lay down the rule that coal is contraband of war, but should rather recognise that in doing so the States are trying to shorten the struggle as much as possible. This means a shorter interruption of legitimate trade. Coal declared contraband, in a word, should mean a speedy return of peace.

The New Company Bill.

There is little doubt that the present Bill, namely, the Companies' Act (1867) Amendment (No. 2) Bill is the outcome of the recommendations of the Departmental

Committee appointed by the Board of Trade in 1894 and the decision in the case of the Kharaskhoma Syndicate. The first object of the measure is to repeal Section 25 of the Companies' Act, 1867, which enacted that all shares should be deemed to have been issued and held subject to the payment of the whole amount thereof in cash, unless it had been otherwise determined by a contract in writing filed with the Registrar of joint stock companies. In the Kharaskhoma case it was decided that, in order to comply with this section, the contract must state the consideration for the shares, and that it was not sufficient to recite in the filed document that by another agreement, not on the file, the shares were agreed to be allotted, for the considerations therein mentioned. But the Lords Justices refused to give any opinion as to the particularity with which that consideration was to be stated. Now to us that seems a very proper decision. What it seems to say is this: "The section must be complied with, not only in the letter, but in the spirit, and the safeguards given by the legislature are not to be frittered away by any technical avoidance of the true meaning of the Act."

However, be that as it may, it is now intended to repeal that section in toto, and after providing in the second section for existing contracts and subsidiary contracts which do not fully disclose the considerations, the Bill goes on to enact that after the commencement of the Act, whenever a company limited by shares makes an issue of shares in its capital, a notice in writing shall be sent to the Registrar within a month of such issue, stating (1) the number, class, and nominal amount of such shares; (2) how many shares were issued on the footing that they were to be paid for in cash; (3) how many were issued as paid up, or partly paid up, for some consideration other than cash. The penalty for default is to be £5 per diem during the time that such default continues.

As far as it goes this seems a move in the right direction, but its steps in that direction are few. We shall now have a clear statement in the case of each company of the bonâ-fide cash shares, and the "other" shares. Undoubtedly it would have been better had the statement been made to include what was the actual consideration, "other than cash," for which the shares were issued. In many companies this would prove entertaining reading. The great fault, to our mind, is not what the Bill does, but what it does not do. Piecemeal legislation such as this is of very little use. So long as these shares, issued for considerations other than cash, can be placed on an equality with cash shares, so long as the imperfect means of getting an inquiry into the state of a company exist, our company law must be still declared to be in a poor and unfinished state.

THE WEST VIRGINIA AND PITTSBURG RAILROAD COMPANY.

Messrs. Brown, Shipley, and Company have invited holders of the bonds of this railway, which is a dependency of the Baltimore and Ohio Company, to send them in to be exchanged for their negotiable certificates not later than the 1st of next month. The bonds went into default on the 1st inst., and it is necessary that the interests of holders should be protected. They cannot therefore do better than accept the help of this eminent firm of American bankers, and the bonds ought to be sent in to it at once. The reorganisation plan of the Baltimore and Ohio is said to be nearly completed, and united action may be necessary to prevent undue advantage being taken of the helpless position of lines like this, which are more or less at the mercy of that company.

DEARER MONEY AND INVESTMENT STOCKS.

The inevitable retreat of first-class investment securities directly money became dearer is now in full progress, as will be seen from the subjoined table, which records the fall so far since the beginning of last July. Readers of the REVIEW have been warned for some time past that money was going to be much dearer this year than usual, and, as a fall in investment stocks is always the natural sequence of higher rates, they will have been well prepared for the pegging back now going on all round. Owing to the long period of cheap money, all gilt-edged securities had been worked up to heights never before attained, and therefore the influence of a stiffer money market will be greater than usual.

STOCK.	July, 1897.		April, 1898.	
	Price.	Yield.	Price.	Yield.
		£ s. d.		£ s. d.
Consols	113	1 18 6	110	2 1 0
British 2½ per cents.	104½	1 19 0	103	2 1 0
Local Loans Stk.	114	1 19 7	110	2 4 1
India 3½ p.c. Stk.	117	2 14 9	112½	2 18 2
India 3 p.c. Stk.	111	2 12 2	105½	2 15 10
India 2½ p.c. Stk.	98	2 11 0	91	2 14 11
Metropolitan 3½ p.c. Stk.	123	2 9 7	116	2 14 10
Metropolitan 3 p.c. Stk.	114	2 9 10	109	2 13 2
Metropolitan 2½ p.c. Stk.	103	2 7 7	99	2 10 9
Birmingham Corp. 3 p.c. Stk.	113	2 10 10	111	2 12 2
Bradford Corp. 3 p.c. Stk.	113½	2 11 2	108	2 14 5
Cardiff Corp. 3 p.c. Stk.	107	2 10 1	103	2 15 5
Glasgow Corp. 3½ p.c. Stk.	113	2 11 6	110	2 14 9
Leicester Corp. 3½ p.c. Stk.	117	2 15 4	115	2 16 8
Liverpool Corp. 3½ p.c. Stk.	136	2 11 5	131	2 13 5
Manchester Corp. 3 p.c. Stk.	113	2 10 6	108	2 13 10
Nottingham Corp. 3 p.c. Stk.	117	2 11 3	111	2 14 0
Canada 3 p.c. Inscribed	104	2 16 8	101	2 19 1
Cape 4 p.c. Consolidated	117	3 2 6	109	3 6 9
Natal 3½ p.c. Stk.	108	2 18 2	105	3 2 1
New South Wales 3½ p.c.	108	3 1 1	103	3 6 6
New Zealand 4 p.c. Cons.	115	3 5 0	110	3 9 7
Queensland 3½ p.c. Stk.	106	3 4 0	103	3 6 3
South Australian 3½ p.c.	113	2 18 11	107	3 3 9
Victoria 3½ p.c.	107	3 2 2	102	3 7 6
Caledonian 4 p.c. Deb. Stk.	153	2 12 4	149	2 13 8
Great Eastern 4 p.c. Deb.	152	2 12 7	140	2 14 10
Great Northern 3 p.c. Deb.	118	2 10 10	113	2 13 1
Great Western 4 p.c. Deb.	158	2 10 4	149	2 13 8
Lancashire and Yorkshire 3 p.c. Deb.	117	2 11 3	112	2 13 6
London and North Western 3 p.c. Deb.	119	2 10 5	115	2 12 2
London and South Western 3 p.c. Deb.	119	2 10 5	114	2 12 8
North British 3 p.c. Deb.	114	2 12 7	107	2 16 1
North Eastern 3 p.c. Deb.	118	2 10 10	113	2 13 1
Great Northern 4 p.c. Guar.	152	2 12 7	144	2 15 6
Great Western 5 p.c. Guar.	190	2 12 7	180	2 15 7
London & North Western 4 p.c. Guar.	154	2 12 0	145	2 15 2
North British 3 p.c. Guar.	111	2 14 0	106	2 16 6
North Eastern 4 p.c. Guar.	153	2 12 4	143	2 15 11
Great Eastern 4 p.c. Pref.	148	2 14 1	141	2 16 9
Great Northern 4 p.c. Pref.	152	2 12 7	142	2 16 4
Great Western 5 p.c. Pref.	189	2 13 0	180	2 15 7
London & North Western 4 p.c. Pref.	152	2 12 7	145	2 15 2
London & South West 3½ p.c. Pref.	133	2 13 0	127	2 15 1
North British 4 p.c. Pref.	144	2 15 6	136	2 18 10
North Eastern 4 p.c. Pref.	152	2 12 7	143	2 15 11
Delhi Umballa Kalka 4 p.c. Deb.	114	3 0 11	111	3 4 1
Eastern Bengal 4 p.c. Deb.	146	2 14 10	137	2 18 5
East Indian 4½ p.c. Deb. Stk.	166	2 14 3	158	2 17 0
Great Indian Penin. 4 p.c. Deb.	150	2 13 4	138	2 18 0
Bass, Ratcliff, & Gretton 5 p.c. Pref.	154	3 4 10	143	3 9 11
Guinness, Son, & Co. 6 p.c. Pref.	194	3 1 11	189	3 3 6
Reid's Brewery, 5 p.c. Pref. Stk.	144	3 9 5	137	3 13 0
Chelsea Water 4½ p.c. Deb. Stk.	164	2 14 10	160	2 16 3
East London 4½ p.c. Deb. Stk.	166	2 14 2	159	2 16 7
Grand Junction 4 p.c. Deb. Stk.	152	2 12 7	145	2 15 2
Lambeth 4 p.c. Deb. Stk.	150	2 13 4	142	2 16 4
New River 4 p.c. Deb. Stk.	154	2 11 11	144	2 15 7

The set-back has little more than commenced as yet, for money promises to be dear throughout the summer, to say the least, while a prolonged struggle over Cuba and a large loan issued over here by the United States is a probable contingency which would mean heavy gold exports and a 5 per cent., or possibly 6 per cent., Bank rate. This, if maintained for any length of time, would induce another 10 or 20 point drop. And we are quite prepared to see it, time given.

THE COAL WAR IN WALES.

Without organisation, without funds, with some of the men already receiving parish relief, with no hope of help but such as workmen in other trades may be willing or able to afford them, the South Wales colliers have finally declared for war against their employers. The speakers at the Cardiff Conference on Monday, at which the final plunge was taken, seemed to have no very clear idea of what they wanted, and no idea at all as to how they may secure what they demand. They were as men groping in the dark, or waiting for miracles and sure of their performance. They first rejected by a majority of 54,000 the proposal to confer plenary powers on their leaders for the purpose of negotiation with the employers, which of course means virtually that they reject negotiation altogether. They spoke like conquerors dictating terms, not like ill-equipped combatants spoiling for the fray. 62,714 voted against any sort of sliding scale; 29,094 were for some shadowy kind of scale which probably they did not themselves comprehend, and could not explain. Nay, so infatuated and foolish in their infatuation are these poor men, that it required all the impassioned eloquence of "Mabon," the leader they refuse to trust implicitly, to induce them to refrain from asking the enginemen and stokers to cease work. That is, they were prepared to drown the collieries, and so, as they imagined, ruin the owners, oblivious of the fact that they were thus destroying the chances of future work for themselves!

Their present demand is for an advance in wages of 10 per cent., to continue for at least three months. It was a "toss-up" whether 20 per cent. should not be demanded, and a very large number voted for the higher figure. But the majority stuck to the lower figure, and so it became the claim of the Conference. It really did not matter much which of the two amounts was chosen; the one is as likely to be granted as the other. Another remarkable feature in the business is that the thoughtless miners declare that the owners can well afford to grant the 10 per cent. because several collieries have conceded it and are now working merrily! It never seems to have occurred to these men that fancy wages may easily be paid where fancy prices are being received for coal. The Scotch miners have had a shilling a day added to their wages because orders that would otherwise have been executed in Wales have been sent to Scotland and the North of England. Of course, as soon as the Welsh dispute is settled—and it is impossible the contest can be very prolonged—the fancy prices will disappear, and so will the fancy wages. It is the strike in the larger number of the pits which has forced up prices and wages in the few that are at work. The sliding scale is now in abeyance, but the Welsh miners are good enough to tell the coal-owners that when the 10 per cent. advance has been granted, they will be ready to have a talk about a new sliding scale; but it must be a leisurely talk. No plenary powers to leaders; and no decision come to until the whole of the hundred or hundred and thirty thousand miners have given judgment on each particular point. These colliers seem to live in a queer world of their own, where they appear to imagine they have only to stretch out their hands to take what they want. They are making up an awkward object lesson for themselves. A strike undertaken so recklessly, without thought or care as to consequences, cannot but fail, leaving only misery as the portion of those who provoked it and of those unhappily dependent upon them.

A "BULL," A "BULL"! MY "COLOURS" FOR A "BULL"!

Mr. Bottomley favoured the mining market with a particularly pungent Caudle lecture preliminary to his departure to look after his racehorses at Newmarket. Apparently, this swaggering understudy Barnato of the hour entertains the belief that there have been "bears" wickedly at work depressing shares of companies that stand subservient to his bidding. In a screed rich with metaphor and brimful of oracular threats, he hurls defiance at all such, and in the same breath whines "Come, buy; come, buy" to the public. Why this wail, printed in all newspapers and sent broadcast through the post with a penny-stamped envelope enclosed to carry the order back? Surely all this pother must be a great mystery to the ordinary bystander. That prices should fall in the present condition of affairs is only natural, and that shares which had been put up so openly by the "rigging" process should sink back at the prospect of a 5 per cent. Bank rate is only the ordinary experience of the Stock Exchange; yea, even when the leader in a "deal" has bought in against the "bear" more than the entire issued capital of the thing "rigged."

Yet all that poor angry Mr. Bottomley can suggest to his humble and devout supporters is contained in the following rules of conduct:—(1) Hold on to your shares; (2) if you have been induced to sell, buy back at once; (3) buy as many more shares as you can afford to pay for; (4) and above all, insist upon delivery. Now, this is a very beautiful programme and simple too—for Mr. Bottomley. In his eyes its chief merit must rest in the assurance it gives that, if carried out, it will afford him and his friends a fine market to realise upon. By his own statement he and his friends had due for delivery to them 80,000 more shares in the Northern Territories Company than were in existence. Accordingly, fresh buyers must, it would seem, purchase now from this clique, and even at £2 a share, or upwards, said clique's profits would be enormous. No doubt the position in regard to other companies of the group is very similar.

We, therefore, cannot refrain from thinking that the following passage in this noble philanthropist's manifesto has slipped in by mistake:—"When a number of men—actuated, as I have said, by motives of avarice or envy—band themselves together, and, callous to the interests of bonâ-fide investors all over the country, stand at nothing to accomplish their ends, you will probably agree with me that they deserve no quarter." The danger lurking in this passage is that the public may apply these remarks to Mr. Bottomley and his friends themselves instead of to the wicked "bears" against whom the hard doom is really pronounced. That would be such a pity, after all the trouble devoted to the manufacture of this brilliant outburst, that we deem it a kindness to show every one concerned just how the thing stands. Are we right, though? Really now, when you ask, we have a doubt. If Bottomley & Co. own all the shares of the "Terrors" Company and 80,000 more, what do they want you and us, good readers, to buy for? The thing is so good, "don't y' know!" True, but can it be that these self-sacrificing beings are so disinterested as to think they have too much of a good thing? We give it up and, being in doubt, shan't buy. Our little moneys are of use to us. They could be none to such a "brillionaire" as Mr. Horatio Bottomley.

MR. HUGH WATT.

It is best to print the following effusion exactly as it stands, although we must apologise for laying such stuff before the readers of the INVESTORS' REVIEW. Perhaps, however, they may thus be enabled to estimate the moral status of the class of men Mr. Watt, in some degree, represents. His epistle indeed, is excellent as a self-revelation, and on that account alone may be forgiven. Its writer confessedly knows nothing either of the INVESTORS' REVIEW or its conductors, and allows his pen to fly along oblivious of the fact that they may know a good deal more about him than they think their readers would be interested to see printed :—

"NORTHERN TERRORS."

To A. J. WILSON,

Editor "Investors' Review."

I have at last succeeded in getting a copy of what any respectable person having regard to the fabric of wilful falsehood it contains would characterise as your lying and disreputable "rag." The term unsavoury is unfortunate in your mouth. I have always been unsavoury to company wreckers, blackmailers, "rag" touts guinea pigs, and other such human vermin which now infest the City. Your article dated 15th inst. indicates both ignorance and rascality, because records exist proving your statements to be wilful falsehoods. I had no official connection with either the Chile or Caratal Companies, as every man not of mushroom growth in the City knows.

The New Chile Company under my presidency became the richest mining proprietary incorporated in London, and its reconstruction has to pay off a large debenture debt and meet previous liabilities. We obtained about £300,000 sterling of bullion, but the costs in Venezuela swamped even one-ounce crushings. I invested about £50,000 in the company, and year by year desired to resign unavailingly because none of the rich holders would take my place. All British mines there have failed, swamped by fines, tariff, transport, &c., &c. Port Darwin Company was not my creation, nor was I vendor. In fact, I was the means of cancelling the vendor's stock, and purchased every share I held therein. Subsequently, having acquired about 90 per cent. of the stock, advanced on mortgage, but offered to forego this for a similar advance by others. Company never got to work, as machinery bought and erected swamped working capital. Mine was offered for sale, but no bid, and I stepped in and paid all debts, taking property (not then of any value) believing, however, therein, and spent a lot of money exploiting territory. Your mala fides is manifest in every line, because you ignore rich returns since 1892, and you seem so debased as to ignore the full particulars of properties acquired, published with official reports and crushings. You know it is a shameless and barefaced falsehood to say the Howley Claim, which you know has only ten acres (one claim) "forms the chief property of the Goldfields Company," which you know has acquired 700 to 800 acres (fifty claims), and six mills and full plants (not one, as in case of Howley); but parting with the last remnant of respectability is, of course, a small matter to you. If you had wanted any facts I possess of properties prior to sale you could have had them, but that would not suit your infamous object.—Yours, HUGH WATT.

ARGENTINE NOTES.

It is absurd that the only market for the sale of cattle and sheep in the whole of Southern Argentina is at Buenos Ayres, and that the farmers of the Rio Negro have to forward all their live stock to that port. They are entirely at the mercy of the Buenos Ayres Great Southern Railway for the carriage of their freights, and in consequence lose from 25 to 30 per cent. on the price of each sheep in sending, to say nothing of the deterioration in value through spending two or three days in a train without food or drink. There was a rumour that the New Zealand Shipping Company were going to start a "frigorifico" at Bahia Blanca, and to call there regularly for live cargo and frozen meat. Why not? The farmers of the neighbourhood could supply plenty of stock to keep at least one freezer going, and would be greatly benefited by such a procedure. In time, there is no reason why Bahia Blanca should not become as great a port as Buenos Ayres, and direct all the shipping of the southern regions.

The outcry made in our English papers against the cruelties and great loss of life suffered by the live stock cattle and sheep shipped from Argentina to England is beginning to have some effect, for we hear that the *Nacion*, an influential Buenos Ayres paper, is sending a member of its staff on an extended tour to report on the methods employed by different countries. He is to go in a steamer carrying a full live stock cargo from Buenos Ayres to Liverpool, visit the various live stock receiving ports here, then go to the States, and recross in a cattle boat to England. Before returning to America he is also to visit the chief ports on the Continent. We hope that the knowledge he will thus acquire will do some good. Speedy reformation is very necessary, otherwise the trade will be hurt.

RAILWAY CAPITAL EXPENDITURE.

A competent statistician, writing in the *Financial Times*, sums up the capital outlay of the English and Scotch railways, as during the fifteen years ended with 1897, in a table which we take the liberty to reprint :—

Company.	Capital expenditure 1883 to 1896 inclusive.	Capital expenditure year 1897.	Capital expenditure 1883 to 1897 inclusive.
	£	£	£
Caledonian	8,556,753	502,904	9,059,657
Furness	292,993	50,743	343,736
Glasgow and South-West	4,874,181	168,089	5,042,270
Great Central	14,666,465	2,371,726	17,038,191
Great Eastern	10,477,444	627,727	11,105,171
Great Northern	9,667,499	1,499,608	11,167,107
Great Northern of Scotland	1,376,521	164,494	1,541,015
Great Western	13,769,470	1,154,832	14,924,302
Highland	2,479,737	247,185	2,726,922
Lancashire and Yorkshire	13,960,433	995,822	14,956,255
London and North-West	16,442,123	905,173	17,347,296
London and South-West	12,089,608	852,182	12,941,790
London, Brighton, and South Coast	2,983,283	292,843	3,276,126
London, Chatham, and Dover	3,182,095	125,044	3,308,139
Metropolitan	1,446,052	147,399	1,593,451
Metropolitan District	1,045,291	14,841	1,060,132
Midland	24,732,949	1,695,004	26,427,953
North British	10,968,395	1,196,987	12,165,362
North-Eastern	10,585,361	580,690	11,166,060
North Staffordshire	438,658	33,508	472,166
South-Eastern	3,404,990	607,602	4,012,592
Total	167,440,301	14,234,403	181,675,693

The writer adds :—

The above indicates the enormous outlay of over 181½ millions during the fifteen years 1883-1897, both inclusive—an average of rather over twelve millions per annum. The Midland still maintains with ease its leading position as the railway which in recent years has expended most on capital account, the next being the North-Western, which is, however, rather more than nine millions behind its rival. And, as our details of the expenditure during 1897 clearly show, there is at present no slackening of the rate of outlay.

We may go further, and allege that there will be no slackening until the companies are brought face to face with the consequences of their extravagance through some decline in their business, or revolt of the trading and travelling community against their exactions. Much of the money thus piled up on these roads represents relief of revenue charges; it is extravagant expenditure at nearly all points, and it creates an illusory industrial prosperity which helps, equally with the lavish expenditure of the Government, to mislead the nation as to the true extent of its wealth and prosperity.

THE FISH OIL AND GUANO SYNDICATE.

Our lively Irish compatriots have taken up this new adventure with great gusto. An enthusiastic meeting was held in Dublin on the 5th inst., at which it was agreed to convert this syndicate, whose capital is £40,000, into a company with a share capital of £250,000 in £1 shares. £200,000 of it is to be distributed to the shareholders, that is, £5 for every £1 original capital. And still £50,000 is left to provide working capital, £10,000 to be issued forthwith at £2 premium per share. Lord Lurgan, the chairman of the meeting, delivered a speech giving a glowing account of the company's prospects. We hope he will prove a true prophet, though he did hold forth in his own country. Various companies in various countries are to be floated to acquire the rights and patents to prepare fish oil and guano, and from these the parent company is to receive handsome sums. What the total capitalisation will be of these various concerns it is not easy to discover, but it was vaguely magnificent and Dunlopist in statement. One company alone is to have a "capital," so-called, of £500,000. We have already seen the prospectus of the American Fisheries Company, which was floated earlier in the year, and it did not inspire us with enthusiasm.

The chief excitement, however, at the meeting was the story of Volenite. This, it is claimed, is a new substance which "is equal to gutta percha and superior to vulcanite." For electrical work its insulating powers are said to be marvellous, and the cost of production is to be the merest trifle. It is very pleasant reading, no doubt, and fortune seems to be within easy grasp for Pat and Mike, and we are sorry to spoil the picture by a hint that there appears to be a good deal to be done before success is secured. Fish oil, fish guano, and volenite may all be wonderful articles of commerce, but they have yet to be proved so. We cannot look with favour on the financial methods of this syndicate. It is not a straightforward action, in our opinion, to tempt people into subscribing for shares in companies with large nominal capitals before any kind of genuine business has been built up for such companies to live by. Our advice, then, is to leave these ventures to those who know all about them, and to read the reports of such meetings as that where Lord Lurgan prophesied at random with a large grain of salt.

Electric Lighting Companies and Local Vestries.

Subjoined is a sensible view of this question, which was dealt with in these columns a fortnight ago. But in this instance we do not know that the Marylebone Vestry can be blamed much. It has been roused to action by the manner in which the Metropolitan Electric Company has abused the monopoly it has hitherto enjoyed within the parish. Probably a fair revision of its tariff would avert the threatened competition :—

To the Editor.

Sir,—A feeling of uneasiness has been created in the market for electric lighting shares by the action of the Marylebone Vestry. The body has signified its intention of applying to Parliament for powers to start lighting by electricity on its own account, and so enter into competition with the Metropolitan Electric Lighting Company, which has put down mains and erected stations for the supply of current in that district. There is a great deal to be said on behalf of local bodies controlling the lighting of their districts, but the Marylebone Vestry's action seems open to question. After allowing the Metropolitan Company to obtain powers for their district and to sink capital in the laying of mains, building of stations, &c., and by their work prove that electric lighting is a commercial success, it does not appear honest for the Vestry to enter into competition by means of the ratepayers' money. Such competition must be one-sided, for naturally the Vestry would, do its utmost to cut into the business as it would not be hampered by the necessity of making ends meet. What the inhabitants would gain in the way of cheaper lighting would be offset by the increased debt that must be incurred before the Vestry's supply could be started. Further, it should not be forgotten that all these companies have the length of their existence defined by Act of Parliament: at the expiry of their powers the Vestry can acquire their stations, plant, &c., at a price entirely depending on the money spent on erecting them, without any addition for goodwill. If the Marylebone Vestry had followed the example of the one in St. Pancras, which refused to give powers to any private enterprise, no objection could be raised to their application. Under these circumstances we have no doubt shareholders in the various electric companies will support their directors in opposing the Marylebone Vestry.

In all this there is a lesson for directors of electric lighting companies. It ought to impress on them that the existence of their companies is limited, and therefore their efforts should be towards economical and careful management, and the building up of good reserves rather than the distribution of fat dividends. By these means prices of electric lighting shares will not be forced up to giddy heights, and when the time comes for them to hand over their trusts they will be able to do so with the knowledge of having done their duty properly and well.

Y. Z.

Distressed Mauritius.

The latest advices from this Colony indicate that matters are going from bad to worse. Already the attention of Mr. Chamberlain has been drawn to the distress prevailing amongst the planters and working population, and a plea has been put forward that similar assistance should be given to Mauritius to that which is now being accorded to the West Indies. Mr. G. D. Coriolis, the Surveyor-General of the Colony and a Member of Council, estimates that the population has to struggle with a deficit of 10,000,000 rupees as the result of its trading for the past three years. The consequence is that capital has been leaving the island, and its available currency has undergone a reduction of at least 2,000,000 rupees, through export as the result of the disasters in 1895. To add to the difficulties, interest is very high. The Mauritius planter, for example, has to pay 15 per cent. for the discount of his paper besides an export duty upon his sugar, whereas the sugar growers in Queensland get their money, it is alleged, at from 3 per cent. to 4 per cent. and have no export duty to pay, the consequence being that they have almost closed Australian markets to Mauritius sugar. To remedy this state of things it is suggested that the Government should be empowered to organise agricultural banks by means of which loans at moderate rates of interest might be made upon the growing crops, under proper security. This is a reasonable proposal, and if the British Government, in its liberality, can see its way to render the planters some further assistance, the difficulties might be surmounted. Failing help, it seems probable that by the end of the present year the Government of the island will be in pretty serious trouble. A deficit of 1,000,000 rupees is estimated as the probable result to it at the end of the present year. As it will not be possible to impose fresh taxes, the only alternative is to reduce expenses, and this must fall upon the Government employés. There ought to be a remedy for this state of things. Mauritius is not played out. All that seems to be required is some further supplies of capital, accessible to the planters at moderate rates of interest. No species of agricultural industry can thrive which has to borrow money at 15 per cent. and pay taxes in addition. Will some member of Parliament kindly jog Mr. Chamberlain's memory upon this matter?

British Trade and Foreign Rivals.

In the current number of the *Economic Review*, Mr. A. W. Flux supplies a needed corrective to the nonsense too glibly talked about the decadence of English trade and commerce. Because things "made in Germany" are making their appearance in places where they had never been before, and anxious consuls and no less anxious protectionists are making the most of what is the undoubted advance in German commerce, must we therefore conclude that British enterprise is dead, or that British commerce is disappearing from the face of the earth? Where is the proof? We have given too much attention to the partial statistics of the "fair traders," whose only nostrum for saving us from foreign rivalry is to exclude it, and thus deprive us of the greatest stimulus we have to exertion and enterprise. There may, as Mr. Flux admits, be evidence of loss or of too slow progress in special directions, but then, on the other hand, "there is a great mass of trade in which sufficient progress is being made to nearly or quite counterbalance" the losses thus made. "Where are the (foreign) gains—in what trades?" There is no explicit answer to these questions. The truth is, our censors and croakers have been looking only at scraps and corners of trade statistics which indicate slight losses here, and partial decreases there, but never take the trouble, perhaps hardly know how to get at the broad results and great volume of our foreign trade. This is what Mr. Flux has attempted to do. He has compared British exports with the most authentic estimate of the exports of the world—that formed by Dr. von Juraschek; and the conclusion he comes to—is bound to come to—is that British trade, though it necessarily fluctuates, sometimes very greatly, has kept, and is still keeping by a long way, its lead in the commerce of the world. Mr. Flux gives in a series of diagrams a vivid picture of his results and conclusions. Among other things he shows us that Germany, though an energetic rival, is far from being our greatest. In some things Belgium's rivalry is more serious, and is not dangerous merely because of the smallness of the country. Our real rival and most powerful competitor is the United States. Her competition is already close. Only within the last fortnight she has carried to the Clyde quantities of pig iron 10s. a ton cheaper than it could be procured at home; while a Clyde shipbuilder has given an order for 5,000 tons of steel ship plates to an American firm, which can send them from the States at a figure much below what the British manufacturer demands. This is a competition that will increase, and will tax our manufacturers' energies to cope with far more than the competition of Germany. America has also vast stores of mineral wealth hardly more than tapped yet. But as yet even her competition need not frighten us. She *may* some day take our place in the van of commerce; but that day is a long way off, and is not certain of ever arriving.

THE PANAWAL TEA COMPANY.

The Secretary-Director of this company does not naturally like our remarks about his company, as the subjoined letter sets forth. At the same time the facts are unfortunately in favour of our contention, although we did not accuse his board of "dividing profits up to the hilt," as he implies in his letter. Does it not, however, stand to reason that the 8 and 10 per cent. dividends of 1894, 1895, and 1896 were ill-advised in face of the fact that only 2 per cent. could be declared for last year, of which nearly one-half was drawn from the balance forward. Mr. Batten should turn to the record of the Eastern Produce Company, which, with a capital cost of about £30 per acre, prefers to set aside about 40 per cent. of profits to reserves, rather than increase its dividend above 7 per cent. If the Panawal Board had followed this policy in past years it would not have had to make such a poor display this time :—

To the Editor.

DEAR SIR,—I have read with some interest the article in your issue of the 8th inst., but, is it entirely just so far as the Panawal Company is concerned?

If your critic had taken the trouble to examine the Report he would have found that the capital cost per acre for "Tea in full bearing" when the company was formed was £52 7s. 7d., as against, on December 31 last, £38 12s. 11d. per acre, showing a reduction in capital cost per acre since the formation of the company of £13 14s. 8d., say about 25 per cent.

The directors might have treated the balance of the proceeds of the sale of Ranegama, less cost of factory, some £500, as profit available for distribution amongst the shareholders, had they not thought it wiser to continue their policy of writing down the cost per acre of the "Tea in full bearing."

I think in common fairness you ought not to have overlooked these facts. Your financial critic on tea does not seem to go into the capital cost per acre of "Tea in full bearing," as shown in each annual report.

If the directors had pursued the policy that you seem to indicate of paying up to the hilt, how could they have written down the cost of "Tea in full bearing" by 25 per cent. since the formation of the company?

He also overlooks the fact that the Coolie Advances are valued in the balance-sheet at 11·41d. per rupee, while the present rate of exchange is about 1s. 4d., a further reserve of some £200, in addition to the £230 "reserve fund," which sums, if taken into account, would further reduce the present capital cost per acre.

Surely for a tea company a better "reserve" (for which your critic clamours) could not well be found than by gradually writing down capital cost per acre.

J. H. BATTEN.

TROUBLES OF AUSTRIAN TRADERS.

"Fair" traders at home should carefully read and inwardly digest the complaints uttered by Austrian manufacturers and traders at a conference which has just been held at Vienna. While our "Fair" traders never miss an opportunity of urging renewed protection in this country and the shutting out of foreign competition, Austrian traders are complaining that high Customs tariffs and the absence of foreign competition are ruining them. There were other complaints, especially of the Austrian iron ring, which was denounced as one of the most serious obstacles to the development of native industry; but the Customs dues "which excluded foreign competition" were looked upon as worst of all, because, in excluding outside competition, they fed and nourished rings and monopolies. The Hungarian Government devotes constant attention to the development of native industry, with the result that trade there is in a tolerably healthy and vigorous condition. But the Austrian Government seems to have no time, perhaps hardly even the opportunity, to consider trade questions. It cannot even get the *ausgleich* with Hungary renewed, though that is considered of the utmost importance for Austrian trade. As for Customs tariffs, the inadequacy of inland navigation and of railway communication, the high railway rates, and the lack of facilities for obtaining credit, the Government might consider how to reform them, but the members of the Reichsrath will discuss nothing but what has been aptly described as the sterile nationality question. It was suggested at the conference that a separate party should be formed, devoting itself exclusively to the interests of trade. An energetic commercial party might do much good. Certain it is that unless Austrian traders and manufacturers set about energetically helping themselves, their condition must get steadily worse. Trade rings and high Customs dues mean trade ruin in the end.

Critical Index to New Investments.

CITY OF SHEFFIELD.

The corporation will receive offers for loans in sums of £100 and upwards, on mortgage of the rates, to be repaid in six months. Interest March 1 and September 1. Corporation is also prepared to receive offers of loans of £50 and upwards on deposit, interest due same date. A mortgage will be granted to depositor, but he will have to pay the *ad valorem* duty of ⅛ per cent. This sort of business is more for insurance companies than for the general public.

JOSEPH CROSFIELD AND SONS, LIMITED.

This company was formed in July, 1896, to acquire the business of Joseph Crosfield & Sons, Bank Quay Soap Works, Warrington, established in Waterloo year. In addition to soap the company are manufacturers of caustic soda, silicate of soda, and chemically-pure glycerine, being contractors to her Majesty's Government for the last-named article. During the past year the businesses of Messrs. D. C. Keeling & Co. and Messrs. Medley and Son, soap manufacturers of Liverpool, have been purchased and absorbed by the company. More working capital is now needed for extensions and additions to the works and plant, and the Manchester and Liverpool District Banking Company are therefore authorised to receive subscriptions for an issue of 20,000 5 per cent. cumulative pre-preference shares of £10 each at £11 per share, being part of an authorised issue of 25,000 shares. The capital already in existence consists of £150,000 ordinary and £150,000 5 per cent. preference shares, all of which is held by the directors and members of the Crosfield family, £150,000 4½ per cent. irredeemable first mortgage debenture stock, and £140,000 4½ per cent.

"A" debenture stock. The new issue, of course, ranks before the existing preference shares, and is entitled to repayment of capital at £11 per share. The assets standing in the books at the date (not given) of the last stock-taking, together with the additional working capital provided by this issue, amount to £772,000, or presumably the assets stood at £552,000. Voisey & Worthington certify the net profits for fifteen months ended February 28, 1898, at £60,000, being at the rate of over £48,000 per annum, while the debenture interest will absorb £12,675, leaving £35,323 to meet the dividend of £10,000 on the pre-preference shares. The company has entered into a contract with Messrs. Williamson, Murray, & Co. relative to this issue, and this may be inspected; but as applicants have to go to Warrington to do so, it is not of much use to intending subscribers in London. We think it would always be well if copies of such contracts could be seen in all cities or towns where subscription lists are opened. The company seems to do a sufficiently profitable business to make the new issue a fair investment, though we should have preferred more details about the assets and a fuller statement regarding profits.

STEVENSON & HOWELL, LIMITED.

Formed to take over from beginning of the year a business of manufacturing chemists, distillers, and importers of essential oils and essences, manufacturers of colours, technical chemists, &c. carried on at Southwark, with branch offices at Manchester and Glasgow, and agencies abroad. Capital £200,000 in £1 shares, one-half ordinary and the other 5 per cent. cumulative preference; 80,000 of latter offered at par; interest March and September. Purchase price £160,000, comprising £80,000 in cash, and £80,000 in ordinary shares; balance of capital reserved to be issued when needed. Premises only leasehold with unexpired terms from 64 to 75 years. Assets of firm, December 31 last, exclusive of goodwill, stated at £72,925, but no particulars given. Chartered accountants certify profits of last ten years continuously progressive; those for 1895 being £15,130; for 1896, £15,737, and for 1897, £17,747; average for the three years £16,205, or sufficient to pay interest on present issue of preference capital four times over. A moderate investment might be made by those who know the business to be good.

Company Reports and Balance-Sheets.

*** *The Editor will be much obliged to the Secretaries of Joint Stock Companies if they would kindly forward copies of Reports and Balance-Sheets direct to the Office of* THE INVESTORS' REVIEW, *Norfolk House, Norfolk-street, W.C., so as to insure prompt notice in these columns.*

THE UNION ASSURANCE SOCIETY.—In 1897 this company enjoyed a gross income of £902,285, being £63,036 more than in 1896. Of this income £454,083 came from the Fire Department, being an increase of £30,565. The Fire Department was worked at a cost of 33·38 per cent. of the premium income and losses paid and outstanding came to 56·4 per cent. Stated in money, the losses were £254,820, and the expenses and commissions £151,787, therefore the profit on the year's operations amounted to £48,058, which was not a strikingly favourable result, and the directors have wisely transferred £75,000 from profit and loss to the fire account in order to create a reserve fund to cover liabilities under current policies, the fire fund remaining at the same figure at the end of the year as at the beginning, namely, £323,539. In the Life Department 3,642 new policies were issued, insuring £1,141,594, and yielding £40,675 in annual premiums, besides £1,931 in single premiums. Of this total a small amount was re-insured, and the net premium income for the year amounted to £330,708, or to £24,270 more than that for 1896. In addition to this the company received £80,147 from interest on invested funds, and £27,797 as profit on investments sold, so that its entire income in this branch amounted to £438,702. Claims absorbed £194,458, including those arising upon twenty-one endowment policies, and expenses and commission took £58,124, being 17·58 per cent. of the premium income, which was fairly high, but still ·39 per cent. below the ratio of the previous year. The net rate of interest actually realised on the total funds, productive and unproductive, was £3 16s. 5d. per cent. after deducting income tax, and the directors say that, with the view to maintain the rate of interest, certain changes in the investments have been made, resulting, amongst other things, in the realisation of the substantial profit above-mentioned. They add, further, that they have satisfied themselves that the values at which the investments stand in the society's books are in every way justified, and that, while no investment has been written up in value, those which have fallen in price have been written down to their market value at the end of the year. This is a fair and straightforward method of dealing with investments. After meeting all outgoing surrenders, cash bonuses, claims, &c., a balance of £175,470 was left, which, being added to the Life Assurance Fund, brought it up to £2,155,329 at the end of the year. The society has a paid-up capital of £180,000, and a Life reserve fund of £350,000, forming additional security to policy-holders over and above the Life Fund already mentioned and the uncalled capital of £270,000. The bulk of the Life and other funds are invested in securities within the United Kingdom, but in the Life Department about £413,000 is invested in Indian, Colonial, and foreign stocks.

THE ANGLO-FRENCH EXPLORATION COMPANY, LIMITED.—The report of this company for the year ended December 31 last does not strike us favourably; for one thing, it is not frank and straightforward. Reading it cursorily, one would imagine that the company was really making way, but it does not appear to be doing anything of the sort. A balance of £96,862 is brought out at the credit of profit and loss, but it is subject to the deduction of £38,344 due to the managing director in South Africa, and to £24,508 written off for "ascertained losses." Deducting the £62,852 thus reached from the credit balance there is only about £34,000 left which could with any stretch be called "profit," and had it not been that a balance of £104,474 remained to the credit of this account from the previous year, and that £50,000 is taken from the reserve fund, although how it could be got out of that we are not told, the directors could not have paid the preference and ordinary dividends, still less have given £27 4s. 5d. to each founders' share of £1. The ordinary shares received 3s. for the year, and the preference shares got, of course, their 6 per cent. When these dividends are paid a balance of £36,196 will be left to carry forward, as against £104,474 brought down. This does not seem to us prosperity, especially as the company does not possess large resources in the shape of funds in hand, and has no separate investments for its reserve, while at the same time it lies under contingent liabilities amounting to £135,237. The directors state that the investments held by the company are as heretofore taken in the balance-sheet at either average cost or balance of cost. We confess we do not know what this means. It, however, was satisfactory to the board, for taken together with the cash then in hand it brought out an excess of assets over called-up capital and liabilities amounting to £460,000, of which £200,000 stands at the credit of the reserve fund. This is really a way of saying that the reserve fund is a mere excrescence or book-keeper's product, and we should very much like to know how the managing director became entitled to his £38,000. There is no information in the report worth a broker's half commission on ten shares.

THE STOCK EXCHANGE.—The report of the managers of this great institution for the year ended March 25 last indicates some reduction in its prosperity. The total of the receipts was £245,631, against £266,955 in the previous year, a reduction of £21,324. Against this, expenses were only reduced £9,870, from £99,497 to £89,629, so that the net revenue for the year was £11,457 less at £156,001. Adding the balance of £33,938 brought forward, there remained £189,939 to be dealt with, and out of this two dividends, one of £3 and the other of £4 10s. per £12 share have been paid, absorbing £150,000 and leaving £34,939 to be carried forward. Receipts from entrance fees fell from £88,830 to £59,421, which was below the average of £66,126 for the past five years. At the date of the report the membership stood at 3,962, and the number of admitted clerks was 2,601, showing an increase of 104 in the membership, and a decrease of fourteen in the clerks. This would indicate an increase in the revenue for the current year. In 1876, when the new deed of settlement took effect, the number of proprietors was 268: it is now 998, and we hope this total will rapidly increase, for the ideal is that every member of the "House" ought to be a proprietor holding one or more shares. The paid-up share capital of the company is £240,000, but it has issued £250,000 3½ per cent. debentures and the total amount of its balance-sheet, including the balance at credit of income account, was £804,980 on March 25 last. The proprietors have £32,210 at the credit of leasehold redemption account and a reserve of £72,566, besides a floating debt of £80,000.

INDO-EUROPEAN TELEGRAPH COMPANY.—The receipts of this company last year amounted to £130,347, as against £123,539 in 1896. Working expenses were a little higher, so that the net profit amounted to £60,968, or an increase of £5,534. The board with characteristic caution increased the amount placed to reserve by £5,000 to £15,000, and then paid the usual dividends and bonus, equal to 10 per cent. for the year, carrying forward £9,073 as against £7,704 brought in. The reserve will then amount to £292,276, and is wholly invested in high-class securities. The amount spent upon the undertaking is written down each year, and now stands at only £363,529. Needless to say, the trading and cash balances are much in favour of the company, and after paying the dividend and meeting trading liabilities, it has nearly £80,000 to its credit on this account.

CITY OF SANTOS IMPROVEMENTS.—The weakness of the Brazilian Exchange has unfavourably affected the revenue of this company, and after writing off £1,843 on this account, the profit for the past year was £7,702. This permitted of the redemption of £591 of debentures and a dividend of 5 per cent. on the preferred ordinary capital. Last year the same dividend was paid, £1,000 being placed to reserve, and £1,675 written off debenture issue expenses. The company has entered into a new water contract, practically on a gold basis, with the State Government and, the new capital having been placed, the works are being rapidly pushed forward. A loan of £24,800 has been raised, and the existing debentures amount to £17,900, which is not a heavy debt for this company with £100,000 of preferred ordinary capital, to say nothing of £35,000 of deferred ordinary. The reserve fund amounts to £7,210, but is wholly in the business.

GREAT NORTHERN TELEGRAPH COMPANY OF COPENHAGEN.—The preliminary working account of this company shows that the traffic receipts for last year, after allowing £17,070 for loss on exchange, amounted to £346,267, or an increase of £13,186. Working expenses were £4,504 larger, but interest and sundries came to very much less, and the net revenue of £324,224 was below that of 1896 by £27,313. The usual £10,000 of debentures are redeemed, and £21,111 is placed to amortisation account, or half the amount so contributed a year ago. Only £77,777 is placed to reserve, or £5,556 less than for 1896, but the dividend is maintained at 10 per cent., and the sum of £61,057 is carried forward, or slightly more than was brought in. The company is in splendid financial condition, for the outstanding debentures only amount to £160,000, and the reserve stands at £1,158,918, being almost wholly invested in high-class securities. Trading balances are of course in favour of the company, and the share capital is only £1,500,000.

ALAGOAS RAILWAY COMPANY.—Although the receipts of this line fell off last year, working expenses were reduced still more, so that the surplus of 89,024 milreis compares with 68,958 milreis for 1896. This profit, however, had to bear £2,596 for charges in England, and this left only £50 as the net profit, as against a net loss of £31 for the preceding year. The Government guarantee, amounting to £41,799, was, however, paid, and this allowed of debenture interest being met, £2,261 of debentures to be redeemed, and dividends amounting to 4 per cent. to be declared upon the ordinary shares. After this the balance forward will be increased by £1,326 to a total of £13,240. It is an unfortunate showing, and no one can be surprised that the position of these Brazilian guaranteed railways is less and less liked.

SAN PAULO GAS COMPANY.—The bad conditions of business in Brazil last year were reflected in the diminution of the revenue of this company by £5,295 to a total of £96,208. In addition, the loss on exchange was greater, amounting to £3,927, but £1,000 of this was met by a deduction from reserve. After placing, as a year ago, £10,000 to contingency account, the net profit was returned as £24,825, or only £1,796 less than the previous year. This permitted of the payment of dividends equal to 10 per cent., and the carrying forward of about the same amount as was brought in. The expenditure upon fresh works, on account of the new contract, is being proceeded with, and it is intended to raise a sum in debentures not exceeding £50,000 to provide funds for this purpose. In the meantime, we might mention that the reserve has diminished by £2,637, and the £20,000 that ought to be in the contingency account has disappeared from the balance-sheet. Doubtless the sums have been used in the new extensions, but nothing is said about them in the report. For all it says, they might have been non-existent.

AUSTRALIAN MORTGAGE, LAND, AND FINANCE COMPANY.—Not only can no progress be reported towards the very fine position formerly occupied by this company, but the shareholders have to face a further reduction of profits which, for 1897, were only £42,649 compared with £54,993 in 1896. The consequence is that the dividend has to be lowered to 7½ per cent. for the year, as against 10 per cent. a year ago, 12½ per cent. for 1895, 15 per cent. for 1893 and 1894, 17½ per cent. for 1892, and 20 per cent. for 1891. It is fortunately seldom that shareholders in a sound and well-managed concern such as this have to abide with such a progressive reduction in dividend, but the directors are not to blame, and in face of the difficulty of getting good business we think they have done very well. The continued decline in profits is the outcome of the policy adopted at the time of the Australian crisis, when not only crippled but diseased financial institutions were assisted along to drag out a miserable existence and to be a mill-stone round the neck of enterprise and progress for years. Apart from this fundamental reason for the continued depression the report tells us that the past season in the Australian Colonies has again been severe, causing a considerable loss in sheep and a poor lambing. Recent advices, however, state that rains have now fallen over the greater part of the colonies, and prospects are, in consequence, brighter. The steady rise in the price of wool, which manifested itself at the opening sales of the year and attained further development during the second series just closed, is also a satisfactory feature. The movements shown by the balance-sheet include a trifling reduction in advances on wool, but an increase of £170,000 in loans on land and stock, which with the value of properties, amount to nearly two millions. Cash in hand and bills receivable now stand for £35,849, whereas a year ago the item included short loans in London, and figured for £283,872. Of the difference another hundred thousand pounds has been put into investments, which with the holding of Consols, now amount to £955,000. On the other side debentures are £77,000 less, and bills payable £93,000 less, against which there is an increase of £180,000 in sundry creditors and customers' balances. The position disclosed is sound enough, and the fact that the total of the balance sheet exceeds 3½ millions, and was under 4 millions at the end of 1892, when the company was paying high dividends, shows how solid the business was then, and how well it has been kept together.

JOHN BARKER & COMPANY, LIMITED.—Although this company pays such a high dividend, we cannot commend the manner in which profits are divided. The gross profit of £148,942 was only £855 more than in 1896, but working expenses were considerably higher. Despite the fact that less was set aside to repairs and depreciation, the net profit of £52,419 was £4,317 less than in 1896. Yet the same dividend of 13¾ per cent. was declared upon the ordinary shares, which permitted a distribution of £2 4s. 6d. per £1 management share, or at the rate of 225 per cent. Only £1,000 was put to reserve out of revenue, as against £7,000 a year ago, and the amount forward is slightly higher. The sum of £60,000 received as premiums upon new shares was certainly placed to reserve, raising its total to £75,000, but the paring down of the allowances for reserve, depreciation, and repairs is not a happy sign. The present year, we believe, has opened badly in this trade, and the company will have to provide dividend upon the £40,000 of new ordinary capital, which if the dividend is to be maintained, will mean an increased charge of about £5,500. The allocations to reserve and depreciation, however, will not surely bear any further reduction. The directors show a remarkable desire to drop off this board.

LONDON TRUST COMPANY.—As usual, this company does not publish a list of its investments, so that the report tells one very little. The £2,013,077 of investments and loans yielded a revenue of £84,083, and after meeting expenses and debenture interest, the balance allows of 4 per cent. being distributed on both preferred and deferred stocks. The sum of £1,546 is placed to reserve, and the balance of £5,257 carried forward is slightly higher than the sum brought in. The amount placed to reserve has been devoted to writing off the value of securities, and so the reserve remains at £40,000. Nothing definite is said about the market value of the securities, the only remark being that the value is slightly better than at the corresponding period of last year. Last year the report stated that the value of securities was slightly less than that of the preceding year, but when that year is referred to, it is found that the only statement about them was to the effect that there was a considerable improvement in the value of securities generally. All this does not bring light as to what the market value of the securities held really is, and this manner of giving information is quite in consonance with the policy of a board that does not publish a list of securities. We never exercise faith in these cases.

HIGHLAND TEA COMPANY OF CEYLON.—For a small company this one's record for last year was not bad. There was a moderate increase in the output, but the average price realised per pound was nearly ½d. less, while exchange, of course, operated against it. The net profit of £2,371 was therefore £200 less, but it permitted the board to distribute 7 per cent. in dividends, or the same as last year, and to write off £260, the balance of the preliminary expenses. In doing this the balance forward was reduced by £129 to only £75. Although last year was a bad one for the industry, we should have preferred to see this company distribute at least 1 per cent. less in dividend, and so have prevented the capital cost of the block rising. It is too freely assumed that matters will mend this year, and companies of this class would have been wiser if they had kept more in hand to meet the uncertainties of the future.

POONAGALLA VALLEY CEYLON COMPANY.—The coffee crop of this company failed almost entirely last year, but that does not mean much. With 53,500 lb. more of tea secured the total revenue fell off £997, as the price of 7¼d. per lb. obtained was nearly 1d. per lb. less. Expenses were higher owing to the special causes affecting the industry, and the result was a gross profit of £1,168, against £2,845 for 1896. After debenture interest and general charges had been met the beggarly net profit of £207 was left. In this parlous state of affairs the board waived their fees, and as £362 was brought forward, a dividend of 3 per cent. was declared, as against 6 per cent. for 1896, and the miserable sum of £44 was carried forward. It would have been better if less had been distributed in dividend last year, and no dividend at all paid this year, for we note that the capital account continues to rise, while liquid assets are very small. Further capital will probably have to be issued, and the poor condition of the company perhaps made worse.

THE DEBENTURE SECURITIES INVESTMENT COMPANY.—We have always liked the frank way in which the affairs of this company have been put before its shareholders. The wisdom of this policy seems to be having its reward, for in the report for the year ended March 31 last we are told that the proprietors allowed the directors not only to pay 4 per cent. on the preferred stock and 5 per cent. on the ordinary stock into which the 40,000 shares of the first issue have been converted, but to set aside £13,350 to the reserve fund, which thus in three years has been raised to £34,150. In addition £210 has been written off preliminary expenses, and all current charges met, a balance of £36 being left to carry forward. Securities have appreciated £3,279 over cost price, but this appreciation is quite rightly not taken into the balance-sheet. A full list of investments is appended to the report, and shows that the money in the company's hands has been widely distributed.

THE FERREIRA GOLD MINING COMPANY.—This is in several respects the model company of the Transvaal as far as gold mining is concerned. It is not such a great company as the Robinson, but its board has followed a much more conservative and satisfactory policy in regard to its capital, which has not been inflated at all. On the contrary, it remains at the modest total of £90,000, and developments have been met very largely out of the revenue. No wonder, therefore, that the dividends have been good and that the shares should stand at a very high premium. Last year the cash profit amounted to £358,700, and a balance of £165,602 was brought forward from the previous year. This gave £524,302 for distribution, and £80,244 of this was expended on capital account. Another £270,000 was devoted to the payment of dividends, and a balance of £174,058 was left to carry forward. The dividends came to 300 per cent. for the year on the paid-up capital. Large amounts were written off for mine development and depreciation, and, with all this allowed for, the total balance at the credit of profit and loss in the balance-sheet is about £430,000. If a long life could be guaranteed to this company it would be the most desirable investment the Rand could offer, but its life will probably be brief.

SUBMARINE CABLES TRUST.—For 1897 the revenue was £23,156, including £159 brought forward. Both the October and April coupons for last year were met, the balance of 10s. due on the April one having been paid in July. The money was also in hand for the coupon due on the 15th inst., which has been duly met. After meeting the expenses of the Trust, which amounted to £1,560, and paying these coupons a balance of £20 is left to be carried forward, so that there is nothing much to come and go upon. The trustees state that they have sold the balance of the Anglo-American Telegraph deferred stock held for the Trust, and got £69,200 for it. This money has been reinvested, in accordance with the Trust Deed. We hope the new investments will help the revenue a bit, but of what do they consist?

ROYAL MAIL STEAM PACKET COMPANY.—The disturbed condition of Brazilian affairs has, of course, had a bad influence on the earnings during the past year, particularly in the second six months, owing to the Government of Brazil curtailing their subventions in aid of immigrations, to stagnation of trade there, and to the bad effect of the further fall in the exchange. In addition, the bad harvest in Argentina, and the condition of West Indian interests were also factors in the decline of freight and passenger receipts. The falling off in the latter compared with 1896 was as much as £30,000, while receipts from freight were £3,800 less, and even Government contracts and postal services yielded rather less, the total earnings being £741,045, as against £776,549. On the other hand, expenditure increased by £5,726, which is moderate, considering that 47,000 additional miles were run. The amount transferred to meet repairs of the Fleet is consequently only £65,000 compared with £95,000 a year ago; the usual sum of £47,700 is carried to insurance account, and £68,698 is written off for depreciation compared with £80,707. With the reduction of £42,000 in these appropriations there is a balance carried forward to profit and loss account of £10,758, against £9,980 in 1896, in spite of increased expenses, and the substantial reduction in receipts. Shareholders again receive two dividends for the year of 30s. each, which absorb £45,000, and £5,000 is transferred from the insurance account to repair and renewal account, which partly makes good the smaller appropriation from profit and loss, and the reserve of the insurance account remains at £250,000, to which it was recently raised. This is not a grand start for the new chairman to make, and the outlook at present does not indicate that the current year will be any better.

UNION STEAMSHIP COMPANY.—The report states that the trade and commerce of South Africa, and in consequence the company's receipts, have been materially affected by the rinderpest and prolonged drought. From this statement, and the fact that the amount available, after providing for depreciation, coal, wages, and other expenses, is £177,922 as compared with £155,142, we may conclude that less has been allowed for depreciation, or else that expenditure has been cut down. It is, however, impossible to learn what has been really done from the few particulars given in the thing the directors call their profit and loss and revenue account. Of this amount £125,000 is transferred to insurance maintenance, wear and tear and reserve account, and a dividend of 5½ per cent. for the year is paid on the share capital. While the reserve and insurance accounts have been further strengthened, the net cost of the ships has been written up from £1,229,927 to £1,341,720, and the net cost of property and plant from £90,178 to £137,565. The dividend is ½ per cent. better than was paid for 1896, but whether the directors are justified in paying it is not clear. It is, however, considered good enough to ask for an addition of £500 to their salary. Direction stands in the present accounts for the fairly substantial sum of £2,417, equal to over 6 per cent. of the dividend paid to shareholders, and the company has not been doing at all brilliantly for several years past.

VIENNA GENERAL OMNIBUS COMPANY.—During the half-year ended December 31 last, the number of omnibuses at work was twenty-eight in excess of 1896, and the receipts increased by 70,676 florins, but the addition to expenses was as much as 127,469 florins. The number of passengers carried rose from 7,621,000 to 8,365,000, and 4½ kilometres were run against 2½, but all this extra work proved expensive, for the average daily earnings per horse dropped from fls. 2.61 to fls. 2·37. Receipts are said to have been affected for several months by many of the leading thoroughfares being broken up by the municipal authorities for laying down a new service of gas pipes, which not only diverted the 'buses from their established routes and turned traffic over to the tram cars, whose lines were left undisturbed, but largely increased the expenses by the extra mileage necessitated by the obstructions. Expenses were also affected by the serious advance in drivers' and conductors' wages, and provender cost more, and although efforts to improve matters were made by keeping down outlay on maintenance of carriages, harness and buildings, the available balance carried to revenue account is only £4,054 compared with £8,787 a year ago, and after paying debenture interest the profit for the half year is £2,062, against £6,590. This profit, added to £8,048 brought forward, gives £10,111, and an interim dividend is to be paid at the rate of 5 per cent. per annum. This is a poor result from a concern having a share and debenture capital of £134,000, but shareholders are cheered by the prospect of increased traffic in the summer from the opening of the International Exhibition, and from the celebrations of the Imperial and Royal Golden Jubilee.

BUENOS AYRES (NEW) GAS COMPANY.—The profit of this company in 1897 was £1,663 less than in 1896, and while debenture interest was a little lower, the sum of £10,335 was written off as depreciation as compared with £7,054 a year ago. The net profit of £34,681 was therefore £4,308 below that of 1896, but the directors were able to declare 6 per cent., or the same dividend as last year, and to carry £792 more forward. There was, however, no allocation to reserve, whereas a year ago £5,000 was placed to that fund. But it is better policy to pay close attention to depreciation rather than heap up a big nominal reserve at the cost may be of the assets. Another wise step has been the writing off of the amount of £13,919, standing to the credit of renewal account, from the sum set down as representing service pipes and meters in use and in stock. Even then the item stands at £54,149, and naturally in time renewals must be needed. In the year, the old £200,000 of 6 per cent. debentures were converted into £220,000 of 4 per cent. debenture stock. The operation, however, appears to have been very costly, for in addition to the increase of £20,000 in principal, £18,906 had to be set down for discount and expenses. There should, however, be a saving of £3,200 a year from the conversion, and it would be prudent to set aside this saving, or a good portion of it, to wipe out the amount, which cannot be considered a satisfactory asset. We notice that the assets have been swelled by Deuda Consolidada, valued at £24,965, and we hope this paper evidently received in payment of the Municipality debt will prove better secured than the old Municipal bonds. The South Barracas Company still appears to be a moderate drain upon the undertaking, but taken as a whole the balance-sheet has improved considerably.

PACIFIC LOAN AND INVESTMENT COMPANY.—After providing for debenture interest and all charges for the past year, the available balance is £19,313, against £20,603 at the end of 1896. The dividend is again 6 per cent., and the reduced balance of £8,063 is carried forward. The directors say that the maintenance of better prices for grain has improved the position of many of the company's borrowers. On the other hand, partial crop failures following years of low prices, and so affecting certain borrowers, have made it needful to effect some further foreclosure, with the result of increasing the total holdings. Sales amounting to £11,892 have been effected during the year at a gain to the company of £4,241, which amount has been passed to the credit of the "Foreclosed Properties Suspense Account." The balance-sheet shows that against £392,900 of debenture stock, the share capital is £187,500 paid up, and £562,500 uncalled, and there is also a reserve fund of £85,000, but this is not separately invested in securities. Amongst the assets, mortgages, loans, &c., have diminished from £534,000 to £510,000, while foreclosed properties have increased from £91,513 to £109,515. With 17 per cent. of their mortgages on their hands the directors should be thinking about improving the look of their balance-sheet, even at the cost of dividend.

WEST FLANDERS RAILWAYS.—The general revenue account of this company for the half-year ended December 31 showed a surplus of £37,324. The sum of £3,529 is set aside to various reserves, in addition to which £4,100 had been spent in redeeming bonds. A supplementary dividend of 2s. 4d. per share was then declared on the preference shares, making the dividend for the year 13s. 4d. per share, and 9s. 3d. per share was distributed on the ordinary shares, making the total return for the year, on those shares, 15s. per share. These are the highest dividends yet declared by the company, and the directors have signalised the event by establishing a general sinking fund, which they started with a contribution of £1,200 for last half-year. The sum put to this fund may, according to circumstances, be either reduced or increased with a view, on the one hand, of maintaining as far as possible the rate of dividend latterly paid, and on the other, of accumulating such a sum as will more completely attain the object of the board and provide for any possible depreciation in the assets of the company. One cannot imagine an English company doing the like.

THE UNITED STATES AND SPAIN.

PRESIDENT MCKINLEY'S ULTIMATUM.

The American President signed the joint resolutions of Congress on Wednesday morning at 11.24, and soon after signed a dispatch containing an ultimatum to Spain. A copy of this was handed to the Spanish Minister at Washington, who immediately demanded his passports, and as promptly received them. The ultimatum was presented to the Spanish Government by General Woodford, the American Minister at Madrid, yesterday evening.

THE SPANISH QUEEN'S SPEECH.

The opening of the Cortes at Madrid on Wednesday afternoon presented a scene of great brilliancy and enthusiasm. The Queen Regent read the Royal speech, sitting on the throne, while the young King occupied a seat near her. The speech is quiet in tone. It begins by acknowledging with gratitude the intervention of the Pope, and the friendly attitude of the Great Powers; and then says:—

> It is possible that an act of aggression is imminent and that neither the sanctity of our right nor the moderation of our conduct nor the express wish of the Cuban people freely manifested may serve to restrain the passions and hatred let loose against the Spanish Fatherland. In anticipation of this critical moment, when reason and justice will have for their support only the Spanish courage and the traditional energy of our people, I have hastened the assembly of the Cortes, and the supreme decision of Parliament will, doubtless, sanction the unalterable resolution of my Government to defend our rights, whatsoever sacrifices may be imposed upon us to accomplish this task. In acting thus in unison with the nation I not only perform the duty which I swore to fulfil when I accepted the Regency, but I also seek to strengthen my mother's heart with the confident belief that the Spanish people will display a force which nothing can shake until the time when it will be given to my son to defend, in person, the honour of the nation and the integrity of its territory.

The following is the concluding paragraph of the speech:—

> Even though the future shows dark before us, even though difficulties surround us, they will not be beyond the powers and energy of the country, which in the end will triumph. With an army and navy whose glorious traditions make courage even more courageous, with a nation united as one man in the face of foreign aggression, with faith in God who has always aided our ancestors in the great crises of our country's history, we shall, with no less honour than of yore, pass through this new crisis, which it is sought to bring upon us by provocations devoid either of reason or justice.

Under the liquidation of the London and Universal Bank, Limited, Mr. Samuel Wheeler, the liquidator, announces that a third and final dividend of 2s. 6d. in the pound has been declared, and that it may be received at his office, 33, Carey-street, any day except Saturday, between 11 and 2.

TRADE AND PRODUCE.

War, the apprehension of which has been such a disturbing element in our increasingly prosperous trade, must now be regarded as close upon us. The American ultimatum was presented to Spain yesterday. Next week may probably witness the commencement of hostilities. It is too soon to venture on an estimate of its probable effect upon trade; but, if it benefits some portions of our business, it must seriously damage others. The shipping industry will, no doubt, be the first to feel its evil effects; and this is all the more unfortunate in that our shippers were evidently entering on an exceptionally busy season; and freights have been going up for some little time. Much will, however, depend on what may be declared contraband of war, and whether either or both combatants contemplate the issue of letters of marque to privateers. There seems a belief or impression that the United States will not do so; perhaps even Spain may also refrain. Nothing certain is known on the subject. The gunmakers of Birmingham will lose nothing by war. It is likely to make good to some extent the loss put upon them by the closing of the Persian Gulf ports to the importation of arms. Wheat dealers may be said to have been preparing for the approaching struggle for some time. Prices have gone up from 1s. to 3s. per quarter within these last ten days, and they are pretty certain now to go up further. It is just possible, however, that the likelihood of war was not responsible for all this rise. Home stocks had undoubtedly diminished a good deal, and large shipments were looked forward to for their replenishment. American dealers have been for some time hurrying off wheat cargoes before the expected declaration of war should interrupt the trade, and a considerable quantity of wheat must now be on the sea on its way here. The cargo market has been kept active for weeks by the steady Continental demand—much of it possibly for the replenishing of Spanish stocks. Prices for spot and futures have alike gone high—about a shilling further advance being netted on Wednesday in spot as well as in futures.

If coal is not declared contraband of war, the disturbance caused in that market by the stupid strike of the Welsh miners would be considerably intensified; for Spain, in the event of war, would require large supplies of coal for her navy. No doubt she has been looking during these last few weeks to the augmentation of her stock of coal, but it is now such a prime necessity in naval warfare that she could hardly have yet got sufficient to carry her very far. But the general expectation seems to be that coal will be declared contraband of war; and, if so, our coalowners will lose many good fat orders, and Spain will be very adversely affected in her naval operations. It may be noted that the Scotch colliers who demanded a shilling a day increase in wages, have had their demand conceded, and so a strike in the Scotch coal trade has not been added to that in South Wales. The owners preferred to pocket the high prices going to entering upon a contest with their workmen.

It does not seem as if the iron trade will be greatly affected by the outbreak of war. Of course, if prolonged, it must affect the imports of raw material; but it will be some time before that can be felt. The general position of the iron trade is excellent. The results of the quarterly meetings are regarded as encouraging, and better rates are quoted in some instances, while, in every case, old rates are well maintained. Scotch iron and steel makers are reported to be so pressed with orders that they can make their own terms, and most of them have a year's work secured. The Glasgow market was surprised—perhaps a little fluttered—by the arrival of a sample of pig-iron from America at 10s. per ton below the price at which it could be got at home. If the sample was up to specification a considerable further importation was expected; but that expectation may not now be fulfilled. Another fact is worth noting. Clyde shipbuilders are very busy, and the demand for ship plates has consequently been large; but British makers have so raised their prices that a Clyde firm placed an order for 5,000 tons of ship plates with an American house on terms lower than he could command here. It is a fact that may show how the wind blows; and British manufacturers may make a note of it. Whether the war will interfere with the delivery of the order remains to be seen. British ship plates have been quoted as high as £5 15s. per ton. Iron settlement prices on Wednesday were:—Scotch, 46s. 1½d.; Cleveland, 40s.; hematite, 49s. 7½d.

Copper, which early last week showed little alteration in value, took a sudden turn upwards towards the end of the week. On Friday the price had risen 10s. per ton from the 7th inst. There was a good deal of buying, apparently in American interests. The reason for the sudden rise is not quite clear. There has been no falling off in imports. Messrs. James Lewis & Son state that up to the 18th the imports had been 4,898 tons, and the deliveries 6,042 tons greater than last year. During the last fortnight stocks have increased 1,113 tons, and the visible supplies 1,452 tons. The larger part of the recent imports have been from the United States, but after to-morrow they must be considerably checked if not altogether cut off. There has been great activity in the market during the week, with an almost continued rise in price. On Wednesday there was at one time a further gain of 5s. to 6s. 3d. per ton, but before the close there was a fall of 2s. 6d. from the highest point. On Second Change, Messrs. Lewis Lazarus & Sons state, 400 tons sold at £51 17s. 6d. and 16s. 3d. cash, £51 18s. 9d. for May 11, and £52 7s. 6d. three months. Settlement price for standard, £51 17s. 6d. net.

Wool is somewhat unsettled. There has been no marked alteration since the last auction sales, and possibly not much may be expected until we have some experience of what the sales opening on May 3 are likely to turn out. Manufacturers did not respond very willingly to the sharp rise in prices at the last sales; and there is not much demand for any but merinos and the finer class of wools. In Leeds the cloth trade is rather dull as yet; but the prospects for the season are considered good, especially in the finer materials. There is depression in Leicester, though the yarn market is fairly active. In Huddersfield, however, there have been numerous orders for inferior and medium worsteds and serges, and for tweeds, which can be made into suitings at low prices, while in the finer makes of plain vicunas and serges and of fancy worsteds there is a steady business, though hardly up to the average, owing to the absence of an active Continental demand. The River Plate wools auction at Liverpool on Wednesday was well attended, and a fair business was done, though at a slight reduction for merinos and crossbreds.

THE PROPERTY MARKET.

The Mart has now recovered from the holidays. These told rather heavily upon business this year, the total for Easter week being only £28,785, in contrast with £62,605 for the same period last year. Yesterday week the total realisation was £15,285, consisting largely of freehold property. This was also the case on Friday, though the total reached only £12,580. Messrs. Dennant & Co. sold a profit rental of £150 for nineteen years, arising from the "Zetland Arms" public-house in Old Brompton-road, for £1,400, and a block of houses in Wallbutton-road, Brockley, held for seventy-seven years, at £1,550. Seven freehold houses in Farningham were disposed of by Messrs. Stimson & Sons for £1,660, and thirteen leasehold houses in Bexley for £2,499. Four freehold shops in High-street, Islington, realised, in the hands of Messrs. Hoppé & Snowdon, £4,620. Messrs. A. J. Sheffield and E. Holsworth also disposed of several lots of freehold property to ready buyers.

If the total sales at the Mart on Monday did not reach a high amount—£15,880—the attendance was good, and business brisk with the auctioneers who had engagements. Again there was a large show of freehold properties. Messrs. Moss & jameson disposed of two freehold shops in Cambridge-road, Kilburn, for £2,740, and Nos. 28, 30, and 32, Andre-road, Battersea, went for £1,350. The total realised by this firm was £5,725. Mr. Alfred Richards sold four freehold residences at Wood Green for £3,600, and Messrs. Egood & Fuller a freehold shop in the Blackfriars-road for £2,320, about thirty-five years' purchase on the present rental. Mr. W. A. Blakemore got rid of three out of four lots offered by him in the City, in Brixton, and at Battersea, at a total of £2,310. Two farms—Wakeham's and Poff's, at Bexhill-on-Sea, of eighteen and twenty acres—were offered as building sites, but failed to attract purchasers, and were withdrawn at £17,500 and £9,250 respectively. The rage for building does not seem to have reached Bexhill yet.

They were very busy at Tokenhouse Yard on Tuesday and the sales for the day amounted to the handsome figure of £52,810. The biggest business was done by Messrs. Wriford & Dixons, who disposed of numerous lots of reversions and freehold property at very high prices. This is not surprising when it is understood that the freehold properties were situated in Holborn, Piccadilly, Leicester-square, Oxford-street, Berwick-street, Wardour-street, and Tottenham Court-road. The Paris Hotel and Restaurant, Berwick-street, freehold, rent £130, went for £3,260. The residence at 14, Dover-street, Piccadilly, also freehold, fetched £5,400, while another freehold residence in Wardour-street brought £3,560. Almost the only lot put up by this firm of auctioneers which remained unsold was the "Coach and Horses" public-house in Carnaby-street, Regent-street. Licensed properties seem to be commanding less and less attention. Five more of them were put up on Tuesday at Masons' Hall Tavern, but not one of them was sold. The rebound from the inflation in this class of property last year has been very severe. It must be noted that Messrs. E. & H. Lumley sold at the Mart the Glebe Farm, of 622 acres, at Stockton, Wilts, the Bishop of Southwark being the purchaser. The property, as we have already stated, was offered on the plan of payment by a deposit of 15 per cent., the balance spread over thirty-five years by equal half-yearly instalments. The successful experiment is likely to be widely followed.

Though the total realisations at the Mart on Wednesday amounted to only £18,750, the business was good. A leasehold residence in Clarence-terrace, Regent's Park, in which Mr. George R. Sims resides, was sold by Messrs. H. E. Foster and Cranfield for £2,250. Mr. T. G. Wharton disposed of a corner block of shop property at Walham Green, covering an area of 4,500 ft., and let on repairing leases, expiring in 1902, at £32 per annum, at £3,025. An enclosure of freehold building land at Teddington, containing nearly 3½ acres, was placed by Mr. E. Pennington, for £2,500, a price that was considered very satisfactory. Messrs. Edwin Fox & Bousfield sold a freehold ground rent of £800 per annum, secured on 54, Pall Mall, with reversion in 76½ years, for £26,700, or about 33½ years' purchase.

Mr. Rhodes has, according to a *Daily Mail* correspondent, completed a big scheme for the removal from Cape Town to Rhodesia of 10,000 Fingoes, in order to augment the supply of native labour for the mines in Rhodesia. The ten Fingo indunas who negotiated the matter have returned from Rhodesia delighted with the terms and with the country. Whole locations will be removed, men, women, children, and cattle, by railway, and the Cape Government is actively assisting in the scheme. Each head of a family will receive a title to ten acres of land, free of taxation, on condition of working a certain portion of every year, a similar arrangement to that made in the Cape Glen Grey Act. The 10,000 Fingoes represent the first batch; more will follow as they are required.

Notice to Subscribers.

Complaints are continually reaching us that the Investors' Review cannot be obtained at this and the other railway bookstall, that it does not reach Scotch and Irish cities till Monday, and that it is not delivered in the City till Saturday morning.

We publish on Friday in time for the Review to be at all Metropolitan bookstalls by at latest 4 p.m., and we believe that it is there then, having no doubt that Messrs. W. H. Smith & Son do their best, but they have such a mass of papers to handle every day that a fresh one may well look almost like a personal enemy and be kept in short supply unless the reading public shows unmistakably that it is wanted. A little perseverance, therefore, in asking for the Investors' Review is all that should be required to remedy this defect.

All London newsagents can be in a position to distribute the paper on Friday afternoon if they please, and here also the only remedy is for subscribers to insist upon having it as soon as published. Arrangements have been made that all our direct City subscribers shall have their copies before 4 p.m. on Friday. As for the provinces, we can only say that the paper is delivered to the forwarding agents in ample time to be in every English and Scotch town, and in Dublin and Belfast, likewise, early on Saturday morning. Those despatched by post from this office can be delivered by the first London mail on Saturday in every part of the United Kingdom.

ADVERTISEMENTS.

All Advertisements are received subject to approval, and should be sent in not later than 5 p.m. on Thursdays.

The advertisements of American Life Insurance Offices are rigorously excluded from the Investors' Review, and have been so since it commenced as a Quarterly Magazine in 1892.

For tariff and particulars of positions open apply to the Advertisement Manager, Norfolk House, Norfolk-street, W.C.

To Correspondents.

The Editor cannot undertake to return rejected communications. Letters from correspondents must, in every case, be authenticated by the name and address of the writer.

Telegraphic Address: "Unveiling, London."

The Investors' Review.

The Week's Money Market.

The discount market perceptibly eased off in the beginning of the week owing to the fair sums in gold arriving from abroad, but the last two days saw a sharp upward turn. Business "outright" became difficult on Wednesday, the rate for such accommodation being then quoted 4¼ per cent., and the majority of the transactions were conducted on the basis of 3⅞ to 4 per cent., "subject to half the advance in the Bank rate." When it was found yesterday that the Bank directors had made no more in the rate there was a little more inclination to take bills, but the rate for three months' remitted paper did not fall below 3⅞ to 4 per cent. The market, indeed, will probably continue to act cautiously in the present state of affairs, and in its present mood would rather lose business, as it is doing, than lock up its resources too freely. The Bank of England has taken a further step towards attracting gold from abroad by making advances free of interest for short periods to importers bringing gold over. The arrangement is understood to have been entered upon at the suggestion of the importing firms, but the mere fact that the Bank of England should adopt such a course has rather tended to increase the cautious attitude of the market. The result has been that on the week the Bank gained quite £500,000 from the foreign movements, and with the Continental exchanges standing at their present height, further arrivals seem probable. The Bank return was therefore much stronger, and were it not for the political uncertainties, a very different state of things would prevail in the market.

The figures in the Bank return do not, it is true, indicate great strength measured by the enormous interests dependent upon its power to meet demands from all the ends of the earth. The reserve is still only £19,688,000, although that is an increase of £1,254,000 on last week, and the "other" deposits, which contain the balances upon which the smooth working of other banks throughout the kingdom with liabilities aggregating £800,000,000 or so depend, are only £36,621,000, or £714,000 more than last week. Yet the position would tend to become easier through the bent of Continental exchanges in our favour, and, had we merely our own imperial interests to look to, the summer might be passed with no advance beyond 4 per cent. But there is a war risk before the market, and the Bank has only £30,270,000 in gold on hand to cover that risk and meet all home demands to boot. Therefore the Bank is still weak and the increase of £834,000 in its stock of gold, £499,000 of it in gold from abroad, since the previous return was made up counts for very little. Happily the Bank remains in control over the market, and can force it to keep rates up whether inclined so to do or not. The "other" securities have actually risen £152,000 this week to £34,239,000, and the balances of the Government departments (public deposits) have been rising also, so that, at £12,675,000, they are £679,000 larger now than they were a week ago. However inconvenient this husbanding of money by the Treasury may be to dealers in credit, it is useful just now to the Bank in helping it to keep a tight grasp over the open market. For all that, the discount houses will do well not to let the fear of a 5 per cent. rate go from before their eyes.

SILVER.

Bar silver late last week dropped to 25⅞d. per ounce for immediate delivery, and although the price recovered to 25 11/16d. per ounce at one time, it is not particularly firm at this quotation. The monetary pressure in India, which at first encouraged purchases of the metal, has rather hurt the market for the metal there, and the quotation in the bazaars has therefore dropped back to 66½. Further discussion went on as to the chance of war affecting market supplies, but there does not seem to be any tangible reason to assume that they would be diminished. Although the balances of the Banks of Bombay and Bengal improved, there has been considerable applications for India Council drafts, chiefly on account of Calcutta. Under this influence the price for transfers has been raised to 1s. 4 3/32d., and the Council has increased the amount offered on Wednesday next to 60 lacs. Treasury balances in India are about at their highest, their total at the end of March amounting to 16 crores, and some relief should be obtained as the total declines. India exchanges have risen 3/32d. to 1s. 4 1/16d., but Chinese rates show an inclination to droop.

BANK OF ENGLAND.

AN ACCOUNT pursuant to the Act 7 and 8 Vict., cap. 32, for the Week ending on Wednesday, April 20, 1898.

ISSUE DEPARTMENT.

	£		£
Notes Issued	44,708,350	Government Debt	11,015,100
		Other Securities	5,784,900
		Gold Coin and Bullion	27,908,350
		Silver Bullion	—
	£44,708,350		£44,708,350

BANKING DEPARTMENT.

	£		£
Proprietors' Capital	14,553,000	Government Securities	13,191,953
Rest	3,177,795	Other Securities	34,239,218
Public Deposits (including Exchequer, Savings Banks, Commissioners of National Debt, and Dividend Accounts)	12,675,148	Notes	17,326,275
Other Deposits	36,620,609	Gold and Silver Coin	2,361,728
Seven Day and other Bills	92,622		
	£67,119,174		£67,119,174

Dated April 21, 1898.

H. G. BOWEN, *Chief Cashier.*

In the following table will be found the movements compared with the previous week, and also the totals for that week and the corresponding return last year:—

Banking Department.

Last Year. April 21.		April 13, 1898.	April 20, 1898.	Increase.	Decrease.
£	Liabilities.	£	£	£	£
3,237,005	Rest	3,170,215	3,177,795	7,580	—
11,656,693	Pub. Deposits	11,996,514	12,675,148	678,634	—
38,856,267	Other do.	35,906,140	36,620,609	714,469	—
142,302	7 Day Bills	93,417	92,622	—	795
	Assets.			Decrease.	Increase.
13,842,586	Gov. Securities	13,197,953	13,191,953	6,000	—
28,701,528	Other do.	34,087,675	34,239,218	—	151,543
25,801,153	Total Reserve	18,433,658	19,688,003	—	1,254,345
				1,406,683	1,406,683
				Increase.	Decrease.
£		£	£	£	£
27,290,895	Note Circulation	27,802,810	27,282,075	—	420,735
51 p.c.	Proportion	38⅝ p.c.	39⅞ p.c.	—	—
2½ "	Bank Rate	4 "	4 "	—	—

Foreign Bullion movement for week £499,000 in.

LONDON BANKERS' CLEARING.

Month of	1898.	1897.	Increase.	Decrease.
	£	£	£	£
January	673,281,000	576,558,000	96,723,000	—
February	648,601,000	597,652,000	50,949,000	—
Week ending				
March 2	190,157,000	177,852,000	12,305,000	—
" 9	134,490,000	126,182,000	8,308,000	—
" 16	174,377,000	148,937,000	25,440,000	—
" 23	129,828,000	118,578,000	11,250,000	—
" 30	170,668,000	158,421,000	12,247,000	—
April 6	186,540,000	147,789,000	38,751,000	—
" 13	112,101,000	154,099,000	—	41,998,000
" 20	168,810,000	92,332,000	76,478,000	—
Total to date	2,490,785,000	2,221,305,000	268,480,000	—

BANK AND DISCOUNT RATES ABROAD.

	Bank Rate.	Altered.	Open Market.
Paris	2	March 14, 1895	1¾
Berlin	4	April 9, 1898	3⅜
Hamburg	4	April 9, 1898	3⅜
Frankfort	4	April 9, 1898	3⅜
Amsterdam	3	April 13, 1897	2¾
Brussels	3	April 28, 1896	2
Vienna	4	January 22, 1896	4¾
Rome	5	August 27, 1895	3
St. Petersburg	5½	January 23, 1898	4¾
Madrid	5	June 17, 1896	4
Lisbon	6	January 25, 1891	6
Stockholm	4	March 3, 1898	3½
Copenhagen	4	January 20, 1898	4
Calcutta	12	February 24, 1898	—
Bombay	13	February 24, 1898	—
New York call money	1 to 1½	—	—

NEW YORK ASSOCIATED BANKS (dollar at 4s.).

	April 16, 1898.	April 9, 1898.	April 2, 1898.	April 17, 1897.
	£	£	£	£
Specie	29,506,000	28,416,000	28,312,000	17,324,000
Legal tenders	11,138,000	11,904,000	12,644,000	20,512,000
Loans and discounts	116,018,000	117,556,000	119,170,000	100,794,000
Circulation	2,787,800	2,776,800	2,771,200	3,090,000
Net deposits	132,704,000	133,968,000	136,443,000	113,772,000

Legal reserve is 25 per cent. of net deposits; therefore the total reserve (specie and legal tenders) exceeds this sum by £7,468,000, against an excess last week of £6,828,000.

BANK OF FRANCE (25 francs to the £).

	April 21, 1898.	April 14, 1898.	April 7, 1898.	April 22, 1897.
	£	£	£	£
Gold in hand	74,312,920	74,178,120	74,319,320	76,772,000
Silver in hand	48,690,800	48,617,720	48,694,480	48,803,000
Bills discounted	33,733,960	33,449,840	30,617,960	*41,799,000
Advances	15,239,880	15,171,080	15,700,560	—
Note circulation	148,173,120	151,102,520	150,324,320	147,307,000
Public deposits	7,369,320	6,911,320	5,576,400	7,160,000
Private deposits	22,854,440	21,160,120	19,578,640	17,598,000

Proportion between bullion and circulation 83 per cent. against 81⅜ per cent. a week ago.

* Includes advances.

FOREIGN RATES OF EXCHANGE ON LONDON.

Place.	Usance.	Last week's.	Latest.	Place.	Usance.	Last week's.	Latest.
Paris	chqs.	25·34½	25·35	Italy	sight	26·87½	27·52
Brussels	chqs.	25·40	25·45	Do. gold prem.	..	106·15	108·05
Amsterdam	short	12·10½	12·14	Constantinople	3 mths	109·30	109·32½
Berlin	short	20·51½	20·53½	B. Ayres gd. pm.	..	165·30	168·80
Do.	3 mths	20·32	20·33	Rio de Janeiro	90 dys	6	5⅜d.
Hamburg	3 mths	20.31	20·32	Valparaiso	90 dys	17⅞	17⅝d.
Frankfort	short	20·52	20·55	Calcutta	T. T.	1/4	1/4 1/16
Vienna	short	12.09	12·10	Bombay	T. T.	1/3 31/32	1/4 1/32
St. Petersburg	3 mths	94.10	94·05	Hong Kong	T. T.	1/10⅜	1/10⅛
New York	60 dys	4·80½	4·80	Shanghai	T. T.	2/5⅜	2/5¼
Lisbon	sight	34⅜	33½d.	Singapore	T. T.	1/10⅜	1/10¼
Madrid	sight	36·32	nom.				

IMPERIAL BANK OF GERMANY (20 marks to the £).

	April 15, 1898.	April 7, 1898.	Mar. 31, 1898.	April 15, 1897.
	£	£	£	£
Cash in hand	43,820,450	43,269,700	44,141,650	43,612,000
Bills discounted	34,501,300	37,171,950	38,514,850	*35,133,000
Advances on stocks	4,385,950	5,240,800	6,210,700	—
Note circulation	56,944,900	60,696,700	64,060,850	54,183,000
Public deposits	24,130,050	22,931,900	22,047,550	21,100,000

* Includes advances.

AUSTRIAN-HUNGARIAN BANK (1s. 8d. to the florin).

	April 15, 1898.	April 7, 1898.	Mar. 31, 1898.	April 15, 1897.
	£	£	£	£
Gold reserve	30,490,833	30,577,750	30,521,166	26,401,000
Silver reserve	10,454,333	10,448,660	10,453,250	10,501,000
Foreign bills	806,416	916,750	1,012,167	—
Advances	1,759,916	1,806,083	1,877,750	—
Note circulation	51,954,583	52,850,416	52,021,750	40,780,000
Bills discounted	11,312,000	12,442,333	12,437,416	*13,122,000

* Includes advances.

NATIONAL BANK OF BELGIUM (25 francs to the £).

	April 14, 1898.	April 7, 1898.	Mar. 31, 1898.	April 15, 1897.
	£	£	£	£
Coin and bullion	4,060,960	4,134,280	4,153,480	4,144,000
Other securities	16,540,080	16,910,360	17,180,880	13,605,000
Note circulation	19,408,400	19,274,790	19,868,080	15,184,000
Deposits	2,553,800	3,174,720	3,412,880	2,707,000

BANK OF SPAIN (25 pesetas to the £).

	April 16, 1898.	April 9, 1898.	April 2, 1898.	April 17, 1897.
	£	£	£	£
Gold	9,761,480	9,643,800	9,631,120	8,528,400
Silver	10,279,200	10,472,880	10,614,600	10,528,000
Bills discounted	25,098,280	24,532,120	24,698,640	7,594,480
Advances and loans........	5,791,080	5,226,040	5,287,440	9,837,600
Notes in circulation	52,189,240	51,614,320	51,074,480	43,233,600
Treasury advances, coupon account	95,000	97,640	79,600	126,840
Treasury balances	72,440	20,200	2,720	229,320

LONDON COURSE OF EXCHANGE.

Place.	Usance.	April 5.	April 14.	April 19.	April 21.
Amsterdam and Rotterdam	short	12·2	12·2½	12·2½	12·3½
Do. do.	3 months	12·3⅜	12·4⅜	12·4½	12·5
Antwerp and Brussels	3 months	25·51¼	25·58¾	25·60¾	25·67½
Hamburg	3 months	20·65	20·74	20·74	20·76
Berlin and German B. Places	3 months	20·66	20·74	20·74	20·77
Paris	cheques	25·31¼	25·35	25·36¼	25·37½
Do.	3 months	25·45	25·50	25·52½	25·53¾
Marseilles	3 months	25·46¼	25·51¼	25·52½	25·53¾
Switzerland................	3 months	25·65	25·67½	25·70	25·72½
Austria....................	3 months	12·16¼	12·25	12·23¾	12·26¼
St. Petersburg	3 months	24$\frac{15}{16}$	24$\frac{13}{16}$	24⅞	24⅞
Moscow	3 months	24⅞	24⅞	24$\frac{13}{16}$	24$\frac{13}{16}$
Italian Bank Places	3 months	27·40	27·35	27·52½	27·50
New York	60 days	49$\frac{1}{16}$	49	49	49
Madrid and Spanish B. P. ..	3 months	33	31⅜	29½	27½
Lisbon	3 months	34⅛	34	33$\frac{3}{16}$	32⅞
Oporto	3 months	34¼	34	33$\frac{3}{16}$	32⅞
Copenhagen................	3 months	18·42	18·42	18·46	18·47
Christiania	3 months	18·42	18·42	18·46	18·48
Stockholm	3 months	18·42	18·43	18·45	18·48

OPEN MARKET DISCOUNT.

	Per cent.
Thirty and sixty day remitted bills	3⅞—4
Three months "	3⅞—4
Four months "	3⅞—4
Six months "	3⅞—4
Three months fine inland bills	4—4¼
Four months "	4—4¼
Six months "	4¼

BANK AND DEPOSIT RATES.

	Per cent.
Bank of England minimum discount rate	4
" " short loan rates	4
Banker's rate on deposits	2½
Bill brokers' deposit rate (call)	2½
" 7 and 14 days' notice	2¾
Current rates for 7 day loans	2½—2¾
" " for call loans	2—2½

Stock Market Notes and Comments.

We have again not much to say this week about the Stock Exchange. It has continued to gnaw its thumbs, in a sense, and to curse the "Yankees" for destroying business. The general feeling throughout the country is on the whole strikingly sympathetic with the American people in their present dispute with Spain, but this is by no means the sentiment prevalent on the Stock Exchange, and it is not wonderful that it should be momentarily angry instead of pleased. This Cuban affair caught our market in full career towards great triumphs in American railroad securities. Jobbers and brokers had loaded themselves up, in many instances, to the utmost of their capacity with these securities, in the full expectation that the development of prosperity in the United States this year would have enabled them to realise at very handsome profits. Instead of profits they now see ghastly losses staring them in the face, and they naturally curse. Nevertheless, they will be quite ready to commence the play again directly affairs seem to take a favourable turn, and for our part we should advise those of our readers who hold American securities to maintain a calm spirit. Good will come to the Union out of this struggle—good and perhaps also evil. Many things may be changed as the result of it, and assuredly it cannot be more than a temporary check to the development of the country's magnificent resources. It is very doubtful, indeed, whether the war will have any appreciable effect in diminishing the prosperity of American railways this year, and should it end speedily in a triumph for the United States naval and military forces, there will be no holding prices back. The risk, therefore, of keeping what one has got seems small, and the chance of an increase in the present loss not very serious.

Outside American "rails" and Spanish bonds, we may say that there has been nothing doing on the Stock Exchange beyond the struggles of speculative investors all over the country to unload what they are no longer able to carry. Readers of this Review know very well that we have insisted, to weariness even, upon the remarkable extent to which a prolonged season of cheap money has allowed the habit of private pawning of securities with banks, for the sake of the margin of interest thus obtained, to be developed. As long as money was cheap we could not point to facts in any number in proof of our statements, and the haughty man of the market scouted us as merely a "theorist," a "pessimist," and so on. Proof in abundance is coming forth now, and will be found by any one who cares to look, in the steady decline which has set in among all investment securities from Consols down to the lowest railway preference treated as investment stock. If any man will take the trouble to compare to-day's prices of British Corporation stocks, Home railways debenture, guaranteed, and preference stocks, or Colonial bonds with those of six months ago, as he can do to a sampling extent in an excellent table contributed on another page of this number, he will find that they have already fallen from 5 per cent. to 10 per cent. Some recent speculators' or syndicators' pets have even depreciated more. For example, the fall in India 2½ per cent. is, we believe, about 13 per cent. In this case weak syndicates who subscribed for the loan when it was issued at fancy prices are at the bottom of the rapid decline; but with old stocks nothing of the kind is at work. There the fall arises from the struggle of multitudes of nominal holders to escape from a position which once brought them profit, but now causes them a loss they are unable to bear. And the bankers who chirpily lent on these "first-class" stocks to all and sundry are now beginning nervously to call in their loans. So steady is the stream of this kind of selling—forced and voluntary—that the jobbers have in many cases a great deal more stock already on their hands than they care to carry, and are certainly in no mood to make further purchases. Consequently, the actual prices sent out night after night in the official list are all more or less hollow; that is to say, the quotation may be, say, 148 to 151, but the man who wishes to sell five thousand stock might, perhaps, find a jobber, after some considerable difficulty, willing to give him 145. In many cases there is no actual practical quotation, as we may call it, in these securities; they simply cannot be sold except at odd times and by driblets. And this is the result merely of an advance in the Bank rate to 4 per cent. What will the consequences be should that rate go to 5 per cent. or 6 per cent.? We must leave the answer to the imaginations of those who have been foolish enough to get caught in this trap.

But if first-class investment securities are being struck by blight in this manner on a very moderate advance in the rates for money, what is going to happen in the more or less purely speculative markets, such as those for De Beers and Rio Tinto shares, for Argentine securities, for Italian bonds, for Transvaal gold mine shares, for Rhodesian shares and Western Australian shares, with all the host of miscellaneous "industrial" shares that have been poured out upon the British public during the last five years? We ask this question, but do not attempt now to answer it. We prefer that readers should ponder over it, and think out an answer for themselves. Who would care to hold shares at the present time in a company which may have nothing in the way of substantial assets to represent the market price of its shares? Have we not been right throughout in protesting against the system of fancy market premiums, which cheap money has allowed to come into existence.

The whole machinery of modern company promotion and premium concoction is now going to be put to the test, but the resulting downfall of it may not be immediate. Readers must not run away with the notion that we expect a crisis next week, or next month : it may not come next year. What we insist upon is—and they will do well to attend to our warning — that the elements of a crisis lie around us on every side, that we are travelling towards a crisis, and that therefore the prudent man will now, while there is time, so arrange his affairs as to make himself safe against the worst that his imagination may conjure up to him as likely to happen when the crisis comes : we are merely speaking common sense. Surely this is plain enough. It is no interest of ours to "croak," for the so-called croaker is always unpopular. We warn and adjure and beseech, because we cannot do otherwise without lying.

He alone is serene in mind just now who owes no man anything, who has not pawned stock with his banker to the limits of his available capital, who has not invested his money in rubbish the touts recommended to him as "good for a rise," "an excellent 10 per cent. investment," or ensnared the simple into by such other garbage of stock phrases as the corrupt hireling may have at command.

The Week's Stock Markets.

Business has come practically to a standstill after a week of suspense, and the downward movement in all departments led by the foreign market is simply a reflection of what has happened on the Paris and other Continental bourses. The Stock Exchange generally has had to come to the conclusion that there is now very little hope of a peaceful solution of the dispute between the United States and Spain, and with the prospects of a rise in the Bank rate in the near future, none of the dealers are very anxious to increase their commitments. Needless to say the latest quotations are the lowest of the week, and in most cases the worst of the year.

Highest and Lowest this Year.		Last Carrying over Price.	BRITISH FUNDS, &c.	Closing Price.	Rise or Fall.
113⅝	109½	—	Consols 2¾ p.c. (Money)...	109¾	− 11/16
113 5/16	109¾	111¼	Do. Account (May 5)	109⅞	− 13/16
106¼	101	104¾	2½ p.c. Stock red. 1905 ...	101½	−2
363	342	—	Bank of England Stock...	344	−3½
117	111¾	113	India 3½ p.c. Stk. red. 1931	112	− ½
109¼	104	105¼	Do. 3 p.c. Stk. red. 1948	104½	− ¼
96⅜	90	92½	Do. 2½ p.c. Stk. red. 1926	90½	− ½

In the market for Home Government securities Consols kept tolerably steady for several days, but eventually gave way in sympathy with the weakness displayed in all other markets, and the 2½ per cent. "Childers" 2¾ per cent., the Indian sterling loans, and Bank of England stock have all participated in the fall. Home corporation issues, Colonial Government and Indian Railway stocks show a considerable decline, but the heaviest falls have taken place in the premier securities of the leading Home Railway companies, large blocks coming on the market, and selling being hardly practical, dealers showing a disinclination to make prices.

The Home Railway market shared in the more cheerful feeling displayed by markets generally on Friday, when the political outlook was promising to take a more favourable turn, and the tendency has been a tolerably firm one since, due more than anything else to the fact that business has continued to be on the smallest possible scale. A collapse, however, occurred on Wednesday, although there was very little stock offering, and the latest quotations are the lowest of the week. Great Eastern has been the principal sufferer, but this was partly accounted for by the announcement of a new issue of capital to the extent of £675,000, and the traffic return was not up to expectations. Great Central issues have also been conspicuously weak, and this is also the case with the stocks of the mineral lines in the Welsh coal district, where the deadlock still continues. Some of the heavy lines expect to benefit by the dislocation of goods traffic during this dispute, and North Eastern Consols have met with rather more support than has fallen to the lot of other stocks in this market.

Highest and Lowest this Year.		Last Carrying over Price.	HOME RAILWAYS.	Closing Price.	Rise or Fall.
186	172½	175⅝	Brighton Def.	173⅞	− ⅞
59½	54⅜	56¼	Caledonian Def.	55⅛	− ½
20⅝	18¼	19¼	Chatham Ordinary	18⅜	− ⅜
77¼	63	67	Great Central Pref.	64½	−2
24⅝	21⅜	22	Do. Def.	21½	− ¼
124½	118¼	121⅝	Great Eastern	118⅝	− 2
61⅜	50⅝	53	Great Northern Def.	51⅜	−1¼
179⅝	169⅜	172	Great Western	169¼	−2¼
51¾	45¼	48⅞	Hull and Barnsley	47¾	− ½
149¼	145½	147½	Lanc. and Yorkshire	145¾	−1½
136⅛	127½	129	Metropolitan	128	−1
31	26¾	27½	Metropolitan District	27	—
88¾	82¾	85	Midland Pref.	83	−1½
95⅝	84⅝	87½	Do. Def.	85¼	−1⅝
93¼	87	88¾	North British Pref.	87¼	−1
47½	41⅜	43¼	Do. Def.	42⅛	− ½
181½	172¾	174¼	North Eastern	173½	+ ⅜
205½	197	199	North Western	197¼	−1¼
117⅛	105⅞	109¼	South Eastern Def.	106⅛	−1⅞
98¾	89	91	South Western Def.	89	−1¾

United States Railroad shares were comparatively steady, with dealings on a very small scale, during the early part of the week, and even the news of the resolution passed by Congress, which amounted practically to a declaration of war against Spain, did not cause much of a fall. Wall-street operators have been adopting a waiting policy, and doing little or nothing beyond marking down quotations a trifle in sympathy with each fresh decline in Spanish stock, and there is evidently a very large speculative account open for the fall on this side.

Highest and Lowest this Year.		Last Carrying over Price.	CANADIAN AND U.S. RAILWAYS.	Closing Prices.	Rise or Fall.
14 5/16	10¾	11¾	Atchison Shares	11	− ½
34	23¼	26½	Do. Pref.	24⅝	−1⅜
15⅝	11⅛	12½	Central Pacific...............	11¼	−1
99¾	87½	92½	Chic. Mil. & St. Paul......	87½	−3⅛
14¼	10⅝	11½	Denver Shares	10⅜	−1
54⅛	41⅞	44¾	Do. Prefd.	42½	−1⅞
16⅝	11¼	12¾	Erie Shares	11⅝	− ⅝
44⅞	30	34	Do. Prefd.	31	−2
110½	100	103	Illinois Central	100	−2
62½	46⅛	51½	Louisville & Nashville ...	47⅛	−2⅞
14½	10¼	11	Missouri & Texas	10¼	− ¾
122¾	108⅛	115	New York Central	111	−2
57¼	43	46¾	Norfolk & West. Prefd....	44¼	−1¾
70⅛	59	64¼	Northern Pacific Prefd....	60⅞	−1⅜
19½	13¾	14⅞	Ontario Shares	14	− ¾
62½	57	58½	Pennsylvania	57¾	− ⅜
12½	8	8¾	Reading Shares	8 1/16	− ⅛
34½	24½	27	Southern Prefd.	25¼	−1⅜
37⅛	18¾	20⅛	Union Pacific	19⅛	− ⅜
20¼	14½	16	Wabash Prefd.	15¼	− ¼
30⅛	21¼	23½	Do. Income Debs....	22	−1
92¾	76	83	Canadian Pacific............	76	−6¼
78½	69⅞	73½	Grand Trunk Guar.	72⅜	− ⅜
69½	57⅛	66½	Do. 1st Pref.	65½	− ⅜
50⅛	37¼	47⅛	Do. 2nd Pref.	45⅜	− ½
25⅛	19¼	22½	Do. 3rd Pref.	21½	− ⅜
105¼	101½	102½	Do. 4 p.c. Deb.	102½	− ½

Canadian Pacific and Grand Trunk stocks opened the week with a firm tone, and a moderate rise was established, only to be lost again, owing to the report that the officials of both companies have returned to Montreal from New York, having failed utterly to arrive at any solution of the rate war. This makes the third failure to come to a settlement of the question, and the prospects are not very encouraging. Both the traffic returns were wonderfully good, especially the Trunk statement, and considering all things the market in the latter company's stocks has been rather a good one. A sharp break quite at the last took place in Canadian Pacific shares, in sympathy with the weakness of the American market.

Highest and Lowest this Year.	Last Carrying over Price.	FOREIGN BONDS.	Closing Price.	Rise or Fall.
94½ 85	88	Argentine 5 p.c. 1886......	85	−1¾
92⅜ 82¾	86½	Do. 6 p.c. Funding	82½	−2
76¾ 64⅛	68¾	Do. 5 p.c. B. Ay. Water	64½	−2½
61¾ 42½	47½	Brazilian 4 p.c. 1889	43½	−2
69⅞ 48	52	Do. 5 p.c. 1895	48	−2½
65 44½	49	Do. 5 p.c. West Minas Ry....................	45	−2½
108¾ 106½	107⅞	Egyptian 4 p.c. Unified...	106⅞	−1
104¾ 100½	104½	Do. 3½ p.c. Pref. ...	100¾ x.d.	−1¼
103 100⅛	101½	French 3 p.c. Rente	100	−1
44¾ 34½	44	Greek 4 p.c. Monopoly...	41¼	−1¾
93 5/16 88¾	92	Italian 5 p.c. Rente	89⅜	−1⅝
100 89	96¾	Mexican 6 p.c. 1888	89	−7
20⅜ 17½	18¾	Portuguese 1 p.c.	17½	−¾
62½ 32¼	47¾	Spanish 4 p.c.	32¼	−11½
45½ 40	41¾	Turkish 1 p.c. "B"	40½	−½
26 7/16 22¾	24⅜	Do. 1 p.c. "C"	23	−½
22 7/16 20	21	Do. 1 p.c. "D"	20	−½
46⅝ 40	45½	Uruguay 3½ p.c. Bonds...	45¼	−½

Matters have steadily gone from bad to worse in the foreign market, and hardly one gleam of sunshine has penetrated through the gloom overhanging the whole list. True, prices rallied to such an extent on Friday that Spanish bonds actually closed the day with an advance of ½; but, as the price has since dropped 10 or 12 points, too much stress need not be laid on the temporary recovery. The Paris Bourse has been demoralised by rumours of serious financial embarrassments, followed by several failures in connection with the mid-monthly settlement. Heavy selling of Spanish bonds from Madrid has been going on all the week, and a number of failures have also been announced from that quarter. Next in importance to the fall in Spanish 4 per cents. is the big drop in all the Mexican Government stocks, due to the forced closing of weak Continental accounts, and sales by German syndicates, who apparently are afraid that Mexico may be drawn into the quarrel between Spain and the United States. All South American stocks, at all dealt in, show a big loss on the week, among which may be mentioned Guatemala bonds, the fall in this case being accentuated by the action of the authorities in fixing the duty on coffee at a lower level than had been agreed upon with the bondholders. Brazilian bonds weakened, but only to a lesser extent, the exchange being tolerably steady.

Highest and Lowest this Year.	Last Carrying over Price.	FOREIGN RAILWAYS.	Closing Price.	Rise or Fall.
100 99½	99½	Argentine Gt. West. 5 p.c. Pref. Stock..................	100	—
158¼ 137	147	B. Ay. Gt. Southern Ord..	137xd	−6¼
78¼ 65	70	B. Ay. and Rosario Ord...	66xd	−3
12¼ 10½	10⅜	B. Ay. Western Ord.	10½	−¼
87¼ 73	77	Central Argentine Ord....	74	−3
92 83	82½	Cordoba and Rosario 6 p.c. Deb.	83	—
95½ 86	87	Cord. Cent. 4 p.c. Deb. (Cent. Nth. Sec.)	86½	−1
61¾ 44	45½	Do. Income Deb. Stk. ...	44½	−1½
25¼ 17	19¼	Mexican Ord. Stk.	17	−2
83½ 70	75	Do. 8 p.c. 1st Pref.	70½	−4

Foreign Railway emissions were again pressed for sale, and the fall amounts to something like six in several instances. Alagoas stocks were especially weak on the unsatisfactory report, and heavy declines have occurred in Buenos Ayres Great Southern, Minas and Rio, Costa Rica, Bahia Blanca Preference, and United Railways of the Havana. The old Mexican companies issues gave way in sympathy with the Government bonds, in spite of a good traffic return and the steadiness of the silver market.

Little has happened of interest in the miscellaneous section, but changes are not all in the downward direction, although nearly so. Crystal Palace debentures show a rise, the scheme of reconstruction having been approved, thereby securing new capital to the extent of £100,000. Royal Mail Steam Packet shares advanced owing to the satisfactory report; and a jump of 5 took place in Daimler Motor, while Lyons' shares have been inquired for on rumours of a 20 per cent. dividend. On the other hand Welsbach issues continue on the down grade; Coats' declined, heavy selling being indulged in by Glasgow operators; P. & O. deferred fell 5, and Anglo-Ceylon Estates 10, and falls are also noticeable in Aerated Bread, British Electric Traction, and Hudson's Bay, while telegraph, electric lighting, gas and water stocks, and most of the tea companies issues show losses. Cycle shares close weak, Dunlop deferred more especially so, and the "split" among the directors of the Syndicate Music Halls has led to a lot of selling of that class of shares. Gas Light and Coke stocks show little change, although it is reported that the company's Bill for converting its various issues is to be opposed at every stage in its passage through the House of Commons.

There was little of interest in markets during the closing hours of the week. Spanish 4 per cents. dropped still lower, making a total loss of 11½ on balance, and the last price was the worst. All foreign stocks closed weak, but there was a slight recovery in Rio Tinto shares. Home Railway stocks were again pressed for sale, with the exception of Brighton "A," which was rather inquired for. Canadian Pacific shares closed flat on heavy selling orders from Berlin, and Mexican Railway issues were very depressed; but Grand Trunk descriptions and United States Railroad shares were somewhat steadier at the last.

Mining and Finance Companies.

The South African market, after a brief period of steadiness, gave way under the influence of Continental sales, which especially affected De Beers, Rand Mines, and one or two of the other favourites of the Paris Bourse, and the result is that prices again mark a considerable fall all round. Western Australian ventures gave way in sympathy, the feature being the collapse of the "Bottomley" group led by Market Trust. Copper shares have been very depressed, Rio Tinto on heavy sales from Paris, the Mount Lyell group on the death of the chairman of the North Mount Lyell Co., and to a lesser extent to the publication of a poor return by the parent company, and Anaconda and Cape Copper and several minor concerns in sympathy with the rest. Indian shares close dull at a moderate decline.

NOTICES.

With reference to the Guatemala debt, the Council of Foreign Bondholders is informed by the Minister of Guatemala in Europe that he has received a telegram from the Minister of Foreign Relations in Guatemala, of which the following is a translation:—"Assembly reduced coffee duty 81. Government disposed to assign other revenues or to enter into arrangements with the bondholders. Make this known.—Anguiano."

The Bank of Montreal will pay, on and after May 2, the half-year's interest due on May 1 on the Province of Quebec 5 per cent. loans of 1874 and 1876.

The British Bank of South America, Limited, notifies the bondholders of the Mogyana Railway Company 5 per cent. debenture loan that the interest thereon due on the 1st prox. will be paid by it on and after Monday, the 2nd prox.

Messrs. Glyn, Mills, Currie, & Co. notify that they are prepared to pay, on the 1st prox., the coupons of the Uruguay 3½ per cent. consolidated debt due on that date.

The Bank of China and Japan, Limited, intend to make, on May 14 next, a final repayment of 10 per cent. to depositors in the Bank of China, Japan, and the Straits, Limited (in liquidation), who will then have received the full amount of their deposits, with interest at 4½ per cent. per annum to above date. This anticipates the date (October 31, 1899) fixed under the reconstruction scheme for final repayment, by about 18 months, which must be gratifying to those concerned in the liquidation, and should induce confidence in the new institution.

The result of the poll of the London and Northern Assets Corporation, Limited, on the resolution for the adoption of the scheme proposed by the directors for the amalgamation of the Corporation with the London & Northern Debenture Corporation, Limited, was to-day declared in favour of the scheme as follows:—For the resolution, 25,593; against, 10,866. Having been passed by both Corporations, the scheme will now be carried into effect as speedily as possible.

An extraordinary general meeting of the Harvey Steel Company of Great Britain, Limited, is to be held at the Westminster Palace Hotel, Victoria-street, Westminster, on April 28, 1898, at 2.30 p.m., to consider the following resolution:—"That each of the existing £10 shares in the company's capital be divided into ten fully paid £1 shares." Should the resolution be passed by a majority it will be submitted to a subsequent extraordinary meeting for confirmation.

Messrs. Glyn, Mills, Currie, & Co. have received a cable from the London and River Plate Bank at Monte Video, announcing the dispatch by mail of a remittance amounting to £5,800 for the service of the Uruguayan 5 per cent. loan of 1896.

Mr. George White was yesterday elected President of the Bristol Stock Exchange.

Dividends Announced.

MISCELLANEOUS.

D. & W. MURRAY, LIMITED.—interim dividend on the ordinary shares at the rate of 7½ per cent. per annum.

BELL'S ASBESTOS COMPANY, LIMITED.—Dividend at the rate of 4 per cent. per annum. £2,338 carried forward.

DUNVILLE & COMPANY, LIMITED.—Interim dividend of 13s. per share for the half-year ended March 31.

GREAT NORTHERN TELEGRAPH COMPANY, COPENHAGEN.—Dividends amounting to 10 per cent. declared, £77,777 added to reserve, and £61,057 carried forward.

ANGLO-CONTINENTAL GOLD SYNDICATE.—12½ per cent. per annum on the ordinary shares.

RUSSIAN PETROLEUM AND LIQUID FUEL COMPANY, LIMITED.—Interim dividends on the preference shares of 6½ per cent. per annum, calculated from the due date of the instalments up to and including March 12, and on the ordinary shares of £1 per share.

NETHERLANDS INCANDESCENT GAS LIGHT COMPANY, LIMITED.—Dividend of 10 per cent.

KAFFIRS CONSOLIDATED INVESTMENT AND LAND COMPANY, LIMITED.—Dividend at the rate of 3d. per share for the month of April.

DE LAMAR MINING COMPANY, LIMITED.—Dividend for the year ended March 31 of 6d. per share.

VICTORIA GOLD MINING ASSOCIATION.—6d. per share.

TRANSVAAL GOLD FIELDS, LIMITED.—1s. per share (5 per cent.) for 1897, £1,500 to be added to reserve, and £127,781 carried forward.

UNITED STATES AND SOUTH AMERICAN TRUST COMPANY, LIMITED.—Dividend recommended at the rate of 5 per cent. on the preferred stock for the half-year, and at the rate of 1 per cent. for the year ended April 4. £1,000 to be added reserve, and balance forward of about £1,400.

NEUCHATEL ASPHALTE COMPANY.—A final dividend of 7s. per share, making, with the interim dividend, a total dividend of 11s. per share for the year 1897.

ALLIANCE INVESTMENT COMPANY.—Directors recommend a dividend of ¼ per cent. remaining unpaid on the preferred stock, and, in addition, a dividend for the half-year ended April 15, at the rate of 4⅜ per cent. per annum, making, with the interim dividend, 4⅜ per cent. for the year on the preferred stock.

RAILWAYS.

NORTHERN PACIFIC.—Quarterly dividend of 1 per cent. on the preferred stock.

TALTAL COMPANY, LIMITED.—Interim dividend for the half-year to December 31 at the rate of 1s. 3d. per share.

MEXICAN NATIONAL, LIMITED.—Dividend of £2 15s. 8d. per cent. on the "A" certificates.

ROHILKUND AND KUMAON RAILWAY.—Dividend for the past half-year of £2 10s. net.

COSTA RICA RAILWAY.—Dividend for the year 1897 of 4s. per share, £8,000 being added to reserve fund, and £6,797 carried forward.

BANKS.

BANK OF MONTREAL.—Dividend for the half-year ended 31st inst., at the rate of 10 per cent. per annum.

BANK OF ADELAIDE.—Dividend at 7 per cent. per annum, £5,000 being added to reserve fund (making it £160,000) and £15,952 carried forward.

BREWERY.

DARTFORD COMPANY, LIMITED.—Interim dividend on the ordinary share capital at the rate of 6 per cent. per annum for the half-year ended March 31.

MINING RETURNS.

BRILLIANT BLOCK.—Crushed 1,131 tons of quartz for a yield of 893 oz. of gold.

CALIFORNIA EXPLORATION.—Crushed 398 tons, bullion produced $3,650, sulphurets estimated $270.

EAGLEHAWK CONSOLIDATED.—Partial clean up 149 oz. of gold.

EAST MURCHISON UNITED.—Great Eastern—1,050 tons of ore crushed; 1,010 oz. of gold obtained. Donegal Lenses—750 tons of ore crushed; 590 oz. of gold obtained.

LUIPAARD'S VLEI.—March crushing—Tons crushed, 3,600, assaying 8⅜ dwt.; gold obtained, 1,150 oz.

OTTOS KOPJE.—7,088 loads washed during the week ended April 14; 179 carats of diamonds won.

PALMAREJO.—Return for March—Crushed 1,800 tons; panned 1,650 tons, producing $45,000.

PREMIER.—625 tons for 317 oz.

AGAMEMNON.—200 tons of ore mined, 225 tons of ore treated, 150 oz. bullion recovered.

BARRETT.—Gold yield for March, 510 oz.

BONANZA.—Results for last month:—From mill—crushed, 5,706 tons; obtained 5,104 oz. of gold. From cyanide and slimes works—treated, 5,611 tons, yielding 3,123 oz. of gold; total, 8,227 oz. of gold.

CHIAPAS.—1,950 tons of ore crushed, yielding 86 tons of concentrates. The stamp mill ran twenty-seven days, crushing 1,550 tons of tailings, yielding 180 oz. of gold.

KLERKSDORP GOLD AND DIAMOND COMPANY.—Results of crushing for March, 700 oz. of gold.

LAKE VIEW CONSOLS.—Clean up for March—Crushed 4,935 tons, yielded 4,402 oz. of gold. Cyanide return: 3,624 tons treated, yielded 2,672 oz. of gold. Concentrates, 25 tons value, 875 oz. of gold. Total return for March, 8,039 oz.

MAY CONSOLIDATED.—The yield of gold during March was 5,715 oz. from 14,500 tons crushed. Cyanide, 2,145 oz. from 8,892 tons. Total for month, 7,860 oz.

MIKADO, ONTARIO.—Further cablegram from the manager states that the output for March should have been 730 oz. of gold instead of 530 oz. as previously advised. This is exclusive of tailings.

SIMMER AND JACK.—Crushed 29,240 tons, obtained 7,781 oz. of gold from mill and 3,010 oz. of gold from tailings by cyanide during the month, also slimes 609 oz.

WORCESTER.—Result of crushing—Main reef, 3,948 tons; south reef, 799 tons; yield of gold, 1,915 oz.; concentrates, 457 oz.; tailings, 516 oz.; total, 2,888 oz.

MOUNT LYELL.—From March 20 to April 6, inclusive, a total quantity of 10,960 tons of ore have been treated: 8,979 tons from open cuts assaying before treatment—copper, 2·98 per cent., silver, 3·21 oz. per ton; gold, 0·196 oz. per ton: 1,983 tons from No. 4 Tunnel assaying before treatment—copper, 7·23 per cent.; silver, 7·58 oz. per ton; gold, 0·059 oz. per ton. The converters have produced during the same period 315 tons of blister copper, containing—copper, 310 tons; silver, 35,733 oz.; gold, 1,689 oz.

ST. JOHN DEL REY MINING COMPANY.—Gold produce, April 1 to 10, £6,296; yield per ton, ·77 of an oz. troy.

WASSAU (GOLD COAST).—602 oz. of bar gold from 557 tons of ore; 22 stamps worked 22 days. Detailed result of February return:—The 10-stamp 750-lb. mill worked 25 days 18 hours; and the 12-stamp 550-lb. mill 22 days 19 hours. Ore crushed, 572½ tons, producing 724½ oz. bar gold, which together with 23½ oz. from pan amalgam, gave 786 oz. standard gold, and realised £3,068 4s. 6d.

MENZIES LADY SHERRY.—Crushed 50 tons for 97 oz.

BELLEVUE PROPRIETARY.—Clean up for fortnight—140 tons crushed for 316 oz.

BURBANK'S BIRTHDAY GIFT.—Crushed 480 tons; yield 660 oz. free gold, exclusive of tailings.

DAY DAWN BLOCK.—Result of crushing for the fortnight ended the 16th inst.—Tons crushed, 1,440; yield of gold, 1,333 oz., including tailings.

DE LAMAR.—Return for March, including clean up of old mill:—Leached, 900 tons; bullion produced from cyanide treatment, $16,413; surplus from clean up of old mill, $6,300; estimated value of ore and mill residues shipped to smelters, $3,824; miscellaneous revenue, $120.

OURO PRETO.—5,629 tons of ore produced 1,731 oz. of gold.

PAHANG CORPORATION.—March returns:—Jeram Lumpong Mill; 1,470 tons of stone crushed, producing 77 tons of black tin; Jeram Batang Mill—775 tons of stone crushed, producing 18½ tons of black tin.

NORTH BOULDER.—405 oz. gold from 447 tons crushed.

VICTORY (CHARTER'S TOWERS).—Crushed 106 tons for 340 oz.

FRANK SMITH DIAMOND.—4,700 loads washed, producing 251 carats.

HYDERABAD (DECCAN).—Output of coal from the Singareni Collieries for four weeks ended March 26 was 29,514 tons.

NEW AUSTRALIAN BROKEN HILL CONSOLS.—17 cwt., containing 2,050 oz. of silver, all from level No. 1.

LAKE VIEW SOUTH.—Crushed 1,300 tons for 321 oz.; also 32 tons concentrates worth 13½ dwt. per ton.

TRAMWAY AND OMNIBUS RECEIPTS.

HOME.

Name.	Period.	Ending.	Amount.	Increase or Decrease on 1897.	Weeks or Months.	Aggregate to Date. Amount.	Aggregate to Date. Inc. or Dec. on 1897.
			£	£		£	£
Aberdeen District ..	Week	Apr. 16	477	+63	—	—	—
Belfast Street	"	" 16	2,850	+791	—	—	—
Birmingham and Aston	"	" 16	573	+123	—	—	—
Birmingham and Midland...........	"	" 16	*776	+186	—	—	—
Birmingham City ..	"	" 16	*4,137	+811	—	—	—
Blessington and Poulaphouca	"	" 17	37	+22	15	150	+34
Bristol Tramways and Carriage	"	" 15	3,273	+1,053	—	—	—
Burnley and District.	"	" 16	314	−80	—	—	—
Bury, Rochdale, and Oldham	"	" 16	916	−22	—	—	—
Croydon............	"	" 16	432	+127	—	—	+1,051
Dublin and Blessington	"	" 17	172	+43	15	1,401	+120
Dublin and Lucan ..	"	" 16	85	+18	16	605	−307
Dublin United......	"	" 15	3,338	+698	—	40,629	+2,903
Edinburgh and District...............	"	" 16	2,445	+379	15	33,636	+3,166
Edinburgh Street ..	"	" 16	678	+134	15	8,762	+1,131
Glasgow............	"	" 16	3,009	+353	—	—	—
Lea Bridge and Leyton	"	" 16	966	+277	—	—	—
London, Deptford, and Greenwich ..	"	" 16	675	+104	—	8,430	+616
London General Omnibus	"	" 16	21,655	+2,538	—	—	—
London Road Car ..	"	" 16	6,740	+711	†	91,910	+5,946
London Southern ..	"	" 16	606	+108	—	—	—
North Staffordshire..	"	" 16	418	−8	—	5,930	+29
Provincial..........	"	" 16	2,928	+519	—	—	—
Southampton	"	" 16	459	+133	—	—	—
South London	"	" 16	*1,950	+267	†	23,969	+1,171
South Staffordshire..	"	" 15	846	+250	15	8,938	+291
Tramways Union ..	Month	March	9,988	+601	3	28,630	+3,346
Wigan and District..	Week	—	317	−30	—	—	—
Woolwich and South East London......	"	" 16	506	+125	†	4,793	+436

* Includes Easter Week. † From January 1.

FOREIGN.

Name.	Period.	Ending.	Amount.	Increase or Decrease on 1897.	Weeks or Months.	Aggregate to Date. Amount.	Aggregate to Date. Inc. or Dec. on 1897.
			£	£		£	£
Anglo-Argentine	Week	Mch. 21	4,711	+707	*	51,030	+4,607
Barcelona	"	Apr. 16	1,125	+5		17,247	−2,156
Barcelona, Ensanche y Gracia	"	" 16	232	+43		2,400	+58
Bordeaux	"	" 15	2,391	+135		29,615	−1,056
Buenos Ayres and Belgrano	Month	Feb.	4,409	+749	*	9,162	+1,273
Buenos Ayres Grand National	Week	Mch. 19	$27,140	+$5,001	†	+	$226,374
Buenos Ayres New..	Month	Jan.	$69,905	−$1,85		$60,905	−$1,852
Calais	Week	Apr. 16	153	+21			
Calcutta............	"	" 16	1,460	+136			
Gothenburg	"	" 6	363	+90			

* From January 1. † From April 1, 1897

Answers to Correspondents.

Questions about public securities, and on all points in company law, will be answered week by week, in the Review, on the following terms and conditions:—

A fee of five shillings must be remitted for each question put, provided they are questions about separate securities. Should a private letter be required, then an extra fee of five shillings must be sent to cover the cost of such letter, the fee then being ten shillings for one query only, and five shillings for every subsequent one in the same letter. While making this concession the Editor will feel obliged if private replies are as much as possible dispensed with. It is wholly impossible to answer letters sent merely "with a stamped envelope enclosed for reply."

Correspondents will further greatly oblige by so framing their questions as to obviate the necessity to name securities in the replies. They should *number* the questions, keeping a copy for reference, thus:—"(1) Please inform me about the present position of the Rowenzori Development Co. (2) Is a dividend likely to be paid soon on the capital stock of the Congo-Sudan Railway?

Answers to be given to all such questions by simply quoting the numbers 1, 2, 3, and so on. The Editor has a rooted objection to such forms of reply as—"I think your Timbuctoo Consols will go up," or "Sell your Slowcoach and Draggem Bonds," because this kind of thing is open to all sorts of abuses. By the plan suggested, and by using a fancy name to be replied to, each query can be kept absolutely private to the inquirer, and no scope whatever be given to market manipulations. Avoid, as names to be replied to, common words, like "investor," "inquirer," and so on, as also "bear" or "bull." Detached syllables of the inquirer's name, or initials reversed, will frequently do as well as anything, so long as the answer can be identified by the inquirer.

The Editor further respectfully requests that merely speculative questions should as far as possible be avoided. He by no means sets himself up as a market prophet, and can only undertake to provide the latest information regarding the securities asked about. This he will do faithfully and without bias.

Replies cannot be guaranteed in the same week if the letters demanding them reach the office of the Investors' Review, Norfolk House, Norfolk-street, W.C., later than the first post on Wednesday mornings.

Next Week's Meetings.

Monday, April 25.

San Sebastian Nitrate	Winchester House, 3 p.m.

Tuesday, April 26.

City of Glasgow Life Assurance ...	Glasgow, 3 p.m.
Day Dawn Block and Wyndham Gold Mining	Cannon-street Hotel, 2 p.m.
Hand in Hand Fire and Life ...	26, New Bridge-street, 1 p.m.
London and Westminster Finance Corporation...	5, Fenchurch-street, noon
London Corn Exchange	Mark-lane, 12.30 p.m.
London Trust...	Cannon-street Hotel, 12.30 p.m.
Pacific Loan and Investment ...	Liverpool, 1.30 p.m.
Sambre and Meuse Railway ...	10, Moorgate-street, 1 p.m.
Sheba Gold Mining Company ...	Winchester House, 2.15 p.m.

Wednesday, April 27.

Athenry and Tham Extension Railway	Dublin, 10.30 a.m.
Australasian Investment	Edinburgh, 12.30 p.m.
Australian and New Zealand Mortgage	Canuon-street Hotel, 1 p.m.
Australian Mortgage Land and Finance	Cannon-street Hotel, noon.
British South African Land and Mining	Metropolitan-chambers, noon.
Great Western of Brazil Railway ...	2, Coleman-street, 1 p.m.
Highland Railway	Inverness Station, 1 p.m.
Highland Tea of Ceylon	16, Philpot-lane, noon.
Manchester Brewery	Manchester, noon.
Oriental Telephone	Cannon-street Hotel, 1 p.m.
Poonagalla Valley (Ceylon)	16, Philpot-lane, 3 p.m.
Royal Mail Steam Packet	Cannon-street Hotel, 1 p.m.
Southwold Railway	17, Victoria-street, S.W., 3 p.m.
Submarine Cables Trust	Winchester House, 3 p.m.
Swedish Association	3, Lothbury, 1.30 p.m.
Union Bank of Scotland	Glasgow, noon.
Union Steamship	Winchester House, noon.

Thursday, April 28.

Alamillos Company	6, Queen-street-place, 12.25 p.m.
Buenos Ayres New Gas	1, East India-avenue, 12.30 p.m.
Debenture Securities Invest. ...	12, Moorgate-street, 2 p.m.
Durban Roodepoort Gold Mining ..	Cannon-street Hotel, 2.30 p.m.
Fortuna Company	6, Queen-street-place, 12.20 p.m.
Fylde Waterworks	Blackpool, noon.
General Steam Navigation	55, Great Tower-street, noon.
John Barke & Co.	Kensington High-street, noon.
Linare's Lead	6, Queen-street-place, 12.15 p.m.
London & Lancashire Fire Insurance	Liverpool, noon.
Salt Union	Winchester House, 3 p.m.

Friday, April 29.

Alagoas Railway	Cannon-street Hotel, 12.30 p.m.
Army & Navy Co-operative Stores...	Westminster Town Hall, 2.30 p.m.
Demerara Railway	Cannon Street Hotel, noon.
Eastern Produce and Estates Co. ..	Winchester-House, noon.
London and Lancashire Life Assurance	67, Cornhill, 1 p.m.
Union Assurance	Winchester House, 1 p.m.

Prices of Mine and Mining Finance Companies' Shares.

Shares £1 each except where otherwise stated

Australian.

Making-Up Price, Apr. 12.	Name	Closing Price.	Rise or Fall.	Making-Up Price, Apr. 12.	Name	Closing Price.	Rise or Fall.
1⅜	Aladdin	1½		⅜	Hannan's Star	5/16	− ⅛
3½	Associated	2¾	− 1/16	4 [illegible]	Ivanhoe, New	4¾	− 1/16
[illegible]	Do. Southern	⅝	− ¼	[illegible]	Kalgurli Mt. & Iron King, 18/	⅞	− 1/16
1¼	Brownhill Extended	1	− 1/16	4 [illegible]	Kalgurli	4¾	− 1/16
1⅛	Burbank's Birthday	1 [illegible]	− ⅛	2 [illegible]	Lady Shenton	2 [illegible]	− 1/16
[illegible]	Central Boulder	⅞	− ⅛	8¼	Lake View Cons.	7⅛	− 1 [illegible]
5/6	Chaffers, 4/	4/9		⅛	Do. Extended	⅝	− 1/16
[illegible]	Colonial Finance, 15/	⅛ dis	− [illegible]	1	Do. South	⅞	− 1/16
—	Crœsus S. United	⅛	− 1/16	1⅜	London & Globe Finance	1¼	− ⅛
1	E. Murchison	1		⅞	London & W.A. Exploration	⅞	− ⅛
5/	Golden Arrow 19/	4/6		[illegible]	Do. Investment	⅝	− ⅛
7½	Golden Horseshoe	6	− 1	⅞	Mainland Consols	⅞	+ 1/16
[illegible]	Golden Link	⅝	− 1/16	⅛	North Boulder, 10/	⅛	− ⅛
19/6	Great Boulder, 2/	16/6	− /9	1 [illegible]	North Kalgurli	1 [illegible]	− ⅛
1⅛	Do. Main Reef, 10/	1 1/16		—	Northern Territories	1¼	− 1⅛
3	Do. Perseverance	2⅞	− [illegible]	2½	Peak Hill	2¼	
[illegible]	Do. South	⅞	− [illegible]	2	South Kalgurli	1⅝	− 1/16
2	Hainault	1⅞	− ⅛	1 [illegible]	W. A. Goldfields	1¼	− ⅛
[illegible]	Hampton Plains	⅞	− ⅛	2 [illegible]	W. A. Joint Stock	1 1/16	− ⅛
7½	Hannan's Brownhill	6¾	− ⅝	1 [illegible]	W. A. Market Trust	10/3	− 6/
[illegible]	Hannan's Oroya	[illegible]		1¼	W. A. Loan & General Fin.	1 1/16	− ⅛
15/	Do. Proprietary	11/	− /3	⅞	White Feather	⅛	− 1/16

South African.

Making-Up Price, Apr. 12.	Name	Closing Price.	Rise or Fall.	Making-Up Price, Apr. 12.	Name	Closing Price.	Rise or Fall.
5¼	Angelo	4⅞	− ⅜	2/6	Lisbon-Berlyn	2/6	
1	Aurora West	1		2¼	May Consolidated	2¼	− 1/16
2¼	Bantjes	[illegible]	− ⅛	4⅛	Meyer and Charlton	4	− ⅛
9/6	Barrett, 10/	8/6	− /6	4	Modderfontein	3¾	− ⅛
3⅛	Bonanza	3⅛		1 [illegible]	New Bultfontein	[illegible]	− ⅛
7/	Buffelsdoorn	⅜	+ /6	3 [illegible]	New Primrose	3⅜	− ⅛
5⅛	City and Suburban, £4	5⅞	− 1/16	1 [illegible]	Nigel	1 1/16	− ⅛
2 [illegible]	Comet (New)	2 [illegible]	− 1/16	—	Nigel Deep	1 1/16	− ⅛
5⅛	Con. Deep Level	3 x.r.		⅞	North Randfontein	⅞	− ⅛
11	Crown Deep	10⅞	− ⅛	5⅛	Nourse Deep	4⅞	− ⅛
12⅜	Crown Reef	12⅛	− ⅛	1¼	Porges-Randfontein	1	− 1/16
26⅛	De Beers, £5	23⅛		20⅛	Rand Mines	26	− 2⅛
3 [illegible]	Driefontein	3⅛	− ⅛	1⅛	Randfontein	1⅛	+ ⅛
5¼	Durban Roodepoort	5⅛	+ ⅛	2⅛	Rietfontein	1¾	− ⅛
3⅛	Do. Deep	3⅛	− ⅛	9¼	Robinson Deep	9⅛	− ⅛
4 [illegible]	East Rand	3⅞	− 1/16	7¼	Do. Gold, £5	7⅛	− ⅛
23⅛	Ferreira	22	− ⅛	[illegible]	Do. Randfontein	⅞	− 1/16
6⅛	Geldenhuis Deep	6⅛		1 [illegible]	Roodepoort Central Deep	1¼	− 1/16
5	Do. Estate	5		6¼	Rose Deep	5⅛	− ⅛
[illegible]	George Goch	⅞		2 [illegible]	Salisbury	2⅛	− ⅛
2⅛	Ginsberg	1 [illegible]	− 1/16	1 [illegible]	Sheba	1⅛	
1 [illegible]	Glencairn	1⅛		3 [illegible]	Simmer and Jack, £5	2⅞	− ⅛
8¼	Goldfields Deep	8¼		3¼	Transvaal Gold	2¾	− ⅛
8⅛	Griqualand West	8	− ⅛	3⅛	Treasury	3	
9	Henry Nourse	8⅞	− ⅛	3 [illegible]	United Roodepoort	3⅛	− ⅛
8	Heriot	7½	− ⅛	1 [illegible]	Van Ryn	1⅞	− 1/16
7⅜	Jagersfontein	7	− ⅛	5 [illegible]	Village Main Reef	5¼	− 1/16
8	Jubilee	7⅞		1⅛	Vogelstruis	1 1/16	− 1/16
4 [illegible]	Jumpers	4⅛	− ⅛	[illegible]	Do. Deep	[illegible]	+ ⅛
2⅛	Kleinfontein	2 1/16	− ⅛	9½	Wemmer	8⅛	− ⅛
3 [illegible]	Knight's	2¾	− 1/16	⅛	West Rand	⅛	
2 [illegible]	Lancaster	2	− [illegible]	5 [illegible]	Wolhuter, £4	5 [illegible]	− 1/16
3	Langlaagte Estate	2⅞	− 1/16	2¼	Worcester	2⅛	− 1/16

Land Exploration and Rhodesian

Making-Up Price, Apr. 12.	Name	Closing Price.	Rise or Fall.	Making-Up Price, Apr. 12.	Name	Closing Price.	Rise or Fall.
2⅛	Anglo-French Ex.	2	− ⅛	[illegible]	Mashonaland Central	⅞	− 1/16
1⅞	Barnato Consolidated	1 [illegible]	− 1/16	6⅛	Matabele Gold Reefs	6 x.r.	− ⅛
[illegible]	Bechuanaland Ex.	⅞		2 [illegible]	Mozambique	2	− 1/16
2 [illegible]	Chartered B.S.A.	2 [illegible]	− ⅛	⅞	Oceana Consolidated	[illegible]	− 1/16
⅜	Clark's Cons.	[illegible]		1 [illegible]	Rhodesia, Ltd.	1 [illegible]	− 1/16
[illegible]	Colenbrander	1/16		4⅛	Do. Exploration	3⅞	− ⅛
4 [illegible]	Cons. Goldfields	3⅞	− 1/16	1⅛	Do. Goldfields	1 [illegible]	− 1/16
1	Do. Pref.	20/		4	S. A. Gold Trust	3 [illegible]	− 1/16
1 [illegible]	Exploration	1 [illegible] x.d.		1	Tati Concessions	⅞	− 1/16
2 [illegible]	Geelong	2¾	− ⅛	⅞	Transvaal Development	[illegible]	− 1/16
[illegible]	Henderson's Est.	[illegible]	− 1/16	[illegible]	United Rhodesia	⅞	− 1/16
1½	Johannesburg Con. In.	1⅜	− ⅛	1½	Willoughby	1 1/16	− 1/16
1	Do. Water	[illegible]	− [illegible]	⅞	Zambesia Explor.	⅞	
1⅞	Mashonaland Agency	1⅛	− ⅛				

Miscellaneous.

Making-Up Price, Apr. 12.	Name	Closing Price.	Rise or Fall.	Making-Up Price, Apr. 12.	Name	Closing Price.	Rise or Fall.
1⅛	Alamillos, £2	1⅛		13/6	Mount Lyell, South	10/6	− 3/3
5⅛	Anaconda, $25	4⅞	− [illegible]	4⅛	Mount Morgan, 17s. 6d.	4	− ⅛
8/	Balaghât, 18/	5/	− 3/	5⅛	Mysore, 10s.	5 [illegible]	− 1/16
13/9	Brilliant, £2	12/3	− 1/3	13/	Mysore Goldfields	12/	− /6
2⅛	Do. St. George's	2 [illegible]	+ 1/16	7/	Do. Reefs, 17/	6/	− 1/
9/6	British Broken Hill	9/6		10/	Do. West	8/6	
2 [illegible]	Broken Hill Proprietary	2 [illegible]	− 1/16	8/	Do. Wynaad	6/	− /6
—	Do. Block 10	3¼		2 [illegible]	Namaqua, £2	2¼	− 1/16
4⅞	Cape Copper, £2	4⅞	− ⅛	3⅛	Nundydroog	3 [illegible]	− ⅛
5	Champion Reef, 10s.	5		3 [illegible]	Ooregum	3⅜	− ⅛
2⅛	Copiapo, £2	2 [illegible]	− [illegible]	3 [illegible]	Do. Pref.	3 [illegible]	− 1/16
3 [illegible]	Coromandel	3		25⅛	Rio Tinto Def., £5	24⅞	− 3
14/	Day Dawn Block	13/6	− /6	6⅛	Do. Pref. £5	5⅞	− ⅛
2 [illegible]	Frontino & Bolivia	2 [illegible]	− [illegible]	17/6	St. John del Rey	16/6	− /6
1⅛	Hall Mines	1 [illegible]		8/9	Taitipu	[illegible]	
2 [illegible]	Libiola, £5	2⅞	− ⅛	7⅛	Tharsis, £2	6⅞	− [illegible]
8	Linares, £3	7⅞	− ⅛	2⅛	Tolima "A," £5	2⅛	
4	Mason & Barry, £3	3 [illegible]		4 [illegible]	Waihi	3 [illegible]	− 1/16
5	Mountain Copper, £5	4⅞	− ⅛	1⅛	Waitekauri	1⅛	− 1/16
13⅛	Mount Lyell, £3	11⅛	− 1⅛	1 [illegible]	Woodstock (N.Z.)	[illegible]	− ⅛
2⅞	Mount Lyell, North	2⅜	− ⅛				

It is understood that the assessment on the Baltimore and Ohio stock under the plan of reorganisation now in course of elaboration will be 20 per cent., and that the holders will receive preferred stock for the amount.

Railway Traffic Returns.

BURMA RAILWAYS. — Receipts for week ending March 19, Rs. 2,27,636; increase, Rs. 20,832. Aggregate from January 1, Rs. 23,89,527; decrease, Rs. 1,01,621.

ALCOY AND GANDIA RAILWAY AND HARBOUR COMPANY.—Traffic for week, April 16:—Ps. 5,050, increase Ps. 80. Aggregate from January 1, Ps. 139,750, increase Ps. 3,880.

WEST FLANDERS RAILWAY.—Gross receipts for week ending April 17, £2,394; increase, £371. Total from January 1, £34,591; increase, £1,319.

WEST OF INDIA PORTUGUESE RAILWAY.—Week ending March 25, Rs. 4,164; increase, Rs. 1,625.

QUEBEC CENTRAL RAILWAY.—Receipts for fourth week of March, $13,473; decrease, $984. Aggregate from July 1, $81,700; decrease, $10,702.

MOBILE AND BIRMINGHAM RAILROAD.—Traffic for fourth week of March, $9,633; increase, $460. Aggregate from July 1, $285,528; decrease, $3,530.

ALGECIRAS (GIBRALTAR) RAILWAY.—Traffic for week ended April 9, Ps. 20,650; increase Ps. 150. Aggregate from july 1, Ps. 816,532; increase, Ps. 24,478.

BENGAL CENTRAL RAILWAY.—Traffic for week ending March 26, Rs. 29,938; increase, Rs. 8,434. Total from January 1, Rs. 247,835; increase, Rs. 27,328.

ASSAM-BENGAL RAILWAY.—Traffic for week ended March 12, Rs. 23,273; decrease, Rs. 958. Aggregate from January 1, Rs. 2,46,909; increase, Rs. 17,815.

PUERTO CABELLO AND VALENCIA RAILWAY.—Traffic receipts for week ending March 11, £1,217; decrease, £243. Aggregate from January 1, £9,675; decrease, £3,244.

DELHI UMBALLA KALKA RAILWAY.—Receipts for week ended April 16, Rs. 29,200; increase Rs. 1,900. Aggregate from january 1, Rs. 5,47,500; increase, 1,51,300.

ROHILKUND AND KUMAON RAILWAY.—Traffic receipts for week ending March 19, Rs. 8,325; decrease, Rs. 6,460. Aggregate from january 1, Rs. 65,285; decrease, Rs. 18,317.

WESTERN OF SANTA FE RAILWAYS.—Gross receipts for week ending April 16, $41,500; increase, $30,910.

CLEATOR AND WORKINGTON.—Gross receipts for the week ending April 16 amounted to £903, an increase of £65. Total receipts from January 1, £15,196; a decrease of £689.

COCKERMOUTH AND KESWICK RAILWAY.—Receipts for the week ending April 16, £905; increase, £167. Aggregate from January 1, £12,450; increase, £1,248.

MANILA RAILWAY.—Receipts for week ending April 16, $18,982; increase, $1,544.

SOUTHERN MAHRATTA RAILWAY.—Receipts for week ended March 26, Rs. 97,416; decrease, Rs. 46,883.

GREAT WESTERN OF BRAZIL RAILWAY.—Traffic for week ending March 12, $30,696; increase, $4,654. Aggregate receipts to date $442,970; increase, $60,111.

VILLA MARIA AND RUFINO RAILWAY.—Traffic for week ending April 16, $4,782; increase, $1,781. Aggregate from january 1, $71,680, increase $309.

The approximate traffic return of the Manchester Ship Canal fo March shows a take of £16,337, as compared with £14,762 for the corresponding month last year, while the total receipts for the three months to date have reached £53,922, as against £46,601 a year ago.

ENGLISH RAILWAYS.

Div. for half years. 1896	1896	1897	1897	Last Balance forward.	Amt. to pay 1 p.c. on Ord. for ½ yr.	NAME.	Date.	Gross Traffic for week: Amt.	Inc. or dec. on 1897.	Inc. or dec. on 1896.	No. of weeks	Gross Traffic for half-year to date: Amt.	Inc. or dec. on 1897.	Inc. or dec. on 1896.	Mileage.	Inc. on 1897.	Working	Prior Charges last ½ year.	Prop. add Cap. Exp. this ½ year
				£	£												%	£	£
10	10	10	10	2,707	5,094	Barry	Apr 16	3,079	−5,339	−4,007	16	133,387	−5,136	+14,312	31	—	8·89	60,665	316,853
nil	nil	nil	nil	—	—	Brecon and Merthyr.. ..	„ 17	1,154	−99	−515	16	23,013	+270	−2,057	61	—	—	—	—
nil	nil	nil	nil	3,979	4,749	Cambrian	„ 17	5,647	+904	+916	*	69,679	+2,176	—	250	—	60·96	63,148	40,000
1¾	1½	2	1¾	1,510	3,150	City and South London ..	„ 17	945	+100	+24	16	16,771	+87	+1,151	3½	—	56·67	5,552	124,000
1	2	1½	2	7,895	13,220	Furness	„ 17	9,061	+582	+589	*	133,118	+3,556	—	139	—	49·88	97,423	20,910
1	1½	½	1	2,207	27,470	Great Cent. (late M., S., & L.)	„ 17	41,637	+353	+3,040	15	635,394	+7,763	+37,094	352½	—	57·17	627,386	1,200,000
3½	4¾	2	5	51,283	62,865	Great Eastern	„ 17	†86,851	−‡5,114	+13,446	15	1,188,113	+41,635	+106122	1,158¼	2	55·35	860,138	250,000
3	5½	3	5	15,094	102,496	Great Northern	„ 17	†94,793	−2,193	+5,657	16	1,489,577	+42,358	+110965	1,071	8	61·36	641,485	750,000
4¾	7½	4¾	7½	31,350	121,981	Great Western	„ 17	†182,150	−6,850	+7,920	15	2,578,470	+38,540	+112980	2,582	21	31·44	1,486,272	800,000
nil	2	nil	1¾	8,951	16,487	Hull and Barnsley	„ 17	6,865	+675	+541	15	96,425	−240	+8,821	73	—	58·21	70,290	52,9..
5	5¾	5	5½	21,495	83,704	Lancashire and Yorkshire ..	„ 17	†98,087	−‡5,901	+7,430	15	1,375,661	+45,576	+52,213	555½	25	56·70	674,745	451,976
4¾	8	4¾	8½	26,243	43,049	Lon., Brighton, & S. Coast	„ 16	†58,914	−‡5,395	+9,388	16	759,701	+30,507	+44,286	476½	—	50·20	407,042	240,735
nil	nil	nil	nil	72,294	56,296	London, Chatham, & Dover	„ 17	†32,471	−‡2,626	+3,309	15	404,092	+14,235	+23,098	185½	—	50·65	367,873	nil
6¼	8	6¼	7¾	89,535	204,068	London and North Western	„ 17	†230,549	−4,157	+4,359	15	3,383,781	+72,557	+180536	1,911½	—	36·92	1,404,534	600,000
5	8½	8¼	8¾	23,038	59,367	London and South Western	„ 17	†84,073	−‡2,768	+13,018	15	1,008,926	+47,115	+68,951	941	6½	51·75	513,740	389,000
2½	6	2½	6½	14,592	6,691	Lon., Tilbury, & Southend	„ 17	†6,736	+1,126	+2,244	16	78,494	+6,216	+13,378	81	—	52·57	39,590	15,000
3½	3¾	3¾	3¾	17,133	26,409	Metropolitan	„ 17	16,767	+706	+1,419	*	247,602	+5,906	—	64	—	43·63	148,047	254,000
nil	nil	nil	nil	4,006	11,250	Metropolitan District ..	„ 17	7,907	+321	—	15	127,900	+4,003	—	13	—	48·70	119,663	38,450
5	7	5½	6½	38,143	174,582	Midland	„ 17	†188,014	−‡7,016	+25,763	16	2,913,555	+38,570	+208900	1,354¾	15½	57·59	1,216,582	690,000
5¾	7½	5¾	7	22,374	138,189	North Eastern	„ 16	†154,896	−‡1,716	+31,685	15	2,119,650	+24,627	+119565	1,597¾	—	58·82	795,077	436,004
7½	7¾	7½	7½	7,061	10,102	North London	„ 17			Not recd.		not	recvd.		12	—	50·90	49,973	7,600
4	5	4	4½	4,745	16,150	North Staffordshire	„ 17	†15,314	−‡371	+1,646	16	249,443	+6,192	+15,094	312	—	55·27	118,142	19,605
10	10	11		1,642	3,004	Rhymney	„ 16	2,505	−2,048	−2,384	16	76,075	−2,619	+4,207	71	—	49·68	29,049	16,700
3	6¾	3½	6¾	4,054	50,215	South Eastern	„ 16	†49,331	−‡2,045	+7,920	*	635,144	+39,449	—	448	—	51·88	380,763	250,000
3½	3½	3½	3½	2,315	25,961	Taff Vale	„ 16	6,125	−8,161	−8,743	16	223,360	−24,152	−10,164	121	—	54·90	94,800	92,000

* From January 1. † Easter week, 1898. ‡ Good Friday week, 1897.

SCOTCH RAILWAYS.

Div. for half years. 1896	1896	1897	1897	Last Balance forward.	Amt. to pay 1 p.c. on Ord. for ½ yr.	NAME.	Date.	Gross Traffic for week: Amt.	Inc. or dec. on 1897.	Inc. or dec. on 1896.	No. of weeks	Gross Traffic for half-year to date: Amt.	Inc. or dec. on 1897.	Inc. or dec. on 1896.	Mileage.	Inc. on 1897.	Working	Prior Charges last ½ year.	Prop. add Cap. Exp. this ½ year
5	5	5½	5	9,544	78,066	Caledonian	Apr. 17	78,160	+ 535	+ 7,314	11	784,525	+ 20,399	—	851½	5	50·38	588,248	441,477
5	5½	5	5	7,364	24,639	Glasgow and South-Western	„ 16	†31,891	+ †2,670	+ 5,511	11	300,138	+ 11,630	—	393½	—	54·69	221,663	196,145
3½	3½	3½	—	1,291	4,600	Great North of Scotland	„ 16	8,416	+ 25	862	11	83,893	− 296	+ 2,126	331	15½	52·03	92,178	60,000
	nil		—	10,477	12,820	Highland	„ 17	9,226	+ 207	+ 976	7	60,175	+ 2,093	—	479¾	27¾	58·63	78,976	,000
	1½	1	1½	819	45,819	North British	„ 17	80,777	+ 3,041	+ 8,914	11	766,640	+ 21,220	—	1,230	23	48·62	944,809	40,800

† Spring Holidays.

IRISH RAILWAYS.

Div. for half years. 1896	1896	1897	1897	Last Balance forward.	Amt. to pay 1 p.c. on Ord. for ½ yr.	NAME.	Date.	Gross Traffic for week: Amt.	Inc. or dec. on 1897.	Inc. or dec. on 1896.	No. of weeks	Gross Traffic for half-year to date: Amt.	Inc. or dec. on 1897.	Inc. or dec. on 1896.	Mileage.	Inc. on 1897.	Working	Prior Charges last ½ year.	Prop. add Cap. Exp. this ½ year
6½	6½	6½	—	5,466	1,790	Belfast and County Down ..	Apr. 15	3,664	+ 1,411	+ 1,647	*	32,296	+ 2,200	—	76½	—	55·58	17,690	10,000
5½	6½	5½	—	—	4,284	Belfast and Northern Counties	„ 15	6,583	+ 1,164	+ 1,807	*	77,026	+ 5,442	—	249	—	—	—	—
	3	2	—	1,418	1,200	Cork, Bandon, and S. Coast† ..	„ 16	1,438	− 61	− 81	*	17,972	− 1,259	—	103	—	54·82	14,436	5,450
	6¾	6½	6¾	38,776	17,816	Great Northern	„ 15	‡17,368	+ 2,471	+ 2,475	15	214,877	+ 2,644	+ 13,182	528	36	50·15	88,068	22,000
	5½	5½	5½	30,339	24,855	Great Southern and Western ..	„ 15	—	—	—	not	received	—	—	603	13	51·45	72,802	46,582
	4	4	4½	11,372	11,850	Midland Great Western ..	„ 15	11,198	+ 1,351	+ 363	15	142,721	+ 6,923	—	538	—	50·31	83,129	1,800
nil	nil	nil	nil	229	2,822	Waterford and Central ..	„ 15	896	+ 147	—	*	12,822	+ 1,504	—	59½	—	53·24	6,858	1,500
nil	nil	nil	nil	1,936	2,987	Waterford, Limerick & W. ..	„ 15	5,978	+ 343	+ 779	*	82,280	+ 3,269	—	350½	—	57·83	42,617	7,075

* From January 1. † Twelve weeks' strike. ‡ Easter

FOREIGN RAILWAYS.

Mileage. Total.	Increase on 1897.	Increase on 1896.	Name	Gross Traffic for Week. Week ending	Amount.	In. or Dec. upon 1897.	In. or Dec. upon 1896.	Gross Traffic to Date. No. of Weeks.	Amount.	In. or Dec. upon 1897.	In. or Dec. upon 1896.
					£	£	£		£	£	£
319	—	—	Argentine Great Western ..	Apr. 8	6,311	+ 504	+ 2,133	40	222,560	− 13,738	− 44,148
76⅝	—	—	Bahia and San Francisco ..	Mar. 19	3,330	+ 881	+ 1,483	12	35,707	+ 12,130	+ 13,741
234	48	84	Bahia Blanca and North West ..	Mar. 20	393	− 151	—	38	29,719	+ 60	—
74	—	—	Buenos Ayres and Ensenada ..	Apr. 17	3,215	− 388	− 864	15	51,993	− 9,105	− 14,094
426	—	—	Buenos Ayres and Pacific ..	Apr. 16	7,659	+ 22	+ 475	41	271,508	− 54,176	+ 6,832
914	1	3	Buenos Ayres and Rosario ..	Apr. 16	13,882	+ 3,064	+ 2,103	15	260,097	+ 69,394	+ 43,401
1,499	30	68	Buenos Ayres Great Southern ..	Apr. 17	29,810	+ 2,526	− 716	41	1,228,661	+ 88,642	+ 175,334
602	107	177	Buenos Ayres Western ..	Apr. 17	11,803	+ 122	− 2,332	41	496,067	− 79,007	− 87,840
845	55	77	Central Argentine ..	Apr. 16	20,239	+ 5,033	+ 3,569	14	333,822	+ 83,041	+ 24,213
197	—	—	Central Bahia ..	Jan. 31*	$133,559	− $3,944	+ $12,758	—	—	—	—
271	—	—	Central Uruguay of Monte Video	Apr. 16	5,002	+ 2,507	+ 426	41	244,661	+ 13,914	− 16,126
228	—	—	Do. Eastern Extension	Apr. 16	1,883	+ 1,204	+ 261	41	52,715	+ 7,527	− 1,476
182	—	—	Do. Northern Extension	Apr. 16	751	+ 416	− 43	41	25,989	+ 75	− 6,988
180	—	—	Cordoba and Rosario ..	Apr. 10	1,840	− 10	− 150	41	87,405	− 15,285	− 1,995
128	—	—	Cordoba Central ..	Apr. 10	$21,000	− $3,630	− $2,610	14	$303,700	− $49,220	− $66,630
549	—	—	Do. Northern Extension	Apr. 10	$47,000	− $12,720	− $100	14	$630,790	− $228,650	− $123,680
137	—	—	Costa Rica ..	Mar. 26	7,304	+ 714	+ 1,423	13	69,797	− 15,448	− 1,151
99	—	—	East Argentine ..	Mar. 6	615	− 150	− 66	10	6,505	− 720	− 579
386	—	6	Entre Rios ..	Apr. 16	2,290	+ 1,324	+ 670	41	66,141	+ 19,475	+ 13,917
555	—	24	Inter Oceanic of Mexico ..	Apr. 9	$63,700	+ $14,400	+ $22,650	40	$2,310,790	+ $364,140	+ $718,860
93	—	—	La Guaira and Caracas ..	Mar. 18	2,461	+ 72	+ 81	12	22,880	− 4,926	− 3,834
321	—	—	Mexican ..	Apr. 16	$88,300	+ $20,300	—	15	$1,230,700	+ $124,350	—
1,846	—	—	Mexican Central ..	Apr. 14	$258,288	+ $376	+ $86,049	15	$3,797,295	+ $89,363	+ $974,852
2,217	—	—	Mexican National ..	Apr. 14	$112,786	+ $18,357	+ $17,995	15	$1,652,503	+ $120,574	+ $319,479
228	—	—	Mexican Southern ..	Apr. 14	$10,000	− $4,917	+ $1,493	2	$24,660	− $5,036	+ 5,390
206	—	—	Minas and Rio ..	Feb. 31*	$128,262	+ $16,417	—	8 mos.	$1,436,813	+ $203,482	—
94	—		N. W. Argentine ..	Apr. 16	1,315	− 82	− 207	15	15,136	− 6,733	− 4,120
242	3	—	Nitrate ..	Apr. 15	18,375	+ 2,188	+ 4,209	13	107,065	+ 1,860	− 42,111
320	—	—	Ottoman ..	Apr. 9	4,483	+ 404	+ 1,010	13	69,786	− 15,969	+ 8,036
77½	—	—	Recife and San Francisco ..	Feb. 19	6,872	+ 807	− 273	8	46,005	+ 1,818	− 6,782
86½	—	—	San Paulo ..	Mar. 13†	20,104	− 3,037	—	10	108,589	− 19,100	—
186	—	—	Santa Fe and Cordova ..	Apr. 16†	1,992	+ 1,031	− 1,270	42	69,171	− 5,374	− 3,411
110	—	—	Western of Havana ..	Apr. 16	2,005	+ 339	+ 1,135	41	73,475	+ 5,893	+ 6,430

* For month ended. † For fortnight ended.

INDIAN RAILWAYS.

Mileage. Total.	Increase on 1897.	Increase on 1896.	Name.	Gross Traffic for Week. Week ending	Amount.	In. or Dec. on 1897.	In. or Dec. on 1896.	Gross Traffic to Date. No. of Weeks.	Amount.	In. or Dec. on 1897.	In. or Dec. on 1896.
862	—	—	Bengal Nagpur ..	Apr. 9	Rs.1.80.000	+Rs.43.846	+Rs.25.696	15	Rs.21.38.651	+Rs.16.865	−R.2.70.639
807	8	63	Bengal and North-Western ..	Mar. 19	Rs.1.26.400	+Rs.23.963	−Rs.244	12	Rs.14.61.314	+Rs.1.91.810	−Rs.24.122
461	—	—	Bombay and Baroda ..	Apr 16	£34,558	+£6,369	−£6,057	16	£385,044	−£8,526	−£147,378
1,885	2	13	East Indian ..	Apr. 16	Rs.12.74.000	+R.1.10.000	+Rs1.94.000	15	Rs.1.89.18.000	+Rs.3.83.000	+R13.32.000
1,491	—	—	Great Indian Penin. ..	Apr. 16	£79,228	+£26,075	−£6,298	16	£1,033,826	+£148,247	−£205,797
736	—	—	Indian Midland ..	Apr. 16	Rs.1.50.640	+Rs.30.311	+Rs.22.964	16	Rs.20.66.704	+Rs.1.24.062	+Rs365.138
840	—	—	Madras ..	Apr 2	£19,983	+£640	+£1,925	13	£250,602	−£14,073	−£7,726
1,043	—	—	South Indian ..	* Mar. 10	Rs.1.67.070	−Rs.2.272	+Rs.1.363	12	Rs.1.673.198	−Rs.239.682	−Rs.37.158

UNITED STATES AND CANADIAN RAILWAYS.

Mileage. Total.	Increase on 1897.	Increase on 1896.	Name.	Gross Traffic for Week. Period Ending.	Amount.	In. or Dec. on 1897.	Gross Traffic to Date. No. of Weeks.	Amount.	In. or Dec. on 1897.
					dols.	dols.		dols.	dols.
917	—	—	Baltimore & Ohio S. Western ..	Apr. 14	136,388	+29,960	40	5,366,184	+570,096
6,568	92	156	Canadian Pacific ..	Apr. 14	451,000	+62,000	14	6,116,000	+1,234,000
922	—	—	Chicago Great Western ..	Apr. 14	88,695	+9,162	40	4,243,288	+532,318
6,169	—	469	Chicago, Mil., & St. Paul ..	Apr. 14	567,000	+105,000	14	8,746,101	+1,341,300
1,685	—	—	Denver & Rio Grande ..	Apr. 14	139,600	+5,600	40	6,407,300	+1,053,400
3,512	—	—	Grand Trunk, Main Line ..	Apr. 14	£77,419	+£9,000	14	£1,075,182	+£110,648
335	—	—	Do. Chic. & Grand Trunk	Apr. 14	£15,586	+£4,176	14	£225,345	+£52,605
189	—	—	Do. Det., G. H. & Mil. ..	Apr. 14	£3,499	−£92	14	£51,609	−£2,897
2,938	—	—	Louisville & Nashville ..	Apr. 14	393,000	+32,000	14	6,020,175	+1,007,620
2,197	137	137	Miss., K., & Texas ..	Apr. 14	206,382	−15,638	40	10,142,918	+520,337
477	—	—	N. Y., Ontario, & W. ..	Apr. 14	65,860	−4,538	40	3,062,567	+91,818
1,570	—	—	Norfolk & Western ..	Apr. 7	225,000	+16,000	39	8,315,000	+886,000
3,499	336	—	Northern Pacific ..	Mar. 21	390,000	+105,000	11	4,070,000	+1,216,000
1,223	—	—	St. Louis S. Western ..	Apr. 14	82,000	+13,000	14	—	—
4,654	—	—	Southern ..	Apr. 14	371,000	+14,000	40	4,997,812	+1,311,443
1,979	—	—	Wabash ..	Apr. 14	253,000	+49,000	14	3,581,406	+722,000

MONTHLY STATEMENTS.

Mileage. Total.	Increase on 1896	Increase on 1895.	Name.	Net Earnings for Month. Month.	Amount.	In. or Dec. on 1897.	In. or Dec. on 1896.	Net Earnings to Date. No. of Months.	Amount.	In. or Dec. on 1897.	In. or Dec. on 1896.
					dols	dols.	dols.		dols.	dols.	dols.
6,935	44	444	Atchison ..	February	746,000	+191,000	+129,318	2	1,240,434	+313,670	−139,884
6,547	103	106	Canadian Pacific ..	February	424,000	+39,000	+19,268	2	940,000	+182,000	+110,318
6,169	—	469	Chicago, Mil., & St. Paul ..	January	757,000	+52,000	−30,713	—	—	—	—
1,685	—	—	Denver & Rio Grande ..	February	219,000	+52,500	+22,731	8	2,244,907	+367,7	−8,088
1,970	—	—	Erie ..	January	471,000	+33,000	−107,852	—	—	—	—
3,512	—	—	Grand Trunk, Main Line ..	February	£56,453	+£13,757	+£25,860	2	£143,853	+£48,041	+64,910
335	—	—	Do. Chic. & Grand Trunk	February	£8,210	+£5,197	+5,595	2	£21,310	+£14,130	+15,582
189	—	—	Do. Det. G. H. & Mil. ..	February	£528	−£1,369	−209	2	£2,328	−£677	+1,459
3,127	—	939	Illinois Central* ..	February	2,177,767	+413,527	+422,489	2	4,481,665	+819,013	+805,758
2,396	—	—	New York Central* ..	February	3,429,000	+128,000	+222,359	2	6,934,000	+490,597	249,393
477	—	—	New York Ontario, & W. ..	February	57,800	−3,800	+19,504	9	833,700	+33,400	+75,492
1,570	—	—	Norfolk & Western ..	February	242,000	+69,000	+43,239	2	525,000	+83,247	+91,585
3,407	—	—	Pennsylvania ..	January	1,259,101	+65,700	+236,000	2	2,511,898	92,400	+345,000
1,055	—	—	Phil. & Reading ..	February	584,382	−44,678	—	8	6,865,102	+446,422	—

* Statement of gross traffic.

Prices Quoted on the London Stock Exchange.

Throughout the INVESTORS' REVIEW middle prices alone are quoted, the object being to give the public the approximate current quotations of every security of any consequence in existence. On the markets the buying and selling prices are both given, and are often wide apart where stocks are seldom dealt in. Other particulars will be found in the INVESTMENT INDEX published quarterly—January, April, July, and October—in connection with this REVIEW, price 2s., by post 2s. 2d. Where dividends are paid only once a year, an *italic* type is used to distinguish them. The London Stock Exchange Official List is quoted in the REVIEW almost entire, only very insignificant issues, or bonds falling due within the next two or three years, being omitted. But the list is subdivided into the leading, or active, stocks, and those less frequently dealt in. The former will be found under the head of "Stock Markets," and with more details than it is possible to give for the bulk of securities. By retaining the file of the INVESTORS' REVIEW any subscriber can follow for himself the movements of securities from week to week, and the INVESTMENT INDEX will from time to time help to fill up deficiencies in the information.

Tea Companies and Mines and Mining Finance Stocks are placed in special lists.

Among the abbreviations used are the following:—S.F. Snk. Fd. *sinking fund*; Certs., *certificates*; Debs. or Dbs., *debentures*; Db. or D.Stk., *debenture stock*; Pf., Prf., or Pref., *preference*; Prefd. or Pfd., *preferred*; Dfd., *deferred*; L. or Ltd., *limited*; Sh., *share*; Ans., *annuities*; Cu. or Cm., *cumulative*; Gu or Guar., *guaranteed*; Bds., *bonds*; S., Sr., or Ser., *series*; In., Ins., Insc., *inscribed*; Dr., Drgs., Drwgs., *drawings*; Stg., Strlg., *sterling*; Lia., *liable to*; Sp., Surp., *surplus*; Per., Perp., *perpetual*; Ln. *lien*; Lo. *loan*.

The dates following the names of securities are the years of issue or of redemption. Where shares are not fully paid up, their nominal amount is given with the name so that investors may know the liability upon them.

BRITISH FUNDS, &c.

Rate.	Name.		Price.
2¾	2¾ p.c.'s (Childers') Red..	1905	103
3	Local Loans Stk.	1912	110
3	Metro. Police Deb. Stk.	1920	105½
—	Red Sea Ind. Tel. Ann.	1908	8½
4	Canada Gv. "Intcl. Rly."	1903	104
4	Do. do. ..	1908	111
4	Do. Bonds	1910	112
4	Do. Bonds	1913	117½
3	Egyptian Gov. Gar.		106½
3	Mauritius Ins. Stk.	1940	114
4	Turkish Guar. 1855		109
11½	Bank of Ireland Stk.		390
3½	India Rupee Paper		61
3½	Do. 1854-5		62
3	Do. 1896-7	1916	55
3½	Isle of Man Deb.		104
3	Do. Deb. Stk...	1919-29	103

CORPORATION AND COUNTY STOCKS.

FREE OF STAMP DUTY.

Rate.	Name.		Price.
3½	Metropolitan Con.	1929	115½
3	Do.	1941	109
2½	Do.	1920-49	99
2½	L.C.C. Con. Stock	1920	98
3½	Comm. of Sewers, Scp., S.F.	1905	106
3½	Corp. of Lond. Bds...	1897-1902	100½
3	Do.	1897-1912	101
3½	Do, Debs. Scp.	S.F. 1916	105
2½	Do., Deb. Stk. Scrip ..	1927-57	98
3	Barnsley	1916-46	105
3	Barry	1914-46	101
3	Bath	1909-34	102
3	Batley	1914-44	101½
3½	Birmingham	1945	117½
3	Do.	1947	111
2½	Do.	1926	98
3	Blackburn	1930	106½
3	Bournemouth	1913-33	103
3½	Bradford	1945	116½
3	Do. Deb. Stock ..	1954	108
3	Brighouse	1916-46	100
3½	Brighton	1946	117
2½	Do.	1957	97
3	Burton-on-Trent	1913-43	101
3	Cambridge	1913-43	103
3½	Cardiff	1935	116½
3	Do.	1914-54	103
3	Cheltenham	1971	107
3	Chichester	1916-46	101
3½	Croydon		134
3	Do.	1940	108½
3	Derby	1920-50	107
3	Devon C.C.	1917-33	104½
3½	Dewsbury	1930	109
3	Do.	1930	103
3	Dorset County	1922-32	105
3	Douglas (I. of Man)	1926	101
3	Dover	1913-43	101
3½	Dublin	1944	113½
3	Eastbourne	1920-40	104
3	Edinburgh	1924	108
2½	Do.	1927	98
2½	Exeter	1917-57	96
3	Glamorgan County	1914-34	104
3½	Glasgow	1914	110½
3	Do.	1921	106½
2½	Do.	1925-40	99
3	Gloster	1915-55	101
3	Grimsby	1913-45	103
3	Hampshire County	1914-34	105½
3	Hanley	1913-43	106
3	Harrogate	1914-34	103
3	Hastings	1915-54	103½
2½	Hertfordshire C.C.	1916-36	98
3	Heston & Isleworth U.D.C.	1915-35	101
3	Huddersfield	1934	107
3½	Hull (1st iss.)		131½
3	Inverness	1914-44	101
3	Ipswich	1952	108½
3	Lancaster	1919-55	103
2½	Leeds	1927	98
3½	Leicester	1934	115
3	Lincoln	1910	102
3½	Liverpool		131½

Corporation, &c. (*continued*):—

Rate.	Name.		Price.
3	Manchester	1941	107½
3	Mansfield	1915-45	100
3½	Middlesbro'	1909	105½
3½	Do.	1911-13	105
3	Do.	1915	104
3	Middlesex C.C.	1915-35	106
3½	Newcastle	1936	118½
3½	Do. Irred.		129½
2½	Do.	1915-36	100
3	Newcastle-under-Lyme..	1909-44	101
3	Newport (Mon.)	1915-55	101½
3	Norwich	1952	110
3	Nottingham		111½
3	Oxford	1951	109½
3	Penzance	1916-46	100½
3	Plymouth	1949	109½
3	Pontypridd U.D.C.	1916-46	98
3	Poole	1915-45	101
3½	Portsmouth 1916	24 & 27	112
3	Do.	1913-33	106½
3	Ramsey	1920-40	100
3	Ramsgate	1915-55	102
3½	Reading		129½
3	Do.	1962	104½
3½	Rhyl U.D.C.	1953	110
3	Richmond (Surrey)	1942	104½
3	River Wear Debt Certs.		100
3	St. Helen's	1915-55	102
3	Scarbro'	1915-50	102
2½	Sheffield	1925-57	96
3	Shipley U.D.C.	1915-35	100
3	Somerset Co.	1923-33	104
3	South Shields	1915-45	100
2½	Southampton	1915-45	102
3	Southend-on-Sea	1916-46	102
3	Staffs C.C.	1915-35	102
3	Stockport	1914-54	103
3	Stockton	1932	104
3	Do.	1915-35	103
3	Surrey Co.	1922-32	105½
3½	Swansea		130
3	Do.	1955	106
3	Taunton	1918-3-9-43	101
3	Tees Conserv. Deb. Stk.	1947	100
3	Thames Conserv. "A" Deb. Stk.	1954	103½
3	Do. "B" Deb. Stk.	1954	103½
3	Torquay	1913-43	101½
3	Tunbridge Wells	1931	101½
3	Tynemouth	1913	99
3	Wakefield	1929	101½
3	Walsall	1932	107½
3	West Bromwich	1930	106½
3½	West Ham	1929	110
3	Do.	1945	105
3	West Sussex C.C.	1915-35	106
3	Weston-s.-Mare Lcl. Bd.	1914-44	100
3	Weymouth & Melc. Regis	1918	101
3	Widnes	1915-55	100
3	Wigan	1921	105
3	Windsor	1918-55	102
3½	Wisbech	1947	113½
3½	Wolverhampton	1932	118
3	Do.	1924-54	107
3	York	1916-41	106½

SUBJECT TO STAMP DUTY.

Rate.	Name.		Price.
3½	Belfast City & Dis. Watr.	1938	114
3	Do. Red Stk.	1953-6	106
3½	Belfast	1924	103
4	Blackburn Con. Deb. Irred.		141½
3½	Do. do. Irred.		130
3½	Bristol		128½
3½	Burnley	1933	114
2½	Chesterfield Gas & Wtr.	1916-46	98
3½	Douglas Town	1921	105
3	Dover Harb. 1st Deb...	1956	104½
3½	Hull (2nd iss.)		128½
4	Leeds Deb.	1927	124
3½	Do.		115½
3	Do.	1927	106
3	Leicester	1919-44	102½
4	Manchester		145
3	Do.	1908	104½
4½	Middlesboro' Mrts.	1908	111
3½	Newark-on-Trent ..	1901-41	96
3½	Sheffield	1898-1916	105½
3½	Do.	1925-36	114
3	Do.	1925	106½
3½	Southampton	S.F.	106
4½	Stockton Morts.	1908	110½
3½	Worcester	1950	109

COLONIAL AND PROVINCIAL GOVERNMENT SECURITIES.

Rate.	Name.		Price.
6	British Columbia	1907	119½
4½	Do. Debs...	1917	111½
3	British Guiana Imgtn. Bds.		98
5	Canada, "Intercol. Rail,"	1903	109
4	Do. (Bonds)	1904-5-6-8	106
4	Do. Reduced	1910	106½
3½	Do. Bnds.	1909-34	103
4	Do. Loan	1910-35	106½
3	Do. Loan	1938	100
6	Cape of G. Hope	1900	—
5	Do.	1900	—
4½	Do. red. by an. draw.		106
4½	Do. 1879		109
4	Do. 1881		108
4	Do.	1917-23	113½
4½	Ceylon		110
4	Do.		106½
4½	Fiji Gov. Deb. Sink. Fd.		101½
4	Jamaica Sink. Fd.	1923	105
5	Manitoba Debs.	1910	113
5	Do. Ster. Bds.	1888	119½
4	Do. Ster. Debs.		106
4	Mauritius, Cons. Debs. 1880....		103½
4½	Natal, Sink. Fd.	1919	118
4	Do. do.	1926	115
3½	Newfoundland Stg. Bds.	1941	97
3½	Do. do. ..	1947	97
3	Do. do.		86½
5	New South Wales	1897-1902	104½
4	Do.	1903-5-8-9-12	105
5	New Zealand	1914	118
5	Do. Cnsls. 1 p.c. per an. Sink. Fd.		103
3½	Nova Scotia Debs.		104
5	Quebec Prov.	1904-6	110
4½	Do. (drgs.)		104
5	Do. Strlg. Bds.	1912	115
4	Do. Strlg. Bds.	1928	110
4	Do. Strlg. Bds.	1934	108
4	Queensland	1913-15	105
4½	St. Lucia Debs.		102½
6	South Australia	1897-1900	103½
6	Do.	1901-1918	119
5	Do.	1911-1920	116
4	Do.	1899-1916	105
4	Do.	1929	108½
4	Do.	1916	106½
4	Do.	1917-18-24	107½
6	Tasmania	1897-1901	104
4	Do. 1908-11,	1913-14-20	107½
5	Trinidad Debs., an. drw. 1 p.c...		106
4	Victoria	1899-1901	101½
4½	Do.	1904	105
4	Do. Rail. Loan	1907	104
4	Do. Loans	1908-13	105
4½	West. Austr. 1 p.c. ac. Sink. Fd.		107
4	Do. do.		106

REGISTERED AND INSCRIBED STOCKS.

No stamp duty except for Canada 4 p.c. Reduced (½ per cent.).

Rate.	Name.		Price.
4	Antigua Insc. Stk. Red.	1919-44	109
3½	Barbados Insc. Stk.	1925-42	107
3	British Colum. Insc. Stk.	1941	101½
4	British Guiana Insc.	1935	118½
4	Canada Stk. Regd. ..	1904-5-6-8	104
4	Do. 4 p.c. (late 5 p.c.) Regd.	1910	106½
3½	Do. 3½ p.c. Stock Regd.	1909-34	103
4	Do. Ln. for 4 milln. stg.	1910-35	106½
3	Do. Stk. Regd.	1938	100
2½	Do. Insc.	1947	90
4	Cape G. Hope Regd. ..	1917-23	113½
4	Do. (Ln. of '83) Insc. ..	1923	113½
4	Do. Cons. Stk. Insc.	1916-36	109
3½	Do. Consol. Insc. Stock	1929-49	106
4	Ceylon Insc. Stock	1934	118½
3	Do.	1940	101
4	Grenada Insc. Stock	1917-42	110
3½	Hong Kong Insc. Stock	1918-43	103½
4	Jamaica Insc. Stock	1934	118
—	Do.	1922-44	98
4	Mauritius Inscribed	1937	118½
4	Natal Consd. Stk. Insc.	1937	113
4	Do.	1937	117½
3½	Do. Inscribed Stock ..	1914-39	105
4	Newfoundland Inscribed	1913-38	106
4	Do.	1935	113
4	Do. Consd. Stk. Ins.	1936	113
4	N. S. Wales Stock Insc.	1933	116
3½	Do.	1924	103
3½	Do.	1918	103
3	Do.	1935	96

Colonial, &c. (*continued*):—

Rate.	Name.		Price.
4	N. Zealnd. Con. Stk. Ins.	1929	110
3½	Do	1940	106
3	Do. Inscribed	1945	98
3	Quebec (Prov.) Ins. Stk.	1937	93
4	Queensland Stock Insc.	1915-24	106½
3½	Do.	1921-4-30	103
3½	Do.	1945	106
3	Do.	1922-47	96
4	St. Lucia Insc. Stock ..	1919-44	112
4	S. Austrln. (1882-7) Reg.	1916-36	107½
3½	Do. In. Stk. Reg.	1939	107
3	Do.	1916-26	99
3/	Do.	1916	98
3½	Tasmanian Insc. Stock ..	1920-40	106
4	Do.	1920-40	116
4	Trinidad Insc. Stock	1917-42	110
3	Do.	1922-44	98
4	Victoria Rly. Loan '81, Inscribed Stock	1907	104
4	Victoria Insc. Stock	1908-13-19	104½
4	Victoria (1883) Ins. Stk.	1920	110
3½	Do. Inscribed Stock	1921-3-6	102
4	Do. do.	1911-26	108
4	W. Austral. Insc. Stock	1934	116½
4	Do.	1911-31	109
3½	Do.	1915-35	104
3	Do.	1915-35	96
3	Do.	1916-36	96

FOREIGN STOCKS, BONDS, &c.

COUPONS PAYABLE IN LONDON.

Last Div.	Name.		Price.
36/	Argentine Ry. Loan 6 p.c.	1881	85½
15/	Do. 5 p.c.	1884	64
30/	Do. N. Cent. Ry. Ext. 5 p.c.	1887-8-9	62
30/	Do. 5 p.c. Trsy. Convs.	1887	64
5/4½	Do. 4½ p.c. Interl. Gld.	1888	61
27/	Do. 4½ p.c. Stlg. Extrl.	1888	61
10/6	Do. 3½ p.c. External ..	1889	46
4	Do. 4 p.c. Ry. Guar. Res....		52
4½	Brazilian	1883	46
4½	Do. Gold	1879	50½
4½	Do.	1888	45
36/	Buenos Ayres	1824	82½
6	Do.	1882-3-6	44
6	Bulgarian	1888	91
6	Do. Mort. Bonds	1892	91
4½	Chilian	1885	72
4½	Do.	1886	73
4½	Do.	1887	72
4½	Do.	1889	80½
5	Do.	1892	83
4½	Do.	1893	72
4½	Do.	1895	70
5	Do.	1896	81
7	Chinese Silver	1894	100
6	Do. Gold	1895	105
6	Do. Apl. '95 bydwgs.	1901-15	108½
5	Do. Red. dwgs. in 36 yr.	1896	97½
5	Do. Do. Regis.	1896	98
1½	Colmbn. 1½ to 3 p.c. Ext. Bds.	1896	17
6	Cordova, Prov.	1886	25
—	Do. Eng. Ass. Certs.		24
—	Do. 6 p.c.	1887-8	25
—	Do. Eng. Ass. Certs.		24
3	Costa Rica "A"		29
2½	Do. "B"		22
3	Danish Gold	1914	98
10/	Ecuador N. Ext. Bds. 4½ p.c. ascn. to 5 p.c.		21
3½	Egypt'n Ins. Stk. lia. Stp. Dty.	1890	100
4	Do. State Domain	1878	103½
4	Do. D. Sanieh, Red. ..	1905	101½
6	Entre Rios	1886-8	31
6	Do. Fndg. Ln. Bds.	1894-1921	31
6	Do. do. Parana City		28
15/	Greek	1881	38
15/	Do.	1884	38
12/	Do. Rentes		31
15/	Do. (Piræus-Larissa Ry.)		37
3/6	Do. Fundg. Loan	1893	40
4	Guatemala Extl. Debt		28½
6	Hawaiian		102½
4	Hungarian Gold Rentes		101
3	Do.	1895	91½
6	Italian Irriga. Guar.		108
5	Do. Maremmana		91
5	Japan 5 p.c.		100½
5	Mexican (Nat. R. Tehuantp c.)..		88½
6	Do. Extrl.	1890	90

Foreign Stocks, &c. (*continued*):—

Last Div.	Name.	Price.
6	Mexican Extrl. 1893	89
5	Do. Intrnl. Cons. Slvr.	36
5	Do Intern. Rd. Bds. 2d. Ser.	36
4	Nicaragua 1886	50
3½	Norwegian, red. 1937, or earlier	98
3	Do. do. 1965, do.	98
3½	Do. 3½ p.c. Bnds.	102
1	Paraguay 1p.c. ris. 3p.c. 1886-96	15
5	Russian, 1822, £ Strlg.	149
3	Do. 1859	95
4	Do. (Nicolas Ry.) 1867-9	102
3	Do. Transcauc. Ry. 1882	94
4	Do. Con. R. R. Bd. Ser. I., 1889	101
4	Do. Do. II., 1889	101
4	Do. Do. III., 1891	102
3½	Do. Bonds	100
4	Do. Ln. (Dvinsk and Vitbsk)	101
6	Salvador 1889	64
—	S Domingo 4s. Unified .. 1980	57½
6	San Luis Potosi Stg. 1889	87
5	San Paulo (Brzl.), Stg. 1888	88½
6	Santa Fé 1883-4	33
—	Do. Eng. Ass. Certs. Dep.	32
5	Do. 1888	43
—	Do. Eng. Ass. Certs. Dpsit.	42
5	Do. (W. Cnt. Col. Rly.) Mrt.	22
5	Do. & Reconq. Rly. Mort.	22
5	Spanish Quickslvr Mort. 1870	100
3½	Swedish 1880	102
3	Do. 1888	98
3	Do. Conversion Loan 1894	98
5	Trans. Gov. Loan Red. 1903-42	102
50/	Tucuman (Prov.) 1888	69
4	Turkish, Secd. on Egypt. Trib.	101
3½	Turkish, Egpt. Trib., Ott. Bd., '94	97
4	Do. Priority 1890	87½
1	Do. Convted Series, "A"	65½
5	Do. Customs Ln. 1886	92½
5	Uruguay Bonds 1896	55
3	Venzuela New Con. Debt 1881	32

COUPONS PAYABLE ABROAD.

Last Div.	Name.	Price.
7	Argentl. Nat. Cedla. Sries, "B".	33
5	Austrian Ster. Rnts., ex 10fl., 1870	94
5	Do. do. do.	84
5	Do. Paper do. 1870	83
5	Do. do. do.	85
4	Do. Gld Rentes 1876	100
2½	Belgian exchange 25fr.	92
3	Do. do.	101
3½	Danish Int., 1887, Rd. 1896	—
2½	Dutch Certs. ex 12 gldrs.	87
3	Do. Bonds	98
3	Do. Insc. Stk.	97
3½	French Rentes	104½
3	Do. 1878, '81-4., Red.	100
3	German Imp. Ln. 1891	95
3	Do. do. 1892-3	95
3	Do. do. 1890-4	96
5	Japan Cons. Ln., '92, 3, & 5, Red.	45
36/9	Prussian Consols	102
3	" Cons. Stg. Ln. 1891	96
4	Rumanian Bds. 1890	—
4	Do. do. 1891	—
4	Utd. States, 1877, Red. 1907	114
4	Do. 1895, 30 yrs.	124
3½	Do. Maschsetts Gl. 1935	113½
3½	Do. Gold Bonds 1923	107½
2	Virginia Cpn. Bds., 3 p.c. from July, 1901	70

BRITISH RAILWAYS.

ORD. SHARES AND STOCKS.

Last Div.	Name.	Price.
10	Barry, Ord.	274½
4	Do. Prefd.	125
6	Do. Defd.	147½
5	Caledonian, Ord.	152
3	Do. Prefd.	97
—	Do. Defd. Ord., No. 1	4½
	Cambrian, Ord	6½
—	Do. Coast Cons.	6½
32/	Cardiff Ry. Pref. Ord.	117
3/	Central Lond. £10 Ord. Sh.	10½
1/9½	Do. do. £6 paid	6½
3½d.	Do. Pref. Half-Shares	1½
1/6	Do. Def. do	4½
1½	City and S. London	69
—	East London, Cons.	6½
2	Furness	63½
2½	Glasgow and S. West. Pfd.	79
2½	Do. do. Dfd.	63
3	Great Central, Ord. 1894	39½
32/0	Do. London Exten.	71
—	Great N. of Scotland, Prfd.	90
—	Do. Dfd.	32
4	Great Northern, Prefd.	118½
—	Do. Consolidated "A"	50
—	Do. do. "B"	191½
2	Highland	79
4	Isle of Wight, Prefd.	120½
3	Do. Defd.	83½
	Lancs. Derbys. and E. Cst.	4
8½	L. Brighton and S. C. Ord.	185
6	Do. Prefd. Ord.	197
30/	Do. Contgt. Rights Certs.	16½
5½	Lond. and S. Western Ord.	222½
4	Do. Preferred	132
6½	Lond., Tilb., and Southend	133½
—	Mersey, £20 shares	½
—	Metropolitan, New Ord.	127
2½	Do. Surplus Lands	94
4	North Cornwall, 4 p.c. Pref.	104½
22/6	Do. Deferred	22½
7½	North London	224½
4½	North Staffordshire	130

British Railways (*continued*):—

Last Div.	Name.	Price.
3/3	Plymouth, Devenport, and S. W. Junc. £10	9
3/	Port Talbot £10 Shares	9
9d.	Rhondda Swns. B. £10 Sh.	5
10	Rhymney, Cons.	265½
4	Do. Prefd.	123
6⅛	Do. Defd.	145½
1½	Scarboro', Bridlington Junc.	47½
6½	South Eastern, Ord	150
6	Do. Pref.	192
3½	Taff Vale	78
25/	Vale of Glamorgan	127½
3	Waterloo & City	136½

LEASED AT FIXED RENTALS.

Last Div.	Name.	Price.
4	Birkenhead	143½
5.19.0	East Lincolnshire	200½
5½	Hamsmith. & City Ord.	192½
4½	Lond. and Blackwll.	161½
4½	Do. £10 4½ p. c. Pref.	161½
56/6	Lond. & Green. Ord.	101
5	Do. 5 p. c. Pref.	174½
5	Nor. and Eastn. £50 Ord.	89
6	Do.	104½
3½	N. Cornwall 3½ p. c. Stk.	124½
4⅞	Nott. & Granthm. R. & C.	142½
3½	Portptk. & Wigtn. Guar. Stk.	121½
9	Vict. Stn. & Pimlico Ord.	312½
4½	Do. 4½ p. c. Pref.	158½
4/	West Lond. £20 Ord. Shs.	14
4⅞	Weymouth & Portld.	160½

DEBENTURE STOCKS.

Last Div.	Name.	Price.
4	Alexandra Dks. & Ry.	132½
3	Barry, Cons.	108
4	Brecon & Mrthyr, New A	127½
4	Do. New B	105
4	Caledonian	148½
4	Cambrian "A"	132½
4	Do. "B"	128½
4	Do. "C"	124½
4	Do. "D"	107½
3	Cardiff Rly.	101½
4	City and S. Lond.	139
3½	Cleator & Working Junc.	118½
3	Devon & Som. "A"	103½
16/3	Do. "B" 4 p. c.	36
—	Do. "C" 4 p. c.	10
4	E. Lond. 2nd Ch. 4 p. c. A	135
6/	Do. 2nd B	67½
—	Do. 3rd Ch. 4 p. c.	18½
—	Do. 4th do.	9½
3½	Do. 1st (3½ p. c.)	128½
2½	Do. 2½ p.c.(Whitech.Exn).	87
4	Forth Bridge	142½
4	Furness	142½
4	Glasgow and S. Western	148
5	Gt. Central	—
4½	Do.	154½
4	Gt. Eastern	146
4	Gt. N. of Scotland	145½
3	Gt. Northern	112
4	Gt. Western	148½
4½	Do.	156½
4½	Do.	165½
5	Do.	183½
2½	Do.	96½
4	Highland	143½
3	Hull and Barnsley	104½
3	Do. 2nd (3-4 p. c).	122
4	Isle of Wight	144½
3	Do. Cent. "A"	92½
4½	Do. "B"	115½
4	Do. "C"	82½
3	Lancs. & Yorkshire	112½
4	Lancs. Derbys. & E. Cst.	123½
4	Lpool St. Hlen's & S. Lancs.	126
4½	Ldn. and Blackwall	155½
4	Ldn. and Greenwich	146
4	Lond., Brighton, &c.	148½
4½	Do.	164½
4½	Lond., Chath., &c., Arb.	153½
4½	Do. "B"	152½
4	Do.	138½
4	Do. 1883	138½
3	Do.	106
3	Lond. & N. Western	114
3	Lond. & S. Westn. "A"	112½
3	Do. Consld.	112½
4	Lond., Til., & Southend	146
—	Mersey, 5 p. c. (Act, 1866)	65
4	Metropolitan	146
4½	Do.	163½
3½	Do.	126½
6	Met. District	207½
4	Do.	139
2½	Midland	94
4½	Mid-Wales "A"	137½
4	Neath & Brecon 1st	129
4	Do. "A 1"	118½
3	North British	109½
3	Do. 1893	107½
3½	N Cornwall, Launcstn, &c.	124½

Debenture Stocks (*continued*):—

Last Div.	Name.	Price.
3	North Eastern	112½
4½	North London	163½
3	N. Staffordshire	111
4	Plym. Devpt. & S.W. Jn.	141½
4	Rhondda and Swan. Bay	130½
4	Rhymney	145
4	South-Eastern	147½
5	Do.	180
3½	Do.	127½
3	Do.	113½
3	Taff Vale	109½
4	Tottenham & For. Gate	144½
3	Vale of Glamorgan	105½
3	West Highld. (Gtd. by N.B.)	107½
4	Wrexham, Mold, &c. "A"	115½
4	Do. "B"	102½
4	Do. "C"	97½

GUARANTEED SHARES AND STOCKS.

Last Div.	Name.	Price.
4	Caledonian	146½
4	Do.	142½
4	Forth Bridge	142
4	Furness 1881	137½
4	Glasgow & S. Western	142½
4	Do. St. Enoch. Rent	142½
6	Gt. Central	199½
4½	Do. 1st Pref.	151½
3½	Do. Pref.	104½
5	Do. Irred. S.Y. Rent	161½
4½	Do. do.	139½
4	Gt. Eastern, Rent	141
5	Do. Metropolitan	176½
4	Do.	141½
4	Gt. N. of Scotland	138½
4	Gt. Northern	142
5	Gt. Western, Rent	177½
5	Do. Cons.	177½
4	Lancs. & Yorkshire	142½
5	L., Brighton & S. C.	177
3½	L., Chat. & D. (Shrtlds.)	110½
4	L. & North Western	143½
4	L. & South Western 1881	144½
4½	Met. District, Ealing Rent	150
4½	Do. Fulham Rent	150
4	Do. Midland Rent	141½
4	Do. Mid. & Dist. Guar.	126½
2½	Midland, Cons. Perp.	91
3	Mid. & G. N. Jt., "A" Rnt.	106
3	N. British, Lien	106
4	Do Cons. Pref. No. 1	139½
3	N. Cornwall, Wadebrge. Gu.	107
4	N. Eastern	142½
5	N. Staff. Trent & M. £20 Shs.	35½
3½	Nott. Suburban Ord.	123½
20/6	S. E. Perp. Ann.	35½
4½	Do. 4½ p.c.	160½
3½	S. Yorks. Junc. Ord.	118½
4½	W. Cornwall (G. W., Br., Ex., & S. Dev. Joint Rent	158½
3	W. Highl. Ord. Stk. (Gua., N.B.)	106½

PREFERENCE SHARES AND STOCKS.

DIVIDENDS CONTINGENT ON PROFIT OF YEAR.

Last Div.	Name	Price.
4½	Alexandra Dks. & Ry. "A"	125½
5	Barry (First)	169½
4	Do. Consolidated	138½
4	Caledonian Cons., No. 1	141½
4	Do. do. No. 2	141½
5	Do. do. 1878	174½
4	Do. Pref. 1884	141
4	Do. do. 1887 (Conv.)	152½
—	Cambrian, No. 1 4 p. c. Pref.	72½
—	Do. No. 2 do.	39½
—	Do. No. 3 do.	19
—	Do. No. 4 do.	10
5	City & S. Lond. £10 shares	15½
—	Do. New	14
4	Furness, Cons. 1881	134½
4	Do. "A" 1881	131½
4	Do. "B" 1883	129½
4	Glasgow & S. Western	141½
4	Do. No. 2	140½
4	Do. 1888	140
4	Do. 1891	140
5	Gt. Central	158½
4	Do.	132½
5	Do. Conv. 1872	153½
5	Do. do. 1874	153½
5	Do. do. 1876	152½
5	Do. do. 1879	151½
5	Do. do. 1881	147½
4	Do. 1889	112½
4	Do. 1891	106½
5	Do. 1894	103
4	Gt. Eastern, Cons.	140½
4	Do. 1886	139½
4	Do. 1881	138½
4	Do. 1884	139½

Preference Shares, &c. (*continued*):—

Last Div.	Name.	Price.
4	Gt. Eastern, Cons. 1887	139½
4	Do. 1888	139½
3½	Do. 1890	121½
3½	Do. 1893	121½
—	Do. (Int. fr. Jan '99) 1893	117½
4	Gt. North Scotland "A"	133½
4	Do. "B"	133½
4	Gt. Northern, Cons.	141½
3	Do. 1896	106
5	Gt. Western Cons.	177
36/11	Hull & Barnsley Red. at 115	107
4	Isle of Wight	133½
3	Lancs. & Yorkshire, Cons.	106½
2/2½	Lanc. Drby & E.C. 5 p.c. £10	10½
—	Do. 5 p.c. 2nd £10	9½
5	Lond., Bright., &c., Cons.	176½
5	Do. 2nd Cons.	175½
4½	Lond., Chat. & Dov. Arbitr.	134½
25/	Do. 2nd Pref. 4½ p.c.	91
4	Lond. & N. Western	142½
4	Lond. & S. Western 1881	142½
4	Do. 1884	142½
3½	Do.	126½
4	Lond., Tilbury & Southend	141½
4	Do. Cons., 1887	141½
4	Do 1891	141½
—	Mersey, 5 p.c. Perp.	—
4	Metropolitan, Perp.	140½
4	Do. 1882	140½
4	Do. Irred.	140½
4	Do. 1887	140½
4	Do. New	140½
4½	Do.	146½
3½	Do.	123½
3	Do. Guar.	101½
2½	Metrop. Dist. Exten 5 p.c.	110
2½	Midland, Perp. Pref.	88½
4	N. British Cons., No. 2	135½
4½	Do. Edin. & Glasgow	151½
5	Do. 1865	167½
5	Do. Conv. 1874	168½
4½	Do. 1875	151½
4½	Do. Conv. 1875	152½
5	Do. do. 1879	168½
4	Do. do. 1884	137½
4	Do. do. 1888	138
4	Do. do. 1890	137½
4	Do. do. 1892	137½
4	N. Eastern	142½
4½	N. Lond., Cons. 1866	174½
4½	Do. 2nd Cons. 1875	160
3	N. Staffordshire	107
4½	Plym. Devpt. & S. W. Junc.	149½
1/5	Port Talbot, &c., 4 p.c. £10 Shares, 4 paid	5
5/	Rhondda & Swansea Bay, 5 p.c. £10 Shares	12½
4	Rhymney, Cons.	140½
4½	S. Eastern, Cons.	157½
5	Do. do.	176½
4	Do. Vested Cos'.	141½
4	Do. 1891	141½
3½	Do. 1893	124½
2	Do. 3 p.c. after July 1900	101½
4	Taff Vale	142½

INDIAN RAILWAYS.

Last Div.	Name.	Paid.	Price.
3½	Assam Bengal, Ld., (3½ p.c. till June 30, then 3 p.c.)	100	101
4/	Barsi Light, Ld., £10 Shs.	10	10½
6	Bengal and N. West., Ld.	100	149½
4/	Do. £10 Shares	10	14½
3/6	Do. 3½ p.c. Cum. Pf. Shs.	10	10½
8½d.	Do.	4	4½
2/3½	Bengal Central, Ld., £10 (3½ p.c. + ½th net earn)	5	5½
3	Bengal Dooars, Ld.	100	116
4	Bengal Nagpr., Lim. (gua. 4 p.c. + 4th sp. pfts.)	100	114
7½	Bombay, Baroda, and C. I. (gua. 5 p.c)	100	214
36/1	Burma, Ld. (gua. 2½ p.c. and ½ p.c. add. till 1901)	100	108½
1/7	Do. £10 Shares		3½
4	Delhi Umb. Kalka, Ld., Gua. 3½ p.c. + net earn.	100	122
4	Do. Deb. Stk., 1890 (1926)	100	111
9/10	Estn. Bengal, "A" An. 1957	—	25
9/	Do. "B" 1957	—	29
4	Do. Gua. Deb. Stock	100	136½
9/7½	East Ind. Ann. "A" (1953)	—	27
8/4½	Do. "C"	—	28
8/11½	Do. "B"	—	
6⅛	Do. Def. Ann. Cap. (gua. 4 p.c. + ½th sp. pfts.)	—	150
115/9	East Ind. Def. Ann. "D"	—	156
4½	East Ind. Irred. Stock	100	158½
5	Gt. Indian Penin., Gua 5 p.c. + ½ surplus profits	100	166½
4	Do. Irred. 4 p.c. Deb. St.	100	136½
4	Indian Mid., Ld. (gua. 4 p.c. + ½th surplus pfts.)	100	114
51/	Madras Guar. + ½ sp. pfts.	100	166
48/6	Do. do.	100	156
46/	Do. do.	100	146
4	Nilgiri, Ld., 1st Deb. Stk.	100	97
4	Oude & Rohil. Db. Stk. Rd.	100	—
5⅛	Rohil. and Kumaon, Ld.	100	132
9/11	Scinde, Punj., and Delhi, "A" Ann., 1958	—	25
9/1	Do. "B" do.	—	29

Indian Railways (*continued*):—

Last Div.	NAME.	Paid.	Price.
4	South Behar, Ld., £10 shs.	100	100
3½	Do. Deb. Stk. Red.	100	101
4½	South Ind., Gu. Deb. Stk.	100	158½
5	South Indian, Ld. (gua. 3 p.c., and ⅓ spls. profits)	100	122½
5	Sthn. Mahratta, Ld. (3½ p.c. & ¼th net earnings)	100	116
4	Do. Deb. Stk. Red.	100	120
3½	Southern Punjab, Ld....	100	106
3½	Do. Deb. Stk. Red.	—	105
5	Nizam's Gua. State, Ld. (†	100	114½
4	Do. Mort. Deb., 1936	100	109
4	Do. do. Reg.	100	108
17/3½	Nizam's Gua. State, Ld., 3½ p.c. Mt. Deb. bearer	—	94½
17/3½	Do. Reg. do. ..	—	93½
5	W. of India Portgese., Ld.	100	68½
5	Do. Deb. Stk., Red	100	99

RAILWAYS.—BRITISH POSSESSIONS.

Last Div.	NAME.	Paid.	Price.
5	Atlantic & N.W. Gua. 1 Mt. Bds., 1937	100	124½
5/3	Buff. & L. Huron Ord. Sh.	10	13½
5½	Do. 1st Mt. Perp. Bds. 1879	100	141½
5½	Do. 2nd Mt. Perp. Bds.	100	141½
—	Calgary & Edmon. 6 p.c. 1st Mt. Stg. Bds. Red..	100	75½
5	Canada Cent. 1st Mt. Bds. Red.	100	103
4	Can. Pacific Pref. Stk.....	100	100
5	Do. Strl. 1st Mt. Deb. Bds. 1915	100	117
3½	Do. Ld. Grnt. Bds., 1938..	100	106
3½	Do. Ld. Grnt. Ins. Stk. ..	100	106
4	Do. Perp. Cons. Deb. Stk.	100	114
5	Do. Algoma Bch. 1st Mt. Bds., 1937	100	121
2	Demerara, Original Stock	100	47
7	Do. Perp. Pref. Stk....	100	155½
9½d.	Do. 4 p.c. Cum. Ext. Pref. £10 Shs.	4	6½
—	Dominion Atlntc. Ord. Stk.	100	33½
5	Do. 5 p.c. Pref. Stk.....	100	97½
4	Do. 1st. Deb. Stk......	100	104½
4	Do. 2nd do. Red.	100	100
—	EmuBay & Mt. Bischoff, Ld.	5	4½
4½	Do. Irred. Deb. Stk....	100	98
nil.	Gd. Trunk of Canada, Stk.	100	7¾
6	Do. 2nd. Equip. Mt. Bds.	100	130½
5	Do. Perp. Deb. Stk.......	100	135½
5	Do. Gt. Westn. Deb. Stk.	100	127½
5	Do. Nthn. of Can. 1st Mt. Bds., 1902	100	102½
4	Do. do. Deb. Stk	100	102
5	Do. G. T. Geor. Bay & L. Erie 1 Mt., 1903	100	104
5	Do. Mid. of Can. Stl. 1st Mt. (Mid. Sec.) 1908....	100	105
5	Do. do. Cons. 1 Mt. Bds. 1912	100	106
5	Do. Mont. & Champ. 1 Mt. Bds., 1902	100	103
	Do. Welln., Grey & Brce. 7 p.c. Bds. 1 Mt.	100	109
—	Jamaica 1st Mtg. Bds. Red.	—	103
—	Manitoba & N. W., 6 p.c. 1st Mt. Bds., Red......	100	—
—	Do. Ldn. Bdhldrs. Certs.	—	—
5	Manitoba S. W. Col. 1 Mt. Bd., 1934 $1,000 price %	—	120
—	Mid. of W. Aust. Ld. 6 p.c. 1 Mt. Dbs., Red.	100	25
4	Do. Deb. Bds., Red.	100	103
4	Nakusp & Slocan Bds., 1918	100	106
3	Natal Zululand Ld. Debs.,	100	77½
5	N. Brunswick 1st Mt. Stg. Bds., 1934	100	121
4	Do. Perp. Cons. Deb. Stk.	100	114
—	N. Zealand Mid., Ld., 5 p.c. 1st Mt. Debs..........	100	35
6	Ontario & Queb. Cap. Stk.	$100	155½
5	Do. Perm. Deb. Stk......	100	142½
—	Qu'Appelle, L. Lake & Sask. 6 p.c. 1 Mt. Bds. Red.	100	41½
	Queb. & L. S. John, 1st Mt. Bds., 1909	100	25½
	Quebec Cent., Prior Ln. Bds., 1908	100	107
1½	Do. 5 p.c. Inc. Bds.	100	39
4	St. Lawr. & Ott. Stl. 1st Mt.	100	113
4	Shuswap & Okan., 1st Mt. Deb. Bds., 1915	100	76
5	Temiscouata, 5 p.c. Stl. 1st Deb. Bds., Red.........	100	9½
5	Do. (S. Franc. Brch.) 5 p.c. Stl. 1 Mt. Db. Bds., 1910	100	10
4	Toronto, Grey & B. 1st Mt.	100	112
1/2	Well. & Mana. £5 Shs. ..	1	½
5	Do. Debs., 1908........	100	110
5	Do. 2nd Debs., 1908....	100	109
5	Do. 3rd do., 1908	100	108
6	Atlan. & St. Law. Shs., 6 p.c.	100	162½
5	Gd. Trunk Mt. Bds., 1934	100	116½
5	Michigan Air Line, 5 p.c. 1st Mt. Bds., 1902......	100	104
4	Minneap., S. P. & Slt. Ste. Mar, 1st Mt. Bds., 1938	$1000	97½

AMERICAN RAILROAD STOCKS AND SHARES.

Last Div.	NAME.	Paid.	Price.
6/	Alab. Gt. Sthn. A 6 p.c. Pref.	10*l.*	9
—	Do. do "B" Ord. ..	10*l.*	2
—	Alabma. N. Orl.-Tex. &c., "A" Pref.	10*l.*	½
—	Do. "B" Def.	10*l.*	½
5½	Atlant. First Lsd. Ls. Rtl. Trust..................	Stk.	97½
—	Baltimore & Ohio Com. ..	$100	16
—	Baltimore Ohio S.W. Pref.	$100	6
—	Chesap. & Ohio Com.	$100	18
—	Chic. Gt. West. 5 p.c. Pref. Stock "A"..........	$100	30½
—	Do. do. Scrip. In.......	—	27
8/3	Do. 4 p.c. Deb. Stk.......	$100	67½
4	Do. Interest in Scrip	$100	63½
$4	Chic. Junc. Rl. & Un. Stk. Yds. Com.	$100	110½
$1½	Do. 6 p.c. Cum. Pref.	$100	114½
$3½	Chic. Mil. & St. P. Pref...	$100	146
7	Cleve. & Pittsburgh......	$10	86½
$1½	Clev., Cincin., Chic., & St. Louis Com.	$100	—
—	Erie 4 p.c. Non-Cum. 1st Pf.	—	31
—	Do. 4 p.c. do. 2nd Pf.	—	17
—	Gt. Northern Pref.	$100	150
$2½	Illinois Cen. Lsd. Lines ..	$100	95½
—	Kansas City, Pitts & G. ..	$100	19
$3	L. Shore & Mich. Sth. C.	$100	185
—	Mex. Cen. Ltd. Com.	$100	5
—	Miss. Kan. & Tex. Pref...	$100	32½
2½	N.Y., Pen. & O. 1st Mt. Tst. Ltd., Ord.	—	48½
4	Do. 1st Mort. Deb. Stk. ..	$100	93½
8	North Pennsylvania	$50	—
—	Northn. Pacific, Com.....	$100	22½
1¾	Pitts. F. Wayne & Chic...	$100	174
—	Reading 1st Pref.	$50	19½
—	Do. 2nd Pref...........	$50	10
—	S. Louis & S. Fran. Com.	$100	6½
—	Do. 2nd Pref.	$100	25
6	St. Louis Bridge 1st Pref..	$100	107
3	Do. 2nd Pref.	$100	50
6	Tunnel Rail. of St. Louis	$100	107
$1½	St. Paul, Min. and Man...	$100	129
—	Southern, Com.	$100	7¾
—	Wabash, Common........	$100	7

AMERICAN RAILROAD BONDS. CURRENCY.

Last Div.	NAME.	Price.
7	Albany & Susq. 1 Con. Mrt. 1906	118
7	Allegheny Val. 1 Mt...... 1910	125½
5	Burling., Cedar Rap. & N. 1 Mt. 1906	109½
5	Canada Southern 1 Mt.... 1908	111
5	Chic. & N. West. Sk. Fd. Db. 1933	117½
5	Do. Deb. Coupon 1921	112½
6	Chicago & Tomah 1905	109½
5	Chic. Burl. & Q. Skg. Fd. 1901	102½
4	Do. Nebraska Ext....... —	98
6	Chic., Mil., & S. Pl., 1 Mt. S.W. Div............. 1909	117½
7	Do. (S. Paul Div.) 1 Mt. 1902	132½
5	Do. (La Cross & D. 1919	112½
7	Do. 1 Mt. (Hast. & Dak.) 1910	127½
5	Do. Chic. & Mis. Riv. 1 Mt. 1926	112½
5	Chic., Rock Is. and Pac. 1 Mt. Ext. 1934	108
6	Det., G. Haven & Mil. Equip 1918	105
6	Do. do. Cons. Mt. 1918	102½
6	Ill. Cent., 1 Mt., Chic. & S. 1898	—
7	Indianap. & Vin., 1 Mt. .. 1908	125
6	Do. do. 2 Mt. .. 1900	100½
6	Lehigh Val., Cons. Mt..... 1923	112½
—	Mexic. Cent., Ln. 2 Cons. Inc. —	5
7	N.Y. Cent. & H.R. Mt. Bonds 1903	119½
5	Do. Deb. 1904	111
6	Penns. Cons. S. F M. 1905	118
4	West Shore, 1 Mt. 2361	110

DITTO—GOLD.

Last Div.	NAME.	Price.
6	Alabama Gt. Sthn. 1 Mt. .. 1908	114
5	Do. Mid. 1 1928	90½
4	Allegheny Val. Gen. Mt. .. 1942	107
4	Atch., Top., & S. Fé Gn. Mt. 1995	89
3	Do. Adj. Mt............ 1995	58½
5	Do. Equipt. Tnst. ...... —	102½
5	Atlantic & Dan. 1 Mt...... 1950	96½
5	Baltimore & Ohio.......... 1925	97½
5	Do. Speyer's Tst. Recpts. 1925	96
5	Do. Cons. Mt. 1988	102½
4½	Do. 4½ p.c. 1 Mt. Term. 1934	82½
4½	Do. Brown Shipley's Dep. Cts. —	82½
5	Balt. Belt 5 p.c. 1 Mort..... 1990	90
4½	Balt. & Ohio S.W. 1 Mt. .. 1990	102½
4½	Do. 4½ p.c. 1 Cons. Mt. 1893 1993	78
—	Do. Inc. Mt. 5 p.c. Cl. A —	29½
—	Do. do. Cl. B —	10
5	Balt. & Ohio S.W. Term 5 p.c. 1942	97½
6	Balt. & Ptmac (Mn. L.) 1 Mt. 1911	124
6	Do. do. (Tunnel) 1 Mt. 1911	126
4	Beech Creek 1 Mt. 1936	109
5	Do 2 Mort. 1936	116
4	Carthage & Adiron 1 Mt... 1981	109

American Railroad Bonds—Gold (*continued*):—

Last Div.	NAME.	Price.
5	Cent. of Georgia 1 Mort. .. 1945	117½
5	Do. Cons. Mt. 1945	90½
5	Cent. of N. Jrsy. Gn. Mt... 1987	112½
6	Central Pacific, 1 Mort. 1898	102
6	Do. Speyer's Certs....... —	106
5	Do. Land Grant 1900	99
5	Chesap. & Ohio 1st Cons. Mt. 1939	113½
4½	Do. Gen. Mt............. 1992	80
6	Chic. & W. Ind. Gen. Mt. Skg. Fd. 1932	120
5	Chic. Mil. & St. Pl. (Chic. & L. Sup.) 1 Mt. 1921	114½
5	Do. Chic. & Pac. W. 1921	117½
5	Do. Wisc. & Minn. 1 Mt. 1921	114½
5	Do. Terminal Mt. 1914	114½
4	Do. General Mt. 1989	106½
5	Chic. St. L. & N. Orleans.. 1951	122½
4	Do. 1 Mort. (Memphis) .. 1951	105½
4	Clevel., Cin., Chic. & St. L., 1 Mt. (Cairo) 1939	90
4	Do. 1 Mt. (Cinc., Wab., & Mich.) 1991	90
4	Do. 1 Col. Tst. Mt. (S. Louis) 1990	96
4	Do. General Mt. 1993	82½
4½	Clevel. & Mar. Mt. 1935	109
4½	Clevel. & Pittsburgh 1942	116½
4½	Do. Series B. 1942	116½
—	Colorado Mid. 1 Mt. 1936	63½
—	Do. Bdhrs.' Comm. Certs. —	63½
4	Dnvr. & R. Gde. 1 Cons. Mt. 1936	91
5	Do. Imp. Mort.......... 1928	90
4	Detroit & Mack. 1 Lien 1995	92½
5	E. Tennes., Virg., & Grgia. Cons. Mt. 1956	111½
5	Elmira, Cort., & Nthn. Mt. 1914	100
4	Erie 1 Cons. Mt. Pr. Ln. .. 1996	89
3	Do. Gen. Lien 1996	70
6	Galvest., Harrisb., &c., 1 Mt.....	107½
5	Georgia, Car. & N. 1 Mt. .. 1929	96
4½	Gd. Rpds & Inda. Ex. 1 Mt. 1941	112½
5	Do. 1 Mt. (Muskegon) .. 1926	39½
3½	Illinois Cent. 1 Mt. 1951	104½
4	Do. 1952	105
4	Do. Cairo Bdge. .. 1950	102
4	Do. 1953	102
4	Do. General Mort. .. 1904	102½
5	Kans. City, Pitts. & G. 1 M. 1923	80
3½	L. Shore & Mich. Southern 1997	109
4½	Lehigh Val. N.Y. 1 Mt..... 1940	103½
5	Lehigh Val. Term. 1 Mt. .. 1941	109½
5	Long Island 1931	117½
5	Do. Deb.......... 1934	102
5	Do. (N. Shore Bch.) 1 Cons. Mt. 1932	94
6	Louisville & Nash. G. Mt.. 1930	120
6	Do. 2 Mt. Sk. Fd. (S. & N. Alabama........ 1910	107
6	Do. 1 Mt. N. Orl. & Mb. 1930	122½
5	Do. 1 Mt. Coll. Tst. ... 1931	102½
4	Do. Unified 1940	86
4½	Do. Mobile & Montgy. 1 Mt. 1945	105½
4	Manhattan Cons. Mt....... 1990	94
4	Mexican Cent. Cons. Mt. .. 1911	64½
—	Do. 1 Cons. Inc, ...	13
6	Mexican Nat. 1 Mt......... 1927	105½
3½	Do. 2 Mt. 6 p.c. Inc. A 1917	54
—	Do. do. B.. 1917	10
3	Do. Matheson's Certs.....	—
3	Michig. Cnt. (Battle Ck. & S.) 1 Mt. 1989	88
6	Minneap. & S. L. 1 Mt. Pacific Ext. 1921	117½
5	Do. 1 Consold......... 1934	104½
4	Minne., Slt. S. M. & A. 1 Mt. 1926	98
5	Minneapolis Westn. 1 Mt... 1911	105½
4	Miss. Kans. & Tex. 1 Mt... 1990	88
4	Do. 2 do. 1990	61
4	Mobile & Birm. Mt. Inc.... 1945	38
5	Do. P. Lien 1945	88
4	Mohawk & Mal. 1 Mt....... 1991	108
5	Montana Cent. 1 Mt. 1937	111½
5	Nashv., Chattan., & S. L. 1 Cons. Mt.................. 1928	102½
5	Nash., Flor., & Shff. Mt... 1937	95½
4	N. Y. & Putnam 1 Cons. Mt. 1993	108
5	N. Y., Brooklyn, & Man. B. 1 Cons. Mt............. 1935	107½
4	N. Y. Cent. & Hud. R. Deb. Certs. 1890 1905	105
4	Do. Ext. Debt. Certs.... 1905	103
7	N. Y., L. Erie, & W. 1 Cons. Mt. (Erie) 1920	139½
7	Do. 1 Con. Mt. Fd. Coup. 1920	137½
5	N. Y., Onto., & W. Cons. 1 Mt...................... 1939	110
4	Do. 4 p.c. Refund. Mt.. 1992	99
5	N. Y. & Rockaway B. 1 Mt. 1927	102½
6	Norfolk & West. Gn. Mt.... 1931	123
6	Do. Imp. & Ext........ 1934	118½
4	Do. 1 Cons. Mt........ —	79
6	N. Pacific Gn. 1 Mt. Ld. Gt. 1921	—
4	Do. P. Ln. Rl. & Ld. Gt. —	95
3	Do. Gn. Ln. Rl. & Ld. Gt. —	60
5	Oregon & Calif. 1 Mt....... 1927	77½
5	Oregon Rl. & Nav. Col. Tst. —	—
6	Panama Skg. Fd. Subsidy.. 1910	102½
4½	Pennsylvania Rlrd. 1913	113
4	Do. Equip. Tst. Ser. A.. 1914	104
4	Do. Cons. Mt............ 1943	112½
4½	Penna. Company 1st Mort. 1921	113
5	Perkiomen 1 Mrt., 2nd ser.. 1918	91½
4½	{ Pitts., C., C., & St. Ls. Con. Mt. G.B., Ser. A } 1940-2	111½
4	Do. Cons. Mort., Ser. D.. 1945	102½
6	Pittsbgh., Cle., & Toledo .. 1922	100½
4	Reading, Phil., & R. Genl. 1997	82
5	Richmond & Dan. Equip. .. 1909	97½
5	Rio Grande Junc. 1st Mort. 1939	94
4	Rio Grande West 1st Tst. Mt. 1939	82½
6	St. Joseph & Gd. Island .. 1925	—
7	S. Louis Bridge 1st Mort .. 1925	134½
5	S. Louis Mchts. Bdge. Term. 1st Mort................. 1930	102½

American Railroad Bonds (*continued*):

Last Div.	NAME.	Price.
4	S. Louis S. West 1st Mort.. 1989	75
—	Do. 4 p.c. 2nd Mort. Inc. 1989	30
—	S. Louis Term. Cupples Sta. & Prop. 1st. Mrt. 4½ p.c. 1902-17	102
4½	St. Paul Minn., & Manit. 1933	109
6	Do. do. 1933	132½
6	Shamokin, Sunbury, &c. 2 Mt. 1925	109
5	S. & N. Alabama Cons. Mt. 1936	97½
5	Southern 1 Cons. Coup. 1994	91
4	Do. E. Tennes Reorg. Lien .. 1938	100
6	S. Pacific of Cal. 1 Mt... 1205-12	110
4½	Trml. Assn. of S. Louis 1 Mt. 1939	110½
5	Do. 1 Cons. Mt.......... 1944	109
5	Texas & Pac. 1 Mt.......... 2000	100½
—	Do. 5 p.c. 2 Mt. Income 2000	30
5	Toledo & Ohio Cent. 1 Mt. West. Div. 1935	102½
4½	Toledo., Walhon., Val., & Ohio 1 Mt. 1931-3	111½
—	Union Pacific 1 Mt. 4 p.c. .. 1947	93
—	Union Pac., Linc., & Color. 1 Mt. 1918	—
4	United N. Jersey Gen. Mt... 1944	115½
6	Vicksbrg., Shrevept., & Pac. Pr. Ln. Mt. 1915	100½
5	Wabash 1 Mt. 1939	106½
4	Wn. Pennsylvania Mt. 1928	109½
5	W. Virga. & Pittsbg. 1 Mt. 1990	82½
5	Wheeling & L. Erie 1 Mt. (Wheelg. Div.) 5 p.c. 1928	90½
5	Do. Extn. Imp. Mt. 1930	90
—	Do. do. Brown Shipley's Cts..	—
5	Willmar & Sioux Falls 1 Mt. 1938	111

STERLING.

Last Div.	NAME.	Price.
6	Alabama Gt. Sthn. Deb..... 1906	104½
5	Do. Gen. Mort. .. 1927-8	99
5	Alabama, N. Orl., Tex. & Pac. 5 p.c. "A" Dbs... 1910-40	99
55/	Do. do. "B" do. 1910-40	52
—	Do. do. "C" do.	19
—	Allegheny Valley 1910	128½
4	Atlantic 1st Leased Line Perp...	98
6	Baltimore and Ohio........ 1902	107
6	Do. do. 1910	117½
5	Do. do. 1877........	96½
—	Do. Morgan's Certs. ..	96½
4½	Do. do. 1933	89½
6	Chicago & Alton Cons. Mt. 1903	112
5	Chic. St. Paul & Kan. City Priority	105
6	Eastn. of Massachusetts 1906	117½
5	Illinois Cent. Skg. Fd.	103
5	Do. 1905	108
3½	Do. 1950	99½
4	Do. 1 Mt. 1951	110
3	Do. 1 Mt. 1951	92½
6	Louisville & Nash., M. C. & L. Div., 1 Mt. 1902	104½
7	Do. 1 Mt. (Memphis & O.)...................... 1901	111
47/4	Mexican Nat. "A" Certs. 5 p.c. Non. cum.	45½
—	Do. "B" Certs....	10
6	N.Y. & Canada 1 Mt...... 1904	111½
6	N. York Cent. & H.R. Mort. 1903	112
4½	N. York, Penns., & Ohio Pr. Ln. Extd. 1935	—
5	Do. Equip. Tst.	103½
5	Do. 5 p.c. Equip. Tst. (1890)	103½
6	Nrthn. Cent. Cons. Gen. Mt. ..	106
6	Pennsylvania Gen. Mt. 1910	125
6	Do. Cons. Skg. Fd. Mt. 1905	113½
3½	Do. Cons. Mt.......... 1945	105½
6	Phil. & Erie Cons. Mort .. 1920	134½
6	Phil. & Reading Gen. Cons. Mort. 1911	126
6	Pittsbg. & Connells. Cons. 1926	116
—	Do. Morgan's Certs....	116
4	St. Paul., Min., & Manitoba (Pac. Extn.) 1940	96½
6	S. & N. Alabama 1903	107½
6	Un. N. Jersey & C. Gen. Mt. 1901	109½

FOREIGN RAILWAYS

Last Div.	NAME.	Paid.	Price.
4/	Alagoas, Ltd., Shs.......	20	4½
5	Do. Deb. Stk., Red. ..	100	42½
6	Antofagasta, Ltd., Stk. ..	100	68
4	Do. Perp. Deb. Stk. ..	100	89
—	Arauco, Ld., Ord. Shs. ..	10	½
—	Do. 10 p.c. Cum. Pref.	10	½
5	Argentine Gt. W., Ld.,	100	72
5	Do. 5 p.c. Cum. Pref. Shs.	100	100
4	Do. 1 Deb. Stk.	100	103
1/0/0	Argentine N.E., Ltd., 6 p.c. Cum. Pref. Stk. ..	100	10
—	Do. 5 p.c. Deb. Stk., Red.	100	29
2/	Arica and Tacna Shs. ..	20	1½
10/	Bahia & San Fcisco, Ld.,	20	9
6/	Do. Timbo. Bch. Shs.	20	4½
12/	Bahia, Blanca, & N.W. Ln. Prf. Cum. 6 p.c. ..	100	50
4	Do. 4 p.c. 1 Deb. Stk., Red.	100	93
6	Barranquilla R. & P., Ld., 6 p.c. 1 Deb. Stk., Red.	100	96

Foreign Railways (*continued*):—

Last Div.	Name.	Paid.	Price.
3/	Bilbao Riv. & Cantabn., Ltd., Ord.	3	5¾
—	Bolivar, Ltd. Shs.	10	1½
6	Do. 6 p.c. Deb. Stk.	100	96½
—	Brazil Gt. Southn. Ltd., 7 p.c. Cum. Pref.	20	1½
6	Do. Perm. Deb. Stk	100	39½
5½	B. Ayres Gt. Southn. Ld., Ord. Stk.	100	138
5	Do. Pref. Stk.	100	133
4	Do. Deb. Stk.	100	115
30/	B. Ayres & Ensen. Port., Ltd., Ord. Stk.	100	63
5	Do. Cum. 1 Pref. Stk.	100	121
6/0/0	Do. 6p.c.Con. Pref.Stk.	100	99
4	Do. Deb. Stk., Irred.	100	113
10⅜	B. Ayres Northern, Ltd., Ord. Stk.	100	265
12½	Do. Pref. Stk.	100	320
5	Do. 5 p.c. Mt. Deb.Stk., Red.	100	113
3/15/0	B. Ayres & Pac., Ld., 7 p.c. 1 Pref. Stk. (Cum.)	100	86
4	Do. 1 Deb. Stk.	100	100
5/5/0	Do. 4½ p.c. 2 Deb. Stk.,	100	89
3	B. Ayres & Rosario, Ltd., Ord. Stk.	100	66
—	Do. New, £20 Shs.	20	—
7/	Do. 7 p.c. Pref. Shs.	10	17
7/	Do. Sunchales Ext.	10	14½
4	Do. Deb. Stk., Red.	100	107
—	B. Ayres & Val. Trans., Ltd., 7 p.c. Cum. Pref.	20	6½
4	Do. 4 p.c. "A" Deb. Stk., Red.	100	71
—	Do. 6 p.c. "B" Deb. Stk. Red.	100	44
3/6	B. Ayres Westn. Ld. Ord.	10	10½
3/	Do. Def. Shs.	10	6½
5	Do. 5 p.c. Pref.	10	12½
4	Do. Deb. Stk.	100	106½
6	Cent.Arg.Deb.Sk. Rd.	100	160½
4	Do. Deb. Stk. Rd.	100	111
6	Cent. Bahia L. Ord. Stk.	100	42
	Do. Deb. Stk., 1934	100	72½
5	Do. Deb. Stk., 1937	100	58
3/6	Cent. Uguy. East. Ext. L. Shs.	10	5½
5	Do. Perm. Stk.	100	111
3/6	Do. Nthn. Ext. L. Sh.	10	4½
5	Do. Perm. Deb. Stk	100	105
3	Do. of Montev. Ltd., Ord. Stk	100	84
6	Do. Perm. Deb. Stk	100	140
10/	Conde d'Eu, Ltd. Ord.	20	7
—	Cordba & Rosar., Ltd., 6 p.c. Pref. Shs.	100	42½
4	Do. 1 Deb. Stk	100	91
7½	Do. 6 p.c. Deb. Stk	100	93
—	Cordba Cent., Ltd., 5 p.c. Cu. 1 Pref. Stk	100	83½
—	Do. 5 p.c. Non-Cum. 2 Pref. Stk	100	46
5	Do. Deb. Stk	100	119
—	Costa Rica, Ltd., Shs.	10	3½
8/	Dna. Thrsa. Chris., Ltd., 7 p.c. Pref. Shs.	20	4
20/	E. Argentine, Ltd	100	40
6	Do. Deb. Stk	100	104
1/1	Egyptn. Dlta. Lgt. Rys., Ltd., £10 Pref. Shs.	8	10½
—	Entre Rios, L., Ord. Shs.	5	¾
—	Do. Cu. 5 p.c. Pref.	5	2½
6/	Gt. Westn. Brazil, Ltd.,	20	9½
6	Do. Perm. Deb. Stk	100	90½
6	Do. Extn. Deb. Stk	100	76½
—	Int.-Oceanic Mex., Ltd., 7 p.c. Pref.	10	1½
4	Do. Deb. Stk	100	80
42/6	Do. 7 p.c. "A" Deb. Sk.	100	67
—	Do. 7 p.c. "B" Deb. Sk.	100	31
5/	La Guaira & Carac.	10	7½
5	Do. 5 p.c. Deb. Sk. Red.	100	100
8/4	Lembg.-Czern.-Jassy	30	24½
1/	Lima, Ltd.	20	2½
—	Manila Ltd. 7 p.c. Cu. Pf.	10	¾
20/6½	Mexican 2nd Pref. 6 p.c.	100	32
6	Do. Perp. Deb. Stk.	100	139
1/0/0	Mexican Sthrn., Ld., Ord.	100	23
—	Do. 4 p.c. 1 Db. Stk. Rd.	100	83
—	Do. 4 p.c. 2 do.	100	61
—	Mid. Urgy., Ltd.	100	18½
5	Do. Deb. Stk.	100	64
12/	Minas & Rio, Ltd.	20	9
5/2	Namur & Liege	20	12½
11/6	Do. Pref.	20	29
13/	Natal & Na. Cruz, Ld., 7 p.c. Cum Pref.	20	6
—	Nitrate Ltd., Ord.	10	5
—	Do. 7 p.c. Pr. Con. Or.	10	3½
—	Do. Def. Conv. Ord.	10	¾
7/	N.-E. Urgy., Ltd., Ord.	10	14½
7/	Do. 7 p.c. Pref.	10	14½
—	N.-W. Argentine Ld., 7 p.c. Pref.	10	2½
6	Do. 6 p.c. 1 Deb. Stk.	100	113
—	Do. 2 Deb. Stk.	100	94
—	N.W. Uruguay 6 p.c. 1 Pref. Stk.	100	17
—	Do. 5 p.c. 2 Pref. Stk.	100	7½
6	Do. 6 p.c. Deb. Stk.	100	80½
22/	Ottoman (Sm. Aid.)	20	14
—	Paraguay Cntl., Ld., 5 p.c. Perm. Deb. Stk.	100	11
—	Piræus, Ath., & Pelo.	275	1½
	Pto. Alegre & N. Hambg Ld., 7 p.c. Pref. Shs.	20	4
6	Do. Mt. Deb. Stk. Red.	100	77½
—	Puerto Cabello & Val. Ld.	10	1½
5	Recife & S. Francisco	100	68
14	R. Claro S. Paulo, Ld., Sh.	10	22½
5	Do. Deb. Stk.	100	125

Foreign Railways (*continued*):—

Last Div.	Name.	Paid.	Price.
5/	Royal Sardinian Pref.	10	12½
5/	Sambre & Meuse	20	18
5/6	Do. Pref.	10	12½
28/	San Paulo Ld.	20	34½
2/9½	Do. New Ord. £10 sh.	6	9½
2/	Do. 5 p.c. Non.Cm.Pref.	10	12
5½	Do. Deb. Stk.	100	133
5	Do. 5 p.c. Deb. Stk	100	127
—	S. Fé & Cordova, Gt. Sthn., Ld., Shares	100	50½
6	Do. Perp. Deb. Stk.	100	121
3/2½	S. Austrian	20	7
10/	Sthn. Braz. R. Gde. do Sul, Ld.	20	7½
6	Do. 6 p. c. Deb. Stk.	100	69½
4	Swedish Centl., Ld., 4 p.c. Deb. Stk.	100	107
5	Do. Pref.	100	100
1/9	Taltal, Ld.	5	2½
—	Uruguay Nthn., Ld. 7 p.c. Pfd. Stk.	100	8
3½	Do. 5 p.c. Deb. Stk.	100	30
—	Villa Maria & Rufino, Ld., 6 p.c. Pref. Shs.	100	20
4	Do. 4 p.c. 1 Deb. Stk.	100	74
6/0/0	Do. 6 p.c. 2 Deb. Stk.	100	47
5/9	West Flanders	8½	21
5/6	Do. 5½ p.c. Pref.	10	18
3/	Wstn. of Havana, Ld.	10	4½

FOREIGN RAILWAY OBLIGATIONS

Per Cent.	Name.	Price.
6	Alagoas Ld., 6 p.c. Deb., Rd.	81
—	Alcoy & Gandia, Ld., 5 p.c. Debs., Red.	25
5	Arauco., Ld., 5 p.c. 1st Mt., Rd.	62½
—	Do. 6 p.c. Mt. Deb., Rd.	42½
6	Brazil G. Sthn., L., Mt. Dbs., Rd.	80½
6	Do. Mt. Dbs. 1893, Rd.	48½
5½	Campos & Caran. Dbs., Rd.	75
6	Central Bahia, L., Dbs., Rd.	90½
5½	Conde d'Eu, L., Dbs., Rd.	76
6	Costa Rica, L., 1st Mt. Dbs., Rd.	107
6	Do. 2nd Dbs., Rd.	88
5	Do. Prior Mt. Db., Rd.	104
6	Cucuta Mt. Dbs., Rd.	101
5½	Donna Thrsa. Cris., L., Dbs., Rd.	68
3	Eastn. of France, £20 Dbs., Rd.	18½
4	Egyptn. Delta Light, L., Db., Rd	92½
—	Espito. Santo & Cara. 5 p.c. Stl. Dbs., Rd.	38
4	Gd. Russian Nic., Rd.	102
5	Inter-Oceanic Mex., L., 5 p.c. Pr. Ln. Dbs., Rd.	103
3	Ital. 3 p.c. Bds. A & B, Rd.	56½
—	Ituana 6 p.c. Debs., 1918	74
—	Leopoldina, 6 p.c. Dbs. £50 Bds.,	21
—	Do. do. Comms. Cert.	21
—	Do. 5 p.c. Stg. Dbs. (1888), Rd.	29
—	Do. do. Comm. Certs.	29
—	Do. 5 p.c. Stg. Dbs. (1890), Rd.	21
—	Do. do. Comms. Certs.	21
—	Macahé & Cam. 5 p.c. Dbs., Rd.	29
—	Do. do. Comms. Certs.	29
—	Do. (Cantagallo), 5 p.c., Red.	29
—	Do. do. Comm. Certs.	29
—	Manila Ltd., 6 p.c. Deb., Red.	23
6	Do. Prior Lien Mt., Rd.	101½
6	Do. Series "B," Rd.	80
7	Matanzas & Sab., Rd.	101½
6	Minas & Rio, L., 6 p.c. Dbs., Rd.	94
5	Mogyana 5 p.c. Deb. Bds., Rd.	103
5	Moscow-Jaros., Rd.	106½
5½	Natal & Na. Cruz Ltd., 5½ p.c. Debs., Red.	83
5	Nitrate, Ltd. Mt. Bds., Red.	79
3	Nthn. France, Red.	18½
4	N. of S. Af. Rep. (Trnsvl.) Gu. Bds. Red.	94½
3	Nthn. of Spain £20 Pri. Obs. Red.	7½
6	Ottmn. (Smy to A.) (Kujk) Asnt. Debs., Red.	109
6	Ottmn. (Seraik.) Asg. Debs. Red.	109
6	Ottmn. (Seraik) Non-Asg. D., Rd	109
5	Ottmn. Kuyjk. Ext. Red.	105
5	Ottmn. Serkeuy. Ext. Red.	101½
5	Ottmn. Tireh Ext. 1910	98
5	Ottmn. Debs, 1886, Red.	97
5	Do. 1888, Red. 1935	97½
5	Do. 1893, Red. 1935	99
5	Ottmn. of Anlia. Debs., Rd.	90½
5	Do. Ser. II	87
4	Ottomn. Smyr. & Cas. Ext. Bds., Red.	83½
3	Paris, Lyon & Medit. (old sys., £20), Red.	18½
3	Paris, Lyon & Medit. (new sys., £20), Red.	18½
50/	Piræus, At. & Pelp., 6 p.c. 1st Mt. Bds., Red.	89½
3	Do. 5 p.c. Mt. Bds., Red.	71
4	Pretoria-Pietbg., Ltd., Red.	93
7	Puerto Cab. & Val., Ltd., 1st Mt. Debs., Red.	86
—	Rio de Jano. & Nthn., Ltd., 6 p.c. £100 Deb., Red.	21
—	Rio de Jano. (Gr. Para.), 5 p.c. 1st Mt. St. £100 Debs., Red.	21
5	Royal Sardinian, A, Rd. £20	11½

Foreign Rly. Obligations (*continued*):—

Per Cent.	Name.	Price.
5	Ryl. Trns.-Afric. 5 p.c. 1st Mt. £100 Bds., Red.	61
7	Sagua La Grande, B pRd.	98
4	Sa. Fe & Cor. G.S., Ld. Pr Ln. Bds.	104
5	Sa. Fe, 5 p.c. 2nd Reg. Dbs.	80
3	South Austrian, £20 Red.	15
3	South Austrian, (Ser. X.)	14½
3	South Italian £20 Obs. (Ser. A to G), Red.	12
3½	S. W. of Venez. (Barq.), Ltd., 7 p.c. 1st Mt. £100 Debs.	55½
5	Taltal, Ltd., 5 p.c. 1st Ch. Debs., Red.	97
5	Utd. Rwys. Havana, Red.	84
3	Wtrn. of France, £20 Red.	18½
6	Wrn. B. Ayres St. Mt. Debs., 1902	108
6	Wrn. B. Ayres, Reg. Cert.	106½
5	Do. Mt. Bds.	122
6	Wtrn. of Havna., Ld. Mt. Dbs., Rd.	97
7	Wrn. Ry. San Paulo Red.	99
—	Wrn. Santa Fe, 7 p.c. Red.	38
2/8	Zafra & Huelva, 3 p.c. Red.	2½

BANKS.

Div.	Name.	Paid.	Price.
2/4½	Agra, Ltd.	6	3½
4/2½	Anglo-Argentine, Ltd., £	7	5½
8 fls.	Anglo-Austrian	120 f	13
6/	Anglo-Californian, Ltd., £20 Shares	10	11
4/	Anglo-Egyptian, Ltd., £	5	6
5/	Anglo-Foreign Bkg., Ltd.	7	8
7/	Anglo-Italian, Ltd.	5	7
7/6	Bk. of Africa, Ltd., £18½	6½	10
20/	Bk. of Australasia	40	49
10/	Bk. of Brit. Columbia	20	20½
25/	Bk. of Brit. N. America	50	64
20/	Bk. of Egypt, Ltd., £25	12½	19
5/	Bk. of Mauritius, Ltd.	10	9
18/	Bk. of N. S. Wales	20	38
4 p.c.	Bk. of N. Zland. Gua. Stk.	100	102
6/	Bk. of Roumania, £20 Shs.	6	7½
2/6	Tarapaca & Ldn., Ltd., £10	5	3½
—	Bque. Fse. de l'Afri. du S.	100 f	3½
f.22.50	Bque. Internatle. de Paris	20	23
6/	Brit. Bk. of S. America, Ltd., £20 Shares	10	10
15/	Capital & Cties., L., £50	10	39
16/	Chart. of India, &c.	20	32½
10/	City, Ltd., £40 Shares	10	20
18/	Colonial, £100 Shares	30	21
10/	Delhi and London, Ltd.	25	—
5/	German of London, Ltd.	10	10½
25/	Hong-Kong & Shanghai	28½	44½
4/	Imperl. of Persia	6½	3½
10/	Imperl. Ottoman, £20 Sh.	10	10½
12/	Intrnatl. of Ldn., Ld., £20	15	11½
20/	Ionian, Ltd.	25	15
16/	Lloyds, Ltd., £50 Shs.	8	30½
10/	Ldn. & Braziln. Ltd., £20	10	16½
44/	Ldn. & County, Ltd., £80	20	100½
9/	Ldn. & Hanseatic, L., £20	10	10½
22/6	Ldn. & Midland, L., £60	12½	53
8/9	Ldn. & Provin., Ltd., £10	5	22½
39/	Ldn. & Riv. Plate, L., £25	15	49
2/1½	Ldn. & San Fcisco, Ltd.	7	4½
28/	Ldn. & Sth. West., L., £50	20	68
26/	Ldn. & Westmins., L., £100	20	54½
5/	Ldn. of Mex. & S. Amer. Ltd., £10 Shs.	6	5½
15/	Ldn. Joint Stk., L., £100	15	33
12/9½	Ldn., Paris & Amer., L. £20	16	25
2/4½	Merchant Bkg., L., £9	4	2½
6/3	Metropn, Ltd., £50 Shs.	5	14½
9/	National, Ltd., £50 Shs.	10	19½
4/3	Natl. of Mexico, $100 Shs.	$40	13
1/3	National of N. Z., L., £7½	2½	2
8/	National S. Afric. Rep.	10	14½
18/10½	National Provcl. of Eng. Ltd., £75 Shs.	10½	50
21/7½	Do. do. £60 Shs.	12	57
6/6	North Eastn., Ltd., £20 Sh.	6	15
19/	Parr's, Ld., £100 Shs.	20	90
12/6	Prov. of Ireland, L., £100	12½	28½
40/	Stand. of S. Afric., L., £100	25	63
12/6	Union of Australia, L., £75	25	26
4 p.c.	Do. do. Ins. Stk. Dep. 1900	100	101
15/6	Union of Ldn., Ltd., £100	15½	35

BREWERIES AND DISTILLERIES.

Div.	Name.	Paid.	Price.
4½	Albion Prp. 1 Mt. Db. Sk.	100	111
4	All Saints', L., Db. Sk. Rd.	100	97
7	Allsopp, Ltd.	100	148
6	Do. Cum. Pref	100	156
4½	Do. Deb. Stk., Red.	100	116
3½	Do. Deb. Stk., Red.	100	101
4½	Alton & Co., L., Db., Rd	100	104
4½	Do. Mt. Bds., 1896	100	103
—	Arnold, Perrett, Ltd.	10	6
6	Do. Cum. Pref.	10	10

Breweries &c. (*continued*):—

Div.	Name.	Paid.	Price.
5½	Arrol, A., & Sons, L., Cum. Pref. Shs.	10	10
4½	Do. 1 Mt. Db. Stk., Rd.	100	104
5	Backus, 1 Mt. Db., Red.	100	59
4	Barclay, Perk., L., Cu. Pf.	10	11½
3½	Do. Mt. Db. Stk., Red.	100	110
—	Barnsley, Ltd.	10	12
6	Do. Cum. Pref.	10	14
1/3	Barrett's, Ltd	2½	1½
1/3	Do. 5 p.c. Pref.	2½	2½
3/	Bartholomay, Ltd.	10	3
8	Do. Cum. Pref.	10	8½
6	Do. Deb.	100	97½
5	Bass, Ratcliff, Ltd., Cum. Pref. Stk.	100	143½
4½	Do. Mt. Db. Stk., Rd.	100	125
4	Bell, J., L., 1 Mt. D. Stk., R	100	100
2/6	Benskin's, L., Cum. Pref.	5	—
4½	Do. 1 Mt. Db. Stk Red.	100	—
4½	Do. "B" Deb. Sk, Rd.	100	—
7/	Bentley's Yorks., Ltd.	10	11½
6/	Do. Cum. Pref.	10	12½
4½	Do. Mt. Debs., Red.	100	110
4½	Do. do. 1892, Red.	100	110
—	Bieckert's, Ltd.	20	2
5	Do. Debs., Red.	100	57
—	Birmingham., Ltd., 6 p.c. Cum. Pref.	5	2½
4½	Do. Mt. Debs., Red.	50	41½
5½	Boardman's, Ld., Cm. Pf.	10	8½
4½	Do., Perp. 1 Mt. Db. Sk.	100	106½
30/9	Brain & Co., Ltd.	100	101
4½	Brakspear, L., 1 D. Stk. Rd	100	109
4	Brandon's, L., 1 D. Stk. R.	100	105½
21/	Bristol (Georges) Ltd.	10	46
6	Do. Cum. Pref.	10	18
5	Do. Mt. Db. Sk. 1888 Rd.	100	115½
17/6	Bristol United, Ltd.	10	35
6	Do. Cum. Pref.	10	16½
4½	Do. Db. Sk. Rd.	100	126
5½	Buckley's, L., C. Pre-prf.	10	10½
4½	Do. 1 Mt. Db. Stk. Rd.	100	106½
4	Bullard & Sns, L., D. Sk. R.	100	105
6	Bushell, Watk., L., C. Pf.	10	14
4½	Do. 1 Mt. Db. Sk. Rd.	100	112
5	Camden, Ltd., Cum. Pref.	10	11½
4½	Do. 1 Mt. Db. Sk. Rd.	100	108
5½	Cameron, Ltd., Cm. Prf.	10	13½
4½	Do. Mort Deb. Stk.	100	108
3½	Do. Perp Mt. Db. Sk.	100	100½
5	Cam'bell, J'stone, L., C. Pf.	5	5
4½	Do. 4½ p.c. 1 Mt. Db. Sk.	100	105
4	Campbell, Praed, L., Per. 1 Mort. Deb. Stk.	100	106
4	Cannon, L., Mt. Db. Stk.	100	109
4	Do. "B" Deb. Stk.	100	104
5	Castlemaine, L., 1 Mt. Db.	100	94
3½	Charrington, Ltd., Mort. Deb. Stk. Red.	100	106
2/	Cheltnhm. Orig., Ltd.	5	7
6	Do. Cum. Pref.	5	7½
4	Do. Debs. Red.	100	106
10/	Chicago, Ltd.	10	3
6	Do. Debs.	100	84½
—	Cincinnati, Ltd.	10	½
—	Do. Cum. Pref.	10	1
10/	City of Baltimore	10	4
16/	Do. 8 p.c. Cum. Pref	10	8
14/	City of Chicago, Ltd.	10	1½
8	Do. Cum. Pref.	10	6
13	City of London, Ltd.	100	205½
5	Do. Cum. Pref.	100	137
4	Do. Mt. Deb. Stk., Rd.	100	112½
2/	Colchester, Ltd.	5	4½
7	Do. Pref.	5	6½
4½	Do. Deb. Stk., Red.	100	109
5	Combe, Ltd., Cum. Pref.	10	14
4	Do. Mt. Db. Stk, Rd.	100	110
3½	Do. Perp. Deb. Stk.	100	107
5	Comm'cial, L., D. Sk., Rd.	100	107½
5	Courage, L., Cm. Pref. Shs.	100	137½
4	Do. Irr. Mt. Deb. Stk.	100	125
3½	Do. Irr. "B" Mt. Db. Sk.	100	104
8/	Daniell & Sons, Ltd.	10	8
7	Do. Cum. Pref.	10	12½
4½	Do. 1 Mt. Perp. Db. Sk.	100	108½
4½	Do. "B" Deb. Stk.	100	102
10d.	Dartford, Ltd.	5	5½
9/9	Do. Cum. Pref.	5	5½
4	Do. 1 Mt. Db. Sk. Rd.	100	99
4	Davenport, Ld., 1 D. Stk.	100	102½
10/	Denver United, Ltd.	10	3½
8	Do. Cum. Pref.	10	7½
6	Do. Debs.	100	96½
4½	Deuchar, L., 1 D. Sk., Rd.	100	106
8/	Distillers, Ltd.	10	23½
4½	Do. Mt. Db. Stk., Rd.	100	115½
—	Dublin Distillers, Ltd.	5	1½
3/	Do. Cum. Pref.	5	4½
4½	Do. Irr. Deb. Stk.	100	—
5	Eadie, Ltd., Cum. Pref.	10	11
4	Do. Irr. 1 Mt. Db. Sk.	100	107
10/	Edinbgh. Utd., Ltd.	10	13
6	Do. Cum. Prf.	10	13½
5	Do. 1 Mt. Dbs.	100	110½
4	Eldridge, Pope, L. D. St. R.	100	107
—	Emerald & Phœnix, Ltd.	10	1½
8	Do. Cum. Pref.	10	4½
6	Empress Ltd., C. Pf.	10	11½
4½	Do. Mt. Deb. Stk.	100	105
10/	Farnham, Ltd.	10	16½
6	Do. Cum. Pref.	10	14½
4	Fenwick, L., 1 D. Sk., Rd.	100	103
4	Flower & Sons, Irr. D. Sk.	100	111
4	Friary, L., 1 Db. Stk., Rd.	100	103½
4	Do. 1 "A" Db. Sk., Rd	100	100
4½	Groves, L., 1 Db. Sk., Rd.	100	110
14	Guinness, Ltd.	100	589
6	Do. Cum. Prf. Stk.	100	189½
5	Do. Deb. Stk., Red.	100	122
5	Hall's Oxford L., Cm. Pf.	5	5½
6/	Hancock, Ld., Cm. Pf. Ord.	10	14
[illegible]	Do. Def. Ord.	10	17½

Breweries, &c. (continued):—

Div.	Name.	Paid.	Price.
6	Hancock, Ld., Cum. Pref.	10	14
4	Do. 1 Deb. Stk., Rd.	100	112
5	Hoare, Ltd. Cum. Pref.	10	12½
5	Do. "A" Cum. Pref.	10	12½
4	Do. Mt. Deb. Stk., Rd.	100	111
3½	Do. do. do. Rd.	100	104
3/6	Hodgson's, Ltd.	5	9½
5	Do. 1 Mt. Db., Red.	—	120½
4	Do. 2 Mt. Db., 1906	—	102
4½	Hopcraft & N., Ltd., 1 Mt. Deb. Stk., Red.	100	103
5	Huggins, Ltd., Cm. Prf.	10	—
4½	Do. 1st D. Stk. Rd.	100	—
4½	Do. "B" Db. Stk. Rd.	100	—
12/	Hull, Ltd.	10	17
7	Do. Cum. Prf.	10	14½
4½	Ind, Coope, L., D. Sk., Rd.	100	118
4	Do. "B" Mt. Db. Stk. Rd.	100	111
8/	Indianapolis, Ltd.	10	3½
8	Do. Cm. Prf.	10	9
5/	Jones, Frank, Ltd.	10	3½
7½	Do. Cum. Pref.	10	7½
5	Do. 1st Mort. Debs.	100	90½
3/	J. Kenward & Ct., Ltd.	5	5½
4½	Kingsbury, L., 1 D. Sk., Rd	100	—
4	Lacon, L., D. Stk., Red.	100	110
4	Do. Irrd. "B" D. Sk.	100	106
4/	Lascelles, Ltd.	5	11
6	Do. Cum. Pref.	5	7½
5	Leney, Ltd., Cum. Pref.	10	11½
4	Do. 1 Mt. Db. Stk. Rd.	100	102
30/7½	Lion, Ltd., £25 shares	17	49½
10/9½	Do. New £10 shares	6	17
6	Do. Perp. Pref.	20	33
4	Do. B. Mt. Db. Sk. Rd.	100	107
4½	Lloyd & Y., Ltd., 1 Mt. Deb. Stk., Rd.	100	100½
4½	Locke & S., Ltd., Irr. 1st Mt. Deb. Stk.	100	101
4½	Lovibond, Ltd., 1st Mt. Deb. Stk., Rd.	100	102½
30/4	Lucas & Co., Ld., Deb. Stk.	100	107
8/	Manchester, Ltd.	10	19½
7	Do. Cum. Pref.	10	17
5	Marston, J., L., Cm. Prf.	10	10½
4	Do. 1 Mt. Db. Sk., Rd.	100	101½
9/	Massey's Burnley, Ltd.	10	17
6	Do. Cum. Pref.	10	14½
4½	McCracken, Ltd., 1 Mt. Deb., 1908	100	59½
5	McEwan, Ltd., Cm. Pref.	10	14
5	Meux, Ltd., Cum. Pref.	10	14
4	Do. Mt. Db. Stk. Red.	100	111
4½	Michell & A., Ltd., 1 Mt. Deb. Stk. Red.	100	105
4½	MileEndDist. Db. Sk. Rd.	100	111
—	Milwaukee & Chic., Ltd.	10	1½
4/	Do. Cum. Pref.	10	5½
4½	Michell, Toms, L., Db.	50	57
6	Morgan, Ltd., Cum. Pref.	10	14½
10/	Nalder & Coll., Ltd.	10	35
6	Do. Cum. Pref.	10	15½
4½	Do. Deb. Red.	100	112
12/	Newcastle, Ltd.	10	19½
6	Do. Cum. Pref.	10	14½
5	Do. 1 Mt. Deb., 1911	100	111½
4	Do. "A" Deb. Stk. Red.	100	104
6	New England, Ltd	10	4½
8	Do. Cum. Pref.	10	9½
6	Do. Debs. Red.	100	101½
4	New London, L., 1 D. Sk.	100	103
7/2	New Westminster, Ltd.	4	10½
2/4½	Do. Pref.	4	6½
—	New York, Ltd.	10	1
—	Do. 8 p.c. Cum. Pref.	10	4½
6	Do. 1 Mt. Deb. Red.	100	77½
5	Noakes, Ld., Cum. Pref.	10	11½
4	Do 1 Mt. Db. Stk., Rd.	100	104
4½	Norfolk, L., "A" D. Sk. Rd.	100	106
10/	Northampton, Ld.	10	16½
7	Do. Cum. Pref.	10	16
6	Do. Cum. Pref.	10	12½
5	Do. 1 Mt. Per. Db. Sk.	100	126
4	Nth. East., L., 1 D. Sk. Rd.	100	102
4½	N. Worcesters., L. Per. 1 Mort. Deb. Stock	100	97½
6	Nottingham, L., Cm. Prf.	10	1½
5	Do. 1 Mt. Deb. Stk., Red.	100	114
17/4	Do. "B" do. Red.	50	112
6/	Ohlsson' Cape, Ld.	5	17
7	Do. Cum. Pref.	5	9
4½	Do. 2nd Cum. Pref.	5	5½
5	Do. Deb. Stk., Red.	100	114
4½	Oldfield, L., 1 Mt. Db. Stk.	100	106
6	Page & Overt., L., Cm. Prf.	10	13½
4½	Do. 1 Mt. Dbs, Red.	100	109
10/	Parker's Burslem, Ltd.	10	24½
6	Do. Cum. Pref.	10	14½
4	Do. 1 Mt. Db. Stk., Red.	100	111
4	Persse, Ld., 1 Mt. Db. Rd.	100	95½
4	Phipps, L., Irr. 1 Db. Stk.	100	113
8	Plymouth, L., Min. Cu. Pf.	10	13½
4½	Do. Mt. Deb. Stk., Red.	100	104½
4½	Pryor, Reid, L., 1 D.S., R.	100	103½
5	Reid's, Ld., Cm. Pref. Stk.	100	137½
4	Do. Mt. Deb. Stk., Red	100	110
3½	Do. "B" Mt. Db. Stk., Rd	100	102
5	Rhondda Val., L., Cu. Pf	10	11
4½	Do. 1 Mt. Deb. Stk., Rd	100	109
5	Robinson, Ld., Cum. Pref.	10	11½
4½	Do. 1 Mt. Perp. Db. Stk.	100	112
4/	Rochdale, Ltd.	10	6
4½	Do. 1 Mt. Deb. Stk.	100	93½
7	Royal, Brentford, Ltd.	10	21½
	Do. Cum. Pref.	10	15
4½	Do. 1 Mt. Dbs. Red	100	107
6/	St. Louis, Ltd.	10	7½
8	Do. Cum. Pref.	10	8½
14/	St. Pauli, Ltd.	10	10
7	Do. Cum Pref.	10	12
4½	Salt (T.), L., 1 Db. Sk. Rd.	100	110
4½	Do. "B" D. Stk. Red	100	107
—	San Francisco, Ltd	10	½
—	Do. 8 p.c. Cum. Pref.	10	½

Breweries, &c. (continued):—

Div.	Name.	Paid.	Price.
4½	Savill Brs., L., D. Sk. Rd.	100	118
4½	Scarboro., Ltd., 1 Db. Stk.	100	101
4	Shaw (Hy.), Ltd., 1 Mt. Db. Stk., Red.	100	104
22/	Showell's, Ltd.	10	32½
7	Do. Cum. Pref.	10	17½
3/	Do. Gun. Shs.	5	7½
4½	Do. Mt. Db. Stk., Red.	100	—
4	Simonds, L., 1 D. Sk., Rd.	100	111
5½	Simson & McP., L., Cu. Pf.	10	9½
4½	Do. 1 Mt. Deb. Stk.	100	99
5/	Smith, Garrett, L., £20 Shs	10	16½
5	Do. Cum. Pref.	20	26
3½	Do. 3½ p.c. Mt. Db. Stk.	100	107
5	Smith's, Tadcster, L., CPf	10	12
4½	Do. Deb. Stk., Red.	100	112
4	Do. Deb. Stk. Red.	100	108
4½	Star, L., 1 M. Db. Stk., Rd.	100	105
4	Steward & P., L., 1 D. Sk.	100	111
9/	Strettons Derby, Ltd.	10	13
6	Do. Cum. Pref.	10	13½
4	Do. Irr. 1 Mt. Db. Stk.	100	103½
4½	Strong, Romsey, L., 1 D. S.	100	115
5	Stroud, L., Db. Sk., Rd.	100	111½
4½	Tadcaster To'er, L., D. Sk.	100	113
8/	Tamplin, Ltd	10	21
6	Do. Cum. Pref.	100	15
4	Do. "A" Db. Sk., Rd.	10	107
6	Thorne, Ltd., Cum. Pref.	10	14
4	Do. Deb. Stk., Red.	100	103½
15/	Threlfall, Ltd.	10	46
6	Do. Cum. Pref.	10	16½
5	Do. 1 Mt. Dbs., Red.	100	116
4	Tollemache, L., D. Sk. Rd.	100	105
4	Truman, Hanb., D. Sk., R.	100	110
3	Do. "B" Mt. Db. Sk., Rd.	100	95
10/	United States, Ltd.	10	9
8	Do. Cum. Pref.	10	11
6	Do. 1 Mt. Deb.	100	105½
6/	Walker & H., Ld., Cm. Prf.	10	11
4½	Do. 1 Mt. Deb. Stk., Red.	100	107
5	Walker, Peter, Ld. Cm. Prf.	10	13½
4	Do. 1 Mt. Dbs, Red.	100	111
4	Wallingford, L., D. Sk. Rd.	100	107
6	Watney, Ld., Cm. Prf. Sk.	100	167
5	Do. Mt. Db. Sk., Rd.	100	115½
4½	Do. "B" Mt. Db. Sk., Rd.	100	111
3½	Do. Mt. Db. Stk.	100	101
5	Watney, D., Ld., Cm. Prf.	10	12½
4½	Do. 1 Mt. Db. Stk.	100	106
10/	Webster & Sons, Ltd.	10	16½
6	Do. Cum. Pref.	10	14
5	Wenlock Ltd Pref.	10	12½
4	Do. 1 Mt. Db. Sk., Rd.	100	107
5	West Cheshire, L., Cu. Pf.	10	10½
4	Do. Irred. 1 Mt. Db. Sk.	100	99
4½	Whitbread, L., Cu. Pf. Sh.	100	124½
4	Do. Db. Stk., Red.	100	110
3½	Do. "B" Db. Stk., Rd.	100	101
9/	Wolverhmpton & D. Ld.	10	17
6	Do. Cum. Pref.	10	13½
4½	Do. 1 Mt. Dbs., Red.	100	108
5½	Worthington, Ld., Cm. Prf.	10	15½
5½	Do. Cum. "B" Pref.	10	13½
4½	Do. Mt. Db. Sk., Rd.	100	113
3½	Do. Irr. "B" Db. Stk.	100	102
10/	Yates's Castle, Ltd.	10	13½
5	Do. Cum. Pref.	10	11
5	Younger W., L., Cu. Pf. Sh.	100	132½

CANALS AND DOCKS.

Last Div.	Name.	Paid.	Price.
4	Birmingham Canal	100	142½
—	E. & W. India Dock	100	20½
—	Do. 4 p.c. Prf. Stk.	100	74
—	Do. P.L. Deb. Stk.	100	100
—	Do. Cons. Deb. Stk.	100	90
40/	G. Junction Ord. Shs.	100	151½
6/	Do. do. Pref.	10	19
4½	King's Lynn Per. Db. Stk.	100	116½
2½	Leeds & L'pool Canal	100	71
2½	Lndn & St. Kath. Dks.	100	55
4½	Do. Pref.	100	136½
4½	Do. Pref., 1878	100	132½
4½	Do. Pref., 1882	100	130
4	Do. Deb. Stk.	100	134½
—	Mchester Ship C. 5 p.c. Pf.	10	1½
3½	Do. 1st Perp. Mt. Deb.	100	98
—	Milford Dks. Db. Stk. "A"	100	18½
3½	Millwall Dk.	100	59
5	Do. Perp. Pref.	100	140½
4½	Do. Pref.	100	105½
5	Do. New Per. Prf., 1887	100	126½
5	Do. Per. Deb. Stk.	100	152½
4/	Newhaven Har.	10	14½
2½	N. Metropolitan	100	66
5	Sharpness Nw. Pf. "A" Sk.	100	144½
4	Do. Deb. Stk.	100	118½
5	Sheffield & S. Yorks Nav. 4½ p.c. Pref Stk.	100	115½
36.432	Suez Canal	20	124
7	Surrey Comcl. Dok., Ord.	100	149½
7	Do. Min. 4 p.c. Pref. "A"	110	150
5	Do. Pref. "B"	100	148½
5	Do do. "C"	100	148½
5	Do. do. "D"	100	144½
4½	Do Deb. Stk.	100	152½

COMMERCIAL, INDUSTRIAL, &c.

Last Div.	Name.	Paid.	Price.
5	Accles, L., 1 Mt. Db., Red.	100	84½
2/6	Aërated Bread, Ltd.	1	12½
—	African Gold Recovery, L.	1	½
2/	Aluminium, L., "A" Shs.	1	2
4½	Do. 1 Mt. Db. Stk., Red.	100	97
5½	Amelia Nitr., L., 1 Mort Deb., Red.	100	82½
7/	Anglo-Chil. Nitrate, Ltd., Cum. Pref.	10	6½
4½	Do. Cons. Mt. Bds., Red.	100	79½
4½	Anglo-Russian Cotton, Ld., 1 Charge Debs., Red.	100	98
11/3	Angus (G., & Co., L.), £10	7½	17
6/	Apollinaris, Ltd.	10	11½
5/	Do. 5 p.c. Cum. Pref.	10	10½
4	Do. Irred. Deb. Stock	100	104
5/	Appleton, French, & S., L.	5	½
3/	Argentine Meat Pres., L., 7 p.c. Pref.	10	2½
5	Argentine Refinry, Db. Rd.	100	98
6d.	Armstrong, Whitw., Ltd.	1	3½
4	Do. Cum. Pref.	5	6½
5	Artisans', Labr. Dwllgs., L.	100	131½
4½	Do. Non-Cm. Prf., 1879	100	132½
4½	Do. do. 1884	100	132½
—	Asbestos & Asbestic, Ltd.	10	7½
2/7½	Ashley-grdns., L., C. Prf.	5	6½
4½	Do. 1 Mt. Deb. Stk.	100	112½
5/	Assam Rly. & Trdng., L., 8 p.c. Cum. Pref. "A"	10	15
—	Do. Deferrd. "B" Shs.	1	4
—	Do. do. (iss. f. pd)	1	3½
8/	Do. Cum. Pre-Prf. "A"	10	14½
6/	Do. New Pref.	10	11½
5	Do. Debs., Red.	100	107
5	Do. Ref. Mort. Debs.	100	109
6	Aust'lian Pastrl, L., Cu. Pf.	10	7
8d.	Aylesbury Dairy, Ltd.	1	1½
4	Do. 4 p.c. Mt. Dbs.	100	104½
10/	Babcock & Wilcox, Ltd.	10	30
6	Do. 6 p.c. Cm. Prf.	10	16
8	Baker (Chs.), L., Cm. Pf.	5	8½
8	Do. "B," Cm. Pref.	5	8
8d.	Barker (John), Ltd.	1	2½
5½	Do. Cum. Pref.	5	7½
4½	Do. Irred. 1 Mt. Db. Stk.	100	130
—	Barnagore Jute, Ltd.	5	3
5	Do. Cum. Pref.	5	4½
7½d.	Belgravia Dairy, Ltd.	1	1½
5/6	Bell (R.) & Co., Ltd.	5	3½
1/	Bell's Asbestos, Ltd.	1	½
5	Do. Mt. Db. Bds., Rd.	100	107
10/	Bengal Mills, Ltd.	10	11
6/	Do. 5 p.c. Cum. Prf.	10	10½
2/5	Benson (J. W.) L., Cm. Pf.	10	10½
4	Do. Perp. Mt. Db. Stk.	100	101
6	Bergvik, L., 6 p.c. Cm. Pf.	10	12½
12/	Do. Dfd.	10	9½
4½	Do. 1 Dbs., Red.	100	103½
5/	Birm'ham Vinegar, Ltd.	5	14½
5	Do. Cum. Pref.	5	5½
4½	Do. 1 Mt. Db. Stk., Rd.	100	109½
5	Boake (A.) L., 5 p.c. Cu. Pf.	10	10½
2/6	Bodega, Ltd.	5	8½
4½	Do. Mt. Deb. Stk., Rd.	100	111
8/	Bottomley & Brs., Ltd.	10	6½
6/	Do. 6 p.c. Pt.	10	9½
8½d.	Bovril, Ltd.	1	½
1/0½	Do. Def.	1	½
6½d	Do. Cum. Pref.	1	1
4½	Do. Deb. Stk.	100	100
5/	Bradbury, Gretrex., Ltd., £10 share	8	14
5/	Do. 5 p.c. Cum. Pref.	10	13½
5/	Brewers' Sugar, L., 5 p.c. Cum. Pref.	10	10½
3/6	Brighton Grd. Hotel, Ld.	5	3½
4	Do Mt. Db. Stk., Red.	100	100½
5	Bristol Hotel & Palm. Co., Ltd. 1st Mt. Red. Deb.	100	105
9½d.	British & Bengton's. Tea Tr. Asc., Ltd.	1	1½
5	Do. Cum. Prf.	5	5½
—	British Deli & Lgkat. Tobacco, Ltd.	1	½
—	Do. Cum. Prf.	1	½
—	British Tea Table, Ltd.	1	2½
5½	Do. Cum. Pref.	1	1½
2/6	Brooke, Ben., & Co., Ltd., Cum. Pref.	5	5½
7/6	Brooke, Bond & Co., Ltd.	5	20
3/	Brown Brs., L., Cum. Pref.	5	5½
10/	Browne & Eagle, Ltd.	10	13½
5	Do. Cum. Pref.	10	13
4	Do. Mrt. Db. Sk., Red.	100	110
20/	Brunner, Mond, & Co., Lt.	0	41
7/	Do. £10 shares	3½	17
7	Do. Cum. Pref.	10	18
7	Do. £10 shares	5	8½
10/	Bryant & May, Ltd.	5	20
3/	Bucknall, H., & Sons, Lt.	5	7
6	Do. Cum Pref.	5	7½
4/	Burke, E. & J., Ltd.	5	7½
6	Do. Cum. Pref.	5	7½
6	Do. Irred. Deb. Stk.	100	155
1/	Burlington Htls. Co., Ltd	1	1½
5	Do. Cum. Pref.	1	1
4	Do. Perp. Deb. Stk.	100	106½
5	Bush, W. J., & Co., Ltd., Cum. Pref.	5	5½
4	Do. 1 Deb. Stk., Red.	100	102
5½	Callard, Stewart, & Watt, Ltd., Cum. Pref.	1	1½
4/	Callender's Cable L., Shs.	5	9½
4½	Do. 1 Deb. Stk., Red.	100	111½
—	Campbell, R., & Sons, Lt.	3	2½
6	Cantareira Water, Bd., Rd	100	99½
5	Do. (2nd issue)	100	90
4	Cartavio Sugar, Ltd., 6 p.c. 1st Debs., Red.	90	82½
9/	Cassell & Co., Ltd., £10	9	15½
5	Causton, Sir J., & Sons, Ltd., Cum. Pref.	10	13½

Commercial, &c. (continued):—

Last Div.	Name.	Paid.	Price.
4	Cent. Prod. Mkt. of B.A. 1st Mt. Str. Debs.	100	81
4	Chappell & Co., Ltd., Mt. Deb. Stk. Red.	100	100
6/	Chicago & N.W. Gran. 8 p.c. Cum. Pref.	10	3
—	Chicago Packing & Prov.	10	6
8	Do. Cum. Pref.	10	10½
6/	City Offices, Ltd	36½	17
3½	Do. Mt. Deb. Stk.	100	108½
7/2½	Cy. London Real Prop., Ltd., £25 shs.	12	19
4/6	Do. £12½ shs.	7½	13½
3½	Do. Deb. Stk. Red.	100	106½
3½	Do. Deb. Stk. Red.	100	105½
3	Do.	100	100½
4/	Cy. of Santos Imprvts., Ltd., 7 p.c. Pref.	10	8½
20/			
8	Clay, Bock, & Co., Ltd.	10	6
6	Do. Cum. Pref.	10	10
20/	Do. Mort. Deb.	100	103½
6	Coats, J. & P., Ltd.	10	55
4½	Do. Cum. Pref.	10	17½
9½d	Do. Deb. Stk. Red.	100	112½
4	Coburg Hotel, Ltd	1	1½
6	Do. Deb. Stk. Red.	100	102
4½	Colonial Consign & Dis., Ltd., Cum. Pref.	5	4½
—	Do. 1st Mort. Debs.	100	96½
4/	Colorado Nitrate, Ltd.	5	½
5	Co. Gen. des Asphtes. de F., Ltd.	6	6½
5	Do, Non-Cm. Prf.	—	5½
5	Cook, J. W., & Co., Ltd., Cum. Pref.	5	5½
5	Cook, T., & Son, Egypt, Ltd., 1st Mt. Deb. Red.	100	111½
—	Cork Co., Ltd., 6 p.c. Cum. Pref.	5	2
5	Cory, W., & Sn, L., Cu. Pf.	5	6½
4	Do. 1st Deb. Stk. Red.	100	108
8½d.	Crisp & Co., Ltd	1	1½
5½	Do. Cum. Pref.	1	1½
—	Crompton & Co., Ltd., 7 p.c. Cum. Pref.	5	2½
5	Do. 1st Mt. Reg. Deb.	—	90½
4/6	Crossley, J., & Sons, Ltd.	5	8½
5	Do. Cum. Pref.	5	6½
—	Crystal Pal. Ord. "A" Stk.	100	7½
—	Do. "B" Red. Stk	100	1½
6	Do. 6 p.c. 1st 1887 Deb. Stk. Red.	100	117½
—	Do. 6 p.c. 2nd 1887 Deb. Stk. Red.	100	46½
—	Do. 6 p.c. 3rd 1887 Deb. Stk. Red.	100	22½
3	Do. 3 p.c. 1st 1893 Deb. Stk.	100	93½
—	Daimler Motor, Ltd	10	9
4/	Dalgety & Co., £20 Shs.	5	5½
4½	Do. Deb. Stk.	100	123
4	Do.	100	115
7/	De Keyser's Ryl. Htl., L.	10	14
5	Do. Cum. Pref.	10	11½
4	Do. Deb. Stk., Red.	100	110
6	Denny, H., & Sons, Ltd., Cum. Pref.	10	14½
5/3	Devas, Routledge & Co., L.	7	8½
5	Dickinson, J., & Co., L., Cum. Pref. Stk.	100	123
4½	Domin. Cottn. Mls., Ltd. Mt. Stg. Dbs.	100	97
6/	Dorman, Long & Co., L.	5	4½
—	Eastmans, Ltd	10	2½
12/	Do. 8 p.c. Cum. Pref.	10	10½
2/6	E. C. Powder, Ltd.	3	5½
1/6	Edison & Swn Utd. Elec. Ltd., "A" £5 Shs.	3	2½
2/6	Do. fully-paid	5	4½
4½	Ekman Pulp & Ppr. Co., Ltd., Mt. Deb., Red.	100	96
1/1½	Electric Construc., Ltd.	2	2½
7	Do. Cum. Pref.	2	3½
2½/	Eley Bros., Ltd.	15	38
—	Elmore's Cop. Deptg., L.	1	½
—	Elmore's Wire Mnfg., L.	2	½
—	Elysée Pal. Hotel Co., L.	5/	½
5 p.c.	Do. 5 p.c. £100 Db., Rd.	70	97½
8½d.	Evans, Ben., & Co., Ltd.	1	1
5	Do. 1 Mt. Db. Sk., Rd.	100	108
1/5½d.	Evans., D. H., & Co., L.	1	2½
6	Do. Cum. Pref.	1	1½
4½	Do. 1 Mt. Db. Sk., Rd.	100	112
2/1	*Evening News*, L., 5 p.c. Cum. Pref.	5	5½
5/3	Evered & Co., L., £10 Sh.	7	12½
7/6	Do.	10	18½
4	Fairbairn Pastoral Co., Aust., L., 1 Mt. Db., Rd.	100	102
6	Fairfield Shipbldg., Ltd., Cum. Pref.	10	10½
4½	Do. Mort. Deb. Stk.	100	109½
6/	Farmer & Co., Ld., 6 p.c. Cum. Pref.	10	13½
10	Field, J. C. & J., Ltd.	10	10
14/	Do. 7 p.c. Cum. Pref.	10	14
1/3	Fordham, W. B., & Sns, Ld.	1	2
5/6	Forest. Warehouse, Ltd.	11	9½
4	Do. Regd. Debs., Rd.	100	103½
3/6	Foster, M. B. & Sons, Ltd.	4	6
5	Do. Pref.	10	11½
9/	Foster, Porter, & Co., L.	10½	15½
4	Fowler, J., & Co. (Leeds), Ltd., 1 Mt. Deb., Red.	100	103½
3/	Fraser & Chalmers, Ltd.	3	2
4½	Free, Rodwell & Co., Ltd., Deb Stk.	100	104½
6½d.	Furness, T., & Co., Ltd., 5½ p.c. Cum. Pref.	1	½
4½	Garside & Co. (of Manchstr), L., 1 Mt. Db. Sk.	100	112
11	Genl. Hydraul Power, L.	100	275

Commercial, &c. (*continued*):—

Last Div.	Name.	Paid.	Price.
8/	Gillman & Spencer, Ltd.	5	2¼
6	Do. Pref.	5	4¼
5	Do. Mort. Debs.	50	51
4	Goldsbro., Mort & Co., L., "A" Deb. Stk., Red.	100	73½
—	Do. 3 p.c. "B" Inc. Deb. Stk., Red	100	14
8/	Gordon Hotels, Ltd.	10	19½
5½	Do. Cum. Pref.	10	14½
4½	Do. Perp. Deb. Stk.	100	137½
4	Do. do.	100	122½
—	Greenwich Inld. Linoleum Co., Ltd.	1	½
7	Greenwood & Batley, Ltd., Cum. Pref.	10	10
7½d.	Hagemann & Co., Ltd., 6 p.c. Cum. Pref.	1	1
—	Hammond, Ltd.	10	¼
—	Do. 8 p.c. Cum. Pref.	10	2½
—	Do. 6 p.c. Cum. Inc. Stk. Red.	100	45
	Hampton & Sons, Ltd., 4 p.c. 1 Mt. Db. St. Red.	100	105
—	Hans Crescent Htl., L., 6 p.c. Cum. Pref.	5	3
4	Do. 1 Mt. Deb. Stk.	100	90
6d.	Harmsworth, Ld., Cm. Pf.	1	1⅛
4/	Harrison, Barber, Ltd.	5	4½
3/	Harrod's Stores, Ltd.	1	4½
2/6	Do. Cum. Pref.	5	7½
5½	Hawaiian Comcl. & Sug. 1 Mt. Debs.	100	91½
5	Hazell, Watson, L., C. P.	10	12
18/	Henley's Teleg., Ltd.	10	22
7	Do. Pref. Shs.	10	19
4½	Do. Mt. Db. Stk., Rd.	100	112½
6	Henry, Ltd.	10	12½
5	Do. Cum. Pref.	10	13½
4½	Do. Mt. Debs., Red.	50	53
6	Hepworth, Ld., Cm. Prf.	10	11
1/4½	Herrmann, Ltd.	1	½
—	Hildesheimer, Ltd.	3	1½
1/2½	Holbrn. & Frasca, Ltd.	1	1½
5	Do. Cum. Pref.	10	11½
4	Do. Deb. Stk.	100	113
6	Home & Col. Stres, L., C. P	5	7½
6	Hood & M.'s Stres., Ltd., Cum. Pref.	1	½
6	Hook, C. T Ltd.	10	6
7/2	Hornsby, Ltd., £10 Shs.	8	3
5/6	Do. 6 p.c. Cm. Pf. Sk.	100	90
—	Hotchks. Ordn., Ltd.	10	1
—	Do. 7 p.c. Cm. Prf	10	4
5	Do. 1 Mt. Dbs., Rd.	100	96½
6	Htl. Cecil, Ld., Cm. Prf.	5	4
4	Do. 1 Mt. D. Sk., R.	100	105½
8/	Heward & Bulgh, Ltd.	10	38
6	Do. Pref.	10	16
4	Do. Deb. Stk., Red.	100	108
5/	Howell, J., Ltd., £5 Shs.	4	9
—	Howell & Js., Ld., £3½ Shs.	3	½
1/6	Humber, Ltd.	1	½
6	Do. Cum. Pref.	1	¾
5/6	Hunter, Wilts., Ltd.	5	7
2/7	Hyam Clthg., Ltd., 5 p.c. Cum. Pref.	5	5½
10/	Impl. Russn. Cotton, L.	5	6
5	Impd. Industl. Dwgs., Ld.	100	130½
6d.	Do. Defrd.	1	1½
23/	Impd. Wood Pave., Ltd.	10	15½
15/	Ind. Rubber, Gutta Per. Telegraph Works, Ltd.	10	21½
4	Do. 1 Mt. Debs., Red.	100	104
6	Intern. Tea, Cum. Pref.	5	6½
10½d.	Jays, Ltd.	1	1½
5½	Do. Cum. Pref.	5	6½
1/2½d.	Jones & Higgins, Ltd.	1	2½
4½	Do. 1 Mt. Db. Sk., Rd.	100	113
5/	Kelly's Directory, Ltd., 5 p.c. Cum. Pref.	10	12½
4	Do. Mort. Db. Sk., Rd.	100	106
—	Kent Coal Explrtn. Ltd.	1	½
9½d.	King, Howmann, Ltd.	1	1½
4/	Kinloch & Co., Ltd.	5	8½
6	Do. Pref.	5	7
5	Lady's Pictorial Pub., Ltd., Cum. Pref.	5	5
—	La Guaira Harb., Ltd., 7 p.c. Deb. Stk.	100	—
—	Do. 2 Mt. 7 p.c. Deb. Bds., Red.	100	—
4/	Lagunas Nitrate, Ltd.	5	1½
2/	Lagunas Syn., Ltd.	5	1
5	Do. 1 Mt. Debs., Red.	100	78½
—	L. Copais Ld., 1 Mt. 6 p.c. Debs., Red.	100	35½
3/	Lautaro Nitrate, Ltd.	5	4
5	Do. 1 Mt. Debs., Red.	—	100
9/	Lawes Chem. L., £10 shs.	9	5½
14/	Do. N. Cm. Min. Pref.	10	12½
—	Leeds Forge, 7 p.c. Cm. Pf.	5	3½
5	Do. 1 Mt. Debs., Red.	50	47
5	Lever Bros., L., Cm. Pf.	10	13½
6	Liberty, L., 6 p.c. Cm. Pf.	10	15
20/	Liebig's, Ltd.	20	75
5	Lilley & Sk., L., Cm. Pf.	5	5½
39/4	Linoleum Manftg Ltd.	5	16
3/	Linotype, Ltd., Pre	5	5½
5/	Do. Def.	5	7½
4/	Lister & Co., Ltd.	10	4
5	Do. Cum. Pref.	10	8½
5/	Liverpool. Nitrate	5	5
—	Liverpool. Warehsg., Ltd	10	3½
5½	Do. Cum. Pref.	10	8½
4	Do. 1 Mt. Db. Stk., Rd.	100	105
5½	Lockharts, Ltd., Cm. Pf.	1	1½
4/6	Ldn. & Til. Lightrage £10	9	6½
6/	Ldn. Comcl. Sale Rms., L.	10	17½
3	Do. 1 Mt. Deb. Stk., Red.	100	103
3	London Nitrate, Ltd.	5	1½
4/	London Nitrate, Ld. 8 p.c. Cm. Min. Pf.	5	3½
8/	London Pavilion, Ltd.	5	6½

Commercial, &c. (*continued*):—

Last Div.	Name.	Paid.	Price.
2/6	London. Produce Clg. Ho., Ltd., £10 Shares	2½	3½
4/	London Stereos., Ltd.	5	3
6d.	Ldn. Un. Laun. L. Cm. Pf.	1	½
8½d.	Louise, Ltd.	1	½
5½	Do. Cum. Pref.	1	½
5/	Lovell & Christmas, Ltd.	5	11½
6	Do. Cum. Pref.	5	7½
4	Do. Mt. Deb. Stk., Red.	100	107
1/3	Lyons, Ltd.	1	4
4½	Do. 1 Mt. Deb., Stk., Rd.	100	111½
10/	Machinery Trust, Ltd.	5	14
4½	Do. 4½ Deb. Stk.	100	104
6	MacLellan, L., Min. C. Pf.	10	9½
5	Do. 1 Mt. Debs., 1900	100	101½
—	McEwan, J. & Co, Ltd.	10	1½
6	Do. Mt. Debs., Red.	100	89½
8	McNamara, L., Cm. Pref.	10	9
7½d.	Maison Virot, Ltd.	1	1½
2/7	Do. 6 p.c. Cum. Pref.	5	4½
5/	Manbré Sacc., L., Cm. Pf.	10	12
10/	Mangan Brze., L., £10 Shs.	6	15½
2/	Mason & Mason, Ltd.	5	2½
6	Do. Cum. Pref.	5	5½
—	Maynards, Ltd.	1	½
6	Do. Cum. Pref.	1	½
9½d.	Mazawattee Tea, Ltd.	1	1½
5	Do. Cum. Pref.	5	5½
6	Mellin's Food Cum. Pref.	5	6½
4½	Met. Ascn. Imp. Dwlgs. L.	100	110
3½	Do. 1 Mt. Deb. Stk.	100	97
5	Metro. Indus. Dwlgs., Ltd.	5	5
4	Do. do. Cum. Pref.	5	5½
5	Metro. Prop., L., Cm. Pf.	5	5½
4½	Do. 1st Mt. Debs. Stk.	100	108½
6	Mexican Cotton 1 Mt. Db.	100	93½
4½	Mid. Class Dwlgs., L., Db.	100	120½
1/	Millars' Karri, Ltd.	1	3½
6	Do. Cum. Pref.	1	1½
5/	Milner's Safe, Ltd.	10	20½
20/	Moir & Son, Ltd., Pref.	5	8½
6	Morgan Cruc., L., Cm. Pf.	10	14½
2/	Morris, B., Ltd.	3½	3½
2/6	Murray L. 5½ p.c. C. Pf.	5	5½
63/4½	Do. 4½ 1 Mt. Db. Sk. Rd.	100	106
—	Natnl. Dwlgs., L., 5 p.c. Pf.	5	1
1/7½	Nat. Safe Dep., Ltd.	4	3½
6	Do. Cum. Pref.	1	1½
—	Native Guano, Ltd.	5	½
—	Nelson Bros., Ltd.	10	2½
5	Do. Deb. Stk., Red.	100	80½
4/	Neuchtel Asph., Ltd.	10	10½
—	New Central Borneo, Ld.	1	—
10d.	New Darvel Tob., Ltd.	18/	1½
1/6	New Explosives, Ltd.	3	3½
5/3½	New Gd. Htl., Bham, L.	5	4
5½	Do. Pref.	5	4½
4	Do. 1 Mt. Db. Stk., Rd.	100	96½
—	New Julia Nitrate, Ltd.	10/	⅛
—	New Ldn. Borneo Tob., L.	16/	½
1/6	New Premier Cycle, Ltd.	1	½
6	Do. 6 p.c. Cum. Pref.	1	½
4½	Do. 4½ p.c. 1 Mt. Db. Rd	100	—
—	New Tamargl. Nitr., Ltd	1	⅛
—	Do. 8 p.c. Cum. Pref.	1	½
6	Do. 6 p.c. 1 Mt. Dbs. Rd.	100	62½
3'78d.	Newnes, G., L., Cm. Prf.	1	1½
1/3	Nitr. Provision, Ltd.	2½	½
24/	Nobel-Dynam., Ltd.	10	18½
—	North Brazn. Sugar, Ltd.	1	½
15/	Oakey, Ltd.	10	31
6	Do. Cum. Pref.	10	17
—	Paccha Jazp. Nitr., Ltd.	5	½
5	Pac. Borax, L., 1 Db. Rd.	100	110
—	Palace Hotel, Ltd.	10	5½
5½	Do. Cum. Pref.	10	8½
4	Do. 1 Mt. Deb. Stk.	100	104
2/6	Palmer, Ltd.	5	1½
6	Do. Cum. Pref.	5	2½
1/2½d	Paquin, Ltd.	1	1
6	Do. Cum. Pref.	5	4½
5½	Parnall, Ltd., Cum. Pref.	1	½
4/6	Pawsons, Ltd., £10 Shs.	6	6½
4	Do. Mt. Debs., Red.	100	106
6	Pearks, G. & T., Ltd., 6 p.c. Cum. Pref.	1	½
9½d.	Pears, Ltd.	1	1½
6	Do. Cum. Pref.	10	14½
5	Do. Deb. Stk.	100	129
5½	Pearson, C. A., L., Cu. Pf.	5	5½
4/3	Peebles, Ltd.	5	7½
5	Do. Cum. Pref.	5	6½
4½	Do. Mt. Deb. Stk. Red.	100	113½
5½	Peek Bros., Ltd., 1 Cum. Pref., Nos. 1-60,000	5	6
3½	Do. 3½ p.c 1 Db. Stk.	100	103½
7½d.	Pegamoid, Ltd.	1	½
—	Phospho-Guano, Ltd.	5	2½
—	Pillsbury-W. Fl. Mills, L.	10	1½
16/	Do. 8 p.c. Cum. Pref.	10	6½
6	Do. 1 Mort. Debs.	100	95½
9½d.	Plummer, Ltd.	1	1½
5	Do. Cum. Pref.	5	5½
7/6	Price's Candle, Ltd.	16	35
6	Priest Marians, L., Cm. Pf.	1	1½
6	Pryce Jones, Ld., Cm. Pf.	5	7½
5	Do. Deb. Stk.	100	122
8½d.	Pullman, Ltd.	1	1½
6d.	Do. Cum. Pref.	1	1½
11¼d.	Raleigh Cycle, Ltd.	1	½
6	Do. Cum. Pref.	1	½
—	Recife Drnge. Ld. 1 Mt. Debs., '??	100	19
6	Redfern, Ltd. Cum. Prf.	10	14
5	Ridgways, Ltd., Cu. Pf.	5	5½
—	R. Janeiro Cy. Imps. Ld.	25	8½
5	Do. Debs.	100	86½
5	Do. 1882-1893	100	86½
11/	R. Jan Fl. Mills, Ltd.	7	6½
5	Do. 1 Mt. Debs., Rd.	100	94
—	Riv. Plate Meat, Ltd.	5	3½
—	Do. Pref.	5	5
8½d.	Roberts, J. R., Ltd.	1	1½

Commercial, &c. (*continued*):—

Last Div.	Name.	Paid.	Price.
5	Roberts 1 Mt. D. Sk., Rd.	100	112
1/4½	Roberts, T. R., Ltd.	1	2½
5	Do. Cum. Pref.	1	1½
3/	Rosario Nit., Ltd.	5	3½
5	Do. Debs., Red.	100	103
5	Do. Huara, Debs.	—	104
1/	Rover Cycle, Ltd.	1	½
6/	Ryl. Aquarium, Ltd.	5	4½
6	Do. Pref.	5	6
5	Ryl. Htl., Edin., Cm. Pf.	1	1½
1/2½	Ryl. Niger, Ltd., £10 Sh.	2	3
6/	Do.	10	15½
—	Russian Petroleum	10	22
—	Do. 6½ p.c. Cm. Prf.	10	11
3/	Ruston, Proctor, Ltd.	10	12
4½	Do. 1 Mort. Debs.	100	104
6/	Sadler, Ltd.	12	7
—	Sal. Carmen Nit., Ltd.	5	4
9d.	Salmon & Gluck., Ltd.	1	1 5/16
	Salt Union, Ltd.	10	1½
1½	Do. 7 p.c. Pref.	10	6
4½	Do. Deb. Stk.	100	101½
4½	Do. "B" Deb. Sk., Rd.	100	97½
—	San Donato Nit., Ltd.	5	½
2/6	San Jorge Nit., Ltd.	5	3½
—	San Pablo Nit., Ltd.	5	½
—	San Sebastn. Nit., Ltd.	5	½
1/9	Sanitas, Ltd	1	2½
—	Sa. Elena Nit., Ltd.	5	½
—	Sa. Rita Nit., Ltd.	5	1½
5/	Savoy Hotel, Ltd.	10	16
7	Do. Pref.	10	14
4	Do. 1 Mt. Deb. Stk.	100	111½
5	Do. Debs., Red	100	102½
5	Do. & Ldn. For. Htl., Ltd., 5 p.c. Debs. Red.	100	99
1½d.	Schweppes, Ltd.	1	1 1/16
—	Do Def.	1	⅜
5	Do. Cum. Pref.	1	1½
4	Do. Deb. Stk.	100	108
1/	Singer Cyc., Ltd.	1	½
5½	Do Cum. Pref.	1	½
—	Smokeless Pwdr., Ltd.	1	½
5½d.	S. Eng. Dairies, Ltd., 6 p.c. Cum. Pref.	1	1½
—	Sowler Thos. L.	1	1
3/4½	Do. 5½ Cm. Pf.	5	5½
4/6	Spencer, Turner, & Co. Ltd	5	8½
5	Do. Cum. Pref.	5	6½
5	Spicer, Ld., 5 p.c. Dbs. Rd.	100	65
4/	Spiers & Pond, Ltd.	10	22½
5	Do. 1 Mt. Debs., Red.	100	117½
5	Do. "A" Db. Stk., Rd.	100	111
5	Do. "B" 1 Db. Stk., Rd.	100	111
4	Do. Fd. "C" 1 Db. S., R.	100	104
7/6	Spratt's, Ltd	5	12½
4	Do. Debs., 1914	—	105
5	Steiner Ld., Cm. Pf.	10	11½
4	Do. 1 Mt. Db. Sk. Rd.	100	106
9/	Stewart & Clydesdale, L.	10	14
6	Do. Cum. Pref.	10	15
35/5	Sulphide Corp.	100	80
1/	Swan & Edgar, L.	1	1½
1/	Sweetmeat Automatic, L.	1	4
2/9	Teetgen, Ltd., Cum. Pref.	5	6
24/	Teleg. Construction., Ld.	12	36½
5	Do. Db. Bds., Rd., 1899	100	103½
3/0½	Tilling, Ld. 5½ p.c. Cm. Prf.	5	6½
4	Do. 4 p.c. 1 Dbs., Rd.	—	104
8½d.	Tower Tea, Ltd.	1	1½
5	Do. Cum. Pref.	5	5½
5	Travers, Ltd., Cum. Pref.	10	12½
4	Do. 1 Mt. Dbs., Rd.	100	105
6	Tucuman Sug., 1 Dbs., Rd.	100	100
4/	United Alkali, Ltd.	10	1½
7	Do. Cum. Pref.	10	7½
5	Do. Mt. Db. Stk., Rd.	100	109½
2½d.	United Horse Shoe, Ltd., Non-Cum. 8 p.c. Pref.	1	⅛
5	Un. Kingm. Tea, Cm. Prf.	5	4½
2/	Un. Lankat Plant., Ltd.	1	2
4/	Un. Limmer Asphlte., Ld.	3	4½
13/	Val de Travers Asph., L.	10	15½
3/	V. den Bergh's, L., Cm. P.	5	6½
6	Walkers, Park., L., C. Pf.	10	3
4½	Do. 1 Mt. Debs., Red.	100	90½
6/	Wallis, Thos. & Co., Ltd.	5	14
6	Do. Cum. Pref.	5	8½
5½	Waring, Ltd., Cum. Pref.	5	5½
4½	Do. 1 Mt. Db. Sk., Red.	100	112
4½	Do. Irred. "B" Db. Stk.	100	105
12/	Waterlow, Dfd. Ord.	10	14½
4/	Do. Pref.	10	14½
3½	Do. Cum. Pref.	10	10½
10/	Waterlow Bros. & L., Ld.	10	9
5	Do. Pref.	10	12½
1/2½	Welford, Ltd.	1	2
4½	Do. Debs., Red.	100	108
1/	Welford's Surrey Dairies, Ltd.	1	1½
7½d.	West London Dairy, Ltd.	1	1
4½	Wharncliffe Dwllgs, L., Pf.	10	11½
18/10	Do. 3 p.c. Irr. Mt. Db. Sk.	100	96
6d.	White, A. J., Ltd.	1	½
6	Do. 6 p.c. Cum. Pref.	1	⅝
4	White, J. Bazley, Ltd., 1 Mort. Debs., Red.	100	99½
5	White, R., Ltd., 1 Mort. Deb. Stock, Red.	100	104½
11/	White, Tomkins, Ltd	10	11½
5	Do. Cum. Pref.	10	11½
6	White, W. N., L., Cm. Pf.	1	1
2/6	Wickens, Pease & Co., L.	5	3½
6	Wilkie, Ltd., Cum. Pref.	10	15½
4/	Willans & Robinson, Ltd.	5	8
6	Do. Cum. Pref.	5	7½
4½	Do. 1 Mt. Db. Stk., Red.	100	108
7½d.	Williamsons, L., Cm. Prf.	1	1½
6	Winterbottm. Book Cloth, Ltd., Cum. Prf.	10	15
3/	Yates, Ltd.	5	6½
6	Do. Cum. Pref.	5	6½
	Young's Paraffin, Ltd.	4	1½

CORPORATION STOCKS—COLONIAL AND FOREIGN.

Per Cent.	Name.	Paid.	Price.
6	Auckland City, '72 1904-24	100	118
6	Do. Cons., '79, Red. 1930	100	138½
5	Do. Deb. Ln., '83..1934-8	100	117
6	Auckland Harb. Debs.	100	111½
5	Do. 1917	100	111
5	Do. 1936	100	116
5½	Balmain Boro' 1914	—	115
5	Boston City (U.S.)	100	102½
5	Do. ..1902	100	105
5	Brunswick Town 5. c. Debs. 1916-20	100	111
15/	B. Ayres City 6 p.c.	100	55
4½	Do. 4½ p.c.	100	74
5	Cape Town, City of	100	113
4	Do. ..1943	100	116
4	Chicago, City of, Gold 1915	—	108
6	Christchurch 1926	100	131½
—	Cordoba City	100	17½
5	Duluth (U.S.) Gold ..1926	—	110
6	Dunedin (Otago) 1925	100	127½
6	Do. 1906	100	113
5	Do. Consols..1908	100	111
4	Durban Insc. Stk. 1944	100	111
4	Essex Cnty., N. Jersey 1926	$100	114½
5	Fitzroy, Melbrne. ..1916-19	100	110
5	Gisborne Harbour 1915	100	110½
4	Greymouth Harbour ..1925	100	110
4	Hamilton 1934	100	108
5	Hobart Town 1918-30	100	116
4	Do. 1940	100	107
4½	Invercargill Boro. Dbs. 1936	100	111
6	Kimberley Boro., S.A. Dbs.	—	102
4	Launceston Twn. Dbs. 1916	100	107
6	Lyttleton, N.Z., Harb. 1929	100	125
4	Melbourne Bd. of Wks. 1921	100	107
5	Melb. City Debs. 1897-1907	100	107½
4½	Do. Debs. 1908-27	100	113½
4	Do. Debs. ..1915-20-22	100	108
5	Melbne. Harb. Bds., 1908-9	100	112
4½	Do. do. 1915	100	110
4	Do. do. 1918-21	100	105
4½	Melbrne. Tms, Dbs. 1914-16	100	113
4½	Do. Fire Brig. Db. 1921	100	108
5	Mexico City Stg.	100	88
4	Moncton N. Bruns. City	100	103
4½	Montevideo	100	59
5	Montreal Stg.	100	104
5	Do. 1874	100	104
5	Do. 1879	100	106
3½	Do. 1933	100	104
3	Do. Perm. Deb. Stk	100	98
4	Do. Cons. Deb. Stk. 1932	100	113
6	Napier Boro. Consolid. 1914	100	119
5	Napier Harb. Debs. ..1920	100	115
5	Do. Debs. ..1928	100	107
6	New Plymouth Harb. Debs. 1909	100	108
6	New York City 1901	—	107½
3½	Do. 1910-26	—	103½
4½	Nth. Melbourne Debs. 1-600 1921	100	105
5	Oamaru Boro. Cons. ..1920	100	101
6	Do. Harb. Bds. (Reg.)	100	74
25/	Do. 6 p.c. (Bearer)..1919	100	35
6	Otago Harb. Deb. Reg.	100	103
6	Do. 1877	100	107
6	Do. 1881 1921	100	115
5	Do. Debs. ..1921	100	107
5	Do. Cons. ..1934	100	105
6	Ottawa City	100	111
6	Do. 1904	100	113½
4½	Do. Debs. ..1913	100	108½
6	Port Elizabeth Waterworks	100	111
5	Port Louis	100	111
5	Prahran Debs. 1917	100	109
4	Do. Debs. 1919	100	102
6	Quebec C. Coupon. 1875 1905	100	112
6	Do. do. 1878 1908	100	116
4½	Do. Debs. 1914-18	100	108
4	Do. Debs. 1923	200	108
3½	Do. Cns. Rg. Stk., Red.	100	101
5	Richmond (Melb.) Dbs. 1917	100	112
4	Rio Janeiro City	100	57
4	Rome City	100	—
4	Do. 2nd to 8th Iss.	100	92
—	Rosario C.	100	26½
—	Do.	100	26½
4	St. Catherine (Ont.) ..1926	100	101
4	St. John, N.B., Debs. 1934	—	103
4½	St. Kilda (Melb) Dbs. 1918-21	100	105
4	St. Louis C. (Miss.)..1911	100	106
4	Do. 1913	100	103½
3'65	Do. 1915	—	110
—	Santa Fé City Debs.	100	21
6	Santos City	100	95
6	Sofia City	100	83
5	Sth. Melbourne Debs. 1915	100	111
4½	Do. Debs. 1919	100	107
5	Sydney City 1904	100	109
4	Do. Debs. 1912-13	100	107
4	Do. do. (1894) ..1919	100	109
7	Timaru Boro. 7 p.c. .. 1910	100	126½
5	Timaru Harb. Debs 1914	100	107
5	Do. Debs. ..1916	100	106
6	Toronto City Wtwks 1904-6	100	114
6	Do. Cons. Debs. ..1898	100	101
5	Do. G. Cns. Dbs. 1919-20	100	118
4	Do. Strlg. 1922-8	100	107
4	Do. Local Improv.	100	102
3½	Do. 1929	100	104
5½	Valparaiso	100	100
4	Vancouver 1931	100	107
4	Do. 1932	100	108
6	Wanganui Harb. Dbs. 1905	100	110
6	Wellington Con. Deb. 1907	100	117
6	Do. Improv., 1879	100	123
6	Do. Wtrwks. Dbs., 1880	100	123
4½	Do. Debs., 1893....1933	100	116
4½	Wellington Harb. 1907	100	104
4	Westport Harb. Dbs. 1925	100	110
6	Winnipeg City Deb. ..1907	—	118
5	Do. 1914	100	119

FINANCIAL, LAND, AND INVESTMENT.

Last Div.	Name.	Paid.	Price.
5	Agency, Ld. & Fin. Aust., Ltd., Mt. Db. Stk., Rd.	100	90½
	Amer. Frehld. Mt. of Lon., Ld., Cum. Pref. Stk.	100	87½
4½	Do. Deb. Stk., Red.	100	93
1/	Anglo-Amer. Db. Cor., L.	2	1
4	Do. Deb. Stk., Red	100	106½
5½	Ang.-Ceylon & Gen. Est., Ltd., Cons. Stk.	100	55
6	Do. Reg. Debs., Red.	100	102½
—	Ang.-Fch. Explorn., Ltd.	1	2
6	Do. Cum. Pref.	1	1⅛
—	Argent. Ld. & Inv., Ltd. £1 Shares	10/	nil
—	Do. Cum. Pref.	4	1¾
1/	Assets Fnders.' Sh., Ltd.,	4	1¾
6/	Assets Realiz., Ltd., Ord.,	5	8¾
5	Do. Cum. Pref.	5	6½
26/	Austrln. Agricl £25 Shs.	21½	63½
—	Aust. N. Z. Mort., Ltd., £10 Shs.	1	1½d.
4½	Do. Deb. Stk., Red.	100	90½
4	Do. Deb. Stk., Red.	100	82½
4½	Australian Est. & Mt., L., 1 Mt. Deb. Stk., Red.	100	104
5	Do. "A" Mort. Deb. Stk., Red.	100	96
2/6	Australian Mort., Ld., & Fin., Ltd. £25 Shs.	5	4
1/6	Do. New, £25 Shs.	3	3
4	Do. Deb. Stk	100	110½
3	Do. Do.	100	85
5	Bengal Presidy. 1 Mort. Deb., Red.	100	106
25/	British Amer. Ld. "A"	1	19
—	Do. "B"	24	7
1/7½	Brit. & Amer. Mt., Ltd. £10 Shs.	2	½
5/	Do. Pref.	10	10
4	Do. Deb. Stk., Red.	100	103
1/3	Brit. & Austrlsn Tst Ln., Ltd. £25 Shs.	2½	⅜
4½	Do. Perm. Debs., Red.	100	103
1½d.	Brit. N. Borneo. £1 Shs.	15/	11/16
2½d.	Do.	1	1
—	Brit. S. Africa	1	2⅞
5	Do. Mt. Deb., Red.	—	96
6	B. Aires Harb. Tst., Red.	100	96
12/6	Canada Co.	1	26
—	Canada N. W. Ld., Ltd.	$25	83½
—	Do. Pref.	$100	$50½
4	Canada Perm. Loan & Sav. Perp. Deb. Stk.	100	99½
—	Curamalan Ld., 1 Mt. 7 p.c. Bds., Red.	—	94½
3/7½	Deb Corp., Ld., £10 Shs	4	3
5	Do. Cum. Pref.	10	11½
4	Do. Perp. Deb. Stk.	100	112
9d.	Deb. Corp. Fders' Sh., Ld.	3	⅜
4/5 7/10	Eastn. Mt. & Agncy, Ld., "A"	10	5½
4½	Do. Deb. Stk., Red.	100	100
5	Equitable Revers. In. Ltd.	100	—
2/6	Exploration, Ltd.	1	1 5/16
/6d.	Freehold Trst. of Austria. Ltd. £10 Shs.	1	¾
4	Do. Perp. Deb. Stk.	100	100
—	Genl. Assets Purchase, Ltd., 5 p.c. Cum. Pref.	10	—
70/	Genl. Reversionary, Ltd.	100	—
3½	Holborn Vi. Land	100	105
3½	House Prop. & Inv.	100	85½
13/	Hudson's Bay	13	20
—	Hyderabad (Deccan)	5	3
4	Impl. Col. Fin. & Agcy. Corp.	100	94½
4½	Impl. Prop. Inv., Ltd., Deb. Stk., Red.	100	91½
2/6	Internatl. Fincial. Soc., Ltd. £7½ Shs.	2½	1½
4	Do. Deb. Stk., Red.	100	99½
1/9½	Ld. & Mtge. Egypt, Ltd. £18 Shs.	3	2¾
5	Do. Debs., Red.	100	103
4½	Do. Debs., Red.	100	102
—	Ld. Corp. of Canada, Ltd.	1	⅜
4½	Ld. Mtge. Bk. of Texas Deb. Stk.	100	—
3½	Ld. Mtge. Bk. Victoria 4½ p.c. Deb. Stk.	100	78
2/9½	Law Debent. Corp., Ltd., £10 Shs.	2	1⅜
4½	Do. Cum. Pref.,	10	12
4	Do. Deb. Stk.	100	112
—	Law Land, L., 4½ Cm. Prf.	5	5½
1/	Ldn. & Australasian Deb. Corp., Ltd., £4 Shs.	2	½
4½	Do. 4½ p.c. Mt. Deb. Stk., Red.	100	99
1/9	Ldn. & Middx. Frhld. Est. £2 Shs.	35/	3
2/6	Lndn. & N. Y. Inv. Corp., Ltd.	5	1⅜
5	Do. 5 p.c. Cum. Pref.	10	8½
1/6	Ldn. & Nth. Assets Corp., Ltd., £2 Shs.	1½	⅜
2	Ldn. & N. Deb. Corp., L.	2	1½
3/6	Ldn. & S. Afric. Explrn. Ltd.	½	13½
2/	Mtge. Co. of R. Plate, Ltd. £10 Shs.	2	3½
4½	Do. Deb. Stk., Red.	100	112
4½	Morton, Rose Est., Ltd., 1st Mort. Debs.	—	101
6/6	Natal Land Col. Ltd.	10	7
4/	Do. 8 p.c. Pref., 1870	5	8
5/6	Natl. Disct. L., £25 Shs.	5	10½
4½	New Impl. Invest., Ltd. Pref. Stk.	100	62½
	New Impl. Invest., Ltd. Def. Stk.	100	9
3½	N. Zld. Assets Real Deb	100	99

Financial, Land, &c. (*continued*) :—

Last Div.	Name.	Paid.	Price.
4	N. Zld. Ln. & Mer. Agcy., Ltd Prf. Ln, Deb. Stk	100	94
2/6	N. Zld. Tst. & Ln. Ltd., £25 Shs.	5	1½
12/6	N. Zld. Tst. & Ln. Ltd., 5 p.c. Cum. Pref.	25	19
—	N. Brit. Australsn. Ltd.	100	6½
—	Do. Irred. Guar.	100	32½
5	Do. Mort. Debs.	100	82½
4½	N. Queensld. Mort. & Inv., Ltd., Deb. Stk.	100	92
—	Oceana Co., Ltd.	—	—
6	Peel Riv., Ld. & Min. Ltd.	100	88½
—	Peruvian Corp., Ltd.	100	2¾
—	Do. 4 p.c. Pref.	100	8½
3	Do. 6 p.c. 1 Mt. Debs., Red.	100	38
—	Queenld. Invest. & Ld. Mort. Pref. Ord. Stk.	100	20
3/7	Queenld. Invest. & Ld. Mort. Ord. Shs.	4	4
4	Queenld. Invest. & Ld. Mort. Perp. Debs.	100	88
3½	Raily. Roll Stk. Tst. Deb., 1903-6	100	100½
50/	Reversiony. Int. Soc., Ltd.	100	—
2/8½	Riv. Plate Trst., Loan & Agcy., L., "A" £10 Shs.	2	4
1/6	Riv. Plate Trst., Loan & Agcy., Ltd., Def. "B"	5	3½
	Riv. Plate Trst., Loan & Agy., L., Db. Stk., Red.	100	109
—	Santa Fé & Cord. Gt. South Land, Ltd.	20	5
—	Santa Fé Land	10	2½
2/	Scot. Amer. Invest., Ltd. £10 Shs.	2	2¾
2½	Scot. Australian Invest., Ltd., Cons.	100	74½
6	Scot. Australian Invest., Ltd., Guar. Pref.	100	135½
5	Scot. Australian Invest., Ltd., Guar. Pref.	100	106½
4	Scot. Australian Invest., Ltd., 4 p.c. Perp. Dbs.	100	105½
5	Sivagunga Zemdy., 1st Mort., Red.	100	101
20/	Sth. Australian	20	52½
3½	Stock Exchange Deb., Rd.	—	101½
—	Strait Develt., Ltd.	1	1/16
2/6	Texas Land & Mt., Ltd. £10 Shs.	2½	3
4½	Texas Land & Mt., Ltd., Deb. Stk., Red.	100	105
—	Transvaal Est. & Dev., L.	1	11/16
—	Transvaal Lands, Ltd., £1 Shs.	15/	½
—	Do. F. P.	1	5/16
—	Transvaal Mort., Loan, & Fin., Ltd., £10 Shs.	2	½
2/	Tst & Agcy. of Austrlsa., Ltd., £10 Shs.	1	2
7/5	Do. Old, fully paid	10	15½
5/7	Do. New, fully paid	10	12½
5	Do. Cum. Pref.	10	12½
3/	Trust & Loan of Canada, £20 Shs.	5	4½
1/9½	Do. New £20 Shs.	3	2¼
—	Tst. & Mort. of Iowa, Ltd., £10 Shs.	2½	½
4½	Do. Deb. Stk. Red.	100	92½
—	Tst., Loan, & Agency of Mexico, Ltd., £10 Shs.	2	½
—	Trsts., Exors, & Sec. Ins. Corp., Ltd., £10 Shs.	7	1½
4	Do. Irred. Deb. Stk.	100	106½
5/	Union Dsc., Ld., £10 Shs.	5	10½
—	Union Mort. & Agcy. of Aust., Ltd., £6 Shs.	2	—
6	Do. Pref. Stk	100	30
—	Do. 6 p. Pref. £6 Shs.	2	½
4½	Do. Deb. Stk	100	92½
4	Do. Deb. Stk	100	85½
5	Do. Deb. Stk. Red.	100	96½
1/6	U.S. Deb. Cor. Ltd., £8 Shs.	1	½
5½	Do. Cum. Pref. Stk.	100	100½
4½	Do. Irred. Deb. Stk.	100	105½
5	U.S. Tst. & Guar. Cor., Ltd., Pref. Stk.	100	77½
6/	Van Dieman's	25	15
4	Walker's Prop. Cor., Ltd., Guar. 1 Mt. Deb. Stk.	100	109
4½	Wstr. Mort. & Inv., Ltd., Deb. Stk.	100	92½

FINANCIAL—TRUSTS.

Last Div.	Name.	Paid.	Price.
1/6	Afric City Prop., Ltd	1	1½
6	Do. Cum. Pref.	1	1 1/16
4	Alliance Invt., Ltd., Cm. 4½ p. c. Prefd.	100	74½
—	Do. Defd	100	13½
4	Do. Deb. Stk. Red.	100	106½
5	Amrcn. Invt., Ltd., Prfd.	100	116½
5	Do. Defd.	100	89½
4	Do. Deb. Stk. Red.	100	116½
4	Army & Navy Invt., Ltd., 5 p.c. Prefd.	100	83½
—	Do. Defd. Stk.	100	16½
4	Do. Deb. Stk.	100	107½
4	Atlas Investment, Ltd., Prefd. Stk.	100	70½
4½	Bankers' Invest., Ltd., Cum. Prefd.	100	105
1/0/0	Do. Defd	100	27½
4	Do. Deb. Stk	100	113
	Brewery & Comml. Inv., Ltd., £10 Shs.	5	6

Financial—Trusts (*continued*) :—

Last Div.	Name.	Paid.	Price.
4	British Investment, Ltd., Cum. Prefd.	100	108
5	Do. Defd.	100	102½
4	Do. Deb. Stk.	100	108½
6	Brit. Steam. Invst., Ltd., Prefd.	100	116½
3/0/0	Do. Defd	100	70½
4½	Do. Perp. Deb. Stk	100	121½
1/9	Car Trust Invst., Ltd., £10 Shs.	2½	2
5	Do. Pref.	100	101
4	Do. Deb. Stk., 1915	100	105
4	Clnl. Sec., Ltd., Prefd.	100	106½
2½	Do. Defd.	100	47½
4	Consolidated, Ltd., Cum. 1st Pref.	100	92
4	Do. 5 p.c. Cm. 2nd do.	100	71½
—	Do. Defd.	100	14½
4½	Do. Deb. Stk.	100	112½
—	Deb. Secs. Invst.	100	105½
—	Do. 4 p.c. Cm. Pf. Sk.	100	106½
4½	Edinburgh Invest., Ltd., Cum. Prefd. Stk.	100	100½
4	Do. Deb. Stk. Red.	100	106½
5	Foreign, Amer. & Gen. Invt., Ltd., Prefd.	100	112½
2	Do. Defd.	100	60½
4	Do. Deb. Stk.	100	115½
5	Foreign & Colonial Invt., Ltd., Prefd.	100	136½
5½	Do. Defd.	100	99½
4½	Gas, Water & Gen. Invt., Cum. Prefd. Stk.	100	86½
3	Do. Defd. Stk.	100	36½
4	Do. Deb. Stk.	100	106
5	Gen. & Com. Invt., Ltd., Prefd. Stk.	100	106½
2	Do. Defd. Stk.	100	36½
4	Do. Deb. Stk.	100	113½
1/9	Globe Telegph. & Tst., Ltd.	10	11½
6	Do. do. Pref.	10	17½
4	Govt. & Genl. Invt., Ld., Prefd.	100	84½
3½	Do. Defd.	100	42½
4½	Govts. Stk. & other Secs. Invt., Ltd., Prefd.	100	88½
1	Do. Defd.	100	26
4½	Do. Deb. Stk.	100	111
4	Do. do.	100	104
4½	Guardian Invt., Ltd., Pfd.	100	87½
—	Do. Defd.	100	19½
4	Do. Deb. Stk.	100	104
5	Indian & Gen. Inv., Ltd., Cum. Prefd.	100	107½
2½	Do. Defd.	100	56
4½	Do. Deb. Stk.	100	121½
5	Indust. & Gen. Tst., Ltd., Unified	100	101½
3½	Do. Deb. Stk. Red.	100	100½
4½	Internat. Invt., Ltd., Cm. Prefd.	100	69½
—	Do. Defd.	100	7½
4	Do. Deb. Stk.	100	101
4	Invest. Tst. Cor. Ltd. Pfd.	100	101
4	Do. Defd.	100	93
4	Do. Deb. Stk. Red.	100	105
5	Ldn. Gen. Invest. Ltd., 5 p.c. Cum. Prefd.	100	109½
7½	Do. Defd.	100	118
4½	Ldn. Scot. Amer. Ltd. Pfd.	100	106½
£3	Do. Defd.	100	59½
4	Do. Deb. Stk.	100	112
4	Ldn. Tst., Ltd., Cum. Prfd. Stk.	100	105
4	Do. Defd. Stk.	100	74½
4	Do. Deb. Stk., Red.	100	108
3½	Do. Mt. Deb. Stk., Red.	100	104
5	Mercantile Invt. & Gen., Ltd., Prefd.	100	111
3	Do. Defd.	100	46½
4	Do. Deb. Stk.	100	112½
4	Merchants, Ltd., Pref. Stk.	100	105½
4	Do. Ord.	100	79
4	Do. Deb. Stk.	100	117½
5	Municipal, Ltd., Prefd.	100	55½
—	Do. Defd.	100	17½
4½	Do. Debs.	100	112
4½	Do. Debs. "B"	100	99½
4½	Do. "C" Deb. Stk.	100	88½
5	New Investment, Ltd. Ord.	100	94½
5	Omnium Invest., Ltd., Pfd.	100	91½
1	Do. Defd.	100	26½
4	Do. Deb. Stk.	100	104
5/	Railway Deb. Tst. Ld., £20 Shs.	10	6½
5	Do. Debs., Red.	100	107½
4½	Do. Deb. Stk., 1911	100	107½
4	Do. do. 1927	100	106½
4	Railway Invst. Ltd., Prefd.	100	111
17/7	Do. Defd.	100	20
8/	Railway Share Trust & Agency "A"	8	6
7½	Do. "B" Pref. Stk.	100	146½
4½	River Plate & Gen. Invt., Ltd., Prefd.	100	104
£3	Do. Defd.	100	50½
5	Scot. Invst., Ltd., Pfd. Stk.	100	94½
1½	Do. Defd.	100	26½
4	Do. Deb. Stk.	100	108
4½	Sec. Scottish Invst., Ltd., Cum. Prefd.	100	86½
£2	Do. Defd. Stk.	100	32
4	Do. Deb. Stk.	100	107½
5/	Sth. Africa Gold Tst., Ltd.	1	3½
6	Do. Cum. Pref	1	1
5½	Do. 1st Debs., Red.	100	102
1/9	Stock Conv. & Invest., Ltd., £5 Shs.	1	1½
4½	Do. do. 4½ p.c. Cm. Prf.	100	113½
2½	Do. Ldn. & N. W. 1st. Charge Prefd.	100	114½
4	Do do. 2nd Chge Prfd.	100	111
32/6	Do. do. Defd. Charge	100	29½
3	Do. N. East. 1 Chge Pfd.	100	91½

Financial—Trusts (*continued*) :—

Last Div.	Name.	Paid.	Price.
37/6	Stock N. East Defd. Chge	100	37
6	Submarine Cables	100	132½
5	U.S. & S. Amer. Invest., Ltd., Prefd.	100	100½
2	Do. Defd.	100	27½
4	Do. Deb. Stk.	100	105½

GAS AND ELECTRIC LIGHTING.

Last Div.	Name.	Paid.	Price.
10/6	Alliance & Dublin Con. 10 p.c. Stand.	10	24
7/6	Do. 7 p.c. Stand.	10	16½
5	Austln. Gas Lght. (Syd.) Debs. 1902	100	106
5	Bay State of N. Jrsy. Sk. Fd. Tst. Bd., Red.	—	92½
3/	Bombay, Ltd.	5	6
2/4½	Do. New	4	5
12	Brentford Cons.	100	295½
9	Do. New	100	225½
5	Do. Pref.	100	142½
4	Do. Deb. Stk.	100	136
11½	Brighton & Hove Gen. Cons. Stk.	100	272½
8½	Do. "A" Cons. Stk.	100	197½
5	Bristol 5 p.c. Max.	100	129½
22/6	British Gas Light, Ltd.	20	55½
11/6	Bromley Gas Consumrs.' 10 p.c. Stand.	10	26
8/6	Do. 7 p.c. Stand.	10	21
—	Brush Electl. Enging., L.	—	1¾
6	Do. 6 p.c. Pref.	—	2¼
4½	Do. Deb. Stk.	100	112
4½	Do. 2 Deb. Stk., Red.	100	103½
5/	B. Ayres (New), Ltd.	10	9½
4	Do. Deb. Stk., Rd.	—	99
18/6	Cagliari Gas & Wtr., Ltd.	20	31
8/	Cape Town & Dist. Gas Light & Coke, Ltd.	10	16½
4½	Do. Pref.	10	12½
6	Do. 1 Mt. Debs. 1910	50	60
4/	Charing Cross & Strand Elec. Sup., Ltd.	5	14
4½	Do. Cum. Pref.	5	6½
3/	Chelsea Elec. Sup., Ltd.	5	10½
4½	Do. Deb. Stk., Red.	100	116
5	Chic. Edis'n Co. 1 Mt., Rd.	$1000	106
20/	City of Ldn. Elec. Lht., L.	10	26½
—	Do. New £10 Shs.	5	18
6	Do. Cum. Pref.	10	18
5	Do. Deb. Stk., Red.	100	131½
13½	Commercial, Cons.	100	332½
10½	Do. New	100	252½
4½	Do. Deb. Stk.	100	155½
14	Continental Union, Ltd.	100	225
11	Do. Pref. Stk.	100	239½
—	County of Lon. & Brush Prov. Elec. Lg., Ltd	10	14½
6	Do. Cum. Pref.	10	15½
14	Croydon Comcl. Gas, Ld., "A" Stk., 10 p.c.	100	312½
11	Do. "B" Stk., 7 p.c.	100	260
5½	Crystal Pal. Dist. Ord. 5 p.c. Stk.	100	130½
5	Do. Pref. Stk.	100	141½
8/	European, Ltd.	10	24
6/	Do.	7½	17½
12½	Gas Light & Ck Cons. Stk., "A" Ord.	100	284½
4	Do. "B" (4 p.c. Max.)	100	120½
10	Do. "C," "D," & "E" (Pref.)	100	310
5	Do. "F" (Pref.)	100	152½
7½	Do. "G" (Pref.)	100	222½
7	Do. "H" (7 p.c. Max.)	100	197½
10	Do. "J" (Pref.)	100	310
6	Do. "K"	100	185½
4	Do. Deb. Stk.	100	133½
4½	Do. do.	100	152½
6	Do. do.	100	204½
8/	Hong Kong & China, Ld.	10	14½
4/	House to House Elec. Light Sup., Ltd.	5	10½
7	Do. Cum. Pref.	5	11½
10	Imperial Continental	100	215½
3½	Do. Deb. Stk., Red	100	104½
2/	Malta & Medit., Ltd.	5	5½
7/	Metrop. Elec. Sup., Ltd.	10	18½
4½	Do. 1 Mt. Deb. Stk.	100	119
5	Metro. of Melbrne. Dbs. 1908-12	100	111
4½	Do. Debs. 1918-22-4	100	103
10/	Monte Video, Ltd.	20	15½
9½	Newcastle-upon-Tyne	100	237½
—	Do. 3½ p.c. Deb. Stk.	100	117½
12/	Notting Hill Elec. Ltg., Ltd.	10	20
4/6	Oriental, Ltd.	5	8½
4/0½	Do. New	4½	7½
10d.	Do. do. [illegible]	1	1½
3/6	Ottoman, Ltd.	5	4½
—	Para, Ltd.	—	—
6	People's Gas Lt. & C. of Chic. 2 Mt. 1904	100	105½
5	River Plate Elec. Lgt. & Trac., Ltd., 1 Deb. Stk.	—	92½
8½	Royal Elec. of Montreal	—	144
4½	Do. 1 Mt. Deb.	100	104
11/	St. James' & Pall Mall Elec. Light, Ltd.	5	18
7	Do. Pref.	5	10½
4	Do. Deb. Stk., Red.	100	108½
10/	San Paulo, Ltd.	10	16½

Gas and Electric (*continued*) :—

Last Div.	Name.	Paid.	Price.
10	Sheffield Unit. Gas Lt. "A"	100	251½
10	Do. "B"	100	251½
10	Do. "C"	100	251½
—	Sth. Ldn. Elec. Sup., Ld.	2	2⅜
5¾	South Metropolitan	100	134½
3	Do. 3 p.c. Deb. Stk.	100	104½
12	Tottenham & Edmonton Gas Lt. & C., "A"	100	290
9	Do. "B"	100	210
7/	Tuscan, Ltd.	10	14
5	Do. Debs., Red.	100	101½
5/	West Ham 10 p.c. Stan.	5	12
8/	Wstmnstr. Elec. Sup., Ld.	5	17

INSURANCE.

Last Div.	Name.	Paid.	Price.
4/	Alliance, £20 Shs.	44/	10¾
10/	Alliance, Mar., & Gen., Ld., £100 Shs.	25	53
19/	Atlas, £50 Shs.	6	31
12/	British & For. Marine, Ld., £20 Shs.	4	23½
7½d.	British Law Fire, Ltd., £10 Shs.	1	1½
7/6	Clerical, Med., & Gen. Life, £25 Shs.	50/	16½
10/	Commercial Union, Ltd., £50 Shs.	5	45½
4	Do. "W. of Eng." Ter. Deb. Stk.	100	110½
£9	County Fire, £100 Shs.	80	190
5/	Eagle, £50 Shs.	5	½
4/	Employrs' Liability, Ltd., £10 Shs.	2	4½
—	Empress, Ltd., £5 Shs.	1	—
21/	Equity & Law, £100 Shs.	6	23
7/6	General Life, £100 Shs.	5	15
4½d.	Gresham Life, £5 Shs.	15/	2½
2/6	Guardian, Ld., £10 Shs.	5	11½
10/	Imperial, Ltd., £20 Shs.	5	29½
5/6	Imperial Life, £20 Shs.	4	6½
6/	Indemnity Mutual Mar., Ltd., £15 Shs.	3	12
1/	Lancashire, £20 Shs.	2	5
7½d.	Law Acc. & Contin., Ltd., £5 Shs.	10/	1
5/	Law Fire, £100 Shs.	2½	18
9½d.	Law Gunr. & Trust, Ltd., £10 Shs.	1	1½
9/	Law Life, £20 Shs.	2	25
2/9	Law Un. & Crown £10Shs	12/	7
4	Do. Deb. Stk., 1942	100	110½
14/6	Legal & General, £50 Shs.	8	15½
9d.	Lion Fire, Ltd., £8½ Shs.	1½	½
14/	Liverpool & London & Globe, Stk.	2	53½
20/	Do. Globe £1 Ann	—	35½
35/	London, £25 Shs.	12½	60½
4/	Lond. & Lanc. Fire, £25Shs	2½	19½
2/	Lond. & Lanc. Life, £25Shs	2	6½
1/	Lond. & Prov. Mar., Ld., £10 Shs.	1	¾
6/	Lond. Guar. & Accident, Ltd., £5 Shs.	2	11½
10/	Marine, Ltd., £25 Shs.	4½	43
2/	Maritime, Ltd., £10 Shs.	2	4½
1/6	Merc. Mar., Ld., £10 Shs.	2½	2½
—	National Marine, Ltd., £9 Shs.	1	½
10/	N. Brit. & Merc., £25 Shs.	6½	42½
20/	Northern, £100 Shs.	10	81
40/	Norwich Union Fire, £100 Shs.	12	126½
10/	Ocean Acc. & Guar., fy. pd.	5	22
2/	Do. £5 Shs.	1	4
7/6	Ocean, Marine, Ltd.	2½	9
2/	Palatine, £10 Shs.	2	3½
2/6	Pelican, £10 Shs.	1	3½
23/	Phoenix, £50 Shs.	5	43
£6	Provident, £100 Shs.	10	31
5/	Railway Pasngrs., £10Shs.	2	8½
2/6	Rock Life, £5 Shs.	10/	4½
8	Royal Exchange	100	360
28/	Royal, £20 Shs.	3	54½
4/	Sun, £10Shs.	10/	11½
3/9	Sun Life, £10 Shs.	7½	14½
6	Thames & Mrsey. Marine, Ltd., £20 Shs.	2	10½
9	Union, £10 Shs.	4	24½
4/	Union Marine, £20 Shs.	2½	8½
12/	Universal Life, £100 Shs.	12	42
2/	World Mar ne, £5 Shs.	2	1½

IRON, COAL, AND STEEL.

Last Div.	Name.	Paid.	Price.
—	Barrow Hæm. Steel, Ltd.	7½	2
9/	Do. 6 p.c. 2nd Pref.	7½	6½
10/	Bolck., Vaugh. & C., Ld.	20	16½
6/	Do. £8 liab	12	9
7/6	Brown, J. & Co., Ltd., £20 Shs.	15	20½
7/6	Consett Iron, Ld., £10Shs.	7½	29½
4/	Do. 8 p.c. Cum. Pref.	5	11
7/6	Ebbw Vale Steel, Iron & Coal, Ltd., £23 Shs.	20	6
15/	General Mining Assn., Ld.	5½	7½
8/	Harvey Steel Co. of Gt. Britain, Ltd.	10	29
5	Lehigh V. Coal 1 Mt. 5 p.c. Guar. Gd. Cp. Bds.	—	95½
42/6	Nantyglo & Blaina Iron, Ltd., Pref.	562	97½
1/	Nerbudda Coal & Iron, Ltd., £3 Shs.	56/	1⁄16
—	Newport Abrcrn. Bk. Vein Steam Coal, Ltd.	10	4½
5/	New Sharlston Coll., Ltd. Pref.	20	9½
4½d.	Nw. Vancvr. Coal & Ld., L.	1	½
2/6	North's Navigation Coll. (1889) Ltd.	5	2½
10/	Do. 10 p.c. Cum. Pref.	5	6½
—	Rhymney Iron, Ltd.	5	1½
	Do. New, £5 Shs.	4½	½
5	Do. Mt. Debs., Red.	100	98½
5	Shelton Irn., Stl. & Cl. Co., Ltd., 1 Chg. Debs., Red.	100	99½
50/	Sth. Hetton Coal, Ltd.	100	—
2/	Vickers & Maxim, Ltd.	1	3½
5	Do. 5 p.c. Prfd. Stk.	100	129½

SHIPPING.

Last Div.	Name.	Paid.	Price.
12/	African Stm. Ship, £20 Shs.	16	10½
15/	Do. Fully-paid	20	14½
5/	Amazon Steam Nav., Ltd.	12½	9
8/	Castle Mail Pakts., Ltd., £20 Shs.	14	16
3½	Do. 1st Deb. Stk., Red.	100	102
6/	China Mutual Steam, Ltd.	5	2½
6	Do. Cum. Pref.	10	9½
10/	Cunard, Ltd.	20	9½
5/	Do. £20 Shs.	10	3½
4½	Furness, Withy, & Co., Ltd., 1 Mt. Dbs., Red.	100	106
6/	General Steam	15	8
5/	Do. 5 p.c. Pref., 1874	10	9
5/	Do. 5 p.c. Pref., 1877	10	8½
26/4½	Leyland & Co., Ltd.	10	19
7/	Do. 7 p.c. Cum. Pref.	10	14½
2/11	Do. 4½ p.c. Cum. Pre-Pf.	3	10½
4	Do. 1st Mt. Dbs., Red.	100	106½
7/6	Mercantile Steam, Ltd.	5	7½
6/4½	New Zealand Ship., Ltd.,	6	5
4	Do. Deb. Stk., Red.	100	104
5/	Orient Steam, Ltd.	10	5
5	P. & O. Steam, Cum. Prefd.	100	149½
19	Do. Defd.	100	234½
3½	Do. Deb. Stk.	100	117
5	Richelieu & Ont., 1st Mt. Debs., Red.	100	100
30/	Royal Mail, £100 Shs.	60	54
2/6	Shaw, Sav., & Alb., Ltd., "A" Pref.	5	5½
5/	Do. "B" Ord.	5	3½
8/	Union Steam, Ltd.	20	20
4/	Do. New £20 Shs.	10	8½
4	Do. Deb. Stk., Red.	100	106
7/	Union of N.Z., Ltd.	10	10
5½	Wilson's & Fur.-Ley., 5½ p.c. Cum. Pref.	10	10½
4½	Do. 1 Mt. Db. Sk., Rd.	100	106½

TELEGRAPHS AND TELEPHONES.

Last Div.	Name.	Paid.	Price.
4	African Direct, Ltd., Mort. Debs., Red.	100	102
—	Amazon Telegraph, Ltd.	10	7½
15/	Anglo-American, Ltd.	100	60½
30/	Do. 6 p.c. Prefd. Ord.	100	110
—	Do. Defd. Ord.	100	12½
3/	Brazilian Submarine, Ltd.	10	16½
5	Do. Debs., 2 Series	100	114

Telegraphs and Telephones (*continued*) :—

Last Div.	Name.	Paid.	Price.
4/	Chili Telephone, Ltd.	5	3½
$1½	Comcial. Cable, $100 Shs.	—	180
4	Do. Stg. 500-yr. Deb. Stk. Red.	100	105
2½d.	Consd. Telpehone Constr., &c., Ltd.	10/	½
6/	Cuba Submarine, Ltd.	10	7
10/	Do. 10 p.c. Pref.	10	15
2/	Direct Spanish, Ltd.	5	4½
5/	Do. 10 p.c. Cum. Pref.	5	10½
4½	Do. Debs.	50	104½
3/	Direct U.S. Cable, Ltd.	20	10½
2/6	Eastern, Ltd.	10	17½
3/	Do. 6 p.c. Cum. Pref.	10	18½
4	Do. Mt. Deb. Stk., Red.	100	128½
2/6	Eastern Exten., Aus., & China, Ltd.	10	18½
5	Do. (Aus. Gov. Sub.) Deb., Red.	100	101
5	Do. do. Bearer	100	101½
4	Do. Mort. Deb. Stk.	100	128½
5	Eastn. & S. Afric., Ltd., Mort. Deb. 1900	100	101
5	Do. Bearer	100	101½
4	Do. Mort. Debs. 1909	100	103½
4	Do. Mort. Debs. (Maur. Subsidy)	25	108½
5/	Grt. Nthn. Copenhagen	10	30
5	Do. Debs., Ser. B., Red.	100	101½
12/6	Indo-European, Ltd.	25	53½
6	London Platino-Brazilian, Ltd., Debs. 1904	100	107½
4/	Montevideo Telph., Ltd., 6 p.c. Pref.	5	2½
3/	National Telephone, Ltd.	5	5½
6/	Do. Cum. 1 Pref.	10	17
6/	Do. Cum. 2 Pref.	10	16
5	Do. Non-Cum. 3 Pref.	5	5½
3½	Do. Deb. Stk., Red.	100	102½
4d.	Oriental Telephone, Ltd.	1	½
4	Pac. & Euro. Tlg. Dbs., Rd.	100	106½
4/	Reuter's, Ltd.	8	8½
5/	Un. Riv. Plate Telph., Ltd.	5	4½
5	Do. Deb. Stk., Red.	100	106½
—	West African Telg., Ltd.	10	4
5	Do. 5 p.c. Mt. Debs., Red.	100	100½
—	W. Coast of America, Ltd.	10	½
3/	Western & Brazilian, Ltd.	15	12
3/	Do. 5 p.c. Pref. Ord.	7½	7½
—	Do. Defd. Ord.	7½	4½
4	Do. Deb. Stk., Red.	100	107½
1/	W. India & Panama, Ltd.	10	½
6/	Do. Cum. 1 Pref.	10	7½
6/	Do. Cum. 2 Pref.	10	6
5	Do. Debs., Red.	100	106½
7	West. Union, 1 Mt. 1902 ($	1000	107½
6	Do. 6 p.c. Stg. Bds., Rd.	100	102½

TRAMWAYS AND OMNIBUS.

Last Div.	Name.	Paid.	Price.
1/6	Anglo-Argentine, Ltd.	5	3½
6	Do. Deb. Stk.	100	127½
4/	Barcelona, Ltd.	10	12
5	Do. Deb., Red.	100	105½
7/6	Belfast Street Trams.	10	16½
—	Blackpl. & Fltwd. Tram., £10 Shs.	8	13
10/	Bordeaux Tram. & O. Ltd.	10	11½
5	Do. Cum. Pref.	10	11
—	Brazilian Street Ry., Ltd.	2	½
—	British Elec. Trac., Ltd.	10	16
—	B. Ayres & Belg. Tram., Ltd., 6 p.c. Cum. Pref.	5	—
6	Do. 1 Deb. Stk.	100	—
—	B. Ayres. Gd. Nat., Ltd., 6 p.c 1 Deb. Bds., Red.	100	54½
5½	Do. Pref. Debs., Red.	100	94½
1/	Calais, Ltd.	5	1
—	Calcutta, Ltd.	10	3½
—	Carthagena & Herr., Ltd.	10	3
5	Do. Deb., Red.	100	90
5	City of B'ham. Trams., Ltd., 5 p.c. Cum. Pref.	5	6
4	Do. 1 Mort. Debs., Rd.	100	106½
3/9	City of B. Ayres, Ltd.	5	7
2/3	Do. Ext. £5 Shs.	3	4½
6	Do. Deb. Stk	100	145
1/4	Edinburgh Street Tram.	4	4
1/	Glasgow Tram. & Omni. Ltd., £9 Shs.	8	3
3/7½	Imperial, Ltd.	6	14½
3/	Lond., Deptfd, & Greenwich, Prefd.	5	3½
nil	Do. Defd.	5	1
10½	Lond. Gen. Omni., Ltd.	100	200
4	Do. Deb., Red.	100	115½

Tramways and Omnibus (*continued*) :—

Last Div.	Name.	Paid.	Price.
4/9½	London Road Car	6	10½
28/6	Do. Red. 1 Mt. Deb. Stk.	100	108½
5	London St. Rly. (Prov., Ont.), Mt. Debs.	100	110
12/6	London St. Trams.	—	2
12/9	London Trams., Ltd.	10	10
6/	Do. Non-Cum. Pref.	10	10½
5	Do. Mt. Db. Stk., Rd.	100	101
5	Lynn & Boston 1 Mt. 1924 $	1000	107
5	Milwaukee Elec. Cons. Mt. $	1000	100½
5	Minneapolis St. 1 Cons. Mt. $	1000	96
5	Montreal St. Dbs., 1908	100	109
4½	Do. Debs., 1922	100	107
6/	Nth. Metropolitan	10	12½
1/9½	Nth. Staffords., Ltd.	6	5
5/6	Provincial, Ltd	10	7
6/	Do. Cum. Pref.	10	13½
5	St. Paul City, 1937 $	1000	96
5	Do. Guar. Twin City Rap. Trans. $	1000	96
5/	Southampton	10	6½
5/	South London	10	5½
7/6	Sunderland, Ltd.	10	6½
4½	Toronto 1 Mt., Red.	100	106
2/6	Tramways Union, Ltd.	5	6½
4½	Do. Deb., Red.	100	109
5/	Vienna General Omnibus.	5	5½
5	Do. 5 p.c. Mt. Deb., Red.	100	103½
4/	Wolverhampton, Ltd	10	6½

WATER WORKS.

Last Div.	Name.	Paid.	Price.
8/	Antwerp, Ltd.	20	22
6/	Cape Town District, Ltd.	5	7
10½	Chelsea	100	325
5	Do. Pref. Stk.	100	178½
4½	Do. Pref. Stk., 1875	100	158½
4½	Do. Deb. Stk.	100	160½
5/6	City St. Petersburg, Ltd.	13	11
5/	Colne Valley	10	15½
4	Do. Deb. Stock	100	137½
£4	Consol. of Rosar., Ltd., 4 p.c. 1 Deb. Stk., Red.	100	92
8	East London	100	225½
4½	Do. Deb. Stk.	100	160
3	Do. Deb. Stk., Red.	100	106
37/6	Grand Junction (Max. 10 p.c.) "A"	50 }	121
18/9	Do. "B"	25 }	
18/9	Do. "C" (Max. 7½ p.c.)	25	55½
35/	Do. "D" (Max. 7 p.c.)	50	104½
4	Do. Deb. Stock	100	145½
13	Kent	100	360½
7	Do. New (Max. 7 p.c.)	100	215½
7/	Kimberley, Ltd.	7	5
6	Do. Debs., Red.	100	104½
6	Do. Deb. Stk., Red.	100	107½
10	Lambeth (Max. 10 p.c.)	100	300½
7½	Do. (Max. 7½ p.c.), 50 & 25	—	230½
4	Do. Deb. Stock	100	142½
3	Do. Red. Deb. Stock	100	103
10/	Montevideo, Ltd.	20	16
5	Do. 1 Deb. Stk.	100	108½
5	Do. 2 Deb. Stk.	100	103½
132/9	New River New	100	442½
4	Do. Deb. Stk.	100	144½
4	Do. Deb. Stk. "B"	100	144½
—	Odessa, Ltd., "A" 6 p.c. Prefd.	20	—
nil	Do. "B" Deferred	20	—
4	Portland Con. Mt. "B," 1927	—	102½
8/	Seville, Ltd.	20	12
5/6	Southend "Addl." Ord.	10	17½
6	Southwark and Vauxhall	100	157½
6	Do. "D" Shares (7½ p.c. max.)	100	154½
5	Do. Pref. Stock	100	176½
4	Do. "A" Deb. Stock	100	144½
3	Staines Resvirs. Jt. Com. Gua. Deb. Stk., Red.	100	106
7/	Tarapaca, Ltd.	10	9½
10	West Middlesex	100	302½
4½	Do. Deb. Stk.	100	162½
3	Do Deb. Stk.	100	106

Prices Quoted on the Leading Provincial Exchanges.

ENGLISH.

In quoting the markets, B stands for Birmingham; Bl for Bristol; M for Manchester; L for Liverpool; and S for Sheffield.

CORPORATION STOCKS.

Chief Market.	Int or Div.	Name.	Amount paid.	Price.
M	3½	Bolton, Red. 1935 ..	100	113½
M	3½	Burnley, Red. 1933..	100	114
M	3½	Bury, Red. 1946	100	116½
L	2½	Liverpool, Red. 1925	100	102½
B	3½	Longton, 1932	100	106
M	4	Oldham Prp. Db. Sk.	100	146
M	£1	Do. Gas & W. Ann.		34½
S	4	Rotherham 4 p.c., Red. 1927...... (£	1 an	112
M	3½	Runcorn Red. 1923..	100	104
S	2½	Sheffield Water Ann.	100	118½
S	3	Do.	3 an	90
L	3½	Southport Red. 1936 {	5 an 100	112
L	3	Do. Red. 1914..	100	102½
M	3	Todmorden, Red. 1914	100	102

RAILWAYS.

Chief Market.	Int or Div.	Name.	Amount paid.	Price.
B	4½	Bridgewater Pref. ..	100	135½
M	1½	Cleator & Workton.	100	76
M	4	Do. 1883 Pref. ..	100	109
L	4	Cockermth. K. & P.	100	113½
L	4	Isle of Man	5	6¾
L	5	Do. Pref.	5	6½
L	3	Liverpool Overhead	10	10¾
L	4	Do. Deb. Stk. ..	100	110
L	5	Do. Pref.	10	16
L	6½	Maryport & Carlisle	100	172
Bl	46/	Neath & Brecon "A"	100	65½
M	4½	Oldham, Ashton, &c.	10	16¾
Bl	5½	Penarth Harbour ..	100	182½
Bl	4	Do. Deb. Stk. ..	100	145
Bl	3½	Do. Deb. Stk. ..	100	127
Bl	1½	Ross & Monmouth..	20	5¾
Bl	6	Do. Pref.	20	42½
M	3	Southport & Cheshire Deb. Stk.	100	104½
M	nil.	Do. Pref.	100	23½
Bl	2½	West Somerset Gu...	100	96½
Bl	5	Wye Val. Deb. Stk.	100	162

BANKS.

Chief Market.	Int or Div.	Name.	Amount paid.	Price.
L	8/	Adelphi, L., £20 Shs.	10	16⅛
L	12/6	Bk of L'ool, L., £100 Sh	12½	39½
B	5/6	Brmnghm. Dis. & C., Ltd., £20 Shs.....	4	10½
B	6/3	Co. of Staffs., L., £40	5	13¾
S	17½	Crompton & Evans, Ltd., £20 Shs	4	15
M	14/	Lancs. & Yorks, Ltd., £20 Shs.....	10	31½
L	30/	Livrpl. Union, Ltd., £100 Shs.	20	60¾
M	24/	Manchester & Co., Ltd., £100 Shs. ..	16	61½
M	20/	Mnchstr. & Livrpool. Dis., Ltd., £60 Shs.	10	51¾
M	1/6	Mer. of Lancashire, Ltd., £20 Shs.....	3	6½
L	16/	Nth. & Sth. Wales, Ltd., £40 Shs.....	10	35¾
B	20/	Notts Joint St., Ltd., £50 Shs..........	10	26¾
S	15	Sheffield Banking, Ltd., £50 Shs.....	17½	51½
S	20	Do. & Rotherham, Ltd., £50 Shs...	8	26¼
S	10	Do. & Hallamsh., Ltd., £100 Shs..	25	56
S	10	Do. Union, Ltd., £40 Shs.........	10	25½
M	12/	Union of Manchester, Ltd., £25 Shs.. ..	11	27½
M	10/	Williams, Deacon, &c. Ltd., £50 Shs.....	8	25¾
Bl	20	Wilts & Dorset, Ltd., £50 Shs..........	10	49½
S	5/6	York City & Co., Ltd., £10 Shs.....	3	13

BREWERIES.

Chief Market.	Int or Div.	Name.	Amount paid.	Price.
B	6	Ansell & Sons Pref.	10	15½
B	5	Do. Debs.	100	110
L	9/	Bent's	10	18½
L	6	Do. Cum. Pref...	10	14¾
L	4½	Do. Deb. Stk. ..	100	111
L	13/6	Birkenhead, £5 paid	5	22½
L	13/6	Do. £10 paid....	10	27½
M	9/	Boddington's	9	19⅛
M	5	Do. Cum. Pref...	10	12¾
M	4	Do. Deb. Stk. ..	100	107½
B	4½	Butler & Co. Db. Stk	100	111
M	6	Chesters' Cum. Pref.	10	13½
M	4½	Do. Debs.	100	109
S	10/	Clarkson's Ord.	10	23
S	6	Do. Cum. Prf. Stk.	10	14
M	4	Dutton & Co. Db. Sk.	100	104
M	4½	Hardy's Crown Debs.	100	111
B	10/	Holt	10	18½
B	5	Do. Cum. Pref...	10	12¾
B	4	Do. Debs.	100	108½
B	12/6	Lichfield	10	—
B	5	Do. Cum. Pref...	10	12
M	5½	Manchester Deb. Stk.	100	142
B	6/	Mitchell, H., & Co.	10	40
B	6	Do. Cum. Pref...	10	15½
Bl	6	Oakhill Pref........	10	16½

Breweries (*continued*):—

Chief Market.	Int. or Div.	Name.	Amount paid.	Price.
M	8/	Springwell	10	10¾
M	7	Do. Pref.	10	13½
Bl	9	Stroud	10	16½
Bl	6	Do. Pref	10	14½
M	6/	Taylor's Eagle......	10	11¼
M	7	Do. Cum. Pref ..	10	13½
M	5½	Do. Deb. Stk. ..	100	117½
S	10	Tennant Bros £20 shs	15	33½
S	10	Wheatley & Bates ..	10	14½
S	6	Do. Cum. Pref.	10	12⅝

CANALS AND DOCKS.

Chief Market.	Int. or Div.	Name.	Amount paid.	Price.
Bl	5	Hill's Dry Dk. &c. £20	18	9
M	4	Manc. Ship Canal 1st Mt. Deb. Stk.	100	104
M	4	Do. 2nd do.	100	103½
L	36/3	Mersey Dck. & Harb.	an.	117½
L	35/	Do.	an.	116½
M	10/	Rochdale Canal	100	36½
B	37/6	Staff. & Worc. Canal	100	74½
B	4½	Do. Deb. Stk....	100	137
Bl	4	Swansea Harb......	100	114
B	27/6	Warwick & Birm. Cnl	100	65½
B	12/6	Do. & Napton do.	100	23

COMMERCIAL & INDUSTRIAL.

Chief Market.	Int. or Div.	Name.	Amount paid.	Price.
L	5	Agua Santa Mt. Debs	100	100
M	8/	Armitage, Sir E. & Sns Ltd..............	10	19
M	4	Do. Deb. 1910 ..	100	101
L	6	Ang. Chil. Nit. 1 Mt. Debs., 1919 ..	100	109½
Bl	11	Bath Stone Firms ..	10	19
M	4/9½	Barlow & Jones, Ltd., £10 Shs.	8	10⅝
B	12/6	Birmgham. Ry. Car.	10	16½
B	6	Do. Pref.	10	15½
B	5/	Do. Small Arms	5	14½
M	£18	Blackpool Pier......	100	277½
M	5	Do. Tower Debs.	50	54½
M	3/	Do. Wi. Gar. & P.	5	4
Bl	10	Bristl. & S. W. R. Wag. £20 Shs..........	3	6½
Bl	8	Do. Wag. & Carri. £10 Shs..........	10	15
M	7/	Crosses & Winkwth. Ltd..............	5	12½
L	5	G. Angus & Co. Pref.	10	13½
Bl	5	Gloster. Carri. & W.		10½
Bl	5	Gt. Wstn. Cttn., Ltd.	20	15
M	6	Hetherington, L. Prf.	10	8½
M	4½	Do. Debs., 1910	100	98½
B	7½d.	Hinks (J. & Son), Ltd.	1	27/6
S	26/	Jessop & Sons, £50 Sh	30	27¾
S	10	Kayser, Ellsn. & Co. L.	5	11¾
S	6	Do. Pref.	5	7¾
M	7/6	Kellner-Partgton., L.	5	14¾
M	4½	Do. Debs., 1914..	100	106
M	5	Kerr Thread, Ltd., Debs.	100	101
B	17/	King's Norton Metal, £10 Shs..........	8½	19½
M	5/	Lancashire & Yorks. Wagon, Ltd.	10	10½
L	10/	Liverpool Exch., Ltd.	20	27½
L	45/	Do. Grain Stge, Ltd.	50	108
L	5/	Do. Rubber, Ltd...	5	5¾
M	9d.	Manchester Bond. Whse., L., £10 Shs.	4½	2½
M	3/9	Do. Comcial. Bldgs., Ltd., £10 Shs.	5	10½
M	4/	Do. No. 2, £10 Shs.	5	10½
M	2/6	Do. No. 3, £10 Shs.	5	7½
M	5/	Do. Corn, &c., Exchange, Ltd.	10	16½
M	4	Do. Debs.	100	126
M	8	Do. Ryl. Exchge, L.	100	237½
B	5/	Midland Rlwy. Car. Wgn., Ld., £20 Sh.	10	14½
Bl	5	Millers & Corys Dbs.	100	100½
B	18/6	Mint, Brgham., Ltd.	5	7½
B	5	Do. Debs.	25	108
B	10/	Nettlefolds, Ltd.....	10	50
B	5	Do. Pref.	10	15½
S	9	Nth. Centrl. Wgn., L.	5	8⅝
B	15/	Patnt. Nut & Bolt, L.	10	34
B	5	Do. Pref.	10	14¾
B	1/	Perry & Co., Ltd. ..	1	27/
B	6d.	Do. Pref.	1	27/
S	10	Round, J., & Co., L., £10 Shs.	6	12
S	15	Rodgers, J., & Sons, L.	100	213
M	18/9	Rylands & Sons, Ltd., £20	15	38½
M	2/6	Do. paid up	20	43½
M	4	Do. Debs. .. 1909	100	106
S	5	Sanderson Brs. & Co., Ltd. Debs.	100	102
M	4½	Schwabe, S., & Co., Ltd., 1 Debs. 1914	100	102
S	7½.	Sheffield Forge & Rolling, Ltd.	10	11½
L	80/	Southport Pier, Ltd.	100	88½
L	2½	Do. W. Gdns., Ltd.	5	3½
Bl	5	Spillers & Bakers, Ltd, £10 Shs.	9	15½
Bl	6	Do. Pref.	10	14½
B	5/	Union Rolling Stock, Ltd., £20 Shs.....	5	7½
M	6/	Victoria Pr., S'port, L.	5	4⅝
Bl	8	Western Wagon & Property, Ltd.....	6	9¾
S	10	Westenholm, G., & Son, Ltd., £25 Shs.	20	22¾
S	6½	Yorksh. Wagon, Ltd.	2	2¾

FINANCIAL, TRUSTS, &c.

Chief Market.	Int. or Div.	Name.	Amount paid.	Price.
M	1/	Manchstr. Trst. £10 Shs.	2	13/9
M	1/3	N. of Eng. T. Deb. & A., Ltd. £10 Shs.	2½	27/3
M	3½	Do. 1 Mt. Debs...	100	97½
L	—	Pacific Ln. & Inv., L.	2½	2¾
L	4	Do. Deb. Stk.....	100	103
L	—	United Trst., L. Prfd.	100	72½
L	—	Do. Deferred....	100	62½

GAS.

Chief Market.	Int. or Div.	Name.	Amount paid.	Price.
Bl	5	Bristol Gas (5 p.c. mx.)	100	128½
Bl	4	Do. 1st Deb.	100	137
S	10	Gt. Grimsby "C" ..	10	201
L	10	Liverpool Utd. "A"	100	235
L	7	Do. "B"......	100	176
L	4	Do. Deb.	100	137
S	10	Sheffield Gas "A," "B," "C"	100	248
B	10½	Wolverhampton	100	230
B	3	Do. 6 p.c. Pref...	100	172

INSURANCE.

Chief Market.	Int. or Div.	Name.	Amount paid.	Price.
M	6	Equitable F. & Acc. £5 Shs.	1	38/6
L	2/	Liverpool Mortgage £10 Shs.	2	1⁵⁄₁₆
M	4/	Mchester. Fire £20 Shs	2	7¾
M	5/	National Boiler & G., Ltd., £10 Shs.	3	13½
L	2/	Reliance Mar., Ltd., £10 Shs.	2	4⁵⁄₁₆
L	4/	Sea, Ltd., £10 Shs...	2	10⁵⁄₁₆
L	8/	Stnd. Mar., L., £20 Sh.	4	8⁵⁄₁₆
L	1/	State Fire, L., £20 Sh.	1	2

COAL, IRON, AND STEEL.

Chief Market.	Int. or Div.	Name.	Amount paid.	Price.
Bl.	12	Albion Stm. Coal ..	10	11½
M	16/9	And. Knowles & S., Ltd., £37½ Shs...	23½	11¾
M	5	Do. Mt. Debs. 1908	100	106½
Bl.	1/½	Ashton V. Iron	100	26
S	12½	Bessemer, Ltd.	10	20⅛
S	5	Do. Pref.	10	12¾
S	12/6	Briggs, H., & Co., "A" £15 Shs....	12½	15½
S	8/6	Do. "B" £15 Shs.	8½	9⅝
S	20	Brown Baley's. Stl., L.	10	32
S	5	Brown, J., & Co., Cum. Pref.	10	13½
S	5	Cammell, C. & Co., Ltd.	85	13⅛
S	5	Do. Pref.	5	6⁵⁄₁₆
M	5	Chatterley Whitfield. Col., Debs., 1905..	100	100½
Bl	—	Davis, D., & Sons, Ld.	10	10
M	5	Evans, R., & Co., Ltd., Deb., 1910 ..	100	101
S	12½	Fox, S., & Co., Ltd., £100 Shs.	80	178½
Bl	10	Gt. Wstn. Col., L., "A"	5	10½
Bl	6	Do. "B"	5	4¾
Bl	3	Main Colliery, Ltd.	10	7½
B	5/	Muntz's Metal, Ltd.	5	8½
B	5	Do. Pref.......	5	6½
M	2/6½	Nth. Lonsd. Iron and Steel, Ltd., £10 Sh.	8½	2½
Bl	6	North's Nav. Coll., Ltd., Debs.	100	106
S	30/	Parkgate Irn. & Stl., Ltd., £100 Shs. ..	75	69½
M	6	Pearson & Knls., Ld., "A" Cum. Pref...	50	46
B	10/	Sandwell Pk. Col., L.	10	17½
M	6/3	Sheepbridge Coal and Iron, Ltd., "A"	25	18¾
M	2/6	Do. "B"	10	7¾
M	5	Do. "C" Gua. Pf.	25	28¾
Bl	4	South Wales Coll., Ltd., "A"	17	8½
S	30/	Staveley Coal & Iron, Ltd., "A" £100 Sh.	60	80¾
S	30/	Do. "C"	60	82
M	1/10½	Tredegar Iron & Cl., Ld., "A" £10 Sh.	7½	2½
M	1½	Do. "B" Stk. ..	100	35
M	6/	Wigan Cl. & Irn., Ld.	10	7
M	4/6	Do. £10 Shs.	7½	4

SHIPPING.

Chief Market.	Int. or Div.	Name.	Amount paid.	Price.
Bl	6	Bristol St. Nav. Pref.	10	11¾
L	15/	Brit. & Af. St. Nav..	10	13½
L	8/10½	British & Estn, Ltd.	6½	2⅝
L	10/	Pacific Stm. Nav., L.	25	24½
L	30/	Wst. Ind. & Pac. St. Ltd., £25 Shs....	20	27½

TRAMWAYS, &c.

Chief Market.	Int. or Div.	Name.	Amount paid.	Price.
B	5/	Brmngh. & Aston, L.	5	11
B	5/	Do. Mid., Ltd. ..	10	7¾
Bl	6/	Bristol Tr. & Car., Ltd..	10	20½
Bl	4/	Do. Debs.	100	122
L	6	I. of Man Elec., L., Pref.	1	1⅛
M	15/	Manchester C. & T, L., "A" £20 Shs.	15	27¾
M	10/	Do. "B"	10	18¾

WATER WORKS.

Chief Market.	Int. or Div.	Name.	Amount paid.	Price.
Bl	7	Bristol	25	62½
Bl	7	Do..............	20	47½
Bl	58/	Do. 7 p.c. max. ..	100	158½
Bl	4½	Do. Pref.	20	32½
Bl	5	Do. Pref.	10	17¾
Bl	3½	Do. Deb.	100	129½
M	10	Fylde "A"........	100	335
M	7	Do. "B"	100	224
B	6	S. Staffs. Ord. "A"	100	165
B	—	Do. "B"	100	164
B	4	Do. Deb. Stk.	100	140
B	5	Do. Pf "A" "B" "C"	100	170
M	£3½	Stockport District ..	100	184½
B	2/	Wolverhampton New	5	6¾

SCOTTISH.

In quoting the markets, E stands for Edinburgh, and G for Glasgow.

RAILWAYS.

Chief Market.	Int. or Div.	Name.	Nom. Amount	Price.
E	6½	Arbroath and Forfar	25	49½
G	1½	Callander and Oban.	10	7⅛
G	4	Do. Deb. Stock	100	148
G	4½	Do. Pref.......	10	14½
G	4	Cathct. Dist. Deb. Stk.	100	148
E	5	Edin. and Bathgate .	100	179½
E	7	Forth & Clyde Junc.	100	222½
G	4	Lanarks. and Ayrsh.	10	13¾
G	4	Do. & Dumbartons.	10	14⅛
G	4	Do. Deb. Stk.	100	149

BANKS.

Chief Market.	Int. or Div.	Name.	Nom. Amount	Price.
G	12	Bank of Scotland ..	100	35
G	16	British Linen	100	49
G	8	Caledonian, Ltd.....	2½	97
G	10	Clydesdale, Ltd.	10	2
G	16	Commercl. of Scot., L.	20	8
G	16	National of Scot. Ld.	100	41
G	8	Royal of Scotland ..	100	233
G	11	Union of Scotland, L.	10	26

BREWERIES.

Chief Market.	Int. or Div.	Name.	Nom. Amount	Price.
E	5	Bernard, Thos. Pref.	10	10
E	5	Bernard, T. & J., Cum. Pref........	10	12
G	20	Highland Distilleries	3½	10⅛

CANALS AND DOCKS.

Chief Market.	Int. or Div.	Name.	Nom. Amount	Price.
G	4	Clyde Nav. 4 p.c....	100	123½
G	3½	Do. 3½ p.c......	100	105
G	3½	Greenock Harb. "A"	100	101
G	2	Do. "B"	100	38½

MISCELLANEOUS.

Chief Market.	Int. or Div.	Name.	Nom. Amount	Price.
G	4½	Alexander & Co. Debs.	100	110½
G	5	Alexander Ferguson & Co. Cum. Pref..	10	11¾
G	5	Baird, H., & Sns. C. P.	10	12½
E	12	Barry, Ostlere, & Co.	7½	12½
E	6	Do. Cum. Pref...	10	15
G	5	Brown, Stewart, Deb.	100	84
E	7½	Broxburn Oil	8½	8½
E	6	Do. Cum. Pref...	10	11⅛
E	7	Edinburgh & Dist. Tram. Cum Pref.	5	9
E	5	Gilroy, Sns, & Co. Dbs.	100	99
G	9	Glasgow Cot. Spin...	6	6
G	30/	Do. Royal Exchg.	46	110
G	—	Pumpherston Oil Pf.	10	8¾
E	7	Scottish Assam Tea	10	11⅛
E	5	Scottish Waggon....	10	12½
G	5	Stoddard & Co. Pref.	10	12⅛

FINANCIAL, LAND, AND INVESTMENT.

Chief Market.	Int. or Div.	Name.	Nom. Amount	Price.
G	1/	Assets Co...........	1	47/
E	4½	Investors' Mort. Pref.	100	98½
E	4	Do. Deb. Stk....	100	102½
E	4	Nthn. Inv. N. Zeal. Deb. Stk.	100	107
E	4	N. of Scot. Canadian Deb. Stk.	100	106
E	4½	Real & Deb. Corp. Deb. Stk.	100	106½

INSURANCE.

Chief Market.	Int. or Div.	Name.	Amount paid.	Price.
G	12/	Caledonian F. & Life	5	36½
G	4/6	City of Glasgow Life	2½	12½
E	19/	Edinburgh Life	20	54½
G	13/1	Life Ass. of Scotland	8⅓	34¼
E	8	Nat. Guar. & Surety	2	52/
G	17½	Scottish Union and National "A"	1	94/
G	17½	Do. "B"	3¼	18½

IRON, COAL, AND STEEL.

Chief Market.	Int. or Div.	Name.	Amount paid.	Price.
E	Nil.	Addie, Coll. Cm. Pref.	10	7¾
E	8/	Arniston Coal	8	12¾
E	2½	Cairntable Gas Coal	8	86/
E	12½	Fife Coal	10	20½
E	5	Do. Cum. Pref.	10	13
G	7	Merry & Cunghame. Cum. Pref.	10	16
G	5	Do. Debentures	100	105½
E	1/9	Niddrie & Benhar Cl.	1½	41/
G	5	Steel Com. of Scotlnd.	—	
	—	"A" Deb. Stk.	100	113
G	6	Do. 2nd Mt. "B"	100	110
E	—	Watson, John	8½	11
E	6	Do. Cum. Pref.	7½	8¼
E	12½	Wilson's & Cly. Coal	3	8¾

IRISH.

In quoting the markets, B stands for Belfast, and D for Dublin.

CORPORATION STOCKS.

Chief Market.	Int. or Div.	Name.	Amount paid.	Price.
B	3½	Belfast, 1921	100	111¼
B	3½	Do. 1912	100	106½
B	3½	Do. 1924	100	106½
B	3	Do. 1955	100	105½
B	3½	Do. Water Com.	100	114½
B	3	Do. do.	100	106
B	3½	Do. Harbour Com.	100	112½
D	3½	Rathmines & Rathgar	100	110
D	3½	Waterford Deb.	100	—

RAILWAYS.

Chief Market.	Int. or Div.	Name.	Amount Paid.	Price.
D	30/	Cork, Bandon, & S.C.	100	77
D	4	Do. Deb.	100	130½
D	4	Do. W. Cork Pref.	100	—
B	65/	Belfast & Northern	100	159½
B	4	Do. Deb.	100	146
B	4	Do. Pref.	100	141½
B	6½	Belfast & C. Down	100	167½
B	4	Do. Deb.	100	147
B	3	Do.	100	107½
B	4½	Do. 4½ Pref. B.	100	150
B	5	Do. Guar.	100	173
D	Nil.	Dublin, Wick. & Wex.	100	31⅞
D	4	Do. Deb.	100	123
D	4½	Do. Deb.	100	—
D	6	Do. Guar.	100	169½
D	4	Do. C. of Dub. Junc.	100	—
D	5	Do. 1860 Pref.	100	120½
D	50/	Do. 1864 Pref.	100	106
D	50/	Do. 1865 Pref.	100	94
B	67/6	Great Northern	100	175
B	4	Do. Deb.	100	147
B	4	Do. Pref. B.	100	143½
B	5½	Gt. South & Western	100	143½
B	4	Do. Deb.	100	148½
B	4	Do. Guar.	100	140
D	45/	Midland Gt. Western	100	114½
D	4	Do. Deb.	100	140
D	4½	Do. Deb.	100	151½
D	4½	Do. Deb.	100	—
D	5	Do. Pref.	100	174
D	4	Do. Pref.	100	137
D	—	Waterford & Central	100	15
D	3	Do. Deb.	100	—
D	3½	Do. Pref.	100	130
D	4	Waterfd. L., & W. Db.	100	135
D	4½	Do. Deb.	100	—
D	4	Do. Pref.	100	130
D	3½	Do. Pref.	100	102

BANKS.

Chief Market.	Int. or Div.	Name.	Amount paid.	Price.
B	50/	Belfast, Old, £125 Shs.	25	126½
P	20/	Do. New, £125 Shs.	25	50⅝
D		Hibernian, £20 Shs.	5	6¾
D	9/	Munster & Leinster £5 Shs.	2	5¼
B	11/	Northern, £50 Shs.	10	26½
D	12/	Royal, £50 Shs.	10	28½
B	5/	Ulster, £15 Shs.	2½	12½

BREWERIES AND DISTILLERIES.

Chief Market.	Int. or Div.	Name.	Amount paid.	Price.
D	10/	Castlebellingham & Drog	10	16½
D	6	Do. Pref.	10	15½
D	4½	Do. Deb.	100	115
B	17/	Dunville & Co.	10	28½
B	6	Irish Distillery, Pref.	10	13
B	5	Do. Deb.	100	110
B	6	J. & J. M'Connell, Pf.	10	15½
B	13/6	Mitchell & Co.	9	19½
B	5	Do. Deb.	10	11½
D	4½	Phœnix Brew. Deb.	100	96
B	6/	Wm. Cowan	10	13½
B	6	Do. Pref.	10	13½
B	8/	Young, King, & Co.	8	14

STEAM AND CANAL.

Chief Market.	Int. or Div.	Name.	Amount paid.	Price.
B	Nil	Belfast Steamship	50	35½
D	10/	British and Irish	50	—
D	15/	City of Dublin	100	61
D	3½	Do. Deb.	100	105
D	30/	Dublin & Lpool. Bldg.	50	73
D	2/6	Dundalk & Newry	10	4½
D	4/	Grand Canal	10	12
D	3	Do. Pref.	10	9½
D	3	Do. Deb.	100	99½
B	30/	Irish Shipowners	100	65
B	3/	Ulster Steamship	5	6

MISCELLANEOUS.

Chief Market.	Int. or Div.	Name.	Amount paid.	Price.
D	3/1	Arnott & Co.	4	7½
D	6	Do. Pref.	4	6⅛
B	8/	Belfast Com. Bldgs.	10	11
B	37/6	Do. Ropework Co.	75	93½
B	5	Do. do. Pref.	10	13
B	2/	Do. Discount Co.	3	43/
B	5	Do. do. Pref.	5	4½
B	10/	Brookfield Linen	25	17½
B	Nil	Coey & Co.	25	4
B	5	Do. Deb.	50	48
B	4½	David Allen & S's Deb.	100	107
D	4/	Dublin Trams	10	19⅛
D	6	Do. Pref.	10	18
D	4	Do. Deb.	100	—
B	6/	Edenderry Spinning	10	9
B	25/	Falls Flax Spinning	25	15
B	17/	Forster, Green, & Co.	10	21
B	9/	Island Spinning	7½	7½
B	8/	Jas. Lindsay & Co.	8	16½
B	1/7½	John Arnott & Co.	4	4½
B	4½	Do. Deb.	50	56
D	5/	Kinahan & Co.	10	11½
D	5½	Do. Pref.	10	11½
D	4½	Do. Deb.	100	109½
B	12/	Kirker & Co.	10	10
B	5/	Leahy, Kelly, & Leahy	5	8½
B	6	Do. Pref.	5	7½
B	4/	Lindsay Bros. Ltd.	8	7½
B	4½	Do. Deb.	50	56½
D	1/	National Assurance	2½	38/
B	10/	Olley & Co.	5	7½
D	1/1½	Patriotic Assurance	2½	29/3
B	3/7½	P. Johnston & Son, L.	6	6½
B	10/	Robertson, F., & Co.	8	23½
B	10	Ulster Marine Insur.	5/	7/
B	15/	York-street Flax	25	33½
B	6	Do. Pref.	10	15½
B	4½	Do. Deb.	100	120

INDIAN AND CEYLON TEA COMPANIES.

Acres Planted.	Crop, 1897.	Paid up Capital.	Share.	Paid up.	Name.	Dividends. 1894.	1895.	1896.	Int. 1897.	Price.	Yield.	Reserve.	Balance Forward.	Working Capital.	Mortgages, Debs. or Pref. Capital not otherwise stated.
	lb.	£	£	£	INDIAN COMPANIES.							£	£	£	£
11,240	3,128,000	120,000	10	3	Amalgamated Estates	—	*	10	5	3⅛	8½	10,000	16,500	D52,950	—
		400,000	10	10	Do. Pref.	—	*	5	‡5	10	5				
10,223	3,560,000	187,160	20	20	Assam	20	20	20	5	59½	6½	55,000	1,730	D11,350	—
6,130	3,278,000	142,500	10	10	Assam Frontier	3	6	6	—	8½	6½	—	286	20,000	82,500
		142,500	10	10	Do. Pref.	6	6	6	3	11½	5½				
2,087	839,000	66,745	5	5	Attaree Khat	12	12	8	3	7½	5½	3,790	4,820	7,770	—
1,633	583,000	78,170	10	10	Borelli	4	4	5	—	8	6½	—	3,256	D270	6,500 Pref.
1,720	812,000	60,825	5	5	British Indian	6	5	5	—	3½	6½	—	2,920	12,300	16,500 Pref.
3,223	2,247,000	114,500	5	5	Brahmapootra	20	18	20	6	13	7½	—	28,440	41,600	
3,754	1,617,000	76,500	10	10	Cachar and Dooars	*	8	7	—	10½	6½	—	1,645	21,240	
		76,500	10	10	Do. Pref.	*	6	6	3	11½	5½				
3,946	2,083,000	72,010	1	1	Chargola	8	7	10	2½	18/	10½	3,000	3,300	—	—
		81,000	1	1	Do. Pref.	7	7	7	3½	1⅛	5½				
1,971	942,000	33,000	5	5	Chubwa	10	8	10	3½	6	8½	10,000	2,043	D5,400	—
		33,000	5	5	Do. Pref.	7	7	7	3½	7	5				
32,250	11,500,000	120,000	10	3	Cons. Tea and Lands	—	*	10	5	3½	7½	65,000	14,240	D191,674	—
		1,000,000	10	10	Do. 1st Pref.	—	*	5	‡5	11⅛	4½				
		400,000	10	10	Do. 2nd Pref.	—	*	7	‡7	12	5½				
2,230	617,000	135,420	20	20	Darjeeling	5½	5½	6	—	22½	5	5,552	1,565	1,700	—
2,114	445,000	60,000	10	10	Darjeeling Cons.	—	—	4/2	—	6	—	—	1,820	—	—
		60,000	10	10	Do. Pref.	—	*	5	2½	9½	5½				
6,660	3,518,000	150,000	10	10	Dooars	12½	12½	12½	2½	18	7	45,000	300	D32,000	—
		75,000	10	10	Do. Pref.	7	7	7	3½	16	4½				
3,367	1,811,000	165,000	10	10	Doom Dooma	11½	10	12½	5	21½	5½	30,000	4,032	—	10,000
1,377	582,000	61,120	5	5	Eastern Assam	5	nil.	4	—	3	6½	—	1,790	—	10,000
4,038	1,675,000	85,000	10	10	East India and Ceylon	*	nil.	7	—	8½	7½	—	1,710	—	—
		85,000	10	10	Do. Pref.	*	6	6	3	11½	5½				
7,500	3,363,000	219,000	10	10	Empire of India	—	*	6/10	2½	11½	—	15,000	—	27,000	—
		219,000	10	10	Do. Pref.	—	*	5	2½	11	4½				
1,180	540,000	94,060	10	10	Indian of Cachar	7	3½	3	—	4½	6½	6,070	—	7,120	—
3,050	824,000	83,500	5	5	Jhanzie	10	10	10	4	8	6½	14,500	1,070	2,700	—
7,980	3,680,000	250,000	10	10	Jokai	10	10	10	5	17½	5½	45,000	990	D9,000	—
		100,000	10	10	Do. Pref.	*	6	6	3	14½	4½				
5,224	1,563,000	100,000	20	20	Jorehaut	20	20	20	—	58½	6½	36,220	2,955	3,000	—
1,547	504,000	65,660	10	8	Lebong	15	15	15	5	16½	7½	9,000	2,150	8,650	—
5,082	1,709,000	100,000	10	10	Lungla	*	10	6	3	8½	6½	—	1,543	D21,000	—
		100,000	10	10	Do. Pref.	*	6	6	3	11½	5½				
2,684	885,000	95,970	10	10	Majuli	7	5	5	—	7	7½	—	2,606	560	—
1,375	380,000	91,840	1	1	Makum	—	—	2	—	1½	1½	—	—	1,200	25,000
2,990	770,000	100,000	1	1	Moabund	—	—	*	—	½	—	—	—	-	—
		50,000	1	1	Do. Pref.	—	—	*	2½	1	5				
1,080	482,000	79,590	10	10	Scottish Assam	7	7	7	—	10½	6½	6,500	800	9,590	—
4,150	1,456,000	100,000	10	10	Singlo	7	8	5	1	8½	5½	—	300	D5,200	—
		80,000	10	10	Do. Pref.	*	6½	6½	3½	13½	5				
	Crop, 1896.				CEYLON COMPANIES.										
7,970	1,743,824	250,000	100	100	Anglo-Ceylon, & Gen.	—	*	5½	—	65	8½	10,992	1,405	D72,844	166,520
1,836	685,741	50,000	10	10	Associated Tea	—	*	5	2½	7½	6½	—	164	2,478	—
		60,000	10	10	Do. Pref.	—	*	6	3	10½	5½				
10,390	4,000,000§	167,380	10	10	Ceylon Tea Plantations	15	15	15	‡15	27	5½	84,500	1,516	D30,819	—
		81,080	10	10	Do. Pref.	7	7	7	‡7	16½	4½				
5,722	1,542,700§	55,260	5	3	Ceylon & Oriental Est.	5	8	7	—	2½	7½	—	230	D2,047	71,000
		46,000	5	5	Do. Pref.	6	6	6	3	5	6				
2,157	801,629	111,330	5	5	Dimbula Valley	—	*	10	5	5½	8½	—	—	1,733	6,250
		62,607	5	5	Do. Pref.	—	*	6	3	6½	4½				
11,496	3,635,000§	298,250	5	5	Eastern Prod. & Est.	3	5	6½	‡7	6½	5½	20,000	11,740	D17,797	102,500
2,193	1,050,000§	22,080	10	10	New Dimbula "A"	10	16	16	4	24	6	11,000	2,024	1,150	8,400
		55,710	10	10	Do. "B"	18	16	16	4	22	7½				
2,572	570,360	100,000	10	10	Ouvah	6	8	6	2	8½	7	4,000	1,151	D1,255	—
2,630	964,963§	200,000	10	10	Nuwara Eliya	—	*	6	‡6	11	5½	—	—	—	30,000
1,720	720,200	41,000	10	10	Scottish Ceylon	15	15	15	5	22	6½	7,000	1,252	D3,970	9,000 Pref.
2,450	750,000§	39,000	10	6	Standard	12½	15	15	‡15	14	6½	9,000	800	D14,012	4,000
		17,000	10	10	Do.	12½	15	15	‡15	22	6½				

* Company formed this year.

Working-Capital Column.—In working-capital column, D stands for *debit*.
† Interim dividends are given as actual distribution made. ‡ *Total* div. § Crop 1897

Printed for the Proprietor by LOVE & WYMAN, LTD., Great Queen Street, London, W.C.; and Published by CLEMENT WILSON at Norfolk House, Norfolk Street, Strand, London, W.C

The Investors' Review

EDITED BY A. J. WILSON.

Vol. I.—No. 17. New Series. | FRIDAY, APRIL 29, 1898. | [Registered as a Newspaper.] | Price 6d. By post, 6½d

Notice to Subscribers.

Complaints are continually reaching us that the INVESTORS' REVIEW cannot be obtained at this and the other railway bookstall, that it does not reach Scotch and Irish cities till Monday, and that it is not delivered in the City till Saturday morning.

We publish on Friday in time for the REVIEW to be at all Metropolitan bookstalls by at latest 4 p.m., and we believe that it is there then, having no doubt that Messrs. W. H. Smith & Son do their best, but they have such a mass of papers to handle every day that a fresh one may well look almost like a personal enemy and be kept in short supply unless the reading public shows unmistakably that it is wanted. A little perseverance, therefore, in asking for the INVESTORS' REVIEW is all that should be required to remedy this defect.

All London newsagents can be in a position to distribute the paper on Friday afternoon if they please, and here also the only remedy is for subscribers to insist upon having it as soon as published. Arrangements have been made that all our direct City subscribers shall have their copies before 4 p.m. on Friday. As for the provinces, we can only say that the paper is delivered to the forwarding agents in ample time to be in every English and Scotch town, and in Dublin and Belfast, likewise, early on Saturday morning. Those despatched by post from this office can be delivered by the first London mail on Saturday in every part of the United Kingdom.

CONTENTS

The Investors' Review.

Hispano-American Sinews of War.

It is hardly a war yet, and impatient sensation lovers among us as well as in the United States are beginning to jeer at Mr. McKinley for what they describe as his absurd attempt to carry on war in a peaceful, merciful, or "benevolent" manner. The "quaker warrior" some wags have already nicknamed him. They should possess their souls in patience, for in all probability sensations in plenty will gratify their craving before many weeks, perhaps before many days, are over. In one sense both Governments seem to have been taken by surprise at the rapidity with which events moved, the United States not least. Neither Power was ready for the fight when war actually broke out. We have said all along that the American Government misunderstood the temper of the Spanish people, and this is now demonstrated to be the just view by the haste with which they commenced the business of war when they found their efforts to deliver Cuba by peaceful ways scouted. Without an army, with a fleet scattered to all the ends of the earth, and without funds in hand, they rushed to the fray and have not yet found the foe. But mistakes and miscalculations of this kind will right themselves very soon in the United States, all the sooner perhaps if they, to begin with, meet with a rebuff or two at sea, as is by no means improbable. Meanwhile, it is interesting, from our point of view, to observe how the two Powers are setting about the provision of money, the sinews of war.

The one country is rich, with, on the whole, a willing population behind its Government; the other is not exactly poor but dominated by a Government which has only a precarious hold on the affections of the people, and has always found the utmost difficulty in raising taxation. To no small extent the measures taken by the two Powers to raise funds illustrate this divergence in their respective positions. A loan of $500,000,000 in 3 per cents., payable "in coin"—that ambiguous phrase which may yet cost the States so much—is expected to be launched in the United States in portions as required, and will doubtless be sold up to a point without difficulty. Also new taxation is to be imposed by doubling the duty on excisable liquors, raising the tobacco excise, and making additions to the stamp duties, and so on. These changes are in all calculated to bring $100,000,000 per annum more into the Treasury. And this is perhaps the best course the Washington Cabinet could have taken, for should the people become accustomed to this internal taxation it may, when peace is restored, afford a basis from which enlightened statesmen can work to get the Customs tariff reduced and a more liberal foreign trade policy established. Hitherto, Protectionist obstruction has always prevented the establishment of the inland revenue on a satisfactory footing. In the meantime, such large measures for meeting war expenses indicate a very deliberate purpose on the part of the Washington Government to carry the struggle to a successful issue, cost what it may. We must now, therefore, at least pay the American people the tribute of being in earnest over this matter. They have made up their minds to drive the Spaniards out of the western hemisphere, and we have not the slightest doubt that they will succeed. Whatever follows, humanity must gain by their triumph.

Spain, on the other hand, betrays her financial straits the moment she tries to find means to fight with. A forced loan of one year's taxes is to be wrung from the people in addition to the ordinary taxation of the year, and the note issue of the Bank of Spain, already so swollen that the peseta is at about 45 per cent. discount, is to be extended by another 500,000,000 pesetas, so that its maximum will amount to two milliards, or £80,000,000 nominal. Not much change in taxation appears to be possible to eke out this dangerous source of "supplies," but the project for re-leasing the Almaden quicksilver mines is revived, and another loan is, if possible, to be raised on the security of a tax upon navigation. Of course this latter loan cannot be anything but an internal one, and we fear it will be very feebly subscribed. Indeed, the bulk of the people cannot have the means with which to subscribe, harried as they will be by the payment of two years' taxation in one, plus the corrupt commissions wrung from them as usual by the tax collector. And the sum obtainable from the Almaden Mines will not go very far. The present loan issued by the Rothschilds only amounted to £3,318,100 originally, and there is still £348,400 of it to be paid off. It is a 5 per cent. loan, and was issued at 80 per cent., with a sinking fund of 1½ per cent. Not much better terms could be obtained now, in the damaged condition of Spanish credit, for a fresh loan on the same security, but let us suppose that, by extending the lease and enlarging the output, if that be possible, Spain managed to get £3,000,000 on this security in the French or English markets: it would be but a drop in the ocean. Now Spanish helplessness in money matters is a main factor in determining the outcome of this conflict. Should the Spaniards make a dash at the American fleet, cripple it, sink it, drive it away from Havana and scour the Atlantic coast of the United States in piratical style with cruisers as privateers—then it is possible, although very improbable, that the United States would hurry to make peace on the terms of the *status quo ante*. On the other hand, should Mr. McKinley's tactics of playing a waiting game, sending relief to the starving inhabitants of Cuba, arming the insurgents and supporting them with a division of United States regulars, keeping strict watch the while over Havana, be capable of being maintained, then long before the autumn Spain must be brought to her knees and obliged to surrender Cuba on any terms or none. She cannot prolong a contest in these days under modern conditions of warfare, and is wholly unable financially to bear the strain of a long-drawn-out blockade.

Stock Market Notes and Comments.

Everybody is still waiting for this war to begin, and business continues nearly at a standstill. So bad is it that some people were expressing the hope that to-morrow might be made a Stock Exchange holiday, seeing that Monday is one by old usage. It is indeed most irksome to be engaged in Stock Exchange business at present. Nothing can be done satisfactorily with a reasonable conviction that profit will result. The "bull" and "bear" are alike nonplussed. It is no use to sell American railroad shares for the fall, because the war might be over in a week or two, and then where would the "bear" be? Equally vain is it to buy them for the rise, because it is possible that the Spaniards might have the first advantage, in which case prices would fall much lower than they are now. And if that applies to American railroads, which were by far the most active market in the Stock Exchange before this Spanish quarrel broke out, it is equally applicable to foreign Government securities. We, indeed, cannot speculate in them because we do not hold any worth speaking of. All, then, the London market can do is to pick up a little as intermediary to the speculations originating in other markets. We do not trust the more rickety classes of Continental securities enough to buy "bulls" of them, and the "bears" of them among us have been so often pickled that they are shy of having another fling; besides, what is the use of selling such stocks as Spanish "fours," or Portuguese 1 per cents. at present quotations? Both these may be worthless, and even if not there is not much to hope for in them in the shape of a rise.

The most perplexing division of the stock markets at the present is that for South American securities. Why should Chilian and Argentine bonds have been slipping back so persistently until just the other day? We can understand the fall in Brazilian bonds, for the wonder has been for a long time how they ever kept the prices they did; but Chili we have always believed to be recuperating, and undoubtedly her successive administrations have made the most strenuous efforts to put and keep her finances in order. The Argentine

Republic, too, we have been preached into believing on the reforming and reviving tack. Only a few months ago the Government of Buenos Ayres solemnly decreed the reconsumption of payment in full upon all classes of the public debt, and entered into arrangements for assuming the derelict debts of the various provinces. It was all rose-water and sweetmeats from the financier's point of view, and yet here the various classes of bonds have been tumbling £1, £2, and £3 a day sometimes, dragging Argentine railways down with them at the very time when their traffics were beginning to improve under the influence of this year's better harvest. What does it all mean? We cannot yet say; but one probable cause of the fall might well be the necessity many great market proppers have recently been under of finding ready money. In other words, the lower prices reached by whole groups of securities together illustrate the solidarity of the financial market-controllers all the world over. Provided no great loss falls upon this body of international financiers at one point, they can usually work all markets according to their will. We know very well, for instance, that the Argentine Republic, although mending in some ways, and gradually filling up and growing richer, is, from the point of view of its Government, by no means in a position to resume full payment of its public debts, still less to load itself up with the provincial debts as an additional burden on the federal Budget. This weakness, however, in no way deterred the financiers who sway the fiscal policy of the Republic from undertaking a campaign to raise the market price of its loans. They had the means to do this, and also to enable the Argentine Government to seem solvent for a time sufficiently long to insure the sale of the bonds they hold to investors the world over, if not at a profit, still at very much less loss than they stood to incur some years ago. We have not the least doubt that, but for the untoward outbreak of this quarrel between the United States and Spain, the financiers in charge of Argentine credit would have successfully concluded the campaign undertaken with this object and once more have handed over large masses of doubtful bonds to investors at high prices, to their own great relief and enrichment. But the Government of Washington has temporarily upset their calculations, has driven Spanish bonds down from 60 or thereabouts to the neighbourhood of 30, and in doing so has forced the international financiers to come to each other's support. Money has already had to be withdrawn from all kinds of enterprises in order to prevent a general breakdown in Latin finance, and Argentina came in for its share of the rebuff. If the war goes on for any length of time we may see much greater depreciation and much more expanded than anything that has yet taken place, although these last few days have seen a pause and a rally. It need hardly be said that a market so dominated, or driven, through the necessities sometimes of the great potentates of finance, is not a market in which the private individual should dabble much. Least of all should he buy when they seem to be doing so.

Since the Chartered meeting, and, above all, since the Boer Government conceded 10s. per case on the price of dynamite, we have had a brisk effort made to put life into South African shares. Rand Mines have been run up a pound or two in spite of the distressed state of the French open market, already almost in the throes of dissolution, and there have been bobbings up of 5s., 10s., or a pound in many other shares of properties or alleged properties.

These movements are like the jerks of a galvanic needle. There is no solidity in them, and they are not as yet backed up by public buying. The utmost that even the Chartered stalwarts have been able to do has been to raise that company's shares by half-a-crown, which was no sooner gained than lost again, although the "rights" to the new issue are valued at 6½d. So long as the masses of share dabblers throughout the country refuse to join in the play instability must be the aspect of the market, and we earnestly hope they will not join. We have again and again given them abundant reasons why they should not, and must unweariedly repeat the advice, for the simple reason that it embodies a profound conviction that prices are, on the average, far too high measured by intrinsic values. And the unfortunate individual who is sitting upon shares at probably much higher prices ought never to "average" with a view to minimise his loss. The policy he ought rather to pursue is to unload a little of his holding on every advance in the market. It is not at all the game of the "bosses" that he should make money out of them, it must never be forgotten. Their object is to increase in wealth at his expense.

We have dealt with one of the Australian puddles elsewhere, and may let it alone here, but may say in regard to Copper shares that we do not much believe in a great increase in copper mining profits through the present war. Shares, led by Rio Tinto ordinary, the most manipulated thing on the Paris Bourse, have been going up, and may continue for some little time to do so. Those who possess any should not wait for the inevitable reaction to let the ardent financiers have them.

Northern "Terrors" Collapse.

On several occasions recently we have drawn attention to the outrageous speculation in the shares of this company, if we can call it a company. It was capitalised nominally at £300,000, and the £1 shares were introduced upon the market at £3. At the mid-April account these shares were carried over at £4 each and had been higher. Between then and the end of last week they fell to less than £1, and disaster has followed, although the jobbers managed to screw up the price to 1¼ for "making-up" purposes on Tuesday. We are not able to state what the resulting differences to be paid are, but the lowest estimate we have heard of is £120,000, and the probability is that the amount will prove to be very much larger. Happily the public are not very much interested in this gamble, and the loss will fall more, if we may so phrase it, on the guilty than on the innocent. Altogether something like forty members, or firms, of the Stock Exchange are involved in the smash, and one firm is said to owe upwards of £70,000 as its share in the loss. Various attempts at a composition have been made, but as we write we cannot say that any of them is in a position to be carried out. The difficulty is to find the money, and in all probability the bursting of this bubble will have been found to mark the end of what we cannot but regard as a nefarious conspiracy upon the credulity of the public.

What astonishes one most is that firms classed as "most respectable" on the Stock Exchange should be found to have voluntarily involved themselves in such a business. That they have done so is an illustration of the ravenous competition for business which goes on amongst the members. No broker or jobber of the least intelligence could have been unaware of the character of those companies of which the Northern Territories was the latest outcome, the ultimate flower, so to say. They were a matter of paper and ink and cheap-Jack oratory throughout. Possibly some substance may have been behind one or two of them, in the shape of mining properties in Western Australia with some little gold to show. Whether that is so or not was really of no consequence to the business in hand, which was to manufacture company after company, with capitals entirely out of proportion to any solid business or industry they might have to do, and, by means of trading in the shares of these companies, to endeavour to draw in large sums of money from the always gullible public. The whole thing was worked by two or three men, and it is quite conceivable that the dealings might have been so arranged as to leave the losses to fall upon the mushroom companies, while the individuals who created them and used them as their tools cleared out with what money there was to be had. The time has not yet come to write the history of this miserable affair, and we are not sure that it could be fully written unless an investigation takes place before an experienced Judge of the High Court. It is, however, alleged that some of the brokers who have been occupied in creating this unsubstantial financial structure are in the position to receive large differences, while some of the companies which have been buyers of the Northern Territories Company's shares are so crippled that the utmost we have heard offered by way of composition is 10s. in the pound. How one set of brokers could be in this position, while another and larger band by dealing for the same group of men have to encounter losses, which in some instances must be unbearable, is more than we can explain, except on the supposition that some members of the "ring" have "ratted" against their partners, and in doing so hastened the consummation certain to come sooner or later to all such squib and cracker company fashioning and share tossing.

There could indeed be but one end to this sort of aërated finance, so attenuated was its substance, the very facility of manufacture and success, up to a point, presaging its sudden collapse one day. A group of individuals allot themselves the shares of successive companies as they are created and start a swarm of brokers to buy and sell for them, or for account of one or other of the set. Little money is requisite in such operations, because the shares need not be paid for. They are all in the family as it were, and Jack buys from Tom, and Tom buys from Dick, and Dick from Ebenezer, until together they sometimes work prices up to quite giddy heights, waiting always for the chance to unload upon the public. When the public, attracted as flies to the candle by the advancing quotations, does buy the band divides great fortunes; but when the public, chilled by many sad experiences, only looks on, the day soon arrives when the whole of the frail structure topples to the ground of its own pithlessness. Then losses have to be borne by the instruments of the market marauders within the market; and there is wailing and blasphemy in place of confidence and the chink of pocketed gold.

We cannot say we feel any pity for the brokers and jobbers, directly, and with foreknowledge of the plot, engaged in furthering this Northern Territories gamble; if they are all ruined and driven from the Stock Exchange it will be good for the moral tone of that body. Many members, however, both brokers and jobbers, are innocently involved in smashes of this sort nearly always. They deal for clients who will buy, or they are drawn into jobbing against their better judgment because the thing is done in their market, and have to suffer for the sins of others. The very fact, however, that a number of innocent people may find themselves drawn into the whirlpool of destruction such collapses create, should stir the Stock Exchange as a body to endeavour to find some means by which financial Dick Turpinism in any shape could be effectually dealt with on its first appearance. There is something altogether anomalous in the freedom with which Stock Exchange habits of business permit operations of this kind to be conducted time and again to their disastrous conclusions. The consciences of the markets will not be moved by this one lesson, but they are going to have some others, perhaps of a sharper description still, and by the time members have run the gauntlet through a series of liquidations, bound to strip numbers of them of all they possess, and to throw not a few out of the Stock Exchange as defaulters, it is not improbable that they will have become awake to the fact that they have other duties to perform in relation to the public than that of mere instruments of money making, so called. We conceive that neither broker nor jobber is justified, for the sake of any commission paid to him, or of any "turn" offered to him on prices, to buy and sell pieces of paper which he must know to be of suspicious origin or altogether worthless. The morality of this kind of business is much on a par with that of the unclean usurer who traffics in forged bills of exchange. It is habit alone which blinds men to the infamy of "rigging" impostures such as the Northern Territories episode has proved to be.

Some Conditions of Modern Warfare.

An American correspondent, in a letter to us dealing with the dispute between the United States and Spain, remarks that the war, if it does come, will be of great scientific interest even if it goes on but for a few weeks in good earnest. When it is over the world will know something of the real value of the various sorts of ironclads, torpedo boats, torpedo destroyers, &c., and of modern fortifications for harbour defences. "It will be odd," he goes on to say, "if after all your incessant war talk, your millions of soldiers, and hundreds of war craft, peaceable America should be the first to have a fight." As we write the probability of a fight has been turned into a certainty, and the prospect of immediate hostilities opens up many possibilities besides those connected with the efficiency of the various engines of destruction modern ingenuity has brought into existence. Already we have had some instruction as to the value of ironclads in the conflict between China and Japan, and the impression left on our mind by that war is that the huge battleship is by no means the ultimate perfection of a vessel of war. But that far-away strife had comparatively small effect upon the economic condition of European nations. It did not disturb Western money markets nor cause Bourse speculators to tremble for their fate at each turn of the strife. Neither Japan nor China were then involved in modern European finance to an extent which could have affected the stability of any market for a single hour. It will be altogether different with the war between the United States and Spain, and already the mere prospect of this war has produced distressing consequences on every Exchange where tokens of public indebtedness are dealt in.

When war is spoken of in the United States the mind naturally goes back to the condition of things existing at the time of the outbreak of strife between the North and the Southern Confederacy thirty-seven years ago. That gigantic struggle produced immense consequences on the industries of the United Kingdom, and profoundly influenced our mercantile credit for some years, but the world was not then linked together by electricity as it is to-day. The first Atlantic cable was not laid till 1865, and it was not until the succeeding year that regular telegraphic communication was established between the two great divisions of the English-speaking people on either side of the Atlantic. Since then this method of instant communication has been established, not only between Europe and America, North and South, but between all parts of the British dominions and the Far East. The whole world over, where civilisation has made only a beginning of existence, this means of inter-communication is now in constant use. So familiar are we with the telegraph in daily life that it is extremely difficult for us to realise what the world was like when communication was slow between distant parts of the earth; when it took nearly a fortnight, for instance, to convey the intelligence of a victory or a defeat in the United States to the English people, or a month to bring similar news from India. Now all the world lives in the open and in constant inter-communion. If there is a heated discussion in the House of Representatives at Washington in the evening of one day we know all about it in outline in London next morning at breakfast time. Rumours fly across the wires as fast as they are generated, and the minds of people here have frequently been perplexed and dismayed, during recent weeks, at the variety of passions at play in the United States alone.

Many effects flow from this facility of intercourse between nation and nation. In some respects it is a most powerful aid in the maintenance of peace. A false rumour does not get time to grow and lay hold upon the imagination of the people as it could do in the old days. It would be impossible now to have a seven years' war over the question of a "Jenkins's ear," cut off seven years before the strife began, which the alleged shearing of it helped to bring on. Witness the calmness which has succeeded the first excitement about the blowing up of the United States cruiser *Maine* in Havana harbour. Report after report about the origin of this lamentable catastrophe has reached us from America with such rapidity that the first horror has been completely dulled, and it is difficult for people here to enter now into the feelings of resentment which appear to play so large a part in drawing the United States into a conflict with Spain. Perhaps this apathy arises to a considerable extent from the general refusal of the English mind to accept the theory that the ship was blown up by a mine laid, treacherously or otherwise, in Havana harbour, and exploded with deliberate intent to destroy the great ship and her crew. Much as we know about Spanish habits of cruelty, and about Spanish Jesuitry in polities, we have all along refused to accept the decision of the American Committee of Inquiry, and of the American people, that it was a mine, no matter how fired, which blew this vessel to pieces. This attitude, perhaps, helps to make us doubt whether Americans believe the theory themselves. Be that as it may, unquestionably, had we only heard of this disaster some time after its occurrence, by letters giving substantial details from the American point of view, it is not improbable that we should have worked ourselves into a white heat of indignation against Spanish treachery. But when assertion and counter assertion came hourly to hand from Madrid and Havana, from Washington and New York, the hubbub created by this conflict of assertion helped to calm the mind, and we are in no danger now of misconstruing the motives which are driving the American people into war, so far at least as the loss of the *Maine* is concerned. Nor can the American people themselves be in that ignorance of Spanish sentiment and Spanish pride which might easily have prevailed but for the instant communication of all that passes in Madrid and throughout Spain to the American newspapers. Certainly, the telegraph may be made to convey lies, and even when it tells the truth passion may distort the truth; but, making all allowances, it does seem to us that this facility for the instantaneous interchange, if only of anathemas, is a help in preventing those misunderstandings arising from ignorance, out of which so many wars have sprung. In the present instance peace has not been brought about by the aid of constant talk across the ocean, but that is because a situation has arisen in Cuba, and in the United States, too strained and difficult to be smoothed down by any interchange of proposals. If Spain had been able to put aside her false pride so far as to sell the island to America, war might have been averted, and Spanish finances put for a time in some kind of order. Failing that, however, and failing a voluntary relinquishment of the island by the Madrid Government, a struggle to drive the Spaniard out was sooner or later inevitable.

More interesting even than the question of the influence of telegraphy in helping nations to keep peace with each other are the effects it produces upon what may be called the international money market. In the good old days rival nations might fall out and pound away at each other for years without materially affecting the well-being of next-door neighbours not actually involved in the conflict. It is otherwise now when the whole world, one may say, is held in mortgage, more or less, in London, Paris, Berlin, Amsterdam, and New York. Undoubtedly the telegraph has brought all markets for dealing in public securities into most intimate relationship. It has done more; it has made all markets cosmopolitan in their transactions according to the degree of their wealth. Hence such an event as a war between two countries like Spain and the United States, whose securities are dealt in on every important Bourse in Europe, produces far-reaching effects upon credit beyond anything previously experienced. We do not suppose that the defeat of Spain will have anything like the momentous consequences which the defeat of France had in 1871. It may, however, be said that France alone then suffered, while other markets gained. The power of London, for example, as the Clearing House pivot on which the world's finance turns, was incalculably enlarged by the Franco-Prussian war. Its consequences were by degrees to bring first French and then German capital here in large amounts. Before the war it was possible that the Paris Bourse might, under enlightened administration, have become the great international market of the world. After the war it was no longer possible; London became undisputed master, and in spite of a valiant struggle of twenty-seven years Paris is to-day, partly because of recent legislation, threatened with a lapse into complete insignificance. And it is just at Paris that the effects of this war over the fate of Cuba will tell with most disastrous consequences. Already the mere rumour of war has brought enormous loss upon French holders of Spanish bonds. The first effect of the war will unquestionably be to throw Spain into bankruptcy as a nation, and bankruptcy, as we have before said, is almost certain to be accompanied by revolution and social disorganisation of a very dangerous kind. Should such domestic upheavals take place in Spain, then the French people will suffer, not merely by the reduction of the market value of Spain's public obligations to rubbish prices, but likewise by the depreciation sure to take place in the securities of the Spanish railways, which are to a large extent now owned in France. The effect, in short, of Spain's defeat, and the consequent collapse of Spanish credit, might be such in France as to hurry on the revolution now, to all appearance, preparing to burst forth there. And the international character of all markets for public securities is already strikingly illustrated in the consequences which are flowing from the destruction of the values of Spanish securities held in France. This has told upon the power of French operators to hold any class of securities. They have been obliged to sell Italian Rente, Rio Tinto and De Beers mine shares and even Egyptian bonds, in order to find the means to meet the strain put upon their resources by the decline in Spanish securities. Again, French weakness has reacted upon our market, and, conjointly with the withdrawals of gold for the United States, has helped to send up the value of money in London high enough to oblige speculative holders of all classes of securities here to become sellers. A general lowering of quotations has occurred through the precarious condition of Spanish finances alone, and when we add to that the effect of a mere prospect of war upon the price of American railroad securities held here, and dealt in in London, Belgium, Holland, and Germany to an extent we cannot estimate, we can partly realise how tremendous consequences might flow instantly from any great disaster in war, no matter to which combatant. The whole world hangs together in a manner it never did before. International credit has been worked up to a degree of delicate permeation throughout all forms of business to an extent never before witnessed in the world's history.

One consolation arises from this. If the world is not too much overburdened by debt, the distribution of the blow to credit caused by any single event or catastrophe prevents that blow from having the destructive effect at one point it might under other conditions have had. In a sense, the risk of revolution in France through the default of Spain may be said to have been sensibly lessened by the facility the telegraph has given to speculators all over the United States to sell "bears" of Spanish "Fours." Every nation, including our own, has joined in this "bear" selling, to no small extent by being instantly, and all at the same time, made aware of the danger impending to Spanish credit. By this action, which has sent Spanish bonds down 45 per cent. in two months, French holders have at last probably found buyers at better prices than could have been secured if their market had been isolated, or if communications had been slow, as in the old days, between Europe and America. The "bear" is obliged to buy back, and in buying supports the market he seeks to destroy. Left to itself, the Paris Bourse, or at least the *Coulisse*, might have almost foundered under the blow administered by the outbreak of war between the United States and Spain. There would have been no outlet for the stock Frenchmen held. It would have fallen in price, and no buyers would have been encountered to arrest the fall. Banks and banking institutions might have collapsed under the strain, bringing such a degree of social misery into existence through their failure as might have thrown France into the hands of socialists and anarchists for a period long enough to destroy her precariously founded republican institutions. This catastrophe, at any rate, has been averted by the free market the rest of the world has lately given French holders of Spanish bonds. They have been able to sell, and in selling to minimize their losses. The bonds they sell pass through the intermediary "bear" purchaser's into other hands all over the world, and should the bonds go lower and lower, as they probably will, the loss will be distributed over such a wide range that it may be borne without producing a breakdown in public credit at any one point. This is a phase of modern finance which must never be lost sight of in estimating the probable consequences of any particular event upon banking stability.

Our Trade and War.—III.

Colonial Expansion.

Our advisers who desire that England should defy the world in general, and its chief Powers in particular, and that we should annex all the unoccupied land left on the globe, from a commercial point of view recommend a policy that is too extended and which savours of reckless commitments beyond the resources of the British firm. The annual profits of our China trade at 5 per cent. would represent annually about £600,000, and of our West African trade, £170,000, or, say, in round figures, £1,000,000. What would a war about either of these countries cost? Possibly some £500,000,000, or our profit on the trade for 500 years to come, in addition to the untold losses that a collision with any Great Power, not to mention three of them at once, would inflict upon our commerce. Let us, therefore, clearly recognise that a war for trade in these directions would be absolute lunacy from a mercantile point of view. Of course war is at times a sad necessity when the honour of the country is involved, but let us be very clear first that such a state of things has arisen, and, in the meantime, like the strong man armed, keep our own house in dignified peace.

So far as foreign possessions are concerned, no one who looks at the map can doubt that England holds the best. If other Powers at the eleventh hour wish to pick up the fragments that are left, let us leave them to do so without an exhibition of childish and paltry jealousy, especially as any gain they may make must necessarily benefit us in some way. With one-third of the world to administer, we have our hands more than full. If in the past, our statesmen wisely refrained from occupying any portion of the mainland of China when the only difficulty would have been the burden of administration, added to our already gigantic responsibilities, it would be obviously unwise in the extreme to undertake such a task and to start a great European war as well.

The policy of colonial expansion on the part of France and of Germany has not had encouraging results. France was earlier in the field and has more valuable possessions, but Greater Germany appears to contain less than 1,000 Germans, notwithstanding its vast size. The fact is that colonies in the tropics or among semi-civilised races in no case bring much grist to the mill. Those of our colonies which are of any use from a trade point of view are in temperate climates, such as North America or Australia. India may appear to be an exception, but is not so when the enormous size, the teeming population, and its advanced civilisation are considered. The natives of India take only 2s. 1¾d. per head of our produce, while our temperate zone colonies take some £3 10s. per head. Our exports to India are swollen by the construction of railways in that Empire, and this may for very many years continue. Apart from this, what do the natives want from us? A rich Bengali Baboo spends 4d. a day on home-grown rice and dresses in white cotton, which will soon be made at home for him. What can the hundreds of millions of Indian poor want from us in a warm climate? Of the exports of British produce, not one-fifth goes to the tropics, the remaining four-fifths mainly going to Europe, the United States, Canada, Australia, and South Africa. If Germany and France wish to bring the waste places of the tropics into order by all means let them do so. If Russia wishes to open up Northern China, it would only be to our benefit. We have practically no trade there now, and after all Russia takes four times per head from us what China does under present circumstances. That Russia, Germany, or France will make much of colonial expansion appears open to doubt, and this affords another reason for the unadvisability of war directed against their policy.

Even if it were true that our wars in the past gave us a colonial empire and our inter-imperial trade of £183,000,000 a year, it does not seem to have been commercially a good investment. A profit of 5 per cent. on that total would be £9,150,000, and of 10 per cent. £18,300,000. Our national debt, due entirely to these wars, has for nearly a century been a fearful burden on our population. Its incidence is now greatly reduced, but it still costs us £28,000,000 a year. From a trade point of view, this looks very like a national loss of £10,000,000 a year. Our Empire must thus be defended on much wider grounds, and is happily most defensible upon them. Nor is it by any means clear that our Empire and our Imperial trade are due to our past wars. In a sense, no doubt, our old conflicts with Spain, and afterwards with France, gave us the mastery of the seas, and thus led to our acquiring our colonies. But the latter would have been useless to us without many other circumstances. In the past, Spain, Portugal, Holland, and France have been the greatest colonial powers in the world, and gained their positions by war. Where are their Empires now, and what good did they ever do them? The two first-named powers were mainly brought to their present sunken position by the burden of extraneous empire—a warning surely to us not to extend our responsibilities too far. Our colonies proper have succeeded, because we had and have a redundant population, and because the discovery of steam power was made in this country where we had the command of coal, iron, and abundant capital. We thus got the start over Continental nations who were immersed in wars, and in their consequences, at a time when we enjoyed (with the break of the Crimean war) over three-quarters of a century of complete European peace. Now that the unification of Germany and Italy, the breaking of the restless spirit of France, and the natural and prodigious advance of Russia in population and civilisation, have all brought about a new and apparently fairly settled balance of power, other nations are treading on our heels. Our old monopoly of external commerce is at an end, our lead in the world's market is gone, and eager foreign rivals dispute every scrap of our trade. Is this a time for bloated armaments, for hasty wars, and possibly for the conscription, particularly when our competitors have made a study of our past and present errors and weaknesses, so as to avoid them all? It is often advanced as a reason for the necessity of opening new markets, by war if necessary, that our old ones are one by one being closed to us, through the Protectionist policy of other nations. What are we to do, under what is called a system of one-sided free trade, when door after door is slammed in our faces? The prophets of ill, as in so many other cases, lament too previously, for such hard things as facts are against them. It is, of course, perfectly true that we should in some respects be much better off if other countries adopted a modern commercial policy, but as it is we do pretty well—in fact, a good deal better than our neighbours. In 1882 our trade with countries doing £10,000,000 a year and upwards with us, in Europe and its existing and former colonies, and with the United States, was £460,000,000. In 1896 the figures rose to £470,000,000, an increase of £10,000,000, although prices had fallen enormously in the interval. It is true that the increase was in our imports, but this simply means that the dividends paid to us on the foreign investment of our profits had risen £10,000,000—a not unsatisfactory tribute paid by other nations to our prosperity. Although this is so far satisfactory, there is unhappily reason to think that foreign nations are gaining ground on us in trade matters.

The Condition of Brazil.

In one sense remarkably little is known about it. For years back the Rio exchange has been declining until it is now well below 6d. per milreis, showing the currency of the country to be at a discount of quite 80 per cent.; and in a general way the public knows that Brazil has not only an extravagant and helpless central Government but a number of more or less corrupt and wasteful State Governments, so that, great though the natural resources of the country are, they are absorbed or scattered so much that both State and Federal Treasuries exist in chronic impecuniosity. The rate of exchange barometer, in short, points straight to national insolvency. In such circumstances the continual puzzle is how Brazil manages to maintain appearances by paying the interest and sinking fund charges on her foreign debt, as well as the guarantees accorded to the subsidised railways, mostly constructed with English money. Some little light is thrown on problems of this kind by the very interesting report of Mr. Consul-General Wagstaff on the trade of Rio de Janeiro for the past year. He points out, for instance, that a commercial crisis has been precipitated by the exclusive attention which Brazilian planters have devoted to coffee growing in the past few years. Seduced by the high prices prevailing some time ago, they went in wholesale for extending the plantation of the shrub, with the consequence that the supply of the berry is now enormously in excess of market requirements. Between 1887 and 1896 the average profit of the planter is estimated by Mr. Wagstaff to have been 150 per cent., and great as the fall in the price of coffee has since been he can still produce it at a profit. Naturally, however, the low prices now ruling have hit the power of the Government to remit to Europe very severely, because, although the export of coffee has risen until last season it reached the total of 9,678,317 bags, it does not yield sufficient to give the Government a large margin to draw upon. And the worst of it is that other sources of wealth have been so completely neglected by a class intent in the pursuit of fortunes in coffee, that the people have to be fed from abroad, and are thus entirely unprepared to encounter misfortune.

Time given, this condition will doubtless improve, and already the cultivation of Indian corn and beans at least is extending, and the planters are becoming awake to the necessity of producing something besides coffee for export. Movement, however, in this wholesome direction takes time, and before it can be carried to the extent necessary to save the country its central Government may founder in bankruptcy, if nothing worse. In vain does the Rio Government struggle along by raising local loans, by floating Treasury bills in London, and perhaps by squeezing further advances out of the Rothschilds, who are as deeply implicated in Brazilian finance as the Barings were in Argentine. The day must come, under present conditions, when it will be impossible for the Government to meet its sterling obligations in Europe, and our impression is that it is not now a day far off. The crisis which has been grinding along in Brazil, for the last four or five years at least, is now breaking out in an acute form in Portugal, with whom, as the mother country, Brazil still maintains intimate relations. Should a collapse happen in Portugal, it must hasten the end in Brazil likewise, and it would not in any way surprise us if the additional strain put upon international credit by the present war were to upset the equilibrium in both countries. We have dwelt only upon the financial aspect of the question, because it is the most pressing, but traders will find a great deal to interest them in Mr. Wagstaff's report, and should give careful heed to his advice with regard to the packing of goods, so as to make them pass the Custom House easily, and study the tariff changes, which to some extent appear to be favourable to a revival of trade. It by no means follows that because the Governments of Brazil, federal and local, may be more or less insolvent, or likely to fall into insolvency, the people are therefore poorer. Under certain circumstances the bankruptcy of a Government might well be a nation's salvation. In the case of Brazil we should not be at all surprised were its collapse as a federal State to lead to the institution of a number of independent Republics. We have spoken only of coffee. What interest have Bahia and Pernambuco in coffee? The question alone suggests cleavage enough to sunder North from South.

Economic and Financial Notes and Correspondence.

Some Consequences of a State of War.

Whether there is to be fighting or Spanish privateering or not—we expect plenty of both—commerce is already beginning to feel the effects of the declared state of hostility between the United States and Spain. Postal communication has been stopped in the United States with Spain and all Spanish Colonies, and the British Postmaster-General has issued a notice that, communication with Cuba being interrupted, letters for Havana and all other places in the island will be detained in the Post Office and not forwarded until some opportunity arises for their safe transmission. Letters, however, directed to be sent by any particular route will be dispatched, although the Postmaster-General has no ground for supposing that they will in consequence secure early delivery. This is perhaps a small matter. Of more importance, however, is the advance in rates of marine insurance. British companies in New York have raised their rates on American bottoms 50 per cent., and in addition they now charge a premium of 10½ per cent. for long voyages, and in some cases as high as 5 per cent. for Transatlantic voyages. These advances are made on account of the uncertain position of the Spanish navy, and because Spanish privateers have been reported on the British coasts. The effect of such high rates will be to send trade more and more into British channels. American ships will no longer be able to sail under their own flag, and the commerce of the port of New York will suffer diminution. American trade, however, as we have frequently pointed out, need not necessarily be much interfered with in bulk by these consequences of a state of war. It will simply be diverted to Canada, for the most part, and perhaps also to Mexico. It is an ill wind that blows nobody good. What a pity the Canadian Government has not got its subsidised line of mail steamers ready. They might have done a roaring trade this summer. Could it not arrange with the Orient, or some other limp company on this side, to fill the gap meanwhile until the chosen contractors have had time to raise the money and build the ships?

Mr. Rhodes—A Correction and Criticism.

With only an imperfect report in an evening newspaper to guide us last week, we somewhat misunderstood Mr. Rhodes's statement with regard to the money spent in what he is pleased to call the development of Rhodesia. In order to put ourselves right we give the correct version in full and shall offer some comments upon it.

First of all there is the money you have spent in the development and conquest of the country which you have named after me. Now that money is roughly not £10,000,000, as Earl Grey, if he will allow me to correct him, has stated, but is roughly about six millions. That I say is a debenture debt. I am speaking to two audiences—not only here to the people of this country, but to the people in that country, which is becoming a self-governing State—just like another State of South Africa—and the money expended in the conquest and development of it should, when those people have become fully a self-governing State, become a debenture debt of the country. We must look at these things broadly. The people who are really going to benefit most by the expenditure of the money in bringing Rhodesia into a condition of civilisation are the people who will come after us so far as settlers are concerned. A new country is very difficult. Everything is raw, everything is difficult, everything is against you. Some of you no doubt have read the stories of the Governors of Australia. When they commenced the state of the country was regarded almost as hopeless. Now it has four millions of people and a revenue of £100,000,000 a year. And with regard to Rhodesia I think it would be unfair to solely debit you or the first people of the country with the total cost of the conquest and development from barbarism to civilisation. The people who benefit by the expenditure should repay it in the form of a public debt, and when the country changes from a Chartered administration, and becomes a self-governing State, it must take over from you what debt you have incurred in connection with the conquest and development of that country. And I feel sure they will do it.

It will be remembered that we challenged Earl Grey's statement at the time and it seems to us that he ought to have at once corrected so glaring an exaggeration. That, however, is his affair and may be left where it stands. Of much more importance is the indication the above extract gives of Mr. Rhodes's intention to lay upon the backs of the inhabitants of Rhodesia, as soon as a decent pretext is given him to do so, a debt of about £6,000,000. How he arrives even at this figure we do not know. Hardly so much has been spent on wars and everything else, if we exclude the 2,000,000 of shares taken as promoter's fee by him and his associates of the De Beers syndicate, which originally projected and carried out the annexation. Including the premiums received on the shares and the debentures, we cannot find that quite £4,000,000 of money has really been put into the territory directly by the company. The inference, therefore, is that Mr. Rhodes does intend to throw the 2,000,000 shares divided up by the promoters into the total "debt." In a common man this proposal would meet with the utmost condemnation, but Mr. Rhodes is *sui generis*, and his cool proposition was greeted with cheers by the enthusiastic shareholders.

From their point of view, indeed, the cheers were justified. If the settlers in the territory of the company can be loaded in this way at the start, and persuaded to pay, say, 5 per cent. upon the "bonds," Chartered shareholders would enter upon a revenue of £300,000 and still possess the whole of their shares on which to receive whatever "profit" could be extracted in addition. That is one way of looking at the proposed transaction, and it heightens our admiration for the splendid impudence which conceived it. It might bear another aspect, however, even for Chartered shareholders, were the debentures given to them for their so-called "expenditure" in the country, including the £3,000,000 swallowed up in the Matabele and Mashona rebellions, to be sold to third parties, for then these third parties would hold a mortgage over the territory which might become extremely burdensome. Shouting shareholders might reflect that this would not be the only debt Rhodesians would have to carry by any means. As we pointed out a fortnight ago, the "progress" they create must provide interest on a railway capital the total of which may soon be another £6,000,000, all of which would come before the Chartered shareholder. And there is all the mining capital in addition which will look for revenue in some shape, with probably mine debentures bringing ever so many other dogs to wrangle over the bone. Hence the estimate put forward by us that £3,000,000 of free revenue—free to be taken from them—would have to be produced by the inhabitants of the country before they could put a bit of bread in their own mouths, so to say, is by no means an exaggerated one, and, however delighted shareholders may be at the prospect, we think sensible people may well hesitate, not once, but many times, before committing their future to a country prospectively eaten into to this extent by its conquerors with their dependents, suckers, and hired chorus of applauders.

Cuban Horrors.

Before giving way freely to the call for "sympathy with Spain," for "money to help Spain to fight," and so on, the City should read the *Daily Chronicle* of Thursday's report of an interview with Mr. G. C. Musgrave, its special correspondent, lately ejected from the island by the Spaniards, and now on his way back again. In this interview Weylerism is set forth in all its horrors of murder, rapine, laying waste, starvation, and every crime the history of Spain as a ruling power has made us familiar with since her conquests in America began. The Spaniard of peace and "good society" may be, generally is, a gentleman in manners and speech. But place him in uncontrolled sway over a number of his fellow men and he oftener than not develops the instinct of the bloodthirsty savage. Weyler, in Cuba, was merely a modern replica of Alva in the Netherlands, probably without Alva's fanaticism, and the worst of it is that the Government of Spain is too weak to be able to keep its agents in order.

"But Mr. Musgrave may be exaggerating." Well, it is easy for our Foreign Office to put his credibility to the test. He tells a story of the murder of a British subject, a Mr. Dalregon, in cold blood. The Spanish soldiers woke him in the middle of the night and shot him dead without a word of explanation. This British subject left a wife and family it would appear, and, if they also have not since been done to death, redress of their wrongs ought to be required of the Spanish Government, unless it can give, or compel General Weyler to give, an explanation of the deed which may remove it from the category of wilful murder.

The Tax on Bills of Exchange.

In his reply to the desultory talk over his Budget, Sir Michael Hicks-Beach passed heedlessly over the suggestion of Sir Samuel Montagu that a committee should be appointed to deal with the question of foreign bills of exchange. Sir Samuel wishes to have the laws and customs regulating these settled by international agreement. We are not sure what he means by that, but on one point he certainly was justified in drawing attention to this subject. Last July, in dealing with it in this Review, we pointed out that the present uniform tax of 1s. per cent. on all bills of exchange, no matter of what currency, was tending directly to destroy our former large business in this negotiable instrument, and to throw payments more and more into the form of sight cheques and telegraphic transfers. As we then pointed out, the stamp on a seven-day bill is equivalent to 2·3 per cent. per annum on the amount of it, a quite absurd impost; and it astonishes us that the Chancellor of the Exchequer, who has been himself a bank director, did not catch at the opportunity Sir Samuel Montagu's suggestion opened up to him to set on foot a movement to remove at least this anomaly. Had he devoted himself to the labour of graduating the stamp duty on bills of exchange so that those of brief currency, up to two months, say, would pay less considerably than those bearing more distant dates of payment, he would have powerfully assisted the bankers of the City to resume and maintain their hold upon this international instrument of commerce. The reform would have been a worthier one in our opinion than the proposed changes in the income tax, or the reduction in the tobacco duty, one of which does not seem to us fiscally sound, and the other nobody has yet said "thank you" for. However, a lowered tobacco duty does appeal in some sense to the masses, even if they get nothing by it, whereas the proper regulation of bill stamps would have seemed to the multitude of the electorate only to touch the pockets of the City—those bulging pockets.

The Rise in Wheat.

If it had been Great Britain herself that had delivered a declaration of war against another Power, there could scarcely have been a greater turmoil among wheat dealers than has prevailed for the last ten days or a fortnight. Prices have gone up with a rush and a bound until business was done at 47s. a quarter, and in one instance, at least, at 48s. That is the highest figure as yet. The average is probably not more than 45s. or 46s., but the tendency is still upward, and it is not impossible that it may soon reach even 50s.—the highest price touched since 1891, when the Russian ukase against the exportation of wheat caused an extraordinary, though happily temporary, excitement in the wheat trade. For the present enormous rise in wheat there seems no adequate reason. Farmers, it is said, hold out because they believe rates will be higher yet. Possibly; but it may easily happen that they may hold out too long, and suffer loss in consequence. For many weeks past the rates for wheat have been firm, with an upward tendency; but until last week the rise was comparatively small, and no fear was entertained of exceptional rates. The imports for the season up to last week were about a million quarters less than those of the same period last year. It was estimated some weeks ago that to keep up stocks to their average level between now and August we should require to import about 10,000,000 quarters. There has also for weeks been an exceptional demand for France and the Continent; but all these causes combined would not have produced a very serious rise in the price had it not been for the bursting of the war cloud between Spain and America.

But that can only be regarded as an excuse or pretence. New York exporters have for weeks been busy sending off large shipments of wheat. Many of them are now on the way. There may be some little delay before these exports are resumed; for the doubt about the attitude of the United States and Spain towards the Declaration of Paris, and the engagement of privateers made shippers timid. But that doubt is now dispelled. Both countries have repudiated privateering; for though Spain reserves to herself a conditional right to resort to it in case of a change of circumstances, nobody believes that she will do so. The war risk fixed by the Marine Insurance Companies on British vessels from the United States and Canada is only 5s. per cent. in contrast with £2 per cent. on ships sailing under the American or Spanish flag. The insurance companies, therefore, have no great apprehension of interference with grain freights in British vessels, so that there can be no solid reason for the extraordinary upward spurt in the price of wheat. It cannot last. There are ample stores of grain in the United States and Canada for our own needs as well as those of the Continent; and these will be forthcoming in due time. Indian wheat, too, and Argentine will soon be abundant on the market. So the reign of the speculative "bull" can only, we believe, be of brief duration.

The Neutrality Proclamation.

This document, to those who expected logical precision and clear definition of what is contraband of war, may be somewhat disappointing, but we do not see that, with a due regard to all the interests concerned, the proclamation could well have been any more clear or precise than it is. It is quite according to precedent. Indeed, in the main, it may be regarded as a veteran that has done duty in several wars. No doubt something more definite was perhaps expected on the question of coal; but had the English Government declared coal contraband of war, its motives would have been misunderstood, and it would certainly have been accused of favouring America at the expense of Spain. If, however, coal is not made contraband of war, her Majesty's subjects are left in no doubt as to how and when it may be supplied to belligerent vessels. Such ships on entering English ports may be supplied with just enough coal to carry them to their nearest home port, and no ship can be supplied a second time within three months, unless by special permission. This may not perhaps be altogether agreeable to coal dealers who hoped for an opportunity of doing a big business with belligerent craft. But no neutrality proclamation would probably have satisfied the aspirations of such gentlemen. What that document has to aim at securing is that there shall be no repetition of the *Alabama* difficulty; and this the proclamation, if impartially carried out, may easily do. It has at least been very effectual in the case of the American gunboat *Somers*, at Falmouth, in regard to which it cannot be said that we have been led astray from the strict path of neutral duty by sympathy or sentiment. Of course there are difficulties in the neutrality proclamation in the way of the unwary, but they are scarcely to be avoided in such a document. The main thing is to insist on its impartial enforcement. Spain may deserve nothing special at our hands, but at least she is entitled to strictly legal and just treatment as a belligerent; and benevolence may be mixed with our neutrality to America without straining official proclamations, which must descend to farce and worse if their provisions are not carried out with the utmost impartiality.

Dutch Petroleum and the Standard Oil Company

We are glad to read in Mr. Consul Robinson's report from Amsterdam that, so far, the attempts of the Standard Oil Company of America to obtain a footing in the petroleum interest of the Dutch East Indies has not met with success. The company sought to buy the shares of the Mocara Enim Company, an important concession in Sumatra, but at an extraordinary general meeting of the latter held in February last to ratify the agreement, the Dutch Government interfered and stated that no concessions would be granted "to a company under the control of the American monster monopoly." Whether the Standard Oil Company will be effectually stopped by such a statement is doubtful, but the Government seems quite determined to resist it to the utmost. "The agitation against the Standard Oil Company's monopoly," says Mr. Robinson, "in so far as this inflicts on this country all the dangers and disasters caused by an exclusive supply of low-flashing oil, is a constantly increasing one." We are delighted to hear it, and, now that Sir Vivian Majendie is dead, hope to see this good example followed vigorously by ourselves—by the people, we mean, not by our Government. It never does anything which savours "of interference with the liberty of the subject," or of the alien, to blow himself and his neighbours to pieces if he chooses.

Agriculture in Germany.

Mr. T. R. Mulvany, H.B.M.'s Consul at Düsseldorf, is evidently a persevering as well as an energetic gentleman; and it will not be his fault apparently if we are not made thoroughly acquainted with all the ways and outcome of German trade and commerce. But he should stick to facts: his theories are of little use where they are not misleading. Here, for instance, as introductory to an interesting paper on German agriculture which he has had compiled by a German gentleman who evidently knows his subject, Mr. Mulvany gravely informs us that while the British farmer has been discouraged and depressed by the difficulties which confront him, the German farmer has made progress "under the less adverse policy of a moderate amount of protection and fair railway freights." Then he speaks of this industry in England and Ireland as being "a hopelessly minous one." Even English farmers, much as they may be given to grumbling, would scarcely agree with such a hopeless statement; and as to the "moderate amount of protection" being a benefit to the German farmer, the voluminous facts marshalled in Mr. Koenig's report seems to us to show that it has nothing to do with the success of agriculture in Germany.

Not only do the State railways give the German farmer the benefit of the "fair railway freights" which are denied to the British agriculturist, but the State provides him with a large number of technical educational establishments where he may be thoroughly fitted for his business. Then there are the State experimental stations, where all sorts of experiments are made for the benefit of the farmer, where also fodder, manures, seeds, and so forth are tested for a merely nominal fee. The transfer of land is almost as simple and easy as that of any commercial commodity. There are few large farms—absolutely none above 500 hectares, or about 1,000 acres. Eleven per cent. of the farms are under four acres, and 44 per cent. from ten to forty acres. This refers more particularly to Westphalia. General workmen and farm labourers are encouraged to acquire land and build their own cottages, with the result that the workers are settled and easily available in the various districts. Fruit-growing adds much to the income of the German farmer, while the English farmer will hardly look at it; and, even if he did, the railways would extract a too great percentage of the profit in freight for carrying the fruit to the central markets. The very moors are cultivated with profit in Germany; and vast tracts of waste land have thus been turned into fruitful districts, growing some of the finest sugar-beetroots to be seen in Germany. Credit banks are also numerous. In all these things the State has been and continues to be helpful. In fact, the German farmer gets so much done for him by the State that he ought to be ashamed to keep the State picking the pockets of the consumers for him under the guise of "protection," moderate or otherwise.

UNFORTUNATE AUSTRIA.

What is Austria coming to? While her commercial men are appealing for legislative reforms in relief of trade, her politicians seem bent on making legislation of any sort impossible. The scenes witnessed in the Reichsrath since its reassembling are enough to make moderate men despair of Parliamentary Government. Three or four deputies who were suspended in one of the many riots in the Reichsrath before Christmas, and were deprived of their official salaries for three days, have won a victory in the law courts. The judges have ordered the salaries to be paid, and thus virtually declare the famous Lex Falkenhayn illegal. Undoubtedly this is a triumph for the Opposition deputies, but instead of accepting it quietly, and setting about the business of the nation like sensible practical men, they celebrate the event by an orgie of riot. They have carried a motion for the impeachment of Count Badeni, the former Premier, by a majority of eight. But to what end? Nothing more will probably be heard of it, unless the absence of impeachment proceedings be made the excuse for further disorder. The sooner commercial men found a commercial party in the Reichsrath the better for themselves and the country. There will be no commercial reforms for them otherwise. Then there is the *Ausgleich* to be settled. Unless it is arranged soon the very union of the dual kingdom will be in jeopardy. There is a colonial party in Austria. It wishes to found a colony in East Asia. It has been casting longing eyes on China, at which every Power but Austria has had its pull, and it proposes to send a Commission to the Far East to inquire how best Austrian interests may be furthered in that distant quarter. The Emperor approves and encourages the project; but what is the use of it if the Reichsrath is to confine itself to miserable wranglings over trifles, leaving the real interests of the country to take care of themselves? Austrian trade is still in swaddling clothes, and without more freedom, it must lose strength until its continued existence may be in danger.

THE COTTON MANUFACTURING INDUSTRY OF MEXICO.

A very interesting and instructive report is that of Mr. Lionel Carden on the subject of the ancient industry which at the present day forms such a profitable source of revenue to the Mexican Government. Practised by the natives for centuries before the Spanish conquest, it was not encouraged or protected under Spanish rule, which strove rather to check any enterprise that might interfere with the trade of the mother country, and not until after the Independence were any efforts made to revive this languishing source of wealth. The first factory was built in 1834, near Puebla, with a view to taking advantage of the abundant jute supply of that district, water being the only motive power used in the earlier stages. It is still the principal power, fuel being very dear, and consequently all, or nearly all, of the sites for subsequent factories were chosen with the view to water, except in one or two instances where other advantages had to be taken into consideration. In 1896 there were 107 factories at work throughout the Republic, with an aggregate of 13,826 horse power, forty-five being worked by water alone, twenty-eight by steam alone, and twenty-eight by steam and water combined, the proportion of steam in these last averaging about 25 per cent. of their total power. The machinery in the same year consisted of 13,660 looms, 448,156 spindles, and 24 printing machines, to which 500 looms were added in 1897, and by the end of this year another 1,200 will be in operation. We are glad to note that English machinery is increasing rapidly in favour on account of its superiority and stability, and that for some years past all the new machinery erected has been of English make. Mexico cannot manage to raise much more than half the raw material required annually in its factories, and imports the rest from the United States, levying a customs duty of about 1d. per lb. The price of the native cotton is also governed by that of the foreign, and in 1896 the mean price per lb. was 20 cents for both Mexican and foreign. The total amount consumed was 53,273,397 lb., at a cost of $10,645,679, or about £1,065,000. The total cost of production, including over $2,000,000 paid in taxation, Mr. Carden estimates at about $18,000,000, and though unable to give the exact profits in the industry, they are generally stated at from 20 to 30 per cent. on the actual capital invested. Up till now Mexico has not been able to supply the local demand for cotton fabrics in her markets, and has had to import low grade price goods from England, but as the manufacturing capacity increases in greater proportion annually than the consumption, it will not be long before the factories will produce all that is required in the country, and enable the people to dispense with our aid. This, however, Mr. Carden points out, is with regard to low-grade goods only, the Mexican operative being incapable of skilled labour and unable to make tissues of finer finish or with any variety of textures. English merchants, instead of losing what trade they have, might greatly increase it by the introduction of new materials direct to the consumer, especially among the poorer classes.

Critical Index to New Investments.

LONDON GENERAL OMNIBUS COMPANY.

Issue of £75,000 4 per cent debentures, being part of £300,000 authorised. Tenders are invited at a minimum of 110 per cent. The stock which is redeemable October 1, 1934, presumably at par, is secured on the freehold and leasehold properties of the company, and interest is due April and October. The paid-up capital is £700,000, and the reserves £165,000, while the net income for past twenty years was equal to £73,577 per annum, and for last year reached £119,856. The directors do not condescend to say what the money is wanted for. Can it be for motors? Whatever it is for we do not approve this piling-up of debenture debt when the main security the company has to offer is short leases, the value of which is being rapidly written up in the balance sheet. Allowing for redemption in thirty-six years, the yield of £3 10s. 3d. per cent. is not at all tempting considering the security. A point to notice is that the trustees for the debenture-holders consist of the chairman, deputy chairman, and another director. Trustees should never be members of the board.

THRELFALL'S BREWERY COMPANY, LIMITED.

This Liverpool and Manchester Brewery is making a further issue of shares. It has an authorised capital of £1,000,000, of which three-fourths is subscribed and paid up. It now offers 7,500 ordinary shares of £10 each at 37½, which should bring to the company's treasury £281,250, but the premium is to be placed to the reserve fund. The money will be used in the business, and in paying for properties recently purchased and in the purchase of further properties. This is a wonderfully good brewery. The new issue has caused the existing shares to fall £3, but as they are still 4½ above what the new shares are offered at, the latter will be promptly taken up by existing shareholders, whose applications will very properly be first considered.

BROOKS & DOXEY, LIMITED.

A Manchester business of textile machinists, founded by Samuel Brooks in 1859, now employs over 1,900 men, and the two establishments cover an area of nearly fifteen acres. Land and buildings, almost freehold, are valued at £168,618, and stock, stores, and work on hand at £77,329, while book-debts are guaranteed to produce £44,500, and patterns, patents, and trade marks are put in for £10,000, nothing being charged for goodwill. This makes a total of £300,448, and the vendors have agreed to accept £300,000, two-thirds of which will be cash. The capital comprises £100,000 in ordinary shares, £100,000 in 5 per cent. preference shares, and £100,000 4 per cent. debenture stock, and the vendors take one third of each class. Accountant's certificate is not satisfactory, merely stating that profits for four years ended December 1896, were sufficient to pay 10 per cent. on ordinary shares. This is as far as we are taken, for the works were almost closed for eight months last year owing to the engineers' and spindle-makers' strikes. It is unfortunate that the business should be offered immediately after such a disastrous year. The business may be good, but there is nothing in the accountant's certificate to prove that it is not a declining one.

NOVELLO & CO., LIMITED.

This company is formed to purchase the well-known music publishing business founded by Vincent Novello in 1811, but the purchase does not include the branch in New York. It is difficult to learn much from the accountant's certificate. No account, it seems, has ever been taken of the machinery and plant, nor has stock been taken of the music, &c., in hand, the profits having always been dealt with irrespective thereof. Then, as regards profits, no details are given beyond the simple fact that during the five years ending December, 1897, they exceeded £100,000, or an average of £20,000 per annum. Assets included in the transfer amount to £270,000, of which book debts represent £34,535; stereotyped and engraved plates, £81,685; and plant, fittings, &c., £40,421. Deducting trade debts, £12,138, to be paid by the company, the goodwill and leaseholds stand for £88,154. The share capital is £270,000 in £10 shares, equally divided into ordinary and 4½ per cent. preference, and £90,000 of the latter is offered to the public at 5s. per share premium. The remainder of the share capital is taken by the vendors, and although we do not see the purchase price stated, we assume it is £270,000 as well as the premium on the shares offered. The accountant's certificate is not at all to our liking, and that the assets are worth the amount stated we should much doubt. Even were the shares offered at par, we see no attraction in them.

L. ROSE & CO., LIMITED.

We have all heard of Rose's "Lime Juice Cordial," and this is the company that makes it. The share capital is £150,000 in 15,000 6 per cent. Cumulative Preference shares of £5 each and 75,000 ordinary shares of £1 each. Preference shares alone are offered for subscription, all the ordinary, with £65,000 in cash being taken by the vendors. No statement of assets is supplied, but profits for past three years are certified at £7,466, £10,986, and £12,061. This shows good progress, and as the preference dividend will require only £4,500, this should be easily forthcoming. But what is the security for the money? and are the West Indies going to be affected by the war? In spite of the excellent profit shown, we should not be surprised if the issue does not meet with a very cordial reception.

E. ROBINSON & SONS, LIMITED.

Company is formed to acquire and extend the thirty-year-old business of tobacco, cigarette, and snuff manufacturers of St. Peter's-gate, Stockport. Capital, £100,000 in £1 shares, 35,000 being 5 per cent. cumulative preference, and the remainder ordinary. Little is said about past profits beyond the fact that for three years ended January 7 last, they amounted to £22,033, or an average of £7,344 per annum, but this does not show whether profits are rising or diminishing. Assets are taken over at £75,000, but of this only £13,001 represents freehold property, and machinery and plant, the remaining £62,000 being made up of book debts, £14,810; stock-in-trade, £30,582; and goodwill, £16,605. The vendors ask £75,000 for the business, which seems a very full price; of this amount £50,000 is to be cash. Interest on the preference shares should be pretty safe on this basis, but still, we have not a high opinion of the concern.

THE GROSVENOR DAIRIES LIMITED.

The company offer £30,000 6 per cent. cumulative preference shares at par for the purpose of buying eight "businesses" owned by the Manor Farm Dairy, Clapham. These "businesses" comprise only ten shops; and although the dairy has been carried on for twenty years, only one year's profits are given, aggregating £4,764, while a Philpot-lane firm value the leases, goodwill, &c., at £30,715, goodwill probably bulking largely. The shares now offered appear to be part of the capital offered last year, which met with only a poor response, and we see no reason why investors should come forward more liberally on the second asking.

Company Reports and Balance-Sheets.

⁂ *The Editor will be much obliged to the Secretaries of Joint Stock Companies if they would kindly forward copies of Reports and Balance-Sheets direct to the Office of* THE INVESTORS' REVIEW, *Norfolk House, Norfolk-street, W.C., so as to insure prompt notice in these columns.*

ECONOMIC LIFE ASSURANCE SOCIETY.—In their seventy-fifth annual report the directors of this mutual office state that 559 policies were completed in the year, insuring £469,777 and yielding £15,161 in new premiums, of which £4,825 were single premiums. Part of this was reinsured, so that the net addition to the premium income was £10,271. The total premium income less reassurance was £225,196. Claims absorbed £287,571, including bonus additions, this being less than 83 per cent. of the amount allowed for according to the Institute Table of Mortality, while the claims were under 72 per cent. of the expected number. A large annuity business is done by this society, and last year £80,822 was received on this account in purchase of eighty-eight annuities aggregating £6,930 per annum. Expenses and commission, after making adjustment for single premiums and the capital received for annuities, was reduced from 13·45 to 12·85 per cent. of the premium income. The rate of interest received on the total funds fell 2d. per cent. to £4 0s. 5d., which is still a very good rate. As the result of the year's business the total funds of the society were increased by £97,000 to £3,783,278, and this large sum is nearly all invested at home, only £552,204 being in Indian and Colonial Government securities and £36,070 in Foreign Government securities. The interest income amounted to £147,219.

THE CITY OF GLASGOW LIFE ASSURANCE COMPANY.—This company's fifty-ninth annual report for the year ended January 20 last states that 1,081 policies were accepted, insuring £627,305, and producing £22,637 in annual premiums. A considerable proportion, however, of this was reinsured, so that the net addition to the company's risk was £508,005, and to the premium income £19,353. Only £1,536 was received as single premiums. The total net premium income is now £213,577, and the income from interest and dividends, &c., was £83,220 last year. The company does a small annuity business, having sold immediate annuities of £1,241 within the year, against which annuities amounting to £939 fell in. Claims in the insurance department, including bonus, amounted to £129,120 net. They arose in consequence of the death of 198 policy holders, and both number and amount are stated by the directors to be again considerably within those expected and provided for by the company's calculations. The total receipts of the year were £306,100, and the disbursements £210,198; this left £95,972 to be added to the accumulated funds, raising them to £2,380,802. The company's investments yield an average interest of £3 15s, 8d. per cent. A committee of directors report that the securities are in perfect order, and that their market value is in excess of the value in the books. The ratio of expenses to premium income exceeded 17·5 per cent., which is high in these days of falling interest and keen competition. The great bulk of the company's funds appear to be judiciously invested in home securities.

OTAGO HARBOUR BOARD.—Mr. Hugh Gourley, the chairman of this board, makes a favourable report on the business of the harbour for the past year, stating that, notwithstanding the large expenditure of £13,000 on the works, the surplus of revenue amounted to £2,664, which raised the credit balance to £7,858. The increase in the revenue was £7,160 he states, but it does not appear to us that this can be the case, because £3,604 is included as proceeds of the sale of debentures. We reckon that capital, but there may be some special reason which we do not know for treating the money differently in these accounts. Assuming that these debentures were capital, then the expenditure of the year would appear to have exceeded the income by £600. The matter is trifling enough seeing that such a large sum was spent on works, and there can be no doubt that the board has an expanding income, so we merely allude to the subject for the sake of clear book-keeping. All the charges on the outstanding debt of £687,400 were fully met, and the board appears to have no floating obligation of any sort. Power has been given by the New Zealand Parliament to expend £11,600 on capital account in the improvement of the harbour, and, no doubt, this is a wise outlay.

THE UNION BANK OF SCOTLAND, LIMITED.—For the year ended April 2 this bank made a profit of £151,039, to which £25,965 has to be added, being the balance brought forward. This gives £177,004 for distribution, and £110,000 of it is set aside to pay a dividend of 11 per cent., or 22s. per share in two equal halves on May 10 and November 10 next; £10,000 is placed to cost of bank premises; and £30,000 added to reserve or rest, making its total £595,000, exclusive of the amount set aside for dividend and the balance forward, which latter amounts to £23,338 after income-tax has been paid. From these figures it is evident that the bank might have easily paid a larger dividend, but the directors have done wisely in strengthening the reserve. Eleven per cent. is a very good return, even on a bank share, and we hope this conservative policy will be adhered to until the reserve at least equals the paid-up capital of £1,000,000. The balance-sheet is well divided up, and indicates both the bills discounted, advances or cash credits, and the loans on securities. In addition, various classes of investments are set out, and show that the bank's money is well administered. The total of the balance-sheet amounts to £14,151,685, the liability on deposits being £11,239,481.

SCHWEPPES, LIMITED.—The directors of this company have issued their first report covering a period of nearly eight months up to December 31 last, being the time of the company's life. In this they state that the net profits came to £40,896, and they think this satisfactory, although it does not allow more than 2 per cent. per annum to be paid on the deferred capital of £350,000, this dividend to be reckoned only from the date of the payment of the final instalment on the shares. In justification of their cheerfulness the directors urge that immediate loss of revenue has arisen from the reduction of the charge to customers for bottles to a uniform rate of 1s. per dozen. Already, they state, this concession has stimulated consumption to such an extent that the sales of the year have increased by upwards of 1,500,000 bottles. It is possible, therefore, that the company may do better in the future. At the same time, there is no getting over the fact that a capitalisation of £1,250,000 is an enormous one for such a business, and to bring it into proper trim a large sum from revenue ought to be devoted each year to writing down goodwill. Unless this is done the company can never be in a position to meet adversity or keen competition from rivals less handicapped.

THE EDINBURGH INVESTMENT TRUST, LIMITED.—For its ninth year, ended March 15 last, this company made a profit of £19,543, after providing for interest and expenses of management, and exclusive of profit on investments sold. Out of this they met the preferred stock dividend, and paid 3 per cent. on the deferred stock for the year, leaving £3,709 to be carried forward, as against £1,594 brought in and included in the total profit just mentioned above. No particulars are furnished with regard to the investments of the company, but the directors state that £428,388 is in stocks and shares of public companies and £271,489 in railway bonds, debentures, &c., and that the total of £699,878 thus reached is distributed over 282 investments, being an average of about £3,480 in each. There appears to be depreciation on these investments, well as the money is distributed, and accordingly the sum of £8,086, realised as profit on the sale of securities during the year, has been applied to meeting depreciation. We should have liked to see some valuation of the securities held.

INDUSTRIAL AND GENERAL TRUST.—The revenue of this Trust in the past year ended March 31 from dividends, interest, and commissions was a little higher, but profit on realisations was less than half the amount obtained in the preceding twelve months. Expenses were slightly lower, and the net balance of £68,916 was £20,504 below that shown a year ago. The usual dividend of 5 per cent. only absorbed £47,125, and the sum of £12,500 was applied to the reduction of the debenture stock rebate and expenses account, and £9,317 put to reserve, raising it to £35,000. The amount carried forward—£4,095—was then about the same as that brought in. The debenture stock rebate and expenses account now amounts to £37,500, the wiping out of which remains as a charge upon the net revenue of future years. The reserve is specially invested in high-class securities. The investments stand at about the same amount in the books, but loans against securities have risen very much, being £66,428, as against £28,001 a year ago. We hope these will prove more fortunate than those of a former generation. A glance through the investments shows that the realisations effected were often well timed, but these operations, we should imagine, tend rather to dilute the quality of the investments. At the same time, there appears to be a tendency to return to the old underwriting devices of what we thought was a bygone era in regard to this Trust. For instance, in the list will be found fresh investments as under :—

	Nominal Amount. £
Monger's West Australian Stores Preference ...	1,555
" " " Ordinary ...	1,270
" " " Founders' ...	127
Mountain Copper Company Shares	11,250
National Electric Free Wiring Company ...	1,570
Schibareff Petroleum Company Preference ...	6,500
" " " Ordinary ...	3,300
Rhodesia Breweries Ordinary	3,000
New Trinidad Lake Asphalte Debentures ...	23,500
	£52,072

These are relatively such large blocks that little short of underwriting business could have induced the company to go into the ventures so heavily. As a matter of fact, they are all hazardous, and no doubt some of them will prove troublesome later on. In the year just passed the company may easily have got rid of more shares of this class, so that commission-shearing operations may have been bigger than these figures would seem to point to. At the same time, the amount mentioned compared with the total investments is not large, but it is not wise to sell good securities, even if they are overvalued in the market, if the money is to be placed in issues of this class.

ABOUKIR COMPANY.—This company has been working since 1888 upon land in Egypt reclaimed by the draining of a large lake. At one time its indebtedness was very considerable, but steady selling of land has at last enabled the reduction of the debenture and loan debt to be taken in hand. The profit and loss account is a rather involved affair, but apparently the revenue was £10,554, chiefly from profit on land sales, against which expenditure for maintenance came to £2,790, interest and salaries to £6,027, and depreciation to £102. The net balance was therefore £1,633, but £2,488 was brought in, and accordingly the directors propose the first dividend in the history of the company of 3 per cent., carrying forward £1,628. It is evidently preparing to pay off more of the debentures and then convert the remaining indebtedness into a form of debt bearing a lower rate of interest. Such a step is urgently needed, for the charge now is about 6 per cent., but the present time is not the best for such an operation, and by waiting a little longer the principal of the debt to be dealt with ought to be further reduced and so facilitate the operation. If that is carried through in a prudent manner, a good portion of the revenue ought to be freed, and regular dividends become a probability.

PACIFIC TRUST ASSOCIATION.—This Liverpool concern has a paid-up share capital of £100,000, and debentures outstanding to the extent of £46,020. Against these it has £105,147 in mortgages and loans upon land in California, Oregon, and Washington, and £36,711 in foreclosed properties. Including £850 brought forward, the total income was £12,421, and after payment of expenses there was a net balance of £4,433. A dividend of 2½ per cent. was declared, and £1,933 carried forward. Profit to the extent of £1,254 obtained on sale of foreclosed properties was put to a special reserve. The ordinary reserve is £5,000.

HIGHGATE HILL TRAMWAYS.—The new company to work this cable line is capitalised upon a sensible footing, £15,000 covering the purchase consideration of the tramway, depôt, machinery, and cars. To find the money for this, £10,000 in shares and £6,000 in 5 per cent. mortgage debentures have been issued, and the company appears to owe but little besides these amounts. Last year the line was worked for eight and a half months, and in that time the revenue was £3,735, which left, after paying debenture interest, a net profit of £308. This permitted a dividend of 6d. per £1 share and the carrying forward of £50. It is claimed, however, that £326 special expenditure was included in the working expenses, and, as presumably this will not recur, it will leave a margin to provide against depreciation in future years.

DOOM DOOMA TEA COMPANY.—This is first amongst the important Indian tea companies to issue its report, and the experience it sets forth does not augur well for the statements of other companies. A total of 1,812,990 lb. of tea was produced, or 38,374 lb. less than the preceding year, and nearly 200,000 lb. below the estimate. Cost of manufacture and bringing the tea to market was increased by the higher exchange and the high price of rice, so that the total cost was 8$\frac{3}{32}$d. per lb., or 1$\frac{1}{4}$d. per lb. above that of 1896. At the same time, the average price obtained was 11$\frac{13}{32}$d. per lb., or $\frac{1}{2}$d. per lb. less than in 1896. The company was, therefore, hit on all sides, and the result was that the profit for the year was only £19,040, as against £31,607 for 1896. Fortunately, the prosperous season in 1896 had been utilised by placing £10,000 to reserve, and so the board are able to declare the same dividend—12½ per cent.—as a year ago, but in doing so they reduced the amount forward by £2,067 to a total of £1,965. The company, however, has a reserve fund of £30,000, and last year must be considered exceptionally bad. The loss on rice incurred by the company amounted to no less than 10 per cent. of the outlay at the gardens, and, of course, this expenditure left nothing to show for it.

LONDON GENERAL INVESTMENT TRUST.—This company has done so well that one rather fears that future years will not show such good results. Upon investments and loans amounting to £245,000 it obtained a revenue in interest and dividends amounting to £15,594, or well nigh 6½ per cent. We are quite prepared to admit that it started at the right time, that is, when prices of securities were low, but even allowing for that circumstance, such a return appears to be abnormal. This is especially the case as in all probability the revenue from certain classes of investments may easily show a falling off this year. The board employed £1,750 of the profits in writing down the cost of certain securities, and £300 more was written off preliminary expenses, the balance providing the preference interest, and 7½ per cent. on the deferred stock, as against 7 per cent. for the two preceding years. It seems a pity that the amount written off preliminary expenses was reduced, as the sum still left in the balance-sheet is £1,900, after the company has been in existence for eight years. The sum of £8,110 was obtained from profit upon realisation of securities, and this has been added to reserve, raising its total to £16,339. It is intended to convert the founders' shares, but in dealing with this matter, it ought to be kept in view that the past year was probably exceptionally favourable for the company. The balance-sheet looks well, loans being rather less, and the only debt of importance being £24,161 for bank loan and overdraft. The securities are said to have a market, or estimated value of £9,392 above the value in the books, which is in addition to the reserve. A good deal of the valuation, however, must be upon estimates, as the securities without an official quotation form a fair portion of the investments.

BELL'S ASBESTOS COMPANY.—The profit-earning character of this business seems to steadily decline, for last year the profits amounted to £10,690, as against £15,772 in 1896, and £28,443 in 1894. The charge for interest and management fees (the directors have evidently been paid in part on a scale dependent upon profits) was less, but the net profit of £5,171 for last year was £4,506 below that in 1896. Fortunately, last year £4,000 was added to reserve, and so the board only reduce the dividend by 1 per cent. to 4 per cent., which enables them to carry forward £2,339, or £371 more. Debentures to the extent of about £3,500 were redeemed in the year, and in certain other respects the report, in the meagre information it supplies, gives evidence of cautious policy; but this, of course, is of little avail if profits continue to run off at the pace they have been doing lately. Some statement, therefore, is needed in order to prevent shareholders from becoming thoroughly disheartened.

Bechuanaland Exploration Company.—After having been in existence ten years this company has paid three dividends, all in one year—1895—amounting to 6s. per share. Upon the strength of that remarkable performance its shares were run up to a high figure, which induced unfortunate holders to subscribe for fresh shares at a fancy figure, and upon the £162,069 netted in this way as premiums the company appears to have been living of late. Last year, with a revenue of £26,734, the expenditure came to £34,651, and so a loss in working of £7,917 was shown. Against that only £1,438, the balance brought in, could be placed, and the remaining £6,478 is left as a debit for the future. The directors are bound to admit at last that the £369,627, standing in the balance-sheet as the company's interest in stocks, shares, and syndicates, must be taken subject to depreciation, and accordingly they have withdrawn £72,069 from the premium account and put it to a "special reserve against depreciation." The future, of course, is stated to be very hopeful, but so it has been declared to be from the beginning of the history, and we note that the company has a liability of £68,713 in connection with its interests in stocks, shares, and syndicates. If these do not turn out better than they have done so far the consequences might be inconvenient. The company has shed one of its founders, for Mr. George Cawston will no longer grace its board. We wonder has he any reason to regret his connection with this singularly unfortunate company.

Hand-in-Hand Fire and Life Insurance Society.—For the past year, the 201st of the society's existence, the out-turn of the fire department has been bad. Losses and expenses, including commission, amounted to £107,107, while net premiums came to only £103,372, consequently there was a loss of £3,735 on the year's business, without taking account of the income from investments. The directors state that this loss has arisen chiefly through the Cripplegate fire of November 19 last, which cost them about £21,000, the largest loss the society has ever had by one fire, except one in 1766, when it lost £25,758 by a fire in Cornhill. In the past ten years, however, a profit of £130,833 has been made, of which £107,361 has been paid in company's returns, and the balance, £23,472, as well as interest, has been added to the accumulated fund. The net fire premiums of the year showed an increase of £3,302, and the loss ratio was £71·2 per cent. In the life department business was better, the new business of 1897 being the largest ever transacted by the society. Five hundred and seventy-three new policies were issued, insuring £351,983, and yielding £13,553 in annual premium. The total net premium income was £182,038, and 135 claims by death absorbed £125,545. The ratio of expenses and commission to premium was just over 12 per cent. After meeting all charges in both branches of the business, the accumulated funds, which include the general fund fire and life, and the life insurance fund under the Act of 1870, were augmented by £14,444 to £2,820,638. Valuation of the life department liabilities has again been made at 3 per cent., and shows an unappropriated surplus of £344,727. Excluding funds invested in reversionary interests, the average rate earned was £3 14s. 6d. The directors express regret at the retirement of Mr. Blenkinsop, the secretary, who has been thirty-seven years in the society's service, twenty-five of them in his present post. All except about £500,000 of the company's funds is invested in home securities of the best class.

The United States and South American Investment Trust Company, Limited.—This company's financial year ends on April 4, and it is now eleven years old. For the period just closed income was £40,687, and outgoings of all kinds, including interest on debenture stock, left £23,232 as net revenue. Adding the £1,009 brought forward, the entire free balance was £24,241. Out of this the preferred stock dividend has been paid and 1 per cent. for the year on the deferred stock, leaving £1,000 to be added to reserve and £1,491 to be carried forward. Considerable particulars are given regarding the company's investments, some of which are showing improvement, and a net profit of £11,258 from sales among them was added to the reserve, raising it to £17,909. From this however, £10,656 has been deducted and written off against securities permanently depreciated in value. Up to now the company's power of investment has been restricted to North and South American securities. Powers, however, have been granted to extend the limits, and the trustees propose to take advantage of them. They seem to be working the Trust with care and judgment on the whole, and some chance of improvement should be given by the recovery of Argentine agriculture and the rise in the prices of many Argentine securities. We are glad to see that the company does not appear to have much money in Brazilian securities, although it has quite enough to give it some trouble. A very full list of investments is appended to the report, including a separate one of securities purchased during the year. From this latter we notice that "extended powers of investment" have already been exercised, as we find Bovril preference shares, Austrian Incandescent shares, Bechuanaland Railway debentures, De Beers shares, Cory & Son's ordinary shares, North Worcestershire Breweries "B" debentures, Scheppes shares, and Welsbach preference and ordinary stock among the items added to the property of the Trust. We do not know that we can commend very cordially the judgment which has dictated some of these purchases.

The Great Boulder Proprietary Gold Mines, Limited.—The year ended December 31 last was a prosperous one for this, the best of all Western Australian mines discovered thus far. The net profit on the year's working was £272,805, exclusive of the small balance brought forward. Dividends aggregating 155 per cent. on the paid-up capital have been, or will be, paid out of these profits, and, in addition, £19,000 has been devoted to writing down machinery and plant, development account, and so on. Large reserves appear to exist in the tailings untreated, the value of which is estimated at £221,640. Reserves of ore have also increased during the year, and the latest advice with regard to the opening of the 400-ft. levels point to the reef being as rich there as it has proved to be nearer the surface. No particular difficulty seems to have been experienced with the supply of water, which has been sufficient to keep the 30-stamp battery working without interruption. Altogether it is a satisfactory report, and we can only trust the prosperity may long continue.

Central Bahia Railway Company.—Comment has been made upon the fact that the earnings of this company have risen by leaps and bounds of late, having been £57,685 in 1892; since when they have risen each year until £147,060 was received last year. One little matter, however, was forgotten in mentioning this, and that is that the exchange is taken throughout at the nominal rate of 27d. per milreis. Now in 1892 the milreis stood about 12½d., while last year the rate was about 7d., so that while £57,685 in 1892 represented £26,500 sterling, £147,060 in 1897 represented only about £38,100. It is not, therefore, surprising to find that working expenses have more than kept pace with the receipts, and that, after paying working expenses in Brazil, a profit of only 203,037 milreis was left, or a beggarly £5,963. Even then London charges, to the extent of £3,075, had to be met, so that the company had to depend almost entirely upon the Government guarantee for the funds to provide debenture interest, sinking fund charges, and dividend. The guarantee was duly paid, amounting to £105,783, and out of this fat sum £44,477 was required for debenture interest, £19,616 for sinking fund, and the balance permitted of a "dividend" of 6 per cent. for the year, £10,116 being carried forward, as against £11,518 brought in. In such circumstances it is only natural that the company has done nothing in regard to extensions. To build at the present time would probably be to do so cheaply, but apparently the worst has not yet been seen in Brazil.

Costa Rica Railway Company.—The new board has considerably improved the look of things. Gross receipts for 1897 were $2,894,547, against $2,618,113 in 1896, while the working expenses were only $1,319,707, compared with $1,503,823, the result in sterling being net receipts of £136,994, or £41,293 more than in the previous year. Debenture interest takes a little more owing to the extra charge on the prior mortgage debentures, and £2,000 is appropriated towards their redemption, but there still remains £50,797, from which a dividend of 4s. per share is to be paid, or 2 per cent., requiring only £36,000. The directors could have paid more, but have wisely put £8,000 to reserve and carry forward £6,797. The measure of improvement compared with 1896 will be seen when we say that the available balance then was £2,849, which naturally did not allow of any dividend being paid, or of anything being placed to reserve. Increases in revenue are reported under nearly every head and the saving in working expenses has reduced their ratio to receipts from 57½ to 45½ per cent. The banana traffic is expanding because growers are getting a better price, and there is a prospect of development of mineral resources which should benefit the line. Altogether, the position of the company has undergone a great change for the better, and in view of the hard work and expense borne by Mr. Herbert Allen in bringing this change about, it is proposed to hand him a special sum of £2,000 out of the past year's profits. A resolution to this effect will be brought forward at the meeting next Thursday, and shareholders will show their gratitude by unanimously approving it.

Buenos Ayres and Ensenada Port Railway Company.—An additional reason for the carrying through of the provisional agreement for the absorption of this company by the Buenos Ayres Great Southern Company is furnished by the report just issued. From this it appears that receipts amounted to £191,732, working expenses to £118,781, and net revenue to £72,951. After adding a few small items the balance allowed the payment of debenture interest, rentals, and the dividend upon the first preference stock, so that the income preference and the ordinary stocks received no distribution. The year must have been an exceptionally bad one, partly owing to the destruction by fire of the company's Central Station, but to a much larger extent to the compulsory removal by the Argentine Government of the company's railway between Casa Amarillâ and the Central Station, and the similar removal of the railway connecting this company's system at the Central Station with the Central Argentine, Pacific, and Rosario Railways at the Retiro. Possibly the strong Buenos Ayres Great Southern Company may be able to arrange matters more satisfactorily with the Government, but at any rate holders of Buenos Ayres and Ensenada securities must be rather glad to sink into the bosom of this greater company.

Mason & Barry, Limited.—This company appears to be working down its reserves of ore, for while 177,549 tons were broken and raised last year, the shipments amounted to 267,290 tons. The stock of ore and copper precipitate in Portugal, too, is only reported as worth £136,681, compared with £207,408 in 1896, and £246,854 in 1895. It is, therefore, a wise policy on the part of the board to pay back more of the capital to the shareholders and also write down assets vigorously. In the year £16,358 was deducted from the value of the works, buildings, plant, railways, piers, and other fixed and movable plant of the undertaking, and the total value of the same is now returned at £123,524. The sum of £4,500 was also written off the shares of La Sabina Company, reducing that asset to £31,700. Beyond these items, the assets of the company consist of its stocks, cash, and a large sum in high-class securities. After making the deduction mentioned the net profit for the past year was £43,406, which allows the directors to declare a dividend of 4s. per share for the year, or about 7 per cent., and carry forward £6,372. Out of the surplus assets it is proposed to repay the shareholders £1 per share, which will require £185,145, and leave the outstanding capital at £370,290.

ORIENT STEAM NAVIGATION COMPANY.—The result of the past year's working is a profit of £77,143, compared with £79,101 made in 1896, but in consequence of the *Garonne* having been sold only £62,213 is carried to reserve for depreciation of steamers against £67,158, so there remains a balance of £14,930 compared with £11,942; and, after paying the same dividend of 5s. per share, the balance carried forward is increased from £282 to £3,269. The fleet stands in the balance-sheet at £1,059,104, against which the reserve for depreciation amounts to £529,023, or just 50 per cent. The outstanding debentures of the company have been reduced from £108,850 to £92,550.

TRADE AND PRODUCE.

There has been nothing seen for many years like the recent excitement in the wheat trade. As soon as war was certain, dealers made haste to raise prices until they attained a height not reached since 1891, when the Russian ukase prohibiting the export of wheat caused a mad rush here for enhanced values until they secured 49s., and even 50s. in some cases, and for a brief day. That excitement was only temporary, and the present turmoil is not likely, we believe, to be of long duration. No doubt wheat has for many weeks been firm, and prices have steadily, though slowly, been going up. They would probably have reached 40s. to 42s. without the incitement of war, but certainly nobody imagined that within a week or ten days the rate for wheat would rise as high as 47s., and even 48s., the figure at which, at least in one or two cases, business was done. Shrewd observers assert that it will yet—and perhaps soon—go up to 50s.; but if it reach that point, it will not long remain there. Evidently, stocks in France and other Continental countries have been allowed to run very low, and exceptional purchases for the Continent have been hardening the market. But now that there is a tolerable certainty that neither of the belligerents in the present war will resort to privateering, and that there will be no interference with grain cargoes in neutral ships, there is no reason why the price should be kept at its present unnatural height. There are ample stocks in the United States and Canada, not to speak of other reserves, and if American vessels cannot bring these over to us, then British and other neutral vessels will. Not that we can look for cheap wheat for the present, nor for some time to come, but we may certainly expect the disappearance of the present inflation. The official New York report shows that exports thence in March last amounted to 15,459,575 bushels, as against 7,901,722 last year, a fact which indicates an exceptionally heavy demand from this side of the Atlantic. If the American exports are continued at anything like the same rate, we can be in no danger of falling short, and the New York figures seem to indicate no diminution in the supplies received there, the total amount for the first two weeks of April having been 7,379,136 bushels, against 3,057,482 last year. This wave of excitement and high pressure in England will probably, therefore, soon run its course, and wheat will settle down to a more rational figure. But as yet the advance goes merrily on. At Mark-lane, on Wednesday, red wheat was quoted at 46s. and white 48s.—the highest it has yet reached in Mark-lane. Provincial sellers in some cases make business impossible by their extravagant demands. The cargo market opened more quietly on Wednesday, but hardened towards the close, and prices were fully maintained, the Continental demand being still good.

At Newcastle yesterday 50s. was asked for white wheat, and even at that figure farmers were holding back.

Otherwise trade has not as yet been seriously disturbed by the war. Birmingham has had inquiries on behalf of America as to the time and price at which 100,000 rifles could be delivered; but no orders followed. There can be none now. In another respect Birmingham will be severely hit by the war. Her trade with Cuba is estimated as worth about £500,000 per annum; but that is now shut off, and in the event of Spain being defeated, it will probably never be recovered. We need not, therefore, be surprised to hear that the war has had an unsettling effect on Birmingham trade. There is little change in the iron trade. Wolverhampton, however, is busy with orders for the Australian and Indian markets. There are plenty of orders in the home trade, and for iron bars the recent advance in price has brought many new orders in the fear that the advance may go further yet. Pig-iron is in great demand, and it seems certain that the price will soon go up. Settlement prices on Monday:—Scotch, 46s. 3d.; Cleveland, 40s. 1½d.; hematite, 50s. In Glasgow, steel and iron manufacturers are busy with old orders, though new ones are not coming in so abundantly as the makers would like. But then the old orders will keep them going for a considerable time yet. There is great firmness in the hematite trade, but somehow, in Barrow-on-Furness at least, the holders of warrant iron are not pushing sales in view of the war and the depression which may follow if long continued. For the present, however, things go well, and prices are firm. Scotch pig-iron advanced at Glasgow on Wednesday to 46s. 7d., but in the afternoon it lost 1½d.; while Cumberland and hematite each gained 1½d. Wednesday's settlement prices—Scotch, 46s. 6d.; Cleveland, 40s. 3d.; hematite, 50s. 6d.

Copper is still on the upward tack, and there is every indication that prices have not yet reached their extreme height. There have been fluctuations, but they are rare, and never violent. At first 'Change on Tuesday about 1,000 tons were sold at £52 10s. to 11s. 3d. for cash and near dates, £52 12s. 6d. and 13s. 9d. for May prompts, £52 15s. to £53 for June dates, and £53 2s. 6d. for three months. These prices were all, however, beaten at second 'Change, when there was nothing below £52 11s. 3d. for cash and near dates, £52 15s. for June 10, £52 17s. 6d. two months, £53 and £53 1s. 3d. three months. Settlement price for standard, £52 12s. 6d. net. At Wednesday's market, however, there was a slight fall after a gain of 2s. 6d. at the opening. About 700 tons were sold for three months, realising £53 2s. 6d., 1s. 3d., and £53. Cash was done at £52 10s., and June 9 at 5s. more. The settlement price was £52 10s. The reduction cannot be regarded as likely to last.

Cotton has been quiet but firm throughout the week. Futures have gone rather higher, but spot has not, and it is hardly thought, from the state of stocks in the cloth-making districts, that there will be any serious further increase in consequence of the war. American supplies are still abundant.

There is little to report in regard to wool. The markets have been inactive, with rather a tendency to depression. There have been no marked alterations in values. Still, reports from the manufacturing districts speak hopefully of a speedy improvement in business. The third series of wool sales open on May 3, and Messrs. Jacomb, Son, & Company give the following as the net quantity available for these sales: New South Wales, 54,000 bales; Queensland, 23,000 bales; Victorian, 37,000 bales; Tasmanian, 6,500 bales; South Australian, 9,500 bales; West Australian, 5,000 bales; New Zealand, 59,000 bales: Cape and Natal, 15,000 bales. The total amount is 209,000. The average daily offerings will be about 12,260 bales.

There is practically no change in the coal market. Some of the non-associated collieries in Wales which had been virtually stopped have resumed, and the output has been increased; but, of course, there is no slackening in the demand, and prices remain as high as ever. There is no sign of an arrangement of the strike. The employers remain firm, as the manifesto they have just issued clearly shows; and they still refuse the 10 per cent. advance, or to resume negotiations unless the men's representatives come armed with plenary powers. As coal has not been declared contraband of war, it is not probable that the Hispano-American war will have any pronounced influence on the market here; but the home demand is quite sufficient to well maintain existing prices, if not to enhance them—at least while the Welsh strike lasts.

Sugar has benefited by the war, temporarily at least, though how long the rise in value may continue it would be hazardous to guess. But the value *has* risen, and that there is some confidence in the immediate future is shown by the hopeful feeling expressed by dealers. The prospects of the world's supplies during the next six months having now become more clearly defined, according to Mr. Czarnikow's circular, and prices being still moderate, the trade are buying freely at an advance of about 3½d. on beet and about 6d. on cane. The tone remains firm, and strong opinions are expressed as to a further improvement; but dealers would do well to exercise considerable caution. In the circumstances we are not surprised to hear that speculation is reviving.

Next Week's Meetings.

MONDAY, MAY 2.

Alliance Investment	Winchester House, noon.
City of Santos Improvements ...	Gresham House, noon.
J. & E. Hall & Co.	23, St. Swithin's-lane, 11 a.m.
North British and New Zealand Invest.	Glasgow, 2 p.m.
Northern American Trust	Dundee, noon.

TUESDAY, MAY 3.

Imperial Continental Gas	Cannon-street Hotel, 2.30 p.m.
Imperial Russian Cotton and Jute ...	Winchester House, 2.30 p.m.
Ionian Bank	93, Bishopsgate-street, 1 p.m.
Law Fire Insurance	114, Chancery-lane, 1 p.m.
London General Investment ...	12, Moorgate-street, noon.
Pacific Trust Association	Liverpool, noon.
United States and South American Trust	Winchester House, noon.

WEDNESDAY, MAY 4.

Buenos Ayres and Ensenada Railway...	Winchester House, 2.30 p.m.
Commercial Union Assurance ...	25, Cornhill, noon.
Doom Dooma Tea	1, Great Winchester-street, 3 p.m.
Scottish Union and National Insurance	Edinburgh, 2 p.m.
Sun Life Assurance	63, Threadneedle-street, 2 p.m.
West Flanders Railway	10, Moorgate-street, 2 p.m.

THURSDAY, MAY 5.

Argentine Land and Investment ...	Winchester House, 1 p.m.
Bell's Asbestos	Cannon-street Hotel, 2.30 p.m.
Caledonian Insurance	Edinburgh, 2.30 p.m.
Costa Rica Railway	Winchester House, 3 p.m.
Highgate Hill Tramways	Winchester House, 2.30 p.m.
Industrial and General Trust ...	Winchester House, noon.
London Platino Brazilian Telegraph	Bloomfield House, 12.30 p.m.
Pelican Life	70, Lombard-street, 1.30 p.m.
William Younger & Co.	Edinburgh, 10 a.m.

FRIDAY, MAY 6.

Anglo-American Debenture Corporation	Cannon-street Hotel, 12.30 p.m.
Central Bahia Railway	Cannon-street Hotel, 2 p.m.
Scottish Australian Mining	Winchester House, noon.
North British and Mercantile Insurance	Edinburgh, noon.

Diary of the War.

April 21.—We propose giving, in the form of a diary, the leading events of this Spanish-American war from day to day, hoping thereby to give a clearer and more concise view of affairs than would be possible in a general weekly review. To-day we reached what is officially understood to be "a state of war." President McKinley's ultimatum was duly presented to Senor Polo de Bernabe, the Spanish Ambassador at Washington, who seemed to be quite prepared for it, and at once sent a note—which was probably written some days before—asking for his passports. At the same time a telegraphic dispatch was sent off to General Woodford at Madrid, directing him to present the ultimatum to the Spanish Government. But Spanish officials were too quick for the American Ambassador. Senor de Bernabe had probably telegraphed to them from Washington that he had received the ultimatum, and before General Woodford had time to wait upon the Spanish Foreign Minister, that functionary informed him that diplomatic relations had been broken off between the two countries. So he asked for his passports, turned the American Legation over to the British Embassy, and left Madrid at four in the afternoon. The Minister was able to leave the Spanish capital without disturbance, but at Valladolid a large crowd collected at the station and stones were thrown at the train; but the passengers got away without injury, though things looked very bad for a while. The ultimatum gave the Spaniards until Saturday the 23rd to withdraw their government and military forces from Cuba.

April 22.—To-day President McKinley's proclamation of the blockade of Cuba is issued. The blockade is to extend along the north coast of Cuba, including all ports between Cardenas, Bahia Honda, and the port of Cienfuegos on the south coast. Early this morning the American fleet which is to enforce the blockade sailed from Key West. After about an hour's sail a Spanish freight steamer was seen steaming up the Mexican Gulf. She was found to be the Buenaventura, laden with timber; was promptly seized and sent off to Key West, the first prize of the war.

April 23.—The blockade declared to be effective. When the American fleet came within about five miles of Havana, several shots were fired from the forts, but they did not reach the ships, and the fire was not returned. Another prize for the Americans! Nothing having been known at Havana of the sailing of the American fleet, or of the blockade, the Spanish liner *Don Pedro* left Havana as usual for San Juan, Porto Rico, and Cadiz. She made a bold attempt to escape the American warships, and was duly pulled up, when near Matanzas. She was despatched to Key West; and soon after her departure, there was a chase after another vessel which, however, turned out to be a Swedish schooner, and she was allowed to proceed on her voyage. President McKinley, having been empowered by Congress to call for volunteers, to-day issued a proclamation asking for 125,000 of these. At first the number was to be 40,000, then it was raised to 100,000. The going up to 125,000 is significant. But we are forgetting. Other two prizes were taken by the American fleet to-day. A small schooner heading for Havana was run down by a gunboat, and her course was involuntarily changed for Key West. Then came the *Miguel Josef*, of the Periello Line, from New Orleans for Barcelona, *vià* Havana, which was captured 100 miles from the latter port.

April 24.—A very important decree is published in the Spanish *Official Gazette*. It is, on the part of Spain, a virtual adhesion to the Declaration of Paris. Indeed, it is declared that the only part of that declaration which Spain refused to recognise was the abolition of privateering, and now, in this decree, the Spanish Government announce that, while they do not intend to issue letters of marque, they reserve the right to do so if circumstances seem to them to justify it. At present, however, a force of auxiliary cruisers will be organised from the mercantile marine to co-operate with the navy according to the needs of the war, but they will be commanded by naval officers. It may be as well to give the regulations laid down by Spain for the observance of maritime law. They are as follow:—

(1) Neutral flags cover the enemy's merchandise except contraband of war.
(2) Neutral merchandise except contraband of war is not seizable under the enemy's flag.
(3) A blockade to be obligatory must be effective, *i.e.*, maintained by a sufficient force to prevent access to the enemy's littoral.

As America some time ago announced her adhesion to the Declaration of Paris and expressed her determination not to issue letters of marque, there should be no fear now of privateers, and neutrals may make themselves tolerably easy on the score of trade. The Foreign Enlistment Act was to-day proclaimed at Hong Kong.

April 25.—War has now been officially and formally declared by the American Congress on the recommendation of the President, dating it from the 21st. Some little trouble may arise from a somewhat hasty order from the British authorities at Hong Kong to two vessels of the United States Squadron to leave the port at once. They left; but the Commodore and the American Consul protested on the ground that, as the American Government had not notified a declaration of war, there was no necessity for such a peremptory order. We fear the Hong Kong authorities are wrong. Two more prizes for the American fleet; but very tiny ones—of little importance to any one except the prize crews, and not much to them. There was an exciting chase of an Italian warship which was sailing into Havana on the 23rd. The American Admiral's flagship, the *New York* was close upon the stranger before her nationality was discovered. Salutes were exchanged, and the exciting incident closed. Submarine mines have been placed in position for the protection of New York.

April 26.—The feature of the day has been the neutrality proclamation issued by Great Britain. It strictly follows precedents, except that the regulation as to the coaling and provisioning of belligerent ships in British harbours is made rather more stringent. No definition of contraband of war is attempted, nor is there a hint given as to whether Government consider coal contraband. But no ships of war of either belligerent in the territorial jurisdiction of the Queen shall be permitted to take in any supplies except provisions that may be necessary for the subsistence of the crew, and so much coal as may be necessary to carry the vessel to the nearest port of her own country, or to some nearer destination she may choose. No more coal can be supplied to the same ship at any of our ports until the lapse of three months, without special permission. An American ship at Falmouth has been the first victim of the proclamation. It could not leave without an addition to the crew, and, as recruiting a crew in this country would have been a breach of the Foreign Enlistment Act, the ship has been laid up at Falmouth until after the war. President McKinley issued a proclamation allowing Spanish vessels in United States ports until May 21 to effect their clearance. The Spanish ships already seized are not to be given up, but to be held pending the decision of the prize courts. The Spanish Transatlantic steamer *Panama* has been captured. A circular issued to the Powers by the Spanish Government declares the real motive of the United States to be annexation. In the Cortes Senor Sagasta declared for a war *à outrance*, and a vote of confidence was adopted.

April 27.—The Chamber at Madrid have been providing the "sinews of war." The special navy credit is to be increased to 90,000,000 pesetas. The Government propose to issue Treasury bonds up to 100,000,000 pesetas, guaranteed on the Almaden quicksilver mines; to issue further bonds guaranteed by the "general resources of the nation"; to negotiate advances with the State monopoly companies; to enforce a year's payment in advance of the land and industrial taxes; to double the floating debt; and to convert the bonds of the External Debt into Internal stocks. The Finance Minister declared he saw no reason for pessimism; and certainly, if Spain can float safely with all this load upon her, she must be in a better position than is generally supposed. Lieutenant Rowan, of the United States Infantry, has been able to land on the east coast of Cuba, and has gone to arrange for the co-operation of the insurgents in the event of an American invasion. The United States Squadron has left Hong Kong for Manilla. It is now said that the 125,000 Volunteers asked for by the President will be at his disposal on Monday next. A Spanish gunboat is said to have captured the American ship *Saranac*, with 1,640 tons of coal. There is a rummour of a duel, off Matanzas, between an American torpedo-boat destroyer and a Spanish torpedo boat, in which the American is said to have retired badly injured.

April 28.—The first "great fight" is reported to-day, though its true dimensions are not yet known probably. The American blockading fleet at Cuba, or rather three of the ships belonging to it, bombarded Matanzas on the 26th apparently, and in half-an-hour the forts at the entrance to the harbour were silenced and dismantled. The Spanish fire from the forts is said to have been wretched, the shots mostly falling short of the fleet. There is said to have been great loss of life among the Spaniards; but of this there is no proof; and it is possible that the "bombardment" may turn out to have been rather a small affair.

THE PROPERTY MARKET.

A total of sales for last week at Tokenhouse-yard of £214,791, as contrasted with £22,760 in the corresponding period of 1897, seems to show conclusively that investors are more than ever turning their attention to building investments, more especially freeholds. One of the most considerable events of the week was the sale on Friday of Ridler's Hotel, Holborn, comprising an area of 6,110 ft., with a rental for the next twenty-eight years of £750. It brought £37,500, or fifty years' purchase. It is understood that the Prudential Assurance Company are the purchasers. Another important sale on Friday consisted of two modern shops in Oxford-street, let on repairing lease at £1,250 per annum, also factory premises in rear of the estimated value of £390 per annum, and held on lease direct from the Duke of Portland. The properties were purchased by Messrs. James Jay (Limited), the tenants of part of the property, at £30,400. Among ground rents the most important transaction was in regard to a rent of £800 a year secured on property in the main Pall Mall, which brought 30¼ years' purchase.

City freeholds when offered for sale at the Mart are sure to attract considerable attention. Two were disposed of on Tuesday. One was offered by Messrs. St. Quintin & Son. It is the property, 79 and 79A, Leadenhall-street, let on lease at £350 per annum, and was sold at £9,050, or nearly twenty-six years' purchase. The second is at 52, Aldgate, let at £150 a year, and was disposed of by Messrs. Ellis & Son for £3,850, or rather over twenty-five years' purchase. A freehold wharf of two acres in Crook's-road, Stratford, was disposed of by Mr. Millard for £4,450. The total of the day's sales was £20,395.

Freeholds were again uppermost at the Mart on Tuesday, when the total of the day's sales went up to £53,892. The leading event of the day was the sale by Messrs. Debenham, Tewson, & Co., of a freehold residential and building estate of 213 acres, known as Burvale, at Hersham, Surrey, which realised a total of £23,370.

The family residence and grounds, with about 81¾ acres of land, brought £12,000; an adjoining block of land, nearly 88½ acres in extent, went for £6,000; Woodlark Farm, over fourteen acres, realised £1,200, and some smaller properties brought £350. Several other minor freeholds were disposed of by the same firm at good prices. There was another City freehold offered by Messrs. Jones, Lang, & Company; it is situated in Basinghall-street, let at £450 a year, and was sold at £9,000. For another freehold residence known as Dernclough, in Wanstead Park, Messrs. Corkett & Henderson found a buyer previous to auction, at a price not stated. Portions of a building estate at Harold Wood, Essex, containing nearly 27½ acres, were sold by the same firm at £2,900. Some freehold ground rents in Kensington and Hammersmith were well sold by Messrs. C. Rawley, Cross, & Co., the total received being £4,552. Mr. C. W. Davies obtained £2,990 for a freehold at Harcott's-gate, Sussex, The Bungalow, with nearly four acres of land.

There was nothing of much importance done at the mart on Wednesday.

Some of the stocks and shares sold by Messrs. W. G. Stanfield & Co. at Bradford, on Monday, are worth noting. The total amount received was over £34,500, and the following are a few of the details:—£5,000 worth 2¾ per cent. British Government consolidated stock, £110 per cent.; £2,100 North-Eastern Railway Consols, £172 per cent.; £2,352 8s. Midland Railway 2½ per cent. stock, £86 15s. per cent.; £2,000 Midland Railway 2½ per cent. preferred ordinary stock, £82 10s. per cent.; £1,845 worth of similar stock, £82 5s. per cent.; £2,000 Midland Railway 2½ per cent. deferred ordinary stock, £84 10s. per cent.; £1,845 Midland Railway 2½ per cent. deferred stock, £84 5s. per cent.

Mr. Alfred Richards had a sale of freehold and leasehold properties at Tottenham on Wednesday evening. The two leasehold lots were bought in, but the freehold—residence and grounds at 60, Silver-street, Edmonton, let at a rental of £52 10s.—was disposed of for £900.

Answers to Correspondents.

Questions about public securities, and on all points in company law, will be answered week by week, in the REVIEW, on the following terms and conditions:—

A fee of FIVE shillings must be remitted for each question put, provided they are questions about separate securities. Should a private letter be required, then an extra fee of FIVE shillings must be sent to cover the cost of such letter, the fee then being TEN shillings for one query only, and FIVE shillings for every subsequent one in the same letter. While making this concession the EDITOR will feel obliged if private replies are as much as possible dispensed with. It is wholly impossible to answer letters sent merely "with a stamped envelope enclosed for reply."

Correspondents will further greatly oblige by so framing their questions as to obviate the necessity to name securities in the replies. They should *number* the questions, keeping a copy for reference, thus:—"(1) Please inform me about the present position of the Rowenzori Development Co. (2) Is a dividend likely to be paid soon on the capital stock of the Congo-Sudan Railway?

Answers to be given to all such questions by simply quoting the numbers 1, 2, 3, and so on. The EDITOR has a rooted objection to such forms of reply as—"I think your Timbuctoo Consols will go up," or "Sell your Slowcoach and Draggem Bonds," because this kind of thing is open to all sorts of abuses. By the plan suggested, and by using a fancy name to be replied to, each query can be kept absolutely private to the inquirer, and no scope whatever be given to market manipulations. Avoid, as names to be replied to, common words, like "investor," "inquirer," and so on, as also "bear" or "bull." Detached syllables of the inquirer's name, or initials reversed, will frequently do as well as anything, so long as the answer can be identified by the inquirer.

The EDITOR further respectfully requests that merely speculative questions should as far as possible be avoided. He by no means sets himself up as a market prophet, and can only undertake to provide the latest information regarding the securities asked about. This he will do faithfully and without bias.

Replies cannot be guaranteed in the same week if the letters demanding them reach the office of the INVESTORS' REVIEW, Norfolk House, Norfolk-street, W.C., later than the first post on Wednesday mornings.

ARDEN.—There is, I am afraid, not much chance in the immediate future of a rise in price. The company suffers from over capitalisation, and has been heavily handicapped by the serious fall in exchange. So far as I can discover, the properties represent more than the value of the debentures. There is no haste to sell, but I think you should do so, if you get a fair opportunity.

NAVAL—(1.) This company is small but respectable. Dividends have fluctuated. In 1890, 8 per cent. was paid, in 1894 only 4 per cent., since then they have risen gradually to 7 per cent. I see no reason against an investment to a small extent if you do not object to a share which is not very marketable; the figure you mention seems quite enough, probably you can get them at a lower price. (2.) You are quite right, I will send you a P. C. showing how you stand.

Dividends Announced.

MISCELLANEOUS.

PACIFIC STEAM NAVIGATION COMPANY.—Final dividend for 1897 of 5s. per share, making 25s. per share for the year.

ALASKA TREADWELL GOLD MINING COMPANY.—37½ cents per share declared.

ALASKA MEXICAN GOLD MINING COMPANY.—10 cents a share.

HALL MINES, LIMITED.—Interim dividend of 1s. per share on the ordinary shares.

ARGENTINE LAND AND INVESTMENT COMPANY, LIMITED.—Dividend of 1¼ per cent (1s. per share).

PORGES RANDFONTEIN GOLD MINING COMPANY, LIMITED.—Dividend of 10 per cent., equal to 2s. per share for 1897.

HOUSE PROPERTY AND INVESTMENT COMPANY, LIMITED.—Balance dividend of £2 5s. per cent. for the year ended March 31, making with interim already paid £4 per cent. for the year.

WRIGHT & GREIG, LIMITED.—Interim at the rate of 12 per cent. per annum on the ordinary shares.

LAKE VIEW CONSOLS, LIMITED.—Second interim dividend of 10s. per share.

NATIONAL SAFE DEPOSIT COMPANY, LIMITED.—Interim dividend at the rate of 4 per cent. per annum on the ordinary shares, and the usual half-yearly dividend on the 6 per cent. preference shares.

BRILLIANT GOLD MINING COMPANY, LIMITED.—6d. per share.

TREASURY GOLD MINES, LIMITED.—10 per cent., equal to 8s. per £4 share.

MILLARS' KARRI AND JARRAH FORESTS, LIMITED.—2s. per share on the ordinary shares.

QUEEN CROSS REEF GOLD MINING COMPANY, LIMITED.—Dividend of 6d. per share.

"EVENING NEWS," LIMITED.—Interim dividend at the rate of 5 per cent. per annum on the preference shares, and at the rate of 12½ per cent. per annum on the ordinary shares.

EASTERN EXTENSION AUSTRALASIA AND CHINA TELEGRAPH, LIMITED.—2s. 6d. per share for the quarter ended December 31, with a bonus of 4s. per share, making a total of 7 per cent. for the year.

BROXBURN OIL COMPANY, LIMITED.—7½ per cent. on the ordinary shares for the past year.

WEST INDIAN AND PANAMA TELEGRAPH COMPANY, LIMITED.—Dividend on the six months ended December 31 of 6d. per share on the ordinary shares.

CEYLON TEA PLANTATIONS COMPANY, LIMITED.—Final dividend of 8 per cent. on the ordinary shares, making 15 per cent. for the year.

LAMBETH WATERWORKS COMPANY.—Dividends at the rate of 10 per cent. and 7½ per cent. per annum respectively on the share capital of the company.

NOBEL DYNAMITE TRUST.—A dividend of 12 per cent. for the year ending April 30 is recommended, carrying forward about £13,000.

LIVERPOOL NITRATE.—Dividend of 5 per cent. announced payable May 14.

SHAW SAVILL & ALBION COMPANY.—Dividend on the preferred and ordinary shares at the rate of 5 per cent. per annum, £5,000 carried to a dividend equalisation fund, and £2,255 carried forward.

EMPLOYERS LIABILITY ASSURANCE CORPORATION.—Dividend of 4s. per share, being at the rate of 10 per cent. per annum, on the paid-up capital, carrying forward £184,641.

RAILWAYS.

SOUTH INDIAN COMPANY, LIMITED.—Dividend out of surplus profits of 20s. per cent., which with the guaranteed interest will make a distribution of £2 10s. for the half-year, or at the rate of 5 per cent. per annum, as compared with 4½ per cent. for the corresponding half of the previous year.

BENGAL CENTRAL, LIMITED.—15s. per cent., which, in addition to the guaranteed interest, will make a distribution for the current half-year of £2 10s. per cent.

BENGAL CENTRAL RAILWAY.—Dividend for the half-year ended December, of 15s. per cent., which, in addition to the guaranteed interest will make a distribution of 2½ per cent. for the current half-year.

INSURANCE.

LANCASHIRE COMPANY.—Dividend for the half-year ended December 31 at the rate of 7½ per cent. per annum. £30,000 to fire reserve out of fire profits.

The Postmaster-General has promised to make the experiment of placing a travelling post-office somewhere near Hyde Park Corner for the collection of telegrams and express messenger services during the season. It will be a great convenience, and may probably become a permanent institution.

Among Mr. E. Schenk's suggestions for increasing the popularity of the Crystal Palace to a dividend-paying point are the improvement of the catering and railway facilities, the construction of a huge skating rink, the encouragement of the theatre, and the attracting of big football and cricket matches to the Palace. Education facilities have apparently no present place in the programme.

Among the articles set forth for sale in the London and South Western Railway Company's annual "clearing sale" is an "artificial leg (new)." Of course it is new; how could a second-hand one get there? Wearers of wooden legs do not take them off for the journey, nor are they likely to walk off in a moment of forgetfulness, neglecting to carry the inert leg with them.

To Correspondents.

The EDITOR cannot undertake to return rejected communications. Letters from correspondents must, in every case, be authenticated by the name and address of the writer.

Telegraphic Address: "Unveiling, London."

The Investors' Review.

The Week's Money Market.

Floating balances continued to accumulate in the market during the week, with the result that day-to-day loans do not command more than 2 per cent., and loans for a week are quoted 2¼ to 2½ per cent. A good deal of the free credit on offer arises from the keeping in hand of balances in connection with the Chinese loan, the final call upon which is due on May 3, the formal transfer of the proceeds to Japan taking place on the 7th of that month. In connection with this payment, Germany has been sending over money freely, as, although a moderate sum will be transferred to Japan at the Imperial Bank of Germany, the bulk of the £12,000,000 will be handed over at the Bank of England. The sums received from Germany have of course gone to swell market balances, and, combined with other arrivals of gold from abroad, add much to the prevailing ease. It is significant, however, that the India Council has all through been able to obtain 3 per cent. for loans running beyond the date of the transfer of the Japanese indemnity.

Dealers in bills have been loth to reduce their discount quotations in the uncertain condition of affairs, but events have been too strong for them. The great ease in the short money market, and the sending of over £1,000,000 in gold into the Bank, have compelled them to gradually reduce their rate to 3¾ per cent. for two and three months' remitted bills, with a fraction over for longer-dated paper. Compared with the 3½ to 4 per cent. quoted all round a week ago, the decline does not appear to be important, but it ought to be recognised that it has taken place in face of a war between two great Powers which threatens, if prolonged, to have wide-reaching results. Indeed, the very manner in which the Bank of England obtained the important accession to its stock of gold must tend to make the market cautious. Not only has it continued to make advances free of interest to importers of the metal, but it has taken the unprecedented step of raising its buying price of gold. Although a little mystery has been imported into its operations in this respect, it is pretty certain that it paid 77s. 9¾d. per ounce for the African gold that came into the market this week, and at the same time yielded ½d. per ounce to the brokers for assay, thus giving way on a little point that has long been disputed. The policy of acting with a freer hand in regard to the attraction of gold is certainly an improvement on the old fixed price stereotyped in the Bank Act of 1844; but under present conditions the Money Market is not sure that the energies of the Bank of England may not have been aroused by some knowledge as to future events that is not generally possessed.

A cautious attitude, therefore, is still maintained in the open market, and is distinctly prudent in view of the monetary difficulties in Spain, Portugal, Italy, and Brazil, called forth or accentuated by recent movements in their exchanges. Sharp fluctuations in the international value of their currencies are bound to add seriously to the burdens of those countries, and it would be premature to assume that further unfavourable developments will not take place. Meantime, the American exchange, which has dominated the position, has risen sharply of late, and withdrawals of gold to New York are no longer possible. It is too early yet to assume that the recovery will be sustained for long, and, meanwhile, the important Continental exchanges are running back rapidly to a position adverse to us.

Endeavours were made to obtain 4 to 4¼ per cent. for fortnightly loans to the Stock Exchange at the settlement, but very little was done at the higher figure, and a certain amount had to be lent below 4 per cent. Even then the reduction in the amount of floating stock proved to be so important that large sums of money were paid back to the loaning bank by intermediaries who had no use for the funds upon the terms demanded. There must, therefore, have been a healthy contraction of stock-running that is particularly opportune at the present juncture, when the future appears to be clouded in so many directions.

On the whole, the Bank return issued yesterday sustains the impression that money will now remain easier, with rates tending to slip back until the war demand for gold stirs them up again. Not only did £1,160,000 in coin and bars come in from abroad, but £350,000 returned from active circulation. This was partly balanced by an increase of £161,000 in the note circulation, but even so the reserve of the banking department is now £1,350,000 larger than it was a week ago at £21,038,000, which raises its proportion to the liabilities to 41¾, notwithstanding a net increase of over £1,000,000 in the deposits. Thanks to this influx of cash and to a decrease of £314,000 in the public deposits, the "other" deposits, which sustain the market balances, have risen to £1,336,000 to £37,957,000, and £304,000 has been paid off on "other" securitities. Their total, however, is still £33,935,000 and shows that by mid-May, perhaps, the Bank will be in a position to reassert its control over the open market. Meanwhile, and apart from upsets to nerves through politics, money should be cheaper; and while it is, a discount will be held up with difficulty.

SILVER.

The market has been decidedly firm this week, not altogether on account of the activity of buyers but rather owing to the reluctance of sellers to part with the metal. The price for immediate delivery has, therefore, risen 1/16d. on the week to 26¼d. per oz., and the two months' forward quotation has advanced ⅛d. to 26 5/16d. per oz., the advance in the Singapore exchange affecting the latter quotation. Buying of late on Eastern account has been almost entirely for the Straits, where the disappearance of the Japanese yen, and the impossibility of obtaining Mexican dollars, lead to more and more British dollars being coined. In regard to Mexican dollars it is interesting to note that the coins, together with silver, are being actually imported into Mexico at the moment. Continental buying has also helped the market, but so far we have heard nothing about purchases on behalf of Spain. The cash balances at the Bank of Spain have fallen away considerably, a matter which might easily encourage its officials to do what they did some years back, that is, use a little gold to buy silver and coin it at about 60d. per ounce, thus converting it into money nominally two and a half times the value of the gold employed. But perhaps Spain is too poor to do even this, and the printing machine will alone stand in the gap. Indian exchanges have fallen to 1s. 3 15/16d. as the cash balances of the two important Presidency banks have risen considerably, and the Bank of Bengal has reduced its rate from 12 per cent. to 11.

BANK OF ENGLAND.

AN ACCOUNT pursuant to the Act 7 and 8 Vict., cap. 32, for the Week ending on Wednesday, April 27, 1898.

ISSUE DEPARTMENT.

	£		£
Notes Issued	46,115,310	Government Debt	11,015,100
		Other Securities	5,784,900
		Gold Coin and Bullion	29,315,310
		Silver Bullion	—
	£46,115,310		£46,115,310

BANKING DEPARTMENT.

	£		£
Proprietors' Capital	14,553,000	Government Securities	13,191,953
Rest	3,184,638	Other Securities	33,935,386
Public Deposits (including Exchequer, Savings Banks, Commissioners of National Debt, and Dividend Accounts)	12,361,186	Notes	18,572,450
Other Deposits	37,956,705	Gold and Silver Coin	2,465,333
Seven Day and other Bills	109,593		
	£68,165,122		£68,165,122

Dated April 28, 1898.

H. G. BOWEN, *Chief Cashier.*

In the following table will be found the movements compared with the previous week, and also the totals for that week and the corresponding return last year:—

Banking Department.

Last Year. April 28.		April 20, 1898.	April 27, 1898.	Increase.	Decrease.
£	Liabilities.	£	£	£	£
3,141,047	Rest	3,177,795	3,184,638	6,843	—
11,220,465	Pub. Deposits	12,675,148	12,361,186	—	313,962
38,903,977	Other do.	36,620,609	37,956,705	1,336,096	—
137,755	7 Day Bills	92,622	109,593	16,971	—
	Assets.			Decrease.	Increase.
13,842,586	Gov. Securities	13,191,953	13,191,953	—	—
28,018,745	Other do.	34,239,218	33,935,386	303,832	—
26,094,913	Total Reserve	19,688,003	21,037,783	—	1,349,780
				1,663,742	1,663,742
				Increase.	Decrease.
£		£	£	£	£
27,199,000	Note Circulation	27,282,075	27,542,860	160,785	—
51⅞ p.c.	Proportion	39⅞ p.c.	41¾ p.c.	—	—
2 "	Bank Rate	4 "	4 "	—	—

Foreign Bullion movement for week £1,160,000 in.

LONDON BANKERS' CLEARING.

Month of	1898.	1897.	Increase.	Decrease.
	£	£	£	£
January	673,281,000	576,558,000	96,723,000	—
February	648,601,000	597,652,000	50,949,000	—
Week ending				
March 2	190,157,000	177,852,000	12,305,000	—
" 9	134,490,000	126,182,000	8,308,000	—
" 16	174,377,000	148,937,000	25,440,000	—
" 23	129,828,000	118,578,000	11,250,000	—
" 30	170,668,000	158,421,000	12,247,000	—
April 6	186,540,000	147,789,000	38,751,000	—
" 13	112,101,000	154,099,000	—	41,998,000
" 20	168,810,000	92,332,000	76,478,000	—
" 27	129,959,000	138,288,000	—	8,329,000
Total to date	2,629,744,000	2,369,593,000	260,151,000	—

BANK AND DISCOUNT RATES ABROAD.

	Bank Rate.	Altered.	Open Market.
Paris	2	March 14, 1895	1⅞
Berlin	4	April 9, 1898	3⅜
Hamburg	4	April 9, 1898	3⅜
Frankfort	4	April 9, 1898	3⅜
Amsterdam	3	April 13, 1897	2¾
Brussels	3	April 28, 1896	2⅝
Vienna	4	January 22, 1896	4⅛
Rome	5	August 27, 1895	3
St. Petersburg	5½	January 23, 1898	4½
Madrid	5	June 17, 1896	4
Lisbon	6	January 25, 1891	6
Stockholm	4	March 3, 1898	4
Copenhagen	4	January 20, 1898	4
Calcutta	11	April 28, 1898	—
Bombay	13	February 24, 1898	—
New York call money	1½ to 2	—	—

NEW YORK ASSOCIATED BANKS (dollar at 4s.).

	April 23, 1898	April 16, 1898.	April 9, 1898.	April 24, 1897.
	£	£	£	£
Specie	31,084,000	29,506,000	28,416,000	17,414,000
Legal tenders	10,682,000	11,138,000	11,904,000	21,176,000
Loans and discounts	114,530,000	116,018,000	117,556,000	100,970,000
Circulation	2,816,000	2,787,800	2,776,800	3,074,000
Net deposits	132,244,000	132,704,000	133,968,000	114,956,000

Legal reserve is 25 per cent. of net deposits; therefore the total reserve (specie and legal tenders) exceeds this sum by £8,705,000, against an excess last week of £7,468,000.

BANK OF FRANCE (25 francs to the £).

	April 28, 1898	April 21, 1898.	April 14, 1898.	April 29, 1897.
	£	£	£	£
Gold in hand	74,375,920	74,312,920	74,178,120	76,885,000
Silver in hand	48,614,320	48,690,800	48,617,720	48,870,000
Bills discounted	36,839,520	33,733,960	33,449,840	*43,958,000
Advances	15,016,800	15,239,880	15,171,080	—
Note circulation	148,438,040	148,173,120	151,102,520	148,841,000
Public deposits	8,035,040	7,569,320	6,911,320	7,422,000
Private deposits	25,655,600	22,554,440	[illegible]	[illegible]

Proportion between bullion and circulation 82⅞ per cent. against 83 per cent. a week ago.

* Includes advances.

FOREIGN RATES OF EXCHANGE ON LONDON.

Place.	Usance.	Last week's.	Latest.	Place.	Usance.	Latest.	Last week's.
Paris	chqs.	25·35	25·30⅝	Italy	sight	26·87½	27·15
Brussels	chqs.	25·45	25·36⅞	Do. gold prem.	..	106·15	107·45
Amsterdam	short	12·14	12·09½	Constantinople	3 mths	109·30	109·15
Berlin	short	20·53½	20·52	B. Ayres gd. pm.	..	165·50	164·80
Do.	3 mths	20·33	20·31	Rio de Janeiro	90 dys	6	5 15/16d.
Hamburg	3 mths	20·32	20·30½	Valparaiso	90 dys	17⅞	17⅞d.
Frankfort	short	20·55	20·51	Calcutta	T. T.	1/4	1/3 15/16
Vienna	short	12·10	12·07	Bombay	T. T.	1/3 15/16	1/3 15/16
St. Petersburg	3 mths	94·05	94·00	Hong Kong	T. T.	1/10¼	1/10¼
New York	60 dys	4·80	4·81¼	Shanghai	T. T.	2/5⅜	2/5⅜
Lisbon	sight	33½d.	30⅞d.	Singapore	T. T.	1/10⅝	1/10⅜
Madrid	sight	nom.	44·50				

IMPERIAL BANK OF GERMANY (20 marks to the £).

	April 23, 1898.	April 15, 1898.	April 7, 1898.	April 23, 1897.
	£	£	£	£
Cash in hand	44,146,250	43,820,450	43,269,700	44,774,000
Bills discounted	35,280,900	34,561,300	37,171,950	*34,028,000
Advances on stocks	3,714,050	4,385,950	5,340,800	—
Note circulation	55,337,100	56,944,900	60,696,700	52,890,000
Public deposits	24,558,350	24,130,050	22,931,900	22,454,000

* Includes advances.

AUSTRIAN-HUNGARIAN BANK (1s. 8d. to the florin).

	April 23, 1898.	April 15, 1898.	April 7, 1898.	April 23, 1897.
	£	£	£	£
Gold reserve	30,116,666	30,490,833	30,577,750	26,448,000
Silver reserve	10,462,916	10,454,333	10,448,660	10,515,000
Foreign bills	709,750	806,416	916,750	—
Advances	1,753,750	1,759,916	1,806,083	—
Note circulation	51,513,833	51,952,583	52,850,416	49,432,000
Bills discounted	11,577,333	11,332,000	12,442,333	*12,843,000

* Includes advances.

NATIONAL BANK OF BELGIUM (25 francs to the £).

	April 21, 1898.	April 14, 1898.	April 7, 1898.	April 22, 1897.
	£	£	£	£
Coin and bullion	4,270,440	4,066,280	4,134,280	4,211,000
Other securities	16,643,080	16,549,080	16,916,360	16,133,000
Note circulation	19,307,200	19,498,400	19,274,720	18,656,000
Deposits	3,056,840	2,553,800	3,174,320	3,090,000

BANK OF SPAIN (25 pesetas to the £).

	April 23, 1898.	April 16, 1898.	April 9, 1898.	April 24, 1897.
	£	£	£	£
Gold	9,719,040	9,761,480	9,643,800	8,528,400
Silver	8,727,600	10,279,200	10,472,880	10,552,560
Bills discounted	27,121,040	25,098,280	24,532,120	7,457,200
Advances and loans	5,695,400	5,791,080	5,226,040	9,963,240
Notes in circulation	52,229,000	52,189,240	51,614,320	43,170,680
Treasury advances, coupon account	564,160	95,000	97,640	263,560
Treasury balances	123,800	72,440	20,200	477,680

LONDON COURSE OF EXCHANGE.

Place.	Usance.	April 19.	April 21.	April 26.	April 28.
Amsterdam and Rotterdam	short	12·2¾	12·3½	12·3	12·2
Do. do.	3 months	12·4½	12·5	12·4⅜	12·4½
Antwerp and Brussels	3 months	25·60⅝	25·67½	25·63¾	25·61¼
Hamburg	3 months	20·74	20·76	20·75	20·72
Berlin and German B. Places	3 months	20·74	20·77	20·75	20·73
Paris	cheques	25·36¼	25·37½	25·35	25·32½
Do.	3 months	25·52½	25·53¾	25·50	25·46¼
Marseilles	3 months	25·52½	25·53¾	25·51¼	25·47½
Switzerland	3 months	25.70	25·72½	25·72½	25·72½
Austria	3 months	12·23¾	12·26¼	12·25	12·23¾
St. Petersburg	3 months	24⅜	24⅞	24⅜	24⅞
Moscow	3 months	24 5/16	24 5/16	24 5/16	24 5/16
Italian Bank Places	3 months	27.52½	27·80	27·60	27·35
New York	60 days	49	49	48⅞	48¾
Madrid and Spanish B. P.	3 months	29½	27¼	25½	25¾
Lisbon	3 months	33 3/16	32½	31½	30¾
Oporto	3 months	33 1/16	32½	31½	30¾
Copenhagen	3 months	18·46	18·47	18·47	18·46
Christiania	3 months	18·46	18·48	18·47	18·46
Stockholm	3 months	18·46	18·48	18·47	18·46

OPEN MARKET DISCOUNT.

	Per cent.
Thirty and sixty day remitted bills	3⅝
Three months "	3⅝—3 11/16
Four months "	3¾
Six months "	3¾
Three months fine inland bills	4
Four months "	4
Six months "	4¼

BANK AND DEPOSIT RATES.

	Per Cent.
Bank of England minimum discount rate	4
" " short loan rates	4
Banker's rate on deposits	2½
Bill brokers' deposit rate (Call)	2½
" 7 and 14 days' notice	2¾
Current rates for 7 day loans	2½—2¾
" " for Call loans	2

The Week's Stock Markets.

"Very little business" has been the daily report from the Stock Exchange, but prices have been marked up pretty considerably, nevertheless, just as they were put down last week. The rise in Consols has been the principal feature, due to the large influx of gold at the Bank; and, although investment business is practically at a standstill, there is a slightly steadier appearance about the list of Home Railway Preference and Debenture stocks. Canadian Railway issues rose sharply on rumours of a settlement of the rate war, but the market for United States securities has been a quiet one. The account was only remarkable for its smallness, and the recovery coming just in time, the making-up prices did not show any serious differences apart from the fall of about fourteen in Spanish 4 per cents.

Highest and Lowest this Year.		Last Carrying over Price.	BRITISH FUNDS, &c.	Closing Price.	Rise or Fall.
113⅛	109¼	—	Consols 2¾ p.c. (Money)...	111½	+1⅜
113 1/16	109½	111½	Do. Account (May 5)	111 9/16	+1 7/16
106¼	101	104¾	2½ p.c. Stock red. 1905 ...	103¼	+1¼
363	341	—	Bank of England Stock...	347½	+3½
117	111⅜	113	India 3½ p.c. Stk. red. 1931	114	+2
109¼	103⅜	105½	Do. 3 p.c. Stk. red. 1948	106½	+2
96⅜	90	92½	Do. 2½ p.c. Stk. red. 1926	92	+1½

Consols show a big rise on the week, due to the easier tendency in the money market, assisted by "bear" closing, the firmness being also shared in by the Indian sterling loans. Colonial Government issues, after a weak opening, recovered, and Home Corporation stocks are firmer, notably London County descriptions. Bank of England stock has risen about 3½.

Home Railway stocks, with one or two exceptions, are higher on balance, but business has again been on the smallest possible scale. The passenger lines have been most in demand, Brighton and South-Eastern deferreds both meeting with a good deal of support; but this does not apply to Chatham first preference, which is quoted lower, and Metropolitan and Great Central preferred have both lost ground. Among the "heavy" lines Great Western advanced slightly, in spite of the poor traffic which was due to the strike, and Midland deferred rose sharply, helped by a good return. South-Western deferred leaves off without much change, but this company's issues were very depressed in the earlier part of the week. Continuation rates ruled lighter, the account disclosing a reduction in the position open. South-Eastern deferred opened at ¼ contango and went to "even"; otherwise rates were inclined to be rather more onerous towards the close, Great Eastern starting "even" and going to ⅜ contango, Brighton A finishing at ½, and North-Eastern at ⅜ contango, after being ⅛ only in each case at the opening.

Highest and Lowest this Year.		Last Carrying over Price.	HOME RAILWAYS.	Closing Price.	Rise or Fall.
186	172½	175½	Brighton Def.	175⅝	+1¼
59¾	54⅛	55⅝	Caledonian Def.	55¾	+ ⅜
20⅝	18¼	18⅜	Chatham Ordinary	18¾	+ ⅜
77⅞	62½	63	Great Central Pref.	63	−1½
24⅝	21⅜	21½	Do. Def.	21¼	− ¼
124½	118	119¾	Great Eastern	118¾	+ ⅜
61½	50⅝	52	Great Northern Def.	52½	+1¼
179⅞	168¼	169¾	Great Western	169⅞	+ ⅜
51¾	45¼	49¼	Hull and Barnsley	50	+2¼
149¼	145	146	Lanc. and Yorkshire	146	+ ¼
136⅛	127¼	127½	Metropolitan	127½	− ½
31	26¾	27¼	Metropolitan District	27¼	+ ¼
88⅞	82⅛	83½	Midland Pref.	83¾	+ ⅝
95⅞	84½	86	Do. Def.	86½	+1¼
93¼	86¾	87¼	North British Pref.	87½	+ ¼
47½	41¾	42⅜	Do. Def.	42⅜	+1½
181½	172¾	173½	North Eastern	173¾	+ ¼
205½	196½	197½	North Western	197⅞	+ ⅜
117⅞	105½	108	South Eastern Def.	108¼	+2½
98⅞	87	88½	South Western Def.	89	—

There is nothing of startling importance to chronicle in the market for United States railroad shares, which closes rather dull after a short period of activity. A moderate demand on home and provincial account was the principal feature and helped to steady quotations during the first part of the week, but business in Wall-street has gradually dwindled away, operators there being rather afraid that the United States Government's need of money might lead to stringency. Towards the close quotations hardened a little in sympathy with the further rise in Canadian Pacific, a feature being the strength of Northern Pacific issues on a good traffic return, and prices on the whole are slightly firmer than a week ago. Continuation rates were round about 5 per per cent., which is ½ per cent. below the general rate last time.

Highest and Lowest this Year.	Last Carrying over Price.	CANADIAN AND U.S. RAILWAYS.	Closing Prices.	Rise or Fall.
14 5/16 10⅜	10½	Atchison Shares	10⅝	− ¼
34 23½	24⅜	Do. Pref.	25¼	+ ⅜
15⅝ 11	11	Central Pacific	11¼	—
99¾ 85½	87¾	Chic. Mil. & St. Paul	88¾	+1¼
14¼ 10	10½	Denver Shares	10¾	+ ¼
54¼ 41½	42½	Do. Prefd.	42⅝	+ ½
16⅝ 11¼	11⅛	Erie Shares	11⅛	—
44⅝ 29⅛	32¾	Do. Prefd.	33⅜	+2⅛
110½ 99	100	Illinois Central	100¼	+ ¾
62½ 45¼	47¾	Louisville & Nashville	48	+ ⅝
14½ 9 13/16	10¼	Missouri & Texas	10⅛	− ⅛
122¾ 108¼	110½	New York Central	111½	+ ½
57¼ 42⅝	45	Norfolk & West. Prefd.	45½	+1¼
70¼ 59	61¾	Northern Pacific Prefd.	63½	+2¼
19½ 13⅜	14	Ontario Shares	14¼	+ ⅛
62½ 56¾	57½	Pennsylvania	57⅛	− ⅛
12½ 7 13/16	8	Reading Shares	8¼	+ ⅜
34¼ 24¼	25⅛	Southern Prefd.	25¾	+ ½
37⅛ 18½	19	Union Pacific	19¾	+ ⅜
20¼ 14½	15½	Wabash Prefd.	15¾	+ ½
30⅛ 21	22	Do. Income Debs.	22	—
92¾ 74	80½	Canadian Pacific	82⅝	+6⅝
78⅝ 69⅞	73¼	Grand Trunk Guar.	73⅜	+1
69¼ 57⅛	67½	Do. 1st Pref.	62½	+2
50⅛ 37¼	47¼	Do. 2nd Pref.	47⅝	+2
25⅛ 19¼	22⅛	Do. 3rd Pref.	22½	+ ½
105½ 101½	102	Do. 4 p.c. Deb.	102	+ ⅛

Canadian Pacific shares, which closed very flat on Thursday, have since gone ahead, the Continental selling coming to a sudden conclusion, and another rumour to the effect that the rate war is again coming to an end has caused an advance of five or six points. A good deal of buying from Montreal has helped the upward move, and much is being said about the big increases to come, owing to the diversion of traffic from the United States over the Canadian roads. Grand Trunk stocks have risen in sympathy and are among the very few which "make up" higher this time than last.

Highest and Lowest this Year.	Last Carrying over Price.	FOREIGN BONDS.	Closing Price.	Rise or Fall.
94½ 84	87	Argentine 5 p.c. 1886	87¾	+2¾
92⅝ 81⅝	85	Do. 6 p.c. Funding	85¼	+3
76¾ 64	67	Do. 5 p.c. B. Ay. Water	68	+3¼
61¾ 41⅛	41½	Brazilian 4 p.c. 1889	44¾	+1¼
69⅞ 46	46	Do. 5 p.c. 1895	49½	+1½
65 42¾	43	Do. 5 p.c. West Minas Ry.	46½	+1¼
108¾ 106¼	107¼	Egyptian 4 p.c. Unified	107¼	+ ¼
104¾ 100½	101	Do. 3½ p.c. Pref.	101¼	+ ¼
103 99¼	100¼	French 3 p.c. Rente	100½	+ ½
44¾ 34½	42½	Greek 4 p.c. Monopoly	43½	+2¼
93 5/16 88¾	90½	Italian 5 p.c. Rente	90⅝	+1¼
100 87½	93	Mexican 6 p.c. 1888	94	+5
20⅞ 16	16⅞	Portuguese 1 p.c.	17¼	− ⅜
62½ 30½	34¼	Spanish 4 p.c.	33⅜	+1¼
45¼ 40	41¼	Turkish 1 p.c. "B"	41½	+1½
26 1/16 22⅝	23½	Do. 1 p.c. "C"	23⅜	+ ⅜
22 1/16 20	20½	Do. 1 p.c. "D"	20⅜	+ ⅜
46⅝ 40	44½	Uruguay 3½ p.c. Bonds	45½	+ ⅜

In the Foreign market Spanish Fours started the week by establishing another "record," the price touching 30½, but on a cessation of sales by Paris speculators a recovery set in, and after fluctuating, at times sharply, within comparatively narrow limits, are finally rather higher than a week ago. Most of the leading inter-Bourse securities have also risen, the closing of accounts open for the fall having imparted a firmer tone all round. Portuguese stock which fell sharply on Saturday, in sympathy with a sudden drop in the Lisbon Exchange, has since partly recovered. Chinese loans are slightly higher. Greek bonds keep very steady, in anticipation of the launching of the new loan, and Russian 4 per cent, and Egyptian Unified are firmer. Among South American stocks Brazilian bonds weakened in sympathy with a falling exchange at Rio, and then advanced to well above last week's closing, and Argentine and Chilian are also firm at the finish, after being very depressed. A slight "bear" squeeze was reported from Paris on Wednesday, the ease of the London money market encouraging buyers. Continuation rates were about 1 per cent. lower than a fortnight ago, Spanish being the exception, the rate in this case being 1 to 3 per cent. against 4 to 5 per cent.

Highest and Lowest this Year.	Last Carrying over Price.	FOREIGN RAILWAYS.	Closing Price.	Rise or Fall.
100 99½	100	Argentine Gt. West. 5 p.c. Pref. Stock	100	—
158¼ 136	140	B. Ay. Gt. Southern Ord.	144	+7
78½ 65	68	B. Ay. and Rosario Ord.	70	+4
12¼ 10¼	10½	B. Ay. Western Ord.	10⅞	+ ¼
87¼ 73	77	Central Argentine Ord.	78⅛	+4½
92 83	82	Cordoba and Rosario 6 p.c. Deb.	83	—
95⅛ 85½	86	Cord. Cent. 4 p.c. Deb. (Cent. Nth. Sec.)	86	− ½
61¾ 42	42½	Do. Income Deb. Stk.	45	+ ⅝
25¼ 16¾	17¼	Mexican Ord. Stk.	18	+1
83½ 69¼	71	Do. 8 p.c. 1st Pref.	71½	+1

Foreign Railway stocks were sold persistently all the week, and it was not until quite the last thing that any support was forthcoming. A rally then occurred in some of the leading Argentine companies, amounting to as much as seven points in Buenos Ayres Great Southern, the rise in the price of wheat being expected to benefit them, and the traffic returns were generally satisfactory. Western of Havana and Manila bonds were almost unsaleable and leave off considerably lower, and falls of 6 have taken place in Conde d'Eu 5½ per cent., and Cordoba Central first preference. Mexican Railway issues were hardly affected by the announcement of the dividend on the first preference, although it was worse even than the market expected.

The Miscellaneous market has been an idle one, the general decline in prices which took place towards the end of last week being due generally to a few sales in a very narrow market. Allsopp preferred ordinary has fluctuated rather wildly, before closing practically without change on balance; Guinness has fallen 20 and Younger preference 2; Threlfall's ordinary weakened on the new issue of capital. Gas stocks were marked down considerably, and insurance companies' issues have been pressed for sale. Schweppes deferred gave way a little more, the dividend of 2 per cent. being considered very poor. Welsbach ordinary improved somewhat on the granting of an official quotation, but realisations have since caused a set back. Among shipping companies a rise of six was recorded in F. Leyland ordinary shares, but Royal Mail lost last week's rise. Russian Petroleum is about two higher; Coats close firm on influential buying from the North; and Anglo-American Telegraph, Hudson's Bay, Liebig's, and Lyons' shares have all improved their position. Declines have taken place in J. Barker debenture, Vickers and Maxim, and Dumont Coffee debentures, and Trust companies' emissions are generally weaker.

There was very little business during the closing hours of the week, and many were the gloomy forebodings as to to-morrow's settlement in the Western Australian Mining market, and a large batch of failures is expected. Other markets were well supported, Consols closing firm on a good Bank return coupled with the further large influx of gold to the Bank. Among Foreign Government stocks Argentine were in strong demand on a fall in the gold premium at Buenos Ayres. Brazilians advanced still further, and Mexican issues finally almost succeeded in wiping out last week's big declines; but Spanish bonds and Rio Tinto shares closed dull on Paris sales. Foreign Railway stocks finished at about the best, and Canadian Pacific and United States Railroad shares were in renewed request, but Grank Trunk stocks gave way just a little at the last.

Mining and Finance Companies.

The South African market, after being tolerably steady, finished up quite firm, under the influence of buying orders from Paris. Various rumours were also made use of to raise quotations, one to the effect that President Kruger was disposed to grant certain concessions with regard to the dynamite monopoly, and the latter statement has now apparently been confirmed, a reduction of 10s. per case being announced. Most of the leading favourites, notably Rand Mines and De Beers, are considerably higher on the week, but Chartered shares have hardly moved. The account being again a small one was easily arranged, rates if anything being rather lighter. Trouble has however been brewing in the West Australian section, and the heavy shake out which occurred towards the close of last week has only been followed by a partial recovery, although Lake View Consols, Great Boulder and Hannan's Brown Hill finally reached a slightly higher level than at the close of business on Thursday last. The Bottomley group has been severely handled, Market Trust getting down into the neighbourhood of 5s, while Northern Territories have shed about 2¾ during the account. So far matters have not been definitely arranged. One or two small failures have already been announced, but more are expected. Copper securities have exhibited great strength, as the price of the metal is expected to go still higher during the war, the latest quotations comparing very favourably with last week's closing.

Prices of Mine and Mining Finance Companies' Shares.

Shares £1 each except where otherwise stated

AUSTRALIAN.

Making-Up Price, Apr. 26.	Name	Closing Price.	Rise or Fall.	Making-Up Price, Apr. 26.	Name	Closing Price.	Rise or Fall.
1½	Aladdin	1½		½	Hannan's Star	7/16	
2¾	Associated	2¾		4 11/16	Ivanhoe, New	5	+ ½
9/16	Do. Southern	½	- ⅛	15/16	Kalgurli Mt. & Iron King, 18/	1	
1	Brownhill Extended	1		4⅜	Kalgurli	4⅝	+ ¼
1⅛	Burbank's Birthday	1 1/16	- ⅛	2 5/16	Lady Shenton	2 5/16	
⅞	Central Boulder	13/16	- 1/16	8⅝	Lake View Cons.	8⅞	+ ¼
5/3	Chaffers, 4/	4/6	- /3	⅝	Do. Extended	⅝	
16/3	Colonial Finance, 15/	½ dis		½	Do. South	½	
—	Crœsus S. United	¼		1 5/16	London & Globe Finance	1 5/16	+ 1/16
⅞	E. Murchison	⅝	- ¼	15/16	London & W. A. Exploration	⅞	
4/6	Golden Arrow 19/	4/	- /6	⅞	Do. Investment	⅞	
6¼	Golden Horseshoe	6½	+ ¼	¾	Mainland Consols	¾	
⅜	Golden Link	⅜		13/16	North Boulder, 10/	9/16	- 3/16
18/9	Great Boulder, 2/	19/	+ 2/6	1¼	North Kalgurli	1 5/16	+ ½
1 3/16	Do. Main Reef, 10/	1 1/16		1 13/16	Northern Territories	1½	- 5/16
2⅝	Do. Perseverance	2¾	+ ⅛	2 7/16	Peak Hill	2½	
½	Do. South	½		1⅝	South Kalgurli	1¾	+ ⅛
1⅜	Hainault	1⅜	+ ⅛	1¼	W. A. Goldfields	1⅜	+ ⅛
11/16	Hampton Plains	⅝		1	W. A. Joint Stock	15/16	- ⅛
7	Hannan's Brownhill	7	+ ⅛	8/9	W. A. Market Trust	4/3	- 6/
5/16	Hannan's Oroya	3/16	- ⅛	½	W. A. Loan & General Fin.	¼	- 3/16
11/16	Do. Proprietary	11/		—	White Feather	½	

SOUTH AFRICAN.

Making-Up Price, Apr. 26.	Name	Closing Price.	Rise or Fall.	Making-Up Price, Apr. 26.	Name	Closing Price.	Rise or Fall.
4⅞	Angelo	5	+ ⅛	2/3	Lisbon-Berlyn	2/	- /6
1	Aurora West	1½	+ ⅛	2⅜	May Consolidated	2⅜	
3⅛	Bantjes	¾	+ 1/16	4	Meyer and Charlton	4⅜	+ ½
8/6	Barrett, 10/	8/	- /6	3 5/16	Modderfontein	3 11/16	+ 1/16
3⅞	Bonanza	4	+ ⅛	13/16	New Bultfontein	1	+ 3/16
5/16	Buffelsdoorn	⅜		3⅜	New Primrose	3⅜	
5½	City and Suburban, £4	5¾		1 5/16	Nigel	1½	+ 3/16
2 5/16	Comet (New)	2 5/16	+ ⅛	—	Nigel Deep	1 3/16	
3¼	Con. Deep Level	3½	+ ¼	5/16	North Randfontein	⅜	+ ½
10¼	Crown Deep	10½		4⅞	Nourse Deep	4⅜	- ⅛
12	Crown Reef	12½		1	Porges-Randfontein	1	
24⅛	De Beers, £5	25½	+ 1⅜	26⅜	Rand Mines	28⅝	+ 2⅛
3⅛	Driefontein	3⅜	+ ⅛	1 5/16	Randfontein	1⅛	- ⅛
5 13/16	Durban Roodepoort	6	+ ⅛	1⅞	Rietfontein	1½	
3 5/16	Do. Deep	3½		9	Robinson Deep	9⅜	
3 11/16	East Rand	4½	+ ½	7⅜	Do. Gold, £5	7⅞	+ ½
22¼	Ferreira	23½	+ 1¼	¾	Do. Randfontein	15/16	+ 3/16
6⅛	Geldenhuis Deep	6¼	+ ⅛	1½	Roodepoort Central Deep	1½	
5	Do. Estate	5½	+ ¼	5⅜	Rose Deep	6¼	+ ½
½	George Goch	½		2⅛	Salisbury	2⅛	
2	Ginsberg	1 13/16		1½	Sheba	1 13/16	+ 1/16
1 13/16	Glencairn	1 11/16	- 1/16	2⅜	Simmer and Jack, £5	2 13/16	+ 1/16
7⅞	Goldfields Deep	8⅛	- ⅛	2 13/16	Transvaal Gold	3	+ ⅛
8	Griqualand West	8		3	Treasury	3 3/16	+ 1/16
8¼	Henry Nourse	8¾	+ ½	3½	United Roodepoort	3⅛	
7½	Heriot	7½		1⅜	Van Ryn	1⅜	- ⅛
7¼	Jagersfontein	7½	+ ¼	5¼	Village Main Reef	5⅝	+ ¼
7⅜	Jubilee	7⅝	+ ¼	1½	Vogelstruis	1 3/16	
4 13/16	Jumpers	5	+ ⅛	½	Do. Deep	13/16	
2	Kleinfontein	2 3/16		8¼	Wemmer	8¼	
2 11/16	Knight's	3½	+ ⅜	½	West Rand	½	
1 13/16	Lancaster	2 1/16	+ 1/16	5⅜	Wolhuter, £4	5½	+ 3/16
2⅞	Langlaagte Estate	3	+ ⅛	2⅝	Worcester	2⅝	

LAND EXPLORATION AND RHODESIAN

2	Anglo-French Ex.	2 1/16	+ 1/16	½	Mashonaland Central	½	
1 7/16	Barnato Consolidated	1 5/16	- ⅛	5⅜	Matabele Gold Reefs	6½	+ ½
11/16	Bechuanaland Ex.	⅝		1 11/16	Mozambique	2	
2¾	Chartered B.S.A.	2 13/16		⅞	Oceana Consolidated	⅞	+ 1/16
¼	Clark's Cons.	3/16		1¼	Rhodesia, Ltd.	1 1/16	
5/16	Colenbrander	5/16		3⅛	Do. Exploration	3⅛	
3 13/16	Cons. Goldfields	4 1/16	+ 1/16	1	Do. Goldfields	1	- 1/16
1	Do. Pref.	20/		3½	S. A. Gold Trust	3½	+ 1/16
1 1/16	Exploration	1 3/16		11/16	Tati Concessions	11/16	+ ⅛
2⅞	Geelong	2 13/16	- 1/16	¾	Transvaal Development	¾	- 1/16
⅜	Henderson's Est.	5/16		½	United Rhodesia	½	
1⅛	Johannesburg Con. In.	1⅜		1	Willoughby	1 1/16	
1/16	Do. Water	1/16		1/16	Zambesia Explor.	1	+
1⅜	Mashonaland Agency	1⅜					

MISCELLANEOUS.

1	Alamillos, £2	1⅛		½	Mount Lyell, South	10/	- /6
4⅞	Anaconda, $25	5	+ ⅛	4	Mount Morgan, 17s. 6d.	4 3/16	+ 1/16
5/6	Balaghât, 18/	7/	+ 2/	4 13/16	Mysore, 10s.	5 3/16	
11/6	Brilliant, £2	12/3		11/6	Mysore Goldfields	10/6	- 1/6
2 1/16	Do. St. George's	2 1/16		5/6	Do. Reefs, 17/	6/	
9/6	British Broken Hill	9/6		8/	Do. West	8/	- /6
2 1/16	Broken Hill Proprietary	2 1/16		6/	Do. Wynaad	5/6	- /6
—	Do. Block 10	3½	- ½	2½	Namaqua, £2	2½	
4⅞	Cape Copper, £2	4 13/16	+ 1/16	3½	Nundydroog	3 1/16	
4 13/16	Champion Reef, 10s.	5		3 5/16	Ooregum	3 5/16	+ 1/16
2½	Copiapo, £2	2 11/16	+ ⅛	3 11/16	Do. Pref.	3 13/16	+ ⅛
3	Coromandel	3		26¼	Rio Tinto Def., £5	27	+ 2½
13/	Day Dawn Block	13/6		6	Do. Pref. £5	6	+ ⅛
2 5/16	Frontino & Bolivia	2 5/16		16/6	St. John del Rey	16 6	
1½	Hall Mines	1 1/16		8/9	Taitipu	⅞	- 1/16
2 7/16	Libiola, £5	2⅞	- ⅛	7	Tharsis, £2	7	+ ⅛
7⅞	Linares, £3	8	+ ⅛	2½	Tolima "A," £5	2½	
4	Mason & Barry, £3	3 13/16		4 5/16	Waihi	4½	+ 1/16
4⅞	Mountain Copper, £5	4⅞		1⅞	Waitekauri	1½	- ⅛
12⅞	Mount Lyell, £3	13	+ 1⅛	1	Woodstock (N.Z.)	1	+ 1/16
2 5/16	Mount Lyell, North	2 11/16	+ 1/16				

TRAMWAY AND OMNIBUS RECEIPTS.

HOME.

Name.	Period.	Ending.	Amount.	Increase or Decrease on 1897.	Weeks or Months.	Aggregate to Date. Amount.	Aggregate to Date. Inc. or Dec. on 1897.
			£	£		£	£
Aberdeen District	Week	Apr. 23	396	-18	—	—	—
Belfast Street	"	" 23	2,111	-657	—	—	—
Birmingham and Aston	"	" 23	432	-184	—	—	—
Birmingham and Midland	"	" 23	622	*-107	—	—	—
Birmingham City	"	" 23	3,606	*-485	—	—	—
Birmingham General	"	" 23	882	-22	—	—	—
Blessington and Poulaphouca	"	" 24	10	-15	16	160	+18
Bristol Tramways and Carriage	"	" 22	7,609	*-353	—	—	—
Burnley and District	"	" 23	308	-27	—	—	—
Bury, Rochdale, and Oldham	"	" 23	800	*-191	—	—	—
Croydon	"	" 23	371	+32	—	—	+1,083
Dublin and Blessington	"	" 24	94	-69	16	1,496	+50
Dublin and Lucan	"	" 25	51	-53	17	656	-360
Dublin United	"	" 22	3,118	-106	—	43,748	+2,796
Dudley and Stourbridge	"	" 23	158	-65	17	2,741	+109
Edinburgh and District	"	" 23	2,435	+224	16	36,071	+3,390
Edinburgh Street	"	" 23	736	+73	16	9,499	+1,205
Glasgow	"	" 23	2,662	‡-348	—	—	—
Harrow-road and Paddington	"	" 23	268	-55	—	—	—
Lea Bridge and Leyton	"	" 23	737	-148	—	—	—
London, Deptford, and Greenwich	"	" 23	576	-73	—	9,006	+543
London General Omnibus	"	" 23	21,165	+596	—	—	—
London Road Car	"	" 23	6,450	-108	†	98,361	+5,918
London Southern	"	" 23	538	-27	—	—	—
North Staffordshire	"	" 23	383	-32	—	6,313	-3
Provincial	"	" 23	2,296	-840	—	—	—
Rossendale Valley	"	" 22	169	-15	—	—	—
Southampton	"	" 23	353	-83	—	—	—
South London	"	" 23	1,716	*-174	†	25,685	+996
South Staffordshire	"	" 22	566	-362	16	9,504	-71
Tramways Union	Month	March	9,958	+661	3	28,030	+3,346
Wigan and District	Week	Apr. 23	270	-18	—	—	—
Woolwich and South East London	"	" 23	352	-114	†	5,145	+338

* Includes Easter Week. † From January 1. ‡ Holiday Week.

FOREIGN.

Name.	Period.	Ending.	Amount.	Increase or Decrease on 1897.	Weeks or Months.	Aggregate to Date. Amount.	Aggregate to Date. Inc. or Dec. on 1897.
			£	£		£	£
Anglo-Argentine	Week	Mch. 28	4,270	+413	*	55,300	+5,110
Barcelona	"	Apr. 23	1,027	-297		18,274	-2,453
Barcelona, Ensanche y Gracia	"	" 23	201	-29		3,601	+79
Bordeaux	"	" 22	2,195	-216		31,810	-1,272
Buenos Ayres and Belgrano	Month	Feb.	4,409	+749	*	9,168	+1,273
Buenos Ayres Grand National	Week	Mch. 26	$26,090	+$3,700	†		+$170,057
Buenos Ayres New	Month	Jan.	$59,905	-$1,852		$69,905	-$1,852
Calais	Week	Apr. 23	125	-34			
Calcutta	"	" 16	1,460	+136			
Gothenburg	"	" 13	384	+81			

* From January 1. † From April 1, 1897.

AFRICAN MINING RETURNS.

Dividends Declared in 1896	1897	1898	Capital Issued.	Nominal Amount of Share.	Name of Company.	Monthly Crushings. January. Tons.	Oz.	Dwt. per ton.	February. Tons.	Oz.	Dwt. per ton.	March. Tons.	Oz.	Dwt. per ton.	Totals. Months.	Ozs.	Profits Declared. Jan.	Feb.	Mar.	Totals. Months.	—	Stamps now Working.
p.c.	p.c.	p.c.	£	£													£	£	£		£	
—	—	25	225,000	1	Angelo	12,657	5,863	9.3	11,615	5,868	11.0	11,701	5,719	9.8	3	17,443	12,636	13,803	12,617	3	39,056	60
—	—	—	130,000	1	Balmoral	12,770	2,318	3.7	11,160	2,015	3.6	—	2,425	—	3	6,758	1,456	544	1,107	3	3,107	60
—	75	50	200,000	1	Bonanza	11,627	8,036	13.8	10,220	7,741	15.1	—	8,227	—	3	24,004	18,430	18,545	20,429	3	58,404	40
—	—	—	550,000	1	Buffelsdoorn	33,118	3,607	2.2	26,688	3,034	2.3	—	2,902	—	3	9,543	—	—	—	—	—	75
—	—	—	133,000	1	Champ d'Or	8,989	3,193	7.0	8,929	2,998	6.7	—	2,968	—	3	9,159	—	—	—	—	—	50
5	15	—	1,360,000	4	City and Suburban	32,345	11,032	6.8	26,990	9,678	7.2	—	11,030	—	3	31,740	18,553	15,451	17,326	3	51,330	160
—	—	—	224,635	1	Comet	9,707	3,231	6.6	8,314	2,968	7.1	8,626	2,928	6.8	3	9,127	4,814	4,812	4,124	3	13,750	40
—	—	—	300,000	1	Crown Deep	42,262	13,429	6.3	39,170	10,248	5.2	40,390	9,718	4.8	3	33,393	17,026	9,086	10,700	3	36,812	160
110	170	100	120,000	1	Crown Reef	34,787	12,110	7.0	23,711	10,332	8.7	—	12,080	—	3	34,522	22,379	19,537	22,656	3	64,572	120
55	80	20	125,000	1	Durban Roodepoort	16,635	6,105	7.2	15,800	6,179	7.1	16,665	6,341	7.6	3	19,625	—	—	—	—	—	80
275	300	—	90,000	1	Ferreira	18,480	12,213	13.2	16,925	12,077	14.3	—	12,299	—	3	36,609	27,775	27,320	27,890	3	82,985	80
12½	45	50	200,000	1	Geldenhuis Estate	34,857	10,088	5.8	30,895	10,019	6.5	—	10,743	—	3	30,850	17,477	18,825	20,838	3	57,138	120
—	30	—	300,000	1	Geldenhuis Deep	35,890	11,493	6.3	41,343	11,366	5.5	48,263	10,774	4.4	3	33,633	17,686	18,414	21,100	3	57,200	190
—	10	—	150,000	1	Gelden. Main Reef	5,734	1,310	4.6	2,100	424	4.0	—	952	—	3	2,686	566	a2,050	241	3	a1,243	30
—	—	—	325,000	1	George Goch	13,691	3,068	4.5	12,356	2,950	4.8	—	3,007	—	3	9,025	—	—	—	—	—	120
—	25	—	160,000	1	Ginsberg	8,795	2,383	5.4	6,669	2,154	6.1	—	2,591	—	3	7,128	4,385	3,191	4,751	3	12,327	40
—	—	—	500,000	1	Glencairn	27,584	6,749	4.9	24,583	6,512	5.3	—	6,958	—	3	20,219	11,107	10,239	10,264	3	31,610	110
30	125	—	125,000	1	Henry Nourse	15,200	7,608	10.0	13,980	7,723	11.0	15,130	8,308	10.9	3	23,638	14,571	16,482	17,452	3	48,505	60
85	100	25	111,864	1	Heriot	15,622	5,832	7.4	14,440	5,737	7.9	—	5,824	—	3	17,393	10,030	9,642	8,705	3	28,377	70
350	500	125	21,000	1	Johan. Pioneer	4,637	3,723	16.0	4,817	3,865	16.0	—	4,105	—	3	11,693	9,950	—	—	1	9,950	30
60	90	25	50,000	1	Jubilee	9,038	3,092	6.8	8,488	2,808	6.6	—	2,798	—	3	8,628	—	—	—	—	—	50
30	60	—	100,000	1	Jumpers	19,246	5,407	5.6	17,510	5,319	6.1	—	5,073	—	3	15,799	6,160	7,150	5,370	3	19,680	100
—	—	—	231,250	1	Kleinfontein	18,212	5,163	5.6	17,290	4,942	5.7	19,061	4,655	4.9	3	14,760	5,441	4,905	4,370	3	14,716	95
—	—	—	312,180	1	Knight's	24,290	5,215	4.3	24,500	5,485	4.4	25,680	5,476	4.3	3	16,176	3,076	—	4,400	2	7,476	120
30	30	—	470,000	1	Langlaagte Estate	37,695	8,692	5.1	27,624	7,840	5.6	31,119	10,191	6.6		26,823	—	—		—	—	120
—	—	—	550,000	1	Lang. Block B.	19,129	4,709	4.9	18,160	4,760	5.2	19,812	4,927	5.0	3	14,402	—	—	—	—	—	80
—	—	—	250,000	1	Langlaagte Star	9,673	4,031	8.3	9,045	3,424	7.5	11,062	3,498	6.3	3	10,953	—	—	—	—	—	30
20	—	—	275,000	1	May Consolidated	22,399	6,509	5.8	20,292	7,371	7.2	23,390	7,860	6.7	3	21,740	8,217	11,768	12,213	3	32,198	100
20	50	—	85,000	1	Meyer and Charlton	14,406	3,910	5.4	13,969	3,935	5.6	—	3,895	—	3	11,740	5,348	5,893	5,596	3	16,837	80
—	—	—	949,620	4	Modderfontein		—	—	7,684	2,835	7.4	—	3,677	—	2	6,512	—	—	—	—	—	60
—	—	—	200,000	1	Nigel	6,970	2,831	8.1	6,083	2,773	8.8	—	2,868	—	3	8,472	—	—	—	—	—	25
—	—	—	300,000	1	Nth. Randfontein	9,801	1,944	3.9	8,514	1,972	4.6	9,892	2,393	4.8	3	6,309	—	—	—	—	—	40
—	—	—	374,934	1	Nourse Deep	13,023	5,400	8.3	11,587	4,642	8.0	13,723	4,860	7.1	3	14,902	7,710	5,604	5,200	3	18,514	60
—	—	—	400,000	1	Paarl Central	9,604	2,535	5.3	10,618	2,540	4.8	11,315	2,611	4.6	3	7,686	—	—	—	—	—	60
—	10	—	487,500	1	Porges Randfontein	11,692	3,981	6.8	11,605	3,532	6.1	12,581	3,541	5.6	3	11,054	—	—	—	—	—	60
—	50	—	300,000	1	Primrose	37,789	9,137	4.8	34,077	8,824	5.2	—	9,484	—	3	27,445	12,463	11,664	12,492	3	36,619	160
—	10	—	165,000	1	Princess Estate	8,688	2,837	6.5	8,610	2,725	6.3	—	2,720	—	3	8,282	2,002	1,850	1,750	3	5,609	40
—	—	—	270,000	1	Rietfontein	4,265	769	3.6	15,130	3,628	4.8	—	2,087	—	3	6,484	—	3,115	—	1	3,115	50
—	—	—	300,000	1	Rietfontein "A"	13,255	5,543	8.4	13,189	5,049	7.6	—	4,737	—	3	15,331	11,145	9,682	7,566	3	28,393	60
12	15	—	2,750,000	5	Robinson	31,440	b15,574	9.9	30,003	b15,203	11.3	—	b16,454	—	3	47,231	36,530	35,000	37,000	3	108,530	120
—	—	—	600,000	1	Robinson R'dfontein	9,700	3,341	6.9	7,944	2,566	6.5	8,177	2,696	6.6	3	8,603	—	—	—	—	—	35
—	—	—	175,000	1	Roodepoort Gold	5,805	1,266	4.4	4,806	950	4.0	—	986	—	3	3,202	52	—	—	—	—	40
25	40	—	150,000	1	Roodepoort United	11,760	4,423	7.5	10,954	4,057	7.4	—	3,922	—	3	12,402	7,240	6,680	5,350	3	19,262	70
—	—	—	400,000	1	Rose Deep	27,058	9,666	7.1	23,149	8,660	7.5	29,424	10,166	6.3	3	23,492	15,900	12,932	15,100	3	43,932	117
—	—	—	100,000	1	Salisbury	8,506	2,497	5.7	8,476	2,462	5.8	—	2,650	—	3	7,539	3,179	—	—	1	3,179	50
20	20	3¾	1,075,000	1	Sheba	11,760	6,400	10.9	10,418	5,930	11.4	—	4,370	—	3	16,700	—	—	—	—	—	120
—	—	—	4,700,000	5	Simmer and Jack	44,760	10,163	4.5	41,030	9,081	4.3	—	11,420	—	3	30,664	—	—	—	—	—	100
—	—	—	235,000	1	Spes Bona	9,100	2,037	4.5	8,894	2,283	5.1	—	2,122	—	3	6,442	451	—	—	1	451	40
—	15	—	35,000	1	Stanhope	4,428	1,058	4.7	4,220	1,054	5.0	—	980	—	3	3,092	—	—	—	—	—	20
—	—	—	604,225	1	Trans. G. M. Est.	14,032	6,600	9.4	9,844	4,145	8.4	18,277	6,769	7.4	3	17,514	10,138	10,400	—	2	20,538	75
—	—	—	540,000	4	Treasury	9,574	3,385	7.5	9,247	3,844	8.3	—	3,813	—	3	11,242	5,876	6,436	6,920	3	19,232	40
—	—	—	300,000	1	Van Ryn	19,942	4,189	4.2	16,701	3,738	4.5	18,713	4,373	4.7	3	12,300	3,518	1,440	—	2	4,958	80
—	—	—	260,000	1	Village Main Reef	6,510	3,499	5.4	13,425	5,356	7.9	12,908	5,964	9.3	3	14,821	—	8,621	8,000	2	16,621	65
75	100	—	80,000	1	Wemmer	10,998	6,072	11.0	10,200	5,803	11.3	12,139	6,243	12.8	3	18,118	13,190	12,561	12,987	3	38,738	50
—	—	—	400,000	1	West Rand	6,879	1,889	5.5	6,075	1,784	5.9	6,665	1,770	5.3	3	5,443	1,374	—	—	1	1,374	30
—	—	—	—	1	Windsor	6,890	1,942	5.6	6,397	1,745	5.4	—	1,844	—	3	5,531	—	—	3,027	1	3,027	40
—	10	—	860,000	4	Wolhuter	22,265	7,559	6.8	21,220	6,675	6.3	—	6,936	—	3	21,170	10,823	9,027	8,452	3	28,302	100
35	30	15	95,722	1	Worcester	5,204	2,023	7.8	4,885	2,888	11.8	—	2,674	—	3	7,585	5,033	4,690	—	2	9,723	40
—	—	—	90,000	1	York	9,483	2,302	4.9	8,271	2,201	5.3	—	—	—	2	4,503	—	—	—	—	—	40

a Loss. b Exclusive of yield from Concentrates bought—1,396 oz. in January, 1,320 oz. in February and 2,913 oz. in March.

MINING RETURNS.

CUMBERLAND.—From Cyanide works:—Tailings works recovered 252 oz. from 920 tons.

IVANHOE.—Clean up March 15, 1,500 oz. gold from 993 tons crushed.

MANGANA (TASMANIA) GOLD REEFS.—380 tons crushed, yield 85 oz. retorted gold.

HIGHLAND CHIEF.—Crushed 65 tons, 34 oz.; concentrates 20 oz. in addition.

LAKE GEORGE.—March return:—6,750 tons of crude sulphide ore furnaced, yielding 267'78 tons of first matte containing 530 oz. of gold, 18,482 oz. of silver, and 87'21 tons of copper; Costs—mining 7'62s., smelting 9'87s., development 1'75s., and handling 53s.

OTTOS KOPJE.—7,518 loads washed during the week ended April 21; 246 carats of diamonds won.

CUDDINGWARRA.—Crushed during past fortnight, 151 tons, yielding 136 oz. of gold; assay of tailings 19 dwt.

BRITISH BROKEN HILL.—Fortnight ended April 21:—3,007 tons crude ore produced 460 tons concentrates, containing 290 tons lead, and 12,598 oz. silver.

CONSOLIDATED MURCHISON.—Crushed 278 tons; obtained 286 oz. of gold.

CRESCENT.—300 tons, 108 oz.

GREAT BOULDER PROPRIETARY.—Tons of ore crushed 1,465, yield 3,319 oz. gold.

ALADDIN'S LAMP.—400 tons of ore crushed, yielding 410 oz.; and two tons of special ore have been shipped, containing 55 oz.

ALASKA TREADWELL.—Bullion shipment, $38,501; ore milled, 20,414 tons; sulphurets treated, 373 tons; bullion from sulphurets, $13,667.

NEW QUEEN.—Result of crushing for past fortnight: 1,220 ft. formation, 420 tons, yielding 310 oz. gold.

ST. JOHN DEL REY.—Gold produced April 11 to 20, £6,7-0; yield per ton, '72 of an oz. troy.

NEW BULTFONTEIN.—Production of diamonds for four weeks ended March 26, 5,900 carats, or an average of 29⅝ carats per 100 loads. For the four weeks ended April 23, 6,700 carats, averaging 30¼ carats per 100 loads.

NORTH-WEST AUSTRALIAN GOLDFIELDS.—Cleaned up April 15, 130 tons. Result, 223 oz. smelted gold.

BAYLEY'S UNITED.—Cyanide plant has treated 894 tons tailings, yielding 808 oz. gold. Treated 179 tons rich ore on hand, yielding 202 oz. of gold.

FRANK SMITH DIAMOND.—3,500 loads washed, producing 247 carats.

MIDDLESEX, W. A.—First clean up from 70 tons, 75 oz.

VICTORIA (CHARTERS TOWERS).—295 tons crushed, yielded 419 oz. gold.

LADY EVELYN.—Crushed 145 tons for 277 oz. gold.

NOTICES.

A sub-branch to the Croydon branch of the Union Bank of London, Limited, will be opened at 76, High-street, South Norwood, on May 2. Permanent premises have been secured at 18, Cromwell-place, South Kensington, and will be opened for business as soon as the necessary alterations are effected.

The directors of the Grand Trunk Railway Company of Canada have decided to give to the holders of the Hamilton and North-Western 6 per cent. first mortgage bonds, maturing on June 1 next, the option until May 10 of accepting £98 of perpetual 4 per cent. consolidated debenture stock for each £100 bond, in addition to the half-year's interest of £3 per cent. payable on June 1. The interest on the 4 per cent. debenture stock is payable quarterly, on January 14, April 14, July 14, and October 14 in each year, by warrants forwarded by post to the holders, and the debenture stock now offered will be entitled to the first quarter's interest, payable on July 14, 1898. The Company will allot, at the price of £102 10s. per £100 of debenture stock, any extra amount of that stock required by bondholders to enable them to register even amounts. Forms for effecting the exchange and any further information can be obtained at the office of the Company, 203, Dashwood-house, New Broad-street, E.C.

The Canada North-West Land Company announce that the sales of farm lands for the quarter to March 31 show an increase of 4,489 acres and £23,862 over the same period last year.

The Bank of England are prepared to receive the coupons due the 30th inst. on the Demerara Railway Company's scrip.

The Council of Foreign Bondholders is prepared to receive the certificates of deposit issued by it against the New Plymouth Harbour Board 6 per Cent. debentures for the purpose of stamping and payment of the coupon due on May 1, 1898.

Messrs. J. Thomson T. Bonar & Co. notify that the coupons due May 1 next, together with the bonds drawn at the final drawing on February 4 last, of the Lehigh and Wilkes-Barre Coal Company's first mortgage 6 per cent. Sterling bonds, will be paid on or after May 2 at their offices, 57½, Old Broad-street, E.C.

The British South Africa Company notifies that forms of application for the 250,000 new shares authorised on the 21st inst. have been posted to shareholders.

On and after April 30 the rate of interest allowed by the Hong Kong and Shanghai Banking Corporation on money placed on deposit for twelve months will be raised to 4 per cent. per annum.

The City Bank, Limited, announces the numbers of the bonds of the Chilian International 6 per cent. loan of 1892, drawn in March last, for payment on July 1.

The directors of the Rio Tinto Company have elected Mr. W. Duff Bruce to be deputy-chairman of the Company.

Railway Traffic Returns.

BURMA RAILWAYS.—Receipts for week ending March 26, Rs. 2,34,945; increase, Rs. 20,880. Aggregate from January 1, Rs. 26,24,472; decrease, Rs. 1,70,741.

ALCOY AND GANDIA RAILWAY AND HARBOUR COMPANY.—Traffic for week, April 23:—Ps. 7,000; increase, Ps. 200. Aggregate from January 1, Ps. 146,750; increase Ps. 4,080.

WEST FLANDERS RAILWAY.—Gross receipts for week ending April 24, £2,100; decrease, £367. Total from January 1, £37,311; increase, £961.

WEST OF INDIA PORTUGUESE RAILWAY.—Week ending April 2, Rs. 6,016; increase, Rs. 2,100. Aggregate from January 1, Rs. 60,060; increase, Rs. 18,301.

QUEBEC CENTRAL RAILWAY.—Receipts for first week of April, $7,088; decrease, $1,758. Aggregate from July 1, $88,789; decrease, $12,461.

MOBILE AND BIRMINGHAM RAILROAD.—Traffic for first week of April, $5,964; increase, $343. Aggregate from July 1, $291,492; decrease, $3,186.

ALGECIRAS (GIBRALTAR) RAILWAY.—Traffic for week ended April 16, Ps. 32,720; increase Ps. 5,100. Aggregate from July 1, Ps. 840,252; increase, Ps. 29,578.

ASSAM-BENGAL RAILWAY.—Traffic for week ended March 19, Rs. 24,058; increase, Rs. 3,543. Aggregate from January 1, Rs. 2,73,119; increase, Rs. 23,430.

PUERTO CABELLO AND VALENCIA RAILWAY.—Traffic receipts for week ending March 18, £986; decrease, £355. Aggregate from January 1, £10,661; decrease, £4,598.

DELHI UMBALLA KALKA RAILWAY.—Receipts for week ended April 23, Rs. 30,600; increase Rs. 2,600. Aggregate from January 1, Rs, 5,78,100; increase, 1,53,900.

ROHILKUND AND KUMAON RAILWAY.—Traffic receipts for week ending March 26, Rs. 15,160; increase, Rs. 5,464. Aggregate from January 1, Rs. 80,318; decrease, Rs. 12,980.

WESTERN OF SANTA FE RAILWAYS.—Gross receipts for week ending April 23, $36,660; increase, $15,110.

MANILA RAILWAY.—Receipts for week ending April 23, $19,938; increase, $7,780. Aggregate from January 1, $311,961; increase, $73,754.

SOUTHERN MAHRATTA RAILWAY.—Receipts for week ended April 2, Rs. 122,575; decrease, Rs. 13,692.

GREAT WESTERN OF BRAZIL RAILWAY.—Traffic for week ending March 19, $28,436; increase, $5,530. Aggregate receipts to date $471,407; increase, $65,641.

VILLA MARIA AND RUFINO RAILWAY.—Traffic for week ending April 23, $5,308; increase, $1,683. Aggregate from January 1, $76,988, increase $1,992.

ANTOFOGASTA (CHILI) AND BOLIVIA RAILWAY.—Traffic receipts for month of March, $447,000; decrease, $55,000.

BOLIVAR RAILWAY.—Receipts for month of March, £5,912; increase, £722. Aggregate for nine months, £18,867; decrease, £7,262.

CLEATOR AND WORKINGTON.—Gross receipts for the week ending April 23 amounted to £1,070, a decrease of £31. Total receipts from January 1, £16,266, a decrease of £720.

COCKERMOUTH AND KESWICK RAILWAY.—Receipts for the week ending April 23, £828; increase, £13. Aggregate from January 1, £13,279; increase, £1,261.

ENGLISH RAILWAYS.

Div. for half years. 1896	1896	1897	1897	Last Balance forward.	Amt. to pay 1 p.c. on Ord. for ½ yr.	NAME.	Date.	Gross Traffic for week: Amt.	Inc. or dec. on 1897.	Inc. or dec. on 1896.	No. of weeks	Gross Traffic for half-year to date: Amt.	Inc. or dec. on 1897.	Inc. or dec. on 1896.	Mileage.	Inc. on 1897.	Working	Prior Charges last ½ year.	Prop. add Cap. Exp. this ½ year
				£	£												%	£	£
10	10	10	10	2,707	5,094	Barry	Apr 23	2,123	−5,407	−5,519	17	135,510	−10,543	+8,793	31	—	8·89	60,665	316,853
nil	nil	nil	nil	—	—	Brecon and Merthyr	,, 24	1,176	−380	−493	17	24,189	−110	−2,550	61	—	—	—	—
nil	nil	nil	nil	3,979	4,749	Cambrian	,, 24	5,336	−381	+698	*	75,015	+1,795	—	250	—	60·96	63,148	40,000
1½	1½	2	1½	1,510	3,150	City and South London ..	,, 24	998	+70	+109	17	17,769	+157	+1,620	3½	—	56·07	5,552	124,000
1	2	1½	2	7,895	13,210	Furness	,, 24	9,371	+452	+779	*	142,489	+4,008	—	139	—	49·88	97,423	80,910
2	1½	½	1	2,207	27,470	Great Cent. (late M.,S.,& L.)	,, 24	48,566	+4,987	+6,161	16	683,960	+12,750	+43,255	352½	—	57·17	627,386	1,200,000
1½	4¾	2	5	51,283	62,865	Great Eastern	,, 24	80,878	−‡6,309	+4,980	16	1,268,991	+35,326	+111102	1,158¼	2	55·35	860,138	250,000
3	5¾	3	5	15,094	102,496	Great Northern	,, 24	97,685	+‡13,641	+6,516	17	1,587,262	+45,999	+117481	1,071	8	61·36	641,485	750,000
4½	7¾	4½	7½	31,350	121,981	Great Western	,, 24	182,070	−‡12610	+4,730	16	2,760,540	+25,830	+117710	2,582	21	31·44	1,486,272	800,000
nil	2	nil	1½	8,951	16,487	Hull and Barnsley	,, 24	9,037	+3,372	+1,614	16	105,462	+3,132	+10,435	73	—	58·21	70,290	52,[illegible]
5	5¾	5	5½	21,495	83,704	Lancashire and Yorkshire ..	,, 24	92,512	−‡3,394	+1,087	16	1,468,173	+42,182	+53,300	555½	25	56·70	674,745	451,976
4½	8	4½	8½	26,243	43,049	Lon., Brighton, & S. Coast	,, 23	52,939	−‡2,430	+3,352	17	812,640	+34,077	+47,638	476½	—	50·20	407,042	240,735
nil	nil	nil	nil	72,294	56,296	London, Chatham, & Dover	,, 24	29,520	−‡1,939	+1,885	16	433,612	+12,296	+14,983	185¼	—	30·65	367,873	nil
6½	8	6½	7¾	89,535	204,068	London and North Western	,, 24	236,708	+12,692	+16,036	16	3,020,489	+85,249	+196572	1,911½	—	56·92	1,404,534	600,000
5	8½	8½	8½	23,038	59,367	London and South Western	,, 24	78,064	−‡3,831	+5,577	16	1,086,990	+43,284	+74,528	941	6½	51·75	513,740	389,000
2½	6	2½	6½	14,592	6,691	Lon., Tilbury, & Southend	,, 24	5,208	−‡1,379	+317	17	83,702	+4,837	+13,695	81	—	52·57	39,590	15,000
3½	3¾	3¾	3¾	17,133	26,409	Metropolitan	,, 24	16,563	−‡402	+1,376	*	264,165	+5,504	—	64	—	43·63	148,047	254,000
nil	nil	nil	nil	4,006	71,250	Metropolitan District ..	,, 24	8,255	+218	−55	16	136,135	+4,251	—	13	—	48·70	119,663	38,450
5	7	5½	6½	38,143	174,582	Midland	,, 24	187,727	−‡754	+15,614	17	3,101,282	+37,813	+224514	1,354¾	15½	57·59	1,216,582	650,000
5½	7½	5½	7	22,374	138,189	North Eastern	,, 23	136,836	−‡14481	−2,811	16	2,256,480	+10,146	+116748	1,597¾	—	58·82	795,077	436,004
7½	7½	7½	7½	7,061	10,102	North London	,, 24		Not recd				not	recvd.	12	—	50·90	40,973	7,600
4	5	4	4½	4,745	16,150	North Staffordshire	,, 24	14,273	−‡1,314	−193	17	263,716	+4,878	+14,901	312	—	55·27	118,142	19,605
10	10	11	10	1,642	3,004	Rhymney	,, 23	2,959	−1,364	−1,916	17	79,034	−3,984	+1,291	71	—	49·68	29,049	16,700
3	6½	3½	6½	4,054	50,215	South Eastern	,, 23	44,650	−‡3,589	+3,043	*	679,794	+35,411	—	448	—	51·88	380,763	250,000
3½	3½	3½	3½	2,315	25,961	Taff Vale	,, 23	6,502	−15,692	−8,252	17	229,862	−33,342	−18,416	121	—	54·90	94,800	92,000

* From January 1. ‡ Good Friday week, 1897.

SCOTCH RAILWAYS.

Div. for half years. 1896	1896	1897	1897	Last Balance forward.	Amt. to pay 1 p.c. on Ord. for ½ yr.	NAME.	Date.	Gross Traffic for week: Amt.	Inc. or dec. on 1897.	Inc. or dec. on 1896.	No. of weeks	Gross Traffic for half-year to date: Amt.	Inc. or dec. on 1897.	Inc. or dec. on 1896.	Mileage.	Inc. on 1897.	Working	Prior Charges last ½ year.	Prop. add Cap. Exp. this ½ year
5	5	5½	5	9,544	78,066	Caledonian	Apr. 24	78,861	− 1,174	+ 5,611	12	863,387	+ 19,225	—	851½	5	50·38	558,248	441,477
5	5½	5	5	7,364	24,639	Glasgow and South-Western	,, 23	30,752	− †634	+ 4,560	12	330,890	+ 10,936	—	393½	—	54·69	221,663	196,145
3½	3½	3½	—	1,291	4,600	Great North of Scotland	,, 23	8,134	+ 23	+ 391	12	92,029	− 273	+ 2,517	331	15½	52·03	92,178	60,000
	nil		—	10,477	12,820	Highland	,, 24	9,338	+ 526	+ 506	8	69,513	+ 2,619	—	479½	27½	58·63	78,976	,000
	1½	1	1½	819	45,819	North British	,, 24	77,600	− 535	+ 3,930	12	844,240	+ 20,685	—	1,230	23	48·62	944,809	40,800

† Holidays, 1897.

IRISH RAILWAYS.

Div. for half years. 1896	1896	1897	1897	Last Balance forward.	Amt. to pay 1 p.c. on Ord. for ½ yr.	NAME.	Date.	Gross Traffic for week: Amt.	Inc. or dec. on 1897.	Inc. or dec. on 1896.	No. of weeks	Gross Traffic for half-year to date: Amt.	Inc. or dec. on 1897.	Inc. or dec. on 1896.	Mileage.	Inc. on 1897.	Working	Prior Charges last ½ year.	Prop. add Cap. Exp. this ½ year
6½	6½	6½	—	5,466	1,790	Belfast and County Down ..	Apr. 22	2,082	− 1,355	+ 71	*	34,377	+ 943	—	76½	—	55·58	17,690	10,000
5½	6½	5½	—	—	4,284	Belfast and Northern Counties	,, 22	5,626	− ‡765	+ 431	*	82,652	+ 4,077	—	249	—	—	—	—
	3	2	—	1,418	1,200	Cork, Bandon, and S. Coast† ..	,, 23	1,423	− 150	+ 101	*	10,395	− 1,419	—	103	—	54·82	14,436	5,450
	6½	6½	6½	18,776	17,316	Great Northern	,, 22	15,811	− ‡1234	+ 1,706	16	230,688	+ 11,410	+ 14,076	528	36	50·15	88,068	22,000
	5½	5½	5½	30,339	24,855	Great Southern and Western ..	,, 22	—	—	—	not	received	—	—	603	13	51·45	72,800	46,582
	4	4	4½	11,372	11,850	Midland Great Western ..	,, 22	11,545	− 151	+ 728	16	154,269	+ 6,772	—	538	—	50·31	83,129	1,800
nil	nil	nil	nil	229	2,822	Waterford and Central ..	,, 22	942	+ 81	—	*	13,764	+ 1,387	—	[illegible]	—	53·84	6,458	1,900
nil	nil	nil	nil	1,936	2,987	Waterford, Limerick & W. ..	,, 22	5,097	− 19	+ 71	*	87,350	+ 3,250	—	350½	—	57·83	42,617	7,075

* From January 1. † Thirteen weeks' strike. ‡ Easter Week, 1897.

FOREIGN RAILWAYS.

Mileage. Total.	Increase on 1897.	Increase on 1896.	Name	Gross Traffic for Week. Week ending	Amount.	In. or Dec. upon 1897.	In. or Dec. upon 1896.	Gross Traffic to Date. No. of Weeks.	Amount.	In. or Dec. upon 1897.	In. or Dec. upon 1896.
					£	£	£		£	£	£
319	—	—	Argentine Great Western ..	Apr. 8	8,311	+ 904	+ 2,133	40	222,560	− 13,738	− 44,141
76⅝	—	—	Bahia and San Francisco ..	Mar. 19	3,330	+ 881	+ 1,483	12	35,707	+ 12,130	+ 13,741
234	48	84	Bahia Blanca and North West ..	Mar. 27	586	− 154	—	39	30,305	− 94	—
74	—	—	Buenos Ayres and Ensenada ..	Apr. 24	3,612	+ 9	− 656	16	55,603	− 9,096	− 14,760
426	—	—	Buenos Ayres and Pacific ..	Apr. 23	9,073	+ 1,093	+ 18	42	280,582	− 53,081	+ 6,851
914	1	3	Buenos Ayres and Rosario ..	Apr. 23	16,804	+ 6,231	+ 3,293	16	276,901	+ 75,625	+ 46,694
1,499	30	68	Buenos Ayres Great Southern ..	Apr. 24	32,664	+ 6,002	+ 3,481	42	1,261,325	+ 94,644	+ 178,815
802	207	177	Buenos Ayres Western	Apr. 24	12,710	+ 666	− 3,180	42	508,777	− 78,341	− 91,022
845	55	77	Central Argentine	Apr. 23	19,940	+ 5,423	+ 3,639	15	353,762	+ 88,464	+ 27,852
297	—	—	Central Bahia	Feb. 31*	$142,798	+ $14,292	+ $1,866	2	$276,357	+ $10,347	+ $14,624
271	—	—	Central Uruguay of Monte Video	Apr. 23	6,720	+ 1,631	+ 390	42	231,381	+ 15,545	− 15,736
208	—	—	Do. Eastern Extension	Apr. 23	2,002	+ 611	+ 390	42	54,717	+ 8,138	− 921
182	—	—	Do. Northern Extension	Apr. 23	774	+ 116	− 68	42	26,763	+ 192	− 7,056
180	—	—	Cordoba and Rosario	Apr. 17	1,710	+ 350	− 60	42	88,805	− 15,045	− 2,365
128	—	—	Cordoba Central	Apr. 17	$21,000	− $2,750	− $2,120	15	$326,700	− $51,970	− $68,730
549	—	—	Do. Northern Extension	Apr. 17	$48,000	− $14,300	− $15,200	15	$678,790	− $242,950	− $138,880
137	—	—	Costa Rica	Apr. 9	7,193	+ 2,310	+ 1,673	14	82,854	− 13,127	− 998
99	—	—	East Argentine	Mar. 13	677	+ 103	+ 131	11	7,285	− 617	− 345
386	—	6	Entre Rios	Apr. 23	2,620	+ 1,565	+ 1,111	42	68,761	+ 21,040	+ 17,028
555	—	24	Inter Oceanic of Mexico	Apr. 23	$67,200	+ $14,500	+ $21,340	41	$2,441,420	+ $391,970	+ $660,690
23	—	—	La Guaira and Caracas	Mar. 25	2,060	− 285	− 1,103	13	24,939	− 5,212	− 4,938
321	—	—	Mexican	Apr. 23	$88,500	+ $145,000	—	16	$1,319,200	+ $138,850	—
1,846	—	—	Mexican Central	Apr. 21	$254,804	+ $44,869	+ $69,128	16	$4,052,099	+ $44,481	+ $1,043,980
2,217	—	—	Mexican National	Apr. 21	$106,644	+ $6,501	+ $22,345	16	$1,759,147	+ $127,075	+ $341,814
228	—	—	Mexican Southern	Apr. 21	$11,800	− $565	+ $2,457	3	$36,460	− $5,675	+ $2,047
106	—	—	Minas and Rio	Feb. 31*	$128,262	+ $16,417	—	8 mos.	$1,436,813	+ $203,482	—
94	—		N. W. Argentine	Apr. 23	1,343	+ 134	+ 72	16	16,479	− 6,507	− 4,051
242	3	—	Nitrate	Apr. 15	18,375	+ 2,188	+ 4,209	13	107,065	+ 1,860	− 42,111
300	—	—	Ottoman	Apr. 16	4,106	− 88	− 99	16	73,893	− 15,227	+ 7,938
77¼	—	—	Recife and San Francisco ..	Feb. 26	6,265	+ 345	− 1,336	9	52,270	+ 2,163	− 8,118
86½	—	—	San Paulo	Mar. 27†	18,471	− 6,090	—	12	127,060	− 25,190	—
186	—	—	Santa Fe and Cordova	Apr. 23	3,022	+ 2,262	− 355	43	72,193	− 3,112	− 3,767
110	—	—	Western of Havana	Apr. 23	1,640	− 292	+ 760	42	75,115	+ 5,601	+ 7,190

* For month ended. † For fortnight ended.

INDIAN RAILWAYS.

Mileage. Total.	Increase on 1897.	Increase on 1896.	Name.	Gross Traffic for Week. Week ending	Amount.	In. or Dec. on 1897.	In. or Dec. on 1896.	Gross Traffic to Date. No. of Weeks.	Amount.	In. or Dec. on 1897.	In. or Dec. on 1896.
862	—	—	Bengal Nagpur	Apr. 23	Rs.1.90.000	+ Rs.64.708	+ Rs. 57.028	17	Rs.25.35.540	+ Rs.1.57.452	− R.1.44.993
827	8	63	Bengal and North-Western ..	Mar. 26	Rs.1.39.120	+ Rs.14.296	+ Rs. 12.476	13	Rs.16.04.225	+ Rs.2.09.897	+ R.1.66.033
461	—	—	Bombay and Baroda	Apr 16	£34,558	+ £6,369	− £6,057	16	£385,044	− £8,526	− £147,378
1,885	2	13	East Indian	Apr. 23	Rs.14.01.000	+ R.2.00.000	+ Rs2.67.000	17	Rs.2.03.19.000	+ Rs.5.83.000	+ R15.99.000
1,491	—	—	Great Indian Penin.	Apr. 16	£79,228	+ £26,075	− £6,298	16	£1,033,826	+ £148,247	− £205.797
736	—	—	Indian Midland	Apr. 23	Rs.1.50.040	+ Rs 8.092	+ Rs.32.159	17	Rs.22.16.744	+ Rs.3.74.868	+ Rs387.293
840	—	—	Madras	Apr 9	£19,983	+ £642	+ £1,905	13	£250,602	− £14,073	− £7,726
1,043	—	—	South Indian	¶ Mar. 19	Rs.1.67.070	− Rs.2.272	+ Rs.1.363	12	Rs.1.673.198	− Rs.239.682	− Rs.37.159

UNITED STATES AND CANADIAN RAILWAYS.

Mileage. Total.	Increase on 1897.	Increase on 1896.	Name.	Gross Traffic for Week. Period Ending.	Amount.	In. or Dec. on 1897.	Gross Traffic to Date. No. of Weeks.	Amount.	In. or Dec. on 1897.
					dols.	dols.		dols.	dols.
917	—	—	Baltimore & Ohio S. Western ..	Apr. 21	135,000	+ 33,000	41	5,101,184	+ 603,096
6,568	92	136	Canadian Pacific	Apr. 21	453,000	+ 87,000	15	6,569,000	+ 1,321,000
922	—	—	Chicago Great Western	Apr. 21	87,590	+ 5,000	41	4,330,878	+ 537,328
6,169	—	469	Chicago, Mil., & St. Paul ..	Apr. 21	564,000	+ 59,000	15	8,748,101	+ 1,341,300
1,685	—	—	Denver & Rio Grande	Apr. 21	146,800	+ 21,100	41	6,554,100	+ 1,074,300
3,512	—	—	Grand Trunk, Main Line ..	Apr. 21	£72,070	+ £530	15	£1,147,252	+ £111,187
335	—	—	Do. Chic. & Grand Trunk	Apr. 21	£13,499	+ £2,485	15	£231,844	+ £55,070
189	—	—	Do. Det., G. H. & Mil. ..	Apr. 21	£3,586	− £291	15	£55,135	− £3,188
2,938	—	—	Louisville & Nashville	Apr. 21	379,000	+ 15,000	15	6,339,175	+ 1,023,620
2,197	137	137	Miss., K., & Texas	Apr. 21	212,511	+ 9,288	41	10,355,429	+ 529,625
477	—	—	N. Y., Ontario, & W.	Apr. 21	62,128	− 2,810	41	3,124,695	+ 89,008
1,570	—	—	Norfolk & Western	Apr. 7	225,000	+ 16,000	39	8,315,000	+ 886,000
3,499	336	—	Northern Pacific	Mar. 21	390,000	+ 103,000	11	4,070,000	+ 1,216,000
1,223	—	—	St. Louis S. Western	Apr. 21	248,000	+ 24,000	21	1,770,400	+ 306,091
4,654	—	—	Southern	Apr. 21	369,000	+ 24,000	41	6,366,812	+ 1,335,443
1,979	—	—	Wabash	Apr. 21	263,000	+ 32,000	15	3,844,406	+ 774,000

MONTHLY STATEMENTS.

Mileage. Total.	Increase on 1896	Increase on 1895.	Name.	Net Earnings for Month. Month.	Amount.	In. or Dec. on 1897.	In. or Dec. on 1896.	Net Earnings to Date. No. of Months.	Amount.	In. or Dec. on 1897.	In. or Dec. on 1896.
					dols	dols.	dols.		dols.	dols.	dols.
6,935	44	444	Atchison	March	904,000	+ 337,000	+ 369,344	3	2,144,434	+ 674,836	+ 229,480
6,547	103	106	Canadian Pacific	February	424,000	+ 39,000	+ 19,268	2	940,000	+ 182,000	+ 110,318
6,169	—	469	Chicago, Mil., & St. Paul ..	March	1,180,000	+ 170,000	+ 65,202	3	2,726,334	+ 225,840	+ 84,122
1,685	—	—	Denver & Rio Grande	February	219,000	+ 52,500	+ 22,731	8	2,244,907	+ 367,7	− 8,088
1,970	—	—	Erie	January	471,000	+ 33,000	− 107,852	—	—	—	—
3,512	—	—	Grand Trunk, Main Line ..	February	£56,453	+ £13,757	+ £23,860	2	£143,853	+ £48,041	+ 64,910
335	—	—	Do. Chic. & Grand Trunk	February	£8,910	+ £5,197	+ 5,595	2	£21,310	+ £14,130	+ 15,582
189	—	—	Do. Det. G. H. & Mil. ..	February	£528	− £1,369	− 207	2	£2,328	− £677	+ 1,459
3,127	—	239	Illinois Central*	February	2,177,767	+ 413,527	+ 422,489	2	4,481,665	+ 819,023	+ 805,759
2,396	—	—	New York Central*	February	3,429,000	+ 128,000	+ 222,359	2	6,934,000	+ 492,597	249,393
477	—	—	New York Ontario, & W. ..	February	57,800	− 3,800	+ 19,304	9	832,700	+ 33,400	+ 75,462
1,570	—	—	Norfolk & Western	February	242,000	+ 69,000	+ 43,259	2	525,000	+ 83,247	+ 91,585
3,407	—	—	Pennsylvania	January	1,359,101	+ 65,700	+ 236,000	2	2,511,898	92,400	+ 345,000
1,055	—	—	Phil. & Reading	February	584,381	− 44,678	—	8	6,865,102	+ 446,422	—

* Statement of gross traffic.

Prices Quoted on the London Stock Exchange.

Throughout the INVESTORS' REVIEW middle prices alone are quoted, the object being to give the public the approximate current quotations of every security of any consequence in existence. On the markets the buying and selling prices are both given, and are often wide apart where stocks are seldom dealt in. Other particulars will be found in the INVESTMENT INDEX published quarterly—January, April, July, and October—in connection with this REVIEW, price 2s., by post 2s. 2d. Where dividends are paid only once a year, an *italic* type is used to distinguish them. The London Stock Exchange Official List is quoted in the REVIEW almost entire, only very insignificant issues, or bonds falling due within the next two or three years, being omitted. But the list is subdivided into the leading, or active, stocks, and those less frequently dealt in. The former will be found under the head of "Stock Markets," and with more details than it is possible to give for the bulk of securities. By retaining the file of the INVESTORS' REVIEW any subscriber can follow for himself the movements of securities from week to week, and the INVESTMENT INDEX will from time to time help to fill up deficiencies in the information.

Tea Companies and Mines and Mining Finance Stocks are placed in special lists.

Among the abbreviations used are the following:—S.F. Snk.Fd. *sinking fund*; Certs., *certificates*; Debs. or Dbs., *debentures*; Db. or D.Stk., *debenture stock*; Pf., Prf., or Pref., *preference*; Prefd. or Pfd., *preferred*; Dfd., *deferred*; L. or Ltd., *limited*; Sh., *share*; Ans., *annuities*; Cu. or Cm., *cumulative*; Gu or Guar., *guaranteed*; Bds., *bonds*; S., Sr., or Ser., *series*; In., Ins., Insc., *inscribed*; Dr., Drgs., Drwgs., *drawings*; Stg., Strlg., *sterling*; Lia., *liable to*; Sp., Surp., *surplus*; Per., Perp., *perpetual*; Ln. *lien*; Lo. *loan*.

The dates following the names of securities are the years of issue or of redemption. Where shares are not fully paid up, their nominal amount is given with the name so that investors may know the liability upon them.

BRITISH FUNDS, &c.

Rate	Name.		Price.
2¾	2¾ p.c.'s (Childers') Red..	1905	103
3	Local Loans Stk.	1912	110
3	Metro. Police Deb. Stk.	1920	105½
—	Red Sea Ind. Tel. Ann.	1908	8½
4	Canada Gv. "Intcl. Rly."	1903	104
4	Do. do. ..	1908	111
4	Do. Bonds	1910	112
4	Do. Bonds	1913	117½
3	Egyptian Gov. Gar.		106½
3	Mauritius Ins. Stk.	1940	114
4	Turkish Guar. 1855		109
11½	Bank of Ireland Stk.		390
3½	India Rupee Paper		61
3½	Do. 1854-5		62
3	Do. 1896-7	1916	55
3½	Isle of Man Deb.		104
3	Do. Deb. Stk...	1919-29	103

CORPORATION AND COUNTY STOCKS.

FREE OF STAMP DUTY.

Rate	Name.		Price.
3½	Metropolitan Con.	1929	117½
3	Do.	1941	110
2½	Do.	1920-49	100
2½	L.C.C. Con. Stock	1920	99
3½	Comm. of Sewers, Scp., S.F.	1905	105
3½	Corp. of Lond. Bds...	1897-1902	100½
3	Do.	1897-1912	101
3½	Do, Debs. Scp. .... S.F.	1916	105
2½	Do., Deb. Stk. Scrip ..	1927-57	98
3	Barnsley	1916-46	105
3	Barry	1914-46	101½
3	Bath	1909-34	102
3	Batley	1914-41	101½
3½	Birmingham	1945	117½
3	Do.	1947	111½
2½	Do.	1926	98
3	Blackburn	1930	106½
3	Bournemouth	1913-33	103
3½	Bradford	1945	116½
3	Do. Deb. Stock ..	1954	108
3	Brighouse..............	1916-46	100
3½	Brighton	1946	117
2½	Do.	1957	97
3	Burton-on-Trent........	1913-43	101
3	Cambridge	1913-43	103
3½	Cardiff	1935	115½
3	Do.	1914-54	103
3	Cheltenham............	1971	107
3	Chichester	1916-46	101
3½	Croydon		131½
3	Do.	1940	103½
3	Derby	1920-50	107
3	Devon C.C..............	1917-33	104½
3½	Dewsbury	1930	109
3	Do.	1930	103
3	Dorset County	1922-32	105
3	Douglas (I. of Man)	1926	101
3	Dover	1913-43	101
3½	Dublin	1944	113½
3	Eastbourne	1920-40	104
3	Edinburgh	1924	108
2½	Do.	1927	98
2½	Exeter	1917-57	96
3	Glamorgan County	1914-34	104
3½	Glasgow	1914	109
3	Do.	1921	104½
2½	Do.	1925-40	98
3	Gloster	1915-55	101
3	Grimsby	1913-45	103
3	Hampshire County	1914-34	105½
3	Hanley	1913-43	105
3	Harrogate	1914-34	103
3	Hastings	1915-54	103½
2½	Hertfordshire C.C.	1916-36	98
3	Heston & Isleworth U.D.C.	1915-35	101
3	Huddersfield	1934	107
3½	Hull (1st iss.)		131½
3	Inverness	1914-44	101
3	Ipswich	1952	108½
3	Lancaster..............	1919-55	103
2½	Leeds	1927	98
3½	Leicester	1934	114½
3	Lincoln...............	1919	102
3½	Liverpool		131

Corporation, &c. (*continued*):—

Rate	Name.		Price.
3	Manchester	1941	107½
3	Mansfield...............	1915-45	100
3½	Middlesbro'............	1909	105½
3½	Do.	1911-13	105
3	Do.	1915	104
3	Middlesex C.C..........	1915-35	106
3½	Newcastle	1936	118½
3½	Do. Irred.		129½
2½	Do.	1915-36	100
3	Newcastle-under-Lyme..	1909-44	101
3	Newport (Mon.)	1915-55	101½
3	Norwich	1952	110
3	Nottingham		111½
3	Oxford	1951	109½
3	Penzance..............	1916-46	100½
3	Plymouth	1942	109½
3	Pontypridd U.D.C.	1916-46	98
3	Poole..................	1915-45	101
3½	Portsmouth........1916	24 & 27	112
3	Do.	1913-33	106½
3	Ramsey	1920-40	100
3	Ramsgate..............	1915-55	102
3½	Reading		129½
3	Do.	1962	103½
3½	Rhyl U.D.C.	1953	110
3	Richmond (Surrey)	1942	104½
3	River Wear Debt Certs.		100
3	St. Helen's	1915-55	102
3	Scarbro'	1915-50	102
2½	Sheffield	1925-57	92½
3	Shipley U.D.C..........	1915-35	100
3	Somerset Co.	1923-33	104
3	South Shields..........	1915-45	100
2½	Southampton	1915-45	102
3	Southend-on-Sea	1916-46	102
3	Staffs C.C.	1915-35	102
3	Stockport..............	1914-54	103
3	Stockton	1932	104
3	Do.	1915-35	103
3	Surrey Co.	1922-32	105½
3½	Swansea		130
3	Do.	1955	106
3	Taunton	1918 3-9-43	101
3	Tees Conserv. Deb. Stk.	1947	100
3	Thames Conserv. "A" Deb. Stk..........	1954	103½
3	Do. "B" Deb. Stk.	1954	103½
3	Torquay	1913-43	101½
3	Tunbridge Wells	1931	102
3	Tynemouth	1913	99
3	Wakefield..............	1929	101½
3	Walsall................	1932	107½
3	West Bromwich........	1930	106½
3½	West Ham	1929	110
3	Do.	1945	105
3	West Sussex C.C.	1915-35	106
3	Weston-s.-Mare Lcl Bd.	1914-44	100
3	Weymouth&Melc. Regis	1918	101
3	Widnes................	1915-55	100
3	Wigan	1921	104½
3	Windsor	1918-55	102
3½	Wisbech	1947	113½
3½	Wolverhampton	1932	117
3	Do.	1924-54	107
3	York	1916-41	106½

SUBJECT TO STAMP DUTY.

Rate	Name.		Price.
3½	Belfast City & Dis. Watr.	1938	114
3	Do. Red Stk.	1953-6	106
3½	Belfast	1924	103
4	Blackburn Con. Deb. Irred.		141½
3½	Do. do. Irred.		130
3½	Bristol		128½
3½	Burnley................	1933	114
2½	Chesterfield Gas & Wtr.	1916-46	98
3½	Douglas Town	1921	106
3	Dover Harb. 1st Deb...	1956	104½
3½	Hull (2nd iss.)		128½
4	Leeds Deb.............	1927	124
3½	Do.		115½
3	Do.	1927	106
3	Leicester	1919-44	103½
4	Manchester..................		145
3	Do.	1928	104½
4½	Middlesboro' Mrts.	1903	111
3½	Newark on-Trent ...	1901-41	96
3½	Sheffield	1898-1916	105½
3½	Do.	1925-36	114
3	Do.	1925	105½
3½	Southampton	S.F.	106
4½	Stockton Morts.........	1908	110½
3½	Worcester..............	1950	100

COLONIAL AND PROVINCIAL GOVERNMENT SECURITIES.

Rate	Name.		Price.
6	British Columbia........	1907	119½
4½	Do. Debs...	1917	111½
3	British Guiana Imgtn. Bds.		98
5	Canada, "Intercol. Rail,"	1903	107½
4	Do. (Bonds)	1904-5-6-8	106
4	Do. Reduced	1910	106½
3½	Do. Bnds.	1909-34	105
4	Do. Loan	1910-35	106½
3	Do. Loan	1938	100
6	Cape of G. Hope	1900	—
5	Do.	1900	—
4½	Do. red. by an. draw.		106
4½	Do. 1879		109
4	Do. 1881		108
4	Do	1917-23	113½
4½	Ceylon		110
4	Do.		106½
4½	Fiji Gov. Deb. Sink. Fd.		101½
4	Jamaica Sink. Fd.	1923	103
5	Manitoba Debs....... ...	1910	113
5	Do. Ster. Bds.	1888	119½
4	Do. Ster. Debs.		106
4	Mauritius, Cons. Debs. 1880....		103½
4½	Natal, Sink. Fd.........	1919	118
4	Do. do.	1926	115
3½	Newfoundland Stg. Bds.	1941	97
3½	Do. do. ..	1947	97
3	Do. do.		86½
5	New South Wales 1897-1902		104½
4	Do.	1903-5-8-9-10	106
5	New Zealand	1914	118
5	Do. Cnsls. 1 p.c. per an. Sink. Fd.		103
3½	Nova Scotia Debs.		104
5	Quebec Prov.	1904-6	110
4½	Do. (drgs.)		104
5	Do. Strlg. Bds.	1912	115
4	Do. Strlg. Bds.	1928	110
4	Do. Strlg. Bds.	1934	108
4	Queensland	1913-15	104½
4½	St. Lucia Debs..................		102½
6	South Australia	1897-1900	103½
6	Do.	1901-1918	119
5	Do.	1911-1920	116
4	Do.	1899-1916	106
4	Do.	1929	108½
4	Do.	1916	106½
4	Do.	1917-18-24	107½
6	Tasmania	1897-1901	104
4	Do. 1908-11,	1913-14-20	107½
5	Trinidad Debs., an. drw. 1 p c...		106
4	Victoria	1899-1901	101½
4½	Do.	1904	105
4	Do. Rail. Loan	1907	104
4	Do. Loans	1908-13	104
4½	West. Austr. 1 p.c. ac. Sink. Fd.		107
4	Do. do.		106

REGISTERED AND INSCRIBED STOCKS.

No stamp duty except for Canada 4 p.c. Reduced (½ per cent.).

Rate	Name.		Price.
4	Antigua Insc. Stk. Red.	1919-44	109
3½	Barbados Insc. Stk.	1925-42	107
3	British Colum. Insc. Stk.	1941	101½
4	British Guiana Insc.....	1935	116½
4	Canada Stk. Regd. ..	1904-5-6-8	104
4	Do. 4 p.c. (late 5 p.c.) Regd.	1910	106½
3½	Do. 3½ p.c. Stock Regd.	1909-34	105
4	Do. Ln. for 4 milln. stg.	1910-35	106½
3	Do. Stk. Regd.	1938	100
2½	Do. Insc..............	1947	89
4	Cape G. Hope Regd. ..	1917-23	113½
4	Do. (Ln. of '83) Insc. ..	1923	113½
4	Do. Cons. Stk. Insc....	1916-36	109
3½	Do. Consol. Insc. Stock	1929-49	106
4	Ceylon Insc. Stock	1934	118½
3	Do.	1940	101
4	Grenada Insc. Stock....	1917-42	110
3½	Hong Kong Insc. Stock	1918-43	103½
4	Jamaica Insc. Stock....	1934	117
—	Do.	1922-44	98
4	Mauritius Inscribed	1937	118½
4	Natal Consd. Stk. Insc.	1927	113
4	Do.	1937	117½
3½	Do. Inscribed Stock..	1914-30	105
4	Newfoundland Inscribed	1913-38	106
4	Do.	1935	113
4	Do. Consd. Stk. Ins.	1936	113
4	N. S. Wales Stock Insc.	1933	116½
3½	Do.	1924	104
3½	Do.	1918	103
3	Do.	1935	96½

Colonial, &c. (*continued*):—

Rate	Name.		Price.
4	N. Zealnd. Con. Stk. Ins.	1929	110
3½	Do	1940	106
3	Do. Inscribed....	1945	99
3	Quebec (Prov.) Ins. Stk.	1937	93
4	Queensland Stock Insc.	1915-24	107½
3½	Do.	1921-4-30	103
3½	Do.	1945	105
3	Do.	1922-47	98
4	St. Lucia Insc. Stock ..	1919-44	112
4	S. Austrln. (1882-7) Reg.	1916-36	108½
3½	Do. In. Stk. Reg.	1939	107
3	Do.	1916-26	99
3/	Do.	1916	99
3½	Tasmanian Insc. Stock..	1920-40	106
4	Do.	1920-40	116
4	Trinidad Insc. Stock....	1917-42	110
3	Do.	1922-44	98
4	Victoria Rly. Loan '81, Inscribed Stock	1907	105
4	Victoria Insc. Stock	1908-13-19	108
4	Victoria (1885) Ins. Stk.	1920	110
3½	Do. Inscribed Stock	1921-3-6	103
4	Do. do.	1911-26	108
4	W. Austral. Insc. Stock	1934	116½
4	Do.	1911-31	109
3½	Do.	1915-38	104
3	Do.	1915-35	96
3	Do.	1916-36	97

FOREIGN STOCKS, BONDS, &c.

COUPONS PAYABLE IN LONDON.

Last Div.	Name.		Price.
36/	Argentine Ry. Loan 6 p.c.	1881	84½
15/	Do. 5 p.c.	1884	63
30/	Do. N. Cent. Ry. Ext. 5 p.c.	1887-8-9	62
30/	Do. 5 p.c. Trsy. Convs.	1887	63
5/4½	Do. 4½ p.c. Interl. Gld.	1888	61
27/	Do. 4½ p.c. Stlg. Extrl.	1888	61
10/6	Do. 3½ p.c. External ..	1889	47
4	Do. 4 p.c. Ry. Guar. Res....		54
4½	Brazilian	1883	46
4½	Do. Gold..........	1879	50½
4½	Do.	1888	45
36/	Buenos Ayres	1824	77½
6	Do.	1882-3-6	44
6	Bulgarian	1888	92
6	Do. Mort. Bonds	1892	92
4½	Chilian	1885	69½
4½	Do.	1886	71
4½	Do.	1887	69½
4½	Do.	1889	78½
5	Do.	1892	80½
4½	Do.	1893	69½
4½	Do.	1895	67
5	Do.	1896	79
7	Chinese Silver	1894	100
6	Do. Gold	1895	105
6	Do. Apl. '95 by dwgs.	1901-15	108½
5	Do. Red. dwgs. in 36 yr.	1896	98
5	Do. Do. Regis.	1896	98
1½	Colmbn. 1½ to 3 p.c. Ext. Bds.	1896	16½
6	Cordova, Prov.	1886	23
—	Do. Eng. Ass. Certs.		22
—	Do. 6 p.c.	1887-8	23
—	Do. Eng. Ass. Certs.		22
3	Costa Rica "A"		29
2½	Do. "B"		22
3	Danish Gold	1914	98
10/	Ecuador N. Ext. Bds. 4½ p.c. ascn. to 5 p.c..................		20
3½	Egypt'n Ins. Stk. lia. Stp. Dty.	1890	100
4	Do. State Domain	1878	103½
4	Do. D. Sanieh, Red. ..	1905	101½
6	Entre Rios...............	1880-8	30
6	Do. Fndg. Ln. Bds.	1894-1921	30
6	Do. do. Parana City......		27½
15/	Greek	1881	39
15/	Do.	1884	39
12/	Do. Rentes..................		33
15/	Do. (Piræus-Larissa Ry.)		37
2/6	Do. Fundg. Loan	1893	43
4	Guatemala Extl. Debt...........		27
6	Hawaiian		102½
4	Hungarian Gold Rentes.........		100½
3	Do.	1895	91½
6	Italian Irriga. Guar.		108
5	Do. Maremmana		91
5	Japan 5 p.c.		100½
5	Mexican (Nat. R. Tehuantp c.)..		88½
6	Do. Extrl.	1890	94

Foreign Stocks, &c. (*continued*):—

Last Div.	Name.	Price.
6	Mexican Extrl. 1893	93
5	Do. Intrnl. Cons. Slvr.	36
5	Do Intern. Rd. Bds. 2d. Ser.	36
4	Nicaragua 1886	47½
3½	Norwegian, red. 1937, or earlier	98
3	Do. do. 1965, do.	98
3½	Do. 3½ p.c. Bnds.	102
1	Paraguay 1p.c. ris. 3p.c. 1886-96	15
5	Russian, 1822, £ Strlg.	149
3	Do. 1859	95
4	Do. (Nicolas Ry.) 1867-9	101
3	Do. Transcauc. Ry. 1882	94
4	Do. Con. R. R. Bd. Ser. I., 1889	101
4	Do. Do. II., 1889	101
4	Do. Do. III., 1891	101
3½	Do. Bonds	100
4	Do. Ln. (Dvinsk and Vitbsk)	99
6	Salvador 1889	64
—	S Domingo 4s. Unified .. 1960	59½
6	San Luis Potosi Stg. 1889	87
5	San Paulo (Brzl.), Stg. 1888	88½
6	Santa Fé 1883-4	32
—	Do. Eng. Ass. Certs. Dep.	31
5	Do. 1888	42
—	Do. Eng. Ass. Certs. Dpsit.	41
5	Do. (W. Cnt. Col. Rly.) Mrt.	22
5	Do. & Reconq. Rly. Mort.	22
5	Spanish Quickslvr Mort. 1870	99
3½	Swedish 1880	102
3	Do. 1888	98
3	Do. Conversion Loan 1894	98
5	Trans. Gov. Loan Red....1903-42	103
59/	Tucuman (Prov.) 1888	67½
4	Turkish, Secd. on Egypt. Trib.	100
3½	Turkish, Egpt. Trib., Ott. Bd., '94	96½
4	Do. Priority 1890	87½
1	Do. Convted Series, "A"	66
5	Do. Customs Ln. 1886	92½
5	Uruguay Bonds 1896	54
3	Venzuela New Con. Debt 1881	31

COUPONS PAYABLE ABROAD.

Last Div.	Name.	Price.
7	Argent. Nat. Cedla. Sries, "B"	32½
5	Austrian Ster. Rnts., ex 10fl., 1870	85
5	Do. do. do.	83
5	Do. Paper do. 1870	83
5	Do. do. do.	85
4	Do. Gld Rentes 1876	100
2½	Belgian exchange 25 fr.	92
3	Do. do.	101
3½	Danish Int., 1887, Rd. 1896	—
2½	Dutch Certs. ex 12 gldrs.	85
3	Do. Bonds	98
3	Do. Insc. Stk.	97
3½	French Rentes	104½
3	Do. 1878, '81-4., Red.	100¼
3	German Imp. Ln. 1891	94½
3	Do. do. 1892-3	94½
3	Do. do. 1890-4	95
5	Japan Cons. Ln., '92, 3, & 5, Red.	45
36/9	Prussian Consols	101
3	" Cons. Stg. Ln. 1891	96
4	Rumanian Bds. 1890	—
4	Do. do. 1891	—
4	Utd. States, 1877, Red. 1907	110
4	Do. 1895, 30 yrs.	122
3½	Do. Maschsetts Gl. 1935	113½
3½	Do. Gold Bonds 1923	107½
2	Virginia Cpn. Bds., 3 p.c. from July, 1901	70

BRITISH RAILWAYS.

ORD. SHARES AND STOCKS.

Last Div.	Name.	Price.
10	Barry, Ord.	274½
4	Do. Prefd.	125
6	Do. Defd.	147½
5	Caledonian, Ord.	151
3	Do. Prefd.	96½
—	Do. Defd. Ord., No. 1	4½
	Cambrian, Ord	6½
—	Do. Coast Cons.	6½
32/	Cardiff Ry. Pref. Ord.	115
3/	Central Lond. £10 Ord. Sh.	10½
1/9½	Do. do. £6 paid	6½
3½d.	Do. Pref. Half-Shares	1½
1/6	Do. Def. do.	4½
1½	City and S. London	68
—	East London, Cons.	6½
2	Furness	63½
2½	Glasgow and S. West. Pfd.	79
2½	Do. do. Dfd.	62
3	Great Central, Ord....1894	39½
32/0	Do. London Exten.	71
—	Great N. of Scotland, Prfd.	90
—	Do. Dfd.	32
4	Great Northern, Prefd.	117½
—	Do. Consolidated "A"	49
—	Do. do. "B"	189½
2	Highland	76½
4	Isle of Wight, Prefd.	120½
3	Do. Defd.	83½
	Lancs. Derbys. and E. Cst.	4
8½	L. Brighton and S. C. Ord.	184
6	Do. Prefd. Ord.	196
30/	Do. Contgt. Rights Certs.	16½
5½	Lond. and S. Western Ord.	220½
4	Do. Preferred	132
6½	Lond., Tilb., and Southend	133½
—	Mersey, £20 shares	½
—	Metropolitan, New Ord.	127½
2½	Do. Surplus Lands	93
4	North Cornwall, 4 p.c. Pref.	104½
18/6	Do. Deferred	22½
7½	North London	222½
4½	North Staffordshire	130

British Railways (*continued*):—

Last Div.	Name.	Price.
3/3	Plymouth, Devenport, and S. W. Junc. £10	9
3/	Port Talbot £10 Shares	9
9d.	Rhondda Swns. B. £10 Sh.	5
10	Rhymney, Cons.	265½
4	Do. Prefd.	123
6½	Do. Defd.	145½
1½	Scarboro', Bridlington Junc.	47½
6½	South Eastern, Ord.	149
6	Do. Pref.	191
3½	Taff Vale	78
25/	Vale of Glamorgan	127½
3	Waterloo & City	134½

LEASED AT FIXED RENTALS.

Last Div.	Name.	Price.
4	Birkenhead	141½
5.19.0	East Lincnshire	200½
3½	Hamsmith. & City Ord.	192½
4½	Lond. and Blackwll.	159½
4½	Do. £10 4½ p. c. Pref.	159½
56/6	Lond. & Green. Ord.	101
5	Do. 5 p. c. Pref.	173½
5	Nor. and Eastn. £50 Ord.	89
6	Do.	104½
3½	N. Cornwall 3½ p. c. Stk.	124½
4½	Nott. & Granthm. R. & C.	140½
3½	Portptk. & Wigtn. Guar. Stk.	121½
9	Vict. Stn. & Pimlico Ord.	312½
4½	Do. 4½ p. c. Pref.	158½
4/	West Lond. £20 Ord. Shs.	14
4½	Weymouth & Portld.	157½

DEBENTURE STOCKS.

Last Div.	Name.	Price.
4	Alexandra Dks. & Ry.	132½
3	Barry, Cons.	107
4	Brecon & Mrthyr, New A	127½
4	Do. New B	106
4	Caledonian	147½
4	Cambrian "A"	132½
4	Do. "B"	127½
4	Do. "C"	122½
4	Do. "D"	107½
3	Cardiff Rly.	100½
4	City and S. Lond.	139
3½	Cleator & Working Junc.	118½
3	Devon & Som. "A"	103½
16/3	Do. "B" 4 p. c.	36
—	Do. "C" 4 p. c.	10
4	E. Lond. and Ch. 4 p. c. A	135
5/	Do. 2nd B	67½
—	Do. 3rd Ch. 4 p. c.	18½
—	Do. 4th do.	9½
3½	Do. 1st (3½ p. c.)	128½
2½	Do. 2½ p.c. (Whitech. Exn)	87
4	Forth Bridge	141½
4	Furness	141½
4	Glasgow and S. Western	146½
5	Gt. Central	—
4½	Do.	153½
4	Gt. Eastern	144½
4	Gt. N. of Scotland	141½
3	Gt. Northern	111½
4	Gt. Western	147½
4½	Do.	156½
4½	Do.	164½
5	Do.	182½
2½	Do.	96½
4	Highland	141½
3	Hull and Barnsley	103½
3	Do. and (3-4 p. c)	122
4	Isle of Wight	142½
3	Do. Cent. "A"	92½
4½	Do. "B"	115½
4	Do. "C"	82½
3	Lancs. & Yorkshire	111½
4	Lancs. Derbys. & E. Cst.	123½
4	Lpool St. Hlen's & S. Lancs.	126
4½	Ldn. and Blackwall	155½
4	Ldn. and Greenwich	143½
4	Lond., Brighton, &c.	148½
4½	Do.	164½
4½	Lond., Chath., &c., Arb.	152½
4½	Do. "B"	152½
4	Do.	138½
4	Do. 1883	138½
3	Do.	106
3	Lond. & N. Western	113
3	Lond. & S. Westn. "A"	112
3	Do. Consld.	112
4	Lond., Til., & Southend	144½
—	Mersey, 5 p. c. (Act, 1866)	65
4	Metropol.tan	144½
4½	Do.	162½
3½	Do.	126½
6	Met. District	207½
4	Do.	139
2½	Midland	93½
4½	Mid-Wales "A"	137½
4	Neath & Brecon 1st	127½
4	Do. "A 1"	117½
3	North British	106½
3	Do. 1893	107½
3½	N Cornwall, Launcstn., &c.	124½

Debenture Stocks (*continued*):—

Last Div.	Name.	Price.
3	North Eastern	112
4½	North London	163½
3	N. Staffordshire	110½
4	Plym. Devpt. & S.W. Jn.	141½
4	Rhondda and Swan. Bay	130½
4	Rhymney	144½
4	South-Eastern	146½
5	Do.	180
3½	Do.	127½
3	Do.	112
3	Taff Vale	108½
4	Tottenham & For. Gate	143½
3	Vale of Glamorgan	105½
3	West Highld. (Gtd. by N. B.)	107
4	Wrexham, Mold, &c. "A"	115½
4	Do. "B"	102½
4	Do. "C"	97½

GUARANTEED SHARES AND STOCKS.

Last Div.	Name.	Price.
4	Caledonian	146½
4	Do.	142½
4	Forth Bridge	141½
4	Furness 1881	137½
4	Glasgow & S. Western	141½
4	Do. St. Enoch. Rent	141½
6	Gt. Central	193½
4½	Do. 1st Pref.	150½
3½	Do. Pref.	104½
5	Do. Irred. S.Y. Rent	161½
4½	Do. do.	139½
4	Gt. Eastern, Rent	140½
5	Do. Metropolitan	176½
4	Do.	140½
4	Gt. N. of Scotland	132½
4	Gt. Northern	141½
5	Gt. Western, Rent	179½
5	Do. Cons.	179½
4	Lancs. & Yorkshire	141½
5	L., Brighton & S. C.	175½
3½	L., Chat. & D. (Shrtlds.)	110½
4	L. & North Western	144½
4	L. & South Western.. 1881	142½
4½	Met. District, Ealing Rent	150
4½	Do. Fulham Rent	150
4	Do. Midland Rent	141½
4	Do. Mid. & Dist. Guar.	126½
2½	Midland, Cons. Perp.	90
3	Mid. & G.N. Jt., "A" Rnt.	106
3	N. British, Lien	105
4	Do Cons. Pref. No. 1	138½
3	N. Cornwall, Wadebrge. Gu.	107
4	N. Eastern	142½
5	N. Staff. Trent & M. £20 Shs.	35½
3½	Nott. Suburban Ord.	123½
20/6	S. E. Perp. Ann.	35½
4½	Do. 4½ p.c.	160½
3½	S. Yorks. Junc. Ord.	118½
4½	W. Cornwall (G. W., Br., Ex., & S. Dev. Joint Rent	157½
3	W. Highl. Ord. Stk. (Gua., N.B.)	105½

PREFERENCE SHARES AND STOCKS.

DIVIDENDS CONTINGENT ON PROFIT OF YEAR.

Last Div.	Name	Price.
4½	Alexandra Dks. & Ry. "A"	125½
5	Barry (First)	167½
4	Do. Consolidated	136½
4	Caledonian Cons., No. 1	141½
4	Do. do. No. 2	140½
5	Do. do. 1878	172½
4	Do. Pref. 1884	140½
4	Do. do. 1887 (Conv.)	152½
—	Cambrian, No. 1 4 p.c. Pref.	72½
—	Do. No. 2 do.	39½
—	Do. No. 3 do.	19
—	Do. No. 4 do.	10
5	City & S. Lond. £10 shares	15½
—	Do. New	13½
4	Furness, Cons. 1881	133
4	Do. ...."A" 1881	131½
4	Do. ...."B" 1883	129½
4	Glasgow & S. Western	140½
4	Do. No. 2	139
4	Do. 1888	139
4	Do. 1891	139
5	Gt. Central	158½
4	Do.	131½
5	Do. Conv. 1872	153½
5	Do. do. 1874	153½
5	Do. do. 1876	152½
5	Do. do. 1879	151½
5	Do. do. 1881	147½
4	Do. 1889	112½
4	Do. 1891	106½
5	Do. 1894	101½
4	Gt. Eastern, Cons.	139
4	Do. 1886	138½
4	Do. 1881	138½
4	Do. 1884	138½

Preference Shares, &c. (*continued*):—

Last Div.	Name.	Price.
4	Gt. Eastern, Cons. 1887	138½
4	Do. 1888	138½
3½	Do. 1890	120½
3½	Do. 1893	120½
—	Do. (Int. fr. Jan '99) 1893	117½
4	Gt. North Scotland "A"	133½
4	Do. "B"	133½
4	Gt. Northern, Cons.	141½
3	Do. 1896	106½
5	Gt. Western Cons.	176½
36/11	Hull & Barnsley Red. at 115	107
4	Isle of Wight	133½
3	Lancs. & Yorkshire, Cons.	106½
2/2½	Lanc. Drby & E.C. 5 p.c. £10	10
—	Do. 5 p.c. 2nd £10	8½
5	Lond., Bright., &c., Cons.	176½
5	Do. 2nd Cons.	175½
4½	Lond., Chat. & Dov. Arbitr.	133½
£5/	Do. 2nd Pref. 4½ p.c.	91
4	Lond. & N. Western	143½
4	Lond. & S. Western .. 1881	142½
4	Do. 1884	141½
3½	Do.	125
4	Lond., Tilbury & Southend	140½
4	Do. Cons., 1887	140½
4	Do 1891	140½
—	Mersey, 5 p.c. Perp.	—
4	Metropolitan, Perp.	140½
4	Do. 1882	140½
4	Do. Irred.	140½
4	Do. 1887	140½
4	Do. New	140½
4½	Do.	146½
3½	Do.	123½
3	Do. Guar.	101½
2½	Metrop. Dist. Exten 5 p.c.	110
2½	Midland, Perp. Pref.	89
4	N. British Cons., No. 2	134½
4½	Do. Edin. & Glasgow	151½
5	Do. 1865	165½
5	Do. Conv. 1874	165½
4½	Do. 1875	150½
4½	Do. Conv. 1875	150½
5	Do. do. 1879	165½
4	Do. do. 1884	136½
4	Do. do. 1888	136½
4	Do. do. 1890	136½
4	Do. do. 1892	136½
4	N. Eastern	142½
4½	N. Lond., Cons. 1866	173½
4½	Do. 2nd Cons. .. 1875	167½
3	N. Staffordshire	106½
4½	Plym. Devpt. & S. W. Junc.	149½
1/5	Port Talbot, &c., 4 p.c. £10 Shares, 4 paid	8
5/	Rhondda & Swansea Bay, 5 p.c. £10 Shares	12½
4	Rhymney, Cons.	140½
4½	S. Eastern, Cons.	158½
5	Do. do.	175½
4	Do. Vested Cos'.	140½
4	Do. 1891	140½
3½	Do. 1893	122½
2	Do. 3 p.c. after July 1900	101½
4	Taff Vale	141½

INDIAN RAILWAYS.

Last Div.	Name.	Paid.	Price.
3½	Assam Bengal, Ld., (3½ p.c. till June 30, then 3 p.c.)	100	100
4/	Barsi Light, Ld., £10 Shs.	10	11
6	Bengal and N. West., Ld.	100	148½
4/	Do. £10 Shares	10	14½
3/6	Do. 3½ p.c. Cum. Pf. Shs.	10	10½
8½d.	Do.	4	4½
2/3½	Bengal Central, Ld., £10 (3½ p.c. + ½th net earn)	5	5½
3	Bengal Dooars, Ld.	100	114
4	Bengal Nagpr., Lim. (gua. 4 p.c. + 4th sp. pfts.)	100	114
7½	Bombay, Baroda, and C. I. (gua. 5 p.c)	100	214
36/1	Burma, Ld. (gua. 2½ p.c. and ½ p.c. add. till 1901)	100	107½
1/7	Do. £10 Shares		3
4	Delhi Umb. Kalka, Ld., Gua. 3½ p.c. + net earn.	100	120
4	Do. Deb. Stk., 1890 (1916)	100	111
9/10	Estn. Bengal, "A" An. 1957	—	25
9/	Do. "B" 1957	—	29
4	Do. Gua. Deb. Stock	100	136½
9/7½	East Ind. Ann. "A" (1953)	—	27
8/4½	Do. "C"	—	28
8/11½	Do. "B"	—	30
6½	Do. Def. Ann. Cap. (gua. 4 p.c. + ½th sp. pfts.)	—	150
115/9	East Ind. Def. Ann. "D"	—	156
4½	East Ind. Irred. Stock	100	158½
5	Gt. Indian Penin., Gua 5 p.c. + ½ surplus profits	100	166½
4	Do. Irred. 4 p.c. Deb. St.	100	136½
4	Indian Mid., Ld. (gua. 4 p.c. + ½th surplus pfts.)	100	114
51/	Madras Guar. + ½ sp. pfts.	100	166
48/6	Do. do.	100	156
46/	Do. do.	100	146
4	Nilgiri, Ld., 1st Deb. Stk.	100	97
4	Oude & Rohil. Db. Stk. Rd.	100	—
5⅛	Rohil. and Kumaon, Ld.	100	132
9/11	Scinde, Punj., and Delhi, "A" Ann., 1958	—	25
9/1	Do. "B" do.	—	

Indian Railways (*continued*):—

Last Div.	NAME.	Paid.	Price.
4	South Behar, Ld., £10 shs.	100	100
3½	Do. Deb. Stk. Red.	100	101
4½	South Ind., Gu. Deb. Stk.	100	158½
5	South Indian, Ld. (gua. 3 p.c., and ¼ spls. profits)	100	122½
5	Sthn. Mahratta, Ld. (3½ p.c. & ⅛th net earnings)	100	115½
4	Do. Deb. Stk. Red.	100	120
3½	Southern Punjab, Ld.	100	106
3½	Do. Deb. Stk. Red.	—	105
5	Nizam's Gua. State, Ld. [†	100	114½
4	Do. Mort. Deb., 1936	100	107
4	Do. do. Reg.	100	106
17/3½	Nizam's Gua. State, Ld., 3½ p.c. Mt. Deb. bearer	—	94½
17/3½	Do. Reg. do. ..	—	93½
5	W. of India Portgese., Ld.	100	68½
5	Do. Deb. Stk., Red	100	99

RAILWAYS.—BRITISH POSSESSIONS.

Last Div.	NAME.	Paid.	Price.
5	Atlantic & N.W. Gua. 1 Mt. Bds., 1937	100	124½
5/3	Buff. & L. Huron Ord. Sh.	10	13½
5½	Do. 1st Mt. Perp. Bds. 1879	100	141½
5½	Do. 2nd Mt. Perp. Bds.	100	141½
—	Calgary & Edmon. 6 p.c. 1st Mt. Stg. Bds. Red..	100	75½
5	Canada Cent. 1st Mt. Bds. Red.	100	103
4	Can. Pacific Pref. Stk.	100	100
5	Do. Strl. 1st Mt. Deb. Bds. 1915	100	116
3½	Do. Ld. Grnt. Bds., 1938..	100	106
3½	Do. Ld. Grnt. Ins. Stk. ..	100	106
4	Do. Perp. Cons. Deb. Stk.	100	114
5	Do. Algoma Bch. 1st Mt. Bds., 1937	100	121
2	Demerara, Original Stock	100	47
7	Do. Perp. Pref. Stk.	100	155½
9½d.	Do. 4 p.c. Cum. Ext. Pref. £10 Shs.	4	6½
—	Dominion Atlntc. Ord. Stk.	100	33½
5	Do. 5 p.c. Pref. Stk.	100	97½
4	Do. 1st. Deb. Stk.	100	103½
4	Do. 2nd do. Red.	100	99
—	Emu Bay & Mt. Bischoff, Ld.	5	4½
4½	Do. Irred. Deb. Stk.	100	98
nil.	Gd. Trunk of Canada, Stk.	100	8
6	Do. 2nd. Equip. Mt. Bds.	100	130½
5	Do. Perp. Deb. Stk.	100	135½
5	Do. Gt. Westn. Deb. Stk.	100	127½
5	Do. Nthn. of Can. 1st Mt. Bds, 1902	100	102½
4	Do. do. Deb. Stk	100	102
5	Do. G. T. Geor. Bay & L. Erie 1 Mt., 1903	100	104
5	Do. Mid. of Can. Stl. 1st Mt. (Mid. Sec.) 1908	100	105
5	Do. do. Cons. 1 Mt. Bds. 1912	100	106
5	Do. Mont. & Champ. 1 Mt. Bds., 1902	100	103
	Do. Welln., Grey & Brce. 7 p.c. Bds. 1 Mt.	100	109
—	Jamaica 1st Mtg. Bds. Red.	—	103
—	Manitoba & N. W., 6 p.c. 1st Mt. Bds., Red	100	—
—	Do. Ldn. Bdhldrs. Certs.	—	—
5	Manitoba S. W. Col. 1 Mt. Bd., 1934 $1,000 price %	—	120
—	Mid. of W. Aust. Ld. 6 p.c. 1 Mt. Dbs., Red.	100	25
4	Do. Deb. Bds., Red.	100	103
4	Nakusp & Slocan Bds., 1918	100	106
3	Natal Zululand Ld. Debs.,	100	77½
5	N. Brunswick 1st Mt. Stg. Bds., 1934	100	121
4	Do. Perp. Cons. Deb. Stk.	100	114
—	N. Zealand Mid., Ld., 5 p.c 1st Mt. Debs.	100	35
6	Ontario & Queb. Cap. Stk.	$100	154½
5	Do. Perm. Deb. Stk	100	142½
—	Qu'Appelle, L. Lake & Sask. 6 p.c. 1 Mt. Bds. Red.	100	40½
	Queb. & L. S. John, 1st Mt. Bds., 1909	100	25½
	Quebec Cent., Prior Ln. Bds., 1908	100	107
1½	Do. 5 p.c. Inc. Bds.	100	39
4	St. Lawr. & Ott. Stl. 1st Mt.	100	113
4	Shuswap & Okan., 1st Mt. Deb. Bds., 1915	100	76
5	Temiscouata, 5 p.c. Stl. 1st Deb. Bds., Red.	100	9½
5	Do. (S. Franc. Brch.) 5 p.c. Stl. 1 Mt. Db. Bds., 1910	100	10
4	Toronto, Grey & B. 1st Mt.	100	112
1/2	Well. & Mana. £5 Shs. ..	1	½
5	Do. Debs., 1908	100	110
5	Do. 2nd Debs., 1908	100	109
5	Do. 3rd do., 1908	100	108
6	Atlan. & St. Law. Shs., 6 p.c.	100	161½
5	Gd. Trunk Mt. Bds., 1934	100	116½
5	Michigan Air Line, 5 p.c. 1st Mt. Bds., 1902	100	104
4	Minneap., S. P. & Slt. Ste. Mar, 1st Mt. Bds., 1938	$1000	97½

AMERICAN RAILROAD STOCKS AND SHARES.

Last Div.	NAME.	Paid.	Price.
6/	Alab. Gt. Sthn. A 6 p.c. Pref.	10/.	9
—	Do. do "B" Ord. ..	10/.	1½
—	Alabma. N. Orl.-Tex. &c., "A" Pref.	10/.	½
—	Do. "B" Def.	10/.	¼
5½	Atlant. First Lsd. Ls. Rll. Trust	Stk.	97½
—	Baltimore & Ohio Com. ..	$100	16
—	Baltimore Ohio S.W. Pref.	$100	6
—	Chesap. & Ohio Com.	$100	18½
—	Chic. Gt. West. 5 p.c. Pref. Stock "A"	$100	30½
—	Do. do. Scrip. In.	—	27
8/3	Do. 4 p.c. Deb. Stk.	$100	67½
4	Do. Interest in Scrip	$100	63½
$4	Chic. Junc. Rl. & Un. Stk. Yds. Com.	$100	108½
$1½	Do. 6 p.c. Cum. Pref.	$100	114½
$3½	Chic. Mil. & St. P. Pref. ..	$100	146
7	Cleve. & Pittsburgh	$10	86
$1½	Clev., Cincin, Chic., & St. Louis Com.	$100	—
—	Erie 4 p.c. Non-Cum. 1st Pf.	—	32½
—	Do. 4 p.c. do. 2nd Pf.	—	16
—	Gt. Northern Pref.	$100	150
$2½	Illinois Cen. Lsd. Lines ..	$100	95½
—	Kansas City, Pitts & G. ..	$100	18
$3	L. Shore & Mich. Sth. C.	$100	185
—	Mex. Cen. Ltd. Com.	$100	5
—	Miss. Kan. & Tex. Pref. ..	$100	32½
2½	N.Y., Pen. & O. 1st Mt. Tst. Ltd., Ord.	—	47½
4	Do. 1st Mort. Deb. Stk. ..	$100	92½
$	North Pennsylvania	$50	—
—	Northn. Pacific, Com.	$100	23½
1½	Pitts. F. Wayne & Chic. ..	$100	174
—	Reading 1st Pref.	$50	19
—	Do. 2nd Pref.	$50	10
—	S. Louis & S. Fran. Com.	$100	6½
—	Do. 2nd Pref.	$100	25
6	St. Louis Bridge 1st Pref. .	$100	107
3	Do. 2nd Pref.	$100	50
6	Tunnel Rail. of St. Louis	$100	107
$1½	St. Paul, Min. and Man. ..	$100	132½
—	Southern, Com.	$100	7½
—	Wabash, Common	$100	7

AMERICAN RAILROAD BONDS. CURRENCY.

Last Div.	NAME.		Price.
7	Albany & Susq. 1 Con. Mrt.	1906	118
7	Allegheny Val. 1 Mt.	1910	125½
5	Burling., Cedar Rap. & N. 1 Mt.	1906	109½
5	Canada Southern 1 Mt.	1908	111
5	Chic. & N. West. Sk. Fd. Db.	1933	117½
5	Do. Deb. Coupon	1921	112½
6	Chicago & Tomah	1905	109½
5	Chic. Burl. & Q. Skg. Fd.	1901	102½
4	Do. Nebraska Ext.	—	98
6	Chic., Mil., & S. Pl., 1 Mt. S.W. Div.	1909	117½
7	Do. (S. Paul Div.) 1 Mt.	1902	132½
5	Do. (La Cross & D.	1919	112½
7	Do. 1 Mt. (Hast. & Dak.)	1910	127½
5	Do. Chic. & Mis. Riv. 1 Mt.	1926	112½
5	Chic., Rock Is. and Pac. 1 Mt. Ext.	1934	108
6	Det., G. Haven & Mil. Equip	1918	105
6	Do. do. Cons. Mt.	1918	102½
6	Ill. Cent., 1 Mt., Chic. & S.	1898	—
7	Indianap. & Vin., 1 Mt. ..	1908	125
6	Do. do. 2 Mt. ..	1900	100½
6	Lehigh Val., Cons. Mt.	1923	112½
—	Mexic. Cent., Ln. 2 Cons. Inc.	—	5
7	N.Y. Cent. & H.R. Mt. Bonds	1903	117½
5	Do. Deb.	1904	107½
6	Penns. Cons. S. F M.	1905	118
4	West Shore, 1 Mt.	2361	110

DITTO—GOLD.

Last Div.	NAME.		Price.
6	Alabama Gt. Sthn. 1 Mt. ..	1908	114
5	Do. Mid. 1	1928	90½
4	Allegheny Val. Gen. Mt. ..	1942	106
4	Atch., Top., & S. Fé Gn. Mt.	1995	87½
3	Do. Adj. Mt.	1995	58
5	Do. Equipt. Tmst.	—	102½
5	Atlantic & Dan 1 Mt.	1950	96½
5	Baltimore & Ohio	1925	95
5	Do. Speyer's Tst. Recpts.	1925	95
5	Do. Cons. Mt.	1988	100
4½	Do. 4½ p.c. 1 Mt. Term.	1934	82½
4½	Do. Brown Shipley's Dep. Cts.	—	82½
5	Balt. Belt 5 p.c. 1 Mort.	1990	85
4½	Balt. & Ohio S.W. 1 Mt. ..	1990	99½
4½	Do. 4½ p.c. 1 Cons. Mt. 1893	1993	75½
—	Do. Inc. Mt. 5 p.c. Cl. A	—	29½
—	Do. do. Cl. B	—	10
5	Balt. & Ohio S.W. Term 5 p.c.	1942	97½
6	Balt. & Ptmac (Mn. L.) 1 Mt.	1911	124
6	Do. do. (Tunnel) 1 Mt.	1911	126
4	Beech Creek 1 Mt.	1936	109
5	Do 2 Mort.	1936	116
4	Carthage & Adiron 1 Mt. ..	1981	109

American Railroad Bonds—Gold (*continued*):—

Last Div.	NAME.		Price.
5	Cent. of Georgia 1 Mort. ..	1945	117½
5	Do. Cons. Mt.	1945	90½
5	Cent. of N. Jrsy. Gn. Mt. ..	1987	113
6	Central Pacific, 1 Mort.	1898	102½
6	Do. Speyer's Certs.	—	106
5	Do. Land Grant	1900	101
5	Chesap. & Ohio 1st Cons. Mt.	1939	113½
4½	Do. Gen. Mt.	1992	77
6	Chic. & W. Ind. Gen. Mt. Skg. Fd.	1932	120
5	Chic. Mil. & St. Pl. (Chic. & L. Sup.) 1 Mt.	1921	114½
5	Do. Chic. & Pac. W.	1921	117½
5	Do. Wisc. & Minn. 1 Mt.	1921	112½
5	Do. Terminal Mt.	1914	114½
4	Do. General Mt.	1989	106½
5	Chic. St. L. & N. Orleans..	1951	122½
4	Do. 1 Mort. (Memphis) ..	1951	105½
4	Clevel., Cin., Chic. & St. L., 1 Mt. (Cairo)	1939	90
4	Do. 1 Mt. (Cinc., Wab., & Mich.)	1991	90
4	Do. 1 Col. Tst. Mt. (S. Louis)	1990	96
4	Do. General Mt.	1993	82½
4½	Clevel. & Mar. Mt.	1935	109
4½	Clevel. & Pittsburgh	1942	116½
4½	Do. Series B.	1942	116½
—	Colorado Mid 1 Mt.	1936	63½
—	Do. Bdhrs.' Comm. Certs.	—	63½
4	Dnvr. & R. Gde. 1 Cons. Mt.	1936	89½
5	Do Imp. Mort.	1928	88
4	Detroit & Mack. 1 Lien	1995	92½
5	E. Tennes., Virg., & Grgia. Cons. Mt.	1956	111½
5	Elmira, Cort., & Nthn. Mt.	1914	100
4	Erie 1 Cons. Mt. Pr. Ln. ..	1996	83½
3	Do. Gen. Lien	1996	68
6	Galvest., Harrisb., &c., 1 Mt.		107½
5	Georgia, Car. & N. 1 Mt. ..	1929	96
4½	Gd Rpds & Inda. Ex. 1 Mt.	1941	112½
5	Do. 1 Mt. (Muskegon) ..	1926	39½
3½	Illinois Cent. 1 Mt.	1951	104½
4	Do.	1952	104½
4	Do. Cairo Bdge. ..	1950	102
4	Do.	1953	102
4	Do. General Mort. ..	1904	102½
5	Kans. City, Pitts. & G. 1 M.	1923	71
3½	L. Shore & Mich. Southern	1997	109
4½	Lehigh Val. N.Y. 1 Mt.	1940	102½
5	Lehigh Val. Term. 1 Mt. ..	1941	109½
5	Long Island	1931	117½
5	Do. Deb.	1934	102
5	Do. (N. Shore Bch.) 1 Cons. Mt.	1932	94
6	Louisville & Nash. G. Mt. ..	1930	120
6	Do. 2 Mt. Sk. Fd. (S. & N. Alabama	1910	107
6	Do. 1 Mt. N Orl. & Mb.	1930	122½
5	Do. 1 Mt. Coll. Tst.	1931	102½
4	Do. Unified	1940	85½
4½	Do. Mobile & Montgy. 1 Mt.	1945	105½
4	Manhattan Cons. Mt.	1990	93
4	Mexican Cent. Cons. Mt. ..	1911	62½
—	Do. 1 Cons. Inc, ...		13
6	Mexican Nat. 1 Mt.	1927	106
3½	Do. 2 Mt. 6 p.c. Inc. A	1917	52½
—	Do. do. B. ..	1917	10
3	Do. Matheson's Certs.		—
3	Michig. Cnt. (Battle Ck. & S.) 1 Mt.	1989	88
6	Minnep. & S. L. 1 Mt. Pacific Ext.	1921	117½
5	Do. 1 Consold.	1934	104½
4	Minne., Slt S. M. & A. 1 Mt.	1926	97
5	Minneapolis Westn. 1 Mt. ..	1911	105½
4	Miss. Kans. & Tex. 1 Mt. ..	1990	86½
4	Do. 2 do.	1990	59
4	Mobile & Birm. Mt. Inc.	1945	38
5	Do. P. Lien	1945	88
4	Mohawk & Mal. 1 Mt.	1991	108
5	Montana Cent. 1 Mt.	1937	111½
5	Nashv., Chattan., & S. L. 1 Cons. Mt.	1928	102½
5	Nash., Flor., & Shff. Mt. ..	1937	92½
4	N. Y. & Putnam 1 Cons. Mt.	1993	108
5	N. Y., Brooklyn, & Man. B. 1 Cons. Mt.	1935	107½
4	N. Y. Cent. & Hud. R. Deb. Certs. 1890	1905	104½
4	Do. Ext. Debt. Certs.	1905	103
7	N. Y., L. Erie, & W. 1 Cons. Mt. (Erie)	1920	139½
7	Do. 1 Con. Mt. Fd. Coup.	1920	137½
5	N. Y., Onto., & W. Cons. 1 Mt.	1939	110
4	Do. 4 p.c. Refund. Mt. ..	1992	99
5	N. Y. & Rockaway B. 1 Mt.	1927	102½
6	Norfolk & West. Gn. Mt.	1931	119½
6	Do. Imp. & Ext.	1934	117½
4	Do. 1 Cons. Mt.	—	78
6	N. Pacific Gn. 1 Mt. Ld. Gt.	1921	—
4	Do. P. Ln. Rl. & Ld. Gt.	—	93
3	Do. Gn. Ln. Rl. & Ld. Gt.	—	59
5	Oregon & Calif. 1 Mt.	1927	76½
5	Oregon Rl. & Nav. Col. Tst.	—	—
6	Panama Skg. Fd. Subsidy..	1910	102½
4½	Pennsylvania Rlrd.	1913	110½
4	Do. Equip. Tst. Ser. A..	1914	104
4	Do. Cons. Mt.	1943	112½
4½	Penna. Company 1st Mort.	1921	110
5	Perkiomen 1 Mrt., 2nd ser. .	1918	91½
4½	Pitts., C., C., & St. Ls. Con. Mt. G. B., Ser. A	1940-2	110
4	Do. Cons. Mort., Ser. D..	1945	102½
6	Pittsbgh., Cle., & Toledo ..	1922	100½
4	Reading, Phil., & R. Genl.	1997	80
5	Richmond & Dan. Equip. ..	1909	97½
5	Rio Grande Junc. 1st Mort.	1939	92½
4	Rio Grande West 1st Tst. Mt.	1939	82½
6	St. Joseph & Gd. Island ..	1925	—
7	S. Louis Bridge 1st Mort	1928	134½
5	S. Louis Mchts. Bdge. Term. 1st Mort.	1930	102½

American Railroad Bonds (*continued*):

Last Div.	NAME.		Price.
4	S. Louis S. West 1st Mort..	1989	75
—	Do. 4 p.c. 2nd Mort. Inc.	1989	30
—	S. Louis Term. Cupples Sta. & Prop. 1st. Mrt. 4½ p.c.	1970-17	102
4½	St. Paul Minn., & Manit.	1933	107½
6	Do. do.	1933	132½
6	Shamokin, Sunbury, &c. 2 Mt.	1925	100
5	S. & N. Alabama Cons. Mt.	1936	97½
5	Southern 1 Cons. Coup.	1994	89
4	Do. E. Tennes Reorg. Lien ..	1938	100
6	S. Pacific of Cal. 1 Mt. ..	1905-12	110
4½	Trml. Assn. of S. Louis 1 Mt.	1939	110½
5	Do. 1 Cons. Mt.	1944	108
5	Texas & Pac. 1 Mt.	2000	100
—	Do. 5 p.c. 2 Mt. Income	2000	30
5	Toledo & Ohio Cent. 1 Mt. West. Div.	1935	102½
4½	Toledo., Walhon., Val., & Ohio 1 Mt.	1931-3	111½
—	Union Pacific 1 Mt. 4 p.c. ..	1947	92
—	Union Pac., Linc., & Color. 1 Mt.	1918	—
4	United N. Jersey Gen. Mt. ..	1944	113½
6	Vicksbrg., Shrevept., & Pac. Pr. Ln. Mt.	1915	100½
5	Wabash 1 Mt.	1939	106½
4	Wn. Pennsylvania Mt.	1928	109½
5	W. Virga. & Pittsbg. 1 Mt.	1990	80
5	Wheeling & L. Erie 1 Mt. (Wheelg. Div.) 5 p.c.	1928	90½
5	Do. Extn. Imp. Mt.	1930	90
—	Do. do. Brown Shipley's Cts. ..		—
5	Willmar & Sioux Falls 1 Mt.	1938	111

STERLING.

Last Div.	NAME.		Price.
6	Alabama Gt. Sthn. Deb.	1906	104½
5	Do. Gen. Mort. ..	1927-8	99
5	Alabama, N. Orl., Tex. & Pac. 5 p.c. "A" Dbs. ..	1910-40	98
55/	Do. do. "B" do.	1910-40	52
—	Do. do. "C" do.		19
—	Allegheny Valley	1910	127½
4	Atlantic 1st Leased Line Perp. ..		98
6	Baltimore and Ohio	1902	106
6	Do. do.	1910	116½
5	Do. do. 1877		94
—	Do. Morgan's Certs. ..		93½
4½	Do. do.	1933	88
6	Chicago & Alton Cons. Mt.	1903	111
5	Chic. St. Paul & Kan. City Priority		105
6	Eastn. of Massachusetts	1906	117½
5	Illinois Cent. Skg. Fd.		103
5	Do.	1905	108
3½	Do.	1950	99½
4	Do. 1 Mt.	1951	110
3	Do. 1 Mt.	1951	92½
6	Louisville & Nash., M. C. & L. Div., 1 Mt.	1902	104½
7	Do. 1 Mt. (Memphis & O.)	1901	111
47/4	Mexican Nat. "A" Certs. 5 p.c. Non. cum.		43½
—	Do. "B" Certs.		9
6	N.Y. & Canada 1 Mt.	1904	111½
6	N. York Cent. & H.R. Mort.	1903	112
4½	N. York, Penns., & Ohio Pr. Ln. Extd.	1935	—
5	Do. Equip. Tst.		103½
5	Do. 5 p.c. Equip. Tst. (1890)		103½
6	Nrthn. Cent. Cons. Gen. Mt. ..		106
6	Pennsylvania Gen. Mt.	1910	124½
6	Do. Cons. Skg. Fd. Mt.	1905	112½
3½	Do. Cons. Mt.	1945	103½
6	Phil. & Erie Cons. Mort ..	1920	132½
6	Phil. & Reading Gen. Cons. Mort.	1911	124½
6	Pittsbg. & Connells. Cons.	1926	114
—	Do. Morgan's Certs.		114
4	St. Paul., Min., & Manitoba (Pac. Extn.)	1940	96
6	S. & N. Alabama	1903	107½
6	Un. N. Jersey & C. Gen. Mt.	1901	109½

FOREIGN RAILWAYS

Last Div.	NAME.	Paid.	Price.
4/	Alagoas, Ltd., Shs.	20	5
5	Do. Deb. Stk., Red. ..	100	42½
6	Antofagasta, Ltd., Stk. ..	100	66
4	Do. Perp. Deb. Stk. ..	100	89
—	Arauco, Ld., Ord. Shs. ..	10	—
—	Do. 10 p.c. Cum. Pref.	10	—
5	Argentine Gt. W., Ld.,	100	71
5	Do. 5 p.c. Cum. Pref. Shs.	100	10
4	Do. 1 Deb. Stk.	100	10
1/0/0	Argentine N.E., Ltd., 6 p.c. Cum. Pref. Stk. ..	100	
—	Do. 5 p.c. Deb. Stk., Red.	100	29
2/	Arica and Tacna Shs. ..	20	1½
10/	Bahia & San Fcisco, Ld.,	20	8
6/	Do. Timbo. Bch. Shs.	20	4½
12/	Bahia, Blanca, & N.W. Ln. Prf. Cum. 6 p.c. ..	100	51
4	Do. 4 p.c. 1 Deb. Stk., Red.	100	92
6	Barranquilla R. & P., Ld., 6 p.c. 1 Deb. Stk., Red.	100	96

Foreign Railways (*continued*):—

Last Div.	Name.	Paid.	Price.
3/	Bilbao Riv. & Cantabn., Ltd., Ord.	3	5½
—	Bolivar, Ltd. Shs.	10	1¾
6	Do. 6 p.c. Deb. Stk.	100	96½
—	Brazil Gt. Southn. Ltd., 7 p.c. Cum. Pref.	20	1½
6	Do. Perm. Deb. Stk	100	40
5½	B. Ayres Gt. Southn. Ld., Ord. Stk.	100	144
5	Do. Pref. Stk.	100	133
4	Do. Deb. Stk.	100	114
30/	B. Ayres & Ensen. Port., Ltd., Ord. Stk.	100	68
5	Do. Cum. 1 Pref. Stk.	100	120
6/0/0	Do. 6p.c.Con. Pref.Stk.	100	99
4	Do. Deb. Stk., Irred.	100	113
10⅛	B. Ayres Northern, Ltd., Ord. Stk.	100	265
12½	Do. Pref. Stk.	100	320
5	Do. 5 p.c. Mt. Deb.Stk., Red.	100	113
3/15/0	B. Ayres & Pac., Ld., 7 p.c. 1 Pref. Stk. (Cum.)	100	86
4	Do. 1 Deb. Stk.	100	100
5/5/0	Do. 4½ p.c. 2 Deb. Stk.	100	89
3	B. Ayres & Rosario, Ltd., Ord. Stk.	100	66
—	Do. New, £20 Shs.	20	—
7/	Do. 7 p.c. Pref. Shs.	10	17
7/	Do. Sunchales Ext.	10	14½
4	Do. Deb. Stk., Red.	100	106
—	B. Ayres & Val. Trans., Ltd., 7 p.c. Cum. Pref.	20	6½
4	Do. 4 p.c. "A" Deb. Stk., Red.	100	71
—	Do. 6 p.c. "B" Deb. Stk. Red.	100	44
3/6	B. Ayres Westn. Ld. Ord.	10	10½
3/	Do. Def. Shs.	10	6½
5	Do. 5 p.c. Pref.	10	12½
4	Do. Deb. Stk.	100	106½
6	Cent. Arg. Deb. Sk. Rd.	100	160½
4	Do. Deb. Stk. Rd.	100	110
6	Cent. Bahia L. Ord. Stk.	100	42
	Do. Deb. Stk., 1934	100	72½
5	Do. Deb. Stk., 1937	100	58
3/6	Cent. Uguy. East. Ext. L. Shs.	10	5½
5	Do. Perm. Stk.	100	111
3/6	Do. Nthn. Ext. L. Sh.	10	4
5	Do. Perm. Deb. Stk.	100	103½
3	Do. of Montev. Ltd., Ord. Stk.	100	82
6	Do. Perm. Deb. Stk.	100	141
10/	Conde d'Eu, Ltd. Ord.	20	7
—	Cordba & Rosar., Ltd., 6 p.c. Pref. Shs.	100	41
4	Do. 1 Deb. Stk.	100	91
75	Do. 6 p.c. Deb. Stk.	100	93
—	Cordba Cent., Ltd., 5 p.c. Cu. 1 Pref. Stk.	100	77½
—	Do. 5 p.c. Non-Cum. 2 Pref. Stk.	100	43½
5	Do. Deb. Stk.	100	119
—	Costa Rica, Ltd., Shs.	10	3½
8/	Dna. Thrsa. Chris., Ltd., 7 p.c. Pref. Shs.	20	3½
20/	E. Argentine, Ltd	100	40
6	Do. Deb. Stk.	100	104
1/1	Egyptn. Dlta. Lgt. Rys., Ltd., £10 Pref. Shs.	8	10½
—	Entre Rios, L., Ord. Shs.	5	¾
—	Do. Cu. 5 p.c. Pref.	5	2½
6/	Gt. Westn. Brazil, Ltd.,	20	9½
6	Do. Perm. Deb. Stk.	100	90½
6	Do. Extn. Deb. Stk.	100	76½
—	Int.-Oceanic Mex., Ltd., 7 p.c. Pref.	10	1½
4	Do. Deb. Stk.	100	80
42/6	Do. 7 p.c. "A" Deb. Sk.	100	67
—	Do. 7 p.c. "B" Deb. Sk.	100	30
5/	La Guaira & Carac.	10	7½
5	Do. 5 p.c. Deb. Sk. Red.	100	100
8/4	Lembg.-Czern.-Jassy	30	24½
2/	Lima, Ltd.	20	2½
—	Manila Ltd. 7 p.c. Cu. Pf.	10	¼
20/6½	Mexican 2nd Pref. 6 p.c.	100	31
6	Do. Perp. Deb. Stk.	100	138
1/0/0	Mexican Sthrn., Ld., Ord.	100	23
—	Do. 4 p.c. 1 Db. Stk. Rd.	100	83
—	Do. 4 p.c. 2 do.	100	61
—	Mid. Urgy., Ltd.	100	18½
5	Do. Deb. Stk.	100	64
12/	Minas & Rio, Ltd.	20	9
5/2	Namur & Liege	20	12½
11/6	Do. Pref.	20	20
13/	Natal & Na. Cruz, Ld., 7 p.c. Cum Pref.	20	6
—	Nitrate Ltd., Ord.	10	5
—	Do. 7 p.c. Pr. Con. Or.	10	3½
—	Do. Def. Conv. Ord.	10	¾
7/	N.-E. Urgy., Ltd., Ord.	10	14½
7/	Do. 7 p.c. Pref.	10	14½
—	N.-W. Argentine Ld., 7 p.c. Pref.	10	2½
6	Do. 6 p.c. 1 Deb. Stk.	100	113
—	Do. 2 Deb. Stk.	100	94
—	N.W. Uruguay 6 p.c. 1 Pref. Stk.	100	17
—	Do. 5 p.c. 2 Pref. Stk.	100	7½
6	Do. 6 p.c. Deb. Stk.	100	80½
22/	Ottoman (Sm. Ald.)	20	13½
—	Paraguay Cntl., Ld., 5 p.c. Perm. Deb. Stk.	100	11
—	Piræus, Ath., & Pelo.	275	1½
	Pto. Alegre & N. Hambg. Ld., 7 p.c. Pref. Shs.	20	4
6	Do. Mt. Deb. Stk. Red.	100	77½
—	Puerto Cabello & Val. Ld.	10	1½
5	Recife & S. Francisco	100	67
14	R. Claro S. Paulo, Ld., Sh.	10	21½
5	Do. Deb. Stk.	100	125
5	Royal Sardinian Ord.	10	11½
5/	Royal Sardinian Pref.	10	12
5/	Sambre & Meuse	20	18
5/6	Do. Pref.	10	12½
28/	San Paulo Ld.	20	33
2/9½	Do. New Ord. £10 sh.	6	9
2/	Do. 5 p.c. Non.Cm.Pref.	10	12
5½	Do. Deb. Stk.	100	133
5	Do. 5 p.c. Deb. Stk.	100	127
—	S. Fé & Cordova, Gt. Sthn., Ld., Shares	100	50½
6	Do. Perp. Deb. Stk.	100	121
3/2½	S. Austrian	20	7
10/	Sthn. Braz. R. Gde. do Sul, Ld.	20	7½
6	Do. 6 p.c. Deb. Stk.	100	69½
4	Swedish Centl., Ld., 4 p.c. Deb. Stk.	100	107
5	Do. Pref.	100	100
1/9	Taltal, Ld.	5	2½
—	Uruguay Nthn., Ld. 7 p.c. Pfd. Stk.	100	8
3½	Do. 5 p.c. Deb. Stk.	100	30
—	Villa Maria & Rufino, Ld., 6 p.c. Pref. Shs.	100	20
4	Do. 4 p.c. 1 Deb. Stk.	100	73
6/0/0	Do. 6 p.c. 2 Deb. Stk.	100	47
5/9	West Flanders	8½	21
5/6	Do. 5½ p.c. Pref.	10	18
3/	Wstn. of Havana, Ld.	10	4

FOREIGN RAILWAY OBLIGATIONS

Per Cent.	Name.	Price.
6	Alagoas Ld., 6 p.c. Deb., Rd.	81
—	Alcoy & Gandia, Ld., 5 p.c. Debs., Red.	24
5	Arauco, Ld., 5 p.c. 1st Mt., Rd.	62½
—	Do. 6 p.c. Mt. Deb., Rd.	42½
6	Brazil G. Sthn., L., Mt. Dbs., Rd.	80½
6	Do. Mt. Dbs. 1893, Rd.	40½
5½	Campos & Caran. Dbs., Rd.	75
6	Central Bahia, L., Dbs., Rd.	90½
5½	Conde d'Eu, L., Dbs., Rd.	70
6	Costa Rica, L., 1st Mt. Dbs., Rd.	104
6	Do. 2nd Dbs., Rd.	88
5	Do. Prior Mt. Db., Rd.	104
6	Cucuta Mt. Dbs., Rd.	101
5½	Donna Thrsa. Cris., L., Dbs., Rd.	68
3	Eastn. of France, £20 Dbs., Rd.	18½
4	Egyptn. Delta Light, L., Db., Rd	98½
—	Espito. Santo & Cara. 5 p.c. Stl. Dbs., Rd.	38
4	Gd. Russian Nic., Rd.	102
5	Inter-Oceanic Mex., L., 5 p.c. Pr. Ln. Dbs., Rd.	102
3	Ital. 3 p.c. Bds. A & B, Rd.	57½
—	Ituana 6 p.c. Debs., 1918	74
—	Leopoldina, 6 p.c. Dbs. £50 Bds.,	21
—	Do. do. Comms. Cert.	21
—	Do. 5 p.c. Stg. Dbs. (1888), Rd.	29
—	Do. do. Comm. Certs.	29
—	Do. 5 p.c. Stg. Dbs. (1890), Rd.	21
—	Do. do. Comms. Certs.	21
—	Macahé & Cam. 5 p.c. Dbs., Rd.	29
—	Do. do. Comms. Certs.	29
—	Do. (Cantagallo), 5 p.c., Red.	29
—	Do. do. Comm. Certs.	29
—	Manila Ltd., 6 p.c. Deb., Red.	22
6	Do. Prior Lien Mt., Rd.	98½
6	Do. Series "B," Rd.	80
7	Matanzas & Sab., Rd.	101½
6	Minas & Rio, L., 6 p.c. Dbs., Rd.	94
5	Mogyana 5 p.c. Deb. Bds., Rd.	103
5	Moscow-Jaros., Rd.	106½
5½	Natal & Na. Cruz Ltd., 5½ p.c. Debs., Red.	83
5	Nitrate, Ltd. Mt. Bds., Red.	78
3	Nthn. France, Red.	19
4	N. of S. Af. Rep. (Trnsvl.) Gu. Bds. Red.	94½
3	Nthn. of Spain £20 Prl. Obs. Red.	7½
6	Ottmn. (Smy to A.)(Kujk) Aant. Debs., Red.	109
6	Ottmn. (Seraik.) Asg. Debs. Red.	109
6	Ottmn. (Seraik.) Non-Asg. D., Rd	109
5	Ottmn. Kuyjk. Ext. Red.	105
5	Ottmn. Serkeuy. Ext. Red.	100½
5	Ottmn. Tireh Ext. 1910	96
5	Ottmn. Debs, 1886, Red.	97
5	Do. 1888, Red. 1935	97½
5	Do. 1893, Red. 1935	99
5	Ottmn. of Anlia. Debs., Rd.	90½
5	Do. Ser. II.	87
4	Ottomn. Smyr. & Cas. Ext. Bds., Red.	83½
3	Paris, Lyon & Medit. (old sys., £20), Red.	18½
3	Paris, Lyon & Medit. (new sys., £20), Red.	18½
30/	Piræus, At. & Pelp., 6 p.c. 1st Mt. Bds., Red.	89½
3	Do. 5 p.c. 2 Mt. Bds., Red.	71
4	Pretoria-Pietbg., Ltd., Red.	93
7	Puerto Cab. & Val., Ltd., 1st Mt. Debs., Red.	83
—	Rio de Jano. & Nthn., Ltd., 6 p.c. £100 Deb., Red.	21
—	Rio de Jano. (Gr. Para.), 5 p.c. 1st Mt. St. £100 Debs., Red.	21
2	Royal Sardinian, A, Rd. £20	11½
3	Royal Sardinian, B., Rd. £20	11½

Foreign Rly. Obligations (*continued*):—

Per Cent.	Name.	Price.
5	Ryl. Trns.-Afric. 5 p.c. 1st Mt. £100 Bds., Red.	61
7	Sagua La Grande, B pRd.	98
4	Sa. Fe & Cor. G.S., Ld. Pr Ln. Bds.	104
5	Sa. Fe, 5 p.c. 2nd Reg. Dbs.	80
3	South Austrian, £20 Red.	15½
3	South Austrian, (Ser. X.)	15
3	South Italian £20 Obs. (Ser. A to G), Red.	12
3½	S. W. of Venez. (Barq.), Ltd., 7 p.c. 1st Mt. £100 Debs.	55½
5	Taltal, Ltd., 5 p.c. 1st Ch. Debs., Red.	97
5	Utd. Rwys. Havana, Red.	83
3	Wtrn. of France, £20 Red.	18½
6	Wrn. B. Ayres St. Mt. Debs., 1902	108
6	Wrn. B. Ayres, Reg. Cert.	106½
5	Do. Mt. Bds.	121
6	Wtrn. of Havna., Ld. Mt. Dbs., Rd.	90
7	Wrn. Ry. San Paulo Red.	99
—	Wrn. Santa Fé, 7 p.c. Red.	38
2/8	Zafra & Huelva, 3 p.c. Red.	2½

BANKS.

Div.	Name.	Paid.	Price.
2/4½	Agra, Ltd.	6	3½
4/2½	Anglo-Argentine, Ltd., £9	7	5½
8 fls.	Anglo-Austrian	120f.	13
6/	Anglo-Californian, Ltd., £20 Shares	10	11
4/	Anglo-Egyptian, Ltd., £15	5	6
5/	Anglo-Foreign Bkg., Ltd.	7	8
7/	Anglo-Italian, Ltd.	5	7
7/6	Bk. of Africa, Ltd., £18¾	6¼	10
20/	Bk. of Australasia	40	49
10/	Bk. of Brit. Columbia	20	20½
25/	Bk. of Brit. N. America	50	64
20/	Bk. of Egypt, Ltd., £25	12½	19
5/	Bk. of Mauritius, Ltd.	10	9
18/	Bk. of N. S. Wales	20	37½
4 p.c.	Bk. of N. Zland. Gua. Stk.	100	102
6/	Bk. of Roumania, £20 Shs.	6	7½
2/6	Tarapaca & Ldn., Ltd., £10	5	3½
—	Bque. Fse. de l'Afri. du S.	100f	3½
f. 22.50	Bque. Internatle. de Paris	20	23
6/	Brit. Bk. of S. America, Ltd., £20 Shares	10	10
16/	Capital & Cties., L., £50	10	39
16/	Chart. of India, &c.	20	31½
10/	City, Ltd., £40 Shares	10	20
18/	Colonial, £100 Shares	30	21
10/	Delhi and London, Ltd.	25	—
5/	German of London, Ltd.	10	10½
25/	Hong-Kong & Shanghai	25½	45½
4/	Imperl. of Persia	6½	3½
10/	Imperl. Ottoman, £20 Shs	10	11
12/	Intrnatl. of Ldn., Ld., £20	15	11
10/	Ionian, Ltd.	25	15
16/	Lloyds, Ltd., £50 Shs.	8	30½
10/	Ldn. & Braziln. Ltd., £20	10	16
44/	Ldn. & County, Ltd., £80	20	100
9/	Ldn. & Hanseatic, L., £20	10	10½
22/6	Ldn. & Midland, L., £60	12½	53
8/9	Ldn. & Provin., Ltd., £10	5	22½
39/	Ldn. & Riv. Plate, L., £25	15	49
2/1½	Ldn. & San Fcisco, Ltd.	7	4½
28/	Ldn. & Sth. West., L., £50	20	68
26/	Ldn. & Westmins., L., £100	20	54½
5/	Ldn. of Mex. & S. Amer., Ltd., £10 Shs.	6	5½
15/	Ldn. Joint Stk., L., £100	15	33
12/9½	Ldn., Paris & Amer., L. £20	16	25
2/4½	Merchant Bkg., L., £9	4	2¾
6/3	Metropn, Ltd., £50 Shs.	5	14½
9/	National, Ltd., £50 Shs.	10	19½
4/5	Natl. of Mexico, $100 Shs.	$40	12½
1/3	National of N. Z., L., £7½	2½	2
3/	National S. Afric. Rep.	10	14½
18/10½	National Provcl. of Eng., Ltd., £75 Shs.	10½	49½
21/7½	Do. do. £60 Shs.	12	56
6/6	North Eastn., Ltd., £20 Shs	6	15
19/	Parr's, Ld., £100 Shs.	20	90
12/6	Prov. of Ireland, L., £100	12½	29½
40/	Stand. of S. Afric., L., £100	25	62
12/6	Union of Australia, L., £75	25	26
4 p.c.	Do. do. Ins. Stk. Dep. 1900	100	101
15/6	Union of Ldn., Ltd., £100	15½	34½

BREWERIES AND DISTILLERIES.

Div.	Name.	Paid.	Price.
4½	Albion Prp. 1 Mt. Db. Sk.	100	111
4	All Saints', L., Db. Sk. Rd.	100	97
7	Allsopp, Ltd.	100	145
6	Do. Cum. Pref	100	155
4½	Do. Deb. Stk., Red.	100	116
3½	Do. Deb. Stk., Red.	100	101
4½	Alton & Co., L., Db., Rd	100	104
4½	Do. Mt. Bds., 1896	100	103
—	Arnold, Perrett, Ltd.	10	6
6	Do. Cum. Pref.	10	10
4½	Do. 1 Mt. Db. Stk., Rd	100	106

Breweries &c. (*continued*):—

Div.	Name.	Paid.	Price.
5½	Arrol, A., & Sons, L., Cum. Pref. Shs.	10	10
4½	Do. 1 Mt. Db. Stk., Rd.	100	104
5	Backus, 1 Mt. Db., Red.	100	59
4	Barclay, Perk., L., Cu. Pf.	10	11½
3½	Do. Mt. Db. Stk., Red.	100	109
—	Barnsley, Ltd.	10	11½
6	Do. Cum. Pref.	10	13½
1/3	Barrett's, Ltd	2½	1½
1/3	Do. 5 p.c. Pref.	2½	2½
3/	Bartholomay, Ltd.	10	2½
8	Do. Cum. Pref.	10	6½
6	Do. Deb.	100	37½
5	Bass, Ratcliff, Ltd., Cum. Pref. Stk.	100	143½
4½	Do. Mt. Db. Stk., Rd.	100	124
4	Bell, J., L., 1 Mt. D. Stk., R	100	100
2/6	Benskin's, L., Cum. Pref.	5	—
4½	Do. 1 Mt. Db. Stk Red.	100	—
4½	Do. "B" Deb. Sk, Rd.	100	—
7/	Bentley's Yorks., Ltd.	10	11½
6/	Do. Cum. Pref.	10	12½
4½	Do. Mt. Debs., Red.	100	110
4½	Do. do. 1892, Red.	100	110
—	Bieckert's, Ltd.	20	2
5	Do. Debs., Red.	100	57
—	Birmingham., Ltd., 6 p.c. Cum. Pref.	5	2½
4½	Do. Mt. Debs., Red.	50	41½
5½	Boardman's, Ld., Cm. Pf.	10	8½
4½	Do., Perp. 1 Mt. Db. Sk.	100	105½
30/9	Brain & Co., Ltd.	100	101
4½	Brakspear, L., 1 D. Stk. Rd	100	108
4	Brandon's, L., 1 D. Stk. R.	100	105½
21/	Bristol (Georges) Ltd.	10	45
6	Do. Cum. Pref.	10	18
5	Do. Mt. Db. Sk. 1888 Rd.	100	175½
17/6	Bristol United, Ltd.	10	35
6	Do. Cum. Pref.	10	16½
4½	Do. Db. Sk. Rd.	100	126
5½	Buckley's, L., C. Pre-prf.	10	10½
4½	Do. 1 Mt. Db. Stk. Rd.	100	104½
4	Bullard & Sns, L., D. Sk. R.	100	104½
6	Bushell, Watk., L., C. Pf.	10	14
4½	Do. 1 Mt. Db. Sk. Rd.	100	112
5	Camden, Ltd., Cum. Pref.	10	11½
4½	Do. 1 Mt. Db. Sk. Rd.	100	106
5½	Cameron, Ltd., Cm. Prf.	10	13½
4½	Do. Mort Deb. Stk.	100	108
3½	Do. Perp Mt. Db. Sk.	100	100½
5	Cam'bell, J'stone, L., C. Pf.	5	5
4½	Do. 4½ p.c. 1 Mt. Db. Sk.	100	105
4	Campbell, Praed, L., Per. 1 Mort. Deb. Stk.	100	106
4	Cannon, L., Mt. Db. Stk.	100	109
4	Do. "B" Deb. Stk.	100	104
5	Castlemaine, L., 1 Mt. Db.	100	94
3½	Charrington, Ltd., Mort. Deb. Stk. Red.	100	106
2/	Cheltnhm. Orig., Ltd.	5	7
6	Do. Cum. Pref.	5	7½
4	Do. Debs. Red.	100	106
10/	Chicago, Ltd.	10	3
6	Do. Debs.	100	84½
—	Cincinnati, Ltd.	10	½
—	Do. Cum. Pref.	10	1
10/	City of Baltimore	10	4
16/	Do. 8 p.c. Cum. Pref	10	8
14/	City of Chicago, Ltd.	10	1
8	Do. Cum. Pref.	10	6
13	City of London, Ltd.	100	205½
5	Do. Cum. Pref.	100	137
4	Do. Mt. Deb. Stk., Rd.	100	112½
2/	Colchester, Ltd.	5	4½
7	Do. Pref.	5	6½
4½	Do. Deb. Stk., Red.	100	109
5	Combe, Ltd., Cum. Pref.	10	13½
4	Do. Mt. Db. Stk, Rd.	100	110
3½	Do. Perp. Deb. Stk.	100	107
5	Comm'cial, L., D. Sk., Rd.	100	107½
5	Courage, L., Cm. Pref. Shs.	100	137½
4	Do. Irr. Mt. Deb. Stk.	100	125
3½	Do. Irr. "B" Mt. Db. Sk.	100	104
8/	Daniell & Sons, Ltd.	10	7½
7	Do. Cum. Pref.	10	12½
4½	Do. 1 Mt. Perp. Db. Sk.	100	107½
4½	Do. "B" Deb. Stk.	100	101
10d.	Dartford, Ltd.	5	5½
9/9	Do. Cum. Pref.	5	5½
4	Do. 1 Mt. Db. Sk. Rd.	100	99
4	Davenport, Ld., 1 D. Stk.	100	101½
10/	Denver United, Ltd.	10	3½
8	Do. Cum. Pref.	10	7½
6	Do. Debs.	100	98½
4½	Deuchar, L., 1 D. Sk., Rd.	100	108
8/	Distillers, Ltd.	10	23½
4½	Do. Mt. Db. Stk., Rd.	100	115½
—	Dublin Distillers, Ltd.	5	1½
3/	Do. Cum. Pref.	5	4½
4½	Do. Irr. Deb. Stk.	100	—
5	Eadie, Ltd., Cum. Pref.	10	11
4	Do. Irr. 1 Mt. Db. Sk.	100	106
10/	Edinbgh. Utd., Ltd.	10	13
6	Do. Cum. Prf.	10	13½
5	Do. 1 Mt. Dbs.	100	110½
4	Eldridge, Pope, L. D. St. R.	100	107
—	Emerald & Phœnix, Ltd.	10	1½
8	Do. Cum. Pref.	10	5½
6	Empress Ltd., C. Pf.	10	11½
4½	Do. Mt. Deb. Stk.	100	106
10/	Farnham, Ltd.	10	17
6	Do. Cum. Pref.	10	14½
4	Fenwick, L., 1 D. Sk., Rd.	100	103
4	Flower & Sons, Irr. D. Sk.	100	111
4	Friary, L., 1 Db. Stk., Rd.	100	103½
4	Do. 1 "A" Db. Sk., Rd	100	100
4½	Groves, L., 1 Db. Sk., Rd.	100	110
14	Guinness, Ltd.	100	560
6	Do. Cum. Prf. Stk.	100	187½
5	Do. Deb. Stk., Red.	100	121
5	Hall's Oxford L., Cm. Pf.	5	5½
6/	Hancock, Ld., Cm. Pf. Ord.	10	14
7/	Do. Def. Ord.	10	17½

Breweries, &c. (*continued*):—

Div.	Name.	Paid.	Price.
6	Hancock, Ld., Cum. Pref.	10	14
4	Do. 1 Deb. Stk., Rd.	100	112
5	Hoare, Ltd. Cum. Pref.	10	12½
5	Do. "A" Cum. Pref.	10	12¼
4	Do. Mt. Deb. Stk., Rd.	100	111
3½	Do. do. do. Rd.	100	104
3/6	Hodgson's, Ltd.	5	9½
5	Do. 1 Mt. Db., Red.	—	120½
4	Do. 2 Mt. Db., 1906	—	102
4½	Hopcraft & N., Ltd., 1 Mt. Deb. Stk., Red.	100	103
5	Huggins, Ltd., Cm. Prf.	10	—
4½	Do. 1st D. Stk. Rd.	100	—
4½	Do. "B" Db. Stk. Rd.	100	—
12/	Hull, Ltd.	10	17
7	Do. Cum. Pref.	10	14½
4½	Ind, Coope, L., D.Sk., Rd.	100	118
4	Do. "B" Mt. Db. Stk. Rd.	100	111
8/	Indianapolis, Ltd.	10	3½
8	Do. Cm. Prf.	10	9
5/	Jones, Frank, Ltd.	10	2½
7½	Do. Cum. Pref.	10	7
5	Do. 1st Mort. Debs.	100	90½
3/	J. Kenward & Co., Ltd.	5	5½
4½	Kingsbury, L., 1 D.Sk., Rd	100	—
4	Lacon, L., D. Stk., Red.	100	110
4	Do. Irrd. "B" D. Sk.	100	106
4/	Lascelles, Ltd.	5	11
6	Do. Cum. Pref.	5	7¾
5	Leney, Ltd., Cum. Pref.	10	11¼
4	Do. 1 Mt. Db. Stk. Rd.	100	102
30/7½	Lion, Ltd., £25 shares	17	49½
10/9½	Do. New £10 shares	6	17
6	Do. Perp. Pref.	20	33
4	Do. B. Mt. Db. Sk. Rd.	100	107
4½	Lloyd & Y., Ltd., 1 Mt. Deb. Stk., Rd.	100	100½
4½	Locke & S., Ltd., Irr. 1st Mt. Deb. Stk.	100	101
4½	Lovibond, Ltd., 1st Mt. Deb. Stk., Rd.	100	102½
30/4	Lucas & Co., Ld., Deb. Stk.	100	107
8/	Manchester, Ltd.	10	19½
7	Do. Cum. Pref.	10	16
5	Marston, J., L., Cm. Prf.	10	10¾
4	Do. 1 Mt. Db. Sk., Rd.	100	101½
9/	Massey's Burnley, Ltd.	10	17
6	Do. Cum. Pref.	10	14½
4½	McCracken, Ltd., 1 Mt. Deb., 1908	100	58½
5	McEwan, Ltd., Cm. Pref.	10	14
5	Meux, Ltd., Cum. Pref.	10	14
4	Do. Mt. Db. Stk. Red.	100	111
4½	Michell & A., Ltd., 1 Mt. Deb. Stk. Red.	100	105
4½	MileEndDist. Db. Sk. Rd.	100	111
—	Milwaukee & Chic., Ltd.	10	1
4/	Do. Cum. Pref.	10	5½
4½	Michell, Toms, L., Db.	50	57
6	Morgan, Ltd., Cum. Pref.	10	14½
10/	Nalder & Coll., Ltd.	10	35
6	Do. Cum. Pref.	10	15¾
4½	Do. Deb. Red.	100	112
12/	Newcastle, Ltd.	10	19½
6	Do. Cum. Pref.	10	14¾
5	Do. 1 Mt. Deb., 1911	100	111½
4	Do. "A" Deb. Stk. Red.	100	104
6	New England, Ltd	10	4½
8	Do. Cum. Pref.	10	9½
6	Do. Debs. Red	100	101½
4	New London, L., 1 D.Sk.	100	103
7/2	New Westminster, Ltd.	4	10½
2/4½	Do. Pref.	4	6½
—	New York, Ltd.	10	1
—	Do. 8 p.c. Cum. Pref.	10	4½
6	Do. 1 Mt. Deb. Red.	100	77½
5	Noakes, Ld., Cum. Pref.	10	11¾
4	Do 1 Mt. Db. Stk., Rd.	100	104
4½	Norfolk, L., "A" D.Sk. Rd	100	106
10/	Northampton, Ld.	10	16½
7	Do. Cum. Pref.	10	16
6	Do. Cum. Pref.	10	12½
5	Do. 1 Mt. Per. Db. Sk.	100	127
4	Nth. East., L., 1 D. Sk. Rd.	100	102
4½	N. Worcesters., L. Per. 1 Mort. Deb. Stock	100	97½
6	Nottingham, L., Cm. Prf.	10	1¼
5	Do. 1 Mt. Deb. Stk., Red.	100	114
17/4	Do. "B" do. Red.	50	112
6/	Ohlsson' Cape, Ld.	5	17
7	Do. Cum. Pref.	5	9
4½	Do. 2nd Cum. Pref.	5	5½
5	Do. Deb. Stk., Red.	100	114
4½	Oldfield, L., 1 Mt. Db. Stk.	100	105
6	Page & Overt., L., Cm. Prf.	10	13½
4½	Do. 1 Mt. Dbs., Red.	100	109
10/	Parker's Burslem, Ltd.	10	24½
6	Do. Cum. Pref.	10	14½
4	Do. 1 Mt. Db. Stk., Red.	100	111
4	Persse, Ld., 1 Mt. Db. Rd.	100	95½
4	Phipps, L., Irr. 1 Db. Stk.	100	113
8	Plymouth, L., Min. Cu. Pf.	10	13½
4½	Do. Mt. Deb. Stk., Red.	100	104½
4½	Pryor, Reid, L., 1 D.S., R.	100	103½
5	Reid's, Ld., Cm. Pref. Stk.	100	136½
4	Do. Mt. Deb. Stk., Red	100	110
3½	Do. "B" Mt. Db. Stk., Rd	100	102
5	Rhondda Val., L., Cu. Pf	10	11
4½	Do. 1 Mt. Deb. Stk., Rd	100	109
5	Robinson, Ld., Cum. Pref.	10	11½
4½	Do. 1 Mt. Perp. Db. Stk.	100	112
4/	Rochdale, Ltd.	10	6
4½	Do. 1 Mt. Deb. Stk.	100	98½
7	Royal, Brentford, Ltd.	10	22
	Do. Cum. Pref.	10	15
4½	Do. 1 Mt. Dbs. Red	100	106
6/	St. Louis, Ltd.	10	3½
8	Do. Cum. Pref.	10	8½
14/	St. Paull, Ltd.	10	10
7	Do. Cum. Pref.	10	12
4½	Salt (T.), L., 1 Db. Sk. Rd.	100	110
4½	Do. "B" Db. Stk. Red	100	106
—	San Francisco, Ltd.	10	½
—	Do. 8 p.c. Cum. Pref.	10	½

Breweries, &c. (*continued*):—

Div.	Name.	Paid.	Price.
4½	Savill Brs., L., D. Sk. Rd.	100	118
4½	Scarboro., Ltd., 1 Db. Stk.	100	101
4	Shaw (Hy.), Ltd., 1 Mt. Db. Stk., Red.	100	104
22/	Showell's, Ltd.	10	32
7	Do. Cum. Pref.	10	17½
3/	Do. Gun. Shs.	5	7½
4½	Do. Mt. Db. Stk., Red.	100	—
4	Simonds, L., 1 D. Sk., Rd.	100	111
5½	Simson & McP., L., Cu. Pf.	10	9½
4½	Do. 1 Mt. Deb. Stk.	100	99
5/	Smith, Garrett, L., £20 Shs	10	16½
5	Do. Cum. Pref.	20	26
3½	Do. 3½ p.c. Mt. Db. Stk.	100	107
5	Smith's, Tadcaster, L., CPf	10	12
4½	Do. Deb. Stk., Red.	100	112
4	Do. Deb. Stk. Red.	100	108
4½	Star, L., 1 M. Db. Stk., Rd.	100	105
4	Steward & P., L., 1 D. Sk.	100	109½
9/	Strettons Derby, Ltd.	10	13
6	Do. Cum. Pref.	10	13½
4	Do. Irr. 1 Mt. Db. Stk.	100	103½
4½	Strong, Romsey, L., 1 D.S.	100	115
5	Stroud, L., Db. Sk., Rd.	100	111½
4½	Tadcaster To'er, L., D.Sk.	100	113
8/	Tamplin, Ltd	10	21
6	Do. Cum. Pref.	100	15
4	Do. "A" Db. Sk., Rd.	10	107
6	Thorne, Ltd., Cum. Pref.	10	14
4	Do. Deb. Stk., Red.	100	103½
15/	Threlfall, Ltd.	10	42
6	Do. Cum. Pref.	10	16½
5	Do. 1 Mt. Dbs., Red.	100	116
4	Tollemache, L., D. Sk. Rd.	100	105
4	Truman, Hanb., D. Sk., R.	100	110
3	Do. "B" Mt. Db. Sk., Rd.	100	95
10/	United States, Ltd.	10	8½
8	Do. Cum. Pref.	10	11
6	Do. 1 Mt. Deb	100	105½
6/	Walker & H., Ld., Cm. Pref.	10	10¾
4½	Do. 1 Mt. Deb. Stk., Red.	100	107
5	Walker, Peter, Ld. Cm. Prf.	10	13½
4	Do. 1 Mt. Dbs. Red.	100	111
4	Wallingford, L., D. Sk. Rd.	100	107
6	Watney, Ld., Cm. Prf. Sk.	100	167
5	Do. Mt. Db. Sk., Rd.	100	115½
4½	Do. "B" Mt. Db. Sk., Rd.	100	111
3½	Do. Mt. Db. Stk.	100	101
5	Watney, D., Ld., Cm. Prf.	10	12½
4½	Do. 1 Mt. Db. Stk.	100	107
10/	Webster & Sons, Ltd.	10	16¾
6	Do. Cum. Pref.	10	14
5	Wenlock Ltd Pref.	10	12
4	Do. 1 Mt. Db. Sk., Rd.	100	108
5	West Cheshire, L., Cu. Pf.	10	10½
4	Do. Irred. 1 Mt. Db. Sk.	100	99
4½	Whitbread, L., Cu. Pf. Sh.	100	124½
4	Do. Db. Stk., Red.	100	110
3½	Do. "B" Db. Stk., Rd.	100	101
9/	Wolverhampton & D. Ld.	10	17
6	Do. Cum. Pref.	10	13½
4½	Do. 1 Mt. Dbs., Red.	100	108
5½	Worthington, Ld., Cm. Prf.	10	15½
5½	Do. Cum. "B" Pref.	10	13¾
4½	Do. Mt. Db. Sk., Rd.	100	113
3½	Do. Irr. "B" Db. Stk.	100	101
10/	Yates's Castle, Ltd.	10	13½
5	Do. Cum. Pref.	10	11
5	Younger W., L., Cu. Pf. Sh.	100	130½

CANALS AND DOCKS.

Last Div.	Name.	Paid.	Price.
4	Birmingham Canal	100	142½
—	E. & W. India Dock	100	20
—	Do. 4 p.c. Prf. Stk.	100	74
—	Do. P.L. Deb. Stk.	100	100
—	Do. Cons. Deb. Stk.	100	89
40/	G. Junction Ord. Shs.	100	150½
6/	Do. do. Pref.	10	19
4½	King's Lynn Per. Db. Stk.	100	116½
2½	Leeds & L'pool Canal	100	71
2½	Lndn & St. Kath. Dks.	100	54
4½	Do. Pref.	100	136½
4½	Do. Pref., 1878	100	132½
4½	Do. Pref., 1882	100	130
4	Do. Deb. Stk.	100	134½
—	Mchester Ship C. 5 p.c. Pf.	10	1½
3½	Do. 1st Perp. Mt. Deb.	100	98
—	Milford Dks. Db. Stk. "A"	100	18½
3½	Millwall Dk.	100	59
5	Do. Perp. Pref.	100	140½
4½	Do. Pref.	100	106½
5	Do. New Per. Prf., 1887	100	126½
5	Do. Per. Deb. Stk.	100	152½
4/	Newhaven Har.	10	14½
2½	N. Metropolitan	100	65
5	Sharpness Nw. Pf. "A" Sk.	100	144½
4	Do. Deb. Stk.	100	118½
5	Sheffield & S. Yorks Nav. 4½ p.c. Pref Stk.	100	115½
36.432	Suez Canal	20	135½
7	Surrey Comcl. Dok., Ord.	100	149½
7	Do. Min. 4 p.c. Pref. "A"	110	150
5	Do. Pref. "B"	100	148½
5	Do do. "C"	100	148½
5	Do. do. "D"	100	144½
4½	Do Deb. Stk.	100	152½

COMMERCIAL, INDUSTRIAL, &c.

Last Div.	Name.	Paid.	Price.
5	Accles, L., 1 Mt. Db., Red.	100	84½
2/6	Aërated Bread, Ltd.	1	12
—	African Gold Recovery, L.	1	¼
2/	Aluminium, L., "A" Shs.	1	2
4½	Do. 1 Mt. Db. Stk., Red.	100	97
5½	Amelia Nitr., L., 1 Mort Deb., Red.	100	82½
7/	Anglo-Chil. Nitrate, Ltd., Cum. Pref.	10	6½
4½	Do. Cons. Mt. Bds., Red.	100	79½
4½	Anglo-Russian Cotton, Ld., 1 Charge Debs., Red.	100	98
11/3	Angus (G., & Co., L.), £10	7½	17
6/	Apollinaris, Ltd.	10	11½
5/	Do. 5 p.c. Cum. Pref.	10	10½
4	Do. Irred. Deb. Stock	100	104
6/	Appleton, French, & S., L.	5	½
3/	Argentine Meat Pres., L., 7 p.c. Pref.	10	2¾
5	Argentine Refinry, Db. Rd.	100	98
6d.	Armstrong, Whitw., Ltd.	1	3½
4	Do. Cum. Pref.	5	6½
5	Artisans', Labr. Dwllgs., L.	100	128½
4½	Do. Non-Cm. Prf., 1879	100	132½
4½	Do. do. 1884	100	132½
—	Asbestos & Asbestic, Ltd.	10	7½
2/7½	Ashley-grdns., L., C. Prf.	5	6½
4½	Do. 1 Mt. Deb. Stk.	100	112½
5/	Assam Rly. & Trdng., L., 8 p.c. Cum. Pref. "A"	10	14½
—	Do. Deferrd. "B" Shs.	1	4
—	Do. do. (iss. f. pd)	1	3½
8/	Do. Cum. Pre-Prf. "A"	10	15
6/	Do. New Pref.	10	11½
5	Do. Debs., Red.	100	107
5	Do. Red. Mort. Debs.	100	109
6	Aust'lian Pastrl, L., Cu. Pf.	10	7
8d.	Aylesbury Dairy, Ltd.	1	1⅛
4	Do. 4 p.c. Mt. Dbs.	100	104½
10/	Babcock & Wilcox, Ltd.	10	29
6	Do. 6 p.c. Cm. Prf.	10	16
8	Baker (Chs.), L., Cm. Pf.	5	8¾
8	Do. "B" Cm. Pref.	5	8
8d.	Barker (John), Ltd.	1	2½
5½	Do. Cum. Pref.	5	7½
4½	Do. Irred. 1 Mt. Db. Stk.	100	127½
—	Barnagore Jute, Ltd.	5	3
5	Do. Cum. Pref.	5	4¾
7½d.	Belgravia Dairy, Ltd.	1	1
5/6	Bell (R.) & Co., Ltd.	5	3½
1/	Bell's Asbestos, Ltd.	1	¾
5	Do. Mt. Db. Bds., Rd.	100	107
10/	Bengal Mills, Ltd.	10	11
6/	Do. 5 p.c. Cum. Prf.	10	10½
2/5	Benson (J.W.) L., Cm. Pf.	10	10¾
4	Do. Perp. Mt. Db. Stk.	100	101
6	Bergvik, L., 6 p.c. Cm. Pf.	10	12½
12/	Do. Dfd.	10	10
4½	Do. 1 Dbs., Red.	100	103½
5/	Birm'ham Vinegar, Ltd.	5	14
5	Do. Cum. Pref.	5	5¼
4½	Do. 1 Mt. Db. Stk., Rd.	100	109½
5	Bonke (A.) L., 5 p.c. Cu. Pf.	10	10¾
2/6	Bodega, Ltd.	5	8¼
4½	Do. Mt. Deb. Stk., Rd.	100	111
8/	Bottomley & Brs., Ltd.	10	6½
6/	Do. 6 p.c. Pt.	10	9½
8½d.	Bovril, Ltd.	1	1¼
1/0½	Do. Def.	1	¾
6½d.	Do. Cum. Pref.	1	1
4½	Do. Deb. Stk.	100	100
5/	Bradbury, Gretrex., Ltd., £10 share	8	14
5/	Do. 5 p.c. Cum. Pref.	10	13½
5/	Brewers' Sugar, L., 5 p.c. Cum. Pref.	10	10½
3/6	Brighton Grd. Hotel, Ld.	5	3½
4	Do Mt. Db. Stk., Red.	100	100½
5	Bristol Hotel & Palm. Co., Ltd. 1st Mt. Red. Deb.	100	105
9½d.	British & Bengton's. Tea Tr. Asc., Ltd.	1	1½
5	Do. Cum. Prf.	5	5¼
—	British Deli & Lgkat. Tobacco, Ltd.	1	½
—	Do. Cum. Prf.	1	½
—	British Tea Table, Ltd.	1	2½
5½	Do. Cum. Pref.	1	1¼
2/6	Brooke, Ben., & Co., Ltd., Cum. Pref.	5	5¾
7/6	Brooke, Bond & Co., Ltd.	5	19
3/	Brown Brs., L., Cum. Pref.	5	5¾
10/	Browne & Eagle, Ltd.	10	13½
5	Do. Cum. Pref.	10	13
4	Do. Mrt. Db. Sk., Red.	100	110
20/	Brunner, Mond, & Co., Lt.	0	41
7/	Do. £10 shares	9	17
7	Do. Cum. Pref.	10	18
7	Do. £10 shares	5	8½
10/	Bryant & May, Ltd.	5	19½
3/	Bucknall, H., & Sons, Lt.	5	7
6	Do. Cum Pref.	5	7¾
4/	Burke, E. & J., Ltd.	5	7½
6	Do. Cum. Pref.	5	7¾
6	Do. Irred. Deb. Stk.	100	155
1/	Burlington Htls. Co., Ltd	1	1½
5	Do. Cum. Pref.	1	1
4	Do. Perp. Deb. Stk.	100	105½
5	Bush, W. J., & Co., Ltd. Cum. Pref.	5	5½
4	Do. 1 Deb. Stk., Red.	100	102
5½	Callard, Stewart, & Watt, Ltd., Cum. Pref.	1	1½
4/	Callender's Cable L., Shs.	5	9½
4½	Do. 1 Deb. Stk., Red.	100	111½
—	Campbell, R., & Sons, Lt.	3	2½
6	Cantareira Water, Bd., Rd	100	98½
5	Do. (2nd issue)	100	90
4	Cartavio Sugar, Ltd., 6 p.c. 1st Debs., Red.	20	82½
9/	Cassell & Co., Ltd., £10	9	15
5	Causton, Sir J., & Sons, Ltd., Cum. Pref.	10	13½

Commercial, &c. (*continued*):—

Last Div.	Name.	Paid.	Price.
4	Cent. Prod. Mkt. of B.A. 1st Mt. Str. Debs.	100	79
4	Chappell & Co., Ltd., Mt. Deb. Stk. Red.	100	103
6/	Chicago & N.W. Gran. 8 p.c. Cum. Pref.	10	3
—	Chicago Packing & Prov.	10	6
8	Do. Cum. Pref.	10	10½
6/	City Offices, Ltd	12	7½
3½	Do. Mt. Deb. Stk.	100	108½
7/2½	Cy. London Real Prop., Ltd., £25 shs.	12	19
4/6	Do. £12½ shs.	7½	13½
3½	Do. Deb. Stk. Red.	100	106½
3½	Do. Deb. Stk. Red.	100	105½
3	Do.	100	100½
4/	Cy. of Santos Imprvts.,		
20/	Ltd., 7 p.c. Pref.	10	8½
8	Clay, Bock, & Co., Ltd.	10	5½
6	Do. Cum. Pref.	10	10
20/	Do. Mort. Deb.	100	103½
6	Coats, J. & P., Ltd.	10	56
4½	Do. Cum. Pref.	10	17½
9½d	Do. Deb. Stk. Red.	100	112½
4	Coburg Hotel, Ltd	1	1½
6	Do. Deb. Stk. Red.	100	102
4½	Colonial Consign & Dis., Ltd., Cum. Pref.	5	4¾
—	Do. 1st Mort. Debs.	100	96½
4/	Colorado Nitrate, Ltd.	5	½
5	Co. Gén. des Asphtes. de F., Ltd.	6	6½
5	Do, Non-Cm. Prf.	—	5½
	Cook, J. W., & Co., Ltd., Cum. Pref.	5	5½
5	Cook, T., & Son, Egypt, Ltd., 1st Mt. Deb. Red.	100	112½
—	Cork Co., Ltd., 6 p.c. Cum. Pref.	5	2
5	Cory, W., & Sn, L., Cu. Pf.	5	6
4	Do. 1st Deb. Stk. Red.	100	108
8½d.	Crisp & Co., Ltd	1	1¾
5½	Do. Cum. Pref.	1	1¼
—	Crompton & Co., Ltd., 7 p.c. Cum. Pref.	5	2½
5	Do. 1st Mt. Reg. Deb.	—	90½
4/6	Crossley, J., & Sons, Ltd.	5	8
5	Do. Cum. Pref.	5	6½
—	Crystal Pal. Ord. "A" Stk.	100	6½
—	Do. "B" Red. Stk	100	1¼
6	Do. 6 p.c. 1st 1887 Deb. Stk. Red.	100	117½
—	Do. 6 p.c. 2nd 1887 Deb. Stk. Red.	100	49½
—	Do. 6 p.c. 3rd 1887 Deb. Stk. Red.	100	22½
3	Do. 3 p.c. 1st 1895 Deb. Stk.	100	92½
—	Daimler Motor, Ltd.	10	8
4/	Dalgety & Co., £20 Shs.	5	5½
4½	Do. Deb. Stk.	100	123
4	Do.	100	115
7/	De Keyser's Ryl. Htl., L.	10	14
5	Do. Cum. Pref.	10	12
4	Do. Deb. Stk., Red.	100	110
6	Denny, H., & Sons, Ltd., Cum. Pref.	10	14½
5/3	Devas, Routledge & Co., L.	7	8½
5	Dickinson, J., & Co., L., Cum. Pref. Stk.	100	123
4½	Domin. Cottn. Mls., Ltd. Mt. Stg. Dbs.	100	97
6/	Dorman, Long & Co., L.	5	4½
—	Eastmans, Ltd	10	2½
12/	Do. 8 p.c. Cum. Pref.	10	10
2/6	E. C. Powder, Ltd.	3	5½
1/6	Edison & Swn Utd. Elec. Ltd., "A" £5 Shs.	3	2½
2/6	Do. fully-paid	5	4½
4½	Ekman Pulp & Ppr. Co., Ltd., Mt. Deb., Red.	100	96
1/1½	Electric Construc., Ltd.	2	2¾
7	Do. Cum. Pref.	2	3¼
25/	Eley Bros., Ltd.	10	38
—	Elmore's Cop. Deptg., L.	1	½
—	Elmore's Wire Mnfg., L.	2	½
—	Elysee Pal. Hotel Co., L.	5/	½
5 p.c.	Do. 5 p.c. £100 Db., Rd.	70	97½
8½d.	Evans, Ben., & Co., Ltd.	1	1
5	Do. 1 Mt. Db. Sk., Rd.	100	108
1/8½d.	Evans, D. H., & Co., L.	1	2½
6	Do. Cum. Pref.	1	1½
4½	Do. 1 Mt. Db. Sk., Rd.	100	112
2/1	*Evening News*, L., 5 p.c. Cum. Pref.	5	5½
5/3	Evered & Co., L., £10 Sh.	7	12½
7/6	Do.	10	13½
4	Fairbairn Pastoral Co., Aust., L., 1 Mt. Db., Rd.	100	102
6	Fairfield Shipbldg., Ltd., Cum. Pref.	10	10½
4½	Do. Mort. Deb. Stk.	100	109½
6/	Farmer & Co., Ld., 6 p.c. Cum. Pref.	10	13½
10	Field, J. C. & J., Ltd.	10	10
14/	Do. 7 p.c. Cum. Pref.	10	14½
1/3	Fordham, W.B., & Sns, Ld.	1	2
5/6	Fore-st. Warehouse, Ltd.	11	9½
4	Do. Regd. Debs., Rd.	100	102½
3/6	Foster, M. B. & Sons, Ltd.	4	6
5	Do. Pref.	10	11½
9/	Foster, Porter, & Co., L.	10½	15½
4	Fowler, J., & Co. (Leeds), Ltd., 1 Mt. Deb., Red.	100	103½
3/	Fraser & Chalmers, Ltd	3	1½
4½	Free, Rodwell & Co., Ltd., Deb Stk.	100	104½
6½d.	Furness, T., & Co., Ltd., 5½ p.c. Cum. Pref.	1	¾
4½	Gartside & Co. (of Manchstr), L., 1 Mt. Db. Sk.	100	112
11	Genl. Hydraul Power, L.	100	[illegible]

Commercial, &c. (*continued*):—

Last Div.	Name.	Paid.	Price.
8/	Gillman & Spencer, Ltd.	5	2½
6	Do. Pref.	5	4¾
5	Do. Mort. Debs.	50	51
4	Goldsbro., Mort & Co., L., "A" Deb. Stk., Red.	100	73½
—	Do. 3 p.c. "B" Inc. Deb. Stk., Red	100	14
8/	Gordon Hotels, Ltd.	10	20
5½	Do. Cum. Pref.	10	14½
4½	Do. Perp. Deb. Stk.	100	137½
4	Do. do.	100	122½
—	Greenwich Inld. Linoleum Co., Ltd.	1	⅛
7	Greenwood & Batley, Ltd., Cum. Pref.	10	10
7½d.	Hagemann & Co., Ltd., 6 p.c. Cum. Pref.	1	1
—	Hammond, Ltd.	10	½
—	Do. 8 p.c. Cum. Pref.	10	2½
—	Do. 6 p.c. Cum. Inc. Stk. Red.	100	45
	Hampton & Sons, Ltd., 4 p.c. 1 Mt. Db. St. Red.	100	105
—	Hans Crescent Htl., L., 6 p.c. Cum. Pref.	5	3
4	Do. 1 Mt. Deb. Stk.	100	90
6d.	Harmsworth, Ld., Cm. Pf.	1	1⅛
4/	Harrison, Barber, Ltd.	5	4½
3/	Harrod's Stores, Ltd.	1	4¾
2/6	Do. Cum. Pref.	5	7½
3½	Hawaiian Comcl. & Sug. 1 Mt. Debs.	100	91½
5	Hazell, Watson, L., C. P.	10	12
18/	Henley's Teleg., Ltd.	10	22
7	Do. Pref. Shs.	10	19
4½	Do. Mt. Db. Stk., Rd.	100	112½
6	Henry, Ltd.	10	12
5	Do. Cum. Pref.	10	13½
4½	Do. Mt. Debs., Red.	50	53
6	Hepworth, Ld., Cm. Prf.	10	11
1/4½	Herrmann, Ltd.	1	¾
—	Hildesheimer, Ltd.	3	1½
1/2½	Holbrn. & Frasca, Ltd.	1	1¼
5	Do. Cum. Pref.	10	11½
4	Do. Deb. Stk.	100	113
6	Home & Col. Stres, L., C.P	5	7½
6	Hood & M.'s Stres., Ltd., Cum. Pref.	1	½
6	Hook, C. T Ltd.	10	6
7/2	Hornsby, Ltd., £10 Shs.	8	3
5/6	Do. 6 p.c. Cm. Pf. Sk.	100	90
—	Hotchks. Ordn., Ltd.	10	1
—	Do. 7 p.c. Cm. Prf.	10	4
5	Do. 1 Mt. Dbs., Rd.	100	96½
6	Htl. Cecil, Ld., Cm. Prf.	5	4
4	Do. 1 Mt. D. Sk., R.	100	105½
8/	Heward & Bulgh, Ltd.	10	38
6	Do. Pref.	10	16
4	Do. Deb. Stk., Red.	100	108
5/	Howell, J., Ltd., £5 Shs.	4	8¾
—	Howell & Js. Ld., £3½ Shs.	3	[illegible]
1/6	Humber, Ltd.	1	[illegible]
6	Do. Cum. Pref.	1	[illegible]
5/6	Hunter, Wilts., Ltd.	5	7
2/7	Hyam Clthg., Ltd., 5 p.c. Cum. Pref.	5	5½
10/	Impl. Russn. Cotton, L.	5	6
5	Impd. Industl. Dwgs., Ld.	100	130½
6d.	Do. Defrd.	1	1½
25/	Impd. Wood Pave., Ltd.	10	15½
15/	Ind. Rubber, Gutta Per. Telegraph Works, Ltd.	10	21½
4	Do. 1 Mt. Debs., Red.	100	104
6	Intern. Tea, Cum. Pref.	5	6½
10½d.	Jays, Ltd.	1	1½
5½	Do. Cum. Pref.	5	6½
1/2½d.	Jones & Higgins, Ltd.	1	2½
4½	Do. 1 Mt. Db. Sk., Rd.	100	113
5/	Kelly's Directory, Ltd., 5 p.c. Cum. Pref.	10	12½
4	Do. Mort. Db. Sk., Rd.	100	106
—	Kent Coal Explrtn. Ltd.	1	½
9½d.	King, Howmann, Ltd.	1	1½
4/	Kinloch & Co., Ltd.	5	8½
6	Do. Pref.	5	7
5	Lady's Pictorial Pub., Ltd., Cum. Pref.	5	5
48/4	La Guaira Harb., Ltd., 5 p.c. Deb. Stk.	100	85
—	Do. 2 Mt. 7 p.c. Deb. Stk., Red.	100	22½
4/	Lagunas Nitrate, Ltd.	5	1½
2/	Lagunas Syn., Ltd.	5	¾
5	Do. 1 Mt. Debs., Red.	100	76
—	L. Copais Ld., 1 Mt. 6 p.c. Debs., Red.	100	35½
3/	Lautaro Nitrate, Ltd.	5	3½
5	Do. 1 Mt. Debs., Red.	—	100
9/	Lawes Chem. L., £10 shs.	9	5½
14/	Do. N. Cm. Min. Pref.	10	12½
—	Leeds Forge, 7 p.c. Cm. Pf.	5	3½
5	Do. 1 Mt. Debs., Red.	50	47
5	Lever Bros., L., Cm. Pf.	10	13½
6	Liberty, L., 6 p.c. Cm. Pf.	10	15
20/	Liebig's, Ltd.	20	77
5	Lilley & Sk., L., Cm. Pf.	5	5½
39/4	Linoleum Manfg Ltd.	5	16
3/	Linotype, Ltd., Pre	5	5½
5/	Do. Def.	5	7½
4/	Lister & Co., Ltd.	10	4
5	Do. Cum. Pref.	10	8½
5/	Liverpool Nitrate	5	4½
—	Liverpool Warehsg., Ltd	10	3½
5½	Do. Cum. Pref.	10	8½
4	Do. 1 Mt. Db. Stk., Rd.	100	105
5½	Lockharts, Ltd., Cm. Pf.	1	1½
4/6	Ldn. & Til. Lightrage £10	9	6½
6/	Ldn. Comcl. Sale Rms., L.	10	17½
3	Do. 1 Mt. Deb. Stk., Red.	100	105
3	London Nitrate, Ltd.	5	1½
4/	London Nitrate, Ld. 8 p.c. Cm. Min. Pf.	5	3½
8/	London Pavilion, Ltd.	5	6½

Commercial, &c. (*continued*):—

Last Div.	Name.	Paid.	Price.
2/6	London Produce Clg. Ho., Ltd., £10 Shares	2½	3½
4/	London Stereos., Ltd.	5	3
6d.	Ldn. Un. Laun. L. Cm. Pf.	1	[illegible]
8½d.	Louise, Ltd.	1	[illegible]
5½	Do. Cum. Pref.	1	[illegible]
5/	Lovell & Christmas, Ltd.	5	11½
6	Do. Cum. Pref.	5	7½
4	Do. Mt. Deb. Stk., Red.	100	107
1/3	Lyons, Ltd.	1	4½
4½	Do. 1 Mt. Deb., Stk., Rd.	100	111½
10/	Machinery Trust, Ltd.	5	13½
4½	Do. 4½ Deb. Stk.	100	104
6	MacLellan, L., Min. C. Pf.	10	9
5	Do. 1 Mt. Debs., 1900	100	101½
—	McEwan, J. & Co., Ltd.	10	1½
6	Do. Mt. Debs., Red.	100	89½
8	McNamara, L., Cm. Pref.	10	9
7½d.	Maison Virot, Ltd.	1	1½
2/7	Do. 6 p.c. Cum. Pref.	5	4½
5/	Manbré Sacc., L., Cm. Pf.	10	12
10/	Mangan Brze., L., £10 Shs.	6	15½
2/	Mason & Mason, Ltd.	5	2½
6	Do. Cum. Pref.	5	5½
—	Maynards, Ltd.	1	[illegible]
6	Do. Cum. Pref.	1	[illegible]
9½d.	Mazawattee Tea, Ltd.	1	1½
5	Do. Cum. Pref.	5	5½
6	Mellin's Food Cum. Pref.	5	6½
4½	Met. Ascn. Imp. Dwlgs. L.	100	110
3½	Do. 1 Mt. Deb. Stk.	100	97
5	Metro. Indus. Dwlgs., Ltd.	5	5
4	Do. do. Cum. Pref.	5	5½
5	Metro. Prop., L., Cm. Pf.	5	5½
4½	Do. 1st Mt. Debs. Stk.	100	108½
6	Mexican Cotton 1 Mt. Db.	100	93½
4½	Mid. Class Dwlgs., L., Db.	100	120½
1/	Millars' Karri, Ltd.	1	3½
6	Do. Cum. Pref.	1	1½
5/	Milner's Safe, Ltd.	10	20½
10/	Moir & Son, Ltd., Pref.	5	8½
6	Morgan Cruc., L., Cm. Pf.	10	14½
2/	Morris, B., Ltd.	3½	3½
2/6	Murray L. 5½ p.c. C. Pf.	5	5½
63/4½	Do. 4½ 1 Mt. Db. Sk. Rd.	100	106
—	Natnl. Dwlgs., L., 5 p.c. Pf.	5	1
1/7½	Nat. Safe Dep., Ltd.	4	3½
6	Do. Cum. Pref.	1	1½
—	Native Guano, Ltd.	5	½
—	Nelson Bros., Ltd.	10	2½
5	Do. Deb. Stk., Red.	100	80½
4/	Neuchtel Asph., Ltd.	10	10½
—	New Central Borneo, Ld.	1	—
10d.	New Darvel Tob., Ltd.	18/	1½
1/6	New Explosives, Ltd.	3	3½
5/3½	New Gd. Htl., Bham, L.	5	4
5½	Do. Pref.	5	4½
4	Do. 1 Mt. Db. Stk., Rd.	100	96½
—	New Julia Nitrate, Ltd.	10/	—
—	New Ldn. Borneo Tob., L.	16/	½
1/6	New Premier Cycle, Ltd.	1	[illegible]
6	Do. 6 p.c. Cum. Pref.	1	½
4½	Do. 4½ p.c. 1 Mt. Db. Rd	100	—
—	New Tamargl. Nitr., Ltd	1	[illegible]
—	Do. 8 p.c. Cum. Pref.	1	[illegible]
6	Do. 6 p.c. 1 Mt. Dbs. Rd.	100	62½
3'78d.	Newnes, G., L., Cm. Prf.	1	1½
1/3	Nitr. Provision, Ltd.	2½	½
24/	Nobel-Dynam., Ltd.	10	18
—	North Brazn. Sugar, Ltd.	1	¼
15/	Oakey, Ltd.	10	31
6	Do. Cum. Pref.	10	17
—	Paccha Jazp. Nitr., Ltd.	5	⅛
5	Pac. Borax, L., 1 Db. Rd.	100	110
—	Palace Hotel, Ltd.	10	5½
5½	Do. Cum. Pref.	10	7
4	Do. 1 Mt. Deb. Stk.	100	102
2/6	Palmer, Ltd.	5	1½
6	Do. Cum. Pref.	5	2½
1/2½d	Paquin, Ltd.	1	[illegible]
6	Do. Cum. Pref.	5	4½
5½	Parnall, Ltd., Cum. Pref.	1	[illegible]
4/6	Pawsons, Ltd., £10 Shs.	6	6½
4	Do. Mt. Debs., Red.	100	106
6	Pearks, G. & T., Ltd., 6 p.c. Cum. Pref.	1	¾
9½d.	Pears, Ltd.	1	1½
6	Do. Cum. Pref.	10	14½
5	Do. Deb. Stk.	100	129
5½	Pearson, C. A., L., Cu. Pf.	5	5½
4/3	Peebles, Ltd.	5	7½
5	Do. Cum. Pref.	5	6½
4½	Do. Mt. Deb. Stk. Red.	100	113½
5½	Peek Bros., Ltd., 1 Cum. Pref., Nos. 1-60,000	5	6½
3½	Do. 3½ p.c. 1 Db. Stk.	100	103½
7½d.	Pegamoid, Ltd.	1	⅝
—	Phospho-Guano, Ltd.	5	2½
—	Pillsbury-W. Fl. Mills, L.	10	1½
16/	Do. 8 p.c. Cum. Pref.	10	6½
6	Do. 1 Mort. Debs.	100	95½
9½d.	Plummer, Ltd.	1	1½
5	Do. Cum. Pref.	5	5½
7/6	Price's Candle, Ltd.	16	34
6	Priest Marians, L., Cm. Pf.	1	1½
6	Pryce Jones, Ld., Cm. Pf.	5	7½
5	Do. Deb. Stk.	100	122
8½d.	Pullman, Ltd.	1	1½
6d.	Do. Cum. Pref.	1	1½
11/	Raleigh Cycle, Ltd.	1	[illegible]
6	Do. Cum. Pref.	1	[illegible]
—	Recife Drnge. Ld. 1 Mt. Debs., R	100	19
6	Redfern Ltd. Cum. Prf.	10	14
5	Ridgways, Ltd., Cu. Pf.	5	5½
—	R. Janeiro Cy. Imps. Ld.	25	8½
5	Do. Debs.	100	86½
5	Do. 1882-1893	100	86½
11/	R. Jan Fl. Mills, Ltd.	7	6½
5	Do. 1 Mt. Debs., Rd.	100	94
—	Riv. Plate Meat, Ltd.	5	3½
—	Do. Pref.	5	5
8½d.	Roberts, J. R., Ltd.	1	1½

Commercial, &c. (*continued*):—

Last Div.	Name.	Paid.	Price.
5	Roberts 1 Mt. D. Sk., Rd.	100	112
1/1½	Roberts, T. R., Ltd.	1	2½
5	Do. Cum. Pref.	1	1½
3/	Rosario Nit., Ltd.	5	3½
5	Do. Debs., Red.	100	103
5	Do. Huara, Debs.	—	104
1/	Rover Cycle, Ltd.	1	¾
6/	Ryl. Aquarium, Ltd.	5	4½
6	Do. Pref.	5	6
5	Ryl. Htl., Edin., Cm. Pf.	1	1½
1/2½	Ryl. Niger, Ltd., £10 Sh.	2	3
6/	Do.	10	15½
—	Russian Petroleum	10	24
—	Do. 6½ p.c. Cm. Prf	10	10½
3/	Ruston, Proctor, Ltd.	10	12
4½	Do. 1 Mort. Debs.	100	104
6/	Sadler, Ltd.	11	7
—	Sal. Carmen Nit., Ltd.	5	3½
9d.	Salmon & Gluck., Ltd.	1	1⅛
	Salt Union, Ltd.	10	1½
1½	Do. 7 p.c. Pref.	10	5½
4½	Do. Deb. Stk.	100	101½
4½	Do. "B" Deb. Sk., Rd.	100	97½
—	San Donato Nit., Ltd.	5	[illegible]
2/6	San Jorge Nit., Ltd.	5	3½
—	San Pablo Nit., Ltd.	5	[illegible]
—	San Sebastn. Nit., Ltd.	5	[illegible]
1/9	Sanitas, Ltd	1	2½
—	Sa. Elena Nit., Ltd.	5	[illegible]
—	Sa. Rita Nit., Ltd.	5	1½
5/	Savoy Hotel, Ltd.	10	16
7	Do. Pref.	10	14
4	Do. 1 Mt. Deb. Stk.	100	111½
5	Do. Debs., Red	100	102½
5	Do. & Ldn. For. Htl., Ltd., 5 p.c. Debs. Red.	100	99
1½d.	Schweppes, Ltd.	1	1½
—	Do Def.	1	[illegible]
5	Do. Cum. Pref.	1	1½
4	Do. Deb. Stk.	100	107
1/	Singer Cyc., Ltd.	1	[illegible]
5½	Do Cum. Pref.	1	[illegible]
—	Smokeless Pwdr., Ltd.	1	⅛
5½d.	S. Eng. Dairies, Ltd., 6 p.c. Cum. Pref.	1	1½
—	Sowler Thos. L.	1	1
3/4½	Do. 5½ Cm. Pf.	5	5½
4/6	Spencer, Turner, & Co. Ltd	5	8½
5	Do. Cum. Pref.	5	6½
5	Spicer, Ld., 5 p.c. Dbs. Rd.	100	65
4/	Spiers & Pond, Ltd.	10	22
5	Do. 1 Mt. Debs., Red.	100	117½
5	Do. "A" Db. Stk., Rd.	100	111
5	Do. "B" 1 Db. Stk., Rd.	100	111
4	Do. Fd. "C" 1 Db. S., R.	100	104
7/6	Spratt's, Ltd	5	12½
4	Do. Debs., 1914	—	105
5	Steiner Ld., Cm. Pf.	10	11½
4	Do. 1 Mt. Db. Sk. Rd.	100	106
9/	Stewart & Clydesdale, L.	10	14
6	Do. Cum. Pref.	10	15
35/5	Sulphide Corp.	100	80
1/	Swan & Edgar, L.	1	1½
1/	Sweetmeat Automatic, L.	1	4
2/9	Teetgen, Ltd., Cum. Pref.	5	6
24/	Teleg. Construction., Ld.	12	36½
5	Do. Db. Bds., Rd., 1899	100	103½
3/0½	Tilling, Ld. 5½ p.c. Cm. Prf.	5	6½
4	Do. 4 p.c. 1 Dbs., Rd.	—	102
8½d.	Tower Tea, Ltd.	1	1½
5	Do. Cum. Pref.	5	5½
5	Travers, Ltd., Cum. Pref.	10	12½
4	Do. 1 Mt. Dbs., Rd.	100	105
5	Tucuman Sug., 1 Dbs., Rd.	100	100
4/	United Alkali, Ltd.	10	1½
7	Do. Cum. Pref.	10	7½
5	Do. Mt. Db. Stk., Rd.	100	108½
2½d.	United Horse Shoe, Ltd., Non-Cum. 8 p.c. Pref.	1	⅛
5	Un. Kingm. Tea, Cm. Prf.	5	4½
2/	Un. Lankat Plant., Ltd.	1	2
4/	Un. Limmer Asphlte., Ld.	3	4½
13/	Val de Travers Asph., L.	10	15½
3/	V. den Bergh's, L., Cm. P.	5	6½
6	Walkers, Park., L., C. Pf.	10	3
4½	Do. 1 Mt. Debs., Red.	100	90½
6/	Wallis, Thos. & Co., Ltd.	5	14
6	Do. Cum. Pref.	5	8½
5½	Waring, Ltd., Cum. Pref.	5	5½
4½	Do. 1 Mt. Db. Sk., Red.	100	112
4½	Do. Irred. "B" Db. Stk.	100	104
12/	Waterlow, Dfd. Ord.	10	14
4/	Do. Pref.	10	14
3½	Do. Cum. Pref.	10	10½
10/	Waterlow Bros. & L., Ld.	10	9
5	Do. Pref.	10	12½
1/2½	Welford, Ltd.	1	2
4½	Do. Debs., Red.	100	109
1/	Welford's Surrey Dairies, Ltd.	1	1½
7½d.	West London Dairy, Ltd.	1	1
4½	Wharncliffe Dwllgs, L., Pf.	10	11½
18/10	Do. 3 p.c. Irr. Mt. Db. Sk.	100	96
6d.	White, A. J., Ltd.	1	¾
6	Do. 6 p.c. Cum. Pref.	1	[illegible]
4	White, J. Bazley, Ltd., 1 Mort. Debs., Red.	100	99½
5	White, R., Ltd., 1 Mort. Deb. Stock, Red.	100	104½
11/	White, Tomkins, Ltd	10	11½
5	Do. Cum. Pref.	10	11½
6	White, W. N., L., Cm. Pf.	1	1
2/6	Wickens, Pease & Co., L.	5	3½
6	Wilkie, Ltd., Cum. Pref.	10	15½
4/	Willans & Robinson, Ltd	5	8
6	Do. Cum. Pref.	5	7½
4½	Do. 1 Mt. Db. Stk., Red.	100	108
7½d.	Williamsons, L., Cm. Prf.	1	1½
6	Winterbottm. Book Cloth, Ltd., Cum. Prf.	10	15
3/	Yates, Ltd.	5	6½
6	Do. Cum. Pref.	5	6½
	Young's Paraffin. Ltd.	4	1½

CORPORATION STOCKS—COLONIAL AND FOREIGN.

Per Cent.	Name.	Paid.	Price.
6	Auckland City, '72 1904-24	100	118
6	Do. Cons., '79, Red. 1930	100	138½
5	Do. Deb. Ln., '83..1934-8	100	117
6	Auckland Harb. Debs.	100	111½
5	Do. 1917	100	111
5	Do. 1936	100	116
5½	Balmain Boro' 1914	—	113½
5	Boston City (U.S.)	100	102½
5	Do. 1902	100	105
5	Brunswick Town 5. c. Debs. 1916-20	100	111
15/	B. Ayres City 6 p.c.	100	51
4½	Do. 4½ p.c.	100	71
5	Cape Town, City of	100	113
4	Do. 1943	100	116
4	Chicago, City of, Gold 1915	—	108
6	Christchurch 1926	100	131½
—	Cordoba City	100	17½
5	Duluth (U.S.) Gold ..1926	—	110
6	Dunedin (Otago) 1925	100	127½
6	Do. 1906	100	113
5	Do. Consols..1908	100	111
4	Durban Insc. Stk. 1944	100	111
4	Essex Cnty., N. Jersey 1906	100	114½
5	Fitzroy, Melbrne...1916-19	100	110
5	Gisborne Harbour 1915	100	110½
4	Greymouth Harbour..1925	100	110
4	Hamilton 1934	100	108
5	Hobart Town 1918-30	100	116
4	Do. 1940	100	107
4½	Invercargill Boro. Dbs. 1936	100	111
6	Kimberley Boro., S.A. Dbs.	—	102
4	Launceston Twn. Dbs. 1916	100	107
6	Lyttleton, N.Z., Harb. 1929	100	125
4	Melbourne Bd. of Wks. 1921	100	107
5	Melb. City Debs. 1897-1907	100	107½
4½	Do. Debs. 1908-27	100	115½
4	Do. Debs...1915-20-22	100	108
5	Melbne. Harb. Bds., 1908-9	100	112
4½	Do. do. 1915	100	110
4	Do. do. 1918-21	100	105
4½	Melbrne. Tms, Dbs. 1914-16	100	113
4½	Do. Fire Brig. Db. 1921	100	108
5	Mexico City Stg.	100	83
4	Moncton N. Bruns. City	100	103
4½	Montevideo	100	50
5	Montreal Stg.	100	104
5	Do. 1874	100	104
5	Do. 1879	100	106
3½	Do. 1933	100	104
3	Do. Perm. Deb. Stk	100	97
4	Do. Cons. Deb. Stk. 1932	100	113
6	Napier Boro. Consolid. 1914	100	119
5	Napier Harb. Debs...1920	100	115
5	Do. Debs...1928	100	107
6	New Plymouth Harb. Debs. 1909	100	108
6	New York City 1901	—	107½
3½	Do. 1910-26	—	103½
4½	Nth. Melbourne Debs. 1-600 1921	100	105
5	Oamaru Boro. Cons...1920	100	101
6	Do. Harb. Bds. (Reg.)	100	74
25/	Do. 6 p.c. (Bearer)..1919	100	35
6	Otago Harb. Deb. Reg.	100	103
6	Do. 1877	100	107
6	Do. 1881..1921	100	115
5	Do. Debs...1921	100	107
5	Do. Cons...1934	100	105
6	Ottawa City	100	111
6	Do. 1904	100	113½
4½	Do. Debs...1913	100	108½
6	Port Elizabeth Waterworks	100	111
5	Port Louis	100	111
5	Prahran Debs. 1917	100	109
4	Do. Debs. 1919	100	102
6	Quebec C. Coupon. 1875 1905	100	112
6	Do. do. 1878 1908	100	116
4½	Do. Debs. 1914-18	100	108
4	Do. Debs. 1923	100	108
3½	Do. Cns. Rg. Stk., Red.	100	101
5	Richmond (Melb.) Dbs. 1917	100	112
4	Rio Janeiro City	100	57
4	Rome City	100	—
4	Do. 2nd to 8th Iss.	100	92
—	Rosario C.	100	26½
—	Do.	100	26½
4	St. Catherine (Ont.)..1926	100	101
4	St. John, N.B., Debs. 1934	—	103
4½	St. Kilda (Melb) Dbs. 1918-21	100	105
4	St. Louis C. (Miss.)..1911	100	106
4	Do. 1913	100	103½
3'65	Do. 1915	—	110
—	Santa Fé City Debs.	100	20
6	Santos City	100	95
6	Sofia City	100	83
5	Sth. Melbourne Debs. 1915	100	111
4½	Do. Debs. 1919	100	107
5	Sydney City 1904	100	109
4	Do. Debs. 1912-13	100	107
4	Do. do. (1894)..1919	100	109
7	Timaru Boro. 7 p.c...1910	100	126½
5	Timaru Harb. Debs 1914	100	107
5	Do. Debs...1916	100	107
6	Toronto City Wtrwks 1904-6	100	114
6	Do. Cons. Debs. ..1898	100	101
5	Do. G. Cns. Dbs. 1919-20	100	118
4	Do. Strlg. 1922-8	100	107
4	Do. Local Improv.	100	102
3½	Do. 1929	100	104
3½	Valparaiso	100	100
4	Vancouver 1931	100	107
4	Do. 1932	100	108
6	Wanganui Harb. Dbs. 1905	100	110
6	Wellington Con. Deb. 1907	100	117
6	Do. Improv., 1879	100	123
6	Do. Wtrwks. Dbs., 1880	100	123
4½	Do. Debs., 1893...1933	100	116
4½	Wellington Harb. 1907	100	104
4	Westport Harb. Dbs. 1925	100	110
6	Winnipeg City Deb...1907	—	118
5	Do. 1914	100	113

FINANCIAL, LAND, AND INVESTMENT.

Last Div.	Name.	Paid.	Price.
5	Agency, Ld. & Fin. Aust., Ltd., Mt. Db. Stk., Rd.	100	90½
	Amer. Frehld. Mt. of Lon., Ld., Cum. Pref. Stk.	100	87½
4½	Do. Deb. Stk., Red.	100	92
1/	Anglo-Amer. Db. Cor., L.	2	1
4	Do. Deb. Stk., Red	100	105½
5½	Ang.-Ceylon & Gen. Est., Ltd., Cons. Stk.	100	55
6	Do. Reg. Debs., Red.	100	102½
—	Ang.-Fch. Explorn., Ltd.	1	2 1/16
6	Do. Cum. Pref.	1	1½
—	Argent. Ld. & Inv., Ltd. £1 Shares	10/	nil
—	Do. Cum. Pref.	4	1¼
1/	Assets Fnders.' Sh., Ltd.,	4	1⅜
6/	Assets Realis., Ltd., Ord.,	5	8½
5	Do. Cum. Pref.	5	6¼
26/	Austrln. Agricl £25 Shs.	21½	63½
—	Aust. N. Z. Mort., Ltd., £10 Shs.	1	1½d.
4½	Do. Deb. Stk., Red.	100	90½
4	Do. Deb. Stk., Red.	100	82½
4½	Australian Est. & Mt., L., 1 Mt. Deb. Stk., Red.	100	103
5	Do. "A" Mort. Deb. Stk., Red.	100	96
2/6	Australian Mort., Ld., & Fin., Ltd. £25 Shs.	5	4½
1/6	Do. New, £25 Shs.	3	3
4	Do. Deb. Stk	100	109½
3	Do. Do.	100	85
5	Bengal Presidy. 1 Mort. Deb., Red.	100	106
25/	British Amer. Ld. "A"	1	19
—	Do. "B"	24	7
1/7½	Brit. & Amer. Mt., Ltd. £10 Shs.	2	½
5/	Do. Pref.	10	10
4	Do. Deb. Stk., Red.	100	103
1/3	Brit. & Austrlsn Tst Ln., Ltd. £25 Shs.	2½	½
4½	Do. Perm. Debs., Red.	100	103
1½d.	Brit. N. Borneo. £1 Shs.	15/	1/16
2½d.	Do.	1	1
—	Brit. S. Africa	1	2 1/16
5	Do. Mt. Deb., Red.	—	96
6	B. Aires Harb. Tst., Red.	100	94
12/6	Canada Co.	1	26
—	Canada N. W. Ld., Ltd.	$25	83½
—	Do. Pref.	$100	350½
4	Canada Perm. Loan & Sav. Perp. Deb. Stk.	100	99½
—	Curamalan Ld., 1 Mt. 7 p.c. Bds., Red.	—	94½
3/7½	Deb Corp., Ld., £10 Shs	4	3
5	Do. Cum. Pref.	10	11¼
4	Do. Perp. Deb. Stk.	100	112
9d.	Deb. Corp. Fders' Sh., Ld.	3	½
4/5 1/10	Eastn. Mt. & Agncy, Ld., "A"	10	5½
4½	Do. Deb. Stk., Red.	100	100
5	Equitable Revers. In. Ltd.	100	—
2/6	Exploration, Ltd.	1	1 1/16
/6d.	Freehold Trst. of Austria. Ltd. £10 Shs.	1	½
4	Do. Perp. Deb. Stk.	100	100
—	Genl. Assets Purchase, Ltd., 5 p.c. Cum. Pref.	10	—
70/	Genl. Reversionary, Ltd.	100	—
2½	Holborn Vi. Land	100	105
2½	House Prop. & Inv.	100	85½
13/	Hudson's Bay	13	19½
—	Hyderabad (Deccan)	5	3
4	Impl. Col. Fin. & Agcy. Corp.	100	92½
4½	Impl. Prop. Inv., Ltd., Deb. Stk., Red.	100	91½
2/6	Internatl. Fincial. Soc., Ltd. £7½ Shs.	2½	1½
4	Do. Deb. Stk., Red.	100	99½
1/9½	Ld. & Mtge. Egypt, Ltd. £18 Shs.	3	2¾
5	Do. Debs., Red.	100	103
4½	Do. Debs., Red.	100	102
—	Ld. Corp. of Canada, Ltd.	1	½
4½	Ld. Mtge. Bk. of Texas Deb. Stk.	100	—
3½	Ld. Mtge. Bk. Victoria 4½ p.c. Deb. Stk.	100	78
2/9½	Law Debent. Corp., Ltd., £10 Shs.	2	1½
4½	Do. Cum. Pref.,	10	12
4	Do. Deb. Stk.	100	114
—	Law Land, L., 4½ Cm. Prf.	5	5½
1/	Ldn. & Australasian Deb. Corp., Ltd., £4 Shs.	2	½
4½	Do. 4½ p.c. Mt. Deb. Stk., Red.	100	99
1/9	Ldn. & Middx. Frhld. Est. £2 Shs.	35/	3
2/6	Lndn. & N. Y. Inv. Corp., Ltd.	5	1¾
5	Do. 5 p.c. Cum. Pref.	10	8½
1/6	Ldn. & Nth. Assets Corp., Ltd., £2 Shs.	1½	½
2	Ldn. & N. Deb. Corp., L.	2	1¼
3/6	Ldn. & S. Afric. Explrn. Ltd.	½	13¼
2/	Mtge. Co. of R. Plate, Ltd. £10 Shs.	2	3
4½	Do. Deb. Stk., Red.	100	112
4½	Morton, Rose Est., Ltd., 1st Mort. Debs.	—	101
0/6	Natal Land Col. Ltd.	10	7½
4/	Do. 8 p.c. Pref., 1870	5	8
5/6	Natl. Disct. L., £25 Shs.	5	10½
4½	New Impl. Invest., Ltd. Pref. Stk.	100	61½
	New Impl. Invest., Ltd. Def. Stk.	100	9
3½	N. Zld. Assets Real Deb.	100	99

Financial, Land, &c. (*continued*):—

Last Div.	Name.	Paid.	Price.
4	N. Zld. Ln. & Mer. Agcy., Ltd Prf. Ln, Deb. Stk	100	94
2/6	N. Zld. Tst. & Ln. Ltd., £25 Shs.	5	1½
12/6	N. Zld. Tst. & Ln. Ltd., 5 p.c. Cum. Pref.	25	19
—	N. Brit. Australsn. Ltd.	100	6½
—	Do. Irred. Guar.	100	32½
5	Do. Mort. Debs.	100	82½
4½	N. Queensld. Mort. & Inv., Ltd., Deb. Stk.	100	93
—	Oceana Co., Ltd.	—	—
6	Peel Riv., Ld. & Min. Ltd.	100	88½
—	Peruvian Corp., Ltd.	100	2¼
—	Do. 4 p.c. Pref.	100	8½
3	Do. 6 p.c. 1 Mt. Debs., Red.	100	38
—	Queensld. Invest. & Ld. Mort. Pref. Ord. Stk.	100	20
3/7	Queensld. Invest. & Ld. Mort. Ord. Shs.	4	4
4	Queensld. Invest. & Ld. Mort. Perp. Debs.	100	88
3½	Raily. Roll Stk. Tst. Deb., 1903-6	100	100½
50/	Reversiony. Int. Soc., Ltd.	100	—
2/8½	Riv. Plate Trst., Loan & Agcy., L., "A" £10 Shs.	2	4
1/6	Riv. Plate Trst., Loan & Agcy., Ltd., Def. "B"	5	3½
	Riv. Plate Trst., Loan & Agy., L., Db. Stk., Red.	100	109
—	Santa Fé & Cord. Gt. South Land, Ltd.	20	5
—	Santa Fé Land	10	2½
2/	Scot. Amer. Invest., Ltd. £10 Shs.	2	2⅜
2½	Scot. Australian Invest., Ltd., Cons.	100	74½
6	Scot. Australinn Invest., Ltd., Guar. Pref.	100	135½
5	Scot. Australian Invest., Ltd., Guar. Pref.	100	106½
4	Scot. Australian Invest., Ltd., 4 p.c. Perp. Dbs.	100	105½
5	Sivagunga Zemdy., 1st Mort., Red.	100	101
20/	Sth. Australian	20	52½
3½	Stock Exchange Deb., Rd.	—	101½
—	Strait Develt., Ltd.	1	1/16
2/6	Texas Land & Mt., Ltd. £10 Shs.	2½	3
4½	Texas Land & Mt., Ltd., Deb. Stk., Red.	100	105
—	Transvaal Est. & Dev., L.	1	5/16
—	Transvaal Lands, Ltd., £1 Shs.	15/	⅜
—	Do. F. P	1	5/16
—	Transvaal Mort., Loan, & Fin., Ltd., £10 Shs.	2	½
2/	Tst & Agcy. of Austrlsa., Ltd., £10 Shs.	1	2
7/5	Do. Old, fully paid	10	15½
5/7	Do. New, fully paid	10	12½
5	Do. Cum. Pref.	10	12½
3/	Trust & Loan of Canada, £20 Shs.	5	4½
1/9½	Do. New £20 Shs.	3	2½
—	Tst. & Mort. of Iowa, Ltd., £10 Shs.	2½	½
4½	Do. Deb. Stk. Red.	100	92½
—	Tst., Loan, & Agency of Mexico, Ltd., £10 Shs.	2	½
—	Trsts., Exors, & Sec. Ins. Corp., Ltd., £10 Shs.	7	1½
4	Do. Irred. Deb. Stk.	100	106½
5/	Union Dsc., Ld., £10 Shs.	5	10½
—	Union Mort. & Agcy. of Aust., Ltd., £6 Shs.	2	—
6	Do. Pref. Stk	100	30
—	Do. 6 p. Pref. £6 Shs.	2	½
4½	Do. Deb. Stk	100	92½
4	Do. Deb. Stk	100	85½
5	Do. Deb. Stk. Red.	100	96½
1/6	U.S. Deb. Cor. Ltd., £8 Shs.	1	½
5½	Do. Cum. Pref. Stk	100	100½
4½	Do. Irred. Deb. Stk	100	105½
5	U.S. Tst. & Guar. Cor., Ltd., Pref. Stk	100	77½
6/	Van Dieman's	25	14
4	Walker's Prop. Cor., Ltd., Guar. 1 Mt. Deb. Stk.	100	109
4½	Wstr. Mort. & Inv., Ltd., Deb. Stk.	100	92½

FINANCIAL—TRUSTS.

Last Div.	Name.	Paid.	Price.
1/6	Afric City Prop., Ltd	1	1½
6	Do. Cum. Pref.	1	1 1/16
4	Alliance Invt., Ltd., Cm. 4½ p. c. Prefd.	100	73½
—	Do. Defd	100	12½
4	Do. Deb. Stk. Red.	100	106½
5	Amrcn. Invt., Ltd., Prfd.	100	114½
5	Do. Defd.	100	88½
4	Do. Deb. Stk. Red.	100	115½
4	Army & Navy Invt., Ltd., 5 p.c. Prefd.	100	81½
—	Do. Defd. Stk.	100	16½
4	Do. Deb. Stk.	100	102½
4	Atlas Investment, Ltd., Prefd. Stk.	100	70½
4½	Bankers' Invest., Ltd., Cum. Prefd.	100	103
1/0/0	Do. Defd	100	22½
4	Do. Deb. Stk	100	110
	Brewery & Comml. Inv., Ltd., £10 Shs.	5	6

Financial—Trusts (*continued*):—

Last Div.	Name.	Paid.	Price.
4	British Investment, Ltd., Cum. Prefd.	100	108
5	Do. Defd.	100	102½
4	Do. Deb. Stk.	100	108½
6	Brit. Steam. Invst., Ltd., Prefd.	100	116½
3/0/0	Do. Defd	100	68½
4½	Do. Perp. Deb. Stk	100	120½
1/9	Car Trust Invst., Ltd., £10 Shs.	2½	2
5	Do. Pref.	100	101
4	Do. Deb. Stk., 1915	100	103
4	Clnl. Sec., Ltd., Prefd.	100	104½
2½	Do. Defd.	100	47½
4	Consolidated, Ltd., Cum. 1st Pref.	100	91
4	Do. 5 p.c. Cm. 2nd do.	100	71½
—	Do. Defd.	100	14½
4½	Do. Deb. Stk.	100	112½
—	Deb. Secs. Invst.	100	105½
—	Do. 4 p.c. Cm. Pf. Sk.	100	106½
4½	Edinburgh Invest., Ltd., Cum. Prefd. Stk.	100	109½
4	Do. Deb. Stk. Red.	100	106½
5	Foreign, Amer. & Gen. Invt., Ltd., Prefd.	100	109½
2	Do. Defd.	100	47½
4	Do. Deb. Stk.	100	115½
5	Foreign & Colonial Invt., Ltd., Prefd.	100	136½
5½	Do. Defd.	100	97½
4½	Gas, Water & Gen. Invt., Cum. Prefd. Stk.	100	84½
3	Do. Defd. Stk.	100	36½
4	Do. Deb. Stk.	100	103
5	Gen. & Com. Invt., Ltd., Prefd. Stk.	100	106½
2	Do. Defd. Stk.	100	36½
4	Do. Deb. Stk.	100	113½
1/9	Globe Telegph. & Tst. Ltd.	10	11½
6	Do. do. Pref.	10	17
4	Govt. & Genl. Invt., Ld., Prefd.	100	84½
3½	Do. Defd.	100	42½
4½	Govts. Stk. & other Secs. Invt., Ltd., Prefd.	100	86½
1	Do. Defd.	100	25
4½	Do. Deb. Stk.	100	111
4	Do. do.	100	104
4½	Guardian Invt., Ltd., Pfd.	100	87½
—	Do. Defd.	100	19½
4	Do. Deb. Stk.	100	104
5	Indian & Gen. Inv., Ltd., Cum. Prefd.	100	107½
2½	Do. Defd.	100	56
4½	Do. Deb. Stk.	100	121½
5	Indust. & Gen. Tst., Ltd., Unified	100	98
3½	Do. Deb. Stk. Red.	100	100½
4½	Internat. Invt., Ltd., Cm. Prefd.	100	65½
—	Do. Defd.	100	7½
4	Do. Deb. Stk.	100	101
4	Invest. Tst. Cor. Ltd. Pfd.	100	100
4	Do. Defd.	100	91
4	Do. Deb. Stk. Red.	100	105
5	Ldn. Gen. Invest. Ltd., 5 p.c. Cum. Prefd.	100	109½
7½	Do. Defd.	100	118
4½	Ldn. Scot. Amer. Ltd. Pfd.	100	104½
£3	Do. Defd.	100	59½
4	Do. Deb. Stk.	100	111
4	Ldn. Tst., Ltd., Cum. Prfd. Stk.	100	102
4	Do. Defd. Stk.	100	72½
4	Do. Deb. Stk., Red.	100	108
3½	Do. Mt. Deb. Stk., Red.	100	104
5	Mercantile Invt. & Gen., Ltd., Prefd.	100	110
3	Do. Defd.	100	44½
4	Do. Deb. Stk.	100	110½
4	Merchants, Ltd., Pref. Stk.	100	104½
4	Do. Ord.	100	77½
4	Do. Deb. Stk.	100	117½
6	Municipal, Ltd., Prefd.	100	55½
—	Do. Defd.	100	17½
4½	Do. Debs.	100	112
4½	Do. Debs. "B"	100	99½
4½	Do. "C" Deb. Stk.	100	88½
5	New Investment, Ltd. Ord.	100	92½
5	Omnium Invest., Ltd., Pfd.	100	91½
1	Do. Defd.	100	26½
4	Do. Deb. Stk.	100	104
5/	Railway Deb. Tst. Ld., £20 Shs.	10	6½
5	Do. Debs., Red.	100	107½
4½	Do. Deb. Stk., 1911	100	107½
4	Do. do. 1927	100	107½
4	Railway Invst. Ltd., Prefd.	100	111
17/7	Do. Defd.	100	19
8/	Railway Share Trust & Agency "A"	8	5½
7½	Do. "B" Pref. Stk.	100	145½
4½	River Plate & Gen. Invt., Ltd., Prefd.	100	104
£3	Do. Defd.	100	50½
5	Scot. Invst., Ltd., Pfd. Stk.	100	94½
3½	Do. Defd.	100	26½
4	Do. Deb. Stk.	100	108
4½	Sec. Scottish Invst., Ltd., Cum. Prefd.	100	86½
£3	Do. Defd. Stk.	100	32
4	Do. Deb. Stk.	100	107½
5/	Sth. Africa Gold Tst., Ltd.	1	3½
6	Do. Cum. Pref	1	1
5½	Do. 1st Debs., Red.	100	102
1/9	Stock Conv. & Invest., Ltd., £5 Shs.	1	1½
4½	Do. do. 4½ p.c. Cm. Prf.	100	112½
3½	Do. Ldn. & N. W. 1st. Charge Prefd.	100	114½
4	Do do. 2nd Chge Prfd.	100	111
32/6	Do. do. Defd. Charge	100	29½
3	Do. N. East. 1 Chge Pfd.	100	91½

Financial—Trusts (*continued*):—

Last Div.	Name.	Paid.	Price.
37/6	Stock N. East Defd. Chge	100	36
6	Submarine Cables	100	138½
5	U.S. & S. Amer. Invest., Ltd., Prefd.	100	97½
2	Do. Defd.	100	25½
4	Do. Deb. Stk.	100	105½

GAS AND ELECTRIC LIGHTING.

Last Div.	Name.	Paid.	Price.
10/6	Alliance & Dublin Con. 10 p.c. Stand.	10	24
7/6	Do. 7 p.c. Stand.	10	16½
5	Austln. Gas Lght. (Syd.) Debs. 1909	100	106
5	Bay State of N. Jrsy. Sk. Fd. Tst. Bd., Red.	—	89½
3/	Bombay, Ltd.	5	6
2/4½	Do. New	4	5
12	Brentford Cons.	100	295½
9	Do. New	100	225½
5	Do. Pref.	100	142½
4	Do. Deb. Stk.	100	136
11½	Brighton & Hove Gen. Cons. Stk.	100	272½
8½	Do. "A" Cons. Stk.	100	197½
5	Bristol 5 p.c. Max.	100	129½
22/6	British Gas Light, Ltd.	20	55½
11/6	Bromley Gas Consumrs.' 10 p.c. Stand.	10	26
8/6	Do. 7 p.c. Stand.	10	21
—	Brush Electl. Enging., L.	—	1⅜
6	Do. 6 p.c. Pref.	—	2½
4½	Do. Deb. Stk.	100	112
4½	Do. 2 Deb. Stk., Red.	100	103½
5/	B. Ayres (New), Ltd.	10	9½
4	Do. Deb. Stk., Rd.	—	99
18/6	Cagliari Gas & Wtr., Ltd.	20	31
8/	Cape Town & Dist. Gas Light & Coke, Ltd.	10	16½
4½	Do. Pref.	10	12½
6	Do. 1 Mt. Debs. 1910	50	60
4/	Charing Cross & Strand Elec. Sup., Ltd.	5	13½
4½	Do. Cum. Pref.	5	6½
3/	Chelsea Elec. Sup., Ltd.	5	10
4½	Do. Deb. Stk., Red.	100	116
5	Chic. Edis'n Co. 1 Mt., Rd.	$1000	106
20/	City of Ldn. Elec. Lht., L.	10	26
—	Do. New £10 Shs.	5	18
6	Do. Cum. Pref.	10	18
5	Do. Deb. Stk., Red.	100	131½
13½	Commercial, Cons.	100	332½
10½	Do. New	100	252½
4½	Do. Deb. Stk.	100	152½
14	Continental Union, Ltd.	100	220
11	Do. Pref. Stk.	100	205
—	County of Lon. & Brush Prov. Elec. Lg., Ltd.	10	14½
6	Do. Cum. Pref.	10	15½
14	Croydon Comcl. Gas, Ld., "A" Stk., 10 p.c.	100	312½
11	Do. "B" Stk., 7 p.c.	100	260
5½	Crystal Pal. Dist. Ord. 5 p.c. Stk.	100	130½
5	Do. Pref. Stk.	100	143½
8/	European, Ltd.	10	24
6/	Do.	7½	17½
12¾	Gas Light & Ck Cons. Stk., "A" Ord.	100	284½
4	Do. "B" (4 p.c. Max.)	100	120½
10	Do. "C," "D," & "E" (Pref.)	100	306½
5	Do. "F" (Pref.)	100	152½
7½	Do. "G" (Pref.)	100	222½
7	Do. "H" (7 p.c. Max.)	100	197½
10	Do. "J" (Pref.)	100	306½
6	Do. "K"	100	184½
4	Do. Deb. Stk.	100	133½
4½	Do. do.	100	152½
6	Do. do.	100	204½
8/	Hong Kong & China, Ld.	10	14½
4/	House to House Elec. Light Sup., Ltd.	5	10½
7	Do. Cum. Pref.	5	11½
10	Imperial Continental	100	215½
3½	Do. Deb. Stk., Red	100	104½
2/	Malta & Medit., Ltd.	5	5½
7/	Metrop. Elec. Sup., Ltd.	10	18
4½	Do. 1 Mt. Deb. Stk.	100	119
5	Metro. of Melbrne. Dbs. 1908-12	100	111
4½	Do. Debs. 1918-22-4	100	108
10/	Monte Video, Ltd.	20	15½
9½	Newcastle-upon-Tyne	100	237½
—	Do. 3½ p.c. Deb. Stk.	100	117½
12/	Notting Hill Elec. Lig., Ltd.	10	19½
4/6	Oriental, Ltd.	5	8½
4/0½	Do. New	4½	7½
10½d.	Do. do. 1897	1	1½
3/6	Ottoman, Ltd.	5	4½
—	Para, Ltd.	—	—
6	People's Gas Lt. & C. of Chic. 2 Mt. 1904	100	105½
5	River Plate Elec. Lgt. & Trac., Ltd., 1 Deb. Stk	—	92½
8½	Royal Elec. of Montreal	—	144
4½	Do. 1 Mt. Deb.	100	104
11/	St. James' & Pall Mall Elec. Light, Ltd.	5	18
7	Do. Pref.	5	10½
4	Do. Deb. Stk., Red.	100	108½
10/	San Paulo, Ltd.	10	16½

Gas and Electric (*continued*):—

Last Div.	Name.	Paid.	Price.
10	Sheffield Unit. Gas Lt. "A"	100	251½
10	Do. "B"	100	251½
10	Do. "C"	100	251½
—	Sth. Ldn. Elec. Sup., Ld.	2	2½
5¼	South Metropolitan	100	133½
3	Do. 3 p.c. Deb. Stk.	100	104½
12	Tottenham & Edmonton Gas Lt. & C., "A"	100	290
9	Do. "B"	100	210
7/	Tuscan, Ltd.	10	13½
5	Do. Debs., Red.	100	101½
5/	West Ham 10 p.c. Stan.	5	12
8/	Wstmnstr. Elec.Sup.,Ld.	5	17

INSURANCE

Last Div.	Name.	Paid.	Price.
4/	Alliance, £20 Shs.	44/	10¼
10/	Alliance, Mar., & Gen., Ld., £100 Shs.	25	53
19/	Atlas, £50 Shs.	6	30½
12/	British & For. Marine, Ld., £20 Shs.	4	23
7½d.	British Law Fire, Ltd., £10 Shs.	1	1½
7/6	Clerical, Med., & Gen. Life, £25 Shs.	50/	16½
10/	Commercial Union, Ltd., £50 Shs.	5	44½
4	Do. "W. of Eng." Ter. Deb. Stk.	100	110½
£9	County Fire, £100 Shs.	80	100
5/	Eagle, £50 Shs.	5	½
4/	Employrs' Liability, Ltd., £10 Shs.	2	4¼
—	Empress, Ltd., £5 Shs.	1	—
21/	Equity & Law, £100 Shs.	6	23
7/6	General Life, £100 Shs.	5	15
4½d.	Gresham Life, £5 Shs.	15/	2½
2/6	Guardian, Ld., £10 Shs.	5	11½
10/	Imperial, Ltd., £20 Shs.	5	29½
3/6	Imperial Life, £20 Shs.	4	6¼
6/	Indemnity Mutual Mar., Ltd., £15 Shs.	3	11
1/	Lancashire, £20 Shs.	2	5
7½d.	Law Acc. & Contin., Ltd., £5 Shs.	10/	¾
5/	Law Fire, £100 Shs.	2½	18
9½d.	Law Guar. & Trust, Ltd., £10 Shs.	1	1½
9/	Law Life, £20 Shs.	2	25
2/9	Law Un. & Crown £10Shs	12/	7
4	Do. Deb. Stk., 1942	100	110½
14/6	Legal & General, £50Shs.	8	15½
9d.	Lion Fire, Ltd., £8½ Shs.	1½	¾
14/	Liverpool & London & Globe, Stk	2	52
10/	Do. Globe £1 Ann	—	35½
35/	London, £25 Shs.	12½	60
4/	Lond. & Lanc. Fire, £25Shs	2½	19½
2/	Lond. & Lanc. Life, £25Shs	2	7
1/	Lond. & Prov. Mar., Ld., £10 Shs.	1	¾
6/	Lond. Guar. & Accident, Ltd., £5 Shs.	2	11½
10/	Marine, Ltd., £25 Shs.	4½	41
2/	Maritime, Ltd., £10 Shs.	2	4
1/6	Merc. Mar., Ld., £10Shs.	2½	2¼
—	National Marine, Ltd., £9 Shs.	1	½
10/	N. Brit. & Merc., £25Shs.	6¼	12
20/	Northern, £100 Shs.	10	81
40/	Norwich Union Fire, £100 Shs.	12	125½
10/	Ocean Acc. & Guar., fy. pd.	5	22
2/	Do. £5 Shs.	1	4
7/6	Ocean, Marine, Ltd.	2½	8½
2/	Palatine, £10 Shs.	2	3½
2/6	Pelican, £10 Shs.	1	3½
21/	Phœnix, £50 Shs.	5	42
£6	Provident, £100 Shs.	10	31
5/	Railway Passngrs., £10Shs.	2	8½
2/6	Rock Life, £5 Shs.	10/	4½
8	Royal Exchange	100	355
18/	Royal, £20 Shs.	3	53½
4/	Sun, £10 Shs.	10/	11¼
3/9	Sun Life, £10 Shs.	7½	14½
6	Thames & Mrsey. Marine, Ltd., £20 Shs.	2	10
9	Union, £10 Shs.	4	24½
4/	Union Marine, £20 Shs.	2½	8½
12/	Universal Life, £100 Shs.	12	42
2/	World Marine, £5 Shs.	2	1½

IRON, COAL, AND STEEL.

Last Div.	Name.	Paid.	Price.
—	Barrow Hæm. Steel, Ltd.	7½	2
9/	Do. 6 p.c. 2nd Pref.	7½	6½
10/	Bolck., Vaugh. & C., Ld.	20	16½
6/	Do. £8 liab.	12	9
7/6	Brown, J. & Co., Ltd., £20 Shs.	15	20
7/6	Consett Iron, Ld., £10Shs.	7½	29½
4/	Do. 8 p.c. Cum. Pref.	5	11
7/6	Ebbw Vale Steel, Iron & Coal, Ltd., £23 Shs.	20	6
15/	General Mining Assn., Ld.	5½	7½
8/	Harvey Steel Co. of Gt. Britain, Ltd.	10	28
5	Lehigh V. Coal 1 Mt. 5 p.c. Guar. Gd. Cp. Bds.	—	95½
42/6	Nantyglo & Blaina Iron, Ltd., Pref.	862	94½
1/	Nerbudda Coal & Iron, Ltd., £3 Shs.	56/	1⁄16
—	Newport Abrcrn. Bk. Vein Steam Coal, Ltd.	10	4½
5/	New Sharlston Coll., Ltd. Pref.	20	9½
4½d.	Nw. Vancvr. Coal & Ld., L.	1	½
2/6	North's Navigation Coll. (1889) Ltd.	5	2½
10/	Do. 10 p.c. Cum. Pref.	5	6½
—	Rhymney Iron, Ltd.	5	1½
	Do. New, £5 Shs.	4½	½
5	Do. Mt. Debs., Red.	100	98½
5	Shelton Irn., Stl. & Cl. Co., Ltd., 1 Chg. Debs., Red.	100	99½
50/	Sth. Hetton Coal, Ltd.	100	—
2/	Vickers & Maxim, Ltd.	1	3¼
5	Do. 5 p.c. Prfd. Stk.	100	127½

SHIPPING.

Last Div.	Name.	Paid.	Price.
12/	African Stm. Ship, £20 Shs.	16	10½
15/	Do. Fully-paid	20	14½
2/	Amazon Steam Nav., Ltd.	12½	9
8/	Castle Mail Pakts., Ltd., £20 Shs.	14	16
3½	Do. 1st Deb. Stk., Red.	100	102
6/	China Mutual Steam, Ltd.	5	2½
6	Do. Cum. Pref.	10	9½
10/	Cunard, Ltd.	20	9½
5/	Do. £20 Shs.	10	3¼
4½	Furness, Withy, & Co., Ltd., 1 Mt. Dbs., Red.	100	107
6/	General Steam	15	8
5/	Do. 5 p.c. Pref., 1874	10	9
5/	Do. 5 p.c. Pref., 1877	10	8½
20/4½	Leyland & Co., Ltd.	10	25
7/	Do. 7 p.c. Cum. Pref.	10	15
2/11	Do. 4½ p.c. Cum. Pre-Pf.	3	10½
4	Do. 1st Mt. Dbs., Red.	100	105½
7/6	Mercantile Steam, Ltd.	5	7½
6/4½	New Zealand Ship., Ltd.,	6	5
4	Do. Deb. Stk., Red.	100	104
5/	Orient Steam, Ltd.	10	5
5	P. & O. Steam, Cum. Prefd.	100	147½
19	Do. Defd.	100	232½
3½	Do. Deb. Stk.	100	117
5	Richelieu & Ont., 1st Mt. Debs., Red.	100	100
30/	Royal Mail, £100 Shs.	60	53
2/6	Shaw, Sav., & Alb., Ltd., "A" Pref.	5	5½
5/	Do. "B" Ord.	5	3½
8/	Union Steam, Ltd.	20	20
4/	Do. New £20 Shs.	10	8½
4	Do. Deb. Stk., Red.	100	106
7/	Union of N.Z., Ltd.	10	10
5½	Wilson's & Fur.-Ley., 5½ p.c. Cum. Pref.	10	10½
4½	Do. 1 Mt. Db. Sk., Rd.	100	106½

*** *Tea Shares will be found in the Special Table following.*

TELEGRAPHS AND TELEPHONES.

Last Div.	Name.	Paid.	Price.
4	African Direct, Ltd., Mort. Debs., Red.	100	102
—	Amazon Telegraph, Ltd.	10	7½
15/	Anglo-American, Ltd.	100	60½
30/	Do. 6 p.c. Prefd. Ord.	100	109½
—	Do. Defd. Ord.	100	12½
3/	Brazilian Submarine, Ltd.	10	16
5	Do. Debs., 2 Series	100	114

Telegraphs and Telephones (*continued*):—

Last Div.	Name.	Paid.	Price.
4/	Chili Telephone, Ltd.	5	3½
$1½	Comcial. Cable, $100 Shs.	—	160
4	Do. Stg. 500-yr. Deb. Stk. Red.	100	105
2½d.	Consd. Telpehone Constr., &c., Ltd.	10/	½
6/	Cuba Submarine, Ltd.	10	6½
10/	Do. 10 p.c. Pref.	10	14½
2/	Direct Spanish, Ltd.	5	4½
5/	Do. 10 p.c. Cum. Pref.	5	10½
4½	Do. Debs.	50	104½
3/	Direct U.S. Cable, Ltd.	20	10½
2/6	Eastern, Ltd.	10	17
3/	Do. 6 p.c. Cum. Pref.	10	18½
4	Do. Mt. Deb. Stk., Red.	100	127
2/6	Eastern Exten., Aus., & China, Ltd.	10	18
5	Do. (Aus. Gov. Sub.) Deb., Red.	100	101
5	Do. do. Bearer	100	101½
4	Do. Mort. Deb. Stk.	100	128½
5	Eastn. & S. Afric., Ltd., Mort. Deb. 1900	100	101
5	Do. Bearer	100	101½
4	Do. Mort. Debs. 1909	100	103½
4	Do. Mort. Debs. (Maur. Subsidy)	25	108½
5/	Grt. Nthn. Copenhagen	10	29½
5	Do. Debs., Ser. B., Red.	100	101½
12/6	Indo-European, Ltd.	25	53½
6	London Platino-Brazilian, Ltd., Debs. 1904	100	107½
4/	Montevideo Telph., Ltd., 6 p.c. Pref.	5	2½
3/	National Telephone, Ltd.	5	5½
6/	Do. Cum. 1 Pref.	10	16
6/	Do. Cum. 2 Pref.	10	16
5	Do. Non-Cum. 3 Pref.	5	5½
3½	Do. Deb. Stk., Red.	100	102½
4d.	Oriental Telephone, Ltd.	1	11⁄16
4	Pac. & Euro. Tlg. Dbs., Rd.	100	106½
4/	Reuter's, Ltd.	8	8½
5/	Un. Riv. Plate Telph., Ltd.	5	4½
5	Do. Deb. Stk., Red.	100	106½
—	West African Telg., Ltd.	10	4
5	Do. 5 p.c. Mt. Debs., Red.	100	100½
—	W. Coast of America, Ltd.	10	½
3/	Western & Brazilian, Ltd.	15	11½
3/	Do. 5 p.c. Pref. Ord.	7½	7½
—	Do. Defd. Ord.	7½	4½
4	Do. Deb. Stk., Red.	100	107½
1/	W. India & Panama, Ltd.	10	½
6/	Do. Cum. 1 Pref.	10	7½
6/	Do. Cum. 2 Pref.	10	6
5	Do. Debs., Red.	100	106½
7	West. Union, 1 Mt. 1902 ($	1000	107½
6	Do. 6 p.c. Stg. Bds., Rd.	100	102½

TRAMWAYS AND OMNIBUS.

Last Div.	Name.	Paid.	Price.
1/6	Anglo-Argentine, Ltd.	5	3½
6	Do. Deb. Stk.	100	125
4/	Barcelona, Ltd.	10	12
5	Do. Deb., Red.	100	105½
7/6	Belfast Street Trams.	10	16½
—	Blackpl. & Fltwd. Tram., £10 Shs.	8	13
10/	Bordeaux Tram. & O. Ltd.	10	11½
5	Do. Cum. Pref.	10	11
—	Brazilian Street Ry., Ltd.	2	½
—	British Elec. Trac., Ltd.	10	16
—	B. Ayres & Belg. Tram., Ltd., 6 p.c. Cum. Pref.	5	—
6	Do. 1 Deb. Stk.	100	—
—	B. Ayres. Gd. Nat., Ltd., 6 p.c 1 Deb. Bds., Red.	100	55½
5½	Do. Pref. Debs., Red.	100	94½
1/	Calais, Ltd.	5	1
—	Calcutta, Ltd.	10	3½
—	Carthagena & Herr., Ltd.	10	3
5	Do. Deb., Red.	100	90
5	City of B'ham. Trams., Ltd., 5 p.c. Cum. Pref.	5	5½
4	Do. 1 Mort. Debs., Rd.	100	106½
3/9	City of B. Ayres, Ltd.	5	7
2/3	Do. Ext. £5 Shs.	3	4½
6	Do. Deb. Stk	100	145
1/6	Edinburgh Street Tram.	4	4
1/	Glasgow Tram. & Omni. Ltd., £9 Shs.	8	3
3/7½	Imperial, Ltd.	6	14½
3/	Lond., Deptfd, & Greenwich, Prefd.	5	3½
nil	Do. Defd.	5	1
10½	Lond. Gen. Omni., Ltd.	100	195
4	Do. Deb., Red.	100	115½

Tramways and Omnibus (*continued*):—

Last Div.	Name.	Paid.	Price.
4/9½	London Road Car	6	10½
28/6	Do. Red. 1 Mt. Deb. Stk.	100	108½
5	London St. Rly. (Prov., Ont.), Mt. Debs.	100	110
12/6	London St. Trams.	—	2
12/9	London Trams., Ltd.	10	10
6/	Do. Non-Cum. Pref.	10	10½
5	Do. Mt. Db. Stk., Rd.	100	102
5	Lynn & Boston 1 Mt. 1924 $	1000	107
5	Milwaukee Elec. Cons. Mt. $	1000	100½
5	Minneapolis St. 1 Cons. Mt $	1000	96
5	Montreal St. Dbs., 1908	100	109
4½	Do. Debs., 1922	100	107
6/	Nth. Metropolitan	10	13
1/9½	Nth. Staffords., Ltd.	6	5
5/6	Provincial, Ltd.	10	7
6/	Do. Cum. Pref.	10	13½
5	St. Paul City, 1937 $	1000	96
5	Do. Guar. Twin City Rap. Trans. $	1000	96
5/	Southampton	10	6½
5/	South London	10	5½
7/6	Sunderland, Ltd.	10	6½
4½	Toronto 1 Mt., Red.	100	106
2/6	Tramways Union, Ltd.	5	6½
4½	Do. Deb., Red.	100	109
5/	Vienna General Omnibus.	5	5½
5	Do. 5 p.c. Mt. Deb., Red.	100	103½
4/	Wolverhampton, Ltd.	10	6½

WATER WORKS.

Last Div.	Name.	Paid.	Price.
8/	Antwerp, Ltd.	20	22
6/	Cape Town District, Ltd.	5	7
10½	Chelsea	100	325
5	Do. Pref. Stk.	100	178½
4½	Do. Pref. Stk., 1875	100	158½
4½	Do. Deb. Stk.	100	160½
5/6	City St. Petersburg, Ltd.	13	11
5/	Colne Valley	10	15½
4	Do. Deb. Stock	100	137½
£4	Consol. of Rosar., Ltd., 4 p.c. 1 Deb. Stk., Red.	100	92
8	East London	100	225½
4½	Do. Deb. Stk.	100	160
3	Do. Deb. Stk., Red.	100	106
37/6	Grand Junction (Max. 10 p.c.) "A"	50	117½
18/9	Do. "B"	25	
18/9	Do. "C" (Max. 7½ p.c.)	25	54½
35/	Do. "D" (Max. 7 p.c.)	50	102½
4	Do. Deb. Stock	100	145½
13	Kent	100	360½
7	Do. New (Max. 7 p.c.)	100	215½
7/	Kimberley, Ltd.	7	5
6	Do. Debs., Red.	100	104½
6	Do. Deb. Stk., Red.	100	107½
10	Lambeth (Max. 10 p.c.)	100	297½
7½	Do. (Max. 7½ p.c.), 50 & 25	—	230½
4	Do. Deb. Stock	100	142½
3	Do. Red. Deb. Stock	100	103
10/	Montevideo, Ltd.	20	16
5	Do. 1 Deb. Stk.	100	108½
5	Do. 2 Deb. Stk.	100	103½
132/9	New River New	100	442½
4	Do. Deb. Stk.	100	144½
4	Do. Deb. Stk. "B"	100	144½
—	Odessa, Ltd., "A" 6 p.c. Prefd.	20	—
nil	Do. "B" Deferred	20	—
4	Portland Con. Mt. "B," 1927	—	102½
8/	Seville, Ltd.	20	12
5/6	Southend "Addl." Ord.	10	17½
6	Southwark and Vauxhall	100	157½
6	Do. "D" Shares (7½ p.c. max.)	100	154½
5	Do. Pref. Stock	100	176½
4	Do. "A" Deb. Stock	100	144½
3	Staines Resvirs. Jt. Com. Gua. Deb. Stk., Red.	100	105
7/	Tarapaca, Ltd.	10	9
10	West Middlesex	100	302½
4½	Do. Deb. Stk.	100	162½
3	Do Deb. Stk.	100	106

Prices Quoted on the Leading Provincial Exchanges.

ENGLISH.

In quoting the markets, B stands for Birmingham; Bl for Bristol; M for Manchester; L for Liverpool; and S for Sheffield.

CORPORATION STOCKS.

Chief Market.	Int or Div.	NAME.	Amount paid.	Price.
M	3½	Bolton, Red. 1935 ..	100	113½
M	3½	Burnley, Red. 1933..	100	114
M	3½	Bury, Red. 1946	100	116½
L	3½	Liverpool, Red. 1925	100	102¼
B	3½	Longton, 1932	100	106
M	4	Oldham Prp. Db. Sk.	100	143
M	£1	Do. Gas&W.Ann.		34½
S	4	Rotherham 4 p.c., Red. 1927...... [£	1 an	112
M	3½	Runcorn Red. 1923..	100	104
S	2¾	Sheffield Water Ann.	100	118½
S	3	Do.	3 an	90
L	3½	Southport Red. 1936 {	5 an 100	112
L	3	Do. Red. 1914..	100	102½
M	3	Todmorden, Red. 1914	100	102

RAILWAYS.

Chief Market.	Int or Div.	NAME.	Amount paid.	Price.
B	4½	Bridgewater Pref. ..	100	135½
M	1¾	Cleator & Workton.	100	76
M	4	Do. 1883 Pref. ..	100	109
L	4	Cockermth. K. & P.	100	113½
L	4	Isle of Man	5	6¾
L	5	Do. Pref.	5	6½
L	3	Liverpool Overhead	10	10¾
L	4	Do. Deb. Stk. ..	100	110
L	5	Do. Pref.	10	16
L	6¼	Maryport & Carlisle	100	172
Bl	45/	Neath & Brecon "A"	100	65½
M	4¾	Oldham, Ashton. &c.	10	16¾
Bl	5¼	Penarth Harbour ..	100	182½
Bl	4	Do. Deb. Stk. ..	100	145
Bl	3½	Do. Deb. Stk. ..	100	127
Bl	1¾	Ross & Monmouth..	20	5¼
Bl	6	Do. Pref.	20	42½
M	3	Southport & Cheshire Deb. Stk.	100	104½
M	nil.	Do. Pref.	100	23½
Bl	2¾	West Somerset Gu...	100	96½
Bl	5	Wye Val. Deb. Stk.	100	162

BANKS.

Chief Market.	Int or Div.	NAME.	Amount paid.	Price.
L	8/	Adelphi, L., £20 Shs.	10	16⅛
L	12/6	Bk of L'pool, L., £100 Sh	12½	39¾
B	5/6	Brmnghm. Dis. & C., Ltd., £20 Shs.....	4	10¾
B	6/3	Co. of Staffs., L., £40	5	13¾
S	17½	Crompton & Evans, Ltd., £20 Shs	4	15
M	14/	Lancs. & Yorks, Ltd., £20 Shs.....	10	31¾
L	30/	Livrpl. Union, Ltd., £100 Shs.	20	60¾
M	24/	Manchester & Co., Ltd., £100 Shs. ..	16	61½
M	20/	Mnchstr. & Livrpool. Dis., Ltd., £60 Shs.	10	51⅝
M	1/6	Mer. of Lancashire, Ltd., £20 Shs.....	3	6½
L	16/	Nth. & Sth. Wales, Ltd., £40 Shs.....	10	35¾
B	20/	Notts Joint St., Ltd., £50 Shs..........	10	26¾
S	15	Sheffield Banking, Ltd., £50 Shs.....	17½	51½
S	20	Do. & Rotherham, Ltd., £50 Shs...	8	26¾
S	10	Do. & Hallamsh., Ltd., £100 Shs..	25	56
S	10	Do. Union, Ltd., £40 Shs.........	10	25½
M	12/	Union of Manchester, Ltd., £25 Shs.. ..	11	27¾
M	10/	Williams, Deacon, &c. Ltd., £50 Shs.....	8	25⅝
Bl	20	Wilts & Dorset, Ltd., £50 Shs..........	10	49½
S	5/6	York City & Co., Ltd., £10 Shs.....	3	12⅝

BREWERIES

Chief Market.	Int or Div.	NAME.	Amount paid.	Price.
B	6	Ansell & Sons Pref.	10	16
B	5	Do. Debs.	100	110
L	9/	Bent's	10	17¾
L	6	Do. Cum. Pref...	10	14½
L	4½	Do. Deb. Stk. ..	100	111
L	13/6	Birkenhead, £5 paid	5	22¼
L	13/6	Do. £10 paid....	10	27½
M	9/	Boddington's	9	19½
M	5	Do. Cum. Pref...	10	12¾
M	4	Do. Deb. Stk. ..	100	107½
B	4½	Butler & Co. Db. Stk	100	111
M	6	Chesters' Cum. Pref.	10	13½
M	4½	Do. Debs.	100	109
S	10/	Clarkson's Ord.	10	23
S	6	Do. Cum. Prf. Stk.	10	14
M	4	Dutton & Co. Db. Sk.	100	104
M	4½	Hardy's Crown Debs.	100	111
B	10/	Holt	10	18
B	5	Do. Cum. Pref...	10	12⅝
B	4	Do. Debs.	100	109½
B	12/6	Lichfield	10	—
B	5	Do. Cum. Pref...	10	12
M	5½	Manchester Deb. Stk.	100	142
B	6/	Mitchell, H., & Co.	10	39½
B	6	Do. Cum. Pref...	10	15½
Bl	6	Oakhill Pref........	10	16½

Breweries (*continued*):—

Chief Market.	Int. or Div.	NAME.	Amount paid.	Price.
M	5/	Springwell	10	10½
M	7	Do. Pref.	10	13½
Bl	9	Stroud	10	16½
Bl	6	Do. Pref	10	14½
M	6/	Taylor's Eagle......	10	11¾
M	7	Do. Cum. Pref ..	10	13½
M	5½	Do. Deb. Stk. ..	100	117½
S	10	Tennant Bros £20 shs	15	33½
S	10	Wheatley & Bates ..	10	14½
S	6	Do. Cum. Pref.	10	12¾

CANALS AND DOCKS.

Chief Market.	Int. or Div.	NAME.	Amount paid.	Price.
Bl	8	Hill's Dry Dk. &c. £20	18	9
M	4	Manc. Ship Canal 1st Mt. Deb. Stk.	100	104
M	4	Do. 2nd do.	100	103½
L	36/3	Mersey Dck. & Harb.	an.	117¾
L	35/	Do.	an.	116½
M	10/	Rochdale Canal	100	36½
B	37/6	Staff. & Worc. Canal	100	74½
B	4½	Do. Deb. Stk....	100	137
Bl	4	Swansea Harb......	100	114
B	27/6	Warwick & Birm. Cnl	100	65
B	12/6	Do. & Napton do.	100	22½

COMMERCIAL & INDUSTRIAL.

Chief Market.	Int. or Div.	NAME.	Amount paid.	Price.
L	5	Agua Santa Mt. Debs	100	100
M	8/	Armitage, Sir E. & Sns Ltd	10	19
M	4	Do. Deb. 1910 ..	100	101
L	6	Ang. Chil. Nit. 1 Mt. Debs., 1919 ..	100	109½
Bl	11	Bath Stone Firms ..	10	19
M	4/9½	Barlow & Jones, Ltd., £10 Shs.	8	10⅝
B	12/6	Birmgham. Ry. Car.	10	16
B	6	Do. Pref.	10	15½
B	5/	Do. Small Arms	5	13½
M	£12	Blackpool Pier......	100	277½
M	5	Do. Tower Debs.	50	54½
M	3/	Do. Wl. Gar. & P.	5	4
Bl	10	Bristl. & S. W. R. Wag. £20 Shs..........	3	6
Bl	8	Do. Wag. & Carri. £10 Shs..........	10	15
M	7/	Crosses & Winkwth. Ltd..............	5	12½
L	5	G. Angus & Co. Pref.	10	13½
Bl	5	Gloster. Carri. & W.		10½
Bl	5	Gt. Wstn. Cttn., Ltd.	20	15
M	6	Hetherington, L. Prf.	10	8½
M	4½	Do. Debs., 1910	100	98½
B	7½d.	Hinks (J. & Son), Ltd.	1	27/
S	20/	Jessop & Sons, £50 Sh	30	27½
S	10	Kayser, Ellsn. & Co. L.	5	11¾
S	6	Do. Pref.	5	7¾
M	7/6	Kellner-Partgton., L.	5	14½
M	4½	Do. Debs., 1914..	100	106
M	5	Kerr Thread, Ltd., Debs..............	100	101
B	17/	King's Norton Metal, £10 Shs..........	8½	19½
M	5/	Lancashire & Yorks. Wagon, Ltd.	10	10½
L	10/	Liverpool Exch., Ltd.	20	27½
L	45/	Do. Grain Stge, Ltd.	50	108
L	5/	Do. Rubber, Ltd...	5	5⅜
M	9d.	Manchester Bond. Whse., L., £10 Shs.	4½	2½
M	3/9	Do. Comcial. Bldgs., Ltd., £10 Shs.	5	10½
M	4/	Do. No. 2, £10 Shs.	5	10½
M	2/6	Do. No. 3, £10 Shs.	5	7½
M	5/	Do. Corn, &c., Exchange, Ltd.	10	16¾
M	4	Do. Debs.	100	126
M	8	Do. Ryl. Exchge, L.	100	237½
B	5/	Midland Rlwy. Car. Wgn., Ld., £20 Sh.	10	14½
Bl	5	Millers & Corys Dbs.	100	100½
B	12/6	Mint, Brgham., Ltd.	5	7⅝
B	5	Do. Debs.	25	108
B	10/	Nettlefolds, Ltd.....	10	49½
B	5	Do. Pref.	10	15½
S	9	Nth. Centrl. Wgn., L.	5	8⅝
B	15/	Patnt. Nut & Bolt, L.	10	34
B	5	Do. Pref.	10	14⅝
B	1/	Perry & Co., Ltd. ..	1	27/6
B	6d.	Do. Pref.	1	27/6
S	10	Round, J., & Co., L., £10 Shs.	6	12
S	15	Rodgers, J., & Sons, L.	100	213
M	18/9	Rylands & Sons, Ltd., £20	15	38½
M	2/6	Do. paid up	20	43½
M	4	Do. Debs. .. 1909	100	106
S	5	Sanderson Brs. & Co., Ltd, Debs.	100	102
M	4½	Schwabe, S., & Co., Ltd., 1 Debs. 1914	100	102
S	7½	Sheffield Forge & Rolling, Ltd.	10	11½
L	80/	Southport Pier, Ltd.	100	88½
L	2½	Do. W. Gdns., Ltd.	5	3½
Bl	5	Spillers & Bakers, Ltd, £10 Shs.	9	16
Bl	6	Do. Pref.	10	14½
B	5/	Union Rolling Stock, Ltd., £20 Shs....	5	7½
M	5/	Victoria Pr., S'port, L.	5	4½
Bl	8	Western Wagon & Property, Ltd.....	6	9½
S	10	Wostenholm, G., & Son, Ltd., £25 Shs.	20	22½
S	6½	Yorksh. Wagon, Ltd.	2	2¾

FINANCIAL, TRUSTS, &c.

Chief Market.	Int. or Div.	NAME.	Amount paid.	Price.
M	1/	Manchstr. Trst. £10 Shs.............	2	13/9
M	1/3	N. of Eng. T. Deb. & A., Ltd. £10 Shs.	2½	27/3
M	3½	Do. 1 Mt. Debs...	100	97½
L	—	Pacific Ln. & Inv., L.	2½	2¾
L	4	Do. Deb. Stk.....	100	103
L	—	United Trst., L. Prfd.	100	72½
L	—	Do. Deferred....	100	62½

GAS.

Chief Market.	Int. or Div.	NAME.	Amount paid.	Price.
Bl	5	Bristol Gas (5 p.c. mx.)	100	128½
Bl	4	Do. 1st Deb.	100	137
S	10	Gt. Grimsby "C" ..	10	201
L	10	Liverpool Utd. "A"	100	235
L	7	Do. "B"......	100	176
L	4	Do. Deb.	100	137
S	10	Sheffield Gas "A," "B," "C"	100	248
B	10½	Wolverhampton	100	230
B	3	Do. 6 p.c. Pref...	100	172

INSURANCE.

Chief Market.	Int. or Div.	NAME.	Amount paid.	Price.
M	6	Equitable F. & Acc. £5 Shs.	1	38/6
L	2/	Liverpool Mortgage £10 Shs.	2	1$\frac{1}{16}$
M	4/	Mchester. Fire £20 Shs	2	7¾
M	5/	National Boiler & G., Ltd., £10 Shs.	3	13½
L	2/	Reliance Mar., Ltd., £10 Shs.	2	4$\frac{1}{16}$
L	4/	Sea, Ltd., £10 Shs...	2	10$\frac{1}{16}$
L	8/	Stnd. Mar., L., £20 Sh.	4	8
L	1/	State Fire, L., £20 Sh.	1	2

COAL, IRON, AND STEEL.

Chief Market.	Int. or Div.	NAME.	Amount paid.	Price.
Bl.	10	Albion Stm. Coal ..	10	11½
M	15/9	And. Knowles & S., Ltd., £37½ Shs. ..	23½	11½
M	5	Do. Mt. Debs. 1908	100	105½
Bl.	1/½	Ashton V. Iron	100	26
S	12½	Bessemer, Ltd.	10	20⅛
S	5	Do. Pref.	10	12½
S	12/6	Briggs, H., & Co., "A" £15 Shs.....	12½	15½
S	8/6	Do. "B" £15 Shs.	8½	9⅜
S	20	Brown Baley's Stl., L.	10	32½
S	5	Brown, J., & Co., Cum. Pref.	10	13⅛
S	5	Cammell, C. & Co., Ltd.	85	12⅝
S	5	Do. Pref.	5	6$\frac{1}{16}$
M	5	Chatterley Whitfield. Col., Debs., 1905..	100	100½
Bl	—	Davis, D., & Sons, Ld.	10	10
M	5	Evans, R., & Co., Ltd., Deb., 1910 ..	100	101
S	12½	Fox, S., & Co., Ltd., £100 Shs.	80	178½
Bl	10	Gt. Wstn. Col., L., "A"	5	10½
Bl	6	Do. "B"	5	4½
Bl	3	Main Colliery, Ltd.	10	7½
B	5/	Muntz's Metal, Ltd.	5	8½
B	5	Do. Pref.......	5	6½
M	2/6½	Nth. Lonsd. Iron and Steel, Ltd., £10 Sh.	8½	2½
Bl	6	North's Nav. Coll., Ltd., Debs.	100	105
S	30/	Parkgate Irn. & Stl., Ltd., £100 Shs. ..	75	69½
M	6	Pearson & Knls., Ld., "A" Cum. Pref...	50	46
B	10/	Sandwell Pk. Col., L.	10	17
M	6/3	Sheepbridge Coal and Iron, Ltd., "A"	25	18½
M	2/6	Do. "B"	10	7½
M	5	Do. "C" Gua. Pf.	25	28½
Bl	4	South Wales Coll., Ltd., "A"	17	8½
S	30/	Staveley Coal & Iron, Ltd., "A" £100 Sh.	60	80¾
S	30/	Do. "C"	60	82
M	1/10½	Tredegar Iron & Cl., Ld., "A" £10 Sh.	7½	2½
M	1½	Do. "B" Stk. ..	100	35
M	6/	Wigan Cl. & Irn., Ld.	10	7
M	4/6	Do. £10 Shs.	7½	4

SHIPPING.

Chief Market.	Int. or Div.	NAME.	Amount paid.	Price.
Bl	6	Bristol St. Nav. Pref.	10	11½
L	15/	Brit. & Af. St. Nav..	10	13½
L	3/10½	British & Estn. Ltd.	6½	3½
L	10/	Pacific Stm. Nav., L.	25	24½
L	30/	Wst. Ind. & Pac. St. Ltd., £25 Shs....	20	26½

TRAMWAYS, &c.

Chief Market.	Int. or Div.	NAME.	Amount paid.	Price.
B	5/	Brmngh. & Aston, L.	5	11
B	5/	Do. Mid., Ltd...	10	7½
Bl	6/	Bristol Tr. & Car., Ltd..	10	20½
Bl	4/	Do. Debs.	100	122
L	6	I. of Man Elec., L., Pref.	1	1$\frac{1}{16}$
M	15/	Manchester C. & T., L., "A" £20 Shs.	15	27½
M	10/	Do. "B"	10	18½

WATER WORKS.

Chief Market.	Int. or Div.	NAME.	Amount paid.	Price.
Bl	7	Bristol	25	62½
Bl	7	Do.	20	47½
Bl	58/	Do. 7 p.c. max. ..	100	158½
Bl	4½	Do. Pref.	20	32½
Bl	5	Do. Pref.	10	17½
Bl	3½	Do. Deb.	100	129½
M	10	Fylde "A"........	100	335
M	7	Do. "B"	100	224
B	6	S. Staffs. Ord. "A"	100	165
B	—	Do. "B"	100	164
B	4	Do. Deb. Stk.	100	140
B	5	Do. Pf "A" "B" "C"	100	170
M	£3½	Stockport District ..	100	184½
B	2/	Wolverhampton New.	5	6½

SCOTTISH.

In quoting the markets, E stands for Edinburgh, and G for Glasgow.

RAILWAYS.

Chief Market.	Int. or Div.	NAME.	Nom. Amount	Price.
E	5½	Arbroath and Forfar	25	49½
G	1¾	Callander and Oban .	10	7$\frac{1}{16}$
G	4	Do. Deb. Stock	100	144
G	4½	Do. Pref.......	10	14½
G	4	Cathct. Dist. Deb. Stk.	100	146
E	5	Edin. and Bathgate .	100	179½
E	7	Forth & Clyde Junc.	100	222½
G	4	Lanarks. and Ayrsh.	10	13⅝
G	4	Do. & Dumbartons.	10	14$\frac{1}{16}$
G	4	Do. Deb. Stk.	100	147

BANKS.

Chief Market.	Int. or Div.	NAME.	Nom. Amount	Price.
G	12	Bank of Scotland ..	100	351
G	16	British Linen	100	494
G	8	Caledonian, Ltd.....	2½	97
G	10	Clydesdale, Ltd.	10	22½
G	16	Commercl. of Scot., L.	20	83
G	16	National of Scot. Ld.	100	408
G	8	Royal of Scotland ..	100	228
G	11	Union of Scotland, L.	10	26½

BREWERIES.

Chief Market.	Int. or Div.	NAME.	Nom. Amount	Price.
E	5	Bernard, Thos. Pref.	10	10½
E	5	Bernard, T. & J., Cum. Pref........	10	12½
G	20	Highland Distilleries	3½	10$\frac{1}{16}$

CANALS AND DOCKS.

Chief Market.	Int. or Div.	NAME.	Nom. Amount	Price.
G	4	Clyde Nav. 4 p.c....	100	123½
G	3½	Do. 3½ p.c.......	100	105
G	3½	Greenock Harb. "A"	100	101
G	2	Do. "B"	100	38½

MISCELLANEOUS.

Chief Market.	Int. or Div.	NAME.	Nom. Amount	Price.
G	4½	Alexander & Co. Debs.	100	110
G	5	Alexander Ferguson, & Co. Cum. Pref..	10	11½
G	5	Baird, H., & Sns. C. P.	10	12½
E	12	Barry, Ostlere, & Co.	7½	12½
E	6	Do. Cum. Pref...	10	14½
G	5	Brown, Stewart, Deb.	100	84
E	7½	Broxburn Oil	5½	8½
E	6	Do. Cum. Pref...	10	11½
E	7	Edinburgh & Dist. Tram. Cum Pref.	5	8⅝
E	5	Gilroy, Sns, & Co. Dbs.	100	99
G	9	Glasgow Cot. Spin...	6	6
G	30/	Do. Royal Exchg.	46	110
G	—	Pumpherston Oil Pf.	10	8½
E	7	Scottish Assam Tea	10	11
E	5	Scottish Waggon....	10	12½
G	5	Stoddard & Co. Pref.	10	12½

FINANCIAL, LAND, AND INVESTMENT.

Chief Market.	Int. or Div.	NAME.	Nom. Amount	Price.
G	1/	Assets Co..........	1	47/
E	4½	Investors' Mort. Pref.	100	96½
E	4	Do. Deb. Stk....	100	102½
E	4	Nthn. Inv. N. Zeal. Deb. Stk.	100	107
E	4	N. of Scot. Canadian Deb. Stk.	100	106
E	4½	Real & Deb. Corp. Deb. Stk.	100	108½

INSURANCE.

Chief Market.	Int. or Div.	Name.	Amount paid.	Price.
G	12/	Caledonian F. & Life	5	36¼
G	4/6	City of Glasgow Life	2½	12¾
E	19/	Edinburgh Life	20	54½
G	13/1	Life Ass. of Scotland	8⅓	34½
E	8	Nat. Guar. & Surety	2	52/
G	17½	Scottish Union and National "A"	1	94/
G	17½	Do. "B"	3¾	18½

IRON, COAL, AND STEEL.

Chief Market.	Int. or Div.	Name.	Amount paid.	Price.
E	Nil.	Addie, Coll. Cm. Pref.	10	7⅝
E	8/	Arniston Coal	8	12¾
E	2½	Cairntable Gas Coal	8	86/
E	12½	Fife Coal	10	20½
E	5	Do. Cum. Pref.	10	13
G	7	Merry & Cunghame. Cum. Pref.	10	16
G	5	Do. Debentures	100	105½
E	1/9	Niddrie & Benhar Cl.	1½	41/
G	5	Steel Com. of Scotlnd	—	
	—	"A" Deb. Stk.	100	113
G	6	Do. and Mt. "B"	100	110
E	—	Watson, John	8½	11½
E	6	Do. Cum. Pref.	7½	8½
E	12½	Wilson's & Cly. Coal	3	8½

IRISH.

In quoting the markets, B stands for Belfast, and D for Dublin.

CORPORATION STOCKS.

Chief Market.	Int. or Div.	Name.	Amount paid.	Price.
B	3½	Belfast, 1921	100	111½
B	3½	Do. 1919	100	106½
B	3½	Do. 1924	100	106¾
B	3	Do. 1955	100	106½
B	3½	Do. Water Com.	100	114½
B	3	Do. do.	100	106
B	3½	Do. Harbour Com.	100	112½
D	3½	Rathmines & Rathgar	100	110
D	3½	Waterford Deb.	100	—

RAILWAYS.

Chief Market.	Int. or Div.	Name.	Amount Paid.	Price.
D	30/	Cork, Bandon, & S.C.	100	77
D	4	Do. Deb.	100	139½
D	4	Do. W. Cork Pref.	100	—
B	65/	Belfast & Northern	100	159
B	4	Do. Deb.	100	146
B	5	Do. Pref.	100	138
B	6½	Belfast & C. Down	100	167½
B	4	Do. Deb.	100	147
B	3	Do.	100	107½
B	4½	Do. 4½ Pref. B.	100	150
B	5	Do. Guar.	100	173
D	Nil.	Dublin, Wick. & Wex.	100	31
D	4	Do. Deb.	100	123
D	4½	Do. Deb.	100	—
D	6	Do. Guar.	100	169½
D	4	Do. C. of Dub. Junc.	100	—
D	5	Do. 1860 Pref.	100	120½
D	50/	Do. 1864 Pref.	100	106
D	50/	Do. 1865 Pref.	100	94
B	67/6	Great Northern	100	174
B	4	Do. Deb.	100	147
B	4	Do. Pref. B.	100	141½
B	5½	Gt. South & Western	100	142
B	4	Do. Deb.	100	147
B	4	Do. Guar.	100	141½
D	45/	Midland Gt. Western	100	113
D	4	Do. Deb.	100	140
D	4½	Do. Deb.	100	151½
D	4½	Do. Deb.	100	—
D	5	Do. Pref.	100	174
D	4	Do. Pref.	100	137
D	—	Waterford & Central	100	15
D	3	Do. Deb.	100	—
D	3½	Do. Pref.	100	130
D	4	Waterfd. L., & W. Db.	100	135
D	4½	Do. Deb.	100	—
D	4	Do. Pref.	100	130
D	3½	Do. Pref.	100	102

BANKS.

Chief Market.	Int. or Div.	Name.	Amount paid.	Price.
B	50/	Belfast, Old, £125 Shs.	25	126½
B	20/	Do. New, £125 Shs.	25	50½
D		Hibernian, £20 Shs.	5	6½
D	2/	Munster & Leinster £5 Shs.	2	5½
B	11/	Northern, £50 Shs.	10	26½
D	12/	Royal, £50 Shs.	10	28½
B	5/	Ulster, £15 Shs.	2½	12⅝

BREWERIES AND DISTILLERIES.

Chief Market.	Int. or Div.	Name.	Amount paid.	Price.
D	10/	Castlebellingham & Drog.	10	16½
D	6	Do. Pref.	10	15⅝
D	4½	Do. Deb.	100	115
B	17/	Dunville & Co.	10	28½
B	6	Irish Distillery, Pref.	10	13
B	5	Do. Deb.	100	110
B	6	J. & J. M'Connell, Pf.	10	15⅛
B	13/6	Mitchell & Co.	9	19½
B	5	Do. Deb.	10	11½
D	4½	Phœnix Brew. Deb.	100	96
B	6/	Wm. Cowan	10	13¼
B	6	Do. Pref.	10	13⅛
B	8/	Young, King, & Co.	8	14

STEAM AND CANAL.

Chief Market.	Int. or Div.	Name.	Amount paid.	Price.
B	Nil	Belfast Steamship	50	35½
D	10/	British and Irish	50	—
D	15/	City of Dublin	100	61½
D	3½	Do. Deb.	100	105
D	30/	Dublin & Lpool. Bldg.	50	73
D	2/6	Dundalk & Newry	10	4½
D	4/	Grand Canal	10	12
D	3	Do. Pref.	10	9½
D	3	Do. Deb.	100	99½
B	30/	Irish Shipowners	100	65
B	3/	Ulster Steamship	5	6

MISCELLANEOUS.

Chief Market.	Int. or Div.	Name.	Amount paid.	Price.
D	3/1	Arnott & Co.	4	7½
D	6	Do. Pref.	4	6⅛
B	8/	Belfast Com. Bldgs.	10	11
B	37/6	Do. Ropework Co.	75	96
B	5	Do. do. Pref.	10	13
B	2/	Do. Discount Co.	3	45/
B	5	Do. do. Pref.	5	4½
B	10/	Brookfield Linen	25	17½
B	Nil	Coey & Co.	25	4
B	5	Do. Deb.	50	48
B	4½	David Allen & S's Deb.	100	107
D	4/	Dublin Trams	10	19¼
D	6	Do. Pref.	10	17½
D	4	Do. Deb.	100	—
B	8/	Edenderry Spinning	10	9
B	25/	Falls Flax Spinning	25	15
B	17/	Forster, Green, & Co.	10	21
B	9/	Island Spinning	7½	7½
B	8/	Jas. Lindsay & Co.	8	16½
B	1/7½	John Arnott & Co.	4	4¼
B	4½	Do. Deb.	50	56
D	5/	Kinahan & Co.	10	11½
D	5½	Do. Pref.	10	11½
D	4½	Do. Deb.	100	109½
B	12/	Kirker & Co.	10	10
B	5/	Leahy, Kelly, & Leahy	5	8½
B	6	Do. Pref.	5	7¾
D	4/	Lindsay Bros. Ltd.	8	7½
B	4½	Do. Deb.	50	56½
D	1/	National Assurance	2½	39/
B	10/	Olley & Co.	5	7¾
D	1/1½	Patriotic Assurance	2½	29/9
B	3/7½	P. Johnston & Son, L.	6	6½
B	10/	Robertson, F., & Co.	8	23½
B	10	Ulster Marine Insur.	5/	7/
B	15/	York-street Flax	25	33½
B	6	Do. Pref.	10	15⅛
B	4½	Do. Deb.	100	120

INDIAN AND CEYLON TEA COMPANIES.

Acres Planted.	Crop, 1897.	Paid up Capital.	Share.	Paid up.	Name.	Dividends. 1894.	1895.	1896.	Int. 1897.	Price.	Yield.	Reserve.	Balance Forward.	Working Capital.	Mortgages, Debs. or Pref. Capital not otherwise stated.
	lb.	£	£	£	INDIAN COMPANIES.							£	£	£	£
11,240	3,128,000	120,000	10	3	Amalgamated Estates	—	*	10	5	3⅝	8¼	10,000	16,500	D52,950	—
		400,000	10	10	Do. Pref.	—	*	5	‡5	9¼	5				
10,223	3,560,000	187,160	20	20	Assam	20	20	20	5	60	6½	55,000	1,730	D11,350	—
6,130	3,278,000	142,500	10	10	Assam Frontier	3	6	6	—	7	8½	—	286	20,000	82,500
		142,500	10	10	Do. Pref.	6	6	6	‡6	11	5⅜				
2,087	839,000	66,745	5	5	Attaree Khat	12	12	8	3	7	6	3,790	4,820	7,770	—
1,633	583,000	78,170	10	10	Borelli	4	4	5	—	7½	6½	—	3,256	D270	6,500 Pref.
1,720	812,000	60,825	5	5	British Indian	6	5	5	—	3½	6½	—	2,920	12,300	16,500 Pref.
3,223	2,247,000	114,500	5	5	Brahmapootra	20	18	20	6	13	7½	—	28,440	41,600	·
3,754	1,617,000	76,500	10	10	Cachar and Dooars	*	8	7	‡7	10½	6½	—	1,645	21,240	·
		76,500	10	10	Do. Pref.	*	6	6	‡6	11½	5½				
3,946	2,083,000	72,010	1	1	Chargola	8	7	10	2½	18/	10½	3,000	3,300	—	—
		81,000	1	1	Do. Pref.	7	7	7	3½	1 1/16	5½				
1,971	942,000	33,000	5	5	Chubwa	10	8	10	‡8	6	6½	10,000	2,043	D5,400	—
		33,000	5	5	Do. Pref.	7	7	7	‡7	6½	5½				
32,250	11,500,000	120,000	10	3	Cons. Tea and Lands	—	*	10	5	3½	7½	65,000	14,240	D191,674	—
		1,000,000	10	10	Do. 1st Pref.	—	*	5	‡5	10½	4½				
		400,000	10	10	Do. 2nd Pref.	—	*	7	‡7	12	5½				
2,230	617,000	135,420	20	20	Darjeeling	5½	5½	6	—	22	5½	5,552	1,565	1,700	—
2,114	445,000	60,000	10	10	Darjeeling Cons.	—	*	4/2	—	6	—	—	1,820	—	—
		60,000	10	10	Do. Pref.	—	*	5	2½	9½	5½				
6,660	3,518,000	150,000	10	10	Dooars	12½	12½	12½	2½	18	7	45,000	300	D32,000	—
		75,000	10	10	Do. Pref.	7	7	7	3½	16½	4½				
3,367	1,811,000	165,000	10	10	Doom Dooma	11½	10	12½	‡12½	20½	6½	30,000	4,032	—	10,000
1,377	582,000	61,120	5	5	Eastern Assam	5	nil.	4	—	2½	6½	—	1,790	—	10,000
4,038	1,675,000	85,000	10	10	East India and Ceylon	*	nil.	7	—	8½	7½	—	1,710	—	—
		85,000	10	10	Do. Pref.	*	6	6	3	11½	5½				
7,500	3,363,000	219,000	10	10	Empire of India	—	*	6/10	2½	11½	—	15,000	—	27,000	—
		219,000	10	10	Do. Pref.	—	*	5	2½	10½	4½				
1,180	540,000	94,060	10	10	Indian of Cachar	7	3½	3	‡2	3½	5½	6,070	—	7,120	—
3,050	824,000	83,500	5	5	Jhanzie	10	10	10	4	8	6½	14,500	1,070	2,700	—
7,980	3,680,000	250,000	10	10	Jokai	10	10	10	5	17½	5½	45,000	990	D9,000	—
		100,000	10	10	Do. Pref.	*	6	6	3	14⅛	4½				
5,224	1,563,000	100,000	20	20	Jorehaut	20	20	20	—	58	6½	36,220	2,955	3,000	—
1,547	504,000	65,660	10	8	Lebong	15	15	15	‡12½	16½	6½	9,000	2,150	8,650	—
5,082	1,709,000	100,000	10	10	Lungla	*	10	6	3	8½	7	—	1,543	D21,000	—
		100,000	10	10	Do. Pref.	*	6	6	3	11	5½				
2,684	885,000	95,970	10	10	Majuli	7	5	5	—	6½	7½	—	2,606	560	—
1,375	380,000	91,840	1	1	Makum	—	—	2	—	1½	1½	—	—	1,200	25,000
2,990	770,000	100,000	1	1	Moabund	—	—	*	—	½	—	—	—	—	—
		50,000	1	1	Do. Pref.	—	—	*	2½	1	5				
1,080	482,000	79,590	10	10	Scottish Assam	7	7	7	—	10½	6½	6,500	800	9,590	—
4,150	1,456,000	100,000	10	10	Singlo	*	8	5	1	8½	6	—	300	D5,800	—
		80,000	10	10	Do. Pref.	*	6½	6½	3½	13½	5				
	Crop, 1896.				CEYLON COMPANIES.										
7,970	1,743,824	250,000	100	100	Anglo-Ceylon, & Gen.	—	*	5½	—	65	8½	10,992	1,405	D72,844	166,520
1,836	685,741	50,000	10	10	Associated Tea	—	*	5	2½	7½	6½	—	164	2,478	—
		60,000	10	10	Do. Pref.	—	*	6	3	10½	5½				
10,390	4,000,000§	167,380	10	10	Ceylon Tea Plantations	15	15	15	‡15	26	5½	84,500	1,516	D30,819	—
		81,080	10	10	Do. Pref.	7	7	7	‡7	16½	4½				
5,722	1,542,700§	55,960	5	3	Ceylon & Oriental Est.	5	8	7	—	2½	7½	—	230	D2,047	71,000
		46,000	5	5	Do. Pref.	6	6	6	3	5	6				
2,157	801,629	111,330	5	5	Dimbula Valley	—	*	10	5	5½	10	—	—	1,733	6,250
		62,607	5	5	Do. Pref.	—	*	6	3	6½	4½				
11,496	3,635,000§	298,250	5	5	Eastern Prod. & Est.	3	5	6½	‡7	6½	5½	20,000	11,740	D17,797	102,500
2,193	1,050,000§	22,080	10	10	New Dimbula "A"	15	16	16	4	24	7	11,000	2,024	1,150	8,400
		55,710	10	10	Do. "B"	18	16	16	4	22	7½				
2,572	570,360	100,000	10	10	Ouvah	6	8	6	2	8	7	4,000	1,151	D1,255	—
2,630	964,963§	200,000	10	10	Nuwara Eliya	—	*	6	‡6	10½xd.	5½	—	—	—	30,000
1,720	720,200	41,000	10	10	Scottish Ceylon	15	15	15	5	22	6½	7,000	1,252	D3,970	9,000 Pref.
2,450	750,000§	39,000	10	6	Standard	12½	15	15	‡15	13xd.	6½	9,000	800	D14,012	4,000
		17,000	10	10	Do.	12½	15	15	‡15	22xd.	6½				

Working-Capital Column.—In working-capital column, D stands for *debit*.

* Company formed this year. † Interim dividends are given as actual distribution made. ‡ *Total* div. § Crop 189

Printed for the Proprietor by Love & Wyman, Ltd., Great Queen Street, London, W.C.; and Published by Clement Wilson at Norfolk House, Norfolk Street, Strand, London, W.C

The Investors' Review

EDITED BY A. J. WILSON.

Vol. I.—No. 18. New Series. | FRIDAY, MAY 6, 1898. | [Registered as a Newspaper.] | Price 6d. By post, 6½d

The Investment Index,

A Quarterly Supplement to the "Investors' Review."

Price 2s. net, 8s. 6d. per annum, post free.

THE INVESTMENT INDEX is an indispensable supplement to the Investors' Review. A file of it enables investors to follow the ups and downs of markets, and each number gives the return obtainable on all classes of securities at recent prices, arranged in a most convenient form for reference. Appended to its tables of figures are criticisms on company balance sheets, State Budgets, &c., similar to those in the Investors' Review.

Regarding it, the *Speaker* says: "The Quarterly 'Investment Index' is probably the handiest and fullest, as it is certainly the safest, of guides to the investor."

"The compilation of securities is particularly valuable."—*Pall Mall Gazette.*

"Its carefully classified list of securities will be found very valuable."—*Globe.*

"At no time has such a list of securities been more valuable than the present."—*Star.*

"The invaluable 'Investors' Index.'"—*Sketch.*

"A most valuable compilation."—*Glasgow Herald.*

Subscription to the "Investors' Review" and "Investment Index," 36s. per annum, post free.

CLEMENT WILSON,
NORFOLK HOUSE NORFOLK STREET, LONDON, W.C.

THE

LAW GUARANTEE AND TRUST SOCIETY, LIMITED.

Capital Subscribed	£1,000,000
do. Paid-up	£100,000
do. Uncalled	£900,000
Reserve Fund	£70,000

FIDELITY GUARANTEES,
On behalf of Managers, Secretaries, Clerks, Cashiers, Collectors, &c.

DEBENTURE INSURANCE.
The advantages of such insurance are as follows:—
1. The Debentures being guaranteed by the Society can be placed at not less than par, thus saving discount.
2. A lower rate of interest is willingly accepted.
3. The Society acting as Trustee for Debenture Holders also adds to the Security.

MORTGAGE INSURANCE.

CONTINGENCY INSURANCE,
In respect of Defects in Title, Lost Documents, Missing Beneficiaries, Re-Marriage, Issue and Name and Arms Risks, &c.

LICENSE INSURANCE.
Mortgagees of Licensed Property should always insure in a substantial Insurance Society against loss they may sustain by depreciation in consequence of the license being lost.

TRUSTEESHIPS for Debenture Holders, and under Wills, Marriage Settlements, &c.

HEAD OFFICE:
49, CHANCERY LANE, LONDON.
CITY OFFICE:
56, MOORGATE STREET, E.C.

CONTENTS

The Investors' Review.

Unhappy Spain.

The first serious encounter between the forces of Spain and those of the United States has resulted in a defeat more overwhelming to the Spaniard than those even who, like ourselves, had no faith in his power of resistance could have imagined possible beforehand. The Spanish fleet in the Philippines has been destroyed, and Manila, with the whole of the islands dependent upon its government, by the time this appears will have passed out of the hands of Spain for ever. A more sudden blow has never been delivered by one Power against another under such conditions, for the United States squadron had to fight the land fortifications and the Spanish ships at one and the same time, and that it overcame both after a very brief conflict is proof of Spain's unpreparedness and decayed vitality almost as much as of American prowess. No wonder that the United States people are elated. That one battle might very well end the war. Not that the present Government in Spain will be willing to evacuate Cuba, and waive all claim to that and others of its possessions in the West Indies merely because it has lost the Philippines. But how long will the present Government continue in Spain? From the first we have insisted that a revolution is ripe there, and that defeat at any point would bring dangerous forces to the surface at any moment. These forces may now explode and overturn the Government. Before another week is over, the Royal Family may have to fly for their lives. Martial law has already been proclaimed in Madrid, the Cortes is in wild rebellion, and unless the Atlantic fleet redeems Spanish "honour" by a victory within a very few days there may be no Government at all in the country.

It does not follow, though, that revolution in Spain will end the war. On the contrary, we should not be surprised if the struggle over Cuba became intensified, although should that happen it cannot be a long struggle. The American people, however, should not become elated too soon. Their rejoicings over Admiral Dewey's victory are natural enough and justifiable, but they must not forget that the task they set themselves to has not yet been seriously begun, and that the Spanish people, in a ferment of revolutionary patriotism, might give them more trouble than the sedate, courtly, but utterly bankrupt Government of Queen Maria Christina. That Government, in short, cannot effectively carry on the war because it is too respectable. It is a Government which struggles to keep up appearances and to pay its way. A less scrupulous Government would have defaulted on the Spanish debt years ago, in order to put itself in funds for the purpose of reasserting its hold over Cuba, and might have done many other questionable deeds with a view to obtain ready money; but the Austrian Princess, Queen Regent of Spain in right of her marriage with the late King Alfonso, had other ideas and followed other traditions, with the consequence that, as we have from the first insisted, this war with the United States had to be faced by her Government in a state of bankruptcy. It is very difficult to give people in this country any idea how poor Spain is. Some help towards forming a conception of it may be obtained by the study of a report on Spanish trade for the past year by Mr. H. W. B. Harrison, commercial attaché to the British Embassy in Madrid, issued the other day by the Foreign Office. But even this conveys only a faint picture of the stagnation and decay which has fallen upon this once mighty people. The Spaniard never has been a trader, nor has any Spanish Government ever risen much above that mental attitude towards traders which characterised the robber barons of the Rhine. Therefore the one idea of every Government, in modern days at least, has been that, if trade seemed to be flourishing, the proper course was to tax it to death, This is called "protection," and all Latin countries are adepts in the system, no matter what their form of government may be; but Spain has had less material to work upon than her neighbours, much less than France for instance, and therefore Spanish trade has become blighted with greater rapidity than even that of Italy. Most of the flourishing sections of her export business are in foreign hands; foreign capital has developed her mines and worked them. The cotton industries of Catalonia are, we believe, partly in French hands, and they, too, seem to be perishing, because there is small outlet for Spanish cotton goods abroad, except in her own possessions, now being torn from her, and now unable to buy anything. So the imports of raw cotton, Mr. Harrison tells us, have been falling off because the internal consumption is declining faster than foreign trade, which, however, was last year larger by about £300,000 than in 1896, perhaps on Government account, the total being under £2,400,000. The increasing poverty of the Spanish people is closing more and more the outlet at home for Spanish manufactures. Half the foreign trade of the country is done with England and France, and English and French capital have put what life there is into that trade. We are her great customers for iron ore, mercury, argentiferous lead, and copper. Her own possessions figure to a very small extent in her commerce and will soon disappear. With a population nearly half that of the United Kingdom the total foreign trade of Spain does not amount to the value of one month's trade of the United Kingdom; it is less than one-twelfth of ours, in short. This smallness is really not to be wondered at when we consider how perfectly innocent of any common-sense views regarding commerce the Spanish mind is. Mr. Harrison gives a *résumé* of the customs duties levied on wheat and flour from the beginning of the present century until now. It is itself a remarkable lesson in how not to do it. Up to 1816, the duty on wheat was less than one peseta per 100 kilos, and for a brief period the duty disappeared altogether, or was scarcely perceptible, a mere registration fee of infinitesimal account. That period, however, lasted only from 1867 to 1869; in the latter year a duty of three pesetas was imposed, and gradually additions have since been made to this tax, until now it amounts to 10½ pesetas on the 100 kilos. No wonder, then, that the people complain of hunger. The greatness of their poverty is eloquently expressed by the smallness of the yield of their customs tariff. With heavy duties, not only on wheat, but on sugar, spirits, cod fish, cocoa, coffee, wheat flour, petroleum, and many other articles, including all kinds of cereals, the total yield of the customs was only £5,222,000 in 1894, and it fell to £4,431,000 in 1896.

No wonder, then, that the Government is bankrupt. But were a revolutionary Government to be set up in Spain, it might prolong the war by defaulting on the debt, seizing the gold and silver in the Bank of Spain, issuing an unlimited amount of paper money, and confiscating the still vast property of the Church. A dictatorship, such as that of the bloodthirsty and rapacious General Weyler, would be just such a Government, restrained by neither law nor tradition, and, until better arises, we must beware of its advent. Glad indeed should we be to look upon the war as at an end, but the overthrow of Sagasta and the flight of the Queen Regent cannot be trusted to stop it. Worse might then follow, and the annihilation of the Spanish fleet in the West Indies would alone place Spain hopelessly at the mercy of her foe. Then civil war would probably break out in the Peninsula between Carlist and Republican—between Heaven knows what faction. Truly, the future is black.

The Real "Defeat" of Russia in China.

It seems to us that the worst thing about the recent developments of Russian policy in China is the effect they have produced on the minds of the English people. If there be one thing more than another which we do not like it is to be cheated or outwitted. If the Russian diplomatists had only remembered the lesson of the events which preceded the Crimean War they might have been warned not to treat the English Foreign Office in the way they have done over Port Arthur and

Ta-lien-wan. No immediate danger of a fight between us and Russia exists, but the tortuous diplomacy of the St. Petersburg Foreign Office has unquestionably laid the foundations of a very dangerous quarrel in the future. Lord Salisbury was taken in, as honest men are always liable to be. He believed the assurances given to him by Count Mouravief, given in the name of the Emperor, although, we hope, not with the Emperor's knowledge and sanction, and imagined that the arrival of Russia at Port Arthur might be accepted as a guarantee that North China would be open to British trade—that the *status quo ante* established by treaty would not be broken in upon. He was assured that no intention whatever lurked behind Russian plans to annex and obtain exclusive control over any part of China. Within a fortnight, or little more, these assurances were utterly falsified, and before many weeks had passed it became painfully evident that Russia intended to make Port Arthur and Ta-lien-wan exclusive Russian possessions, with the consequence that the whole Liaou-tong peninsula, with Manchuria behind it, will soon become another Russian province. This is a lamentable fact, and not less so because it has already compelled England to half-abandon her liberal policy towards China and all nations trading with China. We have never hitherto sought any exclusive privileges there. Where we went all nations were welcome to come to barter their goods and enter into every kind of enterprise. This is all changed, and, as we said some time ago, the policy of the "open door" has given place to a policy of "spheres of influence," and the carrying out of this new system is very likely one of these days to provoke a great war over the partition of China.

Such being the position, it is fortunate for us that there should be a drawing together at the present time of the two great halves of the Anglo-Saxon people. Were nothing else to come out of this lamentable strife between the United States and Spain, that alone would be a signal benefit to mankind. In all probability, when the day of settling disputes in China by the sword does come we shall have no European Power to stand by us. Each one of them able to stand up will be anxious to "grab" something for itself, animated by that passion for "exclusive dealing" which is a mark of their more or less benighted economic condition. Our only possible allies in the Far East are the Japanese, whose interests are so far identical with ours that they desire to have China opened up to their commercial enterprise and trade. In proportion to the intensity of this desire they dread the supremacy there of any Power animated by the jealous commercial spirit of Russia, France, or even Germany, and that fear might stand us in good stead. It is possible, of course, that the Germans might think it to their interest also to stand by us, had we to oppose the encroachments of Russia upon the middle kingdom, or on our liberties of trade in the interior of the Chinese Empire. But we cannot count on this friendship, nor in an absolute way on that of Japan. Hence the importance of having the United States at one with us in this quarrel. It is not often that we are in accord with Mr Cecil Rhodes, but if the opinions ascribed to him in Monday's *Daily Chronicle* are indeed his, then he has given expression to a just sentiment that we hope will come to be universal both in the United States and here at home. Were the American people to recognise that their trade interests are really identical with those of the mother country; that their best chance of expanding their foreign business to an extent worthy of their great industrial capacity and incalculable resources is to join cordially with us in free interchange of commodities, so that they would have access to all our markets, and we access to theirs, then commercial unity would arise between the two nations which might make them irresistible, and not in commerce alone. For we may go further and say that the best chance of preventing war between us and European States, whether in the Far East, or the Near East, or at any other point, would be the knowledge possessed by such States that the Americans and ourselves meant to stand shoulder to shoulder in the quarrel. Russia, for instance, would pause, and probably retreat from any attempt to injure our commerce in China, did her diplomatists understand that the American fleet would fight side by side with ours, were we forced to defend ourselves against such designs by an appeal to arms. It would be a great thing for the world, and for the progress of civilisation in the world, if the Anglo-Saxon people were thus to become as one family all over the earth, ready to stand by each other, not to provoke war, not to range the world in search of territory, but to impose peace upon countries now consumed by jealousy of others and the passion for strife.

Perhaps this is a dream too pleasant and fascinating to be treated as coming within the range of practical politics. It is a dream to cherish, however, and we trust that the United States will learn even by their successes, which were never doubtful in this war, to rise to the dignity of their position and obligations as a great nation. They cannot hold themselves apart from the rest of the world. They have pacific imperial interests which grow in importance with the growth of their population and the ramifications of their trade; and the day is not far distant when they must take their part in settling the quarrels of the world or in preventing them from breaking out. And we think the Russians may be sure that in any strife that may arise between them and us, not through our ill-will or desire to injure them or to hold back their development in any way, but through the tortuous duplicity of their diplomacy, the United States will not stand afar off to see the mother country worsted or put upon.

Not that we shall be unable to give good account of ourselves; many a day and year must elapse before Russia dares to encounter us at sea, build ships of war as she may. The hour of conflict is, therefore, probably far off, but these reflections may be valuable as suggesting to Russian statesmen a better way in which to secure the continued goodwill of England and of English-speaking peoples than the way of deceit. Had the Russian Foreign Office, at the outset, frankly laid before Lord Salisbury the plans of the Emperor, there might have been some grumbling here, and we should not have made the mistake of suggesting the opening of Ta-lien-wan as a treaty port, so as to lay ourselves open to the charge of having been bullied out of a perfectly fair position, but we should in the end have acquiesced. Although probably seeking compensation much in the way we have since been obliged to do, there would have been less friction and less soreness than now exists, and Russian statemen may be well assured that it would have been better for them to have paid the whole Chinese indemnity in exchange for the concessions they have now wrung from the Chinese by bullying with the sword drawn, than to have created an impression in the English mind that their only method in diplomacy is that of the deceiver. The English money market might have been opened to them once more to aid them in their railway building and other progressive works. But they have chosen the baser course, and will assuredly find out the mistake they have made when France breaks down again and leaves them alone with their gigantesque schemes and their native poverty.

The "Tips" Lure.

Tips are of many species, and there is a curious fascination about most forms of them. In our young days an unexpected shilling from some open-handed relation rejoiced our hearts and pockets. That species of tip has to come to an end when we are grown up, but some let its place be taken by a desire for "straight tips" about an outsider in a horse race; others prefer a gamble in a speculative stock or share. There is no doubt the Stock Exchange does offer chances sometimes, and many men who would never dream of backing a horse will take a "tip" from some sanguine friend to buy shares in this or that doubtful undertaking. "Must go to £5," says the friend; "you can get them for 15s., so you know your loss." Very tempting, and perhaps the thing does turn out right once in a way, but how many times do such deals result in losses? It would be difficult to say, but the odds must always be largely against the acceptor of such tips. That this is so is proved by any price list of speculative shares. Compare such a list of to-day with one dated two years back and note the changes. Many names have altogether disappeared, or have been re-christened on reconstruction: it is a simple matter of so many "tips" gone wrong, and some must be the losers.

Tipsters are clever folk, though their art is not a difficult one. They vary in style. Some are bold and unblushing and don't stick at trifles; others are more artistic and seek to convince us almost against our better judgment by adopting an analytical style, giving reasons for their "tip." The Investors' Review has a reputation for "crabbing things," to use a City phrase, perhaps deservedly, and any way we hope we shall have it for some time yet, as in our opinion it is not the duty of a newspaper to encourage folk to rush into schemes of any sort. All we can do is to put salient facts before them and let them use their own judgment. At the same time, we are not crusaders against gambling: that will go on as long as the world continues spinning. Let those who can afford to run risks do so; it is no affair of ours. They do not require our caution. It is the man of moderate means who buys speculatively, more than he can pay for on the strength of some apparent information published by a tipster that we wish to help. After all, they form the majority, and if more caution were shown by them very few of the wild-cat schemes could be successfully carried through.

We will endeavour to describe one or two methods of the tipster, and take the bold, unblushing style first. From away "at the back of beyond" comes a story of a rich gold "find" where the yellow metal is to be got by the handful. The place is far from everywhere; across, it may be, a sandy desert or through some fever-laden jungle, where a white man's existence is a continual struggle with death. That counts for nothing. A syndicate of wise men, hearing of this new Eldorado, put a little cash together and tempt some mining expert to face the danger and visit this wonderful spot. His instructions as to reports are very clear. They must be glowing as to the quantity of gold, and the difficulties of getting it must be minimised. Next we find a company formed with a capital many times the cost of the mine, as of course the property has to be acquired from some native chief. The expert's reports are embodied in enticing prospectuses, but somehow the public is chary and the applications are small. Nevertheless the directors go to allotment, and the shares are assigned to themselves, their friends, and their nominees. Not much good have they got so far; but wait. Presently more glowing accounts come home; paragraphs appear in the papers, pure undiluted puffs, paid for in meal or malt. Then in the market buyers suddenly spring up, and the shares which lay dormant and unknown are forthwith quoted at a premium.

How a premium does tempt the simple mind! In rushes the public, one on top of the other, to buy, and those behind the scenes generously supply all comers. If the puffs are cleverly worked this market may continue for some time, and every effort will be used to this end in order to allow the public to have as many of the shares as possible. Then comes a pause. Very little is said about the shares; everybody is waiting for the future rise which, alas! cometh not. One morning a tired holder tries to sell and cannot do so at the nominal quotation, and gradually the price begins to droop and sometimes disappears. Final scene of all, the company is wound up and decorously forgotten, or if there seems still to be money in it extractable from open pockets, it is reconstructed and the game commences again. Who could be so foolish, the reader asks, as to join such a concern? Surely none could be taken in by such methods? Really now? Have you no certificate in your safe which at one time represented shares, in apparently a valuable property now naught but dust and ashes? If not, you are a lucky individual. Told briefly, these methods seem crude, but what we have said is the usual skeleton of the image, though the features may vary. Excuses are not difficult to make—failure of water, difficulty of transit, &c., all obvious when the scheme was started, but well hidden then or treated with indifference.

More artistic is the analytical puff, or tip, where a plausible show is made to give facts which are in themselves true, and yet those following the tip lose money. Among the many stocks and shares dealt in on the Stock Exchange there are not a few which are seldom heard of. Intrinsically their value may be moderate, or perhaps almost *nil*, but speculatively they have chances. Let us take an example. In the course of its career some big undertaking has fallen on evil times. Money is hard to borrow; the business is good, we are informed, and likely to recover if only a little timely aid were given. Debentures, let us say, are offered to obtain this money, and to induce public subscription a bonus of stock, which will share in the profits if these expand beyond a certain percentage, is given to subscribers. Time goes on and the debentures become a first-rate security, but the bonus stock never reaches the happy position of receiving a dividend. This matters nothing to the original subscriber: his actual money is safe enough, and the bonus can be sold at a low price per cent. to any one who fancies a speculative lock up which may turn out well in the dim and distant future. A market is created to a limited extent by such transactions, but the counter is seldom dealt in. Its price may go up to 10 per cent. and down to 3 per cent. or 4 per cent. in the course of years and no one gain or lose much. But one fine morning a happy idea strikes some sharp City man. He gets together one or two friends, and they quietly purchase a fair amount of this neglected security, which a lot of people consider cheap, but very few care to buy, as it is not easily resold. That is of little consequence to this little group, and after they have got all they think necessary, they manage to get a letter into some paper pointing out the cheapness of the stuff they hold; or, better still, prove to a willing editor that the stock is really below its value, and that with the improved condition of trade a dividend is quite possible in five or six years' time. He takes a hand in the game probably, and when all is ready for the *coup* publishes facts and estimates in his column of news. Presto! the trick is done. In comes the simple outsider to buy his modest amount, followed by others of the same kidney; up goes the price (for the amount of free stock in the market is small), and our friends quietly slip out, editor and all. The rush is soon over, no more support is forthcoming, the price droops, leaving the poor unfortunate follower of the "tip" with a certificate that may some day be worth a few pounds more than he gave for it, and also, which is more probable, may not. The mischief of this trickery is obvious enough. A man sees a particular tip, and noticing the moderate immediate rise that follows it, thinks it means a certain profit, if followed. He does not, perhaps, trouble to watch further that particular "tip's" history, but decides to follow the next one himself. Just as likely as not he makes a profit on his first venture, and then tries another and another, until one day he finds he has put money he can scarcely afford into various stocks and shares which he cannot sell except at serious loss. Is it right for the Press to take such a prominent lead in giving "tips" to their readers, as a prominent section of it does? We do not think it is. By all means criticise, and when a concern is honest say so; but it is not a writer's duty to say "buy this," or "buy that, because it is sure to go up." Such tactics are more often than not the outcome of corrupt designs, and at the best are merely the opinions of individuals who can in no way be held responsible for the harm they may do.

Indian Currency Moonrakers.

Indian merchants and bankers will be prudent in not expecting too much from this latest effort to pave the way for putting Indian currency straight. There are too many politicians, officials, ex-officials, hobbyites, in the committee's composition for any satisfactory conclusion to be reached. A few more men of the stamp of Mr. Hambro, Mr. Robert Campbell, or Mr. W. H. Holland, would have inspired greater hope that the investigation and discussion to be entered upon might at least lead to a recognition of what is and what is not possible. We can now have but a slender stock of this hope, but it is well the committee was appointed. It must, at the worst, serve as a means of gathering to a head, or a heap, the diversified "views" and infallible remedies with the multitude of which the world is now grown weary. Perhaps also, this marshalling of nostrums might have the effect of putting an end to the possibility of writing such despatches as that sent by Lord Elgin's Council to the Secretary of State, and published this week in the latest batch of official correspondence. That sort of effusion can please none but our foes. Of all Indian official deliverances on this subject we never saw one more "up in the moon." Its compiler does not, apparently, bestow one single thought upon the true economic state of India. All the reasoning is founded on an imaginary "power" which, it is assumed, the Government possesses to bring about a "stable rate of exchange" or to beget "confidence in the stability of the rupee" by one dodge or another. Yet at one point the language is frank enough. In order to reach the "gold standard" of perfection these officials pray for, a loan of £20,000,000 effective will be wanted by way of foundation stone, and this, it is computed, will add £550,000 per annum to the foreign obligations of the Indian Government. Good: and how is this addition to the annual charge to help towards a fixed exchange value for the rupee? To say that the twenty millions will not all be wanted at once, and, therefore, that the charge it imposes will be small at first, is only to beg the question.

Would it not be much wiser for these officials, and for this committee, to endeavour first of all to discover what the financial position of India—of the Indian people—really is? Currencies never go wrong and give trouble in any country unless there be something very much amiss with its general health in an economic sense. We see Italy, Spain, Brazil, Portugal, the Argentine Republic, and other States, all more or less involved in precisely the same kind of difficulties which beset India. The possession of a "gold standard" has not saved them from a depreciated exchange, and we are all as ready as a well-crammed schoolboy to give abundant reason why it has not. Can it be that the same causes are at work destroying the credit of India? We think they are, and have for many years said so, but the official stuffs his ears and refuses to hear, piles up the spending, borrows profusely, and finding bad becoming worse still wails louder and louder for the perpetration of this currency trick or another in order to make everything right for evermore. Give him this £20,000,000 and he would go on merrily till it was exhausted, which would not be long, and then blandly come with demand for yet more millions. Each dose of the life-sapping stimulant of borrowed money would only increase the danger of collapse in India and add to our troubles there. What of that, if "the present lot" got their rupees home at 16d. instead of 9d. or 6d., as it might be if extravagance without doles went on unchecked? And India is "happy," says Sir Michael Hicks Beach, and requires nothing of us. Really, really now, have our politicians fallen altogether into a state of hypnotised dotage about this dependency? Would that this Departmental Committee could be expected to brush aside all the drivelling proposals and "appeals" and false arithmetic of bureaucrats and doctrinaires, in order to go straight to the root of the matter, and find out how far India is now loaded beyond her capacity by the excessive weight of the "home charge" her poor and hungry population have to find every day of their lives. What is the average annual surplus of Indian foreign trade, and what proportion does it bear to the annual amount India has to remit to England under all heads, Government, corporate, and private? The answer to this might show that it is retrenchment and economy, not a currency juggling, that India requires to save her Government from insolvency. But we expect this will be the last line of investigation to be entered upon.

But the worst remains to be noticed. Not content with the proposal to foist upon India a gold standard it is in no position to pay for out of its own resources, the Government of Lord Elgin proposes to go a step further and melt down the silver rupees at the rate of 100,000,000 a year and sell the silver bullion in the market. The official theorists foolishly imagine that by confining the sale to India, where they assume the consumption of the metal in an uncoined form averages 60,000,000 rupees' worth per annum, the extra quantity thus thrown on the market can be disposed of at an equivalent price to 1s. 4d. per rupee. It is impossible for us to conceive the attitude of mind this proposal involves, but one thing is plain enough: this Government has no knowledge of the real wants of the Indian people, is absolutely out of touch with the natives, and does not practically know anything about the currency requirements of the country. Such absolute alienation of rulers from ruled is the most melancholy fact of all, and makes us dread the future far more than any actual administrative folly could do. It is perfectly plain to any unprejudiced outsider that if India has to borrow gold to make a standard, that gold is the property of her creditors, and will go back to them as fast as their demands upon it arise. Equally plain is it that if a large quantity of silver rupees is withdrawn from circulation, and melted down and sold, two consequences must follow. The price of silver in the open market will be still further depreciated, to the great loss of the Indian people and Government—a most cruel loss that the people cannot afford—and the trade of India, especially its small retail trade, as we may call it, will soon become hampered to a disastrous extent by the scarcity of coin. What the end of this folly is to be we dare not try to imagine, but it cannot be a good end, and we trust whatever the Departmental Committee may, or may not, sanction, it will stop the execution of this absolutely daft project. If lose India we must, let us do so like men, not as Bedlamites.

Our Trade and War.—IV.

FOREIGN COMPETITION.

The "made in Germany" scare was absurdly exaggerated by the small remnant of benighted Protectionists still among us, but it contained a serious element of truth. As the French army in 1871 went down before the needle gun and superior strategy, so will our international trade fall, unless we move with the times. Not to speak of our deficient technical education, our children have to waste a year of their time on our chaotic system of weights and measures, compared with what they would have to spend if we had the metric system. Then certainly another year is lost by our method or rather absence of method, in spelling. The first is kept up because people say that John Bull must stick to his pound and could never master a kilogramme. Our spelling is not modernised, because the empty pedants who rule us educationally, decree that chaotic spelling is so important as exhibiting the history of our language. For instance, the useless "u" in honour teaches us that the Latin "honor" reached us *viâ* Norman-French, where the "u" was acquired. Our elementary school children spend so much time in learning to spell that few of them get to the Romans or to the Normans, and those who do never acquire any clear ideas about them at all. Superfluous letters in words thus convey no information to them, while they undoubtedly waste time. Then, as if our weights and our spelling were not sufficient burdens for the weak backs of our children, we have the "religious" difficulty to contend with. People so abound in Christian charity that it is impossible to conceive the Church of England or the Roman Catholic child learning his A B C or his arithmetic side by side with the Congregationalist, the Baptist, or the Wesleyan. That A, B, or C, are what they are called, and that two and two make four, are nevertheless absolutely proved facts; but because the sects differ as to a certain number of dogmas (which very few grown persons ever master, even if they say they do) the bulk of our children have to be educated in separate schools, which are naturally inefficient and costly because they are on a small scale, and this is done because the main effort is directed to cram as much catechism as possible into the infant mind. Nor is the state of secondary or of University education better, but rather worse, from a practical point of view, though the so-called "religious" difficulty is not so harmful.

Modern commerce is largely scientific, and with our inferior education we are falling behind in the race. The German scientists have beaten our cane sugar planters, who had a far superior plant and climate to start with. They have annexed the higher branches of the chemical and dye trades. In electrical science, due as it was to the discoveries of Englishmen, the whole of the practical appliances are left to our American brethren, who have given us the electric light, the telephone, and the trolley tram car. In all practical science our sceptre has passed away and the alien sits on our throne. As to our knowledge of foreign tongues, as has been said, our pride is to speak only one language—our own. If we manufacture by rule of thumb, talk English only, and insist that foreigners should muddle their brains with our pounds and ounces, the next step with a nation of world-carriers ought, at any rate, to be to see that our transport arrangements were supremely good. Instead of this, our railway rates are the highest and the most unscientific of those of any of the great trading nations, and our maritime freights are controlled by shipping rings and corners, to the benefit in both cases of our rivals.

There are many signs that all these things are telling seriously against us in the world's markets. It is difficult to compare the amounts of trade returns, because of the enormous drop in prices of late years, but it is possible to do so properly by taking percentages only. Our trade with the British Empire in 1882 was 26·6 per cent. of our whole trade. In 1896 it had fallen to 24·9 per cent. If our colonial transactions had kept up, it would have meant that they would have been some £14,000,000 more—a loss of, perhaps, a profit of £1,400,000 a year to the Empire. This, however, is only a prelude to far worse things, unless we set our house in order, and realise the fact that we have no longer a monopoly, but have to fight for our trade in grim earnest by keeping abreast of the times. If at a time when other nations are learning the advantages of that peace from which we have so long benefited, we plunge into needless wars, which must in any case ruin our trade for years, we shall indeed deserve to forfeit our high place among the nations. Less than a year ago we saw in London streets a patriotic pageant unmatched in history, and which no existing power could attempt to rival. As the Jubilee procession moved along in stately order, with our venerable and venerated Queen as the central figure knitting together the vast and mighty empire that was symbolised, it would have appeared incredible that within a few months any section of the public should have given way to the undignified and senseless panics lately witnessed. If England be but true to herself, if she will move with the age, and live and let live, there need be no fear of the result. The growing trade and increasing prosperity of other nations can only be sources of gain to ourselves, if we have the small amount of nerve necessary to enable us to resist narrow jealousies, absolutely unworthy of a great people.

The following tables give a comprehensive view of our trade with foreign countries, the British Empire, the Tropics, &c. :—

OUR TRADE WITH FOREIGN COUNTRIES ABOVE £20,000,000 A YEAR.

—	Population.	Total Trade per Head.	Imports.	Per Head.	Exports.	Per Head.
		£ s. d.	£	£ s. d.	£	£ s. d.
Russia ...	129,200,000	0 5 6	22,600,000	0 3 8	11,400,000	0 1 10
Sweden and Norway ...	6,200,000	3 0 0	13,800,000	1 19 9½	7,000,000	1 0 2¼
Germany ...	52,200,000	1 3 5	27,500,000	0 10 5¼	33,900,000	0 12 11
Holland ...	4,500,000	9 6 8	29,200,000	6 11 4	12,300,000	2 15 4
Dutch Colonies ...	1,000,000	2 16 0	700,000	0 14 0	2,100,000	2 2 0
Belgium ...	6,000,000	6 18 4	19,200,000	4 4 3	12,300,000	2 14 1
France ...	38,500,000	1 16 8	50,100,000	1 6 0	20,600,000	0 10 8
French Colonies ...	5,000,000	2 12 0	700,000	2 5 7½	800,000	0 6 4½
United States	70,000,000	1 19 6	106,300,000	1 10 4½	32,000,000	0 9 1½
Total ...	143,300,000	2 14 9	270,100,000	1 16 9	132,400,000	0 18 0

OUR FOREIGN TRADE FROM £10,000,000 TO £20,000,000 A YEAR.

		£ s. d.	£	£ s. d.	£	£ s. d.
Denmark & Colonies	2,300,000	6 0 10	10,600,000	4 12 1½	3,300,000	1 8 8½
Spain ...	18,200,000	0 17 3	11,900,000	0 4 2	3,800,000	0 13 1
Spanish Colonies ...	2,500,000	1 1 7	500,000	0 3 11½	2,200,000	0 17 7½
Turkey ...	15,000,000	0 14 1	5,300,000	0 7 0½	5,300,000	0 7 0½
Egypt ...	6,800,000	1 19 5	9,600,000	1 8 2½	3,800,000	0 11 2½
Brazil ...	14,300,000	0 15 3	4,000,000	0 5 7½	6,900,000	0 9 7½
Argentine Republic ...	4,000,000	3 18 6	8,900,000	2 4 6	6,800,000	1 14 0
China ...	400,000,000	0 0 6½	3,000,000	0 0 1½	8,400,000	0 0 5
Total ...	463,100,000	0 4 1	53,800,000	0 2 4	40,500,000	0 1 9

OUR TRADE WITH OTHER FOREIGN COUNTRIES.

		£ s. d.	£	£ s. d.	£	
—	155,000,000	0 7 4	24,700,000	0 3 2	34,600,000	—

OUR TRADE WITH BRITISH POSSESSIONS.

		£ s. d.	£	£ s. d.	£	£ s. d.
N. America	5,500,000	4 4 0	16,400,000	2 19 7½	6,700,000	1 4 4½
West Indies & Guiana	1,600,000	3 8 8	2 [illegible]0,000	1 18 8½	3,100,000	1 0 11½
Australasia ..	4,300,000	12 9 9	29 [illegible],000	6 16 8½	24,300,000	5 13 [illegible]
S. Africa ..	2,400,000	6 16 [illegible]	5 [illegible],000	5 1 4½	14,900,000	1 15 4½
	13,800,000	6 13 1	57,[illegible],000	3 9 4½	49,000,000	3 3 8½
India, Ceylon & Straits ..	312,000,000	0 4 1	32,000,000	0 2 0½	33,900,000	0 2 1½
Other Possessions ..	2,500,000	6 2 5	7,600,000	3 0 3½	7,700,000	3 2 1½
Total ..	327,900,000	0 11 2	93,200,000	0 5 7½	90,600,000	0 5 6½

PROPORTIONS OF OUR TRADE.

FOREIGN.

—	Imports.	Percentage of Total Imports.	Exports.	Percentage of Total Exports.	Total Foreign Trade.	Percentage of Total Trade.
	£		£		£	
1882	313,500,000	75·9	214,300,000	69·9	527,800,000	73·3
1896	348,600,000	78·4	205,700,000	69·4	554,300,000	75·09

TRADE WITH BRITISH EMPIRE.

	£		£		£	
1882	99,400,000	24·06	92,300,000	30·1	191,700,000	26·6
1896	93,200,000	21·09	90,600,000	30·5	183,800,000	24·9

TOTAL TRADE.

—	Imports.	Exports.	Total.	Trade per Head of British and Irish Population.		Total.
				Imports.	Exports.	
	£	£	£	£ s. d.	£ s. d.	£ s. d.
1882	413,000,000	306,600,000	719,600,000	11 14 7	6 17 2	18 11 9
1896	441,800,000	296,300,000	738,100,000	11 3 1	6 1 8	17 4 9

OUR TRADE WITH WEST AFRICA, 1896.

—	Imports.	Exports.	Total.
	£	£	£
Niger	312,000	607,000	919,000
Lagos	1,256,000	562,000	1,818,000
Sierra Leone and Gambia	291,000	381,000	672,000
Total	1,859,000	1,550,000	3,409,000
Foreign	129,000	600,000	779,000
Total W. Africa	1,988,000	2,200,000	4,188,000

Population, British West Africa, 1,600,000.

The Annual Report of the Mutual Life Insurance Company of New York.

We have before us the report of this concern for the year 1897. It is of the usual flaming description, and bears the signature of Mr. D. C. Haldeman, who declares it to be "his privilege" to submit such a statement to British policy holders. We confess we fail to see where the advantage to these individuals comes in ; only it is necessary to read a little between the lines in order to see how hollow the pretences of prosperity are which the company, or its agent here, puts forward. For instance, we are told that the number of policies issued and paid for last year was 55,870, insuring £27,879,046, a total "only once" exceeded by the company. This is wonderful, and the drums may be beaten. Unfortunately, Mr. Haldeman goes on to say that the total number of policies in force at the end of the year was 342,642, insuring £192,115,478, an increase of £3,628,638. This opens a new view of the matter, for, on turning to the claims paid item, we find that this amounted to but £3,122,012. How then comes it that, with nearly £28,000,000 in new policies written, the gross addition to the amount insured was little more than £3,500,000? We fear there is only one explanation. Policies to the enormous amount of £21,000,000 or thereby were, in one form or other, shed off during the year. This is a prodigious waste, but, of course, it means money to the officials, commission agents, and so on, who carry this, for them, gloriously profitable business on. The trade is very dirty and shameful, we may be sure, but it pays some people, else it would not be continued. Surely this is a fair inference from the facts just stated.

Let us look now a moment at the "British branch" business, which does not seem so wonderful after all. By dint of their literature and unscrupulous agents' statements, such as we have exposed on more than one occasion, 3,074 policies were completed in this branch last year, insuring £1,675,387, and yielding £71,011 in new premiums; and it is added that the character of the business is shown by the fact that "the annual discontinuance from all causes, including termination by death, mortality, completion of limited payments and surrenders is only 5 per cent." This is an astounding statement, of which no proof is given. We cannot even guess what it means, and defy anybody to do so on the data supplied.

On comparing, however, the total of the "completed" British business just given with that for the previous year, we are glad to find that it shows a falling off of about £400,000. This does not justify the boast that "the firm hold this office has established in Great Britain is no doubt due to the reputation which the company has always enjoyed, and to its remarkable bonus results, which may be illustrated by reference to some policies still on the books." Indeed; but how about the policies which have become claims and had to be paid? Will Mr. Haldeman produce a few authentic examples from the matured policies of the past year to illustrate the magnificence of these bonuses? We think not; he is more likely to fall back on the "valuable options" which his office professes to give and on the "liberal surrender values" (when there are any) it distributes in circulars with lavish profusion. But why is it that the magnificent "bonuses," stated in general terms as ranging from £1 13s. 6d. per cent. per annum to £5 5s. 1d. per cent., according to the age of the assured, are only to be fingered by holders of small policies up to £1,000, if at all? Where are such bonuses on large policies of £10,000 and upwards? Does money accumulate at a smaller ratio on these large policies than on the small ones? We should be glad to have particulars regarding the return on some of these large policies from an independent source, in order to be able to test the value of Mr. Haldeman's rhetoric.

And what about the "surplus" trotted out at £7,291,210? Is not this a misleading total, seeing that the bulk of the policies in force, all of them in fact up to January, 1898, are valued on a 4 per cent. basis? The company only professes to have earned an average of £4 8s. 6d. per cent. on its investments last year, a falling off of 3s. 1d. per cent. on the return of the year before, and its directors have so far recognised the danger this steadily falling interest creates by resolving to value in future at 3½ per cent. only. They seem afraid, however, to extend this valuation to the whole of their policies, because, if they did so, the above-mentioned actuarial surplus would in a great part disappear. Is it honest or in any way straightforward to parade a fancy figure of this kind arrived at by such questionable arithmetic? We leave the people who run this business to answer, and emphatically warn the public once more to give it a wide berth until a satisfactory answer is forthcoming.

With all their pushing and astounding "liberality," in print, towards the people who find the money to carry this business on, the managers and agents who "run" it are still most of all liberal to themselves, and accordingly the proportion of expenses to premium income was last year as high as ever, namely 25·7. Of course, this includes the expenses of the annuity business, but if we allowed 2½ per cent. off for that, it should still be ample to keep the staff in sleek comfort, not to say pious profusion. The proportion is still large enough also to insure princely incomes to the irresponsible men in New York who have organised this large business and conduct it in a manner wholly and absolutely despotic so far as any policy holder here or in the United States is concerned. There must be an end put to this kind of thing, in England at least, and we shall hammer away at it until public attention is drawn to what will one day prove to be a very shocking scandal should a root-and branch reform fail to take place.

Economic and Financial Notes and Correspondence.

THE FRENCH ELECTIONS AND DEAR BREAD.

It is peculiarly unfortunate for M. Méline and his supporters that the price of wheat should have risen to such an extent in France as to threaten serious disturbances in many parts of the country just on the eve of the General Election. Should the ferment caused by the present state of semi-famine lead to the overthrow of the Protectionist party in France, we, to be sure, should not be sorry, and something better might perhaps take its place. Anything worse than the present *régime* we could hardly imagine, for it is one which makes France a hotbed of revolutionary projects. And the force of the elements of disorder fermenting through the length and breadth of the Republic has been greatly intensified by the refusal of the Government to reduce the enormous import duty on wheat. M. Yves Guyot, in a very striking article entitled "The Feudal Impost," published in last Monday's *Siècle*, calculates that between September 1, 1897, and August 1, 1898, a period of eleven months, the French people will have paid about 150,000,000 francs in wheat duty, an amount which is only 28,000,000 francs under the produce of the stamp duties, and more than 23,000,000 francs larger than the revenue from licences. Again and again in recent weeks M. Méline has been appealed to to issue a decree temporarily reducing, or suspending altogether, the tax of seven francs per quintal on imported wheat, but he has shuffled and hesitated until, though he has at last decided to take the step, it is too late. The stupid obstinacy of the man is just that kind of mental characteristic which does more to nourish discontent with existing institutions than any other kind of administrator would be capable of. M. Méline is feeble all round, and completely in the hands of the agricultural party, or rather in the hands of each band of self-seeking Protectionists in turn, humbly eager to oblige every prescriptive robber at the expense of the dumb community at large. As M. Guyot pertinently observes, this wheat tax enhanced the price of bread to the people by far more than its actual amount, because the flour merchant and baker put a profit on the additional price they have to pay. But it is useless to preach wisdom to M. Méline. He cannot even take warning from the bread riots in Italy, and pours out his wrath on the heads of the bakers with a gusto quite mediæval.

LORD SALISBURY IN SELF-DEFENCE.

The speech of the Prime Minister and Foreign Secretary to the Dames and others of the Primrose League does not strike us as being in his happiest vein, and we regret to see it noted that he looked ill and worn. That he was bold, as usual, in speech, not to say rash in his defence of our recent diplomacy in China, and that with all his boldness could not get over the fact of our having been driven to seize Wei-Hai-Wei because Russia practically scouted the policy of the "open door." Having taken the place, it may be good policy now to vaunt it at the expense of Port Arthur, and it is unquestionably an excellent spot to control the Gulf of Pechili from in time of war; but it is not, as his Lordship seems to imply, a place to turn into a great fortress. We hope, therefore, that his words do not imply large demands for money for this purpose in the near future.

At other points, we think the language of the speech justified. It was fair retort and more to point out that we have gained our ends at some vital points, such as the retention of British control over the Chinese Maritime Customs, the opening of additional ports, and of all the navigable waterways. Whether three years ago concessions like these would have been unattainable may be open tó dispute, but unquestionably when yielding became the fashion with the Chinese Government, we contrived to get a full share of the favours going. And we have China's pledge that no part of the territory of the Yang-tse Valley shall be alienated to any other Power. When the day of dividing up the carcass comes, this pledge may stand us in good stead.

THE UNITED STATES WAR BILL.

We shall be much interested to know what kind of bond Congress is going to allow Mr. Secretary Gage to issue in order to obtain funds to carry on the war with Spain. If they are to be bonds, interest and principal of which are payable merely in "coin," they will have to be kept for home consumption, but if the Senate can be persuaded to sanction a gold bond, they would be eagerly bought up in this country above par, if bearing 3 per cent. interest. In fact, the United States could sell a ten or fifteen millions sterling 2½ per cent. loan to-morrow in London at, or very near, par, if it were distinctly a gold loan. Perhaps necessity may compel the Senate to give up its silver predilections, if not immediately, then at an early date, and it will be a fortunate thing for American credit should it do so, for the war, and what will follow it, is going to be extremely costly. Mr. Gage told the Finance Committee of the Senate on Tuesday that during the next two months the war would increase the Government's expenditure by about $50,000,000, and that at the end of this time the entire amount of currency in the Treasury would be exhausted, including $30,000,000 of the gold reserve. Mr. Gage further declared that the war would diminish revenue, and hence his demand for an authorisation to issue bonds. Apparently the amount for which sanction is asked at the present time is $150,000,000, the whole of which, no doubt, the people of the States could probably themselves subscribe. They, however, would do so at the expense of sales of some of their other investments, with the result that their unquestionable gold securities would come here while they kept the dubious bonds at home. So the principal immediate interest in these provisions and estimates is the clue they give to the possible gold demands of the United States in the near future. In all probability one-third of the money to be raised there, say, £10,000,000, will have to be imported, and the whole of this demand seems likely to come in the first instance on the London market.

LORD CROMER'S REPORT.

Many important points crop up in the interesting and valuable account of the British stewardship in Egypt which this able administrator has made to the Foreign Office. At present, however, we shall touch on one point only, the cost of the Soudan War. Up to now, we gather, the total outlay on this head has been £1,850,000, of which £750,000 has gone into railways and telegraph works of permanent value. Part of this money has been provided out of the "special reserve," and on this there is a deficit of £571,000. Also Egypt appears to owe England £780,000 on account of the advance made in the early part of 1897, and we do not see how these short comings are to be met except by a new loan. The ordinary income and expenditure of the country just about balance each other. To be sure, Egypt is paying off debt and now owes £98,107,000 in funded obligations against £99,386,000 a year ago. Also, there is a sum of £E3,833,000 at the credit of the "general reserve fund," but happily £2,000,000 odd of this is ear-marked to public works, and the balance is in the control of the Powers, so that we cannot touch it. So it appears probable that before long Egypt will require a loan of several millions to put the finances straight. Will the Debt Commissioners sanction this loan?

THE DISTURBANCES IN SIERRA LEONE.

Would it not be well that, when the debate on the Colonial Office vote opens in the House of Commons to-night, the Government should make some definite statement as to the causes of the excitement and turmoil among the revolting natives in Sierra Leone? The latest news about the disturbances at Sherbro is that they have become serious, that a number of Sierra Leoneans have been massacred, that European factories have been plundered, that warehouses have been burned down, and that Bendu is in ruins. Very probably, as Colonial officials say, there is great exaggeration in the accounts received. Bendu may be a very unimportant town, but that is no reason why it should be allowed to be ruined. Whatever exaggeration there may be in the reports, however, fresh troops have to be sent to quell the disturbances. Is there any reason why Government should persist in enforcing the obnoxious hut tax, which is understood to have been the main cause of this extensive and extending revolt, though the mischievous conduct of the native frontier police must also be saddled with a certain amount of responsibility in the matter? It would surely be better to drop the hut tax altogether rather than permit the continuance of a disorder which endangers life and property and completely paralyses such trade as there is in the province. An inquiry into the conduct of the frontier police also would do no harm, and might reveal so much mismanagement, to use a mild term, as to necessitate, if not a disbandment, at least a thorough reorganisation of the force. It is idle to urge that the revolt must be quelled before remedial measures can be taken. Unless the hut tax is abolished, it is not improbable that the quelling of the revolt might be almost equivalent to the extermination of the native population.

UNITED STATES TONNAGE DUES.

It is pleasant to learn that the proposed tax of $2½ per ton on all foreign shipping entering the United States ports has been abandoned by the United States legislature. Mr. McKinley has been peculiarly unfortunate in his Chairman of the Committee of Ways and Means in the House of Representatives. Mr. Dingley's mind is narrow and essentially parochial in its views. He means well, doubtless, according to his lights, but the tariff framed by him and imposed in 1896 upon the country has already produced disastrous results for the revenue, and, what is worse, has caused no small friction and ill-will between merchants and manufacturers here and the American people. In spite of all this, he remains fully convinced that he has done a great deed for his country's good, and was bent on continuing his services in the same direction by clapping a vexatious duty on British ships, for that was really all the proposed tax meant, severe enough to insure immediate success for the Canadian fast line of steamers to be forthwith established. Canada has not been sleeping while recent events have been shaping themselves, and in a few days the public will receive the prospectus of this projected line of steamers, which is to be established with a capital of upwards of £2,000,000. Had Mr. Dingley been a member of the concessionaire company he could not have served its interests better than by getting this tax established. Canadian railways and steamships and Canadian ports would have flourished immensely, thanks to that tax, and the trade of the port of New York must have decayed. Happily this danger has been averted, and when the war is over the friendly rivalry between the United States and Canada will on the Canadian side be sustained by no such adventitious help as the tonnage tax would have given it.

The Russian Naval Programme.

This is much more lavish than the recently announced extra credit of 90,000,000 roubles would have led people to suppose and is thus summarised in an interesting telegram from the St. Petersburg correspondent of the *Times*, published on Wednesday :—

> At present there are building and completing in Russia and abroad altogether six first-class battleships, one of the second-class, one large armoured cruiser, one coast-defence ironclad, four smaller protected cruisers, three gunboats, about seventeen torpedo-boat destroyers, and nine or ten torpedo-boats. The new programme above explained, so far as it goes at present, indicates only six or seven new and large vessels besides the smaller ships. This will hardly exhaust the 90,000,000 roubles, the allotment of which was recently proclaimed with such a flourish of trumpets. The most unusual act of official frankness in publicly announcing this extra credit was not without a purpose, both in Russia and abroad, but it was not noticed at the time that the imperial ukase referring to the matter described the 90,000,000 roubles as being in addition to the increased credit previously granted, which was never made public. Therefore, it is believed that not 90,000,000, but between 120,000,000 and 130,000,000 roubles are at the disposal of the Admiralty this year for naval construction, including the 6,000,000 roubles for this purpose in the annual Budget. Some of it will, no doubt, be spent on increasing and improving the means and tools for shipbuilding.

The Brazilian Budget.

Except by way of historical memoranda there is little use in putting down the figures of this effort in romance. To the best of our recollection Brazil never published completed accounts for any financial year worth the ink they were printed with, and the Republic has in this respect been slavishly faithful to the traditions of the Empire. However, such as they are, we may mention that the President, at the opening of Congress, stated in his Message that the receipts for 1898 would probably amount to 312,000 contos of reis, against 304,800 contos estimated. But the expenditure is also expected to exceed this enlarged income by about 3,500 contos, and we should be greatly surprised, seeing how the exchange has fallen, if the result does not prove to be very much worse than this. Be that as it may, the President is sanguine still and looks for a revenue of 338,120 contos in the current year, 1898-99. What the expenditure is to be the telegraphic summary does not tell us, and probably enough the President does not know. Nor is it made clear whether the extraordinary credits of 60,000 contos opened last year, because Congress would not pass the Income Tax Bill, are included in the estimated expenditure of that year. In fact, we know nothing for a certainty about Brazilian finance from these junks of totals, but at 6d. for the milreis, which is above its present value, the estimated income for the current year is worth only £8,450,000.

Sleepy Somerset House.

In spite of all the examination of witnesses by the Committee upon Company Law, Somerset House continues to doze, leaving company organisers to pursue their own course in regard to making returns. By the section of the Companies' Acts that governs the filing of share registers at Somerset House, it is enacted that a list of shareholders shall be filed within a month of the holding of the first meeting of the company, which is, of course, the statutory meeting which must be held within four months of registration. But, on application this week to see the list of the West Australian Market Trust, we found that it had not been filed. Yet the West Australian Market Trust was registered in July, 1897, so that nine months have elapsed since its formation, and the list of shareholders ought to have been filed about four months back. The penalty for not complying with the law rises to £5 per day, and "every director and manager who shall knowingly and wilfully authorise or permit such default shall incur the like penalty." Hundreds of companies neglect to fulfill this condition, and with this fine harvest at its feet, Somerset House continues comfortably somnolent, while our legislators in their committee-rooms propose new measures of reform, in spite of the evident fact that the old safeguards are wholly ignored by the recalcitrant company promoter.

A Lesson in German Farming.

We can hardly imagine a better tonic for the British farmer, fagged and morose from long and useless crying for the moon in the shape of the protectionist coddling which he can never again receive, and which would only undermine his constitution if he did receive, than to "read, mark, and inwardly digest" the report on German agriculture just issued from the Foreign Office. It is an eminently wholesome and invigorating story of how German farmers have fared in a prolonged struggle with depression, how they have helped themselves, and in turn have been assisted in a perfectly legitimate manner by the State. The root fact and lesson of this little practical essay are that the modern farmer should have a thorough business training; that he must have a sound education, abundant knowledge, scientific and technical; and that he must, to be really successful in the struggle with his home and foreign competitors, be an expert in organisation and administration. In all this the State may be helpful without being demoralising. There is scarcely a University in Germany that has not an agricultural college connected with it. What would Oxford say if it were proposed to add agriculture to its curriculum? Then there are State experimental stations, where all sorts of experiments useful to the farmer are made, where also fodder, manures, seeds, and so forth are tested at a merely nominal fee. There are dairy schools and model dairies all over the country, as well as other means of giving hints or active aid to the agriculturist. The farmers themselves have set up thousands of co-operative societies for mutual assistance in production and sale, especially in dairy farming. They have many credit unions for advancing loans to members at the minimum current interest. These have been admirably managed and immensely beneficial to the farming community.

Turning to England we find nothing of this sort—neither co-operative union nor State assistance. The old "gentleman farmer" is going, is almost gone; but his active, energetic, business successor has not yet arrived. The State has done something in supplying instruction in cheese-making and dairy-farming; but its efforts have been tentative, timid, and somewhat blundering. What a gigantic blunder, for instance, was committed when Parliament two years ago voted something like two millions annually ostensibly to relieve the farmer in some measure from the burden of the rates! The money has been worse than wasted. It has been of no benefit to agriculture; it has given no sensible relief to the farmer; and the landlords alone will reap the ultimate benefit. But suppose such a sum—or half of it—had been devoted to founding agricultural colleges, setting up model dairies, establishing experimental stations, and supplying tests of fodder, manures, seeds, &c., for the benefit of the farmer—why, it must have gone far to revolutionise our agricultural system. With such assistance, added to the natural advantages of soil and climate already his, the English farmer might have been able to struggle successfully against his foreign rival, who is now so steadily encroaching even upon his home markets, especially in the matter of dairy produce, poultry, eggs, cheese, and butter—not to mention the rivalry to which he is being subjected even in beef and mutton. There is surely no insuperable obstacle in the way of the English farmer doing what the German farmer has been able to accomplish—with intelligent assistance.

It is so far satisfactory that the Council of the Central and Associated Chambers of Agriculture, at their meeting on Tuesday, urged that Government should create a central agricultural institution for the purposes of agricultural research, and to act as a centre of union for the whole country. There is here some indication that the farmers are becoming alive to what they really need, while showing a tendency to be less political and more practical. That central institution might become an experimental station, which in time might throw out branches in big agricultural centres, and so bring their benefits to the very doors of the farmers. But will our Government respond favourably? It seems doubtful. They appear to have come to the conclusion that they have done enough for agriculture when they passed that Rating Relief Bill, which can confer no permanent benefit except on the landlords. That seems, at least, the only inference to be drawn from the reception accorded to a deputation that waited on Mr. Chaplin on Tuesday to suggest legislation for checking the importation of adulterated dairy products. There was margarine, for instance; it was often sold for butter, and was invariably coloured like butter. Was it not possible to prohibit this artificial colouring of margarine, so that people might not be deceived into buying it for butter? Mr. Chaplin could see no great use in this. It was true the Government had promised in the Queen's Speech a Food Adulteration Bill, but they had no time to deal with it. The excuse is rather an odd one; for as much time has already been saved on the Irish Local Government Bill as might have almost sufficed for passing the Adulteration Bill. As to the adulteration of foreign milk, Mr. Chaplin is to send a few samples for analysis to Dr. Klein. On the whole, however, his quondam agricultural friends received from him the "cold shoulder." They should take a lesson from Germany, and change their tactics. For the present, they might join with the Chambers of Agriculture in urging the establishment of a Central Institution of Research and Experiment. But they should not stop there. Why should they not insist on the diversion of those two millions going to the landlords for use in the establishment of agricultural colleges, model dairies, and so forth? That way lies fruitful agricultural agitation; only from such reforms can we hope for successful farming.

LLOYD'S "SLIPS" AND THE STAMP ACTS.

A decision of the greatest importance to insurers at Lloyd's was given by Mr. Justice Mathew last week, in the case of The Home Marine Insurance Company v. Smith. It was an action brought to recover a sum of money under a contract of reinsurance underwritten by the defendant in the action and other Lloyd's underwriters. The "slip" was in the following form: "Open Cover. 30—6—97. Dawson Brothers. Cash. Steamer or steamers. United Kingdom and Continent and (or) America. Reinsurance. Rates as per indorsement." A list here followed of the amounts taken by each underwriter, and to each of these amounts the initials of the underwriter were placed. The slip then continued: "F. G. A. and York-Antwerp rules. Deviation clause. Old or new bill of lading, including all risks from warehouse lighterage and until delivered. Negligence clause. £4,000." On the back appeared the steamship lines on which the risks were reinsured, the amount which the plaintiffs reserved as their own risk, and the premiums, taking all risks, and f. p. a.

Now, by the Stamp Act, 1891, a policy of insurance includes every writing whereby any contract of insurance is made or agreed to be made, or is evidenced, and a contract for sea insurance shall not be valid unless the same is expressed in a policy of sea insurance, which is not valid unless it specifies the particular risk or adventure, the names of the subscribers or underwriters, and the sums insured, and, further, it must be for a period not exceeding twelve months. There was no doubt that in this case the sum insured was not mentioned, for the cover, the limit of excess taken on each ship, only applied to each particular case, and there was no mention of what the total amount of the reinsurance would be. The plaintiffs contended that this "slip" or cover note was in fact a policy within the meaning of the Act, and could be stamped on payment of a penalty, and in the alternative they said it was good as a contract to issue a policy.

The learned judge has decided this not to be so, as this note clearly was not a policy. The defendant said his reason for taking this stamp objection was that the plaintiffs had not followed the usual course of business in declaring any excess coming forward by a particular vessel, and providing for premiums and stamps, and obtaining a policy, but that having abstained from making their declarations for a long time, he had failed to receive premiums. Be that as it may, we must thoroughly endorse the statement of his Lordship that the taking of this technical objection by an underwriter at Lloyd's was regrettable. He has found that it was a contract of insurance binding in honour only, and the conduct of underwriters at such an institution as Lloyd's in acting in this way cannot fail to leave a deep impression on the minds of insurers in general.

CEYLON TEA COMPANIES.

Subjoined is a letter, which holders of Ceylon Tea Company shares will do well to read and think over. And not these alone, for is not over-capitalisation the vice of the age?—

To the Editor.

SIR,—Will you kindly permit a poor but industrious planter to comment a little on your admirable article in the REVIEW of April 22 *re* Ceylon tea companies, and if I do not quite agree with you in all you say, I know you will think none the less of me for that.

You make too much of the "loss on rice," which only occurs when supplied by the Colombo agents of the companies concerned with their commissions added. Estates are not bound to supply rice at a fixed price, and as a matter of fact, where the superintendent is at liberty to buy in the best market, there is usually a small gain to the estate in supplying it to coolies.

The other parrot-cry of "exchange" merely means—at 1d. per rupee—4 per cent. added to estate expenditure; not a ruinous item. I own a small estate of about 200 acres, from which I have an average *net* profit of £1,400. Last year it fell to £1,320, there being an additional estate expenditure of £80, owing to rise in the rupee.

With your limited liability companies, *the leakage occurs in London, not in Ceylon*, or in silver fluctuations.

For twenty-five years I was manager of a group of estates, the *gross* annual returns from which were equal to from £20,000 to £25,000 sterling; the total expenditure about £10,000. These were chiefly in the grand old days when coffee was king and the rupee was worth 2s.

Between the absent proprietor and the manager there was perfect confidence, and all went smoothly till the arrival of leaf blight; then for a few years there was but little margin of profit, though with cinchona, &c., we managed to tide over the time of transition without actual loss.

In five years, after planting tea, the *gross* returns again rose to £15,000 sterling, and as the rupee had fallen, the estate could be worked more cheaply.

Now came the day of company mongering.

At first my kindly employer was loth to listen to the overtures of the swaggering promoter. Albeit, he was getting an old man, and the offer of £80 per acre—which was just double his own and my valuation—settled the matter.

Need I say that this transaction was soon followed up by a prospectus, offering to all lucky enough to apply in time shares in the cream of tea estates at the rate of £95 per acre!

Now there are no gulls like the cockney gull: the rush was immediate, and in a few days the shares stood at a premium! But mark the sequel. By a peculiar manipulation 10 per cent. was paid once in a way, with the certain prospect of a yearly diminishing dividend till reconstruction takes place.

This applies to 90 per cent. of the companies formed within the last three years.

In passing through London the other day, I had the privilege of witnessing a meeting of directors. Being but a clod in poorly fitting togs, I was easily ignored, but took mental notes, and came to the conclusion that I had never seen a more pitiable or palpable farce in my life.

There you had six swaggering City men, or pseudo-City men, in faultless frock-coats and high hats, met to concoct some feasible excuse for low dividends.

God help shareholders who depend upon them; but do not blame Ceylon.—Yours faithfully,

MACG.

EXIT THE RESPECTABLES!

The "respectable" part of the City will be much shocked to learn that Sir W. Lawrence Young and Sir Charles Jessel have felt bound to resign their positions on the London board of the Johannesburg Consolidated Investment Company. It is understood that the reason dictating this step is their objection to being the mere nominees of the permanent directorate—Messrs. S. B. Joel, J. B. Joel, and H. Barnato—which under the Articles of Association has power to do whatever it likes with the London board. The two young gentlemen who have just retired appear to have had so little weight in the management of the concern that after a stay of two to three years upon the board, during which time a reconstruction was carried through, they have never been able to obtain the rescinding of the objectionable articles in the constitution of the company. To openly slight two baronets, one of whom is related to the Glyns, is, however, a very serious offence, and now "respectable" people in the City will give up the Barnato group as lost to all decency. But what was the London board of the "Johnnies" Company doing in the years 1895 and 1896, when so much bad business was transacted?

Goldfields of Lydenburg.

Now that these two young gentlemen have more time upon their hands, they might do far worse than give a little information about some of the "properties" of the Barnato group. Take Goldfields of Lydenburg as an instance. In the midst of the mad time in 1895, the shares of this mysterious concern were planted upon dealers in the market at about £7 a piece. It was a Barnato affair, and so the poor dealers took the shares. Since then it has issued one report, which we believe told very little, and no one can learn anything about the affair. What is worse, the old sponsors for the concern have turned round upon it and actually refuse to buy back the shares from the market even at par—£1 apiece! This is the depth of degradation from the market point of view, and the dealers are now seeking for light where darkness black as ink reigns supreme.

Debenture Holders and Preferential Payments.

An important decision was given by Mr. Justice Kekewich last week with regard to the effect of the Preferential Payment in Bankruptcy Amendment Act, 1897. By Section 3 of that enactment, in the winding up of any company under the Companies' Acts, certain debts mentioned in Section 1 of the Preferential Payments in Bankruptcy Act, 1888, amongst which is included income-tax, are, so far as the assets available for the payment of general creditors may be insufficient to meet them, to have priority over the claims of debenture holders or holders of debenture stock under any floating charge created by the company. The point in the case in question, Weekes *v.* The Kent, Sussex, and General Land Society, was whether the Commissioners of Inland Revenue were entitled to a preferential claim for income-tax, the debenture holders having commenced an action for the enforcement of their security prior to the Act coming into operation. The learned judge has held that the Act was not retrospective, following the decision of Mr. Justice Wright *in re* The Waverley Typewriter, Limited. These judgments seem to us to be sound, for certainly, *primâ facie*, an Act is not intended to be retrospective. The Legislature has only by express words interfered with debenture holders if they have not taken steps to realise their securities before the beginning of the Act. This Act of 1897 seems really to form part of, and extend the Act of 1888, which in terms only applies where a winding up has commenced after the beginning of the Act. To use the words of Sir George Jessel, "it is a general rule that when the Legislature alters the rights of parties by taking away or conferring any right of action, its enactments, unless in express terms they apply to pending actions, do not affect them."

The Gas Light and Coke Company.

If a Parliamentary inquiry is conducted into the methods of this company it would be well to examine its policy of accumulating a large balance forward. The last time it had its price of gas at 3s. 1d. per 1,000—between June, 1892, and December, 1895—it kept this high price in force so long that it accumulated a balance of over £200,000, which has enabled the board to maintain the dividends at 12¾ per cent. ever since. Having raised the price of gas in order to meet the increased cost of coal and for other reasons, the directors kept the price up longer than was necessary in order to accumulate a big balance forward, and in this way, during the twelve months ended June, 1894, the company charged nearly 3d. per 1,000 feet more than was necessary in order to effect this purpose. By doing this the dividend was ¾ per cent. lower for that year than if a proper price had been charged, which meant a loss to the shareholders of £38,348, but then the higher price of gas brought in £213,000 more, so that the public were the sufferers by this action. To our mind, the policy is a violation of the sliding scale agreement, and it ought to be carefully inquired into by the committee, if one be appointed.

Profit on Realisations.

The trust companies are just now particularly strong in respect of profit on realisations. Some very wisely do not bring it into their revenue accounts; others do, and it may be said to have a strong influence upon revenue in such instances. Take the Anglo-American Debenture Corporation as an example. Its total income last year was put at £54,568, of which £19,750 came from profit on securities sold and commissions. The commissions probably did not represent much, and if the profit from realisations had been eliminated from the profit and loss account the return would not have been a bright one. The revenue would then have consisted of £34,818, of which £23,880 would have been absorbed by working charges and debenture interest, leaving but £11,018 as net profit. This would have been equal to a dividend of a little under 4 per cent., whereas by taking its profit upon realisations into account, the company was able to write off £7,519 of unsatisfactory assets, and then declare a dividend of 6 per cent., and carry about £5,000 more forward. But, as any one knows who follows the markets, profits upon realisation are an extremely fluctuating form of income, so that no one should treat the revenue of the Anglo-American Debenture Corporation last year as at all typical of the future.

Hotel Cecil.

The board of this company quietly announced last week that the preference interest due on April 30 would not be paid. Our analysis of the accounts in the December number of the Investors' Review must have led the public to expect financial difficulties, but we were under the impression that interest upon the preference capital was guaranteed by the vendors up to January 1 last, so that two months of such interest ought to be in hand. The notice, however, is vaguely worded, and perhaps a payment may be made later on. We are not sanguine, however, about the future of this concern, for its capital of £1,300,000 requires a revenue equal to that of a small sovereign State. Where, we wonder, is this capital placed?

The West Australian Market Trust.

In the present tearful condition of this recently created concern it may be interesting to see what the melancholy monster was supposed to own at the start. According to an agreement dated July 7, 1897, the Joint Stock Institute—that faithful handmaiden of the Bottomley group—kindly transferred to the West Australian Market Trust shares to the nominal value of £500,000, taking in payment therefor £500,000 nominal in shares of the West Australian Market Trust. So particular were the parties joining in this romantic "deal" that a schedule was attached to the agreement specifying the actual shares to be transferred. They were as follows:—

150,000 North-Western Associated Gold Mines.
75,000 West Australian Joint Stock and Finance Corporation.

50,000 Associated Southern Gold Mining Company.
100,000 Westralian Joint Stock Founders'.
25,000 Northern Territories Gold Fields of South Australia.
25,000 Burbank's No. 1 West Gold Mining Company.
25,000 Burbank's No. 1 South Extended Gold Mine.
20,000 West Australian Loan and General Finance Company.
10,000 Fraser South Extended Gold Mine.
20,000 Nil Desperandum Gold Mine.

The shares were all of £1 each fully paid, and were taken at their nominal price. Needless to say, they were all Bottomley shares, and we wonder, after the "spouting geyser" sort of career of the West Australian Market Trust, how many shares in this collection are now actually under the control of its board? An ordinary trust is usually a great hand at borrowing. What, then, may we expect of a "Market Trust"? And yet the shares in the portfolio of this thing of flimsy beauty, put it as delicately as one may, were hardly of a nature to encourage advances, so that any operations of the kind must have been conducted under considerable difficulty. Before, then, any reconstruction of the delicate fabric is attempted, it might be well just for once to woo common sense so far as to begin by finding out whether the Trust really owns the shares it is supposed to possess. If they are of the character set forth in the schedule of July last, there would probably be little advantage in paying for them a second time, by dint of redeeming them from the grip of money-lenders. It might be considerably cheaper in the end to wind up right off.

We pause to note with admiration that the shareholders in the Western Australian Market Trust—who be they, we pray?—met yesterday, and swore by all their gods and their Bottomley to support the shares or die in the faith. But they did not, it would seem, just say straight out, "Reconstruct, and take our 5s. a share to pay up differences with." No, they cheered their chairman to the echo, and well he deserved the din they made, for was not his speech in quite his best "boy-stood-on-the-burning-deck"-vein. "Most despicable and barefaced conspiracy ever formed within the four walls of the city of London"; "felt it his duty to buy up these non-existent shares to steady the market," "rumours of rigging absolutely false" — "we want a quarter of a million of money," the valiant word-slinger went on, "and I myself will find £150,000 of it." Bravo! who says Mr. Bottomley cannot rise to the occasion? Three cheers for him—and a committee of investigation for the Trust, consisting of Mr. Jones, Mr. Preston, Mr. Cutliffe, and Mr. Joy. We are shocked, especially as we know not these men. This will not pay differences, either, on the 12th inst. Ah! we forgot—there is Mr. Bottomley's £150,000. He never fails to plank down the cash—never—never; no matter what they say about the Hansard Union charity fund.

Critical Index to New Investments.

IDRIS & COMPANY, LIMITED.

The business consists principally of the manufacture of table waters, and was originally commenced as far back as 1875, the present company being formed in 1893. The share capital is £150,000, and the directors now offer £70,000 4 per cent. mortgage debenture stock at par. It is redeemable at 105 after September, 1925, on six months' notice. The stock is secured by a first mortgage on properties valued at £56,235 and a floating charge on the undertaking. Profits for the year ended September last are said to have reached £14,340, but, notwithstanding, the security seems far too slender.

FURNESS, WITHY, & COMPANY, LIMITED.

The directors of this West Hartlepool company offer for subscription, at £1 premium, 30,000 5 per cent. cumulative preference shares of £10 each, so that the return to the investor is a few pence over 4½ per cent. The company was incorporated in 1891 to acquire the business of Christopher Furness, proprietor of the Furness line of steamers, and Edward Withy & Company, shipbuilders and repairers and graving dock proprietors. In July, 1896, £450,000 4½ per cent. debentures were issued at 5 premium, while all the ordinary capital of £700,000 is held by Sir Christopher Furness, his co-directors, and friends. Until the reserve fund equals the amount of the outstanding debentures, the dividend on the ordinary shares is limited to 5 per cent. This reserve now stands at £206,900, and the premium on the present issue is to be added to it. Profits for four years are given, but only up to April, 1897, when for that year they were £140,715, against £99,949 to April, 1896, £85,476 in 1895, and £85,959 in 1894. These, however, are gross profits, and the last profit and loss account shows that after deducting expenses, debenture interest, and transferring £70,000 to reserve for depreciation, underwriting, &c., the balance remaining was only £57,161, while the interest on the preference shares now issued will require £15,000. The balance-sheet shows that steamships, freeholds and leaseholds, machinery, &c., stand at £563,246; investments in steamship companies, engine works, dry docks, &c., at £276,099; other investments, not specified, at £236,393; sundry debtors at £420,957, and cash and bills at £302,217. The reserve, we take it, is amount written off steamers to date, while the investments in steamship companies show that this company will suffer in times of depression not only through its own steamers, but through its investments in other companies, and the item "other investments" may mean just anything. The proceeds of the present issue will be devoted to the new developments now in contemplation, and the company has recently acquired a controlling interest in Irvine's Shipbuilding and Dry Docks Company, but no particulars of its standing are supplied. Assuming, however, that the assets of Furness Withy stand near their real value in the balance-sheet, there should be good security for the shares now offered, though we never think 5 per cent. too much for shares in such a concern to yield.

THE NORTH MOUNT LYELL COPPER COMPANY, LIMITED.

This by no means satisfactorily proved company offers for subscription at par an issue of £200,000 5 per cent. first mortgage debentures, redeemable at 105 on June 30, 1908, or at any previous date on six months' notice at 110. They are a first charge on the undertaking and property, and the trust deed provides for the creation of a sinking fund of £20,000 out of profits each year for redemption of the issue by drawings or purchase commencing July 1, 1900, also that the sum of £20,000 shall be deposited with the trustees to meet the first two years' interest. Debenture holders will have the option, to be exercised before July 1, 1900, of exchanging their debentures for fully-paid shares at the rate of seventeen and a half shares for each £100 of debentures. The value of the ore in sight is put at a very high figure, but what is wanted is actual results. The issued share capital is £465,000: where has all this gone? We never had a great deal of faith in this property, and profits will have to be pretty large to make a fair return upon such a mass of capital.

MELLIN'S FOOD COMPANY FOR AUSTRALIA AND NEW ZEALAND, LIMITED.

Share capital £125,000 in £1 shares, of which 100,000 are 6 per cent. cumulative preference, and 25,000 ordinary, the latter, with £50,000 in cash, being taken by Mellin's Food, Limited, the parent company, as purchase price. The latter guarantees the dividend on the preference shares for twenty years, and all we are told about the parent is that its net profits for two years are sufficient to make good the guarantee several times over. So they may be; but there is a good deal of blind faith necessary.

NEW ITALIAN OPERA SYNDICATE, LIMITED.

Another attempt, it seems, is to be made to turn the old Olympic Theatre, or rather the new one, since its rebuilding, to some purpose. "It has long been realised by the lovers of music that the performance of grand opera should not be limited to the 'London Season,'" and therefore grand opera is to be performed for at least six months of the year, and the rest of the time the theatre is to be let for comic opera, American drama, English opera, &c. The share capital is £30,000 in £1 shares, of which 10,000 are offered for subscription, and there is an issue of £20,000 in 5 per cent. first mortgage debenture bonds of £50 each. These are secured by way of floating charge upon the lease and assets and property of the syndicate, and are redeemable at six months' notice at £55 after 1905. The lease is valued at about £50,000, and the vendor, who takes £30,000, including two-thirds of the ordinary shares, values the assets at £20,000. An estimated profit for six months of grand opera of £25,000 is spoken of, but this we need not go into. Too much grand opera is not good for anybody, especially such audiences as are likely to be attracted to the Opera House. A floating charge on the fifty-two year lease, at a rent of £2,250 per annum, must be a fine security, while as to the assets we are inclined to look upon the venture as an effort by Colonel Mapleson, the vendor and operatic director, to dispose of his choice collection, which includes scenery never before used, costumes, jewellery and armour and operas which have never been performed. Grand opera is not likely to make fortunes for investors or restore the fallen ones of the old Olympic.

SPEAR BROTHERS & CLARK, LIMITED.

Share capital, £160,000, in 20,000 ordinary and 12,000 5 per cent. cumulative preference shares of £5 each, with an issue of £50,000 4½ per cent. debenture stock, redeemable at 105 on six months' notice after 1904. Debenture stock and preference shares offered for subscription at par. Bacon-curing firms in Bath and Bristol are to be amalgamated, the Bath business dating back to the early part of the century. Debentures are a fixed charge upon freehold and leasehold premises valued at £24,393, and a floating charge upon the other assets, which include stock-in-trade, £52,166, and plant, &c., £950, an inadequate security for the debenture and preference capital. The statement regarding profits is also unsatisfactory, as all we are told is that the average yearly profits of the whole of the businesses for a given time amount to £12,731. Of the purchase price of £112,510, nearly one-third represents goodwill, and, taken altogether, we think the investment may very well be left to the West of England.

THE YORKSHIRE LAUNDRIES, LIMITED.

Washing there is no doing without, and we should imagine it is pretty profitable work. It ought to be if much of a dividend is to be earned on the capital now offered. It seems that the vendor has bought up nine laundries, and is now selling them at a profit to the company for no less than £167,500, presumably in cash, which hardly suggests confidence. Properties are valued at a lump sum of £166,578, but this includes the goodwill of all the businesses, which for aught investors can tell may represent half the valuation. Profits for 1897 are stated at £12,613, but one year's profits are no good for estimating the qualities of a concern of this sort. The capital now offered consists of £60,000 6 per cent. cumulative preference and £60,000 ordinary shares, all of £1 each, with an issue of £55,000 5 per cent. first mortgage debenture stock, offered at 105. Investors, we think, should pass this by.

Company Reports and Balance-Sheets.

*** *The Editor will be much obliged to the Secretaries of Joint Stock Companies if they would kindly forward copies of Reports and Balance-Sheets direct to the Office of* THE INVESTORS' REVIEW, *Norfolk House, Norfolk-street, W.C., so as to insure prompt notice in these columns.*

THE METROPOLITAN LIFE ASSURANCE SOCIETY.—For the year ended December 31 last, this society issued 188 new policies, insuring £140,940 and yielding £4,404 in new annual, and £2,486 in single, premiums. Claims arose under 155 policies, and took £140,103, both number and amount being well within the estimates. The funds of the society were increased by £9,860 to £2,036,938 at the end of the year, a total which shows a reserve of £37 14s. 11d. against every £100 assured. This society follows the plan of dividing its policies under series, and these series receive abatements on the premiums charged in proportion to their age. At the valuation made for the purpose of fixing the amount of these abatements at the end of last year, the rate of interest was reduced to 3¼ per cent. for all participating, and 3 per cent. for non-participating, policies, instead of 3½ per cent. all round as formerly. The actual cost of this change was £72,230, the whole of which sum was set aside out of the surplus of the years 1892-97. Even then the directors are able to allow abatement of premiums on policies of the first, second, and third series amounting to 71 per cent., 56 per cent., and 41 per cent. respectively, and to reduce those of the fourth series by 30 per cent. when entitled. This left £5,220 to be carried forward unappropriated. The society has never paid any commissions for new business, and the expenses of management, including pensions, amounted for the past year to rather less than 8 per cent. of the premium income. No less than £68,602 was paid in reduction of premiums out of the income of the year. The society's funds are well invested and stand at a price above their book value.

THE GRESHAM LIFE ASSURANCE SOCIETY, LIMITED.—We are sorry to have to class any British Life Office, which should be trustworthy, alongside the three American offices about which we have had, and shall have, so much to say, but it cannot be helped. This Gresham Life Office is run on much the same lines as they are, and exceedingly careful management will be required in the next ten years to prevent it from coming to their predestined end. Its report for last year does show some improvement upon previous ones, and we therefore indulge in the hope that it is now being managed in a way that may enable it to pull round. Expenses, however, still run very high, and amounted to nearly 22 per cent. of the premium income for the year as against rather more than 24 per cent. for 1896. In such circumstances the funds of the society naturally grow at a slower pace than its liabilities. Its total income last year amounted to £1,200,102, of which £946,703 came from premiums and only £199,291 from dividends, &c. These figures of course apply to the life department. Out of this large income about £395,000 net went to pay claims, a little over £60,000 was absorbed by surrenders, and about £211,000 went in expenses and commissions, the result of the whole being that only £341,000 was added to the life funds, raising them to £5,096,233. This is not a very large addition to the invested resources of a company which increased its liabilities on policies last year by £2,803,437. But if the life department is not in a flourishing condition the annuity branch seems to us to be less so. Last year £130,067 was received as purchase money for annuities, bringing the company under a liability of £14,306 per annum on that account, and this business was obtained at a cost of over 8 per cent. of the cash paid in, which surely was a most unreasonable charge. Worse still, the total of the annuity payments for which the company is liable came to £163,255, and when expenses and income tax were added to the outgoings there remained only about £10,000 to be added to the annuity fund out of the whole £130,000 received during the year for new annuities sold. This cannot be sound business, whatever is. The company as a vendor of annuities is living on its past, or from hand to mouth, and will get into trouble before very long unless it mends its ways.

TEXAS LAND AND MORTGAGE COMPANY.—The income of this company was rather less last year, and after interest and working charges had been met the net revenue was £18,103. This permitted of a dividend of 10 per cent., with £2,000 to reserve, £1,500 to a contingent account, and £2,263 forward. The reserve fund will then stand at £75,000, and is wholly invested in high-class securities. In spite of last year having been considered a good one, the foreclosures account increased by £7,256, and now amounts to £64,891. A few years back it was not more than half this total, and it would be a wise step if the board endeavoured to reduce the item either by sales or writing down out of revenue. Interest on loans accrued and interest in arrear, we are glad to see, is £2,660 less, but its total of £19,398 is still too high and must contain a great deal of interest in arrear—often an asset practically worthless in cases of this kind. We would, therefore, rather see these items reduced than further additions made to reserve, for it is no benefit to the shareholders to add to reserve, if certain assets require writing down.

WEST COAST OF AMERICA TELEGRAPH COMPANY.—This reorganised company has not started very grandly. The revenue for the year came to £25,773, and after payment of working charges and debenture interest the sum of £296 was left to be carried forward. The debentures amount to £150,000, bearing interest at 4 per cent., guaranteed by the Brazilian Submarine Company. The latter company, which came to the assistance of the concern when it defaulted, received £37,500 in ordinary shares as a bonus for its guarantees. There are also £20,000 of 4 per cent. income bonds (non-cumulative), which are exchangeable at the option of the holders for ordinary shares. Apparently these bonds received nothing for last year. The balance-sheet is a poor one, but not so bad as the history of the undertaking would lead one to expect.

CONSOLIDATED WATERWORKS COMPANY OF ROSARIO.—This reorganised concern is improving its system, and so its debenture issue has been increased. Revenue, however, did not increase last year, but this is attributed to the depression of trade in Rosario consequent upon the partial failure of the crops for several years in succession. The total revenue was £28,465, and the net profit was £14,570. Of this, £7,215 was absorbed by debenture and loan interest, and the balance permitted of a distribution of 5 per cent. on the 6 per cent. preference shares, and the writing off of £314 from the preliminary expenses account. This last account will then stand at £998, and there is also a doubtful asset in the shape of £3,658 for discount and expenses on issue of debenture stock, which will surely have to be written down out of revenue. Revenue may easily improve this year, but a good deal will have to be done to put the concern upon a sound basis.

ANGLO-AMERICAN DEBENTURE CORPORATION.—Last year this corporation had a total income of £54,568, and after payment of expenses and debenture interest the net revenue was £23,109. Included in the expenses was £7,579 written off expenses of issue of debenture stock and payments to debenture holders on conversion, both of which accounts were extinguished, and therefore the charge will not recur again. On the other hand, £19,750 was received as profit on securities sold, which is a form of revenue that fluctuates and at times disappears altogether. The profit must therefore be considered above the average, and we are glad to note that the board only paid 6 per cent. in dividend, and thereby increased the balance forward by about £5,000 to a total of £18,921. We should have better liked their policy if they had put the extra £5,000 to reserve, and thus raised that fund to £15,430, as they assert that the depreciation upon the investments is about £13,000. Such a policy would have insured the sum being added to the accumulations of the company, which still need the same as it has £492,000 of debenture capital against only £301,000 of share capital, the latter having a liability of £3 per £5 share. The corporation still pursues its short-sighted policy of issuing no list of investments.

ELMORE'S GERMAN AND AUSTRO-HUNGARIAN METAL COMPANY.—After seven years of existence this concern is able to report that

"Elmore's Metall Actiengesellschaft," the German concern working under its tutelage, whose securities constitute the only asset of the English company, barring the extremely delicate item of patents, earned a profit of £3,202. The charges of the English company, however, amounted to £9,293, but these were cleverly arranged for when the capital was written down, and so they are wiped out in a "chartered accountant's" sort of way from the balance-sheet. The needs of the company are shown, however, in the proposal to issue £60,000 of 6 per cent. debenture stock, part of which will be used to redeem the £44,983 of 8 per cent. debenture stock, falling due next July, the balance being used in the business. Of course things are going to be better this year, but we have read something like this some years ago.

SCOTTISH AUSTRALIAN MINING COMPANY.—For the half-year ended December 31 this company was able to declare a dividend at the rate of 2 per cent. per annum, making 2½ per cent. for the whole year. This compares with nil for the two preceding years, but in times gone by the company paid high dividends. The balance forward was also increased by £690 to a total of £2,281. The company must, therefore, have done better, but the report speaks of a further fall in the price of coal in Australia, so that the current year's working may not be so good, although the strike in the South Wales coal trade may yet favourably influence the prices obtained for its coal.

SIMMER AND JACK PROPRIETARY MINES.—With an issued capital of £4,700,000, this company's accounts show a balance of £435,150 to the credit of profit and loss, £353,120 of it described as profit on sale of investments, and £66,574 as the result of the year's mining, certainly not a very brilliant result. The directors point out that crushing has been seriously interfered with during the year. Early in November, the old 100-stamp mill was shut down, and the new mill with 240 stamps will not be fully completed until next month. Part, however, was at work almost immediately after the old mill was closed. In all, 164,06⅘ tons were treated, and gold to the value of £259,704 was won, or about 31s. 8d. per ton crushed. With ore of such low grade expenses are high, the actual result being a profit of 8s. 1·39d. per ton. Not promising, surely. Turning to other items in the accounts, we find that the debenture debt of £500,000 has been reduced to £308,600, and the directors propose to devote part of the proceeds of the sale of investments to its further redemption. In this they are quite right. Money so earned is greatly a matter of luck, and it is only fair to the shareholders that it should be used to get rid of such an incubus. Other details do not seem quite so satisfactory. Among the assets we notice sundry debtors £331,389, an amount the chairman described as liquid, but there ought to have been some explanation of this large sum. Perhaps it represents cash still to be received from the purchasers of the various investments, but we don't know. To shareholders the most interesting part of the chairman's speech is that dealing with the future. He gave several interesting assays, one yielding forty-eight dwts. per ton, another thirty-eight dwts., and so on down to nine dwts. This last is the average figure of the tonnage crushed during 1897; but assays are proverbially rosy. With the new mill in full swing 40,000 tons are expected to be crushed every month. At 8s. per ton profit this means a net revenue of £192,000 for twelve months. To pay 5 per cent. on the nominal capital requires £235,000, which would mean an increase of nearly 3s. per ton in net profits. It is to be hoped the ore will improve sufficiently to give this increase, or that expenses will decrease, else the mine has a poor chance of justifying its present capitalisation. Even a 5 per cent. dividend is little enough at the present price of £3 for the £5 share: mining shares ought to pay a clear 10 per cent. after the holder has put aside enough for a sinking fund.

SCOTTISH CEYLON TEA COMPANY.—This company seems to have suffered severely from the events that interfered with Ceylon tea planters last year. Its tea sold at an average of ¾d. per lb. less than in 1896, and its crop was 12,000 lb. smaller, so that revenue was £2,302 smaller, while, of course, the higher exchange, and we presume the cost of rice, although it is not mentioned, led to an increase of £2,247 in the working charges. Net profit, therefore, was only £4,429, as against £8,976 in 1896, with the result that the dividend was reduced to 10 per cent., as compared with 15 per cent. for 1896, whilst nothing was set aside for depreciation and reserve, and the amount forward was even reduced. The company, however, is a strong one, as its 10 per cent. dividend for such a year shows, and its capital cost works out at only £27 per acre. Virtually, nothing was added to this account during the year, so that the need of a depreciation allowance was not so apparent. Profits may be better next year, but so long as exchange keeps up, which it may do for some time, they are not likely to return to their old figure.

CHARLES BAKER & COMPANY, LIMITED.—Supplying cheap clothing appears to have been profitable, for the profits of this company last year, including £1,113 from Jubilee letting, came to £34,939, and after paying £5,104 for interest, and setting aside £1,457 for depreciation, there was a balance of £25,862, which provided the 8 per cent. on the preference capital, and dividends and bonus equal to 15 per cent. upon the ordinary shares. The balance forward was then increased by £2,308 to a total of £2,513. A considerable amount was received in premiums upon new issues during the year, and, after meeting the cost of such issues, the sum of £2,407 was added to the leasehold redemption fund from this source. That fund will then stand at £7,157, and there is also a reserve of £5,000. Nothing, however, was added to these reserves out of the revenue of the year, and we should have preferred to have seen some such allocation before so high a dividend as 15 per cent. was declared. According to its balance-sheet the company was not too flush with ready cash, and further accumulations out of revenue are necessary if the rate of profit is to be kept up.

NAHALMA TEA ESTATE COMPANY.—With a crop 14,700 lb. below the estimate, this company obtained last year about ½d. per lb. less for its tea, while the cost was about ½d. per lb. higher. The profit was therefore only about ¾d. per lb., as compared with 1¾d. per lb. for 1896, with the result that net profits came to £206, as against £1,467 in 1896. Last September an interim dividend of 2 per cent. had been declared, which absorbed £280, and as £65 was brought in, nothing more could be distributed, the year's operations closing with a debit balance of £8. During the twelve months £600 of debentures were redeemed.

MEXICAN RAILWAY COMPANY.—The report for the second half of last year shows the usual characteristics of better earnings and increased loss on exchange, but considering the stimulating effect the fall in the value of the dollar ought to have on the business of the country the result of the half year's working is not a thing to be proud of. Out of an available balance of £23,958, a dividend on the 8 per cent. first preference stock at the rate of 1⅞ per cent. per annum absorbs £23,944, and this makes the return for the whole year 2 3/16 per cent., giving a yield of just 3 per cent. on the present price of the stock. It is satisfactory to know that compared with the second half of 1896, there was an increase in the revenue derived from every source of railway earnings, local goods and passenger traffic giving $84,513 more, and foreign import traffic $44,419 more. Half the increase, however, went in additional expenses, leaving the net revenue greater by $65,741, and this in turn disappeared as the amount realised in sterling, owing to the lower value of the dollar, was £4,920 less of net revenue than in the half-year with which comparison is made. Referring to the regulations for controlling rates on American traffic to competitive points in Mexico, the report says some modifications have been made by the arbitrators, but certain points are still under consideration. No mention, however, is made of the suggested sliding-scale for regulating rates according to the exchange, so we may conclude the Government is not favourable to the proposal. Satisfactory progress is being made with the harbour works, and the sea-wall on the north and north-west are approaching completion. For the first four months of this year earnings, compared with 1897, show an increase of $153,000, which is satisfactory, but there is nothing to show that exchange may not be again lower, and therefore the company's stocks offer no attraction to buyers.

NEW GENERAL TRACTION COMPANY.—Annual report to March 23, shows an available balance of £15,857, but this is not clear profit, some portion representing balance brought forward and an amount reserved last year in connection with Bills before Parliament. After deducting £2,122, cost of issuing new capital, and paying 6 per cent. on the preference shares, there remains £3,746 to be carried forward. Considering the strides electric traction is making these 6 per cent. preference shares should be a good speculative investment.

Diary of the War.

April 29.—The "great fight" of the 27th at Matanzas is shown by the detailed accounts not to have been so very great after all. It was a nice bit of target practice in which the United States gunners displayed infinitely better marksmanship than the Spaniards. Matanzas harbour is so far protected by a long strip of land, at the outermost point of which the Spaniards were observed to be mounting guns on what is described as a fort, more probably only earthworks, more or less hastily thrown up. The United States ships opened fire at a distance of over two miles, quickly found their mark, and in eighteen minutes—not a second more—the "fort" was in ruins. The Spanish fire was very wild, and not one of the American ships was struck. The Americans ran down a rich prize just off Cardenas—the *Guido*—which was making for Havana with stores for the Spanish army, and a considerable amount of money—believed to be $400,000.

April 30.—Some interesting facts became known to-day. The American liner *Paris*, said to have been chased by Spanish cruisers, and captured, as some supposed, has safely arrived at New York, after an "uneventful voyage." So has one exciting rumour of the early days of the war been disposed of; and another has been as effectually dissipated by the arrival of the *Shenandoah* at Liverpool. This ship was reported captured by the Spaniards. It has a cargo of wheat valued, at present prices, at something like £50,000—a pleasant morsel for Spain if she had secured it. The reports of the "great fight" at Matanzas have been cruelly—we do not say correctly—discounted by the Spanish authorities. The "forts" are declared to have been untouched by the American bombardment; the "great slaughter" of the early telegrams is reduced by Spanish despatches to the killing of one poor mule; and we are gravely assured that at least one funnel of one of the American ships was hit and injured by a Spanish shot. The American authorities now say the bombardment was not ordered from Washington, but that the Admiral's conduct has been approved. The Spanish fleet has at last left Cape de Verd—compelled thereto rather by neutrality contingencies than urgent war policy. But the ships started under "sealed orders."

May 1.—No marked change in the position of the belligerents; but news confirmatory of another bombardment, this time at Cabanas, about thirty or forty miles from Havana. Not a momentous engagement by any means; only undertaken apparently as a test of the strength of the defensive works. A request from Washington representatives of European Powers, as to when Europeans would be notified to leave the island, drew from President McKinley an intimation that, though the bombardment of Havana would not take place at once, it would be advisable that foreigners should leave Cuba before the 4th. It is said the British

Consul at Santiago de Cuba has been mobbed, and an English gunboat has been sent for his protection. The Powers generally have lodged remonstrances at Washington against the tonnage tax clauses of the War Revenue Bill.

May 2.—The sea fight at Manila yesterday (Sunday) morning was evidently a considerable encounter, if not entitled to the epithet of "great." The American squadron reached Manila on Saturday about midnight. They had taken up position by daybreak, and soon after commenced the attack on Forts Cavite and Manila. The Spanish ships took an active part in the defence, and suffered greatly; but so did the American ships. After the conflict had lasted some hours there seems to have been a pause. The Spanish telegrams say the Americans "retired." But the battle was soon renewed, and, though the Madrid despatches say the American squadron "took refuge behind the foreign merchant shipping on the east side of the bay," there seems little doubt the Spaniards were defeated. One of their ships was set on fire; another was blown up. The New York merchants are agitating against the tonnage dues of the War Revenue Bill. They fear that, if the Bill passes as it is, it will drive a good deal of the English, French, and German trade to Canadian ports.

May 3.—Details of the great fight at Manila show that the result has been worse for the Spaniards than was supposed from the first accounts. The American Admiral brought his ships in the darkness opposite Cavite and Manila before the Spanish authorities knew where they were. The fort on Corregidor Island at the entrance of the Bay fired some warning shots *after* the American fleet had passed. No mines seem to have been laid. Neither ships nor forts on the Spanish side had any search lights. The fight was therefore forced upon them when unprepared. They had but a poor fleet—apparently all wooden ships, and of course old. These were all destroyed. Two were burned, one was blown up, and three were sunk to prevent their seizure by the Americans. The loss of life is stated at 400. The Spaniards fought well undoubtedly, but the contest seems to have been hopeless from the first. Through the British Consul at Manila, Admiral Dewey demanded the surrender of all torpedoes, guns, and possession of the cable offices. The demand was refused, and the bombardment at once began. According to the latest news to-day, Manila was in flames and Cavite has been destroyed. Washington is elated; Madrid depressed, inclined to censure, but insists on the Philippines defeat being avenged. Americans seem hastening to the conclusion that this battle may end the war. We do not believe it. Spain has not yet got sense thrashed into her.

May 4.—The United States flag now floats over Manila; and one of the questions most discussed among American politicians is, what shall be done with the Philippines? They will of course be retained under military administration until the conclusion of the war; but after? American jingoes would keep them permanently, as giving the United States a base and excuse for action in China, reckless of European jealousy and the expansion this would give to the Monroe doctrine. But sober American politicians and statesmen do not take that view. President McKinley's opinion is said to be that, after the war, the Philippines may be sold to some European Power—Great Britain by preference—in order to provide an indemnity, which Spain will be in no condition to pay. There is no thought of permitting Spain to reoccupy the islands, else the United States might continue in possession until an indemnity was paid. But the settlement of this question is a matter for the future. We are promised exciting news from Cuba before the week is out. The present object is said to be to seize some port—say Matanzas—and land a sufficient military force to co-operate with the fleet in an attack upon Havana. But as to this there is no certainty. It is announced from Washington that the tonnage tax clause in the War Revenue Bill is to be dropped. Probably the most serious news of the day is the announcement that martial law has been proclaimed in Madrid. This was hardly expected so soon. There has been rioting, but not of an alarming kind apparently; and the *Times* correspondent remarks upon the general quiet and order that reign in Madrid. The Government, however, must know of something that occasions them alarm. Not improbably they fear General Weyler, who is becoming the hero of the baser sort of Madrid jingoes. There need be little doubt that he means mischief, and will not lift a finger to assist the Government who dismissed him from Cuba. If revolutionary trouble breaks out there need be little doubt that this general, who was the author of the awful reconcentrado system, will play a leading part.

May 5.—We are still without news from the American side of the Manila battle, although rumour says that a telegram has been received from Admiral Dewey stating that fifty men were killed in the engagement. Excitement is spreading in Spain, and there was a fierce discussion in the Lower Chamber of the Cortes on the 3rd inst., during which Señor Salmeron, a Republican deputy, strongly attacked the Queen Regent, and was called to order. The Premier made a vigorous reply. General Weyler entered the House while the debate was going on, and took his seat between the Republicans and Carlists. In the Senate the leaders of all parties promised their cordial support to the Government. There have been serious riots in several towns. A state of siege has been proclaimed in Valencia, and bread riots occurred in Talavera. The fishermen at Gijon rose against the fish monopolists, and proved so troublesome that "the troops fired on them in self-defence." The coal-miners in Oviedo are on strike, and a state of siege has been proclaimed there also. Very serious riots are reported from Velasco, where the bakers' shops were pillaged. The dangerous revolutionary fever seems spreading steadily. Rear-Admiral Sampson's fleet, having coaled at Key West, has sailed for unknown regions. The general opinion is that Puertorico is his objective point, and that he proposes to capture that port before the Spanish fleet from Cape de Verd reaches it. There is, however, another rumour that the Spanish fleet has held homeward and is now at Cadiz. It seems probable that the military expedition to Cuba will be delayed until, as a *New York Herald* despatch puts it, "Spain's sea power in the Atlantic has been effectually crushed."

TRADE AND PRODUCE.

It did seem for a time this week as if the extraordinary rise in the price of wheat had been effectually checked, and that the turn downwards had even begun. The reports received on Monday from the provincial markets appeared to make it clear that buyers, though they gave in in a rare case or two in Yorkshire to high demands—one being as much as 53s. per quarter—they were not disposed to go beyond 50s. as a rule, and a good deal of business was done at from 48s. to 50s. Still, at Mark-lane on Monday rather a serious view was taken of the position, and many maintained that, with the diminution of English stocks, the continued demand for the Continent, the possible prolongation of the war, and a somewhat pessimistic view of the supplies to be expected from the United States and Canada—not much is expected from Russia—little if any diminution in rates could be looked for. No advance was, however, asked for on Monday, Friday's prices being firmly maintained. On Tuesday, reductions were noted at several provincial centres; and in the cargo market here there was early in the day a tendency to give way, which resulted later in a slight decrease. The news of the Spanish defeat at Manila seemed to suggest to many that the war would be of shorter duration than was anticipated, and the prospects at the close of the day were regarded as rather against sellers, and it was considered not improbable that further reductions would soon be heard of. At the opening at Mark-lane on Wednesday, however, more strength was shown as well as considerable excitement, and soon the price of English wheat rose 2s., English flour also advancing 1s. 6d. per sack. The supply of American was extremely short, and an advance of 2s. was early quoted. Little credence was given to reports that Mr. Leiter, of Chicago, had agents here prepared to unload large quantities of his "cornered" stock. It was not till later in the day that the news arrived of the suspension by the French Government of the duties on cereals until July 1. This had an immediate and we may almost say a remarkable effect upon the markets, more especially the cargo market. There was an advance of 2s., followed not long after by another of 1s. The principal demand was of course for France, the desire being to get as much as possible forwarded there at once. It was stated that some cargoes intended for the English markets had been re-consigned to France. For Californian near at hand 50s. 9d. was bid, but holders asked as much as 53s. Whether right or wrong, the belief for the present is that the wheat supplies all round are shorter than was at one time thought, though it would be difficult to give a sound reason for the belief. In the first three weeks of April the exports from Atlantic coast ports were 8,389,492 bushels, against 3,588,170 bushels last year, and from Pacific ports 2,529,628 bushels against only 712,871 in the same weeks last year. "Shipments of wheat," says *Dun's Review*, "have been stimulated by fear of interruption, but the great demand shows that foreign needs are not to be satisfactorily met even by the considerable United States surplus. Indeed, there is indication that the world's supply may prove too small even after the American supplies have been exhausted." Certainly the probabilities all point to a maintenance of present prices, and perhaps some advance for at least a few weeks to come. Fortunately the reports of this year's crops continue to be favourable.

No change of importance can be reported in the iron market. On the whole, the tone is healthy, and there is an increasing flow of business. There are fears in some markets that the supply of ore for iron-making from Spain may be cut off altogether, though how that should result we cannot conceive, or, at least, be so enhanced in price as to seriously affect the cost of pig-iron. These fears seem exaggerated; but in their last weekly circular, Messrs. William Jacks & Company say very truly: "The continued heavy consumption of iron in all districts, the decrease in stocks, and the probability that the Spanish-American trouble will interfere with the shipment of American pig-iron to the Continent, as well as with the supplies of ore, are making both consumers and speculators more inclined to buy pig-iron." Hematite will be adversely affected should Spain carry out her scheme for placing a duty on shipping. Birmingham is taking a more cheerful view of the loss of trade from Cuba. It is now pointed out that it has been dwindling steadily for the last two or three years. Local trade is generally brisk, and new orders are coming in satisfactorily. Gun and ammunition makers are now benefiting by the war, and have heavy contracts on hand for the American as well as the Spanish Government. Benefiting by the stoppage of works in Wales, Glasgow steel-makers are insisting on very stiff prices. They ask £5 5s. for angles, £6 15s. for ship-plates, and £6 5s. for boiler-plates. Reports from other iron centres are also satisfactory.

Copper has been strangely dull throughout the week, with a steady fall in price, until Wednesday, when a reaction set in, and values quickly improved. Fully 2,000 tons changed hands, cash realising £51 7s. 6d., 6s. 3d., 8s. 9d., 11s. 3d., May dates £51 10s., 11s. 3d., 8s. 9d., 7s. 6d., one month £61 10s., and three months £52, £51 18s. 9d., 17s. 6d., 16s. 3d., £52 1s. 3d. and 2s. 6d. Settlement price, £51 10s. There is still considerable confidence that the upward movement has not by any means exhausted itself. During the first fortnight of April the total visible supplies exhibited an increase of 1,513 tons upon those reported at the end of March, but there has since been a reduction of 645 tons. The stocks in England and France and afloat from Chili and Australia now stand at 28,891 tons, as compared with 33,793 tons last year, and 38,446 tons at 30th April, 1896. The deliveries last month were 22,943 tons, as against 19,025 tons in April, 1897, and 18,960 tons in the same period of 1896. As the haste to ship as much American copper as possible to Europe before the war broke out greatly reduced stocks, we cannot look for much from that quarter for some time. Refined copper has commanded big prices, high conductivity bars selling up to £59, and cathodes up to £58 delivered at Birmingham.

There is no change in the matter of coal. Wales is still idle, and there is no present prospect of a termination of the strike. There is, indeed, a fear now that the stokers and engine-men may leave work, as they have expressed themselves very much dissatisfied with the increase in wages offered by the employers. Their refusal to work might be serious, as the suspension of pumping would, of course, mean the flooding of the mines; but even if the present engine-men were to leave, it would surely be possible to get others to take their places.

The third series of Colonial wool sales began on Tuesday, when, though the attendance was good and the competition fairly animated, prices of all descriptions of merino wools, according to Messrs. Jacombe, Son & Co., hardly ruled up to the closing rates of last sales, and were occasionally 5 per cent. easier. Fine cross-breds showed no change, but other sorts were on the average 5 per cent. below late auction currency. There is not much stock in the hands of the manufacturers, but trade continues restricted, with little prospect of immediate improvement.

The firmness in the sugar market continues, and with a good trade demand the prices of all kinds of raw sugar have advanced. Yet the direct imports since January 1 are very much larger than at the same period last year, being 29,918 tons against 22,775 tons, and coastwise 9,807 tons, as compared with 3,687. American markets have also advanced, and, as the imports from Cuba have ceased, American refiners may soon have to look to Europe for supplies of beet. According to Messrs. W. Connal & Company's circular a good business has been done in Greenock crushed, and prices have advanced for all qualities 9d. to 1s. In Glasgow on Friday there was a rise of 5s. per ton on sugar, making 15s. for the week. May tenders, and a notion that the American victory in the Philippines may lead to an early termination of the war, has since had a quietening influence on the market. Besides, as Mr. Czarnikow points out in his circular, the trade, having supplied themselves freely during the last fortnight, are less eager purchasers. Still, the general tone remains firm. But the probabilities rather point to further weakening than strengthening. The American market remains firm for spot and near at hand sugars.

THE PROPERTY MARKET.

Last week's sales at the Mart amounted to a total of £157,000—a somewhat diminished but still very satisfactory aggregate. Again freehold and leasehold properties were the mainstay of the market. Very few landed estates have been offered, and these unimportant. Let us hope that such properties are disappearing from the auction room because agriculture is recuperating sufficiently to induce owners to stick to their land. Some important properties were disposed of at the Mart last Friday. Messrs. Protheroe & Morris obtained £8,100 for a block of freehold property, Eltoe House and Church Farm, with about eleven and a half acres, in Church-road, Leyton. Then a number of leasehold houses at Hackney, offered by Messrs. Bunch & Duke, realised £4,500, and the purchaser seemed to have a notion that he might easily dispose of them again at a profit. A block of freehold building land, eleven and a quarter acres in extent, in Hale-lane, Edgware, Middlesex, was disposed of by Messrs. Baker & Sons at £1,260. Mr. T. Westacott also sold a freehold property in Albert-road, Bexhill-on-Sea, rental £100, at £1,500.

On Tuesday the sales totalled only £16,375. Of this sum Mr. J. W. Kennedy contributed £8,030, the price of a block of twenty-four acres of building land at East Ham. That is at the rate of £330 per acre. Messrs. Weatherall & Green obtained £2,750 for half-a-dozen leasehold houses at Clapham, £1,940 for another lot in the same locality, and £1,575 for six plots of building land at Woking, Surrey. A considerable number of lots remained unsold.

To the total amount of £33,230 realised at the Mart on Tuesday, Messrs. Debenham, Tewson, & Company contributed the handsome sum of £27,985. Their lots were all but one freehold and leasehold ground rents, their chief one being a freehold ground rent of £130, at Denmark Hill, Camberwell, reversion in ten and a half years, which went for £15,000. There was a keen competition for the lot. Another was a freehold ground rent of £82 17s., reversion in ninety-four years, at Valmar-road. It realised £2,830. Two freehold houses in Coldharbour-lane fetched £4,760. The leaseholds all sold well. Messrs. Dunn, Homan, & Coverdale also sold some leasehold houses in Compton-road, Canonbury, and Messrs. F. Jolly & Company successfully disposed of a freehold residence in Down's-road, Hackney. Several licensed houses were offered at Masons' Hall Tavern on Tuesday, but only one found a purchaser. It was the Earl of Eglinton, at the corner of Eglinton-road and St. Stephen's-road, Old Ford, held for a term of seventy-one years at a rental of £125 per annum, reduced to £95 by sub-letting. Messrs. J. & M. Johnson & Company were the auctioneers, and the house brought £17,500.

Friday's transactions at the Mart only totalled £21,265, but the business done was good. Messrs. Alfred Savill & Son disposed of thirty acres of freehold land at Stanford-le-Hope, Essex, for £3,000. A freehold residence, with four and three quarters acres of land, at Bexley Heath, was sold by Messrs. Baxter, Payne, & Lepper at £2,900. Over £6,500 was realised by Messrs. Douglas, Young, & Company from lots of freeholds at South Lambeth and Balham. It was a day mainly of bricks and mortar.

Messrs. Edwin Fox and Bousfield announce an important sale of stocks and shares, including freehold estates, comprising parts of a King's share in the New River, £3,000 3 per cent. debenture stock in the same company, and 600 £50 new 7 per cent. shares in the Grand Junction Waterworks Company.

Mr. Alfred Richards announces another sale of gas and water stocks and shares at the Mart on Wednesday next.

Answers to Correspondents.

Questions about public securities, and on all points in company law, will be answered week by week, in the REVIEW, on the following terms and conditions :—

A fee of FIVE shillings must be remitted for each question put, provided they are questions about separate securities. Should a private letter be required, then an extra fee of FIVE shillings must be sent to cover the cost of such letter, the fee then being TEN shillings for one query only, and FIVE shillings for every subsequent one in the same letter. While making this concession the EDITOR will feel obliged if private replies are as much as possible dispensed with. It is wholly impossible to answer letters sent merely "with a stamped envelope enclosed for reply."

Correspondents will further greatly oblige by so framing their questions as to obviate the necessity to name securities in the replies. They should *number* the questions, keeping a copy for reference, thus :—"(1) Please inform me about the present position of the Rowenzori Development Co. (2) Is a dividend likely to be paid soon on the capital stock of the Congo-Sudan Railway ?

Answers to be given to all such questions by simply quoting the numbers 1, 2, 3, and so on. The EDITOR has a rooted objection to such forms of reply as—"I think your Timbuctoo Consols will go up," or "Sell your Slowcoach and Draggem Bonds," because this kind of thing is open to all sorts of abuses. By the plan suggested, and by using a fancy name to be replied to, each query can be kept absolutely private to the inquirer, and no scope whatever be given to market manipulations. Avoid, as names to be replied to, common words, like "investor," "inquirer," and so on, as also "bear" or "bull." Detached syllables of the inquirer's name, or initials reversed, will frequently do as well as anything, so long as the answer can be identified by the inquirer.

The EDITOR further respectfully requests that merely speculative questions should as far as possible be avoided. He by no means sets himself up as a market prophet, and can only undertake to provide the latest information regarding the securities asked about. This he will do faithfully and without bias.

Replies cannot be guaranteed in the same week if the letters demanding them reach the office of the INVESTORS' REVIEW, Norfolk House, Norfolk-street, W.C., later than the first post on Wednesday mornings.

H. E.—I am very sorry to see your list, as I have very little belief in any of the companies you mention. No. 1 has, perhaps, some value behind it, but it is difficult to have faith in any of this group. No. 3, efforts will be made to re-organise with an "assessment" of 20 per cent. to 25 per cent. if it is not wound up compulsorily. You should certainly not average. It is quite likely every artifice will be used to send prices up again ; if so, you should sell slowly, and get rid of your holdings gradually. In the long run I am afraid nearly all will prove worthless, so do not be too patient, but make up your mind to "cut your loss." As I cannot give you a detailed answer about each concern, your remittance is more than sufficient. I am returning the balance.

Next Week's Meetings.

MONDAY, MAY 9.

General Accident Assurance ...	Perth, noon.
Mason & Barry	Cannon-street Hotel, 2 p.m.
Texas Land and Mortgage Company	2, Suffolk House, 2.30 p.m.
Villa Maria and Rufino Railway ...	Winchester House, noon.

TUESDAY, MAY 10.

Equitable Life Assurance	Mansion House-street, 11 a.m.
Felixstowe Dock and Railway ...	66, Lincoln's Inn-fields, 11.30 a.m.
Nohalma Tea Estate...	30, Victoria-street, S.W., 1 p.m.
West Coast of America Telegraph...	Winchester House, noon.

WEDNESDAY, MAY 11.

Eastern Extension Telegraph Company	Winchester House, 2.30 p.m.
Globe and Phœnix Gold Mining ...	12, Old Jewry, noon.
Piggs Peak Development ...	3, Crown-court, noon.
Universal Life Assurance ...	1, King William-street, 1 p.m.

THURSDAY, MAY 12.

Bally Paper Mills	28, Fenchurch-street, 2.30 p.m.
Bombay Gas	6, Drapers Gardens, noon.
Lascells, Tickner & Company ...	Guildford.
Liverpool and London and Globe Insurance	Liverpool, noon.
Metropolitan Life Assurance ...	13, Moorgate-street.
National Provincial Bank of England	112, Bishopsgate-street, noon.
New General Traction	Cannon-street Hotel, noon.
Scottish Ceylon	16, Philpot-lane, noon.
Trust and Agency of Australasia ...	Cannon-street Hotel, 11.30 a.m.

FRIDAY, MAY 13.

Mexican Railway	Cannon-street Hotel, 2.30 p.m.
Union Assurance Society	Winchester House, 1.30 p.m.

Notice to Subscribers.

Complaints are continually reaching us that the Investors' Review cannot be obtained at this and the other railway bookstall, that it does not reach Scotch and Irish cities till Monday, and that it is not delivered in the City till Saturday morning.

We publish on Friday in time for the Review to be at all Metropolitan bookstalls by at latest 4 p.m., and we believe that it is there then, having no doubt that Messrs. W. H. Smith & Son do their best, but they have such a mass of papers to handle every day that a fresh one may well look almost like a personal enemy and be kept in short supply unless the reading public shows unmistakably that it is wanted. A little perseverance, therefore, in asking for the Investors' Review is all that should be required to remedy this defect.

All London newsagents can be in a position to distribute the paper on Friday afternoon if they please, and here also the only remedy is for subscribers to insist upon having it as soon as published. Arrangements have been made that all our direct City subscribers shall have their copies before 4 p.m. on Friday. As for the provinces, we can only say that the paper is delivered to the forwarding agents in ample time to be in every English and Scotch town, and in Dublin and Belfast, likewise, early on Saturday morning. Those despatched by post from this office can be delivered by the first London mail on Saturday in every part of the United Kingdom.

ADVERTISEMENTS.

All Advertisements are received subject to approval, and should be sent in not later than 5 p.m. on Thursdays.

The advertisements of American Life Insurance Offices are rigorously excluded from the Investors' Review, and have been so since it commenced as a Quarterly Magazine in 1892.

For tariff and particulars of positions open apply to the Advertisement Manager, Norfolk House, Norfolk-street, W.C.

To Correspondents.

The Editor cannot undertake to return rejected communications.

Letters from correspondents must, in every case, be authenticated by the name and address of the writer.

Telegraphic Address: "Unveiling, London."

The Investors' Review.

The Week's Money Market.

The short loan market has been full of money during the past seven days, and the chief difficulty has been to find employment for it upon reasonable terms. The rate for day-to-day loans gradually subsided to 1½ to 2 per cent., and no more than 2½ per cent. was demanded upon advances for a week. The position must have been irksome to the "discount houses," which were granting $2\frac{1}{2}$ and $2\frac{3}{4}$ per cent. upon deposits, and found their floating balances commanding such unremunerative rates. The India Council did a small business throughout at 3 per cent. for its loans for about a fortnight, so that the present ease does not delude the market into granting long-term advances at current rates. And already the calling in of balances in connection with the Chinese Loan has begun to harden rates, so that 2 per cent. is now the nearest rate for day-to-day loans.

Discount rates at one time gave way in face of the large arrivals of gold, and on Friday last three months' remitted bills were quoted as low as $3\frac{1}{2}$ per cent. Although gold has since continued to go into the Bank of England each day, the tone has hardened, chiefly because the New York exchange has once again fallen. At the present quotation, it is possible to bid 77s. 10d. per ounce for bar gold on American account, and Japanese yen is usually taken for the same quarter in preference to being sent into the Bank. Therefore, in spite of the fact that no less than £2,163,000 in gold was received by the Bank in the week, the feeling grows stronger that we have not come to an end of the monetary pressure. Arrangements are understood to have been made for the export of considerable amounts of gold to New York, which, if not obtained in the open market, will certainly be taken from the Bank of England. A leading cause of the demand is the enhanced price of wheat, which adds to the indebtedness of Europe to the United States. This circumstance may cause further transfers of the metal here from the Continent, but a good deal of the Continental debt, we fancy, is being liquidated by sales of securities from Paris and Berlin, operations which will throw the responsibility of finding the necessary gold upon this market. We have good reason for stating, too, that a fair portion of the funds to be transferred to the Japanese Government on Saturday next will be withdrawn in the form of gold for Yokohama. This movement will probably lead to the remarkable spectacle of gold coming from, and going to, Japan at the same time, but such an experience is not at all unusual when a country has its currency in an unsettled condition. Should these demands prove as important as is feared in some quarters, we may easily see the bulk of the gold that has recently arrived taken away again, and accordingly the market is wise in refusing to work under $3\frac{5}{8}$ per cent. for remitted bills of the usual dates. Yesterday, the market closed much harder, and had been driven to the Bank, where it borrowed nearly £300,000 at 4 per cent. by the calling in of the Chinese Loan money. Outside rates for call loans rose to 3 per cent., and there is every appearance of increased tightness next week.

This week's Bank returns is all a matter of gold. Through the influx of £2,163,000 from abroad, the banking reserve has been increased by £1,682,000, and the stock of bullion by £1,932,000, the circulation having increased by £480,000 in notes and coin at the end of the month. "Other" deposits have risen £1,314,000 to £39,270,000, and "other" securities have run down £1,167,000 to £32,768,000, thanks to the gold in, and to the decrease of £822,000 in the public deposits or Treasury and departmental balances. These, however, are still £11,539,000. The decline in the "other" securities shows that the Bank's bill case is emptying, and in the actual condition of the market it cannot be filled again. Thanks to the addition to the reserve its total is now £22,720,000, which is equal to $44\frac{1}{2}$ per cent. of the liabilities, compared with $41\frac{3}{4}$ a week ago.

SILVER.

Buying on account of a French mint order in a market thoroughly prepared for the operation was sufficient to cause the price of bars for immediate delivery to rise to $26\frac{1}{4}$d. per ounce last Friday. Immediately the order was completed, every one became a seller, and the price gave way rapidly. The downward movement, too, was accentuated by the publication on Tuesday of the despatch sent home by the Indian Government prior to its Budget statement. A very fair digest of this despatch appeared in the *Sunday Special* three weeks previous, but the market would not credit the extravagant policy therein outlined until it received official confirmation, now amply bestowed. Although it is known that the matter must now be left to the Departmental Committee—whose deliberations may easily run over months—the market was upset by the mere suggestion of the Indian Government that it should melt down rupees and sell the metal thus produced. That India should not buy silver for a year or two—it might be three or four years if we only lend it enough gold—might be a light matter to the Indian Government, but it would mean a further smashing blow to the silver market, and dealers in the metal shuddered at the mere proposal. Accordingly sales were pressed, and the price for immediate delivery has fallen $\frac{3}{4}$d. on the week to 26d. per oz., and the forward quotation is $\frac{5}{8}$d. weaker at $25\frac{11}{16}$d. per oz. Chinese exchanges have responded to the movement, and for the time being the whole market is in a state of uncertainty. Meantime, the Indian exchange has dropped because the stimulant urgently needed in the shape of a big sterling loan is now put off until the committee has reported. The India Council, however, has sold its quota at the declining rates, although trade is reported to be disorganised in India by the plague. The Bank of Bombay has reduced its rate from 13 per cent. to 12.

BANK OF ENGLAND.

AN ACCOUNT pursuant to the Act 7 and 8 Vict., cap. 32, for the Week ending on Wednesday, May 4, 1898.

ISSUE DEPARTMENT.

	£		£
Notes Issued	48,124,010	Government Debt	11,015,100
		Other Securities	5,784,900
		Gold Coin and Bullion	31,324,010
		Silver Bullion	—
	£48,124,010		£48,124,010

BANKING DEPARTMENT.

	£		£
Proprietors' Capital	14,553,000	Government Securities	13,187,953
Rest	3,183,433	Other Securities	32,768,502
Public Deposits (including Exchequer, Savings Banks, Commissioners of National Debt, and Dividend Accounts)	11,538,715	Notes	20,331,030
Other Deposits	39,270,461	Gold and Silver Coin......	2,388,707
Seven Day and other Bills..	130,663		
	£68,676,272		£68,676,272

Dated May 5, 1898.

H. G. BOWEN, *Chief Cashier.*

In the following table will be found the movements compared with the previous week, and also the totals for that week and the corresponding return last year:—

Banking Department.

Last Year. May 5.		April 27, 1898.	May 4. 1898.	Increase.	Decrease.
£	Liabilities.	£	£	£	£
3,135,656	Rest	3,184,638	3,183,433	—	1,205
9,682,730	Pub. Deposits....	12,361,186	11,538,715	—	822,471
39,477,189	Other do.	37,956,705	39,270,461	1,313,755	—
198,405	7 Day Bills	109,593	130,663	21,070	—
	Assets.			Decrease.	Increase.
13,842,586	Gov. Securities ..	13,191,953	13,187,953	4,000	—
27,735,259	Other do.	33,935,386	32,768,502	1,166,804	—
25,469,105	Total Reserve....	21,037,733	22,719,737	—	1,681,954
				2,505,630	2,505,630
				Increase.	Decrease.
£		£	£	£	£
27,584,610	Note Circulation.	27,542,860	27,792,980	250,120	—
$51\frac{3}{4}$ p.c.	Proportion	$41\frac{3}{4}$ p.c.	$44\frac{1}{2}$ p.c.	—	—
$2\frac{1}{2}$ "	Bank Rate	4 "	4 "	—	—

Foreign Bullion movement for week £2,163,000 in.

LONDON BANKERS' CLEARING.

Month of	1898.	1897.	Increase.	Decrease.
	£	£	£	£
January	673,081,000	576,358,000	96,723,000	—
February ..	648,001,000	577,052,000	70,949,000	—
Week ending				
March 2	190,157,000	177,852,000	12,305,000	—
" 9	134,400,000	126,152,000	8,248,000	—
" 16	174,377,000	148,937,000	25,440,000	—
" 23	129,828,000	118,578,000	11,250,000	—
" 30	170,668,000	153,421,000	17,247,000	—
April 6	186,540,000	147,780,000	38,760,000	—
" 13	112,101,000	154,090,000		41,992,000
" 20	168,810,000	92,312,000	76,478,000	—
" 27	122,058,000	131,278,000		8,320,000
May 4	174,037,000	138,967,000	35,070,000	—
Total to date	2,8[illegible],000	2,308,180,000	501,[illegible],000	—

BANK AND DISCOUNT RATES ABROAD.

	Bank Rate.	Altered.	Open Market.
Paris	2	March 14, 1895	1⅞
Berlin	4	April 9, 1898	3⅛
Hamburg	4	April 9, 1898	3⅛
Frankfort	4	April 9, 1898	3⅜
Amsterdam	3	April 13, 1897	2⅞
Brussels	3	April 28, 1896	2⅞
Vienna	4	January 22, 1896	3⅞
Rome	5	August 27, 1895	3
St. Petersburg	5½	January 23, 1898	4½
Madrid	5	June 17, 1896	5
Lisbon	6	January 25, 1891	6
Stockholm	4	March 3, 1898	4
Copenhagen	4	January 20, 1893	4
Calcutta	11	April 28, 1898	—
Bombay	12	May 5, 1898	—
New York call money	2 to 2½	—	—

NEW YORK ASSOCIATED BANKS (dollar at 4s.).

	April 30, 1898.	April 23, 1898	April 16, 1898.	May 1, 1897.
	£	£	£	£
Specie	31,678,000	31,084,000	29,506,000	17,466,000
Legal tenders	10,148,000	10,682,000	11,138,000	21,160,000
Loans and discounts	114,040,000	114,530,000	116,018,000	101,166,000
Circulation	2,850,800	2,816,000	2,787,800	3,000,000
Net deposits	131,700,000	132,244,000	132,704,000	115,372,000

Legal reserve is 25 per cent. of net deposits; therefore the total reserve (specie and legal tenders) exceeds this sum by £8,901,000, against an excess last week of £8,705,000.

BANK OF FRANCE (25 francs to the £).

	May 5, 1898.	April 28, 1898	April 21, 1898.	May 6, 1897.
	£	£	£	£
Gold in hand	74,450,800	74,375,920	74,312,920	77,180,000
Silver in hand	48,733,040	48,614,320	48,690,810	48,929,000
Bills discounted	34,248,520	36,839,520	33,733,960	*42,077,000
Advances	15,736,840	15,016,800	15,239,880	—
Note circulation	149,901,640	148,438,040	148,173,120	148,107,000
Public deposits	5,899,880	8,035,040	7,569,320	6,106,000
Private deposits	24,174,880	25,655,600	22,854,440	19,665,000

Proportion between bullion and circulation 82⅝ per cent. against 82⅞ per cent. a week ago.

* Includes advances.

FOREIGN RATES OF EXCHANGE ON LONDON.

Place.	Usance.	Last week's.	Latest.	Place.	Usance.	Latest.	Last week's.
Paris	chqs.	25'30½	25'34	Italy	sight	27'15	27'12
Brussels	chqs.	25'36½	25'30½	Do. gold prem.	..	107'45	107'17
Amsterdam	short	12'09½	12'10½	Constantinople	3 mths	109'15	109'15
Berlin	short	20'52	20'51	B. Ayres gd. pm.	..	164'80	163'30
Do.	3 mths	20'31	20'32½	Rio de Janeiro	90 dys	5⅜d.	5⅜d.
Hamburg	3 mths	20.30½	20'32	Valparaiso	90 dys	17⅝d.	17 7/16d.
Frankfort	short	20'51	20'51	Calcutta	T. T.	1/3 15/16	1/3⅞
Vienna	short	12.07	12'07½	Bombay	T. T.	1/3 15/16	1/3 15/16
St. Petersburg	3 mths	94.00	93'95	Hong Kong	T. T.	1/10½	1/10
New York	60 dys	4'81½	4'80½	Shanghai	T. T.	2/5⅛	2/5⅛
Lisbon	sight	30⅜d.	30⅜d.	Singapore	T. T.	1/10 13/16	1/10 7/16
Madrid	sight	44'50	51'50				

IMPERIAL BANK OF GERMANY (20 marks to the £).

	April 30, 1898.	April 23, 1898.	April 15, 1898.	April 30, 1897.
	£	£	£	£
Cash in hand	42,442,550	44,146,350	43,820,450	44,193,000
Bills discounted	37,216,650	35,280,900	34,561,300	*36,671,000
Advances on stocks	4,462,600	3,714,050	4,385,950	—
Note circulation	58,116,400	55,337,100	56,944,900	55,578,000
Public deposits	22,135,200	24,558,350	24,130,050	21,857,000

* Includes advances.

AUSTRIAN-HUNGARIAN BANK (1s. 8d. to the florin).

	April 30, 1898.	April 23, 1898.	April 15, 1898.	April 30, 1897.
	£	£	£	£
Gold reserve	29,677,250	30,116,666	30,490,833	26,487,000
Silver reserve	10,441,250	10,462,916	10,454,333	10,498,000
Foreign bills	473,500	709,750	805,416	—
Advances	1,833,750	1,753,750	1,759,916	—
Note circulation	53,799,083	51,513,833	51,052,583	51,313,000
Bills discounted	14,009,916	11,577,333	11,332,000	*11,388,000

* Includes advances.

NATIONAL BANK OF BELGIUM (25 francs to the £).

	April 28, 1898.	April 21, 1898.	April 14, 1898.	April 29, 1897.
	£	£	£	£
Coin and bullion	4,266,480	4,270,440	4,066,280	4,109,000
Other securities	16,307,880	16,643,080	16,540,080	16,600,000
Note circulation	19,662,520	19,307,200	19,498,400	19,315,000
Deposits	2,581,600	3,056,840	2,553,800	2,885,000

BANK OF SPAIN (25 pesetas to the £).

	April 30, 1898.	April 23, 1898.	April 16, 1898.	May 1, 1897.
	£	£	£	£
Gold	9,833,520	9,719,040	9,761,480	8,540,000
Silver	7,131,520	8,727,600	10,279,200	10,484,000
Bills discounted	29,157,680	27,121,040	25,098,280	*18,413,000
Advances and loans	4,795,760	5,695,400	5,791,080	—
Notes in circulation	51,621,800	52,229,000	52,189,240	43,440,000
Treasury advances, coupon account	765,200	564,160	95,000	—
Treasury balances	480,560	123,800	72,440	—

* Including loans.

LONDON COURSE OF EXCHANGE.

Place.	Usance.	April 26.	April 28.	May 3.	May 5.
Amsterdam and Rotterdam	short	12'3	12'2	12'2	12'2
Do. do.	3 months	12'4⅜	12'4½	12'4½	12'4⅜
Antwerp and Brussels	3 months	25'63¾	25'61¼	25'60	25'60
Hamburg	3 months	20'75	20'72	20'72	20'73
Berlin and German B. Places	3 months	20'75	20'73	20'73	20'73
Paris	cheques	25'35	25'32½	25'32½	25'35
Do.	3 months	25'50	25'46¼	25'46¼	25'48¾
Marseilles	3 months	25'51¼	25'47½	25'50	25'50
Switzerland	3 months	25'72½	25'72½	25.73¾	25'72½
Austria	3 months	12'25	12'23¾	12'22½	12'21¼
St. Petersburg	3 months	24⅜	24⅜	24⅜	24⅜
Moscow	3 months	24 13/16	24 13/16	24 13/16	24 13/16
Italian Bank Places	3 months	27'60	27'35	27.40	27'42½
New York	60 days	48⅝	48⅝	48 11/16	48 11/16
Madrid and Spanish B. P.	3 months	25⅛	25⅛	23½	nom.
Lisbon	3 months	31⅛	30⅜	30⅜	29⅞
Oporto	3 months	31⅛	30⅜	30⅜	29⅞
Copenhagen	3 months	18'47	18'46	18'46	18'46
Christiania	3 months	18'47	18'46	18'46	18'46
Stockholm	3 months	18'47	18'46	18'46	18'46

OPEN MARKET DISCOUNT.

	Per cent.
Thirty and sixty day remitted bills	3⅝
Three months "	3 11/16–3¾
Four months "	3¾
Six months "	3¾
Three months fine inland bills	4
Four months "	4
Six months "	4¼

BANK AND DEPOSIT RATES.

	Per cent.
Bank of England minimum discount rate	4
" " short loan rates	4
Banker's rate on deposits	2½
Bill brokers' deposit rate (call)	2½
" 7 and 14 days' notice	2¾
Current rates for 7 day loans	2½–3
" " for call loans	2–3

Stock Market Notes and Comments.

Since we wrote last the Stock Exchange has completed its settlement comfortably enough in all departments excepting the Western Australian. There the troubles of the so-called "Bottomley Group" of wondrous companies still cause much anxiety, and have produced several failures. It was announced at the end of the week that the "difficulties" had been surmounted, and only two more members were declared defaulters when the market opened again on Tuesday. We do not believe in this pretty story, and expect to hear a good deal more of these troubles before they are ended. Much questionable business has been transacted in the shares of these companies, and if everybody had their deserts, a few men, members of the Stock Exchange and outsiders, would soon be cooling their heels in some one or other of her Majesty's prisons. We hope some of them will get there before all is over. Such a patch-up as has now been made is merely a make-believe payment of debts in many cases, for the simple reason that, clever as modern financiers sometimes are, they cannot always make paper perform the functions of gold. Small in some respects though this filthy puddle is, it has shaken the whole Western Australian market, and will make the engineering of advances in the shares dealt in there difficult for some time to come. We therefore think the public should avoid this section of the Stock Exchange as much as possible, at least until the test of time has been applied to it. Six months hence we shall probably know a good deal more about it than we do now.

In other departments the attitude has been more cheerful, and quite a smart advance occurred in American railroad securities on Tuesday, upon the strength of the news from the Philippines. Short-sighted and sanguine people, here and in the States, jumped to the conclusion that the destruction of the Spanish squadron in the Bay of Manila meant the end of the war. They now begin to see that they were wrong, and the clouds are again gathering over not only this department of the Exchange, but of others also. It was easy to overcome, in the Philippines, a number of old ships and forts badly manned and gunned. The task of subduing Cuba and destroying the Atlantic fleet of Spain has still to be accomplished, and we fear it is going to take both time and a great deal of money. Meanwhile trouble is brewing in Spain itself, and default on her public debt may be looked upon as certain next July. A further fall in Spanish bonds is therefore probable. There will be fluctuations, of course, representing the tug-of-war between "bull" and "bear," but the tendency must be downward, and the further the fall progresses the greater the danger of collapse in other directions. Portugal and Brazil are likely to be involved in the ruin of Spain, because their finances have been propped and patched up by substantially the same class of men. The centre of strength for all these States has been the Paris market, and that is now suffering grievously at many points. How long it can continue able to bear the strain put upon it from many quarters we should not like to guess, but it will be prudent for people here interested in stock markets to keep a watchful eye on France. There are more elements of the kind that work to produce an explosion active there at the present hour than have been stirring since 1848.

Home securities, too, will be again adversely affected by the distress elsewhere, and by the necessities of the two Powers at war. The United States will require a great deal of money, and Spain, under whatever Government, must abstract money from the pockets of her creditors if she is to continue the fight. The displacement or loss of funds thus produced cannot but jar on a sensitive market like ours, and so we still think it prudent to advise caution in buying. People are too apt to imagine when they see a rise of one or two pounds in prices that they have missed the opportunity to buy. They may be assured that they are in no danger of doing this just yet in any division of the stock markets. We have to provide for a great many requirements this year outside those arising from the present war, chief amongst these being the higher price we, and all European countries, are paying for bread. This not only demands more money everywhere, but directly impoverishes large sections of the community. As the year progresses we shall feel the effects of this impoverishment and all the unusual demands for money more and more acutely. The last fortnight has made us happy in witnessing large imports of gold, but we forgot that most of this gold came to us either as payment of the German half of the Chinese Loan, or in transit on its way to the States, principally in payment for wheat bought there by Continental nations to supply their unusual deficiency. In short, we stand to lose this gold again, and probably will lose most of it in the autumn, if not sooner. It is not, in other words, a stable foundation on which to build a renewed and permanent advance in public securities. Probably enough, people who have money really to invest can do no harm in purchasing the best classes of domestic securities on a falling market at any time. They may by and bye see lower prices for what they have bought, but these lower prices could be taken advantage of to increase their investments, so as to obtain a higher average rate of interest, and whatever the interest they obtain may be, it is as safe as anything mundane can ever be. We therefore in no way discourage prudent investment, provided it is confined to non-speculative securities of the best class. What we are always endeavouring to do is to discountenance speculation on mere transitory phases of markets whose condition must, from surrounding circumstances, be slippery and treacherous for many months to come.

In spite of the permanent instructions in the REVIEW people continually write to ask us what mine share or group of shares they had best purchase to "make a bit" on. A little reflection should convince them of the futility of this proceeding. We can no more tell what the quality of ninety-nine mines out of 100 may be than we can predict next year's weather. Good and proved mines are visible to everybody, and their quality is emphatically expressed in the price of their shares. So far as we can judge, looking at the matter coldly and without prejudice, there is not a really cheap mine share in the market. A strong combined attempt is being made to induce the public to believe that Witwatersrand shares are now "worth buying for a good rise." Some few may be, as lottery tickets, but as we cannot foretell the prizes in a lottery, we decline to recommend them, and are very sure that most, if not all, the high-priced shares, deep level and other, are at the present moment well above their intrinsic value. What man in his sober senses would pay £30 for a £1 Rand Mines share? They, with many others similarly inflated, may go higher, because the power of the cliques behind them is great, but they are not an "investment" in any sense where they stand, and there is room for a prodigious fall.

The Week's Stock Markets.

Business has again been very restricted, the holiday in London on Monday being followed by the closing of Wall-street on Wednesday. The differences to be met in the Western Australian market caused considerable anxiety for several days, but matters were at length patched or shored up, and fewer failures occurred than was at one time feared. An almost general rise has since taken place, due to re-purchases by "bears," but Spanish bonds are lower, owing to the alarming rumours from Madrid, and Rio Tinto shares have fallen heavily. Consols were weaker on Saturday, on the revival of the American demand for gold, but there has been a recovery since.

Highest and Lowest this Year.		Last Carrying over Price.	BRITISH FUNDS, &c.	Closing Price.	Rise or Fall.
113⅜	109¼	—	Consols 2¾ p.c. (Money)...	111	- ⅜
113 1/16	109½	111¼	Do. Account (June 1)	111⅛	—
106¼	101	104½	2½ p.c. Stock red. 1905 ...	104½	+1¼
363	341	—	Bank of England Stock...	346	-1½
117	111⅜	114	India 3½ p.c. Stk. red. 1931	114	—
109½	103⅜	107½	Do. 3 p.c. Stk. red. 1948	107	+ ½
96⅜	90	92¼	Do. 2½ p.c. Stk. red. 1926	92	—

Consols register a further advance, owing to the large influx of gold into the Bank, and the account disclosed a scarcity of stock, judging by the continuation rate which was only 2—2½ per cent. The proposals of the Indian Government to establish a gold currency caused a sharp rise in the Indian sterling loans, but rupee paper has lost most of the advance which took place at the beginning of the week, the exchange being lower. Colonial Government stocks have picked up a good deal, and the premier securities of the leading Home Railway Companies also show a little recovery.

The Home Railway market has been a firm one, and prices are all marked higher. There is practically no account open just now, so a very little buying caused an advance out of all proportion to the amount of business really transacted. Some persistent buying of "Underground" stocks is the feature, exhibition traffic prospects being the only reason assigned for the sharp rise in Metropolitan Ordinary and New Ordinary; but this inquiry on a market bare of stock was accountable for the rise of several points. Satisfactory traffic returns were published by all the companies with the exception of the Great Western, which is still suffering from the effects of the Welsh coal strike. The passenger lines did especially well last week, and both the Brighton and South-Eastern Companies' deferred stocks have been inquired for, and Great Eastern was also firmer for the same reason.

Highest and Lowest this Year.		Last Carrying over Price.	HOME RAILWAYS.	Closing Price.	Rise or Fall.
186	172½	175¼	Brighton Def.	176¼	+1¼
59¼	54⅝	55⅝	Caledonian Def.	56⅜	+⅜
20⅜	18¼	18¾	Chatham Ordinary	19⅜	+⅛
77¼	62	63	Great Central Pref.	64	+1
24⅝	21¼	21½	Do. Def.	21¾	+½
124½	118	119¼	Great Eastern	119½	+⅛
61⅞	50¾	52	Great Northern Def.	53¼	+1¼
179⅞	168¼	169¾	Great Western	169¼	—
51¾	45¼	49¼	Hull and Barnsley	50½	+½
149¼	145	146	Lanc. and Yorkshire	146½	+½
136¼	127¼	127½	Metropolitan	131¼	+3¾
31	26¾	27¼	Metropolitan District	28	+¾
88¾	82½	83½	Midland Pref.	84¼	+½
95⅝	84½	86	Do. Def.	87¼	+¾
93¼	86¾	87¼	North British Pref.	88½	+1
47½	41¾	42⅞	Do. Def.	43¼	+⅜
181½	172¾	173½	North Eastern	174¼	+¾
205½	196½	197½	North Western	197⅜	—
117⅛	105½	108	South Eastern Def.	109¼	+1
98¾	87	88½	South Western Def.	90½	+1½

The market for United States railroad shares displayed a hesitating tendency during the latter part of last week, and business dwindled away almost to nothing at all. Wall-street operators, however, became very excited on Monday over the news of the victory of the United States fleet off Manila, and a wild rush of buying orders sent prices up from one to four dollars. When the London market reopened on Tuesday it was soon found that only a feeble response was forthcoming, which rather discouraged Wall-street, while profit-taking, in view of the holiday in New York on Wednesday, tended to impart a dull tone. Quotations are nevertheless considerably higher than a week ago, but there is still a decided disinclination on the part of home operators to increase their commitments to any great extent. The Baltimore and Ohio Company defaulted on the 1st inst. on its main line sterling loan, and an early reorganisation scheme is looked for. Canadian Pacific shares were firmer in sympathy with the American market, and a good traffic return, coupled with a satisfactory working statement for March, brought in some buying orders; but the report that the meeting of the trans-continental lines, in order to end the rate war, has been postponed, caused a certain amount of profit-taking.

Highest and Lowest this Year.		Last Carrying over Price.	CANADIAN AND U.S. RAILWAYS.	Closing Prices.	Rise or Fall.
14⅛	10⅜	10½	Atchison Shares	12¼	+1⅜
34	23½	24⅝	Do. Pref.	28⅞	+3⅜
15⅝	11	11	Central Pacific	12½	+1¼
99¾	85½	87¾	Chic. Mil. & St. Paul	95⅝	+6⅝
14¼	10	10½	Denver Shares	11⅛	+1
54¼	41½	42½	Do. Prefd.	47⅛	+4½
16⅜	11¼	11⅛	Erie Shares	13⅜	+1¼
44⅛	29¼	32¾	Do. Prefd.	35	+1⅜
110½	99	100	Illinois Central	104½	+4
62½	45¼	47¾	Louisville & Nashville	53¼	+5¾
14½	9⅞	10¼	Missouri & Texas	11⅜	+1
122⅜	108½	110½	New York Central	118	+6½
57¼	42⅝	45	Norfolk & West. Prefd.	50¾	+5¼
70⅛	59	61⅞	Northern Pacific Prefd.	67¾	+4⅝
19½	13⅜	14	Ontario Shares	15¼	+1⅛
62½	56¼	57½	Pennsylvania	59½	+1⅜
12½	7⅞	8	Reading Shares	9¼	+1
34¼	24¼	25¼	Southern Prefd.	29	+3¼
37⅛	18½	19	Union Pacific	22⅜	+2⅛
20¼	14⅝	15½	Wabash Prefd.	17⅛	+1⅛
30¼	21	22	Do. Income Debs.	24¾	+2¾
92¼	74	80½	Canadian Pacific	85¼	+2⅝
78⅛	69⅞	73¼	Grand Trunk Guar.	73¾	+⅜
69¼	57½	67½	Do. 1st Pref.	67⅝	+¾
50½	37¼	47¾	Do. 2nd Pref.	48¼	+¾
25¼	19¼	22⅜	Do. 3rd Pref.	22⅜	+¼
103¾	101½	102	Do. 4 p.c. Deb.	102¾	+¾

Apart from Spanish bonds the Foreign market has been a firm one, although the Paris Bourse showed some weakness, especially towards the close of last week. The weakness there seems to have been caused by apprehensions of difficulties at the settlement, but rates came out lighter than had been expected, and the account being satisfactorily arranged a firmer tone was soon apparent. Spanish 4 per cents. have of course been depressed, the news of the defeat of the Spanish fleet at Manila, followed by the proclamation of martial law in Madrid, causing a decline down to the lowest point yet touched. Another reason for the weakness is the continued rise in the Madrid exchange, and the proposal to convert the present external into an internal loan was also viewed unfavourably. Although some few of the other inter-Bourse securities have weakened in sympathy, it has not been to any great extent, and the latest quotations are generally higher on balance. Brazilian bonds continue their upward move, the visit of the vice-president to Europe being expected to lead to good results. Argentine and Chilian issues have hardened in sympathy, and Peruvian corporation debentures are higher. Mexican stocks have also been in demand, and now stand about on the level of a few weeks back before the heavy fall occurred.

Highest and Lowest this Year.		Last Carrying over Price.	FOREIGN BONDS.	Closing Price.	Rise or Fall.
94½	84	87	Argentine 5 p.c. 1886	87¾	—
92⅞	81⅝	85	Do. 6 p.c. Funding	85⅜	−⅛
76¾	64	67	Do. 5 p.c. B. Ay. Water	68½	+½
61⅜	41⅛	41½	Brazilian 4 p.c. 1889	43½	−1⅛
69⅞	46	46	Do. 5 p.c. 1895	48⅜	−1
65	42¾	43	Do. 5 p.c. West Minas Ry.	46	−½
108⅝	105½	107¼	Egyptian 4 p.c. Unified	106⅞x.d.	+1¼
104¾	100½	101	Do. 3½ p.c. Pref.	101¼	+½
103	99½	100½	French 3 p.c. Rente	101½	+1
44⅞	34½	42½	Greek 4 p.c. Monopoly	43	−½
93⅞	88¾	90½	Italian 5 p.c. Rente	91	+⅜
100	87½	93	Mexican 6 p.c. 1888	95½	+1½
20⅞	16	16⅞	Portuguese 1 p.c.	17¼	+⅜
62½	29⅜	34¼	Spanish 4 p.c.	30½	−3⅜
45½	40	41¼	Turkish 1 p.c. "B"	44¼	+2½
26⅛	22¾	23⅝	Do. 1 p.c. "C"	24⅝	+1
22⅛	20	20½	Do. 1 p.c. "D"	21⅜	+½
46⅜	40	44¾	Uruguay 3½ p.c. Bonds	45x.d.	+¾

Foreign Railway stocks have been actively dealt in at considerably higher prices, the leading Argentine companies meeting with most support, notably Buenos Ayres and Pacific Prefs. and Central Argentine. Among changes in the adverse direction, a decline of 12½ in Royal Trans-African 5 per cent. First Mortgage bonds is the principal feature. Mexican Railway issues were firmer, owing to the rise in the price of silver, and the subsequent drop in the price of the metal did not cause much of a set-back. Nitrate shares advaneed slightly in spite of a poor traffic return.

Highest and Lowest this Year.		Last Carrying over Price.	FOREIGN RAILWAYS.	Closing Price.	Rise or Fall.
100	99½	100	Argentine Gt. West. 5 p.c. Pref. Stock	100	—
158¼	136	140	B. Ay. Gt. Southern Ord.	143	−1
78½	65	68	B. Ay. and Rosario Ord.	71½	+1½
12¼	10¼	10½	B. Ay. Western Ord.	10½	—
87¼	73	77	Central Argentine Ord.	78¼	—
92	81	82	Cordoba and Rosario 6 p.c. Deb.	81	−2
95½	85½	86	Cord. Cent. 4 p.c. Deb. (Cent. Nth. Sec.)	88½	+2½
61⅞	42	42½	Do. Income Deb. Stk.	49	+4
25¼	16¾	17¼	Mexican Ord. Stk.	18½	+¾
83½	69½	71	Do. 8 p.c. 1st Pref.	73	+1¾

Among Miscellaneous securities, Anglo-American Telegraph stocks have been put up, on the idea that the war will benefit the company; and the debentures of several other kindred concerns have risen for no other reason. Welsbach Gas ordinary rose 6 directly the special settlement was got over; Nobel-Dynamite advanced owing to a satisfactory dividend announcement; Coats and English Sewing Cotton shares have again attracted attention, large buying orders coming from Glasgow; and City Offices 3 per cent. debentures have risen 7 or 8 points. In the Brewery list Guinness shows a rise of 20, and several of the lower-priced American companies' shares have been inquired for. Hotel Cecil preference and debentures fell sharply, owing to the passing of the dividend on the preference; Dumont Coffee issues show a further decline, and United Alkali debentures have been pressed for sale.

The principal feature just at the last was a sharp fall in Consols caused partly by Lord Salisbury's remarks at the Albert Hall, and partly by a poor Bank return. Indian Government stocks also gave way, and left off weak. Among Foreign Government issues Spanish 4 per cents. closed rather above the worst, but still $3\frac{3}{8}$ down on the week, and Rio Tinto shares hardened a little before the close. Argentine and Brazilian bonds fell considerably, and are finally lower than a week ago. United States Railroad shares were actively dealt in on rumours to the effect that Spain had given way, and the last quotations are about the best of the week. Canadian Pacific and Grand Trunk issues closed firm in sympathy.

MINING AND FINANCE COMPANIES.

The South African market has been steady to firm for the greater part of the week, with a duller tendency towards the close. President Kruger's speech at the opening of the Volksraad was considered encouraging, although no indication was given of the nature of forthcoming measures, but it is rumoured that the loan negotiations are progressing satisfactorily. The Paris settlement passing off smoothly, a little support was then forthcoming from that quarter, deep level companies attracting some attention, and most of the better class shares are marked up a little. Western Australian ventures were adversely affected by the state of uncertainty as to whether the various accounts of those mixed up in the Bottomley collapse would be arranged, and during this state of suspense prices crumbled away. It was a relief to all concerned when matters were to a certain extent smoothed over for the time being, but not before several more small failures had been reported. "Northern Terrors" and Market Trust have shed a little more of their already sadly-diminished prices, but a big rise has taken place in Golden Horse Shoe on rumours of some new developments at the mine, and Kalgurli and Hannan's Brown Hill have also gone ahead. There was a more cheerful tone in the general mining market, but no increase in the volume of business. Indian shares keep very steady, and are not often mentioned, although the crushing returns were again good. Copper shares have shown some rather considerable movements, Rio Tinto, after rising steadily, suddenly giving way on a rumour that the Spanish Government intended levying a tax on the metal, and Paris operators taking fright, the price fell sharply.

THE CRÉDIT FONCIER OF FRANCE.

The Governor of this great establishment, which was founded in 1852, and for thirty years stood in the first rank of the most important of those existing in France, is appointed by the Government. The Crédit Foncier was created in order to aid the agricultural population, but it abandoned its primary benevolent character, and, after having undergone several transformations, has become a real bank. Besides its share capital it has issued a debenture capital amounting at the present time to 3,796 million francs nominal value, or 2,951 millions effective value, and possesses a reserve fund of 165 millions. It received the privilege of issuing *obligations à lots* in France at the time of its foundation. It has often been considered by the French to be as trustworthy as the Bank of France itself. Unhappily, it has not been managed with sufficient ability to enable it to maintain its reputation; and during the past fifteen years it has lost its former high position and has become an establishment with no more credit than a secondary bank; investors do not believe that it will ever be able to regain its once prominent standing, and, as a general rule, it no longer enjoys the confidence of French capitalists after having for so long been regarded as the safest of all banks. Space will not allow us to trace here the history of the Crédit Foncier, but we may remind the English investor that its downfall has been brought about solely by its scandalous speculations; and in this we include the speculations in land at Paris and Nice, as well as those conducted on the property market and the Bourse, which have often assumed gigantic proportions. Until the day of its decline, the Crédit Foncier was the main instrument employed by the Government, both under the Third Empire and the Third Republic, for the purpose of influencing the Bourse; and all of the many different ministers who have administered the Financial Department have not only made use of its services, but have scandalously abused them.

But this state of things could not continue indefinitely, and, in 1895, the day came when M. Christophle, the Governor, found it necessary to resign his office in order to avoid revelations perhaps worse than those which had recently been brought to light in the Panama business. The resignation of M. Christophle, who had held the post of Governor for eighteen years, was the direct result of an inquiry made by the Inspectors of Finances into the state of the Crédit Foncier. The responsibility for the irregularities committed under the preceding administration still remains to be explained, but, while we do not in the least take upon ourselves the defence of M. Christophle, we think the Conseil d'Etat is especially blameworthy for having, after due discussion, approved of the statutes submitted to its consideration: for these statutes included the power of dealing in stocks and shares on the Bourse. This was simply equivalent to giving a moral sanction to the future acts, whatever they might be, of this privileged company. For a quarter of a century, it was consequently like an overflowing of the Pactolus; the Crédit Foncier paid enormous dividends to its shareholders running from 15 to 25 per cent., and its shares, of the nominal amount of 500 francs, then only half-paid up, rose above 1,800 francs, the price at which they were exchanged on the Bourse fifteen years ago. The confidence of the public was at that time absolute.

It was only in 1882, at the time that the Crédit Foncier amalgamated with its young rival the Banque Hypothécaire, that its shares were fully paid-up, a sum of twenty-six million francs having been furnished for this purpose by the shareholders of the Banque Hypothécaire. The situation has since altered greatly, and to-day the shares of the Crédit Foncier are obtainable on the market at the much lower price of 660 or 670 francs, and the dividend to be paid to the shareholders for 1897 has just been fixed at twenty-five francs, being a net yield of 3·65 per cent. The real solidity of the Crédit Foncier, however, cannot be doubted; but the shareholders can only expect to increase the present very modest dividend by allowing a new, prudent, honest, and enlightened administration to operate for their benefit. It is indispensable, first of all, that the Government should strictly keep the Crédit Foncier to its true rôle of intermediate agent, and take especial care that the loans of the future are not negotiated without solid security. The confidence of the general public, moreover, has been so much shaken that it can only be restored if the Crédit Foncier renounces its old methods of trying to earn its dividends by means of speculative campaigns. It is absolutely necessary, too, that the new Governor should publish frank and frequent returns showing the real state of business, instead of imitating his precedessor by keeping the true condition of affairs in darkness by issuing ambiguous or incomplete accounts. M. Labeyrie, on the other hand, must, of course, be afforded the necessary time to improve the position as left by M. Christophle. We must say, however, that he appears to have begun the work of amelioration most unfortunately, for last year he instituted two conversions, which were equivalent to a compulsory diminution of interest for the debenture-holders. This has produced a very bad impression, and if M. Labeyrie does not wish to lose his *clientèle* he will avoid such action in the future. An examination of the present situation shows that the rate of interest of the loans of the Crédit Foncier is still too high, compared with the rate of money on the market; and the result is that for four or five years many borrowers have taken advantage of the clause for reimbursement and repaid their debts. That forces the Crédit Foncier to repurchase on the Bourse debentures of a similar amount, and these latter are usually quoted at par; hence there is a loss, which is sometimes serious. The diminution in the employment of the capital and reserves in loans results in an increase in the figure of the securities possessed by the Crédit Foncier, whether they are its own, or only held as guarantees. In 1897, the loans of that nature amounted only to sixty-two and a half millions, against sixty-six in 1896, and seventy-four in 1895 and 1894. On December 31, 1897, the amount of the loans made with the debenture capital was 3,116 million francs. It is quite clear that the profits of the Crédit Foncier still continue to decrease, and that it has great difficulty in fighting against recent economical transformations. The 3 per cent. debentures, of the same type as those of the railways, constitute a heavy burden of redemption for the Crédit Foncier, and, judging from what is being whispered by many well-informed people, we fear that the bearers of these certificates will, in the very near future, be compelled to submit to another conversion. That is not the right method to aid the Crédit Foncier to regain its ancient prestige with investors; but must, on the contrary, result in an avalanche of *valeurs à lots* being thrown on the market, where the buyers will be very few, as there is very little demand now for that class of investment.

TWO MINOR ELECTRIC LIGHT COMPANIES.

In dealing with the important London electric companies, we did not enter upon the prospects of the two new companies working in the London area—the County of London and Brush and the South London. Their works have been so recently put up that the revenue earned was no criterion of their future ability to produce dividends for their shareholders; and so we did not care to deal with them in conjunction with the dividend-paying concerns.

Of the two the South London appears to us to be a very poorly conceived undertaking. Although styled the South London, it possesses, we believe, only the right to supply energy in the Parish of Lambeth, which is not a great area, nor a very promising one. Indeed, the London Electric Supply, which has been working in the South of London for years, did not think it worth while applying to light more than the extreme northern part of the parish, as the prospects of revenue were so poor in its other parts. Then, to the east of this parish for the greater part of its extent lies Camberwell, through the principal streets of which two other electric companies—the County of London and Brush and the London Electric Supply—are laying their cables, and the local authorities would doubtless object to another company entering the district. To the west lies Battersea, in which the local authority is preparing to supply its own light, and Clapham and Streatham, which are already supplied by the County of London and Brush.

Therefore the South London Company's area is small and is likely to remain so, yet it has raised capital to the extent of £113,556 and will doubtless raise more. The cost of the provisional order and preliminary expenses came to the extravagant figure of £47,649; and the manner in which some of the shares were issued was not at all to our liking. With a poor and restricted district and heavily capitalised, the prospects appear to be very unsatisfactory, and the quotation of a considerable premium for the shares must be esteemed an aberration of the market, misled by the influence of the excellent results obtained by the older companies.

The County of London and Brush has a great part of London to work upon, but it is not by any means the best from a revenue-earning point of view. The districts of Clerkenwell and St. Luke's, with the Holborn district, contain business quarters that may consume a certain amount of energy, especially as the Gas Light and Coke Company has raised its price for gas. The larger area of the company's operation is, however, in the South of London, and here it has built a great station to supply the Putney, Wandsworth, Streatham, Clapham, and Tooting Graveney districts. In those parishes, we believe, it has no competitor at present, but then, of course, gas is supplied by the gas company at 2s. 3d. per thousand feet. The company is also laying mains in the parishes of Camberwell, St. George the Martyr, St. Olave's, and Horsleydown, but here it finds a competitor in the shape of the London Electric Supply Corporation, which has its works at Deptford and is thus well able to supply energy in the South of London. The price charged will have to be low in this South London area, as the moderate price of gas will necessitate cheapness in order to obtain even a footing.

The company certainly showed a fair profit last year, but this was drawn mainly from financial operations and a large profit obtained from the sale of its interest in the Bournemouth and Poole Electricity Supply Company. It has considerable interest in two other provincial companies, but although these are profitable ventures the expenditure required upon the London part of the business quite dwarfs their importance. Meantime, the revenue from the two London stations at work has so far been very small, and it seems as if revenue in their cases will take time to grow. Capital expenditure on the other districts, however, is going on, and must be provided for, and it is therefore very probable that the premium of 40 per cent. upon the ordinary shares, which have never yet received a dividend, is too high. It may be years yet before a fair dividend is received upon the shares, while the continual expenditure required by the company to protect its districts must lead to fresh issues of capital from time to time.

MINING RETURNS.

LEICESTER CONSOLIDATED.—4,525 loads washed, producing 151 carats.

WELD HERCULES.—Crushed 237 tons, produced 198 oz. gold. Tailings 6 dwt. per ton.

BELLEVUE PROPRIETARY.—196 tons crushed, yielding 417 oz.

BROKEN HILL PROPRIETARY.—25,019 tons of ore treated, including product from ores purchased, and the output from the refinery was 487,155 oz. silver, 2,390 tons of lead, and 57 tons of antimonial lead (estimated), the copper matte containing 22 tons of copper (estimated) and 22,304 oz. of silver (estimated).

LONDONDERRY.—300 tons crushed for a yield of 582 oz. gold.

OTTOS KOPJE.—7,786 loads washed, 224 carats of diamonds won.

NORTH BURGESS.—Result of last clean up was 232 oz. from 35 tons.

VICTORIA AND QUEEN.—Partial clean up of 520 tons for 961 oz. gold.

HAURAKI.—Crushed 130 tons for 424 oz.

CUDDINGWARRA.—Crushed during month 334 tons of ore, yielding 288 oz. gold; assay of tailings 20 dwt.

BRILLIANT.—2,550 tons of stone crushed for a yield of 3,000 oz. gold.

MELBOURNE DEMOCRAT.—Crushed 295 tons of stone for 247 oz. gold, and 115 tons of mullock for 29 oz. of gold.

PESTARENA UNITED.—452 tons of ore produced 462 oz. of gold.

KOFFYFONTEIN.—Returns for April, 3,151 carats diamonds.

NORTH BOULDER.—324 oz. gold from 342 tons crushed.

LADY SHENTON.—Crushed 600 tons; yield, 1,760 oz. 14 dwt., including 110 oz. 14 dwt. from plates.

BONNIE DUNDEE.—Crushed 153 tons of quartz from the Victory Reef (1,090 ft. formation) for 193 oz. of gold, and 184 tons of quartz from the Victory Reef (1,575 ft. formation) for 214 oz. of gold.

CHAMPION EXTENDED AND HOME RULE.—1,050 tons of ore crushed yielded 821 oz. of gold, including concentrates.

CHAMPION REEF.—Last month's return:—7,470 tons of stone produced 9,170 oz. of gold, 2,380 tons of tailings produced 398 oz. of gold, 4,775 tons of tailings (cyanide process) produced 1,342 oz. of gold.

DAY DAWN BLOCK AND WYNDHAM.—Tons crushed, 1,270; yield of gold, 1,111 oz., including tailings.

DAY DAWN P. C.—Crushing for past fortnight—No. 1 shaft, 320 tons, 355 oz.; No. 3 shaft, 114 tons, 88 oz.

MYSORE WEST AND MYSORE WYNAAD.—Bullion return for April:—Ounces of gold 380, from 1,400 tons of ore crushed.

MOUNT USHER.—100 tons crushed yielded 44 oz. of gold.

COROMANDEL.—Last month's return:—1,200 tons of stone produced 803 oz. of gold; 1,100 tons of tailings (cyanide process) produced 102 oz. of gold.

MYSORE.—Return for April:—7,020 tons of quartz produced 11,383 oz. of gold; 2,765 tons of tailings produced 764 oz. of gold; 1,820 tons of tailings (cyanide process) produced 247 oz. of gold.

IVANHOE.—Clean up for last two weeks, 1,476 oz. of gold from 909 tons crushed; total return for April, 2,977 oz. of gold from 1,902 tons crushed.

NINE REEFS.—900 tons of stone crushed yielded, by amalgamation, 81 oz. of gold; by cyanide process, 59 oz. of gold.

NORSEMAN.—Return for April:—Ounces of gold, 826, from 861 tons of ore crushed.

NUNDYDROOG COMPANY.—April return:—3,010 tons quartz crushed, produced 2,779 oz. of gold; 750 tons of tailings treated yielded 83 oz. of gold; 2,890 tons of tailings treated by cyanide yielded 367 oz. of gold.

OOREGUM.—Last month's return:—5,903 tons of quartz produced 3,563 oz. of gold 4,600 tons of tailings produced 634 oz. of gold.

TOLIMA.—Estimated April returns (60 tons), £2,009.

MOUNT YAGAHONG.—800 tons of ore crushed for a yield of 780 oz. melted gold, exclusive of tailings.

FRANK SMITH DIAMOND.—5,100 loads washed, producing 253 carats.

RAILWAY TRAFFIC RETURNS.

ALCOY AND GANDIA RAILWAY AND HARBOUR COMPANY.—Traffic for week, April 30:—Ps. 8,800; increase, Ps. 400. Aggregate from January 1, Ps. 155,590; increase, Ps. 4,480.

QUEBEC CENTRAL RAILWAY.—Receipts for second week of April, $6,963; decrease, $7,437. Aggregate from July 1, $95,754; decrease, $14,898.

MOBILE AND BIRMINGHAM RAILROAD.—Traffic for second week of April, $6,010; increase, $663. Aggregate from July 1, $297,502; decrease, $2,123.

ALGECIRAS (GIBRALTAR) RAILWAY.—Traffic for week ended April 23, Ps. 24,540; increase, Ps. 7,500. Aggregate from July 1, Ps. 864,792; increase, Ps. 37,078.

WEST FLANDERS RAILWAY.—Gross receipts for week ending April—May 1, £2,339; increase, £42. Total from January 1, £39,610; increase, £1,007.

WEST OF INDIA PORTUGUESE RAILWAY.—Week ending April 6, Rs. 3,930; increase, Rs. 312. Aggregate from January 1, Rs. 63,990; increase, Rs. 18,613.

PUERTO CABELLO AND VALENCIA RAILWAY.—Traffic receipts for week ending March 25, £549; decrease, £124. Aggregate from January 1, £11,911; decrease, £4,722.

DELHI UMBALLA KALKA RAILWAY.—Receipts for week ended April 30, Rs. 28,900; increase, Rs. 1,300. Aggregate from January 1, Rs. 6,07,000; increase, 1,55,200.

ROHILKUND AND KUMAON RAILWAY.—Traffic receipts for week ending April 2, Rs. 10,160; increase, Rs. 403. Aggregate from January 1, Rs. 90,432; decrease, Rs. 12,673.

WESTERN OF SANTA FE RAILWAYS.—Gross receipts for week ending April 30, $46,485; increase, $25,055.

VILLA MARIA AND RUFINO RAILWAY.—Traffic for week ending April 30, $292; increase, $36. Aggregate from January 1, $6,059; increase, $881.

MANILA RAILWAY.—Receipts for week ending April 30, $19,000; increase, $4,387. Aggregate from January 1, $330,961; increase, $78,141.

SOUTHERN MAHRATTA RAILWAY.—Receipts for week ended April 2, Rs. 14,2661; increase, Rs. 10,705.

MIDLAND URUGUAY RAILWAY.—Receipts for month of March, £3,404; decrease £214.

SOUTHERN PACIFIC RAILWAY.—The net earnings for the month of March, $1,525,341; increase, $339,190.

DOMINION ATLANTIC RAILWAY.—Receipts for month of March, $37,760; increase £2,348.

CLEATOR AND WORKINGTON.—Gross receipts for the week ending April 30 amounted to £1,154, an increase of £16. Total receipts from January 1, £17,420, a decrease of £704.

COCKERMOUTH AND KESWICK RAILWAY.—Receipts for the week ending April 30, £842; increase, £74. Aggregate from January 1, £14,121; increase, £1,336.

BENGAL CENTRAL RAILWAY.—Traffic receipts for week ending April 9, Rs. 19,108; increase, Rs. 2,490.

Prices of Mine and Mining Finance Companies' Shares.

Shares £1 each except where otherwise stated.

AUSTRALIAN.

Making-Up Price, Apr. 26.	Name	Closing Price.	Rise or Fall.	Making-Up Price, Apr. 26.	Name	Closing Price.	Rise or Fall.
[illegible]	Aladdin	[illegible]		[illegible]	Hannan's Star	[illegible]	
[illegible]	Associated	[illegible]	+ [illegible]	[illegible]	Ivanhoe, New	[illegible]	+ [illegible]
[illegible]	Do. Southern	[illegible]	+ [illegible]	[illegible]	KalgurliMt.&IronKing,18/	[illegible]	
1	Brownhill Extended	[illegible]	+ [illegible]	[illegible]	Kalgurli	[illegible]	+ [illegible]
[illegible]	Burbank's Birthday	[illegible]		[illegible]	Lady Shenton	[illegible]	+ [illegible]
[illegible]	Central Boulder	[illegible]	− [illegible]	[illegible]	Lake View Cons.	[illegible]	+ [illegible]
5/3	Chaffers, 4/	5/6	+ 1/	[illegible]	Do. Extended	[illegible]	
46/3	Colonial Finance, 15/	[illegible] dis	− [illegible]	[illegible]	Do. South	[illegible]	+ [illegible]
—	Crœsus S. United	[illegible]		[illegible]	London & Globe Finance	[illegible]	
[illegible]	E. Murchison	[illegible]	+ [illegible]	[illegible]	London&W.A.Exploration	[illegible]	+ [illegible]
4/6	Golden Arrow 19/	4/6	+ /6	[illegible]	Do. Investment	[illegible]	+ [illegible]
[illegible]	Golden Horseshoe	[illegible]	+ [illegible]	[illegible]	Mainland Consols	[illegible]	
[illegible]	Golden Link	[illegible]		[illegible]	North Boulder, 10/	[illegible]	+ [illegible]
18/9	Great Boulder, 2/	19/6	+ /6	[illegible]	North Kalgurli	[illegible]	+ [illegible]
[illegible]	Do. Main Reef, 10/	[illegible]	+ [illegible]	[illegible]	Northern Territories	[illegible]	− [illegible]
[illegible]	Do. Perseverance	[illegible]	+ [illegible]	[illegible]	Peak Hill	[illegible]	+ [illegible]
[illegible]	Do. South	[illegible]		[illegible]	South Kalgurli	[illegible]	+ [illegible]
[illegible]	Hainault	[illegible]		[illegible]	W. A. Goldfields	[illegible]	+ [illegible]
[illegible]	Hampton Plains	[illegible]	+ [illegible]	1	W. A. Joint Stock	[illegible]	+ [illegible]
7	Hannan's Brownhill	[illegible]	+ [illegible]	8/9	W. A. Market Trust	4/	− /3
[illegible]	Hannan's Oroya	[illegible]	+ [illegible]	[illegible]	W. A. Loan&General Fin.	[illegible]	+ [illegible]
[illegible]	Do. Proprietary	11/		—	White Feather	[illegible]	

SOUTH AFRICAN.

Making-Up Price, Apr. 26.	Name	Closing Price.	Rise or Fall.	Making-Up Price, Apr. 26.	Name	Closing Price.	Rise or Fall.
[illegible]	Angelo	[illegible]	+ [illegible]	2/3	Lisbon-Berlyn	2/3	+ /3
1	Aurora West	[illegible]		[illegible]	May Consolidated	[illegible]	+ [illegible]
[illegible]	Bantjes	[illegible]	+ [illegible]	4	Meyer and Charlton	4	− [illegible]
8/6	Barrett, 10/	8/6	+ /6	[illegible]	Modderfontein	[illegible]	− [illegible]
[illegible]	Bonanza	[illegible]	+ [illegible]	[illegible]	New Bultfontein	[illegible]	+ [illegible]
[illegible]	Buffelsdoorn	[illegible]		[illegible]	New Primrose	[illegible]	− [illegible]
[illegible]	City and Suburban, £4	[illegible]	+ [illegible]	[illegible]	Nigel	[illegible]	+ [illegible]
[illegible]	Comet (New)	[illegible]	+ [illegible]	—	Nigel Deep	[illegible]	
[illegible]	Con. Deep Level	[illegible]	+ [illegible]	[illegible]	North Randfontein	[illegible]	
[illegible]	Crown Deep	[illegible]	+ [illegible]	[illegible]	Nourse Deep	5	+ [illegible]
12	Crown Reef	[illegible]	+ [illegible]	1	Porges-Randfontein	[illegible]	+ [illegible]
[illegible]	De Beers, £5	[illegible]	+ [illegible]	[illegible]	Rand Mines	[illegible]	+ [illegible]
[illegible]	Driefontein	[illegible]	+ [illegible]	[illegible]	Randfontein	[illegible]	+ [illegible]
[illegible]	Durban Roodepoort	[illegible]	+ [illegible]	[illegible]	Rietfontein	[illegible]	+ [illegible]
[illegible]	Do. Deep	[illegible]	+ [illegible]	9	Robinson Deep	[illegible]	
[illegible]	East Rand	[illegible]	+ [illegible]	[illegible]	Do. Gold, £5	[illegible]	+ [illegible]
[illegible]	Ferreira	[illegible]	+ 1	[illegible]	Do. Randfontein	[illegible]	+ [illegible]
[illegible]	Geldenhuis Deep	7	+ [illegible]	[illegible]	Roodepoort Central Deep	[illegible]	+ [illegible]
5	Do. Estate	[illegible]	+ [illegible]	[illegible]	Rose Deep	[illegible]	+ [illegible]
[illegible]	George Goch	[illegible]	+ [illegible]	[illegible]	Salisbury	3	+ [illegible]
2	Ginsberg	[illegible]	+ [illegible]	[illegible]	Sheba	[illegible]	+ [illegible]
[illegible]	Glencairn	[illegible]	+ [illegible]	[illegible]	Simmer and Jack, £5	[illegible]	+ [illegible]
[illegible]	Goldfields Deep	[illegible]		[illegible]	Transvaal Gold	[illegible]	+ [illegible]
8	Griqualand West	[illegible]	+ [illegible]	3	Treasury	[illegible]	
[illegible]	Henry Nourse	[illegible]	+ [illegible]	[illegible]	United Roodepoort	[illegible]	+ [illegible]
[illegible]	Heriot	[illegible]		[illegible]	Van Ryn	[illegible]	
[illegible]	Jagersfontein	[illegible]	+ [illegible]	[illegible]	Village Main Reef	[illegible]	+ [illegible]
[illegible]	Jubilee	[illegible]	+ [illegible]	[illegible]	Vogelstruis	[illegible]	
[illegible]	Jumpers	[illegible]	+ [illegible]	[illegible]	Do. Deep	[illegible]	
	Kleinfontein	[illegible] x		[illegible]	Wemmer	[illegible]	+ [illegible]
[illegible]	Knight's	[illegible]	+ [illegible]	[illegible]	West Rand	[illegible]	+ [illegible]
[illegible]	Lancaster	[illegible]	+ [illegible]	[illegible]	Wolhuter, £4	[illegible]	
[illegible]	Langlaagte Estate	[illegible]	+ [illegible]	[illegible]	Worcester	[illegible]	

LAND EXPLORATION AND RHODESIAN

Making-Up Price, Apr. 26.	Name	Closing Price.	Rise or Fall.	Making-Up Price, Apr. 26.	Name	Closing Price.	Rise or Fall.
2	Anglo-French Ex.	[illegible]	+ [illegible]	[illegible]	Mashonaland Central	[illegible]	
[illegible]	Barnato Consolidated	[illegible]	+ [illegible]	[illegible]	Matabele Gold Reefs	[illegible]	
[illegible]	Bechuanaland Ex.	[illegible]		[illegible]	Mozambique	2	
[illegible]	Chartered B.S.A.	[illegible]		[illegible]	Oceana Consolidated	[illegible]	
[illegible]	Clark's Cons.	[illegible]		[illegible]	Rhodesia, Ltd.	[illegible]	
[illegible]	Colenbrander	[illegible]		[illegible]	Do. Exploration	[illegible]	+ [illegible]
[illegible]	Cons. Goldfields	[illegible]	+ [illegible]	1	Do. Goldfields	1	
1	Do. Pref.	20/		[illegible]	S. A. Gold Trust	[illegible]	+ [illegible]
[illegible]	Exploration	[illegible]		[illegible]	Tati Concessions	1	+ [illegible]
[illegible]	Geelong	[illegible]		[illegible]	Transvaal Development	[illegible]	+ [illegible]
[illegible]	Henderson's Est.	[illegible]		[illegible]	United Rhodesia	[illegible]	
[illegible]	Johannesburg Con. In.	[illegible]		1	Willoughby	[illegible]	
[illegible]	Do. Water	[illegible]	− [illegible]	[illegible]	Zambesia Explor.	1	
[illegible]	Mashonaland Agency	[illegible]	− [illegible]				

MISCELLANEOUS.

Making-Up Price, Apr. 26.	Name	Closing Price.	Rise or Fall.	Making-Up Price, Apr. 26.	Name	Closing Price.	Rise or Fall.
1	Alamillos, £2	[illegible]		[illegible]	Mount Lyell, South	10/	
[illegible]	Anaconda, $25	[illegible]	+ [illegible]	4	Mount Morgan, 17s. 6d.	[illegible]	+ [illegible]
5/6	Balaghât, 18/	7/		[illegible]	Mysore, 10s.	[illegible]	
11/6	Brilliant, £2	12/3		11/6	Mysore Goldfields	11/6	+ 1/
[illegible]	Do. St. George's	[illegible]	+ [illegible]	5/6	Do. Reefs, 17/	5/6	− /6
9/6	British Broken Hill	9/6		8/	Do. West	7/6	− /6
[illegible]	Broken Hill Proprietary	[illegible]		6/	Do. Wynand	6/	+ /6
—	Do. Block 10	[illegible]		[illegible]	Namaqua, £2	[illegible]	+ [illegible]
[illegible]	Cape Copper, £2	[illegible]	+ [illegible]	[illegible]	Nundydroog	[illegible]	+ [illegible]
[illegible]	Champion Reef, 10s.	5		[illegible]	Ooregum	[illegible]	
[illegible]	Copiapo, £2	[illegible]	+ [illegible]	[illegible]	Do. Pref.	4	+ [illegible]
3	Coromandel	[illegible]	− [illegible]	[illegible]	Rio Tinto Def., £5	[illegible] x	− [illegible]
13/	Day Dawn Block	14/9	+ 1/3	6	Do. Pref. £5	[illegible]	+ [illegible]
[illegible]	Frontino & Bolivia	[illegible]	+ [illegible]	16/6	St. John del Rey	18/	+ 1/6
[illegible]	Hall Mines	[illegible]		8/9	Taitipu	8/	+ /6
[illegible]	Libiola, £5	[illegible]	− [illegible]	7	Tharsis, £2	[illegible]	+ [illegible]
[illegible]	Linares, £3	8		[illegible]	Tolima "A," £5	[illegible]	− [illegible]
4	Mason & Barry, £3	4	+ [illegible]	[illegible]	Waihi	[illegible]	+ [illegible]
[illegible]	Mountain Copper, £5	[illegible]	+ [illegible]	[illegible]	Waitekauri	[illegible]	
[illegible]	Mount Lyell, £3	[illegible]	− [illegible]	[illegible]	Woodstock (N.Z.)	1	
[illegible]	Mount Lyell, North	[illegible]	− [illegible]				

DIVIDENDS ANNOUNCED.

MISCELLANEOUS.

PARKGATE IRON AND STEEL COMPANY.—Further dividend of £3 15s. per share, making with the interim of £1 10s. paid in December last a total of £5 5s. per share, or 7 per cent. per annum.

DARJEELING COMPANY, LIMITED.—5 per cent. £357 carried forward.

MOUNT MORGAN GOLD MINING COMPANY, LIMITED.—6d. per share for the month of April.

GORDON STEAM SHIPPING COMPANY, LIMITED.—5 per cent. for the six months, making with interim of 3 per cent., a total of 8 per cent. for the year.

COMPAGNIE GÉNÉRALE DES ASPHALTES DE FRANCE.—5s. per share on the ordinary shares.

HARMSWORTH BROTHERS, LIMITED.—Interim dividend for the six months ended April 30 at the rate of 5 per cent. per annum on the preference shares, and on the ordinary shares at the rate of 20 per cent. per annum, as compared with 15 per cent. for the same period last year.

EAST MURCHISON UNITED.—1s. per share.

BUENOS AYRES (NEW) GAS COMPANY, LIMITED.—Dividend at the rate of 6 per cent. per annum for 1897, of which 2½ per cent. has already been paid as interim dividend.

LASCELLES, TICKNER, & COMPANY, LIMITED.—Dividend for the year of 9 per cent., in addition to a bonus of 2 per cent. on the ordinary shares, £2,000 placed to reserve, and £1,456 carried forward.

CEYLON PROPRIETARY TEA ESTATES COMPANY, LIMITED.—3 per cent. on the ordinary shares.

ASHLEY GARDENS PROPERTIES.—Interim dividend upon the ordinary shares at the rate of 7 per cent. per annum for the half-year ended March 25.

WORCESTER EXPLORATION AND GOLD MINING COMPANY, LIMITED.—15 per cent.

CLYDESDALE (TRANSVAAL) COLLIERIES.—Interim dividend of 5 per cent.

DALGETY AND COMPANY, LIMITED.—Interim dividend for the half-year ended December 31 of 4s. per share.

LAND AND MORTGAGE COMPANY OF EGYPT.—Dividend for the six months ended March 31, at the rate of 8 per cent. per annum, making with the interim dividend 7 per cent. for the year.

WORCESTER EXPLORATION COMPANY.—A dividend of 15 per cent. has been declared.

WAIHI GOLD MINING COMPANY.—Dividend of 2s. per share on the old shares, and at the rate of 5 per cent. on the new shares.

BREWERIES.

NALDER AND COLLYER'S COMPANY.—Further dividend on the ordinary shares at the rate of 12½ per cent. per annum for the half-year ended March 25, making 12½ per cent. for the year, and in addition a bonus of 5 per cent. on the ordinary shares, £13,000 placed to reserve, and £4,050 carried forward.

WEST CHESHIRE COMPANY, LIMITED.—Interim dividend on the ordinary shares for the half-year ended March 31, at the rate of 7 per cent. per annum, being a similar dividend to that declared for the same period last year.

BANK.

NATIONAL OF AUSTRALASIA.—Dividend for half-year at the rate of 5 per cent. per annum on the preference shares. £37,000 carried forward.

TRAMWAY AND OMNIBUS RECEIPTS.

HOME.

Name.	Period.	Ending.	Amount.	Increase or Decrease on 1897.	Weeks or Months.	Aggregate to Date. Amount.	Aggregate to Date. Inc. or Dec. on 1897.
			£	£		£	£
Aberdeen District	Week	Apr. 30	409	+19	—	—	—
Belfast Street	"	" 30	2,298	+230	—	—	—
Birmingham and Aston	"	" 30	452	+31	—	—	—
Birmingham and Midland	"	" 30	641	+58	—	—	—
Birmingham City	"	" 30	3,667	+221	—	—	—
Birmingham General	"	" 30	885	+118	—	—	—
Blessington and Poulaphouca	"	May 1	8	−12/6	17	168	+18
Bristol Tramways and Carriage	"	Apr. 29	2,694	+402	—	—	—
Burnley and District	"	" 30	297	−36	—	—	—
Bury, Rochdale, and Oldham	"	" 30	787	−29	—	—	—
Croydon	"	" 30	366	+33	—	—	+1,117
Dublin and Blessington	"	May 1	129	−22	17	1,625	+27
Dublin and Lucan	"	Apr. 30	59	−6	18	715	−366
Dublin United	"	" 22	3,118	−106	—	43,748	+2,796
Dudley and Stourbridge	"	" 30	159	+4	18	2,900	+112
Edinburgh and District	"	" 30	2,210	+77	17	38,282	+3,468
Edinburgh Street	"	" 30	589	+34	17	10,089	+1,239
Glasgow	"	" 30	2,758	+32	—	—	—
Harrow-road and Paddington	"	" 30	270	+21	—	—	—
Lea Bridge and Leyton	"	" 30	746	+36	—	—	—
London, Deptford, and Greenwich	"	" 30	583	+23	—	9,591	+566
London General Omnibus	"	" 30	20,993	+97	—	—	—
London Road Car	"	" 30	6,414	−208	†	104,775	+5,839
London Southern	"	" 30	517	−8	—	—	—
North Staffordshire	"	" 30	306	−12	—	6,709	−15
Provincial	"	" 30	2,207	−199	—	—	—
Rossendale Valley	"	" 29	171	+19	—	—	—
Southampton	"	" 30	363	−14	—	—	—
South London	"	" 30	1,710	+27	†	27,396	+1,024
South Staffordshire	"	" 29	579	+29	17	10,083	−43
Tramways Union	Month	March	9,988	+661	3	28,630	+3,346
Wigan and District	Week	Apr. 30	287	+10	—	—	—
Woolwich and South East London	"	" 30	351	+9	†	5,497	+331

† From January 1.

FOREIGN.

Name.	Period.	Ending.	Amount.	Increase or Decrease on 1897.	Weeks or Months.	Aggregate to Date. Amount.	Aggregate to Date. Inc. or Dec. on 1897.
			£	£		£	£
Anglo-Argentine	Week	Apr. 4	4,883	+1,152	*	60,183	+6,203
Barcelona	"	" 30	1,043	−206		19,317	−2,659
Barcelona, Ensanche y Gracia	"	" 30	210	−2		3,811	+27
Bordeaux	"	" 29	2,148	−271		33,058	−1,343
Buenos Ayres and Belgrano	Month	Mch.	5,219	+1,305	*	14,382	+2,578
Buenos Ayres Grand National	Week	Apr. 2	$24,601	+$5,451	†		+ $211,062
Buenos Ayres New	Month	Jan.	$69,003	−$1,852		$69,905	−$1,352
Calais	Week	Apr. 30	140	−30			
Calcutta	"	" 16	1,460	+116			
C'rth'g'na & Herrerias	Month	" —	4,007	+712		18,800	+1,011
Gothenburg	Week	" 13	354	+81			

* From January 1. † From April 1, 1897.

ENGLISH RAILWAYS.

Div. for half years. 1896	1896	1897	1897	Last Balance forward.	Amt. to pay 1 p.c. on Ord. for ½ yr.	NAME.	Date.	Gross Traffic for week: Amt.	Inc. or dec. on 1897.	Inc. or dec. on 1896.	No. of weeks	Gross Traffic for half-year to date: Amt.	Inc. or dec. on 1897.	Inc. or dec. on 1896.	Mileage.	Inc. on 1897.	Working	Prior Charges last ½ year.	Prop. add Cap. Exp. this ½ year
				£	£												%	£	£
10	10	10	10	2,707	5,094	Barry	Apr 30	2,202	−7,325	−6,261	18	137,712	−17,868	+2,532	31	—	8·89	60,665	316,858
nil	nil	nil	nil	—	—	Brecon and Merthyr	May 1	1,081	−420	−660	18	25,271	−536	−3,210	61	—	—	—	—
nil	nil	nil	nil	3,979	4,749	Cambrian	,, 1	5,739	−328	+982	*	80,754	+2,123	—	250	—	60·96	63,148	40,000
1¾	1¾	2	1¾	1,510	3,150	City and South London ..	,, 1	988	+54	+110	18	18,757	+811	+1,730	3½	—	56·67	5,552	124,000
	2	1½	2	7,895	13,220	Furness	,, 1	9,463	+465	+933	*	151,952	+4,473	—	139	—	49·88	97,423	20,910
1	1½	½	1	2,207	27,470	Great Cent. (late M., S., & L.)	,, 1	49,600	+3,774	+4,380	17	733,560	+16,524	+44,818	352½	—	57·17	627,386	1,200,000
1½	4¾	2	5	51,283	62,865	Great Eastern	,, 1	85,266	+6,340	+7,781	17	1,354,257	+41,626	+118883	1,158½	2	55·35	860,138	250,000
3	5½	3	5	15,094	102,496	Great Northern	,, 1	101,374	+3,993	+11,879	18	1,688,636	+49,992	+129260	1,071	8	61·36	641,483	750,000
4½	7½	4¾	7½	31,350	121,981	Great Western	,, 1	181,120	−8,150	+1,190	17	2,941,660	+17,660	+118900	2,582	21	51·44	1,486,272	800,000
nil	2	nil	1½	8,951	16,487	Hull and Barnsley	,, 1	8,700	+1,021	+2,085	17	114,162	+4,153	+12,520	73	—	58·21	70,290	52,5..
5	5¾	5	5½	21,495	83,704	Lancashire and Yorkshire ..	,, 1	94,749	+4,344	+5,048	17	1,562,922	+46,526	+58,348	555½	25	56·70	674,745	451,976
4¾	8	4¾	8½	26,243	43,049	Lon., Brighton, & S. Coast	Apr 30	51,873	−3,872	+838	18	864,513	+30,205	+48,476	476½	—	50·20	407,042	240,735
nil	nil	nil	nil	72,294	56,296	London, Chatham, & Dover	May 1	30,740	+491	+1,980	17	464,352	+12,787	+26,963	185½	—	50·65	367,873	nil
6½	8	6½	7½	89,535	204,068	London and North Western	,, 1	253,093	+8,940	+27,022	17	3,873,582	+94,189	+223594	1,911½	—	56·92	1,404,334	600,000
5	8½	8½	8½	23,038	59,367	London and South Western	,, 1	79,166	+1,061	+8,646	17	1,166,156	+44,345	+83,174	941	6½	51·75	513,740	389,000
2¾	6	2¾	6½	14,592	6,691	Lon., Tilbury, & Southend	,, 1	5,293	+413	+963	18	88,995	+5,250	+14,658	81	—	52·57	39,390	15,000
3½	3¾	3¾	3¾	27,133	26,409	Metropolitan	,, 1	16,247	+276	+905	*	280,412	+5,780	—	64	—	43·63	148,047	254,000
nil	nil	nil	nil	4,006	11,230	Metropolitan District ..	,, 1	8,239	+340	+125	17	146,394	+4,391	—	13	—	48·70	119,663	38,430
5	7	5½	6½	38,143	174,582	Midland	,, 1	194,707	+12,391	+27,245	18	3,295,989	+50,264	+251739	1,354¾	15½	57·59	1,216,582	650,000
5½	7½	5¾	7	22,374	138,189	North Eastern	Apr 30	159,188	+20,835	+15,657	17	2,415,674	+30,981	+132411	1,597¾	—	58·82	795,077	436,904
7¾	7¾	7¾	7½	7,061	10,102	North London	May 1			Not recd			not	recvd.	12	—	50·90	49,973	7,600
4	5	4	4½	4,745	16,150	North Staffordshire	,, 1	15,945	+1,191	+1,163	18	279,661	+6,069	+16,064	312	—	55·27	118,142	19,605
10	10	11	10	1,642	3,004	Rhymney	Apr 30	2,446	−2,787	−2,279	18	81,480	−6,772	+11	71	—	49·68	29,049	16,700
3	6½	3½	6½	4,054	50,215	South Eastern	,, 30	47,164	+1,423	+2,587	*	726,958	+36,477	—	448	—	51·88	380,763	250,000
3½	3½	2½	3½	2,315	25,961	Taff Vale	,, 30	6,668	−9,205	−8,872	18	236,530	−42,547	−27,288	121	—	54·90	94,800	92,000

* From January 1.

SCOTCH RAILWAYS.

1896	1896	1897	1897	Last Balance forward	Amt. to pay 1 p.c. on Ord. for ½ yr.	Name	Date	Amt.	Inc. or dec. on 1897	Inc. or dec. on 1896	No. of weeks	Amt.	Inc. or dec. on 1897	Inc. or dec. on 1896	Mileage	Inc. on 1897	Working	Prior Charges last ½ year	Prop. add Cap. Exp. this ½ year
5	5	5½	5	9,544	78,066	Caledonian	Apr. 24	78,861	− 1,174	+ 5,611	12	863,387	+ 19,225	—	851½	5	50·38	588,248	441,472
5	5½	5	5	7,364	24,639	Glasgow and South-Western	,, 30	30,338	+ 2,011	+ 3,246	13	361,228	+ 12,946	—	393½	—	54·69	221,663	196,145
3½	3½	3½	—	1,291	4,600	Great North of Scotland	,, 30	8,490	− 106	+ 258	13	100,519	− 433	+ 2,775	331	15½	52·03	92,178	60,000
	nil		—	10,477	12,800	Highland	May 1	8,754	− 63	− 389	9	78,267	+ 2,556	—	479¾	27½	58·63	78,976	,000
	1½	1	1½	819	45,819	North British	,, 1	76,653	+ 2,421	+ 3,636	13	920,893	+ 23,206	—	1,230	23	48·62	944,809	40,800

IRISH RAILWAYS.

1896	1896	1897	1897	Last Balance forward	Amt. to pay 1 p.c. on Ord. for ½ yr.	Name	Date	Amt.	Inc. or dec. on 1897	Inc. or dec. on 1896	No. of weeks	Amt.	Inc. or dec. on 1897	Inc. or dec. on 1896	Mileage	Inc. on 1897	Working	Prior Charges last ½ year	Prop. add Cap. Exp. this ½ year
6½	6½	6½	—	5,466	1,790	Belfast and County Down ..	Apr. 29	2,270	+ 40	− 4	*	36,640	+ 983	—	76½	—	55·38	17,690	10,000
5½	6½	5½	—	—	4,284	Belfast and Northern Counties	,, 29	5,340	+ 77	+ 512	*	87,992	+ 4,734	—	249	—	—	—	—
	3	2	—	1,418	1,200	Cork, Bandon, and S. Coast† ..	,, 30	1,434	− 148	− 47	*	20,829	− 1,567	—	103	—	54·82	14,436	5,450
	6¼	6½	6½	38,776	17,816	Great Northern	,, 29	16,578	+ 138	+ 1,662	17	247,266	+ 11,548	+ 16,380	528	36	50·15	88,068	22,000
	5½	5½	5½	30,339	24,855	Great Southern and Western ..	,, 29	—	—	—	not	received	—	—	603	13	51·45	72,802	46,582
	4	4	4½	11,372	11,850	Midland Great Western ..	,, 29	12,244	+ 744	+ 781	17	166,513	+ 7,516	—	538	—	50·31	83,129	1,800
nil	nil	nil	nil	229	2,822	Waterford and Central ..	,, 29	972	+ 1·2	—	*	14,736	+ 1,709	—	59½	—	53·24	6,858	1,500
nil	nil	nil	nil	1,936	2,987	Waterford, Limerick & W. ..	,, 29	5,039	− 261	+ 588	*	92,405	+ 2,989	—	350½	—	57·83	42,617	7,075

* From January 1. † Fourteen weeks' strike.

THE CURRANT TRADE OF THE MOREA.

Since the enforcement of the Retention Law in the Morea the currant trade of that province has become more profitable to all concerned in it. Mr. Consul F. B. Wood in his report states that since 1895, the first year of the law, about 45,000 tons have been retained in the Government stores at Patras, instead of as formerly being exported to become a glut on the market, with a consequent fall in prices. The Government is not allowed to export the percentage of currants given it by the shippers without first reducing them to pulp or syrup, or it may sell them locally for distilling purposes, and so cheaply can it afford to do so that great stimulus has been given to the manufacture of wines and spirits in the country. It is hoped that very shortly all the retention currants will be bought and used by the local distillers.

The old law forbidding the shipment of currants before August 28 will, in all probability, shortly be renewed, and, if so, will greatly benefit the shippers, and also place on the market a better quality than is at present given. The growers during the lapse of this law have gathered their crops before thoroughly matured, and hurried them to the markets in order to obtain the high prices given for first fruits, while the shippers, not knowing when the first shipments would be ready, have wasted much time in port awaiting their cargoes.

To a Maori rising we have long been strangers; but one has occurred among the Hausau natives, and is said to be serious. They have risen in protest against the dog tax. A detachment of artillery, with quick-firing guns, has been sent against the Hausaus, who were threatening the town of Reewene.

An English syndicate has been granted 250,000 acres of land in New Guinea. For what?

According to the *Japan Herald* japan cotton yarns are better in quality than Bombay spinnings, and also somewhat cheaper. As a consequence, they are said to be superseding the Bombay article in China. They were first shipped from japan during the prevalence of the plague in Bombay.

The statement of the foreign trade of the United States for March shows continuous progress. The total exports for the month were valued at $112,817,863, an increase of fully $25,000,000 over March, 1896. The imports, however, showed a decrease of $14,800,000, the total value for the month being $61,507,437. How will the totals for April look after a few weeks of war?

Having recently picked up a knicknack marked "Made in Germany," the Ameer of Afghanistan gravely remarked to Sir Salter Pyne, "Your country is degenerating. England has been sending out bad things, and so, to protect themselves, France and Germany and Russia have decided to mark everything that they manufacture." This is certainly regarding the matter from a novel point of view. What do the "fair" traders say to it?

Early strawberries are being largely exported from France to England. Last year about a thousand tons were landed at Plymouth and Southampton. This year a much larger quantity is expected.

The Victorian Government contemplate carrying out several public works, including an extensive irrigation scheme, at a total cost of over £2,000,000. The money will be raised annually at the rate of £750,000.

The gold exports from Western Australia in April amounted to 84,083 oz., valued at £319,517, as compared with 39,660 oz., valued at £150,709, in the corresponding month of last year.

The gold yield of Tasmania for the quarter ended March 31 amounted to 9,300 oz., being a decrease of 4,000 oz., as compared with the corresponding quarter of last year.

FOREIGN RAILWAYS.

Mileage.			Name	Gross Traffic for Week.				Gross Traffic to Date.			
Total.	Increase on 1897.	Increase on 1896.		Week ending	Amount.	In. or Dec. upon 1897.	In. or Dec. upon 1896.	No. of Weeks.	Amount.	In. or Dec. upon 1897.	In. or Dec. upon 1896.
					£	£	£		£	£	£
929	—	—	Argentine Great Western	Apr. 27	9,765	+ 1,628	+ 1,598	43	259,500	− 53	− 59,616
76½	—	—	Bahia and San Francisco	Mar. 19	3,330	+ 881	+ 1,483	12	35,707	+ 12,130	+ 13,741
234	48	84	Bahia Blanca and North West	Mar. 27	586	− 154	—	39	30,305	− 94	—
74	—	—	Buenos Ayres and Ensenada	May 1	3,345	− 252	− 668	17	58,950	− 9,348	− 15,428
426	—	—	Buenos Ayres and Pacific	Apr. 30	9,131	+ 1,456	− 565	43	289,712	− 51,626	+ 6,284
914	1	3	Buenos Ayres and Rosario	Apr. 30	16,585	+ 4,259	+ 4,351	17	293,486	+ 79,884	+ 31,045
2,499	30	68	Buenos Ayres Great Southern	May 1	33,963	+ 5,308	+ 7,181	43	1,295,288	+ 99,952	+ 185,096
602	107	177	Buenos Ayres Western	May 1	14,451	+ 858	− 2,158	43	523,228	− 77,473	− 93,180
845	55	77	Central Argentine	Apr. 30	23,083	+ 7,702	+ 7,700	16	376,845	+ 96,166	+ 35,532
197	—	—	Central Bahia	Feb. 28*	$142,798	+ $14,291	+ $1,866	2	$276,357	+ $10,347	+ $14,624
271	—	—	Central Uruguay of Monte Video	Apr. 30	7,2[illegible]	+ 2,691	+ 1,551	43	258,669	+ 18,236	− 14,185
228	—	—	Do. Eastern Extension	Apr. 30	1,589	− 248	+ 372	43	56,306	+ 7,890	− 351
182	—	—	Do. Northern Extension	Apr. 30	818	+ 426	+ 113	43	27,581	+ 617	− 6,943
180	—	—	Cordoba and Rosario	Apr. 24	2,435	+ 1,070	+ 505	43	91,240	− 14,175	− 1,865
128	—	—	Cordoba Central	Apr. 24	$25,000	+ $980	+ $2,400	16	$332,200	− $50,990	− $65,830
549	—	—	Do. Northern Extension	Apr. 24	$34,000	− $6,110	− $10,800	16	$732,790	− $249,060	− $149,630
437	—	—	Costa Rica	Apr. 15	8,023	+ 4,643	+ 3,290	15	90,877	− 8,484	+ 4,288
99	—	—	East Argentine	Mar. 13	677	+ 103	+ 131	11	7,285	− 617	− 345
386	—	6	Entre Rios	Apr. 30	2,479	+ 1,341	+ 1,209	43	71,240	+ 22,381	+ 18,237
555	—	24	Inter Oceanic of Mexico	Apr. 30	$63,100	+ $9,580	+ $18,700	42	$2,504,520	+ $401,550	+ $679,750
23	—	—	La Guaira and Caracas	Mar. 25	2,060	− 285	− 1,103	13	24,939	− 5,212	− 4,938
321	—	—	Mexican	Apr. 30	$92,500	+ $14,500	—	17	$1,411,700	+ $153,350	—
1,846	—	—	Mexican Central	Apr. 30‡	$347,012	− $5,176	+ $80,728	18	$4,399,711	+ $39,305	+ $1,124,728
1,217	—	—	Mexican National	Apr 30‡	$146,466	+ $9,482	+ $29,074	18	$1,905,613	+ $136,557	+ $170,898
228	—	—	Mexican Southern	Apr. 30	$14,350	− $5,478	− $153	4	$51,010	− $11,149	+ $7,894
205	—	—	Minas and Rio	Mar. 31*	$161,153	− $9,628	—	9 mos.	$1,597,971	+ $193,854	—
94	—		N. W. Argentine	Apr. 30	1,290	+ 59	− 263	17	17,769	− 6,538	− 4,214
242	3	—	Nitrate	Apr. 15	18,375	+ 2,188	+ 4,209	13	107,065	+ 1,860	− 42,111
320	—	—	Ottoman	Apr. 23	3,284	− 947	− 1,203	16	77,177	− 16,195	+ 6,755
77½	—	—	Recife and San Francisco	Mar. 5	6,397	+ 2,280	+ 105	10	58,668	+ 4,444	− 8,013
86½	—	—	San Paulo	Mar. 27†	18,471	− 6,000	—	12	127,060	− 25,190	—
186	—	—	Santa Fe and Cordova	Apr. 23	3,022	+ 2,262	− 355	43	72,193	− 3,112	− 3,767
110	—	—	Western of Havana	Apr. 23	1,640	− 292	+ 760	42	75,115	+ 5,601	+ 7,190

* For month ended. † For fortnight ended. ‡ For nine days.

INDIAN RAILWAYS.

Mileage.			Name.	Gross Traffic for Week.				Gross Traffic to Date.			
Total.	Increase on 1897.	Increase on 1896.		Week ending	Amount.	In. or Dec. on 1897.	In. or Dec. on 1896.	No. of Weeks.	Amount.	In. or Dec. on 1897.	In. or Dec. on 1896.
862	—	—	Bengal Nagpur	Apr. 23	Rs.1.90.000	+Rs.64.708	+Rs. 57.028	17	Rs.25.35.540	+Rs.1.57.452	−R. 1.44.993
827	8	63	Bengal and North-Western	Apr. 2	Rs.1.55.530	+Rs.24.469	+Rs. 29.513	14	Rs.17.67.074	+Rs.2.41.685	+R. 62.461
461	—	—	Bombay and Baroda	Apr 30	£38,592	+£2,989	−£1,751	18	£465,065	−£3,676	−£149,741
1,885	2	13	East Indian	Apr. 30	Rs.13.62.000	+R.1.38.000	+Rs2.52.000	18	Rs.2.16.81.000	+Rs.7.21.000	+R18.51.000
1,491	—	—	Great Indian Penin.	Apr. 30	£75,781	+£20,228	−£6,381	18	£1,80,331	+£194,119	−£212,904
736	—	—	Indian Midland	Apr. 30	Rs.1.46.310	+Rs.12 701	+Rs.39.555	18	Rs.2.400.271	+Rs.1.82.074	+Rs.464.063
840	—	—	Madras	Apr. 30	£21,084	+£1,192	+£184	18	£331,709	−£19,316	−£5,635
1,043	—	—	South Indian	Apr. 2	Rs.2.10.281	+Rs.48.249	+Rs.37.551	14	Rs.20.42.148	−Rs.201.155	−R2.17.702

UNITED STATES AND CANADIAN RAILWAYS.

Mileage.			Name.	Gross Traffic for Week.			Gross Traffic to Date.		
Total.	Increase on 1897.	Increase on 1896.		Period Ending.	Amount.	In. or Dec. on 1897.	No. of Weeks.	Amount.	In. or Dec. on 1897.
					dols.	dols.		dols.	dols.
917	—	—	Baltimore & Ohio S. Western	Apr. 21	135,000	+33,000	41	5,501,184	+603,096
6,568	92	156	Canadian Pacific	Apr. 30†	573,000	+106,000	16	7,171,000	+1,439,000
922	—	—	Chicago Great Western	Apr. 30†	136,606	+26,468	42	4,467,484	+563,787
6,169	—	469	Chicago, Mil., & St. Paul	Apr. 21	564,000	+59,000	15	8,746,101	+1,341,300
1,685	—	—	Denver & Rio Grande	Apr. 30†	199,400	+35,400	42	6,753,300	+1,109,900
3,512	—	—	Grand Trunk, Main Line	Apr. 30†	£90,874	+£2,584	16	£1,238,126	+£113,771
335	—	—	Do. Chic. & Grand Trunk	Apr. 30†	£16,569	+£2,379	16	£255,413	+£57,469
189	—	—	Do. Det., G. H. & Mil.	Apr. 30†	£4,385	−£334	16	£59,520	−£3,522
2,938	—	—	Louisville & Nashville	Apr. 21	379,000	+18,000	15	6,399,175	+1,025,620
2,197	137	137	Miss., K., & Texas	Apr. 21	212,511	+9,288	41	10,355,429	+329,625
477	—	—	N. Y., Ontario, & W.	Apr. 21	62,128	−2,810	41	3,124,695	+89,008
1,570	—	—	Norfolk & Western	Apr. 21	226,000	+70,000	15	3,444,960	+359,433
3,499	336	—	Northern Pacific	Apr. 21	408,000	+109,000	15	6,044,775	+1,899,552
1,223	—	—	St. Louis S. Western	Apr. 21	82,000	+3,000	21	1,770,400	+306,221
4,654	—	—	Southern	Apr. 21	369,000	+24,000	41	5,366,812	+1,335,443
1,979	—	—	Wabash	Apr. 21	263,000	+52,000	16	3,844,406	+774,000

† For nine days.

MONTHLY STATEMENTS.

Mileage.			Name.	Net Earnings for Month.				Net Earnings to Date.			
Total.	Increase on 1896	Increase on 1895.		Month.	Amount.	In. or Dec. on 1897.	In. or Dec. on 1896.	No. of Months.	Amount.	In. or Dec. on 1897.	In. or Dec. on 1896.
					dols	dols.	dols.		dols.	dols.	dols.
6,935	44	444	Atchison	March	904,000	+337,000	+369,344	3	2,144,434	+674,836	+229,460
6,547	103	206	Canadian Pacific	March	753,000	+253,000	+276,469	3	1,693,000	+415,000	+328,787
6,169	—	469	Chicago, Mil., & St. Paul	March	1,180,000	+170,000	+65,202	3	2,726,334	+225,840	+84,122
1,685	—	—	Denver & Rio Grande	March	267,900	+39,242	+38,942	9	2,512,889	+407,063	+30,946
1,970	—	—	Erie	March	611,000	+53,000	+8,708	3	1,378,800	+92,400	−94,251
3,512	—	—	Grand Trunk, Main Line	March	£102,200	+£14,331	+£31,909	3	£245,953	+£62,372	+100,819
335	—	—	Do. Chic. & Grand Trunk	March	£17,400	+£10,152	+13,357	3	£38,710	+£24,282	+28,039
189	—	—	Do. Det. G. H. & Mil.	March	£4,200	−£1,414	+3,221	3	£6,528	+£737	+6,419
3,127	—	239	Illinois Central*	February	2,177,767	+413,327	+422,489	2	4,481,665	+819,013	+805,758
2,396	—	—	New York Central*	February	3,429,000	+128,000	+222,359	2	6,034,000	+492,507	249,323
477	—	—	New York Ontario, & W.	March	84,600	−4,800	+40,032	9	915,100	+35,200	+115,494
1,570	—	—	Norfolk & Western	March	321,000	+18,000	+110,317	3	826,000	+65,247	+201,902
3,407	—	—	Pennsylvania	January	1,159,101	+65,700	+236,000	2	2,511,898	92,400	+345,000
1,055	—	—	Phil. & Reading	February	584,151	−44,678	—	8	6,805,102	+446,429	—

Prices Quoted on the London Stock Exchange.

Throughout the Investors' Review middle prices alone are quoted, the object being to give the public the approximate current quotations of every security of any consequence in existence. On the markets the buying and selling prices are both given, and are often wide apart where stocks are seldom dealt in. Other particulars will be found in the Investment Index published quarterly—January, April, July, and October—in connection with this Review, price 2s., by post 2s. 2d. Where dividends are paid only once a year, an *italic* type is used to distinguish them. The London Stock Exchange Official List is quoted in the Review almost entire, only very insignificant issues, or bonds falling due within the next two or three years, being omitted. But the list is subdivided into the leading, or active, stocks, and those less frequently dealt in. The former will be found under the head of "Stock Markets," and with more details than it is possible to give for the bulk of securities. By retaining the file of the Investors' Review any subscriber can follow for himself the movements of securities from week to week, and the Investment Index will from time to time help to fill up deficiencies in the information.

Tea Companies and Mines and Mining Finance Stocks are placed in special lists.

Among the abbreviations used are the following:—S.F. Snk. Fd. *sinking fund*; Certs., *certificates*; Debs. or Dbs., *debentures*; Db. or D.Stk., *debenture stock*; Pf., Prf., or Pref., *preference*; Prefd. or Pfd., *preferred*; Dfd., *deferred*; L. or Ltd., *limited*; Sh., *share*; Ans., *annuities*; Cu. or Cm., *cumulative*; Gu or Guar., *guaranteed*; Bds., *bonds*; S., Sr., or Ser., *series*; In., Ins., Insc., *inscribed*; Dr., Drgs., Drwgs., *drawings*; Stg., Strlg., *sterling*; Lia., *liable to*; Sp., Surp., *surplus*; Per., Perp., *perpetual*; Ln. *lien*; Lo. *loan*.

The dates following the names of securities are the years of issue or of redemption. Where shares are not fully paid up, their nominal amount is given with the name so that investors may know the liability upon them.

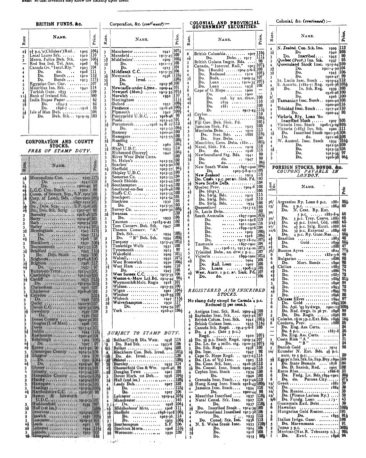

BRITISH FUNDS, &c.

Rate	Name.		Price.
2¾	2¾ p.c.'s (Childers') Red.	1905	104½
3	Local Loans Stk.	1912	110
3	Metro. Police Deb. Stk.	1920	105½
—	Red Sea Ind. Tel. Ann.	1908	8½
4	Canada Gv. "Intcl. Rly."	1903	104
4	Do. do.	1908	111
4	Do. Bonds	1910	112
4	Do. Bonds	1913	117½
3	Egyptian Gov. Gar.		107
3	Mauritius Ins. Stk.	1940	114
4	Turkish Guar. 1855		109
11½	Bank of Ireland Stk.		380
3½	India Rupee Paper		62
3½	Do. 1854-5		62
3	Do. 1896-7	1916	55
3½	Isle of Man Deb.		104
3	Do. Deb. Stk.	1919-29	103

CORPORATION AND COUNTY STOCKS.

FREE OF STAMP DUTY.

Rate	Name.		Price.
3½	Metropolitan Con.	1929	117½
3	Do.	1941	110
2½	Do.	1920-49	99
2½	L.C.C. Con. Stock	1920	98
3½	Comm. of Sewers, Scp., S.F.	1905	106
3½	Corp. of Lond. Bds.	1897-1902	100½
3	Do.	1897-1912	101
3½	Do., Debs. Scp. S.F.	1916	105
2½	Do., Deb. Stk. Scrip	1927-57	98
3	Barnsley	1916-46	105
3	Barry	1914-46	101
3	Bath	1909-34	102
3	Batley	1914-44	101½
3½	Birmingham	1945	117½
3	Do.	1947	111½
2½	Do.	1926	98
3	Blackburn	1930	106½
3	Bournemouth	1915-33	103
3½	Bradford	1945	119½
3	Do. Deb. Stock	1954	108
3	Brighouse	1916-46	100
3½	Brighton	1946	117
2½	Do.	1957	97
3	Burton-on-Trent	1913-43	101
3	Cambridge	1913-43	103
3½	Cardiff	1935	113½
3	Do.	1914-54	103½
3	Cheltenham	1971	107
3	Chichester	1916-46	101
3½	Croydon		131½
3	Do.	1940	105½
3	Derby	1920-50	107
3	Devon C.C.	1917-33	104½
3½	Dewsbury	1939	109
3	Do.	1930	103
3	Dorset County	1929-39	105
3	Douglas (I. of Man)	1926	101
3	Dover	1913-43	101
3½	Dublin	1944	113½
3	Eastbourne	1920-40	104
3	Edinburgh	1924	105½
2½	Do.	1927	97
2½	Exeter	1917-37	96
3	Glamorgan County	1914-34	104
3½	Glasgow	1914	109
3	Do.	1921	104½
2½	Do.	1925-40	99
3	Gloster	1915-55	101
3	Grimsby	1913-45	103
3	Hampshire County	1914-34	105½
3	Hanley	1913-43	103
3	Harrogate	1914-34	103
3	Hastings	1915-54	103½
2½	Hertfordshire C.C.	1910-30	98
3	Heston & Isleworth U.D.C.	1915-35	101
3	Huddersfield	1934	107
3½	Hull (1st iss.)		129½
3	Inverness	1914-44	100
3	Ipswich	1959	108½
3	Lancaster	1929-55	103
2½	Leeds	1927	98
3½	Leicester	1934	114½
3	Lincoln	1919	103
3½	Liverpool		132

Corporation, &c. (*continued*):—

Rate.	Name.		Price.
3	Manchester	1941	107½
3	Mansfield	1915-45	100
3½	Middlesbro'	1909	105½
3½	Do.	1911-13	105
3	Do.	1915	104
3	Middlesex C.C.	1915-35	106
3½	Newcastle	1936	118½
3½	Do. Irred.		120½
2½	Do.	1915-36	100
3	Newcastle-under-Lyme	1909-44	101
3	Newport (Mon.)	1915-55	101½
3	Norwich	1952	110
3	Nottingham		111½
3	Oxford	1951	108½
3	Penzance	1916-46	100½
3	Plymouth	1942	109½
3	Pontypridd U.D.C.	1916-46	98
3	Poole	1915-45	101
3½	Portsmouth 1916	24 & 27	112
3	Do.	1913-33	106½
3	Ramsey	1920-40	100
3	Ramsgate	1915-55	102
3½	Reading		120½
3	Do.	1962	104½
3½	Rhyl U.D.C.	1953	110
3	Richmond (Surrey)	1942	104½
3	River Wear Debt Certs.		100
3	St. Helen's	1915-55	102
3	Scarbro'	1915-50	102
2½	Sheffield	1925-57	94½
3	Shipley U.D.C.	1915-35	100
3	Somerset Co.	1923-33	104
3	South Shields	1915-45	100
2½	Southampton	1915-45	102
3	Southend-on-Sea	1916-46	102
3	Staffs C.C.	1915-35	102
3	Stockport	1914-54	101
3	Stockton	1932	104
3	Do.	1915-35	103
3	Surrey Co.	1922-32	105½
3½	Swansea		130
3	Do.	1955	106
3	Taunton	19183-9-43	102
3	Tees Conserv. Deb. Stk.	1947	100
3	Thames Conserv. "A" Deb. Stk.	1954	108½
3	Do. "B" Deb. Stk.	1954	103½
3	Torquay	1913-43	101½
3	Tunbridge Wells	1931	102
3	Tynemouth	1913	99
3	Wakefield	1929	101½
3	Walsall	1932	107½
3	West Bromwich	1930	106½
3½	West Ham	1929	110
3	Do.	1945	106
3	West Sussex C.C.	1915-35	106
3	Weston-s.-Mare Lcl.Bd.	1914-44	99½
3	Weymouth&Melc. Regis	1918	101
3	Widnes	1915-55	100
3	Wigan	1921	104½
3	Windsor	1918-55	102
3½	Wisbech	1947	113½
3½	Wolverhampton	1932	117
3	Do.	1924-54	107
3	York	1916-41	106½

SUBJECT TO STAMP DUTY.

Rate.	Name.		Price.
3½	Belfast City & Dis. Watr.	1938	114
3	Do. Red Stk.	1953-6	106
4½	Belfast	1904	103
4	Blackburn Con. Deb. Irred.		141½
3½	Do. do. Irred.		130
3½	Bristol		129½
3½	Burnley	1933	114
3	Chesterfield Gas & Wtr.	1916-46	98
3½	Douglas Town	1921	105
3	Dover Harb. 1st Deb.	1936	104½
3½	Hull (2nd iss.)		128½
4	Leeds Deb.	1907	123
3½	Do.		115½
3	Do.	1927	106
3	Leicester	1919-44	103½
4	Manchester		145
3	Do.	1928	104½
4½	Middlesboro' Mrts.	1908	111
3½	Sheffield	1898-1916	105½
3½	Do.	1925-36	114
3	Do.	1925	105½
3½	Southampton	S.F.	106
4½	Stockton Morts.	1908	110½
3½	Worcester	1950	109

COLONIAL AND PROVINCIAL GOVERNMENT SECURITIES.

Rate.	Name.		Price.
6	British Columbia	1907	119½
4½	Do. Debs.	1917	111½
3	British Guiana Imgtn. Bds.		98
5	Canada, "Intercol. Rail,"	1903	107½
4	Do. (Bonds)	1904-5-6-8	105
4	Do. Reduced	1910	107½
3½	Do. Bnds.	1909-34	107
4	Do. Loan	1910-35	107½
3	Do. Loan	1938	102
6	Cape of G. Hope	1900	—
5	Do.	1900	—
4½	Do. red. by an. draw.		108
4½	Do. 1879		110
4	Do. 1881		108
4	Do.	1917-23	113½
4½	Ceylon		110
4	Do.		106½
4½	Fiji Gov. Deb. Sink. Fd.		101½
4	Jamaica Sink. Fd.	1923	103
5	Manitoba Debs.	1910	113
5	Do. Ster. Bds.	1888	119½
4	Do. Ster. Debs.		104
4	Mauritius, Cons. Debs. 1880		103½
4½	Natal, Sink. Fd.	1919	118
4	Do. do.	1926	115
3½	Newfoundland Stg. Bds.	1941	99
3½	Do. do.	1947	99
3	Do. do.		86½
5	New South Wales	1897-1902	104½
4	Do.	1903-5-8-9-12	105
5	New Zealand	1914	118
5	Do. Cnsls. 1 p.c. per an. Sink. Fd.		103
3½	Nova Scotia Debs.		104
5	Quebec Prov.	1904-6	102
4½	Do. (drgs.)		105
5	Do. Strlg. Bds.	1912	115
4	Do. Strlg. Bds.	1928	110
4	Do. Strlg. Bds.	1934	108
4	Queensland	1913-15	105
4½	St. Lucia Debs.		102
6	South Australia	1897-1900	103½
6	Do.	1901-1918	119
5	Do.	1911-1920	116
4	Do.	1899-1916	104
4	Do.	1929	108½
4	Do.	1916	106½
4	Do.	1917-18-24	107½
6	Tasmania	1897-1901	104
4	Do.	1908-11, 1913-14-20	107½
5	Trinidad Debs., an. drw. 1 p c.		107
4	Victoria	1899-1901	101½
4½	Do.	1904	105
4	Do. Rail. Loan	1907	105
4	Do. Loans	1908-13	105
4½	West. Austr. 1 p.c. ac. Sink. Fd.		107
4	Do. do.		106

REGISTERED AND INSCRIBED STOCKS.

No stamp duty except for Canada 4 p.c. Reduced (½ per cent.).

Rate.	Name.		Price.
4	Antigua Insc. Stk. Red.	1919-44	109
3½	Barbados Insc. Stk.	1925-42	107
3	British Colum. Insc. Stk.	1941	101½
4	British Guiana Insc.	1935	116½
4	Canada Stk. Regd.	1904-5-6-8	105
4	Do. 4 p.c. (late 5 p.c.) Regd.	1910	107½
3½	Do. 3½ p.c. Stock Regd.	1909-34	107
4	Do. Ln. for 4 milln. stg.	1910-35	107½
3	Do. Stk. Regd.	1938	102
2½	Do. Insc.	1947	92
4	Cape G. Hope Regd.	1917-23	114
4	Do. (Ln. of '83) Insc.	1923	115
4	Do. Cons. Stk. Insc.	1916-36	112
3½	Do. Consol. Insc. Stock	1929-49	110
4	Ceylon Insc. Stock	1934	120
3	Do.	1940	102
4	Grenada Insc. Stock	1917-42	110
3½	Hong Kong Insc. Stock	1918-43	103½
4	Jamaica Insc. Stock	1934	118
—	Do.	1922-44	98
4	Mauritius Inscribed	1937	118½
4	Natal Consd. Stk. Insc.	1927	116
4	Do.	1937	118½
3½	Do. Inscribed Stock	1914-39	105
4	Newfoundland Inscribed	1913-38	106
4	Do.	1935	113
4	Do. Consd. Stk. Ins.	1936	113
4	N. S. Wales Stock Insc.	1933	118½
3½	Do.	1924	106
3½	Do.	1918	105
3	Do.	1935	98½

Colonial, &c. (*continued*):—

Rate.	Name.		Price.
4	N. Zealnd. Con. Stk. Ins.	1929	112
3½	Do	1940	108
3	Do. Inscribed	1945	96
3	Quebec (Prov.) Ins. Stk.	1937	93
4	Queensland Stock Insc.	1915-24	109
3½	Do.	1921-4-30	104
3½	Do.	1945	106
3	Do.	1922-47	99
4	St. Lucia Insc. Stock	1919-44	112
4	S. Austrln. (1882-7) Reg.	1916-36	108½
3½	Do. In. Stk. Reg.	1939	108
3	Do.	1916-26	100
3/	Do.	1916	100
3½	Tasmanian Insc. Stock	1920-40	108
4	Do.	1920-40	116
4	Trinidad Insc. Stock	1917-42	110
3	Do.	1922-44	98
4	Victoria Rly. Loan '81: Inscribed Stock	1907	105
4	Victoria Insc. Stock	1908-13-19	106
4	Victoria (1883) Ins. Stk.	1920	111
3½	Do. Inscribed Stock	1921-3-6	104
4	Do. do.	1911-26	108
4	W. Austral. Insc. Stock	1934	116½
4	Do.	1911-31	109
3½	Do.	1915-35	104
3	Do.	1915-35	97
3	Do.	1916-36	96½

FOREIGN STOCKS, BONDS, &c.

COUPONS PAYABLE IN LONDON.

Last Div.	Name.		Price
36/	Argentine Ry. Loan 6 p.c.	1881	85½
15/	Do. 5 p.c.	1884	65
30/	Do. N. Cent. Ry. Ext. 5 p.c.	1887-8-9	65
30/	Do. 5 p.c. Trsy. Convs.	1887	65
5/4½	Do. 4½ p.c. Interl. Gld.	1888	63
27/	Do. 4½ p.c. Stlg. Extrl.	1888	64
10/6	Do. 3½ p.c. External	1889	48
4	Do. 4 p.c. Ry. Guar. Res		55½
4½	Brazilian	1883	48
4½	Do. Gold	1879	55½
4½	Do.	1888	47
36/	Buenos Ayres	1824	77½
6	Do.	1882-3-6	46
6	Bulgarian	1888	92
6	Do. Mort. Bonds	1892	92
4½	Chilian	1885	72
4½	Do.	1886	74
4½	Do.	1887	72
4½	Do.	1889	81½
5	Do.	1892	84
4½	Do.	1893	72
4½	Do.	1895	70
5	Do.	1896	82
7	Chinese Silver	1894	97
6	Do. Gold	1895	106
6	Do. Apl. '95 by dwgs.	1901-15	109½
5	Do. Red. dwgs. in 36 yr.	1896	99
5	Do. Do. Regis.	1896	99
1½	Colmbn. 1½ to 3 p.c. Ext. Bds.	1896	16½
6	Cordova, Prov.	1886	25
—	Do. Eng. Ass. Certs.		24
—	Do. 6 p.c.	1887-8	25
—	Do. Eng. Ass. Certs.		24
3	Costa Rica "A"		31
2½	Do. "B"		24
3	Danish Gold	1914	96
10/	Ecuador N. Ext. Bds. 4½ p.c. ascn. to 5 p.c.		20
3½	Egypt'n Ins. Stk. lia. Stp. Dty.	1890	100
4	Do. State Domain	1878	104
4	Do. D. Sanieh, Red.	1905	102
6	Entre Rios	1886-8	33
6	Do. Fndg. Ln. Bds.	1894-1901	30½
6	Do. do. Parana City		27½
15/	Greek	1881	39
15/	Do.	1884	39
12/	Do. Rentes		35
15/	Do. (Piræus-Larissa Ry.)		38
7/6	Do. Fundg. Loan		43
4	Guatemala Extl. Debt		30
6	Hawaiian		102½
4	Hungarian Gold Rentes		101
3	Do.	1895	91½
6	Italian Irriga. Guar.		108
5	Do. Maremmana		91
5	Japan 5 p.c.		102½
5	Mexican (Nat. R. Tehuantp c.)		92½
6	Do. Extrl.	1896	94

Foreign Stocks, &c. (*continued*):—

Last Div.	NAME.	Price
6	Mexican Extrl. 1893	95
5	Do. Intrnl. Cons. Slvr.	36
5	Do Intern. Rd. Bds. 2d. Ser.	36
4	Nicaragua 1886	4½
3½	Norwegian, red. 1937, or earlier	98
3	Do. do. 1965, do.	98
3½	Do. 3½ p.c. Bnds.	102
1	Paraguay 1p.c. ris. 3p.c. 1886-96	15
5	Russian, 1822, £ Strlg.	149
3	Do. 1859	94
4	Do. (Nicolas Ry.) 1867-9 ..	100
3	Do. Transcauc. Ry. 1882 ..	94
4	Do. Con. R. R. Bd. Ser. I., 1889 ..	102
4	Do. Do. II., 1889 ..	102
4	Do. Do. III., 1891 ..	102
3½	Do. Bonds	100
4	Do. Ln. (Dvinsk and Vitbsk)	100½
6	Salvador 1889	64
—	S Domingo 4s. Unified .. 1980	59½
6	San Luis Potosi Stg. 1889	87
5	San Paulo (Brzl.), Stg. 1888	88½
6	Santa Fé 1883-4	35
—	Do. Eng. Ass. Certs. Dep...	34
5	Do. 1888	46
—	Do. Eng. Ass. Certs. Dpsit..	45
5	Do. (W. Cnt. Col. Rly.) Mrt.	25
5	Do. & Reconq. Rly. Mort...	25
5	Spanish Quickslvr Mort. 1870 ..	100½
3½	Swedish 1880	102
3	Do. 1888	98
3	Do. Conversion Loan 1894..	98
5	Trans. Gov. Loan Red...1903-42	103
50/	Tucuman (Prov.) 1888	67½
4	Turkish, Secd. on Egypt. Trib.	101
3½	Turkish, Egpt. Trib., Ott. Bd., '94	97½
4	Do. Priority 1890	89½
1	Do. Convted Series, "A"..	66
5	Do. Customs Ln. 1886	92½
5	Uruguay Bonds 1896	55½
3	Venzuela New Con. Debt 1881	32

COUPONS PAYABLE ABROAD.

Last Div.	NAME.	Price
7	Argent. Nat. Cedla. Sties, "B".	35
5	Austrian Ster. Rnts., ex 10fl., 1870	85
5	Do. do. do.	83
5	Do. Paper do. 1870	83
5	Do. do. do.	83
4	Do. Gld Rentes 1876	100
3	Belgian exchange 25 fr.	100
3½	Danish Int., 1887, Rd. 1896	—
2½	Dutch Certs. ex 12 gldrs.	85
3	Do. Bonds	97
3	Do. Insc. Stk.	96
3½	French Rentes	104½
3	Do. 1878, '81-4., Red.	99
3	German Imp. Ln. 1891	94½
3	Do. do. 1892-3	94½
3	Do. do. 1890-4	95
5	Japan Cons. Ln., '92, 3, & 5, Red.	46
36/9	Prussian Consols	102
3	" Cons. Stg. Ln. 1891	96
4	Rumanian Bds. 1890	—
4	Do. do. 1891	—
4	Utd. States, 1877, Red. 1907	110
4	Do. 1895, 30 yrs.	122
3½	Do. Maschsetts Gl. 1935	113½
3½	Do. Gold Bonds 1923	107½
2	Virginia Cpn. Bds., 3 p.c. from July, 1901	70

BRITISH RAILWAYS.

ORD. SHARES AND STOCKS.

Last Div.	NAME.	Price.
10	Barry, Ord.	274½
4	Do. Prefd.	125
6	Do. Defd.	147½
5	Caledonian, Ord.	153
3	Do. Prefd.	97½
—	Do. Defd. Ord., No. 1	4½
	Cambrian, Ord	5½
—	Do. Coast Cons.	5½
32/	Cardiff Ry. Pref. Ord.	115
3/	Central Lond. £10 Ord. Sh.	10½
1/9½	Do. do. £6 paid	6½
3½d.	Do. Pref. Half-Shares ..	1½
1/6	Do. Def. do	4½
1½	City and S. London	68½
—	East London, Cons.	6½
2	Furness	63½
2½	Glasgow and S. West. Pfd.	81
2½	Do. do. Dfd.	64
3	Great Central, Ord 1894	40
32/0	Do. London Exten.	71
—	Great N. of Scotland, Prfd.	90
—	Do. Dfd.	32
4	Great Northern, Prefd.	118½
—	Do. Consolidated "A"	51
—	Do. do. "B"	189½
2	Highland	76½
4	Isle of Wight, Prefd.	120½
3	Do. Defd.	83½
	Lancs. Derbys. and E. Cst.	4
8½	L. Brighton and S. C. Ord.	185
6	Do. Prefd. Ord.	196
10/	Do. Contgt. Rights Certs.	18½
3½	Lond. and S. Western Ord.	222½
4	Do. Preferred	133
6½	Lond., Tilb., and Southend	133½
—	Mersey, £20 shares	1
—	Metropolitan, New Ord. ..	129½
2½	Do. Surplus Lands	93
4	North Cornwall, 4 p.c. Pref.	104½
18/6	Do. Deferred	22½
7½	North London	222½
4½	North Staffordshire	129

British Railways (*continued*):—

Last Div.	NAME.	Price.
3/3	Plymouth, Devenport, and S. W. Junc. £10	9
3/	Port Talbot £10 Shares ..	9½
9d.	Rhondda Swns. B. £10 Sh.	5
10	Rhymney, Cons.	265½
4	Do. Prefd.	123
6⅛	Do. Defd.	145½
1½	Scarboro', Bridlington Junc.	17½
6½	South Eastern, Ord	149
6	Do. Pref.	191
3½	Taff Vale	80
25/	Vale of Glamorgan	127½
3	Waterloo & City	134½

LEASED AT FIXED RENTALS.

Last Div.	NAME.	Price.
4	Birkenhead	144
5.19.0	East Lincnshire	200½
5½	Hamsmith. & City Ord. ..	192½
4½	Lond. and Blackwll.	160½
4½	Do. £10 4½ p. c. Pref...	160½
56/6	Lond. & Green. Ord.	101
5	Do. 5 p. c. Pref.	173½
5	Nor. and Eastn. £50 Ord...	89
6	Do. ..	104½
3½	N. Cornwall 3½ p. c. Stk...	124½
4⁷⁄₁₆	Nott. & Granthm. R.&C...	140½
3½	Portptk.& Wigtn.Guar.Stk.	121½
9	Vict. Stn. & Pimlico Ord...	312½
4½	Do. 4½ p. c. Pref.	158½
4/	West Lond. £20 Ord. Shs.	14
4⅛	Weymouth & Portld.	157½

DEBENTURE STOCKS.

Last Div.	NAME.	Price.
4	Alexandra Dks. & Ry.	130½
3	Barry, Cons.	107
4	Brecon & Mrthyr, New A	127½
4	Do. New B	105
4	Caledonian	147½
4	Cambrian "A"	132½
4	Do. "B"	127½
4	Do. "C"	122½
4	Do. "D"	107½
3	Cardiff Rly.	100½
4	City and S. Lond.	137½
3½	Cleator & Working Junc...	118½
3	Devon & Som. "A"	103½
16/5	Do. "B" 4 p. c.	36
—	Do. "C" 4 p. c.	10
4	E. Lond. and Ch. 4 p. c. A	135
5/	Do. 2nd B	67½
—	Do. 3rd Ch. 4 p. c. ..	18½
—	Do. 4th do.	9½
3½	Do. 1st (3½ p. c.)	128½
2½	Do. 2½ p.c. (Whitech. Exn)	87
4	Forth Bridge	141½
4	Furness	141½
4	Glasgow and S. Western ..	146½
5	Gt. Central	—
4½	Do.	154½
4	Gt. Eastern	145
4	Gt. N. of Scotland	141½
3	Gt. Northern	111½
4	Gt. Western	148½
4½	Do.	156½
4½	Do.	165½
5	Do.	182½
2½	Do.	96½
4	Highland	141½
3	Hull and Barnsley	104½
3	Do. 2nd (3-4 p. c) ..	122½
4	Isle of Wight	142½
3	Do. Cent. "A" ..	92½
4½	Do. "B"	115½
4	Do. "C"	82½
3	Lancs. & Yorkshire	112
4	Lancs. Derbys. & E. Cst...	123½
4½	Ldn. and Blackwall	155½
4	Ldn. and Greenwich	143½
4	Lond., Brighton, &c.	148½
4½	Do.	165½
4½	Lond., Chath., &c., Arb...	153½
4½	Do. "B" ..	152½
4	Do.	138½
4	Do. 1883....	138½
3	Do.	106
3	Lond. & N. Western	114
3	Lond. & S. Westn. "A" ..	113
3	Do. Consld.	113
4	Lond., Til., & Southend ..	144½
—	Mersey, 5 p. c. (Act, 1866)	65
4	Metropolitan	144½
4½	Do.	162½
3½	Do.	126½
6	Met. District	207½
4	Do.	139
2½	Midland	96
4½	Mid-Wales "A"	137½
4	Neath & Brecon 1st	127½
4	Do. "A 1" ..	117½
3	North British	108
3	Do. 1893	107½
3½	N. Cornwall, Launcstn., &c.	124½
3	North Eastern	112

Debenture Stocks (*continued*):—

Last Div.	NAME.	Price.
4½	North London	163½
3	N. Staffordshire	111
4	Plym. Devpt. & S.W. Jn...	141½
4	Rhondda and Swan. Bay..	130½
4	Rhymney	144½
4	South-Eastern	147
5	Do.	180
3½	Do.	127½
3	Do.	112
3	Taff Vale	108½
4	Tottenham & For. Gate ..	143½
3	Vale of Glamorgan	105½
3	West Highld. (Gtd. by N.B.)	107
4	Wrexham, Mold, &c. "A"	115½
4	Do. "B"	102½
4	Do. "C"	97½

GUARANTEED SHARES AND STOCKS.

Last Div.	NAME.	Price.
4	Caledonian	146½
4	Do.	142½
4	Forth Bridge	141½
4	Furness 1881	137½
4	Glasgow & S. Western	141½
4	Do. St. Enoch, Rent	141½
6	Gt. Central	198½
4½	Do. 1st Pref.	150½
3½	Do. Pref.	104½
5	Do. Irred. S.Y. Rent	161½
4½	Do. do.	139½
4	Gt. Eastern, Rent	140½
5	Do. Metropolitan..	177½
4	Do.	140½
4	Gt. N. of Scotland	138½
4	Gt. Northern	142½
5	Gt. Western, Rent	180½
5	Do. Cons.	180½
4	Lancs. & Yorkshire	143½
5	L., Brighton & S. C.	178½
3½	L., Chat. & D. (Shrtlds.)..	110½
4	L. & North Western	145
4	L. & South Western.. 1881	142½
4½	Met. District, Ealing Rent	150
4½	Do. Fulham Rent	150
4	Do. Midland Rent	141½
4	Do. Mid. & Dist. Guar.	126½
2½	Midland, Cons. Perp.	91
3	Mid.&G.N. Jt., "A" Rnt..	106
3	N. British, Lien	106
4	Do Cons. Pref. No. 1	139
3	N. Cornwall, Wadebrge. Gu.	107
4	N. Eastern	144
5	N. Staff. Trent & M. £20 Shs.	35½
3½	Nott. Suburban Ord.	123½
20/6	S. E. Perp. Ann.	35½
4½	Do. 4½ p.c.	161½
3½	S. Yorks. Junc. Ord.	118½
4½	W. Cornwall (G. W., Br., Ex., & S. Dev. Joint Rent	158½
3	W. Highl. Ord. Stk. (Gua., N.B.)	105½

PREFERENCE SHARES AND STOCKS.

DIVIDENDS CONTINGENT ON PROFIT OF YEAR.

Last Div.	NAME	Price.
4½	Alexandra Dks. & Ry. "A"	125½
5	Barry (First)	167½
4	Do. Consolidated	136½
4	Caledonian Cons., No. 1 ..	141½
4	Do. do. No. 2 ..	140½
5	Do. do. 1878	172½
4	Do. Pref. 1884	140½
4	Do. do. 1887 (Conv.)	152½
—	Cambrian, No. 1 4 p.c. Pref.	72½
—	Do. No. 2 do.	37½
—	Do. No. 3 do.	17½
—	Do. No. 4 do.	9
5	City & S. Lond. £10 shares	15½
—	Do. New	15½
4	Furness, Cons. 1881	133
4	Do. ......"A" 1881	131½
4	Do. ......"B" 1883	129½
4	Glasgow & S. Western	140½
4	Do. No. 2....	138½
4	Do. 1888	139
4	Do. 1891	139
5	Gt. Central	158½
4	Do.	131½
5	Do. Conv..... 1872	153½
5	Do. do. 1874	153½
5	Do. do. 1876	152½
5	Do. do. 1879	151½
5	Do. do. 1881	147½
4	Do. 1889	112½
4	Do. 1891	106½
5	Do. 1894	102½
4	Gt. Eastern, Cons.	138½
4	Do. 1880	138½
4	Do. 1881	138½
4	Do. 1884	138½

Preference Shares, &c. (*continued*):—

Last Div.	NAME.	Price.
4	Gt. Eastern, Cons..... 1887	138½
4	Do. 1888	138½
3½	Do. 1890	120½
3½	Do. 1893	120½
—	Do. (Int. fr. Jan '99) 1893	117½
4	Gt. North Scotland "A" ..	133½
4	Do. "B" ..	133½
4	Gt. Northern, Cons.	141½
3	Do. 1896	106½
5	Gt. Western Cons.	178½
36/11	Hull & Barnsley Red. at 115	107½
4	Isle of Wight	133½
3	Lancs. & Yorkshire, Cons.	107
2/2½	Lanc. Drby & E.C. 5 p.c. £10	10
—	Do. 5 p.c. 2nd £10	9
5	Lond., Bright., &c., Cons.	177½
5	Do. 2nd Cons.	176½
4½	Lond., Chat. & Dov. Arbitr.	134
25/	Do. 2nd Pref. 4½ p.c.	93
4	Lond. & N. Western	144
4	Lond. & S. Western.. 1881	142½
4	Do. 1884	141½
3½	Do.	126
4	Lond., Tilbury & Southend	140½
4	Do. Cons., 1887	140½
4	Do 1891	140½
—	Mersey, 5 p.c. Perp.	—
4	Metropolitan, Perp.	140½
4	Do. 1882	140½
4	Do. Irred.	140½
4	Do. 1887	140½
4	Do. New	140½
4½	Do.	146½
3½	Do.	123½
3	Do. Guar.	101½
2½	Metrop. Dist. Exten 5 p.c.	110
2½	Midland, Perp. Pref.	90
4	N. British Cons., No. 2 ..	135½
4½	Do. Edin. & Glasgow	151½
5	Do. 1865	165½
5	Do. Conv. 1874	166½
4½	Do. 1875	151½
4½	Do. Conv. 1875	151½
5	Do. do. 1879	166½
4	Do. do. 1884	136½
4	Do. do. 1888	136½
4	Do. do. 1890	136½
4	Do. do. 1892	136½
4	N. Eastern	142½
4½	N. Lond., Cons. 1866	173½
4½	Do. 2nd Cons. .. 1875	157½
3	N. Staffordshire	106½
4½	Plym. Devpt. & S. W. Jun...	149½
1/5	Port Talbot, &c., 4 p.c. £10 Shares, 4 paid	5
5/	Rhondda & Swansea Bay, 5 p.c. £10 Shares	12½
4	Rhymney, Cons.	140½
4½	S. Eastern, Cons.	158½
5	Do. do.	177½
4	Do. Vested Cos	140½
4	Do. 1891	140½
3½	Do. 1893	122½
2	Do. 3 p.c. after July 1900	101½
4	Taff Vale	142½

INDIAN RAILWAYS.

Last Div.	NAME.	Paid.	Price.
3½	Assam Bengal, Ld., (3½ p.c. till June 30, then 3 p.c.)	100	100
4/	Barsi Light, Ld., £10 Shs.	10	11
6	Bengal and N. West., Ld	100	148½
4/	Do. £10 Shares	10	14½
3/6	Do. 3½ p.c. Cum. Pf. Shs.	10	10½
5½d.	Do.	4	4½
2/3½	Bengal Central, Ld., £10 (3½ p.c. + ½th net earn)	5	6
3	Bengal Dooars, Ld.	100	114
4	Bengal Nagpr., Lim. (gua. 4 p.c. + 4th sp. pfts.) ..	100	114
7½	Bombay, Baroda, and C. I. (gua 5 p.c)	100	214
36/1	Burma, Ld. (gua. 2½ p.c. and ½ p.c. add. till 1901)	100	107½
1/7	Do. £10 Shares		3
4	Delhi Umb. Kalka, Ld., Gua. 3½ p.c. + net earn.	100	120
4	Do. Deb. Stk., 1890 (1916)	100	111
9/10	Estn. Bengal, "A" An. 1957	—	25
9/	Do. "B" 1957	—	30
4	Do. Gua. Deb. Stock ..	100	136½
9/7½	East Ind. Ann. "A" (1953)	—	27
8/4½	Do. "C"	—	29
8/11½	Do. "B"	—	31
6⅛	Do. Def. Ann. Cap. (gua. 4 p.c. + ½th sp. pfts.)	—	150
115/9	East Ind. Def. Ann. "D"	—	156
4½	East Ind. Irred. Stock ..	100	158½
5	Gt. Indian Penin., Gua 5 p.c. + ½ surplus profits..	100	167½
4	Do. Irred. 4 p.c. Deb. St.	100	136½
4	Indian Mid., Ld. (gua. 4 p.c. + ¼th surplus pfts.)	100	114
31/	Madras Guar. + ½ sp. pfts.	100	166
48/6	Do. do.	100	156
46/	Do. do.	100	146
4	Nilgiri, Ld., 1st Deb. Stk.	100	97
4	Oude & Rohil. Db. Stk. Rd.	100	—
5½	Rohil. and Kumaon, Ld.	100	132
9/11	Scinde, Punj., and Delhi, "A" Ann., 1958	—	85
9/1	Do. "B" do. ..	—	30

Indian Railways (*continued*):—

Last Div.	Name.	Paid.	Price.
4	South Behar, Ld., £10 shs.	100	100
3½	Do. Deb. Stk. Red.	100	101
4½	South Ind., Gu. Deb. Stk.	100	158½
5	South Indian, Ld. (gua. 3 p.c., and ½ spls. profits)	100	122½
5	Sthn. Mahratta, Ld. (3½ p.c. & ¼th net earnings)	100	115½
4	Do. Deb. Stk. Red.	100	120
3½	Southern Punjab, Ld.	100	105
3½	Do. Deb. Stk. Red.	—	104
5	Nizam's Gua. State, Ld. (†	100	114½
4	Do. Mort. Deb., 1936	100	107
4	Do. do. Reg.	100	106
17/3½	Nizam's Gua. State, Ld., 3½ p.c. Mt. Deb. bearer	—	94½
17/3½	Do. Reg. do.	—	93½
5	W. of India Portgese., Ld.	100	68½
5	Do. Deb. Stk., Red	100	99

RAILWAYS.—BRITISH POSSESSIONS.

Last Div.	Name.	Paid.	Price.
5	Atlantic & N.W. Gua. 1 Mt. Bds., 1937	100	124½
5/3	Buff. & L. Huron Ord. Sh.	10	13½
5½	Do. 1st Mt. Perp. Bds. 1879	100	141½
5½	Do. 2nd Mt. Perp. Bds.	100	141½
—	Calgary & Edmon. 6 p.c. 1st Mt. Stg. Bds. Red.	100	75½
5	Canada Cent. 1st Mt. Bds. Red.	100	103
4	Can. Pacific Pref. Stk.	100	100
5	Do. Strl. 1st Mt. Deb. Bds. 1915	100	117
3½	Do. Ld. Grnt. Bds., 1938	100	106
3½	Do. Ld. Grnt. Ins. Stk.	100	106
4	Do. Perp. Cons. Deb. Stk.	100	115
5	Do. Algoma Bch. 1st Mt. Bds., 1937	100	121
2	Demerara, Original Stock	100	47
7	Do. Perp. Pref. Stk.	100	155½
1/10	Do. 4 p.c. Cum. Ext. Pref. £10 Shs.	4	8
—	Dominion Atlntc. Ord. Stk.	100	33½
5	Do. 5 p.c. Pref. Stk.	100	97½
4	Do. 1st. Deb. Stk.	100	103½
4	Do. 2nd do. Red.	100	99
—	EmuBay & Mt. Bischoff, Ld.	5	4½
4½	Do. Irred. Deb. Stk.	100	98
nil.	Gd. Trunk of Canada, Stk.	100	8½
6	Do. 2nd. Equip. Mt. Bds.	100	130½
5	Do. Perp. Deb. Stk.	100	135½
5	Do. Gt. Westn. Deb. Stk.	100	127½
5	Do. Nthn. of Can. 1st Mt. Bds, 1902	100	102½
4	Do. do. Deb. Stk	100	102
5	Do. G. T. Geor. Bay & L. Erie 1 Mt., 1903	100	104
5	Do. Mid. of Can. Stl. 1st Mt. (Mid. Sec.) 1908	100	103
5	Do. do. Cons. 1 Mt. Bds. 1912	100	106
5	Do. Mont. & Champ. 1 Mt. Bds., 1909	100	103
	Do. Welln., Grey & Brce. 7 p.c. Bds. 1 Mt.	100	109
—	Jamaica 1st Mtg. Bds. Red.	—	103
—	Manitoba & N. W., 6 p.c. 1st Mt. Bds., Red	100	—
—	Do. Ldn. Bdhldrs. Certs.	—	—
5	Manitoba S. W. Col. 1 Mt. Bd., 1934 $1,000 price %	—	120
—	Mid. of W. Aust. Ld. 6 p.c. 1 Mt. Dbs., Red.	100	25
4	Do. Deb. Bds., Red.	100	103
4	Nakusp & Slocan Bds., 1918	100	106
3	Natal Zululand Ld. Debs.,	100	77½
5	N. Brunswick 1st Mt. Stg. Bds., 1934	100	121
4	Do. Perp. Cons. Deb. Stk.	100	114
—	N. Zealand Mid., Ld., 5 p.c. 1st Mt. Debs.	100	35
6	Ontario & Queb. Cap. Stk.	$100	154½
5	Do. Perm. Deb. Stk.	100	143½
—	Qu'Appelle, L. Lake & Sask. 6 p.c. 1 Mt. Bds. Red.	100	40½
	Queb. & L. S. John, 1st Mt. Bds., 1909	100	25½
	Quebec Cent., Prior Ln. Bds., 1908	100	107
1½	Do. 5 p.c. Inc. Bds.	100	39
4	St. Lawr. & Ott. Stl. 1st Mt.	100	112
4	Shuswap & Okan., 1st Mt. Deb. Bds., 1915	100	76
5	Temiscouata, 5 p.c. Stl. 1st Deb. Bds., Red.	100	9½
5	Do. (S. Franc. Brch.) 5 p.c. Stl. 1 Mt. Db. Bds., 1910	100	10
4	Toronto, Grey & B. 1st Mt.	100	112
1/2	Well. & Mana. £5 Shs.	1	½
5	Do. Debs., 1908	100	108
5	Do. 2nd Debs., 1908	100	107
5	Do. 3rd do., 1908	100	106
6	Atlnn. & St. Law. Shs., 6 p.c.	100	161½
5	Gd. Trunk Mt. Bds., 1934	100	116½
5	Michigan Air Line, 5 p.c. 1st Mt. Bds., 1902	100	104
4	Minneap., S. P. & Slt. Ste. Mar, 1st Mt. Bds., 1938	$1000	97½

AMERICAN RAILROAD STOCKS AND SHARES.

Last Div.	Name.	Paid.	Price.
6/	Alab. Gt. Sthn. A 6 p.c. Pref.	10*l.*	9
—	Do. do "B" Ord.	10*l.*	1½
—	Alabma. N. Orl.-Tex. &c., "A" Pref.	10*l.*	½
—	Do. "B" Def.	10*l.*	½
5½	Atlant. First Lsd. Ls. Rtl. Trust	Stk.	97½
—	Baltimore & Ohio Com.	$100	17
—	Baltimore Ohio S.W. Pref.	$100	6
—	Chesap. & Ohio Com.	$100	20
—	Chic. Gt. West. 5 p.c. Pref. Stock "A"	$100	30½
—	Do. do. Scrip. In.	—	27
8/3	Do. 4 p.c. Deb. Stk.	$100	67½
4	Do. Interest in Scrip	$100	63½
$4	Chic. Junc. Rl. & Un. Stk. Yds. Com.	$100	113½
$1½	Do. 6 p.c. Cum. Pref.	$100	117
$3½	Chic. Mil. & St. P. Pref.	$100	146
7	Cleve. & Pittsburgh	$10	86
$1½	Clev., Cincin., Chic., & St. Louis Com.	$100	—
—	Erie 4 p.c. Non-Cum. 1st Pf	—	34½
—	Do. 4 p.c. do. 2nd Pf.	—	17
$2½	Gt. Northern Pref.	$100	150
$2½	Illinois Cen. Lsd. Lines	$100	95½
—	Kansas City, Pitts & G.	$100	19
$3	L. Shore & Mich. Sth. C.	$100	190
—	Mex. Cen. Ltd. Com.	$100	5
—	Miss. Kan. & Tex. Pref.	$100	32½
2½	N.Y., Pen. & O. 1st Mt. Tst. Ltd., Ord.	—	47½
4	Do. 1st Mort. Deb. Stk.	$100	92½
4	North Pennsylvania	$50	—
—	Northn. Pacific, Com.	$100	26½
1½	Pitts. F. Wayne & Chic.	$100	174
—	Reading 1st Pref.	$50	21½
—	Do. 2nd Pref.	$50	11½
—	S. Louis & S. Fran. Com.	$100	6
—	Do. 2nd Pref.	$100	24½
6	St. Louis Bridge 1st Pref.	$100	107
3	Do. 2nd Pref.	$100	50
6	Tunnel Rail. of St. Louis	$100	107
$1½	St. Paul, Min. and Man.	$100	132½
—	Southern, Com.	$100	8½
—	Wabash, Common	$100	7

AMERICAN RAILROAD BONDS. CURRENCY.

Last Div.	Name.	Price.
7	Albany & Susq. 1 Con. Mrt. 1906	118
7	Allegheny Val. 1 Mt. 1910	125½
5	Canada Southern 1 Mt. 1908	111
5	Chic. & N. West. Sk. Fd. Db. 1933	117½
5	Do. Deb. Coupon 1921	112½
6	Chicago & Tomah 1905	109½
5	Chic. Burl. & Q. Skg. Fd. 1901	102½
4	Do. Nebraska Ext. —	93
6	Chic., Mil., & S. Pl., 1 Mt. S.W. Div. 1909	117½
7	Do. (S. Paul Div.) 1 Mt. 1902	132½
5	Do. (La Cross & D. 1919	112½
7	Do. 1 Mt. (Hast. & Dak.) 1910	127½
5	Do. Chic. & Mis. Riv. 1 Mt. 1926	112½
5	Chic., Rock Is. and Pac. 1 Mt. Ext. 1934	108
6	Det., G. Haven & Mil. Equip 1918	105
6	Do. do. Cons. Mt. 1918	102½
6	Ill. Cent., 1 Mt., Chic. & S. 1898	—
7	Indianap. & Vin., 1 Mt. 1908	125
6	Do. do. 2 Mt. 1900	100½
6	Lehigh Val., Cons. Mt. 1923	112½
—	Mexic. Cent., Ln. 2 Cons. Inc. —	5
7	N.Y. Cent. & H.R. Mt. Bonds 1903	117½
5	Do. Deb. 1904	107½
6	Penns. Cons. S. F M. 1905	118
4	West Shore, 1 Mt. 2361	110

DITTO—GOLD.

Last Div.	Name.	Price.
6	Alabama Gt. Sthn. 1 Mt. 1908	114
5	Do. Mid. 1 1928	90½
4	Allegheny Val. Gen. Mt. 1942	106
4	Atch., Top., & S. Fé Gn. Mt. 1995	90½
3	Do. Adj. Mt. 1995	61½
5	Do. Equipt. Tmst. —	102½
5	Atlantic & Dan. 1 Mt. 1950	95½
5	Baltimore & Ohio 1925	97
5	Do. Speyer's Tst. Recpts. 1925	97
5	Do. Cons. Mt. 1988	100
4½	Do. 4½ p.c. 1 Mt. Term. 1934	82½
4½	Do. Brown Shipley's Dep. Cts. —	82½
5	Balt. Belt 5 p.c. 1 Mort. 1990	85
4½	Balt. & Ohio S.W. 1 Mt. 1990	100
4½	Do. 4½ p.c. 1 Cons. Mt. 1893 1993	75½
—	Do. Inc. Mt. 5 p.c. Cl. A —	27½
—	Do. do. Cl. B —	10
5	Balt. & Ohio S.W. Term 5 p.c. 1942	97½
6	Balt. & Ptmac (Mn. L.) 1 Mt. 1911	124
6	Do. do. (Tunnel) 1 Mt. 1911	126
4	Beech Creek 1 Mt. 1936	109
4	Carthage & Adiron 1 Mt. 1981	109

American Railroad Bonds—Gold *continued*):—

Last Div.	Name.	Price.
5	Cent. of Georgia 1 Mort. 1945	117½
5	Do. Cons. Mt. 1945	90½
5	Cent. of N. Jrsy. Gn. Mt. 1987	113½
6	Central Pacific, 1 Mort. 1898	102½
6	Do. Speyer's Certs. —	106
5	Do Land Grant 1900	101
5	Chesap. & Ohio 1st Cons. Mt. 1939	114½
4½	Do. Gen. Mt. 1992	78½
6	Chic. & W. Ind. Gen. Mt. Skg. Fd. 1932	120
5	Chic. Mil. & St. Pl. (Chic. & L. Sup.) 1 Mt. 1921	114½
5	Do. Chic. & Pac. W. 1921	117½
5	Do. Wisc. & Minn. 1 Mt. 1921	112½
5	Do. Terminal Mt. 1914	114½
4	Do. General Mt. 1925	106½
5	Chic. St. L. & N. Orleans 1951	122½
4	Do. 1 Mort. (Memphis) 1951	105½
4	Clevel., Cin., Chic. & St. L. 1 Mt. (Cairo) 1939	90
4	Do. 1 Mt. (Cinc., Wab., & Mich.) 1991	90
4	Do. 1 Col. Tst. Mt. (S. Louis) 1990	96
4	Do. General Mt. 1993	82½
4½	Clevel. & Mar. Mt. 1935	109
4½	Clevel. & Pittsburgh 1942	116½
4½	Do. Series B. 1942	116½
—	Colorado Mid. 1 Mt. 1936	63½
—	Do. Bdhrs.' Comm. Certs. —	63½
4	Dnvr. & R. Gde. 1 Cons. Mt. 1936	91½
5	Do Imp. Mort. 1928	91
4	Detroit & Mack. 1 Lien 1995	92½
5	E. Tennes., Virg., & Grgia. Cons. Mt. 1956	111½
5	Elmira, Cort., & Nthn. Mt. 1914	100
4	Erie 1 Cons. Mt. Pr. Ln. 1996	90
3	Do. Gen. Lien 1996	71
6	Galvest., Harrisb., &c., 1 Mt.	107½
5	Georgia, Car. & N. 1 Mt. 1929	96
4½	Gd. Rpds & Inda. Ex. 1 Mt. 1941	112½
5	Do. 1 Mt. (Muskegon) 1926	30½
3½	Illinois Cent. 1 Mt. 1951	104½
4	Do. 1952	104½
4	Do. Cairo Bdge. 1950	102
4	Do. 1953	101
4	Do. General Mort. 1904	102½
5	Kans. City, Pitts. & G. 1 M. 1923	73½
3½	L. Shore & Mich. Southern 1997	109
4½	Lehigh Val. N.Y. 1 Mt. 1940	102½
5	Lehigh Val. Term. 1 Mt. 1941	109½
5	Long Island 1931	117½
5	Do. Deb. 1934	102
5	Do. (N. Shore Bch.) 1 Cons. Mt. 1932	94
6	Louisville & Nash. G. Mt. 1930	120
6	Do. 2 Mt. Sk. Fd. (S. & N. Alabama 1910	107
6	Do. 1 Mt. N. Orl. & Mb. 1930	122½
5	Do. 1 Mt. Coll. Tst. 1931	102½
4	Do. Unified 1940	99
4½	Do. Mobile & Montgy. 1 Mt. 1945	105½
4	Manhattan Cons. Mt. 1990	93
4	Mexican Cent. Cons. Mt. 1911	64½
—	Do. 1 Cons. Inc.	13
6	Mexican Nat. 1 Mt. 1927	106
3½	Do. 2 Mt. 6 p.c. Inc. A 1917	52½
—	Do. do. B. 1917	9
3	Do. Matheson's Certs.	—
3	Michig. Cnt. (Battle Ck. & S.) 1 Mt. 1989	88
6	Minneap. & S. L. 1 Mt. Pacific Ext. 1921	117½
5	Do. 1 Consold. 1934	104½
4	Minne., Slt S. M. & A. 1 Mt. 1926	98
5	Minneapolis Westn. 1 Mt. 1911	105½
4	Miss. Kans. & Tex. 1 Mt. 1990	82½
4	Do. 2 do. 1990	62
4	Mobile & Birm. Mt. Inc. 1945	38
5	Do. P. Lien 1945	88
4	Mohawk & Mal. 1 Mt. 1991	108
5	Montana Cent. 1 Mt. 1937	111½
5	Nashv., Chattan., & S. L. 1 Cons. Mt. 1928	102½
5	Nash., Flor., & Shff. Mt. 1937	92½
4	N. Y. & Putnam 1 Cons. Mt. 1993	108
5	N. Y., Brooklyn, & Man. B. 1 Cons. Mt. 1935	107½
4	N. Y. Cent. & Hud. R. Deb. Certs. 1890 1905	104½
4	Do. Ext. Debt. Certs. 1905	103
7	N. Y., L. Erie, & W. 1 Cons. Mt. (Erie) 1920	139½
7	Do. 1 Con. Mt. Fd. Coup. 1920	137½
5	N. Y., Onto., & W. Cons. 1 Mt. 1939	110
4	Do. 4 p.c. Refund. Mt. 1992	99
6	Norfolk & West. Gn. Mt. 1931	121½
6	Do. Imp. & Ext. 1934	117½
4	Do. 1 Cons. Mt. —	80
6	N. Pacific Gn. 1 Mt. Ld. Gt. 1921	—
4	Do. P. Ln. Rl. & Ld. Gt. —	96
3	Do. Gn. Ln. Rl. & Ld. Gt. —	61
5	Oregon & Calif. 1 Mt. 1927	77
6	Panama Skg. Fd. Subsidy 1910	102½
4½	Pennsylvania Rlrd. 1943	110½
4	Do. Equip. Tst. Ser. A 1914	104
4	Do. Cons. Mt. 1943	112½
4½	Penna. Company 1st Mort. 1921	110½
5	Perkiomen 1 Mrt., 2nd ser. 1918	91½
4½	{ Pitts., C., C., & St. Ls. Con. Mt. G. B., Ser. A } 1940-2	110
4	Do. Cons. Mort., Ser. D. 1945	102½
6	Pittsbgh., Cle., & Toledo 1922	100½
4	Reading, Phil., & R. Genl. 1997	84
5	Richmond & Dan. Equip. 1909	97½
5	Rio Grande Junc. 1st Mort. 1939	92½
4	Rio Grande West 1st Tst. Mt. 1939	82½
7	S. Louis Bridge 1st Mort 1928	134½
5	S. Louis Mchts. Bdge. Term. 1st Mort. 1930	102½
4	S. Louis S. West 1st Mort. 1989	75
—	Do. 4 p.c. 2nd Mort. Inc. 1989	30

American Railroad Bonds (*continued*):

Last Div.	Name.	Price.
—	S. Louis Term. Cupples Sta. & Prop. 1st. Mrt. 4½ p.c. 1902-17	102
4½	St. Paul Minn., & Manit. 1933	107½
6	Do. do. 1933	132½
6	Shamokin, Sunbury, &c. 2 Mt. 1925	100
5	S. & N. Alabama Cons. Mt. 1936	97½
5	Southern 1 Cons. Coup. 1994	91½
4	Do. E. Tennes Reorg. Lien 1938	100
6	S. Pacific of Cal. 1 Mt. 1905-12	110
4½	Trml. Assn. of S. Louis 1 Mt. 1939	110½
5	Do. 1 Cons. Mt. 1944	108
5	Texas & Pac. 1 Mt. 2000	102
—	Do. 5 p.c. 2 Mt. Income 2000	30
5	Toledo & Ohio Cent. 1 Mt. West. Div. 1935	102½
4½	Toledo., Walhon., Val., & Ohio 1 Mt. 1931-3	111½
—	Union Pacific 1 Mt. 4 p.c. 1947	92
—	Union Pac., Linc., & Color. 1 Mt. 1918	—
4	United N. Jersey Gen. Mt. 1944	113½
6	Vicksburg., Shrevept., & Pac. Pr. Ln. Mt. 1915	100½
5	Wabash 1 Mt. 1939	106½
4	Wn. Pennsylvania Mt. 1928	108½
5	W. Virga. & Pittsbg. 1 Mt. 1990	75
5	Wheeling & L. Erie 1 Mt. (Wheelg. Div.) 5 p.c. 1928	90½
5	Do. Extn. Imp. Mt. 1930	90
—	Do. do. Brown Shipley's Cts.	—
5	Willmar & Sioux Falls 1 Mt. 1938	111

STERLING.

Last Div.	Name.	Price.
6	Alabama Gt. Sthn. Deb. 1906	104½
5	Do. Gen. Mort. 1907-8	99
5	Alabama, N. Orl., Tex. & Pac. 5 p.c. "A" Dbs. 1910-40	96½
55/	Do. do. "B" do. 1910-40	52
—	Do. do. "C" do.	19
—	Allegheny Valley 1910	127½
4	Atlantic 1st Leased Line Perp.	98
6	Baltimore and Ohio 1902	106
6	Do. do. 1910	113
5	Do. do. 1877	94
—	Do. Morgan's Certs.	93½
4½	Do. do. 1933	88
6	Chicago & Alton Cons. Mt. 1903	111
5	Chic. St. Paul & Kan. City Priority	106
6	Eastn. of Massachusetts 1906	117½
5	Illinois Cent. Skg. Fd.	103
5	Do. 1903	108
3½	Do. 1950	99½
4	Do. 1 Mt. 1951	110
3	Do. 1 Mt. 1951	92½
6	Louisville & Nash., M. C. & L. Div., 1 Mt. 1902	104½
7	Do. 1 Mt. (Memphis & O.) 1901	111
55/8	Mexican Nat. "A" Certs. 5 p.c. Non. cum.	41
—	Do. "B" Certs.	9
6	N.Y. & Canada 1 Mt. 1904	108½
6	N. York Cent. & H.R. Mort. 1903	112
4½	N. York, Penns., & Ohio Pr. Ln. Extd. 1935	—
5	Do. Equip. Tst.	101½
5	Do. 5 p.c. Equip. Tst. (1890)	103½
6	Nthn. Cent. Cons. Gen. Mt.	106
6	Pennsylvania Gen. Mt. 1910	125
6	Do. Cons. Skg. Fd. Mt. 1905	114
3½	Do. Cons. Mt. 1945	103½
6	Phil. & Erie Cons. Mort 1920	132½
6	Phil. & Reading Gen. Cons. Mort. 1911	122½
6	Pittsbg. & Connells. Cons. 1926	114
—	Do. Morgan's Certs.	114
4	St. Paul., Min., & Manitoba (Pac. Extn.) 1940	96½
6	S. & N. Alabama 1903	104½
6	Un. N. Jersey & C. Gen. Mt. 1901	109½

FOREIGN RAILWAYS

Last Div.	Name.	Paid.	Price.
4/	Alagoas, Ltd., Shs.	20	5
5	Do. Deb. Stk., Red.	100	42½
6	Antofagasta, Ltd., Stk.	100	73
4	Do. Perp. Deb. Stk.	100	91
—	Arauco, Ld., Ord. Shs.	10	—
—	Do. 10 p.c. Cum. Pref.	10	—
5	Argentine Gt. W., Ld.,	100	72
5	Do. 5 p.c. Cum. Pref. Shs.	100	100
4	Do. 1 Deb. Stk.	100	102
1/0/0	Argentine N.E., Ltd., 6 p.c. Cum. Pref. Stk.	100	9½
—	Do. 5 p.c. Deb. Stk., Red.	100	29
2/	Arica and Tacna Shs.	20	1½
10/	Bahia & San Fcisco., Ld.,	20	8½
6/	Do. Timbo. Bch. Shs.	20	4½
12/	Bahia, Blanca, & N.W. Ln. Prf. Cum. 6 p.c.	100	54
4	Do. 4 p.c. 1 Deb. Stk., Red.	100	92
6	Barranquilla R. & P., Ld., 6 p.c. 1 Deb. Stk., Red.	100	96

Foreign Railways (*continued*):—

Last Div.	Name.	Paid.	Price.
3/	Bilbao Riv. & Cantabn., Ltd., Ord.	3	5½
—	Bolivar, Ltd. Shs.	10	1½
6	Do. 6 p.c. Deb. Stk.	100	96½
—	Brazil Gt. Southn. Ltd., 7 p.c. Cum. Pref.	20	1½
6	Do. Perm. Deb. Stk	100	41½
5½	B. Ayres Gt. Southn. Ld., Ord. Stk.	100	144
5	Do. Pref. Stk.	100	134
4	Do. Deb. Stk.	100	115½
20/	B. Ayres & Ensen. Port., Ltd., Ord. Stk.	100	68
5	Do. Cum. 1 Pref. Stk.	100	121
6/0/0	Do. 6p.c. Con. Pref. Stk.	100	99
4	Do. Deb. Stk., Irred.	100	113
10⅛	B. Ayres Northern, Ltd., Ord. Stk.	100	265
12½	Do. Pref. Stk.	100	320
5	Do. 5 p.c. Mt. Deb. Stk., Red.	100	113
3/15/0	B. Ayres & Pac., Ld., 7 p.c. 1 Pref. Stk. (Cum.)	100	94
4	Do. 1 Deb. Stk.	100	101
3/5/0	Do. 4½ p.c. 2 Deb. Stk.	100	90
3	B Ayres & Rosario, Ltd., Ord. Stk.	100	72
—	Do New, £20 Shs.	20	—
7/	Do. 7 p.c. Pref. Shs.	10	17
7/	Do. Sunchales Ext.	10	14½
4	Do. Deb. Stk., Red.	100	106
—	B. Ayres & Val. Trans., Ltd., 7 p.c. Cum. Pref.	20	6½
4	Do. 4 p.c. "A" Deb. Stk., Red.	100	71
—	Do. 6 p.c. "B" Deb. Stk. Red.	100	43
3/6	B. Ayres Westn. Ld. Ord.	10	10½
3/	Do. Def. Shs	10	6½
5	Do. 5 p.c. Pref.	10	12½
4	Do. Deb. Stk.	100	107½
6	Cent. Arg. Deb. Sk. Rd.	100	160½
4	Do. Deb. Stk. Rd.	100	110
6	Cent. Bahia L. Ord. Stk.	100	44½
	Do. Deb. Stk., 1934	100	72½
5	Do. Deb. Stk., 1937	100	58
3/6	Cent. Uguy. East. Ext. L. Shs	10	5½
5	Do. Perm. Stk	100	112
3/6	Do. Nthn. Ext. L. Sh.	10	4
5	Do. Perm. Deb. Stk	100	103½
3	Do. of Montev. Ltd., Ord. Stk	100	85
6	Do. Perm. Deb. Stk	100	141
10/	Conde d'Eu, Ltd. Ord.	20	7
—	Cordba & Rosar., Ltd., 6 p.c. Pref. Shs.	100	41
4	Do. 1 Deb. Stk.	100	90
75	Do. 6 p.c. Deb. Stk.	100	91
—	Cordba Cent., Ltd., 5 p.c. Cu. 1 Pref. Stk	100	78½
—	Do. 5 p.c. Non-Cum. 2 Pref. Stk	100	45
5	Do. Deb. Stk	100	118
—	Costa Rica, Ltd., Shs	10	4½
8/	Dna. Thrsa. Chris., Ltd., 7 p.c. Pref. Shs.	20	3½
20/	E. Argentine, Ltd	100	40
6	Do. Deb. Stk	100	104
1/1	Egyptn. Dlta. Lgt. Rys., Ltd., £10 Pref. Shs.	8	10½
—	Entre Rios, L., Ord. Shs.	5	½
—	Do. Cu. 5 p.c. Pref.	5	3
6/	Gt. Westn. Brazil, Ltd.,	20	8½
6	Do. Perm. Deb. Stk	100	90½
6	Do. Extn. Deb. Stk	100	76½
—	Int.-Oceanic Mex., Ltd., 7 p.c. Pref	10	1½
4	Do. Deb. Stk	100	82
42/6	Do. 7 p.c. "A" Deb. Sk.	100	67
—	Do. 7 p.c. "B" Deb. Sk.	100	30
5/	La Guaira & Carac	10	7½
5	Do. 5 p.c. Deb. Sk. Red.	100	100
12/3	Lembg.-Czern.-Jassy	30	24½
1/	Lima, Ltd.	20	2½
—	Manila Ltd. 7 p.c. Cu. Pf.	10	½
20/6½	Mexican 2nd Pref. 6 p.c.	100	31
6	Do. Perp. Deb. Stk.	100	137
1/0/0	Mexican Sthrn., Ld., Ord.	100	23
—	Do. 4 p.c. 1 Db. Stk. Rd.	100	83
—	Do. 4 p.c. 2 do.	100	61
—	Mid. Urgy., Ltd.	100	18½
5	Do. Deb. Stk	100	62
12/	Minas & Rio, Ltd.	20	8
5/2	Namur & Liege	20	12½
11/6	Do. Pref	20	29
13/	Natal & Na. Cruz, Ld., 7 p.c. Cum Pref.	20	6
—	Nitrate Ltd., Ord.	10	5½
—	Do. 7 p.c. Pr. Con. Or.	10	3½
—	Do. Def. Conv. Ord.	10	½
7/	N.-E. Urgy., Ltd., Ord.	10	14½
7/	Do. 7 p.c. Pref.	10	14½
—	N.-W. Argentine Ld., 7 p.c. Pref.	10	2
6	Do. 6 p.c. 1 Deb. Stk.	100	113
—	Do. 2 Deb. Stk.	100	94
—	N.W. Uruguay 6 p.c. 1 Pref. Stk.	100	17
—	Do. 5 p.c. 2 Pref. Stk.	100	7½
6	Do. 6 p.c. Deb. Stk.	100	80½
22/	Ottoman (Sm. Aid.)	20	13½
—	Paraguay Cntl., Ld., 5 p.c. Perm. Deb. Stk.	100	11
—	Piræus, Ath., & Pelo.	75	1½
	Pto. Alegre & N. Hamb'g Ld., 7 p.c. Pref. Shs.	20	4
6	Do. Mt. Deb. Stk. Red.	100	74½
—	Puerto Cabello & Val. Ld.	10	1½
5	Recife & S. Francisco	100	67
14/	R. Claro S. Paulo, Ld., Sh.	10	21
5	Do. Deb. Stk.	100	125
5	Royal Sardinian Ord	10	11½

Foreign Railways (*continued*):—

Last Div.	Name.	Paid.	Price.
3/	Royal Sardinian Pref.	10	12
5/	Sambre & Meuse	20	18
5/6	Do. Pref.	10	12½
22/	San Paulo Ld.	20	32
2/10½	Do. New Ord. £10 sh.	6	8½
4/8	Do. 5 p.c. Non. Cm. Pref.	10	11½
5½	Do. Deb. Stk.	100	132
5	Do. 5 p.c. Deb. Stk	100	127
—	S. Fé & Cordova, Gt. Sthn., Ld., Shares	100	49½
6	Do. Perp. Deb. Stk.	100	121
3/2½	S. Austrian	20	7
10/	Sthn. Braz. R. Gde. do Sul, Ld.	20	7
6	Do. 6 p.c. Deb. Stk.	100	69½
4	Swedish Centl., Ld., 4 p.c. Deb. Stk.	100	107
5	Do. Pref.	100	98
1/3	Taltal, Ld.	5	2½
—	Uruguay Nthn., Ld. 7 p.c. Pfd. Stk.	100	8
3½	Do. 5 p.c. Deb. Stk.	100	30
—	Villa Maria & Rufino, Ld., 6 p.c. Pref. Shs.	100	18
4	Do. 4 p.c. 1 Deb. Stk.	100	73
6/0/0	Do. 6 p.c. 2 Deb. Stk.	100	46
5/9	West Flanders	8½	21
5/6	Do. 5½ p.c. Pref.	10	18
3/	Wstn. of Havana, Ld.	10	4

FOREIGN RAILWAY OBLIGATIONS

Per Cent.	Name.	Price.
6	Alagoas Ld., 6 p.c. Deb., Rd.	81
—	Alcoy & Gandia, Ld., 5 p.c. Debs., Red.	23
5	Arauco., Ld., 5 p.c. 1st Mt., Rd.	62½
—	Do. 6 p.c. Mt. Deb., Rd.	42½
6	Brazil G. Sthn., L., Mt. Dbs., Rd.	80½
6	Do. Mt. Dbs. 1893, Rd.	48½
5½	Campos & Caran. Dbs., Rd.	75
6	Central Bahia, L., Dbs., Rd.	90
5½	Conde d'Eu, L., Dbs., Rd.	70
6	Costa Rica, L., 1st Mt. Dbs., Rd.	107
6	Do. 2nd Dbs., Rd.	91
5	Do. Prior Mt. Db., Rd.	104
6	Cucuta Mt. Dbs., Rd.	101
5½	Donna Thrsa. Cris., L., Dbs., Rd.	69½
3	Eastn. of France, £20 Dbs., Rd.	18½
4	Egyptn. Delta Light, L., Db., Rd	98½
—	Espito. Santo & Cara. 5 p.c. Stl. Dbs., Rd.	38
4	Gd. Russian Nic., Rd.	102
5	Inter-Oceanic Mex., L., 5 p.c. Pr. Ln. Dbs., Rd.	102
3	Ital. 3 p.c. Bds. A & B, Rd.	57½
—	Ituana 6 p.c. Debs., 1918	74
—	Leopoldina, 6 p.c. Dbs. £50 Bds.,	21
—	Do. do. Comms. Cert.	21
—	Do. 5 p.c. Stg. Dbs. (1888), Rd.	29
—	Do. do. Comm. Certs.	29
—	Do. 5 p.c. Stg. Dbs. (1890), Rd.	21
—	Do. do. Comms. Certs.	21
—	Macahé & Cam. 5 p.c. Dbs., Rd.	29
—	Do. do. Comms. Certs.	29
—	Do. (Cantagallo), 5 p.c., Red.	29
—	Do. do. Comm. Certs.	29
—	Manila Ltd., 6 p.c. Deb., Red.	22
6	Do. Prior Lien Mt., Rd.	98½
6	Do. Series "B," Rd.	80
7	Matanzas & Sab., Rd.	101½
6	Minas & Rio, L., 6 p.c. Dbs., Rd.	95
5	Mogyana 5 p.c. Deb. Bds., Rd.	101
5	Moscow-Jaros., Rd.	105½
5½	Natal & Na. Cruz Ltd., 5½ p.c. Debs., Red.	93
5	Nitrate, Ltd. Mt. Bds., Red.	82
3	Nthn. France, Red.	19
4	N. of S. Af. Rep. (Trnsvl.) Gu. Bds. Red.	94½
3	Nthn. of Spain £20 Pri. Obs. Red.	7
6	Ottmn. (Smy to A.) (Kujk) Asnt. Debs., Red.	106
6	Ottmn. (Seraik.) Asg. Debs. Red.	106
6	Ottmn. (Seraik) Non-Asg. D., Rd	106
5	Ottmn. Kuyjk. Ext. Red.	103
5	Ottmn. Serkeuy. Ext. Red.	100½
5	Ottmn. Tireh Ext. 1910	93
5	Ottmn. Debs, 1886, Red.	97
5	Do. 1888, Red. 1935	97½
5	Do. 1893, Red. 1935	97
5	Ottmn. of Anlia. Debs, Rd.	90½
4	Ottomn. Smyr. & Cas. Ext Bds., Red.	83½
3	Paris, Lyon & Medit. (old sys. £20), Red.	18½
3	Paris, Lyon & Medit. (new sys., £20), Red.	18½
50/	Piræus, At. & Pelp., 6 p.c. 1st Mt. Bds., Red.	89½
3	Do. 5 p.c. Mt. Bds., Red.	69½
4	Pretoria-Pietbg., Ltd., Red.	93
7	Puerto Cab. & Val., Ltd., 1st Mt. Debs., Red.	31
—	Rio de Jano. & Nthn., Ltd., 6 p.c. £100 Deb., Red.	21
—	Rio de Jano. (Gr. Para.), 5 p.c. 1st Mt. St. £100 Debs., Red.	21
[illegible]	Royal Sardinian, A, Rd. £20	11½
3	Royal Sardinian, B., Rd. £20	11½

Foreign Rly. Obligations (*continued*):—

Per Cent.	Name.	Price.
5	Ryl. Trns.-Afric. 5 p.c. 1st Mt. £100 Bds., Red.	48½
4	Sa. Fe & Cur. G.S., Ld. Pr Ln. Bds.	104
5	Sa. Fe, 5 p.c. and Reg. Dbs.	80
3	South Austrian, £20 Red.	15½
3	South Austrian, (Ser. X.)	15
3	South Italian £20 Obs. (Ser. A to G), Red.	12
3½	S.W. of Venez (Barq.), Ltd., 7 p.c. 1st Mt. £100 Debs.	55½
5	Taltal, Ltd., 5 p.c. 1st Ch. Debs., Red.	97
5	Utd. Rwys. Havana, Red.	80½
3	Wtrn. of France, £20 Red.	18½
6	Wrn. B. Ayres St. Mt. Debs., 1902	107
6	Wrn. B. Ayres, Reg. Cert.	106
5	Do. Mt. Bds.	121
6	Wtrn. of Havna., Ld. Mt. Dbs., Rd.	90
7	Wrn. Ry. San Paulo Red.	99
—	Wrn. Santa Fé, 7 p.c. Red.	38
2/8	Zafra & Huelva, 3 p.c. Red.	2½

BANKS.

Div.	Name.	Paid.	Price.
2/4½	Agra, Ltd.	6	3½
4/2½	Anglo-Argentine, Ltd., £9	7	5½
8 fls.	Anglo-Austrian	120f	13
6/	Anglo-Californian, Ltd., £20 Shares	10	11
4/	Anglo-Egyptian, Ltd., £15	5	6
5/	Anglo-Foreign Bkg., Ltd.	7	7½
7/	Anglo-Italian, Ltd.	5	7
7/6	Bk. of Africa, Ltd., £18¾	6¼	10
20/	Bk. of Australasia	40	49
10/	Bk. of Brit. Columbia	20	20½
25/	Bk. of Brit. N. America	50	64
20/	Bk. of Egypt, Ltd., £25	12½	19
5/	Bk. of Mauritius, Ltd.	10	9
18/	Bk. of N. S. Wales	20	37½
4 p.c.	Bk. of N. Zland. Gua. Stk.	100	100
6/	Bk. of Roumania, £20 Shs.	6	7½
2/6	Tarapaca & Ldn., Ltd., £10	5	3½
—	Bque. Fse. de l'Afri. du S.	100f	3½
f.22.50	Bque. Internatle. de Paris	20	23
6/	Brit. Bk. of S. America, Ltd., £20 Shares	10	10
16/	Capital & Cties., L., £50	10	39
20/	Chart. of India, &c.	20	30½
10/	City, Ltd., £40 Shares	10	20
18/	Colonial, £100 Shares	30	21
10/	Delhi and London, Ltd.	25	—
5/	German of London, Ltd.	10	10½
25/	Hong-Kong & Shanghai	28½	45½
4/	Imperl. of Persia	6½	3½
10/	Imperl. Ottoman, £20 Shs	10	11½
12/	Intrnatl. of Ldn., Ld., £20	15	11
10/	Ionian, Ltd.	25	15
16/	Lloyds, Ltd., £50 Shs.	8	31
10/	Ldn. & Braziln. Ltd., £20	10	15½
44/	Ldn. & County, Ltd., £80	20	100
9/	Ldn. & Hanseatic, L., £20	10	10½
22/6	Ldn. & Midland, L., £60	12½	53
8/9	Ldn. & Provin., Ltd., £10	5	22½
39/	Ldn. & Riv. Plate, L., £25	15	49
2/1½	Ldn. & San Fcisco, Ltd.	7	4½
28/	Ldn. & Sth. West., L., £50	20	68
26/	Ldn. & Westmins., L., £100	20	55
5/	Ldn. of Mex. & S. Amer. Ltd., £10 Shs.	6	5½
15/	Ldn. Joint Stk., L., £100	15	33½
12/9½	Ldn., Paris & Amer., L. £20	16	25
2/4½	Merchant Bkg., L., £9	4	2½
6/3	Metropn, Ltd., £50 Shs.	5	14½
9/	National, Ltd., £50 Shs.	10	19½
4/5	Natl. of Mexico, $100 Shs.	$40	12½
1/3	National of N. Z., L., £7½	2½	2
7/	National S. Afric. Rep.	10	13½
18/10½	National Provcl. of Eng. Ltd., £75 Shs.	10½	49½
21/7½	Do. do. £60 Shs	12	56½
6/6	North Eastn., Ltd., £20 Shs	6	15
19/	Parr's, Ld., £100 Shs.	20	90
12/6	Prov. of Ireland, L., £100	12½	29½
40/	Stand. of S. Afric., L., £100	25	63
12/6	Union of Australia, L., £75	25	26
4 p.c.	Do. do. Ins. Stk. Dep 1900	100	101
15/6	Union of Ldn., Ltd., £100	15½	34½

BREWERIES AND DISTILLERIES

Div.	Name.	Paid.	Price.
4½	Albion Prp. 1 Mt. Db. Sk.	100	111
4	All Saints, L., Db. Sk. Rd.	100	97
7	Allsopp, Ltd	100	147
6	Do. Cum. Pref	100	154
4½	Do. Deb. Stk., Red.	100	116
3½	Do. Deb. Stk., Red.	100	101
4½	Alton & Co., L., Db., Rd	100	104
4½	Do. Mt. Bds., 1896	100	103
—	Arnold, Perrett, Ltd.	10	6
6	Do. Cum. Pref.	10	10
4½	Do. 1 Mt. Db. Stk., Rd	100	106

Breweries &c. (*continued*):—

Div.	Name.	Paid.	Price.
5½	Arrol, A., & Sons, L. Cum. Pref. Shs.	10	10
4½	Do. 1 Mt. Db. Stk., Rd.	100	105
5	Backus, 1 Mt. Db., Red.	100	59
4	Barclay, Perk., L., Cu. Pf.	10	11½
3½	Do. Mt. Db. Stk., Red.	100	109
—	Barnsley, Ltd.	10	11½
6	Do. Cum. Pref.	10	13½
1/3	Barrett's, Ltd	2½	1½
1/3	Do. 5 p.c. Pref.	2½	2½
3/	Bartholomay, Ltd.	10	2
8	Do. Cum. Pref.	10	5½
6	Do. Deb.	100	97½
5	Bass, Ratcliff, Ltd., Cum. Pref. Stk.	100	143½
4½	Do. Mt. Db. Stk., Rd.	100	124
4	Bell, J., L., 1 Mt. D. Stk., R	100	100
—	Benskin's, L., Cum. Pref.	5	—
—	Do. 1 Mt. Db. Stk Red.	100	—
—	Do. "B" Deb. Sk, Rd.	100	—
7/	Bentley's Yorks., Ltd.	10	11½
6/	Do. Cum. Pref.	10	12½
4½	Do. Mt. Debs., Red.	100	110
4½	Do. do. 1892, Red.	100	110
—	Bieckert's, Ltd.	20	2
5	Do. Debs., Red.	100	57
—	Birmingham., Ltd., 6 p.c. Cum. Pref.	5	2½
4½	Do. Mt. Debs., Red.	50	39½
5½	Boardman's, Ld., Cm. Pf.	10	8½
4½	Do., Perp. 1 Mt. Db. Sk.	100	105½
30/9	Brain & Co., Ltd.	100	101
4½	Brakspear, L., 1 D. Stk. Red.	100	108
4	Brandon's, L., 1 D. Stk. Red.	100	105½
21/	Bristol (Georges) Ltd.	10	45
6	Do. Cum. Pref.	10	18
5	Do. Mt. Db. Sk. 1888 Rd.	100	115½
17/6	Bristol United, Ltd.	10	35
6	Do. Cum. Pref.	10	16½
4½	Do. Db. Sk. Rd.	100	126
5½	Buckley's, L., C. Pre-prf.	10	10½
4½	Do. 1 Mt. Db. Stk. Rd.	100	104½
4	Bullard & Sons, Ltd., D. Sk. R.	100	104
6	Bushell, Watk., L., C. Pf.	10	14
4½	Do. 1 Mt. Db. Sk. Rd.	100	112
5	Camden, Ltd., Cum. Pref.	10	11½
4½	Do. 1 Mt. Db. Sk. Rd	100	108
5½	Cameron, Ltd., Cm. Prf.	10	13½
4½	Do. Mort Deb. Stk.	100	108
3½	Do. Perp Mt. Db. Sk.	100	100½
5	Campbell, J'stone, L., C. Pf.	5	5
4½	Do. 4½ p.c. 1 Mt. Db. Sk.	100	103
4	Campbell, Praed, L., Per. 1 Mort. Deb. Stk.	100	105
4	Cannon, L., Mt. Db. Stk.	100	109
4	Do. "B" Deb. Stk.	100	104
5	Castlemaine, L., 1 Mt. Db.	100	94
3½	Charrington, Ltd., Mort. Deb. Stk. Red.	100	106
2/	Cheltnhm. Orig., Ltd.	5	7
6	Do. Cum. Pref.	5	7½
4	Do. Debs. Red.	100	106
10/	Chicago, Ltd.	10	3
6	Do. Debs.	100	64½
—	Cincinnati, Cum. Pref.	10	1
10/	City of Baltimore	10	4
16/	Do. 8 p.c. Cum. Pref	10	8
14/	City of Chicago, Ltd.	10	1½
8	Do. Cum. Pref.	10	5½
13	City of London, Ltd.	100	205½
5	Do. Cum. Pref.	100	136
4	Do. Mt. Deb. Stk., Rd.	100	110½
2/	Colchester, Ltd.	5	4½
7	Do. Pref.	5	6½
4½	Do. Deb. Stk., Red.	100	109
5	Combe, Ltd., Cum. Pref.	10	13½
4	Do. Mt. Db. Stk, Rd.	100	110
3½	Do. Perp. Deb. Stk.	100	107
5	Comm'cial, L., D. Sk., Rd.	100	107½
5	Courage, L., Cm. Pref. Shs.	100	137½
4	Do. Irr. Mt. Deb. Stk.	100	125
3½	Do. Irr. "B" Mt. Db. Sk.	100	104
8/	Daniell & Sons, Ltd.	10	7½
7	Do. Cum. Pref.	10	12½
4½	Do. 1 Mt. Perp. Db. Sk.	100	107½
4½	Do. "B" Deb. Stk.	100	99
10d.	Dartford, Ltd.	5	5
2/9	Do. Cum. Pref.	5	5½
4	Do. 1 Mt. Db. Sk. Rd	100	99
4	Davenport, Ld., 1 D. Stk.	100	101½
10/	Denver United, Ltd.	10	3½
8	Do. Cum. Pref.	10	[illegible]
6	Do. Debs.	100	96½
4½	Deuchar, L., 1 D. Sk., Rd.	100	108
8/	Distillers, Ltd.	10	23½
—	Dublin Distillers, Ltd.	5	1½
3/	Do. Cum. Pref.	5	4½
4½	Do. Irr. Deb. Stk.	100	—
5	Eadie, Ltd., Cum. Pref.	10	11
4	Do. Irr. 1 Mt. Db. Sk.	100	106
10/	Edinbgh. Utd., Ltd.	10	13
6	Do. Cum. Prf.	10	13½
4	Eldridge, Pope, L. D. St. R.	100	107
—	Emerald & Phoenix, Ltd.	10	1½
8	Do. Cum. Pref.	10	5½
6	Empress Ltd., C. Pf.	10	11½
4½	Do. Mt. Deb. Stk.	100	106
10/	Farnham, Ltd.	10	17
6	Do. Cum. Pref.	10	14½
4	Fenwick, L., 1 D. Sk., Rd.	100	103
4	Flower & Sons, Irr. D. Sk.	100	111
4	Friary, L., 1 Db. Stk., Rd.	100	103½
4	Do. 1 "A" Db. Sk., Rd	100	100
4½	Groves, L., 1 Db. Sk., Rd.	100	111
14	Guinness, Ltd.	100	560
6	Do. Cum. Prf. Stk.	100	177½
5	Do. Deb. Stk., Red.	100	118
5	Hall's Oxford L., Cm. Pf.	5	5½
6/	Hancock, Ld., Cm. Pf. Ord.	10	14
7/	Do. Def. Ord	10	17½

Breweries, &c. (*continued*) :—

Div.	Name.	Paid.	Price.
6	Hancock, Ld., Cum. Pref.	10	14
4	Do. 1 Deb. Stk., Rd.	100	112
5	Hoare, Ltd. Cum. Pref.	10	12¾
5	Do. "A" Cum. Pref.	10	12½
4	Do. Mt. Deb. Stk., Rd.	100	111
3½	Do. do. do. Rd.	100	104
3/6	Hodgson's, Ltd.	5	9¾
5	Do. 1 Mt. Db., Red.	—	120½
4	Do. 2 Mt. Db., 1906	—	102
4½	Hopcraft & N., Ltd., 1 Mt. Deb. Stk., Red.	100	103
5	Huggins, Ltd., Cm. Prf.	10	—
4½	Do. 1st D. Stk. Rd.	100	—
4½	Do. "B" Db. Stk. Rd.	100	—
12/	Hull, Ltd.	10	17
7	Do. Cum. Pref.	10	14½
4½	Ind, Coope, L., D.Sk., Rd.	100	118
4	Do. "B" Mt. Db. Stk. Rd.	100	111
8/	Indianapolis, Ltd.	10	3
8	Do. Cm. Prf.	10	8½
5/	Jones, Frank, Ltd.	10	2¾
7½	Do. Cum. Pref.	10	6¾
5	Do. 1st Mort. Debs.	100	90½
3/	J. Kenward & Ct., Ltd.	5	5¾
4½	Kingsbury, L., 1 D.Sk., Rd	100	—
4	Lacon, L., D. Stk., Red.	100	110
4	Do. Irrd. "B" D. Sk.	100	106
4/	Lascelles, Ltd.	5	11
6	Do. Cum. Pref.	5	7¾
5	Leney, Ltd., Cum. Pref.	10	11½
4	Do. 1 Mt. Db. Stk. Rd.	100	102
30/7½	Lion, Ltd., £25 shares	17	49½
10/9½	Do. New £10 shares	6	17
6	Do. Perp. Pref.	20	33
4	Do. B. Mt. Db. Sk. Rd.	100	106
4½	Lloyd & Y., Ltd., 1 Mt. Deb. Stk., Rd.	100	100½
4½	Locke & S., Ltd., Irr. 1st Mt. Deb. Stk.	100	102
4½	Lovibond, Ltd., 1st Mt. Deb. Stk., Rd.	100	101½
30/4	Lucas & Co., Ld., Deb. Stk.	100	107
12/	Manchester, Ltd.	10	19
7	Do. Cum. Pref.	10	16½
5	Marston, J., L., Cm. Prf.	10	10¾
4	Do. 1 Mt. Db. Sk., Rd.	100	101½
9/	Massey's Burnley, Ltd.	10	17
6	Do. Cum. Pref.	10	14½
4½	McCracken, Ltd., 1 Mt. Deb., 1908	100	59½
5	McEwan, Ltd., Cm. Pref.	10	14
5	Meux, Ltd., Cum. Pref.	10	14
4	Do. Mt. Db. Stk. Red.	100	111
4½	Michell & A., Ltd., 1 Mt. Deb. Stk. Red.	100	105
4½	Mile End Dist. Db. Sk. Rd.	100	111
—	Milwaukee & Chic., Ltd.	10	1½
4/	Do. Cum. Pref.	10	6½
4½	Michell, Toms, L., Db.	50	57
6	Morgan, Ltd., Cum. Pref.	10	14½
10/	Nalder & Coll., Ltd.	10	35
6	Do. Cum. Pref.	10	15½
4½	Do. Deb. Red.	100	112
12/	Newcastle, Ltd.	10	19½
6	Do. Cum. Pref.	10	14¾
5	Do. 1 Mt. Deb., 1911	100	110½
4	Do. "A" Deb. Stk. Red.	100	104
6	New England, Ltd	10	4½
8	Do. Cum. Pref.	10	9
6	Do. Debs. Red.	100	101½
4	New London, L., 1 D.Sk.	100	103
7/2	New Westminster, Ltd.	4	10¾
2/4½	Do. Pref.	4	6½
—	New York, Ltd.	10	1
—	Do. 8 p.c. Cum. Pref.	10	4½
6	Do. 1 Mt. Deb. Red.	100	77½
5	Noakes, Ld., Cum. Pref.	10	11¾
4	Do 1 Mt. Db. Stk., Rd.	100	106
4½	Norfolk, L., "A" D.Sk.Rd	100	106
10/	Northampton, Ld.	10	16½
7	Do. Cum. Pref.	10	16
6	Do. Cum. Pref.	10	12½
5	Do. 1 Mt. Per. Db. Sk.	100	127
4	Nth. East., L., 1 D. Sk. Rd.	100	102
4½	N. Worcesters., L. Per. 1 Mort. Deb. Stock	100	37½
6	Nottingham, L., Cm. Prf.	10	1½
5	Do. 1 Mt. Deb. Stk., Red.	100	114
17/4	Do. "B" do. Red.	50	112
6/	Ohlsson' Cape, Ld.	5	17
7	Do. Cum. Pref.	5	9
4½	Do. 2nd Cum. Pref.	5	5½
5	Do. Deb. Stk., Red.	100	114
4½	Oldfield, L., 1 Mt. Db. Stk.	100	105
6	Page & Overt., L., Cm. Prf.	10	13½
4½	Do. 1 Mt. Dbs., Red.	100	109
10/	Parker's Burslem, Ltd.	10	24½
6	Do. Cum. Pref.	10	14½
4	Do. 1 Mt. Dr. Stk., Red.	100	111
4	Persse, Ld., 1 Mt. Db. Rd.	100	95½
	Phipps, L., Irr. 1 Db. Stk.	100	113
8	Plymouth, L., Min. Cu. Pf.	10	13½
4½	Do. Mt. Deb. Stk., Red.	100	105½
4½	Pryor, Reid, L., 1 D.S., R.	100	103½
5	Reid's, Ld., Cm. Pref. Stk.	100	136½
4	Do. Mt. Deb. Stk., Red	100	110
3½	Do. "B" Mt. Db. Stk., Rd	100	102
5	Rhondda Val., L., Cu. Pf	10	11
4½	Do. 1 Mt. Deb. Stk., Rd	100	109
5	Robinson, Ld., Cum. Pref.	10	11½
4½	Do. 1 Mt. Perp. Db. Stk.	100	112
4/	Rochdale, Ltd.	10	6
4½	Do. 1 Mt. Deb. Stk.	100	91½
7	Royal, Brentford, Ltd.	10	21
	Do. Cum. Pref.	10	15
4½	Do. 1 Mt. Dbs. Red	100	103
6/	St. Louis, Ltd.	10	3
8	Do. Cum. Pref.	10	8
24/	St. Paul, Ltd.	10	10
7	Do. Cum. Pref.	10	12
4½	Salt (T.), L., 1 Db. Sk. Rd.	100	111
4½	Do. "B" Db. Stk. Red	100	106
—	San Francisco, Ltd.	10	½
—	Do. 8 p.c. Cum. Pref.	10	¾

Breweries, &c. (*continued*) :—

Div.	Name.	Paid.	Price.
4½	Savill Brs., L., D. Sk. Rd.	100	118
4½	Scarboro., Ltd., 1 Db. Stk.	100	101
4	Shaw (Hy.), Ltd., 1 Mt. Db. Stk., Red.	100	104
22/	Showell's, Ltd.	10	32
7	Do. Cum. Pref.	10	17½
3/	Do. Gua. Shs.	5	7¾
4½	Do. Mt. Db. Stk., Red.	100	—
4	Simonds, L., 1 D. Sk., Rd.	100	111
5½	Simson & McP., L., Cu. Pf.	10	9½
4½	Do. 1 Mt. Deb. Stk.	100	98
5/	Smith, Garrett, L., £20 Shs	10	16½
5	Do. Cum. Pref.	20	26
3½	Do. 3½ p.c. Mt. Db. Stk.	100	107
5	Smith's, Tadcster, L., C.Pf	10	12
4½	Do. Deb. Stk., Red.	100	112
4	Do. Deb. Stk. Red.	100	108
4½	Star, L., 1 M. Db. Stk., Rd.	100	103
4	Steward & P., L., 1 D. Sk.	100	108
9/	Strettons Derby, Ltd.	10	13
6	Do. Cum. Pref.	10	13½
4	Do. Irr. 1 Mt. Db. Stk.	100	103½
4½	Strong, Romsey, L., 1 D.S.	100	115
5	Stroud, L., Db. Sk., Rd.	100	111½
4½	Tadcaster To'er, L., D.Sk.	100	113
8/	Tamplin, Ltd	10	21
6	Do. Cum. Pref.	100	15
4	Do. "A" Db. Sk., Rd.	10	105
6	Thorne, Ltd., Cum. Pref.	10	14
4	Do. Deb. Stk., Red.	100	103½
15/	Threlfall, Ltd.	10	43
6	Do. Cum. Pref.	10	16½
5	Do. 1 Mt. Dbs., Red.	100	114
4	Tollemache, L., D. Sk. Rd.	100	105
4	Truman, Hanb., D. Sk., R.	100	110
3	Do. "B" Mt. Db. Sk., Rd.	100	95
10/	United States, Ltd.	10	8½
8	Do. Cum. Pref.	10	11
6	Do. 1 Mt. Deb.	100	105½
6/	Walker & H., Ld., Cm. Prf.	10	10¾
4½	Do. 1 Mt. Deb. Stk., Red.	100	107
5	Walker, Peter, Ld. Cm. Prf.	10	13½
4	Do. 1 Mt. Dbs. Red.	100	111
4	Wallingford, L., D. Sk. Rd.	100	105
6	Watney, Ld., Cm. Prf. Sk.	100	167
5	Do. Mt. Db. Sk., Rd.	100	115½
4½	Do. "B" Mt. Db. Sk., Rd.	100	111
3½	Do. Mt. Db. Stk.	100	101
5	Watney, D., Ld., Cm. Prf.	10	12
4½	Do. 1 Mt. Db. Stk.	100	107
10/	Webster & Sons, Ltd.	10	16¾
6	Do. Cum. Pref.	10	14
5	Wenlock Ltd Pref.	10	11¾
4	Do. 1 Mt. Db. Sk., Rd.	100	106
5	West Cheshire, L., Cu. Pf.	10	10½
4	Do. Irred. 1 Mt. Db. Sk.	100	99
4½	Whitbread, L., Cu. Pf. Sh.	100	123½
4	Do. Db. Stk., Red.	100	109
3½	Do. "B" Db. Stk., Rd.	100	101
9/	Wolverhmpton & D. Ld.	10	17
6	Do. Cum. Pref.	10	13½
4½	Do. 1 Mt. Dbs., Red.	100	107
5½	Worthington, Ld., Cm. Prf.	10	15½
5½	Do. Cum. "B" Pref.	10	13½
4½	Do. Mt. Db. Sk., Rd.	100	113
3½	Do. Irr. "B" Db. Stk.	100	101
10/	Yates's Castle, Ltd.	10	13½
5	Do. Cum. Pref.	10	10¾
5	Younger W., L., Cu. Pf. Sh.	100	125½

CANALS AND DOCKS.

Last Div.	Name.	Paid.	Price.
4	Birmingham Canal	100	142½
—	E. & W. India Dock	100	20
—	Do. 4 p.c. Prf. Stk.	100	74
—	Do. P.L. Deb. Stk.	100	100
—	Do. Cons. Deb. Stk.	100	89
40/	G. Junction Ord. Shs.	100	150½
6/	Do. do. Pref.	10	19
4½	King's Lynn Per. Db. Stk.	100	117½
2½	Leeds & L'pool Canal	100	71
2½	Lndn & St. Kath. Dks.	100	54
4½	Do. Pref.	100	135½
4½	Do. Pref., 1878	100	132½
4½	Do. Pref., 1882	100	130
4	Do. Deb. Stk.	100	134½
—	Mchester Ship C. 5 p.c. Pf.	10	1¾
3½	Do. 1st Perp. Mt. Deb.	100	93
—	Milford Dks. Db. Stk. "A"	100	13½
3½	Millwall Dk.	100	59
5	Do. Perp. Pref.	100	140½
4½	Do. Pref.	100	105½
5	Do. New Per. Prf., 1887	100	126½
5	Do. Per. Deb. Stk.	100	152½
4/	Newhaven Har.	10	14½
2½	N. Metropolitan	100	65
5	Sharpness Nw. Pf. "A" Sk.	100	144½
4	Do. Deb. Stk.	100	118½
5	Sheffld & S. Yorks Nav. 4½ p.c. Pref Stk.	100	115½
36.432	Suez Canal	20	135½
7	Surrey Comcl. Dok., Ord.	100	149½
7	Do. Min. 4 p.c. Pref. "A"	110	150
8	Do. Pref. "B"	100	148½
5	Do do. "C"	100	148½
5	Do. do. "D"	100	144½
4½	Do Deb. Stk.	100	152½

COMMERCIAL, INDUSTRIAL, &c.

Last Div.	Name.	Paid.	Price.
5	Accles, L., 1 Mt. Db., Red.	100	84½
2/6	Aërated Bread, Ltd.	1	12
—	African Gold Recovery, L.	1	¼
2/	Aluminium, L., "A" Shs.	1	2
4½	Do. 1 Mt. Db. Stk., Red.	100	97
5½	Amelia Nitr., L., 1 Mort Deb., Red.	100	82½
7/	Anglo-Chil. Nitrate, Ltd., Cum. Pref.	10	6½
4½	Do. Cons. Mt. Bds., Red.	100	77½
4½	Anglo-Russian Cotton, Ld., 1 Charge Debs., Red.	100	98
11/3	Angus (G., & Co., L.), £10	7½	17
6/	Apollinaris, Ltd.	10	11½
5/	Do. 5 p.c. Cum. Pref.	10	10¾
4	Do. Irred. Deb. Stock	100	104
8/	Appleton, French, & S., L.	5	½
3/	Argentine Meat Pres., L., 7 p.c. Pref.	10	2¾
5	Argentine Refinry, Db. Rd.	100	98
6d.	Armstrong, Whitw., Ltd.	1	3½
4	Do. Cum. Pref.	5	6½
5	Artisans', Labr. Dwllgs., L.	100	128½
4½	Do. Non-Cm. Prf., 1879	100	132½
4½	Do. do. 1884	100	132½
—	Asbestos & Asbestic, Ltd.	10	7½
2/7½	Ashley-grdns., L., C. Prf.	5	6½
4½	Do. 1 Mt. Deb. Stk.	100	112½
5/	Assam Rly. & Trdng., L., 8 p.c. Cum. Pref. "A"	10	14½
—	Do. Deferrd. "B" Shs.	1	4
—	Do. do. (iss. f. pd)	1	3½
8/	Do. Cum. Pre-Prf. "A"	10	15
6/	Do. New Pref.	10	11½
5	Do. Debs., Red.	100	106
5	Do. Red. Mort. Debs.	100	109
6	Aust'lian Pastrl, L., Cu. Pf.	10	7
8d.	Aylesbury Dairy, Ltd.	1	1½
4	Do. 4 p.c. Mt. Dbs.	100	104½
10/	Babcock & Wilcox, Ltd.	10	29
6	Do. 6 p.c. Cm. Prf.	10	16
8	Baker (Chs.), L., Cm. Pf.	5	8¾
8	Do. "B" Cm. Pref.	5	8
2/1	Barker (John), Ltd.	1	2½
5½	Do. Cum. Pref.	5	7½
4½	Do. Irred. 1 Mt. Db. Stk.	100	127½
—	Barnagore Jute, Ltd.	5	3
5	Do. Cum. Pref.	5	4¾
7½d.	Belgravia Dairy, Ltd.	1	1½
5/6	Bell (R.) & Co., Ltd.	5	3½
1/	Bell's Asbestos, Ltd.	1	¾
5	Do. Mt. Db. Bds., Rd.	100	107
10/	Bengal Mills, Ltd.	10	11
6/	Do. 5 p.c. Cum. Prf	10	10½
5/	Benson (J.W.) L., Cm. Pf.	10	10½
4	Do. Perp. Mt. Db. Stk	100	101
6	Bergvik, L., 6 p.c. Cm. Pf	10	12½
12/	Do. Dfd.	10	10½
4½	Do. 1 Dbs., Red.	100	103½
5/	Birm'ham Vinegar, Ltd.	5	14
5	Do. Cum. Pref.	5	5½
4½	Do. 1 Mt. Db. Stk., Rd	100	109½
5	Boake (A.) L., 5 p.c. Cu. Pf.	10	10¾
2/6	Bodega, Ltd.	5	8½
4½	Do. Mt. Deb. Stk., Rd.	100	111
8/	Bottomley & Brs., Ltd.	10	6½
6/	Do. 6 p.c. Pf.	10	9½
8½d.	Bovril, Ltd.	1	[illegible]
1/0½	Do. Def.	1	[illegible]
6½d	Do. Cum. Pref.	1	1
4½	Do. Deb. Stk.	100	100
5/	Bradbury, Gretrex., Ltd., £10 share	8	14
5/	Do. 5 p.c. Cum. Pref.	10	13½
5/	Brewers' Sugar, L., 5 p.c. Cum. Pref.	10	10½
3/6	Brighton Grd. Hotel, Ld.	5	3½
4	Do Mt. Db. Stk., Red.	100	100½
5	Bristol Hotel & Palm. Co. Ltd. 1st Mt. Red. Deb.	100	106
9½d.	British & Bengton's Tea Tr. Asc., Ltd.	1	1½
5	Do. Cum. Prf.	5	5¼
—	British Deli & Lgkat. Tobacco, Ltd.	1	½
—	Do. Cum. Prf.	1	¾
—	British Tea Table, Ltd.	1	2¾
5½	Do. Cum. Pref.	1	1½
2/6	Brooke, Ben., & Co., Ltd., Cum. Pref.	5	5½
7/6	Brooke, Bond & Co., Ltd.	5	19
3/	Brown Brs., L., Cum. Pref.	5	5¾
10/	Browne & Eagle, Ltd.	10	13½
5	Do. Cum. Pref.	10	13
4	Do. Mrt. Db. Sk., Red.	100	110
20/	Brunner, Mond, & Co., Lt.	[illegible]	42
7/	Do. £10 shares	3	17
7	Do. Cum. Pref.	10	18
7	Do. £10 shares	5	8½
10/	Bryant & May, Ltd.	5	19½
3/	Bucknall, H., & Sons, Lt.	5	6½
6	Do. Cum Pref.	5	7½
4/	Burke, E. & J., Ltd.	5	7½
6	Do. Cum. Pref.	5	7½
6	Do. Irred. Deb. Stk.	100	155
1/	Burlington Htls. Co., Ltd	1	1½
5	Do. Cum. Pref.	[illegible]	1
4	Do. Perp. Deb. Stk.	100	105½
5	Bush, W. J., & Co., Ltd. Cum. Pref.	5	5½
4	Do. 1 Deb. Stk., Red.	100	102
5½	Callard, Stewart, & Watt, Ltd., Cum. Pref.	1	1½
4/	Callender's Cable L., Shs.	5	9½
4½	Do. 1 Deb. Stk., Red.	100	111½
—	Campbell, R., & Sons, Lt.	3	2½
6	Cantareira Water, Bd., Rd	100	99½
5	Do. (2nd issue)	100	90
4	Cartavio Sugar, Ltd., 6 p.c. 1st Debs., Red.	90	82½
9/	Cassell & Co., Ltd., £10	9	15
5	Causton, Sir J., & Sons, Ltd., Cum. Pref.	10	13½

Commercial, &c. (*continued*) :—

Last Div.	Name.	Paid.	Price.
4	Cent. Prod. Mkt. of B.A. 1st Mt. Str. Debs.	100	77
4	Chappell & Co., Ltd., Mt. Deb. Stk. Red.	100	103
6/	Chicago & N.W. Gran. 8 p.c. Cum. Pref.	10	3
—	Chicago Packing & Prov.	10	6
8	Do. Cum. Pref.	10	10½
6/	City Offices, Ltd	12	7½
3½	Do. Mt. Deb. Stk.	100	108½
7/2½	Cy. London Real Prop., Ltd., £25 shs.	12	19
4/6	Do. £12½ shs.	7½	13½
3½	Do. Deb. Stk. Red.	100	106½
3½	Do. Deb. Stk. Red.	100	105½
3	Do.	100	100½
4/	Cy. of Santos Imprvts.,		
20/	Ltd., 7 p.c. Pref.	10	8½
8	Clay, Bock, & Co., Ltd.	10	5½
6	Do. Cum. Pref.	10	10
20/	Do. Mort. Deb.	100	103½
20/	Coats, J. & P., Ltd.	10	58
4½	Do. Cum. Pref.	10	17½
9½d	Do. Deb. Stk. Red.	100	112½
4	Coburg Hotel, Ltd.	1	1¼
6	Do. Deb. Stk. Red.	100	102
4½	Colonial Consign & Dis., Ltd., Cum. Pref.	5	4¾
—	Do. 1st Mort. Debs.	100	96½
4/	Colorado Nitrate, Ltd.	5	¼
5	Co. Gén des Asphtes. de F., Ltd.	6	6½
3	Do. Non-Cm. Prf.	—	5¾
	Cook, J. W., & Co., Ltd., Cum. Pref.	5	5½
5	Cook, T., & Son, Egypt, Ltd., 1st Mt. Deb. Red.	100	110½
—	Cork Co., Ltd., 6 p.c. Cum. Pref.	5	2
5	Cory, W., & Sn, L., Cu. Pf.	5	6
4	Do. 1st Deb. Stk. Red.	100	108
1/6	Crisp & Co., Ltd	1	1½
5½	Do. Cum. Pref.	1	1½
—	Crompton & Co., Ltd., 7 p.c. Cum. Pref.	5	2½
5	Do. 1st Mt. Reg. Deb.	—	90½
4/6	Crossley, J., & Sons, Ltd.	5	8
5	Do. Cum. Pref.	5	6½
—	Crystal Pal. Ord. "A" Stk.	100	6½
—	Do. "B" Red. Stk	100	1½
6	Do. 6 p.c. 1st 1887 Deb. Stk. Red.	100	117½
—	Do. 6 p.c. 2nd 1887 Deb. Stk. Red.	100	50½
—	Do. 6 p.c. 3rd 1887 Deb. Stk. Red.	100	22½
3	Do. 3 p.c. 1st 1895 Deb. Stk.	100	92½
—	Daimler Motor, Ltd	10	8
4/	Dalgety & Co., £20 Shs.	5	5½
4½	Do. Deb. Stk.	100	123
4	Do.	100	113
7/	De Keyser's Ryl. Htl., L.	10	14
5	Do. Cum. Pref.	10	12
4	Do. Deb. Stk., Red.	100	110
6	Denny, H., & Sons, Ltd., Cum. Pref.	10	14½
5/3	Devas, Routledge & Co., L.	7	8½
5	Dickinson, J., & Co., L., Cum. Pref. Stk.	100	123
4½	Domin. Cottn. Mls., Ltd. Mt. Stg. Dbs.	100	97
6/	Dorman, Long & Co., L.	5	4½
—	Eastmans, Ltd	10	2½
12/	Do. 8 p.c. Cum. Pref.	10	10
2/5	E. C. Powder, Ltd.	3	5½
1/6	Edison & Swn Utd. Elec. Ltd., "A" £5 Shs.	3	2½
2/6	Do. fully-paid	5	4½
4½	Ekman Pulp & Ppr. Co. Ltd., Mt. Deb., Red.	100	96
7/1½	Electric Construc., Ltd.	2	2½
7	Do. Cum. Pref.	2	3½
2/-	Eley Bros., Ltd.	10	38
—	Elmore's Cop. Deptg., L.	1	¼
—	Elmore's Wire Mnfg., L.	2	⅛
—	Elysée Pal. Hotel Co., L.	5/	[illegible]
5 p.c.	Do. 5 p.c. £100 Db., Rd.	70	97½
8½d.	Evans, Ben., & Co., Ltd.	1	1
5	Do. 1 Mt. Db. Sk., Rd.	100	108
1/3½d.	Evans, D. H., & Co., L.	1	2½
6	Do. Cum. Pref.	1	1½
4½	Do. 1 Mt. Db. Sk., Rd.	100	112
2/6	*Evening News*, L., 5 p.c. Cum. Pref.	5	5½
5/3	Evered & Co., L., £10 Sh.	7	12½
7/6	Do.	10	18½
4	Fairbairn Pastoral Co. Aust., L., 1 Mt. Db., Rd.	100	107
6	Fairfield Shipbldg., Ltd., Cum. Pref.	10	10½
4½	Do. Mort. Deb. Stk.	100	109½
6/	Farmer & Co., Ld., 6 p.c. Cum. Pref.	10	13½
10	Field, J. C. & J., Ltd.	10	10
14/	Do. 7 p.c. Cum. Pref.	10	14½
1/3	Fordham, W. B., & Sns Ld.	7	2
5/6	Fore-st. Warehouse, Ltd.	11	9½
4	Do. Regd. Debs., Rd.	100	103½
3/6	Foster, M. B. & Sons, Ltd.	4	6
5	Do. Pref.	10	11½
9/	Foster, Porter, & Co., L.	10½	15½
4	Fowler, J., & Co. (Leeds) Ltd., 1 Mt. Deb., Red.	100	103½
3/	Fraser & Chalmers, Ltd.	3	1½
4½	Free, Rodwell & Co., Ltd., Deb Stk.	100	104½
6½d.	Furness, T., & Co., Ltd., 5½ p.c. Cum. Pref.	1	¾
4½	Gartside & Co. (of Manchstr), L., 1 Mt. Db. Sk.	100	112
11	Genl. Hydraul Power, L.	100	270

Commercial, &c. (*continued*):—

Last Div.	Name.	Paid.	Price.
8/	Gillman & Spencer, Ltd.	5	2¼
6	Do. Pref.	5	4½
5	Do. Mort. Debs	50	51
4	Goldsbro., Mort & Co., L., "A" Deb. Stk., Red.	100	73½
—	Do. 3 p.c. "B" Inc. Deb. Stk., Red	100	14
8/	Gordon Hotels, Ltd.	10	20
5½	Do. Cum. Pref.	10	14½
4½	Do. Perp. Deb. Stk.	100	137½
4	Do. do.	100	122½
—	Greenwich Inld. Linoleum Co., Ltd.	1	⅜
7	Greenwood & Batley, Ltd., Cum. Pref.	10	10
7½d.	Hagemann & Co., Ltd., 6 p.c. Cum. Pref.	1	1
—	Hammond, Ltd.	10	½
—	Do. 8 p.c. Cum. Pref.	10	2½
—	Do. 6 p.c. Cum. Inc. Stk. Red.	100	45
	Hampton & Sons, Ltd., 4 p.c. 1 Mt. Db. St. Red.	100	105
—	Hans Crescent Htl., L., 6 p.c. Cum. Pref.	5	3
4	Do. 1 Mt. Deb. Stk.	100	90
6d.	Harmsworth, Ld., Cm. Pf.	1	1⅛
4/	Harrison, Barber, Ltd.	5	4½
3/	Harrod's Stores, Ltd.	1	4¾
2/6	Do. Cum. Pref.	5	7½
5½	Hawaiian Comcl. & Sug. 1 Mt. Debs.	100	91½
5	Hazell, Watson, L., C. P.	10	11½
18/	Henley's Teleg., Ltd.	10	22
7	Do. Pref. Shs.	10	19
4½	Do. Mt. Db. Stk., Rd.	100	112½
6	Henry, Ltd.	10	12
5	Do. Cum. Pref.	10	13½
4½	Do. Mt. Debs., Red.	50	53
6	Hepworth, Ld., Cm. Prf.	10	11
1/4½	Herrmann, Ltd.	1	⅞
—	Hildesheimer, Ltd.	3	1½
1/2½	Holbrn. & Frasca, Ltd.	1	1⅛
5	Do. Cum. Pref.	10	11½
4	Do. Deb. Stk.	100	113
6	Home & Col. Stres, L., C.P	5	7½
6	Hood & M.'s Stres., Ltd., Cum. Pref.	1	½
6	Hook, C. T Ltd.	10	6
7/2	Hornsby, Ltd., £10 Shs.	8	3
—	Hotchks. Ordn., Ltd.	10	1
—	Do. 7 p.c. Cm. Prf.	10	4
5	Do. 1 Mt. Dbs., Rd.	100	96½
5	Htl. Cecil, Ld., Cm. Prf.	5	3½
4	Do. 1 Mt. D. Sk., R.	100	100½
8/	Howard & Bulgh, Ltd.	10	39
6	Do. Pref.	10	16
4	Do. Deb. Stk., Red.	100	108
5/	Howell, J., Ltd., £5 Shs.	4	8¾
—	Howell & Js., Ltd., £3½ Shs.	3	⅜
1/6	Humber, Ltd.	1	⅜
6	Do. Cum. Pref.	1	7/16
5/6	Hunter, Wilts., Ltd.	5	7
2/7	Hyam Clthg., Ltd., 5 p.c. Cum. Pref.	5	5½
10/	Impl. Russn. Cotton, L.	5	6
5	Impd. Industl. Dwgs., Ld.	100	130½
6d.	Do. Defrd.	1	1½
25/	Impd. Wood Pave., Ltd.	10	15½
15/	Ind. Rubber, Gutta Per. Telegraph Works, Ltd.	10	21½
4	Do. 1 Mt. Debs., Red.	100	104
6	Intern. Tea, Cum. Pref.	5	6½
10½d.	Jays, Ltd.	1	1½
5½	Do. Cum. Pref.	5	6½
1/2½d.	Jones & Higgins, Ltd.	1	2½
4½	Do. 1 Mt. Db. Sk., Rd.	100	111
5/	Kelly's Directory, Ltd., 5 p.c. Cum. Pref.	10	12½
4	Do. Mort. Db. Sk., Rd.	100	106
—	Kent Coal Expirtn. Ltd.	1	
9½d.	King, Howmann, Ltd.	1	1½
4/	Kinloch & Co., Ltd.	5	8¾
6	Do. Pref.	5	7
5	Lady's Pictorial Pub., Ltd., Cum. Pref.	5	5
48/4	La Guaira Harb., Ltd., 5 p.c. Deb. Stk.	100	85
—	Do. 2 Mt. 7 p.c. Deb. Stk., Red.	100	22½
4/	Lagunas Nitrate, Ltd.	5	1½
2/	Lagunas Syn., Ltd.	5	⅛
5	Do. 1 Mt. Debs., Red.	100	76
—	L. Copais Ld., 1 Mt. 6 p.c. Debs., Red.	100	35½
3/	Lautaro Nitrate, Ltd.	5	4
5	Do. 1 Mt. Debs., Red.	—	100
9/	Lawes Chem. L., £10 shs.	9	5½
14/	Do. N. Cm. Min. Pref.	10	12½
—	Leeds Forge, 7 p.c. Cm. Pf.	5	3½
5	Do. 1 Mt. Debs., Red.	50	44
5	Lever Bros., L., Cm. Pf.	10	13½
6	Liberty, L., 6 p.c. Cm. Pf.	10	15
20/	Liebig's, Ltd.	20	78
5	Lilley & Sk., L., Cm. Pf.	5	5½
39/4	Linoleum Manftg. Ltd.	5	16
3/	Linotype, Ltd., Pre	5	5½
3/	Do. Def.	5	7½
4/	Lister & Co., Ltd.	10	4
5	Do. Cum. Pref.	10	8½
5/	Liverpool. Nitrate	5	4½
—	Liverpool. Warehsg., Ltd	10	3½
5½	Do. Cum. Pref.	10	8½
4	Do. 1 Mt. Db. Stk., Rd.	100	105
5½	Lockharts, Ltd., Cm. Pf.	1	1½
4/6	Ldn. & Til. Lightrage £10	9	6½
6/	Ldn. Comcl. Sale Rms., L.	10	17½
3	Do. 1 Mt. Deb. Stk., Red.	100	103
3	London Nitrate, Ltd.	5	1½
4/	London Nitrate, Ld. 8 p.c. Cm. Min. Pf.	5	3½
8/	London Pavilion, Ltd.	5	6½

Commercial, &c. (*continued*):—

Last Div.	Name.	Paid.	Price.
2/6	London. Produce Clg. Ho., Ltd., £10 Shares	2½	3½
4/	London Stereos., Ltd.	5	3
6d.	Ldn. Un. Laun. L. Cm. Pf.	1	½
8½d.	Louise, Ltd.	1	½
5½	Do. Cum. Pref.	1	½
5/	Lovell & Christmas, Ltd.	5	11½
6	Do. Cum. Pref.	5	7½
4	Do. Mt. Deb. Stk., Red.	100	107
1/3	Lyons, Ltd.	1	4½
4½	Do. 1 Mt. Deb., Stk., Rd.	100	111½
10/	Machinery Trust, Ltd.	5	13½
4½	Do. 4½ Deb. Stk.	100	104
6	MacLellan, L., Min. C. Pf.	10	9
5	Do. 1 Mt. Debs., 1900	100	101½
—	McEwan, J. & Co, Ltd.	10	1½
6	Do. Mt. Debs., Red.	100	89½
8	McNamara, L., Cm. Pref.	10	9
7½d.	Maison Virot, Ltd.	1	1½
2/7	Do. 6 p.c. Cum. Pref.	5	4½
5/	Manbré Sacc., L., Cm. Pf.	10	12
10/	Mangan Brze., L., £10 Shs.	6	15½
2/	Mason & Mason, Ltd.	5	2½
6	Do. Cum. Pref.	5	5½
—	Maynards, Ltd.	1	⅜
6	Do. Cum. Pref.	1	⅝
9½d.	Mazawattee Tea, Ltd.	1	1⅜
5	Do. Cum. Pref.	5	5½
6	Mellin's Food Cum. Pref.	5	6½
4½	Met. Ascn. Imp. Dwlgs. L.	100	110
3½	Do. 1 Mt. Deb. Stk.	100	97
5	Metro. Indus. Dwlgs., Ltd.	5	4½
4	Do. do. Cum. Pref.	5	5½
5	Metro. Prop., L., Cm. Pf.	5	5½
4½	Do. 1st Mt. Debs. Stk.	100	108½
6	Mexican Cotton 1 Mt. Db.	100	93½
4½	Mid. Class Dwlgs., L., Db.	100	120½
1/	Millars' Karri, Ltd.	1	3½
6	Do. Cum. Pref.	1	1⅜
5/	Milner's Safe, Ltd.	10	20½
10/	Moir & Son, Ltd., Pref.	5	8
6	Morgan Cruc., L., Cm. Pf.	10	14½
2/	Morris, B., Ltd.	3½	3½
2/6	Murray L. 5½ p.c. C. Pf.	5	5½
63/4½	Do. 4½ 1 Mt. Db. Sk. Rd.	100	106
—	Natnl. Dwlgs., L., 5 p.c. Pf.	5	1
1/7½	Nat. Safe Dep., Ltd.	4	3½
6	Do. Cum. Pref.	1	1
—	Native Guano, Ltd.	5	½
—	Nelson Bros., Ltd.	10	2½
5	Do. Deb. Stk., Red.	100	80½
4/	Neuchtel Asph., Ltd.	10	10½
—	New Central Borneo, Ld.	1	—
10d.	New Darvel Tob., Ltd.	18/	1½
1/6	New Explosives, Ltd.	3	3
5/3¾	New Gd. Htl., Bham, L.	5	4
5½	Do. Pref.	5	4½
4	Do. 1 Mt. Db. Stk., Rd.	100	96½
—	New Julia Nitrate, Ltd.	10/	—
—	New Ldn. Borneo Tob., L.	16/	½
1/6	New Premier Cycle, Ltd.	1	⅝
6	Do. 6 p.c. Cum. Pref.	1	¾
4½	Do. 4½ p.c. 1 Mt. Db. Rd	100	—
—	New Tamargl. Nitr., Ltd	1	⅛
—	Do. 8 p.c. Cum. Pref.	1	⅜
6	Do. 6 p.c. 1 Mt. Dbs. Rd.	100	62½
3'78d.	Newnes, G., L., Cm. Prf.	1	1½
1/3	Nitr. Provision, Ltd.	2½	¾
24/	Nobel-Dynam., Ltd.	10	18
—	North Brazn. Sugar, Ltd.	1	½
15/	Oakey, Ltd.	10	31
6	Do. Cum. Pref.	10	17
—	Paccha Jazp. Nitr., Ltd.	5	½
5	Pac. Borax, L., 1 Db. Rd.	100	110
—	Palace Hotel, Ltd.	10	5½
5½	Do. Cum. Pref.	10	7
4	Do. 1 Mt. Deb. Stk.	100	102
2/6	Palmer, Ltd.	5	1½
6	Do. Cum. Pref.	5	2½
1/2½d	Paquin, Ltd.	1	⅝
6	Do. Cum. Pref.	5	4
5½	Parnall, Ltd., Cum. Pref.	1	¾
4/6	Pawsons, Ltd., £10 Shs.	6	6½
4	Do. Mt. Debs., Red.	100	106
6	Pearks, G. & T., Ltd., 6 p.c. Cum. Pref.	1	¾
9½d.	Pears, Ltd.	1	1⅛
6	Do. Cum. Pref.	10	14
5	Do. Deb. Stk.	100	129
5½	Pearson, C. A., L., Cu. Pf.	5	5½
4/3	Peebles, Ltd.	5	7½
5	Do. Cum. Pref.	5	6½
4½	Do. Mt. Deb. Stk. Red.	100	113½
5½	Peek Bros., Ltd., 1 Cum. Pref., Nos. 1-60,000	5	6½
3½	Do. 3½ p.c 1 Db. Stk.	100	102½
7½d.	Pegamoid, Ltd.	1	⅝
—	Pillsbury-W. Fl. Mills, L.	10	1⅝
16/	Do. 8 p.c. Cum. Pref.	10	6½
6	Do. 1 Mort. Debs.	100	92½
9½d.	Plummer, Ltd.	1	1½
5	Do. Cum. Pref.	5	5½
7/6	Price's Candle, Ltd.	16	34
6	Priest Marians, L., Cm. Pf.	1	1½
6	Pryce Jones, Ld., Cm. Pf.	5	7½
5	Do. Deb. Stk.	100	122
8½d.	Pullman, Ltd.	1	1½
6d.	Do. Cum. Pref.	1	1½
11/10	Raleigh Cycle, Ltd.	1	⅝
6	Do. Cum. Pref.	1	¾
—	Recife Drnge. Ld. 1 Mt. Debs., R	100	19
6	Redfern, Ltd. Cum. Prf.	10	14
5	Ridgways, Ltd., Cu. Pf.	5	6½
—	R. Janeiro Cy. Imps. Ld.	25	7½
5	Do. Debs.	100	86½
5	Do. 1882-1893	100	86½
11/	R. Jan Fl. Mills, Ltd.	7	6½
5	Do. 1 Mt. Debs., Rd.	100	94
—	Riv. Plate Meat, Ltd.	5	3½
—	Do. Pref.	5	5
8½d.	Roberts, J. R., Ltd.	1	1½
5	Roberts 1 Mt. D. Sk., Rd.	100	112

Commercial, &c. (*continued*):—

Last Div.	Name.	Paid.	Price.
1/1½	Roberts, T. R., Ltd.	1	2½
5	Do. Cum. Pref.	1	1½
3/	Rosario Nit., Ltd.	5	3½
5	Do. Debs., Red.	100	103
1/	Rover Cycle, Ltd.	1	¾
6/	Ryl. Aquarium, Ltd.	5	4½
6	Do. Pref.	5	6
5	Ryl. Htl., Edin., Cm. Pf.	1	1½
1/2½	Ryl. Niger, Ltd., £10 Sh.	2	3
6/	Do.	10	15½
20/	Russian Petroleum	10	23
6½	Do. 6½ p.c. Cm. Prf.	10	10½
3/	Ruston, Proctor, Ltd.	10	12
4½	Do. 1 Mort. Debs.	100	104
6/	Sadler, Ltd.	12	7
—	Sal. Carmen Nit., Ltd.	5	3½
9d.	Salmon & Gluck., Ltd.	1	1⅜
	Salt Union, Ltd.	10	1½
1½	Do. 7 p.c. Pref.	10	6
4½	Do. Deb. Stk.	100	101½
4½	Do. "B" Deb. Sk., Rd.	100	97½
—	San Donato Nit., Ltd.	5	½
5/	San Jorge Nit., Ltd.	5	3½
—	San Pablo Nit., Ltd.	5	½
—	San Sebastn. Nit., Ltd.	5	½
1/9	Sanitas, Ltd	1	2½
—	Sn. Elena Nit., Ltd.	5	½
—	Sa. Rita Nit., Ltd.	5	1½
5/	Savoy Hotel, Ltd.	10	16
7	Do. Pref.	10	14
4	Do. 1 Mt. Deb. Stk.	100	111½
5	Do. Debs., Red	100	102½
5	Do. & Ldn. For. Htl., Ltd., 5 p.c. Debs. Red.	100	99
1½d.	Schweppes, Ltd.	1	1½
—	Do Def.	1	½
5	Do. Cum. Pref.	1	1½
4	Do. Deb. Stk.	100	105
1/	Singer Cyc., Ltd.	1	⅝
5½	Do Cum. Pref.	1	⅞
—	Smokeless Pwdr., Ltd.	1	⅜
5½d.	S. Eng. Dairies, Ltd., 6 p.c. Cum. Pref.	1	1½
—	Sowler Thos. L.	1	½
3/4½	Do. 5½ Cm. Pf.	5	5½
4/6	Spencer, Turner, & Co. Ltd	5	8½
5	Do. Cum. Pref.	5	6½
5	Spicer, Ld., 5 p.c. Dbs. Rd.	100	65
4/	Spiers & Pond, Ltd.	10	22
5	Do. 1 Mt. Debs., Red.	100	117½
5	Do. "A" Db. Stk., Rd.	100	111
5	Do. "B" 1 Db. Stk., Rd.	100	111
4	Do. Fd. "C" 1 Db. S., R.	100	104
7/6	Spratt's, Ltd	5	12½
4	Do. Debs., 1914	—	105
5	Steiner Ld., Cm. Pf.	10	11½
4	Do. 1 Mt. Db. Sk. Rd.	100	106
9/	Stewart & Clydesdale, L.	10	14
6	Do. Cum. Pref.	10	15
35/5	Sulphide Corp.	100	80
1/	Swan & Edgar, L.	1	1½
1/	Sweetmeat Automatic, L.	1	4
2/9	Teetgen, Ltd., Cum. Pref.	5	6
24/	Teleg. Construction., Ld.	12	36½
5	Do. Db. Bds., Rd., 1899	100	103½
3/0½	Tilling, Ld. 5½ p.c. Cm. Prf.	5	6½
4	Do. 4 p.c. 1 Dbs., Rd.	—	103
8½d.	Tower Tea, Ltd.	1	1½
5	Do. Cum. Pref.	5	5½
5	Travers, Ltd., Cum. Pref.	10	12½
4	Do. 1 Mt. Dbs., Rd.	100	105
6	Tucuman Sug., 1 Dbs., Rd.	100	100
4/	United Alkali, Ltd.	10	1½
7	Do. Cum. Pref.	10	8½
5	Do. Mt. Db. Stk., Rd.	100	107½
2½d.	United Horse Shoe, Ltd., Non-Cum. 8 p.c. Pref.	1	½
5	Un. Kingm. Tea, Cm. Prf.	5	4½
2/	Un. Lankat Plant., Ltd.	1	2
4/	Un. Limmer Asphlte., Ld.	3	4½
13/	Val de Travers Asph., L.	10	15½
3/	V. den Bergh's, L., Cm. P.	5	6
6	Walkers, Park., L., C. Pf.	10	3
4½	Do. 1 Mt. Debs., Red.	100	90½
6/	Wallis, Thos. & Co., Ltd.	5	14
6	Do. Cum. Pref.	5	8½
5½	Waring, Ltd., Cum. Pref.	5	5½
4½	Do. 1 Mt. Db. Sk., Red.	100	112
4½	Do. Irred. "B" Db. Stk.	100	104
12/	Waterlow, Dfd. Ord.	10	14
4/	Do. Pref.	10	14
3½	Do. Cum. Pref.	10	10½
10/	Waterlow Bros. & L., Ld.	10	9
5	Do. Pref.	10	12½
1/2½	Welford, Ltd.	1	1⅛
4½	Do. Debs., Red.	100	109
1/	Welford's Surrey Dairies, Ltd.	1	1⅛
7½d.	West London Dairy, Ltd.	1	1
4½	Wharncliffe Dwllgs., L., Pf.	10	11½
18/10	Do. 3 p.c. Irr. Mt. Db. Sk.	100	96
6d.	White, A. J., Ltd.	1	⅜
6	Do. 6 p.c. Cum. Pref.	1	⅝
4	White, J. Bazley, Ltd., 1 Mort. Debs., Red	100	97½
5	White, R., Ltd., 1 Mort. Deb. Stock, Red.	100	104½
11/	White, Tomkins, Ltd	10	11½
5	Do. Cum. Pref.	10	11½
6	White, W. N., L., Cm. Pf.	1	½
2/6	Wickens, Pease & Co., L.	5	3½
6	Wilkie, Ltd., Cum. Pref.	10	15½
4/	Willans & Robinson, Ltd	5	8
6	Do. Cum. Pref.	5	7½
4½	Do. 1 Mt. Db. Stk., Red.	100	108
7½d.	Williamsons, L., Cm. Prf.	1	1½
6	Winterbottm. Book Cloth, Ltd., Cum. Prf.	10	15
3/	Yates, Ltd.	5	6½
6	Do. Cum. Pref.	5	6½
	Young's Paraffin, Ltd.	4	1½

CORPORATION STOCKS—COLONIAL AND FOREIGN.

Per Cent.	Name.	Paid.	Price.
6	Auckland City, '72 1904-24	100	118
6	Do. Cons., '79, Red. 1930	100	135½
5	Do. Deb. Ln., '83..1934-8	100	117
6	Auckland Harb. Debs.	100	111½
5	Do. 1917	100	111
5	Do. 1936	100	116
5½	Balmain Boro' 1914	—	113½
5	Boston City (U.S.)	100	102½
5	Do. 1902	100	105
5	Brunswick Town 5 c. Debs. 1916-20	100	111
15/	B. Ayres City 6 p.c.	100	51
4½	Do. 4½ p.c.	100	71½
5	Cape Town, City of	100	113
4	Do. 1943	100	116
4	Chicago, City of, Gold 1915	—	108
6	Christchurch 1926	100	131½
—	Cordoba City	100	17½
5	Duluth (U.S.) Gold 1926	—	110
6	Dunedin (Otago) 1925	100	127½
6	Do. 1906	100	113
5	Do. Consols 1908	100	111
4	Durban Insc. Stk. 1944	100	111
4	Essex Cnty., N. Jersey 1926	100	114½
5	Fitzroy, Melbrne. 1916-19	100	110
5	Gisborne Harbour 1915	100	109
4	Greymouth Harbour 1925	100	110
4	Hamilton 1934	100	108
5	Hobart Town 1918-30	100	115
4	Do. 1940	100	105
4½	Invercargill Boro. Dbs. 1936	100	111
6	Kimberley Boro., S.A. Debs.	—	102
4	Launceston Twn. Dbs. 1916	100	107
6	Lyttleton, N.Z., Harb. 1929	100	125
4	Melbourne Bd. of Wks. 1921	100	107
5	Melb. City Debs. 1897-1907	100	106½
4½	Do. Debs. 1908-27	100	111½
4	Do. Debs. 1915-20-22	100	106
5	Melbne. Harb. Bds., 1908-9	100	113
4½	Do. do. 1915	100	111
4	Do. do. 1918-21	100	106
4½	Melbrne. Tms, Dbs. 1914-16	100	113
4½	Do. Fire Brig. Db. 1921	100	108
5	Mexico City Stg.	100	89
4	Moncton N. Bruns. City	100	102
4½	Montevideo	100	59
5	Montreal Stg.	100	103
5	Do. 1874	100	103
5	Do. 1879	100	104
3½	Do. 1933	100	102
3	Do. Perm. Deb. Stk.	100	96
4	Do. Cons. Deb. Stk. 1932	100	111
6	Napier Boro. Consolid. 1914	100	119
5	Napier Harb. Debs. 1920	100	115
5	Do. Debs. 1928	100	107
6	New Plymouth Harb. Debs. 1909	100	107
6	New York City 1901	—	107½
3½	Do. 1910-26	—	103½
4½	Nth. Melbourne Debs. 1-6-0 1921	100	105
5	Oamaru Boro. Cons. 1920	100	101
6	Do. Harb. Bds. (Reg.)	100	74
25/	Do. 6 p.c. (Bearer) 1919	100	35
6	Otago Harb. Deb. Reg.	100	103
6	Do. 1877	100	107
6	Do. 1881 1921	100	115
5	Do. Debs. 1921	100	107
5	Do. Cons. 1934	100	105
6	Ottawa City	100	109
6	Do. 1904	100	111½
4½	Do. Debs. 1913	100	108½
6	Port Elizabeth Waterworks	100	111
5	Port Louis	100	111
5	Prahran Debs. 1917	100	109
4	Do. Debs. 1919	100	102
6	Quebec C. Coupon. 1875 1905	100	112
6	Do. do. 1875 1908	100	116
4½	Do. Debs. 1914-18	100	108
4	Do. Debs. 1923	100	108
3½	Do. Cns. Rg. Stk., Red.	100	101
5	Richmond (Melb.) Dbs. 1917	100	112
4	Rio Janeiro City	100	57
4	Rome City	100	—
4	Do. 2nd to 8th Iss.	100	92
—	Rosario C.	100	26½
—	Do.	100	26½
4	St. Catherine (Ont.) 1926	100	101
4	St. John, N.B., Debs. 1934	—	103
4½	St. Kilda (Melb) Dbs. 1918-21	100	105
4	St. Louis C. (Miss.) 1911	100	104
4	Do. 1913	100	103½
3·65	Do. 1915	—	108½
—	Santa Fé City Debs.	100	20
6	Santos City	100	95
6	Sofia City	100	84
5	Sth. Melbourne Debs. 1915	100	111
4½	Do. Debs. 1919	100	107
5	Sydney City 1904	100	109
4	Do. Debs. 1912-13	100	107
4	Do. do. (1894) 1919	100	109
7	Timaru Boro. 7 p.c. 1910	100	128½
5	Timaru Harb. Debs 1914	100	107
5	Do. Debs. 1916	100	107
6	Toronto City Wtwks 1904-6	100	114
5	Do. G. Cns. Dbs. 1919-20	100	118
4	Do. Strlg. 1922-8	100	107
4	Do. Local Improv.	100	102
3½	Do. 1929	100	104
5½	Valparaiso	100	99
4	Vancouver 1931	100	107
4	Do. 1932	100	108
6	Wanganui Harb. Dbs. 1905	100	110
6	Wellington Con. Deb. 1907	100	117
6	Do. Improv., 1879	100	123
6	Do. Wtrwks. Dbs., 1880	100	123
4½	Do. Debs., 1893 1933	100	114
4½	Wellington Harb. 1907	100	104
4	Westport Harb. Dbs. 1925	100	110
6	Winnipeg City Deb. 1907	—	116
5	Do. 1914	100	117

FINANCIAL, LAND, AND INVESTMENT.

Last Div.	Name.	Paid.	Price.
5	Agncy, Ld. & Fin. Aust., Ltd., Mt. Db. Stk., Rd.	100	90½
	Amer. Frehld. Mt. of Lon., Ld., Cum. Pref. Stk.	100	87½
4½	Do. Deb. Stk., Red.	100	92
1/	Anglo-Amer. Db. Cor., L.	2	1
4	Do. Deb. Stk., Red	100	105½
5½	Ang.-Ceylon & Gen. Est., Ltd., Cons. Stk.	100	55
6	Do. Reg. Debs., Red.	100	102½
—	Ang.-Fch. Explorn., Ltd.	1	2¼
6	Do. Cum. Pref.	1	1½
—	Argent. Ld. & Inv., Ltd. £1 Shares	10/	nil
—	Do. Cum. Pref.	4	1½
1/	Assets Fnders.' Sh., Ltd.,	4	1¾
6/	Assets Realis., Ltd., Ord.,	5	8¾
5	Do. Cum. Pref.	5	6¾
26/	Austrln. Agricl £25 Shs.	21½	63½
	Aust. N. Z. Mort., Ltd.,		
4½	Deb. Stk., Red.	100	90½
4	Do. Deb. Stk., Red.	100	82½
4½	Australian Est. & Mt., L., 1 Mt. Deb. Stk., Red.	100	103
5	Do. "A" Mort. Deb. Stk., Red.	100	96
5/	Australian Mort., Ld., & Fin., Ltd. £25 Shs.	5	4½
1/6	Do. New, £25 Shs.	3	3
4	Do. Deb. Stk.	100	109½
3	Do. Do.	100	85
5	Bengal Presidy. 1 Mort. Deb., Red.	100	106
25/	British Amer. Ld. "A"	1	19
—	Do. "B"	24	7
1/7½	Brit. & Amer. Mt., Ltd. £10 Shs.	2	1
5/	Do. Pref.	10	10
4	Do. Deb. Stk., Red.	100	103
1/3	Brit. & Austrln Tst Ln., Ltd. £25 Shs.	2½	¾
4½	Do. Perm. Debs., Red.	100	103
1½d.	Brit. N. Borneo. £1 Shs.	15/	1½
2½d.	Do.	1	¾
—	Brit. S. Africa	1	2½
5	Do. Mt. Deb., Red.	—	97
6	B. Aires Harb. Tst., Red.	100	94
12/6	Canada Co.	1	26
—	Canada N. W. Ld., Ltd.	$25	43½
—	Do. Pref.	$100	350½
4	Canada Perm. Loan & Sav. Perp. Deb. Stk.	100	99½
6	Curamalan Ld., 6 p.c. "A" Scrip	—	92
3/7½	Deb Corp., Ld., £10 Shs	4	3½
5	Do. Cum. Pref.	10	11½
4	Do. Perp. Deb. Stk.	100	112
9d.	Deb. Corp. Fdrs' Sh., Ld.	3	¾
4/5⅜	Eastn. Mt. & Agncy, Ld., "A"	10	5½
4½	Do. Deb. Stk., Red.	100	100
5	Equitable Revers. In. Ltd.	100	—
2/6	Exploration, Ltd.	1	1 1/16
/6d.	Freehold Trst. of Austria. Ltd. £10 Shs.	1	¾
4	Do. Perp. Deb. Stk.	100	100
70/	Genl. Reversionary, Ltd.	100	—
4½	Holborn Vi. Land	100	105
4½	House Prop. & Inv.	100	85½
13/	Hudson's Bay	13	21
—	Hyderabad (Deccan)	5	3
4	Impl. Col. Fin. & Agcy. Corp.	100	92½
4½	Impl. Prop. Inv., Ltd., Deb. Stk., Red.	100	91½
2/6	Internatl. Fincial. Soc., Ltd. £7½ Shs.	2½	1½
4	Do. Deb. Stk., Red.	100	99½
1/9½	Ld. & Mtge. Egypt, Ltd. £18 Shs.	3	2¾
5	Do. Debs., Red.	100	103
4½	Do. Debs., Red.	100	102
—	Ld. Corp. of Canada, Ltd.	1	¾
4½	Ld. Mtge. Bk. of Texas Deb. Stk.	100	—
3½	Ld. Mtge. Bk. Victoria 4½ p.c. Deb. Stk.	100	78
2/9½	Law Debent. Corp., Ltd., £10 Shs.	2	1½
4½	Do. Cum. Pref.,	10	12
4	Do. Deb. Stk.	100	114
—	Law Land, L., 4½ Cm. Prf.	5	5½
1/	Ldn. & Australasian Deb. Corp., Ltd., £4 Shs.	2	¾
4½	Do. 4½ p.c. Mt. Deb. Stk., Red.	100	99
1/9	Ldn. & Middx. Frhld. Est. £2 Shs.	35/	3
2/6	Lndn. & N. Y. Inv. Corp., Ltd.	5	1½
5	Do. 5 p.c. Cum. Pref.	10	6½
1/6	Ldn. & Nth. Assets Corp., Ltd., £2 Shs.	1½	¾
2	Ldn. & N. Deb. Corp., L.	2	1½
3/6	Ldn. & S. Afric. Explrn. Ltd.	½	13
2/	Mtge. Co. of R. Plate, Ltd. £10 Shs.	2	3
4½	Do. Deb. Stk., Red.	100	112
4½	Morton, Rose Est., Ltd., 1st Mort. Debs.	—	99
6/6	Natal Land Col. Ltd.	10	7½
4/	Do. 8 p.c. Pref., 1870	5	8
5/6	Natl. Disct. L., £25 Shs.	5	10½
4½	New Impl. Invest., Ltd. Pref. Stk.	100	61½
	New Impl. Invest., Ltd. Def. Stk.	100	9
3½	N. Zld. Assets Real Deb.	100	99
4	N. Zld. Ln. & Mer. Agcy., Ltd Prf. Ln. Deb. Stk	100	94
2/6	N. Zld. Tst. & Ln. Ltd., 7'£25 Shs.	5	1½

Financial, Land, &c. (*continued*):—

Last Div.	Name.	Paid.	Price.
12/6	N. Zld. Tst. & Ln. Ltd., 5 p.c. Cum. Pref.	25	20
—	N. Brit. Australsn. Ltd.	100	6½
—	Do. Irred. Guar.	100	32½
5	Do. Mort. Debs.	100	82½
4½	N. Queensld. Mort. & Inv., Ltd., Deb. Stk.	100	93
6	Peel Riv., Ld. & Min. Ltd.	100	88½
—	Peruvian Corp., Ltd.	100	2
—	Do. 4 p.c. Pref.	100	9
3	Do. 6 p.c. 1 Mt. Debs., Red.	100	39½
—	Queenld. Invest. & Ld. Mort. Pref. Ord. Stk.	100	20
3/7	Queenld. Invest. & Ld. Mort. Ord. Shs.	4	4
4	Queensld. Invest. & Ld. Mort. Perp. Debs.	100	88
3½	Raily. Roll Stk. Tst. Deb., 1903-6	100	100½
50/	Reversiony. Int. Soc., Ltd.	100	—
2/8½	Riv. Plate Trst., Loan & Agcy., L., "A" £10 Shs.	2	4
1/6	Riv. Plate Trst., Loan & Agcy., Ltd., Def. "B"	5	3½
	Riv. Plate Trst., Loan & Agy., L., Db. Stk., Red.	100	109
—	Santa Fé & Cord. Gt. South Land, Ltd.	20	5
—	Santa Fé Land	10	2½
2/	Scot. Amer. Invest., Ltd. £10 Shs.	2	2¾
2½	Scot. Australian Invest., Ltd., Cons.	100	74½
6	Scot. Australian Invest., Ltd., Guar. Pref.	100	135½
5	Scot. Australian Invest., Ltd., Guar. Pref.	100	106½
4	Scot. Australian Invest., Ltd., 4 p.c. Perp. Dbs.	100	105½
5	Sivagunga Zemdy., 1st Mort., Red.	100	101
20/	Sth. Australian	20	50
3½	Stock Exchange Deb., Rd.	—	101½
—	Strait Develt., Ltd.	1	1/16
2/6	Texas Land & Mt., Ltd. £10 Shs.	2½	3
4½	Texas Land & Mt., Ltd., Deb. Stk., Red.	100	106
—	Transvaal Est. & Dev., L.	1	1/16
—	Transvaal Lands, Ltd., £1 Shs.	15/	½
—	Do. F. P.	1	1/16
—	Transvaal Mort., Loan, & Fin., Ltd., £10 Shs.	2	½
2/	Tst & Agcy. of Austrlsa., Ltd., £10 Shs.	1	2
7/5	Do. Old, fully paid	10	15½
3/7	Do. New, fully paid	10	12½
5	Do. Cum. Pref.	10	12½
3/	Trust & Loan of Canada, £20 Shs.	5	4½
1/9½	Do. New £20 Shs.	3	2½
4½	Tst. & Mort. of Iowa, Ltd., Deb. Stk. Red.	100	92½
—	Tst., Loan, & Agency of Mexico, Ltd., £10 Shs.	2	½
—	Trsts., Exors, & Sec. Ins. Corp., Ltd., £10 Shs.	7	1½
4	Do. Irred. Deb. Stk.	100	106½
3/	Union Dsc., Ld., £10 Shs.	5	10½
6	Union Mort. & Agcy. of Aust., Ltd., Pref. Stk.	100	30
—	Do. 6 p. Pref. £6 Shs.	2	½
4½	Do. Deb. Stk	100	92½
4	Do. Deb. Stk	100	85½
5	Do. Deb. Stk. Red.	100	96½
1/6	U.S. Deb. Cor. Ltd., £8 Shs.	1	½
5½	Do. Cum. Pref. Stk.	100	100½
4½	Do. Irred. Deb. Stk.	100	105½
5	U.S. Tst. & Guar. Cor., Ltd., Pref. Stk.	100	77½
6/	Van Dieman's	25	14
4	Walker's Prop. Cor., Ltd., Guar. 1 Mt. Deb. Stk.	100	109
4½	Wstr. Mort. & Inv., Ltd., Deb. Stk.	100	90½

FINANCIAL—TRUSTS.

Last Div.	Name.	Paid.	Price.
1/6	Afric City Prop., Ltd.	1	1½
6	Do. Cum. Pref.	1	1 1/16
4	Alliance Invt., Ltd., Cm. 4½ p.c. Prefd.	100	73½
—	Do. Defd.	100	12½
4	Do. Deb. Stk. Red.	100	106½
5	Amron. Invt., Ltd., Prfd.	100	114½
5	Do. Defd.	100	88½
4	Do. Deb. Stk. Red.	100	115½
4	Army & Navy Invt., Ltd., 5 p.c. Prefd.	100	81½
—	Do. Defd. Stk.	100	16½
4	Do. Deb. Stk.	100	102½
4	Atlas Investment, Ltd., Prefd. Stk.	100	70½
4½	Bankers' Invest., Ltd., Cum. Prefd.	100	103
1/0/0	Do. Defd.	100	22½
4	Do. Deb. Stk	100	110
	Brewery & Comml. Inv., Ltd., £10 Shs.	5	6

Financial—Trusts (*continued*):—

Last Div.	Name.	Paid.	Price.
4	British Investment, Ltd., Cum. Prefd.	100	107
5	Do. Defd.	100	102½
4	Do. Deb. Stk.	100	108½
6	Brit. Steam. Invst., Ltd., Prefd.	100	116½
3/0/0	Do. Defd	100	69½
4½	Do. Perp. Deb. Stk	100	120½
1/9	Car Trust Invst., Ltd., £10 Shs.	2½	2
5	Do. Pref	100	101
4	Do. Deb. Stk., 1915	100	104
4	Clnl. Sec., Ltd., Prefd.	100	103½
2½	Do. Defd.	100	47½
4	Consolidated, Ltd., Cum. 1st Pref.	100	91
4	Do. 5 p.c. Cm. 2nd do.	100	71½
—	Do. Defd.	100	14½
4½	Do. Deb. Stk.	100	112½
5	Deb. Secs. Invst.	100	101½
4	Do. 4 p.c. Cm. Pf. Sk.	100	104½
4½	Edinburgh Invest., Ltd., Cum. Prefd. Stk.	100	109½
4	Do. Deb. Stk. Red.	100	106½
5	Foreign, Amer. & Gen. Invt., Ltd., Prefd.	100	109½
2	Do. Defd.	100	47½
4	Do. Deb. Stk.	100	115½
5	Foreign & Colonial Invt., Ltd., Prefd.	100	136½
5½	Do. Defd.	100	97½
4½	Gas, Water & Gen. Invt., Cum. Prefd. Stk.	100	85½
3	Do. Defd. Stk.	100	36½
4	Do. Deb. Stk.	100	104
5	Gen. & Com. Invt., Ltd., Prefd. Stk.	100	106½
2	Do. Defd. Stk.	100	36½
4	Do. Deb. Stk.	100	113½
2/6	Globe Telegph. & Tst., Ltd.	10	11½
6	Do. do. Pref.	10	17
4	Govt. & Genl. Invt., Ld., Prefd.	100	84½
3½	Do. Defd.	100	42½
4½	Govts. Stk. & other Secs. Invt., Ltd., Prefd.	100	86½
1	Do. Defd.	100	25
4½	Do. Deb. Stk.	100	111
4	Do. do.	100	104
4½	Guardian Invt., Ltd., Pfd.	100	87½
—	Do. Defd.	100	19½
4	Do. Deb. Stk.	100	104
5	Indian & Gen. Inv., Ltd., Cum. Prefd.	100	107½
2½	Do. Defd.	100	56
4½	Do. Deb. Stk.	100	119½
5	Indust. & Gen. Tst., Ltd., Unified	100	100
3½	Do. Deb. Stk. Red.	100	100½
4½	Internat. Invt., Ltd., Cm. Prefd.	100	65½
—	Do. Defd.	100	7½
4	Do. Deb. Stk.	100	101
4	Invest. Tst. Cor. Ltd. Pfd.	100	100
4	Do. Defd.	100	90
4	Do. Deb. Stk. Red.	100	105
5	Ldn. Gen. Invest. Ltd., 5 p.c. Cum. Prefd.	100	111
7½	Do. Defd.	100	118
4½	Ldn. Scot. Amer. Ltd. Pfd.	100	104½
£3	Do. Defd.	100	59½
4	Do. Deb. Stk.	100	111
4	Ldn. Tst., Ltd., Cum. Prfd. Stk.	100	100
4	Do. Defd. Stk.	100	70½
4	Do. Deb. Stk., Red.	100	107
3½	Do. Mt. Deb. Stk., Red.	100	102½
5	Mercantile Invt. & Gen., Ltd., Prefd.	100	109
3	Do. Defd.	100	44½
4	Do. Deb. Stk.	100	111½
4	Merchants, Ltd., Pref. Stk.	100	104½
4	Do. Ord.	100	80½
4	Do. Deb. Stk.	100	115½
5	Municipal, Ltd., Prefd.	100	55½
—	Do. Defd.	100	17½
4½	Do. Debs.	100	112
4½	Do. Debs. "B"	100	99½
4½	Do. "C" Deb. Stk.	100	88½
5	New Investment, Ltd. Ord.	100	92½
5	Omnium Invest., Ltd., Pfd.	100	91½
1	Do. Defd.	100	26½
4	Do. Deb. Stk.	100	104
5/	Railway Deb. Tst. Ld., £10 Shs.	10	6½
5	Do. Debs., Red.	100	107½
4½	Do. Deb. Stk., 1911	100	107½
4	Do. do. 1927	100	107½
4	Railway Invst. Ltd., Prefd.	100	111
17/7	Do. Defd.	100	19½
8/	Railway Share Trust & Agency "A"	8	5½
7½	Do. "B" Pref. Stk.	100	145½
4½	River Plate & Gen. Invt., Ltd., Prefd.	100	104
£3	Do. Defd.	100	50½
5	Scot. Invst., Ltd., Pfd. Stk.	100	91½
1½	Do. Defd.	100	26½
4	Do. Deb. Stk.	100	106
4½	Sec. Scottish Invst., Ltd., Cum. Prefd.	100	86½
£8	Do. Defd. Stk.	100	82
4	Do. Deb. Stk.	100	107½
5/	Sth. Africa Gold Tst., Ltd.	1	3½
6	Do. Cum. Pref	1	1
5½	Do. 1st Debs., Red.	100	102
1/9	Stock Conv. & Invest., Ltd., £5 Shs.	1	1½
4½	Do. do. 4½ p.c. Cm. Prf.	100	112½
2½	Do. Ldn. & N. W. 1st. Charge Prefd.	100	114½
4	Do do. 2nd Chge Prfd.	100	111
32/6	Do. do. Defd. Charge	100	30
3	Do. N. East. 1 Chge Pfd.	100	90½

Financial—Trusts (*continued*):—

Last Div.	Name.	Paid.	Price.
37/6	Stock N. East Defd. Chge	100	36
6	Submarine Cables	100	138½
5	U.S. & S. Amer. Invest., Ltd., Prefd.	100	97½
2	Do. Defd.	100	25½
4	Do. Deb. Stk.	100	105½

GAS AND ELECTRIC LIGHTING.

Last Div.	Name.	Paid.	Price.
10/6	Alliance & Dublin Con. 10 p.c. Stand.	10	24
7/6	Do. 7 p.c. Stand.	10	16½
5	Austln. Gas Lght. (Syd.) Debs. 1909	100	106
5	Bay State of N. Jrsy. Sk. Fd. Tst. Bd., Red.	—	89½
3/	Bombay, Ltd.	5	6
2/4½	Do. New	4	5
12	Brentford Cons.	100	296½
9	Do. New	100	220
5	Do. Pref.	100	142½
4	Do. Deb. Stk.	100	136
11½	Brighton & Hove Gen. Cons. Stk.	100	272½
8½	Do. "A" Cons. Stk.	100	197½
5	Bristol 5 p.c. Max.	100	129½
22/6	British Gas Light, Ltd.	20	55½
11/6	Bromley Gas Consumrs.' 10 p.c. Stand.	10	26
8/6	Do. 7 p.c. Stand.	10	21
—	Brush Electl. Enging., L.	—	1½
6	Do. 6 p.c. Pref.	—	2½
4½	Do. Deb. Stk.	100	112
4½	Do. 2 Deb. Stk., Red.	100	102½
7/	B. Ayres (New), Ltd.	10	9
4	Do. Deb. Stk., Rd.	—	99
18/6	Cagliari Gas & Wtr., Ltd.	20	31
8/	Cape Town & Dist. Gas Light & Coke, Ltd.	10	16½
4½	Do. Pref.	10	12½
6	Do. 1 Mt. Debs. 1910	50	59
4/	Charing Cross & Strand Elec. Sup., Ltd.	5	13½
4½	Do. Cum. Pref.	5	6½
3/	Chelsea Elec. Sup., Ltd.	5	10
4½	Do. Deb. Stk., Red.	100	115
5	Chic. Edis'n Co. 1 Mt., Rd	$1000	106
20/	City of Ldn. Elec. Lht., L.	10	26½
—	Do. New £10 Shs.	5	18½
6	Do. Cum. Pref.	10	18
5	Do. Deb. Stk., Red.	100	131½
13½	Commercial, Cons.	100	325½
10½	Do. New	100	252½
4½	Do. Deb. Stk.	100	152½
14	Continental Union, Ltd.	100	220
11	Do. Pref. Stk.	100	205
—	County of Lon. & Brush Prov. Elec. Lg., Ltd.	10	14½
6	Do. Cum. Pref.	10	15½
14	Croydon Comcl. Gas, Ld., "A" Stk., 10 p.c.	100	312½
11	Do. "B" Stk., 7 p.c.	100	260
5½	Crystal Pal. Dist. Ord. 5 p.c. Stk.	100	130½
5	Do. Pref. Stk.	100	143½
8/	European, Ltd.	10	24
6/	Do.	7½	17½
12½	Gas Light & Ck Cons. Stk., "A" Ord.	100	282½
4	Do. "B" (4 p.c. Max.)	100	120½
10	Do. "C," "D," & "E" (Pref.)	100	302½
5	Do. "F" (Pref.)	100	152½
7½	Do. "G" (Pref.)	100	222½
7	Do. "H" (7 p.c. Max.)	100	197½
10	Do. "J" (Pref.)	100	302½
6	Do. "K"	100	180½
4	Do. Deb. Stk.	100	133½
4½	Do. do.	100	152½
6	Do. do.	100	204½
8/	Hong Kong & China, Ld.	10	14½
4/	House to House Elec. Light Sup., Ltd.	5	10½
7	Do. Cum. Pref.	5	11½
10	Imperial Continental	100	217½
3½	Do. Deb. Stk., Red	100	104½
2/	Malta & Medit., Ltd.	5	5½
7/	Metrop. Elec. Sup., Ltd.	10	19
4½	Do. 1 Mt. Deb. Stk.	100	119
5	Metro. of Melbrne. Dbs. 1908-12	100	111
4½	Do. Debs. 1918-22-4	100	108
10/	Monte Video, Ltd.	20	15½
9½	Newcastle-upon-Tyne	100	237½
—	Do. 3½ p.c. Deb. Stk.	100	117½
18/	Notting Hill Elec. Ltg., Ltd.	10	19½
4/6	Oriental, Ltd.	5	8½
4/0½	Do. New	4½	7½
10d.	Do. do. 1879	1	1½
3/6	Ottoman, Ltd.	5	4½
6	People's Gas Lt. & C. of Chic. 2 Mt. 1904	100	105½
5	River Plate Elec. Lgt. & Trac., Ltd., 1 Deb. Stk.	—	92½
8s	Royal Elec. of Montreal	—	144
4½	Do. 1 Mt. Deb.	100	104
11/	St. James' & Pall Mall Elec. Light, Ltd.	5	18
7	Do. Pref.	5	10½
4	Do. Deb. Stk., Red.	100	108½
10/	San Paulo, Ltd.	10	16

Gas and Electric (*continued*):—

Last Div.	Name.	Paid.	Price.
10	Sheffield Unit. Gas Lt. "A"	100	251½
10	Do. "B"	100	251½
10	Do. "C"	100	251½
—	Sth. Ldn. Elec. Sup., Ld.	2	2¼
5½	South Metropolitan	100	133½
3	Do. 3 p.c. Deb. Stk.	100	104½
12	Tottenham & Edmonton Gas Lt. & C., "A"	100	290
9	Do. "B"	100	210
7/	Tuscan, Ltd.	10	13½
5	Do. Debs., Red.	100	101½
5/	West Ham 10 p.c. Stan.	5	12
8/	Wstmnstr. Elec. Sup., Ld.	5	17½

INSURANCE.

Last Div.	Name.	Paid.	Price.
4/	Alliance, £20 Shs.	44/	10½
10/	Alliance, Mar., & Gen., Ld., £100 Shs.	25	53
19/	Atlas, £50 Shs.	6	30½
12/	British & For. Marine, Ld., £20 Shs.	4	23
7½d.	British Law Fire, Ltd., £10 Shs.	1	1½
7/6	Clerical, Med., & Gen. Life £25 Shs.	50/	16½
10/	Commercial Union, Ltd., £50 Shs.	5	44½
4	Do. "W. of Eng." Ter. Deb. Stk	100	110½
£9	County Fire, £100 Shs.	80	195
5/	Eagle, £50 Shs	5	½
4/	Employrs' Liability, Ltd., £10 Shs.	2	4
—	Empress, Ltd., £5 Shs.	1	—
21/	Equity & Law, £100 Shs.	6	23
7/6	General Life, £100 Shs.	5	15
4½d.	Gresham Life, £5 Shs.	15/	2½
2/6	Guardian, Ld., £10 Shs.	5	11½
10/	Imperial, Ltd., £20 Shs.	5	29½
5/6	Imperial Life, £20 Shs.	4	6½
6/	Indemnity Mutual Mar., Ltd., £15 Shs.	3	11
1/	Lancashire, £20 Shs.	2	5
7½d.	Law Acc. & Contin., Ltd., £5 Shs.	10/	⅜
3/	Law Fire, £100 Shs.	2½	18
9½d.	Law Guar. & Trust, Ltd., £10 Shs.	1	1⅜
9/	Law Life, £20 Shs.	2	25
2/9	Law Un. & Crown £10Shs	12/	7
4	Do. Deb. Stk., 1942	100	110½
14/6	Legal & General, £50 Shs.	8	15½
9d.	Lion Fire, Ltd., £8½ Shs.	1½	⅜
14/	Liverpool & London & Globe, Stk	2	52
20/	Do. Globe £1 Ann	—	35½
35/	London, £25 Shs.	12½	60
8/	Lond. & Lanc. Fire, £25Shs	2½	18½
2/	Lond. & Lanc. Life, £25Shs	2	7
1/	Lond. & Prov. Mar., Ld., £10 Shs.	1	⅜
6/	Lond. Guar. & Accident, Ltd., £5 Shs.	2	12
10/	Marine, Ltd., £25 Shs.	4½	40½
2/	Maritime, Ltd., £10 Shs.	2	4
1/6	Merc. Mar., Ld., £10 Shs.	2½	2½
—	National Marine, Ltd., £9 Shs.	1	—
20/	N. Brit. & Merc., £25 Shs.	6½	42
20/	Northern, £100 Shs.	10	81
40/	Norwich Union Fire, £100 Shs.	12	125½
10/	Ocean Acc. & Guar., fy. pd.	5	22
2/	Do. £5 Shs.	1	4
7/6	Ocean, Marine, Ltd.	2½	8½
2/	Palatine, £10 Shs.	2	3½
2/6	Pelican, £10 Shs.	1	3½
23/	Phoenix, £50 Shs.	5	42
2/6	Provident, £100 Shs.	10	31
3/	Railway Passngrs., £10Shs.	2	8½
2/6	Rock Life, £5 Shs.	10/	4½
8	Royal Exchange	100	355
18/	Royal, £20 Shs.	3	53½
4/	Sun, £10 Shs.	10/	11
3/9	Sun Life, £10 Shs.	7½	14½
6	Thames & Mrsey. Marine, Ltd., £20 Shs.	2	10½
9	Union, £10 Shs.	4	24½
4/	Union Marine, £20 Shs.	2½	8½
12/	Universal Life, £100 Shs.	12	42
3/	World Marine, £5 Shs.	2	1½

IRON, COAL, AND STEEL.

Last Div.	Name.	Paid.	Price.
—	Barrow Hæm. Steel, Ltd.	7½	2
9/	Do. 6 p.c. 2nd Pref.	7½	6½
10/	Bolck., Vaugh. & C., Ld.	20	16½
6/	Do. £8 liab.	12	9
7/6	Brown, J. & Co., Ltd., £20 Shs.	15	20
7/6	Consett Iron, Ld., £10 Shs.	7½	29½
7/6	Ebbw Vale Steel, Iron & Coal, Ltd., £23 Shs.	20	6
12/6	General Mining Assn., Ld.	5½	7½
8/	Harvey Steel Co. of Gt. Britain, Ltd.	10	27
5	Lehigh V. Coal 1 Mt. 5 p.c. Guar. Gd. Cp. Bds.	—	95½
42/6	Nantyglo & Blaina Iron, Ltd., Pref.	$62	94½
1/	Nerbudda Coal & Iron, Ltd., £3 Shs.	56/	$\frac{1}{16}$
—	Newport Abrcrn. Bk. Vein Steam Coal, Ltd.	10	5½
5/	New Sharlston Coll., Ltd. Pref.	20	9½
4½d.	Nw. Vancvr. Coal & Ld., L.	1	⅛
2/6	North's Navigation Coll. (1889) Ltd.	5	2½
10/	Do. 10 p.c. Cum. Pref.	5	6½
—	Rhymney Iron, Ltd.	5	1½
	Do. New, £5 Shs.	4½	½
5	Do. Mt. Debs., Red.	100	98½
5	Shelton Irn., Stl. & Cl. Co., Ltd., 1 Chg. Debs., Red.	100	99½
50/	Sth. Hetton Coal, Ltd.	100	—
2/	Vickers & Maxim, Ltd.	1	3½
5	Do. 5 p.c. Prfd. Stk.	100	127½

SHIPPING.

Last Div.	Name.	Paid.	Price
12/	African Stm. Ship, £20 Shs.	16	10½
15/	Do. Fully-paid	20	14½
5/	Amazon Steam Nav., Ltd.	12½	9
8/	Castle Mail Pakts., Ltd., £20 Shs.	14	16
3½	Do. 1st Deb. Stk., Red.	100	102
6/	China Mutual Steam, Ltd.	5	2½
6	Do. Cum. Pref.	10	9½
10/	Cunard, Ltd.	20	9½
5/	Do. £20 Shs.	10	3½
4½	Furness, Withy, & Co., Ltd., 1 Mt. Dbs., Red.	100	105
6/	General Steam	15	7½
5/	Do. 5 p.c. Pref., 1874	10	8½
5/	Do. 5 p.c. Pref., 1877	10	8½
26/4½	Leyland & Co., Ltd.	10	25
7/	Do. 7 p.c. Cum. Pref.	10	15
2/11	Do. 4½ p.c. Cum. Pre-Pf.	3	10½
4	Do. 1st Mt. Dbs., Red.	100	106½
7/6	Mercantile Steam, Ltd.	5	7½
6/4½	New Zealand Ship., Ltd.,	6	5
4	Do. Deb. Stk., Red.	100	104
5/	Orient Steam, Ltd.	10	5
5	P. & O. Steam, Cum. Prefd.	100	147½
19	Do. Defd.	100	232½
3½	Do. Deb. Stk.	100	117
5	Richelieu & Ont., 1st Mt. Debs., Red.	100	100
30/	Royal Mail, £100 Shs.	60	51
2/6	Shaw, Sav., & Alb., Ltd., "A" Pref.	5	5
5/	Do. "B" Ord.	5	3½
14/	Union Steam, Ltd.	20	19
7/	Do. New £20 Shs.	10	8½
4	Do. Deb. Stk., Red.	100	106
7/	Union of N.Z., Ltd.	10	10
5½	Wilson's & Fur.-Ley., 5½ p.c. Cum. Pref.	10	10½
4½	Do. 1 Mt. Db. Sk., Rd.	100	106½

**** Tea and Coffee Shares will be found in the Special Table following.*

TELEGRAPHS AND TELEPHONES.

Last Div.	Name.	Paid.	Price.
4	African Direct, Ltd., Mort. Debs., Red.	100	102
—	Amazon Telegraph, Ltd.	10	7½
15/	Anglo-American, Ltd.	100	61½
30/	Do. 6 p.c. Prefd. Ord.	100	111
—	Do. Defd. Ord.	100	14½
3/	Brazilian Submarine, Ltd.	10	16
5	Do. Debs., 2 Series	100	114

Telegraphs and Telephones (*continued*):—

Last Div.	Name.	Paid.	Price.
4/	Chili Telephone, Ltd.	5	3½
$1½	Comcial. Cable, $100 Shs.	—	165
4	Do. Stg. 500-yr. Deb. Stk. Red.	100	104
2½d.	Consd. Telpehone Constr., &c., Ltd.	10/	½
6/	Cuba Submarine, Ltd.	10	6½
10/	Do. 10 p.c. Pref.	10	14½
2/	Direct Spanish, Ltd.	5	4½
5/	Do. 10 p.c. Cum. Pref.	5	10½
4½	Do. Debs.	50	104½
3/	Direct U.S. Cable, Ltd.	20	10½
2/6	Eastern, Ltd.	10	17½
3/	Do. 6 p.c. Cum. Pref.	10	18½
4	Do. Mt. Deb. Stk., Red.	100	125
2/6	Eastern Exten., Aus., & China, Ltd.	10	18½
5	Do. (Aus. Gov. Sub.) Deb., Red.	100	102
5	Do. do. Bearer	100	102½
4	Do. Mort. Deb. Stk.	100	128½
5	Eastn. & S. Afric., Ltd., Mort. Deb. 1900	100	102
5	Do. Bearer	100	102½
4	Do. Mort. Debs. 1909	100	103½
4	Do. Mort. Debs. (Maur. Subsidy)	25	106½
5/	Grt. Nthn. Copenhagen	10	29
5	Do. Debs., Ser. B., Red.	100	101½
12/6	Indo-European, Ltd.	25	51½
6	London Platino-Brazilian, Ltd., Debs. 1904	100	107½
4/	Montevideo Telph., Ltd., 6 p.c. Pref.	5	2½
3/	National Telephone, Ltd.	5	5½
6/	Do. Cum. 1 Pref.	10	16
6/	Do. Cum. 2 Pref.	10	16
5	Do. Non-Cum. 3 Pref.	5	5½
3½	Do. Deb. Stk., Red.	100	102½
8d.	Oriental Telephone, Ltd.	1	½
4	Pac. & Euro. Tlg. Dbs., Rd.	100	106½
4/	Reuter's, Ltd.	8	8½
5/	Un. Riv. Plate Telph., Ltd.	5	4½
5	Do. Deb. Stk., Red.	100	106½
—	West African Telg., Ltd.	10	4
5	Do. 5 p.c. Mt. Debs., Red.	100	100½
—	W. Coast of America, Ltd.	10	½
3/	Western & Brazilian, Ltd.	15	11½
3/	Do. 5 p.c. Pref. Ord.	7½	7½
—	Do. Defd. Ord.	7½	4½
4	Do. Deb. Stk., Red.	100	106½
1/	W. India & Panama, Ltd.	10	½
6/	Do. Cum. 1 Pref.	10	7½
6/	Do. Cum. 2 Pref.	10	6
5	Do. Debs., Red.	100	106½
7	West. Union, 1 Mt. 1902 $	1000	105½
6	Do. 6 p.c. Stg. Bds., Rd.	100	102½

TRAMWAYS AND OMNIBUS.

Last Div.	Name.	Paid.	Price.
1/6	Anglo-Argentine, Ltd.	5	3½
6	Do. Deb. Stk.	100	125
4/	Barcelona, Ltd.	10	11½
5	Do. Deb., Red.	100	105½
7/6	Belfast Street Trams.	10	16½
—	Blackpl. & Fltwd. Tram., £10 Shs.	8	13
10/	Bordeaux Tram. & O., Ltd.	10	11½
5	Do. Cum. Pref.	10	11
—	Brazilian Street Ry., Ltd.	2	½
—	British Elec. Trac., Ltd.	10	16
—	B. Ayres & Belg. Tram., Ltd., 6 p.c. Cum. Pref.	5	—
6	Do. 1 Deb. Stk.	100	—
—	B. Ayres. Gd. Nat., Ltd., 6 p.c 1 Deb. Bds., Red.	100	59½
5½	Do. Pref. Debs., Red.	100	94½
1/	Calais, Ltd.	5	1
—	Calcutta, Ltd.	10	3½
—	Carthagena & Herr., Ltd.	10	5
5	Do. Deb., Red.	100	90
5	City of B'ham. Trams., Ltd., 5 p.c. Cum. Pref.	5	5½
4	Do. 1 Mort. Debs., Rd.	100	106½
3/9	City of B. Ayres, Ltd.	5	6½
2/3	Do. Ext. £5 Shs.	3	4
6	Do. Deb. Stk	100	145
1/4	Edinburgh Street Tram.	4	4
1/	Glasgow Tram. & Omni. Ltd., £9 Shs.	8	3
3/7½	Imperial, Ltd.	6	14½
3/	Lond., Deptfd, & Greenwich, Prefd.	5	3½
nil	Do. Defd.	5	1
10½	Lond. Gen. Omni., Ltd.	100	195
4	Do. Deb., Red.	100	115½

Tramways and Omnibus (*continued*):—

Last Div.	Name.	Paid.	Price.
4/9½	London Road Car	6	10½
28/6	Do. Red. 1 Mt. Deb. Stk.	100	108½
5	London St. Rly. (Prov., Ont.), Mt. Debs.	100	110
12/6	London St. Trams.	—	2
12/9	London Trams., Ltd.	10	10
6/	Do. Non-Cum. Pref.	10	10½
5	Do. Mt. Db. Stk., Rd.	100	101
5	Lynn & Boston 1 Mt. 1924 $	1000	106
5	Milwaukee Elec. Cons. Mt. $	1000	100½
5	Minneapolis St. 1 Cons. Mt $	1000	96
5	Montreal St. Dbs., 1908	100	109
4½	Do. Debs., 1922	100	107
6/	Nth. Metropolitan	—	11
1/9½	Nth. Staffords., Ltd.	6	5
5/0	Provincial, Ltd	10	7
6/	Do. Cum. Pref.	10	13½
5	St. Paul City, 1937 $	1000	96
5	Do. Guar. Twin City Rap. Trans. $	1000	—
5/	Southampton	10	6½
5/	South London	10	5½
7/6	Sunderland, Ltd.	10	6½
4½	Toronto 1 Mt., Red.	100	106
2/6	Tramways Union, Ltd.	5	6½
4½	Do. Deb., Red.	100	109
2/6	Vienna General Omnibus.	5	5½
5	Do. 5 p.c. Mt. Deb., Red.	100	103½
4/	Wolverhampton, Ltd.	10	6½

WATER WORKS.

Last Div.	Name.	Paid.	Price.
8/	Antwerp, Ltd.	20	22½
6/	Cape Town District, Ltd.	5	7
10½	Chelsea	100	325
5	Do. Pref. Stk.	100	178½
4½	Do. Pref. Stk., 1875	100	158½
4½	Do. Deb. Stk.	100	160½
5/6	City St. Petersburg, Ltd.	13	11
5/	Colne Valley	10	15½
4	Do. Deb. Stock	100	137½
£4	Consol. of Rosar., Ltd., 4 p.c. 1 Deb. Stk., Red.	100	91
8	East London	100	225½
4½	Do. Deb. Stk.	100	160
3	Do. Deb. Stk., Red.	100	106
37/6	Grand Junction (Max. 10 p.c.) "A"	50	117½
18/9	Do. "B"	25	
18/9	Do. "C" (Max. 7½ p.c.)	25	54½
35/	Do. "D" (Max. 7 p.c.)	50	102½
4	Do. Deb. Stock	100	142½
13	Kent	100	360½
7	Do. New (Max. 7 p.c.)	100	215½
7/	Kimberley, Ltd.	7	4½
6	Do. Debs., Red.	100	104½
6	Do. Deb. Stk., Red.	100	107½
10	Lambeth (Max. 10 p.c.)	100	297½
7½	Do. (Max. 7½ p.c.), 50 & 25	—	230½
4	Do. Deb. Stock	100	142½
3	Do. Red. Deb. Stock	100	103
10/	Montevideo, Ltd.	20	16
5	Do. 1 Deb. Stk.	100	108½
5	Do. 2 Deb. Stk.	100	103½
132/9	New River New	100	442½
4	Do. Deb. Stk.	100	144½
4	Do. Deb. Stk. "B"	100	144½
4	Portland Con. Mt. "B," 1927	—	102½
8/	Seville, Ltd.	20	12
5/6	Southend "Addl." Ord.	10	17½
6	Southwark and Vauxhall	100	157½
6	Do. "D" Shares (7½ p.c. max.)	100	154½
5	Do. Pref. Stock	100	176½
4	Do. "A" Deb. Stock	100	142½
3	Staines Resvirs. Jt. Com. Gua. Deb. Stk., Red.	100	105
8/	Tarapaca, Ltd.	10	9
10	West Middlesex	100	302½
4½	Do. Deb. Stk.	100	162½
3	Do Deb. Stk.	100	106

INDIAN AND CEYLON TEA COMPANIES.

Acres Planted.	Crop, 1897.	Paid up Capital.	Share.	Paid up.	Name.	Dividends. 1894.	1895.	1896.	Int. 1897.	Price.	Yield.	Reserve.	Balance Forward.	Working Capital.	Mortgages, Debs. or Pref. Capital not otherwise stated.
	lb.	£	£	£	INDIAN COMPANIES.							£	£	£	£
11,240	3,128,000	120,000	10	3	Amalgamated Estates	—	*	10	5	3⅜	8¼	10,000	16,500	D52,950	—
		400,000	10	10	Do. Pref.	—	*	5	‡5	9⅞	5				
10,223	3,560,000	187,160	20	20	Assam	20	20	20	5	60	6⅝	55,000	1,730	D11,350	—
6,150	3,278,000	142,500	10	10	Assam Frontier	3	6	6	—	7	8½	—	286	20,000	82,500
		142,500	10	10	Do. Pref.	6	6	6	‡6	11	5⅜				
2,087	839,000	66,745	5	5	Attaree Khat	12	12	8	3	7	6	3,790	4,820	7,770	—
1,633	583,000	78,170	10	10	Borelli	4	4	5	—	7½	6⅝	—	3,256	D270	6,500 Pref.
1,720	812,000	60,825	5	5	British Indian	6	5	5	—	4	6¼	—	2,920	12,300	16,500 Pref.
3,223	2,247,000	114,500	5	5	Brahmapootra	20	18	20	6	13	7⅝	—	28,440	41,600	*
3,754	1,617,000	76,500	10	10	Cachar and Dooars	*	8	7	‡7	10½	6⅝	—	1,645	21,240	*
		76,500	10	10	Do. Pref.	*	6	6	‡6	11½	5¼				
3,946	2,083,000	72,010	1	1	Chargola	8	7	10	2½	[illegible]	13	3,000	3,300	—	—
		81,000	1	1	Do. Pref.	7	7	7	3½	1⅛	5⅜				
1,971	942,000	33,000	5	5	Chubwa	10	8	10	‡8	5¼xd	6⅞	10,000	2,043	D5,400	—
		33,000	5	5	Do. Pref.	7	7	7	‡7	6⅜	5½				
32,250	11,500,000	120,000	10	3	Cons. Tea and Lands	—	*	10	5	3½	7⅞	65,000	14,240	D191,674	—
		1,000,000	10	10	Do. 1st Pref.	—	*	5	‡5	10½	4⅞				
		400,000	10	10	Do. 2nd Pref.	—	*	7	‡7	12	5⅞				
2,230	617,000	135,420	20	20	Darjeeling	5½	5½	6	‡5	21	4⅞	5,552	1,565	1,700	—
2,114	445,000	60,000	10	10	Darjeeling Cons.	—	—	4/2	—	6	—	—	1,820	—	—
		60,000	10	10	Do. Pref.	—	*	5	2½	9½	5¼				
6,660	3,518,000	150,000	10	10	Dooars	12½	12½	12½	2½	17½	7	45,000	300	D32,000	—
		75,000	10	10	Do. Pref.	7	7	7	3½	16½	4¼				
3,367	1,811,000	165,000	10	10	Doom Dooma	11¼	10	12½	‡12½	21	6⅛	30,000	4,032	—	10,000
1,377	582,000	61,120	5	5	Eastern Assam	½	nil.	4	—	2½	6⅞	—	1,790	—	10,000
4,038	1,675,000	85,000	10	10	East India and Ceylon		nil.	7	—	8½	7⅞	—	1,710	—	—
		85,000	10	10	Do. Pref.	*	6	6	3	11½	5¼				
7,500	3,363,000	219,000	10	10	Empire of India	—	*	6/10	2½	11½	—	15,000	—	27,000	—
		219,000	20	10	Do. Pref.	—	*	5	2½	10½	4⅞				
1,180	540,000	94,060	10	10	Indian of Cachar	7	3½	3	‡2	3½	5½	6,070	—	7,120	—
3,050	824,000	83,500	5	5	Jhanzie	10	10	10	4	7½	7	14,500	1,070	2,700	—
7,980	3,680,000	250,000	10	10	Jokai	10	10	10	5	17½	5⅞	45,000	990	D9,000	—
		100,000	10	10	Do. Pref.	*	6	6	3	14½	4⅛				
5,924	1,563,000	100,000	20	20	Jorehaut	20	20	20	—	58	6⅞	36,220	2,955	3,000	—
1,547	504,000	65,660	10	8	Lebong	15	15	15	‡12½	16½	6⅞	9,000	2,150	8,630	—
5,082	1,709,000	100,000	10	10	Lungla	*	10	6	3	8½	7	—	1,343	D21,000	—
		100,000	10	10	Do. Pref.	*	6	6	3	11	5⅜				
2,684	885,000	95,970	10	10	Majuli	7	5	5	—	6⅛	7⅞	—	2,606	560	—
1,375	380,000	91,840	1	1	Makum	—	—	*	—	1⅛	1⅞	—	—	1,200	25,000
2,990	770,000	100,000	1	1	Moabund	—	—	*	—	¼	—	—	—	—	—
		50,000	1	1	Do. Pref.	—	—	*	2½	1	5				
1,080	482,000	79,590	10	10	Scottish Assam	7	7	7	—	10½	6¼	6,500	800	9,590	—
4,150	1,456,000	100,000	10	10	Singlo	6	8	5	1	8½	6	—	300	D5,200	—
		80,000	10	10	Do. Pref.	*	6½	6½	3½	13½	5				
					CEYLON COMPANIES.										
7,970	1,743,824§	250,000	100	100	Anglo-Ceylon, & Gen.	—	*	5½	—	65	8½	10,992	1,405	D72,844	166,580
1,836	685,741§	50,000	10	10	Associated Tea	—	*	5	2½	7½	6⅝	—	164	2,478	—
		60,000	10	10	Do. Pref.	—	*	6	3	10½	5¾				
10,390	4,000,000	167,380	10	10	Ceylon Tea Plantations	15	15	15	‡15	25xd	6	84,500	1,516	D30,819	—
		81,080	10	10	Do. Pref.	7	7	7	‡7	16½	4¼				
5,722	1,542,700	55,260	5	3	Ceylon & Oriental Est.	5	8	7	—	[illegible]	7⅜	—	230	D2,047	71,000
		46,000	5	5	Do. Pref.	6	6	6	3	5	6				
2,157	801,629§	111,330	5	5	Dimbula Valley	—	*	10	5	5½	10	—	—	1,733	6,250
		62,607	5	5	Do. Pref.	—	*	6	3	6½	4⅞				
11,496	3,635,000	298,250	5	5	Eastern Prod. & Est.	3	5	6½	‡7	6⅛xd	5½	20,000	11,740	D17,797	102,500
2,193	1,050,000	22,080	10	10	New Dimbula "A"	10	16	16	4	24	7	11,000	2,024	1,150	8,400
		55,710	10	10	Do. "B"	18	16	16	4	22	7¼				
2,572	570,360§	100,000	10	10	Ouvah	6	8	6	2	8	7½	4,000	1,151	D1,255	—
2,630	964,963	200,000	10	10	Nuwara Eliya	—	*	6	‡6	10¼xd	5⅞	—	—	—	30,000
1,720	720,200§	41,000	10	10	Scottish Ceylon	15	15	15	‡10	17	6	7,000	1,252	D3,970	9,000 Pref.
2,450	750,000	39,000	10	6	Standard	12½	15	15	‡15	12½	7½	9,000	800	D14,012	4,000
		17,000	10	10	Do.	12½	15	15	‡15	22xd	7				

Working-Capital Column.—In working-capital column, D stands for *debit*.

* Company formed this year. † Interim dividends are given as actual distribution made. ‡ *Total* div. § Crop 1896.

NOTICES.

The numbers are announced of thirty-four 5 per cent. debentures, amounting to £6,800, of the Land and Mortgage Company of Egypt, Limited, which have been drawn for payment at par on May 16.

The Right Hon. W. Lidderdale has been elected Chairman of the Council of Foreign Bondholders, in place of Sir John Lubbock, Bart., M.P., resigned.

The rate of exchange for payment of the coupons of the Chinese 7 per cent. silver loan, due May 1, has been fixed by the Hong-Kong and Shanghai Banking Corporation at 2s. 6d. per tael.

The United Railways of the Havana and Regla Warehouses, Limited, being about to issue debenture stock certificates in exchange for the scrip certificates, have instructed Messrs. J. Henry Schröder & Co. to inform holders of the 5 per cent. (1890) bonds of the United Railways of the Havana who have not yet converted that they should forthwith, and not later than Friday, May 13, send in their bonds for exchange into the 5 per cent. consolidated irredeemable debenture stock in order to enable arrangements to be made for the issue of interest warrants on July 1.

The numbers are announced of 125 bonds of £100 each of the Imperial Government of Persia 6 per cent. loan, 1892, which have been drawn for payment at par on May 14 at the Imperial Bank of Persia.

The Council of Foreign Bondholders have received advices from the agents of the Paraguay bondholders at Asuncion, remitting the instalment of the debt service, due on April 1, paid by the Government for account of the coupon payable on July 1, 1898.

The London Joint Stock Bank, Limited, announces that branches will shortly be opened at 11, Station-parade, Muswell Hill, and 2, Railway-approach, Lower Edmonton, with which latter will be connected sub-branches at Palmer's Green and Winchmore Hill.

The Commissioners of Inland Revenue have entered into an agreement with the Corporation of Bath for the composition of the stamp duties payable on transfers of £68,432 Corporation of Bath 3 per cent. stock. Transfers executed on or after April 1, 1898, will be exempt.

Messrs. J. S. Morgan & Co. inform holders of the Baltimore and Ohio Railroad Company 6 per cent. sterling mortgage bonds (loan of 1874) that the company having made default in payment of the coupon due 1st inst., they think it necessary that holders should forthwith deposit their bonds with them in order that steps may be taken for the protection of their interests. They have also arranged with Messrs. J. P. Morgan & Co., of New York, to act as committee and depositary of the bondholders under the bondholders' agreement of this date, and to issue their negotiable receipts for the bonds deposited. A copy of the agreement, together with the requisite lists to be filled up on deposit, can be obtained at 22, Old Broad-street, E.C.

Baring Brothers & Co., Limited, are prepared to deliver provisional scrip for the new Argentine Government 4 per cent. bonds to be issued for the conversion of the bonds of the City of Buenos Ayres 6 per cent. loan, 1888, deposited with them up to April 30, and represented by their receipts Nos. 1 to 1,280 inclusive.

Messrs. Glyn, Mills, Currie, & Co., announce that they have received cable advice from the London and River Plate Bank at Monte Video announcing the despatch by mail of a remittance amounting to £7,000 for the service of the Uruguayan 5 per cent. loan of 1896.

Messrs. Brown, Shipley, & Co., notify to the holders of the 5 per cent. first mortgage gold bonds, dated April 1, 1890, of the West Virginia and Pittsburgh Railroad Company that the time for depositing bonds with them is extended to June 1 next.

Dundee Natal Coal and Estates Company, Limited.—This undertaking has been reconstituted, and such shareholders in the former Dundee Coal Company as there are in this country are to send in their certificates to the London office, receiving for their £1 shares, £3 10s. in the new company, payable as to £2 10s. in shares, 10s. in cash, and 10s. in cash or shares. The capital of the old company was £100,000 in £1 shares, of which 92,000 were issued.

The Grand Trunk Railway Company of Canada informs holders of the Hamilton and North-Western 6 per cent. first mortgage bonds that all bonds not exchanged for debenture stock by May 10, under the conditions already advertised, will be paid off in cash at par by the company on and after June 1. Bonds must be deposited at the company's offices three clear days before the date of payment.

Baring Brothers & Co., Limited, publish the numbers of 196 bonds of the City of Buenos Ayres 4½ per cent. loan of 1888 which have been drawn by lot. By the terms of the arrangement made in November, 1892, these bonds are payable at par on June 1, 1903, and continue to bear interest until that date.

Holders of certificates for the old first and consolidated mortgage bonds of the Colorado Midland Railroad Company are reminded that the new securities to be given under the plan of reorganization can now be obtained in exchange for such certificates at the banking house of Messrs. Glyn, Mills, Currie, & Co., 67, Lombard-street, E.C. Certificates must be presented by the holder in person, or by his banker or agents. Securities will not be sent by post.

Shareholders in the Suez Canal Company possessing twenty-five or more shares who are desirous of being present at the general meeting to be held on June 7 next must deposit their shares with Messrs. N. M. Rothschild & Sons before June 1, in exchange for which a card of admission to the meeting will be given in due course.

The numbers are published of twenty-three debentures amounting to £2,300 of the Chicago and North-West Granaries Company, Limited, which have been drawn and will be paid off at 10 per cent. premium on July 1 next.

The new issue of 22,000 deferred ordinary shares of £10 each recently offered to the holders of preferred ordinary stock in Samuel Allsopp & Sons, Limited, has been fully subscribed.

The Secretary of Champagne Frères, Limited, begs to notify that the transfer register of the preference shares will be closed from the 7th to the 14th inst., both dates inclusive, for the payment of the half-yearly dividend.

Mr. Lawrence Rawstorne and Mr. Oliver Ormerod Walker have been elected members of the board of directors of the Lancashire Insurance Company, Manchester.

Printed for the Proprietor by Love & Wyman, Ltd., Great Queen Street, London, W.C.; and Published by Clement Wilson at Norfolk House, Norfolk Street, Strand, London, W.C

The Investors' Review

EDITED BY A. J. WILSON.

Vol. I.—No. 19. New Series. | FRIDAY, MAY 13, 1898. | [Registered as a Newspaper.] | Price 6d. By post, 6½d

Notice to Subscribers.

Complaints are continually reaching us that the INVESTORS' REVIEW cannot be obtained at this and the other railway bookstall, that it does not reach Scotch and Irish cities till Monday, and that it is not delivered in the City till Saturday morning.

We publish on Friday in time for the REVIEW to be at all Metropolitan bookstalls by at latest 4 p.m., and we believe that it is there then, having no doubt that Messrs. W. H. Smith & Son do their best, but they have such a mass of papers to handle every day that a fresh one may well look almost like a personal enemy and be kept in short supply unless the reading public shows unmistakably that it is wanted. A little perseverance, therefore, in asking for the INVESTORS' REVIEW is all that should be required to remedy this defect.

All London newsagents can be in a position to distribute the paper on Friday afternoon if they please, and here also the only remedy is for subscribers to insist upon having it as soon as published. Arrangements have been made that all our direct City subscribers shall have their copies before 4 p.m. on Friday. As for the provinces, we can only say that the paper is delivered to the forwarding agents in ample time to be in every English and Scotch town, and in Dublin and Belfast, likewise, early on Saturday morning. Those despatched by post from this office can be delivered by the first London mail on Saturday in every part of the United Kingdom.

CONTENTS

The Investors' Review.

A Chartered Company for Sale, Price £10,000,000.

They want a deal of explaining, these ten millions of Earl Grey's. Mr. Rhodes made still another effort to elucidate them at the meeting of the Bechuanaland Railway Company on Friday last. And from his words we infer that the Chartered Company, being nearly played out as money distiller from British grubs, is to be offered to the nation "cheap at ten millions." No, Mr. Rhodes says, at least not yet—but take the reporter's summary of his own words :—

In the course of his speech at the recent meeting of the shareholders of the Chartered Company, he stated that the debt of that company was, roughly, about £6,000,000, and that his colleague Lord Grey, had stated it at £10,000,000. There appeared to be a contradiction there, but that was not really so, for this reason. He thought that Lord Grey said that the investments in connection with the country had been £10,000,000. They must remember, although the debt of the Chartered Company was £6,000,000, that that company was a guarantee for their railway for £2,000,000. Then there was the Mashonaland Railway, together with the Beira Railway, which was built without guarantee, and there had been telegraphic expenses and other items which would make up £10,000,000. At the same time the real debt of the country was only £6,000,000, and he thought it was wise to clear up the apparent contradiction. The debt, of course, was the money expended in the country in excess of receipts. Of course, the debenture debt of the country was only £1,200,000. He used the word "debt" in the sense of money spent in the country.

Now, in the first place, Lord Grey did not say that the investments "in connection with" Rhodesia had been

£10,000,000. What at all events he is reported to have said was that "the Chartered Company has found £10,000,000 and upwards for developing Rhodesia." We challenged that statement at the time, and the successive explanations of it have only deepened the mystery. Instead of throwing more light on it last Friday, Mr. Rhodes leaves us in greater bewilderment than ever. Assume that the Mashonaland Railway and Beira Railway ultimately cost between them £3,000,000; add this £3,000,000 to the £2,000,000 guaranteed for the Bechuanaland Railway and still we cannot find the figures of Lord Grey. According to the balance-sheet issued with the last report of the Chartered Company, the actual expenditure on what may be called administrative account left a deficit of £1,145,502 at the end of March, 1897, after all the revenues since the company began operations had been credited against the gross outlay. None of the other items in this balance-sheet can be looked upon as expenditure for the development of the country. Amongst the assets held are £25,000 African Lakes Corporation shares, £314,000 Bechuanaland Railway debentures, £500 De Beers' shares, 9,305 Shashi and Macloutsie Exploration and Mining shares, costing £5,788, £895,327 nominal of shares in a variety of mining companies and stocks, stores, &c. Debtors, including the Bechuanaland Railway Company, which owed £329,418, and sundry minor expenditures on concessions go to make up a total of nearly £7,000,000, in large part promoters' flim-flam. Some of the items ought to be written off against the gross expenditure mentioned by Mr. Rhodes and Earl Grey, and boiling the thing down, exclusive of the cost of the Matabeleland rebellion, we cannot discover that £3,000,000 has genuinely been spent in the "development" of the country. Add £3,000,000 to the extra liberal £5,000,000 arrived at above, and the gross total is only £8,000,000. In reality the outlay to date has been very much less, and does not attain to £10,000,000 even if we clap on £3,000,000 for the Matabeleland rebellion. This last amount, as we have repeatedly insisted, ought not to be charged against the Chartered Company at all; it ought to be paid by Mr. Rhodes and his associates, who made what Mr. Chamberlain is now pleased to describe as the "mistake" of raiding into the Transvaal, or of organising a raid from the consequences of which they bolted.

Turn the matter the other way round and deduct from the share capital the £2,000,000 nominal given to the promoters, out of which they may easily have netted their £12,000,000 to £15,000,000, and we cannot find that the company has had more than £5,000,000, up to the date of the share issue last week, to handle in the shape of debenture money, shares, and share premiums subscribed for by the public. If an additional £5,000,000 had been spent on railway extension, then Lord Grey's £10,000,000 would be about reached, but it has not been the custom hitherto to class the railways as a direct expenditure of the company. By doing that there would have been no necessity for the existence of the separate undertakings by which the lines have been, or are being constructed. Indeed, from the point of view of Chartered shareholders it would have been surely much more to the purpose for the company to have built railways with its own money, so that it might have enjoyed the whole of the wonderful net income expatiated upon by Mr. Rhodes at last Friday's meeting. Why were these Mashonaland and Bechuanaland railway companies created, if the Chartered Company is to include their expenditure among its assets, to be claimed for against the British Government when the day comes to saddle upon us the monstrous waste which has been the characteristic of this undertaking from its inception? Taxpayers will be well advised to keep an eye upon this business. They are going to be made to pay for it, of that they may be quite sure; and one of the aims of the promoters of the Chartered Company is unquestionably to keep well before the public a claim of large magnitude to be one day sprung upon the English people, and rushed through Parliament; a Parliament more or less in the hands of the band.

Just consider the attitude of Mr. Chamberlain in this matter. The weakness of his speech on Friday night would have been deplorable had we not already had abundant evidence that in all that relates to Charterland he is the abject tool of Mr. Rhodes. Although he repudiated any compact with that gentleman in regard to this enormous claim, and denied that the Government had sanctioned a guarantee upon a capital of £2,000,000 to extend the Bechuanaland Railway to the Zambesi, it was perfectly evident from the tone of his observations that he only waited to be asked in order to surrender. Look at the manner in which he endeavoured to draw a parallel between this railway—through a barren tropical country totally unfitted for European occupation, where labour must be performed by blacks, practically slaves, if performed at all—and the Canadian Pacific Railway, running through the icy and half-desert wastes of western Canada. His utterances at this point are so remarkable that we think they ought to be quoted here for purposes of future reference. There can, as a contributor demonstrates on another page, be no analogy whatever between these two undertakings, and we go so far as to say that Mr. Chamberlain could not have discovered his pretended analogy except for one of two reasons. Either he is hand and glove with Mr. Rhodes in a plot to engage British credit in this "wild-cat" Central African enterprise, or he was eager for an opportunity to give a good rousing puff to the Canadian Pacific Railway Company, in which he is understood to be a large shareholder. Neither motive was creditable to him. He is attacking Sir William Harcourt, and, in the course of his harangue, speaks as follows:—

> Then the right hon. gentleman goes on to deal with the railway proposal which has been made by Mr. Rhodes and which is under the consideration of her Majesty's Government. The time has not yet come; we have not had time ourselves to consider this proposal. No doubt it will want a great deal of consideration, and I will not anticipate in any way what our decision upon it may be; but this I will say—that to treat a scheme of this kind, even in its inception, as a wild-cat scheme is characteristic of the right hon. gentleman, but is not justified by our colonial history. (Cheers.)
>
> Sir W. Harcourt.—I spoke of the speech. My remarks were not applied simply to the railway. I spoke of the possession of the whole of Africa as a wild-cat scheme. That is the point.
>
> Mr. Chamberlain.—I did not know that cats could scheme, especially wild cats. (Laughter and cries of "Oh.") Then does the right hon. gentleman think that this scheme is one which her Majesty's Government may fairly consider?
>
> Sir W. Harcourt.—They may consider it.
>
> Mr. Chamberlain.—Yes; but I understood the right hon. gentleman represented it as ridiculous from the first. I ask, Sir, is it one atom more ridiculous, for anything the right hon. gentleman knows, than the original proposal to make the Canadian Pacific Railway? (Cheers.) The Canadian Pacific Railway has made the Dominion of

Canada. (Cheers.) What was it before? Indeed, it was nothing but "our lady of snows." At that time the greatest wheat-producing area in the world was nothing more than a desert of prairie, which not even the Indians themselves had passed over. That has been entirely changed by this great railway carried through by a poor colony under extraordinary circumstances, with the greatest enterprise, and, fortunately, with most absolute success. (Cheers.) If the right hon. gentleman wants my opinion, there is nothing more ridiculous and nothing more improbably successful in the proposal now made by Mr. Rhodes than in the proposal of the Canadian Pacific Railway.

Language of this sort compels us to bow the head and blush with shame. Has Parliament indeed fallen so low as to cheer such words, to treat the man who uttered them as intelligent, honourable—a man to respect? Will it swallow this balderdash—insincere, and politically absolutely dishonest balderdash—and vote the guarantee Rhodes demands? Will it endorse the "preferential trade" absurdity and allow the Charterland potentate to embroil us with other nations should the thing he "governs" ever get so far as to have any trade? Yes, we fear it will do all that and more, for it is a Parliament of cravens and hypocrites over this matter. Because "courtly influence" of the highest is said to be behind Mr. Rhodes, no chosen of the free and enlightened electorate dares to speak a word of the truth, unless it be Mr. Labouchere. Side issues are descanted upon, the core of the subject ignored always. What, for example, could be more hollow than the denunciations of slave labour with which Mr. John Ellis opened the debate last Friday. We do not mean that Mr. Ellis was consciously insincere, but he was conscious that this was a safe aspect of the Rhodesian imposture to wax eloquently wroth upon. But his words were vanity, and he ought to know it. We are founding a black slave empire in South Africa, if founding anything at all. Whites cannot labour with the hand there, on the land or in the mines. The labourer must be black, and black labour, for generations to come, perhaps for ever, will in Africa be more or less forced labour. It is so at the De Beers Mine, in the Witwatersrand, among the Boers. Preach and snivel as we may, the fact cannot be gainsaid. A black slave empire! How does that consort with British ideas of freedom? Shall we be eager to buy it up when the group who founded it have—like the two Dukes who have pocketed their share of the "profits" and scuttled off—ceased to care for it because it yields no more plunder?

Our Foreign Trade in April.

Last month the value of our imports rose to £40,246,716, being an increase of £5,110,161 or 14½ per cent. on the figures for the corresponding month in 1897. This is the largest increase yet recorded, much larger than that of the three preceding months of the year put together. Indeed, the total increase for the four months is only £6,552,842, or 4·2 per cent., the total being £159,317,623, against £152,764,781. This would be all right if exports were developing at a corresponding speed, but that is not the case. On the contrary, exports decreased £2,204,111 last month, compared with the corresponding month, or 11·1 per cent., the total having fallen to £17,496,011, against £19,700,122 a year ago. Here again the decline was larger last month than in the whole of the preceding three months taken together, for the total shrinkage, including that of April, is now no more than £3,795,180, or 4·8 per cent. In other words, we sent out goods last month to the value of £75,203,129 as against £78,998,309 in April, 1897. Nor does the decline stop here. Our exports of foreign and colonial merchandise fell off last month by £1,168,928, the total being only £6,139,253. This decline wipes out the previous improvement, and leaves the four months with a decrease of £708,132. As a consequence of this increasing divergence between the two sides of our trading account, the current balance against us has risen from £41,808,315 at the end of April, 1897, to £62,864,469 at the end of last month, a difference the wrong way of £21,056,154.

Before inquiring into the causes of this unfortunate change it may be well to point out its serious effect upon our money market. We cannot flatter ourselves that the great swelling out of our imports is due to the increased profitableness of our investments abroad, for that is not the case. These investments are rather decreasing in value, or, at any rate, there is good reason to believe that they are declining in amount. It may be, indeed, that we are taking payment in goods for some securities, American railroad and other, which we have been exporting of late, but on this point it is impossible to obtain statistics. We shall, therefore, be more prudent in regarding the large gap of nearly £63,000,000 now visible between the value of our imports and that of our exports as a debt which is to be paid in money. Some portion of it must certainly be so paid, unless the balance is redressed soon. Therefore the reasonable presumption is that we shall see drafts made upon our slender stock of gold at no distant date. Already, from one cause and another, these drafts have been very material. Last month we imported gold to the value of £5,072,794, but our exports in the same time amounted to £5,948,806, and since the year began we have imported only £1,532,001 more than we have exported; that is to say, out of £14,331,635 received, £12,799,624 has gone abroad again. These figures are much larger than those for the same period of time in either of the two previous years, and show that if the supply of precious metal is large, the demand also has increased to a very significant extent. The large supply that comes from the mines, at any rate, is in a manner capital returning home, which we are employing as revenue with which to pay our current debts. It may be all right for some time, if this large supply keeps up, but should it not do so, and it has been recently an artificially forced supply to some extent, then a very serious position lies ahead for our money market. We shall have to encounter a heavy export of gold with no adequate set off against it either in the value of goods exported or in fresh supplies of the metal.

Leaving this subject, which will be continually cropping up as the weeks pass, let us now look a little into the causes at work to produce the present somewhat alarming state of our foreign trade. Naturally, one ascribes the heavy increase in import values to the rise in the price of wheat and other cereals, and it partly is so, but not wholly. There has been no increase in the quantity of wheat imported this year up to the end of April; on the contrary, it is smaller than for the same period in either 1897 or 1896, and wheat-flour has not risen in quantity to a compensating extent. Neither have prices as yet much affected values, although it is true that on all kinds of grain, except maize, the total values to date are rather heavier than those of a year ago. On wheat alone the increase on the month has been £716,000, and on the four months £732,000. The full effect of dearer grain, in short, has yet to be felt, and this coming effect makes the present statistical position of our trade all the more significant in the way of a warning. If a slight increase in prices has produced an increase of £2,500,000 in the value of articles of food and drink imported duty free in April, what may we not expect in May, June, and July?

The two largest increases which go towards producing an augmentation of £2,306,194 in the value of raw materials for textile manufactures imported are raw wool and cotton. Wool has risen upwards of £1,340,000 in the month, and cotton about £950,000. It is quite possible that this may be a transitory increase, since for the four months both cotton and wool will show a shortcoming in value, and wool a shortcoming also in quantity compared with a year ago. We need not, therefore, insist upon this excess in one month's figures as a point of danger. In other respects, imports jog on much as usual, with no great swelling out in any total. We wish the same could be said about the decline in exports, but this is decidedly more unsatisfactory from many points of view. Looking through the detailed tables presented by the Board of Trade, it is rare indeed for us to come across a progressive increase in the value of any leading article of British manufacture exported. We are still losing trade with France, Italy, Dutch India, China, Central America, Chile, the Argentine Republic, British West and South Africa, and the foreign West Indies in cotton goods exported. But for the larger shipments to British India our trade in this class of goods would be in a bad way. Even the United States, great as the falling off there has been, shows up better than some of these countries. The position is not quite so bad with linen yarn and linen tissues, but we cannot pronounce the trade in these, or in the similar productions of jute, as in any sure degree progressive; although exports of jute yarn this year considerably surpassed those for the first four months of 1896. Still more unsatisfactory is our woollen trade. In woollen tissues the past three years have exhibited progressive declines on our exports to Germany, Holland, the Argentine Republic, and, of course, the United States, with which our trade in woollen and worsted fabrics is almost ruined by the tariff. There is no progress either with our own dependencies, whether in South Africa, India, Australasia, or North America. Canada has indeed this year taken more worsted tissues from us than in either of the two previous years for the same period of time, but there is a progressive decrease in our exports to Australia and to South Africa. Nor do China and Japan give us any consolation or any European country, except perhaps Belgium, where the export of worsted goods is larger than usual. Germany, Holland, France, Spain, and Italy all take less from us now than they did last year or the year before. Our exports of carpets are non-progressive, and there is little that can be called encouraging in our heavier commerce in iron, copper, or the manufactures thereof. Steel has indeed gone up, but although the total exports of iron and steel, in whole or in part manufactured, are about £400,000 higher in value than for the same time in 1896, they are £527,000 below those for the first four months of 1897. Altogether, the prospect is not particularly cheerful, and unless a change for the better soon ensues, the country has trying times ahead of it—times not at all in harmony with the extravagant scale of national expenditure now fashionable—thanks to the way the nation is dominated by militarism, and misled through a Parliament which inspires anything but respect among thoughtful citizens.

Dear Bread and Revolution.

Is the great boom in wheat checked? There is a lull undoubtedly in the upward rush of prices; but it might perhaps be rash yet to conclude that this lull will be lasting. But it exists, and we cannot help thinking it probable that—barring some unexpected sign that the war is to be more prolonged and desperate than there is any indication of at present—the lull will continue, and that we may soon see at least a slight turn downward in prices. It should not be forgotten that this is not the first lull that has occurred in the feverish speculative excitement in the wheat market so largely caused by the war. For days before the French Government announced the suspension of the import duties on cereals, English markets had been very quiet. In many the price had gone down—not much, but still down—and the tendency seemed likely to continue, when the French suspensory notice afforded a pretext to speculators to send prices bounding up again. No doubt French wheat supplies had run down considerably, and the suspension of the cereal duties was a great inducement to send France as much wheat as she would take. She took a good deal, and is still taking; but in ordinary times the effect of this upon our markets would hardly have been appreciable. It was the war excitement, and the anxiety of speculators to revive the upward movement that supplied the lever that has been forcing up prices during the last eight or ten days. We are somewhat sanguine, then, that this second lull having come upon us, it will not be disturbed so soon as the last, if at all. There is nothing in the war prospects at present that can afford a pretext. Speculators seem to have exhausted themselves—perhaps they are a little frightened. There has been a "slump" in Liverpool, another in New York, and one in Chicago. Our "visible supply" of wheat is only about a million quarters less than it was this time last year, certainly not sufficient to justify such a rise as has recently occurred in wheat. The shipments to Europe have been steadily increasing during the last three weeks; while from India we last week received 195,000 quarters, against 79,000 in the previous week. These supplies from India are the more notable, in that last year at this time we were receiving none at all from that country. There never has been any suggestion that our wheat supplies would give out before the new harvest was gathered in—and it promises to be an excellent one. Our ordinary supplies this year have, no doubt, been sufficiently shrunken to have justified a moderate rise in price, though certainly nothing like the upward rush that has been caused by a skilful use of the war scare by speculators and "corner" men. Although for one brief mad moment the price of wheat in New York touched 190 cents per bushel, equivalent to 63s. per quarter, the highest price at which business has been done in English markets was 57s., and that deal was small and exceptional; 55s. has been occasionally asked, but very rarely conceded. Indeed, the top figure for business dealings may be stated at 50s. to 52s., and at that buyers have only purchased enough for their immediate wants, so confident were they of an early return to lower prices.

Whatever may be the upshot of this pause in the speculative fever, the dearness of bread caused by the really unnatural rise in the price of wheat has brought about a crisis in Italy which is very serious and may be disastrous. It is about three months since the bread riots broke out there, and compelled the Government to suspend until May 1 the duties on cereals. Before May arrived, however, the war had given another turn to the screw, wheat went further up in price, and bread in proportion. The rioting was renewed, and the suspension of the cereal duties had not only to be continued, but the Government had in many cases to supply money to provide food for the famishing rioters. For a time these disturbances, though annoying, were not regarded as formidable, because it was evident the rioters were not organised. It was the cry of the hungry; temporary supplies of bread might have satisfied them, and stopped the fighting. But within a week the aspect of affairs has changed. The Government have no longer to deal with mere bread rioters, but with organised and armed revolutionists. A state of siege has been proclaimed in four of the leading cities. Officially, we are assured that quiet has been restored, and that work in the factories has been resumed. But no confidence is placed in such assurances. The independent news channels are stopped up by the official censor. Parliament is only to be allowed to sit for a fortnight's session. Perhaps this decision was prudent. It will certainly be a relief to the Government, who must have been overwhelmed by interpellations, and might have been overturned in the scrimmage of wordy Parliamentary warfare. But the decision must also be taken as the Ministerial measure of the extreme gravity of the situation. To take, so to say, a whole nation by the throat in this way is, to say the least of it, perilous, and may rather encourage than repress revolution.

To many of us this condition of affairs in Italy is no surprise. Close observers have seen the crisis coming for years. About four years ago, as readers of the INVESTORS' REVIEW may remember, we wrote:—"To save the country and give it a chance to recuperate, a powerful Ministry should reduce the cost of the naval and military services to about one-fourth of its present amount, suspend for ten years all debt amortisation, and pay for a like period only 3 per cent. on the whole of the public debt. . . . . Far better take a manly course of this kind and give the inhabitants of the country contentment, than go forward, with the risk of complete bankruptcy and perhaps revolution ahead." But there was no such powerful Minister then, nor is there one now. The revolution is no longer "ahead." Italy appears to be in the midst of it. There is no way out of it but retrenchment and consequent relief to the taxpayers, freedom and encouragement of trade and industry, and a steady regard for the social welfare of the people, instead of that blasting anxiety to pose as a Great Power which has almost brought ruin to Italy. What has the Triple Alliance done for Italy? Why should she cling to it? She cannot afford such luxuries until she has set her business house in order. But where is the Minister to be found powerful and sagacious enough to initiate and carry out such a programme as is essential for the salvation of Italy—one that must also include negotiations with the Vatican for the settlement of the differences with the Church, at present a ruthless enemy to Italian progress? Such a Minister may, perhaps, yet be found in Italy, but he is not known. Her "statesmen," so far as we know anything of them, are merely rather commonplace officials, ready, like the Marquis di Rudini, to obey the orders of political cliques, but incapable of initiating or carrying out a strong policy. This it is which makes the Italian outlook so black at present.

Spain also has been suffering by the boom in wheat. Bread riots have been very numerous there, but of course, the existing misery has been terribly intensified by the hopeless war into which the Government have been rushed to a considerable extent because of their weak dread of popular indignation if they adhered too tenaciously to a peaceful policy. But the root troubles in Spain are very similar to those of Italy—reckless expenditure and constant borrowing, with a crippled, unhealthy, and declining trade to support it. Spain has very great natural resources, but apparently a hopeless incapacity for making the most of them. She, too, wants strong administrators, with some business capacity, and a turn for the useful rather than the merely ornamental. But the tendency to revolution seems ingrained in the population. They have had a remarkably prolonged time of quiet; but at present they seem waiting for a new revolutionary outburst. It is in the air, visible in the quick-gathering clouds: it may break out at any hour. That it will break out soon there is no doubt; what or who may be thrown to the surface in the *débâcle* is not so clear.

Matabele Gold Reefs.

Now that Rhodesia is supposed to have been quieted and the hardy pioneers in that wonderful area are able to do as they like, the market is paying more attention to the Matabele Gold Reefs group. Although we have no great faith in the gold-bearing character of the reefs of Matabeleland, we are bound to admit that the shareholders in the Matabele Gold Reefs and Estates Company will have a fair run for their money. Formed in October, 1894, with the moderate capital of £112,000, of which only £30,000 was "considered as paid," the company took over 488 gold reef claims and thirty-six farms, aggregating about 221,550 acres, and since then it has acquired a variety of rights, town stands, coal areas, and other concessions, which acquisitions have only caused the capital to be increased to £115,500. The company has not yet paid a dividend owing to the grievous condition of affairs in Matabeleland, but it has floated three subsidiary companies within the last three years: the Matabele Mines, the Geelong Gold, and the West Nicholson. It is an amusing characteristic of the company-creating mind that each of these three companies, which were to work only small sections of the property, had a larger capital than its parent, the amount "considered as paid" in the last named being the mere bagatelle of £170,000. The group who operate the property were not content with subsidiary mines, but they opened their hands widely, and floated in 1895 two companies, the Rhodesia Goldfields and the Rhodesia Concessions. The first named was to invest in shares, and has an issued capital of £100,000 in preferred, and £255,000 in ordinary shares, dividends being paid for about a year on the preferred shares, and then ceasing. The Rhodesia Concessions was to acquire lands and claims, and a small matter of land and mineral grants covering 600 square miles north of the Zambesi was actually acquired. An expedition was sent out, but apparently nothing much more has been done. In the same year—the group was very busy that year—the Rhodesia Agency, Limited, was formed to take over from Messrs. Partridge and Weston Jarvis the agencies of their companies, and to act generally as milking maid to the richly endowed creations of those two gentlemen, who seem to have been the soul and marrow of the affair. For this agreeable purpose a capital of £192,000 was considered necessary, of which £100,000 was presented to the vendors. Through this Rhodesia Agency a complete union was made with the Willoughby's Consols, a group that had been working slightly apart from the Matabele Gold Reefs coterie. Willoughby's Consols owed its inception to Sir John Willoughby, one of the leaders to defeat at Krugersdorp, who kindly transferred concessions obtained by him to two joint-stock affairs—the Willoughby's Mashonaland Expedition Syndicate and the Mashonaland Development Company, and then arranged to amalgamate these concerns into the Willoughby's Consolidated Company with a bloated capital of £713,960, of which £508,500 was "considered as paid." We fail to find any dividend distributed by this company, but it floated two subsidiary concerns—the Matabele Central Estates and the Buluwayo Waterworks. The Matabele Central Estates was strong in land and cattle (it was not explained how the cattle were obtained) and needless to say nothing is heard about its doings. The Buluwayo Waterworks has been building its works, so that little more than the spending of money has been accomplished. In addition, the group took a share with outsiders in the Bembesi District Gold Claims and White's Consolidated, so that the full list of the companies in the group is as follows :—

——	Date of Registration.	Capital issued.	Capital considered as paid.
		£	£
Matabele Gold Reefs ...	30 Oct. 1894	115,500	30,000
Willoughby's Consolidated	12 Dec. "	713,960	508,500
Rhodesia Goldfields... ...	1 Jan. 1895	355,000	—
Rhodesia Concessions ...	1 Mar. "	150,000	100,000
Buluwayo Waterworks ...	3 April "	92,138	62,500
Matabele Central Estates ...	4 April "	100,000	70,000
Bembesi Dist. Gold Claims	29 Aug. "	49,841	13,500
Rhodesia Agency	12 Sept. "	192,000	100,000
Matabele Mines	19 Dec. "	180,000	80,000
White's Consolidated ...	26 June 1896	325,000	275,000
Geelong Gold Mine... ...	29 Jan. 1897	130,000	115,000
West Nicholson Company...	— April 1898	210,000	170,000
		2,609,939	1,524,500

A great fuss is made in the market about the prospects of the subsidiary concerns of the Matabele Gold Reefs; but we must confess that the manner in which they have been capitalised does not lead one to expect very much from them. The Matabele Mines had certainly £100,000 of working capital, but that was more than two years ago, and in the hands of the military men who form the larger number of this group, such an amount cannot be expected to last long. The Geelong Company only seems to have had a working capital of £15,000, while the recently floated West Nicholson Company was endowed with £40,000 for its own purposes. These companies have at the same time to bear the weight of heavy masses of paper capital created in the happy company-promoter's style, and unless the mines prove wonderfully productive they are likely to break down from over-capitalisation. To further handicap the unfortunate concerns they have, we presume, to pay for the attentions of the Rhodesia Agency and Rhodesia Goldfields concerns, whose services would not be lightly valued. Whilst there is a narrow market in them, the shares of these subsidiary concerns are kept at high premiums, but then the hard practical test of regular crushings has not been applied to them, and until that is done, any one who is supplied by the public with the requisite funds can do what he likes with the quotation for a mine.

Although a military group as a whole, the delicate London operations of the coterie seem to be a good deal in the hands of two civilians—Messrs. H. Partridge and A. Weston Jarvis. One or other of these two gentlemen appears upon the Board of each of the companies, and the Rhodesia Agency, which acts as London secretary for the lot, bought up the business of Messrs. Partridge and Weston Jarvis. The members of the group are as follows :—

MR. H. PARTRIDGE, Director of the Matabele Gold Reefs, Matabele Mines, Geelong Gold Mining Company, Rhodesia Agency, Rhodesia Goldfields, Bembesi District Gold Claims, Rhodesia Concessions, Willoughby's Consols, West Nicholson, and White's Consolidated.

MR. A. WESTON JARVIS, Director of the Rhodesia Agency, Buluwayo Waterworks, Willoughby's Consols, and Matabele Central Estates.

COLONEL THE HON. C. G. GATHORNE HARDY, Director of the Matabele Mines, Geelong Gold Mining, Matabele Gold Reefs, Rhodesia Goldfields, Bembesi District Gold Claims, West Nicholson, and Buluwayo Waterworks.

MAJOR S. WYNNE FINCH, Director of the Rhodesia Agency, Rhodesia Goldfields, Bembesi District Gold Claims, Buluwayo Waterworks, Willoughby's Consols, and White's Consols.

SIR JOHN C. WILLOUGHBY, Director of the Rhodesia Goldfields, Buluwayo Waterworks, Matabele Central Estates, White's Consols, and Willoughby's Consols.

MAJOR W. T. E. FOSBERY, Director of the Rhodesia Agency, Rhodesia Concessions, and Matabele Central Estates.

LORD HARRIS, Director of the Matabele Mines and Rhodesia Agency.

MAJOR MAURICE HEANY, Director of the Matabele Gold Reefs, Matabele Mines, Geelong Gold Mining, Rhodesia Goldfields, and West Nicholson.

MR. F. C. SELOUS, Director of the Matabele Gold Reefs, Geelong Gold Mining, and Rhodesia Goldfields.

MR. J. J. HAMILTON, Director of the Matabele Gold Reefs, Geelong Gold Mining, West Nicholson, and Willoughby's Consols.

At the last meeting of the Matabele Gold Reefs Company, the burden of the chairman's speech was the number of fresh companies to be floated this year; at least eight were mentioned. But ordinary men of business would be inclined to wait and see how the dozen already floated in the years 1894 to 1898 got on before adding to the list. Only one of the collection seems to have paid a dividend in that time, and that one was the stock-jobbing concern, which probably grasped a profit in the last Rhodesian "boom." That was the time when Chartereds went up to nearly 10; but let us hope the public will not suffer from such another fit of frenzy, and if that is avoided, the Matabele Gold Reefs group may be asked to show more practical proofs of the riches of their properties than it has hitherto done before money is again given to it to play with.

A Wild-Cat Scheme.

The House of Commons appears to be losing its powers of criticism in respect of geographical and commercial questions. Sir William Harcourt declared the idea of a railway from Cairo to Capetown to be "a wild-cat scheme." Mr. Chamberlain sought to answer him by drawing a parallel between the proposed line and the Canadian Pacific Railway. A more fallacious parallel it would be impossible to imagine; yet no member of the House of Commons made any effort to expose the folly of Mr. Chamberlain's argument.

What is the position of the Canadian Pacific Railway? To begin with, it lies entirely within British territory. It starts, as one may say, from a British port on the east coast of North America, and terminates at a British port on the west coast of North America. It lies throughout in almost the same latitude. It traverses throughout a country which, though cold in the winter months, is perfectly adapted for a population of European origin. From a strategical point of view, it is invaluable, forming as it does a sort of "covered way" between the resources of the east and the west. From a commercial point of view, it is even more invaluable, seeing that the only sea-routes from Nova Scotia to British Columbia are round Cape Horn, or through the Arctic Sea, the former impracticable by reason of its distance, the latter by reason of its interruption by ice. In these conditions is to be found the justification for the trans-continental railway in Canada. There are other trans-continental railways which are similarly justified; for example, the Russian line through Siberia and the trans-continental lines in the United States.

Thus the proposition is perfectly tenable that trans-continental railways are often justifiable, and are capable of being of immense service, both commercially and strategically. But to assert that because certain trans-continental railways are justifiable all trans-continental railways are justifiable is to assert an absurdity. Let us suppose the state of things in Canada to be different. Let us suppose that the greater part of the route from the Atlantic to the Pacific lay through a tropical and unproductive country. Let us suppose that at various points along this route the line touched on the territory of foreign Powers. Let us suppose that the central States of the American Union did not exist, and that they were replaced by an open sea, from the edge of which railway lines from two to three hundred miles in length could be carried to all the points which the Canadian Pacific line now traverses. Under such conditions as those, would any one have regarded a trans-continental line as a sane and reasonable project? Would any one travel by it who could accomplish the journey from the Atlantic to the Pacific in a first-class mail steamer? Would any one send goods along it who could send them by sea? Would any one make use of even half its length who could reach the same point by, say, a voyage of a thousand miles by sea and carriage over three hundred miles by rail? Strategically, moreover, such a line would be more of a danger and anxiety than anything else. To what interruptions might it not be subject! What diplomatic difficulties might it not create!

All this, and much worse than this, it is proposed to do in respect of the line from Capetown to Cairo. It is spoken of in some quarters as a "grand idea." Well, it is a big idea, certainly; but then megalomaniacs have also big ideas—ideas which do not find acceptance because they are obviously insane. This idea of a Capetown to Cairo railway ought, in spite of Mr. Chamberlain's patronage and approval, to be recognised as insane. In order to arrive at this conclusion it is only necessary to consider a few figures.

Regard the line in the first place as a through line from Europe to South Africa. Who would be such a fool as to travel by it, or to forward merchandise by it? At an inside estimate the distance could not be less than 5,000 miles. If you convey goods at the absurdly low rate of a penny per ton per mile, the freight from Cairo would be at least £20 per ton, not including the cost of getting the goods on to the railway first. Well, you can land goods in Capetown from England by steamer for between 50s. and 60s. per ton, and probably in less time than would be occupied in forwarding the same goods, first of all to Cairo, and thence from Cairo to Capetown. The problem would be very little altered if you made Johannesburg your terminus instead of Capetown. Beyond this, unless you are going to raise a diplomatic hurricane by charging considerably more for Continental manufactures than for British, you will be putting an advantage into the hands of your mercantile competitors. At the present time, German manufactures for Africa start from Hamburg, and have to be carried past British shipping ports. How would the case stand if they could be shipped to the northern terminus of your trans-African railway from Trieste, or even Salonika? As regards passengers, what sane person would be willing to exchange a voyage from Southampton to Capetown in a 10,000-ton steamer for a ten or eleven days' roasting in a railway carriage from Port Said to Table Bay? There would be little, if any, gain in point of time; for, even at the best, the journey to Port Said from London would occupy some five days, whereas the newer class of mail steamers now reach Capetown in sixteen days.

Then consider the Capetown-Cairo line in connection with the trade of the interior districts through which it is to pass. At no point will it fail to be in competition with some very much shorter route from the seaboard. Take, first of all, the Soudan. You have a more or less navigable Nile which you are going to make more navigable. You have, moreover, the prospect of a railway from Suakin to Berber even if the Nile below Berber were to fail you. As for the lakes of Central Africa, there is already a railway under construction from Mombasa, and it is much more than likely that the Germans will build a line towards the interior from Dar-es-Salem. Coming further south, the Zambesi is navigable considerably above the point where it is to be crossed by the trans-continental line. The whole of Rhodesia will be supplied from Beira the moment Mr. Rhodes allows the Beira line to be completed. No one ought to know all this better than Mr. Rhodes. Mr. Rhodes, however, is singularly ignorant of all figures that do not square with any job he has on hand. To show the extent to which railways are handicapped wherever there is even partial competition by sea, reference need only be made to what happens at this day in the Cape Colony. From Capetown to Kimberley direct by rail is 647 miles; yet Kimberley merchants prefer to have goods from Capetown sent by sea to Port Elizabeth (450 miles) and thence by rail to Kimberley (484 miles), a total of 934 miles against 647. Even the sixty odd miles difference between the routes to Johannesburg from Port Elizabeth and from East London gives a most decided advantage to the latter port.

From a diplomatic and strategical point of view, the proposed trans-continental line presents most formidable difficulties and disadvantages. The northern terminus of the line in Egypt can never be regarded as safely defensible, having regard to complications that may any day occur through the action of France or Russia, or both. The line itself would be, in fact, a source of weakness to the Empire, requiring the protection of a naval and military force which might well be wanted elsewhere. Beyond this there would always be the possibility of German interruption in the centre of Africa. Some day or other the hold which Great Britain has on the Mediterranean will undergo diminution, and that diminution will come about all the sooner if Great Britain follows the absorptive policy indicated by the proposal for an African trans-continental railway. As for the reports of coal mines on the Zambesi, if they are there they might doubtless be useful for supplying coal to steamers on the Zambesi. But does any reasonable person really suppose that such coal could ever be economically available for export, or that, in respect of South African consumption, it could for an instant compete with known coal mines in the Transvaal and Natal?

In the face of all these facts, a question might well be asked as to the reason for pressing such a proposal on the attention of the nation. The object would seem to be to give to the adventure of an unsuccessful and semi-bankrupt joint-stock company the dignity of a vast and important national enterprise. The Chartered Company evidently desires—this is plain from Mr. Rhodes's speech at the Cannon-street meeting—to be bought out on as advantageous terms as possible; and, with the present balance of parties in the House of Commons, this object can best be secured by extolling and magnifying the greatness and the Imperial importance of the company's achievements and of the gentleman who, as the *Daily News* took care to impress upon us the other day, "*is* the Company." It all comes to this, then—that grave national responsibilities are to be undertaken, national expenditure incurred, national risks encountered, for the sole benefit of Mr. Rhodes, whose previous performances have violated international law, compromised the reputation and honour of the country, and stirred up, in a not unimportant province of the British Empire, enmities and irritations which it will require years to get rid of.

F. Reginald Statham.

Economic and Financial Notes and Correspondence.

The French Elections.

The final opinion about these cannot yet be given, as a large number of second ballots must take place on Sunday week. So far, however, as they have gone returns indicate a serious check to the Méline administration. We cannot call it a defeat just yet, but it is in some respects worse than that, because M. Méline and his Cabinet will have in the new Chamber an uncertain and much weakened majority—no majority at all, in fact, unless the "rallied" Monarchists and Bonapartists habitually vote with M. Méline's avowed supporters. The Radical Republicans and Socialists have increased their numbers at the expense of the Moderate and Progressive Republicans, and what the new Chamber promises to show us is an accentuation of that chaos of parties which made the last Chamber such a futile one. Out of the electoral contest, in short, no party has arisen strong enough to lay hold of power and to carry out a definite programme, be it socialist, monarchical, or honestly republican. Hence what we must expect is a period of wrangling and weakness, where ministries will come and go, combinations form and dissolve, with even greater rapidity than we have been accustomed to see them do in France. Needless to say, weakness, legislative impotence, absence of definiteness of policy in any direction, may prove most disastrous for France. What she requires at the present is a strong and enlightened Government, emancipated from parochial conceptions of statecraft, and delivered from servitude to class interests and factions—a Government able to take the direction of the country's affairs in a bold manner, and capable of lifting them out of the rut where they now crawl. There is no hope of any such arising out of the class of men returned to the new Chamber, and what we should dread is that the civil powers will grow weaker and weaker in the near future, until a dangerous militarism arises to seize power on the pretext of putting down social disorder.

Greek Finance.

Now that the guaranteed Greek loan has been launched in London, Paris, and St. Petersburg, Greek finance will possess fresh interest to investors. The report of Major Law, who has been appointed British delegate to the new Commission of Control, will therefore be read with interest. It has just been issued as a Parliamentary paper, and forms a very careful study of Greek resources. The sum of it is that from now down to 1901, deficits may be looked for under the new arrangement, that for the current year being 10,929,186 drachmi. In 1901 the tide turns, and a slight surplus is estimated to accrue, rising in the succeeding year to 3,647,818 drachmi. This, however, falls to 2,360,120 in 1903, owing to the increase in the amount required to meet the charges undertaken by the Commission of Control. The ordinary expenditure of Greece has to be kept down under 65,000,000 drachmi, except in the current year, when, for various reasons, it will amount to 65,501,326 drachmi. Debt charges will amount on the old loans to 14,218,750 drachmi, the exchange being taken at 1·60 drachmi per franc. This is exclusive, apparently, of 1,440,000 drachmi per annum required by the 1833 loan, which is also guaranteed by France, England, and Russia; and in 1903 the total will rise for the old gold debt to 1,462,530 drachmi as a result of the increase in the sinking fund from 1 per cent. to 2 per cent. Any recovery in the rate of exchange, raising the value of the Greek coin, will take effect in an increase of the amount devoted to debt redemption. From 1900 onwards a minimum annual sum of 2,000,000 drachmi will be devoted to the withdrawal of the forced currency. The accumulated deficit of this and the next two years, amounting to over 17,000,000 drachmi, will be covered by appropriations from the new loan, £800,000 of which is held in reserve for this purpose. There has been no Budget for the past year owing to the war, and 1898, therefore, embraces really twenty-two months, so that the large deficit on that period is not likely to cause serious inconvenience to the Treasury until the beginning of next year, when some money from the guaranteed loan will be employed in filling the gap. By 1903 it is expected that there will be a surplus of about 5,000,000 drachmi even after providing for the supplementary charges, for which the International Commission undertakes no direct responsibilities. The gross revenue for the current year is estimated at 85,556,500 drachmi, and it is calculated that by 1903 the total will have risen to 100,266,500 drachmi. We have no doubt whatever that Greek finance will improve under the new *régime*, and shall be disappointed if the results are not better than this forecast. Of course, much will depend on the recovery of Thessaly from the effects of the late war and the Turkish occupation. But it is a fertile country and possesses an industrious people; and if the farmers are not taxed too severely or robbed, and they certainly will not be robbed under the rule of the Commission, the future promises well.

THE STANDARD OIL COMPANY.

Mr. George Rice, of the Ohio Standard Oil Company, has sent us several publications dealing with the *néfaste* aspect of American commerce presented by the history of this company and the Standard Oil Trust. We dealt fully with the subject in an article last year, founded upon Mr. Demarest Lloyd's book "Wealth and Commonwealth," and need only now mention the fact that Mr. Rice was therein cited as one of the most courageous, indomitable, and unwearied opponents of the abominable combination between railway officials and the Oil Trust group to crush out all opposition and to fill their own pockets. Those interested in this question will find some very valuable documents quoted in the principal pamphlet before us, and at the end of that pamphlet there is a statement showing that the Standard Oil Company in the twenty-five years of its existence has made profits to the extent of $1,000,000,000. Supposing this true, how much did the presidents, vice-presidents, directors, and other officials of the railways in league with this company absorb as theft pure and simple in the same time? Was it another $1,000,000,000, or twice as much? Some enormous amount it certainly was, and a few months ago, Mr. Lloyd wrote to us from Chicago to point out that if English bondholders who have been defrauded by this league were to combine, and bring actions for restitution against these thieves, some of whom rank as amongst the most honoured, as they are the most wealthy, of American citizens, large sums of money might be disgorged. We did not publish that suggestion at the time, because we did not believe a combination of the kind possible, nor that American law courts could be trusted to render speedy judgment in favour of the defrauded railway proprietors in this country or in America. But if the money is there, and if it is recoverable from these men, or their heirs, let the American stock and bond holders themselves commence the fight. People here might then be encouraged to join. Meanwhile, all we can do is to note the fact that this system of robbery and extortion continues to the present hour, that no law, not even the Inter-State Commerce Law, has proved effective to break it down. There are, to-day, railroad presidents in the United States in receipt of large revenues drawn out of the rebates given to the Standard Oil Trust and denied to its rivals. "Exclusive dealing," in short, and fraudulent combination between traders and carriers are as rife to-day in the American Union as ever. Consequently, we have no faith in the lower grades of securities issued by any American railroad. They may seem to afford substantial guarantee of solvency one year and the next prove bankrupt. Only the very best class of bonds are things to be permanently invested in.

THE GAS LIGHT AND COKE COMPANY.

An elaborate reply has been issued by the board of this company to the strictures made upon its policy by Mr. George Livesey, of the South Metropolitan Company, at the recent half-yearly meeting of shareholders. To a considerable extent it is an effective reply, because Mr. Livesey has so many inconsistencies, and has advocated such a variety of views at different periods in his long career that he affords easy game. When the discussion, however, is brought to the point we do not think that it can be very encouraging to Gas Light and Coke stockholders. There is in the directors' reply a sort of undercurrent of admission that things are not going well with the company, and the inference we should draw is, that dividends must decrease rather than increase in the near future. There is no getting over the fact that the company has had to raise the price of gas, after depleting large reserves accumulated out of past profits in a manner which, as we have already pointed out, can hardly be looked upon as fair to the consumer. To raise the price of gas at the very time when electric light competition is, by the directors' own admission, depriving them of a large amount of business, is to decidedly weaken the company's power of effective competition. Nor is there any getting over the further fact that the company is overloaded with capital. We are quite willing to admit that Mr. Livesey does not seem to have been fair in his handling of the capital account. It remains true, none the less, that the expenditure upon new appliances to meet the extension of business has of late years been very heavy, and that the company has now upon it a load of capital amounting to something like £12,000,000, the market value of which is about double this sum. There is no danger, of course, that the company will fall within any measurable period of time into such a position as the London Docks, for instance, now occupy; but there does seem to be a danger that its affairs will slip from bad to worse unless most energetic measures are taken to arrest the decay, and an advance in the price of gas at the present time is decidedly not amongst these measures. Stockholders should come together and appoint a competent committee to look into their affairs while there is yet time.

THE "BROTHERTON GROUP" OF FRAUDS.

It seems to us that the Registrar in Bankruptcy could have come to no other decision than he did in refusing to allow Mr. J. D. Linton and Mr. A. C. L. Fuller their expenses in connection with the inquiry now adjourned. Both these gentlemen were probably innocent of any thought of fraud, but they allowed men intent upon committing fraud, and very gross fraud too, to use them as their tools. That being the case, they cannot complain if now made to suffer pecuniary loss. One consolation should at least be theirs. The fate they now suffer makes them a warning to similarly endowed gentlemen to avoid the toils of the company promoter. Nothing looks easier than to carry on the occupation of a director. It is nice to seem to handle large sums of capital, to execute "contracts," to declare "dividends," and all that sort of thing, but danger lurks beneath the surface often, and the simple-minded man, who is as innocent of a knowledge of business often as of the Chinese language, comes into the City some morning to discover that knaves have used his name to cloak their stealing. A good many more lessons of the kind now taught to these two gentlemen will, we fear, be required before the class from which they come learns effectually the meaning of the monkey, cat, and chestnuts fable. Why has no warrant been applied for and issued against Messrs. Brotherton and Van Ee?

THE CITY OF LONDON ELECTRIC LIGHTING COMPANY AND ITS CALLS.

Dilatory individuals who will not pay their calls must often be a burden to a company secretary, but, at the same time, such official ought to be slow to threaten punitive measures. The secretary of the City of London Electric Lighting Company, however, has been insisting upon the payment of an extravagant penalty for the lapse of memory of certain of his shareholders.

Last November this company issued 10,000 ordinary £10 shares, at a premium of £8 per share, a considerable proportion of which was paid up on allotment, and the first "call" for the balance fell due in March. The usual custom in such cases is to issue a notice of "call" to those who hold the provisional certificates, although such certificates bear upon them the date of said call. Apparently, this was not done in this case, and the first reminder an unfortunate shareholder who had forgotten to pay up received from the company was the following letter :—

City of London Electric Lighting Company,
May 3, 1898.

Issue of 10,000 Ordinary Shares (November, 1897).

DEAR SIR,—I notice that, according to the returns of our bankers, you have not paid the instalment of £6 per share due on the 30th ultimo on your holding of four shares of the above issue. I have to request that the instalment be paid forthwith, together with interest at the rate of 10 per cent. per annum thereon, calculated from the 30th ultimo up to the date of actual payment by you. This payment of interest is necessary as the dividend commenced to accrue on the instalment as from the 30th ultimo, and, as you will remember, the rate of dividend paid last year on the ordinary shares of the company was at the rate of 10 per cent. per annum.—Yours faithfully, (Signed) J. CECIL BULL,
Manager and Secretary.

For a gentleman who professes to be so exact as Mr. Bull, it is remarkable that two important errors should appear in the above letter. The first is that the 30th ultimo would mean April 30, and interest would therefore accrue for only three days. That, however, is a mere clerical blunder, for March 30 was evidently meant. The assumption that the shareholder will receive 10 per cent. upon his money is, however, radically wrong, for as the £10 shares were issued at £8 premium, the yield of a 10 per cent. dividend upon such a payment would only be a little over 5½ per cent. The shareholder, therefore, will presumably receive this yield upon his money, and why should he be asked to pay 10 per cent. upon his call?

As a matter of fact, the laggard shareholder at once tendered the amount called and interest at 5 per cent. on the amount for thirty-five days, but his cheque was rejected, and two days' further interest demanded at the exorbitant rate of 10 per cent. Such cavalier treatment savours of thoughtless insolence, and is, at least, unnecessarily irritating to shareholders who are prone to look upon the secretary as a servant of their company, not its master. Mere courtesy demanded that some premonitory warning should have, in this instance, been issued as to the danger of neglecting a "call," and without having done this, to ask for 10 per cent. interest upon a share that will presumably yield under 6 per cent. is neither politic nor fair.

THE BRINSMEAD SWINDLE.

On Saturday last, at the Old Bailey, Mr. Justice Phillimore dealt out to those who were responsible for this gross fraud well-deserved punishment, varying from five years' penal servitude to six months' hard labour. A sum of no less than £40,000 had been obtained from the public by the accused. Early in 1896 the business of Thomas Edward Brinsmead & Sons had been turned into a company with a capital of £8,000, but after the existence of about a month was wound up voluntarily. The affairs then came into the hands of the present gentlemen, who arranged to bring out a company with a capital of £100,000. £5 was to be the magnificent remuneration of the vendor, who was a clerk of no means whatever, but who signed the necessary documents. He was to allow the new company to acquire his valuable rights for £76,650, which as a matter of fact was to go straight into the pockets of the Consolidated Contracts Corporation, alias Messrs. Ainsworth & Bernard, the promoters. As we have stated above, the public were only fleeced of some £40,000. This worthy vendor, by the way, had guaranteed 8 per cent. to investors in the concern for several years. Another clerk was the purchaser on behalf of the company, and received the like remuneration of £5. We entirely endorse the remarks of the learned judge that this was a fraud of the most gross and monstrous kind. That the public should be ready to subscribe to such concerns as these is wonderful in the extreme, but we are afraid that as long as gullible persons are to be found ready to advance money on such flimsy pretexts, so long will frauds of this kind be committed.

IDLE FADS AND FOOLISH FADDISTS.

The wheat boom has set all sorts of Protectionist hobbyists to work; but especially has it given energy to the good but unreflecting people who try to work on public anxiety by picturing the starving condition of England in case of her being at war, unless we at once set up national granaries for the storage of wheat. These gentlemen have themselves chosen a committee, sent witnesses before it to be examined, and now they have published the report of these unbiassed investigators. Of course they are, with a marvellous unanimity, in favour of these national granaries. They think we ought to have at least 8,000,000 quarters of wheat stored up, and strictly preserved for use in war time. If there were any difficulty about its keeping, portions could be sold off and the stock renewed, say, every three years. In other words, the State would become a huge dealer in grain, and a constant source of disturbance in markets, with a perpetual tendency to increase the price to ordinary consumers. But this, of course, is the real object of this movement. It would be as pleasant to the faddists as a duty on imports. Then, what about the expense? We already pay some seventy millions a year in "war insurance" on our army and navy. But if we set up these granaries, the initial cost would be at least £20,000,000, with a steady and not easily calculable yearly drain thereafter. And there would be endless appeals to sell the stored grain at a cheap rate, or to appropriate it for nothing in case of distress arising anywhere in the country. In short, it would be an infallible measure for keeping up the price of wheat at a cost to the taxpayers of perhaps two or three millions a year, with a tolerable certainty that the stores would be depleted, or out of condition, when war broke out. If we cannot depend on our navy to guard our grain ships in war, what is the use of it?

THE TELEPHONE INQUIRY.

We are not surprised that Sir James Fergusson withdrew his name from the list of the House of Commons Committee to inquire into the administration of the National Telephone Company as soon as he saw it. What does surprise us is that he, a director of the company, should have allowed his name to appear on the list at all. His excuse is that he was urged to do so by several members of the Government. It would be interesting to know who these Ministers were, and what their reasons could be for making so extraordinary a suggestion. The inquiry has been ordered by the Government itself. It is to be held because of the bad service rendered to the public by the company and because of their obstinate refusal to permit of any improvement in that service. The suggestion that Sir James Fergusson should occupy a seat on the committee was thus a suggestion that he should "inquire and report" to the House of Commons upon his own conduct. What were the motives which prompted those particular Ministers to press Sir James to occupy such an anomalous position even against his own inclination? If the Government generally approved of the nomination, it suggests grave suspicion about the whole inquiry.

This Telephone Company, which probably has not a single friend among the commercial men who are perforce its main support, seems to have an inexplicable fascination for politicians and ex-Ministers, as well apparently as actual Ministers. Sir Henry Fowler's election as a director of it was announced about the same time as the Committee of Inquiry was being nominated. Did Sir Henry take office in the interests of the public or of the company? We all know that he is an honourable man, and that he most scrupulously avoids recording his vote in a matter affecting any concern with which he is connected. That is as it ought to be so far as it goes; but is it a judicious step on the part of one of the "great, wise, and eminent" occupants of the Front Opposition Bench to join the directorate of a company whose administration of its affairs has been so unsatisfactory that strongly expressed public opinion has forced the Government and the House of Commons to institute an investigation into its ways? Is Sir Henry Fowler hopeful of improving the administration or of organising a better telephone service for the public? If so, we can only applaud his courage and pray for his success. But a more prudent man and eminent politician would have deferred acceptance of such a directorship until he had seen what might come of the Parliamentary inquiry.

GREAT NORTHERN TELEGRAPH COMPANY.

In dealing with the preliminary figures of the year's working of this company, we noted that the sum received for interest had fallen markedly. A study of the full report discloses that this falling off was a mere matter of account, the board having preferred to carry the interest on investments belonging to the reserve and renewal fund directly to that fund, instead of bringing it into the revenue account. This policy is decidedly the better one, and ought to be pursued by all companies with a large invested reserve. It is stated that in the course of a twelvemonth the whole debt of the company will be extinguished, but it is not clear how this will be effected. The revenue of the company has kept up well, in spite of the reduced rates that followed the decisions of the Buda Pesth Conference; but, of course, events in China have helped the cable traffic. The company advocates strongly a cable being laid to Iceland, for which it has obtained an annual subvention of £5,000 per annum for twenty years from Denmark, but this is not sufficient, and the company has approached the Governments of Great Britain, France, and Russia, with a view to obtaining a veiled subvention from each in the shape of a fixed yearly payment for the transmission of meteorological telegrams. The proposal is ingenious, but a high price cannot be paid for such information.

LAGUNAS NITRATES.

After a lapse of some months we have the judgment in the action brought by the Lagunas Nitrate Company against the Lagunas Syndicate and the executors of the late Colonel North and Maurice Jewell, which to all intents and purposes amounts to a defeat of the plaintiffs. True that Mr. Justice Romer has held that the company is entitled to such damages as they have suffered by the maquina not being ready between June and December, 1894, and by the defects in the water supply up to that time, but that will prove poor consolation to the company, who will have to bear the general costs of the action, which, if rumour speaks correctly, amount to some £30,000.

The action was brought by the company for rescission of the contract of purchase from the syndicate on the ground of misrepresentation in the prospectus, and for damages for breach of contract. Fraud, however, was not alleged against any of the defendants, but it was alleged that they had not shown good faith. The distinction seems to us a very fine one. What in fact the plaintiffs said was, "You have not acted in good faith, and we don't charge bad faith." The present judgment entirely exonerates the defendants from any imputation of want of good faith, and the learned judge has found that they at the time believed, and had reasonable grounds for believing, that the company was acquiring the property at a reasonable price. He has further found that although on June 30, 1894, the property did not in every respect answer to the statements in the prospectus, yet all the defects were remedied by December in that year, and at that time the company had such a property as they bargained for. Any loss that the company may have suffered during that time the defendants are to make good.

Such is the result of the action, which lasted for sixteen days, and it will not be amiss to refer shortly to the circumstances out of which it arose. Colonel North had, prior to 1889, purchased some 4,000 acres in Chili, and in that year sold it to the syndicate for £700 in cash and £109,300 in shares. In 1894 the plaintiff company was formed, and a contract was entered into with the syndicate for purchase at the price of £850,000, which contract it was now sought to set aside. This purchase price was to be paid £300,000 in cash and the balance in shares, which consideration was actually handed over, but it should be mentioned that the vendor syndicate had expended some £360,000 in cash on the property. These facts clearly show how the actual value of speculative properties such as these can rise and fall; but the company having discovered that nitrates are by no means such trumps as they expected, have sought to go back on their arrangement of 1894. It should be further added that the company have continued to work the nitrate right down to the present time, notwithstanding the disputes, and that, too, not only when the syndicate directors were the company directors, but even since they obtained an independent board, and this has been on a commercial scale for the dividend purposes of the company, and not merely to keep the factory open as a going concern. This was amply borne out by the fact that in April, 1897, the directors declared an interim dividend of 4 per cent., the payment of which was only stayed on the suggestion that it might prejudice the action. This being so, without a doubt we think that Mr. Justice Romer came to a right conclusion. The company have certainly, as facts have turned out, not got a good bargain, but in speculations of a kind such as this those who enter on them must expect to take some risk.

THE PARDY GROUP OF MINES.

"A Mining Prospector" in Massi Kessi, South-East Africa, writes to us, under date March 31, to make some statements in regard to these properties which we think it well to lay before shareholders and the public. He deems it remarkable that before passing the amalgamation scheme the shareholders did not send a trustworthy expert to give them a true report upon the properties and upon the work done, to see whether the things bought were really worth the money given or to be given for them. Further, he challenges Mr. Pardy's statement that the Guy Faux reef had been traced through the properties on the range. This, he says, is a mistake, although it is true that drives have been put in in most of the properties, some very nearly through the boundary, and others from three to six hundred feet in length. The reef, however, he asserts has not been cut in any one of them. What they have got of this reef in the Guy Faux property itself is very good, but how far the reef extends to the other properties is a point not yet proved, and its presence in them seems to be doubted on the spot. There are good reefs in that locality, the writer goes on to say, and three have been cut, carrying payable gold three miles north-west of the Guy Faux mine, but these are not yet proved to be in what he calls "Pardy's Ground." The writer also questions the statements made at the shareholders' meeting by the chairman in regard to future expectations, now that the new battery has been erected. The mine, he alleges, has been badly worked and cut about to try to get rich stone, and he doubts whether sufficient of such stone can be found to supply the new battery, at any rate under the present condition of the mine. He further questions the estimate put forward as to the value of the tailings, and does not think Mr. Pardy justified in putting it at £20,000. These are the principal points in this letter, and they deserve to be considered.

AN AMENDE TO THE INDIAN FRONTIER ARMY.

On February 4 last, a stinging paragraph appeared among our notes attacking the humanity of British officers in India, and roundly asserting that they had let the troops fire on women and children in bed at night. The charge was founded on a telegram to the *Times*, published some weeks before, describing how a village had been fired on at night after its inhabitants had come back from the hills. It made no mention of "women and children." We put these there in our ignorance of the frontier people and their habits of life. Naturally, the accusation of cruelty such as this caused indignation, and brought forth evidence that we were wrong. Some of this evidence we now lay before our readers in extracts from a letter from the front written by an officer in command of one of the regiments. It is a very interesting letter, and throws much light on the spirit animating the men who do the fighting. In printing it, we have to apologise and express regret that we should have cast so ugly an imputation upon a service whose traditions have ever been honourable and humane—so far as the business of making war can be humane. Readers may be assured that had we not believed our army to be degenerating and growing savage in these hateful frontier scrimmages, we never should have written as we did. This officer, writing as follows, takes occasion, in rebuking us, to give a most interesting outline of the nature of these frontier operations :—

The case of the Investors' Review is an instance of one of the defects of the telegraph as a channel for information. In the first place, there were no women or children anywhere near the Khyber at the time the paragraph you quote was printed. All true frontier tribes remove their women, children, cattle, and property to some place of safety before troops can arrive, and as they have sentries on the tops of their hills always watching our movements, and a system of beacon signals at night, they are rarely, if ever, surprised. There have been instances (not in this compaign) of our surprising villages when we suddenly crossed the border to punish raids—but in these cases the villagers, if they refuse to surrender, are given time to remove their women and children before the village is fired at. The Afridis of the Khyber had removed their women and children into Afghan territory, to Ningrahar and Jellalabad, long before our troops appeared on the scene, and only three or four weeks ago the Zakka-Khels petitioned that they might be allowed to bring back their families to the Khyber, as they were suffering from the cold and damp of the low-lying ground about Jellalabad. Permission was given, although the Zakkas had not complied with our terms.

No soldiers or camp followers are allowed near Afridi villages where there are women, and this order is very strictly enforced.

An Afridi village is not what Europeans picture to themselves, a collection of smiling cottages, each with its little garden. It is a collection of ten or twelve mud houses, windowless and chimneyless. The backs of the houses form a continuous wall, some 12 ft. or 15 ft. high, and in a corner of the centre is a very strongly built tower, some 30 ft. or 40 ft. high, crenellated, and with machicoulis, embrasures, &c.

The entrance to these towers is a small door 15 ft. from the ground, and you ascend by a small ladder, which is drawn up and the door closed. In large villages every fifteen houses have their tower, because not only are there constant feuds between villages, but between sections of villages, and men are constantly besieged in their towers for weeks together. Provisions are drawn up by a rope, and if a head shows itself it is immediately potted at from the hostile tower. After a time, both sides call a truce for a certain period.

Not many lives are lost in this game as a rule, but now the Afridis have got such good rifles, either they will wipe themselves out or they will get sick of the reign of disorder, and invite the Government to take their country.

The game the Afridis played in the Khyber was similar to that they played in Tirah Maidan, where the camp was surrounded by these little hamlets. The young bloods come down at night, and with their Sniders, Lee-Metfords, and Martinis, shoot into the camp from the towers. Until all these towers were destroyed there was no peace or safety in camp.

No one who has not experienced it himself can realise guerilla warfare in a country like this.

The hillmen in their sandals get about their hills like goats, and from behind good cover shoot into the mass of troops and baggage which have to move along the beds of the ravines. To crown the heights with troops moving parallel to the column is impossible, as the hills are too broken and precipitous. You must send small parties to occupy points on each side while the baggage column passes through. As these parties descend the precipitous hills to join the rear guard, they are followed up by the agile enemy. Ghurkas and frontier troops are best at this work, in which they have practice.

Britishers are helpless bullocks on such hills as these. . . As for the miserable wives of the hillmen whom Mr. Wilson speaks of—may he never fall into their hands: where mutilations occur, the men are generally incited to it by women.

Yet another officer of still higher rank comes down on us and raises a point which was implied perhaps, but certainly not brought directly forward in our unhappy paragraph. His defence of war is vigorous, and it would be our own, if wars must come: the more ruthless and cruel they are, as war, the sooner will they end. But the sternness and cruelty should be in the open fighting, between army and army, not by armed men on the defenceless and weaponless. We do not agree with this writer as to the origin of the recent trans-frontier troubles, but that is not now the question. The question is, did the Army and its leaders pass beyond the bounds of fair warfare in dealing with the hillmen the Civil Government of India had sent them to "punish." On the testimony before us we must frankly admit that so far as women and children went, it did not, and these extracts satisfy us that, given the nature of the war to be waged, the cruelty exhibited towards non-combatants was probably in most cases unavoidable. But let the reader clearly understand that if this exonerates the officers and men in the campaign, as we gladly admit it does, it is in no sense a justification of the Afridi War. The guilt of that, however, lies elsewhere. This second officer says :—

I assume the telegraphic information given as the basis of the comments to be accurate, and I justify it. We are at war with the tribes; it was provoked by them, not by us; the terms which we have declared we will impose are essentially moderate; they are not cruel. The tribes must be brought to submit to them; the sterner the pressure the shorter the agony, and in the end less cruel. . . . If they take refuge in inaccessible hills and snipe our troops and raid our convoys, the only pressure we can bring upon them is by denying them the use of their houses and farms in the cultivated valleys till they submit; . . . but to say that we ought to let them occupy their villages because it is cruel to shell them is about as reasonable as to say that we ought to shoot with blank cartridge from pity at the ghastly wounds our dum-dum bullets cause in the enemy.

War is cruel, and we ought to impose the minimum of cruelty necessary to secure its ends. Mr. Wilson's false assumption is that to deny the use of the lower villages to the tribesmen and their wives and children is not a necessary means of bringing the requisite pressure on the tribes. No one doubts the cruelty of the means any more than one doubts the cruelty of the wounds caused by our shells and bullets.

To justify Mr. Wilson it is necessary to prove, not only the cruelty, but the uselessness of the measure from a military point of view. This he does not attempt to do.

The Fight for the Central Pacific.

We hope shareholders who have not yet done so will lose no time in joining this committee, and in helping it to rescue the property :—

To the Editor.

Sir,—I am instructed to inform you that the Right Hon. Sir William Marriott has joined the Central Pacific Shareholders' Protection Committee.—Yours faithfully,

W. C. Gunner, Secretary.

124, Chancery-lane, Room No. 12,
May 12, 1898.

Drucker v. Hooley.

We must say that we entirely agree with the verdict in this case. The charges made against Mr. Hooley, which in substance and fact amounted to fraud, were unsupported by a tittle of evidence. Doubtless, Mr. Hooley got the best of the bargain with Drucker, but it seems absurd that when, in a business transaction, one person gets the better of another, the one who has the worst of the deal shonld turn round and impute all kinds of *mala fides* to the other without evidence to support the imputation. Both these gentlemen are not unknown in the world of finance. Mr. Drucker admitted he was not a novice, and that he wanted to get rid of these shares. Mr. Hooley simply made the best bargain he could. That was the view of the jury, and we suppose that is the view of all sensible men.

The United Railways of Havana.

We are not responsible for the wording of the notice referred to in the following letter. It did not reach us as an advertisement, but as one of those notices which come to us in shoals through advertising agents for gratuitous insertion. Some effort is made to weed or condense them, but they are not otherwise interfered with, if printed at all. None the less do we regret it, should this particular notice have misled anybody :—

To the Editor.

DEAR SIR,—I beg to draw your attention to an advertisement appearing among the notices on page 664 of the last issue of your REVIEW, in which 1890 bondholders of the United Railways of Havana are informed that they should forthwith send in their bonds for exchange into irredeemable debenture stock. You are probably acquainted with the circumstances of the late issue of irredeemable debenture stock, and the option given to 1890 bondholders to come into the scheme; and you will probably agree with me in thinking that this advertisement is designed, and I am afraid intentionally designed, to create the impression that the conversion is now obligatory. A word of warning from you would prevent the bondholders from being misled. There appears to me to be something very wrong in the form of the present advertisement.—Yours, &c., E. S. C.

THE WEST AFRICAN TROUBLE.

It was just as well that Mr. Davitt orced on a discussion in the House of Commons on the West African trouble. It has relieved the tension and anxiety felt in this country at the prospect of another "little war" in a quarter of doubtful national value, though of undoubtedly pestilential climate. All accounts agreed in describing the situation as serious, and the crisis as critical. Mr. Chamberlain thinks the newspaper reports exaggerated. We hope so. But the most assuring statement he made was that the rainy season, which has almost arrived, will render a fighting campaign impossible for the next four months. This will give time for reflection; and as a special commissioner is to be sent to the disaffected districts to investigate the matters in dispute, it is probable that no future campaign will be required. The special commissioner, not having a personal interest in enforcing the hut tax, may be able to discover a different way of raising the necessary revenue without hurting the *amour-propre* of the Governor, who seemed to consider that the prestige of Great Britain was bound up in enforcing this hut tax of his—at least until a sufficient number of the natives had been killed to coerce the living remainder into submission.

THE WORLD'S OUTPUT OF COAL.

It is a pity that the interesting figures just issued by the Board of Trade in reference to the world's coal supply only come down to 1896; but there seem official difficulties in the way, and we must be content with what we can get. One of the first things that strikes us in perusing these pages is that, though Great Britain still heads the list by a long way, both as producer and exporter, the United States is advancing upon her with accelerated strides, and must by and bye take the lead in her turn. The production in Great Britain increased from 164 million tons in 1883 to 195 millions in 1896, or an increase of about thirty million tons. The United States, however, advanced from 103 millions in 1883 to 171 millions in 1896, which is an increase of about sixty-eight millions. The German output increased from fifty-six to eighty-six millions, or about the same increment as in Great Britain. France, however, only rose from twenty-one to twenty-nine millions, and Belgium from eighteen to twenty-one millions. Although much the heaviest consumer of her coal per head, England, as compared with other countries, seems an almost reckless exporter, as if she were hurrying to get to the end of her reserve of coal. In 1896, for example, she exported forty-five million tons, while Germany limps slowly after with a modest six millions, Belgium being next with four millions, while the United States—like a giant reserving his strength—sends abroad a trifling two and a half millions, precisely the same amount as New South Wales, and half a million more than Japan, whose total production in 1895 was 4,849,000 tons. It should be noted, however, that Canada imports from the United States about half the quantity of coals she consumes. Her own output is now 3,750,000 tons a year, not quite up to New South Wales, which stands at the top of our colonial production with four million tons. But though the amount is yet small, the coal output in the colonies of Victoria, Queensland, and Tasmania is slowly increasing. Even in the Cape and Natal it is steadily advancing, while in India and Canada it has about trebled since 1883. So the bases of the world's coal supply are extending. Every country where the mineral can be found is beginning to bring up at least enough to satisfy its local wants. As Japan's own demand is yet comparatively small, it has entered upon exportation with characteristic energy. Italy is the heaviest importer, taking 90 per cent. of her supply from the United Kingdom; Sweden takes 87 per cent.; Spain 48 per cent.; and Russia, 15.

LORD SALISBURY AT THE COUNTRY BANKERS' DINNER.

He did not raise their spirits on Wednesday night; on the contrary, his utterances were decidedly more gloom-producing than those in the Primrose speech, and seemed to point to a belief on his part that the business of expanding the Empire was in danger of being carried too far. The nation, he said, might be in danger of suffering as bankers suffer when they trade beyond their capital. It is a pity the speech was not reported in full: it would have been such a nice cold douche to the jingoes, and might have helped to check the wild spirit of aggrandisement, at all or any cost, now so fashionable. As it is, bankers, after hearing what his Lordship said, are less disposed than ever to lend money cheap.

Critical Index to New Investments.

LONDON COUNTY BILLS.

Tenders will be received at the Bank of England on Tuesday next for London County bills to the amount of £500,000. They will be dated May 21, and will be payable at six months after date. Payment in full must be made by the 21st inst. This is not a favourable time for the Council to have to borrow, and the discount may be a little higher than usual.

GREEK GUARANTEED 2½ PER CENT. GOLD LOAN OF 1898.

The total amount is £6,800,000, of which £5,004,900 was offered in third parts in London, Paris, and St. Petersburg. Price of issue 100½, 20 per cent. on application, similar instalments on May 24, June 8, and July 5, and 20½ per cent. on August 5. A coupon for six months' interest is payable October 1 next, and a discount of 1½ per cent. per annum is allowed on payments in advance, so that the net price would work out but a shade over par. Scrip issued in any of the three countries may be exchanged for bonds in that, or in either of the other countries, which should facilitate early dealings. The bonds, both principal and interest, will be payable in gold, free of all taxation by the Hellenic Government, and coupons will be payable April 1 and October 1 in pounds sterling, at 25 francs per £, or at roubles 9·375 per £. The loan is guaranteed by the Governments of France, Great Britain, and Russia, and, according to the terms of the convention, the Bank of England and the Russian Banks agreed to take in equal shares £3,333,333 6s. 8d., and they undertook that the same should be subscribed at the price fixed. The Banks of England and Russia and the French banks get a commission of ½ per cent. on the amounts received for their guarantee and services, and an annual commission of ⅛ per cent. on the coupons and drawn bonds paid by them. The amortisation of the loan will be effected by the International Commission of Control, either by drawings at par, commencing in January, 1903, or, if the price is below par, by purchases. These are the essential particulars. From the public point of view the loan has little attraction; it is dear, but it is a trustee investment and should be good for the post-office. Owing to high exchanges and to the prices fixed in the various capitals, it was more profitable to subscribe in Paris and St. Petersburg than in London, and the London portion of the loan was not taken by the general investor, although well covered. Subscriptions were sent to Paris and St. Petersburg because, as Mr. Gibson Bowles stated in his question to Sir M. Hicks Beach on Tuesday, there was a saving in the price of 1 1/16 per cent. in Paris and of 1¼ per cent. in St. Petersburg by doing so. In the end the loan will probably all come to London, as neither France nor Russia can afford to lend at 2½ per cent.

FINE COTTON SPINNERS AND DOUBLERS' ASSOCIATION, LIMITED.

This combination, of which Sir W. H. Houldsworth, Bart., is chairman, is formed to amalgamate thirty-one firms and companies, the factories and mills acquired being upwards of sixty in number. No endeavour to create a monopoly is contemplated, it is said, but the centralisation is expected to lead to considerable economy. Share capital, £2,000,000 in ordinary and £2,000,000 in 5 per cent. cumulative preference shares of £1 each, with first mortgage 4 per cent. debenture stock to the amount of £2,000,000, redeemable after September, 1918, at par, or before then at 10 premium on six months' notice. Two-thirds of each class of capital is issued at par, and of this one-third, with £2,794,250 in cash, goes to make up the purchase price of £4,127,584, of which £774,779 is for stocks and the remainder for the properties. No valuations are supplied, the basis upon which the undertakings have been united being that of profit-earning capacity, computed on a three years' average. Even on the best showing of the accountants, the profits for the last three years, which give an average of £234,337, would only leave 8½ per cent. for the ordinary shares now issued. We are not much impressed with the prospects. The vendors take 66 per cent. of the purchase money in cash, and the absence of valuations is not fair to the public. But the capital has been subscribed, for there are some excellent businesses in the bunch, and with economy the thing may pay.

LEE-METFORD SMALL ARMS AND AMMUNITION COMPANY, LIMITED.

To arms! to arms! ye brave. Hurry up, for Mr. E. T. Hooley has something to sell—fifty-seven patent rights and applications for patents for various rifles, &c. The Lee-Metford patents have from four to five years to run, and those covering the rifles of the new types have on an average a life of from ten to twelve years. The capital is £350,000 in £1 shares—all offered for subscription it will be noticed—and there is an issue of £50,000 4½ per cent. debentures, redeemable after ten years at 110. Mr. Hooley acts as middleman between the Lee Arms Company of America, and the British Magazine Rifle Company, Limited, on the one part, and the present company on the other, and sells the patent rights to the latter for £250,000. The new company also buys from Mr. Hooley works in Birmingham and machinery therein. These were recently purchased for £45,000 in cash, and now the company gives £50,000 for them, payable in the debentures now issued. Very short life the principal patents, did you say? May soon be replaced by a new invention. Quite so; that is why the public are to buy them at this high figure. I don't see any statement about valuations or profits made in the past. My dear sir, you seem to forget this is a Hooley prospectus. Confidence, confidence, sir; if you have not that you are useless for such promotions. But did not Mr. Loraine Fuller give some interesting and straightforward evidence about this rifle before the Registrar in Bankruptcy the other day? Was not the main patent offered to the public for less money a year or so ago?

MANCHESTER LINERS, LIMITED.

This is another of Sir Christopher Furness's projects, which are becoming numerous. Its object is, in the first instance, to run three cargo-carrying steamers between Manchester and Montreal in the summer, and between Manchester and St. John, New Brunswick, in the winter. The share capital is £1,000,000 in £10 shares, half ordinary and half 5 per cent. cumulative preference, and the present issue consists of 17,500 shares of each class. Sir Christopher is to be chairman, and he and his friends will, if necessary, apply for 15,000 of the ordinary shares now issued, or will take a portion of that amount in preference shares if all the ordinary are applied for. A contract has been entered into between Furness, Withy, & Co., Sir Christopher Furness, and the present company, giving option of purchasing three steamers, now being built, for £90,000 each, and Furness, Withy, & Co., of which Sir Christopher is chairman, are to have a commission of 2½ per cent. on the purchase price for services rendered. Moreover, so long as Sir Christopher is chairman of "Manchester Liners," Furness, Withy, & Co. are to prepare plans, &c., and to superintend the construction of new steamers which may be ordered, at a commission of 2½ per cent. on the purchase price, as well as the same commission for valuing and surveying any steamers purchased by the company. We do not see why the new company should be saddled with this arrangement; in fact, we do not at all like this system of linking together various interests in which Sir Christopher is a sharer. But apart from this we should doubt whether the line will get sufficient business to make it a success.

UNITED GRAIN ELEVATORS, LIMITED.

With a capital of £100,000 in £1 shares, 60,000 being ordinary and the remainder 5½ per cent. cumulative preference, this Liverpool promotion is formed to take over as a going concern three businesses, two of which were only started last year, one as recently as October. Profits of two of them for one year and of the other for six months are given at £8,616, after allowing £8,602 for depreciation. There is now offered for subscription 30,000 ordinary and 26,667 preference shares and £20,000 4½ per cent. debentures, all to be had at par. The latter can be redeemed at 105 on six months' notice. Elevators and barges are valued at £62,841, and land and machinery at £4,833, while the purchase price is £100,000, including £71,667 in cash, so that the vendors should get the best of the deal. But if more than ordinary doubts are felt about the debenture interest, the Liverpool Mortgage Insurance Company will ensure the due payment of principal and interest of the debentures at a premium of ½ per cent. We never thought much of Liverpool promotions.

THE SPIRAL GLOBE, LIMITED.

This company is formed to purchase the British, foreign, and colonial patents and rights of Messrs. Dunlap & Quain for their spiral glass cover for electric incandescent lamps. The invention is simple, and consists of a spiral glass rod, having lens-like qualities, and of about one-eighth of an inch in diameter, closely coiled round the bulb of an electric incandescent lamp, the chief advantage claimed being that it more than doubles the effective light emitted, and therefore insures a corresponding economy in the consumption of electric current. Whatever prospect the company had, however, is spoiled by over-capitalisation, the capital being £150,000 in £1 shares, of which one-half is now issued, and the purchase price is as much as £65,000, of which £40,000 is to be cash. In addition, the company has to pay the vendor a further sum of £25,000 in cash on the sale of the foreign patents. Some vendors never know how to ask enough.

Company Reports and Balance-Sheets.

⁂ *The Editor will be much obliged to the Secretaries of Joint Stock Companies if they would kindly forward copies of Reports and Balance-Sheets direct to the Office of* The Investors' Review, *Norfolk House, Norfolk-street, W.C., so as to insure prompt notice in these columns.*

Lankapara Tea Company.—The crop of 643,125 lb. fell 37,000 lb. below the estimate, and the average price of 7½d. per lb. was ⅛d. per lb. below that of 1896, while the higher exchange increased the working charges. The accounts, however, were helped by a rather large sale of tea seed, but this is not a reliable sort of revenue. After meeting charges of all kinds the profit was £4,294, or £944 less than 1896, which must be considered good in view of the unfavourable character of the year. With the sum of £799 brought in, the available total is £5,094, of which £4,000 will be distributed in a dividend of 8 per cent., and £1,084 used to write off the cost of new grants, machinery, and permanent buildings. We are glad to see the property written down to this extent, for it is still highly capitalised, but the trading balances are not in favour of the company, and in all probability the money for a portion of the dividend had to be borrowed, for no less than £10,451 was due to creditors and on "bills payable," while cash only represented £252, and the crop came to £11,283, of which the dividend represented £4,000.

Chardwar Tea Company.—Owing to bad management the working of this company last year was unprofitable. The crop of 179,684 lb. was 56,316 below the estimate, and the price realised per lb. was less. With a revenue of £7,774, expenditure came to £7,974, so the deficit on working the season was £200. The balance of £1,276 was brought forward, and out of this the preference dividend of 6 per cent., requiring £300, was paid, leaving £976 to be carried to the new year. The capitalisation appears to be moderate, but the cost of production is high, that for this year being estimated at $8\frac{7}{16}$d. per lb.

Compagnie Générale des Asphaltes de France.—The profit of this company last year amounted to £9,243, and, including £12,493 brought forward, there was an available total of £21,736. Preference interest absorbed £2,600, and 7s. per £6 share, or about 7 per cent., was distributed in dividends upon the ordinary shares, leaving £12,536 to be carried forward. The profit and loss account is very meagre, so that one cannot tell how the item of depreciation is dealt with year by year. In the balance-sheet, however, there appears £25,120, which has been written off altogether from buildings, plant, machinery, and mines. The total amount standing to the credit of that account is £78,862, of which £33,000 is represented by freehold property and buildings. There is, however, an item of £60,000 for French shares, which we presume represents the concession and mines, and it would be interesting to learn if these shares require to be written down in any way.

SANTA RITA NITRATE COMPANY.—After meeting debenture interest and administrative charges, the net profit of this company last year was £3,996. The sum of £3,865 was absorbed by redemption of mortgage debentures, and although £7,690 was brought forward, the board prudently refrained from paying a dividend, carrying the balance of £7,822 forward. They promise, however, an interim dividend later on, as they have made profitable sales for the current year. The debentures are now reduced to £31,500, but the liquid balances of the company are brought very low, and it would be imprudent to expect much in the way of dividends, especially as the prospects of an agreement amongst the producers are not bright.

TRUST AND AGENCY COMPANY OF AUSTRALASIA.—The profit of £91,913 earned last year was £148 less than in 1896, and in order to provide for a special loss of £7,712 on realisation of a mortgage, £7,500 had to be taken from the reserve. After administrative charges and taxes had been met the net balance was £80,090. Of this £43,750 was absorbed by preference dividend, £18,570 by interest on ordinary capital paid in advance, and the remainder permitted of 20 per cent. in dividends being paid on the ordinary shares and £269 was carried forward. The debentures were reduced in the year by about £10,000 to a total of £382,352, and their amount, compared to the mass of £1,357,870, represented by paid-up share capital, is almost insignificant. The company, however, has felt the burden of the depression in Australia, and it is fortunate that the board were so prudent in the past. As it is, the reserve tends to diminish, and the 20 per cent. dividends (they used to be 22½ per cent.), become more difficult. Last year, however, the company increased its loans, which led to a reduction in the investments in London, but naturally loans in Australia ought to pay it best. There is, however, one startling fact in regard to this concern, and that is, that with £1,722,141 invested on its own account in loans on mortgages, there should be no foreclosure account. In good years such an account might well be absent, but in the time of stress and storm through which Australia is passing some such account must exist. Its absence from the balance-sheet is not a sign of strength, and the sooner it is included the better we shall like it.

THE SCOTTISH UNION AND NATIONAL INSURANCE COMPANY.—In its fire department this company had a net premium revenue of £552,703 last year and paid £305,846 in claims. Expenses, including commission, took £186,389, or about 30 per cent. of the premium income. Deducting these two items from the premium revenue there was a net surplus of £60,469, which was carried to profit and loss account. Shareholders will receive a dividend of 16 per cent. and a bonus of 1½ per cent. out of this, which will absorb £52,000, so that the whole of the net surplus is not paid away; but the company also received over £37,000 for interest on shareholders' capital and reserve and a balance of £26,099 was brought forward from the previous year; therefore the directors are able to carry £5,000 to the fire premium reserve and £35,000 to the general reserve, and still have £30,965 left to carry forward. The business is thus very prosperous in this branch. It is also prosperous in the life branch, where 1,036 policies were issued, insuring £521,262, and yielding £21,055 in new premiums; £40,000 of this total was reinsured. Claims by death took £291,497, and commission and expenses about £42,000, or 13½ per cent. of the premium income. The increase on the life and annuity funds for the year amounted to £108,660, a sum of £15,093 having been received for fresh annuities sold. The company's total funds amount to £4,785,469, a considerable portion of which is invested abroad, £669,687 in United States railway bonds and guaranteed shares, £253,436 in United States municipal and State bonds, and £454,058 in terminable debentures and fixed deposits, besides Colonial and Indian securities of various sorts.

THE GENERAL LIFE ASSURANCE COMPANY.—The board of this company, which now only does life business, having sold its fire business, adopted a prudent course in its quinquennial valuation by reducing the rate of interest to 3 per cent. on all their policies, except assurances effected under special tables and annuities, which are valued at 3½ per cent. In this way 96·4 per cent. of the entire liabilities of the company come under the finer valuation, and the result is an apparent loss to participating policy holders and shareholders of £60,532, which is the difference between the surplus to be anticipated under a 3½ per cent. valuation and one at 3 per cent. In other words, £80,788 is the actuarial surplus, instead of £141,320. Nevertheless, this policy is the right one, and will strengthen the company in the future. It actually earned £4 0s. 3d. on its investments as an average during the past five years, and in the year just closed the rate earned was £4 1s. 3d. Going to the accounts of that year we find the company issued 1,236 policies, insuring £556,703, and yielding £25,468 in premiums. Claims, &c., absorbed £112,339, of which £20,115 was paid by other companies with whom the General Life had effected reinsurance. The deaths were twenty-four below the number expected by the tables of mortality, and £29,831 less was paid away under them than had been estimated for. Nevertheless, the expenses of the company were rather high, being over 19·6 per cent. of the premium income, excluding of course the capital of £11,093 received for seventeen new annuities sold, and notwithstanding the receipt of £58,283 from interest and dividends and £13,557 as profit on investments sold, the life fund was only increased during the year by £117,882. It now amounts to £1,620,319. Shareholders received £7,500 in a dividend and bonus amounting together to 15 per cent. for the year, their share of the surplus being £19,436, which leaves £61,352 for participating policy holders, whose bonus this time will not be large. The money accumulated by the company appears to be very carefully and soundly invested almost entirely in home securities.

YORKSHIRE FIRE AND LIFE INSURANCE COMPANY.—The seventy-fourth annual meeting of the shareholders of this company was held on the 10th inst. at York, Lord Wenlock in the chair, when the report and balance-sheet for the year ending February 28, 1898, were adopted. The net fire premium income amounted to £105,136, against £102,592 in 1897, showing a net increase of £2,544. The losses were £57,577, against £56,166 in 1897, the ratio in both years being almost identical, viz., 54·7 per cent. on the premium income. The net amount carried to profit and loss account, after providing for expenses and outstanding losses, was £21,087. The fire reserve fund remains at £240,000. In the life department 421 new policies were issued for £256,695, against £236,521 last year. The total net premium income was increased to £67,509 from £65,285 in 1897. The claims in this department amounted to £40,654, compared with £30,641 in 1897, and the total funds of the department amounted to £812,971, against £754,728, a net increase of £58,243. The ratio of expenses to premium income was 15·7 per cent. A dividend at the same rate as last year, viz., 9s. per share, or 25 per cent., is paid. The total assets of the company now amount to £1,149,217.

IMPERIAL CONTINENTAL GAS ASSOCIATION.—The profit of this semi-private concern for the half-year ended December 31 was returned as £245,152, or £11,000 less than the corresponding half of 1896, but we note that the contingencies account increased by £109,400, whereas a year ago the addition was only £86,000, so that the gross profit must have been fairly well maintained, and the usual 5 per cent. dividend for the half-year was declared. The sum of £34,000 was added to depreciation, or a little less than a year ago, and the reserve had the usual addition, these funds having stood in the last four half-years as follows :—

	Depreciation.	Reserve.	Contingencies.
	£	£	£
June 30, 1896	911,238	382,000	607,267
December 31, 1896 ...	949,481	387,228	693,205
June 30, 1897	999,099	392,441	761,342
December 31, 1897...	1,033,340	397,335	872,749

The reserve fund is specially invested in Consols, and the depreciation fund in high-class securities, but the contingencies fund is in the business. Trading balances and liquid assets, however, are so favourable that the huge sum is almost all held by the company apart from the general undertaking. Nothing fresh was added at the meeting about the Vienna business, but the chairman seemed to lean to the view that an amicable arrangement was not outside the range of possibilities. At Amsterdam, the undertaking of the association will be taken over by the local authorities next August, who pay 25 per cent. premium upon the capital sunk in the undertaking there. The money thus received will be employed in the redemption of the 4 per cent. debentures, whose amount now is £376,000. The association seems to be extending its operations in Germany, and generally the business appears to be progressive.

INVESTMENT TRUST CORPORATION.—This corporation has done much better than the average trust. In the last five years the deferred stock has received an average dividend of 5 per cent., and the securities are stated to have only a moderate depreciation upon them. This last year the Trust earned upon its investments of £2,753,281 an income of £117,606, or, roughly speaking, 4¼ per cent. upon their cost price. As the total capital is £2,600,000, the rest having been found out of reserve, and £2,080,000 of this capital receives a fixed interest at the rate of 4 per cent., the board were able with this income to meet £10,580 of administrative expenses, pay 5 per cent. in dividend on the £520,000 of deferred stock, and carry £1,500 more forward, raising the total of that item to £25,760. The changes of investments during the year resulted in a small profit, which has been applied in reduction of cost of securities. Apparently the corporation does no loan business, while the board distinctly state that no securities with a liability upon them are held The reserve amounts to £115,000 and the balance forward to £25,760, and after these sums have been deducted from the book cost of the investments, a valuation of the latter made at the date of the report showed a depreciation of 6½ per cent. Upon the total this represents £175,000, so that the item of depreciation is not one to be despised, but a year ago it was 9½ per cent. In spite of this depreciation, the Trust must be considered to have done well, but our commendations must stop at this point, for no list of investments is given, so it is utterly impossible to speak with the slightest degree of accuracy about the position. By an effort we may imagine that past experience proves the investments to be well placed, but who is to say that views have not changed upon the board, leading to the holding of an altogether different class of securities now from those in the hands of the Trust a few years back?

CHICAGO PACKING AND PROVISION COMPANY.—The report of this company tells one little about its position. Last year it apparently earned a larger profit than the year before, as out of the net balance it was able to pay 12 per cent. or one and a half years' interest upon the preference shares, thus wiping off arrears, and then distribute 2 per cent. upon the ordinary shares, leaving £1,050 to be carried forward. In the circumstances we should have thought it would have been prudent to forego the dividend on the ordinary shares, but the directors seem to prefer dividing up closely. The balance-sheet tells nothing, as the chief asset is shares in one or two American companies—it is not clear which—and the balance-sheets of these companies ought to be included in the report. But we have no faith in these Anglo-American industrial concerns, which generally bring loss to the British investor.

THE LIVERPOOL AND LONDON AND GLOBE INSURANCE COMPANY.—In its fire department this company received a premium income of £1,540,706 last year, and it paid, or will pay, £857,714 in losses arising within the year. Losses, in other words, took 55·6 per cent.

of the premiums, and expenses and commission took a further 31 per cent. These deductions left £165,169 as profit, without counting interest earned. In the life department 765 policies, insuring £472,206, were issued, yielding £24,030 in new premiums. The total premium income was £242,139. Claims paid, including bonuses, took £204,262, and expenses amounted to just 10 per cent. of the premium income. The total of the life and annuity funds was increased during the year by £182,943, and now amounts to £5,190,245, but £155,254 of this represents capital received against new annuities amounting to £14,917 sold. The profit and loss account discloses the splendid character of the business as a whole, the net balance being £1,217,733, out of which dividends and a bonus aggregating 36s. per share, or 90 per cent. have been paid, or declared, for the year. The total funds of the company amount to £10,236,133, including not only the life and annuity funds, but the Globe Perpetual Annuity Fund, and the various funds of the fire department. This money is invested to the extent of £1,083,945 in mortgages on property outside the kingdom, and another £1,250,000 or so is invested in United States and Foreign Government securities.

SUN INSURANCE OFFICE (FIRE).—Last year this office's premium income was £1,012,340, or £42,655 more than in the previous year. Losses took £588,296, or 58·11 per cent. of the premiums, and expenses, commission, &c., absorbed £343,252, or 33·91 per cent. of the premiums. After providing the usual reserve of 40 per cent. of the premiums to cover liabilities under current policies, £142,401 is left to be carried to profit and loss. The total amount at the credit of profit and loss amounts to £270,750, and £100,000 of this has been carried to special reserve fund against large individual risks. Out of the balance a dividend of 4s. per share was paid in January last, and another of 4s. 6d. per share will be paid next July, making 85 per cent. on the par value of the share for the year.

THE NITRATE RAILWAYS COMPANY, LIMITED.—Adversity seems to have done this company good. Gross receipts last year came to £443,427, and the net income was £211,043. Measured by percentages, expenses show an increase on the previous year, but measured by the work done they have been reduced, so that the board can claim to have effected considerable economies without impairing efficiency. That is to say, while the total working expenses were 52·34 per cent. of the income last year, against 48·49 per cent. in 1895, the cost per quintal of traffic carried was reduced from 4·10d. to 3.42d., an economy in absolute cost of nearly 17 per cent. A dividend of 3 per cent. is declared on the unconverted ordinary and the preferred shares, which will leave £136,121 to be carried forward, against £119,760 brought in. The directors report that exports of nitrate have not increased since the combination to limit output was dissolved, and they do not anticipate much variation in the volume of traffic to be carried during the present year. The abundant years 1889, 1890, and 1891 are, in short, gone for many a day, if not for ever, and therefore the watchword must be economy, reduction of expenses at all points, and absolute cessation of plundering by officials or anybody else.

THE SCOTTISH AMICABLE LIFE ASSURANCE SOCIETY issued 735 new policies last year, insuring £515,944, and yielding £35,008 in new premiums. Also it sold annuities to the capital value of £71,431. Claims took £226,146, which was "considerably less" than actuarial probabilities indicated. The total income for the year was £456,377, and the total outgo £298,383, which left £157,000 to be added to the net funds, bringing their total up to £3,830,932. Expenses of management, including commission, came to 13·95 per cent. of the premium revenue. The average rate earned on the funds was £4 0s. 9d. per cent. before deducting income tax. No less than £1,744,000 of the funds is invested abroad.

CLEMENT, GLADIATOR, AND HUMBER (FRANCE), LIMITED.—The first report, which only brings us up to September last, hardly fulfils the rosy prospects with which the prospectus abounded. Earl De La Warr, chairman of the Dunlop Company, is also chairman of this undertaking, and amongst its directors is Martin D. Rucker, the managing director of Humber & Company. Clément, Gladiator, &c., is the outcome of the amalgamation of three French cycle businesses, and in the prospectus reference was made to the advantages which must accrue from the amalgamation. The statement about past profits was presented in anything but a clear way, but the profits of the two companies—the Clement and the Gladiator—for the year ended October 1, 1896, were guaranteed by the vendor at £80,000. The results of the French business of Humber & Company had not been ascertained, or at least were not given, but, said the prospectus, "judging from the turnover and the popularity of Humber machines in France, the profits should be very considerable." The prospectus then showed that the preference dividend and 9 per cent. on the ordinary shares would require only £75,000, and added that "the calculation was made without taking into account any profits of the French business of Humber & Company, Limited, which should materially increase the dividend on the ordinary shares." Results do not bear out these anticipations. The actual net profit for the year is only £51,727, the Humber branch, from the date of the incorporation of the company, showing a loss of £8,392, which proves that the statements in the prospectus, to say the least, were beside the mark, and instead of any 9 per cent. dividend, which was to have been materially increased by the profits from the Humber branch, only 5 per cent. is paid, and £4,738 is carried forward. The balance-sheet is not at all encouraging. Amongst the assets, land, buildings, plant, patent rights, and goodwill stand at £714,780, the magnificent sum of £7,694 having been written off for depreciation. If this item was written down by 50 per cent. we should not think it would stand too high. Fixtures, fittings, and stables, less £1,485 written off, represent £13,290, and in addition to all this the works at Nantes and the cycles known as "Phebus" are a separate item for £29,159. Stock-in-trade bulks largely for £71,274, while book debts and bills receiveable stand at the terrible total of £119,036, against which there is a reserve for doubtful debts and bills amounting to £9,181, an item which, did it stand at five times the amount, would probably not be too large for its purpose. But perhaps we are wrong, for the auditors tell us they have compared the balance-sheet and profit and loss account with the books and vouchers, and find them in accordance therewith, which is kind of them. Another reassuring statement is that the stock has been certified by the managing directors, so of course it would not be put too high. Still we must say that the position of Clément, Gladiator, & Humber (France), Limited, if not up to promise, compares very well with most of the cycle companies over here, though we would just make the remark that Mr. Ernest Terah Hooley and his friends displayed keen judgment when they took the £900,000 of purchase money in cash.

NATIONAL PROVINCIAL BANK OF ENGLAND.—Our premier bank did very well last year, the profits, with £67,008 brought in, being £714,649 compared with £667,008 for 1896, when £53,996 was brought in. The directors are therefore able to increase the dividend from 19 to 20 per cent., and while £30,000 was last year transferred to credit of bank premises account, the amount transferred now is £40,000 as well as £5,000 to the provident fund, while the balance carried forward is £2,600 larger at £69,649. Deposits have further grown from £46,788,000 to £48,810,000, and acceptances have increased from £552,900 to £564,000. Cash at Bank of England and at head office and branches has risen from £5,749,000 to £6,459,000, and at call and notice from £4,240,000 to £4,482,000. Amongst the investments, English Government securities have increased from £8,097,000 to £8,132,000, and Indian and Colonial Government, railway debenture, and other securities, from £8,290,000 to £8,599,000. Bills discounted, loans, &c., are some half million up at £25,709,000. This is one of the two great bill-buying banks in London, the other being the London and County, and we wish for statistics' sake it would separate bills from advances in the balance sheet. Thomas George Robinson, Esq., and Selwyn Robert Pryor, Esq., have been elected directors in place of Richard Blaney Wade, Esq., and Duncan Macdonald, Esq., deceased.

WEST INDIA AND PANAMA TELEGRAPH COMPANY.—This undertaking is still lamenting over its subsidies. The subsidy of £2,000 per annum from the Government of Jamaica ceased last March, and now the financial crisis has caused Antigua and St. Kitts to reduce their subsidies from £800 to £600 each for the current year. Under the influence of the depressed condition of West Indian trade the little company, naturally, has not had a good time, the receipts for the half-year ending December 31 being £32,228 against £34,053 in 1896, and the expenses £19,772 against £21,398, being a reduction of about £200 net. The sum of £1,243 is brought forward, but to pay the preference dividends and 6d. per share on the ordinary, £1,000, has to be taken from the reserve, leaving £721 to be carried forward. Having lowered rates to meet the competition of the Bermuda and Jamaica line, the prospects are not at all promising.

IMPERIAL RUSSIAN COTTON AND JUTE FACTORY.—The gross profit of this concern last year amounted to £28,165, and after setting aside £2,494 for depreciation and meeting administrative charges, the net profit was £18,022, to which add £7,270 brought forward. A dividend of 10 per cent. absorbed £13,000, the sum of £5,000 was placed to reserve, and £7,293 was carried forward. The reserve will now amount to £25,000, and with the balance forward, and a debenture premium redemption fund of £1,200, the company has about £33,000 of accumulated profits. Depreciation to the extent of £20,111 has been written off the properties during its history, and their total now stands at £131,222. The trading balances of the company are therefore in a sound condition, and only £29,000 of debentures are out. It is, however, intended to issue at least £20,000 of second debentures in order to provide for the completion of the twine and rope factory, mangling machinery, and other plant in a new department of the business. This will cost about £35,000, the balance being found, we presume, out of the resources of the company.

SOUTHERN BRAZILIAN RIO GRANDE DO SUL RAILWAY COMPANY.—Like most of the Brazilian guaranteed railways, this one works at a loss. Last year its total receipts came to £45,722, and expenditure to £47,365, so that the loss on working was £1,641. This is better than in the two previous years, the loss in 1896 being £3,433, and in 1895 no less than £8,465, but in those years revolutions and floods affected the traffic of the line. The guarantee of the Brazilian Government is, of course, the salvation of the company, and as this amounts to £103,896 for the year, the dividend is relatively high. Including £21,446 brought forward, the sum pays the debenture interest and dividends amounting to 5½ per cent. upon the shares, leaving £26,757 to be carried forward, of which £10,177 has been invested in high-class securities on this side. Apparently nothing is done in the way of debenture redemption, and as the debenture stock amounts to £1,002,384, the prospects in case of whole or even partial default by the Brazilian Government makes one shudder.

SCOTTISH AUSTRALIAN INVESTMENT COMPANY.—There is a miserable tale repeated by this company in its half-yearly report. A net profit of £33,578 is shown, of which £26,061 is absorbed by preference and debenture interest, and the balance of £7,692 permits of a dividend at the rate of 2½ per cent. per annum on the ordinary stock, and the carrying forward of £1,442. The drought in Australia is said to have broken up, but losses of stock at the Gaumain and Nivê Downs Stations have been so severe that the board deem it advisable to take £35,000 from reserve. This latter item is then reduced to £115,000, as against £170,000 a few years back, but it does not matter much, as it never was a very satisfactory item, being wholly in the business. If it were wiped out, and some of the pastoral property written down, it might be better for the concern.

Diary of the War.

May 6.—No war news, unless we regard the landing of ammunition for the Cuban insurgents at a point about seventeen miles from Havana as war news. The expedition consisted of seven men and two horses. They were conveyed in a tug-boat, which was fired upon by some Spanish cavalry from the island. But expedition and ammunition, with several boxes of dynamite, were safely given over to the insurgents commanded by General Gomez. No casualties. Considerable anxiety in United States about the continued silence of Admiral Dewey at Manila. It seems inexplicable. The movements of the Spanish fleet from Cape de Verde are equally mysterious. It is not at Cadiz, as was reported yesterday. The only warships there are preparing to sail in some unknown direction. Admiral Sampson, while aiming at the capture of Puertorico, is to keep a look out for the returning American warship *Oregon*, and an eye on the Spanish fleet when it becomes visible; but at present

"The Spanish fleet cannot be seen,
Because 'tis not in sight."

May 7.—The war continues to present us with but meagre fare in the shape of news. The morning papers, as a rule, devote a large amount of space to rumours, which, in the main, are merely tantalising; while the ingenuity of the evening papers in discovering "startling" intelligence, which is rarely confirmed, is really remarkable, though wearisome. A French liner, sailing for Havana, was brought to and boarded by men from the American warship *Annapolis*. Her captain was warned not to attempt an entry, but he immediately resumed his course; and a shot was then fired across the ship's bows. The vessel itself was seized and taken to Key West. Then the French ambassador at Washington sought her release on the ground that she did not sail on April 23, and could not know of the war, which was only declared on the 25th—though dating from the 21st—and was not notified to foreign Powers until the 27th. These arguments seem to have impressed the United States Government, for orders were issued to release the steamer, and to convey her under escort to Havana. It was only prudent thus to avoid what must have proved an ugly, and perhaps serious, international difficulty. No news from Manila, and American anxiety increasing. One suggestion is that Admiral Dewey may, after destroying the Spanish fleet, have found that his supply of ammunition was not sufficient to reduce the forts, and is thus caught in a sort of trap. Some such notion seems to be entertained at Madrid, and Senor Sagasta talks of sending reinforcements to the Philippines, and still contesting their possession. We must wait for enlightenment. No public hint of peace in Spain, but privately, it is said, moderate and far-seeing politicians are found to suggest that a way should now be sought to open peace negotiations. Probably the only obstacle to action on such suggestions is the fear of ignorant and ill-informed popular indignation. Serious rioting in Murcia. The town hall set on fire the law courts pillaged and fired, the prisoners set free, the telegraph wires cut, a dynamite store looted, and its contents distributed. A serious situation indeed!

May 8.—At last there is news direct from Admiral Dewey. It is brief. He destroyed the Spanish ships; he destroyed the forts at Cavite; has the whole place "in his grip"; but cannot take possession of Manila for want of men. His munitions also, it seems, need replenishing. Not an American sailor was lost, nor an American ship damaged. A most complete victory.

May 9.—The details now received of Admiral Dewey's great achievement at Manila give us as perfect a picture of what occurred as may be desired, and it is but right at once to acknowledge that the American accounts now published fully confirm, in the main, the early reports supplied to us exclusively through Spanish sources. With the exception of the first unfortunate announcement of victory sent out from Madrid, the original story as told in the Spanish despatches is now entirely confirmed. There is no question of the courage of the Spanish forces employed; their skill, however, has not been so conspicuous. Their fleet was no doubt antiquated and worthless as compared with the American fleet, which also included a far larger number of ships than the Spanish. But it is also evident that the Spanish guns on the forts as well as on the fleet were badly served. The firing was extremely wild; the gunners were too eager to "blaze away," as is shown in the fact that only one of the American ships, the *Baltimore*, was badly damaged, the others not at all. The Americans report no loss of life: the wounds were few and trifling. On the Spanish side, on the other hand, the fleet was completely destroyed; the number of killed is believed to be at least 400, and the wounded 600. Admiral Dewey's squadron arrived outside Manila Bay late on the night of Saturday, April 30. Ships were despatched to reconnoitre; but not a Spanish vessel was visible. No outlook was kept. The only consideration, then, for Admiral Dewey was whether he should risk ignoring the submarine mines which ought to have been laid in the Bay. He decided to take the risk. All except the stern lights were extinguished. The vessels proceeded up the south side of the Bay with great caution; and half a dozen of them had passed the Corregidor fort before they were observed. Searchlights seem to have been unknown on the Spanish forts. The American ships went on their course, and arrived opposite the Cavite forts at daybreak on Sunday morning, May 1. The Manila guns opened fire at five miles' range, but did not hit the enemy's ships. The Americans did not reply at once; they manœuvred in search of the Spanish war vessels, which were found at last under the wing of the Cavite forts "in battle array," though steam apparently was not up! At least it was some time before they entered on the fray. The result was as we have stated. It was agreed not to bombard Manila, on condition that its forts remained silent. An American military force is to be sent to Manila as rapidly as possible to enable the Admiral to take possession of the town; and American journals are now again discussing what they are to do with the Philippines. It is significant that the drift of opinion seems now in favour of retaining the islands to give the States a foothold in the Far East, and, as a corollary, to set to work to create a great fleet, with perhaps a great army to follow. Meanwhile, Europe is looking on with increasing interest. Germany seems rather anxious about the future of the Philippines. France, according to the Madrid correspondent of the *Times*, has her eye on the Balearic Islands, and Russia seems inclined, if occasion offers, to lay bands on Ceuta. Twenty years ago this war between the United States and Spain would not have suggested any change of territory except such as the chances of war might have given to one or other of the belligerents; now there is scarcely a European Power that is not apparently formulating claims to "compensation," a *fin de siècle* euphemism for diplomatic "theft."

May 10.—A day of rumour rather than of fact. Commodore Dewey has been thanked by Congress for his achievement at Manila: and a Bill was passed with great promptitude promoting him to the rank of Rear-Admiral. Several of his officers have also been promoted. The Admiral is to receive a sword, and his officers and men medals commemorative of Manila. These are about the only facts there are, except that there has been a renewal of the rioting in Spain. The American expedition against Cuba has been postponed—naturally; for until Admiral Sampson has returned to Havana, the bombardment is not likely to take place, and it is by no means clear where the Admiral and his ships are. They are said to have been seen somewhere to the north of Cape Haytian on Sunday, while seventeen Spanish vessels are reported as having been seen off Puertorico. There have heen many rumours of engagements in the Atlantic, but no confirmation of them. A reconstruction of the Spanish Cabinet seems probable, Senor Sagasta, the Premier, and Senor Moret, the Colonial Minister, being about to retire.

May 11.—The Spanish fleet which sailed some time ago from Cape de Verde has at last been discovered. Not, however, at Puertorico, near which it was said to be on Sunday last, nor anywhere at sea, searching for Admiral Sampson's squadron, but at Cadiz! It has gone home; and there is a strong impression that we shall hear very little more of it. It has been attached to the reserve squadron; but clearly, if the Spanish authorities had believed the ships fit for anything, they would not have brought them to Cadiz, leaving Puertorico open to the American fleet, and the defence of Havana entirely to the troops under General Blanco. This entirely changes the aspect of affairs: Admiral Sampson may run his ships into Puertorico any day. There is practically nothing to stop him. Whether he will then return to Havana is uncertain. If he does, it will not be merely to carry on the somewhat dull work of the blockade; for it seems to have been finally resolved at Washington that a more formidable expedition than was at first contemplated is to be fitted out as soon as possible for the invasion of Cuba. General Miles has gone to Tampa, presumably to prepare this expedition. Some reports speak of its starting before the week is out, or at least early in next week; but if it is ready to start in ten days or a fortnight it will do very well. It is believed in America that the army now to be sent will dispose of General Blanco and his force—said to consist of 60,000 regulars and 30,000 volunteers—by the end of June, and thus be ready to escape from the island before the most dangerous hot weather sets in. Of course, the bombardment of Havana will begin as soon as the American expedition has started. It seems probable that Admiral Sampson may return to conduct this bombardment—unless Puertorico proves a harder nut for him to crack than looks likely at present. A further supply of rifles and ammunition is to be despatched to the Cuban insurgents immediately, to be left at various points on the coast of which these insurgents have the command. At Manila the insurgents are said to be beyond the control of Admiral Dewey as well as the Spanish authorities. The population are represented as starving, and the British residents regard their position as critical. The news from Spain itself is gloomy. A Ministerial crisis seems inevitable. There is some grim talk about a dictator, and General Weyler seems qualifying for the post. There has been more rioting at Alicante and other towns, and it is impossible to say what a day may bring forth in this unhappy country.

May 12.—All is in doubt again about that Spanish Cape de Verde fleet. There has been no confirmation of its arrival at Cadiz, and the report is now regarded with suspicion at Washington. Nothing has been heard of Admiral Sampson, who should have arrived at Puertorico yesterday. Were the Spanish ships watching him after all? The Bill providing for the war expenditure has passed the Spanish Chamber, though its passage was accompanied by a fierce running fire of invective from Republican and Carlist deputies. The Government were sadly riddled. No further serious disturbances are reported from Spain, but the Government is "extending the area subject to martial law." An ominous proceeding. Several smart attempts to land men and arms near Cienfuegos, under cover of the fire of four American ships, were frustated by the Spaniards, and fourteen men were wounded. What the object of these attempts was does not appear. More talk about peace.

To Correspondents.

The Editor cannot undertake to return rejected communications. Letters from correspondents must, in every case, be authenticated by the name and address of the writer.

Telegraphic Address: "Unveiling, London."

*** Owing to pressure on our space, we are compelled again to leave over our table of prices quoted on the leading provincial exchanges.

The Investors' Review.

The Week's Money Market.

Rates on short loans have fluctuated from day to day, but the tone has generally been harder. The calling in of balances on account of the Chinese Loan payment at once cleared the market of its superabundant supplies of cash, and the rate for day-to-day loans became 3½ to 4 on the Friday preceding that payment. On Saturday, the day of the actual transfer of the £11,088,000, the rate fell off to a wobbly 2½ to 3¼ per cent. in expectation of the speedy release of a portion of the funds handed over to the Japanese Government. When, however, these hopes proved ill-founded, and the Stock Exchange settlement caused a little more activity in the short loan market, the rate for day-to-day money rose to 3 to 4 per cent., which has been the comprehensive quotation for the last four days. Recourse had to be made freely to the Bank of England at times, so that on balance the market increased its indebtedness to that institution by about £3,000,000. The India Council renewed small amounts each day at 3½ per cent. for advances of fourteen to eighteen days.

There has been little change in discount rates during the week. On Saturday, the hopes of an early release of Japanese money caused two and three months' remitted bills to be discounted at about 3⅝ to 3$\frac{11}{16}$ per cent., but the news that the Japanese funds will be retained by the Bank of England for a time at once caused a return to the former level of 3$\frac{11}{16}$ to 3¾ per cent., at which quotations the market has remained steady. There appears to be a little splitting of hairs as to the definition of the course adopted by the Bank of England in order to retain possession of the unemployed balances of the Japanese Government, but it seems to be certain that some *quid pro quo* for this advantage has been rendered by the Bank. Its policy in holding fast to the money is well advised, and that it should take the step is only another proof that the old "cast-iron" methods are disappearing under the influence of common sense. At the same time, there does not seem to be reason to assume that no money will be released on this account, for the operation in connection with the investment of Japan in £2,000,000 of the Chinese Loan should bring some money out, while the liabilities of the Japanese Government to shipbuilders are also large, and constantly falling due. Then, if gold is taken to Japan, an endeavour will be made to buy it in the open market, which, if successful, must lead to a further setting free of balances in the Bank of England. Meantime the anxieties of the market are aroused as to the effect of the high price of wheat upon the course of bullion movements. So far the American exchange has moved to only a moderate extent, the demand for gold on that account being restricted to the open market, and even so is only of a languid nature. India, however, is stated to be in a position to ship grain freely, and if anything like the million tons of wheat spoken of as probable is sent by it, there is the chance that an enquiry for the metal may arise in that quarter. The Bank of England certainly gained over £1,000,000 in the week from imports of gold, but the great motive for the arrivals from the Continent—payments on account of the German half of the Chinese loan—is now no longer operative, and ordinary conditions have now come into play. A new Russian loan in Berlin, even if it is in part a conversion, will tend to harden the German money market, and thus weaken our power to draw the metal. There is, therefore, no reason for discount rates to weaken at present, although we are approaching the period when the dull summer season usually has a depressing effect upon them.

Less was heard about repayments of loans by lenders in the Stock Exchange this time, and loans for the settlement ruled about 4 to 4¼ per cent., most business, however, being transacted at the lower figure. The Greek loan, or rather the £1,660,000 offered here, did not excite enthusiasm, as the high exchanges ruling caused the French and Russian portions to be cheaper. After allowing for accrued interest, the price of subscription meant par, and at this figure there was sufficient demand on the part of those who always hunger after "gilt edged" securities to cause applications to the amount of £3,036,000. Allotments, therefore, worked out at about 54 per cent. of the amounts asked for.

Most of the gold, yesterday's Bank returns shows, which came in during the week has been retained in stock, and as notes have come back from circulation as usual in the second week of the month, the banking reserve is larger by £1,093,000 than it was a week ago at £23,813,000. But this has not been nearly enough to enable the market to work as usual and find the Chinese loan money at the same time. It has therefore been obliged to borrow £3,007,000 on "other" securities, raising the total of these once more to £35,775,000. All this money, all the addition to the reserves, and £135,000 paid out from the Government balances, have gone to swell the "other" deposits which have risen £4,246,000 to £43,516,000. The strength of this total is illusory, since the balances of the Japanese Government alone represent perhaps ten millions of it, perhaps more, and as these balances are kept out of the market, the prospect before it is one of dependence on the Bank for weeks, perhaps months, to come. The large increase in the "other" deposits has caused the proportion of reserves to liabilities to fall from 44½ per cent. to 43½.

SILVER.

The price of the metal, after an initial drop to 25⅞d. per ounce, has steadily advanced during the week. At the last quite a rush up occurred in the quotation on an urgent order for spot silver from Paris on account of Spain, and the price for immediate delivery is $\frac{7}{16}$d. higher at 26⅝d. per ounce. The forward has risen ⅜d. to 26¼d. per ounce. It is not clear whether these orders have been completed and sellers, therefore, have been altogether disinclined to press the metal. The Indian exchanges have run up above 1s. 4d., as the business in wheat there is growing more active, and has already caused the Indian money markets to tighten up again. The wheat crop has proved to be very good, and large shipments on this account will, while they last, do more to help the Indian Government towards its ideal of a high exchange than anything that has happened of late. It remains, however, to be seen whether India will prefer to take its differences in silver or gold, in spite of all that Governmeut may do to encourage the latter to go. Under these circumstances, the Council drafts are keenly competed for, and special sales are frequently made.

BANK OF ENGLAND.

An Account pursuant to the Act 7 and 8 Vict., cap. 32, for the Week ending on Wednesday, May 11, 1898.

ISSUE DEPARTMENT.

	£		£
Notes Issued	48,924,770	Government Debt	11,015,100
		Other Securities	5,784,900
		Gold Coin and Bullion	32,124,770
		Silver Bullion	—
	£48,924,770		£48,924,770

BANKING DEPARTMENT.

	£		£
Proprietors' Capital	14,553,000	Government Securities	13,187,953
Rest	3,191,329	Other Securities	35,775,252
Public Deposits (including Exchequer, Savings Banks, Commissioners of National Debt, and Dividend Accounts).....	11,403,473	Notes	21,368,125
Other Deposits	43,516,141	Gold and Silver Coin......	2,444,642
Seven Day and other Bills..	112,029		
	£72,775,972		£72,775,972

Dated May 12, 1898.

H. G. BOWEN, *Chief Cashier.*

In the following table will be found the movements compared with the previous week, and also the totals for that week and the corresponding return last year :—

Banking Department.

Last Year. May 12.		May 4. 1898.	May 11, 1898.	Increase.	Decrease.
£	Liabilities.	£	£	£	£
3,132,282	Rest	3,183,433	3,191,329	7,896	—
10,188,734	Pub. Deposits....	11,538,715	11,403,473	—	135,242
39,446,125	Other do.	39,270,461	43,516,141	4,245,680	—
185,299	7 Day Bills	130,663	112,029	—	18,634
	Assets.			Decrease.	Increase.
13,842,586	Gov. Securities ..	13,187,953	13,187,953	—	—
28,052,106	Other do.	32,768,582	35,775,252	—	3,006,670
25,611,289	Total Reserve....	22,719,737	23,812,767	—	1,093,030
				4,253,576	4,253,576
				Increase.	Decrease.
£		£	£	£	£
27,409,295	Note Circulation.	27,792,980	27,556,645	—	236,335
51⅛ p.c.	Proportion	44½ p.c.	43¼ p.c.	—	—
2 "	Bank Rate	4 "	4 "	—	—

Foreign Bullion movement for week £1,076,000 in.

LONDON BANKERS' CLEARING.

Month of	1898.	1897.	Increase.	Decrease.
	£	£	£	£
January	673,281,000	576,558,000	96,723,000	—
February ..	648,601,000	597,652,000	50,949,000	—
Week ending				
March 2	190,157,000	177,852,000	12,305,000	—
" 9	134,490,000	126,182,000	8,308,000	—
" 16	174,377,000	148,937,000	25,440,000	—
" 23	129,828,000	118,578,000	11,250,000	—
" 30	170,668,000	158,421,000	12,247,000	—
April 6	186,540,000	147,789,000	38,751,000	—
" 13	112,101,000	154,099,000	—	41,998,000
" 20	168,810,000	92,332,000	76,478,000	—
" 27	129,959,000	138,288,000	—	8,329,000
May 4	174,057,000	138,987,000	35,070,000	—
" 11	160,526,000	128,252,000	32,274,000	—
Total to date	2,964,327,000	2,636,832,000	327,495,000	—

BANK AND DISCOUNT RATES ABROAD.

	Bank Rate.	Altered.	Open Market.
Paris	2	March 14, 1895	1⅞
Berlin..	4	April 9, 1898	3⅝
Hamburg	4	April 9, 1898	3⅞
Frankfort	4	April 9, 1898	3⅝
Amsterdam	3	April 13, 1897	2⅝
Brussels	3	April 28, 1896	2¼
Vienna	4	January 22, 1896	3⅜
Rome...............................	5	August 27, 1895	3
St. Petersburg......................	5½	January 23, 1898	4½
Madrid	5	June 17, 1896	5
Lisbon	6	January 25, 1891	6
Stockholm	4	March 3, 1898	4
Copenhagen.........................	4	January 20, 1898	4
Calcutta	11	April 28, 1898	—
Bombay	12	May 5, 1898	—
New York call money	2 to 2½	—	—

NEW YORK ASSOCIATED BANKS (dollar at 4s.).

	May 7, 1898.	April 30, 1898.	April 23, 1898	May 8, 1897.
	£	£	£	£
Specie..........................	31,958,000	31,678,000	31,084,000	17,514,000
Legal tenders	9,806,000	10,148,000	10,682,000	19,824,000
Loans and discounts	114,218,000	114,040,000	114,530,000	100,984,000
Circulation	2,919,800	2,850,800	2,816,000	2,934,000
Net deposits	131,924,000	131,700,000	132,244,000	114,072,000

Legal reserve is 25 per cent. of net deposits; therefore the total reserve (specie and legal tenders) exceeds this sum by £8,783,000, against an excess last week of £8,901,000.

BANK OF FRANCE (25 francs to the £).

	May 12, 1898.	May 5, 1898.	April 28, 1898	May 6, 1897.
	£	£	£	£
Gold in hand....................	74,518,720	74,450,800	74,375,920	78,166,000
Silver in hand	48,839,960	48,733,040	48,614,320	49,000,000
Bills discounted	34,816,040	34,248,520	36,839,520	*41,341,000
Advances	16,934,800	15,736,840	15,016,800	—
Note circulation	147,992,840	149,901,640	148,438,040	146,959,000
Public deposits.................	7,546,280	5,899,880	8,035,040	7,221,000
Private deposits	22,914,840	24,174,880	25,655,600	19,611,000

Proportion between bullion and circulation 83½ per cent. against 82¾ per cent. a week ago.

* Includes advances.

FOREIGN RATES OF EXCHANGE ON LONDON.

Place.	Usance.	Last week's.	Latest.	Place.	Usance.	Last week's.	Latest.
Paris	chqs.	25'34	25'33	Italy	sight	27'12	27'28
Brussels	chqs.	25'39½	25'38	Do. gold prem.	..	107'17	107'70
Amsterdam	short	12'10½	12'10¼	Constantinople..	3 mths	109'15	109'16
Berlin..........	short	20'51	20'50½	B. Ayres gd. pm.	..	163'30	158'30
Do.	3 mths	20'32½	20'32	Rio de Janeiro..	90 dys	5⅝d.	5¾d.
Hamburg	3 mths	20'32	20.30	Valparaiso......	90 dys	17⅜d.	17⅜d.
Frankfort	short	20'51	20'49	Calcutta........	T. T.	1/3⅞	1/4
Vienna	short	12'07½	12.09½	Bombay........	T. T.	1/3⅞	1/4
St. Petersburg..	3 mths	93'95	93.55	Hong Kong	T. T.	1/10	1/10⅛
New York......	60 dys	4'80¾	4'81½	Shanghai	T. T.	2/5½	2/5⅜
Lisbon	sight	30⅛d.	30d.	Singapore	T. T.	1/10⅛	1/10⅛
Madrid	sight	51'50	45'00				

IMPERIAL BANK OF GERMANY (20 marks to the £).

	May 7, 1898.	April 30, 1898.	April 23, 1898.	May 7, 1897.
	£	£	£	£
Cash in hand	42,740,100	42,442,550	44,146,350	44,992,000
Bills discounted	35,671,150	37,216,650	35,286,900	*35,312,000
Advances on stocks........	4,219,350	4,462,600	3,714,050	—
Note circulation	56,454,000	58,116,400	55,337,100	54,105,000
Public deposits..........	22,297,800	22,135,200	24,558,350	20,516,000

* Includes advances.

AUSTRIAN-HUNGARIAN BANK (1s. 8d. to the florin).

	May 7, 1898.	April 30, 1898.	April 23, 1898.	May 7, 1897.
	£	£	£	£
Gold reserve	27,801,083	29,677,250	30,116,666	27,790,000
Silver reserve	10,443,333	10,441,250	10,462,916	10,505,000
Foreign bills............	417,250	473,500	709,750	—
Advances	1,842,916	1,833,750	1,753,750	—
Note circulation	53,063,500	53,799,053	51,513,833	51,265,000
Bills discounted	14,122,500	14,009,916	11,577,333	*14,771,000

* Includes advances.

NATIONAL BANK OF BELGIUM (25 francs to the £).

	May 5, 1898.	April 28, 1898.	April 21, 1898.	May 6, 1897.
	£	£	£	£
Coin and bullion	4,391,480	4,266,480	4,270,440	4,344,000
Other securities	16,738,800	16,397,880	16,643,080	16,349,000
Note circulation	19,528,520	19,662,520	19,307,200	18,659,000
Deposits..................	2,962,400	2,581,600	3,036,840	3,017,000

BANK OF SPAIN (25 pesetas to the £).

	May 8, 1898.	April 30, 1898.	April 23, 1898.	May 8, 1897.
	£	£	£	£
Gold	9,833,520	9,833,520	9,719,040	8,578,000
Silver	3,860,520	7,131,520	8,727,600	6,421,000
Bills discounted	23,978,720	29,157,080	27,121,040	*18,135,000
Advances and loans........	4,893,360	4,795,760	5,695,400	—
Notes in circulation	52,292,320	51,621,600	52,229,000	43,767,000
Treasury advances, coupon account	212,360	765,200	564,160	—
Treasury balances	277,760	180,560	123,800	—

* Including loans.

LONDON COURSE OF EXCHANGE.

Place.	Usance.	May 3.	May 5.	May 10.	May 12.
Amsterdam and Rotterdam	short	12'2	12'2	12'2½	12'2½
Do. do.	3 months	12'4¼	12'4½	12'4⅛	12'4½
Antwerp and Brussels	3 months	25'60	25'60	25'60	25'60
Hamburg..................	3 months	20'72	20'73	20'72	20'72
Berlin and German B. Places	3 months	20'73	20'73	20'72	20'72
Paris	cheques	25'37½	25'35	25'35	25'35
Do.	3 months	25'48¾	25'48¾	25'50	25'50
Marseilles	3 months	25'50	25'50	25'51¼	25'51¼
Switzerland...............	3 months	25.73¾	25'72½	25'72½	25'72½
Austria..................	3 months	12'22½	12'21½	12'26¼	12'25
St. Petersburg	3 months	24⅝	24½	24⅞	24⅞
Moscow	3 months	24⅞	24⅞	24⅞	24⅞
Italian Bank Places	3 months	27.40	27'42½	27'55	27'62½
New York	60 days	4⁸⁄₁₆	4⁸⁄₁₆	4⁸⁄₁₆	4⅞
Madrid and Spanish B. P...	3 months	23½	nom.	24	24½
Lisbon	3 months	30½	29½	29	29½
Oporto	3 months	30½	29½	29	29½
Copenhagen..............	3 months	18'46	18'46	18'46	18'46
Christiania	3 months	18'46	18'46	18'46	18'46
Stockholm	3 months	18'45	18'46	18'46	18'46

OPEN MARKET DISCOUNT.

	Per cent.
Thirty and sixty day remitted bills	3¾
Three months "	3¾ 3⅞
Four months "	3⅞
Six months "	3⅞
Three months fine inland bills	4
Four months "	4
Six months "	4¼

BANK AND DEPOSIT RATES.

	Per cent.
Bank of England minimum discount rate	4
" " short loan rates	4
Banker's rate on deposits	2½
Bill brokers' deposit rate (call)	2½
" 7 and 14 days' notice	2¾
Current rates for 7 day loans	3½
" " for call loans	3¼

Stock Market Notes and Comments.

With the world so full of agitation, wars, hunger, and revolution, it is really wonderful to behold the strength of our markets. We can understand why Home securities should hold up while the agitation which is now spreading over the Continent from Italy and Spain finds as yet no echo here, because our population has not been living for a generation with want as a bosom friend, ground to the dust by excessive taxation, and so exhausted that the slightest extra pressure must drive it to rebel. Wealth has broadened and spread downwards with us, instead of becoming more and more concentrated in few hands as on the Continent, and, to some degree, in the United States. Therefore we are calm; therefore the investing classes can continue to place their accumulations in Home stocks with serenity of mind, and they seek these stocks more and more because of the turmoil beyond our shores. Because they do so the price of our good securities naturally remain high and show elasticity with every dip caused by passing frights.

Abroad, however, the position is very different, and it puzzles the mere onlooker to understand why not only Spanish stock should occasionally show a tendency to recover, and Italian Rente abstain from sinking much, but why even United States railroad stocks should rush away up before the war the Union has entered upon against Spain has been completed to the end of the first act. As regards Continental stocks we cannot but look upon the market for them as most treacherous. They may be kept up in price, or raised in price occasionally, by the struggle between "bull" and "bear," but intrinsically not even French Rentes are worth present figures. The market for all this class of stocks is, therefore, often most difficult to deal in on the Stock Exhange. No man, not the most experienced jobber, can see five minutes ahead. Operators in every part of the civilised world are playing against each other in these securities, to such an extent that the influences affecting the market at any one spot cannot be discovered or traced. A man buys thinking the indications favourable to a rise, and almost before he has entered the bargain selling comes from somewhere and drives the price down. The market is thus at the mercy of a thousand cross currents and side influences, the importance of which no individual can measure.

And of course the very breadth of range, as it were, over which the play extends, may have the effect of sustaining prices for a time, and to a certain extent the credit obtainable in all banking centres can be utilised for the same purpose. So long as the over-burden of profitless securities does not cause a breakdown in credit, markets may simmer and shiver along, devoid of great sensation, but a constant source of perplexity, and now and then of loss. Beyond all these influences, however, there is the dominating one of the insolvency ot Spain and Italy, to say nothing of the, as yet, smothered fermentation in France, Austria, and even Germany. This essential weakness must force prices downwards in the long run and in the main, struggle against the decline as speculators may. And because there is no stability in the financial position, at any rate of any Latin country, we think British investors wise in giving their securities the go by for the present. It is not, in some respects, a good thing for us to be without the possession of large masses of Continental securities at a time like the present, were it for no other reason than that the possession of them would enable us the more easily to draw in whatever amount of gold we required from abroad at any pinch. And the lack of both interest-bearing securities and foreign bills of exchange renders our market, in some respects, extremely weak at the present moment. For all that, and balancing advantages and disadvantages, we are inclined to think that it will be better for the stability of our credit that we should be mostly without this class of investment for a time. Speculators may buy and sell as suits their humour, but the quiet investor should not touch the stocks of any country where revolution may now be raging, or threatening to break out. Scheme and lend as they may, the all-powerful-looking *Haute Banque* cannot always and for ever keep insolvent States from foundering.

United States securities stand in another category. We have always had a weakness for them, in spite of the many disappointments they have given us, and the atrocious frauds that have often been perpetrated upon us by American railroad financiers. Yet it is puzzling to account for the rise in these at present, and we do not believe in its durability. It has not been produced here. Some people may have bought weak bonds during the depression which immediately preceded the outbreak of hostilities with Spain, but the attitude of holders and speculators here has on the whole been hostile, and since prices have risen, we believe selling on this side has decidedly predominated. It is not wonderful that this should be so, for large numbers of people had bought extensively just before the war against Spain began, in the expectation of a great advance, owing to the splendid opportunity shortness of bread in Europe was likely to give American railroads this year. Multitudes, therefore, were caught in the fall, and have been raging ever since. Now that American speculators have lifted prices again, this angered crowd has been flinging its stock away, thereby doing one good thing, at any rate, in fending off to some extent the United States demand for gold. We are not at all sure that they are wrong in taking this course. Indeed, if we were in a similar position we should sell directly we saw our money back, because the rise has come too soon to be enduring. The States have not yet paid for the war, and a large disorganisation in their banking system, as well as in their marketable securities, may occur before the bill is met, even should the war now end because Spain has been eaten to death by its ichneumon ruling classes. Undoubtedly the Union is in a very strong position at present through the splendid prices it is getting for its cereals, and, thanks to this, it may meet its enlarged expenditure much more easily than it could have done one or two years ago. But the railways have "wars" of their own and do their best still to ruin each other for the profit of those in control of them. For all the talk of peace also, we believe the war is going to last long enough and to cost such sums, even if ended soon, as must far more than absorb the advantage given by the poverty of Europe and high prices for wheat. Believing this, we think the time has not yet come to seriously invest in the great bulk of American railroad securities dealt in on this market. Gamble in them if you will and take your chances; but invest in them, no.

Apart from such points as these the markets for the past week present nothing to comment upon. They are all more or less unsatisfactory markets, the best thing about them being the lightness of the speculative account carried on inside the Stock Exchange. So small is this that it is now unprofitable to lend money on stocks in many departments. That is to say, money is dearer from the banker than in the market, and moneylenders inside the Exchange are paying banks 4 per cent. and upwards for money which they are obliged to lend again at 3 per cent. and 3½ per cent. and sometimes less. This smallness of speculation is an excellent thing for the stability of the Exchange, although bad at the moment for the moneylender there, but it is no index whatever to the extent of the speculative account open on the part of the public. How great that is we have no means of gauging, but the smallness of the current speculative business on the Stock Exchange points to a lock up of money on the part of its customers heavy enough to force most of them to abstain from further dabbling. The market is thereby reduced very much to hum-drum investment business, which is not very profitable to the "House," and certainly never picturesque.

We need say nothing further this week about mine shares. They are much where they were, only that the men in control of the South African and Australian markets have been pushing quotations up. How far they will be successful in this we do not know, but in regard to the Australasian section it must not be forgotten that the Bottomley puddle has not yet been cleaned up; and in regard to the South African the splendid return of gold for April must not blind people to the fact that the increase is due to the additional stamps at work and not to richer returns from any of the mines. We should be delighted to see a few more both African and Australian mines entering the dividend list, but fear this will have to be waited for just a little longer.

The Week's Stock Markets.

Stock markets were quiet during the closing hours of last week, and the tone was generally dull owing to the usual amount of realisations in view of the settlement which began on Monday. The present week opened with an increase in business, and the opinion gaining ground that the war is likely to end soon caused a decided rise in United States railroad shares, and the tone became firm in all departments. The reported return of the Spanish fleet to Cadiz was also taken as meaning an early cessation of hostilities, and this led to repurchases by "bears," and even to a certain amount of fresh speculative buying.

Highest and Lowest this Year.		Last Carrying over Price.	BRITISH FUNDS, &c.	Closing Price.	Rise or Fall.
113⅛	109¼	—	Consols 2¾ p.c. (Money)...	110⅞	− ⅛
113 3/16	109½	111¼	Do. Account (June 1)	111⅛	—
106¼	101	104½	2½ p.c. Stock red. 1905 ...	103¾	− ¾
363	341	—	Bank of England Stock...	346	—
117	111⅞	114	India 3½ p.c. Stk. red. 1931	113½	− ½
109¼	103⅜	107½	Do. 3 p.c. Stk. red. 1948	106½	− ½
96⅛	90	92¼	Do. 2½ p.c. Stk. red. 1926	92	—

Consols declined steadily during the earlier part of the week, and other high-class securities were flat, owing to the hardening tendency of the money market, coupled with the rather unsatisfactory feeling produced by Lord Salisbury's recent speech. Then again the issuing of the new Greek loan was thought to be partly responsible for some of the selling, although there was not a great rush for it as far as London was concerned. The firmness of other markets during the last few days, and the slackening of the American inquiry for gold, have, however, imparted a rather firmer appearance to the whole list of gilt-edged securities, the premier stocks of the leading Home railway companies again attracting buyers.

Highest and Lowest this Year.		Last Carrying over Price.	HOME RAILWAYS.	Closing Price.	Rise or Fall.
186	172½	176½	Brighton Def.	177	+ ¾
59¼	54⅞	56½	Caledonian Def.	57	+ ⅜
20⅛	18¼	19¾	Chatham Ordinary	19⅞	+ ¼
77¼	62	65	Great Central Pref.	66½	+ 2½
24⅜	21¼	22	Do. Def.	23	+ 1¼
124½	118	119¼	Great Eastern	119⅞	+ ¾
61¼	50¾	53¾	Great Northern Def.	54¾	+ 1
179⅛	168⅛	170	Great Western	170¼	+ ⅜
51¼	45¼	50⅜	Hull and Barnsley	50¼	− ¼
149¼	145	146	Lanc. and Yorkshire	146¼	+ ¼
136⅛	127¼	131½	Metropolitan	134½	+ 3¼
31	26¾	28	Metropolitan District	28	—
88⅜	82⅛	84½	Midland Pref.	84⅜	+ ½
95⅛	84½	87½	Do. Def.	87¾	+ ½
93¼	86¾	89½	North British Pref.	90	+ 1½
47⅛	41¾	43⅛	Do. Def.	43⅞	+ ⅜
181½	172¾	174½	North Eastern	174¾	+ ¼
205¼	196½	197¾	North Western	197½	+ ½
117⅛	105½	110	South Eastern Def.	111⅛	+ 1⅛
98⅜	87	91½	South Western Def.	93	+ 2½

In Home railway stocks all the Great Central Company's issues have been very firm, in view of the opening of part of the London extension in about another two months' time, and for this reason Metropolitan ordinary and new ordinary have both hardened. The coal war is thought to be drawing to a close, although there is not much indication of it yet. Stock was scarce at the settlement, and the light rates brought in buyers, especially for South Eastern deferred, the latter stock being also helped by a good traffic return, whereas the Brighton Company's "take" was a poor one. South Western deferred has met with considerable support, and so has Great Eastern, a good deal of small investment business being reported.

Owing to the absence of reliable information concerning the war, the market in United States railroad shares became inactive and dull, and remained so until the close of last week. The news that eventually arrived from Manila being of such an eminently satisfactory character promptly led to a large accession of buying orders, and home operators were not slow to follow the lead of Wall-street, and a big rise has been established throughout the whole list. Latest rumours to the effect that Spain is only waiting for a favourable opportunity to sue for peace, and that the war will soon be over, and the like, have all been made the most of to raise prices, and the continued advance in the price of wheat has been another "bull" point. Apparently the trouble in the grain trade that was talked of in New York a few days ago was not as serious as was at first assumed. The Wabash Company's officials in an announcement just published state that "all surplus income will, for the present, be used to pay the floating debt rather than interest on the debenture stock." Canadian Pacific shares have been quiet, but leave off rather higher than last week, and Grand Trunk stocks were only moderately active at a slight advance, the traffic returns in each case being fairly satisfactory.

Highest and Lowest this Year.		Last Carrying over Price.	CANADIAN AND U.S. RAILWAYS.	Closing Prices.	Rise or Fall.
14 5/16	10⅜	12½	Atchison Shares	13¼	+ 1
34	23½	31	Do. Pref.	32¼	+ 3⅜
15⅜	11	13¼	Central Pacific	13¼	+ ⅜
99¾	85½	98	Chic. Mil. & St. Paul	98½	+ 3⅝
14¼	10	12	Denver Shares	12½	+ ⅝
54½	41½	48½	Do. Prefd.	48	+ ⅛
16⅜	11¼	13¾	Erie Shares	13⅜	+ ½
44⅛	29½	36½	Do. Prefd.	36½	+ 1½
110½	99	106¼	Illinois Central	107½	+ 2¾
62½	45¼	55¼	Louisville & Nashville	55¼	+ 2⅜
14½	9 15/16	12	Missouri & Texas	11⅜	+ ⅛
122¾	108½	118½	New York Central	119	+ 1
57¼	42⅞	52	Norfolk & West. Prefd.	52	+ 1¼
70⅛	59	68¼	Northern Pacific Prefd.	67⅞ xd	+ ⅛
19½	13⅜	15¾	Ontario Shares	15½	+ ⅜
62½	56¾	60¼	Pennsylvania	59½ xd	+ 1⅜
12½	7 13/16	9¾	Reading Shares	9⅞	+ ⅛
34½	24¼	30¼	Southern Prefd.	30½	+ 1½
37⅛	18½	24	Union Pacific	23¾	+ 1⅛
20¼	14½	20½	Wabash Prefd.	20	+ 2½
30⅛	21	28½	Do. Income Debs.	28	+ 3¼
92¾	74	86	Canadian Pacific	86½	+ 1
78½	69⅞	74	Grand Trunk Guar.	75½	+ 1¾
69¼	57⅛	68½	Do. 1st Pref.	68⅛	+ 1
50⅜	37¼	49	Do. 2nd Pref.	49⅜	+ 1½
25⅛	19¼	22¾	Do. 3rd Pref.	23¼	+ ⅜
105¾	101½	102½	Do. 4 p.c. Deb.	103¼	+ ½

In the Foreign market the principal features may be shortly stated to consist of a big rise in Brazilian bonds, and a moderate recovery in Spanish "Fours," while in the adverse direction there has been a collapse in Italian Rente. The advance in the Brazilian bonds in the first place was only accounted for by a statement which was alleged to have been made by the President-elect, who is now in Paris, while since then rumours have been flying about that the Brazilian Government has come to terms over the sale of the Central Railway. Various causes have led to the rise in Spanish, coming, as it did, in the face of the news of the total destruction of their fleet at Manila, but the principal reason undoubtedly is that the payment of the coupon on July 1 has been arranged for and the amount remitted, while the publication of the balance-sheet of the Bank of Spain led to a decline in the exchange. There is, moreover, a rumour about to the effect that a new ministry is to be formed in Madrid, and this was viewed favourably. Large blocks of Italian Rente have been thrown on the market, and for several days the news relating to the rioting in Milan was of a very unsatisfactory sort, but on Wednesday all offers of stock were promptly taken up by both German and French operators, and the latest quotation is well above the worst. Egyptian loans were favourably affected by Lord Salisbury's remarks, and an advance has taken place in Transvaal 5 per cents., Japanese, French 3½ per cents., and Chinese gold bonds of 1896. Argentine Government and the various Cedula issues show an all-round improvement, the fall in the exchange (owing to the continued rise in the price of wheat and the large exports that are now taking place), together with the success of the new internal loan, all having a good effect. Continuation rates at the settlement were rather higher if anything, with the exception of Spanish bonds, which were carried over at "even" to 2 per cent., against 2 per cent. last time.

Highest and Lowest this Year.		Last Carrying over Price.	FOREIGN BONDS.	Closing Price.	Rise or Fall.
94½	84	88¾	Argentine 5 p.c. 1886......	89½	+1¾
92⅝	81⅝	86¼	Do. 6 p.c. Funding	87	+1½
76¾	64	69	Do. 5 p.c. B. Ay. Water	70	+1½
61¾	41½	47	Brazilian 4 p.c. 1889	46¾	+3¼
69⅞	46	53	Do. 5 p.c. 1895	53	+4½
65	42¾	48¼	Do. 5 p.c. West Minas Ry..................	48	+2
108¾	105½	107	Egyptian 4 p.c. Unified...	107¼	+ ½
104¾	100½	102	Do. 3½ p.c. Pref. ...	101¼	—
103	99½	101½	French 3 p.c. Rente	101½	—
44¾	34½	42½	Greek 4 p.c. Monopoly...	42½	− ½
93 9/16	88¾	90¼	Italian 5 p.c. Rente	90¼	− ¾
100	87⅛	95½	Mexican 6 p.c. 1888	96½	+1
20⅞	16	17¼	Portuguese 1 p.c.	17¾	+ ⅝
62½	29⅝	32¼	Spanish 4 p.c.	34⅜	+4
45½	40	44	Turkish 1 p.c. "B"	44	− ¼
26 1/16	22¾	24¾	Do. 1 p.c. "C"	24¾	—
22 7/16	20	21¼	Do. 1 p.c. "D"	21⅝	—
46⅝	40	44½	Uruguay 3½ p.c. Bonds...	44½	− ¼

Among Foreign railway stocks, Cordoba Central (Central Northern) 4 per cents. gave way, as the traffic return was again very bad, but most of the leading Argentine issues have regained the losses of the earlier part of the week, and Brazilian and Uruguayan emissions are also firmer at the last. Nitrate Railway shares were bought in anticipation of the report, but profit-taking followed its publication. Mexican issues have been entirely neglected.

Highest and Lowest this Year.		Last Carrying over Price.	FOREIGN RAILWAYS.	Closing Price.	Rise or Fall.
101¼	99	99	Argentine Gt. West. 5 p.c. Pref. Stock.................	101	+1
158¼	136	138½	B. Ay. Gt. Southern Ord..	140 ex. new	—
78½	65	71½	B. Ay. and Rosario Ord...	73½	+2
12¼	10¼	10¾	B. Ay. Western Ord.	11	+ ¼
87¼	73	78	Central Argentine Ord....	79½	+1
92	78½	79	Cordoba and Rosario 6 p.c. Deb.	81	—
95½	85½	87½	Cord. Cent. 4 p.c. Deb. (Cent. Nth. Sec.)	90	+1½
61¾	42	46½	Do. Income Deb. Stk. ...	50	+1
25⅜	16⅜	18¼	Mexican Ord. Stk.	19	+ ½
83½	69½	72¼	Do. 8 p.c. 1st Pref.	73½	+ ¼

In the Miscellaneous market, Anglo-American Telegraph stocks, especially the deferred, have been largely bought, and there is an idea that this war is putting a lot of money into the company's coffers, and that it will mean a dividend of 10s. or £1 on the deferred this year. Russian Oil shares have again been waking up, and the price rose sharply when the resolution for splitting the ordinary into £1 shares was passed at the meeting. Great weakness has been the chief characteristic of the market for cycle ventures, and prices have now gone down to quite rubbish level. A further serious shrinkage is noticeable in Dumont Coffee debentures, and several tea companies' shares mark declines. London General Omnibus ordinary has risen 5, but City Offices 3 per cent. debentures have gone back a little after the recent sharp rise. Some inquiry has sprung up for Eastmans and Hammond Meat shares; Millar's Karri ordinary is higher owing to a satisfactory report, and Pillsbury Washburn Mills preference has risen in connection with the "boom" in wheat. Brewery emissions present few features of note; Guinness preference is 7 lower, and the debentures of several of the other leading companies have fallen 1 each. The directors of Wm. Younger are making a new issue of capital, and the preference stock has risen 4, while the demand for the leading American companies' shares still continues.

United States railroad shares closed flat, due to heavy sales on the part of influential houses, and the news that the return of the Spanish fleet to Cadiz has not yet been satisfactorily confirmed, taken in conjunction with the Spanish Premier's fighting speech on Wednesday night, does not quite bear out the idea that an early termination of the war is imminent. Spanish 4 per cents. also leave off dull, but still show a rise of 4 on the week; but apart from this, the Foreign market was well supported by Continental buying orders. Home railway stocks close firm, especially Metropolitan and Great Central issues, the small investment business being more pronounced. Mexican railway issues rose a little quite at the last in sympathy with the improvement in silver, and several other Foreign Railway stocks again advanced. South African mining shares were adversely affected by a forecast of President Kruger's speech.

Mining and Finance Companies.

Rather more activity has been displayed in the South African market, chiefly on Continental support, and the good Rand output, which is again a record one, tended to encourage operators. Chartered shares drooped after the debate in the House of Commons on Friday, but there has been a recovery since, and most of the leading favourites have added a little to their price during the week. All the leading Western Australian companies' shares mark substantial rises. Especially is this the case with Golden Horse Shoe. The account in this section passed off quietly and without trouble, although it was looked forward to with a considerable amount of apprehension. About the only feature the settlement disclosed was the fact that the account open had again been very largely reduced. The "Bottomley" group has not attracted much attention, Market Trusts, after dropping to 2s., having since slightly recovered, as the hearing of the winding-up petition has been put back for a month. Continuation rates were again round about 8 to 10 per cent., with slightly lower terms on some of the higher-priced shares, which appeared to be rather scarce for delivery.

Among copper-producing concerns, Rio Tinto and Cape show a slight advance, and it is now assumed that the Spanish export duty on the metal will be very moderate. Business remains extremely quiet and other miscellaneous shares show little alteration.

TRADE AND PRODUCE.

A week of extraordinary excitement in the wheat market has ended in comparative quiet, with a pause in the wild fluctuation which has characterised Liverpool, New York, and Chicago, and an apparent check to the pretty steady rise which has lately been taking place in the English provincial markets. Not that sellers have yet shown any pressing desire to sell. On the contrary, the inclination is still to hold on, in the hope of even higher prices. But buyers have been very cautious in their operations throughout the week. They have only bought to supply immediate needs, and have never ceased to show a certain amount of confidence that there would, in no long time, be a turn in the flowing tide. It was felt generally, and sometimes expressed even among sellers, that as soon as there were indications that the war was not likely to be unduly prolonged, wheat would begin to go down; not rapidly perhaps, but still go down to a figure considerably beyond what sanguine holders at present think possible. Many English farmers still hope, perhaps believe, that 60s. per quarter will yet be attained. We hardly think so. Although the price in New York once, in a moment of fierce excitement, touched 190 cents per bushel equivalent to 63s. a quarter, 57s. is the extreme price that has been quoted in the English market, and the dealings at that rate were few and exceptional; 54s. and 55s. have frequently been demanded, but these can hardly be regarded as business quotations; 50s. to 51s. is nearer the mark; and there is no present appearance of a likelihood of going beyond that. The return of the Spanish fleet to home waters may be said to be an open confession of weakness, and so appearances seem to indicate a comparatively early conclusion of the war. Speculation seems to have run its course for the present, and cannot easily, unless something new and unexpected turns up, "resurrect" the excitement of the past ten days. At Mark-lane on Wednesday all was quiet; it was a remarkable contrast to the animation of the previous week. Then the shipments of wheat have considerably increased. "Dornbusch" gives the shipments of bread stuffs to Europe during the week ending May 7 at 1,362,000 quarters, as compared with 1,048,000 quarters in the preceding week, and 983,500 for the week ending April 23. From India, too, the shipments last week amounted to 196,000 quarters, against 79,000 in the previous week, while a year ago we were receiving none at all from India. English farmers, it is believed, hold about 1,300,000 quarters as compared with 2,019,000 last year. There are now on the way to England at least 2,850,000 quarters, while the Continental demand is at least not increasing. According to Dornbusch the "visible supply" on May 1 was 11,800,000 quarters as compared with 12,699,000 quarters last year—a decrease undoubtedly, but not in itself, and without the aid of the war excitement, enough to have run up wheat to the height at which it has been fluttering for some time past. Nobody doubts that there are quite sufficient supplies to carry us over to the new harvest, and of the coming crops we continue to receive the most satisfactory reports. We are inclined to think, therefore, that we have now reached the top price in the wheat boom, and that in a little while prices will begin to settle down to what we may call their natural level.

There has been a fair, though not a very active, business in cotton, and nothing particular has been happening in the markets. The spot market has been quiet. Futures opened on Wednesday a point or so higher, but soon after receded a couple of points, and closed quiet and steady at one and a half to two points net loss. In Manchester things are steady, but the volume of business is not improving; indeed, the manufacturers have had fewer offers with lower prices than at the close of April. The Indian demand is fair, but China buyers are not offering much. On the whole business has a sluggish tendency.

The colonial wool sales are not going off so briskly as the previous series. Better descriptions of merinos and crossbreds are firm, but lower qualities show a decline. Yet a large proportion of the stocks are disposed of and the Continental demand is good. In Huddersfield business last week was more depressed than it has been this year. Scarcely anything is doing with the United States. Business in Leeds is quiet, with little prospect of change.

Copper is still on the down grade; and, in the present condition of the war prospects, it is not likely to improve much. Cash passed on Wednesday at £51 13s., and three months £51 7s. 6d. and 8s. 9d. combined. Settlement price, £51 2s. 6d., as compared with £51 10s. last week. In other metal trades business is well maintained, except perhaps in the Scotch iron warrant market, where, but for the firm tone in the English Midlands, there would probably have been a sensible decline. Shipbuilders continue busy, but new orders are not coming in so freely. Only 12,000 tons of new shipping were placed on the Clyde last month, againt 130,000 tons for March. A general improvement reported in pig iron; and in the Glasgow market on Wednesday more business was done than for a long time, the total turnover being fully 60,000 tons. Scotch rose 1½d., Cleveland 3d., and hematite ½d., while copper was reported idle. The demand for hematite pig iron has greatly improved, and business is done at Barrow-in-Furness, at fuller prices, ranging from 50s. 6d. to 52s. for parcels of mixed Bessemer numbers, net f. o. b. Shipbuilders and marine engineers there are full of work, and the number of new orders coming in is fairly satisfactory. In Birmingham business is reported as fairly healthy, but the scarcity of pig keeps the prices of wrought iron well up. Home demands are increasing in Wolverhampton, colonial business good, and shipping orders for bars, rods, and hoops satisfactory. Trade in South Shropshire excellent. Sellers decline to make any concession, and buyers are now more inclined to operate.

Coal continues in much the same condition, and there will, of course, be no change until a settlement has been made of the South Wales strike. There is now more likelihood of this than there has been for some time. The men have been holding many meetings, and there seems a growing feeling in favour of accepting Mr. Ritchie's suggestion for a conference. Of course, the President of the Board of Trade can only call it at the request of both parties to the dispute. The proposal is to base the conference on the lines of that at which Lord Rosebery presided and succeeded in settling the last great coal dispute.

The linen trade is reported quietly steady at Barnsley, but in Belfast "slow." There are numerous rumours of financial embarrassments, but nothing definite. No improvement announced in the Dundee linen trade, but considerable activity in jute, the outbreak of the plague in Calcutta having caused a rush to secure jute goods, as it is feared that foreign buyers, refusing to deal with India, might take their supplies from Dundee.

THE PROPERTY MARKET.

The total sales for last week at the Mart contrast somewhat with the similar week of last year, the amounts being £119,107 and £142,874 respectively, or a difference of £23,767. There seems no adequate explanation of this drop in business at this season, except that high-class property has been rather scarce in the market recently. The smaller investments offering during the week, however, sold well. The official monthly summary of sales shows some interesting results. At the Mart the sales for last April were considerably in advance of those of last year, being £475,689, as against £399,909. Private contract sales also come out well as compared with last year, £41,615 to £27,248. But the country and suburban sales were only £297,033 this year, while for April, 1897, they were £407,195. Probably this may be largely accounted for by the somewhat remarkable boom in licensed property last year. It has now become almost a drug in the market. Several good properties were disposed of yesterday week, though the total for the day was little above £35,000. Messrs. Stimson & Son ran up a total of £8,000, their chief dealings being in Bermondsey freeholds. Nos. 51, 61, 104, and 106, Spa-road, producing a gross rental of £162 8s., made £2,250, and Nos. 116 and 132, Jamaica-road, gross rental £97 10s., £1,360. Messrs. C. C. and T. Moore had on hand numerous investments in all parts of London, their aggregate being £7,550. A terrace of thirteen dwelling-houses and two shops, Nos. 234 to 262, even, Rotherhithe New-road, Rotherhithe, leasehold for a term of sixty-two and a half years, at ground-rents amounting to £31, gross annual rental £554 8s., fetched £4,990, and other properties also went well. Messrs. Driver, of Holloway, sold the freehold of No. 61, Albion-road, Stoke Newington, let at £125 yearly, for £2,250; and four leasehold houses, Nos. 2, 10, 12, and 14, Pemberton-terrace, Holloway, term fifty-three years, ground-rent £42, rental £160 per annum, for £1,560. The "Three Pigeons" public-house at Brentford went for £5,000. It is a freehold, with a rental of £100, and was submitted by Messrs. Orgill, Marks, & Orgill. Friday's returns were only £12,500, but they included several excellent freeholds. Riverside house and two acres in Staines realised £2,600. Another freehold in Blackfriars-road, of the annual rental of £120, was disposed of by Messrs. Woods & Snelling for £2,300.

With nothing exceptionally high-class on offer, the total of sales at the Mart on Monday, nevertheless, went up as far as £48,527. Mr. Smallpeice had the highest total; but the most interesting of his lots—the Crown lease of the Lowther Arcade, Strand—was withdrawn at £30,000. The actual bidding went from £15,000 to £24,100. Mr. Smallpeice was more successful with some leasehold properties at Campden Hill, Kensington, which produced a total of £11,200. Freehold properties in Gordon-road, Kilburn, bringing in a rental of £348, were sold by Mr. Percival Hodson for £3,550. The "Gun" Tavern in Church-street, Croydon, freehold, rental £150, was sold by Messrs. Blake & Carpenter, at £4,000. A freehold ground rent £125, in Dryden-road, reversion in ninety-eight years, brought £3,000; and another in Mitcham, Surrey, £31 10s., reversion in two years, went for £7,650. Messrs. Elliot, Son, & Boyton obtained excellent prices for leasehold investments at Norwood, Finsbury Park, &c. The lot at Norwood consisted of houses in Church-road, with eighty and a half years to run, a ground rent of £140, and annual rental of £495, and was disposed of for £6,320.

No fewer than nine of the lots offered at the Mart on Tuesday were left unsold, and this accounts for the smallness of the day's total, £19,055. To this total, Messrs. Debenham, Tewson, & Co. contributed £11,750, the price of a city freehold property, at 37, Wood-street, and 5, Little Love-lane, let at £500 per annum. Two leasehold residences in Lexham-gardens, Kensington, were sold by Messrs. Rogers, Chapman, & Thomas, for £2,050; and a freehold ground rent of £12 per annum on property in Larkhall-rise, Clapham, with reversion in three and three-quarter years, was sold by Messrs. Ventom, Bull, & Cooper for £1,266. Three licensed houses changed hands at the Masons' Hall Tavern on Tuesday, and a fourth, the Greyhound Hotel at Croydon, was withdrawn from competition, the owner intimating his willingness to treat privately. The lease and goodwill of the Lord Raglan, in St. Martin's-le-Grand, City, held for a term of forty-nine years at £375 per annum, sold for £40,000. The lease and goodwill of the White Ferry House in Pimlico, with forty years to run at a rent of £150, offered by Messrs. Schofield, Evans, & Loader, changed hands at £37,310. The Lothian Arms, Lothian-road, Camberwell, was disposed of by Mr. William Rolfe for £3,110.

Wednesday's proceedings at the Mart were rather uninteresting, and the day's total only reached £20,029. Mr. Alfred Richards had the largest account, consisting of a number of gas and water shares. Among these were 500 £10 shares in the Southend Waterworks Company, which fetched from £15 5s. to £17 7s. 6d. each, realising a grand total of £7,957.

Next Week's Meetings.

MONDAY, MAY 16.	
Compagnie Générale des Asphaltes	Winchester House, 1 p.m.
Millars' Karri & Jarrah Forests ...	Winchester House, noon.
TUESDAY, MAY 17.	
Chardwar Teas	128, Leadenhall-street, 3 p.m.
Clément, Gladiator & Humber (France)	Hotel Cecil, 2 p.m.
Lankapara Tea	218, Leadenhall-street, 12.30 p.m.
Metropolitan District	Westminster Palace Hotel, 1 p.m.
New Vancouver Coal & Mining ...	12, Old Jewry-chambers, 3 p.m.
West Middlesex Waterworks ...	19, Marylebone-road, noon.
WEDNESDAY, MAY 18.	
Broxburn Oil	Glasgow, 2 p.m.
Investment Trust Corporation ...	Cannon-street Hotel, 2 p.m.
Lebong Tea	93, Cannon-street, 11.30 a.m.
Santa Rita Nitrate	Winchester House, 2 p.m.
Van Diemen's Land	31, Finsbury Circus, noon.
Vizianagoram Mining	Winchester House, noon
West India and Panama Telegraph	Winchester House, noon.
West London Dairy	6, Spring-street, W., 2.30 p.m.
THURSDAY, MAY 19.	
Colney Hatch Gas	New Southgate, 4 p.m.
Land and Mortgage of Egypt ...	Cannon-street Hotel, noon.
Singapore Gas	Cannon-street Hotel, 1 p.m.
Surrey Commercial Gas	106, Fenchurch-street, 1 p.m.
Waterford and Central Ireland Railway	Dublin, 2 and 2.30 p.m.
FRIDAY, MAY 20.	
Burgess Hill Waterworks	Burgess Hill, 6.30 p.m.
Hong Kong and China Gas	Gresham House, noon.
Scottish Australian Investment ...	Winchester House, noon.

Answers to Correspondents.

Questions about public securities, and on all points in company law, as well as on the position of life insurance offices and their promises, will be answered week by week, in the REVIEW, on the following terms and conditions :—

A fee of FIVE shillings must be remitted for each question put, provided they are questions about separate securities. Should a private letter be required, then an extra fee of FIVE shillings must be sent to cover the cost of such letter, the fee then being TEN shillings for one query only, and FIVE shillings for every subsequent one in the same letter. While making this concession the EDITOR will feel obliged if private replies are as much as possible dispensed with. It is wholly impossible to answer letters sent merely "with a stamped envelope enclosed for reply."

Correspondents will further greatly oblige by so framing their questions as to obviate the necessity to name securities in the replies. They should *number* the questions, keeping a copy for reference, thus :—"(1) Please inform me about the present position of the Rowenzori Development Co. (2) Is a dividend likely to be paid soon on the capital stock of the Congo-Sudan Railway?

Answers to be given to all such questions by simply quoting the numbers 1, 2, 3, and so on. The EDITOR has a rooted objection to such forms of reply as—"I think your Timbuctoo Consols will go up," or "Sell your Slowcoach and Draggem Bonds," because this kind of thing is open to all sorts of abuses. By the plan suggested, and by using a fancy name to be replied to, each query can be kept absolutely private to the inquirer, and no scope whatever be given to market manipulations. Avoid, as names to be replied to, common words, like "investor," "inquirer," and so on, as also "bear" or "bull." Detached syllables of the inquirer's name, or initials reversed, will frequently do as well as anything, so long as the answer can be identified by the inquirer.

The EDITOR further respectfully requests that merely speculative questions should as far as possible be avoided. He by no means sets himself up as a market prophet, and can only undertake to provide the latest information regarding the securities asked about. This he will do faithfully and without bias.

Replies cannot be guaranteed in the same week if the letters demanding them reach the office of the INVESTORS' REVIEW, Norfolk House, Norfolk-street, W.C., later than the first post on Wednesday mornings.

MEDICUS.—Many thanks for the pamphlet. There has been a decided rise in the stock since you wrote, and it is now nearly at its full value, as there must be a decrease in the dividend. I think you would be prudent in selling part of your holding at any rate, and so lessen the cost of the balance.

MINING RETURNS.

Messrs. A. Barsdorf & Co. have received a cablegram from the Chamber of Mines of the South African Republic, Johannesburg, stating that the total gold output of all the mines of the Transvaal making returns to the Chamber amounted for April to 353,243 oz., comprising 335,125 oz. for the Witwatersrand district, and 18,118 oz. for the outside districts. The production of the Witwatersrand district was 325,907 oz. in March, 1898, and 235,698 oz. in April, 1897, and of the outside districts 21,736 oz. in March, 1898.

MYALL'S UNITED.—2,100 tons crushed for a yield of 363 oz., tailings assayed 2 dwt. per ton. By cyanide process—1,600 tons of tailings treated, yielding 233 oz.

MENZIES' CRUSOE.—Cyanide process—900 tons tailings; yield, 534 oz. gold; value, £1,600.

ZEEHAN-MONTANA.—Have shipped 230 tons of silver lead ore containing about 136 tons 8 cwt. of lead, and 19,580 oz. of silver.

MOUNT ZEEHAN (TASMANIA).—Have shipped 25 tons of silver lead ore, containing about 17½ tons of lead and 2,075 oz. of silver.

GOLD FIELDS OF MYSORE.—Last month's return :—30 oz. of gold obtained from 660 tons sand, cyanide process; 192 oz. of gold obtained from amalgamation.

HALL MINES (BRITISH COLUMBIA).—4,734 tons of ore smelted, yielding 218 tons matte, containing approximately 92 tons copper, 71,460 oz. silver, 254 oz. gold.

MYSORE REEFS (KANGUNDY).—April return :—686 tons of ore crushed, yielding 192 oz. of gold.

ST. JOHN DEL REY.—Gold produce month of April, £23,380; yield per ton, 0·92 of an ounce troy.

STANHOPE.—Last month's crushing yielded 989 oz.

WAITEKAURI.—During April the mill ran twenty-four days, yielding £4,851 from 1,680 tons.

WEALTH OF NATIONS.—Crushed during April 650 tons, gross yield being 433 oz. of gold.

WORCESTER EXPLORATION AND GOLD.—Last month's crushing yielded 2,961 oz. of gold.

BURMA RUBY.—65,000 loads washed, producing rubies valued at Rs. 77,000.

GLYNN'S LYDENBURG.—From mill: crushed, 1,251 tons; obtained, 510 oz. of fine gold, equal to 556 oz. standard gold. From cyanide works: treated, 840 tons, yielding 173 oz. of fine gold, equal to 189 oz. standard gold.

HIGHLAND CHIEF.—During the last fortnight crushed 120 tons, yielding 70 oz.

JUBILEE.—Last month's return :—Tons crushed, 5,239; ounces obtained, 1,056; tailings yielded 624 oz.

MONTANA.—The total output for April was—gold, 2,000 oz.; and silver, 8,540 oz., obtained from 6,400 tons of ore crushed in the mills and 4,305 tons of tailings from the dams brought under treatment.

OTTO'S KOPJE.—7,031 loads washed during the week ended May 5, 200 carats won, including stones of 12 and 10 carats each.

PIGG'S PEAK.—Crushed, 2,250 tons, for 293 oz.; cyanide, 2,600 tons, for 389 oz.; total yield, £2,300.

TRANSVAAL GOLD MINING ESTATES.—From mill—crushed, 9,796 tons; obtained 3,403 oz. of fine gold, equal to 3,712 oz. standard gold. From outside cyanide works—treated, 2,373 tons, yielding 1,004 oz. of fine gold, equal to 1,095 oz. standard gold.

WAIHI.—For the period ended April 30 the two mills ran twenty-four days, yielding £22,851 from 6,690 tons crushed. In addition £7,100 has been obtained from various crushings at the Victoria Mill before the above period.

WEMMER.—Crushed, 6,863 tons, yielding 4,366 oz.; cyanide plant, 4,600 tons treated, yielding 932 oz.; and from concentrates, 150 tons caught, assaying 135 dwt. per ton.

WITWATERSRANDT (KNIGHT'S).—Crushed, 14,280 tons, yielding 4,253 oz. gold; 8,160 tons cyanide tailings treated, yielding 1,403 oz. gold.

NIGEL.—Last month's return :—1,414 oz. battery; 1,792 oz. cyanide.

BARRETT.—Gold yield for April, 325 oz.

GREAT BOULDER PERSEVERANCE.—Returns from smelting works not yet to hand. Number of tons of ore milled, April—880 tons for 1,044 oz.

HENRY NOURSE.—Crushed 8,655 tons, producing 5,088 oz.; treated 6,450 tons cyanide, producing 3,174 oz.

LANCASTER.—8,041 tons crushed, yielding 2,880 oz.; 5,685 tons of tailings treated, yielding 1,244 oz.

LISBON-BERLYN.—Ore mined, 2,400 tons; ore crushed, 2,400 tons; treated by cyanide, 2,050 tons; fine gold recovered, 600 oz.

NATAL COLLIERIES AND DURBAN COALING STATION.—Output for March—3,152 tons.

SHEBA GOLD.—6,600 tons of ore, 3,003 oz.; 3,600 tons of tailings, 949 oz.; 110 tons of concentrates, 800 oz.

ANGELO.—Tons crushed, 6,836; ounces recovered from mill, 3,377; tons treated by cyanide, 5,606; ounces recovered, 2,595; ounces recovered by products, 14; ounces recovered by slimes, 134.

BONANZA.—From mill—crushed 5,240 tons, obtained 5,074 oz. of gold; from cyanide and slimes works—treated 4,944 tons, yielding 3,041 oz. of gold.

BRILLIANT AND ST. GEORGE UNITED.—Last month's crushing :—3,084 oz. of gold from 9,371 tons of quartz.

CROWN DEEP.—Tons crushed, 20,400; yield in fine gold from mill, 5,812 oz.; tons of sands and concentrates treated by cyanide works, 17,240; yield in fine gold, 4,134 oz.; tons of slimes treated, 2,880; yield in fine gold, 337 oz.

FRONTINO AND BOLIVIA.—Result for April :—Produce value, £11,140.

GEORGE GOCH AMALGAMATED.—During April 8,353 tons were crushed, yielding 1,642 oz. gold, and 1,095 oz. gold from tailings.

GRAND CENTRAL.—Crushed, 4,000 tons, yielding bullion estimated at $62,200; concentrates estimated to realise $22,400.

GREAT BOULDER PROPRIETARY.—Crushing returns for the past fortnight :—Tons of ore crushed, 1,425; yield of gold in ounces, 3,157.

NEW COMET.—Tons crushed, 4,990; ounces recovered from mill, 1,815 treated by cyanide, 4,126; ounces recovered, 1,167; ounces recovered by products, 131; ounces recovered by slimes, 53.

NEW KLEINFONTEIN.—Tons crushed, 10,080; ounces recovered from mill, 3,195; tons treated by cyanide, 7,568; ounces recovered from cyanide, 1,248.

NEW QUEEN.—Result of crushing for past fortnight :—405 tons, yielding 235 oz gold.

NOURSE DEEP.—Tons crushed, 7,423; yield in fine gold from mill, 2,414 oz.; tons of sands and concentrates treated by cyanide works, 5,723; yield in fine gold, 1,556 oz.; total yield in bullion, 4,013 oz., equal to 3,970 oz. fine gold.

ROODEPOORT UNITED MAIN REEF.—Tons crushed, 7,575, produced 3,151 oz.; produce from cyanide, 941 oz.; total, 4,092 oz.

VILLAGE MAIN REEF.—Crushed, 8,480 tons, yielding 5,009 oz. of gold: cyanide, treated 8,470 tons, producing 3,081 oz. of gold.

THE VAN RYN GOLD MINES ESTATE.—Crushed, 11,347 tons, yielded 3,119 oz. bar gold; cyanide works, 8,190 tons of tailings treated, yielded 1,254 oz.

BLOCK "B" LANGLAAGTE.—Production for April :—Mill—ore crushed, 10,943 tons of 2,000 lb.; gold retorted, 2,740 oz. Tailings (cyanide process)—tons treated, 6,750; gold recovered, 1,324 oz. Concentrates (cyanide process)—tons treated, 132; gold recovered, 370 oz.—total gold recovered, 4,434 oz.

CASSEL COAL.—Output for April, 23,580 tons.

CHIAPAS.—1,600 tons of ore crushed, yielding 62 tons of concentrates. The stamp mill ran twenty-six days, crushing 1,350 tons of tailings, yielding 160 oz. gold.

CLYDESDALE (TRANSVAAL) COLLIERIES.—Clydesdale sales for April amount to 20,250 tons.

CROWN REEF.—Output for April :—Yield in smelted gold from mill, 6,934 oz.; from cyanide works, 4,270 oz.; from slimes works, 227 oz.

DE LAMAR.—Return for April :—Beached during the month, 1,831 tons; bullion produced from cyanide treatment, $16,661; surplus from clean up of old mill, $3,000; estimated value of ore shipped to smelters, $2,000.

GELDENHUIS MAIN REEF.—909 tons crushed, yielding 200 oz.; 540 tons treated by cyanide, yielding 129 oz.—total, 329 oz.

GELDENHUIS ESTATE.—Crushed, 16,464 tons; obtained from mill, 6,395 oz.; from concentrates by cyanide, 933 oz.; from tailings by cyanide, 2,700 oz.; from slimes by cyanide, 526 oz.—total, 10,554 oz.

HOPE'S HILL (SOUTHERN CROSS, W.A.).—Crushed, 40 tons for 40 oz.

JUMPERS GOLD.—Results for April :—Crushed, 11,500 tons; obtained from mill, 3,906 oz.; from concentrates by cyanide 649 oz.; from tailings by cyanide, 843 oz.—total, 5,398 oz.

LAKE VIEW CONSOLS.—Clean up for April :—Crushed, 5,670 tons, yielding 5,955 oz. of gold; tailings assay, 10 dwt. 16 gr. per ton; cyanide return 3,498 tons of tailings treated, yielded 2,804 oz. 8 dwt. of gold; tailings (residues) assay, 3 dwt. 23 gr. per ton. Have not cleaned up concentrates and slimes treated during last month. Total return for April (exclusive of concentrates and slimes), 8,759 oz. of gold.

LANGLAAGTE ESTATE.—Mill—ore crushed, 20,068 tons of 2,000 lb.; gold retorted, 7,769 oz.; tailings, cyanide process—tons treated, 12,150; gold recovered, 1,558 oz.; concentrates, cyanide process—tons treated, 624; gold recovered, 1,864 oz.

LANGLAAGTE STAR.—Mill—ore crushed, 4,093 tons of 2,000 lb.; gold retorted, 2,172 oz.; tailings, cyanide process—tons treated, 5,280; gold recovered, 942 oz.

MEYER AND CHARLTON.—Crushed 9,082 tons, producing 2,682 oz. Extracted from tailings, 1,254 oz.

NORTH RANDFONTEIN.—Mill—ore crushed, 6,743 tons of 2,000 lb.; gold retorted, 1,533 oz.; tailings, cyanide process—tons treated, 3,840; gold recovered, 562 oz.; concentrates—cyanide process—tons treated, 55; gold recovered, 130 oz.

NEW GUADALCAZAR QUICKSILVER MINES.—The production of quicksilver for the past month amounts to 7,600 lb. = 101⅓ flasks.

PAARL CENTRAL.—From Mill—crushed 5,785 tons, yielding 1,119 oz. of gold. From cyanide works—treated 3,625 tons, yielding 940 oz.—total 2,059 oz.

PORGES RANDFONTEIN.—Mill—ore crushed, 7,703 tons of 2,000 lb.; gold retorted, 2,463 oz. Tailings, cyanide process—tons treated, 5,625; gold recovered, 679 oz. Concentrates, cyanide process—tons treated, 111; gold recovered, 309 oz.

PRINCESS ESTATE.—Crushed, 6,485 tons; gold won, 1,914 oz.; extracted from tailings, 836 oz.; total, 2,750 oz.

ROBINSON.—Mill—crushed, 14,657 tons of ore, yielded in smelted gold 10,416 oz. From concentrates (by chlorination), 1,160 oz.; from tailings (cyanide process), 3,373; from slimes, 1,430 oz. From concentrates bought (by chlorination), 2,914 oz.

ROBINSON RANDFONTEIN.—Mill—ore crushed, 4,531 tons of 2,000 lb.; gold retorted, 1,982 oz. Tailings (cyanide process)—tons treated, 3,960; gold recovered, 604 oz. Concentrates (cyanide process)—tons treated, 110; gold recovered, 247 oz.

SIMMER AND JACK.—Crushed, 34,780 tons; obtained 9,937 oz. of gold from mill, 3,700 oz. of gold from tailings by cyanide, and 714 oz. of gold from slimes; total, 14,351 oz. of gold during the month of April.

TREASURY GOLD MINES.—Output for April, 5,300 tons, yielded 3,649 oz.

UNITED IVY REEF.—Last month's output was 615 oz.; crushed 1,100 tons.

WEST RAND.—Crushed 3,652 tons, yielded 791 oz.; cyanide treated, 2,734 tons, yielded 675 oz.

WOLHUTER.—Result of operations for April—Crushed, 12,636 tons; total ounces produced by mill and cyanide, 6,823.

BARNATO GROUP OF MINES.—New Primrose, 9,653 oz; Glencairn Main Reef, 6,747 oz.; Ginsberg, 2,875 oz.; Rietfontein A, 4,863 oz.; Roodepoort, 1,138 oz.; Buffelsdoorn, 2,225 oz.; New Spes Bona, 1,894 oz.; Consolidated Main Reef, 2,491 oz. from 6,152 tons battery and 1,186 oz. from 3,456 tons cyanide.

CROWN REEF.—Working results for April—crushed by 120-stamp mill, 15,426 tons. Yield in smelted gold, 6,934 oz.; from 120-stamp cyanide works, 4,270 oz.; from slimes works, 227 oz.

DURBAN-ROODEPOORT.—Results for April—quartz milled, 10,160 tons for 5,076 oz.; tailings treated, 6,640 tons, for 1,152 oz.

FERREIRA.—Results for April—crushed, 10,869 tons; bar gold extracted, 8,136 oz.; concentrates caught, 282 tons; assay value of concentrates, 4 oz. 10 dwt. fine gold per ton, equal to, say, 1,260 oz.; bullion produced from tailings, 3,006 oz.; bullion produced from slimes, 1,114 oz.

FRANK SMITH DIAMONDS.—3,650 loads washed, producing 186 carats.

JUMPERS DEEP.—Tons crushed by eighty stamps, 11,187; yield in fine gold from mill, 4,075 oz.; tons of sands and concentrates treated by cyanide works, 8,374; yield in fine gold from sands and concentrates, 2,095 oz.; total yield in bullion 7,313 oz., equal to 6,170 oz.

MAY CONSOLIDATED.—The yield of gold during April was 5,465 oz., from 13,013 tons crushed. Cyanide, 2,666 oz. from 8,760 tons; total for month, 8,131 oz.

NEW MODDERFONTEIN.—Output for April—7,112 tons yielded 2,928 oz.; cyanide, 912 oz.

ROSE DEEP.—Tons crushed, 15,164; yield in fine gold from mill; 4,666 oz.; tons of sands and concentrates treated by cyanide works, 11,100; yield in fine gold from sands and concentrates, 2,670 oz.; tons of silmes treated, 5,568; yield in fine gold from slimes, 456 oz.; total yield in bullion 10,223 oz., equal to 7,792 oz. fine gold.

YORK.—4,224 tons crushed in April, yielding 877 oz., while 3,510 tons of tailings gave 584 oz., while 3,510 tons of tailings gave 584 oz.—total, 1,461 oz.

ALBION (TRANSVAAL).—Crushed 1,300 tons; yield 372 ozs., 860 tons from stopes; 440 tons from dump.

CHAMP D'OR FRENCH.—Crushed 5,428 tons yielding 2,243 oz. Cyanide, 3,850 tons treated yielding 913 oz. Concentrates 85 ozs.

WINDSOR GOLD MINING COMPANY.—Result for April:—Crushed 3,958 tons, producing 1,224 oz.; obtained by cyanide, 747 oz. Total, 1,971 oz of gold. Profit for month, £3,139.

TRAMWAY AND OMNIBUS RECEIPTS.

HOME.

Name.	Period.	Ending.	Amount.	Increase or Decrease on 1897.	Weeks or Months.	Aggregate to Date. Amount.	Aggregate to Date. Inc. or Dec. on 1897.
			£	£		£	£
Aberdeen District	Week	May 7	536	+58	—	—	—
Belfast Street	"	" 7	2,288	+252	—	—	—
Birmingham and Aston	"	" 7	465	+31	—	—	—
Birmingham and Midland	"	" 7	667	+54	—	—	—
Birmingham City	"	" 7	3,744	+254	—	—	—
Birmingham General	"	" 7	871	+86	—	—	—
Blessington and Poulaphouca	"	" 8	20	+16/	18	178	+19
Bristol Tramways and Carriage	"	" 6	2,478	+206	—	—	—
Burnley and District	"	" 7	315	+23	—	—	—
Bury, Rochdale, and Oldham	"	" 7	852	+30	—	—	—
Croydon	"	" 7	360	+45	—	—	+1,162
Dublin and Blessington	"	" 8	100	+1	18	1,725	+29
Dublin and Lucan	"	" 7	69	−2	19	784	−368
Dublin United	"	" 6	2,973	+62	—	49,699	+2,905
Dudley and Stourbridge	"	" 7	170	+11	19	3,070	+123
Edinburgh and District	"	" 7	2,553	+303	18	40,835	+3,772
Edinburgh Street	"	" 7	690	+109	18	10,779	+1,349
Gateshead and District	Month	April	940	+59	—	—	—
Glasgow	Week	May 7	2,058	+73	—	—	—
Harrow-road and Paddington	"	" 6	239	+65	—	—	—
Lea Bridge and Leyton	"	" 7	735	—	—	—	—
London, Deptford, and Greenwich	"	" 7	589	+8	—	10,180	+574
London General Omnibus	"	" 7	21,406	−42	—	—	—
London Road Car	"	" 7	6,623	−325	†	111,398	+5,469
London Southern	"	" 7	521	−14	—	—	—
North Staffordshire	"	" 7	415	−17	—	7,124	−32
Provincial	"	" 7	2,329	−48	—	—	—
Rossendale Valley	"	" 6	171	−4	—	—	—
Southampton	"	" 7	377	+11	—	—	—
South London	"	" 7	1,725	−15	†	29,121	+1,009
South Staffordshire	"	" 6	577	−16	18	10,661	−58
Tramways Union	Month	April	20,870	+1,149	4	39,500	+4,495
Wigan and District	Week	May 7	312	+176‡	—	—	—
Woolwich and South East London	"	" 7	352	+6	†	5,849	+337

† From January 1. ‡ Strike in 1897.

FOREIGN.

Name.	Period.	Ending.	Amount.	Increase or Decrease on 1897.	Weeks or Months.	Aggregate to Date. Amount.	Aggregate to Date. Inc. or Dec. on 1897.
			£	£		£	£
Anglo-Argentine	Week	Apr. 11	4,544	+350	*	64,727	+6,642
Barcelona	"	" 7	1,122	−150	—	20,439	−2,809
Barcelona, Ensanche y Gracia	"	" 7	219	+3	—	4,030	+30
Bordeaux	"	" 29	2,148	−271	—	33,958	−1,543
Brazilian Street	Month	Mch. (m	lr 51,419	+ mlr 30	47) —	—	—
British Columbia Electric	"	"	$30,729	+$10493	‡	$305,154	—
Do. net	"	"	$10,391	+$4,958	‡	$97,402	—
Buenos Ayres and Belgrano	"	"	5,219	+1,305	*	14,382	+2,578
Buenos Ayres Grand National	Week	Apr. 9	$25,651	+$3,718	†	—	+$25328
Buenos Ayres New	Month	Feb.	$61,322	−$4,402	—	$131,227	−$6,254
Calais	Week	May 7	151	+7	—	—	—
Calcutta	"	Apr. 16	1,460	+136	—	—	—
C'rth'g'na & Herrerias	Month	April	4,607	+712	—	18,809	+1,011
Gothenburg	Week	" 27	325	+20	—	—	—
Lynn and Boston	Month	Mch.	$105,471	+$6,044		$622,228	+$27912
Do. net	"	"	$4,2847	+$6,607		$216,383	+$3,162

* From January 1. † From April 1, 1898. ‡ From April 15, 1897. § From October 1, 1897.

It is announced by the General Post Office that private cipher and code telegrams for the Bank of Italy, Rome, will be accepted.

The Ranfurly Mining Company report the discovery of a seam of cannel coal 3 ft. 3 in. thick at Dungannon, County Tyrone. Mr. Munro, the engineer, expresses the opinion that there are many good seams of coal lower down. If true, the discovery will be a very important one, especially for Belfast; but it will be well to wait a little before jumping to conclusions.

Prices of Mine and Mining Finance Companies' Shares.

Shares £1 each except where otherwise stated.

AUSTRALIAN.

Making-Up Price, May 9.	Name	Closing Price.	Rise or Fall.	Making-Up Price, May 9.	Name	Closing Price.	Rise or Fall.
1¼	Aladdin	1¼		9/16	Hannan's Star	9/16	
3½	Associated	3½	+ 1/16	5 7/16	Ivanhoe, New	5 7/16	+ ¼
1/16	Do. Southern	1/16	− ⅛	15/16	Kalgurli Mt. & Iron King, 15/	¼	
1	Brownhill Extended	1 1/16	+ ⅛	5¼	Kalgurli	5½	+ ¼
1	Burbank's Birthday	1⅛	+ 1/16	2 3/16	Lady Shenton	2 3/16	+ ⅛
½	Central Boulder	9/16	+ ⅛	8⅝	Lake View Cons.	9	+ 7/16
5/	Chaffers, 4/-	5/	− /6	¼	Do. Extended	¼	
1/16	Colonial Finance, 15/	¼ dis		⅛	Do. South	1/16	
¾	Crœsus S. United	¾		1⅛	London & Globe Finance	1 1/16	− ⅛
¼	E. Murchison	½		½	London & W. A. Exploration	½	
4/	Golden Arrow 19/	5/	+ /6	1/16	Do. Investment	¼	
8½	Golden Horseshoe	8⅝	+ ⅛	½	Mainland Consols	½	
1/16	Golden Link	⅛		1/16	North Boulder, 10/	½	
19/9	Great Boulder, 2/	19/ x.		1 1/16	North Kalgurli	1⅛	+ ⅛
1½	Do. Main Reef, 10/	1½		¾	Northern Territories	¾	
2½	Do. Perseverance	2 3/16		2½	Peak Hill	2½	
1/16	Do. South	¾		1¼	South Kalgurli	1 5/16	+ ⅛
1⅛	Hainault	1⅛		1½	W. A. Goldfields	1 7/16	− 1/16
¾	Hampton Plains	¾		1/16	W. A. Joint Stock	¾	− 1/16
7 5/16	Hannan's Brownhill	7 5/16	+ 1/16	2/	W. A. Market Trust	4/	
⅝	Hannan's Oroya	⅝		1/16	W. A. Loan & General Fin.	¼	− 1/16
1½	Do. Proprietary	13/	+ 2/	1/16	White Feather	⅛	

SOUTH AFRICAN.

Making-Up Price, May 9.	Name	Closing Price.	Rise or Fall.	Making-Up Price, May 9.	Name	Closing Price.	Rise or Fall.
5½	Angelo	5⅝	+ 1/16	2/3	Lisbon-Berlyn	2/3	
1	Aurora West	1½		2¼	May Consolidated	2½	+ 1/16
1⅛	Bantjes	1½	+ 1/16	4	Meyer and Charlton	4	
8/6	Barrett, 10/	8/6		3 13/16	Modderfontein	3¾	− ⅛
4 3/16	Bonanza	4 3/16		1 1/16	New Bultfontein	1 1/16	
⅝	Huffelsdoorn	⅝		3 13/16	New Primrose	3⅞	− ⅛
5 13/16	City and Suburban, £4	5⅞		1¼	Nigel	1¼	+ 1/16
2¼	Comet (New)	2⅜	+ ⅛	1¼	Nigel Deep	1½	+ 1/16
3⅜	Con. Deep Level	3⅜		¾	North Randfontein	¾	
11	Crown Deep	11⅛	+ ¼	5	Nourse Deep	5½	+ ½
12½	Crown Reef	12¾	+ ¼	1 1/16	Porges-Randfontein	1 1/16 x	
27	De Beers, £5	27⅜	+ ¼	30½	Rand Mines	30⅝	+ ⅜
3½	Driefontein	4	+ 1/16	1 1/16	Randfontein	1/16	
6½	Durban Roodepoort	6¾	+ ⅛	1 1/16	Rietfontein	1¼	
3 1/16	Do. Deep	3½		9¼	Robinson Deep	9⅜	+ ⅛
4 5/16	East Rand	4½	− 1/16	7⅝	Do. Gold, £5	8⅛	+ ⅛
24½	Ferreira	24½	+ ¼	1 3/16	Do. Randfontein	1	− 1/16
7	Geldenhuis Deep	7¾	+ ¼	1 3/16	Roodepoort Central Deep	1 1/16	+ 1/16
5⅛	Do. Estate	6½	+ ⅛	6⅛	Rose Deep	6⅛	
¾	George Goch	13/16	+ 1/16	3 5/16	Salisbury	3⅜	+ ⅜
2¼	Ginsberg	2½	+ ¼	1⅜	Sheba	1⅜	
1 13/16	Glencairn	1 13/16		3¼	Simmer and Jack, £5	3⅜	+ ⅛
8¾	Goldfields Deep	9	+ ⅛	3 5/16	Transvaal Gold	3⅜	+ ⅛
8⅝	Griqualand West	8⅝	− ¼	3¼	Treasury	3⅜	+ 1/16
9	Henry Nourse	9	+ 3/16	3¼	United Roodepoort	3⅜	+ ⅛
7⅝	Heriot	7¾	+ ¼	1⅛	Van Ryn	1¼	+ ⅛
7⅝	Jagersfontein	7½	− ⅛	5 13/16	Village Main Reef	6 1/16	+ 1/16
8¾	Jubilee	9½	+ 1	1½	Vogelstruis	1⅝	+ 1/16
5 1/16	Jumpers	5⅝		1/16	Do. Deep	⅝	+ 1/16
2 3/16	Kleinfontein	2½	+ 3/16	9½	Wemmer	9⅝	+ ⅛
3½	Knight's	3⅝	+ ⅛	⅞	West Rand	⅞	+ 1/16
2½	Lancaster	2½		5⅞	Wolhuter, £4	5⅞	
3⅛	Langlaagte Estate	3¼	+ 3/16	2½	Worcester	2⅝	+ ⅛

LAND EXPLORATION AND RHODESIAN.

Making-Up Price, May 9.	Name	Closing Price.	Rise or Fall.	Making-Up Price, May 9.	Name	Closing Price.	Rise or Fall.
2⅝	Anglo-French Ex.	2⅝		⅞	Mashonaland Central	⅞	− ⅛
1⅛	Barnato Consolidated	1¼	+ ⅛	6⅛	Matabele Gold Reefs	6⅛	− ⅛
¾	Bechuanaland Ex.	¾		2 3/16	Mozambique	2¼	+ ⅛
2⅞	Chartered B.S.A.	2 15/16		¾	Oceana Consolidated	¾	
¾	Clark's Cons.	11/16	− ⅛	1 1/16	Rhodesia, Ltd.	1½	+ 1/16
11/16	Colenbrander	11/16		4⅝	Do. Exploration	4⅜	− ⅛
4½	Cons. Goldfields	4⅝	+ ⅛	1	Do. Goldfields	1	
1	Do. Pref.	20/		4	S. A. Gold Trust	4 1/16	+ 1/16
1¼	Exploration	1¼	− 1/16	1	Tati Concessions	1 1/16	+ 1/16
2 13/16	Geelong	2 13/16		1/16	Transvaal Development	1/16	
1/16	Henderson's Est.	1/16		13/16	United Rhodesia	¾	
1 13/16	Johannesburg Con. In.	1 13/16	+ 1/16	1 1/16	Willoughby	1 1/16	
¾	Do. Water	¾	+ 1/16	13/16	Zambesia Explor.	1	
1⅛	Mashonaland Agency	1 1/16					

MISCELLANEOUS.

Making-Up Price, May 9.	Name	Closing Price.	Rise or Fall.	Making-Up Price, May 9.	Name	Closing Price.	Rise or Fall.
1	Alamillos, £2	1½		½	Mount Lyell, South	9/	− 1/
5	Anaconda, $25	5	+ 1/16	4 1/16	Mount Morgan, 17s. 6d.	4⅞	+ 1/16
5/6	Balaghât, 18/	6/6	− /6	5 1/16	Mysore, 10s.	5 1/16	
12/	Brilliant, £2	12/3x		11/6	Mysore Goldfields	11/6	
2 3/16	Do. St. George's	2½		5/6	Do. Reefs, 17/	4/6	− 1/
9/6	British Broken Hill	9/6		7/	Do. West	7/	− /6
2⅛	Broken Hill Proprietary	2½		6/	Do. Wynaad	5/6	− /6
3	Do. Block 10	3	− ⅛	2½	Namaqua, £2	2⅝	+ 1/16
5	Cape Copper, £2	5	+ 1/16	3 13/16	Nundydroog	3 13/16	+ ⅛
5	Champion Reef, 10s.	4¾x	+ 1/	3⅝	Ooregum	3⅝	− 1/16
2⅛	Copiapo, £2	2 1/16		3 11/16	Do. Pref.	3 11/16	− 1/16
2 13/16	Coromandel	2 13/16		20½	Rio Tinto Def., £5	20½	+ ⅛
15/	Day Dawn Block	14/9		5⅜	Do. Pref. £5	5 13/16	
2 1/16	Frontino & Bolivia	2¼	+ 1/16	1	St. John del Rey	22	+ 2/
1 1/16	Hall Mines	1 1/16 x		8/9	Taitapu	7/6	− [illegible]
2⅜	Libiola, £5	2⅛	− ⅛	7	Tharsis, £2	6⅛	
8	Linares, £3	7⅞	− ⅛	2¼	Tolima "A," £5	2½	
4	Mason & Barry, £3	4		4⅜	Waihi	4 7/16	+ 1/16
4⅞	Mountain Copper, £5	4⅞		1⅛	Waitekauri	1¼	+ ⅛
12⅝	Mount Lyell, £3	12⅜	− ⅛	⅞	Woodstock (N.Z.)	⅞	− ⅛
2⅞	Mount Lyell, North	2⅞	+ 1/16				

At the annual meeting of the proprietors of the Equitable Life Insurance Society it was resolved to present their president, Mr. Richard Twining, with his portrait in oil. It will ultimately take its place in the board-room among portraits of other officials and directors of the society. Mr. Twining is in his ninety-first year, has been on the board for more than a quarter of a century, and his father and grandfather had also been members of the directorate.

ENGLISH RAILWAYS.

Div. for half years. 1896	1896	1897	1897	Last Balance forward.	Amt. to pay 1 p.c. on Ord. for ½ yr.	Name.	Date.	Gross Traffic for week: Amt.	Inc. or dec. on 1897.	Inc. or dec. on 1896.	No. of weeks	Gross Traffic for half-year to date: Amt.	Inc. or dec. on 1897.	Inc. or dec. on 1896.	Mileage.	Inc. on 1897.	Working	Prior Charges last ½ year.	Prop. add Cap. Exp. this ½ year.
				£	£												%	£	£
10	10	10	10	2,707	5,094	Barry	May 7	2,024	−6,561	−4,124	19	140,636	−24,429	+1,592	31	—	8·89	60,663	316,853
nil	nil	nil	nil	—	—	Brecon and Merthyr	„ 8	1,212	−209	−379	19	26,483	−745	−3,588	61	—	—	—	—
nil	nil	nil	nil	3,979	4,749	Cambrian	„ 8	5,555	+394	+324	*	86,309	+2,517	—	250	—	60·96	63,148	40,000
1⅞	1½	2	1½	1,510	3,150	City and South London ..	„ 8	964	+7	+55	19	19,721	+218	+1,786	3½	—	56·67	5,552	124,000
	2	1½	2	7,895	13,210	Furness	„ 8	9,090	+145	+267	*	161,042	+4,618	—	139	—	49·88	97,423	20,910
1	1½	½	1	2,207	27,470	Great Cent. (late M., S., & L.)	„ 8	48,402	+3,478	+4,409	18	781,962	+20,002	+48,809	352½	—	57·17	627,386	1,200,000
1½	4½	2	5	51,283	62,865	Great Eastern	„ 8	85,561	−180	+7,884	18	1,439,281	+41,486	+120227	1,158½	2	55·35	860,138	250,000
3	5½	3	5	15,094	102,496	Great Northern	„ 8	96,408	+3,024	+8,211	19	1,785,044	+53,016	+137471	1,071	8	61·16	641,485	750,000
4½	7½	4½	7½	31,350	121,981	Great Western	„ 8	178,610	−12,290	−970	18	3,120,270	+5,390	+117930	2,582	21	51·44	1,486,272	800,000
nil	2	nil	1½	8,951	16,487	Hull and Barnsley	„ 8	7,850	+820	+1,494	18	122,012	+4,973	+14,014	73	—	58·21	70,290	52,920
5	5½	5	5½	21,495	83,704	Lancashire and Yorkshire ..	„ 8	96,596	+4,953	+5,108	18	1,639,518	+51,479	+63,456	555½	25	56·70	674,745	451,976
4½	8	4½	8½	26,243	43,049	Lon., Brighton, & S. Coast	„ 7	51,724	−438	+1,953	19	916,237	+29,707	+50,429	476½	—	50·20	407,042	240,735
nil	nil	nil	nil	72,294	56,296	London, Chatham, & Dover	„ 8	29,167	−370	+920	18	493,519	+12,417	+27,883	185½	—	50·65	367,873	nil
6½	8	6½	7½	89,535	204,068	London and North Western	„ 8	230,536	+2,481	+11,210	18	4,113,118	+96,670	+234804	1,911½	—	56·92	1,404,534	600,000
5	8½	5	8½	23,038	59,367	London and South Western	„ 8	73,101	+548	+3,126	18	1,239,257	+44,893	+86,300	941	6½	51·75	313,740	389,000
2½	6	2½	6½	14,592	6,691	Lon., Tilbury, & Southend	„ 8	5,118	−45	+476	19	94,113	+5,205	+13,134	81	—	52·57	39,590	15,000
3½	3½	3½	3½	17,133	26,409	Metropolitan	„ 8	16,436	+307	+1,372	*	296,848	+6,177	—	64	—	43·63	148,047	254,000
nil	nil	nil	nil	4,000	11,250	Metropolitan District ..	„ 8	8,201	+250	+320	18	152,595	+4,841	—	13	—	46·70	119,663	38,430
5	7	5½	6½	38,143	174,582	Midland	„ 8	194,645	+4,010	+22,042	19	3,490,634	+54,214	+273801	1,354¾	15½	57·39	1,216,582	630,000
5½	7½	5½	7	22,374	138,189	North Eastern	„ 7	158,999	+6,406	+15,693	18	2,574,673	+37,387	+148404	1,597¾	—	58·72	795,077	436,004
7½	7½	7½	7½	7,061	10,108	North London	„ 8			Not recd			not	recvd.	12	—	50·90	49,973	7,800
4	5	4	4½	4,745	16,150	North Staffordshire	„ 8	16,737	+334	+1,353	19	296,398	+6,403	+17,417	312	—	55·27	118,142	29,605
10	10	11	10	1,642	3,004	Rhymney	„ 7	1,681	−2,947	−2,592	19	83,162	−9,718	−2,580	71	—	49·68	29,049	16,300
3	6¾	3½	6¾	4,054	50,215	South Eastern	„ 7	50,472	+1,681	+6,343	*	777,430	+38,593	—	448	—	51·88	380,763	250,000
3½	3½	3½	3½	2,315	25,961	Taff Vale	„ 7	6,605	−8,744	−7,507	19	243,135	−51,291	−34,795	121	—	54·90	94,800	92,000

* From January 1.

SCOTCH RAILWAYS.

1896	1896	1897	1897	Last Balance forward	Amt. to pay 1 p.c. on Ord. for ½ yr.	Name	Date	Amt.	Inc. or dec. on 1897	Inc. or dec. on 1896	No. of weeks	Amt.	Inc. or dec. on 1897	Inc. or dec. on 1896	Mileage	Inc. on 1897	Working	Prior Charges	Prop. add Cap. Exp.
5	5	5¼	5	9,544	78,066	Caledonian	May 8	75,786	+ 1,564	—	14	1,018,543	+ 24,514	—	851½	5	50·38	588,248	441,477
5	5½	5	5	7,364	24,639	Glasgow and South-Western	„ 7	28,132	+ 1,032	+ 2,144	14	389,360	+ 13,981	—	393½	—	54·69	221,663	196,245
3½	3½	3½	—	1,291	4,600	Great North of Scotland	„ 7	10,176	+ 522	+ 630	14	110,695	+ 89	+ 3,405	331	15½	52·03	90,178	60,000
	nil		—	10,477	12,820	Highland	„ 8	9,738	+ 389	− 389	10	88,005	+ 2,945	—	479½	27½	58·63	78,976	,080
	1¼	1	1¼	819	45,819	North British	„ 8	74,206	+ 1,675	+ 3,201	14	995,099	+ 24,781	—	1,230	23	48·62	944,809	40,800

IRISH RAILWAYS.

1896	1896	1897	1897	Last Balance forward	Amt. to pay 1 p.c. on Ord. for ½ yr.	Name	Date	Amt.	Inc. or dec. on 1897	Inc. or dec. on 1896	No. of weeks	Amt.	Inc. or dec. on 1897	Inc. or dec. on 1896	Mileage	Inc. on 1897	Working	Prior Charges	Prop. add Cap. Exp.
6½	6½	6½	—	5,466	1,790	Belfast and County Down ..	May 6	2,390	+ 101	− 153	*	30,040	+ 1,085	—	76½	—	55·58	17,690	10,000
5½	6½	5½	—	—	4,284	Belfast and Northern Counties	„ 6	5,092	+ 241	+ 334	*	93,084	+ 4,995	—	249	—	—	—	—
	3	2	—	1,418	1,200	Cork, Bandon, and S. Coast† ..	„ 7	1,353	− 213	− 172	*	22,382	− 1,780	—	103	—	54·82	14,436	5,450
	6½	6½	6½	38,776	17,816	Great Northern	„ 6	16,057	+ 1,187	+ 1,876	18	263,323	+ 12,735	+ 18,456	528	—	50·15	88,068	22,000
	5½	5½	5½	30,339	24,855	Great Southern and Western ..	Apr. 29	—	—	—	not	received	—	—	603	13	51·45	72,802	46,580
	4	4	4½	11,372	11,850	Midland Great Western ..	„ 29	12,111	+ 563	+ 572	18	178,624	+ 8,079	—	538	—	50·31	83,129	1,800
nil	ni	nil	nil	229	2,822	Waterford and Central ..	„ 29	890	+ 24	—	*	15,626	+ 1,733	—	59½	—	53·24	6,858	1,500
nil	ni	nil	nil	1,936	2,987	Waterford, Limerick & W. ..	„ 29	5,013	+ 147	+ 262	*	97,438	+ 3,136	—	350½	—	57·83	42,617	7,075

* From January 1. † Fifteen weeks' strike.

NOTICES.

The numbers are announced of thirty-two 4 per cent. consolidated first mortgage debentures amounting to £3,200 of John Barley White & Brothers, Limited, which have been drawn for payment at 110 per cent. on June 30 next.

Mr. Killingworth Hedges, C.E., has joined the board of the Somzée Greyson Intensified Gaslight Syndicate, Limited.

The offices of the Sheba Gold Mining Company, Limited, have been removed to No. 5, St. Helen's-place, E.C.

Messrs. N. M. Rothschild & Sons announce that a drawing of the Egyptian State Domain mortgage bonds amounting to £206,380 nominal capital will take place this month. The bonds so drawn will cease to bear interest from June 1.

It is announced that the coupons due May 15 on the City of Vancouver (British Columbia) 6 per cent. debentures Nos. 1 to 308 will be paid, on and after the 16th inst., by the Bank of British North America.

Mr. Frank Gardner has been appointed chairman of the British Westralia Syndicate, Limited, in place of the late Mr. Woolf Joel.

Mr. Thomas Morgan Harvey has retired from the firm of Harvey & Greenacre. The business will in future be carried on by the continuing partners under the same style.

The Union Bank of London, Limited, has secured the premises No. 8, High-street, Notting Hill Gate, W., and will open a branch there as soon as the necessary alterations are completed.

The numbers are published of the bonds, amounting to £11,500, of the loan of £347,000 (part of £500,000) of the City of London 3 per cent. bonds (Artisan's Dwelling Act, 1881), which have been drawn to be paid off at par on April 5, 1899.

For the purpose of preparing the dividend payable on the 1st prox., the London and Midland Bank, Limited, notify that the transfer books of the Chesterfield Gas and Water Board 2½ per cent. loan will be closed from May 26 to June 1, both days inclusive.

The monthly balance-sheet issued by the London and Midland Bank, Limited, shows that on May 4 the current deposit and other accounts were £22,073,768; the cash in hand and at the Bank of England, £2,627,981; money at call and short notice, £2,664,416; investments, £4,513,763; the bills of exchange, £2,860,255; advances on current accounts, loans on security, and other accounts, £12,808,032.

The name of the Law Accident and Contingency Insurance Society has been changed to Law Acciden Insurance Society (Limited).

The numbers are announced of 106 Equipment Trust bonds (1890) of the New York, Pennsylvania, and Ohio Railroad Company which have been drawn for payment at par on June 1.

Mr. Walter F. Mills, of the firm of Newson-Smith, Mills, & Co., has been appointed official liquidator of R. N. Cunningham & Co. (Limited), in the place of the late Mr. H. Newson-Smith.

The Mount Lyell Comstock Company (No Liability) has established a London office and branch register of shareholders at 138, Leadenhall-street, London, E.C., and constituted Messrs. D. J. Mackay and David Tweedie the London board.

Applications for £1,660,000, the British portion of the Greek Guaranteed 2½ per cent. loan, were received at the Bank of England on the 10th inst., and amounted to £3,036,500. The allotments were about 54 per cent. of the amounts applied for.

RAILWAY TRAFFIC RETURNS.

Alcoy and Gandia Railway and Harbour Company.—Traffic for week, May 7:—Ps. 6,000; increase, Ps. 100. Aggregate from January 1, Ps. 161,550; increase, Ps. 4,580.

Quebec Central Railway.—Receipts for third week of April, $7,036; decrease, $2,328. Aggregate from July 1, $102,791; decrease, $17,926.

Mobile and Birmingham Railroad.—Traffic for third week of April, $5,671; increase, $141. Aggregate from July 1, $303,174; decrease, $2,381.

Algeciras (Gibraltar) Railway.—Traffic for week ended April 30, Ps. 20,450; increase, Ps. 2,590. Aggregate from July 1, Ps. 885,242; increase, Ps. 39,668.

West Flanders Railway.—Gross receipts for week ending May 8, £2,109; decrease, £480. Total from January 1, £42,905; increase, £466.

West of India Portuguese Railway.—Week ending April 16, Rs. 4,574; increase, Rs. 1,159. Aggregate from January 1, Rs. 68,564; increase, Rs. 19,772.

Puerto Cabello and Valencia Railway.—Traffic receipts for week ending March 25, £549; decrease, £124. Aggregate from January 1, £11,211; decrease, £4,722.

Delhi Umballa Kalka Railway.—Receipts for week ended May 7, Rs. 26,200; decrease, Rs. 1,500. Aggregate from January 1, Rs. 6,33,200; increase, Rs. 1,52,700.

Rohilkund and Kumaon Railway.—Traffic receipts for week ending April 9, Rs. 12,831; increase, Rs. 3,708. Aggregate from January 1, Rs. 1,03,173; decrease, Rs. 9,005.

Western of Santa Fe Railways.—Gross receipts for week ending May 7, $31,161; increase, $6,831.

Villa Maria and Rufino Railway.—Traffic for week ending May 7, $413; increase, $172. Aggregate from January 1, $6,472; increase, $1,053.

Southern Mahratta Railway.—Receipts for week ended April 16, Rs. 1,26,023; decrease, Rs. 11,143.

Bengal Central Railway.—Traffic receipts for week ending April 16, Rs. 15,212; decrease, Rs. 158. Aggregate from January 1, Rs. 312,113; increase, Rs. 43,578.

Cleator and Workington.—Gross receipts for the week ending May 7 amounted to £1,017, an increase of £58. Total receipts from January 1, £18,437, a decrease of £646.

Cockermouth and Keswick Railway.—Receipts for the week ending May 7, £896; increase, £69. Aggregate from January 1, £15,018; increase, £1,406.

Peruvian Corporation Railways.—Receipts for month of April, $240,025; decrease, $21,030.

Burma Railways.—Traffic receipts for week ending April 9, Rs. 1,80,322; decrease Rs. 1,144. Aggregate from January 1, Rs. 30,74,188; decrease, Rs. 80,682.

Assam Bengal Railway.—Traffic receipts for week ending April 9, Rs. 30,465; increase, Rs. 10,726. Aggregate from January 1, Rs. 36,736; increase, Rs. 62,745.

H.H. The Nizam's Guaranteed State Railways.—Traffic receipts from January 1 to April 16 were Rs. 12,05,561; increase, Rs. 71,306.

FOREIGN RAILWAYS.

Mileage. Total.	Increase on 1897.	Increase on 1896.	NAME	GROSS TRAFFIC FOR WEEK. Week ending	Amount.	In. or Dec. upon 1897.	In. or Dec. upon 1896.	GROSS TRAFFIC TO DATE. No. of Weeks.	Amount.	In. or Dec. upon 1897.	In. or Dec. upon 1896.
					£	£	£		£	£	£
319	—	—	Argentine Great Western	May 6	8,073	+ 298	+ 610	45	267,573	+ 245	+ 58,771
76½	—	—	Bahia and San Francisco	Apr. 15	2,987	+ 549	+ 1,083	16	—	—	—
234	48	84	Bahia Blanca and North West	Apr. 10	565	− 420	—	41	31,437	− 802	—
74	—	—	Buenos Ayres and Ensenada	May 8	3,640	− 389	− 485	19	62,590	− 9,737	− 15,913
426	—	—	Buenos Ayres and Pacific	May 7	8,056	+ 535	+ 727	44	297,769	− 51,090	+ 7,012
914	1	3	Buenos Ayres and Rosario	May 7	16,737	+ 4,219	+ 4,093	19	310,223	+ 84,123	+ 55,138
2,499	30	68	Buenos Ayres Great Southern	May 8	27,421	+ 2,372	+ 5,269	44	1,322,709	+ 102,324	+ 191,265
602	107	177	Buenos Ayres Western	May 8	12,461	+ 13	− 3,008	44	535,689	− 77,460	− 96,188
845	55	77	Central Argentine	May 7	22,198	+ 7,456	+ 7,856	19	399,043	+ 103,622	+ 43,408
297	—	—	Central Bahia	Feb. 28*	$142,798	+ $14,201	+ $1,866	2	$276,357	+ $10,347	+ $14,624
271	—	—	Central Uruguay of Monte Video	May 7	6,190	+ 2,469	+ 497	44	264,859	+ 20,705	− 13,668
228	—	—	Do. Eastern Extension	May 7	1,359	+ 582	+ 97	44	57,665	+ 8,472	− 254
282	—	—	Do. Northern Extension	May 7	594	+ 160	− 215	44	28,175	+ 777	− 7,158
180	—	—	Cordoba and Rosario	May 1	2,375	+ 715	+ 330	44	93,615	− 13,460	− 1,530
128	—	—	Cordoba Central	May 1	$25,500	+ $250	− $2,000	18	$377,700	− $30,740	− $67,840
549	—	—	Do. Northern Extension	May 1	$59,500	− $12,900	− $200	18	$792,290	− $261,960	− $149,880
137	—	—	Costa Rica	Apr. 30	6,677	+ 1,921	+ 4,433	18	105,003	− 3,404	+ 11,708
99	—	—	East Argentine	Mar. 27	693	+ 175	+ 23	12	9,053	− 24	+ 179
386	—	6	Entre Rios	May 7	1,776	+ 687	+ 712	44	73,016	+ 23,068	+ 18,983
555	—	24	Inter Oceanic of Mexico	May 7	$56,200	+ $2,940	+ $12,200	43	$2,560,720	+ $404,490	+ $691,950
23	—	—	La Guaira and Caracas	Mar. 25	2,060	− 285	− 1,103	13	24,939	− 5,212	− 4,938
321	—	—	Mexican	May 7	$74,600	+ $4,600	—	19	$1,486,300	+ $157,950	—
1,846	—	—	Mexican Central	May 7	$249,376	− $8,863	+ $63,337	19	$4,649,087	+ $30,442	+ $1,188,845
1,217	—	—	Mexican National	Apr 30‡	$146,466	+ $9,482	+ $29,074	18	$1,905,613	+ $136,557	+ $370,838
228	—	—	Mexican Southern	May 7	$13,048	− $175	+ $4,310	5	$64,058	− $11,324	+ $12,204
106	—	—	Minas and Rio	Mar. 31*	$161,158	− $9,628	—	9 mos.	$1,597,971	+ $193,854	—
94	—		N. W. Argentine	May 7	1,317	+ 5	− 165	19	19,086	− 6,533	− 4,379
242	3	—	Nitrate	Apr. 30†	11,739	− 3,099	− 6,599	18	118,804	− 11,239	− 48,700
320	—	—	Ottoman	Apr. 30	4,114	− 4,350	− 669	18	81,291	− 20,445	+ 6,066
77½	—	—	Recife and San Francisco	Mar. 12	5,896	+ 769	− 1,110	11	64,565	+ 5,204	− 9,121
86½	—	—	San Paulo	Mar. 27†	18,471	− 6,090	—	12	127,060	− 25,190	—
186	—	—	Santa Fe and Cordova	May 7	1,826	+ 862	− 970	45	77,225	+ 5	− 5,330
110	—	—	Western of Havana	May 7	1,530	− 346	+ 170	45	78,357	+ 5,025	+ 8,072

* For month ended. † For fortnight ended. ‡ For nine days.

INDIAN RAILWAYS.

Mileage. Total.	Increase on 1897.	Increase on 1896.	NAME.	GROSS TRAFFIC FOR WEEK. Week ending	Amount.	In. or Dec. on 1897.	In. or Dec. on 1896.	GROSS TRAFFIC TO DATE. No. of Weeks.	Amount.	In. or Dec. on 1897.	In. or Dec. on 1896.
862	—	—	Bengal Nagpur	May 7	Rs.1.65.000	+ Rs.35.638	——	19	Rs.29.26.815	+ Rs.2.87.398	——
827	8	63	Bengal and North-Western	Apr. 9	Rs.1.52.410	+ Rs. 3.957	——	15	Rs.19.32.068	+ Rs.2.58.226	——
461	—	—	Bombay and Baroda	Apr 30	£38,592	+ £2,989	− £1,751	18	£465,065	− £3,676	− £149,741
1,885	1	13	East Indian	May 7	Rs.13.22.000	+ Rs.38.000	+ Rs22.52.000	19	Rs.2.30.03.000	+ Rs.7.59.000	+ R21.03.000
1,491	—	—	Great Indian Penin.	May 7	£76,707	+ £23,660	+ £1,893	19	£1,268,870	+ £220,612	− £208,179
736	—	—	Indian Midland	May 7	Rs.1.51.549	+ Rs. 5.657	+ Rs.43.260	19	Rs.25.63.235	+ Rs.1.99.147	+ Rs.518.738
840	—	—	Madras	Apr. 30	£21,084	+ £1,192	+ £184	18	£331,709	− £19,316	− £5,635
1,043	—	—	South Indian	Apr. 9	Rs.1.65.940	+ Rs. 2.794	+ Rs. 13	15	Rs.22.09.713	− Rs.202.327	− R2.16.064

UNITED STATES AND CANADIAN RAILWAYS.

Mileage. Total.	Increase on 1897.	Increase on 1896.	NAME.	GROSS TRAFFIC FOR WEEK. Period Ending.	Amount.	In. or Dec. on 1897.	GROSS TRAFFIC TO DATE. No. of Weeks.	Amount.	In. or Dec. on 1897.
					dols.	dols.		dols.	dols.
917	—	—	Baltimore & Ohio S. Western	Apr. 30‡	188,674	+ 50,422	42	5,689,546	+ 652,743
6,568	92	156	Canadian Pacific	May 7	507,000	+ 82,000	17	7,678,000	+ 1,521,000
922	—	—	Chicago Great Western	May 7	108,397	+ 27,516	43	4,575,881	+ 591,302
6,169	—	469	Chicago, Mil., & St. Paul	Apr. 30‡	848,000	+ 106,000	16	9,594,101	+ 1,407,300
1,685	—	—	Denver & Rio Grande	May 7	141,900	+ 19,400	43	6,895,400	+ 1,129,300
3,512	—	—	Grand Trunk, Main Line	May 7	£72,504	+ £6,499	17	£1,310,630	+ £120,270
335	—	—	Do. Chic. & Grand Trunk	May 7	£12,678	+ £2,211	17	£268,091	+ £59,680
189	—	—	Do. Det., G. H. & Mil.	May 7	£3,127	− £227	17	£62,647	− £3,749
2,938	—	—	Louisville & Nashville	Apr. 30‡	543,000	+ 68,000	16	6,943,175	+ 1,093,620
2,197	137	137	Miss., K., & Texas	May 7	154,000	− 26,000	43	10,768,428	+ 525,290
477	—	—	N. Y., Ontario, & W.	May 7	55,703	− 4,568	43	3,274,843	+ 89,756
1,570	—	—	Norfolk & Western	Apr. 30‡	213,000	+ 31,000	15	3,657,960	+ 390,433
3,499	336	—	Northern Pacific	Apr. 30‡	574,000	+ 130,000	16	6,618,775	+ 2,029,552
1,223	—	—	St. Louis S. Western	Apr. 30‡	113,000	+ 10,000	16	1,883,400	+ 316,221
4,654	—	—	Southern	Apr. 30‡	493,000	+ 47,000	42	5,859,812	+ 1,382,443
1,979	—	—	Wabash	May 7	235,000	+ 58,000	17	4,498,406	+ 918,000

‡ For nine days.

MONTHLY STATEMENTS.

Mileage. Total.	Increase on 1896	Increase on 1895.	NAME.	NET EARNINGS FOR MONTH. Month.	Amount.	In. or Dec. on 1897.	In. or Dec. on 1896.	NET EARNINGS TO DATE. No. of Months.	Amount.	In. or Dec. on 1897.	In. or Dec. on 1896.
					dols	dols.	dols.		dols.	dols.	dols.
6,935	44	444	Atchison	March	904,000	+ 337,000	+ 369,344	3	2,144,434	+ 674,816	+ 229,460
6,547	103	106	Canadian Pacific	March	753,000	+ 253,000	+ 276,469	3	1,693,000	+ 415,000	+ 315,787
6,169	—	469	Chicago, Mil., & St. Paul	March	1,180,000	+ 170,000	+ 65,202	3	2,726,334	+ 225,840	+ 54,122
1,685	—	—	Denver & Rio Grande	March	567,900	+ 39,242	+ 38,944	9	2,517,889	+ 407,003	+ 30,046
1,970	—	—	Erie	March	611,000	+ 53,000	+ 8,706	3	1,378,600	+ 62,400	− 64,251
3,512	—	—	Grand Trunk, Main Line	March	£102,100	+ £14,331	+ £31,909	3	£245,953	+ £12,372	+ 100,819
335	—	—	Do. Chic. & Grand Trunk	March	£17,400	+ £10,152	+ 13,357	3	£38,710	+ £24,282	+ 28,919
189	—	—	Do. Det. G. H. & Mil.	March	£4,200	− £1,414	+ 3,221	3	£6,528	+ 4,737	+ 6,419
3,127	—	239	Illinois Central	March	759,000	+ 206,000	+ 343,862	3	2,213,704	+ 365,620	+ 549,739
2,396	—	—	New York Central*	April	3,807,000	+ 302,000	+ 394,152	4	‡14,602,000	+ 964,000	—
477	—	—	New York Ontario, & W.	March	84,600	− 4,800	+ 40,032	9	916,300	+ 35,200	+ 115,404
1,570	—	—	Norfolk & Western	March	301,000	+ 18,000	+ 110,317	3	826,000	+ 63,247	+ 201,002
3,407	—	—	Pennsylvania	February	1,359,101	+ 65,700	+ 236,000	2	2,511,898	92,400	+ 345,000
1,055	—	—	Phil. & Reading	March	701,190	+ 50,822	—	9	7,507,293	+ 524,064	—

* Statement of gross traffic.

Prices Quoted on the London Stock Exchange.

Throughout the Investors' Review middle prices alone are quoted, the object being to give the public the approximate current quotations of every security of any consequence in existence. On the markets the buying and selling prices are both given, and are often wide apart where stocks are seldom dealt in. Other particulars will be found in the Investment Index published quarterly—January, April, July, and October—in connection with this Review, price 2s., by post 2s. 2d. Where dividends are paid only once a year, an *italic* type is used to distinguish them. The London Stock Exchange Official List is quoted in the Review almost entire, only very insignificant issues, or bonds falling due within the next two or three years, being omitted. But the list is subdivided into the leading, or active, stocks, and those less frequently dealt in. The former will be found under the head of "Stock Markets," and with more details than it is possible to give for the bulk of securities. By retaining the file of the Investors' Review any subscriber can follow for himself the movements of securities from week to week, and the Investment Index will from time to time help to fill up deficiencies in the information.

Tea Companies and Mines and Mining Finance Stocks are placed in special lists.

Among the abbreviations used are the following:—S. F. Snk. Fd. *sinking fund*; Certs., *certificates*; Debs. or Dbs., *debentures*; Db. or D.Stk., *debenture stock*; Pf., Prf., or Pref., *preference*; Prefd. or Pfd., *preferred*; Dfd., *deferred*; L. or Ltd., *limited*; Sh., *share*; Ans., *annuities*; Cu. or Cm., *cumulative*; Gu or Guar., *guaranteed*; Bds., *bonds*; S., Sr., or Ser., *series*; In., Ins., Insc., *inscribed*; Dr., Drgs., Drwgs., *drawings*; Stg., Strlg., *sterling*; Lia., *liable to*; Sp., Surp., *surplus*; Per., Perp., *perpetual*; Ln. *lien*; Lo. *loan*.

The dates following the names of securities are the years of issue or of redemption. Where shares are not fully paid up, their nominal amount is given with the name so that investors may know the liability upon them.

BRITISH FUNDS, &c.

Rate	Name.	Price.
2¾	2¾ p.c.'s (Childers') Red.. 1905	104¼
3	Local Loans Stk. 1912	110
3	Metro. Police Deb. Stk. 1920	106½
—	Red Sea Ind. Tel. Ann. 1908	8¼
4	Canada Gv. "Intcl. Rly." 1903	104
4	Do. do. .. 1908	111
4	Do. Bonds 1910	112
4	Do. Bonds 1913	117½
3	Egyptian Gov. Gar.	106½
3	Mauritius Ins. Stk. 1940	114
4	Turkish Guar. 1855	109
11½	Bank of Ireland Stk.	390
3½	India Rupee Paper	62
3½	Do. 1854-5	62½
3	Do. 1896-7 1916	55
3½	Isle of Man Deb.	104
3	Do. Deb. Stk... 1919-29	103

CORPORATION AND COUNTY STOCKS.

FREE OF STAMP DUTY.

Rate	Name.	Price.
3½	Metropolitan Con. 1929	117½
3	Do. 1941	110
2½	Do. 1920-49	99
2½	L.C.C. Con. Stock 1920	98
3½	Comm. of Sewers, Scp., S.F. 1905	105
3½	Corp. of Lond. Bds...1897-1902	100½
3	Do. 1897-1919	101
3½	Do., Debs. Scp. ...... S.F. 1916	105
2½	Do., Deb. Stk. Scrip .. 1927-57	98
3	Barnsley 1916-46	105
3	Barry 1914-46	101
3	Bath 1909-34	102
3	Batley 1914-44	101½
3½	Birmingham 1945	117½
3	Do. 1947	111½
2½	Do. 1926	98
3	Blackburn 1930	106½
3	Bournemouth 1913-33	103
3½	Bradford 1943	116½
3	Do. Deb. Stock .. 1954	108
3	Brighouse.............. 1916-46	100
3½	Brighton 1946	117
2½	Do. 1937	96½
3	Burton-on-Trent.......... 1913-43	101
3	Cambridge 1913-43	103
3½	Cardiff 1935	114½
3	Do. 1914-54	103½
3	Cheltenham.......... 1971	106½
3	Chichester 1916-46	101
3½	Croydon	131½
3	Do. 1940	107½
3	Derby 1920-50	106½
3	Devon C.C. 1917-33	104½
3½	Dewsbury 1930	109
3	Do. 1930	103
3	Dorset County 1922-32	105
3	Douglas (I. of Man) 1926	101½
3	Dover 1913-43	101
3½	Dublin 1944	113½
3	Eastbourne 1920-40	104
3	Edinburgh 1924	105½
2½	Do. 1927	97
2½	Exeter 1917-57	96
3	Glamorgan County 1914-34	104
3½	Glasgow 1914	109
3	Do. 1921	104½
2½	Do. 1925-40	98
3	Gloster 1915-55	101
3	Grimsby 1913-43	103
3	Hampshire County 1914-34	105½
3	Hanley 1913-43	103
3	Harrogate 1914-34	103
3	Hastings 1915-54	103½
2½	Hertfordshire C.C. 1916-36	98
3	Heston & Isleworth U.D.C. 1915-35	101
3	Huddersfield 1934	107
3½	Hull (1st iss.)	126½
3	Inverness 1914-44	100
3	Ipswich 1952	107½
3	Lancaster 1919-55	103
2½	Leeds 1927	98
3½	Leicester 1934	114½
3	Lincoln 1910	103
3½	Liverpool	131

Corporation, &c. (*continued*):—

Rate	Name.	Price.
3	Manchester 1941	107½
3½	Middlesbro' 1909	105½
3½	Do. 1911-13	106
3	Do. 1915	104
3	Middlesex C.C. 1915-35	106
3½	Newcastle 1936	118½
3½	Do. Irred.	129½
2½	Do. 1915-36	100
3	Newcastle-under-Lyme.. 1909-44	101
3	Newport (Mon.) 1915-55	101½
3	Norwich 1952	110
3	Nottingham	111½
3	Oxford 1951	109½
3	Penzance 1916-46	100½
3	Plymouth 1949	109½
3	Pontypridd U.D.C. 1916-46	98
3	Poole 1915-45	101
3½	Portsmouth .... 1916 24 & 27	112
3	Do. 1913-33	106
3	Ramsey 1920-40	100
3	Ramsgate 1915-55	102
3½	Reading	125
3	Do. 1969	106
3½	Rhyl U.D.C. 1953	110
3	Richmond (Surrey) 1942	104½
3	River Wear Debt Certs.	100
3	St. Helen's 1915-55	102
3	Scarbro' 1915-50	102
2½	Sheffield 1925-57	94½
3	Shipley U.D.C. 1915-35	100
3	Somerset Co. 1923-33	104
3	South Shields 1915-45	100
2½	Southampton 1915-45	102
3	Southend-on-Sea 1916-46	102
3	Staffs C.C. 1915-35	103½
3	Stockport 1914-54	101
3	Stockton 1932	104
3	Do. 1915-35	103
3	Surrey Co. 1922-32	105½
3½	Swansea	129
3	Do. 1955	106
3	Taunton 1918-3-9-43	102
3	Tees Conserv. Deb. Stk. 1947	100
3	Thames Conserv. "A" Deb. Stk. 1954	103½
3	Do. "B" Deb. Stk. 1954	103½
3	Torquay 1913-43	101½
3	Tunbridge Wells 1931	102
3	Tynemouth 1913	99
3	Wakefield 1929	101½
3	Walsall 1932	107½
3	West Bromwich 1930	106½
3½	West Ham 1929	110
3	Do. 1945	105
3	West Sussex C.C. 1915-35	106
3	Weston-s.-Mare Lcl Bd. 1914-44	99½
3	Weymouth & Melc. Regis 1918	101
3	Widnes 1915-55	100
3	Wigan 1921	104½
3	Windsor 1918-55	102
3½	Wisbech 1947	113½
3½	Wolverhampton 1932	117
3	Do. 1924-54	107
3	York 1916-41	106½

SUBJECT TO STAMP DUTY.

Rate	Name.	Price.
3½	Belfast City & Dis. Watr. 1938	114
3	Do. Red Stk. 1933-6	106
3½	Belfast 1924	103
4	Blackburn Con. Deb. Irred.	141½
3½	Do. do. Irred.	130
3½	Bristol	120½
3½	Burnley 1933	114
2½	Chesterfield Gas & Wtr. 1916-46	98
3½	Douglas Town 1921	105
3	Dover Harb. 1st Deb... 1956	104½
3½	Hull (2nd iss.)	125½
4	Leeds Deb. 1927	123
3½	Do.	115½
3	Do. 1927	106
3	Leicester 1919-44	103½
4	Manchester	145
3	Do. 1928	104½
4½	Middlesboro' Mrts. 1908	111
3½	Sheffield 1898-1916	105½
3½	Do. 1925-36	114
3	Do. 1923	105½
3½	Southampton .... S.F.	106
4½	Stockton Mrts. 1908	110½
3½	Worcester 1950	109

COLONIAL AND PROVINCIAL GOVERNMENT SECURITIES.

Rate	Name.	Price.
6	British Columbia.......... 1907	119½
4½	Do. Debs. .. 1917	111½
3	British Guiana Imgtn. Bds.	96
5	Canada, "Intercol. Rail," 1903	107½
4	Do. (Bonds) 1904-5-6-8	105
4	Do. Reduced 1910	107½
3½	Do. Bnds. 1909-34	107
4	Do. Loan 1910-35	107½
3	Do. Loan 1938	102
6	Cape of G. Hope 1900	—
5	Do. 1900	—
4½	Do. red. by an. draw.	108
4½	Do. 1879	110
4	Do. 1881	108
4	Do. 1917-23	113½
4½	Ceylon	110
4	Do.	106½
4½	Fiji Gov. Deb. Sink. Fd.	101½
4	Jamaica Sink. Fd. 1923	103
5	Manitoba Debs. 1910	113
5	Do. Ster. Bds. 1888	119½
4	Do. Ster. Debs.	104
4	Mauritius, Cons. Debs. 1880...	103½
4½	Natal, Sink. Fd. 1919	118
4	Do. do. 1926	115
3½	Newfoundland Stg. Bds. 1941	99
3½	Do. do. .. 1947	99
3	Do. do.	86½
5	New South Wales 1897-1902	104½
4	Do. 1903-5-8-9-12	106
5	New Zealand 1914	118
5	Do. Cnds. 1 p.c. per an. Sink. Fd.	103
3½	Nova Scotia Debs.	104
5	Quebec Prov. 1904-6	108
4½	Do. (drgs.)	105
5	Do. Strlg. Bds. 1912	115
4	Do. Strlg. Bds. 1928	110
4	Do. Strlg. Bds. 1934	108
4	Queensland 1913-15	105
4½	St. Lucia Debs.	102
6	South Australia 1898-1900	103½
6	Do. 1901-1918	119
5	Do. 1911-1920	116
4	Do. 1899-1916	104
4	Do. 1929	108½
4	Do. 1916	106½
4	Do. 1917-18-24	107½
6	Tasmania 1897-1901	104
4	Do. 1908-11, 1913-14-20	107½
5	Trinidad Debs., an. drw. 1 p.c...	107
4	Victoria 1899-1901	101½
4½	Do. 1904	105
4	Do. Rail. Loan 1907	105
4	Do. Loans 1908-13	105
4½	West. Austr. 1 p.c. ac. Sink. Fd.	107
4	Do. do.	106

REGISTERED AND INSCRIBED STOCKS.

No stamp duty except for Canada 4 p.c. Reduced (½ per cent.).

Rate	Name.	Price.
4	Antigua Insc. Stk. Red. 1919-44	109
3½	Barbados Insc. Stk. 1925-42	107
3	British Colum. Insc. Stk. 1941	101½
4	British Guiana Insc. 1935	116½
4	Canada Stk. Regd. ..1904-5-6-8	105
4	Do. 4 p.c. (late 5 p.c.) Regd. 1910	103
3½	Do. 3½ p.c. Stock Regd. 1909-34	107
4	Do. Ln. for 4 milln. stg. 1910-35	108
3	Do. Stk. Regd. 1938	102
2½	Do. Insc. 1947	92
4	Cape G. Hope Regd. .. 1917-23	114
4	Do. (Ln. of '83) Insc. .. 1923	115
4	Do. Cons. Stk. Insc. 1916-36	112
3½	Do. Consol. Insc. Stock 1929-49	110
4	Ceylon Insc. Stock 1934	120
3	Do. 1940	102
4	Grenada Insc. Stock 1917-42	110
3½	Hong Kong Insc. Stock 1918-43	103½
4	Jamaica Insc. Stock 1934	118
—	Do. 1922-44	98
4	Mauritius Inscribed 1937	118½
4	Natal Consd. Stk. Insc. 1927	116
4	Do. 1937	118½
3½	Do. Inscribed Stock.. 1914-39	105
4	Newfoundland Inscribed 1913-38	106
4	Do. 1935	113
4	[illegible] Consd. Stk. Ins. 1936	113
4	N. S. Wales Stock Insc. 1933	118
3½	Do. 1924	107
3½	Do. 1918	105
3	Do 1935	98

Colonial, &c. (*continued*):—

Rate	Name.	Price.
4	N. Zealnd. Con. Stk. Ins. 1929	112
3½	Do 1940	108
3	Do. Inscribed 1945	99
3	Quebec (Prov.) Ins. Stk. 1937	93
4	Queensland Stock Insc. 1915-24	109
3½	Do. 1921-4-30	104
3½	Do. 1945	106
3	Do. 1922-47	99
4	St. Lucia Insc. Stock .. 1919-44	112
4	S. Austrln. (1882-7) Reg. 1916-36	108½
3½	Do. In. Stk. Reg. 1939	108
3	Do. 1916-26	100
3/	Do. 1916	100
3½	Tasmanian Insc. Stock.. 1920-40	108
4	Do. 1920-40	116
4	Trinidad Insc. Stock 1917-42	110
3	Do. 1922-44	98
4	Victoria Rly. Loan '81 Inscribed Stock 1907	105
4	Victoria Insc. Stock 1908-13-19	106
4	Victoria (1883) Ins. Stk. 1920	111
3½	Do. Inscribed Stock 1921-3-6	104
4	Do. do. 1911-26	108
4	W. Austral. Insc. Stock 1934	116½
4	Do. 1911-31	109
3½	Do. 1915-35	104
3	Do. 1915-35	97
3	Do. 1916-36	97

FOREIGN STOCKS, BONDS, &c.

COUPONS PAYABLE IN LONDON.

Last Div.	Name.	Price.
36/	Argentine Ry. Loan 6 p.c. 1881	85½
15/	Do. 5 p.c. 1884	65
30/	Do. N. Cent. Ry. Ext. 5 p.c. 1887-8-9	65½
30/	Do. 5 p.c. Trsy. Convs. 1887	65
5/4½	Do. 4½ p.c. Interl. Gld. 1888	64
27/	Do. 4½ p.c. Stlg. Extrl. 1888	64
10/6	Do. 3½ p.c. External .. 1889	47
4	Do. 4 p.c. Ry. Guar. Res....	55½
4½	Brazilian 1883	49
4½	Do. Gold 1879	58½
4½	Do. 1888	48
30/	Buenos Ayres 1824	77½
6	Do. 1882-3-6	46
6	Bulgarian 1888	93
6	Do. Mort. Bonds 1892	93
4½	Chilian 1885	72
4½	Do. 1886	73
4½	Do. 1887	72
4½	Do. 1889	81½
5	Do. 1892	84
4½	Do. 1893	72
4½	Do. 1895	70
5	Do. 1896	82
7	Chinese Silver 1894	97
6	Do. Gold 1895	106
6	Do. Apl. '95 by dwgs. 1901-15	109½
5	Do. Red. dwgs. in 36 yr. 1896	93½
5	Do. Do. Regis. 1896	99
1½	Colmbn. 1½ to 3 p.c. Ext. Bds. 1896	17½
6	Cordova, Prov. 1886	24
—	Do. Eng. Ass. Certs.	23
—	Do. 6 p.c. 1887-8	24
—	Do. Eng. Ass. Certs.	23
3	Costa Rica "A"	30
2½	Do. "B"	23
3	Danish Gold 1914	98
10/	Ecuador N. Ext. Bds. 4½ p.c. ascn. to 5 p.c.	20
3½	Egypt'n Ins. Stk. lia. Stp. Dty. 1890	100
4	Do. State Domain 1878	104½
4	Do. D. Sanieh, Red. .. 1905	102½
6	Entre Rios 1886-8	33
6	Do. Fndg. Ln. Bds. 1894-1901	29
6	Do. do. Parana City	22½
15/	Greek 1881	39
15/	Do. 1884	39
12/	Do. Rentes	33
15/	Do. (Piræus-Larissa Ry.)	37
7/6	Do. Fundg. Loan	42
4	Guatemala Extl. Debt	30
6	Hawaiian	102½
4	Hungarian Gold Rentes	101
3	Do. 1895	91½
6	Italian Irriga. Guar.	112
5	Do. Maremmana	91
5	Japan 5 p.c.	103½
5	Mexican (Nat. R. Tehuantp c.)..	92½
6	Do. Extrl. 1890	96

Foreign Stocks, &c. *continued*:—

Last Div.	Name.	Price.
6	Mexican Extrl. 1893	95
5	Do. Intrnl. Cons. Slvr.	36
5	Do Intern. Rd. Bds. 2d. Ser.	36
4	Nicaragua 1886	42¼
3½	Norwegian, red. 1937, or earlier	98
3	Do. do. 1965, do.	98
3½	Do. 3½ p.c. Bnds.	102
1	Paraguay 1p.c. ris. 3p.c. 1886-96	15
5	Russian, 1822, £ Strlg.	149
3	Do. 1859	93
4	Do. (Nicolas Ry.) 1867-9	100
3	Do. Transcauc. Ry. 1882	94
4	Do. Con. R. R. Bd. Ser. I., 1889	103
4	Do. Do. II., 1889	103
4	Do. Do. III., 1891	102
3½	Do. Bonds	101
4	Do. Ln. (Dvinsk and Vitbsk)	101
6	Salvador 1889	62½
—	S Domingo 4s. Unified .. 1980	62
6	San Luis Potosi Stg. 1889	86
5	San Paulo (Brzl.), Stg. 1888	88½
6	Santa Fé 1883-4	36
—	Do. Eng. Ass. Certs. Dep.	35
5	Do. 1888	47
—	Do. Eng. Ass. Certs. Dpsit.	46
5	Do. (W. Cnt. Col. Rly.) Mrt.	24
5	Do. & Reconq. Rly. Mort.	24
5	Spanish Quicksilvr Mort. 1870	99½
3½	Swedish 1880	102
3	Do. 1888	98
3	Do. Conversion Loan 1894	98
5	Trans. Gov. Loan Red....1903-42	106
59/	Tucuman (Prov.) 1888	67½
4	Turkish, Secd. on Egypt. Trib.	102
3½	Turkish, Egpt. Trib., Ott. Bd., '94	97¼
4	Do. Priority 1890	89½
1	Do. Convted Series, "A"	66
5	Do. Customs Ln. 1886	94½
5	Uruguay Bonds 1896	55
3	Venzuela New Con. Debt 1881	32

COUPONS PAYABLE ABROAD.

Last Div.	Name.	Price.
7	Argent. Nat. Cedla. Sries, "B"	35
5	Austrian Ster. Rnts., ex 10fl., 1870	85
5	Do. do. do.	83
5	Do. Paper do. 1870	83
5	Do. do. do.	83
4	Do. Gld Rentes 1876	100
3	Belgian exchange 25 fr.	100
3½	Danish Int., 1887, Rd. 1896	—
2½	Dutch Certs. ex 12 gldrs.	85
3	Do. Bonds	97
3	Do. Insc. Stk.	96
3½	French Rentes	106
3	Do. 1878, '81-4., Red.	99
3	German Imp. Ln. 1891	95
3	Do. do. 1892-3	95
3	Do. do. 1890-4	95
5	Japan Cons. Ln., '92, 3, & 5, Red.	46
35/9	Prussian Consols	102
3	" Cons. Stg. Ln. 1891	96
4	Utd. States, 1877, Red. 1907	112
4	Do. 1895, 30 yrs.	126
3½	Do. Maschsetts Gl. 1935	113½
3½	Do. Gold Bonds 1923	107½
2	Virginia Cpn. Bds., 3 p.c. from July, 1901	69½

BRITISH RAILWAYS.

ORD. SHARES AND STOCKS.

Last Div	Name.	Price.
10	Barry, Ord.	274½
4	Do. Prefd.	125
6	Do. Defd.	147½
5	Caledonian, Ord.	155
3	Do. Prefd.	99
—	Do. Defd. Ord., No. 1	4½
	Cambrian, Ord.	5½
—	Do. Coast Cons.	5½
32/	Cardiff Ry. Pref. Ord.	115
3/	Central Lond. £10 Ord. Sh.	10½
1/9½	Do. do. £6 paid	6½
3½d.	Do. Pref. Half-Shares	1½
1/6	Do. Def. do.	4½
1½	City and S. London	68½
—	East London, Cons.	6½
2	Furness	64½
2½	Glasgow and S. West. Pfd.	81
2½	Do. do. Dfd.	65
3	Great Central, Ord....1894	41
32/0	Do. London Exten.	73
—	Great N. of Scotland, Prfd.	90
—	Do. Dfd.	33
4	Great Northern, Prefd.	119¼
—	Do. Consolidated "A"	52
—	Do. do. "B"	190½
2	Highland	77½
4	Isle of Wight, Prefd.	120½
3	Do. Defd.	83½
	Lancs. Derbys. and E. Cst.	4
8½	L. Brighton and S. C. Ord.	186
6	Do. Prefd. Ord.	197
10/	Do. Contgt. Rights Certs.	18¼
5½	Lond. and S. Western Ord.	225½
4	Do. Preferred	133
6½	Lond., Tilb., and Southend	133½
—	Mersey, £20 shares	½
—	Metropolitan, New Ord.	132½
2½	Do. Surplus Lands	93
4	North Cornwall, 4 p.c. Pref.	104½
12/8	Do. Deferred	22½
7½	North London	223½
4½	North Staffordshire	129

British Railways (*continued*):—

Last Div.	Name.	Price.
3/3	Plymouth, Devenport, and S. W. Junc. £10	9
3/	Port Talbot £10 Shares	9½
9d.	Rhondda Swns. B. £10 Sh.	5
10	Rhymney, Cons.	265½
4	Do. Prefd.	123
6½	Do. Defd.	145½
1½	Scarboro', Bridlington Junc.	47½
6½	South Eastern, Ord.	150
6	Do. Pref.	192
3½	Taff Vale	82
25/	Vale of Glamorgan	127½
3	Waterloo & City	134½

LEASED AT FIXED RENTALS

Last Div.	Name.	Price.
4	Birkenhead	144
5.19.0	East Lincnshire	202½
5½	Hamamith. & City Ord.	192½
4½	Lond. and Blackwll.	160½
4½	Do. £10 4½ p. c. Pref.	160½
56/6	Lond. & Green. Ord.	101
5	Do. 5 p. c. Pref.	173½
5	Nor. and Eastn. £50 Ord.	89
6	Do.	104½
3½	N. Cornwall 3½ p. c. Stk.	124½
4⁷⁄₁₀	Nott. & Granthm. R. & C.	143½
3½	Portptk. & Wigtn. Guar. Stk.	121½
9	Vict. Stn. & Pimlico Ord.	312½
4½	Do. 4½ p. c. Pref.	158½
4/	West Lond. £20 Ord. Shs.	14
4⁹⁄₁₀	Weymouth & Portld.	157½

DEBENTURE STOCKS.

Last Div.	Name.	Price.
4	Alexandra Dks. & Ry.	130½
3	Barry, Cons.	107
4	Brecon & Mrthyr, New A	127½
4	Do. New B	105
4	Caledonian	149
4	Cambrian "A"	132½
4	Do. "B"	127½
4	Do. "C"	122½
4	Do. "D"	107½
3	Cardiff Rly.	100½
4	City and S. Lond.	137
3½	Cleator & Working Junc.	118½
3	Devon & Som. "A"	103½
16/3	Do. "B" 4 p. c.	36
—	Do. "C" 4 p. c.	10
4	E. Lond. 2nd Ch. 4 p. c. A	135
6/	Do. 2nd B	67½
—	Do. 3rd Ch. 4 p. c.	19½
—	Do. 4th do.	9½
3½	Do. 1st (3½ p. c.)	128½
2½	Do. 2½ p.c. (Whitech. Exn)	87
4	Forth Bridge	142½
4	Furness	142½
4	Glasgow and S. Western	147
5	Gt. Central	—
4½	Do.	155½
4	Gt. Eastern	145
4	Gt. N. of Scotland	141½
3	Gt. Northern	111½
4	Gt. Western	149
4½	Do.	156½
4½	Do.	165½
5	Do.	184½
2½	Do.	96½
4	Highland	141½
3	Hull and Barnsley	104½
3	Do. 2nd (3-4 p. c).	122½
4	Isle of Wight	142½
3	Do. Cent. "A"	92½
4½	Do. "B"	115½
4	Do. "C"	82½
3	Lancs. & Yorkshire	112
4	Lancs. Derbys. & E. Cst.	123½
4½	Ldn. and Blackwall	155½
4	Ldn. and Greenwich	144½
4	Lond., Brighton, &c.	148½
4½	Do.	165½
4½	Lond., Chath., &c., Arb.	154½
4½	Do. "B"	153½
4	Do.	138½
4	Do. 1883	138½
3	Do.	106
3	Lond. & N. Western	115
3	Lond. & S. Westn. "A"	113½
3	Do. Consld.	113½
4	Lond., Til., & Southend	144½
—	Mersey, 5 p. c. (Act, 1866)	65
4	Metropolitan	144½
4½	Do.	162½
3½	Do.	126½
6	Met. District	207½
4	Do.	139
2½	Midland	95
4½	Mid-Wales "A"	137½
4	Neath & Brecon 1st	127½
4	Do. "A 1"	117½
3	North British	110
3	Do. 1893	108
7½	N. Cornwall, Launcstn., &c.	124½
	North Eastern	113

Debenture Stocks (*continued*):—

Last Div.	Name.	Price.
4½	North London	163½
3	N. Staffordshire	111
4	Plym. Devpt. & S.W. Jn.	141½
4	Rhondda and Swan. Bay	130½
4	Rhymney	144½
4	South-Eastern	147
5	Do.	182½
3½	Do.	127½
3	Do.	113
3	Taff Vale	103½
4	Tottenham & For. Gate	143½
3	Vale of Glamorgan	105½
3	West Highld. (Gtd. by N.B.)	107
4	Wrexham, Mold, &c. "A"	115½
4	Do. "B"	102½
4	Do. "C"	97½

GUARANTEED SHARES AND STOCKS.

Last Div.	Name.	Price.
4	Caledonian	146½
4	Do.	142½
4	Forth Bridge	142½
4	Furness 1881	137½
4	Glasgow & S. Western	141½
4	Do. St. Enoch, Rent	141½
6	Gt. Central	198½
4½	Do. 1st Pref.	150½
3½	Do. Pref.	104½
5	Do. Irred. S.Y. Rent	161½
4½	Do. do.	139½
4	Gt. Eastern, Rent	142½
5	Do. Metropolitan	177½
4	Do.	141½
4	Gt. N. of Scotland	138½
4	Gt. Northern	143½
5	Gt. Western, Rent	181½
5	Do. Cons.	180½
4	Lancs. & Yorkshire	143½
5	L., Brighton & S. C.	179½
3½	L., Chat. & D. (Shrtlds.)	110½
4	L. & North Western	145
4	L. & South Western .. 1881	144
4½	Met. District, Ealing Rent	150
4½	Do. Fulham Rent	150
4	Do. Midland Rent	141½
4	Do. Mid. & Dist. Guar.	126½
2½	Midland, Cons. Perp.	92
3	Mid. & G. N. Jt., "A" Rnt.	106
3	N. British, Lien	107
4	Do Cons. Pref. No. 1	139
3	N. Cornwall, Wadebrge. Gu.	107
4	N. Eastern	144
5	N. Staff. Trent & M. £20 Shs.	35½
3½	Nott. Suburban Ord.	123½
20/6	S. E. Perp. Ann.	35½
4½	Do. 4½ p.c.	162½
3½	S. Yorks. Junc. Ord.	118½
4½	W. Cornwall (G. W., Br., Ex., & S. Dev. Joint Rent	159½
3	W. Highl. Ord. Stk. (Gua., N.B.)	104½

PREFERENCE SHARES AND STOCKS.

DIVIDENDS CONTINGENT ON PROFIT OF YEAR.

Last Div.	Name	Price.
4½	Alexandra Dks. & Ry. "A"	125½
5	Barry (First)	167½
4	Do. Consolidated	136½
4	Caledonian Cons., No. 1	141½
4	Do. do. No. 2	140½
5	Do. do. 1878	174½
4	Do. Pref. 1884	140½
4	Do. do. 1887 (Conv.)	152½
—	Cambrian, No. 1 4 p.c. Pref.	72½
—	Do. No. 2 do.	37½
—	Do. No. 3 do.	17½
—	Do. No. 4 do.	9
5	City & S. Lond. £10 shares	15½
—	Do. New	14
4	Furness, Cons. 1881	133
4	Do. ...."A" 1881	131½
4	Do. ...."B" 1883	129½
4	Glasgow & S. Western	140½
4	Do. No. 2	140½
4	Do. 1888	139½
4	Do. 1891	139½
5	Gt. Central	158½
4	Do.	131½
5	Do. Conv. 1872	153½
5	Do. do. 1874	153½
5	Do. do. 1876	152½
5	Do. do. 1879	151½
5	Do. do. 1881	147½
4	Do. 1889	112½
4	Do. 1891	106½
5	Do. 1894	105½
4	Gt. Eastern, Cons.	141½
4	Do. 1866	139½
4	Do. 1881	138½
4	Do. 1884	138½

Preference Shares, &c. (*continued*):—

Last Div.	Name.	Price.
4	Gt. Eastern, Cons. 1887	132½
4	Do. 1888	133½
3½	Do. 1890	120½
3½	Do. 1895	120½
—	Do. (Int. fr. Jan '99) 1893	117½
4	Gt. North Scotland "A"	133½
4	Do. "B"	133½
4	Gt. Northern, Cons.	142½
3	Do. 1896	107
5	Gt. Western Cons.	180½
36/11	Hull & Barnsley Red. at 115	107½
4	Isle of Wight	133½
3	Lancs. & Yorkshire, Cons.	102
2/2½	Lanc. Drby & E. C. 5 p.c. £10	10
—	Do. 5 p.c. 2nd £10	9
5	Lond., Bright., &c., Cons.	178½
5	Do. and Cons.	177½
4½	Lond., Chat. & Dov. Arbitr.	136
26/	Do. 2nd Pref. 4½ p.c.	93
4	Lond. & N. Western	145
4	Lond. & S. Western .. 1881	144
4	Do. 1884	143
3½	Do.	126½
4	Lond., Tilbury & Southend	140½
4	Do. Cons., 1887	140½
4	Do 1891	140½
—	Mersey, 5 p.c. Perp.	—
4	Metropolitan, Perp.	140½
4	Do. 1882	140½
4	Do. Irred.	140½
4	Do. 1887	140½
4	Do. New	140½
4½	Do.	146½
3½	Do.	123½
3	Do. Guar.	101½
2½	Metrop. Dist. Exten 5 p.c.	110
2½	Midland, Perp. Pref.	12
4	N. British Cons., No. 2	125½
4½	Do. Edin. & Glasgow	151½
5	Do. 1865	165½
5	Do. Conv. 1874	166½
4½	Do. 1874	151½
4½	Do. Conv. 1875	151½
5	Do. do. 1870	164½
4	Do. do. 1884	126½
4	Do. do. 1888	126½
4	Do. do. 1890	126½
4	Do. do. 1892	126½
4	N. Eastern	145
4½	N. Lond., Cons. 1866	174½
4½	Do. and Cons. .. 1875	157½
3	N. Staffordshire	106½
4½	Plym. Devpt. & S. W. Junc.	149½
1/5	Port Talbot, &c., 4 p.c. £10 Shares, 4 paid	5
5/	Rhondda & Swansea Bay, 5 p.c. £10 Shares	12½
4	Rhymney, Cons.	140½
4½	S. Eastern, Cons.	160½
5	Do. do.	178½
4	Do. Vested Cos'.	140½
4	Do. 1891	140½
3½	Do. 1893	122½
2	Do. 3 p.c. after July 1900	101½
4	Taff Vale	141½

INDIAN RAILWAYS.

Last Div.	Name.	Paid.	Price.
3½	Assam Bengal, Ld., (3½ p.c. till June 30, then 3 p.c.)	100	100
4/	Barsi Light, Ld., £10 Shs.	10	11
6	Bengal and N. West., Ld	100	148½
4/	Do. £10 Shares	10	14½
3/6	Do. 3½ p.c. Cum. Pf. Shs.	10	10½
8½d.	Do.	4	4½
2/3½	Bengal Central, Ld., £10 (3½ p.c. + ¼th net earn)	5	6
3	Bengal Dooars, Ld.	100	114
4	Bengal Nagpr., Lim. (gua. 4 p.c. + 4th sp. pfts.)	100	114
7½	Bombay, Baroda, and C. I. (gua 5 p.c)	100	214
36/1	Burma, Ld. (gua. 2½ p.c. and ½ p.c. add. till 1901)	100	107½
1/7	Do. £10 Shares		3
4	Delhi Umb. Kalka, Ld., Gua. 3½ p.c. + net earn.	100	121
4	Do. Deb. Stk., 1890 (1916)	100	111
9/10	Estn. Bengal, "A" An. 1957	—	25
9/	Do. "B" 1957	—	30
4	Do. Gua. Deb. Stock	100	136½
9/7½	East Ind. Ann. "A" (1953)	—	27
8/4½	Do. "C"	—	28
8/11½	Do. "B"	—	30
6⅛	Do. Def. Ann. Cap. (gua. 4 p.c. + ⅕th sp. pfts.)	—	150
115/9	East Ind. Def. Ann. "D"	—	156
4½	East Ind. Irred. Stock	100	158½
5	Gt. Indian Penin., Gua 5 p.c. + ½ surplus profits	100	167½
4	Do. Irred. 4 p.c. Deb. St.	100	136½
4	Indian Mid., Ld. (gua. 4 p.c. + ¼th surplus pfts.)	100	113
51/	Madras Guar. + ½ sp. pfts.	100	166
43/6	Do. do.	100	156
40/	Do. do.	100	146
4	Nilgiri, Ld., 1st Deb. Stk.	100	97
4	Oude & Rohil. Db. Stk. Rd.	100	—
5½	Rohil. and Kumaon, Ld.	100	132
9/11	Scinde, Punj., and Delhi, "A" Ann., 1958	—	25
9/1	Do. "B" do.	—	30

Indian Railways (*continued*):—

Last Div.	Name.	Paid.	Price.
4	South Behar, Ld., £10 shs.	100	100
3½	Do. Deb. Stk. Red.	100	101
4½	South Ind., Gu. Deb. Stk.	100	158½
5	South Indian, Ld. (gua. 3 p.c., and ½ spls. profits)	100	122½
5	Sthn. Mahratta, Ld. (3½ p.c. & ¼th net earnings)	100	115½
4	Do. Deb. Stk. Red.	100	120
3½	Southern Punjab, Ld.	100	105
3½	Do. Deb. Stk. Red.	—	104
5	Nizam's Gua. State, Ld. [†	100	114½
4	Do. Mort. Deb., 1936	100	107
4	Do. do. Reg.	100	106
17/3½	Nizam's Gua. State, Ld., 3½ p.c. Mt. Deb. bearer	—	94½
17/3½	Do. Reg. do.	—	93½
5	W. of India Portgese., Ld.	100	67½
5	Do. Deb. Stk., Red	100	99

RAILWAYS.—BRITISH POSSESSIONS.

Last Div.	Name.	Paid.	Price.
5	Atlantic & N.W. Gua. 1 Mt. Bds., 1937	100	125½
5/3	Buff. & L. Huron Ord. Sh.	10	13½
5½	Do. 1st Mt. Perp. Bds. 1879	100	141½
5½	Do. 2nd Mt. Perp. Bds.	100	141½
—	Calgary & Edmon. 6 p.c. 1st Mt. Stg. Bds. Red.	100	76½
5	Canada Cent. 1st Mt. Bds. Red.	100	103
4	Can. Pacific Pref. Stk.	100	100½
5	Do. Strl. 1st Mt. Deb. Bds. 1915	100	117
3½	Do. Ld. Grnt. Bds., 1938	100	106
3½	Do. Ld. Grnt. Ins. Stk.	100	106
4	Do. Perp. Cons. Deb. Stk.	100	115
5	Do. Algoma Bch. 1st Mt. Bds., 1937	100	121
2	Demerara, Original Stock	100	47
7	Do. Perp. Pref. Stk.	100	155½
1/10	Do. 4 p.c. Cum. Ext. Pref. £10 Shs.	4	8
—	Dominion Atlntc. Ord. Stk.	100	33½
5	Do. 5 p.c. Pref. Stk.	100	97½
4	Do. 1st. Deb. Stk.	100	103½
4	Do. 2nd do. Red.	100	99
—	EmuBay & Mt. Bischoff, Ld.	5	4½
4½	Do. Irred. Deb. Stk.	100	98
nil.	Gd. Trunk of Canada, Stk.	100	8½
6	Do. 2nd. Equip. Mt. Bds.	100	131½
5	Do. Perp. Deb. Stk.	100	136½
5	Do. Gt. Westn. Deb. Stk.	100	127½
5	Do. Nthn. of Can. 1st Mt. Bds, 1902	100	103½
4	Do. do. Deb. Stk	100	102
5	Do. G. T. Geor. Bay & L. Erie 1 Mt., 1903	100	105
5	Do. Mid. of Can. Stl. 1st Mt. (Mid. Sec.) 1908	100	103
5	Do. do. Cons. 1 Mt. Bds. 1912	100	106
5	Do. Mont. & Champ. 1 Mt. Bds., 1902	100	104
	Do. Welln., Grey & Brce. 7 p.c. Bds. 1 Mt.	100	109
—	Jamaica 1st Mtg. Bds. Red.	—	103
—	Manitoba & N. W., 6 p.c. 1st Mt. Bds., Red	100	—
—	Do. Ldn. Bdhldrs. Certs.	—	—
5	Manitoba S. W. Col. 1 Mt. Bd., 1934 $1,000 price %	—	120
—	Mid. of W. Aust. Ld. 6 p.c. 1 Mt. Dbs., Red.	100	37½
4	Do. Deb. Bds., Red.	100	103
4	Nakusp & Slocan Bds., 1918	100	106
3	Natal Zululand Ld. Debs.,	100	72½
5	N. Brunswick 1st Mt. Stg. Bds., 1934	100	121
4	Do. Perp. Cons. Deb. Stk.	100	114
—	N. Zealand Mid., Ld., 5 p.c. 1st Mt. Debs.	100	35
6	Ontario & Queb. Cap. Stk.	$100	154½
5	Do. Perm. Deb. Stk.	100	143½
—	Qu'Appelle, L. Lake & Sask. 6 p.c. 1 Mt. Bds. Red.	100	40½
	Queb. & L. S. John, 1st Mt. Bds., 1909	100	32
	Quebec Cent., Prior Ln. Bds., 1908	100	107
1½	Do. 5 p.c. Inc. Bds.	100	38
4	St. Lawr. & Ott. Stl. 1st Mt.	100	112
4	Shuswap & Okan., 1st Mt. Deb. Bds., 1915	100	76
5	Temiscouata, 5 p.c. Stl. 1st Deb. Bds., Red.	100	9½
5	Do. (S. Franc. Brch.) 5 p.c. Stl. 1 Mt. Db. Bds., 1910	100	10
4	Toronto, Grey & B. 1st Mt.	100	112
1/9	Well. & Mana. £5 Shs.	1	½
5	Do. Debs., 1908	100	107
5	Do. 2nd Debs., 1908	100	106
5	Do. 3rd do., 1908	100	104
6	Atlan. & St. Law. Shs., 6 p.c.	100	163½
5	Gd. Trunk Mt. Bds., 1934	100	116½
5	Michigan Air Line, 5 p.c. 1st Mt. Bds., 1902	100	104
4	Minneap., S. P. & Slt. Ste. Mar, 1st Mt. Bds., 1938	$1000	98

AMERICAN RAILROAD STOCKS AND SHARES.

Last Div.	Name.	Paid.	Price.
6/	Alab. Gt. Sthn. A 6 p.c. Pref.	10/.	9
—	Do. do "B" Ord.	10/.	1½
—	Alabma. N. Orl.-Tex. &c., "A" Pref.	10/.	½
—	Do. "B" Def.	10/.	¼
5½	Atlant. First Lsd. La. Rtl. Trust	Stk.	97½
—	Baltimore & Ohio Com.	$100	19
—	Baltimore Ohio S.W. Pref.	$100	7
—	Chesap. & Ohio Com.	$100	22
—	Chic. Gt. West. 5 p.c. Pref. Stock "A"	$100	32½
—	Do. do. Scrip. In.	—	30½
8/3	Do. 4 p.c. Deb. Stk.	$100	67½
4	Do. Interest in Scrip	$100	63½
$4	Chic. Junc. Rl. & Un. Stk. Yds. Com.	$100	116½
$1½	Do. 6 p.c. Cum. Pref.	$100	119½
$3½	Chic. Mil. & St. P. Pref.	$100	147½
7	Cleve. & Pittsburgh	$10	86
$1½	Clev., Cincin., Chic., & St. Louis Com.	$100	—
—	Erie 4 p.c. Non-Cum. 1st Pf.	—	36½
—	Do. 4 p.c. do. 2nd Pf.	—	18
$2½	Gt. Northern Pref.	$100	160
$2½	Illinois Cen. Lsd. Lines	$100	95½
—	Kansas City, Pitts & G.	$100	19
$3	L. Shore & Mich. Sth. C.	$100	190
—	Mex. Cen. Ltd. Com.	$100	5
—	Miss. Kan. & Tex. Pref.	$100	36
2½	N.Y., Pen. & O. 1st Mt. Tst. Ltd., Ord.	—	47½
4	Do. 1st Mort. Deb. Stk.	$100	92½
2	North Pennsylvania	$50	—
—	Northn. Pacific, Com.	$100	27½
1½	Pitts. F. Wayne & Chic.	$100	174
—	Reading 1st Pref.	$50	23
—	Do. 2nd Pref.	$50	11½
—	S. Louis & S. Fran. Com.	$100	6
—	Do. 2nd Pref.	$100	25½
6	St. Louis Bridge 1st Pref.	$100	107
3	Do. 2nd Pref.	$100	50
6	Tunnel Rail. of St. Louis	$100	107
$1½	St. Paul, Min. and Man.	$100	137½
—	Southern, Com.	$100	8½
—	Wabash, Common	$100	8

AMERICAN RAILROAD BONDS. CURRENCY.

Last Div.	Name.	Price.
7	Albany & Susq. 1 Con. Mrt. 1906	118
7	Allegheny Val. 1 Mt. 1910	125½
5	Canada Southern 1 Mt. 1908	111
5	Chic. & N. West. Sk. Fd. Db. 1933	117½
5	Do. Deb. Coupon 1921	112½
6	Chicago & Tomah 1905	109½
5	Chic. Burl. & Q. Skg. Fd. 1901	102½
4	Do. Nebraska Ext. —	100
6	Chic., Mil., & S. Pl., 1 Mt. S.W. Div. 1909	117½
7	Do. (S. Paul Div.) 1 Mt. 1902	132½
5	Do. (La Cross & D. 1919	112½
7	Do. 1 Mt. (Hast. & Dak.) 1910	127½
5	Do. Chic. & Mis. Riv. 1 Mt. 1926	112½
5	Chic., Rock Is. and Pac. 1 Mt. Ext. 1934	108
6	Det., G. Haven & Mil. Equip 1918	105
6	Do. do. Cons. Mt. 1918	102½
6	Ill. Cent., 1 Mt., Chic. & S. 1898	—
7	Indianap. & Vin., 1 Mt. 1908	125
6	Do. do. 2 Mt. 1900	100½
6	Lehigh Val., Cons. Mt. 1923	112½
—	Mexic. Cent., Ln. 2 Cons. Inc. —	5
7	N.Y. Cent. & H.R. Mt. Bonds 1903	119½
5	Do. Deb. 1904	109½
6	Penns. Cons. S. F. M. 1905	118
4	West Shore, 1 Mt. 2361	110

DITTO—GOLD.

Last Div.	Name.	Price.
6	Alabama Gt. Sthn. 1 Mt. 1908	114
5	Do. Mid. 1 1928	90½
4	Allegheny Val. Gen. Mt. 1942	106
4	Atch., Top., & S. Fé Gn. Mt. 1995	92½
3	Do. Adj. Mt. 1995	64½
5	Do. Equipt. Tmst. —	102½
5	Atlantic & Dan. 1 Mt. 1950	96½
5	Baltimore & Ohio 1925	100
5	Do. Speyer's Tst. Recpts. 1925	100
5	Do. Cons. Mt. 1988	104
4½	Do. 4½ p.c. 1 Mt. Term. 1934	84
4½	Do. Brown Shipley's Dep. Cts. —	84
5	Balt. Belt 5 p.c. 1 Mort. 1990	85
4½	Balt. & Ohio S.W. 1 Mt. 1990	100
4½	Do. 4½ p.c. 1 Cons. Mt. 1893 1993	75½
—	Do. Inc. Mt. 5 p.c. Cl. A —	27½
—	Do. do. Cl. B —	10
5	Balt. & Ohio S.W. Term 5 p.c. 1942	97½
6	Balt. & Ptmac (Mn. L.) 1 Mt. 1911	124
6	Do. do. (Tunnel) 1 Mt. 1911	126
4	Beech Creek 1 Mt. 1936	109
4	Carthage & Adiron 1 Mt. 1981	109

American Railroad Bonds—Gold (*continued*):—

Last Div.	Name.	Price.
5	Cent. of Georgia 1 Mort. 1945	117½
5	Do. Cons. Mt. 1945	90½
5	Cent. of N. Jrsy. Gn. Mt. 1987	116
6	Central Pacific, 1 Mort. 1898	102½
6	Do. Speyer's Certs. —	106
5	Do. Land Grant 1900	101
5	Chesap. & Ohio 1st Cons. Mt. 1939	116
4½	Do. Gen. Mt. 1992	81
6	Chic. & W. Ind. Gen. Mt. Skg. Fd. 1932	120
5	Chic. Mil. & St. Pl. (Chic. & L. Sup.) 1 Mt. 1921	114½
5	Do. Chic. & Pac. W. 1921	117½
5	Do. Wisc. & Minn. 1 Mt. 1921	112½
5	Do. Terminal Mt. 1914	114½
4	Do. General Mt. 1989	106½
5	Chic. St. L. & N. Orleans 1951	122½
4	Do. 1 Mort. (Memphis) 1951	105½
4	Clevel., Cin., Chic. & St. L., 1 Mt. (Cairo) 1939	90
4	Do. 1 Mt. (Cinc., Wab., & Mich.) 1991	90
4	Do. 1 Col. Tst. Mt. (S. Louis) 1990	95
4	Do. General Mt. 1993	82½
4½	Clevel. & Mar. Mt. 1935	109
4½	Clevel. & Pittsburgh 1942	116½
4½	Do. Series B. 1942	116½
—	Colorado Mid. 1 Mt. 1936	63½
—	Do. Bdhrs.' Comm. Certs. —	63½
4	Dnvr. & R. Gde. 1 Cons. Mt. 1936	94
5	Do Imp. Mort. 1928	93
4	Detroit & Mack. 1 Lien 1995	92½
5	E. Tennes., Virg., & Grgia. Cons. Mt. 1956	111½
5	Elmira, Cort., & Nthn. Mt. 1914	100
4	Erie 1 Cons. Mt. Pr. Ln. 1996	92
3	Do. Gen. Lien 1996	73
6	Galvest., Harrisb., &c., 1 Mt.	107½
5	Georgia, Car. & N. 1 Mt. 1929	96
4½	Gd Rpds & Inda. Ex. 1 Mt. 1941	112½
5	Do. 1 Mt. (Muskegon) 1926	36
3½	Illinois Cent. 1 Mt. 1951	104½
4	Do. 1952	104½
4	Do. Cairo Bdge. 1950	102
4	Do. 1953	101
4	Do. General Mort. 1904	102½
5	Kans. City, Pitts. & G. 1 M. 1923	73½
3½	L. Shore & Mich. Southern 1997	109
4½	Lehigh Val. N.Y. 1 Mt. 1940	102½
5	Lehigh Val. Term. 1 Mt. 1941	109½
5	Long Island 1931	117½
5	Do. Deb. 1934	102
5	Do. (N. Shore Bch.) 1 Cons. Mt. 1932	94
6	Louisville & Nash. G. Mt. 1930	120
6	Do. 2 Mt. Sk. Fd. (S. & N. Alabama 1910	107
6	Do. 1 Mt. N. Orl. & Mb. 1930	122½
5	Do. 1 Mt. Coll. Tst. 1931	102½
4	Do. Unified 1940	90
4½	Do. Mobile & Montgy. 1 Mt. 1945	105½
4	Manhattan Cons. Mt. 1990	97½
4	Mexican Cent. Cons. Mt. 1911	65
—	Do. 1 Cons. Inc,	14
6	Mexican Nat. 1 Mt. 1927	106
3½	Do. 2 Mt. 6 p.c. Inc. A 1917	52½
—	Do. do. B. 1917	9
3	Do. Matheson's Certs.	—
3	Michig. Cnt. (Battle Ck. & S.) 1 Mt. 1989	88
6	Minneap. & S. L. 1 Mt. Pacific Ext. 1921	—
5	Do. 1 Consold. 1934	104½
4	Minne., Slt. S. M. & A. 1 Mt. 1926	98½
5	Minneapolis Westn. 1 Mt. 1911	106½
4	Miss. Kans. & Tex. 1 Mt. 1990	91
4	Do. 2 do. 1990	64
4	Mobile & Birm. Mt. Inc. 1945	38
5	Do. P. Lien 1945	88
4	Mohawk & Mal. 1 Mt. 1991	108
5	Montana Cent. 1 Mt. 1937	111½
5	Nashv., Chattan., & S. L. 1 Cons. Mt. 1928	102½
5	Nash., Flor., & Shff. Mt. 1937	92½
4	N. Y. & Putnam 1 Cons. Mt. 1993	106
5	N. Y., Brooklyn, & Man. B. 1 Cons. Mt. 1935	107½
4	N. Y. Cent. & Hud. R. Deb. Certs. 1890 1905	106
4	Do. Ext. Debt. Certs. 1905	105
7	N. Y., L. Erie, & W. 1 Cons. Mt. (Erie) 1920	142½
7	Do. 1 Con. Mt. Fd. Coup. 1920	139½
5	N. Y., Onto., & W. Cons. 1 Mt. 1939	111
4	Do. 4 p.c. Refund. Mt. 1992	100
6	Norfolk & West. Gn. Mt. 1931	121½
6	Do. Imp. & Ext. 1934	117½
4	Do. 1 Cons. Mt. —	82
6	N. Pacific Gn. 1 Mt. Ld. Gt. 1921	—
4	Do. P. Ln. Rl. & Ld. Gt. —	97
3	Do. Gn. Ln. Rl. & Ld. Gt. —	62
5	Oregon & Calif. 1 Mt. 1927	78½
6	Panama Skg. Fd. Subsidy 1910	102½
4½	Pennsylvania Rlrd. 1913	112
4	Do. Equip. Tst. Ser. A 1914	104
4	Do. Cons. Mt. 1943	112½
4½	Penna. Company 1st Mort. 1921	110½
5	Perkiomen 1 Mrt., 2nd ser. 1918	91½
4½	Pitts., C., C., & St. Ls. Con. Mt. G. B., Ser. A 1940-2	111
4	Do. Cons. Mort., Ser. D 1945	102½
6	Pittsbgh., Cle., & Toledo 1922	100½
4	Reading, Phil., & R. Genl. 1997	86
5	Richmond & Dan. Equip. 1909	97½
5	Rio Grande Junc. 1st Mort. 1939	92½
4	Rio Grande West 1st Tst. Mt. 1939	82½
7	S. Louis Bridge 1st Mort 1928	134½
5	S. Louis Mchts. Bdge. Term. 1st Mort. 1930	102½
4	S. Louis S. West 1st Mort. 1989	75
—	Do. 4 p.c. 2nd Mort. Inc. 1989	30

American Railroad Bonds (*continued*):

Last Div.	Name.	Price.
—	S. Louis Term. Cupples Sta. & Prop. 1st. Mrt. 4½ p.c. 1908-17	102
4½	St. Paul Minn., & Manit. 1933	107½
6	Do. do. 1933	132½
6	Shamokin, Sunbury, &c. 2 Mt. 1925	100
5	S. & N. Alabama Cons. Mt. 1936	97½
5	Southern 1 Cons. Coup. 1994	93½
4	Do. E. Tennes Reorg. Lien 1938	100
6	S. Pacific of Cal. 1 Mt. 1905-12	110
4½	Trml. Assn. of S. Louis 1 Mt. 1939	110½
5	Do. 1 Cons. Mt. 1944	108
5	Texas & Pac. 1 Mt. 2000	104½
—	Do. 5 p.c. 2 Mt. Income 2000	34
5	Toledo & Ohio Cent. 1 Mt. West. Div. 1935	102½
4½	Toledo., Walhon., Val., & Ohio 1 Mt. 1931-3	111½
—	Union Pacific 1 Mt. 4 p.c. 1947	96
—	Union Pac., Linc., & Color. 1 Mt. 1918	—
4	United N. Jersey Gen. Mt. 1944	113½
6	Vicksbrg., Shrevept., & Pac. Pr. Ln. Mt. 1915	100½
5	Wabash 1 Mt. 1939	106½
4	Wn. Pennsylvania Mt. 1928	109½
5	W. Virga. & Pittsbg. 1 Mt. 1990	75
5	Wheeling & L. Erie 1 Mt. (Wheelg. Div.) 5 p.c. 1928	90½
5	Do. Extn. Imp. Mt. 1930	90
—	Do. do. Brown Shipley's Cts.	—
5	Willmar & Sioux Falls 1 Mt. 1938	111

STERLING.

Last Div.	Name.	Price.
6	Alabama Gt. Sthn. Deb. 1906	104½
5	Do. Gen. Mort. 1927-8	98
5	Alabama, N. Orl., Tex. & Pac. 5 p.c. "A" Dbs. 1910-40	98½
55/	Do. do. "B" do. 1910-40	55
—	Do. do. "C" do.	19
—	Allegheny Valley 1910	128½
4	Atlantic 1st Leased Line Perp.	100
6	Baltimore and Ohio 1902	108
6	Do. do. 1910	116
5	Do. do. 1877	97½
—	Do. Morgan's Certs.	97½
4½	Do. do. 1933	90
6	Chicago & Alton Cons. Mt. 1903	111
5	Chic. St. Paul & Kan. City Priority	105
6	Eastn. of Massachusetts 1906	117½
5	Illinois Cent. Skg. Fd.	103
5	Do. 1905	108
3½	Do. 1950	99½
4	Do. 1 Mt. 1951	110
3	Do. 1 Mt. 1951	92½
6	Louisville & Nash., M. C. & L. Div., 1 Mt. 1902	104½
7	Do. 1 Mt. (Memphis & O.) 1901	111
53/8	Mexican Nat. "A" Certs. 5 p.c. Non. cum.	41
—	Do. "B" Certs.	9
6	N.Y. & Canada 1 Mt. 1904	108½
6	N. York Cent. & H.R. Mort. 1903	112
4½	N. York, Penns., & Ohio Pr. Ln. Extd. 1935	—
5	Do. Equip. Tst.	101½
5	Do. 5 p.c. Equip. Tst. (1890)	103½
6	Nrthn. Cent. Cons. Gen. Mt.	106
6	Pennsylvania Gen. Mt. 1910	126
6	Do. Cons. Skg. Fd. Mt. 1905	114½
3½	Do. Cons. Mt. 1945	103½
6	Phil. & Erie Cons. Mort 1920	132½
6	Phil. & Reading Gen. Cons. Mort. 1911	122½
6	Pittsbg. & Connells. Cons. 1926	114
—	Do. Morgan's Certs.	114
4	St. Paul., Min., & Manitoba (Pac. Extn.) 1940	96½
6	S. & N. Alabama 1903	104½
6	Un. N. Jersey & C. Gen. Mt. 1901	109½

FOREIGN RAILWAYS

Last Div.	Name.	Paid.	Price.
4/	Alagoas, Ltd., Shs.	20	5½
5	Do. Deb. Stk., Red.	100	42½
6	Antofagasta, Ltd., Stk.	100	73
4	Do. Perp. Deb. Stk.	100	91
—	Arauco, Ld., Ord. Shs.	10	—
—	Do. 10 p.c. Cum. Pref.	10	—
5	Argentine Gt. W., Ld.,	100	76
5	Do. 5 p.c. Cum. Pref. Shs.	100	100
4	Do. 1 Deb. Stk.	100	102
1/0/0	Argentine N.E., Ltd., 6 p.c. Cum. Pref. Stk.	100	9½
—	Do. 5 p.c. Deb. Stk., Red.	100	28
2/	Arica and Tacna Shs.	20	1½
10/	Bahia & San Fcisco., Ld.,	20	8½
6/	Do. Timbo. Bch. Shs.	20	4½
12/	Bahia, Blanca, & N.W. Ln. Prf. Cum. 6 p.c.	100	53
4	Do. 4 p.c. 1 Deb. Stk., Red.	100	92
6	Barranquilla R. & P., Ld., 6 p.c. 1 Deb. Stk., Red.	100	96

Foreign Railways (*continued*):—

Last Div.	Name.	Paid.	Price.
3/	Bilbao Riv. & Cantabn., Ltd., Ord.	3	5
—	Bolivar, Ltd. Shs.	10	1½
6	Do. 6 p.c. Deb. Stk.	100	96½
—	Brazil Gt. Southn. Ltd., 7 p.c. Cum. Pref.	20	1½
6	Do. Perm. Deb. Stk	100	43
5½	B. Ayres Gt. Southn. Ld., Ord. Stk.	100	141
5	Do. Pref. Stk.	100	134
4	Do. Deb. Stk.	100	116½
30/	B. Ayres & Ensen. Port., Ltd., Ord. Stk.	100	67
5	Do. Cum. 1 Pref. Stk.	100	120
6/0/0	Do. 6p.c.Con. Pref.Stk.	100	99
4	Do. Deb. Stk., Irred.	100	113
10⅝	B. Ayres Northern, Ltd., Ord. Stk.	100	265
12⅝	Do. Pref. Stk.	100	320
5	Do. 5 p.c. Mt. Deb.Stk., Red.	100	113
3/15/0	B. Ayres & Pac., Ld., 7 p.c. 1 Pref. Stk. (Cum.)	100	94
4	Do. 1 Deb. Stk.	100	102
5/5/0	Do. 4½ p.c. 2 Deb. Stk.	100	91
3	B Ayres & Rosario, Ltd., Ord. Stk.	100	73½
—	Do New, £20 Shs.	20	—
7/	Do. 7 p.c. Pref. Shs.	10	17
7/	Do. Sunchales Ext.	10	14½
4	Do. Deb. Stk., Red.	100	107
—	B. Ayres & Val. Trans., Ltd., 7 p.c. Cum. Pref.	20	6½
4	Do. 4 p.c. "A" Deb. Stk., Red.	100	71
—	Do. 6 p.c. "B" Deb. Stk. Red.	100	43
3/6	B. Ayres Westn. Ld. Ord.	10	11
3/	Do. Def. Shs.	10	6½
5	Do. 5 p.c. Pref.	10	12¼
4	Do. Deb. Stk.	100	108
6	Cent. Arg. Deb.Sk. Rd.	100	159½
4	Do. Deb. Stk. Rd	100	110
6	Cent. Bahia L. Ord. Stk.	100	49
	Do. Deb. Stk., 1934	100	72½
5	Do. Deb. Stk., 1937	100	60
3/6	Cent. Uguy. East. Ext. L. Shs	10	5½
5	Do. Perm. Stk.	100	112
3/6	Do. Nthn. Ext. L. Sh.	10	4
5	Do. Perm. Deb. Stk.	100	103½
3	Do. of Montev. Ltd., Ord. Stk.	100	87
6	Do. Perm. Deb. Stk.	100	141
10/	Conde d'Eu, Ltd. Ord.	20	7
—	Cordba & Rosar., Ltd., 6 p.c. Pref. Shs.	100	39
4	Do. 1 Deb. Stk	100	90
75	Do. 6 p.c. Deb. Stk	100	90
—	Cordba Cent., Ltd., 5 p.c. Cu. 1 Pref. Stk	100	78
—	Do. 5 p.c. Non-Cum. 2 Pref. Stk	100	44
5	Do. Deb. Stk	100	118
—	Costa Rica, Ltd., Shs.	10	4½
8/	Dna. Thrsa. Chris., Ltd., 7 p.c. Pref. Shs.	20	3½
20/	E. Argentine, Ltd	100	40
6	Do. Deb. Stk.	100	101
1/2	Egyptn. Dlta. Lgt. Rys., Ltd., £10 Pref. Shs.	8	10
—	Entre Rios, L., Ord. Shs.	5	¾
—	Do. Cu. 5 p.c. Pref.	5	3
6/	Gt. Westn. Brazil, Ltd.,	20	8
6	Do. Perm. Deb. Stk	100	90½
6	Do. Extn. Deb. Stk	100	76½
—	Int.-Oceanic Mex., Ltd., 7 p.c. Pref.	10	1½
4	Do. Deb. Stk	100	83
42/6	Do. 7 p.c. "A" Deb. Sk.	100	67
—	Do. 7 p.c. "B" Deb. Sk.	100	30
5/	La Guaira & Carac	10	7½
5	Do. 5 p.c. Deb. Sk. Red.	100	100
1 1/3	Lembg.-Czern.-Jassy	30	24½
1/	Lima, Ltd.	20	2½
—	Manila Ltd. 7 p.c. Cu. Pf.	10	[illegible]
20/6½	Mexican and Pref. 6 p.c.	100	31
6	Do. Perp. Deb. Stk.	100	137
1/0/0	Mexican Sthrn., Ld., Ord.	100	22
—	Do. 4 p.c. 1 Db.Stk. Rd.	100	83
—	Do. 4 p.c. 2 do.	100	59
—	Mid. Urgy., Ltd.	100	18½
5	Do. Deb. Stk	100	61
12/	Minas & Rio, Ltd.	20	9
5/2	Namur & Liege	20	12½
11/6	Do. Pref.	20	29
13/	Natal & Na. Cruz, Ld., 7 p.c. Cum Pref.	20	6
—	Nitrate Ltd., Ord.	10	5¼
—	Do. 7 p.c. Pr. Con. Or.	10	4¼
—	Do. Def. Conv. Ord.	10	[illegible]
7/	N.-E. Urgy., Ltd., Ord.	10	14¼
7/	Do. 7 p.c. Pref.	10	14½
—	N.-W. Argentine Ld., 7 p.c. Pref.	10	2
6	Do. 6 p.c. 1 Deb. Stk.	100	113
—	Do. 2 Deb. Stk.	100	94
—	N.W. Uruguay 6 p.c. 1 Pref. Stk.	100	17
—	Do. 5 p.c. 2 Pref. Stk.	100	7½
6	Do. 6 p.c. Deb. Stk	100	80½
22/	Ottoman (Sm. Aid.)	20	13½
—	Paraguay Cntl., Ld., 5 p.c. Perm. Deb. Stk.	100	11
—	Piræus, Ath., & Pelo.	275	1½
	Pto. Alegre & N. Hambg Ld., 7 p.c. Pref. Shs.	20	4
6	Do. Mt. Deb. Stk. Red.	100	74½
—	Puerto Cabello & Val. Ld.	10	1½
5	Recife & S. Francisco	100	62½
24/	R. Claro S. Paulo, Ld., Sh.	10	20½
5	Do. Deb. Stk.	100	125
5	Royal Sardinian Ord.	10	11½

Foreign Railways (*continued*):—

Last Div.	Name.	Paid.	Price.
5/	Royal Sardinian Pref.	10	12
5/	Sambre & Meuse	20	18
5/6	Do. Pref.	10	12½
22/	San Paulo Ld.	20	31½
2/10½	Do. New Ord. £10 sh.	6	8½
4/8	Do. 5 p.c. Non.Cm.Pref.	10	11½
5½	Do. Deb. Stk.	100	132
5	Do. 5 p.c. Deb. Stk.	100	127
—	S. Fé & Cordova, Gt. Sthn., Ld., Shares	100	49½
6	Do. Perp. Deb. Stk.	100	120
3/2½	S. Austrian	20	7
10/	Sthn. Braz. R. Gde. do Sul, Ld.	20	7
6	Do. 6 p.c. Deb. Stk.	100	67½
4	Swedish Centl., Ld., 4 p.c. Deb. Stk.	100	107
5	Do. Pref.	100	100½
1/3	Taltal, Ld.	5	2½
—	Uruguay Nthn., Ld. 7 p.c. Pfd. Stk.	100	8
3½	Do. 5 p.c. Deb. Stk.	100	30
—	Villa Maria & Rufino, Ld., 6 p.c. Pref. Shs.	100	18
4	Do. 4 p.c. 1 Deb. Stk.	100	73
6/0/0	Do. 6 p.c. 2 Deb. Stk.	100	46
5/9	West Flanders	8½	21
5/6	Do. 5½ p.c. Pref.	10	18
3/	Wstn. of Havana, Ld.	10	4

FOREIGN RAILWAY OBLIGATIONS

Per Cent.	Name.	Price.
6	Alagoas Ld., 6 p.c. Deb., Rd.	81
—	Alcoy & Gandia, Ld., 5 p.c. Debs., Red.	20
5	Arauco., Ld., 5 p.c. 1st Mt., Rd.	62½
—	Do. 6 p.c. Mt. Deb., Rd.	42½
6	Brazil G. Sthn., L., Mt. Dbs., Rd.	83½
6	Do. Mt. Dbs. 1893, Rd.	49½
5½	Campos & Caran. Dbs., Rd.	72
6	Central Bahia, L., Dbs., Rd.	90
5½	Conde d'Eu, L., Dbs., Rd.	70
6	Costa Rica, L., 1st Mt. Dbs., Rd.	107
6	Do. 2nd Dbs., Rd.	91
5	Do. Prior Mt. Db., Rd.	103
6	Cucuta Mt. Dbs., Rd.	101
5½	Donna Thrsa. Cris., L., Dbs., Rd.	68½
3	Eastn. of France, £20 Dbs., Rd.	18½
4	Egyptn. Delta Light, L., Db., Rd	100
—	Espito. Santo & Cara. 5 p.c. Stl. Dbs., Rd.	38
4	Gd. Russian Nic., Rd.	102
5	Inter-Oceanic Mex., L., 5 p.c. Pr. Ln. Dbs., Rd.	103
3	Ital. 3 p.c. Bds. A & B, Rd.	57½
—	Ituana 6 p.c. Debs., 1918	74
—	Leopoldina, 6 p.c. Dbs. £50 Bds.	21
—	Do. do. Comms. Cert.	21
—	Do. 5 p.c. Stg. Dbs. (1888), Rd.	29
—	Do. do. Comm. Certs.	29
—	Do. 5 p.c. Stg. Dbs. (1890), Rd.	21
—	Do. do. Comms. Certs.	21
—	Macahé & Cam. 5 p.c. Dbs., Rd.	29
—	Do. do. Comms. Certs.	29
—	Do. (Cantagallo), 5 p.c., Red.	29
—	Do. do. Comm. Certs.	29
—	Manila Ltd., 6 p.c. Deb., Red.	20
6	Do. Prior Lien Mt., Rd.	98½
6	Do. Series "B," Rd.	80
7	Matanzas & Sab., Rd.	101½
6	Minas & Rio, L., 6 p.c. Dbs., Rd.	95
5	Mogyana 5 p.c. Deb. Bds., Rd.	101
5	Moscow-Jaros., Rd.	105½
5½	Natal & Na. Cruz Ltd., 5½ p.c. Debs., Red.	90
5	Nitrate, Ltd. Mt. Bds., Red.	88½
3	Nthn. France. Red.	19
4	N. of S. Af. Rep. (Trnsvl.) Gu. Bds. Red.	96
3	Nthn. of Spain £20 Pri. Obs. Red.	7
6	Ottmn. (Smy to A.)(Kujk) Asnt. Debs., Red.	106
6	Ottmn. (Seraik.) Asg. Debs. Red.	106
6	Ottmn. (Seraik) Non-Asg. D., Rd	106
5	Ottmn. Kuyjk. Ext. Red.	103
5	Ottmn. Serkeuy. Ext. Red.	100½
5	Ottmn. Tireh Ext. 1910	98
5	Ottmn. Debs, 1886, Red.	97
5	Do. 1888, Red. 1935	96½
5	Do. 1893, Red. 1935	97
5	Ottmn. of Anlia. Debs., Rd.	90½
4	Ottomn. Smyr. & Cas. Ext Bds., Red.	83½
3	Paris, Lyon & Medit. (old sys., £20), Red.	18½
3	Paris, Lyon & Medit. (new sys., £20), Red.	18½
50/	Piræus, At. & Pelp., 6 p.c. 1st Mt. Bds., Red.	89½
3	Do. 5 p.c. Mt. Bds., Red.	69½
4	Pretoria-Pietbg., Ltd., Red.	93
7	Puerto Cab. & Val., Ltd., 1st Mt. Debs., Red.	81
—	Rio de Jano. & Nthn., Ltd., 6 p.c. £100 Deb., Red.	21
—	Rio de Jano. (Gr. Para.), 5 p.c. 1st Mt. St. £100 Debs., Red.	21
2	Royal Sardinian, A, Rd. £20	12
3	Royal Sardinian, B., Rd. £20	12

Foreign Rly. Obligations (*continued*):—

Per Cent.	Name.	Price.
5	Ryl. Trns.-Afric. 5 p.c. 1st Mt. £100 Bds., Red.	48½
4	Sa. Fe & Cor. G.S., Ld. Pr Ln. Bds.	104
5	Sa. Fe, 5 p.c. and Reg. Dbs.	80
3	South Austrian, £20 Red.	15½
3	South Austrian, (Ser X.)	15½
3	South Italian £20 Obs. (Ser. A to G), Red.	12
3½	S.W. of Venez. (Barq.), Ltd., 7 p.c. 1st Mt. £100 Debs.	55½
5	Taltal, Ltd., 5 p.c. 1st Ch. Debs., Red.	97
5	Utd. Rwys. Havana, Red.	83½
3	Wtrn. of France, £20 Red.	18½
6	Wrn. B. Ayres St. Mt. Debs., 1902	107
6	Wrn. B. Ayres, Reg. Cert.	105
5	Do. Mt. Bds.	121
6	Wtrn. of Havna., Ld. Mt. Dbs., Rd.	90
7	Wrn. Ry. San Paulo Red.	99
—	Wrn. Santa Fé. 7 p.c. Red.	39
2/6	Zafra & Huelva, 3 p.c. Red.	2½

BANKS.

Div.	Name.	Paid.	Price.
2/4½	Agra, Ltd.	6	3½
4/2½	Anglo-Argentine, Ltd., £9	7	5½
8 fls.	Anglo-Austrian	120f	13
6/	Anglo-Californian, Ltd., £20 Shares	10	11
4/	Anglo-Egyptian, Ltd., £15	5	6
5/	Anglo-Foreign Bkg., Ltd.	7	7½
7/	Anglo-Italian, Ltd.	5	7
7/6	Bk. of Africa, Ltd., £15¾	6¼	10½
20/	Bk. of Australasia	40	49
10/	Bk. of Brit. Columbia	20	20
25/	Bk. of Brit. N. America	50	64
20/	Bk. of Egypt, Ltd., £25	12½	19
5/	Bk. of Mauritius, Ltd.	10	9
18/	Bk. of N. S. Wales	20	37½
4 p.c.	Bk. of N. Zland. Gua. Stk.	100	101½
6/	Bk. of Roumania, £20 Shs.	6	7½
2/6	Tarapaca & Ldn., Ltd., £10	5	3½
—	Bque. Fse. de l'Afri. du S.	100f	3½
f.22.50	Bque. Internatle. de Paris	20	23
6/	Brit. Bk. of S. America, Ltd., £20 Shares	10	10
16/	Capital & Cties., L., £50	10	39
20/	Chart. of India, &c.	20	30½
10/	City, Ltd., £40 Shares	10	20
18/	Colonial, £100 Shares	30	21
10/	Delhi and London, Ltd.	25	—
5/	German of London, Ltd.	10	10½
25/	Hong-Kong & Shanghai	28⅛	46
4/	Imperl. of Persia	6⅛	3½
10/	Imperl. Ottoman, £20 Shs	10	11½
12/	Intrnatl. of Ldn., Ld., £20	15	11
10/	Ionian, Ltd.	25	15
16/	Lloyds, Ltd., £50 Shs.	8	31
10/	Ldn. & Brazil. Ltd., £20	10	15½
44/	Ldn. & County, Ltd., £80	20	102
9/	Ldn. & Hanseatic, L., £20	10	10½
22/6	Ldn. & Midland, L., £60	12½	53
8/9	Ldn. & Provin., Ltd., £10	5	22½
39/	Ldn. & Riv. Plate, L., £25	15	49
2/1½	Ldn. & San Fcisco, Ltd.	7	4½
28/	Ldn. & Sth. West., L., £50	20	68
26/	Ldn. & Westmins., L., £100	20	56
3/	Ldn. of Mex. & S. Amer., Ltd., £10 Shs.	6	5½
15/	Ldn. Joint Stk., L., £100	15	34
12/9½	Ldn., Paris & Amer., L. £20	16	25
2/4½	Merchant Bkg., L., £9	4	2½
6/3	Metropn, Ltd., £50 Shs.	5	14½
9/	National, Ltd., £30 Shs.	10	19½
4/5	Natl. of Mexico, $100 Shs.	$40	12½
1/3	National of N. Z., L., £7½	2½	2
8/	National S. Afric. Rep.	10	13½
18/10½	National Provcl. of Eng., Ltd., £75 Shs.	10½	51
21/7½	Do. do. £60 Shs.	12	58½
6/6	North Eastn., Ltd., £20 Shs	6	15
19/	Parr's, Ld., £100 Shs.	20	90
12/6	Prov. of Ireland, L., £100	12½	29½
40/	Stand. of S. Afric., L., £100	25	64
12/6	Union of Australia, L., £75	25	27
4 p.c.	Do. do. Ins. Stk. Dep. 1900	100	101
15.6	Union of Ldn., Ltd., £100	15½	35

BREWERIES AND DISTILLERIES

Div.	Name.	Paid.	Price.
4½	Albion Prp. 1 Mt. Db. Sk.	100	111
4	All Saints, L., Db.Sk. Rd.	100	97
7	Allsopp, Ltd	100	146
6	Do. Cum. Pref	100	153
4½	Do. Deb. Stk., Red	100	116
3½	Do. Deb. Stk., Red.	100	102
4½	Alton & Co., L., Db., Rd	100	105
4½	Do. Mt. Bds., 1896	100	104
—	Arnold, Perrett, Ltd.	10	6
6	Do. Cum. Pref.	10	10
4½	Do. 1 Mt. Db. Stk., Rd	100	106

Breweries &c. (*continued*):—

Div.	Name.	Paid.	Price.
5½	Arrol, A., & Sons, L., Cum. Pref. Shs.	10	10
4½	Do. 1 Mt. Db. Stk., Rd.	100	105
5	Backus, 1 Mt. Db., Red.	100	59
4	Barclay, Perk., L., Cu. Pf.	10	11½
3½	Do. Mt. Db. Stk., Red.	100	109
—	Barnsley, Ltd.	10	11½
6	Do. Cum. Pref.	10	13½
1/3	Barrett's, Ltd.	2½	1½
1/3	Do. 5 p.c. Pref.	2½	2½
3/	Bartholomay, Ltd.	10	2½
8	Do. Cum. Pref.	10	6
6	Do. Deb.	100	97½
5	Bass, Ratcliff, Ltd., Cum. Pref. Stk.	100	142½
4½	Do. Mt. Db. Stk., Rd.	100	124
4	Bell, J., L., 1 Mt. D. Stk., R	100	100
—	Benskin's, L., Cum. Pref.	5	—
—	Do. 1 Mt. Db. Stk Red.	100	—
—	Do. "B" Deb. Sk, Rd.	100	—
7/	Bentley's Yorks., Ltd.	10	10½
6/	Do. Cum. Pref.	10	12½
4½	Do. Mt. Debs., Red.	100	110
4½	Do. do. 1892, Red.	100	110
—	Bieckert's, Ltd.	20	2
5	Do. Debs., Red.	100	57
—	Birmingham., Ltd., 6 p.c. Cum. Pref.	5	2½
4½	Do. Mt. Debs., Red.	50	39½
5½	Boardman's, Ld., Cm. Pf.	10	8½
4½	Do., Perp. 1 Mt. Db.Sk.	100	105½
30/9	Brain & Co., Ltd.	100	101
4½	Brakspear, L., 1 D. Stk. Red.	100	108
4	Brandon's, L., 1 D. Stk. Red.	100	104½
21/	Bristol (Georges) Ltd.	10	45
6	Do. Cum. Pref.	10	17½
5	Do. Mt. Db. Sk. 1888 Rd.	100	115½
17/6	Bristol United, Ltd.	10	35
6	Do. Cum. Pref.	10	16½
4½	Do. Db.Sk. Rd.	100	126
5½	Buckley's, L., C. Pre-prf.	10	10½
4½	Do. 1 Mt. Db. Stk. Rd.	100	104½
4	Bullard & Sons, Ltd., D. Sk. R.	100	104
6	Bushell, Watk., L., C. Pf.	10	14
4½	Do. 1 Mt. Db. Sk. Rd.	100	112
5	Camden, Ltd., Cum. Pref.	10	11½
4½	Do. 1 Mt. Db. Sk. Rd.	100	137
5½	Cameron, Ltd., Cm. Prf.	10	13½
4½	Do. Mort Deb. Stk.	100	108
3½	Do. Perp Mt. Db. Sk.	100	100½
5	Cam'bell, J'stone, L., C.Pf.	5	5
4½	Do. 4½ p.c. 1 Mt.Db.Sk.	100	103
4	Campbell, Praed, L., Per. 1 Mort. Deb. Stk.	100	105
4	Cannon, L., Mt. Db. Stk.	100	109
4	Do. "B" Deb. Stk.	100	104
5	Castlemaine, L., 1 Mt. Db.	100	94
3½	Charrington, Ltd., Mort. Deb. Stk. Red.	100	106
2/	Cheltnhm. Orig., Ltd.	5	7
6	Do. Cum. Pref.	5	7½
4	Do. Debs. Red.	100	106
10/	Chicago, Ltd.	10	2½
6	Do. Debs.	100	84½
—	Cincinnati, Cum. Pref.	10	1
10/	City of Baltimore	10	4
16/	Do. 8 p.c. Cum. Pref	10	8
14/	City of Chicago, Ltd.	10	1½
8	Do. Cum. Pref.	10	6
13	City of London, Ltd.	100	206½
5	Do. Cum. Pref.	100	136
4	Do. Mt. Deb. Stk., Rd.	100	109½
2/	Colchester, Ltd.	5	4½
7	Do. Pref.	5	6½
4½	Do. Deb. Stk., Red.	100	109
5	Combe, Ltd., Cum. Pref.	10	13½
4	Do. Mt. Db. Stk, Rd.	100	110
3½	Do. Perp. Deb. Stk.	100	107
5	Comm'cial, L., D. Sk., Rd.	100	107½
5	Courage, L., Cm. Pref. Shs.	100	137½
4	Do. Irr. Mt. Deb. Stk.	100	125
3½	Do. Irr. "B" Mt. Db. Sk.	100	104
8/	Daniell & Sons, Ltd.	10	7½
7	Do. Cum. Pref.	10	12½
4½	Do. 1 Mt. Perp. Db. Sk.	100	107½
4½	Do. "B" Deb. Stk.	100	99
10d.	Dartford, Ltd.	5	5
2/9	Do. Cum. Pref.	5	5½
4	Do. 1 Mt. Db. Sk. Rd	100	99
4	Davenport, Ld., 1 D. Stk.	100	101½
10/	Denver United, Ltd.	10	3½
8	Do. Cum. Pref.	10	7½
6	Do. Debs.	100	98½
4½	Deuchar, L., 1 D.Sk., Rd.	100	108
8/	Distillers, Ltd.	10	23½
—	Dublin Distillers, Ltd.	5	1½
3/	Do. Cum. Pref.	5	4½
4½	Do. Irr. Deb. Stk.	100	—
5	Eadie, Ltd., Cum. Pref.	10	11
4	Do. Irr. 1 Mt. Db. Sk.	100	106
10/	Edinbgh. Utd., Ltd.	10	13
6	Do. Cum. Prf.	10	13½
4	Eldridge, Pope, L. D. St. R.	100	107
—	Emerald & Phœnix, Ltd.	10	1½
8	Do. Cum. Pref.	10	5½
6	Empress Ltd., C. Pf.	10	11½
4½	Do. Mt. Deb. Stk.	100	105
10/	Farnham, Ltd.	10	17
6	Do. Cum. Pref.	10	[illegible]
4	Fenwick, L., 1 D. Sk., Rd.	100	103
4	Flower & Sons, Irr. D. Sk.	100	111
4	Friary, L., 1 Db. Stk., Rd.	100	103½
4	Do. 1 "A" Db.Sk., Rd	100	100
4½	Groves, L., 1 Db. Sk., Rd.	100	111
14	Guinness, Ltd.	100	530
6	Do. Cum. Prf. Stk.	100	[illegible]
5	Do. Deb. Stk., Red.	100	117
5	Hall's Oxford L., Cm. Pf.	5	5½
6/	Hancock, Ld., Cm. Pf Ord.	10	14
[illegible]	Do. Def. Ord	10	17½

Breweries, &c. (*continued*):—

Div.	Name.	Paid.	Price.
6	Hancock, Ld., Cum. Pref.	10	15½
4	Do. 1 Deb. Stk., Rd.	100	112
5	Hoare, Ltd. Cum. Pref.	10	12¾
5	Do. "A" Cum. Pref.	10	12¼
4	Do. Mt. Deb. Stk., Rd.	100	111
3½	Do. do. do. Rd.	100	104
3/6	Hodgson's, Ltd.	5	9½
5	Do. 1 Mt. Db., Red.	—	119½
4	Do. 2 Mt. Db., 1906	—	102
4½	Hopcraft & N., Ltd., 1 Mt. Deb. Stk., Red.	100	103
5	Huggins, Ltd., Cm. Prf.	10	—
4½	Do. 1st D. Stk. Rd.	100	—
4½	Do. "B" Db. Stk. Rd.	100	—
12/	Hull, Ltd.	10	17
7	Do. Cum. Pref.	10	14½
4½	Ind, Coope, L., D. Sk., Rd.	100	118
4	Do. "B" Mt. Db. Stk. Rd.	100	111
8/	Indianapolis, Ltd.	10	3
8	Do. Cm. Prf.	10	8¾
5/	Jones, Frank, Ltd.	10	2½
7½	Do. Cum. Pref.	10	6½
5	Do. 1st Mort. Debs.	100	90½
3/	J. Kenward & Co., Ltd.	5	5½
4½	Kingsbury, L., 1 D. Sk., Rd	100	—
4	Lacon, L., D. Stk., Red.	100	110
4	Do. Irrd. "B" D. Sk	100	106
4/	Lascelles, Ltd.	5	11¾
6	Do. Cum. Pref.	5	7¾
5	Leney, Ltd., Cum. Pref.	10	11½
4	Do. 1 Mt. Db. Stk. Rd.	100	102
30/7½	Lion, Ltd., £25 shares	17	49½
10/9½	Do. New £10 shares	6	17
6	Do. Perp. Pref.	20	33
4	Do. B. Mt. Db. Sk. Rd.	100	106
4½	Lloyd & Y., Ltd., 1 Mt. Deb. Stk., Rd.	100	100½
4½	Locke & S., Ltd., Irr. 1st Mt. Deb. Stk.	100	103
4½	Lovibond, Ltd., 1st Mt. Deb. Stk., Rd.	100	101½
30/4	Lucas & Co., Ld., Deb. Stk.	100	107
12/	Manchester, Ltd.	10	19
7	Do. Cum. Pref.	10	16½
	Marston, J., L., Cm. Prf.	10	10¾
4	Do. 1 Mt. Db. Sk., Rd.	100	101½
9/	Massey's Burnley, Ltd.	10	17
6	Do. Cum. Pref.	10	14½
4½	McCracken, Ltd., 1 Mt. Deb., 1908	100	59½
5	McEwan, Ltd., Cm. Pref.	10	14
5	Meux, Ltd., Cum. Pref.	10	14
4	Do. Mt. Db. Stk. Red.	100	111
4½	Michell & A., Ltd., 1 Mt. Deb. Stk. Red	100	105
4½	Mile End Dist. Db. Sk. Rd.	100	111
—	Milwaukee & Chic., Ltd.	10	1½
4/	Do. Cum. Pref.	10	6½
4½	Michell, Toms, L., Db.	50	57
6	Morgan, Ltd., Cum. Pref	10	14½
10/	Nalder & Coll., Ltd.	10	35
6	Do. Cum. Pref.	10	15½
4½	Do. Deb. Red.	100	112
12/	Newcastle, Ltd.	10	19½
6	Do. Cum. Pref.	10	14¾
5	Do. 1 Mt. Deb., 1911	100	110½
4	Do. "A" Deb. Stk. Red.	100	105
6	New England, Ltd	10	4½
8	Do. Cum. Pref.	10	9
6	Do. Debs. Red.	100	101½
4	New London, L., 1 D. Sk.	100	103
7/2	New Westminster, Ltd.	4	10
2/4½	Do. Pref.	4	6½
—	New York, Ltd.	10	1
—	Do. 8 p.c. Cum. Pref.	10	4
6	Do. 1 Mt. Deb. Red.	100	77½
5	Noakes, Ld., Cum. Pref.	10	11¼
4	Do 1 Mt. Db. Stk., Rd.	100	105
4½	Norfolk, L., "A" D Sk. Rd	100	106
10/	Northampton, Ld.	10	16½
7	Do. Cum. Pref.	10	16
6	Do. Cum. Pref.	10	12½
5	Do. 1 Mt. Per. Db. Sk.	100	127
4	Nth. East., L., 1 D. Sk. Rd.	100	102
4½	N. Worcesters., L. Per. 1 Mort. Deb. Stock	100	97½
6	Nottingham, L., Cm. Prf.	10	1½
5	Do. 1 Mt. Deb. Stk., Red.	100	114
27/4	Do. "B" do. Red.	50	112
6/	Ohlsson' Cape, Ltd.	5	17
7	Do. Cum. Pref.	5	9
4½	Do. 2nd Cum. Pref.	5	5½
5	Do. Deb. Stk., Red.	100	115
4½	Oldfield, L., 1 Mt. Db. Stk.	100	105
6	Page & Overt., L., Cm. Prf.	10	14
4½	Do. 1 Mt. Dbs., Red.	100	109
10/	Parker's Burslem, Ltd.	10	24½
6	Do. Cum. Pref.	10	14½
4	Do. 1 Mt. Db. Stk., Red.	100	111
4	Persse, Ld., 1 Mt. Db. Rd.	100	95½
	Phipps, L., Irr. 1 Db. Stk.	100	113
8	Plymouth, L., Min. Cu. Pf.	10	13½
4½	Do. Mt. Deb. Stk., Red.	100	106½
4½	Pryor, Reid, L., 1 D S., R.	100	103½
5	Reid's, Ld., Cm. Pref. Stk.	100	136½
4	Do. Mt. Deb. Stk., Red	100	110
3½	Do. "B" Mt. Db. Stk., Rd	100	102
5	Rhondda Val., L., Cu. Pf	10	11
4½	Do. 1 Mt. Deb. Stk., Rd	100	109
5	Robinson, Ld., Cum. Pref.	10	11½
4½	Do. 1 Mt. Perp. Db. Stk.	100	112
4/	Rochdale, Ltd.	10	6
4½	Do. 1 Mt. Deb. Stk.	100	91½
7	Royal, Brentford, Ltd.	10	2½
	Do. Cum. Pref.	10	13
4½	Do. 1 Mt. Dbs. Red	100	103
6/	St. Louis, Ltd.	10	3½
8	Do. Cum. Pref.	10	8½
14/	St. Pauli, Ltd.	10	10
7	Do. Cum Pref.	10	12
4½	Salt (T.), L., 1 Db. Sk. Rd.	100	111
4½	Do. "B" Db. Stk. Red	100	103
—	San Francisco, Ltd	10	½
—	Do. 8 p.c. Cum. Pref.	10	½

Breweries, &c. (*continued*):—

Div.	Name.	Paid.	Price.
4½	Savill Brs., L., D. Sk. Rd.	100	118
4½	Scarboro., Ltd., 1 Db. Stk.	100	101
4	Shaw (Hy.), Ltd., 1 Mt. Db. Stk., Red.	100	104
22/	Showell's, Ltd	10	31
7	Do. Cum. Pref.	10	17½
3/	Do. Gua. Shs.	5	7½
4½	Do. Mt. Db. Stk., Red.	100	—
4	Simonds, L., 1 D. Sk., Rd.	100	111
5½	Simson & McP., L., Cu. Pf.	10	9½
4½	Do. 1 Mt. Deb. Stk.	100	98
5/	Smith, Garrett, L., £20 Shs	10	16½
5	Do. Cum. Pref.	20	26
3½	Do. 3½ p.c. Mt. Db. Stk.	100	107
5	Smith's, Tadcaster, L., C Pf	10	12
4½	Do. Deb. Stk., Red.	100	112
4	Do. Deb. Stk. Red.	100	108
4½	Star, L., 1 M. Db. Stk., Rd.	100	103
4	Steward & P., L., 1 D. Sk.	100	108
9/	Strettons Derby, Ltd.	10	13
6	Do. Cum. Pref.	10	13½
4	Do. Irr. 1 Mt. Db. Stk.	100	104½
4½	Strong, Romsey, L., 1 D. S.	100	115
5	Stroud, L., Db. Sk., Rd.	100	111½
4½	Tadcaster To'er, L., D. Sk.	100	113
8/	Tamplin, Ltd	10	21
6	Do. Cum. Pref.	100	15
4	Do. "A" Db. Sk., Rd.	10	105
6	Thorne, Ltd., Cum. Pref.	10	14
4	Do. Deb. Stk., Red.	100	103½
15/	Threlfall, Ltd.	10	46
6	Do. Cum. Pref.	10	16½
5	Do. 1 Mt. Dbs., Red.	100	114
4	Tollemache, L., D. Sk. Rd.	100	105
4	Truman, Hanb., D. Sk., R.	100	110
3	Do. "B" Mt. Db. Sk., Rd.	100	93
10/	United States, Ltd.	10	8½
8	Do. Cum. Pref.	10	11
6	Do. 1 Mt. Deb.	100	105½
6/	Walker & H., Ld., Cm. Prf.	10	10¼
4½	Do. 1 Mt. Deb. Stk., Red.	100	107
5	Walker, Peter, Ld. Cm. Prf.	10	13½
4	Do. 1 Mt. Dbs. Red.	100	110
4	Wallingford, L., D. Sk. Rd.	100	105
6	Watney, Ld., Cm. Prf. Sk.	100	167
5	Do. Mt. Db. Sk., Rd.	100	115½
4½	Do. "B" Mt. Db. Sk., Rd.	100	111
3½	Do. Mt. Db. Stk.	100	101
5	Watney, D., Ld., Cm. Prf.	10	12
4½	Do. 1 Mt. Db. Stk.	100	107
10/	Webster & Sons, Ltd.	10	16½
6	Do. Cum. Pref.	10	14
5	Wenlock Ltd Pref.	10	11¾
4	Do. 1 Mt. Db. Sk., Rd.	100	105
5	West Cheshire, L., Cu. Pf.	10	10½
4	Do. Irred. 1 Mt. Db. Sk.	100	93
4½	Whitbread, L., Cu. Pf. Sh.	100	123½
4	Do. Db. Stk., Red.	100	103
3½	Do. "B" Db. Stk., Rd.	100	101
9/	Wolverhmpton & D. Ld.	10	17
6	Do. Cum. Pref.	10	13½
4½	Do. 1 Mt. Dbs., Red.	100	103
5½	Worthington, Ld., Cm. Prf.	10	15½
5½	Do. Cum. "B" Pref.	10	13½
4½	Do. Mt. Db. Sk., Rd.	100	113
3½	Do. Irr. "B" Db. Stk.	100	101
10/	Yates's Castle, Ltd	10	13½
5	Do. Cum. Pref.	10	11
5	Younger W., L., Cu. Pf. Sh.	100	123½

CANALS AND DOCKS.

Last Div.	Name.	Paid.	Price.
4	Birmingham Canal	100	142½
—	E. & W. India Dock	100	20
—	Do. 4 p.c. Prf. Stk.	100	74
—	Do. P.L. Deb. Stk.	100	101
—	Do. Cons. Deb. Stk.	100	89
40/	G. Junction Ord. Shs.	100	149½
6/	Do. do. Pref.	10	19
4½	King's Lynn Per. Db. Stk.	100	117½
2½	Leeds & L'pool Canal	100	71
2½	Lndn & St. Kath. Dks.	100	54
4½	Do. Pref.	100	136½
4½	Do. Pref., 1878	100	132½
4½	Do. Pref., 1882	100	130
4	Do. Deb. Stk.	100	133½
—	M'chester Ship C. 5 p.c. Pf.	10	2
3½	Do. 1st Perp. Mt. Deb.	100	93
—	Milford Dks. Db. Stk. "A"	100	13½
3½	Millwall Dk.	100	60
5	Do. Perp. Pref.	100	140½
4½	Do. Pref.	100	106½
5	Do. New Per. Prf., 1887	100	126½
5	Do. Per. Deb. Stk.	100	152½
4/	Newhaven Har.	10	14½
2½	N. Metropolitan	100	65
5	Sharpness Nw. Pf. "A" Sk.	100	141½
4	Do. Deb. Stk.	100	117½
5	Sheffiel & S. Yorks Nav. 4½ p.c. Pref Stk.	100	115½
36.43s	Suez Canal	20	133
7	Surrey Comcl. Dck., Ord.	100	149½
7	Do. Min. 4 p.c. Pref. "A"	110	150
5	Do. Pref. "B"	100	143½
5	Do do. "C"	100	148½
5	Do. do. "D"	100	144½
4½	Do Deb. Stk.	100	152½

COMMERCIAL, INDUSTRIAL, &c.

Last Div.	Name.	Paid.	Price.
5	Accles, L., 1 Mt. Db., Red.	100	84½
2/6	Aërated Bread, Ltd.	1	12
—	African Gold Recovery, L.	1	¼
2/	Aluminium, L., "A" Shs.	1	2
4½	Do. 1 Mt. Db. Stk., Red.	100	97
5½	Amelia Nitr., L., 1 Mort Deb., Red.	100	82½
7/	Anglo-Chil. Nitrate, Ltd., Cum. Pref.	10	6¾
4½	Do. Cons. Mt. Bds., Red.	100	77½
4½	Anglo-Russian Cotton, Ld., 1 Charge Debs., Red.	100	98
11/3	Angus (G., & Co., L.), £10	7½	17
6/	Apollinaris, Ltd.	10	11¾
5/	Do. 5 p.c. Cum. Pref.	10	10¾
4	Do. Irred. Deb. Stock	100	104
5/	Appleton, French, & S., L.	5	—
3/	Argentine Meat Pres., L., 7 p.c. Pref.	10	2¾
5	Argentine Refinry, Db. Rd.	100	98
6d.	Armstrong, Whitw., Ltd.	1	3½
4	Do. Cum. Pref.	5	6½
5	Artisans', Labr. Dwllgs., L.	100	122½
4½	Do. Non-Cm. Prf., 1879	100	132½
4½	Do. do. 1884	100	132½
—	Asbestos & Asbestic, Ltd.	10	7¾
2/7½	Ashley-grdns., L., C. Prf.	5	6½
4½	Do. 1 Mt. Deb. Stk.	100	112½
5/	Assam Rly. & Trdng., L., 8 p.c. Cum. Pref. "A"	10	14
—	Do. Deferrd. "B" Shs.	1	4
—	Do. do. (iss. f. pd)	1	3½
8/	Do. Cum. Pre-Prf. "A"	10	15
6/	Do. New Pref.	10	11½
5	Do. Debs., Red.	100	106
5	Do. Red. Mort. Debs.	100	110
6	Aust'lian Pastrl, L., Cu. Pf.	10	7
8d.	Aylesbury Dairy, Ltd.	1	1½
4	Do. 4 p.c. Mt. Dbs.	100	104½
10/	Babcock & Wilcox, Ltd.	10	29
6	Do. 6 p.c. Cm. Prf.	10	16
8	Baker (Chs.), L., Cm. Pf.	5	8½
8	Do. "B" Cm. Pref.	5	8
2/1	Barker (John), Ltd.	1	2¾
5½	Do. Cum. Pref.	5	7½
4½	Do. Irred. 1 Mt. Db. Stk.	100	127½
—	Barnagore Jute, Ltd.	5	3
5	Do. Cum. Pref.	5	4½
7½d.	Belgravia Dairy, Ltd.	1	1¼
5/6	Bell (R.) & Co., Ltd.	5	3½
1/	Bell's Asbestos, Ltd.	1	¾
5	Do. Mt. Db. Bds., Rd.	100	107
10/	Bengal Mills, Ltd.	10	11
6/	Do. 5 p.c. Cum. Prf.	10	10½
5/	Benson (J.W.) L., Cm. Pf.	10	10½
4	Do. Perp. Mt. Db. Stk.	100	101
6	Bergvik, L., 6 p.c. Cm. Pf.	10	12½
12/	Do. Dfd.	10	10½
4½	Do. 1 Dbs., Red.	100	103½
5/	Birm'ham Vinegar, Ltd.	5	14
5	Do. Cum. Pref.	5	5½
4½	Do. 1 Mt. Db. Stk., Rd.	100	109½
5	Boake (A.) L., 5 p.c. Cu. Pf.	10	10¾
2/6	Bodega, Ltd.	5	8¼
4½	Do. Mt. Deb. Stk., Rd.	100	111
8/	Bottomley & Brs., Ltd.	10	6½
6/	Do. 6 p.c. Pt.	10	9½
8½d.	Bovril, Ltd.	1	1½
1/0½	Do. Def.	1	¾
6½d	Do. Cum. Pref.	1	1
4½	Do. Deb. Stk.	100	100
5/	Bradbury, Gretrex., Ltd., £10 share	8	14
5/	Do. 5 p.c. Cum. Pref.	10	13½
5/	Brewers' Sugar, L., 5 p.c. Cum. Pref.	10	10½
3/6	Brighton Grd. Hotel, Ld.	5	3½
4	Do Mt. Db. Stk., Red.	100	100½
5	Bristol Hotel & Palm. Co. Ltd. 1st Mt. Red. Deb.	100	105
9½d.	British & Bengton's. Tea Tr. Asc., Ltd.	1	1½
5	Do. Cum. Prf.	5	5½
—	British Deli & Lgkat. Tobacco, Ltd.	1	¾
—	Do. Cum. Prf.	1	¾
—	British Tea Table, Ltd.	1	2¾
5½	Do. Cum. Pref.	1	1¼
2/6	Brooke, Ben., & Co., Ltd., Cum. Pref.	5	5¾
7/6	Brooke, Bond & Co., Ltd.	5	19
3/	Brown Brs., L., Cum. Pref.	5	5¾
10/	Browne & Eagle, Ltd.	10	13½
5	Do. Cum. Pref.	10	13
4	Do. Mrt. Db. Sk., Red.	100	110
20/	Brunner, Mond, & Co., Lt.	0	40
7/	Do. £10 shares	3	17
7	Do. Cum. Pref.	10	18
7	Do. £10 shares	5	8½
10/	Bryant & May, Ltd.	5	19¾
3/	Bucknall, H., & Sons, Lt.	5	6¾
6	Do. Cum Pref.	5	7¾
4/	Burke, E. & J., Ltd.	5	7½
6	Do. Cum. Pref.	5	7¾
6	Do. Irred. Deb. Stk.	100	155
1/	Burlington Htls. Co., Ld.	1	1½
5	Do. Cum. Pref.	1	1
4	Do. Perp. Deb. Stk.	100	105½
5	Bush, W. J., & Co., Ltd., Cum. Pref.	5	5½
4	Do. 1 Deb. Stk., Red.	100	102
5½	Callard, Stewart, & Watt Ltd., Cum. Pref.	1	1½
4/	Callender's Cable L., Shs.	5	9½
4½	Do. 1 Deb. Stk., Red.	100	111½
—	Campbell, R., & Sons, Lt.	3	2½
6	Cantareira Water, Bd., Rd	100	93½
5	Do. (2nd issue)	100	87½
4	Cartavio Sugar, Ltd., 6 p.c. 1st Debs., Red.	20	82½
9/	Cassell & Co., Ltd., £10	9	15
5	Causton, Sir J., & Sons, Ltd., Cum. Pref.	10	13¾

Commercial, &c. (*continued*):—

Last Div.	Name.	Paid.	Price.
4	Cent. Prod. Mkt. of B.A. 1st Mt. Str. Debs.	100	77
4	Chappell & Co., Ltd., Mt. Deb. Stk. Red	100	103
6/	Chicago & N.W. Gran. 8 p.c. Cum. Pref.	10	3
—	Chicago Packing & Prov.	10	6
8	Do. Cum. Pref.	10	10½
6/	City Offices, Ltd	12	8
3½	Do. Mt. Deb. Stk.	100	108½
7/2½	Cy. London Real Prop., Ltd., £25 shs.	12	19
4/6	Do. £12½ shs.	7½	13¼
3½	Do. Deb. Stk. Red.	100	106½
3½	Do. Deb. Stk. Red.	100	106½
3	Do.	100	100½
4/	Cy. of Santos Imprvts.,		
20/	Ltd., 7 p.c. Pref.	10	8½
8	Clay, Bock, & Co., Ltd.	10	5½
6	Do. Cum. Pref.	10	9
20/	Do. Mort. Deb.	100	102½
20/	Coats, J. & P., Ltd.	10	59
4½	Do. Cum. Pref.	10	17
9½d	Do. Deb. Stk. Red.	100	112½
4	Coburg Hotel, Ltd	1	1½
6	Do. Deb. Stk. Red.	100	102
	Colonial Consign & Dis., Ltd., Cum. Pref.	5	4½
4½	Do. 1st Mort. Debs.	100	96½
—	Colorado Nitrate, Ltd.	5	½
4/	Co. Gén des Asphtes. de F., Ltd.	6	6½
5	Do. Non-Cm. Prf.	—	5
5	Cook, J. W., & Co., Ltd., Cum. Pref.	5	5½
5	Cook, T., & Son, Egypt, Ltd., 1st Mt. Deb. Red.	100	110½
—	Cork Co., Ltd., 6 p.c. Cum. Pref.	5	2
5	Cory, W., & Sn, L., Cu. Pf.	5	5½
4	Do. 1st Deb. Stk. Red.	100	108
1/6	Crisp & Co., Ltd	1	1½
5½	Do. Cum. Pref.	1	1½
—	Crompton & Co., Ltd., 7 p.c. Cum. Pref.	5	2½
5	Do. 1st Mt. Reg. Deb.	—	90½
4/6	Crossley, J., & Sons, Ltd.	5	8
5	Do. Cum. Pref.	5	6½
—	Crystal Pal. Ord. "A" Stk.	100	6½
—	Do. "B" Red. Stk	100	1½
6	Do. 6 p.c. 1st 1887 Deb. Stk. Red.	100	117½
—	Do. 6 p.c. 2nd 1887 Deb. Stk. Red.	100	49½
—	Do. 6 p.c. 3rd 1887 Deb. Stk. Red.	100	22½
3	Do. 3 p.c. 1st 1893 Deb. Stk.	100	92½
—	Daimler Motor, Ltd	10	7
4/	Dalgety & Co., £20 Shs.	5	6½
4½	Do. Deb. Stk.	100	123
4	Do.	100	113
7/	De Keyser's Ryl. Htl., L.	10	14
5	Do. Cum. Pref.	10	12
4	Do. Deb. Stk., Red.	100	110
6	Denny, H., & Sons, Ltd., Cum. Pref.	10	14½
5/3	Devas, Routledge & Co., L.	7	8½
5	Dickinson, J., & Co., L., Cum. Pref. Stk.	100	123
4½	Domin. Cottn. Mls., Ltd. Mt. Stg. Dbs.	100	97
6/	Dorman, Long & Co., L.	5	4½
—	Eastmans, Ltd	10	2½
12/	Do. 8 p.c. Cum. Pref.	10	10½
2/6	E. C. Powder, Ltd	3	5½
1/6	Edison & Swn Utd. Elec. Ltd., "A" £3 Shs.	3	2½
2/6	Do. fully-paid	5	4½
4½	Ekman Pulp & Ppr. Co., Ltd., Mt. Deb., Red.	100	95
1/1½	Electric Construc., Ltd.	2	2½
7	Do. Cum. Pref.	2	3½
2/	Eley Bros., Ltd.	10	38
—	Elmore's Cop. Deptg., L.	1	¾
—	Elmore's Wire Mnfg., L.	2	¾
—	Elysée Pal. Hotel Co., L.	5/	¾
5 p.c.	Do. 5 p.c. £100 Db., Rd.	70	97½
8½d.	Evans, Ben., & Co., Ltd.	1	1
5	Do. 1 Mt. Db. Sk., Rd.	100	108
1/5½d.	Evans, D. H., & Co., L.	1	2½
6	Do. Cum. Pref.	1	1½
4½	Do. 1 Mt. Db. Sk., Rd.	100	112
2/6	*Evening News*, L., 5 p.c. Cum. Pref.	5	5½
5/3	Evered & Co., L., £10 Sh.	7	12½
7/6	Do.	10	18½
4	Fairbairn Pastoral Co., Aust., L., 1 Mt. Db., Rd.	100	102
6	Fairfield Shipbldg., Ltd., Cum. Pref.	10	10½
4½	Do. Mort. Deb. Stk.	100	110
6/	Farmer & Co., Ld., 6 p.c. Cum. Pref.	10	13½
10	Field, J. C. & J., Ltd.	10	10
14/	Do. 7 p.c. Cum. Pref.	10	11½
1/3	Fordham, W.B., & Sns, Ld.	1	2
5/6	Fore-st. Warehouse, Ltd.	11	9½
4	Do. Regd. Debs., Rd.	100	103½
3/6	Foster, M. B. & Sons, Ltd.	4	6
5	Do. Pref.	10	11½
9/	Foster, Porter, & Co., L.	10½	15½
4	Fowler, J., & Co. (Leeds) Ltd., 1 Mt. Deb., Red.	100	101½
3/	Fraser & Chalmers, Ltd.	3	1½
4½	Free, Rodwell & Co., Ltd., Deb Stk.	100	101½
6½d.	Furness, T., & Co., Ltd., 5½ p.c. Cum. Pref.	1	1
4½	Gartside & Co. (of Manchstr), L., 1 Mt. Db. Sk.	100	111
11	Genl. Hydraul Power, L	100	270

Commercial, &c. (*continued*):—

Last Div.	Name.	Paid.	Price.
8/	Gillman & Spencer, Ltd.	5	2½
6	Do. Pref.	5	4½
5	Do. Mort. Debs.	50	51
4	Goldsbro., Mort & Co., L., "A" Deb. Stk., Red.	100	70½
—	Do. 3 p.c. "B" Inc. Deb. Stk., Red	100	12
8/	Gordon Hotels, Ltd.	10	20
5½	Do. Cum. Pref.	10	14½
4½	Do. Perp. Deb. Stk.	100	138½
4	Do. do.	100	122½
—	Greenwich Inld. Linoleum Co., Ltd.	1	⅛
7	Greenwood & Batley, Ltd., Cum. Pref.	10	10
7½d.	Hagemann & Co., Ltd., 6 p.c. Cum. Pref.	1	1
—	Hammond, Ltd.	10	½
—	Do. 8 p.c. Cum. Pref.	10	3
—	Do. 6 p.c. Cum. Inc. Stk. Red.	100	47½
	Hampton & Sons, Ltd., 4 p.c. 1 Mt. Db. St. Red.	100	105
—	Hans Crescent Htl., L., 6 p.c. Cum. Pref.	5	3
4	Do. 1 Mt. Deb. Stk.	100	90
6d.	Harmsworth, Ld., Cm. Pf.	1	1 1/16
4/	Harrison, Barber, Ltd.	5	4½
3/	Harrod's Stores, Ltd.	1	4⅞
2/6	Do. Cum. Pref.	5	7½
5½	Hawaiian Comcl. & Sug. 1 Mt. Debs.	100	91½
7	Hazell, Watson, L., C. P.	10	11½
18/	Henley's Teleg., Ltd.	10	22
7	Do. Pref. Shs.	10	19
4½	Do. Mt. Db. Stk., Rd.	100	112½
6	Henry, Ltd.	10	12
5	Do. Cum. Pref.	10	13½
4½	Do. Mt. Debs., Red.	50	53
6	Hepworth, Ld., Cm. Prf.	10	—
1/4½	Herrmann, Ltd.	1	½
—	Hildesheimer, Ltd.	3	1½
1/2½	Holbrn. & Frasca, Ltd.	1	1½
5	Do. Cum. Pref.	10	11½
4	Do. Deb. Stk.	100	113
6	Home & Col. Stres., L., C.P	5	7½
6	Hood & M.'s Stres., Ltd., Cum. Pref.	1	½
6	Hook, C. T Ltd.	10	6
7/2	Hornsby, Ltd., £10 Shs.	8	3
—	Hotchks. Ordn., Ltd.	10	1
—	Do. 7 p.c. Cm. Prf.	10	4½
5	Do. 1 Mt. Dbs., Rd.	100	97½
6	Htl. Cecil, Ld., Cm. Prf.	5	3
4	Do. 1 Mt. D. Sk., R.	100	100½
8/	Howard & Bulgh, Ltd.	10	39
6	Do. Pref.	10	16
4	Do. Deb. Stk., Red.	100	108
5/	Howell, J., Ltd., £5 Shs.	4	9
—	Howell & Js., Ltd., £3½ Shs.	3	¼
1/6	Humber, Ltd.	1	⅜
6	Do. Cum. Pref.	1	5/16
5/6	Hunter, Wilts., Ltd.	5	7
2/7	Hyam Clthg., Ltd., 5 p.c. Cum. Pref.	5	5½
10/	Impl. Russn. Cotton, L.	5	6
5	Impd. Industl. Dwgs., Ld.	100	130½
6d.	Do. Defrd.	1	1½
25/	Impd. Wood Pave., Ltd.	10	15½
15/	Ind. Rubber, Gutta Per. Telegraph Works, Ltd.	10	21½
4	Do. 1 Mt. Debs., Red.	100	104
6	Intern. Tea, Cum. Pref.	5	6½
10½d.	Jays, Ltd.	1	1⅛
5½	Do. Cum. Pref.	5	6½
1/2½d.	Jones & Higgins, Ltd.	1	2½
4½	Do. 1 Mt. Db. Sk., Rd.	100	111
5/	Kelly's Directory, Ltd., 5 p.c. Cum. Pref.	10	12¾
4	Do. Mort. Db. Sk., Rd.	100	105
—	Kent Coal Explrtn. Ltd.	1	⅛
9½d.	King, Howmann, Ltd.	1	1½
4/	Kinloch & Co., Ltd.	5	8½
6	Do. Pref.	5	7
5	Lady's Pictorial Pub., Ltd., Cum. Pref.	5	5
48/4	La Guaira Harb., Ltd., 5 p.c. Deb. Stk.	100	85
—	Do. 2 Mt. 7 p.c. Deb. Stk., Red.	100	24
4/	Lagunas Nitrate, Ltd.	5	1½
2/	Lagunas Syn., Ltd.	5	1½
5	Do. 1 Mt. Debs., Red.	100	77½
—	L. Copais Ld., 1 Mt. 6 p.c. Debs., Red.	100	35½
3/	Lautaro Nitrate, Ltd.	5	4
5	Do. 1 Mt. Debs., Red.	—	100
9/	Lawes Chem. L., £10 shs.	9	5½
14/	Do. N. Cm. Min. Pref.	10	12½
—	Leeds Forge, 7 p.c. Cm. Pf.	5	3½
5	Do. 1 Mt. Debs., Red.	50	47
5	Lever Bros., L., Cm. Pf.	10	13½
6	Liberty, L., 6 p.c. Cm. Pf.	10	15
20/	Liebig's, Ltd.	20	78
5	Lilley & Sk., L., Cm. Pf.	5	5½
39/4	Linoleum Manftg Ltd.	5	16
3/	Linotype, Ltd., Pre	5	5½
5/	Do. Def.	5	7½
4/	Lister & Co., Ltd.	10	4
5	Do. Cum. Pref.	10	8½
5/	Liverpool, Nitrate	5	4½
—	Liverpool Warehsg., Ltd	10	3½
5½	Do. Cum. Pref.	10	8½
4	Do. 1 Mt. Db. Stk., Rd.	100	105
5½	Lockharts, Ltd., Cm. Pf.	1	1½
4/6	Ldn. & Til. Lightrage £10	9	6½
6/	Ldn. Comcl. Sale Rms., L.	10	17½
3	Do. 1 Mt. Deb. Stk., Red.	100	103
3	London Nitrate, Ltd.	5	1½
4/	London Nitrate, Ld. 8 p.c. Cm. Min. Pf.	5	3½
4/	London Pavilion, Ltd.	5	6½

Commercial, &c. (*continued*):—

Last Div.	Name.	Paid.	Price.
2/6	London Produce Clg. Ho., Ltd., £10 Shares	2½	3½
4/	London Stereos., Ltd.	5	3
6d.	Ldn. Un. Laun. L. Cm. Pf	1	½
8½d.	Louise, Ltd.	1	½
5½	Do. Cum. Pref.	1	½
5/	Lovell & Christmas, Ltd.	5	11½
6	Do. Cum. Pref.	5	7½
4	Do. Mt. Deb. Stk., Red.	100	107
1/3	Lyons, Ltd.	1	4½
4½	Do. 1 Mt. Deb., Stk., Rd.	100	111½
10/	Machinery Trust, Ltd.	5	13½
4½	Do. 4½ Deb. Stk.	100	104
6	MacLellan, L., Min. C. Pf.	10	9
5	Do. 1 Mt. Debs., 1900	100	101½
—	McEwan, J. & Co, Ltd.	10	1½
6	Do. Mt. Debs., Red.	100	89½
8	McNamara, L., Cm. Pref.	10	9
7½d.	Maison Virot, Ltd.	1	1½
2/7	Do. 6 p.c. Cum. Pref.	5	4½
4/	Manbré Sacc., L., Cm. Pf.	10	12
10/	Mangan Brze., L., £10 Shs.	6	15½
2/	Mason & Mason, Ltd.	5	2½
6	Do. Cum. Pref.	5	5½
—	Maynards, Ltd.	1	½
6	Do. Cum. Pref.	1	½
9½d.	Mazawattee Tea, Ltd.	1	1½
5	Do. Cum. Pref.	5	5½
6	Mellin's Food Cum. Pref.	5	6½
4½	Met. Ascn. Imp. Dwlgs. L.	100	110
3½	Do. 1 Mt. Deb. Stk.	100	—
5	Metro. Indus. Dwlgs., Ltd.	5	4½
4	Do. do. Cum. Pref.	5	5½
5	Metro. Prop., L., Cm. Pf.	5	5½
4½	Do. 1st Mt. Debs. Stk.	100	108½
6	Mexican Cotton 1 Mt. Db.	100	93½
4½	Mid. Class Dwlgs., L., Db.	100	120½
1/	Millars' Karri, Ltd.	1	3½
6	Do. Cum. Pref.	1	1½
5/	Milner's Safe, Ltd.	10	20½
20/	Moir & Son, Ltd., Pref.	5	8
6	Morgan Cruc., L., Cm. Pf.	10	14½
2/	Morris, R., Ltd.	3½	3½
2/6	Murray L. 5½ p.c. C. Pf.	5	5½
63/4½	Do. 4½ 1 Mt. Db. Sk. Rd.	100	106
1/7½	Nat. Safe Dep., Ltd.	4	3½
6	Do. Cum. Pref.	1	1
—	Native Guano, Ltd.	5	½
—	Nelson Bros., Ltd.	10	2½
5	Do. Deb. Stk., Red.	100	80½
4/	Neuchtel Asph., Ltd.	10	10½
10d.	New Darvel Tob., Ltd.	18/	1½
1/6	New Explosives, Ltd.	3	3
5/3½	New Gd. Htl., Bham, L.	5	4
5½	Do. Pref.	5	4½
4	Do. 1 Mt. Db. Stk., Rd.	100	95½
—	New Julia Nitrate, Ltd.	10/	—
—	New Ldn. Borneo Tob., L.	16/	1
1/6	New Premier Cycle, Ltd.	1	1/16
6	Do. 6 p.c. Cum. Pref.	1	½
4½	Do. 4½ p.c. 1 Mt. Db. Rd	100	—
—	New Tamargl. Nitr., Ltd	1	1/16
—	Do. 8 p.c. Cum. Pref.	1	3/16
6	Do. 6 p.c. 1 Mt. Dbs. Rd.	100	62½
3'78d.	Newnes, G., L., Cm. Prf.	1	1½
1/3	Nitr. Provision, Ltd.	2½	½
24/	Nobel-Dynam., Ltd.	10	18½
—	North Brazn. Sugar, Ltd.	1	½
15/	Oakey, Ltd.	10	31
6	Do. Cum. Pref.	10	17½
—	Paccha Jazp. Nitr., Ltd.	5	½
5	Pac. Borax, L., 1 Db. Rd.	100	110
—	Palace Hotel, Ltd.	10	5½
5½	Do. Cum. Pref.	10	7
4	Do. 1 Mt. Deb. Stk.	100	102
2/6	Palmer, Ltd.	5	1
6	Do. Cum. Pref.	5	2½
1/2½d	Paquin, Ltd.	1	½
6	Do. Cum. Pref.	5	4
5½	Parnall, Ltd., Cum. Pref.	1	½
4/6	Pawsons, Ltd., £10 Shs.	6	6½
4	Do. Mt. Debs., Red.	100	106
6	Pearks, G. & T., Ltd., 6 p.c. Cum. Pref.	1	½
9½d.	Pears, Ltd.	1	1½
6	Do. Cum. Pref.	10	14
5	Do. Deb. Stk.	100	129
5½	Pearson, C. A., L., Cu. Pf.	5	5½
4/3	Peebles, Ltd.	5	7½
5	Do. Cum. Pref.	5	6½
4½	Do. Mt. Deb. Stk. Red.	100	113½
5½	Peek Bros., Ltd., 1 Cum. Pref., Nos. 1-60,000	5	6½
3½	Do. 3½ p.c 1 Db. Stk.	100	102½
7½d.	Pegamoid, Ltd.	1	½
—	Pillsbury-W. Fl. Mills, L.	10	2½
16/	Do. 8 p.c. Cum. Pref.	10	7½
6	Do. 1 Mort. Debs.	100	92½
9¾d.	Plummer, Ltd.	1	1½
5	Do. Cum. Pref.	5	5½
7/6	Price's Candle, Ltd.	16	34
6	Priest Marians, L., Cm. Pf.	1	1½
6	Pryce Jones, Ld., Cm. Pf.	5	7½
5	Do. Deb. Stk.	100	122
8½d.	Pullman, Ltd.	1	1½
6d.	Do. Cum. Pref.	1	1½
11/16	Raleigh Cycle, Ltd.	1	½
6	Do. Cum. Pref.	1	½
—	Recife Drnge. Ld. 1 Mt. Debs., R	100	19
6	Rudfern, Ltd. Cum. Prf.	10	14
5	Ridgways, Ltd, Cu. Pf.	5	5½
—	R. Janeiro Cy. Imps. Ld.	25	7½
5	Do. Debs.	100	86½
5	Do. 1882-1893	100	86½
11/	R. Jan Fl. Mills, Ltd.	7	6½
5	Do. 1 Mt. Debs., Rd.	100	94
—	Riv. Plate Meat, Ltd.	5	2½
—	Do. Pref.	5	5
8½d.	Roberts, J. R., Ltd.	1	1½
5	Roberts 1 Mt. D. Sk., Rd.	100	112
1/1½	Roberts, T. R., Ltd.	1	2½
5	Do. Cum. Pref.	1	1½

Commercial, &c. (*continued*):—

Last Div.	Name.	Paid.	Price.
3/	Rosario Nit., Ltd.	5	3½
5	Do. Debs., Red.	100	103
1/	Rover Cycle, Ltd.	1	½
6/	Ryl. Aquarium, Ltd.	5	4½
6	Do. Pref.	5	6
5	Ryl. Htl., Edin., Cm. Pf.	1	1½
1/2½	Ryl. Niger, Ltd., £10 Sh.	2	3
6/	Do.	10	15½
20/	Russian Petroleum	10	24½
6½	Do. 6½ p.c. Cm. Prf	10	10½
3/	Ruston, Proctor, Ltd.	10	12
4½	Do. 1 Mort. Debs.	100	104
6/	Sadler, Ltd.	12	7
—	Sal. Carmen Nit., Ltd.	5	3½
9d.	Salmon & Gluck., Ltd.	1	1 1/16
	Salt Union, Ltd.	10	1⅛
1½	Do. 7 p.c. Pref.	10	6
4½	Do. Deb. Stk.	100	100½
4½	Do. "B" Deb. Sk., Rd.	100	97½
—	San Donato Nit., Ltd.	5	½
5/	San Jorge Nit., Ltd.	5	3½
—	San Pablo Nit., Ltd.	5	½
—	San Sebastn. Nit., Ltd.	5	½
1/9	Sanitas, Ltd	1	2½
—	Sa. Elena Nit., Ltd.	5	½
—	Sa. Rita Nit., Ltd.	5	1½
5/	Savoy Hotel, Ltd.	10	16
7	Do. Pref.	10	14
4	Do. 1 Mt. Deb. Stk.	100	111½
5	Do. Debs., Red	100	102½
5	Do. & Ldn. For. Htl., Ltd., 5 p.c. Debs. Red.	100	90
1½d.	Schweppes, Ltd.	1	1½
—	Do Def.	1	½
5	Do. Cum. Pref.	1	1½
4	Do. Deb. Stk.	100	106
1/	Singer Cyc., Ltd.	1	½
5½	Do Cum. Pref.	1	½
—	Smokeless Pwdr., Ltd.	1	½
5½d.	S. Eng. Dairies, Ltd., 6 p.c. Cum. Pref.	1	1½
	Sowler Thos. L.	1	1
3	Do. 5½ Cm. Pf.	5	5½
4/6½	Spencer, Turner, & Co. Ltd	5	8½
5	Do. Cum. Pref.	5	6½
5	Spicer, Ld., 5 p.c. Dbs. Rd.	100	65
4/	Spiers & Pond, Ltd.	10	22
5	Do. 1 Mt. Debs., Red.	100	118½
5	Do. "A" Db. Stk., Rd.	100	111
5	Do. "B" 1 Db. Stk., Rd.	100	111
4	Do. Fd. "C" 1 Db. S., R.	100	104
7/6	Spratt's, Ltd.	5	12½
4	Do. Debs., 1914	—	105
5	Steiner Ld., Cm. Pf.	10	11½
4	Do. 1 Mt. Db. Sk. Rd.	100	106
9/	Stewart & Clydesdale, L.	10	14
6	Do. Cum. Pref.	10	15
35/5	Sulphide Corp.	100	80
1/	Swan & Edgar, L.	1	1½
1/	Sweetmeat Automatic, L.	1	4
2/9	Teetgen, Ltd., Cum. Pref.	5	6
24/	Teleg. Construction., Ld.	12	36½
5	Do. Db. Bds., Rd, 1899	100	103½
3/0½	Tilling, Ld. 5½ p.c. Cm. Prf.	5	6½
4	Do. 4 p.c. 1 Dbs., Rd.	—	104
8½d.	Tower Tea, Ltd.	1	1½
5	Do. Cum. Pref.	5	5½
5	Travers, Ltd., Cum. Pref.	10	12½
4	Do. 1 Mt. Dbs., Rd.	100	105
6	Tucuman Sug., 1 Dbs., Rd.	100	100
4/	United Alkali, Ltd.	10	2
7	Do. Cum. Pref.	10	8½
5	Do. Mt. Db. Stk., Rd.	100	107½
2½d.	United Horse Shoe, Ltd., Non-Cum. 8 p.c. Pref.	1	½
	Un. Kingm. Tea, Cm. Prf.	5	4½
8/	Un. Lankat Plant., Ltd.	1	2
4/	Un. Limmer Asphlte., Ld.	3	5
13/	Val de Travers Asph., L.	10	15½
3/	V. den Bergh's, L., Cm. P.	5	6½
6	Walkers, Park., L., C. Pf.	10	3
4½	Do. 1 Mt. Debs., Red.	100	90½
6/	Wallis, Thos. & Co., Ltd.	5	14
6	Do. Cum. Pref.	5	8½
5½	Waring, Ltd., Cum. Pref.	5	5½
4½	Do. 1 Mt. Db. Sk., Red.	100	112
4½	Do. Irred. "B" Db. Stk.	100	104
12/	Waterlow, Dfd. Ord.	10	14
4/	Do. Pref.	10	14
3½	Do. Cum. Pref.	10	10½
10/	Waterlow Bros. & L., Ld.	10	9
5	Do. Pref.	10	12½
1/2½	Welford, Ltd.	1	1½
4½	Do. Debs., Red.	100	109
1/	Welford's Surrey Dairies, Ltd.	1	1½
7½d.	West London Dairy, Ltd.	1	1
4½	Wharncliffe Dwllgs, L., Pf.	10	11½
18/10	Do. 3 p.c. Irr. Mt. Db. Sk.	100	96
6d.	White, A. J., Ltd.	1	½
6	Do. 6 p.c. Cum. Pref.	1	½
4	White, J. Bazley, Ltd., 1 Mort. Debs., Red	100	99½
5	White, R., Ltd., 1 Mort. Deb. Stock, Red.	100	104½
11/	White, Tomkins, Ltd.	10	11½
5	Do. Cum. Pref.	10	11½
6	White, W. N., L., Cm. Pf.	1	½
9/6	Wickens, Pease & Co., L.	5	3½
6	Wilkie, Ltd., Cum. Pref.	10	15
4/	Willans & Robinson, Ltd	5	9
6	Do. Cum. Pref.	5	7½
4½	Do. 1 Mt. Db. Stk., Red.	100	108
7½d.	Williamsons, L., Cm. Prf.	1	1½
6	Winterbottm. Book Cloth, Ltd., Cum. Prf.	10	15
3/	Yates, Ltd.	5	6½
6	Do. Cum. Pref.	5	6½
	Young's Paraffin. Ltd.	4	1½

CORPORATION STOCKS—COLONIAL AND FOREIGN.

Per Cent.	Name.	Paid.	Price.
6	Auckland City, '72 1904-24	100	118
6	Do. Cons., '79, Red. 1930	100	135½
5	Do. Deb. Ln., '83..1934-8	100	117
6	Auckland Harb. Debs.	100	111½
5	Do. 1917	100	111
5	Do. 1936	100	114
5½	Balmain Boro' 1914	—	113½
5	Boston City (U.S.)	100	102½
5	Do. ..1902	100	105
5	Brunswick Town 5 c. Debs. 1916-20	100	111
15/	B. Ayres City 6 p.c.	100	51
4½	Do. 4½ p.c.	100	71½
5	Cape Town, City of	100	113
4	Do. ..1943	100	116
4	Chicago, City of, Gold 1915	—	108
6	Christchurch 1926	100	131½
—	Cordoba City	100	17½
5	Duluth (U.S.) Gold ..1926	—	110
6	Dunedin (Otago) 1925	100	127½
6	Do. 1906	100	113
5	Do. Consols..1908	100	111
4	Durban Insc. Stk. 1944	100	111
4	Essex Cnty., N. Jersey 1926	$100	114½
5	Fitzroy, Melbrne. ..1916-19	100	110
5	Gisborne Harbour 1915	100	109
4	Greymouth Harbour..1925	100	110
4	Hamilton 1934	100	108
5	Hobart Town 1918-30	100	115
4	Do. 1940	100	105
4½	Invercargill Boro. Dbs. 1936	100	111
6	Kimberley Boro., S. A. Debs.	—	102
4	Launceston Twn. Dbs. 1916	100	107
6	Lyttleton, N.Z., Harb. 1929	100	125
4	Melbourne Bd. of Wks. 1921	100	107
5	Melb. City Debs. 1897-1907	100	106½
4½	Do. Debs. 1908-27	100	111½
4	Do. Debs...1915-20-22	100	106
5	Melbne. Harb. Bds., 1908-9	100	113
4½	Do. do. 1915	100	111
4	Do. do. 1918-21	100	106
4½	Melbrne. Tms. Dbs. 1914-16	100	113
4½	Do. Fire Brig. Db. 1921	100	108
5	Mexico City Stg.	100	80
4	Moncton N. Bruns. City	100	102
4½	MonteVideo	100	59
5	Montreal Stg.	100	103
5	Do. 1874	100	103
5	Do. 1879	100	104
3½	Do. 1933	100	102
3	Do. Perm. Deb. Stk.	100	95
4	Do. Cons. Deb. Stk. 1932	100	112
6	Napier Boro. Consolid. 1914	100	119
5	Napier Harb. Debs...1920	100	115
5	Do. Debs...1928	100	107
6	New Plymouth Harb. Debs. 1900	100	107
6	New York City 1901	—	107½
3½	Do. 1910-26	—	103½
4½	Nth. Melbourne Debs. 1-600 1921	100	106
5	Oamaru Boro. Cons...1920	100	101
6	Do. Harb. Bds. (Reg.)	100	74
25/	Do. 6 p.c. (Bearer)..1919	100	35
6	Otago Harb. Deb. Reg.	100	103
6	Do. 1877	100	107
6	Do. 1881 1921	100	115
5	Do. Debs. ..1921	100	107
5	Do. Cons. ..1934	100	105
6	Ottawa City	100	101
6	Do. 1904	100	111½
4½	Do. Debs. ..1913	100	108½
6	Port Elizabeth Waterworks	100	111
5	Port Louis	100	111
5	Prahran Debs. 1917	100	109
4	Do. Debs. 1919	100	102
6	Quebec C. Coupon. 1875 1905	100	112
6	Do. do. 1876 1908	100	116
4½	Do. Debs. 1914-18	100	108
4	Do. Debs. 1923	100	108
3½	Do. Cns. Rg. Stk., Red.	100	101
5	Richmond (Melb.) Dbs. 1917	100	112
4	Rio Janeiro City	100	57
4	Rome City	100	—
4	Do. 2nd to 8th Iss.	100	90
—	Rosario C.	100	26½
—	Do.	100	26½
4	St. Catherine (Ont.) ..1926	100	101
4	St. John, N.B., Debs. 1934	—	103
4½	St. Kilda (Melb) Dbs. 1918-21	100	105
4	St. Louis C. (Miss.)..1911	100	104
4	Do. 1913	100	103½
3·65	Do. 1915	—	108½
—	Santa Fé City Debs.	100	20
6	Santos City	100	95
6	Sofia City	100	84
5	Sth. Melbourne Debs. 1911	100	111
4½	Do. Debs....1910	100	107
5	Sydney City 1904	100	100
4	Do. Debs. 1912-17	100	107
4	Do. do. (1894) ..1919	100	109
7	Timaru Boro. 7 p.c...1910	100	126½
5	Timaru Harb. Debs 1914	100	107
5	Do. Debs...1916	100	107
6	Toronto City Wtrwks 1904-6	100	114
5	Do. G. Cns. Dbs. 1919-20	100	118
4	Do. Stelg. 1922	100	107
4	Do. Local Improv.	100	102
3½	Do. 1920	100	104
5½	Valparaiso	100	[illegible]
4	Vancouver 1931	100	107
4	Do. 1932	100	108
6	Wanganui Harb. Dbs. 1915	100	110
6	Wellington Con. Deb. 1907	100	117
6	Do. Improv., 1879	100	123
6	Do. Wtrwks. Dbs. 1880	100	123
4½	Do. Debs. 1893....1933	100	114
4½	Wellington Harb. 1907	100	104
5	Westport Harb. Dbs. 1925	100	110
6	Winnipeg City Deb. ..1907	—	118
5	Do. 1914	100	117

FINANCIAL, LAND, AND INVESTMENT.

Last Div.	Name.	Paid.	Price.
5	Agncy. Ld. & Fin. Aust., Ltd., Mt. Db. Stk., Rd.	100	90½
	Amer. Frehld. Mt. of Lon., Ld., Cum. Pref. Stk.	100	87½
4½	Do. Deb. Stk., Red.	100	92
1/	Anglo-Amer. Db. Cor., L.	2	1
4	Do. Deb. Stk., Red	100	105½
5½	Ang.-Ceylon & Gen. Est., Ltd., Cons. Stk.	100	55
6	Do. Reg. Debs., Red.	100	101½
—	Ang.-Fch. Explorn., Ltd.	1	2¼
6	Do. Cum. Pref.	1	1½
—	Argent. Ld. & Inv., Ltd. £1 Shares	10/	nil
—	Do. Cum. Pref.	4	1½
1/	Assets Fnders.' Sh., Ltd.,	4	1¾
6/	Assets Realis., Ltd., Ord.,	5	8¼
5	Do. Cum. Pref.	5	6½
26/	Austrln. Agricl. £25 Shs.	21½	62½
4½	Aust. N. Z. Mort., Ltd., Deb. Stk., Red.	100	90½
4	Do. Deb. Stk., Red.	100	82½
4½	Australian Est. & Mt., L., 1 Mt. Deb. Stk., Red.	100	103
5	Do. "A" Mort. Deb. Stk., Red.	100	96
5/	Australian Mort., Ld., & Fin., Ltd. £25 Shs.	5	5
1/6	Do. New, £25 Shs.	3	3
4	Do. Deb. Stk.	100	100½
3	Do. Do.	100	85
5	Bengal Presidy. 1 Mort. Deb., Red.	100	106
23/	British Amer. Ld. "A"	1	19
—	Do. "B"	24	7
1/7½	Brit. & Amer. Mt., Ltd. £10 Shs.	2	1
5/	Do. Pref.	10	10
4	Do. Deb. Stk., Red.	100	103
1/3	Brit. & Austrian Tst Ln., Ltd. £25 Shs.	2½	¾
4½	Do. Perm. Debs., Red.	100	104
1½d.	Brit. N. Borneo. £1 Shs.	15/	5/16
2½d.	Do.	1	¾
—	Brit. S. Africa	1	2½
5	Do. Mt. Deb., Red.	—	98
6	B. Aires Harb. Tst., Red.	100	93
12/6	Canada Co.	1	26
—	Canada N. W. Ld., Ltd.	$25	23½
—	Do. Pref.	$100	350½
4	Canada Perm. Loan & Sav. Perp. Deb. Stk.	100	99½
6	Curamalan Ld., 6 p.c. "A" Scrip	—	92
3/7½	Deb Corp., Ld., £10 Shs	4	3½
5	Do. Cum. Pref.	10	11½
4	Do. Perp. Deb. Stk.	100	112
9d.	Deb. Corp. Fders' Sh., Ld.	3	¾
4/5⅛	Eastn. Mt. & Agncy, Ld., "A"	10	5½
4½	Do. Deb. Stk., Red.	100	100
5	Equitable Revers. In. Ltd.	100	—
2/6	Exploration, Ltd.	1	1 1/16
/6d.	Freehold Trst. of Austrla. Ltd. £10 Shs.	1	¾
4	Do. Perp. Deb. Stk.	100	100
70/	Genl. Reversionary, Ltd.	100	—
3½	Holborn Vi. Land	100	105
3½	House Prop. & Inv.	100	85½
13/	Hudson's Bay	13	21
—	Hyderabad (Deccan)	5	3
4	Impl. Col. Fin. & Agcy. Corp.	100	92½
4½	Impl. Prop. Inv., Ltd., Deb. Stk., Red.	100	91½
2/6	Internatl. Fincial. Soc., Ltd. £7½ Shs.	2½	1½
4	Do. Deb. Stk., Red.	100	90½
1/9½	Ld. & Mtge. Egypt, Ltd. £18 Shs.	3	2¾
5	Do. Debs., Red.	100	103
4½	Do. Debs., Red.	100	102
—	Ld. Corp. of Canada, Ltd.	1	¾
4½	Ld. Mtge. Bk. of Texas Deb. Stk.	100	—
3½	Ld. Mtge. Bk. Victoria 4½ p.c. Deb. Stk.	100	78
2/9½	Law Debent. Corp., Ltd., £10 Shs.	2	1¾
4½	Do. Cum. Pref.,	10	11½
4	Do. Deb. Stk.	100	114
—	Law Land, L., 4½ Cm. Prf.	5	5½
1/	Ldn. & Australasian Deb. Corp., Ltd., £4 Shs.	2	½
4½	Do. 4½ p.c. Mt. Deb. Stk., Red.	100	99
1/9	Ldn. & Middx. Frhld. Est. £2 Shs.	35/	3
2/6	Lndn. & N. Y. Inv. Corp., Ltd.	5	1¾
5	Do. 5 p.c. Cum. Pref.	10	6¼
1/6	Ldn. & Nth. Assets Corp., Ltd., £2 Shs.	2½	¾
2	Ldn. & N. Deb. Corp., L.	2	1½
3/6	Ldn. & S. Afric. Explrn. Ltd.	½	12¾
2/	Mtge. Co. of R. Plate, Ltd. £10 Shs.	2	3
4½	Do. Deb. Stk., Red.	100	112
4½	Morton, Rose Est., Ltd., 1st Mort. Debs.	—	99
6/6	Natal Land Col. Ltd.	10	7½
4/	Do. 8 p.c. Pref., 1870	5	8
5/6	Natl. Disct. L., £25 Shs.	5	10¼
4½	New Impl. Invest., Ltd. Pref. Stk.	100	61½
	New Impl. Invest., Ltd. Def. Stk.	100	9
3½	N. Zld. Assets Real Deb.	100	99
4	N. Zld. Ln. & Mer. Agcy., Ltd Prf. Ln. Deb. Stk	100	94
2/6	N. Zld. Tst. & Ln. Ltd., £25 Shs.	5	1½

Financial, Land, &c. (*continued*):—

Last Div.	Name.	Paid.	Price.
12/6	N. Zld. Tst. & Ln. Ltd., 5 p.c. Cum. Pref.	25	20
—	N. Brit. Australsn. Ltd.	100	6½
—	Do. Irred. Guar.	100	32½
5	Do. Mort. Debs.	100	82½
4½	N. Queensld. Mort. & Inv., Ltd., Deb. Stk.	100	93
6	Peel Riv., Ld. & Min. Ltd.	100	88
—	Peruvian Corp., Ltd.	100	2
—	Do. 4 p.c. Pref.	100	9
3	Do. 6 p.c. 1 Mt. Debs., Red.	100	39½
—	Queensld. Invest. & Ld. Mort. Pref. Ord. Stk.	100	20
3/7	Queensld. Invest. & Ld. Mort. Ord. Shs.	4	4
4	Queensld. Invest. & Ld. Mort. Perp. Debs.	100	88
3½	Raily. Roll Stk. Tst. Deb., 1903-6	100	100½
50/	Reversiony. Int. Soc., Ltd.	100	—
2/8½	Riv. Plate Trst., Loan & Agcy., L., "A" £10 Shs.	2	4
1/6	Riv. Plate Trst., Loan & Agcy., Ltd., Def. "B"	5	3½
	Riv. Plate Trst., Loan & Agy., L., Db. Stk., Red.	100	109
—	Santa Fé & Cord. Gt. South Land, Ltd.	20	5
—	Santa Fé Land	10	2½
2/	Scot. Amer. Invest., Ltd. £10 Shs.	2	2½
2½	Scot. Australian Invest., Ltd., Cons.	100	71½
6	Scot. Australian Invest., Ltd., Guar. Pref.	100	135½
5	Scot. Australian Invest., Ltd., Guar. Pref.	100	106½
4	Scot. Australian Invest., Ltd., 4 p.c. Perp. Dbs.	100	105½
5	Sivagunga Zemdy., 1st Mort., Red.	100	101
20/	Sth. Australian	20	50
3½	Stock Exchange Deb., Rd.	—	101½
—	Strait Develt., Ltd.	1	1/16
2/6	Texas Land & Mt., Ltd. £10 Shs.	2½	3
4½	Texas Land & Mt., Ltd., Deb. Stk., Red.	100	105
—	Transvaal Est. & Dev., L.	1	5/16
—	Transvaal Lands, Ltd., £1 Shs.	15/	½
—	Do. F. P.	1	1/16
—	Transvaal Mort., Loan, & Fin., Ltd., £10 Shs.	2	½
2/	Tst & Agcy. of Austrlsa., Ltd., £10 Shs.	1	2
7/5	Do. Old, fully paid	10	15½
5/7	Do. New, fully paid	10	12½
5	Do. Cum. Pref.	10	12½
3/	Trust & Loan of Canada, £20 Shs.	5	4½
1/9½	Do. New £20 Shs.	3	2½
4½	Tst. & Mort. of Iowa, Ltd., Deb. Stk. Red.	100	92½
—	Tst., Loan, & Agency of Mexico, Ltd., £10 Shs.	2	½
—	Trsts., Exors, & Sec. Ins. Corp., Ltd., £10 Shs.	7	1¾
4	Do. Irred. Deb. Stk.	100	106½
5/	Union Dsc., Ld., £10 Shs.	5	10¼
6	Union Mort. & Agcy. of Aust., Ltd., Pref. Stk.	100	30
—	Do. 6 p. Pref. £6 Shs.	2	½
4½	Do. Deb. Stk	100	92½
4	Do. Deb. Stk	100	85½
5	Do. Deb. Stk. Red.	100	96½
1/6	U.S. Deb. Cor. Ltd., £8 Shs.	1	½
5½	Do. Cum. Pref. Stk	100	100½
4½	Do. Irred. Deb. Stk.	100	105½
5	U.S. Tst. & Guar. Cor., Ltd., Pref. Stk.	100	77½
6/	Van Dieman's	25	15
4	Walker's Prop. Cor., Ltd., Guar. 1 Mt. Deb. Stk.	100	109
4½	Wstr. Mort. & Inv., Ltd., Deb. Stk.	100	92½

FINANCIAL—TRUSTS.

Last Div.	Name.	Paid.	Price.
1/6	Afric City Prop., Ltd	1	1½
6	Do. Cum. Pref.	1	1 1/16
4	Alliance Invt., Ltd., Cm. 4½ p.c. Prefd.	100	75½
—	Do. Defd	100	12½
4	Do. Deb. Stk. Red.	100	106½
5	Amrcn. Invt., Ltd., Prfd.	100	114½
5	Do. Defd.	100	88½
4	Do. Deb. Stk. Red.	100	115½
4	Army & Navy Invt., Ltd., 5 p.c. Prefd.	100	81½
—	Do. Defd. Stk.	100	16½
4	Do. Deb. Stk.	100	105½
4	Atlas Investment, Ltd., Prefd. Stk.	100	70½
4½	Bankers' Invest., Ltd., Cum. Prefd.	100	103
1/0/0	Do. Defd	100	23½
4	Do. Deb. Stk	100	111
	Brewery & Comml. Inv., Ltd., £10 Shs.	5	6

Financial—Trusts (*continued*):—

Last Div.	Name.	Paid.	Price.
4	British Investment, Ltd., Cum. Prefd.	100	107
5	Do. Defd.	100	103½
4	Do. Deb. Stk.	100	108½
6	Brit. Steam. Invst., Ltd., Prefd	100	116½
8/0/0	Do. Defd	100	69½
4½	Do. Perp. Deb. Stk	100	120½
1/9	Car Trust Invst., Ltd., £10 Shs.	2½	2
5	Do. Pref	100	101
4	Do. Deb. Stk., 1915	100	104
4	Cinl. Sec., Ltd., Prefd.	100	102½
2½	Do. Defd.	100	45½
4	Consolidated, Ltd., Cum. 1st Pref.	100	92
4	Do. 5 p.c. Cm. and do.	100	71½
—	Do. Defd.	100	14½
4½	Do. Deb. Stk.	100	112½
5	Deb. Secs. Invst.	100	103½
4	Do. 4 p.c. Cm. Pf. Sk.	100	105½
4½	Edinburgh Invest., Ltd., Cum. Prefd. Stk.	100	107½
4	Do. Deb. Stk. Red.	100	106½
5	Foreign, Amer. & Gen. Invt., Ltd., Prefd.	100	112½
2	Do. Defd.	100	43½
4	Do. Deb. Stk.	100	115½
5	Foreign & Colonial Invt., Ltd., Prefd.	100	136½
5½	Do. Defd.	100	99½
4½	Gas, Water & Gen. Invt., Cum. Prefd. Stk.	100	85½
3	Do. Defd. Stk.	100	36½
4	Do. Deb. Stk.	100	104
5	Gen. & Com. Invt., Ltd., Prefd. Stk.	100	106½
2	Do. Defd. Stk.	100	36½
4	Do. Deb. Stk.	100	113½
2/6	Globe Telegph. & Tst., Ltd.	10	11½
6	Do. do. Pref.	10	17
4	Govt. & Genl. Invt., Ld., Prefd.	100	84½
3½	Do. Defd.	100	42½
4½	Govts. Stk. & other Secs. Invt., Ltd., Prefd.	100	86½
1	Do. Defd.	100	25
4½	Do. Deb. Stk.	100	111
4	Do. do.	100	104
4½	Guardian Invt., Ltd., Pfd.	100	87½
—	Do. Defd.	100	19½
4	Do. Deb. Stk.	100	104
5	Indian & Gen. Inv., Ltd., Cum. Prefd.	100	107½
2½	Do. Defd.	100	55
4½	Do. Deb. Stk.	100	119½
5	Indust. & Gen. Tst., Ltd., Unified	100	102
3½	Do. Deb. Stk. Red.	100	99½
4½	Internat. Invt., Ltd., Cm. Prefd.	100	66½
—	Do. Defd.	100	7½
4	Do. Deb. Stk.	100	101
4	Invest. Tst. Cor. Ltd. Pfd.	100	100
4	Do. Defd.	100	90
4	Do. Deb. Stk. Red.	100	105
5	Ldn. Gen. Invest. Ltd., 5 p.c. Cum. Prefd.	100	111½
7½	Do. Defd.	100	120
4½	Ldn. Scot. Amer. Ltd. Pfd.	100	104½
£3	Do. Defd.	100	59½
4	Do. Deb. Stk.	100	111
4	Ldn. Tst., Ltd., Cum. Prfd. Stk.	100	99
4	Do. Defd. Stk.	100	68½
4	Do. Deb. Stk., Red.	100	107
3½	Do. Mt. Deb. Stk., Red.	100	102½
5	Mercantile Invt. & Gen., Ltd., Prefd.	100	109
3	Do. Defd.	100	44½
4	Do. Deb. Stk.	100	111½
4	Merchants, Ltd., Pref. Stk.	100	104½
4	Do. Ord.	100	80½
4	Do. Deb. Stk.	100	115½
5	Municipal, Ltd., Prefd.	100	55½
—	Do. Defd.	100	17½
4½	Do. Debs.	100	111
4½	Do. Debs. "B"	100	99½
4½	Do. "C" Deb. Stk.	100	88½
5	New Investment, Ltd. Ord.	100	92½
5	Omnium Invest., Ltd., Pfd.	100	91½
1	Do. Defd.	100	26½
4	Do. Deb. Stk.	100	104
5/	Railway Deb. Tst. Ld., £10 Shs.	10	6½
5	Do. Debs., Red.	100	107½
4½	Do. Deb. Stk., 1911	100	107½
4	Do. do. 1927	100	106½
4	Railway Invst. Ltd., Prefd.	100	111
11/7	Do. Defd.	100	19½
8/	Railway Share Trust & Agency "A"	8	5½
7½	Do. "B" Pref. Stk.	100	145½
4½	River Plate & Gen. Invt., Ltd., Prefd.	100	104
£3	Do. Defd.	100	50½
5	Scot. Invst., Ltd., Pfd. Stk.	100	91½
7½	Do. Defd.	100	26½
4	Do. Deb. Stk.	100	106
4½	Sec. Scottish Invst., Ltd., Cum. Prefd.	100	89½
£3	Do. Defd. Stk.	100	32
4	Do. Deb. Stk.	100	107½
5/	Sth. Africa Gold Tst., Ltd.	1	4½
6	Do. Cum. Pref	1	1
5½	Do. 1st Debs., Red.	100	102
1/9	Stock Conv. & Invest., Ltd., £5 Shs.	1	1½
4½	Do. do. 4½ p.c. Cm. Prf.	100	113½
3½	Do. Ldn. & N. W. 1st Charge Prefd.	100	114½
4	Do do. 2nd Chge Prfd.	100	111
32/6	Do. do. Defd. Charge	100	30
3	Do. N. East. 1 Chge Pfd.	100	90½

Financial—Trusts (*continued*):—

Last Div.	Name.	Paid.	Price.
37/6	Stock N. East Defd. Chge	100	36
6	Submarine Cables	100	138½
5	U.S. & S. Amer. Invest., Ltd., Prefd.	100	99½
2	Do. Defd.	100	25½
4	Do. Deb. Stk.	100	105½

GAS AND ELECTRIC LIGHTING.

Last Div.	Name.	Paid.	Price.
10/6	Alliance & Dublin Con. 10 p.c. Stand.	10	24
7/6	Do. 7 p.c. Stand.	10	16½
5	Austln. Gas Lght. (Syd.) Debs. 1909	100	106
5	Bay State of N. Jrsy. Sk. Fd. Tst. Bd., Red.	—	89½
3/	Bombay, Ltd.	5	6
2/4½	Do. New	4	5
12	Brentford Cons.	100	292½
9	Do. New	100	217½
5	Do. Pref.	100	142½
4	Do. Deb. Stk.	100	136
11½	Brighton & Hove Gen. Cons. Stk.	100	272½
8½	Do. "A" Cons. Stk.	100	197½
5	Bristol 5 p.c. Max.	100	129½
22/6	British Gas Light, Ltd.	20	55½
11/6	Bromley Gas Consumrs.' 10 p.c. Stand.	10	26
8/6	Do. 7 p.c. Stand.	10	21
—	Brush Electl. Enging., L.	—	1½
6	Do. 6 p.c. Pref.	—	2½
4½	Do. Deb. Stk.	100	112
4½	Do. 2 Deb. Stk., Red.	100	102½
7/	B. Ayres (New), Ltd.	10	9
4	Do. Deb. Stk., Rd.	—	98
12/6	Cagliari Gas & Wtr., Ltd.	20	31
8/	Cape Town & Dist. Gas Light & Coke, Ltd.	10	16½
4½	Do. Pref.	10	12½
6	Do. 1 Mt. Debs. 1910	50	59
4/	Charing Cross & Strand Elec. Sup., Ltd.	5	13½
4½	Do. Cum. Pref.	5	6½
3/	Chelsea Elec. Sup., Ltd.	5	10
4½	Do. Deb. Stk., Red.	100	116
5	Chic. Edis'n Co. 1 Mt., Rd.	$1000	106
20/	City of Ldn. Elec. Lht., L.	10	26½
—	Do. New £10 Shs.	5	18½
6	Do. Cum. Pref.	10	18
5	Do. Deb. Stk., Red.	100	131½
13½	Commercial, Cons.	100	325½
10½	Do. New	100	252½
4½	Do. Deb. Stk.	100	152½
14	Continental Union, Ltd.	100	220
11	Do. Pref. Stk.	100	200
—	County of Lon. & Brush Prov. Elec. Lg., Ltd.	10	14
6	Do. Cum. Pref.	10	15½
14	Croydon Comcl. Gas, Ld., "A" Stk., 10 p.c.	100	312½
11	Do., "B" Stk., 7 p.c.	100	260
5½	Crystal Pal. Dist. Ord. 5 p.c. Stk.	100	130½
5	Do. Pref. Stk.	100	143½
8/	European, Ltd.	10	24
6/	Do.	7½	17½
12½	Gas Light & Ck Cons. Stk., "A" Ord.	100	285½
4	Do. "B" (4 p.c. Max.)	100	120½
10	Do. "C," "D," & "E" (Pref.)	100	302½
5	Do. "F" (Pref.)	100	152½
7½	Do. "G" (Pref.)	100	222½
7	Do. "H" (7 p.c. Max.)	100	197½
10	Do. "J" (Pref.)	100	302½
6	Do. "K"	100	180½
4	Do. Deb. Stk.	100	133½
4½	Do. do.	100	152½
6	Do. do.	100	204½
8/	Hong Kong & China, Ld.	10	14½
4/	House to House Elec. Light Sup., Ltd.	5	10
7	Do. Cum. Pref.	5	11½
10	Imperial Continental	100	217½
3½	Do. Deb. Stk., Red	100	104½
2/	Malta & Medit., Ltd.	5	6½
7/	Metrop. Elec. Sup., Ltd.	10	18½
4½	Do. 1 Mt. Deb. Stk.	100	119
5	Metro. of Melbrne. Dbs. 1908-12	100	111
4½	Do. Debs. 1918-22-4	100	108
10/	Monte Video, Ltd.	20	15½
9½	Newcastle-upon-Tyne	100	237½
—	Do. 3½ p.c. Deb. Stk.	100	117½
12/	Notting Hill Elec. Ltg., Ltd.	10	20
4/6	Oriental, Ltd.	5	8½
4/0½	Do. New	4½	7½
10d½.	Do. do. 1879	1	1½
3/6	Ottoman, Ltd.	5	4½
6	People's Gas Lt. & C. of Chic. 2 Mt. 1904	100	105½
5	River Plate Elec. Lgt. & Trac., Ltd., 1 Deb. Stk.	—	92½
8½	Royal Elec. of Montreal	—	144
4½	Do. 1 Mt. Deb.	100	104
11/	St. James' & Pall Mall Elec. Light, Ltd.	5	18
7	Do. Pref.	5	10½
4	Do. Deb. Stk., Red.	100	108½
10/	San Paulo, Ltd.	10	15½

Gas and Electric (*continued*):—

Last Div.	Name.	Paid.	Price.
10	Sheffield Unit. Gas Lt. "A"	100	251½
10	Do. "B"	100	251½
10	Do. "C"	100	251½
—	Sth. Ldn. Elec. Sup., Ld.	2	2½
5¼	South Metropolitan	100	134½
3	Do. 3 p.c. Deb. Stk.	100	104½
2	Tottenham & Edmonton Gas Lt. & C., "A"	100	290
9	Do. "B"	100	210
7/	Tuscan, Ltd.	10	13½
5	Do. Debs., Red.	100	101½
5/	West Ham 10 p.c. Stan.	5	12
8/	Wstmnstr. Elec. Sup., Ld.	5	16½

INSURANCE

Last Div.	Name.	Paid.	Price.
4/	Alliance, £20 Shs.	44/	10½
20/	Alliance, Mar., & Gen., Ld., £100 Shs.	25	53
19/	Atlas, £50 Shs.	6	30½
12/	British & For. Marine, Ld., £20 Shs.	4	23½
7½d.	British Law Fire, Ltd., £10 Shs.	1	1½
7/6	Clerical, Med., & Gen. Life £25 Shs.	50/	16½
10/	Commercial Union, Ltd., £50 Shs.	5	43½
4	Do. "W. of Eng." Ter. Deb. Stk.	100	110½
£9	County Fire, £100 Shs.	80	196
5/	Eagle, £50 Shs.	5	½
4/	Employers' Liability, Ltd., £10 Shs.	2	4
—	Empress, Ltd., £5 Shs.	1	—
21/	Equity & Law, £100 Shs.	6	23
7/6	General Life, £100 Shs.	5	15
4½d.	Gresham Life, £5 Shs.	15/	2½
2/6	Guardian, Ld., £10 Shs.	5	11
10/	Imperial, Ltd., £20 Shs.	5	29
5/6	Imperial Life, £20 Shs.	4	6½
6/	Indemnity Mutual Mar., Ltd., £15 Shs.	3	11½
1/	Lancashire, £20 Shs.	2	5
7½d.	Law Acc. & Contin., Ltd., £5 Shs.	10/	¾
5/	Law Fire, £100 Shs.	2½	18
9½d.	Law Guar. & Trust, Ltd., £10 Shs.	1	1⅜
9/	Law Life, £20 Shs.	2	25
2/9	Law Un. & Crown £10 Shs	12/	7
4	Do. Deb. Stk., 1942	100	110½
14/6	Legal & General, £50 Shs.	8	15½
9d.	Lion Fire, Ltd., £8½ Shs.	1½	⅞
14/	Liverpool & London & Globe, Stk.	2	52½
20/	Do. Globe £1 Ann	—	35½
35/	London, £25 Shs.	12½	58
8/	Lond. & Lanc. Fire, £25 Shs	2½	18¾
2/	Lond. & Lanc. Life, £25 Shs	2	7
1/	Lond. & Prov. Mar., Ld., £10 Shs.	1	¾
6/	Lond. Guar. & Accident, Ltd., £5 Shs.	2	12
10/	Marine, Ltd., £25 Shs.	4½	41
2/	Maritime, Ltd., £10 Shs.	2	4
1/6	Merc. Mar., Ld., £10 Shs.	2½	2½
10/	N. Brit. & Merc., £25 Shs.	6¼	42½
20/	Northern, £100 Shs.	10	81
40/	Norwich Union Fire, £100 Shs.	12	124½
10/	Ocean Acc. & Guar., fy. pd.	5	22
2/	Do. £5 Shs.	1	4
7/6	Ocean, Marine, Ltd.	2½	8½
2/	Palatine, £10 Shs.	2	3½
2/6	Pelican, £10 Shs.	1	3½
23/	Phoenix, £50 Shs.	5	42
£6	Provident, £100 Shs.	10	32
5/	Railway Psangrs., £10 Shs.	2	8½
2/6	Rock Life, £5 Shs.	10/	4½
8	Royal Exchange	100	355
18/	Royal, £20 Shs.	3	53½
4/	Sun, £10 Shs.	10/	11
3/9	Sun Life, £10 Shs.	7½	14½
6	Thames & Mrsey. Marine, Ltd., £20 Shs.	2	10½
9	Union, £10 Shs.	4	24½
4/	Union Marine, £20 Shs.	2½	8½
12/	Universal Life, £100 Shs.	12	42
2/	World Marine, £5 Shs.	2	1½

IRON, COAL, AND STEEL.

Last Div.	Name.	Paid.	Price.
—	Barrow Hæm. Steel, Ltd.	7½	2
9/	Do. 6 p.c. 2nd Pref.	7½	6½
10/	Bolck., Vaugh. & C., Ld.	20	16½
6/	Do. £8 liab.	12	8½
7/6	Brown, J. & Co., Ltd., £20 Shs.	15	20
7/6	Consett Iron, Ld., £10 Shs.	7½	29½
7/6	Ebbw Vale Steel, Iron & Coal, Ltd., £23 Shs.	20	6½
12/6	General Mining Assn., Ld.	5½	7½
8/	Harvey Steel Co. of Gt. Britain, Ltd.	10	27
5	Lehigh V. Coal 1 Mt. 5 p.c. Guar. Gd. Cp. Bds.	—	95½
42/6	Nantyglo & Blaina Iron, Ltd., Pref.	$62	96
1/	Nerbudda Coal & Iron, Ltd., £3 Shs.	56/	$\frac{1}{16}$
—	Newport Abrcrn. Bk. Vein Steam Coal, Ltd.	10	5½
5/	New Sharlston Coll., Ltd. Pref.	20	9½
4½d.	Nw. Vancvr. Coal & Ld., L.	1	½
2/6	North's Navigation Coll. (1889) Ltd.	5	2½
10/	Do. 10 p.c. Cum. Pref.	5	6½
—	Rhymney Iron, Ltd.	5	1½
	Do. New, £5 Shs.	4½	½
5	Do. Mt. Debs., Red.	100	98½
5	Shelton Irn., Stl. & Cl. Co., Ltd., 1 Chg. Debs., Red.	100	99½
50/	Sth. Hetton Coal, Ltd.	100	—
2/	Vickers & Maxim, Ltd.	1	3½
5	Do. 5 p.c. Prfd. Stk.	100	127½

SHIPPING.

Last Div.	Name.	Paid.	Price
12/	African Stm. Ship, £20 Shs.	16	10½
15/	Do. Fully-paid	20	14½
5/	Amazon Steam Nav., Ltd.	12½	9
8/	Castle Mail Pakts., Ltd., £20 Shs.	14	16
3½	Do. 1st Deb. Stk., Red.	100	102
6/	China Mutual Steam, Ltd.	5	2½
6	Do. Cum. Pref.	10	9½
10/	Cunard, Ltd.	20	9½
5/	Do. £20 Shs.	10	3½
4½	Furness, Withy, & Co., Ltd., 1 Mt. Dbs., Red.	100	106
6/	General Steam	15	7½
5/	Do. 5 p.c. Pref., 1874	10	8½
5/	Do. 5 p.c. Pref., 1877	10	8½
26/4½	Leyland & Co., Ltd.	10	25
7/	Do. 7 p.c. Cum. Pref.	10	15
2/11	Do. 4½ p.c. Cum. Pre-Pf.	3	10½
4	Do. 1st Mt. Dbs., Red.	100	106½
7/6	Mercantile Steam, Ltd.	5	7½
6/4½	New Zealand Ship., Ltd.,	6	5
4	Do. Deb. Stk., Red.	100	104
5/	Orient Steam, Ltd.	10	5
5	P.&O. Steam, Cum. Prefd.	100	147½
19	Do. Defd.	100	232½
3½	Do. Deb. Stk.	100	117
5	Richelieu & Ont., 1st Mt. Debs., Red.	100	100
30/	Royal Mail, £100 Shs.	60	51
2/6	Shaw, Sav., & Alb., Ltd., "A" Pref.	5	5
5/	Do. "B" Ord.	5	4
14/	Union Steam, Ltd.	20	19
7/	Do. New £20 Shs.	10	8½
4	Do. Deb. Stk., Red.	100	106
7/	Union of N.Z., Ltd.	10	10
5½	Wilson's & Fur.-Ley., 5½ p.c. Cum. Pref.	10	10½
4½	Do. 1 Mt. Db. Sk., Rd.	100	106½

*** *Tea Shares will be found in the Special Table following.*

TELEGRAPHS AND TELEPHONES.

Last Div.	Name.	Paid.	Price.
4	African Direct, Ltd., Mort. Debs., Red.	100	102
—	Amazon Telegraph, Ltd.	10	7½
15/	Anglo-American, Ltd.	100	64½
30/	Do. 6 p.c. Prefd. Ord.	100	113½
—	Do. Defd. Ord.	100	16
3/	Brazilian Submarine, Ltd.	10	16
5	Do. Debs., 2 Series	100	114

Telegraphs and Telephones (*continued*):—

Last Div.	Name.	Paid.	Price.
4/	Chili Telephone, Ltd.	5	3½
$1½	Comcial. Cable, $100 Shs.	—	165
4	Do. Stg. 500-yr. Deb. Stk. Red.	100	105
2½d.	Consd. Telpehone Constr., &c., Ltd.	10/	½
6/	Cuba Submarine, Ltd.	10	7
10/	Do. 10 p.c. Pref.	10	15
2/	Direct Spanish, Ltd.	5	4½
5/	Do. 10 p.c. Cum. Pref.	5	10½
4½	Do. Debs.	50	104½
3/	Direct U.S. Cable, Ltd.	20	10½
2/6	Eastern, Ltd.	10	17½
3/	Do. 6 p.c. Cum. Pref.	10	18½
4	Do. Mt. Deb. Stk., Red.	100	125
2/6	Eastern Exten., Aus., & China, Ltd.	10	18½
5	Do. (Aus. Gov. Sub.) Deb., Red.	100	102
5	Do. do. Bearer	100	102½
4	Do. Mort. Deb. Stk.	100	128½
5	Eastn. & S. Afric., Ltd., Mort. Deb. 1900	100	102
5	Do. Bearer	100	102½
4	Do. Mort. Debs. ..1909	100	103½
4	Do. Mort. Debs. (Maur. Subsidy)	25	106½
5/	Grt. Nthn. Copenhagen	10	29
5	Do. Debs., Ser. B., Red.	100	101½
12/6	Indo-European, Ltd.	25	51½
6	London Platino-Brazilian, Ltd., Debs. 1904	100	108½
4/	Montevideo Telph., Ltd., 6 p.c. Pref.	5	2½
3/	National Telephone, Ltd.	5	5½
6/	Do. Cum. 1 Pref.	10	16
6/	Do. Cum. 2 Pref.	10	16
5	Do. Non-Cum. 3 Pref.	5	5½
3½	Do. Deb. Stk., Red.	100	101½
8d.	Oriental Telephone, Ltd.	1	½
4	Pac. & Euro. Tlg. Dbs., Rd.	100	106½
4/	Reuter's, Ltd.	8	8½
5/	Un. Riv. Plate Telph., Ltd.	5	4½
5	Do. Deb. Stk., Red.	100	106½
—	West African Telg., Ltd.	10	4
5	Do. 5 p.c. Mt. Debs., Red.	100	100½
—	W. Coast of America, Ltd.	10	½
3/	Western & Brazilian, Ltd.	15	12½
3/	Do. 5 p.c. Pref. Ord.	7½	7½
—	Do. Defd. Ord.	7½	4½
4	Do. Deb. Stk., Red.	100	106½
1/	W. India & Panama, Ltd.	10	½
6/	Do. Cum. 1 Pref.	10	7½
6/	Do. Cum. 2 Pref.	10	6
5	Do. Debs., Red.	100	106½
7	West. Union, 1 Mt. 1902($	1000	105½
6	Do. 6 p.c. Stg. Bds., Rd.	100	102½

TRAMWAYS AND OMNIBUS.

Last Div.	Name.	Paid.	Price.
1/6	Anglo-Argentine, Ltd	5	3½
6	Do. Deb. Stk.	100	125
4/	Barcelona, Ltd	10	11½
5	Do. Deb., Red.	100	105½
7/6	Belfast Street Trams.	10	16½
—	Blackpl. & Fltwd. Tram., £10 Shs.	8	13
10/	Bordeaux Tram. & O. Ltd.	10	11½
5	Do. Cum. Pref.	10	11
—	Brazilian Street Ry., Ltd.	2	½
—	British Elec. Trac., Ltd.	10	16
—	B. Ayres & Belg. Tram., Ltd., 6 p.c. Cum. Pref.	5	—
6	Do. 1 Deb. Stk.	100	—
—	B. Ayres. Gd. Nat., Ltd., 6 p.c 1 Deb. Bds., Red.	100	58½
5½	Do. Pref. Debs., Red.	100	94½
1/	Calais, Ltd.	5	1
—	Calcutta, Ltd.	10	3½
—	Carthagena & Herr., Ltd.	10	3
5	Do. Deb., Red.	100	90
5	City of B'ham. Trams., Ltd., 5 p.c. Cum. Pref.	5	5½
4	Do. 1 Mort. Debs., Rd.	100	106½
3/9	City of B. Ayres, Ltd	5	6½
2/3	Do. Ext. £5 Shs.	3	4
6	Do. Deb. Stk	100	145
1/4	Edinburgh Street Tram.	4	4
1/	Glasgow Tram. & Omni. Ltd., £9 Shs.	8	3
3/7½	Imperial, Ltd.	6	14½
3/	Lond., Deptfd., & Greenwich, Prefd.	5	3½
nil	Do. Defd.	5	1
10½	Lond. Gen. Omni., Ltd.	100	200
4	Do. Deb., Red.	100	114½

Tramways and Omnibus (*continued*):—

Last Div.	Name.	Paid.	Price.
4/9½	London Road Car	6	10½
28/6	Do. Red. 1 Mt. Deb. Stk.	100	108½
5	London St. Rly. (Prov., Ont.), Mt. Debs.	100	110
12/6	London St. Trams.	—	2
12/9	London Trams., Ltd.	10	10
6/	Do. Non-Cum. Pref.	10	10½
5	Do. Mt. Db. Stk., Rd.	100	99½
5	Lynn & Boston 1 Mt. 1924 $	1000	106
5	Milwaukee Elec. Cons. Mt. $	1000	100½
5	Minneapolis St. 1 Cons. Mt. $	1000	96
5	Montreal St. Dbs., 1908	100	109
4½	Do. Debs., 1922	100	107
6/	Nth. Metropolitan	—	11½
1/9½	Nth. Staffords., Ltd.	6	5
5/6	Provincial, Ltd	10	7
6/	Do. Cum. Pref.	10	13½
5	St. Paul City, 1937 $	1000	96
5	Do. Guar. Twin City Rap. Trans. $	1000	—
5/	Southampton	10	6½
5/	South London	10	5½
7/6	Sunderland, Ltd.	10	6½
4½	Toronto 1 Mt., Red.	100	106
2/6	Tramways Union, Ltd.	5	6½
4½	Do. Deb., Red.	100	109
2/6	Vienna General Omnibus.	5	5½
5	Do. 5 p.c. Mt. Deb., Red.	100	103½
4/	Wolverhampton, Ltd	10	6½

WATER WORKS.

Last Div.	Name.	Paid.	Price.
8/	Antwerp, Ltd.	20	22½
6/	Cape Town District, Ltd.	5	7
10½	Chelsea	100	325
5	Do. Pref. Stk.	100	178½
4½	Do. Pref. Stk., 1875	100	158½
4½	Do. Deb. Stk.	100	160½
5/6	City St. Petersburg, Ltd.	13	11
5/	Colne Valley	10	15½
4	Do. Deb. Stock	100	137½
£4	Consol. of Rosar., Ltd., 4 p.c. 1 Deb. Stk., Red.	100	91
8	East London	100	225½
4½	Do. Deb. Stk.	100	160
3	Do. Deb. Stk., Red.	100	106
37/6	Grand Junction (Max. 10 p.c.) "A"	50	117
18/9	Do. "B"	25	
18/9	Do. "C" (Max. 7½ p.c.)	25	54½
35/	Do. "D" (Max. 7 p.c.)	50	97½
4	Do. Deb. Stock	100	142½
13	Kent	100	360½
7	Do. New (Max. 7 p.c.)	100	215½
7/	Kimberley, Ltd.	7	4½
6	Do. Debs., Red.	100	104½
6	Do. Deb. Stk., Red.	100	107½
10	Lambeth (Max. 10 p.c.)	100	297½
7½	Do. (Max. 7½ p.c.), 50 & 25	—	230½
4	Do. Deb. Stock	100	142½
3	Do. Red. Deb. Stock	100	103
10/	Montevideo, Ltd.	20	16
5	Do. 1 Deb. Stk.	100	108½
5	Do. 2 Deb. Stk.	100	103½
132/9	New River New	100	442½
4	Do. Deb. Stk.	100	144½
4	Do. Deb. Stk. "B"	100	144½
4	Portland Con. Mt. "B," 1927	—	102½
8/	Seville, Ltd.	20	12
5/6	Southend "Addl." Ord.	10	17½
6	Southwark and Vauxhall	100	157½
6	Do. "D" Shares (7½ p.c. max.)	100	154½
5	Do. Pref. Stock	100	176½
4	Do. "A" Deb. Stock	100	141½
3	Staines Resvirs. Jt. Com. Gua. Deb. Stk., Red.	100	105
8/	Tarapaca, Ltd.	10	9
10	West Middlesex	100	302½
4½	Do. Deb. Stk.	100	162½
3	Do Deb. Stk.	100	106

INDIAN AND CEYLON TEA COMPANIES.

Acres Planted.	Crop, 1897.	Paid up Capital.	Share.	Paid up.	Name.	Dividends. 1894.	1895.	1896.	Int. 1897.	Price.	Yield.	Reserve.	Balance Forward.	Working Capital.	Mortgages, Debs. or Pref. Capital not otherwise stated.
	lb.	£	£	£	INDIAN COMPANIES.							£	£	£	£
21,240	3,128,000	120,000	10	3	Amalgamated Estates	—	*	10	5	3¾	8½	10,000	16,500	D52,950	—
		400,000	10	10	Do. Pref.	—	*	5	†5	9¾	5				
20,223	3,560,000	187,160	20	20	Assam	20	20	20	5	60	6¾	55,000	1,730	D11,350	—
6,150	3,278,000	142,500	10	10	Assam Frontier	3	6	6	—	7	8½	—	286	20,000	82,500
		142,500	10	10	Do. Pref.	6	6	6	†6	11	5½				
2,087	839,000	66,745	5	5	Attaree Khat	22	22	8	3	7	6	3,790	4,820	7,770	—
1,633	583,000	78,170	10	10	Borelli	4	4	5	—	7½	6¾	—	3,256	D270	6,500 Pref.
1,720	812,000	60,825	5	5	British Indian	6	5	5	—	4	6¼	—	2,920	12,300	16,500 Pref.
3,223	2,247,000	114,500	5	5	Brahmapootra	20	18	20	6	13	7¾	—	28,440	41,600	·
3,754	1,617,000	76,500	10	10	Cachar and Dooars	*	8	7	†7	10½	6¾	—	1,645	21,240	·
		76,500	10	10	Do. Pref.	*	6	6	†6	11¼	5¼				
3,946	2,083,000	72,010	1	1	Chargola	8	7	10	2½	¾	13	3,000	3,300	—	—
		81,000	1	1	Do. Pref.	7	7	7	3½	1⅛	5½				
1,971	942,000	33,000	5	5	Chubwa	10	8	10	†8	6	6¾	10,000	2,043	D5,400	—
		33,000	5	5	Do. Pref.	7	7	7	†7	6¾	5¼				
32,250	11,500,000	120,000	10	3	Cons. Tea and Lands	—	*	10	5	3¾	7¾	65,000	14,240	D191,674	—
		1,000,000	10	10	Do. 1st Pref.	—	*	5	†5	10⅞	4¾				
		400,000	10	10	Do. 2nd Pref.	—	*	7	†7	12	5¾				
2,230	617,000	135,420	20	20	Darjeeling	5½	5½	6	†5	22	5½	5,552	1,565	1,700	—
2,114	445,000	60,000	10	10	Darjeeling Cons.	—	*	4/2	—	6	—	—	1,820	—	—
		60,000	10	10	Do. Pref.	—	*	5	2½	9½	5¼				
6,660	3,518,000	150,000	10	10	Dooars	12½	12½	12½	2½	18	7	45,000	300	D32,000	—
		75,000	10	10	Do. Pref.	7	7	7	3½	16½	4¼				
3,367	1,811,000	165,000	10	10	Doom Dooma	11½	10	12½	‡12½	20½	6¼	30,000	4,032	—	10,000
1,377	582,000	61,120	5	5	Eastern Assam	5	nil.	4	—	3½	6¾	—	1,790	—	10,000
4,038	1,675,000	85,000	10	10	East India and Ceylon	*	nil.	7	—	8½	7¾	—	1,710	—	—
		85,000	10	10	Do. Pref.	*	6	6	3	11¼	5¼				
7,500	3,363,000	219,000	10	10	Empire of India	—	*	6/10	2½	11¼	—	15,000	—	27,000	—
		219,000	10	10	Do. Pref.	—	*	5	2½	10½	4¾				
1,180	540,000	94,060	10	10	Indian of Cachar	7	3½	3	†2	3½	5¼	6,070	—	7,120	—
3,050	824,000	83,500	5	5	Jhanzie	10	10	10	4	8	6¼	14,500	1,070	2,700	—
7,980	3,680,000	250,000	10	10	Jokai	10	10	10	5	17¾	5¾	45,000	990	D9,000	—
		100,000	10	10	Do. Pref.	*	6	6	3	14¾	4¾				
5,224	1,363,000	100,000	20	20	Jorehaut	20	20	20	—	58	6¾	36,220	2,955	3,000	—
1,547	504,000	65,660	10	8	Lebong	15	15	15	‡12½	16½	6¾	9,000	2,150	8,650	—
5,082	1,709,000	100,000	10	10	Lungla	*	10	6	3	8½	7	—	1,543	D21,000	—
		100,000	10	10	Do. Pref.	*	6	6	3	11	5½				
2,684	885,000	95,970	10	10	Majuli	7	5	5	—	6¾	7¾	—	2,606	560	—
1,375	380,000	91,840	1	1	Makum	—	—	2	—	1⅛	1¾	—	—	1,200	25,000
2,990	770,000	100,000	1	1	Moabund	—	—	*	—	½	—	—	—	—	—
		50,000	1	1	Do. Pref.	—	—	*	2½	1	5				
1,080	482,000	79,590	10	10	Scottish Assam	7	7	7	—	10½	6½	6,500	800	9,590	—
4,150	1,456,000	100,000	10	10	Singlo	5	5	5	1	8½	6	—	300	D5,200	—
		80,000	10	10	Do. Pref.	*	6½	6½	3½	13¾	5				
					CEYLON COMPANIES.										
7,970	1,743,824§	250,000	100	100	Anglo-Ceylon, & Gen.	—	*	5½	—	65	8½	10,992	1,405	D72,844	166,580
2,836	685,741§	50,000	10	10	Associated Tea	—	*	5	2½	7¼	6¾	—	164	2,478	—
		60,000	10	10	Do. Pref.	—	*	6	3	10½	5¾				
10,390	4,000,000	167,380	10	10	Ceylon Tea Plantations	15	15	15	‡15	26	5¾	84,500	1,516	D30,819	—
		81,080	10	10	Do. Pref.	7	7	7	‡7	16½	4¼				
5,722	1,542,700	55,960	5	3	Ceylon & Oriental Est.	5	8	7	—	2¾	7¾	—	230	D2,047	71,000
		46,000	5	5	Do. Pref.	6	6	6	3	5	6				
2,157	801,629§	111,330	5	5	Dimbula Valley	—	*	10	5	5½	10	—	—	1,733	6,250
		62,607	5	5	Do. Pref.	—	*	6	3	6¼	4¾				
11,496	3,635,000	298,250	5	5	Eastern Prod. & Est.	3	5	6½	‡7	6¾xd	5¾	20,000	11,740	D17,797	102,500
2,193	1,050,000	22,080	10	10	New Dimbula "A"	10	16	16	4	24	7	11,000	2,024	1,150	8,400
		55,710	10	10	Do. "B"	18	16	16	4	22	7¼				
2,572	570,360§	100,000	10	10	Ouvah	6	8	6	2	8	7½	4,000	1,151	D1,255	—
2,630	964,963	200,000	10	10	Nuwara Eliya	—	*	6	†6	10½xd	5¾	—	—	—	30,000
1,720	720,200§	41,000	10	10	Scottish Ceylon	15	15	15	‡10	17	6	7,000	1,252	D3,970	9,000 Pref.
2,450	750,000	39,000	10	6	Standard	12½	15	15	‡15	13	7	9,000	800	D14,012	4,000
		17,000	10	10	Do.	12½	15	15	‡15	22xd	7				

* Company formed this year. Working-Capital Column.—In working-capital column, D stands for *debit*. † Interim dividends are given as actual distribution made. ‡ *Total* div. § Crop 1896.

DIVIDENDS ANNOUNCED.

MISCELLANEOUS.

BROKEN HILL PROPRIETARY BLOCK 10 COMPANY, LIMITED.—Dividend No 57 of 2s. per share declared due.

NEW SHARE LOAN COMPANY, LIMITED.—Interim dividend at the rate of 10 per cent. per annum for the half-year ending 31st inst.

SWEETMEAT AUTOMATIC DELIVERY COMPANY, LIMITED.—Interim dividend for the quarter ended March 31, at the rate of 20 per cent. per annum, the same as for the corresponding period of last year.

SILVERTON TRAMWAY COMPANY, MELBOURNE.—2s. per share, payable on June 1.

GRAND HOTEL, MANCHESTER.—Dividend to be paid on the preference shares to March 31, and an Interim dividend at the rate of 8 per cent. per annum upon the ordinary shares for same period.

ASHLEY GARDENS PROPERTIES, LIMITED.—Interim dividend at the rate of 7 per cent. per annum on the ordinary shares for the half-year ended March 31.

PROVINCIAL TRAMWAYS COMPANY, LIMITED.—Interim dividend of 2s. 6d. per share on the ordinary shares for the year ended September 30.

COBURG HOTEL, LIMITED.—Further distribution at the rate of 12 per cent. per annum, which, with the interim dividend, will make a total of 10 per cent. for the year.

PROVINCIAL TRAMWAYS, LIMITED.—Interim dividend of 2s. 6d. per share on the ordinary shares.

BRUNNER, MOND & CO.—25 per cent. on the ordinary shares, and 7 per cent. on the preference shares; balance forward of £82,212.

WESTERN AND BRAZILIAN TELEGRAPH COMPANY, LIMITED.—Payment recommended of 6s. 9d. per share, making, with the interim dividend paid in November last, a total distribution of 3⅜ per cent. for 1897. This will give 6s. 9d. to the ordinary, 6s. to the preferred ordinary, and 9d. to the deferred ordinary shareholders.

REUTER'S TELEGRAM COMPANY.—Dividend of 2½ per cent., making 5 per cent. for the year, placing £5,277 to the reserve fund and carrying forward £411.

GRAND CENTRAL MINING COMPANY, LIMITED.—Interim dividend at the rate of 2s. per share, warrants for which will be posted on 28th inst.

BRILLIANT AND ST. GEORGE UNITED GOLD MINING COMPANY, LIMITED.—1s. per share, payable on 21st inst.

FRASER AND CHALMERS, LIMITED.—5 per cent. on the ordinary shares, payable on 24th inst.

BURBANK'S BIRTHDAY GIFT GOLD MINES, LIMITED.—Interim dividend of 1s. per share. Warrants will be posted on or after 31st inst.

BREWERIES.

STRETTONS DERBY, LIMITED.—Usual interim dividend at the rate of 7 per cent. per annum on the ordinary shares.

RAILWAYS.

SOUTHERN BRAZILIAN RIO GRANDE DO SUL COMPANY, LIMITED.—Dividend, at the rate of 6 per cent. per annum for the second half of 1897; £26,757 carried forward.

DELHI-UMBALLA-KALKA COMPANY, LIMITED.—Interim dividend at the rate of 5½ per cent. per annum for the half-year ended December 31 last, as compared with 3½ per cent. per annum for the corresponding period of 1896.

INSURANCE.

GUARDIAN FIRE AND LIFE.—5s. 6d. per share, making, with the interim dividend 8 per cent. for the year.

UNION ASSURANCE SOCIETY.—Directors have resolved to increase the dividend on the shares from 18s. to £1 per share, payable, 10s. half yearly in January and July, first payment to be made on July 11 next.

MARINE INSURANCE.—Dividend of £2 per share in respect for the year 1895 (the same dividend was paid last year), and £25,000 added to the reserve fund, which will then amount to £575,000. Of the accruing dividend, 10s. per share was paid in January last, and the balance will be Paid on July 11.

BANK.

ANGLO-EGYPTIAN, LIMITED.—Interim dividend of 4s. per share for the half-year ended February 28, payable on June 1.

A telegram from Brisbane states that "informations have been laid against the late directors and auditors of the Queensland National Bank in consequence of revelations of the Inquiry Commissioners."

The gold exported from New Zealand during April amounted to 15,220 oz., of the value of £56,948, as compared with 18,136 oz., of the value of £71,069, in the corresponding month of last year.

Austria has decided not to order a temporary suspension of the corn duties in consequence of the rise in the price of wheat.

The export of gold from the Cape during the month of April amounted to £1,145,520.

The German trade returns for the first quarter of this year show an increase of £3,396,850 in the exports and £8,444,750 in the imports.

Printed for the Proprietor by LOVE & WYMAN, LTD., Great Queen Street, London, W.C.; and Published by CLEMENT WILSON at Norfolk House, Norfolk Street, Strand, London, W.C

The Investors' Review

EDITED BY A. J. WILSON.

Vol. I.—No. 20. New Series. | FRIDAY, MAY 20, 1898. | [Registered as a Newspaper.] | Price 6d. By post, 6½d

CONTENTS

The Investors' Review.

The Passing of Mr. Gladstone.

When this aged statesman retired from office in 1894 we published an appreciation of his career to which there is little now to be added. His public life closed then, but none the less will the nation now mourn his departure, ripe in years though he was; and not the United Kingdom alone: all European peoples may well join in our mourning. He has been so long before the world, and has played so many parts in public life, that we of the younger generation who are familiar only with his later career, and with the apparent failure of the Irish policy to which he committed the Liberal Party in 1885, are apt to overlook some of the most striking and picturesque episodes in his life's history. Far has he travelled from that August day in 1841, when he stood before the electors of Newark, to seek re-election on his appointment as Master of the Mint in Sir Robert Peel's administration, and promised protection to the farmers, "adequate protection, through the means of the sliding scale." When Sir Robert Peel, driven by stress of circumstances and allegiance to the will of the people, became a free trader, Mr. Gladstone went with him, and in this aspect of Sir Robert's character he was a Peelite all his life through. Aristocratic in instincts and tastes, no man of his time listened more attentively to the wishes of the democracy, or more earnestly endeavoured to carry out in legislative enactments what he conscientiously believed to be its mandate. In this respect

Mr. Gladstone was always a follower and fanner of public opinion, seldom the creator of that opinion. Masterful he was in many of his attitudes; self-sacrificing, too, on occasion, and, we believe, always thoroughly conscientious. But his great strength lay in interpreting and bringing home to the common understanding, and, in spreading the knowledge of what he believed to be the policy of the hour most popular with the majority of the electorate. He was the servant of the people always, not their master; and as the people is given frequently to change its views, he also in the course of his long life presented many inconsistencies to the cold-blooded spectator of his words and deeds.

But Mr. Gladstone was not really inconsistent with himself, and we do not believe that he ever changed an opinion for any selfish object. No statesman England ever had displayed a greater sacrifice of self than he did when he made the mistake of obeying the mandate, as he took it to be, of the great body of the Irish people in introducing the Home Rule Bill. Events have proved that to have been a mistake, and those of us who ardently supported him then, for the most part have had since to admit that the Home Rule he meant to bestow upon Ireland was a gift for which the Irish people are, perhaps through no fault of their own, still unripe. Whatever his mistakes were, however, Mr. Gladstone was always, and all through his career, on the side of freedom, public liberty, the enlargement of knowledge, and the spread of wealth among the masses. When he grasped the principles of free trade, it was to assimilate them thoroughly, and he never swerved from them throughout his public life. In a like manner, and in spite of inconsistencies such as his strongly expressed sympathy with the Southern Confederacy at the outbreak of the Civil War in the United States, he never forswore his allegiance to the development of liberty in oppressed nationalities. Ten years after he stood before the electors of Newark as a landlord's man, a high Tory and convinced Protectionist, he was writing those letters about the cruelties of the Government of Naples which stirred a spirit that drove King "Bomba" from his throne; and in 1867, when taxed with his sympathy with the American Confederate States, he gave an explanation which shows that, however his instincts might have misled him, at the time he fully believed severance to be the best policy in the interests alike of State and individual freedom. "My sympathies were then," he wrote, "where they had long before been, where they are now—with the whole American people. I probably, like many Europeans, did not understand the nature and working of the American Union. I had imbibed justly, if erroneously, an opinion that twenty or twenty-four millions of the North would be happier and would be stronger (of course assuming that they would hold together) without the South than with it, and also that the negroes would be much nearer to emancipation under a Southern Government than under the old system of the Union, which had not, at that date, 1862, been abandoned, and which always appeared to me to place the whole power of the North at the command of the slave-holding interests of the South. As far as regards the special or separate interests of England in the matter, I, differing from many others, had always contended that it was best for our interest that the Union should be kept entire."

Some will say that this explanation proves the curious tendency of Mr. Gladstone's mind to a certain form of Jesuitical casuistry, and no doubt his mind was fundamentally ecclesiastical in its cast. He would have been a magnificent administrator as a bishop, and all through his career as a popular politician, at the head of a great Party, he never lost his taste for theological discussion any more than his love of Greek literature. He was not a great writer on any of the subjects that he took up, and his excursions into theological controversy will not be the incidents of his life by which he is likely to be most remembered. But he was a great orator, a man with a heart in him that his audience felt the beating of as they listened to the majestic roll of his eloquence and vehement declamation; and he was more than that: he was a great constructive statesman who has indelibly left his mark upon the laws and economic life of the land and the developments of our nineteenth century civilisation. Sadly, therefore, will the nation he loved so well and served so faithfully bid him a last adieu. All the deeper will be the sorrow as we contrast him with the men he has left behind him. He would have been a stranger in his own house had he lived to sit in the Parliament of to-day, a Parliament so degenerate as to have reduced legislation to an evening frivolity and administration to an emulative stampede in riotous waste. Four times was Mr. Gladstone Prime Minister, and he was plain William Ewart and a poor man to the end. It is best so.

It is the fashion with many, while admitting the departed statesman's greatness in a general way, to add, "but his foreign policy was weak." History, we imagine, will not endorse this verdict, which is merely the parrot repetition of a phrase the maledictions of disappointed quarrellers have dinned into our ears. It is not the time now to review the acts and influence of Mr. Gladstone in this sphere of politics, and he never was Foreign Minister. But at two points in his career he surely displayed imperial statesmanship of the noblest order. The Government of which he was the head in 1872 settled the *Alabama* dispute with the United States by arbitration, and in submitting to arbitration successfully resisted the inclusion of the indirect claims somewhat unscrupulously put forward by the Cabinet of General Grant. Surely that was a splendid deed well done in the interests of humanity. Where would the chance of the now fashionably-desired accord with the States have been to-day had Mr. Gladstone and his colleagues then listened to the war party, and, to gratify diseased vanity, put bloodshed between kindred over a question where we were wrong. And when he bowed before the justice of their position and gave back to the Boers of the Transvaal the freedom Sir Theophilus Shepstone and the Government of Cape Colony had filched from them, did he not open a better age for all the whites in South Africa than further attempts at Boer coercion could have done? Where would the talk of a federated South Africa have been but for that display of statesmanlike magnanimity? The answer is best supplied by the words of Lord Randolph Churchill: "The surrender of the Transvaal and the peace concluded by Mr. Gladstone with the victors of Majuba Hill were at the time, and still are, the object of sharp criticism and bitter denunciation from many politicians at home, *quorum pars parva fui*. Better and more precise information, combined with cool reflection, leads me to the conclusion that, had the British Government of that day taken advantage of its strong military position, and annihilated, as it could easily have done, the Boer forces, it would indeed have regained the Transvaal, but it might have lost Cape Colony."* This is the testimony of a political enemy, and its justness is attested by the peace which has stood the Jameson Raid and many things besides. We might go on, not always in eulogy, not forgetful that good arises out of men's evil, or mistakes, and evil sometimes of their good, even as life wars with death, and death with life, the universe through; but we have said enough for this time. A spirit essentially humane, and courageous in its humanity, has passed from among us for ever. All that is left for us is to mourn from afar, and hush contentions in sympathy for those near and dear to him, who in his loss have seen the light of their lives go out.

The Condition of Italy.

Whether the Marquis di Rudini succeeds in retaining power as the Minister of King Humbert on a policy of military rule or not, does not seem to us to much affect the future of Italy. Revolution has come there, and will stay until it accomplishes its work, repression or no repression. It has been coming for many a long day. Seldom or never have we alluded to Italian financial affairs in the pages of this REVIEW during the past six years, except to point out that all the conditions were making for revolution there. The truth of the matter is that Italian unity was brought about too hastily and too abruptly to weld all the country together as one. From the first the North and South have been jealous of each other, and the North, with its active, industrious population, has despised the South. From the first, clericalism has been as the fly in the ointment, marring all the efforts of the Civil Government to unite the people in allegiance to a superimposed constitutional Government on the British model. And, as Mr. Stillman quite rightly pointed out in last week's *Speaker*, nominal unity was effected without that purification of the system of taxation which alone could have made the central Government seem just to the masses of the people. Throughout Italy privileged classes have all along escaped their fair share of taxation, with the consequence that the steadily augmenting weight of that taxation has fallen with crushing effect upon the backs of the poor. Italy has been filled, almost from the day when it became one State, with cries of hunger and discontent arising from this poverty, and instead of devoting themselves to internal reforms Italian politicians of all shades of opinion, and above all Signor Crispi, spent their energies in trying to make Italy a great military power. In this aspect the new kingdom has all along been like a dwarf trying to keep pace with giants on the march, and now the people have risen in sullen revolt against miseries which have become unendurable. Dear bread was as the touchwood that kindled the fire, but all the materials for a great conflagration have been accumulating this generation back.

What is now really passing within the kingdom we cannot at present know. Telegraphic communication of an independent kind is entirely suppressed, and we are very doubtful if letters telling too much of the truth are allowed to come through the post. We may surmise, however, that displays of military force will be sufficient for the time being, and as long as the troops do not fraternise with the people, to put down open disorder in the cities; but the troops, we feel sure, cannot be counted on to continue this loathsome occupation very long. Already at Naples some soldiers sent to suppress riot fraternised with the rioters, and the same thing is sure to occur in other places, however much the Government may endeavour to distribute the army, so that each division of the troops has to deal with a population to which it is a stranger or antipathetic. But grant that the army is loyal to the House of Savoy and that the Marquis di Rudini, or another, is able to maintain order under martial law, it is none the less beyond the power of all the engines of Government together to force discontented people to work or to pay taxes. The removal of the bread tax itself, which must now be looked upon as permanent—at least, while wheat remains at anything like its present price, no Government in Italy would dare, even behind bayonets, to reimpose the 13s. a quarter duty on imported wheat which was to have been levied again, after a brief interval, from the first of this month. And if taxes fall off, the machinery of Government must come to pieces. The State, in other words, goes towards bankruptcy while maintaining order; and when it is bankrupt the second act of the revolution will come upon the stage. Either the Government, in order to obtain money, will have to force the privileged classes into bearing their full share of the public burdens, or it will have to default on the public obligations of the State; or yet again, it will have to allow the pay of the army on whose loyalty its existence depends from day to day to fall into arrears. Thus the difficulties which any Ministry set up in Italy must be prepared to encounter are only beginning, and the mere reiteration that "all is quiet in Italy," that "perfect order reigns in Milan," that "the disorders" here, there, and everywhere "have been suppressed," means very little. The question is, what can the Government do to so alter the conditions of life for the bulk of the Italian people as to make them contented, and to cease to flee from the country in hundreds of thousands per annum as from a land of pestilence? We are afraid none of the Italian Parliamentary statesmen whose names have been before the public in this generation can be trusted to do much towards solving this question. The position they are in is very similar to that occupied by the last few Ministries of Louis XVI. of France. They may scheme and devise and decree, but the sullen will of the people in the end must prevail. Italy, in short, has entered upon a period of revolution, the ultimate outcome of which no man can foretell. Its end may be the splitting up of the country into hostile republics as of old, or a tyrant may arise to place all the land under his foot. The only thing that appears certain is that the death-knell of the monarchy as now established has begun to ring.

Mr. Chamberlain's Birmingham Speech.

Mr. Secretary Chamberlain must be highly gratified at the success of his address to his supporters in Birmingham last Friday. His words have caused a cackle all over Europe and in the United States which

* "Men, Mines, and Animals in South Africa." p. 23.

exceeds any similar demonstration produced by recent utterances of his chief the Marquis of Salisbury. For a brief moment all men's thoughts were occupied with the attempt to discover what the speaker really intended. They have not benefited much by this exercise, and by the time these words appear most foreign politicians, at least, will probably have given up the attempt. Yet serious consequences might follow such a deliverance. We might even imagine Russian hostility increased by it, for the simple reason that the Czar and his foreign minister may not much relish being compared with the devil. To say that this style of address is not complimentary is little, to call it vulgar is not much, nor is it more adequately described as a "blazing indiscretion"; and yet we may hope that astute Russians understand Mr. Chamberlain and his limitations sufficiently not to be provoked into proceeding right off to the annexation of China. A gentleman who carries his political opinions about with him as a commercial traveller carries samples to suit all customers, eager to meet every requirement chance offers him, is not to be looked upon as a grave and responsible statesman. Sensible people in this country have long ceased to take Mr. Chamberlain that way, and therefore the effect produced by his language in foreign capitals and upon foreign journalists has struck us here as an effect ludicrously out of proportion to the cause. We have been almost as astonished, if not quite so delighted, as he himself doubtless is.

Apparently Mr. Chamberlain's three objects in making this speech—apart from the desire to advertise himself, which is always a dominant consideration with him—were to insult Russia at the same time that he proclaimed the impotence of England as against Russia; to provoke France, so as to render the chances of an agreement with her in the West African dispute, about which not one person in a million in this country knows anything, or cares a brass button, pretty nearly impossible; and to make the most of the fashionable fad of the moment, an "alliance" with the United States. The last of these aims may be praiseworthy enough in itself, but the advocacy of it was so overdone after dinner last Friday, and there are so many reasons why we should have no treaty of alliance with the American Union, that even this part of the speech may do more harm than good. What we require with the United States is friendliness of feeling, accord upon great questions of international policy, and a sympathetic trade rivalry. The last of these objects is yet a long way from attainment, and too great eagerness on our part to solicit a treaty of offensive and defensive alliance with the great Republic might serve to convince its politicians that we sought their support because of our failing strength under our free-trade policy.

Admit, however, that Mr. Chamberlain struck the right note on this point, caught the popular feeling at the flood, as it were, and expressed sentiments which his shrewdness led him to expect immense popular sympathy with, and what shall we say of his hostility towards France? He surely could not imagine that any body of people in this country has the slightest desire that a conflict with France should be provoked over West Africa, or even West Africa and Southern China together. As far as we can judge of the opinion of sensible men in the City of London no imaginable war could at the present time be more unpopular. To be sure the City, like the entire kingdom, is completely ignorant of the nature of the dispute in Africa, and cannot even guess what the French case is, not against us, but against the Royal Niger Company, whose political misdeeds we have fallen heir to at the price of £700,000. But business men do feel that neither in its present trade nor in its potential wealth is the whole of West Africa together worth to us the cost of one month's war with France. And some who know the history of the Royal Niger Company, its high-handed defiance of the Treaty of Berlin in attempting, by its regulations of 1894, to close the navigation of the lower Niger in its own interests, and who remember the hostility which Liverpool has again and again manifested against this company and its questionable mercantile policy, have a shrewd suspicion that the British case may not be so strong as it looks, or as Mr. Chamberlain wishes it to look, and that, therefore, if we quarrel with France over the settlement of boundaries in the Western Soudan, we are recklessly and wilfully doing wrong to injure our nearest neighbour, with whom our commercial interests are very large and becoming more closely interlinked every year. Happily, in our opinion, the danger of war with France is in reality lessened by an outburst like that of the Colonial Secretary. The Marquis of Salisbury is not dead yet, nor driven from his post, and he is a man of peace. Negotiations with France are controlled by him, and with him the ultimate decision rests. Being a man of peace, the probability is that when he has to encounter the strong resentment of the French Government at the attitude of Mr. Chamberlain he will smooth matters down by making greater concessions than, if left to himself, he would either have been asked to do, or have been disposed to accord.

In short, the never-resting conflict waged by the Colonial Secretary against the Prime Minister, a conflict of which the Birmingham speech forms the latest round, may be taken to explain in no small measure the high proficiency which Lord Salisbury has now attained in the art of making "graceful concessions." It is not his desire to embroil the United Kingdom in a great war. He is too able a man not to understand how disastrous such a war would be to our commerce, how deadly its consequences might become to our established institutions. His long experience as a politician has not left him merely a politician; he is capable of measuring some, at least, of the effects which war would produce on our delicate credit system, and could shrewdly guess what the expenditure of £200,000,000 taken out of the capital of the country, all now in active employment, would mean to British industrial supremacy. This being so, there is not much need to be alarmed about this wildly exciting tirade of the Colonial Minister's, even so far as France is concerned. It was not a wise speech, nor the speech of a statesman, and for that very reason, perhaps, the harm it has done will be transitory, or remain only in greater advantages secured by France in the settlement of the reiver's ownership of West Africa.

As to Russia, also, we need not much disturb ourselves. After all, our relations with that great Empire cannot be very much worse than recent events have left them. The traditional policy and suspicion of Russian designs have, under stimulus of recent events, revived to the full in the minds of the people of this country. We may lament this, and do lament it. There may be faults on both sides to account for the increased enmity, although we think the greater fault lies with Russia, so far at least as recent events in China enable us to distribute blame; but we have to accept the facts, much as the whale might accept the enmity of the buffalo. We do not suppose that the anger excited by Mr. Chamberlain's somewhat coarse attack will cause Russia to move one step faster in her march towards the complete absorption of Northern China; and if it quickens the determination of the Czar to absolutely close Ta-lien-wan to British commerce, that is really not much more than we deserve for treating as a trustworthy statesman an expert and clever-tongued man of affairs.

The Rand Mines, Limited, and its Group.—I.

The full reports of this company and of eight of the dependent companies which it finances and controls have now reached this country. They deserve very careful study at the hands of British speculators in mine shares. In his speech at the Rand Mines meeting Mr. Eckstein, the Chairman, made some comments which, we suppose, were meant as an answer to the criticisms passed by us upon the finance of these companies. His remarks seem to us singularly inadequate. It may, however, be well to quote what he says in order that this inadequacy may be the more easily demonstrated.

I have this week been favoured with a marked copy of the last INVESTORS' REVIEW, a paper in which the deep levels are demolished—entirely to the satisfaction of the writer. I think that the best answer would be to attach this article as an appendix to our report, but it will suffice if I refer to two points which show the extraordinary logic and the amazing ignorance of the writer—exceptional even in a professional critic. Because we have framed conservative estimates, because we have fulfilled our promises—says this sagacious writer—there is something mysteriously wrong: we must be picking the eyes out of our mines. That in No. 1 and No. 2 is equally worth preserving. Because we are "sorting our ore," because we are "working close and clean," and are thus "grading up" our ore by exercising every possible care to exclude waste rock—therefore we are robbing the mine and picking its eyes out. It appears that it is a crime to fulfil your promises, and a deception on your fellows to put up extensive and complicated machinery to enable you to reject worthless rock—you ought to mill it and bring down your yield. We have heard from hundreds of independent observers that nowhere in the world is more information given to shareholders and the public than on these fields, and nowhere in the world are the mines so honestly and conscientiously worked in the interests of shareholders; but you cannot please everybody, gentlemen, and one consoles one's self with the reflection, what must be the moral characteristics of the man who starts out with the freehand assumption that a whole community of people whom he does not know are radically dishonest? No, you cannot please everybody, nor is it necessary that you should try to do so, and there is sometimes a little grim amusement derivable from the position when—as now—some of your critics are indicting you—with abundance of evidence, of course—for making out everything worse than it is, so that you may buy up the whole industry, while others charge you with perpetrating an organised boom by forced returns, so that you may foist your worthless stock on a confiding public. The Rand Mines, Limited, which is responsible for the management of the subsidiaries, is not a jobber but an investor. What we have we hold, what we hold is enough. We shall pursue the even tenor of our way, aiming in our work at that level of profit which we reasonably hope to maintain, giving you the facts as we find them, whether it be in the development of our works or in the conditions for which the Government of this State is responsible.

We have no interest whatever of a personal or pecuniary sort in any of these properties; never had; and never intend to have any. The criticisms we pass, therefore, ought at least to be accepted as entirely unprejudiced from this point of view. Our only desire is to place before British investors considerations deemed by us worthy of their attention, in order that they may have some counterpoise to the steadily laudatory comments which fill the English Press from—we regret we have to say it—the *Economist* downwards. Not so very long ago the *Economist* published a remarkable supplement which we have filed for reference, and in which, amongst other things, the value of Rand Mine shares was appraised at 40. In other respects this old and eminently respectable paper has gone so emphatically over to the side of this particular group of South African mines as to give rise to one or two very silly and unjustifiable rumours, the existence which we lament and merely cite as an example of the mischief which may be done by indiscriminate and indiscreet eulogy of enterprises which at the very best must be regarded as highly speculative. All that seems to have happened to the *Economist* is to have lighted upon a contributor endowed with unbounded and unquestioning faith in the enterprises guided by the wisdom of Messrs. Wernher, Beit, & Co.

Let us, who have no bias of any kind, look at the matter simply as a speculation and see what its chances are, measured by the data made public. Mr. Eckstein, as the above extract shows, implicitly admits the truth of our charge that those of the Rand Mines group of mines already in operation do "pick" their ore. We, therefore, need not further labour that point; it is more profitable to turn to the finances of these companies as disclosed in their reports. We have gone through the whole of them very carefully, and have worked out the net revenue they would have to find in order to pay their debenture interest and 5 per cent. on the present market value of their shares. Were we to include the Rand Mines Company itself, at the price, not of 40, but of 30 for its £1 share, and the further capital of, say, £750,000 still required to bring eight of the companies it is financing into full operation, the net revenue necessary to pay 5 per cent. should be about £1,300,000 per annum. This is a rough and ready estimate, but plainly as unfair as rough, and we have no desire to be unfair. It is unfair, because as we shall demonstrate before we have done, the capital of the Rand Mines is in great measure a replica or concentrated essence of the capitals of all the mines which it foster-fathers and controls. To get at a more correct view of the future it will be best to eliminate the Rand Mines altogether, and deal only with the eight companies whose reports are published along with that of the Rand Mines, Limited. The answer may be given in tabular form thus:—

Name.	Price.	Market value of issued capital.	Amount required to pay 5 per cent. on quoted price.
		£	£
Glen Deep	2½	1,250,000	62,500
Rose Deep	6¼	2,500,000	125,000
Geldenhuis Deep.........	7	2,100,000	105,000
Jumper's Deep	4	1,629,164	81 458
Nourse Deep..............	5	1,874,670	93,733
Crown Deep	11	3,300,000	165,000
Langlaagte Deep.........	2½	1,625,000	81,250
D. Roodpt. Deep	3	873,000	43,650
		£15,151,834	£757,501

Upwards of three-quarters of a million, then, will be required to pay 5 per cent. on the market price of the shares of these eight companies, or rather not quite the market price in all cases, but at prices approximately those current as we write: some shares have been falling lately, and we have therefore "estimated low" like a Chancellor of the Exchequer manœuvring for a big surplus. But two omissions affect the value of this table. One is the debts of these companies and the other is their unissued shares. The interest on the debts, taken at 6 per cent. on the average—the Rand Mines, Limited, charges 7 per cent., and some companies have issued debentures as low as 5½ per cent.—comes to over £126,000 per annum. Add this to the amount required to pay 5 per cent. on the issued shares at given prices, and we get a total of £884,000 as the net income these must produce over and above what is required for depreciation, amortisation of debt, and reduction in the capitalised value of wasting properties in order to give 5 per cent. dividend to holders at prices, let us say, near those of the market. As we have no means of knowing whether the unissued shares possessed by most of the companies will be wanted or not, we, for the present, leave them out of account. Our estimate is therefore quite moderate; and now let us see what chance there is of its realisation.

Some little help in this direction is afforded by the number of stamps which the eight companies will have in operation when in full working order. To some extent we have to estimate this total, because it is very problematical whether all the stamps projected could ever be put into operation. Probably not enough black bondmen can ever be found to pick out the quantities of ore necessary to keep them steadily supplied, and in some cases we fear there is not enough ore to pick. Be this as it may, we give the companies the full benefit of their projected equipment, and find that, were the design in each case carried to completion, 1,040 stamps would be at work. The next question is how many tons of ore will one stamp crush per annum, and here again we cannot get an exact figure. Working up averages, however, and allowing about 330 days to the year—for of course the black slaves work Saturday and Sunday, and the mills are only stopped for cleans up—we think it a liberal estimate to put the crushing capacity per stamp at 1,500 tons per annum. For 1,040 stamps working this full time the output, therefore, would be 1,560,000 tons crushed. This would mean a very much larger output of ore from the mines, because, as not only Mr. Eckstein but various mine managers admit in their reports, the ore has to be carefully "sorted." In the Durban Roodepoort Deep, for example, "fully 30 per cent. of the ore mined will be sorted out as waste," the manager informs us, and in the Crown Deep, which is so far the richest of the mines brought into operation, there is also a considerable percentage of waste which may be expected to continue. To get 1,560,000 tons of payable ore would therefore require the extraction of perhaps quite 2,000,000 tons of rock, and, needless to say, this is a very formidable total.

Having arrived at the crushing capacity of 1,040 stamps working 330 days to the year, the next question is: what profit can reasonably be expected per stamp? and here also we have no very definite data. Two of the companies in this group now crushing, the Geldenhuis Deep and the Crown Deep, give very different results. The Geldenhuis Deep showed a profit last year of 12s. 8·256d. per ton, while that of the Crown Deep amounted to 18s. 11·452d. per ton. On this basis, it seems fair to estimate that, under existing conditions, the average profit will be 15s. per ton, and at 15s. per ton 1,560,000 tons of payable ore crushed will come, in round figures, to a net profit of £1,170,000. This, it will be seen, is more than enough to meet the 5 per cent. we have suggested as the minimum yield on the share capital of these companies at the moderate prices we have fixed. But it is not enough to pay 7 per cent. after deducting interest on borrowed capital as at present and without reckoning the £750,000 odd estimated to be still required to bring these eight companies to full fruition. Surely to say this is to demonstrate that there is no justification whatever for the current, or approximately current, prices of most of these shares, if not all. Five per cent. is not a sufficient return on any mining share. Holders of such ought to receive at least 10 per cent., and in addition, large sums ought to be available for depreciation of machinery and mine claims. Up to the present, as far as we can discover, nothing whatever is allowed for depreciation in the Rand Mines' group of properties, and the longer provision of this kind is delayed the heavier must the amount be ultimately set aside from revenue to write the capital cost down. We have given here only the merest outline of the calculations made by us, because it is not wise to burden readers with details of figures; but upon this basis, is it not reasonable to ask what ground the market has for expecting that higher prices ought to rule for the shares of any one of these companies? Our estimate, it must be remembered, is the best possible at all points, a best probably unattainable for years to come, if ever.

Take the Crown Deep as an example. It is the crack company, as we might call it, of the group, and what does its balance-sheet indicate? An extravagant rate of expenditure, machinery and plant alone standing in the books at £297,000, nothing whatever written off for depreciation, a debt of £110,000 to the Rand Mines, Limited, and a dead weight of £200,000 in fully-paid shares given for the claims. If the other shares of this company had not been sold at such extravagant prices as to give the company £500,000 for nothing it must by now have been absolutely helpless. In his report on this company to the directors, the manager estimates that when the bottom levels are reached the returns of the mine will show a decided improvement, although, for some months to come, he does not anticipate that the present yield of about 10 dwts. will be exceeded. But supposing the yield rises to 15 dwts. per ton on the average, will this company be able to pay dividends justifying the present price of the shares? To pay 5 per cent. on these shares plus interest on borrowed capital would require over £170,000 per annum. The profit of the company for the past year was £67,513. Double this and still there is not enough, quadruple it, and the net revenue is not sufficient to give shareholders at £11 per share 10 per cent. of their money, and to provide a reserve and sinking fund to meet the rapid exhaustion of the ore. We shall have a good deal more to say about these subsidiary companies and about the Rand Mines, Limited, itself in our next issue. Meanwhile, the following table exhibits the holdings of the Rand Mines, Limited, in the eight companies we have been dealing with, together with the total number of shares issued and the number in the hands of the public. It is, to our mind, a suggestive table which tempted ones would do well to ponder. Amongst other points which to the simple may appear obscure, it explains why the financiers interested in this group of companies are so lavish in expending capital, or market profits, in costly advertisements of the reports and balance-sheets of these companies. These advertisements at least serve the purpose of bribing the Press to hold its tongue. We trust they do not also conduce to making a free market for the shares. When, we may well ask, did ever the Mysore group of mines have to stoop to such tactics? A "free market"! How can that be with a company like Langlaagte Deep, or Jumpers or Glen or Nourse Deeps? Quotations in all such cases must be fictitious. Let readers note and beware.

Name.	Shares Issued.	Held by Rand Mines, Limited.	Held by Public.
Glen Deep	500,000	251,791	248,209
Rose Deep	400,000	143,720	256,280
Geldenhuis Deep	300,000	122,558	177,442
Jumpers Deep	407,391	270,741	136,650
Nourse Deep	374,934	268,382	106,552
Crown Deep	500,000	232,860	267,140
Langlaagte Deep	650,000	628,700	21,300
Durban Roodepoort Deep	291,000	59,000	232,000

Economic and Financial Notes and Correspondence.

LORD SALISBURY'S SPEECH AND SILENCE.

How hard driven the Prime Minister is at times by the zeal of his irrepressible and irresponsible colleague in the Colonial Office was curiously illustrated on Tuesday night by his Lordship's speech in reply to Lord Kimberley in the House of Lords. He had to say something about China and our position there, and on the spur of the moment, perhaps, he struck a new reason why we have "leased" Wei-Hai-Wei. Here are his interesting words :—

> Who shall say that China is for ever prostrate, because there are not men to give effect to the enormous material and physical forces she is possessed of? I should say what China wants is courage. One of my defences of the occupation of Wei-Hai-Wei is that it had a tendency to strengthen China against despair, and to give her courage, if the occasion should arise, to stand up against her enemies. The danger of allowing the occupation of Port Arthur to take place without any corresponding movement on our side was that China, or, at all events, large classes of Chinamen, would give themselves up to despair, and believe that the domination of one foreigner was the destiny from which it would be impossible to escape. It was our business to tell them that, so far as we were able to prevent it, that destiny would not overtake them. I do not know that we could have done anything better for restoring their courage, and I am quite certain that there was no more effective method of driving them to despair than by allowing Port Arthur to be occupied by the power that already stands over so enormous a portion of their frontier, and threatens them with so large a conquest.

In its way this is the best thing of Lord Salisbury's we have read for a long time and must possess an exquisite flavour of "drollery" to Englishmen in the East. To give "courage" to the Chinese mandarins; yes, that was it. Not your mere vulgar annexation, with a view to the partition of China, not "going one better" in rivalry with Russia. Nothing of the kind. China may be prostrate, as Mr. Chamberlain said, contrariwise to his chief, but "we mean to encourage her to get on her feet again." Excruciatingly humorous is this conception of our lofty mission of civilisation, and how mad we should all be were it to come true.

But what about France and the hissing, terrible Gorgon of her breeding, threatening us in our perambulations up and down the world and athwart it, looking for something more to appropriate? Ah! Lord Salisbury was not asked about this, and so he, wise man that he is, said never a word. German designs in the East, French intrigues in Southern and Western China, those unknown and apparently unknowable burning questions, pondering over which beats Mr. Chamberlain's brain like new wine, all were passed dumbly by. This also is strangely interesting, and may be taken to prove that Club society is quite right when it declares that the Prime Minister coaches his colleague to say the things he does not care to utter himself. Wise fellows these clubbites are, but we humble folk in the City rather wish at times that the punishment of the "branks" had not been abolished for scolds, and that the duties of ministerial exposition were not so very much distributed up.

THE INDIAN CURRENCY COMMITTEE.

Even the business worm will turn, it would seem. Who started the petition which has been influentially signed to present to the Government praying, it to improve the composition of the Indian Currency Committee now sitting, we do not know, but it was a step highly necessary to be taken even if it serves no other purpose than to afford bankers and merchants an opportunity of entering their protest against the manner in which Lord George Hamilton has selected its present members. It is an inexpressible misfortune for India and our interests there that a "fushionless" being of this description should be at the head of the India Office. His Currency Committee is an adequate expression of his own feebleness, as we pointed out at the time it was announced, and of nothing else. There are not more than three men competent for the purpose in view upon it, for we do not consider Sir Henry Fowler in any degree qualified to deal with subtle questions of exchange, and of the relation of a currency to the wants and wealth of a people. And the way Lord George has stuffed upon this committee a majority of incompetent advisers, doctrinaires, and half-pay Indian officials, eager above all things for a high rupee, is nothing short of scandalous. Whether any attention be paid to the petition or not, the Government may rest assured that business men will not forget its conduct in this matter when the next election comes round.

THE LATE MR. OTTOMAR HAUPT.

We join sadly with the *Financial Times* in its expressions of regret over the loss of this gentleman, its Paris correspondent and an able and amiable man. When we knew him—many years ago now—in London, he was an argumentative bimetallist, and defended the heresy with all his fervid Teutonic ingenuity. But he was not a mere German Jew word-slave or dialectic windlestraw. He had sense and reasonableness, and so was able to escape from the snares such entangle themselves in, and to become, as the *Financial Times* says, one of the acutest living defenders of the Gold Standard. Indeed, he went too far for us in this direction also, and his criticisms on all things often lacked balance. But he was a most painstaking writer on bullion and exchange, and quite the greatest authority on arbitrage in his day. His book, "Arbitrages et Parités," has passed through many editions, and the last one, issued in 1894, was a large octavo volume of over 900 pages, packed full of most useful information. We shall very much miss his banking and Continental finance letters to the *Financial Times*, and sincerely mourn his loss.

THE NEW CANADIAN FAST MAIL SERVICE.

Last week's *Syren and Shipping* prints "an advance copy" of the prospectus drawn up, setting forth the object and chief features of this project, and giving some particulars regarding the capital required. It asserts, in doing this, that the prospectus is being circulated for underwriting purposes, and therefore it is really public property. Assuming this to be correct, we find that the entire capital is put at £2,125,000, divided into £700,000 4½ per cent. first mortgage debenture stock, and 140,000 £10 shares, half of which will be called 6 per cent. cumulative preference shares. The odd £25,000 consists of £1 deferred shares thrown to the promoters, and these will take one-third of the remaining profits after 10 per cent. has been paid on the ordinary shares and provision made for a reserve fund, &c. A most fanciful estimate of the profits to be obtained from this new undertaking is embodied in the prospectus, from which it appears that 10 per cent. is certain to be earned on the ordinary shares right off by the help of the Government subsidy of £154,500 to be granted for ten years, and of which Mr. Chamberlain has kindly arranged that we, the taxpayers of this country, should find £51,500.

When this project came up originally we attacked it with severity and described it as a mad project, without the slightest reasonable foundation or hope of profit. We hold that opinion still, although recently we have been mockingly inviting the Canadian Government to hurry up and take its chance while Mr. Dingley was throttling shipping entering United States ports. Mr. Dingley, however, has not been allowed to do this, and such slender chance as his proposed tonnage duty might have given to a scheme of this kind must now be abandoned. There can be no sufficient traffic of a remunerative kind for this line, and it is still only part and parcel of the various enterprises which the Canadian Pacific Railway "ring" have set on foot for the purpose of keeping that undertaking well before the public in an apparently prosperous condition. The Pacific mail service of that company is worked at an enormous loss, and must be so worked because it can never form a large freight-carrying route. If Canada chooses to pay for this kind of luxury, we certainly could have no objection ; but as taxpayers here we have the right, and it is our duty, to protest against the appropriation of our hard-earned money to any extent in furtherance of disastrous projects such as this. Not only is there no prospect of paying traffic for such a line—if for no other reason than because nobody who could help it will go to the winter ports of Canada at Halifax and St. John in order to embark for Europe, or in order to proceed from Europe into the interior of the American continent—but the floating palaces to be put on the route under the contract have no freight capacity to speak of and cannot possibly compete with the slow boats which already occupy the field and prove more than adequate for all the traffic available, even with the stimulus such traffic receives through Portland being their winter port. To this place patriotic Imperialists, and what not, have decreed that the fast mail line must not go. It would be a crime in the eyes of Jingoes on both sides of the water to let it go, at least until money begins to be lost.

We have something else to say, however, about this scheme, and that is to ask on what grounds the projectors of it, the High Commissioner of Canada, Lord Strathcona and Mount Royal and his associates, have agreed to pay down a lump sum of £1,980,000 to the contractors, holders of the "concession," Messrs. Petersen, Tate, & Co., of Newcastle-on-Tyne, they undertaking to deliver four ships by a certain date. What guarantee does this comparatively obscure, and, so far as we can learn, not oppressively wealthy, shipping firm give to the company that it can furnish value for the money? Apparently, four steamers are to be put upon the route of 10,000 tons capacity each, and as the *Syren* points out, this is equivalent to paying for these steamers half a million each. Will Lord Strathcona and Mount Royal venture to maintain that the finest boat that could be built, of the capacity and with the appointments stipulated, ought to cost anything like this sum, and if he cannot do that, is he not lending himself to a miserable job, whereby a number of unknown people in Canada calculate upon pocketing a large amount of money in the shape of solid "profit" —the difference between the real and the lump nominal cost of the vessels? What was to hinder this company, if honestly gone about, to raise its capital in a straightforward manner as wanted, and to contract directly with a shipbuilder or shipbuilders, of character and good repute, for the ships it required to be built, at the market price? We should very much like to hear what a first-class shipbuilder thinks of this part of the business, and for the present we shall leave the subject here, trusting that nobody with any regard for his money will be found to underwrite a penny of the capital until points like these, now dark, are made plain. Had the project been good in itself, the way in which this capital is to be raised and paid away ought to have damned it in the eyes of the investing public.

Germany and China.

There have this week been great doings at Peking in which Prince Henry of Prussia played a leading part. If Germany is slow to open the door for us at Kiao Chau, she has been prompt to throw wide the gates of the Summer Palace. As the *Times'* correspondent puts it, the visit of Prince Henry has "broken down the last barrier hedging the Court of Peking." Henceforth the Palace will be more open to western ideas as well as western personages. The Prince's first visit was to the Dowager Empress, who appeared "unpainted and unveiled" behind a table in the "form of an altar." She was gracious and unembarrassed, as became the real ruler of China ; but the Emperor, poor man, who only nominally rules, was embarrassed and nervous when his turn came to meet the Prince. His hand trembled ; he started when the German escort beat their drums ; but he subsequently regained some of his self-possession. The ordeal was not so terrible as it seemed. The blushing Emperor survived it, and returned to the obscurity of his splendid dwelling. When will he next emerge from this obscurity, and who will then be his interlocutor? What will be the ultimate upshot of this unique visit to Chinese Royalty? Will it remain a mere curiosity, or is it to be an epoch-making incident in the history of China? It would be hard to say. The Empress is now to receive the wives of foreign ministers. Perhaps this is as much as can be expected in the meantime. The occupants of the hitherto sacred palace have to learn to walk. It will be some time before they get accustomed to the hurry-scurry of modern advancement.

But China outside the palace has to go forward with more celerity. Western energy has now a firm grip of the country. There will be protests against the rapidity. There will probably be more rioting such as there has been at Sha-Shi and in other parts of the Yangtse Valley. But these cannot be regarded as of serious importance. The collection of the likin by the Customs authorities is not a popular measure, especially with the ruling mandarins, to whom it means a considerable loss in their customary blackmail. They cannot give that up without a growl. But such riot and grumbling cannot stop the advance of commerce. We have just received the first of our Consular reports from Sha-Shi. It is an interesting, even a picturesque document, and informs us that this port on the Yangtse was opened on September 26, 1896. The foreign community consisted at the end of 1897 of seventeen persons, including two Britons. Of the shipping of the port 56·66 per cent. was British, the remaining 43·34 per cent. Chinese. The value of the native and foreign exports for the year was £20,326, and the imports £27,183. These are the real beginnings of western civilisation on the Yangtse. Their development will be rapid. Here, too, is a most significant achievement—the conclusion of arrangements for the construction and working of an important system of railways. The contract has been given, with the full concurrence of the Chinese Government, to the eminent firm of Messrs. Jardine, Matheson, & Company. The first section, between Shanghai and Nanking, will be begun at once. It is to be 200 miles long; goes through a district of great fertility, as the special correspondent of the *Standard* assures us, and is the first railway in China that has been constructed and worked under British auspices. This is one of the most important steps yet taken in the development of the country. It will be a security for the rapid advancement of trade, in which, however, the shrewd Chinaman will be sure to have his full share.

MR. GEORGE LIVESEY AND THE GAS LIGHT AND COKE (CHARTERED) COMPANY.

We have received a letter and some papers from Mr. Livesey which, taken together, prove that we were misled last week in estimating the value of the Gas Light board's retort to his criticism, and believed him on *ex parte* evidence to be guilty of inconsistency. We are sorry that we should have misconstrued his attitude in any degree, because we have sympathy with the object he has in view. There can be no doubt that the Gas Light Company is in an unsatisfactory position, and it would be a pity were its stockholders to be diverted by anything resembling a personal wrangle from giving their attention to effecting reforms in the present methods of business or system of management, a system we have at some point or other called in question for years back. Left where it is, following the policy now adopted, it must go from bad to worse, and stockholders have to face a further reduction in their dividends. The cardinal error from the public's point of view is raising the price of gas; but that error springs from maladministration under which the company's revenue-earning power has been impaired. It would be a great pity if the largest gas manufacturing company in the world were to drift into a condition where drastic measures and the submission to severe losses in capital and income by the stockholders would alone prove adequate to restore it to health. Upon this question of the price of gas it will be interesting to quote the following extract forming the concluding portion of a letter written by Mr. Livesey and published in the *Journal of Gas Lighting* of the 10th inst. :—

The surest test is the price of gas. The Chartered Company use well over two million tons of coal a year, and water gas in addition, and charge 3s. per 1,000 cubic feet. There is only one concern in the three kingdoms using over 100,000 tons that charges a higher price, viz., Dublin; but theirs is probably the worst district in existence, for they have only about twenty-six customers per mile of main. West Ham comes next with forty-two; while the Chartered Company in 1896 had 140. There is no other large concern charging so much as 3s. I give all those using 20,000 tons and upwards that did so in 1896 (the last return available) :—

		Tons.		Price. s.	d.
Chartered	(about)	2,140,000	(now)	3	0
Dublin		133,000		3	5
West Ham		86,000		3	0
Tottenham	(about)	40,000		3	0
Hastings	"	40,000		3	0
Preston (18-candle gas)	"	40,000	(about)	3	0
Norwich		31,000	"	3	5
Oxford		29,000		3	0
Cork		28,000		3	6
Bournemouth (Gas and Water)		24,000		3	3
Exeter		23,000		3	0
Eastbourne		22,000		3	0
Swansea		21,000		3	0
Mitcham and Wimbledon		21,000		3	8
Folkestone		20,000		3	0
Richmond		20,000		3	0
Tunbridge Wells		20,000		3	0
Guildford		12,000		3	0
Watford		9,000		3	0
Falmouth		3,400	(less 2½ per cent.)	3	0

The above are all companies. There are only two corporations using 20,000 tons or more, and none over 44,000, charging more than 3s. per 1,000 cubic feet, excepting one or two in Scotland that supply 22-candle gas and upwards. There are many small undertakings charging less. I give a few examples, omitting all charging exceptionally low prices, and all the large companies, who charge from 2s. 6d. down to about 1s. 8d. :—

	Tons.	Price. s.	d.
Brentford	141,000	2	11
Crystal Palace District	103,000	2	7
Brighton	75,000	2	9
Croydon	59,000	2	8
Wandsworth and Putney	49,000	2	4
Rochester	41,000	2	6
Kingston	33,000	2	10
Ipswich	23,000	2	10
Scarborough	22,000	2	9
Maidstone	21,000	2	4
Worcester	20,000	2	7
Isle of Thanet	17,000	2	8
Dover	16,000	2	9

None in either list, except Preston and Swansea, is near coalfields, and scarcely any of them can get coal so cheap as the Chartered. Brighton has been harder hit by the electric light than the Chartered. In many of these cases the price has been reduced since 1896—Wandsworth, for instance, to 2s. 2d. per 1,000 cubic feet; but I believe there is no case in the United Kingdom of an increase of price since then, except the solitary Chartered, the greatest gas company in the world. Whether or not this justifies my criticism of the management, I leave your readers to judge. The "Reply" has given no answer.

KRUGER THE UNDAUNTED.

As was natural, on the occasion of his being sworn in as President of the South African Republic for the fourth time Mr. Kruger made an explanation of his future policy and gave a justification of his past. It was a stirring, if somewhat primitive scene, that in the open before the Government House at Pretoria. The houses were decorated, the burghers were armed—perhaps it is their custom—and even the "music that soothes" was not wanting. The members of the Raad were present of course, and so were the public officials. Even the "foreign diplomatic body" graced the scene, and were assured by President Kruger with all the solemnity of a sovereign ruler, that, as it had been in the past, so it would be his desire in the future to remain on friendly terms with all nations. Much of his speech—of which we have as yet only a comparatively brief summary—seems to have been taken up with the grievances of the mining community, who refuse to be comforted by the prospective promises of the President or satisfied with his defence of what he has done in the past. They are rather sulky and sullen, and cannot or will not see that the President has done anything for the mining industry. He is, they say, bringing the country to bankruptcy, and will not listen to their advice as to the way to take to avoid it.

Well, we should not like to pronounce any strong opinion until we have seen the full text of the Presidential address. But certainly it seems that his mining critics are rather too hard upon the President. He was able to show that £200,000 per annum had been taken off the railway charges for the carriage of mining machinery, &c.—a matter of no small moment, one would have thought, to mine-owners. Besides that, there had been reductions in the Customs dues amounting to £750,000 a year, principally affecting the necessaries of life and articles used in mines. There had recently been effected a reduction of ten shillings a case on dynamite, and negotiations were in progress for a further reduction—possibly of five shillings a case. Negotiations had also been entered upon with Portugal as to the supply of labour. These are very substantial concessions, and ought at least to be acknowledged. There was, perhaps, something brusquely naïve in his threat to banks and other institutions which had advanced money to poor people on mortgage, and now threatened to foreclose; but there may be reason for it; and, if he can, as he promises, put a check upon the formation of bogus companies, it is not for miners or any one else connected with the Republic to complain. President Kruger is very conservative—stiffnecked, perhaps, and peradventure rather too prone to boggle about progress and reform; but at least he shows that he is beginning to see the necessity for advancing. He is undaunted by the opposition. The mining interest might make more of the President if they humoured him more. His views as to the promotion of agriculture should be received with something better than sneers. Boers are poor farmers, but if he can help them by irrigation, is it not worth the trial? Agriculture is the real backbone of the country, and, as President Kruger said recently, "When the gold industry has passed away, agriculture will remain the backbone of the country." Gold mining is vastly important, but in the nature of things it is temporary and passing. It will not establish or support a State. Agriculture, which begets trade and commerce, is essential for that. It is desirable for even mine-owners to reflect that in South Africa we cannot at once eject the Dutch. We must live with them and work with them, and business men should carry themselves accordingly.

The Chignecto Railway.

We have received from Mr. A. D. Provand, M.P., a pamphlet containing the history of this unfortunate enterprise and of his endeavours to bring about some settlement with the Canadian Government. It forms a melancholy story, and we have read it with pained surprise. When the project was originally launched we treated it as a highly speculative one and doubted very much whether it would ever pay. It has never been brought to the proof. Owing to the Baring crisis money difficulties arose, and the company could not raise the funds to finish the railway. After it had spent some £750,000 further work was stopped and the Dominion Government, taking advantage of a penal clause in the contract, repudiated its liability to pay any subsidy, and practically confiscated this money. That is the plain English of the transaction in a few words. At the time this ill-fated project was conceived, the people of Canada were in the hands of one of the most daring and unscrupulous gangs of "boodlers" that ever sat upon and sucked the blood out of any people. Morally, therefore, we are disposed to doubt whether Canada could be held responsible for this transaction, looked at from the people's side; but in honour that young nation is bound to take cognizance of the complaints made by investors here who, in all good faith, found so much money, believing that they had to deal with a Government which would keep its engagements even when to do so involved it in loss. The proper course, we imagine, is for the Dominion Government to agree with the representatives of the railway company, and appoint arbitrators to investigate both sides of the case, and settle the amount of damages to be paid. It would be shameful were the matter to rest where it is.

Long's Hotel Company.

An extraordinary circular has been issued by the directors of this company to their shareholders. One of their number, a Mr. Loibl, has undertaken to buy out the company, paying 45s. in cash for each share. Why this offer is made is explained in paragraph 4 of the circular, which runs: "Mr. Loibl, being the lessor to the company of the hotel premises, would on completion take a complete surrender of the lease, and would then be in a position to make arrangements for dealing with the property in a manner more favourable than any open to the company, which is bound by the terms of the existing lease. Mr. Loibl is thus in a position to offer to the company better terms than could be expected from any other purchaser; he will, however, have to make large financial rearrangements, and undertake onerous and uncertain liabilities, and he has requested the directors to state clearly that in making an offer so favourable to the shareholders he expects to reap some personal profit by his subsequent dealings with the property." There is a charming frankness about the conclusion of this quotation that almost disarms criticism. If Mr. Loibl were a generous outsider there might be nothing to say, but we find that that gentleman figures in the original prospectus as the vendor, as well as the lessor of the hotel. Originally the business was floated as a public company in the end of 1888, with a capital of £65,000 in £5 shares, nearly all of which went as purchase money. In 1893 it was found necessary to write off half the capital, reducing the shares to £2 10s. Now, before ten years are over, we find the vendor anxious, or willing, to buy back his old property for less than half what was paid him at the start. True, the lease is ten years shorter, and the business has not been profitable. Why this generosity, then? We have had some startling examples of this method of financing of late, but, somehow, they do not inspire us with much belief in their philanthropy. Before Mr. Loibl's offer is accepted shareholders should insist on further information. Why, as a director of the company, does not Mr. Loibl devote his energies towards making his prospective profit for the benefit of his shareholders? Why cannot he alter the lease as lessor, if that document stands in the way? Two-thirds of the shareholders have agreed to the scheme, the directors state in their circular. It seems to us that the remaining third should refuse their support unless more sufficient reasons for its acceptance are forthcoming, and should combine to force an investigation.

Balance-Sheet Assets.

How often does a company hug as an asset some worthless item in order that the balance-sheet may look well. Such delusive book-keeping is frequently the secret of apparent big reserves, which lapse into uselessness when put to the test. A strong board of directors, however, ought to have none of this, and ought to write off out of a balance-sheet everything which has been lost or become worthless. A good instance of the manner in which the pruning knife must be used at times is furnished by the London and South African Exploration Company. Going back to the end of 1894, it will be found that in addition to the land and houses representing the investment of the company's capital, it had £91,019 of other assets, including £74,070 of debtors for claim leases from two diamond companies, and for surface rents. This large sum of £74,070 swelled out the balance-sheet beautifully, so that the company claimed a balance in hand of £69,024. Since then the board has had to examine into the position of those assets, as the two diamond companies went irretrievably into liquidation and the arrears of surface rents were not met. By liberal writing down the £74,070 of doubtful assets has shrunk to a mere £5,145, and the total assets outside the property and estates has fallen to £60,169, the chief asset now being £31,760 of investments. In this way a wholesome revision has taken place, and, although at a first glance the company looks poorer, it is probably the richer for the pruning down of the book assets, supposing, of course, that the "investments" are well placed. As to this we have no knowledge.

Dividend Payments on Instalments.

Time after time we have pointed out the dangerous manner in which profits can be manipulated under this principle. The report of the Brampton Brewery Company affords still another instance of the deceptive character of the results attained under this system. The company was issued last June, and, of course, some time elapsed before the various denominations of capital were fully paid. The report, however, shows that the profits were taken for the whole twelve months ended March 31 last, and interest was, of course, paid to the vendors for the interregnum, but that did not amount to the difference between the dividend and interest charges actually paid on the company's received capital and the amount the fully-paid capital would have required. By dint of paying the interest charges and a dividend of 8 per cent. to the shares merely upon the amount paid upon them, and a lump sum of £4,661 to the vendors for interest on the purchase money, only £14,773 was absorbed, whereas if the full interest, charges, and dividend for the year had been met, the sum required would have been £17,900. The company certainly did not distribute the difference, putting as it did £2,000 to reserve, and writing £1,117 off preliminary expenses, so no complaint can be made on this head. Still, to the ordinary man the tale went forth that the company, after paying 8 per cent. on the ordinary shares, was able to set aside these sums, whereas, in reality, if it had paid the dividend and interest charges for the whole year, there would only have been a small balance left.

THE SOUTH WALES STRIKE.

It is nearing its end. The colliers have consented at last to give their representatives who may meet the employers the plenary powers these have all along insisted upon. There is, then, a probability of an early meeting of a conference on the lines suggested by the President of the Board of Trade. It would seem also probable that the miners have suffered sufficiently to induce them to be more reasonable in regard to the terms of settlement. The loss they have by their obstinate shortsightedness inflicted upon the community is practically incalculable; but some slight indication of its possible extent may be gathered from the loss of traffic suffered by the three Welsh railways chiefly affected by the dispute. During the last nineteen weeks the receipts of the Taff Vale Railway have been £51,291 less than in the corresponding period of last year. During eighteen weeks the Barry line similarly lost £24,429; and the Rhymney, in nineteen weeks, £9,713. The total decrease is £85,438. The Great Western Railway, which has important mineral branches in South Wales, has also lost about £12,000; and the stocks of each of these lines have gone down a point or two in quotations as compared with last year. But of course this is a "mere fleabite" as contrasted with the loss in wages, the loss to the employers, and the dislocation in business, not only in South Wales, but throughout the country. The worst of it is that this strangely irrational quarrel seems almost to destroy the hope of better things in the future. It was the stupidest and least responsible section of the Welsh colliers that voted this strike in opposition to the advice of the men's most prudent leaders. Fortunately this sort of reckless unintelligent irresponsibility has resulted this time in disastrous failure. It may possibly serve as a lesson. We sincerely hope so, but repeated failures of a similar kind, though not on so gigantic a scale, have gone far to convince us that your "striking" workman is not always, not even generally, the kind of being who can be taught by experience.

"FINANCIAL AGENTS!"

No one will be disposed to quarrel with the sentences pronounced by the Recorder of London on Messrs. Marcus Leon and Blumenthal of eight and six years' penal servitude respectively. The practice followed by these gentlemen was to introduce to each other impecunious persons, and induce them to draw and accept bills, which they subsequently presented to bankers to be discounted as genuine trade bills. They carried on their "business" under the name of Blumenthal & Company and received sums ranging from £25 to £1,000 as commission for these introductions from both drawers and acceptors. After they had managed to discount these bills, and had deducted their commission, the proceeds were equally divided between the drawers and acceptors. When the bill matured the parties went bankrupt, to the no small loss of the unfortunate discounter. The swindles had been carried on since 1886, and no less than £2,000,000 worth of bills had been thus put in circulation. Their operations were brought to light in the bankruptcy proceedings of one Burckhart, who, when in very low water financially, was attracted by the firm's advertisement. The magnitude of the operations and the ease with which they were carried on for nearly twelve years are certainly extraordinary, and it is to be hoped that the exemplary sentences now imposed will have their effect in intimidating rogues who may contemplate similar operations.

BREWERY ISSUES.

We are not surprised that some of the holders of preference shares in the Camden Brewery Company objected to the authorisation to raise £200,000 further in loans or debentures. By incurring such indebtedness, which will certainly be done, the debenture capital of the company will be raised to £350,000, and the share capital will still stand at £270,000, of which only £120,000 is in ordinary shares. The £150,000 of preference capital, therefore, has to stand all risks of the new acquisitions proving unprofitable, while if they bring increased profits the poor preference shareholder will obtain no benefit. The new debenture capital will probably cause an increase of £8,000 per annum in the fixed charges, and, with the prices of public houses at their present level, it is quite conceivable that some of the purchases may prove bad bargains. This £8,000 in interest will, however, have to be paid, and in that case the margin in front of the preference interest might be seriously encroached upon.

THE WORKMEN'S COMPENSATION ACT.

This measure comes into force on July 1 next; and to all appearance it will have an effect upon trade and prices which probably nobody contemplated when the Act was under discussion in Parliament. The insurance companies have been carefully considering the matter, and have arranged a table of rates which are about eight to ten times higher than Mr. Chamberlain and his friends estimated when the Bill was before the House of Commons. The Colonial Secretary has been surprised and even shocked at the presumption of the insurance companies in going so far beyond his calculations; and he has been scolding them in good set terms for what he considers their "ridiculous" conduct in this respect. But we presume the companies will prefer the opinion of their actuaries to that of Mr. Chamberlain, and will continue to be guided by it accordingly. If experience should prove that the rates now adopted are too high, competition may be trusted to bring them down to a more natural level. But so serious a view do the companies take of the character of the risks under the Compensation Act, that they have resolved to deal with them as with fire risks, and to distribute the liability among various companies. Mr. Chamberlain's floutings have fallen on stony ground.

But manufacturers and others would seem to have also come to the conclusion that the insurance companies are seeking too much; and trades are already banding themselves together for the formation of mutual insurance associations. The experiment is not without risk, but with careful, prudent management there is no reason why such associations should not succeed. The railway companies seem to be making no special preparation for their protection under the Act: they are to meet this compensation in the same way as they meet the compensation to passengers in case of accidents. But coalowners are to combine for so much of the cost as it may not be convenient to throw upon the consumer. Engineers, shipbuilders, shipowners, are all contemplating mutual combination, and it is not impossible that the Shipbuilders' and Engineers' Federation will form the nucleus for these trades. These mutual insurance associations seem likely to have another and somewhat far-reaching influence. The combination thus assured among employers will no doubt, in time, be utilised in the settlement of trade and industrial questions. Trade-unionism may or may not be "played out," but it will certainly have now to meet and cope with more and better organisation among the employers than they have ever yet encountered. That is one of the probable effects of the Workmen's Compensation Act which was not contemplated even by its framers. Another effect will apparently have to be faced. The Sheffield coalowners are already asking enhanced rates on renewal of contracts to cover the cost of possible loss under the Compensation Act. Scotch coalowners are said to contemplate similar action, so that no small part of the cost to employers may yet fall on the patient backs of the consumers, including the artisans themselves.

A YEAR OF AMERICAN TRADE.

1897 has been rather a remarkable year in the history of American trade. It opened under somewhat depressing circumstances. The depression of several years seemed continuing, as it had been intensified by the uneasiness and uncertainty connected with the Presidential election. Hopes of improvement were considerable, however, but the signs were slow in coming. We have before us the consular reports for New York, Baltimore, and Chicago; and they all have the same story to tell. The year was well advanced before the hoped-for improvement made its appearance. It was heralded by the great European demand for grain, and the consequent rise in price in America. Indeed, but for this improvement in wheat prices and exports, our Baltimore consul believes that 1897 would have shown a repetition of the stagnation in trade which had characterised the three previous years. Wheat was one of the largest crops that had ever been raised, the return showing over 530,000,000 bushels, an increase of more than 100,000,000 bushels as compared with that of the previous year. The high price obtained for wheat enabled the Western farmers to pay off mortgages, and left them a larger margin for general expenditure, and so set agoing that advance in trade which distinguished the year 1897, and which would have undoubtedly been continued in 1898 but for the check given to it by the outbreak of the war.

According to our New York consul the total value of the exports was the largest on record. In Baltimore there had been a heavy increase in the exports of provisions, lard, and illuminating oil, and an augmentation in copper and tobacco, which, with the enormous export of grain, made 1897 the greatest year for exports in the existence of Baltimore. It was a notable feature of the year, too, that the first shipment of steel rails from the United States to India then took place. They were sent to Calcutta, and were succeeded by another shipment to South Africa; and it would seem that American steel rails are finding their way into several markets where before England had the command. It is also worthy of note that British manufacturers appear to be holding their own in the United States, "except as regards hosiery, linens, and laces." British hosiery has almost disappeared from the American market, having been supplanted by the German article. What may have been the reason for this is not apparent, but it would seem that no effort whatever had been made to regain the trade. Saxon linens are also making inroads on the English trade in that article; and a hint is thrown out that, if English manufacturers were to bring themselves more closely in touch with American wholesale houses, and ascertain the wants of the market, they might probably check the downward tendency, which has not yet advanced very far. In shipping, British vessels seem to keep an easy lead. Of 874 foreign trade vessels entered at the port of Baltimore in 1897, 696 were British. Some time ago, just before the war broke out, Glasgow was somewhat perturbed by the arrival of a cargo of pig iron from America, which was sold at about 10s. a ton below what it could be obtained for in England. It would appear that a continuance of such exports may be expected when the war allows of the resumption of commerce under normal conditions; for the production of pig iron in the United States in 1897 was the largest ever recorded in any previous year. In this, as in many other ways, the loss to America by this war with Spain will be very great.

Critical Index to New Investments.

SOUTHAMPTON CORPORATION.

Capital and Counties Bank offers for tender at a minimum of 101 per cent. an issue of £120,000 2½ per cent. stock. Interest is due January and July, and the stock can be redeemed at par in July, 1915. The money is wanted chiefly for street improvements, sewerage and drainage works, and a new infectious diseases hospital. Population of Southampton is 100,000; rateable value £422,359; and the capital value of the entire undertakings and properties of the Corporation is put at £1,001,982, the existing debt being £518,322. In July, 1895, £100,120 of similar stock was placed at 102½ per cent. and in December, 1896, £100,000 of stock was sold at an average of £101 1s. 6d., or only 1s. 6d. over the minimum. Good as the security is, the present seems hardly the time to offer it, and in spite of a full half year's interest being payable next July, we rather doubt the reception it will receive.

KENSINGTON PALACE MANSIONS, LIMITED.

With a share capital of only £50,000 held by the vendor, an issue is made of £63,000 in 4½ per cent. first mortgage debenture stock at par. It is redeemable at par December, 1975, by sinking fund policies in the Alliance and Sun Companies, the lease expiring in the following March. Property, which is situated in Kensington Gore, is valued at £110,000. The stock appears to be a fair second-rate venture for those who do not mind having no share capital to lean against.

THE BRITANNIA WORKS COMPANY (1898), LIMITED.

This is a reorganisation of the Britannia Works Company, Limited, manufacturers of the well-known Ilford dry plates, films, and photographic papers. Originally established in 1880, the business was carried on as a private concern until December, 1891, when it was converted into a private limited liability company. The capital is £380,000 in 190,000 ordinary and 190,000 6 per cent. cumulative preference shares, of which the vendor takes 60,000 shares of each class and also £260,000 in cash. The company has been very prosperous in the past, the profits for 1894 being £47,994; for 1895, £43,746; for 1896, £46,939; and for 1897, £47,362. We see no reason given why the vendor is selling nor any valuation of the assets. Perhaps, therefore, it would be well to wait awhile and see the first report before investing much in the shares.

COAST DEVELOPMENT COMPANY, LIMITED.

If there be wisdom in the multitude of counsellors this company ought to do well, for it has ten directors residing at different places between Twickenham and Dumbarton. The object is to acquire various undertakings, comprising the Clacton-on-Sea and General Land, Building, and Investment Company, Limited, Belle Steamers, Limited, Clacton-on-Sea Pier Company, Limited, Clacton-on-Sea Hall and Library Company, Limited, and the recently formed Walton-on-the-Naze Pier and Hotel Company, Limited. Share capital is £500,000 in 40,000 5 per cent. cumulative preference and 60,000 ordinary shares of £5 each, of which 9,968 preference and 8,458 ordinary, with an issue of £100,000 4 per cent. first mortgage irredeemable debenture stock are offered at par. The assets acquired from the old companies are stated at £346,717, but some of the things taken over seem very expensive. The Clacton and Walton-on-the-Naze piers stand for £52,112 and five passenger steamers at £124,750, or an average of £24,950 each, and if the remaining assets are valued on this basis we should say the sale will be a very good thing for the old companies. Profits for past three years are certified at £12,575, £15,292, and £17,843, giving an average of £15,237. This refers to the first four companies, and depreciation and interest on capital has yet to be deducted, so that the margin for the ordinary shares on this basis would not be large. The consideration given for the assets is £294,000, viz.: 10,032 preference, and 21,542 ordinary shares, and £136,130 to discharge the liabilities of the old companies. The amalgamated venture offers, we think, small attraction to the prudent investor.

COSTA RICA COFFEE ESTATES, LIMITED.

Of the share capital of £50,000 in £10 shares, one-half is offered for subscription. Company buys a partially developed coffee estate in Costa Rica called "La Canada," comprising an area of about 809 acres, but only sixty acres are in bearing. Purchase price is £14,500 in cash, and £9,500 in shares. Costa Rica coffee may be very fine stuff, but this is not the time to take shares in a coffee company.

HARVEY'S YOKER DISTILLERY, LIMITED.

This will not do under any circumstances. Company is formed to buy a distillery at Yoker, near Glasgow, said to have been successfully carried on for about 150 years. We feel ashamed to admit we never heard of it. Share capital, £90,000 in £1 shares, 50,000 being 5½ per cent. cumulative preference, and the rest ordinary,

The preference are offered with an issue of £40,000 4 per cent. debentures at par. Purchase price is £98,000, including £58,000 in cash, although the distillery is valued at only £46,777. The profit statement is certainly extraordinary. Without deduction for interest on capital, partners' salaries, income tax, depreciation on building and machinery, or for wear and tear on casks, they were for 1894, £3,053; for 1895, £2,812; for 1896, £9,792; and for 1897, £8,271. These profits include a yearly estimated appreciation on the stock of whisky held, and the large increase in profits for the past two years is due to sales of whisky in stock, upon which basis the company is to be floated. The thing is really too funny.

KENT COAST MINERAL WATER COMPANY, LIMITED.

Capital £15,000 in 4½ per cent. debentures, £20,000 in 6 per cent. preference, and £40,000 in ordinary shares, the greater part of which is now offered at par. Six firms in the east of Kent are to be amalgamated, and their net profits, which are given separately for three years, show an average per annum of £4,642. We never thought much of these ginger-pop amalgamations, and the fact that the vendor takes £44,000 in cash out of the £50,000 of purchase money shows that he likewise does not think much of them.

Company Reports and Balance-Sheets.

*** *The Editor will be much obliged to the Secretaries of Joint Stock Companies if they would kindly forward copies of Reports and Balance-Sheets direct to the Office of* THE INVESTORS' REVIEW, *Norfolk House, Norfolk-street, W.C., so as to insure prompt notice in these columns.*

THE EQUITABLE LIFE ASSURANCE SOCIETY.—The annual reports of this society, of which the 136th is now before us, are monotonously good. In 1897 312 new policies were issued insuring £284,809 and yielding £17,723 in new premiums, including £6,702 single premiums. Also fourteen annuities amounting to £907 were granted for £9,559. Claims on 100 policies took £239,965, of which sum £132,450 represented the amount contracted for in the policies and £107,515 bonus additions thereto. But for bonuses aggregating £13,570 surrendered previously, or applied in reduction of premiums, the second of these totals would have been £121,084. In one case the sum assured and bonuses declared together exceeded the original amount assured more than four times over. On forty-nine policies surrendered the surrender values amounted to 83·5 per cent. of the premiums paid. Expenses of management were under 7·3 per cent. of the premium income and less than 4 per cent. of the total income. At the end of the year the accumulated funds amounted to £4,402,281, an increase of £80,748 on the previous year's total. This money is invested in the best stocks and securities, all, with a small exception, within the United Kingdom. It is announced that the Earl of Denbigh has been appointed a director in place of the late Major-General Sim.

LONDON AND SOUTH AFRICAN EXPLORATION COMPANY.—This company has a pretty steady revenue from its lands, but of late years it has been writing off various worthless assets, and so the balance forward diminishes. Thus the sum of £58,785 was brought in, but only £30,603 was carried forward, the reduction being chiefly due to the writing off of £16,438 owing by the Gordon Diamond Company as a bad debt. It should not be passed unnoted that the revenue did not prove sufficient to meet expenses and pay the dividends of the year, which latter amounted to £80,000. With a revenue of £88,078, working expenses came to £19,821, and so the balance had to be reduced by about £11,600 in order that the dividend might be paid. The profits of the company are good, but we should imagine the board would do wisely to return to the dividends of 12s. per share in place of the 16s. per share now distributed each year. Ever since the higher rate has been paid the cash balance of the company has been running off, and, as against £70,887 at the end of 1895, it is now only £30,603.

REUTER'S TELEGRAM COMPANY.—Perhaps owing to political disturbances, this company appears to have done well during 1897, and after working charges had been met, the net profit is £10,687. This permits of a dividend of 5 per cent., the placing of £5,278 to reserve, and the carrying forward of £411. The reserve will then amount to £26,000, but is practically absorbed by the capital expenditure of £27,145 upon establishing an advertisement branch. We should doubt very much whether this branch was a success, and so the reserve should not be treated as a very tangible asset. The balance-sheet in other respects is not particularly strong, so that further additions to reserve ought to be made before the dividend is increased.

ARIZONA COPPER COMPANY.—Burdened with a malodorous past, this company appears to have at last issued safely from the slough, and accordingly its board, which has never failed to take the market view of the position, is apparently going to "run the show for all it is worth." Of the £100,000 of terminable debentures, £37,080 have been redeemed out of profits, a further sum of £47,020 falls due at Whit Sunday, 1899, and the balance of £15,900 can be arranged to be redeemed at that date. From that date, therefore, it is proposed to reconstruct the concern. First, the other debenture issues will be taken in hand, and the "A" 6½ per cent. debenture stock, amounting to £134,908, and the "B" 7 per cent. debenture stock, amounting to £181,239, will be converted into a new 5 per cent. debenture stock. The "A" debenture stock is redeemable at a bonus of 10 per cent., so that the amount of new debenture stock will be just about £330,000. The saving in interest will be, at the start, about £5,000, but 25 per cent. of the net profits are to be used in redemption, so that the initial annual charge of £16,500 for interest ought to diminish. The "A" preference shares of £40,000 will be left untouched to receive 6 per cent. interest, but the few deferred shares out will be merged into the preferred issue, thus constituting a total of £640,000, which will be equally divided into preferred and ordinary stock, the former being entitled to a cumulative 7 per cent. dividend, and the latter taking surplus profits. As the profits for the year ended September 30 amounted to £129,000, it is argued that if this rate be maintained all the charges might be met and £59,626 left for dividend on the new deferred stock, less any sum devoted for improvements and extensions. The scheme seems fair to all concerned, but shareholders should not build too much on profits being maintained at the rate mentioned. The development of new copper mines goes on apace, and the present high quotation of the metal may not last. Still once Whit Sunday, 1899, is passed, and this scheme is agreed to, the fixed charges ought to be so reduced that dividends upon both the preferred and deferred stocks may be reasonably expected.

BRAMPTON BREWERY COMPANY.—This new company earned last year a gross profit of £21,967, and after paying interest on purchase money and on debenture stock the net balance was £11,631. This allowed of the payment of preference interest, a dividend of 8 per cent. on the ordinary shares, the carrying of £2,000 to reserve, the writing off of £1,117, or the whole of the preliminary expenses, and the carrying forward of £473. The dividend and interest upon the various denominations of capital were only paid for the period during which the instalments had been paid up, while the whole profits of the year were taken, the vendors receiving interest for the time during which full payment had not been made to them. The result was a saving of £3,100 to the company, which is precisely the amount set aside to reserve and the wiping out of the preliminary expenses. Dividends on the ordinary shares are not allowed to rise above 8 per cent. until the reserve amounts to £20,000, but we have yet to see whether any substantial surplus above the amount so required will be earned. A little lower dividend than 8 per cent. would please us better.

MALAY PENINSULA COFFEE COMPANY.—A bad record is shown by this new company for its first year of working. The crop was short, prices were low, and the cost of picking and curing the berry was unusually heavy. The result was that there was a loss on working of £1,975, and as £1,450 had been paid away in an interim dividend on the preference shares, the company has to start on its career with a balance to the bad of £3,403. It is stated that less than half the cultivated area is in full bearing, but this implies a heavy cost for upkeep, and as the balance-sheet showed that the company owed more than it possessed in liquid assets the outlook is not encouraging. Everything appears to have banded against this poor company, but we wonder whether its conception was altogether healthy.

W. N. WHITE & COMPANY, LIMITED.—This small concern had a gross profit last year of £13,829, and after payment of administrative charges a sum of £8,370 was left as net profit. One-tenth of this amount is put to reserve, the preference interest of 6 per cent. is paid, and a dividend of 10 per cent. is declared upon the ordinary shares. The chief asset to all appearances is "goodwill," and there does not seem to be any strong desire to accumulate funds in order to reduce the £60,000 at which the "Purchase of the Business, &c." stands.

ROHILKUND AND KUMAON RAILWAY COMPANY.—The company last half-year benefited to a moderate extent by the Frontier War. This caused an increase of Rs. 9,747 in the coaching traffic; which more than covered the diminution of Rs. 4,517 in the goods traffic, chiefly from grain. The net receipts came to £5,630, as against £4,652 in 1896, a great part of the improvement being due to the higher exchange. A dividend of £2 11s. 9d. per cent. is proposed for the half-year, making £5 3s. 6d. for the year, which is the same rate as for the three previous years. The sum of £900 is transferred to the reserve, which will then stand at £8,000. The Secretary of State for India received £279 as his half of surplus profits after 5 per cent. had been paid upon the capital, but in future years the Government will only take the half of surplus profits after the stock has received 6 per cent.

AMERICAN AND GENERAL MORTGAGE AND INVESTMENT CORPORATION.—The revenue of this corporation tends to improve, but it is insufficient to meet the preference interest. That, however, is not so serious a matter as it looks, for there is only £28,718 of deferred capital against £265,000 of preferred shares and debenture and loan debt. For last year the revenue was £11,719, and after administrative charges were met the net balance of £9,272 was arrived at. Of this £1,500 was set aside to meet realised losses, and £500 to write down preliminary expenses; then 3 per cent. in interest was paid upon the 5 per cent. preference shares, leaving £362 to be added to the carry forward, which will be £506. The interest upon the preferred shares is cumulative, and the arrears will now amount to 9 per cent. The real estate business of the company, which is its weakest side, shows some improvement, the loans on mortgage having been reduced £5,740, and the real estate held by £4,771. This has enabled the company to put £6,000 more into investments, which of late have yielded better than land mortgages. Some £4,133 of the real estate is also under contract for sale, so that that item will drop below £40,000. But we fear the best of the lands and mortgages are being redeemed, and to deal with the residuum will be troublesome.

The shifting of investments appears tò have been done with judgment, and they now consist of a much better collection than some time ago. The company has, however, £18,166 of losses realised upon investments to wipe out before its balance-sheet can be considered at all satisfactory. The present dividend ought not to be increased until this item and the £1,000 of preliminary expenses are wiped out, for the real estate is sure to bring more losses later on.

BALAGHAT GOLD MINING COMPANY.—So far as revenue is concerned, the results of this company last year were most disappointing. Only £752 in gold was obtained, and £2,064 from water rents, so that with a small sum from transfer fees, the total revenue was £2,946 against £10,232 of expenditure, making a loss on working of £7,285. Depreciation of plant, machinery, &c., required £3,584, so that the debit balance for the year is £10,870. In the time, however, a good deal of exploration work has been done, and a valuable ore body is claimed to have been found at the 700-feet level south at Tennant's shaft. Powerful pumps have also been put to work at Haine's shaft which had previously been under water up to the 410-feet level, and the water had been lowered at the time of the issue of the report to the 670-feet level. The pumping of the shaft dry to the 800-feet level is not expected to take long, and the board is hopeful that the remaining resources of the company will last until the mill is in a position to make returns. Of this we should be rather dubious unless creditors prove patient, as the balance-sheet at December 31 last only showed free assets of about £1,500.

THE BRITISH TEA TABLE COMPANY.—This company makes up its accounts to March 31 last, and the profit shown is £20,408. All this, however, does not come to the shareholders, because the company did not enter into possession until July 1 last, and had to pay certain moneys over to the vendors. So £14,621 was all that the directors had to distribute. They have paid the preference dividend, and declared a dividend of 1s. 3d. per share on the ordinary shares, which they say is equivalent to about 10 per cent. per annum on the amounts for the time being paid thereon. A balance of £1,509 is left to carry forward. Goodwill stands in the balance-sheet at £130,411, and we should not like to trust the company with much of our money until this has been materially written down.

The report of the CASTNER-KELLNER ALKALI COMPANY, LIMITED, for the period ended March 31 last states that the profit was £9,161 on the working of the first installation of 1,000 horse-power. It is expected that the full output of 4,000 horse-power will be ready within the present year. To meet the final costs of the substantial works being erected an issue of £80,000 5 per cent. first mortgage debenture stock, part of an issue of £100,000 repayable in three years. A sum of £8,677 is carried forward as net profit, and it is hoped that six months hence the profit will be enough to warrant an interim dividend at the rate of 8 per cent. Current expenses look very moderate.

J. W. BENSON, LIMITED.—For the year ended March 31 last the net profit was £56,139, including the dividend of £9,066 from the shares of Hunt & Reskell, Limited, held by the company. Of the total, £7,040 has been carried to general reserve as representing profit earned previous to the incorporation of the company. After meeting prior charges, paying 10 per cent. on the ordinary shares, and adding £4,959 to the general reserve, a balance of £8,820 is left to carry forward. This seems good on a company capitalised at £750,000, but why is the amount devoted to depreciation not stated?

NEW EXPLOSIVES COMPANY, LIMITED.—Net profit for 1897 was £2,601, which, added to £3,593 brought forward, gives £6,194 for appropriation, and the directors pay a 2½ per cent. dividend out of it, leaving £3,944 to go to the new year. Extensive new works are to be ready this month. Delay has been caused by a strike and the engineers' lock out. All the £24,000 of debentures have been "practically" taken up, but the new works will cost about £32,500 when finished. The balance-sheet and profit and loss accounts are full and clear.

MONTEVIDEO GAS COMPANY.—Again this company has had a bad year. The reduction in the price of gas made in 1896 led to considerable loss in revenue, which was accentuated by the political unrest in the city. During the whole of 1897 commercial enterprise was checked by politics, and not until the present provisional Government took office in February this year was there any sign of commercial revival. Revenue was, therefore, about £12,000 less than two years ago, and although working expenses were reduced, the net profit of £18,034 was nearly £10,000 below that of 1895. As a consequence, the sum of £7,136 had to be withdrawn from the contingency fund in order to maintain the dividend at 5 per cent., and, of course, the balance forward of £4,456 also disappeared. The contingency fund, however, will then stand at £18,137, and the insurance fund at £12,500. The reserve, too, will be £64,540, after £9,463 has been deducted for the redemption of debentures. The latter policy is a good one, as they bear interest at 5 per cent., and the company is rich in surplus assets.

TRUST AND LOAN COMPANY OF CANADA.—This high-class company earned in the half-year ended March 31 a net revenue of £10,988, which allowed of a dividend at the usual rate of 6 per cent. per annum, the addition of £619 to reserve, and the addition of a like sum to the balance forward, which amounts to £10,390. The reserve fund, however, had to bear £4,217 for loss on securities realised in Canada and £2,593 for depreciation of investments held in England, but it benefited to the extent of £3,670 from interest and £619 from revenue, so that the net decrease was only £3,629. The company has been steadily meeting moderate losses on realisation of securities in Canada, and although its loans and debentures outstanding have diminished by about £32,000 in the past two years, its net revenue has been maintained. The foreclosure account rises, but it is proportionately small to the live mortgages, and overdue interest is much less.

JHANZIE TEA ASSOCIATION.—Owing to climatic influences the outturn of tea last year was only 825,091 lb., or 202,909 lb. less than the estimate, and 142,816 lb. below the output of the previous year. A fractional higher price, however, was obtained, the average being 10·50d. per lb., as against 10·13d. per lb. in 1896; but the result was that the sales came to £5,334 less, and owing to the higher exchange, which cost the company £1,216, the working expenses were £354 more. Accordingly, the net profits were only £3,933, as against £9,521 in 1896. Such a reduction, we should fancy, was unprecedented in the history of the company, and the board met the emergency by withdrawing £2,000 from reserve, and reducing the dividend from 10 to 8 per cent. That they could then pay such a good rate is proof of the sterling solidity of the concern, for the reserve will then stand at £15,800. At the same time, it was prudent to reduce the dividend, as there is no certainty that the current year will see anything like 10 per cent. earned.

RIVER PLATE GAS COMPANY.—A newly amalgamated concern, it has started with a good year. Gross profits came to £80,662, and after including £30,907 as a balance left over after the settlement of the accounts of the old companies, there was a total of £111,259. The sum of £12,301 was absorbed by debenture interest, £6,751 by administrative salaries, and £4,000 placed as a reserve against bad and doubtful debts. Out of the balance of £87,679, the directors declared dividends equal to 6 per cent. for the year, carried £20,000 to reserve, and wrote off £5,288, the whole of the preliminary expenses, which left £10,966 to be carried forward. It ought to be clearly understood that this was not done wholly out of one year's profits, for the £30,907 brought in from 1896 just accounts for the allocation to reserve and the big carry forward. At the same time bad debts ought not to require—at least we hope not—so much in future years, debenture interest should be less by one-third, and of course preliminary expenses will not recur. There is, however, an unsatisfactory item in the balance-sheet of £27,339 for "discount on issue of debenture stock and premium on redemption" which ought to be written off out of profits. At present the reserve and carry forward may be said to be invested in this intangible fashion, and not until this item disappears can those accumulations be said to be set free for a useful purpose.

WENHOLT ESTATES COMPANY OF AUSTRALIA.—Not a happy record belongs to this company, for in its history of ten years the ordinary shareholders have only received three dividends and they were small. Whatever may have happened in the past the board now seems to be endeavouring to improve the financial position of the concern. Last year was not a favourable year for the Australian pastoral industry, yet after paying £10,000 in debenture interest the company showed a profit, including £5,112 brought forward, of £21,730. Of this £10,973 was used to write off the balance of permanent improvements, £6,500 was absorbed in paying the interest on the preference capital, and £4,256 was left to be carried forward. By this arrangement, the whole of the £54,316 spent in past years as permanent improvements upon the stations and stock is written off, and these will stand in the books at the original value of £500,000. There is a reserve fund of £10,565, but this is practically ear-marked to purchase a new property. The effects of the drought are seen in the diminished number of stock upon the property, but we should imagine that this company has not suffered so severely as others in this respect. If the expected improvement comes this year, a dividend upon the £200,000 of ordinary capital may be in sight, but it would be wise to add to reserves at the same time, and not use these reserves wholly in the business. The experience of the Scottish Australian Investment ought to be a warning on this head, for its £200,000 of reserve is very little assistance in the period of adversity.

CASTLE MAIL PACKETS COMPANY.—Considering that there was some falling off in the trade with South Africa during the past year for reasons well-known, the figures of the balance sheet are satisfactory. Practically all the assets have been written up; the fleet, including payments on account of new steamers, standing at £1,352,479, compared with £1,154,786 a year ago. Property has been raised from £84,868 to £93,014; cash at bankers from £47,443 to £57,338, and investments from £36,501 to £51,000, the total assets standing at £1,763,334, or £232,000 more than in 1896. On the other side, £150,000 of temporary advances have been replaced by £330,000 3½ per cent. debenture stock, which is borrowing cheap enough for such a company, the insurance fund has been raised from £249,390 to £323,476, and the reserve from £125,000 to £135,000. The credit balance is then £27,433 compared with £26,120 a year ago, from which a dividend of 12s. per share is to be paid, making 20s. for the year, as in 1896. Two new large vessels of between 9,000 and 10,000 tons register are being built by the Fairfield Company to pay for which the company will need more money. Opportunity is, therefore, to be taken to rearrange the capital by which the basis will be improved upon which to raise the new capital. In the first place, the balance of £6 will be called upon the 36,000 ordinary shares, less £2 to be credited from the insurance fund, so that the net amount produced will be £144,000. It is also proposed to issue 12,000 preference shares to bring in £240,000. The directors further want powers to issue the balance of the share capital of 22,000 shares, which would make up the entire authorised capital of £1,400,000. We do not think that the present earnings by any means warrant this large increase in the paid-up capital, but in view of growing competition the directors doubtless wish to be in a strong position, no matter how the dividend may be affected.

THE OTAGO AND SOUTHLAND INVESTMENT COMPANY, LIMITED.—Last year the board of this company reduced its liability on debentures by a net sum of £47,960. This has not been done without loss through realisations of securities in New Zealand, but even so it is well done, as the company carries securities representing £165,014 on which it is receiving no interest. Owing to £5,204 lost and to the smallness of the revenue, the debit balance now amounts to £23,869, £14,335 of it accruing last year. Charges have been reduced by £600. The prospect is not over cheerful.

JOHN BAZLEY WHITE & BROTHERS, LIMITED, Cement Manufacturers.—Last year's profits amounted to £89,057, an increase of over £30,000. During the year two additional cement works have been acquired, adding about £35,000 to capital account. On the other side of the balance sheet, freehold and leasehold properties have risen £54,000. Reserve fund is increased by £10,000. Apparently this fund is invested outside the business, but this point is not very clear in the accounts. Goodwill, trade marks, &c., stand as before. £3,410 has been used to redeem debentures. The directors state a fair amount has been written off for depreciation and loss caused by floods. A dividend of 4 per cent. is to be paid on the ordinary shares. Certainly there is an improvement, but with the large capital sunk in the business we should like to see efforts made to reduce the goodwill asset.

MILLARS' KARRI AND JARRAH FORESTS, LIMITED.—The result of the first year's working is quite up to the promise of the prospectus, the profits from trading amounting to £70,121, of which £11,974 is appropriated to property reserve account, and £10,000 to depreciation suspense account, although it is claimed that the works have been maintained in the highest state of efficiency. The ordinary shareholders get a dividend of 3s. per share for the year, or 15 per cent., and £11,930 is carried forward. Reference is made to the large increase in the output of timber, and to cope with the expanding business another 50,000 ordinary shares are to be issued at £1 premium *pro rata* to existing ordinary shares, which will give them a nice little bonus. The number of these wood concerns have increased considerably of late, and we should think there is a good prospect of lively competition in the future.

Diary of the War.

May 13.—Meagre fare in war news. The Spanish Cape Verde squadron is again missing. It has not been at Cadiz; such is the latest assurance. Where is it? Nobody knows, or at least, nobody will tell. It cannot apparently have gone near Porto Rico; for reports are received of Admiral Sampson's bombardment of San Juan, and of the surrender of that port. Two American gunboats and a torpedo-boat, the *Winslow*, having looked into the harbour of Cardenas to ascertain the exact position of the shore batteries, and to attack, if opportunity offered, some Spanish gunboats, had such a hot reception from the forts that they retired. The *Winslow* was badly hit through her boiler, and it was with difficulty that she was towed beyond the range of the Spanish fire. The Americans evidently cannot do what they like on the Cuban coast. The Spaniards there, at least, keep a fairly good look out.

May 14.—Another turn of the kaleidoscope, and a new arrangement of war prospects, necessitating a prompt change of tactics on the part of the Americans. The Cape Verde Spanish fleet is not only not at Cadiz, but has never attempted to go there. It is now discovered that a couple of days ago—Thursday, the 12th—this fleet, moving so noiselessly and escaping observation so cleverly, arrived at Fort de France, Martinique, one of the Lesser Antilles, that it coaled there, or a few miles off at sea, and sailed away again, no man, except the Admiral in command, knows whither. Admiral Sampson, on the same morning, very early, had arrived at Puertorico, and at daybreak bombarded the forts on San Juan. He destroyed them, say some accounts, but his own despatch does not claim so much. It is clear, however, that he inflicted severe damage upon them, receiving comparatively little in return; but he nevertheless withdrew his fleet, and the Spanish report asserts that one of his ships had to be towed away. Previous to bearing down upon Puertorico, Admiral Sampson and fleet had been scouring the seas in search of the Spanish squadron; but the seas he scoured were two or three hundred miles to the north of where the Spaniards had been steaming; and so of course they never met. The question now is, whither has the Spanish fleet sailed? It may have gone towards Puertorico, a not improbable assumption; or it may have sought to intercept the returning American warship *Oregon*, a notso probable assumption for a squadron consisting of at least four large fighting ships and three torpedo boats; or it may have gone by a circuitous route to the south of Jamaica, holding for Havana by the southern and western coast of Cuba. This is the assumption on which the American naval authorities have acted, for they immediately ordered the despatch of the flying squadron under Commodore Schley from Hampton Roads for Havana, to strengthen the somewhat weakened blockading fleet there. It would seem also that the fact of the discovery of the whereabouts of the Cape Verde fleet had been communicated to Admiral Sampson, who immediately sailed from San Juan with the whole or chief part of his fleet, also in the direction of Cuba. If he took all his ships with him, his progress must have been slow, as he had two monitors, and the speed of one of these at least does not exceed twelve knots an hour. Supposing the Spanish fleet is heading for Havana, it is calculated that it might reach that destination by Sunday night. But it is believed that Commodore Schley, with the flying squadron, might reach Havana to-night. If so, he would be in time to meet the Spanish fleet to-morrow (Sunday) night or Monday, and a big naval fight would result. But there is yet another contingency. Admiral Cervera with his Spanish ships may sail for neither of the points indicated, but out into the "ewigkeit" where he has during the last fortnight so adroitly escaped observation. The "moral effect" of such a movement would be great. It would postpone indefinitely the American military expedition to Cuba, for it cannot sail as long as there is a possibility of this erratic Spanish fleet coming down upon it at any moment and from any quarter.

May 15.—Situation much the same as yesterday. The Spanish fleet still invisible. No word from Admiral Sampson. Commodore Schley, it is now said, cannot reach Havana before to-morrow, so that, if Admiral Cervera should get there, say, to-night, he might raise the blockade and get under the shelter of the Havana forts. This might strengthen the defence of Cuba, but it would leave the Americans in command of the sea, and would settle the fate of Puertorico. American papers treat with humorous grimness the suggestion by Mr. Chamberlain of an alliance with the United States. They have no objections to friendly relations, but they refuse to be involved in England's European quarrels.

May 16.—Admiral Cervera's fleet has again upset American calculations. It appeared off Curaçao, one of the Dutch West India Islands, about forty miles north of Venezuela, on Saturday morning. The Spanish Admiral seems to be in no hurry to take refuge anywhere—either Havana or Puertorico, or other port. The American Admiralty seem to think he now aims at Cienfuegos; but that appears doubtful. Of course he might go there or he might proceed round Cuba to Havana. But if he goes to either Cienfuegos, or Havana, or Puertorico, he virtually shuts himself up; and the Americans can concentrate their fleets for his destruction. The tactical success of their Admiral has elated the Spaniards and all suggestion of peace is lost in the cry for a continuation of the war. It is a poor peg on which to hang such a policy, but Spanish depression had become so profound that a small hint of success might easily bring elation. Mr. Chamberlain's speech has made a great sensation on the Continent. It is interpreted as an appeal, *ad misericordiam*, for an alliance with the United States if possible, but, failing that, with any Continental State. None of his critics, however, allow the possibility of alliance. Comment on the speech in American journals is not very profuse. but the suggested Anglo-Saxon alliance is not altogether scouted. France repudiates the notion that anything in the present condition of the West African negotiations justifies the suggestion that there is any danger to peace there.

May 17.—Still searching for the Spanish fleet, which has nowhere been seen since it left Curaçao on Sunday evening, the 11th. Admiral Sampson is watching for it in the Windward Passage. Commodore Schley's position is not quite clear, but he has not gone to Havana. The Spanish Ministry has resigned, and Senor Sagasta is engaged in the reconstruction of the Cabinet; it will continue Liberal, as a Conservative Ministry could not have been formed without a majority in the Chamber, and to risk a general election just now in search of a majority is too dangerous a proceeding to be thought of. The reconstruction of the Ministry means, it seems, "a vigorous prosecution of the war," though how Senor Sagasta is to set about it is not quite clear. The war may be prolonged as long as Admiral Cervera keeps afloat and avoids a battle, but the Home Government cannot afford much assistance to him. The only thing they can do is to send out the reserve fleet at Cadiz to try and find him and render assistance; and as the Admiral in command there has been summoned to Madrid, possibly this step may be in contemplation.

May 18.—Americans still in search of the Spanish fleet, which has called nowhere since its brief rest at Curaçao.

May 19.—Senor Sagasta has succeeded in forming a new ministry, but the Spanish fleet has not been seen again. No news of it whatever.

THE PROPERTY MARKET.

It almost seems as if the supply of property at Tokenhouse-yard were falling below the demand. The quantity disposed of last week brought in a total of £181,356, or £64,220 lower than the total for the corresponding week of 1897. But buyers seem still plentiful, competition keen, and prices are improving. Land, especially for building, is in increasing demand. Fifteen acres in Church End, Finchley, sold last week at £500 per acre; another lot, in smaller parcels, at Barnes, brought over £1,500 per acre; while a farm of about thirty-two acres near Brentwood, in Essex, went for the modest sum of £9 an acre. A freehold estate at Streatham of fifty acres, with seven residences, offered yesterday week by Messrs. Farebrother, Ellis, & Co., did not, however, command the reserve price put upon it, £150,000, or £3,000 an acre, and so was withdrawn. The firm mentioned on the same day sold the freehold of 11, New Burlington-street, Bond-street, for £15,700, and the leasehold professional residence, 34, Bruton-street, for £4,500. Messrs. White & Sons, of Dorking, acting with Messrs. Hampton & Sons, disposed of a freehold residential property known as "Bokefield," at Westcott, Surrey, with ten and a half acres, for £7,600. The remaining supply consisted mostly of bricks and mortar. Messrs. Newbon, Edwards, & Shepherd sold a leasehold residence at Finsbury Park, sixty-nine years unexpired term, at £1,210. A Guardian life policy for £3,800 and profits, life aged 57, was disposed of by Messrs. Vernon & Son for £1,650. Messrs. Stimson & Son got £1,500 for the freehold house, 285, Camberwell-road, and £750 for two freeholds, 212 and 214, St. George's-road, Peckham. Total of the day's sales, £56,255.

Friday was what may be called a good day at the Mart. Several large properties were disposed of at good prices. Messrs. Protheroe

& Morris sold two freehold blocks of building land in Long-lane, Finchley, at £4,210; other two freehold blocks in Squire's-lane, Finchley, at £1,170; and the Ballards'-lane Nursery, area 1a. 1r. 5p., freehold, rent £154 at £2,500. Mr. W. A. Blackmore realised £2,700 on a number of leasehold houses in Percy-road and Thomas-road, Hackney; and Mr. L. Farmer disposed of Brondesbury House, Willesden, and about three acres, unexpired term sixty-one and a half years, at £2,350. A freehold property at Crouch Hill, rent £120, with four plots of land, was sold by Mr. Smallpeice for £4,100; as well as freehold ground rents of £35, reversion in seventy-seven years, at £1,295.

Out of nineteen lots offered at the Mart on Monday six were bought in, and the total of the day's sales only reached £11,900. Messrs. Beale & Capps succeeded in disposing of some leasehold property in Clarendon-gardens, with fifty years to run, ground rent of £28, and rent of £295, at £2,375; other leaseholds in Paddington and Notting Hill at a total of £3,575. The only other important lot was that offered by Messrs. Holcombe, Betts, and West, a freehold residence, with two and a half acres, at Northwood, Middlesex, which brought £2,250.

The excellent business of Tuesday almost made up for the inactivity of Monday. The total sales amounted to £65,415, and some very fine properties were disposed of. Messrs. Farebrother, Ellis, & Company negociated the sale of the late Lady Watkin's riverside residence, "Mount Felix," at Walton-on-Thames, which, with over fifty acres of land, brought £23,500. Messrs. Debenham, Tewson, & Company obtained £12,000 for the freehold of Nos. 362 to 375, Old-street, St. Luke's, covering an area of 8,100 feet, and £6,700 for a freehold building estate of nine acres at Ealing—a very fair figure. Messrs. Walton & Lee disposed of two lots of freehold building land at Surbiton for £3,550. The Leaming House Estate, containing seventy-two and a half acres, at Ullswater, Cumberland, in the Lake District, was placed by Messrs. Bean, Burnett, & Eldridge for £7,600. Messrs. E. and H. Lumley disposed of Great Cliff End Farm at Pegwell Bay, Kent, containing 111½ acres, freehold, at £4,200. This was sold on the system of deferred payment recently introduced by Messrs. Lumley. These are some of the most notable transactions of an active day at the Mart. Two licensed houses were sold at Masons' Hall Tavern on Tuesday—one, the "Cauliflower," a well-known public at Ilford, with stabling and garden, freehold, which Messrs. Orgill, Marks, & Orgill negotiated for £50,000. It is stated that the house has been in the possession of one family for 200 years. The other house was the "Tulip Tree" at Richmond, situated opposite the athletic grounds in the Old Deer Park. For the twenty-seven and a half years' lease, at £60 rent, with goodwill, Messrs. Fleuret, Sons, & Adams obtained £2,640. Mr. Alfred Richards announces a sale of leasehold residences in Islington at the Mart next Monday, and on Tuesday of eleven long leasehold houses, two freehold villas, and a plot of freehold building land in Tottenham.

At the Mart on Wednesday Messrs. Edwin Fox & Bousfield sold portions of an adventurer's share in the New River Company at the rate of over £129,000 per share, and 50 new ordinary shares in the Grand Junction Waterworks Company at prices ranging from £95 to £103 per share. The day's sale at Tokenhouse-yard amounted to £15,810, but the details were of minor interest. Messrs. Douglas Young & Co. were the chief operators, all except one of their lots being sold at an aggregate of £6,305.

TRADE AND PRODUCE.

The tone of the English wheat markets has been very easy during the week, with a decidedly downward tendency. In one or two instances business could only be done at a reduction of 2s. to 3s. a quarter; but as a rule the attitude of buyers and sellers alike has been one of expectancy—the former pretty confident of a decrease in price, and the latter hoping for a yet further increase. These were the views animating Mark-lane until Wednesday last, when the general impression seemed to be that the wheat "boom" must be regarded as at an end, and that the question must now be how far the decrease in price would go. Not far for some time, probably. Indeed, Chicago and New York seem not altogether to have given up hope of a resumption of the upward tendency; but the speculative efforts to produce a rally in prices have been weak and ineffectual. Liverpool responded languidly, and the market fluctuated in a heedless sort of way; but there was no quotable change in values. Yet the demand for the Continent continues. France seems still to take as much as she can get, and many shipments for English ports have again been reconsigned for French ports. Italy also is taking a great deal, and so is Spain. But the supplies keep well up. *Dun's Review* tells us that Western receipts at New York, after averaging less than 2,500,000 bushels per week for four months, a fortnight ago suddenly rose to 3,500,000 bushels. Exports for the same week amounted to 2,094,389 bushels, flour included, against 1,498,167 bushels from Atlantic ports last year, and 559,348 against 99,508 from Pacific ports. This does not look like any shrinkage in supplies from that quarter. Supplies from Russia are also considerable; and from India the reports are that the chief difficulty is to get ships to carry the stocks of wheat and cotton coming in for shipment. The latest English quotations show a decline of 1s. to 3s., but business is far from active. Sellers are not pressing; and it is probable that for some little time yet the current quotations will be fairly well maintained. If the Chicago and New York speculators find, as they seem to be doing at present, that prices cannot be further forced, we may look, in the course of the week, for a gradual reduction, though not a very considerable one. The latest American as well as English market reports indicate growing weakness in the sellers. Wheat is manifestly on the downward grade. The war scare is losing its influence.

Though the shipments of cotton to this country have been well kept up, there is little change in the Liverpool market. The continent, however, being already tolerably well supplied, has lately been taking rather less than the average. As to the new crop, Messrs. Neill Bros. say the reports are, on the whole, favourable. The weather has been rather too dry for some time, but otherwise the conditions are satisfactory.

So far as the wool auctions are concerned, there has been great firmness of tone if no particular rise in price. The main demand, however, would seem to be for the Continent, with some considerable transactions on Russian and even American account. But for the home market the demand has not been so great. Reports from Leicester are inclined to be rather desponding. There is less actual depression than formerly, but the recovery is slow: there is great want of confidence, and the turnover is restricted to the supply of actual needs at very low prices. Spinners, as a rule, have ample supplies on hand. Leeds is more hopeful, the outlook having become brighter than it was some weeks ago. In Huddersfield, though comparatively little has been doing on the spot, travellers' orders are above the average, and repeat orders are so numerous as to have put some strain on the merchants' stocks. On the whole, there seems a more hopeful prospect, but no very strong confidence in the future.

Copper is in a peculiar position. Statistically it stands well. During the past fortnight a reduction of 1,362 tons has taken place in the visible supplies, while stocks show a reduction of 1,762 tons. Still, during this period the price of G. M. B.'s has declined from £52 2s. 6d. to £51 13s. 9d. per ton, a total reduction of 8s. 9d. During this week the market has been flat, with a weak and undecided tone throughout, resulting in a further fall on Wednesday to £51 7s. 9d. for cash, while the best price obtainable for June 10 and other dates nearer the end of the month were £51 8s. 9d. In the afternoon session £51 10s. was paid for two months, but three months, which earlier in the day were dealt in at £51 12s. 6d., receded later to £51 11s. 3d. Settlement price was £51 7s. 6d. The curiosities in the copper position are attributable, first, to an increase of the American output, and to the uncertainty of the war and political situation. The market is pretty certain to fluctuate not a little for some time, but in itself the trade is in a perfectly healthy condition.

The upward movement in pig-iron has been checked by speculation, and on Wednesday there was a sudden drop, Scotch lost 7d., Cleveland 4½d., and hematite 5d. The reports from the iron manufacturing districts show great activity, however. The Glasgow producers of iron and steel have announced a general advance in prices; in Sheffield prices have gone up all round about 2s. per ton. South Shropshire maintains a firm tone; and from Barrow-on-Furness we learn that more activity has been shown, though makers are not booking to a large extent. Still there is a decidedly firm tone, and quotations have advanced, mixed Bessemer numbers being now quoted at 52s. to 53s. 6d. per ton f. o. b. Warrant iron in active demand and holders are very firm. Stocks represent 172,000 tons, and forty-seven furnaces are in blast, as compared with thirty-seven in the corresponding week of last year. More still would be lighted if the supply of native ore were better. Birmingham prices are not considered so satisfactory, though there, too, the tendency is upwards. The great bulk of the Admiralty orders for electro-plate, representing £4,000 to £5,000 value, have been placed in Birmingham. The gunmakers are greatly irritated at the stoppage of the Persian Gulf trade. It represents to them a loss of 25,000 to 30,000 guns per annum; and as neither the German nor Belgian makers suffer by the prohibition put upon English makers, the Birmingham trade will fall into German and Belgian hands. This does seem rather rough upon Birmingham. Glasgow reports activity in all departments. Locomotive engineers are in treaty for some Indian work, and Australia is buying tubes more freely. Offers of American steel plates at moderate rates have been somewhat disconcerting to home producers, who are thus brought face to face with an article, for which they charge about £6 a ton, offered at about £4 12s. Such an outlook is not quite pleasant.

As to coal the fancy prices caused by the strike have begun to fall a little. As the strike itself may probably soon be ended, the downward tendency is likely to continue.

Messrs. Gow, Wilson, & Stanton, in their circular of the 18th, give some figures which they say might at first sight appear to indicate a check in the consumption of British-grown tea in North America, but they do not warrant such a supposition. The increase in the first quarter of 1897 was due to the fear of an alteration in the tea duty. There was a very heavy increase in the Indian tea taken in the first quarter of 1897, nearly the whole being lost during the remaining three quarters, the total quantity for the year being 5,663,244 lb. against 2,587,273 in 1896; the quantity of Ceylon tea was 5,698,596 lb. in 1897, and in 1896 4,354,510 lb., the main portion of the year's increase being contributed in the first quarter. The quantities of Indian tea brought forward at recent auctions show a considerable reduction. The tone continues steady. Buying has been fairly general in Ceylon tea, and the late improvement in price is fully maintained.

Over half a million francs in securities and gold has been stolen from one of the vans of the Paris-Lyon-Méditerranée Company. The driver of the van knew of nothing wrong until, going from the railway station, he had reached the Place de la Bastille, when passers-by drew his attention to the fact that the door at the back of the vehicle was open. He then discovered that two packages had disappeared—one containing securities valued at 480,000 francs and 12,000 francs in gold. The thieves escaped with their booty. Later accounts say that the real value of the securities stolen is about £30,000.

Notes on Books.

Dictionnaire du Commerce, de l'Industrie, et de la Banque. Publié sous la direction de MM. YVES GUYOT et A. RAFFALOVICH. Paris: Guillaumin et Cie., Editeurs. Première Livraison, price three francs; to be completed in two vols., price fifty francs.

We have received the first number of this publication, and give it a cordial welcome. The book is wanted, and its appearance is opportune. The editing of it could not have been in more competent hands than those of MM. Yves Guyot and Arthur Raffalovich, the one of whom is an able economist and an ardent free trader, and the other a financier of wide experience and eminent talent. This first number carries us down to *Allemagne*, the article on which runs on to the next number. It contains also articles on *Abonnement*, by M. Salefranque; *Accidents du Travail*, by M. Maurice Bellom; *Action, Actionnaire*, by MM. L. Guérin et Léantéy; *Admission à la Cote*, by M. Emmanuel Vidal; *Agent de Change, Agiotage*, by M. E. Vidal; *Agriculture*, by M. Louis Passy; *Alaska* and *Alexandrie* (d'Egypte) by M. Ravier; and *Alimentation*, by M. le Dr. Laumonier. It is a very arduous undertaking, and we trust the welcome it will receive from the business public will amply reward those who have had the courage and energy to undertake it.

Fenn on the Funds: Being a Handbook of Pubic Debts, &c. Edited by S. F. VAN OSS, with the assistance of H. H. BASSETT. London: Effingham Wilson.

Our old familiar friend appears in a new dress, and on the whole we think an improved one. Although now elbowed aside by many newer text-books "Fenn on the Funds" still has a place, or ought to have a place, on the reference book-shelf of every banker's and financier's library. It specialises one form of financial knowledge—that relating to the debts of all nations—and in this edition the information about these has been supplemented by a great many facts relating to the revenue and expenditure and trade of many of the countries dealt with. As far as we have been able to estimate by a brief examination the work has been ploddingly well and, on the whole, accurately revised. We are not sure that the publisher was wise in omitting the Bank Act, or, at any rate, the rules of the London Stock Exchange. These latter are very inaccessible to the general public, and "Fenn on the Funds" could always hitherto be relied upon to give a reprint of them up to date. Mr. Van Oss has written an introduction to the book which, though not new, is worth reading and suggestive. In it will be found a summary of all the burdens the civilised and semi-civilised peoples of the world have now to carry in the shape of public debts. They aggregate to the inconceivable total of £6,121,000,000. This mountain, we take it, represents only the interest-bearing debt of the various States dealt with and takes no account of the enormous obligations in the shape of paper money which oppress countries like Spain and Brazil, or which go to form a material part of the national obligations of many other countries, such as France and the United States.

Pelican House, E.C. By G. B. WEST, Author of *Half Hours with the Millionaires.* London: T. Fisher Unwin.

A cleverly written but rather peculiar sort of book. What the author's aim may have been in writing it we know not. It is not apparent. There is no plot, no real story. At the outset we thought it must be intended as a scathing exposure of some scheme of financial rascality. There have been some such schemes. It could certainly do no harm if they were exposed so thoroughly that there could be no hope of resuscitating them, or anything like them. But there is no such exposure of financial villany here. If anything it is a fairly-painted picture of financial imbecility. The particular syndicate whose history is here recorded was the conception of several gentlemen more or less silly, who ought in reason to have come to grief, and very nearly did so, but whom luck befriended, and in the end they retire with flying colours and modestly well-filled purses. The syndicate announced itself ready to combine philanthropy and usurious interest; they advanced sums to impecunious cranks and faddists at 5 per cent. per week interest. What is more remarkable still is that the loans were all repaid, interest as well as principal. Some of the sketches or caricatures, for there is something of both in "Pelican House, E.C.," are cleverly done, but the book is not enthralling. Nay, it is sometimes hard and rather dry reading, and when you come to the end, you can hardly say that you have gained anything, not even amusement, at least in a large way.

Davis's Bulawayo Directory and Handbook to Matabeleland. With Map and Township Plan.

We should hardly have thought that Bulawayo yet required a directory; but this is, it seems, the second issue. The first appeared in March, 1896, just as the Matabele rising was coming to a head, so rapidly does civilisation in these days tread on the heels of disappearing barbarism. There is a good deal of readable matter about "Lobengula and his times," about the "Occupation of Mashonaland," and the Matabele War. A very good map accompanies the book, as well as a ground plan of Bulawayo. The trade directory of Bulawayo is more extensive than might have been thought at first. It has six accountants and auditors, four aerated water manufacturers, five mining agents, nine architects, thirteen attorneys, notaries, and conveyancers—lawyers are always to the front—eleven auctioneers, nine bakers and confectioners, three banks, four drinking bars, four blacksmiths and farriers, only one boarding-house, but twenty-one brokers. There are twenty-eight builders and contractors, but if Bulawayo progresses there should be work for them all. Nine butchers will probably prove enough for the present population, though eleven carpenters does not seem an extravagant supply. There should be work for the half-dozen clothiers and outfitters, whose names are given; and there may be work for the twenty-seven civil and mining engineers. It is to be hoped for the comfort of the population that the two dentists named will be sufficient. We cannot afford space or time to go through the list; but we may further note that there are eight hairdressers, twelve hotels, only two laundries, six insurance offices, twenty-seven merchants and importers, one pawnbroker, one photographer, one high school, one music teacher, and four newspapers.

THE RUMOURED JAPANESE LOAN.

The rumour as to the flotation of a Japanese loan in Europe has been revived, and this time the only thing the authorities can say about it is that the report is premature. We may assume from this that, whether the amount be £15,000,000, or whether it be a smaller sum designed for the relief of "approved public undertakings," Japan is on the point of appealing to the moneylenders. There is no good reason why it should not obtain the accommodation it desires provided it cares to offer a fair price; for the credit of the country is good, and it is progressing, if only slowly, in material wealth. The only fear is that its attempts to force the rate of advance may land it in difficulties. It is satisfactory, however, to note that this year the Government is curbing its desire to be extravagant, and has abandoned some of the more pettifogging of the devices which it initiated last year for the purpose of increasing the revenue. It has not gone in for any radical reform—the commitments which it has made in furtherance of the national ambition to become a great power in the Far East would be quite sufficient to prevent that, even if the cabinet were to show a leaning (which it has not done) in that direction. But at least the Budget for 1898-9 provides for less expenditure than that of 1897-8, and this indicates a recognition by the Ministry of Finance of the fact that the country is not yet equal to the pace proposed in the first flush of success after the war.

What Japan wants just now is some means of remedying the financial stringency that has clogged its footsteps for more than eighteen months past. All the indemnity money has been allocated, and a good deal more in addition. The good effect of the influx has been nullified by the speculative mania, higher taxes, increased wages, and the drain of hard cash caused by over-indulgence in European luxuries of one sort and another; imports are going up at an alarming rate, while exports are now actually on the decline, and the country is at this moment left with about as much money and bullion as it possessed a quarter of a century ago, when the foreign trade was not one-tenth of what it is now. The money at present in London cannot be applied to the relief of this unpleasant situation, for the bulk of it is wanted for the discharge of the country's obligations in Europe, and the balance will be needed to ease the drain occasioned by the alarmingly large exports of gold, which amounted to close upon 5,000,000 yen for February alone. The note issue stands at 350,000,000 yen, and the people are beginning to realise that it is rather too large and that notes are not exactly the same thing to them as gold. Prices have reached an absurdly high level, and enterprise all round is languishing. A loan of £15,000,000 would go a long way in improving matters, provided the money were judiciously handled, and not flung away by the Government in the purchase of more expensive gewgaws for fighting purposes, on which Japan has already spent much more than it can afford. A very sensible way of helping the commercial ventures which are hanging fire for want of capital would be to encourage the investment of European money in them, but until the operation of the new treaties in October next foreigners can have no voice in any Japanese undertaking, and the Japanese themselves have not shown the commercial ability and honesty essential to confidence, while the need of help is very urgent.

To Correspondents.

The Editor cannot undertake to return rejected communications.

Letters from correspondents must, in every case, be authenticated by the name and address of the writer.

Telegraphic Address: "Unveiling, London."

*** Owing to pressure on our space, we are compelled again to leave over our table of prices quoted on the leading provincial exchanges.

CENTRAL PACIFIC RAILROAD.

SHAREHOLDERS' PROTECTION COMMITTEE.

The Right Honourable Sir William Marriott (Chairman).
Aubrey Stanhope, Esq.
M. J. Horgan, Esq., Cork. *F. J. Longton, Esq., Liverpool.
T. Stewart-Jones, Esq., London. *W. Morshead, Esq., London (Deputy-Chairman).
Edward Fox White, Esq., London.

*Committee who protested in March, 1894, against the continuing stoppage by Mr. Huntington of the reduced 2 per cent. dividends.

A meeting of shareholders, favourable to reorganization without assessment, on the basis of the plan which had the approval of Mr. Fairchild, Mr. Bayard, Lord Monkswell, and Sir John Lubbock, as opposed to the Banbury proposals, will be held at Winchester House, Old Broad Street, London, E.C., on Tuesday, the 7th day of June, 1898, at 2.30 p.m.

1. In opposition to the policy and proceedings of (a) Mr. C. P. Huntington, (b) the present Board, and (c) the Banbury Committee.
2. To consider the situation and the measures in progress for the protection of the stockholders.

Meanwhile particulars, with prints of recent correspondence between the Protection Committee and (1) Mr. C. P. Huntington, (2) Mr. Banbury, M.P., and (3) others, may be obtained by shareholders on application to

W. C. GUNNER, Secretary.

124, Chancery Lane—Room No. 12.
19th May, 1898.

The Right Hon. Lord Monkswell has kindly consented to act as Trustee for the stockholders if desired.

SUN LIFE ASSURANCE SOCIETY.

ESTABLISHED 1810.

Funds in hand exceed £3,900,000.
Total Income exceeds £600,000.

The "Perfect Protection" Policy.

LIFE OR ENDOWMENT ASSURANCES

WITH

Relief from payment of Premiums during PERMANENT or temporary illness causing inability to attend to ordinary occupation for at least two consecutive months;

Suspension of payment of Premiums to meet policy-holders' pecuniary convenience;

Immediate payment of half the sum assured on disablement by total loss of eyesight or of two limbs;

AND

Special and attractive Bonus Scheme, providing large reductions or total extinguishment of Premiums payable after age 60.

THE "PERFECT PROTECTION" POLICY affords the most complete and suitable Assurance ever offered to professional and business men dependent upon their own exertions.

Apply for Prospectus giving full particulars to the General Manager.

CHIEF OFFICE

63, THREADNEEDLE STREET, LONDON, E.C.

Notice to Subscribers.

Complaints are continually reaching us that the Investors' Review cannot be obtained at this and the other railway bookstall, that it does not reach Scotch and Irish cities till Monday, and that it is not delivered in the City till Saturday morning.

We publish on Friday in time for the Review to be at all Metropolitan bookstalls by at latest 4 p.m., and we believe that it is there then, having no doubt that Messrs. W. H. Smith & Son do their best, but they have such a mass of papers to handle every day that a fresh one may well look almost like a personal enemy and be kept in short supply unless the reading public shows unmistakably that it is wanted. A little perseverance, therefore, in asking for the Investors' Review is all that should be required to remedy this defect.

All London newsagents can be in a position to distribute the paper on Friday afternoon if they please, and here also the only remedy is for subscribers to insist upon having it as soon as published. Arrangements have been made that all our direct City subscribers shall have their copies before 4 p.m. on Friday. As for the provinces, we can only say that the paper is delivered to the forwarding agents in ample time to be in every English and Scotch town, and in Dublin and Belfast, likewise, early on Saturday morning. Those despatched by post from this office can be delivered by the first London mail on Saturday in every part of the United Kingdom.

ADVERTISEMENTS.

All Advertisements are received subject to approval, and should be sent in not later than 5 p.m. on Thursdays.

The advertisements of American Life Insurance Offices are rigorously excluded from the Investors' Review, and have been so since it commenced as a Quarterly Magazine in 1892.

For tariff and particulars of positions open apply to the Advertisement Manager, Norfolk House, Norfolk-street, W.C.

The Investors' Review.

The Week's Money Market.

Considerable balances were released during the week, and so the short loan market has been comparatively flush of cash. Not only did a portion of the Japanese money come out, but the large inflow of gold increased credits, and the influence in this latter case often came earlier that the actual arrival of the metal, owing to the Bank's system of allowing advances free of interest on shipments. The rate for day to day loans, which a week ago stood at 3 to 4 per cent., has accordingly dropped to 2½ to 3 per cent., and threatens to become weaker if conditions do not change.

Discount rates under these circumstances, had to give way to a moderate extent. Indeed, they would have been very weak if it were not for the political uncertainties of the time. The coin and bullion now totals £36,100,000, which is more than the amount held before the American drain commenced, and is about the same total as was held a year ago when the discount rate stood at 1 per cent. The market, however, has no control over the percentage represented by the amount owned by the Japanese Government; but if it is true that that Government is selling exchange freely against its Bank of England balances, such operations, combined with payments to creditors, must lead to the transfer of a considerable part of the Japanese funds to the market. The American exchange, contrary to general expectation, has risen sharply, and so there is absolutely no demand for gold in the open market, save occasional small orders on account of India. The Bank of England has, therefore, reduced its buying price of bars to the normal figure of 77s. 9d. per ounce, and receives all arrivals of bars. It, however, raised its purchasing price of American eagles to 76s. 5d., and by so doing actually obtained a small parcel on Wednesday. No one, however, attempts to forecast the future by beating down discount rates, and the decline to 3½ to 3$\frac{9}{16}$ per cent. for three months' remitted bills is more the result of the deadweight of these favourable influences than of any disposition to bid freely. The Spanish-American dispute, however, may yet have surprises for the market, and no one is prepared to say that we have seen the end of the gold shipment to America. Whilst the market is still so heavily indebted to the Bank it cannot take too decided an initiative, and if political matters improve, there appears to be the prospect of some large financial schemes being promoted which will draw money out of us. The characteristic of our financial business of late years has been its insularity, but if any proportion of the schemes to develope China and Egypt are put into force, money must leave the country for those purposes. It would therefore be unwise to look for too rapid a decline in discounts, although further weakness is probable.

The issue of £500,000 London County six months' bills was well received, applications to the extent of £2,684,000 being submitted. Tenders at £98 5s. 8½d. received 11 per cent., and the average discount rate for the whole was £3 6s. 9d. per cent. It compared with £1 2s. per cent. for an issue of £600,000 a year ago.

The figures of the Bank return show that the inflow of gold from abroad, and also some returns of gold from circulation, is gradually delivering the market from the grasp of the Bank itself. Altogether £1,521,000 was added to the stock of coin and bullion within the week, £1,384,000 coming from abroad. A few notes also came back to roost, and the reserve of the banking department has consequently been increased by £1,629,000 to £25,441,000. Of this money, £1,465,000 has been utilised to reduce the indebtedness of the market to the Bank, and the "other" deposits are therefore now down to £34,310,000, still a highly respectable total. No advantage has accrued to the "other" deposits which are, indeed, smaller by £380,000 at £43,136,000, because the balances of the Government classed as "public" deposits have risen by £529,000 to £11,933,000, a total even now well above the average at this date. At present, then, the market is not directly enriched by the gold; it is only relieved of strain. A good many more millions' worth of the metal will have to arrive before "cheap money" could again visit us to stay. The poverty of the market is greater than it looks, because the Japanese Government balances, it must never be forgotten, help most materially to swell the total under "other" deposits.

SILVER.

The cessation of Spanish buying caused the price of bars for immediate delivery to drop back last Saturday to 26½d. per ounce. Even at this figure there was no ordinary demand for the East, but the feeling was strong that more Spanish orders would follow, and so no further decline was permitted. This view will probably prove to be correct, and buying, said to be in preparation for another order, has forced the price up again to 26$\frac{5}{16}$d. per ounce. Whilst these orders are about, the market is bound to be unsettled, as being usually of a pressing nature the price paid is a good one, and floating supplies of the metal tend to be absorbed. The Eastern demand, however, is very poor, or else there would have been a much stronger advance. The "forward" quotation, therefore, is no better than 26$\frac{3}{16}$d. per ounce. Indian exchanges have risen to 1s. 4$\frac{1}{32}$d., the banks of Bombay recording a sharp drop in its cash balances as a result of the activity in the grain business. So the Council sells its drafts freely, and since the commencement of April has disposed of nearly £4,000,000. Of course, this is the busy season, but if the wheat business proves to be as large as is hoped, the demand must continue good for some time to come.

BANK OF ENGLAND.

AN ACCOUNT pursuant to the Act 7 and 8 Vict., cap. 32, for the Week ending on Wednesday, May 18, 1898.

ISSUE DEPARTMENT.

	£		£
Notes Issued	50,435,315	Government Debt	11,015,100
		Other Securities	5,784,900
		Gold Coin and Bullion	33,635,315
		Silver Bullion	—
	£50,435,315		£50,435,315

BANKING DEPARTMENT.

	£		£
Proprietors' Capital	14,553,000	Government Securities	13,185,953
Rest	3,206,098	Other Securities	34,310,099
Public Deposits (including Exchequer, Savings Banks, Commissioners of National Debt, and Dividend Accounts)	11,932,659	Notes	22,986,005
Other Deposits	43,135,953	Gold and Silver Coin	2,455,450
Seven Day and other Bills	109,797		
	£72,937,507		£72,937,507

Dated May 19, 1898.

H. G. BOWEN, *Chief Cashier.*

In the following table will be found the movements compared with the previous week, and also the totals for that week and the corresponding return last year:—

Banking Department.

Last Year. May 19.		May 11, 1898.	May 18, 1898.	Increase.	Decrease.
£	Liabilities.	£	£	£	£
3,140,137	Rest	3,191,329	3,206,098	14,769	—
11,494,228	Pub. Deposits	11,403,473	11,932,659	529,185	—
39,500,539	Other do.	43,516,141	43,135,953	—	380,188
182,563	7 Day Bills	112,029	109,797	—	2,232
	Assets.			Decrease.	Increase.
13,922,127	Gov. Securities	13,187,953	13,185,953	2,000	—
28,654,701	Other do.	35,775,252	34,310,099	1,465,153	—
26,293,639	Total Reserve	23,812,767	25,441,455	—	1,628,688
				2,011,108	2,011,108
				Increase.	Decrease.
£		£	£	£	£
27,185,185	Note Circulation	27,556,645	27,449,310	—	107,335
51⅜ p.c.	Proportion	43¼ p.c.	46⅝ p.c.	—	—
2 "	Bank Rate	4 "	4 "	—	—

Foreign Bullion movement for week £1,384,000 in.

LONDON BANKERS' CLEARING.

Month of	1898.	1897.	Increase.	Decrease.
	£	£	£	£
January	673,281,000	576,558,000	96,723,000	—
February	648,601,000	597,652,000	50,949,000	—
March	799,520,000	729 970,000	69,550,000	—
Week ending				
April 6	186,540,000	147,789,000	38,751,000	—
" 13	112,101,000	154,099,000	—	41,998,000
" 20	168,810,000	92,332,000	76,478,000	—
" 27	129,959,000	138,288,000	—	8,329,000
May 4	174,057,000	138,987,000	35,070,000	—
" 11	160,526,000	128,252,000	32,274,000	—
" 18	171,078,000	152,987,000	18,091,000	—
Total to date	3,135,405,000	2,789,819,000	345,586,000	—

BANK AND DISCOUNT RATES ABROAD.

	Bank Rate.	Altered.	Open Market.
Paris	2	March 14, 1895	1⅞
Berlin	4	April 9, 1898	3½
Hamburg	4	April 9, 1898	3¼
Frankfort	4	April 9, 1898	3⅝
Amsterdam	3	April 13, 1897	2¼
Brussels	3	April 28, 1896	2⅞
Vienna	4	January 22, 1896	3⅛
Rome	5	August 27, 1895	3
St. Petersburg	5½	January 23, 1898	4½
Madrid	5	June 17, 1896	5
Lisbon	6	January 25, 1891	6
Stockholm	4	March 3, 1898	4
Copenhagen	4	January 20, 1898	4
Calcutta	11	April 28, 1898	—
Bombay	12	May 5, 1898	—
New York call money	1½ to 2	—	—

NEW YORK ASSOCIATED BANKS (dollar at 4s.).

	May 14, 1898.	May 7, 1898.	April 30, 1898.	May 15, 1897.
	£	£	£	£
Specie	32,678,000	31,058,000	31,678,000	[illegible]
Legal tenders	10,048,000	9,806,000	10,145,000	[illegible]
Loans and discounts	114,734,000	114,218,000	[illegible]	101,100,000
Circulation	2,618,600	2,910,200	[illegible]	[illegible]
Net deposits	[illegible]	131,024,000	[illegible]	114,442,000

Legal reserve is 25 per cent. of net deposits; therefore the total reserve (specie and legal tenders) exceeds this sum by £9,395,000, against an excess last week of £8,783,000.

FOREIGN RATES OF EXCHANGE ON LONDON.

Place.	Usance.	Last week's.	Latest.	Place.	Usance.	Last week's.	Latest.
Paris	chqs.	25'33	25'34	Italy	sight	27'28	27'36
Brussels	chqs.	25'38	25'38	Do. gold prem.	..	107'70	108'15
Amsterdam	short	12'10½	12'10½	Constantinople..	3 mths	109'16	109'20
Berlin.........	short	20'50½	20'47½	B. Ayres gd. pm.	..	158'80	158'30
Do.	3 mths	20'32	20'29	Rio de Janeiro..	90 dys	5⅜d.	5⅜d.
Hamburg	3 mths	20'30	20'29½	Valparaiso......	90 dys	17 7/16d.	17 1/16d.
Frankfort	short	20'49	20'49	Calcutta........	T. T.	1/4	1/4 1/32
Vienna	short	12'09½	12'09	Bombay........	T. T.	1/4 1/32	1/4 1/32
St. Petersburg..	3 mths	93'55	93'75	Hong Kong	T. T.	1/10½	1/10¼
New York......	60 dys	4'81½	4'83½	Shanghai	T. T.	2/5⅜	2/5⅜
Lisbon	sight	30d.	29 7/16d.	Singapore	T. T.	1/10⅜	1/10½
Madrid	sight	45'00	44'10				

IMPERIAL BANK OF GERMANY (20 marks to the £).

	May 14, 1898.	May 7, 1898.	April 30, 1898.	May 15, 1897.
	£	£	£	£
Cash in hand	43,091,550	42,749,100	42,442,550	45,658,000
Bills discounted	33,717,350	35,671,150	37,216,650	*33,931,000
Advances on stocks........	4,090,950	4,219,350	4,462,600	—
Note circulation	54,611,800	56,454,000	58,116,400	52,222,000
Public deposits............	24,561,350	22,297,800	22,135,900	23,917,000

* Includes advances.

AUSTRIAN-HUNGARIAN BANK (1s. 8d. to the florin).

	May 14, 1898.	May 7, 1898.	April 30, 1898.	May 14, 1897.
	£	£	£	£
Gold reserve	29,308,250	29,467,750	29,677,250	27,796,000
Silver reserve	10,454,583	10,443,333	10,441,250	10,508,000
Foreign bills..............	367,666	417,250	473,500	—
Advances	1,834,750	1,842,916	1,833,750	—
Note circulation	52,573,166	53,063,500	53,749,083	51,985,000
Bills discounted	13,731,750	14,122,500	14,009,916	*16,683,000

* Includes advances.

NATIONAL BANK OF BELGIUM (25 francs to the £).

	May 12, 1898.	May 5, 1898.	April 28, 1898.	May 13, 1897.
	£	£	£	£
Coin and bullion	4,240,160	4,391,480	4,266,480	4,143,000
Other securities	16,417,160	16,738,800	16,397,830	15,949,000
Note circulation	19,545,960	19,528,520	19,662,520	18,927,000
Deposits..................	2,476,560	2,962,400	2,581,600	2,420,000

BANK OF SPAIN (25 pesetas to the £).

	May 14, 1898.	May 8, 1898.	April 30, 1898.	May 15, 1897.
	£	£	£	£
Gold	9,833,520	9,833,520	9,833,520	8,649,000
Silver	4,876,440	5,860,520	7,131,520	10,305,240
Bills discounted	30,537,400	28,978,720	29,157,680	8,432,280
Advances and loans........	4,293,120	4,893,360	4,795,760	10,090,560
Notes in circulation	52,718,000	52,292,320	51,621,800	43,772,720
Treasury advances, coupon account	409,240	112,360	765,200	501,320
Treasury balances	359,240	277,760	180,560	727,240

LONDON COURSE OF EXCHANGE.

Place.	Usance.	May 10.	May 12.	May 17.	May 19.
Amsterdam and Rotterdam	short	12'2½	12'2½	12'2½	12'2½
Do. do.	3 months	12'4⅜	12'4½	12'4⅜	12'4⅜
Antwerp and Brussels	3 months	25'60	25'60	25'57½	25'58¾
Hamburg..................	3 months	20'72	20'72	20'70	20'69
Berlin and German B. Places	3 months	20'72	20'72	20'70	20'69
Paris	cheques	25'35	25'35	25'35	25'36¼
Do.	3 months	25'50	25'50	25'48¾	25'50
Marseilles	3 months	25'51¼	25'51¼	25'50	25'51¼
Switzerland................	3 months	25'72½	25'72½	25'72½	25'71¼
Austria..................	3 months	12'26¼	12'25	12'25	12'25
St. Petersburg	3 months	24 11/16	24 11/16	24 11/16	24 11/16
Moscow	3 months	24⅝	24⅝	24⅝	24⅝
Italian Bank Places	3 months	27'55	27'62½	27'77½	27'67½
New York	60 days	48 11/16	48¾	48 11/16	48¾
Madrid and Spanish B. P. ..	3 months	24	24¼	26¼	24½ nom.
Lisbon	3 months	29	29⅛	28¼	28¼
Oporto	3 months	29	29⅛	28½	28¼
Copenhagen................	3 months	18'46	18'46	18'45	18'45
Christiania	3 months	18'46	18'46	18'45	18'45
Stockholm	3 months	18'46	18'46	18'45	18'45

OPEN MARKET DISCOUNT.

	Per cent.
Thirty and sixty day remitted bills	3½
Three months "	3½
Four months "	3½
Six months "	3½—3⅝
Three months fine inland bills	4
Four months "	4
Six months "	4¼

BANK AND DEPOSIT RATES.

	Per cent.
Bank of England minimum discount rate	4
" " short loan rates	4
Banker's rate on deposits	2½
Bill brokers' deposit rate (call)	2½
" 7 and 14 days' notice	2½
Current rates for 7 day loans	2½—3
" " for call loans	2½

Stock Market Notes and Comments.

There is really nothing new to be said about the stock markets this week; they would have been as calm as a mill pond on a summer's day but for the sensation caused by Mr. Chamberlain's speech. That did not disturb us much here on Saturday, but it caused a first-class sensation on the Continental bourses, and induced speculators, in Paris more particularly, to sell with great persistence. The "funk" spread to London, and all this week we have been in a state of grumbling disgust. Business has been made difficult, and prices have kept displaying a tendency to fall which effectively prevents serious people from coming near the market. Now the Stock Exchange never likes to be left to itself. It must have a large public playing upon it, and busy buying and selling, and failing this it falls out of heart and into a mood to accept almost anything with ill-humour. Rumours of the most silly description pass across markets, we may say every hour of the day, and a punter may here and there profit by a momentary rise or fall in some price or other caused by some of these rumours. Generally speaking, however, they have no effect of any kind; people have got too *blasé* to care for the sensational stories they are continually treated to, and in their cynical moments numbers will be heard to declare that even this Spanish-American war is little better than a long-drawn-out farce. How exhausted minds have become through a surfeit of sensations could be measured by the slender results produced on Monday when the tale was put about that Mr. Chamberlain had "resigned." To be sure, nobody in the least imagined him capable of such a step, and in its present mood the market would be much more disposed to believe that he had procured the resignation of Lord Salisbury, so unpopular is his Lordship with the scatter-brained lot we mostly have to do with. Anyway, the story was laughed at and prices lay still. Yet we believe it is a fact that the right hon. gentleman did tender his resignation—to cow his colleagues, of course, and bring Lord Salisbury back to a due state of meekness.

Under such a condition it is useless to pretend to give definite advice of any kind, except to reiterate our well-worn one, "keep away from markets." Nothing is to be gained just now by buying anything, and much may be lost. For the time being, and for various reasons we need not now specify, the money market looks easier, and were circumstances otherwise happy cheaper money would as usual cause prices to advance. But when we see gold pouring into the bank and Consols often falling in price we may be quite sure that markets are not favourable to investors. There is an undercurrent of uneasiness which bars the way to a steady upward movement, and until it has died down or disappeared the prudent will buy sparingly, if at all. Why, even the great Sir Thomas Lipton, it seems, is not able just yet to invest his money. He was paid up this week by the company to which he has transferred his business, and must have the best part of £2,000,000 lying idle at his bankers'. Popular estimate computes him to be worth considerably over £3,000,000 altogether, and he must be a poor, unhappy man with so much money that he does not know what to do with. To let it lie at his bankers always would never do, and yet he does not feel able to invest it on the Stock Exchange; not yet, at any rate. He had better go round the country and pick up a few derelict landed estates and improve them. They will be worth having some day when the young men who are coming on have been taught by bitter experience that it is better to cultivate the soil of their native land than to buy "Chartereds" and play pitch and toss with things like Northern "Terrors," while cursing the Russians and inviting the French to come on.

American geniuses of this sort appear to be still happy in pushing up the prices of their own securities, and we rejoice. It not only allows us to sell, but reduces the danger of heavy demands from New York upon our stock of gold. But really, we see no sense in this action. The war with Spain does not appear to have commenced yet. It almost looks just now as if when it does start Rear-Admiral Dewey might have ground for thinking that he would have done more wisely to have looked in at Manila on his way out to his China station after helping to conquer Cuba than to get trapped their on his way home for the fray. Really, though, there is no knowing but what the Wall-street speculators have got a tip that the whole thing is a joke or mystification intended to cover a "transaction" wherein dollars will go to Spain in exchange for Cuba. In that case—ah! the wind is still in the East and our gift of prophecy is frozen up.

The Week's Stock Markets.

An almost total absence of business has been the general report from markets throughout the week. The uneasiness caused by the aspect of foreign affairs was increased by Mr. Chamberlain's speech at Birmingham on Friday last, and although there was not much selling at any one time, there was, on the other hand, no inclination on the part of operators to increase their commitments during the present unsettled state of things. As there was no support forthcoming from the outside public, prices are lower in all departments, although the slightly steadier tendency on the Continental bourses on Wednesday helped to strengthen markets here which were inclined to harden under the influence of the Premier's speech in the House of Lords on Tuesday night. Consols have come down steadily, and Indian Government stock close flat. Home corporation issues, after being weak, finally show a recovery in several instances, and Colonial Government descriptions also rallied from the lowest points of the week, but Indian railway shares have been depressed and close at the worst.

Highest and Lowest this Year.	Last Carrying over Price.	BRITISH FUNDS, &c.	Closing Price.	Rise or Fall.
113⅛ 109¼	—	Consols 2¾ p.c. (Money)...	110⅞	—
113 1/16 109½	111¼	Do. Account (June 1)	111	− ⅛
106¼ 101	104½	2½ p.c. Stock red. 1905 ...	104	+ ¼
363 341	—	Bank of England Stock...	345	—1
117 111⅜	114	India 3½ p.c. Stk. red. 1931	113¼	— ¼
109¼ 103⅜	107½	Do. 3 p.c. Stk. red. 1948	106¾	+ ¼
96⅜ 90	92¼	Do. 2½ p.c. Stk. red. 1926	91	—1

In the Home railway market, the principal transactions have been in the stocks of the passenger lines, and the fluctuations in the deferred stocks of the Brighton and South Eastern Companies have been considerable. The former company's traffic return was again disappointing, the poor showing being doubtless due to the unsettled weather. Metropolitan ordinary has reacted after last week's sharp rise, and Great Central issues have fallen in sympathy. Great Western gave way,

Highest and Lowest this Year.	Last Carrying over Price.	HOME RAILWAYS.	Closing Price.	Rise or Fall.
186 172½	176½	Brighton Def.	175	−2
59¼ 54⅞	56½	Caledonian Def.	56¼	− ¾
20⅛ 18¼	19¾	Chatham Ordinary	19¼	− ⅝
77¼ 62	65	Great Central Pref.	66	− ½
24⅜ 21¼	22	Do. Def.	22½	− ½
124½ 118	119¼	Great Eastern	119⅜	− ¼
61¼ 50¾	53¼	Great Northern Def.	53¼	−1½
179¼ 168½	170	Great Western	168⅞	−1⅜
51¼ 45¼	50⅜	Hull and Barnsley	49⅞	− ⅜
149¼ 145	146	Lanc. and Yorkshire	145½	−1
136⅛ 127¼	131½	Metropolitan	131	−3½
31 26¾	28	Metropolitan District	27½	− ⅛
88⅜ 82½	84½	Midland Pref.	83¾	−1
95⅛ 84½	87½	Do. Def.	86¼	−1½
93¼ 86¾	89½	North British Pref.	89¼	− ¾
47½ 41¾	43⅛	Do. Def.	43	− ⅛
181½ 172¾	174½	North Eastern	174	− ¾
205¼ 196¼	197¾	North Western	196⅞	−1
117⅛ 105½	110	South Eastern Def.	109⅝	−1⅜
98⅜ 87	91½	South Western Def.	92¼	− ¾

although the traffic return was no worse than it has been at any time during the dead-lock in the Welsh coal district, which still seems to be a long way from being settled. Taff Vale is also lower for the same reason, and the Midland return was a poor one; otherwise the traffics were good. In the present condition of affairs, a very little selling caused a considerable decline, and the closing quotations, although rather above the worst, yet still show a serious depreciation. A certain amount of "pawned" stock has come on the market during the last few days, and helped to still further depress prices; but towards the close a few investment purchases came to hand, and imparted a rather steadier tone.

United States railroad shares were also adversely affected by Mr. Chamberlain's speech, taken in conjunction with the fact that the long-looked-for and decisive action between the American and Spanish fleets is still delayed. A little Continental and local buying steadied the market here for a time, but prices are all lower than a week ago, in common with the decline in other departments. In Wall-street business has been on a small scale, and the little buying that has taken place was of the purely professional type, while the reaction in the price of wheat did not tend to improve matters.

Highest and Lowest this Year.	Last Carrying over Price.	CANADIAN AND U.S. RAILWAYS.	Closing Prices.	Rise or Fall.
14 1/16 10⅜	12½	Atchison Shares	12¼	− ⅞
34 23½	31	Do. Pref.	31½	− ½
15⅝ 11	13¼	Central Pacific	12½	− ¾
99¾ 85½	98	Chic. Mil. & St. Paul	98¼	− ¼
14¼ 10	12	Denver Shares	11½	− ⅝
54¼ 41½	48½	Do. Prefd.	46¼	−1¾
16⅝ 11¼	13¾	Erie Shares	12⅛	−1
44⅛ 29½	36½	Do. Prefd.	34⅞	−1⅜
110½ 99	106¼	Illinois Central	106	−1¼
62½ 45¼	55¼	Louisville & Nashville ...	54½	−1⅜
14½ 9 3/16	12	Missouri & Texas	11	− ⅛
122¼ 108½	118½	New-York Central	117¾	−1¼
57¼ 42⅞	52	Norfolk & West. Prefd....	51	−1
70⅛ 59	68¼	Northern Pacific Prefd....	66⅝	−1
19½ 13⅜	15¾	Ontario Shares	15¼	− ⅛
62½ 56¾	60¼	Pennsylvania	58¾ xd	− ½
12½ 7 3/16	9¾	Reading Shares	9⅛	− ½
34½ 24¼	30¼	Southern Prefd.	29⅜	−1⅛
37⅛ 18½	24	Union Pacific	23	− ⅝
20¼ 14½	20½	Wabash Prefd.	19	−1
30¼ 21	28½	Do. Income Debs....	26½	−1½
92¾ 74	86	Canadian Pacific	85	−1¼
78⅛ 69⅞	74	Grand Trunk Guar.	74⅜	− ⅛
69¼ 57⅛	68½	Do. 1st Pref.	68⅜	− ⅛
50⅛ 37¼	49	Do. 2nd Pref.	48⅞	− ⅛
25⅛ 19¼	22¾	Do. 3rd Pref.	22⅛	− ⅜
105¾ 101½	102⅛	Do. 4 p.c. Deb.	103	− ¼

Canadian Pacific and Grand Trunk issues, after a period of dulness, picked up a little, and when both the companies published good returns there was a smart rally to nearly last week's level. Nothing whatever has yet transpired as to any settlement of the rate war question having been arrived at.

Foreign Government stocks have followed the downward trend of prices reported from all the Continental bourses, which were seriously alarmed by Lord Salisbury's unreported speech, followed as it was immediately after by Mr. Chamberlain's very much reported one. The Paris Bourse especially got into a very nervous state, business consisting chiefly of realisations made in consequence of these disquieting utterances. Spanish 4 per cents. again mark a moderate decline, although once towards the close of last week a little French support was forthcoming, a few "bear" operators closing their accounts. The Madrid exchange shows a further improvement, but any advantage that might have been taken of this fact was more than offset by the news of another Cabinet crisis and a disagreement among the ministers, coupled with rumours of fresh disturbances in Madrid. Italian Rente has attracted much less attention this week than last, and purchases on behalf of the Italian Government, and the report that tranquility is now completely restored in Milan and the other affected districts, has kept the price tolerably steady. Heavy sales of Turkish groups on a very narrow market caused a sharp fall, part of which has since been made up. Chinese loans drooped owing to Mr. Chamberlain's remarks about the state of affairs in the Far East, and Transvaal 5 per cents. fell a little after President Kruger's speech was received here. Apart from Spanish bonds, which show no recovery from the worst point of the week, there is a slightly firmer tone apparent in all inter-Bourse securities at the last, due to repurchases by "bear" operators, who were anxious to close their accounts prior to the holiday yesterday (Ascension Day). In the South American section, Argentine issues all gave way on the news of the increase in the export duty on wheat. Brazilian bonds have hardly moved, the Rio exchange remaining stationary, while the proposal to pay the interest half in gold and half in scrip has met with approval. Among the less prominent securities there has been a fall of 5 in Salvador 6 per cents.

Highest and Lowest this Year.		Last Carrying over Price.	FOREIGN BONDS.	Closing Price.	Rise or Fall.
94½	84	88¾	Argentine 5 p.c. 1886......	87½	−2
92⅝	81⅝	86¼	Do. 6 p.c. Funding	85½	−1½
76¾	64	69	Do. 5 p.c. B. Ay. Water	67½	−2½
61⅝	41½	47	Brazilian 4 p.c. 1889	46	−¼
69⅞	46	53	Do. 5 p.c. 1895	52½	−½
65	42¾	48¼	Do. 5 p.c. West Minas Ry....................	47	−1
108⅜	105½	107	Egyptian 4 p.c. Unified...	107	−¼
104¾	100½	102	Do. 3½ p.c. Pref. ...	102	+¼
103	99½	101½	French 3 p.c. Rente	101	−½
44⅞	34½	42½	Greek 4 p.c. Monopoly...	42	−½
93 3/16	88¾	90¼	Italian 5 p.c. Rente	89 13/16	−7/16
100	87½	95½	Mexican 6 p.c. 1888	96	−½
20⅞	16	17¼	Portuguese 1 p.c.	17¼	−⅛
64½	29⅝	32¼	Spanish 4 p.c.	32½	−1⅝
45½	40	44	Turkish 1 p.c. "B"	43¾	−¾
26 1/16	22¾	24¾	Do. 1 p.c. "C"	24¼	−¼
22 1/16	20	21¼	Do. 1 p.c. "D"	21¼	−¼
46⅝	40	44½	Uruguay 3½ p.c. Bonds...	44¼	−¼

Argentine railway stocks have also been adversely affected by the proposed increase in the export duty on wheat, and although the traffic returns again show substantial gains, there is a considerable shrinkage in prices, especially in Buenos Ayres Great Southern ordinary. On the other hand, rumours of a settlement with the Government caused an inquiry for the Cordoba Central Company's stocks. Nitrate Railway shares have quietly slipped back again to their old level, and the Mexican Company's emissions were sold after the meeting on Friday last.

Highest and Lowest this Year.		Last Carrying over Price.	FOREIGN RAILWAYS.	Closing Price.	Rise or Fall.
101¼	99	99	Argentine Gt. West. 5 p.c. Pref. Stock..................	101	—
158½	134	138½	B. Ay. Gt. Southern Ord..	136	−4
78⅝	65	71½	B. Ay. and Rosario Ord...	72½	−1
12¼	10¼	10¾	B. Ay. Western Ord.	10¾	−¼
87½	73	78	Central Argentine Ord....	78	−1½
92	78	79	Cordoba and Rosario 6 p.c. Deb.	78	−3
95½	85½	87½	Cord. Cent. 4 p.c. Deb. (Cent. Nth. Sec.)	89	−1
61⅝	42	46½	Do. Income Deb. Stk. ...	51½	+1½
25½	16¾	18¼	Mexican Ord. Stk.	18	−1
83½	69½	72½	Do. 8 p.c. 1st Pref.	71½	−2

The Miscellaneous market has been a dull and uninteresting one, and in the majority of cases the changes have been in the downward direction. Among brewery stocks Guinness ordinary fell 10 and Allsopp preferred ordinary 3, but Guinness's preference and Younger preference are both 2 higher. Telegraph companies' issues are lower, as it is feared that some more cable cutting will yet be heard of, but there has been a steady rise amounting to about 15 in Commercial Cable. Gas Light "A" is firmer on the passing of the company's Bill for splitting the stock, but holders of electric lighting companies' shares have taken fright at the possibility of the threatened competition from the local vestries. Among the very few changes in the upward direction a slight improvement in Howell and James is noticeable on the satisfactory meeting. Pillsbury-Washburn Mills ordinary and preference show a urther advance, and P. and O. deferred is 2 igher. On the other hand, Holborn and Frascati ebenture has fallen 4, and La Guaira Harbour debenre 5½. Bryant and May shares gave way owing to the Government inquiry as to the death of several of the company's employés, and British Tea Table ordinary was pressed for sale on the appearance of a discouraging report. Welsbach ordinary is 4 lower.

Almost the only feature during the closing hours of the week was a sudden rise in Consols, a few purchases for cash, and a little "bear" closing being quite sufficient to raise the price fully ½ per cent., as the market appears to be very bare of stock. The Indian Government sterling loan, and one or two of the leading Home corporation stocks also shared in the upward movement. All the Continental bourses being closed to-day (Thursday), business was almost at a standstill, but the tone was fairly steady in the foreign market, Argentine Government and railway bonds being inquired for. United States railroad shares gave way a little more, notably Denver preferred, Louisville and Southern preferred, and Canadian issues were weaker in sympathy. Apart from a further heavy fall in Mount Lyell shares, the mining market was quiet and featureless.

MINING AND FINANCE COMPANIES.

The South African market was not taken with President Kruger's speech, and the Paris Bourse being in such a depressed state, and doing little except send selling orders, jobbers naturally rather hesitated about making prices. On Tuesday, for the first time for nearly a week, there was a little recovery on "bear" closing, but it did not amount to much. Western Australian ventures have been more erratic in their movements, but the net result is to leave prices rather the worse, although the fall rarely amounts to more than about ⅜. "Market Trusts" at one time touched 2s. and then moved up a little. Copper shares all fell sharply, in spite of the large reduction noticeable in the visible supply of the metal. Rio Tinto was particularly weak owing to reported disturbances at the mines, while the fall in Mount Lyell was due to the arrival of a cabled extract of the report. Indian shares are generally a little weaker.

Next Week's Meetings.

MONDAY, MAY 23.

Arnold Perrot & Co....	1, East India-avenue, 3 p.m.
Kimberley Diamond Mining ...	Winchester House, 3.30 p.m.
London and South African Exploration	Winchester House, 3 p.m.
London Bank of Australia	Winchester House, 12.30 p.m.
Malay Peninsula Coffee	138, Leadenhall-street, 1 p.m.
River Plate Gas	Winchester House, 12.30 p.m.

TUESDAY, MAY 24.

Brazilian Street Railway	Gresham House, 2.30 p.m.
Castle Mail Packets Company ...	Cannon-street Hotel, noon.
Lambeth Waterworks	Brixton Hill, noon.
London Corn Exchange (Special) ...	Mark-lane, noon.
Mason & Barry	87, Cannon-street, noon.
Nitrate Railways	Winchester House, noon.
Rohilkund & Kumaon Railway ...	Gresham House, noon.
W. N. White & Co.	Cannon-street Hotel, 12.30 p.m.

WEDNESDAY, MAY 25.

American and General Investment	Winchester House, 3 p.m.
General Life Assurance	103, Cannon-street, 1 p.m.
North Brancepeth Coal	Darlington, noon.
Otago and Southland Investment ...	5, Adam's-court, 11.30 a.m.
Reuter's Telegram Agency	Old Jewry, noon.
Santa Anna Gold Mining	Winchester House, 2 p.m.
Southern Brazilian Rio Grande do Sul	Winchester House, noon.
Weinhold Estate of Australia ...	52, Lombard-street, noon.

THURSDAY, MAY 26

Army and Navy Auxiliary Supply ...	Westminster Town Hall, 2.30 p.m.
Eugene Rimmel	5, Chancery-lane, 4 p.m.
First Scottish American Trust ...	Dundee, noon.
Nobel Dynamite Trust	Winchester House, 1 p.m.
Rock Life	15, New Bridge-street, noon.
San Donato Nitrate	Liverpool, 11 a.m.
Trust and Loan Company of Canada	7, Great Winchester-street, 2 p.m.

FRIDAY, MAY 27.

Ballaghat Valley	Cannon-street Hotel, noon.
astner Kellner Alkali Company ...	Cannon-street Hotel, noon.
Freshwater Yarmouth and Newport Railway	9, Clements-lane, 2 p.m.
Jhanzie Tea Association	14, St. Mary Axe, 2.30 p.m.
King's Norton Metal Company ...	16, Gt. George-street, S.W., noon.
Union Assurance	81, Cornhill, noon.

Answers to Correspondents.

Questions about public securities, and on all points in company law, as well as on the position of life insurance offices and their promises, will be answered week by week, in the Review, on the following terms and conditions :—

A fee of FIVE shillings must be remitted for each question put, provided they are questions about separate securities. Should a private letter be required, then an extra fee of FIVE shillings must be sent to cover the cost of such letter, the fee then being TEN shillings for one query only, and FIVE shillings for every subsequent one in the same letter. While making this concession the Editor will feel obliged if private replies are as much as possible dispensed with. It is wholly impossible to answer letters sent merely "with a stamped envelope enclosed for reply."

Correspondents will further greatly oblige by so framing their questions as to obviate the necessity to name securities in the replies. They should *number* the questions, keeping a copy for reference, thus :—"(1) Please inform me about the present position of the Rowenzori Development Co. (2) Is a dividend likely to be paid soon on the capital stock of the Congo-Sudan Railway ?

Answers to be given to all such questions by simply quoting the numbers 1, 2, 3, and so on. The Editor has a rooted objection to such forms of reply as—"I think your Timbuctoo Consols will go up," or "Sell your Slowcoach and Draggem Bonds," because this kind of thing is open to all sorts of abuses. By the plan suggested, and by using a fancy name to be replied to, each query can be kept absolutely private to the inquirer, and no scope whatever be given to market manipulations. Avoid, as names to be replied to, common words, like "investor," "inquirer," and so on, as also "bear" or "bull." Detached syllables of the inquirer's name, or initials reversed, will frequently do as well as anything, so long as the answer can be identified by the inquirer.

The Editor further respectfully requests that merely speculative questions should as far as possible be avoided. He by no means sets himself up as a market prophet, and can only undertake to provide the latest information regarding the securities asked about. This he will do faithfully and without bias.

Replies cannot be guaranteed in the same week if the letters demanding them reach the office of the Investors' Review, Norfolk House, Norfolk-street, W.C., later than the first post on Wednesday mornings.

J. F. S.—It is not possible to say yet how the company is doing, but it does not appear to be very strong financially. Purchase price was heavy and the issue was not fully subscribed; the underwriters had to take a big percentage. There is very little market, but you may be able to sell your stock. If you can, you should do so even at a discount.

NJOX.—1. Quite good. 2. Such issues must be publicly made. 3. They are only advantageous as temporary investments. 4. They are not very marketable and, as a rule, I think you will find the borrower only has right to give the "cancelling notice." 5. Yes, if you are satisfied with the return. Mortgages on even high-class properties usually yield a little more.

A. J.—1 and 2. Financially, position is moderate, the business, however, appears to be growing. See no reason for selling at present. 3. I have no particulars of this concern. If you will send me copy of report I will look into it. 4. I did not like the prospectus of this concern, but have not seen the first report. An interim dividend was paid in September, which proves nothing. If you can get out reasonably I think you can find something safer. 5. None of the companies controlled by founders of this concern are investments in the proper sense of the word. Your company makes its money to a large extent by market manipulations, which lately have been seldom possible or profitable. I cannot say whether it is right to sell now or not, as it is quite likely efforts will be made to improve this market generally, which will probably be successful, unless politics put a stop to such tactics. 6. Are not worth selling at present prices. Those managing it and others in this group are, I believe, honest, though sanguine. 7. Have you ever noticed the price of the debentures of this company ? The shares are mere gambling counters and, intrinsically, have little value ; but here, again, market operations may be successful. Arrangements are being made to try and put a better face on its prospects, and such is the belief in its future that I should not be surprised to see a rise, but I should not care to guarantee it. Kindly read instructions at the head of this column and note same for your future guidance.

A formidable coal trust is the latest development of the spirit of American monopoly manufacture. We are told that negotiations are now pending in Boston, United States, which, if completed in conformity with the hopes of the negotiators, will result in the discontinuance of some of the largest coal firms doing business in Boston. The scheme is to organise a company which will take over the business of these firms, which handle annually about 1,000,000 tons. This is not quite half the amount of the United States present annual export ; but if the suggested scheme is successful, it may but form the nucleus of more gigantic schemes, which, in course of time, may embrace a large part of the coal output of the States.

The India Council is renewing £2,500,000 of its sterling bills falling due on the 3rd proximo, and tenders for these will be received this day week at the chief cashier's office, Bank of England.

Prices of Mine and Mining Finance Companies' Shares.

Shares £1 each except where otherwise stated.

Australian.

Making-Up Price, May 9.	Name	Closing Price.	Rise or Fall.	Making-Up Price, May 9.	Name	Closing Price.	Rise or Fall.
1½	Aladdin	1½		11/16	Hannan's Star	⅞	+ 1/16
3⅜	Associated	3 3/16	− 1/16	5 5/16	Ivanhoe, New	5 1/16	− ¼
1/16	Do. Southern	1/16		1/16	Kalgurli Mt.&Iron King, 18/	½	
1	Brownhill Extended	1 1/16	− ⅛	5½	Kalgurli	5 1/16	− 11/16
1	Burbank's Birthday	1½		2 3/16	Lady Shenton	2 1/16	− ⅛
⅜	Central Boulder	⅜	− 1/16	8¼	Lake View Cons.	8 1/16	− 1/16
5/	Chaffers, 4/	4/3	− /9	½	Do. Extended	⅜	− ⅛
11/16	Colonial Finance, 15/	½ dis		⅜	Do. South	⅜	− 1/16
⅜	Crœsus S. United	5/16	− 1/16	1¼	London & Globe Finance	1⅛	− 1/16
⅞	E. Murchison	1	+ 1/16	⅜	London & W. A. Exploration	⅜	− 1/16
4/	Golden Arrow 19/	4/3	− /9	1/16	Do. Investment	½	− 1/16
8¼	Golden Horseshoe	8 11/16	+ 7/16	½	Mainland Consols	1/16	− 1/16
11/16	Golden Link	11/16	+ 1/16	11/16	North Boulder, 10/	½	− 1/16
19/9	Great Boulder, 2/	17/6	− 1/9	1 5/16	North Kalgurli	1 1/16	− 1/16
1¼	Do. Main Reef, 10/	1 3/16	− 1/16	⅞	Northern Territories	13/16	− 1/16
2¼	Do. Perseverance	2⅛	− 1/16	2¼	Peak Hill	2¼	
11/16	Do. South	⅝	− 1/16	1⅜	South Kalgurli	1 3/16	− ⅛
1¾	Hainault	1⅝	− ⅛	1¼	W. A. Goldfields	1¼	+ 1/16
⅝	Hampton Plains	11/16	− 1/16	11/16	W. A. Joint Stock	1/16	− 1/16
7 5/16	Hannan's Brownhill	7 1/16	− ¼	2/3	W. A. Market Trust	2/6	− 1/6
⅝	Hannan's Oroya	1/16	− 1/16	⅞	W. A. Loan & General Fin.	⅞	
1/1	Do. Proprietary	10/9	− 2/3	5/16	White Feather	⅜	

South African.

Making-Up Price, May 9.	Name	Closing Price.	Rise or Fall.	Making-Up Price, May 9.	Name	Closing Price.	Rise or Fall.
5½	Angelo	5 1/16	− 1/16	2/3	Lisbon-Berlyn	1/6	− /9
1	Aurora West	1	− ⅛	2¼	May Consolidated	2⅛	− ⅛
1⅛	Bantjes	1	− ⅛	4	Meyer and Charlton	3⅞	− ⅛
8/6	Barrett, 10/	8/6		3 11/16	Modderfontein	3 9/16	− 1/16
4 3/16	Bonanza	4¼	+ 1/16	1 3/16	New Bultfontein	1 1/16	
⅞	Buffelsdoorn	13/16	− 1/16	3 13/16	New Primrose	3⅝	− ⅛
5 5/16	City and Suburban, £4	5⅛	− ⅛	1⅜	Nigel	1⅜	
2¼	Comet (New)	2⅛	− ⅛	1¼	Nigel Deep	1	− ¼
3½	Con. Deep Level	3⅜	− ⅛	⅞	North Randfontein	⅞	
11	Crown Deep	11¼		5	Nourse Deep	4⅞	− ⅛
12⅞	Crown Reef	12⅝	− ¼	1 1/16	Porges-Randfontein	1	− 1/16
27	De Beers, £5	26⅞	− ⅛	30½	Rand Mines	28¾	− 1¾
3⅞	Driefontein	3⅝	− ¼	1 5/16	Randfontein	1 1/16	− ¼
6¼	Durban Roodepoort	6⅛	− ⅛	1 5/16	Rietfontein	1⅛	− ⅛
3 1/16	Do. Deep	3⅛	− ⅛	9¾	Robinson Deep	9⅝	− ⅛
4 11/16	East Rand	4½	− ⅛	7⅞	Do. Gold, £5	8	− ⅛
24½	Ferreira	23⅞	− ⅝	1 3/16	Do. Randfontein	11/16	− 1/16
7	Geldenhuis Deep	7⅜	− ⅛	1 5/16	Roodepoort Central Deep	1⅛	− 1/16
5⅛	Do. Estate	5⅛	− ⅛	6½	Rose Deep	6¼	− ¼
⅞	George Goch	⅞	− 1/16	3 5/16	Salisbury	3 1/16	− 1/16
2⅛	Ginsberg	2⅛	− ⅛	1⅜	Sheba	1⅜	− ⅛
1 11/16	Glencairn	1 9/16	− ⅛	3⅜	Simmer and Jack, £5	3⅛	− ⅛
8⅞	Goldfields Deep	8⅝	− ¼	3 1/16	Transvaal Gold	2 15/16	− 1/16
8½	Griqualand West	8⅝	+ ⅛	3½	Treasury	3⅜	− ⅛
9	Henry Nourse	8⅞	− ⅛	3⅜	United Roodepoort	3¼	− ⅛
7⅝	Heriot	7⅜	− ¼	1⅜	Van Ryn	1 5/16	− 1/16
7⅞	Jagersfontein	7⅝	− ¼	5 11/16	Village Main Reef	5 9/16	− 1/16
8⅞	Jubilee	9⅝		1⅜	Vogelstruis	1 5/16	− 1/16
5 1/16	Jumpers	5	− ⅛	11/16	Do. Deep	⅝	− ⅛
2 5/16	Kleinfontein	2 3/16	− 1/16	9⅞	Wemmer	9⅞	
3⅞	Knight's	3⅝	− ¼	1/16	West Rand	⅞	− ⅛
2⅞	Lancaster	2 9/16	− 3/16	5⅞	Wolhuter, £4	5⅝	− ¼
3⅝	Langlaagte Estate	3⅜	− ¼	2⅝	Worcester	2¾	+ ⅛

Land Exploration and Rhodesian.

Making-Up Price, May 9.	Name	Closing Price.	Rise or Fall.	Making-Up Price, May 9.	Name	Closing Price.	Rise or Fall.
2½	Anglo-French Ex.	2⅛	− ⅜	⅞	Mashonaland Central	⅞	
1⅞	Barnato Consolidated	1 11/16	− 3/16	6¼	Matabele Gold Reefs	5⅞	− ⅜
⅞	Bechuanaland Ex.	13/16	− 1/16	2 3/16	Mozambique	2 1/16	− 1/16
2⅞	Chartered B.S.A.	2 5/16	− ⅛	⅞	Oceana Consolidated	13/16	− 1/16
⅝	Clark's Cons.	5/16		1 1/16	Rhodesia, Ltd.	1⅛	− ⅛
1/16	Colenbrander	⅝	− 1/16	4⅛	Do. Exploration	3⅞	− ¼
4⅜	Cons. Goldfields	4 5/16	− 1/16	1	Do. Goldfields	13/16	− 1/16
1	Do. Pref.	20/6	+ /6	4	S. A. Gold Trust	3⅞	− 1/16
1½	Exploration	1⅜	− ⅛	1	Tati Concessions	1	− 1/16
2 3/16	Geelong	2⅛	− 1/16	11/16	Transvaal Development	⅝	− 1/16
5/16	Henderson's Est.	⅝	− 1/16	11/16	United Rhodesia	⅞	
1 1/16	Johannesburg Con. In.	1 1/16	− ⅛	1 1/16	Willoughby	1	− 1/16
⅞	Do. Water	13/16	− 1/16	13/16	Zambesia Explor.	13/16	− 1/16
1⅜	Mashonaland Agency	1 3/16	− ⅛				

Miscellaneous.

Making-Up Price, May 9.	Name	Closing Price.	Rise or Fall.	Making-Up Price, May 9.	Name	Closing Price.	Rise or Fall.
1	Alamillos, £2	1½		⅞	Mount Lyell, South	7/6	− 1/6
5	Anaconda, $25	4⅞	− ⅛	4 5/16	Mount Morgan, 17s. 6d.	4 3/16	− 1/16
5/6	Balaghât, 18/	6/6		5 1/16	Mysore, 10s.	5	− 1/16
12/	Brilliant, £2	12/	− /3	11/6	Mysore Goldfields	10/6	− 1/
2 3/16	Do. St. George's	2 1/16	− 1/16	5/6	Do. Reefs, 17/	5/6	+ 1/
9/6	British Broken Hill	10/6	+ 1/	7/	Do. West	7/	
2⅜	Broken Hill Proprietary	2⅜		6/	Do. Wynaad	5/6	
3	Do. Block 10	3		2⅝	Namaqua, £2	2 3/16	− 1/16
5	Cape Copper, £2	4 13/16	− 3/16	3 11/16	Nundydroog	3 9/16	− ⅛
5	Champion Reef, 10s.	4 15/16	− 1/16	3½	Ooregum	3⅜	− ⅛
2⅜	Copiapo, £2	2 5/16		3 3/16	Do. Pref.	3 1/16	− ⅛
2 13/16	Coromandel	2⅝	− 3/16	26½	Rio Tinto Def., £5	25⅞	− ⅝
15/	Day Dawn Block	14/9		5⅛	Do. Pref. £5	5 1/16	− 1/16
2 3/16	Frontino & Bolivia	2⅛		1	St. John del Rey	20/	
1 5/16	Hall Mines	1¼	− 1/16	8/9	Taiupu	7/6	
2⅞	Libiola, £5	2⅝	− ¼	7	Tharsis, £2	6⅞	− ⅛
8	Linares, £3	7⅞		2½	Tolima "A," £5	2½	
4	Mason & Barry, £3	4		4⅛	Waihi	4 1/16	− ⅛
4⅜	Mountain Copper, £5	4⅜		1⅜	Waitekauri	1¼	− ⅛
12⅛	Mount Lyell, £3	10⅞	− 1¼	⅞	Woodstock (N.Z.)	¾	− ⅛
2⅝	Mount Lyell, North	2 9/16	− 1/16				

The foreign trade of France during the first four months of 1898 amounted in value to, imports 1,474,144,000 francs, and exports, 1,132,733,000 francs, as compared with imports 1,328,923,000 francs, and exports 1,157,016,000 francs in the corresponding period of last year.

The gold yield of Victoria for April amounted to 65,395 oz.

TRAMWAY AND OMNIBUS RECEIPTS.

HOME.

Name.	Period.	Ending.	Amount.	Increase or Decrease on 1897.	Weeks or Months.	Aggregate to Date.	
						Amount.	Inc. or Dec. on 1897.
			£	£		£	£
Aberdeen District	Week	May 14	437	+35	—	—	—
Belfast Street	"	" 14	2,230	+143	—	—	—
Birmingham and Aston	"	" 7	465	+31	—	—	—
Birmingham and Midland	"	" 14	667	+53	—	—	—
Birmingham City	"	" 14	3,748	+272	—	—	—
Birmingham General	"	" 14	864	+72	—	—	—
Blessington and Poulaphouca	"	" 15	11	+ 7/	19	189	+19
Bristol Tramways and Carriage	"	" 13	2,648	+360	—	—	—
Burnley and District	"	" 14	291	+34	—	—	—
Bury, Rochdale, and Oldham	"	" 14	809	+5	—	—	—
Croydon	"	" 14	367	+69	—	—	+1,231
Dublin and Blessington	"	" 15	120	−1	19	1,845	+28
Dublin and Lucan	"	" 14	74	−3	20	858	−3,371
Dublin United	"	" 13	3,116	+223	—	52,816	+3,128
Dudley and Stourbridge	"	" 14	168	+8	20	3,239	+132
Edinburgh and District	"	" 14	2,381	+211	19	43,216	+3,983
Edinburgh Street	"	" 14	632	+52	19	11,412	+1,402
Gateshead and District	Month	April	940	+59	—	—	—
Glasgow	Week	May 14	2,560	+170	—	—	—
Harrow-road and Paddington	"	" 13	268	—	—	—	—
Lea Bridge and Leyton	"	" 14	756	+30	—	—	—
London, Deptford, and Greenwich	"	" 14	594	+25	—	10,774	+599
London General Omnibus	"	" 14	22,091	+856	—	—	—
London Road Car	"	" 14	6,848	−33	†	118,246	+5,486
London Southern	"	" 14	541	+22	—	—	—
North Staffordshire	"	" 14	399	+7	—	7,523	−24
Provincial	"	" 14	2,274	−109	—	—	—
Rossendale Valley	"	" 13	187	+33	—	—	—
Southampton	"	" 14	387	+18	—	—	—
South London	"	" 14	1,766	+47	†	30,887	+1,056
South Staffordshire	"	" 13	606	+12	19	11,267	−47
Tramways Union	Month	April	10,870	+1,149	4	39,300	+4,495
Wigan and District	Week	May 14	308	+274‡	—	—	—
Woolwich and South East London	"	" 14	354	+6	†	6,204	+343

† From January 1. ‡ Strike in 1897.

FOREIGN.

Name.	Period.	Ending.	Amount.	Increase or Decrease on 1897.	Weeks or Months.	Aggregate Amount.	Inc. or Dec. on 1897.
			£	£		£	£
Anglo-Argentine	Week	Apr. 18	4,676	+647	*	69,403	+7,289
Barcelona	"	May 14	1,114	−271	—	21,553	−3,030
Barcelona, Ensanche y Gracia	"	" 14	214	−10	—	4,244	+20
Bordeaux	"	" 13	2,207	− 29	—	38,435	−1,648
Brazilian Street	Month	Mch.	[mlr 51,419	+ mlr 5047]	—	—	—
British Columbia Electric	"	"	$30,729	+$10493	‡	$305,154	—
Do. net	"	"	$10,391	+$4,958	‡	$97,402	—
Buenos Ayres and Belgrano	"	"	5,219	+1,305	*	14,382	+2,578
Buenos Ayres Grand National	Week	Apr. 16	$26,733	+$4,296	†	—	+$9,610
Buenos Ayres New	Month	Feb.	$61,322	−$4,402	—	$131,227	−$6,254
Calais	Week	May 14	136	−11	—	—	—
Calcutta	"	May 14	1,313	−113	—	—	—
C'rth'g'na & Herrerias	Month	April	4,607	+712	—	18,809	+1,011
Gothenburg	Week	May 11	377	+44	—	—	—
Lynn and Boston	Month	Mch.	$105,471	+$5,944		$622,228	+$27912
Do. net	"	"	$4,2847	+$6,607		$216,383	+$3,162

* From January 1. † From April 1, 1898. ‡ From April 15, 1897. § From October 1, 1897.

A REASON FOR THE PROTECTION OF SMALL BIRDS.

Mr. Consul Hearn, reporting on the state of trade and agriculture in Bordeaux, puts forth a very strong argument in favour of the protection of small birds on the ground that they are the great destroyers of insects among the vines. Last year the vintage was a particularly bad one, partly owing to "atmospheric disturbances," but greatly also to the hordes of cochylis which attacked and ruined the blossoms and fruit, causing a loss in certain important vineyards of some hundreds of casks. Mr. Hearn argues that "the appearance of cochylis is contemporary with the destruction of small birds in the vineyards," and though as against this he has been told that there never were many birds among the vines even before *la chasse* was free to all, there were then no insects, and therefore no *raison d'être* for the birds. "Now the vines are infested with insect life, and if the birds were only allowed they would go to the vines in search of grub, cochylis or other kinds, and obtain for the proprietor a result which no amount of money can accomplish." Many women and children were employed last year to search for and destroy the eggs and larvæ of insects, whereas their natural destroyers, thrushes and starlings, who could have done the work much more effectually, were offered for sale by thousands in the streets of Bordeaux.

RAILWAY TRAFFIC RETURNS.

Alcoy and Gandia Railway and Harbour Company.—Traffic for week, May 14 :—Ps. 7,800 ; the same as last year. Aggregate from January 1, Ps. 169,350 ; Increase, Ps. 4,580.

Quebec Central Railway.—Receipts for fourth week of April, $14,267 ; increase, $695. Aggregate from July 1, $117,058 ; decrease, $16,530.

Mobile and Birmingham Railroad.—Traffic for fourth week of April, $9,573 ; increase, $,2,832. Aggregate from July 1, $312,747 ; increase, $450.

Algeciras (Gibraltar) Railway.—Traffic for week ended May 7, Ps. 23,780 ; increase, Ps. 2,880. Aggregate from July 1, Ps. 908,962 ; increase, Ps. 42,458.

West Flanders Railway.—Gross receipts for week ending May 15, £2,643 ; increase, £656. Total from January 1, £45,633 ; increase, £1,725.

West of India Portuguese Railway.—Week ending April 23, Rs. 4,717 ; increase, Rs. 1,291. Aggregate from January 1, Rs. 73,281 ; increase, Rs. 21,063.

Puerto Cabello and Valencia Railway.—Traffic receipts for week ending April 8, £964 ; decrease, £679. Aggregate from January 1, £12,368 ; decrease, £5,683.

Delhi Umballa Kalka Railway.—Receipts for week ended May 14, Rs. 30,400 ; decrease, Rs. 4,900. Aggregate from January 1, Rs. 6,63,600 ; increase, Rs. 1,58,600.

Manila Railway.—Receipts for week ending May 7, $18,000 ; increase, $3,262. Aggregate from January 1, $348,961 ; increase, $81,403.

Rohilkund and Kumaon Railway.—Traffic receipts for week ending April 16, Rs. 9,770 ; increase, Rs. 506. Aggregate from January 1, Rs. 1,13,539 ; decrease, Rs. 7,903.

Western of Santa Fe Railways.—Gross receipts for week ending May 14, $45,000 ; increase, $21,370.

Villa Maria and Rufino Railway.—Traffic for week ending May 14, $272 ; increase, $58. Aggregate from January 1, $5,744 ; increase, $1,111.

Southern Mahratta Railway.—Receipts for week ended April 23, Rs. 1,14,969 ; decrease, Rs. 21,320.

Bengal Central Railway.—Traffic receipts for week ending April 23, Rs. 17,012 ; decrease, Rs. 1,126. Aggregate from January 1, Rs. 330,548 ; Increase, Rs. 43,875.

Burma Railways.—Traffic receipts for week ending April 16, Rs. 1,46,788 ; increase Rs. 3,316. Aggregate from January 1, Rs. 32,38,143 ; decrease, Rs. 60,199.

Assam Bengal Railway.—Traffic receipts for week ending April 16. Rs. 24,628 ; increase, Rs. 6,941. Aggregate from January 1, Rs. 3,92,894 ; Increase, Rs. 70,216.

H.H. The Nizam's Guaranteed State Railways.—Traffic receipts from January 1 to April 23 were Rs. 13,05,753 ; increase, Rs. 102,374.

Great Western of Brazil.—Traffics receipts for the week ending April 9, $14,651 ; decrease, $4,007. Aggregate from January 1, $532,652 ; increase, $69,560.

Cleator and Workington.—Gross receipts for the week ending May 14 amounted to £1,141, an increase of £8. Total receipts from January 1, £19,578, a decrease of £638.

Cockermouth and Keswick Railway.—Receipts for the week ending May 14, £868 ; Increase, £95. Aggregate from January 1, £15,887 ; increase, £1,502.

MINING RETURNS.

Balmoral Main Reef.—April return :—2,045 oz.

City and Suburban.—Last month's crushings yielded 11,496 oz.

New Rietfontein.—April return :—3,277 oz.

Weld Hercules.—Crushed 295 tons, produced 286 oz. gold. Tailings 6 dwt. per ton.

Transvaal Coal.—April :—Output, 20,500 tons ; profit £1,800.

Victoria (Charters Towers).—265 tons, crushed yielded 367 oz. gold.

Consolidated of Western Australia.—From Yellow Aster Mine a crushing of 30 tons, realising 59 oz. 6 dwt. of smelted gold.

Hannan's Brownhill.—450 tons of sands, 565 tons of slimes treated, 2,300 oz. of gold recovered.

Mikado (Lake of the Woods District), Ontario.—During the twenty-four days ended April 30 the mill crushed 750 tons, yielding 444 oz. of gold.

New Heriot Gold.—Last month's crushing yielded 5,806 oz.

Ottos Kopje Diamond.—4,924 loads washed during the week ended May 12, 143 carats won.

New Zealand Crown.—Tons crushed, 1,667 ; value of bullion, £3,081.

Mount Lyell.—From April 7 to May 4, inclusive, a total quantity of 11,176 tons of ore has been treated, 9,508 tons from open cuts, assaying before treatment—copper, 2·54 per cent. ; silver, 2·57 oz. per ton ; gold, 0·159 oz. per ton. 1,668 tons from No. 4 Tunnel, assaying before treatment—copper, 8·31 per cent. ; silver, 8·99 oz. per ton ; gold, ·077 oz. per ton. The converters have produced during the same period 348 tons of blister copper, containing—copper, 344 tons ; silver, 36,375 oz. ; gold, 1,843 oz.

Anglo-Mexican.—Output for April :—Crushed, 1,671 tons ; $28,363 (U.S. gold) ; 27 days' run. Cyanide plant—tons treated, 620 ; $4,050 (U. S. gold).

Eaglehawk Consolidated.—The yield from last month's working is 189 oz. ; tailings assays average 14½ dwt. per ton.

Hyderabad (Deccan).—Output of coal from the Singareni Collieries for the four weeks ended April 23, 32,069 tons.

Moodie's.—Tons crushed, 1,000 ; ounces obtained, 570.

Pahang Corporation.—April returns :—Jeram Lumpong Mill—1,420 tons of stone crushed, producing 82 tons of black tin. Jeram Batang Mill—810 tons of stone crushed, producing 12 tons (or 17 tons 17* cwt.) of black tin. *Code word mutilated.

Premier Tati Monarch Reef.—Returns for April :—1,450 tons crushed, including 105 tons surface ore, low grade ; yield of retorted gold, 421 oz.

Wentworth Proprietary.—Five weeks' return :—920 tons of ore crushed, yielding 847 oz., and 2 tons rich crude ore shipped, containing 233 oz.

Caylloma Silver.—April production :—10,500 oz. fine silver in export ores, and 12,950 oz. fine silver in bullion.

Day Dawn Block.—Result of crushing for fortnight ended May 14 :—Tons crushed, 1,520 ; yield of gold, 2,034 oz., including tailings.

Day Dawn P.C.—Crushing for two weeks ended May 14 :—No. 1 shaft, 290 tons, 328 oz. ; No. 3 shaft, 120 tons, 100 oz.

New Australian Broken Hill Consols.—Fortnight's output :—1 ton 14 cwt., containing 3,600 oz. of silver.

Ouro Preto.—6,080 tons of ore, produced 1,741 oz. of gold.

St. John Del Rey.—Gold produce May 1 to May 11, £7,458 ; yield per ton, ·77 of an ounce troy.

Labuan and Borneo.—Output, first quality, 700 tons ; second quality, 50 tons.

Frank Smith Diamond.—4,100 loads washed, producing 197 carats.

Highland Chief.—Crushed 155 tons for a yield of 57 oz. gold.

North Boulder.—363 oz. of gold from 343 tons crushed.

Associated Gold of Western Australia.—Ore crushed, 1,700 tons, yielding 1,315 oz. of gold.

The sugar-cane crops in the Cairns district of Queensland are reported to be in good condition. On some farms a yield of fifty tons per acre is expected.

Here is a pretty story of the value of properties held in mortgage by the Argentine National Mortgage Bank. The directors have just had a valuation made of the properties mortgaged to it before the crisis, the owners of which are not paying either interest or amortisation. The result shows that one borrower obtained $250,000 on a property valued officially at $536,000, but of which the actual value is only $1,800.

AFRICAN MINING RETURNS.

Dividends Declared in			Capital Issued.	Nominal Amount of Share.	Name of Company.	Monthly Crushings.											Profits Declared.					Stamps now Working.
						February.			March.			April.			Totals.		Feb.	Mar.	April.	Totals.		
1896	1897	1898				Tons.	Oz.	Dwt. per ton.	Tons.	Oz.	Dwt. per ton.	Tons.	Oz.	Dwt. per ton.	Months.	Ozs.				Months.	—	
p.c.	p.c.	p.c.	£	£													£	£	£		£	
—	—	25	225,000	1	Angelo	11,615	5,868	11.0	11,701	5,712	9.8	12,442	6,120	9.8	4	23,563	13,803	12,617	13,276	4	52,132	60
—	—	—	130,000	1	Balmoral	11,160	2,015	3.6	12,740	2,425	3.8	—	2,045	—	4	8,803	544	1,107	—	3	3,107	50
—	75	50	200,000	1	Bonanza	10,220	7,741	15.1	11,317	8,227	14.5	10,184	8,115	15.9	4	32,119	18,545	20,429	20,639	4	79,043	40
—	—	—	550,000	1	Buffelsdoorn ..	26,688	3,034	2.3	19,097	2,902	3.0	—	2,225	—	4	11,768	—	—	—	—	—	75
—	—	—	133,000	1	Champ d'Or ..	8,929	2,998	6.7	9,357	2,968	6.3	—	3,261	—	4	12,421	—	—	—	—	—	50
5	15	—	1,360,000	4	City and Suburban	26,990	9,678	7.2	32,223	11,030	6.9	—	11,496	—	4	43,236	15,451	17,326	18,620	4	69,950	160
—	—	—	224,635	1	Comet	8,314	2,968	7.1	8,626	2,928	6.8	9,111	3,048	6.6	4	12,175	4,812	4,124	4,832	4	16,562	40
—	—	—	300,000	1	Crown Deep ..	39,170	10,248	5.2	40,390	9,718	4.8	40,520	12,632	6.2	4	46,025	9,086	10,700	13,800	4	50,612	160
210	170	100	120,000	1	Crown Reef.. ..	23,711	10,332	8.7	33,614	12,080	7.2	—	11,431	—	4	45,953	19,537	22,656	19,977	4	84,549	120
55	80	20	125,000	1	Durban Roodepoort	15,800	6,179	7.1	16,665	6,341	7.6	17,250	6,228	7.2	4	25,853	—	—	—	—	—	80
275	300	—	90,000	1	Ferreira	16,925	12,077	14.3	19,723	12,814	13.0	—	13,516	—	4	50,620	27,320	27,890	—	3	82,985	80
12½	45	50	200,000	1	Geldenhuis Estate..	30,895	10,019	6.5	30,686	10,743	7.0	—	10,554	—	4	41,404	18,825	20,838	21,110	4	78,248	120
—	30	—	300,000	1	Geldenhuis Deep ..	41,343	11,366	5.5	48,268	12,810	5.3	47,900	13,124	5.3	4	48,793	18,414	21,100	22,300	4	79,500	190
—	10	—	150,000	1	Gelden. Main Reef	2,100	424	4.0	4,274	952	4.5	1,449	329	4.6	4	3,015	a2,050	241	a1,179	4	a2,322	30
—	—	—	325,000	1	George Goch ..	12,356	2,950	4.8	13,773	3,007	4.3	—	2,737	—	4	11,762	—	—	—	—	—	120
—	25	—	160,000	1	Ginsberg	6,669	2,154	6.1	9,143	2,591	5.6	—	2,875	—	4	10,003	3,191	4,751	5,666	4	17,993	40
—	—	—	500,000	1	Glencairn	24,583	6,512	5.3	27,775	6,958	5.0	—	6,747	—	4	26,566	10,239	10,264	10,040	4	41,650	110
30	125	—	125,000	1	Henry Nourse ..	13,980	7,723	11.0	15,130	8,308	10.9	15,105	8,262	10.9	4	31,900	16,482	17,452	17,646	4	66,151	60
85	100	25	111,864	1	Heriot	14,440	5,737	7.9	15,071	5,824	7.7	—	5,806	—	4	23,199	9,642	8,705	10,221	4	38,598	70
350	500	125	81,000	1	Johan. Pioneer ..	4,817	3,865	16.0	5,600	4,105	14.6	—	4,086	—	4	15,779	—	—	—	1	9,950	30
60	90	25	50,000	1	Jubilee	8,488	2,808	6.6	8,991	2,798	6.2	—	2,580	—	4	11,268	—	—	—	—	—	50
30	60	—	100,000	1	Jumpers	17,510	5,319	6.1	18,620	5,073	5.4	—	5,398	—	4	21,197	7,150	5,370	6,750	4	26,430	100
—	—	—	231,250	1	Kleinfontein ..	17,200	4,942	5.7	19,061	4,655	4.9	17,648	4,443	5.0	4	19,203	4,905	4,370	4,752	4	19,468	95
—	—	—	312,180	1	Knight's	24,560	5,485	4.4	25,680	5,476	4.3	23,440	5,656	4.8	4	21,832	5,380	4,400	5,400	4	16,256	120
30	30	—	470,000	1	Langlaagte Estate..	27,624	7,840	5.6	31,119	10,191	6.6	32,842	11,191	6.8	4	38,014	—		—	—	—	170
—	—	—	550,000	1	Lang. Block B. ..	18,160	4,760	5.2	19,812	4,927	5.0	17,825	4,434	5.0	4	18,836	—	—	—	—	—	80
—	—	—	250,000	1	Langlaagte Star ..	9,045	3,424	7.5	11,062	3,498	6.3	10,273	3,114	6.0	4	14,067	—	—	—	—	—	30
20	—	—	275,000	1	May Consolidated	20,292	7,371	7.2	23,390	7,860	6.7	21,773	8,131	7.4	4	29,871	11,768	12,213	12,985	4	45,183	100
20	50	—	85,000	1	Meyer and Charlton	13,969	3,935	5.6	15,258	3,895	5.1	—	3,936	—	4	15,676	5,893	5,596	5,706	4	22,543	80
—	—	—	949,620	4	Modderfontein ..	7,684	2,835	7.4	12,769	3,677	5.8	—	3,840	—	3	10,352	—	—	—	—	—	60
—	—	—	200,000	1	Nigel	6,283	2,773	8.8	7,440	2,868	7.7	—	3,206	—	4	11,678	—	—	—	—	—	25
—	—	—	300,000	1	Nth. Randfontein..	8,514	1,972	4.6	9,892	2,393	4.8	10,638	2,225	4.2	4	3,534	—	—	—	—	—	40
—	—	—	374,934	1	Nourse Deep ..	11,587	4,642	8.0	13,728	4,860	7.1	13,146	4,913	7.5	4	19,813	5,604	5,200	5,400	4	23,914	60
—	—	—	400,000	1	Paarl Central ..	10,618	2,540	4.8	11,315	2,611	4.6	9,410	2,059	4.4	4	9,745	—	—	—	—	—	60
—	10	—	487,500	1	Porges Randfontein	11,605	3,532	6.1	12,581	3,541	5.6	13,439	3,541	5.3	4	14,595	—	—	—	—	—	60
—	50	—	300,000	1	Primrose	34,077	8,824	5.2	39,945	9,484	4.7	—	9,653	—	4	37,098	11,664	12,492	13,470	4	50,089	160
—	10	—	165,000	1	Princess Estate ..	8,610	2,725	6.3	8,755	2,720	6.1	—	2,730	—	4	11,032	1,850	1,750	1,861	4	7,353	40
—	—	—	270,000	1	Rietfontein	15,130	3,628	4.8	10,878	2,087	3.8	—	2,277	—	4	8,761	3,115	—	—	1	3,115	30
—	—	—	300,000	1	Rietfontein "A" ..	13,189	5,049	7.6	13,553	4,737	7.0	—	4,863	—	4	20,194	9,682	7,566	8,832	4	37,225	60
12	15	—	2,750,000	5	Robinson	30,003	b15,203	11.3	32,690	b16,454	10.0	—	b16,379	—	4	63,610	35,000	37,021	37,500	4	146,051	120
—	—	—	600,000	1	Robinson R'dfontein	7,944	2,566	6.5	8,177	2,696	6.6	8,601	2,833	6.6	4	11,436	—	—	—	—	—	35
—	—	—	175,000	1	Roodepoort Gold ..	4,806	950	4.0	4,527	986	4.4	—	1,138	—	4	4,340	—	—	—	—	—	40
25	40	—	150,000	1	Roodepoort United	10,054	4,057	7.4	13,159	3,922	6.0	—	4,092	—	4	16,494	6,680	5,350	6,138	4	25,400	70
—	—	—	400,000	1	Rose Deep	23,149	8,660	7.5	29,424	10,166	6.3	31,832	10,223	6.4	4	38,715	12,932	15,100	13,500	4	57,432	110
—	—	—	100,000	1	Salisbury	8,476	2,462	5.8	9,147	2,656	5.8	—	2,500	—	4	10,045	—	—	—	1	3,179	50
20	20	3½	1,075,000	1	Sheba	10,418	5,930	11.4	10,790	4,370	8.1	10,310	4,754	9.2	4	21,454	—	—	—	—	—	120
—	—	—	4,700,000	5	Simmer and Jack ..	41,930	9,081	4.3	53,660	11,420	4.3	—	14,351	—	4	45,015	—	—	—	—	—	100
—	—	—	235,000	1	Spes Bona	8,894	2,283	5.1	8,626	2,122	4.9	—	1,894	—	4	8,336	—	547	—	2	998	40
—	15	—	35,000	1	Stanhope	4,220	1,054	5.0	4,690	980	4.2	—	989	—	4	4,081	—	—	—	—	—	20
—	—	—	604,225	1	Trans. G. M. Est...	9,844	4,145	8.4	18,277	6,769	7.4	12,099	4,807	7.9	4	22,321	10,400	13,126	—	3	33,664	75
—	—	—	540,000	4	Treasury	9,247	3,844	8.3	9,744	3,813	7.8	—	3,649	—	4	14,891	6,436	6,920	6,528	4	25,700	40
—	—	—	300,000	1	Van Ryn	16,701	3,738	4.5	18,713	4,373	4.7	19,537	4,373	4.5	4	16,673	1,440	3,100	5,300	4	13,358	80
—	—	—	260,000	1	Village Main Reef..	13,425	5,358	7.9	12,908	5,964	9.3	16,950	8,030	9.4	4	22,851	8,621	8,000	12,000	3	28,621	65
75	100	75	80,000	1	Wemmer	10,200	5,803	11.3	12,139	6,243	12.8	11,363	6,310	11.1	4	24,428	12,561	12,987	12,764	4	51,502	50
—	—	—	400,000	1	West Rand	6,075	1,784	5.9	6,665	1,770	5.3	6,386	1,466	4.6	4	6,909	—	—	—	1	1,374	30
—	—	—	—	1	Windsor	6,397	1,745	5.4	6,562	1,844	5.6	—	1,971	—	4	7,502	2,750	3,027	3,139	3	8,916	40
—	10	—	860,000	4	Wolhuter	21,220	6,675	6.3	23,251	6,036	6.0	—	6,823	—	4	27,993	9,027	8,452	7,097	4	35,399	100
55	30	15	95,722	1	Worcester	4,885	2,888	11.8	4,936	2,674	10.8	—	2,961	—	4	10,546	4,690	4,907	—	3	14,630	40
—	—	—	90,000	1	York	8,271	2,201	5.3	8,796	1,821	4.1	—	1,461	—	4	7,785	—	—	—	—	—	40

a Loss. b Exclusive of yield from Concentrates bought—1,320 oz. in February, 2,913 oz. in March, and 2,914 oz. in April.

SOUTH AFRICAN MINE CRUSHINGS.

The April output is again a record one, the total for the Witwatersand district being 335,125 oz., or 9,218 oz. more than the March total. The outside districts seem a poor lot, yielding only 18,118 oz. last month, compared with 21,736 oz. for March and 23,263 oz. for February. The Rand total for April is just 100,000 oz. more than in the same month last year; but, of course, there are more mines working, and a good many more stamps. Amongst individual crushings last month, the Simmer & Jack Company had an increase of nearly 3,000 oz. compared with March, and the Angelo, Feireira, Nigel, and Langlaagte Estate Companies all did very well. The second crushing of the Jumpers Deep was 2,300 oz. better than the first, and the return of the Village Main Reef Company was more than 2,000 oz. up, but the Crown Reef shows a considerable reduction, and the York return has been continually growing smaller since crushing began. The return of the Transvaal Estates Company moves up and down as usual, the April output showing a decrease, compared with March, of 2,574 oz., because the returns from the Central cyanide works were not included. The Rand output for the current month promises to be less satisfactory, as several of the mines are hampered by shortness of water, and the May Consolidated, which had been doing extremely well, both as regards yield and profits, has unfortunately been already obliged to shut down its mill for want of water.

The evacuation of Thessaly has begun, and the payment of the first instalment of the indemnity will be made to Turkey forthwith.

Mr. Edward Dobson, of Bradford, has been elected President of the Auctioneers' Institute for the ensuing year, while Mr. Allen Drew, the popular member of the firm of Messrs. Debenham, Tewson, & Company, has been elected a member of the Council.

Twenty-seven thousand tons of coal were shipped in April from Newcastle, N.S.W., to San Francisco, and arrangements have now been made for the shipment of 150,000 tons in May. What about the neutrality proclamation?

The first hundred miles of the Uganda Railway have been opened for traffic. The returns have not yet been issued, but a time and fare book has been published. You may travel the whole length of the line for Rs.38 first class, Rs.19 second class, and Rs.3 3a. third class.

ENGLISH RAILWAYS.

Div. for half years 1896	1896	1897	1897	Last Balance forward.	Amt. to pay 1 p.c. on Ord. for ½ yr.	NAME.	Date.	Gross Traffic for week: Amt.	Inc. or dec. on 1897.	Inc. or dec. on 1896.	No. of weeks	Gross Traffic for half-year to date: Amt.	Inc. or dec. on 1897.	Inc. or dec. on 1896.	Mileage.	Inc. on 1897.	Working	Prior Charges last ½ year.	Prop. add Cap. Exp. this ½ year
				£	£												%	£	£
10	10	10	10	2,707	5,094	Barry	M'y 14	3,094	−7,187	−5,677	20	143,730	−31,616	−7,269	31	—	8·89	60,665	316,852
nil	nil	nil	nil	—	—	Brecon and Merthyr	" 15	1,179	−204	−496	20	27,662	−949	−4,084	61	—	—	—	—
nil	nil	nil	nil	3,979	4,749	Cambrian	" 15	5,360	+239	+445	*	91,669	+2,756	—	250	—	60·96	63,148	40,000
1¾	1½	2	1¾	1,510	3,150	City and South London	" 15	958	−42	+94	20	20,679	+176	+1,879	3½	—	56·67	5,552	124,000
	2	1½	2	7,895	13,220	Furness	" 15	9,171	+177	+281	*	170,213	+4,795	—	139	—	49·88	97,423	20,910
1	1½	½	1	2,207	27,470	Great Cent. (late M., S., & L.)	" 15	55,048	+2,995	+3,836	19	837,010	+22,997	+59,064	357½	—	57·17	627,386	1,200,000
2½	4½	2	5	51,283	62,865	Great Eastern	" 15	80,905	+2,439	+5,274	19	1,520,726	+43,925	+131501	1,158½	2	55·35	860,138	250,000
3	5½	3	5	15,094	102,496	Great Northern	" 15	96,569	+2,859	+7,526	20	1,881,613	+55,875	+144977	1,071	8	61·96	641,485	750,000
4½	7½	4½	7½	31,350	121,981	Great Western	" 15	179,560	−10,090	+800	19	3,299,830	−4,700	+118730	2,582	21	51·44	1,486,272	800,000
nil	2	nil	1½	8,951	16,487	Hull and Barnsley	" 15	8,551	+1,801	+2,404	19	130,563	+6,774	+16,418	73	—	58·21	70,290	52,920
5	5½	5	5½	21,495	83,704	Lancashire and Yorkshire	" 15	96,440	+4,383	+6,605	19	1,755,958	+55,862	+70,061	553½	25	56·70	674,745	451,976
4½	8	4½	8½	26,243	43,049	Lon., Brighton, & S. Coast	" 14	50,582	+576	+1,860	20	966,819	+30,343	+52,295	476½	—	50·20	407,042	240,735
nil	nil	nil	nil	72,294	56,296	London, Chatham, & Dover	" 15	28,768	+586	+1,064	19	522,287	+13,003	+28,947	185½	—	50·65	367,873	nil
6½	8	6½	7¾	89,535	204,068	London and North Western	" 15	241,230	+2,622	+16,102	19	4,354,348	+99,292	+251006	1,911½	—	56·92	1,404,534	600,000
5	8½	8½	8½	23,038	59,367	London and South Western	" 15	71,687	−959	+5,283	19	1,310,944	+43,934	+91,583	941	6½	51·75	513,740	389,000
2¾	6	2¾	6½	14,592	6,691	Lon., Tilbury, & Southend	" 15	5,253	+164	+582	20	99,366	+5,369	+15,716	81	—	52·57	39,590	15,000
3½	3¾	3½	3¾	17,133	26,409	Metropolitan	" 15	16,274	+323	+1,564	*	313,122	+6,500	—	64	—	43·63	148,047	254,000
nil	nil	nil	nil	4,006	11,250	Metropolitan District	" 15	8,341	+348	+516	19	160,936	+5,189	—	13	—	48·70	119,663	38,450
5	7	5½	6½	38,143	174,582	Midland	" 15	185,731	+2,974	+19,891	20	3,676,365	+57,188	+293692	1,354½	15½	57·59	1,216,382	650,000
5½	7½	5½	7	22,374	138,189	North Eastern	" 14	156,361	+4,276	+13,537	19	2,731,074	+41,663	+161641	1,597½	—	58·72	795,077	436,004
7¾	7¾	7¾	7½	7,061	10,108	North London	" 15			Not recd			not	recvd.	12	—	50·90	49,973	7,600
4	5	4	4½	4,745	16,150	North Staffordshire	" 15	14,907	−418	+954	20	311,305	+5,985	+18,371	312	—	55·27	118,142	19,605
10	10	11	10	1,642	3,004	Rhymney	" 14	1,776	−3,580	−2,878	20	84,938	−13,998	−5,458	71	—	49·68	29,049	16,700
3	6½	3½	6½	4,054	50,215	South Eastern	" 14	44,290	+1,381	+3,986	*	821,729	+39,306	—	448	—	51·88	380,763	250,000
3½	3½	3½	3½	2,315	25,961	Taff Vale	" 14	6,790	−9,100	−9,007	20	249,925	−60,391	−43,822	121	—	54·90	94,800	92,000

* From January 1.

SCOTCH RAILWAYS.

5	5	5½	5	9,544	78,066	Caledonian	May 15	74,109	+ 2,372	+ 3,285	15	1,065,767	+ 26,886	—	851½	5	50·38	588,248	441,477
5	5½	5	5	7,364	24,639	Glasgow and South-Western	" 14	28,738	+ 1,137	+ 3,415	15	418,118	+ 15,118	—	393½	—	54·69	221,663	196,145
3½	3½	3½	—	1,291	4,600	Great North of Scotland	" 14	8,916	+ 297	+ 492	15	119,611	+ 386	+ 3,897	331	15½	52·03	92,178	60,000
	nil		—	10,477	12,820	Highland	" 15	9,170	− 56	+ 434	11	97,175	+ 2,889	—	479½	27½	58·63	78,976	,000
	1½	1	1½	819	45,819	North British	" 15	75,322	+ 3,910	+ 5,272	15	1,070,421	+ 28,691	—	1,230	23	48·62	944,809	40,800

IRISH RAILWAYS.

6½	6½	6½	—	5,466	1,790	Belfast and County Down	May 13	2,220	+ 11	− 334	*	41,960	+ 1,096	—	76½	—	55·58	17,690	10,000
5½	6½	5½	—	—	4,284	Belfast and Northern Counties	" 13	5,066	− 31	+ 30	*	98,150	+ 4,964	—	249	—	—	—	—
	3	2	—	1,418	1,200	Cork, Bandon, and S. Coast†	" 14	1,413	− 192	− 161	*	23,796	− 1,972	—	103	—	54·82	14,436	5,450
	6½	6½	6½	38,776	17,816	Great Northern	" 13	15,666	− 87	+ 442	19	278,089	+ 12,648	+ 18,898	528	—	50·15	88,068	22,000
	5½	5½	5½	30,339	24,855	Great Southern and Western	" 13	—	—	—	not	received	—	—	603	13	51·45	72,802	46,582
	4	4	4½	11,372	11,850	Midland Great Western	" 13	10,927	− 136	− 37	19	189,553	+ 7,943	—	538	—	50·31	83,129	1,800
nil	ni	nil	nil	229	2,822	Waterford and Central	" 13	810	− 17	—	*	—	—	—	59½	—	53·24	6,858	1,900
nil	ni	nil	nil	1,936	2,987	Waterford, Limerick & W.	" 13	3,848	+ 106	+ 254	*	—	—	—	350½	—	57·83	42,617	7,075

* From January 1. † Sixteen weeks' strike.

DIVIDENDS ANNOUNCED.

MISCELLANEOUS.

PAVILION THEATRE, LIMITED (Mile End).—Interim dividend on the ordinary shares at the rate of 10 per cent. per annum for the half-year ended April 30.

UNION STEAMSHIP COMPANY OF NEW ZEALAND, LIMITED.—An interim dividend at the rate of 5s. per share, and a bonus from insurance fund of 1s. per share for the six months ended March 31, are payable to British shareholders at the company's offices in London on the 25th inst.

LIEBIG'S EXTRACT OF MEAT COMPANY, LIMITED.—Final dividend for 1897 of 15 per cent., making, with the interim, 20 per cent. for the year, being the same dividend as paid last year.

D. JONES, DICKINSON, & COMPANY.—Interim dividend for the six months ended April 2, at the rate of 7 per cent. per annum on the ordinary shares, and 6 per cent. per annum on the preference shares.

ROYAL OAK OF HAURAKI, LIMITED.—Dividend of 3d. per share is payable on the 25th inst.

WEMMER GOLD MINING COMPANY, LIMITED.—75 per cent. has been declared.

BIRMINGHAM MINT.—Dividend of 10 per cent. recommended and a bonus of 2s. 6d. per share for the year ended March 31.

ASSAM COMPANY.—Final dividend of 12½ per cent., making, with the interim dividend, a total of 17½ per cent. for the year.

FULLER'S EARTH UNION, LIMITED.—3 per cent. for the year ended March 31, carrying forward £1,606, as against 2 per cent. and a balance of £1,307 forward.

W. A. LLOYD'S CYCLE FITTINGS, LIMITED.—Interim dividends at the rate of 5 per cent. per annum on the ordinary shares, and at the rate of 7 per cent. per annum on the preference shares for the half-year ended March 31.

BRANSOM, KENT, & COMPANY, LIMITED.—Interim dividend at the rate of 10 per cent. per annum, as previously, for the half-year ended March 31.

HUMBER & COMPANY, LIMITED.—Usual interim dividend on the ordinary shares at the rate of 5 per cent. per annum, to be paid on June 1 next, together with the dividend on the preference shares.

BRITISH TEA TABLE COMPANY, LIMITED.—10 per cent. on the ordinary shares has been declared.

INTERNATIONAL TRUSTEE, ASSETS, AND DEBENTURE CORPORATION.—Interim dividend at the rate of 7 per annum on the ordinary shares for half-year to April 30.

CITY OF LONDON REAL PROPERTY.—Dividend of 8 per cent. for the year, including interim dividend of 3 per cent., on the original shares, leaving £5,769 to be carried forward, and 9 per cent., including interim dividend of 3 per cent., upon the new shares, leaving £9,340 to be carried forward.

WEST LONDON DAIRY COMPANY, LIMITED.—6 per cent. for the year ended March 26.

PEAK HILL GOLDFIELD, LIMITED.—Further interim dividend of 1s. per share.

VIZIANAGARAM MINING COMPANY, LIMITED.—Final dividend for 1897 declared of 2s. per share, making, with the interim of 1s. per share paid in August last, 15 per cent. for the year.

BANKS.

YOKOHAMA SPECIE.—A dividend at the rate of 15 per cent. is proposed, with 274,689 yen carried forward.

THE BANK OF NEW SOUTH WALES announces a dividend at the rate of 9 per cent. per annum for the half-year ended March 31. A balance of £16,942 was carried forward.

ANGLO-ARGENTINE, LIMITED.—Interim dividend at the rate of 4 per cent. per annum for the half-year ended March 31, payable June 8.

BREWERIES.

BEESTON COMPANY, LIMITED.—Interim dividend on the preference shares at the rate of 5½ per cent. per annum, and on the ordinary shares at the rate of 6 per cent. per annum.

CORNBROOK COMPANY, LIMITED.—Interim dividend of 4s. per share on the ordinary shares for the half-year ended March 31.

RAILWAYS.

BENGAL & NORTH-WESTERN, LIMITED.—The accounts for the half-year ended December 31 have been received from India, and subject to audit the net revenue admits of the payment of a dividend of £2 per cent.

BOMBAY, BARODA, AND CENTRAL INDIAN.—Dividend proposed on the consolidated stock at the rate of 7s. 6d. per cent., in addition to the guaranteed interest, making in all a distribution of £2 17s. 6d. per cent. for the half-year, a against £2 16s. for the corresponding period of last year.

EAST INDIAN.—Directors recommend dividend of £1 4s. 6d. per cent. on the deferred annuity capital and deferred annuity capital class D, in addition to the guaranteed interest for the half-year; making a return guaranteed interest and dividend for 1897 of £6 8s.

FOREIGN RAILWAYS.

Mileage. Total.	Increase on 1897.	Increase on 1896.	NAME	Gross Traffic for Week. Week ending	Amount.	In. or Dec. upon 1897.	In. or Dec. upon 1896.	Gross Traffic to Date. No. of Weeks.	Amount.	In. or Dec. upon 1897.	In. or Dec. upon 1896.
					£	£	£		£	£	£
319	—	—	Argentine Great Western	May 13	8,906	+ 889	+ 1,877	46	276,479	+ 1,120	+ 62,103
76½	—	—	Bahia and San Francisco	Apr. 16	2,987	+ 549	+ 1,083	16	—	—	—
234	48	84	Bahia Blanca and North West	Apr. 17	566	− 308	—	42	32,003	− 1,109	—
74	—	—	Buenos Ayres and Ensenada	May 15	2,838	− 763	− 1,415	20	65,428	− 10,500	− 17,328
426	—	—	Buenos Ayres and Pacific	May 14	9,078	+ 1,019	+ 1,853	45	306,847	− 49,172	+ 8,865
914	1	3	Buenos Ayres and Rosario	May 14	17,514	+ 5,801	+ 4,808	20	327,737	+ 89,924	+ 59,946
2,499	30	68	Buenos Ayres Great Southern	May 15	31,180	+ 6,114	+ 8,546	45	1,353,889	+ 108,438	+ 199,811
602	107	177	Buenos Ayres Western	May 15	13,025	+ 2,951	− 1,329	45	548,714	− 75,509	− 97,517
845	55	77	Central Argentine	May 14	21,723	+ 6,987	+ 7,321	20	420,766	+ 110,609	+ 50,729
197	—	—	Central Bahia	Feb. 28*	$142,798	+ $14,291	+ $1,866	2	$276,357	+ $10,347	+ $14,624
271	—	—	Central Uruguay of Monte Video	May 14	6,216	+ 2,962	+ 892	45	271,075	+ 23,667	− 12,796
228	—	—	Do. Eastern Extension	May 14	1,676	+ 923	+ 636	14	59,341	+ 9,395	+ 382
182	—	—	Do. Northern Extension	May 14	758	+ 514	+ 636	45	28,933	+ 1,291	− 6,990
180	—	—	Cordoba and Rosario	May 8	2,065	+ 315	+ 25	45	95,680	− 13,145	− 1,505
128	—	—	Cordoba Central	May 8	$23,000	− $5,330	− $2,500	19	$400,700	− $56,070	− $70,350
549	—	—	Do. Northern Extension	May 8	$46,500	− $20,010	− $7,760	19	$838,790	− $281,970	− $155,640
137	—	—	Costa Rica	May 7	5,926	+ 1,551	+ 2,836	19	110,929	− 1,854	+ 14,624
99	—	—	East Argentine	Apr. 3	782	+ 275	+ 265	13	9,584	+ 251	+ 193
386	—	6	Entre Rios	May 14	2,013	+ 1,116	+ 703	45	75,029	+ 24,184	+ 19,686
555	—	24	Inter Oceanic of Mexico	May 14	$65,900	+ $9,000	+ $20,600	45	$2,626,620	+ $413,490	+ $712,550
23	—	—	La Guaira and Caracas	Apr. 15	2,765	+ 1,045	+ 410	16	31,845	− 4,696	− 4,597
321	—	—	Mexican	May 14	$81,200	+ $6,200	—	20	$1,567,900	+ $164,130	—
2,846	—	—	Mexican Central	May 14	$251,154	− $2,798	− $71,433	20	$4,900,241	+ $27,644	+ $1,259,478
2,217	—	—	Mexican National	May 7	$105,119	− $539	+ $21,180	19	$2,010,213	+ $118,218	+ $391,559
228	—	—	Mexican Southern	May 14	$12,810	− $889	+ $4,067	6	$76,868	− $11,413	− $16,271
106	—	—	Minas and Rio	Mar. 31*	$161,138	− $9,628	—	9 mos.	$1,597,971	+ $193,854	—
94	—	—	N. W. Argentine	May 14	1,280	− 174	− 298	20	19,086	− 6,702	− 4,676
242	3	—	Nitrate	May 13†	14,036	− 1,641	− 13,779	20	131,840	− 2,880	− 62,479
320	—	—	Ottoman	May 7	4,170	− 2,098	+ 445	19	85,461	− 22,641	+ 6,521
77½	—	—	Recife and San Francisco	Mar. 19	5,827	+ 931	− 1,050	11	70,393	+ 6,145	− 10,171
86½	—	—	San Paulo	Apr. 27‡	21,132	− 9,393	—	15	148,192	—	—
186	—	—	Santa Fe and Cordova	May 14	2,922	+ 1,734	+ 308	45	80,147	+ 1,739	− 5,022
110	—	—	Western of Havana	May 14	1,360	− 513	− 390	45	79,717	+ 4,512	+ 7,682

* For month ended. † For fortnight ended. ‡ For three weeks.

INDIAN RAILWAYS.

Mileage. Total.	Increase on 1897.	Increase on 1896.	NAME.	Gross Traffic for Week. Week ending	Amount.	In. or Dec. on 1897.	In. or Dec. on 1896.	Gross Traffic to Date. No. of Weeks.	Amount.	In. or Dec. on 1897.	In. or Dec. on 1896.
862	—	—	Bengal Nagpur	May 14	Rs.1.73.000	+ Rs.41.456	+ Rs.47.263	20	Rs.30.97.742	+ Rs.3.26.780	+ Rs.37.542
827	8	63	Bengal and North-Western	Apr. 16	Rs.1.49.770	− Rs. 2.897	+ Rs.18.698	16	Rs.20.80.001	+ Rs.2.53.492	+ Rs.1.30.816
461	—	—	Bombay and Baroda	May 14	£46,658	+ £12,837	+ £8,290	20	£556,191	+ £27,108	− £136,519
1,885	2	13	East Indian	May 14	Rs.12.99.000	+ Rs.75.000	+ Rs.3.07.000	20	Rs.2.43.02.000	+ Rs.8.34.000	+ Rs.24.10.000
1,491	—	—	Great Indian Penin.	May 14	£87,927	+ £33,146	+ £12,276	20	£1,360,658	+ £257,618	− £192,042
736	—	—	Indian Midland	May 14	Rs.1.86.260	+ Rs.47.466	+ Rs.77.747	20	Rs.27.54.289	+ Rs.2.51.408	+ Rs.601.979
840	—	—	Madras	May 7	£18,160	− £1,742	− £1,467	19	£349,869	− £21,038	− £7,092
1,043	—	—	South Indian	Apr. 16	Rs.1.60.262	− Rs.14.931	− Rs. 7.912	16	Rs.23.69.974	− Rs.217,279	− Rs.23.977

UNITED STATES AND CANADIAN RAILWAYS.

Mileage. Total.	Increase on 1897.	Increase on 1896.	NAME.	Gross Traffic for Week. Period Ending.	Amount.	In. or Dec. on 1897.	Gross Traffic to Date. No. of Weeks.	Amount.	In. or Dec. on 1897.
					dols.	dols.		dols.	dols.
917	—	—	Baltimore & Ohio S. Western	May 7	138,061	+28,547	43	5,827,607	+681,290
6,568	92	156	Canadian Pacific	May 14	501,000	+55,000	18	8,179,000	+1,576,000
922	—	—	Chicago Great Western	May 14	100,759	+16,861	44	4,675,640	+608,163
6,169	—	469	Chicago, Mil., & St. Paul	May 14	637,900	+116,500	18	10,852,001	+1,605,800
1,685	—	—	Denver & Rio Grande	May 14	149,800	+19,800	44	7,045,200	+1,149,100
3,512	—	—	Grand Trunk, Main Line	May 14	£79,349	+£12,064	18	£1,389,979	+£132,334
335	—	—	Do. Chic. & Grand Trunk	May 14	£14,099	+£4,846	18	£283,090	+£64,526
189	—	—	Do. Det., G. H. & Mil.	May 14	£3,376	−£103	18	£66,023	−£3,852
2,938	—	—	Louisville & Nashville	May 7	499,000	+41,000	17	7,442,175	+1,134,600
2,197	137	137	Miss., K., & Texas	May 14	168,000	−22,000	44	10,936,428	+503,290
477	—	—	N. Y., Ontario, & W.	May 14	64,842	−2,285	44	3,338,685	+87,471
1,570	—	—	Norfolk & Western	May 7	209,000	+20,000	17	3,866,960	+410,433
3,499	336	—	Northern Pacific	May 7	414,000	+93,000	17	7,032,775	+2,122,552
1,223	—	—	St. Louis S. Western	Apr. 30‡	113,000	+10,000	16	1,883,400	+316,221
4,654	—	—	Southern	May 7	371,000	+33,000	43	6,230,812	+1,415,443
1,979	—	—	Wabash	May 14	263,000	+52,000	18	4,761,406	+970,000

‡ For nine days.

MONTHLY STATEMENTS.

Mileage. Total.	Increase on 1896	Increase on 1895.	NAME.	Net Earnings for Month. Month.	Amount.	In. or Dec. on 1897.	In. or Dec. on 1896.	Net Earnings to Date. No. of Months.	Amount.	In. or Dec. on 1897.	In. or Dec. on 1896.
					dols	dols.	dols.		dols.	dols.	dols.
6,935	44	444	Atchison	March	904,000	+337,000	+369,344	3	2,144,434	+674,836	+220,460
6,547	103	106	Canadian Pacific	March	753,000	+233,000	+276,469	3	1,693,000	+415,000	+318,787
6,169	—	469	Chicago, Mil., & St. Paul	March	1,180,000	+170,000	+65,202	3	2,720,334	+225,840	+84,122
1,685	—	—	Denver & Rio Grande	March	267,900	+39,242	+38,942	9	2,519,889	+407,063	+30,946
1,970	—	—	Erie	March	611,000	+53,000	+8,708	3	1,378,000	+92,400	−94,251
3,512	—	—	Grand Trunk, Main Line	March	£102,100	+£14,331	+£31,909	3	£245,953	+£62,372	+100,519
335	—	—	Do. Chic. & Grand Trunk	March	£17,400	+£10,152	+13,357	3	£38,710	+£24,282	+28,939
189	—	—	Do. Det. G. H. & Mil.	March	£4,900	−£1,414	+3,221	3	£6,528	+£737	+6,419
3,127	—	239	Illinois Central	March	759,000	+206,000	+343,862	3	2,213,704	+365,620	+349,739
2,396	—	—	New York Central*	April	3,807,000	+302,000	+394,152	4	14,602,000	+964,000	—
477	—	—	New York Ontario, & W.	March	84,600	−4,800	+40,032	9	918,700	+38,200	+115,494
1,570	—	—	Norfolk & Western	March	301,000	+18,000	+110,317	3	826,000	+63,247	+201,902
3,407	—	—	Pennsylvania	February	1,359,101	+65,700	+236,000	2	2,511,898	92,400	+345,000
1,055	—	—	Phil. & Reading	March	702,100	+50,822	—	9	7,567,201	+524,064	—

Prices Quoted on the London Stock Exchange.

Throughout the Investors' Review middle prices alone are quoted, the object being to give the public the approximate current quotations of every security of any consequence in existence. On the markets the buying and selling prices are both given, and are often wide apart where stocks are seldom dealt in. Other particulars will be found in the Investment Index published quarterly—January, April, July, and October—in connection with this Review, price 2s., by post 2s. 2d. Where dividends are paid only once a year, an *italic* type is used to distinguish them. The London Stock Exchange Official List is quoted in the Review almost entire, only very insignificant issues, or bonds falling due within the next two or three years, being omitted. But the list is subdivided into the leading, or active, stocks, and those less frequently dealt in. The former will be found under the head of "Stock Markets," and with more details than it is possible to give for the bulk of securities. By retaining the file of the Investors' Review any subscriber can follow for himself the movements of securities from week to week, and the Investment Index will from time to time help to fill up deficiencies in the information.

Tea Companies and Mines and Mining Finance Stocks are placed in special lists.

Among the abbreviations used are the following:—S.F. Snk.Fd. *sinking fund*; Certs., *certificates*; Debs. or Dbs., *debentures*; Db. or D.Stk., *debenture stock*; Pf., Prf., or Pref., *preference*; Prefd. or Pfd., *preferred*; Dfd., *deferred*; L. or Ltd., *limited*; Sh., *share*; Ans., *annuities*; Cu. or Cm., *cumulative*; Gu or Guar., *guaranteed*; Bds., *bonds*; S., Sr., or Ser., *series*; In., Ins., Insc., *inscribed*; Dr., Drgs., Drwgs., *drawings*; Stg., Strlg., *sterling*; Lia., *liable to*; Sp., Surp., *surplus*; Per., Perp., *perpetual*; Ln. *lien*; Lo. *loan*.

The dates following the names of securities are the years of issue or of redemption. Where shares are not fully paid up, their nominal amount s given with the name so that investors may know the liability upon them.

BRITISH FUNDS, &c.

Rate	Name.	Price.
2¾	2¾ p.c.'s (Childers') Red.. 1905	104½
3	Local Loans Stk. 1912	110
3	Metro. Police Deb. Stk. 1920	105½
—	Red Sea Ind. Tel. Ann. 1908	8½
4	Canada Gv. "Intcl. Rly." 1903	104
4	Do. do. .. 1908	111
4	Do. Bonds 1910	112
4	Do. Bonds 1913	117½
3	Egyptian Gov. Gar.	106
3	Mauritius Ins. Stk. 1940	114
4	Turkish Guar. 1855	109
11½	Bank of Ireland Stk.	365
3½	India Rupee Paper	62
3½	Do. 1854-5	62
3	Do. 1896-7 1916	55
3½	Isle of Man Deb.	104
3	Do. Deb. Stk... 1919-29	103

CORPORATION AND COUNTY STOCKS.

FREE OF STAMP DUTY.

Rate	Name.	Price.
3½	Metropolitan Con. 1929	115½
3	Do. 1941	110
2½	Do. 1920-49	98
2½	L.C.C. Con. Stock 1920	98
3½	Comm. of Sewers, Scp., S.F. 1905	104
3½	Corp. of Lond. Bds...1897-1902	100½
3	Do. 1897-1912	101
3½	Do, Debs. Scp. S.F. 1916	105
2½	Do., Deb. Stk. Scrip .. 1927-57	98
3	Barnsley 1916-46	105
3	Barry 1914-46	101
3	Bath 1909-34	101
3	Batley 1914-44	101½
3½	Birmingham 1945	117½
3	Do. 1947	111½
2½	Do. 1926	98
3	Blackburn 1930	106½
3	Bournemouth 1913-33	103
3½	Bradford 1945	116½
3	Do. Deb. Stock .. 1954	105
3	Brighouse 1916-46	100
3½	Brighton 1946	117
2½	Do. 1957	96½
3	Burton-on-Trent 1913-43	101
3	Cambridge 1913-43	103
3½	Cardiff 1935	114½
3	Do. 1914-54	103½
3	Cheltenham 1971	106½
3	Chichester 1916-46	101
3½	Croydon	131½
3	Do. 1940	106½
3	Derby 1920-50	106½
3	Devon C.C. 1917-33	104½
3½	Dewsbury 1930	109
3	Do. 1930	103
3	Dorset County 1922-32	105
3	Douglas (I. of Man) 1926	101½
3	Dover 1913-43	101
3½	Dublin 1944	113½
3	Eastbourne 1920-40	104
3	Edinburgh 1924	105½
2½	Do. 1927	97
2½	Exeter 1917-57	96
3	Glamorgan County 1914-34	104
3½	Glasgow 1914	109
3	Do. 1921	104½
2½	Do. 1925-40	98
3	Gloster 1915-55	101
3	Grimsby 1913-45	103
3	Hampshire County 1914-34	105½
3	Hanley 1913-43	103
3	Harrogate 1914-34	103
3	Hastings 1915-54	103½
2½	Hertfordshire C.C. 1916-36	98
3	Heston & Isleworth U.D.C. 1915-35	101
3	Huddersfield 1934	107
3½	Hull (1st iss.)	126½
3	Inverness 1914-44	100
3	Ipswich 1932	107½
3	Lancaster 1919-55	103
2½	Leeds 1927	98
3½	Leicester 1934	114½
3	Lincoln 1919	103
3½	Liverpool	131

Corporation, &c. (*continued*):—

Rate	Name.	Price.
3	Manchester 1941	106½
3½	Middlesbro' 1909	105½
3½	Do. 1911-13	105
3	Do. 1915	104
3	Middlesex C.C. 1915-35	106
3½	Newcastle 1936	118½
3½	Do. Irred.	129½
2½	Do. 1915-36	100
3	Newcastle-under-Lyme.. 1909-44	101
3	Newport (Mon.) 1913-53	101½
3	Norwich 1952	110
3	Nottingham	111½
3	Oxford 1951	109½
3	Penzance 1916-46	100½
3	Plymouth 1942	108½
3	Pontypridd U.D.C. 1916-46	98
3	Poole 1915-45	102
3½	Portsmouth ......1916 24 & 27	112
3	Do. 1913-33	106
3	Ramsey 1920-40	100
3	Ramsgate 1915-55	102
3½	Reading	127½
3	Do. 1962	107
3½	Rhyl U.D.C. 1953	110
3	Richmond (Surrey) 1942	104½
3	River Wear Debt Certs.	100
3	St. Helen's 1915-53	102
3	Scarbro' 1915-50	102
2½	Sheffield 1925-57	94½
3	Shipley U.D.C. 1915-35	100
3	Somerset Co. 1923-33	104
3	South Shields 1915-45	100½
2½	Southampton 1915-45	100½
3	Southend-on-Sea 1916-46	101
3	Staffs C.C. 1915-35	103½
3	Stockport 1914-54	101
3	Stockton 1932	104
3	Do. 1915-35	103
3	Surrey Co. 1922-32	105½
3½	Swansea	129
3	Do. 1955	106
3	Taunton 1918 3-9-43	100
3	Tees Conserv. Deb. Stk. 1947	100
3	Thames Conserv. "A" Deb. Stk. 1954	103½
3	Do. "B" Deb. Stk. 1954	103½
3	Torquay 1913-43	101½
3	Tunbridge Wells 1931	102
3	Tynemouth 1913	99
3	Wakefield 1929	101½
3	Walsall 1932	107½
3	West Bromwich 1930	105
3½	West Ham 1929	110
3	Do. 1945	105
3	West Sussex C.C. 1915-35	106
3	Weston-s.-Mare Lcl.Bd. 1914-44	99½
3	Weymouth&Melc. Regis 1918	101
3	Widnes 1915-55	100
3	Wigan 1921	104½
3	Windsor 1918-53	102
3½	Wisbech 1947	113½
3½	Wolverhampton 1932	117
3	Do. 1924-54	107
3	York 1916-41	105½

SUBJECT TO STAMP DUTY.

Rate	Name.	Price.
3½	Belfast City & Dis. Watr. 1938	114
3	Do. Red Stk. 1953-6	106
3½	Belfast 1924	103
4	Blackburn Con. Deb. Irred.	141½
3½	Do. do. Irred.	130
3½	Bristol	129½
3½	Burnley 1933	114
2½	Chesterfield Gas & Wtr. 1916-46	98
3½	Douglas Town 1921	105
3	Dover Harb. 1st Deb... 1956	104½
3½	Hull (2nd iss.)	128½
4	Leeds Deb. 1927	123
3½	Do.	115½
3	Do. 1927	106
3	Leicester 1919-44	103½
4	Manchester	150
3	Do. 1928	104½
4½	Middlesboro' Mrts. 1908	111
3½	Sheffield 1898-1916	106½
3½	Do. 1925-36	114
3	Do. 1995	106½
3½	Southampton S.F.	106
4½	Stockton Morts. 1908	110½
3½	Worcester 1950	109

COLONIAL AND PROVINCIAL GOVERNMENT SECURITIES.

Rate.	Name.	Price.
6	British Columbia 1907	119½
4½	Do. Debs.. 1917	111½
3	British Guiana Imgtn. Bds.	98
5	Canada, "Intercol. Rail," 1903	108
4	Do. (Bonds) 1904-5-6-8	105
4	Do. Reduced 1910	108
3½	Do. Bnds. 1909-34	107
4	Do. Loan 1910-35	108
3	Do. Loan 1938	102
6	Cape of G. Hope 1900	—
5	Do. 1900	—
4½	Do. red. by an. draw.	108
4½	Do. 1879	110
4	Do. 1881	108
4	Dc 1917-23	113½
4½	Ceylon	108
4	Do.	106½
4½	Fiji Gov. Deb. Sink. Fd.	101½
4	Jamaica Sink. Fd. 1923	103
5	Manitoba Debs. 1910	113
5	Do. Ster. Bds. 1928	119½
4	Do. Ster. Debs.	104
4	Mauritius, Cons. Debs. 1880	101½
4½	Natal, Sink. Fd. 1919	118
4	Do. do. 1926	114
3½	Newfoundland Stg. Bds. 1941	99
3½	Do. do. .. 1947	99
3	Do. do.	86½
5	New South Wales 1897-1902	104½
4	Do. 1903-5-8-9-12	106
5	New Zealand 1914	118
5	Do. Cnsls. 1 p.c. per an. Sink. Fd.	103
3½	Nova Scotia Debs.	104
5	Quebec Prov. 1904-6	108
4½	Do. (drgs.)	105
5	Do. Strlg. Bds. 1912	115
4	Do. Strlg. Bds. 1928	110
4	Do. Strlg. Bds. 1934	108
4	Queensland 1913-15	105
4½	St. Lucia Debs.	102
6	South Australia 1898-1900	103½
6	Do. 1901-1918	119
5	Do. 1911-1920	116
4	Do. 1899-1916	104½
4	Do. 1929	108½
4	Do. 1916	106½
4	Do. 1917-18-24	107½
6	Tasmania 1897-1901	104
4	Do. 1908-11, 1913-14-20	107½
5	Trinidad Debs., an. drw. 1 p.c.	107
4	Victoria 1899-1901	102
4½	Do. 1904	105
4	Do. Rail. Loan 1907	106
4	Do. Loans 1908-13	105
4½	West. Austr. 1 p.c. ac. Sink. Fd.	107
4	Do. do.	106

REGISTERED AND INSCRIBED STOCKS.

No stamp duty except for Canada 4 p.c. Reduced (½ per cent.).

Rate	Name	Price
4	Antigua Insc. Stk. Red. 1919-44	110
3½	Barbados Insc. Stk. 1925-42	107
3	British Colum. Insc. Stk. 1941	101½
4	British Guiana Insc. 1935	116½
4	Canada Stk. Regd. 1904-5-6-8	105
4	Do. 4 p.c. (late 5 p.c.) Regd. 1910	108
3½	Do. 3½ p.c. Stock Regd. 1909-34	105
4	Do. Ln. for 4 milln. stg. 1910-35	108
3	Do. Stk. Regd. 1938	102
2½	Do. Insc. 1947	92
4	Cape G. Hope Regd. .. 1917-23	112
4	Do. (Ln. of '83) Insc. .. 1923	115
4	Do. Cons. Stk. Insc. 1916-36	112
3½	Do. Consol. Insc. Stock 1929-49	110
4	Ceylon Insc. Stock 1934	120
3	Do. 1940	102
4	Grenada Insc. Stock 1917-42	110
3½	Hong Kong Insc. Stock 1918-43	103½
4	Jamaica Insc. Stock 1934	118
—	Do. 1922-44	98
4	Mauritius Inscribed 1937	118½
4	Natal Consd. Stk. Insc. 1927	116
4	Do. 1937	118½
3½	Do. Inscribed Stock.. 1914-39	105
4	Newfoundland Inscribed 1913-38	106
4	Do. 1935	113
4	Do. Consd. Stk. Ins. 1936	113
4	N. S. Wales Stock Insc. 1933	117½
3½	Do. 1924	107
3½	Do. 1918	104
3	Do 1935	97

Colonial, &c. (*continued*):—

Rate.	Name.	Price.
4	N. Zealnd. Con. Stk. Ins. 1929	112
3½	Do 1940	107
3	Do. Inscribed.... 1945	99
3	Quebec (Prov.) Ins. Stk. 1937	93
4	Queensland Stock Insc. 1913-24	109
3½	Do. 1921-4-30	104
3½	Do. 1945	106
3	Do. 1922-47	98
4	St. Lucia Insc. Stock .. 1919-44	112
4	S. Austrln. (1882-7) Reg. 1916-36	108½
3½	Do. In. Stk. Reg. 1939	109
3	Do. 1916-26	100
3/	Do. 1916	100
3½	Tasmanian Insc. Stock.. 1920-40	108
4	Do. 1920-40	116
4	Trinidad Insc. Stock.... 1917-42	110
3	Do. 1922-44	98
4	Victoria Rly. Loan '81 Inscribed Stock 1907	105
4	Victoria Insc. Stock 1908-13-19	106
4	Victoria (1883) Ins. Stk. 1920	111
3½	Do. Inscribed Stock 1921-3-6	104
4	Do. do. 1911-26	108
4	W. Austral. Insc. Stock 1934	116½
4	Do. 1911-31	109
3½	Do. 1915-35	104
3	Do. 1913-35	97
3	Do. 1916-36	97

FOREIGN STOCKS, BONDS, &c.

COUPONS PAYABLE IN LONDON.

Last Div.	Name.	Price
36/	Argentine Ry. Loan 6 p.c. 1881	85½
15/	Do. 5 p.c. 1884	64
30/	Do. N. Cent. Ry. Ext. 5 p.c. 1887-8-9	64
30/	Do. 5 p.c. Trsy. Convs. 1887	64
5/4½	Do. 4½ p.c. Interl. Gld. 1888	63
27/	Do. 4½ p.c. Stlg. Extrl. 1888	64
10/6	Do. 3½ p.c. External .. 1889	47
4	Do. 4 p.c. Ry. Guar. Res.	54
4½	Brazilian 1883	48
4½	Do. Gold 1879	59½
4½	Do. 1888	47
35/	Buenos Ayres 1824	80
6	Do. 1882-3-6	46
6	Bulgarian 1888	92
6	Do. Mort. Bonds 1892	92
4½	Chilian 1885	72
4½	Do. 1886	73
4½	Do. 1887	72
4½	Do. 1889	81½
5	Do. 1892	84
4½	Do. 1893	72
4½	Do. 1895	70
5	Do. 1896	83
7	Chinese Silver 1894	96
6	Do. Gold 1895	106
6	Do. Apl. '95 by dwgs. 1901-15	108
5	Do. Red. dwgs. in 36 yr. 1896	98
5	Do. Do. Regis. 1896	98
1½	Colmbn. 1½ to 3 p.c. Ext. Bds. 1896	17
6	Cordova, Prov. 1886	24
—	Do. Eng. Ass. Certs.	23
—	Do. 6 p.c. 1887-8	24
—	Do. Eng. Ass. Certs.	23
3	Costa Rica "A"	30
2½	Do. "B"	23
3	Danish Gold 1914	98
10/	Ecuador N. Ext. Bds. 4½ p.c. ascn. to 5 p.c.	21
3½	Egypt'n Ins. Stk. lia. Stp. Dty. 1890	100
4	Do. State Domain 1878	104½
4	Do. D. Sanieh, Red. .. 1905	102½
6	Entre Rios 1886-8	33
6	Do. Fndg. Ln. Bds. 1894-1921	29
6	Do. do. Parana City	22½
15/	Greek 1881	38
15/	Do. 1884	38
12/	Do. Rentes	32
15/	Do. (Piræus-Larissa Ry.)	37
7/6	Do. Fundg. Loan (1)	41
4	Guatemala Extl. Debt	30
6	Hawaiian	102½
4	Hungarian Gold Rentes	100½
3	Do. 1895	89
6	Italian Irriga. Guar.	108½
5	Do. Maremmana	91
5	Japan 5 p.c.	103
5	Mexican (Nat. R. Tehuantp c.)	92½
6	Do. Extrl. 1890	95

Foreign Stocks, &c. *continued*):—

Last Div.	Name.	Price
6	Mexican Extrl. 1893	95
5	Do. Intrnl. Cons. Slvr.	36
5	Do Intern. Rd. Bds. 2d. Ser.	36
4	Nicaragua 1886..............	42½
3½	Norwegian, red. 1937, or earlier	98
3	Do. do. 1965, do.	98
3½	Do. 3½ p.c. Bnds.	102
1	Paraguay 1p.c. ris. 3p.c. 1886-96	15
5	Russian, 1822, £ Strlg.	149
3	Do. 1859	93
4	Do. (Nicolas Ry.) 1867-9 ..	100
3	Do. Transcauc. Ry. 1882 ..	94
4	Do. Con. R. R. Bd. Ser. I., 1889 ..	103
4	Do. Do. II., 1889 ..	103
4	Do. Do. III., 1891 ..	102
3½	Do. Bonds	100
4	Do. Ln. (Dvinsk and Vitbsk)	100½
6	Salvador 1889................	57½
—	S Domingo 4s. Unified: .. 1980	62
6	San Luis Potosi Stg. 1889	88
5	San Paulo (Brzl.), Stg. 1888	88½
6	Santa Fé 1883-4..............	34
—	Do. Eng. Ass. Certs. Dep...	33
5	Do. 1888	45
—	Do. Eng. Ass. Certs. Dpsit..	44
5	Do. (W. Cnt. Col. Rly.) Mrt.	24
5	Do. & Reconq. Rly. Mort...	24
5	Spanish Quicksilvr Mort. 1870 ..	99½
3½	Swedish 1880	102
3	Do. 1888	98
3	Do. Conversion Loan 1894..	98
5	Trans. Gov. Loan Red...1903-42	105
59/	Tucuman (Prov.) 1888.........	67½
4	Turkish, Secd. on Egypt. Trib.	102
3½	Turkish, Egpt. Trib., Ott. Bd., '94	98
4	Do. Priority 1890.........	89½
1	Do. Convted Series, "A"..	66
5	Do. Customs Ln. 1886......	94½
5	Uruguay Bonds 1896	54
3	Venzuela New Con. Debt 1881	32

COUPONS PAYABLE ABROAD.

Last Div.	Name.	Price
7	Argent. Nat. Cedla. Sries, "B".	33½
5	Austrian Ster. Rnts., ex 10fl., 1870	85
5	Do. do. do.	83
5	Do. Paper do. 1870	83
5	Do. do. do.	83
4	Do. Gld Rentes 1876	100
3	Belgian exchange 25 fr.	100
3½	Danish Int., 1887, Rd. 1896	—
2½	Dutch Certs. ex 12 gldrs.	85
3	Do. Bonds	97
3	Do. Insc. Stk.........	96
3½	French Rentes	104½
3	Do. 1878, '81-4., Red.	99
3	German Imp. Ln. 1891..........	95
3	Do. do. 1892-3	95
3	Do. do. 1890-4	96
5	Japan Cons. Ln., '92: 3, & 5, Red.	46
36/9	Prussian Consols	102
3	" Cons. Stg. Ln. 1891....	96
4	Utd. States, 1877, Red. 1907	112
4	Do. 1895, 30 yrs.	126
3½	Do. Maschsetts Gl. 1935	113½
3½	Do. Gold Bonds 1923	107½
2	Virginia Cpn. Bds., 3 p.c. from July, 1901	69½

BRITISH RAILWAYS.
ORD. SHARES AND STOCKS.

Last Div	Name.	Price.
10	Barry, Ord.	276½
4	Do. Prefd.	125
6	Do. Defd.	150½
5	Caledonian, Ord..........	154
3	Do. Prefd.	99
—	Do. Defd. Ord., No. 1	4½
	Cambrian, Ord...........	5½
—	Do. Coast Cons.	5½
32/	Cardiff Ry. Pref. Ord.	116
3/	Central Lond. £10 Ord. Sh.	10½
1/9½	Do. do. £6 paid......	6½
3½d.	Do. Pref. Half-Shares..	1½
1/6	Do. Def. do........	4½
1½	City and S. London	68½
—	East London, Cons.	6½
2	Furness	65½
2½	Glasgow and S. West. Pfd.	81
2½	Do. do. Dfd.	64
3	Great Central, Ord....1894	41
32/0	Do. London Exten.....	74½
—	Great N. of Scotland, Prfd.	88
—	Do. Dfd.	33
4	Great Northern, Prefd.....	119½
—	Do. Consolidated "A"	50
—	Do. do. "B"	190½
2	Highland	75½
4	Isle of Wight, Prefd.	120½
3	Do. Defd.	83½
	Lancs. Derbys. and E. Cst.	4
8½	L. Brighton and S. C. Ord.	185
6	Do. Prefd. Ord.	197
10/	Do. Contgt. Rights Certs.	18½
5½	Lond. and S. Western Ord.	225½
4	Do. Preferred	133
6½	Lond., Tilb., and Southend	133½
—	Mersey, £20 shares	½
—	Metropolitan, New Ord...	131½
2½	Do. Surplus Lands....	92
4	North Cornwall, 4 p.c. Pref.	104½
13/6	Do. Deferred	22½
7½	North London...........	223½
4½	North Staffordshire	129

British Railways (*continued*):—

Last Div.	Name.	Price.
3/3	Plymouth, Devenport, and S. W. Junc. £10	8½
3/	Port Talbot £10 Shares ..	9½
9d.	Rhondda Swns. B. £10 Sh.	5
10	Rhymney, Cons.	265½
4	Do. Prefd.	123
6⅛	Do. Defd.	145½
1½	Scarboro', Bridlington Junc.	47½
6½	South Eastern, Ord........	150
6	Do. Pref.	192
3½	Taff Vale	81
25/	Vale of Glamorgan........	127½
3	Waterloo & City	134½

LEASED AT FIXED RENTALS

Last Div.	Name.	Price.
4	Birkenhead	144
5.19.0	East Lincnshire..........	202½
5½	Hamsmith. & City Ord. ..	192½
4½	Lond. and Blackwll.	160½
4½	Do. £10 4½ p. c. Pref...	160½
56/6	Lond. & Green. Ord.......	101
5	Do. 5 p. c. Pref.	176½
5	Nor. and Eastn. £50 Ord...	89
6	Do. ..	104½
3½	N. Cornwall 3½ p. c. Stk...	125½
4⅛	Nott. & Granthm. R. & C...	143½
3½	Portptk. & Wigtn. Guar. Stk.	121½
9	Vict. Stn. & Pimlico Ord...	312½
4½	Do. 4½ p. c. Pref....	158½
4/	West Lond. £20 Ord. Shs.	14
4½	Weymouth & Portld......	157½

DEBENTURE STOCKS.

Last Div.	Name.	Price.
4	Alexandra Dks. & Ry.	130½
3	Barry, Cons.	107
4	Brecon & Mrthyr, New A	127½
4	Do. New B	105
4	Caledonian	147
4	Cambrian "A"	132½
4	Do. "B"	127½
4	Do. "C"	119½
4	Do. "D"	107½
3	Cardiff Rly.	100½
4	City and S. Lond.	137
3½	Cleator & Working Junc...	118½
3	Devon & Som. "A"	103½
10/8	Do. "B" 4 p. c.	36
—	Do. "C" 4 p. c.	10
4	E. Lond. and Ch. 4 p. c. A	135
5/	Do. 2nd B	67½
—	Do. 3rd Ch. 4 p. c. ..	19½
—	Do. 4th do.	9½
3½	Do. 1st (3½ p. c.)	128½
2½	Do. 2½ p.c. (Whitech. Exn).	87
4	Forth Bridge	142½
4	Furness	142½
4	Glasgow and S. Western ..	147
5	Gt. Central	—
4½	Do.	155½
4	Gt. Eastern	145
4	Gt. N. of Scotland........	139
3	Gt. Northern	111½
4	Gt. Western	149
4½	Do	156½
4½	Do.	165½
5	Do.	184½
2½	Do.	96½
4	Highland	139
3	Hull and Barnsley	104½
3	Do. and (3-4 p. c)...	122½
4	Isle of Wight	142½
3	Do. Cent. "A"..	92½
4½	Do. "B"	115½
4	Do. "C"	82½
3	Lancs. & Yorkshire	112
4	Lancs. Derbys. & E. Cst...	123½
4½	Ldn. and Blackwall	155½
4	Ldn. and Greenwich......	144½
4	Lond., Brighton, &c.	148½
4½	Do.	165½
4½	Lond., Chath., &c., Arb...	154½
4½	Do. "B"..	153½
4	Do.	137½
4	Do. 1883....	137½
3	Do.	106
3	Lond. & N. Western......	115
3	Lond. & S. Westn. "A" ..	114
3	Do. Consld.	114
4	Lond., Til., & Southend ..	144½
—	Mersey, 5 p. c. (Act, 1866)	65
4	Metropolitan	144½
4½	Do.	162½
3½	Do.	126½
6	Met. District	207½
4	Do.	138½
2½	Midland	95
4½	Mid-Wales "A"	137½
4	Neath & Brecon 1st	127½
4	Do. "A 1" ..	117½
3	North British	109
3	Do. 1893	107
7½	N Cornwall, Launcstn., &c.	125½
	North Eastern..........	113

Debenture Stocks (*continued*):—

Last Div.	Name.	Price.
4½	North London..........	163½
3	N. Staffordshire	111
4	Plym. Devpt. & S.W. Jn...	141½
4	Rhondda and Swan. Bay..	130½
4	Rhymney	144½
4	South-Eastern	147
5	Do.	182½
3½	Do.	127½
3	Do.	113
3	Taff Vale	109½
4	Tottenham & For. Gate ..	143½
3	Vale of Glamorgan	105½
3	West Highld. (Gtd. by N.B.)	106
4	Wrexham, Mold, &c. "A"	113½
4	Do. "B"	101½
4	Do. "C"	97½

GUARANTEED SHARES AND STOCKS.

Last Div.	Name.	Price.
4	Caledonian	146½
4	Do.	142½
4	Forth Bridge	142½
4	Furness 1881	137½
4	Glasgow & S. Western	141½
4	Do. St. Enoch, Rent	141½
6	Gt. Central	198½
4½	Do. 1st Pref.........	150½
3½	Do. Pref.	104½
5	Do. Irred. S.Y. Rent	161½
4½	Do. do.	139½
4	Gt. Eastern, Rent	141½
5	Do. Metropolitan..	177½
4	Do.	142½
4	Gt. N. of Scotland	138½
4	Gt. Northern	143½
5	Gt. Western, Rent	181½
5	Do. Cons.	181½
4	Lancs. & Yorkshire	143½
5	L., Brighton & S. C.......	179½
3½	L., Chat. & D. (Shrtlds.)..	110½
4	L. & North Western	146
4	L. & South Western.. 1881	144
4½	Met. District, Ealing Rent	150
4½	Do. Fulham Rent	150
4	Do. Midland Rent	141½
4	Do. Mid. & Dist. Guar.	127½
2½	Midland, Cons. Perp.	92
3	Mid. & G.N. Jt., "A" Rnt..	106
3	N. British, Lien	107
4	Do Cons. Pref. No. 1	139
3	N. Cornwall, Wadebrge. Gu.	107
4	N. Eastern	144½
5	N. Staff. Trent & M. £20 Shs.	35½
3½	Nott. Suburban Ord.	123½
20/6	S. E. Perp. Ann.	35½
4½	Do. 4½ p.c...........	162½
3½	S. Yorks. Junc. Ord.	118½
4½	W. Cornwall (G. W., Br., Ex., & S. Dev. Joint Rent	159½
3	W. Highl. Ord. Stk. (Gua., N.B.)...............	104½

PREFERENCE SHARES AND STOCKS.

DIVIDENDS CONTINGENT ON PROFIT OF YEAR.

Last Div.	Name	Price.
4½	Alexandra Dks. & Ry. "A"	125½
5	Barry (First)	167½
4	Do. Consolidated......	136½
4	Caledonian Cons., No. 1 ..	141½
4	Do. do. No. 2 ..	141
5	Do. do. 1878	174½
4	Do. Pref. 1884	140½
4	Do. do. 1887 (Conv.)	152½
—	Cambrian, No. 1 4 p.c. Pref.	72½
—	Do. No. 2 do.	37½
—	Do. No. 3 do.	17½
—	Do. No. 4 do.	9
5	City & S. Lond. £10 shares	15½
—	Do. New	14
4	Furness, Cons. 1881	133
4	Do. ......"A" 1881	131½
4	Do. ......"B" 1883	129½
4	Glasgow & S. Western	140½
4	Do. No. 2....	140½
4	Do. 1888	139½
4	Do. 1891	139½
5	Gt. Central	159½
4	Do.	131½
5	Do. Conv..... 1872	153½
5	Do. do. 1874	153½
5	Do. do. 1876	152½
5	Do. do. 1870	151½
5	Do. do. 1881	147½
4	Do. 1889	112½
4	Do. 1891	107½
5	Do. 1894	107½
4	Gt. Eastern, Cons.........	141½
4	Do. 1886	140
4	Do. 1881	138½
4	Do. 1884	138½

Preference Shares, &c. (*continued*):—

Last Div.	Name.	Price.
4	Gt. Eastern, Cons..... 1887	138½
4	Do. 1888	138½
3½	Do. 1890	120½
3½	Do. 1893	120½
—	Do. (Int. fr. Jan '99) 1893	117½
4	Gt. North Scotland "A"..	133½
4	Do. "B"..	133½
4	Gt. Northern, Cons.	142½
3	Do. 1896	107
5	Gt. Western Cons.	180½
36/11	Hull & Barnsley Red. at 115	109
4	Isle of Wight	133½
3	Lancs. & Yorkshire, Cons.	108
2/2½	Lanc. Drby & E.C. 5 p.c. £10	9½
—	Do. 5 p.c. and £10	9½
5	Lond., Bright., &c., Cons.	178½
5	Do. 2nd Cons.	177½
4½	Lond., Chat. & Dov. Arbitr.	136½
20/	Do. 2nd Pref. 4½ p.c.	93
4	Lond. & N. Western......	145
4	Lond. & S. Western.. 1881	144
4	Do. 1884	143
3½	Do.	127½
4	Lond., Tilbury & Southend	140½
4	Do. Cons., 1887	140½
4	Do 1891	140½
—	Mersey, 5 p.c. Perp.	—
4	Metropolitan, Perp.	141½
4	Do. 1882	140½
4	Do. Irred.	140½
4	Do. 1887	140½
4	Do. New........	140½
4½	Do.	146½
3½	Do.	123½
3	Do. Guar.	101½
2½	Metrop. Dist. Exten 5 p.c.	109½
2½	Midland, Perp. Pref.	92
4	N. British Cons., No. 2 ..	135½
4½	Do. Edin. & Glasgow	151½
5	Do. 1865	165½
5	Do. Conv. 1874	166½
4½	Do. 1875	151½
4½	Do. Conv. 1875	151½
5	Do. do. 1870	166½
4	Do. do. 1884	136½
4	Do. do. 1888	136½
4	Do. do. 1890	136½
4	Do. do. 1892	136½
4	N. Eastern	144
4½	N. Lond., Cons.......1866	174½
4½	Do. 2nd Cons. .. 1875	157½
3	N. Staffordshire	106½
4½	Plym. Devpt. & S. W. Junc.	149½
1/5	Port Talbot, &c., 4 p.c. £10 Shares, 4 paid	5
5/	Rhondda & Swansea Bay, 5 p.c. £10 Shares	12
4	Rhymney, Cons..........	140½
4½	S. Eastern, Cons.	160½
5	Do. do.	179
4	Do. Vested Cos'.....	140½
4	Do. 1891	140½
3½	Do. 1893	122½
2	Do. 3 p.c. after July 1900	101½
4	Taff Vale	141½

INDIAN RAILWAYS.

Last Div.	Name.	Paid.	Price.
3½	Assam Bengal, Ld., (3½ p.c. till June 30, then 3 p.c.)	100	100
4/	Barsi Light, Ld., £10 Shs.	10	11
6	Bengal and N. West., Ld	100	148½
4/	Do. £10 Shares	10	14
3/6	Do. 3½ p.c. Cum. Pf. Shs.	10	10½
6½d.	Do.	4	4½
2/3½	Bengal Central, Ld., £10 (3½ p.c. + ¼th net earn)	5	6
3	Bengal Dooars, Ld.	100	114
4	Bengal Nagpr., Lim. (gua. 4 p.c. + 4th sp. pfts.) ..	100	113
7½	Bombay, Baroda, and C. I. (gua 5 p.c)	100	213
36/1	Burma, Ld. (gua. 2½ p.c. and ½ p.c. add. till 1901)	100	106
1/7	Do. £10 Shares		2½
4	Delhi Umb. Kalka, Ld., Gua. 3½ p.c. + net earn.	100	121
4	Do. Deb. Stk., 1890 (1916)	100	111
9/10	Estn. Bengal, "A" An. 1957	—	24
9/	Do. "B" 1957	—	29
4	Do. Gua. Deb. Stock ..	100	135½
9/7½	East Ind. Ann. "A" (1953)	—	26
8/4½	Do. "C"	—	27
8/11½	Do. "B"	—	29
6⅛	Do. Def. Ann. Cap. (gua. 4 p.c. + ½th sp. pfts.)	—	149
115/9	East Ind. Def. Ann. "D"	—	155
4½	East Ind. Irred. Stock ..	100	157½
5	Gt. Indian Penin., Gua 5 p.c. + ½ surplus profits..	100	165½
4	Do. Irred. 4 p.c. Deb. St.	100	136½
4	Indian Mid., Ld. (gua. 4 p.c. + ¼th surplus pfts.)	100	113
51/	Madras Guar. + ½ sp. pfts.	100	165
48/6	Do. do.	100	155
46/	Do. do.	100	145
4	Nilgiri, Ld., 1st Deb. Stk.	100	97
4	Oude & Rohil. Db. Stk. Rd.	100	—
5⅛	Rohil. and Kumaon, Ld.	100	132
9/11	Scinde, Punj., and Delhi, "A" Ann., 1958	—	24
9/1	Do. "B" do. ..	—	29

Indian Railways (*continued*):—

Last Div.	Name.	Paid.	Price.
4	South Behar, Ld., £10 shs.	100	100
3½	Do. Deb. Stk. Red.	100	101
4½	South Ind., Gu. Deb. Stk.	100	157½
5	South Indian, Ld. (gua. 3 p.c., and ½ spls. profits)	100	122½
5	Sthn. Mahratta, Ld. (3½ p.c. & ¼th net earnings)	100	115½
4	Do. Deb. Stk. Red.	100	120
3½	Southern Punjab, Ld.	100	105
3½	Do. Deb. Stk. Red.	—	104
5	Nizam's Gua. State, Ld. (†	100	114½
4	Do. Mort. Deb., 1936	100	107
4	Do. do. Reg.	100	106
17/3½	Nizam's Gua. State, Ld., 3½ p.c. Mt. Deb. bearer	—	94½
17/3½	Do. Reg. do. ..	—	93½
5	W. of India Portgese., Ld.	100	67½
5	Do. Deb. Stk., Red	100	98

RAILWAYS.—BRITISH POSSESSIONS.

Last Div.	Name.	Paid.	Price.
5	Atlantic & N.W. Gua. 1 Mt. Bds., 1937	100	125½
5/3	Buff. & L. Huron Ord. Sh.	10	13½
5½	Do. 1st Mt. Perp. Bds. 1879	100	141½
5½	Do. 2nd Mt. Perp. Bds.	100	141½
—	Calgary & Edmon. 6 p.c. 1st Mt. Stg. Bds. Red..	100	77½
5	Canada Cent. 1st Mt. Bds. Red.	100	103
4	Can. Pacific Pref. Stk.	100	100½
5	Do. Strl. 1st Mt. Deb. Bds. 1915	100	117
3½	Do. Ld. Grnt. Bds., 1938..	100	106
3½	Do. Ld. Grnt. Ins. Stk. ..	100	106
4	Do. Perp. Cons. Deb. Stk.	100	115
5	Do. Algoma Bch. 1st Mt. Bds., 1937	100	121
3	Demerara, Original Stock	100	46
7	Do. Perp. Pref. Stk.	100	152½
1/10	Do. 4 p.c. Cum. Ext. Pref. £10 Shs.	4	8
—	Dominion Atlntc. Ord. Stk.	100	33½
5	Do. 5 p.c. Pref. Stk.	100	97½
4	Do. 1st. Deb. Stk.	100	103½
4	Do. 2nd do. Red.	100	99
—	EmuBay&Mt.Bischoff, Ld.	5	4½
4½	Do. Irred. Deb. Stk. ...	100	98
nil.	Gd. Trunk of Canada, Stk.	100	8½
6	Do. 2nd. Equip. Mt. Bds.	100	131½
5	Do. Perp. Deb. Stk.	100	136½
5	Do. Gt. Westn. Deb. Stk.	100	128½
5	Do. Nthn. of Can. 1st Mt. Bds, 1902	100	103½
4	Do. do. Deb. Stk	100	102
5	Do. G. T. Geor. Bay & L. Erie 1 Mt., 1903	100	105
5	Do. Mid. of Can. Stl. 1st Mt. (Mid. Sec.) 1908	100	103
5	Do. do. Cons. 1 Mt. Bds. 1912	100	106
5	Do. Mont. & Champ. 1 Mt. Bds., 1902	100	104
	Do. Welln., Grey & Brce. 7 p.c. Bds. 1 Mt.	100	109
—	Jamaica 1st Mtg. Bds. Red.	—	103
—	Manitoba & N. W., 6 p.c. 1st Mt. Bds., Red	100	—
—	Do. Ldn. Bdhldrs. Certs.	—	—
5	Manitoba S. W. Col. 1 Mt. Bd., 1934 $1,000 price %	—	120
—	Mid. of W. Aust. Ld. 6 p.c. 1 Mt. Dbs., Red.	100	37½
4	Do. Deb. Bds., Red.	100	103
4	Nakusp & Slocan Bds., 1918	100	106
3	Natal Zululand Ld. Debs.,	100	72½
5	N. Brunswick 1st Mt. Stg. Bds., 1934	100	121
4	Do. Perp. Cons. Deb. Stk.	100	114
—	N. Zealand Mid., Ld., 5 p.c 1st Mt. Debs.	100	35
6	Ontario & Queb. Cap. Stk.	$100	151½
5	Do. Perm. Deb. Stk.	100	141½
—	Qu'Appelle, L. Lake & Sask. 6 p.c. 1 Mt. Bds. Red.	100	40½
	Queb. & L. S. John, 1st Mt. Bds., 1909	100	32
	Quebec Cent., Prior Ln. Bds., 1908	100	107
1½	Do. 5 p.c. Inc. Bds.	100	37
4	St. Lawr. & Ott. Stl. 1st Mt.	100	112
4	Shuswap & Okan., 1st Mt. Deb. Bds., 1915	100	76
5	Temiscouata, 5 p.c. Stl. 1st Deb. Bds., Red.	100	9½
5	Do. (S. Franc. Brch.) 5 p.c. Stl. 1 Mt. Db. Bds., 1910	100	10
4	Toronto, Grey & B. 1st Mt.	100	112
1/2	Well. & Mana. £5 Shs. ..	1	½
5	Do. Debs., 1908	100	107
5	Do. 2nd Debs., 1908	100	106
5	Do. 3rd do., 1908	100	104
6	Atlan. & St. Law. Shs., 6 p.c.	100	163½
5	Gd. Trunk Mt. Bds., 1934	100	116½
5	Michigan Air Line, 5 p.c. 1st Mt. Bds., 1902	100	104
4	Minneap., S. P. & Slt. Ste. Mar, 1st Mt. Bds., 1938	$1000	98

AMERICAN RAILROAD STOCKS AND SHARES.

Last Div.	Name.	Paid.	Price.
6/	Alab. Gt. Sthn. A 6 p.c. Pref.	10/.	9
—	Do. do "B" Ord. ..	10/.	1½
—	Alabma. N. Orl.-Tex. &c., "A" Pref.	10/.	½
—	Do. "B" Def.	10/.	½
5½	Atlant. First Lsd. Ls. Rtl. Trust	Stk.	97½
—	Baltimore & Ohio Com. ..	$100	19
—	Baltimore Ohio S.W. Pref.	$100	7
—	Chesap. & Ohio Com.	$100	11½
—	Chic. Gt. West. 5 p.c. Pref. Stock "A"	$100	32½
—	Do. do. Scrip. In.	—	30½
8/3	Do. 4 p.c. Deb. Stk.	$100	67½
4	Do. Interest in Scrip	$100	63½
$4	Chic. Junc. Rl. & Un. Stk. Yds. Com.	$100	118½
$1½	Do. 6 p.c. Cum. Pref.	$100	119½
$3½	Chic. Mil. & St. P. Pref. ..	$100	147½
7	Cleve. & Pittsburgh	$10	84½
$1½	Clev., Cincin., Chic., & St. Louis Com.	$100	—
—	Erie 4 p.c. Non-Cum. 1st Pf.	—	35½
—	Do. 4 p.c. do. 2nd Pf.	—	18
$2½	Gt. Northern Pref.	$100	160
$2½	Illinois Cen. Lsd. Lines ..	$100	95½
—	Kansas City, Pitts & G. ..	$100	19
$3	L. Shore & Mich. Sth. C.	$100	190
—	Mex. Cen. Ltd. Com.	$100	5
—	Miss. Kan. & Tex. Pref. ..	$100	37½
2½	N.Y., Pen. & O. 1st Mt. Tst. Ltd., Ord.	—	47½
4	Do. 1st Mort. Deb. Stk. ..	$100	92½
8	North Pennsylvania	$50	—
—	Northn. Pacific, Com.	$100	26½
1¾	Pitts. F. Wayne & Chic. ..	$100	174
—	Reading 1st Pref.	$50	22½
—	Do. 2nd Pref.	$50	11½
—	S. Louis & S. Fran. Com.	$100	6
—	Do. 2nd Pref.	$100	25½
6	St. Louis Bridge 1st Pref. .	$100	107
3	Do. 2nd Pref.	$100	50
6	Tunnel Rail. of St. Louis	$100	107
$1½	St. Paul, Min. and Man. ..	$100	137½
—	Southern, Com.	$100	8½
—	Wabash, Common	$100	8

AMERICAN RAILROAD BONDS. CURRENCY.

Last Div.	Name.	Price.
7	Albany & Susq. 1 Con. Mrt. 1906	118
7	Allegheny Val. 1 Mt. 1910	125½
5	Canada Southern 1 Mt. 1908	112½
5	Chic. & N. West. Sk. Fd. Db. 1933	117½
5	Do. Deb. Coupon 1921	112½
6	Chicago & Tomah 1905	109½
5	Chic. Burl. & Q. Skg. Fd. 1901	102½
4	Do. Nebraska Ext. ...... —	100
6	Chic., Mil., & S. Pl., 1 Mt. S.W. Div. 1909	117½
7	Do. (S. Paul Div.) 1 Mt. 1902	132½
5	Do. (La Cross & D. 1919	112½
7	Do. 1 Mt. (Hast. & Dak.) 1910	127½
5	Do. Chic. & Mis. Riv. 1 Mt. 1926	112½
5	Chic., Rock Is. and Pac. 1 Mt. Ext. 1934	108
6	Det., G. Haven & Mil. Equip 1918	105
6	Do. do. Cons. Mt. 1918	102½
6	Ill. Cent., 1 Mt., Chic. & S. 1898	—
7	Indianap. & Vin., 1 Mt. .. 1908	125
6	Do. do. 2 Mt. .. 1900	100½
6	Lehigh Val., Cons. Mt. 1923	114½
—	Mexic. Cent., Ln. 2 Cons. Inc. —	5
7	N.Y. Cent. & H.R. Mt. Bonds 1903	119½
5	Do. Deb. 1904	111½
6	Penns. Cons. S. F M. 1905	118
4	West Shore, 1 Mt. 2361	110

DITTO—GOLD.

Last Div.	Name.	Price.
6	Alabama Gt. Sthn. 1 Mt. .. 1908	114
5	Do. Mid. 1 1928	90½
4	Allegheny Val. Gen. Mt. .. 1942	106
4	Atch., Top., & S. Fé Gn. Mt. 1995	92
3	Do. Adj. Mt. 1995	65
5	Do. Equipt. Tmst. ...... —	102½
5	Atlantic & Dan. 1 Mt. 1950	96½
5	Baltimore & Ohio 1925	100
5	Do. Speyer's Tst. Recpts. 1925	100
5	Do. Cons. Mt. 1988	104½
4½	Do. 4½ p.c. 1 Mt. Term. 1934	84
4½	Do. Brown Shipley's Dep. Cts. —	84
5	Balt. Belt 5 p.c. 1 Mort. 1990	90
4½	Balt. & Ohio S.W. 1 Mt. .. 1990	101
4½	Do. 4½ p.c. 1 Cons. Mt. 1893 1993	74
—	Do. Inc. Mt. 5 p.c. Cl. A —	28½
—	Do. do. Cl. B —	10
5	Balt. & Ohio S.W. Term 5 p.c. 1942	97½
6	Balt. & Ptmac (Mn. L.) 1 Mt. 1911	124
6	Do. do. (Tunnel) 1 Mt. 1911	126
4	Beech Creek 1 Mt. 1936	109
4	Carthage & Adiron 1 Mt. .. 1981	107

American Railroad Bonds—Gold *continued*):—

Last Div.	Name.	Price.
5	Cent. of Georgia 1 Mort. .. 1945	117½
5	Do. Cons. Mt. 1945	90½
5	Cent. of N. Jrsy. Gn. Mt. .. 1987	116
6	Central Pacific, 1 Mort. 1898	102½
6	Do. Speyer's Certs. ...... —	106
5	Do. Land Grant 1900	101
5	Chesap. & Ohio 1st Cons. Mt. 1939	116
4½	Do. Gen. Mt. 1992	81
6	Chic. & W. Ind. Gen. Mt. Skg. Fd. 1932	119½
5	Chic. Mil. & St. Pl. (Chic. & L. Sup.) 1 Mt. 1921	114½
5	Do. Chic. & Pac. W. 1921	117½
5	Do. Wisc. & Minn. 1 Mt. 1921	112½
5	Do. Terminal Mt. 1914	114½
4	Do. General Mt. 1989	106½
5	Chic. St. L. & N. Orleans .. 1951	122½
4	Do. 1 Mort. (Memphis) .. 1951	104
4	Clevel, Cin., Chic. & St. L. 1 Mt. (Cairo) 1939	90
4	Do. 1 Mt. (Cinc., Wab., & Mich.) 1991	90
4	Do. 1 Col. Tst. Mt. (S. Louis) 1990	96
4	Do. General Mt. 1993	80½
4½	Clevel. & Mar. Mt. 1935	109
4½	Clevel. & Pittsburgh 1942	116½
4½	Do. Series B. 1942	116½
—	Colorado Mid. 1 Mt. 1936	63½
—	Do. Bdhrs.' Comm. Certs. —	63½
4	Dnvr. & R. Gde. 1 Cons. Mt. 1936	94
5	Do Imp. Mort. 1928	91
4	Detroit & Mack. 1 Lien 1995	90
5	E. Tennes., Virg., & Grgia. Cons. Mt. 1956	111½
5	Elmira, Cort., & Nthn. Mt. 1914	100
4	Erie 1 Cons. Mt. Pr. Ln. .. 1996	92
3	Do. Gen. Lien 1996	73
6	Galvest., Harrisb., &c., 1 Mt.	107½
5	Georgia, Car. & N. 1 Mt. .. 1929	96
4½	Gd. Rpds & Inda. Ex. 1 Mt. 1941	112½
5	Do. 1 Mt. (Muskegon) .. 1926	39½
3½	Illinois Cent. 1 Mt. 1951	104½
4	Do. 1952	104½
4	Do. Cairo Bdge. .. 1950	102
4	Do. 1953	101
4	Do. General Mort. .. 1904	102½
5	Kans. City, Pitts. & G. 1 M. 1923	73½
3½	L. Shore & Mich. Southern 1997	106½
4½	Lehigh Val. N.Y. 1 Mt. 1940	104
5	Lehigh Val. Term. 1 Mt. .. 1941	110
5	Long Island 1931	117½
5	Do. Deb. 1934	100
5	Do. (N. Shore Bch.) 1 Cons. Mt. 1932	94
6	Louisville & Nash. G. Mt. .. 1930	118½
6	Do. 2 Mt. Sk. Fd. (S. & N. Alabama 1910	107
6	Do. 1 Mt. N. Orl. & Mb. 1930	122½
5	Do. 1 Mt. Coll. Tst. .. 1931	104½
4	Do. Unified 1940	90
4½	Do. Mobile & Montgy. 1 Mt. 1945	111½
4	Manhattan Cons. Mt. 1990	95
4	Mexican Cent. Cons. Mt. .. 1911	65
—	Do. 1 Cons. Inc, ...	14
6	Mexican Nat. 1 Mt. 1927	104
3½	Do. 2 Mt. 6 p.c. Inc. A 1917	52½
—	Do. do. B .. 1917	9
3	Do. Matheson's Certs.	—
3	Michig. Cnt. (Battle Ck. & S.) 1 Mt. 1989	86
6	Minneap. & S. L. 1 Mt. Pacific Ext. 1921	—
5	Do. 1 Consold. 1934	104½
4	Minne., Slt. S. M. & A. 1 Mt. 1926	98½
5	Minneapolis Westn. 1 Mt. .. 1911	105½
4	Miss. Kans. & Tex. 1 Mt. .. 1990	89
4	Do. 2 do. 1990	63
4	Mobile & Birm. Mt. Inc. 1945	38
5	Do. P. Lien 1945	88
4	Mohawk & Mal. 1 Mt. 1991	108
5	Montana Cent. 1 Mt. 1937	111½
5	Nashv., Chattan., & S. L. 1 Cons. Mt. 1928	102½
5	Nash., Flor., & Shff. Mt. .. 1937	92½
4	N. Y. & Putnam 1 Cons. Mt. 1993	108
5	N. Y., Brooklyn, & Man. B. 1 Cons. Mt. 1935	107½
4	N. Y. Cent. & Hud. R. Deb. Certs. 1890 1905	104
4	Do. Ext. Debt. Certs. 1905	106
7	N. Y., L. Erie, & W. 1 Cons. Mt. (Erie) 1920	144½
7	Do. 1 Con. Mt. Fd. Coup. 1920	139½
5	N. Y., Onto., & W. Cons. 1 Mt. 1939	109
4	Do. 4 p.c. Refund. Mt. .. 1992	100
6	Norfolk & West. Gn. Mt. 1931	122½
6	Do. Imp. & Ext 1934	117½
4	Do. 1 Cons. Mt. .... —	82
6	N. Pacific Gn. 1 Mt. Ld. Gt. 1921	—
4	Do. P. Ln. Rl. & Ld. Gt. —	97
3	Do. Gn. Ln. Rl. & Ld. Gt. —	61
5	Oregon & Calif. 1 Mt. 1927	90
6	Panama Skg. Fd. Subsidy .. 1910	102½
4½	Pennsylvania Rlrd. 1913	110
4	Do. Equip. Tst. Ser. A. .. 1914	104
4	Do. Cons. Mt. 1943	112½
4½	Penna. Company 1st Mort. 1921	110½
5	Perkiomen 1 Mrt., 2nd ser. .. 1918	91½
4½	{Pitts., C., C., & St. Ls. Con. Mt. G.B., Ser. A} 1940-2	111
4	Do. Cons. Mort., Ser. D .. 1945	102½
6	Pittsbgh., Cle., & Toledo .. 1922	100½
4	Reading, Phil., & R. Genl. 1997	85
5	Richmond & Dan. Equip. .. 1909	97½
5	Rio Grande Junc. 1st Mort. 1939	90
4	Rio Grande West 1st Tst. Mt. 1939	82½
7	S. Louis Bridge 1st Mort .. 1925	134½
5	S. Louis Mchts. Bdge. Term. 1st Mort. 1930	102½
4	S. Louis S. West 1st Mort. .. 1989	75
—	Do. 4 p.c. 2nd Mort. Inc. 1989	30

American Railroad Bonds (*continued*):

Last Div.	Name.	Price.
4½	S. Louis Term. Cupples Sta. & Prop. 1st. Mrt. 4½ p.c. 1909-17	100
4½	St. Paul Minn., & Manit. 1933	107½
6	Do. do. 1933	132½
6	Shamokin, Sunbury, &c. 2 Mt. 1925	109
5	S. & N. Alabama Cons. Mt. 1936	97½
5	Southern 1 Cons. Coup. 1994	95½
4	Do. E. Tennes Reorg. Lien .. 1938	100
6	S. Pacific of Cal. 1 Mt. .. 1205-12	111
4½	Trml. Assn. of S. Louis 1 Mt. 1939	110½
5	Do. 1 Cons. Mt. 1944	108
5	Texas & Pac. 1 Mt. 2000	102½
—	Do. 5 p.c. 2 Mt. Income 2000	34
5	Toledo & Ohio Cent. 1 Mt. West. Div. 1935	102½
4½	Toledo., Walhon., Val., & Ohio 1 Mt. 1931-3	111½
—	Union Pacific 1 Mt. 4 p.c. .. 1947	98
—	Union Pac., Linc., & Color. 1 Mt. 1918	—
4	United N. Jersey Gen. Mt. .. 1944	113½
6	Vicksbrg., Shrevept., & Pac. Pr. Ln. Mt. 1915	109½
5	Wabash 1 Mt. 1939	106½
4	Wn. Pennsylvania Mt. 1928	106½
5	W. Virga. & Pittsbg. 1 Mt. 1990	75
5	Wheeling & L. Erie 1 Mt. (Wheelg. Div.) 5 p.c. 1928	90½
5	Do. Extn. Imp. Mt. 1930	90
—	Do. do. Brown Shipley's Cts. ..	—
5	Willmar & Sioux Falls 1 Mt. 1938	108

STERLING.

Last Div.	Name.	Price.
6	Alabama Gt. Sthn. Deb. 1906	104½
5	Do. Gen. Mort. .. 1927-8	99
5	Alabama, N. Orl., Tex. & Pac. 5 p.c. "A" Dbs. .. 1910-40	98½
55/	Do. do. "B" do. 1910-40	56
—	Do. do. "C" do.	19
—	Allegheny Valley 1910	130
4	Atlantic 1st Leased Line Perp. ..	100
6	Baltimore and Ohio 1902	108
6	Do. do. 1910	118
5	Do. do. 1877	100
—	Do. Morgan's Certs. ..	100
4½	Do. do. 1933	92½
6	Chicago & Alton Cons. Mt. 1903	111
5	Chic. St. Paul & Kan. City Priority	106
6	Eastn. of Massachusetts 1906	117½
5	Illinois Cent. Skg. Fd.	103
5	Do. 1905	108
3½	Do. 1950	99½
4	Do. 1 Mt. 1951	110
3	Do. 1 Mt. 1951	92½
6	Louisville & Nash., M. C. & L. Div., 1 Mt. 1902	104½
7	Do. 1 Mt. (Memphis & O.) 1902	111
55/8	Mexican Nat. "A" Certs. 5 p.c. Non. cum.	42
—	Do. "B" Certs.	9
6	N.Y. & Canada 1 Mt. 1904	108½
6	N. York Cent. & H.R. Mort. 1903	112
4½	N. York, Penns., & Ohio Pr. Ln. Extd. 1935	—
5	Do. Equip. Tst.	101½
5	Do. 5 p.c. Equip. Tst. (1890)	103½
6	Nrthn. Cent. Cons. Gen. Mt. ..	106
6	Pennsylvania Gen. Mt. 1910	126
6	Do. Cons. Skg. Fd. Mt. 1905	114½
3½	Do. Cons. Mt. 1945	103½
6	Phil. & Erie Cons. Mort .. 1920	132½
6	Phil. & Reading Gen. Cons. Mort. 1911	122½
6	Pittsbg. & Connells. Cons. 1926	116
—	Do. Morgan's Certs.	116½
4	St. Paul., Min., & Manitoba (Pac. Extn.) 1940	97½
6	S. & N. Alabama 1903	104½
6	Un. N. Jersey & C. Gen. Mt. 1901	109½

FOREIGN RAILWAYS

Last Div.	Name.	Paid.	Price.
12/	Alagoas, Ltd., Shs.	20	5
5	Do. Deb. Stk., Red. ..	100	42½
6	Antofagasta, Ltd., Stk. ..	100	72
4	Do. Perp. Deb. Stk. ..	100	90
—	Arauco, Ld., Ord. Shs. ..	10	—
—	Do. 10 p.c. Cum. Pref.	10	—
5	Argentine Gt. W., Ld.,	100	74
5	Do. 5 p.c. Cum. Pref. Shs.	100	101
4	Do. 1 Deb. Stk.	100	102
1/0/0	Argentine N.E., Ltd., 6 p.c. Cum. Pref. Stk. ..	100	9½
—	Do. 5 p.c. Deb. Stk., Red.	100	28
2/	Arica and Tacna Shs. ..	20	1½
10/	Bahia & San Fcisco., Ld.,	20	9
6/	Do. Timbo. Bch. Shs.	20	4½
12/	Bahia, Blanca, & N.W. Ln. Prf. Cum. 6 p.c. ..	100	53
4	Do. 4 p.c. 1 Deb. Stk., Red.	100	92
6	Barranquilla R. & P., Ld., 6 p.c. 1 Deb. Stk., Red.	100	

Foreign Railways (*continued*):—

Last Div.	Name.	Paid.	Price.
3/	Bilbao Riv. & Cantabn., Ltd., Ord.	3	5
—	Bolivar, Ltd. Shs.	10	1⅞
6	Do. 6 p.c. Deb. Stk.	100	96½
—	Brazil Gt. Southn. Ltd., 7 p.c. Cum. Pref.	20	1½
6	Do. Perm. Deb. Stk	100	44
5½	B. Ayres Gt. Southn. Ld., Ord. Stk.	100	136
5	Do. Pref. Stk.	100	133
4	Do. Deb. Stk.	100	117
30/	B. Ayres & Ensen. Port., Ltd., Ord. Stk.	100	65
5	Do. Cum. 1 Pref. Stk.	100	118
6/0/0	Do. 6p.c.Con. Pref.Stk.	100	98
4	Do. Deb. Stk., Irred.	100	114
10⅛	B. Ayres Northern, Ltd., Ord. Stk.	100	265
12⅛	Do. Pref. Stk.	100	320
5	Do. 5 p.c. Mt. Deb. Stk., Red.	100	113
3/15/0	B. Ayres & Pac., Ld., 7 p.c. 1 Pref. Stk. (Cum.)	100	92½
4	Do. 1 Deb. Stk.	100	101
3/5/0	Do. 4½ p.c. 2 Deb. Stk.	100	91
3	B. Ayres & Rosario, Ltd., Ord. Stk.	100	71
7/	Do. 7 p.c. Pref. Shs.	10	17
7/	Do. Sunchales Ext.	10	14½
4	Do. Deb. Stk., Red.	100	107½
—	B. Ayres & Val. Trans., Ltd., 7 p.c. Cum. Pref.	20	6½
4	Do. 4 p.c. "A" Deb. Stk., Red.	100	70
—	Do. 6 p.c. "B" Deb. Stk. Red.	100	43
3/6	B. Ayres Westn. Ld. Ord.	10	10½
3/	Do. Def. Shs.	10	6½
5	Do. 5 p.c. Pref.	10	12½
4	Do. Deb. Stk.	100	108½
6	Cent. Arg. Deb. Sk. Rd.	100	159½
4	Do. Deb. Stk. Rd.	100	110
6	Cent. Bahia L. Ord. Stk.	100	49
	Do. Deb. Stk., 1934	100	72½
5	Do. Deb. Stk., 1937	100	60
3/6	Cent. Uguy. East. Ext. L. Shs.	10	5½
5	Do. Perm. Stk.	100	112
3/6	Do. Nthn. Ext. L. Sh.	10	4
5	Do. Perm. Deb. Stk.	100	103½
3	Do. of Montev. Ltd., Ord. Stk.	100	86
6	Do. Perm. Deb. Stk.	100	141
10/	Conde d'Eu, Ltd. Ord.	20	7
—	Cordba & Rosar., Ltd., 6 p.c. Pref. Shs.	100	33
4	Do. 1 Deb. Stk.	100	89
75	Do. 6 p.c. Deb. Stk.	100	79½
—	Cordba Cent., Ltd., 5 p.c. Cu. 1 Pref. Stk.	100	82
—	Do. 5 p.c. Non-Cum. 2 Pref. Stk.	100	43
5	Do. Deb. Stk.	100	118
4/	Costa Rica, Ltd., Shs.	10	3½
8/	Dna. Thrsa. Chris., Ltd., 7 p.c. Pref. Shs.	20	3½
20/	E. Argentine, Ltd.	100	39
6	Do. Deb. Stk.	100	103
2/1	Egyptn. Dlta. Lgt. Rys., Ltd., £10 Pref. Shs.	8	10
—	Entre Rios, L., Ord. Shs.	5	¾
—	Do. Cu. 5 p.c. Pref.	5	3
6/	Gt. Westn. Brazil, Ltd.,	20	7½
6	Do. Perm. Deb. Stk.	100	90½
6	Do. Extn. Deb. Stk.	100	77½
—	Int.-Oceanic Mex., Ltd., 7 p.c. Pref.	10	1½
4	Do. Deb. Stk.	100	82
42/6	Do. 7 p.c. "A" Deb. Sk.	100	66
—	Do. 7 p.c. "B" Deb. Sk.	100	29
5/	La Guaira & Carac.	10	7½
5	Do. 5 p.c. Deb. Sk. Red.	100	100
13/3	Lembg.-Czern.-Jassy	30	24½
1/	Lima, Ltd.	20	2½
—	Manila Ltd. 7 p.c. Cu. Pf.	10	¾
20/6½	Mexican 2nd Pref. 6 p.c.	100	31
6	Do. Perp Deb. Stk.	100	137
1/0/0	Mexican Sthrn., Ld., Ord.	100	22
—	Do. 4 p.c. 1 Db. Stk. Rd.	100	82
—	Do. 4 p.c. 2 do.	100	59
—	Mid. Urgy., Ltd.	100	18½
5	Do. Deb. Stk.	100	61
12/	Minas & Rio, Ltd.	20	8½
5/2	Namur & Liege	20	12½
11/6	Do. Pref.	20	29
13/	Natal & Na. Cruz, Ld., 7 p.c. Cum Pref.	20	6
—	Nitrate Ltd., Ord.	10	5½
—	Do. 7 p.c. Pr. Con. Or.	10	4
—	Do. Def. Conv. Ord.	10	¾
7/	N.-E. Urgy., Ltd., Ord.	10	15
7/	Do. 7 p.c. Pref.	10	15½
—	N.-W. Argentine Ld., 7 p.c. Pref.	10	2
6	Do. 6 p.c. 1 Deb. Stk.	100	113
—	Do. 2 Deb. Stk.	100	94
—	N.W. Uruguay 6 p.c. 1 Pref. Stk.	100	16
—	Do. 5 p.c. 2 Pref. Stk.	100	7½
6	Do. 6 p.c. Deb. Stk.	100	80½
22/	Ottoman (Sm. Aid.)	20	13½
—	Paraguay Cntl., Ld., 5 p.c. Perm. Deb. Stk.	100	11
—	Piræus, Ath., & Pelo.	275	1½
4/	Pto. Alegre & N. Hambg Ld., 7 p.c. Pref. Shs.	20	4
6	Do. Mt. Deb. Stk. Red.	100	74½
—	Puerto Cabello & Val. Ld.	10	1¾
5	Recife & S. Francisco	00	64½
24/	R. Claro S. Paulo, Ld., Sh.	10	20½
5	Do. Deb. Stk.	100	125
5	Royal Sardinian Ord.	10	11½
5/	Do. Pref.	10	11½

Foreign Railways (*continued*):—

Last Div.	Name.	Paid.	Price.
5/	Sambre & Meuse	20	18
5/6	Do. Pref.	10	12½
22/	San Paulo Ld.	20	31
2/10½	Do. New Ord. £10 sh.	6	8½
4/8	Do. 5 p.c. Non.Cm. Pref.	10	11½
5½	Do. Deb. Stk.	100	132
5	Do. 5 p.c. Deb. Stk.	100	127
—	S. Fé & Cordova, Gt. Sthn., Ld., Shares	100	46
6	Do. Perp. Deb. Stk.	100	119
3/2½	S. Austrian	20	7
10/	Sthn. Braz. R. Gde. do Sul, Ld.	20	7½
6	Do. 6 p.c. Deb. Stk.	100	64½
4	Swedish Centl., Ld., 4 p.c. Deb. Stk.	100	107
5	Do. Pref.	100	100½
1/3	Taltal, Ld.	5	2½
—	Uruguay Nthn., Ld. 7 p.c. Pfd. Stk.	100	8
3½	Do. 5 p.c. Deb. Stk.	100	30
—	Villa Maria & Rufino, Ld., 6 p.c. Pref. Shs.	100	17
4	Do. 4 p.c. 1 Deb. Stk.	100	73
6/0/0	Do. 6 p.c. 2 Deb. Stk.	100	42½
5/9	West Flanders	8½	21
5/6	Do. 5½ p.c. Pref.	10	17
3/	Wstn. of Havana, Ld.	10	4

FOREIGN RAILWAY OBLIGATIONS

Per Cent.	Name.	Price.
6	Alagoas Ld., 6 p.c. Deb., Rd.	82
—	Alcoy & Gandia, Ld., 5 p.c. Debs., Red.	20
5	Arauco., Ld., 5 p.c. 1st Mt., Rd.	62½
—	Do. 6 p.c. Mt. Deb., Rd.	39½
6	Brazil G. Sthn., L., Mt. Dbs., Rd.	80½
6	Do. Mt. Dbs. 1893, Rd.	50
5½	Campos & Caran. Dbs., Rd.	70
6	Central Bahia, L., Dbs., Rd.	90
5½	Conde d'Eu, L., Dbs., Rd.	70
6	Costa Rica, L., 1st Mt. Dbs., Rd.	109
6	Do. 2nd Dbs., Rd.	91
5	Do. Prior Mt. Db., Rd.	103
6	Cucuta Mt. Dbs., Rd.	101
5½	Donna Thrsa. Cris., L., Dbs., Rd.	68½
3	Eastn. of France, £20 Dbs., Rd.	18½
4	Egyptn. Delta Light, L., Db., Rd	100
—	Espito. Santo & Cara. 5 p.c. Stl. Dbs., Rd.	38
4	Gd. Russian Nic., Rd.	102
5	Inter-Oceanic Mex., L., 5 p.c. Pr. Ln. Dbs., Rd.	103
3	Ital. 3 p.c. Bds. A & B, Rd.	57½
—	Ituana 6 p.c. Debs., 1918	72½
—	Leopoldina, 6 p.c. Dbs. £50 Bds.,	21
—	Do. do. Comms. Cert.	21
—	Do. 5 p.c. Stg. Dbs. (1888), Rd.	29
—	Do. do. Comm. Certs.	29
—	Do. 5 p.c. Stg. Dbs. (1890), Rd.	21
—	Do. do. Comms. Certs.	21
—	Macahé & Cam. 5 p.c. Dbs., Rd.	29
—	Do. do. Comms. Certs.	29
—	Do. (Cantagallo), 5 p.c., Red.	29
—	Do. do. Comm. Certs.	29
—	Manila Ltd., 6 p.c. Deb., Red.	21
6	Do. Prior Lien Mt., Rd.	98½
6	Do. Series "B," Rd.	80
7	Matanzas & Sab., Rd.	101½
6	Minas & Rio, L., 6 p.c. Dbs., Rd.	95
5	Mogyana 5 p.c. Deb. Bds., Rd.	101
5	Moscow-Jaros., Rd.	107½
5½	Natal & Na. Cruz Ltd., 5½ p.c. Debs., Red.	73
5	Nitrate, Ltd. Mt. Bds., Red.	86
3	Nthn. France, Red.	19
4	N. of S. Af. Rep. (Trnsvl.) Gu. Bds. Red.	95
3	Nthn. of Spain £20 Pri. Obs. Red.	7½
6	Ottmn. (Smy to A.)(Kujk) Asnt. Debs., Red.	106
6	Ottmn. (Sernik.) Asg. Debs. Red.	106
6	Ottmn. (Sernik) Non-Asg. D., Rd	106
5	Ottmn. Kuyjk. Ext. Red.	103
5	Ottmn. Serkeuy. Ext. Red.	100½
5	Ottmn. Tireh Ext. 1910	98
5	Ottmn. Debs, 1886, Red.	97
5	Do. 1888, Red. 1935	96½
5	Do. 1893, Red. 1935	97
5	Ottmn. of Anlia. Debs., Rd.	90½
4	Ottomn. Smyr. & Cas. Ext. Bds., Red.	83½
3	Paris, Lyon & Medit. (old sys., £20), Red.	18½
3	Paris, Lyon & Medit. (new sys., £20), Red.	18½
50/	Piræus, At. & Pelp., 6 p.c. 1st Mt. Bds., Red.	89½
3	Do. 5 p.c. Mt. Bds., Red.	69½
4	Pretoria-Pietbg., Ltd., Red.	93
7	Puerto Cab. & Val., Ltd., 1st Mt. Debs., Red.	81
—	Rio de Jano. & Nthn., Ltd., 6 p.c. £100 Deb., Red.	21
—	Rio de Jano. (Gr. Para.), 5 p.c. 1st Mt. St. £100 Debs., Red.	21
2	Royal Sardinian, A, Rd. £20	11½
3	Royal Sardinian, B., Rd. £20	11½

Foreign Rly. Obligations (*continued*):—

Per Cent.	Name.	Price.
5	Ryl. Trns.-Afric. 5 p.c. 1st Mt. £100 Bds., Red.	48½
4	Sa. Fe & Cor. G.S., Ld. Pri. n. Bds.	104
5	Sa. Fe, 5 p.c. 2nd Reg. Dbs.	79
3	South Austrian, £20 Red.	15
3	South Austrian, (Ser. X.)	15
3	South Italian £20 Obs. (Ser. A to G), Red.	11½
3½	S.W. of Venez. (Barq.), Ltd., 7 p.c. 1st Mt. £100 Debs.	55½
5	Taltal, Ltd., 5 p.c. 1st Ch. Debs., Red.	97
5	Utd. Rwys. Havana, Red.	84½
3	Wtrn. of France, £20 Red.	18½
6	Wrn. B. Ayres St. Mt. Debs., 1902	106
6	Wrn. B. Ayres, Reg. Cert.	105
5	Do. Mt. Bds.	121
6	Wtrn. of Havna., Ld. Mt. Dbs., Rd.	91
7	Wrn. Ry. San Paulo Red.	99
—	Wrn. Santa Fé, 7 p.c. Red.	41
2/8	Zafra & Huelva, 3 p.c. Red.	2½

BANKS.

Div.	Name.	Paid.	Price.
2/4½	Agra, Ltd.	6	3½
4/2½	Anglo-Argentine, Ltd., £9	7	5½
8 fls.	Anglo-Austrian	120 f	13
6/	Anglo-Californian, Ltd., £20 Shares	10	11
4/	Anglo-Egyptian, Ltd., £15	5	6
5/	Anglo-Foreign Bkg., Ltd.	7	7½
7/	Anglo-Italian, Ltd.	5	7
7/6	Bk. of Africa, Ltd., £18¾	6¼	10½
20/	Bk. of Australasia	40	50
10/	Bk. of Brit. Columbia	20	20
25/	Bk. of Brit. N. America	50	64
20/	Bk. of Egypt, Ltd., £25	12½	18½
5/	Bk. of Mauritius, Ltd.	10	9
18/	Bk. of N. S. Wales	20	37½
4 p.c.	Bk. of N. Zland. Gua. Stk.	100	101½
6/	Bk. of Roumania, £20 Shs.	6	7½
2/6	Tarapaca & Ldn., Ltd., £10	5	3½
—	Bque. Fse. de l'Afri. du S.	100 f	3½
f. 22.50	Bque. Internatle. de Paris	20	23
6/	Brit. Bk. of S. America, Ltd., £20 Shares	10	9½
16/	Capital & Cties., L., £50	10	39
20/	Chart. of India, &c.	20	30
10/	City, Ltd., £40 Shares	10	20
18/	Colonial, £100 Shares	30	21
10/	Delhi and London, Ltd.	25	—
5/	German of London, Ltd.	10	10½
25/	Hong-Kong & Shanghai	28½	45½
4/	Imperl. of Persia	6½	3
10/	Imperl. Ottoman, £20 Shs	10	11½
12/	Intrnatl. of Ldn., Ld., £20	15	11
10/	Ionian, Ltd.	25	15
16/	Lloyds, Ltd., £50 Shs.	8	31
10/	Ldn. & Braziln. Ltd., £20	10	15½
44/	Ldn. & County, Ltd., £80	20	103
9/	Ldn. & Hanseatic, L., £20	10	10½
22/6	Ldn. & Midland, L., £60	12½	53
8/9	Ldn. & Provin., Ltd., £10	5	22
39/	Ldn. & Riv. Plate, L., £25	15	49
2/1½	Ldn. & San Fcisco, Ltd.	7	4½
28/	Ldn. & Sth. West., L., £50	20	68
26/	Ldn. & Westmins., L., £100	20	56½
5/	Ldn. of Mex. & S. Amer., Ltd., £10 Shs.	6	5½
15/	Ldn. Joint Stk., L., £100	15	34½
12/9½	Ldn., Paris & Amer., L. £20	16	25
2/4½	Merchant Bkg., L., £9	4	2½
6/3	Metropn, Ltd., £50 Shs.	5	14½
9/	National, Ltd., £50 Shs.	10	20
4/5	Nntl. of Mexico, $100 Shs.	$40	12½
1/3	National of N. Z., L., £7½	2½	2
3/	National S. Afric. Rep.	10	13½
18/10½	National Provcl. of Eng., Ltd., £75 Shs.	10½	51
21/7½	Do. do. £60 Shs.	12	58½
6/6	North Eastn., Ltd., £20 Shs	6	15
19/	Parr's, Ld., £100 Shs.	20	90
12/6	Prov. of Ireland, L., £100	12½	29½
40/	Stand. of S. Afric., L., £100	25	64
12/6	Union of Australia, L., £75	25	26½
4 p.c.	Do. do. Ins. Stk. Dep. 1900	100	102
15/6	Union of Ldn., Ltd., £100	15½	35

BREWERIES AND DISTILLERIES.

Div.	Name.	Paid.	Price.
4½	Albion Prp. 1 Mt. Db. Sk.	100	111
4	All Saints', L., Db. Sk. Rd.	100	97
7	Allsopp, Ltd.	100	143
6	Do. Cum. Pref	100	151
4½	Do. Deb. Stk., Red.	100	116
3½	Do. Deb. Stk., Red.	100	102
4½	Alton & Co., L., Db., Rd	100	105
4½	Do. Mt. Bds., 1896	100	104
—	Arnold, Perrett, Ltd.	10	6
6	Do. Cum. Pref.	10	10
4½	Do. 1 Mt. Db. Stk., Rd	100	106

Breweries &c. (*continued*):—

Div.	Name.	Paid.	Price
5½	Arrol, A., & Sons, L., Cum. Pref. Shs.	10	10
4½	Do. 1 Mt. Db. Stk., Rd.	100	105
5	Backus, 1 Mt. Db., Red.	100	59
4	Barclay, Perk., L., Cu. Pf.	10	11½
3½	Do. Mt. Db. Stk., Red.	100	109
—	Barnsley, Ltd.	10	11½
6	Do. Cum. Pref.	10	13½
1/3	Barrett's, Ltd.	2½	1½
1/3	Do. 5 p.c. Pref.	2½	2½
3/	Bartholomay, Ltd.	10	2½
8	Do. Cum. Pref.	10	7
6	Do. Deb.	100	97½
5	Bass, Ratcliff, Ltd., Cum. Pref. Stk.	100	142½
4½	Do. Mt. Db. Stk., Rd.	100	124
4	Bell, J., L., 1 Mt. D. Stk., R	100	100
—	Benskin's, L., Cum. Pref.	5	—
—	Do. 1 Mt. Db. Stk Red.	100	—
—	Do. "B" Deb. Sk, Rd.	100	—
7/	Bentley's Yorks., Ltd.	10	16½
6/	Do. Cum. Pref.	10	12½
4½	Do. Mt. Debs., Red.	100	110
4½	Do. do. 1892, Red.	100	110
—	Bieckert's, Ltd.	20	2
5	Do. Debs., Red.	100	57
—	Birmingham., Ltd., 6 p.c. Cum. Pref.	5	2½
4½	Do. Mt. Debs., Red.	50	39½
5½	Boardman's, Ld., Cm. Pf.	10	8½
4½	Do., Perp. 1 Mt. Db. Sk.	100	106½
30/9	Brain & Co., Ltd.	100	101
4½	Brakspear, L., 1 D. Stk. Red.	100	108
4	Brandon's, L., 1 D. Stk. Red.	100	104½
21/	Bristol (Georges) Ltd.	10	44
6	Do. Cum. Pref.	10	17½
5	Do. Mt. Db. Sk. 1888 Rd.	100	115½
17/6	Bristol United, Ltd.	10	35
6	Do. Cum. Pref.	10	16½
4½	Do. Db. Sk. Rd.	100	126
5½	Buckley's, L., C. Pre-prf.	10	10½
4½	Do. 1 Mt. Db. Stk. Rd.	100	104½
4	Bullard & Sons, Ltd., D. Sk. R.	100	104
6	Bushell, Watk., L., C. Pf.	10	14
4½	Do. 1 Mt. Db. Sk. Rd.	100	112
5	Camden, Ltd., Cum. Pref.	10	11½
4½	Do. 1 Mt. Db. Sk. Rd.	100	107
5½	Cameron, Ltd., Cm. Prf.	10	13½
4½	Do. Mort Deb. Stk.	100	108
3½	Do. Perp Mt. Db. Sk.	100	100½
5	Cam'bell, J'stone, L., C. Pf.	5	5
4½	Do. 4½ p.c. 1 Mt. Db. Sk.	100	103
4	Campbell, Praed, L., Per. 1 Mort. Deb. Stk.	100	105
4	Cannon, L., Mt. Db. Stk.	100	109
4	Do. "B" Deb. Stk.	100	104
5	Castlemaine, L., 1 Mt. Db.	100	94
3½	Charrington, Ltd., Mort. Deb. Stk. Red.	100	106
2/	Cheltnhm. Orig., Ltd.	5	7
6	Do. Cum. Pref.	5	7½
4	Do. Debs. Red.	100	106
10/	Chicago, Ltd.	10	3½
6	Do. Debs.	100	84½
—	Cincinnati, Cum. Pref.	10	1
10/	City of Baltimore	10	4
16/	Do. 8 p.c. Cum. Pref	10	8
14/	City of Chicago, Ltd.	10	1½
8	Do. Cum. Pref.	10	6½
13	City of London, Ltd.	100	206½
5	Do. Cum. Pref.	100	136
4	Do. Mt. Deb. Stk., Rd.	100	109½
2/	Colchester, Ltd.	5	4½
7	Do. Pref.	5	6½
4½	Do. Deb. Stk., Red.	100	109
5	Combe, Ltd., Cum. Pref.	10	14
4	Do. Mt. Db. Stk, Rd.	100	110
3½	Do. Perp. Deb. Stk.	100	107
5	Comm'cial, L., D. Sk., Rd.	100	107½
5	Courage, L., Cm. Pref. Shs.	100	137½
4	Do. Irr. Mt. Deb. Stk.	100	125
3½	Do. Irr. "B" Mt. Db. Sk.	100	104
8/	Daniell & Sons, Ltd.	10	7½
7	Do. Cum. Pref.	10	12½
4½	Do. 1 Mt. Perp. Db. Sk.	100	108½
4½	Do. "B" Deb. Stk.	100	99
10d.	Dartford, Ltd.	5	5
2/9	Do. Cum. Pref.	5	5½
4	Do. 1 Mt. Db. Sk. Rd.	100	99
4	Davenport, Ld., 1 D. Stk.	100	101½
10/	Denver United, Ltd.	10	3½
8	Do. Cum. Pref.	10	8
6	Do. Debs.	100	98½
4½	Deuchar, L., 1 D. Sk., Rd.	100	103
8/	Distillers, Ltd.	10	23½
—	Dublin Distillers, Ltd.	5	1½
3/	Do. Cum. Pref.	5	4½
4½	Do. Irr. Deb. Stk.	100	—
5	Eadie, Ltd., Cum. Pref.	10	11
4	Do. Irr. 1 Mt. Db. Sk.	100	106
10/	Edinbgh. Utd., Ltd.	10	13
6	Do. Cum. Prf.	10	13½
4	Eldridge, Pope, L. D. St. R.	100	107
—	Emerald & Phoenix, Ltd.	10	1½
8	Do. Cum. Pref.	10	5½
6	Empress Ltd., C. Pf.	10	11½
4½	Do. Mt. Deb. Stk.	100	106
10/	Farnham, Ltd.	10	17
6	Do. Cum. Pref.	10	14½
4	Fenwick, L., 1 D. Sk., Rd.	100	103
4	Flower & Sons, Irr. D. Sk.	100	111
4	Friary, L., 1 Db. Stk., Rd.	100	103½
4	Do. 1 "A" Db. Sk., Rd	100	100
4½	Groves, L., 1 Db. Sk., Rd.	100	111
14	Guinness, Ltd.	100	570
6	Do. Cum. Prf. Stk.	100	153½
5	Do. Deb. Stk., Red.	100	116
5	Hall's Oxford L., Cm. Pf.	5	5½
6/	Hancock, Ld., Cm. Pf. Ord.	10	14
4	Do. Def. Ord	10	17½

Breweries, &c. (*continued*) :—

Div.	Name.	Paid.	Price.
6	Hancock, Ld., Cum. Pref.	10	15½
4	Do. 1 Deb. Stk., Rd.	100	112
5	Hoare, Ltd. Cum. Pref.	10	12½
5	Do. "A" Cum. Pref.	10	12½
4	Do. Mt. Deb. Stk., Rd.	100	111
3½	Do. do. do. Rd.	100	104
3/6	Hodgson's, Ltd.	5	9½
5	Do. 1 Mt. Db., Red.	—	117½
4	Do. 2 Mt. Db., 1906	—	100
4½	Hopcraft & N., Ltd., 1 Mt. Deb. Stk., Red.	100	103
5	Huggins, Ltd., Cm. Prf.	10	—
4½	Do. 1st D. Stk. Rd.	100	—
4½	Do. "B" Db. Stk. Rd.	100	—
12/	Hull, Ltd.	10	17
7	Do. Cum. Pref.	10	14½
4½	Ind, Coope, L., D. Sk., Rd.	100	118
4	Do. "B" Mt. Db. Stk. Rd.	100	111
8/	Indianapolis, Ltd.	10	3
8	Do. Cm. Prf.	10	8½
5/	Jones, Frank, Ltd.	10	2½
7½	Do. Cum. Pref.	10	6½
5	Do. 1st Mort. Debs.	100	90½
3/	J. Kenward & Co., Ltd.	5	5½
4½	Kingsbury, L., 1 D. Sk., Rd	100	—
4	Lacon, L., D. Stk., Red.	100	110
4	Do. Irrd. "B" D. Sk.	100	106
4/	Lascelles, Ltd.	5	11½
6	Do. Cum. Pref.	5	7½
5	Leney, Ltd., Cum. Pref.	10	11½
4	Do. 1 Mt. Db. Stk. Rd.	100	102
30/7½	Lion, Ltd., £25 shares	17	49½
10/9½	Do. New £10 shares	6	17
6	Do. Perp. Pref.	20	33
4	Do. B. Mt. Db. Sk. Rd.	100	106
4½	Lloyd & Y., Ltd., 1 Mt. Deb. Stk., Rd.	100	100½
4½	Locke & S., Ltd., Irr. 1st Mt. Deb. Stk.	100	103
4½	Lovibond, Ltd., 1st Mt. Deb. Stk., Rd.	100	101½
30/4	Lucas & Co., Ld., Deb. Stk.	100	107
12/	Manchester, Ltd.	10	19
7	Do. Cum. Pref.	10	16½
	Marston, J., L., Cm. Prf.	10	10½
4	Do. 1 Mt. Db. Sk., Rd.	100	101½
7/	Massey's Burnley, Ltd.	10	16½
6	Do. Cum. Pref.	10	14½
4½	McCracken, Ltd., 1 Mt. Deb., 1908	100	59½
5	McEwan, Ltd., Cm. Pref.	10	14
5	Meux, Ltd., Cum. Pref.	10	13½
4	Do. Mt. Db. Stk. Red.	100	111
4½	Michell & A., Ltd., 1 Mt. Deb. Stk. Red.	100	105
4½	Mile End Dist. Db. Sk. Rd.	100	111
—	Milwaukee & Chic., Ltd.	10	1½
4/	Do. Cum. Pref.	10	6½
4½	Michell, Toms, L., Db.	50	57
6	Morgan, Ltd., Cum. Pref.	10	14½
10/	Nalder & Coll., Ltd.	10	35
6	Do. Cum. Pref.	10	15½
4½	Do. Deb. Red.	100	112
12/	Newcastle, Ltd.	10	19½
6	Do. Cum. Pref.	10	14½
5	Do. 1 Mt. Deb., 1911	100	111½
4	Do. "A" Deb. Stk. Red.	100	105
6	New England, Ltd	10	4½
8	Do. Cum. Pref.	10	9
6	Do. Debs. Red	100	101½
4	New London, L., 1 D. Sk.	100	103
7/2	New Westminster, Ltd.	4	10½
9/4½	Do. Pref.	4	6½
—	New York, Ltd.	10	1
—	Do. 8 p.c. Cum. Pref.	10	4
6	Do. 1 Mt. Deb. Red.	100	77½
5	Noakes, Ld., Cum. Pref.	10	11½
4	Do 1 Mt. Db. Stk., Rd.	100	105
4½	Norfolk, L., "A" D. Sk. Rd.	100	106
10/	Northampton, Ld.	10	16½
7	Do. Cum. Pref.	10	15½
6	Do. Cum. Pref.	10	12½
5	Do. 1 Mt. Per. Db. Sk.	100	127
4	Nth. East., L., 1 D. Sk. Rd.	100	102
4½	N. Worcesters., L., Per. 1 Mort. Deb. Stock	100	97½
6	Nottingham, L., Cm. Prf.	10	1½
5	Do. 1 Mt. Deb. Stk., Red.	100	114
17/4	Do. "B" do. Red.	50	112
6/	Ohlsson' Cape, Ld.	5	17
7	Do. Cum. Pref.	5	9
4½	Do. 2nd Cum. Pref.	5	5½
5	Do. Deb. Stk., Red.	100	116
4½	Oldfield, L., 1 Mt. Db. Stk.	100	105
6	Page & Overt., L., Cm. Prf.	10	14
4½	Do. 1 Mt. Dbs., Red.	100	109
10/	Parker's Burslem, Ltd.	10	24½
6	Do. Cum. Pref.	10	14½
4	Do. 1 Mt. Db. Stk., Red.	100	111
4	Persse, Ld., 1 Mt. Db. Rd.	100	95½
	Phipps, L., Irr. 1 Db. Stk.	100	113
8	Plymouth, L., Min. Cu. Pf.	10	13½
4½	Do. Mt. Deb. Stk., Red.	100	106½
4½	Pryor, Reid, L., 1 D.S., R.	100	103½
5	Reid's, Ld., Cm. Pref. Stk.	100	136½
4	Do. Mt. Deb. Stk., Red	100	110
3½	Do. "B" Mt. Db. Stk., Rd	100	102
5	Rhondda Val., L., Cu. Pf	10	11
4½	Do. 1 Mt. Deb. Stk., Rd	100	109
5	Robinson, Ld., Cum. Pref.	10	11½
4½	Do. 1 Mt. Perp. Db. Stk.	100	112
4/	Rochdale, Ltd.	10	6
4½	Do. 1 Mt. Deb. Stk.	100	98½
7	Royal, Brentford, Ltd.	10	22
	Do. Cum. Pref.	10	15
4½	Do. 1 Mt. Dbs. Red	100	105
6/	St. Louis, Ltd.	10	3½
8	Do. Cum. Pref.	10	8½
14/	St. Paull, Ltd.	10	10
7	Do. Cum. Pref.	10	12
4½	Salt (T.), L., 1 Db. Sk. Rd.	100	111
4½	Do. "B" Db. Stk. Red	100	105
—	San Francisco, Ltd.	10	[illegible]
—	Do. 8 p.c. Cum. Pref.	20	[illegible]

Breweries, &c. (*continued*) :—

Div.	Name.	Paid.	Price.
4½	Savill Brs., L., D. Sk. Rd.	100	118
4½	Scarboro., Ltd., 1 Db. Stk.	100	101
4	Shaw (Hy.), Ltd., 1 Mt. Db. Stk., Red.	100	104
22/	Showell's, Ltd.	10	31
7	Do. Cum. Pref.	10	17½
3/	Do. Gua. Shs.	5	7½
4½	Do. Mt. Db. Stk., Red.	100	—
4	Simonds, L., 1 D. Sk., Rd.	100	111
5½	Simson & McP., L., Cu. Pf.	10	9½
4½	Do. 1 Mt. Deb. Stk.	100	97
5/	Smith, Garrett, L., £20 Shs	10	16½
5	Do. Cum. Pref.	20	26
3½	Do. 3½ p.c. Mt. Db. Stk.	100	107
5	Smith's, Tadcster, L., C Pf	10	12
4½	Do. Deb. Stk., Red.	100	112
4	Do. Deb. Stk. Red.	100	108
4½	Star, L., 1 M. Db. Stk., Rd.	100	103
4	Steward & P., L., 1 D. Sk.	100	108
9/	Strettons Derby, Ltd.	10	13
6	Do. Cum. Pref.	10	13½
4	Do. Irr. 1 Mt. Db. Stk.	100	104½
4½	Strong, Romsey, L., 1 D.S.	100	115
5	Stroud, L., Db. Sk., Rd.	100	109½
4½	Tadcaster To'er, L., D. Sk.	100	113
8/	Tamplin, Ltd	10	21
6	Do. Cum. Pref.	100	15
4	Do. "A" Db. Sk., Rd.	10	106
6	Thorne, Ltd., Cum. Pref.	10	14
4	Do. Deb. Stk., Red.	100	103½
15/	Threlfall, Ltd.	10	45
6	Do. Cum. Pref.	10	16
5	Do. 1 Mt. Dbs., Red.	100	114
4	Tollemache, L., D. Sk. Rd.	100	105
4	Truman, Hanb., D. Sk., R.	100	110
3	Do. "B" Mt. Db. Sk., Rd.	100	95
10/	United States, Ltd	10	8½
8	Do. Cum. Pref.	10	11
6	Do. 1 Mt. Deb	100	106½
6/	Walker & H., Ld., Cm. Prf.	10	10½
4½	Do. 1 Mt. Deb. Stk., Red.	100	107
5	Walker, Peter, Ld. Cm. Prf.	10	13½
4	Do. 1 Mt. Dbs. Red.	100	110
4	Wallingford, L., D. Sk. Rd.	100	105
6	Watney, Ld., Cm. Prf. Sk.	100	168
5	Do. Mt. Db. Sk., Rd.	100	115½
4½	Do. "B" Mt. Db. Sk., Rd.	100	111
3½	Do. Mt. Db. Stk.	100	101
5	Watney, D., Ld., Cm. Prf.	10	12
4½	Do. 1 Mt. Db. Stk.	100	107
10/	Webster & Sons, Ltd.	10	16½
6	Do. Cum. Pref.	10	14
5	Wenlock Ltd Pref.	10	11½
4	Do. 1 Mt. Db. Sk., Rd.	100	106
5	West Cheshire, L., Cu. Pf.	10	10½
4	Do. Irred. 1 Mt. Db. Sk.	100	99
4½	Whitbread, L., Cu. Pf. Sh.	100	123½
4	Do. Db. Stk., Red.	100	109
3½	Do. "B" Db. Stk., Rd.	100	101
9/	Wolverhmpton & D. Ld.	10	17
6	Do. Cum. Pref.	10	13½
4½	Do. 1 Mt. Dbs., Red.	100	108
5½	Worthington, Ld., Cm. Prf.	10	15½
5½	Do. Cum. "B" Pref.	10	13½
4½	Do. Mt. Db. Sk., Rd.	100	113
3½	Do. Irr. "B" Db. Stk.	100	101
6/	Yates's Castle, Ltd.	10	13
5	Do. Cum. Pref.	10	11
5	Younger W., L., Cu. Pf. Sh.	100	131½

CANALS AND DOCKS.

Last Div.	Name.	Paid.	Price.
4	Birmingham Canal	100	142½
—	E. & W. India Dock	100	19½
—	Do. 4 p.c. Prf. Stk.	100	74
—	Do. P.L. Deb. Stk.	100	101
—	Do. Cons. Deb. Stk.	100	89
40/	G. Junction Ord. Shs.	100	149½
6/	Do. do. Pref.	10	19
4½	King's Lynn Per. Db. Stk.	100	117½
2½	Leeds & L'pool Canal	100	71
2½	Lndn & St. Kath. Dks.	100	54
4½	Do. Pref.	100	136½
4½	Do. Pref., 1878	100	132½
4½	Do. Pref., 1882	100	130
4	Do. Deb. Stk.	100	132½
—	Mchester Ship C. 5 p.c. Pf.	10	2
3½	Do. 1st Perp. Mt. Deb.	100	98
—	Milford Dks. Db. Stk. "A"	100	18½
3½	Millwall Dk.	100	60
5	Do. Perp. Pref.	100	140½
4½	Do. Pref.	100	106½
5	Do. New Per. Prf., 1887	100	126½
5	Do. Per. Deb. Stk.	100	152½
4/	Newhaven Har.	10	14½
2½	N. Metropolitan	100	65
5	Sharpness Nw. Pf. "A" Sk.	100	141½
4	Do. Deb. Stk.	100	117½
5	Sheffield & S. Yorks Nav. 4½ p.c. Pref Stk.	100	115½
36.432	Suez Canal	20	137
7	Surrey Comml. Dok., Ord.	100	150½
7	Do. Min. 4 p.c. Pref. "A"	110	151½
5	Do. Pref. "B"	100	148½
5	Do do. "C"	100	148½
5	Do. do. "D"	100	144½
4½	Do Deb. Stk.	100	152½

COMMERCIAL, INDUSTRIAL, &c.

Last Div.	Name.	Paid.	Price.
5	Accles, L., 1 Mt. Db., Red.	100	84½
2/6	Aërated Bread, Ltd.	1	12
—	African Gold Recovery, L.	1	⅛
2/	Aluminium, L., "A" Shs.	1	2
4½	Do. 1 Mt. Db. Stk., Red.	100	97
5½	Amelia Nitr., L., 1 Mort Deb., Red.	100	82½
7/	Anglo-Chil. Nitrate, Ltd., Cum. Pref.	10	6½
4½	Do. Cons. Mt. Bds., Red.	100	77½
4½	Anglo-Russian Cotton, Ld., 1 Charge Debs., Red.	100	98
11/3	Angus (G., & Co., L.), £10	7½	17
6/	Apollinaris, Ltd.	10	11½
5/	Do. 5 p.c. Cum. Pref.	10	10½
4	Do. Irred. Deb. Stock	100	104
3/	Argentine Meat Pres., L., 7 p.c. Pref.	10	2½
5	Argentine Refinry, Db. Rd.	100	98
6d.	Armstrong, Whitw., Ltd.	1	3½
4	Do. Cum. Pref.	5	6½
5	Artisans', Labr. Dwllgs., L.	100	128½
4½	Do. Non-Cm. Prf., 1879	100	132½
4½	Do. do. 1884	100	132½
—	Asbestos & Asbestic, Ltd.	10	7½
2/7½	Ashley-grdns., L., C. Prf.	5	6½
4½	Do. 1 Mt. Deb. Stk.	100	113½
5/	Assam Rly. & Trdng., L., 8 p.c. Cum. Pref. "A"	10	14
—	Do. Deferrd. "B" Shs.	1	4
—	Do. do. (iss. f. pd)	1	3½
8/	Do. Cum. Pre-Prf. "A"	10	15
6/	Do. New Pref.	10	11½
5	Do. Debs., Red.	100	106
5	Do. Red. Mort. Debs.	100	110
6	Aust'lian Pastrl, L., Cu. Pf.	10	7
8d.	Aylesbury Dairy, Ltd.	1	1½
4	Do. 4 p.c. Mt. Dbs.	100	104½
10/	Babcock & Wilcox, Ltd.	10	29
6	Do. 6 p.c. Cm. Prf.	10	16
8	Baker (Chs.), L., Cm. Pf.	5	9
8	Do. "B" Cm. Pref.	5	7½
2/1	Barker (John), Ltd.	1	2½
5½	Do. Cum. Pref.	5	7½
4½	Do. Irred. 1 Mt. Db. Stk.	100	126½
—	Barnagore Jute, Ltd.	5	3
5	Do. Cum. Pref.	5	4½
7½d.	Belgravia Dairy, Ltd.	1	1½
5/6	Bell (R.) & Co., Ltd.	5	3½
9½d.	Bell's Asbestos, Ltd.	1	¾
5	Do. Mt. Db. Bds., Rd.	100	106
10/	Bengal Mills, Ltd.	10	11
6/	Do. 5 p.c. Cum. Prf.	10	10½
5/	Benson (J.W.) L., Cm. Pf.	10	10½
4	Do. Perp. Mt. Db. Stk.	100	101
6	Bergvik, L., 6 p.c. Cm. Pf.	10	12½
12/	Do. Dfd.	10	10½
4½	Do. 1 Dbs., Red.	100	103½
5/	Birm'ham Vinegar, Ltd.	5	14
5	Do. Cum. Pref.	5	5½
4½	Do. 1 Mt. Db. Stk., Rd.	100	109½
5	Bonke (A.) L., 5 p.c. Cu. Pf.	10	10½
2/6	Bodega, Ltd.	5	8½
4½	Do. Mt. Deb. Stk., Rd.	100	111
8/	Bottomley & Brs., Ltd.	10	6½
6/	Do. 6 p.c. Pt.	10	9½
8½d.	Bovril, Ltd.	1	1
1/0½	Do. Def.	1	⅝
6½d.	Do. Cum. Pref.	1	1
4½	Do. Deb. Stk.	100	100
5/	Bradbury, Gretrex., Ltd., £10 share	8	14
5/	Do. 5 p.c. Cum. Pref.	10	13½
5/	Brewers' Sugar, L., 5 p.c. Cum. Pref.	10	10½
3/6	Brighton Grd. Hotel, Ld.	5	4
4	Do Mt. Db. Stk., Red.	100	101½
5	Bristol Hotel & Palm. Co., Ltd. 1st Mt. Red. Deb.	100	105
9½d.	British & Bengton's. Tea Tr. Asc., Ltd.	1	1½
5	Do. Cum. Prf.	5	5½
—	British Deli & Lgkat. Tobacco, Ltd.	1	½
—	Do. Cum. Prf.	1	½
—	British Tea Table, Ltd.	1	2½
5½	Do. Cum. Pref.	1	1½
2/6	Brooke, Ben., & Co., Ltd., Cum. Pref.	5	5½
7/6	Brooke, Bond & Co., Ltd.	5	19
3/	Brown Brs., L., Cum. Pref.	5	5½
10/	Browne & Eagle, Ltd.	10	13½
5	Do. Cum. Pref.	10	13
4	Do. Mrt. Db. Sk., Red.	100	110
20/	Brunner, Mond, & Co., Lt.	[illegible]	40
7/	Do. £10 shares	3	17
7	Do. Cum. Pref.	10	18
7	Do. £10 shares	5	8½
10/	Bryant & May, Ltd.	5	18½
3/	Bucknall, H., & Sons, Lt.	5	7
6	Do. Cum Pref.	5	7½
4/	Burke, E. & J., Ltd.	5	7½
6	Do. Cum. Pref.	5	7½
6	Do. Irred. Deb. Stk.	100	155
1/	Burlington Htls. Co., Ltd	1	1½
5	Do. Cum. Pref.	1	1
4	Do. Perp. Deb. Stk.	100	106½
5	Bush, W. J., & Co., Ltd., Cum. Pref.	5	5½
4	Do. 1 Deb. Stk., Red.	100	102
5½	Callard, Stewart, & Watt, Ltd., Cum. Pref.	1	1½
4/	Callender's Cable L., Shs.	5	9½
4½	Do. 1 Deb. Stk., Red.	100	111½
—	Campbell, R., & Sons, Lt.	3	2½
6	Cantareira Water, Bd., Rd	100	99½
5	Do. (2nd issue)	100	87½
4	Cartavio Sugar, Ltd., 6 p.c. 1st Debs., Red.	80	82½
9/	Cassell & Co., Ltd., £10	9	15
5	Causton, Sir J., & Sons, Ltd., Cum. Pref.	10	13½

Commercial, &c. (*continued*) :—

Last Div.	Name.	Paid.	Price.
4	Cent. Prod. Mkt. of B.A. 1st Mt. Str. Debs.	100	74½
4	Chappell & Co., Ltd., Mt. Deb. Stk. Red	100	103
6/	Chicago & N.W. Gran. 8 p.c. Cum. Pref.	10	3
—	Chicago Packing & Prov.	10	6
8	Do. Cum. Pref.	10	10
6/	City Offices, Ltd	12	8
3½	Do. Mt. Deb. Stk.	100	108½
7/2½	Cy. London Real Prop., Ltd., £25 shs.	12	19
4/6	Do. £12½ shs.	7½	13½
3½	Do. Deb. Stk. Red.	100	106½
3½	Do. Deb. Stk. Red.	100	106½
3	Do.	100	100½
6/	Cy. of Santos Imprvts., Ltd., 7 p.c. Pref.	10	8
20/	Clay, Bock, & Co., Ltd.	10	5
8	Do. Cum. Pref.	10	9
6	Do. Mort. Deb.	100	102½
20/	Coats, J. & P., Ltd.	10	58
20/	Do. Cum. Pref.	10	17
4½	Do. Deb. Stk. Red.	100	112½
9½d	Coburg Hotel, Ltd	1	1½
4	Do. Deb. Stk. Red.	100	102
6	Colonial Consign & Dis., Ltd., Cum. Pref.	5	4½
4½	Do. 1st Mort. Debs.	100	96½
—	Colorado Nitrate, Ltd.	5	[illegible]
4/	Co. Gén des Asphtes. de F., Ltd.	6	6
5	Do. Non-Cm. Prf.	—	5
5	Cook, J. W., & Co., Ltd., Cum. Pref.	5	5½
5	Cook, T., & Son, Egypt, Ltd., 1st Mt. Deb. Red.	100	110½
—	Cork Co., Ltd., 6 p.c. Cum. Pref.	5	2
5	Cory, W., & Sn, L., Cu. Pf.	5	5½
4	Do. 1st Deb. Stk. Red.	100	109
1/6	Crisp & Co., Ltd	1	1½
3½	Do. Cum. Pref.	1	1½
—	Crompton & Co., Ltd., 7 p.c. Cum. Pref.	5	2½
5	Do. 1st Mt. Reg. Deb.	—	90½
4/6	Crossley, J., & Sons, Ltd.	5	7½
5	Do. Cum. Pref.	5	6½
—	Crystal Pal. Ord. "A" Stk.	100	6½
—	Do. "B" Red. Stk	100	1½
6	Do. 6 p.c. 1st 1887 Deb. Stk. Red.	100	117½
—	Do. 6 p.c. 2nd 1887 Deb. Stk. Red.	100	49½
—	Do. 6 p.c. 3rd 1887 Deb. Stk. Red.	100	22½
3	Do. 3 p.c. 1st 1893 Deb. Stk.	100	92½
—	Daimler Motor, Ltd	10	6
4/	Dalgety & Co., £20 Shs.	5	5½
4½	Do. Deb. Stk	100	124
4	Do.	100	113
7/	De Keyser's Ryl. Htl., L.	10	14
5	Do. Cum. Pref.	10	12
4	Do. Deb. Stk., Red.	100	110
6	Denny, H., & Sons, Ltd., Cum. Pref.	10	14½
5/3	Devas, Routledge & Co., L.	7	8½
5	Dickinson, J., & Co., L., Cum. Pref. Stk.	100	123
4½	Domin. Cottn. Mls., Ltd. Mt. Stg. Dbs.	100	97
6/	Dorman, Long & Co., L.	5	4½
—	Eastmans, Ltd	10	2½
12/	Do. 8 p.c. Cum. Pref.	10	10½
2/6	E. C. Powder, Ltd	3	5½
1/6	Edison & Swn Utd. Elec. Ltd., "A" £5 Shs.	3	2½
2/6	Do. fully-paid	5	4½
4½	Ekman Pulp & Ppr. Co., Ltd., Mt. Deb., Red.	100	96
1/1½	Electric Construc., Ltd.	2	2½
7	Do. Cum. Pref.	2	3½
25/	Eley Bros., Ltd.	10	37
—	Elmore's Cop. [illegible], L.	1	[illegible]
—	Elmore's Wire Mnfg., L.	2	[illegible]
—	Elysée Pal. Hotel Co., L.	5/	[illegible]
5 p.c.	Do. 5 p.c. £100 Db., Rd.	70	97½
8½d.	Evans, Ben., & Co., Ltd.	1	1
5	Do. 1 Mt. Db. Sk., Rd.	100	108
1/8½d.	Evans, D. H., & Co., L.	1	2½
6	Do. Cum. Pref.	1	1½
4½	Do. 1 Mt. Db. Sk., Rd.	100	112
2/6	*Evening News*, L., 5 p.c. Cum. Pref.	5	5½
5/3	Evered & Co., L., £10 Sh.	7	12½
7/6	Do.	10	18½
4	Fairbairn Pastoral Co., Aust., L., 1 Mt. Db., Rd.	100	102
6	Fairfield Shipbldg., Ltd., Cum. Pref.	10	10½
4½	Do. Mort. Deb. Stk.	100	110
6/	Farmer & Co., Ld., 6 p.c. Cum. Pref.	10	13½
10	Field, J. C. & J., Ltd.	10	10
14/	Do. 7 p.c. Cum. Pref.	10	14½
1/3	Fordham, W.B., & Sns, Ld.	1	2
5/6	Fore-st. Warehouse, Ltd.	11	9½
4	Do. Regd. Debs., Rd.	100	101½
3/6	Foster, M. B. & Sons, Ltd.	4	6
5	Do. Pref.	10	11½
9/	Foster, Porter, & Co., L.	10½	15½
4	Fowler, J., & Co. (Leeds), Ltd., 1 Mt. Deb., Red.	100	103½
3/	Fraser & Chalmers, Ltd	3	1½
4½	Free, Rodwell & Co., Ltd., Deb Stk.	100	104½
6½d.	Furness, T., & Co., Ltd., 5½ p.c. Cum. Pref.	1	1
4½	Gartside & Co. (of Manchstr), L., 1 Mt. Db. Sk.	100	111
11	Genl. Hydraul Power, L.	100	270

Commercial, &c. (continued):—

Last Div.	Name.	Paid.	Price.
8/	Gillman & Spencer, Ltd.	5	2½
6	Do. Pref.	5	4⅞
5	Do. Mort. Debs	50	51
4	Goldsbro., Mort & Co., L., "A" Deb. Stk., Red.	100	69½
—	Do. 3 p.c. "B" Inc. Deb. Stk., Red	100	12
8/	Gordon Hotels, Ltd.	10	19
5½	Do. Cum. Pref.	10	14½
4½	Do. Perp. Deb. Stk.	100	138½
4	Do. do.	100	122½
—	Greenwich Inld. Linoleum Co., Ltd.	1	⅛
7	Greenwood & Batley, Ltd., Cum. Pref.	10	10
7½d.	Hagemann & Co., Ltd., 6 p.c. Cum. Pref.	1	1
—	Hammond, Ltd.	10	⅝
—	Do. 8 p.c. Cum. Pref.	10	3¼
—	Do. 6 p.c. Cum. Inc. Stk. Red.	100	52½
	Hampton & Sons, Ltd., 4 p.c. 1 Mt. Db. St. Red.	100	105
—	Hans Crescent Htl., L., 6 p.c. Cum. Pref.	5	3
4	Do. 1 Mt. Deb. Stk.	100	90
6d.	Harmsworth, Ltd., Cum. Pref.	1	1½
4/	Harrison, Barber, Ltd.	5	4½
3/	Harrod's Stores, Ltd.	1	4½
2/6	Do. Cum. Pref.	5	7¼
5½	Hawaiian Comcl. & Sug. 1 Mt. Debs.	100	91½
5	Hazell, Watson, L., C. P.	10	11½
18/	Henley's Teleg., Ltd.	10	22
7	Do. Pref. Shs.	10	19
4½	Do. Mt. Db. Stk., Rd.	100	112½
6	Henry, Ltd.	10	11½
5	Do. Cum. Pref.	10	13½
4½	Do. Mt. Debs., Red.	50	53
1/4½	Herrmann, Ltd.	1	¾
—	Hildesheimer, Ltd.	3	1½
1/2½	Holbrn. & Frascn, Ltd.	1	1⅛
5	Do. Cum. Pref.	10	11½
4	Do. Deb. Stk.	100	109
6	Home & Col. Stres, L., C.P	5	7½
6	Hood & M.'s Stres., Ltd., Cum. Pref.	1	⅛
6	Hook, C. T Ltd.	10	6
7/2	Hornsby, Ltd., £10 Shs.	8	3
—	Hotchks. Ordn., Ltd.	10	1
—	Do. 7 p.c. Cm. Prf.	10	4½
5	Do. 1 Mt. Dbs., Rd.	100	97½
6	Htl. Cecil, Ld., Cm. Prf.	5	3½
4	Do. 1 Mt. D. Sk., R.	100	100½
8/	Heward & Bulgh, Ltd.	10	39
6	Do. Pref.	10	16
4	Do. Deb. Stk., Red.	100	108
5/	Howell, J., Ltd., £5 Shs.	4	9
—	Howell & Js., Ltd., £3½ Shs.	3	¾
1/6	Humber, Ltd.	1	¾
6	Do. Cum. Pref.	1	11/16
5/6	Hunter, Wilts., Ltd.	5	7
2/7	Hyam Clthg., Ltd., 5 p.c. Cum. Pref.	5	5¾
10/	Impl. Russn. Cotton, L.	5	5½
5	Impd. Industl. Dwgs., Ld.	100	130½
6d.	Do. Defrd.	1	1½
25/	Impd. Wood Pave., Ltd.	10	15½
15/	Ind. Rubber, Gutta Per. Telegraph Works, Ltd.	10	21½
4	Do. 1 Mt. Debs., Red.	100	104
6	Intern. Tea, Cum. Pref.	5	6½
10½d.	Jays, Ltd.	1	1⅜
5½	Do. Cum. Pref.	5	6½
1/2½d.	Jones & Higgins, Ltd.	1	2½
4½	Do. 1 Mt. Db. Sk., Rd.	100	111
5/	Kelly's Directory, Ltd., 5 p.c. Cum. Pref.	10	12¾
4	Do. Mort. Db. Sk., Rd.	100	106
—	Kent Coal Explrtn. Ltd.	1	⅝
9½d.	King, Howmann, Ltd.	1	1½
4/	Kinloch & Co., Ltd.	5	8½
6	Do. Pref.	5	7
5	Lady's Pictorial Pub., Ltd., Cum. Pref.	5	5
48/4	La Guaira Harb., Ltd., 5 p.c. Deb. Stk.	100	79½
—	Do. 2 Mt. 7 p.c. Deb. Stk., Red.	100	24
4/	Lagunas Nitrate, Ltd.	5	1
2/	Lagunas Syn., Ltd.	5	1
5	Do. 1 Mt. Debs., Red.	100	77½
—	L. Copais Ld., 1 Mt. 6 p.c. Debs., Red.	100	35½
3/	Lautaro Nitrate, Ltd.	5	4
5	Do. 1 Mt. Debs., Red.	—	100
9/	Lawes Chem. L., £10 shs.	9	5½
14/	Do. N. Cm. Min. Pref.	10	12½
—	Leeds Forge, 7 p.c. Cm. Pf.	5	3½
5	Do. 1 Mt. Debs., Red.	50	47
5	Lever Bros., L., Cm. Pf.	10	13½
6	Liberty, L., 6 p.c. Cm. Pf.	10	15
20/	Liebig's, Ltd.	20	79
5	Lilley & Sk., L., Cm. Pf.	5	5½
2/6	Linoleum Manftg Ltd.	5	16
3/	Linotype, Ltd., Pre	5	5¾
3/	Do. Def.	5	7½
4/	Lister & Co., Ltd.	10	4
5	Do. Cum. Pref.	10	8½
5/	Liverpool. Nitrate	5	4¾
—	Liverpool. Warehsg., Ltd	10	3½
5½	Do. Cum. Pref.	10	8½
4	Do. 1 Mt. Db. Stk., Rd.	100	105
5½	Lockharts, Ltd., Cm. Pf.	1	1½
4/6	Ldn. & Til. Lightrage £10	9	6½
6/	Ldn. Comcl. Sale Rms., L.	10	17½
3	Do. 1 Mt. Deb. Stk., Red.	100	103
3	London Nitrate, Ltd.	5	1¾
4/	London Nitrate, Ld. 8 p.c. Cm. Min. Pf.	5	3½
8/	London Pavilion, Ltd.	5	6⅛

Commercial, &c. (continued):—

Last Div.	Name.	Paid.	Price.
2/6	London Produce Clg. Ho., Ltd., £10 Shares	2½	3¼
4/	London Stereos., Ltd.	5	3
6d.	Ldn. Un. Laun. L. Cm. Pf.	1	[illegible]
8½d.	Louise, Ltd.	1	[illegible]
5½	Do. Cum. Pref.	1	[illegible]
5/	Lovell & Christmas, Ltd.	5	11½
6	Do. Cum. Pref.	5	7½
4	Do. Mt. Deb. Stk., Red.	100	107
1/3	Lyons, Ltd.	1	4
4½	Do. 1 Mt. Deb., Stk., Rd.	100	111½
10/	Machinery Trust, Ltd.	5	13½
4½	Do. 4½ Deb. Stk.	100	104
6	MacLellan, L., Min. C. Pf.	10	9
5	Do. 1 Mt. Debs., 1900	100	101½
—	McEwan, J. & Co., Ltd.	10	1½
6	Do. Mt. Debs., Red.	100	89½
8	McNamara, L., Cm. Pref.	10	9
7½d.	Maison Virot, Ltd.	1	1⅛
2/7	Do. 6 p.c. Cum. Pref.	5	4
5/	Manbré Sacc., L., Cm. Pf.	10	12
10/	Mangan Brze., L., £10 Shs.	6	15½
2/	Mason & Mason, Ltd.	5	2½
6	Do. Cum. Pref.	5	5½
—	Maynards, Ltd.	1	⅛
6	Do. Cum. Pref.	1	¾
9½d.	Mazawattee Tea, Ltd.	1	1½
5	Do. Cum. Pref.	5	5½
6	Mellin's Food Cum. Pref.	5	6½
4½	Met. Ascn. Imp. Dwllngs., Ltd.	100	110
5	Metro. Indus. Dwlgs., Ltd.	5	4¾
4	Do. do. Cum. Pref.	5	5½
5	Metro. Prop., L., Cm. Pf.	5	5½
4½	Do. 1st Mt. Debs. Stk.	100	108½
6	Mexican Cotton 1 Mt. Db.	100	93½
4½	Mid. Class Dwlgs., L., Db.	100	120½
1/	Millars' Karri, Ltd.	1	2½
6	Do. Cum. Pref.	1	1⅛
5/	Milner's Safe, Ltd.	10	20½
10/	Moir & Son, Ltd., Pref.	5	8
6	Morgan Cruc., L., Cm. Pf.	10	14½
2/	Morris, B., Ltd.	3½	3½
2/6	Murray L. 5½ p.c. C. Pf.	5	5½
63/4½	Do. 4½ 1 Mt. Db. Sk. Rd.	100	106
1/7½	Nat. Safe Dep., Ltd.	4	3½
6	Do. Cum. Pref.	1	1
—	Native Guano, Ltd.	5	½
—	Nelson Bros., Ltd.	10	2½
5	Do. Deb. Stk., Red.	100	80½
7/	Neuchtel Asph., Ltd.	10	10
10d.	New Darvel Tob., Ltd.	18/	1½
1/6	New Explosives, Ltd.	3	3
5/3½	New Gd. Htl., Bham, L.	5	4
5½	Do. Pref.	5	4½
4	Do. 1 Mt. Db. Stk., Rd.	100	96½
—	New Julia Nitrate, Ltd.	10/	—
—	New Ldn. Borneo Tob., L.	16/	1½
1/6	New Premier Cycle, Ltd.	1	11/16
6	Do. 6 p.c. Cum. Pref.	1	¾
4½	Do. 4½ p.c. 1 Mt. Db. Rd	100	—
—	New Tamargl. Nitr., Ltd	1	1/16
—	Do. 8 p.c. Cum. Pref.	1	¼
6	Do. 6 p.c. 1 Mt. Dbs. Rd.	100	62½
3·78d.	Newnes, G., L., Cm. Prf.	1	1
1/3	Nitr. Provision, Ltd.	2½	½
24/	Nobel-Dynam., Ltd.	10	18½
—	North Brazn. Sugar, Ltd.	1	¼
15/	Oakey, Ltd.	10	31
6	Do. Cum. Pref.	10	17½
—	Paccha Jazp. Nitr., Ltd.	5	¼
5	Pac. Borax, L., 1 Db. Rd.	100	110
—	Palace Hotel, Ltd.	10	5½
5½	Do. Cum. Pref.	10	7½
4	Do. 1 Mt. Deb. Stk.	100	102
2/6	Palmer, Ltd.	5	1
6	Do. Cum. Pref.	5	2
1/2½d	Paquin, Ltd.	1	¾
6	Do. Cum. Pref.	5	4
5½	Parnall, Ltd., Cum. Pref.	1	¾
4/6	Pawsons, Ltd., £10 Shs.	6	6½
4	Do. Mt. Debs., Red.	100	106
6	Pearks, G. & T., Ltd., 6 p.c. Cum. Pref.	1	¾
9½d.	Pears, Ltd.	1	1½
6	Do. Cum. Pref.	10	14
5	Do. Deb. Stk.	100	129
5½	Pearson, C. A., L., Cu. Pf.	5	5
4/3	Peebles, Ltd.	5	7¾
5	Do. Cum. Pref.	5	6½
4½	Do. Mt. Deb. Stk. Red.	100	113½
5½	Peek Bros., Ltd., 1 Cum. Pref., Nos. 1-60,000	5	6½
3½	Do. 3½ p.c. 1 Db. Stk.	100	102½
7½d.	Pegamoid, Ltd.	1	¾
—	Pillsbury-W. Fl. Mills, L.	10	3
16/	Do. 8 p.c. Cum. Pref.	10	8
6	Do. 1 Mort. Debs.	100	94½
9½d.	Plummer, Ltd.	1	1½
5	Do. Cum. Pref.	5	5½
7/6	Price's Candle, Ltd.	16	35
6	Priest Marians, L., Cm. Pf.	1	1½
6	Pryce Jones, Ld., Cm. Pf.	5	7½
5	Do. Deb. Stk.	100	122
8½d.	Pullman, Ltd.	1	1½
6d.	Do. Cum. Pref.	1	1⅛
6d.	Raleigh Cycle, Ltd.	1	11/16
6	Do. Cum. Pref.	1	¾
—	Recife Drnge. Ld. 1 Mt. Debs., R	100	19
6	Redfern, Ltd. Cum. Prf.	10	14
5	Ridgways, Ltd., Cu. Pf.	5	5½
—	R. Janeiro Cy. Imps. Ld.	25	6½
5	Do. Debs.	100	85½
5	Do. 1882-1893	100	85½
11/	R. Jan Fl. Mills, Ltd.	7	6½
5	Do. 1 Mt. Debs., Rd.	100	94
—	Riv. Plate Meat, Ltd.	5	2½
—	Do. Pref.	5	5
8½d.	Roberts, J. R., Ltd.	1	1½
5	Roberts 1 Mt. D. Sk., Rd.	100	112
1/4½	Roberts, T. R., Ltd.	1	2½
5	Do. Cum. Pref.	1	1½

Commercial, &c. (continued):—

Last Div.	Name.	Paid.	Price.
3/	Rosario Nit., Ltd.	5	3½
5	Do. Debs., Red.	100	103
1/	Rover Cycle, Ltd.	1	¾
6/	Ryl. Aquarium, Ltd.	5	4½
6	Do. Pref.	5	6
5	Ryl. Htl., Edin., Cm. Pf.	1	1½
1/2½	Ryl. Niger, Ltd., £10 Sh.	2	3
6/	Do.	10	15½
20/	Russian Petroleum	10	23½
6½	Do. 6½ p.c. Cm. Prf.	10	10½
3/	Ruston, Proctor, Ltd.	10	11
4½	Do. 1 Mort. Debs.	100	104
6/	Sadler, Ltd.	12	7
—	Sal. Carmen Nit., Ltd.	5	3½
9d.	Salmon & Gluck., Ltd.	1	1⅜
—	Salt Union, Ltd.	10	1½
1½	Do. 7 p.c. Pref.	10	5½
4½	Do. Deb. Stk.	100	98½
4½	Do. "B" Deb. Sk., Rd.	100	97½
—	San Donato Nit., Ltd.	5	⅛
5/	San Jorge Nit., Ltd.	5	3½
—	San Pablo Nit., Ltd.	5	⅛
—	San Sebastn. Nit., Ltd.	5	⅛
1/9	Sanitas, Ltd	1	2½
—	Sa. Elena Nit., Ltd.	5	¼
—	Sa. Rita Nit., Ltd.	5	1½
5/	Savoy Hotel, Ltd.	10	16
7	Do. Pref.	10	13½
4	Do. 1 Mt. Deb. Stk.	100	111½
5	Do. Debs., Red	100	102½
5	Do. & Ldn. For. Htl., Ltd., 5 p.c. Debs. Red.	100	99
8½d.	Schweppes, Ltd.	1	1½
2½d.	Do Def.	1	½
5	Do. Cum. Pref.	1	1⅛
4	Do. Deb. Stk.	100	106
1/	Singer Cyc., Ltd.	1	¾
5½	Do Cum. Pref.	1	¾
—	Smokeless Pwdr., Ltd.	1	⅛
5½d.	S. Eng. Dairies, Ltd., 6 p.c. Cum. Pref.	1	1½
—	Sowler Thos. L.	1	1
3/4½	Do. 5½ Cm. Pf.	5	5½
4/6	Spencer, Turner, & Co. Ltd	5	8½
5	Do. Cum. Pref.	5	6½
5	Spicer, Ld., 5 p.c. Dbs. Rd.	100	65
4/	Spiers & Pond, Ltd.	10	22
5	Do. 1 Mt. Debs., Red.	100	118½
5	Do. "A" Db. Stk., Rd.	100	111
5	Do. "B" 1 Db. Stk., Rd.	100	111
4	Do. Fd. "C" 1 Db. S., R.	100	104
7/6	Spratt's, Ltd	5	12¾
4	Do. Debs., 1914	—	105
5	Steiner Ld., Cm. Pf.	10	11½
4	Do. 1 Mt. Db. Sk. Rd.	100	106
9/	Stewart & Clydesdale, L.	10	13½
6	Do. Cum. Pref.	10	14½
35/5	Sulphide Corp.	100	80
1/	Swan & Edgar, L.	1	1¼
1/	Sweetmeat Automatic, L.	1	4
2/9	Teetgen, Ltd., Cum. Pref.	5	6
24/	Teleg. Construction., Ld.	12	36½
5	Do. Db. Bds., Rd., 1899	100	103½
3/0½	Tilling, Ld. 5½ p.c. Cm. Prf.	5	6½
4	Do. 4 p.c. 1 Dbs., Rd.	—	105
8½d.	Tower Tea, Ltd.	1	1½
5	Do. Cum. Pref.	5	5½
5	Travers, Ltd., Cum. Pref.	10	12½
4	Do. 1 Mt. Dbs., Rd.	100	105
6	Tucuman Sug., 1 Dbs., Rd.	100	100
4/	United Alkali, Ltd.	10	1½
7	Do. Cum. Pref.	10	8½
5	Do. Mt. Db. Stk., Rd.	100	107½
2½d.	United Horse Shoe, Ltd., Non-Cum. 8 p.c. Pref.	1	¾
5	Un. Kingm. Tea, Cm. Prf.	5	4½
2/	Un. Lankat Plant., Ltd.	1	1½
4/	Un. Limmer Asphite., Ld.	3	5
13/	Val de Travers Asph., L.	10	15½
3/	V. den Bergh's, L., Cm. P.	5	6½
6	Walkers, Park., L., C. Pf.	10	3
4½	Do. 1 Mt. Debs., Red.	100	90½
6/	Wallis, Thos. & Co., Ltd.	5	14
6	Do. Cum. Pref.	5	8½
5½	Waring, Ltd., Cum. Pref.	5	5½
4½	Do. 1 Mt. Db. Sk., Red.	100	112
4½	Do. Irred. "B" Db. Stk.	100	104
12/	Waterlow, Dfd. Ord.	10	14
4/	Do. Pref.	10	14
3½	Do. Cum. Pref.	10	10½
10/	Waterlow Bros. & L., Ld.	10	9
5	Do. Pref.	10	12½
1/2½	Welford, Ltd.	1	1⅛
4½	Do. Debs., Red.	100	109
1/	Welford's Surrey Dairies, Ltd.	1	1½
7½d.	West London Dairy, Ltd.	1	¾
4½	Wharncliffe Dwllgs, L., Pf.	10	11½
18/10	Do. 3 p.c. Irr. Mt. Db. Sk.	100	96
6d.	White, A. J., Ltd.	1	¾
6	Do. 6 p.c. Cum. Pref.	1	⅝
4	White, J. Bazley, Ltd., 1 Mort. Debs., Red	100	99½
5	White, R., Ltd., 1 Mort. Deb. Stock, Red.	100	104½
11/	White, Tomkins, Ltd	10	11½
5	Do. Cum. Pref.	10	11½
6	White, W. N., L., Cm. Pf.	1	¾
2/6	Wickens, Pease & Co., L.	5	2½
6	Wilkie, Ltd., Cum. Pref.	10	15
4/	Willans & Robinson, Ltd	5	3
6	Do. Cum. Pref.	5	7
4½	Do. 1 Mt. Db. Stk., Red.	100	108
7½d.	Williamsons, L., Cm. Prf.	1	1½
6	Winterbottm. Book Cloth, Ltd., Cum. Prf.	10	15
4/6	Yates, Ltd.	5	6
6	Do. Cum. Pref.	5	6½
	Young's Paraffin. Ltd.	4	1½

CORPORATION STOCKS—COLONIAL AND FOREIGN.

Per Cent.	Name.	Paid.	Price.
6	Auckland City, '72 1904-24	100	118
6	Do. Cons., '79, Red. 1930	100	135½
5	Do. Deb. Ln., '83..1934-8	100	117
6	Auckland Harb. Debs.	100	111½
5	Do. 1917	100	111
5	Do. 1936	100	114
5½	Balmain Boro'....1914	—	113½
5	Boston City (U.S.)	100	102½
5	Do. ..1902	100	105
5	Brunswick Town 5. C. Debs. 1916-20	100	111
15/	B. Ayres City 6 p.c.	100	51
4½	Do. 4½ p.c.	100	71½
5	Cape Town, City of	100	113
4	Do. ..1943	100	115
4	Chicago, City of, Gold 1915	—	108½
6	Christchurch 1926	100	131½
—	Cordoba City	100	17½
5	Duluth (U.S.) Gold ..1926	—	110
6	Dunedin (Otago) 1925	100	127½
6	Do. 1906	100	113
5	Do. Consols..1908	100	111
4	Durban Insc. Stk....1944	100	111
4	Essex Cnty., N. Jersey 1926	$100	114½
5	Fitzroy, Melbrne...1916-19	100	110
5	Gisborne Harbour....1915	100	109
4	Greymouth Harbour..1925	100	110
4	Hamilton 1934	100	108
5	Hobart Town 1918-30	100	115
4	Do. 1940	100	105
4½	Invercargill Boro. Dbs. 1936	100	111
6	Kimberley Boro., S. A. Debs.	—	102
4	Launceston Twn. Dbs. 1916	100	107
6	Lyttleton, N.Z., Harb. 1929	100	125
4	Melbourne Bd. of Wks. 1921	100	107
5	Melb. City Debs. 1897-1907	100	106½
4½	Do. Debs. 1908-27	100	111½
4	Do. Debs...1915-20-22	100	106
5	Melbne. Harb. Bds., 1908-9	100	113
4½	Do. do. 1915	100	111
4	Do. do. 1918-21	100	106
4½	Melbne. Tms. Dbs. 1914-16	100	113
4½	Do. Fire Brig. Db. 1921	100	108
5	Mexico City Stg.	100	89½
4	Moncton N. Bruns. City	100	102
4½	Montevideo	100	59
5	Montreal Stg.	100	103
5	Do. 1874	100	103
5	Do. 1879	100	104
3½	Do. 1933	100	102
3	Do. Perm. Deb. Stk	100	96
4	Do. Cons. Deb. Stk. 1932	100	112
6	Napier Boro. Consolid. 1914	100	119
5	Napier Harb. Debs...1920	100	115
5	Do. Debs...1922	100	107
6	New Plymouth Harb. Debs. 1909	100	107
6	New York City 1901	—	109½
3½	Do. 1910-26	—	103½
4½	Nth. Melbourne Debs. 1-600 1921	100	105
5	Oamaru Boro. Cons...1920	100	101
6	Do. Harb. Bds. (Reg.)	100	74
25/	Do. 6 p.c. (Bearer)..1919	100	35
6	Otago Harb. Deb. Reg.	100	103
6	Do. 1877	100	107
6	Do. 1881 1921	100	115
5	Do. Debs. ..1921	100	107
5	Do. Cons. ..1934	100	105
6	Ottawa City	100	109
6	Do. 1904	100	111½
4½	Do. Debs. ..1913	100	108½
6	Port Elizabeth Waterworks	100	111
5	Port Louis	100	111
5	Prahran Debs. 1917	100	109
4	Do. Debs. 1919	100	102
6	Quebec C. Coupon. 1875 1905	100	112
6	Do. do. 1878 1908	100	116
4½	Do. Debs. 1914-15	100	108
4	Do. Debs. 1923	200	108
3½	Do. Cns. Rg. Stk., Red.	100	101
5	Richmond (Melb.) Dbs. 1917	100	112
4	Rio Janeiro City	100	57
4	Rome City	100	—
4	Do. 2nd to 8th Iss.	100	90
—	Rosario C.	100	26½
—	Do.	100	26½
4	St. Catherine (Ont.)..1926	100	101
4	St. John, N.B., Debs. 1934	—	103
4½	St. Kilda (Melb) Dbs. 1918-21	100	105
4	St. Louis C. (Miss.)..1911	100	104
4	Do. 1913	100	103½
3·65	Do. 1915	—	108½
—	Santa Fé City Debs.	100	19
6	Santos City	100	95
6	Sofia City	100	84
5	Sth. Melbourne Debs. 1915	100	111
4½	Do. Debs....1919	100	107
5	Sydney City 1904	100	109
4	Do. Debs. 1912-13	100	107
4	Do. do. (1894)..1919	100	109
7	Timaru Boro. 7 p.c...1910	100	120½
5	Timaru Harb. Debs 1914	100	107
5	Do. Debs...1916	100	107
6	Toronto City Wtwks 1904-6	100	114
5	Do. G. Cns. Dbs. 1919-20	100	118
4	Do. Strlg. 1922-8	100	107
4	Do. Local Improv.	100	102
3½	Do. 1929	100	104
5½	Valparaiso	100	99
4	Vancouver 1931	100	107
4	Do. 1932	100	108
6	Wanganui Harb. Dbs. 1905	100	110
6	Wellington Con. Deb. 1907	100	117
6	Do. Improv., 1879	100	122
6	Do. Wtrwks. Dbs., 1880	100	123
4½	Do. Debs., 1893....1933	100	114
4½	Wellington Harb. 1907	100	104
4	Westport Harb. Dbs. 1925	100	110
6	Winnipeg City Deb...1907	—	118
5	Do. 1914	100	117

FINANCIAL, LAND, AND INVESTMENT.

Last Div.	Name.	Paid.	Price.
5	Agency, Ld. & Fin. Aust., Ltd., Mt. Db. Stk., Rd.	100	90½
	Amer. Frehld. Mt. of Lon., Ld., Cum. Pref. Stk.	100	87½
4½	Do. Deb. Stk., Red.	100	92
2/4½	Anglo-Amer. Db. Cor., L.	2	1
4	Do. Deb. Stk., Red	100	105½
5½	Ang.-Ceylon & Gen. Est., Ltd., Cons. Stk.	100	55
6	Do. Reg. Debs., Red.	100	101½
3/	Ang.-Fch. Explorn., Ltd.	1	2¼
6	Do. Cum. Pref.	1	1½
—	Argent. Ld. & Inv., Ltd. £1 Shares	10/	nil
—	Do. Cum. Pref.	4	1¼
1/	Assets Fnders.' Sh., Ltd.,	4	1¼
6/	Assets Realis., Ltd., Ord.,	5	8¾
5	Do. Cum. Pref.	5	6½
26/	Austrln. Agricl £25 Shs.	21½	62½
4½	Aust. N. Z. Mort., Ltd., Deb. Stk., Red.	100	87½
4	Do. Deb. Stk., Red.	100	82½
4½	Australian Est. & Mt., L., 1 Mt. Deb. Stk., Red.	100	103
5	Do. "A" Mort. Deb. Stk., Red.	100	96
5/	Australian Mort., Ld., & Fin., Ltd. £25 Shs.	5	5½
2/6	Do. New, £25 Shs.	3	3
4	Do. Deb. Stk	100	109½
3	Do. Do.	100	85
5	Bengal Presidy. 1 Mort. Deb., Red.	100	106
25/	British Amer. Ld. "A"	1	19
—	Do. "B"	24	7
1/7½	Brit. & Amer. Mt., Ltd. £10 Shs.	2	1
5/	Do. Pref.	10	10
4	Do. Deb. Stk., Red.	100	103
1/3	Brit. & Austrlsn Tst Ln., Ltd. £25 Shs.	2½	¾
4½	Do. Perm. Debs., Red.	100	104
1½d.	Brit. N. Borneo. £1 Shs.	15/	1/12
2½d.	Do.	1	⅜
—	Brit. S. Africa	1	2½
5	Do. Mt. Deb., Red.	—	93
6	B. Aires Harb. Tst., Red.	100	93
12/6	Canada Co.	1	26
—	Canada N. W. Ld., Ltd.	$25	83½
—	Do. Pref.	$100	150½
4	Canada Perm. Loan & Sav. Perp. Deb. Stk.	100	99½
6	Curamalan Ld., 6 p.c. "A" Scrip	—	92
3/7½	Deb Corp., Ld., £10 Shs	4	3½
5	Do. Cum. Pref.	10	11½
4	Do. Perp. Deb. Stk.	100	111
9d.	Deb. Corp. Fders' Sh., Ld.	3	½
4/5 1/10	Eastn. Mt. & Agncy, Ld., "A"	10	5½
4½	Do. Deb. Stk., Red.	100	98
5	Equitable Revers. In. Ltd.	100	—
2/6	Exploration, Ltd.	1	1½
/6d.	Freehold Trst. of Austrla. Ltd. £10 Shs.	1	¾
4	Do. Perp. Deb. Stk.	100	100
70/	Genl. Reversionary, Ltd.	100	—
2½	Holborn Vi. Land	100	105
3½	House Prop. & Inv.	100	85½
13/	Hudson's Bay	13	20¾
—	Hyderabad (Deccan)	5	2¼
4	Impl. Col. Fin. & Agcy. Corp.	100	92½
4½	Impl. Prop. Inv., Ltd., Deb. Stk., Red.	100	91½
2/6	Internatl. Fincial. Soc., Ltd. £7½ Shs.	2½	1½
4	Do. Deb. Stk., Red.	100	99½
1/9½	Ld. & Mtge. Egypt, Ltd. £18 Shs.	3	2¾
5	Do. Debs., Red.	100	101
4½	Do. Debs., Red.	100	100
—	Ld. Corp. of Canada, Ltd.	1	⅜
4½	Ld. Mtge. Bk. of Texas Deb. Stk.	100	—
3½	Ld. Mtge. Bk. Victoria 4½ p.c. Deb. Stk.	100	78
2/9½	Law Debent. Corp., Ltd., £10 Shs.	2	1½
4½	Do. Cum. Pref.,	10	11½
4	Do. Deb. Stk.	100	114
—	Law Land, L., 4½ Cm. Prf.	5	5½
1/	Ldn. & Australasian Deb. Corp., Ltd., £4 Shs.	2	½
4½	Do. 4½ p.c. Mt. Deb. Stk., Red.	100	99
1/9	Ldn. & Middx. Frhld. Est. £2 Shs.	35/	3
2/6	Lndn. & N. Y. Inv. Corp., Ltd.	5	1¾
5	Do. 5 p.c. Cum. Pref.	10	8½
1/6	Ldn. & Nth. Assets Corp., Ltd., £2 Shs.	1½	¾
2	Ldn. & N. Deb. Corp., L.	2	1½
3/6	Ldn. & S. Afric. Explrn. Ltd.	½	12¾
2/	Mtge. Co. of R. Plate, Ltd. £10 Shs.	2	3
4½	Do. Deb. Stk., Red.	100	112
4½	Morton, Rose Est., Ltd., 1st Mort. Debs.	—	99
6/6	Natal Land Col. Ltd.	10	7
4/	Do. 8 p.c. Pref., 1870	5	8
5/6	Natl. Disct. L., £25 Shs.	5	10½
4½	New Impl. Invest., Ltd. Pref. Stk.	100	61½
	New Impl. Invest., Ltd. Def. Stk.	100	9
3½	N. Zld. Assets Real Deb.	100	99
4	N. Zld. Ln. & Mer. Agcy., Ltd Prf. Ln, Deb. Stk	100	94
2/6	N. Zld. Tst. & Ln. Ltd., £25 Shs.	5	1½

Financial, Land, &c. (*continued*):—

Last Div.	Name.	Paid.	Price.
12/6	N. Zld. Tst. & Ln. Ltd., 5 p.c. Cum. Pref.	25	20
—	N. Brit. Australsn. Ltd.	100	6½
—	Do. Irred. Guar.	100	32½
5	Do. Mort. Debs.	100	82½
4½	N. Queensld. Mort. & Inv., Ltd., Deb. Stk.	100	93
6	Peel Riv., Ld. & Min. Ltd.	100	88½
—	Peruvian Corp., Ltd.	100	2½
—	Do. 4 p.c. Pref.	100	9
3	Do. 6 p.c. 1 Mt. Debs., Red.	100	39
—	Queenld. Invest. & Ld. Mort. Pref. Ord. Stk.	100	20
3/7	Queenld. Invest. & Ld. Mort. Ord. Shs.	4	4
4	Queenld. Invest. & Ld. Mort. Perp. Debs.	100	88
3½	Raily. Roll Stk. Tst. Deb., 1903-6	100	100½
50/	Reversiony. Int. Soc., Ltd.	100	—
2/8½	Riv. Plate Trst., Loan & Agcy., L., "A" £10 Shs.	2	4
1/6	Riv. Plate Trst., Loan & Agcy., Ltd., Def. "B"	5	3½
	Riv. Plate Trst., Loan & Agy., L., Db. Stk., Red.	100	109
—	Santa Fé & Cord. Gt. South Land, Ltd.	20	5
—	Santa Fé Land	10	2½
2/	Scot. Amer. Invest., Ltd. £10 Shs.	2	2¾
2½	Scot. Australian Invest., Ltd., Cons.	100	70½
6	Scot. Australian Invest., Ltd., Guar. Pref.	100	135½
5	Scot. Australian Invest., Ltd., Guar. Pref.	100	106½
4	Scot. Australian Invest., Ltd., 4 p.c. Perp. Dbs.	100	105½
5	Sivagunga Zemdy., 1st Mort., Red.	100	101
20/	Sth. Australian	20	50
3½	Stock Exchange Deb., Rd.	—	101½
—	Strait Develt., Ltd.	1	1/16
2/6	Texas Land & Mt., Ltd. £10 Shs.	2½	2¾
4½	Texas Land & Mt., Ltd., Deb. Stk., Red.	100	106
—	Transvaal Est. & Dev., L.	1	1/16
—	Transvaal Lands, Ltd., £1 Shs.	15/	½
—	Do. F. P.	1	1/16
—	Transvaal Mort., Loan, & Fin., Ltd., £10 Shs.	2	½
2/	Tst & Agcy. of Austrlsa., Ltd., £10 Shs.	1	2
7/5	Do. Old, fully paid	10	15½
5/7	Do. New, fully paid	10	12½
5	Do. Cum. Pref.	10	12½
3/	Trust & Loan of Canada, £20 Shs.	5	4½
1/9½	Do. New £20 Shs.	3	2½
4½	Tst. & Mort. of Iowa, Ltd., Deh. Stk. Red.	100	92½
—	Tst., Loan, & Agency of Mexico, Ltd., £10 Shs.	2	½
—	Trsts., Exors, & Sec. Ins. Corp., Ltd., £10 Shs.	7	1¾
4	Do. Irred. Deb. Stk.	100	106½
5/	Union Dsc., Ld., £10 Shs.	5	10½
6	Union Mort. & Agcy. of Aust., Ltd., Pref. Stk.	100	30
—	Do. 6 p. Pref. £6 Shs.	2	½
4½	Do. Deb. Stk	100	92½
4	Do. Deh. Stk	100	85½
5	Do. Deb. Stk. Red.	100	96½
1/6	U.S. Deb. Cor. Ltd., £8 Shs.	1	½
5½	Do. Cum. Pref. Stk.	100	100½
4½	Do. Irred. Deb. Stk.	100	105½
5	U.S. Tst. & Guar. Cor., Ltd., Pref. Stk.	100	77½
6/	Van Dieman's	25	16
4	Walker's Prop. Cor., Ltd., Guar. 1 Mt. Deb. Stk.	100	109
4½	Wstr. Mort. & Inv., Ltd., Deb. Stk.	100	92½

FINANCIAL—TRUSTS.

Last Div.	Name.	Paid.	Price.
1/6	Afric City Prop., Ltd	1	1½
6	Do. Cum. Pref.	1	1½
4	Alliance Invt., Ltd., Cm. 4½ p. c. Prefd.	100	74½
—	Do. Defd	100	12½
4	Do. Deb. Stk. Red.	100	106½
5	Amrcn. Invt., Ltd., Prfd.	100	114½
5	Do. Defd.	100	88½
4	Do. Deb. Stk. Red.	100	115½
4	Army & Navy Invt., Ltd., 4 p.c. Prefd.	100	81½
—	Do. Defd. Stk.	100	15½
4	Do. Deb. Stk.	100	105½
4	Atlas Investment, Ltd., Prefd. Stk.	100	70½
4½	Bankers' Invest., Ltd., Cum. Prefd.	100	104
1/0/0	Do. Defd	100	27½
4	Do. Deb. Stk	100	111
	Brewery & Comml. Inv., Ltd., £10 Shs.	5	6

Financial—Trusts (*continued*):—

Last Div.	Name.	Paid.	Price.
4	British Investment, Ltd., Cum. Prefd.	100	107
5	Do. Defd.	100	103½
4	Do. Deb. Stk.	100	106½
6	Brit. Steam. Invst., Ltd., Prefd	100	116½
8/0/0	Do. Defd.	100	71½
4½	Do. Perp. Deb. Stk	100	120½
1/9	Car Trust Invst., Ltd., £10 Shs.	2½	2
5	Do. Pref.	100	101
4	Do. Deb. Stk., 1915	100	104
4	Clnl. Sec., Ltd., Prefd.	100	103½
2⅛	Do. Defd.	100	45½
4	Consolidated, Ltd., Cum. 1st Pref.	100	92
4	Do. 5 p.c. Cm. 2nd do.	100	71½
—	Do. Defd.	100	14½
4½	Do. Deb. Stk.	100	112½
5	Deb. Secs. Invst.	100	103½
4	Do. 4 p.c. Cm. Pf. Sk.	100	105½
4½	Edinburgh Invest., Ltd., Cum. Prefd. Stk.	100	105½
4	Do. Deb. Stk. Red.	100	106½
5	Foreign, Amer. & Gen. Invt., Ltd., Prefd.	100	112½
2	Do. Defd.	100	48½
4	Do. Deb. Stk.	100	115½
5	Foreign & Colonial Invt., Ltd., Prefd.	100	136½
5½	Do. Defd.	100	99½
4½	Gas, Water & Gen. Invt., Cum. Prefd. Stk.	100	85½
3	Do. Defd. Stk.	100	36½
4	Do. Deb. Stk.	100	104
5	Gen. & Com. Invt., Ltd., Prefd. Stk.	100	105½
2	Do. Defd. Stk.	100	36½
4	Do. Deb. Stk.	100	111½
2/6	Globe Telegph. & Tst., Ltd.	10	11½
6	Do. do. Pref.	10	16½
4	Govt. & Genl. Invt., Ld., Prefd.	100	84½
3½	Do. Defd.	100	42½
4½	Govts. Stk. & other Secs. Invt., Ltd., Prefd.	100	85½
1	Do. Defd.	100	25
4½	Do. Deb. Stk.	100	111
4	Do. do.	100	104
4½	Guardian Invt., Ltd., Pfd.	100	87½
—	Do. Defd.	100	19½
4	Do. Deb. Stk.	100	104
5	Indian & Gen. Inv., Ltd., Cum. Prefd.	100	108½
2½	Do. Defd.	100	55
4½	Do. Deb. Stk.	100	119½
5	Indust. & Gen. Tst., Ltd., Unified	100	98½
3½	Do. Deb. Stk. Red.	100	98½
4½	Internat. Invt., Ltd., Cm. Prefd.	100	66½
—	Do. Defd.	100	7½
4	Do. Deb. Stk.	100	101
4	Invest. Tst. Cor. Ltd. Pfd.	100	100
4	Do. Defd.	100	90
4	Do. Deb. Stk. Red.	100	105
5	Ldn. Gen. Invest. Ltd., 5 p.c. Cum. Prefd.	100	111½
7½	Do. Defd.	100	121
4½	Ldn. Scot. Amer. Ltd. Pfd.	100	104½
£3	Do. Defd.	100	59½
4	Do. Deb. Stk.	100	111
4	Ldn. Tst., Ltd., Cum. Prfd. Stk.	100	99
4	Do. Defd. Stk.	100	67½
4	Do. Deb. Stk., Red.	100	107
3½	Do. Mt. Deb. Stk., Red.	100	100½
5	Mercantile Invt. & Gen., Ltd., Prefd.	100	110
3	Do. Defd.	100	44½
4	Do. Deb. Stk.	100	111½
4	Merchants, Ltd., Pref. Stk.	100	104½
4	Do. Ord.	100	80½
4	Do. Deb. Stk.	100	115½
5	Municipal, Ltd., Prefd.	100	55½
—	Do. Defd.	100	17½
4½	Do. Debs.	100	111
4½	Do. Debs. "B"	100	99½
4½	Do. "C" Deb. Stk.	100	88½
5	New Investment, Ltd. Ord.	100	92½
5	Omnium Invest., Ltd., Pfd.	100	91½
2	Do. Defd.	100	26½
4	Do. Deb. Stk.	100	106
5/	Railway Deb. Tst. Ld., £20 Shs.	10	6½
5	Do. Debs., Red.	100	107½
4½	Do. Deb. Stk., 1911	100	107½
4	Do. do. 1927	100	106½
4	Railway Invst. Ltd., Prefd.	100	111
17/7	Do. Defd.	100	19½
8/	Railway Share Trust & Agency "A"	8	5½
7½	Do. "B" Pref. Stk.	100	145½
4½	River Plate & Gen. Invt., Ltd., Prefd.	100	104
£3	Do. Defd.	100	50½
5	Scot. Invst., Ltd., Pfd. Stk.	100	91½
7½	Do. Defd.	100	26½
4	Do. Deb. Stk.	100	106
4½	Sec. Scottish Invst., Ltd., Cum. Prefd.	100	89½
£8	Do. Defd. Stk.	100	32
4	Do. Deb. Stk.	100	108½
5/	Sth. Africa Gold Tst., Ltd.	1	3¼
6	Do. Cum. Pref	1	1
5½	Do. 1st Debs., Red.	100	102
1/9	Stock Conv. & Invest., Ltd., £5 Shs.	1	1¾
4½	Do. do. 4½ p.c. Cm. Prf.	100	113½
3½	Do. Ldn. & N. W. 1st. Charge Prefd.	100	114½
4	Do do. 2nd Chge Prfd.	100	111
82/6	Do. do. Defd. Charge	100	30
3	Do. N. East. 1 Chge Pfd.	100	90½

Financial—Trusts (*continued*):—

Last Div.	Name.	Paid.	Price.
37/6	Stock N. East Defd. Chge	100	36
6	Submarine Cables	100	138½
5	U.S. & S. Amer. Invest., Ltd., Prefd.	100	97½
20/	Do. Defd.	100	24½
4	Do. Deb. Stk.	100	105½

GAS AND ELECTRIC LIGHTING.

Last Div.	Name.	Paid.	Price.
10/6	Alliance & Dublin Con. 10 p.c. Stand.	10	24
7/6	Do. 7 p.c. Stand.	10	16½
5	Austln. Gas Lght. (Syd.) Debs. 1909	100	106
5	Bay State of N. Jrsy. Sk. Fd. Tst. Bd., Red.	—	89½
3/	Bombay, Ltd.	5	6
2/4½	Do. New	4	5
12	Brentford Cons.	100	292½
9	Do. New	100	217½
5	Do. Pref.	100	142½
4	Do. Deb. Stk.	100	136
11½	Brighton & Hove Gen. Cons. Stk.	100	272½
8½	Do. "A" Cons. Stk.	100	197½
5	Bristol 5 p.c. Max.	100	129½
22/6	British Gas Light, Ltd.	20	55½
11/6	Bromley Gas Consumrs.' 10 p.c. Stand.	10	26
8/6	Do. 7 p.c. Stand.	10	21
—	Brush Electl. Enging., L.	—	1½
6	Do. 6 p.c. Pref.	—	2½
4½	Do. Deb. Stk.	100	112
4½	Do. 2 Deb. Stk., Red.	100	102½
7/	B. Ayres (New), Ltd.	10	9
4	Do. Deb. Stk., Rd.	—	98
18/6	Cagliari Gas & Wtr., Ltd.	20	31
8/	Cape Town & Dist. Gas Light & Coke, Ltd.	10	16½
4½	Do. Pref.	10	12½
6	Do. 1 Mt. Debs. 1910	50	50
4/	Charing Cross & Strand Elec. Sup., Ltd.	5	13½
4½	Do. Cum. Pref.	5	6½
3/	Chelsea Elec. Sup., Ltd.	5	9½
4½	Do. Deb. Stk., Red.	100	116
5	Chic. Edis'n Co. 1 Mt., Rd.	$1000	105
20/	City of Ldn. Elec. Lht., L	10	24
—	Do. New £10 Shs.	5	16½
6	Do. Cum. Pref.	10	17
5	Do. Deb. Stk., Red.	100	131½
13½	Commercial, Cons.	100	325½
10½	Do. New	100	252½
4½	Do. Deb. Stk.	100	152½
14	Continental Union, Ltd.	100	220
11	Do. Pref. Stk.	100	200
—	County of Lon. & Brush Prov. Elec. Lg., Ltd.	10	12½
6	Do. Cum. Pref.	10	15½
14	Croydon Comcl. Gas, Ld., "A" Stk., 10 p.c.	100	312½
11	Do. "B" Stk., 7 p.c.	100	260
5½	Crystal Pal. Dist. Ord. 5 p.c. Stk.	100	130½
5	Do. Pref. Stk.	100	143½
8/	European, Ltd.	10	24
6/	Do.	7½	17½
12½	Gas Light & Ck Cons. Stk., "A" Ord.	100	294½
4	Do. "B" (4 p.c. Max.)	100	120½
10	Do. "C," "D," & "E" (Pref.)	100	302½
5	Do. "F" (Pref.)	100	152½
7½	Do. "G" (Pref.)	100	228½
7	Do. "H" (7 p.c. Max.)	100	197½
10	Do. "J" (Pref.)	100	302½
6	Do. "K"	100	180½
4	Do. Deb. Stk.	100	133½
4½	Do. do.	100	152½
6	Do. do.	100	204½
8/	Hong Kong & China, Ld.	10	14
4/	House to House Elec. Light Sup., Ltd.	5	9½
7	Do. Cum. Pref.	5	11½
10	Imperial Continental	100	208½
3½	Do. Deb. Stk., Red	100	104½
2/	Malta & Medit., Ltd.	5	5½
7/	Metrop. Elec. Sup., Ltd.	10	17½
4½	Do. 1 Mt. Deb. Stk.	100	119
5	Metro. of Melbrne. Dbs. 1908-12	100	111
4½	Do. Debs. 1918-22-4	100	106
10/	Monte Video, Ltd.	20	15½
9½	Newcastle-upon-Tyne	100	237½
—	Do. 3½ p.c. Deb. Stk.	100	117½
12/	Notting Hill Elec. Ltg., Ltd.	10	19½
4/6	Oriental, Ltd.	5	8½
4/0½	Do. New	4½	7½
10d½.	Do. do. 1879	1	1½
3/6	Ottoman, Ltd.	5	5
6	People's Gas Lt. & C. of Chic. 2 Mt. 1904	100	105½
5	River Plate Elec. Lgt. & Trac., Ltd., 1 Deb. Stk.	—	92½
8s	Royal Elec. of Montreal	—	144
4½	Do. 1 Mt. Deb.	100	104
11/	St. James' & Pall Mall Elec. Light, Ltd.	5	17
7	Do. Pref.	5	10½
4	Do. Deb. Stk., Red.	100	108½
10/	San Paulo, Ltd.	10	15½

Gas and Electric (*continued*):—

Last Div.	Name.	Paid.	Price.
10	Sheffield Unit. Gas Lt. "A"	100	251½
10	Do. "B"	100	251½
10	Do. "C"	100	251½
—	Sth. Ldn. Elec. Sup., Ld.	2	2
5¾	South Metropolitan	100	135½
3	Do. 3 p.c. Deb. Stk.	100	104½
2	Tottenham & Edmonton Gas Lt. & C., "A"	100	290
9	Do. "B"	100	210
7/	Tuscan, Ltd.	10	13½
5	Do. Debs., Red.	100	101½
5/	West Ham 10 p.c. Stan.	5	12
8/	Wstmnstr. Elec. Sup., Ld.	5	15½

INSURANCE.

Last Div.	Name.	Paid.	Price.
4/	Alliance, £20 Shs.	44/	10¼
20/	Alliance, Mar., & Gen., Ld., £100 Shs.	25	53
19/	Atlas, £50 Shs.	6	29
12/	British & For. Marine, Ld., £20 Shs.	4	23½
7½d.	British Law Fire, Ltd., £10 Shs.	1	1½
7/6	Clerical, Med., & Gen. Life £25 Shs.	50/	16½
20/	Commercial Union, Ltd., £50 Shs.	5	43½
4	Do. "W. of Eng." Ter. Deb. Stk.	100	110½
£9	County Fire, £100 Shs.	80	195
5/	Eagle, £50 Shs.	5	½
4/	Employrs' Liability, Ltd., £10 Shs.	2	4
—	Empress, Ltd., £5 Shs.	1	—
21/	Equity & Law, £100 Shs.	6	23
7/6	General Life, £100 Shs.	5	15
4½d.	Gresham Life, £5 Shs.	15/	2½
2/6	Guardian, Ld., £10 Shs.	5	11
10/	Imperial, Ltd., £20 Shs.	5	29
5/6	Imperial Life, £20 Shs.	4	6¾
6/	Indemnity Mutual Mar., Ltd., £15 Shs.	3	11½
1/6	Lancashire, £20 Shs.	2	5
7½d.	Law Acc. & Contin., Ltd., £5 Shs.	10/	¾
12/6	Law Fire, £100 Shs.	2½	17¾
9½d.	Law Guar. & Trust, Ltd., £10 Shs.	1	1¾
9/	Law Life, £20 Shs.	2	25
2/9	Law Un. & Crown £10 Shs	12/	7
4	Do. Deb. Stk., 1942	100	110½
14/6	Legal & General, £50 Shs.	8	15½
9d.	Lion Fire, Ltd., £8½ Shs.	1½	⅞
14/	Liverpool & London & Globe, Stk.	2	53½
20/	Do. Globe £1 Ann	—	35½
35/	London, £25 Shs.	12½	58
8/	Lond. & Lanc. Fire, £25 Shs	2½	18¾
2/	Lond. & Lanc. Life, £25 Shs	2	7
1/	Lond. & Prov. Mar., Ld., £10 Shs.	1	¾
6/	Lond. Guar. & Accident, Ltd., £5 Shs.	2	12
40/	Marine, Ltd., £25 Shs.	4½	42½
2/	Maritime, Ltd., £10 Shs.	2	4
1/6	Merc. Mar., Ld., £10 Shs.	2½	2½
20/	N. Brit. & Merc., £25 Shs.	6¼	42½
20/	Northern, £100 Shs.	10	81
40/	Norwich Union Fire, £100 Shs.	12	124½
20/	Ocean Acc. & Guar., fy. pd.	5	22
2/	Do. £5 Shs.	1	¾
7/6	Ocean, Marine, Ltd.	2½	8½
2/	Palatine, £10 Shs.	2	3½
2/6	Pelican, £10 Shs.	1	3½
23/	Phœnix, £50 Shs.	5	41½
£6	Provident, £100 Shs.	10	32
5/	Railway Psngrs., £10 Shs.	2	8½
2/6	Rock Life, £5 Shs.	10/	4½
8	Royal Exchange	100	352½
28/	Royal, £20 Shs.	3	54½
4/	Sun, £10 Shs.	10/	11½
3/9	Sun Life, £10 Shs.	7½	14½
6	Thames & Mrsey. Marine, Ltd., £20 Shs.	2	10½
9	Union, £10 Shs.	4	24½
4/	Union Marine, £20 Shs.	2½	8¾
12/	Universal Life, £100 Shs.	12	42
2/	World Marine, £5 Shs.	2	1½

IRON, COAL, AND STEEL.

Last Div.	Name.	Paid.	Price.
—	Barrow Hæm. Steel, Ltd.	7½	2
9/	Do. 6 p.c. and Pref.	7½	6½
10/	Bolck., Vaugh. & C., Ld.	20	16½
6/	Do. £8 liab.	12	8¾
7/6	Brown, J. & Co., Ltd., £20 Shs.	15	20
7/6	Consett Iron, Ld., £10 Shs.	7½	29½
7/6	Ebbw Vale Steel, Iron & Coal, Ltd., £23 Shs.	20	6½
12/6	General Mining Assn., Ld.	5½	7½
8/	Harvey Steel Co. of Gt. Britain, Ltd.	10	27
5	Lehigh V. Coal 1 Mt. 5 p.c. Guar. Gd. Cp. Bds.	—	95½
42/6	Nantyglo & Blaina Iron, Ltd., Pref.	$62	96
1/	Nerbudda Coal & Iron, Ltd., £3 Shs.	56/	⅛
—	Newport Abrcrn. Bk. Vein Steam Coal, Ltd.	10	6½
5/	New Sharlston Coll., Ltd. Pref.	20	9½
4½d.	Nw. Vancvr. Coal & Ld., L.	1	⅛
2/6	North's Navigation Coll. (1889) Ltd.	5	2½
10/	Do. 10 p.c. Cum. Pref.	5	6½
—	Rhymney Iron, Ltd.	5	1½
	Do. New, £5 Shs.	4½	¾
5	Do. Mt. Debs., Red.	100	98½
5	Shelton Irn., Stl. & Cl. Co., Ltd., 1 Chg. Debs., Red.	100	99½
50/	Sth. Hetton Coal, Ltd.	100	—
2/	Vickers & Maxim, Ltd.	1	3½
5	Do. 5 p.c. Prfd. Stk.	100	127½

SHIPPING.

Last Div.	Name.	Paid.	Price.
12/	African Stm. Ship, £20 Shs.	16	10½
15/	Do. Fully-paid	20	14½
5/	Amazon Steam Nav., Ltd.	12½	9
8/	Castle Mail Pakts., Ltd., £20 Shs.	14	15½
3½	Do. 1st Deb. Stk., Red.	100	102
6/	China Mutual Steam, Ltd.	5	3
6	Do. Cum. Pref.	10	9½
10/	Cunard, Ltd.	20	9½
5/	Do. £20 Shs.	10	3¾
4½	Furness, Withy, & Co., Ltd., 1 Mt. Dbs., Red.	100	106
6/	General Steam	15	7½
5/	Do. 5 p.c. Pref., 1874	10	8½
5/	Do. 5 p.c. Pref., 1877	10	8½
26/4½	Leyland & Co., Ltd.	10	25
7/	Do. 7 p.c. Cum. Pref.	10	15
2/11	Do. 4½ p.c. Cum. Pre-Pf.	3	10½
4	Do. 1st Mt. Dbs., Red.	100	106½
7/6	Mercantile Steam, Ltd.	5	7½
6/4½	New Zealand Ship., Ltd.,	6	5
4	Do. Deb. Stk., Red.	100	104
5/	Orient Steam, Ltd.	10	4½
5	P. & O. Steam, Cum. Prefd.	100	147½
19	Do. Defd.	100	234½
3½	Do. Deb. Stk.	100	117
5	Richelieu & Ont., 1st Mt. Debs., Red.	100	100
30/	Royal Mail, £100 Shs.	60	51
2/6	Shaw, Sav., & Alb., Ltd., "A" Pref.	5	5
5/	Do. "B" Ord.	5	4
14/	Union Steam, Ltd.	20	19
7/	Do. New £20 Shs.	10	8½
4	Do. Deb. Stk., Red.	100	106
7/	Union of N.Z., Ltd.	10	10
5½	Wilson's & Fur.-Ley., 5½ p.c. Cum. Pref.	10	10½
4½	Do. 1 Mt. Db. Sk., Rd.	100	106½

**** *Tea Shares will be found in the Special Table following.*

TELEGRAPHS AND TELEPHONES.

Last Div.	Name.	Paid.	Price.
4	African Direct, Ltd., Mort. Debs., Red.	100	102
—	Amazon Telegraph, Ltd.	10	7½
15/	Anglo-American, Ltd.	100	64½
30/	Do. 6 p.c. Prefd. Ord.	100	113
—	Do. Defd. Ord.	100	15
3/	Brazilian Submarine, Ltd.	10	15½
5	Do. Debs., 2 Series	100	114

Telegraphs and Telephones (*continued*):—

Last Div.	Name.	Paid.	Price.
4/	Chili Telephone, Ltd.	5	3½
$1½	Comcial. Cable, $100 Shs.	—	180
4	Do. Stg. 500-yr. Deb. Stk. Red.	100	106
2½d.	Consd. Telpehone Constr., &c., Ltd.	10/	¼
6/	Cuba Submarine, Ltd.	10	7½
10/	Do. 10 p.c. Pref.	10	15
2/	Direct Spanish, Ltd.	5	4½
5/	Do. 10 p.c. Cum. Pref.	5	10½
4½	Do. Debs.	50	104½
3/	Direct U.S. Cable, Ltd.	20	10½
2/6	Eastern, Ltd.	10	17
3/	Do. 6 p.c. Cum. Pref.	10	18½
4	Do. Mt. Deb. Stk., Red.	100	125
2/6	Eastern Exten., Aus., & China, Ltd.	10	17¾
5	Do. (Aus. Gov. Sub.) Deb., Red.	100	102
5	Do. do. Bearer	100	102½
4	Do. Mort. Deb. Stk.	100	128½
5	Eastn. & S. Afric., Ltd., Mort. Deb. 1900	100	102
5	Do. Bearer	100	102½
4	Do. Mort. Debs. 1909	100	102½
4	Do. Mort. Debs. (Maur. Subsidy)	25	106½
5/	Grt. Nthn. Copenhagen	10	28½
5	Do. Debs., Ser. B., Red.	100	101½
12/6	Indo-European, Ltd.	25	51½
6	London Platino-Brazilian, Ltd., Debs. 1904	100	108½
4/	Montevideo Telph., Ltd., 6 p.c. Pref.	5	2½
3/	National Telephone, Ltd.	5	5¾
6/	Do. Cum. 1 Pref.	10	16
6/	Do. Cum. 2 Pref.	10	16
5	Do. Non-Cum. 3 Pref.	5	5½
3½	Do. Deb. Stk., Red.	100	101½
8d.	Oriental Telephone, Ltd.	1	½
4	Pac. & Euro. Tlg. Dbs., Rd.	100	106½
4/	Reuter's, Ltd.	8	8½
5/	Un. Riv. Plate Telph., Ltd.	5	4½
5	Do. Deb. Stk., Red.	100	106½
—	West African Telg., Ltd.	10	4
5	Do. 5 p.c. Mt. Debs., Red.	100	100½
—	W. Coast of America, Ltd.	10	¾
3/	Western & Brazilian, Ltd.	15	12
3/	Do. 5 p.c. Pref. Ord.	7½	7½
—	Do. Defd. Ord.	7½	4½
4	Do. Deb. Stk., Red.	100	106½
1/	W. India & Panama, Ltd.	10	¾
6/	Do. Cum. 1 Pref.	10	7½
6/	Do. Cum. 2 Pref.	10	6
5	Do. Debs., Red.	100	106½
7	West. Union, 1 Mt. 1902($	1000	105½
6	Do. 6 p.c. Stg. Bds., Rd.	100	102½

TRAMWAYS AND OMNIBUS.

Last Div.	Name.	Paid.	Price.
1/6	Anglo-Argentine, Ltd.	5	3½
6	Do. Deb. Stk.	100	125
4/	Barcelona, Ltd.	10	11
5	Do. Deb., Red.	100	105½
7/6	Belfast Street Trams.	10	16½
—	Blackpl. & Fltwd. Tram., £10 Shs.	8	12½
10/	Bordeaux Tram. & O. Ltd.	10	11½
5	Do. Cum. Pref.	10	11
—	Brazilian Street Ry., Ltd.	2	¼
—	British Elec. Trac., Ltd.	10	15¾
—	B. Ayres & Belg. Tram., Ltd., 6 p.c. Cum. Pref.	5	—
6	Do. 1 Deb. Stk.	100	—
—	B. Ayres. Gd. Nat., Ltd., 6 p.c 1 Deb. Bds., Red.	100	59½
5½	Do. Pref. Debs., Red.	100	94½
1/	Calais, Ltd.	5	1
—	Calcutta, Ltd.	10	3½
—	Carthagena & Herr., Ltd.	10	2½
5	Do. Deb., Red.	100	90
5	City of B'ham. Trams, Ltd., 5 p.c. Cum. Pref.	5	5½
4	Do. 1 Mort. Debs., Rd.	100	105½
3/9	City of B. Ayres, Ltd.	5	6½
2/3	Do. Ext. £5 Shs.	3	3½
6	Do. Deb. Stk	100	145
1/4	Edinburgh Street Tram.	4	4
1/	Glasgow Tram. & Omni. Ltd., £9 Shs.	8	2½
3/7½	Imperial, Ltd.	6	14½
3/	Lond., Deptfd, & Greenwich, Prefd.	5	3½
nil	Do. Defd.	5	1
10½	Lond. Gen. Omni., Ltd.	100	200
4	Do. Deb., Red.	100	113

Tramways and Omnibus (*continued*):—

Last Div.	Name.	Paid.	Price.
4/9½	London Road Car	6	10½
28/6	Do. Red. 1 Mt. Deb. Stk.	100	109½
5	London St. Rly. (Prov., Ont.), Mt. Debs.	100	110
12/6	London St. Trams.	—	2
12/9	London Trams., Ltd.	10	9
6/	Do. Non-Cum. Pref.	10	10½
5	Do. Mt. Db. Stk., Rd.	100	101
5	Lynn & Boston 1 Mt. 1924 $	1000	104
5	Milwaukee Elec. Cons. Mt. $	1000	100½
5	Minneapolis St. 1 Cons. Mt $	1000	96
5	Montreal St. Dbs., 1908	100	109
4½	Do. Debs., 1922	100	107
6/	Nth. Metropolitan	—	11½
1/9½	Nth. Staffords., Ltd.	6	5
5/0	Provincial, Ltd	10	7
6/	Do. Cum. Pref.	10	14
5	St. Paul City, 1937 $	1000	96
5/	Southampton	10	6½
5/	South London	10	5½
7/6	Sunderland, Ltd.	10	6½
4½	Toronto 1 Mt., Red.	100	106
2/6	Tramways Union, Ltd.	5	6½
4½	Do. Deb., Red.	100	109
2/6	Vienna General Omnibus.	5	5½
5	Do. 5 p.c. Mt. Deb., Red.	100	103½
4/	Wolverhampton, Ltd.	10	6½

WATER WORKS.

Last Div.	Name.	Paid.	Price.
10/	Antwerp, Ltd.	20	22
6/	Cape Town District, Ltd.	5	7
10½	Chelsea	100	325
5	Do. Pref. Stk.	100	178½
4½	Do. Pref. Stk., 1875	100	158½
4½	Do. Deb. Stk.	100	160½
5/6	City St. Petersburg, Ltd.	13	11
5/	Colne Valley	10	15½
4	Do. Deb. Stock	100	137½
£4	Consol. of Rosar., Ltd., 4 p.c. 1 Deb. Stk., Red.	100	91
8	East London	100	227½
4½	Do. Deb. Stk.	100	160
3	Do. Deb. Stk., Red.	100	106
37/6	Grand Junction (Max. 10 p.c.) "A"	50	117½
18/9	Do. "B"	25	
18/9	Do. "C" (Max. 7½ p.c.)	25	54½
35/	Do. "D" (Max. 7 p.c.)	50	97½
4	Do. Deb. Stock	100	142½
13	Kent	100	360½
7	Do. New (Max. 7 p.c.)	100	215½
7/	Kimberley, Ltd.	7	4½
6	Do. Debs., Red.	100	104½
6	Do. Deb. Stk., Red	100	107½
10	Lambeth (Max. 10 p.c.)	100	297½
7½	Do. (Max. 7½ p.c.), 50 & 25	—	230½
4	Do. Deb. Stock	100	142½
3	Do. Red. Deb. Stock	100	103
10/	Montevideo, Ltd.	20	16
5	Do. 1 Deb. Stk.	100	108½
5	Do. 2 Deb. Stk.	100	103½
132/9	New River New	100	437½
4	Do. Deb. Stk.	100	144½
4	Do. Deb. Stk. "B"	100	144½
4	Portland Con. Mt. "B," 1927	—	102½
8/	Seville, Ltd.	20	12
5/6	Southend "Addl." Ord.	10	17½
6	Southwark and Vauxhall	100	157½
6	Do. "D" Shares (7½ p.c. max.)	100	154½
5	Do. Pref. Stock	100	176½
4	Do. "A" Deb. Stock	100	141½
3	Staines Resvirs. Jt. Com. Gua. Deb. Stk., Red.	100	105
8/	Tarapaca, Ltd.	10	9
10	West Middlesex	100	302½
4½	Do. Deb. Stk.	100	162½
3	Do Deb. Stk.	100	106

INDIAN AND CEYLON TEA COMPANIES.

Acres Planted.	Crop, 1897.	Paid up Capital.	Share.	Paid up.	Name.	Dividends. 1894.	1895.	1896.	Int. 1897.	Price.	Yield.	Reserve.	Balance Forward.	Working Capital.	Mortgages, Debs. or Pref. Capital not otherwise stated.
	lb.	£	£	£	**INDIAN COMPANIES.**							£	£	£	£
11,240	3,128,000	120,000	10	3	Amalgamated Estates	—	*	10	5	3¼	9	10,000	16,500	D52,950	—
		400,000	10	10	Do. Pref.	—	*	5	‡5	9¾	5½				
10,223	3,560,000	187,160	20	20	Assam	20	20	20	‡17½	60	5⅝	55,000	1,730	D11,350	—
6,150	3,278,000	142,500	10	10	Assam Frontier	3	6	6	—	7	8½	—	286	20,000	82,500
		142,500	10	10	Do. Pref.	6	6	6	‡6	11	5½				
2,087	839,000	66,745	5	5	Attaree Khat	12	12	8	3	7	6	3,790	4,820	7,770	—
1,633	583,000	78,170	10	10	Borelli	4	4	5	—	7½	6¼	—	3,256	D270	6,500 Pref.
1,720	812,000	60,825	5	5	British Indian	6	5	5	—	4	6¼	—	2,920	12,300	16,500 Pref.
3,223	2,247,000	114,500	5	5	Brahmapootra	20	18	20	‡15	13	6	—	28,440	41,600	.
3,754	1,617,000	76,500	10	10	Cachar and Dooars	*	8	7	‡7	9¾	7	—	1,645	21,240	.
		76,500	10	10	Do. Pref.	*	6	6	‡6	11½	5¼				
3,946	2,083,000	72,010	1	1	Chargola	8	7	10	2½	¾	13	3,000	3,300	—	—
		81,000	1	1	Do. Pref.	7	7	7	3½	1¼	5½				
1,971	942,000	33,000	5	5	Chubwa	10	8	10	‡8	5⅜	6⅝	10,000	2,043	D5,400	—
		33,000	5	5	Do. Pref.	7	7	7	‡7	6⅝	5¼				
30,250	11,500,000	120,000	10	3	Cons. Tea and Lands	—	*	10	5	3⅛	8	65,000	14,240	D191,674	—
		1,000,000	10	10	Do. 1st Pref.	—	*	5	‡5	10⅞	4⅝				
		400,000	10	10	Do. 2nd Pref.	—	*	7	‡7	12	5⅞				
2,230	617,000	135,420	20	20	Darjeeling	5½	5½	6	‡5	21xd	4¾	5,552	1,565	1,700	—
2,114	445,000	60,000	10	10	Darjeeling Cons.	—	*	4/2	—	6	—	—	1,820	—	—
		60,000	10	10	Do. Pref.	—	*	5	2½	9¼	5¼				
6,660	3,518,000	150,000	10	10	Dooars	12½	12½	12½	2½	17½	7¼	45,000	300	D32,000	—
		75,000	10	10	Do. Pref.	7	7	7	3½	16½	4¼				
3,367	1,811,000	165,000	10	10	Doom Dooma	11¼	10	12½	‡12½	20½xd	6¼	30,000	4,032	—	10,000
1,377	582,000	61,120	5	5	Eastern Assam	5	nil.	4	nil	2½	—	—	1,790	—	10,000
4,038	1,675,000	85,000	10	10	East India and Ceylon	4	nil.	7	—	8⅜	7⅞	—	1,710	—	—
		85,000	10	10	Do. Pref.	*	6	6	3	11	5⅜				
7,500	3,363,000	219,000	10	10	Empire of India	—	*	6/10	2½	11¼	—	15,000	—	27,000	—
		219,000	10	10	Do. Pref.	—	*	5	2½	10¾	4⅞				
1,180	540,000	94,060	10	10	Indian of Cachar	7	3½	3	‡2	3⅝	5½	6,070	—	7,180	—
3,050	824,000	83,500	5	5	Jhanzie	10	10	10	‡8	7	5½	14,500	1,070	2,700	
7,980	3,680,000	250,000	10	10	Jokai	10	10	10	5	16	6	45,000	990	D9,000	—
		100,000	10	10	Do. Pref.	*	6	6	3	14½	4¼				
5,224	1,563,000	100,000	20	20	Jorehaut	20	20	20	—	58	6⅞	36,220	2,955	3,000	—
1,547	504,000	65,660	10	8	Lebong	15	15	15	‡12½	16¼xd	6¾	9,000	2,150	8,650	—
5,082	1,709,000	100,000	10	10	Lungla	*	10	6	‡3	7	4⅛	—	1,543	D21,000	—
		100,000	10	10	Do. Pref.	*	6	6	‡6	10½	5⅝				
2,684	885,000	95,970	10	10	Majuli	7	5	5	—	6⅜	7⅞	—	2,606	560	—
1,375	380,000	91,840	1	1	Makum	—	—	2	—	1	1¾	—	—	1,200	25,000
2,990	770,000	100,000	1	1	Monbund	—	—	*	—	⅜	—	—	—	—	—
		50,000	1	1	Do. Pref.	—	—	*	2½	1	5				
1,080	482,000	79,590	10	10	Scottish Assam	7	7	7	—	10⅞	6½	6,500	800	9,590	—
4,150	1,456,000	100,000	10	10	Singlo	*	8	5	1	8	6	—	300	D5,200	—
		80,000	10	10	Do. Pref.	*	6½	6½	3¼	13	5				
					CEYLON COMPANIES.										
7,970	1,743,824§	250,000	100	100	Anglo-Ceylon, & Gen.	—	*	5½	—	55	9½	10,992	2,405	D72,844	166,300
1,836	685,741§	50,000	10	10	Associated Tea	—	*	5	2½	7⅝	6⅝	—	164	2,478	—
		60,000	10	10	Do. Pref.	—	*	6	3	10⅞	5⅝				
10,390	4,000,000	167,380	10	10	Ceylon Tea Plantations	15	15	15	‡15	25	6	84,500	1,516	D30,819	—
		81,080	10	10	Do. Pref.	7	7	7	‡7	16⅝	4⅜				
5,722	1,542,700	55,960	5	3	Ceylon & Oriental Est.	5	8	7	—	9¼	7⅞	—	230	D2,047	71,000
		46,000	5	5	Do. Pref.	6	6	6	3	4⅝	6				
2,157	801,629§	111,330	5	5	Dimbula Valley	—	*	10	5	5⅜	9	—	—	1,733	6,250
		62,607	5	5	Do. Pref.	—	*	6	3	6¼	4⅞				
11,496	3,635,000	298,250	5	5	Eastern Prod. & Est.	3	5	6½	‡7	6	5⅝	20,000	11,740	D17,797	108,900
2,193	1,050,000	22,080	10	10	New Dimbula "A"	10	16	16	4	24	7	11,000	2,024	1,130	8,400
		55,710	10	10	Do. "B"	18	16	16	4	22	7¼				
2,572	570,360§	100,000	10	10	Ouvah	6	8	6	2	8	7½	4,000	1,151	D1,255	—
2,630	964,963	200,000	10	10	Nuwara Eliya	—	*	6	‡6	10½	5⅝	—	—	—	30,000
1,720	720,200§	41,000	10	10	Scottish Ceylon	15	15	15	‡10	17xd	6	7,000	1,252	D3,970	9,000 Pref.
2,450	750,000	39,000	10	6	Standard	12½	15	15	‡15	12⅞	7	9,000	800	D14,012	4,000
		17,000	10	10	Do.	12½	15	15	‡15	22	7				

Working-Capital Column.—In working-capital column, D stands for *debit*.

* Company formed this year. † Interim dividends are given as actual distribution made. ‡ *Total* div. § Crop 1896.

NOTICES.

Baring Brothers & Co., Limited, have received a remittance of £6,968 13s. 4d., in bills on London at ninety days sight, on account of the service of the City of Buenos Ayres 4½ per cent. loan of 1888.

Messrs. Matheson & Co. are prepared to pay, on and after June 1, the prior lien bonds of the Mexican National Railroad Company drawn for payment on that date, at the rate of 4s. 1½d. per dollar, or £206 5s. per bond, provided the bonds shall have been previously left three clear days for verification.

Mr. Arthur Edward Buckler and Mr. Alfred Coote Norman, who since the death of the late Mr. F. L. Gower have been the sole representatives of the firm of Buckler, Norman, & Gower, have taken into partnership Mr. Charles Birch Crisp, and the style of the new firm will be Buckler, Norman, & Crisp.

The coupons due June 1, 1898, of the New York, Pennsylvania, and Ohio Railroad Company issue of £250,000 equipment trust bonds (1890) of £100 each will be paid, on and after June 1, at the offices of the trust. Coupons will be received between the hours of eleven and two (Saturdays excepted), and must be left three clear days for verification.

The half-yearly interest, due June 1, 1898, on the East Argentine Railway Company's £350,000 6 per cent. debentures will be paid on and after that date (less income tax), at the company's bankers, Messrs. Glyn, Mills, Currie, & Co. The transfer books will be closed from the 21st inst. to June 1, both days inclusive, for the preparation of the warrants.

Messrs. Smith, Payne, & Smiths announce that in order to prepare the dividend due July 1 on the Lincoln Corporation stock and the dividend due July 5 on the Ilkeston Corporation stock, the balances will be struck on the night of Wednesday, June 1, and that on and after Thursday, June 2, the stocks will be transferable ex dividend.

Mr. Arthur Goddard, chartered accountant, of St. George's House, Eastcheap, E.C., the liquidator of the Tigerfontein Gold Mines, Limited (in liquidation), notifies that a dividend of five shares in the Rooderand Gold Mining Company, Limited, for every six held in the Tigerfontein Company, is now deliverable at his office, any day except Saturday, between the hours of eleven and one.

The Capital and Counties Bank, Limited, has established a branch at Dover under the management of Mr. H. S. Cundell.

The coupons of the Imperial Japanese Government 5 per cent bonds, due June 1 next, will be paid by the Yokohama Specie Bank, Limited, 120, Bishopsgate-street Within, E.C.

The Rio Tinto Company notify that at the fifth half-yearly drawing of their 4 per cent. bonds, 1895, to be held on the 1st prox., bonds amounting to £28,900 will be drawn, to be paid off at par on July 1.

Messrs. N. M. Rothschild & Sons announce that the dividends due June 1 on the Brazilian 4½ per cent. loan of 1883 and the Egyptian State Domain mortgage bonds will be paid by them on and after that date (Saturdays excepted).

Messrs. Glyn, Mills, Currie, & Co. notify that they are prepared to pay, on and after June 1 next, the coupons of the Mexican external 6 per cent. loan, 1893, due on that date.

It is notified that all creditors in the matter of the Nava Gold Mines Syndicate, Limited (Paris), are to send in their claims by July 4 next to Mr. Julius H. Byrne, of Gracechurch-street, E.C., the liquidator.

The Union Bank of Australia, Limited, notifies that it is prepared to pay, on and after 1st proximo, the half-year's interest due at that date on the Palmerston North (New Zealand) 5 per cent. loan, £50,000.

It is announced that the "Société de Régie des Monopoles de Grèce" will for the future be known as the "Société de Régie des Revenus Affectés au Service de la Dette Publique Hellénique," and that the old shares will shortly be exchangeable for new, and that 12,000 additional shares will be issued.

The Baltimore and Ohio Railroad Company being still in default on the payment of the coupon due March 1 last, Baring Brothers & Co., Limited, are prepared to receive on deposit bonds of the 6 per cent. sterling loan of 1872, in order that steps may be taken for the protection of the bondholders' interests, and to issue negotiable certificates for the bonds so deposited. A copy of the agreement, together with the requisite lists to be filled up on deposit, can be obtained on application at their office.

Messrs. Glyn, Mills, Currie, & Co. have received advice by cable from the London and River Plate Bank at Montevideo announcing the despatch by mail of a remittance amounting to £5,800 for the service of the Uruguay 5 per cent. loan of 1896.

Egyptian State Domain mortgage bonds to the amount of £206,380 nominal capital have been drawn for payment at par on June 1. The drawing consists of all bonds (not previously cancelled by the operation of the sinking fund) comprised in the series of numbers advertised.

The annual general meeting of Holland & Company, Limited, was held on Wednesday, at the Deptford Distillery, S.E., under the presidency of Mr. Cyril Wanklin. The chairman: Profits for the past year, including the amount brought forward, and deducting interest paid on the debentures (£3,625) were £7,107. Of this, it was proposed to place £7,000 to the credit of the debtors' suspense account, reducing it to £5,293. A total of £31,590 had been thus placed since 1895, and the directors hoped that they might be in a position at the end of the current financial year to recommend the payment of a dividend on some portion of the company's share capital. The report and accounts were unanimously adopted. Mr. Wanklin, he retiring director, was re-elected. Subsequently certain special resolutions for deducing the capital of the company by £48,850, and for altering the relations between the preferred and ordinary shares, by converting them into stock were unanimously passed.

In the Dominion House of Commons on Tuesday, Sir Wilfrid Laurier denied the report that Government intended reviving the bonus of the Chignecto Marine Railway. The Government had been asked for compensation as an alternative to the revival of the subsidy, and they had that matter under consideration.

Printed for the Proprietor by LOVE & WYMAN, LTD., Great Queen Street, London, W.C.: and Published by CLEMENT WILSON

The Investors' Review

EDITED BY A. J. WILSON.

Vol. I.—No. 21. New Series. | FRIDAY, MAY 27, 1898. | [Registered as a Newspaper.] | Price 6d. By post, 6½d

CONTENTS

The Investors' Review.

A Falling Money Market.

Within little more than a week the price of loanable capital in the discount market has subsided fully 1 per cent. Before another week passes it may have gone down considerably further, encouraged by the reduction of the Bank rate to 3½ per cent. How has this remarkable change been brought about? By a very simple cause, a cause which illustrates the remarkable influence which operations of credit pure and simple have over the changes of all money markets and of ours in particular. The subscription of the Chinese loan, half in Germany, half here, has brought some £11,000,000 of credit and cash into the London market, most of which might have remained either abroad or unavailable at home for use in the short loan market of the City. The collection of this money caused scarcity of credit during April, and when it was paid into the Bank of England a report was circulated on such good authority that we credited it, that the Bank meant to allow commission or interest upon the money in order to prevent it from getting back into the market. The Bank has done nothing of the kind, and therefore the Japanese Government has been free to lend its large balances wherever it could place them. This has been done so freely that scarcity has given way to plethora, and discount rates had slipped back almost to 2⅛ per cent. before the Bank put its rate down yesterday. Along with the release of these large balances we have had gold flowing steadily into the country, until within the last six weeks the stock at the Bank of England has been increased by about £7,500,000. No doubt a considerable portion of this gold represents the German half of the Chinese loan, which had nearly all to be sent here in order to be paid over at the Bank of England to Japan, but our Bank rate of 4 per cent., and a market rate for a time pretty near that figure, have also been masterful agents to draw in stray amounts of gold from all parts of Europe and from South America, and the over-trading of Japan has brought large sums in gold from the Far East. At the same time the United States demand, which was feared some time ago, has completely died away and gives no indication of revival. Thus the market is being flooded with money in a manner we could scarcely have foreseen some months ago, and is relieved at the same time from fear of export demands to an extent equally impossible to foretell. It only remains haunted by one dread, and that arises from the project of the Indian Government to borrow £20,000,000 in gold for the purpose of establishing a gold standard in India. We fancy this danger also is not immediate, although it is by no means wholly averted.

How comes it that the apparently uncomfortable indebtedness of our trade position at the present time should be completely buried, as it were, beneath indications of wealth, and the unlimited command of capital, such as the recent influx of credit and gold implies? The explanation is to a large extent in the statement already made. By the Chinese loan we have obtained command of quite £5,000,000 of foreign capital, and much of that capital may remain here to be gradually disbursed by Japan in payment of war materials and ships under construction and manufacture in this country, we thus getting an accession of floating wealth which may remain with us. Such products of credit operations serve to off-set any temporary increase in our indebtedness upon the mere balance against us in our current foreign trade. Is all danger, then, of dearer money in the autumn now swept away, and can we look forward to a time of cheap money such as prevailed with very little interruption for five years till last September? We think not, for several reasons. First of all, other credit operations must come into play which will tend to withdraw money from us in the later months of the year. None of the United States or Spanish bills of costs for the war have yet been met. When they do come forward for payment, the United States at least, is certain to require bullion from Europe to a much larger extent than has yet been exhibited. Assume that this bullion is not drawn from us, or that its amount does not exceed the steady imports of the metal from the mines, and there still remains the bread bill of Europe to be paid. Should wheat continue at or near its present price this bill next autumn and winter will be far more difficult to meet than the one for the present harvest year has proved to be, and as not only we ourselves, but France, Italy, Spain, Belgium, and perhaps to some extent Austria, will have to buy wheat abroad, prudence dictates that we should look for adverse exchanges and heavy exports of gold towards the end of the year. Add to this the danger which exists for us at home from the large number of over-capitalised industrial undertakings whose weak position must soon begin to show itself, and without going further we can at once recognise the advisability of not reckoning upon a prolonged time of low rates for money in the future. It will be much more sensible to treat the present ease as to some extent an accidental thing, due to causes of temporary force, and to recognise that the permanent influences of war and dearer food and inflated credit operations on our own and other markets are working for a higher price for loanable capital at no distant date. It may be all very well to enjoy low rates for money while we have them, but it is not advisable to enter into great operations, whether on the Stock Exchange or in commerce, in the belief that credit will remain easy for many weeks in succession.

Perhaps it is just because they see such probabilities ahead that the directors of the Bank only lowered their rate yesterday by ½ per cent. from 4 per cent. to 3½. Had they had no cause to hesitate they would have done better to lower the rate at once to 3 per cent., since the ½ per cent. step leaves the Bank about as far above the open market as it was before. Accepting this as the reason for the hesitation of the Bank Court, there is no fault to be found. Should foreign exchange betray no tendency to go seriously against us during the next few weeks the rate can be further lowered without disturbing the market in any way.

Farewell Words on Mr. Gladstone.

It was inevitable, we suppose, that his body should be buried in State. Unquestionably there has been more genuine feeling behind the demand of the nation that the great statesman's remains should be thus laid to rest in mother earth than is usually found in such cases. Mr. Gladstone's death has touched most hearts, not only at home but in every civilised country, with a sense of personal loss, in its way unexampled. No more eloquent testimony could be given, not, perhaps, to the estimation in which his political career is held, but to the fascination and binding force of his lofty character and pure, simple life. The country was right to claim to do him honour in his death, and yet we have to confess to a feeling that we should have liked best to have thought of his body as resting at Hawarden among his own people, before whom he went out and in, the quiet, unassuming citizen and friend, a perfect gentleman of the olden time; and there is an unconscious lack of consideration for his own family and friends, and above all for his widow, in the delays and parade incident to a great State function, no matter how shorn of its splendour. When all is over, and the ultimate bourne attained, the cry of the bereaved is ever that of the Patriarch Abraham —"Let me bury my dead out of my sight"— and to keep the living and the dead together longer than can be helped is to inflict the most painful strain on those who mourn the most. Well may her children be anxious for their mother in the days that must intervene—much as the ceremony has been hastened —ere Mrs. Gladstone can look her last on the clay of the warrior now at rest whose life she has shared, whose wounds she has dressed and healed nigh these sixty years.

Last week we said a few words about Mr. Gladstone's influence in foreign politics, and now pause only to ask, could any possible testimony to his success in the highest field of such politics be greater than that afforded by the manner in which other nations join with us in tributes to his memory—in mourning his departure. If it be a nobler deed to unite nations in friendship than to part them in jealousy and strife, then are Mr. Gladstone's achievements to be ranked among the greatest of this or any age. To no small extent, perhaps, his personal character accounts for the accord of nations now in speaking well of his memory, but we cannot help thinking also that the long series of brilliant financial reforms, which, begun by Sir Robert Peel, were carried so far to completion by Mr. Gladstone that the path of every Chancellor of the Exchequer who followed him has been defined beforehand, give the true explanation of his power for good—his influence in promoting peace abroad in past years.

There can be no question that the liberation of our trade, a liberation effected chiefly by Mr. Gladstone's measures, opened the way for that increasing intercourse between ourselves and other nations which, leading as it does to a closer interlinking of interests, causes enmity and prejudices to disappear and friendship to take their place. Thanks to the Budgets of 1853, and 1861, '62, and '63, more than to any performances of diplomacy proper, the day approaches, we may hope, when a war between us and any civilised people will be impossible—a crime too fratricidal and ruinous to be committed on any pretext. We say this and hope this, all the fashion of the hour for playing at war and costly provisions for strife notwithstanding. They are but the fevered protests of a dying barbarity.

As M. Yves Guyot finely says in his thoughtful essay on the deceased statesman published in the *Siècle* of the 20th inst.: "Without doubt the Jingoes have reproached him, as they did Cobden and Bright, with not conducting a foreign policy of bombast. He looked a very timid and small personage when, in 1850, in answer to the clanging discourse of Palmerston, in which the famous formula of old Rome had been recalled, *Civis romanus sum*, in justification of his high-handed interference in Eastern and other foreign affairs, Mr. Gladstone pointed out that the civilisation of England was quite another thing to that of Rome. The grandeur of Rome rested on the exploitation of the conquered peoples by their conquerors; war was its only trade, whereas the glory of the Liberals of England in the present century, the immense service which they have rendered to their country and to humanity, has been to demonstrate that civilisation is the product of industrial effort, that the true expansion of a people was that of its productions, of its language, and its ideas, and not that brought about by its soldiers and generals. The policy of Gladstone," he adds, "has been a policy of affranchisement." This is true, and a grander epitaph no man need desire. We have wandered far in recent years from the aged statesman's ideals of international fellowship, but the eclipse is but transitory, and when the nation is again in its right mind they will reassert their sway.

M. Guyot's concluding paragraphs must be given entire :—

"Gladstone has been one of the grand agents of liberty under all its forms, affranchisement of peoples, freedom for the individual. He has delivered his compatriots from numerous imposts, and from more than a hundred millions of debt. He provoked the recognition of ignored rights. This is the true liberal policy. He will remain a great figure, and merit the homage of posterity, because he brought into the world a little more justice than he found there at the threshold of his career.

"Through a depraved worship of force there are men who represent Bismarck as the great statesman of the second half of the nineteenth century. Is it because he incarnates the policy of treachery, brutality, and rapine? He has organised a powerful Germany, apt at destruction, but he has likewise made a retrograde Europe, a Europe crushed beneath the weight of its armaments, shut up in gigantesque barracks, and 'corporalised' in intellect.

"If progress be in direct ratio to the power of man over things, and in inverse ratio to the coercive power of man over man, then Gladstone, from the point of view of politics, has been its grandest auxiliary. While Bismarck will be ranged among the malefactors of humanity, Gladstone will be classed among its benefactors. This is why, in spite of the faults which he has committed, he is the type of statesman whom we ought to take for our ideal."

Hooley Finance.

In the end of last week eulogies appeared in many papers of an invention for jointing tubes of all descriptions by hydraulic pressure. Duly following these puffs, a prospectus was advertised on Monday of the British Hydraulic Jointing Company, Limited. This stated that a company had been formed with a share capital of £1,200,000 in £1 shares, £800,000 of which were to be issued forthwith. Of this £800,000, only £100,000 was set aside for working capital, the balance going in payment of promoter's profits, and for the patents and provisional or other protection taken out in the United Kingdom, France, and Belgium. There are five directors of this company, all men of some position, and, we should judge, men of honour. The Earl of Crawford, who acts as chairman, is undoubtedly a man of some scientific attainments, and, as far as we have ever heard, perfectly incapable of lending himself to any transaction by which the public would run the risk of losing money. Nevertheless, in our opinion, the public will lose money if it subscribes for these shares. We have studied the prospectus carefully and cannot find in it any substantial ground for a belief that the profits from royalties upon and sales of the hydraulic machines can ever be such as to justify such a monstrous capital. From this aspect, indeed, the company is only another of Mr. E. T. Hooley's extraordinary freaks in capital inflation.

At two points we can put the statement in the prospectus to the test of fact. It is stated that the principle can be applied to anything tubular, and after mentioning a number of kinds of tubes, it goes on to mention in particular that the process is applicable to the jointing of aluminium, "which is difficult, if not impossible, to solder or braze." This statement, according to our information, is directly contrary to fact. One eminent firm engaged in the manufacture of aluminium utensils has succeeded in perfecting a solder which holds, and is so strong that, as those who know the metal can suppose, it is easier to break the thing soldered anywhere else than at the joint. Again, further down the prospectus we are told that the process permits of the easy construction of a cycle frame made of thin tubes of aluminium, as no solder or brazing is required, and this will allow of a combination of great strength with extreme lightness. Here also is a statement which we do not consider in accordance with fact. Aluminium by itself is much too soft a metal, and too deficient in toughness, to be suitable for the thin tubes of a cycle frame. Unless strengthened by some alloy, such tubes would collapse with very slight weight or concussion. Now, if such statements as these are unjustifiable in light of actual experience and facts, may we not fairly conclude that many of the others are exaggerated, and that the extraordinary saving of labour claimed for the new invention exists mainly in the imagination of the sanguine promoters. Grant that it does all that it claims for aluminium, is it not already superseded as an invention of utility in relation thereto by the "weldless" frame? All that has appeared about this invention has, we think, come under our eye, and we have never been able to discover in any statement a convincing proof of the extreme utility of the new process. Welding by pressure is not a new thing by any means. Admit, however, that it is all that is claimed for it, and is it possible to imagine such an invention to be worth £800,000? Indeed, Mr. Hooley seems to buy the patents for that sum and sells them for £1,025,000. It is a monstrous price, totally unjustified by anything put forward in favour of the process, and we should imagine sensible people will keep their money in their pockets.

Mr. Hooley has never been a favourite with the investing public in London. He is looked upon in the City as a phenomenon, not as a man of practical sense and business; and his methods of floating companies have never commended themselves to the minds of prudent people. Not so long ago he introduced with the usual flourish of puffery—including, by the way, an article in the *Illustrated London News*, which was printed as an editorial that we were beguiled into reading with a puzzled mind until the key to it was revealed to us at the close—a wonderful improvement on the Jacquard loom. This was such a complete failure that we believe the money subscribed had to be refunded. Recently in Dublin and in London two trials have taken place which should throw a good deal of light on the harum-scarum, slap-bang, bounce-the-market system of finance, so-called, pursued by this enterprising citizen of Nottingham. The trial in Dublin was that of an action brought by the Components Tube Company, Limited, against a shareholder to recover unpaid calls. The verdict was for the defendant, but we believe a new trial has been applied for, and therefore it is not competent for us here to say whether this verdict was just or not. It is, however, permissible to allude to the evidence given. This went to show that the entire promotion of this company was merely a share-rigging affair, and there was a mysterious deposit of £10,000 which was difficult to trace. Whether it was paid or not even the judge, after the trial had ended, did not seem to be sure, and he lamented in his summing up the absence of Mr. Hooley as a witness. "Several points in doubt," said Mr. Justice Gibson, "in the case would have been made clear if Mr. Hooley's evidence could have made it clear by his contradiction. Unfortunately, however, we are afraid, whether from press of business or otherwise, in a case which affected his commercial honour and standing he did not come into the witness box." It would seem that Mr. Hooley is not popular in Dublin, for in his evidence at the still more recent trial held in London, he roundly stated, in answer to Sir Edward Clarke, that he did not care to go to Ireland. "Why," asked Sir Edward, "did you abandon your action against the Grappler Company and pay costs?". "First," answered Mr. Hooley, "because I knew that the company was in such a position that I could not get anything, and, secondly, because I was advised by many people that it would not be wise for me to go to Dublin, and I never shall go unless they fetch me." We quite believe in Mr. Hooley's reluctance to go to Ireland: the Irish have an awkward way of expressing their feelings. In 1896 the humble editor of this Review was told that it might not be safe for him to appear in that capacity on the Dublin Stock Exchange. This was only a joke, of course, but if he might judge by the hot letters he then received denouncing him for warning the public to have nothing to do with the Dunlop Tyre Company, and other cycle company promotions, the unmeasured wrath which must have accumulated now against Mr. Hooley in the Emerald Isle is too formidable to be encountered by an Englishman possessed of respect for his own skin. It would have been better, by the way, if the Irishmen had listened to us instead of Mr. Hooley and his Press in 1896. Thousands of people who are to-day ruined might have been in comfortable circumstances had they taken our disinterested counsel. This, however, is by the way.

Let us look for a moment at the other action just alluded to, which ended abortively last Thursday week in a disagreement of the jury. This was an action brought by a Belfast merchant, named Reid, against Mr. Ernest Terah Hooley and Mr. Martin D. Rucker, charging them with fraud in connection with the Grappler Pneumatic Tyre Company. It seems that this company had originally a small capital of £75,000, upon which no dividend was ever paid. It was an unsuccessful company, in short, and on April 9, 1896, its shares were quoted between 1s. 9d. and 4s. So helpless was it that its end could not, in ordinary course, have been far off at that date, if left to its own devices. Just then, Mr. Hooley and Mr. Rucker appeared on the scene, and, helped by a Mr. Bulger, a Dublin stockbroker—who has resigned his position as deputy chairman of the Dublin Stock Exchange in consequence of the Dublin trial held early in the present month—they entered into negotiations for the purchase of the Grappler Company, offering £4 per share for shares of which it is admitted that the would-be purchasers had picked up large numbers on the market at 2s. each. Before the negotiations came to this point rumour was busy through the Press, and the price of the shares began to creep up. Then the offer in due course became public and the shares flew up. People from all quarters rushed in to buy, feeling sure that they had a good thing, and that they would at least get back £4 per share, according to the offer of the two eminent English provincial financiers. The bargain was never completed. Messrs. Hooley and Rucker preferred to sacrifice a deposit of £25,000 rather than complete it, and Mr. Reid boldly asserts that there was never any intention of completing it, that the whole thing was a mere trick in order to enable the smart Englishmen to unload at fancy prices thousands of shares which they had picked up for next to nothing. As the jury could not agree, we may take it that Mr. Reid did not prove his case. The very fact, however, that opinion was so divided amongst the jurymen as to prevent their agreement should be accepted as a warning by prudent people to give all Hooley promotions a wide berth. Every one of them has been vitiated by the mistake of excessive capitalisation. It has never appeared to us that Mr. Hooley paid the slightest attention to the intrinsic value of any business or patent, or amalgamation of businesses and patents, he undertook to vend. No pretence has ever been made by him of doing this. His one object has been to put as high a capital value upon the thing he wished to sell as he conceived it possible by all manner of blandishments to get the public to subscribe. This may be "smartness" above board, but none the less is it smartness of a very unprofitable description, and the latest instance before us, in this Hydraulic Company's prospectus, of Mr. Hooley's ambitious versatility does nothing whatever to inspire us with deeper confidence in his judgment than we had before.

The Rand Mines, Limited, and its Group.—II.

An error was made in the table at the end of the article on this subject in last week's number: we gave the "shares issued" of eight Rand Mines' creations, and the number of them held by the parent; the balance of them we treated as held "by the public." This is a misleading phrase and unpardonable on our part, seeing that on February 18 we published a table which demonstrated that "the public" had mighty little to do with some at least of these companies. For example, Glen Deep shares are nearly all held by the Rand Mines, Limited, the Goldfields Deep, Limited, and the Consolidated Goldfields of South Africa, Limited. At least they were so held till quite recently, and the Rand Mines, Limited, has increased its holding during the past year. It follows that the market quotation for Glen Deep shares must be purely fictitious. This is also the case with Rose Deep and with Jumpers Deep, although not quite to the same extent, and it is on the whole gratifying to find that the promoter companies seem to have made little progress in unloading their shares on the public last year. At least, we infer this to be the case from the fact that in several instances the Rand Mines, Limited, has had to buy in shares in order to sustain the market price.

Before proceeding to complete what we have to say about the Rand Mines Company itself, let us complete the observations begun last week relative to the extravagant expenditure of its children. We do not merely mean extravagance in advertising, but at all points. What, may we ask, has been done to prevent waste and to check the prices paid for the appliances necessary and for the equipment of the mines? Mr. Eckstein claimed that the management had been thrifty. Has it? We should like to have independent testimony on this point. Last week we noticed in passing a very heavy sum charged against machinery in the case of the Geldenhuis Deep, and the same characteristic is observable throughout the whole of the accounts presented. Thus machinery and plant in the Glen Deep have cost already £55,000, although not even sixty stamps as a beginning have yet been erected. In the Rose Deep, which is at work with 100 stamps, the cost of machinery and plant has been £209,600. In the Jumpers Deep, which was not then working, there are apparently 100 stamps laid down then of 200 projected and for which we have given the company credit in our estimates. Here the machinery and plant have cost £142,000. The 100 stamps of the Nourse Deep are not yet all erected, although the machinery is on the ground, and the same item in this company's accounts stands at over £116,000. In the Crown Deep, whose full equipment was also to be 200 stamps—and all of this has been apparently erected, although all of it cannot be worked—machinery and plant figure for £296,976. The same item in the Langlaagte Deep, whose reports do not indicate that any stamps are yet erected, stands at £59,692, although the general manager in this instance states that it has been deemed advisable to enter into negotiations for the lease of a neighbouring mill with a view to commencing crushing operations at an early date. And in the Durban Roodepoort Deep, where all the 100 stamps are certainly not erected—it being stated that on commencing operations it may be found that it will be impossible to successfully run more than forty stamps during the first few months owing to the difficulties of obtaining a proper supply of natives—the machinery and plant stand at £126,336. These various amounts tot up to a total of £934,797, and we should like to know not only who controls this expenditure, but why the amount of it varies so much in different concerns for apparently the same article. Is the whole of this machinery provided by Messrs. Wernher, Beit, & Co., acting as agents for the companies in the same way as North & Jewell acted for the North group of nitrate companies? Do they pocket handsome commissions upon the orders? If not, how is the business managed? Shareholders in this country assuredly have not the shade of a shadow of real control over any one of these properties, in the shape of directorate, management, expenditure, or anything else.

Mr. Eckstein boasted at the meeting that an immense amount of information was given about South African mines, more than about any other similar undertakings in the world, and, in some respects, his boast was justified. Still, there is a great deal of information which ought to be useful for shareholders to know that is never even hinted at, and we class all the facts about the management of the mines in this category. Essentially, in everything that relates to the business of sinking shafts, putting up machinery, buying stores, selling products, regulating native labour, and so on, these mines are all as much private property as if no single share had ever been sold to the public. It may be all right, of course, and the management may be thrifty and careful, but it may just as well be the reverse, and we think shareholders here, if they are seriously bent upon making incomes out of their investments, ought to do something towards obtaining information upon this most essential side of their business. They will be active in forming committees when too late. Why cannot they act now? Perhaps because for some of these properties, as we have just demonstrated, there are almost no independent shareholders.

A word finally in regard to the accounts of the Rand Mines, Limited, itself. They show a profit last year of £351,364, making the total profits earned to date

£1,694,737. The whole of these profits have, quite rightly, gone into the business as we may say, the money being used to develop the subsidiary companies, and it has nearly all been profit made on transactions in shares. Out of the last year's income, only £55,443 came from dividends earned; the rest was profit on shares sold, the company having parted with some 70,000 shares in five of its companies during the year, replacing them by additional shares in the Glen Deep, Rose Deep, and Geldenhuis Deep. It both bought and sold in the shares of these two latter companies, so that the profit in their case came from stockjobbing pure and simple, not from mere "investment" as Mr. Eckstein would have us believe. The controllers, no doubt, sold when the shares were high, and bought back when they were low. Needless to say, profit of this description is extremely precarious, and cannot be trusted to continue. Meantime the British public may just as well note that the Rand Mines, Limited, owns nearly 2,500,000 shares in twelve different companies, the whole of which it will doubtless be one of these days quite pleased to put on the market at a handsome profit, notwithstanding the assurances so often given that it is an investment and not a speculative company. A sensible man will not be ready to give it the opportunity to sell. Suppose, though, that the whole of these shares could ultimately be realised at £10 each: that would give Rand Mines shareholders back £25,000,000, and at 30 the market capitalisation of the issued shares is under £10,000,000. Is there not great scope here, then, for an increase in the price of these shares? Possibly, but meantime most of the shares held by the company are unsaleable in quantity on the market at any price.

And there is another way of looking at the subject. Accept as true the declaration that the Rand Mines is an investment company, and how much revenue will it require in the shape of dividends on its present holdings to give 5 per cent. to its own shareholders on the capital now issued at £30 per £1 share? Just about £550,000, including the interest on its 5 per cent. debentures, and without making any allowance whatever for depreciation. Now, we proved last week that it will take over three-quarters of a million to provide 5 per cent. on the quoted price of the shares of the eight companies whose reports are appended to those of the Rand Mines, Limited. But this parent holds over 58 per cent. of the entire issued capital of these companies, and cannot hope—as we made clear to all who care to look at facts without prejudice—to draw in anything like £550,000, still less £650,000, which it would require to be in a strong position. Its possible revenue from these companies cannot be expected, within the next five years, if ever, to reach £350,000 per annum. What else, then, has the company to fall back upon? Well, it holds 9,771 £1 shares in the Simmer & Jack West property, 40,330 £4 shares in the Wolhuter Gold Mines, 215,500 £1 shares in the South Rand Company, and 199,763 £1 shares in the Paarl Central Company. Will these give it a quarter of a million a year in revenue as an "investment" company? We doubt it exceedingly, but have not the data by us to form a judgment upon. We do, however, know that there is no market for any of these shares, except the Wolhuter. The Paarl Central Company has never yet done any good, and its shares now stand at a discount of 50 per cent. Simmer and Jack West shares are not in the "active list" at all, nor yet South Rand shares. We can find no quotation for them. In these circumstances, it will be prudent not to count much on revenue from such quarters, and if this source is left out of account what justification do plain facts give to the current quotation for Rand Mines shares? To our thinking, absolutely none. It would not surprise us at all were the company soon to be in want of more money, for nearly a million is, by its own board's estimate, still required to bring its properties into productive condition, including the Rand Exploration Syndicate's wants—a concern whose capital has not yet been issued. Perhaps "reserve shares" will provide this money. If not, the Rand Mines, Limited, must find it, and how is it to do that if the market will not let it unload some of its present holdings? Its one chance of escape seems to be in a "bear" account, and we trust no one will be so mad after reading what we have said as to sell a "bear" of shares in any of these companies. That would be to commit financial suicide. Leave the Rand Mines, Limited, alone for the present with its investments.

Electric Light Companies and Local Authorities.

Slowly has come to the front a very awkward dispute between local authorities and electric lighting corporations. For a number of years, indeed until the last three, the operation of supplying electric energy was considered a highly speculative undertaking, and although a number of companies were formed between 1887 and 1892, only one local body in London—the St. Pancras Vestry—was bold enough to start supplying the energy prior to 1895. In fact, the local authorities of London, although the Electric Lighting Acts gave them full powers in the matter, shrank from the task, and in the absence of action on their part a number of companies were formed to supply energy in the most promising districts of the Metropolis. Before these companies obtained power to operate, their applications had to go before Parliamentary Committees at which the local bodies interested were represented by counsel, who on behalf of their clients caused to be inserted in the orders regulating the working of the companies many onerous conditions, with the view that if a local authority should wish to buy the undertaking at the end of the forty-two years' lease, it might be able to get it cheap and in full working order. They also obtained full protection for the public in regard to the price to be charged for energy and against the danger of a company growing into a monopoly. In this respect they were doing their duty, and although their action in forcing the companies to make heavy provisions for depreciation led to several of them going without dividends for some years, the policy thus pursued has in the end made the electric lighting companies of London much more solid concerns than joint stock undertakings of recent growth usually are. At the same time it should be admitted that the local authorities and the community at large have benefited by the prosperity of the electric lighting companies, inasmuch as the price of energy in every case, save that of the City of London Company, has been reduced materially below the statutory prices allowed to be charged by the companies, although these cannot generally be said to have yet obtained a fair return on the money invested. Taking the leading London companies we find that the average dividend upon their shares since their date of formation has been as follows :—

	First Capital Issue.	Average Dividend over Period. Per Cent.	Last Dividend. Per Cent.
Charing Cross and Strand	1892	5·33	7
Chelsea	1888	2·85	6
City of London	1891	3·64	10
House to House........................	1888	·40	4
London Electric Supply	1887	nil	nil
Kensington and Knightsbridge......	1888	3·80	10
Metropolitan	1887	2·14	6
Notting Hill	1890	1·62	6
St. James's and Pall Mall	1888	6·40*	14½
Westminster	1889	5·22*	12

* In addition dividends paid to founders.

That the new business was not unattended by risk is evident from the poor results obtained by the London Electric Supply, the House to House, and the Notting Hill Companies; and although the St. James's and Pall Mall and Westminster may be cited as instances of prosperity, it ought to be remembered that they have built up their business in face of competition, and that their charges are much below the statutory limits. The local authorities, by assenting to the granting of powers to the various companies, must be considered to have tacitly agreed to the supply of energy being placed in these companies' hands, and in view of the fact that they did not dare to take the responsibility of carrying out the work themselves, they ought to give those who did dare a fair chance. They are not doing so.

Since the electric lighting companies have proved to possess a prosperous industry, that is, within the last two or three years, there has grown up a strong movement amongst the London vestries to take up the work of electric lighting on their own account. They see St. Pancras gaining fair profits from the business, and even some of the other vestries which started later in the day making some profit on it; and accordingly they apparently do not see why they should not plunge in and secure some of the pickings. In this respect they are particularly favoured by having full liberty of action, for the first clause of the Electric Lighting Act of 1888, which amended the first Act of 1882, runs as follows :—

Notwithstanding anything in the Electric Lighting Act, 1882, no provisional order authorising the supply of electricity by any undertakers within the district of any local authority shall be granted by the Board of Trade, except with the consent of such local authority, unless the Board of Trade in any case in which the consent of such local authority is refused are of opinion that, having regard to all the circumstances of the case, such consent ought to be dispensed with, and in such case they shall make a special report, stating the grounds upon which they have dispensed with such consent. The grant of authority to any undertakers to supply electricity within any area, whether granted by licence or by means of a provisional order, shall not in any way hinder or restrict the granting of a licence or provisional order to the local authority, or to any other company or person within the same area.

Fortified behind this clause the vestries of London have stirred in the matter, and after gaining several advantages in minor districts, notably in Newington, the gauntlet has been thrown down to all the electric lighting companies by the Marylebone Vestry applying for powers to set up an electric lighting station in its own parish. For years this parish has been supplied by the Metropolitan Electric Lighting Company, and although that company has not reduced its charge for energy so quickly as others, it is charging well below the statutory price, and its dividends have throughout been moderate.

Now that it has been satisfactorily proved that the supply of electric energy is a paying business, it stands to reason that the local authority can afford to produce the light at a cheaper rate than a company. In the first place it can borrow money under 3 per cent., and then it has no shareholders for whom to earn profits. Standing charges, such as offices, supervision, collection of accounts, &c., are, in a great measure, provided by the existing staff of the vestry, and should adversity fall upon the undertaking there is always the rates to fall back upon. Against these advantages the only off-set is the proviso that capital must be repaid; but we believe this clause has been utilised by vestries in order to reduce depreciation charges, so that it is not really a drawback. Whatever the intention of the framers of the 1888 Act of Parliament might be, to foster competition in such an unfair manner as is now proposed against the pioneers of the industry, looks inequitable at least. In fact, the Board of Trade in a letter dated May 18, 1889, written by Mr. Calcraft to Lord Rosebery, as Chairman of the London County Council—a letter which laid down the principle of granting orders—put great stress on the fact that permission for one company to enter into another's district was only granted upon special conditions, such as a difference in the form of current supplied or the necessity of obtaining access beyond. This policy, however, appears to have now been abandoned, and the Board of Trade has recently granted powers in cases that virtually admit the principle of free competition at all points.

The electric lighting companies are preparing to oppose the application of the Marylebone Vestry when the matter is brought before Parliament, but unfortunately there is an awkward lack of agreement amongst themselves. First of all, we have one company—the County of London and Brush—acting the part of bold buccaneer, and endeavouring to edge its way into every district in which it can obtain a foothold. Then, to make matters worse, we have a group of gentlemen connected with some of the older electric lighting companies—the Westminster and St. James's and Pall Mall—asking Parliament to consent to a scheme for a Central London Supply Company, with a huge station outside London to bring up current at a very high tension, to supply distributing companies or vestries. Such an undertaking would allow a vestry to light its district without the initial expense of building a station. All that would be needed would be to lay mains and arrange for a supply of energy from the Central Electric Supply Company.

In this chaotic condition, which threatens competition all round, there is danger that the capital invested by the pioneers in this great industry will be imperilled, and we think every one who is at all interested in a fair recognition of enterprise and successful organisation ought to support a movement for the settlement of the respective rights upon a satisfactory basis. Parliament ought to appoint a Joint Committee to consider the whole conditions which have arisen since 1888, the date of the last Act, and take such steps as will give investors some certainty as to what they have to expect in subscribing money towards electric lighting enterprises. By preventing the companies from obtaining a freehold right Parliament certainly acted for the public benefit, but if private capital is now to be wasted by the oppressive action of local bodies, the mainspring of enterprise will be taken away, to the great injury of future progress. For the local authority is usually great at garnering the fruits of other men's labours, but it is particularly weak in initiative. On the other hand, to permit free and open competition in such a matter is an impossibility, as the inconvenience to the public is too great. This was found to be the case in regard to gas years ago, and although the districting of London that took place in regard to those companies cannot be considered to have been wisely conducted, it is upon some such principle that Parliament should act in regard to electric lighting. The local authority ought to be put into its proper place as residuary legatee in every case where private enterprise has first supplied the district with energy, whilst competition betwixt company and company ought to be considered sufficient for the interests of the public. Besides, should there be any oppressive action on the part of the electric lighting companies, the local authority has power to appeal to the Board of Trade and enforce a reduction in the price of energy. In regard to this matter the intention of the Board of Trade was to eventually bring in a sliding scale upon the same principle as in use for gas companies, and Mr. Calcraft, in his letter to Lord Rosebery, stated that considering "the electric companies only have a certain tenure of forty-two years, the Board of Trade are of opinion that a price arranged on the basis of a 10 per cent. dividend would not be unreasonable." But how in the world will it be possible for the companies to earn a 10 per cent. dividend, if the local authority, with all its powers of cheapening cost, is to be allowed to enter into competition against them?

West Australian Market Trust Conjurors.

We have never beheld the burlesque of serious finance carried to such an extreme height as it is in this instance. The success with which Mr. Bottomley and his friends continue the play is, perhaps, due to the small amount of interest the public has in the various "companies" paraded before them; but even so one wonders sometimes when the curtain is to ring down on the final scene. In a general way, people know that this Market Trust arose in some mysterious fashion out of the Joint Stock Institute, and that it engaged recently in the strenuous occupation of keeping up the price of the shares of the Northern Territories Gold Mining Company, Limited, at and above £4. When the artificial market in these shares collapsed the Trust immediately found itself very hard up indeed, for after all one cannot keep even burlesque finance a-whirligigging on nothing. For a short space of time things looked very black, but the Bottomley group was equal to the occasion, and "reconstruction" of the Trust was resolved upon at an enthusiastic meeting of Bottomley's henchmen. Unless our memory is at fault, the understanding was, as expressed at that meeting, to liquidate the old Trust, and form a new one, the new one to possess the same amount of nominal capital as the old, but with 15s. or 16s. only paid per £1 share. A committee, therefore, was appointed to report on the condition of the Trust before finally carrying out this arrangement, and the combined effort of this wonderful body is before us.

Usually, when a company gets into difficulties and requires its affairs to be looked into, shareholders are treated to some details about the possessions of the embarrassed concern, and almost invariably have a balance-sheet put before them showing more or less the assets and liabilities to be dealt with. But our "Trust" committee does not condescend to this kind of thing at all. It takes the high-handed way and delivers judgment like a Delphic oracle. It seems there are "assets and liabilities," but the shareholders are told nothing about them, except that Mr. Wreford and his staff "certified" to their existence. What the assets are, how the losses which have brought down the Trust have arisen, what will be done with the money to be called up on the new shares—all these things are wrapped in their original mystery, and the committee merely condescends to state that it has arrived at the conclusion that the present position has been brought about by "causes of an exceptional character," and then proceeds to laud the zeal and wonderful abilities of the chairman, Mr. Horatio Bottomley, who valiantly "supported" the market until the Trust went down beneath his feet. Furthermore, the committee proceeds to say that it has been agreeably surprised at the present position of the company's assets, and signifies its emphatic opinion that the holding of the Trust in Northern Territories' shares is a most important possession. By "personal inquiry and independent expert advice" it comes to the conclusion that the properties owned by this Northern Territories Company, "judged by results already obtained and present developments," are of great value. You ask for facts in support of this: there are none forthcoming. How many stamps are at work, how many men digging out the ore, what money has been spent on developments, what returns has come from gold won? All these things are in the same original darkness shrouding everything about this amazing group of companies.

There is a practical aim, however, behind all this nice language, and that is not only to put the Trust in the position to command 5s. per share in new capital, or say £125,000, but also to put a new creation of preference shares, not, we believe, mentioned previous to the issue of this report, in front of the assessed ordinary shares, to their damnification. What is to be done with the money obtained from these preference shares? There is no information. How many preference shares are to be issued? The report does not say. Will Mr. Bottomley, or his nominees, or the Trust's preferential creditors, if any, receive these shares? Ask the man in the moon—he may know. Is Mr. Bottomley really going to take ordinary shares for the £150,000 stated to have been advanced by him to help the Trust "through the Joint Stock Institute," which we never knew before to be so rich? Perhaps, but we can only guess: there is no definite information. We are merely informed, with an admirable gravity, that he has agreed to accept repayment of this sum entirely in "fully-paid ordinary shares of the new company, taking them at their full face value." But how could some part of the ordinary shares be issued with liability and some not? Will they be ordinary shares with a preferential right to certain dividends, or what? Still we cannot say. It is all as creepy as Mr. Maskelyne's cabinet of mystery. Assuming the public to be uninterested, this is really one of the most comic exhibitions of how to play the great financier with wind instruments we have seen for many a day. Indeed, the only serious thing about it, to our minds, is the fact that two members of the Stock Exchange have signed the report. They surely can hardly expect that the public is going to come in and find the money to pay their losses on data such as we have indicated. If they do, poor fellows, they deserve our most sincere commiseration, and we hereby tender it to them. As for the others, oh, but they are a merry band of most excellent players!

Economic and Financial Notes and Correspondence.

THE WISDOM OF LORD WINDSOR.

This nobleman has very original geographical ideas, but they are highly suitable for the policy of Mr. Rhodes. At a luncheon held in Westminster Palace on Tuesday last his Lordship held forth thus :—

> As to the proposed extension of the great railway from Bulawayo to Lake Tanganyika, he reminded them that Mr. Rhodes had made an application, not for an advance of public money from England, but only for a guarantee. Mr. Rhodes had suggested that the railway should be made in sections, and only the part that was constructed should be guaranteed by the English Government. Whether Mr. Rhodes was correct or not in his figures was a matter with which they had no concern; they had only to think of the advantages that were to be gained by the price that was to be paid by England for giving this guarantee. The price surely was a great railway through the backbone of Africa, and ultimately and inevitably to reach Khartoum and the Nile valley (cheers). This important railway, with all its advantages, was comparable only to the position which Russia now held in Siberia and in Northern Asia in consequence of the great trunk railway which they had created from China to Port Arthur (cheers). This was surely a policy the value of which the English Government must recognise. He felt confident that the scheme would have the countenance and support which it deserved from her Majesty's Government; and they looked with the utmost interest to the decisions which would be come to by them.

There was much more of the same sort with which we need not trouble the reader. According to this sample, we can only suppose that Lord Windsor imagines Africa to be bounded on the one side by a frozen ocean, and to be occupied on the other by a number of great States hostile to the domination of Great Britain. This is highly interesting, and accounts for the zeal shown by the privileged classes in supporting Mr. Rhodes's sublimely ridiculous project for a railway along the mid-rib or backbone of the African continent. And really the reasons set forth in support of the first little bit of guarantee asked for this railway are in admirable keeping with the whole spirit of those who are seeking to load us taxpayers with the cost of the project. These guarantees, indeed, open an endless vista of similar demands on our purses in the not distant future. In the last report of the Chartered Company, figures were given to prove how exceedingly profitable the already existing bit of this railway had proved to be in the few months of its existence, but the directors forgot to state that this profit arose from exceptional traffic which had been long accumulating, and a very different story will doubtless be told after a year or two, unless successive doses of fresh capital can be secured to keep the trains running.

AND THE POSSIBLE DEVELOPMENTS THEREOF.

We can imagine something of this sort coming before us, and being advocated in Parliament and on the platform by the ever-zealous Secretary of State for the Colonies, whose son is deputy chairman of the Bank of Africa, and therefore interested in the development of one at least of our amazing empires there: guarantees, for a loan to import elephants so as to obtain ivory, to be exported on the mid-rib African railway, the native supply being exhausted; for a loan to enable chiefs and kings of black tribes, scattered throughout the territory served by this railway, to pay their fares to visit each other in order to swear blood-brotherhood in the interests of peace; for a loan to provide capital to "natives" so that they may buy clothes, in furtherance of decency after the English model, which clothes would be imported from Cape Town or Port Elizabeth by this railway; for a "temporary advance" to pay for poles and fresh wiring for Mr. Rhodes's "Cape Town to Cairo" telegraph, the old poles having been eaten by the white ants and the wire stolen for ornaments by the unlettered savages; for a loan to provide funds to enable congratulatory messages at so much per word to be sent between Cape Town and Cairo, and for other purposes, in order to enable the telegraph company to show a "net" revenue; for a loan to pay for imported black labour from the Sandwich Islands or other places where such can be found, the native supply having "given out" through exhaustion or emigration into the territories in Africa occupied by Germany, Portugal, France, or Belgium; for a loan to enable settlers to buy new cattle—which would be, like the new blacks, imported at profitable rates over the railway—to replace their old stock, all eaten up or worked out; for a loan to subsidise a company to be formed to exploit the glaciers of Ruenzori and Mount Kenya, in order that the ice might be sent by the railway to Cape Town for export to England, so that we might always have plenty of pure ice for our "Schweppes"; for money to be expended on "barrages," so that all rivers, especially those in the Nile watershed, might be dammed up at convenient places to establish a storage of water, rendered necessary by the depletion of the aforesaid glaciers; for a loan to enable banks to pay dividends on their capital, all locked up in unrealisable securities, such as advances to mines without ore, to farmers without crops, to graziers minus cattle; and, finally, for a loan to provide the means whereby mine companies might buy ore abroad to be brought over the railway, and crushed at mills unable to obtain any ore on the spot worth crushing. These are but a few of the demands we may expect to see sprung upon us as time goes on, in consequence of the zeal Rhodesians exhibit in the development of their African dominion, present and prospective, with money drawn from our pockets.

AS SEEN WITHOUT LORD WINDSOR'S GLASSES.

The *St. James's Gazette* said the other day that the Bechuanaland Railway guarantee had been arranged. This may be premature news, but we have no doubt it is news which will come true. Were it of any use, we might ask Parliament and Ministers to pause before committing the country to such an unwarranted obligation, at least until the utility of the Uganda Railway now building, and which will cost us probably quite £5,000,000, has been proved by experience. It is of no use. If you speak to a Member of Parliament on the subject, and he is frank, he will tell you "We cannot help ourselves: the whole thing is pushed on by the Prince of Wales, and we have got to vote the money." This answer has been given to us, and whether it embodies a slander against the heir to the throne or not, it carries sufficient weight with Members of Parliament to silence them. "They have not the manhood"—to use the phrase of Mr. Gladstone's quoted by Lord Rosebery in his beautiful speech in the House of Lords last Friday—to stand up in their place and say: "This thing is wrong, and must not be." Many fear loss of Court favours—titles, dinner invitations, presentations to Royalty, and so on. Others merely shirk their duty from moral cowardice, and, between them all, this vote will go through, helping to keep a gigantic imposture on its legs a little longer for the fuller rifling of the simple investor's pockets. Of such stuff are your chosen-by-ballot law-makers made, good electors. The day was when Englishmen had souls they called their own—backbone, and moral courage. Has that day gone for ever? Is the company-promoting share-trafficker henceforth to be our lord and master, making even kings and princes bow to his commands?

THE FRENCH ELECTIONS.

It does not seem to us that the new Chamber of Deputies in France just completed by the second ballots of last Sunday promises well for the stability of M. Méline's ministry. Taking the official enumeration, there are only 254 Republican deputies in a Chamber of 581. Adding the Rallied members, who have forsaken their old allegiance to other parties, to the deputies officially classed Republican proper, the majority for the Government in the Chamber is only two. It therefore follows that in order to retain power M. Méline must lean on one or other of the groups with whom the balance of power rests. Should he lean to the Radicals and follow their programme, then he might command 358 votes out of the total 581. A smaller majority would be given to him by the Radical Socialists, and if he inclined to the Socialists pure and simple he might still maintain his place. Should he decide either to do this or to go over to the Reactionaries, it is probable that a large number of his nominal Republican supporters would forsake him. Whatever side he leans towards, power can only be retained by him on a compromise which will make one or other of the smaller factions in the Chamber master of the situation. His position is in most respects similar to that of the Conservative Party with us, only that he has a greater choice of allies than its leaders have, seeing that there are no less than seven groups, or sects, of politicians in the new Chamber, including ten anti-Semites. The Radicals proper have lost twenty-four of their number in the fight, but still form a party of 104; the Reactionaries have also lost, and are now forty-four against fifty-three, but the Radical Socialists, Socialists, and "Rallied" have all increased their voting power, and are reinforced by ten nondescripts classed as Nationalists or anti-Semites. Enumeration of this kind leads us to fear that the new Chamber will be more of a bear garden than the last one, and we fear the Republican Party, ill-assorted at best, will have the greatest difficulty to maintain its position at the head of the government of the country. To some extent it deserves its fate and to be harassed by its factional enemies, for it has displayed a lack of principle and of moral courage quite lamentable to behold. We are sorry, however, for France, which appears to have stormy times ahead, and assuredly cannot count on a season of calm and enlightened progress.

IMMIGRATION OF ALIENS.

Although Lord Hardwicke's Bill for regulating the immigration of aliens was carried on second reading in the House of Lords by a majority of sixty-two, it is not likely that the measure will figure among the Bills passed into law this session. Of course, it is highly desirable to prevent foreign idiots, as well as foreign paupers, from settling down in our midst; but we doubt if this could be accomplished merely by the appointment of a number of Board of Trade inspectors for the detection of insanity or extreme poverty among foreign visitors arriving on our shores. It would involve a considerable immediate expense and a constant future outlay. We doubt if the results would be commensurate with the cost. Alien immigration is not all bad. We do not know that the proportion of idiots or lunatics among them is large. Lord Hardwicke did not attempt to enlighteen us upon the question. But it was shown during the debate in the Lords that the aliens who have fallen to London's share in this immigration have practically set up a new British industry which is worth several millions a year. This is the trade in ready-made clothing, which is largely exported to the United States, among other countries, and the export of which gives employment to an appreciable proportion of British shipping. We do not know that there is any serious outcry against these aliens among our native working population. This is a form of protection that they do not seem to desire.

Yet we are glad to observe the anxiety shown by Lord Salisbury on behalf of the English ratepayer, whose helplessness in protecting himself from heavy fiscal burdens is quite as conspicuous and pathetic as his Lordship described it. But we could have wished that Lord Salisbury's anxiety had been awakened earlier, and to more practical purpose. Had he, for example, reminded Mr. Chaplin of the pathetic figure of the English ratepayer, when that right hon. gentleman was dragooning the House of Commons into conferring an endowment of about two millions a year on English landlords, the Premier would have been conferring a signal service on the pathetically helpless ratepayer who now excites his compassion. And he might still do an equally great service to the Irish ratepayer, who is asked to buy a no doubt excellent measure of local self-government at a capital outlay of £10,000,000, or a yearly cost of £400,000. If Lord Salisbury would but induce his friends the Irish landlords to forego this nice little bit of blackmail, the pathetically helpless Irish ratepayer would no doubt bless him for a great financial relief. A British Prime Minister has endless ways of assisting the pathetically helpless ratepayer. Suppose he were to try to save this "pathetic figure" from one heavy portion of his burden by reducing our naval expenditure by a paltry million or two per annum, or by insisting on making the army really efficient by strong administrative reforms in place of piling up million upon million of extra expenditure without consideration of the wasteful extravagance of thoughtless, if not incompetent officials? These are only a few of the ways in which an anxious Premier might assist the pathetically helpless English ratepayer, any one of which would be infinitely more helpful to him than this shrimp of an Aliens Bill which he has not asked for, and that may probably add to his fiscal burdens rather than reduce them.

A LESSON FROM THE TIRAH CAMPAIGN.

Last week's *India* contains a striking article of Colonel H. B. Hanna's, formerly of the Punjab Frontier Force, and late commanding at Delhi, on this subject. Colonel Hanna is well known as a strenuous opponent of the present Northern Frontier policy of the military party now dominant in India, not only on strategic, but on economic grounds; and in this article he proves to demonstration that there is no danger whatever of an invasion of India by Russia from that quarter of Asia under modern conditions. Assuming that the Russians intend to employ their Transcaspian railway for the purpose of conveying troops and supplies to the frontier of India, so as to invade our dominion there, he points out that the task would really be beyond the capacity of the railway, and of any conceivable railway service Russia could provide. He takes the experience of the Tirah campaign in proof, and his deductions from the incidents of this compaign are so striking that we take the liberty of quoting them pretty well in full, and beg intelligent citizens at home, who have the interests of the Empire seriously at heart, to ponder his words.

Sir William Lockhart's 25,000 men never got further than fifty miles from their rail-head; yet, though they marched in lightest order, and were not encumbered with heavy cannon and pontoons, 75,000 mules and ponies were not too many for their needs in an eight weeks' campaign. Now, Kabul is 170 miles from the Indian frontier, Kandahar 400 from the Indus; so that, if the Russians elect to invade India by the former city, and we assume them to number 150,000 and to take two months to get through the Khyber, they will require 450,000, or, if they prefer to tempt fate by the Bolan, 900,000 mules to bring them within sight of their objective; and however great may be the difference between these numbers and those that would have been needed by the invaders had they begun their march at the Caspian—from the point of view of the safety of India, I think I am entitled to claim that it need not be taken into account.

But, apart from its incapacity to carry the transport of a large army, or to exercise any appreciable influence on its amount, the Transcaspian railway can never materially affect the problem of the defence of India; for when, at enormous expense, it has been extended to Cabul, it will be but single-lined; liable, at many points, to be buried under sand-drifts or snow, and at many others to be swept away by floods; everywhere exposed to attack from Persia and the tribes, requiring, therefore, to be guarded from end to end—a task which, in time of war, would absorb the services of many thousand troops; a railway which must bring not only much of its water but all its fuel from the Caspian; on which it would be impossible to run a dozen trains in each direction per diem; to which if an army once entrusted its fortunes, there could be no alternative means of advance, and along whose entire course destruction must be the fate of forces depending on it for progress, reinforcement, and supply when the inevitable breakdown occurred—inevitable, because no railway, let alone one worked under such an accumulation of adverse circumstances, could bear the strain to which this line would be subjected when the great host which is to wrest India from the British crown is, at last, set in motion.

It may be said that Russia, who has taken 200 years to get half way to India, may be trusted not to endanger her ultimate success by premature action; and that, continuing her slow forward movement, she will so consolidate her power at every stage of her journey, and so multiply her bases of supply, that at the end she will find herself with a large force ready to her hand, and will have nothing to do but to step across the frontier, defeat the Anglo-Indian army, and enter into the enjoyment of all its resources—railways, arsenals, food magazines, &c.—and so escape the transport difficulty altogether. No doubt, if she indulges in the dream of adding India to her empire, these must be her plans; but unless she can convert Transcaspia and Afghanistan into fruitful lands, and—what would be almost as great a miracle—so win the attachment of their peoples as to be able to dispense with troops on her long line of communications (Skobeleff reckoned them at 90,000)—she will find it more difficult and costly to move large forces gradually up to the confines of India than to hold the intermediate territory with the smallest garrison compatible with its own safety, and to do the whole work of marching or railing a big army from the Caspian to the Indus in one, or, at most, two seasons. Geographically, the Indian Government is in a far better position than Russia for extending its authority to Afghanistan; yet it has twice made the attempt and twice relinquished it; not because it could not march its troops to Kandahar and Kabul, but because it could not support them in those cities when it got them there; and though a completed Caspian railway would make it easier for Russia to convey stores of all kinds into Afghanistan, these, so far as they consisted of food and forage, would be consumed by the large garrison she would be compelled to maintain in that country almost as fast as they arrived. And if it would be difficult to accumulate beforehand in Afghanistan any large quantities of grain and bhoosa, and to keep them in good condition for an indefinite number of years, it would be quite impossible to do this, and at the same time to feed, in addition to its garrison, a second and much larger force whilst waiting for a favourable opportunity of attacking India; so that, railway or no railway, the invaders, the invaders' transport, and a large proportion of the invaders' stores, would always have to be drawn at the last possible moment from beyond the Caspian.

But if these things are as I say—and I defy any man to show how they could be different—the conditions of the defence of India have not changed since the days of Lord Lawrence; and there never was, and never can be, any excuse for reversing that statesman's wise, humane, and economical policy.

President Kruger and his German Friends.

Another plain hint seems to have been given to President Kruger that Germany has changed her mind in regard to the Transvaal. The *Journal des Debats* a few days ago published an article rather sharply criticising the President's conduct in regard to reform. The object seemed to be to warn French financiers against listening to the overtures of the Transvaal Plenipotentiary Extraordinary, Dr. Leyds, should he, on his approaching visit to Europe, try to negotiate a new loan. The significant thing, however, is that this article has been reproduced in the semi-official *Norddeutsche Zeitung*. It is significant because the semi-official journal would not have published the article in question had it not received permission from the "powers that be," and these powers would not have accorded their permission had they not practically accepted the views enunciated in the article. This is one of the conveniences of semi-official journalism. It is the straw which shows how the wind blows. The *Kölnische Zeitung* indicated some months ago that the official weathercock had turned towards the north-east; this new publication indicates that the wind is settled in that somewhat nipping direction. It will be well perhaps for Mr. Kruger to seriously ponder the matter. If, as he said at the swearing-in ceremony, his Government is at peace with all nations, it might be well for him to rest content with that happy state of affairs, and not to risk rebuffs by straining the goodwill of his German friends. Domestic matters are more important to him just now than foreign relations. He has, as we have pointed out, made very substantial concessions to the mining industry; perhaps he may yet see his way to make more. But it is possible Dr. Leyds might be found more useful at home than abroad. Economy of administration may be made to serve the purpose of a foreign loan. If "German allies" are cooling, it may be judicious to cultivate the peaceful graces among the neighbours at home. As to the question of suzerainty, which bulks so largely in President Kruger's last despatch to Mr. Chamberlain, it is rather an airy question at best. If he strictly adheres to the Convention, it is rather a straining of words to boggle about suzerainty. Lord Derby never expressed a very clear notion as to its practical application.

City of London Real Property.

This peculiarly constituted affair did remarkably well last year, and, as our company reports show, both the original and new undertakings increased their dividends by 1 per cent. to the highest figures known in their history. Furthermore, both made substantial additions to their reserves out of revenue, with the consequence that the original undertaking shows a reserve of £105,893 and a sinking fund of £30,531, and the new undertaking a reserve of £113,093 and a sinking fund of £22,305. Now the whole of these accumulations are invested in the business, for after the dividends are paid, little more than a working balance in cash is left on the asset side besides the buildings that constitute the *corpus* of the undertakings. Would it not, however, be a wise policy to invest a portion of the reserves (the sinking funds might well be employed in acquiring fresh properties) in securities outside house property? The companies have done very well, and no doubt they earn a better return upon the reserve by using it in the business; but its character as a reserve is somewhat impaired by this policy. A reserve is assumed to be a fund upon which directors can draw should any unforeseen contingency arise. By using it in the business the risks that apply to that business are attached to the reserve, and thus an event that might lead to a diminution in revenue might also impair the value of the reserve. There is a striking instance of this in the case of the Scottish Australian Investment Company, which a few years back claimed a reserve of £185,000. This, however, was wholly in the business, and so, when revenue fell off owing to the drought in Australia, the board found its reserve also impaired, with the result that dividends have had to be reduced more seriously than would probably have been the case if the reserve had been invested in securities.

Will there be Mediation?

The special correspondent of the *Daily News* at Madrid, who speaks with confidence as one who has some authority for his statement, assures us that there is a "possibility of peace at no distant date." The responsible statesmen of Spain, he adds, are prepared to seize the first opportunity for ending the war, provided it be done on terms honourable to Spain. What the conditions of peace should be it is not for the Spanish Government to say yet; but apparently we may infer that Spanish statesmen have considered possible conditions, and will be prepared to disclose them when negotiations are opened. The thing is to procure a mediator. Would any of the European Powers undertake the responsibility? If there be a Power ready to take up the arduous task, if America agrees and Spain is really willing, then there is no reason why the effort should not be made. But we doubt the possibility of success, at least at present. Responsible Spanish statesmen are probably not only willing but anxious for peace, and they would have avoided war altogether if they could. But the question is not so much with Spanish statesmen as with the Spanish crowd. Are they ready or willing for the acceptance of mediation? We very much doubt it. The results of the war, so far, have been too indecisive; and with the Spanish populace ready to make a hero of Admiral Cervera because of his cleverness in dodging the American fleets, they are not likely to be satisfied with a peace which leaves them with a feeling of defeat, yet not complete enough to crush them. The Spanish statesman who at present proposed peace negotiations would, we fear, have but a short lease of power. He would lay himself open to the attacks alike of Republicans and Carlists. General Weyler, also, might probably, in his own interests, stir up the discontent that is but partially hidden just now in Spain. A proposition of peace would probably only prove the immediate forerunner of revolution. Nor is it at all certain that the United States would welcome a proposal for mediation by a neutral Power. Their fighting forces are being daily strengthened, and it would require very favourable conditions indeed to induce them to sheath the sword, which they may feel to have been only half drawn.

JAMAICA'S OUTLOOK NOT SO BAD.

The retiring Governor of Jamaica's report on the island comes as something like a revelation after all the lugubrious representations we have had as to its rapid descent on the road to ruin—unless helped by State doles. Sir Henry A. Blake takes a general survey of Jamaica since he went there, nine years ago; and the general conclusion he draws is that though capitalists may have suffered, the people as a whole are better off than they were. Even the sugar industry he does not consider to have suffered so much as might have been expected. The quantity exported has diminished, but the hardship is not so much in this decrease as in the fall of price. From an average of 12s. to 13s. per cwt. the rate fell gradually to 9s. 3d. per cwt. in 1895. Rum has also declined, but then the colony is not now so dependent on sugar and rum as it used to be, the percentage of these exports to the total trade having declined during the last three years, while that of fruit and other products has materially increased. The loss to capitalists, to which Governor Blake refers, has probably fallen upon those sugar growers who had not the forethought or energy to face the altered circumstances of the sugar markets. In Dominica, another of our West Indian possessions, the planters were more prompt and resourceful; sugar growing has there been gradually supplanted by the cultivation of limes and cocoa. A good deal of attention is now being given also to coffee-planting, and it seems not improbable that tea-growing will likewise be introduced. Thus, while Dominica suffered little from the sugar failure, and has been going forward in a fairly prosperous condition, Jamaica, or rather the sugar-growers there, deficient in initiative and ingenuity, have been losing because they went on in the old groove, and idly cried to the Imperial Government to make good the losses mainly caused by their own want of foresight. There has undoubtedly been a state of depression, to some extent attributable to the terrible drought of about a year ago; but there are many signs of a revival, which might perhaps have been hastened by a little more mental alertness and vigour on the part of the losing capitalists. Jamaica is evidently not so bad as it has been described, and if it will but follow the example of Dominica and others of its neighbours, it may enjoy substantial prosperity.

MINES AS INVESTMENTS.

The subjoined letter is to the point and true, but written somewhat under a mistake so far as we are concerned. We do not seek to demonstrate the value of Rand shares as investments, but to try to find out what they would be worth to the buyer who really regards them as such :—

To the Editor.

SIR,—With all deference to your authority as a reviewer of investment securities, I venture to think your article on the investment value of shares in the Rand Mines, Limited, labours a point which, in spite of anything the chairman says or may hereafter say, does not really exist. No investor could be satisfied with a problematical £1 a share dividend on a share standing at about £30, as foreshadowed by the chairman of the Rand Mines. In an experience of investments extending over the past twenty-five years, I can safely say the prominent mining shares which may be fairly classed as investment securities may be counted on one's fingers. The Mount Morgan mine, the Mysore, Coromandel, Durban-Roodepoort, Waihi, and a few others are bought and sold on their intrinsic merits, but nearly all the other mines currently quoted, including sound properties like Rio Tinto, Mount Lyell, Lake view Consols, Great Boulders, and the best class of South African mines, are chiefly held as speculative investments to be sold again at a profit. Under these circumstances, any calculation as to their investment value, pure and simple, conveys little or nothing to the speculative buyer of shares who is merely interested by market conditions. Intelligent reasoning is neither required nor looked for. Most people infinitely prefer to buy their own experience, and a very costly process they almost invariably find it.—Yours, &c., BROKER.

UNFORTUNATE AUSTRIA.

Is Austria breaking up? The question may seem premature; but undoubtedly events are tending in that direction, and must have serious consequences unless some check is given to the extravagant hatred and miserable fanaticism of the warring races whose sectional differences make union impossible. Nothing is capable of binding them. The influence of the Emperor seems waning; at least he finds it impossible now to smooth over difficulties as he once could. The warring sectaries will listen to no one. They are as venomous and narrow as the fanatical Dervishes of the Soudan. They would rather break up the Empire than look at a compromise on the language question. And the mischief they are doing is not confined to internal broils. It would seem as if Germany were beginning to take sides with the Germans in Austria. At any rate, the relations of the monarchy with Germany, though not perhaps yet to be described as strained, are giving rise to considerable anxiety. We can hardly believe that they will reach the breaking point; but all this internal haggling and quarrelling must ultimately have the effect of greatly weakening Austria's position, perhaps of shaking the basis of the Triple Alliance, already greatly crippled by the weakness and instability of Italy.

But the Triple Alliance is, at present, a minor consideration with Austria. Her danger is in herself: she is bleeding from internal injuries. The language difficulty made the discussion of the Hungarian *Ausgleich* impossible, and the postponement of this discussion seems to have developed a certain dangerous antagonism between the two halves of the monarchy. The estrangement is daily increasing. Hungary dislikes the proposed increase of the navy, she is suspicious of Austria's suggested changes in the direction of a Customs' frontier, and some of her most notable statesmen have been hinting that the unsettled relations between Austria and Hungary might oblige the latter to exercise her constitutional right of regulating her Customs and commercial affairs independently. Only on Tuesday last Baron Banffy, the Hungarian Premier, announced in the Reichstag that it would be impossible, in the present state of affairs in Austria, to discuss the treaty with Hungary before September. This delay bodes no good for either half of the monarchy. Hungary seems drifting apart. The Austrian Reichsrath, which reassembles in a few days, if it devotes itself, as is fully expected, to wrangling over the rival claims of the German and Czech languages to official superiority, is not likely to do anything to stop the widening breach between Austria and Hungary. Yet, of course, the end of such a process can only be the break up of the Empire.

Even prominent commercial men seem to be losing faith in the permanence of the common Customs system of the two countries, while admitting that the severance of existing commercial relations would have the most serious consequences for both. The Austrian commercial outlook is not more hopeful than the political. Count Goluchowsky, the Minister of Foreign Affairs, recently spoke handsomely of the necessity of encouraging the trade and commerce of Austria; but what has he done to enforce his words? Practically nothing, except to insist on the increase of the Austrian navy, which can hardly be regarded as a relief for commerce. It rather adds to existing burdens. The proposed modifications of the Customs union with Hungary could do little for commerce, though much in estranging the two countries. Austrian exports are steadily declining. If Government wish to encourage trade, they had better save the proposed outlay on the navy, and apply the money to the construction of canals say, while devoting their legislative energies to relieving commerce of the antediluvian obstacles which a crusty, rusty bureaucratism delights in keeping in its path. We cannot, however, hope for much unless Austrian merchants and traders take the matter into their own hands, and act with vigour. Evidently, they need expect little from Government or legislature.

Two Lockett-Harvey Companies.

As could only be expected, the Primitiva and San Donato Companies had a miserable showing for last year—both companies confessing to an actual loss on working, so that no dividend was possible. It is amazing, however, to find that with such a state of affairs the directors neglect to inform shareholders of any of the details of working. The profit and loss account of the Primitiva Company, for instance, is as follows :

	£	s.	d.		£	s.	d.
To Interest	36	19	2	By Transfer Fees	5	10	0
To Loss for twelve months ending December 31 ...	8,182	17	6	By net loss for the twelve months ending December 31...........	8,214	6	8
	£8,219	16	8		£8,219	16	8

This tells the suffering shareholder a great deal about how his money has been lost, does it not? Did the directors take their fees? Were those "agency" expenses as large as usual? Questions of this kind at once spring to the mind when the result is set forth, but the report is as silent as the Sphinx on all things. So we think the more.

The War and Trade in America.

Thus far the war has certainly not been ruinous to trade in America. It has been increasing, not diminishing. There was hesitation for a time, some check on industry through dubiety as to what might or might not happen, and a slight feeling of something like panic from fear as to the possibilities of risk from the plunge into the unknown depths of war. But doubt and dread have vanished, and trade goes on increasing steadily. Actual business through clearing houses for the month of April is 26·3 per cent. above last year. Railway earnings for April have been 15·9 per cent. higher than during the same period last year. Some cotton mills have been closed, but that is more owing to over-production than lack of demand. The wool sales have been much below those of last year at the same time, but prices are more firm, and the demand is increasing. The output of pig iron shows no great change; but there is a confident expectation of expansion in business. Prices are firm. Of course Government orders are heavy, but it is not these that keep the industrial situation healthy and vigorous. High prices for wheat have greatly increased the demand for agricultural implements, as well as for locomotives and cars; and many other demands contribute to the general expansion of trade. It would be a mistake, however, to deduce from this that war, under modern conditions, will, on the average, interfere but little with trade and industry. The present war has so far been exceptional. Spain has not been able to maintain even a strong defensive attitude. She has been incapable of making an attack on American ports or American shipping. She may yet be able to do some damage in these directions; but until she does American trade will flourish. It would probably have been very different had a stronger and richer Power been pitted against the United States. Then the dismal prophecies which the course of present events have thus far falsified would probably have been verified, and adventurous speculators might have profited largely, where now they lose heavily, to the advantage of trade and industry.

Germany's Naval Requirements.

One sort of expenditure leads to another. Germany has finally arranged for the indefinite expansion of her fleet. Now she insists on acquiring coaling stations. Prince Henry's voyage to China has shown how thoroughly dependent she is on foreign coaling stations. The semi-official *Post* tells us that the acquisition of Kiao-Chau was a step which will soon have to be followed by other measures for procuring supplies of coal for the German Navy and for the mercantile marine. When coaling stations are discovered and secured then they must be fortified, and there must be a sufficient naval force to protect them. A pretty and far-reaching vista of constantly increasing expenditure is here suggested! But where are the coaling stations to be got, and how are they to be secured? By war? It will not be always possible to lease them as Kiao-Chau has been leased from China. So the cost will go on indefinitely increasing. If Germany insists upon having coaling stations of her "very own," there is, of course, nothing more to be said. She will go on picking them up as she can get them. But if she is not bent on exclusive possession of such stations, why may she not remain content with the coaling stations possessed by Great Britain? Prince Henry was none the worse of obtaining his fuel at English stations. Suppose, then, that an understanding was arrived at with England on the subject? It would be useful for Germany; it would do no harm to England; and it might strengthen the chances of future peace.

The Lungla Tea Company.

We wonder what shareholders of the old Lungla and Shumshernugger Companies now think of the monstrosity that swallowed up those modest little concerns. In the July 1895 number of this Review we protested against the formation of the company upon the lines then proposed, and since then we have strongly condemned the financial policy of the board. By a "juggle" unworthy of the merest trickster a dividend of 10 per cent. was declared in the first report; this was followed by 6 per cent. in the second, and only 3 per cent. in the third, the one just issued. Meantime the worst principles of finance are being followed by the board. Not only are the whole of the extensions being carried out upon borrowed money, and so placed to capital, but the very cost of maintaining those extensions is also put to capital. Consequently, the company owed last December in loans and advances from agents, &c., no less than £60,000, against about £11,000 of liquid assets. No wonder the board proposes to increase the company's borrowing powers, and we should imagine that its present policy must lead to these being added to until the ordinary shareholders no longer possess a substantial interest in the concern. It is a shocking case of mismanagement, and the sooner the shareholders get rid of the present board the better it will be for their chance of saving some shred of their property. Even preliminary expenses still appear in the balance-sheet for £5,166, while the cash in hand was only £199.

Critical Index to New Investments.

CITY OF CAPE TOWN LOAN.

Standard Bank of South Africa receives tenders on May 31, the minimum being 99 per cent., for an issue of £100,000 3½ per cent. debentures. Interest March and September; principal repayable at par March 31, 1948. Borrowing powers upon security of city rates amount to £1,177,604, of which £688,950 has already been issued, and the present is a portion of unissued balance. Money is being used in completion of works, including drainage and sewerage works, water storage, &c. Population of city 64,000, and of suburbs 51,000; property liable to rates £5,690,280; assets of city £1,325,388; no other liabilities beyond loans already stated. Revenue for 1897 was £146,580, expenditure £141,307. Full half-year's interest payable September 30. The security is excellent, and the loan will be well competed for, though the return is less than has hitherto been obtainable on the issues of the city.

CHANCE & HUNT, LIMITED.

This company is formed to acquire the businesses of the Oldbury Alkali Company, Limited, and of Messrs. W. Hunt & Sons, chemical manufacturers. Both concerns have been in existence over fifty years. Share capital is £280,000, in £10 shares, in equal moities of ordinary and 5 per cent. cumulative preference, all of which are held by vendors. Lloyds Bank invites subscriptions for £120,000 4 per cent. first debentures at 102 per cent. They are redeemable after 1918 at 102, or before then at 105 on six months' notice. The purchase price of the businesses is £420,000, while the plant and machinery are valued at only £314,753. The debentures appear a fairly good investment, though we should have thought more of the company if a few figures had been published about past profits.

KALANTAROFF (BAKU) OIL COMPANY, LIMITED.

Capital £50,000 in £1 shares, of which 30,000 are allotted to vendor, 15,000 offered for subscription at par, and balance held in reserve. Property has an area of about four acres, lies in centre of a famous oil-field, and the first productive oil strata is expected to be reached in three months' time. Even if it is, only three-fourths of the output will belong to the company, as the remaining fourth has to be paid to the lessor as a royalty. Lease is for twelve years from June, 1897. How is it that English capital is being constantly sought to develop Russian oil-fields? There must surely be something against them which does not come to light.

BRITISH DYEWOOD AND CHEMICAL COMPANY, LIMITED.

Four old-established firms carrying on business, chiefly in Glasgow, as importers of dyewood and tanning materials and general drysalters are to be amalgamated. They are described as the leading firms in the trade, and their amalgamation is expected to reduce competition and allow of economies being effected. Capital £570,000 in £10 shares, 22,000 being ordinary and 35,000 5 per cent. cumulative preference. Purchase price £570,000, including all the ordinary shares and £350,000 in cash. It therefore comes down to the fact that the company wants to borrow £350,000 at 5 per cent. This would require £17,500 a year for interest, and although no detailed statement of profits is given, the accountants certify that for nearly six years past they averaged £45,182, and the lowest year exceeded £34,000, so that the preference shares should prove a fair investment.

NEWFOUNDLAND IRON ORE COMPANY, LIMITED.

The company is formed to acquire from H. Spencer & Co., Limited, Workington, an under-lease for ninety-nine years of fourteen claims situate in Conception Bay, Newfoundland. The vendor company asks the modest price of £20,000, including £8,000 in cash, for the under-lease, and there is a royalty to be paid of 8d. per ton. A favourable report from an engineer is supplied, and Mr. Joseph Ellis and Mr. J. S. Randles, who visited Newfoundland last year, are thoroughly satisfied with the genuineness of the reports of the wealth of iron ore in the district. These two gentlemen, however, are directors of the vendor company, and it seems strange, if the property is so rich, that the vendor company should not wish to retain the profits. The capital, too, looks ponderous, £150,000 in £1 shares, of which 75,000 shares are now issued.

H. WILLIAMSON, LIMITED.

The business is that of watch and clock manufacturers, jewellers, &c., carried on at Farringdon-road, London, and at Holyhead-road, Coventry. It was established thirty years ago, and in 1892 was converted into a private limited liability company. Profits for past three years are certified at £17,685, £22,442, and £25,242, but the prospectus says the system of making loans to customers has proved very remunerative, and has secured a large increase in the returns. Assets are valued at £280,000, but this includes book debts, £61,890; loans to customers, £38,733; and goodwill, machinery, plant, patent rights, and trade marks, £110,025. The vendors ask £280,000 for the business, of which they will take £180,000 in cash. Capital, £400,000 in £5 shares, half ordinary, and half 5 per cent. cumulative preference. 15,000 shares of each class offered for subscription. Profits show a good margin after paying preference dividend, but the "loans to customers" business seems to involve some risk, and the book debts are heavy, being £15,000 more than the stock-in-trade. The absence of a separate statement as to how much is allowed for goodwill, rights, and marks, suggests the idea that investors are paying a high price for them. No need to hurry to invest here, we imagine.

J. TYLOR & SONS, LIMITED.

Out of a share capital of £200,000, in £10 shares, equally divided into ordinary and 5 per cent. cumulative preference, 6,700 of the latter are offered for subscription. Company is formed to buy the business of T. Tylor & Sons, Limited, established over a century, and carried on at Newgate-street, King's Cross, and Sydney, New South Wales, as hydraulic and sanitary engineers, and brass and iron founders. Profits for last seven years averaged £12,771, and for last year were £13,830. Debentures are being paid off by the old company, and as interest on present issue of preference shares will need only £5,000 there should be a margin large enough to constitute these shares a good investment.

ANGLO-NORWEGIAN KIESELGUHR COMPANY, LIMITED.

Here is an opportunity to take an interest in something quite out of the ordinary, the object of the company being to buy 100 lakes and waterfalls in South Norway which are known to contain deposits of infusorial earth, otherwise known as kieselguhr, or fossil meal, which when dry forms a powder used in the manufacture of nitro-glycerine explosives and in many other ways. The company will also have transferred to it the benefit of options to buy 250 more lakes. The capital is £100,000 in £1 shares, 70,000 being now issued, of which 25,000 are taken by the vendor with £10,000 in cash. We should hardly think this enterprise will appeal to the ordinary investor; it had better be left to those who know something about the powder, which is apparently not at all a new thing, as it is believed to have been used by the Greeks and Romans. We are not impressed.

BRITISH ALUMINIUM COMPANY, LIMITED.

The share capital, all issued, is £300,000, and the directors now offer an issue of £100,000 5 per cent. debentures at par. They are repayable at par January 1, 1900, or can be redeemed on one month's notice at 105, interest being due May and November. Assets of the company are valued at £625,752, but as the debentures are only a floating charge on them, subject to certain mortgages on the freehold portion of the property amounting to £37,400, and to two series of debentures amounting to £100,000, they are far from first-class. Is it not the case that this company is under bond to buy 2,000 tons of aluminium every year from its American competitors to keep them out of our market; and if so, how can it possess a monopoly of the British supply through its patents? We should like to hear what the trade says on this point, and what is thought of the company's own make of aluminium.

AUSTRALIAN HARDWOODS (JARRAH), LIMITED.

This is another Western Australian wood company, the capital of which is put at the substantial figure of £250,000 in £1 shares, three-fifths being 6 per cent. cumulative preference, and the balance ordinary shares. Present issue is 100,000 preference shares. Company acquires Government licences to fell and remove timber over 47,680 acres of the Jarrah forest on the Darling Range in the Murray district, at a rent of £1,505 per annum. An annual net profit of £30,000 is spoken of, and the marketable timber on the estate is valued at £2,200,000, the rising crop of young trees not being taken into consideration. Yet the vendors are content to accept £150,000 for the licences. In comparing this with existing Jarrah companies, it must be borne in mind that this is only leasehold property.

SEPTIMUS PARSONAGE & COMPANY, LIMITED.

The directors offer 31,436 preference shares of £1 each, entitled to a 6 per cent. cumulative dividend, at 1s. per share premium, and 34,297 ordinary shares of £1 each at 2s. 6d. premium, being the balance of the share capital held in reserve. This is an amalgamation of various businesses which took place in 1896, the trade being wholesale wine and spirit merchants. Profits for 1894 were £11,199; for 1895, £12,501; for 1896, £13,964; and for 1897, £14,840. In spite of this, we have not a favourable opinion of the concern.

GIBBS, MEW, & COMPANY, LIMITED.

Company takes over the Anchor Brewery with another brewery business close by conducted under the style of Herbert Mew & Co. Share capital £50,000; 4½ per cent. debenture stock; £50,000 of the latter. £30,000 is offered at par. Assets valued at £57,000; no statement of profits. Stock offers no attraction to investors.

NATIONAL RELIANCE INSURANCE COMPANY, LIMITED.

This is described as a new independent fire office and the capital is £500,000 in £5 shares, of which 500 are to be issued to the founder, James Hewitt, an insurance broker. The other 99,500 shares, on which it is not anticipated more than £1 per share will be called up, are offered for subscription at 5s. premium. The board is but middling, and we regret to say that we do not think there is any opening at present for a new fire office.

BRITISH HYDRAULIC JOINTING COMPANY, LIMITED.

The company is formed to buy from the Hydraulic Joint Syndicate an invention and patent rights relating to improvements in tubular joints and frame joints, the jointing of tubular frames, and of wheel hubs granted to the inventor, Charles Thomas Crowden, of Beeston, Notts., and other subsidiary patents subsequently acquired by the syndicate. By the invention, it is claimed that articles of tubular construction which have to be made in large quantities can be jointed without screwing, soldering, brazing, or heating. The directors do not form what we should by any means call a business board, and no detailed forecast of profits is ventured upon. The capital is put at the substantial figure of £1,200,000 in £1 shares, of which 800,000 are issued. Contracts show that as far back as April, 1897, there was one made between the syndicate and Johnson & Phillips, engineers, of Charlton, Kent, whereby the latter were entitled to an exclusive license to manufacture machinery under the process; then there was one in February, and another in May, 1898, between Johnson & Phillips and E. T. Hooley, whereby the license was bought by E. T. Hooley for £75,000; another, dated May 16, 1898, between the Hydraulic Joint Syndicate and E. T. Hooley, for the sale of the patents for £800,000 in cash and shares, and another on the following day between Hooley and the present company for re-sale of the patents for £1,025,000 in cash and shares. We are not told that of the capital of £400,000 of the syndicate £10 was all that was paid up, or what Hooley made by selling the syndicate shares at a premium during the closing months of last year and in the early part of this year. Neither do we see what Hooley paid for the patent rights—was it £20,000? Assuming that the patents are perfect, we certainly do not see how shareholders are going to get back their money.

Company Reports and Balance-Sheets.

*** *The Editor will be much obliged to the Secretaries of Joint Stock Companies if they would kindly forward copies of Reports and Balance-Sheets direct to the Office of* THE INVESTORS' REVIEW, *Norfolk House, Norfolk-street, W.C., so as to insure prompt notice in these columns.*

CITY OF LONDON REAL PROPERTY COMPANY.—This dual concern fared better than ever last year. The original properties earned a revenue of £51,754, and after interest on debt, administrative charges, £3,194 for sinking fund, and £2,730 for interest on reserve had been met, the balance was £24,862, to which £5,597 brought forward had to be added. A total dividend of 8 per cent. for the year was declared, or 1 per cent. higher than that for 1896, £5,070 was further added to reserve, and £5,769 was left to be carried forward. The reserve fund will then amouut to £105,893, the sinking fund to £30,531, and the fire insurance fund to £1,066, or about 13½ per ceut. of the capital employed. The new properties showed a total revenue of £64,173, and after deduction of interest on debt, administrative charges, £2,775 for sinking, and £2,790 for interest on reserve fund, the net balance is £38,000, to which £8,749 brought forward has to be added. A total dividend of 9 per cent. is declared, or 1 per cent. more than last year, £10,210 is further added to reserve, and £9,540 is left to be carried forward. The reserve will then stand at £113,093, the sinking fund at £22,305, and fire insurance reserve at £1,343, or in all about 13½ per cent. of the capital employed.

PRIMITIVA NITRATE COMPANY.—This unhappy concern was rather more unhappy last year than usual. The oficina was worked during nine months, but owing to the extremely low prices that ruled for nitrate the loss on working amounted to £8,214. No items of the working expenses are given in the profit and loss account, and we certainly think a clear statement in regard to this matter ought to be issued. Shareholders ought to be in a position to know how their money has been spent, and these "North" companies have not been well managed in the past. As a credit balance of £3,540 was brought in, the year closed with a loss since the reconstruction of the company of £4,674. Unless an improvement sets in the company may easily see further difficulties, as it owes £27,253 on bills payable and to sundry creditors. We know, on the other hand, it has stocks of nitrate and iodine, and consignments of nitrate, but these have not always proved the tower of strength that nitrate companies would have us believe.

SAN DONATO NITRATE COMPANY.—This Lockett-Harvey company did badly last year, the loss on working being £2,960, after allowing £1,798 for depreciation. The oficina did not operate during the year, having completed its quota under the combination in 1896, and could not therefore resume work until April, 1897, at which time prices had declined so much that it was decided to wait for an improvement before restarting work. On the break up of the combination in October prices still further declined, and the works have consequently remained closed. A balance of £10,120 was brought in, so that after deduction of the loss of £2,960, there is a balance of £7,160 to carry forward. This, however, is almost entirely locked up in the stocks of nitrate and iodine, which, we believe, do not improve by keeping, and are valued at cost. To restart, therefore, we are afraid will be a matter of difficulty.

WARNER ESTATE, LIMITED.—The process of acquiring further properties, and increasing the scope of this company renders impossible any adequate idea of its revenue-bearing capacity. During the past year 207 more houses were purchased, and a considerable amount in preference shares was issued, so that neither the full revenue nor the full interest charges are shown in the present report. As it is, the gross rental was £27,026, and after deduction of charges the net balance was £12,417, to which £741 was added by the amount brought in. Of the total, £5,027 was required for preference interest, £2,245 was put to reserve, and the remainder permitted of dividends amounting to 6 per cent. upon the ordinary shares. The reserve also benefited by £9,255 in premiums received upon the preference shares, and its total now amounts to £21,000. There is only £10,400 of mortgage and loans, so that the preference shares are well secured.

KING'S NORTON METAL COMPANY.—An excellent showing is made for the year ended March 31. The profit in that time came to £30,468, as against £22,577 in the preceding year, and of the total £5,000 is set aside to form a dividend equalisation reserve and £9,906 to the general reserve. The balance permits of a dividend of 10 per cent. per annum and a bonus of 5 per cent, or 15 per cent. in all, upon the ordinary shares, and the carrying forward of £1,603. The two reserve funds will then amount to £21,000, or quite 11 per cent. of the capital employed. Premiums amounting to £9,000 received from an issue of preference shares, together with £2,463 for depreciation, have been written off capital expenditure, so that although a large sum had been spent on this account in the year, the item stands lower than it did a year ago. The new money from the preference shares has enabled the £19,000 of debenture debt to be extinguished. Trading balances, as may be imagined, are much in favour of the company, being about £32,000 to its advantage after the dividend is paid. It would be a wise step, while prosperity is thus with it, for the board to invest a fair proportion of the reserve outside the business.

WEST AFRICAN TELEGRAPH COMPANY.—This company is slipping into a rather dangerous position. It claims a subsidy of £12,000 per annum from the French Government, in addition to other subsidies, and this French subsidy has not been paid for two years and a half. Yet the board goes on treating it as received, with the result that it has credited revenue in that time with £32,415 never received. This year it has recognised the danger of this policy by writing the amount off reserve, and setting down the amount owing by the French Government as a separate item. The investments of the reserve have not been touched by the operation, the money paid away as surplus revenue being drawn from the trading balances, which instead of being favourable to the company, as in previous years, are now distinctly adverse. Some statement as to the reality or otherwise of the asset of £32,415 ought to be made at the meeting. Meantime, after including the visionary £12,000, the revenue account of the company is poor indeed, being £64,722 for the year, of which £41,077 was swallowed up by working expenses. Out of the net balance of £23,644, which compares with £31,425 for the year 1896; no less than £10,098 is absorbed by interest on debentures, and the sinking fund required £13,633, so that the balance forward had to be reduced by £87 to the meagre sum of £372 in order to make ends meet. By dint of the sinking fund, the debenture issue has been reduced from £304,000 to £200,000, but if no satisfactory arrangement is made with the French Government, or if the revenue does not improve very much, there must come a breakdown in the company's finances.

DOOARS TEA COMPANY.—Good fortune has attended this concern, and its crop of 3,526,473 lb. was 501,007 lb. more than in 1896, the yield per acre being higher. The market price of the tea was lower, but not heavily so, being 7·75d. per lb., as against 8·26d. per lb. in 1896, and this, combined with the heavy cost of working entailed by a higher exchange, caused the profit of £24,486 to be about £5,500 less than in the preceding year. It proved however, sufficient for the directors to maintain their dividend at 12½ per cent., and carry about the same amount forward. Last year, however, the sum of £5,000 was carried to reserve, and the wisdom of this step is seen in the present result. The reserve amounts to £45,000, but the company is poorly financed, and has actually had to borrow £35,100 from the Agra Bank upon a loan against security.

BRITISH INDIAN TEA COMPANY.—The outturn of this company last year was 811,446 lb., or 63,265 lb. below that of the preceding year. The average price of 7·11d. per lb. was slightly lower, while, of course, the higher exchange prevented expenses falling much, so that the profit of £2,685 was just about half that of 1896. The substantial sum of £2,098 was brought forward, and after inclusion of sundry receipts and deduction of income tax, preference interest, and premium on debenture stock, the balance of £3,942 was left, out of which the directors declared a dividend of 5 per cent. This is the same as last year, but the balance forward is only £76, as against £2,098 a year ago. The balances of the company, however, are in a good condition.

YOKOHAMA SPECIE BANK, LIMITED.—In the half-year ended December 31 last this native Japanese bank made a gross profit of 4,747,515 yen, including 251,303 yen brought forward. Of this, 3,440,747 yen went in working expenses, interest on deposits, &c., leaving 1,306,767 yen as net gain. The directors pay out of this a dividend at the rate of 15 per cent. per annum on both the old and new shares, add 200,000 yen to the reserve fund, raising it to 5,964,000 yen, 100,000 yen to the reserve for equalisation of dividends, bringing it to 696,000 yen, set aside 50,000 yen for the contemplated new building, and give 63,328 yen to increase the remuneration of the staff. All this done, 274,870 yen is left to carry to the new half-year. The aggregate of the balance-sheet is 98,548,720 yen, a most respectable total, and the money is fully employed in the bank's current business.

THE LANCASHIRE INSURANCE COMPANY.—In 1897 the life business

of this company yielded £7,836 in new premiums on life policies, and £2,391 was received as capital in payment for annuities sold. The total income of the life branch was £135,370, including £36,414 from interest and dividends. Claims absorbed £68,932, and cash bonuses amounting to £11,913 were paid to policy holders. After deducting £15,384 for commission and expenses, an amount representing about 15½ per cent. of the premium income, and other payments, £35,671 was left to be added to the life fund, raising it to £1,045,646. In the fire department the premium income was £700,832, and claims came to £419,833. Commissions and expenses took £235,723, or nearly 33·7 per cent. of the premium income. The profit after meeting all outgoings was £33,427. Two dividends have been paid, an interim at the rate of 5 per cent., and a final at the rate of 7½ per cent., making 6¼ per cent. for the year 1897. These absorbed £17,062, but the total balance at the credit of profit and loss is £50,895, including the fire department proportion of interest and dividends, and a balance of £3,434 brought forward. Therefore, after payment of the dividends £33,231 is left over, out of which £30,000 is added to the fire reserve, and a balance of £3,231 remains to be carried forward. Life and fire funds together show an increase of £65,468 on the year, and their total, including the shareholders' capital of £273,000, is £1,639,863. The company's funds appear to be well invested, chiefly at home.

Liebig's Extract of Meat Company, Limited.—This company's accounts are made up to September 30 in South America and to March 31 in London. Last year was a prosperous one and shows a steadily augmenting business in Liebig's extract of beef, notwithstanding increasing competition. The profits for the year amount to £122,376, out of which 20 per cent., or £4 per share, is distributed on the ordinary capital, £1 having been paid in February last as interim dividend. £5,000 is carried to reserve, £2,000 to the employés' provident fund, and £8,248 goes to the directors as their 10 per cent. on the profits. This leaves £7,128 to be carried forward. The stock held at Fray Bentos and in Europe seems to be very high indeed, aggregating, inclusive of packing material, £381,628, and the reserve fund of £145,000 is invested only to the extent of £68,000; but the company is unquestionably rich and prosperous, and its sales of produce of all kinds amounted to £306,243 last year.

J. Lyons & Company, Limited.—In their fourth year, ended March 31 last, the directors of this company were able to make a gross profit of £158,586, which compares with £112,333 in the previous year, and shows remarkable progress. The net profit is £44,323, and, adding the amount brought forward, there is £46,548 available for distribution, out of which, after setting aside £9,830 for depreciation and meeting debenture interest, dividends aggregating 15 per cent. have been declared on the ordinary capital. The reserve is increased by £5,000, and after writing off a portion of the outlay for sundry installation expenses at Trocadero, a balance of £1,316 is carried to the new year. All this is very good, but there are one or two items in the balance-sheet we should like to see modified. The £5,000 carried to reserve, for instance, is good in its way, but it is very little against a goodwill item of £39,189, and we are not sure that the £3,670 devoted to depreciation on leasehold premises, whose total cost is £147,555, is sufficient, but there is nothing in the balance-sheet to indicate weakness, except that we think the company owes too much and would do better to reduce its liabilities on loans and its trade debts. These, with the 4½ per cent. first mortgage debenture stock, aggregate £196,590, and are quite £30,000 larger than the paid-up capital. They are very little set off by stock-in-trade and debts due to the company. A larger increase in the business is expected from the new shop, of which the company has secured an eighty years' lease from the Drapers' Company in Throgmorton-street.

The Mint, Birmingham.—In their ninth annual report the directors of this company announce a net profit of £29,893 for the year ended March 31 last, after writing off £1,600 for depreciation. Adding £2,132 brought forward, the available profit is £32,025, and a dividend of 10 per cent is to be paid, together with a bonus of 2s. 6d. per share for the year, making 12½ per cent. in all. Further, £2,000 is written off goodwill, reducing it to £15,000, and £18,000 is added to reserve, raising it to £36,000. A balance of £2,358 will then be left to carry forward. Trade has been satisfactory, the board says, and the company seems well managed; its reserve, of course, will become more real when goodwill disappears. An extraordinary general meeting is called after the ordinary one on June 3 to sanction extensive changes in the articles of association. Dividend payable June 4.

London and San Francisco Bank.—Some recovery of lost ground has taken place, the net profits for the year ending March 31 last amounting to £17,912 or £1,439 more than in the previous year, and as a larger balance was brought in, the amount available is £21,755, being £3,212 more than in 1897. The dividend then was 3 per cent. and it is now raised to 3½ per cent., and the increased balance of £4,605 is carried forward. According to the balance-sheet deposits and bills payable have risen from £690,000 to £900,000, and bills discounted and advances have increased from £1,050,000 to £1,284,000. A year ago it will be remembered the whole of the reserve fund of £50,000 was transferred to doubtful debts' reserve account, which was thus raised to £72,658. This amount has now been reduced to £62,819, which shows that some of the doubtful securities have been realised.

Quebec Central Railway Company.—The working for the past year shows a little improvement compared with 1896, but this is not saying much. Gross earnings came to $457,643 against $397,106, and the working expenses to $309,555 against $268,794, the net revenue in sterling being £30,979 compared with £26,614. More than half the revenue is absorbed by the prior lien bond interest and from the remainder 1½ per cent. is to be paid on the income bonds. The history of this affair is a melancholy record. In 1881 £556,000 of 5 per cent. first mortgage bonds were issued over here, interest being regularly paid by the government of the province until July, 1886, but the following year default took place, and the company was reconstructed, further capital being raised to finish a branch. The old first mortgage bonds, with some others, were changed for income bonds, and £200,000 5 per cent. prior lien bonds were issued, the total of which has been since increased to £350,000. The interest paid on the income bonds for 1889 was 1½ per cent., but until this year only 1 or 1¼ per cent. has been forthcoming, so that the company may be said to be now doing better. According to the balance sheet the reserve contingent fund remains at $60,463, while on the other side there is a trustee account (in suspense) standing for $74,295.

Ruston, Proctor, & Company, Limited.—This company did better in the year ended March 31, and the profit, including £2,024 brought forward, was £32,297. Depreciation was allowed at the rate of 4 per cent. upon plant and machinery, and the amount required was £2,653. Directors' remuneration took £1,000, debenture interest £10,625, and depreciation of furniture £171, leaving £17,847. Out of this a dividend of 5 per cent. was declared, or 1 per cent. better than last year, and £5,347 carried forward. The profits, however, have not returned to the level prior to 1896-7, when 8 per cent. dividends were comfortably declared, fair sums being written off each year from goodwill. This latter item only stands at £9,000, as against an original total of £82,692, and the money thus accumulated has gone to the benefit of the trading balances which are much in favour of the company.

Lungla (Sylhet) Tea Company.—The outturn last year was 1,710,984 lbs., or 154,868 lbs. less than in 1896, but the average price of the crop was rather better at 7·71d. per lb. as against 7·59d. per lb. a year ago. The higher exchange caused working expenses to increase, and charges were higher in other respects, so that the gross profit was £7,608, as against £13,217 a year ago. Including £1,498 brought forward, the available balance was £9,107, and as the preference interest required £6,000, the directors found that the interim dividend of 3 per cent. absorbed the balance except £107, and so no further distribution was possible. The board is going on with extensions under that insensate plan of borrowing from the agents, and having already exhausted the borrowing powers of £50,000, it proposes to increase them to £100,000. Clearly, this is the way to ruin, and the sooner the shareholders stop the directors on their course the better.

Delaware and Hudson Canal Company.—This is a company with a bit of canal ownership and a good deal of railroad control and colliery business in its constitution. Its canal mileage is 108, whilst its controlled railroads have a mileage of 685. The business centres in the anthracite coal traffic, and out of an output of such coal in the States last year of 41,637,863 tons, the Delaware and Hudson Canal produced 3,965,638 tons and transported 1,681,213 tons for other miners, so that it handled in one way or another about 13 per cent. of the anthracite production. The report of the company, however, does not tell one much about how its finances are worked. It certainly contains a table showing the anthracite production of the United States back to 1820, but the most careful study of the report will fail to tell an outsider what rate of dividend is paid upon the stock. The gross receipts of the company were $18,360,051, working expenses came to $13,085,661, and taxes, interest, and rentals absorbed $3,132,968, leaving $2,141,420 as net revenue. The leased lines of the company brought in a profit of 109,506. The managers charged off as depreciation upon canal, boats, and equipment $1,052,875, and for a number of small items $211,814, or a total of $1,264,689. By reference we find the dividend was 5 per cent., which represents $1,750,000, and so we presume the deductions for depreciation and so forth led to a reduction in the surplus, which now stands at $5,128,344. From 1889 to 1896, the company paid 7 per cent. regularly, but for the last two years only 5 per cent. was distributed.

Diary of the War.

May 21.—At last the Spanish fleet has been located. It arrived at Santiago de Cuba, situated in the south-east of the Island of Cuba, late on Sunday night, the 19th. The latest cruise of the fleet was "without incident," and its safe arrival at Santiago de Cuba is hailed as a "victory" at Madrid. A doubtful one. Admiral Cervera has shown himself clever—in avoiding the American fleet; but now that he has shut himself up in Santiago de Cuba it would seem that he must have reached the end of his tether. The harbour at Santiago de Cuba is a powerful defensive position; but, unless the Americans are culpably remiss in their attentions, the Spanish Admiral cannot bring his ships out again except to destruction. In Santiago he can be of no use to Havana. No doubt it will be some little time before the American fleets can concentrate at Santiago de Cuba; but when they do, Admiral Cervera will be imprisoned there—his only consolation being that he has drawn off the bulk of the enemy's ships from Havana. That of course is something. It ensures further delay in the invasion of Cuba. Indeed there is now talk of postponing this invasion until the autumn. This is inevitable; and there seems nothing before the American fleets but the blockade of Havana and watching Admiral Cervera's fleet. In any case there is not much promise of activity in the near future. American Jingoes are very impatient. They imagined beforehand that the war with Spain would be a "walk over" that would not last a month. Now that they see they were both foolish and mistaken in their prophecies, they blame the Government for dilatoriness instead of confessing their own foolishness. The Spanish Ministry has been reconstructed and introduced to the Chamber, all except the new Foreign Minister, Senor Leon y Castillo, who, as ambassador to France, is engaged in negotiations with the French Government which cannot at present be interrupted. They are, Senor Sagasta informed the Cortes, likely to have important consequences which may be made manifest in the near future—perhaps in a few days even. The Spaniards have had many "surprises" of this sort, but none of them has yet come off. But this one may. We shall see.

May 22.—Is Admiral Cervera at Santiago de Cuba? Doubts are now hinted; some American critics see in it a "Spanish ruse," the object of which is by no means clear. There is nothing for it but wait. American naval authorities are much more reticent than they were. There was to be a "great naval battle" yesterday or to day; accounts of it have not yet arrived.

May 23.—There was a report that the "great naval battle" had been fought, but it was untrue. There is now almost as much uncertainty about Admiral Cervera and his squadron as there was before they were supposed to be "bottled up" in Santiago de Cuba. It is not believed that the Admiral will accept battle on the high seas if he can possibly avoid it. But there is a suspicion that he may seek to escape northwards, and perhaps in time be able to attack some of the American Atlantic ports. Admiral Camara is returning immediately to Cadiz to resume command of the Spanish reserve squadron. It is expected to sail soon with "sealed orders."

May 24.—More mystery. American naval authorities *may* know about the positions of the fleets of Admiral Sampson and Commodore Schley, but if so, they do not tell. Nothing, moreover, is known of Admiral Cervera—whether he has left Santiago de Cuba or whether he ever really entered that port being alike uncertain. It would seem, however, that the United States armed cruiser *Oregon* is now safe. It is expected daily at Key West, and will ultimately join Admiral Sampson's squadron. The American War Board are puzzled at Admiral Cervera permitting the *Oregon* to escape. But, though Admiral Cervera is at present a free lance, it may not be at all times expedient for him to go where he would like to be. Serious complaint was made in the Spanish Cortes that American ships were being sailed close to Spanish ports under the Spanish flag. It was resolved to direct the attention of the European Powers to this conduct; and a hint was thrown out that Spain might retaliate by the employment of privateers to prey upon American shipping. A British steamer, *Ardanmhor*, was seized by mistake in the Straits of Florida. It was released at once on arrival at Key West.

May 25.—Plenty of rumours, but no facts. It is said that the American naval authorities now "believe" that Admiral Cervera is in Santiago de Cuba with his squadron, but they do not know; nobody knows. There is said to have been trouble at Manila between Admiral Dewey and the German consul, who threatened to force his way into the town with provisions for the Spaniards. Senor Leon y Castillo has returned to Paris to continue his "negotiations," which are now said to be of a financial rather than a political character. Admiral Montojo will, it is said, be tried by court-martial on charges of cowardice, with being unready for the fight at Manila, and with not making full use of his opportunities. The *Daily News* special correspondent at Madrid asserts that Spain is anxious for peace. It is not, he says, for the Spanish Government to make proposals; but peace, he thinks, need not be delayed much longer if some disinterested Power were to take the matter up. That is rather a sanguine view of the situation.

May 26.—No confirmation yet of the "bottling up" of Admiral Cervera at Santiago de Cuba, though confident rumours circulate to the effect that he is "cornered" there with Admiral Sampson and Commodore Schley watching him. President McKinley has called for 75,000 more volunteers, clear evidence that the authorities are taking a more serious view of the war. It is now declared that Senor Leon y Castillo is conducting no special negotiations with the French Government. At first they were said to be of such a character as to lead to important international results. Then they were said to be of a purely financial character. Now we are told that there have been no negotiations at all. Admiral Camara has left Madrid for Cadiz with the inevitable "sealed orders."

TRADE AND PRODUCE.

Wheat has been very quiet during the week, with a general reduction in price of from 1s. to 2s. per quarter. Not much business has been doing, however, sellers holding out against any further reduction, and buyers rather keeping aloof, in expectation of a further turn in their favour. Attempts at a rally in price were made in New York early in the week; but they had only a momentary success; and since then the tone of the market has been quiet, not to say dull, with a tendency downward. American supplies continue large, and the quantities coming from India are increasing. Stocks in this country keep well up to the average level; but France is still buying largely. Last week she took 192,000 quarters against only 38,000 in the previous week. Imports of Russian have certainly not been large, and the supplies from that quarter seem likely to diminish rather than increase. On the whole it seems probable that the reduction in rates will not go much further, if any. There have been instances of white wheat changing hands as high as 55s.; and in several districts business was done at 51s. to 53s.; but probably 50s. to 51s. is nearer the average, though in some districts the quotations were 48s. to 50s.

There is no change to report in cotton. The spot market is dull, and futures are receding. The visible supply at the beginning of the week was 3,795,000 bales against 3,347,000 bales last year. No increase in business is reported in Manchester, and, owing to the inadequacy of prices offered, only a moderate turnover has been possible. The condition of the trade has been adversely affected by the absence of buying for Calcutta, though for other Indian centres a moderate business has been doing. Very little speculative buying. Spinners are not securing many new contracts. Demand for yarns small, and prices have a downward tendency. The linen trade in Belfast is reported a shade better, with a sensible improvement in orders from the States. Barnsley, however, reports the demand sluggish in every direction, while recent failures have caused some depression in Dundee, and traders are exercising more caution, though the excitement about the Calcutta plague has abated.

At the third series of colonial wool sales, which closed on the 19th inst., competition, Messrs. Jacomb, Son, & Co. inform us, has not been so even and regular as might have been expected, and there have been occasional nightly fluctuations and irregularities observable. Of the quantity catalogued, 10,700 bales were bought in, while 76,000 bales were taken for export. Importers of some 28,000 bales have not met the market at all. As compared with last auctions there was a decline of from 5 to 7½ per cent. in most sorts; indeed, in all except superior Australasian merino wools in the grease which showed an advance of 5 per cent., and superior fine greasy cross-bred wools, which also advanced 5 per cent. Reports from the manufacturing districts are not particularly bright. The demand in Huddersfield has been almost entirely for home consumption, and that not exceptionally active, though prices have remained firm. Serge and worsted coatings, fine vicunas, and fancy worsted trouserings have been in good demand. Tweeds of the soft Saxony make have also received a good deal of attention. Leeds manufacturers are hopeful of the near future; but recent weather has rather interfered with business, and owing to changeableness in the price of colonial wool, buyers and sellers have alike been cautious. There is a strong hope of considerably increased business with Canada. Already numerous orders have been received, conditional, however, on their execution not before the preferential tariff comes into operation in July next. Leicester is still depressed. Prices are irregular, and the few transactions are at quotations lower than at any time for over fifty years. There is no improvement in the yarn market, and new orders are difficult to procure at prices considered profitable.

Copper continues unsettled, fluctuating greatly from day to day. The war, and the probability that it may be more prolonged than was expected, gives scope to speculators, of which they seem to take full advantage. The tax the Spanish Government proposes to place as a war contribution on copper ore—said to be 2 per cent. *ad valorem*—cannot greatly disturb the market; but then, if the war goes on, the duty is almost sure to be increased, and may indeed begin at even a higher figure than that mentioned. There is no doubt that Spain will extract as much as she can in the present emergency from her extensive mineral resources. We may, therefore, look to continued fluctuations in the copper market. On Monday 500 tons were sold on the London Exchange at £51 7s. 6d., 6s. 8d. and 5s. cash, and £51 8s. 9d. and 7s. 6d. three months. The cash price was maintained on Wednesday, but the rates for three months went down 2s. 6d. to £51 5s. and 6s. 3d. for various dates in August, £51 5s. and 7s. 6d. three months. The market closed quiet. Settlement price, £51 5s., the same as on Monday.

Pig iron has this week taken a downward turn. The market has been inactive and featureless, and a drop is recorded in Scotch of 2½d., Cleveland 2d., and hematite 1d. The reverse can only be temporary, for the reports from the manufacturing districts are generally very satisfactory, and the other day a Scotch firm held out for an advance of 7s. 6d. to 10s. a ton on hematite. He did not get it, however, for hematite makers say that the cost of production has increased so much that profits are not so large as they were five months ago, when hematite was 3s. to 4s. per ton cheaper. When dear coal is added to dear ore, they cut in severely upon profits. Scotch pig iron is now down 1s. 2½d. below the top price paid last week.

There is a pretty confident expectation of an early termination of the Welsh coal strike. The colliers have at last relunctantly agreed to confer plenary powers on their delegates, and the conference with the employers seems now certain to meet on an early day. There is a consequent slackening of prices in Newcastle and other coal centres, which have been so greatly benefited by the strike. Shipowners, however, are looking forward to greatly increased business; for as soon as the Welsh collieries resume work, there must be a considerable addition to the export trade. The forward chartering shows that the owners do not believe in low rates before the late autumn at any rate.

The sugar market is still very firm, with every indication of a continuance. The leading feature of the week has been, according to Mr. Czarnikow, another advance of about 2½d., on near deliveries of beet, caused mainly by a demand for America. August, again, is only 1½d. dearer, and new crop only fractionally harder. Granulated sugar has also participated in the improvement, though as yet only to a small extent. The general position is undoubtedly sound, and seems likely to become stronger month by month.

About 43,000 packages of Indian and Ceylon tea were offered in public auction this week. Messrs. Gow, Wilson, & Stanton state that the average price of Indian tea sold on garden account during the past season was 8.67d., against 9d. during the season ended May 31, 1897, and 8¾d. during the season ending May 31, 1896. The total estimated crop of Indian tea for 1898-9 is given as 158,750,000 lbs., and of this amount 140,500,000 lbs., it is calculated, will be available for the United Kingdom. Lower grades of whole leaf Ceylon tea have been specially in demand, the general tone continuing firm, with a slightly hardening tendency. The average price is 7.73d., against 7½d. in the corresponding week of 1897.

Notice to Subscribers.

Complaints are continually reaching us that the INVESTORS' REVIEW cannot be obtained at this and the other railway bookstall, that it does not reach Scotch and Irish cities till Monday, and that it is not delivered in the City till Saturday morning.

We publish on Friday in time for the REVIEW to be at all Metropolitan bookstalls by at latest 4 p.m., and we believe that it is there then, having no doubt that Messrs. W. H. Smith & Son do their best, but they have such a mass of papers to handle every day that a fresh one may well look almost like a personal enemy and be kept in short supply unless the reading public shows unmistakably that it is wanted. A little perseverance, therefore, in asking for the INVESTORS' REVIEW is all that should be required to remedy this defect.

All London newsagents can be in a position to distribute the paper on Friday afternoon if they please, and here also the only remedy is for subscribers to insist upon having it as soon as published. Arrangements have been made that all our direct City subscribers shall have their copies before 4 p.m. on Friday. As for the provinces, we can only say that the paper is delivered to the forwarding agents in ample time to be in every English and Scotch town, and in Dublin and Belfast, likewise, early on Saturday morning. Those despatched by post from this office can be delivered by the first London mail on Saturday in every part of the United Kingdom.

ADVERTISEMENTS.

All Advertisements are received subject to approval, and should be sent in not later than 5 p.m. on Thursdays.

The advertisements of American Life Insurance Offices are rigorously excluded from the INVESTORS' REVIEW, and have been so since it commenced as a Quarterly Magazine in 1892.

For tariff and particulars of positions open apply to the Advertisement Manager, Norfolk House, Norfolk-street, W.C.

To Correspondents.

The EDITOR cannot undertake to return rejected communications.

Letters from correspondents must, in every case, be authenticated by the name and address of the writer.

Telegraphic Address: "Unveiling, London."

The Investors' Review.

The Week's Money Market.

BANK RATE 3½ PER CENT.

The money market has weakened with a vengeance in the past seven days. Not only has the Bank of England failed to make arrangements to control the Japanese funds, but a large proportion of these funds have been lent directly to the market, and this fact, coupled with the continued influx of gold, has quite conquered the unwillingness of brokers and bankers to reduce rates. Each day has seen greater competition to find employment for funds in the market, and this ease, capped by the reduction in the Bank rate to 3½ per cent., has sent the quotation for day to day loans down to 2 per cent., as against 2½ to 3 per cent. a week ago. Loans for a week are now quoted at 2¼ per cent., and the India Council lends with difficulty, until June 3, at 2½ per cent. Upon the reduction in the official minimum, the discount houses brought down their allowance for deposits by ½ per cent. to 2 per cent. for "call," and 2¼ for "notice" money. The joint stock banks, of course, will now allow 2 per cent. on deposits.

Discount quotations have naturally fallen more severely than rates for short loans, as they had been relatively so much higher. Political misgivings were felt to have been overdone, especially in the shape of Mr. Chamberlain's speech, and when it was found that the American exchange rose rather than fell back, the market had perforce to pay attention to the heavy addition to its resources represented by the inflow of gold. In the past seven weeks quite 7½ millions of the metal have come in, which more than obliterates the effect of the recent shipments to New York. The action of the Bank of England in reducing its rate yesterday from 4 to 3½ per cent. was long forestalled by the market, which bid actively for bills throughout the week. Under this influence, the discount rate for three months' remitted paper, which a week ago was 3½ per cent. fell rapidly to 2½ and then to 2⅜ per cent. at which point it is not particularly firm. Foreign exchanges have necessarily moved against this country as a result of this decline, but the fall in their case has not been rapid, and so far there is no sign of the renewal of a gold demand for the Continent. The only quarter for which gold is wanted is India, and, as usual, this want is so moderate that it can hardly be said to be felt. The Bank of England has therefore reduced its buying price of Japanese yen to 76s. 4½d., but, so far, has made no further change in its price for other foreign coins.

The Stock Exchange settlement found plenty of money on offer, and the banks, after starting their rate for loans at 3½ per cent., had to reduce their terms to 3 per cent. Even then lending brokers paid off considerable sums as a consequence of the contraction of the supply of floating stock in the market.

Another increase of £1,103,582 in the banking reserve, bringing its total up to £26,545,000, made a reduction in the bank rate inevitable. The total stock of coin and bullion is now £37,192,000, and there seems to be no present danger that it will be drawn upon for export. The directors of the Bank, therefore, did well to begin to reduce their rate towards the level of the market. In other respects the Bank return for the past week shows very few changes of any moment. The largest is a decrease of £698,000 in the "other" securities which are still, however, £33,612,000. Thanks to the influx of new money, this decrease, representing the balance of the loans due at the Bank and now repaid, has been effected without further drawing upon the "other" deposits. On the contrary, they are now at £43,452,000, £316,000 larger than they were a week ago.

SILVER.

The price of the metal has fluctuated within narrow limits during the past seven days. Starting at 26$\frac{7}{16}$d. per ounce, the price of bars for immediate delivery rose to 26$\frac{9}{16}$d. per ounce on Monday, owing to purchases variously ascribed to "bear" closing and preparation for another Spanish order. Since then it declined, and, with little doing, the quotation dropped back to 26½d. per ounce, and then strengthened to 26⅝d. per ounce. America does not seem inclined to offer freely, and of course the East is still out of the market. Indian exchanges dropped back in the week to 1s. 3$\frac{13}{16}$d. but at the reduced rates the India Council made a fair allotment, and with the announcement that only 50 lacs will be offered next Wednesday, rates have moved up to 1s. 3$\frac{15}{16}$d. Chinese rates remain very dead, but Singapore is maintained at a quotation well above the usual parity with Hong Kong.

BANK OF ENGLAND.

AN ACCOUNT pursuant to the Act 7 and 8 Vict., cap. 32, for the Week ending on Wednesday, May 25, 1898.

ISSUE DEPARTMENT.

	£		£
Notes Issued	51,635,205	Government Debt	11,015,100
		Other Securities	5,784,900
		Gold Coin and Bullion	34,835,205
		Silver Bullion	—
	£51,635,205		£51,635,205

BANKING DEPARTMENT.

	£		£
Proprietors' Capital	14,553,000	Government Securities	13,201,192
Rest	3,207,308	Other Securities	33,612,171
Public Deposits (including Exchequer, Savings Banks, Commissioners of National Debt, and Dividend Accounts)	12,041,738	Notes	24,188,290
Other Deposits	43,452,172	Gold and Silver Coin	2,356,747
Seven Day and other Bills	104,182		
	£73,358,400		£73,358,400

Dated May 26, 1898.

H. G. BOWEN, *Chief Cashier.*

In the following table will be found the movements compared with the previous week, and also the totals for that week and the corresponding return last year:—

Banking Department.

Last Year. May 26.		May 18, 1898.	May 25, 1898.	Increase.	Decrease.
£	Liabilities.	£	£	£	£
3,142,514	Rest	3,206,098	3,207,308	1,210	—
11,799,790	Pub. Deposits	11,932,659	12,041,738	109,079	—
38,783,685	Other do.	43,135,953	43,452,172	316,219	—
155,031	7 Day Bills	109,797	104,182	—	5,615
	Assets.			Decrease.	Increase.
13,956,270	Gov. Securities	13,185,953	13,201,192	—	15,239
28,326,001	Other do.	34,310,099	33,612,171	697,928	—
26,131,769	Total Reserve	25,441,455	26,545,037	—	1,103,582
				1,124,436	1,124,436
				Increase.	Decrease.
£		£	£	£	£
27,179,980	Note Circulation	27,449,310	27,446,915	—	2,395
51⅝ p.c.	Proportion	46⅝ p.c.	47⅞ p.c.	—	—
2 „	Bank Rate	4 „	3½ „	—	—

Foreign Bullion movement for week £1,056,000 in.

LONDON BANKERS' CLEARING.

Month of	1898.	1897.	Increase.	Decrease.
	£	£	£	£
January	673,281,000	576,558,000	96,723,000	—
February	648,601,000	597,652,000	50,949,000	—
March	799,520,000	729,970,000	69,550,000	—
Week ending April 6	186,540,000	147,789,000	38,751,000	—
„ 13	112,101,000	154,099,000	—	41,998,000
„ 20	168,810,000	92,332,000	76,478,000	—
„ 27	129,959,000	138,288,000	—	8,329,000
May 4	174,057,000	138,987,000	35,070,000	—
„ 11	160,526,000	128,252,000	32,274,000	—
„ 18	171,078,000	152,987,000	18,091,000	—
„ 25	131,037,000	116,372,000	14,665,000	—
Total to date	3,266,442,000	2,906,191,000	360,251,000	—

BANK AND DISCOUNT RATES ABROAD.

	Bank Rate.	Altered.	Open Market.
Paris	2	March 14, 1895	1⅞
Berlin	4	April 9, 1898	3
Hamburg	4	April 9, 1898	3
Frankfort	4	April 9, 1898	3¼
Amsterdam	3	April 13, 1897	2¼
Brussels	3	April 28, 1896	2⅝
Vienna	4	January 22, 1898	3⅝
Rome	5	August 27, 1895	3
St. Petersburg	5½	January 23, 1898	4½
Madrid	5	June 17, 1896	5
Lisbon	6	January 25, 1891	6
Stockholm	4	March 3, 1898	4
Copenhagen	4	January 20, 1898	4
Calcutta	11	April 28, 1898	—
Bombay	12	May 5, 1898	—
New York call money	1 to 1½	—	—

NEW YORK ASSOCIATED BANKS (dollar at 4s.).

	May 21, 1898.	May 14, 1898.	May 7, 1898.	May 22, 1897.
	£	£	£	£
Specie	33,880,000	32,688,000	31,958,000	17,660,000
Legal tenders	10,312,000	10,648,000	9,806,000	20,148,000
Loans and discounts	116,306,000	114,734,000	114,218,000	100,990,000
Circulation	2,948,800	2,938,600	2,919,800	2,882,000
Net deposits	136,198,000	133,344,000	131,924,000	114,426,000

Legal reserve is 25 per cent. of net deposits; therefore the total reserve (specie and legal tenders) exceeds this sum by £10,142,500, against an excess last week of £9,395,000.

BANK OF FRANCE (25 francs to the £).

	May 27, 1898.	May 20, 1898.	May 12, 1898.	May 28, 1897.
	£	£	£	£
Gold in hand	74,790,160	74,690,280	74,518,720	79,520,000
Silver in hand	49,083,960	49,010,560	48,839,960	49,204,000
Bills discounted	32,872,000	32,396,680	34,816,040	*42,671,000
Advances	15,412,160	15,474,440	16,934,800	—
Note circulation	146,154,600	146,693,000	147,992,840	148,293,000
Public deposits	8,730,880	7,917,120	7,546,280	7,357,000
Private deposits	28,947,240	23,041,280	22,914,840	19,255,000

Proportion between bullion and circulation 84¾ per cent. against 84⅜ per cent. a week ago.

* Includes advances

FOREIGN RATES OF EXCHANGE ON LONDON.

Place.	Usance.	Last week's.	Latest.	Place.	Usance.	Last week's.	Latest.
Paris	chqs.	25·34	25·29	Italy	sight	27·36	27·17
Brussels	chqs.	25·38	25·33	Do. gold prem.	..	108·15	107·37½
Amsterdam	short	12·10½	12·08¾	Constantinople	3 mths	109·20	109·20
Berlin	short	20·47½	20·46	B. Ayres gd. pm.	..	158·30	163·70
Do.	3 mths	20·29	20·32½	Rio de Janeiro	90 dys	5¾d.	6$\frac{1}{16}$d.
Hamburg	3 mths	20·29½	20·32½	Valparaiso	90 dys	17$\frac{11}{16}$d.	17$\frac{1}{16}$d.
Frankfort	short	20·40	20·48	Calcutta	T. T.	1/4$\frac{1}{32}$	1/3$\frac{31}{32}$
Vienna	short	12·09	12·05	Bombay	T. T.	1/4$\frac{1}{32}$	1/3$\frac{31}{32}$
St. Petersburg	3 mths	93·75	93·70	Hong Kong	T. T.	1/10¼	1/10¼
New York	60 dys.	4·83½	4·84½	Shanghai	T. T.	2/5¾	2/5¾
Lisbon	sight	29$\frac{1}{16}$d.	29¾d.	Singapore	T. T.	1/10¾	1/10⅝
Madrid	sight	44·10	46·08				

IMPERIAL BANK OF GERMANY (20 marks to the £).

	May 23, 1898.	May 14, 1898.	May 7, 1898.	May 22, 1897.
	£	£	£	£
Cash in hand	44,170,500	43,091,550	42,740,200	46,458,000
Bills discounted	33,882,450	35,717,350	35,671,150	*33,209,000
Advances on stocks	4,174,350	4,090,950	4,219,350	—
Note circulation	52,817,400	54,611,800	56,454,000	51,013,000
Public deposits	25,575,400	24,561,350	22,297,800	25,288,000

* Includes advances.

AUSTRIAN-HUNGARIAN BANK (1s. 8d. to the florin).

	May 23, 1898.	May 14, 1898.	May 7, 1898.	May 23, 1897.
	£	£	£	£
Gold reserve	29,108,166	29,308,250	29,467,750	28,081,000
Silver reserve	10,468,166	10,454,583	10,443,333	10,526,000
Foreign bills	331,666	367,666	417,250	—
Advances	1,803,750	1,834,750	1,842,916	—
Note circulation	51,435,666	52,573,166	53,063,500	49,871,000
Bills discounted	12,925,416	13,731,750	14,122,500	*12,104,000

* Includes advances.

NATIONAL BANK OF BELGIUM (25 francs to the £).

	May 19, 1898.	May 12, 1898.	May 5, 1898.	May 20, 1897.
	£	£	£	£
Coin and bullion	4,290,400	4,240,160	4,391,480	4,187,000
Other securities	16,267,400	16,417,160	16,738,800	14,558,000
Note circulation	19,332,080	19,545,960	19,528,520	18,691,000
Deposits	2,550,400	2,476,560	2,962,400	2,600,000

BANK OF SPAIN (25 pesetas to the £).

	May 21, 1898.	May 14, 1898.	May 8, 1898.	May 22, 1897.
	£	£	£	£
Gold	9,833,520	9,833,520	9,833,520	8,667,000
Silver	4,604,880	4,876,440	5,860,520	10,257,360
Bills discounted	30,132,960	30,537,400	28,978,720	9,385,880
Advances and loans	4,831,320	4,293,120	4,893,360	9,520,280
Notes in circulation	52,373,240	52,718,000	52,292,320	43,804,720
Treasury advances, coupon account	469,800	409,240	112,360	527,240
Treasury balances	676,440	359,240	277,760	928,280

LONDON COURSE OF EXCHANGE.

Place.	Usance.	May 17.	May 19.	May 24.	May 26.
Amsterdam and Rotterdam	short	12·2¼	12·2¼	12·2¼	12·2
Do. do.	3 months	12·4½	12·4½	12·4	12·3⅞
Antwerp and Brussels	3 months	25·57½	25·58¾	25·53¾	25·51¼
Hamburg	3 months	20·70	20·69	20·67	20·66
Berlin and German B. Places	3 months	20·70	20·69	20·67	20·66
Paris	cheques	25·35	25·36¼	25·32½	25·31¼
Do.	3 months	25·48¾	25·50	25·46¼	25·45
Marseilles	3 months	25·50	25·51¼	25·47½	25·45
Switzerland	3 months	25·72½	25·71¼	25·67½	25·65
Austria	3 months	12·25	12·25	12·20	12·20
St. Petersburg	3 months	24 11/16	24 11/16	24 11/16	24 11/16
Moscow	3 months	24⅜	24⅜	24⅜	24⅜
Italian Bank Places	3 months	27·77½	27·67½	27·50	27·45
New York	60 days	48 11/16	48¼	48¾	48¾
Madrid and Spanish B. P.	3 months	26½	24½ nom.	25¼	25¼
Lisbon	3 months	28¼	28¼	28	28⅝
Oporto	3 months	28½	28¼	28	28½
Copenhagen	3 months	18·45	18·45	18·46	18·44
Christiania	3 months	18·45	18·45	18·47	18·44
Stockholm	3 months	18·45	18·45	18·47	18·46

OPEN MARKET DISCOUNT.

	Per cent.
Thirty and sixty day remitted bills	2⅜
Three months "	2½
Four months "	2¼
Six months "	2⅝
Three months fine inland bills	2¼
Four months "	2½
Six months "	2¾—3

BANK AND DEPOSIT RATES.

	Per cent.
Bank of England minimum discount rate	3½
" " short loan rates	—
Banker's rate on deposits	2
Bill brokers' deposit rate (call)	2
" 7 and 14 days' notice	2¼
Current rates for 7 day loans	2—2¼
" " for call loans	2¼

Stock Market Notes and Comments.

Cheaper money is already beginning to have its effect upon the price of securities. Political apprehensions still keep Consols down in spite of Government purchases, but should our West African dispute with France be arranged, as reported, the price of this security also will begin to look up. As yet, however, the buying has been what is called professional, and the investing public still keeps away from the markets. It may rush in now that the Bank rate is down, and buy at considerably higher figures than now prevail, because a reduced bank rate means reduced interest on deposits. Investors will let money lie with their bankers when they receive 2½ per cent. upon it, but when the interest falls to 1½ per cent. they seek to place it in permanent securities. It looks, therefore, as if wisdom dictated speedy purchases, and yet we are not disposed to give this advice, because it seems to us the lower rates for money cannot last for any length of time, and even if they do last, there are so many disturbing influences in active operation that we cannot count upon stable markets for three days running. Within our own sphere we may have many alarms during the present summer, and there is always hanging over us the financial difficulties of the Indian Government. The daily or weekly excitements the public mind has been subjected to since this year began have recently turned away people's thoughts from India, a thing never difficult to do, because we do not at the best of times give India much attention. The difficulties of our Government there, however, are none the less real because we ignore them, and every day that passes brings a crisis in Indian finance nearer. In a very short time only the most heroic remedies will avert this crisis, and among these remedies it is very probable that large exports of gold to India will take a prominent place.

Then we have always to bear in mind the effects of dearer grain upon our resources. These likewise have been obscured recently; it is difficult to say how. Contrary to expectation the United States has ceased to draw gold from Europe, either because their expenditure upon war materials in Europe has assumed extraordinary proportions or because Europe's indebtedness is held in suspense. Perhaps also American speculators have been buying their own securities extensively on our markets, and thereby for the time being reducing the power of their country to draw upon Europe's stock of gold. All these causes may be in operation, but it remains true that we cannot pay 40 per cent. to 50 per cent. more for our wheat without feeling the effects of the increased indebtedness thus created upon our money market. What we should expect, therefore, is that mitigating influences such as those mentioned in connection with the American Union may last for the next two or three months, and then that adverse tendencies should reassert themselves with added force. Certainly the longer the present war between the United States and Spain drags on the more liable are we to credit disturbances from some quarter or other. The Spanish Minister of Finance, we notice, is boasting that his country has plenty of resources with which to carry on the fight, and in his position he is doubtless bound to put a bold face on affairs, but unattached observers know better, and are better able to measure the consequences of large increases in the note circulation of the Bank of Spain and in the internal interest-bearing debt. Spain is near collapse already in consequence of this war, and will be quite without resources should it continue another three months. The condition of Italy has also to be borne in mind, not only in regard to our commercial relations with that country, but in view of the consequences which a collapse in its finances would be certain to produce, both in Paris and Berlin. It is impossible to believe that Italy las now situated can continue to meet her debt obligations in full, and almost equally impossible to expect that the Paris Bourse can stand up under successive blows such as have been, or, will be, administered to it by Portugal, Spain, and Italy taken together.

We need not go further afield in discussing the influences from abroad which affect our market, and there is not much new to be said about domestic ones. Speculation is not very active; that is, its manifestations at the best are only sporadic. We have been taking some part in the gamble in American railways, probably as "bears" to our loss, and there is quite a rush of business in Grand Trunk stocks, but of general speculation there is hardly a trace to be found. Each Stock Exchange settlement discloses a smaller demand for money than the last, and in some of the securities which have suffered most, such as Spanish 4 per cents., we have comparatively little interest. It cannot even be said that the British public has done much to raise the price of Argentine Government securities, although it undoubtedly has bought heavily in Argentine railway stocks. The Government debts, therefore, both of Argentina and Brazil, are handled from above, by the financiers who have to find means to sustain the credit of these countries and prevent their falling into difficulties of an irremediable kind. Generally, in the long run, these financiers succeed in their object, and, given cheap money, they are sure to do so now, but up to the present the public, as far as we can learn, is not deeply involved.

Equally dead is speculation in the mining markets. Either the public holds shares at higher prices which it is waiting to see again in order to sell, or shares are possessed in bales by the trusts and finance companies interested. In either case there is no room for fresh play. Prices have been moved up recently by the action of the financiers, but the public has not responded, at least as far as we can discover. We must, however, admit that our acquaintance is not extensive among the class of brokers who cultivate this kind of business. A better test, therefore, than their experience is found in that of the jobbers, who have had for a long time past very little to do either in the "Kaffir Circus" or the Western Australian market. Had there been general speculation going on in these they would have been busy and making money. They are not busy, and on the whole have probably been losing money. We may, consequently, take it as true that speculation is at a very low ebb in these departments, and we hope it will continue so in spite of the lamentations of the dealers. Almost equally stagnant is the business of the miscellaneous market. There is nothing to "go for" in it, as the phrase is. Almost every share dealt in is at a price which repels instead of attracting the man who is careful of his money, and in many instances quotations are entirely artificial, the product of manœuvres on the part of groups or individuals who have inconvenient quantities of shares to dispose of. We hope such will be obliged to keep these shares until the test of time has been applied to the quality of the companies by which they have been created.

The Week's Stock Markets.

Stock markets have been quiet, but firm on the whole. The decline in discount rates, and the closing of accounts by "bears" prior to the settlement which began on Tuesday, were the chief reasons for the moderate rise which has taken place, but as the Stock Exchange will be closed on Saturday next as well as Monday, and the attractions of Epsom have kept many members away this week, business has naturally been on a very small scale.

Consols rose at one time to 111⅝, owing to cheaper money, but the price has slipped back a little since. Most of the leading Colonial Government inscribed stocks have been marked higher in anticipation of an early reduction in the Bank rate, but Home Corporation issues have not participated in the rise, and a fall of 5 in Manchester 4 per cents. is noticeable.

Highest and Lowest this Year.		Last Carrying over Price.	BRITISH FUNDS, &c.	Closing Price.	Rise or Fall.
113⅛	109¼	—	Consols 2¾ p.c. (Money)...	111⅝	+ ⅞
113 5/16	109½	111¼	Do. Account (June 1)	111¾	+ ¾
106¼	101	104½	2½ p.c. Stock red. 1905 ...	104¾	+ ¾
363	341	—	Bank of England Stock...	347½	+2½
117	111⅜	114	India 3½ p.c. Stk. red. 1931	113½	+ ¼
109¼	103⅜	107½	Do. 3 p.c. Stk. red. 1948	106¾	—
96⅝	90	92¼	Do. 2½ p.c. Stk. red. 1926	92	+1

A feature in the Home railway market was the unexpected announcement made by the directors of the Great Western Company of an issue of nearly 2½ millions of new stock. This new capital is wanted for lines in Somersetshire, and a shortening of the route

Highest and Lowest this Year.		Last Carrying over Price.	HOME RAILWAYS.	Closing Price.	Rise or Fall.
186	172½	176	Brighton Def.	177	+2
59¼	54¼	56⅞	Caledonian Def.	57	+ ¼
20⅝	18¼	19¾	Chatham Ordinary	19⅞	+ ½
77¼	62	66	Great Central Pref.	66	—
24⅜	21¼	22⅞	Do. Def.	22½	+ ⅛
124½	118	120	Great Eastern	120⅛	+ ⅜
61⅛	50⅞	54¼	Great Northern Def.	54½	+1¼
179⅝	164¼	166½	Great Western	165x.new	−3¼
51¾	45¼	50¼	Hull and Barnsley	51	+1⅛
149¼	145	146	Lanc. and Yorkshire	146	+ ¼
136⅛	127½	132½	Metropolitan	133	+2
31	26⅞	27¾	Metropolitan District	28⅞	+1⅞
88⅜	82⅛	84½	Midland Pref.	84¾	+1
95⅝	84½	87½	Do. Def.	88⅛	+1⅞
93¼	86⅞	89½	North British Pref.	89¾	+ ½
47½	41¾	43⅛	Do. Def.	43¾	+ ¼
181½	172¾	174½	North Eastern	174¾	+ ¾
205¼	196¼	197¾	North Western	198¼	+1¼
117⅛	105½	111	South Eastern Def.	111¾	+2¼
98⅜	87	92½	South Western Def.	93¼	+1¼

to South Wales is also to be effected. Great Western ordinary promptly fell about 4, but part of this has since been made up, despite the publication of a very bad traffic return due to the continuance of the deadlock in the Welsh coal trade. Apart from a decline in the stocks of several of the mineral lines serving the same district, there is a general advance in the rest of the list, the most prominent rises being in Midland deferred, South-Eastern deferred, and the "underground" stocks. As regards the latter companies the rise was supposed to be due to some fresh electric traction developments, but in addition the District was helped by another good traffic return, coupled with a scarcity of stock for delivery. Considering the bad weather of last week, the traffic returns were fairly good, although the passenger lines suffered somewhat, but the prospects of a fine Whitsuntide has since led to some inquiry. Continuation rates were light, and about the same as last time, with the exception of Metropolitan, on which the contango rose to ¾ per cent., while the account again disclosed a great scarcity of stock generally.

Among United States railroad shares the principal activity has been in Milwaukee, the price going up with a run, and the smallness of the floating stock, of which mention has been made of late, was clearly demonstrated at the settlement by the "back" of ⅛ per cent. which was at one time charged. There has been a scarcity of war rumours, or definite news of any kind, and Wall-street operators have done little, and business continues restricted on this side, the firmer tendency being due more than anything else to the publication of good reports as to the condition of the crops, and the traffic returns again present an excellent showing.

Highest and Lowest this Year.		Last Carrying over Price.	CANADIAN AND U.S. RAILWAYS.	Closing Prices.	Rise or Fall.
14 3/16	10⅜	12⅜	Atchison Shares	12⅞	+ ⅝
34	23½	32	Do. Pref.	32¼	+1¼
15⅜	11	13	Central Pacific	14⅞	+1⅛
102	85½	100⅜	Chic. Mil. & St. Paul	101⅜	+3¼
14¼	10	11⅞	Denver Shares	11⅞	+ ⅜
54¼	41½	48	Do. Prefd.	48⅜	+2⅛
16⅜	11¼	13	Erie Shares	13¼	+⅝
44⅞	29½	36	Do. Prefd.	36⅜	+1⅞
110½	99	106	Illinois Central	107¾	+1⅜
62½	45¼	55½	Louisville & Nashville	56½	+2
14½	9 13/16	11½	Missouri & Texas	11½	+ ½
122¾	108½	118	New York Central	120	+2¼
57¼	42⅞	52¼	Norfolk & West. Prefd.	52½	+1½
70¼	59	67¼	Northern Pacific Prefd.	67⅛	+1¼
19½	13⅜	15½	Ontario Shares	15¾	+ ⅝
62½	56¼	59	Pennsylvania	59½	+ ¼
12½	7 13/16	9	Reading Shares	9¼	+ ¾
34½	24¼	30¼	Southern Prefd.	30¾	+1⅜
37½	18½	23¾	Union Pacific	23⅞	+ ⅛
20½	14⅛	20	Wabash Prefd.	20½	+1½
30¼	21	28¼	Do. Income Debs.	29½	+2⅜
92¾	74	86½	Canadian Pacific	87½	+2⅛
78⅝	69⅞	76¼	Grand Trunk Guar.	77¾	+3¼
73¼	57⅛	70¼	Do. 1st Pref.	73¼	+4⅞
53¼	37¼	51¼	Do. 2nd Pref.	53⅛	+4¼
25¼	19¼	24¼	Do. 3rd Pref.	24⅞	+2
105¾	101½	103	Do. 4 p.c. Deb.	104	+1

About the only information relating to the rate war that has appeared this week is that the committee hopes soon to arrive at a settlement, yet upon the top of this very vague report there has been a large business at rapidly advancing prices, especially in Grand Trunk stocks, but the traffic return caused a partial relapse, although it was a very good one. Canadian Pacific shares followed the upward move, and purchases by Berlin operators also helped to harden the market. The last price, however, is not quite the best of the week.

The foremost place in the Foreign market has been occupied this week by the Brazilian bonds, which have been forced up rapidly. Various rumours have appeared day by day to account for the steady advance; the negotiations between the Government and the house of Rothschild for the sale of the Central Railway were nearly completed, said one report; and then an arrangement for funding for three years the interest on the National Debt in new 5 per cents., to be secured on the Customs revenue, was talked of, but has not been confirmed. The Rio exchange is considerably higher at

6¼d., but this has not prevented some profit taking, and the last prices are well below the best. Argentine issues owe their rise to the remarks made by Dr. Pellegrini at the beginning of the week, and other South American descriptions are firmer in sympathy. Turning to inter-Bourse securities, there has been only a small business, and the ups and downs day by day have finally resulted in slight gains on balance in Spanish and Italian. A rumour was current on Monday that the dispute between England and France in West Africa was nearly settled, but the improvement which followed this report was afterwards lost, an uneasy feeling being produced on the Paris Bourse by the result of the French elections. Then the speeches in the Spanish Cortes, recommending the payment of the coupon in silver, had a depressing effect on Spanish fours for a time. The strength of Italian Rente was due to purchases by an Italian banking syndicate, and the existence of a "bear" account was disclosed at the settlement, judging from the fact that the stock was carried over "even," contrasted with a contango of 3 per cent. last time; but rates were all lower on this occasion.

Highest and Lowest this Year.		Last Carrying over Price.	FOREIGN BONDS.	Closing Price.	Rise or Fall.
94¾	84	89	Argentine 5 p.c. 1886......	89¾	+2¼
92⅝	81⅝	87½	Do. 6 p.c. Funding	88¾	+3¼
76¾	64	69½	Do. 5 p.c. B. Ay. Water	70¾	+3¼
61¾	41⅛	51½	Brazilian 4 p.c. 1889	51⅛	+5½
69⅞	46	58⅛	Do. 5 p.c. 1895	58	+5½
65	42¾	54	Do. 5 p.c. West Minas Ry..................	54⅛	+7½
108⅝	105½	107¼	Egyptian 4 p.c. Unified...	107¼	+ ¼
104⅞	100½	102	Do. 3½ p.c. Pref. ...	102¼	+ ¼
103	99½	101½	French 3 p.c. Rente	101½	+ ½
44¾	34½	42½	Greek 4 p.c. Monopoly...	42½	+ ½
93 9/16	88⅝	91	Italian 5 p.c. Rente	91½	+1 9/16
100	87½	96	Mexican 6 p.c. 1888	97	+1
20⅝	16	17¾	Portuguese 1 p.c.	18	+ ¾
62½	29⅝	34	Spanish 4 p.c.	34½	+2
45⅛	40	44	Turkish 1 p.c. "B"	44⅛	+1½
26 7/16	22¾	24⅝	Do. 1 p.c. "C"	24 13/16	+ 9/16
22 7/16	20	21¼	Do. 1 p.c. "D"	21⅜	+ ⅛
46⅝	40	44½	Uruguay 3½ p.c. Bonds...	45¼	+1

Argentine and other South American railway stocks have been quite active, and a moderate advance has to be reported, the traffic returns again coming well up to expectations. The Mexican companies' issues show an improvement as well, also due to a good traffic, the increase amounting to over $10,000.

Highest and Lowest this Year.		Last Carrying over Price.	FOREIGN RAILWAYS.	Closing Price.	Rise or Fall.
101¾	99	101	Argentine Gt. West. 5 p.c. Pref. Stock..................	101	—
158¼	134	140	B. Ay. Gt. Southern Ord..	141	+5
78½	65	73½	B. Ay. and Rosario Ord...	74	+1½
12¼	10¼	10¾	B. Ay. Western Ord.......	10¾	—
87¼	73	79	Central Argentine Ord....	80½	+2½
92	76	78	Cordoba and Rosario 6 p.c. Deb.	80	+2
95½	85½	89½	Cord. Cent. 4 p.c. Deb. (Cent. Nth. Sec.)	90	+1
61⅞	42	54½	Do. Income Deb. Stk. ...	55½	+4
25¼	16⅛	18¾	Mexican Ord. Stk.	19¾	+1¾
83½	69½	72½	Do. 8 p.c. 1st Pref.	73½xd	+3

Among Miscellaneous stocks changes are few and unimportant. Guinness ordinary is 10 higher, and Allsopp preferred has risen a point or two; otherwise, there has been little or nothing doing in brewery securities. A further slight shrinkage is noticeable in the leading electric lighting companies' shares, and among water stocks Chelsea preference has fallen 6½. G. H. Hammond shares and the income stock have risen rather sharply, the demand being due to a statement that this company is doing well, large orders having been received for canned meat in connection with the Spanish-American war. Lyons' shares rose on the publication of the report, but Maison Virot ordinary and preference have fallen steadily. Vickers and Maxim attracted buyers, presumably on the report of some sort of a working agreement with a leading American firm, but this tale has since been contradicted.

Markets, on the whole, closed firm, the reduction in the Bank rate not having been quite discounted, and professional buying caused an advance in most of the leading Home railway stocks. Consols also advanced sharply, the rise being assisted by the firmness of the Continental bourses, but the most prominent feature was a big rise in Grand Trunk stocks on influential buying from Montreal helped by provincial orders. United States railroad shares were rather dull at the finish, with one or two exceptions, such as Wabash, Central Pacific, and New York Central bonds, which all closed very firm on Amsterdam buying. The call for more volunteers in America was not liked, as it was thought to mean a prolonged struggle with Spain. Among mining ventures, Mount Lyell closed weak, but other copper-producing companies were firmer.

MINING AND FINANCE COMPANIES.

The South African market has been a comparatively firm one for the greater part of the week, chiefly on Continental support, and the settlement disclosing a scarcity of stock, prices were inclined to go ahead. Paris then became a seller, and in the absence of support here there was a set-back, although the latest quotations still show a moderate gain on balance. Rand Mines were carried over "even" at the last, and continuation rates were generally easier, but, as compared with a fortnight ago, there is an all-round shrinkage apparent in the list of prices. A few of the higher-class West Australian shares have been inquired for, on Adelaide account it is said, and where there is a change in price it is generally in favour of holders; but business has simply dwindled away in this department to nearly the vanishing point. Rates of continuation of "Westralians" were in some instances, such as Associated, a little lighter, the account being an extremely small one. Among copper shares Mount Lyell fell away still further, and the price touched 9⅞ when the cable giving the reason for the lower percentage of copper in the ore recently treated was published. It was also rumoured that the heavy sales of these shares was not unconnected with the late Mr. Crotty's holding, at any rate the selling orders came principally from Melbourne. When they ceased the price rallied a little, and then again weakened. Rio Tintos were pressed for sale on Paris account on the news that the Spanish Government will put an export duty on copper of 1½ or 2 per cent., but repurchases have since caused a recovery to quite last week's level.

THE UNITED MATABELE CLAIMS DEVELOPMENT COMPANY, LIMITED.—Very little information is contained in the report of this company for the year to October 31 last, and not much was to be expected, seeing that it has not got to work yet. The directors, however, do inform us that when certain works are completed, about 10,000 tons of ore will be in sight, and that they have obtained the funds for this development on favourable terms. They also proclaim that the assays have been very favourable, there being 250 tons of ore at grass, which give an average assay value of 2 oz. 4 dwt. 8 gr. to the ton. When they have a quarter of a million tons of this ore laid open we shall begin to have hope. In the meantime, expenses seem to be kept down fairly well, and the balance-sheet offers nothing to comment upon.

MAY CONSOLIDATED GOLD MINING COMPANY, LIMITED.—In the year 1897 this company does not seem to have made very much by its operations. Its gross receipts from gold won were £209,480, and £185,791 of this went in expenses, leaving only £23,688 as net profit, but this was really not available as profit, because £20,047 had to be written off for depreciation. A balance of £4,047 was brought in, and after taking credit for sundry small receipts the sum left to carry forward is £8,483; not a large amount on a gross overturn of about £210,000; but then the net return per ton milled was only 3s. 7·023d. Unless the ore gets richer, or expenses are reduced, the future prospects of the company are anything but brilliant, and £179,201 stands in its books as the dead weight of the capital cost of the claims worked. The company seems to owe £32,545 to the National Bank of the South African Republic, and has, of course, no reserves of any sort.

Answers to Correspondents.

Questions about public securities, and on all points in company law, as well as on the position of life insurance offices and their promises, will be answered week by week, in the Review, on the following terms and conditions:—

A fee of five shillings must be remitted for each question put, provided they are questions about separate securities. Should a private letter be required, then an extra fee of five shillings must be sent to cover the cost of such letter, the fee then being ten shillings for one query only, and five shillings for every subsequent one in the same letter. While making this concession the Editor will feel obliged if private replies are as much as possible dispensed with. It is wholly impossible to answer letters sent merely "with a stamped envelope enclosed for reply."

Correspondents will further greatly oblige by so framing their questions as to obviate the necessity to name securities in the replies. They should *number* the questions, keeping a copy for reference, thus:—"(1) Please inform me about the present position of the Rowenzori Development Co. (2) Is a dividend likely to be paid soon on the capital stock of the Congo-Sudan Railway?

Answers to be given to all such questions by simply quoting the numbers 1, 2, 3, and so on. The Editor has a rooted objection to such forms of reply as—"I think your Timbuctoo Consols will go up," or "Sell your Slowcoach and Draggem Bonds," because this kind of thing is open to all sorts of abuses. By the plan suggested, and by using a fancy name to be replied to, each query can be kept absolutely private to the inquirer, and no scope whatever be given to market manipulations. Avoid, as names to be replied to, common words, like "investor," "inquirer," and so on, as also "bear" or "bull." Detached syllables of the inquirer's name, or initials reversed, will frequently do as well as anything, so long as the answer can be identified by the inquirer.

The Editor further respectfully requests that merely speculative questions should as far as possible be avoided. He by no means sets himself up as a market prophet, and can only undertake to provide the latest information regarding the securities asked about. This he will do faithfully and without bias.

Replies cannot be guaranteed in the same week if the letters demanding them reach the office of the Investors' Review, Norfolk House, Norfolk-street, W.C., later than the first post on Wednesday mornings.

Scotus.—The institution is sound, and the form of policy a reasonable one. Its only drawback is the difficulty of realising if you should require the money. Before accepting you should inquire into the "surrender value."

Tonk.—It is not possible to answer your query this week; will send you a letter in the course of a few days.

Rawley.—1. So far as it is possible to judge from published reports, the management is fairly good, and prospects are said to be encouraging. The shares stand now at a fair price; if you are in lower down it would be prudent, I think, to sell, at any rate, part of your holding. I doubt if there will be much activity in this market for some time. 2. My opinion of this concern has been very openly stated in the columns of this paper. The value behind these shares is almost, if not quite, nil, there may, however, be a rally engineered shortly; if so, sell, and have done with it. In any case, don't wait very long. 3. This is in much the same position as 2. Companies with reserves "invested" in shares of speculative undertakings cannot be considered sound. They will prove mere bubbles in the long run. Sell these also on a rise. Efforts will be made to put a better appearance on the position shortly, I expect; if these prove futile, cut your loss.

NEXT WEEK'S MEETINGS.

Tuesday, May 31.

British Indian Tea ... ... 14, St. Mary Axe, 3 p.m.
Dooars Tea ... ... Winchester House, 2 p.m.

Wednesday, June 1.

Coburg Hotel ... ... Coburg Hotel, 12.30 p.m.

Thursday, June 2.

Baily Paper Mills ... ... 28, Fenchurch-street, 2.30 p.m.
Brownlee & Co. ... ... Glasgow, noon.

Friday, June 3.

Lipton, Limited ... ... Cannon-street Hotel, noon.
Mexican National Railway ... ... Winchester House, 2 p.m.

A conference is shortly to be convened, a preliminary to the conclusion of a convention for clearing up all pending controversies between the United States, Canada, and Great Britain. The negotiations are to include the protection of fish on the great lakes and on the North Atlantic fisheries, the alien labour laws and the question of border immigration, mining regulations at Klondike and elsewhere, the seal question, and the subject of reciprocity. A large order, but no doubt seems to exist as to the possibility of executing it.

Prices of Mine and Mining Finance Companies' Shares.

Shares £1 each, except where otherwise stated.

Australian.

Making-Up Price, May 23.	Name	Closing Price.	Rise or Fall.	Making-Up Price, May 23.	Name	Closing Price.	Rise or Fall.
1½	Aladdin	1 1/16	− 1/16	13/16	Hannan's Star	¾	+ ⅛
3¾	Associated	3⅞	+ 1/16	5⅞	Ivanhoe, New	6	+ 1/16
6/	Do. Southern	⅜	− 1/16	⅛	Kalgurli Mt.&IronKing, 18/	⅛	
1 1/16	Brownhill Extended	1 1/16		5 1/16	Kalgurli	5⅝	+ 1/16
1¼	Burbank's Birthday	1¼		2¼	Lady Shenton	2 1/16 x.	+ ⅛
1/16	Central Boulder	1/16	+ 1/16	8 1/16	Lake View Cons.	8¼	+ 1/16
4/6	Chaffers, 4/	5/3	+ 1/	⅝	Do. Extended	⅜	
11/16	Colonial Finance, 15/	¼ dis		5/16	Do. South	⅜	
	Crœsus S. United	⅜	+ 1/16	1¼	London & Globe Finance	1¼	+ ⅛
⅜	E. Murchison	⅜ x.		⅜	London&W.A.Exploration	11/16	− 1/16
5/	Golden Arrow 19/	4/9	+ /6	⅜	Do. Investment	1/16	− 1/16
7¼	Golden Horseshoe	8¼	− 1/16	⅜	Mainland Consols	1/16	
11/16	Golden Link	11/16		⅜	North Boulder, 10/	⅛	
17/6	Great Boulder, 2/	18/3	+ /9	1⅜	North Kalgurli	1 1/16	
1¼	Do. Main Reef, 10/	1 3/16		11/16	Northern Territories	1	+ 1/16
2¼	Do. Perseverance	2⅜	+ ⅛	2¼	Peak Hill	2¼	
⅜	Do. South	7/16	− 1/16	1 3/16	South Kalgurli	1 5/16	
1¼	Hainault	1⅜	+ ⅛	1¼	W. A. Goldfields	1 1/16	− 1/16
11/16	Hampton Plains	11/16		⅜	W. A. Joint Stock	1/16	
7 3/16	Hannan's Brownhill	7⅜	+ 1/16	⅜	W. A. Market Trust	2/3	− /3
⅝	Hannan's Oroya	⅝	+ 1/16	5/16	W. A. Loan&General Fin.	⅛	
11/16	Do. Proprietary	10/9		5/16	White Feather	⅛	

South African.

Making-Up Price, May 23.	Name	Closing Price.	Rise or Fall.	Making-Up Price, May 23.	Name	Closing Price.	Rise or Fall.
5	Angelo	5 1/16		2/	Lisbon-Berlyn	1/9	+ /3
1	Aurora West	11/16	− 1/16	2¼	May Consolidated	2 1/16	+ 1/16
1	Bantjes	15/16	− 1/16	4	Meyer and Charlton	4	+ ⅛
8/6	Barrett, 10/	8/	− /6	3⅜	Modderfontein	3⅜	− 1/16
4 1/16	Bonanza	4¼		1	New Bultfontein	15/16	− ⅛
1/16	Buffelsdoorn	1/16		3⅜	New Primrose	3⅜	
5 1/16	City and Suburban, £4	5¼		1⅜	Nigel	1⅛	− ⅛
2¼	Comet (New)	2⅜	+ ⅛		Nigel Deep	1	
3⅜	Con. Deep Level	3⅜		⅜	North Randfontein	⅜	
11	Crown Deep	11	− ⅛	5	Nourse Deep	5	+ ⅛
12⅜	Crown Reef	12⅜	+ ⅛	1	Porges-Randfontein	1	
26⅜	De Beers, £5	26⅜	+ ⅛	29⅜	Rand Mines	29	+ ⅛
3⅜	Driefontein	3⅜	+ ⅛	1¼	Randfontein	1⅛	− 1/16
6 1/16	Durban Roodepoort	6⅛		1 1/16	Rietfontein	1⅛	
3 1/16	Do. Deep	3⅛		9⅜	Robinson Deep	9⅜	− ⅛
4⅜	East Rand	4⅜	+ ⅛	8	Do. Gold, £5	8	
24	Ferreira	24	+ ⅛	1	Do. Randfontein	⅜	− 1/16
7⅜	Geldenhuis Deep	7⅜	+ ⅛	1 1/16	Roodepoort Central Deep	1⅛	
5⅜	Do. Estate	5⅜	− ⅛	6⅜	Rose Deep	6⅜	
⅜	George Goch	⅜	− ⅛	3 1/16	Salisbury	3	− 1/16
2 1/16	Ginsberg	2⅛		1⅜	Sheba	1⅜	
1⅜	Glencairn	1⅜	+ 1/16	3⅜	Simmer and Jack, £5	3⅜	
8 1/16	Goldfields Deep	8⅛	− ⅛	2 1/16	Transvaal Gold	3	+ 1/16
8⅛	Griqualand West	8⅛		3⅜	Treasury	3⅜	+ ⅛
9	Henry Nourse	9	+ ⅛	3⅜	United Roodepoort	3⅜	+ ⅛
7⅜	Heriot	7 1/16	+ 1/16	1⅜	Van Ryn	1⅜	− 1/16
7⅜	Jagersfontein	7⅜		5 1/16	Village Main Reef	5 11/16	− 1/16
9⅜	Jubilee	9⅜	+ ⅛	1⅜	Vogelstruis	1⅜	+ 1/16
5	Jumpers	4⅜	− ⅛	⅜	Do. Deep	⅜	
2⅜	Kleinfontein	2⅜	+ 1/16	9⅜	Wemmer	9⅜	+ ⅛
3 1/16	Knight's	3⅜		1/16	West Rand	⅜	
2 1/16	Lancaster	2⅜	+ 1/16	5⅜	Wolhuter, £4	5⅜	− ⅛
3⅜	Langlaagte Estate	3⅜		2⅜	Worcester	2⅜	

Land Exploration and Rhodesian.

Making-Up Price, May 23.	Name	Closing Price.	Rise or Fall.	Making-Up Price, May 23.	Name	Closing Price.	Rise or Fall.
2¼	Anglo-French Ex.	2⅜		⅜	Mashonaland Central	⅜	
1 1/16	Barnato Consolidated	1 11/16		5⅜	Matabele Gold Reefs	5⅜	+ ⅛
⅜	Bechuanaland Ex.	11/16		2	Mozambique	2 1/16	
2⅜	Chartered B.S.A.	2⅜	+ 1/16	11/16	Oceana Consolidated	⅜	− 1/16
⅜	Clark's Cons.	⅜	+ 1/16	1⅜	Rhodesia, Ltd.	1 1/16	+ 1/16
⅜	Colenbrander	⅜		4⅜	Do. Exploration	4⅜	+ ⅛
4⅜	Cons. Goldfields	4 1/16		15/16	Do. Goldfields	1	+ 1/16
1 1/16	Do. Pref.	20/6		3⅜	S. A. Gold Trust	3⅜	− ⅛
2⅜	Exploration	1⅜		1	Tati Concessions	1	
2⅜	Geelong	2⅜	+ ⅛	⅜	Transvaal Development	⅜	
1/16	Henderson's Est.	⅜		⅜	United Rhodesia	⅜	
1 1/16	Johannesburg Con. In.	1 1/16		1	Willoughby	1	
⅜	Do. Water	11/16	+ ⅛	15/16	Zambesia Explor.	⅜	− 1/16
1⅜	Mashonaland Agency	1 1/16					

Miscellaneous.

Making-Up Price, May 23.	Name	Closing Price.	Rise or Fall.	Making-Up Price, May 23.	Name	Closing Price.	Rise or Fall.
1	Alamillos, £2	1	− ⅛	⅜	Mount Lyell, South	7/6	
4⅜	Anaconda, $25	4⅜		4⅜	Mount Morgan, 17s. 6d.	4 1/16	+ ⅛
7/	Balaghât, 18/	7/6	+ 1/	4 11/16	Mysore, 10s.	5 11/16	+ 1/16
12/	Brilliant, £2	12/		10/	Mysore Goldfields	9/	− 1/6
2⅜	Do. St. George's	2 1/16		6/3	Do. Reefs, 17/	7/	+ 1/6
10/	British Broken Hill	10/	− /6	7/	Do. West	6/6	− /6
43/	Broken Hill Proprietary	2⅜		5/	Do. Wynaad	5/	− /6
3	Do. Block 10	3		2 1/16	Namaqua, £2	2 1/16	
4⅜	Cape Copper, £2	4⅜	+ 1/16	3⅜	Nundydroog	3⅜	+ 1/16
4 11/16	Champion Reef, 10s.	4⅜	+ 1/16	3⅜	Ooregum	3⅜	
2 11/16	Copiapo, £2	2 1/16		3⅜	Do. Pref.	3 11/16	
2⅜	Coromandel	2 1/16	− 1/16	26⅜	Rio Tinto Def., £5	26	+ ⅛
15/	Day Dawn Block	14/9		5⅜	Do. Pref. £5	5⅜	
2⅜	Frontino & Bolivia	2 1/16	+ 1/16	1	St. John del Rey	20/	
1⅜	Hall Mines	1⅜		7/6	Taitipu	8/9	+ 1/3
2⅜	Libiola, £5	2⅜x		6⅜	Tharsis, £2	6⅜	+ ⅛
7⅜	Linares, £3	7⅜		2	Tolima "A," £5	2	− ⅛
3⅜	Mason & Barry, £3	3⅜x		4⅜	Waihi	4⅜	+ 1/16
4⅜	Mountain Copper, £5	4⅜		1⅜	Waitekauri	1⅜	
10⅜	Mount Lyell, £3	10	− ⅜	⅜	Woodstock (N.Z.)	⅜	
2⅜	Mount Lyell, North	2⅜	+ 1/16				

President McKinley, we are told, is taking great personal interest in pending legislation for the representation of America at the Paris Exhibition of 1900. It may be good for the commerce of the United States, but his more immediate object is to counteract the efforts being made by the French Press to induce the Government to interest itself on behalf of Spain. It is a sagacious move on the President's part—a move that makes for peace.

THE PROPERTY MARKET.

Last week's results at the Tokenhouse Yard Mart were uncommonly good—the total realised having been £238,160, as compared with £135,420 for the corresponding week last year. The leading lots we have already indicated, and need only now refer to some items of interest in the later days of the week. A farm at Hambledon, Bucks, realised about £17 per acre; but some building land in the same locality commanded as high a figure as £150 per acre. Yesterday week Messrs. Stimson & Sons and C. C. & T. Moore had important sales of ground rents and properties, the respective totals of which were £23,565 and £28,325. One freehold ground rent disposed of by the former firm was in Euston-road—£30, with reversion in four and a half years—and fetched £5,525. Another freehold ground rent of £129, offered by the same firm, with reversion twenty-nine and three-quarter years, brought £3,180. A freehold ground rent of £180 at St. John's Hill, reversion in ninety-six years, was sold by Messrs. Moore at £5,030. Messrs. H. E. Foster & Cranfield sold some valuable reversionary interests and policies well, bringing in a total of over £17,000. A reversion to a trust fund of about £13,218, comprising freehold property and Government stocks, life aged sixty-one, brought £6,350. Another reversion to a sum of £30,000 charged upon freehold property at Carlton, in Notts, lives aged sixty-two and fifty-seven, brought £8,000. Three endowment policies in the Scottish Provident for £1,000, and a policy for £200 with profits, life aged fifty-two, sold for £450. Good business was also done at the Mart on Friday. Messrs. G. A. Wilkinson & Son had a long list of improved ground rents at Brixton, and all were sold at high figures. Messrs. Gouldsmith, Son, & Co. sold, amongst other lots, the leasehold premises Nos. 13, 14, and 15, Sloane-street, and 17, 19, and 21, Pavilion-road, Chelsea, for £8,975. Messrs. F. J. Bisley & Sons got good prices for leasehold properties at Bermondsey, Rotherhithe, and Camberwell.

Several rather important sales are announced for the near future at the Mart. There is, for instance, Weir House, on the Middlesex bank of the Thames, at Teddington, which will be offered by Messrs. St. Quinton & Sons on June 6. Cottismore, a freehold residence, with very pleasant grounds, is to be offered during June by Messrs. Debenham, Tewson, & Co.; and Mr. Newman, of Hillingdon, Middlesex, will offer at Shepperton an adjacent building estate, freehold, including the farm known as the Clock House at Hulliford, near the railway station, and within a few minutes' walk of the river. Messrs. Edwin Fox & Bousfield have in hand for offer at the Mart on June 22 two residential properties on the banks of the Thames: Oldfield Cottage, near Maidenhead, and the property known as Hill Lands, built on the hill top overlooking Wargrave-on-Thames. Both seem likely to attract keen bidders. A City building lease, to be offered by Messrs. Baker & Sons on June 17 by order of the Bridgehouse Estate Committee, must also attract some attention. The lease is for thirty years, comprises about 15,600 feet, with a frontage of 197 feet to Finsbury-pavement and a return frontage of 79 feet to West-street. A freehold property in Clerkenwell-road, a building of five floors, containing a floor and area space of 16,437 feet, is to be offered at the Mart on June 28, by Messrs. Bean, Burnett, and Eldridge. On the same day the same firm, in conjunction with Messrs. Jones, Lang, & Co., will offer the building at 10, Wood-street, held on a long ground lease direct from the Corporation of London. Among other notable properties soon to be offered are a valuable mansion at Brighton; Barnside Moor, near Sheffield, well stocked with grouse; the Bonningtons, a freehold residential estate in the parish of Hunsdon, within three miles of Roydon; two freehold estates in the parish of Melksham, known as the Melksham Forest Farm, and the Little Snarlton Farm; an important building estate known as "The Elms and Wellfield Estate," on the top of Muswell Hill, to be offered by Messrs. Edwin Fox & Bousfield on June 15; and the pretty marine residence on the shores of Cardigan Bay, known as Hafod-y-Bryn, now in possession of Mr. Pope, Q.C. Hean Castle, near Tenby, is also to be offered at the Mart on June 28.

Little was doing at the Mart on Monday and Tuesday, the total for the former being £7,490 and for the latter £18,464. On Monday, Messrs. E. Belfield & Co. offered the Mitcham Brewery and thirteen licensed houses for sale, but they were withdrawn, £49,000 being the highest bid. Some improved ground rents at Marylebone, Hyde Park, and Paddington were successfully disposed of by Messrs. Elliott, Son, & Boyton; but this firm failed to obtain a satisfactory price for the Crown lease of Hanover Lodge, Regent's Park, with five acres of ground, which was consequently withdrawn. There was rather more activity on Tuesday, but not much. Messrs. Debenham, Tewson, & Co. disposed of the corner shop and premises, No. 8, Baker-street, Marylebone, for £2,310, a satisfactory figure; while a freehold building estate of fifteen acres at Higham Hill, Walthamstow, was sold by Mr. W. Houghton for £3,000. Messrs. Fuller, Horsey, Sons, and Cassell disposed of the assets, goodwill, and British and foreign letters patent of the Automatic Castor and Wheel Company for £3,000. The remaining properties offered were of minor importance.

Wednesday was Derby Day even at the Mart, and the properties offered were few and unimportant, the total sales for the day only amounting to £4,782. Messrs. Pearce & Son were the only auctioneers present, and disposed of all their lots at fair prices.

The French and Russian portions of the first instalments of the Greek war indemnity were not paid until the 21st inst. The Porte had sent a remonstrance on the subject on the 20th, and was probably beginning to doubt whether the evacuation of Thessaly had not begun too soon.

TRAMWAY AND OMNIBUS RECEIPTS.

HOME.

Name.	Period.	Ending.	Amount.	Increase or Decrease on 1897.	Weeks or Months.	Aggregate to Date. Amount.	Aggregate to Date. Inc. or Dec. on 1897.
			£	£		£	£
Aberdeen District	Week	May 21	461	+13	—	—	—
Belfast Street	"	" 21	2,187	−347	—	—	—
Birmingham and Aston	"	" 21	416	−9	—	—	—
Birmingham and Midland	"	" 21	638	+6	—	—	—
Birmingham City	"	" 21	3,597	−147	—	—	—
Birmingham General	"	" 23	933	+4	—	—	—
Blessington and Poulaphouca	"	" 22	9	−3	20	199	+16
Bristol Tramways and Carriage	"	" 20	2,696	+212	—	—	—
Burnley and District	"	" 21	318	−34	—	—	—
Bury, Rochdale, and Oldham	"	" 21	813	−64	—	—	—
Croydon	"	" 21	322	−31	—	—	+1,200
Dublin and Blessington	"	" 22	106	−10	20	1,952	+17
Dublin and Lucan	"	" 21	70	—	21	928	−371
Dublin United	"	" 20	3,147	+18	—	55,958	+3,147
Dudley and Stourbridge	"	" 21	161	−4	21	3,400	+127
Edinburgh and District	"	" 21	2,632	+146	20	45,849	+4,130
Edinburgh Street	"	" 21	756	+50	20	12,165	+1,452
Gateshead and District	Month	April	910	+59	—	—	—
Glasgow	Week	May 21	2,886	−26	—	—	—
Harrow-road and Paddington	"	" 20	263	−31	—	—	—
Lea Bridge and Leyton	"	" 21	787	−51	—	—	—
London, Deptford, and Greenwich	"	" 21	580	−43	—	11,334	+554
London General Omnibus	"	" 21	21,009	−1771	—	—	—
London Road Car	"	" 21	6,492	−948	†	124,739	+4,565
London Southern	"	" 21	515	−55	—	—	—
North Staffordshire	"	" 21	361	−29	—	7,904	−54
Provincial	"	" 21	2,210	−497	—	—	—
Rossendale Valley	"	" 20	174	−7	—	—	—
Southampton	"	" 21	374	−55	—	—	—
South London	"	" 21	1,702	−140	†	32,589	+915
South Staffordshire	"	" 20	576	−42	20	11,844	−89
Tramways Union	Month	April	10,870	+1,149	4	39,500	+4,495
Wigan and District	Week	May 21	336	+286‡	—	—	—
Woolwich and South East London	"	" 21	346	−73	†	6,551	+270

† From January 1. ‡ Strike in 1897.

FOREIGN.

			£	£		£	£
Anglo-Argentine	Week	Apr. 25	4,451	+538	*	73,854	+7,827
Barcelona	"	May 21	1,120	−231	—	22,673	−3,311
Barcelona, Ensanche y Gracia	"	" 21	222	—	—	4,466	+20
Bordeaux	"	" 20	2,377	−154	—	40,812	−1,802
Brazilian Street	Month	Mch. [m	lr 51,419	+ mlr 50 47]	—	—	—
British Columbia Electric	"	"	$30,729	+$10493	‡	$305,154	—
Do. net	"	"	$10,394	+$4,958	‡	$97,402	—
Buenos Ayres and Belgrano	"	"	5,219	+1,305	*	14,382	+2,578
Buenos Ayres Grand National	Week	Apr. 23	$25,223	+$3,248	†	—	+$12,751
Buenos Ayres New	Month	March	$70,624	−$864	—	$201,851	−$7,119
Calais	Week	May 21	132	+6	—	—	—
Calcutta	"	May 21	1,269	−121	—	—	—
C'rth'g'na & Herrerias	Month	April	4,607	+712	—	18,809	+1,011
Gothenburg	Week	May 11	377	+44	—	—	—
Lynn and Boston	Month	Mch.	$105,471	+$5,944	—	$622,228	+$27912
Do. net	"	"	$4,2847	+$6,607	—	$216,383	+$3,162

* From January 1. † From April 1, 1898. ‡ From April 15, 1897.
§ From October 1, 1897.

MINING RETURNS.

QUEENSLAND MENZIES GOLD MINING COMPANY.—Crushed 227 tons for 673 oz.

CONSOLIDATED MAIN REEF.—2,491 oz. from 6,159 tons battery, and 1,186 oz. from 3,456 tons cyanide.

OTTOS KOPJE.—5,417 loads washed during week ended May 19. 128 carats won.

NEW QUEEN.—Result for past fortnight:—1,220-ft. formation, 390 tons yielding 162 oz gold.

HANNAN'S REWARD.—Clean up No. 10—Crushed on custom 946 tons, the income from which amounted to £1,785.

MOZAMBIQUE CONSOLIDATED.—Result of April crushing:—278 tons crushed, 258 oz. gold. Tailings 3 dwts.

ALASKA MEXICAN.—Return for April:—Bullion shipment $40,992; ore milled 12,958 tons; sulphurets treated 347 tons; bullion from sulphurets $11,987.

VICTORIA (CHARTERS TOWERS).—250 tons crushed, yielded 398 oz. gold.

BAYLEY'S UNITED.—Shipped two tons arsenical pyrites, worth 770 oz. of gold.

BONNIE DUNDEE.—Crushings reported 183 tons for 114 oz. Tributors on Queen Cross Reef formation crushed 95 tons for 107 oz.

CRESCENT.—Result of crushing for the past month, 600 tons, 89 oz.

GREAT BOULDER PROPRIETARY.—Crushing returns for the fortnight ended May 23:—Tons of ore crushed, 1,070; yield of gold in ounces, 2,385.

WELD HERCULES.—Tons crushed, 258; produced, 260 oz. of gold; tailings, 4 dwt. per ton

WASSAU (GOLD COAST).—April returns:—600 oz. of bar gold, from 572 tons of ore; twenty-two stamps worked twenty-two days. Detailed result of March return:—Ore crushed, 557 tons, producing 602 oz. bar gold, which, together with 13 oz. from copper skimmings, is 645½ oz. standard gold, and realised £2,515 12s. 5d.

FRANK SMITH DIAMOND.—3,200 loads washed, producing 170 carats.

PRINCESS ROYAL (CUE).—Clean up from 250 tons gave 178 oz., exclusive of ailings.

ENGLISH RAILWAYS.

Div. for half years. 1896	1896	1897	1897	Last Balance forward.	Amt. to pay 1 p.c. on Ord. for ½ yr.	NAME.	Date.	Gross Traffic for week: Amt.	Inc. or dec. on 1897.	Inc. or dec. on 1896.	No. of weeks	Gross Traffic for half-year to date: Amt.	Inc. or dec. on 1897.	Inc. or dec. on 1896.	Mileage.	Inc. on 1897.	Working	Prior Charges last ½ year.	Prop. add Cap. Exp. this ½ year
				£	£												%	£	£
10	10	10	10	2,707	5,094	Barry	M'y 21	2,608	−6,202	−5,099	21	146,338	−37,818	−12,368	31	—	8·89	60,665	316,853
nil	nil	nil	nil	—	—	Brecon and Merthyr	,, 22	1,101	−389	−579	21	28,763	−1,338	−4,663	61	—	—	—	—
nil	nil	nil	nil	3,979	4,749	Cambrian	,, 22	5,394	−23	−191	*	97,063	+2,733	—	250	—	60·96	63,148	40,000
1⅜	1¾	2	1¾	1,510	3,150	City and South London	,, 22	987	+29	+94	21	21,666	+205	+1,973	3½	—	56·67	5,552	124,000
	2	1½	2	7,895	13,210	Furness	,, 22	9,627	+296	+451	*	179,840	+5,091	—	139	—	49·88	97,423	20,910
1	1½	½	1	2,207	27,470	Great Cent. (late M., S., & L.)	,, 22	53,365	−156	−983	20	890,375	+22,841	+61,217	352½	—	57·17	627,386	1,200,000
1½	4½	2	5	51,283	62,865	Great Eastern	,, 22	79,727	−1,838	−6,771	20	1,600,453	+42,087	+125270	1,158¾	2	55·35	860,138	250,000
3	5½	3	5	15,094	102,496	Great Northern	,, 22	98,385	+2,304	+114	21	1,979,998	+58,179	+145111	1,071	8	61·76	641,485	750,000
4¾	7½	4¾	7½	31,350	121,981	Great Western	,, 22	176,650	−12,220	−24,750	20	3,476,480	−16,920	+93,980	2,582	21	51·44	1,486,272	800,000
nil	2	nil	1½	8,951	16,487	Hull and Barnsley	,, 22	9,062	+1,904	+2,985	20	139,625	+8,678	+19,403	73	—	58·21	70,290	52,920
5	5¼	5	5½	21,495	83,704	Lancashire and Yorkshire	,, 22	96,115	+3,399	−6,358	20	1,852,113	+59,261	+63,703	555½	25	56·70	674,745	451,976
4¾	8	4¾	8½	26,243	43,049	Lon., Brighton, & S. Coast	,, 21	44,071	−3,784	−9,859	21	1,010,890	+26,559	+42,436	476¾	—	50·20	407,042	240,735
nil	nil	nil	nil	72,294	56,296	London, Chatham, & Dover	,, 22	27,948	−763	−3,298	20	550,235	+12,240	+23,649	185¼	—	50·65	367,873	nil
6½	8	6½	7¾	89,535	204,068	London and North Western	,, 22	236,837	+4,164	−13,822	20	4,591,183	+103456	+237184	1,911½	—	56·92	1,404,534	600,000
5	8½	5	8½	23,038	59,367	London and South Western	,, 22	75,294	−2,937	−8,658	20	1,386,238	+40,997	+82,925	941	—	51·75	513,740	389,000
2¾	6	2¾	6¼	14,592	6,691	Lon., Tilbury, & Southend	,, 22	5,100	−392	−675	21	104,466	+4,977	+15,045	81	—	52·57	39,590	15,000
3½	3¾	3¾	3¾	17,133	26,409	Metropolitan	,, 22	16,333	+416	+660	*	329,455	+6,916	—	64	—	43·63	148,047	254,000
nil	nil	nil	nil	4,006	11,250	Metropolitan District	,, 22	8,344	+640	+174	20	169,280	+5,829	—	13	—	48·70	119,663	38,450
5	7	5¼	6¾	38,143	174,582	Midland	,, 22	189,451	+659	−3,768	21	3,865,816	+57,847	+289924	1,354¾	15½	57·39	1,216,380	650,000
5½	7¼	5¾	7	22,374	138,189	North Eastern	,, 21	156,116	+10,048	+14,018	20	2,887,150	+51,711	+175649	1,597¾	—	58·72	795,077	436,704
7½	7¾	7½	7½	7,061	10,102	North London	,, 22			Not recd			not	recvd.	12	—	50·90	49,973	7,600
4	5	4	4½	4,745	16,150	North Staffordshire	,, 22	15,342	+262	+658	20	326,647	+6,247	+19,029	312	—	55·27	118,142	19,605
10	10	11	10	1,642	3,004	Rhymney	,, 21	1,772	−3,753	−3,063	21	86,711	−17,051	−2,520	71	—	49·68	29,049	16,700
3	6⅝	3½	6⅝	4,054	50,215	South Eastern	,, 21	41,782	+287	−4,324	*	863,511	+39,419	—	448	—	51·88	380,763	250,000
3½	3½	2½	3½	2,315	25,961	Taff Vale	,, 21	6,760	−9,588	−7,823	21	256,685	−69,979	−31,645	121	—	54·90	94,800	92,000

* From January 1.

SCOTCH RAILWAYS.

5	5	5½	5	9,544	78,066	Caledonian	May 22	77,809	+1,117	+3,294	16	1,170,462	+28,003	—	851¼	5	50·38	582,248	441,477
5	5¼	5	5	7,364	24,630	Glasgow and South-Western	,, 21	31,273	+933	+2,088	16	449,393	+16,051	—	393½	—	54·69	221,663	196,143
3½	3½	3½	—	1,291	4,600	Great North of Scotland	,, 21	9,269	+29	+866	16	123,880	+415	+4,763	331	15½	52·43	92,178	60,000
	nil		—	10,477	12,820	Highland	,, 22	9,037	−681	+197	12	106,217	+2,208	—	479¾	97¾	58·63	78,976	[illegible]
	1½	1	1½	819	45,819	North British	,, 22	76,163	+1,270	+3,551	16	1,146,584	+29,961	—	1,230	23	48·62	944,809	40,800

IRISH RAILWAYS.

6½	6½	6½	—	5,466	7,790	Belfast and County Down	May 20	2,326	−197	−176	*	43,589	+890	—	76½	—	55·38	17,690	10,000
5½	6½	5½	—	—	4,284	Belfast and Northern Counties	,, 20	4,900	−313	−797	*	103,050	+4,651	—	249	—	—	—	—
	3	2	—	1,418	1,200	Cork, Bandon, and S. Coast†	,, 21	1,632	−57	−20	*	25,429	−2,030	—	103	—	54·82	14,436	5,430
	6⅜	6½	6⅜	38,776	17,816	Great Northern	,, 20	15,101	−608	+627	20	204,003	+12,040	+19,523	528	—	50·15	88,668	22,000
	5½	5½	5½	30,339	24,853	Great Southern and Western	,, 20	—	—	—	not	received	—	—	603	13	51·45	72,800	46,580
	4	4	4½	11,372	11,850	Midland Great Western	,, 20	8,805	−1,548	−1,528	20	198,558	+6,395	—	538	—	50·31	83,129	1,800
nil	ni	nil	nil	229	2,822	Waterford and Central	,, 20	711	−37	—	*	—	—	—	59½	—	53·04	6,858	1,500
nil	ni	nil	nil	1,936	2,987	Waterford, Limerick & W.	,, 20	4,689	+117	+123	*	—	—	—	350½	—	57·63	42,617	7,075

* From January 1. † Seventeen weeks' strike.

NOTICES.

Mr. William Abbott Turnbull and Mr. William McFarlane have been elected directors of the Thames and Mersey Marine Insurance Company, Limited, with seats at the London board.

Lloyds Bank, Limited, will open a branch on Monday next at 35, Cambridge-street, W., under the management of Mr. W. L. Harris.

The Great Northern Railway of America has removed its London office to 21, Cockspur-street, Pall Mall, S.W.

Mr. Nathaniel Spens has joined the board of the Transvaal Mortgage Loan and Finance Company, Limited.

The registered office of Waldon's Find Gold Mines, Limited, is now at 9-10, Fenchurch-street.

Baring Brothers & Company, Limited, have received cable advice from the Banco Comercial, Montevideo, stating that the bank has received from the municipality the sum of $76,000 gold, on account of the service of the City of Montevideo sterling loan of 1888.

The Imperial Ottoman Bank has decided to call in and cancel its certificates of 100 shares, and to replace them by others of twenty-five shares each. Holders are requested, therefore, to deposit their 100-share certificates at once, either in London, Paris, or Constantinople. Dividends will only be paid on coupons of the new certificates.

Manley Hopkins, Son, & Cookes have removed from 32, Cornhill, E.C., to 91, Gracechurch-street.

With reference to the Guatemala External Debt the Council of Foreign Bondholders has received advices from the Banco de Guatemala, dated the 30 ult., enclosing copy of a protest entered by the bank on behalf of the bondholders against the proposed reduction of the export duty on coffee. The protest had been read in the Assembly, and referred to the Finance Committee for consideration.

The Commissioners of Inland Revenue have entered into an agreement with the Corporation of Dover for the composition of the stamp duties payable on transfers of £93,000 Dover Corporation 3 per cent. stock. Transfers executed on or after March 19, 1898, will be exempt.

The agreement for giving effect to the proposed arrangement between the Central Argentine and the Buenos Ayres Northern Railway Companies having now been concluded, subject to the approval of the shareholders of the Central Argentine Company, and to the passing of the Bill now before Parliament, an extraordinary general meeting of the Central Argentine Company has been convened for June 9, to consider resolutions approving the Bill and the agreement, and authorising the creation and issue of 4 per cent. debenture stock for the carrying out of the arrangement and for other purposes.

The Standard Bank of South Africa has opened a branch at St. John's River, Cape Colony.

The Hon. H. C. Gibbs has retired from the board of the Exploration Company, Limited.

The New Zealand Loan and Mercantile Agency Company, Limited, announce that, in order to facilitate the issue of the new certificates under the scheme of readjustment, the transfer registers of the "A" and "B" debenture stocks will be closed from May 31 to June 28, both inclusive.

The numbers are published of 117 debentures of £100 each of the Blake and Knowles Steam Pump Works, Limited, which have been drawn for repayment at 110 on July 1.

We are informed that the Hon. G. A. Burns, of Messrs. G. & J. Burns, shipowners, Glasgow, has joined the board of directors of the Cunard Steamship Company, Limited.

RAILWAY TRAFFIC RETURNS.

ALCOY AND GANDIA RAILWAY AND HARBOUR COMPANY.—Traffic for week, May 21 :—Ps. 5,000; decrease Ps. 3,700. Aggregate from January 1, Ps. 174,350; increase, Ps. 880.

QUEBEC CENTRAL RAILWAY.—Receipts for first week of May, $7,530; decrease, 824. Aggregate from July 1, $124,580; decrease, $16,555.

MOBILE AND BIRMINGHAM RAILROAD.—Traffic for first week of May, $5,792; increase, $1,080. Aggregate from July 1, $318,540; increase, $1,531.

ALGECIRAS (GIBRALTAR) RAILWAY.—Traffic for week ended May 14, Ps. 22,140; increase, Ps. 4,089. Aggregate from July 1, Ps. 911,102; increase, Ps. 46,637.

WEST FLANDERS RAILWAY.—Gross receipts for week ending May 22, £1,967; decrease, £4. Total from January 1, £48,759; increase, £1,726.

WEST OF INDIA PORTUGUESE RAILWAY.—Week ending April 30, Rs. 6,185; increase, Rs. 1,421. Aggregate from January 1, Rs. 79,466; increase, Rs. 22,464.

ROHILKUND AND KUMAON RAILWAY.—Traffic receipts for week ending April 23, Rs. 9,228; increase, Rs. 1,836. Aggregate from January 1, Rs. 1,23,724; decrease, Rs. 5,110.

VILLA MARIA AND RUFINO RAILWAY.—Traffic for week ending May 21, $453; increase, $230. Aggregate from January 1, $7,107; increase, $1,350.

SOUTHERN MAHRATTA RAILWAY.—Receipts for week ended April 30, Rs. 1,21,864; decrease, Rs. 15,417.

BENGAL CENTRAL RAILWAY.—Traffic receipts for week ending April Rs. 32,452; increase, Rs. 16,657. Aggregate from January 1, Rs. 363,000; increase, Rs. 60,532.

BURMA RAILWAYS.—Traffic receipts for week ending April 25, Rs. 1,58,182; decrease Rs. 26,579. Aggregate from January 1, Rs. 34,11,254; decrease, Rs. 71,849.

H.H. THE NIZAM'S GUARANTEED STATE RAILWAYS.—Traffic receipts from January 1 to April 30 were Rs. 13,97,855; increase, Rs. 1,31,708.

CLEATOR AND WORKINGTON.—Gross receipts for the week ending May 21, amounted to £1,152, a decrease of £29. Total receipts from January 1, £20,730, a decrease of £667.

COCKERMOUTH AND KESWICK RAILWAY.—Receipts for the week ending May 21, £846; increase, £9. Aggregate from January 1, £16,734; increase, £1,511.

DELHI UMBALLA KALKA RAILWAY.—Receipts for week ended May 21, Rs. 31,800; increase, Rs. 8,600. Aggregate from January 1, Rs. 6,95,400; increase, Rs. 1,67,200.

WESTERN OF SANTA FE RAILWAYS.—Gross receipts for week ending May 21, $32,940; increase, $21,940.

GREAT WESTERN OF BRAZIL.—Traffics receipts for the week ending April 16, $23,892; increase, $3,685. Aggregate from January 1, $551,544; increase, $73,248,

FOREIGN RAILWAYS.

Mileage.			Name	Gross Traffic for Week.				Gross Traffic to Date.			
Total.	Increase on 1897.	Increase on 1896.		Week ending	Amount.	In. or Dec. upon 1897.	In. or Dec. upon 1896.	No. of Weeks.	Amount.	In. or Dec. upon 1897.	In. or Dec. upon 1896.
					£	£	£		£	£	£
319	—	—	Argentine Great Western ..	May 13	8,906	+ 889	+ 1,877	46	276,479	+ 1,120	+ 62,103
76½	—	—	Bahia and San Francisco ..	Apr. 30	2,754	− 131	− 1,437	18	—	—	—
434	48	84	Bahia Blanca and North West ..	Apr. 24	574	− 175	—	43	32,577	− 1,284	—
74	—	—	Buenos Ayres and Ensenada ..	May 22	3,020	− 538	—	21	68,448	− 11,038	—
426	—	—	Buenos Ayres and Pacific ..	May 21	9,246	+ 1,411	+ 1,575	46	316,094	− 47,760	+ 10,441
914	1	3	Buenos Ayres and Rosario ..	May 21	15,664	+ 3,123	+ 2,909	21	343,401	+ 93,047	+ 62,855
1,499	30	68	Buenos Ayres Great Southern ..	May 22	29,096	+ 5,674	+ 4,991	46	1,382,985	+ 114,112	+ 204,802
602	107	177	Buenos Ayres Western	May 22	10,645	+ 389	− 2,611	46	559,359	− 75,120	− 100,725
845	55	77	Central Argentine..	May 21	21,276	+ 5,736	+ 6,757	21	442,042	+ 116,345	+ 57,486
197	—	—	Central Bahia	Feb. 28*	$142,798	+ $14,291	+ $1,866	2	$276,357	+ $10,347	+ $14,624
271	—	—	Central Uruguay of Monte Video	May 21	5,311	+ 1,550	− 964	46	276,386	+ 25,217	− 13,760
228	—	—	Do. Eastern Extension	May 21	1,086	+ 160	+ 18	46	60,427	+ 9,555	+ 400
182	—	—	Do. Northern Extension	May 21	562	+ 125	− 291	46	29,495	+ 1,416	− 7,245
180	—	—	Cordoba and Rosario	May 15	2,260	+ 560	+ 725	46	97,940	− 12,585	− 760
128	—	—	Cordoba Central	May 15	$23,000	− $220	− $1,000	20	$423,700	− $56,290	− $71,350
549	—	—	Do. Northern Extension	May 15	$46,000	− $17,520	− $7,250	20	$884,790	− $299,490	− $164,890
137	—	—	Costa Rica..	May 14	5,358	+ 803	− 1,580	20	116,287	− 1,051	+ 13,044
99	—	—	East Argentine	Apr. 10	772	+ 136	+ 147	14	10,547	+ 387	+ 531
386	—	6	Entre Rios..	May 21	1,376	+ 393	+ 44	46	76,405	+ 24,577	+ 19,730
555	—	24	Inter Oceanic of Mexico.. ..	May 21	$61,100	+ $10,100	+ $12,420	46	$2,688,770	+ $424,640	+ $726,020
23	—	—	La Guaira and Caracas	Apr. 15	2,765	+ 1,045	+ 410	16	31,845	− 4,696	− 4,597
321	—	—	Mexican	May 21	$79,100	+ $10,100	—	21	$1,646,600	+ $174,250	—
1,846	—	—	Mexican Central	May 21	$249,765	+ $33,227	+ $69,475	21	$5,150,006	+ $30,871	+ $1,328,953
1,217	—	—	Mexican National	May 21	$109,371	− 2,928	+ $23,313	20	—	—	—
228	—	—	Mexican Southern	May 21	$13,069	− $2,907	+ $4,291	7	$89,037	− $14,320	+ $20,562
106	—	—	Minas and Rio	Mar. 31*	$161,158	− $9,628	—	9 mos.	$1,597,971	+ $193,854	—
94	—		N. W. Argentine	May 21	1,140	− 298	− 438	21	20,226	− 7,000	− 4,816
242	3	—	Nitrate	May 15†	14,036	− 1,641	− 13,779	20	132,840	− 2,880	− 62,479
520	—	—	Ottoman	May 14	4,049	+ 131	+ 758	20	89,511	− 22,510	+ 7,280
77½	—	—	Recife and San Francisco ..	Mar. 26	5,021	+ 737	− 1,074	13	75,414	+ 6,851	− 11,245
86½	—	—	San Paulo	Apr. 17‡	21,132	− 9,393	—	15	148,192	—	—
186	—	—	Santa Fe and Cordova	May 21	2,302	+ 814	− 621	46	82,449	+ 2,558	− 5,643
110	—	—	Western of Havana	May 21	1,540	− 322	− 544	46	81,257	+ 4,190	− 7,132

* For month ended. † For fortnight ended. ‡ For three weeks.

INDIAN RAILWAYS.

Mileage.			Name.	Gross Traffic for Week.				Gross Traffic to Date.			
Total.	Increase on 1897.	Increase on 1896.		Week ending	Amount.	In. or Dec. on 1897.	In. or Dec. on 1896.	No. of Weeks.	Amount.	In. or Dec. on 1897.	In. or Dec. on 1896.
862	—	—	Bengal Nagpur	May 21	Rs.1.80.000	+Rs.51.581	+Rs.62.795	21	Rs.32.77.742	+Rs.3.78.361	+Rs1.00.336
827	8	63	Bengal and North-Western ..	Apr. 23	Rs.1.48.700	+Rs. 7.395	—	17	Rs.22.23.670	+Rs.2.55.803	—
461	—	—	Bombay and Baroda	May 21	£47,942	+£11,416	+£9,950	21	£602,168	+£36,559	−£128,533
1,885	2	13	East Indian	May 21	Rs.13.89.000	+Rs1.58.000	+Rs3.64.000	21	Rs.2.56.91.000	+Rs.9.92.000	+Rs7.74.000
1,491	—	—	Great Indian Penin.	May 21	£84,214	+£28,661	+£9,643	21	£1,448,544	+£289,950	−£178,727
736	—	—	Indian Midland	May 21	Rs.2.20.850	+Rs.72.184	+Rs1.18.256	21	Rs.29.74.509	+Rs.3.22.961	+Rs7.18.906
840	—	—	Madras	May 14	£20,258	−£92	+£275	20	£370,137	−£21,140	−£6,807
1,043	—	—	South Indian	Apr. 23	Rs.1.58.012	−Rs.29.361	−Rs.37.153	17	Rs.2.533.241	−Rs.2.41.385	−Rs.55.876

UNITED STATES AND CANADIAN RAILWAYS.

Mileage.			Name.	Gross Traffic for Week.		Gross Traffic to Date.		
Total.	Increase on 1897.	Increase on 1896.		Period Ending.	Amount.	In. or Dec. on 1897.	No. of Weeks.	Amount.	In. or Dec. on 1897.
					dols.	dols.		dols.	dols.
917	—	—	Baltimore & Ohio S. Western ..	May 14	154,036	+42,784	44	5,981,643	+724,074
6,568	92	156	Canadian Pacific	May 21	511,000	+42,000	19	8,690,000	+1,618,000
922	—	—	Chicago Great Western	May 21	97,000	+11,000	45	4,773,640	+619,163
6,169	—	469	Chicago, Mil., & St. Paul ..	May 21	631,000	+109,000	19	11,483,001	+1,714,800
1,685	—	—	Denver & Rio Grande	May 21	148,800	+22,300	45	7,194,000	+1,171,400
3,512	—	—	Grand Trunk, Main Line ..	May 21	£73,933	+£4,077	19	£1,463,912	+£136,411
335	—	—	Do. Chic. & Grand Trunk	May 21	£15,275	+£4,314	19	£298,365	+£58,840
189	—	—	Do. Det., G. H. & Mil...	May 21	£3,152	−£246	19	£69,175	−£4,098
2,938	—	—	Louisville & Nashville	May 14	424,000	+49,000	18	7,866,175	+1,183,620
2,197	137	137	Miss., K., & Texas	May 21	164,000	−3,000	45	11,100,428	+900,290
477	—	—	N. Y., Ontario, & W.	May 14	64,842	−2,285	44	3,338,685	+87,471
1,570	—	—	Norfolk & Western	May 14	244,000	+67,000	18	4,110,960	+477,433
3,499	336	—	Northern Pacific	May 14	441,000	+113,000	17	7,473,775	+2,235,558
1,223	—	—	St. Louis S. Western	May 14	72,000	+5,000	18	1,942,295	+306,928
4,654	—	—	Southern	May 14	395,000	+64,000	44	6,625,812	+1,479,443
1,979	—	—	Wabash	May 21	252,000	+38,000	19	5,013,406	+1,108,000

MONTHLY STATEMENTS.

Mileage.			Name.	Net Earnings for Month.				Net Earnings to Date.			
Total.	Increase on 1896	Increase on 1895.		Month.	Amount.	In. or Dec. on 1897.	In. or Dec. on 1896.	No. of Months.	Amount.	In. or Dec. on 1897.	In. or Dec. on 1896.
					dols	dols.	dols.		dols.	dols.	dols.
6,935	44	444	Atchison	March	904,000	+337,000	+369,344	3	2,144,434	+674,836	+220,460
6,547	103	106	Canadian Pacific	March	753,000	+243,000	+276,469	3	1,693,000	+415,000	+388,787
6,169	—	469	Chicago, Mil., & St. Paul ..	March	1,180,000	+170,000	+65,202	3	2,725,334	+225,840	+84,122
1,685	—	—	Denver & Rio Grande	March	267,900	+39,242	+38,942	9	2,520,889	+407,063	+30,946
1,970	—	—	Erie..	March	611,000	+33,000	+8,708	3	1,378,600	+91,400	−94,751
3,512	—	—	Grand Trunk, Main Line ..	March	£102,100	+£14,331	+£31,909	3	£245,953	+£62,372	+100,819
335	—	—	Do. Chic. & Grand Trunk	March	£17,400	+£10,152	+13,357	3	£38,710	+£24,282	+28,939
189	—	—	Do. Det. G. H. & Mil. ..	March	£4,200	−£1,414	+3,221	3	£6,528	+£737	+6,419
3,127	—	239	Illinois Central	March	759,000	+206,000	+343,862	3	2,213,704	+365,620	+549,739
2,396	—	—	New York Central*	April	3,807,000	+302,000	+394,152	4	14,602,000	+964,000	—
477	—	—	New York Ontario, & W. ..	March	84,600	−4,800	+40,032	9	928,300	+38,200	+115,494
1,570	—	—	Norfolk & Western	March	301,000	+18,000	+110,317	3	826,000	+65,247	+201,902
3,407	—	—	Pennsylvania	February	1,359,101	+65,700	+236,000	2	2,511,898	92,400	+345,000
1,055	—	—	Phil. & Reading	March	701,100	+50,822	—	9	7,567,293	+524,064	—

Prices Quoted on the London Stock Exchange.

Throughout the INVESTORS' REVIEW middle prices alone are quoted, the object being to give the public the approximate current quotations of every security of any consequence in existence. On the markets the buying and selling prices are both given, and are often wide apart where stocks are seldom dealt in. Other particulars will be found in the INVESTMENT INDEX published quarterly—January, April, July, and October—in connection with this REVIEW, price 2s., by post 2s. 2d. Where dividends are paid only once a year, an *italic* type is used to distinguish them. The London Stock Exchange Official List is quoted in the REVIEW almost entire, only very insignificant issues, or bonds falling due within the next two or three years, being omitted. But the list is subdivided into the leading, or active, stocks, and those less frequently dealt in. The former will be found under the head of "Stock Markets," and with more details than it is possible to give for the bulk of securities. By retaining the file of the INVESTORS' REVIEW any subscriber can follow for himself the movements of securities from week to week, and the INVESTMENT INDEX will from time to time help to fill up deficiencies in the information.

Tea Companies and Mines and Mining Finance Stocks are placed in special lists.

Among the abbreviations used are the following:—S.F. Snk.Fd. *sinking fund*; Certs., *certificates*; Debs. or Dbs., *debentures*; Db. or D.Stk., *debenture stock*; Pf., Prf., or Pref., *preference*; Prefd. or Pfd., *preferred*; Dfd., *deferred*; L. or Ltd., *limited*; Sh., *share*; Ans., *annuities*; Cu. or Cm., *cumulative*; Gu or Guar., *guaranteed*; Bds., *bonds*; S., Sr., or Ser., *series*; In., Ins., Insc., *inscribed*; Dr., Drgs., Drwgs., *drawings*; Stg., Strlg., *sterling*; Lia., *liable to*; Sp., Surp., *surplus*; Per., Perp., *perpetual*; Ln. *lien*; Lo. *loan*.

The dates following the names of securities are the years of issue or of redemption. Where shares are not fully paid up, their nominal amount s given with the name so that investors may know the liability upon them.

BRITISH FUNDS, &c.

Rate.	Name.	Price.
2¾	2¾ p.c.'s(Childers')Red.. 1905	104½
3	Local Loans Stk. 1912	110
3	Metro. Police Deb. Stk. 1920	105½
—	Red Sea Ind. Tel. Ann. 1908	8½
4	Canada Gv. "Intcl. Rly." 1903	105½
4	Do. do. .. 1908	111
4	Do. Bonds 1910	112
4	Do. Bonds 1913	117½
3	Egyptian Gov. Gar.	106
3	Mauritius Ins. Stk. 1940	114
4	Turkish Guar. 1855	109
11½	Bank of Ireland Stk.	385
3½	India Rupee Paper	62
3½	Do. 1854-5	62
3	Do. 1896-7 1916	55
3½	Isle of Man Deb.	104
3	Do. Deb. Stk... 1919-29	103

CORPORATION AND COUNTY STOCKS.

FREE OF STAMP DUTY.

Rate.	Name.	Price.
3½	Metropolitan Con. 1929	116½
3	Do. 1941	110
2½	Do. 1920-49	99
2½	L.C.C. Con. Stock 1920	98
3½	Comm. of Sewers, Scp., S.F. 1905	104
3½	Corp. of Lond. Bds...1898-1902	100½
3	Do. 1898-1919	101
3½	Do., Debs. Scp. ...... S.F. 1916	105
2½	Do., Deb. Stk. Scrip .. 1927-57	93
3	Barnsley 1916-46	103
3	Barry 1914-46	101½
3	Bath 1909-34	101
3	Batley 1914-44	101½
3½	Birmingham 1945	113½
3	Do. 1947	111½
2½	Do. 1926	99
3	Blackburn 1930	105½
3	Bournemouth 1913-33	103
3½	Bradford 1945	116½
3	Do. Deb. Stock .. 1954	106
3	Brighouse.............. 1916-46	100
3½	Brighton 1946	117
3	Do. 1957	96½
	Burton-on-Trent......... 1913-43	101
	Cambridge 1913-43	103
	Cardiff 1935	114½
	Do. 1914-54	103½
	Cheltenham.............. 1971	105½
	Chichester 1916-46	101
3½	Croydon	130½
3	Do. 1940	106½
3	Derby 1920-50	105½
3	Devon C.C.............. 1917-33	104½
3½	Dewsbury 1930	109
3	Do. 1930	103
3	Dorset County 1922-32	105
3	Douglas (I. of Man) 1926	101½
3	Dover 1913-43	101
3½	Dublin 1944	113½
3	Eastbourne 1920-40	104
3	Edinburgh 1924	105½
2½	Do. 1927	97
2½	Exeter 1917-57	96
3	Glamorgan County 1914-34	104
3½	Glasgow 1914	109
3	Do. 1921	104½
2½	Do. 1925-40	98
3	Gloster 1915-55	101
3	Grimsby 1913-45	103
3	Hampshire County 1914-34	105½
3	Hanley 1913-43	103
3	Harrogate 1914-34	103
3	Hastings 1915-54	103½
2½	Hertfordshire C.C. 1916-36	98
3	Heston & Isleworth U.D.C. 1915-35	101
3	Huddersfield 1934	107
3½	Hull (1st iss.)	126½
3	Inverness.............. 1914-44	100
3	Ipswich 1959	107½
3	Lancaster.............. 1919-55	103
2½	Leeds 1927	98
3½	Leicester 1934	116½
3	Lincoln.............. 1919	103
3½	Liverpool..............	132

Corporation, &c. (*continued*):—

Rate.	Name.	Price.
3	Manchester 1941	106½
3½	Middlesbro' 1909	105½
3½	Do. 1911-13	105
3	Do. 1915	104
3	Middlesex C.C.......... 1915-35	106
3½	Newcastle 1936	118½
3½	Do. Irred.	129½
2½	Do. 1915-36	100
3	Newcastle-under-Lyme.. 1909-44	101
3	Newport (Mon.) 1915-55	101½
3	Norwich 1952	110
3	Nottingham	112
3	Oxford 1951	109½
3	Penzance 1916-46	100½
3	Plymouth 1942	106½
3	Pontypridd U.D.C. 1916-46	98
3	Poole.............. 1915-45	102
3½	Portsmouth........1916 24 & 27	112
3	Do. 1913-33	106
3	Ramsey 1920-40	100
3	Ramsgate.......... 1915-55	102
3½	Reading	123½
3	Do. 1962	107
3½	Rhyl U.D.C. 1953	110
3	Richmond (Surrey) 1942	104½
3	River Wear Debt Certs.	100
3	St. Helen's 1915-55	102
3	Scarbro' 1915-50	102
2½	Sheffield 1925-57	94½
3	Shipley U.D.C. 1915-35	100
3	Somerset Co. 1923-33	104
3	South Shields.......... 1915-45	105½
2¾	Southampton 1915-45	100½
3	Southend-on-Sea 1916-46	101
3	Staffs C.C. 1915-35	103½
3	Stockport.......... 1914-54	101
3	Stockton 1930	104
3	Do. 1915-35	103
3	Surrey Co. 1922-32	105½
3½	Swansea	120
3	Do. 1955	106
3	Taunton 1918-3-9-43	100
3	Tees Conserv. Deb. Stk. 1947	100
3	Thames Conserv. "A" Deb. Stk.......... 1954	103½
3	Do. "B" Deb. Stk. 1954	102½
3	Torquay 1913-43	101½
3	Tunbridge Wells 1931	102½
3	Tynemouth 1913	99
3	Wakefield.......... 1929	101½
3	Walsall.......... 1932	107½
3	West Bromwich.......... 1930	105
3½	West Ham 1929	110
3	Do. 1945	105
3	West Sussex C.C. 1915-35	106
3	Weston-s.-Mare Lcl Bd. 1914-44	99½
3	Weymouth & Melc. Regis 1918	101
3	Widnes.......... 1915-55	100
3	Wigan 1921	104½
3	Windsor 1918-55	102
3½	Wisbech 1947	113½
3½	Wolverhampton 1932	117
3	Do. 1924-54	107
3	York 1916-41	105½

SUBJECT TO STAMP DUTY.

Rate.	Name.	Price.
3½	Belfast City & Dis. Watr. 1938	114
3	Do. Red Stk. 1953-6	106
3½	Belfast 1924	103
4	Blackburn Con. Deb. Irred.	141½
3½	Do. do. Irred..........	130
3½	Bristol	130½
3½	Burnley 1933	114
2½	Chesterfield Gas & Wtr. 1916-46	98
3½	Douglas Town 1921	105
3	Dover Harb. 1st Deb... 1956	104½
3½	Hull (2nd iss.)	128½
4	Leeds Deb.......... 1927	123
3½	Do.	115½
3	Do. 1927	106
3	Leicester 1919-44	103½
4	Manchester..........	145
3	Do. 1928	104½
4½	Middlesboro' Mrts. 1908	111
3½	Sheffield 1898-1916	105½
3½	Do. 1925-36	114
3	Do. 1925	105½
3½	Southampton .... S.F.	106
4½	Stockton Morts.......... 1908	110½
3½	Worcester.......... 1950	109

COLONIAL AND PROVINCIAL GOVERNMENT SECURITIES.

Rate.	Name.	Price.
6	British Columbia.......... 1907	119½
4½	Do. Debs. .. 1917	111½
3	British Guiana Imgtn. Bds.	98
5	Canada, "Intercol. Rail," 1903	107½
4	Do. (Bonds) 1904-5-6-8	105
4	Do. Reduced........ 1910	108
3½	Do. Bnds. 1909-34	107
4	Do. Loan 1910-35	109
3	Do. Loan 1938	102
6	Cape of G. Hope........ 1900	—
5	Do. 1900	—
4½	Do. red. by an. draw.	108
4½	Do 1870	110
4	Do. 1881	108
4	Do 1917-23	113½
4½	Ceylon	108
4	Do.	106½
4½	Fiji Gov. Deb. Sink. Fd.	102
4	Jamaica Sink. Fd. 1923	103
5	Manitoba Debs...... ... 1910	113
5	Do. Ster. Bds. 1888	119½
4	Do. Ster. Debs.	104
4	Mauritius, Cons. Debs. 1880...	101½
4½	Natal, Sink. Fd........ 1919	118
4	Do. do. 1926	114
3½	Newfoundland Stg. Bds. 1941	100
3½	Do. do. .. 1947	100
3	Do. do.	86½
5	New South Wales 1897-1902	104½
4	Do. 1903-5-8-9-15	105
5	New Zealand 1914	118
5	Do. Cnsls. 1 p.c. per an. Sink. Fd.	103
3½	Nova Scotia Debs.	104
5	Quebec Prov. 1904-6	108
4½	Do. (drgs.)	105
5	Do. Strlg. Bds. 1912	115
4	Do. Strlg. Bds. 1928	110
4	Do. Strlg. Bds. 1934	103
4	Queensland 1913-15	106
4½	St. Lucia Debs..........	102
6	South Australia 1868-1900	103½
6	Do. 1901-1910	119
5	Do. 1911-1925	115½
4	Do. 1896-1916	105
4	Do. 1929	108½
4	Do. 1916	106½
4	Do. 1917-18-24	107½
6	Tasmania 1897-1901	104
4	Do. 1908-11, 1913-14-20	107½
5	Trinidad Debs., an. drw. 1 p.c...	107
4	Victoria 1899-1901	102
4½	Do. 1904	106
4	Do. Rail. Loan 1907	106
4	Do. Loans 1908-13	106
4½	West. Austr. 1 p.c. an. Sink. Fd.	107
4	Do. do.	106

REGISTERED AND INSCRIBED STOCKS.

No stamp duty except for Canada 4 p.c. Reduced (½ per cent.).

Rate.	Name.	Price.
4	Antigua Insc. Stk. Red. 1919-44	110
3½	Barbados Insc. Stk. 1925-42	107
3	British Colum. Insc. Stk. 1941	101½
4	British Guiana Insc..... 1935	116½
4	Canada Stk. Regd. ..1904-5-6-8	105
4	Do. 4 p.c. (late 5 p.c.) Regd. 1910	103
3½	Do. 3½ p.c. Stock Regd. 1909-34	106
4	Do. Ln. for 4 milln. stg. 1910-35	109
3	Do. Stk. Regd. 1938	102
2½	Do. Insc.......... 1947	92
4	Cape G. Hope Regd. .. 1917-23	112
4	Do. (Ln. of '83) Insc. .. 1923	115
4	Do. Cons. Stk. Insc..... 1916-36	112
3½	Do. Consol. Insc. Stock 1929-49	110
4	Ceylon Insc. Stock 1934	120
3	Do. 1940	102
4	Grenada Insc. Stock.... 1917-42	110
3½	Hong Kong Insc. Stock 1918-43	104
4	Jamaica Insc. Stock.... 1934	118
—	Do. 1922-44	98
4	Mauritius Inscribed 1937	118½
4	Natal Consd. Stk. Insc. 1927	117
4	Do. 1937	119
3½	Do. Inscribed Stock.. 1914-39	105
4	Newfoundland Inscribed 1913-38	106
4	Do. 1935	113
4	Do. Consd. Stk. Ins. 1936	113
4	N. S. Wales Stock Insc. 1933	118
3½	Do. 1924	108
3½	Do. 1918	106
3	Do 1935	99

Colonial, &c. (*continued*):—

Rate.	Name.	Price.
4	N. Zealnd. Con. Stk. Ins. 1929	112
3½	Do 1940	107
3	Do. Inscribed.... 1945	99
3	Quebec (Prov.) Ins. Stk. 1937	93
4	Queensland Stock Insc. 1915-24	110
3½	Do. 1921-4-30	105
3½	Do. 1945	106½
3	Do. 1922-47	99
4	St. Lucia Insc. Stock .. 1919-44	113
4	S. Austrln. (1882-7) Reg. 1916-36	108½
3½	Do. In. Stk. Reg. 1939	109
3	Do. 1916-26	100
3/	Do. 1916	100
3½	Tasmanian Insc. Stock.. 1920-40	109
4	Do. 1920-40	116
4	Trinidad Insc. Stock.... 1917-42	110
3	Do. 1922-44	98
4	Victoria Rly. Loan '81, Inscribed Stock 1907	106
4	Victoria Insc. Stock 1908-13-19	107
4	Victoria (1883) Ins. Stk. 1920	112
3½	Do. Inscribed Stock 1921-3-6	105
4	Do. do. 1911-26	109
4	W. Austral. Insc. Stock 1934	116½
4	Do. 1911-31	109
3½	Do. 1915-35	104
3	Do. 1915-35	97
3	Do. 1916-36	98

FOREIGN STOCKS, BONDS, &c.

COUPONS PAYABLE IN LONDON.

Last Div.	Name.	Price.
36/	Argentine Ry. Loan 6 p.c. 1881	87½
15/	Do. 5 p.c. 1884	66½
30/	Do. N. Cent. Ry. Ext. 5 p.c. 1887-8-9	66½
30/	Do. 5 p.c. Trsy. Convs. 1887	65
5/4½	Do. 4½ p.c. Interl. Gld. 1888	64½
27/	Do. 4½ p.c. Stlg. Extrl. 1888	65
10/6	Do. 3½ p.c. External .. 1889	49
4	Do. 4 p.c. Ry. Guar. Res....	57½
4½	Brazilian 1883	56
4½	Do. Gold.......... 1879	60½
4½	Do. 1888	52
30/	Buenos Ayres 1824	80
6	Do. 1882-3-6	47
6	Bulgarian 1888	92
6	Do. Mort. Bonds 1892	92
4½	Chilian 1885	73
4½	Do. 1886	74
4½	Do. 1887	73
4½	Do. 1889	82½
5	Do. 1892	85
4½	Do. 1893	73
4½	Do. 1895	71
5	Do. 1896	84
7	Chinese Silver 1894	96
6	Do. Gold 1895	107
6	Do. Apl. '95 by dwgs. 1901-15	109
5	Do. Red. dwgs. in 36 yr. 1896	99
5	Do. Do. Regis. 1896	99
1½	Colmbn. 1½ to 3 p.c. Ext. Bds. 1896	17
6	Cordova, Prov. 1886	24
—	Do. Eng. Ass. Certs.	23
—	Do. 6 p.c. 1887-8	24
—	Do. Eng. Ass. Certs.	23
3	Costa Rica "A"	30
2½	Do. "B"	23
3	Danish Gold 1914	98
10/	Ecuador N. Ext. Bds. 4½ p.c. ascn. to 5 p.c.	22
3½	Egypt'n Ins. Stk. lia. Stp. Dty. 1890	100
4	Do. State Domain 1878	104½
4	Do. D. Sanieh, Red. .. 1905	102½
6	Entre Rios.......... 1886-8	34
6	Do. Fndg. Ln. Bds. 1894-1921	29
6	Do. do. Parana City	22½
15/	Greek 1881	38
15/	Do. 1884	38
12/	Do. Rentes..........	32
15/	Do. (Piræus-Larissa Ry.)	37
9/6	Do. Fundg. Loan ......(1)-	41
4	Guatemala Extl. Debt..........	29
6	Hawaiian	102
4	Hungarian Gold Rentes........	101
3	Do. 1895	89½
6	Italian Irriga. Guar.	108½
5	Do. Maremmana	91
5	Japan 5 p.c.	103½
5	Mexican (Nat. R. Tehuantp c.)..	92½
6	Do. Extrl. 1890	95

Foreign Stocks, &c. (*continued*):—

Last Div.	Name.	Price
6	Mexican Extrl. 1893	95
5	Do. Intrnl. Cons. Slvr.	36
5	Do Intern. Rd. Bds. 2d. Ser.	36
4	Nicaragua 1886............	42½
3½	Norwegian, red. 1937, or earlier	98
3	Do. do. 1965. do.	97
3½	Do. 3½ p.c. Bnds.........	102
1	Paraguay 1p.c. ris. 3p.c. 1886-96.	15
5	Russian, 1822, £ Strlg.	149
3	Do. 1859	93
4	Do. (Nicolas Ry.) 1867-9 ..	101
3	Do. Transcauc. Ry. 1882 ..	94
4	Do. Con. R. R. Bd. Ser. I., 1889..	103
4	Do. Do. II., 1889..	103
4	Do. Do. III., 1891..	102
3½	Do. Bonds	100
4	Do. Ln. (Dvinsk and Vitbsk)	100½
6	Salvador 1889..............	57½
—	S Domingo 4s. Unified .. 1980	62
6	San Luis Potosi Stg. 1889	88
5	San Paulo (Brzl.), Stg. 1888	86½
6	Santa Fé 1883-4..............	36
—	Do. Eng. Ass. Certs. Dep...	35
5	Do. 1888	48
—	Do. Eng. Ass. Certs. Dpsit..	47
5	Do. (W. Cnt. Col. Rly.) Mrt.	24
5	Do. & Reconq. Rly. Mort...	24
5	Spanish Quicksilvr Mort. 1870 ..	99½
3½	Swedish 1880	102
3	Do. 1888	93
3	Do. Conversion Loan 1894..	98
5	Trans. Gov. Loan Red...1903-42	105
9/	Tucuman (Prov.) 1888..........	66½
54	Turkish, Secd. on Egypt. Trib.	102
5½	Turkish, Egpt. Trib., Ott. Bd., '94	98
4	Do. Priority 1890..........	89½
1	Do. Convted Series, "A"..	66
5	Do. Customs Ln. 1886......	94½
5	Uruguay Bonds 1896	56
3	Venzuela New Con. Debt 1881	32

COUPONS PAYABLE ABROAD.

Last Div.	Name.	Price
7	Argent. Nat. Cedla. Sries, "B".	33½
5	Austrian Ster. Rnts., ex 10fl., 1870	85
5	Do. do. do.	84
5	Do. Paper do. 1870	84
5	Do. do. do.	84
4	Do. Gld Rentes 1876	100
3	Belgian exchange 25 fr.	100
3½	Danish Int., 1887, Rd. 1896	—
2½	Dutch Certs. ex 12 gldrs.	86
3	Do. Bonds	98
3	Do. Insc. Stk.........	97
3½	French Rentes	104½
3	Do. 1878, '81-4., Red.	99
3	German Imp. Ln. 1891..........	95
3	Do. do. 1892-3	95
3	Do. do. 1890-4	96
5	Japan Cons. Ln., '92, 3, & 5, Red.	46
36/9	Prussian Consols	102
3	" Cons. Stg. Ln. 1891....	96
4	Utd. States, 1877, Red. 1907	112
4	Do. 1895, 30 yrs.......	126
3½	Do. Maschsetts Gl. 1935	113½
3½	Do. Gold Bonds 1923	107½
2	Virginia Cpn. Bds., 3 p.c. from July, 1901	69½

BRITISH RAILWAYS.

ORD. SHARES AND STOCKS.

Last Div	Name.	Price.
10	Barry, Ord.	276½
4	Do. Prefd.	125
6	Do. Defd.	150½
5	Caledonian, Ord..........	155
3	Do. Prefd.	99
—	Do. Defd. Ord., No. 1	4½
	Cambrian, Ord............	5½
—	Do. Coast Cons.	5½
32/	Cardiff Ry. Pref. Ord.	115
3/	Central Lond. £10 Ord. Sh.	10½
1/9½	Do. do. £6 paid......	6½
3½d.	Do. Pref. Half-Shares..	1½
1/6	Do. Def. do..........	4½
1½	City and S. London	68½
—	East London, Cons.	6½
2	Furness	65½
2½	Glasgow and S. West. Pfd.	81
2½	Do. do. Dfd.	64
3	Great Central, Ord....1894	41½
32/0	Do. London Exten.....	74½
—	Great N. of Scotland, Prfd.	88
—	Do. Dfd.	33
4	Great Northern, Prefd......	120
—	Do. Consolidated "A"	51
—	Do. do. "B"	190½
2	Highland	75½
4	Isle of Wight, Prefd.	120½
3	Do. Defd.	83½
	Lancs. Derbys. and E. Cst.	4
8½	L. Brighton and S. C. Ord.	185
6	Do. Prefd. Ord.	197
10/	Do. Contgt. Rights Certs.	18½
5½	Lond. and S. Western Ord.	224½
4	Do. Preferred	133
6½	Lond., Tilb., and Southend	133½
—	Mersey, £20 shares	½
—	Metropolitan, New Ord.....	130
2½	Do. Surplus Lands....	92
4	North Cornwall, 4 p.c. Pref.	104½
12/6	Do. Deferred	22½
7½	North London............	223½
4½	North Staffordshire	129

British Railways (*continued*):—

Last Div.	Name.	Price.
3/3	Plymouth, Devenport, and S. W. Junc. £10	8½
3/	Port Talbot £10 Shares ..	9½
9d.	Rhondda Swns. B. £10 Sh.	5
10	Rhymney, Cons..........	265½
4	Do. Prefd.	123
6½	Do. Defd.	145½
1½	Scarboro', Bridlington Junc.	47½
6½	South Eastern, Ord........	150
6	Do. Pref.	191
3½	Taff Vale	81
25/	Vale of Glamorgan........	124½
3	Waterloo & City	134½

LEASED AT FIXED RENTALS

Last Div.	Name.	Price.
4	Birkenhead	144
5.19.0	East Lincnshire..........	202½
5½	Hammsmith. & City Ord. ..	192½
4½	Lond. and Blackwll.	160½
4½	Do. £100 4½ p. c. Pref...	160½
56/6	Lond. & Green. Ord......	101
5	Do. 5 p. c. Pref.	176½
5	Nor. and Eastn. £50 Ord...	89
6	Do. ..	104½
3½	N. Cornwall 3½ p. c. Stk...	125½
4 1/11	Nott. & Granthm. R. & C...	144½
3½	Portptk. & Wigtn. Guar. Stk.	121½
9	Vict. Stn. & Pimlico Ord...	312½
4½	Do. 4½ p. c. Pref....	158½
4/	West Lond. £20 Ord. Shs.	14
4 1/10	Weymouth & Portld.......	157½

DEBENTURE STOCKS.

Last Div.	Name.	Price.
4	Alexandra Dks. & Ry.	128
3	Barry, Cons.	107
4	Brecon & Mrthyr, New A	124½
4	Do. New B	105
4	Caledonian	147
4	Cambrian "A"	132½
4	Do. "B"	127½
4	Do. "C"	119½
4	Do. "D"	107½
3	Cardiff Rly.	100½
4	City and S. Lond.	137
3½	Cleator & Working Junc...	118½
3	Devon & Som. "A"	103½
16/3	Do. "B" 4 p. c.	36
—	Do. "C" 4 p. c.	10
4	E. Lond. 2nd Ch. 4 p. c. A	135
5/	Do. 2nd B	67½
—	Do. 3rd Ch. 4 p. c. ..	19½
—	Do. 4th do.	9½
3½	Do. 1st (3½ p. c.)	128½
2½	Do. 2½ p.c. (Whitech. Exn).	87
4	Forth Bridge	142½
4	Furness	142½
4	Glasgow and S. Western ..	147
5	Gt. Central	—
4½	Do.	155½
4	Gt. Eastern	145
4	Gt. N. of Scotland........	144½
3	Gt. Northern	111½
4	Gt. Western	149
4½	Do	156½
4½	Do.	166
5	Do.	184½
2½	Do.	96½
4	Highland	139
3	Hull and Barnsley	104½
3	Do. 2nd (3-4 p. c)...	122½
4	Isle of Wight	142½
3	Do. Cent. "A"..	92½
4½	Do. "B"	115½
4	Do. "C"	82½
3	Lancs. & Yorkshire	112
4	Lancs. Derbys. & E. Cst...	123½
4½	Ldn. and Blackwall	155½
4	Ldn. and Greenwich......	144½
4	Lond., Brighton, &c.	148½
4½	Do.	165½
4½	Lond., Chath., &c., Arb...	154½
4½	Do. "B"..	153½
4	Do.	137½
4	Do. 1883....	137½
3	Do.	106
3	Lond. & N. Western......	115
3	Lond. & S. Westn. "A" ..	114
3	Do. Consld.	114
4	Lond., Til., & Southend ..	144½
—	Mersey, 5 p. c. (Act, 1866)	65
4	Metropolitan	144½
4½	Do.	162½
3½	Do.	126½
6	Met. District	207½
4	Do.	138½
2½	Midland	95
4½	Mid-Wales "A"	137½
4	Neath & Brecon 1st	127½
4	Do. "A 1" ..	117½
3	North British	109
3	Do. 1893	108
7½	N. Cornwall, Launcstn., &c.	125½
4	North Eastern............	113

Debenture Stocks (*continued*):—

Last Div.	Name.	Price.
4½	North London............	163½
3	N. Staffordshire	111
4	Plym. Devpt. & S.W. Jn...	141½
4	Rhondda and Swan. Bay..	130½
4	Rhymney	144½
4	South-Eastern............	147
5	Do.	182½
3½	Do.	127½
3	Do.	113
3	Taff Vale	109½
4	Tottenham & For. Gate ..	143½
3	Vale of Glamorgan	105½
3	West Highld. (Gtd. by N.B.)	106
4	Wrexham, Mold, &c. "A"	113½
4	Do. "B"	101½
4	Do. "C"	97½

GUARANTEED SHARES AND STOCKS.

Last Div.	Name.	Price.
4	Caledonian	143½
4	Do.	142½
4	Forth Bridge	142½
4	Furness 1881	137½
4	Glasgow & S. Western	141½
4	Do. St. Enoch, Rent	141½
6	Gt. Central	198½
4½	Do. 1st Pref.........	151½
3½	Do. Pref.	104½
5	Do. Irred. S.Y. Rent	161½
4½	Do. do.	139½
4	Gt. Eastern, Rent	142½
5	Do. Metropolitan..	177½
4	Do.	142½
4	Gt. N. of Scotland........	138½
4	Gt. Northern	145
5	Gt. Western, Rent........	182
5	Do. Cons.	182
4	Lancs. & Yorkshire	144
5	L., Brighton & S. C.......	179½
3½	L., Chat. & D. (Shrtlds.)..	110½
4	L. & North Western	146
4	L. & South Western.. 1881	144
4½	Met. District, Ealing Rent	150
4½	Do. Fulham Rent	150
4	Do. Midland Rent	141½
4	Do. Mid. & Dist. Guar.	127½
2½	Midland, Cons. Perp.	92
3	Mid. & G.N. Jt., "A" Rnt..	106
3	N. British, Lien	107½
4	Do Cons. Pref. No. 1	139
3	N. Cornwall, Wadebrge. Gu.	107
4	N. Eastern	144½
5	N. Staff. Trent & M. £20 Shs.	35½
3½	Nott. Suburban Ord.	123½
20/6	S. E. Perp. Ann.	35½
4½	Do. 4½ p.c..........	162½
3½	S. Yorks. Junc. Ord.	118½
4½	W. Cornwall (G. W., Br., Ex., & S. Dev. Joint Rent	159½
3	W. Highl. Ord. Stk. (Gua., N.B.)..................	104½

PREFERENCE SHARES AND STOCKS.

DIVIDENDS CONTINGENT ON PROFIT OF YEAR.

Last Div.	Name	Price.
4½	Alexandra Dks. & Ry. "A"	126½
5	Barry (First)	167½
4	Do. Consolidated......	136½
4	Caledonian Cons., No. 1 ..	142
4	Do. do. No. 2 ..	141
5	Do. do. 1878	175½
4	Do. Pref. 1884	140½
4	Do. do. 1887 (Conv.)	152½
—	Cambrian, No. 1 4 p.c. Pref.	72½
—	Do. No. 2 do.	37½
—	Do. No. 3 do.	17½
—	Do. No. 4 do.	9
5	City & S. Lond. £10 shares	15½
—	Do. New	14
4	Furness, Cons. 1881	133
4	Do. ......"A" 1881	131½
4	Do. ......"B" 1883	129½
4	Glasgow & S. Western	141½
4	Do. No. 2....	140½
4	Do. 1888	139½
4	Do. 1891	139½
5	Gt. Central	159½
4	Do.	131½
5	Do. Conv..... 1872	153½
5	Do. do. 1874	153½
5	Do. do. 1876	152½
5	Do. do. 1879	151½
5	Do. do. 1881	147½
4	Do. 1889	112½
4	Do. 1891	108½
5	Do. 1894	107½
4	Gt. Eastern, Cons.........	141½
4	Do. 1886	140
4	Do. 1881	138½
4	Do. 1884	136½

Preference Shares, &c. (*continued*):—

Last Div.	Name.	Price.
4	Gt. Eastern, Cons..... 1887	138½
4	Do. 1888	138½
3½	Do. 1890	120½
3½	Do. 1893	120½
—	Do. (Int. fr. Jan '99) 1893	117½
4	Gt. North Scotland "A"..	133½
4	Do. "B"..	133½
4	Gt. Northern, Cons.	143
3	Do. 1896	107
5	Gt. Western Cons.........	181
30/11	Hull & Barnsley Red. at 115	109
4	Isle of Wight	133½
3	Lancs. & Yorkshire, Cons.	108
2/2½	Lanc. Drby & E.C. 5 p.c. £10	9½
—	Do. 5 p.c. 2nd £10	9½
5	Lond., Bright., &c., Cons.	178½
5	Do. and Cons.	178½
4½	Lond., Chat. & Dov. Arbitr.	136½
23/	Do. 2nd Pref. 4½ p.c.	93
4	Lond. & N. Western......	145
4	Lond. & S. Western.. 1881	144
4	Do. 1884	143
3½	Do.	127½
4	Lond., Tilbury & Southend	140½
4	Do. Cons., 1887	140½
4	Do 1891	140½
—	Mersey, 5 p.c. Perp.	—
4	Metropolitan, Perp.	141½
4	Do. 1882	140½
4	Do. Irred.	140½
4	Do. 1887	140½
4	Do. New........	140½
4½	Do.	146½
3½	Do.	123½
3	Do. Guar.	101½
2½	Metrop. Dist. Exten 5 p.c.	110
2½	Midland, Perp. Pref.	92
4	N. British Cons., No. 2 ..	136
4½	Do. Edin. & Glasgow	151½
5	Do. 1865	165½
5	Do. Conv. 1874	166½
4½	Do. 1875	151½
4½	Do. Conv. 1875	151½
5	Do. do. 1870	166½
4	Do. do. 1884	136½
4	Do. do. 1888	136½
4	Do. do. 1890	136½
4	Do. do. 1892	136½
4	N. Eastern	144
4½	N. Lond., Cons. 1866	174½
4½	Do. 2nd Cons. .. 1875	157½
3	N. Staffordshire	107
4½	Plym. Devpt. & S. W. Junc.	149½
1/5	Port Talbot, &c., 4 p.c. £10 Shares, 4 paid	5
5/	Rhondda & Swansea Bay, 5 p.c. £10 Shares	11½
4	Rhymney, Cons..........	140½
4½	S. Eastern, Cons.	160½
5	Do. do.	179
4	Do. Vested Cos'.....	141½
4	Do. 1891	140½
3½	Do. 1893	122½
2	Do. 3 p.c. after July 1900	102
4	Taff Vale	141½

INDIAN RAILWAYS.

Last Div.	Name.	Paid.	Price.
3½	Assam Bengal, Ld., (3½ p till June 30, then 3 p.c.)	100	100
4/	Barsi Light, Ld., £10 Shs.	10	11
6	Bengal and N. West., Ld	100	148½
4/	Do. £10 Shares	10	14
3/6	Do. 3½ p.c. Cum. Pf. Shs.	10	10½
8½d.	Do.	4	4½
2/3½	Bengal Central, Ld., £10 (3½ p.c. + ½th net earn)	5	6
3	Bengal Dooars, Ld.	100	114
4	Bengal Nagpr., Lim. (gua. 4 p.c. + 4th sp. pfts.) ..	100	113
7½	Bombay, Baroda, and C. I. (gua 5 p.c)	100	213
36/1	Burma, Ld. (gua. 2½ p.c. and ½ p.c. add. till 1901)	100	106
1/7	Do. £10 Shares		2½
4	Delhi Umb. Kalka, Ld., Gua. 3½ p.c. + net earn.	100	121
4	Do. Deb. Stk., 1890 (1916)	100	111
9/10	Estn. Bengal, "A" An. 1957	—	24
9/	Do. "B" 1957	—	30
4	Do. Gua. Deb. Stock ..	100	135½
9/7½	East Ind. Ann. "A" (1953)	—	26
8/4½	Do. "C"	—	28
8/11½	Do. "B"	—	30
6 1/8	Do. Def. Ann. Cap. (gua. 4 p.c. + ½th sp. pfts.)	—	149
115/9	East Ind. Def. Ann. "D"	—	155
4½	East Ind. Irred. Stock ..	100	157½
5	Gt. Indian Penin., Gua 5 p.c. + ½ surplus profits..	100	165½
4	Do. Irred. 4 p.c. Deb. St.	100	135½
4	Indian Mid., Ld. (gua. 4 p.c. + ½th surplus pfts.)	100	113
51/	Madras Guar. + ½ sp. pfts.	100	165
48/6	Do. do.	100	156
46/	Do. do.	100	146
4	Nilgiri, Ld., 1st Deb. Stk.	100	97½
4	Oude & Rohil. Db. Stk. Rd.	100	—
5 1/10	Rohil. and Kumaon, Ld.	100	132
9/11	Scinde, Punj., and Delhi, "A" Ann., 1958	—	24
9/1	Do. "B" do. ..	—	30

Indian Railways (*continued*):—

Last Div.	Name.	Paid.	Price.
4	South Behar, Ld., £10 shs.	100	100
3½	Do. Deb. Stk. Red.	100	101
4½	South Ind., Gu. Deb. Stk.	100	157½
5	South Indian, Ld. (gua. 3 p.c., and ¼ spls. profits)	100	122½
5	Sthn. Mahratta, Ld. (3½ p.c. & ¼th net earnings)	100	115½
4	Do. Deb. Stk. Red.	100	120
3½	Southern Punjab, Ld.….	100	105
3½	Do. Deb. Stk. Red.	—	104
5	Nizam's Gua. State, Ld. [†	100	114½
4	Do. Mort. Deb., 1936	100	107
4	Do. do. Reg.	100	106
17/3½	Nizam's Gua. State, Ld., 3½ p.c. Mt. Deb. bearer ….	—	94½
17/3½	Do. Reg. do. ..	—	93½
5	W. of India Portgese., Ld.	100	67½
5	Do. Deb. Stk., Red	100	98

RAILWAYS.—BRITISH POSSESSIONS.

Last Div.	Name.	Paid.	Price.
5	Atlantic & N.W. Gua. 1 Mt. Bds., 1937 ……..	100	125½
5/3	Buff. & L. Huron Ord. Sh.	10	13½
5½	Do. 1st Mt. Perp. Bds. 1879	100	141½
5½	Do. 2nd Mt. Perp. Bds.	100	141½
—	Calgary & Edmon. 6 p.c. 1st Mt. Stg. Bds. Red..	100	77½
5	Canada Cent. 1st Mt. Bds. Red. ………………	100	103
4	Can. Pacific Pref. Stk.….	100	100½
5	Do. Strl. 1st Mt. Deb. Bds. 1915 ………………	100	116
3½	Do. Ld. Grnt. Bds., 1938..	100	106
3½	Do. Ld. Grnt. Ins. Stk. ..	100	106
4	Do. Perp. Cons. Deb. Stk.	100	115
5	Do. Algoma Bch. 1st Mt. Bds., 1937 …………	100	121
3	Demerara, Original Stock	100	46
7	Do. Perp. Pref. Stk.…..	100	152½
2/10	Do. 4 p.c. Cum. Ext. Pref. £10 Shs. …………	4	8
—	Dominion Atlntc. Ord. Stk.	100	33½
5	Do. 5 p.c. Pref. Stk.….	100	97½
4	Do. 1st. Deb. Stk.…..	100	103½
4	Do. 2nd do. Red. ……	100	99
—	EmuBay&Mt. Bischoff, Ld.	5	4½
4½	Do. Irred. Deb. Stk.…	100	98
nil.	Gd. Trunk of Canada, Stk.	100	8½
6	Do. 2nd. Equip. Mt. Bds.	100	131½
5	Do. Perp. Deb. Stk.…..	100	136½
5	Do. Gt. Westn. Deb. Stk.	100	128½
5	Do. Nthn. of Can. 1st Mt. Bds., 1902 …………	100	103½
4	Do. do. Deb. Stk …….	100	102
5	Do. G. T. Geor. Bay & L. Erie 1 Mt., 1903 …..	100	105
5	Do. Mid. of Can. Stl. 1st Mt. (Mid. Sec.) 1908 ….	100	104
5	Do. do. Cons. 1 Mt. Bds. 1912	100	106
5	Do. Mont. & Champ. 1 Mt. Bds., 1902 …………	100	104
	Do. Welln., Grey & Brce. 7 p.c. Bds. 1 Mt. ……	100	109
—	Jamaica 1st Mtg. Bds. Red.	—	103
—	Manitoba & N. W., 6 p.c. 1st Mt. Bds., Red ……	100	—
—	Do. Ldn. Bdhldrs. Certs.	—	—
5	Manitoba S. W. Col. 1 Mt. Bd., 1934 $1,000 price %	—	120
—	Mid. of W. Aust. Ld. 6 p.c. 1 Mt. Dbs., Red. ……	100	40
4	Do. Deb. Bds., Red. ….	100	103
4	Nakusp & Slocan Bds., 1918	100	106
3	Natal Zululand Ld. Debs.,	100	72½
5	N. Brunswick 1st Mt. Stg. Bds., 1934 …………	100	121
4	Do. Perp. Cons. Deb. Stk.	100	114
—	N. Zealand Mid., Ld., 5 p.c 1st Mt. Debs.………	100	35
6	Ontario & Queb. Cap. Stk.	$100	151½
5	Do. Perm. Deb. Stk.…..	100	141½
—	Qu'Appelle, L. Lake & Sask. 6 p.c. 1 Mt. Bds. Red.	100	40½
	Queb. & L. S. John, 1st Mt. Bds., 1909 …………	100	32
	Quebec Cent., Prior Ln. Bds., 1908 …………	100	107
1½	Do. 5 p.c. Inc. Bds. ……	100	37
4	St. Lawr. & Ott. Stl. 1st Mt.	100	112
4	Shuswap & Okan., 1st Mt. Deb. Bds., 1915 ………	100	76
5	Temiscouata, 5 p.c. Stl. 1st Deb. Bds., Red.………	100	9½
5	Do. (S. Franc. Brch.) 5 p.c. Stl. 1 Mt. Db. Bds., 1910	100	10
4	Toronto, Grey & B. 1st Mt.	100	112
1/2	Well. & Mana. £5 Shs. ..	1	½
5	Do. Debs., 1908 ……..	100	107
5	Do. 2nd Debs., 1908 ….	100	106
5	Do. 3rd do., 1908 ……	100	104
6	Atlan. & St. Law. Shs., 6 p.c.	100	163½
5	Gd. Trunk Mt. Bds., 1934	100	116½
5	Michigan Air Line, 5 p.c. 1st Mt. Bds., 1902 ……	100	104
4	Minneap., S. P. & S t. Ste. Mar, 1st Mt. Bds., 1938	$1000	98

AMERICAN RAILROAD STOCKS AND SHARES.

Last Div.	Name.	Paid.	Price.
6/	Alab. Gt. Sthn. A 6 p.c. Pref.	10*l.*	9
—	Do. do "B" Ord. ..	10*l.*	1½
—	Alabma. N. Orl.-Tex. &c., "A" Pref. …………	10*l.*	¾
—	Do. "B" Def. …………	10*l.*	¼
5½	Atlant. First Lsd. Ls. Rtl. Trust……………….	Stk.	98½
—	Baltimore & Ohio Com. ..	$100	19
—	Baltimore Ohio S.W. Pref.	$100	7
—	Chesap. & Ohio Com. ….	$100	22½
—	Chic. Gt. West. 5 p.c. Pref. Stock "A"…………	$100	32½
—	Do. do. Scrip. In…….	—	30½
8/3	Do. 4 p.c. Deb. Stk……	$100	67½
4	Do. Interest in Scrip ….	$100	63½
$4	Chic. Junc. Rl. & Un. Stk. Yds. Com. …………	$100	120½
$1½	Do. 6 p.c. Cum. Pref. ….	$100	120½
$3½	Chic. Mil. & St. P. Pref…	$100	149
7	Cleve. & Pittsburgh……	$10	84½
$1½	Clev., Cincin., Chic., & St. Louis Com. …………	$100	—
—	Erie 4 p.c. Non-Cum. 1st Pf.	—	36½
—	Do. 4 p.c. do. 2nd Pf.	—	18
$2½	Gt. Northern Pref. …..	$100	170
$2½	Illinois Cen. Lsd. Lines ..	$100	95½
—	Kansas City, Pitts & G. ..	$100	19
$3	L. Shore & Mich. Sth. C.	$100	190
—	Mex. Cen. Ltd. Com. ….	$100	5
—	Miss. Kan. & Tex. Pref…	$100	37½
2½	N.Y., Pen. & O. 1st Mt. Tst. Ltd., Ord. ……..	—	47½
4	Do. 1st Mort. Deb. Stk. ..	$100	92½
2	North Pennsylvania ……	$50	—
—	Northn. Pacific, Com.….	$100	27½
1½	Pitts. F. Wayne & Chic…	$100	174
—	Reading 1st Pref. ……..	$50	23
—	Do. 2nd Pref. ………..	$50	11½
—	S. Louis & S. Fran. Com.	$100	6
—	Do. 2nd Pref. ……….	$100	25½
6	St. Louis Bridge 1st Pref..	$100	107
3	Do. 2nd Pref. ………..	$100	50
6	Tunnel Rail. of St. Louis	$100	107
$1½	St. Paul, Min. and Man…	$100	137½
—	Southern, Com. ………..	$100	8½
—	Wabash, Common………	$100	8

AMERICAN RAILROAD BONDS. CURRENCY.

Last Div.	Name.	Price.
7	Albany & Susq. 1 Con. Mrt. 1906	118
7	Allegheny Val. 1 Mt.…… 1910	125½
5	Canada Southern 1 Mt. …. 1908	112½
5	Chic. & N. West. Sk. Fd. Db. 1933	117½
5	Do. Deb. Coupon …… 1921	112½
6	Chicago & Tomah …… 1905	109½
5	Chic. Burl. & Q. Skg. Fd. 1901	102½
4	Do. Nebraska Ext.….. —	100
6	Chic., Mil., & S. Pl., 1 Mt. S.W. Div.…………… 1909	117½
7	Do. (S. Paul Div.) 1 Mt. 1902	132½
5	Do. (La Cross & D. …. 1919	114½
7	Do. 1 Mt. (Hast. & Dak.) 1910	127½
5	Do. Chic. & Mis. Riv. 1 Mt. 1926	112½
5	Chic., Rock Is. and Pac. 1 Mt. Ext. ………… 1934	108
6	Det., G. Haven & Mil. Equip 1918	105
6	Do. do. Cons. Mt. 1918	102½
6	Ill. Cent., 1 Mt., Chic. & S. 1898	—
7	Indianap. & Vin., 1 Mt. .. 1908	125
6	Do. do. 2 Mt. .. 1900	100½
6	Lehigh Val., Cons. Mt.…. 1923	114½
—	Mexic. Cent., Ln. 2 Cons. Inc. —	5
7	N.Y. Cent. & H.R. Mt. Bonds 1903	119½
5	Do. Deb. ………… 1904	111½
6	Penns. Cons. S. F M. …. 1905	118
4	West Shore, 1 Mt. …….. 2361	110

DITTO—GOLD.

Last Div.	Name.	Price.
6	Alabama Gt. Sthn. 1 Mt. ..1908	114
5	Do. Mid. 1 …………1928	90½
4	Allegheny Val. Gen. Mt. ..1942	106
4	Atch., Top., & S. Fé Gn. Mt. 1995	95
3	Do. Adj. Mt.………….1995	66
5	Do. Equipt. Tmst. …… —	102½
5	Atlantic & Dan. 1 Mt.…...1950	96½
5	Baltimore & Ohio………..1925	102
5	Do. Speyer's Tst. Recpts. 1925	102
5	Do. Cons. Mt. ……….1988	107½
4½	Do. 4½ p.c. 1 Mt. Term. 1934	84
4½	Do. Brown Shipley's Dep. Cts. —	84
5	Balt. Belt 5 p.c. 1 Mort.….1990	90
4½	Balt. & Ohio S.W. 1 Mt. ..1990	101
4½	Do. 4½ p.c. 1 Cons. Mt. 1893 1993	72½
—	Do. Inc. Mt. 5 p.c. Cl. A —	28
—	Do. do. Cl. B —	10
5	Balt. & Ohio S.W. Term 5 p.c. 1942	97½
6	Balt. & Ptmac (Mn. L.) 1 Mt. 1911	124
6	Do. do. (Tunnel) 1 Mt. 1911	126
4	Beech Creek 1 Mt. ……..1936	109
4	Carthage & Adiron 1 Mt. ..1981	107

American Railroad Bonds—Gold (*continued*):—

Last Div.	Name.	Price.
5	Cent. of Georgia 1 Mort. ..1945	117½
5	Do. Cons. Mt. ……1945	90½
5	Cent. of N. Jrsy. Gn. Mt. ..1987	116
6	Central Pacific, 1 Mort. ….1898	102½
6	Do. Speyer's Certs. …… —	106
5	Do. Land Grant ………1900	101
5	Chesap. & Ohio 1st Cons. Mt. 1939	116
4½	Do. Gen. Mt.…………1992	82
6	Chic. & W. Ind. Gen. Mt. Skg. Fd. ……………1932	119½
5	Chic. Mil. & St. Pl. (Chic. & L. Sup.) 1 Mt. ………1921	114½
5	Do. Chic. & Pac. W. …1921	117½
5	Do. Wisc. & Minn. 1 Mt. 1921	112½
5	Do. Terminal Mt. ……1914	114½
4	Do. General Mt. ………1989	106½
5	Chic. St. L. & N. Orleans..1951	122½
4	Do. 1 Mort. (Memphis) ..1951	104
4	Clevel., Cin., Chic. & St. L. 1 Mt. (Cairo) …………1939	90
4	Do. 1 Mt. (Cinc., Wab., & Mich.) ……………1991	90
4	Do. 1 Col. Tst. Mt. (S. Louis) 1990	96
4	Do. General Mt. ………1993	80½
4½	Clevel. & Mar. Mt. ………1935	109
4½	Clevel. & Pittsburgh ……1942	116½
4½	Do. Series B. …………1942	116½
—	Colorado Mid. 1 Mt. ……1936	63½
—	Do. Bdhrs.' Comm. Certs. —	63½
4	Dnvr. & R. Gde. 1 Cons. Mt. 1936	94
5	Do Imp. Mort.…………1928	91
4	Detroit & Mack. 1 Lien ….1995	90
5	E. Tennes., Virg., & Grgia. Cons. Mt. ……………1956	111½
5	Elmira, Cort., & Nthn. Mt. 1914	100
4	Erie 1 Cons. Mt. Pr. Ln. ..1996	92
3	Do. Gen. Lien …………1996	73
6	Galvest., Harrisb., &c., 1 Mt.….	107½
5	Georgia, Car. & N. 1 Mt. ..1929	96
4½	Gd. Rpds. & Inda. Ex. 1 Mt. 1941	112½
5	Do. 1 Mt. (Muskegon) ..1926	39½
3½	Illinois Cent. 1 Mt. ………1951	104½
4	Do. ……………………1952	104½
4	Do. Cairo Bdge. ..1950	102
4	Do. ……………………1953	101
4	Do. General Mort. ..1904	102½
5	Kans. City, Pitts. & G. 1 M. 1923	73½
3½	L. Shore & Mich. Southern 1997	106½
4½	Lehigh Val. N.Y. 1 Mt.….1940	104
5	Lehigh Val. Term. 1 Mt. ..1941	110
5	Long Island ……………..1931	117½
5	Do. Deb.………..1934	100
5	Do. (N. Shore Bch.) 1 Cons. Mt. ……………1932	94
6	Louisville & Nash. G. Mt. ..1930	119
6	Do. 2 Mt. Sk. Fd. (S. & N. Alabama………..1910	107
6	Do. 1 Mt. N. Orl. & Mb. 1930	122½
5	Do. 1 Mt. Coll. Tst. …1931	104½
4	Do. Unified …………1940	91
4½	Do. Mobile & Montgy. 1 Mt. 1945	111½
4	Manhattan Cons. Mt. ……1990	95
4	Mexican Cent. Cons. Mt. ..1911	65
—	Do. 1 Cons. Inc, …………	14
6	Mexican Nat. 1 Mt. ……..1927	104
3½	Do. 2 Mt. 6 p.c. Inc. A 1917	52½
—	Do. do. B..1917	9
3	Do. Matheson's Certs.….	—
3	Michig. Cnt. (Battle Ck. & S.) 1 Mt. ……………………1989	86
6	Minneap. & S. L. 1 Mt. Pacific Ext. ……………1921	—
5	Do. 1 Consold. ……1934	107½
4	Minne., Slt. S. M. & A. 1 Mt. 1926	100
5	Minneapolis Westn. 1 Mt…1911	105½
4	Miss. Kans. & Tex. 1 Mt…1990	89
4	Do. 2 do. ….1990	63
4	Mobile & Birm. Mt. Inc….1945	38
5	Do. P. Lien ……………1945	88
4	Mohawk & Mal. 1 Mt……1991	108
5	Montana Cent. 1 Mt. ……1937	111½
5	Nashv., Chattan., & S. L. 1 Cons. Mt……………….1928	102½
5	Nash., Flor., & Shff. Mt…1937	92½
4	N. Y. & Putnam 1 Cons. Mt. 1993	108
5	N. Y., Brooklyn, & Man. B. 1 Cons. Mt…………….1935	107½
4	N. Y. Cent. & Hud. R. Deb. Certs. 1890 …………….1905	104
4	Do. Ext. Debt. Certs….1905	106
7	N. Y., L. Erie, & W. 1 Cons. Mt. (Erie) ……………1920	144½
7	Do. 1 Con. Mt. Fd. Coup. 1920	130½
5	N. Y., Onto., & W. Cons. 1 Mt…………………………1939	109
4	Do. 4 p.c. Refund. Mt..1992	100
6	Norfolk & West. Gn. Mt….1931	124
6	Do. Imp. & Ext…………1934	117½
4	Do. 1 Cons. Mt……… —	83
6	N. Pacific Gn. 1 Mt. Ld. Gt. 1921	—
4	Do. P. Ln. Rl. & Ld. Gt. —	98
3	Do. Gn. Ln. Rl. & Ld. Gt. —	62
5	Oregon & Calif. 1 Mt.……1927	80
6	Panama Skg. Fd. Subsidy..1910	102½
4½	Pennsylvania Rlrd. ……..1913	110
4	Do. Equip. Tst. Ser. A..1914	104
4	Do. Cons. Mt…………1943	112½
4½	Penna. Company 1st Mort. 1921	112
5	Perkiomen 1 Mrt., 2nd ser..1918	91½
4½	{ Pitts., C., C., & St. Ls. Con. Mt. G.B., Ser. A } 1940-2	112
4	Do. Cons. Mort., Ser. D..1945	102½
6	Pittsbgh., Cle., & Toledo ..1922	100½
4	Reading, Phil., & R. Genl. 1997	86
5	Richmond & Dan. Equip. ..1909	97½
5	Rio Grande Junc. 1st Mort. 1939	90
4	Rio Grande West 1st Tst. Mt. 1939	84
7	S. Louis Bridge 1st Mort 1925	134½
5	S. Louis Mchts. Bdge. Term. 1st Mort……………1930	102½
4	S. Louis S. West 1st Mort..1989	75
—	Do. 4 p.c. 2nd Mort. Inc. 1989	30

American Railroad Bonds (*continued*):

Last Div.	Name.	Price.
4½	S. Louis Term. Cupples Sta. & Prop. 1st. Mrt. 4½ p.c. 1902-17	100
4½	St. Paul Minn., & Manit. 1933	108½
6	Do. do. 1933	132½
6	Shamokin, Sunbury, &c. 2 Mt. 1925	100
5	S. & N. Alabama Cons. Mt. 1936	97½
5	Southern 1 Cons. Coup. ….1994	95
4	Do. E. Tennes Reorg. Lien ..1938	100
6	S. Pacific of Cal. 1 Mt…1905-12	111
4½	Trml. Assn. of S. Louis 1 Mt. 1939	110½
5	Do. 1 Cons. Mt…………1944	108
5	Texas & Pac. 1 Mt. ………2000	102½
—	Do. 5 p.c. 2 Mt. Income 2000	34
5	Toledo & Ohio Cent. 1 Mt. West. Div. ……………1935	102½
4½	Toledo., Walhon., Val., & Ohio 1 Mt. …………1931-3	111½
—	Union Pacific 1 Mt. 4 p.c. ..1947	96
—	Union Pac., Linc., & Color. 1 Mt. ………………1918	—
4	United N. Jersey Gen. Mt…1944	113½
6	Vicksbrg., Shrevept., & Pac. Pr. Ln. Mt. ……………1915	101½
5	Wabash 1 Mt. ……………1939	106½
4	Wn. Pennsylvania Mt. ….1928	106½
5	W. Virga. & Pittsbg. 1 Mt. 1990	75
5	Wheeling & L. Erie 1 Mt. (Wheelg. Div.) 5 p.c. ….1928	90½
5	Do. Extn. Imp. Mt. ….1930	90
—	Do. do. Brown Shipley's Cts..	—
5	Willmar & Sioux Falls 1 Mt. 1938	108

STERLING.

Last Div.	Name.	Price.
6	Alabama Gt. Sthn. Deb.….1906	104½
5	Do. Gen. Mort. ..1927-8	100
5	Alabama, N. Orl., Tex. & Pac. 5 p.c. "A" Dbs…1910-40	98
55/	Do. do. "B" do. 1910-40	56
—	Do. do. "C" do. ……	19
—	Allegheny Valley ………..1910	130
4	Atlantic 1st Leased Line Perp…	100
6	Baltimore and Ohio ……..1902	108
6	Do. do. ……..1910	119
5	Do. do. 1877…….	102
—	Do. Morgan's Certs. ..	102
4½	Do. do. ……….1933	95
6	Chicago & Alton Cons. Mt. 1903	112
5	Chic. St. Paul & Kan. City Priority …………………….	106
6	Eastn. of Massachusetts ….1906	117½
5	Illinois Cent. Skg. Fd. ……..	103
5	Do. …………1905	108
3½	Do. …………1950	99½
4	Do. 1 Mt. …….1951	112
3	Do. 1 Mt. …….1951	92½
6	Louisville & Nash., M. C. & L. Div., 1 Mt. ……….1902	104½
7	Do. 1 Mt. (Memphis & O.)…………………….1901	112
55/8	Mexican Nat. "A" Certs. 5 p.c. Non. cum. ………	40½
—	Do. "B" Certs….	9
6	N.Y. & Canada 1 Mt. ……1904	108½
6	N. York Cent. & H.R. Mort. 1903	112
4½	N. York, Penns., & Ohio Pr. Ln. Extd. ……………1935	—
5	Do. Equip. Tst. ……..	101½
5	Do. 5 p.c. Equip. Tst. (1890) ………………………	103½
6	Nrthn. Cent. Cons. Gen. Mt. ..	106
6	Pennsylvania Gen. Mt. ….1910	126
6	Do. Cons. Skg. Fd. Mt. 1905	115
3½	Do. Cons. Mt. ……..1945	104
6	Phil. & Erie Cons. Mort ..1920	132½
6	Phil. & Reading Gen. Cons. Mort. ………………1911	122½
6	Pittsbg. & Connells. Cons. 1926	117½
—	Do. Morgan's Certs….	117½
4	St. Paul., Min., & Manitoba (Pac. Extn.) …………1940	98
6	S. & N. Alabama ………..1903	104½
6	Un. N. Jersey & C. Gen. Mt. 1901	109½

FOREIGN RAILWAYS

Last Div.	Name.	Paid.	Price.
12/	Alagoas, Ltd., Shs. ……	20	5½
5	Do. Deb. Stk., Red. ..	100	44½
6	Antofagasta, Ltd., Stk. ..	100	72
4	Do. Perp. Deb. Stk. ..	100	90
—	Arauco, Ld., Ord. Shs. ..	10	—
—	Do. 10 p.c. Cum. Pref.	10	—
5	Argentine Gt. W., Ld.,	100	76
5	Do. 5 p.c. Cum. Pref. Shs.	100	101
4	Do. 1 Deb. Stk. ……	100	102
1/0/0	Argentine N.E., Ltd., 6 p.c. Cum. Pref. Stk. ..	100	9½
—	Do. 5 p.c. Deb. Stk., Red.	100	29
2/	Arica and Tacna Shs. ..	20	1½
10/	Bahia & San Fcisco., Ld.,	20	9
6/	Do. Timbo. Bch. Shs.	20	4½
12/	Bahia, Blanca, & N.W. Ln. Prf. Cum. 6 p.c. ..	100	52
4	Do. 4 p.c. 1 Deb. Stk., Red.	100	92
6	Barranquilla R. & P., Ld., 6 p.c. 1 Deb. Stk., Red.	100	96

Foreign Railways (*continued*):—

Last Div.	Name.	Paid.	Price.
3/	Bilbao Riv. & Cantabn., Ltd., Ord.	3	5
—	Bolivar, Ltd. Shs.	10	1¼
6	Do. 6 p.c. Deb. Stk.	100	96½
—	Brazil Gt. Southn. Ltd., 7 p.c. Cum. Pref.	20	1½
6	Do. Perm. Deb. Stk	100	47
5½	B. Ayres Gt. Southn. Ld., Ord. Stk.	100	140
5	Do. Pref. Stk.	100	133
4	Do. Deb. Stk.	100	117
30/	B. Ayres & Ensen. Port., Ltd., Ord. Stk.	100	66
5	Do. Cum. 1 Pref. Stk.	100	116
6/0/0	Do. 6p.c.Con. Pref.Stk.	100	96
4	Do. Deb. Stk., Irred.	100	113
10⅛	B. Ayres Northern, Ltd., Ord. Stk.	100	265
12½	Do. Pref. Stk.	100	320
5	Do. 5 p.c. Mt. Deb.Stk., Red.	100	113
3/15/c	B. Ayres & Pac., Ld., 7 p.c. 1 Pref. Stk. (Cum.)	100	92½
4	Do. 1 Deb. Stk.	100	102
5/5/0	Do. 4½ p.c. 2 Deb. Stk.	100	92
3	B. Ayres & Rosario, Ltd., Ord. Stk.	100	74
7/	Do. 7 p.c. Pref. Shs.	10	17
7/	Do. Sunchales Ext.	10	14¼
4	Do. Deb. Stk., Red.	100	107½
—	B. Ayres & Val. Trans., Ltd., 7 p.c. Cum. Pref.	20	6½
4	Do. 4 p.c. "A" Deb. Stk., Red.	100	70
—	Do. 6 p.c. "B" Deb. Stk. Red.	100	43
3/6	B. Ayres Westn. Ld. Ord.	10	10¾
3/	Do. Def. Shs.	10	6¾
5	Do. 5 p.c. Pref.	10	12¾
4	Do. Deb. Stk	100	109
6	Cent. Arg. Deb. Sk. Rd.	100	159½
4	Do. Deb. Stk. Rd	100	110
6	Cent. Bahia L. Ord. Stk.	100	50
	Do. Deb. Stk., 1934	100	69½
5	Do. Deb. Stk., 1937	100	60
3/6	Cent. Uguy. East. Ext. L. Shs.	10	5½
5	Do. Perm. Stk.	100	112
3/6	Do. Nthn. Ext. L. Sh.	10	4
5	Do. Perm. Deb. Stk	100	103½
3	Do. of Montev. Ltd., Ord. Stk	100	86
6	Do. Perm. Deb. Stk	100	142
10/	Conde d'Eu, Ltd. Ord.	20	7
—	Cordba & Rosar., Ltd., 6 p.c. Pref. Shs.	100	39
4	Do. 1 Deb. Stk	100	89
75	Do. 6 p.c. Deb. Stk	100	79
—	Cordba Cent., Ltd., 5 p.c. Cu. 1 Pref. Stk	100	83
—	Do. 5 p.c. Non-Cum. 2 Pref. Stk	100	43
5	Do. Deb. Stk	100	118
4/	Costa Rica, Ltd., Shs.	10	3⅝
8/	Dna. Thrsa. Chris., Ltd., 7 p.c. Pref. Shs.	20	3¼
20/	E. Argentine, Ltd	100	40
6	Do. Deb. Stk	100	103
1/1	Egyptn. Dlta. Lgt. Rys., Ltd., £10 Pref. Shs.	8	10
—	Entre Rios, L., Ord. Shs.	5	¾
—	Do. Cu. 5 p.c. Pref.	5	3½
6/	Gt. Westn. Brazil, Ltd.,	20	7½
6	Do. Perm. Deb. Stk.	100	90
6	Do. Extn. Deb. Stk.	100	77½
—	Int.-Oceanic Mex., Ltd., 7 p.c. Pref.	10	1½
4	Do. Deb. Stk.	100	82
42/6	Do. 7 p.c. "A" Deb. Sk.	100	66
—	Do. 7 p.c. "B" Deb. Sk.	100	29
5/	La Guaira & Carac.	10	7½
5	Do. 5 p.c. Deb. Sk. Red.	100	100
11/3	Lembg.-Czern.-Jassy	30	24½
1/	Lima, Ltd.	20	2½
—	Manila Ltd. 7 p.c. Cu. Pf.	10	¾
20/6½	Mexican 2nd Pref. 6 p.c.	100	33
6	Do. Perp Deb. Stk.	100	137
1/0/0	Mexican Sthrn., Ld., Ord.	100	22
—	Do. 4 p.c. 1 Db.Stk.Rd.	100	82
—	Do. 4 p.c. 2 do.	100	59
—	Mid. Urgy., Ltd.	100	18½
5	Do. Deb. Stk.	100	60
12/	Minas & Rio, Ltd.	20	9½
5/2	Namur & Liege	20	12½
11/6	Do. Pref.	20	29
13/	Natal & Na. Cruz, Ld., 7 p.c. Cum Pref.	20	6½
—	Nitrate Ltd., Ord.	10	5
—	Do. 7 p.c. Pr. Con. Or.	10	4
—	Do. Def. Conv. Ord.	10	¾
7/	N.-E. Urgy., Ltd., Ord.	10	15
7/	Do. 7 p.c. Pref.	10	15½
—	N.-W. Argentine Ld., 7 p.c. Pref.	10	2
6	Do. 6 p.c. 1 Deb. Stk.	100	110
—	Do. 2 Deb. Stk.	100	94
—	N.W. Uruguay 6 p.c. 1 Pref. Stk.	100	16
—	Do. 5 p.c. 2 Pref. Stk.	100	7½
6	Do. 6 p.c. Deb. Stk.	100	80
22/	Ottoman (Sm. Aid.)	20	13½
—	Paraguay Cntl., Ld., 5 p.c. Perm. Deb. Stk.	100	10
—	Piræus, Ath., & Pelo.	275	1½
4/	Pto. Alegre & N. Hambg Ld., 7 p.c. Pref. Shs.	20	4
6	Do. Mt. Deb. Stk. Red.	100	74½
—	Puerto Cabello & Val. Ld.	10	1¼
5	Recife & S. Francisco	100	64⅛
24/	R. Claro S. Paulo, Ld., Sh.	10	21
5	Do. Deb. Stk.	100	125
5	Royal Sardinian Ord.	10	11¼
3/	Do. Pref.	10	11¾

Foreign Railways (*continued*):—

Last Div.	Name.	Paid.	Price.
5/	Sambre & Meuse	20	18
5/6	Do. Pref.	10	12½
22/	San Paulo Ld.	20	32½
2/10½	Do. New Ord. £10 sh.	6	9½
4/8	Do. 5 p.c. Non. Cm. Pref.	10	12
5½	Do. Deb. Stk.	100	132
5	Do. 5 p.c. Deb. Stk	100	127
—	S. Fé & Cordova, Gt. Sthn., Ld., Shares	100	43½
6	Do. Perp. Deb. Stk.	100	119
3/2½	S. Austrian	20	7
10/	Sthn. Braz. R. Gde. do Sul, Ld.	20	7½
6	Do. 6 p.c. Deb. Stk.	100	63½
4	Swedish Centl., Ld., 4 p.c. Deb. Stk.	100	107
5	Do. Pref.	100	101
1/3	Taltal, Ld.	5	2½
—	Uruguay Nthn., Ld. 7 p.c. Pfd. Stk.	100	8
3½	Do. 5 p.c. Deb. Stk.	100	30
—	Villa Maria & Rufino, Ld., 6 p.c. Pref. Shs.	100	17
4	Do. 4 p.c. 1 Deb. Stk.	100	73
6/0/0	Do. 6 p.c. 2 Deb. Stk.	100	42½
5/9	West Flanders	8¾	21
5/6	Do. 5½ p.c. Pref.	10	18
3/	Wstn. of Havana, Ld.	10	4½

FOREIGN RAILWAY OBLIGATIONS

Per Cent.	Name.	Price.
6	Alagoas Ld., 6 p.c. Deb., Rd.	84
—	Alcoy & Gandia, Ld., 5 p.c. Debs., Red.	20
5	Arauco., Ld., 5 p.c. 1st Mt., Rd.	60½
—	Do. 6 p.c. Mt. Deb., Rd.	39½
6	Brazil G. Sthn., L., Mt. Dbs., Rd.	80½
6	Do. Mt. Dbs. 1893, Rd.	50
5½	Campos & Caran. Dbs., Rd.	70
6	Central Bahia, L., Dbs., Rd.	90
5½	Conde d'Eu, L., Dbs., Rd.	70
6	Costa Rica, L., 1st Mt. Dbs., Rd.	109
6	Do. 2nd Dbs., Rd.	91
5	Do. Prior Mt. Db., Rd.	103
6	Cucuta Mt. Dbs., Rd.	102
5½	Donna Thrsa. Cris., L., Dbs., Rd.	68½
3	Eastn. of France, £20 Dbs., Rd.	18¾
4	Egyptn. Delta Light, L., Db., Rd	100
—	Espito. Santo & Cara. 5 p.c. Stl. Dbs., Rd.	38
4	Gd. Russian Nic., Rd.	102
5	Inter-Oceanic Mex., L., 5 p.c. Pr. Ln. Dbs., Rd.	103
3	Ital. 3 p.c. Bds. A & B, Rd.	57½
—	Ituana 6 p.c. Debs., 1918	72½
—	Leopoldina, 6 p.c. Dbs. £50 Bds.,	21
—	Do. do. Comms. Cert.	21
—	Do. 5 p.c. Stg. Dbs. (1888), Rd.	29
—	Do. do. Comm. Certs.	29
—	Do. 5 p.c. Stg. Dbs. (1890), Rd.	21
—	Do. do. Comms. Certs.	21
—	Macahé & Cam. 5 p.c. Dbs., Rd.	29
—	Do. do. Comms. Certs.	29
—	Do. (Cantagallo), 5 p.c., Red.	29
—	Do. do. Comm. Certs.	29
—	Manila Ltd., 6 p.c. Deb., Red.	21
6	Do. Prior Lien Mt., Rd.	98½
6	Do. Series "B," Rd.	80
7	Matanzas & Sab., Rd.	101½
6	Minas & Rio, L., 6 p.c. Dbs., Rd.	95
5	Mogyana 5 p.c. Deb. Bds., Rd.	99
5	Moscow-Jaros., Rd.	107½
5½	Natal & Na. Cruz Ltd., 5½ p.c. Debs., Red.	77
5	Nitrate, Ltd. Mt. Bds., Red.	85
3	Nthn. France, Red.	19
4	N. of S. Af. Rep. (Trnsvl.) Gu. Bds. Red.	95
3	Nthn. of Spain £20 Pri. Obs. Red.	7½
6	Ottmn. (Smy to A.)(Kujk) Asnt. Debs., Red.	106
6	Ottmn. (Sernik.) Asg. Debs. Red.	106
6	Ottmn. (Seraik) Non-Asg. D., Rd	106
5	Ottmn. Kuyjk. Ext. Red.	103
5	Ottmn. Serkeuy. Ext. Red.	100½
5	Ottmn. Tireh Ext. 1910	98
5	Ottmn. Debs, 1886, Red.	97
5	Do. 1888, Red. 1935	96½
5	Do. 1893, Red. 1935	97
5	Ottmn. of Anlia. Debs., Rd.	90½
4	Ottomn. Smyr. & Cas. Ext. Bds., Red.	83½
3	Paris, Lyon & Medit. (old sys., £20), Red.	18¾
3	Paris, Lyon & Medit. (new sys., £20), Red.	18¾
50/	Piræus, At. & Pelp., 6 p.c. 1st Mt. Eds., Red.	89½
3	Do. 5 p.c. Mt. Bds., Red.	69½
4	Pretoria-Pietbg., Ltd., Red.	93
7	Puerto Cab. & Val., Ltd., 1st Mt. Debs., Red.	81
—	Rio de Jano. & Nthn., Ltd., 6 p.c. £100 Deb., Red.	21
—	Rio de Jano. (Gr. Para.), 5 p.c. 1st Mt. St. £100 Debs., Red.	21
2	Royal Sardinian, A, Rd. £20	11½
3	Royal Sardinian, B., Rd. £20	11½

Foreign Rly. Obligations (*continued*):—

Per Cent.	Name.	Price.
5	Ryl. Trns.-Afric. 5 p.c. 1st Mt. £100 Bds., Red.	48½
4	Sa. Fe & Cor. G. S., Ld. Pr. Ln. Bds.	104
5	Sa. Fe, 5 p.c. and Reg. Dbs.	79
3	South Austrian, £20 Red.	15
3	South Austrian, (Ser. X.)	15
3	South Italian £20 Obs. (Ser. A to G), Red.	12
3½	S. W. of Venez. (Barq.), Ltd., 7 p.c. 1st Mt. £100 Debs.	52½
5	Taltal, Ltd., 5 p.c. 1st Ch. Debs., Red.	97
5	Utd. Rwys. Havana, Red.	84½
3	Wtrn. of France, £20 Red.	18½
6	Wrn. B. Ayres St. Mt. Debs., 1902	107
6	Wrn. B. Ayres, Reg. Cert.	105
5	Do. Mt. Bds.	121
6	Wtrn. of Havna., Ld. Mt. Dbs., Rd.	91
7	Wrn. Ry. San Paulo Red.	99
—	Wrn. Santa Fé, 7 p.c. Red.	41
2/8	Zafra & Huelva, 3 p.c. Red.	2½

BANKS.

Div.	Name.	Paid.	Price.
2/4½	Agra, Ltd.	6	3¾
4/2½	Anglo-Argentine, Ltd., £9	7	6
8 fls.	Anglo-Austrian	120 fl.	13
6/	Anglo-Californian, Ltd., £20 Shares	10	11
4/	Anglo-Egyptian, Ltd., £15	5	6
5/	Anglo-Foreign Bkg., Ltd.	7	7½
7/	Anglo-Italian, Ltd.	5	7
7/6	Bk. of Africa, Ltd., £18¾	6½	10½
20/	Bk. of Australasia	40	50
10/	Bk. of Brit. Columbia	20	20
25/	Bk. of Brit. N. America	50	64
20/	Bk. of Egypt, Ltd., £25	12½	18½
5/	Bk. of Mauritius, Ltd.	10	9
18/	Bk. of N. S. Wales	20	38
4 p.c.	Bk. of N. Zland. Gua. Stk.	100	101½
6/	Bk. of Roumania, £20 Shs.	6	7½
2/6	Tarapaca & Ldn., Ltd., £10	5	3½
—	Bque. Fse. de l'Afri. du S.	100 f	3½
f. 22.50	Bque. Internatle. de Paris	20	23
6/	Brit. Bk. of S. America, Ltd., £20 Shares	10	9½
16/	Capital & Cties., L., £50	10	39½
20/	Chart. of India, &c.	20	30
10/	City, Ltd., £40 Shares	10	20
18/	Colonial, £100 Shares	30	21
10/	Delhi and London, Ltd.	25	—
5/	German of London, Ltd.	10	10½
25/	Hong-Kong & Shanghai	28½	44½
4/	Imperl. of Persia	6½	3
10/	Imperl. Ottoman, £20 Shs	10	11⅛
12/	Intrnatl. of Ldn., Ld., £20	15	11
10/	Ionian, Ltd.	25	15½
16/	Lloyds, Ltd., £50 Shs.	8	31½
10/	Ldn. & Brazil. Ltd., £20	10	15½
44/	Ldn. & County, Ltd., £80	20	102
9/	Ldn. & Hanseatic, L., £20	10	10½
22/6	Ldn. & Midland, L., £60	12½	53
8/9	Ldn. & Provin., Ltd., £10	5	21½
39/	Ldn. & Riv. Plate, L., £25	15	49
2/1½	Ldn. & San Fcisco, Ltd.	7	4½
28/	Ldn. & Sth. West., L., £50	20	68
26/	Ldn. & Westmins., L., £100	20	56
5/	Ldn. of Mex. & S. Amer., Ltd., £10 Shs.	6	5½
15/	Ldn. Joint Stk., L., £100	15	34
12/9½	Ldn., Paris & Amer., L. £20	16	25
2/4½	Merchant Bkg., L., £9	4	2½
6/3	Metropn, Ltd., £50 Shs.	5	14½
9/	National, Ltd., £50 Shs.	10	20
4/5	Natl. of Mexico, $100 Shs.	$40	12½
1/3	National of N. Z., L., £7½	2½	2
3/	National S. Afric. Rep.	10	13½
18/10½	National Provcl. of Eng., Ltd., £75 Shs.	10½	50½
21/7½	Do. do. £60 Shs.	12	57½
6/6	North Eastn., Ltd., £20 Shs	6	15
19/	Parr's, Ld., £100 Shs.	20	90
12/6	Prov. of Ireland, L., £100	12½	29½
40/	Stand. of S. Afric., L., £100	25	64
12/6	Union of Australia, L., £75	25	26½
4 p.c.	Do. do. Ins. Stk. Dep. 1900	100	102
15/6	Union of Ldn., Ltd., £100	15½	35

BREWERIES AND DISTILLERIES.

Div.	Name.	Paid.	Price.
4½	Albion Prp. 1 Mt. Db. Sk.	100	111
4	All Saints', L., Db. Sk. Rd.	100	97
7	Allsopp, Ltd.	100	145
6	Do. Cum. Pref	100	150
4½	Do. Deb. Stk., Red.	100	116
3½	Do. Deb. Stk., Red.	100	102
4½	Alton & Co., L., Db., Rd	100	105
4½	Do. Mt. Bds., 1896	100	104
—	Arnold, Perrett, Ltd.	10	6
6	Do. Cum. Pref.	10	10
4½	Do. 1 Mt. Db. Stk., Rd	100	106

Breweries &c. (*continued*):—

Div.	Name.	Paid.	Price
5½	Arrol, A., & Sons, L., Cum. Pref. Shs.	10	10
4½	Do. 1 Mt. Db. Stk., Rd.	100	107
5	Backus, 1 Mt. Db., Red.	100	59
4	Barclay, Perk., L., Cu. Pf.	10	11½
3½	Do. Mt. Db. Stk., Red.	100	109
—	Barnsley, Ltd.	10	11½
6	Do. Cum. Pref.	10	13½
1/3	Barrett's, Ltd	2½	1½
1/3	Do. 5 p.c. Pref.	2½	2½
3/	Bartholomay, Ltd.	10	2½
8	Do. Cum. Pref.	10	7
6	Do. Deb.	100	97½
5	Bass, Ratcliff, Ltd., Cum. Pref. Stk.	100	142½
4½	Do. Mt. Db. Stk., Rd.	100	124
4	Bell, J., L., 1 Mt. D. Stk., R	100	100
—	Benskin's, L., Cum. Pref.	5	—
—	Do. 1 Mt. Db. Stk Red.	100	—
—	Do. "B" Deb. Sk, Rd.	100	—
7/	Bentley's Yorks., Ltd.	10	10½
6/	Do. Cum. Pref.	10	12½
4½	Do. Mt. Debs., Red	100	110
4½	Do. do. 1892, Red.	100	110
—	Bieckert's, Ltd.	20	2
5	Do. Debs., Red.	100	57
—	Birmingham., Ltd., 6 p.c. Cum. Pref.	5	2½
4½	Do. Mt. Debs., Red.	50	39½
5½	Boardman's, Ld., Cm. Pf.	10	8½
4½	Do., Perp. 1 Mt. Db. Sk.	100	105½
30/9	Brain & Co., Ltd.	100	101
4½	Brakspear, L., 1 D. Stk. Red.	100	108
4	Brandon's, L., 1 D. Stk. Red.	100	104½
21/	Bristol (Georges) Ltd.	10	44
6	Do. Cum. Pref.	10	17½
5	Do. Mt. Db. Sk. 1888 Rd.	100	115½
17/6	Bristol United, Ltd.	10	35
6	Do. Cum. Pref.	10	16½
4½	Do. Db. Sk. Rd.	100	120
5½	Buckley's, L., C. Pre-prf.	10	10½
4½	Do. 1 Mt. Db. Stk. Rd.	100	104½
4	Bullard & Sons, Ltd., D. Sk. R.	100	104
6	Bushell, Watk., L., C. Pf.	10	14
4½	Do. 1 Mt. Db. Sk. Rd.	100	112
5	Camden, Ltd., Cum. Pref.	10	11½
4½	Do. 1 Mt. Db. Sk. Rd.	100	107
5½	Cameron, Ltd., Cm. Prf.	10	13½
4½	Do. Mort Deb. Stk.	100	108
3½	Do. Perp Mt. Db. Sk.	100	100½
5	Cam'bell, J'stone, L., C. Pf.	5	5
4½	Do. 4½ p.c. 1 Mt. Db. Sk.	100	103
4	Campbell, Praed, L., Per. 1 Mort. Deb. Stk.	100	105
4	Cannon, L., Mt. Db. Stk.	100	109
4	Do. "B" Deb. Stk.	100	104
5	Castlemaine, L., 1 Mt. Db.	100	94
3½	Charrington, Ltd., Mort. Deb. Stk. Red.	100	106
2/	Cheltnhm. Orig., Ltd.	5	6
6	Do. Cum. Pref.	5	7½
4	Do. Debs. Red.	100	106
10/	Chicago, Ltd.	10	3½
6	Do. Debs.	100	84½
—	Cincinnati, Cum. Pref.	10	1
10/	City of Baltimore	10	3½
16/	Do. 8 p.c. Cum. Pref	10	8
14/	City of Chicago, Ltd.	10	1½
8	Do. Cum. Pref.	10	6½
13	City of London, Ltd.	100	206½
5	Do. Cum. Pref.	100	136
4	Do. Mt. Deb. Stk., Rd.	100	109½
2/	Colchester, Ltd.	5	4½
7	Do. Pref.	5	6½
4½	Do. Deb. Stk., Red.	100	109
5	Combe, Ltd., Cum. Pref.	10	14
4	Do. Mt. Db. Stk, Rd.	100	110
3½	Do. Perp. Deb. Stk.	100	107
5	Comm'cial, L., D. Sk., Rd.	100	107½
5	Courage, L., Cm. Pref. Shs.	100	137½
4	Do. Irr. Mt. Deb. Stk.	100	120½
3½	Do. Irr. "B" Mt. Db. Sk.	100	103
8/	Daniell & Sons, Ltd.	10	7
7	Do. Cum. Pref.	10	12
4½	Do. 1 Mt. Perp. Db. Sk.	100	109
4½	Do. "B" Deb. Stk.	100	99
10d.	Dartford, Ltd.	5	5
2/9	Do. Cum. Pref.	5	5½
4	Do. 1 Mt. Db. Sk. Rd.	100	99
4	Davenport, Ld., 1 D. Stk.	100	101½
10/	Denver United, Ltd.	10	3½
8	Do. Cum. Pref.	10	8
6	Do. Debs.	100	98½
4½	Deuchar, L., 1 D. Sk., Rd.	100	109
8/	Distillers, Ltd.	10	23½
—	Dublin Distillers, Ltd.	5	1½
3/	Do. Cum. Pref.	5	4⅛
4½	Do. Irr. Deb. Stk.	100	—
5	Eadie, Ltd., Cum. Pref.	10	11
4	Do. Irr. 1 Mt. Db. Sk.	100	106
10/	Edinbgh. Utd., Ltd.	10	13
6	Do. Cum. Prf.	10	13½
4	Eldridge, Pope, L. D. St. R.	100	110
—	Emerald & Phœnix, Ltd.	10	1½
8	Do. Cum. Pref.	10	5½
6	Empress Ltd., C. Pf.	10	11½
4½	Do. Mt. Deb. Stk.	100	105
10/	Farnham, Ltd.	10	17½
6	Do. Cum. Pref.	10	14½
4	Fenwick, L., 1 D. Sk., Rd.	100	103
4	Flower & Sons, Irr. D. Sk.	100	111
4	Friary, L., 1 Db. Stk., Rd.	100	103½
4	Do. 1 "A" Db. Sk., Rd	100	100
4½	Groves, L., 1 Db. Sk., Rd.	100	111
14	Guinness, Ltd.	100	580
6	Do. Cum. Prf. Stk.	100	185½
5	Do. Deb. Stk., Red.	100	118
5	Hall's Oxford L., Cm. Pf.	5	5½
6/	Hancock, Ld., Cm. Pf. Ord.	10	14
7	Do. Def. Ord.	10	17½

Breweries, &c. (*continued*):—

Div.	Name.	Paid.	Price.
6	Hancock, Ld., Cum. Pref.	10	15½
4	Do. 1 Deb. Stk., Rd.	100	112
5	Hoare, Ltd. Cum. Pref.	10	12½
5	Do. "A" Cum. Pref.	10	12½
4	Do. Mt. Deb. Stk., Rd.	100	111
3½	Do. do. do. Rd.	100	104
3/6	Hodgson's, Ltd.	5	9½
5	Do. 1 Mt. Db., Red.	—	117½
4	Do. 2 Mt. Db., 1906	—	100
4½	Hopcraft & N., Ltd., 1 Mt. Deb. Stk., Red.	100	103
5	Huggins, Ltd., Cm. Prf.	10	—
4½	Do. 1st D. Stk. Rd.	100	—
4½	Do. "B" Db. Stk. Rd.	100	—
12/	Hull, Ltd.	10	17
7	Do. Cum. Pref.	10	14½
4½	Ind, Coope, L., D.Sk., Rd.	100	118
4	Do. "B" Mt. Db. Stk. Rd.	100	110
8/	Indianapolis, Ltd.	10	3
8	Do. Cm. Prf.	10	8½
5/	Jones, Frank, Ltd.	10	2½
7½	Do. Cum. Pref.	10	6½
5	Do. 1st Mort. Debs.	100	90½
3/	J. Kenward & Ct., Ltd.	5	5½
4½	Kingsbury, L., 1 D.Sk., Rd	100	—
4	Lacon, L., D. Stk., Red.	100	110
4	Do. Irrd. "B" D. Sk.	100	106
4/	Lascelles, Ltd.	5	11½
6	Do. Cum. Pref.	5	7½
5	Leney, Ltd., Cum. Pref.	10	11½
4	Do. 1 Mt. Db. Stk. Rd.	100	102
30/7½	Lion, Ltd., £25 shares	17	49½
10/9½	Do. New £10 shares	6	17
6	Do. Perp. Pref.	20	33
4	Do. B. Mt. Db. Sk. Rd.	100	106
4½	Lloyd & Y., Ltd., 1 Mt. Deb. Stk., Rd.	100	100½
4½	Locke & S., Ltd., Irr. 1st Mt. Deb. Stk.	100	103
4½	Lovibond, Ltd., 1st Mt. Deb. Stk., Rd.	100	101½
30/4	Lucas & Co., Ld., Deb. Stk.	100	107
12/	Manchester, Ltd.	10	19
7	Do. Cum. Pref.	10	16½
5/	Marston, J., L., Cm. Prf.	10	10½
4	Do. 1 Mt. Db. Sk., Rd.	100	101½
7/	Massey's Burnley, Ltd.	10	16½
6	Do. Cum. Pref.	10	14½
4½	McCracken, Ltd., 1 Mt. Deb., 1908	100	59½
5	McEwan, Ltd., Cm. Pref.	10	14
5	Meux, Ltd., Cum. Pref.	10	13½
4	Do. Mt. Db. Stk. Red.	100	111
4½	Michell & A., Ltd., 1 Mt. Deb. Stk. Red.	100	105
4½	Mile End Dist. Db. Sk. Rd.	100	111
—	Milwaukee & Chic., Ltd.	10	1½
4/	Do. Cum. Pref.	10	7
4½	Michell, Toms, L., Db.	50	57
6	Morgan, Ltd., Cum. Pref.	10	14½
20/	Nalder & Coll., Ltd.	10	35
6	Do. Cum. Pref.	10	15½
4½	Do. Deb. Red.	100	112
12/	Newcastle, Ltd.	10	19½
6	Do. Cum. Pref.	10	14½
5	Do. 1 Mt. Deb., 1911	100	111½
4	Do. "A" Deb. Stk. Red.	100	105
6	New England, Ltd.	10	4½
8	Do. Cum. Pref.	10	9
6	Do. Debs. Red.	100	101½
4	New London, L., 1 D.Sk.	100	103
7/2	New Westminster, Ltd.	4	10½
2/4½	Do. Pref.	4	6½
—	New York, Ltd.	10	1
—	Do. 8 p.c. Cum. Pref.	10	4
6	Do. 1 Mt. Deb. Red.	100	77½
5	Noakes, Ld., Cum. Pref.	10	11½
4	Do 1 Mt. Db. Stk., Rd.	100	105
4½	Norfolk, L., "A" D Sk. Rd	100	106
10/	Northampton, Ld.	10	16½
7	Do. Cum. Pref.	10	15½
6	Do. Cum. Pref.	10	12½
5	Do. 1 Mt. Per. Db. Sk.	100	127
4	Nth. East., L., 1 D. Sk. Rd.	100	102
4½	N. Worcesters., L. Per. 1 Mort. Deb. Stock	100	57½
6	Nottingham, L., Cm. Prf.	10	1
5	Do. 1 Mt. Deb. Stk., Red.	100	114
17/4	Do. "B" do. Red.	50	112
6/	Ohlsson' Cape, Ld.	5	17
7	Do. Cum. Pref.	5	9
4½	Do. 2nd Cum. Pref.	5	5½
5	Do. Deb. Stk. Red.	100	116
4½	Oldfield, L., 1 Mt. Db. Stk.	100	105
6	Page & Overt., L., Cm. Prf.	10	14
4½	Do. 1 Mt. Dbs., Red.	100	109
10/	Parker's Burslem, Ltd.	10	21½
6	Do. Cum. Pref.	10	15
4	Do. 1 Mt. Db. Stk., Red.	100	111
4	Persse, Ld., 1 Mt. Db. Rd.	100	95½
4	Phipps, L., Irr. 1 Db. Stk.	100	113
8	Plymouth, L., Min. Cu. Pf.	10	13
4½	Do. Mt. Deb. Stk., Red.	100	106½
4½	Pryor, Reid, L., 1 D.S., R.	100	103½
5	Reid's, Ld., Cm. Pref. Stk.	100	136½
4	Do. Mt. Deb. Stk., Red	100	110
3½	Do. "B" Mt. Db. Stk., Rd	100	103
5	Rhondda Val., L., Cu. Pf	10	11
4½	Do. 1 Mt. Deb. Stk., Rd	100	109
5	Robinson, Ld., Cum. Pref.	10	11½
4½	Do. 1 Mt. Perp. Db. Stk.	100	111½
4/	Rochdale, Ltd.	10	6
4½	Do. 1 Mt. Deb. Stk.	100	91½
7	Royal, Brentford, Ltd.	10	21
	Do. Cum. Pref.	10	15
4½	Do. 1 Mt. Dbs. Red	100	10
6/	St. Louis, Ltd.	10	3½
8	Do. Cum. Pref.	10	8½
14/	St. Pauli, Ltd.	10	10
7	Do. Cum. Pref.	10	12
4½	Salt (T.), L., 1 Db. Sk. Rd.	100	112
4½	Do. "B" Db. Stk. Red	100	106
—	San Francisco, Ltd.	10	½
—	Do. 8 p.c. Cum. Pref.	10	½

Breweries, &c. (*continued*):—

Div.	Name.	Paid.	Price.
4½	Savill Brs., L., D. Sk. Rd.	100	118
4½	Scarboro., Ltd., 1 Db. Stk.	100	101
4	Shaw (Hy.), Ltd., 1 Mt. Db. Stk., Red.	100	104
22/	Showell's, Ltd.	10	30½
7	Do. Cum. Pref.	10	17
3/	Do. Gua. Shs.	5	7½
4½	Do. Mt. Db. Stk., Red.	100	—
4	Simonds, L., 1 D. Sk., Rd.	100	111
3½	Simson & McP., L., Cu. Pf.	10	9½
4½	Do. 1 Mt. Deb. Stk.	100	97
5/	Smith, Garrett, L., £20 Shs	10	16½
5	Do. Cum. Pref.	20	26
3½	Do. 3½ p.c. Mt. Db. Stk.	100	106
5	Smith's, Tadcaster, L., CPf	10	12
4½	Do. Deb. Stk., Red.	100	112
4	Do. Deb. Stk. Red.	100	108
4½	Star, L., 1 M. Db. Stk., Rd.	100	103
4	Steward & P., L., 1 D. Sk.	100	109
9/	Strettons Derby, Ltd.	10	13
6	Do. Cum. Pref.	10	13½
4	Do. Irr. 1 Mt. Db. Stk.	100	104½
4½	Strong, Romsey, L., 1 D. S.	100	115
5	Stroud, L., Db. Sk., Rd.	100	109½
4½	Tadcaster To'er, L., D.Sk.	100	113
8/	Tamplin, Ltd.	10	21
6	Do. Cum. Pref.	100	15
4	Do. "A" Db. Sk., Rd.	10	106
6	Thorne, Ltd., Cum. Pref.	10	14
4	Do. Deb. Stk., Red.	100	103½
15/	Threlfall, Ltd.	10	45
6	Do. Cum. Pref.	10	16
5	Do. 1 Mt. Dbs., Red.	100	114
4	Tollemache, L., D. Sk. Rd.	100	105
4	Truman, Hanb., D. Sk., R.	100	110
3	Do. "B" Mt. Db. Sk., Rd.	100	96
10/	United States, Ltd.	10	9
8	Do. Cum. Pref.	10	11
6	Do. 1 Mt. Deb.	100	106½
6/	Walker & H., Ld., Cm. Pf.	10	10½
4½	Do. 1 Mt. Deb. Stk., Red.	100	107
5	Walker, Peter, Ld. Cm. Prf.	10	13½
4	Do. 1 Mt. Dbs. Red.	100	110
4	Wallingford, L., D. Sk. Rd.	100	105
6	Watney, Ld., Cm. Prf. Sk.	100	168
5	Do. Mt. Db. Sk., Rd.	100	115½
4½	Do. "B" Mt. Db. Sk., Rd.	100	111
3½	Do. Mt. Db. Stk.	100	100½
5	Watney, D., Ld., Cm. Prf.	10	12
4½	Do. 1 Mt. Db. Stk.	100	103
10/	Webster & Sons, Ltd.	10	16½
6	Do. Cum. Pref.	10	14
5	Wenlock Ltd Pref.	10	11½
4	Do. 1 Mt. Db. Sk., Rd.	100	105
5	West Cheshire, L., Cu. Pf.	10	10½
4	Do. Irred. 1 Mt. Db. Sk.	100	99
4½	Whitbread, L., Cu. Pf. Sh.	100	123½
4	Do. Db. Stk., Red.	100	109
3½	Do. "B" Db. Stk., Rd.	100	101
9/	Wolverhmpton & D. Ld.	10	17
6	Do. Cum. Pref.	10	13½
4½	Do. 1 Mt. Dbs., Red.	100	103
5½	Worthington, Ld., Cm. Prf.	10	15½
5½	Do. Cum. "B" Pref.	10	13½
4½	Do. Mt. Db. Sk., Rd.	100	113
3½	Do. Irr. "B" Db. Stk.	100	102
6/	Yates's Castle, Ltd.	10	13
5	Do. Cum. Pref.	10	11
5	Younger W., L., Cu. Pf. Sh.	100	133½

CANALS AND DOCKS.

Last Div.	Name.	Paid.	Price.
4	Birmingham Canal	100	140½
—	E. & W. India Dock	100	19½
—	Do. 4 p.c. Prf. Stk.	100	74
—	Do. P. L. Deb. Stk.	100	101
—	Do. Cons. Deb. Stk.	100	89
40/	G. Junction Ord. Shs.	100	147½
6/	Do. do. Pref.	10	19
4½	King's Lynn Per. Db. Stk.	100	117½
2½	Leeds & L'pool Canal	100	71
2½	Lndn & St. Kath. Dks.	100	54
4½	Do. Pref.	100	136½
4½	Do. Pref., 1878	100	132½
4½	Do. Pref., 1882	100	130
4	Do. Deb. Stk.	100	132½
—	Mchester Ship C. 5 p.c. Pf.	10	2
3½	Do. 1st Perp. Mt. Deb.	100	93
—	Milford Dks. Db. Stk. "A"	100	19½
3½	Millwall Dk.	100	60
5	Do. Perp. Pref.	100	140½
4½	Do. Pref.	100	105½
5	Do. New Per. Prf., 1887	100	126½
5	Do. Per. Deb. Stk.	100	152½
4/	Newhaven Har.	10	14½
2½	N. Metropolitan	100	65
5	Sharpness Nw. Pf. "A" Sk.	100	141½
4	Do. Deb. Stk.	100	117½
5	Sheffiel & S. Yorks Nav. 4½ p.c. Pref Stk.	100	115½
36.13?	Suez Canal	20	138½
7	Surrey Comcl. Dok. Ord.	100	150½
7	Do. Min. 4 p.c. Pref. "A"	110	151½
5	Do. Pref. "B"	100	148½
5	Do. do. "C"	100	148½
5	Do. do. "D"	100	144½
4½	Do. Deb. Stk.	100	152½

COMMERCIAL, INDUSTRIAL, &c.

Last Div.	Name.	Paid.	Price.
5	Accles, L., 1 Mt. Db., Red.	100	84½
2/6	Aërated Bread, Ltd.	1	12½
—	African Gold Recovery, L.	1	½
2/	Aluminium, L., "A" Shs.	1	2
4½	Do. 1 Mt. Db. Stk., Red.	100	97
5½	Amelia Nitr., L., 1 Mort Deb., Red.	100	82½
7/	Anglo-Chil. Nitrate, Ltd., Cum. Pref.	10	6½
4½	Do. Cons. Mt. Bds., Red.	100	77½
4½	Anglo-Russian Cotton, Ld., 1 Charge Debs., Red.	100	97
11/3	Angus (G., & Co., L.), £10	7½	17
6/	Apollinaris, Ltd.	10	11½
5/	Do. 5 p.c. Cum. Pref.	10	10½
4	Do. Irred. Deb. Stock	100	103
3/	Argentine Meat Pres., L., 7 p.c. Pref.	10	2½
5	Argentine Refinry, Db. Rd.	100	98
6d.	Armstrong, Whitw., Ltd.	1	3½
4	Do. Cum. Pref.	5	6½
5	Artisans', Labr. Dwligs., L.	100	128½
4½	Do. Non-Cm. Prf., 1879	100	132½
4½	Do. do. 1884	100	132½
—	Asbestos & Asbestic, Ltd.	10	7½
2/7½	Ashley-grdns., L., C. Prf.	5	6½
4½	Do. 1 Mt. Deb. Stk.	100	113½
5/	Assam Rly. & Trdng., L., 8 p.c. Cum. Pref. "A"	10	14
—	Do. Deferrd. "B" Shs.	1	4
—	Do. do. (iss. f. pd)	1	3½
8/	Do. Cum. Pre-Prf. "A"	10	15
6/	Do. New Pref.	10	11½
5	Do. Debs., Red.	100	106
5	Do. Red. Mort. Debs.	100	110
6	Aust'lian Pastrl, L., Cu. Pf	10	7
8d.	Aylesbury Dairy, Ltd.	1	1½
4	Do. 4 p.c. Mt. Dbs.	100	104½
10/	Babcock & Wilcox, Ltd.	10	28
6	Do. 6 p.c. Cm. Prf.	10	16
8	Baker (Chs.), L., Cm. Pf.	5	9
8	Do. "B" Cm. Pref.	5	7½
2/1	Barker (John), Ltd.	1	2½
5½	Do. Cum. Pref.	5	7½
4½	Do. Irred. 1 Mt. Db. Stk.	100	125½
—	Barnagore Jute, Ltd.	5	3
5	Do. Cum. Pref.	5	4½
7½d.	Belgravia Dairy, Ltd.	1	1½
3/9	Bell (R.) & Co., Ltd.	5	3½
9½d.	Bell's Asbestos, Ltd.	1	½
5	Do. Mt. Db. Bds., Rd.	100	106
10/	Bengal Mills, Ltd.	10	11
6/	Do. 5 p.c. Cum. Prf.	10	10½
5/	Benson (J. W.) L., Cm. Pf.	10	10½
4	Do. Perp. Mt. Db. Stk.	100	101
6	Bergvik, L., 6 p.c. Cm. Pf.	10	13
12/	Do. Dfd.	10	10½
4½	Do. 1 Dbs., Red.	100	103½
5/	Birm'ham Vinegar, Ltd.	5	15
5	Do. Cum. Pref.	5	5½
4½	Do. 1 Mt. Db. Stk., Rd.	100	109½
5	Bonke (A.) L., 5 p.c. Cu. Pf.	10	10½
2/6	Bodega, Ltd.	5	8½
4½	Do. Mt. Deb. Stk., Rd.	100	111
8/	Bottomley & Brs., Ltd.	10	6½
6/	Do. 6 p.c. Pf.	10	9½
8½d.	Bovril, Ltd.	1	1
1/0½	Do. Def.	1	½
6½d	Do. Cum. Pref.	1	1
4½	Do. Deb. Stk.	100	100
5/	Bradbury, Gretrex., Ltd., £10 share	8	14
5/	Do. 5 p.c. Cum. Pref.	10	13½
5/	Brewers' Sugar, L., 5 p.c. Cum. Pref.	10	10½
3/6	Brighton Grd. Hotel, Ld.	5	4
4	Do Mt. Db. Stk., Red.	100	101½
5	Bristol Hotel & Palm. Co., Ltd. 1st Mt. Red. Deb.	100	105
9½d.	British & Bengton's. Tea Tr. Asc., Ltd.	1	1½
5	Do. Cum. Prf.	5	5½
—	British Deli & Lgkat. Tobacco, Ltd.	1	½
—	Do. Cum. Prf.	1	½
—	British Tea Table, Ltd.	1	2½
5½	Do. Cum. Pref.	1	1½
2/6	Brooke, Ben., & Co., Ltd., Cum. Pref.	5	5½
7/6	Brooke, Bond & Co., Ltd.	5	19
3/	Brown Bros., L., Cum. Pref.	5	5½
10/	Browne & Eagle Ltd.	10	13½
5	Do. Cum. Pref.	10	13
4	Do. Mrt. Db. Sk., Red.	100	110
20/	Brunner, Mond, & Co., Lt.	2	40
7/	Do. £10 shares	3	16
7	Do. Cum. Pref.	10	17½
7	Do. £10 shares	5	8½
10/	Bryant & May, Ltd.	5	19
3/	Bucknall, H., & Sons, Lt.	5	7
6	Do. Cum Pref.	5	7½
4/	Burke, E. & J., Ltd.	5	7½
6	Do. Cum. Pref.	5	7½
6	Do. Irred. Deb. Stk.	100	155
1/	Burlington Htls. Co., Ltd.	1	1½
5	Do. Cum. Pref.	1	1
4	Do. Perp. Deb. Stk.	100	105½
5	Bush, W. J., & Co., Ltd., Cum. Pref.	5	5½
4	Do. 1 Deb. Stk., Red.	100	102
5½	Callard, Stewart, & Watt, Ltd., Cum. Pref.	1	1½
4/	Callender's Cable L., Shs.	5	9½
4½	Do. 1 Deb. Stk., Red.	100	111½
—	Campbell, R., & Sons, Lt.	3	2½
6	Cantareira Water, Bd., Rd	100	99½
5	Do. (2nd issue)	100	87½
4	Cartavio Sugar, Ltd., 6 p.c. 1st Debs., Red.	90	82½
9/	Cassell & Co., Ltd., £10	9	15
5	Causton, Sir J., & Sons, Ltd., Cum. Pref.	10	13½

Commercial, &c. (*continued*):—

Last Div.	Name.	Paid.	Price.
4	Cent. Prod. Mkt. of B.A. 1st Mt. Str. Debs.	100	76½
4	Chappell & Co., Ltd., Mt. Deb. Stk. Red.	100	103
6/	Chicago & N.W. Gran. 8 p.c. Cum. Pref.	10	3
—	Chicago Packing & Prov.	10	6
8	Do. Cum. Pref.	10	10
6/	City Offices, Ltd.	12	8
3½	Do. Mt. Deb. Stk.	100	108½
7/2½	Cy. London Real Prop., Ltd., £25 shs.	12	22
4/6	Do. £12½ shs.	7½	15
3½	Do. Deb. Stk. Red.	100	106½
3½	Do. Deb. Stk. Red.	100	105½
3	Do.	100	100½
6/	Cy. of Santos Imprvts., Ltd., 7 p.c. Pref.	10	8
20/	Clay, Bock, & Co., Ltd.	10	5
8	Do. Cum. Pref.	10	9
6	Do. Mort. Deb.	100	102½
20/	Coats, J. & P., Ltd.	10	58
20/	Do. Cum. Pref.	10	17
4½	Do. Deb. Stk. Red.	100	112½
9½d	Coburg Hotel, Ltd.	1	1½
4	Do. Deb. Stk. Red.	100	102
6	Colonial Consign & Dis., Ltd., Cum. Pref.	5	4½
4½	Do. 1st Mort. Debs.	100	96½
—	Colorado Nitrate, Ltd.	5	½
4/	Co. Gén des Asphtes. de F., Ltd.	6	6
5	Do. Non-Cm. Prf.	—	5
5	Cook, J. W., & Co., Ltd., Cum. Pref.	5	5½
5	Cook, T., & Son, Egypt, Ltd., 1st Mt. Deb. Red.	100	110½
—	Cork Co., Ltd., 6 p.c. Cum. Pref.	5	2
5	Cory, W., & Sn, L., Cu. Pf.	5	5½
4	Do. 1st Deb. Stk. Red.	100	109
1/6	Crisp & Co., Ltd.	1	1½
5½	Do. Cum. Pref.	1	1½
—	Crompton & Co., Ltd., 7 p.c. Cum. Pref.	5	—
5	Do. 1st Mt. Reg. Deb.	—	90½
4/6	Crossley, J., & Sons, Ltd.	5	7½
5	Do. Cum. Pref.	5	6½
—	Crystal Pal. Ord. "A" Stk.	100	6½
—	Do. "B" Red. Stk	100	1½
6	Do. 6 p.c. 1st 1887 Deb. Stk. Red.	100	117½
—	Do. 6 p.c. 2nd 1887 Deb. Stk. Red.	100	51½
—	Do. 6 p.c. 3rd 1887 Deb. Stk. Red.	100	22½
3	Do. 3 p.c. 1st 1895 Deb. Stk.	100	92½
—	Daimler Motor, Ltd.	10	6
4/	Dalgety & Co., £20 Shs.	5	5½
4½	Do. Deb. Stk.	100	124
4	Do.	100	113
7/	De Keyser's Ryl. Htl., L.	10	13½
5	Do. Cum. Pref.	10	12
4	Do. Deb. Stk., Red.	100	110
6	Denny, H., & Sons, Ltd., Cum. Pref.	10	14½
5/3	Devas, Routledge & Co., L.	7	8½
5	Dickinson, J., & Co., L., Cum. Pref. Stk.	100	123
4½	Domin. Cottn. Mls., Ltd. Mt. Stg. Dbs.	100	97
6/	Dorman, Long & Co., L.	5	4½
—	Eastmans, Ltd.	10	2½
12/	Do. 8 p.c. Cum. Pref.	10	10½
2/6	E. C. Powder, Ltd.	3	5½
1/6	Edison & Swn Utd. Elec. Ltd., "A" £5 Shs.	3	2½
2/6	Do. fully-paid	5	4½
4½	Ekman Pulp & Ppr. Co., Ltd., Mt. Deb., Red.	100	96
1/1½	Electric Construc., Ltd.	2	2½
7	Do. Cum. Pref.	2	3½
2/	Eley Bros., Ltd.	10	37
—	Elmore's Cop. Deptg., L.	1	½
—	Elmore's Wire Mnfg., L.	2	½
—	Elysée Pal. Hotel Co., L.	5/	½
5 p.c.	Do. 5 p.c. £100 Db., Rd.	70	97½
8½d.	Evans, Ben., & Co., Ltd.	1	1
5	Do. 1 Mt. Db. Sk., Rd.	100	108
1/5½d.	Evans, D. H., & Co., L.	1	2½
6	Do. Cum. Pref.	1	1½
4½	Do. 1 Mt. Db. Sk., Rd.	100	112
2/6	*Evening News*, L., 5 p.c. Cum. Pref.	5	5½
5/3	Evered & Co., L., £10 Sh.	7	12½
7/6	Do.	10	18½
4	Fairbairn Pastoral Co., Aust., L., 1 Mt. Db., Rd.	100	102
6	Fairfield Shipbldg., Ltd., Cum. Pref.	10	11
4½	Do. Mort. Deb. Stk.	100	110
6/	Farmer & Co., Ld., 6 p.c. Cum. Pref.	10	13½
10	Field, J. C. & J., Ltd.	10	10½
14/	Do. 7 p.c. Cum. Pref.	10	14½
1/3	Fordham, W.B., & Sns, Ld.	1	2
5/6	Fore-st. Warehouse, Ltd.	11	9½
4	Do. Regd. Debs., Rd.	100	101½
3/6	Foster, M. R. & Sons, Ltd.	4	6
5	Do. Pref.	10	11½
9/	Foster, Porter, & Co., L.	10½	15½
4	Fowler, J., & Co. (Leeds), Ltd., 1 Mt. Deb., Red.	100	103½
3/	Fraser & Chalmers, Ltd.	3	1½
4½	Free, Rodwell & Co., Ltd., Deb Stk.	100	104½
6½d.	Furness, T., & Co., Ltd., 5½ p.c. Cum. Pref.	1	1
4½	Gartside & Co. (of Manchstr), L., 1 Mt. Db. Sk.	100	112
11	Genl. Hydraul Power, L.	100	270

Commercial, &c. (*continued*):—

Last Div.	Name.	Paid.	Price.
8/	Gillman & Spencer, Ltd.	5	2½
6	Do. Pref.	5	4½
5	Do. Mort. Debs.	50	51
4	Goldsbro., Mort & Co., L., "A" Deb. Stk., Red.	100	69½
—	Do. 3 p.c. "B" Inc. Deb. Stk., Red.	100	12
8/	Gordon Hotels, Ltd.	10	19¼
5½	Do. Cum. Pref.	10	14¼
4½	Do. Perp. Deb. Stk.	100	139½
4	Do. do.	100	122½
—	Greenwich Inld. Linoleum Co., Ltd.	1	⅜
7	Greenwood & Batley, Ltd., Cum. Pref.	10	10
7½d.	Hagemann & Co., Ltd., 6 p.c. Cum. Pref.	1	1
—	Hammond, Ltd.	10	¾
—	Do. 8 p.c. Cum. Pref.	10	3½
—	Do. 6 p.c. Cum. Inc. Stk. Red.	100	56½
	Hampton & Sons, Ltd., 4 p.c. 1 Mt. Db. St. Red.	100	105
—	Hans Crescent Htl., L., 6 p.c. Cum. Pref.	5	3
4	Do. 1 Mt. Deb. Stk.	100	90
6d.	Harmsworth, Ltd., Cum. Pref.	1	1½
4/	Harrison, Barber, Ltd.	5	4½
3/	Harrod's Stores, Ltd.	1	4½
2/6	Do. Cum. Pref.	5	7¼
5½	Hawaiian Comcl. & Sug. 1 Mt. Debs.	100	91½
5	Hazell, Watson, L., C. P.	10	11½
18/	Henley's Teleg., Ltd.	10	22
7	Do. Pref. Shs.	10	19
4½	Do. Mt. Db. Stk., Rd.	100	112½
6	Henry, Ltd.	10	11¾
5	Do. Cum. Pref.	10	13½
4½	Do. Mt. Debs., Red.	50	53
1/4½	Herrmann, Ltd.	1	¾
—	Hildesheimer, Ltd.	3	1¾
1/2½	Holbrn. & Frasca, Ltd.	1	1¼
5	Do. Cum. Pref.	10	11½
4	Do. Deb. Stk.	100	109
6	Home & Col. Stres, L., C.P	5	7¼
6	Hood & M.'s Stres., Ltd., Cum. Pref.	1	½
6	Hook, C. T Ltd.	10	6
7/2	Hornsby, Ltd., £10 Shs.	8	3
—	Hotchks. Ordn., Ltd.	10	1
—	Do. 7 p.c. Cm. Prf.	10	4½
5	Do. 1 Mt. Dbs., Rd.	100	97½
6	Htl. Cecil, Ld., Cm. Prf.	5	3½
4	Do. 1 Mt. D. Sk., R.	100	100½
8/	Howard & Bulgh, Ltd.	10	39
6	Do. Pref.	10	16
4	Do. Deb. Stk., Red.	100	108
5/	Howell, J., Ltd., £5 Shs.	4	8¾
—	Howell & Js., Ltd., £3½ Shs.	3	¾
1/6	Humber, Ltd.	1	¾
6	Do. Cum. Pref.	1	⅞
5/6	Hunter, Wilts., Ltd.	5	7
2/7	Hyam Clthg., Ltd., 5 p.c. Cum. Pref.	5	5¾
10/	Impl. Russn. Cotton, L.	5	5½
5	Impd. Industl. Dwgs., Ld.	100	131½
6d.	Do. Defrd.	1	1½
25/	Impd. Wood Pave., Ltd.	10	15½
15/	Ind. Rubber, Gutta Per. Telegraph Works, Ltd.	10	21½
4	Do. 1 Mt. Debs., Red.	100	104
6	Intern. Tea, Cum. Pref.	5	6½
10½d.	Jays, Ltd.	1	1⅝
5½	Do. Cum. Pref.	5	6½
1/2½d.	Jones & Higgins, Ltd.	1	2¼
4½	Do. 1 Mt. Db. Sk., Rd.	100	111
5/	Kelly's Directory, Ltd., 5 p.c. Cum. Pref.	10	12¾
4	Do. Mort. Db. Sk., Rd.	100	106
—	Kent Coal Explrtn. Ltd.	1	⅝
9½d.	King, Howmann, Ltd.	1	1½
4/	Kinloch & Co., Ltd.	5	8¼
6	Do. Pref.	5	7
5	Lady's Pictorial Pub., Ltd., Cum. Pref.	5	5
48/4	La Guaira Harb., Ltd., 5 p.c. Deb. Stk.	100	79½
—	Do. 2 Mt. 7 p.c. Deb. Stk., Red.	100	24
4/	Lagunas Nitrate, Ltd.	5	1
2/	Lagunas Syn., Ltd.	5	1
5	Do. 1 Mt. Debs., Red.	100	79½
—	L. Copais Ld., 1 Mt. 6 p.c. Debs., Red.	100	35½
3/	Lautaro Nitrate, Ltd.	5	4
5	Do. 1 Mt. Debs., Red.	—	100
9/	Lawes Chem. L., £10 shs.	9	5½
14/	Do. N. Cm. Min. Pref.	10	12½
—	Leeds Forge, 7 p.c. Cm. Pf.	5	3½
5	Do. 1 Mt. Debs., Red.	50	47
5	Lever Bros., L., Cm. Pf.	10	13½
6	Liberty, L., 6 p.c. Cm. Pf.	10	15
20/	Liebig's, Ltd.	20	79
5	Lilley & Sk., L., Cm. Pf.	5	5½
2/6	Linoleum Manfg Ltd.	5	16
3/	Linotype, Ltd., Pre	5	5¾
5/	Do. Def.	5	7½
4/	Lister & Co., Ltd.	10	4
5	Do. Cum. Pref.	10	8¼
5/	Liverpool. Nitrate	5	4¾
—	Liverpool. Warehsg., Ltd	10	3
5½	Do. Cum. Pref.	10	8
4	Do. 1 Mt. Db. Stk., Rd.	100	105
5½	Lockharts, Ltd., Cm. Pf.	1	1½
4/6	Ldn. & Til. Lightrage £10	9	6½
6/	Ldn. Comcl. Sale Rms., L.	10	17½
3	Do. 1 Mt. Deb. Stk., Red.	100	103
3	London Nitrate, Ltd.	5	1½
4/	London Nitrate, Ld. 6 p.c. Cm. Min. Pf.	5	3½
8/	London Pavilion, Ltd.	5	6½

Commercial, &c. (*continued*):—

Last Div.	Name.	Paid.	Price.
2/6	London Produce Clg. Ho., Ltd., £10 Shares	2½	3¾
4/	London Stereos., Ltd.	5	3
6d.	Ldn. Un. Laun. L. Cm. Pf.	1	½
8½d.	Louise, Ltd.	1	¾
5½	Do. Cum. Pref.	1	¾
5/	Lovell & Christmas, Ltd.	5	11½
6	Do. Cum. Pref.	5	7¼
4	Do. Mt. Deb. Stk., Red.	100	107
1/3	Lyons, Ltd.	1	4½
4½	Do. 1 Mt. Deb., Stk., Rd.	100	112½
10/	Machinery Trust, Ltd.	5	13½
4½	Do. 4½ Deb. Stk.	100	104
6	MacLellan, L., Min. C. Pf.	10	9
5	Do. 1 Mt. Debs., 1900	100	101½
—	McEwan, J. & Co., Ltd.	10	1½
6	Do. Mt. Debs., Red.	100	89½
8	McNamara, L., Cm. Pref.	10	9
7½d.	Maison Virot, Ltd.	1	¾
2/7	Do. 6 p.c. Cum. Pref.	5	3½
5/	Manbré Sacc., L., Cm. Pf.,	10	12
10/	Mangan Bree., L., £10 Shs.	6	15½
2/	Mason & Mason, Ltd.	5	2¾
6	Do. Cum. Pref.	5	5½
—	Maynards, Ltd.	1	¾
6	Do. Cum. Pref.	1	⅞
9½d.	Mazawattee Tea, Ltd.	1	1¾
5	Do. Cum. Pref.	5	5½
6	Mellin's Food Cum. Pref.	5	6½
4½	Met. Ascn. Imp. Dwllngs., Ltd.	100	110
5	Metro. Indus. Dwlgs., Ltd.	5	4½
4	Do. do. Cum. Pref.	5	5½
5	Metro. Prop., L., Cm. Pf.	5	5½
4½	Do. 1st Mt. Debs. Stk.	100	108½
6	Mexican Cotton 1 Mt. Db.	100	93½
4½	Mid. Class Dwlgs., L., Db.	100	120½
1/	Millars' Karri, Ltd.	1	2¼
6	Do. Cum. Pref.	1	1⅝
5/	Milner's Safe, Ltd.	10	20½
10/	Moir & Son, Ltd., Pref.	5	8
6	Morgan Cruc., L., Cm. Pf.	10	14¾
2/	Morris, R., Ltd.	3½	3½
2/6	Murray L. 5½ p.c. C. Pf.	5	5¾
63/4½	Do. 4½ 1 Mt. Db. Sk. Rd.	100	107
1/7½	Nat. Safe Dep., Ltd.	4	3½
6	Do. Cum. Pref.	1	1
—	Native Guano, Ltd.	5	½
—	Nelson Bros., Ltd.	10	2½
5	Do. Deb. Stk., Red.	100	80½
7/	Neuchtel Asph., Ltd.	10	10
10d.	New Darvel Tob., Ltd.	18/	1½
1/6	New Explosives, Ltd.	3	3
5/3½	New Gd. Htl., Bham, L.	5	4
5½	Do. Pref.	5	4½
4	Do. 1 Mt. Db. Stk., Rd.	100	96½
—	New Julia Nitrate, Ltd.	10/	—
—	New Ldn. Borneo Tob., L.	16/	1½
1/6	New Premier Cycle, Ltd.	1	⅞
6	Do. 6 p.c. Cum. Pref.	1	¾
4½	Do. 4½ p.c. 1 Mt. Db. Rd	100	—
—	New Tamargl. Nitr., Ltd	1	⅛
—	Do. 8 p.c. Cum. Pref.	1	½
6	Do. 6 p.c. 1 Mt. Dbs. Rd.	100	62½
3'78d.	Newnes, G., L., Cm. Prf.	1	1
1/3	Nitr. Provision, Ltd.	2½	¾
24/	Nobel-Dynam., Ltd.	10	18½
—	North Brazn. Sugar, Ltd.	1	¼
15/	Oakey, Ltd.	10	31
6	Do. Cum. Pref.	10	17¼
—	Paccha Jarp. Nitr., Ltd.	5	¼
5	Pac. Borax, L., 1 Db. Rd.	100	110
—	Palace Hotel, Ltd.	10	5½
5½	Do. Cum. Pref.	10	7½
4	Do. 1 Mt. Deb. Stk.	100	103
2/6	Palmer, Ltd.	5	1
6	Do. Cum. Pref.	5	2
1/2½d	Paquin, Ltd.	1	½
6	Do. Cum. Pref.	5	4
5½	Parnall, Ltd., Cum. Pref.	1	⅝
4/6	Pawsons, Ltd., £10 Shs.	6	6½
4	Do. Mt. Debs., Red.	100	106
6	Pearks, G. & T., Ltd., 6 p.c. Cum. Pref.	1	¾
9½d.	Pears, Ltd.	1	1½
6	Do. Cum. Pref.	10	14
5	Do. Deb. Stk.	100	129
5½	Pearson, C. A., L., Cu. Pf.	5	5
4/3	Peebles, Ltd.	5	7¾
5	Do. Cum. Pref.	5	6½
4½	Do. Mt. Deb. Stk. Red.	100	113½
5½	Peek Bros., Ltd., 1 Cum. Pref., Nos. 1-60,000	5	6½
3½	Do. 3½ p.c 1 Db. Stk.	100	102½
7½d.	Pegamoid, Ltd.	1	¾
—	Pillsbury-W. Fl. Mills, L.	10	3
16/	Do. 8 p.c. Cum. Pref.	10	7¾
6	Do. 1 Mort. Debs.	100	94½
9½d.	Plummer, Ltd.	1	1½
5	Do. Cum. Pref.	5	5½
7/6	Price's Candle, Ltd.	16	35
6	Priest Marians, L., Cm. Pf.	1	1½
6	Pryce Jones, Ld., Cm. Pf.	5	7
5	Do. Deb. Stk.	100	122
8½d.	Pullman, Ltd.	1	1½
6d.	Do. Cum. Pref.	1	1½
6d.	Raleigh Cycle, Ltd	1	[illegible]
6	Do. Cum. Pref.	1	¾
—	Recife Drnge. Ld. 1 Mt. Debs., R	100	19
6	Redfern, Ltd. Cum. Prf.	10	14
5	Ridgways, Ltd., Cu. Pf.	5	5½
—	R. Janeiro Cy. Imps. Ld.	25	7
5	Do. Debs.	100	85½
5	Do. 1880-1893	100	85½
11/	R. Jan Fl. Mills, Ltd.	7	6½
5	Do. 1 Mt. Debs., Rd.	100	94
—	Riv. Plate Meat, Ltd.	5	2½
—	Do. Pref.	5	5
8½d.	Roberts, J. R., Ltd.	1	1½
5	Roberts 1 Mt. D. Sk., Rd.	100	112
1/4½	Roberts, T. R., Ltd.	1	2½
5	Do. Cum. Pref.	1	1¼

Commercial, &c. (*continued*):—

Last Div.	Name.	Paid.	Price.
3/	Rosario Nit., Ltd.	5	3½
5	Do. Debs., Red.	100	103
1/	Rover Cycle, Ltd.	1	¾
6/	Ryl. Aquarium, Ltd.	5	4½
6	Do. Pref.	5	6
5	Ryl. Htl., Edin., Cm. Pf.	1	1¼
1/2½	Ryl. Niger, Ltd., £10 Sh.	2	3
6/	Do.	10	15½
20/	Russian Petroleum	10	21½
6½	Do. 6½ p.c. Cm. Prf.	10	10½
3/	Ruston, Proctor, Ltd.	10	11
4½	Do. 1 Mort. Debs.	100	104
6/	Sadler, Ltd.	12	7
—	Sal. Carmen Nit., Ltd.	5	3½
9d.	Salmon & Gluck., Ltd.	1	1⅛
	Salt Union, Ltd.	10	1½
1½	Do. 7 p.c. Pref.	10	5½
4½	Do. Deb. Stk.	100	98½
4½	Do. "B" Deb. Sk., Rd.	100	97½
—	San Donato Nit., Ltd.	5	[illegible]
5/	San Jorge Nit., Ltd.	5	3½
—	San Pablo Nit., Ltd.	5	[illegible]
—	San Sebastn. Nit., Ltd.	5	[illegible]
1/9	Sanitas, Ltd	1	2½
—	Sa. Elena Nit., Ltd.	5	¼
—	Sa. Rita Nit., Ltd.	5	1½
5/	Savoy Hotel, Ltd.	10	16
7	Do. Pref.	10	13½
4	Do. 1 Mt. Deb. Stk.	100	111½
5	Do. Debs., Red	100	102½
5	Do. & Ldn. For. Htl., Ltd., 5 p.c. Debs. Red.	100	99
8½d.	Schweppes, Ltd.	1	1
2½d.	Do Def.	1	½
5	Do. Cum. Pref.	1	1⅛
4	Do. Deb. Stk.	100	105
1/	Singer Cyc., Ltd.	1	½
5½	Do Cum. Pref.	1	⅞
—	Smokeless Pwdr., Ltd.	1	⅜
5½d.	S. Eng. Dairies, Ltd., 6 p.c. Cum. Pref.	1	1¼
—	Sowler Thos. L.	1	1
3/4½	Do. 5½ Cm. Pf.	5	5½
4/6	Spencer, Turner, & Co. Ltd	5	8½
5	Do. Cum. Pref.	5	6½
5	Spicer, Ld., 5 p.c. Dbs. Rd.	100	65
4/	Spiers & Pond, Ltd.	10	21½
5	Do. 1 Mt. Debs., Red.	100	118½
5	Do. "A" Db. Stk., Rd.	100	111
5	Do. "B" 1 Db. Stk., Rd.	100	111
4	Do. Fd. "C" 1 Db. S., R.	100	104
7/6	Spratt's, Ltd	5	12¼
4	Do. Debs., 1914	—	105
5	Steiner Ld., Cm. Pf.	10	11½
4	Do. 1 Mt. Db. Sk. Rd.	100	107
9/	Stewart & Clydesdale, L.	10	13½
6	Do. Cum. Pref.	10	14½
35/5	Sulphide Corp.	100	80
1/	Swan & Edgar, L.	1	1¼
1/	Sweetmeat Automatic, L.	1	4
2/9	Teetgen, Ltd., Cum. Pref.	5	6
24/	Teleg. Construction., Ld.	12	35½
5	Do. Db. Bds., Rd., 1899	100	103½
3/0½	Tilling, Ld. 5½ p.c. Cm. Prf.	5	6½
4	Do. 4 p.c. 1 Dbs., Rd.	—	105
8½d.	Tower Tea, Ltd.	1	1½
5	Do. Cum. Pref.	5	5½
5	Travers, Ltd., Cum. Pref.	10	12½
4	Do. 1 Mt. Dbs., Rd.	100	105
6	Tucuman Sug., 1 Dbs., Rd.	100	100
4/	United Alkali, Ltd.	10	1¾
7	Do. Cum. Pref.	10	8¾
5	Do. Mt. Db. Stk., Rd.	100	107½
2½d.	United Horse Shoe, Ltd., Non-Cum. 8 p.c. Pref.	1	[illegible]
5	Un. Kingm. Tea, Cm. Prf.	5	4½
2/	Un. Lankat Plant., Ltd.	1	1¼
4/	Un. Limmer Asphlte., Ld.	3	5
13/	Val de Travers Asph., L.	10	15½
3/	V. den Bergh's, L., Cm. P.	5	6¼
6	Walkers, Park., L., C. Pf.	10	3
4½	Do. 1 Mt. Debs., Red.	100	90½
6/	Wallis, Thos. & Co., Ltd.	5	14
6	Do. Cum. Pref.	5	8½
5½	Waring, Ltd., Cum. Pref.	5	5½
4½	Do. 1 Mt. Db. Sk., Red.	100	112
4½	Do. Irred. "B" Db. Stk.	100	104
12/	Waterlow, Dfd. Ord.	10	14
4/	Do. Pref.	10	14
3½	Do. Cum. Pref.	10	10½
10/	Waterlow Bros. & L., Ld.	10	9
5	Do. Pref.	10	12
1/2½	Welford, Ltd.	1	1⅛
4½	Do. Debs., Red.	100	109
1/	Welford's Surrey Dairies, Ltd.	1	1⅝
7½d.	West London Dairy, Ltd.	1	1
4½	Wharncliffe Dwllgs, L., Pf.	10	11¾
18/10	Do. 3 p.c. Irr. Mt. Db. Sk.	100	95
6d.	White, A. J., Ltd.	1	[illegible]
6	Do. 6 p.c. Cum. Pref.	1	[illegible]
4	White, J. Bazley, Ltd., 1 Mort. Debs., Red	100	93½
5	White, R., Ltd., 1 Mort. Deb. Stock, Red.	100	104½
11/	White, Tomkins, Ltd	10	11
5	Do. Cum. Pref.	10	11¾
6	White, W. N., L., Cm. Pf.	1	¾
2/6	Wickens, Pease & Co., L.	5	2½
6	Wilkie, Ltd., Cum. Pref.	10	15
4/	Willans & Robinson, Ltd.	5	8
6	Do. Cum. Pref.	5	7
4½	Do. 1 Mt. Db. Stk., Red.	100	109
7½d.	Williamsons, L., Cm. Prf.	1	1⅝
6	Winterbottm. Book Cloth, Ltd., Cum. Prf.	10	15
4/6	Yates, Ltd.	5	6
6	Do. Cum. Pref.	5	6½
	Young's Paraffin, Ltd.	4	1½

CORPORATION STOCKS—COLONIAL AND FOREIGN.

Per Cent.	Name.	Paid.	Price.
6	Auckland City, '72 1904-24	100	115
6	Do. Cons., '79, Red. 1930	100	135½
5	Do. Deb. Ln., '83..1934-8	100	117
6	Auckland Harb. Debs.	100	111½
5	Do. 1917	100	111
5	Do. 1936	100	114
5½	Balmain Boro'........1914	—	113½
5	Boston City (U.S.)	100	102½
5	Do. ..1902	100	105
5	Brunswick Town 5. c. Debs. 1916-20	100	111
4½	B. Ayres City 4½ p.c.	100	71½
5	Cape Town, City of	100	113
4	Do. ..1943	100	115
4	Chicago, City of, Gold 1915	—	108½
6	Christchurch 1926	100	131½
—	Cordoba City	100	17½
5	Duluth (U.S.) Gold ..1926	—	110
6	Dunedin (Otago) 1925	100	127½
6	Do. 1906	100	113
5	Do. Consols..1908	100	111
4	Durban Insc. Stk.....1944	100	111
4	Essex Cnty., N. Jersey 1926	$100	114½
5	Fitzroy, Melbrne...1916-19	100	110
5	Gisborne Harbour....1915	100	109
4	Greymouth Harbour..1925	100	110
4	Hamilton 1934	100	108
5	Hobart Town 1918-30	100	115
4	Do. 1940	100	105
4½	Invercargill Boro. Dbs. 1936	100	111
6	Kimberley Boro., S. A. Debs.	—	102
4	Launceston Twn. Dbs. 1916	100	107
6	Lyttleton, N.Z., Harb. 1929	100	125
4	Melbourne Bd. of Wks. 1921	100	107
5	Melb. City Debs. 1897-1907	100	106½
4½	Do. Debs.....1908-27	100	111½
4	Do. Debs...1915-20-22	100	106
5	Melbne. Harb. Bds., 1908-9	100	112
4½	Do. do. 1915	100	111
4	Do. do. 1918-21	100	106
4½	Melbrne. Tms. Dbs. 1914-16	100	113
4½	Do. Fire Brig. Db. 1921	100	108
5	Mexico City Stg.	100	89½
4	Moncton N. Bruns. City	100	102
4½	Montevideo	100	60
5	Montreal Stg.	100	103
5	Do. 1874	100	103
5	Do. 1879	100	104
3½	Do. 1933	100	102
3	Do. Perm. Deb. Stk.	100	96
4	Do. Cons. Deb. Stk. 1932	100	112
6	Napier Boro. Consolid. 1914	100	119
5	Napier Harb. Debs...1920	100	115
5	Do. Debs...1928	100	107
6	New Plymouth Harb. Debs. 1909	100	107
6	New York City 1901	—	109½
3½	Do. 1910-26	—	103½
4½	Nth. Melbourne Debs. 1-600 1921	100	105
5	Oamaru Boro. Cons...1920	100	101
6	Do. Harb. Bds. (Reg.)	100	74
25/	Do. 6 p.c. (Bearer)..1919	100	35
6	Otago Harb. Deb. Reg.	100	103
6	Do. 1877	100	107
6	Do. 1881 1921	100	115
5	Do. Debs. ..1921	100	107
5	Do. Cons. ..1934	100	105
6	Ottawa City	100	109
6	Do. 1904	100	111½
4½	Do. Debs. ..1913	100	108½
6	Port Elizabeth Waterworks	100	111
5	Port Louis	100	111
5	Prahran Debs. 1917	100	109
4	Do. Debs. 1919	100	102
6	Quebec C. Coupon. 1875 1905	100	112
6	Do. do. 1878 1908	100	116
4½	Do. Debs. 1914-18	100	108
4	Do. Debs. 1923	200	108
3½	Do. Cns. Rg. Stk., Red.	100	101
5	Richmond (Melb.) Dbs. 1917	100	112
4	Rio Janeiro City	100	57
4	Rome City	100	—
4	Do. 2nd to 8th Iss.	100	91
—	Rosario C.	100	26½
—	Do.	100	26½
4	St. Catherine (Ont.) ..1926	100	101
4	St. John, N.B., Debs. 1934	—	103
4½	St. Kilda (Melb) Dbs. 1915-21	100	105
4	St. Louis C. (Miss.)..1911	100	104
4	Do. 1913	100	103½
3'65	Do. 1915	—	108½
—	Santa Fé City Debs.	100	19
6	Santos City	100	95
6	Sofia City	100	84
5	Sth. Melbourne Debs. 1915	100	111
4½	Do. Debs....1919	100	107
5	Sydney City 1904	100	109
4	Do. Debs. 1912-13	100	107
4	Do. do. (1894)..1919	100	109
7	Timaru Boro. 7 p.c...1910	100	126½
5	Timaru Harb. Debs 1914	100	107
5	Do. Debs...1916	100	107
6	Toronto City Wtwks 1904-6	100	114
5	Do. G. Cns. Dbs. 1919-20	100	118
4	Do. Strlg. 1922-8	100	107
4	Do. Local Improv.	100	102
3½	Do. 1929	100	104
5½	Valparaiso	100	[illegible]
4	Vancouver 1931	100	107
4	Do. 1932	100	108
6	Wanganui Harb. Dbs. 1905	100	110
6	Wellington Con. Deb. 1907	100	117
6	Do. Improv., 1879	100	22
6	Do. Wtrwks. Dbs., 1880	100	23
4½	Do. Debs., 1893....1933	100	14
4½	Wellington Harb. 1907	100	04
4	Westport Harb. Dbs. 1925	100	10
6	Winnipeg City Deb...1907	—	18
5	Do. 1914	100	17

FINANCIAL, LAND, AND INVESTMENT.

Last Div.	Name.	Paid.	Price.
5	Agency, Ld. & Fin. Aust., Ltd., Mt. Db. Stk., Rd.	100	90½
	Amer. Frehld. Mt. of Lon., Ld., Cum. Pref. Stk. ..	100	87½
4½	Do. Deb. Stk., Red. ..	100	92
1/4½	Anglo-Amer. Db. Cor., L.	2	1
4	Do. Deb. Stk., Red ..	100	107½
5½	Ang.-Ceylon & Gen. Est., Ltd., Cons. Stk.	100	50
6	Do. Reg. Debs., Red.	100	101½
3/	Ang.-Fch. Explorn., Ltd.	1	2½
6	Do. Cum. Pref.	1	1½
—	Argent. Ld. & Inv., Ltd. £1 Shares	10/	nil
—	Do. Cum. Pref.	4	1½
1/	Assets Fnders.' Sh., Ltd.	4	1½
6/	Assets Realis., Ltd., Ord.	5	8½
5	Do. Cum. Pref.	5	6½
26/	Austrln. Agricl. £25 Shs.	21½	63½
	Aust. N. Z. Mort., Ltd.,		
4½	Deb. Stk., Red.	100	87½
4	Do. Deb. Stk., Red. ..	100	82½
4½	Australian Est. & Mt., L., 1 Mt. Deb. Stk., Red.	100	102
5	Do. "A" Mort. Deb. Stk., Red.	100	96
5/	Australian Mort., Ld., & Fin., Ltd. £25 Shs. ..	5	5
1/6	Do. New, £25 Shs.	3	3
4	Do. Deb. Stk.	100	110
3	Do. Do.	100	85
5	Bengal Presidy. 1 Mort. Deb., Red.	100	106
25/	British Amer. Ld. "A"	1	19
—	Do. "B"	24	7
1/7½	Brit. & Amer. Mt., Ltd. £10 Shs.	2	1
5/	Do. Pref.	10	10
4	Do. Deb. Stk., Red. ..	100	103
1/3	Brit. & Austrlsn. Tst Ln., Ltd. £25 Shs.	2½	1
4½	Do. Perm. Debs., Red.	100	104
1½d.	Brit. N. Borneo. £1 Shs.	15/	½
2½d.	Do.	1	½
—	Brit. S. Africa	1	2½
5	Do. Mt. Deb., Red.	—	99
6	B. Aires Harb. Tst., Red.	100	93
12/6	Canada Co.	1	26
—	Canada N. W. Ld., Ltd.	$25	83½
—	Do. Pref.	$100	150½
4	Canada Perm. Loan & Sav. Perp. Deb. Stk.	100	99½
6	Curamalan Ld., 6 p.c. "A" Scrip	—	92
3/7½	Deb. Corp., Ld., £10 Shs	4	3½
5	Do. Cum. Pref.	10	11½
4	Do. Perp. Deb. Stk.	100	111
9d.	Deb. Corp. Fders' Sh., Ld.	2	½
4/5⅜	Eastn. Mt. & Agncy, Ltd., "A"	10	5½
4½	Do. Deb. Stk., Red.	100	98
5	Equitable Revers. In. Ltd.	100	—
2/6	Exploration, Ltd.	1	1½
/6d.	Freehold Trst. of Austria. Ltd. £10 Shs.	1	½
4	Do. Perp. Deb. Stk.	100	100
70/	Genl. Reversionary, Ltd.	100	—
3½	Holborn Vi. Land	100	105
3½	House Prop. & Inv.	100	85½
13/	Hudson's Bay	13	21½
—	Hyderabad (Deccan)	5	2½
4	Impl. Col. Fin. & Agcy. Corp.	100	92½
4½	Impl. Prop. Inv., Ltd., Deb. Stk., Red.	100	91½
2/6	Internatl. Fincial. Soc., Ltd. £7½ Shs.	2½	1½
4	Do. Deb. Stk., Red.	100	99½
1/9½	Ld. & Mtge. Egypt, Ltd. £18 Shs.	3	2½
5	Do. Debs., Red.	100	101
4½	Do. Debs., Red.	100	100
—	Ld. Corp. of Canada, Ltd.	1	½
4½	Ld. Mtge. Bk. of Texas Deb. Stk.	100	—
3½	Ld. Mtge. Bk. Victoria 4½ p.c. Deb. Stk.	100	78
2/9½	Law Debent. Corp., Ltd., £10 Shs.	2	1½
4½	Do. Cum. Pref.,	10	11½
4	Do. Deb. Stk.	100	117
—	Law Land, L., 4½ Cm. Prf.	5	5½
1/	Ldn. & Australasian Deb. Corp., Ltd., £4 Shs.	2	½
4½	Do. 4½ p.c. Mt. Deb. Stk., Red.	100	99
1/9	Ldn. & Middx. Frhld. Est. £2 Shs.	35/	3
2/6	Lndn. & N. Y. Inv. Corp., Ltd.	5	1½
5	Do. 5 p.c. Cum. Pref.	10	8½
1/6	Ldn. & Nth. Assets Corp., Ltd., £2 Shs.	1½	½
2	Ldn. & N. Deb. Corp., L.	2	1½
3/6	Ldn. & S. Afric. Explrn. Ltd.	1	12½
2/	Mtge. Co. of R. Plate, Ltd. £10 Shs.	2	3
4½	Do. Deb. Stk., Red.	100	112
4½	Morton, Rose Est., Ltd., 1st Mort. Debs.	—	99
6/6	Natal Land Col. Ltd.	10	7
4/	Do. 6 p.c. Pref., 1870	5	8
5/6	Natl. Disct. L., £25 Shs.	5	10½
4½	New Impl. Invest., Ltd. Pref. Stk.	100	62½
	New Impl. Invest., Ltd. Def. Stk.	100	9
3½	N. Zld. Assets Real Deb.	100	93
4	N. Zld. Ln. & Mer. Agcy., Ltd Prf. Ln, Deb. Stk	100	93
2/6	N. Zld. Tst. & Ln. Ltd., £25 Shs.	5	1½

Financial, Land, &c. (*continued*):—

Last Div.	Name.	Paid.	Price.
12/6	N. Zld. Tst. & Ln. Ltd., 5 p.c. Cum. Pref.	25	19
—	N. Brit. Australsn. Ltd.	100	5½
—	Do. Irred. Guar.	100	32½
5	Do. Mort. Debs.	100	82½
4½	N. Queensld. Mort. & Inv., Ltd., Deb. Stk.	100	93
6	Peel Riv., Ld. & Min. Ltd.	100	88½
	Peruvian Corp., Ltd.	100	2½
—	Do. 4 p.c. Pref.	100	9
3	Do. 6 p.c. 1 Mt. Debs., Red.	100	39
—	Queensld. Invest. & Ld. Mort. Pref. Ord. Stk.	100	20
3/7	Queensld. Invest. & Ld. Mort. Ord. Shs.	4	4
4	Queensld. Invest. & Ld. Mort. Perp. Debs.	100	88
3½	Raily. Roll Stk. Tst. Deb., 1903-6	100	100½
50/	Reversiony. Int. Soc., Ltd.	100	—
2/8½	Riv. Plate Trst., Loan & Agcy., L., "A" £10 Shs.	2	4
1/6	Riv. Plate Trst., Loan & Agcy., Ltd., Def. "B"	5	3½
	Riv. Plate Trst., Loan & Agy., L., Db. Stk., Red.	100	109
—	Santa Fé & Cord. Gt. South Land, Ltd.	20	5
—	Santa Fé Land	10	2½
2/	Scot. Amer. Invest., Ltd. £10 Shs.	2	2½
2½	Scot. Australian Invest., Ltd., Cons.	100	70½
6	Scot. Australian Invest., Ltd., Guar. Pref.	100	135½
5	Scot. Australian Invest., Ltd., Guar. Pref.	100	104½
4	Scot. Australian Invest., Ltd., 4 p.c. Perp. Dbs.	100	106½
5	Sivagunga Zemdy., 1st Mort., Red.	100	101
20/	Sth. Australian	20	47½
3½	Stock Exchange Deb., Rd.	—	101½
—	Strait Develt., Ltd.	1	—
2/6	Texas Land & Mt., Ltd. £10 Shs.	2½	2½
4½	Texas Land & Mt., Ltd., Deb. Stk., Red.	100	106
—	Transvaal Est. & Dev., L.	1	½
—	Transvaal Lands, Ltd., £1 Shs.	15/	½
—	Do. F. P.	1	½
—	Transvaal Mort., Loan, & Fin., Ltd., £10 Shs.	2	½
2/	Tst & Agcy. of Austrlsa., Ltd., £10 Shs.	1	2
7/5	Do. Old, fully paid	10	15½
5/7	Do. New, fully paid	10	12½
5	Do. Cum. Pref.	10	12½
3/	Trust & Loan of Canada, £20 Shs.	5	4½
1/9½	Do. New £20 Shs.	3	2½
4½	Tst. & Mort. of Iowa, Ltd., Deb. Stk. Red.	100	92½
—	Tst., Loan, & Agency of Mexico, Ltd., £10 Shs.	2	½
—	Trsts., Exors, & Sec. Ins. Corp., Ltd., £10 Shs.	7	1½
4	Do. Irred. Deb. Stk.	100	106½
5/	Union Dsc., Ld., £10 Shs.	5	10½
6	Union Mort. & Agcy. of Aust., Ltd., Pref. Stk.	100	30
—	Do. 6 p. Pref. £6 Shs.	2	½
4½	Do. Deb. Stk	100	92½
4	Do. Deb. Stk.	100	85½
5	Do. Deb. Stk. Red.	100	96½
1/6	U.S. Deb. Cor. Ltd., £8 Shs.	1	½
5½	Do. Cum. Pref. Stk.	100	100½
4½	Do. Irred. Deb. Stk.	100	105½
5	U.S. Tst. & Guar. Cor., Ltd., Pref. Stk.	100	77½
6/	Van Dieman's	25	16
4	Walker's Prop. Cor., Ltd., Guar. 1 Mt. Deb. Stk.	100	109
4½	Watr. Mort. & Inv., Ltd., Deb. Stk.	100	92½

FINANCIAL—TRUSTS.

Last Div.	Name.	Paid.	Price.
1/6	Afric City Prop., Ltd	1	1½
6	Do. Cum. Pref.	1	1½
4	Alliance Invt., Ltd., Cm. 4½ p.c. Prefd.	100	73½
—	Do. Defd	100	12½
4	Do. Deb. Stk. Red.	100	106½
5	Amrcn. Invt., Ltd., Prfd.	100	117½
5	Do. Defd.	100	88½
4	Do. Deb. Stk. Red.	100	115½
4	Army & Navy Invt., Ltd., 5 p.c. Prefd.	100	81½
—	Do. Defd. Stk.	100	15½
4	Do. Deb. Stk.	100	105½
4	Atlas Investment, Ltd., Prefd. Stk.	100	70½
4½	Bankers' Invest., Ltd., Cum. Prefd.	100	105
1/0/9	Do. Defd	100	27½
4	Do. Deb. Stk	100	112
	Brewery & Comml. Inv., Ltd., £10 Shs.	5	6

Financial—Trusts (*continued*):—

Last Div.	Name.	Paid.	Price.
4	British Investment, Ltd., Cum. Prefd.	100	107
5	Do. Defd.	100	103½
4	Do. Deb. Stk.	100	106½
6	Brit. Steam. Invst., Ltd., Prefd	100	116½
8/0/0	Do. Defd.	100	71½
4½	Do. Perp. Deb. Stk	100	120½
1/9	Car Trust Invst., Ltd., £10 Shs.	2½	2
5	Do. Pref.	100	101
4	Do. Deb. Stk., 1915	100	104
4	Clnl. Sec., Ltd., Prefd.	100	103½
2½	Do. Defd.	100	43½
4	Consolidated, Ltd., Cum. 1st Pref.	100	92
4	Do. 5 p.c. Cm. 2nd do.	100	71½
—	Do. Defd.	100	14½
4½	Do. Deb. Stk.	100	112½
5	Deb. Secs. Invst.	100	103½
4	Do. 4 p.c. Cm. Pf. Sk.	100	105½
4½	Edinburgh Invest., Ltd., Cum. Prefd. Stk.	100	105½
4	Do. Deb. Stk. Red.	100	106½
5	Foreign, Amer. & Gen. Invt., Ltd., Prefd.	100	112½
2	Do. Defd.	100	48½
4	Do. Deb. Stk.	100	115½
5	Foreign & Colonial Invt., Ltd., Prefd.	100	136½
5½	Do. Defd.	100	97½
4½	Gas, Water & Gen. Invt., Cum. Prefd. Stk.	100	85½
2	Do. Defd. Stk.	100	36½
4	Do. Deb. Stk.	100	104
5	Gen. & Com. Invt., Ltd., Prefd. Stk.	100	105½
2	Do. Defd. Stk.	100	36½
4	Do. Deb. Stk.	100	111½
2/6	GlobeTelegph. & Tst., Ltd.	10	11½
6	Do. do. Pref.	10	17
4	Govt. & Genl. Invt., Ld., Prefd.	100	84½
3½	Do. Defd.	100	42½
4½	Govts. Stk. & other Secs. Invt., Ltd., Prefd.	100	88½
1	Do. Defd.	100	25
4½	Do. Deb. Stk.	100	111
4	Do. do.	100	104
4½	Guardian Invt., Ltd., Pfd.	100	89½
—	Do. Defd.	100	19½
4	Do. Deb. Stk.	100	104
5	Indian & Gen. Inv., Ltd., Cum. Prefd.	100	108½
2½	Do. Defd.	100	55
4½	Do. Deb. Stk.	100	119½
5	Indust. & Gen. Tst., Ltd., Unified	100	98½
3½	Do. Deb. Stk. Red.	100	99½
4½	Internat. Invt., Ltd., Cm. Prefd.	100	66½
—	Do. Defd.	100	7½
4	Do. Deb. Stk.	100	101
4	Invest. Tst. Cor. Ltd. Pfd.	100	101
4	Do. Defd.	100	89
4	Do. Deb. Stk. Red.	100	105
5	Ldn. Gen. Invest. Ltd., 5 p.c. Cum. Prefd.	100	111½
7½	Do. Defd.	100	121
4½	Ldn. Scot. Amer. Ltd. Pfd.	100	104½
£3	Do. Defd.	100	59½
4	Do. Deb. Stk.	100	111
4	Ldn. Tst., Ltd., Cum. Prfd. Stk.	100	100
4	Do. Defd. Stk.	100	68½
4	Do. Deb. Stk., Red.	100	107
3½	Do. Mt. Deb. Stk., Red.	100	100½
5	Mercantile Invt. & Gen., Ltd., Prefd.	100	111
3	Do. Defd.	100	44½
4	Do. Deb. Stk.	100	111½
4	Merchants, Ltd., Pref. Stk.	100	104½
4	Do. Ord.	100	80½
4	Do. Deb. Stk.	100	116½
5	Municipal, Ltd., Prefd.	100	52½
—	Do. Defd.	100	17½
4½	Do. Debs.	100	111
4½	Do. Debs. "B"	100	99½
4½	Do. "C" Deb. Stk.	100	88½
5	New Investment, Ltd. Ord.	100	91½
5	Omnium Invest., Ltd., Pfd.	100	92½
1	Do. Defd.	100	26½
4	Do. Deb. Stk.	100	106
5/	Railway Deb. Tst. Ld., £20 Shs.	10	6½
5	Do. Debs., Red.	100	107½
4½	Do. Deb. Stk., 1911	100	107½
4	Do. do. 1927	100	106½
4	Railway Invst. Ltd., Prefd.	100	112
17/7	Do. Defd.	100	20½
8/	Railway Share Trust & Agency "A"	8	5½
7½	Do. "B" Pref. Stk.	100	146½
4½	River Plate & Gen. Invt., Ltd., Prefd.	100	104
£3	Do. Defd.	100	50½
5	Scot. Invst., Ltd., Pfd. Stk.	100	91½
1½	Do. Defd.	100	26½
4	Do. Deb. Stk.	100	106
4½	Sec. Scottish Invst., Ltd., Cum. Prefd.	100	89½
£3	Do. Defd. Stk.	100	32
4	Do. Deb. Stk.	100	108½
5/	Sth. Africa Gold Tst., Ltd.	1	3½
6	Do. Cum. Pref	1	1
5½	Do. 1st Debs., Red.	100	102
1/9	Stock Conv. & Invest., Ltd., £5 Shs.	1	1½
4½	Do. do. 4½ p.c. Cm. Prf.	100	113½
2½	Do. Ldn. & N. W. 1st. Charge Prefd.	100	114½
4	Do do. 2nd Chge Prefd.	100	111
32/6	Do. do. Defd. Charge	100	30
3	Do. N. East. 1 Chge Pfd.	100	90½

Financial—Trusts (*continued*):—

Last Div.	Name.	Paid.	Price.
37/6	Stock N. East Defd. Chge	100	36
6	Submarine Cables	100	138½
5	U.S. & S. Amer. Invest., Ltd., Prefd.	100	97½
20/	Do. Defd.	100	24½
4	Do. Deb. Stk.	100	105½

GAS AND ELECTRIC LIGHTING.

Last Div.	Name.	Paid.	Price.
10/6	Alliance & Dublin Con. 10 p.c. Stand.	10	24
7/6	Do. 7 p.c. Stand.	10	16½
5	Austln. Gas Lght. (Syd.) Debs. 1902	100	107
5	Bay State of N. Jrsy. Sk. Fd. Tst. Bd., Red.	—	89½
3/	Bombay, Ltd	5	6
2/4½	Do. New	4	5
12	Brentford Cons.	100	292½
9	Do. New	100	217½
5	Do. Pref.	100	142½
4	Do. Deb. Stk.	100	136
11½	Brighton & Hove Gen. Cons. Stk.	100	272½
8½	Do. "A" Cons. Stk.	100	197½
5	Bristol 5 p.c. Max.	100	129½
22/6	British Gas Light, Ltd.	20	55½
11/6	Bromley Gas Consumrs.' 10 p.c. Stand.	10	26
8/6	Do. 7 p.c. Stand.	10	21
—	Brush Electl. Enging., L.	—	1½
6	Do. 6 p.c. Pref.	—	2½
4½	Do. Deb. Stk.	100	112
4½	Do. 2 Deb. Stk., Red.	100	102½
7/	B. Ayres (New), Ltd.	10	9
4	Do. Deb. Stk., Rd.	—	98
18/6	Cagliari Gas & Wtr., Ltd.	20	31
8/	Cape Town & Dist. Gas Light & Coke, Ltd.	10	16½
4½	Do. Pref.	10	12½
6	Do. 1 Mt. Debs. 1910	50	50
4/	Charing Cross & Strand Elec. Sup., Ltd.	5	12½
4½	Do. Cum. Pref.	5	6½
3/	Chelsea Elec. Sup., Ltd.	5	9
4½	Do. Deb. Stk., Red.	100	116
5	Chic. Edis'n Co. 1 Mt., Rd.	$1000	106
20/	City of Ldn. Elec. Lht., L	10	25
—	Do. New £10 Shs.	5	17
6	Do. Cum. Pref.	10	17
5	Do. Deb. Stk., Red.	100	131½
13½	Commercial, Cons.	100	325½
10½	Do. New	100	252½
4½	Do. Deb. Stk.	100	152½
14	Continental Union, Ltd.	100	215
11	Do. Pref. Stk.	100	200
—	County of Lon. & Brush Prov. Elec. Lg., Ltd.	10	13½
6	Do. Cum. Pref.	10	15½
14	Croydon Comcl. Gas, Ld., "A" Stk., 10 p.c.	100	312½
11	Do. "B" Stk., 7 p.c.	100	260
5½	Crystal Pal. Dist. Ord. 5 p.c. Stk.	100	127½
5	Do. Pref. Stk.	100	143½
8/	European, Ltd.	10	24
6/	Do.	7½	17½
12½	Gas Light & Ck Cons. Stk., "A" Ord.	100	294½
4	Do. "B" (4 p.c. Max.)	100	120½
10	Do. "C," "D," & "E" (Pref.)	100	302½
5	Do. "F" (Pref.)	100	152½
7½	Do. "G" (Pref.)	100	222½
7	Do. "H" (7 p.c. Max.)	100	197½
10	Do. "J" (Pref.)	100	302½
6	Do. "K"	100	180½
4	Do. Deb. Stk.	100	133½
4½	Do. do.	100	152½
6	Do. do.	100	202½
8/	Hong Kong & China, Ld.	10	14
4/	House to House Elec. Light Sup., Ltd.	5	9½
7	Do. Cum. Pref.	5	11½
10	Imperial Continental	100	212½
3½	Do. Deb. Stk., Red	100	104½
2/	Malta & Medit., Ltd.	5	5½
7/	Metrop. Elec. Sup., Ltd.	10	17
4½	Do. 1 Mt. Deb. Stk.	100	119
5	Metro. of Melbrne. Dbs. 1908-12	100	111
4½	Do. Debs. 1918-22-4	100	108
10/	Monte Video, Ltd.	20	15
9½	Newcastle-upon-Tyne	100	237½
—	Do. 3½ p.c. Deb. Stk.	100	117½
12/	Notting Hill Elec. Ltg., Ltd.	10	19
4/6	Oriental, Ltd.	5	8½
4/0½	Do. New	4½	7½
10d½.	Do. do. 1879	1	1½
3/6	Ottoman, Ltd.	5	5
6	People's Gas Lt. & C. of Chic. 2 Mt. 1904	100	107½
5	River Plate Elec. Lgt. & Trac., Ltd., 1 Deb. Stk.	—	92½
8s	Royal Elec. of Montreal	—	144
4½	Do. 1 Mt. Deb.	100	104
11/	St. James' & Pall Mall Elec. Light, Ltd.	5	16
7	Do. Pref.	5	10½
4	Do. Deb. Stk., Red.	100	108½
10/	San Paulo, Ltd.	10	15½

Gas and Electric (*continued*):—

Last Div.	Name.	Paid.	Price.
10	Sheffield Unit. Gas Lt. "A"	100	251½
10	Do. "B"	100	251½
10	Do. "C"	100	251½
—	Sth. Ldn. Elec. Sup., Ld.	2	2½
5½	South Metropolitan	100	136½
3	Do. 3 p.c. Deb. Stk.	100	101½
2	Tottenham & Edmonton Gas Lt. & C., "A"	100	290
9	Do. "B"	100	210
7/	Tuscan, Ltd.	10	13½
5	Do. Debs., Red.	100	101½
5/	West Ham 10 p.c. Stan.	5	12
8/	Wstmnstr. Elec. Sup., Ld.	5	16

INSURANCE

Last Div.	Name.	Paid.	Price.
4/	Alliance, £20 Shs.	44/	10½
10/	Alliance, Mar., & Gen., Ld., £100 Shs.	25	53
19/	Atlas, £50 Shs.	6	20
12/	British & For. Marine, Ld., £20 Shs.	4	23½
7½d.	British Law Fire, Ltd., £10 Shs.	1	1½
7/6	Clerical, Med., & Gen. Life £25 Shs.	50/	16½
20/	Commercial Union, Ltd., £50 Shs.	5	43½
4	Do. "W. of Eng." Ter. Deb. Stk.	100	110½
£9	County Fire, £100 Shs.	80	196
5/	Eagle, £50 Shs.	5	½
4/	Employrs' Liability, Ltd., £10 Shs.	2	4
—	Empress, Ltd., £5 Shs.	1	—
21/	Equity & Law, £100 Shs.	6	23
7/6	General Life, £100 Shs.	5	15
4½d.	Gresham Life, £5 Shs.	15/	2½
2/6	Guardian, Ld., £10 Shs.	5	10½
20/	Imperial, Ltd., £20 Shs.	5	29
5/6	Imperial Life, £20 Shs.	4	6½
6/	Indemnity Mutual Mar., Ltd., £15 Shs.	3	11½
1/6	Lancashire, £20 Shs.	2	5
7½d.	Law Acc. & Contin., Ltd., £5 Shs.	10/	½
12/6	Law Fire, £100 Shs.	2½	17½
9½d.	Law Guar. & Trust, Ltd., £10 Shs.	1	1½
9/	Law Life, £20 Shs.	2	25
2/9	Law Un. & Crown £10Shs	12/	7
4	Do. Deb. Stk., 1942	100	110½
14/6	Legal & General, £50Shs.	8	15½
9d.	Lion Fire, Ltd., £8½ Shs.	1½	½
24/	Liverpool & London & Globe, Stk	2	53½
10/	Do. Globe £1 Ann	—	35½
35/	London, £25 Shs.	12½	56
8/	Lond. & Lanc. Fire, £25Shs	2½	18½
2/	Lond. & Lanc. Life, £25Shs	2	7
1/	Lond. & Prov. Mar., Ld., £10 Shs.	1	½
6/	Lond. Guar. & Accident, Ltd., £5 Shs	2	12
10/	Marine, Ltd., £25 Shs.	4½	43½
2/	Maritime, Ltd., £10 Shs.	2	4½
1/6	Merc. Mar., Ld., £10 Shs.	2½	2½
20/	N. Brit. & Merc., £25 Shs.	6½	42
20/	Northern, £100 Shs.	10	81
40/	Norwich Union Fire, £100 Shs.	12	125½
10/	Ocean Acc. & Guar., fy. pd.	5	22½
2/	Do. £5 Shs.	1	4
7/6	Ocean, Marine, Ltd.	2½	8½
2/	Palatine, £10 Shs.	2	3½
2/6	Pelican, £10 Shs.	1	3½
23/	Phœnix, £50 Shs.	5	41½
£6	Provident, £100 Shs.	10	32
5/	Railway Psngrs., £10Shs.	2	8½
2/6	Rock Life, £5 Shs.	10/	4½
8	Royal Exchange	100	352½
18/	Royal, £20 Shs.	3	54
4/	Sun, £10Shs.	10/	11½
3/9	Sun Life, £10 Shs.	7½	14½
6	Thames & Mrsey. Marine, Ltd., £20 Shs.	2	10½
0	Union, £10 Shs.	4	24½
4/	Union Marine, £20 Shs.	2½	8½
12/	Universal Life, £100 Shs.	12	42
2/	World Marine, £5 Shs.	2	1½

IRON, COAL, AND STEEL.

Last Div.	Name.	Paid.	Price.
—	Barrow Hæm. Steel, Ltd.	7½	2
9/	Do. 6 p.c. 2nd Pref.	7½	6½
10/	Bolck., Vaugh. & C., Ld.	20	16½
6/	Do. £8 liab.	12	8½
7/6	Brown, J. & Co., Ltd., £20 Shs.	15	20
7/6	Consett Iron, Ld., £10 Shs.	7½	29½
7/6	Ebbw Vale Steel, Iron & Coal, Ltd., £23 Shs.	20	6½
12/6	General Mining Assn., Ld.	5½	7½
8/	Harvey Steel Co. of Gt. Britain, Ltd.	10	27
5	Lehigh V. Coal 1 Mt. 5 p.c. Guar. Gd. Cp. Bds.	—	96
42/6	Nantyglo & Blaina Iron, Ltd., Pref.	$62	96
1/	Nerbudda Coal & Iron, Ltd., £3 Shs.	56/	$\frac{1}{16}$
—	Newport Abrcrn. Bk. Vein Steam Coal, Ltd.	10	6½
5/	New Sharlston Coll., Ltd. Pref.	20	9½
4½d.	Nw. Vancvr. Coal & Ld., L.	1	½
2/6	North's Navigation Coll. (1889) Ltd.	5	2½
10/	Do. 10 p.c. Cum. Pref.	5	6½
—	Rhymney Iron, Ltd.	5	1½
	Do. New, £5 Shs.	4½	½
5	Do. Mt. Debs., Red.	100	98½
5	Shelton Irn., Stl. & Cl. Co., Ltd., 1 Chg. Debs., Red.	100	99½
50/	Sth. Hetton Coal, Ltd.	100	—
2/	Vickers & Maxim, Ltd.	1	3½
5	Do. 5 p.c. Prfd. Stk.	100	126½

SHIPPING.

Last Div.	Name.	Paid.	Price.
12/	African Stm. Ship, £20 Shs.	16	10½
15/	Do. Fully-paid	20	14½
5/	Amazon Steam Nav., Ltd.	12½	8½
8/	Castle Mail Pakts., Ltd., £20 Shs.	14	15½
3½	Do. 1st Deb. Stk., Red.	100	102
6/	China Mutual Steam, Ltd.	5	3
6	Do. Cum. Pref.	10	9½
10/	Cunard, Ltd.	20	9½
5/	Do. £20 Shs.	10	3½
4½	Furness, Withy, & Co., Ltd., 1 Mt. Dbs., Red.	100	106
6/	General Steam	15	7½
5/	Do. 5 p.c. Pref., 1874	10	8½
5/	Do. 5 p.c. Pref., 1877	10	8½
26/4½	Leyland & Co., Ltd.	10	27
7/	Do. 7 p.c. Cum. Pref.	10	14½
2/11	Do. 4½ p.c. Cum. Pre-Pf.	3	10½
4	Do. 1st Mt. Dbs., Red.	100	106½
7/6	Mercantile Steam, Ltd.	5	8
6/4½	New Zealand Ship., Ltd.,	6	4½
4	Do. Deb. Stk., Red.	100	104
5/	Orient Steam, Ltd.	10	4½
5	P.&O. Steam, Cum. Prefd.	100	147½
19	Do. Defd.	100	234½
3½	Do. Deb. Stk.	100	117
5	Richelieu & Ont., 1st Mt. Debs., Red.	100	100
30/	Royal Mail, £100 Shs.	60	51
2/6	Shaw, Sav., & Alb., Ltd., "A" Pref.	5	5½
5/	Do. "B" Ord.	5	4
14/	Union Steam, Ltd.	20	19
7/	Do. New £20 Shs.	10	8
4	Do. Deb. Stk., Red.	100	106
7/	Union of N.Z., Ltd.	10	10
5½	Wilson's & Fur.-Ley., 5½ p.c. Cum. Pref.	10	10½
4½	Do. 1 Mt. Db. Sk., Rd.	100	106½

**** Tea Shares will be found in the Special Table following.*

TELEGRAPHS AND TELEPHONES.

Last Div.	Name.	Paid.	Price.
4	African Direct, Ltd., Mort. Debs., Red.	100	102
—	Amazon Telegraph, Ltd.	10	7½
15/	Anglo-American, Ltd.	100	65½
30/	Do. 6 p.c. Prefd. Ord.	100	114½
—	Do. Defd. Ord.	100	15½
3/	Brazilian Submarine, Ltd.	10	15½
5	Do. Debs., 2 Series	100	114

Telegraphs and Telephones (*continued*):—

Last Div.	Name.	Paid.	Price.
4/	Chili Telephone, Ltd.	5	3½
$1½	Comcial. Cable, $100 Shs.	—	180
4	Do. Stg. 500-yr. Deb. Stk. Red.	100	105
2½d.	Consd. Telpehone Constr., &c., Ltd.	10/	½
6/	Cuba Submarine, Ltd.	10	7
10/	Do. 10 p.c. Pref.	10	15
2/	Direct Spanish, Ltd.	5	4½
5/	Do. 10 p.c. Cum. Pref.	5	10½
4½	Do. Debs.	50	104½
3/	Direct U.S. Cable, Ltd.	20	10½
2/6	Eastern, Ltd.	10	17
3/	Do. 6 p.c. Cum. Pref.	10	18
4	Do. Mt. Deb. Stk., Red.	100	125
2/6	Eastern Exten., Aus., & China, Ltd.	10	17½
5	Do. (Aus. Gov. Sub.) Deb., Red.	100	102
5	Do. do. Bearer	100	102½
4	Do. Mort. Deb. Stk.	100	127½
5	Eastn. & S. Afric., Ltd., Mort. Deb. 1900	100	102
5	Do. Bearer	100	102½
4	Do. Mort. Debs. 1909	100	102½
4	Do. Mort. Debs. (Maur. Subsidy)	25	106½
5/	Grt. Nthn. Copenhagen	10	29
5	Do. Debs., Ser. B., Red.	100	101½
12/6	Indo-European, Ltd.	25	51½
6	London Platino-Brazilian, Ltd., Debs. 1904	100	108½
4/	Montevideo Telph., Ltd., 6 p.c. Pref.	5	2½
3/	National Telephone, Ltd.	5	5½
6/	Do. Cum. 1 Pref.	10	15
6/	Do. Cum. 2 Pref.	10	16
5	Do. Non-Cum. 3 Pref.	5	5½
3½	Do. Deb. Stk., Red.	100	101½
8d.	Oriental Telephone, Ltd.	1	½
4	Pac. & Euro. Tlg. Dbs., Rd.	100	106½
4/	Reuter's, Ltd.	8	8½
5/	Un. Riv. Plate Telph., Ltd.	5	4½
5	Do. Deb. Stk., Red.	100	105½
—	West African Telg., Ltd.	10	4
5	Do. 5 p.c. Mt. Debs., Red.	100	100½
—	W. Coast of America, Ltd.	10	½
3/	Western & Brazilian, Ltd.	15	11½
3/	Do. 5 p.c. Pref. Ord.	7½	7½
—	Do. Defd. Ord.	7½	4½
4	Do. Deb. Stk., Red.	100	105½
1/	W. India & Panama, Ltd.	10	½
6/	Do. Cum. 1 Pref.	10	7½
6/	Do. Cum. 2 Pref.	10	6
5	Do. Debs., Red.	100	106½
7	West. Union, 1 Mt. 1902 ($	1000	105½
6	Do. 6 p.c. Stg. Bds., Rd.	100	102½

TRAMWAYS AND OMNIBUS.

Last Div.	Name.	Paid.	Price.
1/6	Anglo-Argentine, Ltd	5	3½
6	Do. Deb. Stk	100	125
4/	Barcelona, Ltd	10	11
5	Do. Deb., Red.	100	105½
7/6	Belfast Street Trams.	10	16½
—	Blackpl. & Fltwd. Tram., £10 Shs.	8	12½
10/	Bordeaux Tram. & O.. Ltd.	10	11½
5	Do. Cum. Pref.	10	11
—	Brazilian Street Ry., Ltd.	2	½
—	British Elec. Trac., Ltd.	10	15½
—	B. Ayres & Belg. Tram., Ltd., 6 p.c. Cum. Pref.	5	—
6	Do. 1 Deb. Stk.	100	—
—	B. Ayres. Gd. Nat., Ltd., 6 p.c 1 Deb. Bds., Red.	100	59½
5½	Do. Pref. Debs., Red.	100	94½
1/	Calais, Ltd.	5	1
—	Calcutta, Ltd.	10	3½
—	Carthagena & Herr., Ltd.	10	2½
5	Do. Deb., Red.	100	90
5	City of B'ham. Trams., Ltd., 5 p.c. Cum. Pref.	5	5½
4	Do. 1 Mort. Debs., Rd.	100	105½
3/9	City of B. Ayres, Ltd	5	6½
2/3	Do. Ext. £5 Shs.	3	3½
6	Do. Deb. Stk	100	145
1/4	Edinburgh Street Tram.	4	4
1/	Glasgow Tram. & Omni. Ltd., £9 Shs.	8	2½
3/7½	Imperial, Ltd.	6	14½
3/	Lond., Deptfd, & Greenwich, Prefd.	5	3½
nil	Do. Defd.	5	1
10½	Lond. Gen. Omni., Ltd.	100	195
4	Do. Deb., Red.	100	113½

Tramways and Omnibus (*continued*):—

Last Div.	Name.	Paid.	Price.
4/9½	London Road Car	6	10
28/6	Do. Red. 1 Mt. Deb. Stk.	100	109½
5	London St. Rly. (Prov., Ont.), Mt. Debs.	100	110
12/6	London St. Trams.	—	2
12/9	London Trams., Ltd.	10	9
6/	Do. Non-Cum. Pref.	10	10½
5	Do. Mt. Db. Stk., Rd.	100	101
5	Lynn & Boston 1 Mt. 1924 $	1000	104
5	Milwaukee Elec. Cons. Mt. $	1000	100½
5	Minneapolis St. 1 Cons. Mt $	1000	96
5	Montreal St. Dbs., 1908	100	109
4½	Do. Debs., 1922	100	107
6/	Nth. Metropolitan	—	11½
1/9½	Nth. Staffords., Ltd.	6	5
5/6	Provincial, Ltd	10	6½
6/	Do. Cum. Pref.	10	14
5	St. Paul City, 1937 $	1000	96
5/	Southampton	10	6½
5/	South London	10	5½
7/6	Sunderland, Ltd.	10	6½
4½	Toronto 1 Mt., Red.	100	105
2/6	Tramways Union, Ltd.	5	6
4½	Do. Deb., Red.	100	109
2/6	Vienna General Omnibus.	5	5½
5	Do. 5 p.c. Mt. Deb., Red.	100	103½
4/	Wolverhampton, Ltd.	10	6½

WATER WORKS.

Last Div.	Name.	Paid.	Price.
10/	Antwerp, Ltd.	20	22
6/	Cape Town District, Ltd.	5	7½
10½	Chelsea	100	325
5	Do. Pref. Stk.	100	172½
4½	Do. Pref. Stk., 1875	100	152½
4½	Do. Deb. Stk.	100	160½
5/6	City St. Petersburg, Ltd.	13	11
5/	Colne Valley	10	15½
4	Do. Deb. Stock	100	137½
£4	Consol. of Rosar., Ltd., 4 p.c. 1 Deb. Stk., Red.	100	91
8	East London	100	227½
4½	Do. Deb. Stk.	100	160
3	Do. Deb. Stk., Red.	100	105
37/6	Grand Junction (Max. 10 p.c.) "A"	50	117½
18/9	Do. "B"	25	
18/9	Do. "C" (Max. 7½ p.c.)	25	54½
35/	Do. "D" (Max. 7 p.c.)	50	97½
4	Do. Deb. Stock	100	142½
13	Kent	100	360½
7	Do. New (Max. 7 p.c.)	100	215½
7/	Kimberley, Ltd.	7	4½
6	Do. Debs., Red.	100	104½
6	Do. Deb. Stk., Red	100	107½
10	Lambeth (Max. 10 p.c.)	100	297½
7½	Do. (Max. 7½ p.c.), 50 & 25	—	230½
4	Do. Deb. Stock	100	142½
3	Do. Red. Deb. Stock	100	103
10/	Montevideo, Ltd.	20	16
5	Do. 1 Deb. Stk.	100	108½
5	Do. 2 Deb. Stk.	100	103½
132/9	New River New	100	437½
4	Do. Deb. Stk.	100	144½
4	Do. Deb. Stk. "B"	100	144½
4	Portland Con. Mt. "B," 1927	—	102½
8/	Seville, Ltd.	20	12
5/6	Southend "Addl." Ord.	10	17
6	Southwark and Vauxhall	100	157½
6	Do. "D" Shares (7½ p.c. max.)	100	154½
5	Do. Pref. Stock	100	172½
4	Do. "A" Deb. Stock	100	141½
3	Staines Resvirs. Jt. Com. Gua. Deb. Stk., Red.	100	106
8/	Tarapaca, Ltd.	10	8½
10	West Middlesex	100	302½
4½	Do. Deb. Stk.	100	162½
3	Do Deb. Stk.	100	106

INDIAN AND CEYLON TEA COMPANIES.

Acres Planted.	Crop, 1897.	Paid up Capital.	Share.	Paid up.	Name.	Dividends. 1894.	1895.	1896.	Int. 1897.	Price.	Yield.	Reserve.	Balance Forward.	Working Capital.	Mortgages, Debs., or Pref. Capital not otherwise stated.
	lb.	£	£	£	INDIAN COMPANIES.							£	£	£	£
11,240	3,128,000	120,000	10	3	Amalgamated Estates	—	*	10	5	3¼	9	10,000	16,500	D52,950	—
		400,000	10	10	Do. Pref.	—	*	5	‡5	10	5¼				
10,223	3,560,000	187,160	20	20	Assam	20	20	20	‡17½	59½	3¼	55,000	1,730	D11,350	—
6,130	3,278,000	142,500	10	10	Assam Frontier..........	3	6	6	—	7	8½	—	286	20,000	82,500
		142,500	10	10	Do. Pref.	6	6	6	‡6	11	5½				
2,087	839,000	66,745	5	5	Attaree Khat	12	12	8	3	7	6	3,790	4,820	7,770	—
1,633	583,000	78,170	10	10	Borelli	4	4	5	—	7½	6¾	—	3,256	D270	6,500 Pref.
1,720	812,000	60,825	5	5	British Indian	6	5	5	‡5	4	6¼	—	2,920	12,300	16,500 Pref.
3,223	2,247,000	114,500	5	5	Brahmapootra	20	18	20	‡15	13	6	—	28,440	41,600	·
3,754	1,617,000	76,500	10	10	Cachar and Dooars	*	8	7	‡7	9½	7	—	1,645	21,240	·
		76,500	10	10	Do. Pref.	*	6	6	‡6	11½	5¼				
3,946	2,083,000	72,010	1	1	Chargola	8	7	10	2½	1½	13	3,000	3,300	—	—
		81,000	1	1	Do. Pref.	7	7	7	3½	1¼	5¾				
1,971	942,000	33,000	5	5	Chubwa	10	8	10	‡8	5½	7½	10,000	2,043	D5,400	—
		33,000	5	5	Do. Pref.	7,	7	7	‡7	6¼	5½				
32,250	11,500,000	120,000	10	3	Cons. Tea and Lands	—	*	10	5	3½	8	65,000	14,240	D191,674	—
		1,000,000	10	10	Do. 1st Pref.	—	*	5	‡5	10½	4¾				
		400,000	10	10	Do. 2nd Pref.	—	*	7	‡7	12	5¾				
2,230	617,000	135,420	20	20	Darjeeling................	5½	5¼	6	‡5	21	4¾	5,552	1,565	1,700	—
2,114	445,000	60,000	10	10	Darjeeling Cons............	—	—	4/2	—	6	—	—	1,820	—	—
		60,000	10	10	Do. Pref.	—	*	5	2½	9½	5¼				
6,660	3,518,000	150,000	10	10	Dooars	12½	12½	12½	‡12½	17¾	7	45,000	300	D32,000	—
		75,000	10	10	Do. Pref.	7	7	7	‡7	16½	4¼				
3,367	1,811,000	165,000	10	10	Doom Dooma	11¾	10	12½	‡12½	20½	6¾	30,000	4,032	—	10,000
1,377	582,000	61,120	5	5	Eastern Assam	⅝	nil.	4	nil	2¼	—	—	1,790	—	10,000
4,038	1,675,000	85,000	10	10	East India and Ceylon	*	nil.	7	—	8½	7¾	—	1,710	—	—
		85,000	10	10	Do. Pref.	*	6	6	3	11½	5¼				
7,500	3,363,000	219,000	10	10	Empire of India	—	*	6/10	2½	10½	—	15,000	—	27,000	—
		219,000	10	10	Do. Pref.	—	*	5	2½	11	4¾				
1,180	540,000	94,060	10	10	Indian of Cachar	7	3½	3	‡2	3½	5¼	6,070	—	7,120	—
3,050	824,000	83,500	5	5	Jhanzie	10	10	10	‡8	6¾	5¾	14,500	1,070	2,700	
7,980	3,680,000	250,000	10	10	Jokai	10	10	10	5	16	6	45,000	990	D9,000	—
		100,000	10	10	Do. Pref.	*	6	6	3	14½	4¼				
5,224	1,563,000	100,000	20	20	Jorehaut	20	20	20	—	59	6¾	36,220	2,955	3,000	—
1,347	504,000	65,660	10	8	Lebong	15	15	15	‡12½	15½	6¾	9,000	2,150	8,650	—
5,082	1,709,000	100,000	10	10	Lungla	*	10	6	‡3	6½	5	—	1,543	D21,000	—
		100,000	10	10	Do. Pref.	*	6	6	‡6	10½	5¾				
2,684	885,000	95,970	10	10	Majuli	7	5	5	—	6½	7¾	—	2,606	560	—
1,375	380,000	91,840	1	1	Makum	—	—	2	—	1	2	—	—	1,200	25,000
2,990	770,000	100,000	1	1	Moabund	—	—	*	—	¼	—	—	—	—	—
		50,000	1	1	Do. Pref.	—	—	*	2½	1	5				
1,080	482,000	79,590	10	10	Scottish Assam	7	7	7	—	10½	6¼	6,500	800	9,590	—
4,150	1,456,000	100,000	10	10	Singlo....................	6	8	5	1	8	6	—	300	D5,200	—
		80,000	10	10	Do. Pref.	*	6¼	6¼	3½	13	5				
					CEYLON COMPANIES.										
7,970	1,743,824§	250,000	100	100	Anglo-Ceylon, & Gen.	—	*	5½	—	45	11	10,992	1,405	D72,844	166,520
1,836	685,741§	50,000	10	10	Associated Tea	—	*	5	2½	7½	6¾	—	164	2,478	—
		60,000	10	10	Do. Pref.	—	*	6	3	10½	5¾				
10,390	4,000,000	167,380	10	10	Ceylon Tea Plantations ..	15	15	15	‡15	24	6¼	84,500	1,516	D30,819	—
		81,080	10	10	Do. Pref.	7	7	7	‡7	16	4¼				
5,722	1,542,700	55,260	5	3	Ceylon & Oriental Est....	5	8	7	—	2½	7¾	—	230	D2,047	71,000
		46,000	5	5	Do. Pref.	6	6	6	3	4¼	6				
2,157	801,629§	111,330	5	5	Dimbula Valley	—	*	10	5	5½	9	—	—	1,733	6,250
		62,607	5	5	Do. Pref.	—	*	6	3	6¼	4¾				
11,496	3,635,000	298,250	5	5	Eastern Prod. & Est.	3	5	6¼	‡7	5¼	6	20,000	11,740	D17,797	102,500
2,193	1,050,000	22,080	10	10	New Dimbula "A"	10	16	16	4	24	7	11,000	2,024	1,150	8,400
		55,710	10	10	Do. "B"	18	16	16	4	22	7½				
2,572	570,360§	100,000	10	10	Ouvah	6	8	6	2	8	7½	4,000	1,151	D1,255	—
2,630	964,963	200,000	10	10	Nuwara Eliya	—	*	6	‡6	10½	5¾	—	—	—	30,000
1,720	720,200§	41,000	10	10	Scottish Ceylon	15	15	15	‡10	17	6	7,000	1,252	D3,970	9,000 Pref.
2,450	750,000	39,000	10	6	Standard	12½	15	15	‡15	12½	7	9,000	800	D14,012	4,000
		17,000	10	10	Do......................	12½	15	15	‡15	22	7				

Working-Capital Column.—In working-capital column, D stands for *debit*.

* Company formed this year. † Interim dividends are given as actual distribution made. ‡ *Total* div. § Crop 1896.

DIVIDENDS ANNOUNCED.

MISCELLANEOUS.

INTERNATIONAL TRUSTEE, ASSETS, AND DEBENTURE CORPORATION, LIMITED.—Interim dividend for the six months to April 30 at the rate of 7 per cent. per annum on the ordinary shares.

LOCKHART'S, LIMITED.—Final dividend on the ordinary shares at the rate of 11 per cent. per annum, making a total distribution of 8 per cent. for the year, and leaving £1,045 to be carried forward.

CAPE TOWN AND DISTRICT GAS LIGHT AND COKE COMPANY, LIMITED.—Dividend at the rate of 6 per cent. per annum on the ordinary shares for the half-year ended December 31, making 7 per cent. for the year.

ALBION HOTEL, MANCHESTER, LIMITED.—An interim dividend has been paid on the 5 per cent. cumulative preference shares for the half-year ended March 31.

SLATERS, LIMITED.—Interim dividend on the ordinary shares at the rate of 8 per cent. per annum, payable May 28.

KAFFIRS CONSOLIDATED INVESTMENT AND LAND COMPANY, LIMITED.—3d. per share for the month of May.

BRILLIANT GOLD MINING COMPANY, LIMITED.—6d. per share declared, payable on the 7th prox.

SHARRER'S ZAMBESI TRAFFIC COMPANY, LIMITED.—Interim dividend at the rate of 8 per cent. per annum for the nine months ended March 31.

DETROIT TELEPHONE COMPANY.—Quarterly dividend of 2 per cent., being at the rate of 8 per cent. per annum.

HANNAN LAND COMPANY, LIMITED (PALACE HOTEL), KALGOORLIE.—Dividend at the rate of 5 per cent. for the first quarter of 1898 on the paid-up capital of the company.

P. AND O. STEAM NAVIGATION COMPANY.—At the half-yearly meeting, to be held on June 14, the directors will recommend a dividend at the rate of 5 per cent. per annum on the preferred stock, and an interim dividend at the rate of 7 per cent. per annum on the deferred stock of the company.

BROKEN HILL PROPRIETARY BLOCK 10 COMPANY, LIMITED.—Warrants for dividend No. 57 of 2s. per share have been posted.

BRAZILIAN SUBMARINE TELEGRAPH COMPANY, LIMITED.—Interim dividend of 3s. per share for the quarter ended March 31, payable on June 24.

OXFORD MUSIC HALL, LIMITED.—Dividend at the rate of 12 per cent. per annum for the half-year ended April 30, and a bonus of 2s. per share.

KYNOCH, LIMITED.—Dividend at the rate of 10 per cent. per annum on the ordinary shares to be recommended.

CAPE COPPER COMPANY, LIMITED.—Interim dividend of 3s. per share on the cumulative preference and ordinary shares, payable July 1.

FOSTER & BIRD, LIMITED, KING'S LYNN.—Dividend at the rate of 4 per cent. per annum for the past six months.

CAPE COPPER.—Interim dividend of 3s. per share.

BANKS.

LONDON AND RIVER PLATE, LIMITED.—Interim dividend of 7 per cent. for the half-year ended March 31.

BREWERIES.

WOLVERHAMPTON AND DUDLEY.—Interim dividend on the ordinary shares for the half-year ended March 31 at the rate of 8 per cent. per annum.

NEWCASTLE BREWERIES.—An interim dividend at the rate of 8 per annum on the ordinary shares for half-year ended April 30.

LEEDS AND WAKEFIELD BREWERY.—Directors declared an interim dividend of 7 per cent. per annum on the ordinary shares for the half-year ending March 31.

INSURANCE.

NORWICH AND LONDON ACCIDENT ASSOCIATION.—Interim dividend of 5s. per share, being at the rate of 10 per cent. per annum.

Referring to the concession of 250,000 acres in British New Guinea to the Somers Vine-Lowles syndicate, it is understood that the Queensland Government will ask Mr. Chamberlain to advise the Queen to withold her assent until the Australian colonies are able to express their views.

The wheat export season in Karachi promises to be the heaviest on record. The produce already bought for shipment will, it is said, require twenty-two trains daily until the end of August.

A Mr. McLaughlin, a Chicago dealer, is said to have successfully established a "corner" in oats throughout British Columbia. Dealers expect to have to pay 50 cents.

It has been stated in the House of Commons, by Mr. Curzon, that the conference on the Sugar Bounties is expected to meet on June 7. We shall know soon who the British delegates are to be.

It is reported from Pretoria that negotiations are proceeding between the Transvaal Government and a Continental financial group for a State loan of £6,000,000 to be issued at 98 at 4 per cent.

Printed for the Proprietor by LOVE & WYMAN, LTD., Great Queen Street, London, W.C.; and Published by CLEMENT WILSON at Norfolk House, Norfolk Street, Strand, London, W.C

The Investors' Review

EDITED BY A. J. WILSON.

Vol. I.—No. 22. New Series. | FRIDAY, JUNE 3, 1898. | [Registered as a Newspaper.] | Price 6d. By post, 6½d

The Investment Index,

A Quarterly Supplement to the "Investors' Review."

Price 2s. net. 8s. 6d. per annum, post free.

THE INVESTMENT INDEX is an indispensable supplement to the Investors' Review. A file of it enables investors to follow the ups and downs of markets, and each number gives the return obtainable on all classes of securities at recent prices, arranged in a most convenient form for reference. Appended to its tables of figures are criticisms on company balance sheets, State Budgets, &c., similar to those in the Investors' Review.

Regarding it, the *Speaker* says: "The Quarterly 'Investment Index' is probably the handiest and fullest, as it is certainly the safest, of guides to the investor."

"The compilation of securities is particularly valuable."—*Pall Mall Gazette.*

"Its carefully classified list of securities will be found very valuable."—*Globe.*

"At no time has such a list of securities been more valuable than the present."—*Star.*

"The invaluable 'Investors' Index.'"—*Sketch.*

"A most valuable compilation."—*Glasgow Herald.*

Subscription to the "Investors' Review" and "Investment Index," 36s. per annum, post free.

CLEMENT WILSON,
NORFOLK HOUSE NORFOLK STREET, LONDON, W.C.

THE

LAW GUARANTEE AND TRUST SOCIETY, LIMITED.

Capital Subscribed	£1,000,000
do. Paid-up	£100,000
do. Uncalled	£900,000
Reserve Fund	£70,000

FIDELITY GUARANTEES,
On behalf of Managers, Secretaries, Clerks, Cashiers, Collectors, &c.

DEBENTURE INSURANCE.
The advantages of such insurance are as follows:—
1. The Debentures being guaranteed by the Society can be placed at not less than par, thus saving discount.
2. A lower rate of interest is willingly accepted.
3. The Society acting as Trustee for Debenture Holders also adds to the Security.

MORTGAGE INSURANCE.

CONTINGENCY INSURANCE,
In respect of Defects in Title, Lost Documents, Missing Beneficiaries, Re-Marriage, Issue and Name and Arms Risks, &c.

LICENSE INSURANCE.
Mortgagees of Licensed Property should always insure in a substantial Insurance Society against loss they may sustain by depreciation in consequence of the license being lost.

TRUSTEESHIPS for Debenture Holders, and under Wills, Marriage Settlements, &c.

HEAD OFFICE:
49, CHANCERY LANE, LONDON.
CITY OFFICE:
56, MOORGATE STREET, E.C.

CONTENTS

The Investors' Review.

War and American Securities.

At last we have some definite news regarding the war between the United States and Spain. It seems to be established that the Spanish fleet has taken refuge in the difficult-of-access port of Santiago de Cuba. This is the end of the "brilliant strategy" of the Spanish Admiral, about which we have seen so many discussions and laudations during the last fortnight. He has displayed the strategy of the fox, and has taken to earth, as we may say, without daring to face the enemy at any point. In all probability Commodore Schley is right in his prediction that the Spanish ships will never get out again, for the entrance of Santiago seems to be so narrow that ships can only get out and in in single file, and clearly any attempt on the part of Admiral Cervera to pass out again could be frustrated by a very small number of vessels keeping guard over the exit from the harbour. And it is possible that the knowledge of the American Admiral that the harbour of Santiago was, in this way, a trap enabled the Spanish fleet to get into it unobserved. It would never have entered into the mind of a fighter that an enemy, who also meant to fight, would hide himself in such a dangerous position. We may assume, then, that there is extremely little probability of a great naval battle now. The Spanish fleet is bottled up, or the greater part of it, and may be either captured or destroyed by a combined land and sea attack. It will not be conquered and sunk in the open ocean, nor will it now have the least chance to conquer there or anywhere else. This is a pitiful end to so much Spanish bravado, but we fear it is the only end now to be looked for. A repulse of the first United States attack can only defer, it cannot avert, the doom.

So the question now comes to be, is the war likely to end sooner in consequence of this? At the first sight the appropriate answer seems to be yes. When, however, we consider the task which is before the United States and the season of the year at which it is to be undertaken, as well as the extreme unpreparedness of her raw levies for active operations in the field, we are inclined to lean to the opinion that the Spanish tactics may prolong the struggle. Had Admiral Sampson been fortunate enough to encounter the Spanish fleet at sea and thrash it well before it took refuge in port, we might have seen Spain reduced at once to the necessity of negotiating for peace. Her Government has no resources out of which to equip a fresh fleet, and could not possibly hope to hold out in Cuba without the assistance such a fleet alone might give. All the world would have cried out against Spanish cruelty had Marshal Blanco obstinately persisted in maintaining a defiant attitude in Havana after such a catastrophe. Now, however, the mere possibility that Admiral Cervera might get out again, and the fact that his fleet has not yet been destroyed, encourages the authorities both in Cuba and in Madrid to go on making a show of war, in the hope that something may turn up to let them off with "honour." A piteous wail goes round the Courts of Europe about once a week, and is heard in the newspapers in the shape of rumours that this, that, and the other "Power" or combination of Powers is going to intervene on behalf of Spain. One is almost ashamed to think how much these exhibitions show that Spain has sunk into real cowardliness while still indulging in the braggart language her politicians and military men treated us to. There is, we are almost persuaded, no genuine intention to fight so far as Spain is concerned, and if there be any fight, whether around Santiago or Havana, it will be because the Spaniards there have no choice but to defend themselves. In the meantime, what is called "war" will drag on, and the United States will have to incur an enormous expenditure of men and money in occupying the island. We really see no other alternative. It is exaggeration, of course, to say that the American Government has already spent over £60,000,000 on this conflict to be, but before her Government has driven out the Spaniards, the expenditure may well attain a total much exceeding that sum. Decidedly it would have been cheaper in the long run for the United States to have bought the island, and it certainly would have been far more profitable for Spain and her creditors. Spanish pride, however, would not allow her to accept a sum by which Spain would have been magnificently put in funds and able to pay her debts. It is better, from the point of view of the old "Castilian honour," to go bankrupt and defraud the humble creditor than to sacrifice the chance to dream of the age when Spain was great.

Coming to what is, from our point of view, the practical question, how does this prospect affect American securities? Not very favourably, in our opinion; at least not in the near future. By and bye, when the war is over, and the Spaniard cleared out of the West Indies, as he is bound to be, there might come a great trade revival in the American Union which would lift numbers of her railroad securities, of her municipal and land company bonds, even of her brewery companies' shares, into a much more satisfactory position than they now hold. There is "a long row to hoe" before that time arrives, in our opinion, and, thinking this, we hardly deem it prudent to buy any of these classes of securities just now in the hope of immediate profit. Peace seems to have been, in market phrase, already "discounted" on the Stock Exchange, so that its actual attainment might very well be followed by a collapse in markets. For the United States will be in some ways an entirely different country at the end of this war to what it was before the war began. It will be a country with international responsibilities. In one sense, it always has had these responsibilities, but the habit of its political thought was to pass them by and ignore them. No interference with the affairs of distant nations was countenanced by any party in the body politic. Now this will all be changed—must be changed. The United States will have to keep the Philippines when they have conquered them, as they will, as well as Cuba and Porto Rico; and in holding Cuba they become one of the Great Powers with whom the destinies of the world's future rests. This will necessitate the creation of at least a large navy, in order that the great Republic may be able to speak with authority when international questions in which it is interested come up for settlement; and the creation and maintenance of a great navy must involve many changes in taxation, as well as some difference in the habits and conditions of life for the American people. Once embarked upon a large naval expenditure there is no knowing where the Union may travel to. Public burdens will be increased, and the development of the country perhaps be in some directions arrested. Even if not, and we hope not, it will be just as well for us as mere investors to wait for a time to see what is likely to ensue from the present endeavour of the Union to put an end to a state of affairs in Cuba which has been more or less a nuisance to it ever since the Declaration of Independence. The States had to undertake this job, and we believe good will come to them for having undertaken it, but the good may neither be an overflowing treasury nor an immediate expansion in commercial prosperity.

The Development of China.

It seems to us that the most important lesson to be learned from Mr. Consul Bourne's valuable report on the trade of Central and Southern China has been somewhat overlooked. It would be advisable for those who are contemplating the investment of money in the syndicates and companies which are being organised to "open up" China to read this report with great care. We have seen lately statements put in circulation that most valuable concessions—the building of railways, working of mines, &c. — have been obtained by English capitalists, or English and Italian combined, and the quotations for the "first crop" shares of some of these embryo companies are already extremely high. We earnestly hope that these preliminary flourishes do not signify a thoughtless speculation on the part of the public, in which they could only lose the whole or the greater part of their money. That China is in some respects a great country, with an immense, very poor and hard-working population, is true, but it is a country whose development cannot be forced. The largest province which Mr. Bourne visited, that of Su-chuan, has a population, according to some reckoners, of 70,000,000, and it may in reality amount to 50,000,000, or half the entire probable population of the African continent. Into this province British goods at present find their way with difficulty by the Yang-tse river. All over China our productions might find a greater market than they do now, were the facilities of transport greater and the taxation more honestly, moderately, and intelligently applied, but what a deal these desiderata imply.

Yet there is one great distinction between the position of China in relation to trade and that of Africa. While the African for the most part requires no clothes by reason of the climate, all over China cotton clothing is worn by the people, in greater or less quantities according to the season of the year. At present in provinces like Su-chuan and others of Central and Southern China much of the cloth worn is of native manufacture, and of late years a great increase has taken place in the export of coarser Indian yarn to be woven up into cotton clothes by the native hand-loom weavers, whose wages, Mr. Bourne calculates, come to about 1s. 6d. a week in our money. Also in some parts of China native capitalists have endeavoured to establish cotton mills, and it is probable that in the near future mills under European management, and supplied with the modern appliances of machinery by European capital, will spring up in various parts of the Yang-tse Valley more particularly, and supply a large part of the native demand for the coarser kinds of goods. We in this country can only hope to continue to supply the well-to-do few in China with the finer kinds of cloths that the East, whether Chinese or Indian, is in no position at present to supply. Some day, perhaps, our most formidable competitors for this trade may be the Japanese. At present their competition is not sensibly felt, but there is a certain amount of rivalry between our manufacturers and those of the United States, and in course of time we may have to fight hard not merely to extend our trade, but to retain what we already possess.

Remarks like these, however, deal only with the more superficial aspects of the great question now forced upon us by the changed conditions appertaining to our relations with the great, but perhaps moribund, Chinese Empire. Capitalists here dream of spreading a network of railways over the great territory of that Empire, of digging out its minerals, of which there are plenty all over the more upland portions of the country it would seem; and it is probable that we shall be invited to subscribe the capital for this and the other enterprises, destined to bring large returns, we shall be told, to the men bold enough to be first in the field. We are unable to see the grounds for this sanguine view of these developments, either in the present condition of China, or in the possibilities of the near future. A country where the cost of labour is so low that swarms of heavy-laden porters are able to make a beast's living by carrying goods over difficult mountain passes in order to escape payment of a local tax, which may not in the worst case amount to 5 per cent. on the value of the goods, does not seem to be a country ripe for railway development. Transport unquestionably requires to be improved, but we think the efforts at improvement should be directed in the first instance to the waterways. There is the Yang-tse River itself, for example, which is navigable for 1,000 miles from the sea up to Hankow by ocean-going steamers, but a little beyond that becomes a rapid stream, sometimes flowing with great swiftness, in a narrow channel between gorges for a distance of 100 miles. All goods have to be hauled through these rapids by gangs of men, sometimes as many as 300 being attached to one boat. The labour is prodigious and cruel—"no slaves ever did such work"—and yet so extremely poor is the bulk of the population of China that there seems to be no difficulty whatever in obtaining any number of men to carry on this traffic.

It seems to us that if this stretch of rapids on the great river could be made navigable by steam vessels, either by clearing the channel at various points, or by aiding these steamers with tow ropes and chains at difficult rapids, a stimulus of great value would at once be given to the trade of Western China. Beyond Kuei-Chou the river opens out again, except at one or two points; and it or its feeders are navigable to boats for many hundreds of miles all over the province of Su-chuan, and down, one may say, into the province of Yun-nan, at present supplied with European goods, English and other, through the French territory of Tong-king.

Were our capitalists to devote their attention to enterprises of this kind, and obtained the permission of the Pekin Government to put steamers on all the navigable waterways of the Yang-tse basin, as well as on the Yang-tse itself as far as it is opened to navigation, greater help would be given to the development of trade with the interior of China than anything we can for many a long day hope for from the construction of railways anywhere in the Empire. Probably tramway lines and light railways might be useful at various points to bring goods to the nearest port, but we doubt if even these should be at once undertaken until some other means of existence is found, such as work in mills, foundries, and mines, for the swarms of labourers who may be thrown out of work by such a revolution. Mr. Bourne suggests one way by which a great deal of good might be done, not only to our own trade, but to the industries of China themselves. In dealing with that great province, Su-chuan, he points out that it is unable to import goods sufficient in value to balance the value of its exports, and that consequently exchange with the coast is always in its favour. This leads him to infer that if British merchants would train assistants and representatives in the Chinese language and in knowledge of business, and send these up to the interior to, as it were, tap the splendid resources of the Great Red Basin of Su-chuan that province might become in a position to export enormous quantities of its products for which there is now no outlet. What it chiefly sends now is opium, but the inhabitants who cultivate, as so many of the Chinese do, their land like a garden, would be able to supply much larger quantities of silk, of insect wax, of wool, bristles, hides, fur, feathers, and probably many other articles, now either exported in small quantities or not at all. As this export trade developed so would the import.

What is wanted there and elsewhere is guidance, and the stimulus of minds more enlightened, less conservative, and better educated in the world's wants than the highest classes of the natives. After a time, when the trade in the products of the soil in this and other parts of the interior had been developed, it might be well to lay hold of the mineral wealth to be found there, and as the necessity arose for coal and iron more particularly, railways might be constructed which would enable the products of the mines to be utilised more economically than is possible now. For a time, however, the great waterways of China must remain the principal channels of communication between the interior of the country and the coast. Goods will pass up and down not only the Yang-tse River but the West and South Rivers and the Hoang-Ho, which are either navigable for great distances or can be made navigable. At present, as we have said, the principal part of European trade with the south of China, that at any rate with Yun-nan, goes through Tong-king *viâ* the Red River, or through Hong-Kong *viâ* the West River, and it is probable that if the French adopted a liberal policy towards this transit trade they could control almost the whole of it in the south-west of China, to the exclusion not only of Hong-Kong but of the Burma route, over which we talk of throwing a railway connecting Yun-nan with Eastern Burma. At present, however, the French, who have been very energetic in compelling the Chinese to abandon their local squeezes and allow goods to go through under transit pass to their destination, have almost counterbalanced the advantage thus obtained by the heavy taxation they themselves levy on all goods other than their own passing through their territory into China. As long as this obstructive policy is adhered to the opportunity is given to us to develop our business with that part of the Empire either from Burma or through Canton and Hong-Kong, or by the Yang-tse River, made navigable up to Sui-Fu for steamboats.

But before anything can be done there will be a great deal of friction to be overcome in dealing with the arbitrary local taxation everywhere hampering trade throughout China. We have not space here, nor is it necessary, to go into the details of "likin" dues, of "Fu-shui" and "Kuan-shui," and the various forms of taxation applied, in various degrees of arbitrariness, to traffic from beyond sea passing into the country, but we may mention one example that Mr. Bourne gives. "There are," he says, "twelve likin barriers between Chinkiang and Huai-an Kuan on the Grand Canal, a distance of about 130 miles, and there are thirty-six customs and likin barriers on the Grand Canal between Chinkiang and Chi-ning Chow. Goods pay likin at every other barrier unless under transit pass. The rate for a piece of grey shirtings, according to the printed likin tariff, is about 4·2d. a piece at every other barrier, equivalent to 33 per cent. *ad valorem*, for a distance of 130 miles." This may be an extreme instance, but it serves to illustrate the gigantic task which is before the Imperial maritime customs service in straightening out this tangle of impositions, for many of them are nothing less. We shall not be in the least surprised to find that riots, and even more serious disturbances, may occur within the next few months, or years, in various parts of China as a result of the efforts of European administrators to bring order out of chaos and enforce free transit of goods throughout the country on one payment of a fixed duty covering all these petty local exactions. Such a reform means money taken out of the official pockets.

There is a great deal more of interest in this instructive and valuable report, but we have gone as far with it now as we have space for and must leave it with this recommendation: before putting much money in any Chinese enterprise, however tempting, investors in this country should carefully weigh the information publications like this give them. They cannot master that information without coming to the conclusion that the development of China must be a slow and laborious undertaking, subject to many disappointments and many set-backs. A new relationship is coming into force there between European countries and the Chinese, and it is not going to be established in a day or in many years. But it is worth establishing, and if we are alive to our mercantile interests, active and energetic, we might even at this late day be able to find compensation for the decadence of India in the development of China. Anyway, this is a better piece of work to try to do than any offered by "Empire expanding" among naked savages in tropical climates, into which we have been drawn by the blandishments of the dishonest company promoter.

The Confiscation Bill of the Council of Foreign Bondholders.

So the House of Commons Committee has found the preamble of this Bill proved. We are sorry for this, because it means that the Bill will go through unless vigorously blocked and opposed in the House, as private bills seldom are. It is a Bill for the confiscation of property and for the erection of a co-optative "Council" into an irresponsible oligarchy empowered to negotiate debt compositions with foreign States. In its old form, and thanks to its defective constitution, the Council did incalculable mischief to the creditors of defaulting foreign States. In its new it can hardly help being completely pernicious, the mere tool of the loan monger and "market scooper"—of the men and firms that trade upon national insolvencies and make fortunes out of defaults and compositions.

We have read the proceedings of the Committee on the Bill promoted by Sir John Lubbock, and find the common opinion expressed by the witnesses is that a reconstruction is necessary; but the evidence presents some striking features of disagreement. To the extent of our knowledge points should have been made which were in some cases passed over by both parties. One, relating to the original subscriptions, was referred to by one witness under some disadvantage. He was not free to open an argument. As the founders of the Corporation were to receive services free, but were to profit by the fees paid by those (not members of the Corporation) to whom services were rendered, the subject is important to original subscribers. Let us, therefore, retell the story in a few words.

The subscriptions of founders were received upon that basis; but when a Royal Charter was found by the "promoters" to be unobtainable the funds provided were disposed of in a way that deprived the founders of the advantages promised in the shape of profits to themselves. No consent was asked for, and the information that this had been done was only given after registration under limited liability (without the word limited) had been effected. The founders were (according to the reports of the Council meetings in 1873 and 1874) urged to give up the idea of profits, because the Council would act "gratuitously." Later on, the Council ceased to act "gratuitously."

It appears that the founders of the Corporation, when the one part of the agreement upon which they had subscribed (the return of £100 from moneys earned by means of the capital sum they had provided) had been fulfilled, were so doubtful of the further value in their certificates of permanent membership, that some certificates were sold as all but valueless—two to clerks of the Corporation at the prices of £1 and £3 each. It was stated before the Committee that these transactions caused anxiety. The witness who offered this evidence said he feared that certificates might be bought up by a clique and the purposes of the foundation of the association defeated; and he proposed to refer to the newspapers in support of his view, but that was objected to.

We have taken some care to look up the newspaper reports of the Corporation meetings as well as the reports of the Council. It is evident to any intelligent reader of those documents that the idea of a division of profits was merely a suggestion made with the object of giving them value. They were to become a desirable property in the hands of holders of foreign bonds, who were to be moved (by that or some other means) to influence and act upon the members of the Council in what concerned foreign bonds. The newspaper criticisms to which Sir John Lubbock so emphatically objects, will, if perused, show that the Council has not acted upon the lines laid down at the public meetings held in 1868 and 1869. It was and is objected that holders of foreign bonds are not adequately represented upon the Council, and that the Council has become an agency for the exoneration of defaulting foreign States from their liabilities. The co-optive system has been attacked at successive meetings of the Corporation, because the Council has practically aided defaulting Governments to impose their own terms upon their creditors. Does Sir John Lubbock propose to remedy this cardinal failure? It was not even mentioned before the Committee. Will he go on as before? Having introduced new men without any provision that they hold foreign bonds, or represent holders of such, will he renew under the provisions of his Bill that condition of things which the public Press and the Stock Exchange alike deprecate? To this question the evidence laid before the Committee affords no answer.

The next subject is that relating to the great number of transfers of certificates of permanent membership referred to in No. 53 of the INVESTORS' REVIEW, September, 1897, and No. 6 (new series) February 11, 1898. It is well known that many members of the Stock Exchange have unsuccessfully sought to acquire certificates by means of applications at the Council House. The Council have failed, although the subject has been discussed at public meetings of the Corporation, to offer facilities to purchasers of certificates offered for sale by keeping a list accessible to inquirers. Has Mr. Cooper, the secretary of the Council, been employed by the direction or at the request of Sir John Lubbock or others, members of the Council, in procuring certificates during 1895, 1896, and 1897 for friends or acquaintances for voting purposes at the meeting called to approve the Bill in November, 1897; and, of the purchasers enrolled as members during those three years, how many did, consequently, vote for the Bill? We cannot say, but we do know that some certificates were sold on the Stock Exchange, and we take it that their purchasers did not vote with the Council. Our inquiry, however, relates more particularly to the action of the secretary, and is whether he acted for or by the instructions of members of the Council. If he did, we leave it to any of our readers to say whether votes acquired by his action were rightly and honourably made use of. This matter ought to have been brought before the Committee, and ought now to be inquired into as it has not yet been examined. Was there no means of compelling Mr. Cooper to give evidence, even though he was not called by the counsel for the Bill? No evidence was offered showing how the Council had taken upon itself to act directly in opposition to the interests of bondholders, and in opposition to the principles set out *ab origine* to be adhered to.

Sir John Lubbock was allowed to refer to the "votes of thanks" the Council had received from foreign bondholders. Should he not have been questioned whether the resolutions for those votes had or had not been prepared by the secretary of the Council, and whether the bondholders had or had not been asked to bring them forward? Whether they were or were not spontaneous votes? We are inclined to ask, further, whether the farce that the division of profits is the one object of dissentients was not too elaborately played? The certificate holders found the money to enable the Council to enter upon the protection of holders of foreign bonds, reserving certain advantages to themselves. The Council undertook to act and would only consent to act "gratuitously." The "promoters" did not, according to the evidence of a very positive character, call their co-founders together to ask their consent to registration under limited liability, doing away with the advantages they had reserved to themselves. The promoters acted first and urged afterwards, that as the Council would only act on the "gratuitous" principle, so the subscribers of funds must be content to receive £100 back, with 5 per cent. interest, whenever the money might come in wherewith to pay. Money did not come in at first, and shares, or bonds, whichever or however called, were sold at prices much below £100. Peru, a very much mismanaged business, was the cause of this. But the Council got tired of the gratuitous principle. One of its members declared afterwards that a quorum could not be easily got together when no fees were allowed to the Council. The Council, however, resisted any departure from the gratuitous principle on the part of the general body of members, who were told of the services of the eminent men placed at their disposal for the paltry sum of £100 a year each.

The Council next took opportunity—or its apologists did—to represent those who stated that, having subscribed funds to establish business, they wished to profit by the advantages they had stipulated for as "covetous," or asking what they had no right to. This question of right to assets has been discussed, according to the reports of the Corporation, and the suspension of a solution agreed to as being at that time premature. We ask, for we do not suppose that Sir John Lubbock was consulted concerning the earlier proceedings by which the advantages to subscribers were thrown over without their consent, whether Sir John Lubbock or the Council can honestly say or feel that they are doing justice in using the influence of their position and their names in forcing the general body of proprietors to a decision by a vote of Parliament, when they have taken those proprietors by surprise in the preparation—it may almost be said secretly—of a Bill which no one of them could study, digest, and act against, if so minded, in the five days during which action was possible? The evidence shows the great disadvantages under which the Bill was opposed. The learned counsel opposed to the Bill made a strong case; but the system, foresight, and preparation of the case for the Bill, with the admission of its opponents that a reconstruction is necessary, led—it seems to us naturally—to the decision come to that the preamble has been proved. Given that Sir John Lubbock held the purse-strings, that he had taken every care to exclude those opposed to the Bill from any material means save those derived from the introduction of their hands to their breeches' pockets, and it is no wonder that he succeeds so far. The public spirit of the opponents to the Bill is to be praised. The individual interest of each individual proprietor being so small, it is wonderful that any could be brought together to bear an expense out of all proportion to that interest. The public Press, the Stock Exchange, and individual bondholders have repeatedly expressed their disapprobation of the way in which English holders of foreign bonds have been guided by the Council into disastrous compromises, but all this was left out of sight.

We ask whether the Council do not place an excessive number of their own members upon bondholders' committees, and whether they, the Council, or their secretary, do not negotiate in place of the bondholders' committee itself? Whether the choice of agents is, or is not, made with 'adequate prevision? Whether the Council, in fact, does not predominate in all arrangements of the kind? The general idea is that committees are powerless, and the Bill will place them absolutely in the power of the Council.

Because this is so, we have no hesitation in the expression of a sincere hope that the Bill, in its present form, will not pass. It would violate principle in deciding as to the property rights of the subscribers without evidence. It would perpetuate a system which has proved injurious to the interests of the holders of foreign bonds. It would create the evil, long ago foreseen—an institution where, if the funds could not be divided, they could be applied in pensions, fees, and salaries to functionaries, who would do no good, but infinite harm, should they continue to relieve, on easy terms, foreign defaulting States from their liabilities.

To sum up, the course followed has been to divert subscribers' money so that they get neither profits nor other advantages. Having bagged the profits, the next step the Council took was to devote them to the payment of salaries or fees to its own members. And now as a final wind up it is proposed by this Bill that the accumulated unspent profits of the business shall be declared not to belong to those who self-denyingly subscribed funds to establish the Corporation, but to the small body which alone has hitherto gained by its existence. Parliament is called upon to summarily violate the rights of property, and the process of trying the case and sifting claims in the Law Courts is carefully avoided. Why, by the way, was the Committee left in ignorance of the remarkable case relating to fees brought against Sir John Lubbock and his friends on the Council and settled by them on the threshold of the Court rather than face the ordeal of a trial? The whole story has an evil odour, but it is quite in keeping with the system whereby the Council has been made a close borough, a clique of commission earners, from which representative holders of foreign bonds are carefully excluded. Will Parliament now elevate this body, whose conduct in the past has brought loss on tens of thousands of innocent people, into the position of a sort of offshoot of the Foreign Office, and endow it with a quasi-statutory authority to negotiate and meddle in the affairs of people deprived of all control over it, and who would doubtless do much better if left to their own initiative? We can hardly believe it possible, and yet adroitness and choice of opportunities can do so much, and Members of Parliament are so indifferent and ignorant that, if vigorous opposition is not organised, with a little smiling and dining the mischief may be done. What, we wonder, has Lord Salisbury to say to the invasion of his functions by this proposed new body, to be started on its career with money not its own?

The Drought in Australia and Australian Finance.

An interesting article in the *Australasian Insurance and Banking Record* for April last informs us that the long drought in the Australian colonies has had a disastrous effect on their stock of sheep. The writer estimates that in 1897 alone New South Wales lost nearer 8,000,000 sheep than 6,500,000 to 7,000,000, and this loss fell at the end of a period of three years during each of which immense numbers of sheep perished of hunger and thirst. The other colonies suffered in the same way, so that enormous although their whole stock is now, it is less than it was four years ago. In 1891 the total stock of sheep in the colonies of Australia and New Zealand was 124,500,000, and in 1893 120,000,000. It is now estimated at 104,000,000. We must not stop to dwell on the morality of the shepherding which brings this condition of affairs about, nor on the cruelty displayed in the overstocking of sheep runs to so reckless an extent that a year or two of drought, such as must always be reckoned upon in Australia, causes the wretched animals to die by millions. Habit has made the Australian mind callous to this kind of suffering, and the death of a few millions of sheep by the most painful of all scourges, hunger and thirst, causes no more emotion than the destruction of so many flies by the first frost in autumn.

The economic side of the matter, however, touches everybody, both in the colonies and here, most nearly, and it is a very interesting subject to dwell upon. Unfortunately, the writer of the article gives us comparatively little data to go upon in estimating the probable effects of the prolonged droughts upon the finances of the colonial Governments, and, still more, upon the solvability of the land companies and agency companies in whose hands almost the whole business now is. But a table is supplied exhibiting the value of the Australian wool clip from 1880-81 down to the current year. From this we gather that since 1890 there has been almost no progress made in the output of Australian wool, so far as values go. In 1892-3 and 1895-6 the total values reached

£23,504,000 and £23,175,000 respectively, but in all the other years since 1889 the value of the crop, measured by selling prices in London, has fluctuated between £22,100,000 and £22,846,000, the lowest total being that estimated for the current year, 1897-8. In quantities also the progress has been remarkably small compared with that of the first half of the period under review, and it has declined every year since 1894-5. This is a most serious matter, and must bear severely upon the power of some, at least, of these settlements to maintain their position as solvent-looking communities. Were it not for the gold, which has been found in considerable quantities in most of these colonies, we fear it would have been impossible for them to stand up under the disasters which one after another have fallen upon them. Even this gold, however, will not always sustain the people in their endeavour to pay the interest they owe to creditors here, both on their public debts and on their private obligations to finance and land companies; and at any rate the struggle required to meet these obligations, public and private, must be increasingly severe as time goes on, gold or no gold. The population is expanding very slowly, immigration having all but ceased. The great mass of the people is falling into increasing poverty rather than rising in the scale of comfort; work is scarce in many parts of Australia, scantily peopled though the settlements all are, and not even the rigorous, and some think imprudent, economy practised in Victoria enables the community there to recover from the deadly blow administered to it by the financial crisis of 1893.

Most of these settlements continue, if their statistics are to be relied on, to import more than they export. This means that they continue to contract new debts, because, to be in a sound position, they ought to export much more than they import, in order to have the means wherewith to pay their debt interest in London. Their wool and gold, cheese and butter, timber and coal, horses and cattle, dead meat and hides, are about the only things they have with which to pay their debts; and if they do not export some fifteen or sixteen million pounds' worth more of these products per annum than the entire value of their imports they must somewhere and somehow be again running deeper into debt. The question is where and how? Debts, involving fresh burdens upon these settlements, must be accumulating, although they are not coming here to any great extent for loans, West Australia alone displaying dangerous activity in this direction. Where, then, are they getting the money? Are they depleting their banking balances? Are they sinking deeper into debt to the finance companies and banks? Is, in short, a new crisis in preparation for these colonies through their still improvident expenditure?

We have not the data before us with which to answer these questions, and probably no data will be forthcoming until another crisis does come; but we must never forget that a very substantial reserve fund was in a manner created for the people in most of these colonies by the methods taken to deal with the banks which stopped payment in 1893. The deposits then annexed and turned into shares, in spite of the amounts absolutely lost before the date of their appropriation, must have materially assisted the people in sustaining through the intervening years the struggle to appear solvent. And if the insolvencies of 1893 and earlier or later have from this point of view assisted in this direction, so also has every fresh supply of capital obtained here, no matter on what pretence. Pastoral properties turned into limited companies whose shares and debentures have been sold in London; mining companies created here and floated with large capitals, some portion of which is paid over to the Australian prospectors and promoters; mercantile businesses turned into limited liability companies in order to enable them to find money to pay off loans to banks and for other reasons. All these have contributed towards the "emergency fund," as we may call it, out of which the settlements sustain themselves and still continue to appear solvent to the eyes of the world.

But beyond all this there must be some hidden source out of which the severe losses of the past few years have been temporarily made good. It was not in the power of these colonies, not even of New South Wales, strong by comparison to the others as it is, to encounter the frightful havoc produced by the drought of the past three years without betraying great weakness and instability in credit institutions, unless the banks and finance companies and land companies had found means to make advances to enable the people to tide over the bad time. In themselves the colonists did not possess the resources for doing this, could not have done so, since the drought came upon them soon after the banking crisis had swept the means of so many of them altogether away. Nor were they aided by better prices for their products or by new channels of trade. Unless, therefore, a time of great prosperity should forthwith arise for all these colonies—larger crops of wool and better prices, outlets in the East and in Europe for their agriculture and dairy produce, large supplies of bullion from their mines, and so on—we must in all prudence look for a renewal of the same class of credit breakdowns which devastated them all in 1893. They cannot go on bearing the load they do, meeting the competition they have to encounter in the sale of their productions and enduring the loss produced by dry seasons without once again showing that they have overburdened themselves in the time of their exuberant youth to an extent which has left them without resources or without adequate recuperative power in times of difficulty. The unfortunate thing about all these colonies is that they have such a dead weight of debt to carry that even good years do not allow them to raise their heads out of the slough into which they have cast themselves. The best their people can do in such years is to wipe out a little of the losses accumulated during the bad years. They cannot soar above their burdens and become free of debt, either as individuals or States.

Economic and Financial Notes and Correspondence.

The Financial Troubles of Spain.

It did not require any gift of prophecy to foretell that Spain would not long have entered upon a state of war before she became bankrupt, and already her practical bankruptcy is beginning to show its fruits. The paper money of the Bank of Spain has sunk so far in value that it has become a paying speculation to pass in these notes to the Bank to be exchanged into silver, in order that the silver might be sent out of the country and sold for its bullion price. So severe already has been the depletion of the Bank's small stock of silver on this account that between May 8 and 21 more than £1,250,000 of the metal had been withdrawn from the Bank, and the latest return showed a stock of only £4,330,000. The note circulation, taken at the conventional exchange, amounts to about £52,500,000 ; the Finance Minister, Senor Puigcerver, was therefore a very reckless man when he declared that the Bank had silver enough to exchange for all notes presented. It would not have that even if it bought silver, and coined it to the extent of the entire stock of gold still in its possession. It has been buying silver with somebody's gold in London, and the London bullion dealers have treated Spain precisely like a bankrupt. If the gold was at hand to pay for the silver bought, the silver was sold ; not otherwise.

In order to stop the drain of silver created in the way described, a law has been passed by the Cortes prohibiting its export altogether as a criminal offence. As Senor Calzado declared, this law is absolutely futile, but it has been passed to try to "quiet the public mind," and thus indirectly stop the drain of silver. It will not stop that drain—nothing can stop it in the present position of the paper money, which is at a discount fully greater than that of silver coins compared with the market price of the bullion. Years ago Spain lost all her gold money in circulation, and was only able to maintain a small gold reserve in the Bank by continually forcing out more and more notes. Now it is to lose apparently both that gold and what remains of its silver. When the whole of this bullion is gone what will be its position? What guarantee can it offer to any creditor? What security for a loan? Will the French bankers, desperate as their position must be in relation to Spain's debts, really have the courage to make an advance of £10,000,000, or any amount, however small, on any security that Spain can now offer? Do not these questions serve to indicate how perfectly hollow the pretences of solvency put forward by the present Government of this unhappy country have been for the last ten years at least? Spain is bankrupt, hopelessly bankrupt, and her bankruptcy is about to be made patent to the whole world. Happily for us, we have not believed in her solvency in this country for many a long day. The last default and rearrangement of her debt whereby the public creditor was cheated out of something like half his capital, an arrangement made and carried through by the Council of Foreign Bondholders in 1882, sufficed to cure the British investor of any disposition to again intrust his money to Spanish keeping.

In these circumstances it will be interesting to see how the Spanish Government fares in its attempt to contract a new loan of one thousand million pesetas in 4 per cent. bonds. This is nominally forty millions sterling, and the Bank of Spain is going to be entrusted with the sale of the bonds, utilising "its clients and correspondents at home and abroad to place the new issue." On what grounds can it expect to accomplish this gigantic feat? The existing market value of the sterling foreign debt of Spain stands around 33 per cent. of the nominal value, but the Spanish Government cannot expect to obtain the current market price for a new issue of the proposed dimensions—cannot hope to receive even 30 per cent. The loan, therefore, if sold, would not bring in more than fifteen millions at most, and how long will fifteen millions last at the present rate of Spain's war expenditure? We should judge not longer than eight or nine weeks. In other words, the situation is just about as hopeless as it well could be, and the longer it continues the more striking will be the folly of the Queen Regent's Government in continuing a conflict which it has not strength to sustain. But then it dare not yet make peace.

The Debt of Brazil.

It has been announced that an arrangement has been satisfactorily concluded for funding interest on the debt of the Republic of Brazil during the next three years. Instead of receiving cash for the interest due on this debt the creditors will get 5 per cent. funding bonds after the Argentine manner, and these bonds alone will receive interest in cash, secured upon the customs of Rio de Janeiro in the first instance, and on the customs of other ports should that be necessary. Doubtless this arrangement was the only alternative to complete default upon the foreign debt of Brazil. We cannot, however, say that we relish the plan very much. It gives a temporary breathing time, and prevents that discredit which an open suspension of payment would bring about ; therefore it also enables the loan mongers who conduct the finances of this Republic to manœuvre and struggle so as to bring about an appearance of solvency, such as will enable them once more to sell Brazilian loans to the investing classes of Europe. We may take this, indeed, to be the primary object. Such an arrangement as this is not undertaken for philanthropy or in the interests of the people of Brazil, but merely for the sake of the finance houses, whose occupation would be gone, and whose loss might be severe, did the States they nurse and choke the life out of with debt absolutely default. As to permanent benefit to Brazil from this arrangement we confess we can see none. At the end of the three years the debt will be increased by six or seven million pounds nominal, and Brazil will not be one single milreis better for this extra burden. Her enormous paper money circulation will not have been reduced, nor yet her heavy internal debt, and the more remote consequence of all this appears to us to be a break up of the loose-jointed Republic into fragments, and possibly the annexation of parts of it by foreign Powers such as Germany. Meantime, the market price of Brazilian bonds can perhaps be sustained on the bourses, and that, at any rate, may keep European financiers from despairing about recovering their losses out of investors' pockets.

The Affairs of the Central Pacific Railroad Company.

Mr. Morshead's committee—the Shareholders' Protection Committee—has sent us copies of a correspondence which it has had, or rather tried to have, with the Californian railroad "Boss" Huntington, and with Mr. F. C. Banbury, M.P. Neither of these men have answered the letters of Mr. Morshead. They probably thought it not worth their while. Nevertheless, in our opinion, if Central Pacific shareholders here, who have been robbed and defrauded in a manner so cold-hearted and shameless by the group of scamps who devised and built the Southern Pacific line at their expense, would only heartily stand together and support Mr. Morshead's committee, they probably have now a better chance of obtaining some of their money back than at any previous time since it was misappropriated in millions. They cannot themselves compel the thieves to make restitution, but the United States Government can, and its disposition is now so friendly to England and Englishmen as to make it advisable for those who have grievances against American citizens to strike the iron while hot. We published the Californian official presentment of the Central Pacific frauds in the Investors' Review for June and July of last year. Those who care to look that up and refresh their memories with it will find it curious and suggestive. The scandal it recites the history of is such as no Government could face, were the moral responsibility for permitting such iniquities to be committed once brought home to it. It is a specious theory that the big thieves ought to be let off, and only the small ones punished, and it has been a disastrous one many a time for the British investor.

Indian Currency.

The subjoined note, extracted from the financial columns of the *Indian Daily News*, shows what the business community in India thinks about the proposals of the Simla Government for giving an artificial standard of value to the silver rupee. It is a view in full accord with that of business men in this country, but for that very reason, perhaps, the officials despise it. It is their misfortune rather than their crime to have been so mis-educated as to be quite incapable of taking a practical, common-sense view of business affairs.

Let no one be deluded as to the ultimate result of the new currency policy. Ten crores of rupees are to be taken from the currency reserve, to be melted up, and to be sold in India as bullion. It is expected that the ten crores will realise six crores, which are to be taken from the pockets of the people and locked up in the currency reserve treasuries. The difference of four crores is to be made up by £2,700,000 (the equivalent at 1s. 4d.) in gold, to be borrowed in London and placed also in the reserve treasuries. This will constitute one year's operations. Then the next year, or if in the meantime gold has not rushed into the country, the policy will be repeated, and a further six crores of rupees will be withdrawn from circulation, and so on. Now let there be no mistake as to the effect of this upon the money market. Already for the past two years we have experienced the devastating effects of a contracted currency, but these, serious although they have been, will be as nothing compared to the intense stringency which the new policy will produce. It must not be forgotten that it is not the Government's intention to provide sovereigns to fill the void caused in circulating medium; this is to be left for the public to do. That some gold might be forced out to India under the scheme we admit, but it would only be sent in cases of dire necessity. How could the investing public at home be expected to invest in industries in India when these industries are being strangled through the contraction of the currency, now to be greatly accelerated, and absolutely ruinous rates of interest which the accelerated contraction would produce.

AMERICAN AND CANADIAN HARMONIES.

There was reason for the congratulations offered by the Opposition in the Dominion House of Commons on Wednesday to the Laurier Ministry for the success which had attended their negotiations for the appointment of an International Commission for the settlement of all pending differences between the United States and Canada. There was perhaps some reason also for the complaint of the Leader of the Opposition that the public men of the United States have scarcely understood the Canadians or sympathised with them as they might have done. But there was a great deal more reason for Sir Wilfred Laurier's suggestion that whatever the relations of the two States might have been in the past, it would be as well, at present, not to inquire too curiously who had been in the wrong and who in the right. The past may be forgotten. The new agreement will be of great advantage to Canada; it is a significant and gratifying indication of the cordial relations now existing between the United States and Great Britain, and probably Sir Wilfred is right in anticipating that the influence of these improved relations will extend "wherever there are nations which acknowledge the sovereignty of England." At any rate, there is ample ground for the general satisfaction expressed at the conclusion of this important agreement and at the evidence it affords of the very friendly feelings which animate the United States towards this country. At present there need be no talk of an alliance. That may or may not come. But there should be no serious difficulty in maintaining and strengthening the good understanding now established between the two great English-speaking countries. For ourselves, we are somewhat sceptical about the uses of treaty alliances. They are like written constitutions, apt to bring to the front, at moments of excitement, points of difference which, in the intimacy of diplomatic intercourse, would hardly be felt as serious obstacles to a good understanding. For the present, however, we cannot but be pleased with the early prospect of seeing irritating questions, not supremely important in themselves, but containing infinite possibilities of dangerous disagreement, finally settled in a spirit of friendly compromise. The three main questions are—seals, fishing rights, and tariff; and the importance of the tariff question will be easily appreciated when it is stated that at present more than a third of Canada's exports are taken by the United States, while more than a half of her imports are from the United States. The existing revenue laws seem framed merely to check and frustrate trade. In the present state of feeling there should be no difficulty in arranging a system which will reciprocally develop the trade of both countries, and so intertwine their various interests as to render future differences all but impossible.

Is there room also for the hope that the closer contact between Great Britain and America now likely to prevail may help to modify the craze there for "exclusive" tariffs? We are inclined to think so. The results of the Dingley tariff have been anything but an unmixed blessing to the trade of the United States. In some instances, at least, their home trade has been more damaged by it than the foreign trade against which it was meant to militate. It is probable that the irritation which has existed so long against this country may have unconsciously inspired these hostile tariffs. With the partial or total disappearance of this sense of irritation may there not therefore come a disposition to reconsider the tariff question, and to lean towards that freedom of trade which would be more beneficial to the United States than to foreign countries trading with it? That the American Government have no objections to special arrangements with other countries is shown by the convention just concluded with France. This convention is all the more significant in that it has been concluded at a time when the relations between the two countries seemed to be getting somewhat strained. By the convention the Dingley tariff is so far suspended, the most favoured nation clause is introduced, and France grants to the United States reciprocal advantages in the importation of pork, lard, and kindred products, which had recently been subjected to an increase of duty. The new arrangements are already in force, and the reductions in favour of France are estimated at two and a half million francs. But the arrangement is most satisfactory as indicating that improved relations exist with France as well as with England, and that America is showing more appreciation of the advantage of suspending rather than extending tariff restrictions. Let us hope that America is rapidly learning the lesson that these tariff restrictions are unmitigated evils, and had better be swept away altogether.

THE TRADE OF JAPAN IN 1897.

An interesting report on this subject has been issued by the Foreign Office, compiled by Mr. A. H. Lay, assistant Japanese secretary to her Majesty's Legation in Tokio. As was to be expected, the figures he quotes show a large increase both in imports and exports. The total of the imports amount to £22,828,683, and the total of the exports to £16,398,212. This is an increase of £4,075,294 in the imports, and of £3,769,190 in the exports compared with the returns for 1896. Japan, therefore, is extending her trade with great rapidity, but not quite on safe lines. Indeed, as Mr. Lay points out, the position of the country is fully worse than even these figures reveal, because imports are taken into the returns at the original cost of the goods at the place of production. Add 15 per cent. to this, and we obtain a total of £26,269,968 as the true cost of her imports to Japan. Assume that the same addition has to be made to the value of the exports as representing the profit to the exporter, and still the trading account of the country is in a position very far from sound. Japan, notwithstanding the large sums of money paid to her by China as indemnity, is rapidly assuming the position of a debtor State. Her Government owes money abroad, and her people have no foreign investments to set against this debt. The nation, therefore, depends upon its trade for the means to pay its way, and it cannot go on buying goods to a larger extent than the value of its sales of goods abroad without falling into a position of great danger at home. A continuance of imports largely in excess of the value of the exports must mean, before long, a steady drain upon Japan's metallic money, and if continued long enough it would throw the country into the disastrous chaos of a forced paper currency. We hope better of Japan and of Japanese energy and ability than such an end to her finances would lead us to imply; and it is no doubt the case that the money obtained from China explains to a considerable extent the excess of imports at present. Great prudence and energy, however, will be requisite to prevent the country from continuing to be extravagant, when the means justifying her in a measure in being so have been exhausted.

THE ITALIAN TROUBLE.

The Ministerial crisis in Italy seems to show that the real lesson of the recent revolutionary riots has not been learned by the ruling politicians. The Marquis di Rudini has quarrelled with some of his colleagues because he either cannot or will not recognise the profoundly disturbing influence which the vicious economic condition of Italy exercises upon the fortunes of the country. It was hunger that led to the recent rioting; the Marquis di Rudini seems to see in these riots only the hand and head of the designing priest. The Government have been active in suspending ecclesiastical newspapers, in suppressing Catholic clubs and other semi-ecclesiastical associations. Now it may be perfectly true that the priests have been active and crafty agitators. The Archbishop of Milan was culpable in fleeing from Milan just at the moment when the rioting commenced. The Pope was certainly very mild in his rebuke of the Archbishop, and seemed specially anxious to turn the occasion to the detriment of the civil government. But to begin a struggle with the Vatican now would serve no good purpose. On the contrary, it might do considerable mischief. It would raise the cry of persecution, and help rather to strengthen than weaken the ecclesiastical authorities. We have very little doubt that the priests have, in a way, been agitating against the Government, and doing their best to foment discontent; but the Italian Government have supplied them with a most fertile field for activity in oppressive taxation, extravagant expenditure, and constant endeavours to play the Great Power, even if the country is ruined in the process. The Government may close every Catholic club and suspend every ecclesiastical journal in Italy, but they will be no nearer a solution of their accumulating difficulties. Rather will they be further from it, for priestly irritation would only be intensified and priestly agitation redoubled. The first duty of the Italian Government is to encourage the development of trade and industry, to relieve it from the heavy taxation which is choking it, to reduce the national expenditure, and to moderate Imperial pretensions. Only thus can they free themselves from apprehensions of priestly machinations and of that revolutionary movement which will dog their steps until they have forsaken their present methods of administration and assumed the proper functions of industrial government.

RUSSIAN SHIPPING INNOVATIONS.

The law promulgated at St. Petersburg the other day relating to Russian registry for foreign-built ships is likely to prove a rather good thing for British shipbuilders, and a rather bad thing for British shipowners. All the maritime nations of the Continent have for long been possessed with a desire to strengthen their several mercantile marines, and Germany is the only one which finds itself in a position to produce first-class steam and sailing vessels capable of comparing, for cheapness of construction and general efficiency, with British-built ships. Even Germany cannot do this with no aid whatever, and as for France, Italy, and Austria, they have found their aggregate tonnage decline year by year in spite of the generous support accorded through the medium of bounties not only for construction but for navigation as well. France, indeed, offers to the world the pleasing spectacle of a bounty system that is self-destructive. Its shipbuilders are granted allowances on the basis of tonnage and (in the case of steamers) horse power on all the vessels they turn out of their yards; but all the advantage that might be supposed to be derived from this is swallowed up by the heavy cost of materials of construction, and as for the navigation bounties—which take the form of a premium for every thousand miles traversed by French-built ships between home and foreign ports—they are rendered nugatory in large measure because of the large initial outlay, though it remains that the French shipowner has a far better chance of making money out of the system than the French shipbuilder.

Russia has refrained from adopting this policy. It is unable to produce modern vessels on a commercial basis, but it has endeavoured hitherto to afford some degree of protection for its own industry, such as it is, by charging a duty on ships acquired from abroad for the foreign trade and by imposing stringent regulations for the control of the coastwise and inland sea trades. The latter it proposes to aid still further by the imposition of duties which in the case of iron sailing vessels purchased from abroad will run to twenty gold roubles per ton, and in the case of steamers twenty roubles per ton in addition to three gold roubles per square foot of boiler heating surface. But foreign-going vessels of iron and steel will be exempted from a tonnage tax for ten years from July 1, old style; and it is here that the British shipbuilder will have a look in. Some of the vessels to be acquired will no doubt be second-hand, and of a character which it will cause their present owners no pang to part with at a fair figure. But probably the better half will consist of new vessels, mostly steamers, which, along with the second-hand ones, will be employed in competition with British ships in trade to and from Russian ports.

THE WELSH STRIKE.

The end of the South Wales coal dispute, we fear, is not so near as was expected. All that can be said of the conference between employers and colliers at Cardiff is that points of disagreement were more conspicuous than points of agreement. The employers adhere, at least in principle, to the sliding scale arrangement. The men suggested a conciliation board, composed of owners and colliers, with an umpire to be called in in the event of disagreement. The employers, however, emphatically rejected the proposition. Nor would they listen to the demand for an immediate advance of 10 per cent. in wages, in view of the high cost of working and of the fact that many of the collieries had been worked at a loss. The price received for coal from time to time had always been and must continue to be the factor governing wages, whether in the exact form of the agreement recently in force or not. The reply of the workmen to this was that the wages should regulate the price of the commodity rather than the price of the commodity wages. This is rather an ancient notion, which would be comfortable and comforting for most of us if only it could be generally applied. But that is impossible. The masters would doubtless be glad to apply it also in arranging the scale of profits, but do what traders—colliery owners and others—will, prices will rise and fall, and if wages—and profits, say—are only to be subject to a rise, it does not seem clear how business could be conducted, at least under such conditions as those to which we have been accustomed. Attempts have been made to regulate autocratically the rate of wages, but they have invariably failed, and if workmen were strong enough to enforce such a provision as that suggested by the Welsh colliers, they would have to prepare themselves for a very serious contraction, if not extinction, of the trade done by the United Kingdom. The result, indeed, would be disastrous for both masters and men. But the conference has been adjourned until Saturday. Let us hope the workmen will by that time have more carefully considered their suggestions, will have discovered their impracticability, and be ready to accept some more rational scheme. If not, there seems nothing for it but the indefinite prolongation of the strike. The employers spoke with emphasis and decision; and it can hardly be expected that they will waste time and effort in the discussion of crude fallacies such as were served up by the colliers' representatives at Cardiff on Tuesday.

Another Chilian Loan!

We regret to see the announcement in the papers that the Chilian Government is endeavouring to raise yet another loan, a loan in Germany of 80,000,000 marks, or say in round figures £4,000,000. Amid all the afflictions through which this interesting and progressive Republic has been passing we have stuck by her and spoken well of her, hoping the best and believing in the honesty of her administration. To a great extent we adhere still to the opinions on this point so often expressed in this Review. At the same time a feeling of doubt, if not of alarm, begins to occupy the mind lest Chili should be plunging into debt beyond her depth. Including her internal burdens, her public debt now approaches £20,000,000, which is heavy for a population of less than three and a half millions. Indeed, the present burden of the State could not be carried but for the fact that Chili has obtained for many years a large revenue from the heavy export duty she levies on nitrate of soda, a product she fell heir to after the war with Peru. Out of the total revenue of less than 80,000,000 pesos, nearly 40,000,000 pesos came last year, or was estimated to come, from this nitrate export duty. But there is reason to fear that the trade in this alkali has been much injured and impeded in development by this taxation, and we cannot at present regard the revenue from this source as other than precarious. Even if it were an assured revenue, surely great weakness is exhibited by the determination now expressed to pledge it specially for a loan. This means that a valuable security is to be taken away from the existing debts of the Republic, a security pledged to them, and we are sorry to see the Chilians entering upon such a doubtful course. Sorry also are we to find that they cannot do without more European money for a few years. They must be suffering from causes of depletion which are unknown to us. Perhaps the resolute adherence to an honourable endeavour to restore their currency to a fixed gold valuation of 1s. 6d. per dollar, or peso, has something to do with these continually recurring appeals of the Government to the European moneylender. We trust patriotic Chilians will earnestly endeavour to direct their country's interests into a better way in the near future. If they fail in this the Republic runs in danger of going the way of so many of its neighbours.

The Capture of Lake Tsad.

Of what has our Colonial Office been thinking? Where has Mr. Chamberlain, where Sir Ellis Ashmead-Bartlett been, that a French expedition has been allowed quietly to slip into possession of Lake Tsad, or Chad—the exact spelling being, of course, a matter of minor importance? The essential thing is that a huge lake in the north of Africa, in the Soudan itself, has been captured by the French, when, according to all proper Imperial notions, it ought to have been included among the infinite number and variety of Imperial claims we have been assiduously pegging out all over the world for our especial posterity. How posterity can get on without it it is difficult to conceive. What Sir Ellis Ashmead-Bartlett's feelings must have been when he read of the success of the Gentil mission we almost shudder to think. What he may say to the Colonial Office when he has summed up the full measure of its negligence in this momentous matter we leave to the imagination of others. The Colonial Secretary must prepare to face searching questions on the subject, and the Colonial officials had better immediately look up the geography of the region. It is a wonderful lake. It covers some 10,000 square miles in the dry season; and in the wet expands to some four or five times that extent. It has no natural outlet, but occasionally flows over into a great sunken plain 300 miles to the north-east. How many mills might not be kept grinding by such a volume of water! No gold is yet reported to have been discovered; but that, no doubt, only awaits the shrewd labours of a keen-witted syndicate clever at prospecting and at drawing up prospectuses. If there be difficulties in the way of constructing a railway from Lake Tsad to Khartoum or Cairo, natural canals abound, and their extension would offer no serious obstacles to enterprising syndicates. There are numerous islands in the vicinity, with a considerable population of semi-amphibious negroes. These may be cannibals now, but doubtless they could easily be converted into an imposing army of cheap and willing labourers. Why was such a noble possession allowed to fall into the hands of mere Frenchmen? Must we indeed regard it as theirs hopelessly beyond dispute? Is not the whole Soudan and all that to it appertains clearly within our sphere of influence? Mr. Chamberlain should be up and doing. Another warlike speech at Birmingham might help us. Some portion of the Reserve might be called out. But if Lake Tsad is permitted to be annexed by the French without protest or demand for "compensation," how can we avert the reproach and scathing scorn of posterity?

Industrial and General Trust.

It was a graceful and a wise measure of this board to withdraw the resolution which would have altered the Articles of Association so as to lead to the cessation of the publication of the list of investments. After the painful history of the old company it would have led to all sorts of anxieties as to the management of the board, and would have certainly caused the stocks of the Trust, which we consider to have improved much in intrinsic value of late years, to deteriorate in public opinion. Criticism has certainly been directed to the list of investments—we ourselves sharply criticised certain holdings—but we fancy the board would be the first to admit that the securities we picked out were not even of mediocre value. Criticism of this kind is precisely what a trust board requires, and it was the absence of it that assisted the previous board to play ducks and drakes with the money of their shareholders.

Protection Shackles in Germany.

Germany, if we may trust our Baden consul's diagnosis of the situation, is bent on more thoroughly shackling her home trade than it even now is. The urgent calls for this policy originate, as they mostly do elsewhere, with the landed interest. That wants higher duties on agricultural imports. This seems most surprising in Germany, of all places; for probably in no other country, as we have before shown, is so much done for the encouragement of agriculture and the assistance and education of the agriculturists. Better equipped for the struggle of industrial life than their competitors in other countries, why should German farmers insist on the coddling of protective imposts, and avow themselves eager to accept the enervating influence of State alms? Natural laziness may account for much; but what is there in agriculture which makes so many of its followers calmly insist that it cannot possibly stand on its own legs: it must be propped? German foreign merchants are showing no slackening of energy or enterprise; but what would happen if they were to demand a subvention from Government, because they find it difficult to make big enough fortunes in these times of increasing foreign competition? Their claim would be at least as reasonable as that of the farmer. But it is expected that the German Government will grant the demands of the native agriculturist as soon as existing treaty engagements permit. Mendicity is to be encouraged. The industrial classes may complain, but they will have to pay, though they may ask for and receive the fatal gift of higher duties on foreign manufactures, so that German home business may the more thoroughly be crippled. It is the old vicious cycle. Our consul thinks the result will be that Germany "will become more and more dependent for her export trade upon Great Britain and the British colonies." Of course it will. Yet our "fair" traders would have us throw away such advantages by adopting the Protective system ourselves. But we know too well the blasting influence of such a policy. Only hard experience apparently will teach Germany. Her profound philosophy seems hardly to include political economy. It is unfortunate for her; but she might easily know better and do better if she would.

The Exploration Company.

The resignation of the Hon. H. C. Gibbs from the board of this company is probably of no immediate interest, but the fact may come to be important when the history of this concern is written. The quotations of the mining issues of the Exploration Company still seem to suffer from dry rot, or the dribbling out of shares upon a market reluctant to purchase, and since our article upon the company in the issue of January 21 last, there has been considerable depreciation, as the following table, which we bring up to date, sets forth:—

	Price at or about Special Settlement.	Highest Price.	Price Jan. 20.	Present Price.
Anaconda Copper ...	6½	7¾	5 13/16	5
Aroha Gold Mines ...	1¼	1¾	⅛	1s. 6d.
Beacon Gold Mines ...	15/16	1	⅛	—
Cons. Goldfields N. Zealand	4	4⅝	2⅜	2
Grand Central	2 5/16	3¼	1⅜	1 1/16
Lake George Mines ...	2 11/16	2⅞	2½	¾
Norseman Gold Mine ...	7/16 pm.	2	⅜	7/16
New Zealand Crown ...	2 1/16	2¼	⅜	¾
New Zealand Exploration	*	3⅜	¾	¾

* No price obtainable about this date.

As we explained on January 21, the Special Settlement usually fixed the date of the commencement of market activity in these shares, which generally were issued without the advertisement of a prospectus. Launched usually at a high premium, the quotation advanced further after the Special Settlement and then seemed to experience a "burst up," with the melancholy result set forth in the prices now current for the shares. The above table is clear proof that a buyer of Exploration specialities should not come early into the market, and we should imagine that those who do not touch the shares at all will get off best. Yet there are people in the City who speak of the Exploration Company with bated breath, as if it were one of the solid buttresses to trade and commerce!

The Suez Canal.

Though the directors of the Suez Canal Company, in their report to the meeting of shareholders to be held in Paris next week, announce a falling off in traffic for 1897 of over £260,000, the report cannot, on the whole, be considered an unsatisfactory one. Much of this diminution in traffic is attributable to temporary causes, such as the famine and plague in India and the decrease caused in Australian traffic by the drought and the great mortality in cattle. This temporary character of the diminution of the traffic is further shown by the fact that, so far, this year's returns indicate a substantial increase over those of the corresponding period of last year. The trade from the Far East in 1897 showed a decided improvement, the movement in trade from that region to Europe and America having risen from 2,408,100 tons in 1895 to 2,738,000 tons in 1897. In this connection Japan stands out conspicuously; for while in 1895 only two Japanese vessels passed through the canal, last year there were thirty-four. The receipts for last year amounted to £3,024,281, and the expenses to £1,451,660—showing an excess of receipts over expenditure of £1,572,621. Adding to this £35,607 from the special, and £28,324 from the ordinary reserve, the directors are able to recommend a dividend of £3 12s., or about 2s. less than that of last year. As the reserve fund is still £107,193 in excess of the statutory amount, the result can scarcely be regarded as other than satisfactory. £124,165 has been spent during the year in repairs—chiefly in widening and deepening the canal, both matters of great importance as seen in the ease with which the large steamers of 10,000 tons on the Australian service passed through the canal last year. The Japanese ironclads *Fuji* and *Yashima* also went safely through the canal—a fact which seems to show that it may become useful in time of war for the Power that can seize it and hold it. As we have said, the returns for this year are very favourable up to the present, and if we look to the increasing shipments of wheat from India, and the opening of additional ports in China to European commerce, as well as the construction of new railways in that empire, the returns of the Suez Canal Company should show a steady improvement during the present year.

Harried Uruguay.

It will surprise no one to learn, as we do from Mr. Consul Grenfell's report to the Foreign Office, that the trade and commerce of Uruguay for 1897 showed a serious falling off as compared with the previous year. Trade and revolution never do agree; but at least the revolution of last year in Uruguay, though disastrous for a time, may be regarded as having been not altogether wanting in beneficent influence. It broke with a bad past. Trade had been dwindling for years in consequence of the oppressive taxation to which the country had been subjected. The Dictator Cuertas seems at least in a fair way to put a stop to that; for the first step of his administration has been to insist on economy all round, and the removal of obnoxious taxes. Our consul seems to have confidence in the new provisional President, and to believe in the honesty of his efforts to open the way for expansion of trade and the reduction of taxation. If President Cuertas continues as he has been doing for the past year, the revolution will have been a real blessing for Uruguay. The great shrinkage in the trade of 1897 is shown in the diminution of the imports; and as this falling off was most conspicuous in soft goods, of which Great Britain is the chief exporter to Uruguay, she is of course the greatest sufferer by the present decline in trade. The shringage in the exports has been even greater. There is every indication, however, that the check to trade will only be temporary. Confidence has already been restored, and business has resumed its normal state. More land has been brought under cultivation; and the agricultural outlook seems generally good. Very interesting details are given of the value of articles imported from Great Britain, the United States, Germany, France, and Belgium; but it need only be noted that England still maintains a good lead in the trade as a whole. The Uruguayan trade returns for this year will be looked for with considerable interest; for if they turn out as well as it is hoped, it will give assurance not only of a genuine revival of trade, but of the honesty of the Dictator in relieving the country of an incubus which was slowly killing trade and commerce and reducing Uruguay to a desert.

Trade in the Cyclades.

It is pleasant to hear from our consul in Syra, who discourses hopefully on the trade of the Cyclades, that the international financial control now established may prove a blessing in disguise to Greece. At least the trading community are glad of it as likely to bring about the reform of a defective fiscal system, and so to raise the credit of the country abroad, while benefiting trade at home. It is no less pleasant to find our consul —who should be a good authority—looking forward with confidence to a steady revival of trade and commerce in Greek ports after the somewhat ruthless interruption of the war. But there is one thing which Mr. Consul W. H. Cottrell insists upon. If British traders are to reap the full benefit of the revival of trade in Greece and Crete, they must be prepared to send competent commercial travellers, with abundant samples, to tempt the Greek dealers. It is all very well to sneer at consular agents, who are accused of dwelling on this theme as a handy means of explaining the cause of British decline abroad. That, we are assured, is a great mistake. Neither French nor German dealers treat the matter with that ignorant impatience; for no sooner was the "war scare" over than French and German commercial men appeared on the scene, primed with samples and glib in the Greek language, and contrived to do a good trade. Only one British firm had listened to the repeated appeals of the consuls, and sent a representative. This was a Paisley firm, and its experience may possibly be sufficiently encouraging to induce others to follow the example. We hope so. In these days it will not do to neglect what may hitherto have been regarded even as insignificant markets.

SOME INDIAN RAILWAY COMPANIES.

The reports so far issued referring to the operations during the second half of last year are more satisfactory than might have been expected considering the widespread effects of the plague and famine. The business of the Bombay, Baroda, and Central India Company naturally suffered a good deal, but the other lines make a very respectable showing, as will be seen from the following figures :—

	Gross Receipts.	Working Expenses.	Proportion of Expenses to Receipts.		Net Earnings.
			Dec. 1897.	Dec. 1896.	
Bengal & North W.	Rs. +141,726	+ 76,442	48·84	48·55	+ 65,284
Bengal Central	Rs. +169,836	+ 61,232	54·68	60·83	+108,603
Bombay Baroda, &c.	Rs. −191,104	+251,553	54·98	52·68	−442,657
Madras	£ + 24,191	+ 1,126	48·68	50·83	+ 23,065
South Indian	Rs. +207,149	+154,304	54·20	53·23	+ 52,846
Southern Mahratta.	Rs. +217,214	+158,342	60·72	60·08	+ 58,872

Surplus profits come out very well, and these have been brought home at a rate of exchange more favourable to the companies than for some time past, with the result that in three cases out of four, shareholders receive increase dividends :—

—	Surplus Profits.		Available for dividend.		Dividend for half-year.	
	1897.	1896.	1897.	1896.	Dec. 1897.	Dec. 1896.
	Rs.	Rs.	£	£	per cent.	per cent.
Bengal and North Western	731,158	705,823	43,329	40,673	2	1¾
Bengal Central......	77,440	50,289	4,154	3,134	2½	£2 6s.
Bombay, Baroda, &c.	204,321	334,560	—	—	2½	£2 16s.
Madras	3,615	—	—	—	—	—
South Indian........	258,820	146,418	16,523	13,559	2¾	2¼
Southern Mahratta ..	383,416	366,327	25,379	22,891	2½	2¼

Taking the Bombay and Baroda Company first, as being the most important, we find a reduction in the number of passengers carried on the company's line of as much as 1,376,000, or nearly 23 per cent. ; the decrease in coaching receipts being £54,005. This is due to the continued prevalence of causes that adversely affected the traffic in the previous half-year, the principal being the plague, and the consequent restrictions on travel and fairs enforced under Government orders in districts served by the company's lines. Goods traffic, however, did much better, there being an increase of 29,935 tons carried and of £14,969 in receipts, although trade had not recovered from its previous condition of local depression, and the bountiful crops resulting from the favourable rains of the monsoon had not become available for purposes of export, so that the actual effects of the changing condition of the company's district upon its business were but slight and showed only partial improvement. The quantity of grain carried was 13,015 tons against 7,082 tons in 1896, of other food grains 68,327 tons against 35,465 tons, and of salt 53,981 tons against 44,574 tons ; but of cotton only 14,573 tons were carried against 22,607 tons, and of oil seeds 37,369 tons against 42,678 tons in 1896. This left a net decrease in receipts of £38,896, but in spite of this revenue charges increased by £26,510, of which £30,000 was in carriage and wagon expenses, and was due to charges for renewal of vehicles unavoidably postponed from the previous half year, owing to the non-arrival of English materials required, while expenditure on the change of bridge girders in progress represented £38,078 against £35,458 in 1896. Net earnings per train mile were only 3s. 7d. against 4s. 8d. in 1896, and the net profit for the half year fell short by Rs.237,893 of the amount required to meet interest on the guaranteed stock and bonds and the usual contribution to the provident fund. On its own line, therefore, the company did badly, but the State lines worked for Government, did very much better, there being an increase in receipts, and a saving in expenses, so that the net earnings were Rs.4,702,737 as compared with Rs.4,431,873 in 1896. In fact, the whole of the company's surplus profits is derived from the State lines and amount to Rs.204,321 against Rs.143,462, which improvement, and the better exchange rate largely offsets the poor result on the company's own line.

The South Indian Company did better than in the corresponding period, and with the higher exchange is able to pay ½ per cent. more dividend. The Madras Company also makes a better display. Practically the whole of the increase in gross revenue is retained as net, the result being that the Company is at last able to show a surplus after providing for the guaranteed interest. The surplus is small, Rs.7,231, of which the Company's share is one-half. On the Southern Mahratta line traffic continues to grow, the gross receipts being the largest in its history ; but expenses have grown nearly as fast, so the increase in net is less than Rs.60,000, and the same dividend is paid as in 1896. Passenger traffic fell off largely owing to the plague, but merchandise traffic was much larger, the increase being 22 per cent. in receipts and nearly 11 per cent. in weight, due chiefly to larger movements of food grains owing to famine. The Bengal Central did well and puts up its dividend a little. The increase in receipts is pretty equally divided between passengers, goods and sundries and while nearly all items under expenses show an increase, the total is little more than one-third of the improvement in earnings. The Company's receipts, however, do not expand very rapidly. Neither do the earnings of the Bengal and North Western Company grow much considering the increase in mileage, but it is a line worked cheaply, this and the Madras having the lowest percentage of expenses to receipts in the list. The Company did moderately well during the past half year having a large increase in third class passengers, due mainly to increased attendance at fairs and to the extra mileage open. Merchandise traffic was smaller owing to the grain scarcity, but goods carried on the steamers increased through the continued imports of Burma rice. The higher exchange rate, however, enables the Company to pay a trifle more in the way of dividend, which should assist it with its proposal to raise £750,000 more capital for rolling stock, workshops, and new extensions.

THE BANK OF FRANCE.

The Bank of France, which is not so old as the Bank of England, was created by Napoleon the First. It commenced operations in 1800, with a capital of 30,000,000 francs, in order to aid in the reorganisation of public credit, so unsettled by the Revolution, and to facilitate commercial transactions, for the rate of interest, as a rule, then oscillated between 12 and 20 per cent. It had also to advance to the Government the sums necessary for war. It soon fell into difficulties, and nearly failed in 1805, and also in 1848 and 1865 ; it did not enjoy a normal and progressive course before 1870. In consequence of the suppression of local banks in 1848, it alone possesses the right to issue banknotes. Its present capital is 182,500,000 francs, divided into 182,500 registered shares of 1,000 francs. It does not now, as was the case at first, limit itself to issuing paper money, but practises most of the ordinary operations of financial companies. The Governor, nominated by the State, is assisted by two vice-governors and the Assemblée Générale, composed of the 200 largest shareholders, who elect the Conseil Général, which is formed of fifteen regents and three censors ; the Governor (now M. Pallain) presides at the meetings of the General Council, and alone has the right to sign all treaties and conventions. Without going into details, we may mention that in 1897 the business of the Bank amounted to 15,308,125,000 francs, giving a profit allowing of a dividend of 109 francs, against 115 in 1896. Its shares, now quoted at 3,600 francs, valued 6,500 francs in 1881 and 1882, when the profits were more than one million per week and a dividend from 250 to 290 francs was distributed. This increase in the profits was chiefly due to the crisis brought about by the failure of the Union Générale. As a rule, the Bank has afforded its shareholders dividends varying from 8 to 12 per cent., but since 1889, when it risked losing two and a half millions in advancing by command of the Finance Minister 140 millions to the Comptoir d'Escompte, its business has been constantly diminishing. It must be remembered, however, that the Bank did not wish its business to appear too flourishing, and it willingly renounced the idea of maintaining its shares at their old level, because excessive profits would have served as a valuable argument against it at the time of the negotiations for the renewal of its privilege.

Without speaking of the monopoly, we shall simply consider the Bank from a financial point of view. Its metallic reserve has taken such proportions that any monetary crisis would find it admirably prepared. The reserve gold amounts to £74,500,000 and that of silver to £48,500,000. A diminution of only about £7,000,000 has occurred in the gold reserve since the end of October, 1897, the time when the withdrawals of gold from the Bank of France commenced. Paris maintains its rate of discount invariable at 2 per cent., and the financial world did not appear at all agitated by the withdrawal of several hundred million francs required for the purchase of cereals. The latest weekly balance-sheets do not lead one to suppose that the Bank will be obliged to modify its rate, and Paris looks unconcerned on the present situation while seeing that the reserves of the European banks will suffer somewhat when business in America resumes its normal course. The total value of the banknotes in circulation exceeds the cash in reserve by £26,500,000, which is not contrary to its statutes. The rate of discount of the Bank has been 2 per cent. only for several years. The importance of the metallic reserve seems to have completely freed France from the influence of the Bank of England, and it appears, in fact, that the Bank of France has foreseen all the difficulties to be overcome. It is well to remember that the month of May is usually that in which its reserve attains its highest level, but the present year may be regarded as exceptional, for the payments have been, and will still be, somewhat abnormal. If at any moment the situation should cause legitimate anxiety, the Bank would certainly renounce artificial means, and employ without hesitation a really efficacious defence—that of raising its rate.

For the moment, however, it is not feared that any grave disturbance will result from the present situation. The Government has hitherto acted too strongly and directly on the Bank, but it will do well to profit by past experience and allow it henceforth to observe more strictly the ordinary laws of banking, instead of battling with difficulties by special expedients and trusting to mere chance. The cheque rate on London, now at 25·34, is favourable to England; but Paris can support some loss of gold without trouble, and if its reserve should diminish, no great danger will at present arise. The Bank is the sole depository in France of the precious metals, and from its reserve depends absolutely the degree of facility of its operations abroad. But it must not be overlooked that a monetary crisis affects it in a peculiar manner, for it suffers all the inconveniences of bimetallism. Compelled to receive specie in silver as repayments, it cannot pay with it, owing to the fact that operations with foreign countries can only be conducted in gold, and that home commerce prefers notes. As soon as the Bank puts a large amount of silver into circulation it is returned to it again, the public finding it too heavy and cumbersome. The condition of the B.D.F., then, apparently so strong, requires in fact great prudence and much care in treatment. Gold constitutes but two-thirds of its total reserve, and of what proportions of silver coin and bar silver the other third is composed is not known.

In the event of a crisis, the Bank would pay out silver money at home which the French people are obliged to receive at its nominal value, but it could not thus utilise its silver bars, the law and international conventions prohibiting their transformation into coin. The only thing the Bank could do would be to sell them for their real value on the market, that is to say, at a loss of at least 55 per cent., which would represent a loss equal to more than twice its capital, for there is more than a third of its metallic reserve which it cannot make use of. To furnish and maintain gold in its safes and to dispense with the necessity of raising the Bank rate to defend itself against withdrawals of gold, the State pays in banknotes and silver exclusively the salaries of its functionaries, and the bills of its contractors, as well as the coupons of the holders of Government stock, and the agents of the Treasury remit to the Bank all the gold received by them. The balance-sheet of the Bank, that all the financiers of the world consult assiduously, and which is the only source of authentic information offered to the public, teaches nothing during a crisis concerning the outgoings of gold; it simply indicates the difference between the demand for gold by commerce and the remittances effected by the Treasury, and the drainage is performed clandestinely. It is to be hoped that the optimist previsions of M. Méline will be realised, and that an abundant harvest will exempt France from the necessity of again spending large sums abroad as it has had to do during the past two years. It is affirmed that she possesses more gold and silver in coin than all the rest of Europe together, and that her metallic capital exceeds 8,000 million francs, of which about 5,500 millions is in gold. Thus France has more gold than is really necessary, and it would be profitable for her to part with some of it, which is, moreover, what the Bank is trying to bring about. The premium on gold imposed by the Bank, which was 3 per cent. at the end of 1896, fell to par about the middle of 1897, but rose again towards the end of that year to 4 per cent., and is now as much as 5 per cent. On the other hand, the Bank easily maintains its gold reserve at such a high level through the increase of its commercial exportations, and the interest received in gold on foreign investments. It is, of course, impossible to foretell what America will require, and how far it will be possible to protect the metallic reserves of the Old World against the assaults which are, or will be, made on them; but the situation of the Bank of France shows that its reserve is not appreciably exhausted by the payment for very exceptional quantities of grain, and its immediate available resources, which it was feared would disappear, remain abundant.

Critical Index to New Investments.

THE GOLDSMITHS' AND SILVERSMITHS' COMPANY, LIMITED.

This is a new company, with a share capital of £600,000 in 60,000 £5 5 per cent. cumulative preference and £300,000 £1 ordinary shares. Only the preference shares are offered for subscription, the price asked being par. All the ordinary shares are taken by the vendors in part payment of the price of £600,000 to be given for the business. A certificate of five years' profits is given, signed by Price, Waterhouse, & Co., and it shows rapid progress. No valuation of the assets is supplied, which is a pity, as we think the character of the business could have well stood this publicity, but these preference shares ought to be a very fair industrial investment.

PLYMOUTH CORPORATION STOCK.

Tenders will be received by the National Provincial Bank of England on Tuesday next for an issue of £385,000 2½ per cent. stock, which will be entitled to a full six months' dividend on September 30 next. It is redeemable at par in 1958, or on three months' notice from February, 1918. Minimum price of issue 98 per cent. Money is wanted chiefly for reproductive works, including extension of waterworks and markets, of tramways, electric lighting, &c., and also to pay off part of the existing debt, which amounts to £1,038,688. Population is estimated at 100,000, and the rateable value of the borough is £409,844. At the price the issue does not look very tempting, but it is a trustee stock, and will be assisted by the fall in the value of money.

THE (NEW) CONVALMORE-GLENLIVET AND SCAPA DISTILLERIES, LIMITED.

The capital is put at £135,000 in £10 shares, of which 7,500 are 5 per cent. cumulative preference and the remainder ordinary. The object is to acquire two Highland malt distilleries for £114,945 in cash, and the stocks of whisky and casks are to be purchased at a valuation. We see no inducement to investors this side of the border.

PIGGS PEAK DEVELOPMENT COMPANY, LIMITED.

The company announce an issue of £50,000 7 per cent. first mortgage debentures at par. They can be converted after June, 1900, at 103, and those not previously redeemed are to be paid off at this price on June 30, 1908. The security is a first mortgage on property and concessions of about 40,000 acres in Swaziland, South Africa. With such a history as the company has, none but the bravest speculator will, we imagine, come forward.

Company Reports and Balance-Sheets.

*** *The Editor will be much obliged to the Secretaries of Joint Stock Companies if they would kindly forward copies of Reports and Balance-Sheets direct to the Office of* THE INVESTORS' REVIEW, *Norfolk House, Norfolk-street, W.C., so as to insure prompt notice in these columns.*

ROCK LIFE ASSURANCE COMPANY.—Last year, the ninety-second of this company's existence, 1,010 new policies were issued, insuring £506,903, and yielding £20,257 in new premiums. A small part of this was reinsured. The total premium income of the company was £149,389 net, and it paid in claims and bonuses £109,786, the claims arising on ninety-six deaths, which was fifty-eight below the actuarial expectation. Expenses and commissions took 20 per cent. of the premium income, which was high. The income from interest and dividends was £79,348, £44,086 of which was received on the capital stock paid up and "subscribed." Including the money received for annuities sold, the total income of the company was thus £294,000, and after meeting all outgoings, surrenders, bonuses, &c.,

the funds were increased at the year's end by £54,000. This is a small increase out of such a large revenue, but in addition to heavy current expenses the company had £38,302 to pay in annuities, and paid a dividend bonus of £25,000 to the proprietors out of £44,086 received as interest on their capital. The company's funds, including "subscription" and paid-up capital, amounting to £1,052,057, amounted to £3,191,046, and is well invested, principally at home.

LONDON SCOTTISH AMERICAN TRUST.—The revenue of this Trust improved in every way last year, and, including £603 brought forward, the total income was £70,073. After meeting debenture interest and management expenses, the balance permitted of the placing of £16,000 to reserve, the payment of preference interest and the usual dividend of 3 per cent. on the deferred stock, leaving £1,170 to be carried forward. Included in the income was £7,895 from profit on realisation of securities and £2,757 premium on debenture stock, so that only a little more than £5,000 was put to reserve out of revenue. We should prefer to see such items of income kept out of revenue altogether, as the better managed Trusts have always done. The reserves now amount to £30,000—they are split into four, but they all mean the same thing—and the investments amount to £1,284,227, upon which there is a depreciation of about 6 per cent., after deducting the reserve. The securities are mostly United States issues, so that the depreciation of about £75,000 thus admitted may easily be wiped off later on. Owing to paying off of debenture bonds and loans, the Trust has actually £85,000 less debt than two years ago, so that it has done very well to reduce the depreciation, for it is often the case that the better issues are sold when money is wanted. Unfortunately, the board does not publish its list of investments, so that one dare not recommend its stocks as an investment.

BRAZILIAN SUBMARINE TELEGRAPH COMPANY.—The revenue from messages in the past half-year amounted to £97,448, as against £86,608 in the corresponding half of 1896, and with a little more received from miscellaneous sources the total income was £100,300, of which £26,166 was absorbed by working expenses, and after interest and other charges had been met, the net balance of £69,580 was left. Two interim dividends, making the usual 3 per cent. for the half-year, are declared, the Jubilee bonus to the staff absorbed £4,139, the sum of £25,000 is added to reserve, and £8,662 is carried forward. A closer working arrangement is being arranged with the Western and Brazilian Telegraph Company, and thus the bickering that has gone on for so long between the two concerns should come to an end. The reserve fund amounts to £919,236, of which £689,637 is invested in high-class securities, and £240,340 in shares of other telegraph companies. These, however, yield a poor return, about 2 per cent., and their chief value probably is represented in the control obtained over subsidiary lines. Trading balances, however, are very much in favour of the company.

DUMONT COFFEE COMPANY.—Although there is no dividend on the ordinary capital, nor any allocation to reserve, we like the report just issued by this company better than the one of twelve months back. The profits amounted to £54,425, and with £11,411 brought forward the disposable sum was £65,836. Out of this £51,989 was absorbed by interest on debenture and preference capital and the remaining £13,847 was carried forward, the directors stating that they thought it was more prudent to do so than to declare a small dividend on the ordinary shares. This is the first sign of prudence that we have noted on the part of this board, and let us hope that the caution thus lately instilled into them will be for the benefit of the undertaking. Undoubtedly the company has had to meet considerable difficulties, for the average price of Santos coffee last year was only 31s. 7d. per cwt, as against 51s. 10d. per cwt. in 1896, and an average of about 78s. per cwt. for the four preceding years. This only shows what an astute financier the vendor was, and as we believe he has been selling the shares he received in payment whenever it was possible, the future may not be too pleasant. Still the board has done the right thing, and, with a fairly clean balance-sheet and closer attention to management, the preference shares and debentures may yet prove a tolerable investment.

TINGRI TEA COMPANY.—Last year this company must be considered to have done poorly, for the net revenue was £2,847, as against £4,059 in 1896. With £752 brought forward the disposable balance was £3,600, which allowed of a dividend of 5 per cent., as against 6 per cent. a year ago, and the carrying forward of £775. There is an excellent report from Mr. Magor, one of the board, who has just visited the property.

RAJMAI TEA COMPANY.—Contrary to the experience of most Indian companies, this concern obtained a much better profit for last year. The result of the operations was a surplus of £8,783, which with £4,793 brought forward gave £13,576 to deal with. Dividends amounting to 10 per cent. for the year were proposed, and the balance forward was increased to £7,976. A good deal of the improvement was due to the purchase of a new property at the end of 1896.

MALTA AND MEDITERRANEAN GAS COMPANY.—This company had to meet the competition of the electric light at Malta, and at the same time the Corfu undertaking was sold two years ago, so that no revenue was received from that station. Compared with two years ago, the sale of gas in 1897-8 diminished by £9,015, and residuals also realised less, so that the total revenue of £26,417 was £9,537 below that of 1895-6. Working expenses were less all round, but thanks chiefly to an improvement in exchange, upon which account only £388 had to be provided, as against £4,837 two years ago, the net profit of £9,734 was actually £195 better than in 1895-96. Dividends on the two issues of preference shares were paid, the usual distribution of 6 per cent. upon the ordinary shares was made, and after £1,500 had been put to reserve, the balance of £827 carried forward was about half the amount brought in. The reserve fund now amounts to £4,191, and is wholly invested, besides which there is a reserve account of £4,805. Investments to the value of £6,104 are also held on account of the realisation of the Corfu property, and as the balances of the company are good, the board may possibly continue the process of reducing the loans on debentures, which now only amount to £19,400, and upon which 5 per cent. interest has apparently to be paid.

BACKUS AND JOHNSTON'S BREWERY COMPANY.—The profits of this reconstructed company improved very remarkably last year, being £10,692, as against £4,882 in 1896, and £263 in 1895. Let us hope the improvement is healthy. Out of these profits certain exceptional outlays had to be met, such as two years' directors' fees, and £1,718 for expenses of conversion of debentures, while debenture interest was larger than it will be in future. Altogether about £3,500 of exceptional expenditure was provided for, and after setting aside £1,568 for depreciation, the balance permitted of a distribution of 1 per cent. on the income stock. If profits keep up, this latter stock ought to receive more in the shape of dividends, but the value of the report would be increased if some particulars of the Lima expenditure were added.

ROSBACH SPRINGS, LIMITED.—This is a tiny company not yet got into full working order, and last year there was a debit balance of £482 on the profit and loss account. It is stated in the report that an agency has been opened for the sale of this company's Natural Sparkling Water in the United States, and from this much is expected. Here the company is impeded by the monopolies established through the connection of hotels with the Appolinaris Company, and in other ways.

BANK OF MONTREAL.—This great bank does not publish a report, at least not in England. But its balance-sheet for the year ended April 30 last is before us, and it shows a total of £13,509,104, of which £2,465,736 is capital paid up, and £1,232,659 "rest" or reserve. The note circulation amounts to £1,143,286, against which the bank holds, £524,096 in gold and silver coin, as well as £583,157 in Government demand notes. The deposits aggregate £8,346,000, of which £2,440,739 bears no interest. The profits for the year were £259,993, and £182,242 was brought forward. After paying two dividends of 5 per cent. each, £195,659 is left to be carried forward. The balance-sheet is not very well divided up, and we cannot say under which heading the large amount of drafts issued by the head office on its London branch is embraced. Loans and advances, of a total of £8,079,146, are all in one item.

GUARDIAN FIRE AND LIFE ASSURANCE COMPANY, LIMITED.—Last year the new life business of this company consisted in the issue of 704 new policies, insuring £413,789, and producing £15,918 in new premiums, of which £1,975 represented single premiums. A small amount of these risks was reinsured. The company also received £21,252 for £1,491 of annuities granted. Claims on 158 policies with bonuses took £135,857, number and amount being within expectations, and expenses and commissions came to about 14½ per cent. of the premium income. Interest income was £109,559. The life funds were increased by £167,000 during the year, and now amount to £2,956,239, chiefly invested at home. In the fire department the premium income was £342,161, and the losses £233,849, the income being about £2,800 less, and the losses £31,000 larger than in the previous year. Losses, *i.e.*, came to 68·34 per cent. of the premiums, against 58·75 per cent. in 1896. Expenses and commissions took £122,186, or 35·71 per cent. of the premiums, against 34·4 per cent. the previous year, and consequently, owing to the Cripplegate fire, the year's business resulted in a loss of £13,544. But the fire fund gave an income of £20,381, and £1,031 was realised as profit on investments sold, consequently a net balance of £7,868 remained to be carried to the credit of profit and loss. The total funds of this department stand at £525,850. Including balance brought forward, and £13,200, the year's proportion of life profits, together with £40,286 received as interest on investments, the total available for division is £94,144, and £80,000 of this is taken to pay dividends aggregating 8 per cent. on the share capital. This leaves £14,144 to be carried forward, plus the final portion of the life profits appropriated to the proprietors, as per last quinquennial valuation. Were the company less rich it would feel the inroads made by big fires the more. As it is, good years will now be wanted to sustain the dividend.

THE SOUTH AUSTRALIAN COMPANY.—The sixty-second annual report of this company for the year to April 30 last in England and to December 31 last in South Australia is of the usual complexion. But for the fact that the company is old and solidly based, with excellent possessions in houses, land, and wharves in the colony, it must have suffered greatly from the effects of the appalling drought which has affected all these Australian settlements for several years back. As it is, the revenue was slightly reduced, but not really very much. In spite of the drought the yield of wheat in South Australia amounted to 3 bushels and 46 lb. per acre, an average which left 19,000 tons for export. This was better than in the previous year, but the effect of the drought was none the less most disastrous, especially on market gardens near Adelaide, and several of the company's tenants there had to surrender their leases. Nevertheless, the land sales were by no means stopped, several farms having been disposed of during the year at fair prices, chiefly to tenants, although attempts to sell by auction proved a failure. Allowing for a slight increase in the rent-roll and a decrease in the revenue from the wharves, the gross income of the year was much about the same as in 1896 and amounted to £32,703. After meeting all expenses a balance of £28,861 was left, out of which the directors paid the usual 10 per cent. dividend, or 40s. per share. This left £461 to be carried forward.

NERBUDDA COAL AND IRON COMPANY.—After thirty-eight years of a chequered career, the board of this company appeal to the shareholders to provide fresh capital, and thus save the property. Last year the working led to a loss of £625, which follows upon smaller losses in the two preceding years. The old mines of the company are admitted to be worked out, and they are not considered worth carrying on after the heavy rains of this season. The company, however, has opened out a new field, and the coal obtained from there is claimed to have stood severe trials by the Great Indian Peninsula Railway Company. The latter has contracted to take 14,000 tons of the coal this year, and other customers are expected to bring up the sale to 18,000 to 20,000 tons for the year. Later on the new field is expected to yield easily 40,000 tons per annum. But in order to make the new field available considerable expenditure will have to be effected, and the board, therefore, propose to issue shortly £10,000 in preference shares. It is a miserable statement after nearly forty years of work, but we presume the best thing for the shareholders to do will be to find this fresh money and thus give the old undertaking another chance.

INDO-CHINA STEAM NAVIGATION COMPANY.—A distinct improvement is seen in the past year's working compared with 1896, the net earnings amounting to £80,575 against £28,956. Depreciation absorbs £43,362 compared with £40,260, and £3,086 has had to be provided out of revenue for loss in exchange, whereas last year there was a gain on exchange account of £3,919, which was transferred to an exchange reserve. The directors recommend a dividend of 5 per cent., leaving £1,370 to be carried forward, whereas last year there was no dividend, although £16,318 was transferred from underwriting account to profit and loss. The improvement is due to better freight rates and to the increased tonnage of the fleet.

THE PROPERTY MARKET.

The business done in the Auction Mart last week seems almost trifling, when compared with the corresponding week last year, the totals being £87,881 and £368,919 respectively. But it has to be noted that last year, in anticipation of the Jubilee, the May sales were heavy, while last week's sales were affected by the Derby and by the Whitsuntide holidays. The next few weeks will probably see a considerable difference in business, and probably by the end of June the balance against this year may be reversed. The property offered last week was also, for the most part, confined to small investments, for which, although the demand was good, the amounts received are not conducive to big totals. Yesterday week there was an excellent supply of minor properties, but only one ran into four figures. This was No. 1, Hercules-road, Holloway, with range of stabling, leasehold for fifty-four years at £9 9s. per annum ground rent, rental £142, for which Mr. T. G. Wharton secured a purchaser at £1,500. Among other lots placed by the same auctioneer were :—Nos. 3, 5, 13, 15, and 17, Hercules-road, held for the same term as No. 1, subject to ground rents amounting to £26 5s., £1,395; Nos. 31 to 34, Market-terrace, East Ham, freehold, rental £165, £2,975; and No. 87, Darenth-road, Stamford Hill, held for eighty-six and a half years, ground rent £10, £715. Messrs. Fuller, Horsey, Sons, & Cassell sold the leasehold dwelling-houses, Nos. 1 to 15 (odd), and 2 to 32 (even), Barrow-road, Streatham, held for eighty years at £176 8s. ground rent, and producing £825 per annum, for £6,725; four dwelling-houses, Nos. 28, 30, 38, and 40, Elms-road, Clapham, leasehold for eighty-two years, at a ground rent of £44, and let at rentals amounting to £217 10s. yearly, for £1,840; four leasehold dwelling-houses, Nos. 69 to 75 (odd), Brynmaer-road, Battersea, term sixty-two years, ground rent £25 18s., rental £140 10s., for £1,180; and several other lots. Messrs. Stimson & Sons, and Newbon, Edwards, & Shephard were very successful with a number of Metropolitan and suburban investments, all of their lots finding purchasers at good prices, their respective totals being £6,075 and £4,180. Altogether the proceeds of the day amounted to £43,440. Some leasehold properties offered on Friday by Mr. A. J. Sheffield sold well.

Messrs. Newbon, Edwards, & Shephard announce for to-day at the Mart the sale of an important long leasehold estate at Tottenham, comprising 115 private houses, twenty-eight houses and shops, and building land, as well as leasehold and freehold properties in Notting Hill. On Monday next Mr. Alfred Richards is to sell gas and water stocks and shares in the Aldershot Gas and Water Company, Harrow and Stanmore Gas Company, Barnet District Gas and Water Company, and the Melton Mowbray Gas Light and Coke Company.

Business after the holidays was resumed at the Mart on Wednesday, but the attendance was moderate, and a quiet tone prevailed. Neither were the properties offered of first-class importance (eight remained unsold), and the total for the day only amounted to £16,330. Some freeholds at Hounslow were disposed of by Mr. Thomas Woods at a total of £7,125, and two freehold ground rents at Earl's Court, offered by the Messrs. Woods, brought £3,775.

TRADE AND PRODUCE.

The downward tendency in wheat has now been confirmed. There was a good attendance at Mark-lane on Wednesday, and sellers held firmly to the prices of the previous Friday for some time; but no business was done, and it by-and-bye became evident that no business could be done without a fall in price, and a reduction of 1s. per quarter soon after took place. Flour fell 1s. per sack. This is but repeating what has happened in the provincial markets during the week. Farmers were very reluctant to give way, and in some cases prices were maintained; but in most instances a reduction of from 1s. to 2s. was submitted to. The tone throughout was dull, and business inactive. It is improbable that activity will be restored until there has been a further fall, though much now depends on the reports as to the coming crop. So far they have been excellent, with very few exceptions. The heavy demand for France has slackened. It is understood that it has now a sufficient supply on hand to last until the beginning of August at any rate. The amount of wheat and flour imported into France from August, 1897, to the end of April, 1898, is believed to have reached the unprecedented quantity of 6,507,000 quarters. At present there is on passage to France about 1,500,000 quarters. The shipments to Europe during the week have exceeded 1,300,000 quarters, of which some 250,000 quarters come from India. The quantities shipped from America continue large. According to *Dun's Review*, the exports from Atlantic ports have in three weeks been 7,955,586 bushels, against 4,778,742 bushels last year, and from Pacific ports 1,738,123 bushels, against 610,637 bushels at same period last year. It would seem, then, that our further supplies, at least up to the beginning of August, are pretty well assured; and the nearer we approach the harvest the more generous will the "corner" men be in disposing of their stocks. They can hope for no further increase in prices now. While the urgent demand for France has suddenly ceased, the markets at Antwerp and Hamburg have ruled very dull. The price of bread in London has come down to 6½d., but until the exhaustion of bakers' present stocks, the reduction is not likely to go further. It is improbable, however, that it will be long delayed. Millers are complaining of continued slackness. The supplies into the United Kingdom last week were: Wheat, 282,164 quarters; flour, 99,521 sacks. Less wheat but more flour was sent from America for Europe last week, so that the total breadstuffs shipped represented a falling off of 50,000 quarters. Extraordinary prices are still quoted for May wheat in America, and the July option is held at a high price considering the large crop that is expected to begin arriving during that month.

Cotton is reported firm in New York, with a good export demand, and prices firm, but at home business continues very quiet, the holidays having of course increased the dulness this week. Want of activity in the cloth market is reported from Manchester, and, though prices remain firm, an attempt to advance them at once checked business. The orders executed for India are unimportant, and there is practically no demand from Calcutta. But the tone of the home market on the whole continues firm. Nottingham reports little alteration in the lace trade, but the general demand is declared to be disappointing, and the home demand is as yet below the average.

Rather better reports reach us as to wool. At Huddersfield both manufacturers and merchants have been busy, mostly for the home trade. There is little alteration in price, but the turnover has been growing for a month past, and the clearance of best black goods was last week beyond all precedent. Mill operations are on a larger scale than at any previous period of the year. The United States trade is described as almost a blank, and American reports do not encourage any hope of improvement there. There has been some unsettled feeling in the Canadian market, but that is regarded as temporary. There is a more hopeful tone at Leeds, and rather less depression in Leicester, though there prices continue at a very low level. On the whole, however, the tendency is towards improvement.

Though the statistical position of copper continues strong, with stocks standing at only 27,800 tons against 33,700 at the same date last year, the market is still fluctuating, with the tendency rather downward. During May the price of G. M. B.'s fell 11s. 3d., while stocks declined 1,452 tons, and the total visible supplies 1,100 tons. These reductions, however, as Messrs. Lewis, Lazarus, & Co. remind us, took place during the first fortnight, and the second half of May shows an increase in both positions. There was rather an improved tone at the morning market on Wednesday, but that disappeared at the afternoon session, and there was a decline of 2s. 6d. on the day. Settlement price £51. Cash and near dates £50 17s. 6d; three months £51 1s. 3d.

Very satisfactory reports are received of the iron and steel trades, though at Wolverhampton business is said to be restricted, and makers are rather indifferent as to inquiries for the execution of expiring bargains, looking forward to paying more for pig iron. There is a healthy home demand, and export houses offer good indents. In best bars there is a steady business, and merchant and common qualities are in frequent request. Glasgow reports all departments fully employed. In Sheffield the position is highly satisfactory; so at Newcastle, Birmingham, and Barrow-in-Furness. Orders are steadily flowing in, and prices are everywhere well maintained. Yet the pig-iron market is reported quiet, and in Glasgow on Wednesday, Scotch, Cleveland, and hematite each lost 1½d. Trade, however, is in a thoroughly healthy condition, and the prospects for the future are excellent.

As to coal there is now some doubt. A tendency to a decline in prices had appeared in some quarters in view of the early termination of the Welsh strike; but after the Cardiff conference on Tuesday a settlement is not by any means so certain. In these circumstances prices are well maintained, and some large railway contracts, it is understood, will only be renewed at an advance.

The Corean Government is showing its independence in an admirable way. It has decided to open three more ports, and to make Sing Yang an open market.

The steamer *Umbria* has left New York with £82,000 in specie for London.

Diary of the War.

May 27.—Nothing new. How wearisome the iteration! Impatience in America; excited irritation in Spain. Admiral Cervera not discovered for certain, but it is "believed" he is in Santiago de Cuba. It is the only plausible inference; for had he been cruising at sea all this time he must have called somewhere for coal, and so must have been heard of. But if he be in Santiago, why so much uncertainty about the fact?

May 28.—Continued doubt as to the position of the hostile fleets. Gloom deepening in Spain as it becomes more and more evident that no help will be obtained in Europe. Another Ministerial crisis seems approaching in Madrid.

May 29.—A day of terrible rumour. Admiral Cervera had escaped from Santiago de Cuba with his ships, destroyed the American fleet, killed Admiral Sampson, and set off on a further career of destruction. The rumour came from Jamaica, but has not been confirmed, and is not likely to be confirmed. Another rumour is that Washington authorities are to send balloons to Commodore Schley to be used in finding out whether the Spanish Admira is in Santiago or not.

May 30.—The strange rumour that Admiral Cervera had escaped from Santiago de Cuba, and destroyed the American fleet, has certainly not been confirmed, nor does it seem to be believed anywhere, but it still circulates in a mysterious way in Madrid, in Washington, and New York. But the absurdest rumours gain strength when no direct news is available. The possibilities of peace are discussed by the Madrid papers, but none of them seems to see how steps can be taken by Spain in that direction. "Honour" is not yet satisfied. There is no truculence in the tone of the journals, however; they clearly wish for peace, and would welcome an intervention which might even seem to force peace upon Spain. But Spain herself cannot yet act. To do so would be to raise the spectre of revolution. Another bad reverse might, however, have the same effect.

May 31.—Nothing but rumours. Commodore Schley had seen Admiral Cervera's ships in Santiago Harbour, says one, and was determined not to allow them to escape. But telegrams are still being received from the Commodore at Cienfuegos, so that he can hardly be at Santiago as well. At Washington, says the *Times'* correspondent, there is a pronounced feeling of uncertainty about the Spanish squadron. President McKinley is anxious; and the American intelligence department can hardly be complimented on its smartness. The Madrid Ministry seem to be getting a little alarmed about the increasing exportation of silver. People are becoming somewhat timid about banknotes, and there has been a slight run on the bank for silver coins, most of which are exported. The Finance Minister has been authorised to draw up a Bill preventing this exportation. Several nonsensical rumours about negotiations for an alliance between England and the United States.

June 1.—There is even yet no certainty that Admiral Cervera and his squadron are "bottled up" at Santiago de Cuba; but apparently American war authorities are acting on the belief that the Spanish Admiral has been securely trapped. The expedition for the invasion of Cuba, it is said, will leave Tampa immediately, and may even be at the island on Saturday. General Miles is reported as having left Washington to assume the command. Another rumour—vague and suspicious-looking—is that Admiral Cervera had attempted to escape from Santiago, was at once attacked by the American fleet, and after a sharp encounter retired to the harbour again. The forts of Santiago, as well as the ships, were attacked, and the firing for a time was "very heavy." The news, however, has not been confirmed. It is said that the sailing of the Cadiz fleet has been postponed in consequence of the discovery of defects in the torpedo-boats.

June 2.—The Spaniards claim a victory. There are, however two sides to the story; and we rather think the American side the more plausible. The broad facts seem to be these. Two torpedo-boats crept out of the harbour of Santiago on Sunday night, evidently with the intention of blowing up one or two of the American warships. The boats, however, were discovered by the look out on the *Texas*, search-lights were turned upon them, and shot and shell immediately fired. Other American ships took part in the fray, and the upshot was that the torpedo boats, though coming within 500 yards of the *Texas*, ran back to harbour without launching a single torpedo. The other story is that Commodore Schley attacked the forts at Santiago on Tuesday afternoon, bombarded them for ninety minutes, did no harm, and retired rather the worse for the encounter. The probability is that Commodore Schley made a reconnaissance in force towards Santiago harbour to ascertain, if possible, the strength of the forts and ships there, and that, having satisfied his curiosity, he retired. However that may be, the engagement does not seem to have been a very big one, and there seems nothing to justify the Spanish claim to a victory. Altogether, however, the presence of Admiral Cervera and his squadron in Santiago harbour appears now to be satisfactorily established. It is presumed that the force for the invasion of Cuba is being got together at Tampa, but only routine news is allowed to escape from that camp.

Herr Jan Szczepanik, the young inventor of the telectroscope, announces another invention which, if it can do what is represented, will work a revolution in the textile industry. It is the application of photography to the production of stencil plates for the Jacquard loom. In figured textiles, at present, the designer must fill up millions of squares before the stencil plates can be punched, but by employing ruled screens on photographic glass plates, the inventor claims to be able to weave direct from the original design, with the aid of electricity.

Notes on Books.

L'Affaire Dreyfus. Le Procès Zola devant la Cour d'Assises de la Seine et la Cour de Cassation (7 février, 23 février—31 mars, 2 avril, 1898). Compte-Rendu Sténographique "in extenso" et Documents Annexes. Paris: Aux Bureaux du *Siècle*, 12, Rue de la Grange-Batelière, et P. V. Stock, Editeur, 8, 9, 10, 11, Galerie du Théâtre Français (Palais Royal).

These two volumes will possess considerable historic value dealing, as they do, with a question which is not only agitating France at the present hour from end to end, but is of great interest in every civilised country, as embodying the struggle between civil liberty, freedom of the citizen, and classes or sects bent on domination. Those, therefore, who care to go through these two volumes will find them full of dramatic interest and very lively human documents indeed. At the end of the work, and elsewhere, fac-similes are given of the memorandum on which Captain Dreyfus was condemned, and also of sundry writings of the Commandant Walsin-Esterhazy. It does not require an expert to prove that the memorandum attributed to Dreyfus is in Esterhazy's handwriting. For people who cannot go through this large work there is a little pamphlet drawn up by M. Yves Guyot, called "L'Innocent et le Traitre," which gives a brief history of the case from the beginning This is well worth reading and ought to be translated so as to be available for the general public here. M. Guyot has thrown himself into this case with a single-mindedness that we think places him on a higher pedestal than even M. Zola himself; for in order to fight for justice in this instance, he has had in great measure to sacrifice his career as an elected political leader in France. He did not become a candidate at the last election, because, as he frankly said, nowhere in France could he have found a seat as the avowed champion of the unjustly condemned Alsatian Jew, Captain Dreyfus. Not only was he obliged to stand aside for this reason, but he has had to endure all manner of base accusations hurled at his head by the faction which supports the army in its violent defiance of justice and civil freedom. He is accused of being the mouthpiece of a syndicate formed to discredit the army and so forth. But M. Guyot has stuck manfully to what he believes to be his duty, and we can only hope that the day is not distant when the principles advocated by him will triumph and he with them.

The Mining Manual for 1898. Edited by WALTER R. SKINNER.

The tenth issue of this volume appears as complete as its predecessors, and if possible more comprehensive than ever. The secretaries of companies registered abroad are now included in its pages, there is also a dictionary of mining terms, and the care with which the whole has been compiled makes it a reliable book of reference for all things appertaining to mines and mining. Mr. W. R. Skinner, in his preface, gives some interesting statistics of the returns of gold from the various mining centres, from which we may quote the following table showing the world's production for the past three years:—

	1897. Oz.	1896. Oz.	1895. Oz.
Australasia	2,924,153	2,376,132	2,365,165
South Africa	3,034,675	2,286,084	2,287,773
United States	2,946,300	2,283,445	2,273,580
Russia	1,200,000	1,150,000	1,250,000
India	389,790	321,523	250,640
Other countries	1,860,000	1,747,000	1,798,000
	12,354,918	10,164,184	10,225,158
value	£43,859,958	£36,082,653	£36,299,310

We have received a sheet containing general and comparative tables of the world's statistics, which has been compiled by Mr. Jules Ayer, and is published by Effingham Wilson at the price of 2s. net. The statistics are wonderfully complete, and must have been compiled with great labour. Owing to the method of arrangement the figures are readily available for reference and may be hung on the walls in the offices of bankers, financiers, and others interested in international statistics with great advantage, embracing as they do the areas of the various countries or states of the globe, their population, religions, military and naval power, financial position, railway and telegraphic mileage, &c.

Chili is said to be negotiating a loan of 80,000,000 marks in Germany, secured on the nitrate deposits of Iquique and Tarapaca.

Notice to Subscribers.

Complaints are continually reaching us that the INVESTORS' REVIEW cannot be obtained at this and the other railway bookstall, that it does not reach Scotch and Irish cities till Monday, and that it is not delivered in the City till Saturday morning.

We publish on Friday in time for the REVIEW to be at all Metropolitan bookstalls by at latest 4 p.m., and we believe that it is there then, having no doubt that Messrs. W. H. Smith & Son do their best, but they have such a mass of papers to handle every day that a fresh one may well look almost like a personal enemy and be kept in short supply unless the reading public shows unmistakably that it is wanted. A little perseverance, therefore, in asking for the INVESTORS' REVIEW is all that should be required to remedy this defect.

All London newsagents can be in a position to distribute the paper on Friday afternoon if they please, and here also the only remedy is for subscribers to insist upon having it as soon as published. Arrangements have been made that all our direct City subscribers shall have their copies before 4 p.m. on Friday. As for the provinces, we can only say that the paper is delivered to the forwarding agents in ample time to be in every English and Scotch town, and in Dublin and Belfast, likewise, early on Saturday morning. Those despatched by post from this office can be delivered by the first London mail on Saturday in every part of the United Kingdom.

ADVERTISEMENTS.

All Advertisements are received subject to approval, and should be sent in not later than 5 p.m. on Thursdays.

The advertisements of American Life Insurance Offices are rigorously excluded from the INVESTORS' REVIEW, and have been so since it commenced as a Quarterly Magazine in 1892.

For tariff and particulars of positions open apply to the Advertisement Manager, Norfolk House, Norfolk-street, W.C.

To Correspondents.

The EDITOR cannot undertake to return rejected communications.

Letters from correspondents must, in every case, be authenticated by the name and address of the writer.

Telegraphic Address: "Unveiling, London."

The Investors' Review.

The Week's Money Market.

BANK RATE 3 PER CENT.

The weakness of the money market made further rapid progress during the past seven days. In addition to lending money on the market, the Japanese Government bid so energetically for the India sterling bills that the whole amount went to it at the remarkably low figure of $2\frac{1}{4}$ per cent. The bills taken being for twelve months, the release of at least £2,500,000 of the Japanese funds becomes more absolute than if the course of merely lending its balances on the market for short dates had been persisted in.

With a further large sum thus to be released, and with money coming out from other sources there was naturally a swift drop down in rates for short loans to $1\frac{1}{2}$ to $1\frac{3}{4}$ per cent., as against 2 per cent. current a week ago. The India Council, too, was only able to lend small amounts each day, and its rate gradually dropped to $1\frac{5}{8}$ per cent. for loans for about three weeks. The reduction in the Bank rate yesterday to 3 per cent. hardly affected rates, but the discount houses have reduced their allowance on deposits by $\frac{1}{2}$ per cent. to $1\frac{1}{2}$ per cent. for "call" and $1\frac{3}{4}$ per cent. for "notice" money. The joint stock banks also brought down their deposit rate by $\frac{1}{2}$ per cent. to $1\frac{1}{2}$ per cent.

Large additions to floating balances in the market both from home and foreign sources have had an even more marked influence upon discount rates in the course of the week than on the rates for loans. Competition became very keen for bills, and each day saw discount quotations decline until Wednesday, when at one time three months' remitted paper was quoted a "weak" $1\frac{7}{8}$ per cent. After that, however, a steadier tone prevailed in spite of the further reduction in the Bank rate from $3\frac{1}{2}$ to 3 per cent., and rates have hardened slightly. The New York exchange has fallen back rather quickly, and the ease in money here has produced a demand for gold on Russian account, which has raised the quotation of bar gold outside to 77s. $10\frac{1}{2}$d. per ounce, and sweeps off the major part of the gold arrivals, although the Bank of England continues to offer a price above its usual price for the metal. American houses have also begun to offer bills freely again, which looks as if the weakness in discounts had reached its limit for the time. But, even allowing for these circumstances, there does not seem any prospect of the market becoming distinctly harder, save in the event of an energetic demand for gold from New York. The Continental demand for gold is seldom a pressing demand, and Japan cannot be counted on as a prominent bidder now that it has locked up so much of its funds. No strong demand, therefore, can be expected to come upon this market except from America, and with the coin and bullion at the Bank of England standing at over thirty-seven millions, and the quiet summer season approaching, it will be difficult to maintain rates short of such a demand. We on the whole look, then, for a short period of comparative quiet in the Money Market, and it will be very welcome. The violent fall in rates which has marked the past fortnight is not wholesome in any sense, or indicative of a position of real strength. Should it be followed, after a brief time, by an equally sharp upward movement, the consequences must be distressing in many directions. As far as we can form any definite opinion the next movement should be upward, for influences are already apparent adverse to a further decline in the Bank rate. But when it does come we trust the advance will neither be severe nor unduly sudden.

The £2,500,000 of India sterling bills were competed for with great vigour, the applications amounting to no less than £18,834,000. As we have said, the whole issue went to one quarter, in twelve months' bills, at 2⅛ per cent., and it is known that this quarter represented Japan. Such a rate was about ½ per cent. more favourable to the Indian Government than could have been obtained from the open market on paper of the same usance, for it demanded 2⅛ to 2¼ per cent. on three months' bills. An issue of £100,000 3½ per cents. by the City of Capetown was fairly well received, the amount being covered about two and a quarter times, tenders at £100 1s. per cent., or £1 1s. above the minimum, receiving in full. The last issue of 4 per cents. by this Corporation realised an average price of £100 1s.

This week's Bank return is weaker than last at several points. The banking reserve is down £499,000 to £26,046,000, and "other" deposits have declined as much as £1,047,000 to £42,405,000. These changes, however, are not material to the position of the market, being due in part to the outflow of currency at the end of the month. Further, the market has paid the Bank on one account or another £962,000 in reduction of the total of the "other" securities to £32,650,000. Had gold not come in from abroad to the value of £401,000, the reserve must have shrunk nearly £900,000, in which case the rate would scarcely have been lowered to 3 per cent. As it is there is nothing in these figures to encourage an expectation of prolonged cheap money.

SILVER.

The Spanish demand for the metal is becoming an important factor in the market. Not only has it cleared off a certain proportion of the floating supply, but at times it becomes most pressing for more, so that the usual market haggle has to be dispensed with. In these conditions the ordinary dealers in the metal are thus put about at times to cover operations previously entered upon, and for the last day or two in May quite a scramble ensued for the metal. The opening of the month did not see any real relaxation in the quotation, and the price of bars for immediate delivery at 27⅛d. per ounce is ⅛d. above what it was a week ago. With a special demand of this character upsetting ordinary conditions it is impossible to speak with any degree of confidence about the future. Spain will continue to buy silver while it is able, for it represents in coined pesetas nearly two and a half times its value as bullion to that needy Government. But we are afraid that its ability to turn honest, or other, pennies in this way is approaching an end, and when the inevitable *curso forzoso* comes into play, the motive to purchase silver will no longer exist. The market is now particularly hard, but no one knows when the source of the firmness may disappear, and so the forward price is no better than 26⅞d. per ounce. The India Council sold its drafts at a higher figure, and, in face of large applications, the amount offered next week is reduced to forty lacs. This reduction of 50 per cent. in a fortnight is rather rapid in view of the sixteen millions sterling to be realised this year, as, although close upon four and a half millions has been obtained in a little over two months, it is the best period of the whole year for their sales. The Bank of Bengal had reduced its minimum from 11 per cent. to 10.

BANK OF ENGLAND.

AN ACCOUNT pursuant to the Act 7 and 8 Vict., cap. 32, for the Week ending on Wednesday, June 1, 1898.

ISSUE DEPARTMENT.

	£		£
Notes Issued	51,585,970	Government Debt	11,015,100
		Other Securities	5,784,900
		Gold Coin and Bullion	34,785,970
		Silver Bullion	—
	£51,585,970		£51,585,970

BANKING DEPARTMENT.

	£		£
Proprietors' Capital	14,553,000	Government Securities	13,306,642
Rest	3,160,271	Other Securities	32,649,625
Public Deposits (including Exchequer, Savings Banks, Commissioners of National Debt, and Dividend Accounts)	11,780,209	Notes	23,806,925
Other Deposits	42,405,514	Gold and Silver Coin	2,237,343
Seven Day and other Bills	103,606		
	£72,002,600		£72,002,600

Dated June 2, 1898.

H. G. BOWEN, *Chief Cashier.*

In the following table will be found the movements compared with the previous week, and also the totals for that week and the corresponding return last year:—

Banking Department.

Last Year. June 2.		May 25, 1898.	June, 1898.	Increase.	Decrease.
£	Liabilities.	£	£	£	£
3,110,200	Rest	3,207,308	3,160,271	—	47,037
11,052,085	Pub. Deposits	12,041,738	11,780,209	—	261,529
38,700,828	Other do.	43,452,172	42,405,514	—	1,046,658
184,743	7 Day Bills	104,182	103,606	—	576
	Assets.			Decrease.	Increase.
13,911,171	Gov. Securities	13,201,192	13,306,642	—	105,450
28,443,344	Other do.	33,612,171	32,649,685	962,486	—
25,246,341	Total Reserve	26,545,037	26,046,273	498,764	—
				1,461,250	1,461,250
				Increase.	Decrease.
£		£	£	£	£
27,579,890	Note Circulation	27,446,915	27,777,045	330,130	—
50⅜ p.c.	Proportion	47⅞ p.c.	48 p.c.	—	—
2 "	Bank Rate	3½ "	3 "	—	—

Foreign Bullion movement for week £401,000 in.

LONDON BANKERS' CLEARING.

Month of	1898.	1897.	Increase.	Decrease.
	£	£	£	£
January	673,281,000	576,558,000	96,723,000	—
February	648,601,000	597,652,000	50,949,000	—
March	799,520,000	729,970,000	69,550,000	—
April	597,410,000	532,508,000	64,902,000	—
Week ending				
May 4	174,057,000	138,987,000	35,070,000	—
" 11	160,526,000	128,252,000	32,274,000	—
" 18	171,078,000	152,987,000	18,091,000	—
25	131,037,000	116,372,000	14,665,000	—
June 1	155,655,000	166,981,000	—	11,326,000
Total to date	3,422,097,000	3,073,172,000	348,925,000	—

BANK AND DISCOUNT RATES ABROAD.

	Bank Rate.	Altered.	Open Market.
Paris	2	March 14, 1895	1¾
Berlin	4	April 9, 1898	3¼
Hamburg	4	April 9, 1898	3¼
Frankfort	4	April 9, 1898	3⅛
Amsterdam	3	April 13, 1897	2½
Brussels	3	April 28, 1896	2¼
Vienna	4	January 22, 1896	3⅝
Rome	5	August 27, 1895	3
St. Petersburg	5½	January 23, 1898	5½
Madrid	5	June 17, 1896	5
Lisbon	6	January 25, 1891	6
Stockholm	5	May 18, 1898	4
Copenhagen	4	January 20, 1898	4
Calcutta	10	June 2, 1898	—
Bombay	12	May 5, 1898	—
New York call money	1 to 1½	—	—

NEW YORK ASSOCIATED BANKS (dollar at 4s.).

	May 28, 1898.	May 21, 1898.	May 14, 1898.	May 29, 1897.
	£	£	£	£
Specie	34,772,000	33,880,000	32,688,000	17,795,000
Legal tenders	10,708,000	10,312,000	10,048,000	20,308,000
Loans and discounts	117,946,000	116,306,000	114,734,000	101,502,000
Circulation	2,947,400	2,948,800	2,938,600	2,866,000
Net deposits	139,202,000	136,198,000	133,344,000	115,120,000

Legal reserve is 25 per cent. of net deposits; therefore the total reserve (specie and legal tenders) exceeds this sum by £10,739,500, against an excess last week of £10,142,500.

BANK OF FRANCE (25 francs to the £).

	June 2, 1898.	May 27, 1898.	May 20, 1898.	June 3, 1897.
	£	£	£	£
Gold in hand	74,678,480	74,790,160	74,690,280	79,520,000
Silver in hand	49,145,120	49,073,960	49,010,560	49,204,000
Bills discounted	34,400,720	32,872,000	32,306,680	*47,671,000
Advances	15,520,200	15,412,160	15,474,440	—
Note circulation	148,695,320	146,154,600	146,693,000	148,231,000
Public deposits	8,953,840	8,730,880	7,017,120	7,337,000
Private deposits	21,302,880	21,047,240	21,041,280	[illegible]

Proportion between bullion and circulation 83·27 per cent. against 84⅜ per cent. a week ago.

* Includes advances

FOREIGN RATES OF EXCHANGE ON LONDON.

Place.	Usance.	Last week's.	Latest.	Place.	Usance.	Last week's.	Latest.
Paris	chqs.	25·29	25·28	Italy	sight	27·17	27·19
Brussels	chqs.	25·33	25·31½	Do. gold prem.	..	107·37½	107·40
Amsterdam	short	12·08½	12·08	Constantinople	3 mths	109·20	109·12½
Berlin	short	20·46	20·44	B. Ayres gd. pm.	..	163·70	163·20
Do.	3 mths	20·32½	20·33	Rio de Janeiro	90 dys	6½d.	7¼d.
Hamburg	3 mths	20·32½	20·33	Valparaiso	90 dys	17⅛d.	17¾d.
Frankfort	short	20·46	20·44	Calcutta	T. T.	1/3$\frac{15}{16}$	1/4
Vienna	short	12·05	12·04½	Bombay	T. T.	1/3$\frac{15}{16}$	1/4$\frac{1}{32}$
St. Petersburg	3 mths	93·70	93·80	Hong Kong	T. T.	1/10¼	1/10⅛
New York	60 dys	4·84½	4·83¾	Shanghai	T. T.	2/5⅞	2/6
Lisbon	sight	28⅜d.	28$\frac{1}{16}$d.	Singapore	T. T.	1/10⅝	1/10$\frac{11}{16}$
Madrid	sight	46·08	46·25				

NATIONAL BANK OF BELGIUM (25 francs to the £).

	May 26, 1898.	May 19, 1898.	May 12, 1898.	May 27, 1897.
	£	£	£	£
Coin and bullion	4,207,440	4,290,400	4,240,160	4,067,000
Other securities	16,397,800	16,267,400	16,417,160	16,151,000
Note circulation	19,407,800	19,332,080	19,545,960	18,684,000
Deposits	2,590,040	2,550,400	2,476,560	2,843,000

BANK OF SPAIN (25 pesetas to the £).

	May 28, 1898.	May 21, 1898.	May 14, 1898.	May 29, 1897.
	£	£	£	£
Gold	9,833,520	9,833,520	9,833,520	8,667,000
Silver	4,333,800	4,604,880	4,876,440	10,257,360
Bills discounted	31,047,000	30,132,960	30,537,400	9,385,880
Advances and loans	4,245,800	4,831,320	4,293,120	9,520,280
Notes in circulation	52,906,720	52,373,240	52,718,000	43,804,720
Treasury advances, coupon account	493,400	467,800	409,240	527,240
Treasury balances	824,120	676,440	359,240	928,080

LONDON COURSE OF EXCHANGE.

Place.	Usance.	May 19.	May 24.	May 26.	June 2.
Amsterdam and Rotterdam	short	12·2½	12·2¼	12·2	12·2
Do. do.	3 months	12·4⅜	12·4	12·3⅞	12·3⅞
Antwerp and Brussels	3 months	25·58¾	25·53¾	25·51¼	25·50
Hamburg	3 months	20·69	20·67	20·66	20·64
Berlin and German B. Places	3 months	20·69	20·67	20·66	20·64
Paris	cheques	25·36¼	25·32½	25·31¼	25·30
Do.	3 months	25·50	25·46¼	25·45	25·43¾
Marseilles	3 months	25·51¼	25·47½	25·45	25·43¾
Switzerland	3 months	25·71¼	25·67½	25·65	25·62½
Austria	3 months	12·25	12·20	12·20	12·20
St. Petersburg	3 months	24$\frac{11}{16}$	24$\frac{11}{16}$	24$\frac{11}{16}$	24$\frac{11}{16}$
Moscow	3 months	24⅝	24⅝	24⅝	24⅝
Italian Bank Places	3 months	27·67½	27·50	27·45	27·50
New York	60 days	48½	48¾	48¾	48¾
Madrid and Spanish B. P.	3 months	24½ nom.	25¼	25½	25½
Lisbon	3 months	28½	28	28⅛	28⅜
Oporto	3 months	28½	28	28½	28⅜
Copenhagen	3 months	18·45	18·46	18·44	18·42
Christiania	3 months	18·45	18·47	18·44	18·43
Stockholm	3 months	18·45	18·47	18·46	18·45

OPEN MARKET DISCOUNT.

	Per cent.
Thirty and sixty day remitted bills	1$\frac{13}{16}$—1⅞
Three months "	1⅞—2
Four months "	2—2⅛
Six months "	2—2⅛
Three months fine inland bills	2¼—2⅜
Four months "	2¼—2⅜
Six months "	2½—3

BANK AND DEPOSIT RATES.

	Per cent.
Bank of England minimum discount rate	3
" " short loan rates	—
Banker's rate on deposits	1½
Bill brokers' deposit rate (call)	1½
" 7 and 14 days' notice	1¾
Current rates for 7 day loans	1½—1¾
" " for call loans	1½

Stock Market Notes and Comments.

As we write, business has hardly been resumed on the Stock Exchange. It is not likely to become active, either, until the public mind has overcome what may be called the "Chamberlain funk." As far as we can judge that still dominates, at all events, the speculative class of individual, and it is all the more powerful because nobody can in the least guess why there should be such a ferment among politicians as Mr. Chamberlain's wild words led us to think existed. The French difficulty in West Africa, which was at first blamed for the disturbance of the Colonial Secretary's peace of mind, is in a fair way to disappear and there does not seem to be any new trouble going on between us and our neighbour across the Channel. Neither have we any immediate or acute difference with Russia, except the one Mr. Chamberlain's words caused, and that has, the newspapers say, been conjured away by the explanations and apologies of the Prime Minister, who as usual has to act the peacemaker. No alliance between us and the United States for the purpose of annexing those parts of the world still unclaimed by other Powers, or for other objects, has been talked about, and it is unlikely that we can be drawn into any conflict over disputes amongst the members of the Triple Alliance. We have not heard yet of any plot to annex Spain, nor is Austria in a condition to reassert her sway over any part of disunited Italy. Guess as we may, it is impossible to discover a reason for the extraordinary outbursts politicians, headed by Mr. Chamberlain, every other day treat the nation to. But, as we have said, the vague and the indefinite increase the popular apprehension, and at the present time there is no man sworn at on the Stock Exchange more often or more vigorously than the Secretary of State for the Colonies. He is, in fact, blamed more than he deserves, because even had he held his tongue, we cannot see where active business was to come from.

At all points markets are beset by a prospect of a troubled future. There is no motive for buying any foreign security, not even Brazilian bonds, under the proposed scheme for paying old debts with new. It is, on the contrary, probable enough that the financial difficulties of more than one State will bear with increasing severity upon the resources of the bourses during the remainder of this year, and in the collapse of Spain or Italy the entire structure of international State credit may be put to a severe strain. Home securities, again, still appear to us, and no doubt to most people who can look at the subject with a calm mind, too high in price. The position of our foreign commerce does not warrant us in looking for a recovery in the prices of Home railway stocks to the level of 1896, and when we take into account the effect of dearer bread upon the spending capacity of the masses of the people it seems probable that passenger receipts will suffer this year, or at any rate give no compensation for the decline in goods receipts. Despite cheaper money, then, the probability is that no solid advance can be looked for this summer in the prices of the ordinary stocks of our Home railways, and these form by far the largest interest which our stock markets deal in.

Considerable activity continues to be displayed in the market for United States railroad shares and speculative bonds, but it is the activity produced by the "bull" and the "bear." Perhaps some of the bonds tossed about between London and New York, or New York and Amsterdam, may be worth purchasing as speculative investments just now, such as the so-called prior lien bonds of the Northern Pacific or Erie Companies, the two issues of the Missouri Company, Union Pacific 4 per cents., or Southern 5 per cents. Yet, although the prospects of these and similar issues may be fair, at present there are none of them so cheap as to admit of large operations for the rise in them. And as for the shares, they have mostly reached points which we should not consider representative of their permanent value. Doubtless, the state of war in which the United States now find themselves gives a great impulse to many kinds of traffic, and will benefit the railways accordingly, but there can be no greater mistake than to look upon these transitory gains as permanent. The prudent speculator will be more inclined to count upon a reaction when the war is over, when the special traffic ends and the country is obliged to economise in order to make up the large deficit created by the strife.

It is not necessary to continue this weekly survey further, for we have always to harp on the same string. Not even in the miscellaneous market is there any appreciable scope for an advance in prices, although speculation does linger in some corners of this department and manages to get considerable excitement out of such creations as Welsbach stock and Russian Oil shares. In a general way, however, we cannot honestly say that we see reason for an advance in the prices of good securities of the miscellaneous class any more than the others, and as for those not good, or indifferently good, the probability is that as the autumn approaches they will see lower prices than now prevail.

The truth of the matter is that our great accumulation of banking capital is preying upon itself, and sadly requires a new outlet. It is not profitable, and cannot in the long run benefit anybody, to employ this capital in raising the price of existing securities higher and higher without reference to the intrinsic qualities, or future developments affecting the intrinsic qualities, of these securities. The end of this kind of business must be very heavy losses, which would at once begin to disclose themselves were a genuine outlet found on a large scale for our waste capital in new directions. If we come to open up China, for instance, with our capital and business knowledge and skill in conducting great enterprises, and to draw away millions of money in that direction, the effect must be to lower prices all round on the Stock Exchange, because part of the means now employed in sustaining them will be drawn off for use elsewhere. The mischief of all large recent financial operations in which we have been engaged lies in the fact that they have not tended to withdraw capital from us for investment abroad. Our Colonial loans, our Indian loans, and some, at any rate, of our advances to countries like Chili and Japan, have mostly remained here to meet bills falling due for goods bought or interest on previous debts, and thus such concentrations and "fixings" of capital have had the effect of stimulating our markets by putting more means into bankers' hands to be used for forcing up prices. The new loans, &c., subscribed have not had the effect of denuding the market and sending prices down.

Should, however, a really large outlet be found for our capital abroad, and should it begin to be drafted away in large amounts for use out of the country, the whole aspect of our stock markets would at once be changed, and not even the steady influx of new gold from the mines could be trusted to be sufficient to sustain prices on the Stock Exchange, and at the same time to cover the demands made upon us by our fresh commitments abroad. There may be no immediate probability of such a new development as this, and it certainly does not enter into the thoughts of the ordinary dealer in securities; still, we must weigh all chances in estimating the future, and it is by no means improbable that a change in the direction indicated will occur in one form or another before many months have passed by. If we merely send gold to India, as the Simla Government desires, the effect we speak of will be produced in a moderate degree, and our market is so sensitive that the mere anticipation of such an export of gold materially assisted in depressing prices during the months of April and May. Whatever lies ahead, business in stocks and shares cannot, it seems to us, be genuinely large and good with prices at their present height. Dear money has not lasted long enough, nor brought markets down far enough, to encourage the general public to renew its "dabbling" habits, nor yet to invest with liberality.

The Week's Stock Markets.

Holidays have monopolised most of the time and attention of members, and they have been spread over nearly the whole of the week; consequently the volume of fresh business has been extremely small. The general tone continues good owing to the ease of money, the market for United States railroad shares being the only really active one, but a moderate improvement in the whole list of investment stocks is noticeable. Indian railway and Home railway premier stocks have been most in favour, but Colonial Government issues, and the leading Home corporation and county stocks have also been marked up steadily. Consols have more than recovered the dividend just deducted, and the "carry over" disclosed a reduction in the "bear" account, the rate being no more than 2 per cent.

Highest and Lowest this Year.	Last Carrying over Price.	BRITISH FUNDS, &c.	Closing Price.	Rise or Fall.
113⅛ 109¼	—	Consols 2¾ p.c. (Money)...	111 7/16 xd	+ ⅜
113 5/16 109½	111⅞	Do. Account (July 1)	111 9/16 xd	+ ½
106¼ 101	105	2½ p.c. Stock red. 1905 ...	104⅝xd	+ ½
363 341	—	Bank of England Stock...	350	+2½
117 111⅜	114	India 3½ p.c. Stk. red. 1931	114¼xd	+1¼
109¼ 103⅝	107	Do. 3 p.c. Stk. red. 1948	107½xd	+1½
96⅞ 90	93	Do. 2½ p.c. Stk. red. 1926	92¼xd	+1⅛

The finer weather prevailing towards the close of last week was responsible for the moderate rise in Home railway stocks, and the returns containing the first part of the Whitsuntide traffic were on the whole satisfactory, the greatest disappointments being the Brighton, South-Eastern, and North-Western Companies figures, all of which show a falling off compared with the week before the holiday last year. Changes in the list are unimportant, Great Western showing a further decline, the new stock now being called only 4¾ premium, and Metropolitan ordinary also fell rather sharply and only partially recovered. Metropolitan District ordinary has again met with support, the supply of stock showing a further shrinkage.

Highest and Lowest this Year.	Last Carrying over Price.	HOME RAILWAYS.	Closing Price.	Rise or Fall.
186 172½	176	Brighton Def.	176¾	—
59¼ 54⅛	56¾	Caledonian Def.	57⅛	+ ⅛
20⅞ 18¼	19¼	Chatham Ordinary	19⅞	—
77¼ 62	66	Great Central Pref.	66½	+ ¼
24⅜ 21¼	22⅜	Do. Def.	22¼	− ⅛
124½ 118	120	Great Eastern	120⅛	—
61½ 50¾	54¼	Great Northern Def.	55	+ ½
179⅞ 163⅜	166½	Great Western	164⅛	− ⅜
51¼ 45¼	50¼	Hull and Barnsley.........	51½	+ ½
149¼ 145	146	Lanc. and Yorkshire......	146	—
136⅛ 127¼	132½	Metropolitan	131½	−1½
31 26¾	27¼	Metropolitan District......	29¼	+ ¾
88¾ 82⅞	84½	Midland Pref.	85¾	+ ⅝
95⅝ 84½	87¾	Do. Def.	88⅜	+ ⅝
93¼ 86¾	89⅝	North British Pref.	89½	− ¼
47½ 41¾	43⅝	Do. Def.	44⅝	+ ⅜
181½ 172¾	174½	North Eastern...............	175¼	+ ½
205½ 196¼	197¾	North Western	198½	+ ⅝
117⅛ 105½	111	South Eastern Def.	112	+ ¼
98¾ 87	92½	South Western Def.	94	+ ½

The market for United States railroad shares, although the most active one in the Stock Exchange just now, is still not much troubled with outside business, although the demand for bonds is said to be keener now than for a long time past, both on Continental and New York account. There has accordingly been a steady rise day by day in this class of security, but the absence of any definite news as to what is really going on in Cuban waters continues to prevent any very great increase in speculative business. The principal support has again been given to Milwaukee shares, which mark a further substantial gain, and Union Pacific, Louisville and Nashville, and Northern Pacific preferred are all considerably higher. Last week's eastbound traffic from Chicago amounted to 102,000 tons, while for the corresponding period of last year the tonnage carried amounted to only 49,000 tons. Grand Trunk stocks have been the most conspicuous feature of the week, and the present prices are the highest of the year. The April working statement came out better than even the most sanguine estimates, and the preferences advanced by leaps and bounds, while the prior charge and debenture stocks have also risen considerably. Canadian Pacific shares have not been quite so active, but still mark an advance, the revenue statement for April being about what the market had expected, and the news that the company has obtained control of the Minneapolis and St. Louis road was considered to be a favourable point, as it is expected to prove a valuable extension.

Highest and Lowest this Year.		Last Carrying over Price.	CANADIAN AND U.S. RAILWAYS.	Closing Prices.	Rise or Fall.
14 5/16	10⅞	12¾	Atchison Shares	13⅛	+ ¼
34	23½	32	Do. Pref.	33¾	+1
15⅝	11	13	Central Pacific...............	14¾	+ ⅞
105	85½	100¾	Chic. Mil. & St. Paul......	104⅛	+2½
14¼	10	11⅞	Denver Shares	12⅛	+ ⅜
54⅛	41½	48	Do. Prefd.	49	+1⅝
16⅝	11¼	13	Erie Shares	13¾	+ ⅞
44⅞	29½	36	Do. Prefd.	37⅝	+ ⅝
110½	99	106	Illinois Central	108¾	+1
62½	45¼	55½	Louisville & Nashville ...	58⅛	+1⅝
14½	9 1/16	11½	Missouri & Texas	11⅞	+ ⅜
122¾	108½	118	New York Central	120¼	+ ½
57¼	42⅞	52¼	Norfolk & West. Prefd....	54⅛	+1¾
70¼	59	67¼	Northern Pacific Prefd....	70	+2⅛
19½	13⅝	15½	Ontario Shares	15⅞	+ ⅜
62½	56¼	59	Pennsylvania	60	+ ½
12½	7 1/16	9	Reading Shares	9¾	+ ½
34¼	24½	30¼	Southern Prefd.	32¼	+1½
37⅛	18⅛	23¾	Union Pacific	25⅛	+1⅜
20⅝	14⅝	20	Wabash Prefd.	20⅛	—
30⅛	21	28¼	Do. Income Debs....	29⅜	+ ⅜
92⅞	74	86⅛	Canadian Pacific............	87⅛	+ ⅜
79½	69¼	76¼	Grand Trunk Guar.	78⅜	+ ⅝
76¼	57⅛	70¼	Do. 1st Pref.	75⅜	+2⅜
57½	37¼	51¼	Do. 2nd Pref.	56⅜	+3½
26¼	19¼	24¼	Do. 3rd Pref.	25⅛	+1
105¾	101½	103	Do. 4 p.c. Deb.	104½	+ ½

All the Continental bourses were favourably affected by the reduction in the Bank rate here last week, and the firmer tone has lasted. The remarks made by the French President on Sunday, when he declared that France was resolved to observe the strictest neutrality with regard to the war between America and Spain, still further helped the upward movement. Italian Rente has been one of the weak spots in the foreign market, the difficulties in the Cabinet, which at one time threatened to assume serious proportions, sending down the price rather sharply, but a moderate reaction followed when the syndicate which has lately been supporting the market was again seen to be a buyer. Spanish 4 per cents. have not fluctuated much, or received much attention, but the price, which had been dwindling away, recovered quickly when Paris operators began buying, their action following the announcement of the prohibition of silver exports from Spain, and the news that the new loan is now thought to be practically arranged for. The settlement on the Paris Bourse, which commenced on Wednesday, was easily arranged, money being very abundant and rates again much lower. This encouraged speculators, and prices were sent over higher, about the only exception being Turkish groups, which declined on Vienna sales, from which quarter

Highest and Lowest this Year.		Last Carrying over Price.	FOREIGN BONDS.	Closing Price.	Rise or Fall.
94½	84	89	Argentine 5 p.c. 1886......	90¾	+1
92⅝	81⅝	87½	Do. 6 p.c. Funding	89¾	+ ½
70¾	64	69½	Do. 5 p.c. B. Ay. Water	72½	+1½
61⅝	41⅛	51½	Brazilian 4 p.c. 1889	52⅝	+1
69⅝	46	58⅛	Do. 5 p.c. 1895	59½	+1½
65	42¾	54	Do. 5 p.c. West Minas Ry..................	56	+1½
108¾	105½	107½	Egyptian 4 p.c. Unified...	107½	+ ¼
104¾	100½	102	Do. 3½ p.c. Pref. ...	102½	+ ¼
103	99½	101½	French 3 p.c. Rente	101½	—
44⅞	34⅛	42½	Greek 4 p.c. Monopoly...	42½	—
93 9/16	88¾	91	Italian 5 p.c. Rente	91½	—
100	87½	96	Mexican 6 p.c. 1888	97	—
20⅝	16	17¾	Portuguese 1 p.c.	18½	+ ½
62⅞	29⅝	34	Spanish 4 p.c.	34¼	− ¼
43⅛	40	44	Turkish 1 p.c. "B"	44⅛	—
26 1/16	22¾	24⅜	Do. 1 p.c. "C"	24¾	− 1/16
22 1/16	20	21½	Do. 1 p.c. "D"	21 1/16	− 1/16
46⅞	40	44½	Uruguay 3½ p.c. Bonds...	45½	—

a report of troubles in Servia emanated. Greek bonds, Chinese 1895 and 1896, and Hungarian 4 per cents. have been inquired for, but other inter-bourse stocks are unaltered and hardly mentioned. Some profit taking after the recent rapid rise in Brazilian bonds caused a temporary set-back, but it was short-lived, and the Rio exchange, again moving up, helped in the recovery which followed the announcement made on Wednesday that the proposals for paying the coupons of the debt for three years in 5 per cent. funding bonds have been accepted. Argentine Government and the various Cedulas advanced steadily and close nearly at the best, the resumption of full dividend payments at a comparatively early date being no doubt one of the inducements held out to attract investors, already partly influenced by the improvement shown in the revenue returns of the Republic due to the big rise in the price of wheat. Chilian bonds moved up in sympathy, but Uruguay 3½ per cents. were inclined to weaken.

Highest and Lowest this Year.		Last Carrying over Price.	FOREIGN RAILWAYS.	Closing Price.	Rise or Fall.
103	99	101	Argentine Gt. West. 5 p.c. Pref. Stock.................	103	+2
158½	134	140	B. Ay. Gt. Southern Ord..	142	+1
78½	65	73½	B. Ay. and Rosario Ord...	74	—
12¼	10¼	10¾	B. Ay. Western Ord.	11	+ ¼
87¼	73	79	Central Argentine Ord....	82	+1½
92	76	78	Cordoba and Rosario 6 p.c. Deb.	80	—
95½	85½	89½	Cord. Cent. 4 p.c. Deb. (Cent. Nth. Sec.)	90	—
61½	42	54½	Do. Income Deb. Stk. ...	56	+ ½
25¼	16½	18¾	Mexican Ord. Stk.	20	+ ¼
83½	69½	72½	Do. 8 p.c. 1st Pref.	73½	—

Argentine railway stocks advanced steadily in sympathy with the rise in Government bonds, and the good traffics which are again published stimulated buyers. Other South American companies' emissions have also been well supported, and business in this market has been quite brisk. The old Mexican Company's stocks were not much affected, either by the good traffic return or the rise in the price of silver.

In the Miscellaneous market a good deal of time has been absorbed in arranging the Lipton and English Sewing Cotton special settlements, which were very heavy. The rate on Lipton was 2d. to 3d., and that on "Cottons" 3d., both for the end of June. There was a decline in the price of the latter company's shares, owing to the heavy contango and the disclosing of a weak "bull" account. Welsbach ordinary has come into favour again; Coats' ordinary has met with a good deal of support from Glasgow operators, and Anglo-American and one or two other telegraph companies' issues mark rises, Commercial Cable stock rising 5. A slight scare was administered to holders of Russian and Schibaieff Petroleum shares by the publication of statements questioning the validity of the titles of the various petroleum companies working the Russian oil fields, but the reassuring reports which promptly followed prevented anything very serious happening. One or two other movements of importance are noticeable, Dunlop debentures falling 5 (to 65), New River stock 5, and Savoy Hotel ordinary and preference ½ to 1, but on the other hand Guinness has risen 10, Allsopp preferred ordinary 2, and the preference 3, and several other brewery debentures 1, while Harvey Steel ordinary and Fairfield Shipbuilding preference have also advanced.

Markets closed with a slightly irregular tendency. Foreign Government stocks were well supported, all the Continental bourses sending over higher quotations, and Brazilian bonds were strong on the fresh rise in the Rio exchange. Spanish 4 per cents. closed almost without change on the week, and Italian Rente finally recovered the whole of the earlier loss. United States railroad shares presented a ragged appearance at the last, but the bond list shows an unbroken string of rises, the steady inquiry for all the leading descriptions being the feature. Foreign railway stocks closed dull, and Grand Trunk issues also suffered a little and closed below the best. Among Home railways, Midland and Hull and Barnsley left off firm, but Metropolitan ordinary was a weak market.

Mining and Finance Companies.

The South African market has presented a deserted appearance, and prices have been left to take care of themselves. Changes are therefore trivial. In West Australian ventures Golden Horse Shoe is the feature, the news of the striking of a rich lode bringing in several buyers, and South Kalgurli and Hainault also show a rise on the week, Adelaide again sending over a few buying orders. Among copper-producing concerns Mount Lyell shares rose sharply, the dividend being up to expectations, and the news of the starting of another furnace more than counterbalanced the effect produced by the announcement of a new issue of capital. Indian shares keep very firm, especially Mysore.

ONTARIO'S GOLD RESOURCES.

The province of Ontario is making progress in the production of gold. In other minerals, if we except nickel and copper, it did nothing remarkable last year, and its gold total will not bear comparison with that of British Columbia. But at least it shows a really considerable percentage increase, and the progress made in the five or six years during which the province has been engaged in this branch of mining activity has been relatively rapid. The output in 1897 amounted to 11,412 oz., which compares with 7,154 oz. in the preceding twelve months, 3,038 oz. in 1895, 2,022 oz. in 1894, and 1,695 oz. in 1893—in all 25,321 oz. for the five years. But perhaps the most striking feature of the position is not the present aggregate, but the outlook for the immediate future. It is only within the past three years or so that the authorities have made any systematic study of the auriferous rocks of the province, and it is only now that prospectors, encouraged by the discoveries and conjectures of Dr. Coleman, are beginning to take up claims in the districts more particularly associated with gold—the Upper Seive, Shoal Lake, Manitou, and Lake of the Woods regions. Last year 1,255 locations, representing 115,800 acres, were sold or leased, compared with 1,026 locations of 93,821 acres, for the five previous years; while the new companies formed, nearly every single one for gold mining purposes, numbered 140, with an authorised capital of 101,531,000 dollars, compared with 146 companies with 62,529,000 dollars during the preceding nine years.

NEXT WEEK'S MEETINGS.

MONDAY, JUNE 6.

Arizona Copper	Edinburgh, 12.30 p.m.
City of London Real Property ...	110, Cannon-street, 1 p.m.
Clogher Valley Railway	Aughnacloy, 12.30 p.m.
J. Lyons & Co.	Trocadero Restaurant, noon.
Quebec Central Railway	5, Gt. Winchester-street, noon.
Warner Estate	Norfolk-Street, Strand, 3 p.m.

TUESDAY, JUNE 7.

Bengal and North Western Railway	Winchester House, noon.
Leibig's Extract of Meat	Cannon-street Hotel, 2 p.m.
London Scottish American Trust ...	Cannon-street Hotel, noon.
Norwich Union Fire	Norwich, noon.
Royal Bank of Scotland	Edinburgh, 2 p.m.
Russian Petroleum	Winchester House, noon.
Suez Canal	Paris.

WEDNESDAY, JUNE 8.

Backus and Johnston's Brewery ...	Winchester House, 2 p.m.
Brazilian Submarine Telegraph ...	Winchester House, noon.
Grand Junction Waterworks ...	21, Surrey-street, W.C., 2 p.m.
Madras Railway	61, New Broad-street, 1 p.m.
Milner's Safe	Winchester house, 2 p.m.
Nerbudda Iron and Coal	Gresham House, noon.
South Australian Company	54-5, London Wall, noon.
Southern Mahratta Railway ...	44, Finsbury Circus, noon.
Southern Punjab Railway	Cannon-street Hotel, 1 p.m.
Sun Insurance...	63, Threadneedle-street, 2 p.m.

THURSDAY, JUNE 9.

Indo-China Steam Navigation ...	29, Cornhill, 2 p.m.
Torquay Hotel	Torquay, 3 p.m.
Victory Gold Mining...	Winchester House, 2 p.m.

FRIDAY, JUNE 10.

Bombay, Baroda, and Central India Railway	Cannon-street Hotel, 1 p.m.
Dumont Coffee	Winchester House, 11.30 a.m.
Northern Assurance	Aberdeen, noon.
Streeter & Co....	18, New Bond-street, 3 p.m.

A. J. WHITE, LIMITED (MOTHER SIEGEL'S SYRUP) made a net profit of £88,988 in the first year of its existence, ended March 31 last. This pays preference dividend, gives 10 per cent. on the ordinary shares, and allows £11,773 to be carried forward after £5,000 has been set aside to be invested in first-class securities as the nucleus of a reserve fund. The directors state that they have decided to waive their right to 25 per cent. of the profits after 10 per cent. has been distributed on the ordinary shares, in order to assist in the establishment of the reserve fund. This is a very commendable decision. Nothing in the balance-sheet calls for observation, but we think the profit and loss account might be a little more detailed.

Answers to Correspondents.

Questions about public securities, and on all points in company law, as well as on the position of life insurance offices and their promises, will be answered week by week, in the REVIEW, on the following terms and conditions:—

A fee of FIVE shillings must be remitted for each question put, provided they are questions about separate securities. Should a private letter be required, then an extra fee of FIVE shillings must be sent to cover the cost of such letter, the fee then being TEN shillings for one query only, and FIVE shillings for every subsequent one in the same letter. While making this concession the EDITOR will feel obliged if private replies are as much as possible dispensed with. It is wholly impossible to answer letters sent merely "with a stamped envelope enclosed for reply."

Correspondents will further greatly oblige by so framing their questions as to obviate the necessity to name securities in the replies. They should *number* the questions, keeping a copy for reference, thus:—"(1) Please inform me about the present position of the Rowenzori Development Co. (2) Is a dividend likely to be paid soon on the capital stock of the Congo-Sudan Railway?

Answers to be given to all such questions by simply quoting the numbers 1, 2, 3, and so on. The EDITOR has a rooted objection to such forms of reply as—"I think your Timbuctoo Consols will go up," or "Sell your Slowcoach and Draggem Bonds," because this kind of thing is open to all sorts of abuses. By the plan suggested, and by using a fancy name to be replied to, each query can be kept absolutely private to the inquirer, and no scope whatever be given to market manipulations. Avoid, as names to be replied to, common words, like "investor," "inquirer," and so on, as also "bear" or "bull." Detached syllables of the inquirer's name, or initials reversed, will frequently do as well as anything, so long as the answer can be identified by the inquirer.

The EDITOR further respectfully requests that merely speculative questions should as far as possible be avoided. He by no means sets himself up as a market prophet, and can only undertake to provide the latest information regarding the securities asked about. This he will do faithfully and without bias.

Replies cannot be guaranteed in the same week if the letters demanding them reach the office of the INVESTORS' REVIEW, Norfolk House, Norfolk-street, W.C., later than the first post on Wednesday mornings.

W. D.—(*g*) Apply for return of application money at once. Capital impertinently large, no chance of success. (*a*) There is little hope for this concern, sell if you can. (*b*) (*c*) Both mere counters, sell if any opportunity offers. (*d*) So far the Company has been a miserable failure; if you can send me a copy of the report of investigation committee appointed last year, I will look into it. (*e*) Sell. I have no faith in this concern. (*f*) I am afraid you will find it difficult to get rid of these shares, but you should try. The Company's prospects are not brilliant.

SECURITY.—They are a very fair bond, though certainly not equal to a home security of a similar nature. If your powers permit, I see no reasonable objection to a purchase.

MINING RETURNS.

BAYLEY'S UNITED.—Cyanide plant treated 887 tons tailings yielding 802 oz. gold.

NEW BULTFONTEIN.—The production of diamonds for three weeks and two days, ended May 21, amounted to 5,900 carats, or an average of 30½ carats per 100 loads.

VICTORIA AND QUEEN.—Crushed 550 tons for 943 oz.

ALASKA TREADWELL GOLD.—Return for April:—Bullion shipment, $42,389; ore milled, 22,266 tons; sulphurets treated, 314 tons; of bullion there came from sulphurets $11,968.

BRILLIANT BLOCK.—Have crushed during six weeks 1,932 tons of quartz for a yield of 1,531 oz.

BROKEN HILL PROPRIETARY reports that 23,472 tons of ore were treated for the four weeks ended May 26, 1898, including product from ores purchased, and that the output from the refinery was 1,095 oz. gold (estimated), 461,682 oz. silver, 2,606 tons of lead, and 53 tons antimonial lead (estimated), the copper matte containing 26 tons of copper (estimated) and 26,245 oz. silver (estimated).

EAST MURCHISON UNITED.—Great Eastern.—Clean up May 17, 1,620 tons of ore crushed, 1,100 oz. of gold obtained. Donegal Leases.—390 tons of ore crushed, 356 oz. of gold obtained.

OTTOS KOPJE DIAMOND.—6,818 loads washed during week ended May 26; 152 carats won.

HAURAKI.—Crushed 150 tons producing 403 oz.

ALADDIN'S LAMP.—510 tons of ore crushed, yielding 472 oz., and one ton of special ore has been shipped containing 68 oz.

DAY DAWN BLOCK AND WYNDHAM.—Result of crushing for the fortnight ended May 28:—Tons crushed, 1,500; yield of gold, 1,533 oz., including tailings.

EAGLEHAWK CONSOLIDATED.—General clean up yielded for the last fortnight 189 oz.

FRANK SMITH DIAMOND MINES.—3,700 loads washed, producing 177 carats.

MELBOURNE DEMOCRAT.—Crushed 330 tons of ore, producing 127 oz. of gold.

NEW AUSTRALIAN BROKEN HILL CONSOLS.—Fortnight's output:—Three tons, containing 6,600 oz. of silver.

MENZIES MINING AND EXPLORATION.—During month of March and following month, 284 tons crushed, 193 oz. Month of May, 100 tons crushed, 169 oz. Since when 30 tons crushed. Treated by cyanide 180 tons, 50 oz.

BRITANNIA (MOUNT MALCOLM DISTRICT).—Crushed 580 tons, yielding 734 oz.

BRILLIANT.—2,250 tons of stone has been crushed for a yield of 2,300 oz. of gold.

BONNIE DUNDEE.—Crushed 109 tons of quartz for 100 oz. of gold.

DAY DAWN P. C.—For fortnight ended May 28:—Crushing No. 3 shaft 430 tons, 824 oz.

GREAT EASTERN COLLIERIES.—Last month's output, 14,700.

HIGHLAND CHIEF.—For the last fortnight crushed 140 tons for a yield of 49 oz.

KOFFYFONTEIN.—Returns for May, 3,550 carats.

LONDONDERRY.—Crushed 450 tons for a yield of 675 oz.

MOUNT USHER.—Fifty-two tons ore crushed, 55 oz. gold.

MYALLS UNITED.—Crushed 1,600 tons of ore for a yield over the plates of 307 oz. bullion; with 2½ dwt. per ton in the tailings; by the cyanide process 1,700 tons tailings were treated for a yield of 264 oz. of bullion.

CENTRAL BOULDER.—Number of tons milled 370, total yield 487 ounces.

NORSEMAN GOLD MINES.—Return for month of May, 1,015 oz. from 715 tons crushed. Expenses £1,650, profit £1,950.

Prices of Mine and Mining Finance Companies' Shares.

Shares £1 each, except where otherwise stated.

Australian.

Making-Up Price, May 23.	Name	Closing Price.	Rise or Fall.	Making-Up Price, May 23.	Name	Closing Price.	Rise or Fall.
1½	Aladdin	1½	+ 1/16	15/16	Hannan's Star	⅞	
3⅜	Associated	3 3/16	− 1/16	5⅝	Ivanhoe, New	6 5/16	+ 1/16
6/	Do. Southern	5/16	+ 1/16	⅜	Kalgurli Mt. & Iron King, 18/	⅜	
1 1/16	Brownhill Extended	1	− 1/16	5 3/16	Kalgurli	5 5/16	+ ⅛
1½	Burbank's Birthday	1½		2¼	Lady Shenton	2¼	− 1/16
5/16	Central Boulder	¼	− 1/16	8 15/16	Lake View Cons.	9 1/16	+ ⅛
4/6	Chaffers, 4/	5/6	+ /3	¼	Do. Extended	¼	
13/16	Colonial Finance, 15/	¾	+ ¼	13/16	Do. South	13/16	− 1/16
	Crœsus S. United	½		1½	London & Globe Finance	25/6	+ /6
⅜	E. Murchison	⅜		¾	London & W. A. Exploration	11/16	
5/	Golden Arrow 19/	4/9		¾	Do. Investment	¾	+ ⅛
7⅞	Golden Horseshoe	9 1/16	+ 13/16	¾	Mainland Consols	5/16	
13/16	Golden Link	13/16		⅜	North Boulder, 10/	1/16	− 1/16
27/6	Great Boulder, 2/	18/3		1½	North Kalgurli	1 5/16	+ ⅛
1½	Do. Main Reef, 10/	1 5/16		¾	Northern Territories	¾	− 1/16
2⅜	Do. Perseverance	2 11/16	− 1/16	2¼	Peak Hill	2¼	− ⅛
¾	Do. South	13/16	+ ⅛	1 3/16	South Kalgurli	2¼	+ 1/16
1¾	Hainault	2¼	+ ⅛	1½	W. A. Goldfields	1 3/16	
13/16	Hampton Plains	13/16		⅜	W. A. Joint Stock	5/16	
7⅜	Hannan's Brownhill	7⅜	+ ½	⅝	W. A. Market Trust	2/6	+ /3
¾	Hannan's Oroya	13/16	+ 1/16	5/16	W. A. Loan & General Fin.	5/16	+ 1/16
11/16	Do. Proprietary	11/	+ /3	5/16	White Feather	5/16	− 1/16

South African.

Making-Up Price, May 23.	Name	Closing Price.	Rise or Fall.	Making-Up Price, May 23.	Name	Closing Price.	Rise or Fall.
5	Angelo	5 1/16		2/	Lisbon-Berlyn	1/9	
1	Aurora West	15/16		2⅜	May Consolidated	2⅜	+ 1/16
1	Bantjes	15/16		4	Meyer and Charlton	3⅞	− ⅛
8/6	Barrett, 10/	8/		3½	Modderfontein	3 9/16	+ 1/16
4 1/16	Bonanza	4⅛	− ⅛	1	New Bultfontein	1 1/16	+ ⅛
5/16	Buffelsdoorn	5/16		3⅜	New Primrose	3⅜	
5 1/16	City and Suburban, £4	5¼	+ ½	1½	Nigel	1⅝	+ ⅛
2⅜	Comet (New)	2⅜			Nigel Deep	1	
3⅜	Con. Deep Level	3⅜		⅝	North Randfontein	½	− ⅛
11	Crown Deep	11½	+ ½	5	Nourse Deep	5	
12¼	Crown Reef	12⅝		1	Porges-Randfontein	15/16	− 1/16
26¾	De Beers, £5	27	+ ¼	20½	Rand Mines	20¾	+ ¼
3⅜	Driefontein	3⅜		1½	Randfontein	1⅜	
6 1/16	Durban Roodepoort	6¼		1 3/16	Rietfontein	1¼	
3 3/16	Do. Deep	3⅛	− ⅛	9½	Robinson Deep	9⅜	− ⅛
4⅜	East Rand	4⅜		8	Do. Gold, £5	8	
24	Ferreira	24¼	+ ¼	1	Do. Randfontein	¾	
7⅝	Geldenhuis Deep	7⅝		1 3/16	Roodepoort Central Deep	1 5/16	+ ⅛
5⅜	Do. Estate	5 5/16	− 1/16	6¼	Rose Deep	6	− ¼
¾	George Goch	¾		3 3/16	Salisbury	2⅞	− ⅛
2 3/16	Ginsberg	2 1/16	− 1/16	1½	Sheba	1½	
1⅜	Glencairn	1⅜		3¼	Simmer and Jack, £5	3⅜	+ ⅛
8 3/16	Goldfields Deep	8¼		2 11/16	Transvaal Gold	2 11/16	− 1/16
8½	Griqualand West	8½		3⅜	Treasury	3⅜	
9	Henry Nourse	9		3⅜	United Roodepoort	3⅜	
7⅞	Heriot	7⅞	− 1/16	1¼	Van Ryn	1½	
7⅞	Jagersfontein	7⅞		5 13/16	Village Main Reef	6	+ 1/16
9⅜	Jubilee	9½	+ ½	1½	Vogelstruis	1 5/16	− 1/16
5	Jumpers	4⅞		¾	Do. Deep	¾	
2⅜	Kleinfontein	2 5/16	− 1/16	9⅝	Wemmer	9⅝	
3 3/16	Knight's	3 5/16	+ 1/16	15/16	West Rand	⅞	
2 5/16	Lancaster	2⅜		5⅜	Wolhuter, £4	5¼	
3⅜	Langlaagte Estate	3⅜		2⅜	Worcester	2⅜	

Land Exploration and Rhodesian.

Making-Up Price, May 23.	Name	Closing Price.	Rise or Fall.	Making-Up Price, May 23.	Name	Closing Price.	Rise or Fall.
2¼	Anglo-French Ex.	2 5/16	+ 1/16	¾	Mashonaland Central	¾	
1 13/16	Barnato Consolidated	1 13/16		5⅜	Matabele Gold Reefs	5¼	− ⅛
¾	Bechuanaland Ex.	13/16		2	Mozambique	2 1/16	
2⅝	Chartered B.S.A.	2⅝		13/16	Oceana Consolidated	⅞	
¾	Clark's Cons.	11/16	− 1/16	1½	Rhodesia, Ltd.	1 5/16	
3/16	Colenbrander	3/16	− 1/16	4⅜	Do. Exploration	4⅜	
4¼	Cons. Goldfields	4 1/16		15/16	Do. Goldfields	1	
1 1/16	Do. Pref.	20/6		3⅜	S. A. Gold Trust	3 5/16	− 1/16
1½	Exploration	1 5/16	− 1/16	1	Tati Concessions	1	
2¼	Geelong	2⅛		½	Transvaal Development	½	
5/16	Henderson's Est.	⅜		⅝	United Rhodesia	⅝	
1 1/16	Johannesburg Con. In.	1 1/16		1	Willoughby	1⅛	+ ⅛
¾	Do. Water	¾	− 1/16	13/16	Zambesia Explor.	¾	
1½	Mashonaland Agency	1 1/16					

Miscellaneous.

Making-Up Price, May 23.	Name	Closing Price.	Rise or Fall.	Making-Up Price, May 23.	Name	Closing Price.	Rise or Fall.
1	Alamillos, £2	1		¼	Mount Lyell, South	5/16	+ 1/16
4⅞	Anaconda, $25	5	+ ⅛	4½	Mount Morgan, 17s. 6d.	4 1/16	
7/	Balaghât, 18/	7/	− /6	4 13/16	Mysore, 10s.	5 1/16	+ ¼
12/	Brilliant, £2	12/6	+ /6	20/	Mysore Goldfields	1/16	
2½	Do. St. George's	2½x		6/3	Do. Reefs, 17/	6/	− 1/
10/	British Broken Hill	10/		7/	Do. West	5/	− 1/6
43/	Broken Hill Proprietary	2½		5/	Do. Wynaad	3/16	− 1/16
3	Do. Block 10	3		2 1/16	Namaqua, £2	2⅛	+ 1/16
4⅛	Cape Copper, £2	4⅛		3⅜	Nundydroog	3⅜	
4 11/16	Champion Reef, 10s.	4 9/16	− 1/16	3⅜	Ooregum	3 5/16	− 1/16
2 1/16	Copiapo, £2	2⅛	+ 1/16	3⅜	Do. Pref.	3⅜	− 1/16
2⅜	Coromandel	2 5/16		26½	Rio Tinto Def., £5	26 9/16	+ 1/16
15/	Day Dawn Block	15/	+ /3	5⅞	Do. Pref. £5	6	+ ⅛
2⅛	Frontino & Bolivia	2 3/16		1	St. John del Rey	20/	
1⅛	Hall Mines	1⅛		7/6	Taitipu	¼	+ 1/16
2⅜	Libiola, £5	2⅜		6¼	Tharsis, £2	6⅛	− ⅛
7⅜	Linares, £3	7¼	− ⅛	2	Tolima "A," £5	2	
3⅜	Mason & Barry, £3	3⅜		4⅝	Waihi	4 11/16	+ 1/16
4⅞	Mountain Copper, £5	4⅜	− ½	1½	Waitekauri	1½	
10¼	Mount Lyell, £3	10¼	+ ⅜	⅝	Woodstock (N.Z.)	⅝	
2⅜	Mount Lyell, North	2¼	− ⅛				

RAILWAY TRAFFIC RETURNS.

Mobile and Birmingham Railroad.—Traffic for second week of May, $5,250; decrease, $252. Aggregate from July 1, $323,791; increase, $1,278.

Algeciras (Gibraltar) Railway.—Traffic for week ended May 21, Ps. 26,610; increase, Ps. 3,255. Aggregate from July 1, Ps. 957,712; increase, Ps. 49,892.

West Flanders Railway.—Gross receipts for week ending May 29, £2,021; increase, £41. Total from January 1, £51,014; increase, £1,771.

West of India Portuguese Railway.—Week ending May 7, Rs. 5,492; increase, Rs. 963. Aggregate from January 1, Rs. 84,958; increase, Rs. 23,427.

Villa Maria and Rufino Railway.—Traffic for week ending May 28, $318; increase, $96. Aggregate from January 1, $7,515; increase, $1,446.

Southern Mahratta Railway.—Receipts for week ended May 7, Rs. 1,18,733; decrease, Rs. 31,187.

Bengal Central Railway.—Traffic receipts for week ending May 7, Rs. 17,858; increase, Rs. 1,214. Aggregate from January 1, Rs. 382,590; increase, Rs. 63,478.

Manila Railway.—Receipts for week ending May 21, $18,000; increase, $3,262. Aggregate from January 1, $382,061; increase, $83,831.

Delhi Umballa Kalka Railway.—Receipts for week ended May 28, Rs. 29,500; increase, Rs. 6,000. Aggregate from January 1, Rs. 7,24,900; increase, Rs. 1,73,900.

Western of Santa Fe Railways.—Gross receipts for week ending May 28, $16,120; increase, $3,360.

Great Western of Brazil.—Traffics receipts for the week ending April 23, $20,353; increase, $2,861. Aggregate from January 1, $571,897; increase, $76,110.

Southern Pacific Railway.—The net earnings for the month of April, $1,552,750; increase, $394,030.

Cleator and Workington.—Gross receipts for the week ending May 28, amounted to £1,058, a decrease of £12. Total receipts from January 1, £21,788, a decrease of £679.

Cockermouth and Keswick Railway.—Receipts for the week ending May 28, £969; increase, £187. Aggregate from January 1, £17,703; increase, £1,698.

Rohilkund and Kumaon Railway.—Traffic receipts for week ending April 30, Rs. 8,222; decrease, Rs. 248. Aggregate from January 1, Rs. 1,32,304; decrease, Rs. 5,000.

Assam Bengal Railway.—Traffic receipts for week ending April 30, Rs. 24,557; increase, Rs. 5,441. Aggregate from January 1, Rs. 4,44,754; increase, Rs. 82,082.

Burma Railways.—Traffic receipts for week ending April 30, Rs. 1,98,044; increase Rs. 22,211. Aggregate from January 1, Rs. 36,32,920; decrease, Rs. 26,916.

Antofagasta and Bolivia Railway.—Traffic receipts for month of April $424,000; decrease, $40,000. Aggregate from January 1, $1,526,000; decrease, $164,000.

TRAMWAY AND OMNIBUS RECEIPTS.

HOME.

Name.	Period.	Ending.	Amount.	Increase or Decrease on 1897.	Weeks or Months.	Aggregate to Date. Amount.	Aggregate to Date. Inc. or Dec. on 1897.
			£	£		£	£
Aberdeen District	Week	May 28	464	+25	—	—	—
Belfast Street	"	" 28	2,327	+39	—	—	—
Birmingham and Aston	"	" 21	446	−9	—	—	—
Birmingham and Midland	"	" 28	729	+102	—	—	—
Birmingham City	"	" 28	4,154	+508	—	—	—
Birmingham General	"	" 28	986	+84	—	—	—
Blessington and Poulaphouca	"	" 29	15	+3	21	215	+19
Bristol Tramways and Carriage	"	" 27	2,653	+180	—	—	—
Burnley and District	"	" 26	339	+7	—	—	—
Bury, Rochdale, and Oldham	"	" 28	839	+17/	—	—	—
Croydon	"	" 28	393	+77	—	—	+1,277
Dublin and Blessington	"	" 29	132	+14	21	2,085	+32
Dublin and Lucan	"	" 28	75	—	22	1,003	−371
Dublin United	"	" 27	3,244	+45	—	59,202	+3,192
Dudley and Stourbridge	"	" 28	171	+9	22	3,571	+135
Edinburgh and District	"	" 28	2,700	+372	21	48,550	+4,908
Edinburgh Street	"	" 28	707	+95	21	12,875	+1,548
Gateshead and District	Month	April	940	+59	—	—	—
Glasgow	Week	May 28	3,033	+204	—	—	—
Harrow-road and Paddington	"	" 27	290	+3	—	—	—
Lea Bridge and Leyton	"	" 28	283	+136	—	—	—
London, Deptford, and Greenwich	"	" 28	644	+26	—	11,908	+490
London General Omnibus	"	" 28	24,568	+2,583	—	—	—
London Road Car	"	" 28	7,593	+391	†	132,333	+4,879
London Southern	"	" 28	630	+97	—	—	—
North Staffordshire	"	" 28	394	−20	—	8,298	−74
Provincial	"	" 28	2,620	−4	—	—	—
Rossendale Valley	"	" 27	179	+5	—	—	—
Southampton	"	" 28	427	−181	—	—	—
South London	"	" 28	1,935	−156	†	34,525	+1,072
South Staffordshire	"	" 27	601	−14	21	12,445	−103
Tramways Union	Month	April	10,870	+1,149	4	39,500	+4,495
Wigan and District	Week	May 28	304	+239‡	—	—	—
Woolwich and South East London	"	" 28	443	+3	†	6,994	+273

† From January 1. ‡ Strike in 1897.

FOREIGN.

Name.	Period.	Ending.	Amount.	Increase or Decrease on 1897.	Weeks or Months.	Aggregate to Date. Amount.	Aggregate to Date. Inc. or Dec. on 1897.
			£	£		£	£
Anglo-Argentine	Week	May 2	4,312	+215	*	78,166	+8,042
Barcelona	"	" 28	1,055	−393	—	23,728	−3,704
Barcelona, Ensanche y Gracia	"	" 28	213	−21	—	4,679	−1
Bordeaux	"	" 27	2,270	−85	—	43,082	−1,887
Brazilian Street	Month	Mch.	[illegible]	+ mlr 50 47)	—	—	—
British Columbia Electric	"	"	$30,729	+$10493	‡	$305,154	—
Do. net	"	"	$10,392	+$4,958	‡	$97,400	—
Buenos Ayres and Belgrano	"	April	5,090	+3,645	*	19,472	+3,368
Buenos Ayres Grand National	Week	" 23	$25,223	+$3,248	†	—	+$12,751
Buenos Ayres New	Month	March	$70,624	−$864	—	$801,851	−$7,119
Calais	Week	May 28	144	+13	—	—	—
Calcutta	"	" 28	1,167	−120	—	—	—
C'rth'g'na & Herrerias	Month	April	4,607	+712	—	18,809	+1,022
Gothenburg	Week	May 11	377	+44	—	—	—
Lynn and Boston	Month	Mch.	$105,471	+$6,044	—	$622,228	+$27972
Do. net	"	"	$42,847	+$6,607	—	$216,383	+$3,162

* From January 1. † From April 1, 1898. ‡ From April 15, 1897. § From October 1, 1897.

ENGLISH RAILWAYS.

Div. for half years. 1896	1896	1897	1897	Last Balance forward.	Amt. to pay 1 p.c. on Ord. for ½ yr.	NAME.	Date.	Gross Traffic for week: Amt.	Inc. or dec. on 1897.	Inc. or dec. on 1896.	No. of weeks	Gross Traffic for half-year to date: Amt.	Inc. or dec. on 1897.	Inc. or dec. on 1896.	Mileage.	Inc. on 1897.	Working	Prior Charges last ½ year.	Prop. add Cap. Rap. this ½ year
				£	£												%	£	£
10	10	10	10	2,707	5,094	Barry	M'y 28	2,675	−6,417	−4,099	22	149,013	−44,235	−16,467	31	—	8·89	60,665	316,853
nil	nil	nil	nil	—	—	Brecon and Merthyr.. ..	,, 29	1,281	−599	−533	22	30,044	−1,937	−5,196	61	—	—	—	—
nil	nil	nil	nil	3,979	4,749	Cambrian	,, 29	6,395	+276	+940	*	103,458	+3,009	—	250	—	60·96	63,148	40,000
1¾	1¾	2	1¾	1,510	3,150	City and South London ..	,, 29	1,012	+83	+170	22	22,678	+288	+2,143	3½	—	56·67	5,552	124,000
	2	1½	2	7,895	13,220	Furness	,, 29	9,977	+859	+515	*	189,817	+5,950	—	139	—	49·88	97,423	20,910
1	1½	½	1	2,207	27,470	Great Cent. (late M., S., & L.)	,, 29	55,717	+4,969	+4,410	21	946,092	+27,810	+62,586	352½	—	57·17	627,386	1,200,000
1½	4¾	2	5	51,283	62,865	Great Eastern	,, 29	†95,433	+17,146	+8,331	21	1,695,886	+59,233	+133601	1,158½	2	55·35	860,138	250,000
3	5¾	3	5	15,094	102,496	Great Northern	,, 29	†104,676	+12,188	+13,721	22	2,084,674	+70,367	+158832	1,073	10	61·36	641,465	750,000
4¾	7¾	4¾	7½	31,350	121,981	Great Western	,, 29	†205,990	+17,660	+18,380	21	3,682,470	+740	+112360	2,582	21	51·44	1,486,272	800,000
nil	2	nil	1¾	8,951	26,487	Hull and Barnsley	,, 29	8,371	+718	+2,311	21	147,996	+9,396	+21,714	73	—	58·21	70,290	52,920
5	5¾	5	5½	21,495	83,704	Lancashire and Yorkshire ..	,, 29	†108,269	+17,096	−20,219	21	1,960,382	+76,357	+43,484	535½	25	56·70	674,745	451,976
4¾	8	4¾	8½	26,243	43,049	Lon., Brighton, & S. Coast	,, 28	§165,472	+18,932	+9,460	22	1,076,632	+45,491	+51,896	476½	—	50·20	407,042	240,735
nil	nil	nil	nil	72,294	55,296	London, Chatham, & Dover	,, 29	†34,495	+5,097	+1,073	21	584,730	+17,337	+23,649	185½	—	50·65	367,873	nil
6½	8	6¾	7¾	89,535	204,068	London and North Western	,, 29	†269,901	+40,370	+38,527	21	4,861,086	+143826	+275711	1,911½	—	56·92	1,404,534	600,000
5	8½	8½	8½	23,038	59,367	London and South Western	,, 29	§189,210	+13,548	+6,221	21	1,475,448	+54,545	+89,146	941	—	51·75	513,740	389,000
2¾	6	2¾	6¼	14,592	6,691	Lon., Tilbury, & Southend	,, 29	†16,333	+918	−1,282	22	110,799	+5,895	+13,759	81	—	52·57	39,590	15,000
3½	3¾	3¾	3½	17,133	26,409	Metropolitan	,, 29	16,850	+627	+143	*	346,305	+7,543	—	64	—	43·63	148,047	254,000
nil	nil	nil	nil	4,006	11,250	Metropolitan District ..	,, 29	8,901	+317	+395	21	178,181	+6,146	—	13	—	48·70	119,663	38,450
5	7	5½	6½	38,143	174,582	Midland	,, 29	†215,531	+30,023	+30,023	22	4,081,347	+87,870	+340830	1,354½	15½	57·39	1,216,582	650,000
5¼	7½	5¾	7	22,374	138,189	North Eastern	,, 28	†164,853	+14,913	+4,215	21	3,052,003	+66,624	+179874	1,597¾	—	58·72	795,077	436,904
7½	7½	7½	7½	7,061	10,102	North London	,, 29			Not recd			not	recvd.	12	—	50·90	49,973	7,600
4	5	4	4½	4,745	16,150	North Staffordshire	,, 29	16,194	+736	+309	21	342,841	+6,983	+19,338	312	—	55·27	118,142	19,605
10	10	11	10	1,642	3,004	Rhymney	,, 28	1,827	−3,005	−2,673	22	88,538	−20,056	−11,193	71	—	49·68	29,049	16,700
3	6¾	3½	6¾	4,054	50,215	South Eastern	,, 28	†50,258	+6,933	+2,311	*	913,769	+46,613	—	448	—	51·88	380,763	250,000
3½	3½	3½	3½	2,315	25,961	Taff Vale	,, 28	6,009	−10,022	−7,742	22	262,784	−80,001	−59,387	121	—	54·90	94,800	91,000

* From January 1. § Derby Week. † Week before Whit Monday.

SCOTCH RAILWAYS.

5	5	5¼	5	9,544	78,066	Caledonian	May 29	80,697	+ 3,058	+ 3,370	17	1,251,158	+31,061	—	851½	5	50·38	588,248	441,477
5	5½	5	5	7,364	24,639	Glasgow and South-Western	,, 28	29,548	+ 927	+ 504	17	478,941	+16,978	—	393½	—	54·69	221,663	196,145
3½	3½	3½	—	1,291	4,600	Great North of Scotland	,, 28	9,174	− 160	+ 96	17	138,054	+ 255	+ 4,859	331	15½	52·03	92,178	60,000
	nil		—	10,477	12,820	Highland	,, 29	9,948	+ 266	+ 598	13	116,160	+ 2,374	—	479½	27¾	58·63	78,976	,000
	1½	1	1½	819	45,819	North British	,, 29	77,951	+ 4,217	+ 1,633	17	1,224,535	+34,178	—	1,230	23	48·62	944,809	40,800

IRISH RAILWAYS.

6½	6½	6½	—	5,466	1,790	Belfast and County Down ..	May 27	2,593	− 539	− 433	*	46,182	+ 360	—	76½	—	55·38	17,690	10,000
5½	6½	5½	—	—	4,284	Belfast and Northern Counties	,, 27	5,591	− 239	− 565	*	108,641	+ 4,412	—	249	—	—	—	—
	3	2	—	1,418	1,200	Cork, Bandon, and S. Coast† ..	,, 21	1,267	− 231	− 223	*	26,696	− 2,262	—	103	—	54·82	14,436	5,450
	6¾	6½	6¾	38,776	17,816	Great Northern	,, 21	15,311	− 113	− 106	21	309,404	+ 11,927	+19,419	528	—	50·15	88,068	22,000
	5½	5½	5½	30,339	24,855	Great Southern and Western ..	,, 27	—	—	—	not	received	—	—	603	13	51·45	72,802	46,582
	4	4	4½	11,372	11,850	Midland Great Western ..	,, 27	9,908	− 721	− 576	21	208,987	+ 6,395	—	538	—	50·31	83,129	1,800
nil	ni	nil	nil	229	2,822	Waterford and Central ..	,, 27	711	− 10	—	*	—	—	—	59½	—	53·24	6,858	1,500
nil	ni	nil	nil	1,936	2,987	Waterford, Limerick & W. ..	,, 27	4,507	− 399	− 346	*	—	—	—	350½	--	57·83	42,647	7,075

* From January 1. † Seventeen weeks' strike.

NOTICES.

Northern Pacific Railroad general first mortgage bonds for $43,200 were drawn on the 13th inst. for payment on July 1 at 110 per cent. The amount of such coupon bonds outstanding and undrawn is now reduced to $3,214,000.

All interest in the business of Richard Quincey & Son has passed to Edmund de Quincey Quincey and Richard de Quincey Quincey, sons of Roger de Q. Quincey.

Messrs. George Trollope & Sons give notice that, her Majesty's Commissioners of Works having acquired and pulled down No. 15, Parliament-street, Westminster, which had been occupied by their firm since 1777, they have opened new offices at 24, Mount-street, Grosvenor-square, and at 5, Victoria-street, Westminster.

Coupons of the bonds of the St. Lawrence and Ottawa Railway falling due on June 15 will be paid, on and after that date, at the London office of the Canadian Pacific Railway Company, 1, Queen Victoria-street, E.C.

Messrs. Arthur G. Morrish and Francis O. Grant have amalgamated their businesses under the style of Morrish, Grant, & Co.

The amount of Northern Pacific Railroad general first mortgage bonds recently drawn for redemption is $432,000, not $43,200, as previously stated.

The numbers are published of $432,000 Northern Pacific Railroad general first mortgage bonds, which have been drawn for repayment on July 1 next at 110 per cent.

Notice is given to the holders of Railway Equipment Company of Minnesota 6 per cent. bonds dated June 1, 1891, that the Atlantic Trust Company will receive, at its New York office, until July 11, offers for the sale of the bonds to the amount of $50,000 at not exceeding par and interest to the date of payment. If $50,000 in amount of the bonds are not offered for sale the trustee will redeem by lot bonds to the amount not offered, in accordance with the provisions of the deed of trust.

Baring Brothers & Co., Limited, announce that all unconverted Russian 5 per cent. Transcaucasian Railroad (formerly Poti-Tiflis Railroad) bonds still in circulation are called in for repayment on July 5. Bonds should be presented on or before June 20.

The directors of the Mount Lyell Mining and Railway Company, Limited, have announced their attention to issue 25 000 of the unissued shares, in the proportion of one share for each ten shares held at £3 per share premium (£6 per share), to all shareholders whose names shall be on the registers on June 15.

The London Joint Stock Bank, Limited, announces that branches at Muswell Hill and Lower Edmonton, and sub-branches at Winchmore Hill and Palmer's Green, are now open.

Messrs. J. S. Morgan & Co., and Messrs. J. P. Morgan & Co., in referring to their circular of February 19, 1898, offering to exchange various New York Central and Hudson River Railroad Company bonds for the new 3½ per cent. gold mortgage bonds of 1997 of the same company, now give notice that their offer to supply the new bonds at 103½ and interest will be withdrawn on the 10th inst., after which date the rate will be 104 and interest. New York Central 4 per cent debentures of 1905 will be received at 103·08 ex coupon due June 1.

The numbers are announced of eight bonds of £100 each of the Matanzas and Sabanilla (Cuba) Railroad 7 per cent. loan for £300,000, which have been acquired by purchase and are withdrawn from circulation; also of ninety-two bonds of £100 each which have been drawn for payment on June 15, and will, together with the half-yearly interest due on that date, be paid at the counting-house of Messrs. J. Henry Schröder & Co.

The numbers are published of the first mortgage bonds of the Nitrate Railways Company, Limited, which have been drawn for redemption at the rate of 105 per cent. on July 1.

Mr. Luis Camacho announces the numbers of twenty-two bonds of the Mexican 6 per cent. consolidated external loan of 1893, which have been purchased and cancelled.

The Western Australian Bank has opened a branch at Leonora, Western Australia.

Messrs. R. Anderson & Co., of 14, Cockspur-street, Charing-cross, have opened a City office at 15, Great Winchester-street.

Mr. Douglas M. Hogg's connection with Hogg, Curtis, Campbell, & Co. having ceased, the power granted to him to sign "per procuration" has been withdrawn. Mr. Colin Algernon Campbell, eldest son of Mr. William Middleton Campbell, will henceforward sign for the firm "per procuration."

DIVIDENDS ANNOUNCED.

MISCELLANEOUS.

MOUNT LYELL MINING AND RAILWAY COMPANY, LIMITED.—Dividend of 4s. has been declared, payable on July 1.

MOUNT MORGAN GOLD MINING COMPANY, LIMITED.—6d. per share for the month of May, payable on June 1.

VICTORY (CHARTERS TOWERS) GOLD MINING, LIMITED.—6d. per share has been declared, payable on June 23.

TINGRI TEA COMPANY.—Dividend for past year is 5 per cent., and the board carry forward £776.

J. L. BRAGG, LIMITED.—Interim dividend of 7 per cent. per annum for the half-year ended April 30.

RAJMAI TEA COMPANY, LIMITED.—Final dividend of 5 per cent., making 10 per cent. for the year, with £7,077 carried forward.

BROKEN HILL WATER SUPPLY, LIMITED.—6d. per share, payable on July 1.

BREWERY.

UNITED STATES COMPANY.—Directors recommend further distribution of 5 per cent. on the ordinary shares, making 10 per cent. for the year ended March 31, payable on July 1.

RAILWAYS.

SOUTH AUSTRIAN COMPANY.—Dividend for 1897 has been fixed at 3f. Coupon No. 15 will be paid at the rate of 2s. 4½d. per share.

DELHI UMBALLA KALKA COMPANY, LIMITED.—Interim dividend for the half-year ended December 31 of £2 15s. per cent., payable on June 1.

ANGLO-CHILIAN NITRATE AND RAILWAYS.—Dividend of 14s. per share on the preference shares.

INSURANCE.

ALLIANCE MARINE AND GENERAL ASSURANCE COMPANY, LIMITED.—Dividend for the year will be declared at annual meeting on 22nd inst. of 30s. per share, and a bonus of 10s. per share. An interim dividend of 10s. per share having been paid on January 1, there remains a balance of 30s. per share, which will be paid on July 1.

FOREIGN RAILWAYS.

Mileage. Total.	Increase on 1897.	Increase on 1896.	NAME	GROSS TRAFFIC FOR WEEK. Week ending	Amount.	In. or Dec. upon 1897.	In. or Dec. upon 1896.	GROSS TRAFFIC TO DATE. No. of Weeks.	Amount.	In. or Dec. upon 1897.	In. or Dec. upon 1896.
					£	£	£		£	£	£
319	—	—	Argentine Great Western ..	May 27	6,775	+ 1,299	+ 879	47	283,254	− 4,181	+ 56,219
76½	—	—	Bahia and San Francisco ..	Apr. 30	2,754	− 131	− 1,437	18	—	—	—
234	48	84	Bahia Blanca and North West ..	May 1	592	− 29	—	44	33,169	− 1,313	—
75	1	—	Buenos Ayres and Ensenada ..	May 29	2,884	− 1,524	—	22	71,332	− 12,562	—
426	—	—	Buenos Ayres and Pacific ..	May 28	9,056	+ 1,728	+ 1,784	47	325,150	− 46,031	+ 12,225
914	—	3	Buenos Ayres and Rosario ..	May 28	14,178	+ 2,550	+ 1,880	22	357,579	+ 95,597	+ 64,735
1,499	30	68	Buenos Ayres Great Southern ..	May 29	25,441	+ 6,467	+ 5,128	47	1,403,426	+ 120,579	+ 209,930
602	107	177	Buenos Ayres Western	May 29	10,100	+ 101	− 3,123	47	569,459	− 75,019	− 103,850
845	55	77	Central Argentine	May 28	17,355	+ 3,836	+ 2,766	22	459,397	+ 120,181	+ 60,252
297	—	—	Central Bahia	Feb. 28*	$142,798	+ $14,291	+ $1,866	2	$276,357	+ $10,347	+ $14,624
271	—	—	Central Uruguay of Monte Video	May 28	4,375	+ 944	− 1,342	47	280,761	+ 26,161	− 15,101
228	—	—	Do. Eastern Extension	May 28	994	+ 2	− 80	47	61,421	+ 9,557	+ 320
282	—	—	Do. Northern Extension	May 28	455	+ 123	− 403	47	29,950	+ 1,539	− 7,642
180	—	—	Cordoba and Rosario	May 22	2,055	− 160	+ 380	47	99,995	− 12,745	− 400
228	—	—	Cordoba Central	May 22	$19,500	− $6,262	− $4,000	21	$443,200	− $62,550	− $75,350
549	—	—	Do. Northern Extension	May 22	$47,000	− $20,000	− $15,210	21	$931,790	− $319,490	− $180,100
137	—	—	Costa Rica	May 29	4,869	+ 592	+ 550	48	125,702	+ 257	+ 12,726
99	—	—	East Argentine	Apr. 17	1,001	+ 497	+ 127	35	11,548	+ 884	+ 658
366	—	6	Entre Rios	May 28	1,061	+ 160	− 144	47	77,466	+ 24,737	+ 19,586
555	—	24	Inter Oceanic of Mexico	May 28	$60,500	+ $10,780	+ $18,400	47	$2,749,270	+ $435,420	+ $744,420
23	—	—	La Guaira and Caracas	Apr. 15	2,765	+ 1,045	+ 410	16	31,845	− 4,696	− 4,597
321	—	—	Mexican	May 28	$75,700	+ $8,700	—	22	$1,722,300	+ $182,950	—
1,846	—	—	Mexican Central	May 21	$249,765	+ $33,227	+ $69,475	21	$5,150,006	+ $50,871	+ $1,328,953
1,217	—	—	Mexican National	May 21	$109,371	− $2,928	+ $23,313	20	—	—	—
228	—	—	Mexican Southern	May 31‡	$16,980	− $1,164	+ $5,447	8	$106,917	− $15,483	+ $26,009
206	—	—	Minas and Rio	Mar. 31*	$161,758	− $9,628	—	9 mos.	$1,597,971	+ $193,854	—
94	—		N. W. Argentine	May 28	1,118	− 263	− 752	22	21,344	− 8,518	− 7,122
242	3	—	Nitrate	May 31†	18,520	+ 2,552	− 7,211	22	151,360	− 318	− 69,690
320	—	—	Ottoman	May 21	4,713	+ 235	+ 1,079	21	94,244	− 22,264	+ 8,359
77½	—	—	Recife and San Francisco ..	Apr. 2	5,768	+ 1,610	+ 209	14	81,182	+ 8,461	− 11,036
86½	—	—	San Paulo	May 1‡	17,518	− 2,487	—	17	165,710	—	—
186	—	—	Santa Fe and Cordova	May 28	1,767	+ 667	− 658	47	84,216	+ 3,225	− 6,208
110	—	—	Western of Havana	May 28	1,380	− 462	− 370	47	82,637	+ 3,728	− 6,762

* For month ended. † For fortnight ended. ‡ For ten days ended.

INDIAN RAILWAYS.

Mileage. Total.	Increase on 1897.	Increase on 1896.	NAME.	GROSS TRAFFIC FOR WEEK. Week ending	Amount.	In. or Dec. on 1897.	In. or Dec. on 1896.	GROSS TRAFFIC TO DATE. No. of Weeks.	Amount.	In. or Dec. on 1897.	In. or Dec. on 1896.
862	—	—	Bengal Nagpur	May 21	Rs.1.80.000	+Rs.51.581	+Rs.62.795	21	Rs.32.77.742	+Rs.3.78.361	+Rs1.00.336
827	8	63	Bengal and North-Western ..	Apr. 30	Rs.1.65.210	+Rs.23,039	+Rs.17,301	18	Rs.23.86.415	+Rs.2.76.370	+Rs1.31,868
461	—	—	Bombay and Baroda	May 28	£44,458	+£5,565	+£0,660	22	£647.791	+£43,290	−£120,482
1,885	2	13	East Indian	May 28	Rs.13.21.000	+Rs1.22.000	+Rs3.01.000	22	Rs.2.70.12.000	+Rs.11.14.000	+R30.75.000
1,491	—	—	Great Indian Penin.	May 28	£73,847	+£14,667	+£2,642	22	£1,526,637	+£308,863	−£171,839
736	—	—	Indian Midland	May 28	Rs.1.73.805	+ Rs.9.860	+Rs.66.475	22	Rs.31.53.376	+Rs.3.37.882	+R27.90.360
840	—	—	Madras	May 21	£18,608	−£1,375	−£1,100	21	£388,745	−£22,515	−£5,907
1,043	—	—	South Indian	Apr. 30	Rs.1.71.270	−Rs.6,698	−Rs.32.439	18	Rs.27.13.305	−Rs.2.39.289	−R1.69.522

UNITED STATES AND CANADIAN RAILWAYS.

Mileage. Total.	Increase on 1897.	Increase on 1896.	NAME.	GROSS TRAFFIC FOR WEEK. Period Ending.	Amount.	In. or Dec. on 1897.	GROSS TRAFFIC TO DATE. No. of Weeks.	Amount.	In. or Dec. on 1897.
					dols.	dols.		dols.	dols.
917	—	—	Baltimore & Ohio S. Western ..	May 21	145,073	+38,398	45	6,126,716	+762,472
6,568	92	156	Canadian Pacific	May 21	511,000	+42,000	19	8,690,000	+1,618,000
922	—	—	Chicago Great Western	May 21	97,000	+11,000	45	4,773,640	+619,163
6,169	—	469	Chicago, Mil., & St. Paul ..	May 21	631,000	+109,000	19	11,483,001	+1,714,800
1,685	—	—	Denver & Rio Grande	May 21	148,800	+22,300	45	7,194,000	+1,171,400
3,512	—	—	Grand Trunk, Main Line ..	May 21	£73,033	+£4,077	19	£1,463,912	+£136,412
335	—	—	Do. Chic. & Grand Trunk	May 21	£15,275	+£4,314	19	£296,365	+£68,840
189	—	—	Do. Det., G. H. & Mil...	May 21	£3,152	−£246	19	£69,175	−£4,098
2,938	—	—	Louisville & Nashville	May 21	432,000	+54,000	19	8,298,175	+1,237,620
2,197	137	137	Miss., K., & Texas	May 21	164,000	−3,000	45	11,100,428	+500,290
477	—	—	N. Y., Ontario, & W.	May 21	63,000	−7,000	45	3,401,685	+80,471
1,570	—	—	Norfolk & Western	May 21	235,000	+21,000	19	4,345,960	+498,433
3,499	336	—	Northern Pacific	May 21	461,000	+128,000	19	7,473,775	+2,363,552
1,223	—	—	St. Louis S. Western	May 21	67,000	−8,000	19	2,009,295	+298,928
4,654	—	—	Southern	May 21	438,000	+100,000	19	7,063,812	+1,579,443
1,979	—	—	Wabash	May 21	252,000	+38,000	19	5,013,406	+1,108,000

MONTHLY STATEMENTS.

Mileage. Total.	Increase on 1896	Increase on 1895.	NAME.	NET EARNINGS FOR MONTH. Month.	Amount.	In. or Dec. on 1897.	In. or Dec. on 1896.	NET EARNINGS TO DATE. No. of Months.	Amount.	In. or Dec. on 1897.	In. or Dec. on 1896.
					dols	dols.	dols.		dols.	dols.	dols.
6,935	44	444	Atchison	April	798,000	+319,000	+239,679	4	2,942,434	+993,836	+469,139
6,547	103	106	Canadian Pacific	April	717,000	+90,000	+225,790	4	2,410,000	+505,000	+612,557
6,169	—	469	Chicago, Mil., & St. Paul ..	April	759,000	+19,000	−17,197	4	3,495,334	+244,840	+76,915
1,685	—	—	Denver & Rio Grande	March	267,900	+39,242	+38,942	9	2,512,889	+407,063	+30,946
1,970	—	—	Erie..	April	534,000	+17,000	+45,487	4	1,932,600	+109,400	−48,760
3,512	—	—	Grand Trunk, Main Line ..	April	£114,098	+£16,224	+£20,710	4	£360,051	+£78,596	+£123,507
335	—	—	Do. Chic. & Grand Trunk	April	£11,526	+£6,424	+£5,660	4	£50,236	+£30,706	+£34,378
189	—	—	Do. Det. G. H. & Mil. ..	April	£4,016	+£390	+£2,125	4	£10,544	+£1,127	+£8,744
3,127	—	239	Illinois Central	March	759,000	+206,000	+343,862	3	2,213,704	+363,680	+549,739
2,396	—	—	New York Central*	April	3,807,000	+302,000	+394,152	4	14,602,000	+964,000	—
477	—	—	New York Ontario, & W. ..	April	62,100	−14,700	−13,161	10	980,400	+23,500	+102,339
1,570	—	—	Norfolk & Western	March	301,000	+18,000	+187,400	3	826,000	+65,247	+201,908
3,407	—	—	Pennsylvania	April	1,524,200	+12,000	+236,000	4	5,672,228	+121,300	+575,900
1,055	—	—	Phil. & Reading . ..	March	701,190	+50,822	—	9	7,567,293	+524,064	—

* Estimated [illegible]

Prices Quoted on the London Stock Exchange.

Throughout the INVESTORS' REVIEW middle prices alone are quoted, the object being to give the public the approximate current quotations of every security of any consequence in existence. On the markets the buying and selling prices are both given, and are often wide apart where stocks are seldom dealt in. Other particulars will be found in the INVESTMENT INDEX published quarterly—January, April, July, and October—in connection with this REVIEW, price 2s., by post 2s. 2d. Where dividends are paid only once a year, an *italic* type is used to distinguish them. The London Stock Exchange Official List is quoted in the REVIEW almost entire, only very insignificant issues, or bonds falling due within the next two or three years, being omitted. But the list is subdivided into the leading, or active, stocks, and those less frequently dealt in. The former will be found under the head of "Stock Markets," and with more details than it is possible to give for the bulk of securities. By retaining the file of the INVESTORS' REVIEW any subscriber can follow for himself the movements of securities from week to week, and the INVESTMENT INDEX will from time to time help to fill up deficiencies in the information.

Tea Companies and Mines and Mining Finance Stocks are placed in special lists.

Among the abbreviations used are the following:—S. F. Snk. Fd. *sinking fund*; Certs., *certificates*; Debs. or Dbs., *debentures*; Db. or D.Stk., *debenture stock*; Pf., Prf., or Pref., *preference*; Prefd. or Pfd., *preferred*; Dfd., *deferred*; L. or Ltd., *limited*; Sh., *share*; Ans., *annuities*; Cu. or Cm., *cumulative*; Gu or Guar., *guaranteed*; Bds., *bonds*; S., Sr., or Ser., *series*; In., Ins., Insc., *inscribed*; Dr., Drgs., Drwgs., *drawings*; Stg., Strlg., *sterling*; Lia., *liable to*; Sp., Surp., *surplus*; Per., Perp., *perpetual*; Ln. *lien*; Lo. *loan*.

The dates following the names of securities are the years of issue or of redemption. Where shares are not fully paid up, their nominal amount s given with the name so that investors may know the liability upon them.

BRITISH FUNDS, &c.

Rate.	Name.	Price.
2¾	2¾ p.c.'s (Childers') Red.. 1905	105
3	Local Loans Stk. 1912	111
3	Metro. Police Deb. Stk. 1920	105½
—	Red Sea Ind. Tel. Ann. 1908	8½
4	Canada Gv. "Intcl. Rly." 1903	105½
4	Do. do. .. 1908	111
4	Do. Bonds 1910	112
4	Do. Bonds 1913	117½
3	Egyptian Gov. Gar.	106
3	Mauritius Ins. Stk. 1940	114
4	Turkish Guar. 1855	109
12½	Bank of Ireland Stk.	385
3½	India Rupee Paper	62
3½	Do. 1854-5	62
3	Do. 1896-7 1916	55
3½	Isle of Man Deb.	104
3	Do. Deb. Stk... 1919-29	103

CORPORATION AND COUNTY STOCKS.

FREE OF STAMP DUTY.

Rate.	Name.	Price.
3½	Metropolitan Con. 1929	117
3	Do. 1941	110
2½	Do. 1920-49	99
2½	L.C.C. Con. Stock 1920	98
3½	Comm. of Sewers, Scp., S.F. 1905	104
3½	Corp. of Lond. Bds...1898-1902	100½
3	Do. 1898-1912	101
3½	Do., Debs. Scp. ...... S.F. 1916	105
2½	Do., Deb. Stk. Scrip .. 1927-57	98
3	Barnsley 1916-46	103
3	Barry 1914-46	101½
3	Bath 1909-34	101
3	Batley 1914-44	101½
3½	Birmingham 1945	118½
3	Do. 1947	111½
2½	Do. 1926	99
3	Blackburn 1930	106½
3	Bournemouth 1913-33	103
3½	Bradford 1945	116½
3	Do. Deb. Stock .. 1954	107
3	Brighouse.............. 1916-46	100
3½	Brighton 1946	117
	Do. 1957	96½
	Burton-on-Trent........ 1913-43	101
	Cambridge 1913-43	103
	Cardiff 1935	114½
	Do. 1914-54	103½
	Cheltenham.......... 1971	105½
	Chichester 1916-46	101
	Croydon	130½
3	Do. 1940	106½
3	Derby 1920-50	106½
3	Devon C.C.......... 1917-33	104½
3½	Dewsbury 1930	109
3	Do. 1930	103
3	Dorset County 1922-32	106
3	Douglas (I. of Man) 1926	101½
3	Dover 1913-43	101
3½	Dublin 1944	113½
3	Eastbourne 1920-40	104
3	Edinburgh 1924	105½
2½	Do. 1927	97
2½	Exeter 1917-57	96
3	Glamorgan County 1914-34	104
3½	Glasgow 1914	109
3	Do. 1921	104½
2½	Do. 1925-40	98
3	Gloster 1915-55	101
3	Grimsby 1913-45	103
3	Hampshire County 1914-34	106½
3	Hanley 1913-43	103
3	Harrogate 1914-34	103
3	Hastings 1915-54	103½
2½	Hertfordshire C.C. 1916-36	98
3	Heston & Isleworth U.D.C. 1915-35	101
3	Huddersfield 1934	107
3½	Hull (1st iss.)	126½
3	Inverness 1914-44	100
3	Ipswich 1952	107½
3	Lancaster 1919-55	103
2½	Leeds 1927	98
3½	Leicester 1934	116
3	Lincoln 1919	103
3½	Liverpool	132

Corporation, &c. (*continued*):—

Rate.	Name.	Price.
3	Manchester 1941	107½
3½	Middlesbro' 1909	105½
3½	Do. 1911-13	105
3	Do. 1915	104
3	Middlesex C.C. 1915-35	106
3½	Newcastle 1936	118½
3½	Do. Irred.	129½
2½	Do. 1915-36	100
3	Newcastle-under-Lyme.. 1909-44	101
3	Newport (Mon.) 1915-55	101½
3	Norwich 1952	110
3	Nottingham	112
3	Oxford 1951	109½
3	Penzance 1916-46	100½
3	Plymouth 1942	106½
3	Pontypridd U.D.C. 1916-46	98
3	Poole 1915-45	102
3½	Portsmouth ....1916 24 & 27	112
3	Do. 1913-33	106
3	Ramsey 1920-40	100
3	Ramsgate 1915-55	102
3½	Reading	123
3	Do. 1962	107
3½	Rhyl U.D.C. 1953	110
3	Richmond (Surrey) 1942	104½
3	River Wear Debt Certs.	100
3	St. Helen's 1915-55	102
3	Scarbro' 1915-50	102
2½	Sheffield 1925-57	94½
3	Shipley U.D.C. 1915-35	100
3	Somerset Co. 1923-33	104
3	South Shields 1915-45	100½
2¾	Southampton 1915-45	100½
3	Southend-on-Sea 1916-46	101
3	Staffs C.C. 1915-35	103½
3	Stockport 1914-54	101
3	Stockton 1932	104
3	Do. 1915-35	103
3	Surrey Co. 1922-32	105½
3½	Swansea	129
3	Do. 1955	106
3	Taunton 1918-3-9-43	100
3	Tees Conserv. Deb. Stk. 1947	100
3	Thames Conserv. "A" Deb. Stk. 1954	103½
3	Do. "B" Deb. Stk. 1954	103½
3	Torquay 1913-43	101½
3	Tunbridge Wells 1931	102
3	Tynemouth 1913	99
3	Wakefield 1929	101½
3	Walsall 1932	107½
3	West Bromwich........ 1930	105
3½	West Ham 1929	110
3	Do. 1945	105
3	West Sussex C.C. 1915-35	106
3	Weston-s.-Mare Lcl Bd. 1914-44	99½
3	Weymouth & Melc. Regis 1918	101
3	Widnes 1915-55	100
3	Wigan 1921	104½
3	Windsor 1918-55	102
3½	Wisbech 1947	113½
3½	Wolverhampton 1932	117
3	Do. 1924-54	107
3	York 1916-41	105½

SUBJECT TO STAMP DUTY.

Rate.	Name.	Price.
3½	Belfast City & Dis. Watr. 1938	114
3	Do. Red Stk. 1953-6	106
3½	Belfast 1924	103
4	Blackburn Con. Deb. Irred.	141½
3½	Do. do. Irred.	130
3½	Bristol	130½
3½	Burnley 1933	114
2½	Chesterfield Gas & Wtr. 1916-46	96
3½	Douglas Town 1921	105
3	Dover Harb. 1st Deb... 1956	104½
3½	Hull (2nd iss.)	128½
4	Leeds Deb. 1927	123
3½	Do.	115½
3	Do. 1927	106
3	Leicester 1919-44	103½
4	Manchester	145
3	Do. 1928	104½
4½	Middlesboro' Mrts. 1908	111
3½	Sheffield 1898-1916	105½
3½	Do. 1925-36	114
3	Do. 1925	105½
3½	Southampton .... S.F.	106
4½	Stockton Morts. 1908	110½
3½	Worcester 1930	109

COLONIAL AND PROVINCIAL GOVERNMENT SECURITIES.

Rate.	Name.	Price.
6	British Columbia.......... 1907	119½
4½	Do. Debs... 1917	111½
3	British Guiana Imgtn. Bds.	98
5	Canada, "Intercol. Rail," 1903	107½
4	Do. (Bonds) 1904-5-6-8	105
4	Do. Reduced 1910	109
3½	Do. Bnds. 1909-34	107
4	Do. Loan 1910-35	109
3	Do. Loan 1938	103
6	Cape of G. Hope 1900	—
5	Do. 1900	—
4½	Do. red. by an. draw.	108
4½	Do 1879	108
4	Do. 1881	107
4	Do 1917-23	113
4½	Ceylon	108
4	Do.	106½
4½	Fiji Gov. Deb. Sink. Fd.	101½
4	Jamaica Sink. Fd. 1923	103
5	Manitoba Debs.......... 1910	113
5	Do. Ster. Bds. 1888	119½
4	Do. Ster. Debs.	105
4	Mauritius, Cons. Debs. 1880....	101½
4½	Natal, Sink. Fd.......... 1919	118
4	Do. do. 1926	114
3½	Newfoundland Stg. Bds. 1941	100
3½	Do. do. .. 1947	100
3	Do. do.	86½
5	New South Wales 1897-1902	104½
4	Do. 1903-5-8-9-12	106
5	New Zealand 1914	118
5	Do. Cnsls. 1 p.c. per an. Sink. Fd.	103
3½	Nova Scotia Debs.	104
5	Quebec Prov. 1904-6	108
4½	Do. (drgs.)	105
5	Do. Strlg. Bds. 1912	115
4	Do. Strlg. Bds. 1928	110
4	Do. Strlg. Bds. 1934	108
4	Queensland 1913-15	107
4½	St. Lucia Debs.	102
6	South Australia 1898-1900	103½
6	Do. 1901-1918	119
5	Do. 1911-1920	115½
4	Do. 1899-1916	104½
4	Do. 1929	108½
4	Do. 1916	106½
4	Do. 1917-18-24	107½
6	Tasmania 1897-1901	104
4	Do. 1908-11, 1913-14-20	107½
5	Trinidad Debs., an. drw. 1 p c...	107
4	Victoria 1899-1901	102½
4½	Do. 1904	106
4	Do. Rail. Loan 1907	106
4	Do. Loans 1908-13	106
4½	West. Austr. 1 p.c. ac. Sink. Fd.	107
4	Do. do.	106

REGISTERED AND INSCRIBED STOCKS.

No stamp duty except for Canada 4 p.c. Reduced (½ per cent.).

Rate.	Name.	Price.
4	Antigua Insc. Stk. Red. 1919-44	111
3½	Barbados Insc. Stk. 1925-42	107
3	British Colum. Insc. Stk. 1941	100½
4	British Guiana Insc..... 1935	116½
4	Canada Stk. Regd. ..1904-5-6-8	105
4	Do. 4 p.c. (late 5 p.c.) Regd. 1910	109
3½	Do. 3½ p.c. Stock Regd. 1909-34	107
4	Do. Ln. for 4 milln. stg. 1910-35	109
3	Do. Stk. Regd. 1938	103
2½	Do. Insc. 1947	92
4	Cape G. Hope Regd. — 1917-23	113
4	Do. (Ln. of '83) Insc. — 1923	115
4	Do. Cons. Stk. Insc..... 1916-36	113
3½	Do. Consol. Insc. Stock 1929-49	110
4	Ceylon Insc. Stock 1934	120
3	Do. 1940	103
4	Grenada Insc. Stock.... 1917-42	110
3½	Hong Kong Insc. Stock 1918-43	104
4	Jamaica Insc. Stock.... 1934	118
—	Do. 1922-44	99
4	Mauritius Inscribed 1937	118½
4	Natal Consd. Stk. Insc. 1927	117
4	Do. 1937	119
3½	Do. Inscribed Stock.. 1914-39	106
4	Newfoundland Inscribed 1913-38	107
4	Do. 1935	114
4	Do. Consd. Stk. Ins. 1936	114
4	N. S. Wales Stock Insc. 1933	119
3½	Do. 1924	109
3½	Do. 1918	106
3	Do 1915	100

Colonial, &c. (*continued*):—

Rate.	Name.	Price.
4	N. Zealnd. Con. Stk. Ins. 1929	114
3½	Do 1940	108
3	Do. Inscribed.... 1945	99
3	Quebec (Prov.) Ins. Stk. 1937	93
4	Queensland Stock Insc. 1915-24	110½
3½	Do. 1921-4-30	106
3½	Do. 1945	108
3	Do. 1922-47	99
4	St. Lucia Insc. Stock .. 1919-44	114½
4	S. Austrln. (1882-7) Reg. 1916-36	110½
3½	Do. In. Stk. Reg. 1939	110
3	Do. 1916-26	102
3/	Do. 1916	102
3½	Tasmanian Insc. Stock.. 1920-40	109
4	Do. 1920-40	116
4	Trinidad Insc. Stock.... 1917-42	110
3	Do. 1922-44	99
4	Victoria Rly. Loan '81, Inscribed Stock 1907	106
4	Victoria Insc. Stock 1908-13-19	107
4	Victoria (1883) Ins. Stk. 1920	113
3½	Do. Inscribed Stock 1921-3-6	107
4	Do. do. 1911-26	109
4	W. Austral. Insc. Stock 1934	116½
4	Do. 1911-31	109
3½	Do. 1915-35	105
3	Do. 1915-35	98
3	Do. 1916-36	98

FOREIGN STOCKS, BONDS, &c.

COUPONS PAYABLE IN LONDON.

Last Div.	Name.	Price.
36/	Argentine Ry. Loan 6 p.c. 1881	87½
15/	Do. 5 p.c. 1884	68
30/	Do. N. Cent. Ry. Ext. 5 p.c. 1887-8-9	68½
30/	Do. 5 p.c. Trsy. Convs. 1887	67
5/4½	Do. 4½ p.c. Interl. Gld. 1888	65
27/	Do. 4½ p.c. Stlg. Extrl. 1888	66
10/6	Do. 3½ p.c. External .. 1889	49
4	Do. 4 p.c. Ry. Guar. Res....	59
4½	Brazilian 1883	56
4½	Do. Gold.......... 1879	65½
4½	Do. 1888	55
36/	Buenos Ayres 1824	80
6	Do. 1882-3-6	48
6	Bulgarian 1888	93
6	Do. Mort. Bonds 1892	93
4½	Chilian 1885	76
4½	Do. 1886	77
4½	Do. 1887	76
4½	Do. 1889	83½
5	Do. 1892	89
4½	Do. 1893	75
4½	Do. 1895	73
5	Do. 1896	88
7	Chinese Silver 1894	97
6	Do. Gold 1895	107
6	Do. Apl. '95 by dwgs. 1901-15	109
5	Do. Red. dwgs. in 36 yr. 1896	99
5	Do. Do. Regis. 1896	99
1½	Colmbn. 1½ to 3 p.c. Ext. Bds. 1896	17
6	Cordova, Prov. 1886	25
—	Do. Eng. Ass. Certs.	24
—	Do. 6 p.c. 1887-8	25
—	Do. Eng. Ass. Certs.	24
3	Costa Rica "A"	30
2½	Do. "B"	24
3	Danish Gold 1914	98
10/	Ecuador N. Ext. Bds. 4½ p.c. ascn. to 5 p.c.	22
3½	Egypt'n Ins. Stk. lia. Stp. Dty. 1890	100
4	Do. State Domain 1878	102½
4	Do. D. Sanieh, Red. .. 1905	102½
6	Entre Rios.......... 1886-8	34
6	Do. Fndg. Ln. Bds. 1894-1921	29
6	Do. do. Parana City......	22½
15/	Greek 1881	39
15/	Do. 1884	39
12/	Do. Rentes..........	33
15/	Do. (Piræus-Larissa Ry.)	37
2/6	Do. Fundg. Loan ......(1) -	41
4	Guatemala Extl. Debt..........	29
6	Hawaiian	102
4	Hungarian Gold Rentes........	101½
3	Do. 1895	89½
6	Italian Irriga. Guar.	108½
5	Do. Maremmana	91
5	Japan 5 p.c.	101½
5	Mexican (Nat. R. Tehuantp c.)..	94½
6	Do. Extrl. 1893	96½

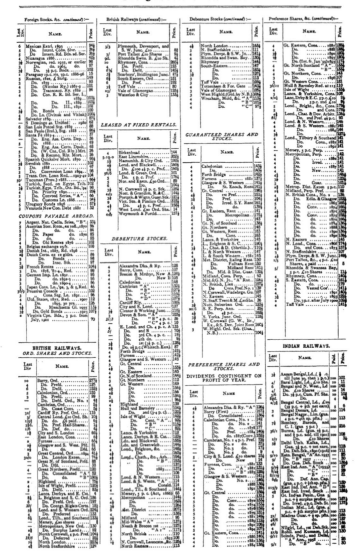

Foreign Stocks, &c. *continued*) :—

Last Div.	NAME.	Price
6	Mexican Extrl. 1893	94¼
5	Do. Intrnl. Cons. Slvr.	36¼
5	Do Intern. Rd. Bds. 2d. Ser.	36½
4	Nicaragua 1886	42½
3½	Norwegian, red. 1937, or earlier	98
3	Do. do. 1965, do.	97
3½	Do. 3½ p.c. Bnds.	102
1	Paraguay 1p.c. ris. 3p.c. 1886-96	15
5	Russian, 1822, £ Strlg.	149
3	Do. 1859	93
4	Do. (Nicolas Ry.) 1867-9	101
3	Do. Transcauc. Ry. 1882	94
4	Do. Con. R. R. Bd. Ser. I., 1889	103½
4	Do. Do. II., 1889	103½
4	Do. Do. III., 1891	102
3½	Do. Bonds	100
4	Do. Ln. (Dvinsk and Vitbsk)	100¼
6	Salvador 1889	87½
—	S Domingo 4s. Unified .. 1980	62
6	San Luis Potosi Stg. 1889	88
5	San Paulo (Brzl.), Stg. 1888	86½
6	Santa Fé 1883-4	37
—	Do. Eng. Ass. Certs. Dep.	36
5	Do. 1888	49
—	Do. Eng. Ass. Certs. Dpsit.	48
5	Do. (W. Cnt. Col. Rly.) Mrt.	26
5	Do. & Reconq. Rly. Mort.	26
5	Spanish Quickslvr Mort. 1870	99½
3½	Swedish 1880	102
3	Do. 1888	97
3	Do. Conversion Loan 1894	98
5	Trans. Gov. Loan Red...1903-42	104
50/	Tucuman (Prov.) 1888	66½
4	Turkish, Secd. on Egypt. Trib.	102
3½	Turkish, Egpt. Trib., Ott. Bd., '94	98
4	Do. Priority 1890	89½
1	Do. Convted Series, "A"	66
5	Do. Customs Ln. 1886	94½
5	Uruguay Bonds 1896	57½
3	Venzuela New Con. Debt 1881	32

COUPONS PAYABLE ABROAD.

Last Div.	NAME.	Price
7	Argent. Nat. Cedla. Sries, "B"	33½
5	Austrian Ster. Rnts., ex 10fl., 1870	86
5	Do. do. do.	84
5	Do. Paper do. 1870	85
5	Do. do. do.	85
4	Do. Gld Rentes 1876	102
3	Belgian exchange 25fr.	100
3½	Danish Int., 1887, Rd. 1896	—
2½	Dutch Certs. ex 12 gldrs.	86
3	Do. Bonds	98
3	Do. Insc. Stk.	97
3½	French Rentes	104½
3	Do. 1878, '81-4., Red.	99
3	German Imp. Ln. 1891	95
3	Do. do. 1892-3	95
3	Do. do. 1890-4	96
5	Japan Cons. Ln., '92, 3, & 5, Red.	46
36/9	Prussian Consols	102
3	" Cons. Stg. Ln. 1891	96
4	Utd. States, 1877, Red. 1907	112
4	Do. 1895, 30 yrs.	126
3½	Do. Maschsetts Gl. 1935	113½
3½	Do. Gold Bonds 1923	107½
2	Virginia Cpn. Bds., 3 p.c. from July, 1901	70

BRITISH RAILWAYS.
ORD. SHARES AND STOCKS.

Last Div	NAME.	Price.
10	Barry, Ord.	277½
4	Do. Prefd.	125
6	Do. Defd.	152½
5	Caledonian, Ord.	155
3	Do. Prefd.	99
—	Do. Defd. Ord., No. 1	4½
	Cambrian, Ord.	5½
—	Do. Coast Cons.	5½
32/	Cardiff Ry. Pref. Ord.	115
3/	Central Lond. £10 Ord. Sh.	10½
1/9½	Do. do. £6 paid	6½
3½d.	Do. Pref. Half-Shares	1½
1/6	Do. Def. do.	4½
1½	City and S. London	69½
—	East London, Cons.	6½
2	Furness	65½
2½	Glasgow and S. West. Pfd.	81
2½	Do. do. Dfd.	65
3	Great Central, Ord....1894	41½
32/0	Do. London Exten.	74½
—	Great N. of Scotland, Prfd.	88
—	Do. Dfd.	33
4	Great Northern, Prefd.	120
—	Do. Consolidated "A"	52
—	Do. do. "B"	190½
2	Highland	75½
4	Isle of Wight, Prefd.	120½
3	Do. Defd.	83½
—	Lancs. Derbys. and E. Cst.	4
8½	L. Brighton and S. C. Ord.	186
6	Do. Prefd. Ord.	197
10/	Do. Contgt. Rights Certs.	18½
5½	Lond. and S. Western Ord.	224½
4	Do. Preferred	133
6½	Lond., Tilb., and Southend	133½
—	Mersey, £20 shares	¾
—	Metropolitan, New Ord.	130
2½	Do. Surplus Lands	92
4	North Cornwall, 4 p.c. Pref.	104½
18/6	Do. Deferred	22½
7½	North London	223½
4½	North Staffordshire	129

British Railways (*continued*) :—

Last Div.	NAME.	Price.
3/3	Plymouth, Devenport, and S. W. Junc. £10	8½
3/	Port Talbot £10 Shares	9½
9d.	Rhondda Swns. B. £10 Sh.	4½
10	Rhymney, Cons.	265½
4	Do. Prefd.	123
6¼	Do. Defd.	145½
1½	Scarboro', Bridlington Junc.	47½
6½	South Eastern, Ord.	151
6	Do. Pref.	192
3½	Taff Vale	80
25/	Vale of Glamorgan	125½
3	Waterloo & City	133½

LEASED AT FIXED RENTALS.

Last Div.	NAME.	Price.
4	Birkenhead	144
5.19.0	East Lincnshire	202½
5½	Hamsmith. & City Ord.	192½
4½	Lond. and Blackwll.	160½
4½	Do. £100 4½ p. c. Pref.	160½
56/6	Lond. & Green. Ord.	101
5	Do. 5 p. c. Pref.	176½
5	Nor. and Eastn. £50 Ord.	89
6	Do.	104½
3½	N. Cornwall 3½ p. c. Stk.	125½
4½	Nott. & Granthm. R. & C.	144½
3½	Portptk. & Wigtn. Guar. Stk.	121½
9	Vict. Stn. & Pimlico Ord.	312½
4½	Do. 4½ p. c. Pref.	158½
4/	West Lond. £20 Ord. Shs.	14
4½	Weymouth & Portld.	157½

DEBENTURE STOCKS.

Last Div.	NAME.	Price.
4	Alexandra Dks. & Ry.	128
3	Barry, Cons.	107
4	Brecon & Mrthyr, New A	124½
4	Do. New B	105
4	Caledonian	148
4	Cambrian "A"	132½
4	Do. "B"	127½
4	Do. "C"	119½
4	Do. "D"	107½
3	Cardiff Rly.	100½
4	City and S. Lond.	137
3½	Cleator & Working Junc.	118½
3	Devon & Som. "A"	103½
16/3	Do. "B" 4 p. c.	36
—	Do. "C" 4 p. c.	10
4	E. Lond. 2nd Ch. 4 p. c. A	135
8/	Do. 2nd B	70½
—	Do. 3rd Ch. 4 p. c.	19½
—	Do. 4th do.	9½
3½	Do. 1st (3½ p. c.)	128½
2½	Do. 2½ p.c. (Whitech. Exn).	87
4	Forth Bridge	142½
4	Furness	142½
4	Glasgow and S. Western	143
5	Gt. Central	—
4½	Do.	155½
4	Gt. Eastern	145
4	Gt. N. of Scotland	144½
3	Gt. Northern	112
4	Gt. Western	149
4½	Do	156½
4½	Do.	166
5	Do.	184½
2½	Do.	96½
4	Highland	139
3	Hull and Barnsley	104½
3	Do. 2nd (3-4 p. c).	122½
4	Isle of Wight	142½
3	Do. Cent. "A"	92½
4½	Do. "B"	115½
4	Do. "C"	82½
3	Lancs. & Yorkshire	112
4	Lancs. Derbys. & E. Cst.	123½
4½	Ldn. and Blackwall	155½
4	Ldn. and Greenwich	144½
4	Lond., Brighton, &c.	148½
4½	Do.	165½
4½	Lond., Chath., &c., Arb.	154½
4½	Do. "B"	153½
4	Do.	137½
4	Do. 1883	137½
3	Do.	106
3	Lond. & N. Western	115
3	Lond. & S. Westn. "A"	114
3	Do. Consld.	114
4	Lond., Til., & Southend	144½
—	Mersey, 5 p. c. (Act, 1866)	65
4	Metropolitan	144½
4½	Do.	162½
3½	Do.	126½
6	Met. District	207½
4	Do.	138½
2½	Midland	96
4½	Mid-Wales "A"	137½
4	Neath & Brecon 1st	127½
4	Do. "A 1"	117½
3	North British	110
3	Do. 1893	108
3½	N. Cornwall, Launcstn., &c.	125½
	North Eastern	113

Debenture Stocks (*continued*) :—

Last Div.	NAME.	Price.
4½	North London	163½
3	N. Staffordshire	111
4	Plym. Devpt. & S. W. Jn.	141½
4	Rhondda and Swan. Bay	130½
4	Rhymney	144½
4	South-Eastern	147
5	Do.	183½
3½	Do.	127½
3	Do.	113
3	Taff Vale	109½
4	Tottenham & For. Gate	143½
3	Vale of Glamorgan	106½
3	West Highld. (Gtd. by N. B.)	106½
4	Wrexham, Mold, &c. "A"	113½
4	Do. "B"	101½
4	Do. "C"	97½

GUARANTEED SHARES AND STOCKS.

Last Div.	NAME.	Price.
4	Caledonian	143½
4	Do.	143½
4	Forth Bridge	142½
4	Furness 1881	137½
4	Glasgow & S. Western	141½
4	Do. St. Enoch, Rent	141½
6	Gt. Central	198½
4½	Do. 1st Pref.	151½
3½	Do. Pref.	104½
5	Do. Irred. S.Y. Rent	161½
4½	Do. do.	139½
4	Gt. Eastern, Rent	141
5	Do. Metropolitan	175½
4	Do.	143
4	Gt. N. of Scotland	138½
4	Gt. Northern	145
5	Gt. Western, Rent	183
5	Do. Cons.	183
4	Lancs. & Yorkshire	145
5	L., Brighton & S. C.	180½
3½	L., Chat. & D. (Shrtlds.)	110½
4	L. & North Western	147
4	L. & South Western .. 1881	145
4½	Met. District, Ealing Rent	150
4½	Do. Fulham Rent	150
4	Do. Midland Rent	141½
4	Do. Mid. & Dist. Guar.	130½
2½	Midland, Cons. Perp.	93
3	Mid. & G. N. Jt., "A" Rnt.	106½
3	N. British, Lien	107½
4	Do Cons. Pref. No. 1	139
3	N. Cornwall, Wadebrge. Gu.	107
4	N. Eastern	145
5	N. Staff. Trent & M. £20 Shs.	36
3½	Nott. Suburban Ord.	123½
20/6	S. E. Perp. Ann.	35½
4½	Do. 4½ p.c.	162½
3½	S. Yorks. Junc. Ord.	118½
4½	W. Cornwall (G. W., Br., Ex., & S. Dev. Joint Rent	160½
3	W. Highl. Ord. Stk. (Gua., N.B.)	104½

PREFERENCE SHARES AND STOCKS.

DIVIDENDS CONTINGENT ON PROFIT OF YEAR.

Last Div.	NAME	Price.
4½	Alexandra Dks. & Ry. "A"	126½
5	Barry (First)	167½
4	Do. Consolidated	136½
4	Caledonian Cons., No. 1	142
4	Do. do. No. 2	141
5	Do. do. 1878	177
4	Do. Pref. 1884	140½
4	Do. do. 1887 (Conv.)	152½
—	Cambrian, No. 1 4 p.c. Pref.	72½
—	Do. No. 2 do.	37½
—	Do. No. 3 do.	17½
—	Do. No. 4 do.	9
5	City & S. Lond. £10 shares	15½
—	Do. New	14
4	Furness, Cons. 1881	133
4	Do. ......"A" 1881	131½
4	Do. ......"B" 1883	129½
4	Glasgow & S. Western	141½
4	Do. No. 2	140½
4	Do. 1888	139½
4	Do. 1891	139½
5	Gt. Central	159½
4	Do.	131½
5	Do. Conv..... 1872	153½
5	Do. do. 1874	153½
5	Do. do. 1876	152½
5	Do. do. 1879	151½
5	Do. do. 1881	149½
4	Do. 1889	112½
4	Do. 1891	108½
5	Do. 1894	107½
4	Gt. Eastern, Cons.	141½
4	Do. 1886	140½
4	Do. 1881	138½
4	Do. 1884	138½

Preference Shares, &c. (*continued*) :—

Last Div.	NAME.	Price.
4	Gt. Eastern, Cons.....1887	138½
4	Do. 1888	138½
3½	Do. 1890	120½
4½	Do. 1893	120½
—	Do. (Int. fr. Jan '99) 1893	117½
4	Gt. North Scotland "A"	133½
4	Do. "B"	133½
4	Gt. Northern, Cons.	143
3	Do. 1896	107
5	Gt. Western Cons.	181
36/11	Hull & Barnsley Red. at 115	110
4	Isle of Wight	133½
3	Lancs. & Yorkshire, Cons.	108
2/2½	Lanc. Drby & E.C. 5 p.c. £10	8½
—	Do. 5 p.c. 2nd £10	8½
5	Lond., Bright., &c., Cons.	178½
5	Do. 2nd Cons.	178½
4½	Lond., Chat. & Dov. Arbitr.	136½
25/	Do, 2nd Pref. 4½ p.c.	93
4	Lond. & N. Western	146
4	Lond. & S. Western .. 1881	145
4	Do. 1884	144
3½	Do.	127½
4	Lond., Tilbury & Southend	141
4	Do. Cons., 1887	141
4	Do 1891	141
—	Mersey, 5 p.c. Perp.	—
4	Metropolitan, Perp.	142
4	Do. 1880	141
4	Do. Irred.	141
4	Do. 1887	141
4	Do. New	141
4½	Do.	146½
3½	Do.	123½
3	Do. Guar.	101½
2½	Metrop. Dist. Exten 5 p.c.	110
2½	Midland, Perp. Pref.	92
4	N. British Cons., No. 2	136
4½	Do. Edin. & Glasgow	152½
5	Do. 1865	165½
5	Do. Conv. 1874	166½
4½	Do. 1875	152½
4½	Do. Conv. 1875	152½
5	Do. do. 1870	166½
4	Do. do. 1884	136½
4	Do. do. 1888	136½
4	Do. do. 1890	136½
4	Do. do. 1892	136½
4	N. Eastern	145
4½	N. Lond., Cons. 1866	174½
4½	Do. 2nd Cons. .. 1875	157½
3	N. Staffordshire	107
4½	Plym. Devpt. & S. W. Junc.	149½
1/5	Port Talbot, &c., 4 p.c. £10 Shares, 4 paid	5
5/	Rhondda & Swansea Bay, 5 p.c. £10 Shares	11½
4	Rhymney, Cons.	140½
4½	S. Eastern, Cons.	161½
5	Do. do.	179
4	Do. Vested Cos'.	141½
4	Do. 1891	140½
3½	Do. 1893	122½
2	Do. 3 p.c. after July 1900	102½
4	Taff Vale	141½

INDIAN RAILWAYS.

Last Div.	NAME.	Paid.	Price.
3½	Assam Bengal, Ld., (½ .c. till June 30, then 3 p.c.)	100	101
4/	Barsi Light, Ld., £10 Shs.	10	11
6	Bengal and N. West., Ld	100	148
4/	Do. £10 Shares	10	14
3/6	Do. 3½ p.c. Cum. Pf. Shs.	10	10½
8½d.	Do.	4	4½
2/3½	Bengal Central, Ld., £10 (3½ p.c. + ½th net earn)	5	6
3	Bengal Dooars, Ld.	100	114
4	Bengal Nagpr., Lim. (gua. 4 p.c. + ¼th sp. pfts.)	100	113
7½	Bombay, Baroda, and C. I. (gua 5 p.c)	100	216
36/1	Burma, Ld. (gua. 2½ p.c. and ½ p.c. add. till 1901)	100	108
1/7	Do. £10 Shares		3½
3½	Delhi Umb. Kalka, Ld., Gua. 3½ p.c. + net earn.	100	118
4	Do. Deb. Stk., 1890 (1916)	100	111
9/10	Eatn. Bengal, "A" An. 1957	—	35
9/	Do. "B" 1957	—	30
4	Do. Gua. Deb. Stock	100	138½
9/7½	East Ind. Ann. "A" (1953)	—	27
8/4½	Do. "C"	—	29
8/11½	Do. "B"	—	31
6⅞	Do. Def. Ann. Cap. (gua. 4 p.c. + ⅕th sp. pfts.)	—	150
115/9	East Ind. Def. Ann. "D"	—	156
4½	East Ind. Irred. Stock	100	188½
5	Gt. Indian Penin., Gua 5 p.c. + ½ surplus profits	100	167½
4	Do. Irred. 4 p.c. Deb. St.	100	137½
4	Indian Mid., Ld. (gua. 4 p.c. + ¼th surplus pfts.)	100	113
51/	Madras Guar. + ½ sp. pfts.	100	166
48/6	Do. do.	100	157
46/	Do. do.	100	146
4	Nilgiri, Ld., 1st Deb. Stk.	100	98
51/9	Rohil. and Kumaon, Ld.	100	130
9/11	Scinde, Punj., and Delhi, "A" Ann., 1958	—	25
9/1	Do. "B" do.	—	30

Indian Railways (*continued*):—

Last Div.	Name.	Paid.	Price.
4	South Behar, Ld., £10 shs.	100	100
3½	Do. Deb. Stk. Red.	100	101
4½	South Ind., Gu. Deb. Stk.	100	158½
5	South Indian, Ld. (gua. 3 p.c., and ½ spls. profits)	100	122½
5	Sthn. Mahratta, Ld. (3½ p.c. & ½th net earnings)	100	115½
4	Do. Deb. Stk. Red.	100	121
3½	Southern Punjab, Ld.	100	105
3½	Do. Deb. Stk. Red.	—	104
5	Nizam's Gua. State, Ld. (†	100	114½
4	Do. Mort. Deb., 1936	100	107
4	Do. do. Reg.	100	106
17/3½	Nizam's Gua. State, Ld., 3½ p.c. Mt. Deb. bearer	—	94½
17/3½	Do. Reg. do. ..	—	93½
5	W. of India Portgese., Ld.	100	68½
5	Do. Deb. Stk., Red	100	98

RAILWAYS.—BRITISH POSSESSIONS.

Last Div.	Name.	Paid.	Price.
5	Atlantic & N.W. Gua. 1 Mt. Bds., 1937	100	126½
5/3	Buff. & L. Huron Ord. Sh.	10	13½
5½	Do. 1st Mt. Perp. Bds. 1879	100	143½
5½	Do. 2nd Mt. Perp. Bds.	100	143½
—	Calgary & Edmon. 6 p.c. 1st Mt. Stg. Bds. Red..	100	78½
5	Canada Cent. 1st Mt. Bds. Red.	100	103
4	Can. Pacific Pref. Stk.	100	101
5	Do. Strl. 1st Mt. Deb. Bds. 1915	100	117
3½	Do. Ld. Grnt. Bds. 1938..	100	108
3½	Do. Ld. Grnt. Ins. Stk. ..	100	107
4	Do. Perp. Cons. Deb. Stk.	100	115
5	Do. Algoma Bch. 1st Mt. Bds., 1937	100	121
3	Demerara, Original Stock	100	46
7	Do. Perp. Pref. Stk.	100	152½
2/10	Do. 4 p.c. Cum. Ext. Pref. £10 Shs.	4	8
—	Dominion Atlntc. Ord. Stk.	100	33½
5	Do. 5 p.c. Pref. Stk.	100	97½
4	Do. 1st. Deb. Stk.	100	105½
4	Do. 2nd do. Red.	100	99
1/3	Emu Bay & Mt. Bischoff, Ld.	5	4½
4½	Do. Irred. Deb. Stk ...	100	98
nil.	Gd. Trunk of Canada, Stk.	100	9½
6	Do. 2nd. Equip. Mt. Bds.	100	133
5	Do. Perp. Deb. Stk... ..	100	138½
5	Do. Gt. Westn. Deb. Stk.	100	130½
5	Do. Nthn. of Can. 1st Mt. Bds, 1902	100	103½
4	Do. do. Deb. Stk	100	103
5	Do. G. T. Geor. Bay & L. Erie 1 Mt., 1903	100	105
5	Do. Mid. of Can. Stl. 1st Mt. (Mid. Sec.) 1908	100	105
5	Do. do. Cons. 1 Mt. Bds. 1912	100	107
5	Do. Mont. & Champ. 1 Mt. Bds., 1902	100	104
	Do. Welln., Grey & Brce. 7 p.c. Bds. 1 Mt.	100	109
—	Jamaica 1st Mtg. Bds. Red.	—	103
—	Manitoba & N. W., 6 p.c. 1st Mt. Bds., Red	100	—
—	Do. Ldn. Bdhldrs. Certs.	—	—
5	Manitoba S. W. Col. 1 Mt. Bd., 1934 $1,000 price %	—	118
—	Mid. of W. Aust. Ld. 6 p.c. 1 Mt. Dbs., Red.	100	40
4	Do. Deb. Bds., Red.	100	103
4	Nakusp & Slocan Bds., 1918	100	106
3	Natal Zululand Ld. Debs.,	100	72½
5	N. Brunswick 1st Mt. Stg. Bds., 1934	100	121
4	Do. Perp. Cons. Deb. Stk.	100	114
—	N. Zealand Mid., Ld., 5 p.c. 1st Mt. Debs..........	100	35
6	Ontario & Queb. Cap. Stk.	$100	151½
5	Do. Perm. Deb. Stk......	100	143½
—	Qu'Appelle, L. Lake & Sask. 6 p.c. 1 Mt. Bds. Red.	100	40½
	Queb. & L. S. John, 1st Mt. Bds., 1909	100	22
	Quebec Cent., Prior Ln. Bds., 1908	100	107
1½	Do. 5 p.c. Inc. Bds.	100	37
4	St. Lawr. & Ott. Stl. 1st Mt.	100	112
4	Shuswap & Okan., 1st Mt. Deb. Bds., 1915	100	76
5	Temiscouata, 5 p.c. Stl. 1st Deb. Bds., Red.	100	9½
5	Do. (S. Franc. Brch.) 5 p.c. Stl. 1 Mt. Db. Bds., 1910	100	10
4	Toronto, Grey & B. 1st Mt.	100	112
1/2	Well. & Mana. £5 Shs. ..	1	½
5	Do. Debs., 1908	100	105
5	Do. 2nd Debs., 1908	100	104
5	Do. 3rd do., 1908	100	103
6	Atlan. & St. Law. Shs., 6 p.c.	100	163½
5	Gd. Trunk Mt. Bds., 1934	100	116½
5	Michigan Air Line, 5 p.c. 1st Mt. Bds., 1902	100	104
4	Minneap., S. P. & S t. Ste. Mar, 1st Mt. Bds., 1938	$1000	93

AMERICAN RAILROAD STOCKS AND SHARES.

Last Div.	Name.	Paid.	Price.
6/	Alab. Gt. Sthn. A 6 p.c. Pref.	10l.	9
—	Do. do "B" Ord. ..	10l.	1½
—	Alabma. N. Orl.-Tex. &c., "A" Pref.	10l.	½
—	Do. "B" Def.	10l.	½
5½	Atlant. First Lsd. Ls. Rtl. Trust....................	Stk.	98½
—	Baltimore & Ohio Com. ..	$100	20
—	Baltimore Ohio S.W. Pref.	$100	7
—	Chesap. & Ohio Com.	$100	22½
—	Chic. Gt. West. 5 p.c. Pref. Stock "A"	$100	32½
—	Do. do. Scrip. In.......	—	30½
8/3	Do. 4 p.c. Deb. Stk.......	$100	67½
4	Do. Interest in Scrip	$100	63½
$4	Chic. Junc. Rl. & Un. Stk. Yds. Com.	$100	121½
$1½	Do. 6 p.c. Cum. Pref.	$100	120½
$3½	Chic. Mil. & St. P. Pref...	$100	149
7	Cleve. & Pittsburgh	$10	84½
$1½	Clev., Cincin., Chic., & St. Louis Com.	$100	—
—	Erie 4 p.c. Non-Cum. 1st Pf.	—	31½
—	Do. 4 p.c. do. 2nd Pf.	—	18
$2½	Gt. Northern Pref.	$100	180
$2½	Illinois Cen. Lsd. Lines ..	$100	95½
—	Kansas City, Pitts & G. ..	$100	19
$3	L. Shore & Mich. Sth. C.	$100	190
—	Mex. Cen. Ltd. Com.	$100	5
—	Miss. Kan. & Tex. Pref...	$100	37½
2½	N.Y., Pen. & O. 1st Mt. Tst. Ltd., Ord.	—	47½
4	Do. 1st Mort. Deb. Stk. ..	$100	92½
8	North Pennsylvania	$50	—
—	Northn. Pacific, Com.....	$100	23½
1½	Pitts. F. Wayne & Chic...	$100	174
—	Reading 1st Pref.	$50	23½
—	Do. 2nd Pref.	$50	12
—	S. Louis & S. Fran. Com.	$100	6
—	Do. 2nd Pref.	$100	25½
6	St. Louis Bridge 1st Pref..	$100	107
3	Do. 2nd Pref.	$100	50
6	Tunnel Rail. of St. Louis	$100	107
$1½	St. Paul, Min. and Man...	$100	147½
—	Southern, Com.	$100	9½
—	Wabash, Common..........	$100	8

AMERICAN RAILROAD BONDS. CURRENCY.

Last Div.	Name.	Price.
7	Albany & Susq. 1 Con. Mrt. 1906	118
7	Allegheny Val. 1 Mt....... 1910	127½
5	Canada Southern 1 Mt..... 1908	112½
5	Chic. & N. West. Sk. Fd. Db. 1933	117½
5	Do. Deb. Coupon 1921	112½
6	Chicago & Tomah 1905	109½
5	Chic. Burl. & Q. Skg. Fd. 1901	102½
4	Do. Nebraska Ext....... —	100
6	Chic., Mil., & S. Pl., 1 Mt. S.W. Div... 1909	117½
7	Do. (S. Paul Div.) 1 Mt. 1902	132½
5	Do. (La Cross & D. 1919	114½
7	Do. 1 Mt. (Hast. & Dak.) 1910	127½
5	Do. Chic. & Mis. Riv. 1 Mt. 1926	112½
5	Chic., Rock Is. and Pac. 1 Mt. Ext. 1934	108
6	Det., G. Haven & Mil. Equip 1918	105
6	Do. do. Cons. Mt. 1918	102½
6	Ill. Cent., 1 Mt., Chic. & S. 1898	—
7	Indianap. & Vin., 1 Mt. .. 1908	125
6	Do. do. 2 Mt. .. 1900	100½
6	Lehigh Val., Cons. Mt..... 1923	114½
—	Mexic. Cent., Ln. 2 Cons. Inc. —	5
7	N.Y. Cent. & H.R. Mt. Bonds 1903	119½
5	Do. Deb. 1904	111½
6	Penns. Cons. S. F M. 1905	114½
4	West Shore, 1 Mt. 2361	110

DITTO—GOLD.

Last Div.	Name.	Price.
6	Alabama Gt. Sthn. 1 Mt. ..1908	114
5	Do. Mid. 1 1928	90½
4	Allegheny Val. Gen. Mt. ..1942	107½
4	Atch., Top., & S. Fé Gn. Mt. 1995	94½
3	Do. Adj. Mt...............1995	67
5	Do. Equipt. Tmst. ...... —	102½
5	Atlantic & Dan 1 Mt.......1950	96½
5	Baltimore & Ohio..........1925	102
5	Do. Speyer's Tst. Recpts. 1925	102
5	Do. Cons. Mt. 1988	107½
4½	Do. 4½ p.c. 1 Mt. Term. 1934	86½
4½	Do. Brown Shipley's Dep. Cts. —	86½
5	Balt. Belt 5 p.c. 1 Mort.....1990	92½
4½	Balt. & Ohio S.W. 1 Mt. ..1990	102
4½	Do. 4½ p.c. 1 Cons. Mt. 1893 1993	73½
—	Do. Inc. Mt. 5 p.c. Cl. A —	28
—	Do. do. Cl. B —	10
5	Balt. & Ohio S.W. Term 5 p.c. 1942	97½
6	Balt. & Ptmac (Mn. L.) 1 Mt. 1911	124
6	Do. do. (Tunnel) 1 Mt. 1911	126
4	Beech Creek 1 Mt. 1936	109
4	Carthage & Adiron 1 Mt...1981	107

American Railroad Bonds—Gold *continued*):—

Last Div.	Name.	Price.
5	Cent. of Georgia 1 Mort. ..1945	117½
5	Do. Cons. Mt. 1945	90½
5	Cent. of N. Jrsy. Gn. Mt...1987	116
6	Central Pacific, 1 Mort. 1890	102½
6	Do. Speyer's Certs....... —	106
5	Do. Land Grant 1900	101
5	Chesap. & Ohio 1st Cons. Mt. 1939	116
4½	Do. Gen. Mt...............1992	83
6	Chic. & W. Ind. Gen. Mt. Skg. Fd. 1932	119½
5	Chic. Mil. & St. Pl. (Chic. & L. Sup.) 1 Mt. 1921	114½
5	Do. Chic. & Pac. W. 1921	117½
5	Do. Wisc. & Minn. 1 Mt. 1921	112½
5	Do. Terminal Mt. 1914	114½
4	Do. General Mt. 1989	106½
5	Chic. St. L. & N. Orleans..1951	120
4	Do. 1 Mort. (Memphis) ..1951	104
4	Clevel., Cin., Chic. & St. L., 1 Mt. (Cairo)..............1939	90
4	Do. 1 Mt. (Cinc., Wab., & Mich.) 1991	90
4	Do. 1 Col. Tst. Mt. (S. Louis) 1990	95
4	Do. General Mt. 1993	80½
4½	Clevel. & Mar. Mt. 1935	109
4½	Clevel. & Pittsburgh 1942	116½
4½	Do. Series B. 1942	116½
—	Colorado Mid. 1 Mt. 1936	63½
—	Do. Bdhrs.' Comm. Certs. —	63½
4	Dnvr. & R. Gde. 1 Cons. Mt. 1936	96
5	Do Imp. Mort.............1928	92
4	Detroit & Mack. 1 Lien 1995	90
5	E. Tennes., Virg., & Grgia. Cons. Mt. 1956	111½
5	Elmira, Cort., & Nthn. Mt. 1914	100
4	Erie 1 Cons. Mt. Pr. Ln. ..1996	93
3	Do. Gen. Lien 1996	76
6	Galvest., Harrisb., &c., 1 Mt....	110
5	Georgia, Car. & N. 1 Mt. ..1929	96
4½	Gd. Rpds & Indn. Ex. 1 Mt. 1941	112½
5	Do. 1 Mt. (Muskegon) ..1926	39½
3½	Illinois Cent. 1 Mt. 1951	104½
4	Do. 1952	104½
4	Do. Cairo Bdge. ..1950	102
4	Do. 1953	102
4	Do. General Mort. ..1904	102½
5	Kans. City, Pitts. & G. 1 M. 1923	73½
3½	L. Shore & Mich. Southern 1997	106½
4½	Lehigh Val. N.Y. 1 Mt.....1940	104
5	Lehigh Val. Term. 1 Mt. ..1941	110
5	Long Island 1931	117½
5	Do. Deb. 1934	100
5	Do. (N. Shore Bch.) 1 Cons. Mt. 1932	92½
6	Louisville & Nash. G. Mt. ..1930	120
6	Do. 2 Mt. Sk. Fd. (S. & N. Alabama 1910	107
6	Do. 1 Mt. N. Orl. & Mb. 1930	1 5½
5	Do. 1 Mt. Coll. Tst. 1931	1 4½
4	Do. Unified 1940	9½
4½	Do. Mobile & Montgy. 1 Mt. 1945	11½
4	Manhattan Cons. Mt. 1990	9½
4	Mexican Cent. Cons. Mt. ..1911	67
—	Do. 1 Cons. Inc, ...	15
6	Mexican Nat. 1 Mt..........1927	104
3½	Do. 2 Mt. 6 p.c. Inc. A 1917	52½
—	Do. do. B..1917	9
3	Michig. Cnt. (Battle Ck. & S.) 1 Mt. 1980	85
5	Minneap. & S. L. 1 Consold. 19 4	107½
4	Minne., Slt S. M. & A. 1 Mt. 1920	100
5	Minneapolis Westn. 1 Mt...1911	105½
4	Miss. Kans. & Tex. 1 Mt...1990	91
4	Do. 2 do. 1990	63
4	Mobile & Birm. Mt. Inc....1945	38
5	Do. P. Lien..............1945	88
4	Mohawk & Mal. 1 Mt.......1991	108
5	Montana Cent. 1 Mt. 1937	111½
5	Nashv., Chattan., & S. L. 1 Cons. Mt...................1928	102½
5	Nash., Flor., & Shff. Mt...1937	95½
4	N. Y. & Putnam 1 Cons. Mt. 1993	108
5	N. Y., Brooklyn, & Man. B. 1 Cons. Mt..................1935	107½
4	N. Y. Cent. & Hud. R. Deb. Certs. 1890 1905	104
4	Do. Ext. Debt. Certs....1905	106
7	N. Y., L. Erie, & W. 1 Cons. Mt. (Erie) 1920	144½
7	Do. 1 Con. Mt. Fd. Coup. 1920	139½
5	N. Y., Onto., & W. Cons. 1 Mt......................1939	109
4	Do. 4 p.c. Refund. Mt...1992	100
6	Norfolk & West. Gn. Mt....1931	124
6	Do. Imp. & Ext..........1934	117½
4	Do. 1 Cons. Mt........ —	84
6	N. Pacific Gn. 1 Mt. Ld. Gt. 1921	—
4	Do. P. Ln. Rl. & Ld. Gt. —	99
3	Do. Gn. Ln. Rl. & Ld. Gt. —	63
5	Oregon & Calif. 1 Mt.......1927	80
6	Panama Skg. Fd. Subsidy..1910	102½
4½	Pennsylvania Rlrd. 1913	110
4	Do. Equip. Tst. Ser. A..1914	104
4	Do. Cons. Mt............1943	112½
4½	Penna. Company 1st Mort. 1921	113½
5	Perkiomen 1 Mrt., 2nd ser..1918	91½
4½	Pitts., C., C., & St. Ls. Con. Mt. G. B., Ser. A 1940-2	112
4	Do. Cons. Mort., Ser. D..1945	102½
6	Pittsbgh., Cle., & Toledo ..1922	100½
4	Reading, Phil., & R. Genl. 1997	86
5	Richmond & Dan. Equip. ..1909	97½
5	Rio Grande Junc. 1st Mort. 1939	90
4	Rio Grande West 1st Tst. Mt. 1939	87½
7	S. Louis Bridge 1st Mort 1929	134½
5	S. Louis Mchts. Bdge. Term. 1st Mort................1930	102½
4	S. Louis S. West 1st Mort..1989	75
—	Do. 4 p.c. 2nd Mort. Inc. 1989	30
4½	S. Louis Term. Cupples Sta. & Prop. 1st. Mrt. 4½ p.c. 1902-17	100
4½	St. Paul Minn., & Manit. 1933	110

American Railroad Bonds (*continued*):

Last Div.	Name.	Price.
6	St. Paul, Minn., & Manit. 1933	132½
6	Shamokin, Sunbury, &c. 2 Mt. 1925	109
5	S. & N. Alabama Cons. Mt. 1936	102
5	Southern 1 Cons. Coup. 1994	96
4	Do. E. Tennes Reorg. Lien ..1938	100
6	S. Pacific of Cal. 1 Mt...1905-12	111
4½	Trml. Assn. of S. Louis 1 Mt. 1939	112½
5	Do. 1 Cons. Mt..........1944	109
5	Texas & Pac. 1 Mt.........2000	104½
—	Do. 5 p.c. 2 Mt. Income 2000	36½
5	Toledo & Ohio Cent. 1 Mt. West. Div. 1935	102½
4½	Toledo., Walhon., Val., & Ohio 1 Mt. 1931-3	111½
—	Union Pacific 1 Mt. 4 p.c. ..1947	97
—	Union Pac., Linc., & Color. 1 Mt. 1918	—
4	United N. Jersey Gen. Mt...1944	115½
6	Vicksbrg., Shrevept., & Pac. Pr. Ln. Mt. 1915	102½
5	Wabash 1 Mt. 1939	110
4	Wn. Pennsylvania Mt. 1928	106½
5	W. Virga. & Pittsbg. 1 Mt. 1990	75
5	Wheeling & L. Erie 1 Mt. (Wheelg. Div.) 5 p.c......1928	90½
5	Do. Extn. Imp. Mt. 1930	90
—	Do. do. Brown Shipley's Cts...	—
5	Willmar & Sioux Falls 1 Mt. 1938	110

STERLING.

Last Div.	Name.	Price.
6	Alabama Gt. Sthn. Deb. 1906	104½
5	Do. Gen. Mort. ..1927-8	98
5	Alabama, N. Orl., Tex. & Pac. 5 p.c. "A" Dbs...1910-40	99
5s/	Do. do. "B" do. 1910-40	55
—	Do. do. "C" do.	19
—	Allegheny Valley 1910	130
4	Atlantic 1st Leased Line Perp...	100
6	Baltimore and Ohio 1902	108
6	Do. do. 1910	120
5	Do. do. 1877........	104
—	Do. Morgan's Certs. ..	104
4½	Do. do. 1933	96
6	Chicago & Alton Cons. Mt. 1903	112
5	Chic. St. Paul & Kan. City Priority	106½
6	Eastn. of Massachusetts....1906	117½
5	Illinois Cent. Skg. Fd.	103
5	Do. 1905	106
3½	Do. 1950	99½
4	Do. 1 Mt. 1951	112
3	Do. 1 Mt. 1951	92½
6	Louisville & Nash., M. C. & L. Div., 1 Mt. 1902	104½
7	Do. 1 Mt. (Memphis & O.)........................1901	112
55/8	Mexican Nat. "A" Certs. 5 p.c. Non. cum.	40½
—	Do. "B" Certs....	9
6	N.Y. & Canada 1 Mt.......1904	118
6	N. York Cent. & H.R. Mort. 1903	112
4½	N. York, Penns., & Ohio Pr. Ln. Extd. 1935	—
5	Do. Equip. Tst.	101½
5	Do. 5 p.c. Equip. Tst. (1890)	101½
	Nrthn. Cent. Cons. Gen. Mt. ..	106
6	Pennsylvania Gen. Mt. 1910	126
6	Do. Cons. Skg. Fd. Mt. 1905	116½
3½	Do. Cons. Mt. 1945	104
6	Phil. & Erie Cons. Mort ..1920	132½
6	Phil. & Reading Gen. Cons. Mort. 1911	120½
6	Pittsbg. & Connells. Cons. 1926	117½
—	Do. Morgan's Certs....	117½
4	St. Paul., Min., & Manitoba (Pac. Extn.) 1940	100
6	S. & N. Alabama 1903	104½
6	Un. N. Jersey & C. Gen. Mt. 1901	109½

FOREIGN RAILWAYS

Last Div.	Name.	Paid.	Price.
12/	Alagoas, Ltd., Shs.	20	6
5	Do. Deb. Stk., Red. ..	100	45½
6	Antofagasta, Ltd., Stk. ..	100	72
4	Do. Perp. Deb. Stk. ..	100	90
—	Arauco, Ld., Ord. Shs. ..	10	—
—	Do. 10 p.c. Cum. Pref.	10	—
5	Argentine Gt. W., Ld.,	100	79
5	Do. 5 p.c. Cum. Pref. Shs.	100	102
4	Do. 1 Deb. Stk.	100	104
1/0/0	Argentine N.E., Ltd., 6 p.c. Cum. Pref. Stk. ..	100	9½
—	Do. 5 p.c. Deb. Stk., Red.	100	29
2/	Arica and Tacna Shs. ..	20	1½
10/	Bahia & San Fcisco., Ld.,	20	10
6/	Do. Timbo. Bch. Shs.	20	4½
12/	Bahia, Blanca, & N.W. Ln. Prf. Cum. 6 p.c. ..	100	53
4	Do. 4 p.c. 1 Deb. Stk., Red.	100	92
6	Barranquilla R. & P., Ld., 6 p.c. 1 Deb. Stk., Red.	100	96

Foreign Railways (*continued*):—

Last Div.	Name.	Paid.	Price.
3/	Bilbao Riv. & Cantabn., Ltd., Ord.	3	5
—	Bolivar, Ltd. Shs.	10	1½
6	Do. 6 p.c. Deb. Stk.	100	96½
—	Brazil Gt. Southn. Ltd., 7 p.c. Cum. Pref.	20	1½
6	Do. Perm. Deb. Stk	100	48
5½	B. Ayres Gt. Southn. Ld., Ord. Stk.	100	142
5	Do. Pref. Stk.	100	133
4	Do. Deb. Stk.	100	117
30/	B. Ayres & Ensen. Port., Ltd., Ord. Stk.	100	66
5	Do. Cum. 1 Pref. Stk.	100	116
6/0/0	Do. 6p.c. Con. Pref. Stk.	100	96
4	Do. Deb. Stk., Irred.	100	113
10⅛	B. Ayres Northern, Ltd., Ord. Stk.	100	265
12½	Do. Pref. Stk.	100	320
5	Do. 5 p.c. Mt. Deb. Stk., Red.	100	113
3/15/0	B. Ayres & Pac., Ld., 7 p.c. 1 Pref. Stk. (Cum.)	100	92½
4	Do. 1 Deb. Stk.	100	102
5/5/0	Do. 4½ p.c. 2 Deb. Stk.	100	92
3	B. Ayres & Rosario, Ltd., Ord. Stk.	100	74
7/	Do. 7 p.c. Pref. Shs.	10	17
7/	Do. Sunchales Ext.	10	14½
4	Do. Deb. Stk., Red.	100	107½
—	B. Ayres & Val. Trans., Ltd., 7 p.c. Cum. Pref.	20	6½
4	Do. 4 p.c. "A" Deb. Stk., Red.	100	70
—	Do. 6 p.c. "B" Deb. Stk. Red.	100	43
3/6	B. Ayres Westn. Ld. Ord.	10	11
3/	Do. Def. Shs	10	6½
5	Do. 5 p.c. Pref.	10	12½
4	Do. Deb. Stk	100	110
6	Cent. Arg. Deb. Sk. Rd.	100	159½
4	Do. Deb. Stk. Rd	100	110
6	Cent. Bahia L. Ord. Stk.	100	50
	Do. Deb. Stk., 1934	100	69½
5	Do. Deb. Stk., 1937	100	60
3/6	Cent. Uguy. East. Ext. L. Shs	10	5½
5	Do. Perm. Stk.	100	112
3/6	Do. Nthn. Ext. L. Sh.	10	4
5	Do. Perm. Deb. Stk	100	103½
3	Do. of Montev. Ltd., Ord. Stk	100	86
6	Do. Perm. Deb. Stk	100	143
10/	Conde d'Eu, Ltd. Ord.	20	7
—	Cordba & Rosar., Ltd., 6 p.c. Pref. Shs.	100	40
4	Do. 1 Deb. Stk	100	90
7½	Do. 6 p.c. Deb. Stk	100	80
—	Cordba Cent., Ltd., 5 p.c. Cu. 1 Pref. Stk	100	84
—	Do. 5 p.c. Non-Cum. 2 Pref. Stk	100	43
5	Do. Deb. Stk	100	118
4/	Costa Rica, Ltd., Shs	10	3½
8/	Dna. Thrsa. Chris., Ltd., 7 p.c. Pref. Shs.	20	3½
20/	E. Argentine, Ltd	100	40
6	Do. Deb. Stk	100	100
1/1	Egyptn. Dlta. Lgt. Rys., Ltd., £10 Pref. Shs.	8	10
—	Entre Rios, L., Ord. Shs.	5	⅞
—	Do. Cu. 5 p.c. Pref.	5	3½
6/	Gt. Westn. Brazil, Ltd.,	20	7½
6	Do. Perm. Deb. Stk	100	92
6	Do. Extn. Deb. Stk	100	75½
—	Int.-Oceanic Mex., Ltd., 7 p.c. Pref.	10	1½
4	Do. Deb. Stk	100	83
42/6	Do. 7 p.c. "A" Deb. Sk.	100	67
—	Do. 7 p.c. "B" Deb. Sk.	100	29
5/	La Guaira & Carac	10	7½
5	Do. 5 p.c. Deb. Sk. Red.	100	100
13/3	Lembg.-Czern.-Jassy	30	24½
1/	Lima, Ltd.	20	2½
—	Manila Ltd. 7 p.c. Cu. Pf.	10	¼
20/6½	Mexican 2nd Pref. 6 p.c.	100	33
6	Do. Perp Deb. Stk.	100	137
1/0/0	Mexican Sthrn., Ld., Ord.	100	22
—	Do. 4 p.c. 1 Db. Stk. Rd.	100	82
—	Do. 4 p.c. 2 do.	100	59
—	Mid. Urgy., Ltd.	100	18½
4	Do. Deb. Stk.	100	60
12/	Minas & Rio, Ltd.	20	10
5/2	Namur & Liege	20	12½
11/6	Do. Pref.	20	29
13/	Natal & Na. Cruz, Ld., 7 p.c. Cum Pref.	20	6½
—	Nitrate Ltd., Ord.	10	5
—	Do. 7 p.c. Pr. Con. Or.	10	4
—	Do. Def. Conv. Ord.	10	¾
7/	N.-E. Urgy., Ltd., Ord.	10	15
7/	Do. 7 p.c. Pref.	10	15½
—	N.-W. Argentine Ld., 7 p.c. Pref.	10	2
6	Do. 6 p.c. 1 Deb. Stk.	100	110
—	Do. 2 Deb. Stk.	100	94
—	N.W. Uruguay 6 p.c. 1 Pref. Stk.	100	16
—	Do. 5 p.c. 2 Pref. Stk.	100	7½
6	Do. 6 p.c. Deb. Stk.	100	80
22/	Ottoman (Sm. Aid.)	20	13½
—	Paraguay Cntl., Ld., 5 p.c. Perm. Deb. Stk.	100	10
—	Piræus, Ath., & Pelo.	275	1½
4/	Pto. Alegre & N. Hambg. Ld., 7 p.c. Pref. Shs.	20	4
6	Do. Mt. Deb. Stk. Red.	100	74½
—	Puerto Cabello & Val. Ld.	10	1½
5	Recife & S. Francisco	100	64½
24/	R. Claro S. Paulo, Ld., Sh.	10	22½
5	Do. Deb. Stk.	100	125
5	Royal Sardinian Ord.	10	11½
3/	Do. Pref.	10	11¾

Foreign Railways (*continued*):—

Last Div.	Name.	Paid.	Price.
5/	Sambre & Meuse	20	18
5/6	Do. Pref.	10	12½
22/	San Paulo Ld.	20	34
2/10½	Do. New Ord. £10 sh.	6	10
4/8	Do. 5 p.c. Non. Cm. Pref.	10	12½
5½	Do. Deb. Stk.	100	132
5	Do. 5 p.c. Deb. Stk	100	127
—	S. Fé & Cordova, Gt. Sthn., Ld., Shares	100	49
6	Do. Perp. Deb. Stk.	100	119
3/2½	S. Austrian	20	7
12/	Sthn. Braz. R. Gde. do Sul, Ld.	20	7½
6	Do. 6 p.c. Deb. Stk.	100	65
4	Swedish Centl., Ld., 4 p.c. Deb. Stk.	100	107
5	Do. Pref.	100	101
1/3	Taltal, Ld.	5	2½
—	Uruguay Nthn., Ld. 7 p.c. Pfd. Stk.	100	8
3½	Do. 5 p.c. Deb. Stk.	100	30
—	Villa Maria & Rufino, Ld., 6 p.c. Pref. Shs.	100	17
4	Do. 4 p.c. 1 Deb. Stk.	100	73
6/0/0	Do. 6 p.c. 2 Deb. Stk.	100	42½
5/9	West Flanders	8¾	21
5/6	Do. 5½ p.c. Pref.	10	18
3/	Wstn. of Havana, Ld.	10	4½

FOREIGN RAILWAY OBLIGATIONS

Per Cent.	Name.	Price.
6	Alagoas Ld., 6 p.c. Deb., Rd.	84
—	Alcoy & Gandia, Ld., 5 p.c. Debs., Red.	20
5	Arauco., Ld., 5 p.c. 1st Mt., Rd.	60½
—	Do. 6 p.c. Mt. Deb., Rd.	39½
6	Brazil G. Sthn., L., Mt. Dbs., Rd.	80½
6	Do. Mt. Dbs. 1893, Rd.	51
5½	Campos & Caran. Dbs., Rd.	70
6	Central Bahia, L., Dbs., Rd.	90
5½	Conde d'Eu, L., Dbs., Rd.	71
6	Costa Rica, L., 1st Mt. Dbs., Rd.	109
6	Do. 2nd Dbs., Rd.	91
5	Do. Prior Mt. Db., Rd.	103
6	Cucuta Mt. Dbs., Rd.	102
5½	Donna Thrsa. Cris., L., Dbs., Rd.	70
3	Eastn. of France, £20 Dbs., Rd.	18½
4	Egyptn. Delta Light, L., Db., Rd	100
—	Espito. Santo & Cara. 5 p.c. Stl. Dbs., Rd.	38
4	Gd. Russian Nic., Rd.	102
5	Inter-Oceanic Mex., L., 5 p.c. Pr. Ln. Dbs., Rd.	103
3	Ital. 3 p.c. Bds. A & B, Rd.	57½
—	Ituana 6 p.c. Debs., 1918	72½
—	Leopoldina, 6 p.c. Dbs. £50 Bds.,	23
—	Do. do. Comms. Cert.	23
—	Do. 5 p.c. Stg. Dbs. (1888), Rd.	32
—	Do. do. Comm. Certs.	32
—	Do. 5 p.c. Stg. Dbs. (1890), Rd.	23
—	Do. do. Comms. Certs.	23
—	Macahé & Cam. 5 p.c. Dbs., Rd.	32
—	Do. do. Comms. Certs.	32
—	Do. (Cantagallo), 5 p.c., Red.	32
—	Do. do. Comm. Certs.	32
—	Manila Ltd., 6 p.c. Deb., Red.	21
6	Do. Prior Lien Mt., Rd.	100½
6	Do. Series "B," Rd.	80
7	Matanzas & Sab., Rd.	101½
6	Minas & Rio, L., 6 p.c. Dbs., Rd.	96
5	Mogyana 5 p.c. Deb. Bds., Rd.	99
5	Moscow-Jaros., Rd.	105½
5½	Natal & Na. Cruz Ltd., 5½ p.c. Debs., Red.	77
5	Nitrate, Ltd. Mt. Bds., Red.	88
3	Nthn. France, Red.	19
4	N. of S. Af. Rep. (Trnsvl.) Gu. Bds. Red.	95
3	Nthn. of Spain £20 Pri. Obs. Red.	7½
6	Ottmn. (Smy to A.)(Kujk) Asnt. Debs., Red.	106
6	Ottmn. (Seraik.) Asg. Debs. Red.	106
6	Ottmn. (Seraik.) Non-Asg. D., Rd	106
5	Ottmn. Kuyjk. Ext. Red.	103
5	Ottmn. Serkeuy. Ext. Red.	100½
5	Ottmn. Tireh Ext. 1910	98
5	Ottmn. Debs, 1886, Red.	97
5	Do. 1888, Red. 1935	96½
5	Do. 1893, Red. 1935	97
5	Ottmn. of Anlia. Debs., Rd.	90½
4	Ottomn. Smyr. & Cas. Ext. Bds., Red.	83½
3	Paris, Lyon & Medit. (old sys., £20), Red.	18¾
3	Paris, Lyon & Medit. (new sys., £20), Red.	18¾
30/	Piræus, At. & Pelp., 6 p.c. 1st Mt. Bds., Red.	90
3	Do. 5 p.c. Mt. Bds., Red.	74
4	Pretoria-Pietbg., Ltd., Red.	93
7	Puerto Cab. & Val., Ltd., 1st Mt. Debs., Red.	81
—	Rio de Jano. & Nthn., Ltd., 6 p.c. £100 Deb., Red.	23
—	Rio de Jano. (Gr. Para.), 5 p.c. 1st Mt. St. £100 Debs., Red.	23
2	Royal Sardinian, A, Rd. £20	11½
3	Royal Sardinian, B., Rd. £20	11¾

Foreign Rly. Obligations (*continued*):—

Per Cent.	Name.	Price.
5	Ryl. Trns.-Afric. 5 p.c. 1st Mt. £100 Bds., Red.	48½
4	Sa. Fe & Cor. G.S., Ld. Pr. Ln. Bds.	104
5	Sa. Fe, 5 p.c. 2nd Reg. Dbs.	78
3	South Austrian, £20 Red.	15
3	South Austrian, (Ser. X.)	15
3	South Italian £20 Obs. (Ser. A to G), Red.	12
3½	S.W. of Venez. (Barq.), Ltd., 7 p.c. 1st Mt. £100 Debs.	52½
5	Taltal, Ltd., 5 p.c. 1st Ch. Debs., Red.	97
5	Utd. Rwys. Havana, Red.	94½
3	Wtrn. of France, £20 Red.	18¾
6	Wrn. B. Ayres St. Mt. Debs., 1902	107
6	Wrn. B. Ayres, Reg. Cert.	105
5	Do. Mt. Bds.	121
6	Wtrn. of Havna., Ld, Mt. Dbs., Rd.	92
7	Wrn. Ry. San Paulo Red.	100
—	Wrn. Santa Fé, 7 p.c. Red.	42
2/8	Zafra & Huelva, 3 p.c. Red.	2½

BANKS.

Div.	Name.	Paid.	Price.
2/4½	Agra, Ltd.	6	3½
2/9½	Anglo-Argentine, Ltd., £9	7	5½
8 fls.	Anglo-Austrian	120 fl	13
6/	Anglo-Californian, Ltd., £20 Shares	10	11
4/	Anglo-Egyptian, Ltd., £15	5	6
5/	Anglo-Foreign Bkg., Ltd.	7	7½
7/	Anglo-Italian, Ltd.	5	7
7/6	Bk. of Africa, Ltd., £18¾	6¼	10½
20/	Bk. of Australasia	40	50
10/	Bk. of Brit. Columbia	20	19½
25/	Bk. of Brit. N. America	50	64
20/	Bk. of Egypt, Ltd., £25	12½	18½
5/	Bk. of Mauritius, Ltd.	10	9
18/	Bk. of N. S. Wales	20	36½
4 p.c.	Bk. of N. Zland. Gua. Stk.	100	101½
6/	Bk. of Roumania, £20 Shs.	6	7½
2/6	Tarapaca & Ldn., Ltd., £10	5	3½
—	Bque. Fse. de l'Afri. du S.	100f	3½
f.22.50	Bque. Internatle. de Paris	20	23
6/	Brit. Bk. of S. America, Ltd., £20 Shares	10	10
16/	Capital & Ctiea., L., £50	10	40
20/	Chart. of India, &c.	20	30
10/	City, Ltd., £40 Shares	10	20
18/	Colonial, £100 Shares	30	21
10/	Delhi and London, Ltd.	25	—
5/	German of London, Ltd.	10	10½
25/	Hong-Kong & Shanghai	28½	45
4/	Imperl. of Persia	6¼	3½
10/	Imperl. Ottoman, £20 Shs	10	11¾
12/	Intrnatl. of Ldn., Ld., £20	15	11
10/	Ionian, Ltd.	25	15½
16/	Lloyds, Ltd., £50 Shs.	8	31½
10/	Ldn. & Brazil. Ltd., £20	10	16½
44/	Ldn. & County, Ltd., £80	20	102
9/	Ldn. & Hanseatic, L., £20	10	10½
22/6	Ldn. & Midland, L., £60	12½	53
8/9	Ldn. & Provin., Ltd., £10	5	21½
21/	Ldn. & Riv. Plate, L., £25	15	48½
2/1½	Ldn. & San Fcisco, Ltd.	7	4½
28/	Ldn. & Sth. West., L., £50	20	68
26/	Ldn. & Westmins., L., £100	20	56½
5/	Ldn. of Mex. & S. Amer., Ltd., £10 Shs.	6	5½
15/	Ldn. Joint Stk., L., £100	15	34
12/9½	Ldn., Paris & Amer., L. £20	16	25
2/4½	Merchant Bkg., L., £9	4	2¾
6/3	Metropn, Ltd., £50 Shs.	5	14½
9/	National, Ltd., £50 Shs.	10	20
5/11	Natl. of Mexico, $100 Shs.	$35	11
1/3	National of N. Z., L., £7½	2½	2
3/	National S. Afric. Rep.	10	13½
18/10½	National Provcl. of Eng., Ltd., £75 Shs.	10½	50½
21/7½	Do. do. £60 Shs.	12	57½
6/6	North Eastn., Ltd., £20 Shs	6	15
19/	Parr's, Ld., £100 Shs.	20	89½
12/6	Prov. of Ireland, L., £100	12½	29½
40/	Stand. of S. Afric., L., £100	25	64
12/6	Union of Australia, L., £75	25	26½
4 p.c.	Do. do. Ins. Stk. Dep. 1900	100	103
15/6	Union of Ldn., Ltd., £100	15½	35

BREWERIES AND DISTILLERIES.

Div.	Name.	Paid.	Price.
4½	Albion Prp. 1 Mt. Db. Sk.	100	111
4	All Saints, L., Db. Sk. Rd.	100	97
7	Allsopp, Ltd	100	147
6	Do. Cum. Pref	100	153
4½	Do. Deb. Stk., Red.	100	116
3½	Do. Deb. Stk., Red.	100	102
4½	Alton & Co., L., Db., Rd	100	107
4½	Do. Mt. Bds., 1896	100	105
—	Arnold, Perrett, Ltd.	10	6
6	Do. Cum. Pref.	10	10
4½	Do. 1 Mt. Db. Stk., Rd	100	107

Breweries &c. (*continued*):—

Div.	Name.	Paid.	Price.
5½	Arrol, A., & Sons, L., Cum. Pref. Shs.	10	10
4½	Do. 1 Mt. Db. Stk., Rd.	100	107
5	Backus, 1 Mt. Db., Red.	100	59
4	Barclay, Perk., L., Cu. Pf.	10	11½
3½	Do. Mt. Db. Stk., Red.	100	109
—	Barnsley, Ltd.	10	11½
6	Do. Cum. Pref.	10	13½
1/3	Barrett's, Ltd	2½	1½
1/3	Do. 5 p.c. Pref.	2½	2½
3/	Bartholomay, Ltd	10	2½
8	Do. Cum. Pref.	10	7
6	Do. Deb.	100	97½
5	Bass, Ratcliff, Ltd., Cum. Pref. Stk.	100	142½
4½	Do. Mt. Db. Stk., Rd.	100	124
4	Bell, J., L., 1 Mt. D. Stk., R	100	100
—	Benskin's, L., Cum. Pref.	5	—
—	Do. 1 Mt. Db. Stk Red.	100	—
—	Do. "B" Deb. Sk, Rd.	100	—
7/	Bentley's Yorks., Ltd.	10	10½
6/	Do. Cum. Pref.	10	12½
4½	Do. Mt. Debs., Red.	100	110
4½	Do. do. 1892, Red.	100	110
—	Bieckert's, Ltd.	20	2
5	Do. Debs., Red.	100	57
—	Birmingham., Ltd., 6 p.c. Cum. Pref.	5	2½
4½	Do. Mt. Debs., Red.	50	39½
5½	Boardman's, Ld., Cm. Pf.	10	8½
4½	Do., Perp. 1 Mt. Db. Sk.	100	104½
30/9	Brain & Co., Ltd.	100	101
4½	Brakspear, L., 1 D. Stk. Red.	100	108
4	Brandon's, L., 1 D. Stk. Red.	100	104½
21/	Bristol (Georges) Ltd.	10	44
6	Do. Cum. Pref.	10	17½
5	Do. Mt. Db. Sk. 1888 Rd.	100	115½
17/6	Bristol United, Ltd.	10	35
6	Do. Cum. Pref.	10	16½
4½	Do. Db. Sk. Rd.	100	120½
5½	Buckley's, L., C. Pre-prf.	10	10½
4½	Do. 1 Mt. Db. Stk. Rd.	100	104½
4	Bullard & Sons, Ltd., D. Sk. R.	100	104
6	Bushell, Watk., L., C. Pf.	10	14
4½	Do. 1 Mt. Db. Sk. Rd.	100	112
5	Camden, Ltd., Cum. Pref.	10	11½
4½	Do. 1 Mt. Db. Sk. Rd.	100	107
5½	Cameron, Ltd., Cm. Prf.	10	13
4½	Do. Mort Deb. Stk.	100	106
3½	Do. Perp Mt. Db. Sk.	100	98½
5	Cam'bell, J'stone, L., C. Pf.	5	6
4½	Do. 4½ p.c. 1 Mt. Db. Sk.	100	103
4	Campbell, Praed, L., Per. 1 Mort. Deb. Stk.	100	105
4	Cannon, L., Mt. Db. Stk.	100	109
4	Do. "B" Deb. Stk.	100	102
5	Castlemaine, L., 1 Mt. Db.	100	94
3½	Charrington, Ltd., Mort. Deb. Stk. Red.	100	106
2/	Cheltnhm. Orig., Ltd.	5	6
6	Do. Cum. Pref.	5	7½
4	Do. Debs. Red.	100	106
10/	Chicago, Ltd.	10	3½
6	Do. Debs.	100	84½
—	Cincinnati, Cum. Pref.	10	1
10/	City of Baltimore	10	3½
16/	Do. 8 p.c. Cum. Pref	10	8
14/	City of Chicago, Ltd.	10	1½
8	Do. Cum. Pref.	10	6½
13	City of London, Ltd.	100	206½
5	Do. Cum. Pref.	100	136
4	Do. Mt. Deb. Stk., Rd.	100	108½
2/	Colchester, Ltd.	5	4½
7	Do. Pref.	5	6½
4½	Do. Deb. Stk., Red.	100	109
5	Combe, Ltd., Cum. Pref.	10	14
4	Do. Mt. Db. Stk, Rd.	100	110
3½	Do. Perp. Deb. Stk.	100	107
5	Comm'cial, L., D. Sk., Rd.	100	107½
5	Courage, L., Cm. Pref. Shs.	100	137½
4	Do. Irr. Mt. Deb. Stk.	100	125½
3½	Do. Irr. "B" Mt. Db. Sk.	100	104
6/	Daniell & Sons, Ltd.	10	7
7	Do. Cum. Pref.	10	12
4½	Do. 1 Mt. Perp. Db. Sk.	100	109
4½	Do. "B" Deb. Stk.	100	99
10d.	Dartford, Ltd.	5	5
2/9	Do. Cum. Pref.	5	5½
4	Do. 1 Mt. Db. Sk. Rd.	100	99
4	Davenport, Ld., 1 D. Stk.	100	101½
10/	Denver United, Ltd.	10	3½
8	Do. Cum. Pref.	10	8
6	Do. Debs.	100	98½
4½	Deuchar, L., 1 D. Sk., Rd.	100	109
8/	Distillers, Ltd.	10	23½
—	Dublin Distillers, Ltd.	5	1½
6	Do. Cum. Pref.	5	4½
4½	Do. Irr. Deb. Stk.	100	—
5	Eadie, Ltd., Cum. Pref.	10	11½
4	Do. Irr. 1 Mt. Db. Sk.	100	107
10/	Edinbgh. Utd., Ltd.	10	13
6	Do. Cum. Prf.	10	13½
4	Eldridge, Pope, L. D. St. R.	100	110
—	Emerald & Phœnix, Ltd.	10	1½
8	Do. Cum. Pref.	10	5½
6	Empress Ltd., C. Pf.	10	11½
4½	Do. Mt. Deb. Stk.	100	103
10/	Farnham, Ltd.	10	17½
6	Do. Cum. Pref.	10	14½
4	Fenwick, L., 1 D. Sk., Rd.	100	103
4	Flower & Sons, Irr. D. Sk.	100	111
4	Friary, L., 1 Db. Stk., Rd.	100	103½
4	Do. 1 "A" Db. Sk., Rd	100	100
4½	Groves, L., 1 Db. Sk., Rd.	100	111
14	Guinness, Ltd.	100	580
6	Do. Cum. Prf. Stk.	100	185½
5	Do. Deb. Stk., Red.	100	119
5	Hall's Oxford L., Cm. Pf.	5	5½
6/	Hancock, Ld., Cm. Pf. Ord.	10	14
7/	Do. Def. Ord	10	17½

Breweries, &c. (*continued*) :—

Div.	Name.	Paid.	Price.
6	Hancock, Ld., Cum. Pref.	10	15
4	Do. 1 Deb. Stk., Rd.	100	110
5	Hoare, Ltd. Cum. Pref...	10	12¾
5	Do. "A" Cum. Pref..	10	12¼
4	Do. Mt. Deb. Stk., Rd.	100	112
3½	Do. do. do. Rd.	100	104
3/6	Hodgson's, Ltd.	5	9½
5	Do. 1 Mt. Db., Red..	—	117½
4	Do. 2 Mt. Db., 1906..	—	100
4½	Hopcraft & N., Ltd., 1 Mt. Deb. Stk., Red. ..	100	103
5	Huggins, Ltd., Cm. Prf..	10	—
4½	Do. 1st D. Stk. Rd...	100	—
4½	Do. "B" Db. Stk. Rd.	100	—
12/	Hull, Ltd.	10	17
7	Do. Cum. Pref.	10	14½
4½	Ind, Coope, L., D.Sk., Rd.	100	119
4	Do. "B" Mt. Db. Stk. Rd.	100	110
8/	Indianapolis, Ltd.	10	3
8	Do. Cm. Prf.	10	8½
5/	Jones, Frank, Ltd.......	10	2½
7½	Do. Cum. Pref.	10	6½
5	Do. 1st Mort. Debs. ..	100	90½
3/	J. Kenward & Ct., Ltd...	5	5¼
4½	Kingsbury, L., 1 D.Sk., Rd	100	—
4	Lacon, L., D. Stk., Red.	100	110
4	Do. Irrd. "B" D. Sk.	100	106
7/	Lascelles, Ltd.	5	11½
6	Do. Cum. Pref.	5	7½
5	Leney, Ltd., Cum. Pref.	10	11½
4	Do. 1 Mt. Db. Stk. Rd.	100	102
30/7½	Lion, Ltd., £25 shares..	17	49½
10/9½	Do. New £10 shares..	6	17
6	Do. Perp. Pref.	20	33
4	Do. B. Mt. Db. Sk. Rd.	100	106
4½	Lloyd & Y., Ltd., 1 Mt. Deb. Stk., Rd.	100	100½
4½	Locke & S., Ltd., Irr. 1st Mt. Deb. Stk.........	100	103
4½	Lovibond, Ltd., 1st Mt. Deb. Stk., Rd.	100	101½
30/4	Lucas&Co., Ld., Deb.Stk.	100	107
12/	Manchester, Ltd.	10	19
7	Do. Cum. Pref.	10	16½
5/	Marston, J., L., Cm. Prf.	10	10½
4	Do. 1 Mt. Db. Sk., Rd.	100	101½
7/	Massey's Burnley, Ltd...	10	16½
6	Do. Cum. Pref.	10	14½
4½	McCracken, Ltd., 1 Mt. Deb., 1908............	100	59½
5	McEwan, Ltd., Cm. Pref.	10	14
5	Meux, Ltd., Cum. Pref..	10	13½
4	Do. Mt. Db. Stk. Red.	100	111
4½	Michell & A., Ltd., 1 Mt. Deb. Stk. Red....	100	105
4½	MileEndDist.Db.Sk.Rd.	100	111
—	Milwaukee & Chic., Ltd.	10	1¾
4/	Do. Cum. Pref.	10	7
4½	Michell, Toms, L., Db...	50	57
6	Morgan, Ltd., Cum. Pref.	10	14½
25/	Nalder & Coll., Ltd.....	10	34
6	Do. Cum. Pref..	10	15½
4½	Do. Deb. Red...	100	112
12/	Newcastle, Ltd.	10	19½
6	Do. Cum. Pref.......	10	14½
5	Do. 1 Mt. Deb., 1911	100	111½
4	Do. "A" Deb.Stk.Red.	100	105
6	New England, Ltd.......	10	4½
8	Do. Cum. Pref......	10	9
6	Do. Debs. Red.......	100	101½
4	New London, L., 1 D.Sk.	100	103
7/2	New Westminster, Ltd..	4	10
2/4½	Do. Pref........	4	6½
—	New York, Ltd.	10	1
—	Do. 8 p.c. Cum. Pref.	10	4
6	Do. 1 Mt. Deb. Red.	100	77½
5	Noakes, Ld., Cum. Pref.	10	12
4	Do 1 Mt. Db. Stk., Rd.	100	105
4½	Norfolk, L., "A" D.Sk.Rd.	100	106
10/	Northampton, Ld.	10	16½
7	Do. Cum. Pref......	10	15½
6	Do. Cum. Pref......	10	12½
5	Do. 1 Mt. Per. Db.Sk.	100	127
4	Nth.East., L., 1 D.Sk.Rd.	100	100
4½	N. Worcesters., L. Per. 1 Mort. Deb. Stock	100	35½
6	Nottingham, L., Cm. Prf.	10	1½
5	Do. 1 Mt. Deb.Stk., Red.	100	114
17/4	Do. "B" do. Red.	50	112
6/	Ohlsson' Cape, Ld.......	5	17
7	Do. Cum. Pref.	5	9
4½	Do. 2nd Cum. Pref.	5	5½
5	Do. Deb. Stk., Red.	100	116
4½	Oldfield, L., 1 Mt. Db.Stk.	100	106
6	Page & Overt., L., Cm. Prf.	10	13½
4½	Do. 1 Mt. Dbs, Red.	100	109
10/	Parker's Burslem, Ltd. ..	10	24½
6	Do. Cum. Pref.	10	15
4	Do. 1 Mt. Db. Stk., Red.	100	112
4	Persse, Ld., 1 Mt. Db. Rd.	100	95½
	Phipps, L., Irr. 1 Db. Stk.	100	113
8	Plymouth, L., Min.Cu.Pf.	10	13
4½	Do. Mt. Deb. Stk., Red.	100	106½
4½	Pryor, Reid, L., 1 D.S., R.	100	103½
5	Reid's, Ld., Cm. Pref. Stk.	100	136½
4	Do. Mt. Deb. Stk., Red	100	110
3½	Do. "B" Mt. Db.Stk., Rd	100	102
5	Rhondda Val., L., Cu. Pf	10	11
4½	Do. 1 Mt. Deb. Stk., Rd	100	109
5	Robinson, Ld., Cum. Pref.	10	11½
4½	Do. 1 Mt. Perp. Db. Stk.	100	111½
4/	Rochdale, Ltd...........	10	6
4½	Do. 1 Mt. Deb. Stk...	100	98½
7	Royal, Brentford, Ltd. ..	10	22
	Do. Cum. Pref. ..	10	15
4½	Do. 1 Mt. Dbs. Red	100	106
6/	St. Louis, Ltd...........	10	3½
8	Do. Cum. Pref....	10	8½
14/	St. Pauli, Ltd.	10	10
7	Do. Cum. Pref....	10	12
4½	Salt (T.), L., 1 Db. Sk. Rd.	100	112
4½	Do. "B" Db.Stk.Red	100	107
—	San Francisco, Ltd.......	10	½
—	Do. 8 p.c. Cum. Pref...	10	½

Breweries, &c. (*continued*) :—

Div.	Name.	Paid.	Price.
4½	Savill Brs., L., D. Sk. Rd.	100	118
4½	Scarboro., Ltd., 1 Db. Stk.	100	101
4	Shaw (Hy.), Ltd., 1 Mt. Db. Stk., Red.........	100	104
22/	Showell's, Ltd...........	10	31
7	Do. Cum. Pref.	10	17
3/	Do. Gua. Shs.	5	7½
4½	Do. Mt. Db. Stk., Red.	100	—
4	Simonds, L., 1 D. Sk., Rd.	100	111
5½	Simson & McP., L., Cu. Pf.	10	9½
4½	Do. 1 Mt. Deb. Stk. ..	100	97
5/	Smith, Garrett, L., £20 Shs	10	16½
5	Do. Cum. Pref.	20	26
3½	Do. 3½ p.c. Mt. Db. Stk.	100	107
5	Smith's, Tadcaster, L., C Pf	10	12
4½	Do. Deb. Stk., Red. ..	100	112
4	Do. Deb. Stk. Red. ..	100	108
4½	Star, L., 1 M. Db. Stk., Rd.	100	103
4	Steward & P., L., 1 D. Sk.	100	109
7/	Strettons Derby, Ltd.....	10	13
6	Do. Cum. Pref.	10	13
4	Do. Irr. 1 Mt. Db. Stk.	100	104½
4½	Strong, Romsey, L., 1 D. S.	100	115
5	Stroud, L., Db. Sk., Rd.	100	109½
4½	Tadcaster To'er, L., D.Sk.	100	113
8/	Tamplin, Ltd............	10	21
6	Do. Cum. Pref.	100	15
4	Do. "A" Db. Sk., Rd.	10	106
6	Thorne, Ltd., Cum. Pref.	10	14
4	Do. Deb. Stk., Red...	100	103½
15/	Threlfall, Ltd.	10	45
6	Do. Cum. Pref.	10	16½
5	Do. 1 Mt. Dbs., Red.	100	114
4	Tollemache, L., D. Sk. Rd.	100	103
4	Truman, Hanb., D. Sk., R.	100	110
3	Do. "B" Mt. Db. Sk., Rd.	100	95
10/	United States, Ltd.......	10	9
8	Do. Cum. Pref.......	10	11
6	Do. 1 Mt. Deb........	100	106½
6/	Walker & H., Ld., Cm. Prf.	10	10½
4½	Do. 1 Mt. Deb. Stk., Red.	100	107
5	Walker, Peter, Ld. Cm. Prf.	10	13½
4	Do. 1 Mt. Dbs. Red. ..	100	110
4	Wallingford, L., D.Sk.Rd.	100	105
6	Watney, Ld., Cm. Prf. Sk.	100	169
5	Do. Mt. Db. Sk., Rd.	100	115½
4½	Do. "B" Mt. Db. Sk., Rd.	100	111
3½	Do. Mt. Db. Stk.	100	101
5	Watney, D., Ld., Cm. Prf.	10	12
4½	Do. 1 Mt. Db. Stk. ..	100	108
10/	Webster & Sons, Ltd. ..	10	16½
6	Do. Cum. Pref. ..	10	14
5	Wenlock Ltd Pref.	10	11½
4	Do. 1 Mt. Db. Sk., Rd.	100	106
5	West Cheshire, L., Cu. Pf.	10	10½
4	Do. Irred. 1 Mt. Db. Sk.	100	99
4½	Whitbread, L., Cu. Pf. Sh.	100	123½
4	Do. Db. Stk., Red.	100	109
3½	Do. "B" Db. Stk., Rd.	100	100
8/	Wolverhmpton & D. Ld..	10	16½
6	Do. Cum. Pref.......	10	13½
4½	Do. 1 Mt. Dbs., Red.	100	106
5½	Worthington, Ld., Cm. Prf.	10	15½
5½	Do. Cum. "B" Pref.	10	13½
4½	Do. Mt. Db. Sk., Rd.	100	113
3½	Do. Irr. "B" Db. Stk.	100	102
6/	Yates's Castle, Ltd.......	10	13
5	Do. Cum. Pref.......	10	11
5	Younger W., L., Cu. Pf. Sh.	100	133½

CANALS AND DOCKS.

Last Div.	Name.	Paid.	Price.
4	Birmingham Canal	100	140½
—	E. & W. India Dock	100	19
—	Do. 4 p.c. Prf. Stk.....	100	74
—	Do. P.L. Deb. Stk.....	100	101
—	Do. Cons. Deb. Stk. ..	100	89
40/	G. Junction Ord. Shs...	100	147½
6/	Do. do. Pref.......	10	19
4½	King's Lynn Per. Db. Stk.	100	117½
2½	Leeds & L'pool Canal....	100	71
2½	Lndn & St. Kath. Dks...	100	54
4½	Do. Pref.............	100	136½
4½	Do. Pref., 1878	100	132½
4½	Do. Pref., 1882	100	130
4	Do. Deb. Stk.	100	132½
—	Mchester Ship C. 5 p.c. Pf.	10	1¼
3½	Do. 1st Perp. Mt. Deb.	100	98
—	Milford Dks. Db.Stk."A"	100	18½
3½	Millwall Dk.............	100	60
5	Do. Perp. Pref.	100	140½
4½	Do. Pref.	100	106½
5	Do. New Per. Prf., 1887	100	126½
5	Do. Per. Deb. Stk....	100	152½
4/	Newhaven Har.	10	14½
2½	N. Metropolitan	100	66
5	Sharpness Nw. Pf."A"Sk.	100	141½
4	Do. Deb. Stk.	100	117½
5	Sheffiel & S. Yorks Nav. 4½ p.c. Pref Stk.......	100	115½
36.432	Suez Canal..............	20	138½
7	Surrey Comcl. Dok., Ord.	100	150½
7	Do. Min. 4 p.c. Pref. "A"	110	151½
5	Do. Pref. "B"........	100	148½
5	Do do. "C"........	100	148½
5	Do. do. "D"........	100	144½
4½	Do Deb. Stk.	100	152½

COMMERCIAL, INDUSTRIAL, &c.

Last Div.	Name.	Paid.	Price.
5	Accles, L., 1 Mt. Db., Red.	100	84½
2/6	Aërated Bread, Ltd.	1	12½
—	African Gold Recovery, L.	1	¼
2/	Aluminium, L., "A" Shs.	1	2
4½	Do. 1 Mt. Db. Stk., Red.	100	97
5½	Amelia Nitr., L., 1 Mort Deb., Red............	100	82½
7/	Anglo-Chil. Nitrate, Ltd., Cum. Pref............	10	6¾
4½	Do. Cons. Mt. Bds., Red.	100	77½
4½	Anglo-Russian Cotton, Ld., 1 Charge Debs., Red.	100	98
11/3	Angus (G., & Co., L.), £10	7½	17
6/	Apollinaris, Ltd.	10	11½
5/	Do. 5 p.c. Cum. Pref.	10	10½
4	Do. Irred. Deb. Stock	100	103
3/	Argentine Meat Pres., L., 7 p.c. Pref............	10	2¾
5	Argentine Refinry, Db. Rd.	100	98
6d.	Armstrong, Whitw., Ltd.	1	3½
4	Do. Cum. Pref.	5	6½
5	Artisans', Labr. Dwllgs., L.	100	128½
4½	Do. Non-Cm. Prf., 1879	100	133½
4½	Do. do. 1884	100	132½
—	Asbestos & Asbestic, Ltd.	10	7½
2/7½	Ashley-grdns., L., C. Prf.	5	6½
4½	Do. 1 Mt. Deb. Stk.	100	113½
5/	Assam Rly. & Trdng., L., 8 p.c. Cum. Pref. "A"	10	14
—	Do. Deferrd. "B" Shs.	1	4
—	Do. do. (iss.f.pd)	1	3½
8/	Do. Cum. Pre-Prf. "A"	10	15
6/	Do. New Pref.........	10	11½
5	Do. Debs., Red.	100	106
5	Do. Red. Mort. Debs.	100	110
6	Aust'lian Pastrl, L., Cu. Pf.	10	7
8d.	Aylesbury Dairy, Ltd. ..	1	1½
4	Do. 4 p.c. Mt. Dbs.	100	104½
10/	Babcock & Wilcox, Ltd.	10	28
6	Do. 6 p.c. Cm. Prf.	10	16
8	Baker (Chs.), L., Cm. Pf.	5	9
8	Do. "B" Cm. Pref.	5	7½
2/1	Barker (John), Ltd.	1	2½
5½	Do. Cum. Pref.	5	7½
4½	Do. Irred. 1 Mt. Db. Stk.	100	125½
2/6	Barnagore Jute, Ltd.....	5	2½
5	Do. Cum. Pref.	5	4½
7½d.	Belgravia Dairy, Ltd. ..	1	1½
5/6	Bell (R.) & Co., Ltd.....	5	4
9½d.	Bell's Asbestos, Ltd.	1	⅝
5	Do. Mt. Db. Bds., Rd.	100	106
10/	Bengal Mills, Ltd.	10	11
6/	Do. 5 p.c. Cum. Prf.	10	10½
5/	Benson (J.W.) L., Cm. Pf.	10	10½
4	Do. Perp. Mt. Db. Stk.	100	101
6	Bergvik, L., 6 p.c. Cm. Pf.	10	13
12/	Do. Dfd.	10	10½
4½	Do. 1 Dbs., Red. ..	100	105½
5/	Birm'ham Vinegar, Ltd.	5	15
5	Do. Cum. Pref.	5	5½
4½	Do. 1 Mt. Db. Stk., Rd.	100	109½
5	Boake (A.) L., 5 p.c. Cu. Pf.	10	10½
2/6	Bodega, Ltd.............	5	8½
4½	Do. Mt. Deb. Stk., Rd.	100	111
12/	Bottomley & Brs., Ltd...	10	6
6/	Do. 6 p.c. Pt.	10	9
8½d.	Bovril, Ltd.	1	1
1/0½	Do. Def.	1	⅞
6½d	Do. Cum. Pref...	1	1
4½	Do. Deb. Stk. ..	100	100
5/	Bradbury, Gretrex., Ltd., £10 share	8	14
5/	Do. 5 p.c. Cum. Pref.	10	13½
5/	Brewers' Sugar, L., 5 p.c. Cum. Pref............	10	10½
3/6	Brighton Grd. Hotel, Ld.	5	4
4	Do Mt. Db.Stk., Red.	100	102
5	Bristol Hotel & Palm.Co., Ltd. 1st Mt. Red. Deb.	100	105
6d.	British & Bengton's. Tea Tr. Asc., Ltd.	1	1½
5	Do. Cum. Prf.	5	5½
—	British Deli & Lgkat. Tobacco, Ltd.	1	½
—	Do. Cum. Prf.	1	½
1/3	British Tea Table, Ltd...	1	2½
5½	Do. Cum. Pref.......	1	1½
2/6	Brooke, Ben., & Co., Ltd., Cum. Pref.............	5	5½
7/6	Brooke, Bond & Co., Ltd.	5	19
3/	Brown Brs., L., Cum. Pref.	5	5½
10/	Browne & Eagle, Ltd. ..	10	13½
5	Do. Cum. Pref.	10	13
4	Do. Mrt. Db. Sk., Red.	100	110
30/	Brunner, Mond, & Co., Lt.	0	38
10/	Do. £10 shares.......	3	14½
7	Do. Cum. Pref.......	10	17
7	Do. £10 shares.......	5	8½
10/	Bryant & May, Ltd.	5	19
3/	Bucknall, H., & Sons, Lt.	5	7
6	Do. Cum Pref........	5	7½
4/	Burke, E. & J, Ltd.	5	7½
6	Do. Cum. Pref.......	5	7½
6	Do. Irred. Deb. Stk...	100	155
1/	Burlington Htls. Co., Ltd	1	1½
5	Do. Cum. Pref.	1	1
4	Do. Perp. Deb. Stk. .	100	105½
5	Bush, W. J., & Co., Ltd.. Cum. Pref.	5	5½
4	Do. 1 Deb. Stk., Red.	100	102
5½	Callard, Stewart, & Watt, Ltd., Cum. Pref.......	1	1½
4/	Callender's Cable L., Shs.	5	10
4½	Do. 1 Deb. Stk., Red.	100	111½
—	Campbell, R., & Sons, Lt.	3	2½
6	Cantareira Water, Bd., Rd	100	99½
5	Do. (2nd issue)	100	87½
4	Cartavio Sugar, Ltd., 6 p.c. 1st Debs., Red. ..	80	82½
9/	Cassell & Co., Ltd., £10	9	15
5	Causton, Sir J., & Sons Ltd., Cum. Pref......	10	13½

Commercial, &c. (*continued*) :—

Last Div.	Name.	Paid.	Price.
4	Cent. Prod. Mkt. of B.A. 1st Mt. Str. Debs.	100	76½
4	Chappell & Co., Ltd., Mt. Deb. Stk. Red....	100	103
6/	Chicago & N.W. Gran. 8 p.c. Cum. Pref......	10	3
4/	Chicago Packing & Prov.	10	6
8	Do. Cum. Pref....	10	10
6/	City Offices, Ltd........	12	8
3½	Do. Mt. Deb. Stk...	100	108½
7/2½	Cy. London Real Prop., Ltd., £25 shs.	12	22
4/6	Do. £12½ shs.........	7½	15
3½	Do. Deb. Stk. Red...	100	108½
3½	Do. Deb. Stk. Red...	100	105½
3	Do.	100	100½
6/	Cy. of Santos Imprvts., Ltd., 7 p.c. Pref.......	10	8
20/	Clay, Bock, & Co., Ltd...	10	5
8	Do. Cum. Pref.......	10	9
6	Do. Mort. Deb.......	100	102½
20/	Coats, J. & P., Ltd.....	10	60
20/	Do. Cum. Pref.	10	17½
4½	Do. Deb. Stk. Red.	100	112½
9½d	Coburg Hotel, Ltd......	1	1½
4	Do. Deb. Stk. Red.	100	102
6	Colonial Consign & Dis., Ltd., Cum. Pref.......	5	4½
4½	Do. 1st Mort. Debs..	100	96½
—	Colorado Nitrate, Ltd. ..	5	⅛
5/	Co. Gén. des Asphtes. de F., Ltd.............	6	6
5	Do, Non-Cm. Prf. ..	—	5
5	Cook, J. W., & Co., Ltd., Cum. Pref...........	5	5½
5	Cook, T., & Son, Egypt, Ltd., 1st Mt. Deb. Red.	100	110½
—	Cork Co., Ltd., 6 p.c. Cum. Pref...........	5	2
5	Cory, W., & Sn, L., Cu. Pf.	5	5¾
4	Do. 1st Deb. Stk. Red.	100	109
1/6	Crisp & Co., Ltd........	1	1½
5½	Do. Cum. Pref......	1	1½
—	Crompton & Co., Ltd., 7 p.c. Cum. Pref.......	5	—
5	Do. 1st Mt. Reg. Deb.	—	90½
4/6	Crossley, J., & Sons, Ltd.	5	8
5	Do. Cum. Pref....	5	6½
—	Crystal Pal. Ord. "A" Stk.	100	6½
—	Do. "B" Red. Stk	100	1½
6	Do. 6 p.c. 1st 1887 Deb. Stk. Red. ..	100	117½
—	Do. 6 p.c. 2nd 1887 Deb. Stk. Red. ..	100	51½
—	Do. 6 p.c. 3rd 1887 Deb. Stk. Red. ..	100	22½
3	Do. 3 p.c. 1st 1895 Deb. Stk.........	100	92½
—	Daimler Motor, Ltd.....	10	6
4/	Dalgety & Co., £20 Shs.	5	5½
4½	Do. Deb. Stk........	100	124
4	Do.	100	112
7/	De Keyser's Ryl. Htl., L.	10	13½
5	Do. Cum. Pref......	10	12
4	Do. Deb. Stk., Red..	100	110
6	Denny, H., & Sons, Ltd., Cum. Pref............	10	14½
5/3	Devas, Routledge & Co., L.	7	8½
5	Dickinson, J., & Co., L., Cum. Pref. Stk.	100	123
4½	Domin. Cottn. Mls., Ltd. Mt. Stg. Dbs.	100	97
6/	Dorman, Long & Co., L.	5	4½
—	Eastmans, Ltd..........	10	3
12/	Do. 8 p.c. Cum. Pref.	10	11
2/6	E. C. Powder, Ltd.......	3	5½
1/6	Edison & Swn Utd. Elec. Ltd., "A" £5 Shs....	3	2½
2/6	Do. fully-paid	5	4½
4½	Ekman Pulp & Ppr. Co., Ltd., Mt. Deb, Red..	100	96
1/1½	Electric Construc., Ltd..	2	2½
7	Do. Cum. Pref.......	2	3½
25/	Eley Bros., Ltd.	10	37
—	Elmore's Cop. Deptg., L.	1	⅛
—	Elmore's Wire Mnfg., L.	2	⅛
—	Elysée Pal. Hotel Co., L.	5/	⅞
5 p.c.	Do. 5 p.c. £100 Db., Rd.	70	97½
8½d.	Evans, Ben., & Co., Ltd.	1	1
5	Do. 1 Mt. Db. Sk., Rd.	100	108
1/5½d.	Evans, D. H., & Co., L.	1	2½
6	Do. Cum. Pref.......	1	1½
4½	Do. 1 Mt. Db. Sk., Rd.	100	112
2/6	*Evening News*, L., 5 p.c. Cum. Pref............	5	5½
5/3	Evered & Co., L., £10 Sh.	7	12½
7/6	Do.	10	18
4	Fairbairn Pastoral Co., Aust., L., 1 Mt. Db., Rd.	100	102
6	Fairfield Shipbldg., Ltd., Cum. Pref............	10	11½
4½	Do. Mort. Deb. Stk..	100	111
6/	Farmer & Co., Ld., 6 p.c. Cum. Pref............	10	13½
10	Field, J. C. & J., Ltd. ..	10	10½
14/	Do. 7 p.c. Cum. Pref.	10	14½
1/3	Fordham, W.B., & Sns, Ld.	1	2
3/6	Fore-st. Warehouse, Ltd.	11	9½
4	Do. Regd. Debs., Rd.	100	101½
3/6	Foster, M. B. & Sons, Ltd.	4	6
5	Do. Pref....	10	11½
9/	Foster, Porter, & Co., L.	10½	15½
4	Fowler, J., & Co. (Leeds), Ltd., 1 Mt. Deb., Red.	100	103½
3/	Fraser & Chalmers, Ltd..	3	1½
4½	Free, Rodwell & Co., Ltd., Deb Stk..............	100	104½
6½d.	Furness, T., & Co., Ltd., 5½ p.c. Cum. Pref.		1
4½	Gartside & Co. (of Manchstr), L., 1 Mt. Db. Sk.	100	112
11	Genl. Hydraul Power, L.	100	273

Commercial, &c. (*continued*):—

Last Div.	Name.	Paid.	Price.
8/	Gillman & Spencer, Ltd.	5	2½
6	Do. Pref.	5	4½
5	Do. Mort. Debs.	50	51
4	Goldsbro., Mort & Co., L., "A" Deb. Stk., Red.	100	69½
—	Do. 3 p.c. "B" Inc. Deb. Stk., Red.	100	12
8/	Gordon Hotels, Ltd.	10	19½
5½	Do. Cum. Pref.	10	14½
4½	Do. Perp. Deb. Stk.	100	139½
4	Do. do.	100	122½
—	Greenwich Inld. Linoleum Co., Ltd.	1	¼
7	Greenwood & Batley, Ltd., Cum. Pref.	10	10
7½d.	Hagemann & Co., Ltd., 6 p.c. Cum. Pref.	1	1
—	Hammond, Ltd.	10	¾
—	Do. 8 p.c. Cum. Pref.	10	3½
—	Do. 6 p.c. Cum. Inc. Stk. Red.	100	56½
	Hampton & Sons, Ltd., 4 p.c. 1 Mt. Db. St. Red.	100	105
—	Hans Crescent Htl., L., 6 p.c. Cum. Pref.	5	3
4	Do. 1 Mt. Deb. Stk.	100	90
6d.	Harmsworth, Ltd., Cum. Pref.	1	1¼
4/	Harrison, Barber, Ltd.	5	4½
3/	Harrod's Stores, Ltd.	1	4¼
2/6	Do. Cum. Pref.	5	7½
5½	Hawaiian Comcl. & Sug. 1 Mt. Debs.	100	91½
5	Hazell, Watson, L., C. P.	10	11½
18/	Henley's Teleg., Ltd.	10	22
7	Do. Pref. Shs.	10	19
4½	Do. Mt. Db. Stk., Rd.	100	112½
6	Henry, Ltd.	10	11½
5	Do. Cum. Pref.	10	13
4½	Do. Mt. Debs., Red.	50	51
1/4½	Herrmann, Ltd.	1	¾
—	Hildesheimer, Ltd.	3	1½
1/2½	Holbrn. & Frasca, Ltd.	1	1½
5	Do. Cum. Pref.	10	11½
4	Do. Deb. Stk.	100	109
6	Home & Col. Stres, L., C.P	5	7½
6	Hood & M.'s Stres., Ltd., Cum. Pref.	1	¼
6	Hook, C. T Ltd.	10	6
7/2	Hornsby, Ltd., £10 Shs.	8	3
—	Hotchks. Ordn., Ltd.	10	1
—	Do. 7 p.c. Cm. Prf.	10	4½
5	Do. 1 Mt. Dbs., Rd.	100	97½
6	Htl. Cecil, Ld., Cm. Prf.	5	3½
4	Do. 1 Mt. D. Sk., R.	100	100½
8/	Heward & Haigh, Ltd.	10	39
6	Do. Pref.	10	16
4	Do. Deb. Stk., Red.	100	108
5/	Howell, J., Ltd., £5 Shs.	4	8½
—	Howell & Js., Ltd., £3½ Shs.	3	¾
6d.	Humber, Ltd.	1	¾
6	Do. Cum. Pref.	1	½
5/6	Hunter, Wilts., Ltd.	5	7
2/7	Hyam Clthg., Ltd., 5 p.c. Cum. Pref.	5	5½
10/	Impl. Russn. Cotton, L.	5	5¼
5	Impd. Industl. Dwgs., Ld.	100	131½
6d.	Do. Defrd.	1	1½
25/	Impd. Wood Pave., Ltd.	10	15½
15/	Ind. Rubber, Gutta Per. Telegraph Works, Ltd.	10	21½
4	Do. 1 Mt. Debs., Red.	100	104
6	Intern. Tea, Cum. Pref.	5	6½
10½d.	Jays, Ltd.	1	1½
5½	Do. Cum. Pref.	5	6½
1/2½d.	Jones & Higgins, Ltd.	1	2¼
4½	Do. 1 Mt. Db. Sk., Rd.	100	111
5/	Kelly's Directory, Ltd., 5 p.c. Cum. Pref.	10	12½
4	Do. Mort. Db. Sk., Rd.	100	106
—	Kent Coal Explrtn. Ltd.	1	¾
9½d.	King, Howmann, Ltd.	1	1½
4/	Kinloch & Co., Ltd.	5	8½
6	Do. Pref.	5	7
5	Lady's Pictorial Pub., Ltd., Cum. Pref.	5	5
48/4	La Guaira Harb., Ltd., 5 p.c. Deb. Stk.	100	79½
—	Do. 2 Mt. 7 p.c. Deb. Stk., Red.	100	25½
4/	Lagunas Nitrate, Ltd.	5	1
2/	Lagunas Syn., Ltd.	5	1
5	Do. 1 Mt. Debs., Red.	100	79½
—	L. Copais Ld., 1 Mt. 6 p.c. Debs., Red.	100	35½
3/	Lautaro Nitrate, Ltd.	5	4
5	Do. 1 Mt. Debs., Red.	—	100
9/	Lawes Chem. L., £10 shs.	9	5½
14/	Do. N. Cm. Min. Pref.	10	12½
—	Leeds Forge, 7 p.c. Cm. Pf.	5	3½
5	Do. 1 Mt. Debs., Red.	50	47
5	Lever Bros., L., Cm. Pf.	10	13½
6	Liberty, L., 6 p.c. Cm. Pf.	10	15
20/	Liebig's, Ltd.	20	79
5	Lilley & Sk., L., Cm. Pf.	5	5½
2/6	Linoleum Manftg Ltd.	5	16
3/	Linotype, Ltd., Pre	5	5½
5/	Do. Def.	5	7½
4/	Lister & Co., Ltd.	10	4
5	Do. Cum. Pref.	10	8½
5/	Liverpool Nitrate	5	4½
—	Liverpool Warehsg., Ltd	10	3
5½	Do. Cum. Pref.	10	7½
4	Do. 1 Mt. Db. Stk., Rd.	100	106
5½	Lockharts, Ltd., Cm. Pf.	1	1¼
4/6	Ldn. & Til. Lightrage £10	9	6½
6/	Ldn. Comcl. Sale Rms., L.	10	17½
3	Do. 1 Mt. Deb. Stk., Red.	100	103
3	London Nitrate, Ltd.	5	1½
4/	London Nitrate, Ld. 8 p.c. Cm. Min. Pf.	5	3½
8/	London Pavilion, Ltd.	5	6

Commercial, &c. (*continued*):—

Last Div.	Name.	Paid.	Price.
2/6	London Produce Clg. Ho., Ltd., £10 Shares	2½	3½
4/	London Stereos., Ltd.	5	3
7½d.	Ldn. Un. Laun. L. Cm. Pf.	1	¾
8½d.	Louise, Ltd.	1	¾
5½	Do. Cum. Pref.	1	¾
5/	Lovell & Christmas, Ltd.	5	11½
6	Do. Cum. Pref.	5	7½
4	Do. Mt. Deb. Stk., Red.	100	107
1/3	Lyons, Ltd.	1	4½
4½	Do. 1 Mt. Deb., Stk., Rd.	100	111½
10/	Machinery Trust, Ltd.	5	14
4½	Do. 4½ Deb. Stk.	100	104
6	MacLellan, L., Min. C. Pf.	10	9
5	Do. 1 Mt. Debs., 1900	100	101½
—	McEwan, J. & Co., Ltd.	10	1½
6	Do. Mt. Debs., Red.	100	89½
8	McNamara, L., Cm. Pref.	10	9
7½d.	Maison Virot, Ltd.	1	¾
2/7	Do. 6 p.c. Cum. Pref.	5	3½
5/	Manbré Sacc., L., Cm. Pf.	10	11½
10/	Mangan Brze., L., £10 Shs.	6	15½
2/	Mason & Mason, Ltd.	5	2½
6	Do. Cum. Pref.	5	5½
—	Maynards, Ltd.	1	¾
6	Do. Cum. Pref.	1	¾
9½d.	Mazawattee Tea, Ltd.	1	1½
5	Do. Cum. Pref.	5	5½
6	Mellin's Food Cum. Pref.	5	6½
4½	Met. Ascn. Imp. Dwlings., Ltd.	100	110
5	Metro. Indus. Dwlgs., Ltd.	5	4½
4	Do. do. Cum. Pref.	5	5½
5	Metro. Prop., L., Cm. Pf.	5	6½
4½	Do. 1st Mt. Debs. Stk.	100	108½
6	Mexican Cotton 1 Mt. Db.	100	93½
4½	Mid. Class Dwlgs., L., Db.	100	120½
2/	Millars' Karri, Ltd.	1	2½
6	Do. Cum. Pref.	1	1½
5/	Milner's Safe, Ltd.	10	20
10/	Moir & Son, Ltd., Pref.	5	8
6	Morgan Cruc., L., Cm. Pf.	10	14½
2/	Morris, B., Ltd.	3½	2½
2/6	Murray L. 5½ p.c. C. Pf.	5	5½
63/4½	Do. 4½ 1 Mt. Db. Sk. Rd.	100	107
1/7½	Nat. Safe Dep., Ltd.	4	3½
6	Do. Cum. Pref.	1	1
—	Native Guano, Ltd.	5	¾
—	Nelson Bros., Ltd.	10	2½
5	Do. Deb. Stk., Red.	100	80½
7/	Neuchtel Asph., Ltd.	10	10
10d.	New Darvel Tob., Ltd.	18/	1½
1/6	New Explosives, Ltd.	3	3½
5/3½	New Gd. Htl., Bham, L.	5	4
5½	Do. Pref.	5	4½
4	Do. 1 Mt. Db. Stk., Rd.	100	96½
—	New Julia Nitrate, Ltd.	10/	—
—	New Ldn. Borneo Tob., L.	16/	1½
1/6	New Premier Cycle, Ltd.	1	¾
6	Do. 6 p.c. Cum. Pref.	1	¾
4½	Do. 4½ p.c. 1 Mt. Db. Rd	100	—
—	New Tamargl. Nitr., Ltd	1	¾
—	Do. 8 p.c. Cum. Pref.	1	¾
6	Do. 6 p.c. 1 Mt. Dbs. Rd.	100	62½
3'78d.	Newnes, G., L., Cm. Prf.	1	1
1/3	Nitr. Provision, Ltd.	2½	½
24/	Nobel-Dynam., Ltd.	10	18½
—	North Brazn. Sugar, Ltd.	1	¼
15/	Oakey, Ltd.	10	31
6	Do. Cum. Pref.	10	17½
—	Paccha Jarp. Nitr., Ltd.	5	¾
5	Pac. Borax, L., 1 Db. Rd.	100	110
—	Palace Hotel, Ltd.	10	5½
5½	Do. Cum. Pref.	10	7½
4	Do. 1 Mt. Deb. Stk.	100	103
2/6	Palmer, Ltd.	5	3½
6	Do. Cum. Pref.	5	2
1/2½d	Paquin, Ltd.	1	¾
6	Do. Cum. Pref.	5	4
5½	Parnall, Ltd., Cum. Pref.	1	¾
4/6	Pawsons, Ltd., £10 Shs.	6	6½
4	Do. Mt. Debs., Red.	100	106
6	Pearks, G. & T., Ltd., 6 p.c. Cum. Pref.	1	¾
9½d.	Pears, Ltd.	1	1½
6	Do. Cum. Pref.	10	14
5	Do. Deb. Stk.	100	129
5½	Pearson, C. A., L., Cu. Pf.	5	4½
4/3	Peebles, Ltd.	5	7½
5	Do. Cum. Pref.	5	6½
4½	Do. Mt. Deb. Stk. Red.	100	113½
5½	Peek Bros., Ltd., 1 Cum. Pref., Nos. 1-60,000	5	6½
3½	Do. 3½ p.c. 1 Db. Stk.	100	102½
7½d.	Pegamoid, Ltd.	1	¾
—	Pillsbury-W. Fl. Mills, L.	10	3½
16/	Do. 8 p.c. Cum. Pref.	10	7½
6	Do. 1 Mort. Debs.	100	94½
9½d.	Plummer, Ltd.	1	1½
5	Do. Cum. Pref.	1	5½
7/6	Price's Candle, Ltd.	16	35
6	Priest Marians, L., Cm. Pf.	1	1½
6	Pryce Jones, Ld., Cm. Pf.	5	7
5	Do. Deb. Stk.	100	122
8½d.	Pullman, Ltd.	1	1½
6d.	Do. Cum. Pref.	1	1½
6d.	Raleigh Cycle, Ltd.	1	¾
6	Do. Cum. Pref.	1	¾
—	Recife Drnge. Ld. 1 Mt. Debs., R	100	19
6	Redfern, Ltd. Cum. Prf.	10	14
5	Ridgways, Ltd., Cu. Pf.	5	5½
—	R. Janeiro Cy. Imps. Ld.	25	7
5	Do. Debs.	100	85½
5	Do. 1882-1893	100	83½
11/	R. Jan Fl. Mills, Ltd.	7	6½
5	Do. 1 Mt. Debs., Rd.	100	94
—	Riv. Plate Meat, Ltd.	5	2½
—	Do. Pref.	5	5
8½d.	Roberts, J. R., Ltd.	1	1½
5	Roberts 1 Mt. D. Sk., Rd.	100	111
1/1½	Roberts, T. R., Ltd.	1	2½
5	Do. Cum. Pref.	1	1½

Commercial, &c. (*continued*):—

Last Div.	Name.	Paid.	Price.
3/	Rosario Nit., Ltd.	8	3½
5	Do. Debs., Red.	100	103
1/	Rover Cycle, Ltd.	1	¾
6/	Ryl. Aquarium, Ltd.	5	4½
6	Do. Pref.	5	6
5	Ryl. Htl., Edin., Cm. Pf.	1	1¼
1/9½	Ryl. Niger, Ltd., £10 Sh.	2	3
6/	Do.	10	15
20/	Russian Petroleum	10	23
6½	Do. 6½ p.c. Cm. Prf	10	10½
3/	Ruston, Proctor, Ltd.	10	11
4½	Do. 1 Mort. Debs.	100	104
6/	Sadler, Ltd.	12	7
—	Sal. Carmen Nit., Ltd.	5	3½
9d.	Salmon & Gluck., Ltd.	1	1¼
	Salt Union, Ltd.	10	1½
1½	Do. 7 p.c. Pref.	10	5½
4½	Do. Deb. Stk.	100	98½
4½	Do. "B" Deb. Sk., Rd.	100	97½
—	San Donato Nit., Ltd.	5	¾
5/	San Jorge Nit., Ltd.	5	3½
—	San Pablo Nit., Ltd.	5	¾
—	San Sebastn. Nit., Ltd.	5	¾
1/9	Sanitas, Ltd	1	2½
—	Sa. Elena Nit., Ltd.	5	¾
—	Sa. Rita Nit., Ltd.	5	1½
5/	Savoy Hotel, Ltd.	10	15
7	Do. Pref.	10	13
4	Do. 1 Mt. Deb. Stk.	100	111½
5	Do. Debs., Red	100	102½
5	Do. & Ldn. For. Htl., Ltd., 5 p.c. Debs. Red.	100	99
8½d.	Schweppes, Ltd.	1	1
2½d.	Do Def.	1	¾
5	Do. Cum. Pref.	1	1¼
4	Do. Deb. Stk.	100	106
1/	Singer Cyc., Ltd.	1	¾
5½	Do Cum. Pref.	1	¾
—	Smokeless Pwdr., Ltd.	1	¾
5½d.	S. Eng. Dairies, Ltd., 6 p.c. Cum. Pref.	1	1½
—	Sowler Thos. L.	1	1
3/4½	Do. 5½ Cm. Pf.	5	5½
4/6	Spencer, Turner, & Co. Ltd	5	8½
5	Do. Cum. Pref.	5	6½
5	Spicer, Ld., 5 p.c. Dbs. Rd.	100	65
4/	Spiers & Pond, Ltd.	10	21½
5	Do. 1 Mt. Debs., Red.	100	118½
5	Do. "A" Db. Stk., Rd.	100	111
5	Do. "B" 1 Db. Stk., Rd.	100	111
4	Do. Fd. "C" 1 Db. S., R.	100	104
7/6	Spratt's, Ltd	5	12½
4	Do. Debs., 1914	—	105
5	Steiner Ld., Cm. Pf.	10	11½
4	Do. 1 Mt. Db. Sk. Rd.	100	107
6/	Stewart & Clydesdale, L.	10	13½
6	Do. Cum. Pref.	10	14½
35/5	Sulphide Corp.	100	80
1/	Swan & Edgar, L.	1	1½
1/	Sweetmeat Automatic, L.	1	3½
2/9	Teetgen, Ltd., Cum. Pref.	5	6
24/	Teleg. Construction., Ld.	12	35½
5	Do. Db. Bds., Rd., 1899	100	103½
3/0½	Tilling, Ld. 5½ p.c. Cm. Prf.	5	6½
4	Do. 4 p.c. 1 Dbs., Rd.	—	105
8½d.	Tower Tea, Ltd.	1	1½
5	Do. Cum. Pref.	5	5½
5	Travers, Ltd., Cum. Pref.	10	12½
4	Do. 1 Mt. Dbs., Rd.	100	106
6	Tucuman Sug., 1 Dbs., Rd.	100	100
4/	United Alkali, Ltd.	10	2
7	Do. Cum. Pref.	10	9
5	Do. Mt. Db. Stk., Rd.	100	107½
2½d.	United Horse Shoe, Ltd., Non-Cum. 8 p.c. Pref.	1	¾
5	Un. Kingm. Tea, Cm. Prf.	5	4½
2/	Un. Lankat Plant., Ltd.	1	2
4/	Un. Limmer Asphlte., Ld.	3	5
13/	Val de Travers Asph., L.	10	15½
3/	V. den Bergh's, L., Cm. P.	5	6½
6	Walkers, Park., L., C. Pf.	10	3
4½	Do. 1 Mt. Debs., Red.	100	90½
6/	Wallis, Thos. & Co., Ltd.	5	14
6	Do. Cum. Pref.	5	8½
5½	Waring, Ltd., Cum. Pref.	5	5½
4½	Do. 1 Mt. Db. Sk., Red.	100	112
4½	Do. Irred. "B" Db. Stk.	100	104
12/	Waterlow, Dfd. Ord.	10	14
4/	Do. Pref.	10	14
3½	Do. Cum. Pref.	10	10½
10/	Waterlow Bros. & L., Ld.	10	9
5	Do. Pref.	10	12
1/2½	Welford, Ltd.	1	1½
4½	Do. Debs., Red.	100	109
3/	Welford's Surrey Dairies, Ltd.	1	1½
7½d.	West London Dairy, Ltd.	1	1
4½	Wharncliffe Dwllgs., L., Pf.	10	11½
18/10	Do. 3 p.c. Irr. Mt. Db. Sk.	100	96
6d.	White, A. J., Ltd.	1	1
6	Do. 6 p.c. Cum. Pref.	1	¾
4	White, J. Bazley, Ltd., 1 Mort. Debs., Red.	100	99½
5	White, R., Ltd., 1 Mort. Deb. Stock, Red.	100	104½
11/	White, Tomkins, Ltd	10	10½
5	Do. Cum. Pref.	10	11½
5	White, W. N., L., Cm. Pf.	1	¾
2/6	Wickens, Pease & Co., L.	5	2½
6	Wilkie, Ltd., Cum. Pref.	10	15
4/	Willans & Robinson, Ltd.	5	8
6	Do. Cum. Pref.	5	7
4½	Do. 1 Mt. Db. Stk., Red.	100	107
7½d.	Williamsons, L., Cm. Prf.	1	1½
6	Winterbottm. Book Cloth, Ltd., Cum. Prf.	10	15
4/6	Yates, Ltd.	5	6
6	Do. Cum. Pref.	5	6½
	Young's Paraffin. Ltd.	4	1½

CORPORATION STOCKS—COLONIAL AND FOREIGN.

Per Cent.	Name.	Paid.	Price.
6	Auckland City, '72 1904-24	100	115
6	Do. Cons., '79, Red. 1930	100	136½
5	Do. Deb. Ln., '83..1934-8	100	117
6	Auckland Harb. Debs.	100	111½
5	Do. 1917	100	112
5	Do. 1936	100	114
3½	Balmain Boro' ... 1914	—	113½
5	Boston City (U.S.)	100	102½
5	Do. ..1902	100	105
5	Brunswick Town 5. c. Debs. ...1916-20	100	111
4½	B. Ayres City 4½ p.c.	100	69
5	Cape Town, City of	100	113
4	Do. ..1943	100	115
4	Chicago, City of, Gold 1915	—	108½
6	Christchurch ...1926	100	131½
—	Cordoba City	100	17½
5	Duluth (U.S.) Gold ..1906	—	110
6	Dunedin (Otago) ...1925	100	127½
6	Do. ...1906	100	113
5	Do. Consols..1908	100	111
4	Durban Insc. Stk. ...1944	100	111
4	Essex Cnty., N. Jersey 1926	$100	114½
5	Fitzroy, Melbrne...1916-19	100	110
5	Gisborne Harbour....1915	100	109
4	Greymouth Harbour..1925	100	110
4	Hamilton ...1934	100	108
5	Hobart Town 1918-30	100	115
4	Do. 1940	100	105
4½	Invercargill Boro. Dbs. 1936	100	111
6	Kimberley Boro., S. A. Debs.	—	102
4	Launceston Twn. Dbs. 1916	100	105
6	Lyttleton, N.Z., Harb. 1929	100	125
4	Melbourne Bd. of Wks. 1921	100	107
5	Melb. City Debs. 1897-1907	100	106½
4½	Do. Debs. ...1908-27	100	111½
4	Do. Debs...1915-20-22	100	105
5	Melbne. Harb. Bds., 1908-9	100	112
4½	Do. do. ...1915	100	111
4	Do. do. ...1918-21	100	105
4½	Melbrne. Tms. Dbs. 1914-16	100	113
4½	Do. Fire Brig. Db. 1921	100	103
5	Mexico City Stg.	100	93
4	Moncton N. Bruns. City	100	102
5	Montevideo	100	60
5	Montreal Stg.	100	108
5	Do. 1874	100	103
5	Do. 1879	100	104
3½	Do. ...1933	100	102
3	Do. Perm. Deb. Stk	100	96
4	Do. Cons. Deb. Stk. 1932	100	112
6	Napier Boro. Consolid. 1914	100	119
5	Napier Harb. Debs...1920	100	115
5	Do. Debs...1928	100	107
6	New Plymouth Harb. Debs. ...1909	100	107
6	New York City ...1901	—	108½
3½	Do. ... 1910-26	—	103½
4½	Nth. Melbourne Debs. 1-600 1921	100	105
5	Oamaru Boro. Cons...1920	100	101
6	Do. Harb. Bds. (Reg.)	100	74
25/	Do. 6 p.c. (Bearer)..1919	100	36
6	Otago Harb. Deb. Reg.	100	103
6	Do. 1877	100	107
6	Do. 1881 ...1921	100	115
5	Do. Debs. ..1921	100	107
5	Do. Cons. ..1934	100	105
6	Ottawa City	100	109
6	Do. ...1904	100	111½
4½	Do. Debs. ..1913	100	108½
6	Port Elizabeth Waterworks	100	111
5	Port Louis	100	111
5	Prahran Debs. ...1917	100	109
4	Do. Debs. ...1919	100	102
6	Quebec C. Coupon. 1873 1905	100	112
6	Do. do. 1878 ...1908	100	116
4½	Do. Debs. ...1914-18	100	108
4	Do. Debs. ...1923	100	108
3½	Do. Cns. Rg. Stk., Red.	100	101
5	Richmond (Melb.) Dbs. 1917	100	112
4	Rio Janeiro City	100	58
4	Rome City	100	—
4	Do. 2nd to 8th Iss.	100	92
—	Rosario C.	100	23½
—	Do.	100	23½
4	St. Catherine (Ont.)..1926	100	101
4	St. John, N.B., Debs. 1934	—	103
4½	St. Kilda (Melb) Dbs. 1918-21	100	105
4	St. Louis C. (Miss.)..1911	100	104
4	Do. ...1913	100	103½
3'65	Do. ...1915	—	103½
—	Santa Fé City Debs.	100	19
6	Santos City	100	95
6	Sofia City	100	84
5	Sth. Melbourne Debs. 1915	100	111
4½	Do. Debs. ...1919	100	107
5	Sydney City ...1904	100	109
4	Do. Debs. 1912-13	100	107
4	Do. do. (1894)..1919	100	109
7	Timaru Boro. 7 p.c...1920	100	136½
5	Timaru Harb. Debs 1914	100	107
5	Do. Debs...1916	100	107
6	Toronto City Wtwks 1904-6	100	114
5	Do. G. Cns. Dbs. 1919-20	100	118
4	Do. Strlg. ...1922-8	100	107
4	Do. Local Improv.	100	108
3½	Do. ...1929	100	105
5½	Valparaiso	100	99
4	Vancouver ...1931	100	107
4	Do. ...1932	100	103
6	Wanganui Harb. Dbs. 1905	100	110
6	Wellington Con. Deb. 1907	100	117
6	Do. Improv., 1879	100	122
6	Do. Wtrwks. Dbs., 1880	100	128
4½	Do. Debs., 1893...1933	100	114
4½	Wellington Harb. ...1907	100	104
4	Westport Harb. Dbs. 1925	100	110
6	Winnipeg City Deb...1907	—	119
5	Do. ...1914	100	117

FINANCIAL, LAND, AND INVESTMENT.

Last Div.	Name.	Paid.	Price.
5	Agncy, Ld. & Fin. Aust., Ltd., Mt. Db. Stk., Rd.	100	90½
	Amer. Frehld. Mt. of Lon., Ld., Cum. Pref. Stk.	100	87½
4½	Do. Deb. Stk., Red.	100	92
1/4½	Anglo-Amer. Db. Cor., L.	2	1
4	Do. Deb. Stk., Red	100	107½
5½	Ang.-Ceylon & Gen. Est., Ltd., Cons. Stk.	100	50
6	Do. Reg. Debs., Red.	100	101½
3/	Ang.-Fch. Explorn., Ltd.	1	2 1/16
6	Do. Cum. Pref.	1	[illegible]
—	Argent. Ld. & Inv., Ltd. £1 Shares	10/	nil
—	Do. Cum. Pref.	4	1½
1/	Assets Fnders.' Sh., Ltd.,	4	1½
6/	Assets Realiz., Ltd., Ord.,	5	8½
5	Do. Cum. Pref.	5	6½
26/	Austrln. Agricl. £25 Shs.	21½	63½
4½	Aust. N. Z. Mort., Ltd., Deb. Stk., Red.	100	87½
4	Do. Deb. Stk., Red.	100	82½
4½	Australian Est. & Mt., L., 1 Mt. Deb. Stk., Red.	100	102½
5	Do. "A" Mort. Deb. Stk., Red.	100	96
5/	Australian Mort., Ld., & Fin., Ltd. £25 Shs.	5	5
1/6	Do. New, £25 Shs.	3	3
4	Do. Deb. Stk.	100	110
3	Do. Do.	100	85
5	Bengal Presidy. 1 Mort. Deb., Red.	100	106
25/	British Amer. Ld. "A"	1	19
—	Do. "B"	24	7
1/7½	Brit. & Amer. Mt., Ltd. £10 Shs.	2	1
5/	Do. Pref.	10	10
4	Do. Deb. Stk., Red.	100	103
1/3	Brit. & Austrlsn Tst Ln., Ltd. £25 Shs.	2½	¾
4½	Do. Perm. Debs., Red.	100	104
1½d.	Brit. N. Borneo. £1 Shs.	15/	9/16
2½d.	Do.	1	¾
—	Brit. S. Africa	1	2¾
5	Do. Mt. Deb., Red.	—	99
6	B. Aires Harb. Tst., Red.	100	94½
12/6	Canada Co.	1	26
—	Canada N. W. Ld., Ltd.	$25	83½
—	Do. Pref.	$100	$50½
4	Canada Perm. Loan & Sav. Perp. Deb. Stk.	100	99½
6	Curamalan Ld., 6 p.c. "A" Scrip	—	92
3/7½	Deb Corp., Ld., £10 Shs	4	3½
5	Do. Cum. Pref.	10	11½
4	Do. Perp. Deb. Stk.	100	111
9d.	Deb. Corp. Fders' Sh., Ld.	3	½
4/5 1/5	Eastn. Mt. & Agncy, Ld., "A"	10	5½
4½	Do. Deb. Stk., Red.	100	98
5	Equitable Revers. In. Ltd.	100	—
2/6	Exploration, Ltd.	1	1½
/6d.	Freehold Trst. of Austrla. Ltd. £10 Shs.	1	¾
4	Do. Perp. Deb. Stk.	100	100
70/	Genl. Reversionary, Ltd.	100	—
3½	Holborn Vi. Land	100	105
4½	House Prop. & Inv.	100	84½
13/	Hudson's Bay	13	21½
—	Hyderabad (Deccan)	5	2¼
4	Impl. Col. Fin. & Agcy. Corp.	100	92½
4½	Impl. Prop. Inv., Ltd., Deb. Stk., Red.	100	91½
2/6	Internatl. Fincial. Soc., Ltd. £7½ Shs.	2¼	1½
4	Do. Deb. Stk., Red.	100	99½
2/4½	Ld. & Mtge. Egypt, Ltd. £18 Shs.	3	2¾
5	Do. Debs., Red.	100	101
4½	Do. Debs., Red.	100	100
—	Ld. Corp. of Canada, Ltd.	1	½
4½	Ld. Mtge. Bk. of Texas Deb. Stk.	100	—
3½	Ld. Mtge. Bk. Victoria 4½ p.c. Deb. Stk.	100	78
2/9½	Law Debent. Corp., Ltd., £10 Shs.	2	1½
4½	Do. Cum. Pref.,	10	12
4	Do. Deb. Stk.	100	115
—	Law Land, L., 4½ Cm. Prf.	5	5½
1/	Ldn. & Australasian Deb. Corp., Ltd., £4 Shs.	2	¼
4½	Do. 4½ p.c. Mt. Deb. Stk., Red.	100	99
1/9	Ldn. & Middx. Frhld. Est. £2 Shs.	35/	3
2/6	Lndn. & N. Y. Inv. Corp., Ltd.	5	1¾
5	Do. 5 p.c. Cum. Pref.	10	8¼
1/6	Ldn. & Nth. Assets Corp., Ltd., £2 Shs.	1½	¾
2	Ldn. & N. Deb. Corp., L.	2	1¼
3/6	Ldn. & S. Afric. Explrn. Ltd.	½	12¾
2/	Mtge. Co. of R. Plate, Ltd. £10 Shs.	2	3
4½	Do. Deb. Stk., Red.	100	112
4½	Morton, Rose Est., Ltd., 1st Mort. Debs.	—	99
6/6	Natal Land Col. Ltd.	10	7
4/	Do. 8 p.c. Pref., 1870	5	8
5/6	Natl. Disct. L., £25 Shs.	5	10½
4½	New Impl. Invest., Ltd. Pref. Stk.	100	62½
	New Impl. Invest., Ltd. Def. Stk.	100	9
3½	N. Zld. Assets Real Deb.	100	99
4	N. Zld. Ln. & Mer. Agcy., Ltd Prf. Ln, Deb. Stk	100	93
2/6	N. Zld. Tst. & Ln. Ltd., £25 Shs.	5	1½

Financial, Land, &c. (*continued*):—

Last Div.	Name.	Paid.	Price.
12/6	N. Zld. Tst. & Ln. Ltd., 5 p.c. Cum. Pref.	25	19
—	N. Brit. Australsn. Ltd.	100	5
—	Do. Irred. Guar.	100	32½
5	Do. Mort. Debs.	100	82½
4½	N. Queensld. Mort. & Inv., Ltd., Deb. Stk.	100	93
6	Peel Riv., Ld. & Min. Ltd.	100	88½
—	Peruvian Corp., Ltd.	100	2½
—	Do. 4 p.c. Pref.	100	9
3	Do. 6 p.c. 1 Mt. Debs., Red.	100	39½
—	Queenld. Invest. & Ld. Mort. Pref. Ord. Stk.	100	20
3/7	Queenld. Invest. & Ld. Mort. Ord. Shs.	4	4
4	Queenld. Invest. & Ld. Mort. Perp. Debs.	100	88
3½	Raily. Roll Stk. Tst. Deb., 1903-6	100	100½
50/	Reversiony. Int. Soc., Ltd.	100	—
2/8½	Riv. Plate Trst., Loan & Agcy., L., "A" £10 Shs.	2	4
1/6	Riv. Plate Trst., Loan & Agcy., Ltd., Def. "B"	5	3½
	Riv. Plate Trst., Loan & Agy., L., Db. Stk., Red.	100	109
—	Santa Fé & Cord. Gt. South Land, Ltd.	20	5
—	Santa Fé Land	10	2½
2/	Scot. Amer. Invest., Ltd. £10 Shs.	2	2¾
2½	Scot. Australian Invest., Ltd., Cons.	100	68½
6	Scot. Australian Invest., Ltd., Guar. Pref.	100	136½
5	Scot. Australian Invest., Ltd., Guar. Pref.	100	104½
4	Scot. Australian Invest., Ltd., 4 p.c. Perp. Dbs.	100	105½
5	Sivagunga Zemdy., 1st Mort., Red.	100	101
20/	Sth. Australian	20	47½
3½	Stock Exchange Deb., Rd.	—	101½
—	Strait Develt., Ltd.	1	—
2/6	Texas Land & Mt., Ltd. £10 Shs.	2½	2¾
4½	Texas Land & Mt., Ltd., Deb. Stk., Red.	100	104
—	Transvaal Est. & Dev., L.	1	½
—	Transvaal Lands, Ltd., £1 Shs.	15/	7/16
—	Do. F. P.	1	½
—	Transvaal Mort., Loan, & Fin., Ltd., £10 Shs.	2	1/16
2/	Tst & Agcy. of Austrlsa., Ltd., £10 Shs.	1	2
7/5	Do. Old, fully paid	10	15½
5/7	Do. New, fully paid	10	12½
5	Do. Cum. Pref.	10	12¾
3/	Trust & Loan of Canada, £20 Shs.	5	4¾
1/9⅜	Do. New £20 Shs.	3	2½
4½	Tst. & Mort. of Iowa, Ltd., Deb. Stk. Red.	100	92½
—	Tst., Loan, & Agency of Mexico, Ltd., £10 Shs.	2	¼
—	Trsts., Exors, & Sec. Ins. Corp., Ltd., £10 Shs.	7	1¾
4	Do. Irred. Deb. Stk.	100	106½
5/	Union Dsc., Ld., £10 Shs.	5	10½
6	Union Mort. & Agcy. of Aust., Ltd., Pref. Stk.	100	30
—	Do. 6 p. Pref. £6 Shs.	2	¼
4½	Do. Deb. Stk	100	92½
4	Do. Deb. Stk	100	85½
5	Do. Deb. Stk. Red.	100	96½
1/6	U.S. Deb. Cor. Ltd., £8 Shs.	1	¼
5½	Do. Cum. Pref. Stk.	100	100½
4½	Do. Irred. Deb. Stk.	100	105½
5	U.S. Tst. & Guar. Cor., Ltd., Pref. Stk.	100	77½
8/	Van Dieman's	25	16½
4	Walker's Prop. Cor., Ltd., Guar. 1 Mt. Deb. Stk.	100	109
4½	Wstr. Mort. & Inv., Ltd., Deb. Stk.	100	92½

FINANCIAL—TRUSTS.

Last Div.	Name.	Paid.	Price.
1/6	Afric City Prop., Ltd	1	1½
6	Do. Cum. Pref.	1	1¼
4	Alliance Invt., Ltd., Cm. 4½ p. c. Prefd.	100	74
—	Do. Defd	100	12½
4	Do. Deb. Stk. Red.	100	104½
5	Amren. Invt., Ltd., Prfd.	100	119½
5	Do. Defd.	100	88½
4	Do. Deb. Stk. Red.	100	113½
4	Army & Navy Invt., Ltd., 5 p.c. Prefd.	100	82½
—	Do. Defd. Stk.	100	15½
4	Do. Deb. Stk.	100	106½
4	Atlas Investment, Ltd., Prefd. Stk.	100	70½
4½	Bankers' Invest., Ltd., Cum. Prefd.	100	103½
1/0/0	Do. Defd.	100	26½
4	Do. Deb. Stk	100	112
	Brewery & Comml. Inv., Ltd., £10 Shs.	5	6

Financial—Trusts (*continued*):—

Last Div.	Name.	Paid.	Price.
4	British Investment, Ltd., Cum. Prefd.	100	107
5	Do. Defd.	100	103
4	Do. Deb. Stk.	100	108½
6	Brit. Steam. Invst., Ltd., Prefd	100	116½
3/0/0	Do. Defd	100	73½
4½	Do. Perp. Deb. Stk	100	120½
1/9	Car Trust Invst., Ltd., £10 Shs.	2½	2
5	Do. Pref.	100	101
4	Do. Deb. Stk., 1915	100	104
4	Clnl. Sec., Ltd., Prefd.	100	103½
2½	Do. Defd.	100	43½
4	Consolidated, Ltd., Cum. 1st Pref.	100	90
4	Do. 5 p.c. Cm. 2nd do.	100	68½
—	Do. Defd.	100	14½
4½	Do. Deb. Stk.	100	112½
5	Deb. Secs. Invst.	100	103½
4	Do. 4 p.c. Cm. Pf. Sk.	100	105½
4½	Edinburgh Invest., Ltd., Cum. Prefd. Stk.	100	105½
4	Do. Deb. Stk. Red.	100	106½
5	Foreign, Amer. & Gen. Invt., Ltd., Prefd.	100	112½
2	Do. Defd.	100	48½
4	Do. Deb. Stk.	100	113½
5	Foreign & Colonial Invt., Ltd., Prefd.	100	136½
5½	Do. Defd.	100	97½
4½	Gas, Water & Gen. Invt., Cum. Prefd. Stk.	100	85½
3	Do. Defd. Stk.	100	36½
4	Do. Deb. Stk.	100	104
5	Gen. & Com. Invt., Ltd., Prefd. Stk.	100	105½
2	Do. Defd. Stk.	100	36½
4	Do. Deb. Stk.	100	111½
2/6	Globe Telegph. & Tst., Ltd.	10	11½
6	Do. do. Pref.	10	17
4	Govt. & Genl. Invt., Ld., Prefd.	100	84½
3½	Do. Defd.	100	41½
4½	Govts. Stk. & other Secs. Invt., Ltd., Prefd.	100	85½
1	Do. Defd.	100	25
4½	Do. Deb. Stk.	100	111
4	Do. do.	100	104
4½	Guardian Invt., Ltd., Pfd.	100	89½
—	Do. Defd.	100	19½
4	Do. Deb. Stk.	100	104
5	Indian & Gen. Inv., Ltd., Cum. Prefd.	100	108½
2½	Do. Defd.	100	58
4½	Do. Deb. Stk.	100	119½
5	Indust. & Gen. Tst., Ltd., Unified	100	98½
3½	Do. Deb. Stk. Red.	100	99½
4½	Internat. Invt., Ltd., Cm. Prefd.	100	66½
—	Do. Defd.	100	7½
4	Do. Deb. Stk.	100	101
4	Invest. Tst. Cor. Ltd. Pfd.	100	101
6	Do. Defd.	100	86
4	Do. Deb. Stk. Red.	100	105
25/	Ldn. Gen. Invest. Ltd., 5 p.c. Cum. Prefd.	100	110½
37/6	Do. Defd.	100	120
4½	Ldn. Scot. Amer. Ltd. Pfd.	100	104½
£3	Do. Defd.	100	59½
4	Do. Deb. Stk.	100	111
4	Ldn. Tst., Ltd., Cum. Prfd. Stk.	100	100
4	Do. Defd. Stk.	100	68½
4	Do. Deb. Stk., Red.	100	107
3½	Do. Mt. Deb. Stk., Red.	100	100½
5	Mercantile Invt. & Gen., Ltd., Prefd.	100	111
3	Do. Defd.	100	44½
4	Do. Deb. Stk.	100	111½
4	Merchants, Ltd., Pref. Stk.	100	104½
4	Do. Ord.	100	80½
4	Do. Deb. Stk.	100	116½
6	Municipal, Ltd., Prefd.	100	57½
—	Do. Defd.	100	17½
4½	Do. Debs.	100	111
4½	Do. Debs. "B"	100	99½
4½	Do. "C" Deb. Stk.	100	92½
5	New Investment, Ltd. Ord.	100	91½
5	Omnium Invest., Ltd., Pfd.	100	92½
1	Do. Defd.	100	26½
4	Do. Deb. Stk.	100	105
5/	Railway Deb. Tst. Ld., £20 Shs.	10	6½
5	Do. Debs., Red.	100	107½
4½	Do. Deb. Stk., 1911	100	107½
4	Do. do. 1927	100	105½
4	Railway Invst. Ltd., Prefd.	100	114½
17/7	Do. Defd.	100	20½
8/	Railway Share Trust & Agency "A"	8	5½
7½	Do. "B" Pref. Stk.	100	146½
4½	River Plate & Gen. Invt., Ltd., Prefd.	100	104
£3	Do. Defd.	100	50½
5	Scot. Invst., Ltd., Pfd. Stk.	100	91½
1½	Do. Defd.	100	26½
4	Do. Deb. Stk.	100	106
4½	Sec. Scottish Invst., Ltd., Cum. Prefd.	100	80½
£3	Do. Defd. Stk.	100	32
4	Do. Deb. Stk.	100	108½
5/	Sth. Africa Gold Tst., Ltd.	1	3½
6	Do. Cum. Pref	1	1
5½	Do. 1st Debs., Red.	100	103
1/9	Stock Conv. & Invest., Ltd., £5 Shs.	1	1½
4½	Do. do. 4½ p.c. Cm. Prf.	100	113½
3½	Do. Ldn. & N. W. 1st. Charge Prefd.	100	113½
4	Do do. 2nd Chge Prfd.	100	111
82/6	Do. do. Defd. Charge	100	30
3	Do. N. East. 1 Chge Pfd.	100	90½

Financial—Trusts (*continued*):—

Last Div.	Name.	Paid.	Price.
37/6	Stock N. East Defd. Chge	100	36
6	Submarine Cables	100	136½
5	U.S. & S. Amer. Invest., Ltd., Prefd.	100	97½
20/	Do. Defd.	100	24½
4	Do. Deb. Stk.	100	103½

GAS AND ELECTRIC LIGHTING.

Last Div.	Name.	Paid.	Price.
10/6	Alliance & Dublin Con. 10 p.c. Stand.	10	24
7/6	Do. 7 p.c. Stand.	10	16½
5	Austln. Gas Lght. (Syd.) Debs. 1902	100	108
5	Bay State of N. Jrsy. Sk. Fd. Tst. Bd., Red.	—	89½
3/	Bombay, Ltd.	5	5½
2/4½	Do. New	4	4½
12	Brentford Cons.	100	292½
9	Do. New	100	217½
5	Do. Pref.	100	142½
4	Do. Deb. Stk.	100	136
11½	Brighton & Hove Gen. Cons. Stk.	100	272½
8½	Do. "A" Cons. Stk.	100	197½
5	Bristol 5 p.c. Max.	100	129½
22/6	British Gas Light, Ltd.	20	55½
11/6	Bromley Gas Consumrs.' 10 p.c. Stand.	10	26
8/6	Do. 7 p.c. Stand.	10	21
—	Brush Electl. Enging., L.	—	1¼
6	Do. 6 p.c. Pref.	—	2½
4½	Do. Deb. Stk.	100	112
4½	Do. 2 Deb. Stk., Red.	100	102½
7/	B. Ayres (New), Ltd.	10	9
4	Do. Deb. Stk., Rd.	—	99
18/6	Cagliari Gas & Wtr., Ltd.	20	31
8/	Cape Town & Dist. Gas Light & Coke, Ltd.	10	15½
4½	Do. Pref.	10	12
6	Do. 1 Mt. Debs. 1910	50	59
4/	Charing Cross & Strand Elec. Sup., Ltd.	5	12½
4½	Do. Cum. Pref.	5	6½
3/	Chelsea Elec. Sup., Ltd.	5	9
4½	Do. Deb. Stk., Red.	100	116
5	Chic. Edis'n Co. 1 Mt., Rd.	$1000	106
20/	City of Ldn. Elec. Lht., L.	10	25
—	Do. New £10 Shs.	5	17
6	Do. Cum. Pref.	10	17
5	Do. Deb. Stk., Red.	100	131½
13½	Commercial, Cons.	100	324½
10½	Do. New	100	252½
4½	Do. Deb. Stk.	100	152½
14	Continental Union, Ltd.	100	215
11	Do. Pref. Stk.	100	200
—	County of Lon. & Brush Prov. Elec. Lg., Ltd.	10	13½
6	Do. Cum. Pref.	10	15½
14	Croydon Comcl. Gas, Ld., "A" Stk., 10 p.c.	100	312½
11	Do. "B" Stk., 7 p.c.	100	260
5½	Crystal Pal. Dist. Ord. 5 p.c. Stk.	100	127½
5	Do. Pref. Stk.	100	143½
8/	European, Ltd.	10	24
6/	Do.	7½	17½
12¾	Gas Light & Ck Cons. Stk., "A" Ord.	100	286½
4	Do. "B" (4 p.c. Max.)	100	120½
10	Do. "C," "D," & "E" (Pref.)	100	262½
5	Do. "F" (Pref.)	100	152½
7½	Do. "G" (Pref.)	100	222½
7	Do. "H" (7 p.c. Max.)	100	197½
10	Do. "J" (Pref.)	100	302½
6	Do. "K"	100	180½
4	Do. Deb. Stk.	100	133½
4½	Do. do.	100	152½
6	Do. do.	100	202½
8/	Hong Kong & China, Ld.	10	14
4/	House to House Elec. Light Sup., Ltd.	5	6½
7	Do. Cum. Pref.	5	11½
10	Imperial Continental	100	212½
3½	Do. Deb. Stk., Red	100	104½
2/	Malta & Medit., Ltd.	5	5½
7/	Metrop. Elec. Sup., Ltd.	10	16½
4½	Do. 1 Mt. Deb. Stk.	100	119
5	Metro. of Melbrne. Dbs. 1908-12	100	111
4½	Do. Debs. 1912-22-4	100	103
10/	Monte Video, Ltd.	20	18
9½	Newcastle-upon-Tyne	100	257½
—	Do. 3½ p.c. Deb. Stk.	100	117½
12/	Notting Hill Elec. Ltg., Ltd.	10	19
3/6	Oriental, Ltd.	5	7½
3/1½	Do. New	4½	7
8½d.	Do. do. 1874	1	1½
3/6	Ottoman, Ltd.	5	5
6	People's Gas Lt. & C. of Chic. 2 Mt. 1904	100	105½
5	River Plate Elec. Lgt. & Trac., Ltd., 1 Deb. Stk.	—	92½
8	Royal Elec. of Montreal	—	144
4½	Do. 1 Mt. Deb.	100	104
11/	St. James' & Pall Mall Elec. Light, Ltd.	5	16½
7	Do. Pref.	5	10½
4	Do. Deb. Stk., Red.	100	109
10/	San Paulo, Ltd.	10	15½

Gas and Electric (*continued*):—

Last Div.	Name.	Paid.	Price.
10	Sheffield Unit. Gas Lt. "A"	100	251½
10	Do. "B"	100	251½
10	Do. "C"	100	251½
—	Sth. Ldn. Elec. Sup., Ld.	2	2½
5¼	South Metropolitan	100	136½
3	Do. 3 p.c. Deb. Stk.	100	101½
2	Tottenham & Edmonton Gas Lt. & C., "A"	100	290
9	Do. "B"	100	210
7/	Tuscan, Ltd.	10	13½
5	Do. Debs., Red.	100	101½
5/	West Ham 10 p.c. Stan.	5	12
8/	Wstmnstr. Elec. Sup., Ld.	5	16½

INSURANCE.

Last Div.	Name.	Paid.	Price.
4/	Alliance, £20 Shs.	44/	10½
10/	Alliance, Mar., & Gen., Ld., £100 Shs.	25	53
19/	Atlas, £50 Shs.	6	29
12/	British & For. Marine, Ld., £20 Shs.	4	23½
7½d.	British Law Fire, Ltd., £10 Shs.	1	1½
7/6	Clerical, Med., & Gen. Life £25 Shs.	50/	16½
20/	Commercial Union, Ltd., £50 Shs.	5	43½
4	Do. "W. of Eng." Ter. Deb. Stk.	100	110½
£9	County Fire, £100 Shs.	80	195
5/	Eagle, £50 Shs.	5	½
4/	Employrs' Liability, Ltd., £10 Shs.	2	3½
—	Empress, Ltd., £5 Shs.	1	—
21/	Equity & Law, £100 Shs.	6	23
7/6	General Life, £100 Shs.	5	15
4½d.	Gresham Life, £5 Shs.	15/	2½
2/6	Guardian, Ld., £10 Shs.	5	10½
10/	Imperial, Ltd., £20 Shs.	5	29
5/6	Imperial Life, £20 Shs.	4	6½
6/	Indemnity Mutual Mar., Ltd., £15 Shs.	3	11½
1/6	Lancashire, £20 Shs.	2	5
7½d.	Law Acc. & Contin., Ltd., £5 Shs.	10/	½
12/6	Law Fire, £100 Shs.	2½	17½
9½d.	Law Guar. & Trust, Ltd., £10 Shs.	1	1½
9/	Law Life, £20 Shs.	2	25
2/9	Law Un. & Crown £10Shs	12/	7
4	Do. Deb. Stk., 1942	100	109½
14/6	Legal & General, £50Shs.	8	15½
9d.	Lion Fire, Ltd., £8½ Shs.	1½	½
22/	Liverpool & London & Globe, Stk.	2	52½
10/	Do. Globe £1 Ann	—	35½
35/	London, £25 Shs.	12½	56
8/	Lond. & Lanc. Fire, £25Shs	2½	18½
2/	Lond. & Lanc. Life, £25Shs	2	7
1/	Lond. & Prov. Mar., Ld., £10 Shs.	1	½
6/	Lond. Guar. & Accident, Ltd., £5 Shs.	2	12
10/	Marine, Ltd., £25 Shs.	4½	43½
2/	Maritime, Ltd., £10 Shs.	2	4½
1/6	Merc. Mar., Ld., £10 Shs.	2½	2½
10/	N. Brit. & Merc., £25Shs.	6¼	42
20/	Northern, £100 Shs.	10	81
40/	Norwich Union Fire, £100 Shs.	12	126½
10/	Ocean Acc. & Guar., fy. pd.	5	22½
2/	Do. £5 Shs.	1	3½
7/6	Ocean, Marine, Ltd.	2½	8½
2/	Palatine, £10 Shs.	2	3½
2/6	Pelican, £10 Shs.	1	3½
21/	Phoenix, £50 Shs.	5	41½
£6	Provident, £100 Shs.	10	32
5/	Railway Passngrs., £10Shs.	2	8½
2/6	Rock Life, £5 Shs.	10/	4½
8	Royal Exchange	100	382½
13/	Royal, £20 Shs.	3	54
4/	Sun, £10 Shs.	10/	11½
3/9	Sun Life, £10 Shs.	7½	14½
6	Thames & Mrsey. Marine, Ltd., £20 Shs.	2	10½
0	Union, £10 Shs.	4	24½
4/	Union Marine, £20 Shs.	2½	8½
12/	Universal Life, £100 Shs.	12	42
2/	World Marine, £5 Shs.	2	1½

IRON, COAL, AND STEEL.

Last Div.	Name.	Paid.	Price.
—	Barrow Hæm. Steel, Ltd.	7½	2
9/	Do. 6 p.c. 2nd Pref.	7½	6½
10/	Bolck., Vaugh. & C., Ld.	20	16½
6/	Do. £8 liab	12	8½
7/6	Brown, J. & Co., Ltd., £20 Shs.	15	20
7/6	Consett Iron, Ld., £10 Shs.	7½	29½
7/6	Ebbw Vale Steel, Iron & Coal, Ltd., £23 Shs.	20	6½
12/6	General Mining Assn., Ld.	5½	7½
8/	Harvey Steel Co. of Gt. Britain, Ltd.	10	23
5	Lehigh V. Coal 1 Mt. 5 p.c. Guar. Gd. Cp. Bds.	—	96
42/6	Nantyglo & Blaina Iron, Ltd., Pref.	862	96
1/	Nerbudda Coal & Iron, Ltd., £3 Shs.	56/	—
—	Newport Abrcrn. Bk. Vein Steam Coal, Ltd.	10	6½
8/	New Sharlston Coll., Ltd. Pref.	20	9½
4½d.	Nw. Vancvr. Coal & Ld., L.	1	½
2/6	North's Navigation Coll. (1889) Ltd.	5	2½
10/	Do. 10 p.c. Cum. Pref.	5	6½
—	Rhymney Iron, Ltd.	5	1½
	Do. New, £5 Shs.	4½	—
5	Do. Mt. Debs., Red.	100	98½
5	Shelton Irn., Stl. & Cl. Co., Ltd., 1 Chg. Debs., Red.	100	99½
50/	Sth. Hetton Coal, Ltd.	100	—
2/	Vickers & Maxim, Ltd.	1	3½
5	Do. 5 p.c. Prfd. Stk.	100	126½

SHIPPING.

Last Div.	Name.	Paid.	Price
12/	African Stm. Ship, £20Shs.	16	10½
15/	Do. Fully-paid	20	14½
5/	Amazon Steam Nav., Ltd.	10½	8½
12/	Castle Mail Pakts., Ltd., £20 Shs.	14	15
3½	Do. 1st Deb. Stk., Red.	100	102
3/	China Mutual Steam, Ltd.	5	3
6	Do. Cum. Pref.	10	9½
10/	Cunard, Ltd.	20	9½
5/	Do. £20 Shs.	10	3½
4½	Furness, Withy, & Co., Ltd., 1 Mt. Dbs., Red.	100	106
6/	General Steam	15	7½
5/	Do. 5 p.c. Pref., 1874	10	8½
5/	Do. 5 p.c. Pref., 1877	10	8½
26/4½	Leyland & Co., Ltd.	10	27
7/	Do. 7 p.c. Cum. Pref.	10	14½
2/11	Do. 4½ p.c. Cum. Pre-Pf.	3	10½
4	Do. 1st Mt. Dbs., Red.	100	104½
7/6	Mercantile Steam, Ltd.	5	8
6/4½	New Zealand Ship., Ltd.,	6	4½
4	Do. Deb. Stk., Red.	100	104
5/	Orient Steam, Ltd.	10	4½
5	P.&O. Steam, Cum. Prefd.	100	147½
19	Do. Defd.	100	234½
3½	Do. Deb. Stk.	100	117
5	Richelieu & Ont., 1st Mt. Debs., Red.	100	100
30/	Royal Mail, £100 Shs.	60	51
2/6	Shaw, Sav., & Alb., Ltd., "A" Pref.	5	5½
5/	Do. "B" Ord.	5	4
14/	Union Steam, Ltd.	20	19
7/	Do. New £20 Shs.	10	8
4	Do. Deb. Stk., Red.	100	106
6/	Union of N.Z., Ltd.	10	9½
5½	Wilson's & Fur.-Ley., 5½ p.c. Cum. Pref.	10	10½
4½	Do. 1 Mt. Db. Sk., Rd.	100	106½

*** *Tea Shares will be found in the Special Table following.*

TELEGRAPHS AND TELEPHONES.

Last Div.	Name.	Paid.	Price.
4	African Direct, Ltd., Mort. Debs., Red.	100	102
—	Amazon Telegraph, Ltd.	10	7½
15/	Anglo-American, Ltd.	100	65½
30/	Do. 6 p.c. Prefd. Ord.	100	115½
—	Do. Defd. Ord.	100	15½
3/	Brazilian Submarine, Ltd.	10	15½
5	Do. Debs., 2 Series	100	114

Telegraphs and Telephones (*continued*):—

Last Div.	Name.	Paid.	Price.
4/	Chili Telephone, Ltd.	5	3½
$12	Comcial. Cable, $100 Shs.	—	185
4	Do. Stg. 500-yr. Deb. Stk. Red.	100	105
2½d.	Consd. Telpehone Constr., &c., Ltd.	10/	½
6/	Cuba Submarine, Ltd.	10	7
10/	Do. 10 p.c. Pref.	10	15
2/	Direct Spanish, Ltd.	5	4½
5/	Do. 10 p.c. Cum. Pref.	5	10½
4½	Do. Debs.	50	104½
3/	Direct U.S. Cable, Ltd.	20	10½
2/6	Eastern, Ltd.	10	17½
3/	Do. 6 p.c. Cum. Pref.	10	18½
4	Do. Mt. Deb. Stk., Red.	100	126
2/6	Eastern Exten., Aus., & China, Ltd.	10	17½
5	Do. (Aus. Gov. Sub.) Deb., Red.	100	102
5	Do. do. Bearer	100	102½
4	Do. Mort. Deb. Stk.	100	127½
5	Eastn. & S. Afric., Ltd., Mort. Deb. 1900	100	102
5	Do. Bearer	100	102½
4	Do. Mort. Debs. 1909	100	102½
4	Do. Mort. Debs. (Maur. Subsidy)	25	106½
5/	Grt. Nthn. Copenhagen	10	29
5	Do. Debs., Ser. B., Red.	100	101½
12/6	Indo-European, Ltd.	25	52
6	London Platino-Brazilian, Ltd., Debs. 1904	100	110
4/	Montevideo Telph., Ltd., 6 p.c. Pref.	5	2½
3/	National Telephone, Ltd.	5	5½
6/	Do. Cum. 1 Pref.	10	15
6/	Do. Cum. 2 Pref.	10	15
5	Do. Non-Cum. 3 Pref.	5	5½
3½	Do. Deb. Stk., Red.	100	104
3d.	Oriental Telephone, Ltd.	1	½
4	Pac. & Euro. Tlg. Dbs., Rd.	100	106½
4/	Reuter's, Ltd.	8	8½
5/	Un. Riv. Plate Telph., Ltd.	5	4½
5	Do. Deb. Stk., Red.	100	105½
—	West African Telg., Ltd.	10	4
5	Do. 5 p.c. Mt. Debs., Red.	100	100½
—	W. Coast of America, Ltd.	10	[illegible]
3/	Western & Brazilian, Ltd.	15	12½
3/	Do. 5 p.c. Pref. Ord.	7½	7
—	Do. Defd. Ord.	7½	4
4	Do. Deb. Stk., Red.	100	105½
6d.	W. India & Panama, Ltd.	10	[illegible]
6	Do. Cum. 1 Pref.	10	7½
6	Do. Cum. 2 Pref.	10	6
5	Do. Debs., Red.	100	107½
7	West. Union, 1 Mt. 1902 ($	1000	106½
6	Do. 6 p.c. Stg. Bds., Rd.	100	103

TRAMWAYS AND OMNIBUS.

Last Div.	Name.	Paid.	Price.
1/6	Anglo-Argentine, Ltd	5	3½
6	Do. Deb. Stk.	100	125
4/	Barcelona, Ltd	10	11
5	Do. Deb., Red.	100	105½
7/6	Belfast Street Trams.	10	16½
—	Blackpl. & Fltwd. Tram., £10 Shs.	8	12½
10/	Bordeaux Tram. & O., Ltd.	10	11½
5	Do. Cum. Pref.	10	11
—	Brazilian Street Ry., Ltd.	2	½
—	British Elec. Trac., Ltd.	10	15½
—	B. Ayres & Belg. Tram., Ltd., 6 p.c. Cum. Pref.	5	—
6	Do. 1 Deb. Stk.	100	—
—	B. Ayres. Gd. Nat., Ltd., 6 p.c. 1 Deb. Bds., Red.	100	59½
5½	Do. Pref. Debs., Red.	100	94½
1/	Calais, Ltd.	5	1
—	Calcutta, Ltd.	10	3½
—	Carthagena & Herr., Ltd.	10	2½
5	Do. Deb., Red.	100	90
5	City of B'ham. Trams., Ltd., 5 p.c. Cum. Pref.	5	5½
4	Do. 1 Mort. Debs., Rd.	100	105½
3/9	City of B. Ayres, Ltd.	5	6½
2/3	Do. Ext. £5 Shs.	3	3½
6	Do. Deb. Stk	100	145
1/4	Edinburgh Street Tram.	4	4
1/	Glasgow Tram. & Omni. Ltd., £6 Shs.	8	2½
3/7½	Imperial, Ltd.	6	14½
3/	Lond., Deptfd, & Greenwich, Prefd.	5	3½
nil	Do. Defd.	5	1
10½	Lond. Gen. Omni., Ltd.	100	195
4	Do. Deb., Red.	100	113½

Tramways and Omnibus (*continued*):—

Last Div.	Name.	Paid.	Price.
4/9½	London Road Car	6	10
28/6	Do. Red. 1 Mt. Deb. Stk.	100	109½
5	London St. Rly. (Prov., Ont.), Mt. Debs.	100	110
12/6	London St. Trams.	—	2
12/9	London Trams., Ltd.	10	9
6/	Do. Non-Cum. Pref.	10	10½
5	Do. Mt. Db. Stk., Rd.	100	101
5	Lynn & Boston 1 Mt. 1924 $	1000	104
5	Milwaukee Elec. Cons. Mt. $	1000	100½
5	Minneapolis St. 1 Cons. Mt. $	1000	96
5	Montreal St. Dbs., 1908	100	109
4½	Do. Debs., 1922	100	107
6/	Nth. Metropolitan	—	11½
1/9½	Nth. Staffords., Ltd.	6	5
2/6	Provincial, Ltd	10	6½
6/	Do. Cum. Pref.	10	14
5	St. Paul City, 1937 $	1000	96
5/	Southampton	10	6½
5/	South London	10	5½
7/6	Sunderland, Ltd.	10	6½
4½	Toronto 1 Mt., Red.	100	105
2/6	Tramways Union, Ltd.	5	6½
4½	Do. Deb., Red.	100	109
2/6	Vienna General Omnibus.	5	5½
5	Do. 5 p.c. Mt. Deb., Red.	100	103½
4/	Wolverhampton, Ltd	10	5½

WATER WORKS.

Last Div.	Name.	Paid.	Price.
20/	Antwerp, Ltd.	20	22
6/	Cape Town District, Ltd.	5	7½
10½	Chelsea	100	325
5	Do. Pref. Stk.	100	172½
4½	Do. Pref. Stk., 1875	100	152½
4½	Do. Deb. Stk.	100	159½
5/6	City St. Petersburg, Ltd.	13	10½
5/	Colne Valley	10	15½
4	Do. Deb. Stock	100	137½
£4	Consol. of Rosar., Ltd., 4 p.c. 1 Deb. Stk., Red.	100	91
8	East London	100	227½
4½	Do. Deb. Stk.	100	160
3	Do. Deb. Stk., Red.	100	105
37/6	Grand Junction (Max. 10 p.c.) "A"	50	117½
18/9	Do. "B"	25	
18/9	Do. "C" (Max. 7½ p.c.)	25	54½
35/	Do. "D" (Max. 7 p.c.)	50	97½
4	Do. Deb. Stock	100	142½
13	Kent	100	360½
7	Do. New (Max. 7 p.c.)	100	215½
7/	Kimberley, Ltd.	7	4½
6	Do. Debs., Red.	100	104½
6	Do. Deb. Stk., Red.	100	107½
10	Lambeth (Max. 10 p.c.)	100	297½
7½	Do. (Max. 7½ p.c.), 50 & 25	—	230½
4	Do. Deb. Stock	100	142½
3	Do. Red. Deb. Stock	100	103
10/	Montevideo, Ltd.	20	16
5	Do. 1 Deb. Stk.	100	108½
5	Do. 2 Deb. Stk.	100	103½
132/6	New River New	100	432½
4	Do. Deb. Stk.	100	144½
4	Do. Deb. Stk. "B"	100	141½
4	Portland Con. Mt. "B," 1927	—	103½
8/	Seville, Ltd.	20	18
5/6	Southend "Addl." Ord.	10	17
6	Southwark and Vauxhall	100	157½
6	Do. "D" Shares (7½ p.c. max.)	100	154½
5	Do. Pref. Stock	100	172½
4	Do. "A" Deb. Stock	100	141½
3	Staines Resvirs. Jt. Com. Gua. Deb. Stk., Red.	100	106
8/	Tarapaca, Ltd.	10	8½
10	West Middlesex	100	302½
4½	Do. Deb. Stk.	100	162½
3	Do Deb. Stk.	100	105

Prices Quoted on the Leading Provincial Exchanges.

ENGLISH.

In quoting the markets, B stands for Birmingham; Bl for Bristol; M for Manchester; L for Liverpool; and S for Sheffield.

CORPORATION STOCKS.

Chief Market.	Int or Div.	Name.	Amount paid.	Price.
M	3½	Bolton, Red. 1935 ..	100	113½
M	3½	Burnley, Red. 1933..	100	114
M	3½	Bury, Red. 1946	100	116½
L	2½	Liverpool, Red. 1925	100	102½
B	3½	Longton, 1932	100	106
M	4	Oldham Prp. Db. Sk.	100	143
M	£1	Do. Gas&W.Ann.		34½
S	4	Rotherham 4 p.c., Red. 1927......[£	1 an	112
M	3½	Runcorn Red. 1923..	100	104
S	2½	Sheffield Water Ann.	100	118½
S	3	Do.	3 an	90
L	3½	Southport Red. 1936	5 an 100	112
L	3	Do. Red. 1914..	100	102½
M	3	Todmorden, Red. 1914	100	102

RAILWAYS.

Chief Market.	Int or Div.	Name.	Amount paid.	Price.
Bl	4½	Bridgewater Pref. ..	100	135½
M	1½	Cleator & Workton.	100	76
M	4	Do. 1883 Pref. ..	100	109
L	4	Cockermth. K. & P.	100	113½
L	4	Isle of Man	5	6½
L	5	Do. Pref.	5	6½
L	3	Liverpool Overhead	10	10½
L	4	Do. Deb. Stk. ..	100	110
L	5	Do. Pref.	10	16
L	6½	Maryport & Carlisle	100	172
Bl	45/	Neath & Brecon "A"	100	65½
M	4½	Oldham, Ashton, &c.	10	16½
Bl	5½	Penarth Harbour ..	100	182½
Bl	4	Do. Deb. Stk. ..	100	145
Bl	3½	Do. Deb. Stk. ..	100	127
Bl	1½	Ross & Monmouth..	20	5½
Bl	6	Do. Pref.	20	42½
M	3	Southport & Cheshire Deb. Stk.	100	103
M	nil.	Do. Pref.	100	23½
Bl	2½	West Somerset Gu...	100	96
Bl	5	Wye Val. Deb. Stk.	100	162

BANKS.

Chief Market.	Int or Div.	Name.	Amount paid.	Price.
L	8/	Adelphi, L., £20 Shs.	10	16½
L	12/6	Bk of L'pool, L., £100 Sh	12½	39
B	5/6	Brmnghm. Dis. & C., Ltd., £20 Shs.....	4	10⅛
B	6/3	Co. of Staffs., L., £40	5	13½
S	17½	Crompton & Evans, Ltd., £20 Shs	4	15
M	14/	Lancs. & Yorks, Ltd., £20 Shs.....	10	31½
L	30/	Livrpl. Union, Ltd., £100 Shs.	20	60½
M	24/	Manchester & Co., Ltd., £100 Shs. ..	16	60½
M	20/	Mnchstr. & Livrpool. Dis., Ltd., £60 Shs.	10	51½
M	1/6	Mer. of Lancashire, Ltd., £20 Shs.....	3	6½
L	16/	Nth. & Sth. Wales, Ltd., £40 Shs.....	10	35½
B	20/	Notts Joint St., Ltd., £50 Shs..........	10	26½
S	15	Sheffield Banking, Ltd., £50 Shs.....	17½	51½
S	20	Do. & Rotherham, Ltd., £50 Shs...	8	27
S	10	Do. & Hallamsh., Ltd., £100 Shs..	25	68½
S	10	Do. Union, Ltd., £40 Shs.........	10	25 1/16
M	12/	Union of Manchester, Ltd., £25 Shs.. ..	11	27½
M	10/	Williams, Deacon, &c. Ltd., £50 Shs.....	8	25½
Bl	20	Wilts & Dorset, Ltd., £50 Shs..........	10	50
S	5/6	York City & Co., Ltd., £10 Shs.....	3	12½

BREWERIES.

Chief Market.	Int or Div.	Name.	Amount paid.	Price.
B	6	Ansell & Sons Pref.	10	16
B	5	Do. Debs.	100	110
L	9/	Bent's............	10	18½
L	6	Do. Cum. Pref...	10	14½
L	4½	Do. Deb. Stk. ..	100	111
L	5/	Birkenhead, £5 paid	5	22½
L	5/	Do. £10 paid....	10	27
M	9/	Boddington's	9	19
M	5	Do. Cum. Pref...	10	12½
M	4	Do. Deb. Stk. ..	100	107½
B	4½	Butler & Co. Db. Stk	100	111
M	6	Chesters' Cum. Pref.	10	13
M	4½	Do. Debs.	100	108½
S	10/	Clarkson's Ord.	10	22½
S	6	Do. Cum. Prf. Stk.	10	14
M	4	Dutton & Co. Db. Sk.	100	104
M	4½	Hardy's Crown Debs.	100	111
B	10/	Holt	10	17½
B	5	Do. Cum. Pref...	10	12½
B	4	Do. Debs.	100	108½
B	12/6	Lichfield	10	—
B	5	Do. Cum. Pref...	10	12
M	3½	Manchester Deb. Stk.	100	141
B	6/	Mitchell, H., & Co.	10	39
B	6	Do. Cum. Pref...	10	15½
Bl	6	Oakhill Pref........	10	16

Breweries (continued):—

Chief Market.	Int. or Div.	Name.	Amount paid.	Price.
M	5/	Springwell	10	10½
M	7	Do. Pref.	10	13½
Bl	9	Stroud	10	16½
Bl	6	Do. Pref......	10	14½
M	6/	Taylor's Eagle......	10	11½
M	7	Do. Cum. Pref ..	10	13½
M	5½	Do. Deb. Stk. ..	100	117½
S	10	Tennant Bros £20 shs	15	33½
S	10	Wheatley & Bates ..	10	14½
S	6	Do. Cum. Pref.	10	12½

CANALS AND DOCKS.

Chief Market.	Int. or Div.	Name.	Amount paid.	Price.
Bl	8	Hill's Dry Dk. &c. £20	18	9
M	4	Manc. Ship Canal 1st Mt. Deb. Stk.	100	105½
M	4	Do. 2nd do.	100	103½
L	36/3	Mersey Dck. & Harb.	an.	117½
L	35/	Do.	an.	116½
M	10/	Rochdale Canal	100	36½
B	37/6	Staff. & Worc. Canal	100	75½
B	4½	Do. Deb. Stk....	100	137
Bl	4	Swansea Harb......	100	112
B	27/6	Warwick & Birm. Cnl	100	65
B	12/6	Do. & Napton do.	100	22½

COMMERCIAL & INDUSTRIAL.

Chief Market.	Int. or Div.	Name.	Amount paid.	Price.
L	5	Agua Santa Mt. Debs	100	101½
M	12/	Armitage, Sir E. & Sns Ltd..............	10	18½
M	4	Do. Deb. 1910 ..	100	103
L	6	Ang. Chil. Nit. 1 Mt. Debs., 1919 ..	100	109½
Bl	11	Bath Stone Firms ..	10	19
M	4/9½	Barlow & Jones, Ltd., £10 Shs.	8	10½
B	12/6	Birmgham. Ry. Car.	10	15
B	6	Do. Pref.	10	15½
B	5/	Do. Small Arms	5	12½
M	£12	Blackpool Pier......	100	277½
M	5	Do. Tower Debs.	50	54½
M	3/	Do. Wi. Gar. & P.	5	4
Bl	10	Bristl. & S.W.R. Wag. £20 Shs..........	3	6
Bl	8	Do. Wag. & Carri. £10 Shs..........	10	15
M	7/	Crosses & Winkwth. Ltd...............	5	12½
L	5	G. Angus & Co. Pref.	10	13½
Bl	5	Gloster. Carri. & W.		9½
Bl	5	Gt. Wstn. Cttn., Ltd.	20	15
M	6	Hetherington, L. Prf.	10	9½
M	4½	Do. Debs., 1910	100	97
B	7½d.	Hinks (J. & Son), Ltd.	1	30/
S	26/	Jessop & Sons, £50 Sh	30	27½
S	10	Kayser, Ellsn. & Co. L.	5	11½
S	6	Do. Pref.	5	7½
M	7/6	Kellner-Partgton., L.	5	14½
M	4½	Do. Debs., 1914..	100	106
M	5	Kerr Thread, Ltd., Debs.	100	101
B	17/	King's Norton Metal, £10 Shs...........	8½	23
M	5/	Lancashire & Yorks. Wagon, Ltd.	10	10½
L	10/	Liverpool Exch., Ltd.	20	27½
L	45/	Do. Grain Stge, Ltd.	50	108
L	5/	Do. Rubber, Ltd...	5	5½
M	9d.	Manchester Bond. Whse., L., £10 Shs.	4½	2½
M	2/9	Do. Comcial. Bldgs., Ltd., £10 Shs.	5	10½
M	4/	Do. No. 2, £10 Shs.	5	10½
M	2/6	Do. No. 3, £10 Shs.	5	7½
M	5/	Do. Corn, &c., Exchange, Ltd.	10	16½
M	4	Do. Debs.	100	126
M	8	Do. Ryl. Exchge, L.	100	237½
B	5/	Midland Rlwy. Car. Wgn., Ld., £20 Sh.	10	15
Bl	5	Millers & Corys Dbs.	100	100½
B	12/6	Mint, Brgham., Ltd.	5	8½
B	5	Do. Debs.	25	108
B	10/	Nettlefolds, Ltd.....	10	48
B	5	Do. Pref.	10	15½
S	9	Nth. Centrl. Wgn., L.	5	9
B	15/	Patnt. Nut & Bolt, L.	10	32½
B	5	Do. Pref.	10	14½
B	1/	Perry & Co., Ltd. ..	1	24/9
B	6d.	Do. Pref.	1	27/
S	10	Round, J., & Co., L., £10 Shs.	6	12
S	15	Rodgers, J., & Sons, L.	100	235
M	18/9	Rylands & Sons, Ltd., £20	15	38½
M	2/6	Do. paid up	20	42½
M	4	Do. Debs. ..1909	100	106
S	5	Sanderson Brs. & Co., Ltd. Debs.	100	101½
M	4½	Schwabe, S., & Co., Ltd., 1 Debs. 1914	100	102
S	7½	Sheffield Forge & Rolling, Ltd.	10	11½
L	80/	Southport Pier, Ltd.	100	95½
L	—	Do. W. Gdns., Ltd.	5	—
Bl	25	Spillers & Bakers, Ltd, £10 Shs.	9	15½
Bl	6	Do. Pref.	10	14½
B	5/	Union Rolling Stock, Ltd., £20 Shs.....	5	7½
M	5/	Victoria Pr., S'port, L.	5	4½
Bl	8	Western Wagon & Property, Ltd.....	6	9½
S	10	Wostenholm, G., & Son, Ltd., £25 Shs.	20	22½
S	6½	Yorksh. Wagon, Ltd.	2	2½

FINANCIAL, TRUSTS, &c.

Chief Market.	Int. or Div.	Name.	Amount paid.	Price.
M	1/	Manchstr. Trst. £10 Shs...............	2	13/3
M	1/3	N. of Eng. T. Deb. & A., Ltd. £10 Shs.	2½	26/3
M	3½	Do. 1 Mt. Debs...	100	97½
L	—	Pacific Ln. & Inv., L.	2½	2½
L	4	Do. Deb. Stk.....	100	103
L	—	United Trst., L. Prfd.	100	72½
L	—	Do. Deferred....	100	62½

GAS.

Chief Market.	Int. or Div.	Name.	Amount paid.	Price.
Bl	5	Bristol Gas (5 p.c. mx.)	100	129
Bl	4	Do. 1st Deb.	100	136
S	10	Gt. Grimsby "C" ..	10	201
L	10	Liverpool Utd. "A"	100	237
L	7	Do. "B"......	100	179
L	4	Do. Deb.	100	137
S	10	Sheffield Gas "A," "B," "C"	100	248
B	10½	Wolverhampton	100	230
B	3	Do. 6 p.c. Pref. ..	100	171

INSURANCE.

Chief Market.	Int. or Div.	Name.	Amount paid.	Price.
M	6	Equitable F. & Acc. £5 Shs.	1	37/6
L	2/	Liverpool Mortgage £10 Shs.	2	1⅛
M	4/	Mchester. Fire £20 Shs..............	2	7½
M	5/	National Boiler & G., Ltd., £10 Shs.	3	13½
L	2/	Reliance Mar., Ltd., £10 Shs.	2	4 1/16
L	4/	Sea, Ltd., £10 Shs...	2	9 1/16
L	8/	Stnd. Mar., L., £20 Sh.	4	7 1/16
L	1/	State Fire, L., £20 Sh.	1	1½

COAL, IRON, AND STEEL.

Chief Market.	Int. or Div.	Name.	Amount paid.	Price.
Bl.	12	Albion Stm. Coal ..	10	—
M	13/9	And. Knowles & S., Ltd., £37½ Shs. ..	23½	11½
M	5	Do. Mt. Debs. 1908	100	105½
Bl.	1/½	Ashton V. Iron	100	26
S	12½	Bessemer, Ltd.	10	20½
S	5	Do. Pref.	10	12½
S	12/6	Briggs, H., & Co., "A" £15 Shs.....	12½	15½
S	8/6	Do. "B" £15 Shs.	8½	10½
S	20	Brown Baley's. Stl., L.	10	32 1/16
S	5	Brown, J., & Co., Cum. Pref.	10	13
S	5	Cammell, C. & Co., Ltd.	85	12½
S	5	Do. Pref.	5	6½
M	5	Chatterley Whitfield. Col., Debs., 1905..	100	100½
Bl	—	Davis, D., & Sons, Ld.	10	10
M	5	Evans, R., & Co., Ltd., Deb., 1910 ..	100	101
S	12½	Fox, S., & Co., Ltd., £100 Shs.	80	181
Bl	10	Gt. Wstn. Col., L., "A"	5	10½
Bl	6	Do. "B"	5	4½
Bl	8	Main Colliery, Ltd.	10	7½
B	5/	Muntz's Metal, Ltd.	5	8
B	5	Do. Pref.......	5	6½
M	2/6½	Nth. Lonsd. Iron and Steel, Ltd., £10 Sh.	8½	2½
Bl	6	North's Nav. Coll., Ltd., Debs.	100	105
S	30/	Parkgate Irn. & Stl., Ltd., £100 Shs. ..	75	77
M	6	Pearson & Knls., Ld., "A" Cum. Pref...	50	46
B	10/	Sandwell Pk. Col., L.	10	17½
M	6/3	Sheepbridge Coal and Iron, Ltd., "A"	25	18½
M	2/6	Do. "B"	10	7½
M	5	Do. "C" Gua. Pf.	25	28½
Bl	4	South Wales Coll., Ltd., "A"	17	8½
S	30/	Staveley Coal & Iron, Ltd., "A" £100 Sh.	60	81½
S	30/	Do. "C"	60	84
M	1/10½	Tredegar Iron & Cl., Ld., "A" £10 Sh.	7½	2½
M	1½	Do. "B" Stk. ..	100	35
M	6/	Wigan Cl. & Irn., Ld.	10	7
M	4/6	Do. £10 Shs.	7½	4

SHIPPING.

Chief Market.	Int. or Div.	Name.	Amount paid.	Price.
Bl	6	Bristol St. Nav. Pref.	10	11½
L	15/	Brit. & Af. St. Nav..	10	14
L	5/10½	British & Estn, Ltd.	6½	3½
L	10/	Pacific Stm. Nav., L.	25	23½
L	30/	Wst. Ind. & Pac. St. Ltd., £25 Shs....	20	28½

TRAMWAYS, &c.

Chief Market.	Int. or Div.	Name.	Amount paid.	Price.
B	5/	Brmngh. & Aston, L.	5	1½
B	5/	Do. Mid., Ltd. ..	10	7½
Bl	6/	Bristol Tr. & Car., Ltd..............	10	21
Bl	4/	Do. Debs.	100	122
L	6	I. of Man Elec., L., Pref.	1	1⅛
M	15/	Manchester C. & T., L., "A" £20 Shs.	15	27
M	10/	Do. "B"	10	18½

WATER WORKS.

Chief Market.	Int. or Div.	Name.	Amount paid.	Price.
Bl	7	Bristol	25	62
Bl	7	Do...............	20	47½
Bl	58/	Do. 7 p.c. max. ..	100	158½
Bl	4½	Do. Pref.	20	31½
Bl	5	Do. Pref.	10	17½
Bl	3½	Do. Deb.	100	124½
M	10	Fylde "A"	100	330
M	7	Do. "B"	100	221
B	6	S. Staffs. Ord. "A"	100	170
B	—	Do. "B"	100	170
B	4	Do. Deb. Stk.	100	140
B	5	Do. Pf "A" "B" "C"	100	170
M	£3½	Stockport District ..	100	184½
B	9/	Wolverhampton New	5	6½

SCOTTISH.

In quoting the markets, E stands for Edinburgh, and G for Glasgow.

RAILWAYS.

Chief Market.	Int. or Div.	Name.	Nom. Amount	Price.
E	5½	Arbroath and Forfar	25	49½
G	1½	Callander and Oban.	10	7⅛
G	4	Do. Deb. Stock	100	142
G	4½	Do. Pref.......	10	14½
G	4	Cathct. Dist. Deb. Stk.	100	144
E	5	Edin. and Bathgate .	100	179½
E	7	Forth & Clyde Junc.	100	222½
G	4	Lanarks. and Ayrsh.	10	14
G	4	Do. & Dumbartons.	10	13½
G	4	Do. Deb. Stk.	100	145

BANKS.

Chief Market.	Int. or Div.	Name.	Nom. Amount	Price.
G	12	Bank of Scotland ..	100	351½
G	16	British Linen	100	488
G	8	Caledonian, Ltd.....	2½	97/
G	10	Clydesdale, Ltd.	10	23½
G	16	Commercl. of Scot., L.	20	86
G	16	National of Scot. Ld.	100	411
G	8	Royal of Scotland ..	100	232
G	11	Union of Scotland, L.	10	25½

BREWERIES.

Chief Market.	Int. or Div.	Name.	Nom. Amount	Price.
E	5	Bernard, Thos. Pref.	10	10½
E	5	Bernard, T. & J., Cum. Pref........	10	12½
G	20	Highland Distilleries	3½	10½

CANALS AND DOCKS.

Chief Market.	Int. or Div.	Name.	Nom. Amount	Price.
G	4	Clyde Nav. 4 p.c....	100	121½
G	3½	Do. 3½ p.c.......	100	104
G	3½	Greenock Harb. "A"	100	100½
G	2	Do. "B"	100	37

MISCELLANEOUS.

Chief Market.	Int. or Div.	Name.	Nom. Amount	Price.
G	4½	Alexander & Co. Debs.	100	107½
G	5	Alexander Ferguson & Co. Cum. Pref..	10	11⅛
G	5	Baird, H., & Sns. C.P.	10	12
E	12	Barry, Ostlere, & Co.	7½	12
E	6	Do. Cum. Pref...	10	14½
G	5	Brown, Stewart, Deb.	100	81½
E	7½	Broxburn Oil	8½	8½
E	6	Do. Cum. Pref...	10	10½
E	7	Edinburgh & Dist. Tram. Cum. Pref.	5	8½
E	5	Gilroy, Sns, & Co. Dbs.	100	96½
G	9	Glasgow Cot. Spin...	6	6
G	30/	Do. Royal Exchg.	46	110
G	—	Pumpherston Oil Pf.	10	8½
E	7	Scottish Assam Tea	10	10½
E	5	Scottish Waggon....	10	12½
G	5	Stoddard & Co. Pref.	10	11½

FINANCIAL, LAND, AND INVESTMENT.

Chief Market.	Int. or Div.	Name.	Nom. Amount	Price.
G	1/	Assets Co...........	1	45/6
E	4½	Investors' Mort. Pref.	100	96½
E	4	Do. Deb. Stk....	100	102
E	4	Nthn. Inv. N. Zeal. Deb. Stk.	100	106½
E	4	N. of Scot. Canadian Deb. Stk.	100	104
E	4½	Real & Deb. Corp. Deb. Stk.	100	106½

INSURANCE.

Chief Market.	Int. or Div.	Name.	Amount paid.	Price.
G	14/	Caledonian F. & Life	5	35½
G	4/6	City of Glasgow Life	2½	12⅝
E	19/	Edinburgh Life	20	54⅞
G	13/2	Life Ass. of Scotland	8⅓	35
E	8	Nat. Guar. & Surety	2	52/6
G	17½	Scottish Union and National "A"	1	89/9
G	17½	Do. "B"	3⅓	17⅞

IRON, COAL, AND STEEL.

Chief Market.	Int. or Div.	Name.	Amount paid.	Price.
E	Nil.	Addie, Coll. Cm. Pref.	10	7¾
E	8/	Arniston Coal	8	13¾
E	2½	Cairntable Gas Coal	8	86/
E	12½	Fife Coal	10	20
E	5	Do. Cum. Pref.	10	12½
G	7	Merry & Cunghame. Cum. Pref.	10	15¾
G	5	Do. Debentures	100	103½
E	1/9	Niddrie & Benhar Cl.	1½	38/
G	5	Steel Com. of Scotlad	—	
	—	"A" Deb. Stk.	100	110½
G	6	Do. and Mt. "B"	100	107
E	6/	Watson, John	8½	10¼
E	6	Do. Cum. Pref.	7½	7¾
E	12½	Wilson's & Cly. Coal	3	8¾

IRISH.

In quoting the markets, B stands for Belfast, and D for Dublin.

CORPORATION STOCKS.

Chief Market.	Int. or Div.	Name.	Amount paid.	Price.
B	3½	Belfast, 1927	100	109
B	3½	Do. 1912	100	106½
B	3½	Do. 1924	100	108½
B	3	Do. 1955	100	106½
B	3½	Do. Water Com.	100	114½
B	3	Do. do.	100	106
B	3½	Do. Harbour Com.	100	110½
D	3½	Rathmines & Rathgar	100	110
D	3½	Waterford Deb.	100	—

RAILWAYS.

Chief Market.	Int. or Div.	Name.	Amount Paid.	Price.
D	30/	Cork, Bandon, & S.C.	100	76
D	4	Do. Deb.	100	139½
D	4	Do. W. Cork Pref.	100	—
B	65/	Belfast & Northern	100	158½
B	4	Do. Deb.	100	146
B	4	Do. Pref.	100	134
B	6½	Belfast & C. Down	100	166½
B	4	Do. Deb.	100	147
B	3	Do.	100	107½
B	4½	Do. 4½ Pref. B.	100	150
B	5	Do. Guar.	100	170
D	Nil.	Dublin, Wick. & Wex.	100	29
D	4	Do. Deb.	100	120
D	4½	Do. Deb.	100	—
D	6	Do. Guar.	100	160
D	4	Do. C. of Dub. Junc.	100	113
D	5	Do. 1860 Pref.	100	—
D	50/	Do. 1864 Pref.	100	—
D	50/	Do. 1865 Pref.	100	—
B	67/6	Great Northern	100	177½
B	4	Do. Deb.	100	147
B	4	Do. Pref. B.	100	140½
B	5½	Gt. South & Western	100	142
B	4	Do. Deb.	100	142
B	4	Do. Guar.	100	141½
D	45/	Midland Gt. Western	100	111½
D	4	Do. Deb.	100	138
D	4½	Do. Deb.	100	145
D	4½	Do. Deb.	100	—
D	5	Do. Pref.	100	165
D	4	Do. Pref.	100	134
D	—	Waterford & Central	100	15
D	3	Do. Deb.	100	102
D	3½	Do. Pref.	100	130
D	4	Waterfd. L., & W. Db.	100	135
D	4½	Do. Deb.	100	—
D	4	Do. Pref.	100	129
D	3½	Do. Pref.	100	101

BANKS.

Chief Market.	Int. or Div.	Name.	Amount paid.	Price.
B	50/	Belfast, Old, £125 Shs.	25	123
B	20/	Do. New, £125 Shs.	25	48
D		Hibernian, £20 Shs.	5	6¼
D	2/	Munster & Leinster £5 Shs.	2	5¼
B	11/	Northern, £50 Shs.	10	26½
D	12/	Royal, £50 Shs.	10	29½
B	5/	Ulster, £15 Shs.	2½	12½

BREWERIES AND DISTILLERIES.

Chief Market.	Int. or Div.	Name.	Amount paid.	Price.
D	6/	Castlebellingham & Drog	10	—
D	6	Do. Pref.	10	15½
D	4½	Do. Deb.	100	115
B	17/	Dunville & Co.	10	27½
B	6	Irish Distillery, Pref.	10	13½
B	5	Do. Deb.	100	110
B	6	J. & J. M'Connell, Pf.	10	15¼
B	9/	Mitchell & Co.	9	19½
B	5	Do. Deb.	10	11
D	4½	Phœnix Brew. Deb.	100	96
B	8/	Wm. Cowan	10	12½
B	6	Do. Pref.	10	13
B	8/	Young, King, & Co.	8	14

STEAM AND CANAL.

Chief Market.	Int. or Div.	Name.	Amount paid.	Price.
B	Nil	Belfast Steamship	50	36½
D	10/	British and Irish	50	—
D	20/	City of Dublin	100	—
D	3½	Do. Deb.	100	—
D	30/	Dublin & Lpool. Bldg.	50	72
D	2/6	Dundalk & Newry	10	4½
D	4/	Grand Canal	10	11½
D	3	Do. Pref.	10	9¼
D	3	Do. Deb.	100	99½
B	30/	Irish Shipowners	100	65
B	3/	Ulster Steamship	5	6½

MISCELLANEOUS.

Chief Market.	Int. or Div.	Name.	Amount paid.	Price.
D	3/1	Arnott & Co.	4	7¼
D	6	Do. Pref.	4	6½
B	8/	Belfast Com. Bldgs.	10	11
B	37/6	Do. Ropework Co.	75	94½
B	5	Do. do. Pref.	10	12½
B	2/	Do. Discount Co.	3	45/
B	5	Do. do. Pref.	5	4½
B	10/	Brookfield Linen	25	17
B	Nil	Coey & Co.	25	4
B	5	Do. Deb.	50	48
B	4½	David Allen & S's Deb.	100	107½
D	4/	Dublin Trams	10	19
D	6	Do. Pref.	10	17½
D	4	Do. Deb.	100	—
B	6/	Edenderry Spinning	10	9
B	25/	Falls Flax Spinning	25	15
B	17/	Forster, Green, & Co.	10	21
B	9/	Island Spinning	7½	7½
B	8/	Jas. Lindsay & Co.	8	16½
B	1/7½	John Arnott & Co.	4	4¼
B	4½	Do. Deb.	50	56
D	5/	Kinahan & Co.	10	11½
D	5½	Do. Pref.	10	11½
D	4½	Do. Deb.	100	—
B	12/	Kirker & Co.	10	10
B	5/	Leahy, Kelly, & Leahy	5	8½
B	6	Do. Pref.	5	7
B	4/	Lindsay Bros. Ltd.	5	7½
B	4½	Do. Deb.	50	56½
D	1/6	National Assurance	2½	—
B	10/	Olley & Co.	5	7¼
D	1/1½	Patriotic Assurance	2½	31/
B	3/7½	P. Johnston & Son, L.	6	6½
B	10/	Robertson, F., & Co.	8	22½
B	10	Ulster Marine Insur.	5/	7/
B	15/	York-street Flax	25	33½
B	6	Do. Pref.	10	15½
B	4½	Do. Deb.	100	117

INDIAN AND CEYLON TEA COMPANIES.

Acres Planted.	Crop, 1897.	Paid up Capital.	Share.	Paid up.	Name.	Dividends. 1894.	1895.	1896.	Int. 1897.	Price.	Yield.	Reserve.	Balance Forward.	Working Capital.	Mortgages, Debs. or Pref. Capital not otherwise stated.
	lb.	£	£	£	INDIAN COMPANIES.							£	£	£	£
11,240	3,128,000	120,000	10	3	Amalgamated Estates	—	*	10	5	3½	9	10,000	16,500	D52,950	—
		400,000	10	10	Do. Pref.	—	*	5	‡5	9¼	5½				
10,223	3,360,000	187,160	20	20	Assam	20	20	20	‡17½	59½	5½	55,000	1,730	D11,350	—
6,150	3,278,000	142,500	10	10	Assam Frontier	3	6	6	—	7	8½	—	286	20,000	82,500
		142,500	10	10	Do. Pref.	6	6	6	‡6	11	5½				
2,087	839,000	66,745	5	5	Attaree Khat	12	12	8	3	7	6	3,790	4,820	7,770	—
1,633	583,000	78,170	10	10	Borelli	4	4	5	—	7½	6½	—	3,256	D270	6,500 Pref.
1,770	812,000	60,825	5	5	British Indian	6	5	5	‡5	3¾xd	6½	—	2,920	12,300	16,500 Pref.
3,223	2,247,000	114,500	5	5	Brahmapootra	20	18	20	‡15	12¾xd	6	—	28,440	41,600	·
3,754	1,617,000	76,500	10	10	Cachar and Dooars	*	8	7	‡7	9½	7	—	1,645	21,240	·
		76,500	10	10	Do. Pref.	*	6	6	‡6	11½xd	5½				
3,946	2,083,000	72,010	1	1	Chargola	8	7	10	2½	¾	13	3,000	3,300	—	—
		81,000	1	1	Do. Pref.	7	7	7	3½	1¼	5½				
1,971	942,000	33,000	5	5	Chubwa	10	8	10	‡8	5½	7½	10,000	2,043	D5,400	—
		33,000	5	5	Do. Pref.	7	7	7	‡7	6½	5½				
32,250	11,500,000	120,000	10	3	Cons. Tea and Lands	—		10	5	3½	8	65,000	14,240	D191,674	—
		1,000,000	10	10	Do. 1st Pref.	—	*	5	‡5	10½	4½				
		400,000	10	10	Do. 2nd Pref.	—	*	7	‡7	11½	5½				
2,230	617,000	135,420	20	20	Darjeeling	5½	5½	6	‡5	21	4½	5,552	1,565	1,700	—
2,114	445,000	60,000	10	10	Darjeeling Cons.	—		4/2	—	6	—	—	1,820	—	—
		60,000	10	10	Do. Pref.	—	*	5	2½	9½	5½				
6,660	3,518,000	150,000	10	10	Dooars	12½	12½	12½	‡12½	18	7	45,000	300	D32,000	—
		75,000	10	10	Do. Pref.	7	7	7	‡7	16½	4½				
3,367	1,811,000	165,000	10	10	Doom Dooma	11¼	10	12½	‡12½	20xd	6¼	30,000	4,032	—	10,000
1,377	582,000	61,120	5	5	Eastern Assam	5	nil.	4	nil	2½	—	—	1,790	—	10,000
4,038	1,675,000	85,000	10	10	East India and Ceylon	5	nil.	7	—	8½	7½	—	1,710	—	—
		85,000	10	10	Do. Pref.	*	6	6	‡6	11xd	5½				
7,500	3,363,000	219,000	10	10	Empire of India	—	*	6/10	2½	10½	—	15,000	—	27,000	—
		219,000	10	10	Do. Pref.	—	*	5	2½	11	4½				
1,180	540,000	94,060	10	10	Indian of Cachar	7	3½	3	‡2	3½	5½	6,070	—	7,120	—
3,050	824,000	83,500	5	5	Jhanzie	10	10	10	‡8	6½xd	6	14,500	1,070	2,700	—
7,980	3,680,000	250,000	10	10	Jokai	10	10	10	5	16	6	45,000	990	D9,000	—
		100,000	10	10	Do. Pref.	*	6	6	‡6	14½	4½				
5,224	1,563,000	100,000	20	20	Jorehaut	20	20	20	—	39	6½	36,220	2,955	3,000	—
1,547	504,000	65,660	10	8	Lebong	15	15	15	‡12½	15½xd	6¼	9,000	2,150	8,650	—
5,082	1,709,000	100,000	10	10	Lungla	5	10	6	‡3	6	5	—	1,543	D21,000	—
		100,000	10	10	Do. Pref.	*	6	6	‡6	10½	5½				
2,684	885,000	95,970	10	10	Majuli	7	5	5	—	6½	7½	—	2,606	560	—
1,375	380,000	91,840	1	1	Makum	—	—	2	—	1	2	—	—	1,200	25,000
2,990	770,000	100,000	1	1	Moabund	—	—	*	—	½	—	—	—	-	—
		50,000	1	1	Do. Pref.	—	—	*	2½	1	5				
1,080	482,000	79,590	10	10	Scottish Assam	7	7	7	—	10½	6½	6,500	800	9,590	—
4,150	1,456,000	100,000	10	10	Singlo	5	8	5	1	8	6	—	300	D5,200	—
		80,000	10	10	Do. Pref.	*	6½	6½	3½	13	5				
					CEYLON COMPANIES.										
7,070	1,743,824§	250,000	100	100	Anglo-Ceylon, & Gen.	—	*	5½	—	45	11	10,992	1,405	D72,844	166,580
1,836	685,741§	50,000	10	10	Associated Tea	—	*	5	2½	7½	6½	—	164	2,478	—
		60,000	10	10	Do. Pref.	—	*	6	3	10½	5½				
10,390	4,000,000	167,380	10	10	Ceylon Tea Plantations	15	15	15	‡15	23½	6½	84,500	1,316	D30,819	—
		81,080	10	10	Do. Pref.	7	7	7	‡7	16½	4½				
5,788	1,542,700	55,260	5	3	Ceylon & Oriental Est.	5	8	7	—	2½	7½	—	230	D2,047	71,000
		46,000	5	5	Do. Pref.	6	6	6	3	4½	6				
2,157	801,629§	111,330	5	5	Dimbula Valley	—	*	10	5	5½	9	—	—	1,733	6,250
		62,607	5	5	Do. Pref.	—	*	6	3	6½	4½				
11,496	3,635,000	298,250	5	5	Eastern Prod. & Est.	3	5	6½	‡7	5½	6½	20,000	11,740	D17,797	108,500
2,193	1,050,000	22,080	10	10	New Dimbula "A"	10	16	16	4	24	7	11,000	2,024	1,150	8,400
		55,710	10	10	Do. "B"	18	16	16	4	22	7½				
2,572	570,360§	100,000	10	10	Ouvah	6	8	6	2	8	7½	4,000	1,151	D1,255	—
2,630	964,963	200,000	10	10	Nuwara Eliya	—	*	6	‡6	10½	5½	—	—	—	30,000
1,720	708,533	41,000	10	10	Scottish Ceylon	15	15	15	‡10	17	8	7,000	1,252	D3,970	9,000 Pref.
2,450	750,000	39,000	10	6	Standard	12½	15	15	‡15	12½	7	9,000	800	D14,012	4,000
		17,000	10	10	Do.	12½	15	15	‡15	22	7				

Working-Capital Column.—In working-capital column, D stands for *debit.*

* Company formed this year. † Interim dividends are given as actual distribution made. ‡ *Total* div. § Crop 1896.

Printed for the Proprietor by Love & Wyman, Ltd., Great Queen Street, London, W.C.; and Published by Clement Wilson at Norfolk House, Norfolk Street, Strand, London, W.C.

The Investors' Review

EDITED BY A. J. WILSON.

Vol. I.—No. 23. New Series. | FRIDAY, JUNE 10, 1898. | [Registered as a Newspaper.] | Price 6d. By post, 6½d

CONTENTS

The Investors' Review.

Our Wasteful National Expenditure.

Business was resumed on Monday by the House of Commons with, amongst other things, a debate on this subject which ought to do good. Unhappily, nothing is more difficult at the present time than to get people to pay any attention to the waste of the nation's substance now so fashionable. We have reached a gross revenue, as Sir William Harcourt pointed out in his most interesting speech, of nearly £117,000,000, twelve of which we hand back to the local authorities, or to landlords and voluntary schools without one penny of advantage to the local ratepayer. On the contrary, this money stimulates local spending bodies to extravagance, and rates keep advancing in rural and urban districts, until they now press very severely in many places upon the great majority of those who have to meet them. In most cases the extravagance is accompanied by local borrowing which, in some quarters, has become almost colonial in its recklessness, and has already told with marked effect upon the standing of many of our municipal securities in the market. These are all much cheaper than they were two years ago, and the tendency for them is to sink still lower in price. We might expect that intelligent citizens would take note of these things, and become earnest in pressing upon their representatives in Parliament the necessity to economise. The reverse of this appears to be the truth. Parliament spends money as a fountain gushes out water, and nobody seems to care the slightest thing about it.

To those who can look back even for ten years, the contrast between the present attitude of the nation towards excessive expenditure and that old fashion of economy and carefulness, once the glory of the Liberal Party, is sufficiently startling to bewilder the mind. The truth appears to be that the disease of transpontine Imperialism, as fostered by that charlatan statesman, Lord Beaconsfield, has crept over our mental faculties like a fungus, rendering us incapable of realising in what direction the nation is drifting. From no economic point of view whatever is there justification to be found for the habits of extravagance now prevailing. Let us apply a very simple test to them. The Jingoes are continually harping upon the necessity for "a great fleet" to protect our commerce and maintain our Imperial domination in all parts of the world. They have so successfully preached this pernicious doctrine that we have now an expenditure upon the Navy amounting to nearly £24,000,000. The average for the five years ended with March 31, 1874, was under £10,000,000. In other words, we have increased the national outlay under this head by more than 140 per cent. in less than thirty years. An increase not quite so phenomenal, but almost equally unjustifiable, has taken place in the outlay upon the army. It ranged from about £13,500,000 and £15,000,000, including part cost of small wars, between 1870 and 1874, and it is about £19,250,000 for the current financial year. Putting the two branches of the Service together, we find an increase of fully 72 per cent. in the outlay compared with what it was in the early seventies.

What justification is there for this monstrous outlay in the expansion of our trade? None whatever. If we take the figures of our imports and exports for the five years ended with 1874 we do not find the slightest evidence that they have expanded in a manner at all proportionate to the increase in our military and naval outlay. The average value of the imports for those five years was about £346,000,000. For 1897 their total value was about £451,000,000. This shows an increase of £105,000,000, or about 30 per cent., as compared with an increase of 72 per cent. in the cost of our military and naval establishments. But there has been practically no increase in the exports since 1874. The average for the five years ended then, including foreign and colonial merchandise re-exported, was £290,000,000, and for last year the total was only £294,000,000, an increase of about 1½ per cent. There is nothing, in fact, more serious about the present business position of the nation than this stagnation of our exports, especially when placed alongside the comparatively steady increase in our imports. No doubt the volume or bulk of the goods manufactured by us and sent out of the country has increased possibly 20 per cent. to 25 per cent., comparing now with a quarter of a century ago; but this increase, when placed alongside the diminished monetary return, may imply, and probably does imply, considerably reduced profits, while the steady expansion of our imports means either that we are living more and more on the proceeds of our capital invested abroad, or that we are pledging and expending capital and assets accumulated in the past, in order to maintain extravagant habits of living. Look at the question from whatever point we may, it is perfectly obvious that the extension of our Empire, and the horrible drain upon our resources which Jingoism has succeeded in imposing under pretence of providing for the maintenance and safety of this Empire, finds no justification in the figures of our commerce.

Our own distinct opinion, formed many years ago and confirmed by constant observation, is that the hideously wasteful expenditure of the nation as it now stands is being met to an increasing extent out of capital. We know very well that the proceeds of the "Death Duties" are a direct levy upon capital, but in an indirect manner the income tax also, to no insignificant extent, represents the same thing, and so do part at least of the proceeds of our Customs duties. Assume that the expansiveness of our imports is due to returns from the investment of British moneys abroad, and how far can we say that the wealth thus placed out at interest is permanently invested with safety, and to be relied on as a continuous source of income?

The answer to this question, it seems to us, must be that the bulk of our foreign investments are of a most transitory and unreliable character; and anybody who looks to the position of our debt-burdened dependencies abroad, without prejudice and in the calm light of reason, must come to the conclusion that very little of a catastrophe would be required to upset the equilibrium of every one of them, and in doing so to dry up at once the source of our apparently abounding and inexhaustible revenue. The "clever idiots," to use an expressive Americanism, who direct the nation in its insane policy of military expenditure and "Imperial" expansion, emit the most blood-curdling shouts, speaking metaphorically, over the danger we should be in in time of war through the stoppage of some of our food supplies. "What would England do," they bellow in all keys of real, or more probably simulated, terror, "were the fleets of her enemies to prevent the regular supply of grain from reaching her shores? The people would starve; there would be revolution and bloodshed and heaven knows what." Language of this kind is stupid enough, even when honest, and unjustified by any sane view of our position. It is scarcely possible to imagine a modern war which could prevent us from receiving all the food we required through one channel or another.

There is, however, a real danger of starvation which these pestilent creatures overlook altogether, and which they are, by their mischievous and misdirected energy, doing their best to make imminent for us all, and that is the danger that we may be unable to find the means to pay for sufficient food were our trade once deranged and our credit system breached by the consequences of a great war. In plain English, as we have again and again insisted, and must continue to insist until the nation becomes aware of the gulf towards which it is plunging, a war on a great scale in which we might be involved would probably at once stop the flow of interest from every one of our colonies and dependencies, because we should have no money to lend them to pay interest with. In regard to them we are most emphatically at the present moment living upon capital. They pay us interest which we advance to them under loans, raised upon various pretexts, but whose real purpose is to keep them from stopping payment. We revel in the income thus supplied and think we are happily living upon their earnings, when we are in actual fact eating up our own capital.

How long this can go on no man dare venture to predict. It is pretty sure to continue as long as our credit system in London is able to keep the appearances of solvency untainted and unbroken in these dependencies, but we may be perfectly certain that if we had to go to war with France or Russia or Germany, or with any two European countries combined, and had to draw off capital from our money market in order to sustain the cost of this war, the immediate consequence would be a suspension of payment, partial or complete, by India, by every colony in Australasia, and probably by the Cape of Good Hope, Natal, and Canada as well, not to mention minor possessions of ours, all of which we have carefully wrapped up in a Nessus shirt of debt. Will the nation look at matters a little in this light, instead of giving the ear continually to those men who bawl every day into the ears that more and more money must be spent on the navy "to make us strong," that the army must be increased by this and that number of battalions and batteries of guns and regiments of cavalry, and so on, lest we be caught napping? Sir Charles Dilke takes a leading part in this hounding the nation to its destruction, and we venture to say that he ought to know better and to be ashamed of himself for helping to conduct such a campaign—a campaign of destruction—which must end in throwing this country back far more than it could ever possibly advance were it to take possession of the entire African continent and half China within the next five years. Nor is throwing back the worst of it. We are positively so encumbering ourselves with armour as to be placed out of all capacity to fight. We are drawing our national revenue out of capital more and more every year, and probably this explains why the nation accepts its fate with such apparent apathy. Were it really a national income taken out of incomes of the people the outcry for reduction in the burdens might have been irresistible long ago. As it is, we shall arise some day and discover that we have consumed our resources in riotous living, spent them upon useless ironclads we can neither arm, man, coal, nor put food and powder in, that our army is a phantom, and that the nation stands cheek by jowl with starvation, because it has not the wherewithal left to purchase foreign grain.

Indian Financial Gymnastics.

A fit of economy must be coming over the India Office, for the annual effusion of the Secretary of State in explanation of the Budget has been reduced to ten pages and a cover. Perhaps the figures usually appended to it will be given in detail in the British reprint of the Indian Budget, a reprint, by-the-bye, which ought not to be necessary if a sufficient number of the original document, printed as a "Gazette extraordinary" in Calcutta, were imported for the use of Members of Parliament and the general public. Taking this memorandum as it stands, though, we are rather glad that no more money than was absolutely necessary has been wasted upon it. It tells us nothing new, and its shiftings, tossings, and arrangements of the Budget figures do not tend to anybody's enlightenment, if that "body" wants to know how it really stands with India. The usual parade is made of the saving by exchange, the "economies" in this and that, and the extra revenue from t'other, with hopes of nice sums from arrears of rent which fell behind in famine years, and, of course, "a surplus"—bless it when it comes! But no particular attention is drawn to the significant fact that the trade of India has declined steadily during the last three years. The exports of merchandise were 1,143 odd millions of rupees in 1895, about 1,004 millions of rupees in 1896, and little more than 976 millions last year. The famine, &c., is of course officially condemned to bear the blame of this decline, not the barrier set up by the artificially high exchange. But why did not famine force imports also down. If the people had less to sell how could they increase their buying? The truth is that exports were depressed and imports stimulated by the abnormal exchange, and consequently the balance on the commercial account in favour of India has fallen from, say, 414 million rupees in the first year named to 240 millions in the last. Including the movement of treasure both ways, the decline has been from Rs. 323,000,000 to Rs.106,000,000, and, to meet all demands, Government and private, India requires a favourable trade balance of 450 to 500 million rupees every year. This curtailment of the favourable trade balance is one of the most brilliant and striking results imaginable of the Indian Government's currency policy in closing the mints. It compels an increase in European borrowings, and the wisdom of a Solomon is not required to enable an unwarped mind to understand that this progress downwards by the "primrose way" of debt and ever more debt, has only to go on a few years longer to bring the Indian Empire to the end of its tether. Nevertheless, the officials can go on dreaming of "savings by exchange" and constructing surpluses which are never realised, and all the time be earnest only in discovering fresh pretexts and excuses for adding to the debt. They are going to add Rs.30,000,000 this year to the rupee debt of India and at least some £2,750,000 net to the sterling debt in England. Since March, 1896, the paper money has been augmented by Rs.20,000,000—which are less hurtful to Indian credit than they might be if they could be got into circulation—by six millions sterling in bills of exchange raised to meet current expenditure in England and still afloat, and by seventy millions of rupees of interest-bearing debt launched in India and up to now in the hands mostly of the first subscribers, besides smaller borrowings on the part of the railway companies. As long as this free borrowing can go on the Indian Government can manufacture surpluses of a sort most years and boast that it is rich.

But if there was not much enlightenment in the Secretary of State's Memorandum, we may perhaps find it well supplemented in the debate on the Indian Budget which took place on Tuesday in the House of Commons. Thanks to the necessity the Indian Government lies under to obtain power to raise a loan "not exceeding £10,000,000" here, this debate came thus early instead of at the very tail of the Parliamentary session. The change has not been one of good augury for the affairs of India. It has always been an excuse hitherto that, owing to the period in the session when the Indian Budget was discussed, it never got thoroughly looked into. Well, we have had the debate early this year, and it was more perfunctory than ever. The members were conspicuous for their absence, so that Lord George Hamilton spoke to nearly empty benches, and the few who remained to take part in the debate never once, if we except Mr. McLean and Sir William Wedderburn, lifted the debate into a plane above that of the mere routine official. And it is significant of the attitude of the British public towards the population of India that most of the newspapers suppressed Sir W. Wedderburn's appeal for inquiry into the condition of the ryots. Lord George's explanation of the Budget was clear and straightforward from his point of view, which is the bureaucratic one, but reading it one would never suppose that there was anything in the shape of danger to our rule in India from the poverty and discontent of its population or in the extravagance of its Government. He boasted that although in the past three years famine, plague, earthquake, and war had cost the Indian Budgets upwards of Rs.243,000,000, the deficit for that period was under Rs.61,000,000, so that Rs.182,000,000 had come from the current revenue. Also he was mighty proud of the fact that during the famine about 829,000,000 units had been fed, being an average of 1,814,000 per day for fifteen months, and he was reasonably and fairly elated at this feat.

Nevertheless, India has to borrow more and more heavily as time goes on, and we may well ask how her deficits would have been filled without these borrowings? We have stated the net borrowing intentions of the present year as far as the Memorandum enables us to gather them, and the mind which is not befogged with official glosses can easily understand how it is that revenue keeps up and that obligations of India in London are partially met, while from £6,000,000 to £10,000,000 of fresh money continues to be poured by us into the country at the call of the Indian Government. That the people are being impoverished by this steady imposition of foreign capital upon them, capital which imposes continually additional burdens for interest, never appears to be suspected by the ordinary mind. So far is it from being so that we find Sir Henry Fowler boasting, in that singularly wooden and pretentious speech delivered by him in the debate, that although the total charges of the Indian Government payable here may amount "to £15,000,000 or £16,000,000" (they are really more, but that does not matter to a great mind like Sir Henry's) "when one analyses that amount one finds that the railway loans, interest, and management will represent next year £8,815,000 of the £16,000,000, which," as he triumphantly exclaims, "is no drain upon India, as it is paid out of the revenues of the railways." Indeed, Sir Henry, and pray how are the "revenues of the railways" collected in India converted into sterling money payable in London? Is it not by the sale of Indian produce, and is not this Indian produce furnished by the labour of the people of India; and if the amount of these exports in excess of the imports be insufficient to cover the annual charges payable here by the Indian Government, must not commerce be disarranged? Are not these railway charges, in other words, a form of indirect taxation, which may be crushing in its weight upon the Indian people? Even if it is sufficient, does not all this produce exported from India, in order that its proceeds may be devoted to meeting Government charges here, imply that the profits of the trade go not to the producer, not to the cultivator and humble taxpayer, but into the Exchequer, and is not the real question that the Government has to investigate the question whether the strain thus placed upon the natives of India is or is not altogether in excess of their capacity to bear it?

We have no doubts upon these points, and have not had a doubt this many a year. We find proofs continually accumulating that the burdens are excessive, and not least in the news which comes from India by all mouths and mails regarding the increasing disaffection of the people. Their hatred of our rule is becoming so intense as to be an imminent danger to our position there, and unless the whole system of Indian finance is changed, it seems to us that our governors may soon have to deal with a strike of the population against our dominion which will be far more difficult to cope with than any mutiny of armed men could be. Passive resistance will take the place of active warfare against us; in sheer despair the weary Indian will lie down and die rather than be ground to the dust any longer by our exactions, and the still more ruthless exactions of the moneylenders whom we have made the dronebees of the Indian community.

In order to really fathom the depth of the stupidity which is manifested in many quarters by people who profess to know India and Indian affairs, we must go outside the dreary and hollow House of Commons debate, and look at what a person who might be deemed unprejudiced has to say on the subject of Indian "wealth." In last week's *Economist* an "East Indian Merchant" delivered himself of an attack upon Sir Robert Giffen, a portion of which we will here quote, partly because the "views" Sir Robert gracefully attributes to the City in his letters, and which this letter writer attacks, are exactly those which we have been hammering away at these many years back, and especially during the past six years in the pages of this Review. In a manner, therefore, we are defending our own position when we take up the cudgels against this Eastern merchant. Here is the paragraph;—

A "poor" and "debtor" country, not so rich even as Egypt, which, Sir Robert says, has got Cook's tourists: not to be compared with a creditor country like France, one of the richest in the world. Now, a "debtor," on a balance of transactions, I take to be one who has to find, and a "creditor" one who has to receive money to square the account. Is it not, then, a notorious fact, of which Sir Robert Giffen and the "City," whose views he says he represents, seem to be unaware, that India for the past sixty years has gone on receiving millions on millions of gold and millions on millions of silver? In the House of Commons, on March 29 last, Sir Samuel Montagu said: "There is an enormous quantity of gold in India, which has been estimated at over £300,000,000, and I feel sure from my knowledge of what has been sent to India during the last fifty years that £300,000,000 is even below the mark." That, besides tons upon tons of silver, has been received by "a poor and debtor" country, which has paid not only for all this great mass of bullion, but for all her other indebtedness as well. In the last official year to March 31, the returns of which are just to hand, famine notwithstanding, the net imports of gold were forty-nine millions of rupees, and of silver eighty-four millions. But then, Sir Robert suggests that if not a poor country as a whole, it has a poor population. There is such a lot of them, such a large divisor, that, however big the dividend, the quotient is small. Now, I hold with the immortal Micawber, that wealth is relative. "Annual income," he says, "twenty pounds; annual expenditure, nineteen nineteen six; result, happiness. Annual income, twenty pounds; annual expenditure, twenty ought six; result, misery." The former position, I take it, describes the normal condition of the frugal, industrious, and saving peasantry of both France and India. Says Sir Robert Giffen: "France is clearly not an example for India in this matter." It seems to me that no two countries, both in soil and people, have industrially more in common. If Sir Robert Giffen wants relative poverty, in the Micawber sense, I think he will find it nearer home.

This, to be sure, is very eloquent and striking, but if the

enthusiastic writer had paused to look a little below the surface he would have found that the "tons upon tons" of silver, and "millions on millions" of gold which India has imported afford no proof whatever that India is growing richer, but the contrary. If a country is rich, in the sense of wealth disseminated more and more amongst the people, it buys increasing quantities of articles of consumption or luxury. Bullion is not what it wants, but merchandise; and the fact that India prefers bullion to merchandise in such large amounts demonstrates that the small class which is enriched through the peace we secure for the whole country, or through their participation in the commerce we have established, is a hoarding class which imports gold and silver to hide it away, having no use for our merchandise and no scope for the employment of their gains as fructifying capital in domestic industries, by reason of the utter poverty of the masses beneath them. Looked at in their true light, these bullion imports of India are perhaps the most emphatic condemnation of our rule which could be adduced. One might have imagined that a merchant would have been the first to see this, and that the mere fact that, assuming him to be an importer of goods into India, he found only an extremely limited outlet for these goods, at the same time that gold and silver continued to pour into the country, might have warned him of something wrong in the body economic. But no, he cites this bullion movement as a proof that the "wealth" of India, of the Indian people, is great and expanding. The wealth of a class may be, doubtless is. The zemindars and other landowners, the moneylenders, the mercantile houses of native origin, and a comparatively small number of people engaged in professions and industries in the cities and on the railways, may all be making money; indeed, some of them must be; but it is money of no use to them, except to turn into ornaments or to hoard as coin or bullion. They accumulate it and bury it, and it is as much lost to us, and to any beneficial employment for the development of India, as if it had been all sunk in the Indian Ocean. All the while that the few heap up this useless gold and silver the great multitude of the people sinks into deeper and deeper poverty. But the merchant never thought of that, nor does the serene official.

Some Company-Mongering Flotsam.

Among the flood of new ventures that were launched last year, not a few were of a kind that did not appeal to the public. Indeed much of the going to allotment and issuing letters of regret must have partaken rather of the character of a farce. Companies thus badly received are often slow to file their lists of shareholders at Somerset House, but there is a limit to the indulgence granted by that long-suffering institution, and so long a time has now elapsed that reluctant promoters have been compelled to disgorge their information. A visit to that shrine of company knowledge has enabled us to look into the position of a few of these new creations, and we must say that the company promoter does not seem to have fared very well. First on our list is

HOOD AND MOORE'S STORES.

This represents a collection of corn and forage shops which was brought out as a company in December 9, 1895. The capital is, or was, £150,000 in £1 shares, divided equally into preference and ordinary, and the £75,000 of preference shares were offered for subscription. Bearing in mind the uninviting fate that has befallen similar issues, it is not surprising to find that two-thirds of the amount offered went into the following twenty-two names:—

Preference.

	No. of Shares.
Industrial and General Trust	2,500
H. Evans	3,000
A. F. G. Gardner	1,000
G. A. Touch...	2,500
T. Pim	3,000
Hon. C. N. Lawrence	3,000
W. C. Slaughter	650
Sir R. Quain	500
H. P. Norton	3,000
A. J. Simpson	1,000
H. Lavarack	1,000
Jessie Touch	2,500
G. Taylor	1,500
New Imperial Investment	2,500
W. May	3,000
J. E. Touch...	3,000
Hon. H. A. Lawrence	2,940
W. Robertson	1,800
Hon. Mrs. C. Lawrence	950
W. Lander	1,900
G. M. Simmonds	2,640
H. P. Weaver	1,000

Ordinary.

Alan F. G. Gardner	35,000
G. W. Hood	10,000
C. Moore	10,000
T. R. Moore	10,000

It is a significant circumstance that since the prospectus was issued, Mr. J. E. Touch has become a director, and he, with Mr. G. A. Touch, Mrs. Jessie Touch, Mr. W. C. Slaughter, the Industrial and General Trust, the Hons. C. N., H. A., and Mrs. C. Lawrence, and Messrs. W. Robertson and W. Lander, of the Imperial Ottoman Bank, represent a little coterie who have taken over 21,000 of the shares amongst them. Did the issue flag, and the Touches and their following come to the rescue? If so, they have not been very happy in their choice, for the £1 preference shares are now quoted about 10s. Another peculiarity of the issue is this: that Mr. A. F. G. Gardner, whose name did not appear in the prospectus, took no less than £35,000 of the ordinary shares. They are, we should imagine, worthless, so it does not matter to the public.

MONGER'S WEST AUSTRALIAN STORES.

Issued as a company in May, 1897, this concern was to buy up the store business of J. H. Monger & Co., Limited, and the stores, hotel, and transport business of the West Australian Goldfields, both, of course, in Western Australia. The former business was being managed by Dalgety & Co., Limited, owing to the decease of the former owner, and there might have been a good reason for the formation of this concern, which, however, was quite spoiled, from an investment point of view, by one fact. The businesses were first sold to the Colonial Industries Company, Limited, which then re-sold to Monger's West Australian Stores, Limited, at a profit not stated. Now, five out of the seven directors of the latter company were directors or shareholders in the Colonial Industries Company, and thus arranged the purchase and sale for themselves. It is a position that no honourable man should have taken without disclosing the profit netted. The capital was fixed at £255,000 in £1 shares, of which £5,000 were founders' and the balance was equally divided into ordinary and preference shares. In May, 1897, there were 66,500 preference, 66,750 ordinary, and a few of the founders' shares offered for subscription. The result does not seem to have been a great success in the way of subscriptions from the public :—

	No. of Shares. Pref.	Ord.	Founders'.
A. A. Baumann	500	—	—
B. H. Blyth	—	1,000	5
Lord Crawshaw	1,000	3,000	40
J. Craven	1,205	1,025	62
L. Craven	500	500	10
A. Chalk	—	1,000	10
Colonial Industries, Limited	3,505	470	2,269
A. G. Dalgety	—	2,000	20
General Assets Trust ...	500	—	5
E. T. Hooley...	—	1,000	20
W. Henty	600	510	31
Industrial and General Trust	1,705	1,270	277
H. W. Jefferson	905	760	46
N. C. Ogle	—	1,015	30
S. Pope	—	510	15
J. Reixach	2,000	—	40
R. Stapley	300	510	23
W. Smith	300	255	15
Scottish Colonial Goldfields	300	255	15
Trustees, Executors, and Sec. Insurance	—	1,525	45
Stock Conversion and Investment Trust	1,205	—	32
London and Australasian Debenture Corporation ...	600	—	16
United States Debenture Corporation	1,505	—	40
G. W. Wolff	1,505	1,280	77
G. S. Woodman	1,203	1,525	127
West Australian Goldfields	20,000	—	400
G. Younger	1,205	510	47
J. Younger	1,205	510	47

Roughly speaking, this short list contains about half the capital, and, noting the similarity in the number of shares held, it is presumable that underwriters had to take up a considerable percentage. The Industrial & General Trust again figures largely, and it has drawn in its train the other trusts that meekly follow its lead. One would almost fancy that the gay old times of Winchester House finance are beginning to be repeated. Mr. E. T. Hooley is not the Ernest Terah of Dunlop and other notorious examples, but is Mr. Edward Timothy Hooley, chief manager to Dalgety & Co., Limited, a gentleman who, we imagine, would not think himself flattered just now by being mistaken for that brilliant financier, now under a cloud.

THE BRITISH DU BOIS MANUFACTURING COMPANY.

In May, 1897, this concern was issued with the modest capital of £100,000, and there was a decided cycle-finance flavour about the promotion, although the article to be produced was lead traps. No less than two companies had to combine in producing the affair, but the shares were not relished by the public, who apparently subscribed very moderately. Leading holders are contained in the following list :—

	No. of shares.
Reed Exploration Syndicate	470
E. S. Torrey	30,900
J. B. Purchase	4,000
C. K. Vokins...	920
A. Du Cros	4,000
A. P. Du Cros	4,000
F. Purchase	1,523
Du Bois Manufacturing Company	30,000
W. H. Purchase	1,000
F. D. Barker...	1,100
C. E. Hill	1,880
P. E. Pilditch	940
J. Lang	3,200
E. K. Purchase	4,940
A. J. Reed	940

These few names account for about £80,000 of the capital. The Du Bois Manufacturing Company was, of course, the vendor, and Mr. E. S. Torrey is chairman of the British Du Bois Company, Mr. E. K. Purchase is a director, and Messrs. J. B. and F. Purchase are probably members of the firm of John B. and F. Purchase, who are solicitors to the company. Mr. J. B. Purchase, by-the-bye, is a director of the Dunlop Pneumatic Tyre, and thus the connection between those interested in the concern and the Messrs. Du Cros seems to be rather close. Mr. C. K. Vokins is the auditor, so that the "family party" in this company appears to hold a large proportion of the capital. The shares are included in the official list, but at present the compilers of that compendium have not ventured upon a quotation.

JARRAHDALE JARRAH FOREST AND RAILWAYS.

Created in October, 1897, this speculative undertaking offered £100,000 in £10 preference shares, the £200,000 of ordinary capital going to the vendors. The preference capital does not appear to have been taken up to any extent by the latter, but some significant names appear as holders of a fair proportion of the issue. We give the holdings in sterling, as the shares are £10 each :—

	Preferred. £
London and Chicago Contract Corporation ...	7,270
Omnium Investment Trust	230
Debenture Securities Investment	1,000
Brewery and Commercial Trust...	1,000
United Discount and Securities Company ...	1,000
London General Investment	1,200
City of London Contract Corporation	7,850
Government and General Investment	220
Imperial Colonial Finance and Agency ...	250
J. R. Ellerman	250
H. O'Hagan	1,000
T. O'Hagan	2,000
C. Morrison	6,500

In these thirteen names stands, therefore, nearly one-third of the total issue. The London and Chicago Contract Corporation and the City of London Contract Corporation are the pet trusts of the two Messrs. O'Hagan, whose record as company promoters is not a happy one. The Debenture Securities Investment, Brewery and Commercial Trust, United Discount and Securities, and London General Investment are companies that are submissive to Mr. J. R. Ellerman, who seems to have joined hands with the brothers O'Hagan in the floating of this concern. The other trusts probably came in as underwriters. The shares are fairly maintained, standing about par, but then this is the "heyday" of Jarrah companies.

MAISON VIROT, LIMITED.

The last issue of the André Mendel group. 70,000 ordinary £1 shares of the company were offered to the public last July at £1 10s. each. The response to this appeal cannot be considered to have been favourable, and the leading holders of the ordinary shares are as follows :—

	No. of shares.
A. von André	2,916
M. Abrahams	1,[illegible]0

	No. of shares.
C. Krebs	3,000
E. McLoughlin	1,700
W. Mendel	15,753
C. Meyer	1,000
W. Nocton	1,000
J. H. Parks	1,000
E. Seligman	500

Thus two-fifths of the issue is in nine names, and of these no less than 17,669 shares are in the names of Messrs. A. von André and W. Mendel, who are the leading members of the issuing firm of André, Mendel & Co. In the meantime, the quotation of these ordinary shares has fallen to ¾ to 1, so that the poor public who subscribed at 1½ must be having a bad time. Of course, Messrs. André and Mendel obtained their shares at a very different figure, and so they can probably be philosophically indifferent to the fall in the market price.

Our Foreign Trade in May.

No change for the better is to be seen in the figures of this trade for the past month. In order that readers may understand how it is going we have compiled the subjoined summary of tables, which will enable them to follow the movement of our commerce out and in, both for the month and for the five months of this year and the preceding two years :—

IMPORTS IN MAY.

	1896. £	1897. £	1898. £
Merchandise	33,349,988	36,346,438	37,706,378
Gold	2,608,212	3,527,593	8,241,182
Silver	1,194,310	1,415,008	925,297
Total	37,152,510	41,289,039	46,872,857

EXPORTS.

	1896. £	1897. £	1898. £
British and Irish Produce ...	18,835,243	19,322,146	17,891,354
Foreign and Colonial Produce	4,748,642	4,954,692	5,106,534
Gold	1,613,902	2,291,196	1,598,971
Silver	1,182,195	1,640,918	933,641
Total	26,379,982	28,208,952	25,530,500
Excess value of imports over exports	10,772,528	13,080,087	21,342,357

IMPORTS FOR FIVE MONTHS ENDED MAY 31.

	1896. £	1897. £	1898. £
Merchandise	181,325,730	189,031,470	196,987,003
Gold	11,729,517	13,084,856	22,572,817
Silver	6,019,087	6,743,877	4,956,426
Total	199,074,334	208,860,203	224,516,246

EXPORTS.

	1896. £	1897. £	1898. £
British and Irish Produce	98,585,679	98,320,455	93,024,483
Foreign and Colonial Merchandise	25,166,803	26,912,849	26,356,559
Gold	8,892,585	9,941,848	14,398,605
Silver	5,934,714	6,189,521	5,784,708
Total	138,579,784	141,364,673	139,564,355
Excess of imports over exports	60,494,550	67,495,530	84,951,891

By these figures it will be seen that, including everything, the adverse balance on the month's trade was £21,342,000, and on the five months' trade about £85,000,000 this year. Compared with the two previous years this shows a progressive increase in badness, but we do not wish to magnify too much the significance of this widening gap between what we buy and what we are able to sell, because it is just possible that the causes producing it may be temporary. We know, for example, that wheat has been much dearer this year than last, and, indeed, the cost of cereals accounts for the whole May increase in our imports over the totals of a year ago. We imported, for example, rather less wheat last month than in May, 1896, but the cost of this smaller quantity was fully £1,100,000 in excess of last year's. In other words, while wheat in 1896 cost us about 6s. 9d. per cwt. it cost us last month 11s. In the same way maize, of which we import enormous quantities, principally from the United States, Canada, and Roumania, has risen in price from about 3s. 2¼d. per cwt. a year ago to 4s. 5¼d. Assuming this rise to be temporary there is no reason why the divergence between our imports and exports, so far as it is dependent on dear grain, should not soon begin to grow less. In the meantime, however, it must not be lost sight of that we are, up to date, nearly £24,500,000 to the bad compared with 1896, and about £17,500,000 worse than in 1897. As the adverse balance is a continuous one it ought to follow that this autumn, if we have no extraordinary resource to fall back upon, bullion will again have to be exported, or securities sold for export, in order to make good the additional deficit; because it may fairly be assumed that the returns from our foreign investments have not increased in volume at a sufficient pace to meet the extra demand upon the nation's purse.

The worst part of the entire trading account undoubtedly continues to be the stagnation of our exports. Had they been increasing ever so little there would have been ground for believing that our larger current expenditure abroad was bearing its legitimate fruit in the larger purchases of our foreign customers. As yet this has not been the case. The total exports for the month of British and Irish produce are worse than those for either of the two preceding Mays, and including foreign and colonial merchandise, and gold and silver, the exhibit is not very materially improved. But there was one working day less this May than last, owing to Whitsuntide, and we must not make too much of one month. If we take the totals for the five months a progressive decrease is to be seen, although it is very slight indeed this year as compared with 1896. And it may, of course, be that sufficient time has not yet elapsed to enable our larger expenditure on foreign products, principally foreign foods, to tell upon the buying power of our customers abroad. We must guard ourselves, therefore, from drawing too gloomy a conclusion from the actual position of our foreign commerce. It stagnates unquestionably, but there are many circumstances at work to make it backward, not least of which is the poverty that has overtaken Continental nations, through their extravagant Budgets, through bad harvests, or, as in the case of Spain, Italy, and Greece, through threatening social upheavals and wars. In the Far East, also, Chinese trade has never recovered from the effects of the war with Japan, and is not likely to recover so long as the former great export of Chinese tea to this country keeps on its way to disappear. In our exports of cotton manufactures it remains true that, but for the heavy shipments to India—shipments which require watching because they are unhealthily stimulated by an inflated rate of exchange, and which may lead to serious mercantile difficulties—a sensible decline would be visible, because nowhere else is adequate compensation for the loss of business, with China and the United States more particularly, being found. Our woollen trade with the United States goes from bad to worse, until it threatens to disappear in some classes of goods, and there also fresh outlets have not arisen in adequate absorbing power. Our Australian colonies do not buy more, but rather less; in fact, our own dependencies outside India are not helping us very much to meet an adverse trade balance at the present time, in spite of their liberal contributions of bullion. The iron trade is recovering somewhat, especially machinery and mill-work, but a melancholy array of declines is visible in all our other great branches of export, even in raw materials; for last month foreign customers took away £220,000 worth less of our coal than in May, 1897. For all this, we are inclined to limit the moralising on our trade position for the present to a warning against over-confidence in regard to the maintenance of "cheap money" during the autumn. If these trade figures mean anything, they mean that we shall have to draw on our stock of gold then to pay for the excessive amount of imports now reaching this country.

Wheat on the Down Grade.

The effect of the "war scare" on the price of wheat has ended, and things are rapidly getting into a more natural condition. The war itself never really did interfere with the supply, but there was a fear that it might, and that gave the speculators and the "corner" men the opportunity to operate for their own advantage. But the prophets who prognosticated a continued dire scarcity in wheat and a rise in price to at least 60s. a quarter have proved mistaken. The scarcity even now is not so very terrible to contemplate, for the attraction of high prices has brought supplies in great abundance, and from quarters where wheat for export was not believed to exist. The arrivals for last week amounted to the extraordinary amount of 1,663,000 quarters, and to that amount Russia, who was supposed to have none to spare, contributed no less than 584,000 quarters; the United States, 543,000; and India, 377,000. What further supplies Russia may be able to afford we are not in a position to say; but the American exports still continue abnormally large, and there is no reason to expect any immediate diminution in their volume. In the week ending May 28, the Atlantic exports of wheat, flour included, amounted to 3,726,442 bushels, against 1,536,607 at the same time last year. It is true the Pacific exports fell to 92,184 bushels, against 314,955 last year; but that deficiency is not at all disquieting in face of the quantities coming from Atlantic ports. Wheat receipts at the West again, according to *Dun's Review*, do not diminish, but run far beyond those of a year ago; for the week mentioned they were 4,625,253 bushels, against 2,969,173 at the same period last year. In the four weeks from both coasts the exports have been 13,691,874 bushels, against 5,704,334 last year. As to future supplies from America there seems no present reason to fear, and as to the condition of the coming crop, all accounts, including the official returns, agree in the estimate that the wheat yield will this year be remarkably large, in spite of the acknowledged deficiency in California. The harvest has already begun in several of the Western States, and some parcels forwarded to New York from Texas confirm the estimate as to the quality of the wheat. Our supplies from India are more likely to increase than diminish; and, taking these and other sources of supply into account, we need, we think, have no fear of the future. Of the home crops we have also, on the whole, favourable reports, and at least a full average crop is counted upon.

In these circumstances, it was, of course, inevitable that there should be a fall in prices. Last week there was a decline in American descriptions of about 2s. 6d., and the loss has certainly not been recovered this week. In the English provincial markets the universal tendency was downwards, and the drop up to the present amounts to from 2s. to 3s. per quarter. The decline has been wrung from the sellers. They stood out bravely for a long time against all reduction; but buyers were equally dogged, and it in time became evident that, if business was to be done at all, reductions must be submitted to. The feeling in Mark-lane on Wednesday was very despondent. But it is doubtful if the decline will be allowed to go very much further—not, at least, until we have more precise information about the amount and quality of the coming crop. Speculators are evidently very uncertain about the future. There have been great fluctuations in New York and Liverpool, but it is very seldom that rises are long maintained. Options also fluctuate greatly, but the tendency is to keep on a low level, though on Wednesday there was in New York some upward reaction. For some Manitoban wheat almost due, 49s. 6d. has been paid, and a parcel just shipped, 48s., while 47s. 3d. and 47s. 6d. have been paid for May-June shipment. For September-October shipment there have been sellers of No. 1 Northern at 33s. 6d. and of Kansas at 33s. 9d. On the whole, however, we are inclined to think that, unless the coming crops greatly exceed in quantity and quality present estimates and anticipations, the price of wheat will not go very far under 40s. per quarter. The war may not greatly interfere with our supplies of wheat; but if much prolonged, as seems not improbable, it must exercise a certain adverse influence on prices. There seems, then, every indication that the present "fat year" on which the Chancellor of the Exchequer recently congratulated the English farmers may be followed by another—not perhaps so very fat as this, but still not so very lean as they have for some time been accustomed to.

On the important question of the price of bread, not very much can be said. One reduction from 7d. to 6½d. has already taken place. It might by this time have easily been followed by another of equal amount; but bakers, like farmers, have been slow to move on the down grade. Their excuse is that, having bought in stocks at the higher figures reigning a week or two ago they cannot make a further reduction until these stocks have been exhausted. That in itself is plausible enough and reasonable enough; but we should not have thought that prudent bakers would have bought largely when prices were at the fever heat of a fortnight ago. They are more likely to have bought only to supply present and pressing needs; so that the most adventurous purchasers among them cannot now have big stocks of the dear wheat. They urge also, however, that it is not sure that the present downward tendency will continue, that there may not indeed be a sudden turn in the opposite direction. The facts we have just stated, however, certainly point in the opposite direction. As far as ordinary intelligence can discern the price will go down rather than up; and even cautiously prudent bakers might risk a further reduction in the price of bread without immediate serious loss, or any great danger of being caught in some sudden upward swirl of prices. They cannot long defer following the downward tendency in the price of wheat.

New South Wales Trade Statistics.

A correspondent has sent us the subjoined extract from a Colonial newspaper; which one he has omitted to inform us, but we judge it to be a Sydney paper :—

A week or two back we quoted some adverse comments on New South Wales conditions in Mr. A. J. Wilson's new financial paper, founded on a set of figures greatly erroneous. We anticipated that the next issue would contain a correction of the mistake, discovered by some representative of the colony. But no one has been on the alert, or Mr. Wilson is not taken as a serious authority, for nothing of the kind has been published, and it still remains before the London public on the authority of the INVESTORS' REVIEW that the colony in 1897 had an excess of imports amounting to £2,500,000, instead of an excess of exports amounting to £1,983,000. The case is represented as four millions and a half sterling against the colony. Is there any wonder, with such statements prominently under the notice of investors, that New South Wales securities should have within six weeks lost the relative advantage they then had over those of the other colonies? This makes it apparent why our securities should have fallen more than those of New Zealand and South Australia, and brought them to the level of the stocks of this colony. On looking at the figures we find that the INVESTORS' REVIEW took the trade of Sydney to represent that of the whole colony. The real difference is shown in the following statement :—

	Imports.	Exports.	Excess of Imports or Exports.
Sydney	£15,229,128	£12,281,109	Excess of Imp. £2,948,019
Colony	15,051,000	17,034,543	Excess of Exp. 1,983,000

The Sydney figures are simply the aggregate value of the imports and exports without regard to the re-exports, and obviously cannot be quoted as representative of the net trade of the colony—that is, the imports for home consumption and the exports of its own produce. This is really represented in the second line (Mr. Coghlan's figures), which show an excess of exports amounting to £1,983,000. Sydney undoubtedly does the bulk of the foreign trade of the colony; but, as an expert, Mr. Wilson ought to have known that the trade of a capital does not count as that of all the colony. No one would think of treating the imports and exports of London as representing the trade of the United Kingdom, or of setting its imports as against its total exports to furnish an illustration of its solvency. Yet that is equivalent to what has been done.

Part III. of the "Statistical Register," dealing with commerce, has just been published by Mr. Coghlan. The main features of the trade of the colony have already been published. The following figures show the value of the imports, exports, and total trade per head of population for the past four years :—

	Imports.	Exports.	Total.
1894 ...	... £12 15 5	... £16 12 7	... £29 8 0
1895 ...	... 12 12 11	... 17 6 11	... 29 19 10
1896 ...	... 15 19 4	... 17 17 4	... 33 16 8
1897 ...	... 16 11 10	... 18 2 6	... 34 14 4

These figures indicate improvement, though not very rapid. The drought seriously affected the trade, particularly the export trade.

It is with much regret that we thus, for the first time, learn of our mistake with reference to the trade of New South Wales; but we cannot help thinking that the mistake was a very pardonable one, seeing that to the best of our recollection no indication whatever was given in the newspaper from which we quoted that the figures referred only to the trade of Sydney or to the trade of the colony minus re-exports, we are not even now sure which.

And there is another reason why the blunder was not so serious as it looks in the eyes of colonial journalists, and that is the obvious unreality of these figures, whether as we took them or as now given. As will be seen from the extract quoted above, New South Wales claims to have exported produce last year to the value of £18 2s. 6d. per head of the population, and to have imported £16 11s. 10d. worth per head. We have often expressed our doubts as to the genuineness of these totals, and will once more state some of the grounds for them. Probably even Australians will grant that their territories and industries are not quite so well developed as those of the United Kingdom, and that their wealth, however much it may bulk in the statistical compilations sent us, is not so great as our own. Moreover, they can hardly deny that the great strength of England consists in the magnificent foreign trade which she does, not only with her colonies, but with all parts of the world, civilised and uncivilised. Also it cannot be gainsaid that in the matter of industrial products the United Kingdom has an immense variety of articles to offer to its customers, while the colonies have nothing except raw produce. Great as our trade is, however, we only managed to import £12 10s. worth of goods and bullion per head of the population in the past year, taking that population at 40,000,000. We include bullion because it figures on both sides of the account in the New South Wales returns, as in those of all the Australasian colonies. Our imports last year thus fell fully £4 per head below those of New South Wales, which is a sufficiently remarkable fact in itself; and it is still worse with the record of our exports. These, including re-exports of foreign and colonial merchandise, and also bullion, only amounted to about £8 11s. per head last year, or, say, £9 10s. per head less than the per head value of the exports of New South Wales as set forth above. There must be something very far wrong in colonial statistics which produce a disparity like this. We are New South Wales's creditors, drawing two and a half to three millions or more from it in hard cash every year, and yet it can spend £4 a head more per annum on foreign goods than we are able to do with all our advantages.

In the articles written by us during 1892-93 upon the finances of these Australasian colonies we pointed out that their official figures were unreliable in many respects, and as far as regards the statistics of trade, specially so, the same article being counted several times over as it passed out and in across the frontier of different colonies, and was returned in the trade statistics of each. Probably enough the same cause of misleading returns prevails to-day, but we cannot help thinking that there is at least one other. Last week, for instance, in mentioning the decline in the value of the Australasian wool crop, we quoted figures, presumably taken from official returns, which showed that the value entered in colonial returns was worked out upon the price of the wool in the London market. This is an entirely misleading way of stating export values, and we fear in some instances even this false standard is not adhered to, but that the wool is sometimes entered at prices which the exporter imagines he ought to receive; and if such a practice is followed with wool it doubtless is so with other articles. Until the obscurity on this point is satisfactorily cleared up we must be pardoned for laying very little stress upon the apparent excess value on exports over imports shown by the figures quoted above. For, obviously, if exports are overvalued in a systematic way, as well as duplicated in various returns, neither the colonist nor the statistician here can have any true conception of the position of the foreign trade of these settlements.

The true test value of a crop of wool is the price which it fetches on the markets of the various colonies. Doubtless there may often be no market on the spot in the true sense of the term to apply this test by, because the pastoral industries of the colonies, and most of their other industries, are conducted on credit in such a manner that the finance companies and banks have control of the entire production and need not in any way locally compete against each other. Competition only arises when the wool reaches Europe, and has to be sold against our home supply and the supplies from South America, the Cape, and other parts of the world. It may, therefore, be an excuse for the colonial statistician that he has no local test of any reliability to apply, and that the London market price is the only genuine measure available. Even so, 15 per cent. at least ought to be deducted from totals thus arrived at to cover freight, insurance, commissions, and other expenses incident to conducting trade.

Still another test may be applied to these figures. We may compare them with those of the United States, which is a country much more developed than Australia, and, although more hampered by tariffs than New South Wales, still a country full of industrial capacities and resources well organised, such as no Australasian settlement can boast of. The figures of the United States' foreign trade for past year have not yet reached us from the Statistical Bureau in Washington, but we have those for 1896 before us, and they indicate that the value of the imports of the American Union was about £2 3s. 2d. per head in that year, and the value of the exports £2 10s. Is it possible to trust figures such as those New South Wales presents us with in view of a fact like that? We think not.

And there is still another source of doubt. When we turn to our own statistics, which are probably on the whole the most accurate in the world, we find that our total exports to the entire Australasian group only amounted to £24,355,000 in 1896, and that our imports from there were only worth £29,402,000. New South Wales took less than £6,400,000 of our goods in 1896. Where did her other imports come from which brought the total up to £15,000,000? A great deal more light is wanted on this point, and until it is forthcoming we must continue to treat these Australasian statistics with deep distrust, as all works of the fancy ought to be treated when thrust into the domain of facts.

Let it be admitted, however, that the figures are approximately correct, and that New South Wales last year succeeded in exporting nearly £2,000,000 worth more of her own and other colonies' goods than she imported, and still the situation of the colony is not satisfactory. At a moderate estimate, her obligations payable in London, in the shape of interest on the public debt and of interest on corporate capital borrowed or raised in this country, amounts to £3,000,000 a year. Indeed, we believe it to be considerably more, counting in the cost of carrying her goods over sea to and fro, but put it at £3,000,000, and the trade of the country does not, on the very best exhibit possible, show a sufficient margin to cover this obligation without allowing anything in the way of profit to the trader. It follows, therefore, that New South Wales, strongest colony of the group though it be, must continue to live by the help of the English moneylender. The people, whether as individuals or as an infant nation, cannot pay their way.

The writer whose paragraph we quote does us too much honour in ascribing to the statement we made the fall which took place in New South Wales securities at the early part of the year. It was not our criticism which brought that about, but the fact that the colony had just issued a fresh loan on this market about the time money with us began to advance in price, and the weight of this loan, which was not then all placed with investors, but lying mostly in the hands of middlemen, was sufficient to press down the quotations for the previously issued stocks of the colony. Now that money in London has become cheaper again these stocks have gone up, and they will continue at high prices until once again money becomes dear. We should like serious colonial politicians to note this fact. It is a warning to them, or ought to be a warning, of the fate that will overtake them should money ever become so dear in London as to paralyse our lending power. When a crisis breaks out here which stops our capacity to go on manufacturing credit for these dependencies at their demand, every colony in the group will find itself unable to meet its engagements. This is not a prophecy or any mere "croaking"; it is the strict logical conclusion to be drawn from the circumstances of the case. While they borrow here New South Wales and the other colonies will continue to make an appearance of meeting their obligations; when borrowing becomes impossible their bankruptcy will declare itself, and when overtaken by that bankruptcy, miscalculations or misinterpretations of statistics imperfectly presented, and in whose genuineness at the best we have extremely little faith, can count for very little. But how soon is a credit upset coming in England? We may not guess, but let colonial politicians note this one significant fact: when money was 4 per cent. in the City of London, and looked like going to 5 per cent., the securities of all these settlements not only declined in price, but became absolutely unsaleable at any price, except in minute amounts. The market seemed to be literally gorged with them until it could hold no more. If 4 per cent. did this, what will 5 or 6 per cent. do?

Economic and Financial Notes and Correspondence.

"WITH A HOOLEY, HOOLEY, HO!"

We knew it must be so. The subjoined paragraph is cut from the *St. James's Gazette* of Wednesday, and it gives the opening scene in the story of a comedy of company-making which should deepen in interest as it unfolds. We need not say that Mr. Hooley's resolution takes us in no way by surprise, and we feel sure it cannot be a shock to our readers. But we do not at all desire to jump upon the poor fellow, and are fully disposed to believe that Mr. Beyfus, his lawyer, spoke only the literal truth when he assured Mr. Registrar Brougham that his client had not made very large sums through his promotions, and that "he had been victimised to an extent which would be quite a revelation to the public." We who have amusedly watched the play from the first could not but be amazed now and then at the childlike, or childish, simplicity of the man. He allowed the schemer with something to vend to humbug him, and he was pounced upon by troops of aristocratic and "society" people, whose impecunious pretentiosity is ever forcing them to hunt down every creature from whom they think money may be wrung. They "subscribed" for shares in his companies, lent him their names on promise of gain, "underwrote" on commission like furies, and when unable to sell their allotment letters at a premium, or to wriggle out of their contracts, got him to back their bills for the calls, or left him to "finance" the stew as best he could. In return they made him a member of the Carlton Club, got him baptised by a bishop, it is said, and fooled his vanity to the point which was fatal to the frog in the fable. Now that he is "down" they will turn their backs upon him and forget his existence, if their creditors will allow them—not so much because they are specially cruel or selfish beyond their class and kind, as because their hunger compels them to be ceaselessly on the prowl for some other victim to suck dry.

At the Bankruptcy Court to-day, Mr. Registrar Brougham, upon the application of Messrs. Beyfus & Beyfus, solicitors, made a receiving order in the case of Ernest Terah Hooley, who has presented his petition, describing himself as of Hill-street, Berkeley-square; of Risley Hall, near Derby; and of Papworth Hall, in the county of Cambridge, company promoter, carrying on business at the Midland Grand Hotel, St. Pancras, and at the Royal Insurance-buildings, Nottingham.

Mr. Beyfus, in making his application, said he regretted to have to ask his Honour to make a receiving order on a petition presented by Mr. E. T. Hooley, whose name was well known through the magnitude of the affairs in which he had been engaged. He desired to state that this step had only been taken by Mr. Hooley after making the most enormous sacrifices and solely in consequence of the necessity of preserving the assets for the general body of creditors instead of allowing some individuals to obtain payment at the expense of others. Mr. Hooley had no doubt that if he had been met in a reasonable way by some of the most pressing of his creditors, this step would have been unnecessary. There seemed to have been a perfect run upon him, and in consequence of the enormous amount of claims which had been made, for which he was totally unprepared, it was perfectly impossible for him to do justice to bonâ-fide creditors while having to attend to the mass of litigation with which he was threatened. It was impossible at present to say what were the liabilities. No doubt they would be very large, but, on the other hand, the assets also were very large, and would no doubt show a good result. This must depend a great deal upon their realisation, which was another reason for coming to the court, so that this might be effected without any undue sacrifice. Looking at the amount which would be involved, Mr. Beyfus said he thought it right to add that he was not prepared, at present, to state whether any scheme would be propounded, as this was a matter which would require the gravest consideration. It was due to Mr. Hooley to say that from what he (Mr. Beyfus) could learn he had not personally reaped the benefit of the very large sums which had been made in connection with some of his promotions, and that he had been victimised to an extent which would be quite a revelation to the public. Now that he had presented his petition he would do his best to have a statement prepared and laid before his creditors at the earliest possible moment.

Inquiry at the Midland Grand Hotel this morning elicited the information that Mr. Hooley and the whole of his staff have left the place.

Mr. Ernest Terah Hooley is in his thirty-ninth year, having been born at Long Eaton, Derbyshire, in 1859. He is the only son of Mr. Terah Hooley, and was married in 1882. His education was private, and he started life as a stockbroker in Nottingham, afterwards becoming a financier; and it was in this sphere that he became famous. Among other enterprises he has floated are the Dunlop Tyre, Bovril, Schweppe, Humber, and Singer Companies. He presented St. Paul's Cathedral with a gold Communion Service. He owns estates in Derbyshire, Cambridgeshire, Huntingdonshire, Essex, Wiltshire, and Scotland.

After reading the above pregnant little story, it does not seem unreasonable to suggest that the Chapter of St. Paul's Cathedral ought to take immediate steps to have that brilliant service of communion plate included among the assets available for Mr. Hooley's creditors. This is the seemly and honest course to follow, and the sooner it is adopted the better will it be for the credit of the Church. Apart from this episode, which involves a question of decency and public morals, the subject which interests us most may be indicated best by the question, "What bank, or banks, will lose most by this failure"? We have from the first appearance of this meteoric financier among us been curious on this point, and now look forward to receiving enlightenment. Money from somewhere he must have had in heaps. Who gave it to him? There will be surprises in the answer to this question, unless we are more than usually mistaken.

IS THE PETROLEUM COMMITTEE CORRUPT?

In its issue of Tuesday last the *Star* newspaper brought two charges of the most damning character against Mr. Jesse Collings in his capacity as chairman of this committee. First, it declared that he was "safeguarding the Standard Oil Trust" by deliberately delaying the issue of the committee's report; and, secondly, as corollary to this, it accused him on the authority of the *Times* of incorporating in his draft views practically identical with those expounded by the late Sir Vivian Majendie, "an official who was notoriously influenced by the pundits of the Standard Oil Trust." To allow no one to mistake its meaning the *Star* winds up its article in these words:—"Mr. Collings is merely quibbling when he professes a tender interest in 'trades which employ petroleum for other purposes than illumination.' Let him exempt them from the general law, if he likes, as gunsmiths and quarries and mines are exempted from the laws as to explosives. But let him not sacrifice the lives of the poor to fill the coffers of John D. Rockefeller."

It is impossible to exaggerate the significance of language like this applied to a public man. If it has any definite meaning, it amounts to an insinuation that Mr. Collings has been "bought up," "nobbled," or in some way "squared" by the Standard Oil Trust. Is he going to sit down in supineness under such an accusation. Will his colleagues in Parliament allow him to pass it by in silence? A more odious innuendo from all points of view could not be imagined, for it implies that this man, who has hitherto posed as the friend of the poor —the old "three acres and a cow" champion, in fact— is allowing himself to be made a tool of by a foreign trading organisation which cares no more for human lives than if men were no better than beetles. It is a perfectly abominable thing that insinuations of this kind should be bandied about so constantly in connection with the Standard Oil Trust's murdering and fire-raising explosive oils, but if Mr. Collings sits still under the attack of the *Star*, and if he does get his committee to report that the true cure for the horrible slaughter and waste of property now allowed to go on unchecked—not even protested against by the over-fat and careless "ring" insurance companies—is to invent a safety lamp and not to properly refine the oil meant for illumination, why then we fear we shall come to think pretty much as the *Star* seems to think now. Yet no, the scantiness of Mr. Collings's understanding will even then be the safeguard of his honour.

AUSTRALIAN FEDERATION.

We have taken, it must be confessed, but a slender interest in the agitation which has been going on throughout the Australian colonies on this question. It does not seem to us that a genuine federation can be within the range of practical politics, with these settlements situated as they are. The motive pushing the agitation on is plain enough, in some at least of these settlements, and we are not surprised that Victoria, South Australia, and Tasmania gave more or less large, although insufficient, majorities in favour of the project, or that it should have been rejected by a very halting poll in New South Wales. New South Wales is regarded with envious eyes, quite unreasonably, by some of the other settlements, who would be very glad to see it take up a portion of their debt burdens. To shift the load of the debt, in short, is the mainspring of this agitation. The Victorians, who are being dragged down towards despair by the horrible pressure of their debts, seized upon the scheme, doubtless with the hope that some kind of mixing up would be accomplished, whereby the various colonial debts, including their own, would be refunded into one large stock, and erected into a trustee security here, so that it might be emitted at or near 2½ per cent. By an arrangement of this kind the Victorians would not only shift part of their burden on to New South Wales, but the gross weight of that burden would be in itself reduced. From some points of view we should have no objection to this course being taken, although we do not consider that even such a stock is good enough to be stamped a "trustee" security, but it is impossible to federate on a mere re-arrangement of the debts basis. Dozens of other questions must crop up, with their jealousies and conflict of interests, which for a long time yet will render any real fusion of these various infant "States" on the model of the United States Federal Republic almost impossible. When the colonies have developed and have compounded with their creditors once or twice more they may reach a more reasonable frame of mind on railway management, local legislative independence, multiplicity of office-holders and so forth, and be willing to sacrifice individual pride of "nationality" in order to become merged in one considerable and promising State. At present any such union is impossible.

The New York Life Insurance Company.

Mr. John M. McCall has courteously sent us some interesting statistics and the fifty-third annual report of this company, being that for 1897. We gladly bear witness, as we have already done, to the fulness of detail in which this company sets forth its investments, and to the superior quality, as far as we are able to judge, of its investments as a whole, compared with those of its rival American companies. If we have any criticism to make it is that too much of the money seems to us to be invested in real estate, which of course would be impossible of realisation were a genuine pinch to come for money, and much of which may very well be overvalued now. Assume, however, that the investments are all first-class, and that the company, as viewed from its own standpoint, is in a sound financial position, it still seems to us that a great deal more information is wanted before we can say that its policies are good investments here. The money drawn from here is all invested in the States, and British policy-holders have no special lien on any part of it—on any of the securities. Moreover, the business of this company is run on the same lines that the other American companies have made us familiar with.

The great bulk, that is to say, of its "new" business never lives to become old, and we remain quite unable to understand how this can be if the business is that of genuine life insurance. We could understand something at least of the peculiarity of American business did this and other companies lend largely on their own policies. It might then be that an enormous number of merely temporary policies would be taken out, which, having served their end, would be dropped as a matter of course in a year or two; but this company does not lend freely on its policies, although it does more in this way than its rivals known here. It is against the habits of all such companies to encourage this practice, and if their policies are taken out for the purpose of raising loans elsewhere, as might be the case with the Mutual, which has the New York Guaranty and Trust Company to work its lending business by, there is still no accounting either for the waste in policies or the cost of new business. Policies raised to form collateral security for loans ought not to be costly to procure, because that is a business which would come to the companies mostly of its own accord, so to speak. This New York Life Company did $135,556,000 worth of new insurance last year, and lost $87,359,000 by death, maturity, surrender, expiry, &c. Thus nearly 64½ per cent. of the gain by the new business disappeared in the loss of the old, and only $14,053,000 of this consisted in claims paid on matured policies. No wonder that in such circumstances and in spite of nearly 25½ per cent. of the premium income going in commissions and expenses, the company should have had $13,982,000 to add to its funds at the end of the year. Much of that money represented somebody's loss. We shall soon return to this subject.

Resources of Natal.

It was a pretty picture that Sir W. Hely-Hutchinson drew of Natal to the London Chamber of Commerce on Monday. Not that the lecture was a search after the picturesque in language. It was rather a plain statement of facts as to the present position of the youngest of our self-governing colonies; but that position is, on the whole, so good, and has been so sturdily won, that the interested reader cannot help taking with him a pleasant impression of Natal. It seems to have an almost ideal climate. Europeans can live and thrive in it; consumptives may be benefited by it; blacks luxuriate in it; and tea and sugar keep much of the not very luxuriant coast region cultivated like a garden. And sugar in Natal is a paying speculation. It is not protected by the ruinous bounty system, but it is to some extent by an import duty which, if the sugar fields expand, the growers may feel themselves strong enough to dispense with. The imports in 1897 amounted to £5,983,589, while the exports were only £1,621,932.

This means a heavy bill to meet and pay even if we assume, as is indeed the case, that a large portion of the import total represents mere transit trade; but it is inevitable in a young colony, and while Natal was the first of the South African colonies to build a railway—of two miles in length—she has now 466 miles of open line; and the income from the railways is enough to pay the interest on the public debt of £8,020,000, incurred mostly in remunerative public works. More than that, the railways last year contributed £208,271 in reduction of taxation. These railways must yet become a valuable property and remain a perennial source of income to the growing colony. With nearly 800,000 acres of land under cultivation, it is a matter of surprise that Natal should have to import such quantities of preserved and frozen provisions, as well as grain and flour. Something must be wanting in its agricultural development, but that fault can and doubtless will be mended. And as to its coal, it seems to have a great future. Of course the quality varies; but there is excellent household coal, and that for steam purposes is only 10 to 15 per cent. worse than the best Welsh. It is already a thriving trade, and as new seams of coal are being discovered its steady expansion is inevitable. The steam coal can be supplied for £1, where the Welsh article would cost 40s. Durban, a city and port reclaimed from the sea sand, has already become a coaling station for the mercantile marine, and will probably soon become a naval coaling station as well. With fairly careful administration, and a rigid determination to keep down the debt, except when incurred for remunerative necessities, Natal's future seems the brightest among any of the South African States. There is no race-trouble as yet. Though there are 700,000 Kaffirs in the colony, they seem quiet and contented; and with 60,000 Europeans, and only 5,000 Dutch, there seems no reason to dread racial differences.

Company Cobbling.

For manipulation of assets we presume no one can beat the board of a mining development company. One of these concerns with the accompanying area of mining claims, grazing land, and water rights has only to spend a few thousands, perhaps hundreds, in opening out a likely or unlikely reef, and, presto! they can claim to have an asset worth £100,000, £200,000, or just what valuation the board likes to put upon it. The shares of this newly-born babe may be peddled out to the public, distributed to the shareholders as a bonus, or retained in the treasury—an American phrase this—in order to add to the beauty of the balance-sheet. If gold could only be won as easily as companies can be manufactured, the race of mining millionaires would be greatly extended.

And the production of companies in this manner

serves a good many ends. Take for instance Willoughby's Consols, which owns 4,451 gold mining claims, 554,000 acres of land, 206 building sites in Bulawayo, Umtali, and Victoria, besides interests in the Zambesi and Tuli coalfields. The issued capital of this huge conglomerate is £813,960, and, needless to say, since the company was formed in 1894 no dividend has been paid. But some little time back the directors took 217 mining claims, and out of them formed two fresh companies—the Bonsor and the Dunraven—with an aggregate capital of £340,000. This capital was all paper, and of course the shareholders in the Willoughby's Consols possessed nothing more by the formation of these two companies than they did before. But the board had now fresh divisible entities which could perhaps be rendered vendable, and so it magnanimously distributes to the shareholders one share in each of these two companies to every holder of twenty-five shares in Willoughby's Consols. The value of these bits of paper is problematical, but on face value it represents a bonus of 8 per cent., and of course takes away from the parent company the stain of paying no dividend. This nicely sugared bolus, however, contains, as usually is the case, an unpleasant core in the shape of a further issue of shares by the two embryonic companies, which the shareholders are asked to subscribe at par. The sum of £20,000 in each case is proposed to be issued, so that by distributing 64,000 fully paid shares "for nothing," it is hoped to obtain £40,000 in cash from the shareholders on the other shares to be paid for. It is far better from the board point of view to do this than to say that Willoughby's Consols wanted to raise £40,000 more capital, and after all it does not cost much to print a few additional nicely decorated certificates. To an outsider the operation is very much akin to the proceeding of the Irishman who lengthened a garment by cutting a piece off the top and sewing it on the bottom. But then latter-day finance is very much of this pattern. And who knows but what good may come of it? At present the maxim is, "If you want gold manufacture shares." Some day it may come to be, "If you want to lose gold buy shares."

THE GERMAN SUGAR TRADE.

With the help of bounties and other things the sugar trade of Germany seems to be rapidly losing the elasticity and expansion which at one time characterised it. According to our Consul at Stettin, beet growing is one of the few German industries that did not participate last year in the economic progress so noticeable in the country, and no branch of trade had to fight for its existence so strenuously as the sugar business. This struggle still continues; and Mr. Powell, our consul, thinks that it was only the general prosperity of German commerce that prevented the industry from failing completely. This is a serious statement, and a very striking indication that the bounty system weakens rather than strengthens industry. To what is the falling off said to be attributable? The total production of sugar in Germany last year was over 180,000 tons more than in the previous year, but it is significant that the quantity exported was 280,000 tons above that of the year before. While the home trade is diminishing greatly, the export business is steadily increasing. That, of course, is the result of the bounty system, as the bonus is only paid on exported sugar. But other damaging influences have been at work. These are the new Bourse law and the prohibition of time bargains. These latter have been forbidden by the German legislature because of their gambling character. But really, there is very little, if any, of the gamble about them. If a trader agrees to sell wheat, say, or sugar, or any other commodity, at a certain price three months hence, it is because he has satisfied himself, by calculations of the crop prospects and otherwise, that he can do so without loss, and probably with considerable gain. The element of chance scarcely enters into it at all. No trader or manufacturer can omit a careful consideration of the possible future course of the markets; and, though he may make no "time bargains," his care and shrewdness in making calculations as to the prospective values of the materials he uses form an important element in his success in business. The prohibition of time bargains has, Mr. Powell assures us, driven German capitalists from the sugar markets, which have fallen largely into the hands of foreigners, who are thus able to keep prices down. Over-production, uncertainty in regard to the Cuba crops, and the new United States tariff, which not only raised the duty, but imposed a differential duty on sugar from countries which granted export bounties, also seriously affected the industry in Germany. The trade is clearly in a bad way in spite of the bounties, whose only real use has been to show their utter worthlessness, or worse, as a protection to industry. It now, however, seems doubtful if the Brussels Conference, which opened on Tuesday, will result in the abolition of the bounties. The French cling to the "secret bounties," and Austrians and Hungarians declare they cannot renounce preference bounties in consequence of German competition. Then some Germans oppose abolition on the ground that it would render the competition of cane sugar more formidable. How strangely do people, otherwise sagacious and shrewd, cling to the most obvious fallacies, even when the mischief they are doing is made manifest by the injury wrought on the "protected" trade.

THE GUARDIAN FIRE AND LIFE INSURANCE COMPANY.

In dealing with this company's annual report we remarked last week that it was only its wealth which prevented it from feeling the smart of heavy fire losses more than it does. In this remark we were not quite accurate. Looking back for the last six or seven years we find that the company has suffered a great deal and has to all appearances drifted into a position where its wealth cannot quite save its shareholders from greater disappointments than they have yet experienced. Take a few figures as an example. In 1891 the fire business resulted in a loss of nearly 2 per cent., in 1892 in a loss of over 4 per cent., and in 1893 in a loss of 2·3 per cent. The next three years, 1894-5-6, show gains of 5·8 per cent., 11·6 per cent. and 5·9 per cent. respectively; but last year again resulted in a loss of 4·1 per cent. For the whole seven years, therefore, the company has been more or less slipping backwards, the profit on 1895 alone being in any degree approximate to what the company should enjoy as an average minimum. No wonder that its dividend has had to be reduced, or that its business, allowing even for the lopping off of the American part of it, should be on the decline. In 1890 the premium income was £579,000. Last year it was only £342,000, and in the same time the fire fund has fallen from £761,000 to £633,000. It fell off £43,000 last year, and in the circumstances we think that the payment of the dividend, which took £80,000, was hardly justified by the record. The company will have to brace itself up and mend its ways if it is not to be distanced in the race by stronger and better-managed concerns.

THE SOUTH WALES STRIKE.

The industrial contest in South Wales seems at present further from settlement than ever. The men's delegates received plenary powers for concluding an arrangement, but they presented demands to the employers which they knew could not be accepted. They asked for an immediate 10 per cent. advance, which the employers have from the first declared their inability to grant. There was no hint at modification, or to the possibility of accepting less. They complain of the want of a conciliatory spirit in the employers; but in what have the colliers shown conciliation? They began the war without funds, without organisation; and yet they now seek rather to dictate terms than invite discussion. Besides the 10 per cent. advance, the men asked for a conciliation or wages board, with an umpire to come in and take the decision out of the hands of the board when the delegates forming it could not agree. Now this, too, the employers had emphatically declared their inability to accept, and the workmen's delegates must have known that in presenting these demands they were merely taking measures for the prolongation of the strike. If that was their object they seem to have completely attained it. Yet every week but increases the sacrifices of the men, not to mention the employers or the trade of the district, which is suffering all round. Business in Cardiff is at a standstill. It will take many months, perhaps years, to recover from the blow struck by this strike at trade. The local railways up to May 28 had lost by diminution of traffic alone £146,000; but if we remember that, previous to the strike, the returns of these companies were weekly increasing, the actual loss to them may be reckoned at a considerably higher figure. The Great Western has also been a loser of over £60,000. This must all tell seriously on the dividends of these companies. Of course, in other districts coal-owners and colliers are both reaping a rich harvest by the enforced idleness and stagnation in South Wales. Is it not about time that Welsh colliers were considering these things, and asking themselves whether it was not time that they should give some indication of a spirit of conciliation and compromise? They cannot gain by delay; they only make a settlement more difficult and less satisfactory for themselves.

British Business Methods.

So much has been said in consular reports for some time on the want of adaptability and push among British merchants in their foreign trade, that we welcome the enterprise of a news agency in trying to get the views of British merchants themselves on the matter. But we can hardly say that the result, so far, has been entirely satisfactory. It is said that considerable friction exists between British consuls and British merchants—which seems to imply a serious charge against the consuls of being actuated, to some extent, by personal feelings in drawing up their reports. That, however, is a matter which might be cleared up and remedied by a little exertion on the part of the Foreign Office. If such friction does exist a remedy ought to be sought for. It is the opinion of one merchant that Continental traders are ready to undertake risks which no English exporter would incur, and that German trade, if apparently expanding, is not flourishing, because heavy losses have been incurred in consequence of the cheap and risky business done abroad. If that be so, then German travellers are much less shrewd than they ought to be. Still another merchant who was interviewed, however, admitted that a little spurring was required, that English travellers were not good linguists, but that British merchants have really as much trade as they can manage. This last remark points the moral of many a consular criticism. It seems to account in some measure for the want of push, for the want of care in studying markets, indifferent packing, and the absence of trade circulars in the language and currency system of those to whom they are addressed. The careless confidence implied in the assurance that the British merchant has really as much trade as he can manage virtually leaves the door open to more wideawake competitors, who move energetically, know the wants of their customers, and adapt themselves to their ways. If German traders have lost by bad or risky debts, it will teach them greater care and discrimination in the future. They have already shown a considerable capacity for learning from experience, but the English trader, with his confident assurance of having as much trade as he can manage, may soon find that he is losing that which he has for want of freer and more intelligent intercourse with his customers. If our foreign trade is ample and good, it will not continue so unless carefully tended. There is danger of loss from over-confidence as well as from want of discrimination in undertaking risks.

Chinese Liberality and Eccentricity.

The Government of China has lost no time in conceding the demands of France for "compensation" for the murder of Père Berthollet, the Catholic missionary. The condemnation of the culprits, or some who may pass for culprits, the punishment of the authorities, an indemnity of 100,000 francs, the erection of a commemorative church on the spot where the murder was committed, and the concession for a railway line connecting the treaty port of Pak-hoi, in the province of Kwang-tung with the valley of the West River at Nanning-fu. These were the French demands, and the Tsung-li-Yamen has conceded every one of them. They were highly practical. The Church is benefited, the French nation is benefited, and the representatives of the murdered priest, if any are alive, will doubtless get their share of the 100,000 francs. But what does China think of it all? The Tsung-li-Yamen may well be getting tired of saying "Yes" because they dare not say "No." May there, therefore, be truth in the story current that the Emperor has consented to flee from Peking, and set up his household gods in the far-off capital of Shen-si, So-gan-fu. It is not impossible. This city was the capital of China before the Manchus made their appearance there. It is situated on the banks of a river which, though 2,500 miles in length, is wholly unnavigable. It is 600 miles from Peking, and can only be reached by caravan. No battleship can approach it. The "mailed fist" might be shown in vain once the Emperor were safely ensconced at So-gan-fu. Ambassadors would be useless. As in Chitral, we might spend loads of money in making roads to get troops to So-gan-fu. But if that were done, the Emperor might come to the resolution to slip over the frontier into Tibet, which is close at hand. Certainly this "flitting" to So-gan-fu, if really resolved upon, would practically mean the forsaking of the country to the tender mercies of the European Powers. But perhaps his Majesty the Emperor thinks it just as well that these Powers should take what they want as that he should have, every other week, to go through the painful, if somewhat farcical, formality of graciously granting concessions or drawing up "leases." It is altogether a queer story, and probably it would be as well to wait for official confirmation before pinning our faith to its accuracy.

Our Trade with Switzerland.

While our exports to Switzerland during the past year ran up in value to two millions sterling, we received from her in exchange nearly six millions. Not a very promising kind of speculation. The worst of it is that the disproportion seems permanent. Germany, on the other hand, sends Switzerland twelve millions, and receives in return only seven millions, a very substantial and paying account for Germany. Though the Swiss finances are in a sound condition, and the expenditure is prudently restrained, Switzerland has her financial worries. She proposed the conversion of her 1887 loan, bearing 3½ per cent. interest, into one issued at par, and carrying only 3 per cent. interest. But the operation did not succeed, not more than half the amount having been taken up. This was a great surprise and disappointment. There seemed no competent cause for it, though in some quarters it was attributed to the policy of nationalising the railways, and the apprehension of the public as regards the £40,000,000 required for that operation. Another matter which is somewhat troubling Swiss traders is the possible ultimate result of the denunciation of the British treaties with Germany and Belgium, as there is no guarantee in the future in regard to the treatment of Swiss goods in the British colonies. Switzerland must lose her present assured position under the terms of her treaty of 1855 with Great Britain, while Canada will be placed in a better position to compete with European countries. What if Canada in her new and improved position were to enter into competition with Switzerland in the condensed milk trade? She might easily do it, and the Swiss dairy farmers could not well afford the loss of British custom for this commodity. Switzerland may well, in the circumstances, feel some alarm; and, according to the report from the British Legation, in which the state of Swiss trade in 1897 is discussed, "more liberal terms for British goods may, it is hoped, result from the readjustment entailed by the present policy of Great Britain."

Critical Index to New Investments.

CITY OF AMSTERDAM THREE PER CENT. BONDS.

Lloyds Bank are authorised to receive subscriptions for an issue of about £1,433,333 bonds at 95¾ per cent., which includes 3 per cent. interest from April 1. The loan is raised for the purchase by the city from the Imperial Continental Gas Association of the existing gas works and undertaking in Amstersdam, the income from which, judging from past years, will be sufficient to provide a surplus towards the municipal revenues beyond the amount required for the service of this loan. Existing debt of the city, the population of which is 506,277, is £6,456,200, and the annual ordinary income £1,070,000. The loan is redeemable at par by annual drawings of one-thirtieth part, commencing in 1900, but power is reserved to at any time redeemed it at par. The city pledges all its corporate assets as security for the due payment of the drawn bonds and coupons, both free of taxes. Amsterdam is a wealthy city, and the bonds are well worth the attention of investors satisfied with a yield of 3⅛ per cent.

BOMBAY, BARODA, AND CENTRAL INDIA RAILWAY COMPANY.

Tenders will be received by the company up to noon on Wednesday next for an issue of £400,000 3 per cent. debentures guaranteed by the Secretary of State for India. The minimum price is fixed at par; debentures will be dated July 8, and will run for three, five, or seven years from that date. Interest is payable in sterling, January 8 and July 8.

GREAT NORTHERN AND CITY RAILWAY COMPANY.

Another attempt is made to float this enterprise, the former effort having been in the early part of 1895, when the public did not take at all kindly to it. The share capital is £1,560,000 in £10 shares equally divided into preferred ordinary "A" shares and deferred ordinary "B" shares, the whole of which are offered at par. On the previous occasion the capital was £1,500,000 in one class of share, of which two-thirds only were offered. The board has been strengthened, and now includes Sir Charles Scotter and Sir Allen Sarle, but surely a more practical man could have been obtained than Sir Francis Knollys. The line will be three miles long, and run from Finsbury Park to Moorgate-street, with three intermediate stations. The motive power will be electricity, and both tunnels will be 16 ft. in diameter, thus taking the Great Northern Company's heaviest suburban trains. After the "A" shares have received a dividend in any year of 4 per cent., the "B" shares are to have 5 per cent., remaining profits to be participated in rateably. The Great Northern Railway Company guarantees the new concern a minimum annual payment of £20,000 for traffic carried, while S. Pearson & Sons, Limited, the contractors, guarantee 4 per cent. on the "A" and 3 per cent. on the "B" shares during the period they work the railway, not exceeding three years after opening of the line, which will help it over what may prove its most difficult time. With the continued growth of suburban traffic, and the ever-increasing desire for quicker transport, we should think the line woutd attract sufficient business to make the venture a success. The Great Northern guarantee is less than on the former occasion, but it represents two-thirds of the dividend on the "A" shares, so they at least seem worth the attention of investors.

LEOPOLDINA RAILWAY COMPANY, LIMITED.

This company, which has a share capital of £5,500,000, made up from conversions of old bonds, was formed to consolidate several Brazilian railways, comprising a system of 1,326 miles. It now offers an issue of £1,300,000 4 per cent. debenture stock at 85 per cent., forming part of an aggregate amount which shall not exceed two-thirds of the share capital. Interest due January and July. The stock is a first charge on the property and undertaking and can be redeemed at par after January 1, 1928, on six months' notice. On acquiring possession, the company had to compromise certain preferential claims and arranged to pay £700,000 of 4 per cent. debenture stock, as well as £250,000 in cash, so that apparently only £350,000 is left for repairs and improvements, which it was last year estimated would require £984,000. It is anticipated that when these repairs are completed the debenture stock may reach £2,000,000. Brazilian securities have been out of favour with investors for some time past, in view of the arrangements being made to allow the Government to make an easy default upon its debt, but the stock now offered, yielding almost 4⅝ per cent., and being a first charge on the railway, should prove a satisfactory investment, though, of course, existing bondholders of the railway are wiped out.

KHEDIVIAL MAIL STEAMSHIP AND GRAVING DOCK COMPANY, LIMITED.

Company is formed to buy the steamers, docks, and other properties belonging to the Egyptian Government, and known as the Poste Khedivieh Administration, which has been sold to Messrs. Allen, Alderson, & Co., of Alexandria, and Mr. Frank Reddaway, of Manchester, who are the vendors. The Egyptian Government grants the company an annual subsidy of £6,150 for fifteen years; while the total revenue from ships, docks, and workshops is estimated at £30,525 per annum. The share capital of the company is £300,000, in 40,000 5½ per cent. cumulative preference shares of £5 each, and 100,000 ordinary shares of £1 each. The preference shares are now offered, together with an issue of £100,000 4½ per cent. first mortgage debenture bonds, at par. The latter are redeemable on June 30, 1918 at par, but can be paid off at any time on six months' notice at 110. All the ordinary shares, with £175,000 in cash, go to the vendors as purchase money. Sir Auckland Colvin is chairman, and the board includes Sir John Stokes of the Suez Canal Company. This seems a fair venture, and as the vendors take all the ordinary shares, a moderate investment in the preference shares or debenture bonds should turn out all right.

NEW BRIGHTON TOWER AND RECREATION COMPANY, LIMITED.

The company was formed in 1896, and now owns thirty-six acres of freehold land. Six per cent. preference shares to the amount of £175,000 were then subscribed, and since then £100,000 of 4 per cent. first mortgage debentures have been placed. Subscriptions are now asked for 125,000 £1 ordinary shares at a premium of 5s. each, upon which a dividend of 10 per cent. (exclusive of premium) is guaranteed from June 30 next to September 30, 1901, for the payment of which equivalent funds have been deposited with the bankers. These shares are offered on behalf of the vendors who were entitled to the shares on the transfer of the estate, but preferred to postpone their issue until the undertaking was completed. By their patience they will be rewarded with £31,250 in the shape of premiums if the shares are subscribed, which is very fine interest for two years. The "guarantee" may act as a bait, but it is a venture that may well be left to Brighton, Old and New.

LONDON, YUKON, AND BRITISH COLUMBIAN MINING AND INVESTMENT CORPORATION.

With a share capital of £175,000 in £1 shares, of which 47,000 go to the vendors with £62,000 in cash, this company is formed to carry on the business of a prospecting, exploration, mining, and financial corporation. Prospects are truly magnificent, and some may no doubt be realised as these sort of undertakings generally do pretty well in their early years; the point is not to hold the shares too long.

GEORGE GALE AND COMPANY, LIMITED.

Company was formed in 1888 to take over a brewery and wine and spirit business at Horndean, Southsea, and Newport (Isle of Wight), and the share capital is £75,000. Applications are invited for an issue of £60,000 4 per cent. first mortgage debentures at par. They are redeemable twenty years after allotment at 110 per cent., and are a first mortgage on freehold and leasehold properties valued at £90,400. Profits for last three years, after adding tho saving of rental by purchase of freeholds, are certified at £7,453 in 1895, £6,016 in 1896, and £6,612 in 1897. The business is old established, over forty years, but the security is not particularly fine, and the profit statement does not indicate a very progressive trade. Still there would be a large margin after paying debenture interest, and the debentures may therefore be set down as a fair third-class investment.

GOLDSMITHS' AND SILVERSMITHS' ALLIANCE, LIMITED.

Since the prospectus appeared we have been asked several questions about it. We pointed out last week that the omission of a valuation of the assets was against the company, and this is one of the points inquired about. Would it not be as well for the directors to give some statement showing the value of the stock-in-trade? Is it a fact or not that two of the vendors are owners of a small private concern which is to some extent a rival of this company? We hear that the capital asked has been largely over-subscribed, but it is not too late for a little more information on these points.

Company Reports and Balance-Sheets.

*** *The Editor will be much obliged to the Secretaries of Joint Stock Companies if they would kindly forward copies of Reports and Balance-Sheets direct to the Office of* THE INVESTORS' REVIEW, *Norfolk House, Norfolk-street, W.C., so as to insure prompt notice in these columns.*

EMPIRE OF INDIA AND CEYLON TEA COMPANY.—The profits of this company in 1897 amounted to £30,471, which permitted of a dividend of 9 per cent., as against 10 per cent. a year ago. The balance forward, however, had to be reduced from £429 to £143. In spite of the high dividend the balance-sheet is not particularly good, and the reserve actually was debited with a proportion of the income tax. This is a novelty in company accounts, but shows the ingenuity of a board when pressed, for without the £500 thus obtained, the 9 per cent. dividend would not have been possible. The directors would have done better if they had declared a dividend of 7 per cent., and put the balance to reserve.

BORELLI TEA COMPANY.—Another sufferer from the earthquake. The crop was 92,426 lb. under the estimate, and the net profit only came to £2,901, as against £4,153 a year ago. The directors had, therefore, to reduce the dividend by 1 per cent. to 4 per cent., and then could only carry forward £2,557, or £534 less than a year ago. The company has no reserve, and we presume the heavy cost of renewing and repairing buildings damaged by the earthquake will have to be found from other sources.

KYNOCH, LIMITED.—This blown-out concern has gone into two speculative businesses—that of supplying cycle components and soap and candles—and the balance-sheet does not seem to have improved by the operation. No less than £103,697 is owing to sundry creditors, and there is an advance on mortgage on the mills, while the debtors' item only stands at £98,652. The cash in hand, indeed, was only £329, in order to meet dividends amounting to about £36,000, so that the addition to the capital now proposed seems very necessary. The profits for the year ended April 6 are stated to have been £50,160, which allowed of a 10 per cent. dividend and the carrying forward of £8,444. But stock-in-trade is returned in the balance-sheet at £241,906, and this is a suspicious item when you are dealing with a soap, cycle components, ammunition company. We must see more of this company before being ready to think much of its shares in the present form.

SUN INSURANCE COMPANY.—In 1897 this company received in premiums £1,012,340, being an increase of £42,655. Of this sum losses absorbed £588,296, or 58·11 per cent., and expenses and commission took £343,252, or 33·91 per cent. Including £387,873 brought forward and £78,671 income from investments, and deducting the usual 40 per cent. reserve for unexpired risks, there is a balance of £142,401 carried to profit and loss account, making a total of £270,749. Of this sum the directors have devoted £100,000 to the creation of a special reserve fund to cover the liabilities incurred by retaining large amounts on individual risks, £8,000 has been transferred to the pension account, increasing it to £40,728, and dividends absorb £102,000, leaving a balance of £58,731 to be carried forward. The investments are good and mostly domestic.

THE BRITISH LINEN COMPANY BANK.—This large Scotch bank did not last year come into a windfall of £103,000 as profit on sales of investments, and therefore its net profits were about £84,000 less than those of the previous year. Nevertheless, the outcome was exceedingly satisfactory, and enabled the directors to pay another dividend of 18 per cent. per annum, namely, 8 per cent. at Christmas and 10 per cent. now. A balance of £44,355 was brought in, and after writing £5,000 off cost of bank premises, £66,109 is left to be carried forward. Including the reserve fund of £1,500,000 and the pensions reserve fund of £100,000, created a year ago, the report says that the undivided profits will now amount to £1,666,109. Is this quite accurate? Should not part of the reserve fund be ascribed to the heavy premiums received on recent issues of new shares? In one sense, of course, these premiums are profit, but not in the ordinary sense of money saved out of current earnings. The paid-up capital remains at £1,250,000, and the liabilities of the bank on deposits and current account balances were, at the date of the balance-sheet, April 15 last, £11,981,277. The bank was also liable for £656,229 on acceptances, and its note circulation amounted to £889,809. Among its principal assets are "gold and silver coin, notes of other banks, cash balances with London bankers, and money at call or short notice in London," all put in one heap, which amounts to £1,770,777. This does not strike us as an excessive cash reserve, and does not compare very favourably with similar entries in the balance-sheets of English banks which have no note circulation, but perhaps the call and notice money, which is not cash, is of small account in the total. Besides its cash and credit out at interest, the bank holds about £4,300,000 of fixed investments, all of an improved description. Its bills discounted and advances amounted to £5,781,212, and its short term loans on stocks and other securities to £3,756,498. The securities held against the acceptances balances the amount of them. These are the principle heads of the balance-sheet and we have nothing to say about them. Business appears to be of quite the ordinary character, so much so that the profit-earning capacity of the bank remains something above the common.

NEW ZEALAND TRUST AND LOAN COMPANY.—From the balance-sheet made up to the end of last year the company appears to have in no way improved upon the unsatisfactory position disclosed a year ago. It has £1,206,739 invested on mortgage in New Zealand, against £1,323,000 at the end of 1896, but the admitted contingent loss, which was then £81,467, has only been reduced to £81,441, while the reserve has declined from £128,000 to £124,091, because it has been drawn upon to provide the amount paid to Mr. Hunter upon his retirement, as well as the expenses incurred in connection with calling capital home for the redemption of debentures and the inspector's special visit to this country. Deducting the contingent loss through depreciation in securities, the net reserve is only £42,550, which is a very small margin. The balance-sheet would have looked better if these items had been charged against the year's revenue, but this would have affected the dividend come what may. The net profits for the year, with £1,827 brought forward, were £34,060, which provides the preference dividend and 5 per cent. on the ordinary shares, and leaves £11,560 to be carried forward. But it has been usual to charge the revenue account with provision for the preference dividend six months in advance. This represents £12,500, so it has been done this time. The directors say they have materially reduced expenses, but the full effect is not seen in the present account. The sooner they reduce the dividend on the ordinary shares the sooner will they display wisdom.

Diary of the War.

June 3.—Some details of the cannonade at Santiago de Cuba have been vouchsafed us. American accounts still assert that Commodore Schley engaged in a reconnaissance to discover the strength of the forts and masked batteries at Santiago; that he discovered this by destroying them; and retired without damage. The Spanish Minister of Marine assures us that Admiral Cervera was present at the "battle," and that it was through his superior strategy that the fight was won. The American reports seem most plausible; but it is impossible to ascertain with certainty what did occur.

June 4.—The Cadiz squadron is reported to have sailed, but of course its destination is unknown. It is said that the Americans are preparing to despatch an expedition of 15,000 men to Puertorico under General Sir Fitzhugh Lee. Messages received by Berlin business firms from representatives in Manila state that there is no symptom of insurrection in the town, and that there is a plentiful supply of food from the interior. The natives and the Spanish troops live almost entirely upon rice. The European residents, however, feel the want of various articles of food which can no longer be imported. Commerce and industry are, of course, at a standstill.

June 5.—Another engagement is reported as having taken place at Santiago de Cuba on Friday the 3rd, but the accounts received are very contradictory. What seems to have occurred is that two or three of the American warships fired on the Morro and other forts at Santiago, while a cruiser guided the *Merrimac*, an old Transatlantic trader and coal ship, towards the harbour, the object being to sink the hulk so as to block the entrance. The *Merrimac* would appear to have turned over and sunk sooner than was expected. At any rate, American despatches speak of the event as a "check" to the Navy, though there seems no doubt about the sinking of the *Merrimac*. It was manned by a volunteer crew of eight or ten men, who were drowned according to American accounts, but were taken prisoners according to Spanish despatches. The Spaniards speak of the sunken ship as a cruiser, and claim credit for having sent her to the bottom. The firing from the Spanish forts is said to have greatly improved.

June 6.—For once we have prompt confirmation of a notable action in the present war. Admiral Sampson, in a brief despatch to the Navy Board at Washington, confirms the sinking of the *Merrimac* at Santiago de Cuba, and gives us to understand that the operation was more important and more completely accomplished than seemed indicated in the first accounts. It was conducted by Naval Instructor Hobson and a crew of seven men. So impressed was Admiral Cervera—leaving no doubt now as to his whereabouts—with the bravery of these eight men that he sent an officer with a flag of truce to inform the American Admiral that they had all been saved, and were prisoners of war, two of them having been slightly wounded. Steps were immediately taken to arrange for the exchange of these prisoners for a like number of Spaniards who are prisoners of war at Atlanta. They have certainly succeeded admirably in a very notable achievement. There can be no further doubt that Admiral Cervera is in Santiago with his squadron, and that they are most effectually "bottled up" there by the sinking of the *Merrimac*. And there is the end of Admiral Cervera's magnificent strategy. He has sailed deliberately into a trap of his own seeking. Perhaps he could not help himself. Cruising in the open sea implies a great waste of coal, and perhaps his only hope of getting a new supply was to go to Santiago. Probably, however, he did not at first contemplate being shut up there. But now he and his ships are rendered useless. The *Epoca*, of Madrid, publishes an article reciprocating what it regards as the *New York Herald's* plea for ending the war, but the peace must be secured on "honourable terms" for Spain. It may be noted that the sinking of the *Merrimac* was regarded in Madrid as a Spanish victory. There was great rejoicing in consequence until the real facts were published.

June 7.—Little additional news. Much praise for Lieutenant Hobson, who sank the *Merrimac* at Santiago de Cuba, and for the chivalrous appreciation by Admiral Cervera of the bravery of Lieutenant Hobson and his crew. In Madrid they have now awakened to the fact that the sinking of the *Merrimac* was not a "victory" for Spain; but they take comfort from the statement that the sunken vessel does not entirely block the harbour, and is to be blown up by dynamite. There is a report in Washington that Sir Julian Pauncefote has asked what terms of peace the United States would grant to Spain; and the reply was that the Spaniards must evacuate Cuba, and give the United States Puertorico in lieu of a war indemnity. On these conditions the Philippine Islands would be restored to Spain.

June 8.—News of another attack on the forts at Santiago de Cuba, which the Americans claim to have completely demolished. Morro Castle is described as a heap of ruins. While the bombardment was in progress—it was stopped, by the way, while the American seamen went to dinner—it was observed that the *Reina Mercedes* was trying to blow up the sunken *Merrimac*, and so to clear the harbour entrance; but a shell from the attacking fleet hit the *Reina Mercedes* so hard that she had to be abandoned where she lay. It seems also that an American force landed, and, in conjunction with the insurgents, made an attack on the fortifications from the land side. The fact of the landing is indirectly confirmed by Admiral Cervera's despatch, which states that the Spanish troops lost three officers killed, and one wounded, while seventeen soldiers were wounded. A Havana despatch states that a landing was attempted, but was repulsed. There has been considerable fighting in Manila between the rebels and the Spanish troops, in which the advantage remained with the former. Their leader is said to have declared himself confident of taking the city, and proposes to set up a government under an American protectorate. Spain still writes and speaks of peace, but takes no step in that direction herself. She pleads that the European Powers should come to her rescue.

June 9.—No further definite news as to operations at Santiago de Cuba; but American despatches point out that these operations were not undertaken for the purpose of taking the town, or to force an entrance to the harbour. They were entered upon as a sort of practice for the fleet, and for testing the strength of the Spanish batteries. In this respect they are regarded as having been perfectly successful. The Spaniards still insist that the Americans were "repulsed," but admit greater damage to the defences than Admiral Sampson seems to have realised. The Spanish Captain-General of Manila describes the situation there as very serious. The revolt is described as general. The United States expeditionary force for Santiago de Cuba left Tampa on Wednesday, and may reach its destination some time to-night or to-morrow. If so, we may look immediately for the delivery of the real attack on Santiago, and so for the first big engagement of this somewhat dilatory war.

THE PROPERTY MARKET.

Last week's total of sales at the Mart was low, £86,680, as compared with the corresponding period of last year, £129,745; but that is accounted for by the holidays and by the smaller character of the investments offered. The returns for the month of May were £1,594,905, as compared with £1,258,694 last year. The most notable sale at the Mart last Friday was that of Messrs. Newbon, Edwards, & Shephard, including a number of leasehold houses and shops and freehold building land at Tottenham, known as the Russell Estate, which produced the fine total of £26,890. Messrs. Protheroe & Morris, Messrs. Dowsett, Knight, & Co., and Messrs. Cronk added fair quotas to the day's total of £37,741.

Monday's business at the Mart did not begin the week well. The total of the day's sales amounted to £19,586; and of the twenty-one lots offered, nine were returned unsold. Only three of the lots sold went into four figures. Of these, two improved rentals under perpetual Corporation leases, arising from the "Clarendon" public-house, Oxford-street, and shop property adjoining, offered by Mr. W. Rolfe, produced £14,300—the former bringing £7,900, and the latter £6,400. Mr. Alfred Richards obtained a total of £4,396 for various gas and water shares.

Several properties of some importance offered at the Mart on Tuesday had to be withdrawn. Among these was the Hafod-y-Bryn, belonging to Mr. S. Pope, Q.C. Icklington Hall Estate, Mildenhall, Suffolk, comprising 5,000 acres, offered by Messrs. Walton & Lee, was withdrawn at the moderate price of £35,500, and a freehold building estate of forty-three acres, at Upper Tooting, offered by the same firm, was also withdrawn at the somewhat high figure of £56,000. Wray Castle, however, on the banks of Lake Windermere, was disposed of for £25,000. As it was stated that £60,000 had been expended on the castle alone, and that there are 800 acres of land attached to it, the price can hardly be described as extravagant. Messrs. Ellis & Son sold freehold offices at 21, Water-lane, City, covering an area of 530 square feet, and let on lease at £120 per annum, at £2,830. The same firm disposed of the business premises, 47, Eastcheap, leasehold for a term of sixty-four years at £80 ground rent, for £2,000. A freehold residence known as Fox Hall, in Baker-street, Enfield, with about two and a half acres of land, submitted by Mr. Alfred Richards, changed hands at £3,025. The total for the day reached £49,500. At the Masons' Hall Tavern the licensed house, the Crown, High-street, Kensington, was sold for £35,000.

The results of Wednesday's business at the Mart only totalled £23,755, but the attendance was fair, and the competition good. Messrs. Douglas, Young, & Co. top the list with an aggregate of £10,420, their principal lot being a block of freehold building land in High-road, Ilford, which realised £5,250. Another consisted of leasehold houses in Westbourne-grove, and brought in £2,010. Messrs. Edwin Fox & Bousfield's sale of stocks and shares attracted a good many visitors.

A very important sale of landed estate has just been accomplished by Messrs. Millar, Son, & Co., Grafton-street, Bond-street, W. It is that of the domain known as Gregynog, Newtown, Montgomery. It is residential, sporting, and agricultural, comprising over 1,800 acres. The mansion is a fine building in the Early English style, and there are 195 farms on the estate, with about fifty cottages. The price obtained for it is said to be satisfactory, though the amount is not given.

TRADE AND PRODUCE.

Reports from trade centres are just a little "mixed." They are not exactly discouraging as a rule, and in some cases—as in shipbuilding—they are confidant, buoyant, and hopeful; but suggestions crop up here and there as to some checking influence, ill-defined, and not very palpable. It may be only the influence of the Whitsun holidays that has not yet exhausted itself. These holidays prolong themselves unduly in some trade centres, as they have a habit of doing in the House of Commons. We merely note the hints and suggestions. We do not think they point to any serious slackening in trade. The dulness in the wheat markets continues. There was quite a feeling of depression in Mark-lane on Wednesday, and dealers offered wheat and flour at a shilling reduction from previous market; but even at this decline, comparatively little business was done. The unsettled and somewhat gloomy feeling was somewhat intensified by a report that one of the most respected Mark-lane houses was in difficulties. The dulness has also characterised the English provincial markets, where there was a fall of from two to three shillings on the week. Futures fluctuated a good deal, but the tendency was lower; and so it was with options, until Wednesday at all events, when there was a slight upward reaction, though it was not strongly maintained. We are still disposed to think that there will be some further decline, though probably not to a very serious extent. It will be some time before we come near the figures of a year ago. New crop reports from America continue favourable. The harvest is almost general in the Western States, and some parcels of new wheat from Texas have already appeared in the New York market. As to supplies for the immediate future, those from America seem still large. More may be expected from Russia, and India is still exporting pretty liberally. Stocks of English wheat are getting low; but harvest prospects are considered very good, especially should June prove warm, and favour us with a little more sunshine than he has hitherto done.

The Irish linen trade is in a critical condition. Several houses in and about Belfast have collapsed, with liabilities estimated in some quarters as high as £750,000, and very moderate hopes are entertained as to the realisations. Five shillings in the pound is about the highest figure stated. The more substantial Ulster houses have weathered the storm pretty successfully; but business, they assert, has been thoroughly demoralised, and these better houses have suffered indirectly in their returns from being unable to sell unless they entered into competition with a class who had nothing of their own to lose. Considerable quantities of goods have been disposed of in London and Manchester, agents freely admitting that they were instructed to sell in order to secure funds to stave off the evil day.

Metals are still active, and trade prospects are good. Copper has suffered reverses, though there is an undertone of firmness, and on Wednesday prices rather improved. There is, however, some uncertainty, not to say uneasiness, as to what Spain may do in the way of imposing war duties, and no real improvement in prices can be looked for just now. The latest quotations for copper are £51 3s. 9d. three months, and £50 17s. 8d. cash. The iron and steel trades show moderate activity. Sheffield steel works and cast steel makers are busy with good Continental orders, but new ones are coming rather sparingly. In Glasgow steel-makers cannot deliver material fast enough; so busy are they that they were obliged to decline tendering for a large quantity of plates for a foreign Government. There is great firmness in hematite pig-iron. New labour troubles are threatened. The Glasgow malleable iron makers are very busy, but there is some danger that work may be stopped by a strike. It is in the coal industry, however, that the greatest danger lurks. The Welsh strike seems to have been prolonged indefinitely. Negociations have been entirely suspended. Members of the Miners' Federation are at present taking a ballot as to the propriety of lodging a demand for 10s. advance in wages. The result will be known in the beginning of next week; and if the demand is made, the chances are the mine-owners will refuse to concede the advance. In that case there would probably be another strike—a calamity that would prove very disastrous in the present condition of trade.

In a review of the tea trade during the past year, to May 31, Messrs. W. J. & H. Thompson utter some useful words of warning to growers in India and Ceylon. Messrs. Thompson urge these growers to modify the policy of making the heaviest crops possible, irrespective of quality. China may yet again become a competitor, especially if the superior character of the Indian and Ceylon teas is not sustained. Messrs. Thompson, therefore, think the truest wisdom of the growers is not to work for heavier crops, but to pay the closest attention to improvement in quality. Thus only can they maintain the lead they have secured in the tea market. Very sound advice, indeed, and, if the Indian and Ceylon tea-growers do not take it to heart, they may live to rue it.

The Paris *Coulisse* credit establishments have resolved on emigrating to Brussels. About a hundred million francs have been subscribed as a guarantee fund.

Notice to Subscribers.

Complaints are continually reaching us that the Investors' Review cannot be obtained at this and the other railway bookstall, that it does not reach Scotch and Irish cities till Monday, and that it is not delivered in the City till Saturday morning.

We publish on Friday in time for the Review to be at all Metropolitan bookstalls by at latest 4 p.m., and we believe that it is there then, having no doubt that Messrs. W. H. Smith & Son do their best, but they have such a mass of papers to handle every day that a fresh one may well look almost like a personal enemy and be kept in short supply unless the reading public shows unmistakably that it is wanted. A little perseverance, therefore, in asking for the Investors' Review is all that should be required to remedy this defect.

All London newsagents can be in a position to distribute the paper on Friday afternoon if they please, and here also the only remedy is for subscribers to insist upon having it as soon as published. Arrangements have been made that all our direct City subscribers shall have their copies before 4 p.m. on Friday. As for the provinces, we can only say that the paper is delivered to the forwarding agents in ample time to be in every English and Scotch town, and in Dublin and Belfast, likewise, early on Saturday morning. Those despatched by post from this office can be delivered by the first London mail on Saturday in every part of the United Kingdom.

ADVERTISEMENTS.

All Advertisements are received subject to approval, and should be sent in not later than 5 p.m. on Thursdays.

The advertisements of American Life Insurance Offices are rigorously excluded from the Investors' Review, and have been so since it commenced as a Quarterly Magazine in 1892.

For tariff and particulars of positions open apply to the Advertisement Manager, Norfolk House, Norfolk-street, W.C.

NOTICES.

THE STOCK EXCHANGE.—NOTICE.

NO MEMBER OF THE STOCK EXCHANGE is ALLOWED to ADVERTISE for business purposes, or to issue circulars to persons other than his own principals.

Persons who advertise as Brokers or Share Dealers are not Members of The Stock Exchange, or under the control of the Committee.

A List of Members of The Stock Exchange who are Stock and Share Brokers may be seen at the Bartholomew-lane entrance of the Bank of England, or obtained on application to EDWARD SATTERTHWAITE,
Secretary to the Committee of the Stock Exchange.

Committee Room, The Stock Exchange, London, E.C.

ABRIDGED PROSPECTUS.

The LIST will be OPENED on MONDAY, June 13th, and CLOSED at or before 4 p.m. on TUESDAY, the 14th.

CITY OF AMSTERDAM THREE PER CENT. BONDS.

ISSUE of Fl.17,200,000 (about £1,433,333).

LLOYDS BANK LIMITED, London (in conjunction with Messrs. Lippmann, Rosenthal & Co., Amsterdam), are authorised to RECEIVE SUBSCRIPTIONS for the above BONDS at £95 15s. per Fl.1,200 (£100 nominal), which includes interest at 3 per cent. from the 1st April.

Payable—£5 0 0 on Application.
£40 15 0 on Allotment.
£50 0 0 on 11th July.

Payment in full may be made on allotment under discount at the rate of 3 per cent. per annum.

The Loan is redeemable at par by means of annual drawings of one-thirtieth part of the whole Loan, to commence in 1900, and to take place in August of every succeeding year until the whole Loan is redeemed.

The object of the Loan is to provide funds for the purchase by the City from the Imperial Continental Gas Association of the existing gas works and undertaking in Amsterdam; the income arising from which, judging from the results of past years, will be sufficient to provide a substantial surplus towards the municipal revenues beyond the amount required for the service of this Loan.

The existing debt of the City of Amsterdam, the population of which on the 1st of April, 1898, was 506,775, is Fl.77,474,400 (say £6,456,200), and the annual ordinary income of the City is about Fl.12,840,000 (say £1,070,000).

The Bonds will be to bearer in the following amounts—

Fl.12,000	Equivalent at the exchange of 12 Fl. to the £, at which Dutch issues are quoted on the London Stock Exchange.	£1,000 0 0
6,000		500 0 0
1,200		100 0 0
1,000		83 6 8
100		8 6 8

bearing Coupons due 1st April and 1st October. The Coupon due 1st October, 1898, will be for a full six months' Dividend.

Coupons will be payable at the Counting House of Messrs. Lippmann, Rosenthal & Co., and at the Nederlandsche Bank, Amsterdam, or will be negotiable at Lloyds Bank Limited, 72, Lombard-street, London, at the exchange of the day, but in any case at a rate not less favourable to the holder than Fl.12.15 per £.

Application will be made to the London Stock Exchange for a settlement and quotation in due course.

Full Prospectuses can be obtained from Lloyds Bank Limited, 72, Lombard-street, or any of the Branches of the Bank; and from Messrs. Hichens, Harrison & Co., 41, Threadneedle-street, or Messrs. Steer, Lawford & Co., 3, Drapers'-gardens.

THE UNION DISCOUNT COMPANY OF LONDON, LIMITED.

Capital Subscribed	£1,300,000
Paid-up	650,000
Reserve Fund	250,000

NOTICE IS HEREBY GIVEN that the Rates of Interest allowed on money on deposit are this day Reduced, as follows:—At call to One per cent.; at Seven and Fourteen days' notice to One-and-a-Quarter per cent. The Company discounts approved bank and mercantile acceptances, receives money on deposit at rates advertised from time to time in the London daily papers, and grants loans on approved negotiable securities.

39, Cornhill, 9th June, 1898. CHRISTOPHER R. NUGENT, Manager.

To Correspondents.

The Editor cannot undertake to return rejected communications.

Letters from correspondents must, in every case, be authenticated by the name and address of the writer.

Telegraphic Address: "Unveiling, London."

The Investors' Review.

The Week's Money Market.

A further sharp decline has taken place this week in rates for short loans. The large sum released by the Japanese Government, and the continued influx of gold, combine to render market balances available for lending more and more plentiful. With a diminishing foreign trade and less speculative activity in the stock markets, the difficulty of employing the sums placed at the disposal of dealers in money becomes aggravated, so that day to day loans now command in the afternoons, no more than ½ per cent., while the all-day rate is no better than ¾ per cent., as against 1½ per cent. a week ago. The India Council has had to further reduce its terms and now obtains a mere 1¼ per cent. for its advances until the end of the month. Although the Bank rate was left at 3 per cent. yesterday, the discount houses have reduced their allowances for money on deposit by ½ per cent. to 1 per cent. for "call," and 1¼ per cent. for "notice." and had no choice but to do so.

Discount rates have also dropped steadily each day, and the "fine" rate for three months' remitted paper is no better than 1 5/16 to 1⅜ per cent., as compared with about 1⅞ per cent. a week ago. The Continental demand for gold has not proved sufficiently pressing to outbid India, which has taken the bulk of the metal arriving during the week. This outflow to the East is becoming a feature that will need watching. Whether it be the result of the currency policy of the Indian Government or not, the purchases of the yellow metal by India, compared with the old favourite silver, have for some time past been becoming relatively more important than they used to be. This has happened in spite of the fact that much of the silver imported into India is really taken there for coinage at the Bombay Mint, in order to be sent to the Straits Settlements.

If the Indian hoarder, or the dealer in the bazaars, is turning to gold instead of silver, the change may play an important part in the developments of our money market. Be this as it may, gold has been steadily bought for India this week at about 77s. 10½d. per ounce, a price above what the Continent could afford to pay. The arrivals of sovereigns, however, and the return of cash from circulation led to a favourable Bank return; but this has not been followed by a further decline in the Bank rate, the Directors evidently considering that they had moved quite rapidly enough in reducing their minimum two weeks running. Unless something meanwhile happens, a reduction to 2½ or 2 per cent. next Thursday seems inevitable. The American exchange tends to rise rather than decline, and without a demand from that quarter, the weakness in our market is likely to make further progress.

The Stock Exchange settlement showed that less stock was being carried there than ever, and although 2½ per cent. was as a rule asked for loans for the fortnight, a good deal of business was done at 2¼ per cent. An issue of £385,000 two and three-quarter per cent. stock by the Plymouth Corporation was poorly received. Only £441,200 was applied for, and the average price of £98 3s. 8d. was no more than 3s. 8d. above the minimum. This was quite what we expected, municipal loans having fallen a little out of favour of late.

The temporary nature of the dip in the reserve of the

Banking Department last week was demonstrated by the figures in yesterday's Bank return. They show an increase of £1,290,000 in this reserve, which now stands at £27,336,000. Gold to the value of £406,000 only came in from abroad, but it was supplemented by £565,000 in coin, and £318,000 in notes returned from the internal circulation. Money to the amount of £869,000 has also been released by the Treasury and Government Departments bringing "public" deposits down to £10,911,000, and as the market had nothing more to pay off at the Bank all these sums have gone to augment the "other" deposits, which have increased £2,148,000 to £44,554,000, a total that sufficiently accounts for the depressed and limp condition of the credit market; the more so as the agents of the Japanese Government continue ready lenders of its balances. Yesterday the Bank lost £597,000 net in gold exported.

SILVER.

After rising to 27½d. per ounce at the end of last week, the price of bar silver for immediate delivery fell back on Tuesday to 27d. per ounce, owing to a cessation in the demand for Spain. The next day orders again came in from that quarter, and the quotation has risen to 27½d. per ounce. The sudden weakness on this temporary falling off in a special demand shows how dependent the market is upon this extraneous source of support, and although the continued run for cash upon the Bank of Spain may at times cause Spanish buying to become more urgent, the inevitable result of the run cannot be far distant, a result which would stop the bank's power to buy most summarily. At the same time, there has been a certain amount of "bear" selling for forward dates which should act as some sort of a protection to the market against the loss of Spanish orders in the near future. The "forward" quotation is almost nominal at 26½d. per ounce. Indian exchanges at one time were weak, coming at 1s. 3¼d., but hardened up again when it was found that the India Council refused to allot transfers below 1s. 4d. Chinese rates have moved up to a moderate extent, but they are well below the quotations at which silver could be taken at a profit.

BANK OF ENGLAND.

AN ACCOUNT pursuant to the Act 7 and 8 Vict., cap. 32, for the Week ending on Wednesday, June 8, 1898.

ISSUE DEPARTMENT.

	£		£
Notes Issued	52,341,525	Government Debt	11,015,100
		Other Securities	5,784,900
		Gold Coin and Bullion	35,541,525
		Silver Bullion	—
	£52,341,525		£52,341,525

BANKING DEPARTMENT.

	£		£
Proprietors' Capital	14,553,000	Government Securities	13,306,642
Rest	3,163,070	Other Securities	32,647,542
Public Deposits (including Exchequer, Savings Banks, Commissioners of National Debt, and Dividend Accounts)	10,911,226	Notes	24,882,800
Other Deposits	44,553,870	Gold and Silver Coin	2,453,185
Seven Day and other Bills	109,003		
	£73,290,169		£73,290,169

Dated June 9, 1898.

H. G. BOWEN, *Chief Cashier.*

In the following table will be found the movements compared with the previous week, and also the totals for that week and the corresponding return last year:—

Banking Department.

Last Year. June 9.		June 1, 1898.	June 8, 1898.	Increase.	Decrease.
£	Liabilities.	£	£	£	£
3,094,000	Rest	3,160,271	3,163,070	2,799	—
10,898,233	Pub. Deposits	11,780,209	10,911,226	—	868,983
38,883,817	Other do.	42,405,514	41,553,870	2,148,356	—
171,271	7 Day Bills	103,606	109,003	5,397	—
	Assets.			Decrease.	Increase.
13,911,171	Gov. Securities	13,306,642	13,306,642	—	—
28,437,370	Other do.	32,649,685	32,647,542	2,143	—
25,252,200	Total Reserve	26,046,273	27,335,985	—	1,289,712
				2,158,695	2,158,695
				Increase.	Decrease.
£		£	£	£	£
27,359,960	Note Circulation.	27,777,045	27,458,725	—	318,320
50¾ p.c.	Proportion	48 p.c.	49¾ p.c.	—	—
2 "	Bank Rate	3 "	3 "	—	—

Foreign Bullion movement for week £406,000 in.

LONDON BANKERS' CLEARING.

Month of	1898.	1897.	Increase.	Decrease.
	£	£	£	£
January	673,281,000	576,558,000	96,723,000	—
February	648,601,000	597,652,000	50,949,000	—
March	799,520,000	729,970,000	69,550,000	—
April	597,410,000	532,508,000	64,902,000	—
Week ending				
May 4	174,057,000	138,987,000	35,070,000	—
" 11	160,526,000	128,252,000	32,274,000	—
" 18	171,073,000	152,987,000	18,091,000	—
25	131,037,000	116,372,000	14,665,000	—
June 1	155,655,000	166,981,000	—	11,326,000
" 8	139,048,000	111,213,000	27,835,000	—
Total to date	3,561,145,000	3,184,385,000	376,760,000	—

BANK AND DISCOUNT RATES ABROAD.

	Bank Rate.	Altered.	Open Market.
Paris	2	March 14, 1895	1¾
Berlin	4	April 9, 1898	3¾
Hamburg	4	April 9, 1898	3¾
Frankfort	4	April 9, 1898	3¾
Amsterdam	3	April 13, 1897	2½
Brussels	3	April 28, 1896	2¾
Vienna	4	January 22, 1896	3[illegible]
Rome	5	August 27, 1895	3
St. Petersburg	5½	January 23, 1898	5½
Madrid	5	June 17, 1896	5
Lisbon	6	January 25, 1891	6
Stockholm	5	May 18, 1898	4
Copenhagen	4	January 20, 1898	4
Calcutta	10	June 2, 1898	—
Bombay	12	May 5, 1898	—
New York call money	1 to 1½	—	—

NEW YORK ASSOCIATED BANKS (dollar at 4s.).

	June 4, 1898.	May 28, 1898.	May 21, 1898.	June 5, 1897.
	£	£	£	£
Specie	35,100,000	34,772,000	33,880,000	17,862,000
Legal tenders	10,820,000	10,768,000	10,312,000	20,264,000
Loans and discounts	120,324,000	117,946,000	116,306,000	102,384,000
Circulation	2,946,200	2,947,400	2,948,800	2,864,000
Net deposits	141,884,000	139,202,000	136,198,000	116,252,000

Legal reserve is 25 per cent. of net deposits; therefore the total reserve (specie and legal tenders) exceeds this sum by £10,449,000, against an excess last week of £10,739,500.

BANK OF SPAIN (25 pesetas to the £).

	June 4, 1898.	May 28, 1898.	May 21, 1898.	June 5, 1897.
	£	£	£	£
Gold	9,833,520	9,833,520	9,833,520	8,724,680
Silver	4,209,480	4,333,800	4,604,880	10,241,520
Bills discounted	31,387,160	31,047,000	30,132,000	9,422,560
Advances and loans	4,481,520	4,245,800	4,831,340	9,665,160
Notes in circulation	52,551,760	52,206,720	52,373,240	44,016,520
Treasury advances, coupon account	895,840	493,400	469,800	629,640
Treasury balances	1,322,960	824,120	676,440	1,300,840

NATIONAL BANK OF BELGIUM (25 francs to the £).

	June 2, 1898.	May 26, 1898.	May 19, 1898.	June 3, 1897.
	£	£	£	£
Coin and bullion	4,430,400	4,207,440	4,290,400	4,263,000
Other securities	16,489,680	16,397,800	16,267,400	16,274,000
Note circulation	19,144,080	19,407,800	19,332,080	18,403,000
Deposits	3,137,600	2,590,040	2,550,400	3,419,000

IMPERIAL BANK OF GERMANY (20 marks to the £).

	May 31, 1898.	May 23, 1898.	May 14, 1898.	May 29, 1897.
	£	£	£	£
Cash in hand	43,158,850	44,170,500	43,091,550	45,035,000
Bills discounted	34,821,000	33,882,450	35,717,350	*35,[illegible]74,000
Advances on stocks	4,462,650	4,174,350	4,090,[illegible]	—
Note circulation	53,892,300	52,817,400	54,011,800	52,[illegible],000
Public deposits	24,648,850	25,573,400	24,501,350	26,[illegible]

* Includes advances.

AUSTRIAN-HUNGARIAN BANK (1s. 8d. to the florin).

	May 31, 1898.	May 23, 1898.	May 14, 1898.	May 31, 1897.
	£	£	£	£
Gold reserve	29,032,000	29,108,166	29,308,250	28,500,000
Silver reserve	10,474,250	10,468,100	10,434,[illegible]	10,[illegible]74,000
Foreign bills	223,416	231,666	307,[illegible]	—
Advances	1,831,750	1,803,750	1,[illegible]34,700	—
Note circulation	51,622,083	51,435,666	52,573,[illegible]	[illegible]
Bills discounted	13,225,216	12,025,416	13,[illegible]	*11,[illegible]

* Includes advances.

BANK OF FRANCE (25 francs to the £).

	June 9, 1898.	June 2, 1898.	May 27, 1898.	June 10, 1897.
	£	£	£	£
Gold in hand	74,936,520	74,678,480	74,790,160	79,560,000
Silver in hand	49,355,120	49,145,120	49,083,960	49,104,000
Bills discounted	28,043,480	34,409,720	32,872,000	*37,819,000
Advances	15,477,880	15,529,200	15,412,160	—
Note circulation	145,639,880	148,695,320	146,154,600	145,703,000
Public deposits	8,290,400	8,953,840	8,730,880	7,352,000
Private deposits	19,731,800	21,392,880	23,947,240	18,738,000

Proportion between bullion and circulation 85⅜ per cent. against 83½ per cent. a week ago.

* Includes advances.

FOREIGN RATES OF EXCHANGE ON LONDON.

Place.	Usance.	Last week's.	Latest.	Place.	Usance.	Last week's.	Latest.
Paris	chqs.	25'28	25'27	Italy	sight	27'19	27'10
Brussels	chqs.	25'31½	25'29	Do. gold prem.	..	107'40	107'15
Amsterdam	short	12'08	12'06½	Constantinople	3 mths	109'12½	109'15
Berlin	short	20'44	20'44	B. Ayres gd. pm.	..	163'20	163'80
Do.	3 mths	20'33	20'32	Rio de Janeiro	90 dys	7½d.	7⅜d.
Hamburg	3 mths	20'33	20'31	Valparaiso	90 dys	17⅜d.	17$\frac{1}{16}$d.
Frankfort	short	20'44	20'38	Calcutta	T. T.	1/4	1/3$\frac{31}{32}$
Vienna	short	12'04½	12'01½	Bombay	T. T.	1/4$\frac{1}{32}$	1/3$\frac{31}{32}$
St. Petersburg	3 mths	93'80	93'90	Hong Kong	T. T.	1/10⅜	1/10⅜
New York	60 dys	4'83⅞	4'84⅞	Shanghai	T. T.	2/6	2/6⅜
Lisbon	sight	28$\frac{1}{16}$d.	29½d.	Singapore	T. T.	1/10$\frac{11}{16}$	1/10⅝
Madrid	sight	46'25	45'47½				

LONDON COURSE OF EXCHANGE.

Place.	Usance.	May 26.	June 2.	June 9.	June 11.
Amsterdam and Rotterdam	short	12'2	12'2	12'2	12'2
Do. do.	3 months	12'3⅞	12'3⅞	12'3½	12'3½
Antwerp and Brussels	3 months	25'51¼	25'50	25'46¼	25'46¼
Hamburg	3 months	20'66	20'64	20'62	20'60
Berlin and German B. Places	3 months	20'66	20'64	20'62	20'60
Paris	cheques	25'31½	25'30	25'30	25'28¾
Do.	3 months	25'45	25'43¾	25'42½	25'42½
Marseilles	3 months	25'45	25'43¾	25'43¾	25'42½
Switzerland	3 months	25'65	25'62½	25'63¾	25'60
Austria	3 months	12'20	12'20	12'18¾	12'16¼
St. Petersburg	3 months	24$\frac{11}{16}$	24$\frac{11}{16}$	24$\frac{11}{16}$	24$\frac{11}{16}$
Moscow	3 months	24⅝	24⅝	24⅝	24⅝
Italian Bank Places	3 months	27'45	27'50	27'42½	27'37½
New York	60 days	48⅞	48⅞	48$\frac{11}{16}$	48$\frac{11}{16}$
Madrid and Spanish B. P.	3 months	25½	25⅜	25½	nom.
Lisbon	3 months	28⅛	28⅛	28⅞	29½
Oporto	3 months	28⅛	28⅛	28⅞	29½
Copenhagen	3 months	18'44	18'42	18'41	18'40
Christiania	3 months	18'44	18'43	18'42	18'40
Stockholm	3 months	18'46	18'45	18'44	18'43

OPEN MARKET DISCOUNT.

	Per cent.
Thirty and sixty day remitted bills	1⅝—1¾
Three months "	1⅝—1¾
Four months "	1¾—1⅞
Six months "	1⅞—2
Three months fine inland bills	1⅞—2
Four months "	2—2¼
Six months "	2¼—2½

BANK AND DEPOSIT RATES.

	Per cent.
Bank of England minimum discount rate	3
" " short loan rates	—
Banker's rate on deposits	1½
Bill brokers' deposit rate (call)	1
" 7 and 14 days' notice	1½
Current rates for 7 day loans	1
" " for call loans	¾

Stock Market Notes and Comments.

This is account week on the Stock Exchange and consequently it is a week more or less dead as regards new business. In fact, business has not been resumed to any extent since the holidays, and the account to settle is a very small one. That lying ahead of us is what is called a "nineteen day" account, and we may therefore see some lively movements during the rest of this month. It is a tradition, or superstition, on the Stock Exchange that "long accounts," as they are called, always produce either excited speculation in some quarter or nice little messes, or both. There is not much chance of the latter at present, greatly though the market would benefit by a good scouring out of some of the riff-raff element it contains. The only direction in which we see indications of what might be called a large gamble is in United States and Canadian railways. These have been going up in price, with small pauses and set-backs, pretty rapidly for some time back, and now that money has fallen diseasedly cheap, it is more than probable that a combined effort will be made to give outsiders who buy "a good run" for their money. We might infer this for another reason. It appears, as far as we can gather, that much of the recent advance has been the work of speculators on the other side of the Atlantic. Brokers and dealers here tell us that the English public has not yet joined in the gamble to any great extent. Until the other week, at least, people here sold rather than bought, because there is always in the early part of an American railroad boom a tired division of people, who have been holding on to depreciated securities for perhaps years back, until they have become absolutely sick of the phrase "American railroad bond" or share, and are eager to dispose of their property at any loss which is less than the one they had made up their minds to endure.

Looking at the subject in a philosophical spirit, we may say that speculation in American railroad securities, whether United States or Canadian, always follows a regular course from the bottom upwards, and from the top downwards. As a preliminary to the rise, there is always a more or less prolonged time of stagnation and decay, during which scandals multiply, railroad companies pass into the hands of the receivers, bondholders discover that their securities have no value, reorganisations get effected at immense profit to the financiers, and the outlook is most of the time painted in most gloomy colours. During this time prices either sink very low or become altogether shadowy, it being often impossible to deal in a great many stocks at the nominal market quotation or any quotation. As the end of this dark period approaches speculators across the Atlantic begin to buy, and the newspapers commence the publication of reassuring assertions; but this does not go very far until a greater or less number of the roads which were derelict have been reorganised. Then, when in the process of reorganisation a few large capitalists in the United States have acquired possession of immense quantities of bonds and shares at quite frivolous prices, the campaign for the advance begins in solid earnest. Traffic returns become wonderfully good, working expenses phenomenally low, and prophecies of dividends appear, pointing to a coming value on the market for bonds or shares the miserable holders of which had long since been resigned to write off as not worth the paper they were printed on. All the time these favourable symptoms are developing, American speculators buy steadily, until they succeed sometimes in pretty well clearing our European markets of any floating stock, or remains of old ruinous "investments," to be had. As we have said, for a considerable time it is very easy to do this, because of the willingness of sickened holders on this side to part with stuff they had lost so much money by. And for a time the British public looks on indifferent. The business is left to the Stock Exchange itself, or pretty much. Members of that institution may and do share in the preliminary upward movement, and hop out and in as accounts come and go, pocketing what profits they can make out of each other, or out of short-winded operators in Wall-street. But it is all a hollow sort of affair until John Bull rises to the bait, and charges, full bodied, down on the Exchange. When this great change comes, and the British public commences to buy, at first slowly, and with an air if anything indifferent and sceptical, the "boom" has begun. A new multitude, which has not the scars of old wounds to contemplate, seeing prices always advancing, soon learns to entertain the opinion that there "must be something good" in this or the other security after all. From this mere "view, don't y' know," to the possession of a firm, settled conviction that these things are first-class investments well worth buying at the high prices current, is only a week or two, or month or two's time according to circumstances, and soon a roaring, ever-increasing horde dashes into markets, eager to secure the valuable bond or share on which a dividend is about to be, or has been, declared. On this the Americans, whose safes were jammed up with this paper, throw it back to us again at magnificent profits;

and go on their way rejoicing to victories new. Having accomplished this splendid feat, things begin to get bad again, usually, in the United States. Traffic earnings fall off, or a "rate war" breaks out—outcome often of some nefarious concession of low rates to trusts and other trading companies—expenses mount up, and by and bye it is once again discovered that a mysterious "floating debt" has developed itself, without anybody knowing anything about it. At the end of the downward sweep another crop of bankruptcies and reorganisations becomes the proper order of harvesting. At present we are in the comparatively middle region of the upward movement, and the British public has not yet arrived at the full conviction that "Norfolks," "Northern Pacifics," "Atchisons," "Missouries," "Southerns," and "Eries" are the very things to speculate in in order to make fortunes. But they are getting that way, and will soon be stoically staking their money and losing it just as they have always done.

No other market except that for railways is worth wasting two sentences upon. There is a Rhodesian "boom" on the way, we are told. Some mines are going to be furnished with machinery, and there are to be wonderful crushings, with an astonishing amount of ounces to the ton in the early autumn, or as soon as the often-washed-away Bulawayo Railway carries the stamps up. Then "look out for a rise," the market tipsters tell us, and we hope holders of these shares will light upon it and sell when it comes.

The oddest thing about the foreign Government bond section is that some addlepates among us have "gone bulls" of Spanish 4 per cents. "Worth 45," they sapiently aver. Perhaps they mean shillings; perhaps they were "bears" early; perhaps—no, we really cannot guess the motive. But we know these enterprising "Johnnies" will have a mighty time to wait for their profits.

The Week's Stock Markets.

Business remains very quiet on the Stock Exchange, but a little more support has been forthcoming from the general public, owing to the absence of political alarms coupled with the fall in the value of money. The market for United States railroad shares has again been the most active one, being well supported by Wall-street for a time, but profit taking has been the order of the day just towards the close, and prices on the whole show a slight loss on balance. Foreign Government stocks, with one or two exceptions, keep firm, owing to the steadiness of the Continental bourses, and the chief and almost the only feature in the mining market has been the rise in some of the higher-priced Western Australian shares. Consols were exceptionally weak, although the further decline in discount rates increased the demand for investment stocks. Home railway issues, after being let alone for several days, finally hardened, and then again weakened in several instances. The settlement was not by any means troublesome, and rates were of the lightest description.

Highest and Lowest this Year.		Last Carrying over Price.	BRITISH FUNDS, &c.	Closing Price.	Rise or Fall.
113⅛	109¼	—	Consols 2¾ p.c. (Money)...	111⅝	− 1/16
113 5/16	109½	111¾	Do. Account (July 1)	111⅝	− 1/16
106¼	101	105	2½ p.c. Stock red. 1905 ...	105	+ ⅜
363	341	—	Bank of England Stock...	354½	+4½
117	111⅝	114	India 3½ p.c. Stk. red. 1931	113¾	− ½
109¼	103⅝	107	Do. 3 p.c. Stk. red. 1948	106¾	− ¾
96⅝	90	93	Do. 2½ p.c. Stk. red. 1926	92	− ½

Among Home Government and other "gilt-edged" securities there has been a steady advance in the 2½ per cents., Local Loans, and Bank stock, but large blocks of Consols have come on the market, and the price has dwindled, while all the Indian Government sterling loans exhibit a loss on the week. The announcement of the new Indian loan seems to have been the principal reason for the decline in Consols and the Indian loans. Most of the leading Colonial Government inscribed stocks mark rises, and a further appreciation in the leading Home railway companies' premier securities is noticeable.

Highest and Lowest this Year.		Last Carrying over Price.	HOME RAILWAYS.	Closing Price.	Rise or Fall.
186	172½	177	Brighton Def.	176½	—
59¼	54⅛	57¼	Caledonian Def.	58¼	+1¼
21¾	18¼	20¾	Chatham Ordinary	21¼	+1½
77¼	62	67	Great Central Pref.	67	+ ⅛
24⅝	21¼	22⅞	Do. Def.	22⅞	—
124½	118	121	Great Eastern	121¼	+1¼
61⅝	50⅞	55	Great Northern Def.	55⅝	+ ⅝
179⅝	163⅜	164¼	Great Western	164⅞	+ ⅜
51⅝	45¼	51½	Hull and Barnsley	51⅞	+ ½
149¼	145	145¾	Lanc. and Yorkshire	146	—
136⅛	127¼	132	Metropolitan	131⅞	+ ¼
31	26⅝	28¾	Metropolitan District	28¼	− ½
88⅜	82⅛	85½	Midland Pref.	85⅛	+ ½
95⅜	84¼	88¼	Do. Def.	88½	− ⅜
93¼	86⅞	89½	North British Pref.	89⅝	+ ¼
47½	41¾	44⅛	Do. Def.	44⅛	+ ⅜
181½	172¼	177¼	North Eastern	177½	+2¼
205½	196¼	198½	North Western	198¾	+ ½
117⅞	105½	113½	South Eastern Def.	113¾	+1¾
98¾	87	93¾	South Western Def.	94	—

In the Home railway market business was inactive during the greater part of the week, and with one or two exceptions changes are unimportant, the prospects of stock being scarce for delivery at the settlement and the cheapness of money not leading to any very great increase in the number of transactions. Chatham and South Eastern stocks rose sharply on a report of some sort of a new working arrangement (for dealing with the Paris Exhibition traffic, said one rumour, which seems a little premature), but the advance in Chatham second preference was due more than anything else to the prospect of an increased dividend this time. North Eastern Consols met with a good deal of support, the traffic being a very fine one, and Great Eastern hardened when it was found that the stock after being carried over "even" at first finally went to ¼ "back." Metropolitan ordinary gave way, it being stated that a Bill for a line between Ealing and High Wycombe has been deposited giving the Great Central Company a connection with the District. There was also a heavier contango this account, the rate being fully ½ per cent. The recent rapid rise in Metropolitan District ordinary seems to have been carried too far, and the inevitable relapse has since taken place. Lancashire and Yorkshire was slightly weaker on the news of the collision on their system, and a decline has also to be recorded in Waterloo and City, some holders, it is believed, having sold out to reinvest in the Great Northern and City Electric Company. The traffic returns were all considered satisfactory.

Highest and Lowest this Year.		Last Carrying over Price.	CANADIAN AND U.S. RAILWAYS.	Closing Prices.	Rise or Fall.
14 5/16	10⅝	14	Atchison Shares	13⅞	+ ⅜
34⅝	23½	34⅜	Do. Pref.	34	+ ¼
15⅝	11	14¼	Central Pacific	14¼	− ¼
105	85½	103¾	Chic. Mil. & St. Paul	103	−1⅛
14¼	10	13⅜	Denver Shares	13¼	+ ⅜
54¼	41½	52½	Do. Prefd.	52½	+2⅜
16⅝	11¼	14⅜	Erie Shares	14⅜	+ ¾
44⅝	29¼	38⅞	Do. Prefd.	38⅝	+1
110½	99	108½	Illinois Central	108	− ⅜
62½	45¼	57½	Louisville & Nashville ...	57	−1⅛
14½	9 15/16	12½	Missouri & Texas	12¼	+ ⅜
122¾	108¼	120	New York Central	119½	− ⅜
57¼	42⅞	55½	Norfolk & West. Prefd.	55	+ ⅜
72⅝	59	72	Northern Pacific Prefd.	71⅞	+1⅞
19½	13⅝	16¾	Ontario Shares	16¼	+ ⅜
62½	56¾	59½	Pennsylvania	59¼	− ¼
12½	7 13/16	10¼	Reading Shares	10¼	+ ½
34¼	24¼	33½	Southern Prefd.	33⅛	+ ⅛
37⅜	18½	26	Union Pacific	25½	—
20¾	14⅝	20½	Wabash Prefd.	20¼	− ¼
30¼	21	29¼	Do. Income Debs.	29¼	− ⅜
92¾	74	89	Canadian Pacific	88⅝	+1⅛
79⅝	69⅞	79¼	Grand Trunk Guar.	79⅝	+1
70⅝	57⅞	76½	Do. 1st Pref.	76¼	+ ⅝
58¼	37¼	58	Do. 2nd Pref.	58	+1⅝
26¾	19¼	26½	Do. 3rd Pref.	26½	+ ⅜
107	101½	105½	Do. 4 p.c. Deb.	106½	+2

New York operators have done their best throughout the week to keep up the prices of United States railroad shares to last week's level, but realisations on this side in view of the settlement caused an almost general relapse, and then Wall-street followed the lead of London, while the absence of very reliable information from the seat of war has tended to restrict business. Union Pacific, Northern Pacific, Southern preferred, and Denver preferred have been the most active counters, but Milwaukee and Louisville and Nashville shares have again attracted a considerable amount of attention, but at slightly lower prices than those ruling at the end of last week. In the bond list there has again been a steady and continuous advance, Wall-street being a large buyer, and a better demand on Home account was also reported. The account was an easy one, money rarely being more than 3 per cent., but stock was found to be rather more plentiful than on the last occasion, Milwaukee this time being carried over "even."

Holders of Grand Trunk stocks had an unpleasant surprise when the traffic return showing an increase of about £700 only was published, whereas the market was going for an increase of anything up to £20,000. The price of the first and second preference stocks came down rapidly, and, recovered afterwards on large buying orders from Montreal, and, as is usually the case, these orders were at once taken to mean that the rate war was going to be settled in a hurry. Up to the present, however, the only arrangement arrived at is said to be one for restoring at an early date the rates east of Chicago. Canadian Pacific shares have been rather neglected, and leave off without much change on the week.

Highest and Lowest this Year.		Last Carrying over Price.	FOREIGN BONDS.	Closing Price.	Rise or Fall.
94½	84	90¼	Argentine 5 p.c. 1886......	89¾	−1
92⅝	81⅝	88¾	Do. 6 p.c. Funding	88	−1¼
76¾	64	71¾	Do. 5 p.c. B. Ay. Water	71¼	−1
61⅞	41⅛	54	Brazilian 4 p.c. 1889	53	+ ½
69⅝	46	61¼	Do. 5 p.c. 1895	60¾	+1¼
65	42¾	56	Do. 5 p.c. West Minas Ry....................	56	—
108⅞	105½	107¼	Egyptian 4 p.c. Unified...	108	+ ⅛
104¾	100½	103	Do. 3½ p.c. Pref. ...	103¼	+ ¾
103	99½	101½	French 3 p.c. Rente	101⅛	—
44⅝	34½	43½	Greek 4 p.c. Monopoly...	43½	+1
93 9/16	88¾	92½	Italian 5 p.c. Rente	92⅝	+ ⅛
100	87½	97¾	Mexican 6 p.c. 1888	98½	+1¼
20⅞	16	18¾	Portuguese 1 p.c.	18¼	+ ¾
62¼	29⅝	36	Spanish 4 p.c.	33¼	− ⅞
46⅛	40	45¼	Turkish 1 p.c. "B"	46	+1¼
26 1/16	22¾	25¾	Do. 1 p.c. "C"	25¼	+1¼
22 1/16	20	21¼	Do. 1 p.c. "D"	21½	+ 9/16
46⅝	40	45	Uruguay 3½ p.c. Bonds...	44⅝	− ⅛

In the Foreign market the principal feature was the strength of the Brazilian bonds, the further rise in the exchange causing re-purchases by "bears," and it is stated that the funding scheme has now been practically accepted by the Brazilian Government. Argentine and Chilian stocks, however, have been flat, rumours that war was imminent between these countries over the western boundary question again cropping up. In addition to this, the action of the Chilian Government in endeavouring to launch some £500,000 in Treasury bills on the London market helped still further to depress the whole list of Chilian bonds. Among inter-Bourse securities, the notification that the July coupon will be paid entirely in gold caused a little bear closing, and this, and the scarcity of stock, helped to raise the price of Spanish 4 per cents., but the rise was not maintained, and the Paris Bourse withdrawing all support, the price drooped in the face of selling orders from Madrid, presumably on behalf of the Bank of Spain. Italian Rente advanced on Berlin purchases. Turkish groups rose somewhat sharply on conversion rumours, and Ottoman Bank shares were bought on the announcement of a satisfactory dividend. Egyptian and Greek loans are slightly higher, and this also applies to Portuguese stock. Continuation rates were very light, Italian being carried over "even," Spanish at about 1 per cent., and Argentine and Brazilian at from 1 to 3 per cent.

Highest and Lowest this Year.		Last Carrying over Price.	FOREIGN RAILWAYS.	Closing Price.	Rise or Fall.
105	99	105	Argentine Gt. West. 5 p.c. Pref. Stock..................	105	+2
158½	134	140½	B. Ay. Gt. Southern Ord..	140	−2
78⅞	65	73⅞	B. Ay. and Rosario Ord...	73½	− ⅜
12¼	10⅛	10⅛	B. Ay. Western Ord.	11	—
87¼	73	81½	Central Argentine Ord....	82½	+ ½
92	76	79	Cordoba and Rosario 6 p.c. Deb.	80	—
95⅜	85½	90	Cord. Cent. 4 p.c. Deb. (Cent. Nth. Sec.)	90	—
61¾	42	53½	Do. Income Deb. Stk. ...	53½	−2½
25¼	16¾	20¼	Mexican Ord. Stk.	21½	+1⅛
83½	69½	75	Do. 8 p.c. 1st Pref.	77	+3⅛

Among Foreign railway issues changes have been numerous, and generally in the upward direction, the principal rises having taken place in Argentine Great Western, East Argentine, and the Leopoldina group, but Buenos Ayres Northern has fallen 5, and Cordoba Central income stock is also rather lower. A smart rise has occurred in the old Mexican Company's first preference and ordinary, and Inter-Oceanic "A" debenture, owing to the rise in silver.

The most prominent change in the list of Miscellaneous securities is a big rise in Allsopp preferred ordinary, due to the light continuation rate and the shortness of stock. Suez Canal shares rose sharply on the satisfactory meeting, and P. & O. deferred on the publication of their report. Gas Light "A" is 3 higher, and rises have also occurred in Aerated Bread, Callender's Cable, and Fairfield Shipbuilding preference. Hudson's Bay shares declined, the dividend not being up to expectations, and falls ranging from 2 to 10 are noticeable in Asbestos and Asbetic ordinary, General Hydraulic Power, United Alkali debenture, and Welsbach ordinary. Electric lighting companies' shares have slipped back a little more; and several tea companies' emissions are weaker, the reports, which are now coming out, showing up rather badly. Very little notice was taken of Mr. Hooley's failure, and the effect upon prices was practically nil. Russian Petroleum ordinary shares are now being dealt in on a £1 basis, the quotation being about 2½.

Markets closed the week quietly, the reported settlement of the Niger question, and rumours of the fall of Manila having little or no effect on prices. Consols picked up a little at the last, and home railway stocks closed strong, especially the Scottish and southern lines. Grand Trunk issues were put up a little towards the close in anticipation of a good traffic, and Canadian Pacific shares were favourably influenced by the contradiction of the rumour of a new issue of capital. United States railroad shares closed firm, especially Northern Pacific preferred and Denver preferred; and Milwaukee and Louisville both recovered from the worst points of the week, although still finishing below last Thursday's level. Among Foreign Government bonds, Spanish 4 per cents. closed weak on Paris sales, and Brazilian and Chilian issues were also weaker at the last for the same reason.

Mining and Finance Companies.

Taking the mining market as a whole, there has been little or nothing doing, speculation being almost at a standstill, and the business, what there was of it, was of the purely professional type. Western Australian shares exhibit a few substantial gains, notably Hainault, Hannan's Brown Hill, and Golden Horse Shoe, on buying orders from Adelaide, and the settlement disclosing a rather short supply of stock, rates were light, a small "back" being at one time paid on Golden Horse Shoe. Indian shares were well supported, the returns for May being good; but among copper-producing companies prices are if anything slightly weaker.

SOME HOOLEY COMPANIES AND THEIR RESULTS.

In the brief time which has elapsed since this wonderful promoter braved his fate and put the Bankruptcy Court between him and his creditors, we have had slender opportunity to put together a skeleton record of his feats. Such as it is, however, the following table will prove interesting to many people and not without instruction to some :—

CYCLE CONCERNS.

Name of Company.	Nominal Capital. £	Present Market Value. £	Depreciation, *i.e.*, loss to public. £
Amalgamated Tyres... ...	1,000,000	150,000	850,000
„ Debentures ...	300,000	No price obtainable.	
Austral Cycle Agency ...	110,000	110,000	—
Bagot Tyre	141,000	No price obtainable.	
Clement Gladiator & Humber	700,000	180,000	520,000
Clement Gladiator Preference	200,000	No price obtainable.	
Components' Tube	150,000	30,000	120,000
Cycle Manufacturers' Tube	250,000	25,000	225,000
Dunlop Pneumatic Tyre ...	1,000,000	775,000	225,000
„ Preference	1,000,000	700,000	300,000
„ Deferred	2,000,000	750,000	1,250,000
„ Debenture	550,000	385,000	165,000
Dunlop (France)	650,000	85,000	565,000
Humber & Co.	250,000	120,000	130,000
„ Preference... ...	250,000	170,000	80,000
Humber & Co. (America) ...	75,000	No market price obtainable.	
Humber & Co. (Portugal) ...	80,435		
Humber & Co. (Russia) ...	75,000		
Humber & Co. (Extension) ...	175,000	35,000	140,000
Singer Cycle Co.	400,000	170,000	230,000
„ Preference... ...	200,000	135,000	65,000
„ Debenture... ...	200,000	No price obtainable.	
Swift Cycle Co.	200,000	95,000	105,000
„ Preference... ...	100,000	80,000	20,000
„ Debenture ...	75,000	No price obtainable.	

OTHER COMPANIES :—

	Nominal Capital. £	Present Market Value. £	Depreciation, *i.e.*, loss to public. £
Blaisdell Pencils	60,000	No price obtainable.	
„ Preference... ...	40,000		
Bovril	750,000	750,000	—
„ Preference	500,000	500,000	—
„ Deferred	750,000	450,000	300,000
„ Debenture	500,000	500,000	—
British Hydraulic Jointing ...	800,000	No price obtainable.	
British Embroidery Machine	250,000	Money returned to applicants.	
Dee Estates	250,000	No price obtainable.	
„ Preference... ...	175,000		
„ Debenture	175,000		
English Sewing Cotton ...	750,000	1,030,000	280,000*
„ Preference... ...	750,000	797,000	47,000*
„ Debenture	750,000	No price obtainable.	
Lee-Metford Small Arms ...	350,000	Money returned to applicants.	
„ Debenture	50,000		
Schweppes	300,000	300,000	—
„ Preference... ...	300,000	300,000	—
„ Deferred	350,000	132,000	218,000
„ Debenture	300,000	318,000	18,000*
Trafford Park Estates ...	650,000	No price obtainable.	
„ Debenture	350,000	315,000	35,000
United Ordnance and Engineering	275,000	No price obtainable.	
United Ordnance and Engineering, Preference ...	275,000		
United Ordnance and Engineering, Debenture ...	250,000		

* Improvement in value.

In considering these two tables it should be remembered that the cycle companies represent usually the earlier efforts of the industrious Mr. Hooley, and therefore sufficient time has elapsed in their case for his vicious methods of finance to work their full effect. The other companies were of a later date, and time has not brought its inevitable harvest in the shape of that depreciation in value such issues merit. Then the worst of them, perhaps—things like Blaisdell Pencils and Dee Estates—are precisely those that have no quotation at all. As far as our information allows, the two tables may be summarised in the following manner.

Sixteen cycle issues with a nominal capital of ...	£8,875,000
value at prices obtainable	3,885,000
Loss to public if it held the issues	£4,990,000
Ten issues of other companies with a nominal capital of	£4,850,000
value at prices obtainable	4,642,000
Loss to public if it held the issues	£208,000

If the latter group is going to follow the example of the cycle companies there is plenty of worry and disappointment for the sanguine holder in the future.

THE CENTRAL PACIFIC RAILWAY COMPANY.

The following is a full report of the portion of Mr. Morshead's speech of June 7, which was briefly reported in the *Financial News* of the 8th. It deserves attentive perusal, and if the stockholders of the company here would only join their fellow sufferers in the States in adopting the course here recommended, they might not only save their property, but administer a lesson to the unscrupulous financiers by whom they have been so often and so systematically robbed, which would do good for all time to come :—

"After the address of Sir William Marriott little can be usefully said on the present occasion of the past history of the Central Pacific Railroad, but you may like to hear, from one of the shareholders who protested in 1894 against the latest and continuing aggression of Mr. C. P. Huntington, a few observations as to our present position and the measures which are in progress for the protection of our investments. Millions of English capital have been lost in American railroads during the last few years, but as an investor in Erie, Atchison, Louisville, and Nashville, Central Pacific, and one or two others, I have no hesitation in saying that so far as my researches have extended, the greatest sufferer by far at the hands of American plutocrats has been the Central Pacific Railroad of California. Four large fortunes, amounting in each case to many millions sterling, have been carved out of its assets by Mr. C. P. Huntington and his three associates, Messrs. Stanford, Hopkins, and Crocker. Fortunately for us, however, the Government and people of the United States, who advanced large subsidies and made extensive land grants to the promoters, are our fellow sufferers. Our property, which, since the sale of the promoters' interests in Europe, has been systematically sucked dry by the vampire company of which Mr. Huntington is president, is the security for £11,000,000 sterling of public money belonging to the Government and people of the United States. This fact suggested to the Fairchild-Lubbock and Protection Committees a short, simple, and practical plan for liquidation of the Government debt and the recovery of the property by the action of the Government. It provides by foreclosure, receivers, and application of the sinking funds, for reorganisation without assessment on a solvency basis, payment of the Government debt, and restoration of the property to its owners with independent control. Evidence and advices from America show that by the adoption of this plan the road could at once pay 4 per cent. on all its liabilities and substantial dividends on the shares. The plan, which had the approval of Mr. Fairchild, Sir John Lubbock, and Lord Monkswell, and is supported by mass meetings at San Francisco, the independent shareholders in America, and the populist Press, has been submitted by your committee to the authorities at Washington, and has met with a friendly and favourable reception. The Banbury proposals, which in our judgment are ruinous to our interests, involve the loss of an opportunity, which can never recur, of rescuing our property by the action of the Government. With the assent of the shareholders, without any money contribution, and their dissent from the plans of Mr. Huntington and his board, which has just been re-elected by the votes of the Banbury committee, your committee are of opinion that success is assured, and we are confident of your assent when the facts are known. The Banbury committee have been publicly challenged to explain them, and we pause for a reply. Frequent communications by letter and cable are passing between the Protection Committee and our supporters at Washington, New York, Rochester, and San Francisco, and the more the shareholders are acquainted with the facts the greater will be the certainty of saving the property. In conclusion, I am in a position to assure you that your committee has a reserve of strength sufficient, in my opinion, with your assent, to insure success, and that our strength will be utilised in defence of our property before any further interference therewith by Mr. Huntington's board or the Banbury committee will be tolerated by the shareholders to whom the facts are known."

THE ST. LOUIS TERMINAL CUPPLES STATION AND PROPERTY COMPANY.—According to advices received the earnings of this company derived from rentals of the terminal warehouses from March 15, 1897 (date of incorporation), to May 1, 1898 (13½ months) were as follows :—Receipts, $311,739.71 (including only two month's rent from four new buildings just completed, which are all leased ; expenses, $58,070.50 ; net earnings, $243,669.21 ; interest on $3,000,000 4½ per cent. first mortgage gold bonds, $151,875.00 ; surplus, $91,794.21. In addition to usual fire insurance this company now also insures its rents.

Answers to Correspondents.

Questions about public securities, and on all points in company law, as well as on the position of life insurance offices and their promises, will be answered week by week, in the REVIEW, on the following terms and conditions:—

A fee of FIVE shillings must be remitted for each question put, provided they are questions about separate securities. Should a private letter be required, then an extra fee of FIVE shillings must be sent to cover the cost of such letter, the fee then being TEN shillings for one query only, and FIVE shillings for every subsequent one in the same letter. While making this concession the EDITOR will feel obliged if private replies are as much as possible dispensed with. It is wholly impossible to answer letters sent merely "with a stamped envelope enclosed for reply."

Correspondents will further greatly oblige by so framing their questions as to obviate the necessity to name securities in the replies. They should *number* the questions, keeping a copy for reference, thus:—"(1) Please inform me about the present position of the Rowenzori Development Co. (2) Is a dividend likely to be paid soon on the capital stock of the Congo-Sudan Railway?

Answers to be given to all such questions by simply quoting the numbers 1, 2, 3, and so on. The EDITOR has a rooted objection to such forms of reply as—"I think your Timbuctoo Consols will go up," or "Sell your Slowcoach and Draggem Bonds," because this kind of thing is open to all sorts of abuses. By the plan suggested, and by using a fancy name to be replied to, each query can be kept absolutely private to the inquirer, and no scope whatever be given to market manipulations. Avoid, as names to be replied to, common words, like "investor," "inquirer," and so on, as also "bear" or "bull." Detached syllables of the inquirer's name, or initials reversed, will frequently do as well as anything, so long as the answer can be identified by the inquirer.

The EDITOR further respectfully requests that merely speculative questions should as far as possible be avoided. He by no means sets himself up as a market prophet, and can only undertake to provide the latest information regarding the securities asked about. This he will do faithfully and without bias.

Replies cannot be guaranteed in the same week if the letters demanding them reach the office of the INVESTORS' REVIEW, Norfolk House, Norfolk-street, W.C., later than the first post on Wednesday mornings.

R. K.—1. There has already been a very substantial rise in all the issues of this road, and I do not think they are now tempting for an investor. If you wish to speculate wait until a flat day and then buy. There are chances of ups and downs which may give you opportunities of getting a profit, but if you lose your money don't blame me. 2. How can any one answer this question? If it were possible to foresee the financial effects of the present struggle it would be fairly easy to predict. In my opinion, the market at the present moment is inflated. It is quite likely it may remain so and some of the cheaper shares rise, as trade is on the whole good, but any sudden stringency for money would bring prices down with a run.

TONK.—The debenture issue should be safe enough, but I am not very much in favour of the preference shares. The company's career has been a chequered one; recently it has done better, thanks to some of the schemes it has been interested in turning out profitable. Its own business is run very close, and at present prices the preference shares seem rather dear.

NEW CLUB.—As the company has been at work not much more than six months in its present form, it is too soon to say that it is on a firm basis. Its directorate is fair—some of the members are connected with prominent firms in that country, but everything depends on the maintenance of traffic. For the first six months the receipts show well, but the debenture debt is heavy, and a buyer of the ordinary shares accepts considerable risk.

SHARK.—No doubt the accounts look well, but every effort has been made to make them appear so. The directors are not a very strong lot. Several of the businesses absorbed were weak, and this is the principal cause of the company finding it difficult to place its shares. The whole affair looks like having a struggle for existence. There is not enough solidity about the assets.

MINING RETURNS.

AUSTRALIA UNITED MINING COMPANY.—Crushed 345 tons, yielding 715 oz.

MYSORE WEST AND MYSORE WYNAAD.—Return for May:—381 oz. gold from 4,500 tons ore crushed.

NINE REEFS COMPANY.—Gold return for May:—900 tons of stone crushed yielded by amalgamation 51 oz. of gold; by cyanide process, 68 oz. of gold.

NORSEMAN GOLD MINES.—Return for May:—Ounces of gold, 1,015, from 715 tons of ore crushed.

HALL MINES, LIMITED (BRITISH COLUMBIA).—2,902 tons of ore smelted, yielding 123 tons matte, containing approximately 47 tons copper; 38,780 oz. silver; 216 oz. gold.

CHAMPION REEF GOLD OF INDIA.—Last month's return:—7,640 tons of stone produced 9,183 oz.; 2,445 tons of tailings produced 598 oz.; 6,105 tons (cyanide process) produced 1,569 oz.

COROMANDEL GOLD.—Last month's return:—1,200 tons of stone produced 701 oz.; 1,900 tons of tailings (cyanide process) 100 oz.

NEW COMET GOLD.—Crushing for last month:—Tons crushed, 5,080; ounces recovered from mill, 1,991; tons treated by cyanide, 4,007; ounces recovered, 1,146.

NUNDYDROOG COMPANY.—May return:—3,040 tons of quartz produced 2,809 oz.; 800 tons of tailings produced 95 oz.; and 3,016 tons (cyanide process) 336 oz.

TOLIMA MINING.—Estimated returns for May (65 tons), £2,000.

NORTH BOULDER.—Crushing for past fortnight:—385 oz. gold from 433 tons crushed.

PRINCESS ROYAL (CUE).—Clean up from 200 tons gave 141 oz. (exclusive of tailings).

CENTRAL BOULDER.—320 tons ore milled produced 487 oz.

NEW PINOS ALTOS.—Bullion shipped for May, £3,200. Estimated profit, £300.

KOMATA REEFS.—Preliminary clean up for four weeks, 400 tons, £1,660.

MENZIES' CONSOLIDATED.—554 tons crushed, yielding 725 oz.

TOKATEA CONSOLS.—96 oz. from 44 tons crushed.

UNITED IVY REEF.—985 tons crushed, produced 670 oz.

TWIN LAKES PLACERS.—Result for May:—Estimated value of bullion produced, $4,000.

OOREGUM.—5,797 tons quartz produced 3,704 oz. of gold; 4,700 tons of tailings produced 749 oz. gold.

CONSOLIDATED GOLDFIELDS OF N. Z.—New Progress mill treated 2,650 tons, yielding £4,700.

OTTOS KOPJE.—4,912 loads washed; 195 carats of diamonds won, including one stone of 31 carats.

IVANHOE.—Clean up for May:—1,751 tons crushed yielded 2,823 oz. gold. Average assay of tailings, 13 dwt. per ton.

HANNAN'S OROVA.—Crushed 891 tons, yielded 544 oz. gold.

MENZIES GOLD REEFS PROPRIETARY.—Crushed 51 tons ore, 61 oz. Cyanide process, 1,100 tons (yield) 730 oz.

MYSORE.—Return for May:—7,045 tons of quartz produced 11,633 oz. of gold; 1,910 tons of tailings produced 373 oz. of gold; 6,447 tons of tailings (cyanide process) produced 416 oz. of gold; obtained from old plates and sands, dismantling Nos. 1 and 3 mill and Nos. 2 and 3 tailings, 5,270 oz. of gold.

NIGEL.—Last month's crushing yielded:—Battery 1,605 oz.; cyanide 1,607 oz.

STANHOPE.—May crushing yielded 918 oz.

LADY EVELYN.—364 tons crushed for 513 oz. gold.

WEALTH OF NATIONS (in liquidation).—640 tons crushed yielded 396 oz. gold.

PADDINGTON CONSOLS (in liquidation).—1,290 tons crushed yielded 780 oz. gold.

GRASKOP.—First crushing 471 tons, yielding 430 oz.

SONS OF GWALIA.—940 tons quartz crushed, yielded 958 oz.

ANGELO GOLD.—Tons crushed, 6,944; ounces from mill, 3,566; tons cyanided, 5,413; ounces recovered from cyanide, 2,095.

BRILLIANT AND ST. GEORGE UNITED.—Crushed 2,257 tons of quartz for 3,209 oz. of gold.

BARRETT GOLD.—May yield: 670 oz.

BURMA RUBY.—Result for May:—39,000 loads washed, producing rubies valued at Rs.61,000.

GREAT BOULDER PERSEVERANCE GOLD.—May return:—Milled 879 tons for 1,035 oz.; smelted, 300 tons for 752 oz.

GOLD FIELDS OF MYSORE.—Last month's return: 41 oz. obtained from 750 tons sand, cyanide process; 181 oz. from amalgamation.

HENRY NOURSE GOLD.—Crushed 8,500 tons, producing 5,130 oz.; 6,170 tons cyanide treated, yielding 3,186 oz.

LANCASTER GOLD.—8,390 tons crushed, yielding 2,954 oz.; 5,145 tons of tailings treated, yielding 1,160 oz.

MONTANA.—Output for May:—Gold, 3,030 oz., and silver, 20,680 oz. obtained from 6,725 tons of ore crushed in the mills and 11,864 tons of tailings from the dams brought under treatment.

NEW QUEEN GOLD.—Crushing for past fortnight, 400 tons, yielding 190 oz.

PIGG'S PEAK DEVELOPMENT.—Crushed, 2,400 tons for 390 oz.; cyanided, 2,600 tons for 510 oz.

STANHOPE GOLD.—Last month's crushing yielded 918 oz.

ST. JOHN DEL REY.—Gold produce for May, £23,400; yield per ton, ·90 of an oz. troy.

SHEBA GOLD.—9,000 tons of ore, 3,070 oz.; 4,690 tons of tailings, 1,020 oz.; 155 tons of concentrates, 1,295 oz.

WAITEKAURI GOLD.—During the month ended May 21 mill yielded £4,329 from 1,805 tons.

WAIHI GOLD.—During the month ended May 28 6,130 tons of ore yielded £18,708.

WEALTH OF NATIONS.—Crushed 640 tons, gross yield 396 oz. gold.

BEACON GOLD.—Return for May:—Oz. of gold, 262, approximate, from 548 tons of ore crushed.

DRIEFONTEIN CONSOLIDATED.—Tons crushed, 13,250; ounces recovered, 3,757; tons treated by cyanide, 12,069; ounces recovered, 3,665.

GRAND CENTRAL.—Crushed 5,150 tons, yielding bullion $60,700. Concentrates estimated at $20,300.

PESTARENA UNITED.—503 tons produced 543 oz. of gold; 305 tons tailings concentrates (cyanide process) produced 260 oz.

SALISBURY GOLD MINING.—Last month's crushing yielded 1,700 oz.

ROODEPOORT UNITED MAIN REEF.—Crushed 6,653 tons, producing 3,157 oz.; cyanide, 621 oz.

VAN RYN GOLD MINES.—Crushed 12,012 tons, yielded 3,156 oz. gold. Cyanide works: 7,980 tons of tailings treated yielded 1,201 oz.

WEMMER GOLD MINING COMPANY.—Crushed 6 945 tons, yielding 4,424 oz. Cyanide plant, 4,750 tons treated, yielding 957 oz., and from concentrates, 139 tons caught, assaying 100 dwt. per ton.

VICTORIA (CHARTERS TOWERS).—295 tons crushed, yielded 513 oz. gold.

PREMIER.—438 tons crushed for 403 oz.

BURBANK'S BIRTHDAY GIFT.—Crushed 910 tons, yielding 1,238 oz. gold, exclusive of tailings.

BONANZA.—From mill—crushed, 5,453 tons; obtained, 5,474 oz. of gold. From cyanide and slimes works—treated, 5,447 tons, yielding 2,475 oz. of gold.

CONSOLIDATED MURCHISON.—Crushed, 505 tons; obtained 509 oz.

CROWN DEEP.—Tons crushed by 160 stamps, 22,946: yield in fine gold from mill, 6,092 oz.; tons of sands and concentrates treated by cyanide works, 18,419; yield in fine gold from sands and concentrates, 4,185 oz.; tons of slimes treated, 3,797; yield in fine gold from slimes, 70 oz.

DE LAMAR.—During May 2,796 tons leached; bullion produced from cyanide treatment, $22,000; surplus from clean-up of old mill, $5,819; estimated value of ore shipped to smelters, $1,100; miscellaneous revenue, $180; total produce for May, $29,099.

FERREIRA GOLD.—Crushed, 11,006 tons; bar gold extracted, 8,297 oz.; concentrates caught, 250 tons; assay value of concentrates, 5 oz. 5 dwt. fine gold per ton, equal to say 1,312 oz.; bullion produced from tailings, 3,016 oz.; bullion produced from slimes, 420 oz.; total gold from all sources, 13,045 oz.

GELDENHUIS DEEP.—Tons crushed by 190 stamps, 23,750; yield in fine gold from mill, 7,257 oz.; tons of sands and concentrates treated by cyanide works, 17,220; yield in fine gold, 3,540 oz.; tons of slimes treated, 5,742; yield in fine gold, 417 oz.

GLYNN'S LYDENBURG.—From mill.—Crushed, 1,583 tons, obtained 615 oz. of fine gold, equal to 671 oz. standard gold. From cyanide works.—Treated, 1,008 tons, yielding 266 oz. of fine gold, equal to 290 oz. standard gold. From slimes works (two months' working).—Treated 772 tons, yielding 268 oz. of fine gold, equal to 292 oz. standard gold. By products (and balance from April).—332 oz. of fine gold, equal to 362 oz. standard gold; total, 1,481 oz. fine gold, equal to 1,615 oz. standard gold.

GREAT BOULDER.—Return for the fortnight ended June 6:—Tons of ore crushed, 1,410; yield of gold in ounces, 3,076.

HANNAN'S VIRGINIA.—Crushed, 350 tons; yielded 88 oz. gold.

JUMPER'S DEEP.—Tons crushed by 80 stamps, 11,571; yield in fine gold from mill, 4,107 oz.; tons of sands and concentrates treated by cyanide works, 8,395; yield in fine gold from sands and concentrates, 2,410 oz.

LUIPAARD'S VLEI.—During May the mill crushed 3,035 tons, yielding 1,433.

MEYER AND CHARLTON.—Crushed, 9,184 tons; gold won, 2,680 oz.; extracted from tailings, 1,323 oz.

NEW KLEINFONTEIN.—Tons crushed, 10,240; ounces recovered from mill, 3,347; tons treated by cyanide, 7,369; ounces recovered from cyanide, 1,162.

NEW MODDERFONTEIN.—Output for May:—7,178 tons; yielded, 3,107 oz.; cyanide, 1,137 oz.

ROSE DEEP.—Tons crushed by 122 stamps, 14,824; yield in fine gold from mill, 5,466 oz.; tons of sands and concentrates treated by cyanide works, 9,802; yield in fine gold from sands and concentrates, 2,149 oz.; tons of slimes treated, 4,443; yield in fine gold from slimes, 455 oz. Total yield in bullion ounces, 10,106; equal to 8,090 oz. fine gold.

WORCESTER.—Last month's crushing yielded 2,764 oz.

QUEEN CROSS REEF.—Crushed 350 tons for 414 oz.

JUBILEE.—1,200 oz. of gold obtained from 3,115 tons crushed. Tailings, 330 oz. Mill working 17 days.

Prices of Mine and Mining Finance Companies' Shares.

Shares £1 each, except where otherwise stated.

AUSTRALIAN.

Making-Up Price, June 8.	Name	Closing Price.	Rise or Fall.	Making-Up Price, June 8.	Name	Closing Price.	Rise or Fall.
1 3/16	Aladdin	1 1/8	+ 1/8	3/8	Hannan's Star	3/8	
3 3/8	Associated	3 7/16	+ 1/8	6 1/4	Ivanhoe, New	6 5/16	+ 1/8
5/	Do. Southern	1/4	− 1/16	7/16	Kalgurli Mt. & Iron King, 18/	1/2	+ 1/8
1	Brownhill Extended	1		5 3/4	Kalgurli	6 1/4	+ 5/16
1 1/16	Burbank's Birthday	1 1/16	+ 1/16	2 1/16	Lady Shenton	2 1/8	− 1/8
5/8	Central Boulder	3/4	+ 1/8	9 1/16	Lake View Cons.	9 3/8	+ 5/16
6/	Chaffers, 4/	6/	+ /6	7/16	Do. Extended	3/8	
11/16	Colonial Finance, 15/	3/4		3/8	Do. South	7/16	+ 1/8
1/4	Crœsus S. United	3/8	+ 1/8	1 1/16	London & Globe Finance	25/6	
5/8	E. Murchison	5/8		11/16	London & W. A. Exploration	11/16	
4/9	Golden Arrow 19/	4/9		7/16	Do. Investment	1/2	
10 1/16	Golden Horseshoe	9 7/8	+ 1/8	1/2	Mainland Consols	1/16	
3/4	Golden Link	3/4	+ 1/16	3/4	North Boulder, 10/	11/16	+ 1/8
18/6	Great Boulder, 2/	19/	+ /9	1 1/4	North Kalgurli	1 1/4	+ 1/16
1 1/16	Do. Main Reef, 10/	15/16	+ 1/8	11/16	Northern Territories	1/16	
3 1/8	Do. Perseverance	3 1/4	+ 1/8	2 3/8	Peak Hill	2 3/8	
5/8	Do. South	3/4	+ 1/16	2 3/8	South Kalgurli	2 3/8	+ 1/8
3	Hainault	2 7/8	+ 1/8	1 3/16	W. A. Goldfields	1 3/16	
11/16	Hampton Plains	11/16		1/2	W. A. Joint Stock	1/2	+ 1/16
8 3/8	Hannan's Brownhill	8 1/2	+ 1/8	2/	W. A. Market Trust	2/6	
1 1/2	Hannan's Oroya	1 1/2	+ 1/16	1/2	W. A. Loan & General Fin.	1/2	+ 1/16
1/16	Do. Proprietary	12/6	+ 1/6	3/16	White Feather	3/16	

SOUTH AFRICAN.

Making-Up Price, June 8.	Name	Closing Price.	Rise or Fall.	Making-Up Price, June 8.	Name	Closing Price.	Rise or Fall.
5 1/4	Angelo	5 1/4	+ 1/16	2/	Lisbon-Berlyn	1/9	
1	Aurora West	1/16		2 1/16	May Consolidated	2 3/8	
1	Bantjes	7/8	− 1/16	3 3/16	Meyer and Charlton	3 3/8	
9/	Barrett, 10/	8/6	+ /6	3 3/8	Modderfontein	3 3/8	− 1/16
4 1/4	Bonanza	4 1/4	+ 1/8	5/8	New Bultfontein	9/16	− 1/8
5/6	Buffelsdoorn	5/16	− 1/8	3 3/8	New Primrose	3 3/8	− 1/8
5 1/16	City and Suburban, £4	5 1/4		1 3/8	Nigel, 15/	1 3/8	
2 3/8	Comet (New)	2 3/8			Nigel Deep	1	
3 1/4	Con. Deep Level	3 1/4		9/16	North Randfontein	1/2	
11 1/4	Crown Deep	11 1/4	+ 1/4	5	Nourse Deep	5	
13	Crown Reef	13	+ 1/4	1 1/8	Porges-Randfontein	11/16	− 1/8
27 1/4	De Beers, £5	27 1/4	+ 1/8	29 3/8	Rand Mines	29	− 1/8
3 1/16	Driefontein	3 1/4	+ 1/4	1 3/8	Randfontein	1 1/16	− 1/16
6 1/4	Durban Roodepoort	6 1/4		1 11/16	Rietfontein	1 1/2	
3 1/16	Do. Deep	3 1/2		9	Robinson Deep	9	− 1/8
4 1/16	East Rand	4 1/2		8	Do. Gold, £5	8	
24 1/2	Ferreira	24 1/2	+ 1/2	5/8	Do. Randfontein	5/8	
7 1/4	Geldenhuis Deep	7 1/4		1 1/4	Roodepoort Central Deep	1 1/4	− 1/16
5 1/16	Do. Estate	5 1/16	+ 1/4	6 1/4	Rose Deep	6 1/4	+ 1/8
5/8	George Goch	11/16	− 1/16	3 1/16	Salisbury	3 1/4	+ 1/8
2 1/16	Ginsberg	2 1/8	+ 1/16	1 1/4	Sheba	1 1/4	
1 1/4	Glencairn	1 3/8		3 3/8	Simmer and Jack, £5	3 3/8	+ 1/8
8 1/4	Goldfields Deep	8	− 1/8	2 1/4	Transvaal Gold	2 1/4	− 1/16
8 1/16	Griqualand West	8 1/4		3 3/8	Treasury	3 3/8	
9 1/16	Henry Nourse	9 1/2	+ 1/2	3 3/8	United Roodepoort	3 1/4	
7 1/16	Heriot	7 3/4		1 3/8	Van Ryn	1 3/8	
7 1/4	Jagersfontein	7 1/4	− 1/4	6 5/16	Village Main Reef	6 1/4	+ 1/4
9 3/8	Jubilee	9 3/8	− 1/4	1 1/4	Vogelstruis	1 1/4	+ 1/16
5	Jumpers	5	+ 1/8	5/8	Do. Deep	11/16	+ 1/16
2 1/4	Kleinfontein	2 1/16		10	Wemmer	10	+ 1/8
3 1/4	Knight's	3 1/4	+ 1/16	11/16	West Rand	9/16	+ 1/16
2 3/8	Lancaster	2 3/8		5 3/16	Wolhuter, £4	5 1/4	
3 1/16	Langlaagte Estate	3	− 1/8	2 1/2	Worcester	2 3/8	

LAND EXPLORATION AND RHODESIAN.

Making-Up Price, June 8.	Name	Closing Price.	Rise or Fall.	Making-Up Price, June 8.	Name	Closing Price.	Rise or Fall.
2 1/16	Anglo-French Ex.	2 1/16		5/8	Mashonaland Central	5/8	
1 1/4	Barnato Consolidated	1 1/16		5 3/4	Matabele Gold Reefs	5 3/4	
1/2	Bechuanaland Ex.	7/16		2 1/16	Mozambique	2 1/4	+ 1/16
2 1/4	Chartered B.S.A.	2 3/8		1 1/2	Oceana Consolidated	1 1/16	+ 1/16
1/2	Clark's Cons.	1/2	+ 1/16	1 5/16	Rhodesia, Ltd.	1 1/4	− 1/16
5/8	Colenbrander	9/16		4 3/8	Do. Exploration	4 3/8	
4 1/16	Cons. Goldfields	4 1/16		15/16	Do. Goldfields	1	
1 1/16	Do. Pref.	20/6		3 3/8	S. A. Gold Trust	3 1/4	− 1/16
1 1/4	Exploration	1 3/8	+ 1/16	7/16	Tati Concessions	7/16	− 1/16
2 1/4	Geelong	2 1/4		1/2	Transvaal Development	1/2	
9/16	Henderson's Est.	5/8	+ 1/8	1/2	United Rhodesia	1/2	
1 1/4	Johannesburg Con. In.	1 1/16		1 1/4	Willoughby	1 3/8	
9/16	Do. Water	9/16	− 1/16	5/8	Zambesia Explor.	5/8	
1 1/4	Mashonaland Agency	1 1/16					

MISCELLANEOUS.

Making-Up Price, June 8.	Name	Closing Price.	Rise or Fall.	Making-Up Price, June 8.	Name	Closing Price.	Rise or Fall.
1	Alamillos, £2	1		1/2	Mount Lyell, South	5/8	− 1/16
4 3/8	Anaconda, $25	4 5/16	− 1/16	4 1/16	Mount Morgan, 17s. 6d.	4 1/4	+ 1/16
6/3	Balaghât, 18/	9/	+ 2/	5 3/8	Mysore, 10s.	5 1/4	+ 1/16
12/	Brilliant, £2	12/6		8/	Mysore Goldfields	5/8	− 1/16
2 1/4	Do. St. George's	2 1/4		5/6	Do. Reefs, 17/	5/9	− 3d
9/6	British Broken Hill	8/9	− 1/3	3/9	Do. West	5/	− 1/6
2 1/4	Broken Hill Proprietary	2 1/16	+ 1/8	2/9	Do. Wynaad	5/16	− 1/16
3	Do. Block 10	3		2 1/4	Namaqua, £2	2 5/16	+ 1/16
4 1/4	Cape Copper, £2	4 1/4		3 5/16	Nundydroog	3 1/4	
4 1/4	Champion Reef, 10s.	4 3/8	+ 1/16	3 1/16	Ooregum	3 1/4	+ 1/16
2 1/4	Copiapo, £2	2 1/4		3 1/16	Do. Pref.	3 3/8	
2 3/8	Coromandel	2 3/8	− 1/16	26 1/2	Rio Tinto £5	26 1/16	− 1/8
15/	Day Dawn Block	15/		6	Do. Pref. £5	6	
2 1/16	Frontino & Bolivia	2 1/16		1	St. John del Rey	20/	
1 1/16	Hall Mines	1 1/16	− 1/16	8/9	Taitipu	1/16	− 1/16
2 1/4	Libiola, £5	2 1/4		6 1/4	Tharsis, £2	6 1/4	
7 1/4	Linares, £3	7 1/4		2 1/4	Tolima "A," £5	2	
3 1/4	Mason & Barry, £3	3 1/4		4 3/8	Waihi	4 5/16	
4 1/4	Mountain Copper, £5	4 3/8		1 1/4	Waitekauri	1 1/4	
10 1/4	Mount Lyell, £3	10 1/4	− 1/8	16/3	Woodstock (N.Z.)	11/16	+ 1/16
2 1/4	Mount Lyell, North	2 1/4					

NOTICES.

The Council of Foreign Bondholders are advised by the London and River Plate Bank that they are this day in receipt of the following cable message from their MonteVideo branch, dated the 1st inst.:—"We have remitted by to-day's mail to Glyn, Mills, Currie, & Co., £34,600 for the service of the Uruguay 3½ per cent. debt." This remittance represents the 45 per cent. of the Customs receipts for the second fortnight of May.

The committee appointed at a public meeting held on August 4, 1897, to protect the interests of the holders of the first mortgage 7 per cent. gold bonds of the Busk Tunnel Railway Company requests holders of such bonds to forthwith deposit the same with the agents, Messrs. C. J. Hambro & Son, 70, Old Broad-street, E.C., where copies of the committee's report as to the present position can be obtained, and the form of certificate to be issued by the committee against deposited bonds can be inspected.

With reference to the death of Mr. George Jackson, which took place on May 24, Messrs. Jackson Brothers and Cory intimate that the business will be carried on by the surviving partner, Mr. Walter Jackson, under the same style and in the same manner as heretofore.

The New Victoria Consols Gold Mining Company (no liability) has opened a London registry office and agency at 70, Cornhill, and Messrs. Stonehams and Wethereds, Limited, have been appointed London agents.

Messrs. Glyn, Mills, Currie, and Co. have received advice by cable from the London and River Plate Bank at MonteVideo announcing the despatch by mail of a remittance amounting to £4,200 for the service of the Uruguay 5 per cent. loan of 1896.

Of the West Virginia and Pittsburgh 5 per cent. gold bonds, the coupon on which, due April 1 last, was passed by the lessees, the Baltimore and Ohio Railroad Company, nearly 70 per cent. have now been deposited with Messrs. Brown, Shipley, & Co.

The transfer books of the 4 per cent. debenture stock of the Buenos Ayres and Rosario Railway Company, closed from the 6th to 18th inst., for the preparation of warrants for payment of the half-year's interest due July 1.

The English Association of American Bond and Share Holders, Limited, will act on behalf of depositing bondholders in the Wheeling and Lake Erie Railway Company in receiving and forwarding deposited bonds. Copies of the plan of reorganisation can be obtained at the office, 5, Great Winchester-street, London, E.C.

Messrs. John Venn and John Dalton Venn, carrying on business as notaries public under the style or firm of "John Venn," at 50, Gresham House, E.C., and 8, St. Martin's-place, Trafalgar-square, W.C., are not, and have not at any time been, in any way connected in business with Mr. W. E. Venn, notary public, of 2, Pope's Head-alley, Cornhill, against whom a receiving order was made on the 2nd inst.

Messrs. Stewart Brothers & Spencer have admitted Mr. Percy Malcolm Stewart into partnership.

TRAMWAY AND OMNIBUS RECEIPTS.

HOME.

Name.	Period.	Ending.	Amount.	Increase or Decrease on 1897.	Weeks or Months.	Aggregate to Date. Amount.	Aggregate to Date. Inc. or Dec. on 1897.
			£	£		£	£
Aberdeen District	Week	June 4	492	+8	—	—	—
Belfast Street	"	" 4	2,268	−125	—	—	—
Birmingham and Aston	"	" 4	851	+365	—	—	—
Birmingham and Midland	"	" 4	813	+166	—	—	—
Birmingham City	"	" 4	4,199	+432	—	—	—
Birmingham General	"	" 4	901	+76	—	—	—
Blessington and Poulaphouca	"	" 5	43	+27	22	258	+46
Bristol Tramways and Carriage	"	" 3	3,717	+255	—	—	—
Burnley and District	"	" 4	387	+42	—	—	—
Bury, Rochdale, and Oldham	"	" 4	975	+87	—	—	—
Croydon	"	" 4	418	+61	—	—	+1,338
Dublin and Blessington	"	" 5	183	+58	22	2,268	+90
Dublin and Lucan	"	" 4	143	+68	23	1,143	−303
Dublin United	"	" 3	3,574	+547	—	62,777	+3,239
Dudley and Stourbridge	"	" 4	253	+80	23	3,824	+215
Edinburgh and District	"	" 4	2,600	+183	22	51,150	+4,686
Edinburgh Street	"	" 4	743	+63	22	13,619	+1,612
Gateshead and District	Month	May	935	+66	—	—	—
Glasgow	Week	June 4	3,073	+4	—	—	—
Harrow-road and Paddington	"	" 3	344	+70	—	—	—
Lea Bridge and Leyton	"	" 4	1,077	+313	—	—	—
London, Deptford, and Greenwich	"	" 4	703	+64	—	12,611	+554
London General Omnibus	"	" 4	23,734	+148	—	—	—
London Road Car	"	" 4	7,409	−409	†	139,743	+4,678
London Southern	"	" 4	685	+105	—	—	—
North Staffordshire	"	" 4	431	−3	—	8,729	−77
Provincial	"	" 4	3,183	+374	—	—	—
Rossendale Valley	"	" 3	202	+37	—	—	—
Southampton	"	" 4	551	+118	—	—	—
South London	"	" 4	2,042	+168	†	36,367	+1,240
South Staffordshire	"	" 3	869	+252	22	13,315	+149
Sunderland	"	" 5	440	+158	—	—	—
Swansea	"	" 3	322	+37	—	—	—
Tramways Union	Month	April	10,870	+1,149	4	39,100	+4,495
Wigan and District	Week	May 28	304	+239‖	—	—	
Woolwich and South East London	"	June 4	547	+139	†	7,542	+412

† From January 1. ‖ Strike in 1897.

FOREIGN.

Name.	Period.	Ending.	Amount.	Increase or Decrease on 1897.	Weeks or Months.	Aggregate to Date. Amount.	Aggregate to Date. Inc. or Dec. on 1897.
			£	£		£	£
Anglo-Argentine	Week	May 9	4,504	+564	*	82,670	+8,606
Barcelona	"	June 4	1,230	−270	—	24,958	−3,974
Barcelona, Ensanche y Gracia	"	" 4	244	+3	—	4,023	+2
Bordeaux	"	" 3	2,465	−109	—	45,547	−1,990
Brazilian Street	Month	April [m	lr46,055	+3,671	—	—	—
British Columbia Electric	"	"	$30,729	+$10403	‡	$305,134	—
Do. net	"	"	$10,391	+$4,958	‡	$97,402	—
Buenos Ayres and Belgrano	"	April	5,090	+3,645	*	19,472	+3,368
Buenos Ayres Grand National	Week	May 7	$23,500	+$1,615	†	—	+$17,163
Buenos Ayres New	Month	March	$70,624	−$504	—	$201,851	−$7,119
Calais	Week	June 4	181	+33	—	—	—
Calcutta	"	" 4	1,092	−277	—	—	—
C'rth'g'na & Herrerias	Month	May	3,600	+173	—	22,418	+1,184
Gothenburg	Week	May 25	408	+38	—	—	—
Lynn and Boston	Month	April	$105,596	+$2,087	7	$727,825	+$30000
Do. net	"	"	$40,418	+$1,912	7	$256,801	+$5,064
Twin City Rapid	"	"	$165,803	+$10411	4	$653,223	+$43012
Do. Net	"	"	$82,670	+$7,350	4	$317,420	+$41589

* From January 1. † From April 1, 1898. ‡ From April 15, 1897.
§ From October 1, 1897

ENGLISH RAILWAYS.

Div. for half years. 1896	1896	1897	1897	Last Balance forward.	Amt. to pay 1 p.c. on Ord. for ½ yr.	NAME.	Date. †	Gross Traffic for week: Amt.	Inc. or dec. on 1897.	Inc. or dec. on 1896.	No. of weeks	Gross Traffic for half-year to date: Amt.	Inc. or dec. on 1897.	Inc. or dec. on 1896.	Mileage.	Inc. on 1897.	Working	Prior Charges last ½ year.	Prop. add Cap. Exp. this ½ year
				£	£												%	£	£
10	10	10	10	2,707	5,094	Barry	June 4	2,586	−6,629	−4,181	23	131,598	−30,837	−20,648	31	—	8·89	60,665	316,853
nil	nil	nil	nil	—	—	Brecon and Merthyr	" 5	1,230	−285	−417	23	31,274	−2,222	−5,613	61	—	—	—	—
nil	nil	nil	nil	3,079	4,740	Cambrian	" 5	6,307	+752	+1,157	*	109,785	+3,761	—	250	—	60·96	63,148	40,000
1¾	1½	2	1¾	1,510	3,150	City and South London ..	" 5	949	+4	+19	23	23,627	+292	+2,162	3¼	—	56·67	5,552	124,000
	2	1½	2	7,895	13,210	Furness	" 5	9,949	+320	+1,193	*	199,766	+6,270	—	139	—	49·88	97,423	20,910
1	1½	½	1	2,207	27,470	Great Cent. (late M., S., & L.)	" 5	51,150	−2,608	−157	22	997,242	+25,202	+62,429	352½	—	57·17	627,386	1,200,000
1½	4½	2	5	51,283	62,865	Great Eastern	" 5	94,735	+528	+18,782	22	1,790,641	+39,761	+152383	1,158¼	2	55·35	860,138	230,000
3	5¼	3	5	15,094	109,406	Great Northern	" 5	95,898	−7,346	+12,644	23	2,180,572	+63,092	+171476	1,073	10	51·36	641,483	750,000
4½	7½	4½	7½	31,350	121,981	Great Western	" 5	187,070	−19,340	+8,460	22	3,269,540	−18,600	+120820	2,589	21	51·44	1,486,272	800,000
nil	2	nil	1½	8,951	16,487	Hull and Barnsley	" 5	6,348	−747	+203	22	154,344	+8,649	+21,939	73	—	58·21	70,290	52,920
5	5¾	3	5½	21,495	83,704	Lancashire and Yorkshire ..	" 5	122,760	+15,986	+32,379	22	2,083,142	+92,343	+75,863	555½	25	56·70	674,745	451,076
4¾	8	4½	8½	26,243	43,040	Lon., Brighton, & S. Coast	" 4	63,760	−5,897	+931	23	1,140,392	+39,594	+52,827	476¾	—	50·20	407,042	240,735
nil	nil	nil	nil	72,294	56,296	London, Chatham, & Dover	" 5	33,380	−1,061	+5,323	22	618,560	+16,276	+30,045	185¼	—	50·65	367,873	nil
6¼	8	6¼	7¾	89,535	204,068	London and North Western	" 5	239,125	−32,417	+13,253	22	5,100,211	+211409	+288964	1,911½	—	56·92	1,404,534	600,000
5	8½	5	8½	23,038	59,367	London and South Western	" 5	86,511	−3,138	+14,314	22	1,561,957	+51,407	+103460	941	—	51·75	513,740	389,000
2¾	6	2¾	6½	14,592	6,691	Lon., Tilbury, & Southend	" 5	8,187	+1,637	+5,279	23	118,986	+5,537	+16,667	81	—	52·57	39,590	15,000
3½	3¾	3¾	3¾	17,133	26,409	Metropolitan	" 5	17,444	+826	+2,100	*	363,749	+8,369	—	64	—	43·63	148,047	254,000
nil	nil	nil	nil	4,006	11,250	Metropolitan District ..	" 5	8,477	+429	+521	22	186,658	+6,573	—	13	—	48·70	119,663	38,430
5	7	5½	6½	38,143	174,582	Midland	" 5	181,767	−17,043	+3,539	23	4,263,114	+70,827	+344369	1,354¾	15½	57·59	1,216,562	650,000
5½	7½	5¾	7	22,374	138,189	North Eastern	" 4	182,205	+21,054	+55,683	22	2,234,208	+87,678	+235559	1,597¾	—	58·72	795,077	436,004
7½	7½	7½	7½	7,061	10,102	North London	" 5	9,098	+24	+642	22	207,176	−1,267	—	12	—	50·90	49,973	7,600
4	5	4	4¾	4,745	16,150	North Staffordshire	" 5	16,428	−67	+1,411	23	359,269	+6,916	+20,749	312	—	55·27	118,142	19,605
10	10	11	10	1,642	3,004	Rhymney	" 4	1,845	−3,507	−3,203	23	90,384	−23,563	−14,396	71	—	49·68	29,049	16,700
3	6⅛	3½	6⅛	4,054	50,213	South Eastern	" 4	58,726	+5,365	+10,779	*	972,495	+33,412	—	448	—	51·88	380,763	250,000
3½	3½	1½	3½	2,315	25,961	Taff Vale	" 4	7,003	−6,776	−9,770	23	269,787	−89,771	−66,153	121	—	54·90	94,800	92,000

* From January 1. † Includes Whit Monday.

SCOTCH RAILWAYS.

5	5	5½	5	9,544	78,066	Caledonian	June 5	80,036	+ 2,087	+ 13,114	18	1,331,194	+ 33,148	—	851½	5	50·38	388,248	441,477
5	5½	5	5	7,364	24,639	Glasgow and South-Western	" 4	32,659	+ 800	+ 5,543	18	511,600	+ 17,780	—	393¼	—	54·69	221,663	196,145
3½	3½	3½	—	1,291	4,600	Great North of Scotland	" 4	9,388	+ 20	+ 1,469	18	147,449	+ 884	+ 6,322	331	15½	52·03	92,178	60,000
	nil		—	10,477	12,820	Highland	" 5	10,954	− 15	—	14	126,414	+ 2,339	—	479¾	27¾	58·63	78,976	,000
	1½	1	1½	819	45,819	North British	" 5	78,838	+ 5,370	+ 9,557	18	1,303,373	+ 39,554	—	1,230	23	48·62	944,809	40,800

IRISH RAILWAYS.

6½	6½	6½	—	5,466	1,790	Belfast and County Down ..	June 3	2,553	− 303	− 184	*	48,735	+ 56	—	76½	—	55·58	17,690	10,000
3¾	6½	3¾	—	—	4,284	Belfast and Northern Counties	" 3	5,379	− 182	+ 608	*	114,290	+ 4,230	—	249	—	—	—	—
	3	2	—	1,418	1,903	Cork, Bandon, and S. Coast† ..	" 4	1,371	− 92	+ 165	*	28,068	− 2,336	—	103	—	54·82	14,436	5,432
	6½	6½	6½	38,776	17,816	Great Northern	" 3	16,736	+ 432	+ 1,316	22	326,140	+ 12,359	+ 20,935	528	—	50·15	88,068	22,000
	5½	5½	5½	30,339	24,853	Great Southern and Western ..	" 3	—	—	—	not	received	—	—	603	13	51·45	72,802	46,582
	4	4	4½	11,379	11,830	Midland Great Western ..	" 3	—	—	not	22	received	—	—	538	—	50·31	83,129	1,800
nil	ni	nil	nil	220	2,802	Waterford and Central ..	" 3	881	− 73	—	*	—	—	—	59½	—	53·24	6,258	1,500
nil	ni	nil	nil	1,936	2,987	Waterford, Limerick & W. ..	" 3	4,582	+ 12	+ 131	*	—	—	—	350½	—	57·83	42,617	7,075

* From January 1. † Seventeen weeks' strike.

NEXT WEEK'S MEETINGS.

MONDAY, JUNE 13.

Bargang Tea	138, Leadenhall-street, noon.
Beyrouth Waterworks	17, Throgmorton-street, 3 p.m.
Dickson & Mann	Armadale, 11 a.m.
Great Boulder Perseverance ...	32, Old Jewry, noon.
North Western of Uruguay Railway	Winchester House, noon.
Royal Insurance	Liverpool, 11 a.m.

TUESDAY, JUNE 14.

Bengal Nagpur Railway	Gresham House, 2.30 p.m.
Chester's Brewery	Manchester, noon.
Commercial Bank of Scotland ...	Edinburgh, 1 p.m.
Malta and Mediterranean Gas ...	60, Gracechurch-street, noon.
Manila Railway	Winchester House, 2 p.m.
Mungledye Tea	138, Leadenhall-street, 2.30 p.m.
New Zealand Trust and Loan ...	9, King William-street, noon.
Peninsular and Oriental Steam Navigation	Leadenhall-street, 1 p.m.
Southwark and Vauxhall Water ...	Southwark Bridge-road, 1 p.m.

WEDNESDAY, JUNE 15.

Bengal Central Railway	Gresham House, 2.30 p.m.
Borelli Tea	138, Leadenhall-street, 2.30 p.m.
General Life Assurance	103, Cannon-street, 1 p.m.
Grand Junction Waterworks ...	65, South Molton-street, W., noon.
Kynoch	Birmingham, noon.
Read'* Drift Land	Winchester House, noon.

THURSDAY, JUNE 16.

Arica and Tacna Railway	31, Lombard-street, 1.30 p.m.
Empire of India and Ceylon Tea ...	Winchester House, 1 p.m.
Sambre and Meuse Railway ...	10, Moorgate-street, 11 a.m.

FRIDAY, JUNE 17.

Great Indian Peninsula Railway ...	Winchester House, 12.30 p.m.
Indian and General Trust ...	Winchester House, 1 p.m.

Messrs. N. M. Rothschild & Sons publish the numbers of 663 bonds, amounting to £66,300, of the Spanish quicksilver mortgage loan, which have been drawn for payment at par on July 1.

RAILWAY TRAFFIC RETURNS.

MOBILE AND BIRMINGHAM RAILROAD.—Traffic for third week of May, $4,808; decrease, $1,916. Aggregate from July 1, $328,559; increase, $62.

ALGECIRAS (GIBRALTAR) RAILWAY.—Traffic for week ended May 28, Ps. 39,200; increase, Ps. 22,702. Aggregate from July 1, Ps. 906,914; increase, Ps. 72,594.

WEST FLANDERS RAILWAY.—Gross receipts for week ending June 5, £2,119; increase, £123. Total from January 1, £53,093; increase, £1,892.

WEST OF INDIA PORTUGUESE RAILWAY.—Week ending May 14, Rs. 8,240; increase, Rs. 4,091. Aggregate from January 1, Rs. 93,200; increase, Rs. 27,318.

VILLA MARIA AND RUFINO RAILWAY.—Traffic for week ending June 4, $386; increase, $60. Aggregate from January 1, $7,841; increase, $1,506.

SOUTHERN MAHRATTA RAILWAY.—Receipts for week ended May 14, Rs. 1,23,343; decrease, Rs. 29,874.

BENGAL CENTRAL RAILWAY.—Traffic receipts for week ending May 14, Rs. 14,838; decrease, Rs. 502. Aggregate from January 1, Rs. 369,902; increase, Rs. 62,450.

DELHI UMBALLA KALKA RAILWAY.—Receipts for week ended June 4, Rs. 28,800; increase, Rs. 4,900. Aggregate from January 1, Rs. 7,53,700; increase, Rs. 1,78,100.

ALCOY AND GANDIA RAILWAY AND HARBOUR COMPANY.—Traffic for week, June 4:—Ps. 10,500; decrease Ps. 2,500. Aggregate from January 1, Ps. 190,000; decrease, Ps. 6,870.

WESTERN OF SANTA FE RAILWAYS.—Gross receipts for week ending June 4, $16,360; increase, $3,025.

GREAT WESTERN OF BRAZIL.—Traffics receipts for the week ending April 30, $22,597; decrease, $2,375. Aggregate from January 1, $394,494; increase, $73,735.

ROHILKUND AND KUMAON RAILWAY.—Traffic receipts for week ending May 7, Rs. 9,716; increase, Rs. 2,173. Aggregate from January 1, Rs. 1,44,244; decrease, Rs. 603.

ASSAM BENGAL RAILWAY.—Traffic receipts for week ending May 7, Rs. 23,409; increase, Rs. 5,703. Aggregate from January 1, Rs. 4,69,383; increase, Rs. 86,005.

BURMA RAILWAYS.—Traffic receipts for week ending May 7, Rs. 1,99,084; increase Rs. 2,669. Aggregate from January 1, Rs. 38,57,261; increase, Rs. 1,070.

QUEBEC CENTRAL RAILWAY.—Traffic receipts for third week of May, $7,882; decrease, $256. Aggregate from January 1, $143,056, decrease, $15,536.

BOLIVIA RAILWAY.—Traffic return for month of April, £1,017; decrease, £2,445. Aggregate from July 1, £20,257; decrease, £9,334.

NORTH WESTERN OF URUGUAY.—Traffic receipts for month of May, $15,000; increase, $3,823. Aggregate from January 1, $73,741; increase, $17,172.

CLEATOR AND WORKINGTON.—Gross receipts for the week ending June 4 amounted to £1,027, an increase of £9. Total receipts from January 1, £22,815, a decrease of £670.

COCKERMOUTH AND KESWICK RAILWAY.—Receipts for the week ending June 4, £1,215; increase, £287. Aggregate from January 1, £18,918; increase, £1,986.

The managing director of the Anaconda Copper Mining Company informs us that the fire at the mines is now under control.

Mr. Bertram Stuart Strnus has retired from the firm of Hale & Son, and the business will be conducted by the remaining partners.

FOREIGN RAILWAYS.

Mileage. Total.	Increase on 1897.	Increase on 1896.	Name	Gross Traffic for Week. Week ending	Amount.	In. or Dec. upon 1897.	In. or Dec. upon 1896.	Gross Traffic to Date. No. of Weeks.	Amount.	In. or Dec. upon 1897.	In. or Dec. upon 1896.
					£	£	£		£	£	£
819	—	—	Argentine Great Western ..	May 27	6,775	+ 1,299	+ 879	47	283,254	— 4,181	+ 56,219
76½	—	—	Bahia and San Francisco ..	Apr. 30	2,754	— 131	— 1,437	18	—	—	—
234	48	84	Bahia Blanca and North West..	May 8	523	— 101	—	45	33,692	— 1,414	—
75	1	—	Buenos Ayres and Ensenada ..	June 5	2,925	— 1,010	—	23	74,257	—	—
426	—	—	Buenos Ayres and Pacific ..	June 4	7,457	+ 1,018	+ 752	48	332,606	— 45,015	+ 13,070
914	—	3	Buenos Ayres and Rosario ..	June 4	14,782	+ 3,928	+ 3,422	23	372,361	+ 99,525	+ 68,157
2,499	30	68	Buenos Ayres Great Southern ..	June 5	24,150	+ 537	+ 5,785	48	1,432,376	+ 121,116	+ 215,715
602	107	177	Buenos Ayres Western	June 5	11,254	— 144	+ 827	48	530,713	— 75,163	— 103,033
845	55	77	Central Argentine..	June 4	17,821	+ 2,505	+ 2,688	23	477,218	+ 122,686	+ 62,940
297	—	—	Central Bahia	Apr. 30*	$155,590	+ $35,560	+ $57,258	4	$581,140	+ $60,760	+ $87,881
271	—	—	Central Uruguay of Monte Video	June 4	5,790	+ 1,987	+ 523	48	286,551	+ 28,148	— 14,578
208	—	—	Do. Eastern Extension	June 4	934	+ 169	+ 36	48	62,355	+ 9,726	+ 356
182	—	—	Do. Northern Extension	June 4	509	+ 212	— 336	48	30,459	+ 1,753	— 7,758
180	—	—	Cordoba and Rosario	June 5	1,635	— 705	— 715	48	103,570	— 13,085	— 1,235
128	—	—	Cordoba Central	June 5	$21,000	— $10,740	— $13,500	23	$482,330	— $88,400	— $101,210
549	—	—	Do. Northern Extension	June 5	$52,000	— $12,780	— $13,350	23	$1,028,000	— $358,780	— $210,470
137	—	—	Costa Rica..	June 4	3,979	— 159	— 189	23	129,681	+ 98	+ 12,537
99	—	—	East Argentine	Apr. 17	1,001	+ 497	+ 127	15	11,548	+ 884	+ 658
886	—	6	Entre Rios..	June 4	1,188	+ 332	— 34	48	78,654	+ 25,069	+ 19,652
555	—	24	Inter Oceanic of Mexico.. ..	June 4	$59,600	+ $10,210	+ $17,620	48	$2,808,870	+ $445,630	+ $762,040
23	—	—	La Guaira and Caracas	Apr. 29	1,573	— 724	—	18	35,814	— 4,781	—
321	—	—	Mexican	June 4	$79,900	+ $11,900	—	23	$1,802,200	+ $194,850	—
1,846	—	—	Mexican Central	May 31‡	$396,475	+ $40,667	+ $147,315	22	$5,556,481	+ $91,538	+ $1,476,268
2,217	—	—	Mexican National	May 31‡	$145,451	— $3,955	+ $37,840	22	$2,360,391	+ $82,193	+ $462,112
228	—	—	Mexican Southern	June 7	$11,560	— $2,189	+ $4,262	9	$118,477	— $17,673	+ $30,271
206	—	—	Minas and Rio	Apr. 30*	$142,119	— $22,067	—	10 mos.	$1,740,090	+ $171,787	—
94	—		N. W. Argentine	June 4	1,333	+ 385	— 27	23	22,677	+ 53	— 7,197
242	3	—	Nitrate	May 31†	18,520	+ 2,552	— 7,211	22	151,360	— 328	— 69,690
320	—	—	Ottoman	May 28	3,531	+ 345	+ 1,73	22	97,775	— 24,931	+ 8,532
77½	—	—	Recife and San Francisco ..	Apr. 9	3,846	— 325	— 326	15	85,029	+ 8,167	— 13,687
86¼	—	—	San Paulo	May 1‡	17,518	— 2,487	—	17	165,710	—	—
186	—	—	Santa Fe and Cordova	June 4	1,545	+ 630	— 140	48	85,761	+ 3,855	— 6,348
110	—	—	Western of Havana	June 4	1,518	— 334	— 102	48	84,155	+ 3,394	— 6,666

* For month ended. † For fortnight ended. ‡ For ten days ended.

INDIAN RAILWAYS.

Mileage. Total.	Increase on 1897.	Increase on 1896.	Name.	Gross Traffic for Week. Week ending	Amount.	In. or Dec. on 1897.	In. or Dec. on 1896.	Gross Traffic to Date. No. of Weeks.	Amount.	In. or Dec. on 1897.	In. or Dec. on 1896.
862	—	—	Bengal Nagpur	June 4	Rs.1.31.000	+ Rs.16.691	+ Rs.20.324	23	Rs.35.96.966	+ Rs.4.61.026	+ Rs.1.22.693
827	8	63	Bengal and North-Western ..	May 7	Rs.1.47.270	— Rs.13,714	— Rs.637	19	Rs.25.34.491	+ Rs.2.63.464	+ Rs.22.79.948
461	—	—	Bombay and Baroda	May 28	£44,458	+ £5,565	+ £6,800	22	£647,791	+ £43,290	— £120,482
1,885	2	13	East Indian	June 4	Rs.12.28.000	+ Rs.64.000	+ Rs.1.76.000	23	Rs.2.82.40.000	+ Rs.11.78.000	+ Rs.32.51.000
1,491	—	—	Great Indian Penin.	June 4	£61,453	+ £7,064	+ £960	23	£1,591,436	+ £319,273	— £167,533
736	—	—	Indian Midland	June 4	Rs.1.71.280	+ Rs.34.408	+ Rs.65.627	23	Rs.33.30.818	+ Rs.3.78.451	+ Rs.18.62.151
840	—	—	Madras	May 21	£18,608	— £1,375	— £1,100	21	£388,745	— £22,515	— £5,907
1,043	—	—	South Indian	May 7	Rs.1.70.240	— Rs.10,307	— Rs.12.153	19	Rs.28.85.439	— Rs.2.47.706	— Rs.2.79.770

UNITED STATES AND CANADIAN RAILWAYS.

Mileage. Total.	Increase on 1897.	Increase on 1896.	Name.	Gross Traffic for Week. Period Ending.	Amount.	In. or Dec. on 1897.	Gross Traffic to Date. No. of Weeks.	Amount.	In. or Dec. on 1897.
					dols.	dols.		dols.	dols.
917	—	—	Baltimore & Ohio S. Western ..	May 31‡	192,858	+ 45,084	46	6,318,574	+ 807,556
6,568	92	156	Canadian Pacific	May 31‡	710,000	+ 102,000	20	9,400,000	+ 1,688,000
922	—	—	Chicago Great Western	May 31‡	137,805	+ 1,806	46	4,912,228	+ 621,554
6,169	—	469	Chicago, Mil., & St. Paul ..	May 31‡	866,000	+ 89,000	20	11,483,001	+ 1,714,800
1,685	—	—	Denver & Rio Grande	May 31‡	201,000	+ 30,000	46	7,395,000	+ 1,201,400
3,512	—	—	Grand Trunk, Main Line ..	May 31‡	£97,146	— £2,912	20	£1,561,058	+ £133,499
335	—	—	Do. Chic. & Grand Trunk	May 31‡	£18,727	+ £3,724	20	£317,092	+ £72,564
189	—	—	Do. Det., G. H. & Mil...	May 31‡	£4,565	— £102	20	£73,740	— £4,200
2,938	—	—	Louisville & Nashville	May 31‡	559,000	— 4,000	20	8,857,175	+ 1,233,620
2,197	137	137	Miss., K., & Texas	May 31‡	280,376	+ 49,248	46	11,381,495	+ 548,904
477	—	—	N. Y., Ontario, & W.	May 31‡	96,916	+ 91	46	3,498,507	+ 80,685
1,570	—	—	Norfolk & Western	May 31‡	202,000	— 11,000	20	4,547,960	+ 487,433
3,499	336	—	Northern Pacific	May 31‡	602,000	+ 131,000	20	8,075,775	+ 2,494,552
1,223	—	—	St. Louis S. Western	May 31‡	130,000	+ 26,000	20	2,139,295	+ 324,928
4,654	—	—	Southern	May 31‡	533,000	+ 66,000	20	7,596,812	+ 1,645,430
1,979	—	—	Wabash	May 31‡	371,000	+ 62,000	46	12,116,430	+ 1,170,000

‡ For ten days ended.

MONTHLY STATEMENTS.

Mileage. Total.	Increase on 1896	Increase on 1895.	Name.	Net Earnings for Month. Month.	Amount.	In. or Dec. on 1897.	In. or Dec. on 1896.	Net Earnings to Date. No. of Months.	Amount.	In. or Dec. on 1897.	In. or Dec. on 1896.
					dols	dols.	dols.		dols.	dols.	dols.
6,935	44	444	Atchison	April	798,000	+ 319,000	+ 239,679	4	2,942,434	+ 993,836	+ 469,139
6,547	103	106	Canadian Pacific	April	717,000	+ 90,000	+ 225,790	4	2,410,000	+ 505,000	+ 612,557
6,169	—	469	Chicago, Mil., & St. Paul ..	April	759,000	+ 19,000	— 17,197	4	3,495,334	+ 244,840	+ 76,915
1,685	—	—	Denver & Rio Grande	April	264,200	+ 11,797	+ 38,988	10	2,777,080	+ 418,782	+ 69,915
1,970	—	—	Erie..	April	554,000	+ 17,000	+ 45,487	4	1,932,600	+ 100,400	— 48,760
3,512	—	—	Grand Trunk, Main Line ..	April	£114,098	+ £16,224	+ £26,710	4	£360,051	+ £78,596	+ £123,527
335	—	—	Do. Chic. & Grand Trunk	April	£11,526	+ £6,424	+ £5,660	4	£50,236	+ £30,706	+ £34,378
189	—	—	Do. Det. G. H. & Mil. ..	April	£4,016	+ £390	+ £2,125	4	£10,544	+ £1,127	+ £8,744
3,127	—	239	Illinois Central	March	759,000	+ 206,000	+ 343,862	3	2,213,704	+ 365,620	+ 549,739
2,396	—	—	New York Central*	April	3,807,000	+ 302,000	+ 394,152	4	14,602,000	+ 964,000	—
477	—	—	New York Ontario, & W. ..	April	62,100	— 14,700	— 13,161	10	980,400	+ 23,500	+ 102,333
1,570	—	—	Norfolk & Western	April	237,000	+ 40,000	+ 96,237	4	1,063,000	+ 105,340	+ 298,139
3,407	—	—	Pennsylvania	April	1,524,200	+ 12,900	+ 236,000	4	5,672,228	+ 121,300	+ 575,900
1,055	—	—	Phil. & Reading	April	623,155	— 12,799	—	10	8,190,448	+ 511,265	—

Prices Quoted on the London Stock Exchange.

Throughout the INVESTORS' REVIEW middle prices alone are quoted, the object being to give the public the approximate current quotations of every security of any consequence in existence. On the markets the buying and selling prices are both given, and are often wide apart where stocks are seldom dealt in. Other particulars will be found in the INVESTMENT INDEX published quarterly—January, April, July, and October—in connection with this REVIEW, price 2s., by post 2s. 2d. Where dividends are paid only once a year, an *italic* type is used to distinguish them. The London Stock Exchange Official List is quoted in the REVIEW almost entire, only very insignificant issues, or bonds falling due within the next two or three years, being omitted. But the list is subdivided into the leading, or active, stocks, and those less frequently dealt in. The former will be found under the head of "Stock Markets," and with more details than it is possible to give for the bulk of securities. By retaining the file of the INVESTORS' REVIEW any subscriber can follow for himself the movements of securities from week to week, and the INVESTMENT INDEX will from time to time help to fill up deficiencies in the information.

Tea Companies and Mines and Mining Finance Stocks are placed in special lists.

Among the abbreviations used are the following:—S.F. Snk. Fd. *sinking fund*; Certs., *certificates*; Debs. or Dbs., *debentures*; Db. or D.Stk., *debenture stock*; Pf. Prf., or Pref., *preference*; Prefd. or Pfd., *preferred*; Dfd., *deferred*; L. or Ltd., *limited*; Sh., *share*; Ans., *annuities*; Cu. or Cm., *cumulative*; Gu or Guar., *guaranteed*; Bds., *bonds*; S., Sr., or Ser., *series*; In., Ins., Insc., *inscribed*; Dr., Drgs., Drwgs., *drawings*; Sg., Strlg., *sterling*; Lia., *liable to*; Sp., Surp., *surplus*; Per., Perp., *perpetual*; Ln. *lien*; Lo. *loan*.

The dates following the names of securities are the years of issue or of redemption. Where shares are not fully paid up, their nominal amount is given with the name so that investors may know the liability upon them.

BRITISH FUNDS, &c.

Rate.	Name.	Price.
2¾	2¾ p.c.'s (Childers') Red.. 1905	105
3	Local Loans Stk. 1912	111
3	Metro. Police Deb. Stk. 1920	104½
—	Red Sea Ind. Tel. Ann. 1908	8¼
4	Canada Gv. "Intcl. Rly." 1903	106¼
4	Do. do. .. 1908	111
4	Do. Bonds 1910	112
4	Do. Bonds 1913	117½
3	Egyptian Gov. Gar.	106
3	Mauritius Ins. Stk. 1940	113
4	Turkish Guar. 1855	109
11½	Bank of Ireland Stk.	385
3½	India Rupee Paper	62
3½	Do. 1854-5	62½
3	Do. 1896-7 1916	55
3½	Isle of Man Deb.	104
3	Do. Deb. Stk... 1919-29	103

CORPORATION AND COUNTY STOCKS.

FREE OF STAMP DUTY.

Rate.	Name.	Price.
3½	Metropolitan Con. 1929	117
3	Do. 1941	111
2½	Do. 1920-49	99
2½	L.C.C. Con. Stock 1920	98
3½	Comm. of Sewers, Scp., S.F. 1905	104
3½	Corp. of Lond. Bds...1898-1902	100½
3	Do. 1898-1917	101
3½	Do., Debs. Scp. ...... S.F. 1916	105
2½	Do., Deb. Stk. Scrip .. 1927-57	97½
3	Barnsley 1916-46	103
3	Barry 1914-46	101½
3	Bath 1909-34	101½
3	Batley 1914-41	101½
3½	Birmingham 1946	116½
3	Do. 1947	110½
2½	Do. 1926	98
3	Blackburn 1930	106½
3	Bournemouth 1913-33	103
3½	Bradford 1945	116½
3	Do. Deb. Stock .. 1934	107
3	Brighouse.............. 1916-46	100
3½	Brighton 1946	117
	Do. 1957	96½
	Burton-on-Trent........ 1913-43	101½
	Cambridge 1913-43	102
	Cardiff 1935	114½
	Do. 1914-54	103
	Cheltenham............ 1971	105½
	Chichester 1926-46	101
	Croydon	128½
3	Do. 1940	107½
3	Derby 1920-50	106½
3	Devon C.C.............. 1917-33	104½
3½	Dewsbury 1930	109
3	Do. 1930	103
3	Dorset County 1922-32	106
3	Douglas (I. of Man) 1926	101½
3	Dover 1913-43	101½
3½	Dublin 1944	111½
3	Eastbourne 1920-40	104
3	Edinburgh 1924	105½
2½	Do. 1927	97
2½	Exeter 1917-57	96
3	Glamorgan County 1914-34	103
3½	Glasgow 1914	109
3	Do. 1921	104½
2½	Do. 1925-40	98
3	Gloster 1915-55	101
3	Grimsby 1913-45	103
3	Hampshire County 1914-34	105½
3	Hanley 1913-43	102½
3	Harrogate 1914-34	103
3	Hastings 1915-54	102½
2½	Hertfordshire C.C. 1916-36	98
3	Heston & Isleworth U.D.C. 1915-35	101
3	Huddersfield 1934	107
3½	Hull (1st iss.)	125½
3	Inverness 1914-44	100
3	Ipswich 1952	107½
3	Lancaster.............. 1919-55	103
2½	Leeds 1927	98
3½	Leicester 1934	116
3	Lincoln................ 1919	102
3½	Liverpool	131

Corporation, &c. (*continued*):—

Rate.	Name.	Price.
3	Manchester 1941	107½
3½	Middlesbro' 1909	105½
3½	Do. 1911-13	105
3	Do. 1915	104
3	Middlesex C.C.......... 1915-35	105
3½	Newcastle 1936	112½
3½	Do. Irred.	129½
2½	Do. 1915-36	100
3	Newcastle-under-Lyme.. 1909-44	100
3	Newport (Mon.) 1915-55	100½
3	Norwich 1952	110
3	Nottingham	113
3	Oxford 1951	108½
3	Penzance 1916-46	100½
3	Plymouth 1942	106½
3	Pontypridd U.D.C. 1916-46	98
3	Poole.................. 1915-45	101
3½	Portsmouth........1916 24 & 27	111
3	Do. 1913-33	105
3	Ramsey 1920-40	99
3	Ramsgate.............. 1915-55	102
3½	Reading	123
3	Do. 1962	106
3½	Rhyl U.D.C. 1953	110
3	Richmond (Surrey) 1942	104½
3	River Wear Debt Certs.	100
3	St. Helen's 1915-55	102
3	Scarbro' 1915-50	102
2½	Sheffield 1925-57	94½
3	Shipley U.D.C. 1915-35	100
3	Somerset Co. 1923-33	104
3	South Shields 1915-45	100½
2½	Southampton 1915-45	100½
3	Southend-on-Sea 1916-46	101
3	Staffs C.C. 1915-35	104½
3	Stockport.............. 1914-54	101
3	Stockton 1932	104
3	Do. 1915-35	103
3	Surrey Co. 1922-32	105½
3½	Swansea	128
3	Do. 1955	105
3	Taunton 1918 3-9-43	101
3	Tees Conserv. Deb. Stk. 1947	100
3	Thames Conserv. "A" Deb. Stk.............. 1954	102½
3	Do. "B" Deb. Stk. 1954	102½
3	Torquay 1913-43	100½
3	Tunbridge Wells 1931	102
3	Tynemouth 1913	99
3	Wakefield.............. 1929	101½
3	Walsall................ 1932	107½
3	West Bromwich........ 1930	105
3½	West Ham 1929	110
3	Do. 1945	105
3	West Sussex C.C. 1915-35	106
3	Weston-s.-Mare Lcl. Bd. 1914-44	99½
3	Weymouth&Melc. Regis 1918	100
3	Widnes................ 1915-55	100
3	Wigan 1921	104½
3	Windsor 1918-55	102½
3½	Wisbech 1947	113½
3½	Wolverhampton 1932	117
3	Do. 1924-54	107
3	York 1916-41	106½

SUBJECT TO STAMP DUTY.

Rate.	Name.	Price.
3½	Belfast City & Dis. Watr. 1938	114
3	Do. Red Stk. 1953-6	106
3½	Belfast 1924	103
4	Blackburn Con. Deb. Irred.	141½
3½	Do. do. Irred..............	130
3½	Bristol	130½
3½	Burnley.................. 1933	114
2½	Chesterfield Gas & Wtr. 1916-46	96
3½	Douglas Town 1921	105
3	Dover Harb. 1st Deb... 1956	104½
3½	Hull (2nd iss.)	128½
4	Leeds Deb.............. 1927	123
3½	Do.	115½
3	Do. 1927	106
3	Leicester 1919-44	103½
4	Manchester..................	145
3	Do. 1928	104½
4½	Middlesboro' Mrts. 1908	111
3½	Sheffield 1898-1916	100½
3½	Do. 1925-36	114
3	Do. 1935	103½
3½	Southampton .... S.F.	106
4½	Stockton Morts......... 1908	110½
3½	Worcester.............. 1950	109

COLONIAL AND PROVINCIAL GOVERNMENT SECURITIES.

Rate.	Name.	Price.
6	British Columbia.......... 1907	119½
4½	Do. Debs.. 1917	111½
3	British Guiana Imgtn. Bds.	98
5	Canada, "Intercol. Rail," 1903	107½
4	Do. (Bonds) 1904-5-6-8	106
4	Do. Reduced 1910	110
3½	Do. Bnds. 1909-34	107
4	Do. Loan 1910-35	110
3	Do. Loan 1938	103
6	Cape of G. Hope 1900	—
5	Do. 1900	—
4½	Do. red. by an. draw.	108
4½	Do 1879	108
4	Do. 1881	107
4	Do 1917-23	113
4½	Ceylon	108
4	Do.	106½
4½	Fiji Gov. Deb. Sink. Fd.	101½
4	Jamaica Sink. Fd. 1923	103
5	Manitoba Debs........ 1910	113
5	Do. Ster. Bds. 1888	119½
4	Do. Ster. Debs.	105
4	Mauritius, Cons. Debs. 1880...	101½
4½	Natal, Sink. Fd........ 1919	118
4	Do. do. 1926	114
3½	Newfoundland Stg. Bds. 1941	100
3½	Do. do. .. 1947	100
3	Do. do.	97
5	New South Wales 1897-1902	104½
4	Do. 1903-5-8-9-12	106
5	New Zealand 1914	118
5	Do. Cnsls. 1 p.c. per an. Sink. Fd.	103
3½	Nova Scotia Debs.	104
5	Quebec Prov. 1904-6	108
4½	Do. (drgs.)	105
5	Do. Strlg. Bds. 1919	115
4	Do. Strlg. Bds. 1928	110
4	Do. Strlg. Bds. 1934	108
4	Queensland 1913-15	108
4½	St. Lucia Debs................	102
6	South Australia 1898-1900	103½
6	Do. 1901-1918	119
5	Do. 1911-1920	115½
4	Do. 1899-1916	104½
4	Do. 1929	108½
4	Do. 1916	106½
4	Do. 1917-18-24	110
6	Tasmania 1897-1901	104
4	Do. 1908-11, 1913-14-20	107½
5	Trinidad Debs., an. drw. 1 p.c...	107
4	Victoria 1899-1901	102½
4½	Do. 1904	107
4	Do. Rail. Loan 1977	107
4	Do. Loans 1908-13	106
4½	West. Austr. 1 p.c. an. Sink. Fd.	107
4	Do. do.	106

REGISTERED AND INSCRIBED STOCKS.

No stamp duty except for Canada 4 p.c. Reduced (½ per cent.).

Rate.	Name.	Price.
4	Antigua Insc. Stk. Red. 1919-44	111
3½	Barbados Insc. Stk. 1925-42	107
3	British Colum. Insc. Stk. 1941	100½
4	British Guiana Insc..... 1935	116½
4	Canada Stk. Regd. ..1904-5-6-8	106
4	Do. 4 p.c. (late 5 p.c.) Regd. 1910	110
3½	Do. 3½ p.c. Stock Regd. 1909-34	107
4	Do. Ln. for 4 milln. stg. 1910-35	110
3	Do. Stk. Regd. 1938	103
2½	Do. Insc.................. 1947	92
4	Cape G. Hope Regd. ... 1917-23	114
4	Do. (Ln. of '83) Insc. .. 1923	117
4	Do. Cons. Stk. Insc.... 1916-36	114
3½	Do. Consol. Insc. Stock 1929-49	109
4	Ceylon Insc. Stock 1934	120
3	Do. 1940	103
4	Grenada Insc. Stock.... 1917-42	110
3½	Hong Kong Insc. Stock 1918-43	104
4	Jamaica Insc. Stock.... 1934	118
—	Do. 1922-44	98
4	Mauritius Inscribed 1937	118½
4	Natal Consd. Stk. Insc. 1927	117
4	Do. 1937	119
3½	Do. Inscribed Stock.. 1914-39	106
4	Newfoundland Inscribed 1913-38	106
4	Do. 1935	114
4	Do. Consd. Stk. Ins. 1936	114
4	N. S. Wales Stock Insc. 1933	118
3½	Do. 1924	109
3½	Do. 1918	107
3	Do 1935	100

Colonial, &c. (*continued*):—

Rate.	Name.	Price.
4	N. Zealnd. Con. Stk. Ins. 1929	115
3½	Do 1940	107
3	Do. Inscribed.... 1945	99
3	Quebec (Prov.) Ins. Stk. 1937	95
4	Queensland Stock Insc. 1915-24	109
3½	Do. 1921-4-30	104½
3½	Do. 1945	107
3	Do. 1922-47	98
4	St. Lucia Insc. Stock .. 1919-44	114½
4	S. Austrln. (1882-7) Reg. 1916-36	110½
3½	Do. In. Stk. Reg. 1939	110
3	Do. 1916-26	102
3/	Do. 1916	102
3½	Tasmanian Insc. Stock.. 1920-40	108
4	Do. 1920-40	115
4	Trinidad Insc. Stock.... 1917-42	110
3	Do. 1922-44	99
4	Victoria Rly. Loan '81, Inscribed Stock 1907	105
4	Victoria Insc. Stock 1908-13-19	108
4	Victoria (1883) Ins. Stk. 1920	111½
3½	Do. Inscribed Stock 1921-3-6	105½
4	Do. do. 1911-26	108
4	W. Austral. Insc. Stock 1934	116½
4	Do. 1911-31	109
3½	Do. 1915-35	105
3	Do. 1915-35	98
3	Do. 1916-36	98

FOREIGN STOCKS, BONDS, &c.

COUPONS PAYABLE IN LONDON.

Last Div.	Name.	Price.
36/	Argentine Ry. Loan 6 p.c. 1881	86½
15/	Do. 5 p.c. 1884	68
30/	Do. N. Cent. Ry. Ext. 5 p.c. 1887-8-9	68
30/	Do. 5 p.c. Trsy. Convs. 1887	66
5/4½	Do. 4½ p.c. Interl. Gld. 1888	64
27/	Do. 4½ p.c. Stlg. Extrl. 1888	66
10/6	Do. 3½ p.c. External .. 1889	48
4	Do. 4 p.c. Ry. Guar. Res....	68
4½	Brazilian 1883	67
4½	Do. Gold.......... 1879	69½
4½	Do. 1888	57
36/	Buenos Ayres 1824	80
6	Do. 1882-3-6	48
6	Bulgarian 1888	94
6	Do. Mort. Bonds 1892	94
4½	Chilian 1885	74
4½	Do. 1886	75
4½	Do. 1887	74
4½	Do. 1889	80½
5	Do. 1890	86
4½	Do. 1893	72
4½	Do. 1895	71
5	Do. 1896	86
7	Chinese Silver 1894	97
6	Do. Gold 1895	107
6	Do. Apl. '95 by dwgs. 1901-15	109
5	Do. Red. dwgs. in 36 yr. 1896	99
5	Do. Do. Regis. 1896	99
1½	Colmbn. 1½ to 3 p.c. Ext. Bds. 1896	17
6	Cordova, Prov. 1886	[illegible]
—	Do. Eng. Ass. Certs.	[illegible]
—	Do. 6 p.c. 1887-8	[illegible]
—	Do. Eng. Ass. Certs.	[illegible]
3	Costa Rica "A"	[illegible]
2½	Do. "B"	[illegible]
3	Danish Gold 1914	[illegible]
10/	Ecuador N. Ext. Bds. 4½ p.c. ascn. to 5 p.c.	[illegible]
3½	Egypt'n Ins. Stk. lia. Stp. Dty. 1890	100
4	Do. State Domain 1898	103½
4	Do. D. Sanieh, Red. .. 1905	103
6	Entre Rios.............. 1886-8	[illegible]
6	Do. Fndg. Ln. Bds. 1894-1902	[illegible]
6	Do. do. Parana City....	[illegible]
15/	Greek 1881	40
15/	Do. 1884	40
10/	Do. Rentes..................	[illegible]
15/	Do. (Piræus-Larissa Ry.)	[illegible]
3/6	Do. Fundg. Loan	[illegible]
4	Guatemala Extl. Debt..........	[illegible]
6	Hawaiian	[illegible]
4	Hungarian Gold Rentes........	[illegible]
3	Do. 1895	[illegible]
6	Italian Irrign. Guar.	[illegible]
5	Do. Maremmana	[illegible]
5	Japan 5 p.c.	[illegible]
5	Mexican (Nat. R. Tehuantep ec....	[illegible]
6	Do. Extl. 1890	[illegible]

Foreign Stocks, &c. (*continued*):—

Last Div.	Name.	Price
6	Mexican Extrl. 1893	95½
5	Do. Intrnl. Cons. Slvr.	36½
5	Do Intern. Rd. Bds. 2d. Ser.	36½
4	Nicaragua 1886	42½
3½	Norwegian, red. 1937, or earlier	98
3	Do. do. 1965, do.	98
3½	Do. 3½ p.c. Bnds.	102
1	Paraguay 1p.c. ris. 3p.c. 1886-96	15
5	Russian, 1822, £ Strlg.	149
3	Do. 1850	93
4	Do. (Nicolas Ry.) 1867-9	102
3	Do. Transcauc. Ry. 1882	94
4	Do. Con. R. R. Bd. Ser. I., 1889	104
4	Do. Do. II., 1889	104
4	Do. Do. III., 1891	102
3½	Do. Bonds	100
4	Do. Ln. (Dvinsk and Vitbsk)	101½
6	Salvador 1889	57½
—	S Domingo 4s. Unified: .. 1980	62
6	San Luis Potosi Stg. 1889	94
5	San Paulo (Bral.), Stg. 1888	86½
6	Santa Fé 1883-4	36
—	Do. Eng. Ass. Certs. Dep.	35
5	Do. 1888	48
—	Do. Eng. Ass. Certs. Dpsit.	47
5	Do. (W. Cnt. Col. Rly.) Mrt.	26
5	Do. & Reconq. Rly. Mort.	26
5	Spanish Quickslvr Mort. 1870	100½
3½	Swedish 1880	102
3	Do. 1888	98
3	Do. Conversion Loan 1894	98
5	Trans. Gov. Loan Red... 1903-42	106
59/	Tucuman (Prov.) 1888	66½
4	Turkish, Secd. on Egypt. Trib.	102
3½	Turkish, Egpt. Trib., Ott. Bd., '94	96½
4	Do. Priority 1890	91½
1	Do. Convted Series, "A"	66
5	Do. Customs Ln. 1886	94½
5	Uruguay Bonds 1896	57
3	Venzuela New Con. Debt 1881	32

COUPONS PAYABLE ABROAD.

Last Div.	Name.	Price
7	Argent. Nat. Cedla. Sries, "B".	34
5	Austrian Ster. Rnts., ex 10fl., 1870	86
5	Do. do. do.	84
5	Do. Paper do. 1870	85
5	Do. do. do.	85
4	Do. Gld Rentes 1876	102
3	Belgian exchange 25 fr.	100
3½	Danish Int., 1887, Rd. 1896	—
2½	Dutch Certs. ex 12 gldrs.	88
3	Do. Bonds	99
3	Do. Insc. Stk.	98
3½	French Rentes	105
3	Do. 1878, '81-4., Red.	100
3	German Imp. Ln. 1891	95
3	Do. do. 1892-3	95
3	Do. do. 1890-4	96
5	Japan Cons. Ln., '92, 3, & 5, Red.	46
36/9	Prussian Consols	102
3	" Cons. Stg. Ln. 1891	96
4	Utd. States, 1877, Red. 1907	114
4	Do. 1895, 30 yrs.	126
3½	Do. Maschsetts Gl. 1935	113½
3½	Do. Gold Bonds 1923	107½
2	Virginia Cpn. Bds., 3 p.c. from July, 1901	71

BRITISH RAILWAYS.

ORD. SHARES AND STOCKS.

Last Div	Name.	Price.
10	Barry, Ord.	277½
4	Do. Prefd.	125
6	Do. Defd.	152½
5	Caledonian, Ord.	156
3	Do. Prefd.	99½
—	Do. Defd. Ord., No. 1	5
	Cambrian, Ord	5½
—	Do. Coast Cons.	5½
32/	Cardiff Ry. Pref. Ord.	113
3/	Central Lond. £10 Ord. Sh.	10½
1/9½	Do. do. £6 paid	6
3½d.	Do. Pref. Half-Shares	1½
1/6	Do. Def. do	4½
1½	City and S. London	69½
—	East London, Cons.	7
2	Furness	65½
2½	Glasgow and S. West. Pfd.	81
2½	Do. do. Dfd.	65
3	Great Central, Ord.... 1894	41½
32/0	Do. London Exten.	74½
—	Great N. of Scotland, Prfd.	88
—	Do. Dfd.	34
4	Great Northern, Prefd.	120½
—	Do. Consolidated "A"	52
—	Do. do. "B"	191
2	Highland	75½
4	Isle of Wight, Prefd.	120½
3	Do. Defd.	83½
—	Lancs. Derbys. and E. Cst.	4
8½	L. Brighton and S. C. Ord.	186
6	Do. Prefd. Ord.	197
10/	Do. Contgt. Rights Certs.	18½
5½	Lond. and S. Western Ord.	226½
4	Do. Preferred	133
6½	Lond., Tilb., and Southend	134½
—	Mersey, £20 shares	½
—	Metropolitan, New Ord.	129
2½	Do. Surplus Lands	92
4	North Cornwall, 4 p.c. Pref.	104½
13/6	Do. Deferred	22½
7½	North London	224½
4½	North Staffordshire	128

British Railways (*continued*):—

Last Div.	Name.	Price.
3/3	Plymouth, Devenport, and S. W. Junc. £10	8½
3/	Port Talbot £10 Shares	9½
9d.	Rhondda Swns. B. £10 Sh.	4½
10	Rhymney, Cons.	265½
4	Do. Prefd.	123
6¼	Do. Defd.	145½
1½	Scarboro', Bridlington Junc.	47½
6½	South Eastern, Ord	152
6	Do. Pref.	192
3½	Taff Vale	79
25/	Vale of Glamorgan	125½
3	Waterloo & City	131½

LEASED AT FIXED RENTALS.

Last Div.	Name.	Price.
4	Birkenhead	144
5.19.0	East Lincnshire	202½
5½	Hamsmith. & City Ord.	192½
4½	Lond. and Blackwll.	161
4½	Do. £100 4½ p. c. Pref.	161
56/6	Lond. & Green. Ord.	101
5	Do. 5 p. c. Pref.	176½
5	Nor. and Eastn. £50 Ord.	89
6	Do.	104½
3½	N. Cornwall 3½ p. c. Stk.	126½
4½	Nott. & Granthm. R. & C.	145½
3½	Portptk. & Wigtn. Guar. Stk.	121½
9	Vict. Stn. & Pimlico Ord.	312½
4½	Do. 4½ p. c. Pref.	160½
4/	West Lond. £20 Ord. Shs.	14
4½	Weymouth & Portld.	157½

DEBENTURE STOCKS.

Last Div.	Name.	Price.
4	Alexandra Dks. & Ry.	128
3	Barry, Cons.	107
4	Brecon & Mrthyr, New A	124½
4	Do. New B	105
4	Caledonian	148
4	Cambrian "A"	132½
4	Do. "B"	127½
4	Do. "C"	119½
4	Do. "D"	107½
3	Cardiff Rly.	101½
4	City and S. Lond.	137
3½	Cleator & Working Junc.	118½
3	Devon & Som. "A"	103½
16/8	Do. "B" 4 p. c.	36
—	Do. "C" 4 p. c.	10
4	E. Lond. and Ch. 4 p. c. A	135
6/	Do. 2nd B	70½
—	Do. 3rd Ch. 4 p. c.	20½
—	Do. 4th do.	9½
3½	Do. 1st (3½ p. c.)	128½
2½	Do. 2½ p.c. (Whitech. Exn)	87
4	Forth Bridge	142½
4	Furness	142½
4	Glasgow and S. Western	143
5	Gt. Central	—
4½	Do.	156½
4	Gt. Eastern	145
4	Gt. N. of Scotland	144½
3	Gt. Northern	113
4	Gt. Western	150
4½	Do	157½
4½	Do.	166
5	Do.	185
2½	Do.	96½
4	Highland	140½
3	Hull and Barnsley	104½
3	Do. 2nd (3-4 p. c).	124½
4	Isle of Wight	142½
3	Do. Cent. "A"	92½
4½	Do. "B"	115½
4	Do. "C"	82½
3	Lancs. & Yorkshire	113
4	Lancs. Derbys. & E. Cst.	123½
4½	Ldn. and Blackwall	155½
4	Ldn. and Greenwich	144½
4	Lond., Brighton, &c.	148½
4½	Do.	165½
4½	Lond., Chath., &c., Arb.	155½
4½	Do. "B"	154½
4	Do.	137½
4	Do. 1883	137½
3	Do.	106
3	Lond. & N. Western	116
3	Lond. & S. Westn. "A"	114½
3	Do. Consld.	114½
4	Lond., Til., & Southend	144½
—	Mersey, 5 p. c. (Act, 1866)	65
4	Metropolitan	144½
4½	Do.	162½
3½	Do.	126½
6	Met. District	208½
4	Do.	138½
2½	Midland	95
4½	Mid-Wales "A"	137½
4	Neath & Brecon 1st	127½
4	Do. "A 1"	117½
3	North British	110
3	Do. 1893	108½
7½	N. Cornwall, Launcstn., &c.	126½
	North Eastern	113

Debenture Stocks (*continued*):—

Last Div.	Name.	Price.
4½	North London	163½
3	N. Staffordshire	112
4	Plym. Devpt. & S.W. Jn.	141½
4	Rhondda and Swan. Bay	130½
4	Rhymney	144½
4	South-Eastern	148
5	Do.	184
3½	Do.	127½
3	Do.	113
3	Taff Vale	109½
4	Tottenham & For. Gate	143½
3	Vale of Glamorgan	105½
3	West Highld. (Gtd. by N. B.)	106½
4	Wrexham, Mold, &c. "A"	113½
4	Do. "B"	101½
4	Do. "C"	97½

GUARANTEED SHARES AND STOCKS.

Last Div.	Name.	Price.
4	Caledonian	143½
4	Do.	143½
4	Forth Bridge	142½
4	Furness 1881	137½
4	Glasgow & S. Western	141½
4	Do. St. Enoch, Rent	141½
6	Gt. Central	198½
4½	Do. 1st Pref.	151½
3½	Do. Pref.	108
5	Do. Irred. S.Y. Rent	163½
4½	Do. do.	140½
4	Gt. Eastern, Rent	142
5	Do. Metropolitan	175½
4	Do.	143½
4	Gt. N. of Scotland	138½
4	Gt. Northern	145
5	Gt. Western, Rent	184
5	Do. Cons.	184
4	Lancs. & Yorkshire	145
5	L., Brighton & S. C.	181½
3½	L., Chat. & D. (Shrtlds.)	110½
4	L. & North Western	148
4	L. & South Western .. 1881	145
4½	Met. District, Ealing Rent	150
4½	Do. Fulham Rent	150
4	Do. Midland Rent	141½
4	Do. Mid. & Dist. Guar.	130½
2½	Midland, Cons. Perp.	93
3	Mid. & G. N. Jt., "A" Rnt.	107
3	N. British, Lien	107½
4	Do Cons. Pref. No. 1	139
3	N. Cornwall, Wadebrge. Gu.	107
4	N. Eastern	146
5	N. Staff. Trent & M. £20 Shs.	36
3½	Nott. Suburban Ord.	123½
20/6	S. E. Perp. Ann.	35½
4½	Do. 4½ p.c.	162½
3½	S. Yorks. Junc. Ord.	118½
4½	W. Cornwall (G. W., Br., Ex., & S. Dev. Joint Rent	160½
3	W. Highl. Ord. Stk. (Gua., N.B.)	104½

PREFERENCE SHARES AND STOCKS.

DIVIDENDS CONTINGENT ON PROFIT OF YEAR.

Last Div.	Name	Price.
4½	Alexandra Dks. & Ry. "A"	126½
5	Barry (First)	169½
4	Do. Consolidated	137½
4	Caledonian Cons., No. 1	142
4	Do. do. No. 2	141
5	Do. do. 1878	177
4	Do. Pref. 1884	140½
4	Do. do. 1887 (Conv.)	150½
—	Cambrian, No. 1 4 p.c. Pref.	72½
—	Do. No. 2 do.	37½
—	Do. No. 3 do.	17½
—	Do. No. 4 do.	9
5	City & S. Lond. £10 shares	15½
—	Do. New	14
4	Furness, Cons. 1881	133
4	Do. ...... "A" 1881	131½
4	Do. ...... "B" 1883	129½
4	Glasgow & S. Western	141½
4	Do. No. 2	140½
4	Do. 1888	139½
4	Do. 1891	139½
5	Gt. Central	159½
4	Do.	132½
5	Do. Conv. 1872	153½
5	Do. do. 1874	153½
5	Do. do. 1876	152½
5	Do. do. 1879	151½
5	Do. do. 1881	149½
4	Do. 1889	112½
4	Do. 1891	108½
5	Do. 1894	109½
4	Gt. Eastern, Cons.	142½
4	Do. 1886	140½
4	Do. 1881	138½
4	Do. 1884	138½

Preference Shares, &c. (*continued*):—

Last Div.	Name.	Price.
4	Gt. Eastern, Cons. 1887	138½
4	Do. 1888	138½
3½	Do. 1890	120½
3½	Do. 1893	120½
—	Do. (Int. fr. Jan '99) 1893	117½
4	Gt. North Scotland "A"	133½
4	Do. "B"	133½
4	Gt. Northern, Cons.	144
3	Do. 1896	107
5	Gt. Western Cons.	181½
36/11	Hull & Barnsley Red. at 115	110
4	Isle of Wight	133½
3	Lancs. & Yorkshire, Cons.	108
2/2½	Lanc. Drby & E.C. 5 p.c. £10	9½
—	Do. 5 p.c. 2nd £10	9
5	Lond., Bright., &c., Cons.	180½
5	Do. 2nd Cons.	179½
4½	Lond., Chat. & Dov. Arbitr.	136
25/	Do. 2nd Pref. 4½ p.c.	96
4	Lond. & N. Western	147
4	Lond. & S. Western .. 1881	145
4	Do. 1884	144
3½	Do.	127½
4	Lond., Tilbury & Southend	141½
4	Do. Cons., 1887	141½
4	Do 1891	141½
—	Mersey, 5 p.c. Perp.	—
4	Metropolitan, Perp.	142½
4	Do. 1882	140½
4	Do. Irred.	141½
4	Do. 1887	141½
4	Do. New	141½
4½	Do.	146½
3½	Do.	123½
3	Do. Guar.	101½
2½	Metrop. Dist. Exten 5 p.c.	111
2½	Midland, Perp. Pref.	92
4	N. British Cons., No. 2	136
4½	Do. Edin. & Glasgow	153
5	Do. 1865	165½
5	Do. Conv. 1874	166½
4½	Do. 1875	153
4½	Do. Conv. 1875	153
5	Do. do. 1870	166½
4	Do. do. 1884	136½
4	Do. do. 1888	136½
4	Do. do. 1890	136½
4	Do. do. 1892	136½
4	N. Eastern	145
4½	N. Lond., Cons. 1866	174½
4½	Do. 2nd Cons. .. 1875	157½
3	N. Staffordshire	107
4½	Plym. Devpt. & S. W. Junc.	149½
1/5	Port Talbot, &c., 4 p.c. £10 Shares, 4 paid	5
5/	Rhondda & Swansea Bay, 5 p.c. £10 Shares	11
4	Rhymney, Cons.	140½
4½	S. Eastern, Cons.	161½
5	Do. do.	180
4	Do. Vested Cos'.	141½
4	Do. 1891	140½
3½	Do. 1893	122½
2	Do. 3 p.c. after July 1900	102½
4	Taff Vale	141½

INDIAN RAILWAYS.

Last Div.	Name.	Paid.	Price.
3½	Assam Bengal, Ld., (3½ p.c. till June 30, then 3 p.c.)	100	102
4/	Barsi Light, Ld., £10 Shs.	10	11
6	Bengal and N. West., Ld	100	148
4/	Do. £10 Shares	10	14
3/6	Do. 3½ p.c. Cum. Pf. Shs.	10	10½
8½d.	Do.	4	6½
2/3½	Bengal Central, Ld., £10 (3½ p.c. + ¼th net earn)	5	6
3	Bengal Dooars, Ld.	100	114
4	Bengal Nagpr., Lim. (gua. 4 p.c. + 4th sp. pfts.)	100	114
7½	Bombay, Baroda, and C. I. (gua 5 p.c)	100	216
36/1	Burma, Ld. (gua. 2½ p.c. and ½ p.c. add. till 1901)	100	108
1/7	Do. £10 Shares		3½
5½	Delhi Umb. Kalka, Ld., Gua. 3½ p.c. + net earn.	100	120
4	Do. Deb. Stk., 1890 (1916)	100	111
9/10	Estn. Bengal, "A" An. 1957	—	25
9/	Do. "B" 1957	—	30
4	Do. Gua. Deb. Stock	100	134½
9/7½	East Ind. Ann. "A" (1953)	—	28
8/4½	Do. "C"	—	29
8/11½	Do. "B"	—	31
6⅛	Do. Def. Ann. Cap. (gua. 4 p.c. + ⅕th sp. pfts.)	—	151
115/9	East Ind. Def. Ann. "D"	—	157
4½	East Ind. Irred. Stock	100	156½
5	Gt. Indian Penin., Gua 5 p.c. + ½ surplus profits	100	169½
4	Do. Irred. 4 p.c. Deb. St.	100	137½
4	Indian Mid., Ld. (gua. 4 p.c. + ¼th surplus pfts.)	100	114
51/	Madras Guar. + ½ sp. pfts.	100	167
48/6	Do. do.	100	158
46/	Do. do.	100	148
4	Nilgiri, Ld., 1st Deb. Stk.	100	98
51/9	Rohil. and Kumaon, Ld.	100	130
9/11	Scinde, Punj., and Delhi, "A" Ann., 1958	—	25
9/1	Do. "B" do.	—	30

Indian Railways (*continued*):—

Last Div.	Name.	Paid.	Price.
4	South Behar, Ld., £10 shs.	100	100
3½	Do. Deb. Stk. Red.	100	101
4½	South Ind., Gu. Deb. Stk.	100	156½
5	South Indian, Ld. (gua. 3 p.c., and ⅓ spls. profits)	100	122½
5	Sthn. Mahratta, Ld. (3½ p.c. & ¼th net earnings)	100	116½
4	Do. Deb. Stk. Red.	100	121
3½	Southern Punjab, Ld.	100	105
3½	Do. Deb. Stk. Red.	—	104
5	Nizam's Gua. State, Ld. ..	100	114½
4	Do. Mort. Deb., 1936	100	108
4	Do. do. Reg.	100	106
17/3½	Nizam's Gua. State, Ld., 3½ p.c. Mt. Deb. bearer	—	95½
17/3½	Do. Reg. do. ..	—	93½
5	W. of India Portgese., Ld.	100	68½
5	Do. Deb. Stk., Red	100	99

RAILWAYS.—BRITISH POSSESSIONS.

Last Div.	Name.	Paid.	Price.
5	Atlantic & N.W. Gua. 1 Mt. Bds., 1937	100	126½
5/3	Buff. & L. Huron Ord. Sh.	10	13½
5½	Do. 1st Mt. Perp. Bds. 1879	100	143½
5½	Do. 2nd Mt. Perp. Bds.	100	143½
—	Calgary & Edmon. 6 p.c. 1st Mt. Stg. Bds. Red..	100	82½
5	Canada Cent. 1st Mt. Bds. Red.	100	103
4	Can. Pacific Pref. Stk.	100	101
5	Do. Strl. 1st Mt. Deb. Bds. 1915	100	117
3½	Do. Ld. Grnt. Bds. 1938..	100	108
3½	Do. Ld. Grnt. Ins. Stk. ..	100	107
4	Do. Perp. Cons. Deb. Stk.	100	115
5	Do. Algoma Bch. 1st Mt. Bds., 1937	100	122
3	Demerara, Original Stock	100	46
7	Do. Perp. Pref. Stk.	100	152½
1/10	Do. 4 p.c. Cum. Ext. Pref. £10 Shs.	4	8
—	Dominion Atlntc. Ord. Stk.	100	33½
5	Do. 5 p.c. Pref. Stk.....	100	97½
4	Do. 1st. Deb. Stk......	100	105½
4	Do. 2nd do. Red.	100	99
1/3	EmuBay&Mt.Bischoff, Ld.	5	4½
4½	Do. Irred. Deb. Stk....	100	98
nil.	Gd. Trunk of Canada, Stk.	100	9⅜
6	Do. 2nd. Equip. Mt. Bds.	100	133
5	Do. Perp. Deb. Stk.......	100	138½
5	Do. Gt. Westn. Deb. Stk.	100	130½
5	Do. Nthn. of Can. 1st Mt. Bds., 1902	100	103½
4	Do. do. Deb. Stk	100	103
5	Do. G. T. Geor. Bay & L. Erie 1 Mt., 1903	100	105
5	Do. Mid. of Can. Stl. 1st Mt. (Mid. Sec.) 1908....	100	108
5	Do.do.Cons.1 Mt.Bds.1912	100	107
5	Do. Mont. & Champ. 1 Mt. Bds., 1902	100	104
	Do. Welln., Grey & Brce. 7 p.c. Bds. 1 Mt.	100	109
—	Jamaica 1st Mtg. Bds. Red.	—	102
—	Manitoba & N. W., 6 p.c. 1st Mt. Bds., Red	100	—
—	Do. Ldn. Bdhldrs. Certs.	—	—
5	Manitoba S. W. Col. 1 Mt. Bd., 1934 $1,000 price %	—	119
—	Mid. of W. Aust. Ld. 6 p.c. 1 Mt. Dbs., Red.	100	42½
4	Do. Deb. Bds., Red.	100	103
4	Nakusp& Slocan Bds., 1918	100	106
3	Natal Zululand Ld. Debs.,	100	72½
5	N. Brunswick 1st Mt. Stg. Bds., 1934	100	121
4	Do. Perp. Cons. Deb. Stk.	100	114
—	N. Zealand Mid., Ld., 5 p.c 1st Mt. Debs..........	100	35
6	Ontario & Queb. Cap. Stk.	$100	151½
5	Do. Perm. Deb. Stk......	100	143½
—	Qu'Appelle, L. Lake & Sask. 6p.c. 1 Mt. Bds. Red.	100	40½
	Queb. & L. S. John, 1st Mt. Bds., 1909	100	32
	Quebec Cent., Prior Ln. Bds., 1908	100	107
1½	Do. 5 p.c. Inc. Bds.	100	37
4	St. Lawr. & Ott. Stl. 1st Mt.	100	112
4	Shuswap & Okan., 1st Mt. Deb. Bds., 1915	100	76
5	Temiscouata, 5 p.c. Stl. 1st Deb. Bds., Red.	100	9½
5	Do. (S. Franc. Brch.) 5 p.c. Stl. 1 Mt. Db. Bds., 1910	100	10
4	Toronto, Grey & B. 1st Mt.	100	112
1/	Well. & Mana. £5 Shs. ..	1	¾
5	Do. Debs., 1908	100	105
5	Do. 2nd Debs., 1908	100	104
5	Do. 3rd do., 1908	100	103
6	Atlan. & St. Law. Shs., 6 p.c.	100	163½
5	Gd. Trunk Mt. Bds., 1934	100	116½
5	Michigan Air Line, 5 p.c. 1st Mt. Bds., 1902	100	104
4	Minneap., S. P. & S t. Ste. Mar, 1st Mt. Bds., 1938	$1000	100

AMERICAN RAILROAD STOCKS AND SHARES.

Last Div.	Name.	Paid.	Price.
6/	Alab. Gt. Sthn. A 6 p.c. Pref.	10/.	9½
—	Do. do "B" Ord. ..	10/.	1½
—	Alabma. N. Orl.-Tex. &c., "A" Pref.	10/.	⅜
—	Do. "B" Def.	10/.	¼
5½	Atlant. First Lsd. La. Rtl. Trust....................	Stk.	98½
—	Baltimore & Ohio Com. ..	$100	20
—	Baltimore Ohio S.W. Pref.	$100	7
—	Chesap. & Ohio Com.	$100	24
—	Chic. Gt. West. 5 p.c. Pref. Stock "A"	$100	34
—	Do. do. Scrip. In.......	—	30½
8/3	Do. 4 p.c. Deb. Stk.......	$100	67½
4	Do. Interest in Scrip	$100	63½
$4	Chic. Junc. Rl. & Un. Stk. Yds. Com.	$100	122½
$1½	Do. 6 p.c. Cum. Pref.	$100	120½
$3½	Chic. Mil. & St. P. Pref...	$100	149
7	Cleve. & Pittsburgh......	$10	86
$1½	Clev., Cincin., Chic., & St. Louis Com.	$100	—
—	Erie 4 p.c. Non-Cum. 1st Pf.	—	38½
—	Do. 4 p.c. do. 2nd Pf.	—	20
$2½	Gt. Northern Pref.	$100	180
$2½	Illinois Cen. Lsd. Lines ..	$100	97½
—	Kansas City, Pitts & G. ..	$100	19
$3	L. Shore & Mich. Sth. C.	$100	190
—	Mex. Cen. Ltd. Com.	$100	5
—	Miss. Kan. & Tex. Pref...	$100	38½
2½	N.Y., Pen. & O. 1st Mt. Tst. Ltd., Ord.	—	47½
4	Do. 1st Mort. Deb. Stk. ..	$100	92½
8	North Pennsylvania	$50	—
—	Northn. Pacific, Com.....	$100	31½
1½	Pitts. F. Wayne & Chic...	$100	175
—	Reading 1st Pref.	$50	24½
—	Do. 2nd Pref.	$50	12½
—	S. Louis & S. Fran. Com.	$100	8
—	Do. 2nd Pref.	$100	33
6	St. Louis Bridge 1st Pref..	$100	107
3	Do. 2nd Pref.	$100	50
6	Tunnel Rail. of St. Louis	$100	107
$1½	St. Paul, Min. and Man...	$100	147½
—	Southern, Com.	$100	9½
—	Wabash, Common	$100	8

AMERICAN RAILROAD BONDS. CURRENCY.

Last Div.	Name.		Price.
7	Albany & Susq. 1 Con. Mrt.	1906	118
7	Allegheny Val. 1 Mt......	1910	127½
5	Canada Southern 1 Mt.	1908	112½
5	Chic. & N. West. Sk. Fd. Db.	1933	120½
5	Do. Deb. Coupon	1921	117½
6	Chicago & Tomah	1905	109½
5	Chic. Burl. & Q. Skg. Fd.	1901	102½
4	Do. Nebraska Ext.......	—	100½
6	Chic., Mil., & S. Pl., 1 Mt. S.W. Div..............	1909	117½
7	Do. (S. Paul Div.) 1 Mt.	1902	132½
5	Do. (La Cross & D.	1919	114½
7	Do. 1 Mt. (Hast. & Dak.)	1910	127½
5	Do. Chic. & Mis. Riv. 1 Mt.	1926	—
6	Det., G. Haven & Mil. Equip	1918	105
6	Do. do. Cons. Mt.	1918	102½
6	Ill. Cent., 1 Mt., Chic. & S.	1898	—
7	Indianap. & Vin., 1 Mt. ..	1908	125
6	Do. do. 2 Mt. ..	1900	100½
6	Lehigh Val., Cons. Mt....	1923	114½
—	Mexic. Cent., Ln. 2 Cons. Inc.	—	5
7	N.Y. Cent. & H.R. Mt. Bonds	1903	120½
5	Do. Deb.	1904	111½
6	Penns. Cons. S. F M.	1905	114½
4	West Shore, 1 Mt.	2361	111

DITTO—GOLD.

Last Div.	Name.		Price.
6	Alabama Gt. Sthn. 1 Mt. ..	1908	114
5	Do. Mid. 1	1928	90½
4	Allegheny Val. Gen. Mt. ..	1942	107½
4	Atch., Top., & S. Fé Gn. Mt.	1995	95½
3	Do. Adj. Mt.............	1995	68½
5	Do. Equipt. Tmst.	—	102½
5	Atlantic & Dan. 1 Mt......	1950	96½
5	Baltimore & Ohio..........	1925	105½
5	Do. Speyer's Tst. Recpts.	1925	105½
5	Do. Cons. Mt.	1988	110
4½	Do. 4½ p.c. 1 Mt. Term.	1934	90
4½	Do. Brown Shipley's Dep. Cts.	—	90
5	Balt. Belt 5 p.c. 1 Mort....	1990	97½
4½	Balt. & Ohio S.W. 1 Mt. ..	1990	104
4½	Do. 4½ p.c. 1 Cons. Mt. 1893	1993	76½
—	Do. Inc. Mt. 5 p.c. Cl. A	—	29
—	Do. do. Cl. B	—	10
5	Balt. & Ohio S.W. Term 5 p.c.	1942	97½
6	Balt. & Ptmac (Mn. L.) 1 Mt.	1911	124
6	Do. do. (Tunnel) 1 Mt.	1911	126
4	Beech Creek 1 Mt.	1936	109
4	Carthage & Adiron 1 Mt...	1981	107

American Railroad Bonds—Gold (*continued*):—

Last Div.	Name.		Price.
5	Cent. of Georgia 1 Mort. ..	1945	117½
5	Do. Cons. Mt.	1945	90½
5	Cent. of N. Jray. Gn. Mt. ..	1987	117½
6	Central Pacific, 1 Mort.	1898	102½
6	Do. Speyer's Certs.	—	106
5	Do. Land Grant	1900	104
5	Chesap. & Ohio 1st Cons. Mt.	1939	117½
4½	Do. Gen. Mt.	1992	86
6	Chic. & W. Ind. Gen. Mt. Skg. Fd.	1932	119½
5	Chic. Mil. & St. Pl. (Chic. & L. Sup.) 1 Mt.	1921	114½
5	Do. Chic. & Pac. W.	1921	117½
5	Do. Wisc. & Minn. 1 Mt.	1921	112½
5	Do. Terminal Mt.	1914	114½
4	Do. General Mt.	1989	108
5	Chic. St. L. & N. Orleans..	1951	120
4	Do. 1 Mort. (Memphis) ..	1951	104
4	Clevel., Cin., Chic. & St. L., 1 Mt. (Cairo)	1939	90
4	Do. 1 Mt. (Cinc., Wab., & Mich.)	1991	90
4	Do. 1 Col. Tst. Mt. (S. Louis)	1990	95
4	Do. General Mt.	1993	80½
4½	Clevel. & Mar. Mt.	1935	109
4½	Clevel. & Pittsburgh	1942	116½
4½	Do. Series B.	1942	116½
—	Colorado Mid. 1 Mt.	1936	65½
—	Do. Bdhrs.' Comm. Certs.	—	55½
4	Dnvr. & R. Gde. 1 Cons. Mt.	1936	98
5	Do. Imp. Mort.	1928	94
4	Detroit & Mack. 1 Lien	1995	90
5	E. Tennes., Virg., & Grgia. Cons. Mt.	1956	111½
5	Elmira, Cort., & Nthn. Mt.	1914	100
4	Erie 1 Cons. Mt. Pr. Ln. ..	1996	95
3	Do. Gen. Lien	1996	76½
6	Galvest., Harrisb., &c., 1 Mt.		110
5	Georgia, Car. & N. 1 Mt. ..	1929	96
4½	Gd. Rpds. & Inda. Ex. 1 Mt.	1941	112½
5	Do. 1 Mt. (Muskegon) ..	1926	39
3½	Illinois Cent. 1 Mt.	1951	104½
4	Do.	1952	104½
4	Do. Cairo Bdge. ..	1950	102
4	Do.	1953	102
4	Do. General Mort. ..	1904	102½
5	Kans. City, Pitts. & G. 1 M.	1923	73½
3½	L. Shore & Mich. Southern	1997	106½
4½	Lehigh Val. N.Y. 1 Mt....	1940	105½
5	Lehigh Val. Term. 1 Mt. ..	1941	112
5	Long Island	1931	117½
5	Do. Deb.	1934	100
5	Do. (N. Shore Bch.) 1 Cons. Mt.	1932	92½
6	Louisville & Nash. G. Mt. ..	1930	121
6	Do. 2 Mt. Sk. Fd. (S. & N. Alabama...........	1910	107
6	Do. 1 Mt. N. Orl. & Mb.	1930	125½
5	Do. 1 Mt. Coll. Tst. ..	1931	106
4	Do. Unified	1940	93
4½	Do. Mobile & Montgy. 1 Mt.	1945	111½
4	Manhattan Cons. Mt.	1990	98
4	Mexican Cent. Cons. Mt. ..	1911	68
—	Do. 1 Cons. Inc, ...		15
6	Mexican Nat. 1 Mt..........	1927	106
3½	Do. 2 Mt. 6 p.c. Inc. A	1917	52½
—	Do. do. B..	1917	9
3	Michig. Cnt. (Battle Ck. & S.) 1 Mt.	1989	86
5	Minneap. & S. L. 1 Consold.	1934	107½
4	Minne., Slt. S. M. & A. 1 Mt.	1926	100
5	Minneapolis Westn. 1 Mt...	1911	105½
4	Miss. Kans. & Tex. 1 Mt. ..	1990	90
4	Do. 2 do.	1990	65
4	Mobile & Birm. Mt. Inc.....	1945	38
5	Do. P. Lien	1945	88
4	Mohawk & Mal. 1 Mt.	1991	108
5	Montana Cent. 1 Mt.......	1937	111½
5	Nashv., Chattan., & S. L. 1 Cons. Mt	1928	102½
5	Nash., Flor., & Shff. Mt. ..	1937	95½
4	N. Y. & Putnam 1 Cons. Mt.	1993	108
5	N. Y., Brooklyn, & Man. B. 1 Cons. Mt	1935	107½
4	N. Y. Cent. & Hud. R. Deb. Certs. 1890	1905	106
4	Do. Ext. Debt. Certs.	1905	106
7	N. Y., L. Erie, & W. 1 Cons. Mt. (Erie)	1920	144½
7	Do. 1 Con. Mt. Fd. Coup.	1920	139½
5	N. Y., Onto., & W. Cons. 1 Mt.	—	109
4	Do. 4 p.c. Refund. Mt...	1992	101½
6	Norfolk & West. Gn. Mt....	1931	124
6	Do. Imp. & Ext..........	1934	117½
4	Do. 1 Cons. Mt.	—	85
6	N. Pacific Gn. 1 Mt. Ld. Gt.	1921	—
4	Do. P. Ln. Rl. & Ld. Gt.	—	100
3	Do. Gn. Ln. Rl. & Ld. Gt.	—	64
5	Oregon & Calif. 1 Mt.......	1927	36
6	Panama Skg. Fd. Subsidy ..	1910	102½
4½	Pennsylvania Rlrd.	1943	112
4	Do. Equip. Tst. Ser. A ..	1914	104
4	Do. Cons. Mt.	1943	112½
4½	Penna. Company 1st Mort.	1921	115
5	Perkiomen 1 Mrt., 2nd ser..	1918	91½
4½	Pitts., C., C., & St. Ls. Con. Mt. G. B., Ser. A	1940-2	114½
4	Do. Cons. Mort., Ser. D..	1945	102½
6	Pittsbgh., Cle., & Toledo ..	1922	100½
4	Reading, Phil., & R. Genl.	1997	88
5	Richmond & Dan. Equip. ..	1909	97½
5	Rio Grande Junc. 1st Mort.	1939	90
4	Rio Grande West 1st Tst. Mt.	1939	90
7	S. Louis Bridge 1st Mort ..	1928	134½
5	S. Louis Mchts. Bdge. Term. 1st Mort.	1930	102½
4	S. Louis S. West 1st Mort..	1989	75½
—	Do. 4 p.c. 2nd Mort. Inc.	1989	30
4½	S. Louis Term. Cupples Sta. & Prop. 1st. Mrt. 4½ p.c.	1902-17	100
4½	St. Paul Minn., & Manit.	1933	111

American Railroad Bonds (*continued*):

Last Div.	Name.		Price.
6	St. Paul, Minn., & Manit.	1933	132½
6	Shamokin, Sunbury, &c. 2 Mt.	1925	109
5	S. & N. Alabama Cons. Mt.	1936	102
5	Southern 1 Cons. Coup.	1994	98
4	Do. E. Tennes Reorg. Lien ..	1938	100
6	S. Pacific of Cal. 1 Mt...	1905-12	111
4½	Trml. Assn. of S. Louis 1 Mt.	1939	112
5	Do. 1 Cons. Mt...........	1944	109
5	Texas & Pac. 1 Mt..........	2000	106½
—	Do. 5 p.c. 2 Mt. Income	2000	38
5	Toledo & Ohio Cent. 1 Mt. West. Div.	1935	102½
4½	Toledo., Walhon., Val., & Ohio 1 Mt.	1931-3	111½
—	Union Pacific 1 Mt. 4 p.c. ..	1947	98
—	Union Pac., Linc., & Color. 1 Mt.	1918	—
4	United N. Jersey Gen. Mt...	1944	117½
6	Vicksbrg., Shrevept., & Pac. Pr. Ln. Mt.	1915	102½
5	Wabash 1 Mt.	1939	110
4	Wn. Pennsylvania Mt.	1928	106½
5	W. Virga. & Pittsbg. 1 Mt.	1990	77½
5	Wheeling & L. Erie 1 Mt. (Wheelg. Div.) 5 p.c.	1928	92½
5	Do. Extn. Imp. Mt.	1930	90
—	Do. do. Brown Shipley's Cts...		—
5	Willmar & Sioux Falls 1 Mt.	1938	118

STERLING.

Last Div.	Name.		Price.
6	Alabama Gt. Sthn. Deb....	1906	104½
5	Do. Gen. Mort. ..	1927-8	98
5	Alabama, N. Orl., Tex. & Pac. 5 p.c. "A" Dbs...	1910-40	100
55/	Do. do. "B" do.	1910-40	57
—	Do. do. "C" do.		19
—	Allegheny Valley	1910	132
4	Atlantic 1st Leased Line Perp...		100
6	Baltimore and Ohio	1909	110
6	Do. do.	1910	122
5	Do. do. 1877........		105½
—	Do. Morgan's Certs. ..		105½
4½	Do. do.	1933	98
6	Chicago & Alton Cons. Mt.	1903	112
5	Chic. St. Paul & Kan. City Priority		106½
6	Eastn. of Massachusetts....	1906	117½
5	Illinois Cent. Skg. Fd.		104
5	Do.	1905	106
3½	Do.	1950	98½
4	Do. 1 Mt.	1951	114
3	Do. 1 Mt.	1951	93½
6	Louisville & Nash., M. C. & L. Div., 1 Mt.	1902	104½
7	Do. 1 Mt. (Memphis & O.)......................	1901	112
55/8	Mexican Nat. "A" Certs. 5 p.c. Non. cum.		40½
—	Do. "B" Certs.....		9
6	N.Y. & Canada 1 Mt.......	1904	116
6	N. York Cent. & H.R. Mort.	1903	112
4½	N. York, Penns., & Ohio Pr. Ln. Extd.	1935	—
5	Do. Equip. Tst.		101½
5	Do. 5 p.c. Equip. Tst. (1890)		101½
6	Nrthn. Cent. Cons. Gen. Mt. ..		106
6	Pennsylvania Gen. Mt.	1910	126
6	Do. Cons. Skg. Fd. Mt.	1905	116½
3½	Do. Cons. Mt.	1945	105
6	Phil. & Erie Cons. Mort ..	1920	134½
6	Phil. & Reading Gen. Cons. Mort.	1911	122½
6	Pittsbg. & Connells. Cons.	1926	117½
—	Do. Morgan's Certs....		117½
4	St. Paul., Min., & Manitoba (Pac. Extn.)	1940	100
6	S. & N. Alabama	1903	104½
6	Un. N. Jersey & C. Gen. Mt.	1901	109½

FOREIGN RAILWAYS

Last Div.	Name.	Paid.	Price.
12/	Alagoas, Ltd., Shs.	20	6½
5	Do. Deb. Stk., Red. ..	100	45½
6	Antofagasta, Ltd., Stk. ..	100	73
4	Do. Perp. Deb. Stk. ..	100	90
—	Arauco, Ld., Ord. Shs. ..	10	—
—	Do. 10 p.c. Cum. Pref.	10	—
5	Argentine Gt. W., Ld.,	100	84
5	Do. 5 p.c. Cum. Pref. Shs.	100	105
4	Do. 1 Deb. Stk.	100	104
1/0/0	Argentine N.E., Ltd., 6 p.c. Cum. Pref. Stk. ..	100	9½
—	Do. 5 p.c. Deb. Stk., Red.	100	20
2/	Arica and Tacna Shs. ..	20	1½
10/	Bahia & San Fcisco., Ld.,	20	10½
6/	Do. Timbo. Bch. Shs.	20	5
12/	Bahia, Blanca, & N.W. Ln. Prf. Cum. 6 p.c. ..	100	52
4	Do. 4 p.c. 1 Deb. Stk., Red.	100	92
6	Barranquilla R. & P., Ld., 6 p.c. 1 Deb. Stk., Red.	100	96

Foreign Railways (*continued*):—

Last Div.	Name.	Paid.	Price.
3/	Bilbao Riv. & Cantabn., Ltd., Ord.	3	5
—	Bolivar, Ltd. Shs.	10	1½
6	Do. 6 p.c. Deb. Stk.	100	96½
—	Brazil Gt. Southn. Ltd., 7 p.c. Cum. Pref.	20	1½
6	Do. Perm. Deb. Stk	100	52
5½	B. Ayres Gt. Southn. Ld., Ord. Stk.	100	141
5	Do. Pref. Stk.	100	133
4	Do. Deb. Stk.	100	117
30/	B. Ayres & Ensen. Port., Ltd., Ord. Stk.	100	66
5	Do. Cum. 1 Pref. Stk.	100	117
6/0/0	Do. 6p.c.Con. Pref.Stk.	100	96
4	Do. Deb. Stk., Irred.	100	113
10⅛	B. Ayres Northern, Ltd., Ord. Stk.	100	260
12½	Do. Pref. Stk.	100	320
5	Do. 5 p.c. Mt. Deb.Stk., Red.	100	113
3/15/0	B. Ayres & Pac., Ld., 7 p.c. 1 Pref. Stk. (Cum.)	100	92½
4	Do. 1 Deb. Stk.	100	102½
5/5/0	Do. 4½ p.c. 2 Deb. Stk.	100	93
3	B. Ayres & Rosario, Ltd., Ord. Stk.	100	73½
7/	Do. 7 p.c. Pref. Shs.	10	17
7/	Do. Sunchales Ext.	10	14½
4	Do. Deb. Stk., Red.	100	108½
—	B. Ayres & Val. Trans., Ltd., 7 p.c. Cum. Pref.	20	6½
4	Do. 4 p.c. "A" Deb. Stk., Red.	100	70
—	Do. 6 p.c. "B" Deb. Stk. Red.	100	44
3/6	B. Ayres Westn. Ld. Ord.	10	11
3/	Do. Def. Shs	10	6½
5	Do. 5 p.c. Pref.	10	12½
4	Do. Deb. Stk	100	111
6	Cent.Arg.Deb.Sk.Rd.	100	159½
4	Do. Deb. Stk. Rd	100	110
6	Cent. Bahia L. Ord. Stk.	100	50
	Do. Deb. Stk., 1934	100	69½
5	Do. Deb. Stk., 1937	100	60
3/6	Cent. Uguy. East. Ext. L. Shs	10	5½
5	Do. Perm. Stk.	100	112
3/6	Do. Nthn. Ext. L. Sh.	10	4
5	Do. Perm. Deb. Stk	100	104
3	Do. of Montev. Ltd., Ord. Stk	100	86
6	Do. Perm. Deb. Stk	100	143
10/	Conde d'Eu, Ltd. Ord.	20	7
—	Cordba & Rosar., Ltd., 6 p.c. Pref. Shs.	100	40
4	Do. 1 Deb. Stk	100	90
75	Do. 6 p.c. Deb. Stk	100	80
—	Cordba Cent., Ltd., 5 p.c. Cu. 1 Pref. Stk	100	84
—	Do. 5 p.c. Non-Cum. 2 Pref. Stk	100	43
5	Do. Deb. Stk	100	118
4/	Costa Rica, Ltd., Shs	10	3½
8/	Dna. Thrsa. Chris., Ltd., 7 p.c. Pref. Shs.	20	3½
20/	E. Argentine, Ltd	100	44
6	Do. Deb. Stk	100	102
1/1	Egyptn. Dlta. Lgt. Rys., Ltd., £10 Pref. Shs.	8	10
—	Entre Rios, L., Ord. Shs.	5	½
—	Do. Cu. 5 p.c. Pref.	5	3
6/	Gt. Westn. Brazil, Ltd.,	20	8
6	Do. Perm. Deb. Stk	100	93
6	Do. Extn. Deb. Stk	100	75½
—	Int.-Oceanic Mex., Ltd., 7 p.c. Pref.	10	1½
4	Do. Deb. Stk	100	83
42/6	Do. 7 p.c. "A" Deb. Sk.	100	71
—	Do. 7 p.c. "B" Deb. Sk.	100	31
5/	La Guaira & Carac.	10	7½
5	Do. 5 p.c. Deb. Sk. Red.	100	103
13/3	Lembg.-Czern.-Jassy	30	24½
1/	Lima, Ltd.	20	2½
—	Manila Ltd. 7 p.c. Cu. Pf.	10	½
20/6½	Mexican and Pref. 6 p.c.	100	33
6	Do. Perp Deb. Stk.	100	139
1/0/0	Mexican Sthrn., Ld., Ord.	100	22
—	Do. 4 p.c. 1 Db.Stk.Rd.	100	84
—	Do. 4 p.c. 2 do.	100	59
—	Mid. Urgy., Ltd.	100	18½
5	Do. Deb. Stk.	100	59
12/	Minas & Rio, Ltd.	20	10½
5/2	Namur & Liege	20	12½
11/6	Do. Pref.	20	29
13/	Natal & Na. Cruz, Ld., 7 p.c. Cum Pref.	20	7
—	Nitrate Ltd., Ord.	10	5½
—	Do. 7 p.c. Pr. Con. Or.	10	4
—	Do. Def. Conv. Ord.	10	½
7/	N.-E. Urgy., Ltd., Ord.	10	15
7/	Do. 7 p.c. Pref.	10	15½
—	N.-W. Argentine Ld., 7 p.c. Pref.	10	2
6	Do. 6 p.c. 1 Deb. Stk.	100	110
—	Do. 2 Deb. Stk.	100	94
—	N.W. Uruguay 6 p.c. 1 Pref. Stk.	100	16
—	Do. 5 p.c. 2 Pref. Stk.	100	7½
6	Do. 6 p.c. Deb. Stk.	100	80
22/	Ottoman (Sm. Aid.)	20	13½
—	Paraguay Cntl., Ld., 5 p.c. Perm. Deb. Stk.	100	10
—	Piræus, Ath., & Pelo.	275	1½
4/	Pto. Alegre & N. Hambg Ld., 7 p.c. Pref. Shs.	20	4
6	Do. Mt. Deb. Stk. Red.	100	74½
—	Puerto Cabello & Val. Ld.	10	1½
5	Recife & S. Francisco	100	65½
24/	R. Claro S. Paulo, Ld., Sh.	10	23
5	Do. Deb. Stk.	100	125
5	Royal Sardinian Ord.	10	11½
5/	Do. Pref.	10	11½

Foreign Railways (*continued*):—

Last Div.	Name.	Paid.	Price.
5/	Sambre & Meuse	20	18
5/6	Do. Pref.	10	12½
22/	San Paulo Ld.	20	34
2/10½	Do. New Ord. £10 sh.	6	10
4/8	Do. 5 p.c. Non.Cm.Pref.	10	12½
5½	Do. Deb. Stk.	100	133
5	Do. 5 p.c. Deb. Stk	100	127
—	S. Fé & Cordova, Gt. Sthn., Ld., Shares	100	49
6	Do. Perp. Deb. Stk.	100	119
3/2½	S. Austrian	20	7
12/	Sthn. Braz. R. Gde. do Sul, Ld.	20	8½
6	Do. 6 p.c. Deb. Stk.	100	66
4	Swedish Centl., Ld., 4 p.c. Deb. Stk.	100	107
5	Do. Pref.	100	101
1/3	Taltal, Ld.	5	2½
—	Uruguay Nthn., Ld. 7 p.c. Pfd. Stk.	100	8
3½	Do. 5 p.c. Deb. Stk.	100	30
—	Villa Maria & Rufino, Ld., 6 p.c. Pref. Shs.	100	17
4	Do. 4 p.c. 1 Deb. Stk.	100	73
6/0/0	Do. 6 p.c. 2 Deb. Stk.	100	42½
5/9	West Flanders	8½	21
5/6	Do. 5½ p.c. Pref.	10	18
3/	Wstn. of Havana, Ld.	10	4½

FOREIGN RAILWAY OBLIGATIONS

Per Cent.	Name.	Price.
6	Alagoas Ld., 6 p.c. Deb., Rd.	84
—	Alcoy & Gandia, Ld., 5 p.c. Debs., Red.	20
5	Arauco., Ld., 5 p.c. 1st Mt., Rd.	64½
—	Do. 6 p.c. Mt. Deb., Rd.	39½
6	Brazil G. Sthn., L., Mt. Dbs., Rd.	88½
6	Do. Mt. Dbs. 1893, Rd.	52
5½	Campos & Caran. Dbs., Rd.	70
6	Central Bahia, L., Dbs., Rd.	89½
5½	Conde d'Eu, L., Dbs., Rd.	71
6	Costa Rica, L., 1st Mt. Dbs., Rd.	109
6	Do. 2nd Dbs., Rd.	91
5	Do. Prior Mt. Db., Rd.	104
6	Cucuta Mt. Dbs., Rd.	102
5½	Donna Thrsa. Cris., L., Dbs., Rd.	71
3	Eastn. of France, £20 Dbs., Rd.	18½
4	Egyptn. Delta Light, L., Db., Rd	100
—	Espito. Santo & Cara. 5 p.c. Stl. Dbs., Rd.	38
4	Gd. Russian Nic., Rd.	102
5	Inter-Oceanic Mex., L., 5 p.c. Pr. Ln. Dbs., Rd.	103
3	Ital. 3 p.c. Bds. A & B, Rd.	57½
—	Ituana 6 p.c. Debs., 1918	72½
—	Leopoldina, 6 p.c. Dbs. £50 Bds.,	25
—	Do. do. Comms. Cert.	25
—	Do. 5 p.c. Stg. Dbs. (1888), Rd.	35
—	Do. do. Comm. Certs.	35
—	Do. 5 p.c. Stg. Dbs. (1890), Rd.	25
—	Do. do. Comms. Certs.	25
—	Macahé & Cam. 5 p.c. Dbs., Rd.	35
—	Do. do. Comms. Certs.	35
—	Do. (Cantagallo), 5 p.c., Red.	35
—	Do. do. Comm. Certs.	35
—	Manila Ltd., 6 p.c. Deb., Red.	21
6	Do. Prior Lien Mt., Rd.	100½
6	Do. Series "B," Rd.	80
7	Matanzas & Sab., Rd.	101½
6	Minas & Rio, L., 6 p.c. Dbs., Rd.	97
5	Mogyana 5 p.c. Deb. Bds., Rd.	100
5	Moscow-Jaros., Rd.	105½
5½	Natal & Na. Cruz Ltd., 5½ p.c. Debs., Red.	76
5	Nitrate, Ltd. Mt. Bds., Red.	87
3	Nthn. France, Red.	19
4	N. of S. Af. Rep. (Trnsvl.) Gu. Bds. Red.	96
3	Nthn. of Spain £20 Pri. Obs. Red.	7½
6	Ottmn. (Smy to A.)(Kujk.) Asnt. Debs., Red.	106
6	Ottmn. (Sernik.) Asg. Debs. Red.	106
6	Ottmn. (Seraik.) Non-Asg. D., Rd	106
5	Ottmn. Kuyjk. Ext. Red.	104
5	Ottmn. Serkeuy. Ext. Red.	101½
5	Ottmn. Tireh Ext. 1910	98
5	Ottmn. Debs, 1886, Red.	97
5	Do. 1888, Red. 1935	98½
5	Do. 1893, Red. 1935	97
5	Ottmn. of Anlia. Debs., Rd.	90½
4	Ottomn. Smyr. & Cas. Ext. Bds., Red.	83½
3	Paris, Lyon & Medit. (old sys., £20), Red.	18¾
3	Paris, Lyon & Medit. (new sys., £20), Red.	18¾
50/	Piræus, At. & Pelp., 6 p.c. 1st Mt. Bds., Red.	90
3	Do. 5 p.c. Mt. Bds., Red.	74
4	Pretoria-Pietbg., Ltd., Red.	93
7	Puerto Cab. & Val., Ltd., 1st Mt. Debs., Red.	81
—	Rio de Jano. & Nthn., Ltd., 6 p.c. £100 Deb., Red.	25
—	Rio de Jano. (Gr. Para.), 5 p.c. 1st Mt. St. £100 Debs., Red.	25
2	Royal Sardinian, A, Rd. £20	11½
3	Royal Sardinian, B., Rd. £20	11½

Foreign Rly. Obligations (*continued*):—

Per Cent.	Name.	Price.
5	Ryl. Trns.-Afric. 5 p.c. 1st Mt. £100 Bds., Red.	48½
4	Sa.Fe&Cor.G.S.,Ld.PrLn.Bds.	104
5	Sa. Fe, 5 p.c. 2nd Reg. Dbs.	78
3	South Austrian, £20 Red.	15
3	South Austrian, (Ser. X.)	15
3	South Italian £20 Obs. (Ser. A to G), Red.	12
3½	S.W. of Venez. (Barq.), Ltd., 7 p.c. 1st Mt. £100 Debs.	50½
5	Taltal, Ltd., 5 p.c. 1st Ch. Debs., Red.	100
5	Utd. Rwys. Havana, Red.	85½
3	Wtrn. of France, £20 Red.	18¾
6	Wrn. B. Ayres St. Mt. Debs., 1902	107
6	Wrn. B. Ayres, Reg. Cert.	106
5	Do. Mt. Bds.	122
6	Wtrn. of Havna., Ld, Mt. Dbs., Rd.	93
7	Wrn. Ry. San Paulo Red.	108½
—	Wrn. Santa Fé, 7 p.c. Red.	42
2/8	Zafra & Huelva, 3 p.c. Red.	2½

BANKS.

Div.	Name.	Paid.	Price.
2/4½	Agra, Ltd.	6	3½
2/9½	Anglo-Argentine, Ltd., £9	7	5½
8 fls.	Anglo-Austrian	120f	13
6/	Anglo-Californian, Ltd., £20 Shares	10	11
4/	Anglo-Egyptian, Ltd., £15	5	6
5/	Anglo-Foreign Bkg., Ltd.	7	7½
7/	Anglo-Italian, Ltd.	5	7
7/6	Bk. of Africa, Ltd., £18¾	6½	10½
20/	Bk. of Australasia	40	50
10/	Bk. of Brit. Columbia	20	19½
25/	Bk. of Brit. N. America	50	64
20/	Bk. of Egypt, Ltd., £25	12½	18½
5/	Bk. of Mauritius, Ltd.	10	9
18/	Bk. of N. S. Wales	20	36½
4 p.c.	Bk. of N. Zland. Gua. Stk.	100	103
6/	Bk. of Roumania, £20 Shs.	6	7½
2/6	Tarapaca & Ldn., Ltd., £10	5	3½
—	Bque. Fse. de l'Afri. du S.	100f	3½
f.22.50	Bque. Internatle. de Paris	20	23
6/	Brit. Bk. of S. America, Ltd., £20 Shares	10	10½
16/	Capital & Cties., L., £50	10	40
20/	Chart. of India, &c.	20	30
10/	City, Ltd., £40 Shares	10	20
18/	Colonial, £100 Shares	30	21
10/	Delhi and London, Ltd.	25	—
5/	German of London, Ltd.	10	10½
25/	Hong-Kong & Shanghai	28½	45½
4/	Imperl. of Persia	6½	3½
10/	Imperl. Ottoman, £20 Shs	10	12½
12/	Internatl. of Ldn., Ld., £20	15	11
10/	Ionian, Ltd.	25	15½
16/	Lloyds, Ltd., £50 Shs.	8	31½
10/	Ldn. & Brazln. Ltd., £20	10	17
44/	Ldn. & County, Ltd., £80	20	102
9/	Ldn. & Hanseatic, L., £20	10	10½
22/6	Ldn. & Midland, L., £60	12½	53
8/9	Ldn. & Provin., Ltd., £10	5	21½
21/	Ldn. & Riv. Plate, L., £25	15	50
2/1½	Ldn. & San Fcisco, Ltd.	7	4½
28/	Ldn. & Sth. West., L., £50	20	68
26/	Ldn. & Westmins., L., £100	20	57½
5/	Ldn. of Mex. & S. Amer., Ltd., £10 Shs.	6	5½
15/	Ldn. Joint Stk., L., £100	15	34
12/9½	Ldn., Paris & Amer., L. £20	16	25
2/4½	Merchant Bkg., L., £9	4	2½
6/3	Metropn, Ltd., £30 Shs.	5	14½
9/	National, Ltd., £50 Shs.	10	20
5/11	Natl. of Mexico, $100 Shs.	$35	12
1/3	National of N. Z., L., £7½	2½	2
5/	National S. Afric. Rep.	10	13½
18/10½	National Provcl. of Eng., Ltd., £75 Shs.	10½	50½
21/7½	Do. do. £60 Shs.	12	57½
6/6	North Eastn., Ltd., £20 Shs	6	15
19/	Parr's, Ld., £100 Shs.	20	89½
12/6	Prov. of Ireland, L., £100	12½	29½
40/	Stand. of S. Afric., L., £100	25	64
12/6	Union of Australia, L., £75	25	27
4 p.c.	Do. do. Ins. Stk. Dep. 1900	100	103
15/6	Union of Ldn., Ltd., £100	15½	35

BREWERIES AND DISTILLERIES.

Div.	Name.	Paid.	Price.
4½	Albion Prp. 1 Mt. Db. Sk.	100	111
4	All Saints', L., Db.Sk.Rd.	100	97
7	Allsopp, Ltd.	100	153
6	Do. Cum. Pref	100	154½
4½	Do. Deb. Stk., Red.	100	117
3½	Do. Deb. Stk., Red.	100	103
4½	Alton & Co., L., Db., Rd	100	107
4½	Do. Mt. Bds., 1896	100	105
—	Arnold, Perrett, Ltd.	10	6
6	Do. Cum. Pref.	10	10
4½	Do. 1 Mt. Db. Stk., Rd	100	107

Breweries &c. (*continued*):—

Div.	Name.	Paid.	Price
5½	Arrol, A., & Sons, L., Cum. Pref. Shs.	10	10
4½	Do. 1 Mt. Db. Stk., Rd.	100	107
5	Backus, 1 Mt. Db., Red.	100	99
4	Barclay, Perk., L., Cu. Pf.	10	11½
3½	Do. Mt. Db. Stk., Red.	100	100
—	Barnsley, Ltd.	10	11½
6	Do. Cum. Pref.	10	13½
1/3	Barrett's, Ltd	2½	1½
1/3	Do. 5 p.c. Pref.	2½	2½
3/	Bartholomay, Ltd.	10	2½
8	Do. Cum. Pref.	10	7
6	Do. Deb.	100	97½
5	Bass, Ratcliff, Ltd., Cum. Pref. Stk.	100	143
4½	Do. Mt. Db. Stk., Rd.	100	124
4	Bell, J., L., 1 Mt. D. Stk., R	100	100
—	Benskin's, L., Cum. Pref.	5	—
—	Do. 1 Mt. Db. Stk Red.	100	—
—	Do. "B" Deb. Sk, Rd.	100	—
7/	Bentley's Yorks., Ltd.	10	10½
6/	Do. Cum. Pref.	10	12½
4½	Do. Mt. Debs., Red.	100	110
4½	Do. do. 1892, Red.	100	110
—	Bieckert's, Ltd.	20	2
5	Do. Debs., Red.	100	57
—	Birmingham., Ltd., 6 p.c. Cum. Pref.	5	2½
4½	Do. Mt. Debs., Red.	50	39½
5½	Boardman's, Ld., Cm. Pf.	10	8½
4½	Do., Perp. 1 Mt. Db. Sk.	100	104½
30/9	Brain & Co., Ltd.	100	101
4½	Brakspear, L., 1 D. Stk. Red.	100	108
4	Brandon's, L., 1 D. Stk. Red.	100	104½
21/	Bristol (Georges) Ltd.	10	45
6	Do. Cum. Pref.	10	17½
5	Do. Mt. Db. Sk. 1888 Rd.	100	115½
17/6	Bristol United, Ltd.	10	35
6	Do. Cum. Pref.	10	16½
4½	Do. Db.Sk.Rd.	100	120½
5½	Buckley's, L., C. Pre-prf.	10	10½
4½	Do. 1 Mt. Db. Stk. Rd.	100	104½
4	Bullard & Sons, Ltd., D. Sk. R.	100	105
6	Bushell, Watk., L., C. Pf.	10	14
4½	Do. 1 Mt. Db. Sk. Rd.	100	112
5	Camden, Ltd., Cum. Pref.	10	11½
4½	Do. 1 Mt. Db. Sk. Rd.	100	107
5½	Cameron, Ltd., Cm. Prf.	10	13
4½	Do. Mort Deb. Stk.	100	106
3½	Do. Perp Mt. Db. Sk.	100	98½
5	Cam'bell, J'stone, L., C. Pf.	5	5
4½	Do. 4½ p.c. 1 Mt. Db. Sk.	100	103
4	Campbell, Praed, L., Per. 1 Mort. Deb. Stk.	100	105
4	Cannon, L., Mt. Db. Stk.	100	109
4	Do. "B" Deb. Stk.	100	102
5	Castlemaine, L., 1 Mt. Db.	100	94
3½	Charrington, Ltd., Mort. Deb. Stk. Red.	100	106
2/	Cheltnhm. Orig., Ltd.	5	6
6	Do. Cum. Pref.	5	7½
4	Do. Debs. Red.	100	106
10/	Chicago, Ltd.	10	3½
6	Do. Debs.	100	84½
—	Cincinnati, Cum. Pref.	10	1
10/	City of Baltimore	10	3½
16/	Do. 8 p.c. Cum. Pref	10	8
14/	City of Chicago, Ltd.	10	1½
8	Do. Cum. Pref.	10	6½
13	City of London, Ltd.	100	206½
5	Do. Cum. Pref.	100	136
4	Do. Mt. Deb. Stk., Rd.	100	109½
2/	Colchester, Ltd.	5	4½
7	Do. Pref.	5	6½
4½	Do. Deb. Stk., Red.	100	109
5	Combe, Ltd., Cum. Pref.	10	14
4	Do. Mt. Db. Stk, Rd.	100	110
3½	Do. Perp. Deb. Stk.	100	107
5	Comm'cial, L., D. Sk., Rd.	100	107½
5	Courage, L., Cm. Pref. Shs.	100	137½
4	Do. Irr. Mt. Deb. Stk.	100	124½
3½	Do. Irr. "B" Mt. Db. Sk.	100	105
8/	Daniell & Sons, Ltd.	10	7
7	Do. Cum. Pref.	10	12
4½	Do. 1 Mt. Perp. Db. Sk.	100	109½
4½	Do. "B" Deb. Stk.	100	99
10d.	Dartford, Ltd.	5	5
2/9	Do. Cum. Pref.	5	5½
4	Do. 1 Mt. Db. Sk. Rd.	100	99
4	Davenport, Ld., 1 D. Stk.	100	101½
10/	Denver United, Ltd.	10	3½
8	Do. Cum. Pref.	10	8½
6	Do. Debs.	100	98½
4½	Deuchar, L., 1 D.Sk., Rd.	100	102
8/	Distillers, Ltd.	10	24
—	Dublin Distillers, Ltd.	5	1½
6	Do. Cum. Pref.	5	4½
4½	Do. Irr. Deb. Stk.	100	—
5	Eadie, Ltd., Cum. Pref.	10	11½
4	Do. Irr. 1 Mt. Db. Sk.	100	106
10/	Edinbgh. Utd., Ltd.	10	13½
6	Do. Cum. Prf.	10	13½
4	Eldridge, Pope, L. D. St. R.	100	107
—	Emerald & Phœnix, Ltd.	10	1½
8	Do. Cum. Pref.	10	8½
6	Empress Ltd., C. Pf.	10	11½
4½	Do. Mt. Deb. Stk.	100	103
10/	Farnham, Ltd.	10	17½
6	Do. Cum. Pref.	10	14½
4	Fenwick, L., 1 D. Sk., Rd.	100	103
4	Flower & Sons, Irr. D. Sk.	100	111
4	Friary, L., 1 Db. Stk., Rd.	100	103½
4	Do. 1 "A" Db. Sk., Rd	100	100
4½	Groves, L., 1 Db. Sk., Rd.	100	111
14	Guinness, Ltd.	100	590
6	Do. Cum. Prf. Stk.	100	155½
5	Do. Deb. Stk., Red.	100	119½
8	Hall's Oxford L., Cm. Pf.	5	5½
6/	Hancock, Ld., Cm. Pf. Ord.	10	14
7/	Do. Def. Ord	10	17½

Breweries, &c. (continued):—

Div.	Name.	Paid.	Price.
6	Hancock, Ld., Cum. Pref.	10	15
4	Do. 1 Deb. Stk., Rd.	100	110
5	Hoare, Ltd. Cum. Pref.	10	12½
5	Do. "A" Cum. Pref.	10	12¼
4	Do. Mt. Deb. Stk., Rd.	100	112
3½	Do. do. do. Rd.	100	104
3/6	Hodgson's, Ltd.	5	9½
5	Do. 1 Mt. Db., Red.	—	117½
4	Do. 2 Mt. Db., 1906	—	100
4½	Hopcraft & N., Ltd., 1 Mt. Deb. Stk., Red.	100	103
5	Huggins, Ltd., Cm. Prf.	10	—
4½	Do. 1st D. Stk. Rd.	100	—
4½	Do. "B" Db. Stk. Rd.	100	—
12/	Hull, Ltd.	10	17
7	Do. Cum. Pref.	10	14½
4½	Ind, Coope, L., D. Sk., Rd.	100	119
4	Do. "B" Mt. Db. Stk. Rd.	100	110
8/	Indianapolis, Ltd.	10	3
8	Do. Cm. Prf.	10	8½
5/	Jones, Frank, Ltd.	10	2½
7½	Do. Cum. Pref.	10	6½
5	Do. 1st Mort. Debs.	100	90½
3/	J. Kenward & Co., Ltd.	5	5½
4½	Kingsbury, L., 1 D. Sk., Rd	100	—
4	Lacon, L., D. Stk., Red.	100	110
4	Do. Irrd. "B" D. Sk.	100	106
7/	Lascelles, Ltd.	5	11½
6	Do. Cum. Pref.	5	7½
5	Leney, Ltd., Cum. Pref.	10	11½
4	Do. 1 Mt. Db. Stk. Rd.	100	102
30/7½	Lion, Ltd., £25 shares	17	49½
10/9½	Do. New £10 shares	6	17
6	Do. Perp. Pref.	20	33
4	Do. B. Mt. Db. Sk. Rd.	100	106
4½	Lloyd & Y., Ltd., 1 Mt. Deb. Stk., Rd.	100	100½
4½	Locke & S., Ltd., Irr. 1st Mt. Deb. Stk.	100	103
4½	Lovibond, Ltd., 1st Mt. Deb. Stk., Rd.	100	101½
30/4	Lucas & Co., Ld., Deb. Stk.	100	107
12/	Manchester, Ltd.	10	19
7	Do. Cum. Pref.	10	16½
5/	Marston, J., L., Cm. Prf.	10	10½
4	Do. 1 Mt. Db. Sk., Rd.	100	101½
7/	Massey's Burnley, Ltd.	10	16½
6	Do. Cum. Pref.	10	14½
4½	McCracken, Ltd., 1 Mt. Deb., 1908	100	59½
5	McEwan, Ltd., Cm. Pref.	10	14
5	Meux, Ltd., Cum. Pref.	10	13½
4	Do. Mt. Db. Stk. Red.	100	111
4½	Michell & A., Ltd., 1 Mt. Deb. Stk. Red.	100	105
4½	Mile End Dist. Db. Sk. Rd.	100	111
—	Milwaukee & Chic., Ltd.	10	1½
4/	Do. Cum. Pref.	10	7½
4½	Michell, Toms, L., Db.	50	57
6	Morgan, Ltd., Cum. Pref.	10	14½
25/	Nalder & Coll., Ltd.	10	34
6	Do. Cum. Pref.	10	15½
4½	Do. Deb. Red.	100	112
12/	Newcastle, Ltd.	10	19½
6	Do. Cum. Pref.	10	15
5	Do. 1 Mt. Deb., 1911	100	111½
4	Do. "A" Deb. Stk. Red.	100	106
6	New England, Ltd	10	4½
8	Do. Cum. Pref.	10	9
6	Do. Debs. Red.	100	101½
4	New London, L., 1 D. Sk.	100	103
7/2	New Westminster, Ltd.	4	10
2/4½	Do. Pref.	4	6½
—	New York, Ltd.	10	1
—	Do. 8 p.c. Cum. Pref.	10	4
6	Do. 1 Mt. Deb. Red.	100	77½
5	Noakes, Ld., Cum. Pref.	10	12
4	Do. 1 Mt. Db. Stk., Rd.	100	105
4½	Norfolk, L., "A" D. Sk. Rd.	100	106
20/	Northampton, Ld.	10	17
7	Do. Cum. Pref.	10	15½
6	Do. Cum. Pref.	10	12½
5	Do. 1 Mt. Per. Db. Sk.	100	127
4	Nth. East., L., 1 D. Sk. Rd.	100	100
4½	N. Worcesters., L. Per. 1 Mort. Deb. Stock	100	85½
6	Nottingham, L., Cm. Prf.	10	1½
5	Do. 1 Mt. Deb. Stk., Red.	100	114
17/4	Do. "B" do. Red.	50	112
6/	Ohlsson' Cape, Ld.	5	17½
7	Do. Cum. Pref.	5	9
4½	Do. 2nd Cum. Pref.	5	5½
5	Do. Deb. Stk., Red.	100	117
4½	Oldfield, L., 1 Mt. Db. Stk.	100	106
6	Page & Overt., L., Cm. Prf.	10	13½
4½	Do. 1 Mt. Dbs., Red.	100	109
10/	Parker's Burslem, Ltd.	10	24½
6	Do. Cum. Pref.	10	15
4	Do. 1 Mt. Db. Stk., Red.	100	112
4	Persse, Ld., 1 Mt. Db. Rd.	100	95½
	Phipps, L., Irr. 1 Db. Stk.	100	113
8	Plymouth, L., Min. Cu. Pf.	10	13½
4½	Do. Mt. Deb. Stk., Red.	100	106½
4½	Pryor, Reid, L., 1 D.S., R.	100	103½
5	Reid's, Ld., Cm. Pref. Stk.	100	136½
4	Do. Mt. Deb. Stk., Red	100	110
3½	Do. "B" Mt. Db. Stk., Rd	100	102
5	Rhondda Val., L., Cu. Pf	10	11
4½	Do. 1 Mt. Deb. Stk., Rd	100	109
5	Robinson, Ld., Cum. Pref.	10	11½
4½	Do. 1 Mt. Perp. Db. Stk.	100	111½
4/	Rochdale, Ltd.	10	6
4½	Do. 1 Mt. Deb. Stk.	100	98½
7	Royal, Brentford, Ltd.	10	22
	Do. Cum. Pref.	10	15
4½	Do. 1 Mt. Dbs. Red	100	105
6/	St. Louis, Ltd.	10	3½
8	Do. Cum. Pref.	10	8½
14/	St. Pauli, Ltd.	10	10
7	Do. Cum. Pref.	10	12
4½	Salt (T.), L., 1 Db. Sk. Rd.	100	112
4½	Do. "B" Db. Stk. Red	100	107
—	San Francisco, Ltd	10	½
—	Do. 8 p.c. Cum. Pref.	10	¼

Breweries, &c. (continued):—

Div.	Name.	Paid.	Price.
4½	Savill Brs., L., D. Sk. Rd.	100	118
4½	Scarboro., Ltd., 1 Db. Stk.	100	101
4	Shaw (Hy.), Ltd., 1 Mt. Db. Stk., Red.	100	104
22/	Showell's, Ltd.	10	32½
7	Do. Cum. Pref.	10	17½
3/	Do. Gua. Shs.	5	7½
4½	Do. Mt. Db. Stk., Red.	100	—
4	Simonds, L., 1 D. Sk., Rd.	100	111
5½	Simson & McP., L., Cu. Pf.	10	9½
4½	Do. 1 Mt. Deb. Stk.	100	97
5/	Smith, Garrett, L., £20 Shs	10	16½
5	Do. Cum. Pref.	20	26
3½	Do. 3½ p.c. Mt. Db. Stk.	100	107
5	Smith's, Tadcster, L., C Pf	10	12
4½	Do. Deb. Stk., Red.	100	112
4	Do. Deb. Stk. Red.	100	108
4½	Star, L., 1 M. Db. Stk., Rd.	100	103
4	Steward & P., L., 1 D. Sk.	100	109
7/	Strettons Derby, Ltd.	10	13
6	Do. Cum. Pref.	10	13
4	Do. Irr. 1 Mt. Db. Stk.	100	104½
4½	Strong, Romsey, L., 1 D.S.	100	115
5	Stroud, L., Db. Sk., Rd.	100	109½
4½	Tadcaster To'er, L., D. Sk.	100	113
8/	Tamplin, Ltd	10	21
6	Do. Cum. Pref.	100	15
4	Do. "A" Db. Sk., Rd.	10	106
6	Thorne, Ltd., Cum. Pref.	10	14
4	Do. Deb. Stk., Red.	100	103½
15/	Threlfall, Ltd.	10	45
6	Do. Cum. Pref.	10	16½
5	Do. 1 Mt. Dbs., Red.	100	114
4	Tollemache, L., D. Sk. Rd.	100	103
4	Truman, Hanb., D. Sk., R.	100	111
3	Do. "B" Mt. Db. Sk., Rd.	100	95
10/	United States, Ltd.	10	9
8	Do. Cum. Pref.	10	11
6	Do. 1 Mt. Deb.	100	106½
6/	Walker & H., Ld., Cm. Prf.	10	10½
4½	Do. 1 Mt. Deb. Stk., Red.	100	108
5	Walker, Peter, Ld. Cm. Prf.	10	13½
4	Do. 1 Mt. Dbs. Red.	100	110
4	Wallingford, L., D. Sk. Rd.	100	105
6	Watney, Ld., Cm. Prf. Sk.	100	169
5	Do. Mt. Db. Sk., Rd.	100	115½
4½	Do. "B" Mt. Db. Sk., Rd.	100	111
3½	Do. Mt. Db. Stk.	100	101
5	Watney, D., Ld., Cm. Prf.	10	12
4½	Do. 1 Mt. Db. Stk.	100	108
10/	Webster & Sons, Ltd.	10	16½
6	Do. Cum. Pref.	10	14
5	Wenlock Ltd Pref.	10	11½
4	Do. 1 Mt. Db. Sk., Rd.	100	106
5	West Cheshire, L., Cu. Pf.	10	10½
4	Do. Irred. 1 Mt. Db. Sk.	100	99
4½	Whitbread, L., Cu. Pf. Sh.	100	123½
4	Do. Db. Stk., Red.	100	110
3½	Do. "B" Db. Stk., Rd.	100	101
8/	Wolverhmpton & D. Ld.	10	18
6	Do. Cum. Pref.	10	13½
4½	Do. 1 Mt. Dbs., Red.	100	108
5½	Worthington, Ld., Cm. Prf.	10	15½
5½	Do. Cum. "B" Pref.	10	13½
4½	Do. Mt. Db. Sk., Rd.	100	113
3½	Do. Irr. "B" Db. Stk.	100	102
6/	Yates's Castle, Ltd.	10	13
5	Do. Cum. Pref.	10	11
5	Younger W., L., Cu. Pf. Sh.	100	134

CANALS AND DOCKS.

Last Div.	Name.	Paid.	Price.
4	Birmingham Canal	100	140½
—	E. & W. India Dock	100	19
—	Do. 4 p.c. Prf. Stk.	100	74
—	Do. P.L. Deb. Stk.	100	101
—	Do. Cons. Deb. Stk.	100	89
40/	G. Junction Ord. Shs.	100	147½
6/	Do. do. Pref.	10	19
4½	King's Lynn Per. Db. Stk.	100	117½
2½	Leeds & L'pool Canal	100	71
2½	Lndn & St. Kath. Dks.	100	54
4½	Do. Pref.	100	136½
4½	Do. Pref., 1878	100	132½
4½	Do. Pref., 1882	100	130
4	Do. Deb. Stk.	100	132½
—	Mchester Ship C. 5 p.c. Pf.	10	1½
3½	Do. 1st Perp. Mt. Deb.	100	98
—	Milford Dks. Db. Stk. "A"	100	18½
3½	Millwall Dk.	100	60
5	Do. Perp. Pref.	100	140½
4½	Do. Pref.	100	106½
5	Do. New Per. Prf., 1887	100	126½
5	Do. Per. Deb. Stk.	100	152½
4/	Newhaven Har.	10	14½
2½	N. Metropolitan	100	67
5	Sharpness Nw. Pf. "A" Sk.	100	141½
4	Do. Deb. Stk.	100	115½
5	Sheffiel & S. Yorks Nav. 4½ p.c. Pref Stk.	100	115½
36.43*	Suez Canal	20	143½
7	Surrey Comcl. Dok., Ord.	100	150½
7	Do. Min. 4 p.c. Pref. "A"	110	151½
5	Do. Pref. "B"	100	146½
5	Do do. "C"	100	148½
5	Do. do. "D"	100	144½
4½	Do Deb. Stk.	100	152½

COMMERCIAL, INDUSTRIAL, &c.

Last Div.	Name.	Paid.	Price.
5	Accles, L., 1 Mt. Db., Red.	100	84½
2/6	Aërated Bread, Ltd.	1	12½
—	African Gold Recovery, L.	1	⅛
2/	Aluminium, L., "A" Shs.	1	2
4½	Do. 1 Mt. Db. Stk., Red.	100	97
5½	Amelia Nitr., L., 1 Mort Deb., Red.	100	82½
7/	Anglo-Chil. Nitrate, Ltd., Cum. Pref.	10	6½
4½	Do. Cons. Mt. Bds., Red.	100	77½
4½	Anglo-Russian Cotton, Ld., 1 Charge Debs., Red.	100	98
11/3	Angus (G., & Co., L.), £10	7½	17
6/	Apollinaris, Ltd.	10	11½
5/	Do. 5 p.c. Cum. Pref.	10	10½
4	Do. Irred. Deb. Stock	100	103
3/	Argentine Meat Pres., L., 7 p.c. Pref.	10	2½
5	Argentine Refinry, Db. Rd.	100	98
6d.	Armstrong, Whitw., Ltd.	1	3½
4	Do. Cum. Pref.	5	6½
5	Artisans', Labr. Dwllgs., L.	100	126
4½	Do. Non-Cm. Prf., 1879	100	134
4½	Do. do. 1884	100	134
—	Asbestos & Asbestic, Ltd.	10	3½
2/7½	Ashley-grdns., L., C. Prf.	5	6½
4½	Do. 1 Mt. Deb. Stk.	100	113½
5/	Assam Rly. & Trdng., L., 8 p.c. Cum. Pref. "A"	10	14
—	Do. Deferrd. "B" Shs.	1	4
—	Do. do. (iss. f. pd)	1	3½
8/	Do. Cum. Pre-Prf. "A"	10	15
6/	Do. New Pref.	10	11½
5	Do. Debs., Red.	100	106
5	Do. Red. Mort. Debs.	100	110
6	Aust'lian Pastrl, L., Cu. Pf.	10	7
8d.	Aylesbury Dairy, Ltd.	1	1½
4	Do. 4 p.c. Mt. Dbs.	100	104½
10/	Babcock & Wilcox, Ltd.	10	28
6	Do. 6 p.c. Cm. Prf.	10	16
8	Baker (Chs.), L., Cm. Pf.	5	9
8	Do. "B" Cm. Pref.	5	7½
2/1	Barker (John), Ltd.	1	2½
5½	Do. Cum. Pref.	5	7½
4½	Do. Irred. 1 Mt. Db. Stk.	100	125½
2/6	Barnagore Jute, Ltd.	5	2½
5	Do. Cum. Pref.	5	4½
7½d.	Belgravia Dairy, Ltd.	1	1½
5/6	Bell (R.) & Co., Ltd.	5	4
9½d.	Bell's Asbestos, Ltd.	1	⅞
5	Do. Mt. Db. Bds., Rd.	100	106
10/	Bengal Mills, Ltd.	10	11
6/	Do. 4 p.c. Cum. Prf.	10	10½
5/	Benson (J. W.) L., Cm. Pf.	10	10½
4	Do. Perp. Mt. Db. Stk.	100	101
6	Bergvik, L., 6 p.c. Cm. Pf.	10	12½
12/	Do. Dfd.	10	11
4½	Do. 1 Dbs., Red.	100	105½
5/	Birm'ham Vinegar, Ltd.	5	15
5	Do. Cum. Pref.	5	5½
4½	Do. 1 Mt. Db. Stk., Rd.	100	109½
5	Boake (A.) L., 5 p.c. Cu. Pf.	10	10½
2/6	Bodega, Ltd.	5	8½
4½	Do. Mt. Deb. Stk., Rd.	100	111
12/	Bottomley & Brs., Ltd.	10	6
6/	Do. 6 p.c. Pt.	10	9
8½d.	Bovril, Ltd.	1	1
1/0½	Do. Def.	1	⅞
6½d.	Do. Cum. Pref.	1	1⅛
4½	Do. Deb. Stk.	100	101
5/	Bradbury, Gretrex., Ltd., £10 share	8	14
5/	Do. 5 p.c. Cum. Pref.	10	13½
5/	Brewers' Sugar, L., 5 p.c. Cum. Pref.	10	10½
3/6	Brighton Grd. Hotel, Ld.	5	4
4	Do Mt. Db. Stk., Red.	100	102
5	Bristol Hotel & Palm. Co., Ltd. 1st Mt. Red. Deb.	100	105
6d.	British & Bengton's Tea Tr. Asc., Ltd.	1	1½
5	Do. Cum. Prf.	5	5½
—	British Deli & Lgkat. Tobacco, Ltd.	1	½
—	Do. Cum. Prf.	1	½
1/3	British Tea Table, Ltd.	1	2½
5½	Do. Cum. Pref.	1	1½
2/6	Brooke, Ben., & Co., Ltd., Cum. Pref.	5	5½
7/6	Brooke, Bond & Co., Ltd.	5	19
3/	Brown Brs., L., Cum. Pref.	5	5½
10/	Browne & Eagle, Ltd.	10	13½
5	Do. Cum. Pref.	10	13
4	Do. Mrt. Db. Sk., Red.	100	110
32/	Brunner, Mond, & Co., Lt.	0	37
10/	Do. £10 shares	3	14½
7	Do. Cum. Pref.	10	17
7	Do. £10 shares	5	8½
10/	Bryant & May, Ltd.	5	18½
3/	Bucknall, H., & Sons, Lt.	5	7
6	Do. Cum. Pref.	5	7½
4/	Burke, E. & J., Ltd.	5	7½
6	Do. Cum. Pref.	5	7½
6	Do. Irred. Deb. Stk.	100	155
1/	Burlington Htls. Co., Ltd.	1	1½
5	Do. Cum. Pref.	1	1
4	Do. Perp. Deb. Stk.	100	106½
5	Bush, W. J., & Co., Ltd., Cum. Pref.	5	5½
4	Do. 1 Deb. Stk., Red.	100	102
5½	Callard, Stewart, & Watt, Ltd., Cum. Pref.	1	1½
4/	Callender's Cable L., Shs.	5	10½
4½	Do. 1 Deb. Stk., Red.	100	111½
—	Campbell, R., & Sons, Lt.	3	2½
6	Cantareira Water, Bd., Rd	100	90½
5	Do. (2nd issue)	100	87½
4	Centavio Sugar, Ltd., 6 p.c. 1st Debs., Red.	90	82½
9/	Cassell & Co., Ltd., £10	9	15
5	Causton, Sir J., & Sons, Ltd., Cum. Pref.	10	13½

Commercial, &c. (continued):—

Last Div.	Name.	Paid.	Price.
4	Cent. Prod. Mkt. of B.A. 1st Mt. Str. Debs.	100	78
4	Chappell & Co., Ltd., Mt. Deb. Stk. Red.	100	103
6/	Chicago & N.W. Gran. 8 p.c. Cum. Pref.	10	3
4/	Chicago Packing & Prov.	10	6
8	Do. Cum. Pref.	10	10
6/	City Offices, Ltd.	12	8
3½	Do. Mt. Deb. Stk.	100	108½
7/2½	Cy. London Real Prop., Ltd., £25 shs.	12	22
4/6	Do. £12½ shs.	7½	15
3½	Do. Deb. Stk. Red.	100	106½
3½	Do. Deb. Stk. Red.	100	105½
3	Do.	100	100½
6/	Cy. of Santos Imprvts., Ltd., 7 p.c. Pref.	10	8
20/	Clay, Bock, & Co., Ltd.	10	5
8	Do. Cum. Pref.	10	9
6	Do. Mort. Deb.	100	104
20/	Coats, J. & P., Ltd.	10	60
20/	Do. Cum. Pref.	10	17½
4½	Do. Deb. Stk. Red.	100	113
9½d.	Coburg Hotel, Ltd	1	1½
4	Do. Deb. Stk. Red.	100	102
6	Colonial Consign & Dis., Ltd., Cum. Pref.	5	4½
4½	Do. 1st Mort. Debs.	100	86½
—	Colorado Nitrate, Ltd.	5	3
5/	Co. Gén. des Asphtes. de F., Ltd.	6	6
5	Do. Non-Cm. Prf.	—	5
5	Cook, J. W., & Co., Ltd., Cum. Pref.	5	5½
5	Cook, T., & Son, Egypt, Ltd., 1st Mt. Deb. Red.	100	120½
—	Cork Co., Ltd., 6 p.c. Cum. Pref.	5	2
5	Cory, W., & Sn, L., Cu. Pf.	5	5½
4	Do. 1st Deb. Stk. Red.	100	109
1/6	Crisp & Co., Ltd	1	1½
5½	Do. Cum. Pref.	1	1½
—	Crompton & Co., Ltd., 7 p.c. Cum. Pref.	5	—
5	Do. 1st Mt. Reg. Deb.	—	90½
4/6	Crossley, J., & Sons, Ltd.	5	6
5	Do. Cum. Pref.	5	6½
—	Crystal Pal. Ord. "A" Stk.	100	6½
—	Do. "B" Red. Stk	100	1½
6	Do. 6 p.c. 1st 1887 Deb. Stk. Red.	100	117½
—	Do. 6 p.c. 2nd 1887 Deb. Stk. Red.	100	81½
—	Do. 6 p.c. 3rd 1887 Deb. Stk. Red.	100	22½
3	Do. 3 p.c. 1st 1895 Deb. Stk.	100	98½
—	Daimler Motor, Ltd	10	6
4/	Dalgety & Co., £20 Shs.	5	5½
4½	Do. Deb. Stk.	100	124
4	Do.	100	112
7/	De Keyser's Ryl. Htl., L.	10	13½
5	Do. Cum. Pref.	10	12
4	Do. Deb. Stk., Red.	100	110
6	Denny, H., & Sons, Ltd., Cum. Pref.	10	14½
5/3	Devas, Routledge & Co., L.	7	8½
5	Dickinson, J., & Co., L., Cum. Pref. Stk.	100	123
4½	Domin. Cottn. Mls., Ltd. Mt. Stg. Dbs.	100	97
6/	Dorman, Long & Co., L.	5	4½
—	Eastmans, Ltd	10	3
12/	Do. 8 p.c. Cum. Pref.	10	11
2/6	E. C. Powder, Ltd.	3	5½
1/6	Edison & Swn Utd. Elec. Ltd., "A" £5 Shs.	3	2½
2/6	Do. fully-paid	5	4½
4½	Ekman Pulp & Ppr. Co., Ltd., Mt. Deb., Red.	100	98
1/1½	Electric Construc., Ltd.	2	2½
7	Do. Cum. Pref.	2	2½
2½/	Eley Bros., Ltd.	10	37
—	Elmore's Cop. Depsg., L.	1	½
—	Elmore's Wire Mnfg., L.	2	½
—	Elysée Pal. Hotel Co., L.	5/	½
5 p.c.	Do. 5 p.c. £100 Db., Rd.	70	97½
8½d.	Evans, Ben., & Co., Ltd.	1	1
5	Do. 1 Mt. Db. Sk., Rd.	100	108
1/8½d.	Evans, D. H., & Co., L.	1	2½
6	Do. Cum. Pref.	1	1½
4½	Do. 1 Mt. Db. Sk., Rd.	100	112
2/6	*Evening News*, L., 5 p.c. Cum. Pref.	5	5½
5/3	Evered & Co., L., £10 Sh.	7	13½
7/6	Do.	10	13
4	Fairbairn Pastoral Co., Aust., L., 1 Mt. Db., Rd.	100	108
6	Fairfield Shipbldg., Ltd., Cum. Pref.	10	11½
4½	Do. Mort. Deb. Stk.	100	111
6/	Farmer & Co., Ld., 6 p.c. Cum. Pref.	10	13½
10	Field, J. C. & J., Ltd.	10	10½
14/	Do. 7 p.c. Cum. Pref.	10	14½
1/3	Fordham, W.B., & Sns, Ld.	1	2
5/6	Fore-st. Warehouse, Ltd.	11	9½
4	Do. Regd. Debs., Rd.	100	101½
3/6	Foster, M. B. & Sons, Ltd.	4	6
5	Do. Pref.	10	11½
9/	Foster, Porter, & Co., L.	10½	15
4	Fowler, J., & Co. (Leeds), Ltd., 1 Mt. Deb., Red.	100	103½
3/	Fraser & Chalmers, Ltd.	3	1½
4½	Free, Rodwell & Co., Ltd., Deb Stk.	100	104½
6½d.	Furness, T., & Co., Ltd., 5½ p.c. Cum. Pref.		1
4½	Gartside & Co. (of Manchstr), L., 1 Mt. Db. Stk.	100	113
11	Genl. Hydraul Power, L.	100	260

Commercial, &c. (continued):—

Last Div.	Name.	Paid.	Price.
8/	Gillman & Spencer, Ltd.	5	2½
6	Do. Pref.	5	4½
5	Do. Mort. Debs	50	51
4	Goldsbro., Mort & Co., L., "A" Deb. Stk., Red.	100	69½
—	Do. 3 p.c. "B" Inc. Deb. Stk., Red	100	12
8/	Gordon Hotels, Ltd.	10	20
5½	Do. Cum. Pref.	10	14½
4½	Do. Perp. Deb. Stk.	100	140½
4	Do. do.	100	122½
—	Greenwich Inld. Linoleum Co., Ltd.	1	½
7	Greenwood & Batley, Ltd., Cum. Pref.	10	10
7½d.	Hagemann & Co., Ltd., 6 p.c. Cum. Pref.	1	1
—	Hammond, Ltd.	10	¾
—	Do. 8 p.c. Cum. Pref.	10	3½
—	Do. 6 p.c. Cum. Inc. Stk. Red.	100	56½
	Hampton & Sons, Ltd., 4 p.c. 1 Mt. Db. St. Red.	100	105
—	Hans Crescent Htl., L., 6 p.c. Cum. Pref.	5	3
4	Do. 1 Mt. Deb. Stk.	100	90
6d.	Harmsworth, Ltd., Cum. Pref.	1	1½
4/	Harrison, Barber, Ltd.	5	4½
3/	Harrod's Stores, Ltd	1	4½
2/6	Do. Cum. Pref.	5	7½
5½	Hawaiian Comcl. & Sug. 1 Mt. Debs.	100	91½
5	Hazell, Watson, L., C. P.	10	11½
18/	Henley's Teleg., Ltd.	10	22
7	Do. Pref. Shs.	10	19
4½	Do. Mt. Db. Stk., Rd.	100	112½
6	Henry, Ltd.	10	11½
5	Do. Cum. Pref.	10	13
4½	Do. Mt. Debs., Red.	50	51
1/4½	Herrmann, Ltd.	1	¾
—	Hildesheimer, Ltd.	3	1¼
1/2½	Holbrn. & Frasca, Ltd.	1	1½
5	Do. Cum. Pref.	10	12
4	Do. Deb. Stk.	100	110
6	Home & Col. Stres, L., C.P	5	7½
6	Hood & M.'s Stres., Ltd., Cum. Pref.	1	½
6	Hook, C. T Ltd.	10	6
7/2	Hornsby, Ltd., £10 Shs.	8	3
—	Hotchks. Ordn., Ltd.	10	1
—	Do. 7 p.c. Cm. Prf.	10	4½
5	Do. 1 Mt. Dbs., Rd.	100	97½
6	Htl. Cecil, Ld., Cm. Prf.	5	3½
4	Do. 1 Mt. D. Sk., R.	100	100½
8/	Howard & Bulgh, Ltd.	10	39
6	Do. Pref.	10	16
4	Do. Deb. Stk., Red.	100	108
5/	Howell, J., Ltd., £5 Shs.	4	8½
—	Howell & Js., Ltd., £3½ Shs.	3	¾
6d.	Humber, Ltd.	1	¾
6	Do. Cum. Pref.	1	[illegible]
5/6	Hunter, Wilts., Ltd.	5	7
2/7	Hyam Clthg., Ltd., 5 p.c. Cum. Pref.	5	5¾
10/	Impl. Russn. Cotton, L.	5	5½
5	Impd. Industl. Dwgs., Ld.	100	131½
6d.	Do. Defrd.	1	1½
25/	Impd. Wood Pave., Ltd.	10	15½
15/	Ind. Rubber, Gutta Per. Telegraph Works, Ltd.	10	21½
4	Do. 1 Mt. Debs., Red.	100	104
6	Intern. Tea, Cum. Pref.	5	6½
10½d.	Jays, Ltd.	1	1½
5½	Do. Cum. Pref.	5	6½
1/2½d.	Jones & Higgins, Ltd.	1	2¼
4½	Do. 1 Mt. Db. Sk., Rd.	100	111
5/	Kelly's Directory, Ltd., 5 p.c. Cum. Pref.	10	12¾
4	Do. Mort. Db. Sk., Rd.	100	106
—	Kent Coal Explrtn. Ltd.	1	⅝
9½d.	King, Howmann, Ltd.	1	1½
4/	Kinloch & Co., Ltd.	5	8¼
6	Do. Pref.	5	7
5	Lady's Pictorial Pub., Ltd., Cum. Pref.	5	5
48/4	La Guaira Harb., Ltd., 5 p.c. Deb. Stk.	100	79½
—	Do. 2 Mt. 7 p.c. Deb. Stk., Red.	100	25½
4/	Lagunas Nitrate, Ltd.	5	1
2/	Lagunas Syn., Ltd.	5	1
5	Do. 1 Mt. Debs., Red.	100	79½
—	L. Copais Ld., 1 Mt. 6 p.c. Debs., Red.	100	35½
3/	Lautaro Nitrate, Ltd.	5	4½
5	Do. 1 Mt. Debs., Red.	—	100
9/	Lawes Chem. L., £10 shs.	9	5½
14/	Do. N. Cm. Min. Pref.	10	12½
—	Leeds Forge, 7 p.c. Cm. Pf.	5	3½
5	Do. 1 Mt. Debs., Red.	50	47
5	Lever Bros., L., Cm. Pf.	10	13½
6	Liberty, L., 6 p.c. Cm. Pf.	10	15
20/	Liebig's, Ltd.	20	79
5	Lilley & Sk., L., Cm. Pf.	5	5½
2/6	Linoleum Manftg Ltd.	5	16
3/	Linotype, Ltd., Pre	5	5¾
5/	Do. Def.	5	7½
4/	Lister & Co., Ltd.	10	4
5	Do. Cum. Pref.	10	8½
5/	Liverpool. Nitrate	5	5
—	Liverpool. Warehsg., Ltd	10	3
5½	Do. Cum. Pref.,	10	7½
4	Do. 1 Mt. Db. Stk., Rd.	100	105
5½	Lockharts, Ltd., Cm. Pf.	1	1½
4/6	Ldn. & Til. Lightrage £10	9	6½
6/	Ldn. Comcl. Sale Rms., L.	10	17½
3	Do. 1 Mt. Deb. Stk., Red.	100	103
3	London Nitrate, Ltd.	5	1¾
4/	London Nitrate, Ld. 8 p.c. Cm. Min. Pf.	5	3½
8/	London Pavilion, Ltd.	5	6

Commercial, &c. (continued):—

Last Div.	Name.	Paid.	Price.
2/6	London. Produce Clg. Ho., Ltd., £10 Shares	2½	3½
4/	London Stereos., Ltd.	5	3
7½d.	Ldn. Un. Laun. L. Cm. Pf.	1	¾
8½d.	Louise, Ltd.	1	¾
5½	Do. Cum. Pref.	1	¾
5/	Lovell & Christmas, Ltd.	5	11½
6	Do. Cum. Pref.	5	7½
4	Do. Mt. Deb. Stk., Red.	100	107
1/3	Lyons, Ltd.	1	4½
4½	Do. 1 Mt. Deb., Stk., Rd.	100	111½
10/	Machinery Trust, Ltd.	5	14
4½	Do. 4½ Deb. Stk.	100	104
6	MacLellan, L., Min. C. Pf.	10	9
5	Do. 1 Mt. Debs., 1900	100	101½
—	McEwan, J. & Co, Ltd.	10	1½
6	Do. Mt. Debs., Red.	100	89½
8	McNamara, L., Cm. Pref.	10	9
7½d.	Maison Virot, Ltd.	1	¾
2/7	Do. 6 p.c. Cum. Pref.	5	3½
5/	Manbré Sacc., L., Cm. Pf.,	10	11½
10/	Mangan Brze., L., £10 Shs.	6	16
2/	Mason & Mason, Ltd.	5	2½
6	Do. Cum. Pref.	5	5½
—	Maynards, Ltd.	1	½
6	Do. Cum. Pref.	1	⅞
9½d.	Mazawattee Tea, Ltd.	1	1½
5	Do. Cum. Pref.	5	5½
6	Mellin's Food Cum. Pref.	5	6½
4½	Met. Ascn. Imp. Dwllngs., Ltd.	100	111
5	Metro. Indus. Dwlgs., Ltd.	5	4½
4	Do. do. Cum. Pref.	5	5½
5	Metro. Prop., L., Cm. Pf.	5	5½
4½	Do. 1st Mt. Debs. Stk.	100	108½
6	Mexican Cotton 1 Mt. Db.	100	93½
4½	Mid. Class Dwlgs., L., Db.	100	120½
2/	Millars' Karri, Ltd.	1	3
6	Do. Cum. Pref.	1	1½
5/	Milner's Safe, Ltd.	10	20
10/	Moir & Son, Ltd., Pref.	5	8
6	Morgan Cruc., L., Cm. Pf.	10	14½
2/	Morris, B., Ltd.	3½	3
2/6	Murray L. 5½ p.c. C. Pf.	5	5½
63/4½	Do. 4½ 1 Mt. Db. Sk. Rd.	100	107
1/7½	Nat. Safe Dep., Ltd.	4	3½
6	Do. Cum. Pref.	1	1
—	Native Guano, Ltd.	5	½
—	Nelson Bros., Ltd.	10	2½
5	Do. Deb. Stk., Red.	100	80½
7/	Neuchtel Asph., Ltd.	10	10
10d.	New Darvel Tob., Ltd.	18/	1½
1/6	New Explosives, Ltd.	3	3½
5/3½	New Gd. Htl., Bham, L.	5	4
5½	Do. Pref.	5	4½
4	Do. 1 Mt. Db. Stk., Rd.	100	96½
—	New Julia Nitrate, Ltd.	10/	—
—	New Ldn. Borneo Tob., L.	16/	1½
1/6	New Premier Cycle, Ltd.	1	1/16
6	Do. 6 p.c. Cum. Pref.	1	½
4½	Do. 4½ p.c. 1 Mt. Db. Rd	100	—
—	New Tamargl. Nitr., Ltd	1	1/16
—	Do. 8 p.c. Cum. Pref.	1	½
6	Do. 6 p.c. 1 Mt. Dbs. Rd.	100	62½
3'78d.	Newnes, G., L., Cm. Prf.	1	1
1/3	Nitr. Provision, Ltd.	2½	½
24/	Nobel-Dynam., Ltd.	10	18½
—	North Brazn. Sugar, Ltd.	1	½
15/	Oakey, Ltd.	10	30
6	Do. Cum. Pref.	10	17½
—	Paccha Jazp. Nitr., Ltd.	5	½
5	Pac. Borax, L., 1 Db. Rd.	100	110
—	Palace Hotel, Ltd.	10	5½
5½	Do. Cum. Pref.	10	7½
4	Do. 1 Mt. Deb. Stk.	100	103
—	Palmer, Ltd	5	½
6	Do. Cum. Pref.	5	2
1/2½d	Paquin, Ltd.	1	½
6	Do. Cum. Pref.	5	4
5½	Parnall, Ltd., Cum. Pref.	1	½
4/6	Pawsons, Ltd., £10 Shs.	6	6½
4	Do. Mt. Debs., Red.	100	106
6	Pearks, G. & T., Ltd., 6 p.c. Cum. Pref.	1	⅝
9½d.	Pears, Ltd.	1	1½
6	Do. Cum. Pref.	10	14
5	Do. Deb. Stk.	100	129
5½	Pearson, C. A., L., Cu. Pf.	5	4½
4/3	Peebles, Ltd.	5	7½
5	Do. Cum. Pref.	5	6½
4½	Do. Mt. Deb. Stk. Red.	100	113½
5½	Peek Bros., Ltd., 1 Cum. Pref., Nos. 1-60,000	5	6½
3½	Do. 3½ p.c 1 Db. Stk.	100	102½
7½d.	Pegamoid, Ltd.	1	½
—	Pillsbury-W. Fl. Mills, L.	10	3½
16/	Do. 8 p.c. Cum. Pref.	10	7½
6	Do. 1 Mort. Debs.	100	94½
9½d.	Plummer, Ltd.	1	1½
5	Do. Cum. Pref.	5	5½
17/6	Price's Candle, Ltd.	16	36
6	Priest Marians, L., Cm. Pf.	1	1
6	Pryce Jones, Ld., Cm. Pf.	5	7
5	Do. Deb. Stk.	100	122
8½d.	Pullman, Ltd.	1	1½
6d.	Do. Cum. Pref.	1	1½
6d.	Raleigh Cycle, Ltd.	1	1/16
6	Do. Cum. Pref.	1	½
—	Recife Drnge. Ld. 1 Mt. Debs., R	100	18
6	Redfern, Ltd. Cum. Prf.	10	14
5	Ridgways, Ltd., Cu. Pf.	5	5½
—	R. Janeiro Cy. Imps. Ld.	25	8
5	Do. Debs.	100	85
5	Do. 1880-1893	100	83½
11/	R. Jan Fl. Mills, Ltd.	7	6½
5	Do. 1 Mt. Debs., Rd.	100	94
—	Riv. Plate Meat, Ltd.	5	2½
—	Do. Pref.	5	5
8½d.	Roberts, J. R., Ltd.	1	1½
5	Roberts 1 Mt. D. Sk., Rd.	100	111
1/4½	Roberts, T. R., Ltd.	1	2½
5	Do. Cum. Pref.	1	1½

Commercial, &c. (continued):—

Last Div.	Name.	Paid.	Price.
3/	Rosario Nit., Ltd.	5	3½
5	Do. Debs., Red.	100	103
1/	Rover Cycle, Ltd.	1	⅝
6/	Ryl. Aquarium, Ltd.	5	4½
6	Do. Pref.	5	6
5	Ryl. Htl., Edin., Cm. Pf.	1	1½
1/2½	Ryl. Niger, Ltd., £10 Sh.	2	2½
6/	Do.	10	14½
20/	Russian Petroleum	10	
6½	Do. 6½ p.c. Cm. Prf.	10	
3/	Ruston, Proctor, Ltd.	10	11½
4½	Do. 1 Mort. Debs.	100	106
6/	Sadler, Ltd.	12	7
—	Sal. Carmen Nit., Ltd.	5	3½
9d.	Salmon & Gluck., Ltd.	1	1⅝
	Salt Union, Ltd.	10	1½
1½	Do. 7 p.c. Pref.	10	5½
4½	Do. Deb. Stk.	100	99½
4½	Do. "B" Deb. Sk., Rd.	100	97½
—	San Donato Nit., Ltd.	5	½
5/	San Jorge Nit., Ltd.	5	3½
—	San Pablo Nit., Ltd.	5	½
—	San Sebastn. Nit., Ltd.	5	½
1/9	Sanitas, Ltd	1	2½
—	Sa. Elena Nit., Ltd.	5	½
—	Sa. Rita Nit., Ltd.	5	1½
5/	Savoy Hotel, Ltd.	10	15
7	Do. Pref.	10	13
4	Do. 1 Mt. Deb. Stk.	100	111½
5	Do. Debs., Red	100	102½
5	Do. & Ldn. For. Htl., Ltd., 5 p.c. Debs. Red.	100	99
8½d.	Schweppes, Ltd.	1	1
2½d.	Do Def.	1	½
5	Do. Cum. Pref.	1	1 1/16
4	Do. Deb. Stk.	100	106
1/	Singer Cyc., Ltd.	1	½
5½	Do Cum. Pref.	1	½
—	Smokeless Pwdr., Ltd.	1	½
5½d.	S. Eng. Dairies, Ltd., 6 p.c. Cum. Pref.	1	1½
—	Sowler Thos. L.	1	1
3/4½	Do. 5½ Cm. Pf.	5	5½
4/6	Spencer, Turner, & Co. Ltd	5	8½
5	Do. Cum. Pref.	5	6½
5	Spicer, Ld., 5 p.c. Dbs. Rd.	100	65
4/	Spiers & Pond, Ltd.	10	21½
5	Do. 1 Mt. Debs., Red.	100	118½
5	Do. "A" Db. Stk., Rd.	100	111
5	Do. "B" 1 Db. Stk., Rd.	100	112½
4	Do. Fd. "C" 1 Db. S., R.	100	104
7/6	Spratt's, Ltd	5	12½
4	Do. Debs., 1914	—	105
5	Steiner Ld., Cm. Pf.	10	11½
4	Do. 1 Mt. Db. Sk. Rd.	100	107
9/	Stewart & Clydesdale, L.	10	13
6	Do. Cum. Pref.	10	14½
35/5	Sulphide Corp.	100	80
1/	Swan & Edgar, L.	1	1½
1/	Sweetmeat Automatic, L.	1	3½
2/9	Tuetgen, Ltd., Cum. Pref.	5	6
24/	Teleg. Construction., Ld.	12	35½
5	Do. Db. Bds., Rd., 1899	100	103½
3/0½	Tilling, Ld. 5½ p.c. Cm. Prf.	5	6½
4	Do. 4 p.c. 1 Dbs., Rd.	—	105
8½d.	Tower Tea, Ltd.	1	1½
5	Do. Cum. Pref.	5	5½
5	Travers, Ltd., Cum. Pref.	10	12½
4	Do. 1 Mt. Dbs., Rd.	100	105
6	Tucuman Sug., 1 Dbs., Rd.	100	100
4/	United Alkali, Ltd.	10	2
7	Do. Cum. Pref.	10	9
5	Do. Mt. Db. Stk., Rd.	100	109½
2¼d.	United Horse Shoe, Ltd., Non-Cum. 8 p.c. Pref.	1	1/16
5	Un. Kingm. Tea, Cm. Prf.	5	4½
2/	Un. Lankat Plant., Ltd.	1	2
4/	Un. Limmer Asphlte., Ld.	3	5
13/	Val de Travers Asph., L.	10	15½
3/	V. den Bergh's, L., Cm. P.	5	6½
6	Walkers, Park., L., C. Pf.	10	3
4½	Do. 1 Mt. Debs., Red.	100	90½
6/	Wallis, Thos. & Co., Ltd.	5	14
6	Do. Cum. Pref.	5	8½
5½	Waring, Ltd., Cum. Pref.	5	5½
4½	Do. 1 Mt. Db. Sk., Red.	100	112
4½	Do. Irred. "B" Db. Stk.	100	104
12/	Waterlow, Dfd. Ord.	10	14
4/	Do. Pref.	10	14
3½	Do. Cum. Pref.	10	10½
10/	Waterlow Bros. & L., Ld.	10	9
5	Do. Pref.	10	12
1/2½	Welford, Ltd.	1	1½
4½	Do. Debs., Red.	100	109
1/	Welford's Surrey Dairies, Ltd.	1	1½
7½d.	West London Dairy, Ltd.	1	1
4½	Wharncliffe Dwllgs, L., Pf.	10	11½
18/10	Do. 3 p.c. Irr. Mt. Db. Sk.	100	96
6d.	White, A. J., Ltd.	1	½
6	Do. 6 p.c. Cum. Pref.	1	⅝
4	White, J. Bazley, Ltd., 1 Mort. Debs., Red	100	99½
5	White, R., Ltd., 1 Mort. Deb. Stock, Red.	100	104½
11/	White, Tomkins, Ltd	10	10½
5	Do. Cum. Pref.	10	11½
6	White, W. N., L., Cm. Pf.	1	⅝
2/6	Wickens, Pease & Co., L.	5	2½
6	Wilkie, Ltd., Cum. Pref.	10	15
4/	Willans & Robinson, Ltd.	5	3
6	Do. Cum. Pref.	5	7
4½	Do. 1 Mt. Db. Stk., Red.	100	107
7½d.	Williamsons, L., Cm. Prf.	1	1½
6	Winterbottm. Book Cloth, Ltd., Cum. Prf.	10	15
4/6	Yates, Ltd.	5	6
6	Do. Cum. Pref.	5	6½
	Young's Paraffin. Ltd.	4	1½

CORPORATION STOCKS—COLONIAL AND FOREIGN.

Per Cent.	Name.	Paid.	Price.
6	Auckland City, '72 1904-24	100	115
6	Do. Cons., '79, Red. 1930	100	135½
5	Do. Deb. Ln., '83..1934-8	100	117
6	Auckland Harb. Debs.	100	111½
5	Do. 1917	100	112
5	Do. 1936	100	114
5½	Balmain Boro'.......1914	—	113½
5	Boston City (U.S.)	100	102½
5	Do. ..1902	100	106
5	Brunswick Town 5. c. Debs. 1916-20	100	111
4½	B. Ayres City 4½ p.c.	100	69
5	Cape Town, City of	100	113
4	Do. ..1943	100	115
4	Chicago, City of, Gold 1915	—	112
6	Christchurch 1926	100	131½
—	Cordoba City	100	17½
5	Duluth (U.S.) Gold ..1926	—	110
6	Dunedin (Otago) 1925	100	127½
6	Do. 1926	100	113
5	Do. Consols..1908	100	111
4	Durban Insc. Stk.....1944	100	111
4	Essex Cnty., N. Jersey 1926	100	114½
5	Fitzroy, Melbrne...1916-19	100	110
5	Gisborne Harbour....1915	100	109
4	Greymouth Harbour..1925	100	110
4	Hamilton 1934	100	108
5	Hobart Town 1918-30	100	115
4	Do. 1940	100	105
4½	Invercargill Boro. Dbs. 1936	100	111
6	Kimberley Boro., S. A. Debs.	—	102
4	Launceston Twn. Dbs. 1916	100	106
6	Lyttleton, N.Z., Harb. 1929	100	125
4	Melbourne Bd. of Wks. 1921	100	107
5	Melb. City Debs. 1897-1907	100	106½
4½	Do. Debs. 1908-27	100	111½
4	Do. Debs...1915-20-22	100	106
5	Melbne. Harb. Bds., 1908-9	100	112
4½	Do. do. 1915	100	111
4	Do. do. 1918-21	100	106
4½	Melbrne. Tms, Dbs. 1914-16	100	113
4½	Do. Fire Brig. Db. 1921	100	108
5	Mexico City Stg.	100	91½
4	Moncton N. Bruns. City	100	102
5	Montevideo	100	61
5	Montreal Stg.	100	103
5	Do. 1874	100	103
5	Do. 1879	100	104
3½	Do. 1933	100	102
3	Do. Perm. Deb. Stk	100	96
4	Do. Cons. Deb. Stk. 1932	100	112
6	Napier Boro. Consolid. 1914	100	119
5	Napier Harb. Debs...1920	100	115
5	Do. Debs...1928	100	107
6	New Plymouth Harb. Debs. 1909	100	107
6	New York City 1901	—	109½
3½	Do. 1910-26	—	103½
4½	Nth. Melbourne Debs. 1-600 1921	100	105
5	Oamaru Boro. Cons...1920	100	101
6	Do. Harb. Bds. (Reg.)	100	74
25/	Do. 6 p.c. (Bearer)..1919	100	35
6	Otago Harb. Deb. Reg.	100	103
6	Do. 1877	100	107
6	Do. 1881 1921	100	115
5	Do. Debs. ..1921	100	107
5	Do. Cons. ..1934	100	105
6	Ottawa City	100	109
6	Do. 1904	100	111½
4½	Do. Debs. ..1913	100	108½
6	Port Elizabeth Waterworks	100	111
5	Port Louis	100	111
5	Prahran Debs. 1917	100	109
4	Do. Debs. 1919	100	102
6	Quebec C. Coupon. 1875 1905	100	112
6	Do. do. 1878 1908	100	116
4½	Do. Debs. 1914-18	100	108
4	Do. Debs. 1923	100	108
3½	Do. Cns. Rg. Stk., Red.	100	101
5	Richmond (Melb.) Dbs. 1917	100	112
4	Rio Janeiro City	100	59
4	Rome City	100	—
4	Do. 2nd to 8th Ise.	100	92
—	Rosario C.	100	25
—	Do.	100	25
4	St. Catherine (Ont.) ..1926	100	101
4	St. John, N.B., Debs. 1934	—	103
4½	St. Kilda (Melb) Dbs. 1918-21	100	105
4	St. Louis C. (Miss.)..1911	100	104
4	Do. 1913	100	103½
3'65	Do. 1915	—	108½
—	Santa Fé City Debs.	100	19
6	Santos City	100	95
6	Sofia City	100	84
5	Sth. Melbourne Debs. 1915	100	111
4½	Do. Debs....1916	100	107
5	Sydney City 1904	100	100
4	Do. Debs. 1912-13	100	107
4	Do. do. (1894)..1910	100	109
7	Timaru Boro. 7 p.c...1910	100	126½
5	Timaru Harb. Debs 1914	100	107
5	Do. Debs...1915	100	107
6	Toronto City Wtwks 1904-6	100	114
5	Do. G. Cns. Dbs. 1910-20	100	113
4	Do. Strlg. 1922-8	100	107
4	Do. Local Improv.	100	104
3½	Do. 1929	100	104
3½	Valparaiso	100	99
4	Vancouver 1931	100	107
4	Do. 1932	100	108
6	Wanganui Harb. Dbs. 1905	100	107
6	Wellington Con. Deb. 1907	100	117
6	Do. Improv., 1879	100	122
6	Do. Wtrwks. Dbs., 1880	100	123
4½	Do. Debs., 1893....1913	100	114
4½	Wellington Harb. 1907	100	104
4	Westport Harb. Dbs. 1925	100	110
6	Winnipeg City Deb...1907	—	119
5	Do. 1914	100	117

FINANCIAL, LAND, AND INVESTMENT.

Last Div.	Name.	Paid.	Price.
5	Agncy, Ld. & Fin. Aust., Ltd., Mt. Db. Stk., Rd.	100	90½
	Amer. Frehld. Mt. of Lon., Ld., Cum. Pref. Stk. ..	100	87½
4½	Do. Deb. Stk., Red. ..	100	92
1/4½	Anglo-Amer. Db. Cor., L.	2	1
4	Do. Deb. Stk., Red ..	100	109¼
⅛	Ang.-Ceylon & Gen. Est., Ltd., Cons. Stk.	100	50
6	Do. Reg. Debs., Red.	100	101½
3/	Ang.-Fch. Explorn., Ltd.	1	2⅛
6	Do. Cum. Pref.	1	1⅛
—	Argent. Ld. & Inv., Ltd. £1 Shares	10/	nil
—	Do. Cum. Pref.	4	1⅜
1/	Assets Fnders.' Sh., Ltd.,	4	1⅜
6/	Assets Realiz., Ltd., Ord.,	5	8⅞
5	Do. Cum. Pref.	5	6½
26/	Austrln. Agricl. £25 Shs.	21½	63½
4½	Aust. N. Z. Mort., Ltd., Deb. Stk., Red.	100	87½
4	Do. Deb. Stk., Red. ..	100	82½
4½	Australian Est. & Mt., L., 1 Mt. Deb. Stk., Red.	100	102½
5	Do. "A" Mort. Deb. Stk., Red.	100	96
5/	Australian Mort., Ld., & Fin., Ltd. £25 Shs. ..	5	5
1/6	Do. New, £25 Shs...	3	3
4	Do. Deb. Stk........	100	110
3	Do. Do.	100	85
5	Bengal Presidy. 1 Mort. Deb., Red.	100	106
25/	British Amer. Ld. "A"	1	19
—	Do. "B"	24	7
1/7½	Brit. & Amer. Mt., Ltd. £10 Shs.	2	1
5/	Do. Pref.	10	10
4	Do. Deb. Stk., Red. ..	100	103
1/3	Brit. & Austrlsn Tst Ln., Ltd. £25 Shs.	2½	¾
4½	Do. Perm. Debs., Red.	100	104
1½d.	Brit. N. Borneo. £1 Shs.	15/	1/16
2½d.	Do.	1	¾
—	Brit. S. Africa	1	2⅛
5	Do. Mt. Deb., Red.	—	99
6	B. Aires Harb. Tst., Red.	100	94½
12/6	Canada Co.	1	26
—	Canada N. W. Ld., Ltd.	$25	83½
—	Do. Pref..........	$100	$50½
4	Canada Perm. Loan & Sav. Perp. Deb. Stk...	100	99½
6	Curamalan Ld., 6 p.c. "A" Scrip	—	92
3/7½	Deb Corp., Ld., £10 Shs	4	3½
5	Do. Cum. Pref.	10	11½
4	Do. Perp. Deb. Stk...	100	110
9d.	Deb. Corp. Fders' Sh., Ld.	3	½
4/3¾	Eastn. Mt. & Agncy, Ld., "A"	10	5½
4½	Do. Deb. Stk., Red.	100	98
5	Equitable Revers. In. Ltd.	100	—
2/6	Exploration, Ltd.	1	1⅜
/6d.	Freehold Trst. of Austria. Ltd. £10 Shs.	1	¾
4	Do. Perp. Deb. Stk...	100	100
70/	Genl. Reversionary, Ltd.	100	—
3½	Holborn Vi. Land	100	106
4½	House Prop. & Inv.	100	84½
13/	Hudson's Bay	13	20½
—	Hyderabad (Deccan)	5	2½
4	Impl. Col. Fin. & Agcy. Corp.	100	92½
4½	Impl. Prop. Inv., Ltd., Deb. Stk., Red.	100	91½
2/6	Internatl. Fincial. Soc., Ltd. £7½ Shs.	2½	1½
4	Do. Deb. Stk., Red..	100	99½
2/4½	Ld. & Mtge. Egypt, Ltd. £18 Shs.	3	2½
5	Do. Debs., Red.	100	101
4½	Do. Debs., Red.	100	100
—	Ld. Corp. of Canada, Ltd.	1	½
4½	Ld. Mtge. Bk. of Texas Deb. Stk.	100	—
3½	Ld. Mtge. Bk. Victoria 4½ p.c. Deb. Stk.	100	78
2/9½	Law Debent. Corp., Ltd., £10 Shs.	2	1½
4½	Do. Cum. Pref., ...	10	12
4	Do. Deb. Stk.	100	113½
—	Law Land, L., 4½ Cm. Prf.	5	5½
1/	Ldn. & Australasian Deb. Corp., Ltd., £4 Shs. ..	2	½
4½	Do. 4½ p.c. Mt. Deb. Stk., Red.	100	99
1/9	Ldn. & Middx. Frhld. Est. £2 Shs.	35/	3
2/6	Lndn. & N. Y. Inv. Corp., Ltd.	5	1½
5	Do. 5 p.c. Cum. Pref...	10	8½
1/6	Ldn. & Nth. Assets Corp., Ltd., £2 Shs.	1½	¾
2	Ldn. & N. Deb. Corp., L.	2	1½
3/6	Ldn. & S. Afric. Explrn. Ltd.	½	12½
2/	Mtge. Co. of R. Plate, Ltd. £10 Shs.	2	3
4½	Do. Deb. Stk., Red...	100	113
4½	Morton, Rose Est., Ltd., 1st Mort. Debs.	—	99
6/6	Natal Land Col. Ltd. ..	10	7
4/	Do. 8 p.c. Pref., 1870..	5	8
5/6	Natl. Disct. L., £25 Shs.	5	10½
4½	New Impl. Invest., Ltd. Pref. Stk.	100	66½
	New Impl. Invest., Ltd. Def. Stk.	100	9½
3½	N. Zld. Assets Real Deb.	100	101
4	N. Zld. Ln. & Mer. Agcy., Ltd Prf. Ln, Deb. Stk	100	93
2/6	N. Zld. Tst. & Ln. Ltd., £25 Shs.	5	1½

Financial, Land, &c. (*continued*):—

Last Div.	Name.	Paid.	Price.
12/6	N. Zld. Tst. & Ln. Ltd., 5 p.c. Cum. Pref.	25	19
—	N. Brit. Australsn. Ltd...	100	5
—	Do. Irred. Guar.....	100	32½
5	Do. Mort. Debs.....	100	82½
4½	N. Queensld. Mort. & Inv., Ltd., Deb. Stk.	100	93
6	Peel Riv., Ld. & Min. Ltd.	100	88½
—	Peruvian Corp., Ltd.	100	6⅛
—	Do. 4 p.c. Pref.	100	9½
3	Do. 6 p.c. 1 Mt. Debs., Red.	100	41
—	Queensld. Invest. & Ld... Mort. Pref. Ord. Stk...	100	20
3/7	Queensld. Invest. & Ld. Mort. Ord. Shs.	4	4
4	Queensld. Invest. & Ld. Mort. Perp. Debs.	100	88
3½	Raily. Roll Stk. Tst. Deb., 1903-6	100	100½
50/	Reversiony. Int. Soc., Ltd.	100	—
2/8½	Riv. Plate Trst., Loan & Agcy., L., "A" £10 Shs.	2	4
1/6	Riv. Plate Trst., Loan & Agcy., Ltd., Def. "B"	5	3½
	Riv. Plate Trst., Loan & Agy., L., Db. Stk., Red.	100	109
—	Santa Fé & Cord. Gt. South Land, Ltd.	20	5
—	Santa Fé Land	10	2½
2/	Scot. Amer. Invest., Ltd. £10 Shs.............	2	2½
2½	Scot. Australian Invest., Ltd., Cons.	100	69½
6	Scot. Australian Invest., Ltd., Guar. Pref.	100	136½
5	Scot. Australian Invest., Ltd., Guar. Pref.......	100	107½
4	Scot. Australian Invest., Ltd., 4 p.c. Perp. Dbs.	100	105½
5	Sivagunga Zemdy., 1st Mort., Red.	100	101
20/	Sth. Australian..........	20	45½
3½	Stock Exchange Deb., Rd.	—	102½
—	Strait Develt., Ltd.......	1	—
2/6	Texas Land & Mt., Ltd. £10 Shs.	2½	2½
4½	Texas Land & Mt., Ltd., Deb. Stk., Red.	100	104
—	Transvaal Est. & Dev., L.	1	½
—	Transvaal Lands, Ltd., £1 Shs.	15/	⅛
—	Do. F. P...........	1	¾
—	Transvaal Mort., Loan, & Fin., Ltd., £10 Shs. ..	2	1/16
2/	Tst & Agcy. of Austrlsa., Ltd., £10 Shs.........	1	2
7/5	Do. Old, fully paid ..	10	15½
5/7	Do. New, fully paid..	10	12½
5	Do. Cum. Pref.......	10	12½
3/	Trust & Loan of Canada, £20 Shs.............	5	4½
1/9½	Do. New £20 Shs....	3	2½
4½	Tst. & Mort. of Iowa, Ltd., Deb. Stk. Red...	100	93
—	Tst., Loan, & Agency of Mexico, Ltd., £10 Shs.	2	½
—	Trsts., Exors, & Sec. Ins. Corp., Ltd., £10 Shs..	7	1½
4	Do. Irred. Deb. Stk.	100	106½
3/	Union Dsc., Ld., £10 Shs.	5	10½
6	Union Mort. & Agcy. of Aust., Ltd., Pref. Stk.	100	30
—	Do. 6 p. Pref. £6 Shs.	2	½
4½	Do. Deb. Stk.........	100	92½
4	Do. Deb. Stk.........	100	85½
5	Do. Deb. Stk. Red...	100	96½
1/6	U.S. Deb. Cor. Ltd., £8 Shs...................	1	¾
5½	Do. Cum. Pref. Stk..	100	100½
4½	Do. Irred. Deb. Stk..	100	105½
5	U.S. Tst. & Guar. Cor., Ltd., Pref. Stk.......	100	77½
8/	Van Dieman's	25	16
4	Walker's Prop. Cor., Ltd., Guar. 1 Mt. Deb. Stk..	100	109
4½	Wstr. Mort. & Inv., Ltd., Deb. Stk.	100	92½

FINANCIAL—TRUSTS.

Last Div.	Name.	Paid.	Price.
1/6	Afric City Prop., Ltd...	1	1⅜
6	Do. Cum. Pref.......	1	1⅛
4	Alliance Invt., Ltd., Cm. 4½ p.c. Prefd.	100	74½
—	Do. Defd............	100	12½
4	Do. Deb. Stk. Red...	100	104½
5	Amrcn. Invt., Ltd., Prfd.	100	119½
5	Do. Defd.	100	88½
4	Do. Deb. Stk. Red...	100	114½
4	Army & Navy Invt., Ltd., 5 p.c. Prefd.	100	82½
—	Do. Defd. Stk.	100	15½
4	Do. Deb. Stk.	100	106½
4	Atlas Investment, Ltd., Prefd. Stk.	100	70½
4½	Bankers' Invest., Ltd., Cum. Prefd.	100	103½
1/0/0	Do. Defd............	100	24½
4	Do. Deb. Stk........	100	114
	Brewery & Comml. Inv., Ltd., £10 Shs.........	5	6

Financial—Trusts (*continued*):—

Last Div.	Name.	Paid.	Price.
4	British Investment, Ltd., Cum. Prefd.	100	107
5	Do. Defd.	100	104
4	Do. Deb. Stk.	100	107½
6	Brit. Steam. Invst., Ltd., Prefd	100	118½
3/0/0	Do. Defd..........	100	73
4½	Do. Perp. Deb. Stk ..	100	120½
1/9	Car Trust Invst., Ltd., £10 Shs...............	2½	2
5	Do. Pref.	100	99
4	Do. Deb. Stk., 1915..	100	104
4	Cinl. Sec., Ltd., Prefd. ..	100	102½
3½	Do. Defd.	100	43½
4	Consolidated, Ltd., Cum. 1st Pref.	100	90
4	Do. 5 p.c. Cm. 2nd do.	100	68½
—	Do. Defd.	100	14½
4½	Do. Deb. Stk.	100	112½
5	Deb. Secs. Invst.........	100	103½
4	Do. 4 p.c. Cm. Pf. Sk.	100	105½
4½	Edinburgh Invest., Ltd., Cum. Prefd. Stk........	100	105½
4	Do. Deb. Stk. Red.	100	106½
5	Foreign, Amer. & Gen. Invt., Ltd., Prefd.	100	112½
2	Do. Defd.	100	48½
4	Do. Deb. Stk.	100	113½
5	Foreign & Colonial Invt., Ltd., Prefd.	100	136½
5½	Do. Defd.	100	96½
4½	Gas, Water & Gen. Invt., Cum. Prefd. Stk.......	100	86½
3	Do. Defd. Stk.	100	36½
4	Do. Deb. Stk.	100	104
5	Gen. & Com. Invt., Ltd., Prefd. Stk.............	100	103½
2	Do. Defd. Stk.	100	36½
4	Do. Deb. Stk.	100	111½
2/6	GlobeTelegph. & Tst., Ltd.	10	11½
6	Do. do. Pref.	10	17
4	Govt. & Genl. Invt., Ld., Prefd.	100	83½
3½	Do. Defd.	100	41½
4½	Govts. Stk. & other Secs. Invt., Ltd., Prefd.	100	86½
1	Do. Defd.	100	25
4½	Do. Deb. Stk.	100	112
4	Do. do.	100	104
4½	Guardian Invt., Ltd., Pfd.	100	89½
—	Do. Defd.	100	19½
4	Do. Deb. Stk.	100	104
5	Indian & Gen. Inv., Ltd., Cum. Prefd.	100	110½
2½	Do. Defd.	100	61
4½	Do. Deb. Stk.	100	119½
5	Indust. & Gen. Tst., Ltd., Unified	100	90½
3½	Do. Deb. Stk. Red.	100	99½
4½	Internat. Invt., Ltd., Cm. Prefd.................	100	66½
—	Do. Defd.	100	7½
4	Do. Deb. Stk.	100	101
4	Invest. Tst. Cor. Ltd. Pfd.	100	102
6	Do. Defd.	100	85
4	Do. Deb. Stk. Red.	100	105
25/	Ldn. Gen. Invest. Ltd., 5 p.c. Cum. Prefd.	100	110½
37/6	Do. Defd.	100	120
4½	Ldn. Scot. Amer. Ltd. Pfd.	100	108½
£3	Do. Defd.	100	59½
4	Do. Deb. Stk.	100	111
4	Ldn. Tst., Ltd., Cum. Prfd. Stk.	100	100
4	Do. Defd. Stk.	100	68½
4	Do. Deb. Stk., Red.	100	107
3½	Do. Mt. Deb. Stk., Red.	100	100½
5	Mercantile Invt. & Gen., Ltd., Prefd.	100	111
3	Do. Defd.	100	44½
4	Do. Deb. Stk.	100	110½
4	Merchants, Ltd., Pref. Stk.	100	104½
4	Do. Ord.	100	80½
4	Do. Deb. Stk.	100	116½
6	Municipal, Ltd., Prefd...	100	52½
—	Do. Defd.	100	17½
4½	Do. Debs.	100	111
4½	Do. Debs. "B".....	100	99½
4½	Do. "C" Deb. Stk.	100	94½
5	New Investment, Ltd. Ord.	100	91½
5	Omnium Invest., Ltd., Pfd.	100	92½
2	Do. Defd....	100	26½
4	Do. Deb. Stk.	100	106
5/	Railway Deb. Tst. Ld., £20 Shs...............	10	6½
5	Do. Debs., Red. ..	100	107½
4½	Do. Deb. Stk., 1911	100	107½
4	Do. do. 1927	100	106½
4	Railway Invst. Ltd., Prefd.	100	115
17/7	Do. Defd.	100	20½
8/	Railway Share Trust & Agency "A"..........	8	6½
7½	Do. "B" Pref. Stk.	100	146½
4½	River Plate & Gen. Invt., Ltd., Prefd.	100	104
£3	Do. Defd.	100	50½
5	Scot. Invst., Ltd., Pfd. Stk.	100	91
2½	Do. Defd...	100	26½
4	Do. Deb. Stk.	100	106
4½	Sec. Scottish Invst., Ltd., Cum. Prefd.	100	89½
£3	Do. Defd. Stk.	100	32
4	Do. Deb. Stk.	100	106½
5/	Sth. Africa Gold Tst., Ltd.	1	3½
6	Do. Cum. Pref	1	1
3½	Do. 1st Debs., Red.	100	103
1/9	Stock Conv. & Invest., Ltd., £5 Shs.	1	1½
4½	Do. do. 4½ p.c. Cm. Prf.	100	115½
3½	Do. Ldn. & N. W. 1st. Charge Prefd.	100	113½
4	Do do. 2nd Chge Prfd.	100	111
32/6	Do. do. Defd. Charge	100	31
3	Do. N. East. 1 Chge Pfd.	100	90½

Financial—Trusts (*continued*):—

Last Div.	Name.	Paid.	Price.
37/6	Stock N. East Defd. Chge	100	37
6	Submarine Cables	100	138½
5	U.S. & S. Amer. Invest., Ltd., Prefd.	100	96½
20/	Do. Defd.	100	24½
4	Do. Deb. Stk.	100	103½

GAS AND ELECTRIC LIGHTING.

Last Div.	Name.	Paid.	Price.
10/6	Alliance & Dublin Con. 10 p.c. Stand.	10	24
7/6	Do. 7 p.c. Stand...	10	16½
5	Austln. Gas Lght. (Syd.) Debs. 1902	100	108
5	Bay State of N. Jrsy. Sk. Fd. Tst. Bd., Red. ..	—	88½
3/	Bombay, Ltd............	5	5½
2/4½	Do. New	4	4½
12	Brentford Cons.	100	292½
9	Do. New	100	217½
5	Do. Pref.	100	142½
4	Do. Deb. Stk. ..	100	136
11½	Brighton & Hove Gen. Cons. Stk.	100	272½
8½	Do. "A" Cons. Stk.	100	197½
5	Bristol 5 p.c. Max.	100	129½
22/6	British Gas Light, Ltd.	20	55½
11/6	Bromley Gas Consumrs.' 10 p.c. Stand.	10	26
8/6	Do. 7 p.c. Stand...	10	21
—	Brush Electl. Enging., L.	—	2
6	Do. 6 p.c. Pref.	—	2½
4½	Do. Deb. Stk.	100	112
4½	Do. 2 Deb. Stk., Red.	100	102½
7/	B. Ayres (New), Ltd. ..	10	9
4	Do. Deb. Stk., Rd. ..	—	98
18/6	Cagliari Gas & Wtr., Ltd.	20	21
8/	Cape Town & Dist. Gas Light & Coke, Ltd.	10	15½
4½	Do. Pref.	10	12
6	Do. 1 Mt. Debs. 1910	50	60
4/	Charing Cross & Strand Elec. Sup., Ltd....	5	12½
4½	Do. Cum. Pref.	5	6½
3/	Chelsea Elec. Sup., Ltd.	5	9
4½	Do. Deb. Stk., Red.	100	116
5	Chic. Edis'n Co. 1 Mt., Rd.	$1000	106
20/	City of Ldn. Elec. Lht., L.	10	25
—	Do. New £10 Shs...	5	17
6	Do. Cum. Pref.	10	17
5	Do. Deb. Stk., Red.	100	131½
13½	Commercial, Cons.	100	324½
10½	Do. New	100	252½
4½	Do. Deb. Stk.	100	152½
14	Continental Union, Ltd.	100	215
11	Do. Pref. Stk.	100	200
—	County of Lon. & Brush Prov. Elec. Lg., Ltd.	10	13½
6	Do. Cum. Pref.	10	15½
14	Croydon Comcl. Gas, Ld., "A" Stk., 10 p.c...	100	312½
11	Do. "B" Stk., 7 p.c.	100	260
5½	Crystal Pal. Dist. Ord. 5 p.c. Stk.	100	127½
5	Do. Pref. Stk.	100	143½
8/	European, Ltd.	10	24
6/	Do.	7½	17½
12½	Gas Light & Ck Cons. Stk., "A" Ord.	100	289½
4	Do. "B" (4 p.c. Max.)	100	120½
10	Do. "C," "D," & "E" (Pref.)	100	302½
5	Do. "F" (Pref.)	100	152½
7½	Do. "G" (Pref.)	100	222½
7	Do. "H" (7 p.c. Max.)	100	197½
10	Do. "J" (Pref.)......	100	302½
6	Do. "K"	100	182½
4	Do. Deb. Stk.	100	133½
4½	Do. do.	100	152½
6	Do. do.	100	202½
8/	Hong Kong & China, Ld.	10	14
4/	House to House Elec. Light Sup., Ltd. ..	5	9½
7	Do. Cum. Pref.	5	11
10	Imperial Continental ..	100	212½
3½	Do. Deb. Stk., Red ..	100	104½
2/	Malta & Medit., Ltd. ..	5	5½
7/	Metrop. Elec. Sup., Ltd.	10	15½
4½	Do. 1 Mt. Deb. Stk.	100	119
5	Metro. of Melbrne. Dbs. 1908-12	100	111
4½	Do. Debs.. 1918-22-4	100	108
10/	Monte Video, Ltd.	20	15
9½	Newcastle-upon-Tyne ..	100	237½
—	Do. 3½ p.c. Deb. Stk.	100	117½
18/	Notting Hill Elec. Ltg., Ltd.	10	18½
3/6	Oriental, Ltd...........	5	7½
3/1½	Do. New	4½	6½
8½d.	Do. do. 1879	1	1½
3/6	Ottoman, Ltd.	5	5
6	People's Gas Lt. & C. of Chic. 2 Mt.....1904	100	106½
5	River Plate Elec. Lgt. & Trac., Ltd., 1 Deb. Stk.	—	92½
$2	Royal Elec. of Montreal	—	144
4½	Do. 1 Mt. Deb. ..	100	104
11/	St. James' & Pall Mall Elec. Light, Ltd. ..	5	16½
7	Do. Pref.	5	10
4	Do. Deb. Stk., Red.	100	108½
10/	San Paulo, Ltd.	10	15½

Gas and Electric (*continued*):—

Last Div.	Name.	Paid.	Price.
10	Sheffield Unit. Gas Lt. "A"	100	251½
10	Do. "B"	100	251½
10	Do. "C"	100	251½
—	Sth. Ldn. Elec. Sup., Ld.	2	2½
5½	South Metropolitan	100	138½
3	Do. 3 p.c. Deb. Stk.	100	102½
2	Tottenham & Edmonton Gas Lt. & C., "A"	100	290
9	Do. "B"	100	210
7/	Tuscan, Ltd.	10	13½
5	Do. Debs., Red.	100	101½
5/	West Ham 10 p.c. Stan.	5	12
8/	Wstmnstr. Elec. Sup., Ld.	5	16

INSURANCE.

Last Div.	Name.	Paid.	Price.
4/	Alliance, £20 Shs.	44/	10½
10/	Alliance, Mar., & Gen., Ld., £100 Shs.	25	53
19/	Atlas, £50 Shs.	6	29
12/	British & For. Marine, Ld., £20 Shs.	4	23
7½d.	British Law Fire, Ltd., £10 Shs.	1	1½
7/6	Clerical, Med., & Gen. Life £25 Shs.	50/	16½
20/	Commercial Union, Ltd., £50 Shs.	5	43½
4	Do. "W. of Eng." Ter. Deb. Stk.	100	110½
£9	County Fire, £100 Shs.	80	195
5/	Eagle, £50 Shs.	5	½
4/	Employrs' Liability, Ltd., £10 Shs.	2	3½
—	Empress, Ltd., £5 Shs.	1	—
21/	Equity & Law, £100 Shs.	6	23
7/6	General Life, £100 Shs.	5	15
4½d.	Gresham Life, £5 Shs.	15/	2½
2/6	Guardian, Ld., £10 Shs.	5	10½
10/	Imperial, Ltd., £20 Shs.	5	29
5/6	Imperial Life, £20 Shs.	4	6½
6/	Indemnity Mutual Mar., Ltd., £15 Shs.	3	11½
1/6	Lancashire, £20 Shs.	2	4½
7½d.	Law Acc. & Contin., Ltd., £5 Shs.	10/	¾
12/6	Law Fire, £100 Shs.	2½	17½
9½d.	Law Guar. & Trust, Ltd., £10 Shs.	1	1½
9/	Law Life, £20 Shs.	2	25
2/9	Law Un. & Crown £10 Shs	12/	7
4	Do. Deb. Stk., 1942	100	108½
14/6	Legal & General, £50 Shs.	8	15½
9d.	Lion Fire, Ltd., £8½ Shs.	1½	¾
22/	Liverpool & London & Globe, Stk	2	52½
10/	Do. Globe £1 Ann	—	35
35/	London, £25 Shs.	12½	57
8/	Lond. & Lanc. Fire, £25 Shs	2½	18½
2/	Lond. & Lanc. Life, £25 Shs	2	7
1/	Lond. & Prov. Mar., Ld., £10 Shs.	1	½
6/	Lond. Guar. & Accident, Ltd., £5 Shs.	2	12
10/	Marine, Ltd., £25 Shs.	4½	44
2/	Maritime, Ltd., £10 Shs.	2	4½
1/6	Merc. Mar., Ld., £10 Shs.	2½	2½
20/	N. Brit. & Merc., £25 Shs.	6½	42
20/	Northern, £100 Shs.	10	81
40/	Norwich Union Fire, £100 Shs.	12	127½
20/	Ocean Acc. & Guar., fy. pd.	5	22½
2/	Do. £5 Shs.	1	3½
7/6	Ocean, Marine, Ltd.	2½	8½
2/	Palatine, £10 Shs.	2	3½
2/6	Pelican, £10 Shs.	1	3½
23/	Phœnix, £50 Shs.	5	41½
£6	Provident, £100 Shs.	10	32
5/	Railway Psngrs., £10 Shs.	2	8½
2/6	Rock Life, £5 Shs.	10/	4½
8	Royal Exchange	100	360½
18/	Royal, £20 Shs.	3	54½
4/	Sun, £10 Shs.	10/	11½
3/9	Sun Life, £10 Shs.	7½	14½
6	Thames & Mrsey. Marine, Ltd., £20 Shs.	2	10½
0	Union, £10 Shs.	4	24½
4/	Union Marine, £20 Shs.	2½	8½
12/	Universal Life, £100 Shs.	12	42
2/	World Marine, £5 Shs.	2	1½

IRON, COAL, AND STEEL.

Last Div.	Name.	Paid.	Price.
—	Barrow Hæm. Steel, Ltd.	7½	1½
9/	Do. 6 p.c. 2nd Pref.	7½	6½
10/	Bolck., Vaugh. & C., Ld.	20	16½
6/	Do. £8 liab.	12	8½
7/6	Brown, J. & Co., Ltd., £20 Shs.	15	20
7/6	Consett Iron, Ld., £10 Shs.	7½	29
7/6	Ebbw Vale Steel, Iron & Coal, Ltd., £23 Shs.	20	6
18/6	General Mining Assn., Ld.	5½	7½
1/7½	Harvey Steel Co. of Gt. Britain, Ltd.	10	2½
5	Lehigh V. Coal 1 Mt. 5 p.c. Guar. Gd. Cp. Bds.	—	98
42/6	Nantyglo & Blaina Iron, Ltd., Pref.	$62	96
1/	Nerbudda Coal & Iron, Ltd., £3 Shs.	56/	—
—	Newport Abrcrn. Bk. Vein Steam Coal, Ltd.	10	6½
5/	New Sharlston Coll., Ltd. Pref.	20	9½
4½d.	Nw. Vancvr. Coal & Ld., L.	1	½
2/6	North's Navigation Coll. (1889) Ltd.	5	2½
10/	Do. 10 p.c. Cum. Pref.	5	6½
—	Rhymney Iron, Ltd.	5	1½
	Do. New, £5 Shs.	4½	1
5	Do. Mt. Debs., Red.	100	98½
5	Shelton Irn., Stl. & Cl. Co., Ltd., 1 Chg. Debs., Red.	100	99½
50/	Sth. Hetton Coal, Ltd.	100	—
2/	Vickers & Maxim, Ltd.	1	3½
5	Do. 5 p.c. Prfd. Stk.	100	125½

SHIPPING.

Last Div.	Name.	Paid.	Price.
12/	African Stm. Ship, £20 Shs.	16	10½
15/	Do. Fully-paid	20	14½
5/	Amazon Steam Nav., Ltd.	12½	8½
12/	Castle Mail Pakts., Ltd., £20 Shs.	14	15
3½	Do. 1st Deb. Stk., Red.	100	102
6/	China Mutual Steam, Ltd.	5	3
6	Do. Cum. Pref.	10	9½
10/	Cunard, Ltd.	20	9½
5/	Do. £20 Shs.	10	3½
4½	Furness, Withy, & Co., Ltd., 1 Mt. Dbs., Red.	100	106
6/	General Steam	15	7½
5/	Do. 5 p.c. Pref., 1874	10	8½
5/	Do. 5 p.c. Pref., 1877	10	8½
26/4½	Leyland & Co., Ltd.	10	27
7/	Do. 7 p.c. Cum. Pref.	10	14½
2/11	Do. 4½ p.c. Cum. Pre-Pf.	3	10½
4	Do. 1st Mt. Dbs., Red.	100	104½
7/6	Mercantile Steam, Ltd.	5	8
6/4½	New Zealand Ship., Ltd.,	6	4½
4	Do. Deb. Stk., Red.	100	104
5/	Orient Steam, Ltd.	10	4½
5	P. & O. Steam, Cum. Prefd.	100	147½
19	Do. Defd.	100	235½
3½	Do. Deb. Stk.	100	117
5	Richelieu & Ont., 1st Mt. Debs., Red.	100	100
30/	Royal Mail, £100 Shs.	60	51
2/6	Shaw, Sav., & Alb., Ltd., "A" Pref.	5	5½
5/	Do. "B" Ord.	5	4
14/	Union Steam, Ltd.	20	19
7/	Do. New £20 Shs.	10	8
4	Do. Deb. Stk., Red.	100	107
6/	Union of N.Z., Ltd.	10	9½
5½	Wilson's & Fur.-Ley., 5½ p.c. Cum. Pref.	10	10½
4½	Do. 1 Mt. Db. Sk., Rd.	100	106½

*** *Tea Shares will be found in the Special Table following.*

TELEGRAPHS AND TELEPHONES.

Last Div.	Name.	Paid.	Price.
4	African Direct, Ltd., Mort. Debs., Red.	100	102
—	Amazon Telegraph, Ltd.	10	7½
15/	Anglo-American, Ltd.	100	65½
30/	Do. 6 p.c. Prefd. Ord.	100	115½
—	Do. Defd. Ord.	100	16
3/	Brazilian Submarine, Ltd.	10	15½
5	Do. Debs, 2 Series	100	114

Telegraphs and Telephones (*continued*):—

Last Div.	Name.	Paid.	Price.
4/	Chili Telephone, Ltd.	5	3
$1½	Comcial. Cable, $100 Shs.	—	185
4	Do. Stg. 500-yr. Deb. Stk. Red.	100	106
2½d.	Consd. Telpehone Constr., &c., Ltd.	10/	½
6/	Cuba Submarine, Ltd.	10	7
10/	Do. 10 p.c. Pref.	10	15
2/	Direct Spanish, Ltd.	5	4½
5/	Do. 10 p.c. Cum. Pref.	5	10½
4½	Do. Debs.	50	104½
3/	Direct U.S. Cable, Ltd.	20	10½
2/6	Eastern, Ltd.	10	17½
3/	Do. 6 p.c. Cum. Pref.	10	18½
4	Do. Mt. Deb. Stk., Red.	100	126
6/6	Eastern Exten., Aus., & China, Ltd.	10	17½
5	Do. (Aus. Gov. Sub.) Deb., Red.	100	102
5	Do. do. Bearer	100	102½
4	Do. Mort. Deb. Stk.	100	127½
5	Eastn. & S. Afric., Ltd., Mort. Deb. 1900	100	102
5	Do. Bearer	100	102½
4	Do. Mort. Debs. 1909	100	102½
4	Do. Mort. Debs. (Maur. Subsidy)	25	106½
5/	Grt. Nthn. Copenhagen	10	29½
5	Do. Debs., Ser. B., Red.	100	101½
12/6	Indo-European, Ltd.	25	51½
6	London Platino-Brazilian, Ltd., Debs. 1904	100	109½
4/	Montevideo Telph., Ltd., 6 p.c. Pref.	5	2½
3/	National Telephone, Ltd.	5	5½
6/	Do. Cum. 1 Pref.	10	15
6/	Do. Cum. 2 Pref.	10	16
5	Do. Non-Cum. 3 Pref.	5	5½
3½	Do. Deb. Stk., Red.	100	103½
8d.	Oriental Telephone, Ltd.	1	½
4	Pac. & Euro. Tlg. Dbs., Rd.	100	106½
4/	Reuter's, Ltd.	8	8½
5/	Un. Riv. Plate Telph., Ltd.	5	4½
5	Do. Deb. Stk., Red.	100	105½
—	West African Telg., Ltd.	10	4
5	Do. 5 p.c. Mt. Debs., Red.	100	100½
—	W. Coast of America, Ltd.	10	½
3/	Western & Brazilian, Ltd.	15	12½
3/	Do. 5 p.c. Pref. Ord.	7½	7½
—	Do. Defd. Ord.	7½	4½
4	Do. Deb. Stk., Red.	100	105½
6d.	W. India & Panama, Ltd.	10	½
6	Do. Cum. 1 Pref.	10	7½
6	Do. Cum. 2 Pref.	10	6
5	Do. Debs., Red.	100	107½
7	West. Union, 1 Mt. 1902 ($	1000	107½
6	Do. 6 p.c. Stg. Bds., Rd.	100	102½

TRAMWAYS AND OMNIBUS.

Last Div.	Name.	Paid.	Price.
1/6	Anglo-Argentine, Ltd.	5	3½
6	Do. Deb. Stk	100	125
4/	Barcelona, Ltd.	10	11
5	Do. Deb., Red.	100	106½
7/6	Belfast Street Trams.	10	16½
—	Blackpl. & Fltwd. Tram., £10 Shs.	8	12½
10/	Bordeaux Tram. & O. Ltd.	10	12
5	Do. Cum. Pref.	10	11
—	Brazilian Street Ry., Ltd.	9	½
—	British Elec. Trac., Ltd.	10	15½
—	B. Ayres & Belg. Tram., Ltd., 6 p.c. Cum. Pref.	5	—
6	Do. 1 Deb. Stk.	100	—
—	B. Ayres. Gd. Nat., Ltd., 6 p.c 1 Deb. Bds., Red.	100	60½
5½	Do. Pref. Debs., Red.	100	94½
1/	Calais, Ltd.	5	1
—	Calcutta, Ltd.	10	3½
—	Carthagena & Herr., Ltd.	10	2½
5	Do. Deb., Red.	100	90
5	City of B'ham. Trams., Ltd., 5 p.c. Cum. Pref.	5	5½
4	Do. 1 Mort. Debs., Rd.	100	105½
3/9	City of B. Ayres, Ltd.	5	6½
2/3	Do. Ext. £5 Shs.	3	3½
6	Do. Deb. Stk	100	145
1/4	Edinburgh Street Tram.	4	4
1/	Glasgow Tram. & Omni. Ltd., £9 Shs.	8	2½
3/7½	Imperial, Ltd.	6	14½
3/	Lond., Deptfd, & Greenwich, Prefd.	5	3½
nil	Do. Defd.	5	1
10½	Lond. Gen. Omni., Ltd.	100	196
4	Do. Deb., Red.	100	113½

Tramways and Omnibus (*continued*):—

Last Div.	Name.	Paid.	Price.
4/9½	London Road Car	6	10
28/6	Do. Red. 1 Mt. Deb. Stk.	100	109½
5	London St. Rly. (Prov., Ont.), Mt. Debs.	100	110
12/6	London St. Trams.	—	2
12/9	London Trams., Ltd	10	9
6/	Do. Non-Cum. Pref.	10	10
5	Do. Mt. Db. Stk., Rd.	100	101
5	Lynn & Boston 1 Mt. 1924 $	1000	104
5	Milwaukee Elec. Cons. Mt. $	1000	100½
5	Minneapolis St. 1 Cons. Mt $	1000	96
5	Montreal St. Dbs., 1908	100	109
4½	Do. Debs., 1922	100	107
6/	Nth. Metropolitan	—	11½
1/9½	Nth. Staffords., Ltd.	6	5
2/6	Provincial, Ltd	10	6½
6/	Do. Cum. Pref.	10	14
5	St. Paul City, 1937 $	1000	96
5/	Southampton	10	6½
5/	South London	10	5½
7/6	Sunderland, Ltd.	10	6½
4½	Toronto 1 Mt., Red.	100	105
2/6	Tramways Union, Ltd.	5	6½
4½	Do. Deb., Red.	100	109
2/6	Vienna General Omnibus.	5	5
5	Do. 5 p.c. Mt. Deb., Red.	100	103½
4/	Wolverhampton, Ltd	10	6

WATER WORKS.

Last Div.	Name.	Paid.	Price.
10/	Antwerp, Ltd.	20	22
6/	Cape Town District, Ltd.	5	½
10½	Chelsea	100	322
5	Do. Pref. Stk.	100	172
4½	Do. Pref. Stk., 1875	100	152½
4½	Do. Deb. Stk.	100	159½
5/6	City St. Petersburg, Ltd.	13	10½
5/	Colne Valley	10	15½
4	Do. Deb. Stock	100	137½
£4	Consol. of Rosar., Ltd., 4 p.c. 1 Deb. Stk., Red.	100	91
8	East London	100	227½
4½	Do. Deb. Stk.	100	160
3	Do. Deb. Stk., Red.	100	105
37/6	Grand Junction (Max. 10 p.c.) "A"	50	117½
18/9	Do. "B"	25	
18/9	Do. "C" (Max. 7½ p.c.)	25	54½
35/	Do. "D" (Max. 7 p.c.)	50	97½
4	Do. Deb. Stock	100	142½
13	Kent	100	360½
7	Do. New (Max. 7 p.c.)	100	215½
7/	Kimberley, Ltd.	7	4½
6	Do. Debs., Red.	100	104½
6	Do. Deb. Stk., Red.	100	107½
10	Lambeth (Max. 10 p.c.)	100	297½
7½	Do. (Max. 7½ p.c.), 50 & 25	—	230½
4	Do. Deb. Stock	100	142½
3	Do. Red. Deb. Stock	100	103
10/	Montevideo, Ltd.	20	16
5	Do. 1 Deb. Stk.	100	108½
5	Do. 2 Deb. Stk.	100	103½
132/9	New River New	100	434½
4	Do. Deb. Stk.	100	143½
4	Do. Deb. Stk. "B"	100	143½
4	Portland Con. Mt. "B," 1927	—	102½
8/	Seville, Ltd.	20	12
5/6	Southend "Addl." Ord.	10	17
6	Southwark and Vauxhall	100	157½
6	Do. "D" Shares (7½ p.c. max.)	100	154½
5	Do. Pref. Stock	100	172½
4	Do. "A" Deb. Stock	100	141½
3	Staines Resvirs. Jt. Com. Gua. Deb. Stk., Red.	100	106
8/	Tarapaca, Ltd.	10	8½
10	West Middlesex	100	302½
4½	Do. Deb. Stk.	100	162½
3	Do Deb. Stk.	100	105

INDIAN AND CEYLON TEA COMPANIES.

Acres Planted.	Crop, 1897.	Paid up Capital.	Share.	Paid up.	Name.	Dividends. 1894.	1895.	1896.	1897.	Price.	Yield.	Reserve.	Balance Forward.	Working Capital.	Mortgages, Debs. or Pref. Capital not otherwise stated.
	lb.	£	£	£	INDIAN COMPANIES.							£	£	£	£
11,240	3,128,000	120,000	10	3	Amalgamated Estates	—	*	10	15	3½	9	10,000	16,500	D52,950	—
		400,000	10	10	Do. Pref.	—	*	5	5	9¾	5¼				
10,223	3,560,000	187,160	20	20	Assam	20	20	20	17½	59	6	55,000	1,730	D11,350	—
6,150	3,278,000	142,500	10	10	Assam Frontier	3	6	6	—	7	8¼	—	286	20,000	82,500
		142,500	10	10	Do. Pref.	6	6	6	6	11	5¼				
2,087	830,000	66,745	5	5	Attaree Khat	12	12	8	5	5	5	3,790	4,820	7,770	—
1,633	583,000	78,170	10	10	Borelli	4	4	5	4	7	6	—	3,256	D270	6,500 Pref.
1,720	812,000	60,825	5	5	British Indian	6	5	5	5	3¾	6⅝	—	2,922	12,300	16,300 Pref.
3,223	2,047,000	114,500	5	5	Brahmapootra	20	18	20	15	12¾	6¼	—	28,440	41,600	
3,754	1,617,000	76,500	10	10	Cachar and Dooars	*	8	7	7	9¾	7	—	1,645	21,240	
		76,300	10	10	Do. Pref.	*	6	6	6	11½	5¼				
3,946	2,083,000	72,010	1	1	Chargola	8	7	10	12½	1	13¾	3,000	3,300	—	—
		81,000	1	1	Do. Pref.	7	7	7	13½	1⅛	5¼				
1,971	942,000	33,000	5	5	Chubwa	10	8	10	8	5½	7¼	10,000	2,043	D5,400	—
		33,000	5	5	Do. Pref.	7	7	7	7	6½	5¼				
,250	11,500,000	120,000	10	3	Cons. Tea and Lands	—	*	10	15	3⅛	8	65,000	14,240	D191,674	—
		1,000,000	10	10	Do. 1st Pref.	—	*	5	5	10¾	4⅝				
		400,000	10	10	Do. 2nd Pref.	—	*	7	7	11⅞	5⅞				
2,030	617,000	133,420	20	20	Darjeeling	5½	5½	6	5	21	4¾	5,552	1,565	1,700	—
2,114	445,000	60,000	10	10	Darjeeling Cons.	—	*	4/2	nil	nom.	—	—	1,820	—	—
		60,000	10	10	Do. Pref.	—	*	5	5	9½	5¼				
6,660	3,518,000	150,000	10	10	Dooars	12½	12½	12½	12½	18	7	43,000	300	D32,000	—
		75,000	10	10	Do. Pref.	7	7	7	7	16⅞	4¼				
3,367	1,811,000	165,000	10	10	Doom Dooma	11½	20	12½	12½	20	6¼	30,000	4,032	—	10,000
1,377	582,000	61,120	5	5	Eastern Assam	5	nil.	4	nil	2¼	—	—	1,790	—	10,000
4,038	1,675,000	85,000	10	10	East India and Ceylon	*	nil.	7	—	7	10	—	1,710	—	—
		85,000	10	10	Do. Pref.	*	6	6	6	11xd	5¼				
7,500	3,363,000	219,000	10	10	Empire of India	—	*	6/10	9	10¾	8¼	15,000	—	27,000	—
		219,000	10	10	Do. Pref.	—	*	5	5	10¾	4¾				
1,180	540,000	94,060	10	10	Indian of Cachar	7	3½	3	2	3½	5¾	*6,070	—	7,120	—
3,050	824,000	83,500	5	5	Jhanzie	10	10	10	8	6⅛xd	6	14,500	1,070	2,700	
7,980	3,680,000	250,000	10	10	Jokai	10	10	10	15	16	6	45,000	990	D9,000	—
		100,000	10	10	Do. Pref.	*	6	6	6	14½	4¼				
5,024	1,563,000	100,000	20	20	Jorehaut	20	20	20	—	59	6⅝	36,220	2,055	3,000	—
1,547	504,000	65,660	10	8	Lebong	15	15	15	12½	15¾xd	6⅝	9,000	2,150	8,650	—
5,082	1,709,000	100,000	10	10	Lungla	*	10	6	3	6	5	—	1,543	D21,000	—
		100,000	10	10	Do. Pref.	*	6	6	6	10	6				
2,684	885,000	95,970	10	10	Majuli	7	5	5	—	6½	7¾	—	2,606	560	—
1,275	380,000	91,840	1	1	Makum	—	—	2	—	1	2	—	—	1,200	25,000
2,990	770,000	100,000	1	1	Moabund	—	—	[illegible]	—	[illegible]	—	—	—	-	—
		50,000	1	1	Do. Pref.	—	—	*	12½	⅞	11				
1,080	482,000	79,590	10	10	Scottish Assam	7	7	7	—	10¾	6½	6,500	800	9,590	—
4,150	1,456,000	100,000	10	10	Singlo	*	8	5	11	8	6	—	300	D5,800	—
		80,000	10	10	Do. Pref.	*	6½	6½	12½	13	5				
					CEYLON COMPANIES.										
7,070	1,743,824§	250,000	100	100	Anglo-Ceylon, & Gen.	—	*	5½	—	45	11	10,992	1,405	D72,844	166,580
1,836	685,741§	50,000	10	10	Associated Tea	—	*	5	12½	7¾	6⅝	—	164	2,478	—
		60,000	10	10	Do. Pref.	—	*	6	13	10¾	5¾				
10,390	4,000,000	167,380	10	10	Ceylon Tea Plantations	15	15	15	15	23½	6⅜	84,500	1,516	D30,819	—
		81,080	10	10	Do. Pref.	7	7	7	7	16¾	4¼				
5,722	1,542,700	55,260	5	3	Ceylon & Oriental Est.	5	8	7	—	2¾	7¼	—	230	D2,047	71,000
		46,000	5	5	Do. Pref.	6	6	6	13	4¾	6				
2,157	801,629§	111,330	5	5	Dimbula Valley	—	*	10	15	5½	9	—	—	1,733	6,250
		62,607	5	5	Do. Pref.	—	*	6	13	6¼	4⅞				
11,496	3,635,000	298,230	5	5	Eastern Prod. & Est.	3	5	6½	7	5¾	6¼	20,000	11,740	D17,797	102,500
2,193	1,050,000	22,080	10	10	New Dimbula "A"	10	16	16	14	24	7	11,000	2,024	1,150	8,400
		55,710	10	10	Do. "B"	18	16	16	14	22	7½				
2,572	570,360§	100,000	10	10	Ouvah	6	8	6	12	8	7¼	4,000	1,151	D1,255	—
2,630	964,963	200,000	10	10	Nuwara Eliya	—	*	6	6	10½	5¾	—	—	—	30,000
1,720	708,533	41,000	10	10	Scottish Ceylon	15	15	15	10	17	6	7,000	1,252	D3,970	9,000 Pref.
2,450	750,000	39,000	10	6	Standard	12½	15	15	15	12¾	7	9,000	800	D14,011	4,000
		17,000	10	10	Do.	12½	15	15	15	22	7				

Working-Capital Column.—In working-capital column, D stands for *debit*.

* Company formed this year. † Interim dividends are given as actual distribution made. ‡ Interim div. only. § Crop 1896.

DIVIDENDS ANNOUNCED.

MISCELLANEOUS.

Anglo-Chilian Nitrate and Railway Company, Limited.—Dividend of 14s. per preference share.

New Hudson Cycle Company, Limited.—Interim dividend at the rate of 6 per cent. on the preference shares.

New Hudson Cycle Extension.—Dividend at the rate of 10 per cent. for the past fifteen months.

Singer Cycle Company, Limited.—Interim dividend at the rate of 5 per cent. per annum on the ordinary shares for the six months ended March 31, 1898.

Boston Steam Trawling.—10 per cent.

Ro al Electric Company of Montreal.—2 per cent. for the quarter ended May 31.

Webster's Brickworks, Limited.—Dividend at the rate of 6 per cent.

Western and Brazilian Telegraph Company, Limited.—Dividend of 6s. 9d. per share, making, with the dividend paid in November, £3 5s. per cent. for the year.

Craven's Caledonia Gold Mining Company (Charters Towers).—3d. per share.

Grand Junction Waterworks Company.—Dividend at the rate of 7½ per cent. on the A, B, and C shares, and at the rate of 7 per cent. on the D shares.

New Zealand Trust and Loan Company, Limited.—2s. 6d. per share, making, with the interim dividend paid in December, 5 per cent. for the year.

Great Boulder Perseverance Gold Mining Company, Limited.—4s. per share.

Hudson's Bay Company.—Dividend of 13s. per share.

Indian and General Investment Trust, Limited.—3 per cent. on the deferred stock.

City and Suburban Gold Mining and Estate Company, Limited.—7½ per cent.

New Zealand and River Plate Land Mortgage Company, Limited.—Interim dividend at the rate of 5 per cent. per annum.

Electric and General Investment Company, Limited.—Further dividend on the ordinary shares at the rate of 30 per cent. per annum, and a bonus of 10 per cent., making, with the interim dividend, 35 per cent. for the year. A dividend of £50 on each founder's share, with £20 per share from the founder's share reserve fund.

Commercial Cable Company.—Quarterly dividend of 1¾ per cent.

Brilliant and St. George United Gold Mining Company.—Dividend of 9d. per share.

New Heriot Gold Mining Company, Limited.—25 per cent.

Zeehan Montana Mine, Limited.—Further dividend of 9d. per share.

Boston Deep Sea Fishing and Ice Company, Limited.—10 per cent.

Gold Patents Company, Limited.—Interim dividend of 5 per cent. payable to shareholders registered on June 30.

Rio De Janeiro Flour Mills and Granaries, Limited.—Interim dividend at the rate of 5s. per share will be paid on the 15th inst.

Victoria and Queen Gold Mining Company, Limited.—1s. per share payable on the 23rd inst.

British and Foreign Marine Insurance Company.—Interim dividend of 8s. per share for the half-year.

Tower Tea.—A final dividend of 1s. 10½d. on ordinary shares, making with the interim dividend 8¾ per cent. for year.

Wolhuter Gold Mines.—A half-yearly dividend of 4s. per share, and an interim dividend of 2s. per share have been declared.

Associated Gold Mines of Western Australia.—Interim dividend at the rate of 2s. per share.

RAILWAYS.

Bengal Dooars Railway Company, Limited.—Dividend of 3½ per cent. for the six months ended December 31, making 5 per cent. for the year.

Alabama Great Southern Railway Company, Limited.—Interim dividend of 3 per cent. on the "A" preference shares.

INSURANCE.

Royal Insurance Company.—Dividend of 20s. per share, making, with the 18s. paid in December last, 38s. for the year.

Norwich Union Fire Insurance Society.—Dividend of £2 per share, and bonus of £1.

Northern Assurance Company.—Further dividend of £1 5s. per share, and bonus of 15s.

British and Foreign Marine Insurance Company, Limited.—Interim dividend of 8s. per share for the half-year.

SHIPPING.

British India Steam Navigation Company, Limited.—Dividend at the rate of 10 per cent. for the year.

Peninsular and Oriental Steam Navigation Company.—Usual interim dividend at the rate of 5 per cent. per annum on the preferred and 7 per cent. on the deferred stock.

BREWERIES.

Chesters Brewery Company, Limited.—5 per cent., making with the interim dividend already paid, 8 per cent. for the year.

Westlake's, Limited.—Interim dividend at the rate of 8 per cent. per annum payable on and after the 13th inst.

BANKS.

Imperial of Persia.—Interim dividend for the half-year ended March 20 of 3s. per share will be payable on and after the 28th inst.

The numbers are published of the 6 per cent. bonds of £100 each of the Cantareira Water Supply and Drainage Company of the City of Sao Paulo, drawn for payment at the British Bank of South America on July 1.

Messrs. N. M. Rothschild and Sons announce that under the operation of the sinking fund bonds of the Brazilian 4½ per cent. loan of 1883, amounting to £90,000 nominal capital, of the Chilian 4½ per cent. loan of 1887, amounting to £12,700 nominal capital, and of the Chilian 5 per cent. loan of 1896, amounting to £24,700 nominal capital, have been purchased.

The Investors' Review

EDITED BY A. J. WILSON.

Vol. I.—No. 24. New Series. | FRIDAY, JUNE 17, 1898. | [Registered as a Newspaper.] | Price 6d. By post, 6½d

CONTENTS

The Investors' Review.

The Looming Conflict in China.

The Marquis of Salisbury made an eminently wise and sensible speech on Tuesday to the deputation that waited upon him with reference to the construction of railways and other matters in China. He did well to remind the nation that British progress has been a thing of private enterprise in the past, and his profession of faith in the power of British energy and resources to win against all enemies, in spite of adverse tariffs, was thoroughly opportune. Nevertheless, we fear events will be too many for his Lordship, and for any Government that may have the handling of British interests in China in the near future. And in spite of the desirability that British railway construction in China, as elsewhere, should be carried out by private enterprise and capital, it seems not improbable that the action of other Powers commercially hostile to us, and full of sullen resentment at our free trade prosperity, may gradually force us into active efforts at annexation in various parts of that empire. Russian aggression, as we may call it without question, in Northern China drove us to obtain the lease of Wei-Hai-Wei; German and French pretensions in Central and Southern China have hurried forward the occupation of those portions of the mainland of China opposite Hong-Kong, which have long been considered necessary to the safety of the island, and now the latest news from China, sent by the always well-informed correspondent of the *Times* in Pekin, probably heralds the occupation by us of some point of vantage in the Yang-tse Valley. It is all very well for Lord Salisbury to say that we have not surrendered any of our rights in China under the existing Treaty of Tientsin and that we do not intend to surrender any of them. If, however, Russia and France, using Belgium as a cat's-paw and financial agent, proceed to the construction of a railway between Pekin and Hankau it is perfectly obvious that we shall have to assert our rights to the freedom of trade through Central China in a manner quite incompatible with pacific representations to the Chinese Government, or with the slow development of the empire by private capital. Private enterprise, in short, cannot hold its own against imperial "mailed fists." In a telegram dated the 14th inst. the *Times* correspondent says :—

The British Government cannot be ignorant that the Peking-Hankau Railway as now being negotiated is not a commercial line, but is controlled by hostile political considerations and is destined to thwart British action in the Yang-tse Valley. The Belgian Minister is merely acting for the Russian and French Legations. China is thus deluded into giving the contract to Belgium as a small, unaggressive Power. She has hitherto repudiated all intention to place the railway so constructed within the power of Russia and France, but now the Tsung-li-Yamên officially admits that the three Legations have been acting conjointly.

It becomes more and more imperative for England to define her sphere of interest in the Yang-tse region, and to insist upon the right of first refusal as to all railways there. If it is too late for her to veto the *pseudo* Belgian railway scheme, she must demand first refusal in case the contract be transferred.

The truth is that France, Germany, and above all Russia, have designs upon China totally antagonistic to our liberal trade policy. They are all exclusive traders, and they see China helpless, a derelict among nations, endowed with splendid natural resources, filled with a dense and most industrious population, and the sight is an irresistible temptation to them to enter in and take possession. By one pretext or another they will seize lines of communication and gradually block the way to the extension of British commerce. The question for us, therefore, is, shall we enter into this conflict and battle with the whole of our enemies at once, or shall we retire from the contest bit by bit protesting. Probably neither course will be actually adopted. It is much more likely that we shall take a middle line, not actively fighting these Powers at any point, but sturdily resisting their encroachments as long as we can. In doing this, as we have said, it may be necessary for us to seize, or lease, as the phrase is, more than one place in the Yang-tse Valley, and political considerations might even drive us into building that extremely difficult and costly line of railway between Burma and Western China. We hope, however, that much of this kind of counter aggression will not be forced upon us at present. Our hands are full enough, and, as Lord Salisbury said, we have quite as much territory already as we can govern; he might have added, as we have the means to develop. Had our hands been less full elsewhere we might, in the interests of our Indian Empire as well as of our own commerce, have taken a more resolute attitude in regard to the partition of China now apparently imminent. As it is, the waiting game appears to be the only one really open to us—waiting and watching, and as we do so laying hold of such positions as may be available for us in the assertion of our undoubted rights, so as to be ready for the day when these militant appropriators and exclusive traders fall out amongst themselves, as they certainly will do.

Another thing we must be careful to do, since this attitude has been forced upon us, is to see that no British money is given to Belgium or Russia to help them to build their projected railways. Let France find the money if she can. If isolation in trade is to be the fashion with these military Continental Powers, let us practise isolation in the investment of our capital. There, at least, we are still strong above all these Powers put together, and if Russia and Germany do enter upon ambitious projects of railway building in China it is not at all improbable that we may yet buy their roads at bankrupt prices. We do not believe that exclusive trading, combined with the exhausting strain of universal military service, is going to win in the industrial struggle of the world; nor do we believe that France is capable of finding the money for Russia to carry out her ambitious schemes all over the northern half of the Chinese Empire, nor yet France and Belgium together. Let none of our money, then, go there, except to further enterprises of our own, and they will not be long, any of these Powers or all of them, before they come to the end of their tether. In the meantime, it is consoling to notice that events are shaping more and more towards a gradual fusion of interests, and co-operation between the United States and ourselves in the Pacific. From this point of view it is excellent news to hear that the Germans are sending a squadron of observation to Manila, with a view perhaps to raise objections to the presence of the United States there as ruler by right of conquest. By all means let the Germans assume an attitude of protest there. In doing so they will more and more alienate the United States from Continental Europe and help to convince American statesmen that England alone, with her free, impartial and liberal commercial policy, can be their friend, can help them to obtain a share in the great trade which the development of China, now to be begun and by one means or another carried out, is sure to create.

The United States "War Revenue" Measures.

It does not seem to us that the United States Legislature has acted altogether wisely in the provisions it has made for paying the cost of the war with Spain. Details of the measure are not yet to hand, but we are able to gather from the outlines telegraphed from time to time, and from the observations in the American newspapers, that the Government is empowered to have recourse to borrowing much more than to prolific sources of new taxation. Sensibly enough, both Houses of Congress have recognised the futility of putting on more tariff duties. This is cheering, because a tacit recognition of the failure of the Dingley Tariff. In this respect, however, the legislators probably could not help themselves, for, without counting anything for the cost of war, the deficit produced mainly by this tariff in the current year's income may reach nearly £15,000,000. The Government of Washington, in short, has begun the war with an empty Treasury, and already would have had to resort freely to the moneylender had it not possessed a considerable unspent balance remaining out of the last credit-sustaining loan raised by President Cleveland. In such circumstances, as the New York *Financial Chronicle* has pointed out in a wise and thoughtful criticism of the Government proposals, the true policy to have pursued was one of abundant taxation levied upon internal sources of revenue. These have lain almost untouched by the fiscal policy of the United States, which has prevailed since the time of the Civil War until now. The country meanwhile has advanced enormously in wealth and population; it therefore ought to have been a comparatively easy matter for the Government and Legislature to open out large sources of revenue in the form of internal taxes. At one point only were they barred; they could not impose an income tax in face of the decision of the Supreme Court in 1895 that such a tax is unconstitutional. Short of this, they might have done much in the way of stamp duties and legacy and succession duties, as well as in taxes upon the gross profits of corporations, to find the bulk of the war expenditure out of revenue.

In reality they have done very little, so little that we are disposed to doubt whether the resulting revenue will amount to the estimated $100,000,000. There is to be a duty of 10 cents per pound on tea, an article the consumption of which is still very moderate in the States, and a stamp tax is to be imposed on all speculative sales of stocks or produce, but how the character of the sales is to be determined we do not know. Further, an excise tax of one-fourth of 1 per cent. is to be imposed on the gross receipts of the Sugar Refining Corporations and on the Standard Oil Trust, when such gross receipts exceed a quarter of a million dollars per annum. The proposed tonnage duty has been abandoned, and what else there is to take its place we cannot say; but if these are all, or the main, new taxes imposed we believe they will prove to be as thoroughly inadequate as they are undoubtedly, at some points, vicious in principle. The singling out of two of the particular businesses conducted as monopolies and the striking at them with an infinitesimal tax of a vexatious character is a concession to the "populist" vote, but not in any sense a wise step. Such a tax may in itself be defensible enough, but it ought to have been imposed upon all corporations or on none. It might then have been graduated so that the larger ones paid a higher percentage than the smaller, but it ought not to have been imposed, nominally as a special punishment on two of the most conspicuously successful monopolies, in reality as a thing so light as to give occasion to the mocker. There was also an increase of the beer duty proposed, and we believe this proposal has been retained. There could be nothing to say against that, nor yet against a considerable increase in the duties upon alcoholic drinks of every description, or on tobacco. Assume that the additional tax on beer is prolific, and still we must come to the conclusion that no sufficient provision has been made in new taxation by Congress for the cost of the war, no provision at all commensurate with the capacity of the people to bear taxation.

But if the taxation imposed is insufficient, and therefore an indication of weak-kneedness on the part of the Government and Legislature, what is to be said of the concessions made to the silverites in the proposal to coin monthly $1,500,000 out of the silver in the Treasury? This measure cannot possibly do any good and it may do an infinity of harm. The silver already coined lies idle in the Treasury. At the end of April, the last date we have, there were 401,323,414 million coined dollars lying there, the public preferring notes. It is impossible to force this debased money into circulation: the people are not used to it, and would not have it even if they were accustomed to handle coin instead of paper, because they regard all the paper money in circulation, even the silver certificates, as payable in gold. To add to this coinage is only to embarrass the Treasury, and to open the door to an inflation of the paper money which has already gone far enough to produce dangerous confusion in the United States currency. There are, in addition to the silver, nearly $100,000,000 worth of bars also lying in the Treasury, purchased under the Sherman Act, and it is this bullion which the Government now propose to coin at the rate of $18,000,000 per annum. The question of seigniorage is stated to have been left in abeyance as long as this rate of coinage continues. It was unnecessary to say anything about it, because the mere fact of coining the metal into dollars stamps it with a fictitious value in the books of the Treasury nearly 100 per cent. in excess of the market value, and notes representing the nominal, not real, value of the metal can be issued. Thus in ten years' time, when the coinage of this bullion at the proposed rate is about completed, the United States Government will have converted about $100,000,000 worth of bars into, say, $175,000,000 worth of silver dollars, against which paper money may be forced into circulation.

We cannot imagine a greater folly than this, and that it should be perpetrated at a time like the present, when it is of vital importance to the States that their credit abroad should be maintained at the highest possible point, is nothing short of exasperating. What can they have been thinking of, these members of the House of Representatives, when they so far backed down to the Senate's demands as to adopt a scheme like this into the war Ways and Means Act? Its ultimate practical effect must be to force the United States back upon silver, the discredited metal, as their national standard. Should this new measure be carried out to its full limit as indicated by the bullion in the Treasury, and should the seigniorage or profit on the dollars already coined be also availed of to issue more paper money, the States must become a silver country whether the people like it or not, and may reach that low-grade credit standard only as a half-way step to becoming a forced paper country.

Meantime, all these provisions together will not go very far towards paying for the present war. As the *Chronicle* points out in the article already alluded to, the first year of the Civil War cost the Northern States $431,000,000, and in some respects the present war will be much more costly while it lasts. Everything has had to be got ready in feverish haste, and therefore at extravagant cost. Two expeditions on land will soon be at work, one in the Philippines and the other in Cuba, in addition to the two fleets. Money, therefore, has been and will be poured out like water, and had taxes to the amount of $400,000,000 of estimated yield been imposed the revenue would still have been insufficient to meet the outlay in the year 1898. This is recognised by the Government and another weak measure is the consequence. Power is taken to raise new funded debt to the amount of $400,000,000, or, say, £80,000,000, and half of this is issued now in 3 per cent. bonds—not gold bonds, but bonds of the usual ambiguous type as to payment. No doubt the money will at once be forthcoming—indeed, banks and people are tumbling over each other after it—because American banks and large classes of the American people are at present flush of money, but when the second half of the loan comes to be offered, as it will have to be before many weeks are over, the nation's free resources may not be so abundant, and in order to fill the subscription, securities which can be sold abroad will then have to be offered in Europe so as to obtain the necessary funds. The provision for coining fresh silver money is not calculated to increase the appetite of European investors even for United States railroad gold bonds. Average minds are unable to distinguish between the risks these bonds carry and the risk of payment in silver attached to the debt of the Government. Mr. McKinley's administration has, therefore, allowed itself to be seriously handicapped by this new "coin" loan at several points. Had Congress authorised the raising of a gold loan, the whole of the money might have been found in Europe —in London—in twenty-four hours. Congress has not given this authorisation, and the money to pay for the war must be raised at home. Securities which can be marketed abroad will have to be exported, and they will come upon a bad market, created by the distrust originating in the subservience of Congress to the Silver Party in the Union. For the present, enthusiasm for the war in the United States will carry off the distrust this shilly-shallying policy is calculated to engender, and the weakness displayed by Congress in keeping taxes light, and in providing that posterity shall bear the brunt of this war, may excite little comment. But here, where we are not in the swirl of passions stirred up by the war, the effect of these measures will be immediate; and it will make itself visible on our stock markets, where the activity in "American rails," up to the present, has not been produced by the investments of British money in American railroad securities, but merely, as we have often explained, by the preparations of the market for such investments to come.

We are sorry to write in this strain, but there is no help for it. The Washington Government and Legislature have been weak, lamentably weak, in their fiscal provisions, before a great national crisis. A manlier course would have dictated a minimum of borrowing and heavy taxation, so that the men who sanctioned and made the war should have paid for it. An upright policy would have forbidden further truckling to the Silver Party; and we are perfectly sure that if Mr. McKinley had had the courage to demand legislation on these lines, and to declare emphatically that the war must be paid by taxation, and that he would not issue more bonds payable in cash without specifying the metal, the enthusiasm of the people would have so backed him up that both Senate and House of Representatives would have been compelled to do his bidding. As it is, when the war is over the people of the States will once more find themselves entangled in a whirlpool of currency blunders and fiscal ineptitudes, out of which they may well see no way of escape, except by repudiation of the hitherto acknowledged moral obligation to pay all Government debts in gold of a fixed standard.

Wonder-Working Argentine Finance.

According to summaries which have reached this country the message of the President of the Argentine Republic, delivered at the opening of Congress last month, contained two statements which seem irreconcilable. On the business of the year, as we might call it, the national income and expenditure showed a net deficit of about $9,160,000 gold; nevertheless, the accumulated deficits of previous years, which amounted to $52,273,318 paper, are said to have been "reduced to $39,000,000" at the end of the year. How this was done seems to be a mystery in Argentina itself, and it is doubly a mystery here. If the year 1897 ended in a considerable deficit one would naturally expect to see this deficit added to those accumulated in previous years. This does not seem to have been the case. It must have been subtracted and a good deal more besides, in order to arrive at the brilliant result disclosed in President Uriburu's essay. Or was it merely funded by the issue or sale of various descriptions of bonds of which the Federal Treasury appears to keep on hand a supply to be used in emergencies? We really cannot say until the detailed figures are before us, and even then perhaps the matter will not be clear.

One thing, however, is perfectly plain, the Argentine Republic is not now paying its way and has not paid its way any year since the bankruptcy of 1890. It has dodged and shuffled along—snatching up funds here and there, increasing the paper money, or neglecting to reduce it, grabbing bonds in the Treasury to be sold more or less surreptitiously, raising forced loans, taking shares in the National Bank into account as cash, and so on. Why this trouble should have been taken to seem solvent we cannot guess, except on one supposition. The Government is permanently anxious to resume once more the dangerous habit of coming to European markets for loans. Possibly it is unfair to ascribe this desire altogether to the initiative of the politicians; they may have been merely the tools and instruments of European financiers in adopting the policy conducive to this end. Undoubtedly they were tools and fools in resuming full payment of interest on the various bonds of the national debt when the Treasury was continually wrestling with deficits. It was, of course, hoped by these means to "restore confidence" in Europe, so as to permit large fresh funding loan operations to be entered into on the London, Paris, and other money markets.

And the motive of the financiers for dictating this course is as plain as a pikestaff. They have had to nurse Argentine deficits for nine years now, and in the process have incurred very considerable engagements which they cannot hope to liquidate except by means of money drawn from the investor. Argentina itself will never repay them. Its rulers would, doubtless, be quite prepared to hand them paper to any amount, but paper does not liquidate debts; it only swells them, and if hard cash has to be given continually by the nursing financiers in exchange for this paper, the day does at last arrive when their resources are used up. They become bankrupt and the Government they have been coddling with them. This is the inevitable finale ahead of the Argentine Government and its backers at the present moment, unless the public in Europe with money in its pockets can be persuaded to exchange its cash for the mountains of paper now piled up in the safes of enterprising banks and finance-houses who have kept Argentina going as an apparently solvent State. At present we see no prospect of the public becoming easily persuaded to do this. To put matters straight, we estimate that about £10,000,000 as a minimum is required, and to enable Argentina to maintain a solvent aspect before the world for another eight or nine years, provision ought to be made for borrowing at least £15,000,000 net in London or elsewhere.

To dribble out a loan of hers in small amounts might be possible, but any attempt to raise even £5,000,000 at once would probably meet with very scanty success. We believe the last loan of the neighbouring Republic of Uruguay still remains mostly in the hands of the financiers who created it, and, therefore, these same financiers have to continue to keep Uruguayan credit on its legs. That is a comparatively light enterprise, but to keep Argentina going and to hold a large loan, unplaced, at the same time that continual fresh advances had to be made, might prove a task too great for the strength of the houses implicated. For our part, we should be glad if it did prove too much. These nursing financiers are a curse of nations. They entice them into debt, and wind obligations about them till they become corrupt and paralysed. Could we only bring about the bankruptcy and complete extinction of a few of these malodorous and heartless financiers many a country would get a little breathing time. Apart from this side of its affairs, the Argentine Republic is making considerable progress in many directions, but it can never be sure of holding that progress while corruption sits atop, forging new fetters faster than the strength of the community can grow up to be equal even to bearing the old.

Collapse of the Wheat Corner.

The collapse of the Leiter wheat corner was inevitable sooner or later. Corners never have succeeded, probably never will, and certainly never should. As a chain is only as strong as its weakest link, so a combination in wheat, or anything else, against the public interest, can only be as strong as the weakest conspirator who joins the combination. A few weeks ago young Mr. Leiter was supposed to have realised a profit of at least five million dollars. His losses, however, have swallowed up his gains, and on Monday his options were hastily closed. Instead of his five million dollars profit, Mr. Leiter only escapes the mortification of an assignment in bankruptcy by placing his cash wheat in the hands of trustees. There seems little doubt that one of the causes of the crash was that at least one member of the combination holding wheat in the North-West had broken faith and was trying to save himself at the expense of his co-conspirators. It is also understood that Mr. Leiter's father had refused to back him longer, thus forcing him to sell his holdings, which he did on Monday, throwing on the Chicago market alone between eight and ten million bushels, mostly for September. This caused a fall of 11 cents in the market and completed the ruin of Mr. Leiter. In a letter which he published a few weeks ago defending his action in connection with this wheat corner, Mr. Leiter said: "All I have done was to back my own judgment." Experience has now shown him that he rested on a broken reed. He has helped to force up the price of wheat to a purely fancy height, thoroughly demoralised the markets, and in encouraging reckless speculation among others has indirectly brought ruin on them as well as himself. Some failures have already taken place here in consequence of the wheat gamble, and probably more may follow, though we are not disposed to think that the evil effects of the collapse on this side the Atlantic will be very serious.

It would be more curious than useful to enter upon an inquiry as to the causes of young Mr. Leiter's failure to accomplish what more mature heads than his have attempted and failed in. They are inherent in all such vicious enterprises. His failure is not a matter of regret to anybody, nor a matter of surprise to any one who has carefully considered the rise and fall of previous corners. But, though there may have been treachery on the part of some of his fellow-conspirators, the main cause of failure lay in Mr. Leiter's own conduct. He held on too long, became latterly too reckless, trusting more to mere chance than to reasonable probability. It is said that, if he had remained satisfied with his May commitments, and retired from the struggle then, he might have retired with very handsome fortune. Perhaps so; but his was case in which "appetite grows with what it feeds on." Having been successful in May, he straightway proceeded to bind himself with June commitments. He began laying the foundations for a corner in July wheat. The war scare had greatly helped him—to his ruin. While his cornering operations had secured an advance on May quotations to \$1.09¼, the war panic rapidly drove the quotation for May delivery up to \$1.50 per bushel, a figure not reached during the previous twenty years. So he went on committing himself hopelessly for June, July, and September futures. He tied himself hand and foot—he could not extricate himself. He could not see, probably did not consider, that the war scare would only be temporary, and by the time that the glowing reports about the growing crops began to be received, he had so committed himself that he could only wait and hope for a miracle. He was caught in his own trap. The reports as to the coming crops improved; the influence of the war scare vanished; supplies of wheat unlooked for by poor Mr. Leiter or his friends came pouring in, not only from the States, but from Canada, from India, from Argentina, and even from Russia. It was impossible long to ward off the inevitable fall. English farmers and dealers struggled against it; Mr. Leiter went on "manipulating" prices with, for a time, a superficial show of success. But you cannot go on struggling against natural forces; the longer the conflict the more sure and the greater must be your discomfiture. This is what Mr. Leiter has found. He loses all he possessed, and a good deal more. How his creditors may fare will depend very much upon how far the senior Mr. Leiter may be willing to come to his assistance. But it must go very hard with many banks and other firms who have been "in the swim;" and the harder it is, the better it will be, if the lesson of the utter futility of such foolishly ambitious enterprises is to be driven home as it ought to be. But unfortunately fools are not taught by experience, and wise men "fight shy" of corners—especially wheat corners.

It is too soon yet to estimate the effect likely to be produced by the collapse on the English markets. Its worst effects will probably be felt in Liverpool, where on Tuesday there was a serious panic, and wheat fell over a shilling per cental. But there was a slight rally before the close, and it may be that the decline has touched bottom. Undoubtedly, however, this Leiter collapse will accentuate the downward tendency which has been prevalent in the English markets for the last fortnight or three weeks. At Spalding, for example, on Tuesday, there was a fall of 4s. per quarter on the top of another fall of 3s. on the previous Tuesday. Wheat which a fortnight ago would have commanded 46s. to 48s., or perhaps 50s., may now be had for from 38s. to 40s. Hard Manitoba is offered for September as low as 31s., while white Indian, May-June, is offered at 36s. 6d. Even at these prices buyers hold aloof. But then this is a time of some excitement, and a good deal of uncertainty. Though dealers generally feel relieved at the collapse of the Leiter corner, which, as one expressed it, had been hanging over the trade "like a great black cloud," there still remains an element of uncertainty which will tend to make sellers as well as buyers cautious, at least for a time. Three or four weeks ago wheat was being offered —and not pressed—at 55s. and 56s. per quarter. If any merchants or farmers, as bereft of ordinary common sense and insight as was Mr. Leiter, then bought stocks as a speculation, they must now be serious losers, if they be not completely undone. But we doubt if such speculators were numerous, and we are inclined to think that the decline in the price of wheat will not go much further at present. And what about the price of bread? Why are bakers so slow in moving downward? If wheat is not likely to decline much further at present, there is certainly not the slightest possibility of its going up. Whatever Leiter's folly may be made an excuse for, it cannot be put forward as an excuse for the continuance of dear bread.

Legal Aspects of the Workmen's Compensation Act.

On July 1 all contracts whereby a workman relinquishes any right to compensation from his employer for personal injuries arising out of and in the course of his employment shall terminate under conditions specified in the Act. The liability imposed by the Act is exceedingly wide, for the employer will be liable to compensate his workman for all injuries caused in the course of the employment. How the accident happened appears to be quite immaterial, and in three cases only does the master seem to be exempted from his liability, viz., where the injury was due to the serious and wilful misconduct of the workman himself, where the accident in question did not arise in the course of the employment, or where such employment was not within the meaning of the Act. However, there will be no liability for trivial injuries, as the employer will not have to pay compensation unless the injury disables the workman from earning full wages for at least two weeks.

Now, what is the employment to which this Act applies, and upon which the workman must be engaged to enable him to recover under the new enactment? Section 7 applies the Act to employment by the "undertakers" on, in, or about a railway, factory, mine, quarry, or engineering work, to employment on, in, or about any building exceeding thirty feet in height, being constructed or repaired by means of scaffolding, or being demolished, or on any building upon which machinery driven by steam, water, or other mechanical power is being used for its construction, repair, or demolition. Thus, a building being pulled down which is above thirty feet, although no scaffolding or machinery is being used, it is submitted, will be within the Act, though when such building has been brought within the thirty feet limit, the employment would cease so to be.

Having thus stated what employment is within this Statute, one must shortly consider how these words are defined in themselves which make up the definition. The "undertaker" in the case of a railway is the company, but where factories, quarries, or laundries are concerned, it means the occupier within the meaning of the Factory Acts; and in the case of a mine the owner within the Mines Acts, 1872 and 1887. However, if it is an engineering work, or a building, the person liable is the one who undertakes the construction or repair. In the same section, railways, factories, mines, and quarries are defined, and the same meaning is to be given to those words as they bear in the Acts regulating their use and working.

Although by no means exhaustive, the foregoing will show the enormous number of industrial concerns which will come within the field and range of this enactment, but before leaving this part of the subject it is worth while shortly considering what the compensation payable will amount to. Where total or partial incapacity arises, a weekly payment not exceeding 50 per cent. of the average weekly earnings, but in any case not exceeding £1 a week, is to be made, and as there is no limitation in the Act this may have to be continued during the whole of the injured man's life. In the case of death there are three scales. Where there are dependants wholly dependent upon the deceased, the amount payable is between £300 and £150, according to the rate of wages, but any weekly payments which have been made may be deducted. If, however, they are only partially dependent, then the amount is to be fixed by arbitration, but may not exceed the above limits. Where no one is left, then the medical and funeral expenses of the deceased need only be paid, but they must not exceed £10. This is practically the legal liability created by the new Act, but it will only furnish the workman with an alternative and extended remedy, for his rights at Common Law and under the Employer's Liability Act of 1880 will only be slightly affected, if at all. Next week we hope to treat shortly with the limited power of contracting out conferred by this Act, the schemes thereunder, and the powers of the arbitrator in the case of disputes.

Economic and Financial Notes and Correspondence.

THE APPROACH OF POLITICAL CHAOS IN FRANCE.

So "Le Père la Ruine" has gone at last. He was a well-meaning man, M. Méline, but weak, and therefore he deserves ill of his country. Subservient to each class interest in turn, he has pleased none, and ended by exciting general distrust, not to say contempt—contempt much more than hatred. The agriculturists despise and blame him because his violent protectionism has still further sterilised their industry instead of causing it to expand and become more profitable. The military faction mocks at him, and plotted his overthrow, because he meekly allowed it to put its foot on his neck, and saw him bid justice defiance at its bidding. To the clerical host he has ceased to be a *persona grata* because he had not the strength of will or of character boldly to set up a despotism and proclaim himself dictator by the grace of an unpatriotic ultramontane Church. Socialists have most cause of all to bless him, for he has done more by enacting measures calculated to grind the faces of the poor, to propagate their doctrines of anarchy and revolution than any Minister France has had since the restoration of the Republic. Yet they will be as ready as the rest to revile him. Alone among the numerous interests and parties he has tried to serve and appease, the anti-Semites may have a good word for him, because he was with them at the last and to the last. In obedience to them he has driven many of the Jews out of Paris, and by so doing has rendered life more difficult for the "native Frenchman" domiciled there. Miserable indeed is the lot of a politician who has to stoop so low as this in order to hold on to the semblance of power. Because he has thus fallen, because he has all through his tenure of office been the conscientious lacquey in other men's hands, M. Méline goes back to his obscurity unlamented, unblest.

But what is to happen in France now that this weak, amiable man of good feeling and no fixed political principles has gone? His helpless subserviency to reactionary factions has resulted in bringing into existence a House of Representatives which is nothing but a cock-pit of factions. We do not see how it will be possible for M. Ribot, M. Bourgeois, or any mere constructor of Ministries to get together, and keep together, a working majority out of such unfusable materials. If Republicans of all shades outside the purely Socialist-Anarchist were to coalesce and support a Ministry devoted to healing the wounds the nation has suffered through the raids made upon its substance and liberties by the protectionists, of all types, there might be hope that peace and contentment would be in some measure restored to the nation. But there is no prospect of any such self-denying union being accomplished. What we may look for rather is a greater activity than ever in the intrigues of cliques, groups, and emissaries of reaction. No sooner will one combination be formed than all the factions excluded from it will set to work to stir up discord within it or to form still other combinations with the view to the overthrow of the one for the moment in power. Amid the clash and dust of Party conflicts the interests of the nation will be lost sight of, and what is even more lamentable, the opportunity to place before the country a policy of enlightened reform and civil and industrial emancipation will be denied to every Ministry that may be set up. The teachings of reason and the demands of justice will be smothered in the babel of contending partisans intent on yelling each other down. A dissolution, which seems unavoidable, and the election of a fresh Chamber gives, for this reason, small prospect of the evolution of a majority inspired by a nobler political ideal. We fear the future is lowering and stormy for France, and sad are we to think so.

THE PROSPECTS OF THE MONEY MARKET.

As far as is visible at present our money market has entered upon a period of calm which may last for two or three months. At no point is it seriously threatened, bearing in mind the help it receives from the new gold continually pouring in from Africa, Australia, India, and other places. Whatever requirements Japan may have the power to make effective can be met out of the open market. Russia has lately betrayed a tendency to take gold, but this cannot, we should think, develop much energy, unless fresh Russian loans are floated on the Continent. Her trade position does not give her command of our bullion market. Austrian buying has ceased and it is by no means improbable that a large hoard accumulated by the Imperial Government in Vienna may be exported again. The political troubles of the empire undoubtedly tend that way, and the wealth of the country is not great enough to admit of its retaining the gold, except by costly artificial means. No other European country can take the metal from us, and there is nothing to be feared from the small demands which might arise from Egypt or South America. To get our gold most countries that want it would have to borrow the means to buy it.

This is becoming true even of the United States, whose people have, so far as we are concerned at the present time, cancelled a considerable portion of Europe's indebtedness to them for cereals by the purchase of their railroad securities. At the same time, when serious danger does next arise to our market it is probable that it will come from this quarter, because the expenses of the war with Spain will involve the selling back to Europe of large amounts of these same securities. We do not think that the new Government loan will be subscribed, or held, to any extent here, whatever finance houses may do, and do reasonably enough; but it may become necessary for the Union to raise money in Europe, to enable its own people to subscribe for this and other loans, by the sale of other stocks for which we can afford a market. Also the collapse of the great "corner" in wheat might produce a large temporary indebtedness on the part of Europe to the States, some of which would be paid in gold. From this quarter, however, we do not expect much immediate demand, and therefore think that our money market will remain more or less stagnant for the summer months. Beyond that it is quite useless to attempt to prophesy. All we can hope for is calmness, without confidence.

THE PETROLEUM QUESTION.

Whatever may be the decision of the Parliamentary Committee now professing to investigate this subject, we trust the public will not let it rest until a thorough and common-sense reform is brought about. And we even make an appeal to the insurance companies. They ought not to sit silent and supine at a time when a question of such vital importance to millions of people, and of no small consequence to their own bankers' balances also, is under discussion. Except the *Star* and, we think, the *Chronicle*, none of the London papers have done much to stir up public opinion on this subject, and we actually have to go to the United States for the facts most intimately bearing upon it. For example, in the latest circular by Mr. George Rice, of Marietta, Ohio, which has reached us, we find extracts from a report of the London County Council issued in January last that we do not happen to have seen published by or commented upon in the leading London newspapers. According to this, the London fires caused by petroleum lamp accidents in the five years ended with 1897 amounted to 12½ per cent. of the total number of fires; but 30 per cent. of the lives lost by fires during the same period came from this cause. And these figures do not represent the entire truth, for the report goes on to say that only seventy-eight deaths from lamp accidents were during the past three years reported by the Fire Brigade, whereas 115 such deaths came to the knowledge of the chief of the department from various sources, and the report adds:—

> It is also necessary to point out that, in addition to these reported accidents, there are numerous small fires of daily occurrence which do not come to the knowledge of the Fire Brigade. Many of these small fires had, however, come to the knowledge of the fire insurance companies, and I understand that the claims made in respect of these small fires, unreported by the Fire Brigade, outnumber the reported cases; and that, of these unreported small fires, more than 50 per cent. are caused by petroleum lamp accidents. There are also unquestionably a very large number of petroleum lamp accidents which are not in any way recorded.

No wonder that in such circumstances the County Council should advocate compulsory measures to prevent this wholesale destruction of human life. What these measures are Mr. Rice indicates with great precision in the remaining portion of his circular. To be sure, this gentleman has his knife into the Standard Oil Trust always, and his main purpose always is to smash that Trust, and to expose its abominations. He is, however, perfectly justified in this retaliatory warfare, for the Trust has done its utmost to crush and ruin him. And the fact that this is his attitude does not lessen the value of his testimony or of his recommendations in regard to good burning oils, because he is probably the most experienced refiner of oil in the world; certainly, in the United States no man bears a higher character in this capacity than he does. What, then, does he recommend? Oils, he states, should be sold by weight. This would tend to insure quality and would overcome those extraordinary shortages which occur on sale by measure. A good burning oil should not be of less weight than 795 degrees specific gravity, or 46 degrees Beaumé; and should be prime white in colour or better. The fire test should not be less than 150 degrees, nor the flash test less than 120 degrees—tested by the Abel or Tagliabue Close Cap. This would insure safety and decrease insurance rates.

But it may be said that fineness of this description would greatly increase the cost of the oil to the consumer. Mr. Rice answers that it only costs three-eighths of a cent a gallon, that is, less than one halfpenny, to refine illuminating oils, and less than this to manufacture the high price grades, owing to less cost of labour, fuel, and acids. This cost of manufacture added to the cost of crude ($1\frac{1}{8}$ cents a gallon), with a quarter of a cent pipeage to refineries, makes the total cost of a gallon of oil in its manufactured state $1\frac{3}{4}$ cents, *i.e.*, less than a penny. The public, he says, has paid to the Standard Oil Monopoly hundreds of millions of dollars for oil in excess of the natural price, to the extent of the rebates allowed by the railroads to the Trust. This is true, but we are not concerned just now with that aspect of the question. If Mr. Rice's estimates are to be trusted, and we think they are, there can be no reason whatever, apart from that furnished by the greed of a corrupt monopoly, why safe oils of the high standard demanded should not be sold at prices which would make them accessible to the poorest. As a matter of fact, the Scotch oils now, which are refined to a flash standard of 105 degrees, and therefore practically as safe as water, can be had at prices which compete with the crude explosive stuff thrust upon the community by the American monopolist corporation. It is time that this sort of thing should be put an end to, and if the Government will not move, the people must take the law into its own hands and refuse absolutely to accept these dangerous oils from the retailer. Were this systematically done there would be a speedy end to the criminal waste of property and life which now goes on unchecked. We call upon the fire insurance corporations to aid in bringing about this reform. It is their interest to do so, unless they are so rich that they do not care what they lose.

We cannot do better than quote the following from yesterday's *Star*, which, if it correctly describes the drift of Mr. Collings's draft report, should lead to immediate action on the part of those who are more anxious to save lives than to harass English traders :—

> We have reason to believe that great stress is laid in Mr. Collings's draft report submitted to the Petroleum Committee on the damage which the raising of the flash-point would inflict upon those trades which use petroleum in manufacturing processes. No such injury can possibly result, for the simple reason that all these trades, without exception, use petroleum spirit (*under* 73 deg. flash-point), which would be entirely unaffected by legislation directed to raising the flash-point of petroleum oil, all of which has a flash-point of 73 deg. or higher. Petroleum spirit is still obtainable for trade processes, although it is far below the existing flash-point of 73 deg.; it would be equally procurable if the flash-point were fixed at 105 deg. Raising the flash-point, would only affect lamp oil, and especially the lamp oil of the Standard Oil Trust. We admit that a law regulating lamps would harass English traders, but that is what the *Times* says Mr. Jesse Collings proposes to substitute for flash-point reform.

The Electric Lighting Debate.

With its usual absence of knowledge, Parliament gave the London electric lighting companies a good drubbing on Tuesday last. The opposition raised on their behalf to the Bill authorising the Bermondsey and Marylebone Vestries to lay down mains and supply energy in their districts was treated by the House as a flagrant attempt to set up a monopoly. Now, amongst temperate supporters of the lighting companies there has been no desire to create such a monopoly, and a due regard has been paid to the competitive tendencies of the Electric Lighting Acts. But after all there is such a thing as justice, and it is indubitably unfair to allow the vestries, after private enterprise has borne the burden and toil of creating a business and demonstrating its paying character, to step in and harass the joint stock concerns. Let competition between one joint stock company and another be fostered if the public so desire, for these compete on the same footing. The companies are all leaseholders and therefore have the same liability to prepare for the end of their concession. But the vestry is virtually a freeholder, and so ought always to be able to work cheaper, quite apart from the other economies at its command, in the shape of low interest charges, lighter cost of installation, and cheaper administration. It is all very well to hark back to the Act of 1888, but it should be remembered that one important change has been effected since that Act was passed, which we believe modifies the position to a very important extent. After urgent representations, local bodies have obtained the right to spread the repayment of loans created in order to supply the electric light over a much longer period than is usually allowed. This concession in itself is a great relief to the local bodies, especially at the start, when expenses are heavy and revenue is light, and must be considered a direct incentive for them to compete with companies working in their districts. If conditions have been altered in this respect, surely the electric lighting companies are justified in asking for an alteration on the other side that shall prevent private enterprise being placed entirely at the mercy of public authorities.

Absolutism in Austria.

Count Thun has been no more successful than his predecessor in reconciling the crazy Nationalists on the language question. The Reichsrath, after a few noisy sittings, has been again adjourned by Imperial decree. Of course, the Emperor had no choice in the matter; it may be regarded as almost fortunate that such an exceptional clause existed in the constitution as enabled him to substitute absolutism for anarchy. For the jarrings and warrings of the rival Nationalists rendered the Reichsrath worse than useless—it made it ridiculous. The adjournment was therefore inevitable; but what of the future? This adjournment by Imperial decree cannot be kept up for ever, yet who can now hope for anything from the reassembling of the Reichsrath? The *Ausgleich* was not so much as mentioned in the Imperial Parliament while it remained in session, and undoubtedly this delay in adopting the working arrangement between Austria and Hungary is weakening the ties that bind the two countries together. It is indeed doubtful whether, if the Emperor Francis Joseph were to die during the present crisis, Hungary would not at once declare her independence. She is becoming accustomed to the notion, and not only is the *Ausgleich* in virtual abeyance, but the Austrian and Hungarian deputations have not been able to agree as to the proportion of the respective contributions of the two countries towards the common expenditure. The friction between the two is steadily increasing. The disintegration of Austria may therefore almost be said to have begun.

The leaders of the Austrian-German party openly declare their intention to seek reincorporation with the Fatherland. Of course the notion is officially scouted in Germany, and we have no doubt it is really distasteful to the German Government at present, but no one can tell what changes of view a continuance of this racial agitation may develop. Many dangers threaten Austria; but until this senseless quarrel between Germans and Slavs is arranged—and of that there is no present hope—

Austria can do nothing to ward them off, or to solidify her domestic or international position. As to trade and commerce, progress in these is impossible while the Empire is distracted over the discussion of nice linguistic points of divergence which mediæval schoolmen would scarcely have considered worth exercising their ingenuity upon. But while these modern schoolmen quarrel and squabble over trifles, the country grows leaner and weaker, until there are suspicions that some of Austria's neighbours are beginning, at least in imagination, to peg out claims in portions of her territory which may conceivably be useful to their posterity. Democracy can play queer cantrips at times. The suspension of the Reichsrath only gives the Government a short lull. If they cannot come to terms with the rival Nationalists there seems nothing for it but to continue the reign of absolutism. Would that satisfy the Germans?

The Meaning of Seigniorage.

The matter of the seigniorage on silver in the United States is not generally understood, or perhaps it would be better to say that the total in question is not generally recognised. The Act of July 14, 1890, known as the Sherman Silver Purchase Act, and since repealed only as respects the purchasing section, requires the Secretary of the Treasury to purchase silver bullion to the aggregate amount of 4,500,000 oz., or so much thereof as might be offered, in each month, at the market price, not exceeding $1 for 371¼ grs. of pure silver, and to issue in payment Treasury notes, redeemable in coin, and a legal tender in payment of all debts, public and private, except where otherwise expressly stipulated in the contract, and receivable for all dues, and when so received, reissuable. The Act required that the Secretary should coin each month 2,000,000 oz. of the bullion so purchased until July 1, 1891, and after that date to coin so much as might be necessary to provide for the redemption of the Treasury notes, and "any gain on seigniorage arising from such coinage shall be accounted for and paid into the Treasury." On May 1 there were in the Treasury 109,355,514 oz., of the coinage value of $141,363,089, the seigniorage being $42,488,427. There have been coined from 59,319,168·53 oz. of silver 76,639,157 standard silver dollars, on which the seigniorage is $19,645,376. Up to May 13 last, there had been redeemed $53,536,722 of Treasury notes issued in purchase of bullion, there were in the Treasury 5,427,059 standard silver dollars available for the redemption of an equal amount of Treasury notes, and there were outstanding such notes to the extent of $102,394,280. The Treasury notes are payable in coin, at the option of the Secretary of the Treasury, but, in order not to discredit silver, the cheaper money, the Secretary has redeemed them in gold, when so demanded. Thus these notes operate the same as greenbacks to deplete the Treasury of its gold, and are so many links in that endless chain against which President Cleveland so strongly protested. While the silver certificates issued against the seigniorage are redeemable in silver, they increase by the sum of $42,000,000 the amount of currency which the Treasury is compelled to keep as good as gold, although intrinsically of inferior value.

Compounding Founders' Shares.

Another electric lighting company—the Metropolitan—has compounded with the holders of its founders' shares. On the whole we do not think the terms agreed upon were satisfactory, and fear that for some time to come this company will suffer from the enormous amount of new capital injected into it by the operation. It is not as if the founders' shares had even received a dividend, for they were only to share after 7 per cent. had been distributed upon the ordinary shares, and so far the highest dividend received by these latter has been 6 per cent. No doubt, however, exists that better dividends will be paid shortly, perhaps even this year, and since these wretched founders' shares form an irremovable part of the capital, the board was perhaps wise in proposing a composition.

But the terms proposed seem to be excessively favourable to the holders of founders' shares. There are to have the right to subscribe for 225 £10 ordinary shares at par for every one founders' share held, and as there are 100 founders' shares the arrangement involves the issue of £225,000 more capital. This represents just two-fifths of the present capital, and although hard cash is a good thing, it may be difficult for the company to find profitable employment for the huge sum thus thrown at its head. Of course, when its useful employment is accomplished the burden taken up by the company will be a little less troublesome, but we do not believe that the operation can ever prove profitable to the present ordinary shareholder.

The cash thus supplied by the "converting founders" could very well have been raised piecemeal by debenture issues as wanted, but supposing it to be worth 4 per cent. to the company—a high figure when such debentures can be issued at 3½ per cent.—the relief per annum to the fixed charges of the company would be £9,000. Deducting this amount from the balance due to the founders if 10 per cent. were declared upon the new capital of £225,000, we get a sum of £13,500 paid to them as pure bonus on account of their founders' rights. If the same dividend were declared upon the present capital the amount payable to the founders would be £9,310. If the dividend were 12 per cent. the new shares would receive £18,000 after deduction of £9,000 for interest, while the founders under their original rights would have obtained only £15,200.

In no circumstance can we imagine the ordinary shareholder benefiting by this liberality to the founder, and we do not think much of the suggestion that these privileged shareholders could have interfered with the financial working of the company. That, to a great extent, is under the control of the Board of Trade auditors, who would prevent any undue division of profits, as it is their especial duty to see that the *corpus* of the undertaking is well maintained. As things have gone, the company has to face increased competition loaded with this incubus of fresh share capital, and it will have a hard struggle to improve upon recent dividends. Of course the founders will not care very much about this, for they can net a comfortable bonus by selling the new shares in the market.

Japan's Gold Standard.

It is freely stated that Japan will use some portion of the indemnity money now in London for the rehabilitation of its gold standard. This may or may not be true, but it is pretty certain that if something heroic is not done the country will soon be depleted of the whole stock of its gold. It will be remembered that a gold standard was adopted in Japan as from October 1 last, and 62,000,000 yen of new gold coins were minted, this quantity being thought ample for the use of the people and for the proper carrying on of a foreign trade in which an excess of imports over exports had already become chronic. We have received the official returns to April 1, and they show that down to that time the country had shipped abroad no less than 39,063,000 yen in gold, or nearly two-thirds of its whole new gold currency, and, in addition to this, it has exported some 20,000,000 of silver yen, which were withdrawn from circulation for the purpose of being reminted into subsidiary coins. The latter, probably, shows more forcibly than the former the real position of the finances of the country, because if the Government had not found its gold supply inadequate, it would not have parted with these silver coins, which were intended for recoinage to replace to some extent the large number of small paper notes now in circulation.

The paper money in circulation is of the nominal value of between 350,000,000 and 400,000,000 yen, and the Government's notion in issuing this relatively vast quantity appears to have been extremely hazy. In their desire to carry out the ambitious programme of naval and military extension inaugurated after the war, the authorities have so recklessly used these paper yen that the rates of labour and prices of commodities have increased two or even three fold, till the common people find themselves so flush of this spurious currency that nothing but foreign food and foreign products will satisfy them—for which the country has to pay in solid cash. It is in this way that the imports are increased, while the price of labour is so high that the Japanese cannot employ it profitably in manufacturing, as hitherto, in the production of goods for export, and, as a consequence, this side is going down steadily month by month. In April imports reached the large total of 25,809,751 yen, whereas the exports only amounted to 10,947,502 yen, being an excess of imports over exports of 14,862,249 yen. The excess of exports over the imports of coin and bullion amounted to 14,481,137 yen, leaving a balance unpaid for of only 381,102 yen. Meanwhile the foreign loan hangs fire. It has already been decided that the land will stand no further taxation, and one or two small loans have been decided upon on the security of productive works. But the financial condition of the country is worse than ever.

The Niger Settlement.

We are glad that it has arrived, but never doubted its arrival. The idea of two nations like England and France going to war about a wretched bit of territory, or a "town" or two, in Africa, was too absurd to bear serious discussion. As far as the semi-official and other reports go, the settlement seems to have been arrived at by the usual way of making mutual concessions; and really, where neither country had any very lofty right to the territory in dispute this was the only sensible course to take. We have no sympathy at all with those who are nagging already at Lord Salisbury for "giving way," and it does not appear to us that anything beyond reason has been conceded to the French. They had a right to the free navigation of the Lower Niger under the Treaty of Berlin. It was our Royal Niger Company which tried to bar their way here, and its action doubtless provoked the French to attempt retaliations up country. The right to navigate necessarily implies the right to have stations on the river. It was therefore proper to make this concession also to them. Equally proper was it to allow them to retain Niki as a sort of half-way post between their coast territory of Dahomey and the upper regions of the river where they have undisputed sway. Altogether, we are glad that the settlement has been made, and sincerely congratulate the Marquis of Salisbury on the common sense which has distinguished, as far as we can judge, his treatment of this small question—small, but irritating as the sting of the mosquito.

The Position of New Zealand.

We have come across, in the *Wairarapa Times*, a very sensible article on the finances of this colony which we summarise and commend to the study of colonists in general. After pointing out that the excess of New Zealand exports over imports have gradually decreased, so that instead of amounting to £3,955,714 as in 1889-90—the year ending on September 30—it has fallen to £1,852,097 last year, the writer goes on to indicate how this decline bears upon the country's prosperity. In the year ended September 30 last, he says New Zealand exported £9,626,936 worth of goods, and if it had had no external debt and been self-contained this would have been so much gain to the country. Imports, however, were valued at £7,774,839, and when these were paid for there was still a balance of £1,852,000 left to the good. This looks very well until we remember that, as the writer puts it, the colonists have to find annually a sum not far short of £3,250,000 to pay interest on their public debt and private obligations to the outside moneylender, Mr. John Bull. Adding this amount, which we think under rather than over the mark, to the value of the exports the apparent surplus is turned into a deficiency of nearly £1,400,000. How, the writer asks, was this money obtained? The only way was by borrowing, and that is exactly how the transaction was completed.

Confronted by a hard fact of this description, the folly of the Seddon Government in boasting of closing the year with a "surplus" becomes conspicuous enough, and the writer of this article shows that it is a hollow pretence, this surplus, even on the Budget exhibit. Any fool can make a parade of prosperity when borrowed money is available for him to do so with, and New Zealand behaves like a splendid fool in this respect. Not only is the country steadily going backwards, because getting deeper in debt, but it seems to be misled in a most shameless manner by those in charge of its public affairs. The railway "surplus," we are told, does not exist; it is produced by charging to "unauthorised" outlay and on capital account items that any joint stock company would have met out of the revenue. The apparent profit is thus most fictitious and the system of book-keeping which enables it to be shown is simply scandalous.

By borrowing and borrowing, on this pretext and the other, labour can be employed, and of course the money disbursed in wages goes to swell the import totals, as the people who receive the wages must live. But when the days of borrowing are over what will the position of the settlement be? That is the true question which all colonists have to ponder, and we need not again press home the answer. They may, however, just consider one point. Leaving out of account altogether the principal of the debt, treating it as something which never will be paid and which nobody ever intends to pay, could New Zealand, on the existing basis of its trade, population, and industrial development, meet the mere interest burdens upon its various debts for twelve months without any assistance from the foreign money-lenders? It could not. The immediate consequence of a cessation of the loan-raising policy which Seddon and his colleagues have lived and flourished by in their ingenious, but also in their shameless, manner would be the bankruptcy of the State and the ruin of the community for a generation to come. Or might it not be the community's salvation? The way it now pursues is the way of inanition and death.

The "Sharpshooter" Gunboat.

We quote the following from an obscure corner of Tuesday's *Daily News* and should like very much to know where this useless vessel was built. Who was responsible for her? She is only about four years old and already, apparently, is in such a bad way that the only thing to do with her is to either sell her for old iron or take her to pieces and build her over again. How many vessels of this description are we getting into the Navy under the present demoniacal haste to have the greatest number of ships in the world, no matter of what quality? The taxpayers have to find the money for these failures, and Parliament is just as helpless as a congregation of field mice to prevent them from being swindled by having foisted into the fleet abortions such as this. Can the Press do nothing to expose, and, by putting to shame bunglers and worse, to stop this kind of thing? Somebody appears to want hanging. "A question or two in the House?" Nay, that would not do any good; the House only knows how to vote away money, and cares nothing for the position of those who pay it. "Waste and come to want" seems to be the modern political motto :—

Her Majesty's torpedo-gunboat *Sharpshooter*, which has been a source of so much trouble and expense ever since she was first commissioned, has been surveyed at Devonport, and it is found that she is generally in a very bad state. It was known that her machinery, as a result of her continuous running on instructional duties, was defective, but it is now discovered that her hull, magazine, and other compartments need such extensive repairs to fit her for further service that it is doubtful if she is worth the expense that would be involved. It was intended that she should take part in the forthcoming naval manœuvres, but there is now no possibility of her doing so, for even if it is decided to keep her in commission she cannot be got ready for sea until September next at the earliest.

THE ROCK LIFE INSURANCE COMPANY.

A fortnight ago, in dealing with the figures of this company, we expressed some doubt as to the meaning of certain entries in its balance-sheet. Since then we have been trying to get some light on this subject, and will now state the facts as far as we have ascertained them. It appears that originally this company had a share capital consisting of 200,000 shares, on which 10s. per share was called up. This still appears in the balance-sheet as a paid-up capital of £100,000. For many years, however, thanks to a proviso in its constitution and to the prosperity of its business, the company was able to pay dividends of 7s. or 8s. per share, as we are informed, and the consequence was that the price of those shares rose to £7 and upwards. This by itself might not have mattered very much. It is the tendency of life insurance companies to make large profits on small emissions of capital if they are successful at all; but some time ago the company obtained power to invest in its own shares, and we believe it has bought back half these shares at a price something like £7 10s. apiece. Hence the entry in the balance-sheet of "subscription capital stock," which amounts to £1,059,000, including the paid-up capital of £100,000. That is to say, £950,000 of this sum represents the book value of the shares bought in.

At present these shares are not worth much more than £4 10s., and there has consequently been much loss upon them as an investment. Part of this loss has been written off, but the shares still stand in the balance-sheet of the company at about £546,000, which we estimate to be about £80,000 above what they are worth taken at their actual market value. As far as we can see, no provision whatever has been made for this depreciation. Why did the auditors allow an item of this kind to escape their notice when they signed the balance-sheet? They give no certificate at all, but that does not exempt them from a charge of carelessness which might become of serious import to the insured if anything went wrong with the company. And it is not a particularly prosperous company, because its constitution handicaps it. Under that constitution one-third of the net profits goes to the proprietors. This is a very serious preventive, indeed, to the obtaining of new business, because it necessarily reduces the amount of bonus which can be given to the policy holders. As the ratio of expenses to premium income is also fairly high, it follows that the company makes little or no progress, and the best thing that could happen to it would be amalgamation with a more vigorous concern, upon lines which would deliver its business from the burden of dead capital and of shareholders' claims it now has to carry and meet. The shareholders, in fact, ought to sell the business for what it is worth and divide the proceeds as far as these can be claimed to represent a return of capital.

WEST AUSTRALIAN TIMBER.

The subjoined letter, coming from Banbury, West Australia, may serve as a useful warning to investors against listening too readily to the blandishments of the touter for West Australian timber companies :—

To the Editor.

SIR,—You will be doing only a simple act of Justice if you warn investors in Britain against putting their money into timber workings here when the concern is so overloaded with capital as are those lately floated in England to work Karri and Jarrah. The business is a sound one fairly treated, but it will not carry such capital as £250,000 and £300,000, as is usual in these companies. Like the gold mines of Coolgardie, which were similarly overloaded, it will only lose the money invested. Africa has paid big prices lately for timber, and hence the present prosperity, but competition is bringing these down, and then ruin. I say £50,000 is ample capital for a mill, and £49,000 of that should be working capital, and then the thing is sound; over this amount merely fattens speculators.

KARRI AND JARRAH.

EXCURSION IN THE CONGO STATE.

Mr. Consul Pickersgill takes a sanguine view of the future of the Congo Independent State; for in his report just presented to the Foreign Office he declares his conviction that the time is fast approaching when Cook's tourists may be personally conducted from Angola to Stanley Falls without wild adventures. The anticipation is hardly consistent with his own experience. There may be no wild adventures, it is true, but there seems to be considerable abundance and variety of malarial fevers, from which few escape and very many die. It is estimated that of every ten whites who become officers of the State, nine are either buried or invalided within three years, while it is calculated that the employés of the largest Belgian trading company, who number 120, only maintain an average service of seven months out of the twenty-four for which they contract. Even in the absence of "wild adventures," these facts are not likely to encourage an inroad of tourists. Though there must be considerable trade done in the Congo State, Mr. Pickersgill says comparatively little about that, but devotes a large portion of his space to a consideration of how the white invasion has affected the black aborigines. Equatorial Africa is certainly not a white man's country; without the assistance of the blacks he would have to give up the country altogether. We doubt if there would be much loss if he did so, and left the fever-stricken land to its original inhabitants. But the Belgians seem determined to stick to it; and they have taken the "civilisation" of the black in hand with a persistency which may, on the whole, be commended, though some of their methods do not seem to be particularly wise. There is too much drilling and more martinetism than there need be; but withal the blacks thrive. There is no active discontent apparent. They are well fed, and more wealthy than they could have been before they became habituated to regular work as porters or labourers in the factories. Their womenkind get more "finery," but it would also seem that they are neglecting more and more the cultivation of their little plots of ground. Their villages are being deserted, and if factories increase in number, the natives will doubtless cluster more and more round these in their small huts. The liquor traffic is very vigorously restricted; and there is every indication that the supply of black labour will be well kept up. If the Government looks sharply after the blacks, they look equally carefully after the taxes. Everything has to pay official toll. "Nothing," say the missionaries, "is free except the fevers," and they have a way of asserting their freedom which not even bureaucrats can withstand.

THE BRUSSELS BOURSE.

The migration of a large section of the open stock market of Paris to Brussels attaches a new interest to the Bourse of that city. We, therefore, extract some particulars about its constitution from our interesting and valuable French contemporary *Le Moniteur des Tirages Financiers* of the 9th instant. The Brussels Bourse, it states, is a free market held in a building owned by the municipality of the city. All that is required from those who desire to act as brokers or *Agents de Change* in this building is a payment of 240 francs to the City Treasury for each principal in a firm, and of 120 francs for each employé of such firm or individual broker. Further, the applicant for admission has to satisfy the Commission of the Bourse that he has never been declared a defaulter and has never suffered any condemnation.

It is not, our contemporary adds, the intention of the immigrants from Paris to enter into competition with the Belgian brokers. They have subscribed a fund of one hundred million francs in order to conduct on a solid basis of capital precisely the same business which they have been accustomed to do in Paris, and they will not deal in specially Belgian securities. Under these limitations we can well believe that "the welcome accorded" to four delegates sent by the *Coulisse* to arrange matters in Brussels "has been particularly warm." The municipality has seen in them "the advent of the goose with the golden eggs. A hundred millions of francs! It is enormous." And it is not all. Sundry Berlin firms, almost equally harassed by the new German laws for the regulation of operations on the Bourse, also contemplate a like transfer of their business to this free market. As London is ready to enter into close relations with these houses it follows that Brussels is on the way to become a great international stock mart.

MR. HOOLEY "IN 'ERCLES VEIN."

Yes, he means to clean out the Augean stable of City Press corruption, not by turning rivers into it, but by playing upon it with the search light of Truth. He has vowed the vow, and behold it recorded in the pages of the *Daily Telegraph* of Friday and Monday last. Here are his words, as taken down by the faithful reporter. Read and tremble, ye bribed ones and blackmailers! We rejoice, but also with trembling, lest the valiant financier's courage should at the last moment fail. Indeed, we have grounds for doubting his "pluck," for he has given no reply to the offer we at once made to him to publish at our own risk whatever fully established and authenticated particulars of bribery and blackmailing he could furnish. We made this offer a week ago, and shall give him still a week to think over it.

"Ask me any questions you like," said Mr. Hooley. "Never mind how straight they are."

"Well, Mr. Hooley, the public would, I think, wish to know to what causes you attribute your present position."

"It is principally due to actions for which I am really not responsible, and the depreciation of the value of cycle securities generally. But first of all, let me say I am not insolvent. I have £400,000 to the good if the estate be properly realised. I have half a million of freeholds."

* * *

"The estate will principally be freeholds—houses, lands, and cattle. There are Risley Hall, Derbyshire, 1,000 acres; this one at Papworth, Cambridgeshire, where I farm 1,000 acres; then 14,000 acres in Wiltshire; 3,500 acres in Essex, which I purchased of Lady Warwick; 8,000 acres in Scotland; 300 acres in the Isle of Wight, next to Osborne; and 1,000 houses in the Midlands, in the Nottingham district."

* * *

"I have not a penny piece in the world."

* * *

"I have gone on paying blackmail until I am sick of it. As soon as I am ready with my statement I am going to give a list of all the people I have paid blackmail to, with the several amounts so paid. A certain class of newspapers have gone for me; they have turned round upon me lately. So I went to the Official Receiver and I turned over everything to him. I made no settlement on my wife for her benefit, nor have I made any for the benefit of our seven children."

* * *

"I made £3,000,000 in hard cash. But I did not make these three millions for myself. There were a lot of people standing in with me; but all these men deserted me when I wanted their support at the finish.

"The chief reason why I filed my petition is to put myself right with the public. When all the papers that have drawn thousands of pounds out of me turned against me I could never have brought out another company. I now intend to show how I promoted companies, how much I paid, and to whom I paid the money, and I am confident I shall receive more sympathy and good than I have yet done. You quite see that I could never bring another company out when they (the papers) were all going for me, don't you?"

* * *

"It has been said of you that you did not manage companies; you only bought and sold them?"

"That is so. I don't say that I can manage a business. I have never said so. I am a dealer—a born dealer. I never worked the businesses at all."

"And having bought a business and sold a business——"

"I had nothing further to do with it. Why should I?"

"Well, what about the man who may have taken shares on the strength of your name?"

"Well, he was a fool," said Mr. Hooley curtly. "That is the truth." He continued: "If I acquire a business for a million, and divide it into debentures, preference, and ordinary shares, and so cut it up for the public, and sell it piece-meal, I am entitled to my profit, am I not? Supposing I buy a business for a million and sell it for £1,100,000, is that too much?"

"Then you do not consider that the public have a right to look to you for the ultimate success of the business you sell to them?"

"Not at all," was the candid reply. "But none of my companies are rotten. Every one is a good going business."

"You do not know what period may elapse before you can put a statement before your creditors?"

"No, I do not; but every effort will be made to get it ready as speedily as possible. I am now working at it myself, and I hope to have the assistance of my solicitor at the end of the week; but he is so pressed with work and inquiries on all sides, and there are such numbers of matters to investigate, and such an enormous amount of detail to go through, that he tells me that it is quite impossible to fix any precise time in which the statement should be forthcoming. I may say I do not consider I have any private debts."

"Will there be a large number of creditors?"

"I should not think there will be fifty."

"And not one of these fifty creditors belongs to the 'widow and the orphan' class—the small investors?"

"Oh, dear no. You see, I have been the man to make the contracts. I have divided the profits with other people, and I have got left in the cart, with all the actions. It is very hard on me. I could name a man who has made through me in gold—not in shares—£797,000, and another who has made £500,000. There are plenty of men who made £100,000 apiece; and some of the solicitors I have employed have made big fortunes out of me alone. I won't say much about this, because probably there will be further investigation in regard to them. I think it fair to add that this remark does not apply to Messrs. Beyfus & Beyfus. In fact, as I told Mr. Beyfus only a few months ago, if he had been acting for me from the first I should have had a million of money in the bank instead of being in this position."

* * *

Reiterating his policy, Mr. Hooley said:—"There was a run upon me. I have paid off £150,000 liabilities in five months. If a man is to devote his life to fighting lawsuits he had better get his position ascertained at once. If I remained in business six months longer they would leave nothing for the Official Receiver. I am going to put myself right with the public before I start again, and when they have heard all, they will see that I have been victimised, and will say, 'That fellow has been badly treated.' just look at what I have recently experienced. There was an attack made upon me in connection with the Beeston Pneumatic Tyre Company. I volunteered to give evidence, with the result that the Judge found that there was not the slightest imputation against me; but this meant my having to devote many hours with the eminent counsel I employed, not to speak of the large fees I had to pay them. Then, again, a few weeks ago I had a claim for very heavy damages, in connection with which, on the eve of the trial, I was asked for £25,000, and £500 costs. Mr. Beyfus told me I should win, and I did win, without paying a penny; but there again I had heavy responsibility, and what is of far more consequence, the worry and trouble incidental to the litigation. And so it would be to the end. Why, I have had a so-called respectable paper come to me at half-past eleven at night with proofs of two articles—the one would cost me £1,000, and the other nothing, and I was to choose which of the two should appear in the morning. No, nothing will frighten me. I have been offered £10,000 a year to work for a syndicate—composed of the very men who have been pressing me. This business of mine is going to cause a hubbub, I fancy."

So much for the first interview. The threats it contained made a bit of a sensation, as well they might, and the *Telegraph* reporter sought Mr. Hooley a second time. He found him busy, with four secretaries classifying the people and papers he meant to expose, dealing with and replying to "4,000 letters" he had received, many of them containing money he was sending back, and altogether in first-rate fighting condition. Here is the concluding portion of the cross-examination that followed:—

"And you will not shorten your black list in any one particular?"

"No; I am so satisfied that the step I have taken will put me right with the public that nothing would prevent my going through with it. I have four secretaries at work in getting at the details of all money I have paid in blackmail during the last three years; and, by the way, let me add that I am perfectly satisfied, after the interview I had with Mr. Brougham, the Official Receiver, that he will investigate to the utmost each separate case. And, incidentally, I may state that I have seen in the papers that Mr. Wreford has been mentioned as a suitable trustee on account of his former connection with the Bankruptcy Court. I may say that I know nothing about this nomination."

"Mr. Hooley, can you explain this? I have heard people say that a weak point in your explanation is that you consented at all to pay what you call blackmail."

"Well, show me any company promoter who does not. There is not one in the City who does not have to submit to the system. They make you pay according to the profit you are receiving. The profit is very well known. According to his profits so the promoter has to pay the blackmailer."

"Then it is a system of sharing profits which is in vogue?"

"With this difference. Though the promoter may make a loss, the blackmailer gets his cash down in advance. I am referring to the gutter Press."

"You did not pay blackmail that these papers should disseminate lies to mislead the public, did you?"

"No; that they should not tell lies about me. I venture to say most emphatically that, however genuine the company, if these men were not paid they would make an attack upon it. Let me give you an instance. I remember to have seen once an advertisement in a leading daily paper to this effect: 'Before investing in —— Company, read such and such a newspaper, on such a date.' The company referred to was mine. In the interval I paid what was asked as blackmail, and the result was that when the paper appeared it contained a favourable article, instead of the damning one which the public had been led to expect. I should like you to quite understand that the money for the majority of industrial companies does not come from London. We are all inclined to think that London is the place that supplies their capital; but it is nothing of the kind. The bulk comes from the provinces, and if you get an attack made upon you in the London Press, it is certain to be copied into fifty provincial journals, not perhaps of the highest class."

"But you have your remedy against unjustifiable attacks—libels—in the law courts?"

"A company promoter cannot always be in court, although he may win every time. And there is a way of damaging a thing while still keeping within the four corners of the law. These men know it well. But I may say I never paid one penny in blackmail to the provincial Press. I think I ought to state that all the blackmailing papers are confined to London. They are not to be found in the provinces. But I want to confine myself to these remarks. As to my private affairs, I do not wish to add anything to what I have already told the public until my statement is before my creditors."

"So, finally, Mr. Hooley, I take it that your correspondence shows how anxious the public is that the blackmailing system should be exposed?"

"Yes. I only wish a powerful paper would take up the matter. Why should not the Government appoint a commission to investigate it? They have done so in regard to moneylending. I can assure you that if they did so in respect of blackmailing in business, what I have already indicated would be as nothing compared with the revelations that would then be made.

"By the way," added Mr. Hooley, as we closed the conversation before strolling in the well-kept park to the trim cricket-ground and meadows where the cattle were grazing, in which the fallen financier takes such keen delight, "I want to say one word more."

"Yes."

"I shall take it as a favour if the *Daily Telegraph* would permit me to say with what pain I have read the references to the gift made by me to St. Paul's Cathedral. When I offered it I was fully justified in so doing. My means thoroughly warranted it, and I think it perfectly disgusting that any question should be now raised in regard to it. These people may just as well call into question the thousands of pounds I have given in charity and for public objects."

Critical Index to New Investments.

UNITED STATES GOVERNMENT LOAN.

Messrs. Seligman Bros., the fiscal agents for the State Department of the United States of America, are prepared to receive and transmit free of charge applications for the war loan of £40,000,000 at par, New York. The bonds bear 3 per cent. interest and are redeemable in coin after ten years, and are repayable August 1, 1918. This is, of course, not an "issue" on this side, but the offer is made to oblige the many Americans resident in this country, or others who may wish to possess some of the bonds.

THE BRAZILIAN FUNDING SCHEME.

The arrangement for permitting Brazil to make default in the most respectable way possible is now made public. For three years, from July 1 next to June 30, 1901, the interest on the whole of the foreign debt, and the amounts payable annually for railway guarantees will be discharged in 5 per cent. funding bonds, and for this purpose Messrs. N. M. Rothschild & Sons are authorised to issue £10,000,000 of such bonds. For the purpose of future reference we append the loans to be included in the scheme:—The 4½ per cent. loan of 1883, the 4½ per cent. loan of 1888, the 4 per cent. loan of 1889, the 5 per cent. loan of 1895, the Western of Minas Railroad Company 5 per cent. guaranteed loan of 1893, and the internal 4½ per cent. gold loan of 1879. The unfortunate railways who are to have their guarantees paid in funding bonds are set forth in an advertisement in another page. Full advantage is to be, of course, taken to escape from the sinking funds and redemption, and not for thirteen years will they be resumed. The new bonds are to be secured on the Rio de Janeiro Customs revenues, and, if these are insufficient, on the other ports of the Union. These for 1897 at a sevenpenny exchange were £2,683,333, and the total of the Union at the same exchange was £7,116,666.

On and after January 1, 1899, and *pari passu* with the issue of funding bonds, the Government will deposit in Rio de Janeiro in trust with the London and River Plate Bank, the London and Brazilian Bank, and the Brazilianische Bank für Deutschland, the equivalent of the said bonds in current paper money at the exchange of 18d., and the paper money equivalent to the bonds issued from July 1 to December 31, 1898, will be deposited in the same manner during a period of three years commencing January 1, 1899. The paper money deposited will either be withdrawn from circulation and destroyed, or (if and when the exchange is favourable) will be applied in the purchase of bills on London in favour of Messrs. N. M. Rothschild & Sons, to be placed to the credit of a fund towards the future payment in gold of the interest on the loans and railway guarantees. The funding bonds will be free from all Brazilian taxes. Thus again is British capital treated contemptuously by a South American Republic, but we deserve our fate for trusting money in such a quarter.

SMITH, GARRETT, & CO., LIMITED.

Williams Deacon and Manchester and Salford Bank offer £83,170 3½ per cent. perpetual mortgage debenture stock, being part of a total of £400,000, of which £216,830 has been already issued. Subscription price, 105 per cent.; interest due April and October. The stock is a first mortgage on the undertaking; profits last year were £56,387; and the assets in the last balance-sheet, including £97,000 uncalled capital, amounted to £837,137. Safe, but expensive, the yield being only £3 11s. 4d. per cent.

HALL & WOODHOUSE, LIMITED.

This company takes over the brewery business carried on by Messrs. Hall & Woodhouse at Blandford and Ansty, in Dorset, together with the neighbouring business of Messrs. Godwin Bros., of the Durweston Brewery. Ansty Brewery was established in 1777, and the Blandford Brewery was acquired fifteen years ago, and there are now 115 licensed houses attached to the concern. Share capital is £100,000, which, with £100,000 in cash, is taken by the vendors. The public are invited to subscribe at par for £100,000 4 per cent. first mortgage debenture stock, redeemable from July 1, 1918, at 108 per cent. Breweries, plant, &c., are valued at £188,476, though the Ansty property appears to be only leasehold, while the profits of the two have grown steadily from £7,571 in 1892 to £11,003 in 1897. Taking the three last years, the average is £10,784, which, with £2,500 estimated profits from the Durweston business, will give a total of £13,284, or more than sufficient to pay the debenture interest three times over. Apart from the fact that the issue exceeds in amount the share capital, the debenture stock seems, as brewery things go, safe, and a fair investment.

COBOURG, NORTHUMBERLAND, AND PACIFIC RAILWAY COMPANY.

Issue of £151,200 5 per cent. perpetual first mortgage debentures of £100 each at 102 per cent. They are a first charge on the railway now being constructed from the Port of Cobourg on Lake Ontario to a junction with the Ontario and Quebec section of the Canadian Pacific at the Central Ontario Junction, only forty-nine miles in length, at the rate of £3,086 per mile. The C. P. leases and works the line as part of its system for 999 years, providing rolling stock and equipment and paying rates and taxes, and pays the C. N. and P. Co. 40 per cent. of gross earnings without deduction whatever. Municipal corporations on the route have subscribed a bonus towards construction of the line of £19,238, and with the same object the Canadian Government has given a free grant of £32,261. The line will be largely used for the carriage of coal required by the Canadian Pacific Railway and various industries. It will be shipped from the Pennsylvania fields to Port Charlotte, Lake Ontario, and transferred in barges to the C. N. & P. Railway, thus saving over 100 miles. An estimate is made that the net amount receivable from the C. P. Company will be £13,132, or nearly double the amount required to pay the interest on the debentures. This may have an effect on the Grand Trunk Company's coal traffic, but it cannot prove a serious matter. Estimates of traffic are not often fulfilled, especially by these small lines, and the debentures offered do not seem at all attractive. If the line is to be so profitable, why did not the Canadian Pacific Company build it itself?

BRITISH WALL PAPER COMPANY, LIMITED.

Five firms are to be amalgamated, Mitchell, Arnott, & Co., Limited, of Lancashire, Dublin, and Belfast; W. G. Wilkins & Co., Limited, of Derby; Walker, Carver, & Co., Limited, of Pendleton; David Walker, of Middleton; and the Heywood Paper Staining Company. The land, buildings, machinery, designs, and general stores are valued at £132,343, while stock-in-trade is put at £40,657, and trade marks and goodwill at £65,877, which makes up the purchase price of £238,878, and of this the vendors are content to take £159,253 in cash. All there is to learn about profits is that for the two years ending August, 1897, which is nearly a year ago, they averaged annually £18,456, before deducting interest and directors' salaries. Share capital is £300,000 in £5 shares, half ordinary and half 6 per cent. cumulative preference, with an issue of £100,000 4½ per cent. debenture stock, redeemable after September 1, 1908, at par, or before then at 5 premium. The preference shares and debenture stock are offered at par, and 15,925 of the ordinary are taken by the vendors in part payment. The interest of the prospectus would have been increased had a list of the discounts allowed of late years been given. As it is, we think little of the security for the debenture stock, and do not see any for the preference shares. Without running much risk of losing a promising investment we should let this go by.

ELECTRO-CHEMICAL COMPANY, LIMITED.

This company has a share capital of £200,000, of which £130,000 has been issued as preference shares and paid up. It was formed in 1894, and claims to have been the first to work on an extensive scale the electrolytic decomposition of salt, for the manufacture of caustic soda, bleach, chlorate of potash, and other chlorine products, for the use of paper makers and others. The company now offer at par £28,500 6 per cent. first mortgage debentures, being balance of £40,000, the remaining £11,500 having been allotted to directors and shareholders. They are redeemable at any time at 105, or at par on July 1, 1910. Farebrother, Ellis, & Co. value the property and works at £73,100, but this does not tell much. The point is that although the works have been in operation for two years the company is unable to show any profits. They may be in course of incubation, but, so far, prospects do not seem encouraging. The trustees for the debenture holders should be independent of the board of directors.

VICTORIA STREET PROPERTIES, LIMITED.

A number of sets of flats, offices, &c., known as Albert Mansions, Victoria-street, Westminster, are to be acquired. They are leasehold, and have seventy-one to eighty-seven years to run at a ground rent of £5,000, and have been valued at £128,000. The share capital is £100,000 in £5 shares, in equal parts of ordinary and 5 per cent. cumulative preference shares. Applications are now invited for an issue of £87,500 4½ per cent. first mortgage debentures at par, part of a total of £120,000. They are redeemable at par by sinking fund before the expiration of the respective leases. Purchase price is not stated, but vendors take £80,000 of the share capital, and it is said that of the debenture issue £7,500 will be working capital, so it may be assumed the cash price is put at the substantial figure of another £80,000. Rents will increase when the unoccupied places are let, but at present the actual rentals are only £7,205, to meet £9,000 for ground rent and interest, to say nothing of expenses, so this can hardly be looked on as a first-class investment.

THE GILL McDOWELL JARRAH COMPANY, LIMITED.

With a capital of £250,000 in £1 shares, equally divided into ordinary and 6 per cent. cumulative preference, of which 83,334 shares of each class are offered for subscription, this venture is brought out to buy a varied assortment of forest estates, timber yard, railway rolling stock, live stock, saw mills, &c. The purchase price is £116,668 in cash and £83,332 in shares, which says much for the sovereigns in preference to the shares. Before long we anticipate that competition will eat considerably into the profits of these Jarrah wood undertakings. For some time past there has been an exceptionally good demand for this wood, and upon the strength of this companies are being formed with capitals three or four times their proper size.

Company Reports and Balance-Sheets.

*** *The Editor will be much obliged to the Secretaries of Joint Stock Companies if they would kindly forward copies of Reports and Balance-Sheets direct to the Office of* The Investors' Review, *Norfolk House, Norfolk-street, W.C., so as to insure prompt notice in these columns.*

Edward & John Burke, Limited.—The profits of this prosperous concern have been declining of late, and the dividend of 7½ per cent. declared for the year ended April 30 last compares with 8 per cent. for 1896-7, and 9 per cent. for the three years preceding. The profits in the past twelve months were so disappointing that the board had to transgress the canons of good financial management by declaring the final dividend at a less rate than the interim distribution. The amount forward was also reduced by £5,657 to the still substantial total of £15,978. Under these circumstances it might be good policy on the part of the directors to increase the information afforded in the report. As it is, there is no shadow of a profit and loss account, the only payments stated beyond interest and dividends being income-tax and managing director's salary, directors' fees and trustees' fees. The text is no more communicative, the only remark being that "the directors have pleasure in submitting their annual report and balance-sheet," a statement which we should even question so far as "pleasure" is concerned. Still the balance-sheet is a good one, for only £24,396 is owing to trade and other creditors, which is offset by sundry debtors amounting to £26,455. Then come £13,751 of bills receivable, £56,448 of cash, and no less than £120,562 in investments, held principally on account of the reserve of £100,000.

Pestarena United Gold Mining.—The hope of a dividend by the long-suffering stock-holders of this concern has been disappointed by the requirements of the property. Although a profit of £9,707 was claimed after debenture interest had been met, the arrangements for providing adequate machinery to a newly developed mine upon the property had to be taken into account. The directors, therefore, intend to pay off the outstanding £6,750 of debentures, with their bonus of 20 per cent., equal together to £8,100, and issue new debentures to the amount of £15,000, bearing interest at 6½ per cent., and repayable at 105 per cent. by annual instalments of not more than £2,500 a year. The charge will thus be £3,550 per annum, which should leave a fair margin for dividends if profits keep up, but depreciation ought also to be taken into account, a matter apparently unheeded.

Attaree Khat Tea Company.—Another sufferer by the Indian earthquake, this company has come through the ordeal with rather an effort. The crop of 852,250 lb. was 75,750 lb. below the estimate, but only 22,000 lb. below that of last year. The average price of 8¼d. per lb. obtained was, however, 1d. per pound less, so that profits only came to £2,678, as against £4,823 for 1896. The directors wisely reduced their dividend to 5 per cent. as compared with 8 per cent. a year ago, and carried forward £4,113, or only £706 less. As it is, the balance-sheet shows that the board has placed the upkeep of the area under immature plants to capital, which is a vicious principle that, if carried out extensively, will tend to injure the tea industry permanently.

Anglo-Chilian Nitrate and Railway Company.—In spite of the lower tariff, the railway receipts of this company were well maintained, and as working expenses were lower, the net profit on this account last year was £68,359, as against £59,344 in 1896. Trading profits in regard to nitrate and iodine only came to £4,430, as compared with £13,986 in 1896 and £55,638 in 1895. Indeed, this part of the business must have been carried on at a loss if fair deduction were made for depreciation, and it is to be hoped that the railway maintenance is not being starved in order to make profits look better. As it was, after meeting administrative charges, mortgage, and other interest, and £12,500 for "commutation of five-sevenths of the commission payable under the consignment contracts of 1890," the net balance was £20,705. The sum of £12,360 was brought forward, which gave £33,065 available for distribution, and permitted of a dividend of 14s. per share upon the preferred shares, and the carrying forward of £8,565. The Oficina Peregrina was completed last year, and its trial working proved eminently satisfactory. The undertaking is burdened with heavy interest charges, and its balance-sheet is none too satisfactory, but improvement has been effected of late, and it is to be hoped that if the nitrate and iodine profits increase, care will be taken to clear off the unsatisfactory items.

Asbestos and Asbestic Company.—There is a strong Bryant & May flavour about this company, but its start cannot be said to have been propitious. Although the large sum of £446,647 was paid for the undertaking, no less than £37,108 had to be spent last year in new buildings, plant, and other equipment. In doing this it has pretty well used up all its spare resources, for the assets outside the undertaking, less outstanding liabilities, are really very little. On the thirteen months' working, the directors claim that a profit of £2,180 has been earned after setting aside £3,541 for depreciation, but no profit and loss account is supplied, and the affair is very much mixed up with two American companies, which may mean that its finances are peculiar. The promises set forth in the prospectus of course have not been fulfilled, and the company has not been able even to supply contract quantities to the H. W. Johns Company alluded to in the prospectus. The intention of working the mill by water power had to be abandoned, and part of the outlay on capital account was occasioned by the installation of additional plant and machinery to be worked by steam. All this looks as if the board went into the undertaking with very little knowledge about the affair, and the only gleam of comfort is that they will issue a circular in October stating the results of the working of the current half-year.

Frank Jones Brewing Company.—The brewing business in the United States is something altogether different to the brewing trade here. This large company, in spite of efforts in years gone by to increase its sale, has to confess to a diminishing trade. The sales of ale and porter in the last few years have been as follows :—

1893 ...	... 274,537 barrels.	1896 ...	... 234,251 barrels.
1894 ...	... 250,071 „	1897 ...	... 222,883 „
1895 ...	... 286,016 „		

Thus, with the exception of 1895, when a peculiar and temporary spurt took place, the sales have steadily declined, and the net trade profits have also diminished, having been £81,016 for 1894 and £50,960 for 1897. The last total only permitted debenture and preference interest to be met, by drawing £3,211 from the balance forward, so that the ordinary shareholders promise to fare badly indeed. Last May the price of beer was reduced $1 per barrel, and since September it is said that sales have steadily increased, but the United States Government is proposing to increase the beer duty by $1 per barrel to $2 per barrel, and this impost will surely affect the trade to a certain extent. The board of this company has done much to improve the balance-sheet, but we are afraid that the over-capitalisation at the start will prove too much for them, and cause the concern to sink into the ooze of disrepute.

St. John del Rey Mining Company.—This company is doing much better, and the returns of gold per month seem lately to have attained an altogether improved position. There is, however, a difficulty looming ahead in the shape of a threatened shortage of water. The rainfall last wet season was only forty-seven inches against an average for the three preceding years of seventy inches. The manager, therefore, fears that during some of the months of the dry season there will be insufficient water for the needs of the mine. To lessen this danger, new engines have been sent out, and arrangements will be made for the water from the Cubango Rego to be brought down to the mine. With 82,761 tons crushed, the yield was 51,101 oz. of gold, and after meeting working expenses, duty and tax on gold, and London charges, the net profit for the year was £53,238. Bond interest took £19,763, and dividends equal to 1s. per share were declared, requiring £22,787, thus leaving £10,688. This sum has been written off establishment and interest charges during construction, the total amount written off to date being £21,134, reducing their total to £41,767. The money so set free, together with £21,295, the amount of bonds converted into shares, has enabled the directors to reduce the bond and debenture indebtedness of the company from £215,000 to £170,000. It still, however, entails a heavy charge, for over £18,000 was paid in interest last year upon the £190,000 of debt, while a Bank loan of £20,000 also exists. If profits improve, every effort should be made to improve the finances, and then the interest charge might be reduced.

Waihi Gold Mining Company.—This company has prospered during the past year, but we do not fancy that the best advantage is being taken of these higher profits. In the year £144,345 was obtained in the shape of gold, and expenses amounted to £62,023, leaving a net profit of £82,322, to which had to be added £22,751 brought forward. The sum of £3,000 was placed to depreciation, and £11,618 to reserve, and £64,000 was distributed in four dividends of 2s. each, or 40 per cent. on the capital. The balance forward of £20,162 was then £2,580 less than that brought in. To replace the money spent on capital account in opening up the mine, and completing the works at the Victoria Mill, the capital was doubled by the creation of 160,000 new shares of £1 each, which were taken by the shareholders at par. This will put the company in good funds, but we doubt whether the old rate of dividend can be distributed, for that would mean £128,000 per annum, and profits, although they have lately increased, have not increased enough to allow this. Besides, we consider the company does not lay by sufficient out of profits. To increase development and stamping power is only to hasten the decay of the property, and the allowance for depreciation ought therefore to be increased.

THE ANTOFAGASTA (CHILI) AND BOLIVIA RAILWAY COMPANY, LIMITED.—The report of the directors of this company for the year to December 31 last reads well. Gross traffic receipts were down a little as compared with those of 1896, being $5,389,602, as against $,5439,153; still the company was able, by the help of the net receipts from the waterworks, and of its proportion of the money received from the Chilian Government as payment of compensation for loss during the civil war, to show a net revenue of £186,418, as compared with £184,581 in 1896. It therefore paid the charges on the debenture stock, and the 6 per cent. dividend on capital stock, together with all administration charges, and had £14,718 over to be handed to the Huanchaca Company in reduction of the amount advanced by it in past years to meet the stock dividend. This is much more satisfactory than the agitation started some time ago in Paris, in the interests of Huanchaca shareholders, would have led us to expect. The only drawback appears to be that traffic receipts are still falling off somewhat, perhaps because of a reduction in the business of the Huanchaca mine. That property, however, only provided 43·37 per cent. of the entire traffic last year, so that the basis of the company's business is steadily broadening, and the directors state that the latest report from the Huanchaca mine announces a large output of payable ore from its western workings, so that its portion of traffic should not shrink much more. There is nothing whatever, in short, in the facts as here presented to justify any disturbance in existing arrangements between the railway and the mining company, nor is there anything to induce Antofagasta stockholders to throw away their stock at low prices at the instigation of French "bears." The accounts seem to be straightforward, and give no indication that a floating debt of any description is being piled up, while the company now owes only £73,700 to the Huanchaca Company on account of advances. If there is anything wrong we cannot discover it in the published accounts or report. But we have no reason to believe that anything is wrong.

ALLIANCE MARINE AND GENERAL ASSURANCE COMPANY, LIMITED.—In the year ended December 31 last the profit made on the underwriting account was £43,325. Adding various other balances, including interest on investments, the amount available at credit of profit and loss was £72,427, out of which a dividend of 30s. and a bonus of 10s., making 40s. per share, or 8 per cent., has been declared, of which 30s. is payable on the first proximo.

THE COLONIAL MUTUAL LIFE ASSURANCE SOCIETY, LIMITED, reports that 2,777 policies, insuring £784,870 were accepted last year, yielding an annual revenue of £27,253. Claims have matured by death under 296 policies, on 276 lives, amounting to £102,206, including bonuses. A sum of £40,332 has been paid for endowments matured under 180 policies. By the death of annuitants under eight policies, the society has been relieved of the payment of £378 per annum. The total funds of the society show an increase of £112,369 13s. 1d., and now amount to £2,153,342. The rate of interest yielded by the funds (after deduction of amount to credit of investment fluctuation fund) has been £4 4s. per cent. No further particulars are before us.

THE SCOTTISH AMICABLE LIFE ASSURANCE SOCIETY.—In the year ended December 31 last this company issued 735 new policies, insuring about £516,000, of which £41,000 was reinsured. The total income amounted to £456,377, of which £236,420 came from premiums and £148,440 from interest, &c., while £71,431 was capital received against annuities sold. Claims took £226,146 less than the expected amount, and expenses and commission absorbed £32,977, or 13·95 per cent. of the premium income. As result, therefore, the society's funds were increased by £157,994 in the course of the year, and now amount to £3,830,932. Out of this comfortable total about £1,744,000 is invested abroad, and rather heavily invested, in American railroad bonds and Indian and Colonial municipal securities. The Scotch, however, have a leaning that way, and are more venturesome often than the English in seeking large interest.

AUSTRALIAN ESTATES AND MORTGAGE COMPANY.—No improvement is shown by the accounts, rather the other way; for a year ago 1 per cent. was paid on the share capital of £1,250,000; now it gets nothing, the drought being put forward as the reason. There has, however, been an improvement in the value of wool, and useful rains have fallen: they generally do when the report of an Australian mortgage company is drawn up. This undertaking has properties and stock and loans on mortgages figuring in the balance-sheet for £3,464,132, and has debenture stock issued to the amount of £2,300,000, so that out of £115,783, being the year's revenue, debenture interest absorbs £109,500 and the reduced balance of £5,366 is carried forward. This is an offshoot of the Union Mortgage and Agency Company of Australia, who are the managing agents. The concern is going from bad to worse, and unless things mend in Australia the debenture interest is threatened.

GRAND JUNCTION WATERWORKS COMPANY.—The company continues to do a steady and progessive business. Total receipts for the half-year ended March 31 were £107,623, against £106,714 in 1897, and £102,949 in 1896. Expenses on maintenance have been larger, whilst special expenditure in connection with the lowering of mains has cost less, but on the whole expenditure absorbed rather more than in the corresponding period, and so does debenture interest. The balance available is £47,536, against £46,592, and the same dividends are therefore declared, of 7½ per cent. per annum on the "A," "B," and "C" shares, and 7 per cent. per annum on the "D" issue.

CALLENDER'S CABLE AND CONSTRUCTION COMPANY.—We gave this company a good word when it was formed in 1894, and we are therefore glad to see that it is turning out so well. The available balance for 1897 is £24,746, of which £4,050 is utilised in paying debenture interest, and £3,000 is appropriated for depreciation of machinery and plant. From the remainder it is proposed to pay a dividend of 10s. per share for the year with a bonus of 2s. 6d. per share, and to carry forward £5,196. This will make a distribution of 12½ per cent., compared with 10 per cent. in former years. The recent expenditure on buildings, plant, and machinery has proved most beneficial to the business, and has enabled the company to produce better and cheaper cables than at any time in the past.

BANK OF BRITISH WEST AFRICA.—A gross profit for last year of £10,289 is not immense, for £7,541 is absorbed in charges; £167 is allowed for depreciation of offices, &c., and £477 is placed to reserve. Fortunately the capital is small, so that the dividend at the rate of 10 per cent. per annum, making 8 per cent. for the year, absorbs only £1,129. Deposits amount to £191,282, while bills and advances represent £128,016.

BARGANG TEA COMPANY.—Bargang, the larger garden cultivated by this company, produced considerably less, but this was almost made up by a larger crop from Kettela, the other garden. Unfortunately, the produce of the latter averaged about 1½d. per lb. less, so that income was nearly £8,900 lower, and expenditure was actually £300 more. The net profit of £1,818 was therefore £1,097 below that of 1896, which compelled the board to reduce the dividend from 7½ to 5 per cent., but by doing this they were able to increase the balance forward from £865 to £1,076. This is a wise step, for the company has no reserve, and already owes too much, everything realisable in the balance-sheet being borrowed against.

READ'S DRIFT LAND COMPANY.—After an existence of nearly ten years, this company, bounteously endowed with land in South Africa, shows accounts going from bad to worse. No less than 182,000 acres of land are owned by the concern, which was an offshoot of the London and South African Exploration Company, and presumably ought to have had the advice of men experienced in ways South African. Yet for last year the loss on working, after the directors had waived their fees, was no less than £1,520, and compares with a loss of £558 in 1896, and of £948 in 1895. Altogether the debit balance to date is brought up to £5,650, and there does not seem to be any growth in receipts that might lead one to hope for better things in the future. The search for minerals on the land was abandoned a year ago, and the other business of the company does not appear particularly profitable.

MUNGLEDYE TEA COMPANY.—This is one of the companies that was most seriously affected by the earthquake last year in Assam. As a consequence, the crop only amounted to 290,194 lb., as against 533,189 lb. in 1896. The price per pound was fairly maintained, but expenses, partly owing to exchange and partly owing to the earthquake, were actually higher, so that the working of the year ended with a loss of £8,091. This poor company has always been in an impecunious condition. Its balance forward, after paying the final dividend for 1896, was £4, and every scrap of liquid assets had been borrowed against, so that the result is further borrowing. Consequently, the agents have had to provide £2,500; the bank, £3,978; and every one else has had to lend a hand, so that the trading liabilities amount to £16,000, as against unsold tea and debtors, amounting to about £5,000. We are afraid that the difference of £11,000 will have to be settled by some issue of capital, and so this poor, unhappy company will become poorer and unhappier. If only a real reserve had been created years ago—not a mere addition to block—the concern might have met this crisis in a more satisfactory manner. And yet there are people going about saying that the strong companies should pull down their reserves in order to maintain dividends at the abnormal level of 1895-6.

Diary of the War.

June 10.—Port Guantanamo, or Port Cumberland, lying some forty miles to the east of Santiago, has been bombarded by Admiral Sampson's fleet, and the forts destroyed. They were abandoned by the Spaniards, as well as the village of Caimamera, though it lies too far up the harbour to have suffered from the United States shells. This is doubtless in preparation for the proposed landing somewhere near Santiago, by destroying the chances of a flank movement on the American troops. But there is no further news as to when these may land. Indeed, it seems doubtful if they have yet left Tampa. There was a bit of a row yesterday in the Madrid Chamber, raised by the receipt of a despatch from the Captain-General of the Philippines appealing urgently for reinforcements, and describing the situation at Manila as desperate. The insurgents had closed round the capital, and the Captain-General evidently considered it hopeless to meet them.

The Madrid deputies got into a somewhat fantastic fury, and blamed the Government for not having sent the necessary reinforcements before. Senor Sagasta recommended calmness and manly fortitude in the presence of disaster, but deputies must have their fling. The leader of the Conservatives offered Government the support of his party, but Senor Romero Robledo, in highly dramatic tones, declared it was not a time to beg for mercy, or intervention, or treaties, but to die, in order that, if all is to perish, the national honour may at least be saved. After such a deliverance, doubtless Senor Robledo enjoyed his dinner. Clearly Don Quixote has left a few descendants in Spain.

June 11.—Admiral Sampson has sent two of his ships, the *Marblehead* and the *Yankee*, to take possession of the outer bay of Guantanamo. The Spanish deputies have become more calm, and yesterday discussed the business of the war estimates in place of "gushing" over the state of Manila, which is still desperate. The rebels may enter into possession of it at any moment. The Captain-General seems to have retired with his troops to the citadel, where he may make a desperate resistance, though scarcely a successful one, for he can hardly depend upon even the troops that still follow him. The "reserve" fleet at Cadiz has not yet sailed, though the Minister of Marine has gone to expedite preparations. It seems destined for Manila; but evidently the fate of that town will be settled before the Cadiz fleet can get half-way to the Philippines. The Washington House of Representives has passed the War Revenue Bill, which provides for the coinage of 1,500,000 silver dollars a month—a veritable Silverite triumph.

June 12.—Little news. Another "test bombardment" is reported—that of Baiquiri, fifteen miles east of Santiago de Cuba. It is to be presumed that all these "test bombardments" are made with a view to decide upon the place at which the military expedition from Tampa will seek a landing, or perhaps to distract the attention of the Spaniards and to puzzle them as to where the landing may be attempted. For it is now hinted that this attempt will not be made first at Santiago, but somewhere else which will greatly surprise the Spaniards, perhaps at Cienfuegos, which, if captured, would paralyse communications between Havana and Santiago, and would serve as a base of supplies for the American forces in the event of a siege of Havana. American plans seem now pretty well matured. We are said to be on the eve of the most important events of the war, but we are in ignorance whether the Tampa expedition has yet sailed. Some say it has, and that big events are due in a day or two. We can only wait and see. A significant fact is recorded as to the small use of the great monitor class of vessels in actual warfare. One of this class, the *Monterey*, was despatched a few days ago from San Francisco for Manila, the harbour of which, it is asserted, it could have defended against a hostile fleet. But it had to take refuge in San Diego, damaged by storm and short of fuel. It is to return to San Francisco because its short experience at sea has shown that the monster cannot safely undertake a voyage of 6,000 miles across the Pacific. If that be so, how many "monitors" of the British navy would prove useless in similar circumstances? Much talk of peace in Madrid journals—talk which seems intended to familiarise the people with the subject, or induce them to ask for a termination of the war, of which, however, there is yet no sign. But there are strange rumours of the mysterious passage of packets and parcels from the Royal Palace at Madrid, as if in preparation for a Royal flight.

June 13.—We have now full confirmation of the occupation by American marines of the harbour of Guantanamo. Even Madrid admits it. The Spanish troops fled with considerable promptitude, leaving even the national flag in a ditch. Thus an excellent landing place and a base for supplies have been secured by the United States fleet; but it is just pssible that the expedition from Tampa may seek to effect a landing at some point nearer Santiago. That expedition, it seems, did leave Tampa on Wednesday, but was ordered back in consequence of a rumour that four Spanish warships were moving mysteriously somewhere in the open sea, and might make an attack on the transport vessels packed with troops and stores. This proceeding was hardly creditable to the judgment of the American authorities; for where were the four Spanish warships to come from? However, the scare is said to be at an end, the expedition has started again, and may possibly reach Cuba tomorrow. Admiral Sampson is in constant communication with the insurgents, has conveyed to them large supplies of arms, and has otherwise arranged for their co-operation in the attack upon Santiago. Maximo Gomez has refused to come to any agreement with General Blanco. More fighting is reported in the Philippines, near Manila, the result of which is not yet known. It is now reported that the scheme submitted to Admiral Dewey by the rebel leader, Aguinaldo, before leaving for the Philippines with the American squadron was to set up a Republic there under a joint American and European Protectorate, a plan which might perhaps avoid international complications. There is still a great deal of discussion at Madrid on the critical situation in the Philippines.

June 14.—The Key West expedition has really sailed. It steamed away at daybreak on Monday, and is expected to reach Cuba on Thursday. Whether it will "pull up" at Santiago is, of course, not known. The small force of marines at Guantanamo has had some severe fighting with a Spanish force that attacked them. The attack began on Saturday afternoon and was continued until Sunday morning. Several of the American marines were killed, and reinforcements have been sent them from the *Marblehead*; but no doubt is entertained as to their ability to maintain their position.

June 15.—The position of the small force of marines at Guantanamo is causing some little anxiety at Washington. They are constantly harassed by the Spaniards, and not a night passes but they have to fight hard and long against their assailants. Slight reinforcements have been sent them, but they cannot be regarded as safe until the arrival of the Key West expedition, about which there is no further definite news. A navy lieutenant, who has somehow been making explorations of the harbour of Santiago—a daring exploit surely—has ascertained that all Admiral Cervera's ships are in that port. As a sample of the sort of news on which Madrid curiosity is fed, it may be noted that there the fact of American troops having been landed at Guantanamo is denied. Practically the whole of the German East Asiatic fleet is now concentrated in the Philippines, and Berlin papers infer that this indicates a determination to intervene in certain eventualities. It has also been suggested by certain ingenious Spaniards that, by granting some advantages to Germany, in the Philippines and elsewhere, it may be possible to secure the services of the Triple Alliance in behalf of Spain! No doubt Germany will be glad of a coaling station in the Philippines if she can get it.

June 16.—The American marines at Guantanamo are evidently in a "tight place," but they hold on tenaciously, though they have to fight nightly for it. As yet the Spanish force sent against them is small; but if a larger is gathered, and were to attack in the night time, when the fleet could be of no use, it would be bad for the marines. They need apparently expect no help from the Tampa expedition for some time yet. The last of it has left, but it seems detained in mid-ocean for some as yet unexplained reason. It is not yet in sight of Cuba; and if the marines at Guantanamo were to be swallowed up by a big Spanish force before the troops reach there, the heather in the States would be on fire with a vengeance. How is it that every movement connected with the American troops is so dilatory? General Augustin, Captain-General at Manila, has sent another despatch to Madrid representing his position as very grave. He does not say he has concentrated his force in the citadel; but it seems practically to amount to that. Manila is closely surrounded by the rebels.

THE PROPERTY MARKET.

Last week turned out to be a very busy one at the Mart, and the sales produced the considerable total of £180,816, or about £66,766 in excess of the corresponding week last year. There seemed small demand for large estates; small class residential properties and ground rents commanded more attention. A piece of building land consisting of nine and three-quarter acres at Southampton was sold at about £800 per acre, a very good price in the circumstances. The freehold ground rent of £232 per annum secured on the premises occupied by Messrs. Doulton & Co. till 1939 was sold by Messrs. Arber, Rutter, & Waghorn for £16,000, the purchasers being the British Empire Mutual Life Assurance Company. This is close upon seventy years' purchase and pays 1⅜ per cent. Messrs. Millar, Son, & Co. were the biggest operators on Friday. A freehold ground rent of £25 in St. John's Wood, reversion in thirty-six and a quarter years, was sold by them for £1,220. A freehold residence at Burwash, Sussex, with over nine acres of land, went for £1,750; and Thackhams Farm, comprising fully seventy-three acres, was knocked down at £2,500, or about £45 an acre. Seven copyhold houses in Hampstead, offered by Mr. T. B. Westacott, with a total rental of £175, fetched £1,000. Several Essex farm properties are to be offered to-day at the Mart by Messrs. Humbert & Flint. There will also be offered to-day a fine property at Aldenham, Herts, comprising mansion, well-timbered garden and grounds, and 108 acres of undulating park and pasture land.

Some excellent properties were disposed of at the Mart on Monday, when the total of the day's sales ran up to £88,549. The Compton Steam Brewery, at Little Compton, Warwick, with thirty tied houses, was sold by Messrs. Alfred Thomas, Reger, & Miles for £35,200. Messrs. Hampton and Sons put up three lots, and sold two of them, the freehold of No. 7, George-street, Hanover-square, realising £7,250, and a residential property at Aston, Herts, £2,800. Licensed properties at Newbury, Herts, were put up by three different auctioneers. Messrs. W. R. Nicholas & Co. secured £3,000 for The Broadway, Hunt's Bar, public-house; £2,800 for the Old London Apprentice; and £1,450 for the Gun, on Wash Common. Messrs. Dreweatt & Watson netted £1,500 for the Tiger, Bartholomew-street, and £2,500 for the Black Boy's Hotel; while Mr. E. W. Neate secured £1,000 for the Cross Keys and residence adjoining. Messrs. King & Chasemore submitted a number of lots of land in Sussex, of which a farm of 200 acres at Rudgwick, and several enclosures of about twenty-eight and a quarter acres, at Slinfold, changed hands at £3,000 and £1,125 respectively. Some improved ground rents arising from properties in Orme-court, Bayswater, amounting to £630 per annum net, put up by Messrs. Barker & Neale, made £16,390, or an average of about twenty-six years' purchase, which must be accounted a very high price.

Mr. H. McCalmont, M.P. for East Cambs., has placed his Bishopswood Estate, in the counties of Hereford and Gloucester, in the market, and it will be submitted to auction at the Mart on Thursday, the 23rd inst., by Messrs. Trollope. This important residential and sporting property extends over upwards of 2,000 acres, of which about 600 acres are wood, and is placed in a lovely part of the country, famous for its grand scenery. The mansion is of a picturesque character, and on a moderate scale.

A total of over £75,000 of sales at the Mart on Tuesday, with a very small percentage of the lots offered remaining unsold, indicated large and lively business. Chief among the day's transactions was the sale by Messrs. Driver & Co. of the Welford Estate, in the Pytchley Hunt district of Northamptonshire, comprising about 1,055 acres, with a rent roll of £1,200 a year, which went at the excellent figure of £25,000, or about twenty-four years' purchase. Messrs. Dean, Barnett, & Oldridge disposed of the freehold "Ivy House" public house, at Hoxton, for £5,460.

Messrs. Field and Sons had a formidable list of freehold and leasehold properties, all of which were sold except one; and the large crowd which thronged their rooms during the day was excellent evidence of the popularity of this class of investments. A number of leasehold houses, in Lansdowne-gardens, South Lambeth, brought £5,880; two freehold houses in Borough High-street, £5,900; another freehold in the same quarter, £2,020; and three freehold buildings in Anerley, £2,260. A freehold property of forty acres at Arkley, Herts, was sold by Messrs. Harland & Son for rather over £6,000. A leasehold residence in William-street, Lowndes-square, was disposed of by Messrs. Rogers, Chapman, & Thomas, at £3,870. At Masons' Hall Tavern, the freehold of the Rose and Crown public-house and Nos. 15 to 25, odd, Gundulph-street, Lambeth, producing an annual rental of £140, offered by Mr. Matthew Miles, changed hands at £5,560. Messrs. Daniel Watney & Sons announce for the 30th inst. the sale of Nos. 5 and 6, Throgmorton-street and No. 7, Shorter's-court. It is an important property, occupies a fine position adjoining the Stock Exchange and Parr's Bank, and covers an area of 2,000 superficial feet. Two freeholds in Soho are to be offered on Monday next by Messrs. Drew & Son, of Richmond.

The Mart looked deserted on Wednesday and was dull as ditch-water as compared with the lively activity of the two previous days. Nine lots were offered, but only three were sold. The total of the day's sales was £3,580. What had come over the Mart? Ascot may probably help to explain. The only transaction worth noting was the disposal by Messrs. Giddy & Giddy of a residential property at Walton-on-Thames for £2,550.

Mr. Alfred Richards announces a sale of £20,000 5 per cent. perpetual debenture stock of the Crystal Palace District Gas Company at the Mart on Wednesday, June 29.

TRADE AND PRODUCE.

With the Leiter collapse we have dealt at some length in another part of this REVIEW, but we may here state that Mr. Leiter has written a very complacent letter, in which he is good enough to explain that the wheat recently under his control is now "in strong hands and present holders will not lose anything." This would, no doubt, be consoling if true; but, as in Liverpool, for instance, Tuesday's decline in price represented a total loss of £37,000 on the day, the holders there are not likely to be in appreciative sympathy with Mr. Leiter's confidence. Tuesday's decline in Liverpool amounted to 1s. 0½d. per cental. Futures are dealt with in loads, and a decline of 1d. per cental means a loss on a load of £20. Tuesday's record reduction represented a loss of £250 per load; and on 150 loads the total decline for the day represented a value for the day of £37,000. On Wednesday, however, though there was still excitement, there was less of panic feeling. Prices were fluctuating in futures, but there was a loss of 3½d. in first call on July, a loss which was only partially recovered at the close. But the market had become more quiet in tone. Business in spot wheats was slow, without change in quotations. Liverpool, as will be seen, has been hard hit, but no failures are reported. Mr. Armour has now the control of Mr. Leiter's American cash stocks of wheat, believed to aggregate 6,000,000 bushels. There is some uncertainty about the control of the Continental and English stocks, but apparently, these, too, have now come under the control of Mr. Armour, who is said to have entered on a "big blind pool" with the two Leiters, senior and junior. If so, there will no doubt be further attempts to jockey the markets, but with the splendid crop prospects there can be no increase in prices. "There will," says Mr. Leiter, in the letter to which we refer above, "be no loss on the wheat, either in cash or future options, that was provided for in to-day's settlement. As to the amount of my profits or loss I have nothing to say." As to these the public will not be greatly interested, so long as there is no prospect of these speculators succeeding in raising values. The Leiter wheat boom, it may be remarked, has lasted about a year and six weeks. He himself computed its probable existence at fourteen months, and he modestly estimated his own profits at $3,000,000. The lowest price he paid for wheat was in June, 1867, when he gave 64⅜c. per bushel. The price on May 10 of this year was $1·85. The droop in the English provincial markets has continued, and ranges from 3s. to 5s. per quarter; but white wheat is still quoted at 42s., red at 40s., the quotation in only one case falling so low as 38s.

Of trade generally not much need be said. Copper is still unsettled and declining. Closing values on Wednesday were £50 3s. 9d. cash and £50 8s. 9d., three months. Settlement price, £50 5s. The price has not touched £51 for a week. From all the iron centres we have excellent reports of activity and increasing business. Glasgow expects a contract for 10,000 tons of steel plates for the Australian Government, for which early delivery cannot be promised. Over £6 is in some cases being paid for ship plates and £6 10 for boiler plates, and wages have been increased 5 per cent. Wolverhampton reports business in a healthy state, and the receipt of many orders during the past week; so with Birmingham and Sheffield. In spite of the coal strike, trade in Swansea has been very active—the imports during the last week showing an increase of 5,000 and the exports nearly 25,000 tons, a very vigorous state of affairs indeed.

As the Welsh coal strike seems now to have been prolonged indefinitely, the colliers declaring that they will have none of the sliding scale, and the owners being equally vigorous in insisting that they must have it; as the non-associated colliers who have been working at a 10 per cent. advance in wages are now striking for a further advance of 15 per cent., it is not surprising to hear that in other coal districts the whole talk is of an increase in price. It is believed that current railway and gas contracts will only be renewed at an advance of 6d. per ton on last year's figures. There is an increased demand for household coal for London, the exceptional chilliness of the season having, of course, greatly increased the consumption.

Wool is looking better, but it has a long way to go yet before it can be said to be in a healthy condition. The London market has been a good deal unsettled by recent failures in the "top" trade in Bradford. But Messrs. Charles Balme & Co. take a rather more cheerful view of the state of affairs. An opinion seems to be gaining ground that the recent depression which has clouded the ultimate markets has reached its limit. Stocks are being more firmly held in consequence. Trade in Leeds is reported better than for weeks past; and Leicester shows a further recovery from the extreme depression, though there is little or no speculation. The list for the next wool sales, on the 28th, has been closed, and the total left available for these is stated at 265,000 bales, compared with 282,000 for the corresponding series last year. Messrs. Jacomb, Son, & Co. believe that "the heavy proportionate supply of cross-bred descriptions will probably, in the absence, meanwhile, of any marked improvement in consumption, operate adversely to any rise in prices for these, but an active inquiry for merinos may be confidently looked for." The price of mohair has been sensibly higher during the last few days in consequence of some increased activity in the demand. The tone in the cotton market has rather improved, but the general condition is one of dulness. Little doing in linens.

Transactions in sugar during the week have been unusually limited, and the demand for refined continues unsatisfactory. The statistical position should give more confidence, and there is likely soon to be a further considerable shrinkage in the old supplies. Transactions in cane have also been small.

NEXT WEEK'S MEETINGS.

MONDAY, JUNE 20.	
Assam Company	5, Laurence Pountney Hill, 2 p.m.
Attaree Khat Tea	138, Leadenhall-street, 2.30 p.m.
British Linen Company Bank ...	Edinburgh, 1 p.m.
Matlock Waterworks	Derby, 4 p.m.
Mysore Reefs (Kangundy)	6, Queen-street Place, 11 a.m.
Wallarah Coal...	3, East India Avenue, 11 a.m.
Young's Paraffin	Glasgow, noon.
TUESDAY, JUNE 21.	
Bank of British W. Africa	Liverpool, 1 p.m.
E. & J. Burke...	Dublin, noon.
Espirito Santo and Caravellos Railway	Winchester House, noon.
Frank Jones Brewing	Winchester House, noon.
William Cory & Sons	Cannon-street Hotel, 11 a.m.
WEDNESDAY, JUNE 22.	
Alliance Marine and General Assurance...	Capel Court, 12.15 p.m.
Bank of Roumania	7, Great Winchester-street 12.30 p.m.
Montreal Waterworks	49, Chancery-lane, 2.30 p.m.
Pestarena United Gold	6, Queen-street Place, 11.30 a.m.
Royal Exchange Assurance	Royal Exchange, noon.
THURSDAY, JUNE 23.	
African Banking Corporation ...	Cannon-street Hotel, 12.30 p.m.
Chelsea Waterworks...	Commercial-road, 1 p.m.
Metropolitan District Railway ...	Westminster Palace Hotel.
St. John del Rey	Cannon-street Hotel, 2 p.m.
FRIDAY, JUNE 24.	
Jokai Assam Tea	St. Mary Axe, 2.30 p.m.
SATURDAY, JUNE 25.	
Harrow and Stanmore Railway ...	1, Southampton-street, noon.

A new station is to be erected on the Metropolitan Railway between King's Cross and Farringdon-street. The intended site is at the point where Farringdon-road and Rosebery-avenue cross each other. It will be in the midst of a crowded population, and should be of great benefit to the locality.

Rumours come from British Honduras of a reduction of the Government establishment, and of cutting down expenses generally, owing to the possible deficit which may occur at the end of the present financial year. We hope the reports are well founded. It is gratifying to find any of our colonies courageously preparing to meet deficits by reductions in expenditure, for which there is probably ample room.

According to the official returns, the imports into France during the first five months of the current year amounted in value to 1,860,165,000 francs, as compared with 1,639,655,000 francs in the corresponding period of last year. The exports amounted to 1,376,612,000 francs, against 1,509,562,000 francs in 1897.

The Emergency Bill for the appropriation of $473,151 to pay the Behring Sea Award to Great Britain passed both Houses at Washington on Tuesday.

UNITED STATES OF BRAZIL FUNDING SCHEME.

The Government of the United States of Brazil, having decided to fund for three years, namely, from the 1st of July, 1898 to the 30th of June, 1901, both inclusive, the Interest on the External Debt, the Interest on the 4½ per cent. Internal Gold Loan of 1879 and also certain amounts payable annually for Railway Guarantees, His Excellency the Minister of Finance, acting in conformity with Laws No. 401 of the 11th of September, 1846, No. 427 of the 9th of December, 1896, No. 428 of the 10th of December, 1896, and No. 489 of the 15th of December, 1897, has authorised Messrs. N. M. Rothschild & Sons to issue an amount not exceeding £10,000,000 nominal Capital, 5 per cent. Funding Bonds specially secured by the Customs Revenues, as hereinafter mentioned.

The following LOANS will be included in the Funding Scheme :—

The 4½ per cent. Loan of 1883.
The 4½ per cent. Loan of 1888.
The 4 per cent. Loan of 1889.
The 5 per cent. Loan of 1895.
The Western of Minas Railroad Company 5 per cent. Guaranteed Loan of 1893.
The Internal 4½ per cent. Gold Loan of 1879 ;

And also the amounts GUARANTEED to the following Railways :—

The Alagoas Railway Company (Linha Principal).
The Alagoas Railway Company (Ramal da Assembleá).
The Great Western of Brazil Railway Company.
The Conde d'Eu Railway Company.
The Central Bahia Railway Company.
The Brazil Great Southern Railway Company.
The Bahia and San Francisco Railway Company (Timbó Branch).
The Donna Theresa Christina Railway Company.
Southern Brazilian Rio Grande do Sul Railway Company.
Companhia Mogyana.
The Minas and Rio Railway Company.
The Natal and Nova Cruz Railway Company.
Compagnie Générale de Chemins de fer Brésiliens (Paranaguá à Curitiba).
Compagnie Générale de Chemins de fer Brésiliens (Prolongamentos e Ramaes).
Compagnie des Chemins de fer Sud-Ouest Brésiliens (Linha de Santa Maria a Cruz Alta).
Compagnie des Chemins de fer Sud-Ouest Brésiliens (Linha de Cruz Alta a Uruguay).
The Bahia and San Francisco Railway Company.
The Recife and San Francisco Railway Company.
Chemin de fer São Paulo and Rio Grande.

The Sinking Funds and Redemption of the Loans will be suspended for thirteen years from the 1st of July, 1898.

The said 5 per cent. Funding Bonds will be specially secured by the Rio de Janeiro Customs Revenues, on which they will be a first charge after provision has been made for the amount required for Interest and repayment of the £2,000,000 five per cent. Treasury Bills issued in January, 1898, which are repayable at the rate of £500,000 every six months, the first amount being due on the 1st of July, 1898. The Bonds will also be secured by the Customs Revenues of the other ports of the Union, should the Rio de Janeiro Customs at any time prove insufficient.

According to the Official Returns the Customs Revenues of the Federal Capital amounted, for the year 1897, to 92,000 Contos of Reis, equivalent, at the Exchange of 7d., to £2,683,333 and at the Exchange of 8d., to £3,066,666.

The total Customs Revenues of the Union, including the above, amounted to 244,000 Contos of Reis, equivalent, at the Exchange of 7d., to £7,116,666, and at the Exchange of 8d., to £8,133,333.

On and after the 1st of January, 1899, and *pari passu* with the issue of Funding Bonds the Government will deposit in Rio de Janeiro in Trust with the London and River Plate Bank, Limited, the London and Brazilian Bank, Limited, and the Brazilianische Bank für Deutschland, the equivalent of the said Bonds in current paper money at the exchange of 18d., and the paper money equivalent to the Bonds issued from the 1st of July to the 31st of December, 1898, will be deposited in the same manner during a period of three years commencing the 1st of January, 1899.

The paper money deposited will either be withdrawn from circulation and destroyed, or, if and when the Exchange is favourable will be applied in the purchase of Bills on London in favour of Messrs. N. M. Rothschild & Sons, to be placed to the credit of a Fund towards the future payment in Gold of the Interest on the Loans and the Railway Guarantees.

The 5 per cent. Funding Bonds will be free from all Brazilian Taxes.

The Bonds will be to bearer in sums of £20, £100, £500, and £1,000 each, with Coupons for Interest at the rate of 5 per cent. per annum payable quarterly, on the 1st of January, the 1st of April, the 1st of July, and the 1st of October, in London, in pounds sterling; and in Paris, Amsterdam, Brussels, and Hamburg, at the exchange of the day on London.

The Bonds will be redeemed by an Accumulative Sinking Fund of one-half per cent. per annum, to be applied half yearly by purchase of Bonds, when the price is under par, and when at or above par by drawings. The Redemption of the Bonds by means of the Sinking Fund, will commence at the end of ten years from the 30th of June, 1901, but the Government reserves the right to pay off the Loan at par at any time.

This Funding Scheme was formulated with the approval of Dr. Campos Salles, President-Elect of the Republic, who during his recent Visit to London was in constant communication with his Government on the subject; and before his departure His Excellency expressed his satisfaction with the scheme and added his assurance that during his term of office, he would do all in his power to place the finances of Brazil on a sound basis, and to restore the credit of his country.

The following are the conditions to be observed by holders of Bonds of the before enumerated Loans for the funding of their Coupons, which are to be presented as they become due up to the 30th of June, 1901, inclusive.

In exchange for their Coupons, holders will receive a receipt for the amount lodged.

These receipts must be presented in amounts of not less than £20 to be exchanged for Scrip, which will be afterwards exchanged for Bonds of the 5 per cent. Funding Loan.

The smallest denomination of Bond being £20, Certificates will be given for fractional parts of £20, and these fractional Certificates may afterwards be exchanged for Scrip or Bonds in like manner with the Receipts, that is to say, in amounts of not less than £20.

No interest will be paid on the Receipts or fractional Certificates, but the Scrip or Bonds given in exchange for Receipts or Certificates will bear Interest from the due date of the Coupons for which the Receipts were issued.

Receipts and Certificates for Coupons due on different dates must be kept separate when presented for exchange into Scrip. Only Receipts and Certificates for Coupons due on the same date can be used together in making up the amount to be exchanged for Scrip or Bonds.

New Court, E.C., 15th of June, 1898.

MESSRS. SELIGMAN BROS., Fiscal Agents for the State Department of the United States of America, are prepared to receive and transmit to the Treasury, free of charge, applications for the UNITED STATES GOVERNMENT LOAN of TWO HUNDRED MILLION DOLLARS ($200,000,000) at par New York.

The Bonds bear interest at the rate of Three per Cent. per annum from August 1st, 1898, and are redeemable in coin at the pleasure of the Government after ten years, and repayable August 1st, 1918.

Individual applications for 500 dollars or less will probably be allotted in full in order of priority, and must be paid in full on application; rebate of interest being allowed till August 1st.

On amounts exceeding 500 dollars a deposit of two per cent. is required. Allotment in this case will take place after July 14th; payments to be made as to twenty per cent. ten days after allotment, balance in four instalments at intervals of forty days, or applicant may anticipate payments.

18, Austin Friars, E.C.
June 14th, 1898.

To Correspondents.

The Editor cannot undertake to return rejected communications.

Letters from correspondents must, in every case, be authenticated by the name and address of the writer.

Telegraphic Address: "Unveiling, London."

The Investors' Review.

The Week's Money Market.

Money has remained very plentiful in the Short Loan market, and day to day loans have stood at about ¾ per cent. throughout the week. "Fixtures," too, are quoted little higher, and the India Council only obtains 1¼ per cent. for its advances by extending loans over the end of the half-year. As the end of the month approaches, a little more demand for cash is certain to make itself felt, but there is not likely to be any pressure of importance.

A slightly harder tone has prevailed in the discount market, chiefly owing to the fact that more bills have been about. The breakdown of the wheat "corner" and the issue at last of the United States war loan have both contributed towards this increased offering of bills, while the difficulties in the grain markets have added a slight tinge of anxiety about credit. Only one corn-dealer's failure has so far been announced, and London is supposed to have stood clear from the wretched gamble, but Liverpool is involved to a certain extent, so that a feeling of relief is experienced from the knowledge that the broken-down speculator in the States is still remitting funds. Under these conditions discount rates have hardened to just an appreciable extent so that 1⅜ to 1½ is quoted for 60-day bills, and 1$\frac{7}{16}$ to 1½ per cent. for three months' paper, as compared with an easy 1⅜ per cent. all round a week ago. The withdrawal of £767,000 in Japanese yen from the Bank of England also had a strengthening influence late last week, but the Continental demand for gold subsequently weakened, so that over a third of the African arrival was secured by the Bank of England at about 77s. 9½d. per ounce, the balance going to Russia and India. Since then the price has risen to 77s. 10d. on an increased demand for Russia.

This week's Bank return is uninteresting, and need not detain us long. "Other" securities show an increase of £626,000, making this total £33,274,000, and the inference is that the Bank has been investing largely to employ its surplus moneys. The market has certainly not been borrowing. All the loss in gold by export, £519,000, has been covered by the return of coin from circulation, and more, for the total stock of bullion is up £161,000 to £38,156,000. Notes have also come back, so that the reserve of the Banking department is up £303,000 to £27,639,000. Had not tax collecting added £583,000 to the "Public" deposits, the market would have been in possession of a large additional amount of credit in consequence of these changes. As it is, "Other" deposits are up only £355,000 to £44,909,000—a quite sufficient total.

SILVER.

For the last seven days Spain has not ostensibly entered the Silver Market as a buyer, and the quotation for bars at one time declined to 26⅞d. per ounce. A slightly firmer tone has prevailed in the last few days, with the result that the price has recovered to 26$\frac{11}{16}$d. per ounce. The hope is naturally entertained that Spain will again enter the market, while, as we are past the middle of the month, "bear" operators are becoming desirous to close up their accounts. The "bear" position, however, is not considered to be very heavy. Money is cheaper in India, as is shown by the drop of 2 per cent. in the Bank of Bombay's rate to 10 per cent. and 1 per cent. in that of the Bank of Bengal, to 9 per cent., with the result that there is more disposition to buy silver. Much, however, will depend upon the course of exchange, but so far the India Council has been able to maintain its policy of only selling transfers at 1s. 4d. per rupee. It has sold so largely up to the present that it can afford to stand out if necessary for a time, but we have yet to see the effect of the high exchange upon the Indian export trade.

Since the commencement of the financial year on April 1 the India Council has sold Rs.7,36,85,406 realising £4,900,588. As the Budget estimated for £16,000,000 to be drawn in the year, this means that, at 1s. 4d. per rupee, some forty-six lacs must, in future, be sold per week in order to obtain the amount.

BANK OF ENGLAND.

AN ACCOUNT pursuant to the Act 7 and 8 Vict., cap. 32, for the Week ending on Wednesday, June 15, 1898.

ISSUE DEPARTMENT.

	£		£
Notes Issued	52,492,675	Government Debt	11,015,100
		Other Securities	5,784,900
		Gold Coin and Bullion	35,692,675
		Silver Bullion	—
	£52,492,675		£52,492,675

BANKING DEPARTMENT.

	£		£
Proprietors' Capital	14,553,000	Government Securities	13,328,051
Rest	3,180,301	Other Securities	33,273,747
Public Deposits (including Exchequer, Savings Banks, Commissioners of National Debt, and Dividend Accounts)	11,494,625	Notes	25,175,650
Other Deposits	44,908,893	Gold and Silver Coin	2,463,452
Seven Day and other Bills	104,081		
	£74,240,900		£74,240,900

* Dated June 16, 1898.

H. G. BOWEN, *Chief Cashier.*

In the following table will be found the movements compared with the previous week, and also the totals for that week and the corresponding return last year:—

Banking Department.

Last Year. June 16.		June 8, 1898.	June 15, 1898.	Increase.	Decrease.
£	Liabilities.	£	£	£	£
3,098,906	Rest	3,163,070	3,180,301	17,231	—
11,260,076	Pub. Deposits	10,911,226	11,494,625	583,399	—
38,936,166	Other do.	44,553,870	44,908,893	355,023	—
163,869	7 Day Bills	109,003	104,081	—	4,922
	Assets.			Decrease.	Increase.
13,948,356	Gov. Securities	13,306,642	13,328,051	—	21,409
28,230,650	Other do.	32,647,542	33,273,747	—	626,205
25,833,011	Total Reserve	27,335,985	27,639,102	—	303,117
				955,653	955,653
				Increase.	Decrease.
£		£	£	£	£
27,287,840	Note Circulation	27,458,725	27,317,025	—	141,700
51½ p.c.	Proportion	49½ p.c.	49 p.c.	—	—
2 "	Bank Rate	3 "	3 "	—	—

· Foreign Bullion movement for week £519,000 out.

LONDON BANKERS' CLEARING.

Month of	1898.	1897.	Increase.	Decrease.
	£	£	£	£
January	673,281,000	576,558,000	96,723,000	—
February	648,601,000	597,652,000	50,949,000	—
March	799,520,000	729,970,000	69,550,000	—
April	597,410,000	532,508,000	64,902,000	—
Week ending				
May 4	174,057,000	138,987,000	35,070,000	—
" 11	160,526,000	128,252,000	32,274,000	—
" 18	171,078,000	152,987,000	18,091,000	—
25	131,037,000	116,372,000	14,665,000	—
June 1	155,655,000	166,981,000	—	11,326,000
" 8	139,048,000	111,213,000	27,835,000	—
" 15	164,537,000	148,402,000	16,135,000	—
Total to date	3,725,682,000	3,332,787,000	392,895,000	—

BANK AND DISCOUNT RATES ABROAD.

	Bank Rate.	Altered.	Open Market.
Paris	2	March 14, 1895	1¾
Berlin	4	April 9, 1898	3⅜
Hamburg	4	April 9, 1898	3⅜
Frankfort	4	April 9, 1898	3⅜
Amsterdam	3	April 13, 1897	2⅝
Brussels	3	April 28, 1896	2¾
Vienna	4	January 22, 1896	4
Rome	5	August 27, 1895	3
St. Petersburg	5½	January 23, 1898	5½
Madrid	5	June 17, 1896	5
Lisbon	6	January 25, 1891	6
Stockholm	5	May 18, 1898	4½
Copenhagen	4½	June 2, 1898	4½
Calcutta	9	June 16, 1898	—
Bombay	10	June 16, 1898	—
New York call money	1¼ to 1½	—	—

NEW YORK ASSOCIATED BANKS (dollar at 4s.).

	June 11, 1898.	June 4, 1898.	May 28, 1898.	June 12, 1897.
	£	£	£	£
Specie	35,836,000	35,100,000	34,772,000	17,854,000
Legal tenders	11,142,000	10,820,000	10,708,000	20,922,000
Loans and discounts	122,152,000	120,324,000	117,946,000	102,745,000
Circulation	2,943,800	2,946,200	2,947,400	2,850,000
Net deposits	144,842,000	141,884,000	139,272,000	117,022,000

Legal reserve is 25 per cent. of net deposits; therefore the total reserve (specie and legal tenders) exceeds this sum by £10,767,500, against an excess last week of £10,449,000.

BANK OF SPAIN (25 pesetas to the £).

	June 11, 1898.	June 4, 1898.	May 28, 1898.	June 12, 1897.
	£	£	£	£
Gold	9,833,520	9,833,520	9,833,520	8,832,000
Silver	4,228,040	4,269,480	4,333,800	10,359,000
Bills discounted	31,701,640	31,387,160	31,047,000	—
Advances and loans	3,878,720	4,481,520	4,245,800	19,244,000
Notes in circulation	52,756,360	52,551,760	52,206,720	44,237,000
Treasury advances, coupon account	879,960	895,840	493,400	—
Treasury balances	1,373,760	1,320,960	824,120	—

NATIONAL BANK OF BELGIUM (25 francs to the £).

	June 9, 1898.	June 2, 1898.	May 26, 1898.	June 10, 1897.
	£	£	£	£
Coin and bullion	4,355,120	4,430,400	4,207,440	4,104,000
Other securities	15,895,760	16,469,880	16,397,800	16,024,000
Note circulation	19,084,440	19,144,060	19,407,800	18,477,000
Deposits	2,546,640	3,137,600	2,590,040	2,985,000

IMPERIAL BANK OF GERMANY (20 marks to the £).

	June 7, 1898.	May 31, 1898.	May 23, 1898.	June 5, 1897.
	£	£	£	£
Cash in hand	43,594,650	43,158,850	44,170,500	46,771,000
Bills discounted	33,530,850	34,821,000	33,862,450	*35,447,000
Advances on stocks	4,458,300	4,462,650	4,174,350	—
Note circulation	52,583,350	53,892,300	52,817,400	50,304,000
Public deposits	25,087,450	24,048,850	25,575,400	28,683,000

* Includes advances.

AUSTRIAN-HUNGARIAN BANK (1s. 8d. to the florin).

	June 7, 1898.	May 31, 1898.	May 23, 1898.	June 5, 1897.
	£	£	£	£
Gold reserve	29,028,084	29,032,000	29,108,166	28,778,000
Silver reserve	10,484,250	10,474,250	10,468,166	10,525,000
Foreign bills	304,416	223,416	331,666	—
Advances	1,859,500	1,821,750	1,803,750	—
Note circulation	5,168,900	51,802,083	51,435,666	50,367,000
Bills discounted	13,231,583	13,225,916	12,925,416	*11,407,000

* Includes advances.

BANK OF FRANCE (25 francs to the £).

	June 16, 1898.	June 9, 1898.	June 2, 1898.	June 17, 1897.
	£	£	£	£
Gold in hand	75,011,960	74,936,520	74,673,480	79,900,000
Silver in hand	49,390,640	49,355,120	49,145,120	49,169,000
Bills discounted	26,487,880	28,043,480	34,409,720	*37,402,000
Advances	15,431,160	15,477,880	15,529,200	—
Note circulation	145,191,760	145,639,880	148,605,320	143,101,000
Public deposits	8,758,720	8,200,400	8,053,840	7,219,000
Private deposits	18,068,800	19,741,800	21,392,880	18,429,000

Proportion between bullion and circulation 85⅝ per cent. against 83⅝ per cent. a week ago.

* Includes advances

FOREIGN RATES OF EXCHANGE ON LONDON.

Place.	Usance.	Last week's.	Latest.	Place.	Usance.	Last week's.	Latest.
Paris	chqs.	25·27	25·26	Italy	sight	27·10	27·02
Brussels	chqs.	25·29	25·27½	Do. gold prem.	..	107·15	107·02½
Amsterdam	short	12·06½	12·07½	Constantinople	3 mths	109·15	109·15
Berlin	short	20·44	20·40½	B. Ayres gd. pm.	..	103·80	103·70
Do.	3 mths	20·32	20·30	Rio de Janeiro	90 dys	7$\frac{5}{16}$d.	7¼d.
Hamburg	3 mths	20·31	20·30	Valparaiso	90 dys	17$\frac{1}{16}$d.	17$\frac{5}{16}$d.
Frankfort	short	20·38	20·38	Calcutta	T. T.	1/3$\frac{15}{16}$	1/3$\frac{15}{16}$
Vienna	short	12·01½	12·00½	Bombay	T. T.	1/3$\frac{15}{16}$	1/3$\frac{15}{16}$
St. Petersburg	3 mths	93·90	94·00	Hong Kong	T. T.	1/10½	1/10½
New York	60 dys	4·84½	4·83½	Shanghai	T. T.	2/6½	2/6½
Lisbon	sight	29½d.	29½d.	Singapore	T. T.	1/10½	1/10½
Madrid	sight	45·47½	46·77				

LONDON COURSE OF EXCHANGE.

Place.	Usance.	June 7.	June 9.	June 14.	June 16.
Amsterdam and Rotterdam	short	12·2	12·2	12·2	12·2
Do. do.	3 months	12·3½	12·3½	12·3½	12·3¾
Antwerp and Brussels	3 months	25·46¼	25·46¼	25·43¾	25·43¾
Hamburg	3 months	20·62	20·60	20·62	20·61
Berlin and German B. Places	3 months	20·62	20·60	20·62	20·62
Paris	cheques	25·30	25·28¾	25·27½	25·27½
Do.	3 months	25·42½	25·42½	25·41¼	25·40
Marseilles	3 months	25·43¾	25·42½	25·41¼	25·41¼
Switzerland	3 months	25·63¾	25·60	25·57½	25·57½
Austria	3 months	12·18¾	12·16¼	12·16¼	12·15
St. Petersburg	3 months	24 15/16	24 15/16	25	25
Moscow	3 months	24⅞	24⅞	24 15/16	24 15/16
Italian Bank Places	3 months	27·42½	27·37½	27·30	27·31¼
New York	60 days	48 13/16	48 13/16	48 13/16	48 13/16
Madrid and Spanish B. P.	3 months	25½	nom.	25 1/16	25
Lisbon	3 months	28¾	29¼	29	29½
Oporto	3 months	28¾	29¼	29	29½
Copenhagen	3 months	18·41	18·40	18·38	18·37
Christiania	3 months	18·42	18·40	18·38	18·37
Stockholm	3 months	18·44	18·43	18·41	18·40

OPEN MARKET DISCOUNT.

	Per cent.
Thirty and sixty day remitted bills	1¾ —1⅞
Three months ,,	1¾ —1 13/16
Four months ,,	1⅞
Six months ,,	2
Three months fine inland bills	2
Four months ,,	2 —2⅛
Six months ,,	2⅛ —2¼

BANK AND DEPOSIT RATES.

	Per cent.
Bank of England minimum discount rate	3
,, ,, short loan rates	—
Banker's rate on deposits	1½
Bill brokers' deposit rate (call)	1
,, 7 and 14 days' notice	1¼
Current rates for 7 day loans	1
,, ,, for call loans	¾

Stock Market Notes and Comments.

It is dreary work trudging round the City just now to find out whether anything is going on. Each man's face is longer than his neighbour's and business of a general kind is very poor indeed. The pockets of the public are empty and their spirits are low. In vain do the jobbers put up prices here and there. Nobody responds and they have to let them tumble back again. When, however, markets in a general way fall into this condition, as they invariably do after each wild orgie of gambling by the public, there are often little spots where something of the old activity can be seen, either real or simulated, and for the past week the idle spectators have been a good deal amused by the revival of the old Chatham and South-Eastern embracing and perpetual love story, with its accompanying spurt in Chatham ordinary and second preference stocks. Intrinsically, Chatham ordinary stock is worthless, and as an investment pure and simple we should consider the second preference very dear at 50.

But that does not matter at all to the gambler when he has set his heart upon driving up prices, so this week he has got second Chatham preference up to 101, and the ordinary up to 23, and he talks glibly of new "pooling" arrangements between the South-Eastern and Chatham, either concluded or just about to be concluded, and favourable, of course, to the smaller company. Prophecies of a possible dividend on the ordinary stock are also diligently circulated, and there is quite a hubbub and bustle in a small way over the matter. It is, we imagine, about the one hundred and fiftieth time in our brief life that we have found the same story trotted out, and have been gently tickled on the bump of covetousness by the same estimates. And the beauty of it is that one never knows when the "fusion" and manufacture of Chatham dividends might come true, especially now that the genial Mr. James Staats Forbes is getting old. He might really wish to do something to distinguish himself by way of winding up his long and rather sterile connection with the Chatham Company.

Looking away from such chances and probabilities to the actual position of this unfortunate concern, the only feeling such market episodes as we have described excites is one of amazement that any human being possessed of enough brains to keep him outside a lunatic asylum could ever dream of buying any of its lower securities, even on a pretence that they might be investments. The low physical condition of the property is notorious. It is probably now the most inefficient and poorly equipped line in England: certainly it is the worst of any of the large companies. The condition of its stations is a disgrace to its management; its rolling stock is old and dirty, and for the most part shockingly lighted, notwithstanding the efforts which have been made lately to improve it out of borrowed money. At a moderate estimate, as we have again and again said, 10 per cent. to 20 per cent. more of the gross receipts of the line ought to be spent every year, for probably the next ten years, to bring it into a state of moderate efficiency, and we do not believe that it could be kept in that state in future years for much less than 60 per cent. of the gross receipts. The public knows, or ought to know, that there is now a million, or nearly, of capital, represented by nothing except obsolete steamboats, which ought to be written off—and so on. What use is there in running over the catalogue, or in warning the public that the net revenue this half-year may not be so tremendous after all, since the company is engaged in patching up and repainting one or two of its suburban stations; a most serious thing to a concern which probably has not spent 5s. on paint for some of these places in the last twenty years? We make this recital simply to warn people who may be ignorant and unsuspecting against having anything to do with the present gamble for the rise in these stocks. It is, in reality, no better than an impudent fraud which men with any pretensions to honesty ought to be ashamed to take any share in. The Chatham and Dover Company is to-day, in all essentials of good finance, an insolvent concern, and the dividends it does pay are not paid squarely out of net income, but evolved through the simple process of starving the up-keep and allowing the property to go to ruin.

Of course the Stock Exchange must have some little excitement or perish altogether in times like these, and it naturally falls back on some home security or other when all else fails, and everything else is failing it at present. The activity of a week ago in American railroad securities has died down considerably this week, because the market soon tired of keeping up the play by itself. It is all very well to run up prices if you know that the man in the street, or in the provinces, is eagerly waiting to buy what you have to sell, but if one jobber merely buys of or sells to another the play soon becomes not only fatiguing but mighty expensive. There is not much inducement to the public to buy American railroad securities just at present, fine "traffics" or no fine "traffics," and we do not believe it will buy much, confronted as it is by the shifty policy of the Washington Government in regard to the currency. The foreign bond market is equally torpid at the present moment, apparently because a large portion of the Paris open market, or *coulisse*, is in process of transference to Brussels. M. Méline, "Father Ruin," as he is well called, has succeeded in more than half strangling the Paris Bourse, and the loss of Paris, in consequence, promises to be the gain of Brussels. A guarantee fund of £4,000,000 is said to have been subscribed by the expatriated *coulissiers*, and arrangements have been entered into whereby the arbitragists in London will transfer part of their business to Brussels. In further preparation for this the two places are being put in communication by telephone. Until the "flitting" has been completed, and the new market in Belgium organised, we cannot expect much activity in foreign Government bonds—unless a revolution breaks out somewhere and one or more bankrupt States tumble openly into default. That might happen any day with Spain or Italy, although the despotic power now trying to rule Italy is going to issue another loan to stave off the inevitable if it can.

Something, though, of the dead calm which hangs over markets is due to a feeling that has entered into men's minds that some catastrophe of a financial kind is going to happen somewhere. There is a spirit of apprehension and unrest abroad which appears to seek gratification in, if it does not originate through dread of, some credit upheaval. This may be the mere result of want of business, and we must not lay too much stress upon it, but the feeling exists and is in no way conducive to active markets.

The Week's Stock Markets.

On the Stock Exchange investment securities have been firm owing to the abundance of money, but there has been little speculative business. The completing of the settlement occupied the attention of members nearly up to the close of last week, and the attractions of Ascot have thinned the attendance very considerably this week. No support has been forthcoming from the Paris Bourse, the Ministerial crisis, and the arranging for the removal of the *coulisse* to Brussels tending to restrict business. Consols dropped at one time to 111 and then recovered to about last Thursday's level; other gilt-edged securities have hardly moved.

Highest and Lowest this Year.		Last Carrying over Price.	BRITISH FUNDS, &c.	Closing Price.	Rise or Fall.
113⅛	109¼	—	Consols 2¾ p.c. (Money)...	111⅞	—
113 9/16	109½	111¾	Do. Account (July 1)	111 7/16	+ 1/16
106¼	101	105	2½ p.c. Stock red. 1905 ...	105	—
363	341	—	Bank of England Stock...	352½	−2
117	111⅝	114	India 3½ p.c. Stk. red. 1931	113¼	− ½
109¼	103⅜	107	Do. 3 p.c. Stk. red. 1948	107	+ ¼
96⅞	90	93	Do. 2½ p.c. Stk. red. 1926	92	—

Interest in the Home railway market has again centred in Chatham and South-Eastern stocks. Nothing new has transpired in reference to the alleged "pooling" arrangement between these companies, but a considerable saving in expenses is expected to be the outcome of the present negotiations, "sufficient, in fact, to bring Chatham ordinary in sight of a dividend," while in some quarters an actual amalgamation is thought to be not altogether improbable. The whole thing may be froth, but a substantial rise has taken place in all the stocks of these companies, Chatham second preference touching par. Great Western has made up a little of the ground lost during the past fortnight despite the poor traffic, and the new stock now stands at about 8 premium. North-Western and Hull and Barnsley both benefited by good traffic returns, but a further decline is noticeable in Waterloo City stock. Several of the premier issues have again been marked up from 1 to 3 points.

Highest and Lowest this Year.		Last Carrying over Price.	HOME RAILWAYS.	Closing Price.	Rise or Fall.
186	172½	177	Brighton Def.	177¼	+1½
59¼	54⅝	57¼	Caledonian Def.	58⅛	− ⅜
23¼	18¼	20¾	Chatham Ordinary	23	+1¼
77¼	62	67	Great Central Pref.	67	—
24⅜	21¼	22¾	Do. Def.	22¾	—
124½	118	121	Great Eastern	121⅝	+ ⅝
61½	50¾	55	Great Northern Def.	55¾	+ ⅜
179⅛	163⅞	164¼	Great Western	166¾	+2
52¾	45¼	51½	Hull and Barnsley.........	52½	+ ¾
149¼	145	145¾	Lanc. and Yorkshire......	146½	+ ½
136⅛	127¼	132	Metropolitan	132	+ ¼
31	26⅜	28¾	Metropolitan District......	29¼	+ ½
88⅝	82⅜	85½	Midland Pref.	86¾	+ ¾
95⅜	84½	88¼	Do. Def.	89	+ ½
93¼	86⅜	89⅞	North British Pref.	90	+ ¼
47½	41¾	44⅝	Do. Def.	45⅛	+ ¼
181½	172¾	177¼	North Eastern...............	178¼	+ ¾
205⅛	196¼	198½	North Western	199⅜	+ ⅞
117⅜	105½	113⅛	South Eastern Def.	114¾	+1
98⅜	87	93¾	South Western Def.	94	—

After one or two brief rallies, the list of United States railroad shares finally exhibits an almost general decline, the most conspicuous fall being in Louisville and Nashville. Fears are now expressed that the expected dividend will not be declared, and the alarming rumours concerning the outbreak of yellow fever in Mississippi brought out a good many selling orders. The collapse of the Leiter wheat corner on Monday was followed by heavy sales of railroad securities by Chicago houses connected with the wheat trade, and Liverpool firms have since been selling heavily. Rumours of German interference in the Philippines was another disturbing element, and considerable sales were made on New York account early in the week to provide funds for taking up the new Government bonds. A little buying on home and Continental account has since been apparent, the good Government crop reports encouraging operators for the rise, but this did not extend far, and the downward trend of prices continued to the close. There has been an almost entire absence of rumours, good, bad, or indifferent.

Another poor traffic knocked the Grand Trunk market to pieces, and the Canadian Pacific Company's return was not over-grand. Consequently, although prices leave off rather above the worst points touched, they still show a considerable decline since last Thursday.

Highest and Lowest this Year.		Last Carrying over Price.	CANADIAN AND U.S. RAILWAYS.	Closing Prices.	Rise or Fall.
14 5/16	10⅜	14	Atchison Shares	13½	− ¼
35¼	23½	34⅜	Do. Pref.	33¾	− ¼
15⅝	11	14¾	Central Pacific..............	14¼	—
105	85½	103¾	Chic. Mil. & St. Paul......	102⅜	− ⅜
14¼	10	13⅝	Denver Shares	13¼	—
54⅛	41½	52½	Do. Prefd.	52¾	+ ¼
16⅝	11¼	14⅜	Erie Shares	14	− ½
44⅝	29½	38¼	Do. Prefd.	36¾	−1¾
110½	99	108½	Illinois Central	107¾	− ¾
62½	45¼	57⅝	Louisville & Nashville ...	54	−3
14½	9 15/16	12½	Missouri & Texas	11⅛	− ⅜
122¾	108½	120	New York Central	119¼	− ¼
57¼	42⅞	55½	Norfolk & West. Prefd....	53¾	−1⅝
72½	59	72	Northern Pacific Prefd....	70⅝	−1⅜
19½	13⅜	16⅜	Ontario Shares	15⅞	− ⅜
62½	50¾	59¼	Pennsylvania	59⅜	− ⅜
12½	7 11/16	10¼	Reading Shares	10	− ¼
34½	24¼	33½	Southern Prefd.	30½	−2⅝
37⅛	18½	26	Union Pacific	24⅝	−1⅜
20¾	14½	20½	Wabash Prefd.	19⅜	− ⅜
30¼	21	29¼	Do. Income Debs....	27⅞	−1⅜
92¾	74	89	Canadian Pacific...........	88	− ⅜
79⅝	69⅞	79¼	Grand Trunk Guar.	77¼	−2¼
76⅛	57⅛	76½	Do. 1st Pref.	72⅛	−3⅜
58⅜	37¼	58	Do. 2nd Pref.	53	−5
26¾	19¼	26½	Do. 3rd Pref.	23⅞	−2⅝
107	101½	105½	Do. 4 p.c. Deb.	105⅜	− ⅜

Foreign Government stocks have presented a neglected appearance all the week, and the volume of business has shrunk to small dimensions. Paris operators are still very much upset by the *coulisse* difficulty, and seem disinclined to increase their commitments until some sort of a definite arrangement is arrived at. The settlement of the West African dispute was almost unnoticed, and had no effect on this market. Turkish issues have been in good demand, it being anticipated that the total extinction of the "A" group at an early date will bring about an improvement in the position of the remaining groups and perhaps their conversion. Trans-

Highest and Lowest this Year.		Last Carrying over Price.	FOREIGN BONDS.	Closing Price.	Rise or Fall.
94½	84	90¼	Argentine 5 p.c. 1886......	90¼	+ ½
92⅝	81⅝	88¼	Do. 6 p.c. Funding	88¼	+ ¼
76¾	64	71¾	Do. 5 p.c. B. Ay. Water	72	+ ¼
61¾	41⅛	54	Brazilian 4 p.c. 1889	53¼	+ ¼
69⅞	46	61¼	Do. 5 p.c. 1895	60½	− ¼
65	42¾	56	Do. 5 p.c. West Minas Ry..................	55¾	− ¼
108¾	105⅛	107⅛	Egyptian 4 p.c. Unified...	108	—
104¾	100½	103	Do. 3½ p.c. Pref. ...	103	− ¼
103	99½	101½	French 3 p.c. Rente	101½	—
44⅞	34½	43½	Greek 4 p.c. Monopoly...	43½	—
93 9/16	88¾	92½	Italian 5 p.c. Rente	92⅜	—
100	87½	97¾	Mexican 6 p.c. 1888	98	− ¼
20⅞	16	18¾	Portuguese 1 p.c.	18⅞	− ⅛
62⅛	29⅜	30	Spanish 4 p.c.	33 13/16	− 1/16
47	40	45½	Turkish 1 p.c. "B"	46⅜	+ ¼
26⅞	22½	25¾	Do. 1 p.c. "C"	26⅜	+ ½
22⅜	20	21¾	Do. 1 p.c. "D"	22⅜	+ ⅝
46⅜	40	45	Uruguay 3½ p.c. Bonds...	44½	+ ⅛

actions in Spanish fours were fewer this week, and the price remains almost unchanged. Chinese bonds are slightly harder, and Ottoman Bank shares show a further advance. Among South American descriptions the Brazilian loans weakened when the funding scheme was published, and Chilian bonds were again pressed for sale, a bad impression having been created by the various explanatory statements relating to the recent issue of Chilian Treasury bills.

Highest and Lowest this Year.		Last Carrying over Price.	FOREIGN RAILWAYS.	Closing Price.	Rise or Fall.
105¼	99	105	Argentine Gt. West. 5 p.c. Pref. Stock	105	—
158¼	134	140½	B. Ay. Gt. Southern Ord.	139	−1
78½	65	73½	B. Ay. and Rosario Ord.	72	−1½
12¼	10¼	10⅞	B. Ay. Western Ord.	10¾	−¼
87¼	73	81½	Central Argentine Ord.	80	−2½
92	76	79	Cordoba and Rosario 6 p.c. Deb.	79	−1
95½	85½	90	Cord. Cent. 4 p.c. Deb. (Cent. Nth. Sec.)	90	—
61½	42	53½	Do. Income Deb. Stk.	53	−½
25½	16½	20¼	Mexican Ord. Stk.	20	−1½
83½	69½	75	Do. 8 p.c. 1st Pref.	74½	−2½

In the Foreign railway market Brazil Great Southern 6 per cent. and United of Havana 5 per cent. both mark rises of 3, but losses of from 1 to 2½ have to be recorded in Central Bahia, Cordoba and Rosario preference, ditto 4 per cents., and Santa Fé and Cordoba second debentures. Mexican Railway ordinary and preference have lost about what they gained last week, the traffic return only showing a small increase of $600, and Mexican Central 4 per cents. are likewise rather weaker.

An idle market is the Miscellaneous one just now, but in spite of this fact there has been a further influx of jobbers into it which speaks badly for other markets. Investment business is almost at a standstill, and the few changes of importance that have been registered are due to exceptional circumstances. The second reading of the Electric Lighting Provisional Orders Bill was followed by an all-round fall in the leading electric lighting companies' shares, with the exception of those of the City of London Company, which were inquired for on the prospects of the corporation taking over the property at an early date. A steady advance has been marked in the stocks of Combe, Watney, and Reid's breweries, the three great concerns which are on the point of amalgamating. E. C. Powder ordinary fell sharply when a dividend of 4s. 6d. (compared with 10s. last year) was announced, and Apollinaris issues were weaker, the "carry forward" being smaller than was expected. Dumont Coffee debentures fell 3 as the result of the meeting, but a rapid recovery has nearly wiped out last week's "slump" in Asbestos and Asbestic. London Produce Clearing House shares were sold on the dividend, and Sanitas shares on the proposed increase in the capital of the company. Liebig has risen 2, and Dunlop debentures 2½.

Home railway stocks closed the week with a firm tendency. Notably North Western, North Eastern, and Great Eastern. United States railway shares hardened a little just before the finish, a cessation of selling orders from Liverpool being reported, and at the same time a good many small orders came to hand, so that the latest quotations were well above the worst, and in the case of Denver preferred, a small rise on the week was established. Among foreign Government bonds a recovery in Argentine, Brazilian, and Chilian issues took place quite at the last, but Spanish and Turkish groups were sold from Paris, and Argentine railway stocks left off weak.

Mining and Finance Companies.

The South African market has been stagnant, features there are none, and the changes on balance are altogether too trivial for notice. Professional operators tried to put prices up a little when the Rand output was announced, but the attractions of Ascot have proved much too powerful this week, and with a very thin attendance of members prices naturally drooped. Paris support was conspicuous by its entire absence. Among Western Australian companies, a little mild excitement was caused by the reported "jumping" of the Golden Horse Shoe Mine, and holders rushed to sell, but a partial recovery came about when the rumour was officially denied. No other changes have taken place worthy of mention, and Adelaide orders have not troubled the market much. A sharp fall in Mount Lyell shares is the most prominent feature in the miscellaneous mining market. Vague rumours are afloat to account for the decline, one report being that an expert or two employed by a big London house have been reporting unfavourably on the property, but last month's return was not much liked, and the fall in the price of copper has been another adverse factor. Rio Tinto shares are also slightly weaker, Paris operators having been too much occupied with the *coulisse* problem to give any support even to their favourite counters. Nundydroog shares drooped a little on the new issue of capital, but other Indian companies' emissions are firmer, Mysore especially on a cable from the mine announcing the discovery of a new reef.

TRAMWAY AND OMNIBUS RECEIPTS.

HOME.

Name.	Period.	Ending.	Amount.	Increase or Decrease on 1897.	Weeks or Months.	Aggregate to Date. Amount.	Inc. or Dec. on 1897.
			£	£		£	£
Aberdeen District	Week	June 11	506	−11	—	—	—
Belfast Street	"	" 11	2,579	+132*	—	—	—
Birmingham and Aston	"	" 11	441	−145*	—	—	—
Birmingham and Midland	"	" 11	647	−142*	—	—	—
Birmingham City	"	" 11	3,809	−452*	—	—	—
Birmingham General	"	" 11	900	−128*	—	—	—
Blessington and Poulaphouca	"	" 12	21	−27*	23	279	+19
Bristol Tramways and Carriage	"	" 10	2,899	−466*	—	—	—
Burnley and District	"	" 11	328	−77*	—	—	—
Bury, Rochdale, and Oldham	"	" 11	905	−209*	—	—	—
Croydon	"	" 11	395	−75*	—	—	+1,263
Dublin and Blessington	"	" 12	134	−81*	23	2,403	+9
Dublin and Lucan	"	" 11	65	−55*	24	1,212	−358
Dublin United	"	" 10	3,350	−194*	—	66,127	+3,545
Dudley and Stourbridge	"	" 11	168	−85*	24	3,992	+130
Edinburgh and District	"	" 11	2,659	+223	23	53,810	+4,909
Edinburgh Street	"	" 11	736	+48	23	14,377	+1,657
Gateshead and District	Month	May	935	+66*	—	—	—
Glasgow	Week	June 11	3,010	+109	—	—	—
Harrow-road and Paddington	"	" 11	186	+8*	—	—	—
Lea Bridge and Leyton	"	" 11	928	+13*	—	—	—
London, Deptford, and Greenwich	"	" 11	646	−57*	—	13,257	+483
London General Omnibus	"	" 11	24,358	+285*	—	—	—
London Road Car	"	" 11	7,634	−422*	†	147,378	+4,317
London Southern	"	" 11	654	+5*	—	—	—
North Staffordshire	"	" 11	390	−57*	—	9,119	−134
Provincial	"	" 11	2,978	−324*	—	—	—
Rossendale Valley	"	" 10	203	−28*	—	—	—
Southampton	"	" 11	443	−196	—	—	—
South London	"	" 11	1,896	−177*	†	38,463	+1,062
South Staffordshire	"	" 10	556	−372*	23	13,872	−222
Sunderland	"	" 5	440	+158*	—	—	—
Swansea	"	" 3	322	+37*	—	—	—
Tramways Union	Month	May	12,823	+1,655	5	52,333	+6,150
Wigan and District	Week	June 11	265	+150‡*	—	—	
Woolwich and South East London	"	" 11	433	+108*	†	7,976	+304

* Whit week, 1897. ‡ Strike in 1897.

FOREIGN.

Name.	Period.	Ending.	Amount.	Increase or Decrease on 1897.	Weeks or Months.	Aggregate to Date. Amount.	Inc. or Dec. on 1897.
			£	£		£	£
Anglo-Argentine	Week	May 26	4,390	+638	*	87,260	+9,244
Barcelona	"	June 11	1,226	−424	—	26,184	−4,398
Barcelona, Ensanche y Gracia	"	" 11	241	−19	—	5,164	−17
Bordeaux	"	" 10	2,468	−233	—	48,015	−2,229
Brazilian Street	Month	April [m	lr46,055	+3,871	—	—	—
British Columbia Electric	"	"	$30,729	+$10493	‡	$305,154	—
Do. net	"	"	$10,394	+$4,958	‡	$97,402	—
Buenos Ayres and Belgrano	"	April	5,090	+3,645	*	19,472	+3,368
Buenos Ayres Grand National	Week	May 14	$23,455	+$2,066	†	—	+$20,370
Buenos Ayres New	Month	March	$70,624	−$864	—	$201,851	−$7,119
Calais	Week	June 11	181	+5	—	—	—
Calcutta	"	" 11	1,224	−111	—	—	—
C'rth'g'na & Herrerias	Month	May	3,600	+173	—	22,418	+1,184
Gothenburg	Week	May 25	408	+38	—	—	—
Lynn and Boston	Month	April	$105,596	+$2,087	7	$727,825	+$30000
Do. net	"	"	$40,418	+$1,912	7	$256,801	+$5,064
Twin City Rapid	"	"	$165,803	+$10411	4	$653,223	+$43912
Do. Net	"	"	$82,690	+$9,356	4	$317,429	+$42582

* From January 1. † From April 1, 1898. ‡ From April 15, 1897. § From October 1, 1897.

Answers to Correspondents.

Questions about public securities, and on all points in company law, as well as on the position of life insurance offices and their promises, will be answered week by week, in the REVIEW, on the following terms and conditions :—

A fee of FIVE shillings must be remitted for each question put, provided they are questions about separate securities. Should a private letter be required, then an extra fee of FIVE shillings must be sent to cover the cost of such letter, the fee then being TEN shillings for one query only, and FIVE shillings for every subsequent one in the same letter. While making this concession the EDITOR will feel obliged if private replies are as much as possible dispensed with. It is wholly impossible to answer letters sent merely "with a stamped envelope enclosed for reply."

Correspondents will further greatly oblige by so framing their questions as to obviate the necessity to name securities in the replies. They should *number* the questions, keeping a copy for reference, thus :—"(1) Please inform me about the present position of the Rowenzori Development Co. (2) Is a dividend likely to be paid soon on the capital stock of the Congo-Sudan Railway?

Answers to be given to all such questions by simply quoting the numbers 1, 2, 3, and so on. The EDITOR has a rooted objection to such forms of reply as—"I think your Timbuctoo Consols will go up," or "Sell your Slowcoach and Draggem Bonds," because this kind of thing is open to all sorts of abuses. By the plan suggested, and by using a fancy name to be replied to, each query can be kept absolutely private to the inquirer, and no scope whatever be given to market manipulations. Avoid, as names to be replied to, common words, like "investor," "inquirer," and so on, as also "bear" or "bull." Detached syllables of the inquirer's name, or initials reversed, will frequently do as well as anything, so long as the answer can be identified by the inquirer.

The EDITOR further respectfully requests that merely speculative questions should as far as possible be avoided. He by no means sets himself up as a market prophet, and can only undertake to provide the latest information regarding the securities asked about. This he will do faithfully and without bias.

Replies cannot be guaranteed in the same week if the letters demanding them reach the office of the INVESTORS' REVIEW, Norfolk House, Norfolk-street, W.C., later than the first post on Wednesday mornings.

S.E.E.—(*a*) Yes, thoroughly good. (*b*) Yes, quite safely. (*c*) I cannot say that. The price might recede a little in a time of dear money, but so would prices for everything. (*d*) Nothing that I can see would affect the dividend on this stock, which seems to me as safe as anything in the list, although the company is not well managed just now.

MINE.—The company is not a "shady" one, but it was over-capitalised at the start, and its shares are still, to a very large extent, in the hands of the underwriters. This prevents any rise from taking place and sends the price down directly money becomes difficult to borrow. As money is now cheap there is no reason for immediate selling, but I do not look for any substantial improvement.

NOMEN.—Your questions are a little too hypothetical to be easy to answer; but I do not think (1) that Government or municipal enterprise will hurt the company in the near future. It has fought, coerced, and, I fear, bribed itself into too strong a position. 2. No likelihood of this at all at present. 3. No, not "decidedly risky," so far, at least, as the preference shares are concerned. 4. No, I cannot advise immediate sale. The shares are fairly safe, but I do not look for any appreciable rise in them. Only the present moment is not favourable to selling.

A. J.—You shall have a reply by letter.

LIBERAL.—There is a fair probability of a temporary jump, I think, but only that. A permanent improvement, though, does not at present appear probable, as I do not see how the country is going to raise another loan.

JERMYN.—Fall due to state of affairs in Italy, and to the lower prices now obtainable for the company's products. I think for this year at least, and perhaps for two or three years, dividends may be reduced, but the property is solid enough, and after a time the price of the stock ought to improve. No accounts are published.

The Trustees, Executors, and Securities Insurance Corporation, Limited, publishes the numbers of the bonds of the City of Mexico 5 per cent. loan of 1889, which have been drawn for repayment at par on July 1, 1898. The drawn bonds should be left three clear days for examination.

The English Association of American Bond and Share Holders, Limited, 5, Great Winchester-street, E.C., notify that they are now prepared to purchase (at the current rate of exchange) the coupons due July 1, 1898, on the prior lien bonds of the Mobile and Birmingham Railroad Company.

The National Bank of New Zealand, Limited, will pay the half-year's interest due on 1st prox. on the City of Auckland 5 per cent. loan for £200,000.

The Commercial Bank of Australia, Limited, will pay the interest due July 1 on the Melbourne Tramways Trust 4½ per cent. loans. Coupons must be left three clear days for examination.

The business of the *Spectator* has been converted into a private limited liability company for family reasons.

Mr. Cecil F. Parr, deputy-chairman, has been appointed chairman of Parr's Bank, Limited, in place of the late Lord Playfair.

The London Committee of the shareholders of the Central Pacific Railroad Company announce that a general meeting of the holders of the certificates issued by them will be held in Winchester House, on Tuesday, the 28th inst at 2 o'clock p.m.

At a meeting of the Board of Directors of the Delhi Umballa Kalka Railway Company, Limited, held on 9th inst., Robert Steel, Esq., C.S.I., was elected a director of the company.

Prices of Mine and Mining Finance Companies' Shares.

Shares £1 each, except where otherwise stated.

AUSTRALIAN.

Making-Up Price, June 8.	Name	Closing Price.	Rise or Fall.	Making-Up Price, June 8.	Name	Closing Price.	Rise or Fall.
1 1/16	Aladdin	1 3/8		3/4	Hannan's Star	5/8	
3 1/2	Associated	3 5/16	– 1/4	6 5/8	Ivanhoe, New	6 3/4	+ 1/16
5/	Do. Southern	1/4		9/16	Kalgurli Mt. & Iron King, 18/	11/16	+ 1/16
1	Brownhill Extended	1		5 7/8	Kalgurli	5 3/4	– 1/8
1 1/16	Burbank's Birthday	1	– 1/16	2 1/16	Lady Shenton	1 15/16	– 1/8
3/8	Central Boulder	5/16	– 1/16	9 7/16	Lake View Cons.	9 3/16	– 1/4
6/	Chaffers, 4/	6/		9/16	Do. Extended	7/16	+ 1/16
11/16	Colonial Finance, 15/	1/4 dis.	+ 1/4	7/8	Do. South	1	+ 1/16
1/2	Crœsus S. United	3/8		1 1/16	London & Globe Finance	23/9	– 1/9
1/8	E. Murchison	1/8		15/16	London & W.A. Exploration	7/8	+ 1/16
4/9	Golden Arrow 19/	5/		1/4	Do. Investment	3/16	– 1/16
10 1/16	Golden Horseshoe	9 1/2	– 3/8	1/8	Mainland Consols	1/16	
3/4	Golden Link	11/16	– 1/16	7/8	North Boulder, 10/	3/4	– 1/16
18/6	Great Boulder, 2/	17/6	– 1/6	1 1/4	North Kalgurli	1 3/16	+ 1/16
1 1/16	Do. Main Reef, 10/	1 1/16	– 1/8	11/16	Northern Territories	11/16	– 1/8
3 1/4	Do. Perseverance	2 15/16	– 1/16	2 3/8	Peak Hill	2 1/2	+ 1/8
3/8	Do. South	3/8		2 3/8	South Kalgurli	2 7/16	+ 1/16
3	Hainault	3 1/4	+ 1/4	1 1/16	W. A. Goldfields	1 1/16	+ 1/16
11/16	Hampton Plains	11/16		3/4	W. A. Joint Stock	11/16	– 1/16
8 13/16	Hannan's Brownhill	8 3/4	+ 1/8	2/	W. A. Market Trust	2/	– /6
1 1/2	Hannan's Oroya	11/16	– 1/16	3/4	W. A. Loan & General Fin.	11/16	– 1/16
1/16	Do. Proprietary	11/6	– 1/	1/16	White Feather	1/16	

SOUTH AFRICAN.

Making-Up Price, June 8.	Name	Closing Price.	Rise or Fall.	Making-Up Price, June 8.	Name	Closing Price.	Rise or Fall.
5 1/4	Angelo	5 1/4	+ 1/8	2/	Lisbon-Berlyn	1/9	
1	Aurora West	15/16		2 1/2	May Consolidated	2 1/16	+ 1/16
1	Bantjes	15/16	+ 1/16	3 11/16	Meyer and Charlton	3 3/4	
9/	Barrett, 10/	9/	+ /6	3 1/2	Modderfontein	3 1/2	
4 1/4	Bonanza	4	– 1/4	11/16	New Bultfontein	11/16	
5/6	Buffelsdoorn	5/16		3 3/4	New Primrose	3 3/4	
5 1/16	City and Suburban, £4	5 1/4	+ 1/4	1 3/8	Nigel, 15/	1 3/8	
2 1/4	Comet (New)	2 1/16	– 1/16		Nigel Deep	11/16	– 1/16
3 1/4	Con. Deep Level	3	– 1/4	9/16	North Randfontein	1/2	
11 5/8	Crown Deep	11 3/4	+ 1/8	5	Nourse Deep	5	
13	Crown Reef	12 7/8	– 1/8	11/16	Porges-Randfontein	11/16	
27 3/8	De Beers, £5	27 9/16	+ 1/16	29 1/4	Rand Mines	29 5/16	+ 1/16
3 1/16	Driefontein	3 1/16	– 1/16	1 3/8	Randfontein	1 5/16	
6 1/4	Durban Roodepoort	6 5/16	+ 1/16	1 11/16	Rietfontein	1 1/4	– 3/8
3 1/16	Do. Deep	3 1/16	+ 1/16	9	Robinson Deep	9 1/4	+ 3/8
4 1/16	East Rand	4 1/16	+ 1/16	8	Do. Gold, £5	8 1/4	+ 1/4
24 1/4	Ferreira	24 1/4	+ 1/2	3/4	Do. Randfontein	3/4	
7 1/4	Geldenhuis Deep	7 1/4	+ 1/8	1 1/4	Roodepoort Central Deep	1 1/4	
5 11/16	Do. Estate	5 11/16		6 1/4	Rose Deep	6 1/4	
1/2	George Goch	1/16	– 1/8	3 1/16	Salisbury	3 1/16	+ 1/16
2 1/16	Ginsberg	2 1/4	+ 1/4	1 1/4	Sheba	1 1/4	
1 3/4	Glencairn	1 3/4		3 3/4	Simmer and Jack, £5	3 3/4	
8 1/4	Goldfields Deep	8 1/4	+ 3/8	2 1/4	Transvaal Gold	2 1/4	– 1/16
8 1/16	Griqualand West	8 1/4		3 3/4	Treasury	3 3/4	
9 1/16	Henry Nourse	9 1/4	+ 1/4	3 1/4	United Roodepoort	3 1/4	
7 1/16	Heriot	7 1/4		1 1/4	Van Ryn	1 5/16	+ 1/16
7 1/4	Jagersfontein	7 1/4	– 3/8	6 1/16	Village Main Reef	6 1/16	– 1/16
9 3/8	Jubilee	9 3/8	+ 1/8	1 3/4	Vogelstruis	1 1/4	+ 1/4
5	Jumpers	5		3/4	Do. Deep	3/4	+ 1/16
2 3/4	Kleinfontein	2 1/2	– 1/16	10	Wemmer	10 1/4	+ 1/4
3 1/4	Knight's	3 3/4	+ 3/8	1 1/4	West Rand	1	– 1/16
2 1/4	Lancaster	2 3/8		5 1/16	Wolhuter, £4	5 1/16	+ 1/16
3 1/16	Langlaagte Estate	3		2 1/4	Worcester	2 1/4	

LAND EXPLORATION AND RHODESIAN.

Making-Up Price, June 8.	Name	Closing Price.	Rise or Fall.	Making-Up Price, June 8.	Name	Closing Price.	Rise or Fall.
2 1/16	Anglo-French Ex.	2 1/2	– 1/16	3/4	Mashonaland Central	3/4	
1 3/8	Barnato Consolidated	1 5/16		5 7/8	Matabele Gold Reefs	5 3/4	– 1/8
3/4	Bechuanaland Ex.	3/4	+ 1/16	2 1/16	Mozambique	2 1/16	+ 1/16
2 1/4	Chartered B.S.A.	2 1/4		13/16	Oceana Consolidated	13/16	
1/4	Clark's Cons.	1/4		1 1/16	Rhodesia, Ltd.	1 1/16	+ 1/16
1/4	Colenbrander	1/16		4 1/4	Do. Exploration	4	– 1/8
4 1/16	Cons. Goldfields	4 1/16		15/16	Do. Goldfields	1	
1 1/16	Do. Pref.	21/	+ /6	3 1/4	S. A. Gold Trust	3 1/16	+ 1/16
1 3/8	Exploration	1 3/8		11/16	Tati Concessions	11/16	
2 3/4	Geelong	2 3/4		1/4	Transvaal Development	1/4	
1/16	Henderson's Est.	1/8		3/4	United Rhodesia	3/4	
1 1/4	Johannesburg Con. In.	1 1/4	– 1/16	1 1/4	Willoughby	1 1/16	– 1/16
1/16	Do. Water	1	+ 1/16	3/4	Zambesia Explor.	3/4	
1 3/8	Mashonaland Agency	1 1/16					

MISCELLANEOUS.

Making-Up Price, June 8.	Name	Closing Price.	Rise or Fall.	Making-Up Price, June 8.	Name	Closing Price.	Rise or Fall.
1	Alamillos, £2	1		1/4	Mount Lyell, South	1/16	+ 1/16
4 3/4	Anaconda, $25	4 11/16	+ 1/8	4 1/16	Mount Morgan, 17s. 6d.	4 1/16	+ 1/16
6/3	Balaghât, 18/	9/		5 3/4	Mysore, 10s.	5 11/16	– 1/16
12/	Brilliant, £2	12/	– /6	8/	Mysore Goldfields	9/	+ 1/6
2 1/2	Do. St. George's	2 3/8	+ 1/8	5/6	Do. Reefs, 17/	6/	+ /3
9/6	British Broken Hill	8/9		3/9	Do. West	6/	+ 1/
2 1/8	Broken Hill Proprietary	2 1/16		2/9	Do. Wynaad	4/6	+ /9
3	Do. Block 10	3		2 3/4	Namaqua, £2	2 1/4	+ 1/16
4 3/4	Cape Copper, £2	4 1/16	– 1/16	3 13/16	Nundydroog	3 13/16	+ 1/16
4 3/4	Champion Reef, 10s.	4 11/16	+ 1/16	3 1/16	Ooregum	3 1/16	+ 1/16
2 1/4	Copiapo, £2	2 1/4		3 1/16	Do. Pref.	3 1/4	+ 1/8
2 3/4	Coromandel	2 3/4		26 1/4	Rio Tinto £5	25 11/16	– 1/8
15/	Day Dawn Block	15/		6	Do. Pref. £5	6	
2 1/16	Frontino & Bolivia	2 1/4	– 1/16	1	St. John del Rey	20/	
1 1/16	Hall Mines	1 1/16		8/9	Taitipu	3/4	+ 1/16
2 1/2	Libiola, £5	2 1/2		6 1/4	Tharsis, £2	6 1/4	
7 1/2	Linares, £3	7 1/4	+ 1/4	1 1/2	Tolima "A," £5	2	
3 3/4	Mason & Barry, £3	3 3/4		4 3/8	Waihi	4 3/8	– 1/16
4 3/8	Mountain Copper, £5	4 1/4	+ 1/8	1 1/4	Waitekauri	1 1/4	
10 1/2	Mount Lyell, £3	9 1/4	– 1 1/4	16/3	Woodstock (N.Z.)	[illegible]	
2 3/8	Mount Lyell, North	2	– 3/8				

The quarterly coupons of the Mexican external 6 per cent. loan of 1890; the Mexican Government Consolidated External 6 per Cent. Loan of 1888; and the United States of Mexico (San Luis Potosi) 6 per cent. loan, and drawn bonds of the latter issue, due July 1, can now be presented for payment on that or any subsequent day at the counting-house of Messrs. Antony Gibbs & Sons, 15, Bishopsgate-street, Within. Coupons and drawn bonds must be left three clear days for examination. The numbers of the bonds of the two first named loans, purchased on the market in accordance with the redemption schemes, will shortly be published.

The Rio Tinto Company, Limited, announce payment of the drawn Bonds and Coupons on their 4 per cent. First Mortgage bonds due 1st prox. They invite holders to present coupons and drawn bonds at once.

Notes on Books.

Le Marché Financier en 1897–1898. Par Arthur Raffalovich, Correspondant de l'Institut. Paris: Librairie Guillaumin et Cie.

This annual volume grows larger with each publication and increases also in value. At present we can merely notice its issue and must reserve analysis of some of the excellent essays it contains until another opportunity. In the meantime, however, we may say that no other book published, so far as we know, gives such full and reliable accounts of the financial position and economic progress of Russia as this does. And the essays on France, Germany, Austria, Spain, and Italy are all most valuable for reference purposes in spite of their occasional optimism. Appended to the chapters dealing specially with various countries of the world, as usual, are interesting monographs on the precious metals and on monetary questions in which statistics relating to the production of gold, monetary circulations in various countries, and so on, are embodied. Altogether Mr. Raffalovich is to be congratulated on the ability, industry, and discretion with which this annual volume is put together.

La Question des Limites Chilo-Argentines. Par HENRI S. DELACHAUX. Paris: Armand Colin et Cie., Editeurs, 5, Rue de Mézières.

This short paper loses somewhat of its interest to us in being the reply to another article we have not seen, by Dr. Steffen. Taken by itself, however, it is an exceedingly clear and able exposition of the nature of the dispute between the Argentine and Chilian Republics over the question of the boundary of their territories. M. Delachaux, who dates his article from La Plata, goes over the history of this long dispute in a very clear and careful manner, showing that it has its origin in the ignorance of the old Spanish viceroys and their officials. When South America from Paraguay on the east and from Panama on the west was Spanish territory, the tide of immigration naturally worked its way inwards from great centres of communication with Europe, such as the Rio de la Plata and the ports of the Pacific. The Chilian population, hemmed in by the Andes, naturally worked their way south much more rapidly than those of Buenos Ayres, which had a vast breadth of territory to spread themselves over, and the Chilians consequently came first in contact with Patagonia, but there was never any delimitation of the boundaries of the two provinces, and when the question came ultimately to be taken up, the data upon which the boundary could be fixed were extremely vague. Out of ignorance of the past the present difficulty has arisen, and dispute has raged around the point whether the boundary was to be fixed by the highest peaks of the Andes, as far as the Andes went south, or by the watershed. M. Delachaux clearly proves that the watershed theory is impracticable, because many streams arise in the Andes and flow eastward for a time only to be driven back towards the Pacific by obstructions created principally through ice action. Towards the south the difficulty was increased by the occupation of the Straits of Magellan by the Chilians. The whole dispute, however, is now in a fair way to be completely settled, and the writer of this interesting essay winds up with the expression of a confident opinion that in the near future the hardy Chilian pioneer will meet the Argentine workman and seal a bond of everlasting friendship at the completely settled boundary of their respective territories. We trust this prophecy will prove accurate, for nothing could be more disastrous to all South America than a dispute leading to blows between these two great Republics.

MINING RETURNS.

BARNATO GROUP.—Outputs for May:—New Primrose, 9,967 oz.; Ginsberg, 3,044 oz.; New Spes Bona, 1,844 oz.; Roodepoort, 1,303 oz.; Balmoral Main Reef, 1,633 oz.; Glencairn Main Reef, 8,430 oz.; New Rietfontein Estate, 2,161 oz.; Rietfontein "A," 4,316 oz.; Buffelsdoorn Estate, 2,863 oz.; Consolidated Main Reef Mines and Estate, 2,472 oz. from 6,163 tons battery, 1,186 oz. from 4,200 tons cyanide.

EAGLEHAWK CONSOLIDATED.—300 tons, yielding 177 oz. of gold for the last fortnight.

GELDENHUIS.—Crushed 17,523 tons; obtained from mill, 6,396 oz.; from concentrates by cyanide, 928 oz.; from tailings, 2,710 oz.; from slimes, 663 oz.

GEORGE GOCH.—8,844 tons crushed, yielding 1,428 oz. gold, and 1,078 oz. of gold from tailings.

HANNAN'S BROWNHILL.—Old Mill, 615 tons sands, and 450 tons slimes treated; 2,600 oz. of gold recovered.

JUMPERS.—Results for May:—Crushed 12,000 tons, obtained from mill, 4,028 oz. of gold; obtained from concentrates by cyanide, 60 oz. of gold; obtained from tailings by cyanide, 1,378 oz. of gold.

NEW GUADALCAZAR QUICKSILVER.—The production of quicksilver for the past month amounts to 9,800 lb. = 130½ flasks.

NOURSE DEEP.—Tons crushed by sixty stamps, 7,611; yield in fine gold, 2,209 oz. Tons of sands and concentrates treated by cyanide works, 5,940; yield in fine gold, 1,851 oz.; total yield in bullion ounces, 4,891, equal to 4,060 oz. fine gold.

PAARL CENTRAL.—Results for May:—From mill, crushed 6,593 tons; yielding 2,352 oz. of gold. From cyanide: treated 4,505 tons, yielding 920 oz. of gold.

PREMIER TATI MONARCH REEF.—1,650 tons crushed, including 290 tons surface low grade ore; yield of retorted gold, 382 oz. Tailings not treated.

PRINCESS ESTATE.—Result for May:—Crushed 5,660 tons, producing 1,958 oz.; 4,135 tons treated by cyanide yielded 841 oz.

VILLAGE MAIN REEF.—Total yield from all sources, approximately, 8,728 oz. of gold.

WITWATERSRANDT GOLD (KNIGHTS).—Mill ran twenty-six days, crushing 16,450 tons, yielding 4,812 oz. of gold; 12,580 tons cyanide tailings treated yielding 1,699 oz. gold.

BLOCK B LANGLAAGTE.—Mill—ore crushed, 10,680 tons of 2,000 lb.; gold retorted, 2,662 oz. Tailings, cyanide process—tons treated, 6,300; gold recovered, 1,265 oz. Concentrates, cyanide process—tons treated, 176; gold recovered, 375 oz.

CASSEL COAL.—Output for May, 20,530 tons.

CITY AND SUBURBAN.—Last month's crushing yielded 11,510 oz.

CROWN REEF.—Crushed, 16,181 tons; yield in smelted gold from mill, 6,860 oz. from cyanide works, 3,784 oz.; from slimes works, 496 oz.

DURBAN-ROODEPOORT.—Quartz milled, 10,210 tons; recovered, 5,072 oz.; tailings treated, 7,020 tons for 1,218 oz.

GELDENHUIS MAIN REEF.—2,100 tons crushed, yielding 503 oz.; 1,320 tons treated by cyanide, yielding 170 oz.

LANGLAAGTE.—Ore crushed, 24,704 tons of 2,000 lb.; gold retorted, 8,147 oz. Tailings, cyanide process—tons treated, 13,950; gold recovered, 1,968 oz. Concentrates, cyanide process—tons treated, 747; gold recovered, 1,889 oz.

LANGLAAGTE STAR.—Ore crushed, 5,274 tons of 2,000 lb.; gold retorted, 1,629 oz. Tailings, cyanide process—tons treated, 4,380; gold recovered, 626 oz. Concentrates, cyanide process—tons treated, 60; gold recovered, 118 oz.

LE CHAMP D'OR.—Crushed, 5,392 tons, yielding 2,170 oz.; cyanide—3,675 tons treated, yielding 833 oz.; concentrates, 76 oz.

OTTOS KOPJE.—6,398 loads washed during the week ended June 9, 207 carats won.

NEW HERIOT.—Last month's crushing yielded 4,639 oz.

NORTH RANDFONTEIN.—Mill—ore crushed, 4,592 tons of 2,000 lb.; gold retorted, 1,069 oz. Tailings, cyanide process—tons treated, 2,640; gold recovered, 365 oz. Concentrates, cyanide process—tons treated, 70; gold recovered, 150 oz.

PORGES RANDFONTEIN.—Mill—ore crushed, 7,630 tons of 2,000 lb.; gold retorted, 2,364 oz. Tailings, cyanide process—tons treated, 5,258; gold recovered, 622 oz. Concentrates, cyanide process—tons treated, 118; gold recovered, 407 oz.

ROBINSON DEEP.—8,620 tons yielded 5,389 oz. of gold; 5,000 tons were treated by cyanide, yielding 2,350 oz.

ROBINSON RANDFONTEIN.—Mill—ore crushed, 5,500 tons of 2,000 lb.; gold retorted, 1,948 oz. Tailings, cyanide process—tons treated, 3,960; gold recovered, 564 oz. Concentrates, cyanide process—tons treated, 88; gold recovered, 204 oz.

SIMMER AND JACK.—Crushed, 35,140 tons; obtained 10,604 oz. of gold from mill; 4,204 oz. of gold from tailings by cyanide, and 726 oz. of gold from slimes.

TREASURY.—Output for May, 5,612 tons; yielded 3,574 oz.

WEST RAND.—Crushed 3,600 tons, yielded 698 oz.; cyanide—treated 2,685 tons, yielded 569 oz.

WINDSOR.—From mill—crushed, 4,030 tons; obtained 1,271 oz. From cyanide works—obtained, 835 oz.

DIORITE KING (W. A.)—Clean up for the months of April and May—154 oz. of gold from 100 tons crushed.

GOLD REEFS OF WEST AFRICA.—Crushed during May, 280 tons of ore, which have yielded about 315 oz. of gold. The gold produced for the months of March and April realised £2,613.

LISBON-BERLYN.—Ore mined, 2,050 tons; ore crushed, 2,150 tons; treated by cyanide, 2,000 tons; fine gold recovered, 640 oz.

MOUNT LYELL.—From May 5 to June 1, inclusive, a total quantity of 12,300 tons of ore has been treated, 11,602 tons from open cuts assaying before treatment—copper, 3·24 per cent.; silver, 3·75 oz. per ton; gold, ·169 oz. per ton; 698 tons from No. 4 tunnel assaying before treatment—copper, 7·00 per cent.; silver, 8·22 oz. per ton; gold, ·088 oz. per ton. The converters have produced during same period 372 tons of blister copper containing—copper, 367 tons; silver, 44,992 oz.; gold, 2,007 oz.

NEW ZEALAND CROWN.—During May 1,823 tons mined, and 1,664 tons crushed. Value of bullion, £3,442.

YORK.—4,594 tons of ore crushed in May, yielding 1,325 oz., while 3,510 tons of tailings gave 692 oz.

CAYLLOMA SILVER.—May production, 19,250 oz. in export ores and 500 oz. in bullion.

FRONTINO AND BOLIVIA.—Produce value £9,523.

HYDERABAD DECCAN.—The output of coal from the Sinareni Collieries for the four weeks ended May 21 was 32,386 tons.

LAKE VIEW CONSOLS.—Crushed, 5,526 tons, yielding 4,867 oz.; by cyanide, 3,370 tons of tailings treated, yielded 2,668 oz.; 2,045 tons of slimes treated yielded 717 oz.; concentrates, 25 tons, value 624 oz. of gold; sulphides shipped, 95 tons, value 293 oz. of gold.

ROBINSON.—Mill crushed 15,191 tons of ore, yielding in smelted gold 10,049 oz.; from concentrates, by chlorination, 1,198 oz.; from tailings, cyanide process, 3,430 oz.; from slimes, 952 oz.; from concentrates bought, by chlorination, 2,673 oz.

WENTWORTH GOLDFIELDS.—800 tons of ore have been crushed, yielding 1,015 oz., and one ton of rich crude ore has been shipped containing 180 oz.

MOUNT CHARLOTTE GOLD.—Crushed 300 tons yielding 120 oz.

CENTRAL BOULDER.—Second return—135 tons, 151 oz.

PRINCESS ROYAL (CUE).—Clean up from 260 tons gave 176 oz.

NOURSE DEEP.—For three months ending April 30:—Ore developed, 14,324 tons; ore mined, 26,992 tons. Total yield, fine gold 12,125,033 oz. Profit per ton 14s. 0·490d. Capital expenditure, £16,797.

GEORGE GOCH GOLD.—Result for May:—8,844 tons crushed, yielded 1,428 oz. of gold, and 1,078 oz. from tailings.

NEW PRIMROSE.—9,967 oz.; profit, £14,515.

GINSBERG.—3,044 oz.; profit, £5,937

NEW SPES BONA.—1,844 oz.

ROODEPOORT.—1,303 oz.

BALMORAL MAIN REEF.—1,633 oz.

GLENCAIRN MAIN REEF.—6,430 oz.; profit, £9,317.

NEW RIETFONTEIN.—2,161 oz.

RIETFONTEIN "A."—4,316 oz.; profit, £6,752.

BUFFELSDOORN ESTATE.—2,863 oz.

CONSOLIDATED MAIN REEF.—2,472 oz. from 6,163 tons, crushed. 1,186 oz. from 4,200 tons cyanide.

TRANSVAAL.—From mill:—Crushed, 9,257 tons; obtained 3,262 oz. of fine gold, equal to 3,559 oz. standard gold. From outside cyanide works:—Treated, 2,150 tons, yielding 883 oz. of fine gold, equal to 963 oz. standard gold. From central cyanide works:—Treated (during last two months), 8,080 tons, yielding 2,600 oz. of fine gold, equal to 2,836 oz. standard gold.

The directors of the English and Scottish Law Life Assurance Association have, on the retirement of Mr. G. F. Hardy, F.I.A., from the position of actuary, appointed Mr. James Douglas Watson to that position, Mr. Hardy continuing his connection with the association as consulting actuary.

The London committee of the shareholders of the Central Pacific Railroad Company announce that a general meeting of the holders of the certificates issued by them will be held in Winchester House, on Tuesday, the 28th inst., at 2 o'clock p.m.

The numbers are published of bonds of the State of San Luis Potosi (United States of Mexico) 6 per cent. loan, which have been drawn for payment on July 1 at Messrs. Antony Gibbs & Sons', Bishopsgate-street Within.

AFRICAN MINING RETURNS.

Dividends Declared in 1896	1897	1898	Capital Issued.	Nominal Amount of Share.	Name of Company.	Monthly Crushings. March. Tons.	Oz.	Dwt. per ton.	April. Tons.	Oz.	Dwt. per ton.	May. Tons.	Oz.	Dwt. per ton.	Totals. Months.	Ozs.	Profits Declared. Mar.	April.	May.	Totals. Months.	—	Stamps now Working.
p.c.	p.c.	p.c.	£	£													£	£	£		£	
—	—	25	225,000	1	Angelo	11,701	5,712	9.8	12,442	6,120	9.8	12,357	6,561	10.6	5	30,124	12,617	13,276	—	4	52,132	60
—	—	—	130,000	1	Balmoral	12,740	2,425	3.8	10,260	2,045	3.9	—	1,633	—	5	10,436	1,107	—	—	3	3,107	40
—	75	50	200,000	1	Bonanza	11,317	8,227	14.5	10,184	8,115	15.9	10,900	7,949	14.6	5	40,068	20,429	20,639	19,763	5	98,866	40
—	—	—	550,000	1	Buffelsdoorn ..	19,097	2,902	3.0	18,088	2,225	2.4	—	2,863	—	5	14,631	—	—	—	—	—	65
—	—	—	133,000	1	Champ d'Or ..	9,357	2,968	6.3	9,278	3,176	6.8	9,067	3,079	6.8	5	15,432	—	—	—	—	—	50
5	15	7½	1,360,000	4	City and Suburban	32,223	11,030	6.9	32,099	11,496	7.1	—	11,510	—	5	54,746	17,326	18,620	18,893	5	88,843	160
—	—	—	224,635	1	Comet	8,626	2,928	6.8	9,111	3,048	6.6	—	3,137	—	5	15,312	4,124	4,832	—	4	18,582	40
—	—	—	300,000	1	Crown Deep ..	40,390	9,718	4.8	40,520	12,632	6.2	45,192	12,945	5.7	5	58,970	10,700	13,800	16,100	5	66,712	160
210	170	100	120,000	1	Crown Reef	33,614	12,080	7.2	27,337	11,431	8.4	—	11,140	—	5	57,093	22,656	19,977	20,497	5	104,046	120
55	80	40	125,000	1	Durban Roodepoort	16,665	6,341	7.6	17,250	6,228	7.2	—	6,290	—	5	32,143	—	—	—	—	—	80
275	300	—	90,000	1	Ferreira	19,723	12,814	13.0	25,556	13,437	10.5	—	13,045	—	5	63,665	27,890	—	—	3	82,985	80
12½	45	50	200,000	1	Geldenhuis Estate ..	30,686	10,743	7.0	32,218	10,554	6.5	—	10,697	—	5	52,101	20,838	21,110	—	4	78,248	120
—	30	—	300,000	1	Geldenhuis Deep ..	48,268	12,810	5.3	47,900	13,124	5.3	46,712	13,277	5.7	5	62,070	21,100	22,300	23,100	5	102,600	190
—	10	—	150,000	1	Gelden. Main Reef	4,274	952	4.5	1,449	329	4.6	3,420	673	3.9	5	3,688	241	a1,179	a184	5	a2,506	30
—	—	—	325,000	1	George Goch ..	13,773	3,007	4.3	13,909	2,737	3.9	—	2,506	—	5	14,268	—	—	—	—	—	120
—	25	—	160,000	1	Ginsberg	9,143	2,591	5.6	9,382	2,875	6.1	—	3,044	—	5	13,047	4,731	5,666	5,937	5	23,930	40
—	—	—	500,000	1	Glencairn	27,775	6,958	5.0	25,686	6,747	5.3	—	6,430	—	5	33,396	10,264	10,040	9,317	5	50,967	110
30	125	—	125,000	1	Henry Nourse ..	15,130	8,308	10.9	15,105	8,262	10.9	14,670	8,316	12.7	5	40,216	17,452	17,646	17,633	5	83,784	60
85	100	50	111,864	1	Heriot	15,071	5,824	7.7	14,862	5,306	7.8	—	4,659	—	5	27,858	8,705	10,221	5,958	5	44,556	70
350	500	275	21,000	1	Johan. Pioneer ..	5,600	4,105	14.6	5,148	4,086	15.9	—	—	—	4	15,779	—	—	—	1	9,950	30
60	90	25	50,000	1	Jubilee	8,991	2,798	6.2	8,150	2,580	6.3	—	1,552	—	5	12,820	—	—	—	-	—	50
30	60	—	100,000	1	Jumpers	18,620	5,073	5.4	18,760	5,398	5.7	—	6,009	—	5	27,206	5,370	6,750	8,315	5	34,745	100
—	—	—	231,250	1	Kleinfontein ..	19,061	4,655	4.9	17,648	4,443	5.0	17,609	4,509	5.1	5	23,712	4,370	4,752	—	4	19,468	95
—	—	—	312,180	1	Knight's	25,680	5,476	4.3	23,440	5,656	4.8	29,030	6,511	4.5	5	28,343	4,400	5,400	7,100	5	25,356	120
30	30	—	470,000	1	Langlaagte Estate ..	31,119	10,191	6.6	32,842	11,191	6.8	39,401	12,014	6.1	5	50,028		—	—	—	—	190
—	—	—	550,000	1	Lang. Block B. ..	19,812	4,927	5.0	17,825	4,434	5.0	17,256	4,303	5.0	5	23,139	—	—	—	—	—	80
—	—	—	250,000	1	Langlaagte Star ..	11,062	3,498	6.3	10,273	3,114	6.0	9,294	2,373	5.1	5	16,440	—	—	—	—	—	35
20	—	—	275,000	1	May Consolidated	23,390	7,860	6.7	21,773	8,131	7.4	—	—	—	4	29,871	12,213	12,985	—	4	45,183	100
20	50	25	85,000	1	Meyer and Charlton	15,258	3,895	5.1	14,727	3,936	5.3	—	4,003	—	5	19,679	5,596	5,706	5,663	5	28,206	80
—	—	—	949,620	4	Modderfontein ..	12,769	3,677	5.8	11,631	3,840	6.6	—	4,244	—	4	14,596	—	—	—	—	—	60
—	—	—	200,000	1	Nigel	7,440	2,868	7.7	7,428	3,206	8.6	—	3,212	—	5	14,890	—	—	—	—	—	25
—	—	—	300,000	1	Nth. Randfontein ..	9,892	2,393	4.8	10,638	2,225	4.2	7,302	1,584	4.3	5	10,118	—	—	—	—	—	40
—	—	—	374,934	1	Nourse Deep ..	13,728	4,860	7.1	13,146	4,913	7.5	13,551	4,891	7.2	5	24,706	5,200	5,400	4,500	5	28,414	60
—	—	—	400,000	1	Paarl Central ..	11,315	2,611	4.6	9,410	2,059	4.4	11,098	2,272	4.1	5	12,017	—	—	—	—	—	60
—	10	—	487,500	1	Porges Randfontein	12,581	3,541	5.6	13,439	3,541	5.3	13,006	3,393	5.2	5	17,988	—	—	—	—	—	60
—	50	—	300,000	1	Primrose	39,945	9,484	4.7	37,241	9,653	5.2	—	9,967	—	5	47,065	12,492	13,470	14,515	5	64,604	160
—	10	—	165,000	1	Princess Estate ..	8,755	2,720	6.1	9,250	2,730	5.9	9,795	2,799	5.7	5	13,831	1,750	1,861	—	4	7,353	40
—	—	—	270,000	1	Rietfontein	10,878	2,087	3.8	10,047	2,277	4.5	—	2,161	—	5	10,922	—	65	—	2	3,180	50
—	—	—	300,000	1	Rietfontein "A" ..	13,553	4,737	7.0	13,904	4,863	7.0	—	4,316	—	5	24,510	7,566	8,832	6,752	5	43,977	60
22	15	—	2,750,000	5	Robinson	32,690	b16,454	10.0	32,666	b16,379	10.0	—	b15,629	—	5	79,239	37,021	37,500	38,000	5	184,051	120
—	—	—	600,000	1	Robinson R'dfontein	8,177	2,606	6.6	8,601	2,833	6.6	9,448	2,716	5.7	5	14,152	—	—	—	—	—	40
—	—	—	175,000	1	Roodepoort Gold ..	4,527	986	4.4	4,846	1,138	4.7	—	1,303	—	5	5,643	—	233	—	1	233	40
25	40	25	150,000	1	Roodepoort United	13,159	3,922	6.0	12,704	4,092	6.4	—	3,778	—	5	20,272	5,350	6,138	6,255	5	31,655	70
—	—	—	400,000	1	Rose Deep	29,424	10,166	6.3	31,832	10,223	6.4	29,069	10,106	6.9	5	48,821	15,100	13,500	14,700	5	72,132	122
—	—	—	100,000	1	Salisbury	9,147	2,636	5.8	8,036	2,506	6.2	—	1,700	—	5	11,745	—	3,157	—	2	6,336	50
20	20	3½	1,075,000	1	Sheba	10,700	4,370	8.1	10,310	4,754	9.2	13,775	5,305	7.7	5	26,759	—	—	—	—	—	120
—	—	—	4,700,000	5	Simmer and Jack ..	53,660	11,490	4.3	64,580	14,351	4.4	—	15,536	—	5	60,551	—	—	—	—	—	100
—	—	—	235,000	1	Spes Bona	8,626	2,122	4.9	8,944	1,894	4.2	—	1,844	—	5	10,180	547	413	—	3	1,411	40
—	15	—	35,000	1	Stanhope	4,690	980	4.2	4,140	989	4.8	—	918	—	5	4,999	—	—	—	—	—	20
—	—	—	604,225	1	Trans. G. M. Est. ..	18,277	6,769	7.4	12,099	4,807	7.9	19,487	7,358	7.5	5	20,679	13,126	4,934	—	4	38,598	75
—	—	10	540,000	4	Treasury	9,744	3,813	7.8	10,600	3,649	6.9	—	3,574	—	5	18,465	6,920	6,328	6,120	5	31,680	40
—	—	—	300,000	1	Van Ryn	18,713	4,373	4.7	19,537	4,373	4.5	19,992	4,357	4.4	5	21,030	3,100	5,300	—	4	13,358	80
—	—	—	260,000	1	Village Main Reef ..	12,908	5,964	9.3	16,950	8,030	9.4	—	8,728	—	5	31,579	8,000	12,000	13,000	4	41,621	65
75	100	75	80,000	1	Wemmer	12,139	6,243	12.8	11,363	6,310	11.1	11,834	6,076	12.7	5	30,504	12,987	12,764	12,075	5	63,577	50
—	—	—	400,000	1	West Rand	6,665	1,770	5.3	6,386	1,466	4.6	6,285	1,267	4.0	5	8,176	—	—	—	1	1,374	30
—	—	—	—	1	Windsor	6,362	1,844	5.6	7,198	1,971	5.5	—	2,106	—	5	9,608	3,027	3,139	3,243	4	12,139	40
—	10	7½	860,000	4	Wolhuter	23,251	6,036	6.0	21,286	6,823	6.4	—	7,186	—	5	35,179	8,452	7,097	9,009	5	44,408	100
55	30	15	95,722	1	Worcester	4,936	2,674	10.8	5,000	2,631	10.5	—	2,764	—	5	13,310	4,907	—	—	3	14,630	40
—	—	—	90,000	1	York	8,796	1,821	4.1	7,734	1,461	3.8	8,104	2,017	4.9	5	9,802	—	—	—	—	—	40

a Loss. b Exclusive of yield from Concentrates bought—2,913 oz. in March, 2,914 oz. in April, and 2,673 oz. in May.

AFRICAN MINE CRUSHINGS.

The May output of the Witwatersrand again supplies a "record," the total being 344,160 oz., compared with 335,125 oz. in April. In the outside districts the yield was 20,856 ozs. as compared with 18,118 oz. Amongst individual mines much better results were given by the Angelo, Jumpers, Jumpers Deep, Langlaagte Estate Modderfontein, Sheba, Simmer & Jack, Village Main Reefs, Knights and York Companies. But the increased yield is often due to more stamps being in use, for the Langlaagte Company had twenty more stamps at work and the Robinson Randfontein and Langlaagte Star Companies five more each. On the other hand, the Balmoral Company had ten stamps less in use, and the Robinson group of mines again refer to the great scarcity of native workmen at the mines. Among the companies which gave poor results may be mentioned the Balmoral, Glencairn, Jubilee, Langlaagte Star, Heriot, North Randfontein, Rietfontein "A," and Salisbury. The May Company owing to shortness of water appears to have yielded nothing. On the whole, the total output grows slowly, and the improvement, month by month, is due to more stamps being at work or to more companies crushing, and not to richer ore being dealt with. Thus last month's output was larger by 9,035 oz. than the April return, but the Robinson Deep made a return for the first time which accounts for 7,739 oz. of this increase, while the Drietfontein Company, which made its first return for April as 1,500 oz., has got into better working form, and increased its output for May to 7,422 oz. So if allowance is made for these two new crushers the returns from the old companies were less instead of showing any increase.

The interest due July 1 next on the Brazilian Government Treasury bills, dated January 1, 1898, also Series A of these bills, due July 1, amounting to £500,000, will be paid by Messrs. N. M. Rothschild & Sons on and after the 1st prox.

The British Bank of South America, Limited, notify to holders of the 6 per cent. debenture bonds of the Cantareira Water Supply and Drainage Company of the City of Sao Paulo that the interest thereon due on the 1st proximo will be paid by them on and after that date, together with the bonds drawn for redemption on the 1st inst.

Messrs. Blake, Boissevain, & Co. are pay, on and after the 1st prox., the sterling coupons of the City of Providence 5 per cent. water loan bonds due on that date. They will also pay the coupons then due on the 5 per cent. collateral trust gold bonds of the Chicago Junction Railways and Union Stockyards Company at the fixed rate of £5 2s. 6d. per coupon of 25 dollars.

Messrs. Rothbarth & Co. have removed from 9, Southwark-street, S.E., to 18, St. Thomas-street, Borough, S.E.

Mr. Robert Steel has been elected a director of the Delhi Umballa Kalka Railway Company, Limited.

ENGLISH RAILWAYS.

Div. for half years. 1896	1896	1897	1897	Last Balance forward.	Amt. to pay 1 p.c. on Ord. for ½ yr.	Name.	Date. †	Gross Traffic for week: Amt.	Inc. or dec. on 1897.	Inc. or dec. on 1896.	No. of weeks	Gross Traffic for half-year to date: Amt.	Inc. or dec. on 1897.	Inc. or dec. on 1896.	Mileage.	Inc. on 1897.	Working	Prior Charges last ½ year.	Prop. add Cap. Exp. this ½ year
				£	£												%	£	£
10	10	10	10	2,707	5,094	Barry	J'ne 11	2,699	−5,066	−5,388	24	154,297	−55,923	−26,036	31	—	8·89	60,665	316,853
nil	nil	nil	nil	—	—	Brecon and Merthyr	" 12	1,173	−536	−443	24	32,447	−2,778	−6,056	61	—	—	—	—
nil	nil	nil	nil	3,979	4,749	Cambrian	" 12	5,441	−628	+185	*	115,228	+3,133	—	250	—	60·96	63,148	40,000
1½	1½	2	1½	1,310	3,150	City and South London ..	" 12	931	+51	+54	24	24,558	+343	+2,216	3¼	—	56·67	5,552	124,000
	2	1½	2	7,895	13,220	Furness	" 12	9,944	+186	+1,215	*	209,710	+6,456	—	139	—	49·88	97,423	20,910
1	1½	½	1	2,207	27,470	Great Cent. (late M.,S.,& L.)	" 12	53,307	+4,936	+3,361	23	1,050,549	+30,138	+64,867	352½	—	57·17	627,386	1,200,000
1½	4¾	2	5	51,283	62,865	Great Eastern	" 12	83,009	−9,880	+5,696	23	1,873,650	+49,881	+158079	1,158½	2	55·35	860,138	250,000
3	5½	3	5	15,094	102,496	Great Northern	" 12	95,775	+9,676	+9,614	24	2,276,347	+72,697	+181090	1,073	10	61·36	641,485	750,000
4¾	7½	4¾	7½	31,350	121,981	Great Western	" 12	179,140	−22,200	−9,200	23	4,048,680	−40,800	+111620	2,582	21	51·44	1,486,272	800,000
nil	2	nil	1½	8,951	16,487	Hull and Barnsley	" 12	8,866	+2,776	+1,374	23	163,210	+11,425	+23,313	73	—	58·21	70,290	52,900
5	5¾	5	5½	21,495	83,704	Lancashire and Yorkshire ..	" 12	99,401	−18,611	+6,493	23	2,182,543	+73,732	+83,056	555½	25	56·70	674,745	451,976
4¾	8	4¾	8½	26,243	43,049	Lon., Brighton, & S. Coast	" 11	54,508	−4,713	+3,051	24	1,194,000	+34,881	+55,878	476½	—	50·20	407,042	240,735
nil	nil	nil	nil	72,294	56,296	London, Chatham, & Dover	" 12	30,100	−1,825	+899	23	648,660	+14,451	+30,944	185½	—	50·65	367,873	nil
6½	8	6½	7¾	89,535	204,068	London and North Western	" 12	241,631	−10,429	+9,122	23	5,341,832	+121838	+298086	1,911½	—	56·92	1,404,534	600,000
5	8½	8¼	8¼	23,038	59,367	London and South Western	" 12	77,305	−5,770	+5,522	23	1,639,264	+45,637	+108982	941	—	51·75	513,740	389,080
2½	6	2½	6½	14,592	6,691	Lon., Tilbury, & Southend	" 12	6,164	−2,300	+747	24	125,150	+5,232	+17,414	81	—	52·57	39,590	15,000
3½	3¾	3¾	3¾	17,133	26,409	Metropolitan	" 12	17,357	+135	+1,729	*	381,106	+8,504	—	64	—	43·63	148,047	254,000
nil	nil	nil	nil	4,006	11,250	Metropolitan District ..	" 12	8,116	−275	−29	23	194,774	+6,300	—	13	—	48·70	119,663	38,450
5	7	5½	6½	38,143	174,582	Midland	" 12	206,594	+45,737	+39,963	24	4,469,708	+110564	+384332	1,354¾	15½	57·59	1,216,582	650,000
5½	7½	5¾	7	22,374	138,189	North Eastern	" 11	138,561	−34,113	+4,494	23	3,372,769	+53,565	+231075	1,597¾	—	58·82	795,077	436,204
7⅛	7⅛	7⅛	7½	7,061	10,102	North London	" 12	8,988	+50	+325	23	216,164	−1,217	—	12	—	50·90	49,973	7,600
4	5	4	4¾	4,745	16,150	North Staffordshire	" 12	14,302	−3,259	−557	24	373,571	+3,637	+20,192	312	—	55·27	118,142	19,605
10	10	11	10	1,642	3,004	Rhymney	" 11	1,649	−2,367	−3,341	24	92,033	−25,930	−17,737	71	—	49·68	29,049	16,700
	6¾	3½	6¾	4,054	50,215	South Eastern	" 11	51,486	−5,248	—	*	1,023,981	+48,646	—	448	—	51·88	380,763	250,000
3½	3½	2½	3½	2,315	25,961	Taff Vale	" 11	5,821	−8,241	−10,233	24	275,668	−98,012	−76,386	121	—	54·90	94,800	92,000

* From January 1. † Includes Whit Monday, 1897.

SCOTCH RAILWAYS.

5	5	5½	5	9,544	78,066	Caledonian	June 12	74,670	+ 1,109	+ 5,129	19	1,405,864	+ 34,957	—	851½	5	50·38	588,248	441,477
5	5½	5	5	7,364	24,639	Glasgow and South-Western	" 11	30,967	+ 540	+ 2,067	19	542,567	+ 18,320	—	393½	—	54·69	221,663	196,245
3½	3½	3½	—	1,291	4,600	Great North of Scotland	" 11	9,098	+ 249	+ 818	19	156,540	+ 333	+ 7,139	331	15½	52·03	92,178	60,000
	nil		—	10,477	12,820	Highland	" 12	10,046	− 68	+ 54	15	136,460	+ 2,291	—	479¾	27½	58·63	78,976	,000
	1½	1	1½	819	45,819	North British	" 12	75,125	+ 2,040	+ 4,076	19	1,378,498	+ 41,591	—	1,230	23	48·62	944,809	40,800

IRISH RAILWAYS.

6½	6½	6½	—	5,466	1,790	Belfast and County Down ..	June 10	2,531	− 479	− 347	*	51,967	− 423	—	76½	—	35·58	17,690	10,000
5½	6½	5½	—	—	4,284	Belfast and Northern Counties	" 10	5,058	− 590	− 240	*	119,278	+ 3,640	—	249	—	—	—	—
	3	2	—	1,418	1,900	Cork, Bandon, and S. Coast† ..	" 11	1,647	− 271	− 220	*	99,715	− 2,627	—	103	—	54·82	14,436	5,450
	6½	6½	6½	38,776	17,816	Great Northern	" 10	15,223	− 1,597	+ 450	23	341,363	+ 10,762	+ 21,385	528	—	50·15	88,068	22,000
	5½	5½	5½	30,339	24,855	Great Southern and Western ..	" 3	—	—	—	not	received	—	—	603	13	51·45	72,802	46,582
	4	4	4½	11,372	11,850	Midland Great Western ..	" 10	10,848	− 785		23	231,610	+ 7,092	− 1,991	338	—	50·31	83,129	1,800
nil	nil	nil	nil	229	2,822	Waterford and Central ..	" 10	871	+ 23	+ 11	*	—	—	—	59½	—	53·24	6,858	1,900
nil	nil	nil	nil	1,936	2,987	Waterford, Limerick & W. ..	" 3	4,382	+ 17	+ 131	*	—	—	—	350½	--	57·83	42,617	7,075

* From January 1. † Seventeen weeks' strike.

DIVIDENDS ANNOUNCED.

MISCELLANEOUS.

Browne & Eagle, Limited.—Interim dividend of 6s. on the ordinary shares, payable on 30th inst. Warrants posted at same time for six months' interest on preference shares and debenture stock.

Distiller's Company, Limited.—12s. per share, together with a bonus of 5s. per share, payable on August 1.

Copiapo Mining Company, Limited.—2s. per share, payable on and after the 21st inst.

Durban-Roodepoort Gold Mining Company, Limited.—Interim dividend of 4s. per share, payable on June 30.

Meyer and Charlton Gold Mining Company, Limited.—25 per cent. has been declared for the six months ending June 30.

Birmingham Mutascope, Limited.—Interim dividend at the rate of 5 per cent. on the paid-up capital for the month of May.

Roodepoort United Main Reef, Limited.—Dividend No. 29 declared, payable to shareholders registered on June 30.

Wilkie & Soames, Limited.—Dividend at the rate of 13 per cent. per annum on the ordinary shares, making, with the interim dividend, 9 per cent. for the year.

Australia United Mining Company, Limited.—Interim dividend of 1s. per share.

Dundee Coal and Estates Company.—Quarterly dividend of 2½ per cent. payable on July 1.

Australia United Mining Company, Limited.—Interim dividend of 1s. per share.

Apollinaris and Johannis.—Final dividend on the ordinary shares of 3 per cent., making with the interim dividend a total of 6 per cent. for the year.

London Produce Clearing House.—An interim dividend at the rate of 6 per cent. per annum.

Eastmans.—Dividend of 6 per cent. on the preference shares.

Frontino and Bolivia Gold Mining Company.—A dividend of 2s. per share.

National Mortgage and Agency of New Zealand.—Interim dividend at the rate of 5 per cent. per annum will be paid on July 8.

INSURANCE.

Ocean Marine Company, Limited.—Interim dividend of 2s. 6d. per share, being at the rate of 10 per cent. per annum.

Merchants' Marine Company, Limited.—Interim dividend at the rate of 6 per cent. per annum for the half-year ended June 30.

Reliance Marine Company, Limited.—Interim dividend of 2s. per share, being at the rate of 10 per cent. per annum.

Maritime Marine Company, Limited.—Interim dividend of 2s. per share.

BREWERIES.

Showell's Stockport, Limited.—Interim dividend for the half-year ended March 30 at the rate of 5 per cent. per annum on the preference shares, and 5 per cent. per annum on the ordinary shares.

RAILWAY TRAFFIC RETURNS.

Algeciras (Gibraltar) Railway.—Traffic for week ended June 4, Ps. 26,790; increase, Ps. 4,903. Aggregate from July 1, Ps. 1,023,704; increase, Ps. 77,099.

West Flanders Railway.—Gross receipts for week ending June 12, £2,037; increase, £164. Total from January 1, £36,267; increase, £2,065.

West of India Portuguese Railway.—Week ending May 21, Rs. 4,325; increase, Rs. 393. Aggregate from January 1, Rs. 97,525; increase, Rs. 27,911.

Villa Maria and Rufino Railway.—Traffic for week ending June 11, £446; increase, £60. Aggregate from January 1, £8,087; increase, £1,566.

Bengal Central Railway.—Traffic receipts for week ending May 21, Rs. 14,689; decrease, Rs. 2,023. Aggregate from January 1, Rs. 4,18,737; increase, Rs. 67,573.

Delhi Umballa Kalka Railway.—Receipts for week ended June 11, Rs. 30,600; increase, Rs. 5,700. Aggregate from January 1, Rs. 7,84,300; increase Rs. 1,78,600.

Alcoy and Gandia Railway and Harbour Company.—Traffic for week, June 11:—Ps. 12,200; increase Ps. 100. Aggregate from January 1, Ps. 203,200; decrease, Ps. 6,770.

Western of Santa Fé Railways.—Gross receipts for week ending June 11, $22,820; increase, $7,050.

Great Western of Brazil.—Traffic receipts for the week ending May 7, $20,410; increase, $6,614. Aggregate from January 1, $614,904; increase, $80,349.

Rohilkund and Kumaon Railway.—Traffic receipts for week ending May 14, Rs. 8,135; decrease, Rs. 875. Aggregate from January 1, Rs. 1,54,408; increase, Rs. 551.

Assam Bengal Railway.—Traffic receipts for week ending May 14, Rs. 21,747; increase, Rs. 639. Aggregate from January 1, Rs. 4,90,509; increase, Rs. 86,223.

Burma Railways.—Traffic receipts for week ending May 14, Rs. 1,88,590; decrease Rs. 10,391. Aggregate from January 1, Rs. 40,45,441; decrease, Rs. 9,731.

Cleator and Workington.—Gross receipts for the week ending June 11 amounted to £1 129, an increase of £232. Total receipts from January 1, £23,944, a decrease of £438.

Cockermouth and Keswick Railway.—Receipts for the week ending June 11, £1,044; decrease, £83. Aggregate from January 1, £19,963; increase, £1,903.

The owners of the principal match factories in Italy have agreed to an arrangement establishing a practical monopoly. It is approved by the Finance Minister, who anticipates a considerable increase from the tax on matches. The match maker gets his monopoly, and all advantages arising therefrom; but there is no compensating consideration for the poor consumer who pays!

FOREIGN RAILWAYS.

Mileage.			Name	Gross Traffic for Week.				Gross Traffic to Date.			
Total.	Increase on 1897.	Increase on 1896.		Week ending	Amount.	In. or Dec. upon 1897.	In. or Dec. upon 1896.	No. of Weeks.	Amount.	In. or Dec. upon 1897.	In. or Dec. upon 1896.
					£	£	£		£	£	£
319	—	—	Argentine Great Western ..	June 10	7,361	+ 1,037	+ 1,547	49	298,715	− 1,238	+ 59,937
76½	—	—	Bahia and San Francisco ..	Apr. 30	2,754	− 131	− 1,437	18	—	—	—
234	48	84	Bahia Blanca and North West..	May 8	523	− 101	—	45	33,692	− 1,414	—
75	1	—	Buenos Ayres and Ensenada ..	June 12	2,843	+ 313	—	24	77,100	+ 13,884	—
426	—	—	Buenos Ayres and Pacific ..	June 11	8,056	+ 2,147	+ 1,930	49	340,662	− 42,867	+ 14,905
914	—	3	Buenos Ayres and Rosario ..	June 11	12,409	− 421	+ 481	24	384,770	+ 99,104	+ 68,630
2,499	30	68	Buenos Ayres Great Southern ..	June 12	21,867	+ 697	− 1,831	49	1,454,443	+ 121,813	+ 213,882
602	107	177	Buenos Ayres Western	June 12	10,073	+ 33	+ 664	49	590,786	− 75,130	− 101,369
845	55	77	Central Argentine..	June 11	14,400	+ 748	− 696	24	491,618	+ 123,434	+ 62,244
197	—	—	Central Bahia	Apr. 30*	$155,590	+ $35,560	+ $57,258	4	$581,140	+ $60,760	+ $87,881
271	—	—	Central Uruguay of Monte Video	June 11	4,946	+ 1,266	− 554	49	291,497	+ 29,414	− 15,132
228	—	—	Do. Eastern Extension	June 11	948	− 62	− 68	49	63,303	+ 9,664	+ 288
182	—	—	Do. Northern Extension	June 11	544	− 502	− 235	49	31,003	+ 851	− 7,993
180	—	—	Cordoba and Rosario	June 5	1,635	− 705	− 715	48	103,570	− 13,085	− 1,235
128	—	—	Cordoba Central	June 5	$21,000	− $10,740	− $13,500	23	$482,330	− $86,400	− $101,210
549	—	—	Do. Northern Extension	June 5	$52,000	− $12,780	− $13,330	23	$1,028,000	− $358,780	− $210,470
137	—	—	Costa Rica..	June 11	3,613	− 686	− 607	24	133,294	− 588	+ 11,930
99	—	—	East Argentine	May 1	1,062	+ 496	+ 69	16	13,802	+ 2,131	+ 1,007
386	—	6	Entre Rios..	June 11	1,044	+ 128	− 266	49	79,698	+ 25,197	+ 19,286
555	—	24	Inter Oceanic of Mexico.. ..	June 11	$57,200	+ $5,080	+ $13,560	49	$2,866,070	+ $450,710	+ $775,650
23	—	—	La Guaira and Caracas	Apr. 29	1,573	− 724	—	18	35,814	− 4,781	—
321	—	—	Mexican	June 11	$78,600	+ $600	—	24	$1,880,800	+ $192,450	—
2,846	—	—	Mexican Central	June 7	$266,001	+ $7,408	+ $96,445	23	$5,812,482	+ $98,946	+ $1,572,713
1,217	—	—	Mexican National	June 7	$99,718	+ $3,653	+ $16,708	23	$2,460,109	+ $85,846	+ $478,820
228	—	—	Mexican Southern	June 14	$11,730	− $141	+ $4,192	10	$130,507	− $17,814	+ $34,463
206	—	—	Minas and Rio	Apr. 30*	$142,119	− $22,067	—	10 mos.	$1,740,090	+ $171,787	—
94	—		N. W. Argentine	June 11	1,496	− 254	− 410	22	24,173	− 9,147	− 8,153
242	3	—	Nitrate	May 31†	18,520	+ 2,552	− 7,211	22	151,360	− 318	− 69,690
320	—	—	Ottoman	June 4	2,888	− 1,451	− 1,468	23	100,663	− 23,382	+ 7,064
77½	—	—	Recife and San Francisco ..	Apr. 16	4,144	+ 1,020	− 2,283	16	89,173	+ 9,186	− 15,970
86½	—	—	San Paulo	May 15†	15,798	− 7,558	—	18	181,508	—	—
186	—	—	Santa Fe and Cordova	June 11	1,432	+ 344	− 455	49	87,193	+ 4,199	− 6,603
110	—	—	Western of Havana	June 11	1,445	− 301	− 175	49	85,600	+ 3,093	+ 6,485

* For month ended. † For fortnight ended.

INDIAN RAILWAYS.

Mileage.			Name.	Gross Traffic for Week.				Gross Traffic to Date.			
Total.	Increase on 1897.	Increase on 1896.		Week ending	Amount.	In. or Dec. on 1897.	In. or Dec. on 1896.	No. of Weeks.	Amount.	In. or Dec. on 1897.	In. or Dec. on 1896.
862	—	—	Bengal Nagpur	June 4	Rs.1.31.000	+Rs.16.691	+Rs.29.324	23	Rs.35.96.966	+Rs.4.61.026	+Rs1.22.693
897	8	63	Bengal and North-Western ..	May 14	Rs.1.64.120	+Rs.9.345		20	Rs.26.96.385	+Rs.2.70.581	—
461	—	—	Bombay and Baroda	June 11	£37,214	+£6,374	+£11,120	23	£734,099	+£63,181	−£96,641
1,885	2	13	East Indian	June 11	Rs.11.36.000	+Rs.52.000	+Rs1.36.000	24	Rs.2.93.76.000	+Rs.11.26.000	+R33.87.000
1,491	—	—	Great Indian Penin.	June 11	£65,239	+£16,009	+£13,505	24	£1,662,678	+£341,256	−£148,025
736	—	—	Indian Midland	June 11	Rs.1.86.050	+Rs.46.888	+Rs.86.359	24	Rs.35.14.610	+Rs.4.23.083	+Rs9.46.254
840	—	—	Madras	June 11	£19,983	+£92	+£366	23	£450,161	−£22,800	−£4,900
1,043	—	—	South Indian	May 14	Rs.1.71.244	−Rs.27,410	−Rs.10.502	20	Rs.30.59.099	−Rs.2.72.701	−Rs2.87.68

UNITED STATES AND CANADIAN RAILWAYS.

Mileage.			Name.	Gross Traffic for Week.			Gross Traffic to Date.		
Total.	Increase on 1897.	Increase on 1896.		Period Ending.	Amount.	In. or Dec. on 1897.	No. of Weeks.	Amount.	In. or Dec. on 1897.
					dols.	dols.		dols.	dols.
917	—	—	Baltimore & Ohio S. Western ..	June 7	131,526	+17,780	47	6,449,600	+825,336
6,568	92	156	Canadian Pacific	" 7	512,000	+43,000	21	9,945,000	+1,764,000
922	—	—	Chicago Great Western	" 7	86,141	−5,281	47	4,998,369	+616,273
6,169	—	469	Chicago, Mil., & St. Paul ..	" 7	657,000	+47,000	21	12,140,001	+1,761,800
1,685	—	—	Denver & Rio Grande	" 7	149,800	+17,300	47	7,544,800	+1,218,900
3,512	—	—	Grand Trunk, Main Line ..	" 7	£69,098	−£192	21	£1,630,156	+£131,587
335	—	—	Do. Chic. & Grand Trunk	" 7	£14,411	+£2,879	21	£331,503	+£75,393
189	—	—	Do. Det., G. H. & Mil...	" 7	£2,798	−£534	21	£76,538	−£4,734
2,938	—	—	Louisville & Nashville	" 7	423,000	+37,000	21	9,280,175	+1,270,620
2,197	137	137	Miss., K., & Texas	" 7	165,345	+6,300	47	11,546,840	+555,204
477	—	—	N. Y., Ontario, & W.	" 7	63,112	−5,777	47	3,561,619	+74,908
1,570	—	—	Norfolk & Western	" 7	221,000	+6,000	21	4,768,960	+493,433
3,499	336	—	Northern Pacific	" 7	395,000	+55,000	21	8,470,775	+2,549,552
1,223	—	—	St. Louis S. Western	" 7	82,000	+12,000	21	2,221,295	+336,928
4,654	—	—	Southern	" 7	384,000	+41,000	21	7,980,812	+1,686,430
1,979	—	—	Wabash	" 7	244,000	+20,000	47	12,360,430	+1,190,000

MONTHLY STATEMENTS.

Mileage.			Name.	Net Earnings for Month.				Net Earnings to Date.			
Total.	Increase on 1896	Increase on 1895.		Month.	Amount.	In. or Dec. on 1897.	In. or Dec. on 1896.	No. of Months.	Amount.	In. or Dec. on 1897.	In. or Dec. on 1896.
					dols	dols.	dols.		dols.	dols.	dols.
6,935	44	444	Atchison	April	708,000	+319,000	+230,670	4	2,942,434	+993,836	+469,139
6,547	103	106	Canadian Pacific	April	717,000	+90,000	+225,790	4	2,410,000	+505,000	+612,557
6,169	—	469	Chicago, Mil., & St. Paul ..	April	759,000	+19,000	−17,197	4	3,495,334	+244,840	+76,915
1,685	—	—	Denver & Rio Grande	April	264,200	+11,727	+38,988	10	2,777,080	+416,762	+69,915
1,970	—	—	Erie..	April	554,000	+17,000	+45,487	4	1,912,600	+100,400	−45,760
3,512	—	—	Grand Trunk, Main Line ..	April	£114,098	+£16,224	+£26,710	4	£360,051	+£78,596	+£123,527
335	—	—	Do. Chic. & Grand Trunk	April	£11,526	+£6,424	+£5,660	4	£50,236	+£30,706	+£34,578
189	—	—	Do. Det. G. H. & Mil. .	April	£4,016	+£390	+£2,125	4	£10,544	+£1,127	+£8,744
3,127	—	239	Illinois Central	April	531,000	+170	+95,770	4	2,744,704	+535,402	+645,518
2,396	—	—	New York Central*	April	3,807,000	+302,000	+394,152	4	14,602,000	+964,000	—
477	—	—	New York Ontario, & W. ..	April	62,100	−14,700	−13,161	10	980,400	+23,500	+102,333
1,570	—	—	Norfolk & Western	April	237,000	+40,000	+96,237	4	1,063,000	+105,340	+298,139
3,407	—	—	Pennsylvania	April	1,524,200	+12,900	+236,000	4	5,672,228	+121,300	+375,900
1,055	—	—	Phil. & Reading . ..	April	623,155	−12,700	—	10	8,100,448	+511,265	—

* Statement of gross traffic.

Prices Quoted on the London Stock Exchange.

Throughout the INVESTORS' REVIEW middle prices alone are quoted, the object being to give the public the approximate current quotations of every security of any consequence in existence. On the markets the buying and selling prices are both given, and are often wide apart where stocks are seldom dealt in. Other particulars will be found in the INVESTMENT INDEX published quarterly—January, April, July, and October—in connection with this REVIEW, price 2s., by post 2s. 2d. Where dividends are paid only once a year, an *italic* type is used to distinguish them. The London Stock Exchange Official List is quoted in the REVIEW almost entire, only very insignificant issues, or bonds falling due within the next two or three years, being omitted. But the list is subdivided into the leading, or active, stocks, and those less frequently dealt in. The former will be found under the head of "Stock Markets," and with more details than it is possible to give for the bulk of securities. By retaining the file of the INVESTORS' REVIEW any subscriber can follow for himself the movements of securities from week to week, and the INVESTMENT INDEX will from time to time help to fill up deficiencies in the information.

Tea Companies and Mines and Mining Finance Stocks are placed in special lists.

Among the abbreviations used are the following:—S.F. Snk.Fd. *sinking fund*; Certs., *certificates*; Debs. or Dbs., *debentures*; Db. or D.Stk., *debenture stock*; Pf. Prf., or Pref., *preference*; Prefd. or Pfd., *preferred*; Dfd., *deferred*; L. or Ltd., *limited*; Sh., *share*; Ans., *annuities*; Cu. or Cm., *cumulative*; Gu. or Guar., *guaranteed*; Bds., *bonds*; S., Sr., or Ser., *series*; In., Ins., Insc., *inscribed*; Dr., Drgs., Drwgs., *drawings*; Stg., Strlg., *sterling*; Lia., *liable to*; Sp., Surp., *surplus*; Per., Perp., *perpetual*; Ln. *lien*; Lo. *loan*.

The dates following the names of securities are the years of issue or of redemption. Where shares are not fully paid up, their nominal amount is given with the name so that investors may know the liability upon them.

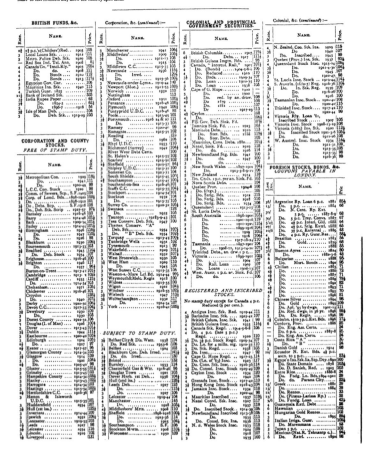

BRITISH FUNDS, &c.

Rate.	Name.	Price.
2¾	2¾ p.c.'s (Childers') Red.. 1905	108
3	Local Loans Stk. 1912	111
3	Metro. Police Deb. Stk. 1920	108
—	Red Sea Ind. Tel. Ann. 1908	8½
4	Canada Gv. "Intcl. Rly." 1903	105½
4	Do. do. .. 1908	111
4	Do. Bonds 1910	112
4	Do. Bonds 1913	117½
3	Egyptian Gov. Gar.	106
3	Mauritius Ins. Stk. 1940	113
4	Turkish Guar. 1855	109
11½	Bank of Ireland Stk.	335
3½	India Rupee Paper	62
3½	Do. 1854-5	62½
3	Do. 1896-7 1916	54
3½	Isle of Man Deb.	104
3	Do. Deb. Stk... 1919-29	103

CORPORATION AND COUNTY STOCKS.

FREE OF STAMP DUTY.

Rate.	Name.	Price.
3½	Metropolitan Con. 1929	118½
3	Do. 1941	111
2½	Do. 1920-49	99
2½	L.C.C. Con. Stock 1920	98
3½	Comm. of Sewers, Scp., S.F. 1905	104
3½	Corp. of Lond. Bds... 1898-1902	100½
3	Do. 1898-1912	101
3½	Do., Debs. Scp. .... S.F. 1916	105
2½	Do., Deb. Stk. Scrip .. 1927-57	97½
3	Barnsley 1916-46	103
3	Barry 1914-46	101½
3	Bath 1909-34	101½
3	Batley 1914-44	101½
3½	Birmingham 1946	116½
3	Do. 1947	110½
2½	Do. 1926	98
3	Blackburn 1930	106½
3	Bournemouth 1913-33	103
3½	Bradford 1945	116½
3	Do. Deb. Stock .. 1934	107
3	Brighouse 1916-46	100
3½	Brighton 1946	117
	Do. 1957	96½
	Burton-on-Trent 1913-43	101½
	Cambridge 1913-43	102½
	Cardiff 1935	115½
	Do. 1914-54	103
	Cheltenham 1971	105½
	Chichester 1916-46	101
	Croydon	128½
3	Do. 1940	107½
3	Derby 1920-50	106½
3	Devon C.C. 1917-33	104½
3½	Dewsbury 1930	109
3	Do. 1930	103
3	Dorset County 1922-32	106
3	Douglas (I. of Man) 1926	100½
3	Dover 1913-43	101½
3½	Dublin 1944	111½
3	Eastbourne 1920-40	103½
3	Edinburgh 1924	106½
2½	Do. 1927	97
2½	Exeter 1917-57	96
3	Glamorgan County 1914-34	103
3½	Glasgow 1914	109
3	Do. 1921	104½
2½	Do. 1925-40	98
3	Gloster 1915-55	101½
3	Grimsby 1913-45	103
3	Hampshire County 1914-34	105½
3	Hanley 1913-43	102½
3	Harrogate 1914-34	103
3	Hastings 1915-54	102½
2½	Hertfordshire C.C. 1926-36	97
3	Heston & Isleworth U.D.C. 1915-35	101
3	Huddersfield 1934	107
3½	Hull (1st iss.)	125½
3	Inverness 1914-44	100
3	Ipswich 1952	106½
3	Lancaster 1919-55	103
2½	Leeds 1927	98
3½	Leicester 1934	116
3	Lincoln 1919	102
3½	Liverpool	131

Corporation, &c. (*continued*):—

Rate.	Name.	Price.
3	Manchester 1941	106½
3½	Middlesbro' 1909	105½
3½	Do. 1911-13	105
3	Do. 1915	104
3	Middlesex C.C. 1915-35	105
3½	Newcastle 1936	118½
3½	Do. Irred.	129½
2½	Do. 1915-36	100½
3	Newcastle-under-Lyme.. 1919-44	100
3	Newport (Mon.) 1915-53	100½
3	Norwich 1952	110
3	Nottingham	113
3	Oxford 1951	108½
3	Penzance 1916-46	100½
3	Plymouth 1942	106½
3	Pontypridd U.D.C. 1916-46	98
3	Poole 1915-45	101
3½	Portsmouth ....1916 24 & 27	111
3	Do. 1913-33	105
3	Ramsey 1920-40	99
3	Ramsgate 1915-55	102
3½	Reading	125
3	Do. 1962	105
3½	Rhyl U.D.C. 1953	110
3	Richmond (Surrey) 1942	104½
3	River Wear Debt Certs.	100
3	St. Helen's 1915-55	102
3	Scarbro' 1915-50	102
2½	Sheffield 1925-57	94½
3	Shipley U.D.C. 1913-35	100
3	Somerset Co. 1923-33	104
3	South Shields 1915-45	107½
2½	Southampton 1915-45	100½
3	Southend-on-Sea 1916-46	101
3	Staffs C.C. 1915-35	104½
3	Stockport 1914-54	101
3	Stockton 1939	104
3	Do. 1915-35	103
3	Surrey Co. 1922-32	105½
3½	Swansea	128
3	Do. 1955	105
3	Taunton 1918 3-9-43	101
3	Tees Conserv. Deb. Stk. 1947	100
3	Thames Conserv. "A" Deb. Stk. 1954	102½
3	Do. "B" Deb. Stk. 1954	102½
3	Torquay 1913-43	100½
3	Tunbridge Wells 1931	102
3	Tynemouth 1913	99
3	Wakefield 1929	101½
3	Walsall 1932	107½
3	West Bromwich 1930	105
3½	West Ham 1929	110
3	Do. 1945	105
3	West Sussex C.C. 1915-35	106
3	Weston-s.-Mare Lcl. Bd. 1914-44	99½
3	Weymouth & Melc. Regis 1918	100
3	Widnes 1915-55	100
3	Wigan 1921	104½
3	Windsor 1918-53	102½
3½	Wisbech 1947	113½
3½	Wolverhampton 1932	117
3	Do. 1924-54	107
3	York 1916-41	105½

SUBJECT TO STAMP DUTY.

Rate.	Name.	Price.
3½	Belfast City & Dis. Watr. 1938	114
3	Do. Red Stk. 1953-6	106
3½	Belfast 1924	103
4	Blackburn Con. Deb. Irred.	141½
3½	Do. do. Irred.	130
3½	Bristol	132
3½	Burnley 1933	114
2½	Chesterfield Gas & Wtr. 1916-46	96
3½	Douglas Town 1921	103
3	Dover Harb. 1st Deb... 1956	104½
3½	Hull (2nd iss.)	128½
4	Leeds Deb. 1927	123
3½	Do.	115½
3	Do. 1927	106
3	Leicester 1919-44	104
4	Manchester	145
3	Do. 1928	103½
4½	Middlesboro' Mrts. 1908	110
3½	Sheffield 1898-1916	100½
3½	Do. 1925-36	114
3	Do. 1925	104½
3½	Southampton .... S.F.	106
4½	Stockton Mrts. 1908	110½
3½	Worcester 1950	109

COLONIAL AND PROVINCIAL GOVERNMENT SECURITIES.

Rate.	Name.	Price.
6	British Columbia 1907	119½
4½	Do. Debs... 1917	111½
3	British Guiana Imgtn. Bds.	98
5	Canada, "Intercol. Rail," 1903	107½
4	Do. (Bonds) 1904-5-6-8	106
4	Do. Reduced 1910	110
3½	Do. Bnds. 1909-34	107
4	Do. Loan 1910-35	110
3	Do. Loan 1938	103
6	Cape of G. Hope 1900	—
5	Do. 1900	—
4½	Do. red. by an. draw.	108
4½	Do 1879	108
4	Do. 1881	107
4	Do 1917-23	113
4½	Ceylon	108
4	Do.	106½
4½	Fiji Gov. Deb. Sink. Fd.	103½
4	Jamaica Sink. Fd. 1923	105
5	Manitoba Debs. 1910	113
5	Do. Ster. Bds. 1888	119½
4	Do. Ster. Debs.	105
4	Mauritius, Cons. Debs. 1880...	101½
4½	Natal, Sink. Fd. 1919	118
4	Do. do. 1926	114
3½	Newfoundland Stg. Bds. 1941	100
3½	Do. do. .. 1947	100
3	Do. do.	97
5	New South Wales 1897-1902	104½
4	Do. 1903-5-8-9-12	106
5	New Zealand 1914	118
5	Do. Cnsls. 1 p.c. per an. Sink. Fd.	103
3½	Nova Scotia Debs.	104
5	Quebec Prov. 1904-6	108
4½	Do. (drgs.)	105
5	Do. Strlg. Bds. 1912	115
4	Do. Strlg. Bds. 1928	110
4	Do. Strlg. Bds. 1934	108
4	Queensland 1913-15	108
4½	St. Lucia Debs.	102
6	South Australia 1898-1900	103½
6	Do. 1901-1918	119
5	Do. 1911-1926	115½
4	Do. 1899-1916	104½
4	Do. 1929	108½
4	Do. 1916	106½
4	Do. 1917-18-24	110
6	Tasmania 1897-1901	104
4	Do. 1908-11, 1913-14-20	107½
5	Trinidad Debs., an. drw. 1 p c...	107
4	Victoria 1899-1901	102½
4½	Do. 1904	107
4	Do. Rail. Loan 1907	107
4	Do. Loans 1908-13	107
4½	West. Austr. 1 p.c. an. Sink. Fd.	107
4	Do. do.	106

REGISTERED AND INSCRIBED STOCKS.

No stamp duty except for Canada 4 p.c. Reduced (½ per cent.).

Rate.	Name.	Price.
4	Antigua Insc. Stk. Red. 1919-44	111
3½	Barbados Insc. Stk. 1925-42	107
3	British Colum. Insc. Stk. 1941	99
4	British Guiana Insc. 1935	116½
4	Canada Stk. Regd. ..1904-5-6-8	106
4	Do. 4 p.c. (late 5 p.c.) Regd. 1910	110
3½	Do. 3½ p.c. Stock Regd. 1909-34	107
4	Do. Ln. for 4 milln. stg. 1910-35	110
3	Do. Stk. Regd. 1938	103
2½	Do. Insc. 1947	92
4	Cape G. Hope Regd. .. 1917-23	114
4	Do. (Ln. of '83) Insc. .. 1923	117
4	Do. Cons. Stk. Insc. 1916-36	114
3½	Do. Consol. Insc. Stock 1929-49	109
4	Ceylon Insc. Stock 1934	120
3	Do. 1940	104
4	Grenada Insc. Stock.... 1917-42	110
3½	Hong Kong Insc. Stock 1918-43	104
4	Jamaica Insc. Stock.... 1934	118
—	Do. 1922-44	98
4	Mauritius Inscribed 1937	119½
4	Natal Consd. Stk. Insc. 1927	117
4	Do. 1937	119
3½	Do. Inscribed Stock.. 1914-39	106
4	Newfoundland Inscribed 1913-38	106
4	Do. 1935	113
4	Do. Consd. Stk. Ins. 1936	113
4	N. S. Wales Stock Insc. 1933	118
3½	Do. 1924	109
3½	Do. 1918	107
3	Do 1935	100

Colonial, &c. (*continued*):—

Rate.	Name.	Price.
4	N. Zealnd. Con. Stk. Ins. 1929	115
3½	Do 1940	107
3	Do. Inscribed.... 1945	99
3	Quebec (Prov.) Ins. Stk. 1937	93½
4	Queensland Stock Insc. 1915-24	109½
3½	Do. 1921-4-30	104½
3½	Do. 1945	107
3	Do. 1922-47	98
4	St. Lucia Insc. Stock .. 1919-44	114½
4	S. Austrln. (1882-7) Reg. 1916-36	110½
3½	Do. In. Stk. Reg. 1939	109
3	Do. 1916-26	100
3/	Do. 1916	100
3½	Tasmanian Insc. Stock.. 1920-40	108
4	Do. 1920-40	115
4	Trinidad Insc. Stock.... 1917-42	110
3	Do. 1922-44	99
4	Victoria Rly. Loan '81, Inscribed Stock 1907	105
4	Victoria Insc. Stock 1908-13-19	108
4	Victoria (1883) Ins. Stk. 1920	112½
3½	Do. Inscribed Stock 1921-3-6	105½
4	Do. do. 1911-26	108
4	W. Austral. Insc. Stock 1934	116½
4	Do. 1911-31	109
3½	Do. 1915-35	105
3	Do. 1915-35	98
3	Do. 1916-36	99

FOREIGN STOCKS, BONDS, &c.

COUPONS PAYABLE IN LONDON.

Last Div.	Name.	Price.
36/	Argentine Ry. Loan 6 p.c. 1881	85½
15/	Do. 5 p.c. 1884	68
30/	Do. N. Cent. Ry. Ext. 5 p.c. 1887-8-9	68
30/	Do. 5 p.c. Trsy. Convs. 1887	67
5/4½	Do. 4½ p.c. Interl. Gld. 1888	64
27/	Do. 4½ p.c. Stlg. Extrl. 1888	65
10/6	Do. 3½ p.c. External .. 1889	48
4	Do. 4 p.c. Ry. Guar. Res....	58½
4½	Brazilian 1883	56
4½	Do. Gold.......... 1879	68
4½	Do. 1888	55
36/	Buenos Ayres 1824	80
6	Do. 1882-3-6	48
6	Bulgarian 1888	95
6	Do. Mort. Bonds 1892	95
4½	Chilian 1885	71
4½	Do. 1886	72
4½	Do. 1887	71
4½	Do. 1889	79½
5	Do. 1892	82
4½	Do. 1893	71
4½	Do. 1895	70
5	Do. 1896	81
7	Chinese Silver 1894	98
6	Do. Gold 1895	109
6	Do. Apl. '95 by dwgs. 1901-15	111
5	Do. Red. dwgs. in 36 yr. 1896	99½
5	Do. Do. Regis. 1896	99
1½	Colmbn. 1½ to 3 p.c. Ext. Bds. 1896	17½
6	Cordova, Prov. 1886	25
—	Do. Eng. Ass. Certs.	24
—	Do. 6 p.c. 1887-8	25
—	Do. Eng. Ass. Certs.	24
3	Costa Rica "A"	30
2½	Do. "B"	24
3	Danish Gold 1914	98
10/	Ecuador N. Ext. Bds. 4½ p.c. ascn. to 5 p.c.	23½
3½	Egypt'n Ins. Stk. lia. Stp. Dty. 1890	100
4	Do. State Domain 1878	103½
4	Do. D. Sanieh, Red. .. 1905	103
6	Entre Rios 1886-8	34
6	Do. Fndg. Ln. Bds. 1894-1921	29
6	Do. do. Parana City	22½
15/	Greek 1881	39
15/	Do. 1884	39
12/	Do. Rentes	33
15/	Do. (Piræus-Larissa Ry.)	38
7/6	Do. Fundg. Loan	42½
4	Guatemala Extl. Debt	28
6	Hawaiian	102
4	Hungarian Gold Rentes	102
3	Do. 1895	89½
6	Italian Irriga. Guar.	108½
5	Do. Maremmana	93
5	Japan 5 p.c.	102
5	Mexican (Nat. R. Tehuantp c.)..	94½
6	Do. Extrl. 1890	98

Foreign Stocks, &c. (*continued*):—

Last Div.	NAME.	Price.
6	Mexican Extrl. 1893	95½
5	Do. Intrnl. Cons. Slvr.	36½
5	Do Intern. Rd. Bds. 2d. Ser.	36½
4	Nicaragua 1886...............	42½
3½	Norwegian, red. 1937, or earlier	98
3	Do. do. 1965, do.	98
3½	Do. 3½ p.c. Bnds.........	102
1	Paraguay 1p.c. ris. 3p.c. 1886-96	17
5	Russian, 1822, £ Strlg.	149
3	Do. 1859..................	93
4	Do. (Nicolas Ry.) 1867-9 ..	102
3	Do. Transcauc. Ry. 1882 ..	92
4	Do. Con. R. R. Bd. Ser. I., 1889..	104
4	Do. Do. II., 1889..	104
4	Do. Do. III., 1891..	102
3½	Do. Bonds	100
4	Do. Ln. (Dvinsk and Vitbsk)	101½
6	Salvador 1889.................	57½
—	S Domingo 4s. Unified: .. 1980	62
6	San Luis Potosi Stg. 1889	94
5	San Paulo (Brzl.), Stg. 1888	86½
6	Santa Fé 1883-4...............	35
—	Do. Eng. Ass. Certs. Dep...	35
5	Do. 1888	48
—	Do. Eng. Ass. Certs. Dpsit..	47
5	Do. (W. Cnt. Col. Rly.) Mrt.	25
5	Do. & Reconq. Rly. Mort...	25
5	Spanish Quickslvr Mort. 1870 ..	101½
3½	Swedish 1880	102
3	Do. 1888	98
3	Do. Conversion Loan 1894..	98
5	Trans. Gov. Loan Red...1903-42	106
59/	Tucuman (Prov.) 1888..........	66½
4	Turkish, Secd. on Egypt. Trib.	103
3½	Turkish, Egpt. Trib., Ott. Bd., '94	99½
4	Do. Priority 1890.........	92
1	Do. Convted Series, "A"..	66
5	Do. Customs Ln. 1886......	96½
5	Uruguay Bonds 1896	57
3	Venzuela New Con. Debt 1881	32

COUPONS PAYABLE ABROAD.

Last Div.	NAME.	Price.
7	Argent. Nat. Cedla. Sries, "B".	33½
5	Austrian Ster. Rnts., ex 10fl., 1870	86
5	Do. do. do.	84
5	Do. Paper do. 1870	85
5	Do. do. do.	85
4	Do. Gld Rentes 1876	102
3	Belgian exchange 25fr.	100
3½	Danish Int., 1887, Rd. 1896	—
2½	Dutch Certs. ex 12 gldrs.	88
3	Do. Bonds	99
3	Do. Insc. Stk........	98
3½	French Rentes	105
3	Do. 1878, '81-4., Red.	100
3	German Imp. Ln. 1891..........	95
3	Do. do. 1892-3	95
3	Do. do. 1890-4	96
5	Japan Cons. Ln., '92, 3, & 5, Red.	47
36/9	Prussian Consols	102
3	" Cons. Stg. Ln. 1891....	96
4	Utd. States, 1877, Red. 1907	113
4	Do. 1895, 30 yrs.......	127
3½	Do. Maschsetts Gl. 1935	113½
3½	Do. Gold Bonds 1923	107½
2	Virginia Cpn. Bds., 3 p.c. from July, 1901	71

BRITISH RAILWAYS.

ORD. SHARES AND STOCKS.

Last Div	NAME.	Price.
	Barry, Ord.	277½
	Do. Prefd.	12½
	Do. Defd.	150½
	Caledonian, Ord...........	153
	Do. Prefd.	110½
	Do. Defd. Ord., No. 1	5
	Cambrian, Ord...........	5½
	Do. Coast Cons.	5½
	Cardiff Ry. Pref. Ord.	113
	Central Lond. £10 Ord. Sh.	10
	Do. do. £6 paid......	6
	Do. Pref. Half-Shares..	1½
	Do. Def. do.........	5
	City and S. London	69½
	East London, Cons.	7½
	Furness	65½
	Glasgow and S. West. Pfd.	82
	Do. do. Dfd.	65
	Great Central, Ord....1894	41½
	Do. London Exten.....	75½
	Great N. of Scotland, Prfd.	88
	Do. Dfd.	34
	Great Northern, Prefd.....	120½
	Do. Consolidated "A"	53
	Do. do. "B"	191½
	Highland	75½
	Isle of Wight, Prefd.	120½
	Do. Defd.	83½
	Lancs. Derbys. and E. Cst.	4
	L. Brighton and S. C. Ord.	186
	Do. Prefd. Ord.	197
	Do. Contgt. Rights Certs.	18½
	Lond. and S. Western Ord.	226½
	Do. Preferred	134
	Lond., Tilb., and Southend	134½
	Mersey, £20 shares	½
	Metropolitan, New Ord...	129
	Do. Surplus Lands....	92
4	North Cornwall, 4 p.c. Pref.	104½
12/6	Do. Deferred	22½

British Railways (*continued*):—

Last Div.	NAME.	Price.
3/3	Plymouth, Devenport, and S. W. Junc. £10	8½
3/	Port Talbot £10 Shares ..	9½
9d.	Rhondda Swns. B. £10 Sh.	4½
10	Rhymney, Cons.	265½
4	Do. Prefd.	123
6½	Do. Defd.	145½
1½	Scarboro', Bridlington Junc.	47½
6½	South Eastern, Ord.........	153
6	Do. Pref.	192
3½	Taff Vale	79
25/	Vale of Glamorgan.........	125½
3	Waterloo & City	125½

LEASED AT FIXED RENTALS.

Last Div.	NAME.	Price.
4	Birkenhead	146
5.19.0	East Lincnshire...........	202½
5½	Hamsmith. & City Ord. ..	192½
4½	Lond. and Blackwll.	161½
4½	Do. £100 4½ p. c. Pref...	161½
56/6	Lond. & Green. Ord........	101
5	Do. 5 p. c. Pref.	176½
5	Nor. and Eastn. £50 Ord...	90
6	Do. ..	104½
3½	N. Cornwall 3½ p. c. Stk...	126½
4½	Nott. & Granthm. R. & C...	145½
3½	Portptk. & Wigtn. Guar. Stk.	121½
9	Vict. Stn. & Pimlico Ord...	312½
4½	Do. 4½ p. c. Pref.....	160½
4/	West Lond. £20 Ord. Shs.	14
4½	Weymouth & Portld.......	157½

DEBENTURE STOCKS.

Last Div.	NAME.	Price.
4	Alexandra Dks. & Ry.	128
3	Barry, Cons.	107
4	Brecon & Mrthyr, New A	124½
4	Do. New B	105
4	Caledonian	148
4	Cambrian "A"	135½
4	Do. "B"	130½
4	Do. "C"	120½
4	Do. "D"	107½
3	Cardiff Rly.	102½
4	City and S. Lond.	137
3½	Cleator & Working Junc...	118½
3	Devon & Som. "A"	103½
16/3	Do. "B" 4 p. c.	36
—	Do. "C" 4 p. c.	10
4	E. Lond. 2nd Ch. 4 p. c. A	136
8/	Do. 2nd B	70½
—	Do. 3rd Ch. 4 p. c. ..	22½
—	Do. 4th do.	11½
3½	Do. 1st (3½ p. c.)	128½
2½	Do. 2½ p.c. (Whitech. Exn)	87
4	Forth Bridge	142½
4	Furness................	140½
4	Glasgow and S. Western ..	143
5	Gt. Central	—
4½	Do.	156½
4	Gt. Eastern	146
4	Gt. N. of Scotland.......	144½
3	Gt. Northern	113
4	Gt. Western...........	151
4½	Do	157½
4½	Do.	166½
5	Do.	185
2½	Do.	96½
4	Highland	140½
3	Hull and Barnsley	104½
3	Do. 2nd (3-4 p. c)...	121½
4	Isle of Wight	142½
3	Do. Cent. "A"..	92½
4½	Do. "B"	115½
4	Do. "C"	82½
3	Lancs. & Yorkshire	112
4	Lancs. Derbys. & E. Cst...	123½
4½	Ldn. and Blackwall	155½
4	Ldn. and Greenwich......	144½
4	Lond., Brighton, &c.	148½
4½	Do.	165½
4½	Lond., Chath., &c., Arb...	156½
4½	Do. "B"..	154½
4	Do.	137½
4	Do. 1883....	137½
3	Do.	106
3	Lond. & N. Western......	117
3	Lond. & S. Westn. "A" ..	115
3	Do. Consld.	115
4	Lond., Til., & Southend ..	145
—	Mersey, 5 p. c. (Act, 1866)	65
4	Metropolitan	146½
4½	Do.	162½
3½	Do.	126½
6	Met. District	208½
4	Do.	138½
2½	Midland	95
4½	Mid-Wales "A"	137½
4	Neath & Brecon 1st	125½
4	Do. "A 1" ..	117½
3	North British	111
3	Do. 1893	109

Debenture Stocks (*continued*):—

Last Div.	NAME.	Price.
4½	North London............	163½
3	N. Staffordshire	112
4	Plym. Devpt. & S.W. Jn...	141½
4	Rhondda and Swan. Bay..	130½
4	Rhymney	144½
4	South-Eastern...........	148
5	Do.	184½
3½	Do.	127½
3	Do.	113
3	Taff Vale	108½
4	Tottenham & For. Gate ..	143½
3	Vale of Glamorgan	105½
3	West Highld. (Gtd. by N.B.)	107½
4	Wrexham, Mold, &c. "A"	113½
4	Do. "B"	101½
4	Do. "C"	97½

GUARANTEED SHARES AND STOCKS.

Last Div.	NAME.	Price.
4	Caledonian	143½
4	Do.	143½
4	Forth Bridge	142½
4	Furness 1881	136½
4	Glasgow & S. Western	143
4	Do. St. Enoch, Rent	141½
6	Gt. Central	198½
4½	Do. 1st Pref.........	152½
3½	Do. Pref.	108
5	Do. Irred. S.Y. Rent	164½
4½	Do. do.	140½
4	Gt. Eastern, Rent	143
5	Do. Metropolitan..	175½
4	Do.	144
4	Gt. N. of Scotland	138½
4	Gt. Northern	146
5	Gt. Western, Rent	185
5	Do. Cons.	185
4	Lancs. & Yorkshire	146
5	L., Brighton & S. C.	183
3½	L., Chat. & D. (Shrtlds.)..	110½
4	L. & North Western	148
4	L. & South Western.. 1881	146
4½	Met. District, Ealing Rent	151½
4½	Do. Fulham Rent	151½
4	Do. Midland Rent	141½
4	Do. Mid. & Dist. Guar.	130½
2½	Midland, Cons. Perp.	94
3	Mid. & G.N. Jt., "A" Rnt..	107
3	N. British, Lien	108½
4	Do Cons. Pref. No. 1	139
3	N. Cornwall, Wadebrge. Gu.	107
4	N. Eastern	146
5	N. Staff. Trent & M. £20 Shs.	36
3½	Nott. Suburban Ord.	123½
20/6	S. E. Perp. Ann.	35½
4½	Do. 4½ p.c.	162½
3½	S. Yorks. Junc. Ord.	118½
4½	W. Cornwall (G. W., Br., Ex., & S. Dev. Joint Rent	161½
3	W. Highl. Ord. Stk. (Gua., N.B.)	104½

PREFERENCE SHARES AND STOCKS.

DIVIDENDS CONTINGENT ON PROFIT OF YEAR.

Last Div.	NAME	Price.
4½	Alexandra Dks. & Ry. "A"	126½
5	Barry (First)	169½
4	Do. Consolidated......	137½
4	Caledonian Cons., No. 1 ..	143
4	Do. do. No. 2 ..	141
5	Do. do. 1878	177
4	Do. Pref. 1884	141
4	Do. do. 1887 (Conv.)	150½
—	Cambrian, No. 1 4 p.c. Pref.	72½
—	Do. No. 2 do.	37½
—	Do. No. 3 do.	17½
—	Do. No. 4 do.	9
5	City & S. Lond. £10 shares	15½
—	Do. New	14
4	Furness, Cons. 1881	131½
4	Do. ......"A" 1881	129½
4	Do. ......"B" 1883	127½
4	Glasgow & S. Western	143
4	Do. No. 2....	141
4	Do. 1888	139½
4	Do. 1891	139½
5	Gt. Central	159½
4	Do.	133½
5	Do. Conv..... 1872	154
5	Do. do. 1874	153½
5	Do. do. 1876	153½
5	Do. do. 1879	151
5	Do. do. 1881	149½
4	Do. 1889	112½
4	Do. 1891	108½
5	Do. 1894	108½
4	Gt. Eastern, Cons.........	142½
4	Do. 1886	141½
	Do. 1881	139½

Preference Shares, &c. (*continued*):—

Last Div.	NAME.	Price.
4	Gt. Eastern, Cons.... 1887	139½
4	Do. 1888	139½
3½	Do. 1890	120½
3½	Do. 1893	120½
—	Do. (Int. fr. Jan '99) 1893	117½
4	Gt. North Scotland "A"..	133½
4	Do. "B"..	133½
4	Gt. Northern, Cons.	145
3	Do. 1896	108
5	Gt. Western Cons.	123
30/11	Hull & Barnsley Red. at 115	113
4	Isle of Wight	133½
3	Lancs. & Yorkshire, Cons.	109
2/2½	Lanc. Drby & E.C. 5 p.c. £10	9½
—	Do. 5 p.c. 2nd £10	9
5	Lond., Bright., &c., Cons.	182
5	Do. 2nd Cons.	181
4½	Lond., Chat. & Dov. Arbitr.	137½
20/	Do. 2nd Pref. 4½ p.c.	101
4	Lond. & N. Western......	147
4	Lond. & S. Western.. 1881	146
4	Do. 1884	145
3½	Do.	127½
4	Lond., Tilbury & Southend	141½
4	Do. Cons., 1887	141½
4	Do 1891	141½
—	Mersey, 5 p.c. Perp.	—
4	Metropolitan, Perp.	143
4	Do. 1882	140½
4	Do. Irred.	141½
4	Do. 1887	141½
4	Do. New........	141½
4½	Do.	146½
3½	Do.	123½
3	Do. Guar.	101½
2½	Metrop. Dist. Exten 5 p.c.	111
2½	Midland, Perp. Pref.	92
4	N. British Cons., No. 2 ..	137
4½	Do. Edin. & Glasgow	153
5	Do. 1865	165½
5	Do. Conv. 1874	166½
4½	Do. 1875	153
4½	Do. Conv. 1875	153
5	Do. do. 1870	166½
4	Do. do. 1884	136½
4	Do. do. 1888	136½
4	Do. do. 1890	136½
4	Do. do. 1892	136½
4	N. Eastern	146
4½	N. Lond., Cons. 1866	174½
4½	Do. 2nd Cons. .. 1875	157½
3	N. Staffordshire	108
4½	Plym, Devpt. & S. W. Junc.	149½
1/5	Port Talbot, &c., 4 p.c. £10 Shares, 4 paid	5
5/	Rhondda & Swansea Bay, 5 p.c. £10 Shares	11
4	Rhymney, Cons.	140½
4½	S. Eastern, Cons.	161½
5	Do. do.	181
4	Do. Vested Cos	141½
4	Do. 1891	140½
3½	Do. 1893	124½
2	Do. 3 p.c. after July 1900	103
4	Taff Vale	138

INDIAN RAILWAYS.

Last Div.	NAME.	Paid.	Price.
3½	Assam Bengal, Ld., (2½ p. c. till June 30, then 3 p.c.)	100	102
4/	Barsi Light, Ld., £10 Shs.	10	10½
4	Bengal and N. West., Ld	100	145
4/	Do. £10 Shares	10	13½
3/6	Do. 3½ p.c. Cum. Pf. Shs.	10	10
8½d.	Do.	4	6
2/3½	Bengal Central, Ld., £10 (3½ p.c. + ½th net earn)	5	6
7	Bengal Dooars, Ld.	100	111
4	Bengal Nagpr., Lim. (gua. 4 p.c. + 4th sp. pfts.) ..	100	114
7½	Bombay, Baroda, and C. I. (gua 5 p.c)	100	220
36/1	Burma, Ld. (gua. 2½ p.c. and ½ p.c. add. till 1901)	100	109
1/7	Do. £10 Shares		3½
5½	Delhi Umb. Kalka, Ld., Gua. 3½ p.c. + net earn.	100	122
4	Do. Deb. Stk., 1890 (1910)	100	111
9/10	Estn. Bengal, "A" An. 1957	—	25
9/	Do. "B" 1957	—	30
4	Do. Gua. Deb. Stock ..	100	134½
9/7½	East Ind. Ann. "A" (1953)	—	28
8/4½	Do. "C"	—	29
8/11½	Do. "B"	—	31
6½	Do. Def. Ann. Cap. (gua. 4 p.c. + ½th sp. pfts.)	—	151
115/9	East Ind. Def. Ann. "D"	—	157
4½	East Ind. Irred. Stock ..	100	158½
5	Gt. Indian Penin., Gua. 5 p.c. + ½ surplus profits..	100	160½
4	Do. Irred. 4 p.c. Deb. St.	100	137½
4	Indian Mid., Ld. (gua. 4 p.c. + ½th surplus pfts.)	100	114
5	Madras Guar. + ½ sp. pfts.	100	164
4½	Do. do.	100	155
4½	Do. do.	100	145
4	Nilgiri, Ld., 1st Deb Stk.	100	98
51/9	Rohil. and Kumaon, Ld.	100	130
9/11	Scinde, Punj., and Delhi, "A" Ann., 1958	—	25

Indian Railways (*continued*):—

Last Div.	Name.	Paid.	Price.
4	South Behar, Ld., £10 shs.	100	100
3½	Do. Deb. Stk. Red.	100	101
4½	South Ind., Gu. Deb. Stk.	100	156½
5	South Indian, Ld. (gua. 3 p.c., and ½ spls. profits)	100	122½
5	Sthn. Mahratta, Ld. (3½ p.c. & ¼th net earnings)	100	114½
4	Do. Deb. Stk. Red.	100	121
3½	Southern Punjab, Ld.	100	105
3½	Do. Deb. Stk. Red.	—	104
5	Nizam's Gua. State, Ld. ..	100	115½
4	Do. Mort. Deb., 1936	100	108
4	Do. do. Reg.	100	106
17/3½	Nizam's Gua. State, Ld., 3½ p.c. Mt. Deb. bearer	—	95½
17/3½	Do. Reg. do. ..	—	93½
5	W. of India Portgese., Ld.	100	73
5	Do. Deb. Stk., Red	100	101

RAILWAYS.—BRITISH POSSESSIONS.

Last Div.	Name.	Paid.	Price.
5	Atlantic & N.W. Gua. 1 Mt. Bds., 1937	100	126½
5/3	Buff. & L. Huron Ord. Sh.	10	13½
5½	Do. 1st Mt. Perp. Bds. 1879	100	143½
5½	Do. 2nd Mt. Perp. Bds.	100	143½
—	Calgary & Edmon. 6 p.c. 1st Mt. Stg. Bds. Red..	100	83½
5	Canada Cent. 1st Mt. Bds. Red.	100	103
4	Can. Pacific Pref. Stk.	100	102
5	Do. Strl. 1st Mt. Deb. Bds. 1915	100	118
3½	Do. Ld. Grnt. Bds. 1938..	100	107
3½	Do. Ld. Grnt. Ins. Stk. ..	100	107
4	Do. Perp. Cons. Deb. Stk.	100	113
5	Do. Algoma Bch. 1st Mt. Bds., 1937	100	122
3	Demerara, Original Stock	100	47½
7	Do. Perp. Pref. Stk.	100	152½
1/10	Do. 4 p.c. Cum. Ext. Pref. £10 Shs.	4	8
—	Dominion Atlntc. Ord. Stk.	100	33½
5	Do. 5 p.c. Pref. Stk.....	100	97½
4	Do. 1st. Deb. Stk.......	100	105½
4	Do. 2nd do. Red.	100	99
1/3	Emu Bay & Mt. Bischoff, Ld.	5	4½
4½	Do. Irred. Deb. Stk....	100	98
nil.	Gd. Trunk of Canada, Stk.	100	8½
6	Do. 2nd. Equip. Mt. Bds.	100	133
5	Do. Perp. Deb. Stk......	100	130½
5	Do. Gt. Westn. Deb. Stk.	100	131½
5	Do. Nthn. of Can. 1st Mt. Bds., 1902	100	103½
4	Do. do. Deb. Stk	100	103
5	Do. G. T. Geor. Bay & L. Erie 1 Mt., 1903	100	105
5	Do. Mid. of Can. Stl. 1st Mt. (Mid. Sec.) 1908	100	106
5	Do. do. Cons. 1 Mt. Bds. 1912	100	108
5	Do. Mont. & Champ. 1 Mt. Bds., 1902	100	104
	Do. Welln., Grey & Brce. 7 p.c. Bds. 1 Mt.	100	110
—	Jamaica 1st Mtg. Bds. Red.	—	102
—	Manitoba & N. W., 6 p.c. 1st Mt. Bds., Red	100	—
—	Do. Ldn. Bdhldrs. Certs.	—	—
5	Manitoba S. W. Col. 1 Mt. Bd., 1934 $1,000 price %	—	119
—	Mid. of W. Aust. Ld. 6 p.c. 1 Mt. Dbs., Red.	100	42½
4	Do. Deb. Bds., Red.	100	104
4	Nakusp & Slocan Bds., 1918	100	106
3	Natal Zululand Ld. Debs.,	100	72½
5	N. Brunswick 1st Mt. Stg. Bds., 1934	100	121
4	Do. Perp. Cons. Deb. Stk.	100	112
—	N. Zealand Mid., Ld., 5 p.c 1st Mt. Debs.	100	35
6	Ontario & Queb. Cap. Stk.	$100	151½
5	Do. Perm. Deb. Stk......	100	144½
—	Qu'Appelle, L. Lake & Sask. 6 p.c. 1 Mt. Bds. Red.	100	40
	Queb. & L. S. John, 1st Mt. Bds., 1909	100	34
	Quebec Cent., Prior Ln. Bds., 1908	100	107
1½	Do. 5 p.c. Inc. Bds.	100	37
4	St. Lawr. & Ott. Stl. 1st Mt.	100	111
4	Shuswap & Okan., 1st Mt. Deb. Bds., 1915	100	76
5	Temiscouata, 5 p.c. Stl. 1st Deb. Bds., Red.	100	9½
5	Do. (S. Franc. Brch.) 5 p.c. Stl. 1 Mt. Db. Bds., 1910	100	12
4	Toronto, Grey & B. 1st Mt.	100	112
1/	Well. & Mana. £5 Shs. ..	1	½
5	Do. Debs., 1908	100	105
5	Do. 2nd Debs., 1908	100	104
5	Do. 3rd do., 1908	100	103
6	Atlan. & St. Law. Shs., 6 p.c.	100	163½
5	Gd. Trunk Mt. Bds., 1934	100	116½
5	Michigan Air Line, 5 p.c. 1st Mt. Bds., 1902	100	104
4	Minneap., S. P. & S t. Ste. Mar, 1st Mt. Bds., 1938	$1000	100

AMERICAN RAILROAD STOCKS AND SHARES.

Last Div.	Name.	Paid.	Price.
6/	Alab. Gt. Sthn. A 6 p.c. Pref.	10/.	9½
—	Do. do "B" Ord. ..	10/.	1½
—	Alabma. N. Orl.-Tex. &c., "A" Pref.	10/.	½
—	Do. "B" Def.	10/.	½
5½	Atlant. First Lnd. Ln. Rtl. Trust	Stk.	98½
—	Baltimore & Ohio Com. ..	$100	20
—	Baltimore Ohio S.W. Pref.	$100	7
—	Chesap. & Ohio Com.	$100	23
—	Chic. Gt. West. 5 p.c. Pref. Stock "A"	$100	34
—	Do. do. Scrip. In.......	—	30½
8/3	Do. 4 p.c. Deb. Stk.......	$100	67½
4	Do. Interest in Scrip	$100	63½
$4	Chic. Junc. Rl. & Un. Stk. Yds. Com.	$100	122½
$1½	Do. 6 p.c. Cum. Pref.	$100	121½
$3½	Chic. Mil. & St. P. Pref...	$100	152½
7	Cleve. & Pittsburgh	$10	86
$1½	Clev., Cincin., Chic., & St. Louis Com.	$100	—
—	Erie 4 p.c. Non-Cum. 1st Pf.	—	37½
—	Do. 4 p.c, do. 2nd Pf.	—	20
$2½	Gt. Northern Pref.	$100	180
$4	Illinois Cen. Lsd. Lines ..	$100	92½
—	Kansas City, Pitts & G. ..	$100	19
$3	L. Shore & Mich. Sth. C.	$100	190
—	Mex. Cen. Ltd. Com.	$100	5
—	Miss. Kan. & Tex. Pref...	$100	38½
2½	N.Y., Pen. & O. 1st Mt. Tst. Ltd., Ord.	—	47½
4	Do. 1st Mort. Deb. Stk. ..	$100	92½
$	North Pennsylvania	$50	—
—	Northn. Pacific, Com.....	$100	29½
1½	Pitts. F. Wayne & Chic...	$100	172
—	Reading 1st Pref.	$50	24
—	Do. 2nd Pref.	$50	12
—	S. Louis & S. Fran. Com.	$100	8
—	Do. 2nd Pref.	$100	33
6	St. Louis Bridge 1st Pref..	$100	103½
3	Do. 2nd Pref.	$100	47½
6	Tunnel Rail. of St. Louis	$100	104
$1½	St. Paul, Min. and Man...	$100	147½
—	Southern, Com.	$100	8½
—	Wabash, Common	$100	8

AMERICAN RAILROAD BONDS. CURRENCY.

Last Div.	Name.		Price.
7	Albany & Susq. 1 Con. Mrt.	1906	118
7	Allegheny Val. 1 Mt.......	1910	127½
5	Canada Southern 1 Mt.....	1908	110½
5	Chic. & N. West. Sk. Fd. Db.	1933	120½
5	Do. Deb. Coupon	1921	117½
6	Chicago & Tomah	1905	109½
5	Chic. Burl. & Q. Skg. Fd.	1901	102½
4	Do. Nebraska Ext.......	—	100½
6	Chic., Mil., & S. Pl., 1 Mt. S.W. Div.	1909	114½
7	Do. (S. Paul Div.) 1 Mt.	1902	129½
5	Do. (La Cross & D.	1919	112½
7	Do. 1 Mt. (Hast. & Dak.)	1910	124½
5	Do. Chic. & Mis. Riv. 1 Mt.	1926	—
6	Det., G. Haven & Mil. Equip	1918	105
6	Do. do. Cons. Mt.	1918	102½
6	Ill. Cent., 1 Mt., Chic. & S.	1898	—
7	Indianap. & Vin., 1 Mt. ..	1908	125
6	Do. do. 2 Mt. ..	1900	100½
6	Lehigh Val., Cons. Mt.	1923	114½
—	Mexic. Cent., Ln. 2 Cons. Inc.	—	5
7	N.Y. Cent. & H.R. Mt. Bonds	1903	117½
5	Do. Deb.	1904	111
6	Penns. Cons. S. F M.	1905	114½
4	West Shore, 1 Mt.	2361	109

DITTO—GOLD.

Last Div.	Name.	Price.
6	Alabama Gt. Sthn. 1 Mt. ..1908	111
5	Do. Mid. 1 1928	92
4	Allegheny Val. Gen. Mt. ..1942	107½
4	Atch., Top., & S. Fé Gn. Mt. 1995	95½
3	Do. Adj. Mt. 1995	67½
5	Do. Equipt. Tmst. ...... —	102½
5	Atlantic & Dan. 1 Mt. 1950	94
5	Baltimore & Ohio 1925	105½
5	Do. Speyer's Tst. Recpts. 1925	106½
5	Do. Cons. Mt. 1988	110
4½	Do. 4½ p.c. 1 Mt. Term. 1934	90
4½	Do. Brown Shipley's Dep. Cts. —	90
5	Balt. Belt 5 p.c. 1 Mort. 1990	97½
4½	Balt. & Ohio S.W. 1 Mt. ..1990	102½
4½	Do. 4½ p.c. 1 Cons. Mt. 1893 1993	75½
—	Do. Inc. Mt. 5 p.c. Cl. A —	29
—	Do. do. Cl. B —	10
5	Balt. & Ohio S.W. Term 5 p.c. 1942	97½
6	Balt. & Ptmac (Mn. L.) 1 Mt. 1911	124
6	Do. do. (Tunnel) 1 Mt. 1911	122½
4	Beech Creek 1 Mt. 1936	107

American Railroad Bonds—Gold (*continued*):—

Last Div.	Name.	Price.
5	Cent. of Georgia 1 Mort. ..1945	118
5	Do. Cons. Mt. 1945	90½
5	Cent. of N. Jrsy. Gn. Mt...1987	115½
6	Central Pacific, 1 Mort. 1898	102
6	Do. Speyer's Certs. ...... —	102½
5	Do. Land Grant 1900	104
5	Chesap. & Ohio 1st Cons. Mt. 1939	117½
4½	Do. Gen. Mt. 1992	86
6	Chic. & W. Ind. Gen. Mt. Skg. Fd. ... .1932	119½
5	Chic. Mil. & St. Pl. (Chic. & L. Sup.) 1 Mt. 1921	112½
5	Do. Chic. & Pac. W. 1921	114½
5	Do. Wisc. & Minn. 1 Mt. 1921	109½
5	Do. Terminal Mt. 1914	112½
4	Do. General Mt. 1989	106
5	Chic. St. L. & N. Orleans..1951	122½
4	Do. 1 Mort. (Memphis) ..1951	104
4	Clevel., Cin., Chic. & St. L. 1 Mt. (Cairo) 1939	87½
4	Do. 1 Mt. (Cinc., Wab., & Mich.) 1991	88
4	Do. 1 Col. Tst. Mt. (S. Louis) 1990	96
4	Do. General Mt. 1993	80½
4½	Clevel. & Mar. Mt. 1935	109
4½	Clevel. & Pittsburgh 1942	116½
4½	Do. Series B. 1942	116½
—	Colorado Mid. 1 Mt. 1936	65½
—	Do. Bdhrs.' Comm. Certs. —	65½
4	Dnvr. & R. Gde. 1 Cons. Mt. 1936	96
5	Do Imp. Mort. 1928	94
4	Detroit & Mack. 1 Lien 1995	90
5	E. Tennes., Virg., & Grgia. Cons. Mt. 1956	111½
5	Elmira, Cort., & Nthn. Mt. 1914	100
4	Erie 1 Cons. Mt. Pr. Ln. ..1996	93
3	Do. Gen. Lien 1996	74
6	Galvest., Harrisb., &c., 1 Mt.	110
5	Georgia, Car. & N. 1 Mt. ..1929	94
4½	Gd. Rpds & Inda. Ex. 1 Mt. 1941	110
5	Do. 1 Mt. (Muskegon) ..1926	39½
3½	Illinois Cent. 1 Mt. 1951	102½
4	Do. 1952	105
4	Do. Cairo Bdge. ..1950	102
4	Do. 1953	103
4	Do. General Mort. ..1904	100½
5	Kans. City, Pitts. & G. 1 M. 1923	73½
3½	L. Shore & Mich. Southern 1997	106½
4½	Lehigh Val. N.Y. 1 Mt. 1940	103½
5	Lehigh Val. Term. 1 Mt. ..1941	112
5	Long Island 1931	116
5	Do. Deb. 1934	100
5	Do. (N. Shore Bch.) 1 Cons. Mt. 1932	95½
6	Louisville & Nash. G. Mt..1930	121
6	Do. 2 Mt. Sk. Fd. (S. & N. Alabama 1910	107
6	Do. 1 Mt. N. Orl. & Mb. 1930	122½
5	Do. 1 Mt. Coll. Tst. 1931	106
4	Do. Unified 1940	91
4½	Do. Mobile & Montgy. 1 Mt. 1945	111½
4	Manhattan Cons. Mt. 1990	98
4	Mexican Cent. Cons. Mt. ..1911	67½
—	Do. 1 Cons. Inc, ...	15
6	Mexican Nat. 1 Mt. 1927	106
3½	Do. 2 Mt. 6 p.c. Inc. A 1917	47½
—	Do. do. B..1917	—
3	Michig. Cnt. (Battle Ck. & S.) 1 Mt. 1989	86
5	Minneap. & S. L. 1 Consold. 1934	107½
4	Minne., Slt. S. M. & A. 1 Mt. 1926	101½
5	Minneapolis Westn. 1 Mt...1911	102½
4	Miss. Kans. & Tex. 1 Mt...1990	90
4	Do. 2 do. 1990	65
4	Mobile & Birm. Mt. Inc....1945	58
5	Do. P. Lien 1945	86
4	Mohawk & Mal. 1 Mt. 1991	108
5	Montana Cent. 1 Mt. 1937	109½
5	Nashv., Chattan., & S. L. 1 Cons. Mt. 1928	102½
5	Nash., Flor., & Shff. Mt...1937	96½
4	N. Y. & Putnam 1 Cons. Mt. 1993	108
5	N. Y., Brooklyn, & Man. B. 1 Cons. Mt. 1935	107½
4	N. Y. Cent. & Hud. R. Deb. Certs. 1890 1905	106
4	Do. Ext. Debt. Certs. 1905	106
7	N. Y., L. Erie, & W. 1 Cons. Mt. (Erie) 1920	144½
7	Do. 1 Con. Mt. Fd. Coup. 1920	139½
5	N. Y., Onto., & W. Cons. 1 Mt. .... —	109
4	Do. 4 p.c. Refund. Mt..1992	101½
6	Norfolk & West. Gn. Mt....1931	124
6	Do. Imp. & Ext 1934	117½
4	Do. 1 Cons. Mt. .... —	84
6	N. Pacific Gn. 1 Mt. Ld. Gt. 1921	—
4	Do. P. Ln. Rl. & Ld. Gt. —	99
3	Do. Gn. Ln. Rl. & Ld. Gt. —	64
5	Oregon & Calif. 1 Mt. 1927	85½
6	Panama Skg. Fd. Subsidy..1910	102½
4½	Pennsylvania Rlrd. 1913	112
4	Do. Equip. Tst. Ser. A..1914	104
4	Do. Cons. Mt. 1943	112½
4½	Penna. Company 1st Mort. 1921	112½
5	Perkiomen 1 Mrt., 2nd ser..1918	91½
4½	Pitts., C., C., & St. Ls. Con. Mt. G.B., Ser. A 1940-2	114½
4	Do. Cons. Mort., Ser. D..1945	102½
6	Pittsbgh., Cle., & Toledo ..1922	100½
4	Reading, Phil., & R. Genl. 1997	86
5	Richmond & Dan. Equip. ..1909	97½
5	Rio Grande Junc. 1st Mort. 1939	90
4	Rio Grande West 1st Tst. Mt. 1939	80
7	S. Louis Bridge 1st Mort 1925	134½
5	S. Louis Mchts. Bdge. Term. 1st Mort. 1930	102½
4	S. Louis S. West 1st Mort..1989	76½
—	Do. 4 p.c. 2nd Mort. Inc. 1989	30
4½	S. Louis Term. Cupples Sta. & Prop. 1st. Mrt. 4½ p.c. 1902-17	100

American Railroad Bonds (*continued*

Last Div.	Name.	Price.
6	St. Paul, Minn., & Manit. 1933	120½
6	Shamokin, Sunbury, &c. 2 Mt. 1925	106
5	S. & N. Alabama Cons. Mt. 1936	102
5	Southern 1 Cons. Coup. 1994	95
4	Do. E. Tennes Reorg. Lien ..1938	100
6	S. Pacific of Cal. 1 Mt...1905-12	111
4½	Trml. Assn. of S. Louis 1 Mt. 1939	112
5	Do. 1 Cons. Mt. 1944	109
5	Texas & Pac. 1 Mt. 2000	106½
—	Do. 5 p.c. 2 Mt. Income 2000	40
5	Toledo & Ohio Cent. 1 Mt. West. Div. 1935	102½
4½	Toledo., Walhon., Val., & Ohio 1 Mt. 1931-3	109½
4	Union Pacific 1 Mt. 4 p.c. ..1947	97
—	Union Pac., Linc., & Color. 1 Mt. 1918	—
4	United N. Jersey Gen. Mt...1944	117½
6	Vicksbrg., Shrevept., & Pac. Pr. Ln. Mt. 1915	102½
5	Wabash 1 Mt. 1939	110
4	Wn. Pennsylvania Mt. 1928	106½
5	W. Virga. & Pittsbg. 1 Mt. 1990	77½
5	Wheeling & L. Erie 1 Mt. (Wheelg. Div.) 5 p.c. 1928	92½
5	Do. Extn. Imp. Mt. 1930	90
—	Do. do. Brown Shipley's Cts...	—
5	Willmar & Sioux Falls 1 Mt. 1938	110

STERLING.

Last Div.	Name.	Price.
6	Alabama Gt. Sthn. Deb. 1906	104½
5	Do. Gen. Mort. ..1927-8	98
5	Alabama, N. Orl., Tex. & Pac. 5 p.c. "A" Dbs...1910-40	101
55/	Do. do. "B" do. 1910-40	58½
—	Do. do. "C" do.	19½
—	Allegheny Valley 1910	132
4	Atlantic 1st Leased Line Perp...	100
6	Baltimore and Ohio 1902	110
6	Do. do. 1910	122½
5	Do. do. 1877........	105½
—	Do. Morgan's Certs. ..	105½
4½	Do. do. 1933	98
6	Chicago & Alton Cons. Mt. 1903	112
5	Chic. St. Paul & Kan. City Priority	106½
6	Eastn. of Massachusetts 1906	117½
5	Illinois Cent. Skg. Fd.	104
5	Do. 1905	106
3½	Do. 1950	99½
4	Do. 1 Mt. 1951	114
3	Do. 1 Mt. 1951	93½
6	Louisville & Nash., M. C. & L. Div., 1 Mt. 1902	107½
7	Do. 1 Mt. (Memphis & O.) 1901	110
55/8	Mexican Nat. "A" Certs. 5 p.c. Non. cum.	40½
—	Do. "B" Certs.	9
6	N.Y. & Canada 1 Mt. 1904	118
6	N. York Cent. & H.R. Mort. 1903	112
4½	N. York, Penna., & Ohio Pr. Ln. Extd. 1935	—
5	Do. Equip. Tst.	101½
5	Do. 5 p.c. Equip. Tst. (1890)	101½
6	Nrthn. Cent. Cons. Gen. Mt. ..	106
6	Pennsylvania Gen. Mt. 1910	127½
6	Do. Cons. Skg. Fd. Mt. 1905	116½
3½	Do. Cons. Mt. 1945	105
6	Phil. & Erie Cons. Mort ..1920	134½
6	Phil. & Reading Gen. Cons. Mort. 1911	122½
6	Pittsbg. & Connells. Cons. 1926	117½
—	Do. Morgan's Certs.	117½
4	St. Paul., Min., & Manitoba (Pac. Extn.) 1940	101
6	S. & N. Alabama 1903	106½
6	Un. N. Jersey & C. Gen. Mt. 1901	109½

FOREIGN RAILWAYS

Last Div.	Name.	Paid.	Price.
12/	Alagoas, Ltd., Shs.	20	6½
5	Do. Deb. Stk., Red. ..	100	45½
6	Antofagasta, Ltd., Stk. ..	100	72
4	Do. Perp. Deb. Stk. ..	100	90
—	Arauco, Ld., Ord. Shs. ..	20	—
—	Do. 10 p.c. Cum. Pref.	20	—
5	Argentine Gt. W., Ld.,	100	83
5	Do. 5 p.c. Cum. Pref. Shs.	100	105
4	Do. 1 Deb. Stk.	100	104
1/0/0	Argentine N.E., Ltd., 6 p.c. Cum. Pref. Stk. ..	100	9½
—	Do. 5 p.c. Deb. Stk., Red.	100	29
2/	Arica and Tacna Shs. ..	20	1½
10/	Bahia & San Fcisco., Ld.,	20	10½
6/	Do. Timbo. Bch. Shs.	20	5
12/	Bahia, Blanca, & N.W. Ln. Prf. Cum. 6 p.c. ..	100	52
4	Do. 4 p.c. 1 Deb. Stk., Red.	100	91
6	Barranquilla R. & P., Ld.,		

Foreign Railways (*continued*):—

Last Div.	Name.	Paid.	Price.
3/	Bilbao Riv. & Cantabn., Ltd., Ord.	3	5
—	Bolivar, Ltd. Shs.	10	1¾
6	Do. 6 p.c. Deb. Stk.	100	96½
—	Brazil Gt. Southn. Ltd., 7 p.c. Cum. Pref.	20	1¾
6	Do. Perm. Deb. Stk	100	55
5½	B. Ayres Gt. Southn. Ld., Ord. Stk.	100	140
5	Do. Pref. Stk.	100	133
4	Do. Deb. Stk.	100	117½
30/	B. Ayres & Ensen. Port., Ltd., Ord. Stk.	100	66
5	Do. Cum. 1 Pref. Stk.	100	117
6/0/0	Do. 6p.c.Con. Pref.Stk.	100	96
4	Do. Deb. Stk., Irred.	100	113
10⅝	B. Ayres Northern, Ltd., Ord. Stk.	100	260
12½	Do. Pref. Stk.	100	320
5	Do. 5 p.c. Mt. Deb.Stk., Red.	100	113
3/15/0	B. Ayres & Pac., Ld., 7 p.c. 1 Pref. Stk. (Cum.)	100	92½
4	Do. 1 Deb. Stk.	100	101
5/5/0	Do. 4½ p.c. 2 Deb. Stk.	100	93
3	B. Ayres & Rosario, Ltd., Ord. Stk.	100	72½
7/	Do. 7 p.c. Pref. Shs.	10	17
7/	Do. Sunchales Ext.	10	14½
4	Do. Deb. Stk., Red.	100	106½
—	B. Ayres & Val. Trans., Ltd., 7 p.c. Cum. Pref.	20	6½
4	Do. 4 p.c. "A" Deb. Stk., Red.	100	70
—	Do. 6 p.c. "B" Deb. Stk. Red.	100	45
3/6	B. Ayres Westn. Ld. Ord.	10	11
3/	Do. Def. Shs.	10	6½
5	Do. 5 p.c. Pref.	10	13
4	Do. Deb. Stk	100	111½
6	Cent. Arg. Deb. Sk. Rd.	100	159½
4	Do. Deb. Stk. Rd	100	110
6	Cent. Bahia L. Ord. Stk.	100	46½
	Do. Deb. Stk., 1934	100	69½
5	Do. Deb. Stk., 1937	100	60
3/6	Cent. Uguy. East. Ext. L. Shs	10	5½
5	Do. Perm. Stk.	100	112
3/6	Do. Nthn. Ext. L. Sh.	10	4
5	Do. Perm. Deb. Stk.	100	104
3	Do. of Montev. Ltd., Ord. Stk	100	85
6	Do. Perm. Deb. Stk	100	143
10/	Conde d'Eu, Ltd. Ord.	20	7
—	Cordba & Rosar., Ltd., 6 p.c. Pref. Shs.	100	38
4	Do. 1 Deb. Stk.	100	89
7½	Do. 6 p.c. Deb. Stk.	100	79
—	Cordba Cent., Ltd., 5 p.c. Cu. 1 Pref. Stk.	100	84
—	Do. 5 p.c. Non-Cum. 2 Pref. Stk	100	43
5	Do. Deb. Stk.	100	118
4/	Costa Rica, Ltd., Shs	10	3½
8/	Dna. Thrsa. Chris., Ltd., 7 p.c. Pref. Shs.	20	3½
20/	E. Argentine, Ltd	100	46
6	Do. Deb. Stk	100	102
1/1	Egyptn. Dlta. Lgt. Rys., Ltd., £10 Pref. Shs.	8	10½
—	Entre Rios, L., Ord. Shs.	5	¾
—	Do. Cu. 5 p.c. Pref.	5	2½
6/	Gt. Westn. Brazil, Ltd.,	20	8
6	Do. Perm. Deb. Stk.	100	93
	Do. Extn. Deb. Stk.	100	75½
—	Int.-Oceanic Mex., Ltd., 7 p.c. Pref.	10	1⅛
4	Do. Deb. Stk	100	83
42/6	Do. 7 p.c. "A" Deb. Sk.	100	70
—	Do. 7 p.c. "B" Deb. Sk.	100	30
5/	La Guaira & Carac.	10	7½
5	Do. 5 p.c. Deb. Sk. Red.	100	103
13/3	Lembg.-Czern.-Jassy	30	24½
1/	Lima, Ltd.	20	2½
—	Manila Ltd. 7 p.c. Cu. Pf.	10	¾
20/6½	Mexican 2nd Pref. 6 p.c.	100	74
6	Do. Perp Deb. Stk.	100	136½
1/0/0	Mexican Sthrn., Ld., Ord.	100	22
—	Do. 4 p.c. 1 Db. Stk. Rd.	100	84½
—	Do. 4 p.c. 2 do.	100	59
—	Mid. Urgy., Ltd.	100	17½
5	Do. Deb. Stk.	100	58
12/	Minas & Rio, Ltd.	20	10
5/2	Namur & Liege	20	12½
11/6	Do. Pref	20	29
13/	Natal & Na. Cruz, Ld., 7 p.c. Cum Pref.	20	6½
—	Nitrate Ltd., Ord.	10	5½
—	Do. 7 p.c. Pr. Con. Or.	10	4
—	Do. Def. Conv. Ord.	10	¾
7/	N.-E. Urgy., Ltd., Ord	10	14½
7/	Do. 7 p.c. Pref.	10	15½
—	N.-W. Argentine Ld., 7 p.c. Pref.	10	2
6	Do. 6 p.c. 1 Deb. Stk.	100	110
—	Do. 2 Deb. Stk.	100	94
—	N.W. Uruguay 6 p.c. 1 Pref. Stk.	100	16
—	Do. 5 p.c. 2 Pref. Stk.	100	7½
6	Do. 6 p.c. Deb. Stk	100	76½
22/	Ottoman (Sm. Aid.)	20	13
—	Paraguay Cntl., Ld., 5 p.c. Perm. Deb. Stk.	100	10
—	Piræus, Ath., & Pelo.	75	1½
4/	Pto. Alegre & N. Hambg Ld., 7 p.c. Pref. Shs.	20	4
6	Do. Mt. Deb. Stk. Red.	100	74½
—	Puerto Cabello & Val. Ld.	10	1½
5	Recife & S. Francisco	100	64½
14/	R. Claro S. Paulo, Ld., Sh.	10	23
5	Do. Deb. Stk.	100	125
5	Royal Sardinian Ord	10	11½
5/	Do. Pref.	10	11½

Foreign Railways (*continued*):—

Last Div.	Name.	Paid.	Price.
5/	Sambre & Meuse	20	18
5/6	Do. Pref.	10	12½
22/	San Paulo Ld.	20	34
2/10½	Do. New Ord. £10 sh.	6	10
4/8	Do. 5 p.c. Non.Cm.Pref.	10	12½
5½	Do. Deb. Stk.	100	133
5	Do. 5 p.c. Deb. Stk	100	127
—	S. Fé & Cordova, Gt. Sthn., Ld., Shares	100	49
6	Do. Perp. Deb. Stk.	100	119
3/2½	S. Austrian	20	7
12/	Sthn. Braz. R. Gde. do Sul, Ld.	20	9
6	Do. 6 p.c. Deb. Stk.	100	67
4	Swedish Centl., Ld., 4 p.c. Deb. Stk.	100	107
5	Do. Pref.	100	101
1/3	Taltal, Ld.	5	2½
—	Uruguay Nthn., Ld. 7 p.c. Pfd. Stk.	100	8
3½	Do. 5 p.c. Deb. Stk.	100	30
—	Villa Maria & Rufino, Ld., 6 p.c. Pref. Shs.	100	17
4	Do. 4 p.c. 1 Deb. Stk.	100	71
6/0/0	Do. 6 p.c. 2 Deb. Stk.	100	42½
5/9	West Flanders	8½	21
5/6	Do. 5½ p.c. Pref.	10	18
3/	Wstn. of Havana, Ld.	10	4½

FOREIGN RAILWAY OBLIGATIONS

Per Cent.	Name.	Price.
6	Alagoas Ld., 6 p.c. Deb., Rd.	84
—	Alcoy & Gandia, Ld., 5 p.c. Debs., Red.	20
5	Arauco., Ld., 5 p.c. 1st Mt., Rd.	64½
—	Do. 6 p.c. Mt. Deb., Rd.	38½
6	Brazil G. Sthn., L., Mt. Dbs., Rd.	80½
6	Do. Mt. Dbs. 1893, Rd.	52
5½	Campos & Caran. Dbs., Rd.	70
6	Central Bahia, L., Dbs., Rd.	89½
5½	Conde d'Eu, L., Dbs., Rd.	71
6	Costa Rica, L., 1st Mt. Dbs., Rd.	110
6	Do. 2nd Dbs., Rd.	91
5	Do. Prior Mt. Db., Rd.	104
6	Cucuta Mt. Dbs., Rd.	102
5½	Donna Thrsa. Cris., L., Dbs., Rd.	71
3	Eastn. of France, £20 Dbs., Rd.	18½
4	Egyptn. Delta Light, L., Db., Rd	101
—	Espito. Santo & Cara. 5 p.c. Stl. Dbs., Rd.	38
4	Gd. Russian Nic., Rd.	102
5	Inter-Oceanic Mex., L., 5 p.c. Pr. Ln. Dbs., Rd.	103
3	Ital. 3 p.c. Bds. A & B, Rd.	57½
—	Ituana 6 p.c. Debs., 1918	72½
—	Manila Ltd., 6 p.c. Deb., Red.	21
6	Do. Prior Lien Mt., Rd.	100½
6	Do. Series "B," Rd.	80
7	Matanzas & Sab., Rd.	101½
6	Minas & Rio, L., 6 p.c. Dbs., Rd.	97
5	Mogyana 5 p.c. Deb. Bds., Rd.	101
5	Moscow-Jaros., Rd.	105½
5½	Natal & Na. Cruz Ltd., 5½ p.c. Debs., Red.	75½
5	Nitrate, Ltd. Mt. Bds., Red.	87
3	Nthn. France, Red.	19½
4	N. of S. Af. Rep. (Trnsvl.) Gu. Bds. Red.	96
3	Nthn. of Spain £20 Pri. Obs. Red.	7½
6	Ottmn. (Smy to A.)(Kujk) Asnt. Debs., Red.	105
6	Ottmn. (Seraik.) Asg. Debs. Red.	106
6	Ottmn. (Seraik) Non-Asg. D., Rd	106
5	Ottmn. Kuyjk. Ext. Red.	104
5	Ottmn. Serkeuy. Ext. Red.	102
5	Ottmn. Tireh Ext. 1910	98
5	Ottmn. Debs, 1886, Red.	97½
5	Do. 1888, Red. 1935	98½
5	Do. 1893, Red. 1935	97
5	Ottmn. of Anlia. Debs., Rd.	83½
4	Ottomn. Smyr. & Cas Ext Bds., Red.	83½
3	Paris, Lyon & Medit. (old sys., £20), Red.	19
3	Paris, Lyon & Medit. (new sys., £20), Red.	18¾
50/	Piræus, At. & Pelp., 6 p.c. 1st Mt. Bds., Red.	89½
3	Do. 5 p.c. Mt. Bds., Red.	74
4	Pretoria-Pietbg., Ltd., Red.	93
7	Puerto Cab. & Val., Ltd., 1st Mt. Debs., Red.	01
3	Royal Sardinian, A, Rd. £20	12
3	Royal Sardinian, B., Rd. £20	12
5	Ryl. Trns.-Afric. 5 p.c. 1st Mt. £100 Bds., Red.	48½
4	Sa. Fe & Cor. G.S., Ld. Pr Ln. Bds.	104
5	Sa. Fe, 5 p.c 2nd Reg. Dbs.	75
3	South Austrian, £20 Red.	15½
3	South Austrian, (Ser X.)	15
3	South Italian £20 Obs. (Ser. A to G), Red.	12
3½	S.W. of Venez (Barq.), Ltd., 7 p.c. 1st Mt. £100 Debs.	46½
5	Taltal, Ltd., 5 p.c. 1st Ch. Debs., Red.	100
5	Utd. Rwys. Havana, Red.	87½
3	Wstn. of France, £20 Red.	19

Foreign Rly. Obligations (*continued*):—

Per Cent.	Name.	Price.
6	Wrn. B. Ayres St. Mt. Debs., 1902	107
6	Wrn. B. Ayres, Reg. Cert.	106
5	Do. Mt. Bds.	122
6	Wtrn. of Havna., Ld, Mt. Dbs., Rd.	93
7	Wrn. Ry. San Paulo Red.	101
—	Wrn. Santa Fé. 7 p.c. Red.	42
2/8	Zafra & Huelva, 3 p.c. Red.	2½

BANKS.

Div.	Name.	Paid.	Price.
2/4½	Agra, Ltd.	6	3½
2/0½	Anglo-Argentine, Ltd., £4	7	5½
8 fls.	Anglo-Austrian	120f	13
6/	Anglo-Californian, Ltd., £20 Shares	10	11
4/	Anglo-Egyptian, Ltd., £15	5	6
5/	Anglo-Foreign Bkg., Ltd.	7	7½
7/	Anglo-Italian, Ltd	5	7
7/6	Bk. of Africa, Ltd., £18¾	6¼	10½
20/	Bk. of Australasia	40	50
10/	Bk. of Brit. Columbia	20	19½
25/	Bk. of Brit. N. America	50	63
20/	Bk. of Egypt, Ltd., £25	12½	18½
5/	Bk. of Mauritius, Ltd.	10	9
18/	Bk. of N. S. Wales	20	36½
4 p.c.	Bk. of N. Zland. Gua. Stk.	100	102½
6/	Bk. of Roumania, £20 Shs.	6	7½
2/6	Tarapaca & Ldn., Ltd., £10	5	3½
—	Bque. Fse. de l'Afri. du S.	100f	3½
f.22.50	Bque. Internatle. de Paris	20	23
6/	Brit. Bk. of S. America, Ltd., £20 Shares	10	10½
16/	Capital & Cties., L., £50	10	40½
20/	Chart. of India, &c.	20	30
10/	City, Ltd., £40 Shares	10	20
18/	Colonial, £100 Shares	30	21
10/	Delhi and London, Ltd.	25	—
5/	German of London, Ltd.	10	10½
25/	Hong-Kong & Shanghai	28½	45
4/	Imperl. of Persia	6½	3½
10/	Imperl. Ottoman, £20 Shs	10	12½
12/	Intrnatl. of Ldn., Ld., £20	15	11
10/	Ionian, Ltd.	25	15½
16/	Lloyds, Ltd., £50 Shs.	8	31½
10/	Ldn. & Braziln. Ltd., £20	10	17½
44/	Ldn. & County, Ltd., £80	20	101½
9/	Ldn. & Hanseatic, L., £20	10	10½
22/6	Ldn. & Midland, L., £60	12½	53
8/9	Ldn. & Provin., Ltd., £10	5	21½
21/	Ldn. & Riv. Plate, L., £25	15	51
2/1½	Ldn. & San Fcisco, Ltd.	7	4
28/	Ldn. & Sth. West., L., £50	20	68
26/	Ldn. & Westmins., L., £100	20	58
5/	Ldn. of Mex. & S. Amer., Ltd., £10 Shs.	6	5½
15/	Ldn. Joint Stk., L., £100	15	34
12/9½	Ldn., Paris & Amer., L. £20	16	25
2/4½	Merchant Bkg., L., £9	4	2½
6/3	Metropn, Ltd., £50 Shs.	5	14½
9/	National, Ltd., £50 Shs.	10	20
3/11	Natl. of Mexico, $100 Shs.	$35	12
1/3	National of N. Z., L., £7½	2½	2
3/	National S. Afric. Rep.	10	13½
18/10½	National Provcl. of Eng., Ltd., £75 Shs.	10½	50½
21/7½	Do. do. £60 Shs.	12	57½
6/6	North Eastn., Ltd., £20 Shs	6	15
19/	Parr's, Ld., £100 Shs.	20	89½
12/6	Prov. of Ireland, L., £100	12½	29½
40/	Stand. of S. Afric., L., £100	25	64
12/6	Union of Australia, L., £75	25	26½
4 p.c.	Do. do. Ins. Stk. Dep. 1900	100	104
15/6	Union of Ldn., Ltd., £100	15½	35

BREWERIES AND DISTILLERIES.

Div.	Name.	Paid.	Price.
4½	Albion Prp. 1 Mt. Db. Sk.	100	111
4	All Saints', L., Db. Sk. Rd.	100	97
7	Allsopp, Ltd	100	153
6	Do. Cum. Pref	100	155½
4½	Do. Deb. Stk., Red.	100	117
3½	Do. Deb. Stk., Red.	100	103
4½	Alton & Co., L., Db., Rd	100	107
4½	Do. Mt. Bds., 1896	100	105
—	Arnold, Perrett, Ltd.	10	6
6	Do. Cum. Pref.	10	10
4½	Do. 1 Mt. Db. Stk., Rd	100	107

Breweries &c. (*continued*):—

Div.	Name.	Paid.	Price
5½	Arrol, A., & Sons, L. Cum. Pref. Shs.	10	10
4½	Do. 1 Mt. Db. Stk., Rd.	100	107
5	Backus, 1 Mt. Db., Red.	100	59
4	Barclay, Perk., L., Cu. Pf.	10	11½
3½	Do. Mt. Db. Stk., Red.	100	108
—	Barnsley, Ltd.	10	10½
6	Do. Cum. Pref.	10	13
1/3	Barrett's, Ltd	2½	1½
1/3	Do. 5 p.c. Pref.	2½	2½
3/	Barthelomay, Ltd.	10	2½
8	Do. Cum. Pref.	10	7
6	Do. Deb.	100	97½
5	Bass, Ratcliff, Ltd., Cum. Pref. Stk.	100	142½
4½	Do. Mt. Db. Stk., Rd.	100	124
4	Bell, J., L., 1 Mt. D. Stk., R	100	100
—	Benskin's, L., Cum. Pref.	5	—
—	Do. 1 Mt. Db. Stk Red.	100	—
—	Do. "B" Deb. Sk, Rd.	100	—
7/	Bentley's Yorks., Ltd.	10	10½
6/	Do. Cum. Pref.	10	12½
4½	Do. Mt. Debs., Red.	100	110
4½	Do. do. 1892, Red.	100	110
—	Bieckert's, Ltd.	20	2
5	Do. Debs., Red.	100	56
—	Birmingham., Ltd., 6 p.c. Cum. Pref.	5	2½
4½	Do. Mt. Debs., Red.	50	39½
5½	Boardman's, Ld., Cm. Pf.	10	8½
4½	Do., Perp. 1 Mt. Db. Sk.	100	104½
30/9	Brain & Co., Ltd.	100	101
4½	Brakspear, L., 1 D. Stk. Red.	100	108
4	Brandon's, L., 1 D. Stk. Red.	100	104½
21/	Bristol (Georges) Ltd.	10	45
6	Do. Cum. Pref.	10	17½
5	Do. Mt. Db. Sk. 1888 Rd.	100	115½
17/6	Bristol United, Ltd.	10	35
6	Do. Cum. Pref.	10	16½
4½	Do. Db. Sk. Rd.	100	120½
5½	Buckley's, L., C. Pre-prf.	10	10½
4½	Do. 1 Mt. Db. Stk. Rd.	100	104½
4	Bullard & Sons, Ltd., D. Sk. R.	100	105
6	Bushell, Watk., L., C. Pf.	10	14
4½	Do. 1 Mt. Db. Sk. Rd.	100	112
5	Camden, Ltd., Cum. Pref.	10	11½
4½	Do. 1 Mt. Db. Sk. Rd.	100	107
5½	Cameron, Ltd., Cm. Prf.	10	13
4½	Do. Mort Deb. Stk.	100	106
3½	Do. Perp Mt. Db. Sk.	100	98½
5	Camp'bell, J'stone, L., C. Pf.	5	5
4½	Do. 4½ p.c. 1 Mt. Db. Sk.	100	103
4	Campbell, Praed, L., Per. 1 Mort. Deb. Stk.	100	105
4	Cannon, L., Mt. Db. Stk.	100	109
4	Do. "B" Deb. Stk.	100	102
5	Castlemaine, L., 1 Mt. Db.	100	94
3½	Charrington, Ltd., Mort. Deb. Stk. Red.	100	106
2/	Cheltnhm. Orig., Ltd.	5	6
6	Do. Cum. Pref.	5	7½
4	Do. Debs. Red.	100	106
10/	Chicago, Ltd.	10	3½
6	Do. Debs.	100	84½
—	Cincinnati, Cum. Pref.	10	1
10/	City of Baltimore	10	3½
16/	Do. 8 p.c. Cum. Pref	10	8
14/	City of Chicago, Ltd.	10	1½
8	Do. Cum. Pref.	10	6½
13	City of London, Ltd.	100	206½
5	Do. Cum. Pref.	100	136
4	Do. Mt. Deb. Stk., Rd.	100	109½
2/	Colchester, Ltd.	5	4½
7	Do. Pref.	5	6½
4½	Do. Deb. Stk., Red.	100	109
5	Combe, Ltd., Cum. Pref.	10	14½
4	Do. Mt. Db. Stk, Rd.	100	111
3½	Do. Perp. Deb. Stk.	100	108
5	Comm'cial, L., D. Sk., Rd.	100	107½
5	Courage, L., Cm. Pref. Shs.	100	137½
4	Do. Irr. Mt. Deb. Stk.	100	124½
3½	Do. Irr. "B" Mt. Db. Sk.	100	105
8/	Daniell & Sons, Ltd.	10	7
7	Do. Cum. Pref.	10	12
4½	Do. 1 Mt. Perp. Db. Sk.	100	103½
4½	Do. "B" Deb. Stk.	100	99
10d.	Dartford, Ltd.	5	5
2/9	Do. Cum. Pref.	5	5½
4	Do. 1 Mt. Db. Sk. Rd	100	99
4	Davenport, Ld., 1 D. Stk.	100	101½
10/	Denver United, Ltd.	10	3½
8	Do. Cum. Pref.	10	8½
6	Do. Debs.	100	98½
4½	Deuchar, L., 1 D. Sk., Rd.	100	109
8/	Distillers, Ltd.	10	25
—	Dublin Distillers, Ltd.	5	1½
6	Do. Cum. Pref.	5	4½
4½	Do. Irr. Deb. Stk.	100	—
5	Eadie, Ltd., Cum. Pref.	10	11½
4	Do. Irr. 1 Mt. Db. Sk.	100	107
10/	Edinbgh. Utd., Ltd.	10	13½
6	Do. Cum. Prf.	10	13½
4	Eldridge, Pope, L. D. St. R.	100	106½
—	Emerald & Phoenix, Ltd.	10	1½
8	Do. Cum. Pref.	10	6
6	Empress Ltd., C. Pf.	10	11½
4½	Do. Mt. Deb. Stk.	100	103
10/	Farnham, Ltd.	10	17½
6	Do. Cum. Pref.	10	14½
4	Fenwick, L., 1 D. Sk., Rd.	100	103
4	Flower & Sons, Irr. D. Sk.	100	111
4	Friary, L., 1 Db. Stk., Rd.	100	103½
4	Do. 1 "A" Db. Sk., Rd	100	100
4½	Groves, L., 1 Db. Sk., Rd.	100	111
14	Guinness, Ltd.	100	590
6	Do. Cm. Prf. Stk.	100	185½
5	Do. Deb. Stk., Red.	100	120
5	Hall's Oxford L., Cm. Pf.	5	5½
6/	Hancock, Ld., Cm. Pf. Ord.	10	14
[illegible]	Do. Def. Ord	10	17½

Breweries, &c. (*continued*) :—

Div.	Name.	Paid.	Price.
6	Hancock, Ld., Cum. Pref.	10	15
4	Do. 1 Deb. Stk., Rd.	100	110
5	Hoare, Ltd. Cum. Pref.	10	12¾
5	Do. "A" Cum. Pref.	10	12¼
4	Do. Mt. Deb. Stk., Rd.	100	113
3½	Do. do. do. Rd.	100	104
3/6	Hodgson's, Ltd.	5	9¾
5	Do. 1 Mt. Db., Red.	—	117½
4	Do. 2 Mt. Db., 1906	—	100
4½	Hopcraft & N., Ltd., 1 Mt. Deb. Stk., Red.	100	103
5	Huggins, Ltd., Cm. Prf.	10	—
4½	Do. 1st D. Stk. Rd.	100	—
4½	Do. "B" Db. Stk. Rd.	100	—
12/	Hull, Ltd.	10	17
7	Do. Cum. Pref.	10	14½
4½	Ind, Coope, L., D.Sk., Rd.	100	119
4	Do. "B" Mt. Db. Stk. Rd.	100	110
8/	Indianapolis, Ltd.	10	3
8	Do. Cm. Prf.	10	8¾
5/	Jones, Frank, Ltd.	10	2½
7½	Do. Cum. Pref.	10	6½
5	Do. 1st Mort. Debs.	100	90½
3/	J. Kenward & Co., Ltd.	5	5¾
4½	Kingsbury, L., 1 D.Sk., Rd	100	—
4	Lacon, L., D. Stk., Red.	100	110
4	Do. Irrd. "B" D. Sk.	100	107
7/	Lascelles, Ltd.	5	11½
6	Do. Cum. Pref.	5	7¾
5	Leney, Ltd., Cum. Pref.	10	11½
4	Do. 1 Mt. Db. Stk. Rd.	100	102
30/7½	Lion, Ltd., £25 shares	17	49½
10/9½	Do. New £10 shares	6	17
6	Do. Perp. Pref.	20	33
4	Do. B. Mt. Db. Sk. Rd.	100	107
4½	Lloyd & Y., Ltd., 1 Mt. Deb. Stk., Rd.	100	100½
4½	Locke & S., Ltd., Irr. 1st Mt. Deb. Stk.	100	103
4½	Lovibond, Ltd., 1st Mt. Deb. Stk., Rd.	100	101½
30/4	Lucas&Co., Ld., Deb.Stk.	100	107
12/	Manchester, Ltd.	10	19
7	Do. Cum. Pref.	10	16½
5/	Marston, J., L., Cm. Prf.	10	10¾
4	Do. 1 Mt. Db. Sk., Rd.	100	101½
7/	Massey's Burnley, Ltd.	10	16½
6	Do. Cum. Pref.	10	14¼
4½	McCracken, Ltd., 1 Mt. Deb., 1908	100	59½
5	McEwan, Ltd., Cm. Pref.	10	14
5	Meux, Ltd., Cum. Pref.	10	14½
4	Do. Mt. Db. Stk. Red.	100	111
4½	Michell & A., Ltd., 1 Mt. Deb. Stk. Red.	100	106
4½	MileEndDist.Db.Sk.Rd.	100	111
—	Milwaukee & Chic., Ltd.	10	1¾
4/	Do. Cum. Pref.	10	6¾
4½	Michell, Toms, L., Db.	50	57
6	Morgan, Ltd., Cum. Pref.	10	14½
25/	Nalder & Coll., Ltd.	10	34
6	Do. Cum. Pref.	10	15¾
4½	Do. Deb. Red.	100	112
12/	Newcastle, Ltd.	10	19½
6	Do. Cum. Pref.	10	15
5	Do. 1 Mt. Deb., 1911	100	111½
4	Do. "A" Deb.Stk.Red.	100	106½
6	New England, Ltd.	10	4¼
8	Do. Cum. Pref.	10	9
6	Do. Debs. Red.	100	101½
4	New London, L., 1 D.Sk.	100	103
7/2	New Westminster, Ltd.	4	10
2/4½	Do. Pref.	4	6½
—	New York, Ltd.	10	¾
—	Do. 8 p.c. Cum. Pref.	10	4
6	Do. 1 Mt. Deb. Red.	100	77½
5	Noakes, Ld., Cum. Pref.	10	12
4	Do. 1 Mt. Db. Stk., Rd.	100	106
4½	Norfolk, L., "A" D.Sk.Rd.	100	106
10/	Northampton, Ld.	10	17
7	Do. Cum. Pref.	10	15½
6	Do. Cum. Pref.	10	12½
5	Do. 1 Mt. Per. Db.Sk.	100	127
4	Nth.East., L., 1 D.Sk.Rd.	100	100
4½	N. Worcesters., L. Per. 1 Mort. Deb. Stock	100	96½
6	Nottingham, L., Cm. Prf.	10	1½
5	Do. 1 Mt.Deb.Stk., Red.	100	114
17/4	Do. "B" do. Red.	50	112
6/	Ohlsson' Cape, Ld.	5	18
7	Do. Cum. Pref.	5	9
4½	Do. 2nd Cum. Pref.	5	5½
5	Do. Deb. Stk., Red.	100	117
4½	Oldfield, L., 1 Mt. Db.Stk.	100	106
6	Page & Overt., L., Cm. Prf.	10	13¾
4½	Do. 1 Mt. Dbs., Red.	100	109
10/	Parker's Burslem, Ltd.	10	24½
6	Do. Cum. Pref.	10	15
4	Do. 1 Mt. Db. Stk., Red.	100	112
4	Persse, Ld., 1 Mt. Db. Rd.	100	95½
	Phipps, L., Irr. 1 Db. Stk.	100	113
8	Plymouth, L., Min.Cu.Pf.	10	13½
4½	Do. Mt. Deb. Stk., Red.	100	106½
4½	Pryor, Reid, L., 1 D.S., R.	100	102½
5	Reid's, Ld., Cm. Pref. Stk.	100	136½
4	Do. Mt. Deb. Stk., Red	100	111
3½	Do. "B" Mt.Db.Stk., Rd	100	104
5	Rhondda Val., L., Cu. Pf	10	11
4½	Do. 1 Mt. Deb. Stk., Rd	100	109
5	Robinson, Ld., Cum. Pref.	10	11
4½	Do. 1 Mt. Perp. Db. Stk.	100	111
4/	Rochdale, Ltd.	10	6
4½	Do. 1 Mt. Deb. Stk.	100	98
7	Royal, Brentford, Ltd.	10	22
	Do. Cum. Pref.	10	13
4½	Do. 1 Mt. Dbs. Red	100	105
6/	St. Louis, Ltd.	10	3
8	Do. Cum. Pref.	10	8
14/	St. Paull, Ltd.	10	10
7	Do. Cum. Pref.	10	12
4½	Salt (T.), L., 1 Db. Sk. Rd.	100	113
4½	Do. "B" Db.Stk. Red	100	107
—	San Francisco, Ltd	10	
—	Do. 8 p.c. Cum. Pref.	10	

Breweries, &c. (*continued*) :—

Div.	Name.	Paid.	Price.
4½	Savill Brs., L., D. Sk. Rd.	100	118
4½	Scarboro., Ltd., 1 Db. Stk.	100	101
4	Shaw (Hy.), Ltd., 1 Mt. Db. Stk., Red.	100	104
22/	Showell's, Ltd.	10	33
7	Do. Cum. Pref.	10	17¼
3/	Do. Gua. Shs.	5	7¾
4½	Do. Mt. Db. Stk., Red.	100	—
4	Simonds, L., 1 D. Sk., Rd.	100	111
5½	Simson & McP., L., Cu. Pf.	10	9½
4½	Do. 1 Mt. Deb. Stk.	100	97
5/	Smith, Garrett, L., £20Shs	10	16½
5	Do. Cum. Pref.	20	26
3½	Do. 3½ p.c. Mt. Db. Stk.	100	107
5	Smith's, Tadcster, L., CPf	10	12
4½	Do. Deb. Stk., Red.	100	112
4	Do. Deb. Stk. Red.	100	108
4½	Star, L., 1 M. Db.Stk., Rd.	100	103
4	Steward & P., L., 1 D. Sk.	100	110
7/	Strettons Derby, Ltd.	10	13
6	Do. Cum. Pref.	10	13
4	Do. Irr. 1 Mt. Db.Stk.	100	104½
4½	Strong, Romsey, L., 1 D.S.	100	113
5	Stroud, L., Db. Sk., Rd.	100	106
4½	Tadcaster To'er, L., D.Sk.	100	113
8/	Tamplin, Ltd	10	21
6	Do. Cum. Pref.	100	15
4	Do. "A" Db. Sk., Rd.	10	106
6	Thorne, Ltd., Cum. Pref.	10	14
4	Do. Deb. Stk., Red.	100	103½
15/	Threlfall, Ltd.	10	45
6	Do. Cum. Pref.	10	16½
5	Do. 1 Mt. Dbs., Red.	100	114
4	Tollemache, L., D. Sk. Rd.	100	103
4	Truman, Hanb., D. Sk., R.	100	111
3	Do. "B" Mt. Db.Sk., Rd.	100	95
10/	United States, Ltd.	10	9
8	Do. Cum. Pref.	10	11
6	Do. 1 Mt. Deb.	100	106½
6/	Walker&H., Ld., Cm. Prf.	10	10¾
4½	Do. 1 Mt. Deb. Stk., Red.	100	108
5	Walker, Peter, Ld. Cm. Prf.	10	13½
4	Do. 1 Mt. Dbs. Red.	100	110
4	Wallingford, L., D.Sk. Rd.	100	105
6	Watney, Ld., Cm. Prf. Sk.	100	170
5	Do. Mt. Db. Sk., Rd.	100	117½
4½	Do. "B" Mt. Db.Sk., Rd.	100	114
3½	Do. Mt. Db. Stk.	100	104
5	Watney, D., Ld., Cm. Prf.	10	12
4½	Do. 1 Mt. Db. Stk.	100	108
10/	Webster & Sons, Ltd.	10	16¾
6	Do. Cum. Pref.	10	14
5	Wenlock Ltd Pref.	10	12
4	Do. 1 Mt. Db. Sk., Rd.	100	106
5	West Cheshire, L., Cu. Pf.	10	10½
4	Do. Irred. 1 Mt. Db.Sk.	100	99
4½	Whitbread, L., Cu. Pf. Sh.	100	123½
4	Do. Db. Stk., Red.	100	110
3½	Do. "B" Db. Stk., Rd.	100	101
8/	Wolverhmpton & D. Ld.	10	18
6	Do. Cum. Pref.	10	13½
4½	Do. 1 Mt. Dbs., Red.	100	108
5½	Worthington, Ld., Cm. Prf.	10	15½
5½	Do. Cum. "B" Pref.	10	13¼
4½	Do. Mt. Db. Sk., Rd.	100	113
3½	Do. Irr. "B" Db. Stk.	100	102
6/	Yates's Castle, Ltd.	10	13
5	Do. Cum. Pref.	10	11
5	Younger W., L., Cu. Pf.Sh.	100	134½

CANALS AND DOCKS.

Last Div.	Name.	Paid.	Price.
4	Birmingham Canal	100	141½
—	E. & W. India Dock	100	19
—	Do. 4 p.c. Prf. Stk.	100	74
—	Do. P L. Deb. Stk.	100	101
—	Do. Cons. Deb. Stk.	100	89
40/	G. Junction Ord. Shs.	100	145½
6/	Do. do. Pref.	10	19
4½	King's Lynn Per. Db. Stk.	100	117½
2½	Leeds & L'pool Canal	100	71
2½	Lndn & St. Kath. Dks.	100	54
4½	Do. Pref.	100	137½
4½	Do. Pref., 1878	100	132½
4½	Do. Pref., 1882	100	130½
4	Do. Deb. Stk.	100	132½
—	Mchester Ship C. 5 p.c. Pf.	10	1¾
3½	Do. 1st Perp. Mt. Deb.	100	93
—	Milford Dks. Db. Stk. "A"	100	18½
3½	Millwall Dk.	100	60½
5	Do. Perp. Pref.	100	140½
4½	Do. Pref.	100	106½
5	Do. New Per. Prf., 1887	100	126½
5	Do. Per. Deb. Stk.	100	152½
4/	Newhaven Har.	10	14½
2½	N. Metropolitan	100	70
5	Sharpness Nw. Pf. "A" Sk.	100	141½
4	Do. Deb. Stk.	100	115½
5	Sheffiel & S. Yorks Nav. 4½ p.c. Pref Stk.	100	115½
36.432	Suez Canal	20	143½
7	Surrey Comcl. Dok., Ord.	100	150½
7	Do. Min. 4 p.c. Pref. "A"	110	151½
5	Do. Pref. "B"	100	148½
5	Do do. "C"	100	148½
5	Do. do. "D"	100	144½
4½	Do Deb. Stk.	100	152½

COMMERCIAL, INDUSTRIAL, &c.

Last Div.	Name.	Paid.	Price.
5	Accles, L., 1 Mt. Db., Red.	100	84½
2/6	Aërated Bread, Ltd.	1	13
—	African Gold Recovery, L.	1	½
2/	Aluminium, L., "A" Shs.	1	2¼
4½	Do. 1 Mt. Db. Stk., Red.	100	97
5½	Amelia Nitr., L., 1 Mort Deb., Red.	100	82½
7/	Anglo-Chil. Nitrate, Ltd., Cum. Pref.	10	7¾
4½	Do. Cons. Mt. Bds., Red.	100	79
4½	Anglo-Russian Cotton, Ld., 1 Charge Debs., Red.	100	98
11/3	Angus (G., & Co., L.), £10	7½	17
6/	Apollinaris, Ltd.	10	11
5/	Do. 5 p.c. Cum. Pref.	10	10½
4	Do. Irred. Deb. Stock	100	103
3/	Argentine Meat Pres., L., 7 p.c. Pref.	10	2¾
5	Argentine Refinry, Db. Rd.	100	98
6d.	Armstrong, Whitw., Ltd.	1	3½
4	Do. Cum. Pref.	5	6½
5	Artisans', Labr. Dwllgs., L.	100	126
4½	Do. Non-Cm. Prf., 1879	100	133½
4½	Do. do. 1884	100	132½
—	Asbestos & Asbestic, Ltd.	10	4¼
2/7½	Ashley-grdns., L., C. Prf.	5	6½
4½	Do. 1 Mt. Deb. Stk.	100	113½
5/	Assam Rly. & Trdng., L., 8 p.c. Cum. Pref. "A"	10	14
—	Do. Deferrd. "B" Shs.	1	4
—	Do. do. (iss.f.pd)	1	3½
8/	Do. Cum. Pre-Prf. "A"	10	15
6/	Do. New Pref.	10	11½
5	Do. Debs., Red.	100	106
5	Do. Red. Mort. Debs.	100	110
6	Aust'lian Pastrl, L., Cu. Pf.	10	7
8d.	Aylesbury Dairy, Ltd.	1	1½
4	Do. 4 p.c. Mt. Dbs.	100	104½
10/	Babcock & Wilcox, Ltd.	10	28
6	Do. 6 p.c. Cm. Prf.	10	16
8	Baker (Chs.), L., Cm. Pf.	5	9
8	Do. "B" Cm. Pref.	5	7¾
2/1	Barker (John), Ltd.	1	2¾
5½	Do. Cum. Pref.	5	7¾
4½	Do. Irred. 1 Mt. Db. Stk.	100	125½
2/6	Barnagore Jute, Ltd.	5	2¾
5	Do. Cum. Pref.	5	4½
7½d.	Belgravia Dairy, Ltd.	1	1¼
5/6	Bell (R.) & Co., Ltd.	3	4
9½d.	Bell's Asbestos, Ltd.	1	¾
5	Do. Mt. Db. Bds., Rd.	100	106
10/	Bengal Mills, Ltd.	10	11
6/	Do. 5 p.c. Cum. Prf.	10	10½
5/	Benson (J.W.) L., Cm. Pf.	10	10½
4	Do. Perp. Mt. Db. Stk.	100	101
6	Bergvik, L., 6 p.c. Cm. Pf.	10	12½
12/	Do. Dfd.	10	11
4½	Do. 1 Dbs., Red.	100	105½
5/	Birm'ham Vinegar, Ltd.	5	15
5	Do. Cum. Pref.	5	5¾
4½	Do. 1 Mt. Db. Stk., Rd.	100	109½
5	Boake (A.) L., 5 p.c. Cu. Pf.	10	10¾
2/6	Bodega, Ltd.	5	8¾
4½	Do. Mt. Deb. Stk., Rd.	100	111
12/	Bottomley & Brs., Ltd.	10	6
6/	Do. 6 p.c. Pt.	10	9
8½d.	Bovril, Ltd.	1	1
1/0½	Do. Def.	1	½
6½d.	Do. Cum. Pref.	1	1⅛
4½	Do. Deb. Stk.	100	101
5/	Bradbury, Gretrex., Ltd., £10 share	8	14
5/	Do. 5 p.c. Cum. Pref.	10	13½
5/	Brewers' Sugar, L., 5 p.c. Cum. Pref.	10	10½
3/6	Brighton Grd. Hotel, Ld.	5	4
4	Do Mt. Db. Stk., Red.	100	102
5	Bristol Hotel & Palm. Co., Ltd. 1st Mt. Red. Deb.	100	104
6d.	British & Bengton's. Tea Tr. Asc., Ltd.	1	1
5	Do. Cum. Prf.	5	5½
—	British Deli & Lgkat. Tobacco, Ltd.	1	¾
—	Do. Cum. Prf.	1	¾
1/3	British Tea Table, Ltd.	1	2½
5½	Do. Cum. Pref.	1	1¼
2/6	Brooke, Ben., & Co., Ltd., Cum. Pref.	5	5¾
7/6	Brooke, Bond & Co., Ltd.	5	19
3/	Brown Brs., L., Cum. Pref.	5	5½
10/	Browne & Eagle, Ltd.	10	13½
5	Do. Cum. Pref.	10	13
4	Do. Mrt. Db. Sk., Red.	100	110
20/	Brunner, Mond, & Co., Lt.	0	37
10/6	Do. £10 shares	3½	14½
7	Do. Cum. Pref.	10	17
7	Do. £10 shares	5	8½
10/	Bryant & May, Ltd.	5	13¾
3/	Bucknall, H., & Sons, Lt.	5	7
6	Do. Cum Pref.	5	7¾
4/	Burke, E. & J., Ltd.	5	7½
6	Do. Cum. Pref.	5	7½
6	Do. Irred. Deb. Stk.	100	155
1/	Burlington Htls. Co., Ltd	1	1¾
5	Do. Cum. Pref.	1	1
4	Do. Perp. Deb. Stk.	100	105½
5	Bush, W. J., & Co., Ltd., Cum. Pref.	5	5½
4	Do. 1 Deb. Stk., Red.	100	102
5½	Callard, Stewart, & Watt, Ltd., Cum. Pref.	1	1½
4/	Callender's Cable L., Shs.	5	10½
4½	Do. 1 Deb. Stk., Red.	100	111½
—	Campbell, R., & Sons, Lt.	3	2¾
6	Cantareira Water, Bd., Rd	100	99½
5	Do. (2nd issue)	100	87½
4	Caravio Sugar, Ltd., 6 p.c. 1st Debs., Red.	20	82½
9/	Cassell & Co., Ltd., £10	9	15
5	Causton, Sir J., & Sons, Ltd., Cum. Pref.	10	13¾

Commercial, &c. (*continued*) :—

Last Div.	Name.	Paid.	Price.
4	Cent. Prod. Mkt. of B.A. 1st Mt. Str. Debs.	100	80
4	Chappell & Co., Ltd., Mt. Deb. Stk. Red.	100	103
6/	Chicago & N.W. Gran. 8 p.c. Cum. Pref.	10	3
4/	Chicago Packing & Prov.	10	6
8	Do. Cum. Pref.	10	10
6/	City Offices, Ltd.	12	8
3½	Do. Mt. Deb. Stk.	100	108½
12/	Cy. London Real Prop., Ltd., £25 shs.	12	21½
9/	Do. £12½ shs.	7½	14½
3¾	Do. Deb. Stk. Red.	100	107½
3½	Do. Deb. Stk. Red.	100	105½
3	Do.	100	100½
6/	Cy. of Santos Imprvts., Ltd., 7 p.c. Pref.	10	8
20/	Clay, Bock, & Co., Ltd.	10	5
8	Do. Cum. Pref.	10	9
6	Do. Mort. Deb	100	103½
20/	Coats, J. & P., Ltd.	10	61
6/	Do. Cum. Pref.	10	18
4½	Do. Deb. Stk. Red.	100	112½
1/2½	Coburg Hotel, Ltd	1	1¾
4	Do. Deb. Stk. Red.	100	102
6	Colonial Consign & Dis., Ltd., Cum. Pref.	5	4¾
4½	Do. 1st Mort. Debs.	100	96½
—	Colorado Nitrate, Ltd.	5	¾
5/	Co. Gén des Asphtes de F., Ltd.	6	6
5	Do. Non-Cm. Prf.	—	5
5	Cook, J. W., & Co., Ltd., Cum. Pref.	5	5¾
5	Cook, T., & Son, Egypt, Ltd., 1st Mt. Deb. Red.	100	110½
—	Cork Co., Ltd., 6 p.c. Cum. Pref.	5	2
5	Cory, W., & Sn, L., Cu. Pf.	5	5¾
4	Do. 1st Deb. Stk. Red.	100	109
1/6	Crisp & Co., Ltd.	1	1½
5½	Do. Cum. Pref.	1	1¼
—	Crompton & Co., Ltd., 7 p.c. Cum. Pref.	5	—
5	Do. 1st Mt. Reg. Deb.	—	90½
4/6	Crossley, J., & Sons, Ltd.	5	8
5	Do. Cum. Pref.	5	6½
—	Crystal Pal. Ord. "A" Stk.	100	6¾
—	Do. "B" Red. Stk	100	1¾
6	Do. 6 p.c. 1st 1887 Deb. Stk. Red.	100	117½
—	Do. 6 p.c. 2nd 1887 Deb. Stk. Red.	100	51½
—	Do. 6 p.c. 3rd 1887 Deb. Stk. Red.	100	22½
3	Do. 3 p.c. 1st 1895 Deb. Stk.	100	92½
—	Daimler Motor, Ltd.	10	6
4/	Dalgety & Co., £20 Shs.	5	5½
4½	Do. Deb. Stk	100	124
4	Do.	100	112
7/	De Keyser's Ryl. Htl., L.	10	13½
5	Do. Cum. Pref.	10	12
4	Do. Deb. Stk., Red.	100	110
6	Denny, H., & Sons, Ltd., Cum. Pref.	10	14½
5/3	Devas, Routledge & Co., L.	7	8¾
5	Dickinson, J., & Co., L., Cum. Pref. Stk.	100	123
4½	Domin. Cottn. Mls., Ltd. Mt. Stg. Dbs.	100	97
6/	Dorman, Long & Co., L.	5	4¾
—	Eastmans, Ltd	10	2¾
12/	Do. 8 p.c. Cum. Pref.	10	11
2/6	E C. Powder, Ltd.	3	4
1/6	Edison & Swn Utd. Elec. Ltd., "A" £5 Shs.	3	2½
2/6	Do. fully-paid	5	4½
4½	Ekman Pulp & Ppr. Co., Ltd., Mt. Deb., Red.	100	96
1/1½	Electric Construc., Ltd.	2	2¾
7	Do. Cum. Pref.	2	3½
25/	Eley Bros., Ltd.	10	37
—	Elmore's Cop. Deptg., L.	1	¾
—	Elmore's Wire Mnfg., L.	2	¾
—	Elysée Pal. Hotel Co., L.	3/	¾
5 p.c.	Do. 5 p.c. £100 Db., Rd.	70	97½
8½d.	Evans, Ben., & Co., Ltd.	1	1
5	Do. 1 Mt. Db. Sk., Rd.	100	110
1/8½d.	Evans., D. H., & Co., L.	1	2½
6	Do. Cum. Pref.	1	1¼
4½	Do. 1 Mt. Db. Sk., Rd.	100	112
2/6	*Evening News*, L., 5 p.c. Cum. Pref.	5	5¾
5/3	Evered & Co., L., £10 Sh.	7	12½
7/6	Do.	10	18
4	Fairbairn Pastoral Co., Aust., L., 1 Mt. Db., Rd.	100	102
6	Fairfield Shipbldg., Ltd., Cum. Pref.	10	11½
4½	Do. Mort. Deb. Stk	100	112½
6/	Farmer & Co., Ld., 6 p.c. Cum. Pref.	10	13½
12/	Field, J. C. & J., Ltd.	10	10
7/	Do. 7 p.c. Cum. Pref.	10	14
1/3	Fordham, W.B., & Sns, Ld.	1	2
5/6	Fore-st. Warehouse, Ltd.	11	9½
4	Do. Regd. Debs., Rd.	100	103½
3/6	Foster, M. B. & Sons, Ltd.	4	6
5	Do. Pref.	10	11½
9/	Foster, Porter, & Co., L.	10½	16
4	Fowler, J., & Co. (Leeds), Ltd., 1 Mt. Deb., Red.	100	103½
3/	Fraser & Chalmers, Ltd.	3	1¾
4½	Free, Rodwell & Co., Ltd. Deb Stk.	100	10½
6½d.	Furness, T., & Co., Ltd., 5½ p.c. Cum. Pref.		1
4½	Gartside & Co. (of Manchstr), L., 1 Mt. Db. Sk.	100	113
11	Genl. Hydraul Power, L.	100	260

Commercial, &c. (*continued*):—

Last Div.	Name.	Paid.	Price.
8/	Gillman & Spencer, Ltd.	5	2½
6	Do. Pref.	5	4½
5	Do. Mort. Debs.	50	51
4	Goldsbro., Mort & Co., L., "A" Deb. Stk., Red.	100	69½
—	Do. 3 p.c. "B" Inc. Deb. Stk., Red	100	12
8/	Gordon Hotels, Ltd.	10	20
5½	Do. Cum. Pref.	10	14½
4½	Do. Perp. Deb. Stk.	100	140½
4	Do. do.	100	122½
—	Greenwich Inld. Linoleum Co., Ltd.	1	½
7	Greenwood & Batley, Ltd., Cum. Pref.	10	10
7½d.	Hagemann & Co., Ltd., 6 p.c. Cum. Pref.	1	1
—	Hammond, Ltd.	10	½
—	Do. 8 p.c. Cum. Pref.	10	2¼
—	Do. 6 p.c. Cum. Inc. Stk. Red.	100	56½
	Hampton & Sons, Ltd., 4 p.c. 1 Mt. Db. St. Red.	100	105
—	Hans Crescent Htl., L., 6 p.c. Cum. Pref.	5	3
4	Do. 1 Mt. Deb. Stk.	100	90
6d.	Harmsworth, Ltd., Cum. Pref.	1	1½
4/	Harrison, Barber, Ltd.	5	4¼
3/	Harrod's Stores, Ltd.	1	4¼
2/6	Do. Cum. Pref.	5	6⅝
5½	Hawaiian Comcl. & Sug. 1 Mt. Debs.	100	91½
5	Hazell, Watson, L., C. P.	10	11½
18/	Henley's Teleg., Ltd.	10	22
7	Do. Pref. Shs.	10	19
4½	Do. Mt. Db. Stk., Rd.	100	112½
6	Henry, Ltd.	10	11¾
5	Do. Cum. Pref.	10	13
4½	Do. Mt. Debs., Red.	50	51
1/4½	Herrmann, Ltd.	1	¾
—	Hildesheimer, Ltd.	3	1½
1/2½	Holbrn. & Frasca, Ltd.	1	1⅛
5	Do. Cum. Pref.	10	12
4	Do. Deb. Stk.	100	110
6	Home & Col. Stres, L., C.P	5	7⅜
6	Hood & M.'s Stres., Ltd., Cum. Pref.	1	½
6	Hook, C. T Ltd.	10	6
7/2	Hornsby, Ltd., £10 Shs.	8	3
—	Hotchks. Ordn., Ltd.	10	1
—	Do. 7 p.c Cm. Prf.	10	4¾
5	Do. 1 Mt. Dbs., Rd.	100	97½
6	Htl. Cecil, Ld., Cm. Prf.	5	3¼
4	Do. 1 Mt. D. Sk., R.	100	100½
8/	Howard & Bulgh, Ltd.	10	39
6	Do. Pref.	10	16
4	Do. Deb. Stk., Red.	100	108
5/	Howell, J., Ltd., £5 Shs.	4	8½
—	Howell & Js., Ltd., £3½ Shs.	3	¾
6d.	Humber, Ltd.	1	[illegible]
6	Do. Cum. Pref.	1	[illegible]
5/6	Hunter, Wilts., Ltd.	5	7
2/7	Hyam Clthg., Ltd., 5 p.c. Cum. Pref.	5	5¾
10/	Impl. Russn. Cotton, L.	5	6
5	Impd. Industl. Dwgs., Ld.	100	131½
6d.	Do. Defrd.	1	1¼
25/	Impd. Wood Pave., Ltd.	10	15½
25/	Ind. Rubber, Gutta Per. Telegraph Works, Ltd.	10	21½
4	Do. 1 Mt. Debs., Red.	100	104
6	Intern. Tea, Cum. Pref.	5	6½
10½d.	Jays, Ltd.	1	1⅜
5½	Do. Cum. Pref.	5	6½
1/2½d.	Jones & Higgins, Ltd.	1	2¼
4½	Do. 1 Mt. Db. Sk., Rd.	100	111
5/	Kelly's Directory, Ltd., 5 p.c. Cum. Pref.	10	12½
4	Do. Mort. Db. Sk., Rd.	100	107
—	Kent Coal Explrtn. Ltd.	1	⅞
9½d.	King, Howmann, Ltd.	1	1⅛
4/	Kinloch & Co., Ltd.	5	8¼
6	Do. Pref.	5	7
5	Lady's Pictorial Pub., Ltd., Cum. Pref.	5	5
18/4	La Guaira Harb., Ltd., 5 p.c. Deb. Stk.	100	79½
15/	Do. 2 Mt. 7 p.c. Deb. Stk., Red.	100	25½
4/	Lagunas Nitrate, Ltd.	5	1
2/	Lagunas Syn., Ltd.	5	1
5	Do. 1 Mt. Debs., Red.	100	82½
—	L. Copais Ld., 1 Mt. 6 p.c. Debs., Red.	100	35½
3/	Lautaro Nitrate, Ltd.	5	4½
5	Do. 1 Mt. Debs., Red.	—	100
9/	Lawes Chem. L., £10 shs.	9	5¼
14/	Do. N. Cm. Min. Pref.	10	12½
—	Leeds Forge, 7 p.c. Cm. Pf.	5	4
5	Do. 1 Mt. Debs., Red.	50	48
5	Lever Bros., L., Cm. Pf.	10	13½
6	Liberty, L., 6 p.c. Cm. Pf.	10	15
20/	Liebig's, Ltd.	20	81
5	Lilley & Sk., L., Cm. Pf.	5	5¼
2/6	Linoleum Manfg Ltd.	5	16
3/	Linotype, Ltd., Pre	5	5⅜
5/	Do. Def.	5	7¼
4/	Lister & Co., Ltd.	10	4
5	Do. Cum. Pref.	10	8½
5/	Liverpool. Nitrate	5	5
—	Liverpool. Warehsg., Ltd	10	3
5½	Do. Cum. Pref.	10	7¼
4	Do. 1 Mt. Db. Stk., Rd.	100	105
5½	Lockharts, Ltd., Cm. Pf.	1	1¼
4/6	Ldn. & Til. Lightrage £10	9	6¾
6/	Ldn. Comcl. Sale Rms., L.	10	17½
3	Do. 1 Mt. Deb. Stk., Red.	100	103
3	London Nitrate, Ltd.	5	1½
4/	London Nitrate, Ld. 8 p.c. Cm. Min. Pf.	5	3½
8/	London Pavilion, Ltd.	5	7

Commercial, &c. (*continued*):—

Last Div.	Name.	Paid.	Price.
2/6	London Produce Clg. Ho., Ltd., £10 Shares	2½	3½
4/	London Stereos., Ltd.	5	3
7½d.	Ldn. Un. Laun. L. Cm. Pf.	1	⅞
8½d.	Louise, Ltd.	1	[illegible]
5½	Do. Cum. Pref.	1	[illegible]
5/	Lovell & Christmas, Ltd.	5	11½
6	Do. Cum. Pref.	5	7½
4	Do. Mt. Deb. Stk., Red.	100	107
1/3	Lyons, Ltd.	1	4
4½	Do. 1 Mt. Deb., Stk., Rd.	100	111½
10/	Machinery Trust, Ltd.	5	14½
4½	Do. 4½ Deb. Stk.	100	105
6	MacLellan, L., Min. C. Pf.	10	9
5	Do. 1 Mt. Debs., 1900	100	101½
—	McEwan, J. & Co., Ltd.	10	1½
6	Do. Mt. Debs., Red.	100	89½
8	McNamara, L., Cm. Pref.	10	9
7½d.	Maison Virot, Ltd.	1	¾
2/7	Do. 6 p.c. Cum. Pref.	5	3¼
4/	Manbré Sacc., L., Cm. Pf.	10	11½
10/	Mangan Brze., L., £10 Shs.	6	16
2/	Mason & Mason, Ltd.	5	2¾
6	Do. Cum. Pref.	5	5½
—	Maynards, Ltd.	1	⅞
6	Do. Cum. Pref.	1	[illegible]
9½d.	Mazawattee Tea, Ltd.	1	1⅜
5	Do. Cum. Pref.	5	5¼
6	Mellin's Food Cum. Pref.	5	6¼
4½	Met. Ascn. Imp. Dwlings., Ltd.	100	108
5	Metro. Indus. Dwlgs., Ltd.	5	4¾
4	Do. do. Cum. Pref.	5	5¼
5	Metro. Prop., L., Cm. Pf.	5	5½
4½	Do. 1st Mt. Debs. Stk.	100	107½
6	Mexican Cotton 1 Mt. Db.	100	93½
4½	Mid. Class Dwlgs., L., Db.	100	120½
2/	Millars' Karri, Ltd.	1	3
6	Do. Cum. Pref.	1	1⅜
5/	Milner's Safe, Ltd.	10	20½
10/	Moir & Son, Ltd., Pref.	5	8
6	Morgan Cruc., L., Cm. Pf.	10	14½
1/	Morris, B., Ltd.	3¼	3
2/6	Murray L. 5½ p.c. C. Pf.	5	5¼
63/4½	Do. 4½ 1 Mt. Db. Sk. Rd.	100	107
1/7½	Nat. Safe Dep., Ltd.	4	3½
6	Do. Cum. Pref.	1	1
—	Native Guano, Ltd.	5	½
—	Nelson Bros., Ltd.	10	2¼
5	Do. Deb. Stk., Red.	100	80½
7/	Neuchtel Asph., Ltd.	10	10
10d.	New Darvel Tob., Ltd.	18/	1½
1/6	New Explosives, Ltd.	3	3
5/3¾	New Gd. Htl., Bham, L.	5	4½
5½	Do. Pref.	5	4½
4	Do. 1 Mt. Db. Stk., Rd.	100	96½
—	New Julia Nitrate, Ltd.	10/	—
—	New Ldn. Borneo Tob., L.	16/	1½
1/6	New Premier Cycle, Ltd.	1	[illegible]
6	Do. 6 p.c. Cum. Pref.	1	¾
4½	Do. 4½ p.c. 1 Mt. Db. Rd	100	—
—	New Tamargl. Nitr., Ltd	1	[illegible]
—	Do. 8 p.c. Cum. Pref.	1	½
6	Do. 6 p.c. 1 Mt. Dbs. Rd.	100	62½
3·78d.	Newnes, G., L., Cm. Prf.	1	1
1/3	Nitr. Provision, Ltd.	2½	¾
24/	Nobel-Dynam., Ltd.	10	17½
—	North Brazn. Sugar, Ltd.	1	¼
15/	Oakey, Ltd.	10	30
6	Do. Cum. Pref.	10	17½
—	Paccha Jazp. Nitr., Ltd.	5	¼
5	Pac. Borax, L., 1 Db. Rd.	100	110
—	Palace Hotel, Ltd.	10	5¼
5½	Do. Cum. Pref.	10	7½
4	Do. 1 Mt. Deb. Stk.	100	103
—	Palmer, Ltd.	5	¾
6	Do. Cum. Pref.	5	2
1/2½d	Paquin, Ltd.	1	⅞
6	Do. Cum. Pref.	5	4
5½	Parnall, Ltd., Cum. Pref.	1	⅞
4/6	Pawsons, Ltd., £10 Shs.	6	6½
4	Do. Mt. Debs., Red.	100	106
6	Pearks, G. & T., Ltd., 6 p.c. Cum. Pref.	1	⅞
9½d.	Pears, Ltd.	1	1½
6	Do. Cum. Pref.	10	14
5	Do. Deb. Stk.	100	129
5½	Pearson, C. A., L., Cu. Pf.	5	4¾
4/3	Peebles, Ltd.	5	7¼
5	Do. Cum. Pref.	5	6½
4½	Do. Mt. Deb. Stk. Red.	100	113½
5½	Peek Bros., Ltd., 1 Cum. Pref., Nos. 1-60,000	5	6¼
3½	Do. 3½ p.c 1 Db. Stk.	100	102½
7½d.	Pegamoid, Ltd.	1	⅞
—	Pillsbury-W. Fl. Mills, L.	10	3½
16/	Do. 8 p.c. Cum. Pref.	10	7¾
6	Do. 1 Mort. Debs.	100	94½
9½d.	Plummer, Ltd.	1	1⅛
5	Do. Cum. Pref.	5	5½
17/6	Price's Candle, Ltd.	16	36
6	Priest Marians, L., Cm. Pf.	1	1½
6	Pryce Jones, Ld., Cm. Pf.	5	7
5	Do. Deb. Stk.	100	122
8½d.	Pullman, Ltd.	1	1½
6d.	Do. Cum. Pref.	1	1½
6d.	Raleigh Cycle, Ltd.	1	[illegible]
6	Do. Cum. Pref.	1	¾
—	Recife Drnge. Ld. 1 Mt. Debs., R	100	18
6	Redfern, Ltd. Cum. Prf.	10	14
5	Ridgways, Ltd., Cu. Pf.	5	5¼
—	R. Janeiro Cy. Imps. Ld.	25	8
5	Do. Debs.	100	85
5	Do. 1882-1893	100	83½
5%	R. Jan Fl. Mills, Ltd.	7	6
5	Do. 1 Mt. Debs., Rd.	100	94
—	Riv. Plate Meat, Ltd.	5	2½
—	Do. Pref.	5	5
8½d.	Roberts, J. R., Ltd.	1	1½
5	Roberts 1 Mt. D. Sk., Rd.	100	111
1/4½	Roberts, T. R., Ltd.	1	2½
5	Do. Cum. Pref.	1	1½

Commercial, &c. (*continued*):—

Last Div.	Name.	Paid.	Price.
3/	Rosario Nit., Ltd.	5	3½
5	Do. Debs., Red.	100	103
1/	Rover Cycle, Ltd.	1	½
6/	Ryl. Aquarium, Ltd.	5	4½
6	Do. Pref.	5	6
5	Ryl. Htl., Edin., Cm. Pf.	1	1½
1/2½	Ryl. Niger, Ltd., £10 Sh.	2	2¾
6/	Do.	10	14½
20/	Russian Petroleum	10	
6½	Do. 6½ p.c. Cm. Prf.	10	
10/	Ruston, Proctor, Ltd.	10	11½
4½	Do. 1 Mort. Debs.	100	105
6/	Sadler, Ltd.	12	7
—	Sal. Carmen Nit., Ltd.	5	4
9d.	Salmon & Gluck., Ltd.	1	1⅛
	Salt Union, Ltd.	10	1½
1½	Do. 7 p.c. Pref.	10	5½
4½	Do. Deb. Stk.	100	100½
4½	Do. "B" Deb. Sk., Rd.	100	97½
—	San Donato Nit., Ltd.	5	½
5/	San Jorge Nit., Ltd.	5	3½
—	San Pablo Nit., Ltd.	5	½
—	San Sebastn. Nit., Ltd.	5	¼
1/9	Sanitas, Ltd	1	2½
—	Sa. Elena Nit., Ltd.	5	½
—	Sa. Rita Nit., Ltd.	5	2¾
5/	Savoy Hotel, Ltd.	10	15
7	Do. Pref.	10	13
4	Do. 1 Mt. Deb. Stk.	100	109½
5	Do. Debs., Red	100	102½
5	Do. & Ldn. For. Htl., Ltd., 5 p.c. Debs. Red.	100	99
8½d.	Schweppes, Ltd.	1	1½
2½d.	Do Def.	1	½
5	Do. Cum. Pref.	1	1⅛
4	Do. Deb. Stk.	100	106
6d.	Singer Cyc., Ltd.	1	[illegible]
5½	Do Cum. Pref.	1	[illegible]
—	Smokeless Pwdr., Ltd.	1	[illegible]
5½d.	S. Eng. Dairies, Ltd., 6 p.c. Cum. Pref.	1	1¼
—	Sowler Thos. L.	1	1
3/4½	Do. 5½ Cm. Pf.	5	5½
4/6	Spencer, Turner, & Co. Ltd	5	8¾
5	Do. Cum. Pref.	5	6½
5	Spicer, Ld., 5 p.c. Dbs. Rd.	100	69
4/	Spiers & Pond, Ltd.	10	21½
5	Do. 1 Mt. Debs., Red.	100	118½
5	Do. "A" Db. Stk., Rd.	100	111
5	Do. "B" 1 Db. Stk., Rd.	100	112½
4	Do. Fd. "C" 1 Db. S., R.	100	104
7/6	Spratt's, Ltd	5	12½
4	Do. Debs., 1914	—	105
5	Steiner Ld., Cm. Pf.	10	11½
4	Do. 1 Mt. Db. Sk. Rd.	100	107
9/	Stewart & Clydesdale, L.	10	13
6	Do. Cum. Pref.	10	14½
35/5	Sulphide Corp.	100	80
1/	Swan & Edgar, L.	1	1½
1/	Sweetmeat Automatic, L.	1	4
2/9	Teetgen, Ltd., Cum. Pref.	5	6
24/	Teleg. Construction., Ld.	12	36½
5	Do. Db. Bds., Rd., 1899	100	103½
3/0½	Tilling, Ld. 5½ p.c. Cm. Prf.	5	6½
4	Do. 4 p.c. 1 Dbs., Rd.	—	105
8½d.	Tower Tea, Ltd.	1	1½
5	Do. Cum. Pref.	5	5¾
5	Travers, Ltd., Cum. Pref.	10	12½
4	Do. 1 Mt. Dbs., Rd.	100	105
6	Tucuman Sug., 1 Dbs., Rd.	100	100
4/	United Alkali, Ltd.	10	2
7	Do. Cum. Pref.	10	9
5	Do. Mt. Db. Stk., Rd.	100	109½
2½d.	United Horse Shoe, Ltd., Non-Cum. 8 p.c. Pref.	1	[illegible]
5	Un. Kingm. Tea, Cm. Prf.	5	4½
2/	Un. Lankat Plant., Ltd.	1	2
4/	Un. Limmer Asphlte., Ld.	3	5
13/	Val de Travers Asph., L.	10	15½
3/	V. den Bergh's, L., Cm. P.	5	6½
6	Walkers, Park., L., C. Pf.	10	2½
4½	Do. 1 Mt. Debs., Red.	100	90½
6/	Wallis, Thos. & Co., Ltd.	5	14
6	Do. Cum. Pref.	5	8¼
5½	Waring, Ltd., Cum. Pref.	5	5⅜
4½	Do. 1 Mt. Db. Sk., Red.	100	112
4½	Do. Irred. "B" Db. Stk.	100	104
12/	Waterlow, Dfd. Ord.	10	14
4/	Do. Pref.	10	14
3½	Do. Cum. Pref.	10	10½
10/	Waterlow Bros. & L., Ld.	10	9
5	Do. Pref.	10	12
1/2½	Welford, Ltd.	1	1½
4½	Do. Debs., Red.	100	109
1/	Welford's Surrey Dairies, Ltd.	1	1⅛
7½d.	West London Dairy, Ltd.	1	1
4½	Wharncliffe Dwllgs, L., Pf.	10	11½
18/10	Do. 3 p.c. Irr. Mt. Db. Sk.	100	96
1/	White, A. J., Ltd.	1	¾
6	Do. 6 p.c. Cum. Pref.	1	[illegible]
4	White, J. Bazley, Ltd., 1 Mort. Debs., Red	100	93½
5	White, R., Ltd., 1 Mort. Deb. Stock, Red.	100	104½
11/	White, Tomkins, Ltd	10	10½
5	Do. Cum. Pref.	10	11½
6	White, W. N., L., Cm. Pf.	1	[illegible]
3/	Wickens, Pease & Co., L.	5	2½
6	Wilkie, Ltd., Cum. Pref.	10	15
4/	Willans & Robinson, Ltd.	5	8
6	Do. Cum. Pref.	5	7
4½	Do. 1 Mt. Db. Stk., Red.	100	107
7½d.	Williamsons, L., Cm. Prf.	1	1½
6	Winterbottm. Book Cloth, Ltd., Cum. Prf.	10	15
4/6	Yates, Ltd.	5	6
6	Do. Cum. Pref.	5	6½
	Young's Paraffin. Ltd.	4	1½

CORPORATION STOCKS—COLONIAL AND FOREIGN.

Per Cent.	Name.	Paid.	Price.
6	Auckland City, '72 1904-24	100	115
6	Do. Cons., '79, Red. 19..	100	135½
5	Do. Deb. Ln., '83..1934-8	100	117
6	Auckland Harb. Debs.	100	111½
5	Do. 1917	100	112
5	Do. 1936	100	114
5½	Balmain Boro' ...1914	—	113½
5	Boston City (U.S.)	100	102½
5	Do. ..1902	100	105
5	Brunswick Town 5 c. Debs. ...1916-20	100	111
4½	B. Ayres City 4½ p.c.	100	69
5	Cape Town, City of	100	113
4	Do. ..1943	100	115
4	Chicago, City of, Gold 1915	—	112
6	Christchurch ...1926	100	131½
—	Cordoba City	100	17½
5	Duluth (U.S.) Gold ..1926	—	110
6	Dunedin (Otago) ...1925	100	127½
6	Do. ...1926	100	113
5	Do. Consols..1908	100	111
4	Durban Insc. Stk. ...1944	100	111
4	Essex Cnty., N. Jersey 1926	$100	114½
5	Fitzroy, Melbrne...1916-19	100	110
5	Gisborne Harbour...1915	100	109
4	Greymouth Harbour..1925	100	110
4	Hamilton ...1934	100	108
5	Hobart Town ...1918-30	100	115
4	Do. ...1940	100	105
4½	Invercargill Boro. Dbs. 1936	100	111
6	Kimberley Boro., S. A. Debs.	—	102
4	Launceston Twn. Dbs. 1916	100	105
6	Lyttleton, N.Z., Harb. 1929	100	125
4	Melbourne Bd. of Wks. 1921	100	107
5	Melb. City Debs. 1897-1907	100	106½
4½	Do. Debs. ...1908-27	100	111½
4	Do. Debs...1915-20-22	100	105
5	Melbne. Harb. Bds., 1908-9	100	112
4½	Do. do. ...1915	100	111
4	Do. do. ...1918-21	100	106
4½	Melbrne. Tms, Dbs. 1914-16	100	113
4½	Do. Fire Brig. Db. 1921	100	103
5	Mexico City Stg.	100	91½
4	Moncton N. Bruns. City	100	102
5	Montevideo	100	61
5	Montreal Stg.	100	103
5	Do. 1874	100	103
5	Do. 1879	100	104
3½	Do. ...1933	100	103
3	Do. Perm. Deb. Stk	100	96
4	Do. Cons. Deb. Stk. 1932	100	112
6	Napier Boro. Consolid. 1914	100	119
5	Napier Harb. Debs...1920	100	115
5	Do. Debs...1928	100	107
6	New Plymouth Harb. Debs. ...1900	100	107
6	New York City ...1901	—	109½
3½	Do. ...1910-26	—	103½
4½	Nth. Melbourne Debs. 1-600 1921	100	105
5	Oamaru Boro. Cons...1920	100	101
6	Do. Harb. Bds. (Reg.)	100	74
25/	Do. 6 p.c. (Bearer)..1919	100	35
6	Otago Harb. Deb. Reg.	100	103
6	Do. 1877	100	107
6	Do. 1881 ...1921	100	115
5	Do. Debs. ..1921	100	107
5	Do. Cons. ..1934	100	105
6	Ottawa City	100	109
6	Do. ...1904	100	111½
4½	Do. Debs. ..1913	100	108½
6	Port Elizabeth Waterworks	100	111
5	Port Louis	100	111
5	Prahran Debs. ...1917	100	109
4	Do. Debs. ...1919	100	102
6	Quebec C. Coupon. 1875 1905	100	112
6	Do. do. 1878 ...1908	100	116
4½	Do. Debs. ...1914-18	100	108
4	Do. Debs. ...1923	100	108
3½	Do. Cns. Rg. Stk., Red.	100	100
5	Richmond (Melb.) Dbs. 1917	100	112
4	Rio Janeiro City	100	59
4	Rome City	100	—
4	Do. 2nd to 8th Iss.	100	93
—	Rosario C.	100	25
—	Do.	100	25
4	St. Catherine (Ont.) ..1926	100	101
4	St. John, N.B., Debs. 1934	—	103
4½	St. Kilda (Melb) Dbs. 1918-21	100	105
4	St. Louis C. (Miss.)..1911	100	104
4	Do. ...1913	100	103½
3·65	Do. ...1915	—	108½
—	Santa Fé City Debs.	100	19
6	Santos City	100	95
6	Sofia City	100	84
5	Sth. Melbourne Debs. 1915	100	111
4½	Do. Debs. ...1919	100	107
5	Sydney City ...1904	100	100
4	Do. Debs. 1912-13	100	107
4	Do. do. (1894) . 1919	100	109
7	Timaru Boro. 7 p.c...1910	100	126½
5	Timaru Harb. Debs 1914	100	107
5	Do. Debs...1916	100	107
6	Toronto City Wtrwks 1904-6	100	114
5	Do. G. Cns. Dbs. 1919-20	100	115
4	Do. Strlg. ...1922-8	100	107
4	Do. Local Improv.	100	104
3½	Do. ...1929	100	104
5½	Valparaiso	100	100
4	Vancouver ...1931	100	107
4	Do. ...1932	100	103
6	Wanganui Harb. Dbs. 1905	100	107
6	Wellington Con. Deb. 1907	100	117
6	Do. Improv., 1879	100	122
6	Do. Wtrwks. Dbs., 1880	100	123
4½	Do. Debs., 1893...1933	100	114
4½	Wellington Harb. ...1907	100	104
4	Westport Harb. Dbs. 1925	100	110
6	Winnipeg City Deb...1907	—	119
5	Do. ...1914	100	117

FINANCIAL, LAND, AND INVESTMENT.

Last Div.	Name.	Paid.	Price.
5	Agncy, Ld. & Fin. Aust., Ltd., Mt. Db. Stk., Rd.	100	90½
	Amer. Frehld. Mt. of Lon., Ld., Cum. Pref. Stk. ..	100	87½
4½	Do. Deb. Stk., Red. ..	100	92
1/4½	Anglo-Amer. Db. Cor., L.	2	1
4	Do. Deb. Stk., Red ..	100	108½
	Ang.-Ceylon & Gen. Est., Ltd., Cons. Stk.	100	50
6	Do. Reg. Debs., Red.	100	101½
3/	Ang.-Fch. Explorn., Ltd.	1	2⅛
6	Do. Cum. Pref.	1	1⅛
—	Argent. Ld. & Inv., Ltd. £1 Shares	10/	nil
—	Do. Cum. Pref.	4	1¼
1/	Assets Fnders.' Sh., Ltd.,	4	1½
6/	Assets Realis., Ltd., Ord.,	5	8¼
5	Do. Cum. Pref.	5	6½
26/	Austrln. Agricl £25 Shs.	21½	63½
	Aust. N. Z. Mort., Ltd.,		
4½	Deb. Stk., Red.	100	87½
4	Do. Deb. Stk., Red. ..	100	80½
4½	Australian Est. & Mt., L., 1 Mt. Deb. Stk., Red.	100	103
5	Do. "A" Mort. Deb. Stk., Red.	100	96
5/	Australian Mort., Ld., & Fin., Ltd. £25 Shs. ..	5	5½
1/6	Do. New, £25 Shs...	3	3½
4	Do. Deb. Stk	100	110
3	Do. Do.	100	85
5	Bengal Presidy. 1 Mort. Deb., Red.	100	107
25/	British Amer. Ld. "A"	1	21
—	Do. "B"	24	7
1/7½	Brit. & Amer. Mt., Ltd. £10 Shs.	2	1
5/	Do. Pref.	10	9½
4	Do. Deb. Stk., Red. ..	100	103
1/3	Brit. & Austrlsn Tst Ln., Ltd. £25 Shs.	2½	¾
4½	Do. Perm. Debs., Red.	100	104
1½d.	Brit. N. Borneo. £1 Shs.	15/	⅜
2½d.	Do.	1	⅜
—	Brit. S. Africa	1	2¾
5	Do. Mt. Deb., Red.	—	100
6	B. Aires Harb. Tst., Red.	100	94
12/6	Canada Co.	1	27
—	Canada N. W. Ld., Ltd.	$25	13½
—	Do. Pref.	$100	552
4	Canada Perm. Loan & Sav. Perp. Deb. Stk...	100	99½
6	Curamalan Ld., 6 p.c. "A" Scrip	—	92
3/7½	Deb Corp., Ld., £10 Shs	4	3½
5	Do. Cum. Pref.	10	11½
4	Do. Perp. Deb. Stk...	100	110
9d.	Deb. Corp. Fders' Sh., Ld.	3	¼
4/5⅞	Eastn. Mt. & Agncy, Ld., "A"	10	5½
4½	Do. Deb. Stk., Red.	100	98
5	Equitable Revers. In. Ltd.	100	—
2/6	Exploration, Ltd.	1	1½
/6d.	Freehold Trst. of Austrla. Ltd. £10 Shs.	1	¾
4	Do. Perp. Deb. Stk...	100	100
70/	Genl. Reversionary, Ltd.	100	—
3½	Holborn Vi. Land	100	105
4½	House Prop. & Inv.	100	84½
13/	Hudson's Bay	13	20½
—	Hyderabad (Deccan)	5	3
4	Impl. Col. Fin. & Agcy. Corp.	100	92½
4½	Impl. Prop. Inv., Ltd., Deb. Stk., Red.	100	91½
2/6	Internatl. Fincial. Soc., Ltd. £7½ Shs.	2½	1½
4	Do. Deb. Stk., Red...	100	99½
2/4½	Ld. & Mtge. Egypt, Ltd. £18 Shs.	3	2¾
5	Do. Debs., Red.	100	101
4½	Do. Debs., Red.	100	100
—	Ld. Corp. of Canada, Ltd.	1	¼
4½	Ld. Mtge. Bk. of Texas Deb. Stk.	100	—
3½	Ld. Mtge. Bk. Victoria 4½ p.c. Deb. Stk.	100	78
2/9½	Law Debent. Corp., Ltd., £10 Shs.	2	1¾
4½	Do. Cum. Pref., ...	10	12
4	Do. Deb. Stk.	100	113½
—	Law Land, L., 4½ Cm. Prf.	5	5¼
1/	Ldn. & Australasian Deb. Corp., Ltd., £4 Shs. ..	2	½
4½	Do. 4½ p.c. Mt. Deb. Stk., Red.	100	99
1/9	Ldn. & Middx. Frhld. Est. £2 Shs.	35/	3
2/6	Lndn. & N. Y. Inv. Corp., Ltd.	5	1¾
5	Do. 5 p.c. Cum. Pref...	10	8¼
1/6	Ldn. & Nth. Assets Corp., Ltd., £2 Shs.	1½	½
2	Ldn. & N. Deb. Corp., L.	2	1¼
3/6	Ldn. & S. Afric. Explrn. Ltd.	1	12¾
2/	Mtge. Co. of R. Plate, Ltd. £10 Shs.	2	3
4½	Do. Deb. Stk., Red...	100	113
4½	Morton, Rose Est., Ltd., 1st Mort. Debs.	—	99
6/6	Natal Land Col. Ltd. ..	10	7
4/	Do. 8 p.c. Pref., 1870..	5	8½
5/6	Natl. Disct. L., £25 Shs.	5	10¾
4½	New Impl. Invest., Ltd. Pref. Stk.	100	66½
	New Impl. Invest., Ltd. Def. Stk.	100	9
3½	N. Zld. Assets Real Deb.	100	101
4	N. Zld. Ln. & Mer. Agcy. Ltd. Prf. Ln. Deb. Stk	100	93
2/6	N. Zld. Tst. & Ln. Ltd., £25 Shs.	5	1¾

Financial, Land, &c. (*continued*):—

Last Div.	Name.	Paid.	Price.
12/6	N. Zld. Tst. & Ln. Ltd., 5 p.c. Cum. Pref.	25	19
—	N. Brit. Australsn. Ltd...	100	4
—	Do. Irred. Guar.	100	32½
5	Do. Mort. Debs.	100	82½
4½	N. Queensld. Mort. & Inv., Ltd., Deb. Stk.	100	93
6	Peel Riv., Ld. & Min. Ltd.	100	90
—	Peruvian Corp., Ltd.	100	2¾
—	Do. 4 p.c. Pref.	100	9½
3	Do. 6 p.c. 1 Mt. Debs., Red.	100	41
—	Queensld. Invest. & Ld. Mort. Pref. Ord. Stk...	100	20
3/7	Queensld. Invest. & Ld. Mort. Ord. Shs.	4	4
4	Queensld. Invest. & Ld. Mort. Perp. Debs.	100	88
3½	Raily. Roll Stk. Tst. Deb., 1903-6	100	100½
50/	Reversiony. Int. Soc., Ltd.	100	—
2/8½	Riv. Plate Trst., Loan & Agcy., L., "A" £10 Shs.	2	4
1/6	Riv. Plate Trst., Loan & Agcy., Ltd., Def. "B"	5	3½
	Riv. Plate Trst., Loan & Agy., L., Db. Stk., Red.	100	109
—	Santa Fé & Cord. Gt. South Land, Ltd.	20	5
—	Santa Fé Land	10	2½
2/	Scot. Amer. Invest., Ltd. £10 Shs.	2	2¾
2½	Scot. Australian Invest., Ltd., Cons.	100	69½
6	Scot. Australian Invest., Ltd., Guar. Pref.	100	136½
5	Scot. Australian Invest., Ltd., Guar. Pref.	100	108½
4	Scot. Australian Invest., Ltd., 4 p.c. Perp. Dbs.	100	106½
5	Sivagunga Zemdy., 1st Mort., Red.	100	101
20/	Sth. Australian	20	48½
3½	Stock Exchange Deb., Rd.	—	101½
—	Strait Develt., Ltd.	1	—
2/6	Texas Land & Mt., Ltd. £10 Shs.	2½	2¾
4½	Texas Land & Mt., Ltd., Deb. Stk., Red.	100	104
—	Transvaal Est. & Dev., L.	1	⅛
—	Transvaal Lands, Ltd., £1 Shs.	15/	1/16
—	Do. F. P.	1	⅛
—	Transvaal Mort., Loan, & Fin., Ltd., £10 Shs. ..	2	1/16
2/	Tst & Agcy. of Austrlsa., Ltd., £10 Shs.	1	2
7/5	Do. Old, fully paid ..	10	15½
5/7	Do. New, fully paid ..	10	12½
5	Do. Cum. Pref.	10	12½
3/	Trust & Loan of Canada, £20 Shs.	5	4½
1/9½	Do. New £20 Shs. ...	3	2½
4½	Tst. & Mort. of Iowa, Ltd., Deb. Stk. Red...	100	92½
—	Tst., Loan, & Agency of Mexico, Ltd., £10 Shs.	2	¼
—	Trsts., Exors, & Sec. Ins. Corp., Ltd., £10 Shs..	7	1½
4	Do. Irred. Deb. Stk.	100	106½
5/	Union Dsc., Ld., £10 Shs.	5	10¾
6	Union Mort. & Agcy. of Aust., Ltd., Pref. Stk.	100	30
—	Do. 6 p. Pref. £6 Shs.	2	¾
4½	Do. Deb. Stk	100	92½
4	Do. Deb. Stk	100	85½
5	Do. Deb. Stk. Red...	100	96½
1/6	U.S. Deb. Cor. Ltd., £8 Shs.	1	¾
5½	Do. Cum. Pref. Stk .	100	100½
4½	Do. Irred. Deb. Stk..	100	105½
5	U.S. Tst. & Guar. Cor., Ltd., Pref. Stk.	100	77½
8/	Van Dieman's	25	16
4	Walker's Prop. Cor., Ltd., Guar. 1 Mt. Deb. Stk..	100	109
4½	Wstr. Mort. & Inv., Ltd., Deb. Stk.	100	92½

FINANCIAL—TRUSTS.

Last Div.	Name.	Paid.	Price.
1/6	Afric City Prop., Ltd ...	1	1½
6	Do. Cum. Pref.	1	1⅛
4	Alliance Invt., Ltd., Cm. 4½ p. c. Prefd.	100	74½
—	Do. Defd.	100	12½
4	Do. Deb. Stk. Red...	100	104½
5	Amrcn. Invt., Ltd., Prfd.	100	119½
5	Do. Defd.	100	88½
4	Do. Deb. Stk. Red...	100	114½
2	Army & Navy Invt., Ltd., 5 p.c. Prefd.	100	82½
—	Do. Defd. Stk.	100	15½
4	Do. Deb. Stk.	100	106½
4	Atlas Investment, Ltd., Prefd. Stk.	100	70½
4½	Bankers' Invest., Ltd., Cum. Prefd.	100	103
1/0/0	Do. Defd.	100	24½
4	Do. Deb. Stk.	100	114
	Brewery & Comml. Inv., Ltd., £10 Shs.	5	6

Financial—Trusts (*continued*):—

Last Div.	Name.	Paid.	Price.
4	British Investment, Ltd., Cum. Prefd.	100	107
5	Do. Defd.	100	103½
4	Do. Deb. Stk.	100	107½
6	Brit. Steam. Invst., Ltd., Prefd	100	120
5/0/0	Do. Defd.	100	75
4½	Do. Perp. Deb. Stk ..	100	120½
1/9	Car Trust Invst., Ltd., £10 Shs.	2½	2
5	Do. Pref.	100	99
4	Do. Deb. Stk., 1915..	100	104
4	Clnl. Sec., Ltd., Prefd. ..	100	102½
2⅓	Do. Defd.	100	43½
4	Consolidated, Ltd., Cum. 1st Pref.	100	91
4	Do. 5 p.c. Cm. 2nd do.	100	68½
—	Do. Defd.	100	14½
4½	Do. Deb. Stk.	100	112½
5	Deb. Secs. Invst.	100	103½
4	Do. 4 p.c. Cm. Pf. Sk.	100	105½
4½	Edinburgh Invest., Ltd., Cum. Prefd. Stk.	100	105½
4	Do. Deb. Stk. Red.	100	106½
5	Foreign, Amer. & Gen. Invt., Ltd., Prefd.	100	112½
2	Do. Defd.	100	47½
4	Do. Deb. Stk.	100	113½
5	Foreign & Colonial Invt., Ltd., Prefd.	100	137½
5½	Do. Defd.	100	96½
4½	Gas, Water & Gen. Invt., Cum. Prefd. Stk.	100	86½
8	Do. Defd. Stk.	100	37½
4	Do. Deb. Stk.	100	104
5	Gen. & Com. Invt., Ltd., Prefd. Stk.	100	103
8	Do. Defd. Stk.	100	36½
4	Do. Deb. Stk.	100	111½
2/6	Globe Telegph. & Tst., Ltd.	10	11¾
6	Do. do. Pref.	10	17
4	Govt. & Genl. Invt., Ld., Prefd.	100	83½
3½	Do. Defd.	100	41½
4½	Govts. Stk. & other Secs. Invt., Ltd., Prefd.	100	86½
1	Do. Defd.	100	25
4½	Do. Deb. Stk.	100	112
4	Do. do.	100	104
4½	Guardian Invt., Ltd., Pfd.	100	89½
—	Do. Defd.	100	19½
4	Do. Deb. Stk.	100	104
5	Indian & Gen. Inv., Ltd., Cum. Prefd.	100	110½
2½	Do. Defd.	100	61
4½	Do. Deb. Stk.	100	119½
5	Indust. & Gen. Tst., Ltd., Unified	100	98½
3½	Do. Deb. Stk. Red.	100	99½
4½	Internat. Invt., Ltd., Cm. Prefd.	100	66½
—	Do. Defd.	100	7
4	Do. Deb. Stk.	100	101
4	Invest. Tst. Cor. Ltd. Pfd.	100	101½
6	Do. Defd.	100	85
4	Do. Deb. Stk. Red.	100	104
25/	Ldn. Gen. Invest. Ltd., 5 p.c. Cum. Prefd.	100	111½
27/6	Do. Defd.	100	120
4½	Ldn. Scot. Amer. Ltd. Pfd.	100	106½
£3	Do. Defd.	100	58½
4	Do. Deb. Stk.	100	111
4	Ldn. Tst., Ltd., Cum. Prfd. Stk.	100	100
4	Do. Defd. Stk.	100	67½
4	Do. Deb. Stk., Red.	100	107
3½	Do. Mt. Deb. Stk., Red.	100	100½
5	Mercantile Invt. & Gen., Ltd., Prefd.	100	111
3	Do. Defd.	100	44½
4	Do. Deb. Stk.	100	110½
4	Merchants, Ltd., Pref. Stk.	100	104½
4	Do. Ord.	100	80½
4	Do. Deb. Stk.	100	117½
3½	Municipal, Ltd., Prefd...	100	48½
—	Do. Defd.	100	17
4½	Do. Debs.	100	111
4½	Do. Debs. "B"	100	99½
4½	Do. "C" Deb. Stk.	100	94½
5	New Investment, Ltd. Ord.	100	91½
5	Omnium Invest., Ltd., Pfd.	100	92½
1	Do. Defd.	100	26½
4	Do. Deb. Stk.	100	106
5/	Railway Deb. Tst. Ld., £20 Shs.	10	6½
5	Do. Debs., Red. ..	100	108½
4½	Do. Deb. Stk., 1911	100	107½
4	Do. do. 1927	100	106½
4	Railway Invst. Ltd., Prefd.	100	115
17/7	Do. Defd.	100	22½
8/	Railway Share Trust & Agency "A"	8	6½
7½	Do. "B" Pref. Stk.	100	148
4½	River Plate & Gen. Invt., Ltd., Prefd.	100	104
£3	Do. Defd.	100	50½
5	Scot. Invst., Ltd., Pfd. Stk.	100	91½
1½	Do. Defd...	100	26½
4	Do. Deb. Stk.	100	106
4½	Sec. Scottish Invst., Ltd., Cum. Prefd.	100	89½
£3	Do. Defd. Stk.	100	32
4	Do. Deb. Stk.	100	106½
5/	Sth. Africa Gold Tst., Ltd.	1	3½
6	Do. Cum. Pref	1	1
5½	Do. 1st Debs., Red.	100	104
1/9	Stock Conv. & Invest., Ltd., £3 Shs.	1	1¾
4½	Do. do. 4½ p.c. Cm. Prf.	100	115½
2½	Do. Ldn. & N. W. 1st. Charge Prefd.	100	113½
4	Do do. 2nd Chge Prfd.	100	111
33/6	Do. do. Defd. Charge	100	31
3	Do. N. East.: Chge Pfd.	100	81½
87/6	Stock N. East Defd. Chge	100	41
6	Submarine Cables	100	138½
5	U.S. & S. Amer. Invest., Ltd., Prefd.	100	96½
20/	Do. Defd.	100	24½
4	Do. Deb. Stk.	100	103½

GAS AND ELECTRIC LIGHTING.

Last Div.	Name.	Paid.	Price.
10/6	Alliance & Dublin Con. 10 p.c. Stand.	10	24
7/6	Do. 7 p.c. Stand...	10	16½
5	Austln. Gas Lght. (Syd.) Debs. 1902	100	108
5	Bay State of N. Jrsy. Sk. Fd. Tst. Bd., Red. ..	—	92
3/	Bombay, Ltd.	5	5½
2/4½	Do. New	4	4½
12	Brentford Cons.	100	292½
9	Do. New	100	217½
5	Do. Pref.	100	142½
4	Do. Deb. Stk. ..	100	132½
11½	Brighton & Hove Gen. Cons. Stk.	100	272½
8½	Do. "A" Cons. Stk.	100	197½
5	Bristol 5 p.c. Max.	100	129½
22/6	British Gas Light, Ltd.	20	56½
11/6	Bromley Gas Consumrs.' 10 p.c. Stand.	10	26
8/6	Do. 7 p.c. Stand...	10	21
—	Brush Electl. Enging., L.	—	1½
6	Do. 6 p.c. Pref.	—	2½
4½	Do. Deb. Stk.	100	112
4½	Do. 2 Deb. Stk., Red.	100	102½
7/	B. Ayres (New), Ltd. ..	10	9½
4	Do. Deb. Stk., Rd. ..	—	90
18/6	Cagliari Gas & Wtr., Ltd.	20	31
6/	Cape Town & Dist. Gas Light & Coke, Ltd.	10	15½
4½	Do. Pref.	10	12
6	Do. 1 Mt. Debs. 1910	50	50
4/	Charing Cross & Strand Elec. Sup., Ltd.	5	12½
4½	Do. Cum. Pref.	5	6½
3/	Chelsea Elec. Sup., Ltd.	5	8½
4½	Do. Deb. Stk., Red.	100	116
5	Chic. Edis'n Co. 1 Mt., Rd.	$1000	106
20/	City of Ldn. Elec. Lht., L.	10	26½
—	Do. New £10 Shs...	5	18½
6	Do. Cum. Pref.	10	17
5	Do. Deb. Stk., Red.	100	130½
13½	Commercial, Cons.	100	324½
10½	Do. New	100	252½
4½	Do. Deb. Stk.	100	150½
10	Continental Union, Ltd.	100	206½
11	Do. Pref. Stk.	100	197½
—	County of Lon. & Brush Prov. Elec. Lg., Ltd.	10	13½
6	Do. Cum. Pref.	10	15
14	Croydon Comcl. Gas, Ld., "A" Stk., 10 p.c. ..	100	312½
11	Do. "B" Stk., 7 p.c.	100	260
5½	Crystal Pal. Dist. Ord. 5 p.c. Stk.	100	127½
5	Do. Pref. Stk.	100	143½
8/	European, Ltd.	10	24
6/	Do.	7½	17½
12½	Gas Light & Ck Cons. Stk., "A" Ord.	100	297½
4	Do. "B" (4 p.c. Max.)	100	120½
10	Do. "C," "D," & "E" (Pref.)	100	304½
5	Do. "F" (Pref.)	100	152½
7½	Do. "G" (Pref.)	100	222½
7	Do. "H" (7 p.c. Max.)	100	197½
10	Do. "J" (Pref.)	100	302½
6	Do. "K"	100	184½
4	Do. Deb. Stk.	100	131½
4½	Do. do.	100	150½
6	Do. do.	100	202½
8/	Hong Kong & China, Ld.	10	14
4/	House to House Elec. Light Sup., Ltd. ..	5	9
7	Do. Cum. Pref.	5	11
10	Imperial Continental ..	100	212½
3½	Do. Deb. Stk., Red ..	100	104½
2/	Malta & Medit., Ltd. ..	5	5½
7/	Metrop. Elec. Sup., Ltd.	10	15½
4½	Do. 1 Mt. Deb. Stk.	100	119½
5	Metro. of Melbrne. Dbs. 1908-12	100	111
4½	Do. Debs...1918-22-4	100	108
10/	Monte Video, Ltd.	20	14½
9½	Newcastle-upon-Tyne ..	100	237½
—	Do. 3½ p.c. Deb. Stk.	100	117½
12/	Notting Hill Elec. Ltg., Ltd.	10	18
3/6	Oriental, Ltd.	5	7¾
3/1½	Do. New	4½	6½
8½d.	Do. do. 1879	1	1⅛
3/6	Ottoman, Ltd.	5	5
6	People's Gas Lt. & C. of Chic. 2 Mt. 1904	100	105½
5	River Plate Elec. Lgt. & Trac., Ltd., 1 Deb. Stk.	—	89½
8⅔	Royal Elec. of Montreal	—	144
4½	Do. 1 Mt. Deb. ..	100	104
11/	St. James' & Pall Mall Elec. Light, Ltd. ..	5	16½
7	Do. Pref.	5	9½
4	Do. Deb. Stk., Red.	100	108½
10/	San Paulo, Ltd.	10	15½

Gas and Electric (*continued*):—

Last Div.	Name.	Paid.	Price.
10	Sheffield Unit. Gas Lt. "A"	100	251½
10	Do. "B"	100	251½
10	Do. "C"	100	251½
—	Sth. Ldn. Elec. Sup., Ld.	2	2¼
5¾	South Metropolitan	100	140½
3	Do. 3 p.c. Deb. Stk.	100	102½
2	Tottenham & Edmonton Gas Lt. & C., "A"	100	290
9	Do. "B"	100	210
7/	Tuscan, Ltd.	10	13½
5	Do. Debs., Red.	100	101½
5/	West Ham 10 p.c. Stan.	5	12
8/	Wstmnstr. Elec. Sup., Ld.	5	15½

INSURANCE.

Last Div.	Name.	Paid.	Price.
4/	Alliance, £20 Shs.	44/	10¾
10/	Alliance, Mar., & Gen., Ld., £100 Shs.	25	53
19/	Atlas, £50 Shs.	6	29
12/	British & For. Marine, Ld., £20 Shs.	4	23
7½d.	British Law Fire, Ltd., £10 Shs.	1	1½
7/6	Clerical, Med., & Gen. Life £25 Shs.	50/	16½
20/	Commercial Union, Ltd., £50 Shs.	5	43½
4	Do. "W. of Eng." Ter. Deb. Stk.	100	110½
£9	County Fire, £100 Shs.	80	195
5/	Eagle, £50 Shs.	5	½
4/	Employrs' Liability, Ltd., £10 Shs.	2	3¾
—	Empress, Ltd., £5 Shs.	1	—
21/	Equity & Law, £100 Shs.	6	23
7/6	General Life, £100 Shs.	5	15
4½d.	Gresham Life, £5 Shs.	15/	2½
5/6	Guardian, Ld., £10 Shs.	5	10½
10/	Imperial, Ltd., £20 Shs.	5	29
5/6	Imperial Life, £20 Shs.	4	6¾
6/	Indemnity Mutual Mar., Ltd., £15 Shs.	3	11½
1/6	Lancashire, £20 Shs.	2	4¾
7½d.	Law Acc. & Contin., Ltd., £5 Shs.	10/	¾
12/6	Law Fire, £100 Shs.	2½	17½
9½d.	Law Guar. & Trust, Ltd., £10 Shs.	1	1½
9/	Law Life, £20 Shs.	2	24½
2/9	Law Un. & Crown £10Shs	12/	7
4	Do. Deb. Stk., 1942	100	109½
14/6	Legal & General, £50 Shs.	8	15½
9d.	Lion Fire, Ltd., £8½ Shs.	1½	¾
22/	Liverpool & London & Globe, Stk.	2	52½
10/	Do. Globe £1 Ann	—	35
35/	London, £25 Shs.	12½	57
8/	Lond. & Lanc. Fire, £25Shs	2½	19
2/	Lond. & Lanc. Life, £25Shs	2	7
1/	Lond. & Prov. Mar., Ld., £10 Shs.	1	½
6/	Lond. Guar. & Accident, Ltd., £5 Shs.	2	12
10/	Marine, Ltd., £25 Shs.	4½	44
2/	Maritime, Ltd., £10 Shs.	2	4½
1/6	Merc. Mar., Ld., £10 Shs.	2½	2½
10/	N. Brit. & Merc., £25 Shs.	6¼	42
20/	Northern, £100 Shs.	10	81
40/	Norwich Union Fire, £100 Shs.	12	125½
10/	Ocean Acc. & Guar., fy. pd.	5	22½
2/	Do. £5 Shs.	1	3½
7/6	Ocean, Marine, Ltd.	2½	8½
2/	Palatine, £10 Shs.	2	3½
2/6	Pelican, £10 Shs.	1	3½
23/	Phoenix, £50 Shs.	5	41½
£6	Provident, £100 Shs.	10	32
5/	Railway Passngrs., £10Shs.	2	8½
2/6	Rock Life, £5 Shs.	10/	4½
8	Royal Exchange	100	350
18/	Royal, £20 Shs.	3	54½
4/6	Sun, £10Shs.	10/	11½
3/9	Sun Life, £10 Shs.	7½	14½
6	Thames & Mrsey. Marine, Ltd., £20 Shs.	2	10½
0	Union, £10 Shs.	4	24½
4/	Union Marine, £20 Shs.	2½	9
12/	Universal Life, £100 Shs.	12	42
2/	World Marine, £5 Shs.	2	1½

IRON, COAL, AND STEEL.

Last Div.	Name.	Paid.	Price.
—	Barrow Hæm. Steel, Ltd.	7½	1¾
9/	Do. 6 p.c. 2nd Pref.	7½	6½
10/	Bolck., Vaugh. & C., Ld.	20	16½
6/	Do. £8 liab.	12	9½
7/6	Brown, J. & Co., Ltd., £20 Shs.	15	20½
7/6	Consett Iron, Ld., £10Shs.	7½	29
7/6	Ebbw Vale Steel, Iron & Coal, Ltd., £23 Shs.	20	6
18/6	General Mining Assn., Ld.	5½	7½
1/7½	Harvey Steel Co. of Gt. Britain, Ltd.	10	2½
5	Lehigh V. Coal 1 Mt. 5 p.c. Guar. Gd. Cp. Bds.	—	96
42/6	Nantyglo & Blaina Iron, Ltd., Pref.	$62	96
1/	Nerbudda Coal & Iron, Ltd., £3 Shs.	56/	—
6/	Newport Abercrn. Bk. Vein Steam Coal, Ltd.	10	6½
5/	New Sharlston Coll., Ltd. Pref	20	10
4½d.	Nw. Vancvr. Coal & Ld., L.	1	½
2/6	North's Navigation Coll. (1889) Ltd.	5	2½
10/	Do. 10 p.c. Cum. Pref.	5	6½
—	Rhymney Iron, Ltd.	5	1½
	Do. New, £5 Shs.	4½	1
5	Do. Mt. Debs., Red.	100	99½
5	Shelton Irn., Stl. & Cl. Co., Ltd., 1 Chg. Debs., Red.	100	100½
50/	Sth. Hetton Coal, Ltd.	100	—
2/	Vickers & Maxim, Ltd.	1	3½
5	Do. 5 p.c. Prfd. Stk.	100	125½

SHIPPING.

Last Div.	Name.	Paid.	Price
12/	African Stm. Ship, £20 Shs.	16	10½
15/	Do. Fully-paid	20	14½
5/	Amazon Steam Nav., Ltd.	12½	8½
12/	Castle Mail Pakts., Ltd., £20 Shs.	14	15
3½	Do. 1st Deb. Stk., Red.	100	102
6/	China Mutual Steam, Ltd.	5	3
6	Do. Cum. Pref.	10	10
20/	Cunard, Ltd.	20	9½
5/	Do. £20 Shs.	10	3½
4½	Furness, Withy, & Co., Ltd., 1 Mt. Dbs., Red.	100	106
6/	General Steam	15	7½
5/	Do. 5 p.c. Pref., 1874	10	8½
5/	Do. 5 p.c. Pref., 1877	10	8½
26/4½	Leyland & Co., Ltd.	10	26
7/	Do. 7 p.c. Cum. Pref.	10	14½
2/11	Do. 4½ p.c. Cum. Pre-Pf.	3	10½
4	Do. 1st Mt. Dbs., Red.	100	104½
7/6	Mercantile Steam, Ltd.	5	8
6/4½	New Zealand Ship., Ltd.,	6	4½
4	Do. Deb. Stk., Red.	100	104
5/	Orient Steam, Ltd.	10	4½
5	P. & O. Steam, Cum. Prefd.	100	147½
19	Do. Defd.	100	235½
3½	Do. Deb. Stk.	100	117
5	Richelieu & Ont., 1st Mt. Debs., Red.	100	100
30/	Royal Mail, £100 Shs.	60	51
2/6	Shaw, Sav., & Alb., Ltd., "A" Pref.	5	5½
5/	Do. "B" Ord.	5	4
14/	Union Steam, Ltd.	20	19
7/	Do. New £20 Shs.	10	8½
4	Do. Deb. Stk., Red.	100	108
6/	Union of N.Z., Ltd.	10	9½
5½	Wilson's & Fur.-Ley., 5½ p.c. Cum. Pref.	10	10½
4½	Do. 1 Mt. Db. Sk., Rd.	100	106½

_ *Tea Shares will be found in the Special Table following.*

TELEGRAPHS AND TELEPHONES.

Last Div.	Name.	Paid.	Price.
4	African Direct, Ltd., Mort. Debs., Red.	100	102
—	Amazon Telegraph, Ltd.	10	7½
15/	Anglo-American, Ltd.	100	65½
30/	Do. 6 p.c. Prefd. Ord.	100	116½
—	Do. Defd. Ord.	100	16½
3/	Brazilian Submarine, Ltd.	10	15½
5	Do. Debs, 2 Series	100	114

Telegraphs and Telephones (*continued*):—

Last Div.	Name.	Paid.	Price.
4/	Chili Telephone, Ltd.	5	3
$1½	Comcial. Cable, $100 Shs.	—	185
4	Do. Stg. 500-yr. Deb. Stk. Red.	100	106
2½d.	Consd. Telpehone Constr., &c., Ltd.	10/	½
6/	Cuba Submarine, Ltd.	10	7
10/	Do. 10 p.c. Pref.	10	15
2/	Direct Spanish, Ltd.	5	4½
5/	Do. 10 p.c. Cum. Pref.	5	10½
4½	Do. Debs.	50	104½
3/	Direct U.S. Cable, Ltd.	20	10½
2/6	Eastern, Ltd.	10	17½
3/	Do. 6 p.c. Cum. Pref.	10	19
4	Do. Mt. Deb. Stk., Red.	100	125
6/6	Eastern Exten., Aus., & China, Ltd.	10	17¾
5	Do. (Aus. Gov. Sub.) Deb., Red.	100	102
5	Do. do. Bearer	100	102½
4	Do. Mort. Deb. Stk.	100	127½
5	Eastn. & S. Afric., Ltd., Mort. Deb. 1900	100	102
5	Do. Bearer	100	102½
4	Do. Mort. Debs. 1909	100	102½
4	Do. Mort. Debs. (Maur. Subsidy)	25	106½
5/	Grt. Nthn. Copenhagen	10	29½
5	Do. Debs., Ser. B., Red.	100	101½
12/6	Indo-European, Ltd.	25	51½
6	London Platino-Brazilian, Ltd., Debs. 1904	100	109½
4/	Montevideo Telph., Ltd., 6 p.c. Pref.	5	2½
3/	National Telephone, Ltd.	5	5¾
6/	Do. Cum. 1 Pref.	10	16
6/	Do. Cum. 2 Pref.	10	16
5	Do. Non-Cum. 3 Pref.	5	5½
3½	Do. Deb. Stk., Red.	100	103½
8d.	Oriental Telephone, Ltd.	1	⅝
4	Pac. & Euro. Tlg. Dbs., Rd.	100	106½
4/	Reuter's, Ltd.	8	8½
5/	Un. Riv. Plate Telph., Ltd.	5	4½
5	Do. Deb. Stk., Red.	100	105½
—	West African Telg., Ltd.	10	4
5	Do. 5 p.c. Mt. Debs., Red.	100	100½
—	W. Coast of America, Ltd.	10	½
6/9	Western & Brazilian, Ltd.	15	12
6/	Do. 5 p.c. Pref. Ord.	7½	7½
9d.	Do. Defd. Ord.	7½	4½
4	Do. Deb. Stk., Red.	100	105½
6d.	W. India & Panama, Ltd.	10	½
6	Do. Cum. 1 Pref.	10	7½
6	Do. Cum. 2 Pref.	10	6
	Do. Debs., Red.	100	107½
7	West. Union, 1 Mt. 1902($	1000	107½
6	Do. 6 p.c. Stg. Bds., Rd.	100	102½

TRAMWAYS AND OMNIBUS.

Last Div.	Name.	Paid.	Price.
1/6	Anglo-Argentine, Ltd.	5	3½
6	Do. Deb. Stk.	100	125
4/	Barcelona, Ltd	10	11
5	Do. Deb., Red.	100	105½
7/6	Belfast Street Trams.	10	16½
—	Blackpl. & Fltwd. Tram., £10 Shs.	8	12½
10/	Bordeaux Tram. & O. Ltd.	10	12½
5	Do. Cum. Pref.	10	11
—	Brazilian Street Ry., Ltd.	2	½
—	British Elec. Trac., Ltd.	10	16
—	B. Ayres & Belg. Tram., Ltd., 6 p.c. Cum. Pref.	5	—
6	Do. 1 Deb. Stk.	100	—
—	B. Ayres. Gd. Nat., Ltd., 6 p.c 1 Deb. Bds., Red.	100	60½
5½	Do. Pref. Debs., Red.	100	94½
1/	Calais, Ltd.	5	1
—	Calcutta, Ltd.	10	3½
—	Carthagena & Herr., Ltd.	10	2½
5	Do. Deb., Red.	100	90
5	City of B'ham. Trams., Ltd., 5 p.c. Cum. Pref.	5	5
4	Do. 1 Mort. Debs., Rd.	100	105½
3/9	City of B. Ayres, Ltd.	5	6½
2/3	Do. Ext. £5 Shs.	3	3½
6	Do. Deb. Stk	100	145
1/4	Edinburgh Street Tram.	4	4
1/	Glasgow Tram. & Omni. Ltd., £9 Shs.	8	2½
3/7½	Imperial, Ltd.	6	14½
3/	Lond., Deptfd., & Greenwich, Prefd.	5	3½
nil	Do. Defd.	5	1
10½	Lond. Gen. Omni., Ltd.	100	195
4	Do. Deb., Red.	100	113½

Tramways and Omnibus (*continued*):—

Last Div.	Name.	Paid.	Price.
4/9½	London Road Car	6	10
28/6	Do. Red. 1 Mt. Deb. Stk.	100	109½
5	London St. Rly. (Prov., Ont.), Mt. Debs.	100	110
12/6	London St. Trams.	—	2
12/9	London Trams., Ltd	10	9
6/	Do. Non-Cum. Pref.	10	10
5	Do. Mt. Db. Stk., Rd.	100	101
5	Lynn & Boston 1 Mt. 1924 $	1000	104
5	Milwaukee Elec. Cons. Mt. $	1000	100½
5	Minneapolis St. 1 Cons. Mt $	1000	96
5	Montreal St. Dbs., 1908	100	109
4½	Do. Debs., 1922	100	107
6/	Nth. Metropolitan	—	11½
1/9½	Nth. Staffords., Ltd.	6	5
2/6	Provincial, Ltd	10	6½
6/	Do. Cum. Pref.	10	14
5	St. Paul City, 1937 $	1000	96
5/	Southampton	10	6½
5/	South London	10	5½
7/6	Sunderland, Ltd.	10	6½
4½	Toronto 1 Mt., Red.	100	105
2/6	Tramways Union, Ltd.	5	6½
4½	Do. Deb., Red.	100	109
2/6	Vienna General Omnibus.	5	5
5	Do. 5 p.c. Mt. Deb., Red.	100	103½
4/	Wolverhampton, Ltd	10	6

WATER WORKS.

Last Div.	Name.	Paid.	Price.
10/	Antwerp, Ltd.	20	22
6/	Cape Town District, Ltd.	5	7½
10½	Chelsea	100	322½
5	Do. Pref. Stk.	100	174½
4½	Do. Pref. Stk, 1875	100	152½
4½	Do. Deb. Stk.	100	159½
5/6	City St. Petersburg, Ltd.	11	10½
5/	Colne Valley	10	15½
4	Do. Deb. Stock	100	137½
£4	Consol. of Rosar., Ltd., 4 p.c. 1 Deb. Stk., Red.	100	91
8	East London	100	227½
4½	Do. Deb. Stk.	100	160
3	Do. Deb. Stk., Red.	100	105
37/6	Grand Junction (Max. 10 p.c.) "A"	50	117½
18/9	Do. "B"	25	
18/9	Do. "C" (Max. 7½ p.c.)	25	54½
35/	Do. "D" (Max. 7 p.c.)	50	97½
4	Do. Deb. Stock	100	142½
13	Kent	100	360½
7	Do. New (Max. 7 p.c.)	100	215½
7/	Kimberley, Ltd.	7	4
6	Do. Debs., Red.	100	104½
6	Do. Deb. Stk., Red	100	107½
10	Lambeth (Max. 10 p.c.)	100	297½
7½	Do. (Max. 7½ p.c.), 50 & 25	—	230½
4	Do. Deb. Stock	100	142½
3	Do. Red. Deb. Stock	100	103
10/	Montevideo, Ltd.	20	16
5	Do. 1 Deb. Stk.	100	110½
5	Do. 2 Deb. Stk.	100	104½
132/9	New River New	100	434½
4	Do. Deb. Stk.	100	143½
4	Do. Deb. Stk. "B"	100	143½
4	Portland Con. Mt. "B," 1927	—	102½
8/	Seville, Ltd.	20	12
5/6	Southend "Addl." Ord.	10	17
6	Southwark and Vauxhall	100	162½
6	Do. "D" Shares (7½ p.c. max.)	100	154½
5	Do. Pref. Stock	100	172½
4	Do. "A" Deb. Stock	100	141½
3	Staines Resvirs. Jt. Com. Gua. Deb. Stk., Red.	100	105
8/	Tarapaca, Ltd.	10	8½
10	West Middlesex	100	297½
4½	Do. Deb. Stk.	100	161½
3	Do Deb. Stk	100	105

INDIAN AND CEYLON TEA COMPANIES.

Acres Planted.	Crop, 1897.	Paid up Capital.	Share.	Paid up.	Name.	Dividends. 1894.	1895.	1896.	1897.	Price.	Yield.	Reserve.	Balance Forward.	Working Capital.	Mortgages, Debs. or Pref. Capital not otherwise stated.
	lb.	£	£	£	INDIAN COMPANIES.							£	£	£	£
11,240	3,128,000	120,000	10	3	Amalgamated Estates	—	*	10	‡5	3½	9	10,000	16,500	D52,950	—
		400,000	10	10	Do. Pref.	—	*	5	5	9½xd	5¼				
10,223	3,560,000	187,160	20	20	Assam	20	20	20	17½	59½	6	55,000	1,730	D11,350	—
6,150	3,278,000	142,500	10	10	Assam Frontier	3	6	6	nil	—	—	—	286	20,000	82,500
		142,500	10	10	Do. Pref.	6	6	6	4	10	4				
2,087	839,000	66,745	5	5	Attaree Khat	12	12	8	5	5	5	3,790	4,820	7,770	—
1,633	583,000	78,170	10	10	Borelli	4	4	5	4	7	6	—	3,256	D270	6,500 Pref.
1,720	812,000	60,825	5	5	British Indian	6	5	5	5	3½xd	7½	—	2,920	12,300	16,500 Pref.
3,223	2,247,000	114,500	5	5	Brahmapootra	20	18	20	15	12½	6	—	28,440	41,600	·
3,754	1,617,000	76,500	10	10	Cachar and Dooars	*	8	7	7	9½	7	—	1,645	21,240	·
		76,500	10	10	Do. Pref.	*	6	6	6	11	5½				
3,946	2,083,000	72,010	1	1	Chargola	8	7	10	5	⅞	8	3,000	3,300	—	—
		81,000	1	1	Do. Pref.	7	7	7	7	1⅛	5⅞				
1,971	942,000	33,000	5	5	Chubwa	10	8	10	8	5⅞	7¼	10,000	2,043	D5,400	—
		33,000	5	5	Do. Pref.	7	7	7	7	6⅛	5¾				
,250	11,500,000	120,000	10	3	Cons. Tea and Lands	—	*	10	‡5	3⅞	8	65,000	14,240	D191,674	—
		1,000,000	10	10	Do. 1st Pref.	—	*	5	5	10⅝xd	4¾				
		400,000	10	10	Do. 2nd Pref.	—	*	7	7	11⅛xd	5¾				
2,230	617,000	135,420	20	20	Darjeeling	5½	5½	6	5	21	4¾	5,552	1,565	1,700	—
2,114	445,000	60,000	10	10	Darjeeling Cons.	—	*	4/2	nil	5	—	—	1,820	—	—
		60,000	10	10	Do. Pref.	—	*	5	5	9⅛xd	5½				
6,660	3,518,000	150,000	10	10	Dooars	12½	12½	12½	12½	17⅞xd	7⅛	45,000	300	D32,000	—
		75,000	10	10	Do. Pref.	7	7	7	7	16⅛	4¾				
3,367	1,811,000	165,000	10	10	Doom Dooma	11¾	10	12½	12½	20	6⅛	30,000	4,032	—	10,000
1,377	582,000	61,120	5	5	Eastern Assam	5	nil.	4	nil	2¼	—	—	1,790	—	10,000
4,038	1,675,000	85,000	10	10	East India and Ceylon	¾	nil.	7	3	6	8	—	1,710	—	—
		85,000	10	10	Do. Pref.	*	6	6	6	11	5¾				
7,500	3,363,000	219,000	10	10	Empire of India	—	*	6/10	9	10¼	8¾	15,000	—	27,000	—
		219,000	10	10	Do. Pref.	—	*	5	5	10½	4¾				
1,180	540,000	94,060	10	10	Indian of Cachar	7	3½	3	2	4	5	6,070	—	7,120	—
3,050	824,000	83,500	5	5	Jhanzie	10	10	10	8	6¼	6	14,500	1,070	2,700	—
7,980	3,680,000	250,000	10	10	Jokai	10	10	10	8	15¾	6¼	45,000	990	D9,000	—
		100,000	10	10	Do. Pref.	*	6	6	6	14¾	4¼				
5,224	1,563,000	100,000	20	20	Jorehaut	20	20	20	—	58¾	6¾	36,220	2,955	3,000	—
1,547	504,000	65,660	10	8	Lebong	15	15	15	12½	15½xd	6¾	9,000	2,150	8,650	—
5,082	1,709,000	100,000	10	10	Lungla	5	10	6	3	6	5	—	1,543	D21,000	—
		100,000	10	10	Do. Pref.	*	6	6	6	10¼	5¾				
2,684	885,000	95,970	10	10	Majuli	7	5	5	nil	6	7¾	—	2,606	560	—
1,375	380,000	91,840	1	1	Makum	—	—	2	—	1	2	—	—	1,200	25,000
2,990	770,000	100,000	1	1	Moabund	—	—	*	—	⅜	—	—	—	-	—
		50,000	1	1	Do. Pref.	—	—	*	12½	⅞	5¾				
1,080	482,000	79,590	10	10	Scottish Assam	7	7	7	—	10¼	6¾	6,500	800	9,590	—
4,150	1,456,000	100,000	10	10	Singlo	6	8	5	‡1	8	6	—	300	D5,200	—
		80,000	10	10	Do. Pref.	*	6½	6¼	13½	13½	5				
					CEYLON COMPANIES.										
7,970	1,743,824§	250,000	100	100	Anglo-Ceylon, & Gen.	—	*	5½	—	45	11	10,992	1,405	D72,844	166,680
1,836	685,741§	50,000	10	10	Associated Tea	—	*	5	10½	7½	6¾	—	164	2,478	—
		60,000	10	10	Do. Pref.	—	*	6	13	10¾	5¾				
10,390	4,000,000	167,380	10	10	Ceylon Tea Plantations	15	15	15	15	23¾	6¼	84,500	1,516	D30,819	—
		81,080	10	10	Do. Pref.	7	7	7	7	16⅞	4⅛				
5,722	1,542,700	55,260	5	3	Ceylon & Oriental Est.	5	8	7	—	2¾	7¼	—	230	D2,047	71,000
		46,000	5	5	Do. Pref.	6	6	6	13	5	6				
2,157	801,629§	111,330	5	5	Dimbula Valley	—	*	10	15	5¼	9	—	—	1,733	6,250
		62,607	5	5	Do. Pref.	—	*	6	13	6⅞	4¾				
11,496	3,635,000	298,250	5	5	Eastern Prod. & Est.	3	5	6¼	7	5¾	6¼	20,000	11,740	D17,797	102,500
2,293	1,050,000	22,080	10	10	New Dimbula "A"	10	16	16	‡4	24	7	11,000	2,024	1,150	8,400
		55,710	10	10	Do. "B"	18	16	16	‡4	22	7¼				
2,572	570,360§	100,000	10	10	Ouvah	6	8	6	4	8	7½	4,000	1,151	D1,255	—
2,630	964,963	200,000	10	10	Nuwara Eliya	—	*	6	6	10⅛	5¾	—	—	—	30,000
1,720	708,533	41,000	10	10	Scottish Ceylon	15	15	15	10	17	6	7,000	1,252	D3,970	9,000 Pref.
2,450	750,000	39,000	10	6	Standard	12½	15	15	15	12¾	7	9,000	800	D14,012	4,000
		17,000	10	10	Do.	12½	15	15	15	22	7				

Working-Capital Column.—In working-capital column, D stands for *debit*.

* Company formed this year. † Interim dividends are given as actual distribution made. ‡ Interim div. only. § Crop 1896.

NOTICES.

According to certified statistics compiled by the Credit Index Company, Limited the number of failures in the United Kingdom for the week ended June 11 was 193 including nine not yet registered, being an increase of forty-four as compared with the corresponding week in 1897.

The Commissioners of Inland Revenue have entered into an agreement for the composition of the stamp duties payable on transfers of the further issue of £100,000 Metropolitan Police debenture stock, in accordance with the provisions contained in Section 115 of the Stamp Act, 1891.

It is announced that arrangements are being made for amalgamating the brewery firms of Messrs. Combe, Messrs. Watney, and Messrs. Reid, and that at an early date they will all be under one management.

Sir Lionel E. Darell has joined the board of the Capital and Counties Bank, Limited.

Mr. J. Lawson Johnston has accepted the chairmanship of Bovril, Limited, which has been vacated by the death of Lord Playfair. Viscount Duncannon will now occupy the vice-chair.

The coupons falling due on June 15, 1898, on the Greek 5 per cent. loan of 1890 (Piræus-Larissa Railway) bonds should be presented at the office of Messrs. C. J. Hambro & Son, 70, Old Broad-street, for payment of 32 per cent. in gold of their face value, in accordance with Article 2 of the International Greek Law of Control.

The numbers are announced of bonds of the Sivagunga Zemindary sterling loan to the amount of £8,100 which have been drawn for payment at par on July 1.

A branch of the National Bank, Limited, will be opened on the 1st proximo at No. 23, Baker-street, W., under the management of Mr. J. G. K. Wales, formerly manager at Harrow-road branch.

Bonds amounting to £960 of the Chilian International 6 per cent. loan of 1892, drawn in Paris in March last, will be paid on July 1 at the City Bank, Limited, Threadneedle-street.

Messrs. Grindlay & Co. have removed to 54, Parliament-street.

Mr. D. N. Shaw, of 20, Bishopsgate-street Within, has been appointed a director of George Ingham & Co., Limited.

The Conde d'Eu Railway Company publishes the numbers of the 5½ per cent. debenture bonds which have been purchased for redemption and cancelled.

The Indian and General Investment Trust, Limited, publishes the numbers of the first mortgage 6 per cent. gold bonds of the Acadia Pulp and Paper Mills, Limited, which have been drawn for payment at $1,090 per bond on July 1.

The numbers are published of the 5 per cent. mortgage debentures of the Argentine Refinery Company, amounting to £3,800 which have been drawn at the offices of the River Plate Trust Loan and Agency Company for repayment at par on July 1, with accrued interest to June 30.

Messrs. J. Henry Schröder & Co. publish the numbers of twenty-three bonds of £100 each of the issue of £200,000 5½ per cent. bonds of the City of Valparaiso, which have been acquired by purchase and cancelled. The half-yearly interest due July 1 next on the above issue will be paid by Messrs. J. Henry Schröder & Co. on and after that date.

Messrs. Glyn, Mills, Currie, & Co. announce that the fourth half-yearly amortisation of the Uruguay 5 per cent. loan of 1896 will take place by public tender in London on the 21st inst., the amount applicable being £9,014. They are therefore prepared to receive tenders of bonds for redemption, forms for which may be obtained at 67, Lombard-street, E.C.

The directors of the New Comet Gold Mining Company, Limited, recommend that debentures to the extent of £200,000 should be created, of which £175,000 shall be issued at par with the right to convert for a period of two years from the date of issue into shares at £3 10s. It will be necessary to increase the capital from £225,000 to £275,000, so as to create shares for the conversion of the debentures, and an extraordinary general meeting has been convened for July 18 to pass the necessary resolutions.

On and after June 15, the offices of The West of India Portuguese Guaranteed Railway Company, Limited, will be at 4, Coleman-street, E.C.

Mr. Hooley has some time since ceased to have any connection with the undertaking known as Hooley and Dee Lands, and the bankruptcy of Mr. Hooley will not affect the estate of the Dee Estates Company, Limited.

An extraordinary general meeting of the Nundydroog Company, Limited, will be held on June 22 for the purpose of considering a resolution for increasing the capital of the company to £242,000, by the issue of 22,000 shares of £1 each, at a premium of £2 each. It is proposed that these shares be offered to the shareholders *pro rata*—viz., one new share for every ten old shares.

The Eastern Telegraph Company, Limited, notify that the cable between Mozambique and Lorenzo Marquez became interrupted on Tuesday evening. As the cable between San Thome and Loanda has been interrupted off the mouth of the Congo since the 3rd inst., this last interruption cuts off all telegraphic communication with South Africa. The repairing ship has left for Mozambique, and it is hoped that the cable will be restored in four days. Meanwhile all telegrams will be sent on from Mozambique to Lorenzo Marquez by mail leaving on the 17th inst., and will be re-telegraphed from the latter place to destination if the cable is not restored before the mail arrives at Lorenzo Marquez.

A drawing of the debentures of the Municipal Corporation of the Port Louis (Mauritius) 5 per cent. loans will take place at the counting-house of Messrs. Chalmers, Guthrie, & Co. (bankers of the Corporation), of 9, Idle-lane, E.C., on the 30th inst.

Messrs. Lumsden & Myers notify that they have removed from 18, Finch-lane to 29, Cornhill, E.C.

The numbers are published of the 5 per cent. mortgage debentures of the Argentine Refinery Company amounting to £3,800, which have been drawn at the offices of the River Plate Trust Loan and Agency Company for repayment at par on July 1, with accrued interest to June 30.

The first batch of letters of allotment and regret for the issue of 300,000 5 per cent. preference shares of the Goldsmiths' and Silversmiths' Company, Limited, were posted on Wednesday.

The Trustees, Executors, and Securities Insurance Corporation, Limited, publishes the numbers of the bonds of the City of Mexico 5 per cent. loan of 1889, which have been drawn for repayment at par on July 1.

Printed for the Proprietor by LOVE & WYMAN, LTD., Great Queen Street, London, W.C.; and Published by CLEMENT WILSON at Norfolk House, Norfolk Street, Strand, London, W.C.

The Investors' Review

EDITED BY A. J. WILSON.

Vol. I.—No. 25. New Series. | FRIDAY, JUNE 24, 1898. | [Registered as a Newspaper.] | Price 6d. By post, 6½d

CONTENTS

The Investors' Review.

Is the Stock Exchange Rotten?

Week by week the burden of our tale about the Stock Exchange is "want of business." "We haven't done a bargain for days" some brokers will candidly admit, not once in a way but often. "Only made the cost of the day's wires" is another form in which the scarcity of orders is emphasised, and there is no doubt that, exaggerated as these statements may be, the markets have had for a long time back comparatively little to do. One cause of the absence of a public we have harped on till we are weary: prices are so high that they positively retard business. We had hoped that dear money would last long enough to bring about such a fall as would have induced the public to come in again, and at least buy for investment. It has not lasted long enough, and directly the jobbers on the Stock Exchange saw rates for money begin to fall they put up again the prices which they had lowered to protect themselves against sellers as much as in consequence of actual sales. We are speaking, of course, about good, or believed-in, securities alone, in regard to which the action of the jobbers is often much like that of the shopkeeper who slams his door in the face of his customers. No inducement whatever is held out to investors to come in as buyers of any class of security. The moment credit becomes cheap, prices are lifted above people's reach, until purchases can only be effected at figures which involve a certainty of loss of capital the moment credit again becomes difficult to obtain on easy, or on any, terms.

To blame the members of the Stock Exchange for this credit-sustained "boycott" of the investor would not be just. They cannot well help themselves. Banks enable them to carry on their business in this way, nay, tempt them to do so, and they merely obey the artificial forces and laws of supply and demand which our system of credit has brought into existence. But we have not covered the whole field in dealing with this particular cause of the want of orders. After all, the chief source of a stock-jobber's or stock-broker's income is not usually investment, but speculation. The Stock Exchange would not have half its present membership were it dependent upon the mere investor, who sells what he had previously bought and delivers the thing sold to the buyer, or who comes with fresh money in his hand to be placed out to advantage. Speculation in all forms, from the mere gamble of the individual who bets in prices for the rise or the fall, who stakes money on "options" as on a horse or a dog or a cricket match, to the more solid operations of the man who buys with his own money, or on his own credit, in expectation that an advance in the price will enable a profit to be secured, constitutes the main business of the Stock Exchange, and it is this which has been so terribly curtailed for more than a year past. Why is it so? The causes are various, and many of them are totally beyond the markets' control, such as the already mentioned price-forcing abundance of money, or the failure of South African mining and other speculations to yield the predicted fat returns. Others, however, appear to us to be the direct offspring of stock market habits of business, and as such they deserve the most careful and anxious attention of the upright members of the Stock Exchange and their committee.

From what we are about to say, it must not be understood that we consider the members of the Stock Exchange as a body so many thieves. On the contrary, we not only believe, but know the great majority of them to be fair and honourable traders, quite as incapable of doing a mean or dishonest action as any similar body of men in the world. We say this absolutely without reserve, and with all the greater emphasis because it is our strong opinion that customs and methods of business are growing more and more prevalent on the Stock Exchange whose effect is to put the honest majority of the members thereof at the mercy of the dishonest and unscrupulous minority. It is the thievish portion of the membership—a very small portion in number, perhaps, but still it is a sensible portion—which is more and more giving the Stock Exchange its character before the world. "We do not originate the swindles that come upon the market," members always argue in self-defence. "Why, then, should we be held responsible? Why can't the public distinguish?" There is cogency in this argument, but it does not cover the whole field, as a moment's reflection should enable even a broker to understand, prejudiced as he naturally is, and must be, in favour of the body to which he belongs.

It is perfectly true that a comparatively small number of the swindles by which the public has been so cruelly victimised, especially since the virulent disease of company mania and premium hunting took possession of it, have originated in the Stock Exchange. Equally true is it, however, that these swindles are nearly all effected by means of the facilities this great market affords, often in defiance of its own rules, to the outside thief. Is it any wonder, therefore, that the people whose pockets have been rifled by "dealings for the coming out," "dealings for the special settlement," "pocket orders," fraudulent simulations of a market demand, &c., &c., for this and the other trash or dishonest concoction, should blame the instrument by which these rascalities are effected far more than the scoundrels who play upon it? We could instance many examples illustrative of the point now insisted upon, and as answer to this question, but the law of libel forbids a too close or detailed adhesion to the truth, for the law of libel is the knave's best and most potent shield. Readers of this Review, however, can have no difficulty in putting two and two together for themselves, and should they not care to do this they need only have a little patience. An abundance of illustrative examples is nearly ready for presentment, and both the bankruptcy and the criminal courts will soon be busy unfolding tales of crime and imposture, all rendered successful, so far as they have been a success hitherto, by the freedom with which the habits and unwritten laws of the Stock Exchange allowed scheming blackguards outside to effect their purpose. When the day of exposure comes, and it is not now far off for some of the carrion, we should not be surprised to see a few members of the Stock Exchange in the criminal dock submitting to sentences of penal servitude, and we have a pretty confident hope that a few of the worst class of company-promoting lawyers will also be there. Take him all round, the City rogue-lawyer is perhaps the basest and most loathsome of all the ghouls in human shape who come there to live by plunder, and batten on ignorance and greed, but his greater infamy cannot exonerate the Stock Exchange from blame, and unless its honest members bestir themselves and compel reforms they will find themselves involved in the obloquy which is about to fall on some of their fellows, whose heads are now held high, and in whose pockets are the wages of crime.

The truth is that any line of conduct approaching to the upright and honest has come to be almost "bad form" on the Stock Exchange. So long as certain outward semblances of respectability are paid deference to, it is open to a member of the Stock Exchange, broker or jobber, to commit almost any crime he has a mind to against the pockets of the outside public. He may join with the lowest kind of thieves outside in making sham prices for the shares of sham companies, he may take "underwriting" commissions and "plant" the shares or stock he has subscribed for on his still trusting clients. When it "suits his book" or the game of his companions in robbery, he may run a price down or run it up. For a fee he can be persuaded to hand in names of sham allottees to the committee of the Stock Exchange, so as to get it to grant a settling day and perhaps a quotation for shares he knows to be not worth the transfer fee. Jobbers, also, may buy and sell in a perfect understanding that the bargains they do are in all their essentials shams. The scamps who are "working" or "making" the market—shifting prices about, that is, and generally upward, so as to induce the public to believe that a genuine demand exists—send one broker confederate in to the Exchange to buy and another to sell at prices arranged beforehand, and the jobber either pockets his "turn on the deal" or, as a partner in the swindle, contracts to do the entire job for a fixed share in the "swag"—the money absorbed from the "gull" public.

But all this and much more goes on under the decent forms of regular and legitimate business. A broker who is a member of the Stock Exchange may take part in foisting a swindle on the public, but he must not advertise his name in the newspapers, except on prospectuses. That is a capital crime, perpetration of which would involve expulsion. Most other rules of the Stock Exchange may be set at defiance, or dodged with impunity, but this one must not be violated, for fear of confounding a most respectable body of men with keepers of "bucket shops." The forms of bargaining, according to prescribed rules, must also be adhered to; that not only promotes discipline, but salves the conscience should the substance of the transaction be a fraud, or a thing on nodding acquaintance with fraud. By the rules of the "House," dealings in letters of allotment are not recognised, but the rule is ignored in practice, and is, indeed, rendered nugatory by that other rule, in virtue of which bargains of any sort cannot be annulled except on proof of fraud or wilful misrepresentation. By the same rule, quotations in the Stock Exchange official list are forbidden to the shares of a company which has not been floated upon a prospectus publicly advertised; yet some of the worst and most brutally callous swindles of the past and of the present day have been perpetrated by the aid of the machinery, and with the active assistance of members of the Stock Exchange in complete contempt of this rule—witness the "boom" and collapse of the Barnato companies. Share lists compiled in derision are taken as genuine, and the rule that two-thirds of the number of shares offered to the public must be genuinely allotted is, by this and other means, made a dead letter. Companies with a foreign domicile which exempts them from British laws, whose share registers cannot be inspected, and whose meetings are held abroad, can be laid before the public here, through the Stock Exchange, with perfect ease.

To add to the facilities in these and other ways given to unscrupulous members of the Stock Exchange—driven perhaps sometimes into dishonest ways by stress of hunger—to bring the institution into disrepute, and injure the honest majority, the utmost care is taken to shield the whole body of its dealings from public criticism, and still more from actions-at-law by wronged "outsiders." The affairs of defaulters are wound up inside the Exchange, without public interference or criticism, and we fear in these proceedings the interests of the public are not unfrequently forgotten. Transactions which might bring scandal; robberies of securities, frauds, participation in plots to defraud, the invasion of the province of the broker by the jobber, and *vice versâ*—all such things are, as much as possible, hushed up for the sake of that "respectability," which is of the essence of the game. And still the honest members go grumbling on, paying their thirty guineas per annum for the "privilege" of belonging to a body so lamentably ill-regulated, and meekly wonder every day of their lives why "business should be so bad." "We have done nothing wrong," they say; "our business is conducted most respectably and regularly; it is these thieves outside who victimise the public and us—not we ourselves who do evil." Unfortunately for them the public is less and less disposed to accept this view, and as its distrust of Stock Exchange methods increases—methods exhibited to it with greatest prominence in the misdeeds of the brigand element in the membership—business will grow worse. Things have already come to such a pass that the individual speculator has almost no chance against the rings, cliques, or syndicates who control prices. At the best of times the chances are, thanks to the regular demands of the market, at least five to one against him. But under modern developments—syndicates, groups, gambling "trusts," and so forth—they may easily be a thousand to one against the isolated operator, and the wealth the market snatches to itself on such odds is shared only by the few who are "in" with the wire pullers. The writer of this article can speak now from a long and varied experience of the City and of Stock Exchange business, and it is his opinion that the plain, ordinary citizen who takes to stock speculation as a means of "making money" courts his own ruin. He himself would as soon think of deliberately putting his hand into the fire as of perpetrating "a time bargain on open account" on the Stock Exchange in any security, so fully persuaded is he that the odds are bound to be against his success. As we said at the outset, we do not blame the Stock Exchange, as a whole or alone, for such a state of things as this implies; but in the judgment impending upon it the innocent will have to bear condemnation with the guilty, unless they take steps so to reform the practices of the institution of which they are members as to give the honest man therein at least an equal chance with the thief. Is the Stock Exchange rotten, then? No, not quite, but it is rotting in places, and the rot must spread, because the one and only effective deterrent to financial crime it furnishes is the initial cost to the criminal. What good can come to an institution which allows its members, if they so choose, to regulate their morals by the size of the fees they exact for the use of their names and services, often in pretty exact ratio to the magnitude of the fraud to be perpetrated?

We must close this already too long article here and leave the discussion of specific reforms to a future day.

Brazil and the Rothschilds.

Default has come, and it has long been foreseen by independent observers. The City has received with comparative indifference the intimation that interest upon the external debt of Brazil will, for the next three years, be paid in paper and that sinking funds are to be suspended for thirteen years. Probably this attitude is due to the fact that there is not an extensive holding of Brazilian Government bonds on the Stock Exchange. Owing to the public's faith in the name of Rothschild there are still considerable amounts of these bonds held throughout the country, and, of course, the capital of the Brazilian guaranteed railways, dealt with in another column, is nearly all held here. There was really, however, no room for any disturbance in the market, because it has for some time been perfectly obvious that the central Government responsible for these loans and guarantees could not possibly continue to pay in cash. It has not squarely paid in cash for many years back. In their letter to the President-elect of the Republic, published in last Monday's *Times*, Messrs. Rothschild declare that they have "always been proud and content to see Brazil faithfully fulfilling all her engagements." If this is so, the firm's pride must be easily gratified, for it itself has been the one and only sustainer of Brazilian credit. The Brazilian Government has never made the smallest attempt to pay its way.

What have the loans issued during, say, the past ten years been for, if not to keep Brazilian "credit" on its legs? Can Messrs. Rothschild point to any substantial gain that the Brazilian nation has received through the issue of these loans? Has the Western of Minas Railway, for example, ever been built, for which a loan of £3,700,000 nominal was raised in 1893? Surely they cannot have forgotten the scandal which arose in connection with this loan, or have overlooked the remarks made about it by Mr. Frederic Harford, second secretary in her Majesty's Legation at Rio, in his report on the finances of Brazil for the years 1890 to 1893. Perhaps it may be as well to quote his observations here just to remind the public and Messrs. Rothschild how this kind of "credit" maintenance has been manipulated. Mr. Harford's words are at least a curious commentary on that further remark in their letter to Dr. Campos Salles, President-elect of Brazil, to the effect that the credit of a country constitutes, after all, "its greatest power." We can quite imagine a financier believing this to be true, but should be very sorry for England if there were nothing better behind its "credit" than loan emissions such as the following describes:—

The motives which led the Government to raise a loan in the name of the Oeste de Minas Railway are thus explained in the report of the Minister of Finance. More than £1,500,000 having been remitted to London in order to satisfy the charges of the Treasury, amongst which figured the payment (part) of the £1,000,000 borrowed of Messrs. Rothschild in 1892, the Government recognised the necessity of effecting a foreign loan in order to avoid its having to appear as a buyer in the exchange market, which is now more sensitive than ever, and Congress not having authorised the raising of a loan by the Government itself, it was arranged with the above company to float a loan in their name, the product of which was to be placed at the disposal of the Treasury agency in London. A loan of £3,700,000 nominal was accordingly negotiated through the medium of Messrs. Rothschild at 80 per cent. and 5 per cent. interest guaranteed by the Government. This loan produced, at 77 per cent., the sum of £2,849,000 net, and, by arrangement with the company, was taken over by the Brazilian Government at the exchange of 20d., the equivalent of which is 34,188,000 milreis. The difference of 3 per cent. (between 80 and 77 per cent.) is presumably for the commission and expenses connected with the raising of the loan.

The shareholders of the railway company can hardly be congratulated on obtaining a loan on such onerous conditions, which, on the other hand, appears to be very advantageous to the Government, who receive the sum of £2,849,000 in gold bought at 20d. to the milreis, and at the same time only undertakes to pay the company, as they require it, 34,188,000 milreis in currency, which, at the present exchange (end of July) of about 12d. is worth but £1,794,000. Unless, therefore, the exchange in the meantime rises above 20d., the Government secure a double advantage. The consideration received by the company is the guarantee of the interest on the nominal capital, which at 5 per cent. amounts to £185,000 per annum, and their good offices in negotiating the loan. Calculated on what the company will actually receive, they will be paying at the rate of nearly 10 per cent. per annum.

Some excitement was caused in Rio by the announcement that the application for a quotation of the above loan of £3,700,000 had been refused by the committee of the London Stock Exchange, and that a settling day only had been granted. The reason for this unusual step would appear to be in the irregularities alleged to have been discovered in the allotment of scrip to subscribers. Some applicants are said to have received the amount they applied for in full, while others did not take any allotment at all. £7,000,000 was nominally applied for, but only £2,650,000 was apparently actually allotted; and the bonds, which at first were quoted at 82 per cent., or 2 per cent. premium, have lately been quoted at 7½ per cent. discount.

The Budget law for 1893 allotted, as a special credit, the sum of 9,335,000 milreis for the interest and repayment of the loan of £1,000,000 contracted in April, 1892, with Messrs. Rothschild at 97, that firm receiving 3 per cent. commission. But if remitted from Brazil the amount allotted would be largely exceeded, owing to the depreciation of the currency, and no doubt the product of the Oeste de Minas Loan will be partly devoted to this purpose. The sum of £12,500 was payable as interest in September and December, 1892, and March, 1893; and on April 1, 1893, a first instalment of £300,000 was due, the balance of £700,000 being payable in July and October of this year, in order to effect the final amortisation of the loan.

It was reported in June that the Government were buying up the bonds of the 4½ per cent. gold internal loan of 1879, of which only 25,629,500 milreis remained in circulation on March 31, 1893. The reason given was that this would facilitate the floating of the Oeste de Minas Railway loan. In any case, the sum of £300,000 in specie was forwarded to London on June 1. In July the Government bought up a considerable amount of the 6 per cent. loan of 1868, paying up to 2,000 milreis for the bonds, and there is now very little of this loan outstanding.—Foreign Office Reports, No. 1321, 1894, pp. 17-19.

Is there not a moral question behind loan raisings of this, of every, description which has never been properly brought into view? Are we not allowed, in virtue of this, to ask what right Messrs. Rothschild, or any loan-issuing house, has to forge fetters in this manner for communities, without really consulting these communities, and with no apparent object except their own gain? It appears to us that this kind of finance is root and branch, not exactly immoral but non-moral, in precisely the same sense that usurious lending to impecunious individuals is. Nations are bought and sold under the guise of issues of bonds just as slaves used to be, and the only check upon the activity of this buying and selling is in such crises as the one which has now overtaken Brazil. When it is no longer possible to emit loans that the public will buy an enslaved nation gets a chance of release—a breathing time. Brazil, it will be said, gets such a chance under this debt-funding arrangement, but we are not so sure of that. There is not, to our thinking, the slightest probability that the new President will have much more power to introduce economies and reforms in the administration of Brazil than his predecessors, or the late Emperor, had. He will talk sweet words and promise much, but his power to do much is very limited. Therefore Brazil is likely to go on in the old way, making a fancy Budget showing a surplus at the beginning of the year, and voting away and wasting sufficient money during the year to realise a more or less extensive deficit at the end. In three years' time, therefore, the position will be so much worse than it is now by the amount of the freely accumulated further deficits and of the funding bonds issued to pay the interest upon the public debt. The end will thus, in all probability, be complete default, undisguised.

This is not a cheerful prospect, and we venture to think that the interests of what may be called the *morale* of high finance would have been much better served by Messrs. Rothschild, if they had, ten years or more ago, refused to issue any more Brazilian loans. Assuredly they themselves, we take it, would to-day have been the richer, had they adopted that nobler line of policy, for none of the loans since, and including, that of

1889, can have been a market success, profitable to the firm. On the contrary, we should imagine, judging by signs and appearances discernible to those who watch markets as a matter of daily routine, that each of these loans have been left to a greater or less extent upon the hands of its issuers, and that no small amount of money belonging to the great House of Rothschild must now be wrapped up in that Brazilian "credit" the London branch of it is so solicitous to see "restored." But for some such position we can scarcely understand what was to be gained by this three years' suspension of cash payments, modelled on the Argentine plan. There can be no substantial hope in the minds of the devisers of this plan that it will do any good. Brazil drifts along and will, by-and-bye—as we said in 1892, when this REVIEW first gave us the opportunity to say what we thought about such things without fear or favour—drift asunder. Her weakness, indeed, as a federal republic lies in the absence of what may be called prescriptive authority in the central Government. It has little real power and can do little real good. The will to check abuses may be there, but the necessary force is not. Presidents and Ministers must bribe, or wink at bribery and corruption, to be permitted to live; and in matters of taxation the range of the federal powers is much limited by the rights and wants of the individual States. Hence the mainstay of Brazilian national finance has all along been the Customs tariff and paper money, two sources of the means to "pay the way" with about as helpful to the solid development of a nation's wealth as choke-damp is healthy to a miner. Is it not time Messrs. Rothschild recognised the bitter truth in this matter? The *moratorium* they have thrown at bondholders and railway debenture holders, like scraped bones to a Pariah dog, can serve no good end for Brazil, and cannot possibly afford the Rothschilds a chance to sell out—not in England at least—but may be a piece of gross cruelty to the inhabitants of Brazil.

By way of wind up to this homily we append a table of the loans affected by this desperate expedient. There are six loans, it will be seen, and they are all held in Europe, even the so-called "internal" loan of 1879, either by the public or by the issuing house and its allies. On these loans, by which upwards of £38,000,000 was raised or sought to be raised, the depreciation to-day is over £16,500,000. Add the market loss on the railway capital, dealt with in another article, and we arrive at a total loss of nearly £22,000,000. It is an ugly picture:—

Issues Loans.	Outstanding amount.	Value at price of issue.	Present value in market.	Depreciation to date.
	£	£	£	£
Brazilian 4½ per cent. 1883	3,382,000	3,009,980	1,758,740	1,251,240
Brazilian 4½ per cent. 1888	5,393,100	5,231,307	2,804,412	2,426,895
Brazilian 4 per cent. 1889	18,533,300	17,679,970	9,266,650	8,413,320
Brazilian 5 per cent. 1895	7,398,000	6,488,300	4,280,840	2,207,460
Brazilian 5 per cent. West of Minas	3,710,000	2,968,000	1,966,300	1,001,700
Brazilian 4½ per cent. Internal 1879	2,702,925	2,702,925	1,486,595	1,216,330
	41,119,025	38,080,482	21,563,537	16,516,945

The Sources of Press Corruption.

No reply has come from Mr. Hooley to our offer to publish what he is pleased to call his list of blackmailing City journalists. We never expected one, because it did not seem to us possible that a man in Mr. Hooley's position could dare to expose fully the methods by which a promoter's business is more or less generally conducted. The question raised by his splenetic outbursts, however, is one of too great importance to be allowed to rest without comment, and we propose to say some frank and straightforward things upon it which the public may note, or otherwise, as it pleases. Unquestionably, there is a great deal of journalistic corruption in the City, but bad as things are it is not yet possible to "blackmail" an honest man there, although it may be nearly impossible to float a company on honest lines. But the root of the corruption is not in the working journalist. He is merely the instrument, and very often has no chance of being straight and clean even if he would. As a matter of fact, the majority of the humble men who provide "money articles" and financial notes for all sorts and qualities of newspapers are just as honest as any other class in the ranks of the journalistic profession. The most obvious proof that they are so is furnished by their poverty. Rarely indeed do we come across an instance of a man becoming rich by corruptly practising the arts of the decoy in financial journalism. Year in and out the same men trudge the same monotonous round amongst the offices of banks and brokers and financiers in the City, gathering information for the purpose of retailing it again to newspaper readers. They were poor when they began this work, and, being as a rule scantily paid and precariously located, for no City journalist is sure of his position, as even the meanest bank clerk who does his duty can be, they remain poor to the end of the chapter. In the whole of our now somewhat lengthened experience of the City, we cannot call to mind more than two or three men who have risen to affluence, or apparent affluence, through prostituting their pen and such talents as they might possess to the service of corrupt finance. This much it is necessary to say in defence of a hardworking and painstaking class of men, upon whom baffled financiers, like this conceited Hooley, and self-righteous moralists, who know nothing of the City and its ways, would cast the whole obloquy of the financial prostitution in City journalism.

Who, then, are the men principally responsible for the corruption which undoubtedly does prevail to an extent far greater than the public supposes, or than even the outpourings of Mr. Hooley's baffled vanity would lead it to suppose? When we come to analyse the matter, the principal sinner, we imagine, will be found to be this public itself, which poses as the chief sufferer. It does not want, as a rule, to be told the truth, this public; it wants to have something pointed out to it that it can "make money" by dealing in. The simple investor, in other words, counts for very little in City finance, and is seldom or ever thought of. Those who rush to subscribe for shares in this, that, or the other company generally do so because actuated by the greed of the gambler. They wish to get first "in," so as to be in a position to sell at a profit to others less early on the scene than themselves. Such is the motive usually dominant in people who dabble in company shares, apply for allotments and so on, and it is to this spirit that the promoter caters. His endeavour is to manufacture something which will "catch on," and in order to do this with success he has to enlist the Press on his side, so as to get it either to put attractive pictures of wealth to come before a crowd of premium hunters, as unfathomable in its stupidity as it is insatiable in its craving for money made without effort, or to take effective steps to gag it. Were the public of a careful mind, and satisfied to place its savings in good securities, the promoter would have very little scope, and many financial journals neither *raison d'être* nor income. It is just because this spirit of carefulness does not exist—except now and again when some prevailing fashion in swindles has enabled successful schemers to carry away immense masses of the country's savings, leaving the cheated ones in a virtuous fit of the blues—that the company promoter can carry on his sooty trade with such habitual success.

In all essentials the average promoter of joint stock companies is a thief, neither more nor less. Sometimes he is a sneak-thief, sometimes a bold highwayman who robs without mask; but always his object is to get money regardless of morals. He does not take up a business with a view to converting it into a joint stock company on lines which will ensure it solidity and permanence, and give, it may be, steady modest profits to its stockholders, but to see how much he can make out of it. In order to succeed at all he may have to employ accountants base enough to dress up figures as bidden in such a way that a large amount of hidden gain is wrapped up in the capital. "Profits" are to this end habitually "cooked," stocks overvalued, and risks minimised. Naturally, starting on such a basis, the promoter is very sensitive to anything in the nature of criticism, no matter how obscure the quarter from which it comes. It is essential to market success—his own and the inner "ring's" speedy unloading—that no doubt of any kind should be allowed to come between the mind of the public—intent also upon speedy profits through allotments sold to catch the dangled premiums—and the bait, because the slightest breath of suspicion causes the ravening mob to hang back. "What if the premium on the shares disappeared before we get a chance to sell out," it says to itself, this mob. At all costs this kind of fear must be prevented and the truth kept back. So the promoter must lay himself out to "nobble" the newspapers as a first step to success. It is merely a question of money. We are sorry to say that newspaper proprietors of all ranks have become more or less completely the company promoters' and loanmongers' tools and allies, simply because it at present pays them to be these. So much is this the case, and so large has the revenue from the advertising of company prospectuses become of late years, that there are not three daily newspapers in London at the present time whose editors would dare systematically to analyse, in the interests of truth and fair dealing, the adventures so lavishly blazoned in their columns. The editor who did that would find his shrift short, because independent criticism of the kind the public ought to have might curtail revenue. He prefers, then, to hold his hand and let the iniquities pass. Is it any wonder, with this initial combination of promoter and newspaper proprietor—all prevailing and all powerful—against him that the humble working journalist should sometimes hold out his hand for a bribe in passing? Can he be blamed if he does become corrupt and sell his pen when he finds some of the purse-proudest in the land doing the like, and taking the money of the fraudulent or other company promoter with both hands, on the tacit understanding that it shall secure him from anything like effective criticism, above all from criticism timed to be of use to the public? Displays of righteous censure after he has collected the "swag" the promoter seldom cares a straw for. But if the highest class of journals can be silenced in this way, and systematically silenced, so that only now and again is a tribute paid to uprightness by a "slating" bestowed upon some peculiarly atrocious attempt at fleecing the public, payment for the advertisements of which may be doubtful, how is it to be expected that the struggling lower ranks of papers will make any attempt to guide the public? The public, as we have said, mostly does not thank them for guidance. It is far easier, therefore, to go with the stream and far more profitable as well. In fact, the profit is often something infinitely greater than any mere revenue from advertisements ever is to such papers, if the business is only judiciously worked. The *Daily Chronicle* has been making some observations about the prevalence of the habit, quite recent in growth, of inserting reports of company meetings in the news columns of weekly papers as if they were independent and the paper's own, when, as a matter of fact, they are paid for as advertisements, and paid for on a high scale, too. But this is one of the smallest services which an easy-going newspaper proprietor can render to the gentlemen interested in selling companies' shares in bales and at higher prices than their intrinsic quality justifies. Nor is it the best-paid service. It frequently is little more to a paper than a gratuitous help to a fictitious circulation. So many copies of the issue in which a report appears are bought to be sent to the company's shareholders, and there the transaction ends. But this kind of corruption, if corruption it be, scarcely affects the company promoter. He is, more often than not, done with his companies before they get to the half-yearly meeting stage, and the services he requires from the newspaper proprietor are of a different and altogether more artistic kind. It may be necessary for him to pay smartly for the insertion of false price quotations, daily or weekly, in the newspapers in order to mislead the public, or, should a mine be in question, to fee proprietors to insert sham cablegrams from the region where the "shaft" is supposed to be. Sham assays and so on have also their price in print. We have heard of as much as £100 being paid for the publication of a single lie of the "rich strike" description, not covering two inches of space in the paper that printed it. The story may be false—and it can be true. Not only must sham quotations and telegrams be provided for by hard cash handed over to newspaper proprietors of a certain class, but heavy fees are exacted by them for the insertion of laudatory paragraphs and leaders, or for puffing items that look like news. More insidious still is the practice which has grown up quite within recent years of filling the "answers to correspondents" columns of daily and weekly newspapers that admit such with bogus advice. Non-existent correspondents are recommended "to buy Blowhards: they are going pounds higher," to "sell Gingerbreads: the thing has petered out," to "hold jujubes for a recovery," and so on, through the whole repertory of the market tout's gibberish. The "pudding-headed" public, rendered swinishly stupid by its lust after the "profits" of dice-throwing—and the dice loaded too—reads these false statements and delusive recommendations and rises to the bait as a fish to the fly.

These are only a few of the ways in which the Press is put at the service of the company promoter, but enough has been said to indicate how difficult it would be for any individual promoter, no matter how lofty his intentions, to turn round upon the people he has subsidised and suborned and expose their practices. Why should he be driven to do such things if his purpose was honest—if he asked nothing more for the companies he had to sell than they were really worth? We are afraid there can be no satisfactory answer to this question of a kind it would be prudent to print. But before leaving this subject for the present it may be well to mention that there is a lower class still of journals in the City, if a lower class be possible, and this is the class which is owned and carried on by some financier or firm of financiers, or company or group of companies, for a definite purpose, that purpose being a systematic puffing of all their own wares, and sometimes an equally systematic abuse of those who cry these wares down, or venture to speak a word of truth about them. There are "bull" organs and "bear" organs of this type sold along the kerbstones round the Stock Exchange—and seldom much elsewhere—whose lives are ephemeral, but which are always provided with the funds necessary to bring them into life and keep them there by some capitalist, or would-be capitalist. Of this class are most of the papers devoted specially to South African and Australian mining finance. Very few of these could live by their own vitality, not having circulation enough or advertisements enough to enable them to pay; but as subsidised frauds, or as blackmailing agencies pure and simple, they come and go, leading a precarious and rather malodorous existence, in the course of which they may have been effective in helping the Barnatos and such like to lighten the purses of the British public of a good many hundreds of thousands of pounds, if not of millions. And they are not all "kerbstone" journals either which flourish, or have flourished by such service.

Wherever we dip beneath the surface in the financial Press of London, and of the greater Press not specially financial which devotes a portion of its space to City affairs, we are sure to find more or less trace of the corrupting power of the financier. We should not call the bulk of this Press a blackmailing Press exactly, although some journals live partly by that most degraded method of obtaining money; it is more a "milking" Press, a Press that exacts toll from the company promoter, in order to purchase its silence, or in order that its columns may be open to say just exactly what the promoter wishes at the time he wishes it, and nothing else. From the high "respectability" of the best papers pressed into the service of the financier in this way to the lowest depth of the worst is only a matter of degree; the moral principle underlying the conduct of the best of them is not essentially different from that animating the veriest gutter imp of journalism. Is there any cure for this state of things? We fancy not, unless the public itself intervenes. When its moral standard becomes higher, the Press which serves it will rise similarly to the height demanded of it, and we shall have some little cleansing of the foul places now cankering the sources of the nation's wealth. With a public supine and indifferent, intent above all things on gambling, this elevation is not to be looked for, and no matter what homilies are read to us—no matter how far the wealth of the people may be consumed by the fraudulent and dishonest financier of the City—corrupt journalism will flourish and fill its pockets; at all events until some great financial crisis comes and sweeps it and its suborners and dupes out of existence together.

Arbitration under the Workmen's Compensation Act.

Under the new Act the power of contracting out of its provisions will be very limited. If the Registrar of Friendly Societies certifies that any scheme of compensation or insurance is on the whole not less favourable to the general body of workmen than the provisions of the Act, then, until the certificate is revoked, the employer may contract with his workmen that the scheme shall be substituted for the relief given by the Act. No scheme is to be so certified which contains an obligation upon the workmen to join it as a condition of their hiring, and before certifying the Registrar is to take steps to ascertain the views of both the employer and employed. It will thus be seen that the Act will apply notwithstanding any contract made to the contrary, except as above stated, and all agreements which are at present subsisting, whereby the workman relinquishes his right to compensation for injuries in the course of his employment, so far as they would relate to rights under this Act, will come to an end as provided for in Section 10. Nothing, however, affects the right to contract out of the rights given by the Common Law or the Employers' Liability Act of 1880, and all existing contracts relating to those rights, or any that may be entered into hereafter, would remain in full force.

Then as to the arbitration which is provided for by the Act in cases where disputes arise. By the second schedule which contains the machinery for settling disputes by means of an arbitrator, there can be five different kinds of this tribunal. Firstly, if a representative committee exists with power of settling matters under this statute which may arise between the employer and employed, if neither party objects the dispute shall be referred to them. Otherwise, if no agreement can be arrived at within three months, there shall be appointed a single arbitrator agreed on between the parties, or in the absence of such agreement, the matter is to go before the County Court judge of the district, who, however, where authorised by the Lord Chancellor, may appoint an arbitrator who shall have all the powers of a County Court judge and shall be paid by the Treasury. The fifth or last kind is only to be appointed where an arbitrator has died, or refused or become unable to act, and in such a case a judge of the High Court in Chambers may appoint. Any question of law which arises during a dispute may be stated by the arbitrator for the decision of the County Court judge, from whom an appeal will lie under conditions to the Court of Appeal.

There seems to be a curious omission in the provisions of the statute. By Section 4 of the schedule the provisions of the Arbitration Act, 1889, are excluded from all arbitrations under this Act. The County Court judge and the arbitrator appointed by him can compel witnesses to attend, and documents to be produced, but the other three kinds of tribunal have no powers of this kind. Only one explanation can be given of this state of affairs, and that is the intention of the Legislature to practically compel disputes to be referred to these two official kinds of arbitrators. That they would undoubtedly be the better tribunals for both parties is beyond dispute, and it must be presumed that the statute, although giving wide scope for other means of settling disputes, leans more strongly to the forum to which it has given these most necessary powers. The memorandum of award, however, given by the committee or agreed arbitrator can be enforced as a County Court judgment.

Costs incident to the arbitration are to be in the absolute discretion of the arbitrator, and any amount awarded as compensation shall be paid on the receipt of the person to whom it is directly payable, and no solicitor or agent shall have as against such person any claim or lien upon that sum, except it is submitted as to the amount actually awarded by the arbitrator or County Court judge in respect of costs. These latter considerations would, of course, only apply to solicitor and client costs, as those incurred between the parties would, as stated, be in the entire power of the arbitrator.

We have thus attempted to indicate the salient features of the new Act. It is a statute teeming and bristling with difficulties at every point. To what extent it will be a subject of litigation only time can show, but the few points we have stated here and in our issue of last week, which are by no means exhaustive, will amply demonstrate, not only the immense importance to all employers and their workpeople of the Act, but the difficulties surrounding its application. It certainly looks as if it will be "good for the lawyers," whoever else it may benefit.

The Brazilian Railways and the Default.

The fact that the Brazilian Government proposes to pay its railway guarantees for the next three years in funding bonds is a serious matter for the Brazilian guaranteed railways. These lines are in a railway sense most miserable concerns, the only important companies being those that work without a guarantee. Not one of the guaranteed lines earns anything like the interest upon its debenture capital, and the majority of the companies operate at an absolute loss. That is to say, supposing the guarantees were to cease altogether, and the directors were bound to work under prevailing conditions, they would save money by laying up their trains and letting the line go to wrack and ruin. And in this instance we are not dealing with roads built yesterday without developed traffic, and which have been spending money with a view to such development. That was the position of many of the Argentine railways when the storm of 1889-90 fell upon them, and their recrudescence of late years has been, in a measure, the result of the money spent, perhaps too freely, but still in the right direction, just prior to the Argentine default. But every one of the Brazilian guaranteed railways given in our list below was built before 1887, and the majority have been at work for about twenty years. Nor has there been much in the way of extension, for almost without exception the lines have remained as originally projected. Whether it be due to the lack of energy in the boards, the tiresome character of the Government regulations, or the unsettled character of the country, the fact remains that the Brazilian guaranteed railways have been signally unprogressive. Scattered up and down the country, without much connection one with the other, and often without any objective point, their only advantage is that they usually connect a part of the interior with a port on the sea-board. To compare the traffic of one of these lines with a fair-sized Argentine railway is like comparing the Highland Railway with the London and North-Western. Even if comparison is made with the fine system of lines in San Paulo, which has been chiefly built up without Government guarantees, the puerile character of these subsidised roads is distressingly apparent. To show that our remarks on this point are not overstrained, in the following table we give the result of last year's working of the various Brazilian guaranteed companies :—

	Date of Formation.	Duration of Guarantee.	Net Revenue or loss on Working Line.	Received from Government as Guarantee.	Spent in Redemption of Debentures.
		Years.	£	£	£
Alagoas ...	1881	30	90	39,254	4,657
Bahia and San Francisco ...	1858	90	36,829*	126,000	nil
Do., Timbo Branch ...	1887	30	5,897*	17,886	nil
Brazil Great Southern ...	1883	30	9,771*†	40,500	4,675
Central Bahia	1875	30	2,846	102,708	19,616
Conde d'Eu ...	1875	30	5,682*	51,406	7,744
Donna Theresa Christina ...	1880	30	7,017*	44,173	9,200
Great Western of Brazil ...	1872	30	442	39,375	nil
Minas and Rio	1880	30	3,700	122,025	17,400
Natal and Nova Cruz... ...	1878	30	7,381*	43,281	13,175
Recife and San Francisco ...	1854	90	6,849	80,282	14,000
Southern Brazilian ...	1883	30	1,641*	103,896	nil

* Loss. † Accounts only up to December, 1896; nothing later.

The Mogyana Company is not included, as this line is guaranteed by the Paulista Company, the Government guarantee being its least important safeguard. There is also the Porto Alegre and New Hamburg line, but its guarantee is merely that of one of the States. Roughly speaking, it may be assumed that the railways spend each year the amount received in guarantee upon paying debenture interest, redeeming debenture debt, and paying dividends upon their share capital. The Bahia and San Francisco has no debenture capital, while that of the Recife and San Francisco is insignificant. In the other instances, the debenture debt is very considerable, and there appears to be little chance of its redemption before the end of the concession. Taking the value of the funding bonds to be received at their best value—80 per cent.—it is clear that the companies will receive only four-fifths of their guarantees in the next three years. The debenture capital of the companies will naturally claim to have its interest paid in full, so that the fund for the shareholders will be trenched upon severely, and when these funding bonds come to be realised it may well prove that they will only net 60 to 70 per cent. of their face value. Argentine 4 per cent. Rescission bonds, for instance, are no more than 58, and Argentina, in the eyes of some people, is supposed to have purged its offences.

The boards of the companies will be naturally inclined to fall upon the sinking funds in their time of necessity, and, by suspending these, obtain some measure of financial relief. But here again the short duration of many of the guarantees will raise a serious obstacle to such a course. The debenture holder can only look for a chance of obtaining his principal back in full by means of these sinking funds, and many of the lines have only seven to twelve years of their guarantee to run. For holders of the debentures to permit the sinking fund to be suspended for three years would diminish the amount repaid, and so a bitter source of dispute exists. How the difficulties of the position will be met it is impossible to say. One condition ought to follow the default of the Government, and that is, that those companies which do earn profits should be allowed to retain them. Under the present system the Government takes all net profits, meantime paying the guarantee in gold. Then the companies ought to have more freedom in working, in regard to tariffs, and in other matters. The raising of the tariff in order to meet the fall in exchange has not proved so efficacious in some cases as had been hoped, but at least the boards of the companies ought to have the right to put this remedy for poor receipts into force to see whether their revenue accounts would not be thereby improved.

Reforms of this character, if permitted, can only bring slight amelioration to the position, and the fact remains that most of the companies are drifting towards the end of their concessions with such a miserable revenue at their command that the cessation of the guarantee must render them bankrupt. The default of the Brazilian Government aggravates an already unsound position, and may lead to awkward disputes. It is not, therefore, surprising to find the prices of Brazilian railway securities running away, and the following table sets forth the depreciation that has fallen on British capital invested in this form in Brazil :—

	Nominal amount of issue.	Value at price of issue.	Value at present market price.	Deprecia-tion at present market price.
	£	£	£	£
Alagoas shares ...	300,000	300,000	97,500	202,500
Do. 5 per cent. deb. stock ...	167,700	167,700	83,385	84,315
Do. 6 per cent. debs.	185,320	185,320	155,652	29,668
Brazil Great Southern......	225,000	225,000	16,875	208,125
Do. 6 per cent. deb. stock ...	195,000	195,000	97,500	97,500
Do. 6 per cent. mort. debs....	208,300	187,470	166,840	20,630
Do. 6 per cent. mort. debs., 1893	45,918	39,015	32,130	6,885
Bahia and San Francisco	1,800,000	1,800,000	810,000	990,000
Do. Timbo Branch	270,000	270,000	67,500	202,500
Central Bahia ...	671,260	671,260	295,328	375,932
Do. 6 per cent. debs............	446,500	446,500	294,690	151,810
Do. 5 per cent. debs............	80,000	72,000	43,200	28,800
Do. 6 per cent. deb. bonds ...	223,560	223,560	196,680	26,880
Conde d'Eu	925,000	425,000	148,750	276,250
Do. 5½ per cent. debs............	235,500	230,790	161,490	69,300
Donna Theresa Christina	308,940	308,940	54,064	254,876
Do. 5½ per cent. debs............	226,300	211,774	148,190	63,584
Great Western of Brazil	300,000	300,000	120,000	180,000
Do. 6 per cent. debs............	306,250	306,250	291,604	14,646
Do. Extension 6 per cent. debs............	177,000	177,000	132,750	44,250
Minas and Rio ...	1,000,000	1,000,000	500,000	500,000
Do. 6 per cent. debs.	552,500	569,175	530,400	38,775
Mogyana debs. ...	379,200	326,112	379,200*	53,088
Natal and Nova Cruz	250,000	250,000	75,000	175,000
Do. 5½ per cent. debs............	209,400	188,460	141,300	47,160
Recife and San Francisco ...	1,200,000	1,200,000	744,000	456,000
Southern Brazilian Rio Grande	600,000	600,000	240,000	360,000
Do. 6 per cent. deb. stock ...	999,355	999,355	659,538	339,817
Total......	11,887,003	11,875,681	6,683,566	5,192,115

* Increase in value.

Three or four of the railways possess issues of deferred shares, but these only represented company-promoters' capital, and they never had a serious market nor can a quotation for them now be found, so we have ignored these issues. Only one issue in the list shows any appreciation in value, and that is simply because the line is not dependent upon its guarantee, but upon an opulent local company—the Paulista.

Economic and Financial Notes and Correspondence.

WORRIED FRANCE.

The Ministerial crisis in France still continues and has left the country for ten days without a government. To outsiders this *impasse* looks much as if the country were ripening for another Dictator, and possibly it is only saved from this fate by the lack of any soldier, or tinsel and feathers godling of an adventurer, capable of playing the part of a Dictator with sufficient *éclat* to please the multitude. We hope the country will continue to lack this kind of saviour, but it seems probable that it will have to go through the turmoil of another general election before it can hope to have a parliamentary party numerous enough and strong enough to establish and maintain a representative government. One after another the men who have been summoned by M. Faure to form a Ministry have had to give up the attempt, because they are unable to get together enough supporters out of the fragments of parties into which the Chamber of Deputies is divided to ensure a majority for three weeks running, nay, even for three days. We must not despair of France on this account, for, as M. Guyot observes, in a very pungent article written by him in the *Siècle* the other day on that pretentious, somewhat stupid, and much over-praised book of Mr. Bodley's on France, it is to the credit of the electorate that M. Méline was unable to count on a majority in the new Chamber. "If," he says, "the electors have not given a majority to Minister Méline, in spite of all the means employed, it is a proof of their independence. They have voted as they wanted to, not as ordered. In some departments they voted for Radicals simply as a protest against the administrative and clerical alliance, which was thrust upon them." Perhaps the next Chamber might be less faction torn, at any rate the experiment will have to be tried. This one, as we have said from the first, will give a reliable majority to no party leader France now has. And the stain of the Dreyfus iniquity damages them all.

THE SPANISH DEBT COUPON.

Nothing could well be more silly than the arrangements the Spanish Government has made for paying the July coupon on the funded debt—unless it be the lies daily concocted and retailed about the war to a population that cannot read. As the Government has really no money of any kind, except bank notes, and must therefore borrow the gold required to meet the coupon, it has decided to economise the payment by giving domestic creditors paper, and gold to foreign ones alone. Said foreign holders of the 4 per cents. must present them, coupons and all, to financial agents. The bonds thus presented have to be stamped, and the domicile of the owner stated, and all this has to be done before the 30th inst. After that we suppose out-in-the-colds will have to take paper. It is a ridiculous arrangement, but may bring some money into the British Exchequer, because bonds presented here to claim payment of the July coupon in gold will have to be stamped with the English 10s. per cent. duty. And we may be quite sure that many a patriotic Spaniard will be able to procure an English domicile for his bonds in order to avoid fingering Bank of Spain notes. The Government had much better have thrown up the sponge at once.

The Daira Sanieh Properties.

Monday's *Times* announced that the Egyptian Government had effected the sale of these properties for £6,431,500, the actual amount of the Daira debt. Buyers will pay £500,000 in cash on August 1, to remain as guarantee until the contract has been completed, bearing meanwhile 3½ per cent. interest. In July, 1899, a further payment of £2,150,000 becomes due. Annual payments of £310,000 will be made until 1905, when the entire price will be paid off. With each payment an equivalent amount of property will be transferred to the buyers, who are bound to resell within seven years and to give half the net profit to the Government. It is stipulated that this profit shall not be under 20 per cent., and so on. The estates thus handed over to private enterprise as against State control comprise 256,000 acres of excellent land, estimated to be worth £6,850,000; also nine sugar factories, 375 miles of agricultural railroads, and other available properties. To Egypt the benefit of the sale is said to be the payment of £500,000 right off, and the extinction of a costly international administration entirely independent of Government control. Where the purchasers "get the pull" is not yet apparent.

The Baltimore and Ohio Railroad.

The plan under which this property is to be set on its feet again has now been made public, and as far as we can say at present it appears to be a thorough and on the whole equitable plan. There are to be $70,000,000 worth of 3½ per cent. prior lien bonds secured on the main line, $63,000,000 4 per cent. bonds secured by first mortgage on all property not covered by the prior lien bonds, $40,000,000 of preferred stock, and $35,000,000 of common stock, making in all a capitalisation of $208,000,000, or about £42,000,000.

This looks on the whole moderate, and if the reorganisation syndicate is able to effect an exchange of the old bonds for new in a thorough manner the Baltimore and Ohio may once again emerge from the unhappy position which past mismanagement, or worse, placed it in. Messrs. Speyer Brothers will have the business in hand here, and they are backed up by such financial strength both on this side and in America as will insure abundance of capital for carrying out the plan. They have behind them a strong syndicate which has subscribed $30,000,000 on terms that in the circumstances cannot be deemed onerous. The agents of all the loans have agreed to support the scheme, and so should the bondholders.

All the securities of the old company proper are embraced in the scheme and, so far as we can judge, are offered very fair terms. The object of the committee has been to cut down the fixed charges so that they will be well within the earning power of the road in bad years. According to the investigation of Mr. Stephen Little the average net income of the property during a period of seven years and two months has been $7,234,000 per annum, less average taxes amounting to $437,000. The real net revenue, therefore, averaged about $6,800,000, and the fixed charges under the new scheme will amount to $6,252,351 annually, thus leaving a very considerable margin even on the net earnings for the year ended June 30, 1887, which was a poor year and gave only $6,594,000. The estimated earnings for the year ending on the 30th inst., not including taxes, but including miscellaneous income, is about $7,976,000. Therefore the pruning knife has been rigorously applied, and the plan deals, as far as we can judge, with the various classes of bonds quite fairly. All get so much cash, representing arrears of interest, and they are converted into a consolidated prior lien 3½ per cent. mortgage of which they receive either dollar for dollar, or a slight premium, together with small bonuses in the 4 per cent. bonds, and in the new preferred stock. Baltimore and Ohio terminal bonds, and Akron and Chicago bonds do not receive any 3½ per cent. stock, nor do the 4½ per cent. bonds of the Philadelphia branch, but they receive fair treatment, and the two first have allotments of preferred stock given to them. Assessments amounting to $2 per share on the old first preferred stock, and $20 per share each on the second preferred and common stocks, will be levied, and the mortgages are executed for larger amounts of all the bonds than the reorganisation plan actually requires. Thus, on the present issue of prior lien bonds the surplus will be $926,910, and a right is reserved to issue an amount not exceeding $5,000,000 additional of these bonds at a rate not exceeding a million a year, after January 1, 1902. Of the second mortgage bonds there are $7,000,000 worth reserved for the new company, and $6,000,000 are set aside to repay the 5 per cent. bonds of the Baltimore Belt line. Also the company will have $5,000,000 in reserve unissued of the new preferred stock, besides some remainder perhaps of the common stock. It is thus hedged on every side pretty well, and, with upright management, ought to enter upon a career of more assured prosperity than it has enjoyed for many years. An annual audit of accounts is provided for.

More About the Oil Flash Point.

Mr. Jesse Collings, Chairman of the Petroleum Committee, has so far gained his aim that his draft report has been accepted for consideration by the Committee, in preference to that of Mr. Ure, who strongly recommended that the flashing point of petroleum should be raised to 100 degrees. This does not mean that Mr. Collings's report will necessarily be adopted; but we fear it must be taken to indicate that the majority of the Committee do not attach so much importance to a consideration of the flashing point of oil as they ought to do. Mr. Collings thinks that if they raised the flash point they would increase the price of oil, and thus inflict a hardship on the poor people who mostly use it. Even if that were true it might not be wise to insist on cheapening the facilities for killing people; but it is not true, as the Petroleum Committee can easily find out for themselves; for the Russian oil, of which there is an abundant supply, has a flash point of 100 degrees, and costs no more than the coarse refuse called oil of the Standard Oil Trust. This latter, we believe, is a product which Americans themselves decline to use for purposes of illumination; and so the dangerous stream has been turned on this country, and thus far our legislators seem to have been wonderfully attentive to the wishes of the Trust in respect to the flash point and other matters.

For, although Mr. Jesse Collings considers it would be a novelty in English legislation, Sir James Fergusson, who is in a bit of a difficulty just now before another Committee, could tell him that, not so many years ago, the flash point of oil in this country was fixed at 110, and that it was only by a series of very suspicious manœuvres that it was ultimately lowered to 73. Sir James Fergusson then occupied the position Mr. Collings does now as Under-Secretary for the Home Office. Three leading chemists were appointed to consider this question of the flashing point, whether it might be lowered below 110 degrees, to which the Petroleum Association objected. It was agreed that it might be lowered to 100 degrees if an efficient tester were used. But the Petroleum Association disliked this efficient tester, and Sir James Fergusson, assisted by Professor, afterwards Sir F., Abel, sanctioned the use of an inferior one, which Sir F. Abel some time after declared to have proved "untrustworthy, unreliable, and susceptible to manipulation." We cannot go over the whole strange story as told by the *Star*; but the upshot was that, by a process which Sir James Fergusson and the Petroleum Association can best explain, the flash point was reduced to 73 degrees. This was in 1879; and since that time the number of oil fires has steadily increased. Last year there were forty deaths from lamp explosions alone; and these explosions were all attributable to the low flash point, which Mr. Jesse Collings, in his wisdom, wishes to make permanent.

It is mere puerility to say that the loss of life from the low flash point has not been satisfactorily proved, for to our mind nothing has been more clearly established, and the evidence laid before the Petroleum Committee on this point is strong enough to satisfy any person of ordinary intelligence. But Mr. Jesse Collings seems always to have the fear of the Standard Oil Trust before him. If he is anxious not to increase the price of oil—a very foolish anxiety, as we have shown—he has no such scruples in regard to the price of lamps, about which he proposes to lay down a series of regulations which cannot be enforced, and would not, even if enforced, prevent explosions where low-flash oil is used. Mr. Collings professes to make these proposals on the recommendation of the Oil Trade Protection Association, but why does he carefully suppress the fact that that association itself declares that improved lamps will be of little use without the raising of the flash-ing point? We cannot understand the persistency with which the manifest dangers of the low flash point are ignored by persons in authority. Nor can we understand why, when considering the question of testers and the flash point, Sir James Fergusson listened rather to the advice of the Petroleum Association than to that of the Fire Protection Committee, and the strong representations of such an eminent authority as Professor Attfield. It almost looks as if, behind it all, there was some occult authority exercising an influence prejudicial to the public interest. If the present Petroleum Committee rest content with the 73 deg. flash point, and the House of Commons accept its recommendations, then the long agitation will have to be continued until the labours of this futile committee have been overturned, and the flash point has been increased to at least 100 deg.

Through the *Times* of Wednesday, Mr. Jesse Collings gives what he seems to consider a crushing reply to his critics. There is, he says, no legal flash point for oil as an illuminant; the flash point is merely to fix "the dividing line between petroleum oil and petroleum spirit." This is sad and rather futile quibbling. It is of no consequence what the legal meaning of the flash point may be. What we know is that oil with a flash point of 73 deg. is dangerously explosive; that the use of it as an illuminant has caused a great many deaths in London alone during the last few years; and that Parliament ought to prohibit the use of such oil as an illuminant in order to avoid continued loss of life from the same cause. If, as Mr. Collings says, somebody has made a mistake as to the legal meaning of the flash point, is that any excuse for our permitting the continuance of a state of affairs which we know leads to enormous loss of life? Mr. Jesse Collings was not elected chairman of the Petroleum Committee to give us a legal definition of the flash point; but to find out the best means for avoiding a loss of life which has shocked everybody but the Standard Oil Trust. If Mr. Collings was in the pay of that strange corporation he could hardly serve its ends more zealously than he has recently been doing.

THE GREAT NORTHERN AND CITY RAILWAY.

It is a pity that this company failed to get its capital subscribed, but we are bound to say that it was not put before the public so attractively as it might have been. Professing to be a sort of relief line to the Great Northern, there was yet no Great Northern director on the board, and the money was asked for without any guarantee of interest from the big company whose trains it was to run straight into the City. In these circumstances, it is not to be wondered at that the market abstained from underwriting the share capital, or that the applications made by the public were few in number—less than 900—and small in amount. The line, however, is one which ought to be made, and for which a great suburban traffic should be forthcoming when made. We hope, therefore, that the Great Northern board may see its way to assist, so that the money may be found on favourable terms. Failing it—and we can understand the reluctance of directors, the capital commitments of whose own line are so threateningly large, to have any outside obligation thrust upon them—the Great Northern and City Company might apply to the Midland and see what it can do. It also wants some relief for its Kentish Town Moorgate-street traffic, and might be glad to give assistance to such a line as this was meant to be, particularly with the Sheffield—we beg its pardon, the Great Central Company—about to come into competition.

MORE CAPITAL FOR THE CHATHAM COMPANY.

We still wait for the announcement of the fooling arrangement—or should it be "pooling"?—between the South-Eastern and Chatham Companies. The suspense is delicious for the jobbers: the "yea" and "nay," and "to-night" and "to-morrow" rumours give them many little ups and downs whereby money may be made. But we have not had to wait for proof of the Chatham Company's necessities. As we have more than once sadly opined, the extravagance of the directors in repainting and repolishing Camberwell Station, and in making a beginning in Brixton, was sure to have a terrible effect on the capital account, and lo and behold! out came these said directors with a demand for £300,000, to be raised in 3 per cent. debenture stock, offered at 103. And they will get the cash, too, such a merry, easy-going world is it for those who know how to humour it.

THE AMERICAN TREASURY POSITION.

The position of the American Treasury is a matter of interest to us just now. On June 1, the net cash balance was $195,754,815, a decrease in the month of over $20,000,000. The amount of free gold was $171,818,055, a decrease of $9,420,082. The excess of expenditure for the month was nearly $18,000,000, and for the eleven months $24,531,337. The extraordinary expenditure on account of the war, which is made apparent in the Treasurer's statement for May, will show a very large increase from this time forward. The national receipts for May prove to have been $30,074,818, or about $300,000 over the total of the same month of last year; while the expenditure reached $47,849,900, that is to say, nearly $18,000,000 in excess of the revenue. For the eleven months of the fiscal year the incomings have been $371,001,768, against $310,600,020 for the same period of 1896-7. Customs receipts contribute $135,260,000, a decrease of $19,000,000, due, of course, to the Dingley tariff, which is proving a fine revenue reducer; internal revenue $153,260,000, an increase of $20,000,000; and miscellaneous $82,460,000, an increase of nearly $60,000,000 referable to the receipts from the sale of the Pacific railroads. The expenditure has aggregated $395,523,105, an increase over 1897 of $53,000,000. Except Indians and interest on the public debt every item shows an increase. That for the War Department is the largest, amounting to over $36,000,000, the greater part of which was incurred for the army. The increase for the navy was about $18,000,000, and for pensions $5,000,000. It is pointed out that notwithstanding the large expenditures made necessary in the

War and Navy Departments in consequence of the war, the expenditure for pensions, which may be regarded as regular liability, is equal to more than 33 per cent. of the entire disbursements, and after the present war has been terminated we can look for still heavier annual appropriations under this head. The condition of the national debt is as follows:—Interest-bearing debt, $847,367,410; debt on which interest has ceased since maturity, $1,264,850; debt bearing no interest, $384,896,315; total $1,233,528,575. This, however, does not include $563,799,933 in certificates and Treasury notes outstanding, which are off-set by an equal amount of cash in the Treasury. But it is considerable enough, and the new war loan now being floated will increase the interest-bearing portion by 25 per cent.

The Rock Life Insurance Company.

Last week a stupid blunder slipped into our note on this company. Happily it does not affect the essential point raised therein, but none the less must it be set right. We said that the company had bought back half its shares at a price of £7 10s. apiece or something like that, and the context implied that these had cost £1,059,000, which, of course, is an absurdity. The company did buy back its shares in the manner described, but these would only have cost it £750,000 had they all been bought at the price mentioned by us, which was an outside price casually mentioned. As a matter of fact, however, these shares really cost only £546,000, so that their average price must have been much less than £7 10s., and the £1,059,000 which figures in the balance-sheet represents, all but the paid-up capital of £100,000, accumulated profits out of which the share purchase was made. The company, in short, dates from the good old days when insurance business was carried on for the benefit of the insurer not the insured. Hence this immense surplus, and it has been suggested to us that the simplest way to lift the company out of its more or less water-logged position would be for the directors to employ some portion of the balance of this large accumulation of money in purchasing the other half of the share capital, and cancelling it, so as to turn the "Rock" into a mutual company. By doing that, the whole of the profits would then accrue to policy-holders instead of two-thirds, as at present arranged, or, allowing for half of the capital bought in, the profit on which is the policy-holders' property, five-sixths. Do the policy-holders receive this profit in reversion, or in cash?

Sir James Fergusson, the Post Office, and the Telephone Company.

How far do we owe it to Sir James Fergusson, M.P., that the Post Office officials have for the last six years been strengthening the monopoly of the Telephone Company, and doing their utmost to discourage competition in this branch of the public service? The question is one which everybody who reads Sir James's evidence before the Telephone Committee must put to himself. The facts, so far, seem to be these. In 1892 Sir James Fergusson was Postmaster-General. Just before leaving office he presented, on behalf of the Post Office, an agreement contemplating an arrangement of telephonic exchange areas to the chairman of the National Telephone Company for signature. The Chairman at first refused to sign, but subsequently did so on receiving, as alleged, an assurance from Sir James that the revision of the areas would be conducted in a reasonable manner.

This assurance was not embodied in the agreement; but it, or something like it, seems to have become well known to the Post Office officials having charge of this business, and they appear to have adopted the view that they were under some obligation at the request of the company to extend these areas though the agreement said nothing on the subject. In fact, the assurance, understanding, or whatever it was, was looked upon as tending to discourage competition; and so it was acted upon throughout to the great benefit of the Telephone Company, though certainly not to the advantage of the public. How did this extraordinary understanding arise? It must be admitted that Sir James Fergusson was quite frank in giving his evidence. He did not know of such an understanding. He could recollect of no conversation which could have justified it; but he admitted he had a relative on the board of directors of the National Telephone Company when the areas were being revised, and in 1896 he joined the board himself.

Sir James's own view was that competition should not be encouraged if the company did their duty, seeing that they would become delegates of the Post Office; but he had no recollection of anything being said on the subject. Then how could the active belief in this non-competition understanding have arisen? Who instilled it into the minds of the Post Office authorities? The agreement itself expressly excludes monopoly and reserves the right of the Post Office to compete with the company or to license others to do so. Yet the postal officials, in arranging about the areas, went beyond the agreement to an "understanding," the origin of which nobody so far has been able to explain, and in their new arrangements solemnly, in the teeth of the signed agreement, discouraged competition in the interests of the company. We take it for granted that the Telephone Committee will probe this matter to the bottom. It is a duty they cannot escape. As for Sir James Fergusson, we imagine that by this time he is thoroughly convinced that a Minister of the Crown, presiding over a department so commercially important as the Post Office, ought not to enter into dealings with a company on whose board sits a relative of his own; or, if circumstances should compel him to do so, that he should be careful to see that the resulting agreement is alone consulted by the postal officials, to the exclusion of mysterious "understandings," which can be used to set aside definite and precisely worded contracts.

Electric Lighting Shares.

Quite apart from the question whether the Marylebone Vestry obtains its Bill or not, we think the decline in the prices of London electric lighting shares has been overdone. There is too great a tendency at the moment to judge them harshly, as before there was a tendency to overrate their excellence. Take, for instance, the matter of the vendors' shares and their obliteration. Although we have not agreed with all the schemes, and personally detest founders' shares as financial enormities, yet it should not be forgotten that the founders in the case of these companies did far more for them than the drones who usually get hold of such shares do. In the case of the electric lighting companies we believe the founders' rights represented many services and outlays incurred in the promotion of the concerns which the Board of Trade would not permit to be placed to capital account, as would have certainly been done in any other type of company. Then the founders' have in each case had to subscribe for a large amount of capital, with an attendant amount of risk, only making their profit by the premium in the market, when premiums came.

But to go back to the matter of the depreciation we find that the shares of the leading companies have fallen to the following extent this year:—

	Highest Price.	Present Price.	Fall.
Charing Cross and Strand	15	11½	3½
Chelsea	12¼	8	4¼
City of London	30¾	25½	5¼
County of London	16	12½	3½
House to House	11⅞	8½	3⅜
Metropolitan	21¾	14½	7¼
Notting Hill	20½	15½	5
St. James's and Pall Mall	19½	15½	4
Westminster	18¾	14¾	4

Such a decline does not seem in our opinion warranted, even if the Marylebone Vestry carries its Bill without modification, of which we are by no means certain.

For, after all, there are only two other companies working in London besides the Metropolitan—the House to House and Notting Hill—which have their districts to themselves. It would be a very different matter for the local authorities in Westminster, the Strand, or any of those important districts, to apply for power to light the area under their control, when two companies are already working in the same area. For one thing, the mere matter of public convenience must be studied, and then the existing companies cannot be obliterated by a stroke of the pen. The Vestry may, therefore, easily shrink from embarking upon a highly competitive business, when, by waiting quietly, the concerns so working will drop comfortably into its hands at practically break-up value.

Finally, the great cheapening of the electric light which is so near at hand will cause its use to become more general, and it is open to question, quite apart from the point of justice, whether in a district like Marylebone the Vestry and a company will not both find plenty of work for a long time without encroaching too much upon one another's business. It takes a great deal of time to build up a business of this kind, and the local authority, as the premier London Vestry in this matter has found out, is obliged to work cautiously lest it find an ugly deficit in its accounts, which, although it may be filled up by raising the rates does not lead to amicable relations between the ratepayers and their representatives. Holders of electric lighting shares, therefore, should not be too eager to get rid of them, for there is at the least a fair prospect of a remunerative business being obtained, while the competition may not prove so terrible as some imagine.

THE WATERLOO AND CITY RAILWAY.

Within the last few weeks the stock of this company has fallen from 139 to 116 or so without any apparent reason. Why should holders have all at once begun to discover that this line is not going to be so prosperous as was expected? We are not sure that holders in the ordinary sense did discover this, and rather believe that the selling comes from what we may call the middlemen or intermediaries who have not been successful in feeding out their subscription amounts to the public. If this is the case these people deserve to suffer because there can be no doubt that the price of the stock was driven much too high. Nothing in the South-Western Company's guarantee, nor yet in the prospectus of the line, warranted a price of 139 nor yet of 130 for this stock, and it could never have reached such a height except by manipulation.

The time is at hand when the weakness of the company's position as an immediate dividend earner must become apparent. On the 27th of next month the liberty to pay 3 per cent. interest out of capital comes to an end, that liberty having been granted for five years only, which period expires then. It was, of course, expected that the line would have been in full working order before this date, but its construction has been in places more difficult than was estimated, and, worse than that, the company has been imprudent in its arrangements for obtaining a terminus in the City. It made a contract with the Central of London Railway, now in course of construction, in virtue of which it is to share that company's terminus at the Royal Exchange; but unfortunately this terminus is still a long way from completion, and consequently the Waterloo and City Company finds itself in the position of having a road with no City outlet to it. We believe a temporary station is being hastily constructed, somewhere about Bucklersbury or the Mansion House, but it will be a station without lifts, and therefore one to be avoided by elderly and gouty City gentlemen on their way to and from their offices.

No wonder that the company's stock has gone down amid such circumstances. We believe it will go further down still before it reaches the price at which an investor would be safe to put money into it, for some time must elapse after the line is in full working condition, and years may slip past before the dividend upon the share capital can get much beyond the 3 per cent. guaranteed minimum. It may be well to remind investors that, under the contract with the South-Western Railway Company, this 3 per cent. is a first charge on the gross receipts for all the capital, share and loan, raised by the company, and doubtless in the course of time the 45 per cent. of the gross receipts which the South-Western is bound to pay as a minimum to the Waterloo and City Company will give the ordinary stock more than this 3 per cent., but it is too early yet to counsel investors to purchase on that distant prospect.

THE FRANK JONES BREWING COMPANY.

At the meeting of the shareholders of this company, held on Tuesday last, an immense amount of virtue was displayed. So great was it that could it be condensed, bottled up, and preserved in ice it would serve any ordinary humdrum company for half-a-dozen years at least; but there was need of it all on this occasion, for the directors had to confess that the company was unable to pay any dividend on its ordinary shares. The gross profits fell to £76,500 for the year, a decrease of £29,000 or so on those of the previous year. But such as it was it was an honest profit, the chairman and other directors repeatedly assured the shareholders. Depreciation had been allowed for to the full and repairs and renewals had even increased £2,155 on the figure for 1896. In all their explanations, however, the directors carefully omitted any mention of the over-capitalisation of the company. It is one of the Trustees, Executors, &c. Corporation's productions, and in a manner did that promoter organisation credit, for, unlike many of its other babies, the Frank Jones Brewing Company has paid dividends on its ordinary shares every year until now. Indeed, for the first five years of the company's life it bravely gave 10 per cent. to the ordinary shareholder, then, in 1893-4, the dividend fell to 7 per cent., and in the following year to 6 per cent., jumping to 8 per cent. in 1895-6 only to fall again to 5 per cent. in 1896-7, and now to zero.

Low prices for beer, incident to greater competition, are assigned as the cause of this decline; anything, in fact, except the true cause, which is that the money asked for the business was at the outset about half a million more than it ought to have been. If the company had been started with a capital of even a million it might have defied competitors, and have held a fair position as an investment through evil times and times prosperous, but with £1,300,000 it has been handicapped against concerns more lightly burdened, and we fear there is no substantial prospect for its shareholders of a speedy return to 10 per cent. The end, in spite of the directors' optimism, is much more likely to be reconstruction. The chairman declared that the additional tax of $1 per barrel, making $2 in all, to be now levied upon beer in the United States is to be universally charged against the consumer. This also is great virtue, but we have not much faith in it. The power of the brewer to do this will be regulated by competition, and it need not surprise the shareholders of this company should they this time next year be told that owing to the pressure of this additional taxation profits have been so much reduced as to put the preference dividend in jeopardy.

THE MUNICIPAL TRUST.

Mr. Auldjo Jamieson has taken the bold course of issuing a circular announcing his resignation from the board of this company, and every one who favours sound finance must cordially endorse the position he takes up. At the time when the reduction in capital was proposed we thought his views were a little strained, but the action of the board since certainly justifies him in his present action. The proposal as to the capital was that £57,540 be written off the preferred stock, and £89,380 off the deferred stock, thus reducing the aggregate from £511,150 to £364,230. Various difficulties arose that prevented the scheme being carried through before the accounts were made up on February 28 last, and despite this fact the board proceeded to divide the revenue up to the hilt in paying a dividend of 3½ per cent. on the original preferred stock. Yet a considerable amount of depreciation had accrued in the twelve months, which, if allowed for, would have swallowed up more than half the sum distributed in dividend, and the auditor drew attention to the serious matter thus involved. The Trust is ploughing through a world of trouble in connection with its American water and light companies, and this is certainly not the time to weaken its financial standing.

A Touching Lesson on "How not to do it."

Poor Spain! How chivalrous in "honour"; how destitute of foresight! How swift to dance on top of "the golden hours," how slow to think of, slower yet to prepare, for the "rainy day." Yet how perilous the position of a nation whose pointless struggles against a desperate fate only provoke our pity—who wails for peace, and is yet timidly doubtful whether "honour" is sufficiently satisfied to allow her to accept it! Spanish statesmen, with full knowledge of the country's poverty and military and naval unpreparedness, dreaded this war, yet dared not avert or avoid it for fear that revolution would undo them. Even revolutionists, however, hesitate to move; for, if they see how the whirlwind may be let loose, they do not perceive the power that is to restrain or guide it. Events may yet force revolution, probably will; but who is there that can exert the strength to escape from the subsequent maelstrom, and assert the power of ruling the miserable warring elements that may remain? Was ever nation in more desperate case—more paralysed by fear—not the wretched fear of the coward, but the timidity born of the absence of that higher courage which would dare boldly to accept defeat that is inevitable in order to save not honour alone, but some of its worldly possessions and support? Is prudence always cowardly or devoid of honourable feeling? Has Spanish administration been so excellent in the past that she can retrieve her honour only by completing the ruin that her own misgovernment has begun?

Take her relations with the Philippines, for example. What has made them so easy a prey to the American navy and the native rebels? It is pitiable to read the recent accounts of how the rebellious natives have closed round the Spanish troops and driven them into Manila to their last resort in the Citadel—poor soldiers fasting, yet fighting and raging lest they have to submit to those contemned insurrectionary natives! And the home government, when it might have done something for the safety of the Philippines, shirked its responsibilities. A previous governor of the colony has told the Madrid Cortes how he appealed for reinforcements to save the Archipelago, and received no reply to his appeals. An arrangement was then made with Aguinaldo, the rebel leader, by which he quitted the colony, and the revolt was pronounced at an end. But he now insists that certain reforms were promised and have never been executed, and that so he is free in honour to return and fight the question out under more favourable auspices. Sharp questions have been asked in Madrid as to who was responsible for not sending the reinforcements asked for before the war broke out; but they receive no answer. Ministers repudiate the alleged promise of reforms, as if the mere suggestion of reform must be resented as an insult. Spanish honour takes no note of progress and advancement. It is a product of two or three hundred years ago, and feels itself bound to reject whatever has happened since then. The rights of the colonists is a phrase apparently without meaning to Spanish statesmen. They know of no rights but those of the conqueror; and the present war is their Nemesis. They are giving us a touching lesson indeed on "how not to do it." They left the Philippines to their fate; and that fate has been to fall into the hands of the despised natives.

Spaniards in Madrid, however, seem now to have recognised that their army in the Philippines has been beaten. Whether they see yet that the colony is lost to them is doubtful. They have been appealing to Germany to "name her price" and take it, if she would only bring the Triple Alliance to the help of Spain, as if two at least of the members of the Triple Alliance at present had not enough to do to keep themselves afloat to prevent active interference in the affairs of other nations. But appeals of this sort seem to soothe the Spanish imagination. It has a look of doing something. Of course, the world must understand that Spanish honour cannot so far demean itself as to make even a frank and rational proposal to such a foe as the United States. But the "Powers" ought to know the sensitiveness of Spanish punctilio. Why do they not make a movement for saving Spain from humiliation? The Spaniards probably begin to feel aggrieved because the Powers remain stolidly immobile. Unfortunate Spaniards! They are ready to believe anything; they refuse to think of defeat until they cannot longer ignore it; and then only regard it apparently as a temporary discomfiture. It might be amusing if it were not so sad—so infantile. Living apparently in a world of "make believe," of illusion and delusion, they have let the world and its opportunities slip; and now, when action is forced upon them, they seem equally wanting in brains and money to help themselves. Their "honour" pricks them only to stand and be thrashed, because blood-letting is somehow considered necessary for saving that fastidious punctilio of honour which, combined with childish ignorance and careless impotence, has been the plague and the ruin of Spain.

New South Wales Trade Statistics.

The following letter states the case for these statistics fairly enough, but it does not convince us that the figures are true, nor yet that the colonists can afford to spend at the rate the import totals imply. All is, perhaps, really explained by the enormous total of the colony's debt—a total, we venture to think, deserving a much stronger epithet than "regrettable":—

To the Editor.

Sir,—The apparent high rate of imports may be accounted for. New countries lack more than old ones: thus Western Australia imports per head of population are over double those of New South Wales. Colonial wages being probably double those paid in England, the people spend liberally. Private expenditure in New South Wales is estimated at £8 per head higher than the United Kingdom, and £5 per head higher than the United States. Again, the declared value of imports in Sydney, if they cover freight and charges, would be much higher than at the London port of shipment, and this should be discounted in comparing British and Colonial expenditure per head. Regarding the high rate of exports per head, the staple exports, 1896, were wool, ten millions sterling, gold and specie six and a half millions. As wool is a high-priced item, say 9d. per lb., it alone to one and a quarter million of inhabitants gives £8 per head, and if the United States export staples were wool values they would amount to six times more than they do, so that a comparison between the two is not fair. *Re* wool prices being taken at London rates, more than half the wool is competed for at auction by foreign and home buyers, so that the reason is not clear why London prices should be taken; but the charges, I take it, were deducted.

After seasons of drought the colony usually enjoys good seasons, and with the elasticity of youth bad times are soon recovered from. The public debt of New South Wales is sixty-one millions, and its amount is regrettable, as the country, the grand free gift of England, has potentialities for wealth with but moderate borrowing. Thirty-seven millions of the debt is in the State railways, which are worked by the Government, and yield a net profit of one and a quarter millions sterling per annum, or 3⅝ per cent. on the capital expended. The Crown lands yield annually over one million sterling for rents and instalments of purchase money, thus lightening the burden of taxation. Enclosing tables New South Wales trade, 1896, also a book on railway system of the colony, I am, Sir, your obedient servant,

Colonist.

St. Leonards, June 21, 1898.

Mr. John Miles (a director of the New River Company) has been elected to the vacant seat on the board of the Gas Light and Coke Company, caused by the death of the Hon. Henry Noel.

Stock Market Notes and Comments.

So much is being said by us elsewhere this week on the Stock Exchange, and on incidents connected therewith, that it would neither be useful nor expedient to make a long discourse under this head. We could not do so if we tried, because week by week the markets grow thinner, less substantial, and more devoid of incident. Going round the City one hears nothing but grumbling, and if experience did not teach one to know better, the feeling created would be that Stock Exchange business was going to wrack and ruin—ending in a knock-out sale. Nothing of the kind is happening or going to happen. All that the grumbling means is that we have a little more dulness, perhaps, than summer usually brings, and that the volatile minds of the market are somewhat more depressed than usual in consequence.

The wonder to us always is that markets keep so firm and steady as they do with so many causes of depression influencing them from every side. So well are prices supported that the victory of the Silver Party in the United States has done nothing to depress American railroad securities, nor yet the collapse of the Leiter wheat corner. Buying here has unquestionably been checked by these incidents, and the latter especially has forced provincial operators for the rise to sell some of their favourite United States stocks, as well as Grand Trunk and Canadian Pacific issues, but there has been no important decline, except in the "Trunk" market, and we see no indication that any serious decline is about to take place. So far as outward appearances go, markets seem likely to drag along in much their present position, one which only gives rise to daily movements out of which it is hardly possible for the smartest jobber to make "a turn" for himself. The Canadian "rate war" seems to have been worked for all it was worth, and when it does come to an end, as we are periodically told it has, there may be no gamblers left to care.

But if American securities can be steady in spite of adverse circumstances, and of a Spanish war which shows no sign of ending, what shall we say of the stocks of France, Italy, and Spain; these surely are not worth their present quotations, for each one of these countries seems to be charged with explosive elements that might burst and work devastation upon their "credit" respectability, of which some of them have little left. Well, for one reason, there is nobody doing much in any of these securities at present. The Paris market is in a state of suspended animation, and we do not expect to see the ejected swarm of its outside brokers, to be organised in Brussels, in full working order before September or October. Dealings being in this way stopped, or nearly, there is not much to influence prices, as we in this country do not possess enough of any of these stocks, except perhaps Italian, to "bang" and "dint" market quotations with. It is well for us that we are not heavily committed to Spanish bonds or Italian Rente, and not bad for us that we possess comparatively little French securities. A storm is unquestionably gathering amongst the democracies of the Continent the effects of which no man can in the least foretell, and we may be thankful if we are able to stand clear while the tempest rages. No matter where the eye is turned on the Continent indications of coming trouble are seen to abound; whether in Russia with its plots, in Germany, with its rapidly triumphing Socialism—a Socialism which means the subversion of empire and of public order—in Austria, storm-tossed by the fragments of races hating each other with a perfect hatred, in France, where no party in the Republic seems able to develop strength enough to take control of its destinies, in Italy, where a crisis has almost been reached that compels the King to choose between absolutism and abdication, and in Spain whose fate needs no description. Clouds and earth tremors are seen and felt everywhere. Yet amid all these indications of approaching disturbance and upheaval stock markets remain calm and prices continue good. It is wonderful, the greatest testimony to the power of credit to defy the elements, so to say, the world has ever witnessed. Should, however, this mighty structure of pure credit be broken down at any one point—it is better perhaps not to go into that just yet. Let us look cheerful and whistle for the next "boom." "But the amount of money some fellows must have lost!" What of it? Let us make believe they haven't.

We have still nothing to say about mine shares. Renewed activity cannot be predicted in them, nor yet another collapse, unless the "New Courtly" and other selling of De Beers means something more than a mud-rush, or the scuttling of the life directors after the fashion set by the Consolidated Goldfields "buy out." The market, though, is dead. People are sitting on what they have, hoping against hope, or, in a few cases, thankful that their investments are still yielding such interest as they do; but confidence and energy are gone and the dreams of wealth are over. It would take a cataclysm, like the discovery that what was left in De Beers was *all* mud, to rouse the "Kaffir Circus" out of its discontented somnolence. Some day that news will doubtless come, since diamonds do not grow on mulberry trees—to use Mr. Cecil Rhodes's favourite simile—but we do not expect it quite yet and De Beers shares may go up again. What we more immediately wait for is the next display of fireworks in the "London and Globe" finance group.

In the miscellaneous market the inflated capitals of so many of the recent companies, Hooley's and others, are gradually sinking to their proper value, and in some instances may go below that value before all is done. We see nothing at all worth buying yet amongst that class of security. Let the underwriters and syndicates bear the burden and the loss, and wait. Opportunity will yet come, where companies have vitality; where they have none it is better for the public not to be in at the death. And deaths will be pretty numerous before long in this region of the promoter's activity.

Critical Index to New Investments.

NOTTINGHAM JOINT STATION STOCK.

The Great Northern and Great Central Railway Acts of 1897 authorised the constitution of the new passenger station at Nottingham as a separate undertaking under the management of a committee appointed by the two companies. Authority was given to raise a separate capital not exceeding £1,000,000, the interest being guaranteed by the two companies jointly. The amounts payable by the two companies will be rent and a working expense taking priority of their interest and dividends. The net earnings of the two companies distributed last year as interest and dividend exceeded three millions sterling. Messrs. Glyn, Mills, & Co. invite subscriptions for £750,000 3 per cent. stock at the price of 107 per cent., interest being payable February and August. Being guaranteed in perpetuity, the stock takes high rank and is a trustee stock. At the price it yields £2 16s. per cent. and will be readily taken. Shareholders in the two railway companies will receive first consideration.

LONDON CHATHAM AND DOVER RAILWAY COMPANY.

Tenders will be received by the board up to 10 a.m. on Wednesday next for £300,000 of this company's 3 per cent. debenture stock, the minimum price being 103 per cent. In 1897 balance of net revenue after deducting all interest accruing on existing debenture stocks and other fixed charges, amounted to upwards of £357,000. Present issue, which will have prior claim on balance of net revenue in future years, is understood to be for the purpose of taking up Lloyds bonds, and will exhaust the company's borrowing powers.

TYNE IMPROVEMENT REDEEMABLE STOCK.

Issue of £500,000 3½ per cent. stock redeemable at par between July, 1918, and July, 1952, inclusive. Messrs. Barclay & Co. are instructed to receive tenders up to 2 p.m. on Thursday next, the minimum being par. The commissioners are authorised to borrow £4,800,000 of which they have borrowed £4,253,631, and of this all but £107,080, which has priority, ranks *pari passu*. The gross revenue of the Tyne Consolidated Fund has grown from £306,565 in 1893 to £346,617 in 1897, and the surplus revenue from £43,167 to £59,427, while as to the trade of the Tyne the imports have steadily increased from 1,697,928 tons in 1882 to 2,015,830 tons last year, and the exports from 9,770,215 tons to 13,779,830 tons. As an investment the security is sound but does not warrant any fancy premium. The tenders were opened yesterday and amounted to £525,310 at prices varying from the minimum to 110, one tender for £300 being put in at this price. Tenders at £100 received about 94 per cent. and those above in full. The average price obtained was only £100 3s. 2d.

W. BUTLER & CO., LIMITED.

Having a share capital of £450,000 and £100,000 of 4½ per cent. first mortgage debenture stock, redeemable January 5, 1906, at 105 per cent., the directors offer for subscription an issue of £250,000 4 per cent. mortgage debenture stock at 105 per cent. Interest is payable January and July and the stock is redeemable on six months' notice from January 5, 1913, at 110 per cent. Company was registered in 1891 to take over the private partnership of W. Butler & Co., brewers and maltsters, Springfield Brewery, Wolverhampton, and since then the business has grown considerably, the present issue being made to pay off existing loans and to provide for further extension as opportunity offers. Stock is a first mortgage on properties, freehold and leasehold, acquired since May, 1891, and which have cost the company £301,630. Assets of the company are stated at £842,221, of which £547,738 represents freehold breweries and properties. Net profits for past three years were £40,777, £48,810, and £55,228, the average for the last seven years being £43,842 per annum. The business is described as one of the oldest established, and like other brewery properties seems to have been worked up by the continued purchase of public houses at high prices. The present issue of debentures, however, appears to be fairly secured as such things go

YATES'S CASTLE BREWERY, LIMITED.

The existing company was incorporated in 1896, and took over a company doing business in Manchester, Liverpool, Birkenhead, Lancaster, &c. The share capital, fully issued, amounts to £250,000, and there exists £100,000 5 per cent. first mortgage debentures, and £75,000 4½ per cent. mortgage debenture stock, both redeemable in 1902. Company now offers £100,000 4 per cent. irredeemable mortgage debenture stock at par, part of a total of £350,000, of which £175,000 can only be issued to redeem existing debenture stocks. Price of the new stock is par, and interest is payable January and July. It will be secured by a first mortgage on certain freehold and leasehold properties, not covered by the present trust deeds, costing £150,000. Assets in the last balance-sheet were stated at £496'670, and profits for past three years have averaged £26,344, while the interest on the whole of the debenture stock, including that now issued, will require only £12,375. In view of the debentures ranking before this issue being paid off in three and a half years, the stock now offered looks well secured.

J. MARSTON, THOMPSON, & SONS, LIMITED.

From the prospectus it appears that J. Marston & Son, Limited, of Horninglow Brewery, Burton-on-Trent, recently acquired the business of John Thompson & Son, Limited, also of Burton-on-Trent. For the purpose of providing the cash portion of the purchase money, and for paying for other recently acquired properties, there is now issued £160,000 4½ per cent. first mortgage "A" debenture stock at 102 per cent. It is redeemable at 110 from July 1, 1920, on six months' notice. The security seems enough at present. Profits for last year were £32,824, interest on the existing debenture stock and mortgages and on the present issue will require but £11,648, and thirst abides.

DAVEY, PAXMAN, & COMPANY, LIMITED.

The London Trust invite subscriptions for an issue of £100,000 4 per cent. first mortgage debenture stock in this company, at 102 per cent., redeemable at 105 from January 1, 1910, on six months' notice. Interest January and July. The business is that of engineers and boilermakers of Colchester, and a considerable business is done with the Admiralty, War Office, India Office, and with colonial and foreign Governments. It has become necessary to erect new shops, and to provide additional plant and working capital, for which £30,000 of the present issue will be appropriated. Share capital is £250,000 in £10 shares, of which 15,000 are taken by the vendors and the remainder held in reserve. Assets comprise freeholds, works, plant, &c., valued at £77,867 and stock-in-trade, cash, bills receivable, &c., at £67,265. No profits are published, but an accountant certifies that average annual profits, without deducting interest on capital, for the last four years are sufficient to pay debenture stock interest more than four times over. Purchase price is £221,400, of which £71,000 will be cash. In the absence of figures regarding profits it is not possible to judge whether the business is flourishing or declining, but apart from this the debenture stock looks a fair investment.

BAKU RUSSIAN PETROLEUM COMPANY, LIMITED.

This company is formed to purchase and amalgamate as going concerns petroleum properties owned by Messrs. G. M. Arafelloff & Co. and Messrs. Boudagoff Brothers & Co., consisting of 260 acres in Southern Russia. The purchase price is £1,250,000 entirely in cash, and the capital is £1,500,000 in £1 shares in equal parts of ordinary and 5½ per cent. cumulative preference. Sir James Kitson, Bart., is the chairman, and himself and three other members of the board are directors of the Russian Petroleum and Liquid Fuel Company, the shares of which were recently run up so high that they had to be divided. Although the agent in London of the Russian Ministry of Finance is satisfied that the company has now complied with all the requirements of the Russian law, a definite arrangement has not been arrived at. Even if it is, and the fields should turn out to be worth the enormous price asked for them, the venture is highly speculative and should not be touched except by those who care to risk their money.

PRIMITIVA GAS COMPANY OF BUENOS AYRES.

Messrs. James Capel & Co. invite subscriptions for £200,000 5 per cent. first debentures, being part of an authorised total of £300,000, at £101 per debenture. Interest is due June and December, and principal and interest are payable in London in sterling. Debentures are secured by a trust deed whereby they become a first floating charge on the entire undertaking. They will be redeemable by a cumulative sinking fund within twenty years, but they may be purchased and cancelled at or under 105; otherwise will be drawn at this price, at which the company has the option to redeem the whole at any time on six months' notice. The company was formed in 1855, and is said to have an unbroken record of success Share capital $4,000,000, national currency, and the dividend, which was 15 per cent. for 1892, has steadily advanced to 24 per cent. for 1897; in addition to which there are reserves, taken from profits, amounting to $1,100,000. The company has recently gone in for electric lighting, and this has created a floating debt which at the end of last year amounted to £110,000 and the present issue is to provide for this, and also for further extension. We see no valuation of the company's assets given, but the revenue for last year is stated at £77,268, whereas debenture interest and sinking fund will need only £17,000, so that the debentures appear to be a good speculative 5 per cent. investment.

HYDRO-INCANDESCENT GAS LIGHT COMPANY, LIMITED.

Company buys British, Indian, Australasian, South African and Canadian patent rights of this light, and the benefits of a licence from the Welsbach Company, whereby the latter undertakes for five years to manufacture and sell the apparatus for half the gross receipts. It is not very clear what the advantages of the light are, but they are said to be very great, and to more nearly approximate the sun's rays, shades of colour being as readily distinguishable as in the daylight. The capital is £200,000 in £1 shares, all of which are offered, and the purchase price is £180,000 payable in cash, the vendors apparently, like ourselves, having a poor opinion of the shares.

HOTEL AND CLUB INVESTMENT COMPANY, LIMITED.

Investors are offered an issue of £150,000 4½ per cent. first mortgage debentures at par, which is being made for the purpose of redeeming the existing debentures of the company and for other purposes. The debentures are of £50 each and are redeemable after 1908 at £52 10s. on six months' notice. We do not know who holds the existing debentures,; none of the £100,000 of share capital is offered, and the purchase price for the concern is not given. We also fail to see any statement of net profits, and the freehold securities, about which so much is made, have apparently to be bought if the debenture money is subscribed. The Brighton surveyor who values the properties, wines, stores, &c., went over the assets, we should imagine, first with the right eye and then with the left and added the two valuations together. This is not by any means an investment.

VENICE HOTELS, LIMITED.

The object of this promotion is to buy various hotels with a view to amalgamation and stop existing competition. The profit statement of three of the hotels needs to be studied to be appreciated. The capital is £200,000 in 28,000 6 per cent. cumulative preference shares of £5 each and 60,000 ordinary shares of £1 each. The latter are taken by the vendors with £100,000 in cash, and if they make nothing out of the shares they ought to come well out of the deal provided the capital is subscribed. It is said that of the £115,000 now offered £75,000 has been already subscribed in Venice, and we should certainly leave the remaining £40,000 to be found by that beautiful city.

JEREMIAH ROTHERHAM & CO., LIMITED.

This is the well-known and old established business of wholesale and retail drapers and general warehousemen of Shoreditch, which the vendors offer to the public for £500,000, and of this they are willing to accept no less than £316,668 in cash. Before deducting £95,362 for trade liabilities the company takes over property, &c., valued at £595,362, but of this heavy amount as much as £484,058 is represented by stock, book debts, goodwill, fixtures, furniture, plant, horses, vans, harness, and utensils, the freehold premises being valued at only £91,575. The share capital is £400,000 in £1 shares, equally divided into ordinary and 5 per cent. cumulative preference, 133,334 shares of each class being offered. An issue is also made of £150,000 4 per cent. first mortgage debenture stock, of which £100,000 is offered at par. Profits for the three years ended January 15, 1898, are given at £38,093, £35,130, and £40,112. The average shows 7 per cent. on the ordinary shares, and a surplus of £7,779, which is very good, but the security is scarcely adequate for the debenture stock, let alone the preference capital. The shares may be received with favour because the business is well known, but the securities are in our opinion not of the nature in which we care to recommend an investment.

Company Reports and Baiance-Sheets.

⁂ *The Editor will be much obliged to the Secretaries of Joint Stock Companies if they would kindly forward copies of Reports and Balance-Sheets direct to the Office of* THE INVESTORS' REVIEW, *Norfolk House, Norfolk-street, W.C., so as to insure prompt notice in these columns.*

THE MOUNT LYELL MINING AND RAILWAY COMPANY, LIMITED.—We have now received the reports and balance-sheet of this important mine for the six months ended March 31 last. From these we learn that the net profit for the half-year was £84,250, of which £77,185 came from smelting operations and £7,065 from the railway. During the half-year, however, the company paid away £100,000 in the shape of two dividends of 4s. each upon the 250,000 shares issued.. This payment in excess of revenue is, no doubt, justified by the fact that a considerable sum in profits had accumulated and been temporarily devoted to capital purposes in the early stages of the company's history. As fresh issues of shares get sold this money is released and is being distributed. Also the company has now six furnaces at work and has ordered another nest of five furnaces, whose aggregate capacity will be equal to that of the present six. The presumption, therefore, is that there will be such an enlarged output of copper as will enable the directors to maintain the present rate of dividend, even should the quality of the ore contiпue low. Last half-year the average assay of copper per ton was 4·25 per cent., of silver 3·69 oz., and of gold 0·177 oz. on the "wet weight" of the ore. Since smelting began the average value of copper per ton has been 45·1 per cent., of silver 3·92 oz., and of gold 0·185 oz. It is obvious, therefore, that the quality of the ore has somewhat fallen off, and the manager in his very straightforward report upon the ore body as far as discovered does not encourage the expectation that a great improvement can be looked for in future. Pockets of rich ore may be found between the 4th and 5th tunnels, but on the average the yield of metals is not, it would seem, expected to be much better than it is now. Enlarged output alone must be looked to as the reliable source of enlarged revenue, and it is estimated by Mr. Sticht, the manager, that there are about 1,781,300 tons of good paying ore above the No. 4 level, and in addition considerable quantities of poor ore, which may be utilised to some extent in smelting the richer. This is enough to keep a mine going for years to come, but not enough to encourage excessive gambling in its shares. At present, however, a dead set is being made on these shares, in the interests, it is said, of the people engaged in an attempt to monopolise the supply of copper. We can see nothing in the report or accounts to warrant any holder in throwing his shares away at the prompting of the "bears"—of sellers who depress the market in the hope of buying back, or of "loading up" and getting control cheap.

THE GELDENHUIS ESTATE AND G. M. COMPANY (ELANDSFONTEIN No. 1), LIMITED.—This Transvaal limited company has issued its report for the year ended March 31 last, from which it appears that the payment of No. 12 dividend left the profit and loss account with a debit balance of nearly £450. This is a small matter, from one point of view, but the balance-sheet is not particularly clear on the position of the capital account. Apparently large sums are being continually added to the capital expenditure of the mine, but these are not systematically brought out in the accounts, and we cannot say whether the £49,651 the board has deemed it advisable to write off for "depreciation" last year is anything like an adequate amount. This question is the more important, because working costs are being reduced and were only 19s. 2·654d. last year as against 20s. 8·879d. the previous year. Would this current expenditure be so low if revenue were properly charged with every item that ought in well-regulated accounts to go there? On the answer to this question depends the further one—whether or not the revenue is being stretched and strained to pay high dividends. And plainly there is no reserve whatever. More than the last shilling has been paid away, and the "depreciation" item merely goes against new capital outlay.

DISTILLERS COMPANY.—Prudence in the past has brought this company to a very comfortable position. Despite the rise of mushroom distilleries the profits for the year ended May 14 amounted to £210,466, as against £206,482 in the preceding year. After payment of interest and administrative charges, £60,000 was placed to depreciation and reserve, £10,000 to fire insurance, and dividends and bonus amounting to 12½ per cent. for the year were proposed, £15,486 being carried forward, or about the same as a year ago. The sum of £30,000 has been written off the cost of works out of the depreciation and reserve account, and by the persistent following of this policy the land and buildings and plant and utensils are about £75,000 below what they stood at in 1891, although profits have risen by one-third in the period. A prudent step, too, is seen in the reduction by one-half of the stock of spirits, grain, &c., and a consequent increase in the cash.

MAJULI TEA COMPANY.—The season was unfavourable and the crop of 899,411 lb. was about 11,000 lb. below the estimate, but about 24,000 lb. above that of 1896. The average price of 9⅝d. per lb. was 5/16d. per lb. below that of 1896, so that the net profit of £3,574 was £1,202 less than in the previous twelve months. This sum would have provided a fair dividend, for the capital is only £95,970, but the cost of recent extensions and their upkeep has locked up all the floating cash of the concern, and so the directors state that no dividend can be paid until the £8,244 recently spent upon extensions is replaced by a fresh issue of capital. In the present state of the Indian tea industry we should say, "Do not attempt to issue fresh capital," but this saying will seem foolishness to the dividend-declaring director and the impatient shareholder. As it is the board seem to aim at issuing £20,000 of preference capital, and thus to perpetuate the mistake made of extending too freely.

SALAR DEL CARMEN SYNDICATE.—This concern does not open its record very brightly. Last year was devoted chiefly to building its oficina, and £60,729 was spent upon the affair, while as it had paid £105,000 for the oficina "Santa Lucia," the properties stand in its books for £165,959. A profit of £2,342 was made out of a few weeks' working, which was more than swallowed up by debenture interest. Administration expenses took £2,250 more, and "Preliminary expenses, and expenses of issue, and discount on debentures" stand for £11,091, an enormous total. There is a cash item of £7,070, but that is not much, while £20,000 of creditors and bills payable will have to be met, and whether the nitrate trade improves or not, the interest upon the £80,000 of debentures will have to be found. It is altogether a most unsatisfactory statement, and while the board appears to be sitting down quietly to await the re-construction of another combination the liabilities of the concern tend to grow.

EDINBURGH EMPIRE PALACE, LIMITED.—Apparently this company has made a poor venture in regard to the University Hotel but after setting aside £302 as loss upon realisation of furnishings the net profit for the year was £3,972. The board very unwisely maintained the dividend at 10 per cent., so that the balance forward was £228 less than brought in. The reserve, too, is little more than half what it was a few years back, and the goodwill remains at the high figure of £7,000. In spite of the lofty dividend this is the high road to trouble, and no one ought to know that better than Mr. Moss. To pay the final dividend borrowing will have to take place, as the cash in hand is £179, while the dividend requires £2,100.

GLASGOW EMPIRE PALACE.—The accounts of this concern look better than those of the "Palace" in the sister city. Profits last year came to £12,169, and after distribution of dividends amounting to 15 per cent. for the year, the balance forward was increased from £1,472 to £4,685. This in itself is a fair reserve, and in addition £535 was written off the expenditure upon furniture, &c. In spite of this, however, that item tends to grow, and it should be remembered that theatrical decorations and properties are not a life-long investment.

NATIONAL MODEL DWELLINGS COMPANY.—A derelict of the Liberator smash. The board of this, a small concern, is doing its best to bring matters round. Out of the net profit of £6,503 the sum of £129 was placed to mortgage redemption fund, £50 as a reserve against bad debts, and £698 was written off commissions and charges in connection with the transfer of mortgages. To the balance of £1,819 had to be added £1,621 brought forward, out of which the board took £1,000 to place to mortgage redemption fund, and then declared a dividend of 1¼ per cent., leaving £600 to be carried forward. The directors have paid off £1,000 of mortgage in the year and will pay another £1,000 shortly. The reserve for bad debts ought to be sufficient for its purpose, and there will then only remain £698, the balance of the commissions, &c., upon transfer of mortgages to wipe out in order to clear off the unsatisfactory items in the balance-sheet. The mortgages ought, however, to be reduced still further.

OHLSSON'S CAPE BREWERIES.—The very satisfactory profit of £57,326 was earned by this concern in the year ended March 31. The sum of £20,000 is placed to reserve and dividends and bonus amounting to 18 per cent. for the year were declared, leaving £1,895 to be carried forward. The reserve will now amount to £75,000, and the balance appears to be a strong one, no less than £24,841 being invested, while trading balances are all in favour of the company. The profit and loss account is very meagre, the amount set aside for depreciation not even being stated.

TAMPLIN & SON'S BREWERY, BRIGHTON.—The profits of this concern are maintained at a high figure, the gross profit last year being no less than £52,116. After payment of expenses, including £2,879 for repairs and £3,389 for depreciation, the net balance is £29,501. The sum of £7,000 is placed to reserve, and dividends equal to 10 per cent. for the year are paid upon the ordinary shares, leaving £2,898 to be carried forward. The total reserves of the company amount to about £50,000, as against £375,000 of share and debenture capital. The balance-sheet is good, the company owning no less than £31,718 of investments, while trading balances are very much in its favour.

THE WESTERN MORTGAGE AND INVESTMENT COMPANY, LIMITED.—This concern seems to require overhauling. Last year, its year ends on March 31, it made a net loss of £13,157, and the business seems to be most expensively conducted. There are only three directors, one of whom, Mr. Andrew Williamson, just appointed, is a member of the firm of Smith & Williamson that acts as the company's managers—and who therefore is, as a director, where he has no business to be—but directors' fees, office expenses, &c., in London came last year to £4,296. Then "losses on real estate and loans fully realised, including American agent's commission on sales"—a most reprehensible jumble of items which ought to be separated—took another £4,851. Law charges in England, £986, have to be added to this, and as the interest on debentures and deposits took nearly £11,000, while the income amounted to £7,725 only, the loss is easily stated as above. For whose benefit is a wasting business of this sort carried on if not for that of the officials? The shareholders merely pay calls, and behold the debit balance against them swelling in amount year by year. It is now nearly £73,000, allowing for a "profit" credited on purchases of the company's own debentures for extinction. The shareholders ought to come together and organise themselves with a view to ending this state of affairs. All the capital will soon be called up, and dissipated at the rate of "progress" now established if they sit still and do nothing.

MUNICIPAL TRUST COMPANY.—The income of this concern continues to shrink in a miserable fashion. For the year ended February 28 it was £30,041, and after payment of working charges and debenture interest the net balance of £9,949 was left, which, including £513 brought forward, gave a total of £10,462. This sum was practically absorbed in paying a dividend of 3½ per cent. on the preferred stock, in spite of the statement by the auditor that £9,682 of depreciation upon the value of the investments ought to be debited to revenue account. In the year no less than £5,942 was added to the depreciation from realised losses on bonds sold or cancelled on foreclosure. This amount of money was admittedly lost, and yet this board proceeds to divide up every scrap of the balance it claims to represent net revenue. No wonder Mr. Auldjo Jamieson is compelled to resign his seat, and we consider the payment of the dividend at the rate of 3½ per cent. a grave mistake.

BROOKE, BOND, & CO., LIMITED.—Prosperity continues to bless this company, and the profit of £32,128 was shown for the year ended May 31. Out of this £10,000 was written off goodwill, £5,000 placed to reserve, and the balance permitted of dividends equal to 15 per cent. for the year. The substantial sum of £4,170 was then carried forward, or a little less than the sum brought in. The board continues to make the best use of the accumulation, having redeemed £1,400 of debentures, and invested £8,623 in purchasing the freehold of their warehouse premises. Goodwill and trademarks have been written down from £100,000 to £36,000 in the course of the company's existence, and the reserve now stands at £32,000. There is also an insurance and contingency fund of £932. We are afraid such prudence and foresight is becoming old-fashioned, but only let the Hooleyised Bovril-Welsbach-Appollinaris-British Tea Table concerns run on for a while longer, and then the weight of water is bound to tell its tale.

Diary of the War.

June 17.—News received that Caimamera has again been shelled by American warships, and no doubt the harbour works were further damaged. No more fighting reported at Guantanamo. The expedition from Tampa has not arrived, and, of course, no forward movement is possible until these troops are available. As to German warships at Manila, the German Government protests that it has no intention of deviating from the strict rules of neutrality.

June 18.—Another—the third—bombardment of the outworks of the harbour of Santiago de Cuba took place two days ago. The Americans claim to have dismantled the western batteries, and to have inflicted heavy loss on the Spaniards. The latter declare they only lost three killed and ten wounded. The Spanish position at Manila is described as desperate. The city is surrounded by the insurgents, but they do not, it is said, intend to deliver their final attack until the arrival of the American troops; and they were expected on the 10th. The Cadiz fleet is reported to have really sailed, but, of course, its destination is not known. A hint to Germany. The Washington Government refuses to believe that Germany has any intention of intervening in the Philippines, but that any attempt on her part to take steps with a view to secure a harbour there would "quickly solidify American opinion in favour of taking and keeping all Spanish possessions in Eastern waters."

June 19.—General Shafter's expedition is at sea, but no news of it since its start from Tampa. It may arrive in the neighbourhood of Santiago on Tuesday, and it seems probable that the attempt to land will be made a little to the east or to the west of that harbour. Punta Cabrera, ten miles to the west of Santiago, was bombarded on Friday, the 17th, when it was ascertained that the defences had recently been strengthened, and that the place was held by a considerable body of Spanish troops. There are rumours of dissensions among American military authorities, but nothing that can be regarded as authentic.

June 20.—The capitulation of Manila is only a question of time, The Spanish Captain-General confesses he cannot now prevent it. the native insurgents have so hemmed him in. Indeed, it is probable that the surrender would have taken place ere now had not Admiral Dewey been anxious to postpone it until the arrival of the American troops. He might then exercise a more perfect control of the situation; but if the American expedition is delayed much longer it is possible the rebels may hasten events. The matter is at present virtually in their hands. Nothing known of the Cadiz squadron. Washington does not believe that it will make for the American coast; but who can tell? It would now be useless to make for the Philippines, and certain Madrid critics hint that it has gone for a cruise to amuse the Spanish public, that it has no direct objective, and has no hope of achieving great results. Perhaps so; but it is singular that that should be said in Madrid. Much talk of peace, but no action taken. The Catalan Union of Barcelona published a manifesto urging peace rather than the ruin of the country; but that manifesto has been much more discussed in London than in Madrid.

June 21.—Exchange of prisoners refused by the Cuban Captain-General; so the plucky Lieut. Hobson, who sank the *Merrimac*, will remain in prison with his intrepid colleagues. The American authorities express surprise at this decision after the opinion voluntarily expressed by Admiral Cervera; but the explanation given in Madrid is that these prisoners, without in any way acting as spies, must have seen too much of the harbour and defences of Santiago to make it discreet to liberate them. In that view, no prisoners could ever be given up. The last heard of the Cadiz squadron is that it had reached Cartagena, and was comfortably berthed there, but what for nobody can say. A New York despatch avers that Admiral Camara had left Cartagena for Cadiz, which, if true, would seem to indicate that something has gone wrong with the ships, and that he deems it necessary to consult with the Admiralty at Madrid as to future operations; or, perhaps, as to how he is to go on doing nothing but burning coal? No announcement yet of the arrival of General Shafter's expedition at Santiago.

June 22.—General Shafter, with his military expedition, has arrived off Cuba. He has had a consultation with Admiral Sampson, and preparations will no doubt be made soon for the landing near Santiago. The transports keep well off the coast. It is announced from Havana that General Blanco is to send six battalions of troops to protect the Spanish coast. Manila despatches describe a fight between the native rebels and three thousand mixed troops under General Monet. The fighting extended over three days, the General was killed, the native levies joined the rebels, and about 500 Spanish troops had to surrender. There are reports of the revolt of native troops in other districts. Don Carlos has been unbosoming himself to a newspaper interviewer, and if his statements are to be taken seriously, he will endeavour, when peace comes with the United States, to grind his own axe, and stir up civil war in the Carlist interest. Barcelona papers are strongly urging the immediate conclusion of peace. The Geneva Red Cross Convention has been accepted by both Governments in this war; and America has fitted up a ship called the *Solace* as a floating ambulance. This is said to be the first Government vessel of any nation which has been commissioned under the Red Cross Convention.

June 23.—American troops have landed at Aguadores, near Santiago, under cover of the guns of the American fleet. There was a considerable force of Spaniards, who were attacked in the rear by about 1,000 Cubans; and after the warships had shelled the shore, the American troops landed, driving the Spaniards towards the Cubans. The invading force landed without suffering any loss. There is a strong feeling of indignation in the United States as to the refusal of General Blanco to liberate Lieutenant Hobson and his colleagues in exchange for Spanish prisoners. The Senate has passed a resolution demanding more information on the subject. The Cadiz fleet has not gone back, we are told, and Admiral Camara, we are assured, cannot possibly return to Madrid, because he announced before leaving that he would never return until the flag had been steeped in American blood. To go back before he had attained that distinction, therefore, would be to invite riot in Madrid. Very likely; but the admiral will find little American blood at the Canaries, where, it is said, we shall next here of him. It does look a little as if the Cadiz squadron were on a mere tour for the purpose of beguiling the Spanish people into the notion that something is being done, while all the time nothing is to be attempted. A strange story is told in the *Daily News* as to the practical capitulation of Manila, not to the American fleet, but to the Germans. The latter objected to a bombardment by the Americans, as they had no force to protect the Germans in Manila; so the bombardment was postponed until the arrival of American troops. When, however, General Augustin found himself so hard pressed by the native rebels he appealed to the foreign warships—all except the Americans—to land a force sufficient to protect the lives of the inhabitatants against the insurgents. This, it is asserted, has been done, and the German Admiral Diedrichs is in command of the landing force. The story seems, to say the least, an extremely doubtful one. The landing could not have been effected without the knowledge of Admiral Dewey, and he would certainly, if he had not vetoed the scheme altogether, at any rate have insisted on taking part in the landing. It is hardly conceivable that the other Powers would have acted in this way without consultation with the American admiral, for surely that would have been an act of war. Ex-President Cleveland, in a recent address, declared strongly against a policy of external expansion and annexation.

TRADE AND PRODUCE.

If the Leiter-Armour "big blind poolists" hoped to recover some at least of the losses of the wheat corner, they must have been sadly disappointed by the results of the past week. "The best laid schemes o' mice and men gang aft agley," and the cornerers of wheat must be finding so to their cost. The slump continued in England, and in New York the "bears" have managed to frustrate nearly every attempt at a rally. Rumours current as to damage to growing wheat by rain in some of the South Western States had one day the effect of causing a slight rise, but the reports were not trustworthy, and have been found to be wrong. The exports from America continue as large as ever. They seem, indeed, getting larger. For the week ending June 11, the Atlantic exports, flour included, were 4,206,273, against 1,634,602 last year, an amount probably larger than any week this year. Nor is there the slightest hint as to serious falling off in the supplies. The official reports of the coming harvest are excellent, and the future seems pretty well secured. The average price of wheat in England last week is given as 42s. 4d., as compared with 45s. 4d. for the previous week. We doubt if the average for this week can be above 40s. There has been little business doing in the English markets, but nothing has been done except at a reduction of from 2s. to 4s. per quarter. Flour was 1s. to 2s. cheaper. Futures rule low. Some near dates have been offered at 38s. to 41s., but no transactions reported. August-September, however, can be had at 31s., though September-October is quoted at 38s. 6d. French wants seem now to be satisfied, more of the American and other cargoes now coming to English ports. It is fully understood that the French dubes will be reimposed at the date fixed, July 1; but the probability is that the suspension will continue both in Italy and Spain. Neither Government can afford to resume these imposts at present; the discontent caused might be serious. Wednesday's markets showed a tendency to harden, and 6d. advance was demanded in London; but buyers did not respond. They still hold aloof. New York was again dominated by the "bears" for a good part of the session, and prices fluctuated considerably, and closed flat on good crop reports. Nothing seems to indicate the possibility of maintaining increased rates for the present. We are too near the harvest, and old stocks are still too considerable to warrant an advance.

Otherwise our trade reports are not so full of encouragement and confidence as they have been for some time. In Glasgow, though shipbuilding continues abnormally active, and iron and steel manufacture, in spite of the adverse influence of the manipulating iron "ring," is as busy as may be, they are beginning to speculate as to whether they have not reached the crest of the wave of active prosperity. The speculation seems to us premature; at least, there are as yet no signs of a downward tendency. Wool continues very quiet; only in Leicester is an improvement recorded in all the most fashionable descriptions of home and colonial produce, but even there prices continue abnormally low. Cotton continues dull and spiritless; and in linens, though Dundee reports a slight improvement, Belfast records none, and Barnsley is emphatically quiet. There is no activity anywhere, and no sign yet of an early marked improvement.

Copper shows no great sign of revival, yet the visible supplies are considerably lower. The bi-monthly statistics show a decrease in the visible supply of 434 tons, and prices have fallen £2 15s. during the last six weeks. What is the reason of this excessive fall, seeing that consumption is larger than production? There seems some sort of mystery about it. Speculation is absent, say Messrs. Morrison, Kekewich & Co., in their circular, and "it suits dealers to keep down prices until they have secured some large lines of refined which they are in treaty for." That is somewhat oracular; but more follows. "Manufacturers," we are told, "complain that fresh orders are not coming in, but directly the standard market hardens we shall see more activity." We must wait for enlightenment, it seems; but meantime we may note some renewed activity in the market on Wednesday, with a recovery of 3s. 9d. per ton. On first 'Change 700 tons were placed at £49 17s. 6d. and 18s. 9d. cash, and on second 'Change cash purchases ruled much the same, with £50 5s. and 3s. 9d. for three months.

No change in reference to the Welsh strike. There has been a suggestion that peace might be concluded on the basis of a 5s. advance in wages, and a reversion to the sliding scale. Meanwhile, the non-associated owners have granted another 10 per cent. advance to their colliers, making a total of 20 per cent. since the beginning of the strike. As this increase, however, is in most cases to be contributed to the strike fund, this is only encouraging continued resistance. The owners must, however, see it to be for their advantage to grant the increase. The building of ships for the Navy was very much delayed last year by the engineers' strike; and now we have the autumn manœuvres stopped from difficulties as to steam coal caused by the Welsh strike. We are getting on. We may yet have the workmen insisting on stopping actual war until wages had been satisfactorily adjusted. But in that case, if they could but check the war, we should not mind. At present, however, this constant interference with the course of trade is very detrimental, and must tend, in the long run, to lower wages. Of course in the districts unaffected by the strike, coal is still advancing in price. From all the iron centres we have very favourable reports. All the works are busy, orders are coming in fairly well, and there is every prospect of continued activity.

There is, as yet, no revival in the demand for sugar, and consumers, according to Mr. Czarnikow, seem to have this spring contracted larger supplies than was expected. It is difficult to sell even at a moderate reduction. Home consumption is going on satisfactorily; but the excess in imports of foreign refined increases.

Debenture interest coupons of the National Mortgage and Agency Company of New Zealand, due July 1, will be paid at the Bank of Scotland in London.

DIVIDENDS ANNOUNCED.

LONDON AND SOUTH AFRICAN EXPLORATION COMPANY.—Dividend of 3s. per share for quarter ending the 30th inst.

MYSORE GOLD MINING COMPANY.—Interim dividend of 4s. 6d. per share.

DENVER AND RIO GRANDE RAILROAD COMPANY.—Semi-annual dividend of 1½ per cent. on the preferred stock.

JOHN BROWN & COMPANY.—Further dividend on the ordinary shares of 12s. 6d. per share, making with the interim dividend paid 6¼ per cent. for the year.

NATIONAL MORTGAGE AND AGENCY OF NEW ZEALAND.—Interim dividend at the rate of 5 per cent. per annum.

WILLIAM JONES & SONS.—Dividend for the eleven months ended March 31 last at the rate of 8 per cent. per annum.

DE LAMAR MINING COMPANY.—Dividend of 6d. per share.

EAST INDIA AND CEYLON TEA COMPANY.—Dividend on the ordinary shares at the rate of 3 per cent.

EAST INDIAN RAILWAY COMPANY.—Dividend for the half-year at the rate of £1 4s. 6d. per cent. on the deferred annuity capital, and the deferred annuity capital class "D," in addition to the guaranteed interest of £2 per cent. The return of guaranteed interest and dividend for 1897 is at the rate of £6 8s. per cent. on the deferred annuity capital and the deferred annuity capital class "D," as compared with £5 3s. 6d. for 1896.

GREAT NORTHERN (U.S.) RAILWAY COMPANY.—Quarterly dividend of 1½ per cent. on the preferred stock, and a quarterly dividend of 1½ per cent. on the St. Paul Minneapolis and Manitoba Railway Company's 6 per cent. guaranteed shares.

GLASGOW EMPIRE PALACE.—Dividend of 20 per cent.

DISTILLERS COMPANY.—Dividend of 12s. per share, which, with the interim dividend of 8s. per share, makes the usual dividend for the year, 20 per cent.; and a bonus of 5s. per share.

GREENWOOD & BATLEY.—Dividend of 7 per cent. on the cumulative preference shares.

SCOTTISH ASSAM TEA COMPANY.—Dividend of 5 per cent.

CORDOBA CENTRAL RAILWAY COMPANY.—Dividend £5 per cent. on the 5 per cent. cumulative first preference stock.

KAFFIRS CONSOLIDATED INVESTMENT AND LAND COMPANY.—Interim dividend of 3d. per share for the month of June.

BRILLIANT GOLD MINING COMPANY.—Dividend of 6d. per share.

SHROPSHIRE BREWERY COMPANY.—Dividend of 5 per cent per annum on the preference shares, and interest at 4 per cent. per annum on the debenture stock.

NEW AFRICAN COMPANY.—Dividend of 12½ per cent.

LA GUAYRA AND CARACAS RAILWAY.—Dividend at the rate of 5 per cent. per annum.

ASSETS REALISATION COMPANY.—Interim dividend at the rate of 8 per cent. per annum on the ordinary shares.

BANK OF NEW SOUTH WALES.—Dividend at the rate of 9 per cent. per annum.

OHLSSON'S CAPE BREWERIES.—Final dividend of 6 per cent. on the ordinary shares, making 12 per cent. for the year, and a bonus of 6s. per share.

MESSAGERIES MARITIMES COMPANY.—Dividend of 25 francs per share of 500 francs.

DANE'S DISCOUNT COMPANY.—Interim dividend at the rate of 10 per cent. per annum for the three months ending June 30.

WITWATERSRANDT GOLD MINING COMPANY (KNIGHT'S).—Interim dividend of 15 per cent.

GLENCAIRN'S MAIN REEF GOLD MINING COMPANY.—Interim dividend of 15 per cent.

NEW PRIMROSE GOLD MINING COMPANY.—Half-yearly dividend of 25 per cent.

GINSBERG GOLD MINING COMPANY.—Half-yearly dividend of 20 per cent.

RIETFONTEIN "A."—Interim dividend of 15 per cent.

JOHANNESBURG ESTATE COMPANY.—A dividend of 2½ per cent. for the six months ending June 30.

SOUTH AFRICAN BREWERIES.—Dividend for the half-year ended March 31 of 7½ per cent. on the ordinary shares, making 12½ per cent. for the year.

ROBINSON GOLD MINING COMPANY.—An interim dividend of 7 per cent. for the half-year ending June 30.

GELDENHUIS DEEP.—An interim dividend of 30 per cent. for the half-year ending June 30, being at the rate of 60 per cent. per annum.

VICTORIA GOLD MINING ASSOCIATION (CHARTERS TOWERS).—Dividend of 6d. per share.

CHICAGO JUNCTION RAILWAYS AND UNION STOCK YARDS COMPANY.—Dividend of 1½ per cent. on the preferred, and dividend of 4 per cent. on the common stock.

ELECTRIC AND GENERAL INVESTMENT COMPANY.—Further dividend at the rate of 30 per cent. per annum for the six months ended May 31, and a bonus of 10 per cent. for the year, making a total of 35 per cent. for the year upon the capital paid up on the ordinary shares. Dividend of £30 per share and a bonus of £20 per share on the founders' shares, and a further £20 per share out of the proceeds of investments sold and dividends received in respect of the founders' share reserve fund, making a total distribution of £70 per founders' share.

HENRY NOURSE GOLD MINING COMPANY.—Dividend (No. 4) of 75 per cent. (15s. per share).

CHILIAN NATIONAL AMMUNITION COMPANY.—A dividend at the rate of 7½ per cent. per annum.

SHEBA GOLD MINING COMPANY.—A dividend of 6d. per share.

JOHANNESBURG WATERWORKS, ESTATE, AND EXPLORATION COMPANY.—A dividend of 7½ per cent.

NUNDYDROOG COMPANY.—An interim dividend of 2s. per share.

JUMPER'S GOLD MINING COMPANY.—A dividend of 30 per cent.

ANGLO-MEXICAN MINING COMPANY.—A dividend of 1s. per share.

MAHOR RANI TEA.—A dividend of 2½ per cent. on the ordinary shares.

UNITED DISCOUNT AND SECURITIES COMPANY.—Interim dividend on the ordinary shares at the rate of 6 per annum.

EASTERN EXTENSION, AUSTRALASIA AND CHINA TELEGRAPH COMPANY.—Interim dividend for the quarter ended March 31 last, of 2s. 6d. per share.

BROOKE, BOND & CO.—Dividend at the rate of 15 per cent. per annum.

TAMPLIN & SON'S BREWERY.—Dividend on the ordinary shares at the rate of 12 per cent. per annum, making with the interim dividend 10 per cent. for the year.

UNITED STATES BREWING COMPANY.—Final dividend of 5 per cent. on the ordinary shares.

ROYAL EXCHANGE ASSURANCE CORPORATION.—Dividend of £10 per cent. for the half-year ending at Midsummer.

AMAZON STEAM NAVIGATION COMPANY.—Dividend of 2 per cent. making a total dividend for the year of 4 per cent.

COLONIAL BANK.—Dividend at the rate of 6 per cent. for the half-year ended December 31.

FERREIRA GOLD MINING COMPANY.—Dividend of 150 per cent.

LONDON AND PROVINCIAL MARINE INSURANCE COMPANY.—Dividend at the rate of 10 per cent. per annum for the half-year ending June 30.

DENVER UNITED BREWERIES.—Final dividend of 8s. per share on the 8 per cent. preference shares.

STOCK CONVERSION AND INVESTMENT TRUST.—Interim dividend of 9d. per share on the ordinary shares.

The trustees for the debenture holders of the Catalinas Warehouses and Mole Company of Buenos Ayres 5 per cent. mortgage debentures for £979,500 have received funds sufficient to make a distribution of £1 per cent., being balance of interest due October 1, 1893, and the same will be paid by the London and River Plate Bank, Limited, 7, Princes-street, London, E.C., on and after June 30, 1898, on presentation of the certificates of deposit of the outstanding bonds, which must be left three clear days for examination.

The Mount Lyell Mining and Railway Company, Limited.—In consequence of the publicity given to recent rumours of an unfavourable nature in regard to the company's mines and undertaking, the London directors, having cabled to the board in Melbourne for information, have heard in reply that there are no grounds for any unfavourable rumours and that everything is proceeding satisfactorily.

The directors of the Nizam Guaranteed State Railways Company, Limited, have elected Sir Andrew R. Scoble to the seat on the board vacated by the death of the late General Alexander Fraser.

Notice to Subscribers.

Complaints are continually reaching us that the INVESTORS' REVIEW cannot be obtained at this and the other railway bookstall, that it does not reach Scotch and Irish cities till Monday, and that it is not delivered in the City till Saturday morning.

We publish on Friday in time for the REVIEW to be at all Metropolitan bookstalls by at latest 4 p.m., and we believe that it is there then, having no doubt that Messrs. W. H. Smith & Son do their best, but they have such a mass of papers to handle every day that a fresh one may well look almost like a personal enemy and be kept in short supply unless the reading public shows unmistakably that it is wanted. A little perseverance, therefore, in asking for the INVESTORS' REVIEW is all that should be required to remedy this defect.

All London newsagents can be in a position to distribute the paper on Friday afternoon if they please, and here also the only remedy is for subscribers to insist upon having it as soon as published. Arrangements have been made that all our direct City subscribers shall have their copies before 4 p.m. on Friday. As for the provinces, we can only say that the paper is delivered to the forwarding agents in ample time to be in every English and Scotch town, and in Dublin and Belfast, likewise, early on Saturday morning. Those despatched by post from this office can be delivered by the first London mail on Saturday in every part of the United Kingdom.

ADVERTISEMENTS.

All Advertisements are received subject to approval, and should be sent in not later than 5 p.m. on Thursdays.

The advertisements of American Life Insurance Offices are rigorously excluded from the INVESTORS' REVIEW, and have been so since it commenced as a Quarterly Magazine in 1892.

For tariff and particulars of positions open apply to the Advertisement Manager, Norfolk House, Norfolk-street, W.C.

To Correspondents.

The EDITOR cannot undertake to return rejected communications.

Letters from correspondents must, in every case, be authenticated by the name and address of the writer.

Telegraphic Address: "Unveiling, London."

The Investors' Review.

The Week's Money Market.

Contrary to general experience, money becomes more plentiful as the end of the month approaches. Although we are at the turn of the quarter, day to day loans can be easily obtained at ½ per cent. per annum, while seven day advances command no more than ¾ per cent. Indeed, the India Council only gets 1 per cent. for loans up to July 4, to the eve, that is, of the Government dividend payments. Such rates pretty well represent low water-mark, and yet floating supplies will be added to after July 5.

It has been impossible to maintain discount rates in face of the abundance of money, and the quotation for three months remitted bills slipped back to 1¾ per cent., in spite of the efforts of the banks, who do not care to do business on this basis with the official minimum at 3 per cent. Sixty-day paper, indeed, has been taken as low as 1¼ per cent., and the absence of a reduction in the Bank rate appears to have little importance to the market. Even the gold demand is sluggish, and while Russia outbid all comers, including the Bank of England, for the Cape gold last week, it is a doubtful point whether it can afford to pay 77s. 10d. for the arrival just upon due. A withdrawal of £102,000 in German coin from the Bank of England took place early this week, but it was not an ordinary exchange operation, and since then the Berlin cheque has moved in our favour. According to present appearances the market should not anticipate the Government dividends to any material extent by borrowings at the Bank, and thus its resources will be added to after the first week in July. The Bank rate will then, we fear, be forced down, whether the directors think the change prudent or not.

Yesterday's Bank return was in all respects humdrum. The reserve has risen £320,000 to £27,959,000 within the week, but none of this money has gone to the credit of the market. "Other" deposits, indeed, have declined £313,000 to £44,596,000 because "Public" deposits, or Government balances, have risen £560,000 to £12,055,000, and because "Other" securities have declined £210,000 to £33,063,000. Gold still flows back from circulation—from Scotland partly—but it will go out again at the end of the month. The total stock of coin and bullion is now £38,490,000 or £334,000 more than it was a week ago, and only £46,000 is due to net imports of the metal from abroad.

SILVER.

Welcome support was given to the market by further Spanish buying. This caused the price of bars for immediate delivery, which had drooped in the interval to 26 11/16d. per oz., to at once jump up to 27⅛d. per oz., at which it has remained steady since. The buying is not very persistent but it has been enough to clear off supplies, and keep the market firm. Buying from the East is not pressing, as China has been shipping silver of late, and India seems to require less than it used to do. After July 1 Japanese silver yen will no longer be exchangeable for gold, and it is therefore to be assumed that the Straits Settlements will not require so much silver in the future. The withdrawal of silver yen from those dependencies has led to a persistent demand for silver to be minted into British dollars, but of course the vacuum thus created must in a great measure have been filled, and now that the inducement to ship silver yen to Japan is withdrawn, the vacuum should not reappear. Meantime the silver yen thus returned to Japan has been promptly defaced and dumped down somewhere is China, so that the shipments from that quarter to India are explained to a certain extent. Money continues to grow easier in India and the Bank of Bombay has reduced its rate by 1 per cent. to 9, thus bringing itself into line with the Bank of Bengal.

Since the commencement of the financial year on April 1 the India Council has sold Rs. 7,36,85,406, realising £5,087,920. As the Budget estimated for £16,000,000 to be drawn in the year, this means that, at 1s. 4d. per rupee, a little less than 41 lacs must, in future, be sold per week in order to obtain the amount.

BANK OF ENGLAND.

AN ACCOUNT pursuant to the Act 7 and 8 Vict., cap. 32, for the Week ending on Wednesday, June 22, 1898.

ISSUE DEPARTMENT.

	£		£
Notes Issued	52,788,895	Government Debt	11,015,100
		Other Securities	5,784,900
		Gold Coin and Bullion	35,988,875
		Silver Bullion	—
	£52,788,895		£52,788,875

BANKING DEPARTMENT.

	£		£
Proprietors' Capital	14,553,000	Government Securities	13,476,051
Rest	3,185,998	Other Securities	33,063,346
Public Deposits (including Exchequer, Savings Banks, Commissioners of National Debt, and Dividend Accounts)	12,054,967	Notes	25,458,155
Other Deposits	44,595,911	Gold and Silver Coin	2,501,258
Seven Day and other Bills	108,934		
	£74,498,810		£74,498,810

Dated June 23, 1898.

H. G. BOWEN, *Chief Cashier.*

In the following table will be found the movements compared with the previous week, and also the totals for that week and the corresponding return last year :—

Banking Department.

Last Year. June 23.		June 15, 1898.	June 22, 1898.	Increase.	Decrease.
£	Liabilities.	£	£	£	£
3,101,430	Rest	3,180,301	3,185,998	5,697	—
11,943,967	Pub. Deposits	11,494,625	12,054,967	560,342	—
38,795,704	Other do.	44,908,893	44,595,911	—	312,982
162,091	7 Day Bills	104,081	108,934	4,853	—
	Assets.			Decrease.	Increase.
13,948,356	Gov. Securities	13,328,051	13,476,051	—	148,000
28,707,672	Other do.	33,273,747	33,063,346	210,401	—
25,900,164	Total Reserve	27,639,102	27,959,413	—	320,311
				781,293	781,293
				Increase.	Decrease.
£		£	£	£	£
27,503,845	Note Circulation.	27,317,025	27,330,720	13,695	—
50⅜ p.c.	Proportion	49 p.c.	49½ p.c.	—	—
2 "	Bank Rate	3 "	3 "	—	—

Foreign Bullion movement for week £46,000 in.

LONDON BANKERS' CLEARING.

Month of	1898.	1897.	Increase.	Decrease.
	£	£	£	£
January	673,281,000	576,558,000	96,723,000	—
February	648,601,000	597,652,000	50,949,000	—
March	799,520,000	729,970,000	69,550,000	—
April	597,410,000	532,508,000	64,900,000	—
Week ending				
May 4	174,057,000	138,987,000	35,070,000	—
" 11	160,526,000	128,252,000	32,274,000	—
" 18	171,078,000	152,987,000	18,091,000	—
25	131,037,000	116,372,000	14,665,000	—
June 1	155,655,000	166,981,000	—	11,326,000
" 8	139,048,000	111,213,000	27,835,000	—
" 15	164,537,000	148,402,000	16,135,000	—
" 22	124,723,000	102,454,000	22,269,000	—
Total to date	3,850,405,000	3,435,241,000	415,164,000	—

BANK AND DISCOUNT RATES ABROAD.

	Bank Rate.	Altered.	Open Market.
Paris	2	March 14, 1895	1⅝
Berlin	4	April 9, 1898	3⅜
Hamburg	4	April 9, 1898	3⅜
Frankfort	4	April 9, 1898	3⅜
Amsterdam	3	April 13, 1897	2¼
Brussels	3	April 28, 1896	2¼
Vienna	4	January 22, 1896	4
Rome	5	August 27, 1895	3
St. Petersburg	5½	January 23, 1898	5½
Madrid	5	June 17, 1896	5
Lisbon	6	January 25, 1891	6
Stockholm	5	May 18, 1898	4½
Copenhagen	4½	June 2, 1898	4½
Calcutta	9	June 16, 1898	—
Bombay	9	June 23, 1898	—
New York call money	1 to 1½	—	—

NEW YORK ASSOCIATED BANKS (dollar at 4s.).

	June 18, 1898.	June 11, 1898.	June 4, 1898.	June 19, 1897.
	£	£	£	£
Specie	36,582,000	35,836,000	35,100,000	18,010,000
Legal tenders	11,822,000	11,142,000	10,820,000	21,274,000
Loans and discounts	122,068,000	122,152,000	120,324,000	103,710,000
Circulation	2,937,400	2,943,800	2,946,200	2,798,000
Net deposits	146,196,000	144,842,000	141,884,000	118,506,000

Legal reserve is 25 per cent. of net deposits; therefore the total reserve (specie and legal tenders) exceeds this sum by £11,855,000, against an excess last week of £10,767,500.

BANK OF SPAIN (25 pesetas to the £).

	June 18, 1898.	June 11, 1898.	June 4, 1898.	June 19, 1897.
	£	£	£	£
Gold	9,833,560	9,833,520	9,833,520	8,878,920
Silver	4,313,640	4,228,040	4,209,480	10,452,920
Bills discounted	33,820,800	31,701,640	31,387,160	9,758,640
Advances and loans	3,692,360	3,878,720	4,481,520	9,600,640
Notes in circulation	52,584,880	52,736,360	52,551,760	44,047,000
Treasury advances, coupon account	—	879,960	895,840	113,640
Treasury balances	1,717,720	1,373,760	1,328,960	1,766,120

NATIONAL BANK OF BELGIUM (25 francs to the £).

	June 16, 1898.	June 9, 1898.	June 2, 1898.	June 17, 1897.
	£	£	£	£
Coin and bullion	4,399,120	4,355,120	4,430,400	4,191,000
Other securities	15,796,480	15,895,760	16,489,880	15,763,000
Note circulation	19,054,400	19,084,440	19,144,080	18,387,000
Deposits	2,455,000	2,546,640	3,137,600	2,858,000

IMPERIAL BANK OF GERMANY (20 marks to the £).

	June 15, 1898.	June 7, 1898.	May 31, 1898.	June 15, 1897.
	£	£	£	£
Cash in hand	44,528,150	43,594,650	43,158,850	46,771,000
Bills discounted	32,565,250	33,530,850	34,821,000	*35,447,000
Advances on stocks	4,528,800	4,458,300	4,460,650	—
Note circulation	52,002,450	52,583,350	53,892,300	50,304,000
Public deposits	26,028,150	25,087,450	24,648,850	28,683,000

* Includes advances.

AUSTRIAN-HUNGARIAN BANK (1s. 8d. to the florin).

	June 15, 1898.	June 7, 1898.	May 31, 1898.	June 15, 1897.
	£	£	£	£
Gold reserve	29,057,585	29,028,084	29,032,000	29,448,000
Silver reserve	10,505,750	10,484,250	10,474,250	10,547,000
Foreign bills	205,083	304,416	223,416	—
Advances	1,839,666	1,859,500	1,831,750	—
Note circulation	51,690,366	5,168,900	51,862,083	49,638,000
Bills discounted	12,756,583	13,231,583	13,225,916	*10,434,000

* Includes advances.

BANK OF FRANCE (25 francs to the £).

	June 23, 1898.	June 16, 1898.	June 9, 1898.	June 24, 1897.
	£	£	£	£
Gold in hand	75,236,600	75,011,960	74,936,520	80,245,000
Silver in hand	49,497,880	49,390,640	49,355,120	49,314,000
Bills discounted	26,252,520	26,487,880	28,043,480	*36,316,000
Advances	15,464,000	15,431,160	15,477,880	—
Note circulation	143,230,640	145,191,760	145,639,880	142,796,000
Public deposits	9,706,920	8,738,720	8,290,400	8,097,000
Private deposits	19,840,000	18,068,800	19,711,800	19,405,000

Proportion between bullion and circulation 87 per cent. against 85½ per cent. a week ago.

* Includes advances.

FOREIGN RATES OF EXCHANGE ON LONDON.

Place.	Usance.	Last week's.	Latest.	Place.	Usance.	Last week's.	Latest.
Paris	chqs.	25·26	25·26	Italy	sight	27·02	27·10
Brussels	chqs.	25·27½	25·27	Do. gold prem.	..	107·02½	107·15
Amsterdam	short	12·07¾	12·04¾	Constantinople	3 mths	109·15	109·20
Berlin	short	20·40½	20·39¼	B. Ayres gd. pm.	..	163·70	170·80
Do.	3 mths	20·30	20·39	Rio de Janeiro	90 dys	7⅞d.	7⅛d.
Hamburg	3 mths	20·30	20·30½	Valparaiso	90 dys	17⅛d.	17d.
Frankfort	short	20·38	20·37	Calcutta	T. T.	1/3⅝	1/3⅝
Vienna	short	12·00¼	11·99¾	Bombay	T. T.	1/3⅝	1/3⅝
St. Petersburg	3 mths	94·00	93·95	Hong Kong	T. T.	1/10½	1/11
New York	60 dys	4·83½	4·84	Shanghai	T. T.	2/6½	2/6¾
Lisbon	sight	29⅝d.	29⅜d.	Singapore	T. T.	1/10⅜	1/10½
Madrid	sight	46·77	47·60				

LONDON COURSE OF EXCHANGE.

Place.	Usance.	June 14.	June 16.	June 21.	June 23.
Amsterdam and Rotterdam	short	12·2	12·2	12·1¼	12·1¼
Do. do.	3 months	12·3½	12·3¾	12·3¼	12·3¼
Antwerp and Brussels	3 months	25·43¾	25·43¾	25·43¾	25·43¾
Hamburg	3 months	20·62	20·61	20·62	20·61
Berlin and German B. Places	3 months	20·62	20·62	20·62	20·61
Paris	cheques	25·27½	25·27½	25·28¾	25·27½
Do.	3 months	25·41¼	25·40	25·42½	25·41¼
Marseilles	3 months	25·41¼	25·41¾	25·43¾	25·41¼
Switzerland	3 months	25·57½	25·57½	25·57½	25·57½
Austria	3 months	12·16¼	12·15	12·13¾	12·15
St. Petersburg	3 months	25	25	25	25
Moscow	3 months	24 11/16	24 11/16	24 11/16	24 11/16
Italian Bank Places	3 months	27·30	27·31¼	27·37½	27·37½
New York	60 days	48 13/16	48 13/16	48⅞	48⅞
Madrid and Spanish B. P.	3 months	25 1/16	25	25	24⅞
Lisbon	3 months	29	29⅛	28⅞	29
Oporto	3 months	29	29⅛	28⅞	29
Copenhagen	3 months	18·38	18·37	18·35	18·35
Christiania	3 months	18·38	18·37	18·35	18·35
Stockholm	3 months	18·41	18·40	18·35	18·35

OPEN MARKET DISCOUNT.

	Per cent.
Thirty and sixty day remitted bills	1½
Three months "	1½—1⅝
Four months "	1⅝
Six months "	1⅞
Three months fine inland bills	1¾
Four months "	2
Six months "	2¼

BANK AND DEPOSIT RATES.

	Per cent.
Bank of England minimum discount rate	3
" " short loan rates	—
Banker's rate on deposits	1½
Bill brokers' deposit rate (call)	1
" 7 and 14 days' notice	1¼
Current rates for 7 day loans	1
" " for call loans	

The Week's Stock Markets.

The general tendency of markets this week has been dull, business simply stagnating, and no improvement is looked for until the present account has dragged to an end. Complaints are heard on all sides of the utter indifference of the general public, the falling off in investment business being most pronounced. The abandonment of the naval manœuvres was viewed with perfect unconcern, and there have been no alarmist reports to disturb markets in the slightest degree.

Among Home Government securities Consols drooped from day to day, and touched 111 1/16, after which the price reacted a little. A sensational drop of about 11 in Bank of England stock was simply due to the fact that a parcel of stock was pressed for sale, and although the amount was not very large, the market, being such a narrow one, allowed the price to give way as stated. A greater part of the fall has, however, since been made up. Another notable move has been in Great Indian Peninsula railway stock, which rose about 9 on the chairman stating at the meeting that the Government intended acquiring the line.

Highest and Lowest this Year.		Last Carrying over Price.	BRITISH FUNDS, &c.	Closing Price.	Rise or Fall.
113⅛	109¼	—	Consols 2¾ p.c. (Money)...	111 3/16	— 1/16
113 1/16	109½	111⅝	Do. Account (July 1)	111 3/16	— ¼
106¼	101	105	2½ p.c. Stock red. 1905 ...	104¾	— ¼
363	341	—	Bank of England Stock...	350	—2½
117	111⅝	114	India 3½ p.c. Stk. red. 1931	112¾	— ½
109¼	103⅝	107	Do. 3 p.c. Stk. red. 1948	106½	— ⅓
96⅝	90	93	Do. 2½ p.c. Stk. red. 1926	92	—

Most of the business in the Home railway market has been in the stocks of the Continental lines. South Eastern deferred was rushed up to over 115, and then as suddenly collapsed, the "bull and bear" struggle going on as merrily as ever. Chatham issues also moved rather erratically, the much-talked-of official announcement still hanging fire. The Chatham directors have, however, taken advantage of the present state of affairs to launch the balance of their unissued debentures, but this had little or no effect on prices. Waterloo and City ordinary has lost a further eight or nine points, some delay in opening the line for traffic being feared, and rumour says the borrowing powers of the company are exhausted, so there seems a possibility of holders having to forego their interest for a time. The failure of the Great Northern and City undertaking was also somewhat of a damper to those interested in similar ventures. Great Central issues are all lower, despite the official announcement that the line will be open for coal traffic on July 25, and Metropolitan ordinary is weaker in sympathy. One of the firmest stocks in the whole list has been Hull and Barnsley, the traffic return showing a substantial increase. The Great Western "take" is again most melancholy reading, and the stock has fallen still more, but the other traffic statements were considered satisfactory, due allowance being made for the inflated figures caused by the Jubilee celebrations last year.

Highest and Lowest this Year.		Last Carrying over Price.	HOME RAILWAYS.	Closing Price.	Rise or Fall.
186	172½	177	Brighton Def.	176¾	— ¼
59¼	54⅜	57½	Caledonian Def.	57⅝	— ⅛
23½	18¼	20¾	Chatham Ordinary	22	—1
77½	62	67	Great Central Pref.	66	—1
24⅝	21¼	22¾	Do. Def.	22¼	— ½
124½	118	121	Great Eastern	121	— ⅜
61¼	50¾	55	Great Northern Def.	54⅞	— ¼
179⅛	163⅝	164¼	Great Western	165½	—1¼
54⅝	45¼	51½	Hull and Barnsley	53¼	+ ¾
149¼	145	145¾	Lanc. and Yorkshire	146	— ½
136⅛	127½	132	Metropolitan	130½	—1¼
31	26⅜	28¾	Metropolitan District	28¾	— ½
88¾	82⅛	85½	Midland Pref.	87	+ ½
95⅝	84½	88¼	Do. Def.	88¼	— ½
93¼	86¾	89½	North British Pref.	89¾	— ¼
47½	41¾	44⅜	Do. Def.	44½	— ⅜
181½	172¾	177¼	North Eastern	177¾	— ¾
205¼	196¼	198½	North Western	199½	— ⅛
117⅛	105½	113½	South Eastern Def.	113½	—1¼
98¾	87	93¾	South Western Def.	93	—1

In the market for United States railroad shares there was some inquiry during the earlier part of the week for Chesapeake and Ohio on amalgamation rumours, and Union Pacific on the prospects of a full dividend on the preferred. Other stocks have met with little support, the fall in wheat causing a weak tone to prevail in Wall-street, and a sharp break in Baltimore and Ohio shares, on the publication of the reorganisation scheme, led to a moderate decline in practically the whole of the active list. This does not apply to gold bonds, which have again been inquired for at higher prices.

Highest and Lowest this Year.		Last Carrying over Price.	CANADIAN AND U.S. RAILWAYS.	Closing Prices.	Rise or Fall.
14 1/16	10⅜	14	Atchison Shares	13½	—
35¼	23½	34⅜	Do. Pref.	34¼	+ ⅛
15⅝	11	14¾	Central Pacific	14	— ¼
105	85½	103⅜	Chic. Mil. & St. Paul	102⅝	—
14¼	10	13⅜	Denver Shares	13½	— ½
54¼	41½	52½	Do. Prefd.	52¼	— ½
16⅜	11¼	14⅜	Erie Shares	13¾	— ¼
44⅜	29½	38⅞	Do. Prefd.	36¾	— ⅜
110½	99	108½	Illinois Central	107	— ⅜
62½	45¼	57½	Louisville & Nashville	53⅞	— ¼
14½	9 1/16	12½	Missouri & Texas	11⅛	—
122¾	108½	120	New York Central	119½	+ ½
57¼	42⅞	55½	Norfolk & West. Prefd.	53⅜	—
72½	59	72	Northern Pacific Prefd.	71	+ ⅜
19½	13⅜	16⅜	Ontario Shares	15⅜	— ¼
62½	56¾	59½	Pennsylvania	59⅜	—
12½	7 1/16	10¼	Reading Shares	9⅝	— ⅜
34⅛	24¼	33½	Southern Prefd.	30¾	+ ⅜
37⅜	18½	20	Union Pacific	23½	— ¼
20¾	14½	20½	Wabash Prefd.	10½	— ¼
30¼	21	29¼	Do. Income Debs.	27½	— ¼
92¾	74	89	Canadian Pacific	86½	—1¾
79⅝	69⅝	79¼	Grand Trunk Guar.	70½	— ⅜
76⅜	57½	70½	Do. 1st Pref.	72½	— ⅜
58¾	37½	58	Do. 2nd Pref.	51½	—1¼
26¾	19¼	26½	Do. 3rd Pref.	22¼	—1½
107	101½	105½	Do. 4 p.c. Deb.	105⅜	— ¼

Canadian Pacific shares started the week by falling about 4, due to heavy sales by Liverpool firms, the traffic return being a great disappointment to every one, while the rumour of a further issue of preferential capital was again freely circulated. Buying orders coming to hand from Montreal put a little better complexion on things, and the old story of the war rate being nearly settled has again been trotted out. Grand Trunk emissions gave way on sales from the North, but afterwards advanced and more than wiped out the earlier losses.

Highest and Lowest this Year.		Last Carrying over Price.	FOREIGN BONDS.	Closing Price.	Rise or Fall.
94¼	84	90¼	Argentine 5 p.c. 1886......	90	− ¼
92⅞	81⅝	88¾	Do. 6 p.c. Funding	87	−1¾
76¾	64	71¾	Do. 5 p.c. B. Ay. Water	71	−1
61⅞	41⅛	54	Brazilian 4 p.c. 1889	53	− ⅛
69⅞	46	61⅛	Do. 5 p.c. 1895	60½	—
65	42¾	56	Do. 5 p.c. West Minas Ry..................	55	− ¾
108¾	105½	107½	Egyptian 4 p.c. Unified...	108	—
104¾	100½	103	Do. 3½ p.c. Pref. ...	103	—
103	99½	101½	French 3 p.c. Rente	102	+ ½
44⅞	34½	43½	Greek 4 p.c. Monopoly...	44	+ ½
93⁹⁄₁₆	88¾	92½	Italian 5 p.c. Rente	92¾	+ ⅜
100	87⅝	97¾	Mexican 6 p.c. 1888	98½	+ ½
20⅞	10	18¾	Portuguese 1 p.c.	18⅝	− ⅛
62¼	29⅝	36	Spanish 4 p.c.	33⅝	−³⁄₁₆
47	40	45½	Turkish 1 p.c. "B"	45⅝	− ⅝
26⅞	22¾	25¼	Do. 1 p.c. "C"	26¼	− ⅛
22⅞	20	21¾	Do. 1 p.c. "D"	22¹⁄₁₆	− ¹⁄₁₆
46⅞	40	45	Uruguay 3½ p.c. Bonds...	44½	− ½

If business has been on a small scale here, Paris operators have done still less, and apart from a sharp fall in Brazilian bonds during the earlier part of the week, most of which has since been made good, there has been little of interest happening. The Brazilian funding scheme has met with a good deal of adverse criticism, and that and a fall in the Rio exchange caused the earlier decline, but some Continental buying helped to put up prices again. Spanish 4 per cents. are weaker after a temporary rise; the latest advices from Madrid taking a less hopeful view of peace prospects, while vague rumours of the Queen Regent's proposed abdication were afloat. Further, the announcement that the coupon will only be paid in gold to foreigners was not much liked, and the price drooped a little more. Turkish groups have also lost ground, trouble in Albania being talked of, and the Ministerial crisis in Italy led to some selling of Italian Rente. Other changes are mostly in the downward direction, due to the weakness of the Paris Bourse on Wednesday, the general impression there now being that the *coulisse* will have ceased to exist by the end of the month. Argentine Government bonds gave way in face of the steady rise in the gold premium at Buenos Ayres.

Highest and Lowest this Year.		Last Carrying over Price.	FOREIGN RAILWAYS.	Closing Price.	Rise or Fall.
105½	99	105	Argentine Gt. West. 5 p.c. Pref. Stock..................	105	—
158½	134	140½	B. Ay. Gt. Southern Ord..	139	—
78⅝	65	73⅝	B. Ay. and Rosario Ord...	71½	− ½
12¼	10¼	10¼	B. Ay. Western Ord.......	10¼	—
87¾	73	81½	Central Argentine Ord....	79½	− ½
92	76	79	Cordoba and Rosario 6 p.c. Deb.	78	−1
95½	85½	90	Cord. Cent. 4 p.c. Deb. (Cent. Nth. Sec.)	90	—
61⅞	42	53½	Do. Income Deb. Stk. ...	50½	−2½
25½	16⅞	20¼	Mexican Ord. Stk.	20	—
83½	69½	75	Do. 8 p.c. 1st Pref.........	74½	−2½

All the leading Brazilian railway companies' stocks are lower than a week ago, in sympathy with the fall in Government bonds, and most of the other movements in foreign railways have been in an adverse direction. Cordoba Central (Central Northern) income stock fell sharply after the report appeared, but the latest price shows some recovery from the worst point touched.

In the Miscellaneous market the selling of all kinds of electric lighting companies' shares went on apace for several days, but there are now indications that holders do not intend throwing away any longer, and a slightly harder tendency is apparent. Apollinaris issues have given way still more, the principal cause of dissatisfaction with the report being the tiny amount placed to reserve. Ebbw Vale shares fell 1½, the report just out showing the disastrous results of the coal strike in South Wales, as far as this company is concerned. Cycle shares keep very weak, and there are few buyers for this class of security just now; but a good business has again been transacted in brewery companies' issues. Marshall and Snelgrove debentures have risen steadily, and rises are also marked in Lipton debenture, London Tramways 4½ per cent. "B" debenture (which is 6 higher) and Brunner, Mond. On the other hand Trafford Park debentures have fallen 7, Brentford Gas 10, and Welsbach 3½.

Home railway stocks closed weak, due to realisations in view of the settlement which begins on Monday, and Grank Trunk stocks were pressed for sale, the market looking for a big decrease in the traffic this week. United States railroad shares left off very firm, on both home and Wall-street buying, especially Atchison, New York Central, Northern Pacific, and Southern. Foreign Government bonds were also well supported at the last, notably Brazilian and Italian. In the mining section, there was a slight rally in De Beers diamond shares, but the Mount Lyell group closed flat at about the worst.

Mining and Finance Companies.

The South African market has again presented a lifeless appearance, and the interruption of cable communication with the Cape did not tend to improve matters. A batch of dividend announcements hardly attracted attention, that of the Henry Nourse Company being the only one to cause any inquiry for shares, and changes are again of the usual unimportant type; but a reported "mud-rush" in the mine led to a little selling of De Beers. Among Western Australian ventures some of the higher-priced shares met with support, notably Golden Horse Shoe, a scarcity of stock at the settlement being expected. London and Globe shares have been a weak market, the report being looked for with a certain amount of apprehension. Among Indian companies, Mysore and Nundydroog advanced on the satisfactory dividends, and other kindred concerns were firm. The Mount Lyell group has again exhibited great weakness, and the directors' assurance that "everything is all right at the mine" did not prevent many holders taking fright and throwing their shares on the market.

NEXT WEEK'S MEETINGS.

Monday, June 27.

Moabund Tea Company ... ... 138, Leadenhall-street, 2.30 p.m.
Solar del Carmen Nitrate ... ... Winchester House, noon.
Asbestos and Asbestic ... ... Cannon-street Hotel, 3 p.m.
Puerto Cabello and Valencia Railway ... ... 60, New Broad-street, 2.30 p.m.
La Guaira and Caracas Railway ... 60, New Broad-street, 2 p.m.

Tuesday, June 28.

Nahor Rani Tea ... ... 138, Leadenhall-street, noon.
Ohlsson's Cape Breweries ... ... Winchester House, 3 p.m.
South African Exploring ... ... 15, Copthall-avenue, 1 p.m.
Cordoba Central Railway Company Winchester House, noon.
Electric and General Investment ... Winchester House, 3 p.m.
John Brown & Co. ... ... Savile-street, East Sheffield, noon.

Wednesday, June 29.

Brooke, Bond, & Co. ... ... Winchester House, noon.
East Indian Railway... ... ... Cannon-street Hotel, noon.
Imperial Ottoman Bank ... ... Winchester House, 1 p.m.
United States Brewing ... ... Winchester House, 11 a.m.
New Options Company ... ... 6, Queen-street-place, noon.
Amazon Steam Navigation ... ... Cannon-street Hotel, noon.

Thursday, June 30.

Tamplin & Son's Brewery ... ... Phœnix Brewery, Brighton, 3 p.m.
Marine Insurance ... ... 29, Old Broad-street, 1 p.m.
Canada Company ... ... 1, East India-avenue, 1.30 p.m.
Rickmansworth and Uxbridge Water 42, Poultry, 12.30.
Tolmia Mining ... ... Winchester House, 12.30 p.m.
Transvaal Gold Mining Estates ... Cannon-street Hotel, 3.30 p.m.
Western Mortgage and Investment Institute of Chartered Accountants, Moorgate-place, E.C.

Messrs. J. Lewens and Hauser Brothers have removed to 5, Great Tower-street, E.C.

Prices of Mine and Mining Finance Companies' Shares.

Shares £1 each, except where otherwise stated.

AUSTRALIAN.

Making-Up Price, June 8.	Name	Closing Price.	Rise or Fall.	Making-Up Price, June 8.	Name	Closing Price.	Rise or Fall.
1 1/16	Aladdin	1⅜		¾	Hannan's Star	¾	
3⅜	Associated	3 5/16		6⅝	Ivanhoe, New	6⅝	− ⅛
5/	Do. Southern	¼		7/16	KalgurliMt.&IronKing, 18/	7/16	− ⅛
1	Brownhill Extended	1		5⅞	Kalgurli	5⅞	
1 1/16	Burbank's Birthday	1⅛	+ ⅛	2 1/16	Lady Shenton	2 1/16	+ ⅛
⅛	Central Boulder	⅛	− 1/16	9 1/16	Lake View Cons.	9⅛	− 1/16
6/	Chaffers, 4/	5/6	− /6	5/16	Do. Extended	5/16	
11/16	Colonial Finance, 15/	½ dis.		1	Do. South	1	
¾	Crœsus S. United	¾		1 1/16	London & Globe Finance	23/	− /9
¼	E. Murchison	¼		13/16	London&W.A.Exploration	¾	
4/9	Golden Arrow 19/	3/6	− 1/6	5/16	Do. Investment	5/16	
20 1/16	Golden Horseshoe	20⅛	+ ⅛	½	Mainland Consols	5/16	
⅝	Golden Link	11/16		⅝	North Boulder, 10/	⅝	
18/6	Great Boulder, 2/	17/6		1⅛	North Kalgurli	1⅛	+ 1/16
1 1/16	Do. Main Reef, 10/	1⅛	− 1/16	11/16	Northern Territories	⅝	+ 1/16
3⅛	Do. Perseverance	2⅞	− 1/16	2⅛	Peak Hill	2⅛	+ ⅛
⅝	Do. South	⅝		2⅛	South Kalgurli	2 1/16	− ⅛
3	Hainault	3	− ⅛	1 1/16	W. A. Goldfields	1 1/16	− ⅛
11/16	Hampton Plains	7/16	− ⅛	¾	W. A. Joint Stock	11/16	
8⅞	Hannan's Brownhill	8⅞	+ ⅛	2/	W. A. Market Trust	2/	
2⅛	Hannan's Oroya	1 5/16		¾	W. A. Loan&General Fin.	11/16	
5/16	Do. Proprietary	10/6	− 1/	1 1/16	White Feather	5/16	

SOUTH AFRICAN.

Making-Up Price, June 8.	Name	Closing Price.	Rise or Fall.	Making-Up Price, June 8.	Name	Closing Price.	Rise or Fall.
5½	Angelo	5 5/16	+ 1/16	2/	Lisbon-Berlyn	1/9	
1	Aurora West	1	+ 1/16	2 1/16	May Consolidated	2⅛	− 1/16
1	Bantjes	11/16		3 5/16	Meyer and Charlton	3⅜	
9/	Barrett, 10/	8/6	− /6	3⅜	Modderfontein	3⅜	
4⅜	Bonanza	4 5/16	+ 1/16	11/16	New Bultfontein	11/16	
5/6	Buffelsdoorn	5/16		3⅞	New Primrose	3⅞	
5 1/16	City and Suburban, £4	5⅛	+ ⅛	1⅛	Nigel, 15/	1 3/16	+ 1/16
2⅜	Comet (New)	2 5/16			Nigel Deep	11/16	
3⅛	Con. Deep Level	3		¾	North Randfontein	11/16	− 1/16
11⅛	Crown Deep	11⅛	− ⅛	5	Nourse Deep	4⅞	− ⅛
13	Crown Reef	13⅛	+ ⅛	1½	Porges-Randfontein	1½	
27⅛	De Beers, £5	26⅝	− ½	29⅝	Rand Mines	29⅝	+ 1/16
3 5/16	Driefontein	3 5/16		1⅛	Randfontein	1 1/16	
6⅞	Durban Roodepoort	6⅞	− 1/16	1 5/16	Rietfontein	1 5/16	+ 1/16
3 1/16	Do. Deep	3 1/16		9	Robinson Deep	9⅛	
4 5/16	East Rand	4⅜	+ 1/16	8	Do. Gold, £5	8	− ⅛
24⅜	Ferreira	24⅜		⅞	Do. Randfontein	⅞	
7⅞	Geldenhuis Deep	7⅞	− ⅛	1½	Roodepoort Central Deep	1½	
5⅜	Do. Estate	5⅜		6⅛	Rose Deep	6⅛	
⅞	George Goch	15/16		3 1/16	Salisbury	3 1/16	
2 1/16	Ginsberg	2⅛	+ ⅛	1½	Sheba	1½	− ⅛
1⅜	Glencairn	1 5/16	+ 1/16	3⅝	Simmer and Jack, £5	3⅝	+ ⅛
8⅞	Goldfields Deep	8⅞		2⅛	Transvaal Gold	2⅛	− 1/16
8 1/16	Griqualand West	8⅛		3⅜	Treasury	3 5/16	+ 1/16
9 1/16	Henry Nourse	9⅝	+ ½	3⅛	United Roodepoort	3⅛	
7 1/16	Heriot	7⅛	+ ⅛	1⅛	Van Ryn	1 1/16	− ⅛
7⅜	Jagersfontein	7⅜		6 1/16	Village Main Reef	6 1/16	− ⅛
9⅜	Jubilee	9⅜		1⅛	Vogelstruis	1⅛	
5	Jumpers	5		⅜	Do. Deep	⅜	
2⅞	Kleinfontein	2⅞		10	Wemmer	10⅛	+ ⅛
3⅜	Knight's	3⅜		1½	West Rand	1½	
2⅛	Lancaster	2⅛		5 5/16	Wolhuter, £4	5⅜	+ 1/16
3 1/16	Langlaagte Estate	3		2⅛	Worcester	2⅛	

LAND EXPLORATION AND RHODESIAN.

Making-Up Price, June 8.	Name	Closing Price.	Rise or Fall.	Making-Up Price, June 8.	Name	Closing Price.	Rise or Fall.
2 1/16	Anglo-French Ex.	2⅛		⅞	Mashonaland Central	13/16	+ 1/16
2⅛	Barnato Consolidated	1⅞	− 1/16	5⅞	Matabele Gold Reefs	5⅝	− ⅛
⅞	Bechuanaland Ex.	⅞		2⅝	Mozambique	2½	− 1/16
2⅞	Chartered B.S.A.	2 13/16	− 1/16	1½	Oceana Consolidated	1½	
⅞	Clark's Cons.	⅞		1 5/16	Rhodesia, Ltd.	1 3/16	− ⅛
⅞	Colenbrander	13/16		4⅛	Do. Exploration	4	
4 3/16	Cons. Goldfields	4 3/16		11/16	Do. Goldfields	11/16	− 1/16
2 1/16	Do. Pref.	21/		3⅝	S. A. Gold Trust	3⅝	− 1/16
1⅛	Exploration	1⅛		11/16	Tati Concessions	11/16	
2⅛	Geelong	2⅛		⅝	Transvaal Development	⅝	
5/16	Henderson's Est.	⅜		⅝	United Rhodesia	5/16	− 1/16
1⅛	Johannesburg Con. In.	1⅛	+ ⅛	1⅜	Willoughby	1 5/16	
11/16	Do. Water	11/16	− 1/16	⅞	Zambesia Explor.	13/16	− 1/16
1⅜	Mashonaland Agency	1 3/16					

MISCELLANEOUS.

Making-Up Price, June 8.	Name	Closing Price.	Rise or Fall.	Making-Up Price, June 8.	Name	Closing Price.	Rise or Fall.
1	Alamillos, £2	1		¼	Mount Lyell, South	5/16	
4⅞	Anaconda, $25	5	+ 1/16	4 1/16	Mount Morgan, 17s. 6d.	4 1/16	
6/3	Balaghât, fully paid	9/		5⅝	Mysore, 10s.	5⅝	+ 1/16
12/	Brilliant, £2	10/	− 2/	8/	Mysore Goldfields	9/	
2⅛	Do. St. George's	2⅛		5/6	Do. Reefs, 17/	6/	
9/6	British Broken Hill	8/9		3/9	Do. West	6/	
2⅛	Broken Hill Proprietary	2 1/16		2/9	Do. Wynaad	4/6	
3	Do. Block 10	3		2⅜	Namaqua, £2	2⅜	
4⅜	Cape Copper, £2	4⅜	+ 1/16	3⅞	Nundydroog	4	+ 1/16
4⅞	Champion Reef, 10s.	4⅞	− 1/16	3 1/16	Ooregum	3 1/16	
2⅞	Copiapo, £2	2⅞		3 1/16	Do. Pref.	3⅛	
2⅝	Coromandel	2⅝		26⅛	Rio Tinto £5	25⅝	− 1/16
15/	Day Dawn Block	15/		6	Do. Pref. £5	6 1/16	+ 1/16
2 1/16	Frontino & Bolivia	2⅝	− ⅛	1	St. John del Rey	20/	
1 1/16	Hall Mines	1⅛	+ 1/16	8/9	Taitipu	1/16	− 1/16
2⅞	Libiola, £5	2	− ⅛	6⅛	Tharsis, £2	6⅛	
7⅞	Linares, £3	7⅜	− ⅛	1⅛	Tolima "A," £5	2	
3⅞	Mason & Barry, £3	3⅞		4⅜	Waihi	4 1/16	+ 1/16
4⅜	Mountain Copper, £5	4⅜	− ⅛	1⅞	Waitekauri	1⅞	− ⅛
10⅛	Mount Lyell, £3	8⅞	− ⅛	16/3	Woodstock (N.Z.)	⅞	− 1/16
2⅛	Mount Lyell, North	1⅞	− ⅛				

The coupons falling due on July 1, 1897, of the Greek 5 per cent. loans of 1881 and 1884 should be presented at the office of Messrs. C. J. Hambro & Son for payment of 32 per cent. in gold of their face value, in accordance with Article 2 of the International Greek Law of Control. The coupons falling due on July 1, 1897, of the Greek 4 per cent. Monopoly loan of 1887 should be presented at the office of Messrs. C. J. Hambro & Son for payment of 43 per cent. in gold of their face value, in accordance with Article 2 of the International Greek Law of Control. Messrs. C. J. Hambro & Son also inform the holders of the scrip of the Greek 5 per cent. funding loan of 1893 that it should be presented for payment of 40 per cent. in gold of the interest due July 1, 1898, in accordance with Article 2 of the International Greek Law of Control.

TRAMWAY AND OMNIBUS RECEIPTS.

HOME.

Name.	Period.	Ending.	Amount.	Increase or Decrease on 1897.	Weeks or Months.	Aggregate to Date. Amount.	Aggregate to Date. Inc. or Dec. on 1897.
			£	£		£	£
Aberdeen District	Week	June 18	523	+45	—	—	—
Belfast Street	"	" 18	2,356	+227	—	—	—
Birmingham and Aston	"	" 18	452	+14	—	—	—
Birmingham and Midland	"	" 18	646	+52	—	—	—
Birmingham City	"	" 18	3,744	+203	—	—	—
Birmingham General	"	" 18	917	+72	—	—	—
Blessington and Poulaphouca	"	" 19	16	+5	24	296	+24
Bristol Tramways and Carriage	"	" 17	2,835	+390	—	—	—
Burnley and District	"	" 18	309	nil	—	—	—
Bury, Rochdale, and Oldham	"	" 18	800	−165	—	—	—
Croydon	"	" 18	374	−55	—	—	+1,208
Dublin and Blessington	"	" 19	129	+14	24	2,532	+23
Dublin and Lucan	"	" 18	68	−8	25	1,280	−386
Dublin United	"	" 17	3,461	+24	—	69,389	+3,369
Dudley and Stourbridge	"	" 18	170	+11	25	4,163	+142
Edinburgh and District	"	" 18	2,674	+272	24	56,484	+5,382
Edinburgh Street	"	" 18	794	+167	24	15,172	+1,827
Gateshead and District	Month	May	935	+66	—	—	—
Glasgow	Week	June 18	2,957	+20	—	—	—
Harrow-road and Paddington	"	" 17	290	+4	—	—	—
Lea Bridge and Leyton	"	" 18	850	+125	—	—	—
London, Deptford, and Greenwich	"	" 18	614	−40	—	13,871	+443
London General Omnibus	"	" 18	23,509	−4,055	—	—	—
London Road Car	"	" 18	7,309	−2,039	†	154,687	+2,819
London Southern	"	" 18	613	+35	—	—	—
North Staffordshire	"	" 18	389	−30	—	9,508	−164
Provincial	"	" 18	2,543	−201	—	—	—
Rossendale Valley	"	" 17	176	−26	—	—	—
Southampton	"	" 18	434	+1	—	—	—
South London	"	" 18	1,818	−185	†	40,282	+877
South Staffordshire	"	" 17	608	+17	24	14,481	−204
Sunderland	"	" 17	294	−37	—	—	—
Swansea	"	" 17	281	−8	—	—	—
Tramways Union	Month	May	12,833	+1,655	5	52,333	+6,190
Wigan and District	Week	June 18	272	+11‡	—	—	
Woolwich and South East London	"	" 18	419	+21	†	8,395	+326

† From January 1. ‡ Strike in 1897.

FOREIGN.

Name.	Period.	Ending.	Amount.	Increase or Decrease on 1897.	Weeks or Months.	Aggregate to Date. Amount.	Aggregate to Date. Inc. or Dec. on 1897.
			£	£		£	£
Anglo-Argentine	Week	May 27	4,459	+775	*	91,719	+20,019
Barcelona	"	June 18	1,213	−434	—	27,397	−4,832
Barcelona, Ensanche y Gracia	"	" 18	239	−22	—	5,403	−39
Bordeaux	"	" 17	2,373	−163	—	50,388	−2,392
Brazilian Street	Month	April (m	lr46,055	+3,871	—	—	—
British Columbia Electric	"	"	$30,729	+$10493	‡	$305,154	—
Do. net	"	"	$10,392	+$4,958	‡	$97,402	—
Buenos Ayres and Belgrano	"	April	5,090	+3,645	*	19,472	+3,36
Buenos Ayres Grand National	Week	May 28	$23,219	+$2,935	†	—	+$27,456
Buenos Ayres New	Month	March	$70,624	−$864	—	$201,851	−$7,119
Calais	Week	June 18	135	−56	—	—	—
Calcutta	"	" 18	1,240	−127	—	—	—
C'rth'g'na&Herrerias	Month	May	3,609	+173	—	22,418	+1,184
Gothenburg	Week	June 15	384	+33	—	—	—
Lynn and Boston	Month	April	$105,396	+$2,087	7	$777,825	+$30000
Do. net	"	"	$40,418	+$1,912	7	$256,801	+$5,064
Twin City Rapid	"	"	$165,803	+$10411	4	$653,223	+$43912
Do. Net	"	"	$82,679	+$9,356	4	$317,429	+$42582

* From January 1. † From April 1, 1898. ‡ From April 15, 1897. § From October 1, 1897.

The Southern Pacific Company will, after July 1 next, against delivery to it at its office in New York of dividend warrants No. 34, appertaining to certificates of stock of the Central Pacific Railroad Company, pay to the persons presenting the same one-half of 1 per cent. of the par value of the stock represented by such certificates respectively.

John Moit & Son, Limited, have taken more commodious offices at Nos. 9 and 10, Great Tower-street, London, E.C.

The numbers are announced of four bonds of £100 each of the Pernambuco Water Company, for redemption on and after July 1, at the offices of Messrs. Knowles & Foster, 48, Moorgate-street, E.C.

Messrs. J. S. Morgan & Co. announce that the coupons due on July 1 next on the bonds issued of the Argentine Government 6 per cent. funding loan of 1891 will be paid at the rate of 5 per cent. on and after that date.

Messrs. Stern Brothers will pay the coupon due on July 1 on the Argentine 3½ per cent. external sterling, 1889, bonds at the rate of 60 per cent. of their nominal value.

Coupon No. 23, due on July 1, on the bonds of the Nicaraguan Railways 6 per cent. loan of 1886, will be paid on and after that date at the City Bank, Limited, Threadneedle-street, E.C., at the reduced rate of 4 per cent. per annum, according to the arrangement of September 17, 1895.

The Bank of New Zealand notifies that the nineteenth annual drawing of debentures, to be paid off on September 30, of the Otago Harbour Board 6 per cent. loan for £350,000 will take place on June 27.

The Union Bank of Australia, Limited, notify that they are prepared to pay, on and after 5th proximo, the half-year's interest due on the debentures of the Canterbury (N. Z.) Church Property Trustees' loan, £50,000.

The Colonial Bank of Australasia, Limited, Melbourne, notifies that the coupons due on July 1 next on loans Nos. 2 and 3 of the Town of Brunswick (near Melbourne), will be paid by its London agents, the London Joint Stock Bank, Limited, 5, Princes-street, E.C.

ENGLISH RAILWAYS.

Div. for half years. 1896	1896	1897	1897	Last Balance forward.	Amt. to pay 1 p.c. on Ord. for ½ yr.	Name.	Date.	Gross Traffic for week: Amt.	Inc. or dec. on 1897.	Inc. or dec. on 1896.	No. of weeks.	Gross Traffic for half-year to date: Amt.	Inc. or dec. on 1897.	Inc. or dec. on 1896.	Mileage.	Inc. on 1897.	Working	Prior Charges last ½ year.	Prop. add Cap. Exp. this ½ year.
				£	£												%	£	£
10	10	10	10	2,707	5,094	Barry	J'ne 18	3,094	−6,135	−4,489	25	157,391	−62,058	†−30,525	31	—	48·89	60,665	316,853
nil	nil	nil	nil	—	—	Brecon and Merthyr	,, 19	919	−897	−697	25	33,366	†−3,450	−6,953	61	—	—	—	—
nil	nil	nil	nil	3,979	4,749	Cambrian	,, 19	5,775	+287	+477	*	121,003	+3,420	—	250	—	60·96	63,148	40,000
1⅝	1½	2	1½	1,310	3,150	City and South London	,, 19	974	−119	+138	25	25,532	+224	+2,354	3¼	—	56·67	5,557	124,000
	2	1½	2	7,895	13,210	Furness	,, 19	10,005	+877	+1,538	*	219,715	+7,333	—	139	—	49·88	97,423	20,910
1	1¼	½	1	2,207	27,470	Great Cent. (late M., S., & L.)	,, 19	55,960	+4,751	+4,996	24	1,106,509	+34,889	+70,881	357½	—	57·17	627,386	1,200,000
1½	4¾	2	5	51,283	62,865	Great Eastern	,, 19	86,133	+2,070	+5,129	24	1,959,783	+51,931	+263208	1,158¾	2	55·35	860,138	257,000
3	5¾	3	5	13,094	102,496	Great Northern	,, 19	98,066	+4,128	+11,398	25	2,374,413	+76,825	+192488	1,073	10	61·36	641,485	750,000
4½	7½	4¾	7½	31,350	121,981	Great Western	,, 19	186,930	−24,820	+3,380	24	4,935,610	−65,020	+168040	2,582	21	51·44	1,486,272	800,000
nil	2	nil	1½	8,951	16,487	Hull and Barnsley	,, 19	9,748	+2,765	+3,109	24	172,958	+14,190	+26,422	73	—	58·21	70,290	58,920
5	5½	5	5½	21,495	83,704	Lancashire and Yorkshire	,, 19	97,324	+1,322	+3,878	24	2,079,867	+75,054	+86,914	555½	25	56·70	674,745	451,976
4¼	8	4½	8½	26,243	43,049	Lon., Brighton, & S. Coast	,, 18	54,004	−60	+4,293	25	1,248,904	+34,821	+60,171	476¾	—	50·20	407,042	240,735
nil	nil	nil	nil	72,294	56,206	London, Chatham, & Dover	,, 19	31,025	−941	+380	24	679,685	+13,510	+31,324	185¾	—	50·65	367,873	nil
6½	8	6½	7½	89,335	204,068	London and North Western	,, 19	245,086	−14,769	+17,910	24	5,586,918	+117669	+316005	1,911¼	—	56·92	1,404,534	600,000
5	8½	8½	8½	93,038	59,367	London and South Western	,, 19	99,303	−3,586	+1,224	24	1,738,567	+42,051	+110016	941	—	51·75	513,740	380,000
2¾	6	2½	6½	14,592	6,691	Lon., Tilbury, & Southend	,, 19	6,708	−126	−3	25	131,358	+5,106	+17,411	81	—	52·57	39,590	15,000
3¼	3¾	3¾	3¾	17,133	26,409	Metropolitan	,, 19	18,436	−175	+3,049	*	399,542	+8,329	—	64	—	43·63	148,047	254,000
nil	nil	nil	nil	4,006	11,250	Metropolitan District	,, 19	8,220	−2,770†	+482	24	202,994	+3,521†	—	13	—	48·70	119,663	38,450
5	7	5¼	6½	38,143	174,582	Midland	,, 19	109,199	+12,343	+33,173	25	4,668,907	+128907	+417805	1,354¼	15¼	57·59	1,216,582	690,000
5¾	7½	5¾	7	22,374	138,189	North Eastern	,, 18	161,486	+21,198	+11,836	24	3,534,235	+74,763	+249911	1,597¾	—	58·82	795,077	436,904
7⅝	7⅝	7⅝	7¼	7,061	10,102	North London	,, 19	8,095	−743	+507	24	225,159	−1,960	—	12	—	50·90	49,973	7,600
4	3	4	4½	4,745	16,150	North Staffordshire	,, 19	15,017	+941	−736	25	388,588	+4,398	+19,456	312	—	55·27	118,142	19,605
10	10	11	10	1,640	3,004	Rhymney	,, 18	1,585	−3,749	−3,472	25	93,619	−20,679	−21,209	71	—	49·68	29,049	16,700
	6⅜	3½	6½	4,054	30,213	South Eastern	,, 18	54,109	+456	+2,848	*	1,078,083	+48,661	—	448	—	51·88	380,763	250,000
3½	3½	3½	3½	2,315	25,961	Taff Vale	,, 18	6,643	−7,822	−7,918	25	282,251	−105834	−84,304	121	—	54·90	94,800	92,000

* From January 1. † Includes extra traffic preceding Jubilee week.

SCOTCH RAILWAYS.

Div. for half years. 1896	1896	1897	1897	Last Balance forward.	Amt. to pay 1 p.c. on Ord. for ½ yr.	Name.	Date.	Gross Traffic for week: Amt.	Inc. or dec. on 1897.	Inc. or dec. on 1896.	No. of weeks.	Gross Traffic for half-year to date: Amt.	Inc. or dec. on 1897.	Inc. or dec. on 1896.	Mileage.	Inc. on 1897.	Working	Prior Charges last ½ year.	Prop. add Cap. Exp. this ½ year.
5	5	5¾	5	9,544	78,066	Caledonian	June 19	77,286	+ 2,022	+ 6,348	20	1,483,151	+ 36,279	—	851½	5	50·38	588,248	441,477
5	5½	5	5	7,364	24,639	Glasgow and South-Western	,, 18	30,950	+ 1,023	+ 1,350	20	573,517	+ 19,343	—	393½	—	54·69	221,663	196,145
3¼	3½	3½	—	1,291	4,600	Great North of Scotland	,, 18	8,911	+ 196	− 25	20	165,451	+ 799	+ 7,114	331	15¾	52·03	92,178	60,000
	nil		—	10,477	12,820	Highland	,, 19	10,571	+ 99	+ 489	16	147,031	+ 2,390	—	470½	27¾	58·63	78,976	[illegible]
	1½	1	1½	819	45,819	North British	,, 19	77,871	+ 4,410	+ 6,680	20	1,436,369	+ 46,004	—	1,230	23	48·62	944,809	40,800

IRISH RAILWAYS.

Div. for half years. 1896	1896	1897	1897	Last Balance forward.	Amt. to pay 1 p.c. on Ord. for ½ yr.	Name.	Date.	Gross Traffic for week: Amt.	Inc. or dec. on 1897.	Inc. or dec. on 1896.	No. of weeks.	Gross Traffic for half-year to date: Amt.	Inc. or dec. on 1897.	Inc. or dec. on 1896.	Mileage.	Inc. on 1897.	Working	Prior Charges last ½ year.	Prop. add Cap. Exp. this ½ year.
6½	6½	6½	—	5,466	1,700	Belfast and County Down	June 17	2,763	+ 164	− 1,347	*	54,030	− 259	—	76½	—	55·58	17,690	10,000
5½	6½	5½	—	—	4,284	Belfast and Northern Counties	,, 10	5,058	− 590	− 240	*	119,978	+ 3,640	—	249	—	—	—	—
	3	2	—	1,418	1,200	Cork, Bandon, and S. Coast†	,, 18	1,500	− 92	− 292	*	31,015	− 2,760	—	103	—	54·82	14,436	5,450
	6½	6½	6½	38,776	17,816	Great Northern	,, 17	16,685	− 71	+ 1,124	24	358,048	+ 10,691	+ 22,509	528	—	50·15	88,068	22,000
	5½	5½	5½	30,339	24,855	Great Southern and Western	,, 3	—	—	—	not	received	—	—	603	13	51·45	72,600	46,380
	4	4	4½	11,379	11,850	Midland Great Western	,, 17	12,960	+ 766	+ 658	24	244,570	+ 7,858	− 1,333	538	—	50·31	83,129	7,800
nil	ni	nil	nil	220	2,822	Waterford and Central	,, 17	738	− 60	− 78	*	—	—	—	59½	—	53·24	6,858	1,500
nil	n	nil	nil	1,936	2,987	Waterford, Limerick & W.	,, 17	4,643	− 614	− 130	*	—	—	—	350½	—	57·83	42,617	7,075

* From January 1. † Seventeen weeks' strike.

RAILWAY TRAFFIC RETURNS.

Algeciras (Gibraltar) Railway.—Traffic for week ended June 12, Ps. 25,103; increase, Ps. 658. Aggregate from July 1, Ps. 1,048,807; increase, Ps. 77,757.

West Flanders Railway.—Gross receipts for week ending June 19, £2,072; increase, £37. Total from January 1, £50,340; increase, £2,106.

Quebec Central Railway.—Traffic receipts for fourth week of May, $16,386; increase, $3,330. Aggregate from January 1, $150,442, decrease, $12,186.

Villa Maria and Rufino Railway.—Traffic for week ending June 18, £335; increase, £174. Aggregate from January 1, £8,442; increase, £1,610.

Bengal Central Railway.—Traffic receipts for week ending May 28, Rs. 25,982; increase, Rs. 8,585. Aggregate from January 1, Rs. 4,44,719; increase, Rs. 76,157.

Delhi Umballa Kalka Railway.—Receipts for week ended June 18, Rs. 26,400; increase, Rs. 500. Aggregate from January 1, Rs. 8,10,700; increase Rs. 1,79,100.

Alcoy and Gandia Railway and Harbour Company.—Traffic for week, June 18, Ps. 11,200; decrease Ps. 3,800. Aggregate from January 1, Ps. 214,400; decrease, Ps. 10,570.

Western of Santa Fe Railways.—Gross receipts for week ending June 18, $12,103; decrease, $1,287.

Burma Railways.—Traffic receipts for week ending May 21, Rs. 1,67,879; decrease Rs. 13,439. Aggregate from January 1, Rs. 42,14,964; decrease, Rs. 21,526.

Cleator and Workington.—Gross receipts for the week ending June 18 amounted to £1,158, an increase of £80. Total receipts from January 1, £25,102, a decrease of £368.

Cockermouth and Keswick Railway.—Receipts for the week ending June 18, £1,044; increase, £116. Aggregate from January 1, £21,008; increase, £2,019.

MINING RETURNS.

St. John Del Rey.—Gold produce, June 1 to 20, £6,900; yield per ton, ·86 of an ounce troy.

Menzies Alpha Leases.—44 tons crushed, yielding 228 oz.

Wassau (Gold Coast) Mining Company, Limited.—May return:—445 oz. gold, from 515 tons ore. April return:—Ore crushed, 530 tons, producing 599¼ oz. bar gold, which gave 622 oz. standard gold.

Goldfields of Surinam.—Result of preliminary washing—214 oz. of gold.

Weld Hercules.—Tons crushed, 233; produced 240 oz. of gold; tailings, 3 dwt. per ton.

Great Boulder.—Shipped 3,076 oz. gold; estimated value £12,611.

British Gold Mines of Mexico.—Crushed during May, 680 tons yielding $5,750 U.S.A. Profit $1,480 U.S.A., and, in addition, there has been shipped 33 tons of rich silver lead ore.

Associated Gold Mines of Western Australia.—Ore crushed 2,300 tons, yielding 1,838 oz.

North Boulder.—366 oz. gold from 390 tons crushed.

New Queen Gold Mining Company.—Results for past fortnight, 390 tons crushed, yielding 210 oz. gold.

Fairview.—450 tons crushed during twenty days, yielding $5,000.

Crescent.—500 tons crushed, yielding 85 oz.

Melbourne Democrat.—152 oz. gold from 290 tons ore crushed.

Anglo-Mexican.—Crushed 1,860 tons, $27,550 (U. S. gold); 1,165 tons treated by cyanide $20,650 (U. S. gold).

Florence.—Clean up yielded 131 oz. gold.

Day Dawn P. C.—595 tons crushed, yielding 691 oz.

Mikado.—Clean up for May produced 169 oz. from 536 tons of ore.

Menzies "Crusoe."—80 tons crushed yielded 184 oz.

Frank Smith Diamond Mines.—3,650 loads washed, producing 231 carats.

Great Boulder Proprietary Gold Mines.—Returns for fortnight ended June 20:—Tons of ore crushed, 1,440; yield of gold, 3,005 oz.

Otto's Kopje Diamond Mines.—6,745 loads washed; 169 carats of diamonds won.

Ouro Preto Gold Mines of Brazil.—May return:—6,293 tons of ore produced 1,651 oz. of gold.

Victoria (Charters Towers).—290 tons crushed yielded 466 oz. gold.

Premier.—472 tons crushed for 516 oz.

Victory (Charters Towers).—Crushed 115 tons for 299 oz.

Red Hill (W. A.) Syndicate.—5 cwts. cleaned up; result 550 oz.

Mysore West and Wynaad.—1,500 tons crushed yielded 381 oz.

New Options Company.—Big Gun, 43 ton 86 oz.; Extended, 15 tons 18 oz.; Cannon, 30 tons 26 oz.

Pahang Corporation.—Jeram Lumpong Mill, 1,550 tons of stone crushed, producing 74 tons of black tin; Jeram Batang Mill, 840 tons of stone crushed, producing 12 tons of black tin.

Peak Hill Goldfield.—As the result of treating by battery amalgamation only, 346 tons of kaolin and quartz ore in their natural proportions, 1,258 oz. of smelted gold have been yielded.

Moodie's.—980 tons crushed yielded 615 oz.

Moanataiari.—Crushed 974 tons. Yield over the plates 290 oz. value £794. Concentrates 21 tons value £79.

Mount Zeehan.—50 tons of silver lead ore shipped, containing about 30 tons of lead, and 4,500 oz. of silver.

Zeehan-Montana.—165 tons of silver lead ore shipped, containing about 99 tons of lead, and 14,850 oz. of silver.

The Bank of New Zealand notifies that the twentieth annual drawing of the bonds of the Auckland Harbour 6 per cent. loan of £150,000 will take place at its offices on July 6, and that the bonds then drawn (the numbers of which will be duly advertised) will be paid by it on presentation on January 10, 1899, on which date interest thereon will cease to accrue. The bonds must be left three clear days for examination before payment.

In consequence of the rebuilding of the premises, the offices of the Colonial Bank will, on the 20th inst., be removed to temporary premises at 118 Bishopsgate-street Within, E.C.

INDIAN AND CEYLON TEA COMPANIES.

Acres Planted.	Crop, 1897.	Paid up Capital.	Share.	Paid up.	Name.	Dividends. 1894.	1895.	1896.	1897.	Price.	Yield.	Reserve.	Balance Forward.	Working Capital.	Mortgages, Debs. or Pref. Capital not otherwise stated.
	lb.	£	£	£	INDIAN COMPANIES.							£	£	£	£
11,240	3,128,000	120,000	10	3	Amalgamated Estates	—	*	10	‡5	3½	9	10,000	16,500	D52,950	—
		400,000	10	10	Do. Pref.	—	*	5	5	9¼xd	5¼				
10,223	3,560,000	187,160	20	20	Assam	20	20	20	17½	59	6	55,000	1,730	D11,350	—
6,150	3,278,000	142,500	10	10	Assam Frontier	3	6	6	nil	—	—	—	286	20,000	12,500
		142,500	10	10	Do. Pref.	6	6	6	4	10	4				
2,087	839,000	66,745	5	5	Attaree Khat	12	12	8	5	5	5	3,790	4,820	7,770	—
1,633	583,000	78,170	10	10	Borelli	4	4	5	4	7	6	—	3,256	D270	6,500 Pref.
1,720	812,000	60,825	5	5	British Indian	6	5	5	5	3½	7½	—	2,920	12,300	16,500 Pref.
3,223	2,247,000	114,500	5	5	Brahmapootra	20	18	20	15	12	6¼	—	28,440	41,600	·
3,754	1,617,000	76,500	10	10	Cachar and Dooars	*	8	7	7	9	7¾	—	1,645	21,240	·
		76,500	10	10	Do. Pref.	*	6	6	6	11	5½				
3,946	2,083,000	72,020	1	1	Chargola	8	7	10	5	1	8	3,000	3,300	—	—
		81,000	1	1	Do. Pref.	7	7	7	7	1¼	5¾				
1,971	942,000	33,000	5	5	Chubwa	10	8	10	8	5½	7¼	10,000	2,043	D5,400	—
		33,000	5	5	Do. Pref.	7	7	7	7	6¼	5½				
,250	11,500,000	120,000	10	3	Cons. Tea and Lands	—	*	10	‡5	3¼	8	65,000	14,240	D191,674	—
		1,000,000	10	10	Do. 1st Pref.	—	*	5	5	10¼	4¾				
		400,000	10	10	Do. and Pref.	—	*	7	7	11¾	5¾				
2,230	617,000	135,420	20	20	Darjeeling	5½	5½	6	5	21	4¾	5,552	1,565	1,700	—
2,114	445,000	60,000	10	10	Darjeeling Cons.	—	*	4/2	nil	5	—	—	1,820	—	—
		60,000	10	10	Do. Pref.	—	*	5	5	9½	5¼				
6,660	3,518,000	150,000	10	10	Dooars	12½	12½	12½	12½	17¾	7¼	45,000	300	D32,000	—
		75,000	10	10	Do. Pref.	7	7	7	7	16¼	4¼				
3,367	1,811,000	165,000	10	10	Doom Dooma	11¾	20	12½	12½	19¾	6¼	30,000	4,032	—	10,000
1,377	582,000	61,120	5	5	Eastern Assam	½	nil.	4	nil	2¼	—	—	1,790	—	10,000
4,038	1,675,000	85,000	10	10	East India and Ceylon	*	nil.	7	3	6	8	—	1,710	—	—
		85,000	10	10	Do. Pref.	*	6	6	6	11	5¼				
7,500	3,363,000	219,000	10	10	Empire of India	—	*	6/10	9	10½	8¼	15,000	—	27,000	—
		219,000	10	10	Do. Pref.	—	*	5	5	11	4½				
1,180	540,000	94,060	10	10	Indian of Cachar	7	3½	3	2	3¾	5¼	6,070	—	7,120	—
3,050	824,000	83,500	5	5	Jhanzie	10	10	10	8	6¼	6	14,500	1,070	2,700	
7,980	3,680,000	250,000	10	10	Jokai	10	10	10	8	14½	6¼	45,000	990	D9,000	—
		100,000	10	10	Do. Pref.	*	6	6	6	14½	4¼				
5,224	1,563,000	100,000	20	20	Jorehaut	20	20	20	—	57	7	36,220	2,955	3,000	—
2,547	504,000	65,660	10	8	Lebong	15	15	15	12½	15½xd	6¾	9,000	2,150	8,650	—
5,082	1,709,000	100,000	10	10	Lungla	5	10	6	3	6	5	—	2,543	D21,000	—
		100,000	10	10	Do. Pref.	*	6	6	6	10¼	5¾				
2,684	885,000	95,970	10	10	Majuli	7	5	5	nil	5	—	—	2,606	560	—
1,375	380,000	91,840	1	1	Makum	—	—	2	—	1	2	—	—	1,200	25,000
2,990	770,000	100,000	1	1	Monbund	—	—	*	—	¾	—	—	—	—	—
		50,000	1	1	Do. Pref.	—	—	*	‡2½	¾	5¾				
2,080	482,000	79,590	10	10	Scottish Assam	7	7	7	—	9¾	5½	8,500	800	9,590	—
4,150	1,456,000	100,000	10	10	Singlo	7	8	5	‡1	8¼	5¾	—	300	D5,200	—
		80,000	10	10	Do. Pref.	*	6½	6½	‡3½	13	5				
					CEYLON COMPANIES.										
7,970	1,743,824§	250,000	100	100	Anglo-Ceylon, & Gen.	—	*	5½	—	45	11	10,992	1,405	D72,844	166,520
1,836	685,741§	50,000	10	10	Associated Tea	—	*	5	‡2½	7¼	6¾	—	164	2,478	—
		60,000	10	10	Do. Pref.	—	*	6	‡3	10¾	5¾				
20,390	4,000,000	167,380	10	10	Ceylon Tea Plantations	15	15	15	15	23	6½	84,500	1,516	D30,819	—
		81,080	10	10	Do. Pref.	7	7	7	7	16¼	4¼				
5,722	1,542,700	55,260	5	3	Ceylon & Oriental Est.	5	8	7	—	2¾	7¼	—	230	D2,047	71,000
		46,000	5	5	Do. Pref.	6	6	6	‡3	5	6				
2,157	801,629§	111,330	5	5	Dimbula Valley	—	*	10	‡5	5½	9	—	—	1,733	6,230
		62,607	5	5	Do. Pref.	—	*	6	‡3	6	5				
11,496	3,635,000	298,250	5	5	Eastern Prod. & Est.	3	5	6½	7	5½	6½	20,000	11,740	D17,797	102,500
2,193	1,050,000	22,080	10	10	New Dimbula "A"	12	16	16	‡4	24	7	11,000	2,024	1,150	8,400
		55,710	10	10	Do. "B"	18	16	16	‡4	22	7¼				
2,572	570,360§	100,000	10	10	Ouvah	6	8	6	4	8	7¼	4,000	1,151	D1,255	—
2,630	964,963	200,000	10	10	Nuwara Eliya	—	*	6	6	10¼	6	—	—	—	30,000
1,720	708,533	41,000	10	10	Scottish Ceylon	15	15	15	10	17	6	7,000	1,252	D3,970	9,000 Pref.
2,450	750,000	39,000	10	6	Standard	12½	15	15	15	12½	7	9,000	800	D14,012	4,000
		17,000	10	10	Do.	12½	15	15	15	22	7				

Working-Capital Column.—In working-capital column, D stands for *debit*.
* Company formed this year. † Interim dividends are given as actual distribution made. ‡ Interim div. only. § Crop 1896.

NOTICES.

Messrs. Matheson & Co., 2, Lombard-street, will pay on and after July 1 coupon No. 23 on the Hawaiian Government 6 per cent. loan of 1886, due on that date. Coupons must be left three clear days for verification.

The Crédit Lyonnais, 40, Lombard-street, E.C., is prepared to receive for payment on July 1, 1898, the coupon and drawn bonds of the Imperial Chinese 4 per cent. Loan, 1895.

The Crédit Lyonnais, Lombard-street, is prepared to receive for payment coupons due July 1 on the Province of Quebec 4 per cent. loan of 1866.

The coupons of the Long Island Railroad 5 per cent. consolidated mortgage bonds due July 1 in New York will be cashed on and after that date, at the exchange of $4·85 per £, at the counting house of Messrs. Robert Benson & Co., 66, New Broad-street.

The Bank of England informs holders of fully-paid scrip of the Greek Guaranteed £2 10s. per cent. gold loan of 1898 that they may exchange the same for stock free of expense. Holders of bonds which have not been stamped with the English impressed Inland Revenue stamp of 10s. per cent. may effect a like exchange, also free of expense. Holders of bonds stamped with the 10s. stamp must pay 12s. 6d. per cent. (Commutation Stamp Duty) if they wish to exchange the same for stock.

Sir William Dunn, M.P., has resigned his seat on the directorate of Parr's Bank, Limited.

We understand that the business of E. Uzielli & Co., of 123, Bishopsgate-street, and Lloyd's, E.C., insurance brokers, has for family reasons been converted into a company. No shares are or will be issued to the public.

The numbers are announced of bonds of the Wellington, Grey, and Bruce Railway Company, which have been drawn, and will be paid at par, at the offices of the Grand Trunk Railway Company in Montreal, or at Dashwood-house, New Broad-street, on July 1. It is also announced that the estimated earnings of the railway for the half-year ending 30th inst., applicable to meet interest on the company's bonds, will admit of the payment of £1 19s. 6d. on each £100 bond, and that this payment will be applied as follows, viz. :—14s. 7d. in final discharge of Coupon No. 36, due July, 1888; and £1 4s. 11d. on account of Coupon No. 37, due January 1, 1889, and will be made on July 1 next at the agency of the company.

Messrs. Glyn, Mills, Currie, & Co. have received advice by cable from the London and River Plate Bank at Montevideo announcing the despatch by mail of a remittance amounting to £4,400 for the service of the Uruguay 5 per cent. loan of 1896.

Messrs. Robarts, Lubbock, & Co. announce that, in accordance with the Law of Congress of November 16, 1895, the coupon, due the 1st prox., of the External Debt of Paraguay will be paid on and after that date at the rate of 2 per cent. per annum.

The numbers are announced of sixty-eight debentures of £100 each of the Tucuman Sugar Company drawn on June 16, for redemption on July 1 next, at the banking-house of Messrs. Glyn, Mills, Currie, & Co., 67, Lombard-street, E.C.

Baring Brothers & Co., Limited, are instructed by the Portuguese Government to pay the coupons of the Portuguese 3 per cent. exterior bonds, due on July 1, at one-third of their face value. No certificates for the residue will be issued.

The Council of Foreign Bondholders are advised by the London and River Plate Bank that they are this day in receipt of the following cable message from their Montevideo branch dated the 16th inst. :—"We have remitted by to-day's mail to Glyn, Mills, Currie & Co. £36,700 for the service of the Uruguay 3½ per cent. debt."

Mr. Walter James has removed to 13, Fish-street Hill, E.C.

The Sulphide Corporation (Ashcroft's Process, Limited) has removed to Finsbury-house, Blomfield-street, E.C.

Messrs. R. Raphael & Sons announce that the coupons due on July 1 next of the Piræus, Athens, and Peloponnesus Railway 5 per cent. bonds will be paid at the rate of 3 per cent. per annum.

The Taltal Railway Company, Limited, announces that, in connection with the sinking fund for redemption of the company's 5 per cent. debentures, no drawing of bonds will take place this year, the required number having been purchased in the market, as provided by the trust deed.

On and after July 1 the London office of the Witwatersrand Gold Mining Company, Limited (Knight's), will be removed to 96, Gresham-house, Old Broad-street, London, E.C., and Mr. John S. Sheldrick has been appointed London secretary.

Messrs. Clarke & Co., of St. Petersburg, announce that they have decided to close their London branch, conducted under the style of Alexr. Fr Clarke & Co. Mr. Frans Ofverberg, of 8, Crosby-square, will continue to represent them in London.

The numbers are announced of bonds amounting to £40,400 of the Egyptian guaranteed 3 per cent. loan, which have been drawn and will be paid off at par at the offices of Messrs. N. M. Rothschild & Sons on September 1 next.

Messrs. Speyer Brothers announce that the coupon due July 1 on the Central Pacific Railroad (California and Oregon Division) bonds issued by them will be paid on and after that date at their offices.

Baring Brothers & Co., Limited, have received a remittance of £20,587 19s. 7d. in bills on London at ninety days' sight on account of the service of the City of Buenos Ayres 4½ per cent. sterling loan of 1888.

Baring Brothers & Co., Limited, give notice that they are authorised to receive and forward to New York the subscriptions of stockholders to the new issue of preferred stock of the Great Northern Railway Company of Minnesota, U.S.A., and to receive payment therefore as provided in the circular of the company dated New York, June 10, 1898, copies of which may be obtained at their counting-house.

The fourth half-yearly amortisation of the bonds of the Oriental Republic of Uruguay 5 per cent. loan, 1896, took place on Tuesday at the banking-house of Messrs. Glyn, Mills, Currie, & Co., by public tender, the amount to be applied being £9,614 5s. Tenders amounted to £74,200, ranging from £55 14s. 6d. to £58 per cent. Tenders of £17,200 at £55 14s. 6d. were accepted.

The Government of the colony of Victoria, Australia, announce that, in connection with the Department of Mines, they have opened an office and museum at 8, Victoria-chambers, Westminster, London, S.W., where all information relating to the mines and minerals of Victoria can be obtained free.

The Stock Conversion and Investment Trust (Limited and Reduced) notifies that the reduction of capital has received the sanction of the Court. The ordinary shares are thus reduced from £5 shares £1 paid to £2 shares with £1 paid and £1 reserve liability.

Mr. G. Auldjo Jamieson has issued a circular to the shareholders of the Municipal Trust Company (Limited and Reduced), stating that he feels obliged to resign his seat on the board, as he believes the course they have determined on as to payment of dividends to be illegal, and also detrimental to the interest of the holders of the company's deferred stock.

FOREIGN RAILWAYS.

Mileage. Total.	Increase on 1897.	Increase on 1896.	Name	Gross Traffic for Week. Week ending	Amount.	In. or Dec. upon 1897.	In. or Dec. upon 1896.	Gross Traffic to Date. No. of Weeks.	Amount.	In. or Dec. upon 1897.	In. or Dec. upon 1896.
					£	£	£		£	£	£
319	—	—	Argentine Great Western ..	June 10	7,361	+ 1,037	+ 1,547	49	298,715	− 1,238	+ 59,937
76½	—	—	Bahia and San Francisco ..	Apr. 30	2,754	− 131	− 1,437	18	—	—	—
234	48	84	Bahia Blanca and North West..	May 22	518	+ 131	—	46	34,605	− 1,434	—
75	1	—	Buenos Ayres and Ensenada ..	June 19	2,919	+ 487	—	25	80,019	+ 13,397	—
426	—	—	Buenos Ayres and Pacific ..	June 18	6,604	+ 1,201	+ 461	50	347,267	− 41,667	+ 15,368
284	—	3	Buenos Ayres and Rosario ..	June 18	13,143	+ 1,399	+ 1,311	25	397,913	+ 100,513	+ 100,503
2,499	30	68	Buenos Ayres Great Southern ..	June 19	22,047	+ 3,172	+ 2,984	50	1,476,490	+ 124,985	+ 216,866
602	107	177	Buenos Ayres Western	June 19	9,249	+ 617	− 773	50	600,035	− 74,513	− 203,140
845	55	77	Central Argentine..	June 18	15,335	+ 2,296	+ 37	25	506,953	+ 125,730	+ 62,281
297	—	—	Central Bahia	Apr. 30*	$155,590	+ $35,560	+ $57,258	4	$581,140	+ $60,760	+ $87,881
272	—	—	Central Uruguay of Monte Video	June 18	4,683	+ 1,340	− 863	50	296,180	+ 30,754	− 15,905
218	—	—	Do. Eastern Extension	June 18	982	+ 273	+ 17	50	64,285	+ 9,937	+ 305
182	—	—	Do. Northern Extension	June 18	618	+ 205	− 183	50	31,621	+ 1,056	− 8,176
180	—	—	Cordoba and Rosario	June 12	1,430	− 500	− 1,050	49	104,500	− 14,085	− 2,785
128	—	—	Cordoba Central	June 12	$22,500	− $6,270	− $16,000	24	$504,830	− $92,670	− $117,210
549	—	—	Do. Northern Extension	June 12	$56,000	− $17,320	− $19,890	24	$1,084,300	− $376,100	− $230,060
237	—	—	Costa Rica..	June 11	3,613	− 686	− 607	24	133,294	− 588	+ 11,930
99	—	—	East Argentine	May 1	1,062	+ 496	+ 69	16	13,802	+ 2,131	+ 1,007
386	—	6	Entre Rios..	June 18	1,012	+ 250	− 279	50	80,710	+ 25,447	+ 19,007
555	—	24	Inter Oceanic of Mexico.. ..	June 18	$53,700	+ $8,070	+ $8,700	50	$2,919,770	+ $457,780	+ $784,300
23	—	—	La Guaira and Caracas	May 20	1,760	− 607	—	21	41,428	− 6,161	—
321	—	—	Mexican	June 18	$79,700	+ $9,200	—	24	$1,960,500	+ $204,650	—
1,846	—	—	Mexican Central	June 14	$257,548	+ $1,796	+ $82,325	24	$6,070,030	+ $100,742	+ $1,655,038
1,217	—	—	Mexican National	June 14	$104,667	+ $3,020	+ $22,719	24	$2,564,776	+ $58,866	+ $501,539
228	—	—	Mexican Southern	June 14	$11,730	− $141	+ $4,192	10	$130,507	− $17,814	+ $34,463
306	—	—	Minas and Rio	Apr. 30*	$142,119	− $22,067	—	10 mos.	$1,740,090	+ $171,787	—
94	—		N. W. Argentine	June 11	1,496	− 254	− 410	22	24,173	− 9,147	− 8,153
242	3	—	Nitrate	June 15	13,476	− 5,117	− 13,692	22	164,360	− 5,448	− 83,858
300	—	—	Ottoman	June 4	2,888	− 1,451	− 1,468	23	100,663	− 23,382	+ 7,064
77½	—	—	Recife and San Francisco ..	Apr. 23	4,072	+ 469	− 1,713	17	93,245	+ 9,655	− 17,683
86½	—	—	San Paulo	May 15†	15,798	− 7,558	—	18	181,508	—	—
186	—	—	Santa Fe and Cordova	June 18	1,355	+ 274	− 478	51	88,548	+ 4,473	− 7,082
110	—	—	Western of Havana	June 18	1,495	− 327	− 335	50	87,025	+ 2,766	+ 6,150

* For month ended. † For fortnight ended.

INDIAN RAILWAYS.

Mileage. Total.	Increase on 1897.	Increase on 1896.	Name.	Gross Traffic for Week. Week ending	Amount.	In. or Dec. on 1897.	In. or Dec. on 1896.	Gross Traffic to Date. No. of Weeks.	Amount.	In. or Dec. on 1897.	In. or Dec. on 1896.
862	—	—	Bengal Nagpur	June 11	Rs.1.31.000	+ Rs.11.134	+ Rs.40.731	24	Rs.37.27.966	+ Rs.4.63.204	+ Rs.22.47.885
827	8	63	Bengal and North-Western ..	May 14	Rs.1.64.120	+ Rs.9.345		20	Rs.26.96.385	+ Rs.2.70.581	—
461	—	—	Bombay and Baroda	June 18	£29,333	− £12	+ £8,374	24	£765,332	+ £65,069	− £86,167
1,885	2	13	East Indian	June 18	Rs.11.56.000	+ Rs.43.000	+ Rs.22.27.000	25	Rs.3.05.32.000	+ Rs.11.69.000	+ R36.14.000
1,491	—	—	Great Indian Penin.	June 18	£53,763	+ £9,102	+ £3,493	25	£1,719,410	+ £353,336	− £141,563
736	—	—	Indian Midland	June 18	Rs.1.80.040	+ Rs.33.928	+ Rs.81.509	25	Rs.36.89.294	+ Rs.4.51.802	+ R10.17.178
840	—	—	Madras	June 11	£19,983	+ £92	+ £366	23	£450,161	− £22,800	− £4,900
1,043	—	—	South Indian	May 21	Rs.1.66.564	− Rs.34.144	− Rs.31.299	21	Rs.32.25.663	− Rs.3.06.845	− Rs3.19.165

UNITED STATES AND CANADIAN RAILWAYS.

Mileage. Total.	Increase on 1897.	Increase on 1896.	Name.	Gross Traffic for Week. Period Ending.	Amount.	In. or Dec. on 1897.	Gross Traffic to Date. No. of Weeks.	Amount.	In. or Dec. on 1897.
					dols.	dols.		dols.	dols.
917	—	—	Baltimore & Ohio S. Western ..	June 14	129,514	+ 13,860	48	6,579,114	+ 839,196
6,568	92	156	Canadian Pacific	" 7	512,000	+ 43,000	21	9,945,000	+ 1,764,000
922	—	—	Chicago Great Western	" 7	86,141	− 5,281	47	4,998,369	+ 616,273
6,169	—	469	Chicago, Mil., & St. Paul ..	" 7	657,000	+ 47,000	21	12,140,001	+ 1,761,800
1,685	—	—	Denver & Rio Grande	" 14	156,300	+ 20,800	48	7,701,100	+ 1,239,700
3,512	—	—	Grand Trunk, Main Line ..	" 14	£71,645	− £1,254	22	£1,701,801	+ £130,333
335	—	—	Do. Chic. & Grand Trunk	" 14	£14,299	+ £2,336	22	£343,802	+ £77,729
189	—	—	Do. Det., G. H. & Mil...	" 14	£3,126	− £529	22	£79,664	− £5,203
2,938	—	—	Louisville & Nashville	" 7	423,000	+ 37,000	21	9,280,175	+ 1,270,620
2,197	137	137	Miss., K., & Texas	" 14	154,704	+ 6,494	48	11,701,504	+ 561,698
477	—	—	N. Y., Ontario, & W.	" 14	70,137	− 5,378	48	3,631,756	+ 69,530
1,570	—	—	Norfolk & Western	" 7	221,000	+ 6,000	21	4,768,960	+ 493,433
3,499	336	—	Northern Pacific	" 7	395,000	+ 55,000	21	8,470,775	+ 2,549,552
1,223	—	—	St. Louis S. Western	" 7	82,000	+ 12,000	21	2,221,295	+ 336,928
4,654	—	—	Southern	" 7	384,000	+ 41,000	21	7,980,812	+ 1,686,430
2,079	—	—	Wabash	" 7	244,000	+ 20,000	47	12,360,430	+ 1,190,000

MONTHLY STATEMENTS.

Mileage. Total.	Increase on 1896	Increase on 1895.	Name.	Net Earnings for Month. Month.	Amount.	In. or Dec. on 1897.	In. or Dec. on 1896.	Net Earnings to Date. No. of Months.	Amount.	In. or Dec. on 1897.	In. or Dec. on 1896.
					dols	dols.	dols.		dols.	dols.	dols.
6,935	44	444	Atchison	April	798,000	+ 319,000	+ 239,679	4	2,942,434	+ 993,836	+ 469,130
6,547	103	206	Canadian Pacific	April	717,000	+ 90,000	+ 225,790	4	2,410,000	+ 305,000	+ 612,557
6,169	—	469	Chicago, Mil., & St. Paul ..	April	759,000	+ 19,000	− 17,197	4	3,495,334	+ 244,840	+ 76,915
1,685	—	—	Denver & Rio Grande	April	264,200	+ 11,727	+ 38,988	10	2,777,080	+ 418,782	+ 69,925
1,970	—	—	Erie..	April	554,000	+ 17,000	+ 45,487	4	1,932,600	+ 109,400	− 48,760
3,512	—	—	Grand Trunk, Main Line ..	April	£114,098	+ £16,224	+ £26,710	4	£360,051	+ £78,596	+ £123,587
335	—	—	Do. Chic. & Grand Trunk	April	£11,526	+ £6,424	+ £5,660	4	£50,236	+ £30,706	+ £34,378
189	—	—	Do. Det. G. H. & Mil. ..	April	£4,016	+ £390	+ £2,125	4	£10,544	+ £1,127	+ £8,744
3,127	—	239	Illinois Central	April	531,000	+ 170	+ 95,779	4	2,744,704	+ 535,402	+ 645,518
2,396	—	—	New York Central*	April	3,837,000	+ 302,000	+ 394,152	4	14,602,000	+ 964,000	—
477	—	—	New York Ontario, & W. ..	April	62,100	− 14,700	− 13,161	10	980,400	+ 23,500	+ 102,333
1,570	—	—	Norfolk & Western	April	237,000	+ 40,000	+ 96,237	4	1,063,000	+ 105,340	+ 298,137
3,407	—	—	Pennsylvania	April	1,524,200	+ 12,900	+ 236,000	4	5,672,228	+ 121,300	+ 575,900
1,055	—	—	Phil. & Reading	April	692,155	− 12,700	—	10	8,190,448	+ 511,265	—

* Statement of gross traffic.

Prices Quoted on the London Stock Exchange.

Throughout the INVESTORS' REVIEW middle prices alone are quoted, the object being to give the public the approximate current quotations of every security of any consequence in existence. On the markets the buying and selling prices are both given, and are often wide apart where stocks are seldom dealt in. Other particulars will be found in the INVESTMENT INDEX published quarterly—January, April, July, and October—in connection with this REVIEW, price 2s., by post 2s. 2d. Where dividends are paid only once a year, an *italic* type is used to distinguish them. The London Stock Exchange Official List is quoted in the REVIEW almost entire, only very insignificant issues, or bonds falling due within the next two or three years, being omitted. But the list is subdivided into the leading, or active, stocks, and those less frequently dealt in. The former will be found under the head of "Stock Markets," and with more details than it is possible to give for the bulk of securities. By retaining the file of the INVESTORS' REVIEW any subscriber can follow for himself the movements of securities from week to week, and the INVESTMENT INDEX will from time to time help to fill up deficiencies in the information.

Tea Companies and Mines and Mining Finance Stocks are placed in special lists.

Among the abbreviations used are the following:—S.F. Snk.Fd. *sinking fund*; Certs., *certificates*; Debs. or Dbs., *debentures*; Db. or D.Stk., *debenture stock*; Pf. Prf., or Pref., *preference*; Prefd. or Pfd., *preferred*; Dfd., *deferred*; L. or Ltd., *limited*; Sh., *share*; Ans., *annuities*; Cu. or Cm., *cumulative*; Gu or Guar., *guaranteed*; Bds., *bonds*; S., Sr., or Ser., *series*; In., Ins., Insc., *inscribed*; Dr., Drgs., Drwgs., *drawings*; Stg., Strlg., *sterling*; Lia., *liable to*; Sp., Surp., *surplus*; Per., Perp., *perpetual*; Ln. *lien*; Lo. *loan*.

The dates following the names of securities are the years of issue or of redemption. Where shares are not fully paid up, their nominal amount is given with the name so that investors may know the liability upon them.

BRITISH FUNDS, &c.

Rate.	Name.	Price.
2¾	2¾ p.c.'s (Childers') Red.. 1905	105
3	Local Loans Stk. 1912	111
3	Metro. Police Deb. Stk. 1920	105
—	Red Sea Ind. Tel. Ann. 1908	8¼
4	Canada Gv. "Intcl. Rly." 1903	105¼
4	Do. do. .. 1908	111
4	Do. Bonds 1910	112
4	Do. Bonds 1913	117½
3	Egyptian Gov. Gar.	106
3	Mauritius Ins. Stk. 1940	113
4	Turkish Guar. 1855	109
£1½	Bank of Ireland Stk.	385
3½	India Rupee Paper	62
3½	Do. 1854-5	62½
3	Do. 1896-7 1916	54
3½	Isle of Man Deb.	104
3	Do. Deb. Stk... 1919-29	103

CORPORATION AND COUNTY STOCKS.
FREE OF STAMP DUTY.

Rate.	Name.	Price.
3½	Metropolitan Con. 1929	117½
3	Do. 1941	110
2½	Do. 1920-49	99
2½	L.C.C. Con. Stock 1920	98
3½	Comm. of Sewers, Scp., S.F. 1905	104
3½	Corp. of Lond. Bds.. 1898-1908	100½
3	Do. 1898-1919	101
3½	Do, Debs. Scp. ...... S.F. 1916	106
2½	Do., Deb. Stk. Scrip .. 1927-57	97½
3	Barnsley 1916-46	103
3	Barry 1914-46	100½
3	Bath 1909-34	101½
3	Batley 1914-44	100½
3½	Birmingham 1946	116½
3	Do. 1947	110½
2½	Do. 1926	98
3	Blackburn 1930	104½
3	Bournemouth 1913-33	102
3½	Bradford 1945	116½
3	Do. Deb. Stock .. 1954	107
3	Brighouse 1916-46	100
3½	Brighton 1946	117
2½	Do. 1957	96½
3	Burton-on-Trent 1913-43	100½
3	Cambridge 1913-43	102½
3½	Cardiff 1935	115½
3	Do. 1914-54	103
3	Cheltenham 1971	105½
3	Chichester 1916-46	101
3½	Croydon	128½
3	Do. 1940	107½
3	Derby 1920-50	105½
3	Devon C.C. 1917-33	104½
3½	Dewsbury 1930	109
3	Do. 1930	103
3	Dorset County 1922-32	106
3	Douglas (I. of Man) 1926	100½
3	Dover 1913-43	101½
3½	Dublin 1944	111½
3	Eastbourne 1920-40	103½
3	Edinburgh 1924	105½
2½	Do. 1927	97
2½	Exeter 1917-57	96
3	Glamorgan County 1914-34	103
3½	Glasgow 1914	109
3	Do. 1921	104½
2½	Do. 1925-40	98
3	Gloster 1915-55	101½
3	Grimsby 1913-45	103
3	Hampshire County 1914-34	105½
3	Hanley 1913-43	102½
3	Harrogate 1914-34	102
3	Hastings 1915-54	103
2½	Hertfordshire C.C. 1916-36	97
3	Heston & Isleworth U.D.C. 1915-35	101
3	Huddersfield 1934	106
3½	Hull (1st iss.)	127½
3	Inverness 1914-44	100
3	Ipswich 1952	106½
3	Lancaster 1919-55	101
2½	Leeds 1927	97
3½	Leicester 1934	114
3	Lincoln 1910	102
3½	Liverpool	131

Corporation, &c. (*continued*):—

Rate.	Name.	Price.
3	Manchester 1941	107½
3½	Middlesbro' 1909	107½
3½	Do. 1911-13	105
3	Do. 1915	104
3	Middlesex C.C. 1915-35	105
3½	Newcastle 1936	116½
3½	Do. Irred.	127½
2½	Do. 1915-36	99½
3	Newcastle-under-Lyme.. 1909-44	100
3	Newport (Mon.) 1915-55	100½
3	Norwich 1952	110
3	Nottingham	113
3	Oxford 1951	108½
3	Penzance 1916-46	100½
3	Plymouth 1942	105
3	Pontypridd U.D.C. 1916-46	98
3	Poole 1915-45	101
3½	Portsmouth ....1916 24 & 27	111
3	Do. 1913-33	105
3	Ramsey 1920-40	99
3	Ramsgate 1915-55	102
3½	Reading	123
3	Do. 1962	106
3½	Rhyl U.D.C. 1953	110
3	Richmond (Surrey) 1942	103½
3	River Wear Debt Certs.	99
3	St. Helen's 1915-55	102
3	Scarbro' 1915-50	101
2½	Sheffield 1925-57	94½
3	Shipley U.D.C. 1915-35	99
3	Somerset Co. 1923-33	104
3	South Shields 1915-45	100½
2½	Southampton 1915-45	99½
3	Southend-on-Sea 1916-46	100
3	Staffs C.C. 1915-35	104½
3	Stockport 1914-54	101
3	Stockton 1932	104
3	Do. 1915-35	103
3	Surrey Co. 1922-32	105½
3½	Swansea	128
3	Do. 1955	106
3	Taunton 1918-39-43	101
3	Tees Conserv. Deb. Stk. 1947	99
3	Thames Conserv. "A" Deb. Stk. 1954	102½
3	Do. "B" Deb. Stk. 1954	102½
3	Torquay 1913-43	100½
3	Tunbridge Wells 1931	102½
3	Tynemouth 1913	99
3	Wakefield 1929	101½
3	Walsall 1932	105½
3	West Bromwich 1930	105
3½	West Ham 1929	110
3	Do. 1945	105
3	West Sussex C.C. 1915-35	106
3	Weston-s.-Mare Lcl.Bd. 1914-44	99½
3	Weymouth&Melc. Regis 1918	100
3	Widnes 1915-55	100
3	Wigan 1921	105½
3	Windsor 1918-55	102½
3½	Wisbech 1947	113½
3½	Wolverhampton 1932	117
3	Do. 1924-54	107
3	York 1916-41	104

SUBJECT TO STAMP DUTY.

Rate.	Name.	Price.
3½	Belfast City & Dis. Watr. 1938	114
3	Do. Red Stk. 1953-6	105
3½	Belfast 1924	103
4	Blackburn Con. Deb. Irred.	140
3½	Do. do. Irred.	128
3½	Bristol	132
3½	Burnley 1933	114
2½	Chesterfield Gas & Wtr. 1916-46	96
3½	Douglas Town 1921	103
3	Dover Harb. 1st Deb... 1936	104½
3½	Hull (2nd iss.)	127½
4	Leeds Deb. 1927	121½
3½	Do.	113½
3	Do. 1927	104
3	Leicester 1919-44	103
4	Manchester	145
3	Do. 1928	103½
4½	Middlesboro' Mrts. 1908	110
3½	Sheffield 1898-1916	100½
3½	Do. 1925-36	114
3	Do. 1925	104½
3½	Southampton .... S.F.	104½
4½	Stockton Morts. 1908	110½
3½	Worcester 1950	109

COLONIAL AND PROVINCIAL GOVERNMENT SECURITIES.

Rate.	Name.	Price.
6	British Columbia 1907	119½
4½	Do. Debs... 1917	111½
3	British Guiana Imgtn. Bds.	98
5	Canada, "Intercol. Rail," 1903	108½
4	Do. (Bonds) 1904-5-6-8	106
4	Do. Reduced 1910	110
3½	Do. Bnds. 1909-34	107
4	Do. Loan 1910-35	110
3	Do. Loan 1938	103
6	Cape of G. Hope 1900	—
5	Do. 1900	—
4½	Do. red. by an. draw.	108
4½	Do 1879	108
4	Do. 1881	107
4	Do 1917-23	113
4½	Ceylon	108
4	Do.	106½
4½	Fiji Gov. Deb. Sink. Fd.	103½
4	Jamaica Sink. Fd. 1923	105
5	Manitoba Debs 1910	113
5	Do. Ster. Bds. 1888	119½
4	Do. Ster. Debs.	105
4	Mauritius, Cons. Debs. 1880....	101½
4½	Natal, Sink. Fd. 1919	118
4	Do. do. 1926	114
3½	Newfoundland Stg. Bds. 1941	100
3½	Do. do. .. 1947	100
3	Do. do.	87
5	New South Wales 1897-1902	104½
4	Do. 1903-5-8-9-12	106
5	New Zealand 1914	118
5	Do. Cnsls. 1 p.c. per an. Sink. Fd.	103
3½	Nova Scotia Debs.	104
5	Quebec Prov. 1904-6	108
4½	Do. (drgs.)	105
5	Do. Strlg. Bds. 1919	115
4	Do. Strlg. Bds. 1928	110
4	Do. Strlg. Bds. 1934	108
4	Queensland 1913-15	108
4½	St. Lucia Debs.	102
6	South Australia 1898-1900	103½
6	Do. 1901-1918	119
5	Do. 1911-1920	115½
4	Do. 1899-1916	104½
4	Do. 1929	108½
4	Do. 1916	106½
4	Do. 1917-18-24	110
6	Tasmania 1897-1901	104
4	Do. 1908-11, 1913-14-20	107½
5	Trinidad Debs., an. drw. 1 p c...	107
4	Victoria 1899-1904	102½
4½	Do. 1904	107
4	Do. Rail. Loan 1907	107
4	Do. Loans 1908-13	107
4½	West. Austr. 1 p.c. ac. Sink. Fd.	107
4	Do. do.	106

REGISTERED AND INSCRIBED STOCKS.

No stamp duty except for Canada 4 p.c. Reduced (½ per cent.).

Rate.	Name.	Price.
4	Antigua Insc. Stk. Red. 1919-44	111
3½	Barbados Insc. Stk. 1925-42	107
3	British Colum. Insc. Stk. 1941	99
4	British Guiana Insc. 1935	114½
4	Canada Stk. Regd. ..1904-5-6-8	106
4	Do. 4 p.c. (late 5 p.c.) Regd. 1910	108
3½	Do. 3½ p.c. Stock Regd. 1909-34	107
4	Do. Ln. for 4 milln. stg. 1910-35	108
3	Do. Stk. Regd. 1938	102
2½	Do. Insc. 1947	92
4	Cape G. Hope Regd. — 1917-23	114
4	Do. (Ln. of '83) Insc. .. 1923	117
4	Do. Cons. Stk. Insc. 1916-36	114
3½	Do. Consol. Insc. Stock 1929-49	108
4	Ceylon Insc. Stock 1934	120
3	Do. 1940	105
4	Grenada Insc. Stock 1917-42	110
3½	Hong Kong Insc. Stock 1918-43	104
4	Jamaica Insc. Stock 1934	118
—	Do. 1922-44	98
4	Mauritius Inscribed 1937	118½
4	Natal Consd. Stk. Insc. 1937	117
4	Do. 1937	119
3½	Do. Inscribed Stock.. 1914-39	106
4	Newfoundland Inscribed 1913-38	106
4	Do. 1935	113
4	Do. Consd. Stk. Ins. 1936	113
4	N. S. Wales Stock Insc. 1933	117
3½	Do. 1924	109
3½	Do. 1918	107
3	Do 1935	100

Colonial, &c. (*continued*):—

Rate.	Name.	Price.
4	N. Zealnd. Con. Stk. Ins. 1929	114
3½	Do 1940	106
3	Do. Inscribed 1945	98
3	Quebec (Prov.) Ins. Stk. 1937	94
4	Queensland Stock Insc. 1915-24	109½
3½	Do. 1921-4-30	104½
3½	Do. 1945	107
3	Do. 1922-47	98
4	St. Lucia Insc. Stock .. 1919-44	114½
4	S. Austrln. (1882-7) Reg. 1916-36	110½
3½	Do. In. Stk. Reg. 1939	109
3	Do. 1916-26	100
3/	Do. 1916	100
3½	Tasmanian Insc. Stock .. 1920-40	108
4	Do. 1920-40	115
4	Trinidad Insc. Stock 1917-42	110
3	Do. 1922-44	98
4	Victoria Rly. Loan '81, Inscribed Stock 1907	105
4	Victoria Insc. Stock 1908-13-19	108
4	Victoria (1885) Ins. Stk. 1920	112½
3½	Do. Inscribed Stock 1921-3-6	105
4	Do. do. 1911-26	108
4	W. Austral. Insc. Stock 1934	114½
4	Do. 1911-31	109
3½	Do. 1915-35	105
3	Do. 1915-35	99
3	Do. 1916-36	99

FOREIGN STOCKS, BONDS, &c.
COUPONS PAYABLE IN LONDON.

Last Div.	Name.	Price.
36/	Argentine Ry. Loan 6 p.c. 1881	85½
15/	Do. 5 p.c. 1884	68
30/	Do. N. Cent. Ry. Ext. 5 p.c. 1887-8-9	67½
30/	Do. 5 p.c. Trsy. Convs. 1887	67
5/4½	Do. 4½ p.c. Interl. Gld. 1888	64
27/	Do. 4½ p.c. Stlg. Extrl. 1888	65
10/6	Do. 3½ p.c. External .. 1889	48
4	Do. 4 p.c. Ry. Guar. Res	58
4½	Brazilian 1883	53
4½	Do. Gold 1879	55½
4½	Do. 1888	53
36/	Buenos Ayres 1824	80
6	Do. 1882-3-6	
6	Bulgarian 1888	96
6	Do. Mort. Bonds 1892	95
4½	Chilian 1885	72
4½	Do. 1886	73
4½	Do. 1887	72
4½	Do. 1889	79½
5	Do. 1892	83
4½	Do. 1893	72
4½	Do. 1895	71
5	Do. 1896	82
7	Chinese Silver 1894	98
6	Do. Gold 1895	109
6	Do. Apl. '95 by dwgs. 1901-15	112
5	Do. Red. dwgs. in 36 yr. 1896	99½
5	Do. Do. Regis. 1896	99
1½	Colmbn. 1½ to 3 p.c. Ext. Bds. 1896	17½
6	Cordova, Prov. 1886	25
—	Do. Eng. Ass. Certs.	24
—	Do. 6 p.c. 1887-8	22
—	Do. Eng. Ass. Certs.	24
3	Costa Rica "A"	36
2½	Do. "B"	23
3	Danish Gold 1914	99
10/	Ecuador N. Ext. Bds. 4½ p.c. ascn. to 5 p.c.	24
3½	Egypt'n Ins. Stk. lia. Stp. Dty. 1890	100
4	Do. State Domain 1878	103½
4	Do. D. Sanieh, Red. .. 1905	103
6	Entre Rios 1886-8	34
6	Do. Fudg. Ln. Bds. 1894-1921	29
6	Do. do. Parana City	22½
15/	Greek 1881	39
15/	Do. 1884	39
12/	Do. Rentes	33
15/	Do. (Piræus-Larissa Ry.)	37
2/6	Do. Fundg. Loan	42½
4	Guatemala Extl. Debt	29
6	Hawaiian	102
4	Hungarian Gold Rentes	102
3	Do. 1895	88½
6	Italian Irriga. Guar.	104½
5	Do. Maremmana	94
5	Japan 5 p.c.	102
5	Mexican (Nat. R. Tehuantp c.)..	94½
6	Do. Extrl. 1890	96½

Foreign Stocks, &c. (*continued*):—

Last Div.	Name.	Price.
6	Mexican Extrl. 1893	95½
5	Do. Intrnl. Cons. Slvr.	36½
5	Do. Intern. Rd. Bds. 2d. Ser.	36½
4	Nicaragua 1886..........	42½
3½	Norwegian, red. 1937, or earlier	97½
3	Do. do. 1965, do.	98½
3½	Do. 3½ p.c. Bnds.	103
1	Paraguay 1p.c. ris. 3p.c. 1886-96	17
5	Russian, 1822, £ Strlg.	149
3	Do. 1859	93
4	Do. (Nicolas Ry.) 1867-9 ..	102
3	Do. Transcauc. Ry. 1882 ..	92
4	Do. Con. R. R. Bd. Ser. I., 1889..	104
4	Do. Do. II., 1889..	104
4	Do. Do. III., 1891..	102
3½	Do. Bonds	100
4	Do. Ln. (Dvinsk and Vitbsk)	101½
6	Salvador 1889..........	57½
—	S Domingo 4s. Unified: .. 1980	62
6	San Luis Potosi Stg. 1889	94
5	San Paulo (Brzl.), Stg. 1888	86½
6	Santa Fé 1883-4..........	36
—	Do. Eng. Ass. Certs. Dep...	35
5	Do. 1888..........	48
—	Do. Eng. Ass. Certs. Dpsit..	47
5	Do. (W. Cnt. Col. Rly.) Mrt.	24
6	Do. & Reconq. Rly. Mort...	24
5	Spanish Quicksilvr Mort. 1870 ..	101½
3½	Swedish 1880	102
3	Do. 1888	99
3	Do. Conversion Loan 1894..	90
5	Trans. Gov. Loan Red...1903-42	106
50/	Tucuman (Prov.) 1888..........	66½
4	Turkish, Secd. on Egypt. Trib.	103
3½	Turkish, Egpt. Trib., Ott. Bd., '94	99½
4	Do. Priority 1890..........	92
1	Do. Convted Series, "A"..	66
5	Do. Customs Ln. 1886......	96½
5	Uruguay Bonds 1896	57
3	Venzuela New Con. Debt 1881	32

COUPONS PAYABLE ABROAD.

Last Div.	Name.	Price.
7	Argent. Nat. Cedla. Sries, "B".	33
5	Austrian Ster. Rnts., ex 10fl., 1870	96
5	Do. do. do.	84
5	Do. Paper do. 1870	85
5	Do. do. do.	85
4	Do. Gld Rentes 1876	102
3	Belgian exchange 25 fr.	100
3½	Danish Int., 1887, Rd. 1896	—
2½	Dutch Certs. ex 12 gldrs.	87
3	Do. Bonds	98
3	Do. Insc. Stk..........	97
3½	French Rentes	105
3	Do. 1878, '81-4., Red.	100
3	German Imp. Ln. 1891..........	95
3	Do. do. 1892-3	95
3	Do. do. 1890-4	96
5	Japan Cons. Ln., '92, 3, & 5, Red.	45
36/9	Prussian Consols	102
3	" Cons. Stg. Ln. 1891....	96
4	Utd. States, 1877, Red. 1907	113
4	Do. 1895, 30 yrs.	128
3½	Do. Maschsetts Gl. 1935	113½
3½	Do. Gold Bonds 1923	107½
2	Virginia Cpn. Bds., 3 p.c. from July, 1901	71

BRITISH RAILWAYS.

ORD. SHARES AND STOCKS.

Last Div	Name.	Price.
10	Barry, Ord.	276½
4	Do. Prefd.	125
6	Do. Defd.	150½
5	Caledonian, Ord..........	158
3	Do. Prefd.	100½
—	Do. Defd. Ord., No. 1	5
	Cambrian, Ord............	4½
—	Do. Coast Cons.	4½
32/	Cardiff Ry. Pref. Ord.	114
3/	Central Lond. £10 Ord. Sh.	10
1/9½	Do. do. £6 paid......	6
3½d.	Do. Pref. Half-Shares..	1½
1/6	Do. Def. do..........	4½
1½	City and S. London	69½
—	East London, Cons.	7½
2	Furness	65½
2½	Glasgow and S. West. Pfd.	82
2½	Do. do. Dfd.	65
3	Great Central, Ord....1894	40½
32/0	Do. London Exten. ...	73½
—	Great N. of Scotland, Prfd.	88
—	Do. Dfd.	34
4	Great Northern, Prefd....	120
—	Do. Consolidated "A"	52
—	Do. do. "B"	191½
2	Highland	75½
4	Isle of Wight, Prefd.	120½
3	Do. Defd.	83½
—	Lancs. Derbys. and E. Cst.	3½
8½	L. Brighton and S. C. Ord.	187
6	Do. Prefd. Ord.	197
10/	Do. Contgt. Rights Certs.	18½
5½	Lond. and S. Western Ord.	225½
4	Do. Preferred	134
6½	Lond., Tilb., and Southend	134½
—	Mersey, £20 shares	½
—	Metropolitan, New Ord. ..	129
2½	Do. Surplus Lands....	91
4	North Cornwall, 4 p.c. Pref.	104½
28/6	Do. Deferred	22½
7½	North London............	224½
4½	North Staffordshire	128

British Railways (*continued*):—

Last Div.	Name.	Price.
3/3	Plymouth, Devenport, and S. W. Junc. £10	8½
3/	Port Talbot £10 Shares ..	9½
9d.	Rhondda Swns. B. £10 Sh.	4½
10	Rhymney, Cons.	265½
4	Do. Prefd.	123
6½	Do. Defd.	145½
1½	Scarboro', Bridlington Junc.	47½
6½	South Eastern, Ord........	152
6	Do. Pref.	192
3½	Taff Vale	79
25/	Vale of Glamorgan........	127½
3	Waterloo & City	117½

LEASED AT FIXED RENTALS.

Last Div.	Name.	Price.
4	Birkenhead	146
5.10.0	East Lincnshire..........	202½
5½	Hamsmith. & City Ord. ..	192½
4½	Lond. and Blackwll.	161½
4½	Do. £100 4½ p. c. Pref...	161½
36/6	Lond. & Green. Ord.......	102
5	Do. 5 p. c. Pref.	176½
5	Nor. and Eastn. £50 Ord...	90
6	Do. ..	104½
3½	N. Cornwall 3½ p. c. Stk...	126½
4 7/8	Nott. & Granthm. R. & C...	145½
3½	Portptk. & Wigtn. Guar. Stk.	121½
9	Vict. Stn. & Pimlico Ord...	312½
4½	Do. 4½ p. c. Pref....	160½
4/	West Lond. £20 Ord. Shs.	14
4	Weymouth & Portld......	157½

DEBENTURE STOCKS.

Last Div.	Name.	Price.
4	Alexandra Dks. & Ry.	128
3	Barry, Cons.	107
4	Brecon & Mrthyr, New A	124½
4	Do. New B	105
4	Caledonian	148
4	Cambrian "A"	135½
4	Do. "B"	130½
4	Do. "C"	120½
4	Do. "D"	107½
3	Cardiff Rly.	103½
4	City and S. Lond.	137
3½	Cleator & Working Junc...	118½
3	Devon & Som. "A"	103½
10/3	Do. "B" 4 p. c.	36
—	Do. "C" 4 p. c.	10
4	E. Lond. and Ch. 4 p. c. A	136
6/	Do. 2nd B	70½
—	Do. 3rd Ch. 4 p. c. ..	22½
—	Do. 4th do.	11½
3½	Do. 1st (3½ p. c.)	128½
2½	Do. 2½ p.c. (Whitech. Exn)	87
4	Forth Bridge	142½
4	Furness	140½
4	Glasgow and S. Western ..	143
5	Gt. Central	—
4½	Do.	156½
4	Gt. Eastern	146
4	Gt. N. of Scotland..........	144½
3	Gt. Northern	113
4	Gt. Western..............	151
4½	Do	158½
4½	Do.	166½
5	Do.	185½
2½	Do.	96½
4	Highland	140½
3	Hull and Barnsley	104½
3	Do. 2nd (3-4 p. c)...	126
4	Isle of Wight	142½
3	Do. Cent. "A"..	92½
4½	Do. "B"	115½
4	Do. "C"	82½
3	Lancs. & Yorkshire	112
4	Lancs. Derbys. & E. Cst..	123½
4½	Ldn. and Blackwall	155½
4	Ldn. and Greenwich......	144½
4	Lond., Brighton, &c.	148½
4½	Do.	166½
4½	Lond., Chath., &c., Arb. ..	156½
4½	Do. "B" ..	154½
4	Do.	138½
4	Do. 1883....	138½
3	Do.	106
3	Lond. & N. Western......	117
3	Lond. & S. Westn. "A" ..	115
3	Do. Consld.	115
4	Lond., Til., & Southend ..	145
—	Mersey, 5 p. c. (Act, 1866)	65
4	Metropolitan	146
4½	Do.	162½
3½	Do.	126½
6	Met. District	208½
4	Do.	138½
2½	Midland	96
4½	Mid-Wales "A"	137½
4	Neath & Brecon 1st	122½
4	Do. "A 1" ..	117½
3	North British	111
3	Do. 1893	109
3½	N. Cornwall, Launcstn., &c.	126½
4	North Eastern............	114

Debenture Stocks (*continued*):—

Last Div.	Name.	Price.
4½	North London..............	163½
3	N. Staffordshire	112
4	Plym. Devpt. & S.W. Jn...	141½
4	Rhondda and Swan. Bay..	130½
4	Rhymney	144½
4	South-Eastern............	148
5	Do.	184½
3½	Do.	127½
3	Do.	114
3	Taff Vale	108½
4	Tottenham & For. Gate ..	143½
3	Vale of Glamorgan	105½
3	West Highld. (Gtd. by N.B.)	107½
4	Wrexham, Mold, &c. "A"	113½
4	Do. "B"	101½
4	Do. "C"	97½

GUARANTEED SHARES AND STOCKS.

Last Div.	Name.	Price.
4	Caledonian	143½
4	Do.	143½
4	Forth Bridge	142½
4	Furness 1881	136½
4	Glasgow & S. Western	143
4	Do. St. Enoch, Rent	141½
6	Gt. Central	198½
4½	Do. 1st Pref........	152½
3½	Do. Pref.	108½
5	Do. Irred. S.Y. Rent	164½
4½	Do. do.	140½
4	Gt. Eastern, Rent	143
5	Do. Metropolitan..	175½
4	Do.	145
4	Gt. N. of Scotland........	138½
4	Gt. Northern	146
5	Gt. Western, Rent........	185
5	Do. Cons.	185
4	Lancs. & Yorkshire	146
5	L., Brighton & S. C.......	184
3½	L., Chat. & D. (Shrtlds.)..	110½
4	L. & North Western	149
4	L. & South Western.. 1881	146
4½	Met. District, Ealing Rent	151½
4½	Do. Fulham Rent	151½
4	Do. Midland Rent	141½
4	Do. Mid. & Dist. Guar.	130½
2½	Midland, Cons. Perp.	94
3	Mid. & G. N. Jt., "A" Rnt..	107
3	N. British, Lien	109
4	Do Cons. Pref. No. 1	139
3	N. Cornwall, Wadebrge. Gu.	107
4	N. Eastern	146
5	N. Staff. Trent & M. £20 Shs.	36
3½	Nott. Suburban Ord.	123½
20/6	S. E. Perp. Ann.	35½
4½	Do. 4½ p.c...........	162½
3½	S. Yorks. Junc. Ord.	118½
4½	W. Cornwall (G. W., Br., Ex., & S. Dev. Joint Rent	162
3	W. Highl. Ord. Stk. (Gua., N.B.)..................	105

PREFERENCE SHARES AND STOCKS.

DIVIDENDS CONTINGENT ON PROFIT OF YEAR.

Last Div.	Name	Price.
4½	Alexandra Dks. & Ry. "A"	126½
5	Barry (First)	169½
4	Do. Consolidated......	137½
4	Caledonian Cons., No. 1 ..	143
4	Do. do. No. 2 ..	141
5	Do. do. 1878	177
4	Do. Pref. 1884	141
4	Do. do. 1887 (Conv.)	150½
—	Cambrian, No. 1 4 p.c. Pref.	72½
—	Do. No. 2 do.	37½
—	Do. No. 3 do.	17½
—	Do. No. 4 do.	9
5	City & S. Lond. £10 shares	15½
—	Do. New	14
4	Furness, Cons. 1881	131½
4	Do. ......"A" 1881	129½
4	Do. ......"B" 1883	127½
4	Glasgow & S. Western	143
4	Do. No. 2....	141
4	Do. 1888	139½
4	Do. 1891	139½
5	Gt. Central	159½
4	Do.	133½
5	Do. Conv..... 1872	154½
5	Do. do. 1874	153½
5	Do. do. 1876	153½
5	Do. do. 1879	152
5	Do. do. 1881	149½
4	Do. 1889	112½
4	Do. 1891	108½
5	Do. 1894	106½
4	Gt. Eastern, Cons..........	143
4	Do. 1886	141½
4	Do. 1881	139½
4	Do. 1884	139½

Preference Shares, &c. (*continued*):—

Last Div.	Name.	Price.
4	Gt. Eastern, Cons..... 1887	139½
4	Do. 1888	139½
3½	Do. 1890	120½
3½	Do. 1893	120½
—	Do. (Int. fr. Jan '99) 1893	117½
4	Gt. North Scotland "A"..	133½
4	Do. "B"..	133½
4	Gt. Northern, Cons.	146
3	Do. 1896	108
5	Gt. Western Cons.	184
36/11	Hull & Barnsley Red. at 115	113
4	Isle of Wight	133½
3	Lancs. & Yorkshire, Cons.	109
2/2½	Lanc. Drby & E.C. 5 p.c. £10	9½
—	Do. 5 p.c. 2nd £10	9
5	Lond., Bright., &c., Cons.	182
5	Do. and Cons.	181
4½	Lond., Chat. & Dov. Arbitr.	137½
25/	Do. 2nd Pref. 4½ p.c.	100
4	Lond. & N. Western......	146
4	Lond. & S. Western.. 1881	146
4	Do. 1884	145
3½	Do.	127½
4	Lond., Tilbury & Southend	141½
4	Do. Cons., 1887	141½
4	Do 1891	141½
—	Mersey, 5 p.c. Perp.	—
4	Metropolitan, Perp.	143
4	Do. 1882	140½
4	Do. Irred.	141½
4	Do. 1887	141½
4	Do. New........	141½
4½	Do.	146½
3½	Do.	123½
3	Do. Guar.	101½
2½	Metrop. Dist. Exten 5 p.c.	111
2½	Midland, Perp. Pref.	93
4	N. British Cons., No. 2 ..	137
4½	Do. Edin. & Glasgow	153
5	Do. 1865	165½
5	Do. Conv. 1874	166½
4½	Do. 1875	153
4½	Do. Conv. 1875	153
5	Do. do. 1870	166½
4	Do. do. 1884	136½
4	Do. do. 1888	136½
4	Do. do. 1890	136½
4	Do. do. 1892	136½
4	N. Eastern	146
4½	N. Lond., Cons. 1866	174½
4½	Do. 2nd Cons. .. 1875	157½
3	N. Staffordshire	108
4½	Plym. Devpt. & S. W. Junc.	149½
1/5	Port Talbot, &c., 4 p.c. £10 Shares, 4 paid	5
5/	Rhondda & Swansea Bay, 5 p.c. £10 Shares	11
4	Rhymney, Cons..........	140½
4½	S. Eastern, Cons.	162½
5	Do. do.	180
4	Do. Vested Cos	141½
4	Do. 1891	141½
3½	Do. 1893	124½
2	Do. 3 p.c. after July 1900	103½
4	Taff Vale	138½

INDIAN RAILWAYS.

Last Div.	Name.	Paid.	Price.
3½	Assam Bengal, Ld., (3½ c. till June 30, then 3 p.c.)	100	102
4/	Barsi Light, Ld., £10 Shs.	10	10½
4	Bengal and N. West., Ld	100	145
4/	Do. £10 Shares	10	13½
3/6	Do. 3½ p.c. Cum. Pf. Shs.	10	10½
8½d.	Do.	4	6
2/3½	Bengal Central, Ld., £10 (3½ p.c. + ¼th net earn)	5	6
7	Bengal Dooars, Ld.	100	111
4	Bengal Nagpr., Lim. (gua. 4 p.c. + 4th sp. pfts.) ..	100	114
7½	Bombay, Baroda, and C. I. (gua 5 p.c)	100	220
36/1	Burma, Ld. (gua. 2½ p.c. and ½ p.c. add. till 1901)	100	109
1/7	Do. £10 Shares		3½
5½	Delhi Umb, Kalka, Ld., Gua. 3½ p.c. + net earn.	100	123
4	Do. Deb. Stk., 1890 (1916)	100	111
9/10	Estn. Bengal, "A" An. 1957	—	25
9/	Do. "B" 1957	—	30
4	Do. Gua. Deb. Stock ..	100	134½
9/7½	East Ind. Ann. "A" (1953)	—	27
8/4½	Do. "C"	—	28
8/11½	Do. "B"	—	30
6⅞	Do. Def. Ann. Cap. (gua. 4 p.c. + ⅕th sp. pfts.)	—	150½
115/9	East Ind. Def. Ann. "D"	—	157
4½	East Ind. Irred. Stock ..	100	167½
5	Gt. Indian Penin., Gua 5 p.c. + ½ surplus profits..	100	167½
4	Do. Irred. 4 p.c. Deb. St.	100	138½
4	Indian Mid., Ld. (gua. 4 p.c. + ¼th surplus pfts.)	100	114
5	Madras Guar. + ½ sp. pfts.	100	162
4½	Do. do.	100	153
4½	Do. do.	100	143
4	Nilgiri, Ld., 1st Deb. Stk.	100	98
51/9	Robil. and Kumaon, Ld.	100	130
9/11	Scinde, Punj., and Delhi, "A" Ann., 1958	—	25
9/1	Do. "B" do. ..	—	30

Indian Railways (*continued*):—

Last Div.	Name.	Paid.	Price.
4	South Behar, Ld., £10 shs.	100	100
3½	Do. Deb. Stk. Red.	100	101
4½	South Ind., Gu. Deb. Stk.	100	156½
5	South Indian, Ld. (gua. 3 p.c., and ¼ spls. profits)	100	122½
5	Sthn. Mahratta, Ld. (3½ p.c. & ⅛th net earnings)	100	113½
4	Do. Deb. Stk. Red.	100	121
3½	Southern Punjab, Ld.....	100	105
3½	Do. Deb. Stk. Red.	—	104
5	Nizam's Gua. State, Ld...	100	117½
4	Do. Mort. Deb., 1936	100	108½
4	Do. do. Reg.	100	107
17/3½	Nizam's Gua. State, Ld., 3½ p.c. Mt. Deb. bearer	—	95½
17/3½	Do. Reg. do. ..	—	93½
5	W. of India Portgese., Ld.	100	75
5	Do. Deb. Stk., Red	100	102

RAILWAYS.—BRITISH POSSESSIONS.

Last Div.	Name.	Paid.	Price.
5	Atlantic & N.W. Gua. 1 Mt. Bds., 1937	100	126½
5/3	Buff. & L. Huron Ord. Sh.	10	13½
5½	Do. 1st Mt. Perp. Bds. 1879	100	143½
5½	Do. 2nd Mt. Perp. Bds.	100	143½
—	Calgary & Edmon. 6 p.c. 1st Mt. Stg. Bds. Red..	100	83½
5	Canada Cent. 1st Mt. Bds. Red.	100	103
4	Can. Pacific Pref. Stk.....	100	102
5	Do. Strl. 1st Mt. Deb. Bds. 1915	100	118
3½	Do. Ld. Grnt. Bds. 1938..	100	108½
3½	Do. Ld. Grnt. Ins. Stk. ..	100	107
4	Do. Perp. Cons. Deb. Stk.	100	113
5	Do. Algoma Bch. 1st Mt. Bds., 1937	100	122
3	Demerara, Original Stock	100	47½
7	Do. Perp. Pref. Stk.....	100	152½
1/10	Do. 4 p.c. Cum. Ext. Pref. £10 Shs.	4	8
—	Dominion Atlntc. Ord. Stk.	100	33½
5	Do. 5 p.c. Pref. Stk.....	100	97½
4	Do. 1st. Deb. Stk......	100	105½
4	Do. 2nd do. Red.	100	100
1/3	EmuBay&Mt.Bischoff, Ld.	5	4½
4½	Do. Irred. Deb. Stk ...	100	98
nil.	Gd. Trunk of Canada, Stk.	100	8½
6	Do. 2nd. Equip. Mt. Bds.	100	133
5	Do. Perp. Deb. Stk......	100	140½
5	Do. Gt. Westn. Deb. Stk.	100	131½
5	Do. Nthn. of Can. 1st Mt. Bds , 1902	100	104½
4	Do. do. Deb. Stk	100	104
5	Do. G. T. Geor. Bay & L. Erie 1 Mt., 1903	100	105
5	Do. Mid. of Can. Stl. 1st Mt. (Mid. Sec.) 1908	100	106
5	Do.do.Cons.1 Mt.Bds. 1912	100	108
5	Do. Mont. & Champ. 1 Mt. Bds., 1902	100	104
	Do. Welln., Grey & Brce. 7 p.c. Bds. 1 Mt.	100	110
—	Jamaica 1st Mtg. Bds. Red.	—	103
—	Manitoba & N. W., 6 p.c. 1st Mt. Bds., Red	100	—
—	Do. Ldn. Bdhldrs. Certs.	—	—
5	Manitoba S. W. Col. 1 Mt. Bd., 1934 $1,000 price %	—	119
—	Mid. of W. Aust. Ld. 6 p.c. 1 Mt. Dbs., Red.	100	42½
4	Do. Deb. Bds., Red.	100	104
4	Nakusp & Slocan Bds., 1918	100	106
3	Natal Zululand Ld. Debs.,	100	72½
5	N. Brunswick 1st Mt. Stg. Bds., 1934	100	121
4	Do. Perp. Cons. Deb. Stk.	100	112
—	N. Zealand Mid., Ld., 5 p.c. 1st Mt. Debs...........	100	35
6	Ontario & Queb. Cap. Stk.	$100	151½
5	Do. Perm. Deb. Stk......	100	144½
—	Qu'Appelle, L. Lake & Sask.6p.c.1 Mt.Bds.Red.	100	40
	Queb. & L. S. John, 1st Mt. Bds., 1909	100	39½
	Quebec Cent., Prior Ln. Bds., 1908	100	107
2½	Do. 5 p.c. Inc. Bds.	100	36
4	St. Lawr. & Ott. Stl. 1st Mt.	100	111
4	Shuswap & Okan., 1st Mt. Deb. Bds., 1915	100	76
5	Temiscouata, 5 p.c. Stl. 1st Deb. Bds., Red.........	100	9½
5	Do. (S. Franc. Brch.) 5 p.c. Stl. 1 Mt. Db. Bds., 1910	100	12
4	Toronto, Grey & B. 1st Mt.	100	112
1/	Well. & Mana. £5 Shs. ..	1	½
5	Do. Debs., 1908	100	108
5	Do. 2nd Debs., 1908	100	104
5	Do. 3rd do., 1908	100	103
6	Atlan. & St. Law. Shs., 6 p.c.	100	163½
5	Gd. Trunk Mt. Bds., 1934	100	116½
5	Michigan Air Line, 5 p.c. 1st Mt. Bds., 1902	100	104
4	Minneap., S. P. & S t. Ste. Mar, 1st Mt. Bds., 1938	$1000	100

AMERICAN RAILROAD STOCKS AND SHARES.

Last Div.	Name.	Paid.	Price.
6/	Alab. Gt. Sthn. A 6 p.c. Pref.	10/.	9½
—	Do. do "B" Ord. ..	10/.	1½
—	Alabma. N. Orl.-Tex. &c., "A" Pref.	10/.	¾
—	Do. "B" Def.	10/.	¼
5½	Atlant. First Lsd. Ls. Rtl. Trust................	Stk.	98½
—	Baltimore & Ohio Com. ..	$100	20
—	Baltimore Ohio S.W. Pref.	$100	7
—	Chesap. & Ohio Com.	$100	23½
—	Chic. Gt. West. 5 p.c. Pref. Stock "A"	$100	34
—	Do. do. Scrip. In.......	—	30½
8/3	Do. 4 p.c. Deb. Stk.......	$100	67½
4	Do. Interest in Scrip	$100	63½
$4	Chic. Junc. Rl. & Un. Stk. Yds. Com.	$100	121½
$1½	Do. 6 p.c. Cum. Pref.	$100	119½
$3½	Chic. Mil. & St. P. Pref...	$100	152½
7	Cleve. & Pittsburgh......	$10	87½
$1½	Clev., Cincin., Chic., & St. Louis Com.	$100	—
—	Erie 4 p.c. Non-Cum. 1st Pf.	—	36½
—	Do. 4 p.c. do. 2nd Pf.	—	20
$2½	Gt. Northern Pref.	$100	180
$4	Illinois Cen. Lsd. Lines ..	$100	92½
—	Kansas City, Pitts & G. ..	$100	19
$3	L. Shore & Mich. Sth. C.	$100	190
—	Mex. Cen. Ltd. Com.	$100	5
—	Miss. Kan. & Tex. Pref...	$100	38½
2½	N.Y., Pen. & O. 1st Mt. Tst. Ltd., Ord.	—	47½
4	Do. 1st Mort. Deb. Stk. ..	$100	92½
2	North Pennsylvania	$50	—
—	Northn. Pacific, Com.....	$100	29½
1½	Pitts. F. Wayne & Chic...	$100	172½
—	Reading 1st Pref.	$50	93½
—	Do. 2nd Pref..........	$50	12
—	S. Louis & S. Fran. Com.	$100	8
—	Do. 2nd Pref.	$100	33
6	St. Louis Bridge 1st Pref..	$100	104
3	Do. 2nd Pref.........	$100	47½
6	Tunnel Rail. of St. Louis	$100	104
$1½	St. Paul, Min. and Man...	$100	147½
—	Southern, Com.	$100	8½
—	Wabash, Common........	$100	8

AMERICAN RAILROAD BONDS. CURRENCY.

Last Div.	Name.	Price.
7	Albany & Susq. 1 Con. Mrt. 1906	118
7	Allegheny Val. 1 Mt....... 1910	127½
5	Canada Southern 1 Mt..... 1908	110½
5	Chic. & N. West. Sk. Fd. Db. 1933	120½
5	Do. Deb. Coupon 1921	117½
6	Chicago & Tomah 1905	109½
5	Chic. Burl. & Q. Skg. Fd. 1901	102½
4	Do. Nebraska Ext....... —	100½
6	Chic., Mil., & S. Pl., 1 Mt. S.W. Div............. 1909	114½
7	Do. (S. Paul Div.) 1 Mt. 1902	129½
5	Do. (La Cross & D. 1919	112½
7	Do. 1 Mt. (Hast. & Dak.) 1910	124½
5	Do. Chic. & Mis. Riv. 1 Mt. 1926	—
6	Det., G. Haven & Mil. Equip 1918	105
6	Do. do. Cons. Mt. 1918	102½
6	Ill. Cent., 1 Mt., Chic. & S. 1898	—
7	Indianap. & Vin., 1 Mt. .. 1908	125
6	Do. do. 2 Mt. .. 1900	100½
6	Lehigh Val., Cons. Mt..... 1923	114½
—	Mexic. Cent., Ln. 2 Cons. Inc. —	5
7	N.Y. Cent. & H.R. Mt. Bonds 1903	117½
5	Do. Deb. 1904	111½
6	Penns. Cons. S. F M. 1905	114½
4	West Shore, 1 Mt. 2361	109

DITTO—GOLD.

Last Div.	Name.	Price.
6	Alabama Gt. Sthn. 1 Mt. ..1908	111
5	Do. Mid. 1 1928	92
4	Allegheny Val. Gen. Mt. ..1942	107½
4	Atch., Top., & S. Fé Gn. Mt. 1995	95½
3	Do. Adj. Mt.............1995	68
5	Do. Equipt. Tmst. .... —	105
5	Atlantic & Dan. 1 Mt.......1950	94
5	Baltimore & Ohio...........1925	107
5	Do. Speyer's Tst. Recpts. 1925	107
5	Do. Cons. Mt. 1988	112½
4½	Do. 4½ p.c. 1 Mt. Term. 1934	90
4½	Do. Brown Shipley's Dep. Cts. —	90
5	Balt. Belt 5 p.c. 1 Mort.....1990	97½
4½	Balt. & Ohio S.W. 1 Mt. ..1990	103
4½	Do. 4½ p.c. 1 Cons. Mt. 1893 1993	76½
—	Do. Inc. Mt. 5 p.c. Cl. A —	29
—	Do. do. Cl. B —	10
5	Balt. & Ohio S.W. Term 5 p.c. 1942	97½
6	Balt. & Ptmac (Mn. L.) 1 Mt. 1911	124
6	Do. do. (Tunnel) 1 Mt. 1911	122½
4	Beech Creek 1 Mt. 1936	107
4	Carthage & Adiron 1 Mt...1981	107

American Railroad Bonds—Gold (*continued*):—

Last Div.	Name.	Price.
5	Cent. of Georgia 1 Mort. ..1945	117½
5	Do. Cons. Mt. 1945	90½
5	Cent. of N. Jrsy. Gn. Mt...1987	114½
6	Central Pacific, 1 Mort. 1898	102
6	Do. Speyer's Certs. ...... —	102½
5	Do. Land Grant 1900	104
5	Chesap. & Ohio 1st Cons. Mt. 1939	117½
4½	Do. Gen. Mt.............1992	86
6	Chic. & W. Ind. Gen. Mt. Skg. Fd. 1932	119½
5	Chic. Mil. & St. Pl. (Chic. & L. Sup.) 1 Mt. 1921	112½
5	Do. Chic. & Pac. W. 1921	117½
5	Do. Wisc. & Minn. 1 Mt. 1921	109½
5	Do. Terminal Mt. 1914	112½
4	Do. General Mt. 1989	106
5	Chic. St. L. & N. Orleans..1951	122½
4	Do. 1 Mort. (Memphis) ..1951	104
4	Clevel., Cin., Chic. & St. L. 1 Mt. (Cairo) 1939	88
4	Do. 1 Mt. (Cinc., Wab., & Mich.) 1991	88
4	Do. 1 Col. Tst. Mt. (S. Louis) 1990	96
4	Do. General Mt. 1993	80½
4½	Clevel. & Mar. Mt. 1935	109
4½	Clevel. & Pittsburgh 1942	119
4½	Do. Series B. 1942	120
—	Colorado Mid. 1 Mt. 1936	65½
—	Do. Bdhrs.' Comm. Certs. —	65½
4	Dnvr. & R. Gde. 1 Cons. Mt. 1936	96
5	Do Imp. Mort...........1928	94
4	Detroit & Mack. 1 Lien 1995	90
5	E. Tennes., Virg., & Grgia. Cons. Mt. 1956	111½
5	Elmira, Cort., & Nthn. Mt. 1914	100
4	Erie 1 Cons. Mt. Pr. Ln. ..1996	93
3	Do. Gen. Lien 1996	74
6	Galvest., Harrisb., &c., 1 Mt.....	110
5	Georgia, Car. & N. 1 Mt. ..1929	94
4½	Gd. Rpds & Inda. Ex. 1 Mt. 1941	110
5	Do. 1 Mt. (Muskegon) ..1926	39½
3½	Illinois Cent. 1 Mt. 1951	102½
4	Do. 1952	105
4	Do. Cairo Bdge. ..1950	102
4	Do. 1953	103
4	Do. General Mort. ..1904	100½
5	Kans. City, Pitts. & G. 1 M. 1923	74
3½	L. Shore & Mich. Southern 1997	106½
4½	Lehigh Val. N.Y. 1 Mt.....1940	103½
5	Lehigh Val. Term. 1 Mt. ..1941	112
5	Long Island 1931	116
5	Do. Deb...........1934	100
5	Do. (N. Shore Bch.) 1 Cons. Mt. 1932	95½
6	Louisville & Nash. G. Mt...1930	121
6	Do. 2 Mt. Sk. Fd., (S. & N. Alabama.........1910	107
6	Do. 1 Mt. N. Orl. & Mb. 1930	122½
5	Do. 1 Mt. Coll. Tst. ...1931	106
4	Do. Unified 1940	91
4½	Do. Mobile & Montgy. 1 Mt. 1945	111½
4	Manhattan Cons. Mt. 1990	98
4	Mexican Cent. Cons. Mt. ..1911	67
—	Do. 1 Cons. Inc, ...	14
6	Mexican Nat. 1 Mt..........1927	106
3½	Do. 2 Mt. 6 p.c. Inc. A 1917	47½
—	Do. do. B..1917	—
3	Michig. Cnt. (Battle Ck. & S.) 1 Mt. 1989	86
5	Minneap. & S. L. 1 Consold. 1934	107½
4	Minne., Slt. S. M. & A. 1 Mt. 1926	101½
5	Minneapolis Westn. 1 Mt...1911	102½
4	Miss. Kans. & Tex. 1 Mt...1990	90
4	Do. 2 do. 1990	65
4	Mobile & Birm. Mt. Inc....1945	38
5	Do. P. Lien 1945	86
4	Mohawk & Mal. 1 Mt.......1991	108
5	Montana Cent. 1 Mt.......1937	109½
5	Nashv., Chattan., & S. L. 1 Cons. Mt..................1928	102½
5	Nash., Flor., & Shff. Mt...1937	95½
4	N. Y. & Putnam 1 Cons. Mt. 1993	108
5	N. Y., Brooklyn, & Man. B. 1 Cons. Mt..............1935	107½
4	N. Y. Cent. & Hud. R. Deb. Certs. 1890 1905	106
4	Do. Ext. Debt. Certs.....1905	106
7	N. Y., L. Erie, & W. 1 Cons. Mt. (Erie) 1920	144½
7	Do. 1 Con. Mt. Fd. Coup. 1920	142½
5	N. Y., Onto., & W. Cons. 1 Mt......................... —	109
4	Do. 4 p.c. Refund. Mt...1992	101½
6	Norfolk & West. Gn. Mt.....1931	125½
6	Do. Imp. & Ext.........1934	120
4	Do. 1 Cons. Mt......... —	84
6	N. Pacific Gn. 1 Mt. Ld. Gt. 1921	—
4	Do. P. Ln. Rl. & Ld. Gt. —	99
3	Do. Gn. Ln. Rl. & Ld. Gt.. —	63½
5	Oregon & Calif. 1 Mt........1927	94½
6	Panama Skg. Fd. Subsidy..1910	105½
4½	Pennsylvania Rlrd. 1913	112
4	Do. Equip. Tst. Ser. A..1914	104
4	Do. Cons. Mt............1943	112½
4½	Penna. Company 1st Mort. 1921	112½
5	Perkiomen 1 Mrt., 2nd ser...1918	91½
4½	{ Pitts., C., C., & St. Ls. Con. Mt. G. B., Ser. A } 1940-2	114½
4	Do. Cons. Mort., Ser. D..1945	104½
6	Pittsbgh., Cle., & Toledo ..1922	105½
4	Reading, Phil., & R. Genl. 1997	86
5	Richmond & Dan. Equip. ..1909	97½
5	Rio Grande Junc. 1st Mort. 1936	90
4	Rio Grande West 1st Tst. Mt. 1939	88
7	S. Louis Bridge 1st Mort 1928	134½
5	S. Louis Mchts. Bdge. Term. 1st Mort.................1930	102½
4	S. Louis S. West 1st Mort..1989	76½
—	Do. 4 p.c. 2nd Mort. Inc. 1989	30
4½	S. Louis Term. Cupples Sta. & Prop. 1st. Mrt. 4½ p.c. 1902-17	100
4½	St. Paul Minn., & Manit. 1933	109

American Railroad Bonds (*continued*):—

Last Div.	Name.	Price.
6	St. Paul, Minn., & Manit. 1933	129½
6	Shamokin, Sunbury, &c. 2 Mt. 1925	106
5	S. & N. Alabama Cons. Mt. 1936	102
5	Southern 1 Cons. Coup. 1994	96
4	Do. E. Tennes Reorg. Lien ..1938	100
6	S. Pacific of Cal. 1 Mt...1905-12	111½
4½	Trml. Assn. of S. Louis 1 Mt. 1939	112
5	Do. 1 Cons. Mt..........1944	109
5	Texas & Pac. 1 Mt...........2000	106½
—	Do. 5 p.c. 2 Mt. Income 2000	39
5	Toledo & Ohio Cent. 1 Mt. West. Div. 1935	102½
4½	Toledo., Walhon., Val., & Ohio 1 Mt. 1931-5	109½
4	Union Pacific 1 Mt. 4 p.c. ..1947	97
—	Union Pac., Linc., & Color. 1 Mt. 1918	—
4	United N. Jersey Gen. Mt...1944	117½
6	Vicksbrg., Shrevept., & Pac. Pr. Ln. Mt. 1915	102½
5	Wabash 1 Mt. 1939	110
4	Wn. Pennsylvania Mt. 1928	106½
5	W. Virga. & Pittsbg. 1 Mt. 1990	77½
5	Wheeling & L. Erie 1 Mt. (Wheelg. Div.) 5 p.c. 1928	96
5	Do. Extn. Imp. Mt.....1930	90
—	Do. do. Brown Shipley's Cts...	—
5	Willmar & Sioux Falls 1 Mt. 1938	110

STERLING.

Last Div.	Name.	Price.
6	Alabama Gt. Sthn. Deb.....1906	104½
5	Do. Gen. Mort. ..1927-8	98
5	Alabama, N. Orl., Tex. & Pac. 5 p.c. "A" Dbs...1910-40	101
55/	Do. do. "B" do. 1910-40	59
—	Do. do. "C" do.	20½
—	Allegheny Valley 1910	132
4	Atlantic 1st Leased Line Perp...	100
6	Baltimore and Ohio.........1902	110
6	Do. do. 1910	123½
5	Do. do. 1877.........	106½
—	Do. Morgan's Certs. ..	106½
4½	Do. do. 1933	100
6	Chicago & Alton Cons. Mt. 1903	112
5	Chic. St. Paul & Kan. City Priority	106½
6	Eastn. of Massachusetts....1906	117½
5	Illinois Cent. Skg. Fd.	104
5	Do. 1905	104
3½	Do. 1950	99½
4	Do. 1 Mt. 1951	114
3	Do. 1 Mt. 1951	93½
6	Louisville & Nash., M. C. & L. Div., 1 Mt. 1902	107
7	Do. 1 Mt. (Memphis & O.)........................1901	110
55/8	Mexican Nat. "A" Certs. 5 p.c. Non. cum.	40½
—	Do. "B" Certs.....	9
6	N.Y. & Canada 1 Mt.......1904	110
6	N. York Cent. & H.R. Mort. 1903	112
4½	N. York, Penna., & Ohio Pr. Ln. Extd. 1935	—
5	Do. Equip. Tst.	101½
5	Do. 5 p.c. Equip. Tst. (1890)	101½
6	Nrthn. Cent. Cons. Gen. Mt. ..	106
6	Pennsylvania Gen. Mt. 1910	127½
6	Do. Cons. Skg. Fd. Mt. 1905	116½
3½	Do. Cons. Mt..........1945	105
6	Phil. & Erie Cons. Mort ..1920	134½
6	Phil. & Reading Gen. Cons. Mort. 1911	124
6	Pittsbg. & Connells. Cons. 1926	119½
—	Do. Morgan's Certs.....	119½
4	St. Paul., Min., & Manitoba (Pac. Extn.) 1940	101
6	S. & N. Alabama...........1903	106½
6	Un. N. Jersey & C. Gen. Mt. 1901	108½

FOREIGN RAILWAYS

Last Div.	Name.	Paid.	Price.
12/	Alagoas, Ltd., Shs.......	20	6½
5	Do. Deb. Stk., Red. ..	100	45½
6	Antofagasta, Ltd., Stk. ..	100	74
4	Do. Perp. Deb. Stk. ..	100	91
—	Arauco, Ld., Ord. Shs. ..	10	—
—	Do. 10 p.c. Cum. Pref.	10	—
5	Argentine Gt. W., Ld.,	100	83
5	Do. 5 p.c. Cum. Pref. Shs.	100	105
4	Do. 1 Deb. Stk.	100	104
1/0/0	Argentine N.E., Ltd., 6 p.c. Cum. Pref. Stk. ..	100	94
—	Do. 5 p.c. Deb. Stk., Red.	100	29
2/	Arica and Tacna Shs. ..	20	1½
10/	Bahia & San Fcisco., Ld.,	20	8½
6/	Do. Timbo. Bch. Shs.	20	5
12/	Bahia, Blanca, & N.W. Ln. Prf. Cum. 6 p.c. ..	100	52
4	Do. 4 p.c. 1 Deb. Stk., Red.	100	91
6	Barranquilla R. & P., Ld., 6 p.c. 1 Deb. Stk., Red.	100	96

Foreign Railways (*continued*):—

Last Div.	Name.	Paid.	Price.
3/	Bilbao Riv. & Cantabn., Ltd., Ord.	3	5
—	Bolivar, Ltd. Shs.	10	1½
6	Do. 6 p.c. Deb. Stk.	100	96½
—	Brazil Gt. Southn. Ltd., 7 p.c. Cum. Pref.	20	1¼
6	Do. Perm. Deb. Stk	100	51
5½	B. Ayres Gt. Southn. Ld., Ord. Stk.	100	139
5	Do. Pref. Stk.	100	133
4	Do. Deb. Stk.	100	118
30/	B. Ayres & Ensen. Port., Ltd., Ord. Stk.	100	66
5	Do. Cum. 1 Pref. Stk.	100	117
6/0/0	Do. 6p.c.Con. Pref.Stk.	100	96
4	Do. Deb. Stk., Irred.	100	113
10⅓	B. Ayres Northern, Ltd., Ord. Stk.	100	260
10½	Do. Pref. Stk.	100	320
5	Do. 5 p.c. Mt. Deb.Stk., Red.	100	113
3/15/0	B. Ayres & Pac., Ld., 7 p.c. 1 Pref. Stk. (Cum.)	100	91½
4	Do. 1 Deb. Stk.	100	101
5/5/0	Do. 4½ p.c. 2 Deb. Stk.	100	92
3	B. Ayres & Rosario, Ltd., Ord. Stk.	100	71½
7/	Do. 7 p.c. Pref. Shs.	10	17
7/	Do. Sunchales Ext.	10	14½
4	Do. Deb. Stk., Red.	100	107
12/	B. Ayres & Val. Trans., Ltd., 7 p.c. Cum. Pref.	20	6½
4	Do. 4 p.c. "A" Deb. Stk., Red.	100	70
—	Do. 6 p.c. "B" Deb. Stk. Red.	100	45
3/6	B. Ayres Westn. Ld. Ord.	10	10½
3/	Do. Def. Shs.	10	6½
5	Do. 5 p.c. Pref.	10	13
4	Do. Deb. Stk	100	112
6	Cent.Arg. Deb.Sk. Rd.	100	159½
4	Do. Deb. Stk. Rd.	100	110
6	Cent. Bahia L. Ord. Stk.	100	46½
	Do. Deb. Stk., 1934	100	67½
5	Do. Deb. Stk., 1937	100	59
3/6	Cent. Uguy. East. Ext. L. Shs.	10	5½
5	Do. Perm. Stk.	100	112
3/6	Do. Nthn. Ext. L. Sh.	10	4
5	Do. Perm. Deb. Stk.	100	104
3	Do. of Montev. Ltd., Ord. Stk	100	85
6	Do. Perm. Deb. Stk.	100	143
10/	Conde d'Eu, Ltd. Ord.	20	7
—	Cordba & Rosar., Ltd., 6 p.c. Pref. Shs.	100	38
4	Do. 1 Deb. Stk.	100	89
75	Do. 6 p.c. Deb. Stk.	100	78
—	Cordba Cent., Ltd., 5 p.c. Cu. 1 Pref. Stk.	100	83
—	Do. 5 p.c. Non-Cum. 2 Pref. Stk.	100	43
5	Do. Deb. Stk.	100	118
4/	Costa Rica, Ltd., Shs.	10	3½
8/	Dna. Thrsa. Chris., Ltd., 7 p.c. Pref. Shs.	20	3½
20/	E. Argentine, Ltd.	100	46
6	Do. Deb. Stk.	100	103
1/1	Egyptn. Dlta. Lgt. Rys., Ltd., £10 Pref. Shs.	8	10½
—	Entre Rios, L., Ord. Shs.	5	½
—	Do. Cu. 5 p.c. Pref.	5	2½
6/	Gt. Westn. Brazil, Ltd.,	20	8
6	Do. Perm. Deb. Stk.	100	93
6	Do. Extn. Deb. Stk.	100	75½
—	Int.-Oceanic Mex., Ltd., 7 p.c. Pref.	10	1½
4	Do. Deb. Stk.	100	83
42/6	Do. 7 p.c. "A" Deb. Sk.	100	69
—	Do. 7 p.c. "B" Deb. Sk.	100	30
5/	La Guaira & Carac.	10	7½
5	Do. 5 p.c. Deb. Sk. Red.	100	103
13/3	Lembg.-Czern.-Jassy	30	24½
1/	Lima, Ltd.	20	2½
—	Manila Ltd. 7 p.c. Cu. Pf.	10	¾
20/6½	Mexican 2nd Pref. 6 p.c.	100	33
6	Do. Perp Deb. Stk.	100	138½
1/0/0	Mexican Sthrn., Ld., Ord.	100	22
—	Do. 4 p.c. 1 Db.Stk.Rd.	100	85
—	Do. 4 p.c. 2 do.	100	59
—	Mid. Urgy., Ltd.	100	17½
4	Do. Deb. Stk.	100	57
12/	Minas & Rio, Ltd.	20	9
5/2	Namur & Liege	20	12½
11/6	Do. Pref.	20	29
13/	Natal & Na. Cruz, Ld., 7 p.c. Cum Pref.	20	6
—	Nitrate Ltd., Ord.	10	5½
—	Do. 7 p.c. Pr. Con. Or.	10	4
—	Do. Def. Conv. Ord.	10	½
7/	N.-E. Urgy., Ltd., Ord.	10	14½
7/	Do. 7 p.c. Pref.	10	15½
—	N.-W. Argentine Ld., 7 p.c. Pref.	10	2
6	Do. 6 p.c. 1 Deb. Stk.	100	110
—	Do. 2 Deb. Stk.	100	94
—	N.W. Uruguay 6 p.c. 1 Pref. Stk.	100	16
—	Do. 5 p.c. 2 Pref. Stk.	100	7½
6	Do. 6 p.c. Deb. Stk.	100	75½
22/	Ottoman (Sm. Aid.)	20	13
—	Paraguay Cntl., Ld., 5 p.c. Perm. Deb. Stk.	100	10
—	Piræus, Ath., & Pelo.	275	2
4/	Pto. Alegre & N. Hambg. Ld., 7 p.c. Pref. Shs.	20	3½
6	Do. Mt. Deb. Stk. Red.	100	74½
—	Puerto Cabello & Val. Ld.	10	1½
5	Recife & S. Francisco	100	60
24/	R. Claro S. Paulo, Ld., Sh.	10	23
5	Do. Deb. Stk.	100	127
5	Royal Sardinian Ord.	10	11½
5/	Do. Pref.	10	11½

Foreign Railways (*continued*):—

Last Div.	Name.	Paid.	Price.
5/	Sambre & Meuse	20	18
5/6	Do. Pref.	10	12½
22/	San Paulo Ld.	20	33½
2/10½	Do. New Ord. £10 sh.	6	9½
4/8	Do. 5 p.c. Non.Cm.Pref.	10	12
5½	Do. Deb. Stk.	100	133
5	Do. 5 p.c. Deb. Stk.	100	123
—	S. Fé & Cordova, Gt. Sthn., Ld., Shares	100	49
6	Do. Perp. Deb. Stk.	100	119
3/9½	S. Austrian	20	7
12/	Sthn. Braz. R. Gde. do Sul, Ld.	20	8
6	Do. 6 p.c. Deb. Stk.	100	65
4	Swedish Centl., Ld., 4 p.c. Deb. Stk.	100	107
5	Do. Pref.	100	101
1/3	Taltal, Ld.	5	2½
—	Uruguay Nthn., Ld. 7 p.c. Pfd. Stk.	100	8
3½	Do. 5 p.c. Deb. Stk.	100	30
—	Villa Maria & Rufino, Ld., 6 p.c. Pref. Shs.	100	17
4	Do. 4 p.c. 1 Deb. Stk.	100	71
6/0/0	Do. 6 p.c. 2 Deb. Stk.	100	42½
3/9	West Flanders	8½	21
5/6	Do. 5½ p.c. Pref.	10	18
3/	Wstn. of Havana, Ld.	10	4½

FOREIGN RAILWAY OBLIGATIONS

Per Cent.	Name.	Price.
6	Alagoas Ld., 6 p.c. Deb., Rd.	84
—	Alcoy & Gandia, Ld., 5 p.c. Debs., Red.	20
5	Arauco., Ld., 5 p.c. 1st Mt., Rd.	64½
—	Do. 6 p.c. Mt. Deb., Rd.	39½
6	Brazil G. Sthn., L., Mt. Dbs., Rd.	80½
6	Do. Mt. Dbs. 1893, Rd.	51
5½	Campos & Caran. Dbs., Rd.	70
6	Central Bahia, L., Dbs., Rd.	87½
5½	Conde d'Eu, L., Dbs., Rd.	71
6	Costa Rica, L., 1st Mt. Dbs., Rd.	110
6	Do. 2nd Dbs., Rd.	91
5	Do. Prior Mt. Db., Rd.	104
6	Cucuta Mt. Dbs., Rd.	102
5½	Donna Thrsa. Cris., L., Dbs., Rd.	71
3	Eastn. of France, £20 Dbs., Rd.	18½
4	Egyptn. Delta Light, L., Db., Rd	101
—	Espito. Santo & Cara. 5 p.c. Stl. Dbs., Rd.	38
4	Gd. Russian Nic., Rd.	102
5	Inter-Oceanic Mex., L., 5 p.c. Pr. Ln. Dbs., Rd.	103
3	Ital. 3 p.c. Bds. A & B, Rd.	57½
—	Ituana 6 p.c. Debs., 1918	72½
—	Manila Ltd., 6 p.c. Deb., Red.	21
6	Do. Prior Lien Mt., Rd.	100½
6	Do. Series "B," Rd.	80
7	Matanzas & Sab., Rd.	99½
6	Minas & Rio, L., 6 p.c. Dbs., Rd.	97
5	Mogyana 5 p.c. Deb. Bds., Rd.	101
5	Moscow-Jaros., Rd.	105½
5½	Natal & Na. Cruz Ltd., 5½ p.c. Debs., Red.	75½
5	Nitrate, Ltd. Mt. Bds., Red.	87
3	Nthn. France, Red.	19½
4	N. of S. Af. Rep. (Trnsvl.) Gu. Bds. Red.	96
3	Nthn. of Spain £20 Pri. Obs. Red.	7½
6	Ottmn. (Smy to A.)(Kujk) Asnt. Debs., Red.	107
6	Ottmn. (Seraik.) Asg. Debs. Red.	107
6	Ottmn. (Seraik.) Non-Asg. D., Rd	107
5	Ottmn. Kuyjk. Ext. Red.	105
5	Ottmn. Serkeuy. Ext. Red.	102
5	Ottmn. Tireh Ext. 1910	98
5	Ottmn. Debs, 1886, Red.	98½
5	Do. 1888, Red. 1935	98½
5	Do. 1893, Red. 1935	97
5	Ottmn. of Anlia. Debs., Rd.	90½
4	Ottomn. Smyr. & Cas Ext. Bds., Red.	84
3	Paris, Lyon & Medit. (old sys., £20), Red.	19
3	Paris, Lyon & Medit. (new sys., £20), Red.	18½
30/	Piræus, At. & Pelp., 6 p.c. 1st Mt. Bds., Red.	89½
3	Do. 5 p.c. Mt. Bds., Red.	71½
4	Pretoria-Pietbg., Ltd., Red.	93
7	Puerto Cab. & Val., Ltd., 1st Mt. Debs., Red.	81
3	Royal Sardinian, A, Rd. £20	12
3	Royal Sardinian, B., Rd. £20	12
5	Ryl. Trns.-Afric. 5 p.c. 1st Mt. £100 Bds., Red.	48½
4	Sa. Fe & Cor. G.S., Ld. Pr Ln. Bds.	104
5	Sa. Fe, 5 p.c. 2nd Reg. Dbs.	75
3	South Austrian, £20 Red.	15½
3	South Austrian, (Ser. X.)	15
3	South Italian £20 Obs. (Ser. A to G), Red.	12
3½	S.W. of Venez. (Barq.), Ltd., 7 p.c. 1st Mt. £100 Debs.	43½
5	Taltal, Ltd., 5 p.c. 1st Ch. Debs., Red.	100
5	Utd. Rwys. Havana, Red.	88½
3	Wstn. of France, £20 Red.	19

Foreign Rly. Obligations (*continued*):—

Per Cent.	Name.	Price.
6	Wrn. B. Ayres St. Mt. Debs., 1902	108
6	Wrn. B. Ayres, Reg. Cert.	107
5	Do. Mt. Bds.	122
6	Wtrn. of Havna., Ld, Mt. Dbs., Rd.	94
7	Wrn. Ry. San Paulo Red.	101
—	Wrn. Santa Fé, 7 p.c. Red.	41
2/8	Zafra & Huelva, 3 p.c. Red.	2½

BANKS.

Div.	Name.	Paid.	Price.
2/4½	Agra, Ltd.	6	3½
2/9½	Anglo-Argentine, Ltd., £9	7	6
8 fls.	Anglo-Austrian	120 fl	13
6/	Anglo-Californian, Ltd., £20 Shares	10	11
4/	Anglo-Egyptian, Ltd., £15	5	6
5/	Anglo-Foreign Bkg., Ltd.	7	7½
7/	Anglo-Italian, Ltd.	5	7
7/6	Bk. of Africa, Ltd., £18¾	6¼	10½
20/	Bk. of Australasia	40	50
10/	Bk. of Brit. Columbia	20	19½
25/	Bk. of Brit. N. America	50	64
20/	Bk. of Egypt, Ltd., £25	12½	18
5/	Bk. of Mauritius, Ltd.	10	9
18/	Bk. of N. S. Wales	20	36½
4 p.c.	Bk. of N. Zland. Gua. Stk.	100	102½
6/	Bk. of Roumania, £20 Shs.	6	7½
2/6	Tarapaca & Ldn., Ltd., £10	5	3½
—	Bque. Fse. de l'Afri. du S.	100 f	3½
f.22.50	Bque. Internatle. de Paris	20	23
6/	Brit. Bk. of S. America, Ltd., £20 Shares	10	10½
16/	Capital & Cties., L., £50	10	40½
20/	Chart. of India, &c.	20	30½
10/	City, Ltd., £40 Shares	10	20
18/	Colonial, £100 Shares	30	20½
10/	Delhi and London, Ltd.	25	—
5/	German of London, Ltd.	10	10½
25/	Hong-Kong & Shanghai	28½	46
4/	Imperl. of Persia	6½	3½
10/	Imperl. Ottoman, £20 Shs	10	12½
12/	Intrnatl. of Ldn., Ld., £20	15	11
20/	Ionian, Ltd.	25	15½
16/	Lloyds, Ltd., £50 Shs.	8	31½
10/	Ldn. & Brasiln. Ltd., £20	10	17½
44/	Ldn. & County, Ltd., £80	20	101
9/	Ldn. & Hanseatic, L., £20	10	10½
22/6	Ldn. & Midland, L., £60	12½	53
8/9	Ldn. & Provin., Ltd., £10	5	21½
21/	Ldn. & Riv. Plate, L., £25	15	51
2/9½	Ldn. & San Fcisco, Ltd.	7	4
28/	Ldn. & Sth. West., L., £50	20	68½
26/	Ldn. & Westmins., L., £100	20	58
5/	Ldn. of Mex. & S. Amer., Ltd., £10 Shs.	6	5½
15/	Ldn. Joint Stk., L., £100	15	34
12/9½	Ldn., Paris & Amer., L. £20	16	25
2/4½	Merchant Bkg., L., £9	4	2½
6/3	Metropn, Ltd., £50 Shs.	5	14½
9/	National, Ltd., £50 Shs.	10	20½
5/11	Natl. of Mexico, $100 Shs.	$35	12
1/3	National of N. Z., L., £7½	2½	2
12/	National S. Afric. Rep.	10	14
18/10½	National Provcl. of Eng., Ltd., £75 Shs.	10½	50½
21/7½	Do. do. £60 Shs.	12	57½
6/6	NorthEastn., Ltd., £20 Shs	6	15
19/	Parr's, Ld., £100 Shs.	20	88½
12/6	Prov. of Ireland, L., £100	12½	29½
40/	Stand. of S. Afric., L., £100	25	64
12/6	Union of Australia, L., £75	25	26½
4 p.c.	Do. do. Ins. Stk. Dep. 1900	100	104
15/6	Union of Ldn., Ltd., £100	15½	35

BREWERIES AND DISTILLERIES.

Div.	Name.	Paid.	Price.
4½	Albion Prp. 1 Mt. Db. Sk.	100	111
4	All Saints', L., Db.Sk.Rd.	100	97
7	Allsopp, Ltd	100	152
6	Do. Cum. Pref	100	155½
4½	Do. Deb. Stk., Red	100	117
3½	Do. Deb. Stk., Red	100	103
4½	Alton & Co., L., Db., Rd	100	107
4½	Do. Mt. Bds., 1896	100	105
—	Arnold, Perrett, Ltd.	10	6
6	Do. Cum. Pref.	10	10
4½	Do. 1 Mt. Db. Stk., Rd	100	107

Breweries &c. (*continued*):—

Div.	Name.	Paid.	Price.
5½	Arrol, A., & Sons, L., Cum. Pref. Shs.	10	10
4½	Do. 1 Mt. Db. Stk., Rd.	100	108
5	Backus, 1 Mt. Db., Red.	100	89
4	Barclay, Perk., L., Cu. Pf.	10	11½
3½	Do. Mt. Db. Stk., Red.	100	109
—	Barnsley, Ltd.	10	11
6	Do. Cum. Pref.	10	13½
1/3	Barrett's, Ltd	2½	1½
1/3	Do. 5 p.c. Pref.	2½	2½
3/	Bartholomay, Ltd.	10	3½
8	Do. Cum. Pref.	10	6½
6	Do. Deb.	100	96
5	Bass, Ratcliff, Ltd., Cum. Pref. Stk.	100	142½
4½	Do. Mt. Db. Stk., Rd.	100	124
4	Bell, J., L., 1 Mt. D.Stk., R	100	100
—	Benskin's, L., Cum. Pref.	5	—
—	Do. 1 Mt. Db. Stk Red.	100	—
—	Do. "B" Deb. Sk, Rd.	100	—
7/	Bentley's Yorks., Ltd.	10	10½
6/	Do. Cum. Pref.	10	13½
4½	Do. Mt. Debs., Red.	100	110
4½	Do. do. 1892, Red.	100	110
—	Bieckert's, Ltd.	20	2
5	Do. Debs., Red.	100	56
—	Birmingham., Ltd., 6 p.c. Cum. Pref.	5	3½
4½	Do. Mt. Debs., Red.	50	38½
5½	Boardman's, Ld., Cm. Pf.	10	8½
4½	Do., Perp. 1 Mt. Db. Sk.	100	104½
30/9	Brain & Co., Ltd.	100	101
4½	Brakspear, L., 1 D. Stk. Red.	100	108
4	Brandon's, L., 1 D. Stk. Red.	100	108½
21/	Bristol (Georges) Ltd.	10	45
6	Do. Cum. Pref.	10	17½
5	Do. Mt. Db. Sk. 1888 Rd.	100	116½
17/6	Bristol United, Ltd.	10	35
6	Do. Cum. Pref.	10	16½
4½	Do. Db.Sk.Rd.	100	121½
5½	Buckley's, L., C. Pre-prf.	10	10½
4½	Do. 1 Mt. Db. Stk. Rd.	100	106½
4	Bullard & Sons, Ltd., D. Sk. R.	100	104½
6	Bushell, Watk., L., C. Pf.	10	13½
4½	Do. 1 Mt. Db. Sk. Rd.	100	112
5	Camden, Ltd., Cum. Pref.	10	11½
4½	Do. 1 Mt. Db. Sk. Rd.	100	107
5½	Cameron, Ltd., Cm. Prf.	10	13
4½	Do. Mort. Deb. Stk.	100	107
3½	Do. Perp Mt. Db. Sk.	100	98½
5	Cam'bell, J'stone, L., C. Pf.	5	5
4½	Do. 4½ p.c. 1 Mt. Db. Sk.	100	104
4	Campbell, Praed, L., Per. 1 Mort. Deb. Stk.	100	108
4	Cannon, L., Mt. Db. Stk.	100	110
4	Do. "B" Deb. Stk.	100	108
5	Castlemaine, L., 1 Mt. Db.	100	96
3½	Charrington, Ltd., Mort. Deb. Stk. Red.	100	107
2/	Cheltnhm. Orig., Ltd.	5	6
6	Do. Cum. Pref.	5	7½
4	Do. Debs. Red.	100	106
10/	Chicago, Ltd.	10	2½
6	Do. Debs.	100	84½
—	Cincinnati, Cum. Pref.	10	1
10/	City of Baltimore	10	3½
16/	Do. 8 p.c. Cum. Pref	10	7½
14/	City of Chicago, Ltd.	10	1½
8	Do. Cum. Pref.	10	6½
13	City of London, Ltd.	100	206½
5	Do. Cum. Pref.	100	136
4	Do. Mt. Deb. Stk., Rd.	100	108½
2/	Colchester, Ltd.	5	4½
7	Do. Pref.	5	6½
4½	Do. Deb. Stk., Red.	100	109
5	Combe, Ltd., Cum. Pref.	10	14½
4	Do. Mt. Db. Stk, Rd.	100	113
3½	Do. Perp. Deb. Stk.	100	108
5	Comm'cial, L., D. Sk., Rd.	100	107½
5	Courage, L., Cm. Pref. Shs.	100	137½
4	Do. Irr. Mt. Deb. Stk.	100	128½
3½	Do. Irr. "B" Mt. Db. Sk.	100	106
8/	Daniell & Sons, Ltd.	10	7
7	Do. Cum. Pref.	10	12
4½	Do. 1 Mt. Perp. Db. Sk.	100	108½
4½	Do. "B" Deb. Stk.	100	99
10d.	Dartford, Ltd.	5	5½
2/9	Do. Cum. Pref.	5	5½
4	Do. 1 Mt. Db. Sk. Rd.	100	99
4	Davenport, Ld., 1 D. Stk.	100	101½
10/	Denver United, Ltd.	10	3½
8	Do. Cum. Pref.	10	8½
6	Do. Debs.	100	78½
4½	Deuchar, L., 1 D.Sk., Rd.	100	109
8/	Distillers, Ltd.	10	25
—	Dublin Distillers, Ltd.	5	3½
6	Do. Cum. Pref.	5	4½
4½	Do. Irr. Deb. Stk.	100	—
5	Eadie, Ltd., Cum. Pref.	10	11½
4	Do. Irr. 1 Mt. Db. Sk.	100	107
10/	Edinbgh. Utd., Ltd.	10	13½
6	Do. Cum. Prf.	10	13½
4	Eldridge, Pope, L. D. St. R.	100	107
—	Emerald & Phœnix, Ltd.	10	1½
8	Do. Cum. Pref.	10	6
6	Empress Ltd., C. Pf.	10	11½
4½	Do. Mt. Deb. Stk.	100	103
10/	Farnham, Ltd.	10	17½
6	Do. Cum. Pref.	10	14½
4	Fenwick, L., 1 D. Sk., Rd.	100	103
4	Flower & Sons, Irr. D. Sk.	100	111
4	Friary, L., 1 Db. Stk., Rd.	100	103½
4	Do. 1 "A" Db. Sk., Rd	100	100
4½	Groves, L., 1 Db. Sk., Rd.	100	111
14	Guinness, Ltd.	100	590
6	Do. Cum. Prf. Stk.	100	185½
5	Do. Deb. Stk., Red.	100	120
5	Hall's Oxford L., Cm. Pf.	5	5½
6/	Hancock, Ld., Cm. Pf. Ord.	10	14
7	Do. Def. Ord	10	17½

Breweries, &c. (*continued*) :—

Div.	Name.	Paid.	Price.
6	Hancock, Ld., Cum. Pref.	10	15
4	Do. 1 Deb. Stk., Rd.	100	110
5	Hoare, Ltd. Cum. Pref...	10	12½
5	Do. "A" Cum. Pref..	10	12
4	Do. Mt. Deb. Stk., Rd.	100	113
3½	Do. do. do. Rd.	100	104
3/6	Hodgson's, Ltd.	5	9½
5	Do. 1 Mt. Db., Red..	—	117½
4	Do. 2 Mt. Db., 1906..	—	100
4½	Hopcraft & N., Ltd., 1 Mt. Deb. Stk., Red. ..	100	103
5	Huggins, Ltd., Cm. Prf..	10	—
4½	Do. 1st D. Stk. Rd...	100	—
4½	Do. "B" Db. Stk. Rd.	100	—
12/	Hull, Ltd.	10	17
7	Do. Cum. Pref.	10	14½
4½	Ind, Coope, L., D.Sk., Rd.	100	119
4	Do. "B" Mt. Db. Stk. Rd.	100	110
8/	Indianapolis, Ltd.	10	3
8	Do. Cm. Prf.	10	8½
5/	Jones, Frank, Ltd.......	10	2½
7½	Do. Cum. Pref.	10	6½
5	Do. 1st Mort. Debs. ..	100	90½
3/	J. Kenward & Ct., Ltd...	5	5½
4½	Kingsbury, L., 1 D.Sk., Rd	100	—
4	Lacon, L., D. Stk., Red.	100	110
4	Do. Irrd. "B" D. Sk.	100	107
7/	Lascelles, Ltd.	5	11½
6	Do. Cum. Pref.	5	7½
5	Leney, Ltd., Cum. Pref.	10	11½
4	Do. 1 Mt. Db. Stk. Rd.	100	102
30/7½	Lion, Ltd., £25 shares..	17	49½
10/9½	Do. New £10 shares..	6	17
6	Do. Perp. Pref.	20	33
4	Do. B. Mt. Db. Sk. Rd.	100	107
4½	Lloyd & Y., Ltd., 1 Mt. Deb. Stk., Rd.	100	100½
4½	Locke & S., Ltd., Irr. 1st Mt. Deb. Stk.	100	103
4½	Lovibond, Ltd., 1st Mt. Deb. Stk., Rd.	100	101½
30/4	Lucas & Co., Ld., Deb. Stk.	100	107
12/	Manchester, Ltd.	10	19
7	Do. Cum. Pref.	10	16½
5/	Marston, J., L., Cm. Prf.	10	10½
4	Do. 1 Mt. Db. Sk., Rd.	100	101½
7/	Massey's Burnley, Ltd...	10	16½
6	Do. Cum. Pref.	10	14½
4½	McCracken, Ltd., 1 Mt. Deb., 1908............	100	61½
5	McEwan, Ltd., Cm. Pref.	10	14
5	Meux, Ltd., Cum. Pref..	10	14½
4	Do. Mt. Db. Stk. Red.	100	112
4½	Michell & A., Ltd., 1 Mt. Deb. Stk. Red....	100	105
4½	Mile End Dist. Db. Sk. Rd.	100	111
—	Milwaukee & Chic., Ltd.	10	1½
4/	Do. Cum. Pref.	10	6½
4½	Michell, Toms, L., Db...	50	57
6/	Morgan, Ltd., Cum. Pref.	10	14½
25/	Nalder & Coll., Ltd.	10	34
6	Do. Cum. Pref..	10	15½
4½	Do. Deb. Red...	100	112
12/	Newcastle, Ltd.	10	20
6	Do. Cum. Pref.......	10	15
5	Do. 1 Mt. Deb., 1911	100	111½
4	Do. "A" Deb. Stk. Red.	100	106½
6	New England, Ltd......	10	4½
8	Do. Cum. Pref.......	10	9
6	Do. Debs. Red......	100	101½
4	New London, L., 1 D.Sk.	100	104
7/2	New Westminster, Ltd..	4	10
2/4½	Do. Pref........	4	6½
—	New York, Ltd.	10	½
—	Do. 8 p.c. Cum. Pref.	10	3½
6	Do. 1 Mt. Deb. Red.	100	77½
5	Noakes, Ld., Cum. Pref.	10	11½
4	Do. 1 Mt. Db. Stk., Rd.	100	106
4½	Norfolk, L., "A" D.Sk. Rd.	100	109
10/	Northampton, Ld.	10	17
7	Do. Cum. Pref......	10	15½
6	Do. Cum. Pref......	10	12½
5	Do. 1 Mt. Per. Db. Sk.	100	127
4	Nth. East., L., 1 D.Sk. Rd.	100	100
4½	N. Worcesters., L. Per. 1 Mort. Deb. Stock	100	96½
6	Nottingham, L., Cm. Prf.	10	1½
5	Do. 1 Mt. Deb. Stk., Red.	100	114
17/4	Do. "B" do. Red.	50	112
6/	Ohlsson' Cape, Ld.......	5	18½
7	Do. Cum. Pref.	5	9
4½	Do. 2nd Cum. Pref.	5	5½
5	Do. Deb. Stk., Red.	100	117
4½	Oldfield, L., 1 Mt. Db. Stk.	100	106
6	Page & Overt., L., Cm. Prf.	10	13½
4½	Do. 1 Mt. Dbs, Red.	100	109
10/	Parker's Burslem, Ltd. ..	10	24½
6	Do. Cum. Pref.	10	15
4	Do. 1 Mt. Dr. Stk., Red.	100	112
4	Persse, Ld., 1 Mt. Db. Rd.	100	95½
	Phipps, L., Irr. 1 Db. Stk.	100	113
8	Plymouth, L., Min. Cu. Pf.	10	14
4½	Do. Mt. Deb. Stk., Red.	100	109½
4½	Pryor, Reid, L., 1 D.S., R.[illegible]	100	102½
5	Reid's, Ld., Cm. Pref. Stk.	100	137½
4	Do. Mt. Deb. Stk., Red	100	111
3½	Do. "B" Mt. Db. Stk., R[illegible]	100	105
5	Rhondda Val., L., Cu. Pf	10	11
4½	Do. 1 Mt. Deb. Stk., Rd	100	109
5	Robinson, Ld., Cum. Pref.	10	11½
4½	Do. 1 Mt. Perp. Db. Stk.	100	111½
4/	Rochdale, Ltd...........	10	6
4½	Do. 1 Mt. Deb. Stk...	100	98½
7	Royal, Brentford, Ltd. ..	10	22
	Do. Cum. Pref. ..	10	15
4½	Do. 1 Mt. Dbs. Red	100	105
6/	St. Louis, Ltd...........	10	3½
8	Do. Cum. Pref. ...	10	8½
14/	St. Pauli, Ltd.	10	10
7	Do. Cum. Pref...	10	12
4½	Salt (T.), L., 1 Db. Sk. Rd.	100	113
4½	Do. "B" Db. Stk. Red	100	107
—	San Francisco, Ltd.......	10	½
—	Do. 8 p.c. Cum. Pref...	10	½

Breweries, &c. (*continued*) :—

Div.	Name.	Paid.	Price.
4½	Savill Brs., L., D. Sk. Rd.	100	118
4½	Scarboro., Ltd., 1 Db. Stk.	100	101
4	Shaw (Hy.), Ltd., 1 Mt. Db. Stk., Red.	100	104
22/	Showell's, Ltd.	10	32½
7	Do. Cum. Pref.	10	17½
3/	Do. Gua. Shs.	5	7½
4½	Do. Mt. Db. Stk., Red.	100	—
4	Simonds, L., 1 D. Sk., Rd.	100	111
5½	Simson & McP., L., Cu. Pf.	10	9½
4½	Do. 1 Mt. Deb. Stk. ..	100	97
5/	Smith, Garrett, L., £20 Shs	10	16½
5	Do. Cum. Pref.	20	26
3½	Do. 3½ p.c. Mt. Db. Stk.	100	107
5	Smith's, Tadcster, L., C Pf	10	12
4½	Do. Deb. Stk., Red. ..	100	112
4	Do. Deb. Stk. Red. ..	100	108
4½	Star, L., 1 M. Db. Stk., Rd.	100	103
4	Steward & P., L., 1 D. Sk.	100	110
7/	Strettons Derby, Ltd.	10	13
6	Do. Cum. Pref.	10	13
4	Do. Irr. 1 Mt. Db. Stk.	100	104½
4½	Strong, Romsey, L., 1 D.S.	100	113
5	Stroud, L., Db. Sk., Rd.	100	106
4½	Tadcaster To'er, L., D.Sk.	100	112
8/	Tamplin, Ltd	10	21½
6	Do. Cum. Pref.	100	15
4	Do. "A" Db. Sk., Rd.	10	106
6	Thorne, Ltd., Cum. Pref.	10	14
4	Do. Deb. Stk., Red...	100	103½
15/	Threlfall, Ltd.	10	45
6	Do. Cum. Pref.	10	16½
5	Do. 1 Mt. Dbs., Red.	100	115
4	Tollemache, L., D. Sk. Rd.	100	103
4	Truman, Hanb., D. Sk., R.	100	111
3	Do. "B" Mt. Db. Sk., Rd.	100	95
10/	United States, Ltd.......	10	9
8	Do. Cum. Pref.	10	11
6	Do. 1 Mt. Deb........	100	106½
6/	Walker & H., Ld., Cm. Prf.	10	10½
4½	Do. 1 Mt. Deb. Stk., Red.	100	109
5	Walker, Peter, Ld. Cm. Prf.	10	13½
4	Do. 1 Mt. Dbs. Red. ..	100	110
4	Wallingford, L., D.Sk. Rd.	100	105
6	Watney, Ld., Cm. Prf. Sk.	100	171
5	Do. Mt. Db. Sk., Rd.	100	121½
4½	Do. "B" Mt. Db. Sk., Rd.	100	118½
3½	Do. Mt. Db. Stk.	100	105
5	Watney, D., Ld., Cm. Prf.	10	12
4½	Do. 1 Mt. Db. Stk. ..	100	108
10/	Webster & Sons, Ltd. ..	10	16½
6	Do. Cum. Pref. ..	10	14
5	Wenlock Ltd Pref.	10	12
4	Do. 1 Mt. Db. Sk., Rd.	100	106
5	West Cheshire, L., Cu. Pf.	10	10½
4	Do. Irred. 1 Mt. Db. Sk.	100	99
4½	Whitbread, L., Cu. Pf. Sh.	100	123½
4	Do. Db. Stk., Red.	100	110
3½	Do. "B" Db. Stk., Rd.	100	101
8/	Wolverhmpton & D. Ld..	10	18
6	Do. Cum. Pref.......	10	13½
4½	Do. 1 Mt. Dbs., Red.	100	108
5½	Worthington, Ld., Cm. Prf.	10	15½
5½	Do. Cum. "B" Pref.	10	13½
4½	Do. Mt. Db. Sk., Rd.	100	113
3½	Do. Irr. "B" Db. Stk.	100	102
6/	Yates's Castle, Ltd.......	10	13
5	Do. Cum. Pref.	10	11
5	Younger W., L., Cu. Pf. Sh.	100	134½

CANALS AND DOCKS.

Last Div.	Name.	Paid.	Price.
4	Birmingham Canal	100	141½
—	E. & W. India Dock	100	19
—	Do. 4 p.c. Prf. Stk.....	100	74
—	Do. P.L. Deb. Stk.....	100	102
—	Do. Cons. Deb. Stk. ..	100	89
40/	G. Junction Ord. Shs...	100	145½
6/	Do. do. Pref.......	10	19
4½	King's Lynn Per. Db. Stk.	100	117½
2½	Leeds & L'pool Canal	100	69
2½	Lndn & St. Kath. Dks. ..	100	54
4½	Do. Pref............	100	137½
4½	Do. Pref., 1878	100	132½
4½	Do. Pref., 1882	100	130
4	Do. Deb. Stk.	100	132½
—	Mchester Ship C. 5 p.c. Pf.	10	1½
3½	Do. 1st Perp. Mt. Deb.	100	100
—	Milford Dks. Db. Stk. "A"	100	19
3½	Millwall Dk.............	100	60
5	Do. Perp. Pref.	100	140½
4½	Do. Pref.	100	106½
5	Do. New Per. Prf., 1887	100	126½
5	Do. Per. Deb. Stk.....	100	152½
4/	Newhaven Har.	10	14½
2½	N. Metropolitan	100	70
5	Sharpness Nw. Pf. "A" Sk.	100	141½
4	Do. Deb. Stk.	100	115½
5	Sheffiel & S. Yorks Nav. 4½ p.c. Pref Stk.......	100	115½
36.432	Suez Canal..............	20	145
7	Surrey Comcl. Dok., Ord.	100	147½
7	Do. Min. 4 p.c. Pref. "A"	110	148½
5	Do. Pref. "B"........	100	148½
5	Do do. "C"........	100	148½
5	Do. do. "D"........	100	144
4½	Do Deb. Stk.	100	152½

COMMERCIAL, INDUSTRIAL, &c.

Last Div.	Name.	Paid.	Price.
5	Accles, L., 1 Mt. Db., Red.	100	84½
2/6	Aërated Bread, Ltd.	1	13
—	African Gold Recovery, L.	1	½
2/	Aluminium, L., "A" Shs.	1	2½
4½	Do. 1 Mt. Db. Stk., Red.	100	97
5½	Amelia Nitr., L., 1 Mort Deb., Red..............	100	82½
7/	Anglo-Chil. Nitrate, Ltd., Cum. Pref..............	10	7½
4½	Do. Cons. Mt. Bds., Red.	100	79
4½	Anglo-Russian Cotton, Ld., 1 Charge Debs., Red.	100	98
11/3	Angus (G., & Co., L.), £10	7½	17
6/	Apollinaris, Ltd.	10	10
5/	Do. 5 p.c. Cum. Pref.	10	10
4	Do. Irred. Deb. Stock	100	101
3/	Argentine Meat Pres., L., 7 p.c. Pref..............	10	2½
5	Argentine Refinry, Db. Rd.	100	98
6d.	Armstrong, Whitw., Ltd.	1	3½
4	Do. Cum. Pref.	5	6½
5	Artisans', Labr. Dwllgs., L.	100	126
4½	Do. Non-Cm. Prf., 1879	100	134
4½	Do. do. 1884	100	132½
—	Asbestos & Asbestic, Ltd.	10	5
2/7½	Ashley-grdns., L., C. Prf.	5	6½
4½	Do. 1 Mt. Deb. Stk.	100	113½
5/	Assam Rly. & Trdng., L., 8 p.c. Cum. Pref. "A"	10	14
—	Do. Deferrd. "B" Shs.	1	4
—	Do. do. (iss. f. pd)	1	3½
8/	Do. Cum. Pre-Prf. "A"	10	15
6/	Do. New Pref.........	10	11½
5	Do. Debs., Red.	100	106
5	Do. Red. Mort. Debs.	100	110
6	Aust'lian Pastrl, L., Cu. Pf.	10	7
8d.	Aylesbury Dairy, Ltd. ..	1	1½
4	Do. 4 p.c. Mt. Dbs.	100	104½
10/	Babcock & Wilcox, Ltd.	10	28
6	Do. 6 p.c. Cm. Prf.	10	16
8	Baker (Chs.), L., Cm. Pf.	5	9
8	Do. "B" Cm. Pref.	5	7½
2/1	Barker (John), Ltd.	1	2½
5½	Do. Cum. Pref.	5	7½
4½	Do. Irred. 1 Mt. Db. Stk.	100	125½
2/6	Barnagore Jute, Ltd.....	5	2½
5	Do. Cum. Pref.	5	4½
7½d.	Belgravia Dairy, Ltd. ..	1	1½
5/6	Bell (R.) & Co., Ltd....	5	4
9½d.	Bell's Asbestos, Ltd. ...	1	½
5	Do. Mt. Db. Bds., Rd.	100	106
10/	Bengal Mills, Ltd.	10	11
6/	Do. 5 p.c. Cum. Prf	10	10½
5/	Benson (J.W.) L., Cm. Pf	10	10½
4	Do. Perp. Mt. Db. Stk.	100	101
6	Bergvik, L., 6 p.c. Cm. Pf	10	12½
12/	Do. Dfd.	10	11
4½	Do. 1 Dbs., Red. ..	100	105½
5/	Birm'ham Vinegar, Ltd.	5	15
5	Do. Cum. Pref. ...	5	5½
4½	Do. 1 Mt. Db. Stk., Rd.	100	109½
5	Boake (A.) L., 5 p.c. Cu. Pf.	10	10½
2/6	Bodega, Ltd.............	5	8½
4½	Do. Mt. Deb. Stk., Rd.	100	111
12/	Bottomley & Brs., Ltd...	10	6
6/	Do. 6 p.c. Pt.	10	9
8½d.	Bovril, Ltd.	1	1
1/0½	Do. Def.	1	½
6½d.	Do. Cum. Pref...	1	1½
4½	Do. Deb. Stk. ..	100	101
5/	Bradbury, Greatrex., Ltd., £10 share	8	14
5/	Do. 5 p.c. Cum. Pref.	10	13½
5/	Brewers' Sugar, L., 5 p.c. Cum. Pref.............	10	10½
3/6	Brighton Grd. Hotel, Ld.	5	4
4	Do Mt. Db. Stk., Red.	100	102
5	Bristol Hotel & Palm Co., Ltd. 1st Mt. Red. Deb.	100	104
6d.	British & Bengton's. Tea Tr. Asc., Ltd.	1	1
5	Do. Cum. Prf.	5	5½
—	British Deli & Lgkat. Tobacco, Ltd.	1	½
—	Do. Cum. Prf.	1	½
1/3	British Tea Table, Ltd...	1	2½
5½	Do. Cum. Pref.......	1	1½
2/6	Brooke, Ben., & Co., Ltd., Cum. Pref.............	5	5½
7/6	Brooke, Bond & Co., Ltd.	5	19
3/	Brown Brs., L., Cum. Pref.	5	5½
10/	Browne & Eagle, Ltd. ..	10	13½
5	Do. Cum. Pref.	10	13
4	Do. Mrt. Db. Sk., Red.	100	110
30/	Brunner, Mond, & Co., Lt.	0	38
10/6	Do. £10 shares.......	3½	14½
7	Do. Cum. Pref.......	10	18
7	Do. £10 shares.......	5	8½
10/	Bryant & May, Ltd.	5	18½
3/	Bucknall, H., & Sons, Lt.	5	7
6	Do. Cum Pref........	5	7½
4/	Burke, E. & J., Ltd.	5	7½
6	Do. Cum. Pref.......	5	7½
6	Do. Irred. Deb. Stk...	100	155
1/	Burlington Htls. Co., Ltd	1	1½
5	Do. Cum. Pref.	1	1
4	Do. Perp. Deb. Stk. ..	100	105½
5	Bush, W. J., & Co., Ltd., Cum. Pref.	5	5½
4	Do. 1 Deb. Stk., Red.	100	102
5½	Callard, Stewart, & Watt, Ltd., Cum. Pref.......	1	1½
4/	Callender's Cable L., Shs.	5	11
4½	Do. 1 Deb. Stk., Red.	100	111½
—	Campbell, R., & Sons, Lt.	3	2½
6	Cantareira Water, Bd., Rd	100	99½
5	Do. (2nd issue)	100	87½
4	Cartavio Sugar, Ltd., 6 p.c. 1st Debs., Red. ..	20	82½
9/	Cassell & Co., Ltd., £10	9	15
5	Causton, Sir J., & Sons Ltd., Cum. Pref.......	10	13½

Commercial, &c. (*continued*) :—

Last Div.	Name.	Paid.	Price.
4	Cent. Prod. Mkt. of B.A. 1st Mt. Str. Debs.	100	80
4	Chappell & Co., Ltd., Mt. Deb. Stk. Red....	100	103
6/	Chicago & N.W. Gran. 8 p.c. Cum. Pref.......	10	3
4/	Chicago Packing & Prov.	10	6
8	Do. Cum. Pref....	10	10
6/	City Offices, Ltd........	12	8
3½	Do. Mt. Deb. Stk...	100	108½
12/	Cy. London Real Prop., Ltd., £25 shs.	12	21½
9/	Do. £12½ shs.........	7½	14½
3½	Do. Deb. Stk. Red...	100	107½
3½	Do. Deb. Stk. Red..	100	105½
3	Do.	100	100½
6/	Cy. of Santos Imprvts., Ltd., 7 p.c. Pref.......	10	2
20/	Clay, Bock, & Co., Ltd...	10	5
8	Do. Cum. Pref.......	10	9
6	Do. Mort. Deb.......	100	104
20/	Coats, J. & P., Ltd.....	10	60
6/	Do. Cum. Pref.	10	18
4½	Do. Deb. Stk. Red.	100	113½
1/2½	Coburg Hotel, Ltd.......	1	1½
4	Do. Deb. Stk. Red.	100	102
6	Colonial Consign & Dis., Ltd., Cum. Pref.	5	4½
4½	Do. 1st Mort. Debs..	100	96½
—	Colorado Nitrate, Ltd. ..	5	½
5/	Co. Gén. des Asphtes. de F., Ltd...............	6	6
5	Do, Non-Cm. Prf. ..	—	5
5	Cook, J. W., & Co., Ltd., Cum. Pref...........	5	5½
5	Cook, T., & Son, Egypt, Ltd., 1st Mt. Deb. Red.	100	110½
—	Cork Co., Ltd., 6 p.c. Cum. Pref...........	5	2
5	Cory, W., & Sn, L., Cu. Pf.	5	5½
4	Do. 1st Deb. Stk. Red.	100	109
1/6	Crisp & Co., Ltd........	1	1½
5½	Do. Cum. Pref......	1	1½
—	Crompton & Co., Ltd., 7 p.c. Cum. Pref.......	5	—
5	Do. 1st Mt. Reg. Deb.	—	90½
4/6	Crossley, J., & Sons, Ltd.	5	8
5	Do. Cum. Pref....	5	6½
—	Crystal Pal. Ord. "A" Stk.	100	6½
—	Do. "B" Red. Stk	100	1½
6	Do. 6 p.c. 1st		
—	1887 Deb. Stk. Red. ..	100	117½
	Do. 6 p.c. 2nd		
—	1887 Deb. Stk. Red. ..	100	51½
	Do. 6 p.c. 3rd		
—	1887 Deb. Stk. Red. ..	100	22½
3	Do. 3 p.c. 1st		
—	1895 Deb. Stk.........	100	92½
	Daimler Motor, Ltd.....	10	6
4/	Dalgety & Co., £20 Shs.	5	5½
4½	Do. Deb. Stk........	100	125
4	Do.	100	112
7/	De Keyser's Ryl. Htl., L.	10	13½
5	Do. Cum. Pref......	10	12
4	Do. Deb. Stk., Red..	100	110
6	Denny, H., & Sons, Ltd., Cum. Pref............	10	14½
5/3	Devas, Routledge & Co. L.	7	8½
5	Dickinson, J., & Co., L., Cum. Pref. Stk.	100	123
4½	Domin. Cottn. Mls., Ltd. Mt. Stg. Dbs.	100	97
6/	Dorman, Long & Co., L.	5	4½
—	Eastmans, Ltd..........	10	2½
12/	Do. 8 p.c. Cum. Pref.	10	11
2/6	E. C. Powder, Ltd......	3	4½
1/6	Edison & Swn Utd. Elec. Ltd., "A" £5 Shs....	3	2½
2/6	Do. fully-paid	5	4½
4½	Ekman Pulp & Ppr. Co., Ltd., Mt. Deb, Red..	100	96
1/1½	Electric Construc., Ltd..	2	2½
7	Do. Cum. Pref.......	2	3½
25/	Eley Bros., Ltd.	10	37
—	Elmore's Cop. Deptg., L.	1	½
—	Elmore's Wire Mnfg., L.	1	½
—	Elysée Pal. Hotel Co., L.	5/	½
5 p.c.	Do. 5 p.c. £100 Db., Rd.	70	97½
8½d.	Evans, Ben., & Co., Ltd.	1	1
5	Do. 1 Mt. Db. Sk., Rd.	100	110
1/8½d.	Evans., D. H., & Co., L.	1	2½
6	Do. Cum. Pref.......	1	1½
4½	Do. 1 Mt. Db. Sk., Rd.	100	112
2/6	*Evening News*, L., 5 p.c. Cum. Pref...........	5	5½
5/3	Evered & Co., L., £10 Sh.	7	12½
7/6	Do.	10	18
4	Fairbairn Pastoral Co., Aust., L., 1 Mt. Db., Rd.	100	102
6	Fairfield Shipbldg., Ltd., Cum. Pref..........	10	11½
4½	Do. Mort. Deb. Stk .	100	113½
6/	Farmer & Co., Ld., 6 p.c. Cum. Pref............	10	13½
12/	Field, J. C. & J., Ltd. ..	10	10
14/	Do. 7 p.c. Cum. Pref.	10	14
1/3	Fordham, W.B., & Sns, Ld.	1	2
5/6	Fore-st. Warehouse, Ltd.	11	9½
4	Do. Regd. Debs., Rd.	100	104
3/6	Foster, M. B. & Sons, Ltd.	4	6
5	Do. Pref....	10	11
9/	Foster, Porter, & Co., L.	10½	16
4	Fowler, J., & Co. (Leeds), Ltd., 1 Mt. Deb., Red.	100	103½
3/	Fraser & Chalmers, Ltd..	3	1½
4½	Free, Rodwell & Co., Ltd., Deb Stk.............	100	104½
6½d.	Furness, T., & Co., Ltd., 5½ p.c. Cum. Pref.		1
4½	Gartside & Co. (of Manchstr), L., 1 Mt. Db. Sk.	100	113
11	Genl Hydraul Power, L.	100	[illegible]

Commercial, &c. (*continued*):—

Last Div.	Name.	Paid.	Price.
8/	Gillman & Spencer, Ltd.	5	2½
6	Do. Pref.	5	4½
5	Do. Mort. Debs.	50	51
4	Goldsbro., Mort & Co., L., "A" Deb. Stk., Red.	100	69½
—	Do. 3 p.c. "B" Inc. Deb. Stk., Red.	100	12
8/	Gordon Hotels, Ltd.	10	20½
5½	Do. Cum. Pref.	10	14½
4½	Do. Perp. Deb. Stk.	100	140½
4	Do. do.	100	122½
—	Greenwich Inld. Linoleum Co., Ltd.	1	⅛
7	Greenwood & Batley, Ltd., Cum. Pref.	10	10
7½d.	Hagemann & Co., Ltd., 6 p.c. Cum. Pref.	1	1
—	Hammond, Ltd.	10	⅜
—	Do. 8 p.c. Cum. Pref.	10	2¼
—	Do. 6 p.c. Cum. Inc. Stk. Red.	100	56½
	Hampton & Sons, Ltd., 4 p.c. 1 Mt. Db. St. Red.	100	105
—	Hans Crescent Htl., L., 6 p.c. Cum. Pref.	5	3
4	Do. 1 Mt. Deb. Stk.	100	90
6d.	Harmsworth, Ltd., Cum. Pref.	1	1½
4/	Harrison, Barber, Ltd.	5	4½
3/	Harrod's Stores, Ltd.	1	4⅝
2/6	Do. Cum. Pref.	5	7
5½	Hawaiian Comcl. & Sug. 1 Mt. Debs.	100	94½
5	Hazell, Watson, L., C. P.	10	11½
18/	Henley's Teleg., Ltd.	10	22
7	Do. Pref. Shs.	10	19
4½	Do. Mt. Db. Stk., Rd.	100	112½
6	Henry, Ltd.	10	11¾
5	Do. Cum. Pref.	10	13
4½	Do. Mt. Debs., Red.	50	51
1/4½	Herrmann, Ltd.	1	¾
—	Hildesheimer, Ltd.	3	1¼
1/2½	Holbrn. & Frasca, Ltd.	1	1⅛
5	Do. Cum. Pref.	10	12
4	Do. Deb. Stk.	100	110
6	Home & Col. Stres., L., C. P.	5	7⅝
6	Hood & M.'s Stres., Ltd., Cum. Pref.	1	⅛
6	Hook, C. T. Ltd.	10	6
7/2	Hornsby, Ltd., £10 Shs.	8	3
—	Hotchks. Ordn., Ltd.	10	1
—	Do. 7 p.c. Cm. Prf.	10	4½
5	Do. 1 Mt. Dbs., Rd.	100	97½
6	Htl. Cecil, Ld., Cm. Prf.	5	3½
4	Do. 1 Mt. D. Sk., R.	100	100½
8/	Howard & Bulgh, Ltd.	10	38
6	Do. Pref.	10	16
4	Do. Deb. Stk., Red.	100	108
5/	Howell, J., Ltd., £5 Shs.	4	8¾
—	Howell & Js., Ltd., £3½ Shs.	3	⅜
6d.	Humber, Ltd.	1	½
6	Do. Cum. Pref.	1	¾
5/6	Hunter, Wilts., Ltd.	5	7
2/7	Hyam Clthg., Ltd., 5 p.c. Cum. Pref.	5	5¾
10/	Impl. Russn. Cotton, L.	5	6
5	Impd. Industl. Dwgs., Ld.	100	131½
6d.	Do. Defrd.	1	1¼
25/	Impd. Wood Pave., Ltd.	10	15½
15/	Ind. Rubber, Gutta Per. Telegraph Works, Ltd.	10	21½
4	Do. 1 Mt. Debs., Red.	100	104
6	Intern. Tea, Cum. Pref.	5	6½
10½d.	Jays, Ltd.	1	1½
5½	Do. Cum. Pref.	5	6½
1/2½d.	Jones & Higgins, Ltd.	1	2½
4½	Do. 1 Mt. Db. Sk., Rd.	100	111
5/	Kelly's Directory, Ltd., 5 p.c. Cum. Pref.	10	13
4	Do. Mort. Db. Sk., Rd.	100	107
—	Kent Coal Explrtn. Ltd.	1	⅛
9½d.	King, Howmann, Ltd.	1	1½
4/	Kinloch & Co., Ltd.	5	8¼
6	Do. Pref.	5	7
5	Lady's Pictorial Pub., Ltd., Cum. Pref.	5	5
48/4	La Guaira Harb., Ltd., 5 p.c. Deb. Stk.	100	79½
15/	Do. 2 Mt. 7 p.c. Deb. Stk., Red.	100	25½
4/	Lagunas Nitrate, Ltd.	5	1
2/	Lagunas Syn., Ltd.	5	1
5	Do. 1 Mt. Debs., Red.	100	82½
—	L. Copais Ld., 1 Mt., 6 p.c. Debs., Red.	100	35½
3/	Lautaro Nitrate, Ltd.	5	4½
5	Do. 1 Mt. Debs., Red.	—	100
9/	Lawes Chem. L., £10 shs.	9	5½
14/	Do. N. Cm. Min. Pref.	10	12½
—	Leeds Forge, 7 p.c. Cm. Pf.	5	4
5	Do. 1 Mt. Debs., Red.	50	48
5	Lever Bros., L., Cm. Pf.	10	13½
6	Liberty, L., 6 p.c. Cm. Pf.	10	15
20/	Liebig's, Ltd.	20	82
5	Lilley & Sk., L., Cm. Pf.	5	5½
2/6	Linoleum Manftg. Ltd.	5	16
3/	Linotype, Ltd., Pref.	5	5½
5/	Do. Def.	5	7¼
4/	Lister & Co., Ltd.	10	4
5	Do. Cum. Pref.	10	8½
5/	Liverpool Nitrate	5	5
—	Liverpool Warehsg., Ltd	10	3
5½	Do. Cum. Pref.	10	7½
4	Do. 1 Mt. Db. Stk., Rd.	100	106
5½	Lockharts, Ltd., Cm. Pf.	1	1½
4/6	Ldn. & Til., Lightrage £10	9	6½
6/	Ldn. Comcl. Sale Rms., L.	10	17½
3	Do. 1 Mt. Deb. Stk., Red.	100	103
3	London Nitrate, Ltd.	5	1½
4/	London Nitrate, Ld. 8 p.c. Cm. Min. Pf.	5	3½
8/	London Pavilion, Ltd.	5	7

Commercial, &c. (*continued*):—

Last Div.	Name.	Paid.	Price.
2/6	London Produce Clg. Ho., Ltd., £10 Shares	2½	3½
4/	London Stereos., Ltd.	5	3
7½d.	Ldn. Un. Laun. L. Cm. Pf.	1	⅞
8½d.	Louise, Ltd.	1	⅝
5½	Do. Cum. Pref.	1	⅝
5/	Lovell & Christmas, Ltd.	5	11½
6	Do. Cum. Pref.	5	7½
4	Do. Mt. Deb. Stk., Red.	100	107
1/9	Lyons, Ltd.	1	3½
4½	Do. 1 Mt. Deb., Stk., Rd.	100	113½
10/	Machinery Trust, Ltd.	5	14½
4½	Do. 4½ Deb. Stk.	100	106
6	MacLellan, L., Min. C. Pf.	10	9
5	Do. 1 Mt. Debs., 1900	100	101½
—	McEwan, J. & Co., Ltd.	10	1
6	Do. Mt. Debs., Red.	100	90½
8	McNamara, L., Cm. Pref.	10	9
7½d.	Maison Virot, Ltd.	1	⅝
2/7	Do. 6 p.c. Cum. Pref.	5	3½
4/	Manbré Sacc., L., Cm. Pf.	10	11¾
10/	Mangan Brze., L., £10 Shs.	6	16
2/	Mason & Mason, Ltd.	5	2½
6	Do. Cum. Pref.	5	5½
—	Maynards, Ltd.	1	⅛
6	Do. Cum. Pref.	1	⅝
9½d.	Mazawattee Tea, Ltd.	1	1½
5	Do. Cum. Pref.	5	5½
3/	Mellin's Food Cum. Pref.	5	6⅜
4½	Met. Ascn. Imp. Dwllngs., Ltd.	100	108
5	Metro. Indus. Dwlgs., Ltd.	5	4½
4	Do. do. Cum. Pref.	5	5½
5	Metro. Prop., L., Cm. Pf.	5	5½
4½	Do. 1st Mt. Debs. Stk.	100	107½
6	Mexican Cotton 1 Mt. Db.	100	93½
4½	Mid. Class Dwlgs., L., Db.	100	120½
2/	Millars' Karri, Ltd.	1	3
6	Do. Cum. Pref.	1	1½
5/	Milner's Safe, Ltd.	10	20½
10/	Moir & Son, Ltd., Pref.	5	8
6	Morgan Cruc., L., Cm. Pf.	10	14½
1/	Morris, R., Ltd.	3½	3
2/6	Murray L. 5½ p.c. C. Pf.	5	5½
63/4½	Do. 4½ 1 Mt. Db. Sk. Rd.	100	107
1/7½	Nat. Safe Dep., Ltd.	4	3½
6	Do. Cum. Pref.	1	1
—	Native Guano, Ltd.	5	½
—	Nelson Bros., Ltd.	10	2½
5	Do. Deb. Stk., Red.	100	80½
7/	Neuchtel Asph., Ltd.	10	10
10d.	New Darvel Tob., Ltd.	18/	1½
1/6	New Explosives, Ltd.	3	3
5/3½	New Gd. Htl., Bham, L.	5	4
5½	Do. Pref.	5	4½
4	Do. 1 Mt. Db. Stk., Rd.	100	96½
—	New Julia Nitrate, Ltd.	10/	—
—	New Ldn. Borneo Tob., L.	16/	1½
1/6	New Premier Cycle, Ltd.	1	1/16
6	Do. 6 p.c. Cum. Pref.	1	½
4½	Do. 4½ p.c. 1 Mt. Db. Rd	100	—
—	New Tamargl. Nitr. Ltd	1	1/16
—	Do. 8 p.c. Cum. Pref.	1	⅛
6	Do. 6 p.c. 1 Mt. Dbs. Rd.	100	62½
3·78d.	Newnes, G., L., Cm. Prf.	1	1
1/3	Nitr. Provision, Ltd.	2½	½
24/	Nobel-Dynam., Ltd.	10	17½
—	North Brazn. Sugar, Ltd.	1	⅛
15/	Oakey, Ltd.	10	30
6	Do. Cum. Pref.	10	17½
—	Paccha Jazp. Nitr., Ltd.	5	⅛
5	Pac. Borax, L., 1 Db. Rd.	100	110
—	Palace Hotel, Ltd.	10	5½
5½	Do. Cum. Pref.	10	7½
4	Do. 1 Mt. Deb. Stk.	100	103
—	Palmer, Ltd.	5	½
6	Do. Cum. Pref.	5	2
1/2½d	Paquin, Ltd.	1	¾
6	Do. Cum. Pref.	5	4
5½	Parnall, Ltd., Cum. Pref.	1	¾
4/6	Pawsons, Ltd., £10 Shs.	6	6½
4	Do. Mt. Debs., Red.	100	106
6	Pearks, G. & T., Ltd., 6 p.c. Cum. Pref.	1	⅞
9½d.	Pears, Ltd.	1	1½
6	Do. Cum. Pref.	10	14
5	Do. Deb. Stk.	100	129
5½	Pearson, C. A., L., Cu. Pf.	5	4½
4/3	Peebles, Ltd.	5	8
5	Do. Cum. Pref.	5	6½
4½	Do. Mt. Deb. Stk. Red.	100	113½
5½	Peek Bros., Ltd., 1 Cum. Pref., Nos. 1-60,000	5	6½
3½	Do. 3½ p.c. 1 Db. Stk.	100	102½
7½d.	Pegamoid, Ltd.	1	⅞
—	Pillsbury-W. Fl. Mills, L.	10	3
16/	Do. 8 p.c. Cum. Pref.	10	7½
6	Do. 1 Mort. Debs.	100	94½
9½d.	Plummer, Ltd.	1	1½
5	Do. Cum. Pref.	5	5½
17/6	Price's Candle, Ltd.	16	36
6	Priest Marians, L., Cm. Pf.	1	1½
6	Pryce Jones, Ld., Cm. Pf.	5	7
5	Do. Deb. Stk.	100	122
8½d.	Pullman, Ltd.	1	1½
6d.	Do. Cum. Pref.	1	1½
6d.	Raleigh Cycle, Ltd	1	1/16
6	Do. Cum. Pref.	1	½
—	Recife Drnge. Ld. 1 Mt. Debs., R.	100	18
6	Redfern, Ltd. Cum. Prf.	10	14
5	Ridgways, Ltd., Cu. Pf.	5	5⅜
—	R. Janeiro Cy. Imps. Ld.	25	8
5	Do. Debs.	100	85
5	Do. 1882-1893	100	83½
5%	R. Jan Fl. Mills, Ltd.	7	6
5	Do. 1 Mt. Debs., Rd.	100	94
—	Riv. Plate Meat, Ltd.	5	2½
—	Do. Pref.	5	5
8½d.	Roberts, J. R., Ltd.	1	1⅜
5	Roberts 1 Mt. D. Sk., Rd.	100	111
1/1½	Roberts, T. R., Ltd.	1	2½
5	Do. Cum. Pref.	1	1½

Commercial, &c. (*continued*):—

Last Div.	Name.	Paid.	Price.
3/	Rosario Nit., Ltd.	5	3½
5	Do. Debs., Red.	100	103
1/	Rover Cycle, Ltd.	1	⅜
6/	Ryl. Aquarium, Ltd.	5	4½
6	Do. Pref.	5	6
5	Ryl. Htl., Edin., Cm. Pf.	1	1½
1/2½	Ryl. Niger, Ltd., £10 Sh.	2	2¾
6/	Do.	10	15
20/	Russian Petroleum	10	
6½	Do. 6½ p.c. Cm. Prf.	10	
10/	Ruston, Proctor, Ltd.	10	11½
4½	Do. 1 Mort. Debs.	100	108
6/	Sadler, Ltd.	12	7
—	Sal. Carmen Nit., Ltd.	5	4
9d.	Salmon & Gluck., Ltd.	1	1½
	Salt Union, Ltd.	10	1⅛
1½	Do. 7 p.c. Pref.	10	5½
4½	Do. Deb. Stk.	100	101½
4½	Do. "B" Deb. Sk., Rd.	100	98
—	San Donato Nit., Ltd.	5	½
5/	San Jorge Nit., Ltd.	5	3½
—	San Pablo Nit., Ltd.	5	½
—	San Sebastn. Nit., Ltd.	5	⅜
1/9	Sanitas, Ltd	1	2¼
—	Sa. Elena Nit., Ltd.	5	½
—	Sa. Rita Nit., Ltd.	5	2½
5/	Savoy Hotel, Ltd.	10	15
7	Do. Pref.	10	13
4	Do. 1 Mt. Deb. Stk.	100	109½
5	Do. Debs., Red	100	102½
5	Do. & Ldn. For. Htl., Ltd., 5 p.c. Debs. Red.	100	99
8½d.	Schweppes, Ltd.	1	1½
2½d.	Do. Def.	1	⅝
5	Do. Cum. Pref.	1	1 1/16
4	Do. Deb. Stk.	100	106
6d.	Singer Cyc., Ltd.	1	½
5½	Do. Cum. Pref.	1	⅝
—	Smokeless Pwdr., Ltd.	1	⅛
5½d.	S. Eng. Dairies, Ltd., 6 p.c. Cum. Pref.	1	1½
—	Sowler Thos. L.	1	1
3/4½	Do. 5½ Cm. Pf.	5	5½
4/6	Spencer, Turner, & Co. Ltd	5	8¾
5	Do. Cum. Pref.	5	6½
5	Spicer, Ld., 5 p.c. Dbs. Rd.	100	69
4/	Spiers & Pond, Ltd.	10	21½
5	Do. 1 Mt. Debs., Red.	100	118½
5	Do. "A" Db. Stk., Rd.	100	111
5	Do. "B" 1 Db. Stk., Rd.	100	112½
4	Do. Fd. "C" 1 Db. S., R.	100	104
7/6	Spratt's, Ltd	5	12½
4	Do. Debs., 1914	—	105
5	Steiner Ld., Cm. Pf.	10	11½
4	Do. 1 Mt. Db. Sk. Rd.	100	107
9/	Stewart & Clydesdale, L.	10	13
6	Do. Cum. Pref.	10	15
35/5	Sulphide Corp.	100	80
1/	Swan & Edgar, L.	1	1½
1/	Sweetmeat Automatic, L.	1	4
2/9	Teetgen, Ltd., Cum. Pref.	5	6
24/	Teleg. Construction., Ld.	12	36½
5	Do. Db. Bds., Rd., 1899	100	103½
3/0½	Tilling, Ld. 5½ p.c. Cm. Prf.	5	6½
4	Do. 4 p.c. 1 Dbs., Rd.	—	106
8½d.	Tower Tea, Ltd.	1	1½
5	Do. Cum. Pref.	5	5½
5	Travers, Ltd., Cum. Pref.	10	12½
4	Do. 1 Mt. Dbs., Rd.	100	105
6	Tucuman Sug., 1 Dbs., Rd.	100	100
4/	United Alkali, Ltd.	10	2
7	Do. Cum. Pref.	10	9
5	Do. Mt. Db. Stk., Rd.	100	109½
2½d.	United Horse Shoe, Ltd., Non-Cum. 8 p.c. Pref.	1	1/16
5	Un. Kingm. Tea, Cm. Prf.	5	4½
2/	Un. Lankat Plant., Ltd.	1	2
4/	Un. Limmer Asphlte., Ld.	3	5
13/	Val de Travers Asph., L.	10	15½
3/	V. den Bergh's, L., Cm. P.	5	6½
6	Walkers, Park., L., C. Pf.	10	2½
4½	Do. 1 Mt. Debs., Red.	100	90½
6/	Wallis, Thos. & Co., Ltd.	5	14
6	Do. Cum. Pref.	5	8½
5½	Waring, Ltd., Cum. Pref.	5	5⅜
4½	Do. 1 Mt. Db. Sk., Red.	100	112
4½	Do. Irred. "B" Db. Stk.	100	104
12/	Waterlow, Dfd. Ord.	10	14
4/	Do. Pref.	10	14
3½	Do. Cum. Pref.	10	10½
10/	Waterlow Bros. & L., Ld.	10	9
5	Do. Pref.	10	12
1/2½	Welford, Ltd.	1	1½
4½	Do. Debs., Red.	100	109
1/	Welford's Surrey Dairies, Ltd.	1	1⅜
7½d.	West London Dairy, Ltd.	1	1
4½	Wharncliffe Dwllgs., L., Pf.	10	11½
18/10	Do. 3 p.c. Irr. Mt. Db. Sk.	100	96
1/	White, A. J., Ltd.	1	¾
6	Do. 6 p.c. Cum. Pref.	1	1/16
4	White, J. Bazley, Ltd., 1 Mort. Debs., Red.	100	99½
5	White, R., Ltd., 1 Mort. Deb. Stock, Red.	100	104½
11/	White, Tomkins, Ltd	10	10½
5	Do. Cum. Pref.	10	11½
6	White, W. N., L., Cm. Pf.	1	⅝
5/	Wickens, Pease & Co., L.	5	2½
6	Wilkie, Ltd., Cum. Pref.	10	15
4/	Willans & Robinson, Ltd.	5	8
6	Do. Cum. Pref.	5	7
4½	Do. 1 Mt. Db. Stk., Red.	100	107
7½d.	Williamsons, L., Cm. Prf.	1	1⅜
6	Winterbottm. Book Cloth, Ltd., Cum. Prf.	10	15
4/6	Yates, Ltd.	5	6
6	Do. Cum. Pref.	5	6½
	Young's Paraffin. Ltd.	4	1½

CORPORATION STOCKS—COLONIAL AND FOREIGN.

Per Cent.	Name.	Paid.	Price.
6	Auckland City, '72 1904-24	100	115
6	Do. Cons., '79, Red. 1930	100	135½
5	Do. Deb. Ln., '83..1934-8	100	117
6	Auckland Harb. Debs.	100	111½
5	Do. 1917	100	113½
5	Do. 1936	100	114
5½	Balmain Boro' 1914	—	113½
5	Boston City (U.S.)	100	102½
5	Do. ..1902	100	105
5	Brunswick Town 5. c. Debs. 1916-20	100	111
4½	B. Ayres City 4½ p.c.	100	69
5	Cape Town, City of	100	113
4	Do. ..1943	100	115
4	Chicago, City of, Gold 1915	—	110
6	Christchurch 1926	100	131½
—	Cordoba City	100	17
5	Duluth (U.S.) Gold ..1926	—	110
6	Dunedin (Otago) 1925	100	127½
6	Do. 1906	100	116
5	Do. Conso's..1908	100	111
4	Durban Insc. Stk.....1944	100	109
4	Essex Cnty., N. Jersey 1926	$100	114½
5	Fitzroy, Melbrne...1916-19	100	110
5	Gisborne Harbour....1915	100	109
4	Greymouth Harbour..1925	100	110
4	Hamilton 1934	100	108
5	Hobart Town 1918-30	100	115
4	Do. 1940	100	105
4½	Invercargill Boro. Dbs. 1936	100	111
6	Kimberley Boro., S. A. Debs.	—	102
4	Launceston Twn. Dbs. 1916	100	105
6	Lyttleton, N.Z., Harb. 1929	100	125
4	Melbourne Bd. of Wks. 1921	100	107
5	Melb. City Debs. 1897-1907	100	106½
4½	Do. Debs. 1908-27	100	111½
4	Do. Debs...1915-20-22	100	106
5	Melbne. Harb. Bds., 1908-9	100	112
4½	Do. do. 1915	100	111
4	Do. do. 1918-21	100	106
4½	Melbrne. Tms. Dbs. 1914-16	100	113
4½	Do. Fire Brig. Db. 1921	100	108
5	Mexico City Stg.	100	92½
4	Moncton N. Bruns. City	100	102
5	Montevideo	100	61
5	Montreal Stg.	100	103
5	Do. 1874	100	103
5	Do. 1879	100	104
3½	Do. 1933	100	103
3	Do. Perm. Deb. Stk.	100	96
4	Do. Cons. Deb. Stk. 1932	100	112
6	Napier Boro. Consolid. 1914	100	119
5	Napier Harb. Debs...1920	100	115
5	Do. Debs...1928	100	107
6	New Plymouth Harb. Debs. 1909	100	107
6	New York City 1901	—	108½
3½	Do. 1910-26	—	103½
4½	Nth. Melbourne Debs. 1-600 1921	100	105
5	Oamaru Boro. Cons...1920	100	101
6	Do. Harb. Bds. (Reg.)	100	74
25/	Do. 6 p.c. (Bearer)..1919	100	35
6	Otago Harb. Deb. Reg.	100	103
6	Do. 1877	100	107
6	Do. 1881 1921	100	115
5	Do. Debs. ..1921	100	107
5	Do. Cons. ..1934	100	105
6	Ottawa City	100	109
6	Do. 1904	100	111½
4½	Do. Debs. ..1913	100	108½
6	Port Elizabeth Waterworks	100	111
5	Port Louis	100	111
5	Prahran Debs. 1917	100	109
4	Do. Debs. 1919	100	102
6	Quebec C. Coupon. 1875 1905	100	113
6	Do. do. 1878 1908	100	117
4½	Do. Debs. 1914-18	100	108
4	Do. Debs. 1923	100	108
3½	Do. Cns. Rg. Stk., Red.	100	100
5	Richmond (Melb.) Dbs. 1917	100	112
4	Rio Janeiro City	100	58
4	Rome City	100	—
4	Do. and to 8th Iss.	100	93
—	Rosario C.	100	25
—	Do.	100	25
4	St. Catherine (Ont.)..1926	100	101
4	St. John, N.B., Debs. 1934	—	103
4½	St. Kilda (Melb) Dbs. 1918-21	100	105
4	St. Louis C. (Miss.)..1911	100	104
4	Do. 1913	100	103½
3·65	Do. 1915	—	108½
—	Santa Fé City Debs.	100	19
6	Santos City	100	95
6	Sofia City	100	98
5	Sth. Melbourne Debs. 1915	100	111
4½	Do. Debs....1919	100	107
5	Sydney City 1904	100	110
4	Do. Deb. 1912-13	100	107
4	Do. do. (1894)..1919	100	109
7	Timaru Boro. 7 p.c...1910	100	126½
5	Timaru Harb. Debs 1914	100	107
5	Do. Debs...1916	100	107
6	Toronto City Wtwks. 1904-6	100	114
5	Do. G. Cns. Dbs. 1919-20	100	118
4	Do. Strlg. 1922-8	100	107
4	Do. Local Improv.	100	104
3½	Do. 1929	100	105
5½	Valparaiso	100	100
4	Vancouver 1931	100	107
4	Do. 1932	100	108
6	Wanganui Harb. Dbs. 1905	100	107
6	Wellington Con. Deb. 1907	100	117
6	Do. Improv., 1879	100	123
6	Do. Wtrwks. Dbs., 1880	100	123
4½	Do. Debs., 1893....1933	100	114
4½	Wellington Harb. 1907	100	104
4	Westport Harb. Dbs. 1925	100	110
6	Winnipeg City Deb...1907	—	119
5	Do. 1914	100	117

FINANCIAL, LAND, AND INVESTMENT.

Last Div.	Name.	Paid.	Price.
5	Agncy, Ld. & Fin. Aust., Ltd., Mt. Db. Stk., Rd.	100	90½
	Amer. Frehld. Mt. of Lon., Ld., Cum. Pref. Stk.	100	87½
4½	Do. Deb. Stk., Red.	100	93
1/4½	Anglo-Amer. Db. Cor., L.	2	1
4	Do. Deb. Stk., Red	100	108½
	Ang.-Ceylon & Gen. Est., Ltd., Cons. Stk.	100	50
6	Do. Reg. Debs., Red.	100	101½
3/	Ang.-Fch. Explorn., Ltd.	1	2 3/16
6	Do. Cum. Pref.	1	11/16
—	Argent. Ld. & Inv., Ltd. £1 Shares	10/	nil
—	Do. Cum. Pref.	4	1½
1/	Assets Fnders.' Sh., Ltd.,	4	1⅜
6/	Assets Realis., Ltd., Ord.,	5	8¾
5	Do. Cum. Pref.	5	6¾
26/	Austrln. Agricl £25 Shs.	21½	63½
	Aust. N. Z. Mort., Ltd.,		
4½	Deb. Stk., Red.	100	87½
4	Do. Deb. Stk., Red.	100	80½
4½	Australian Est. & Mt., L., 1 Mt. Deb. Stk., Red.	100	103
5	Do. "A" Mort. Deb. Stk., Red.	100	96
5/	Australian Mort., Ld., & Fin., Ltd. £25 Shs.	5	5¼
1/6	Do. New, £25 Shs.	3	3½
4	Do. Deb. Stk	100	111
3	Do. Do.	100	85
5	Bengal Presidy. 1 Mort. Deb., Red.	100	107
25/	British Amer. Ld. "A"	1	22
—	Do. "B"	24	7
1/7½	Brit. & Amer. Mt., Ltd. £10 Shs.	2	1
5/	Do. Pref.	10	10
4	Do. Deb. Stk., Red.	100	103
1/3	Brit. & Austrlsn Tst Ln., Ltd. £25 Shs.	2½	¾
4½	Do. Perm. Debs., Red.	100	104
1¼d.	Brit. N. Borneo. £1 Shs.	15/	¾
2½d.	Do.	1	¾
—	Brit. S. Africa	1	2¼
5	Do. Mt. Deb., Red.	—	100
6	B. Aires Harb. Tst., Red.	100	93
12/6	Canada Co.	1	27
—	Canada N. W. Ld., Ltd.	$25	$3½
—	Do. Pref.	$100	$52
4	Canada Perm. Loan & Sav. Perp. Deb. Stk.	100	99½
6	Curamalan Ld., 6 p.c. "A" Scrip	—	92
3/7½	Deb Corp., Ld., £10 Shs	4	3½
5	Do. Cum. Pref.	10	11½
4	Do. Perp. Deb. Stk.	100	110
9d.	Deb. Corp. Fders' Sh., Ld.	3	½
4/5 1/10	Eastn. Mt. & Agncy, Ld., "A"	10	5½
4½	Do. Deb. Stk., Red.	100	98
5	Equitable Revers. In. Ltd.	100	—
2/6	Exploration, Ltd.	1	1⅜
/6d.	Freehold Trst. of Austrla. Ltd. £10 Shs.	1	¾
4	Do. Perp. Deb. Stk.	100	100
70/	Genl. Reversionary, Ltd.	100	—
3½	Holborn Vi. Land	100	105
4½	House Prop. & Inv.	100	84½
13/	Hudson's Bay	13	20½
—	Hyderabad (Deccan)	5	3
4	Impl. Col. Fin. & Agcy. Corp.	100	92½
4½	Impl. Prop. Inv., Ltd., Deb. Stk., Red.	100	91½
2/6	Internatl. Fincial. Soc., Ltd. £7½ Shs.	2½	1½
4	Do. Deb. Stk., Red.	100	99½
2/4½	Ld. & Mtge. Egypt, Ltd. £18 Shs.	3	2¾
5	Do. Debs., Red.	100	101
4½	Do. Debs., Red.	100	100
—	Ld. Corp. of Canada, Ltd.	1	½
4½	Ld. Mtge. Bk. of Texas Deb. Stk.	100	—
3½	Ld. Mtge. Bk. Victoria 4½ p.c. Deb. Stk.	100	78
2/9½	Law Debent. Corp., Ltd., £10 Shs.	2	1¾
4½	Do. Cum. Pref.,	10	12
4	Do. Deb. Stk.	100	113½
—	Law Land, L., 4½ Cm. Prf.	5	5
1/	Ldn. & Australasian Deb. Corp., Ltd., £4 Shs.	2	½
4½	Do. 4½ p.c. Mt. Deb. Stk., Red.	100	99
1/9	Ldn. & Middx. Frhld. Est. £2 Shs.	35/	3
2/6	Lndn. & N. Y. Inv. Corp., Ltd.	5	1¾
5	Do. 5 p.c. Cum. Pref.	10	8¼
1/6	Ldn. & Nth. Assets Corp., Ltd., £2 Shs.	1½	¾
2	Ldn. & N. Deb. Corp., L.	2	1¾
3/6	Ldn. & S. Afric. Explrn. Ltd.	½	12¾
2/	Mtge. Co. of R. Plate, Ltd. £10 Shs.	2	3
4½	Do. Deb. Stk., Red.	100	113
4½	Morton, Rose Est., Ltd., 1st Mort. Debs.	—	100
6/6	Natal Land Col. Ltd.	10	7
4/	Do. 8 p.c. Pref., 1870	5	8½
5/6	Natl. Disct. L., £25 Shs.	5	10½
4½	New Impl. Invest., Ltd. Pref. Stk.	100	67½
	New Impl. Invest., Ltd. Def. Stk.	100	9
3½	N. Zld. Assets Real Deb.	100	101
4	N. Zld. Ln. & Mer. Agcy., Ltd Prf. Ln, Deb. Stk	100	93
2/6	N. Zld. Tst. & Ln. Ltd., £25 Shs.	5	1¾

Financial, Land, &c. (*continued*):—

Last Div.	Name.	Paid.	Price.
12/6	N. Zld. Tst. & Ln. Ltd., 5 p.c. Cum. Pref.	25	20
—	N. Brit. Australsn. Ltd.	100	4
—	Do. Irred. Guar.	100	32½
5	Do. Mort. Debs.	100	82½
4½	N. Queensld. Mort. & Inv., Ltd., Deb. Stk.	100	93
6	Peel Riv., Ld. & Min. Ltd.	100	90
—	Peruvian Corp., Ltd.	100	2¾
—	Do. 4 p.c. Pref.	100	9
3	Do. 6 p.c. 1 Mt. Debs., Red.	100	40
—	Queenld. Invest. & Ld. Mort. Pref. Ord. Stk.	100	20
3/7	Queenld. Invest. & Ld. Mort. Ord. Shs.	4	4
4	Queenld. Invest. & Ld. Mort. Perp. Debs.	100	90
3½	Raily. Roll Stk. Tst. Deb., 1903-6	100	100½
50/	Reversiony. Int. Soc., Ltd.	100	—
2/8½	Riv. Plate Trst., Loan & Agcy., L., "A" £10 Shs.	2	4
1/6	Riv. Plate Trst., Loan & Agcy., Ltd., Def. "B"	5	3½
	Riv. Plate Trst., Loan & Agy., L., Db. Stk., Red.	100	110
—	Santa Fé & Cord. Gt. South Land, Ltd.	20	5
—	Santa Fé Land	10	2½
2/	Scot. Amer. Invest., Ltd. £10 Shs.	2	2¾
2½	Scot. Australian Invest., Ltd., Cons.	100	69½
6	Scot. Australian Invest., Ltd., Guar. Pref.	100	136½
5	Scot. Australian Invest., Ltd., Guar. Pref.	100	108½
4	Scot. Australian Invest., Ltd., 4 p.c. Perp. Dbs.	100	105½
5	Sivagunga Zemdy., 1st Mort., Red.	100	101
20/	Sth. Australian	20	48½
3½	Stock Exchange Deb., Rd.	—	101½
—	Strait Develt., Ltd.	1	—
2/6	Texas Land & Mt., Ltd. £10 Shs.	2½	2¾
4½	Texas Land & Mt., Ltd., Deb. Stk., Red.	100	104
—	Transvaal Est. & Dev., L.	1	½
—	Transvaal Lands, Ltd., £1 Shs.	15/	1/16
—	Do. F. P.	1	⅛
—	Transvaal Mort., Loan, & Fin., Ltd.; £10 Shs.	2	1/16
2/	Tst & Agcy. of Austrlsa., Ltd., £10 Shs.	1	1¾
7/5	Do. Old, fully paid	10	15½
5/7	Do. New, fully paid	10	12½
5	Do. Cum. Pref.	10	12¾
3/	Trust & Loan of Canada, £20 Shs.	5	4½
1/9½	Do. New £20 Shs.	3	2¼
4½	Tst. & Mort. of Iowa, Ltd., Deb. Stk. Red.	100	92½
—	Tst., Loan, & Agency of Mexico, Ltd., £10 Shs.	2	½
—	Trsts., Exors, & Sec. Ins. Corp., Ltd., £10 Shs.	7	1½
4	Do. Irred. Deb. Stk.	100	106½
5/	Union Dsc., Ld., £10 Shs.	5	10¾
6	Union Mort. & Agcy. of Aust., Ltd., Pref. Stk.	100	30
—	Do. 6 p. Pref. £6 Shs.	2	½
4½	Do. Deb. Stk	100	92½
4	Do. Deb. Stk	100	85½
5	Do. Deb. Stk. Red.	100	96½
1/6	U.S. Deb. Cor. Ltd., £8 Shs.	1	½
5½	Do. Cum. Pref. Stk.	100	100½
4½	Do. Irred. Deb. Stk.	100	106½
5	U.S. Tst. & Guar. Cor., Ltd., Pref. Stk.	100	77½
8/	Van Dieman's	25	16
4	Walker's Prop. Cor., Ltd., Guar. 1 Mt. Deb. Stk.	100	109
4½	Wstr. Mort. & Inv., Ltd., Deb. Stk.	100	92½

FINANCIAL—TRUSTS.

Last Div.	Name.	Paid.	Price.
1/6	Afric City Prop., Ltd.	1	1½
6	Do. Cum. Pref.	1	1 1/16
4	Alliance Invt., Ltd., Cm. 4½ p. c. Prefd.	100	72½
—	Do. Defd	100	12½
4	Do. Deb. Stk. Red.	100	104½
5	Amrcn. Invt., Ltd., Prfd.	100	120½
5	Do. Defd.	100	88½
4	Do. Deb. Stk. Red.	100	114½
2	Army & Navy Invt., Ltd., 5 p.c. Prefd.	100	84½
—	Do. Defd. Stk.	100	15½
4	Do. Deb. Stk.	100	107½
4	Atlas Investment, Ltd., Prefd. Stk.	100	70½
4½	Bankers' Invest., Ltd., Cum. Prefd.	100	103
1/0/0	Do. Defd	100	24½
4	Do. Deb. Stk	100	114
	Brewery & Comml. Inv., Ltd., £10 Shs.	5	6

Financial—Trusts (*continued*):—

Last Div.	Name.	Paid.	Price.
4	British Investment, Ltd., Cum. Prefd.	100	108
5	Do. Defd.	100	103½
4	Do. Deb. Stk.	100	107½
6	Brit. Steam. Invst., Ltd., Prefd	100	121
3/0/0	Do. Defd	100	71
4½	Do. Perp. Deb. Stk	100	123
1/9	Car Trust Invst., Ltd., £10 Shs.	9½	2
5	Do. Pref.	100	98
4	Do. Deb. Stk., 1915	100	104
4	Clnl. Sec., Ltd., Prefd.	100	103½
2½	Do. Defd.	100	43
4	Consolidated, Ltd., Cum. 1st Pref.	100	92
4	Do. 5 p.c. Cm. and do.	100	68½
—	Do. Defd.	100	14½
4½	Do. Deb. Stk.	100	112½
5	Deb. Secs. Invst.	100	105½
4	Do. 4 p.c. Cm. Pf. Sk.	100	105½
4½	Edinburgh Invest., Ltd., Cum. Prefd. Stk.	100	105½
4	Do. Deb. Stk. Red.	100	106½
5	Foreign, Amer. & Gen. Invt., Ltd., Prefd.	100	114½
2	Do. Defd.	100	47½
4	Do. Deb. Stk.	100	113½
5	Foreign & Colonial Invt., Ltd., Prefd.	100	137½
5½	Do. Defd.	100	96½
4½	Gas, Water & Gen. Invt., Cum. Prefd. Stk.	100	87½
5	Do. Defd. Stk.	100	37½
4	Do. Deb. Stk.	100	104
5	Gen. & Com. Invt., Ltd., Prefd. Stk.	100	103½
2	Do. Defd. Stk.	100	35½
4	Do. Deb. Stk.	100	111½
2/6	Globe Telegph. & Tst., Ltd.	10	11¼
6	Do. do. Pref.	10	17
4	Govt. & Genl. Invt., Ld., Prefd.	100	83½
3½	Do. Defd.	100	41½
4½	Govts. Stk. & other Secs. Invt., Ltd., Prefd.	100	86½
1	Do. Defd.	100	25
4½	Do. Deb. Stk.	100	112
4	Do. do.	100	104
4½	Guardian Invt., Ltd., Pfd.	100	89½
—	Do. Defd.	100	19½
4	Do. Deb. Stk.	100	104
5	Indian & Gen. Inv., Ltd., Cum. Prefd.	100	110½
2½	Do. Defd.	100	61
4½	Do. Deb. Stk.	100	120½
5	Indust. & Gen. Tst., Ltd., Unified	100	98½
3½	Do. Deb. Stk. Red.	100	99½
4½	Internat. Invt., Ltd., Cm. Prefd.	100	64½
—	Do. Defd.	100	7½
4	Do. Deb. Stk.	100	99
4	Invest. Tst. Cor. Ltd. Pfd.	100	100½
6	Do. Defd.	100	85
4	Do. Deb. Stk. Red.	100	104
25/	Ldn. Gen. Invest. Ltd., 5 p.c. Cum. Prefd.	100	111½
27/6	Do. Defd.	100	120
4½	Ldn. Scot. Amer. Ltd. Pfd.	100	106½
£3	Do. Defd.	100	60½
4	Do. Deb. Stk.	100	111
4	Ldn. Tst., Ltd., Cum. Prfd. Stk.	100	101
4	Do. Defd. Stk.	100	67½
4	Do. Deb. Stk., Red.	100	107½
3½	Do. Mt. Deb. Stk., Red.	100	100½
5	Mercantile Invt. & Gen., Ltd., Prefd.	100	113
3	Do. Defd.	100	48½
4	Do. Deb. Stk.	100	110½
4	Merchants, Ltd., Pref. Stk.	100	104½
4	Do. Ord.	100	80½
4	Do. Deb. Stk.	100	117½
3½	Municipal, Ltd., Prefd.	100	48
—	Do. Defd.	100	17½
4½	Do. Debs.	100	111
4½	Do. Debs. "B"	100	99½
4½	Do. "C" Deb. Stk.	100	94½
5	New Investment, Ltd. Ord.	100	93½
5	Omnium Invest., Ltd., Pfd.	100	92½
1	Do. Defd.	100	26½
4	Do. Deb. Stk.	100	106
5/	Railway Deb. Tst. Ld., £20 Shs.	10	6½
5	Do. Debs., Red.	100	108½
4½	Do. Deb. Stk., 1911	100	107½
4	Do. do. 1927	100	106½
4	Railway Invst. Ltd., Prefd.	100	115
17/7	Do. Defd.	100	22
8/	Railway Share Trust & Agency "A"	8	6½
7½	Do. "B" Pref. Stk.	100	148
4½	River Plate & Gen. Invt., Ltd., Prefd.	100	104
£3	Do. Defd.	100	50½
5	Scot. Invst., Ltd., Pfd. Stk.	100	91½
1½	Do. Defd.	100	26½
4	Do. Deb. Stk.	100	106
4½	Sec. Scottish Invst., Ltd., Cum. Prefd.	100	89½
£2	Do. Defd. Stk.	100	32
4	Do. Deb. Stk.	100	106½
5/	Sth. Africa Gold Tst., Ltd.	1	3½
6	Do. Cum. Pref	1	1
5½	Do. 1st Debs., Red.	100	104
1/9	Stock Conv. & Invest., Ltd., £5 Shs.	1	1½
4½	Do. do. 4½ p.c. Cm. Prf.	100	115½
2½	Do. Ldn. & N. W. 1st. Charge Prefd.	100	113½
4	Do do. 2nd Chge Prfd.	100	111
57/6	Do. do. Defd. Charge	100	32
3	Do. N. East. 1 Chge Pfd.	100	91½

Financial—Trusts (*continued*):—

Last Div.	Name.	Paid.	Price.
57/6	Stock N. East Defd. Chge	100	40
6	Submarine Cables	100	138½
5	U.S. & S. Amer. Invest., Ltd., Prefd.	100	97½
20/	Do. Defd.	100	24½
4	Do. Deb. Stk.	100	103½

GAS AND ELECTRIC LIGHTING.

Last Div.	Name.	Paid.	Price.
10/6	Alliance & Dublin Con. 10 p.c. Stand.	10	24
7/6	Do. 7 p.c. Stand.	10	16½
5	Austin. Gas Lght. (Syd.) Debs. 1909	100	108
5	Bay State of N. Jrsy. Sk. Fd. Tst. Bd., Red.	—	92½
3/	Bombay, Ltd.	5	6
2/4½	Do. New	4	4½
12	Brentford Cons.	100	282½
9	Do. New	100	215
5	Do. Pref.	100	142½
4	Do. Deb. Stk.	100	122½
11½	Brighton & Hove Gen. Cons. Stk.	100	270½
8½	Do. "A" Cons. Stk.	100	197½
5	Bristol 5 p.c. Max.	100	129½
22/6	British Gas Light, Ltd.	20	55
11/6	Bromley Gas Consumrs.' 10 p.c. Stand.	10	26
8/6	Do. 7 p.c. Stand.	10	21
—	Brush Electl. Enging., L.	—	½
6	Do. 6 p.c. Pref.	—	2½
4½	Do. Deb. Stk.	100	113
4½	Do. 2 Deb. Stk., Red.	100	102½
7/	B. Ayres (New), Ltd.	10	9½
4	Do. Deb. Stk., Rd.	—	100
18/6	Cagliari Gas & Wtr., Ltd.	20	31½
6/	Cape Town & Dist. Gas Light & Coke, Ltd.	10	15½
4½	Do. Pref.	10	12
6	Do. 1 Mt. Debs. 1910	50	59
4/	Charing Cross & Strand Elec. Sup., Ltd.	5	11½
4½	Do. Cum. Pref.	5	6½
3/	Chelsea Elec. Sup., Ltd.	5	8
4½	Do. Deb. Stk., Red.	100	116
5	Chic. Edis'n Co. 1 Mt., Rd.	$1000	106
20/	City of Ldn. Elec. Lht., L.	10	25½
—	Do. New £10 Shs.	5	18
6	Do. Cum. Pref.	10	15½
5	Do. Deb. Stk., Red.	100	129½
13½	Commercial, Cons.	100	322½
10½	Do. New	100	252½
4½	Do. Deb. Stk.	100	150½
10	Continental Union, Ltd.	100	209½
11	Do. Pref. Stk.	100	197½
—	County of Lon. & Brush Prov. Elec. Lg., Ltd.	10	17½
6	Do. Cum. Pref	10	14½
14	Croydon Comcl. Gas, Ld., "A" Stk., 10 p.c.	100	312½
11	Do. "B" Stk., 7 p.c.	100	260
5½	Crystal Pal. Dist. Ord. 5 p.c. Stk.	100	128½
5	Do. Pref. Stk.	100	143½
8/	European, Ltd.	10	24
6/	Do.	7½	17½
12½	Gas Light & Ck Cons. Stk., "A" Ord.	100	294½
4	Do. "B" (4 p.c. Max.)	100	120½
10	Do. "C," "D," & "E" (Pref.)	100	304½
5	Do. "F" (Pref.)	100	152½
7½	Do. "G" (Pref.)	100	222½
7	Do. "H" (7 p.c. Max.)	100	197½
10	Do. "J" (Pref.)	100	302½
6	Do. "K"	100	184½
4	Do. Deb. Stk.	100	131½
4½	Do. do.	100	150½
6	Do. do.	100	200½
8/	Hong Kong & China, Ld.	10	14
4/	House to House Elec. Light Sup., Ltd.	5	8½
7	Do. Cum. Pref.	5	10
10	Imperial Continental	100	209½
3½	Do. Deb. Stk., Red	100	104½
2/	Malta & Medit., Ltd.	5	5½
7/	Metrop. Elec. Sup., Ltd.	10	14½
4½	Do. 1 Mt. Deb. Stk.	100	119
5	Metro. of Melbrne. Dbs. 1908-12	100	111
4½	Do. Debs. 1918-22-4	100	106
10/	Monte Video, Ltd.	20	14½
9½	Newcastle-upon-Tyne	100	237½
—	Do. 3½ p.c. Deb. Stk.	100	117½
12/	Notting Hill Elec. Ltg., Ltd.	10	15½
3/6	Oriental, Ltd.	5	7½
2/1½	Do. New	4½	6½
8½d.	Do. do. 1876	1	1½
3/6	Ottoman, Ltd.	5	5
6	People's Gas Lt. & C. of Chic. 1 Mt. 1904	100	105½
5	River Plate Elec. Lgt. & Trac., Ltd., 1 Deb. Stk.	—	85½
8½	Royal Elec. of Montreal	—	144
4½	Do. 1 Mt. Deb.	100	104
11/	St. James' & Pall Mall Elec. Light, Ltd.	5	15½
7	Do Pref.	5	9½
4	Do. Deb. Stk., Red.	100	100½
10/	San Paulo, Ltd.	10	15

Gas and Electric (*continued*):—

Last Div.	Name.	Paid.	Price.
10	Sheffield Unit. Gas Lt. "A"	100	251½
10	Do. "B"	100	251½
10	Do. "C"	100	251½
—	Sth. Ldn. Elec. Sup., Ld.	2	2½
5¼	South Metropolitan	100	140½
3	Do. 3 p.c. Deb. Stk.	100	101½
2	Tottenham & Edmonton Gas Lt. & C., "A"	100	290
9	Do. "B"	100	210
7/	Tuscan, Ltd.	10	13½
5	Do. Debs., Red.	100	101¼
5/	West Ham 10 p.c. Stan.	5	12
8/	Wstmnstr. Elec. Sup., Ld.	5	14½

INSURANCE.

Last Div.	Name.	Paid.	Price.
4/	Alliance, £20 Shs.	44/	10½
10/	Alliance, Mar., & Gen., Ld., £100 Shs.	25	53
19/	Atlas, £50 Shs.	6	29
12/	British & For. Marine, Ld., £20 Shs.	4	24
7½d.	British Law Fire, Ltd., £10 Shs.	1	1½
7/6	Clerical, Med., & Gen. Life £25 Shs.	50/	16½
20/	Commercial Union, Ltd., £50 Shs.	5	43½
4	Do. "W. of Eng." Ter. Deb. Stk.	100	110½
£9	County Fire, £100 Shs.	80	196
5/	Eagle, £50 Shs.	5	½
4/	Employrs' Liability, Ltd., £10 Shs.	2	3½
—	Empress, Ltd., £5 Shs.	1	—
21/	Equity & Law, £100 Shs.	6	23
7/6	General Life, £100 Shs.	5	15
4½d.	Gresham Life, £5 Shs.	15/	2½
5/6	Guardian, Ld., £10 Shs.	5	10½
10/	Imperial, Ltd., £20 Shs.	5	29½
5/6	Imperial Life, £20 Shs.	4	6½
6/	Indemnity Mutual Mar., Ltd., £15 Shs.	3	11½
1/6	Lancashire, £20 Shs.	2	4½
7½d.	Law Acc. & Contin., Ltd., £5 Shs.	10/	½
12/6	Law Fire, £100 Shs.	2½	17½
9½d.	Law Guar. & Trust, Ltd., £10 Shs.	1	1½
9/	Law Life, £20 Shs.	2	24½
2/9	Law Un. & Crown £10Shs	12/	7
4	Do. Deb. Stk., 1942	100	109½
14/6	Legal & General, £50Shs.	8	15½
9d.	Lion Fire, Ltd., £8½ Shs.	1½	½
22/	Liverpool & London & Globe, Stk.	2	52
10/	Do. Globe £1 Ann	—	35
35/	London, £25 Shs.	12½	56
8/	Lond. & Lanc. Fire, £25Shs	2½	19
2/	Lond. & Lanc. Life, £25Shs	2	7
1/	Lond. & Prov. Mar., Ld., £10 Shs.	1	½
6/	Lond. Guar. & Accident, Ltd., £5 Shs.	2	12
10/	Marine, Ltd., £25 Shs.	4½	44
2/	Maritime, Ltd., £10 Shs.	2	4½
1/6	Merc. Mar., Ld., £10 Shs.	2½	2½
10/	N. Brit. & Merc., £25 Shs.	6¼	42
20/	Northern, £100 Shs.	10	81
40/	Norwich Union Fire, £100 Shs.	12	125½
10/	Ocean Acc. & Guar., fy. pd.	5	22½
2/	Do. £5 Shs.	1	3½
7/6	Ocean, Marine, Ltd.	2½	8½
2/	Palatine, £10 Shs.	2	3½
2/6	Pelican, £10 Shs.	1	3½
23/	Phœnix, £50 Shs.	5	41½
£6	Provident, £100 Shs.	10	32
5/	Railway Psangrs., £10Shs.	2	8½
2/6	Rock Life, £5 Shs.	10/	4½
8	Royal Exchange	100	350
18/	Royal, £20 Shs.	3	55
4/6	Sun, £10 Shs.	10/	11½
3/9	Sun Life, £10 Shs.	7½	15
6	Thames & Mrsey. Marine, Ltd., £20 Shs.	2	10½
6	Union, £10 Shs.	4	24½
4/	Union Marine, £20 Shs.	2½	9
12/	Universal Life, £100 Shs.	12	42
2/	World Marine, £5 Shs.	2	1½

IRON, COAL, AND STEEL.

Last Div.	Name.	Paid.	Price.
—	Barrow Hæm. Steel, Ltd.	7½	1½
9/	Do. 6 p.c. and Pref.	7½	6½
10/	Bolck., Vaugh. & C., Ld.	20	17
6/	Do. £8 liab.	12	9½
7/6	Brown, J. & Co., Ltd., £20 Shs.	15	20
7/6	Consett Iron, Ld., £10Shs.	7½	28½
7/6	Ebbw Vale Steel, Iron & Coal, Ltd., £23 Shs.	20	5½
12/6	General Mining Assn., Ld.	5½	7½
1/7½	Harvey Steel Co. of Gt. Britain, Ltd.	10	2½
5	Lehigh V. Coal 1 Mt. 5 p.c. Guar. Gd. Cp. Bds.	—	96
42/6	Nantyglo & Blaina Iron, Ltd., Pref.	862	96
1/	Nerbudda Coal & Iron, Ltd., £3 Shs.	56/	—
6/	Newport Abrcrn. Bk. Vein Steam Coal, Ltd.	10	6½
5/	New Sharlston Coll., Ltd. Pref.	20	10
4½d.	Nw. Vancvr. Coal & Ld., L.	1	½
2/6	North's Navigation Coll. (1889) Ltd.	5	2½
10/	Do. 10 p.c. Cum. Pref.	5	6½
—	Rhymney Iron, Ltd.	5	1½
	Do. New, £5 Shs.	4½	1
5	Do. Mt. Debs., Red.	100	99½
5	Shelton Irn., Stl. & Cl. Co., Ltd., 1 Chg. Debs., Red.	100	100½
50/	Sth. Hetton Coal, Ltd.	100	—
2/	Vickers & Maxim, Ltd.	1	3½
5	Do. 5 p.c. Prfd. Stk.	100	125½

SHIPPING.

Last Div.	Name.	Paid.	Price.
12/	African Stm. Ship, £20 Shs.	16	10½
15/	Do. Fully-paid	20	14½
5/	Amazon Steam Nav., Ltd.	12½	8½
12/	Castle Mail Pakts., Ltd., £20 Shs.	14	15
3½	Do. 1st Deb. Stk., Red.	100	102
6/	China Mutual Steam, Ltd.	5	3
6	Do. Cum. Pref.	10	0
20/	Cunard, Ltd.	20	9½
5/	Do. £20 Shs.	10	3½
4½	Furness, Withy, & Co., Ltd., 1 Mt. Dbs., Red.	100	107
6/	General Steam	15	7½
5/	Do. 5 p.c. Pref., 1874	10	8½
5/	Do. 5 p.c. Pref., 1877	10	8½
26/4½	Leyland & Co., Ltd.	10	26
7/	Do. 7 p.c. Cum. Pref.	10	14½
2/11	Do. 4½ p.c. Cum. Pre-Pf.	3	10½
4	Do. 1st Mt. Dbs., Red.	100	104½
7/6	Mercantile Steam, Ltd.	5	8
6/4½	New Zealand Ship., Ltd.,	6	4½
4	Do. Deb. Stk., Red.	100	104
5/	Orient Steam, Ltd.	10	4½
5	P. & O. Steam, Cum. Prefd.	100	147½
19	Do. Defd.	100	235½
3½	Do. Deb. Stk.	100	117
5	Richelieu & Ont., 1st Mt. Debs., Red.	100	100
30/	Royal Mail, £100 Shs.	60	51
2/6	Shaw, Sav., & Alb., Ltd., "A" Pref.	5	5½
5/	Do. "B" Ord.	5	4
14/	Union Steam, Ltd.	20	19
7/	Do. New £20 Shs.	10	8½
4	Do. Deb. Stk., Red.	100	108
6/	Union of N.Z., Ltd.	10	5½
5½	Wilson's & Fur.-Ley., 5½ p.c. Cum. Pref.	10	10½
4½	Do. 1 Mt. Db. Sk., Rd.	100	108½

*** *Tea Shares will be found in the Special Table following.*

TELEGRAPHS AND TELEPHONES.

Last Div.	Name.	Paid.	Price.
4	African Direct, Ltd., Mort. Debs., Red.	100	102
—	Amazon Telegraph, Ltd.	10	7
15/	Anglo-American, Ltd.	100	65½
30/	Do. 6 p.c. Prefd. Ord.	100	116½
—	Do. Defd. Ord.	100	16½
3/	Brazilian Submarine, Ltd.	10	15½
5	Do. Debs., 2 Series	100	114

Telegraphs and Telephones (*continued*):—

Last Div.	Name.	Paid.	Price.
4/	Chili Telephone, Ltd.	5	3
$8½	Comcial. Cable, $100 Shs.	—	185
4	Do. Stg. 500-yr. Deb. Stk. Red.	100	106
2½d.	Consd. Telpehone Constr., &c., Ltd.	10/	½
6/	Cuba Submarine, Ltd.	10	7
10/	Do. 10 p.c. Pref.	10	15
2/	Direct Spanish, Ltd.	5	4½
5/	Do. 10 p.c. Cum. Pref.	5	10½
4½	Do. Debs.	50	104½
3/	Direct U.S. Cable, Ltd.	20	10½
2/6	Eastern, Ltd.	10	17½
3/	Do. 6 p.c. Cum. Pref.	10	19
4	Do. Mt. Deb. Stk., Red.	100	125
6/6	Eastern Exten., Aus., & China, Ltd.	10	17½
5	Do. (Aus. Gov. Sub.) Deb., Red.	100	102
5	Do. do. Bearer	100	102½
4	Do. Mort. Deb. Stk.	100	126
5	Eastn. & S. Afric., Ltd., Mort. Deb. 1900	100	102
5	Do. Bearer	100	102½
4	Do. Mort. Debs. 1909	100	102½
4	Do. Mort. Debs. (Maur. Subsidy)	25	105½
5/	Grt. Nthn. Copenhagen	10	30
5	Do. Debs., Ser. B., Red.	100	101½
12/6	Indo-European, Ltd.	25	51½
6	London Platino-Brazilian, Ltd., Debs. 1904	100	109½
4/	Montevideo Telph., Ltd., 6 p.c. Pref.	5	2½
3/	National Telephone, Ltd.	5	5½
6/	Do. Cum. 1 Pref.	10	16
6/	Do. Cum. 2 Pref.	10	16
5	Do. Non-Cum. 3 Pref.	5	5½
3½	Do. Deb. Stk., Red.	100	103½
8d.	Oriental Telephone, Ltd.	2	½
4	Pac. & Euro. Tlg. Dbs., Rd.	100	106½
4/	Reuter's, Ltd.	8	8½
5/	Un. Riv. Plate Telph., Ltd.	5	4½
5	Do. Deb. Stk., Red.	100	105½
—	West African Telg., Ltd.	10	4
5	Do. 5 p.c. Mt. Debs., Red.	100	100½
—	W. Coast of America, Ltd.	10	½
6/9	Western & Brazilian, Ltd.	15	11½
6/	Do. 5 p.c. Pref. Ord.	7½	7½
9d.	Do. Defd. Ord.	7½	4½
4	Do. Deb. Stk., Red.	100	105½
5d.	W. India & Panama, Ltd.	10	½
6	Do. Cum. 1 Pref.	10	7½
6	Do. Cum. 2 Pref.	10	6
	Do. Debs., Red.	100	107½
7	West. Union, 1 Mt. 1902 $	1000	107½
6	Do. 6 p.c. Stg. Bds., Rd.	100	102½

TRAMWAYS AND OMNIBUS.

Last Div.	Name.	Paid.	Price.
1/6	Anglo-Argentine, Ltd.	5	3½
6	Do. Deb. Stk.	100	125
4/	Barcelona, Ltd.	10	10½
5	Do. Deb., Red.	100	105½
7/6	Belfast Street Trams.	10	16½
—	Blackpl. & Fltwd. Tram., £10 Shs.	8	12½
10/	Bordeaux Tram. & O. Ltd.	10	13
5	Do. Cum. Pref.	10	11
—	Brazilian Street Ry., Ltd.	2	½
—	British Elec. Trac., Ltd.	10	16½
—	B. Ayres & Belg. Tram., Ltd., 6 p.c. Cum. Pref.	5	—
6	Do. 1 Deb. Stk.	100	—
—	B. Ayres. Gd. Nat., Ltd., 6 p.c 1 Deb. Bds., Red.	100	60½
5½	Do. Pref. Debs., Red.	100	94½
1/	Calais, Ltd.	5	1
—	Calcutta, Ltd.	10	3½
—	Carthagena & Herr., Ltd.	10	2½
5	Do. Deb., Red.	100	90
5	City of B'ham. Trams., Ltd., 5 p.c. Cum. Pref.	5	5
4	Do. 1 Mort. Debs., Rd.	100	105½
3/9	City of B. Ayres, Ltd.	5	6½
2/3	Do. Ext. £5 Shs.	3	3½
6	Do. Deb. Stk	100	142½
1/4	Edinburgh Street Tram.	4	4
1/	Glasgow Tram. & Omni. Ltd., £9 Shs.	8	2½
3/7½	Imperial, Ltd.	6	14
3/	Lond., Deptfd, & Greenwich, Prefd.	5	3½
nil	Do. Defd.	5	1
10½	Lond. Gen. Omni., Ltd.	100	196
4	Do. Deb., Red.	100	113½

Tramways and Omnibus (*continued*):—

Last Div.	Name.	Paid.	Price.
4/9½	London Road Car	6	10
28/6	Do. Red. 1 Mt. Deb. Stk.	100	109½
5	London St. Rly. (Prov., Ont.), Mt. Debs.	100	110
12/6	London St. Trams.	—	2
12/9	London Trams., Ltd	10	9
6/	Do. Non-Cum. Pref.	10	10½
3	Do. Mt. Db. Stk., Rd.	100	101
5	Lynn & Boston 1 Mt. 1924 $	1000	106
5	Milwaukee Elec. Cons. Mt. $	1000	100½
5	Minneapolis St. 1 Cons. Mt $	1000	96
5	Montreal St. Dbs., 1908	100	109
4½	Do. Debs., 1922	100	107
6/	Nth. Metropolitan	—	11½
1/9½	Nth. Staffords., Ltd.	6	5
2/6	Provincial, Ltd	10	6½
6/	Do. Cum. Pref.	10	14
5	St. Paul City, 1937 $	1000	96
5/	Southampton	10	6½
5/	South London	10	5½
7/6	Sunderland, Ltd.	10	6½
4½	Toronto 1 Mt., Red.	100	105
2/6	Tramways Union, Ltd.	5	6½
4½	Do. Deb., Red.	100	109
2/6	Vienna General Omnibus.	5	5
5	Do. 5 p.c. Mt. Deb., Red.	100	103½
4/	Wolverhampton, Ltd.	10	8½

WATER WORKS.

Last Div.	Name.	Paid.	Price.
10/	Antwerp, Ltd.	20	22
6/	Cape Town District, Ltd.	5	7½
10½	Chelsea	100	322½
5	Do. Pref. Stk.	100	174½
4½	Do. Pref. Stk., 1875	100	152½
4½	Do. Deb. Stk.	100	159½
3/6	City St. Petersburg, Ltd.	12	10½
5/	Colne Valley	10	15½
4	Do. Deb. Stock	100	137½
£4	Consol. of Rosar., Ltd., 4 p.c. 1 Deb. Stk., Red.	100	91
8	East London	100	227½
4½	Do. Deb. Stk.	100	160
3	Do. Deb. Stk., Red.	100	105
37/6	Grand Junction (Max. 10 p.c.) "A"	50	118½
18/9	Do. "B"	25	
18/9	Do. "C" (Max. 7½ p.c.)	25	54½
35/	Do. "D" (Max. 7 p.c.)	50	97½
4	Do. Deb. Stock	100	142½
13	Kent	100	360½
7	Do. New (Max. 7 p.c.)	100	215½
7/	Kimberley, Ltd.	7	4½
6	Do. Debs., Red.	100	104½
6	Do. Deb. Stk., Red.	100	107½
10	Lambeth (Max. 10 p.c.)	100	289½
7½	Do. (Max. 7½ p.c.), 50 & 25	—	230½
4	Do. Deb. Stock	100	142½
3	Do. Red. Deb. Stock	100	103
10/	Montevideo, Ltd.	20	16
5	Do. 1 Deb. Stk.	100	110½
5	Do. 2 Deb. Stk.	100	104½
132/9	New River New	100	434½
4	Do. Deb. Stk.	100	143½
4	Do. Deb. Stk. "B"	100	143½
4	Portland Con. Mt. "B," 1927	—	102½
8/	Seville, Ltd.	20	12
5/6	Southend "Addl." Ord.	10	17
6	Southwark and Vauxhall	100	167½
6	Do. "D" Shares (7½ p.c. max.)	100	154½
5	Do. Pref. Stock	100	172½
4	Do. "A" Deb. Stock	100	142½
3	Staines Resvirs. Jt. Com. Gua. Deb. Stk., Red.	100	105
8/	Tarapaca, Ltd.	10	8½
10	West Middlesex	100	297½
4½	Do. Deb. Stk.	100	163½
3	Do Deb. Stk	100	105

REORGANIZATION

OF

THE BALTIMORE AND OHIO RAILROAD COMPANY.

The undersigned Committee, at the request of holders of a large amount of the securities, has been for a long time past engaged in an examination of the affairs of The Baltimore and Ohio System and the relative value and earning capacity of the various lines comprised therein, with a view to formulating a plan of reorganization therefore which should fairly recognise the rights of all security holders, and at the same time bring the fixed charges of the reorganized Company safely within the net earning capacity of the system. Much time and attention have been devoted to acquiring full and accurate information as to all details, including a careful examination of the Company's accounts for the period of nine years and six months, made by Mr. Stephen Little on behalf of the Committee. The aim of the Committee has been to formulate a plan for the reorganization of the system which should accomplish the following results:

(*a*) The reduction of the fixed charges to a limit safely within the net earning capacity of the reorganised properties;

(*b*) Adequate capital for present and future requirements;

(*c*) The payment of floating debt and provision for existing car-trust obligations;

(*d*) The preservation of the integrity of the system as far as the same can be economically and advantageously accomplished and such control of the reorganized Company as shall secure a satisfactory management of the property for a period of years.

Having these objects in view, a plan has been prepared and Messrs. Speyer & Co., and Messrs. Kuhn, Loeb & Co., of New York, and Messrs. Speyer Brothers, of London, have been selected by the Committee to act as Reorganization Managers to carry out the plan.

Messrs. Louis Fitzgerald, Henry Budge, Edward R. Bacon, and William A. Read, have been appointed an Advisory Committee to continue and complete the work of the Reorganization Committee and to consult and co-operate with the Reorganization Managers. Any vacancy in the Advisory Committee occasioned by death, resignation, or otherwise, may be filled by the joint action of the Reorganization Managers, and of the remaining Members of the Advisory Committee.

The undersigned recommend the prompt acceptance of the plan, believing that its consummation will result to the best interests of all security holders, and will place this important property upon a sound and conservative basis.

NEW YORK, June 22, 1898.

LOUIS FITZGERALD,
AUGUST BELMONT,
EDWARD R. BACON,
HENRY BUDGE,
EUGENE DELANO,
WILLIAM A. READ,
HOWLAND DAVIS,

Reorganization Committee.

To the Holders of the following Bonds, Coupons, and Stocks:

Baltimore and Ohio Railroad Company Bonds, Loan of 1853, Extended to 1935 at Four Per Cent.
Baltimore and Ohio Railroad Company 100-Year Five Per Cent. Consolidated Mortgage Bonds of 1888.
Baltimore and Ohio Railroad Company Sterling Six Per Cent. Loan of 1872, Due March 1, 1902.
Baltimore and Ohio Railroad Company Sterling Six Per Cent. Loan of 1874, Due May 1, 1910.
Baltimore and Ohio Railroad Company Six Per Cent. Loan of 1879, Due April 1, 1919 (Account Parkersburg Branch Railroad Company).
Baltimore and Ohio Railroad Company Five Per Cent. Bonds, Loan of 1885 (Account Pittsburgh and Connellsville Railroad Company).
Baltimore and Ohio Railroad Company Four and One-Half Per Cent. Terminal Mortgage Bonds of 1894.
Baltimore and Ohio Railroad Company Sterling Four and One-Half Per Cent. Loan of 1883, Philadelphia Branch.
Baltimore and Ohio Railroad Company Sterling Five Per Cent. Loan of 1877, Due June 1, 1927 (Account Baltimore and Ohio and Chicago Railroad Company).
Baltimore and Ohio Railroad Company First Preferred Stock.
Baltimore and Ohio Railroad Company Second Preferred Stock.
Baltimore and Ohio Railroad Company Common Stock.
Pittsburgh and Connellsville Railroad Company First Mortgage Bonds, Extended to 1946 at Four Per Cent.
Pittsburgh and Connellsville Railroad Company First Mortgage Seven Per Cent. Bonds, Due July 1, 1898.
Pittsburgh and Connellsville Railroad Company Six Per Cent. Consolidated Mortgage Bonds.
Akron and Chicago Junction Railroad Company First Mortgage Five Per Cent. Bonds.
Akron and Chicago Junction Railroad Company Preferred Stock.
Washington City and Point Lookout Railroad Company Six Per Cent. Bonds.
Matured and Unpaid Coupons, and claims for interest on registered bonds, appertaining to any of the above-named Bonds, except those of the Washington City and Point Lookout Railroad Company may be deposited separate from the Bonds as hereinafter stated.

As stated in the foregoing announcement of the Re-organization Committee, a plan has been prepared, with our joint approval and co-operation, for the re-organization of the Baltimore and Ohio Railroad Company's System; and in conformity with an arrangement with the Committee, the undersigned have undertaken to act as Re-organization Managers to carry out the plan.

The plan provides for the creation of the following new securities:—

FIRST

70,000,000 Dols. PRIOR LIEN THREE AND ONE-HALF PER CENT. GOLD BONDS, DUE 1925.

These bonds will bear interest from July 1, 1898, and are to be secured by a mortgage upon the Main Line and Branches, Parkersburg Branches and Pittsburgh Division when acquired by the New Company, covering about 1,017 miles of first track, and about 904 miles of second, third and fourth tracks and sidings and also all the equipment now owned by the Company of the value of upwards of 20,000,000 dols. or hereafter acquired in any manner except by the use of the 34,000,000 dols. reserved First Mortgage Bonds, as hereinafter stated.

The right will be reserved to issue, after January 1st, 1902, not to exceed 5,000,000 dols. additional of these bonds, at the rate of not exceeding 1,000,000 dols. a year, for the enlargement, betterment or extension of the properties covered by the Prior Lien Mortgage, or for the acquisition of additions thereto.

In case delay should occur in acquiring any of the said lines of railway, the execution of the plan will not for that reason necessarily be postponed, but the existing bonds upon such line deposited under the plan may be pledged under the Prior Lien Mortgage, as security for the bonds issued thereunder, until such line of railway shall be acquired by the New Company and subjected to the lien of said mortgage.

The Prior Lien Bonds are to be applied as follows:—

	Dols.
In partial exchange for existing bonds	60,073,090
Purchased by Syndicate to provide cash requirements of plan ...	9,000,000
	69,073,090
For contingencies (any surplus to New Company)	926,910
	70,000,000

SECOND.

63,000,000 Dols. FIRST MORTGAGE FIFTY-YEAR FOUR PER CENT. GOLD BONDS.

These bonds will bear interest from July 1st, 1898, and are to be secured by a mortgage which will be a first lien on the Philadelphia, Chicago, and Akron divisions and branches, and the Fairmont, Morgantown, and Pittsburgh Railroad, covering about 570 miles of first track, and about 332 miles of second, third and fourth tracks and sidings, and also on the properties now included in the present Baltimore and Ohio Terminal Mortgage of 1894, when said lines and properties are acquired by the New Company: also on the Baltimore Belt Railroad, if and when the same shall be acquired by the New Company; and a lien subject to the Prior Lien Mortgage upon the lines, property and equipment covered by the latter.

The right will be reserved to increase the amount of these bonds to 90,000,000 dols. for the enlargement, betterment, or extension of the railroads and properties covered by the Prior Lien Mortgage and also those covered by the First Mortgage, or for the acquisition of extensions or additions thereto or equipment for use thereon, at the rate of not exceeding 1,500,000 dols. a year for the first four years after the organization of the New Company and at the rate of not exceeding 1,000,000 dols. a year thereafter. The right will also be reserved to call in and redeem all or any part of the First Mortgate Bonds after twenty-five years, at 105, and also to issue not to exceed 75,000,000 dols. additional of said bonds or such lesser amount as may be required to retire the Prior Lien bonds when due.

In case delay should occur in acquiring any of the said lines of railway or properties to be included under the First Mortgage as above stated, the execution of the plan will not for that reason necessarily be postponed, but the existing bonds upon such line or property deposited under the plan may be pledged under the First Mortgage, as security for the bonds issued thereunder, until such line or property shall be acquired by the New Company, and subjected to the lien of said First Mortgage.

The First Mortgage Bonds are to be applied as follows:—

	Dollars.
In partial exchange for existing bonds	36,384,535
Purchased by Syndicate to provide cash requirements of plan ...	12,450,000
For contingencies (any surplus to New Company)	1,165,465
	50,000,000
Reserve for New Company	7,000,000
	57,000,000
Reserve to be issued only to retire Baltimore Belt Line 5s. ...	6,000,000
	63,000,000

NOTE.—The properties covered by the Baltimore Belt Line mortgage will be leased at a rental equivalent to interest at 4 per cent. on the existing Belt Line 5 per cent. bonds which is to be in full payment of said interest. The rental agreement will provide that in consideration of the rental the New Company shall have an option to purchase all the said Belt Line 5 per cent. bonds at par and accrued interest at any time within five years on sixty (60) days' notice, and that, in case the Company shall not purchase such bonds within the five years specified, it will at the termination of that period assume the ultimate payment, when due, of the principal of such bonds.

THIRD.

40,000,000 Dols. FOUR PER CENT. NON-CUMULATIVE PREFERRED STOCK.

This stock will be entitled to receive non-cumulative dividends at the rate of 4 per cent. per annum before the payment of any dividend on the Common Stock. This stock will be applied as follows:—

	Dols.
For Reorganization purposes	17,218,700
Purchased by Syndicate to provide cash requirements of plan ...	16,450,000
For adjustment with various outstanding bondholders' and stockholding interests, contingencies, &c., &c. (any surplus to New Company)	1,331,300
	35,000,000
Reserve for New Company...	5,000,000
	40,000,000

FOURTH.

35,000,000 Dols. COMMON STOCK.

This stock will be applied as follows:—

	Dols.
For Reorganization purposes	31,178,000
For adjustment outstanding securities, contingencies, &c. (any surplus to New Company)	3,822,000
	35,000,000

In order to establish such control of the Reorganized Company as shall secure a satisfactory management of the property for a period of years, both classes of stock of the New Company (except such shares as may be disposed of to qualify directors) shall be vested in the following five Voting Trustees for the period of five years:— William Salomon, Abraham Wolff, J. Kennedy Tod, Louis Fitzgerald, and C. H. Coster, although the Voting Trustees in their discretion may deliver their stock at an earlier date as provided in the Trust Agreement. In the meanwhile the Voting Trustees are to deliver their certificates in the usual form.

As stated in the plan, holders of First and Second Preferred and Common Stock of the Baltimore and Ohio Railroad Company may purchase from the Syndicate new preferred and common stock, by depositing their old stocks with the Mercantile Trust Company, or the London and Westminster Bank, Limited, its agency in London, on the following terms: as consideration for shares of the New Company depositors of B. & O. First Preferred Stock must pay 2 dols. per share deposited; depositors of B. & O. Second Preferred Stock must pay 20 dols. per share deposited; and depositors of B. & O. Common Stock must pay 20 dols. per share deposited. Such payments must be made by depositors in not less than three instalments, at least thirty days apart, when and as called for by advertisement published in each instance at least twice a week for two weeks in at least two daily newspapers in New York, Baltimore, and London respectively.

Deposited bonds must carry all coupons and claims for interest on registered bonds maturing on or after July 1, 1898 (except the First Mortgage Six Per Cent. Bonds of the Washington City and Point Lookout Railroad Company, must also carry all matured and unpaid coupons). All matured and unpaid coupons and claims for interest on registered bonds (excepting the unpaid coupons on the First Mortgage Six Per Cent. Bonds of the Washington City and Point Lookout Railroad Company) may be deposited separate from the bonds, and the same will be paid in cash as soon as practicable after the plan is declared operative, with interest on such coupons and claims for interest at the rate of five per cent. per annum from the date of maturity up to the date when the same are finally paid. Interest will also be paid in cash upon the completion of the reorganization on all deposited bonds (excepting the First Mortgage Six per Cent. Bonds of the Washington City and Point Lookout Railroad Company) at the rate provided in the old Bonds up to July 1, 1898, from the coupon date last preceding.

The Syndicate will purchase such coupons and claims for interest on registered bonds matured prior to July 1, 1898, from holders who do not desire to deposit the same under the plan (provided and so soon as the bonds to which the coupons or claims of interest appertain have been deposited) at their face value with interest at the rate of five per cent. per annum from the respective dates of maturity of such coupons or claims for interest to date of purchase, provided such coupons and claims for interest shall be presented for sale to the Syndicate at the office of the Mercantile Trust Company in New York or at its London agency above mentioned on or before July 22, 1898.

The basis of exchange of existing bonds and of sale of new stock is shown in the following table:—

Existing Bonds and Stock to be Deposited.	Each 1,000 dols. or £200 Receives: *Cash.	New Prior Lien 3½% Bonds.	New First Mtge. 4% Bonds.	New Pfd. Stock Trust Certificates.	New Common Stock Trust Certificates.	Actual Percentage for Sterling Issues Figured at 4·8666 Dols.: New Prior Lien 3½% Bonds.	New First Mtge. 4% Bonds.	New Pfd. Stock Trust Certificates.
	Dols.	Dols.	Dols.	Dols.	Dols.	%	%	%
Baltimore & Ohio Loan of 1853, Extended ...	10·00	1,025	125	140				
" " Consolidated Mortgage, 5 per cent. ...	20·83	1,050	125	85				
" " Sterling Loan of 1872 ...	19·47	1,020	120	40	......	104·79	12·33	4·12
" " Sterling Loan of 1874 ...	9·73	1,120	120	160	......	115·07	12·33	26·44
" " Parkersburg Branch Bonds ...	15·00	1,050	125					
Pittsburgh & Connellsville, 1st Extended 4s. ...	20·00	1,025	125	40				
Pittsburgh & Connellsville, 1st 7s., not Extended ...	35·00	1,000	125					
Baltimore & Ohio 5s., Loan of 1885 ...	20·83	1,000	125	100				
Pittsburgh & Connellsville Consolidated Mortgage 6 per cent. Bonds ...	29·20	1,025	120	200	......	105·31	12·33	20·55
Chicago Division, 5 per cent. ...	4·06	100	1,070	100	......	10·27	109·93	10·27
Philadelphia Division, 4½ per cent. ...	10·95	......	1,000	265	......	......	102·74	27·22
Baltimore & Ohio 4½ per cent. Terminal Bonds of 1894 ...	3·75	......	1,000					
Akron & Chicago Junction Bonds ...	8·33	......	1,000	250				
Akron & Chicago Junction, Preferred Stock...	......	......	......	250	1,000			
Washington City and Point Lookout Bonds ...	......	......	......	500	1,000			
Depositors of old 1st Preferred Stock may purchase from Syndicate, on payment of 2 dols. per share deposited ...	......	......	......	525	750			
Depositors of old 2nd Preferred Stock may purchase from Syndicate, on payment of 20 dols. per share deposited ...	......	......	......	200	1,500			
Depositors of old Common Stock may purchase from Syndicate, on payment of 20 dols. per share deposited ...	......	......	......	200	1,000			

* Interest at the rate provided in the old bonds, from the date of the last matured coupon next preceding July 1, 1898, up to the date when the new bonds begin to bear interest, namely, July 1, 1898 (exclusive of previously matured coupons otherwise provided for as stated below).

The Syndicate has agreed to purchase for cash, upon the plan being declared operative, all Baltimore and Ohio Railroad Company One-Hundred-Year Five Per Cent. Consolidated Mortgage Bonds deposited under the plan, whose holders prefer to accept cash rather than to take the new securities, at the price (in New York) of 110 and interest accrued and unpaid since the maturity of the last-paid coupon, provided the depositors of such bonds shall signify their election to receive cash as above stated, by presenting their Certificates of Deposit at the office of the Mercantile Trust Company in New York or at its London agency above specified, within sixty days from the time the plan shall actually be issued, to be stamped as electing to accept such cash payment. Such depositors will thereupon be entitled to receive such cash payment so soon as the plan is declared operative, upon surrender of their Certificates of Deposit so stamped.

	Dols.
The fixed charges of the Company for the year ending June 30, 1897, as reported by the Receivers, were ...	7,771,111
The annual fixed charges, upon completion of the reorganization and retirement of existing bonds as proposed, it is estimated, will be ...	6,252,351
Decrease of annual fixed charges ...	1,518,760

The Company, as shown by Mr. Stephen Little's expert examination and report, dated July 11th, 1896, from September 30th, 1888, to November 30th, 1895, a period of seven years and two months, earned, net, including miscellaneous income, a yearly average of 7,234,000 dols., without deduction, however, of average taxes amounting to 437,000 dols.

		Dols.
The net earnings for the year ending June 30th, were including miscellaneous income ...		6,593,990
(For the fiscal year ending June 30, 1897, equipment of the Company valued on its books at 1,155,829·95, dols. was put out of service and charged, not to operating expenses, but to "Profit and Loss," because it represented the depreciation of a number of years. As against this, however, extraordinary expenses—estimated at not less than 750,000 dols.—for the maintenance of the property generally, were incurred during the year, and charged to operation. For the year 1898, as stated in the annual report of last year, all equipment when put out of service, is replaced with equipment of equal value, as shown on the books of the Company, and the cost thereof charged to "Maintenance of Equipment.")		
The net earnings from the property for the present fiscal year (April, May and June approximated) have (notwithstanding liberal charges for maintenance), as compared with the same period of the preceding fiscal year, increased ...	1,443,909	
Miscellaneous income decreased ...	62,114	
Net increase ...		1,381,795
Estimated net earnings for the fiscal year ending June 30, 1898, including miscellaneous income (Taxes not deducted, they being included in fixed charges) ...		7,975,785

from which, however, will have to be deducted the sum of about 251,000 dols., representing the decrease in the amount of miscellaneous income which will be occasioned by the proposed sale of securities in the treasury and the cancellation of sinking-fund investments under the reorganization. The fixed charges of the new Company will thus be well within the past net income of the property—even that of the last fiscal year of extreme depression. The new Company will be relieved from floating debt and the embarrassment of car and wheelage trust payments and will start, not only with a substantial working cash capital, but also with power to provide facilities for the increase of business. The bye-laws of the new Company will provide that its accounts shall be audited annually by accountants of established reputation.

A Syndicate has been formed to furnish the cash required to provide for unpaid interest, existing car trusts, receiver's certificates, floating debt, and other outstanding obligations, improvement, equipment, working capital, and other purposes of the new Company, and also to purchase new securities not taken by holders of certain of the existing bonds.

The Mercantile Trust Company of New York will act as Depositary under the plan, and the London and Westminster Bank, Limited, will act as its agent for the purpose of receiving deposits in London, England. All holders of bonds and stock affected by the plan may deposit their securities, on and after June 30, 1898, either with the Mercantile Trust Company, at its office, No. 120, Broadway, in the City of New York, or at its agency, the London and Westminster Bank, Limited, 41, Lothbury, London, England, and will receive reorganization certificates of deposit therefor. Application will be made in due course to list such certificates of deposit upon the New York and London Stock Exchanges.

Participation under the plan of reorganization in any respect whatsoever is dependent upon the deposit of securities as above within such time as may be fixed by the Managers, and the plan will embrace only securities so deposited. Copies of the agreement and plan of reorganization are now ready for distribution, and all security holders are invited to obtain them from the undersigned, or from the Depositary or its London agency, as all depositors are bound thereby, without regard to this circular; and the plan and agreement set forth in detail many features which it is impracticable to condense into this circular, but which are of much importance to security holders.

We believe that the prompt consummation of the plan will result to the best interests of all security holders, and will place the administration of this property on a sound and conservative basis. Any further information connected with the reorganization which may be desired by security holders will be furnished on application at the offices of any of the undersigned, or at the office of the Depositary or its London Agency.

Dated New York, June 22, 1898.

SPEYER & CO.,
30, Broad Street, New York.
KUHN, LOEB & CO.,
27, Pine Street, New York.
SPEYER BROTHERS,
7, Lothbury, London.
} Reorganization Managers.

SEWARD, GUTHRIE & STEELE,
EVARTS, CHOATE & BEAMAN,
FRESHFIELDS & WILLIAMS, London,
Counsel to Reorganization Managers.

To the Holders of Bonds or Stocks of the following-named Railroad Companies:—

Columbus and Cincinatti Midland Railroad Company.
Central Ohio Railroad Company.
Newark, Somerset and Straitsville Railroad Company.
Sandusky, Mansfield and Newark Railroad Company.
Schuylkill River, East Side Railroad Company.
Winchester and Potomac Railroad Company.
Winchester and Strasburg Railroad Company.

Referring to the plan and agreement for the reorganization of the Baltimore and Ohio Railroad Company, dated June 22, 1898, holders of the securities of the above-named railroads are requested to communicate at once with the undersigned Advisory Committee, giving the amount of their holdings, and stating how the same are held.

In order to deal with the holders of these leased-line securities, it is deemed necessary to consider each case separately and upon its merits. After hearing from the holders of a large proportion of each class of securities, the matter of adjustment will be considered.

LOUIS FITZGERALD,
EDWARD R. BACON,
HENRY BUDGE,
WILLIAM A. READ,
} Advisory Committee.

WILLIAM C. GULLIVER,
Counsel to Advisory Committee.

ALVIN W. KRECH, Secretary,
120, Broadway, New York.

BALTIMORE AND OHIO RAILROAD COMPANY.

SIX PER CENT. STERLING MORTGAGE BONDS, LOAN OF 1874.

London and New York,
22nd June, 1898.

To the Holders of Certificates issued under the Bondholders' Agreement dated 3rd May, 1898.

Referring to our Circular of 3rd May, 1898, in which the holders of the above described bonds were invited to deposit them, so that all necessary steps might be taken for the protection of their interests, we have now to state that a Plan has been issued for the reorganization of the Baltimore and Ohio Railroad Company.

This Plan, in our opinion, fully recognises the rights of the 6 per cent. Sterling Mortgage Bonds of 1874. The terms thereby secured for them are entirely satisfactory to us, and we feel that they should be to you, and that the bonds we represent should be deposited under said Plan.

Pursuant to the Bondholders' Agreement of 3rd May, 1898, under which your bonds are deposited, and especially to Articles Fourth and Fifth (subdivision 6 thereof), it is necessary before we take any further steps in the line indicated that we shall have the Assent of 60 per cent. in amount of the holders of the above-named certificates.

As you will see on examination of the Plan, the offer to the 6 per cent. Sterling Mortgage Bonds of 1874 is, for each £200 Bond—

1,120 dols. in new Prior Lien 3½ per cent. Gold bonds due 1945 (equal at 4·8666 to 115·07 dols. per cent.), bearing interest from 1st July, 1898.
120 dols. in new First Mortgage 4 per cent. Gold bonds due 1948 (equal at 4·8666 to 12·33 dols. per cent.), bearing interest from 1st July, 1898.
160 dols. in new 4 per cent. non-cumulative Preferred Stock Trust Certificates (equal at 4·8666 to 16·44 dols. per cent.).
9 11/100 dols. in cash, on completion of the reorganization, for interest to 1st July, 1898.

The Coupon on the present Bonds, due 1st May, 1898, namely, £6 per Bond, with interest thereon at 5 per cent. per annum, to be likewise paid in cash as soon as practicable after the Plan is declared operative; or, if the holder so desires, such Coupon will be purchased by a Syndicate for cash as soon as the Bond has been deposited, but not after 22nd July, 1898, at its face value, with interest at 5 per cent. per annum.

If you agree with the views herein expressed, and the offer made is satisfactory to you, will you please sign the "Assent" which may be obtained at the offices of Messrs. J. S. Morgan & Co., 22, Old Broad Street, London, E.C., and return it with the least possible delay to them.

J. S. MORGAN & CO.
J. P. MORGAN & CO.

BALTIMORE AND OHIO RAILROAD COMPANY.

FIVE PER CENT. BONDS DUE 1927, SECURED BY "CHICAGO DIVISION" MORTGAGE OF MAY 29th, 1877.

London and New York,
22nd June, 1898.

To the Holders of Certificates issued under the Bondholders' Agreement dated July 17th, 1897.

Referring to our Circular of July 22nd, 1897, in which the holders of the above described bonds were invited to deposit them, so that all necessary steps might be taken for the protection of their interests, we have now to state that a Plan has been issued for the reorganization of the Baltimore and Ohio Railroad Company.

This Plan, in our opinion, fully recognises the rights of the Baltimore and Ohio "Chicago Division" Bonds. The terms thereby secured for them are entirely satisfactory to us, and we feel that they should be to you, and that the bonds we represent should be deposited under said Plan.

Pursuant to the Bondholders' Agreement of July 17th, 1897, under which your bonds are deposited, and especially to Articles Fourth and Fifth (subdivision 6 thereof), it is necessary before we take any further steps in the line indicated that we shall have the Assent of 60 per cent. in amount of the holders of the above-named certificates.

As you will see on examination of the Plan, the offer to the Baltimore and Ohio "Chicago Division" bondholders is, for each £200 Bond—

100 dols. in new Prior Lien 3½ per cent. Gold bonds due 1925, (equal at 4·8666 to 10·27 dols. per cent.) bearing interest from 1st July, 1898.
1,070 dols. in new First Mortgage 4 per cent. Gold bonds due 1948, (equal at 4·8666 to 109·93 dols. per cent.) bearing interest from 1st July, 1898.
100 dols. in new 4 per cent. non-cumulative Preferred Stock Certificates (equal at 4·8666 to 10·27 dols. per cent.).
4 88/100 dols. in cash, on completion of the reorganization, for interest to 1st July, 1898

The Coupons on the present Bonds, due 1st December, 1897, and 1st June, 1898, namely, £10 per Bond, with interest thereon at 5 per cent. per annum, to be likewise paid in cash as soon as practicable after the plan is declared operative; or, if the holder so desires, such Coupons will be purchased by a Syndicate for cash as soon as the Bond has been deposited, but not after 22nd July, 1898, at their face value, with interest at 5 per cent. per annum.

If you agree with the views herein expressed, and the offer made is satisfactory to you, will you please sign the "Assent" which may be obtained at the offices of Messrs. J. S. Morgan & Co., 22, Old Broad Street, London, E.C. and return it with the least possible delay to them.

J. S. MORGAN & CO.
J. P. MORGAN & CO.

BALTIMORE AND OHIO RAILROAD COMPANY.

FIVE PER CENT. CONSOLIDATED MORTGAGE BONDS,

Issued under Mortgage dated December 19th, 1887.
(Known as Bonds of 1988.)

New York,
22nd June, 1898.

To the Holders of Certificates issued under the Bondholders' Agreement dated 1st November, 1897.

Referring to our Circular of 1st November, 1897, in which we invited the holders of the above-described bonds to deposit them, so that we might take all necessary steps for the protection of their interests, we have now to state that a Plan has been issued for the reorganization of the Baltimore and Ohio Railroad Company.

This Plan, in our opinion, fully recognises the rights of the Consolidated Bonds. The terms thereby secured for them are entirely satisfactory to us, and we feel that they should be to you, and that the bonds we represent should be deposited under said Plan.

Pursuant to the Bondholders' Agreement of 1st November, 1897, under which your bonds are deposited, and especially to Articles Fourth and Fifth (subdivision 6 thereof), it is necessary before we take any further steps in the line indicated that we shall have the Assent of 75 per cent. in amount of the holders of the above-named certificates.

As you will see on examination of the Plan, the offer to the Consolidated Mortgage bondholders for each present bond of 1,000 dols. with all unpaid coupons or interest is substantially—

1,050 dols. in new Prior Lien 3½ per cent. Gold bonds due 1925, bearing interest from 1st July, 1898.
125 dols. in new First Mortgage 4 per cent. Gold bonds due 1948, bearing interest from 1st July, 1898.
85 dols. in new 4 per cent. non-cumulative Preferred Stock Trust Certificates.
20 83/100 dols. in Cash, on completion of reorganization, for interest to 1st July, 1898.

or, at the option of depositors (to be signified within 60 days after the Plan shall actually be issued),

1,100 dols. cash for principal, together with cash for all accrued interest to time of payment, such payment to be made upon the Plan being declared operative.

If you agree with the views herein expressed, and the offer made is satisfactory to you, will you please sign the "Assent" which may be obtained at the offices of Messrs. J. P. Morgan & Co., 23, Wall Street, New York, and return it with the least possible delay to them.

Holders of our certificates desiring to accept the cash offer for the principal of the bonds represented thereby, will please so signify at the foot of the Assent. In all other cases we shall understand that they elect to accept the new securities for the principal of the present bonds.

J. P. MORGAN & CO.
BROWN, BROTHERS & CO.
BARING, MAGOUN & CO.

London, 22nd June, 1898.

Having jointly made an issue of the above-described bonds in this market, under date of 15th May, 1888, simultaneously with that made in New York by our respective representatives, who have signed the above Circular, we strongly recommend all holders of certificates for such bonds to assent to the terms proposed for the bonds under the Plan of Reorganization. Signed "Assents" may be sent to Messrs. J. S. Morgan & Co., 22, Old Broad Street, London, E.C.

J. S. MORGAN & CO.
BROWN, SHIPLEY & CO.
BARING BROTHERS & CO., Limited.

PITTSBURGH AND CONNELLSVILLE RAILROAD COMPANY.

SIX PER CENT. CONSOLIDATED MORTGAGE BONDS DUE 1926, AND GUARANTEED BY THE BALTIMORE AND OHIO RAILROAD COMPANY.

London and New York,
22nd June, 1898.

To the Holders of Certificates issued under the Bondholders' Agreement dated July 15th, 1897.

Referring to our circular of July 22nd, 1897, in which the holders of the above-described bonds were invited to deposit them so that all necessary steps might be taken for the protection of their interests, we have now to state that a Plan has been issued for the reorganization of the Baltimore and Ohio Railroad Company, including the railroad and property of the Pittsburgh & Connellsville Railroad Company.

This Plan, in our opinion, fully recognises the rights of the Pittsburgh and Connellsville Consolidated Bonds. The terms thereby secured for them are entirely satisfactory to us, and we feel that they should be to you, and that the bonds we represent should be deposited under said Plan.

Pursuant to the Bondholders' Agreement of July 22nd, 1897, under which your bonds are deposited, and especially to Articles Fourth and Fifth (subdivision 6 thereof), it is necessary before we take any further steps in the line indicated that we shall have the Assent of 60 per cent. in amount of the holders of the above-named certificates.

As you will see on examination of the Plan, the offer to the Pittsburgh and Connellsville Consolidated Mortgage bondholders is, for each £200 bond—

1,025 dols. in new Prior Lien 3½ per cent. Gold bonds due 1925 (equal at 4·8666 to 105·31 dols. per cent.) bearing interest from 1st July, 1898.
120 dols. in new First Mortgage 4 per cent. Gold bonds due 1948 (equal at 4·8666 to 12·33 dols. per cent.) bearing interest from 1st July, 1898.
200 dols. in new 4 per cent. non-cumulative Preferred Stock Trust Certificates (equal at 4·8666 to 20·56 dols. per cent.)
29 30/100 dols. in cash, on completion of the reorganization, for interest to 1st July, 1898.

The coupons on the present bonds, due 1st July, 1897, and 1st January, 1898, namely, £12 per boud, with interest thereon at 5 per cent. per annum to be likewise paid in cash as soon as practicable after the Plan is declared operative; or, if the holder so desires, such coupons will be purchased by a Syndicate for cash as soon as the bond has been deposited, but not after 22nd July, 1898, at their face value, with interest at 5 per cent. per annum.

If you agree with the views herein expressed, and the offer made is satisfactory to you, will you please sign the "Assent" which may be obtained at the offices of Messrs. J. S. Morgan & Co., 22, Old Broad Street, London, E.C., and return it with the least possible delay to them.

J. S. MORGAN & CO.
J. P. MORGAN & CO.

To Holders of Receipts issued by the undersigned for

BALTIMORE AND OHIO RAILROAD COMPANY'S FIVE PER CENT. BONDS, LOAN OF 1885.

Pursuant to the Bondholders' Agreement of April 10th, 1896, we the undersigned hereby give notice that a Plan and Agreement for the Re-organization of the Baltimore and Ohio Railroad Company, dated June 22nd, 1898, has been prepared, and has been adopted and approved by us, and we hereby recommend the same for the acceptance of the Bondholders. Copies of the said Plan and Agreement have been duly lodged at the offices of Speyer & Co., New York, and Speyer Brothers, London, for inspection by the holders of our receipts issued under said Bondholders' Agreement of April 10th, 1896.

The plan provides that each 1,000 dols. of the above Bonds will, on the completion of the re-organization, be entitled to receive:—

In New Prior Lien 3½ per Cent. Bonds	1,000	dols.
,, 1st Mortgage 4 per Cent. Bonds	125	,,
,, Preferred Stock Trust Certificates	100	,,
In Cash (representing interest accrued from February 1st, 1898, to July 1st, 1898)	20·83	,,

The New Prior Lien and 1st Mortgage Bonds are to bear interest from July 1st, 1898.

Any receipt-holders who do not assent to such Plan and Agreement of Re-organization may withdraw their bonds and coupons represented by our receipts at any time on or before July 21st, 1898, upon the surrender of such receipts, without expense. All receipt-holders who shall not withdraw their bonds and coupons on or before July 21st, 1898, above stated, shall be conclusively deemed to have assented to said Plan and Agreement of Re-organization, and will be bound thereby, and the undersigued will thereupon deposit thereunder all of such bonds and coupons not so withdrawn, in exchange for Re-organization Certificates of Deposit issued under said Plan and Agreement.

SPEYER & CO.
SPEYER BROTHERS, } Depositaries.

Dated, June 22nd, 1898.

BALTIMORE AND OHIO RAILROAD SIX PER CENT. BONDS OF 1872.

To the Holders of Certificates issued under the Bondholders' Agreement of 16th May, 1898.

A plan having been issued, dated the 22nd June, 1898, for the reorganization of the Baltimore & Ohio Railroad, by which satisfactory provision is in our opinion made for the rights of the above Bonds, we shall deposit under the said plan all Bonds deposited with us under the Bondholders' Agreement of the 16th ultimo, provided that such deposit is assented to, as provided in the said agreement, by the holders of Sixty per Cent. in amount of our Certificates. Any holders of Certificates who wish to dissent must give us written notice within two weeks from the 4th of July next. Forms of assent and copies of the plan may be obtained from us by holders of our Certificates.

BARING BROTHERS & CO., LIMITED,
June 22nd, 1898. 8, Bishopsgate, Within.

Founders Court, London, E.C.,
22nd June, 1898.

To the Holders of our Certificates of Deposit for the

BALTIMORE & OHIO RAILROAD COMPANY'S FIRST MORTGAGE FOUR AND A-HALF PER CENT. STERLING BONDS OF 1883

Issued under the Bondholders' Agreement dated 1st October, 1897.

A proposed Plan and Agreement for the Reorganization of the Baltimore and Ohio Railroad Company, dated 22nd June, 1898, has been most carefully considered by us, under which, each of the above bonds will receive 1,000 dols. New First Mortgage Four per Cent. Gold Bonds, and 265 dols. in New Preferred Stock in exchange for each £200 First Mortgage Four and a half per Cent. Sterling Bond 1883. We recommend the same to you for your prompt acceptance.

Under your Bondholders' Agreement of 1st October, 1897, it is provided that if there shall be proposed to our satisfaction any Scheme of Reorganization or Readjustment, we may, with the assent (to be manifested by express approval, or by a failure within two weeks to express dissent), of the holders of certificates of deposit representing sixty per cent. in amount of the deposited bonds, come in under such reorganization.

The Plan and Agreement is deemed satisfactory by us. We request therefore your assent thereto in writing.

Unless, within two weeks from the date of mailing this notice to you and of the first advertisement of this notice in two London newspapers, you notify us of your dissent, we will presume, conclusively, that you have assented to our deposit of your bonds under said Plan and Agreement of Reorganization.

Your bonds will accordingly be deposited by us, if 60 per cent. of the bonds with us deposited shall assent in writing to the deposit under said Plan and Agreement.

If notified by any depositor within two weeks from the date hereof, in writing of his dissent, we will return him the bonds deposited with us, upon surrender of our Certificates of Deposit, thus ending all future obligation to such dissenting bondholder,

If we are not notified of your dissent within the time named, upon receipt by us in exchange for your bonds of certificates of deposit issued under said Plan and Agreement of Reorganization, we will deliver the same to you, without further charge, upon surrender to us of our own certificates.

We solicit most earnestly a very prompt expression, in writing, of your assent or dissent. Unless notified to the contrary by you, we will deposit all coupons of assenting bonds maturing prior to 1st July, 1898, upon depositing such bonds under the Plan.

Having thus obtained for depositing bondholders the opportunity to secure terms of settlement deemed satisfactory by us, we notify you that after the expiration of two weeks from the mailing of this notice and first advertisement thereof, our only duty under the Bondholders' Agreement of 1st October, 1897, will be either to return their bonds to depositing holders who have theretofore signified their desire to withdraw the same, or to surrender to such depositing bondholders as, within that period, shall have assented either expressly or by a failure to dissent, the certificates of deposit which will be issued under said Plan and Agreement of Reorganization, and if the coupons are ordered to be sold, to pay to them any cash received therefor.

In no event will any certificates be delivered by us, saving upon return to us of own certificates of deposit.

Annexed hereto is a form of written assent to the proposed Plan and Agreement of Reorganization.

It is our desire that all assenting bondholders will deliver at the earliest moment after the certificates have been received by us under the Plan and Agreement, their own certificates of deposit with us for exchange. We will be ready, after such exchange, to accept the certificates of deposit thus to you delivered, to be held, in case the Plan and Agreement shall be declared thereafter inoperative, upon the understanding that we will demand in lieu thereof your bonds deposited under said Plan and Agreement, and shall hold said bonds under the original Agreement of 1st October, 1897.

Yours faithfully,
BROWN, SHIPLEY & CO.

STERLING.

FORM OF ASSENT.

As the owner of Brown, Shipley & Company's Certificate(s) of Deposit for Four and a-Half per Cent. First Mortgage Sterling Bonds of 1883 of the Baltimore & Ohio Railway Company, deposited under an Agreement endorsed thereon, No. (s)......................... said Certificate being for £.................... bond(s) assent is given to a deposit by Brown, Shipley & Company, Committee of the said First Mortgage Sterling Bonds of 1883, covered by said Certificate, under a proposed Plan and Agreement for the Reorganization of the Baltimore & Ohio Railway Company, in accordance with the terms of said Plan and Agreement, of which a copy has been received.

(Signature)

....

Founders Court, London, E.C.,
22nd June, 1898.

To the Holders of our certificates of deposit for the

BALTIMORE & OHIO RAILROAD COMPANY'S FIRST MORTGAGE FOUR-AND-A-HALF PER CENT. GOLD TERMINAL BONDS OF 1894

Issued under Bondholders' Agreement, dated 30th September, 1897.

A proposed Plan and Agreement for the Reorganization of the Baltimore and Ohio Railroad Company, dated 22nd June, 1898, has been most carefully considered by us, under which each of the above bonds will receive 1,000 dols. in New First Mortgage 4 per cent. Gold Bonds of the Baltimore and Ohio Railroad Company in exchange for each 1,000 dols. 4½ per cent. Terminal Bonds. We recommend the same to you for your prompt acceptance.

Under your Bondholders' Agreement of September 30th, 1897, it is provided that if there shall be proposed to our satisfaction any Scheme of Reorganization or Readjustment, we may, with the assent (to be manifested by express approval, or by a failure within two weeks to express dissent), of the holders of certificates of deposit representing sixty per cent. in amount of the deposited bonds, come in under such reorganization.

The Plan and Agreement is deemed satisfactory by us. We request therefore your assent thereto in writing.

Unless, within two weeks from the date of mailing this notice to you and of the first advertisement of this notice in two London newspapers, you notify us of your dissent, we will presume, conclusively, that you have assented to our deposit of your bonds under said Plan and Agreement of Reorganization.

your bonds will accordingly be so deposited by us, if sixty per cent. of the bonds with us deposited, shall assent in writing to the deposit under said Plan and Agreement.

If notified by any depositor within two weeks from the date hereof, in writing of his dissent, we will return him the bonds deposited with us, upon surrender of our Certificates of Deposit, thus ending all future obligation to such dissenting bondholder.

If we are not notified of your dissent within the time named, upon receipt by us in exchange for your bonds, of certificates of deposit issued under said Plan and Agreement of Reorganization, we will deliver the same to you, without further charge, upon surrender to us of our own certificates.

We solicit most earnestly a very prompt expression, in writing, of your assent or dissent. Unless notified to the contrary by you, we will deposit all coupons of assenting bonds maturing prior to first July, 1898, upon depositing such bonds under the Plan.

Having thus obtained for depositing bondholders the opportunity to secure terms of settlement deemed satisfactory by us, we notify you that after the expiration of two weeks from the mailing of this notice and first advertisement thereof, our only duty under the Bondholders' Agreement of 30th September, 1897, will be either to return their bonds to depositing holders who have theretofore signified their desire to withdraw the same, or to surrender to such depositing bondholders as, within that period, shall have assented either expressly or by a failure to dissent, the certificates of deposit which will be issued under said Plan and Agreement of Reorganization, and if the coupons are ordered to be sold, to pay to them any cash received therefor.

In no event will any certificates be delivered by us, saving upon return to us of our own certificates of deposit.

Annexed hereto is a form of written assent to the proposed Plan and Agreement of Reorganization.

It is our desire that all assenting bondholders will deliver at the earliest moment after the certificates have been received by us under the Plan and Agreement, their own certificates of deposit with us for exchange. We will be ready, after such exchange, to accept the certificates of deposit thus to you delivered, to be held, in case the Plan and Agreement shall be declared thereafter inoperative, upon the understanding that we will demand in lieu thereof your bonds deposited under said Plan and Agreement, and shall hold said bonds under the original Agreement of 30th September, 1897.

Yours faithfully,
BROWN, SHIPLEY & CO.

TERMINAL.

FORM OF ASSENT.

As the Owner of Brown, Shipley & Company's Certificate(s) of Deposit for dols...................Four and a-Half per Cent. First Mortgage Terminal Gold Bonds of the Baltimore & Ohio Railroad Company, deposited under an Agreement endorsed thereon No.(s) ....I[we] assent to a deposit by Brown, Shipley & Company, Committee of the said First Mortgage Terminal Gold Bonds covered by said Certificate, under a proposed Plan and Agreement for the Reorganization of the Baltimore & Ohio Railroad Company, in accordance with the terms of said Plan and Agreement of which a copy has been received.

(Signature)

....

BELT.

Founders Court, London, E.C.,
22nd June, 1898.

To the Holders of our Certificates of Deposit for the

FIRST MORTGAGE FIVE PER CENT. GOLD BONDS OF THE BALTIMORE BELT RAILROAD COMPANY,

Issued under our Bondholders' Agreement, dated 1st November, 1897.

The proposed Plan and Agreement for the Reorganization of the Baltimore and Ohio Railroad Company, dated 22nd June, 1898, has been most carefully considered by us. We recommend the same to you for your prompt acceptance.

Such Plan provides that the property of the Baltimore Belt Railroad Company is to be leased to the New Company to be formed, at a rental sufficient to pay interest at the rate of Four per centum per annum upon the Baltimore Belt Line bonds. The arrangement is to date from July 1st, 1898, and the payment of interest at the rate of Four per centum after that date is to be in full of all interest due and payable upon such bonds thereafter. Interest at the rate of Five per centum per annum will be paid up to July 1st, 1898, with interest upon overdue coupons, upon the completion of the reorganization.

The Plan further provides that in consideration of the agreement to pay such rental, the holders of said Baltimore Belt Line bonds shall agree that the new Company shall have the option for five years from July 1st, 1898, to purchase said Belt Line bonds at par and accrued interest at any time, upon sixty days' notice of their intention to do so, and that if this option be not exercised within the said period, the the new Company will assume the ultimate payment of the principal of said bonds when due. The form of the proposed lease and agreement with the new Company, covering the arrangement, will be subject to the approval of our Counsel. In order to make the arrangement effective, the holders of the Baltimore Belt Line bonds must present the same to be stamped, and the arrangement will not become operative until the holders of all such Baltimore Belt Line bonds outstanding, or such lesser amount as the Reorganization Managers or the new Company shall approve, shall have consented thereto and presented their bonds for stamping accordingly.

Under your Bondholders' Agreement of November 1st, 1897, it is provided that if at any time there should arise an opportunity for arrangement or settlement considered favourable by us, we may, with the assent (to be manifested by express approval or by a failure within two weeks to express dissent) of the holders of our certificates of deposit representing sixty per cent. in amount of the deposited bonds, make such arrangement and settlement.

The Plan and Agreement present an opportunity for a settlement and arrangement of your claims which we deem favourable. We request, therefore, your assent thereto in writing. Unless within two weeks from the date of mailing this notice to you, and of the first advertisement of this notice in two London newspapers, you notify us of your dissent, we shall presume conclusively that you have assented to the proposed arrangement and to the stamping of your bonds as assenting thereto, as provided by the proposed lease and agreement above mentioned.

Your bonds will accordingly be so presented by us for stamping if 60 per cent. of the bonds deposited with us shall assent in writing to the proposed arrangement, and the same shall become operative by the assent of the requisite amount of outstanding bonds as above stated.

If notified by any depositor within two weeks from the date hereof in writing of his dissent, we shall return him the bonds deposited with us upon surrender of our certificates of deposit, thus ending all future obligation to such dissenting bondholder.

We solicit most earnestly a very prompt expression of your assent or dissent.

Having thus obtained for depositing bondholders the opportunity to secure terms of settlement deemed satisfactory by us, we notify you that after the expiration of two weeks from the mailing of this notice and the first advertisement, our only duty under the Bondholders' Agreement of November 1st, 1897, will be either to return their bonds to depositing holders who have theretofore signified their desire to withdraw the same, or to surrender to such depositing bondholders as within that period shall have assented, either expressly or by failure to dissent, the deposited bonds duly stamped as assenting to the proposed arrangement. In no event will any securities be delivered by us save upon the return to us of our own certificates of deposit.

Annexed hereto is a form of written acceptance of the proposed arrangement.

In case the proposed lease and agreement should not become operative, the deposited bonds will not be stamped, and we shall hold the same under the original agreement of November 1st, 1897.

BROWN, SHIPLEY & CO.

BELT.

FORM OF ASSENT.

First Mortgage Five per Cent. Gold Bonds of the Baltimore Belt Railroad Company, dated 16th September, 1890, Bondholders' Agreement, 1st November, 1897.

As the owner(s) of Messrs. Brown, Shipley & Company's Certificate(s) of Deposit for First Mortgage Five per Cent. Gold Bonds of the Baltimore Belt Railroad Company, deposited under an agreement endorsed thereon No.(s)........................ said Certificate(s) for dols...................of bonds, assent is given to the arrangement as communicated to me[us] by Messrs. Brown, Shipley & Company proposed in regard to said bonds under the Plan and Agreement for the Reorganization of the Baltimore & Ohio Railroad; and Messrs. Brown, Shipley & Company are authorised to present the First Mortgage Five per Cent. Gold Bonds of the Baltimore Belt Railroad Company covered by said Certificate(s) to be stamped in accordance therewith, and with said Plan and Agreement of Reorganization, copy of which has been received.

(Signature)

....

Date........................ . 1898.

Printed for the Proprietor by LOVE & WYMAN, LTD., Great Queen Street, London, W.C.; and Published by CLEMENT WILSON at Norfolk House, Norfolk Street, Strand, London, W.C.

The Investors' Review

EDITED BY A. J. WILSON.

Vol. I.—No. 26. New Series. | FRIDAY, JULY 1, 1898. | [Registered as a Newspaper.] | Price 6d. By post, 6½d

PUBLISHED TO-DAY.

No. XIII of the

INVESTMENT INDEX,

A QUARTERLY SUPPLEMENT

TO THE

Investors' Review.

It will contain, in addition to a complete list of the securities quoted on the London Stock Exchange and a selected list of securities quoted on provincial Stock Exchanges, with the return they give to investors at current prices, so classified that the range of interest desired can be picked out at once, notes on the present aspect of money and stock markets, and also suggestions as to how investments may be made with reasonable probability of safety.

In the appendix a commencement will be made with the formation of a *catalogue raisonné* designed to give at a glance the quality of each security dealt with.

Orders should be sent in early, as it is not proposed to supply this supplement except to subscribers.

Price TWO SHILLINGS net per Number,

Or by Post Two SHILLINGS AND TWOPENCE. Subscription Price, 8/6 per Annum.

CLEMENT WILSON,

NORFOLK HOUSE, NORFOLK STREET, W.C.

THE

LAW GUARANTEE AND TRUST SOCIETY, LIMITED.

Capital Subscribed	£1,000,000
do. Paid-up	£100,000
do. Uncalled	£900,000
Reserve Fund	£70,000

FIDELITY GUARANTEES,

On behalf of Managers, Secretaries, Clerks, Cashiers, Collectors, &c.

DEBENTURE INSURANCE.

The advantages of such Insurance are as follows:—

1. The Debentures being guaranteed by the Society can be placed a[illegible] loss than par, thus saving discount.
2. [illegible] rate of interest is willingly accepted.
[illegible]iety acting as Trustee for Debenture Holders also adds Security.

[illegible]GAGE INSURANCE.

[illegible]NGENCY INSURANCE,

[illegible] of Defects in Title, Lost Documents, Missing Bene-fi[illegible]ries, Re-Marriage, Issue and Name and Arms Risks, &c.

LICENSE INSURANCE.

Mortgagees of Licensed Property should always insure in a substantial Insurance Society against loss they may sustain by depreciation in consequence of the license being lost.

TRUSTEESHIPS for Debenture Holders, and under Wills, Marriage Settlements, &c.

HEAD OFFICE:

49, CHANCERY LANE, LONDON.

CITY OFFICE:

56, MOORGATE STREET, E.C.

CONTENTS

The Investors' Review.

Our "Gift" to Egypt.

Unquestionably we have a great inheritance, and we are dissipating it right royally. It is unnecessary to go over here the story of this Soudan conquest—how it was begun without warning and how each statement made regarding it as it went on has been falsified by the event to such an extent that, had deception been deliberately intended, the Government could not have varied further from the truth than it has actually done. We do not accuse her Majesty's Ministers of falsehood aforethought in this matter; they are more probably victims of a policy of drift. Nobody called for this Soudan conquest; it was instigated by Slatin Pasha and commenced in order to give ambitious British officers something to win "laurels" by. And now, as this REVIEW has said from the outset, we have to meet the cost, for, of course, the remission of £798,802 advanced to Egypt to help to pay the bill for this fighting is only the second instalment of our *largesse* to that country. We have always maintained that Egypt could not afford to conquer the Soudan, and could not maintain authority in it when conquered. There cannot be the slightest doubt that this is the true view to take. We have had to give Egypt about £800,000 now, and we shall have, every war year that follows, to present her with similar gifts of greater or less amount. The picture which the Chancellor of the Exchequer drew of Egyptian prosperity is largely a fictitious one, but had it been true his equally vivid description of the desolation which Mahdist rule has brought upon Dongola, and doubtless on all the rest of the territories cursed by that pestilence, is sufficient to demonstrate to us that there can be no revenue from the Soudan worth reckoning upon for many a day to come. We shall have to pay for conquering it and to pay for garrisoning it. Possibly a few Egyptian officials may get their salaries out of the Cairo Treasury, but that will be about all, unless the development of Egypt, upon which we pride ourselves, not unfairly, is to be arrested, and the country allowed to sink back into barbarism, and its Government into penury. The prospect is not an enticing one, but it is quite in accordance with the anticipations of people who have kept their heads throughout this "Imperialist expansion" mania, which is driving the ship of State on the rocks. Yet only eighty-one members of the Opposition could be mustered to vote against this gift, and once more it was demonstrated that there is no genuine opposition in this Parliament. As a Parliament it is an invertebrate thing, unworthy of respect, and rapidly losing the confidence of thinking men. All it can do, apparently, is to vote away money and entangle us in excessive expenditure of every description. The very same evening on which this £800,000 loan to Egypt—it was a loan a year ago—was remitted, the House cheerfully sanctioned a loan of £10,000,000 to India. Had it been £20,000,000 the voting would have been just the same, the debate just as drivelly and slipshod. The day is coming when the British people will have to treat this kind of liberality also as "gifts" from itself, for the money raised for India will never be paid back. What cares the average M.P. for that? He storks it around Palace-yard, in Society, and plays the great man big with fate, and his scrap of a soul is content to behold him bawling and voting as the crowd bids.

The same number of the *Times* which gave Sir Michael Hicks-Beach's fancy picture of the wonderful prosperity and resources of Egypt—resources which made it out of the question that any further appeal could be made to the overflowing British purse and open British hand—presented, from its Cairo correspondent, a little of the other side of the picture. He writes with reference to freight charges in Egypt, a question brought to the front in an appeal made by the British Chamber of Commerce of Alexandria for relief. There is, it seems, serious mischief to the country and its commerce caused by the heavy tolls levied on boats passing bridges and locks on the Nile and its canals. These charges, this correspondent states, amount in some cases to as much as three-fourths of the obtainable freights, and have caused the almost total disappearance of the large fleet of cargo boats which formerly participated so greatly in the carrying trade of the Delta. It appears that the railways, thanks to this taxation, have stolen the traffic of the boats, and it is now becoming a traffic even railways are totally unable to cope with. Blame for the block of goods is laid upon the strain caused by the Soudan expedition, but that only brought the mischief to a head, and as the correspondent points out, the railway administration has no resources out of which to increase its facilities. It is limited strictly to 43½ per cent. of the gross receipts for working expenses, with the addition of another 1½ per cent. as a sort of capital reserve. This, the writer justly observes, is a mere derisory provision, when it is remembered that the total of 45 per cent. of the gross receipts thus arrived at has to bear the cost of constructing new lines, bridges, stations, and other works which in other countries would appertain to capital account. So the railway has had to get a dole from the Commission of the Public Debt. It has got £100,000 as a free grant and is allowed to spend on capital account the balance of credits open since 1892 and amounting to £1,514,000—this, however, is to be repaid with interest. Even so the traffic cannot be provided for. The moral of this tale comes, as it should, at the end. All that the water taxes yield is £100,000 a year, and were they remitted it is roughly estimated that £50,000 more from traffic earnings would be diverted from the railway into the pockets of the boat owners. The water traffic, which is the best and must be the cheapest for heavy goods, would, in short, revive, and blocks in the warehouses and on the lines would be less frequent, if not at an end; but, though the Government recognises the evil of taxation on transport and the injustice of the present system, it cannot afford to grant even this small relief "during the financial pressure caused by the Soudan War." An appropriate and timely exhibition of riches this, is it not? Can it be that our ardent "developers" in Egypt are making the same mistake as our Children of the Mist bureaucrats of Simla—thinking that because they themselves are pretty comfortable, and growing on the whole better off, the people they rule must be. It is a kind of mistake which has often been fatal to empires.

Fire Insurance Companies' Exactions.

Attention was drawn to this subject the other day by the *Daily News*, and, as it punningly remarked, the question is a "burning" one. No large fire occurs in the City of London, and we may say in any densely built city in the Kingdom, without the fire insurance companies seizing the opportunity to raise their rates. In consequence of the Cripplegate fire it seems that these offices have now raised their charges for insuring warehouses in that part of the City to 31s. per cent. A partner in a firm of manufacturers told the *Daily News* that when he first insured thirty years ago the rate was 3s. per cent., and that before the Cripplegate fire it had been raised to 13s. 6d. to 15s. per cent., and now it is 31s. per cent. Naturally there is a strong feeling of indignation excited by this excessively screwed-up tariff, and the opinion appears to prevail that there is no escape from such exactions except by way of municipal insurance. Municipal insurance, ho[illegible] is perfectly impossible so long as the old[illegible] London proper is governed by an u[illegible] corrupt and altogether irresponsible med[illegible] poration. Even were that corporation [illegible], it is doubtful whether the County Council, endowed with municipal powers for the whole Metropolitan area, could take the matter up, and deal with it in a satisfactory way, unless it fell heir, as the citizens should, to the property of the Livery companies which are now among the greatest anomalies in these islands. Vested interests of all kinds are so powerful, and the landlord interest above all, that genuine municipal fire insurance seems a thing to dream of, not a thing to be realised.

Again and again attempts are made to cope with the tyranny of the combined fire insurance companies by starting rivals, and within the last few months more than one of these new companies have come into existence, notwithstanding the fact that their predecessors in the same field have invariably proved failures. Either they have collapsed altogether, or they are forced to join the combination. From this point of view also there is absolutely no remedy that we can discover. The old combinations are too powerful, and they possess enormous revenues from invested funds as well as in the shape of insurance premiums on private dwellings, which are rarely burned down. Both these sources of income are almost entirely wanting to a new company. An insurance manager once told the writer that it would pay the companies handsomely to insure the furniture of private houses at 6d. per cent. per annum, instead of the usual 1s. 6d. or 2s., could they do that business by itself alone. Possibly the great extension in the use of low-grade, explosive mineral oils imported from America has in recent years somewhat altered the balance by increasing the number of fires in private dwellings, but it has not yet done so to the extent of 50 per cent. in the amount of the claims, else the companies would either have been howling, or putting up their rates, or both; and we are therefore tolerably safe in saying that at least one-half of the net premiums now exacted from private householders goes to enable the companies to meet the losses created by big fires in warehouses and industrial centres. Possessing, in addition to their investments, such revenue to fall back upon, what chance is there for a new company which can do none of this kind of business, or, at least, none to speak of, for years after it is established? There is none. It has to draw its revenue altogether from the more risky kind of fire insurance, which has to be effected by the owners of factories and warehouses such as are now complaining of the rates levied upon them. And even such risks must be taken by the new competitor absolutely, because one of the most effective means which the old companies have of crushing an upstart rival is to refuse to do any business with it. A new company cannot reinsure any of its risks with the old combination of companies until it charges the "ring" scale of premiums, and thereby becomes one of their number. For such reasons as these the enterprise of founding and establishing a new fire insurance company is almost a hopeless one, and the victims of the monopoly must either grin and bear their burdens or remain uninsured.

One way out, indeed, might be found. We have frequently drawn attention in the pages of this REVIEW to the enormous expenses of fire insurance business. As far as we can recollect, there is not a single fire company which is able to conduct its business at a cost appreciably below one-third of the premium income. In not a few the expenses of management and commissions together exceed 35 per cent. of the premium income. This naturally adds in a most important degree to the cost of insurance, and if merchants and manufacturers could hit upon some method or system of mutual insurance whereby the greater part of this heavy expenditure could be done away with, they might be able not only to cover their risks at a moderate premium, but to force down the rates of the monopolist companies.

Why mutual insurance of fire risks has never been successfully carried out on a large scale is more than we can understand; but possibly one difficulty lies in the fact that a great many of the policies effected with the companies represent over-insurance. Statistics are not available to test this point, but the number of cases of arson which come into Court tend to prove that the habit of over-insurance is much more prevalent than it ought to be under any system of commercial morality capable of facing the light of day. Now, mutual insurance could not possibly hope to succeed unless all the firms who combine and pool their funds to give protection to each other against fire act in perfect honesty. Directly any firm in the combination made an attempt to effect policies at exaggerated values or on unreal assets, true mutuality is undermined and must collapse. Probably enough, the wealthy offices which form the monopoly ring in fire insurance are lax and easy in this matter, and suffer themselves to be imposed upon without too much inquiry so long as they can make the business pay. But if this be the case, then the great advance in the scale of premiums charged is not altogether their fault. Even high premiums may represent, to a considerable percentage, extra risks which have to be incurred owing to the dishonesty of the insurers. This is a point of view which requires further elucidation, and we should be very glad indeed if some insurance manager would enable us to throw light upon it. There must be many cases where dishonesty is suspected by the insurance offices which it is not worth their while to fight, law being such a costly thing, and the verdict of juries so uncertain. Is there no office which keeps a private record of these cases capable of being worked up in statistical form, without names, so as to enable us to judge to what extent an improvement in the probity and conscientiousness of insurers might conduce to moderation in the scale of premiums charged?

FIRE INSURANCE BUSINESS IN 1897:—

Name of Company.	Fire Premiums.	Fire Losses.	Percentage of Losses.	Inc. or Dec. as compared with previous year.	Percentage of Expenses.	Total Percentage of Outgo to Premiums.
British Law	57,256	29,768	52.0	− 3.1	44.0	96.0
Norwich Union... ...	887,109	539,245	60.8	− 1.4	34.6	95.4
Equitable	198,728	111,354	56.0	− 7.2	36.3	92.3
Palatine...	690,377	419,416	60.7	− 8.3	37.0	97.7
Law Union	96.902	37,278	38.4	+ 2.2	33.1	71.5
Law Fire...	148,559	63,887	43.0	− 0.5	31.9	74.9
Alliance	536,651	290,988	54.2	+ 1.6	35.8	90.0
Yorkshire	105,136	57,577	54.7	Same	35.0	89.7
County	274,631	99,828	36.3	− 10.9	33.5	69.8
London Assurance ...	385,006	209,232	54.3	+ 7.3	35.2	89.5
Atlas	357,520	205,017	57.3	+ 7.6	35.7	93.0
Scottish Union	552,703	305,845	55.4	− 2.6	33.7	89.1
Union	454,683	254,819	56.4	− 7.2	34.5	90.9
Caledonian	406,927	225,934	55.5	− 2.2	34.9	90.4
Liverpool, London, and Globe	1,540,706	857,714	55.6	+ 0.7	34.0	89.6
North British and Mercantile	1,433,829	809,605	56.5	+ 2.2	34.4	90.9
Royal	2,007,012	1,102,264	55.1	+ 0.9	34.0	89.1
Lancashire	700,832	419,833	59.9	Same	35.4	95.3
Commercial Union ..	1,074,746	586,931	54.6	− 1.6	36.4	91.0
Imperial	611,278	356,045	58.2	+ 4.5	37.0	95.2
Lion	188,185	119,433	63.4	+ 5.3	38.0	101.4
Guardian...	342,160	233,848	68.3	+ 9.6	35.8	104.1
London and Lancashire	839,970	418,579	49.8	− 5.1	35.6	85.4
Manchester	850,599	491,754	57.8	− 1.6	34.9	92.7
National of Ireland ...	288,003	200,694	70.0	− 0.3	32.4	102.4
Hand-in-Hand	103,371	73,571	71.2	+ 20.7	32.4	103.6
Kent	76,106	35,319	46.4	+ 8.4	38.9	85.3
Northern...	662,097	361,467	54.6	− 3.1	36.3	90.9
Royal Exchange ...	344,199	189,695	55.1	+ 2.8	37.9	93.0
Sun	1,012,340	588,296	58.1	+ 6.1	33.9	92.0
Phœnix	1,114.888	665,408	59.6	+ 0.7	32.9	92.5
State	62,993	32,900	52.2	+ 4.1	39.3	91.5

The above table, extended from that published by the *Standard* last Friday, gives at a glance the position of the revenue and expenditure of the fire companies for the past year. It shows that not one of them works its business for less than 30 per cent. of the premium income, and very few of them have as much as 10 per cent. of that income left after meeting expenses and losses. The fattest companies are the few which, like the County Fire, possess a business in the best class of domestic risks—private houses and furniture—and do little outside that. Four offices last year paid away more than they received in premiums.

Company Promoters' Flotsam.

Our recent investigations at Somerset House have been more with a view to obtain knowledge about certain companies, in regard to which interest attaches owing to events that have happened after their formation. Much of the information must have been known before, but in view of eventualities it will be helpful to publish details about the principal holdings in some of these concerns.

Cooper, Cooper, & Co., Limited.

Formed in October, 1895, to take over a few tea and coffee selling businesses, the modest capital of £80,000 in £1 shares was issued, of which £20,000 in ordinary shares went to the vendors, and the balance of £60,000 in preference shares was offered to the public. Apparently the company was well received, and although its future is not particularly hopeful little attention would have been attracted to its affairs, had it not been for the ill-advised proposal to amalgamate it with the Ceylon and Oriental Estates. The latter is an old-established concern that has lived through its peck of troubles, and looked as if it might develop into a sound undertaking. The same cannot be said about Cooper, Cooper, & Co., Limited, for it has not been in existence three years, and its tenure of life must still be regarded as of a fragile character. As the proposal seemed to be all in favour of this company, we append its list of leading shareholders :—

	No. of Shares. Preferred.	Ordinary.
T. Meares	858	7,720
C. H. Meares	1	200
J. Wolfe	150	—
E. H. Absolom	—	3,960
A. Wood	1,500	—
Clarke & Philpot	148	—
Whelan & Higginson	2,249	—
J. Young	868	7,920
B. W. Absolom	940	—
A. Absolom	150	—

Messrs. T. Meares, J. Young, and E. H. Absolom figured as vendors in the prospectus, and their large holding of ordinary shares is thus accounted for. Messrs. J. Wolfe and Clarke & Philpot, although appearing as holders of small amounts, did a large amount of transferring, and the remainder of the names seem to be connected with the promoters. For the £20,000 of ordinary shares to be exchanged into shares of a conglomerate concern would be to at once give them a market, and thus enable an asset of problematical value to be turned into hard cash if desired.

New Trinidad Lake Asphalte Company.

We have found the debentures of this concern figuring so frequently in the list of holdings of Trust companies that we have taken the liberty of glancing at a list of its shareholders. It may first be mentioned that the company was brought out in December, 1897, with Panmure Gordon, Hill, & Co., as its brokers, and Ashurst Morris, Crisp, & Co. as its solicitors. The most active of the directors appeared to be also on the board of the vending company, and the prospectus contained some rather remarkable statements. The share capital was fixed at £500,000 in shares of £10 each, which were all taken by the vendor in part payment for the property. The issue of debentures was for £400,000, but as no list of such holders had to be registered at Somerset House, it is impossible to say into whose hands they have all fallen. A large amount we know is in the hands of various Trusts, which points to the possibility of underwriters having had to take up their quotas. The leading shareholders in the company are as follows :—

	£
J. J. Albright	19,250
Mrs. S. F. Albright	1,230
A. L. Barber	150,420
B. L. Barber	30
J. L. Barber	350
D. L. Barber	300
Barber Asphalte Paving Company	17,180
W. E. Barker	4,380
L. F. Benson	4,740
C. P. Benson	120
M. E. Benson	140
A. Brown & Sons	5,160
Mrs. J. E. Carew...	4,930
H. A. Greig	19,110
J. G. Douglas	12,350
E. Hayes	10,060
R. R. Hefford	3,760
C. H. Finlayson	13,670
Montgomerie National Bank	4,430
New York and Trinidad Asphalte Company	5,040
J. W. Previté	28,350
L. G. Previté	300
E. J. Previté	120
J. W. McCarthy	3,820
M. Stevens	7,920
E. B. Warren	37,240

Messrs. J. W. Previté and A. L. Barber are directors of the Trinidad Asphalte Company, which was the vending company. Most of the shareholders reside in the United States, and the company has all the appearance of one of those gaseous productions favoured by American financiers.

North Worcestershire Breweries.

This was a queer brewery promotion, the whole of the £200,000 of share capital, excepting the seven shares for the signatories and the qualification for the directors, being issued in part payment of purchase money. Upon this slender basis a debenture debt of £250,000 in $4\frac{1}{2}$ per cent. first mortgage debenture stock was issued in May, 1896, at £103 per cent. Since then the gods have not dealt kindly with the concern and the debenture stock is now quoted at 86 per cent., and prospects look poor. Who are the unfortunate holders of the debenture stock we know not, but it may be of interest to record the list of shareholders, as these, we believe, were in many cases connected with the promoters of the affair. The important holdings were as follows :—

	Ordinary. £	Preference. £
T. H. Myring	3,430	—
A. Yorke	—	1,000
W. H. Simpkiss	—	1,000
M. E. Wingfield	1,310	—
Stanley Boulter	—	98,000

	Ordinary.	Preference.
	£	£
Sir W. H. Humphrey ...	28,500	—
G. Simmons	500	—
H. B. Praed	500	—
R. Cobay	500	—
F. R. Garrard	500	—
T. Taylor	500	—
C. J. Fauvel	500	—
Bankers Investment Trust ...	1,000	—
T. H. Weguelin	20,000	—
A. H. Blundell	2,000	—
S. R. Emerson	1'000	—
Gwelo Exploration and Development	500	—
A. E. Whitaker	30,000	—
H. S. Blaydes	1,500	—
J. W. Brett	500	—
M. B. Praed ... ... } H. H. Twining ... ... }	2,550	—

Messrs. Simmons, H. B. Praed, R. Cobay, F. R. Garrard, and T. Taylor are directors of the unfortunate affair, the latter being apparently the chief vendor. Mr. M. B. Praed is a trustee for the debenture holders, but his holding shown is in connection with his post as joint manager of the Inns of Court Branch of Lloyds Bank, and he evidently enjoys the enviable position of lending upon securities for which he is trustee to the debenture holders. He therefore ought to know all about the company. Mr. C. J. Fauvel is, or was, an important personage in the Gwelo Exploration and Development Company, the investment of whose funds in this brewing company was the subject of much remark. The Bankers' Investment Trust has Mr. H. B. Praed as a director, and Mr. F. Praed as secretary, hence its affection for the investment, which we believe is extended to the debentures. The holding of £98,000 in preference shares by Mr. Stanley Boulter is a little large, although we are afraid the share capital is not of much account. We have no handy moral to rub in, and this must do for the present week.

Chinese Mineral Wealth.

There appears to be some confusion, due, no doubt, to a similarity in the names of two distinct provinces, as to the location of the Chinese coal concession recently granted. Honan and Hunan are the two provinces, and both of them boast of deposits of considerable magnitude, but Honan is the one to be associated with the operations of the Anglo-Italian syndicate. It is the province contiguous to Shansi, which is by far the richest of all Chinese mineral-bearing districts, and the coming scene of the development work of other concessionaires. Honan has been but very imperfectly surveyed, and it is probable from the geological character of the country, that numerous beds will some day be discovered whose existence is at present unsuspected. But there are already several places where mining, on the primitive lines general throughout the Celestial Empire, is carried on, and the principal of these are Lushan and Juchau, in the central portion of the province and Honanfu and Taihang-shan in the north. These last are the localities in which European enterprise and European machinery are to be brought into play for the benefit of China as well as of the foreign syndicate. The kind of fuel yielded by both is anthracite, the seams of which appear to be a continuation of those for which Shansi is famous—at any rate, the quality of the Taihang-shan fuel is equal to that of Eastern Shansi, and is clean, solid, and very lustrous into the bargain. The Chinese have made no systematic attempt to work these or any other of their coal deposits to the full extent, and it is really doubtful if they could do so with their existing rude appliances even if they were so minded. Besides, they have laboured under the disadvantage of not being able to market any very considerable output because of the lack of ready and cheap communication with distant places, especially with the coast. In Taihang-shan alone there are usually about 100 shafts or apologies for shafts in operation, and four or five times that number abandoned. The Chinese way is to penetrate no further into the earth, sometimes vertically and sometimes (as in parts of Shansi) on an inclined plane, than a couple of hundred feet or so; and then to open up new ground. The beds in the northern prefectures of Honan range in thickness from 3 ft. to 30 ft. or more, and the whole province does not at present turn out more than 300,000 tons in a year—a total that might be increased tenfold with better facilities for production and distribution. These coal beds, it may be mentioned, occur as in Shansi, in close proximity to inexhaustible quantities of iron ore, much of which is of high quality.

The coalfields of Hunan are much more extensive than those of Honan, and compare on this basis with Shansi, though this last province has an advantage in that all its known beds are of good quality, whereas about half the Hunan fuel is scarcely worth marketing at any distance. The coal-bearing area of this particular province covers 21,000 square miles, about one-half of which is workable. It is divided into fairly equal portions—the anthracite seams running along the Lui River, and the bituminous seams of the Siang River neighbourhood. There is a good demand for the former variety, and consignments go as far as Hankow by river boats along the Yang-tse-Kiang; but the Siang River coal is consumed locally, and, generally speaking, any resident of the district who desires some simply goes to the mines and takes it. The abundance of croppings, and the ease of following a bed down an inclined plane, have caused a great many mines to be opened in succession, and little trouble to be taken to continue operations to any great depth. In the same province are several less important coalfields, the chief of which are those of Sin-chau-fu and Yuen-chau-fu. In Shansi are deposits covering an area of over 14,000 square miles, and it is estimated that the quantity of coal, "equal to the best Pennsylvania," waiting to be mined in this one province alone of the Chinese Empire is 630,000,000,000 tons—enough to last the world at the present rate of consumption for two thousand years to come. Moreover, these deposits are favourably located for working on a plateau about 2,500 ft. above sea level in the south-eastern part of the province; the seams are mostly from 20 ft. to 30 ft. thick; and there is an abundance of labour phenomenally cheap.

Furthermore, iron ore occurs in several strata of the coal beds, and there are numerous kinds, though the only one now employed by the natives is one that melts easily without flux, and is a mixture of clay, iron ore, spathic ore, and hematite. The two chief places in which the manufacture is carried on now are Tse-chau-fu and Ping-ting-chau, and the quality of the iron turned out is generally allowed to be excellent in spite of the very primitive methods employed, and this result is attributable of course to the excellent character of the raw material. Honan also boasts of large deposits of iron ore, which occurs in conjunction with, or in proximity to, the coal measures. The same metal is found in many other parts of the empire—in Shantung, where there are large bodies of black oxide; in Chi-li, where it occurs with the coal; and in Hunan, Shen-se, and Kansu. No efforts have ever been made to gauge the extent of the iron ore deposits of the various provinces, but for those of Shansi and Honan we have the word of Baron von Richthofen, who examined them more exhaustively than any other Western scientist, that they are practically as inexhaustible as the coal measures. That same authority estimated the area of all the known Chinese coalfields investigated by himself alone at 400,000 square miles. But those now about to be worked in Shansi and Honan alone cover 20,000 square miles, with about 900,000,000,000 tons of workable coal; and, pending the opening up of the country, this quantity is enough to be going on with.

Economic and Financial Notes and Correspondence.

THE NEW FRENCH MINISTRY.

At last, after struggling for a fortnight, the dominant Parliamentary groups in the new French Chamber have allowed a Ministry to be constructed under the leadership of the respectable and highly honourable M. Brisson. We hope it will last three weeks, and shall be agreeably surprised if it lasts three months. It is a Ministry of shirking and shunting. No issue really before the country is squarely met in the skeleton programme it has put forth. It is not going to settle the shameful Dreyfus-Esterhazy affair; it is going to allow the corn duties to replace themselves; it is to maintain protection rigorously; constitutional revision is to be temporarily postponed, and the income tax to be proposed will not be upon the sliding scale principle. A Ministry of this kind, without much character, full of contradictory elements, and in essential particulars resting upon dishonesty, cannot endure. It is a Ministry, in the first place, intent upon pleasing the military faction which stands behind all authority in France and compels President and Legislature to bow to its behests. We can augur no good from such a mummery, and the best thing, perhaps, that could happen to it would be speedy disaster. If it lasts as long as M. Méline's administration did—an event in the highest degree improbable—it will have brought France very close to an internal convulsion which might be almost equivalent to revolution, and give the signal all over Europe for the overthrow of the worn-out system of Government it now exists under in restlessness. Meantime, the best we can say of M. Brisson's is that it may be better than no Ministry at all, because the absence of one must, in a very few weeks' time, have brought about some kind of dictatorship. France, we hope, will be spared that scourge, whatever happens; and yet what is to happen there? Things cannot go on as they are now. Shams of all kinds must die—of a violent death or otherwise.

THE UNITED STATES REVENUE BILL.

Full details of this measure have now reached this country and prove it to be rather an elaborate affair, full of minute provisions and small taxes whose value may turn out to lie not so much in the amount they yield as in the principle they establish. The tax on tobacco and its manufacturers, for example, is only to be 6d. in the pound and on cigars about 9s. a thousand. Bankers and brokers of various descriptions are to pay licence duties of moderate amount. Theatres, museums, and concert halls are also to pay a licence-tax, and circuses too; in fact, all kinds of places of public entertainment down to billiard rooms and bowling alleys are to be levied upon for the cost of this war. This licence system is extended to dealers in and manufacturers of tobacco also, but in no instance is the tax a very large one; it may be irritating, but it certainly will not be very productive. In addition to this tobacco tax and these licence duties and the extra dollar per thirty-two gallon barrel on beer, a variety of stamp duties are instituted with considerable skill and care, and some of which may be fairly productive. Telegraphic messages, for instance, are to be stamped with a one-cent stamp each. Broker's contract notes must bear a ten-cent, or 5d. stamp. Telephonic messages also come within the sweep of the revenue collector, and a tax is to be levied of one cent for each message or conversation held in this manner. The penny stamp is imposed upon all cheques, drafts, &c., drawn upon bankers, and on inland bills of exchange there is to be a tax of a penny per hundred dollars. On foreign bills of exchange or letters of credit, which interest us more, the stamp is to be double this amount, or 2d. per hundred dollars. The people are also to pay for stamps on patent medicines, perfumery, "chewing gum" or "substitutes thereof," &c., &c., and of course there is to be the populist tax of ¼ of 1 per cent. on the gross receipts of the Standard Oil Trust and the American Sugar Refining Company. We need not go into further details, because the great bulk of these new imposts are of a purely domestic character, and have an interest for us merely as indicating the line by which some far-seeing United States administration may ultimately seek to compensate the Federal Treasury for revenue lost, or apparently lost, by the establishment of lower customs duties, or their abolition.

CITY CORPORATION "PURITY."

Some people may affect surprise at the revelations in this week's issue of *London*: we cannot. This paper boldly tells the story of how an ex-Lord Mayor, Savory by name, in his zeal for the pure white light of electricity within the bounds of that tiny segment of the great Metropolis over which the turtle and old port band presides, granted a monopoly to the City of London Electric Lighting Company which may last for ever and a day. It is a longish story, and we must refer readers to *London* itself for the details; but briefly it amounts to a charge of conspiracy to defraud the citizens levelled against certain men. Ex-Lord Mayor Savory is accused of taking a leading part. First, there was a "pioneer" company—really a promoting syndicate, which had a nominal capital of £100,000 in £50 shares. Its "chief promoters were Sir Joseph Savory, Lord Mayor and a member of the Streets Committee, and a Mr. Cecil Braithwaite, stockbroker." Six members of the Commission of Sewers are also stated to have been shareholders, and Mr. Nathan Rothschild held £5,000 of the capital.

Within six months this pioneer company had transferred the rights the Corporation had allowed it to acquire to the City of London Company, which started with a capital of £1,300,000. Only half the pioneer company's capital is said to have been paid up, but it received £150,000 from the City Company. The gains of its shareholders need not have ended with this pretty deal, as most of them took shares in the new company, with which they must have done pretty well. It is interesting to note that Mr. W. H. Pannell, chartered accountant, apparently figured in the business in the double capacity of a Commissioner of Sewers and auditor to both the pioneer company and the City of London. What is perhaps worst of all about the transaction is the way in which the absolute monopoly of the City Company is secured to it indefinitely, to the exclusion of all competitors. Nominally the lease is only for twenty-one years, but this term does not commence to run until the company has completed the lighting of the "side streets" of the City. It will never do that, we may be sure. Well may *London* say that "the whole spirit and letter of legislation on electric lighting has been undermined." It is a fit result of this kind of greasy jobbery that the privileged company should be able to charge, as Mr. Brooke-Hitching states, 12s. 8d. per lamp as against 8s. 5d. by the Metropolitan Company, and 7d. per unit of electricity as compared with 6d. and even 4d. elsewhere. The light could easily be supplied at 3d. per unit, but citizens have the compensation of a Lord Mayor's pageant, and, say, half a million's worth of dinners a year, which a few of them help to eat.

MR. HOOLEY'S BANKRUPTCY.

We are pleased to learn that the first meeting of this wonderful man's creditors is to be held at the Bankruptcy-buildings, Carey-street, on the 6th inst. before Mr. H. Brougham, the official receiver appointed by the Court, and, further, that the bankrupt's public examination is to be held on the 27th inst. The latter date is rather far off, but probably it is about the earliest that could be fixed upon owing to the very mixed mass of affairs to be dealt with. We really wish, though, that in the meantime Mr. Hooley would either publish that terrible list of blackmailers and bribe receivers of the Press which he keeps flourishing about, or hold his tongue. His attitude in publishing general charges here and there, without bringing them to the proof, causes the dispassionate observer to set him down as a vain braggart rather than a man of courage really anxious to do the straight thing and expose what is unquestionably a hideous blot on our Press.

He has not even been content with scattering innuendoes and gross charges to all and sundry in this country, absolutely without proof, but must needs publish them in the United States as well. We warn him that he cannot gain any sympathy by this conduct nor any credit for fair play either. As we said last week, there are some honest journalists yet, and Mr. Hooley may depend upon it that, if he continues his present undefinable course, it will not be a lash of woollen cords they will lay upon his back when he gives them the opportunity to strike out. While giving him this unasked advice might we also suggest that it would be somewhat in accordance with the fitness of things if he were to restrain the ardent benevolence of Mrs. Hooley, upon whom he declared he had made no settlements, and who, like himself, we presume, is "without a penny in the world." Her princely gift of £150 to some local hospital or charity the other day excited nasty comments, and if bounties of the kind must be bestowed they had better henceforth be so in secret, not with vulgar advertisement. We say this with no feeling of ill-will to the man, about whom, indeed, we know nothing except what he himself has proclaimed to the world. He has never excited any such feeling in our mind, could not possibly have done so, for his all-too-brief public career has afforded us from time to time a great deal of genuine fun. Beyond challenge he has been the most mirth-provoking company promoter we have ever encountered in all our experience.

THE CENTRAL PACIFIC RAILROAD COMPANY.

The Banbury Committee called a meeting of the British shareholders in this unhappy concern which was duly held last Tuesday. Mr. Banbury himself presided and entered into various interesting and ingenious explanations of the conduct of his committee and its position. We give him every credit for sincerity, and believe that he thinks a great work has been done. None the less was his discourse a very depressing one to those who look for stalwart defence of public morals and private interests at the hands of self-selected or other representatives of invested capital. Mr. Banbury missed the real point at issue between himself and the Shareholders' Protection Committee—usually called the Morshead Committee by way of depreciating its value—and he omitted all reference to the fact brought out in Mr. Bretherton's circular that the dividends now paid to the Central Pacific shareholders by Mr. Huntington, as a sop to keep them quiet, never appear in the Central Pacific accounts at all, but are an advance made to the company by Mr. Huntington for his own purpose, to be claimed from it, with usury, on the first opportunity. This is a small scandal, but an intolerable one of its kind, and even by itself proves the Banbury Committee to be an aggregation of fatuities totally incapable of squarely standing up to the gigantic swindlers who have gutted the Central Pacific for their own profit. Mr. Bretherton, himself a director of the Central Pacific, declares that the "mission" of Sir Rivers Wilson has been an absolute failure, and that to all appearances the line remains as much in Mr. Huntington's hands to-day as it did before. That is, at least, what we take to be the meaning of his statements, and they are most serious, not only for the Banbury Committee, so called, but for all proprietors of American railroads in this country.

In view of such statements and facts it is idle for Mr. Banbury to claim credit for having secured a majority of the shareholders sufficient to enable his committee to turn Mr. Huntington out of the control of the Central Pacific. Even if he has that power, the committee has, by its own chairman's confession, been very dilatory in exercising it, for he was unable to announce to the meeting that the power of attorney by which Mr. Huntington holds the Central Pacific Company's board in the hollow of his hand had yet been revoked. It is to be, he says, and ought to have been ashamed to say it after all these months, after all the light that has been poured upon this Central Pacific infamy by authentic documents proving the fraud by which the Southern Pacific Company of Kentucky has become its destroyer. The true question, indeed, is how long are shareholders here in American railroads of all classes to allow themselves to be supinely defrauded by whatever scamp, or group of scamps, in the States chooses to lay hold of their property? Assuredly as long as misdeeds like those of the Californian group of which this man Huntington is now almost the sole survivor are condoned, as the Banbury Committee would condone them, so long will the British investor be robbed with impunity and without thought of mercifulness. If the shareholders of the Central Pacific Company will absolutely refuse to sanction any patch up of its affairs until the whole iniquity of the Southern Pacific lease and of the frauds in connection with the building of the Southern Pacific with the Central Company's stockholders' money has been exposed ard restitution obtained, then a better day will dawn for the British investor in a'l such securities. It is because we desire to see this better day that we have again and again supported Mr. Morshead, and urged stockholders to rally round him in this matter. We are satisfied that if they made a resolute stand now, and laid their hardships and losses before the Government of Washington, which is, happily, directly interested in the property on account of its debt of nearly $60,000,000 to the Federal Treasury, they would put in motion a power capable of forcing the Stanford-Crocker-Huntington group to refund a portion, at least, of the countless millions stolen from their pockets. If they shirk this admittedly difficult enterprise and allow a white-washing process to be gone through—let bygones be bygones, as the phrase is—then the robbery will continne, and the supine British investor will continue to deserve what he gets.

UNHAPPY ITALY.

There are certainly as yet no signs of improvement in the general condition of Italy. It is seething with discontent, and unfortunately the politicians seem incapable of concentrating attention even on what is best for removing the causes of this discontent. It has been stated as highly creditable to King Humbert that he refused to confer on the Marquis di Rudini the virtual dictatorship for which he at one time asked. We do not suppose the King himself would claim any credit in the matter. Let us hope that he would rather have resented the request as an insult than hesitated about refusing to grant it. But in the matter of the trial and sentence of the Milanese rioters and others, the King sanctioned proceedings which were undoubtedly more dictatorial than judicial. Why should the rioters have been tried by court-martial at all? Was it so necessary to follow these disorderly scenes with swift punishment to the ringleaders that the trials could not be left to the ordinary judges? And where was the justice of submitting to military officers the nice questions involved in discriminating what writings during the last three or four years may have incited the rioters of a few months ago? Editors of various journals have been sentenced to terms of imprisonment varying from three to six years—the latter with solitary confinement—because articles inciting to disturbance were published in their journals several years back. No complaint had been made of these writings at the time; and now when the writers have been prosecuted their cases were not submitted to trained and experienced civil judges, but to military officers, who would probably sneer at what they regard as the word-spinning and hair-splitting of your judicial luminaries, and delight in the rough and ready justice of the drum-head court-martial. It is a sad come-down for Italy thus to set up the military power even in the seat of Justice. If not fallen to a dictatorship, it is far on the road to one. It almost recalls the times—or, at least, the ways—of King Bomba. It has been a terrible business to form a new Ministry; and now that it has been done, we find a general at its head. What does it mean? It seems as if among the rulers of Italy nothing was thought of but knocking heads down in the interest of "law and order," whilst the greatest dangers to this "law and order" lie in the oppressive taxation and the extravagant expenditure which none among the administrators seems to think of mitigating.

The Raising of the Flash Point.

We may commiserate Mr. Jesse Collings. He has been sadly used by certain members of the Petroleum Committee, who first voted in support of his draft report, and then, on consideration of the clause dealing with the flash point, turned against him. It is somewhat unfortunate that these gentlemen did not at first show a better appreciation of this point; for it is the crux of the whole question, and though Sir Vivian Majendie, who should have known better, threw dust in the eyes of the committee on the subject, yet abundant evidence was placed before them showing the danger that lurks in the deadly 73 deg. flash point. But if the conversion of these two members of the committee has been slow, it seems to have been sure, and we shall now have a report presented to the House of Commons showing frankly the dangers of the low flash point and the simple and easy remedy which in a few weeks may be provided by Parliament for at least a prompt diminution in the number of fatalities caused by oil with a low flash point. Though, therefore, we may commiserate Mr. Collings, in one way, we must congratulate him in another. He has, by the action of these two members of the Petroleum Committee, been saved from himself, and perhaps from the Standard Oil Trust. He was incurring a very grave responsibility from which he has been relieved by the second vote of the committee, and it is to be hoped he will accept his defeat with a good grace, and allow us to discard the low flash point—which experience has shown to be responsible for a yearly increasing number of deaths—in order to try whether the high flash point will not work an improvement. Taking the lowest view of the matter, this is surely worth a trial. In writing this we assumed that there would be no going back upon the decision the committee had come to upon the raising of the flash point. But it would appear that our confidence may turn out to have been misplaced. By what seems a rather discreditable trick, an effort was made at the meeting of the committee on Wednesday to practically reduce the flash point to 85 deg. It was introduced on the storage clauses, and as two of the supporters of the high flash point were absent there was a serious danger of the resolution being carried. The opposition raised, however, was so vigorous that the hour of adjournment had arrived before a division could be taken. The committee resumes its sitting to-day, when it will be seen whether the trick will succeed. In itself the proposal is as ingenious as if drawn up by the Standard Oil Trust.

But we cannot congratulate Mr. Collings on the belated assistance the *Times* has sought to render him in the article on the subject which it published on Monday. That article begs the question from first to last. It disdainfully casts aside as a mere "rhetorical statement" a demonstration that in at least one State of the American Union—that of Iowa—where a high flash point is insisted upon by law, there has not been a single one of our familiar lamp fatalities during the last fourteen or fifteen years. It is easy to dispose of all proofs of anything, if such a stubborn and well-sustained fact as that is to be treated merely as a "rhetorical statement." But the *Times* shows itself equally at sea about the flash point itself. It assumes that the 73 deg., Abel test, is equivalent to 100 deg.; and it further assumes—for it confesses it does not know—that if the 100 deg. flash point is enforced, it will be equivalent to 130 deg. But as the *Times* confesses ignorance on the subject, we may dismiss its assertion as a mere "rhetorical statement," not to be seriously considered without further proof. It is very much on a level with the hints and suggestions thrown out in the "explanations" furnished previously to the *Times* by Mr. Jesse Collings, who has never yet shown that he had any lucid views or conclusions on the subject. He suggests difficulties without attempting proofs. Here again is an awkward fact which the *Times* brushes aside with characteristic ignorance and impetuosity. In Scotland they use oil with a high flash point, and accidents are there very rare indeed—almost unknown. That would seem an irresistible argument in favour of the high flash point. But no. The *Times* has a clear and convincing explanation. The average of intelligence is far higher among the Scottish working-classes than in English towns. That is all. Of course you cannot legislate against mere invincible stupidity; but as Scotch intelligence has whatever advantage may be derived from a high flash point, would it not be prudent, before confessing ourselves baffled by English unintelligence, to try whether it might not be assisted in some measure by the higher flash point?

Marvellous Australian Prosperity.

Really, those Budget framers in New South Wales and Victoria ask us to believe a little too much. New South Wales especially is in a boastful mood. The revenue is going to be greater than the estimate, everything is doing well, and the Treasury abounding in wealth. All this in spite of three years of drought, immense losses of stock on the sheep runs—loss estimated at fifteen to twenty millions of sheep alone—and consequent tremendous reductions in wool freights besides other drawbacks. Is it really possible to credit that a small community, which has been wrestling with the consequences of a great, though smothered, bankruptcy for five years back, the whole of whose capital, with very small exception, is drawn from abroad, and whose public debt is stupendous, should be able to display this elasticity? We candidly say that the picture is too roseate for us to contemplate without the gravest possible suspicion. Much the same may be said of Victoria, where the acting Governor, Chief Justice Sir John Madden, met Parliament with a similar glowing description of the wonderful "progress" and resources of the country. The "economy exercised in past years," he said, "has placed the finances on a sound basis. Revenue was steadily increasing, although there had been no increase in taxation." The moral of it all was—and therein lies our suspicion—that this improvement in revenue warrants "a more liberal expenditure for the future"; therefore a scheme has been prepared for "extensive public works and the early construction of railways." Thus it will all end in the same way—another loan from John Bull.

CHATHAM AND DOVER DEBENTURE STOCK.

It was evidently high time that this company came to an agreement with its stronger rival, for it is at the end of its credit tether. This is proved by the announcement that the £300,000 debenture stock offered by it at 103 had not been all sold. Only £167,780 was tendered for or £132,220 less than the sum required, and the highest price offered was 106. This is a change since this time last year, when £150,000 of the same stock was offered at the same minimum and all allotted at an average price of £107 15s. 10d. Evidently the opinion of careful investors has come to be the same as ours, which is something to be thankful for, because this company is essentially in an insolvent position. It must now be in rather an awkward fix also, because it has not obtained enough money by the sale of its debenture stock to pay off the outstanding Lloyds bonds, which amount to £231,375. Also the company has a floating debt of nearly half a million, carried on the security of sundry debentures bearing various rates of interest from 2¾ to 3½. This debt might become very inconvenient if money took a dear fit for any length of time and we are not at all sure that it has not been inconvenient during the last six months. Meekness and a willingness to obliterate himself in these circumstances may well be the only attitude left for Mr. James Staats Forbes to assume. What a melancholy failure this man's career has been!

PUNCTURED "DUNLOPS."

The report of this company for the year ended March 31 last excites various emotions according to the point from which it is viewed. To a mere outsider it is calculated to afford no small amusement, to a shareholder considerable chagrin. We are perforce obliged to take the amusing view. From the first we looked upon this company as one of the drollest productions of promoters' ingenuity modern times have seen. It represented company inflation of the "Hey, diddle diddle" order, and it is quite laughable to see the way in which the directors, having such a concern to deal with, strive to put a bold face upon it. "We have made £484,000 profit last year," they exclaim, including £20,000 brought forward, and they have proceeded to distribute this with what appears to be a lavish hand—£50,000 to "patent reserve fund," £50,000 to a "special" reserve account —presumably a disguised method of providing for losses on bad investments—and £70,000 to a general reserve account, to say nothing of £23,000 held back to meet unpaid rebates. This looks magnificent until we turn back to the previous exhibit. That, to be sure, covered a period of eighteen months' trading, but if we assume the profit on this period to have been equally distributed, we should still have about £660,000 as the gain for the year ended March 31, 1897, against £484,000 for the past year; so the drop has been nearly £200,000 in one year, and the boast that the company has made "the largest sum, apart from the sale of investments, ever realised by it" in any one year, hardly seems much to the purpose. We do not know, indeed, how this modest profit of £480,000 odd is made up, for the balance-sheet describes it as coming from "royalties, net profit on trading, including dividends on investments received or accrued, &c.," really a droll mixture which we have not the means of analysing. It may be all in hand, this profit, and it may not. We should rather think it is not, because this same balance-sheet mentions an item of £207,062 due to "sundry creditors, including bank over-draft." Why is a bank over-draft required if the company has such a prodigious amount of money in hand as profit? It is all very funny.

Comic in their way also are the appropriations to reserve, and the omission of any assignment of money in reduction of goodwill. In the previous year the directors with a large hand placed £320,000 or thereby aside against goodwill; this year nothing goes there, but £50,000 is set aside to what is called a "patent" reserve, said patents standing in the balance-sheet, along with goodwill, at the globular total of £4,263,000, a delightfully fancy figure which we hope shareholders enjoy the contemplation of. No explanation is given of the mysterious increase of £147,000 in the value of the investments "at cost" now held, the total of which is £407,000; nor do the directors condescend to say why with such a dead weight for goodwill and patents some £14,000 should have been added to the cost of freehold and leasehold premises during the year and some £15,000 net to the cost of machinery and plant. These two items now figure for £125,000, and if we add "sundry debtors" £352,000, and the stocks in hand £165,000, together with the investments, worth, say, at a venture, £200,000, we arrive at something less than £850,000, which, at a liberal estimate, might be taken as the approximate gross value of the entire concern with the water squeezed out. Less than a million all told, in short, is what the swollen-out balance-sheet of nearly £5,500,000 boils down to on examination. That being so, we should hardly consider ourselves worthy the name of prophet in saying that in all probability the deferred shares have seen the last dividend they will ever get. It is only 5 per cent. now, or half what they got a year ago, but holders may be thankful they have got anything at all. Only the most skilful book-keeping could have produced this much for them, and even skill in book-keeping cannot insure a continuance of such bounty. We laugh? Why should we not? The shareholders scouted our advice when earnestly and seriously given to them and preferred to play the fool.

THE SOUTH WALES STRIKE.

There is no complaint to be made of the want of moderation in the speeches made in the House of Commons on Friday on the subject of the South Wales strike. It was quite evident that there was a general feeling of anxiety that the dispute should be settled, and that nothing should be said which might tend to retard that settlement. But is there any hope of achieving this result by following any of the suggestions made? We doubt it. Mr. Ritchie somewhat reluctantly indicated his willingness to take steps for naming a conciliator or conciliation board if appealed to by one of the disputants. Such an application has already been made on behalf of the men. But when the conciliator or conciliation board has been appointed, what more can Mr. Ritchie do? Evidently nothing. The strike will then be no nearer an end than now; it may possibly be further from that than ever. The employers have stated with perfect frankness their determination not to submit to outside interference. They reiterated this determination a few days ago when Lord Dunraven suggested the convening of a conference at Dunraven Castle. There is no doubt they will equally resolutely decline to appear before Mr. Ritchie's conciliator or conciliation board. Is it not, therefore, a mere waste of time to insist on action which can lead to nothing? A great deal was said as to whether the dispute could be called a strike or a lock out. It is surely of no consequence which you call it. But there is no doubt the colliers were in this case the first to throw down the challenge. They refused to renew the sliding scale after a certain date; the mine owners retaliated—they could do nothing else—by intimating the termination of all contracts at that date. The men have stated their terms; the employers have rejected these and laid down their own. It is idle for the colliers now to appeal to the House of Commons or the Board of Trade. Can they, after the experience of the engineers, expect thus to coerce the employers into accepting what they have from the first denounced? If that is the expectation of the colliers, they will find themselves greatly mistaken. The question is a very practical one, and will have to be approached in a practical spirit. Some compromise is yet possible; but the workmen must be prepared to discuss its terms with the mine owners, and to trust to their representatives to make the best bargain they can. Surely the colliers have lost enough themselves to induce them now to listen to reason?

EXPANSION OF GERMAN TRADE.

While encouraging aquatics—"which steel the nerves and strengthen the character"—at Cuxhaven, the German Emperor has taken the opportunity to confer with merchants of the Hause Towns, who have convinced him of the necessity of "powerfully supporting trans-oceanic trade." "Wherever German commerce goes," he told his hearers, "it can be sure of the protection and vigorous support of the authorities of the Empire." Trade seems to respond to the Imperial encouragement, as some statistics just issued from our Foreign Office concerning the last quarter's business seems conclusively to show. Germany has suffered considerably under the Dingley Tariff, which has, for example, caused a falling off in the exports to the United States of sugar alone of £650,000; but the loss has been largely counterbalanced by the cultivation of markets in the East Indies and in the British colonies. The result is a total increase in the exports for the first quarter of this year of £3,664,300 as compared with the similar quarter of last year. Take the exports of German iron, for example. There was an increase in those to the East Indies of 8,700 tons; to England and the Netherlands of 31,000 tons; and to China and Japan of 5,000 tons. The general result is striking when we compare it with the outcome of English and French trade. In the first quarter of 1898, English exports showed a diminution of about £1,600,000 as compared with the first quarter of last year; while France in the same way indicated a decrease of £625,000. These figures may have but a passing significance; but it is well we should note them. What is there to explain the great rise in German exports for the quarter, as compared with the fall in English exports? We have not the materials yet for arriving at a reasonable conclusion; but the facts are striking, and may give our merchants matter for reflection. Are we losing all that Germany has been gaining in the way of trade with the East Indies and our colonies generally? Or is Germany making business of a risky character, which may one day cause an ugly crash?

Reports on this subject accumulate almost too quickly to overtake; but the tenor of all is the same—that Germany is going ahead with great energy. Sir Charles Oppenheimer, our Consul-General at Frankfort-on-Main, in his report to the Foreign Office expands on the subject with something of the warmth of romance. But he gives England some comfort. He warns us not to take the "remarks of some newspapers" as representing the opinion of the German people. In the main Germans "foster the sincere wish to see the agreeable and lucrative commercial relations with England continue undisturbed." Nay, he knows that "the German even to-day looks upon the English nation with the greatest respect, and never forgets that it has been his tutor in trade, as well as in commerce and politics." Is this not pleasantly encouraging? It is agreeable also to be assured that the Diet will take the same point of view when the new commercial treaty is presented for acceptance. English trade with Germany is still large; that country is, economically speaking, the most important market for England. British goods, we are assured, are willingly bought by the classes that know how to judge, "because they are looked upon as practical, solid, and agreeable." Paris has fallen from her predominance in fashion, and her place has been taken by London. But English manufacturers must push their goods as the Germans do, by the establishment of agencies, with managers familiar with the country's ways, else they may find themselves shut out by the United States, whose manufacturers have of late been showing increased attention to the German markets.

Perhaps, however, the most striking feature in recent reports on German trade is the fierceness with which German traders fight for protective tariffs and the alacrity with which the Government often listen to their demands. There is wool, of which about 170,000 tons are required yearly for the country's wants. Only about 20,000 tons can be produced at home. Yet these home producers sought the Government to protect them from the bloated foreigner who could run up such a quantity as 170,000 tons. Their appeal was not listened to, for a wonder; but the wool combers, on declaring that woollen yarn could be produced of as good quality in Germany as in England, got an immediate prohibition put upon the free importation of foreign woollen yarn in single or more threads. German ironworkers have already secured preferential railway rates to the detriment of English exporters. Every German industry seems putting in a claim for the erection of a wire fence around its little industrial plot. The only person who never seems to assert himself or lift his voice in protest is the consumer. Nobody hesitates about stealing from him, or getting the Government to do it for them; but he submits with the patience of the sheep to be fleeced and robbed. The agricultural party demand the temporary abolition of commercial treaties, and the adoption of "tariff autonomy"—that is, the fixing of customs-rates suitable for all home industries, commercial treaties then to be negotiated at rates considerably above this minimum tariff. More than this, there is still a considerable party anxious for the establishment of a European coalition against America with her Dingley tariff, as if America were not herself suffering about as much as her trade competitors by the action of that wretched system. For the present Germany seems protection mad. Until she has recovered her senses somewhat, her trade expansion can hardly be altogether sound or assured. England can at least look upon the odd struggle with comparative calmness, while she sees her honest admirer, but stern competitor, trying her best to "kill the goose that lays the golden eggs."

THE TRADE OF HANKOW AND ITS LESSONS.

Mr. Consul R. Warren's report on the trade of Hankow for 1897 vividly illustrates the importance of the battle royal now being fought at Peking on the question of railway concessions. The construction of railways is of course of great importance to China; but, even for China herself the question as to which Power shall construct the lines has become of equal if not more importance. Hankow, for example, is a very important Chinese trade centre. Though its export tea trade, only a few years ago its most considerable in extent and value, has enormously diminished, and is likely practically to vanish altogether, yet the gross value of the trade of Hankow for 1897 was the highest on record. It has thus already more than made up in other exports for the loss on tea. Now a "Belgian" syndicate has been in negotiation with the Chinese Government for the construction of the Peking-Hankow Railway. If it were really a Belgian syndicate who proposed building the railway with Belgian capital, no objection could be raised. But the capital is to be supplied by the Russo-Chinese Bank—that is, by Russia itself—and the Belgian Minister proposes that France should be appointed arbitrator in all disputes that may arise. In truth, Belgium in this matter would be but the cat's-paw of Russia and France — principally the former — who would have control of the railway, and so control the great and growing trade of Hankow. It would gradually cease to be a world's port, and end in being a mere Russian port in the narrowest sense. British trade would immediately suffer; so would the Japanese, as well as that of America and every country but Russia, and perhaps France. In truth, we must always remember that behind this struggle for railway concessions lies the larger and wider and more far-reaching struggle between Protection and Free Trade. We have no fear of the ultimate result; but it is essential that in China, at present, our Foreign Office should show a proper appreciation of the nature of the struggle, and should energetically protest against concessions for railways, at least within British spheres of influence, coming under the control of rabidly Protectionist countries. That at the present moment is of more importance to Great Britain than is the addition of several big warships to our Navy.

As we have said, the trade of Hankow increased enormously during 1897; but, unfortunately, British trade did not largely participate in the advancement. Our shipping still keeps the lead, and is increasing it, but otherwise, for the most part, British trade shows a decline. In the import of foreign goods, the British share is about 50 per cent. of the total imports. The tea trade is in the hands of Russian merchants. Germany has the best part of the "muck and truck" trade, in which are included hides, tallow, wax, gallnuts, bristles, &c. Her merchants do a large business, and are content with very small profits—perhaps also are not always so particular as they might be as to the stability of their customers. Even in cotton goods and yarns our imports show a falling off, while Japanese imports are increasing. Indeed, Japan is becoming our most formidable trade rival in that part of China; and it is a striking fact that since 1895 the imports of Japanese yarn have jumped from 150 cwt. in that year to no less than 52,636 cwt. in 1897. India also is suffering from Japanese competition; while America has gained somewhat at our expense in cotton goods. We shall have apparently to watch other things as well as railways if we are to keep up our trade position in China.

The Great Boulder Company and its Milling Company.

The elaborate statement issued by the board of the Great Boulder Proprietary Company in regard to the formation and contracts with the Boulder Milling Company suffices by itself to condemn them utterly. According to this, the Great Boulder Company possesses already slimes and tailings valued at £240,000. More of these slimes and tailings must accumulate and their treatment was a matter of importance. Instead of making arrangements in the ordinary manner for their treatment, the board admits that it formed another company, the Boulder Milling Company, which was to work a new process invented by a Mr. Köneman. The vendors of the new company received £3,000 in cash, presumably from the Great Boulder Company, and 19,992 shares out of 20,000 shares forming the total capital of the Boulder Milling Company. Then the Great Boulder Company, or rather its board, agreed to take up £20,000 in debentures of the new company, and had half the 19,992 shares transferred to it. So that the Great Boulder Company provided the whole of the cash to carry the matter through, but only possessed half the shares. Then Mr. Köneman is to receive the substantial salary of £2,000 per annum, and the board of the Milling Company is to take 10 per cent. of its profits.

Upon this foundation the Great Boulder hands over its tailings and slimes to the Milling Company, which is to treat them, and after deducting 3 dwt. of gold per ton for working expenses, the Great Boulder Company receives 60 per cent. of the gold extracted and the Milling Company 40 per cent. So that after providing all the capital, allowing a generous margin for working cost, and a good salary for the patentee, the Great Boulder shareholders will be permitted to take three-fifths of the gold produced out of their own tailings and slimes. A reasonable board would have paid a royalty to Mr. Köneman upon his process—it might by chance turn out a failure—and so have obtained for the shareholders all the profits for themselves, for when the £2,000 to Mr. Köneman, the 3 dwt. of gold for working cost, and the 10 per cent. of profits to the Milling Company's board are added together, it would probably represent all that would have to be paid for the treatment of the tailings and slimes after allowing for a royalty charge. But then, you see, Messrs. A. R. Robertson and Gamble North, directors of the Great Boulder Company, are directors of the Milling Company, together with Mr. Lane, the mining expert of the company. The history of the board does not state what becomes of the half of the capital of the Milling Company not taken by the Great Boulder Company. Presumably it goes to Mr. Köneman and his friends, and *who are his friends?*

American Minerals.

The United States continues to make strikingly rapid progress in the production of minerals, and the value of the output for last year is estimated at $678,966,644. Compared with 1896 this figure represents little more than a nominal advance owing to the low range of prices ruling for coal, iron, and some other contributories; but compared with 1895, we have an increase of 8 per cent. even on the valuation basis, while a very cursory glance at the statistics shows that, if measured by the quantity alone, the progress in the last two years has been very appreciable. The principal item is coal, of which the yield in 1897 was 200,257,243 "short" tons of 2,000 lb., equivalent to 178,801,110 "long" tons of 2,240 lb. The previous best year was 1895, when the output reached 172,426,000 long tons. In the intervening year, 1896, the total fell away to 162,503,570 tons as an inevitable result of the commercial depression which marked the second half. As evidence of the progress made by America in the last fifteen years as a coal producer, we may state that in 1890 the yield was 140,883,000 tons, and in 1883 102,868,000 tons. It is to be noted, however, that prices last year established a record for lowness, the average for all kinds, bituminous, anthracite and cannel being only 4s. 2$\frac{3}{4}$d. per ton against 4s. 9$\frac{1}{4}$d. in 1895, 5s. 2$\frac{3}{4}$d. in 1890, and 6s. 5$\frac{1}{2}$d. in 1883. On the basis of quantity produced America still comes next to the United Kingdom, our own output last year having exceeded 203,000,000 tons in spite of the indirect injury occasioned by the engineers' strike. It cannot be said, however, that we have increased our production of coal in the past fifteen years in the same ratio as America, for our total in 1883 was 163,737,327 tons, and it is quite possible that in three or four years more we may have to take second place among the world's coal producers.

Second in value among American minerals last year was iron. The output of ore is not stated, but the pig iron produced was 9,652,680 tons, valued at $92,677,312. This total has been surpassed on one or two previous occasions, the conditions last year not having been altogether favourable to production until the operation of the Dingley tariff. Gold, which ranks third, is credited in the estimates before us at $59,210,795, this being the value of the 2,864,576 fine ounces said to have been obtained. For 1896 the output was 2,568,132 oz., value $53,088,000. These last figures are those of the director of the Mint Bureau at Washington, and may be accepted as approximately accurate. The figures for 1897, however, are subject to revision, and are probably in excess of the actual total. Preliminary estimates of America's gold production have a way of overstating the case, though there is no question that last year saw an improvement on its predecessor. Among the other minerals to which we may refer are copper, of which the yield in the twelve months was 510,190,719 lb., an increase of over 30,000,000 lb.; petroleum, valued at $44,804,962; silver, 56,457,292 troy oz., of a commercial value of $33,755,815, against 58,834,800 oz., commercial value $39,654,655, in 1896; and lead 197,718 tons (an increase of 23,000 tons over 1896), of the value of $11,784,098. It is interesting to note that, on the basis of values the United States has a mineral output twice as large as the United Kingdom.

Dairy Produce in England.

Something has been done for the encouragement of dairy farming in this country, but not enough yet to keep at bay active and vigorous foreign and colonial competitors. More public money might be spent to much better purpose on technical instruction and help for

British farmers than in "relieving" landlords, or in practically bootless efforts to make our navy equal to facing a "world in arms." We are an industrial country, and while a "war insurance" may be necessary, we may easily pay too much for it. The Government of Canada teaches us a most important lesson in this respect. Of course, the "war insurance" question does not worry her as it does the mother country, but by the constant encouragement and instruction she has provided for dairy farming she has become, in several things, our most formidable competitor. In cheese alone, for instance, as we learn from Messrs. W. Weddel & Co.'s review, Canada sent us last year 76,350 tons, or 34,000 tons more than in 1890, the United States coming next with 31,581 tons. The United States used to take the lead in cheese importation, but Canada is rapidly elbowing her out, while the home maker has to struggle on, with but scant encouragement and a big "war insurance" bill, making but an indifferent show among his more fortunate rivals. The last year was a favourable one for the production of milk, with the result that there was a great increase in the home manufacture of butter and cheese, and as the colonial and foreign supply continued undiminished, the season was distinguished from all its predecessors by the unprecedentedly low prices which prevailed. The total imports of butter and cheese showed an increase last year of 9,000 and 17,924 tons respectively, as compared with the previous year. Much of the increase came from our colonies. In butter, for example, the imports from Australia, Canada, and New Zealand amounted to 19,014 tons, against 15,426 tons in 1896. But there has been a marked falling off in the shipments of this article from Germany during the last few years. The supplies from Belgium and France were also diminished; but from Denmark they considerably increased. The home farmer has been fighting valiantly against this competition, but not with success. His rivals have the advantage of him in the wide application of the co-operative principle in farming, and the means they have of saving labour. Take the case of a large butter factory, where a single churn makes 6 cwt. to 10 cwt. of butter. Think of the small amount of labour involved in this operation, as compared with that of the forty to fifty farmers' wives in this country, who, according to Messrs. Weddel, would take half a day to make the same quantity, and then spend another half or whole day in going to the market to sell it. Evidently the British dairy farmer has still somewhat primitive notions. However Government may have neglected him, he has excellent pastures, is close to the markets, and ought not to have allowed himself to be so far beaten as he has been.

It may be worth noting that the *Bulletin de la Société des Agriculteurs* has been taking the Normandy butter-makers very severely to task for the deterioration apparent in the quality of their butter. Nearly 170 samples sent to the recent Paris show from the best farms in the typical districts of Normandy are declared to have shown little uniformity of character. They ranged in quality from very good to very indifferent, and this irregularity is exercising an adverse influence upon the sale of this Normandy product. Normandy has many advantages for dairy farmers; but in butter is being beaten in the French markets by the Charente, Vendée, and Poitou, and in the English markets by Denmark and Norway. Normandy farmers, therefore, like the British, are rated for falling behind the times. In the most successful butter-making districts in France, co-operation in dairy-farming has been adopted, and is extending year by year. These co-operative factories produce the best butter—this seems the universal experience—more uniform in character and quality. Normandy has no such factory, nor, so far as we know, has Great Britain. Is it not time our farmers were bethinking themselves of the desirability of trying the experiment?

A new narrow-gauge railway is to be constructed to join the Engadine with the other valleys of the Canton of Grisons. The Swiss Federal Assembly has approved a grant of 8,000,000 francs for the purpose.

THE REST OF THE INDIAN RAILWAY REPORTS.

With half-a-dozen Indian railway reports we dealt a month ago, and the outcome of the working was shown to be satisfactory. The reports since issued show equally good results, except in the case of the Great Indian Peninsula, which suffered severely from the plague and famine, the company having to bear the full brunt of both in Western India. Traffic as a whole gives evidence of continued expansion, and many of the companies have had a heavy carriage of troops to put against the falling off in passenger traffic:—

—	Gross Receipts.	Working Expenses.	Percentage of expenses to receipts.		Net earnings + increase or − decrease.
			Dec. 1897.	Dec. 1896.	
Bengal Dooars	Rs. + 9,604	− 716	41·41	44·26	+ 10,321
Bengal Nagpur	Rs. − 40,543	− 170,228	60·00	61·80	+ 129,686
East Indian	Rs. + 2,328,289	− 152,407	28·39	31·39	+ 2,480,696
Great Indian Peninsula	£ − 68,670	+ 79,386	75·09	64·48	− 148,056
Indian Midland ...	Rs. + 136,465	+ 64,519	58·76	59·30	+ 71,956
Nizam's Guaranteed	Rs. + 293,146	+ 77,002	46·99	50·72	+ 216,143

As will be seen below, the East Indian Company is able to increase its dividend substantially, and the Bengal Dooars by ½ per cent. The Nizam's Guaranteed Company also has better net profits, and the Indian Midland Company calls upon the Government for less.

—	Surplus Profits.		Available for Dividend.		Dividend for Half-year.	
	1897.	1896.	1897.	1896.	Dec. 1897.	Dec. 1896.
	Rs.	Rs.	£	£	per cent.	per cent.
Bengal Dooars ..	—	—	7,267	5,731	3½	3
Bengal Nagpur	‡1,550,875	‡1,544,448	—	—	2	2
East Indian .. .	1,185,137	571,462	79,007	35,193	£3 4 6*	£2 10 9
Great Indian Peninsula ..	£‡332,000	£‡184,000	—	—	2½	2½
Indian Midland	‡1,034,772	‡1,218,409	—	—	2	2
Nizam's Guaranteed .	Rs.1,980,424	958,345	63,489	48,907	2½	2½

‡ Short of Guaranteed Interest.
* On Deferred Annuity Capital and Annuity Class "D."

The best showing is made by the East Indian Company, which, reckoning the rupee in each year at 1s. 2½d., has an increase of £140,000 for the half-year in gross receipts, and a saving of £9,000 in expenses, the increase in net for the six months being £150,000, and for the whole year just upon £300,000. The percentage of expenses to receipts has now been worked down to the remarkably low figure of less than 28½ per cent., which means that of the gross revenue from the 6½ million miles run, nearly three-fourths is secured as net, an excellent thing for the stockholders here, but how about the working staff and the native customers? In coaching traffic there was an increase of 61,000 passengers, and of Rs.579,193 in receipts. Famine and plague were adverse influences affecting this class of traffic, and the improvement shown is entirely due to the carriage of the military to the North West Frontier, which also accounts for Rs.250,000 of the increase from parcels. In goods traffic there was an increase of 86,000 tons, and in minerals of 256,000 tons, the addition to revenue being Rs.1,660,000. Of Indian corn and cotton less was carried, but there were good increases both in quantity and revenue from hides and skins, oils, cotton piece goods, railway, plant, rice, oil seed, and sugar. In wheat there was an increase of 43,852 tons and Rs.432,301 in receipts, which was far above the average for a second half-year, weight and earnings having been only twice exceeded since 1890. Strange, too, is it to learn that the bulk of the traffic was derived from the famine-stricken districts. Stocks were held back for higher prices, but the imports of cheap rice from Burma and the success of the monsoon food crop beat holders, and instead of supplying famine districts they had to find other markets. Altogether the company did so well that it is able to pay £1 4s. 6d. per cent. for the half-year on the deferred annuity capital and the class "D" annuity capital in addition to the guaranteed interest. This will make £6 8s. per cent. for the whole year, compared with £5 3s. 6d. for 1896, and is the best return since 1891, when the surplus dividend and interest reached £6 17s. 3d. per cent.

The Nizam's Guaranteed State Railway continues to do very well, having a large increase in receipts for the past half-year, of which nearly three-fourths has been saved as rict. The company, of course, suffered in passenger traffic through the plague, but the loss was much more than made up from the increase in goods and mineral traffic, and the results of the working are the best the company has ever had. The Government guarantee expires June 25, 1904, by which time the company should be very well able to run alone. Since 1889 gross earnings have risen from Rs.2,334,133 to Rs.3,777,153 in 1897, or fully 60 per cent., whilst the ratio of expenditure has been worked down from 66·15 per cent. to 46·52 per cent., and it is claimed that the full earning power of the railway has not yet been reached. At present the net amount divisable would pay £2 7s. per cent., or only 3s. less than the guaranteed interest. More capital will have to be raised next year, but this is perhaps inevitable in view of the continued building of new lines.

THE INDIAN MIDLAND COMPANY also did very well during the past six months, the gross earnings being the largest on record and exceeded three millions of rupees. The increase was entirely on the main line, coaching traffic yielding Rs.102,540 more, owing to the carriage of troops, while goods traffic increased by Rs.149,027, though this was considerably reduced by decreases on the branch lines. The present position is that the interest charges for the six months amount to Rs.2,102,686, of which the net earnings of the company equal about one-half; but the net earnings are distinctly growing. In the past half-year they were Rs.1,067,914 against Rs.941,798 in 1896, Rs.740,238 in 1895, Rs.973,864 in 1894, and Rs.617,204 in 1893. The company has a good deal of extension work on hand and a capital account already overdrawn.

THE BENGAL DOOARS is only a small concern of thirty-six miles and the company has no guarantee. It is, however, doing fairly well and pays 3½ per cent. for the half-year, or ½ per cent. more than in the corresponding period, in spite of being put to extra expense through the earthquake, and the reserve fund has been raised to £1,500. Little expansion of traffic can be looked for until the 122 miles of line now on hand have been constructed, towards which purpose further capital was recently raised.

THE BENGAL NAGPUR COMPANY enjoys a 4 per cent. guarantee and appears to be a long way off standing on its own legs, being fully a million and a half short of meeting the half-year's guaranteed interest. Some extensions are to be opened, if ready, in 1900, and with a view to building feeder lines some 600 miles have recently been surveyed. Passenger traffic during the past half-year suffered considerably from the plague and famine, and there was a smaller emigration of coolies to the Assam tea gardens, whilst the increase in the goods traffic receipts was slight in spite of a much larger coal traffic.

THE GREAT INDIAN PENINSULA COMPANY, which renders its accounts in sterling, makes an exceptionally bad display, the receipts being £68,670 less and the expenses £79,386 more than in 1896. The decrease in net revenue for the half-year is therefore £148,057, and for the whole year the falling off is as much as £574,878. During the past half-year there was a decrease of £75,372 in coaching traffic, although the carriage of troops and military baggage brought in £14,852 more, while in the goods traffic there was an improvement of £10,639. The falling off in passenger traffic is ascribed to the plague and consequent quarantine regulations. In the expenditure there was a saving of £19,000 under the head of maintenance, but carriage and wagon expenses increased by £68,000; locomotive by £18,000; and traffic and other charges by over £11,000. Train miles run were 339,955 more than in 1896, and of this increase 150,378 miles was due to coaching, it having been found impossible to adjust the train service required under the exceptional circumstances of the half-year, so as to reduce the passenger train mileage in the ratio of receipts. The result of the working is that only Rs.3,045,682 is transferred to Government towards meeting the guaranteed interest compared with Rs.4,556,187. Fortunately the current half-year promises much better results, the increase in receipts to the middle of June being £353,000. It is practically certain that the Government will exercise its right of buying up this railway next year, the terms being a sum equivalent to the average market value of the capital stock in the three preceding years. Of course it is hoped the purchase will be conducted on very much the same lines as in the case of the East Indian Railway, which would be a very good thing for the shareholders, but they cannot make sure of it yet. India itself has no say in the matter.

The failure of the banking firm of Charles Hopkinson & Sons, of 3, Regent-street, S.W., was announced on Tuesday. It is not of very great importance, as the business of the bank, which was established in 1796, was not very large. No authentic statement of its affairs has yet been published, but the deficiency will be considerable.

Critical Index to New Investments.

WOLVERHAMPTON AND DUDLEY BREWERIES, LIMITED.

This company offers £100,000 of 4 per cent. irredeemable "A" mortgage debenture stock at par. Share capital is £150,000, and there is already an issue of £100,000 4½ per cent. first mortgage debentures in existence. The stock now offered is secured upon ninety-three freehold, two copyhold, and one long leasehold licensed houses and certain unlicensed property acquired since the incorporation of the company and valued at £140,485, and it will also be a floating second charge upon the assets which secure the existing debentures. Profits for three years ended September last are given as £15,098, £20,178, and £27,973, the average being £21,083, which, after paying "A" debenture interest would leave £16,580, so that the new stock seems secure as long as brewery property keeps up.

PLYMOUTH BREWERIES, LIMITED.

Having already £175,665 of 4½ per cent. debenture stock against an issued share capital of only £116,547, the directors now offer £60,000 of 4 per cent. mortgage debenture stock (part of a total of £150,000) at par. It will be redeemable at 105 after the end of next year on six months' notice. Of this issue all but £3,278 will be used in paying off certain liabilities and loans incurred in the purchase of new properties, including the Torquay Brewing and Trading Company. The value of the assets securing the present issue is said to be £208,801, while the net profits have grown from £7,872 in 1895 to £8,583 in 1897 after paying debenture interest. The assets seem to have been valued upon a pretty liberal scale, and how much is represented by goodwill ought not to have been hidden up with freehold and leasehold properties. The debenture stock is not by any means a first-class investment.

JOSEPH THORLEY, LIMITED.

Share capital of £200,000, half ordinary and half 5½ per cent. cumulative preference, is taken by the vendor. The public is invited to subscribe for £60,000 4½ per cent. first mortgage debenture stock, part of a total of £80,000, at 105 per cent. It is redeemable on six months' notice after 1911 at 110 per cent. Leasehold property, plant, &c., are valued at £56,065, and the stock, book debts, &c., at £38,390. No figures about profits are supplied, but it is stated that for the last three years they have been sufficient each year to pay interest on the debenture stock now issued "many times over." Thorley's food for cattle we have all heard of and it may be a good business, but the security for the debenture stock seems none too large.

KING & MORTIMER, LIMITED.

For any one who wants a downright speculative venture, this ought to be suitable. The object of the company is to buy businesses in London or elsewhere, and to develop them into stores. For a start the grocery businesses of Robert King in South Kensington and George Mortimer in Fulham-road have been secured, and a lovely profit statement "on the present basis" is supplied. The capital is £160,000 in £16,000 5½ per cent. preference shares of £5 each, and 80,000 ordinary shares of £1 each, of which 50,000 ordinary are allotted to the vendors, with £60,000 in cash, with which to pay for the businesses. There is also an issue of £40,000 4½ per cent. mortgage debenture stock, which, with the preference shares, is offered at par. The directors will not take any fees until the preference dividend has been paid, which speaks well for the preference shares, but surely, if the concern is as good as made out, giving 50,000 ordinary shares just for transferring the businesses to the public is a remarkably liberal price to pay the vendors. If they get much of this sort of work they ought to grow rich; but King and Mortimer are not likely to have undervalued their properties, so what represents the £140,000 of capital beyond what they receive?

SOUTHPORT OPERA HOUSE AND WINTER GARDENS, LIMITED.

The object of this company is to buy the freehold property known as the Southport Winter Gardens, including the opera house, &c. A Manchester firm values the property, when extensions estimated to cost £60,000 are carried out, at £228,039, and the average income for the last three years is said to have been £23,913. The share capital is £150,000 in £1 shares, of which £130,000 is issued in equal parts of ordinary and 5 per cent. cumulative preference shares, and £75,000 of 4 per cent. debenture stock is offered at par, being part of a total of £100,000. Purchase price is £144,200, subject to an existing mortgage and bond. The vendor does not appear to want any of this sum in shares, and if they are not good enough for him it would be well for the public to leave them alone. To our mind the affair will be crushed by the weight of its capital.

HAMBLET'S BLUE BRICK COMPANY, LIMITED.

Company is formed to acquire from the end of March the old-established brick business of Joseph Hamblet, at West Bromwich, known as the Piercy Brick and Tile Works, together with freehold land and premises extending to over 130 acres. The value of the freeholds, mineral rights, plant, and stock is reported to be £133,018, and the profits for three years ended March last are certified at £10,624, £11,793, and £15,526. Share capital is £60,000 in ordinary and £60,000 in 6 per cent. cumulative preference, with an issue of £60,000 4½ per cent. first mortgage debentures redeemable at 105 after June, 1910, on six months' notice. Purchase price is £180,000, which includes all the ordinary and 10,000 preference shares, with £110,000 in cash. Such a high price is not justified and advantage seems to have been taken of the sudden increase of nearly £4,000 in last year's profits to get rid of the business to the public.

WEST'S PATENT POTTERY AND MACHINE COMPANY, LIMITED.

With the object of buying patents to make flower pots, jam pots, jars, basins, &c., of any plastic material, glass, &c., this company is brought out with a capital of £100,000 in £1 shares, of which the vendors take 55,000 shares and £25,000 in cash, leaving £20,000, if subscribed, for working capital. Assets are referred to, though no value is mentioned, but some lofty estimates are indulged in regarding profits and dividends. It may suit some people.

CONTINENTAL SPARKLETS COMPANY, LIMITED.

Formed with a capital of £240,000 in £1 shares, half ordinary and half 7 per cent. non-cumulative preference, the company acquires sole rights in "Aerators" (Système Sterné), in France, Russia, Belgium, Denmark, Norway and Sweden, Spain, and Luxemburg. The "sparklets" are small steel capsules filled with carbonic acid gas, which, used with a certain bottle and stopper costing 3s., will enable consumers to aerate anything at a moment's notice. Ten sparklets will cost about a shilling. The vendors have appointed the directors, and some of them will receive remuneration from the vendors or promoters in consideration of guaranteeing the subscription of a portion of the capital, and applications for shares will be received only on the footing that no objection is taken on the ground of the directors being so appointed or that they do not constitute an independent board. If this clause is the means of keeping a good many people out of the concern its insertion will have justified itself. A dividend of 25 per cent. is spoken of on the ordinary shares, with a surplus of £11,600 carried forward, and only on the realisation of this estimate should we think the purchase price of £170,000 moderate. There seems a deal of aeration already introduced into the capital as well as into the estimate of future profits and the purchase price.

THE DUTCH THREE PER CENT. LOAN.

Its nominal amount in Dutch money is 57,815,000 florins and in English £4,818,000. It is a 3 per cent. loan in bonds, the bearer secured on the revenues of the Kingdom of the Netherlands, and is offered to British investors at 97 per cent. by Messrs. Speyer Bros. and the Union Bank of London. Redemptions by a 1 per cent. sinking fund, which may be increased, take place by drawings at par or by purchase under par. Applications must be sent in before 4 p.m. on Tuesday next. The loan is not particularly cheap, but the security is about as good as any Europe has to offer.

WELDONS, LIMITED.

This company has been formed to buy the businesses of fashion publishers and pattern manufacturers carried on by Messrs. C. E. Weldon & Co. A whole platoon of newspapers is owned by it, the combined circulation of which is stated to exceed ten million copies per annum. Sir George Newnes is to be chairman of the company, and it will have a share capital of £380,000 in 40,000 5 per cent. £5 cumulative preference shares, and 180,000 £1 ordinary shares. All the capital is offered for subscription at par. We should have liked more particulars about the assets. As it is, the mere statement of the accountants, Messrs. Whinney, Smith, & Whinney, that the average profits for the three years ended December 31 last, amounted to £29,621, or nearly £20,000 more than the preference dividend requires, may be good to day and not so good next year. One thing is satisfactory, there is no debt.

We have received from the Agent-General of New South Wales two voluminous publications: "The Wealth and Progress of New South Wales, 1896-7"; and "The New South Wales Statistical Register." Both contain a large amount of interesting and valuable information bearing on the progress and expansion of the colony.

Company Reports and Balance-Sheets.

*** *The Editor will be much obliged to the Secretaries of Joint Stock Companies if they would kindly forward copies of Reports and Balance-Sheets direct to the Office of* THE INVESTORS' REVIEW, *Norfolk House, Norfolk-street, W.C., so as to insure prompt notice in these columns.*

GILROY SONS & COMPANY, LIMITED.—For the sixth year in succession, the year ended May 31 last, this company has failed to pay any dividend on its ordinary shares, but it meets the preference dividend still and has £3,879 left to be carried forward subject to directors' and auditors' fees. No great detail is afforded in the accounts, but they are clear enough, and we notice that the reserve fund is partly invested. It amounts to £20,000 and the investments stand at £11,312. What the company suffers from is the common complaint of over-capitalisation. It would evidently do very well, even in bad times, were the £175,000 of ordinary share capital out of the way.

ROYAL INSURANCE COMPANY.—In its fire branch this company is the largest in the United Kingdom and probably in the world, but we shall not enter into details regarding this part of its business, because the essential features of it are summarised in a table printed on another page. All we need mention here is that after meeting all outgoings £233,343 were left out of the total premium income of over £2,000,000 to be carried to profit and loss account. The life department also did a large business, insuring £1,028,408 within the year, which amount yielded premiums of £45,427. The total income from premiums was £448,039, and the interest from investments, exclusive of the annuity fund, was £189,152. Claims absorbed £385,510. Only a small business was done in annuities, £55,210 being received for new ones granted. After payment of all claims and expenses, the life and annuity funds were increased by £209,366, and amount to £5,539,264. The expenses of the life business came to 12·6 per cent. of the premium income. Out of the profits of the year dividends aggregating 38s. per share, or 63·333 per cent., have been or will be paid. Adding the proprietors' funds, the fire funds, the reserve fund, &c., to the other possessions of the company, its total assets amount to £9,686,582, and they are all stated together in the balance-sheet, the life investments not being separated from those pertaining to other branches of the business or belonging to the proprietors. Out of this large sum £1,747,760 is invested in mortgages within the United Kingdom, and rather more than £2,000,000 has been placed in various United States securities, including no less than £538,705 in freehold buildings. This last seems a very large item, and we are not sure that the £723,000 committed to United States railway mortgage bonds is a perfectly satisfactory feature in the investment account. Assuming it to be so, the money of the company appears to be pretty solidly distributed, and the auditors certify that the present aggregate market value of the real estate and mortgages in the United States and Australia is at present "in excess of the amounts in the balance-sheet." How they arrive at the value of the mortgages we cannot quite guess.

ROYAL EXCHANGE ASSURANCE COMPANY.—Last year this company did a net new business in the life department amounting to £689,569, or £132,170 more than in 1896, a progressive increase. The net addition this business made to the premium income was about £37,500, and the total premium income was £196,070. Interest earned amounted to £80,744, being £4 1s. 5d. per cent. on the life funds. Expenses and management and commission were 14·9 per cent. of the premium income, and the directors consider this moderate "in view of the high percentage which the new premiums bear to renewals." Sixty-eight new annuities were sold for £60,832. Claims paid took £163,545, an amount considerably less than actuarial expectation. The fire business of the year resulted in a profit of £414,102, including interest and dividends on the fire funds, but we do not go into details. In the marine department, the result was a loss on the year's working, which not only wiped away the £3,881 balance of profit and loss from 1896, but reduced the marine fund from £146,368 to £131,270. Out of the profits of the fire department, however, the profits for 1896 that is to say, those for the past year being carried forward, a dividend of 14 per cent. was paid on the capital stock, leaving the accumulated balance at the credit of profit and loss £702,156, which was about £4,000 less than at the beginning of the year. This company very properly separates its life insurance balance-sheet from the general balance-sheet, and shows a total under that head of £2,091,481. The life fund was increased at the end of the year by £61,000, and now amounts to £2,053,892. This money is invested for the most part within the United Kingdom only, £156,292 appearing in United States first mortgage gold and sterling bonds. The aggregate assets of the company amount to £4,405,712, and the assets of the portions of it not in the life account appear also to be very well and carefully laid out.

NORTHERN ASSURANCE COMPANY.—For the year 1897 this company's new life business amounted to 997 policies, insuring £477,742 net and yielding £17,004 in annual and £1,692 in single premiums. The total premium income of the year was £246,650 and the total income from all sources £361,684. Claims absorbed £186,486 and expenses of management and commissions were kept down to the usual 10 per cent. of the premiums received, thanks to the wealth of the fire branch. At the end of the year the life funds, amounting to £3,362,297, showed an increase of £200,008, but this included the £72,092 received for annuities sold. Although it is a good and steady life business this company does, it is nothing to the fire business, whose premium income last year was £662,097, a large total, although a decrease of £37,909 on the previous year. Details need not be given here either. Profit, after making the usual provisions for current risks, was £83,996, added to which are £60,337 interest on investments not belonging to the life funds, and £65,989, being the balance brought forward from 1896. This gives a gross disposable balance of £210,322, out of which dividends and bonus aggregating £3 per share or 30 per cent. have been declared, leaving £107,085 to be carried forward. In reality the dividend is 60 per cent. on the capital found by the stock holders, half of the £10 per share paid having been made up out of the profits. This company follows the example of the Royal and does not separate its life funds in the balance-sheet given to the public from its other accounts. According to this balance-sheet, its aggregate assets amounted at the end of the year to £5,324,630, and of this about £800,000 is invested in Indian and colonial government, provincial, and municipal securities, and about £920,000 in the same classes of various foreign securities.

KENT FIRE INSURANCE COMPANY, AND UNITED KENT LIFE ASSURANCE AND ANNUITY INSTITUTION OR COMPANY, LIMITED.—This double-barrelled company's fire business is small, and the essential particulars are given elsewhere. At the end of the year the fire fund amounted to £309,678, having been increased by £5,874 within the year. A dividend of 7 per cent. was paid on the shareholders' capital. In the life branch 170 policies were issued, insuring £78,200, and giving £2,854 in premium income. Claims paid took £30,904, and expenses and commission came to £17 1s. 8d. per cent. of the premium income. After paying all claims, annuities, and expenses—the company does a small annuity business—the funds of this branch were increased by £16,981, and now amount to £660,661, or about "50 per cent. of the total sum assured with bonus added." Interest at the rate of £4 2s. per cent. was earned on the invested moneys.

RIVER PLATE FRESH MEAT COMPANY.—The very satisfactory profit of £33,784 was shown by this company for the year ended April 30. After placing £10,000 to reserve a dividend on the ordinary shares of 6 per cent., as against no dividend a year ago, was declared, and £1,184 is carried forward. The reserves of the company will then amount to £35,000, and although trading credits are necessarily large, balances on the whole appear to be favourable to the company. The reserve, however, is wholly in the business, which is rather a pity, as it is a fluctuating business. The company is about to issue £42,100 more 6 per cent. debentures, raising the total to £100,000, as against £250,000 of share capital.

MOABUND TEA COMPANY.—This company has suffered from earthquake, a bad season, and the meretricious attentions of the capital-balloonist. Formerly a strong concern, the capital was increased to £150,000 in 1896, holders of ordinary and preference shares receiving two for one. Owing to the exceptionally bad season the profit amounted to £2,834, which just allowed of the payment of the preference interest, amounting to £2,500, and the carrying forward of a modest balance. The interest on the old preference capital was only £834 per annum, so that the ordinary shareholders will have reason to anathematise the clever gentlemen who induced them to commit the foolhardy conversion of 1896. The balance-sheet is quite in keeping with the conduct of the board, about £34,000 being owed to various creditors against about £18,000 of liquid assets. Further trouble is being prepared for the future by adding £10,514, the cost of upkeep of 1,312 acres of new gardens, to capital account, or just about £8 per acre. Yet the unhappy concern is already too highly capitalised.

UNITED RIVER PLATE TELEPHONE COMPANY.—The revenue of this company steadily improves, so that its gross receipts in the year ended March 31 were about £7,000 above those of the preceding year. The company also enjoyed a windfall in the shape of £6,240 refunded by the municipality on account of taxes paid in previous years, and the board therefore increased the dividend from 5 per cent. to 6, placed £3,000 to depreciation fund, and £10,000 to start a reserve, and then carried the substantial balance of £6,955 forward. The balance-sheet shows a very satisfactory position, no less than £44,054 being invested, but an item of £8,209 on account of conversion of debentures should be written off as quickly as possible.

UNITED STATES BREWING COMPANY.—The profits of this concern have been well maintained, and in the year ended March 31, after allowing £21,250 for repairs and renewals, and £12,465 for depreciation, the net profit was £110,364. Administrative charges and debenture interest required £22,170, and after including £5,065 brought forward, the net balance was £88,194. Preference interest took £28,000, and the 10 per cent. dividend upon the ordinary shares a further £35,000, which allowed £10,000 to be placed to reserve, and £15,194 to be carried forward, or nearly £10,000 more than was brought in. The reserve will then amount to £130,000, and has been employed as capital in the business, with the result that the properties item stands at a less sum than in 1892. The directors carry forward the large balance this year in view of the doubling of the tax upon beer in order to meet the expenses of the war. This company has a far better record than the other American brewing concerns, but there is one thing that might receive attention. No statement is made of the amount allowed for bad debts, which is a very important matter in the American brewing business, and we note the debtors item in the last six years has risen from £136,881 to £219,540, while profits show only a little addition. Mortgages are certainly included in the item, so that the increase may be perfectly natural, but a distinct statement as to the amount set aside each year against bad debts would be an improvement.

NAHOR RAIN TEA COMPANY.—The poor results of 1897 only left a net profit of £1,095, which allowed payment of the preference interest and a dividend of 2½ per cent. on the ordinary shares, as against 10 per cent. in recent years. The balance-sheet is not strong, but this apparently does not matter, as the shareholders have agreed to sell the company for £85,000, as against a total capital of £40,419. They must be bold people who buy on this basis, but we wonder whether Nahor Rain shareholders will get cash or paper? Some of Mr. Hooley's exploits left shareholders poorer than before he plied his bellows.

THE HUDSON'S BAY COMPANY.—The report and balance-sheet of this company for the year ended May 31 last, which covers the trading in Canada to the end of 1896, can disappoint only those who discounted the future and bought shares some time ago, at prices a three years' gold boom might perhaps justify. As a matter of fact, the business done in the period covered by the report was not particularly flourishing. The general trade was affected adversely by the unfavourable condition of business throughout America, and profits were lower in consequence. Also the company had a smaller quantity of furs to deal with, and a still more diminished supply is looked for in the present year. Prices, however, were better, so that the loss in money was not serious. Land sales show an improvement, no doubt as a result of the gold excitement all over North-Western Canada. The company sold 37,923 acres of farm land at an average of $4 85 per acre, which was slightly cheaper than the price obtained the year before, but only 10,784 acres were sold then. Town lots, on the other hand, went off much less freely. The sum of the matter is that the accounts show a profit of £69,373, to which £21,999 has to be added, brought forward from last year. Out of this a dividend of 13s. per share, or 5 per cent., is paid for the year, leaving £26,373 to be carried forward.

AMAZON STEAM NAVIGATION COMPANY.—This undertaking is going from bad to worse. Profits for 1896 were £21,846, but for last year they came to only £9,423, yet £20,208 is to be scattered amongst the shareholders as dividend, the difference being made up of £787 less carried forward, and £10,000 taken from the reserve, although this fund is at the same time drawn upon for £12,969 to adjust the value of stores in Brazil upon a sterling basis. The reserve is consequently reduced to £52,000. The fall in the exchange not only caused a loss of over £9,000, but it was necessary to increase wages in order to avoid trouble. Another point was the very low state of the river, the company having at one time seven steamers aground, and these cost £5,000 to refloat. Moreover, some of the voyages included in the Federal contract have become unremunerative, owing to the exchange, and efforts are being made to get them modified. Altogether the company's position is not a happy one, though for all that we do not see any wisdom is paying dividends out of reserve, especially as nothing beyond a few special credits is written off for depreciation of the fleet, and £9,800 of investments in Consols have been sold out. The position is decidedly weaker than it used to be, and it is becoming a question whether the property, if realised, would allow the repayment of capital in full.

ASSAM RAILWAYS AND TRADING COMPANY.—We are afraid that we shall always be too muddle-headed to understand the working of this company. The railways form the chief asset of the company as they represent half the capital expenditure. So prosperous were these railways that the board had to spend £11,681 in substituting cast-iron sleepers for wooden ones, in order to reduce the net revenue and so obtain the Government subsidy of £7,083. After this curious operation had been carried through, the net revenue from the railways was only £24,561 as against £29,203 in 1896. The line, no doubt, was improved by having better sleepers, but the general revenue account was not. The company spent a large amount upon the petroleum works, and the directors now conclude that the profitable development of the oilfields can best be secured by a separate organisation. They have accordingly taken steps to form a new and independent company. Let us hope that the new company will be a bit stronger than the Makimo Tea Company, which owed its existence to the same initiative, for this wretched concern has paid very little in the way of dividend, and distinguished itself last year by paying nothing at all. Before they have got rid of one source of expenditure, the board entered manfully into another large outlay, having subscribed for 5,000 shares in the Brahmaputra-Sultanpur Branch Railway Company at a cost of about £33,000. Whether the investment will prove lucrative has yet to be seen, but we should imagine it was quite a venture. Coming back to the revenue account we find that profit on general trading was £2,754 less, the Rivers Steam Navigation shares yielded the same revenue, the £20,000 of tea shares produced nothing against £400 in the preceding year, and the investment in the Brahmaputra-Sultanpur Railway produced £86. The total revenue was therefore £58,652 against £66,415 in 1896. The improvement in exchange helped the company considerably, with the result that the net revenue of £51,319 was only £4,088 below that of 1896. This, however, was quite sufficient to compel the board, after paying prior charges, to reduce the distribution on the preference "A" shares to 4½ per cent. for the year as against 6 per cent. for 1896. As the nominal rate upon these shares is 8 per cent. the company drifts deeper and deeper into arrear, so that the total owing on this account is no less than £316,050.

APOLLINARIS AND JOHANNIS, LIMITED.—When we first read over the report of this company's board for the first year of its existence a certain wonder arose in the mind as to why the sheet should have been withheld so carefully from certain portions of the press. This feeling vanished as we looked closer. To all appearance the new company did first rate last year—its year closes on March 31—seeing that it was able to pay no less than 5 per cent. on its ordinary shares—all wind or aërated water. We candidly, never thought it would get so far towards a show of prosperity and great wealth. But a closer look starts the question. Did it really get thus far? Leave the smooth statement of the report—the delightful gloss of the Hunyadi Janos action, and such like—on one side, and look at such accounts as the board in its graciousness provides, and we find that the profit and loss account does not contain what must have been the heaviest part of the expenses. The dividend received from the old "Polly" company, and its German parent came to £173,057, and "johnnies" water yielded £8,808. Add £129 from interest, and we get a total of £181,993 against which only £4,442 is set down as outgoings for directors' and trustees' fees and office expenses. All the cost of advertising the new "Apenta" water was, it seems, paid out of a fund left to the company by the proprietors of the old Apollinaris Company, who must be fellows of an unprincely generosity. And what about the cost of advertising the Apollinaris and Johannis waters? Ah, that was borne by the respective companies. Was it? We really do not know. Things are mixed a bit, and we shall be able to speak more freely a year hence. At present, all we can be quite sure about is that the report and account of this double-springed company does not permit the public or its shareholders to know whether the profits exhibited are genuine or not. We should sell on the no-information were we among the proprietors. Not being so, we smile and wait developments.

IMPERIAL OTTOMAN BANK.—There were no little financial operations during 1897 to swell profits, and they therefore amounted to only £275,278, or £22,000 less than in 1896. The dividend is consequently again only 5 per cent., compared with 6 per cent. for 1895 and 8 per cent. for 1894, the African mining year. According to the figures of the balance-sheet the note circulation has increased £125,000, and bills payable £253,000, but the fixed deposits are down £850,000, and current accounts nearly £800,000. Stock of cash is considerably larger, while investments are down over a million, thus denoting preparedness when business grows brisker. At the annual meeting the chairman told the shareholders that for the future their bank must look for profits more to the commercial development of the country than to financial operations, so that for some time to come we shall not look for any increase in dividend.

NATIONAL BANK OF NEW ZEALAND.—This bank did very well last year, the gross profits reaching £75,015 compared with £69,374 for 1896, the available balance being £29,195 against £26,157. The directors again put £10,000 to reserve, raising it to £40,000, and in addition to the usual dividend of 5 per cent. they are able to pay a bonus of 1 per cent. and to still carry forward a slightly increased balance. The deposits are nearly £70,000 up at £2,208,900, while the increase in bills discounted and advances is £62,000 at £2,383,500.

UNION MORTGAGE AND AGENCY COMPANY OF AUSTRALIA.—The end seems to be within measurable distance. Profit for 1897 came to £35,627 which, added to £13,354 brought forward and £24,607 representing interest received, gives a total of £73,590. All of this except £8,752 goes in expenses and debenture interest, and this balance is carried forward, being £4,600 smaller than the amount brought in. The directors have transferred from reserve £100,000 to provide for ascertained losses and others likely to arise in respect of securities which it may be found expedient to realise. So the shrivelling process goes on. The reserve is now down to £75,000 against a share capital of £933,000 and a debenture debt of £987,000. As usual, Kemp, Ford, & Co. state in their certificate that no valuation has been made of the assets, which stand at the amount shown in the books. This is probably at 50 per cent. above their real value.

JOKAI (ASSAM) TEA COMPANY.—Relatively this company did exceedingly well last year, for the crop was 230,000 lb. larger than 1896, and actually higher than the estimate. The average sale price was only ·27d. per lb. less, while cost of production was actually lower, so that the net profit of 1·83d. per lb. compared with 1·92d. per lb. in 1896. The reduction in expenses was effected, however, by dint of transferring £5,340 from reserve to meet loss upon rice, which is a way of meeting trouble sideways. The net profit, including £1,558 brought forward, amounted to £29,333, but there was more preference capital to pay interest upon, and so the dividend upon the ordinary shares was reduced to 8 per cent., which enabled the amount forward to be increased to £4,300. We are glad to see this reduction in the distribution, for we have had the feeling for some time past that the company had been straining itself in order to maintain the 10 per cent. dividends, and this lower declaration will give its finances a little rest. Such a heavy loss on rice is not likely to occur again, and meantime the reserve benefited by £14,940 in premiums upon new shares, so that its total now stands at £54,600, and is wholly invested outside the business.

Diary of the War.

June 24.—The landing of General Shafter's military force began on Wednesday morning, the 22nd, and by night about 6,000 men were put on shore without a hitch. The coast line and the country for some miles inland were shelled by the fleet before the troops started to land. The Cuban insurgents co-operated with the Americans, who promptly occupied the country for about six miles round. The Spaniards offered no real opposition to the landing. They were obliged, according to the Madrid accounts, to retire to avoid being out-flanked.

June 25.—The American troops on the 24th proceeded by forced marches westwards, and by noon had reached and occupied Juragua, about ten to fifteen miles east of Santiago. The advance was covered by Cuban skirmishers, and the Spaniards, evidently in accordance with instructions, retired almost without firing a shot, though there was a slight skirmish between the flank of a Spanish retreating column and an American reconnoitring party. The Spanish force left Juragua so precipitately that they had no time to burn the town as they intended, but they had done some damage to the railway locomotives and rolling stock. The Spaniards seem to be concentrating at Sevilla, about six miles west of Juragua, and it is expected that they will make their first serious stand there against the American troops. An engagement is not anticipated for some days. The Americans have been somewhat fagged by their forced marches, and they will probably rest at Juragua for some time and have their supplies replenished there. General Lawton is in command of the American force and General Linares of the Spanish. The landing of American troops at Cuba has made a profound impression at Madrid, deepened by the receipt of a despatch from Admiral Cervera at Santiago, describing the situation as critical, and stating that he was preparing for the despatch of as many sailors and marines from his ships as could be spared to take part in the land fighting. It would thus seem that General Blanco has not been able to forward so many battalions as he promised to meet the Americans. It may be doubted, therefore, if the coming fight at Sevilla will be a very severe one. The Spaniards seem to be as badly prepared on land as at sea. The rumours as to the landing of German and other foreign marines at Manila are, as we guessed, now shown to be baseless. The Government at Washington have received satisfactory assurances that Germany had not contemplated any such serious step. The Spanish Minister of Marine has admitted that the destination of the Cadiz squadron is the Philippines. It is sailing thence so leisurely, however, that it seems impossible that it can arrive in time to be of any service. There was some very plain speaking in the Spanish Senate on Thursday. Senor Fernando Gonzales roundly declared in favour of peace, and referred to the chastisement which had fallen upon them as deserved. "For everything that happened now, the whole country, the people, the different parties, the Government, were responsible." The official defence was a bitter attack upon the conduct of the United States in treacherously trying to seize Cuba under the pretext of humanitarianism. It is the pitiful cry of senile pride and conscious impotence. By the way, it is hinted from Washington that, as soon as it is known that the Cadiz squadron has entered the Suez Canal on its voyage to Manila, a few fast cruisers will be detached from Admiral Sampson's fleet, and sent to bombard Spanish ports in the Mediterranean. If so, it would probably do more to hasten peace than anything that has yet happened. If the war is thus brought pretty nearly home to the Madrilese, they may be able to take a rather more practical view of the necessity for concluding peace.

June 26.—Without much rest at Juragua, some portion at least of the American forces have held on westward, and some skirmishing has been reported. The "first battle" indeed is mentioned, in which the Americans lost considerably, but there are no details.

June 27.—The fighting has been almost continuous from Wednesday the 22nd until Saturday the 25th. The Spaniards were steadily driven back upon Santiago; but they undoubtedly fought well, and inflicted severe losses on their enemies. The sharpest fight of all would seem to have been that between the Cubans and Spaniards. The result for long seemed doubtful, though in the end the Cubans prevailed and the Spaniards retired. Another sharp encounter was precipitated by the carelessness of the rough riders—or cowboys—who strode through a narrow part of the wood without throwing out skirmishers or taking the slightest thought of the possibility of an ambuscade. So they incontinently fell into one; and many were killed before they had fully realised the misfortune that had befallen them. Though surprised, however, they quickly rallied, and finally drove back the Spaniards. There was no "battle"—only skirmishing—at Sevilla. The Americans have pretty well closed round Santiago, but the attack upon it cannot take place until the artillery has been brought up, and that is a slow process in consequence of the nature of the roads. The Cadiz squadron has reached Port Said, where it is to "await orders." The British battleship *Illustrious* has been sent to Lisbon to watch over British interests in the Peninsula—a step which is taken to indicate a belief at the Admiralty that the United States may carry out the threat to send cruisers to bombard Spanish ports.

June 28.—The American forces are now within sight of Santiago; but they are resting, partly because they have been taught caution by their experience of the 24th, but mainly because they cannot advance to the assault of the town until the arrival of the artillery. The Spaniards have thrown out entrenchments far in front of Santiago. These seem to be very formidable, and in each case they are defended by barbed wire fencing, which must increase the dangers of an assault. Besides these, the Spaniards have erected block-houses on every hill or eminence commanding the roads to Santiago. Thirty-four of these have been counted. General Shafter is, therefore, very properly making his preparations very cautiously for the assault. It will be a more difficult business than the impulsive rough riders are willing to admit. The Cadiz squadron still at Port Said. The Egyptian Government refuse to supply it with coal, on the protest of the United States Consul. It is officially announced from Washington that a squadron is to be detached from Admiral Sampson's fleet, under the command of Commodore Watson, to bombard Spanish ports in the Mediterranean. These threats of carrying the war home to Spain seem to have made little impression in Madrid. They declare that such bombardment would be a barbarous outrage against international law. The Madrilese are silly folk.

June 29.—Preparations for the assault on Santiago continue, but the date of attack has, it is rumoured, been postponed for a week. A careful examination of the defensive works has convinced General Shafter that the work will be severe, and it is probable he will wait for reinforcements of troops as well perhaps as of artillery. The Americans have advanced to within three miles of Santiago, and the city's water supply is said to have been cut off. Two new blockades have been proclaimed. The first includes all ports on the south coast of Cuba from Cape Frances to Cape Cruz; the second closes San Juan. The Governor-General of the Philippines declares the situation at Manila to be as "grave as ever." Aguinaldo had asked him to surrender to avoid further loss of life, but he treated the demand with contempt. Some complaint is made that the presence of German warships has prevented the surrender of Manila, which, but for the moral support thus afforded, would have submitted to Admiral Dewey long ere this. The rumour of a possible landing of German marines is renewed, but it is not confirmed. Admiral Camara and his Cadiz squadron seem to have settled down at Port Said, at least for a few days. The ships have not been allowed to take in any coal yet.

June 30.—Preparations for a general advance on Santiago continue, but General Shafter is determined not to hurry matters. He has reported to General Miles that the town might be taken in forty-eight hours, but it would involve considerable loss. The Spanish defences are formidable. General Merritt has sailed from San Francisco to take command of the American military forces in the Philippines. He is to issue a manifesto announcing that he will, as representative of the United States, establish a provisional Government, and that his authority must be respected. Americans are viewing German action at Manila with considerable suspicion. Admiral Camara has entered the Suez Canal with his big warships, but the torpedo boat destroyers he is said to have left behind, as if confessing that his voyage to the Philippines was a mere farce. The Spaniards resent the American threat to bombard Spanish ports in the Mediterranean, and are said to have become more warlike than ever.

TRADE AND PRODUCE.

The Workmen's Compensation Act comes into force to-day; and not a merchant, manufacturer, or trader but who has for months been discussing the probable effect it will have on trade. Most of them have taken rather a serious view of the Act; and coalowners gravely considered whether it might not be necessary to abolish discounts in order to recoup them to some extent for the cost of the measure. But a decision on this question seems to have been postponed for the present. Most of the larger firms have combined in schemes of mutual insurance. Smaller firms have had to deal with insurance companies, which for some time have been showing a disposition to lower premiums for policies of this nature. There will probably be less heard of the Act now for some time. It will no doubt get a fair trial, but if it is found to be as costly as many anticipate, an agitation will certainly arise for some modification of its provisions.

As a rule trade has been fairly good during the past week, with an improving tendency, and some confidence in the outlook, but no exceptional activity. In some branches complaint is heard that new orders are not coming in sufficiently freely to make up for the old being sent out. Wheat is still, for the fifth week, on the down grade. The same story is told at every English market, at the various Continental centres, and in America, where the "corner" manipulators have themselves been "cornered." There has been no rise, and no possibility of a rise. The manipulators have now to take what they can get; and with considerable stocks in hand, and the prospect of the coming crop being about a hundred million bushels better than last year's, the chance of securing enhanced prices has utterly disappeared. In the English markets there has been very little doing even at the reduced figures. Sellers are generally anxious to do business, but buyers as persistently hold aloof. Prices have not yet touched bottom. The average for last week is stated at 40s. 8d. Last year for the same week the average was 27s.; in 1896 it was 24s. 10d.; in 1895, 26s. 1d.; and in 1894, 24s. 1d. How far it may yet fall it would be risky to prophesy. June has not been quite so favourable for the English crops as was hoped; but the crop reports continue at least fairly good. The amount of wheat sown this year is, we believe, considerably larger than last year. The New York market was reported firm on Wednesday, with a slight rise, but it is not at all likely to be maintained.

The fourth series of colonial wool sales opened on Tuesday. The available total—we take the figures from Messrs. Jacomb, Son, & Co.'s circular—was 265,000 bales as compared with 282,000 bales for the corresponding series last year. The biddings were animated, not to say keen, but mainly for best merinos and medium and fine cross-breds, which showed an improvement of nearly 5 per cent. In the coarser grades of cross-breds there was a downward tendency. South African wools—not very plentiful—sold without change. Huddersfield reports a sudden dropping off of the summer trade, the deficit being chiefly in the London and Irish trading. Leeds makes a similar remark. We can scarcely wonder at London purchases being checked, for London can hardly be said to have had a summer trade this year. If the warmth of the last day or two continues, it will take Metropolitan dealers all their time to clear out such stocks as they have on hand. This must have been rather an anxious season for most of them. Reports from manufacturing centres, however, are cheerful in tone, and hold out good prospects. There has been a brisk trade with Canada, an improving business with South America, though comparatively little with Australia. Cotton also is looking up, both here and in America, and Manchester speaks more hopefully of the future. If Calcutta would but improve there would be a prompt access of activity. As it is, prices are well maintained. The linen business continues very quiet without change in rates.

Copper is still subject to considerable fluctuations, and on Tuesday business was done so low as £49 6s. 3d. cash, £49 8s. 9d. for early July, and £49 15s. and 12s. 6d. three months. Prices rose a little at the afternoon session, and on Wednesday sales were effected for cash at £49 11s. 3d., and £49 13s. 9d. up to £50 for July prompts, and £49 16s. 3d. to £50 3s. 9d. for three months. American quotations continue somewhat low, and it is doubtful if we can yet look for that steady upward turn which has been expected for weeks, and which seems so amply justified by visible supplies.

From the iron trade centres reports are, on the whole, satisfactory. Work is generally plentiful, though in Sheffield some complaints are heard that orders are not coming in so rapidly as they did a few months ago; but the tone as a rule is firm, and the cost of raw material is sending prices up in some quarters. Glasgow locomotive builders have secured some important orders for Indian railways, amounting to no fewer than 137 engines. The shops were already busy before these orders arrived, and they are now assured of continuous steady work for months to come. The steel-workers' year, now closing, has been the best ever experienced. Prices have been good throughout, and promise to be better in the year that is approaching. The shipbuilding yards are yet fully employed, and will be so for some time, but new orders have recently become somewhat scarcer. At Wolverhampton and Newcastle equally favourable reports are heard. Prices of raw and manufactured iron are both strong.

No practical change in the coal market, but the probability of a settlement of the Welsh dispute seems rather more hopeful—not so much because Mr. Ritchie has agreed to appoint a conciliator as because the colliers themselves are taking action to have a ballot as to whether the sliding scale as a wage regulator shall be renewed or not. It is believed that the ballot, if taken, will show an overwhelming majority in favour of a sliding scale and a 5 per cent. advance in the wage rate. A stoppage of the Yorkshire pits is now threatened in consequence of strikes among the pit lads and pony drivers, who are asking for a 10 per cent. advance; already 5,000 men are idle.

Answers to Correspondents.

Questions about public securities, and on all points in company law, as well as on the position of life insurance offices and their promises, will be answered week by week, in the REVIEW, on the following terms and conditions:—

A fee of FIVE shillings must be remitted for each question put, provided they are questions about separate securities. Should a private letter be required, then an extra fee of FIVE shillings must be sent to cover the cost of such letter, the fee then being TEN shillings for one query only, and FIVE shillings for every subsequent one in the same letter. While making this concession the EDITOR will feel obliged if private replies are as much as possible dispensed with. It is wholly impossible to answer letters sent merely "with a stamped envelope enclosed for reply."

Correspondents will further greatly oblige by so framing their questions as to obviate the necessity to name securities in the replies. They should *number* the questions, keeping a copy for reference, thus:—"(1) Please inform me about the present position of the Rowenzori Development Co. (2) Is a dividend likely to be paid soon on the capital stock of the Congo-Sudan Railway?

Answers to be given to all such questions by simply quoting the numbers 1, 2, 3, and so on. The EDITOR has a rooted objection to such forms of reply as—"I think your Timbuctoo Consols will go up," or "Sell your Slowcoach and Draggem Bonds," because this kind of thing is open to all sorts of abuses. By the plan suggested, and by using a fancy name to be replied to, each query can be kept absolutely private to the inquirer, and no scope whatever be given to market manipulations. Avoid, as names to be replied to, common words, like "investor," "inquirer," and so on, as also "bear" or "bull." Detached syllables of the inquirer's name, or initials reversed, will frequently do as well as anything, so long as the answer can be identified by the inquirer.

The EDITOR further respectfully requests that merely speculative questions should as far as possible be avoided. He by no means sets himself up as a market prophet, and can only undertake to provide the latest information regarding the securities asked about. This he will do faithfully and without bias.

Replies cannot be guaranteed in the same week if the letters demanding them reach the office of the INVESTORS' REVIEW, Norfolk House, Norfolk-street, W.C., later than the first post on Wednesday mornings.

LUSK.—Not at the present price. Pounds lower they may still be a good investment, because the threatened opposition cannot come to much for years, and may never do so. Just now buying cannot be recommended in that particular share.

SAMOHT.—The shares you name are very good, but dear at the price. You must remember that the dividends on the ordinary shares have fluctuated sharply, and once, lately, disappeared altogether. That being so, a preference share at 45 per cent. premium is not tempting, and certainly could not be guaranteed to keep its price for the next ten years. Nothing on earth could, though.

What is his Majesty the King of the Belgians really aiming at? He is credited, though not on specially high authority, with having a mission at Peking trying to obtain a supply of Chinese coolie labourers for the Congo State. We thought labourers were plentiful on the Congo. In return for coolies, however, the King offers to send 10,000 negroes from the Congo country, who, it is urged, could be formed into a valuable fighting force under Belgian officers. Is Belgium anxious to undertake the task of reorganising the Chinese army?

KINGDOM OF THE NETHERLANDS.

ISSUE OF 57,815,000 FLORINS THREE PER CENT. DUTCH GOVERNMENT LOAN,
Authorised by the Law of June 9th, 1898.

MESSRS. SPEYER BROTHERS
AND
THE UNION BANK OF LONDON, LIMITED,

are authorised by His Excellency the Dutch Minister of Finance to receive Subscriptions for the above Loan, bearing Interest from September 1st, 1898.

The price of issue in London is 97 per cent., equal to £97 per Fl. 1,200 (£100 nominal), payable as follows:

£5 per Fl. 1,200 on Application.
20 ,, ,, ,, ,, Allotment.
35 ,, ,, ,, ,, August 29th, 1898.
37 ,, ,, ,, ,, October 3rd, 1898.

£97 per Fl. 1,200 (£100 nominal).

Payment in full may be made on Allotment or on August 29th, under discount at the rate of 3 per cent. per annum. In default of payment of any instalment, the amount previously paid will be subject to forfeiture.

Scrip Certificates "to bearer" will be issued in exchange for the Letter of Allotment. These Certificates, when fully paid, will be exchanged as soon as possible after September 1st against definitive Bonds.

The bonds will be "to bearer" in amounts of Fl. 1,000, Fl. 500, and Fl. 100 each, with half-yearly Coupons due March 1st and September 1st, payable in Amsterdam, and also at the Union Bank of London, Limited, at the exchange of the day. The Bonds may be exchanged in Amsterdam at any time for a like amount of 3 per Cent. Inscribed Government Stock.

The Law of June 9th, 1898, declares that a sum equal to the present Loan shall be provided for by an annual accumulative sinking fund of 1 per cent., commencing in 1899, and that this Fund shall from time to time be applied either by purchases or by drawings at par of any part of the then outstanding 3 per Cent. Dutch Loan. The Government reserves to itself the right to increase the Sinking Fund at any time.

The same law provides that the interest on Bonds drawn ceases from the day they are payable, and such drawn Bonds, if not presented for payment within ten years from their due date, will be forfeited.

These Bonds are similar in every respect to those now officially quoted in London, Amsterdam, Paris, and Frankfort-on-Maine.

The Subscription will be opened simultaneously in Amsterdam and Brussels.

The Subscription in London will be opened on Tuesday, July 5th, 1898, and close at or before 4 o'clock on the same day.

Applications for the Bonds must be made on the annexed form, either to Messrs. Speyer Brothers, 7, Lothbury, London, E.C., or to The Union Bank of London, Limited, 2, Princes Street, London, E.C.

The allotment of the Loan will be made as early as possible after the subscription is closed.

A translation of the Law of June 9th, 1898, may be inspected at the office of Messrs. Freshfields & Williams, 31, Old Jewry, E.C.

London, E.C., June 30th, 1898.

KINGDOM OF THE NETHERLANDS.

ISSUE OF 57,815,000 FLORINS THREE PER CENT. DUTCH GOVERNMENT LOAN.

To Messrs. Speyer Brothers and The Union Bank of London, Limited, London.

............request that you will allot........ ......Fl.......... .. ..in the above Loan, on which............enclose the required deposit of £5 per Fl. 1,200, viz., £..................., in accordance with the Prospectus issued by you, dated June 30th, 1898, and......... engage to accept the said Bonds, or any smaller amount you may allot........., and to make the payments thereon in accordance with the Prospectus.

Signature ....
Name in full ....
Address in full..
....
Date.. 1898.

THE LONDON AND MIDLAND BANK, LIMITED.

NOTICE IS HEREBY GIVEN that the Rate of Interest allowed on Deposits at seven days' call at the Head Office and London Branches, will be One per cent. until further notice.

E. H. HOLDEN, General Manager.

52, Cornhill, E.C., June 30th, 1898.

MARTIN'S BANK, LIMITED.

NOTICE IS HEREBY GIVEN that the Rate of Interest on Deposits with this Bank, subject to seven days' notice, will be One per cent. per annum from this date until further notice.

LUKE HANSARD, Manager.

68, Lombard Street, E.C., June 30th, 1898.

THE CITY BANK, LIMITED.

NOTICE IS HEREBY GIVEN that the present Rate of Interest on Deposits with this Bank, subject to seven days' notice, is One per cent. per annum.

DAVID G. H. POLLOCK, } Joint General
LEWIS S. M. MUNRO, } Managers.

Threadneedle Street, June 30th, 1898.

LONDON AND SOUTH WESTERN BANK, LIMITED.

NOTICE IS HEREBY GIVEN that the Rate of Interest allowed at the Head office and Metropolitan branches of this Bank on Deposits repayable at seven days' notice, is this day reduced to One per cent. per annum.

JOHN WILLIAMS, } Joint General
ROBERT WOODHAMS, } Managers.

Head Office, 168, 169, and 170, Fenchurch Street, E.C.,
June 30th, 1898.

THE MANCHESTER & LIVERPOOL DISTRICT BANKING COMPANY, LIMITED (LONDON OFFICE).

NOTICE IS HEREBY GIVEN that the Rate of Interest allowed on Deposit Accounts at this Office will be One per cent. until further notice.

THOS. FERGUSSON, Manager.

75, Cornhill, E.C., June 30th, 1898.

THE LONDON JOINT STOCK BANK, LIMITED.

NOTICE IS HEREBY GIVEN that the Rate of Interest allowed at the Head Office and Branches of this Bank on Deposits, subject to seven days' notice of withdrawal, is this day reduced to One per cent. per annum.

W. F. NARRAWAY, General Manager.

3, Princes Street, Mansion House, June 30th, 1898.

To Correspondents.

The Editor cannot undertake to return rejected communications.

Letters from correspondents must, in every case, be authenticated by the name and address of the writer.

Telegraphic Address: "Unveiling, London."

The Investors' Review.

The Week's Money Market.

BANK RATE 2½ PER CENT.

After having been at about ½ per cent. for the greater part of the week, the rate for short loans has moved up to 1 to 2 per cent. The firmness, of course, is simply due to the end of the half-year when the London banks have to make up their balances all on one day, instead of taking various dates over a period of ten days, as is done at the end of each intermediate month in the half-year, on the "patent safety" Lidderdale plan. The demand for short loans was so strong that a few borrowers went to the Bank of England and paid 3 or 2½ per cent. for advances just into July. Probably the sum thus borrowed did not exceed the amount withdrawn by the India Council, which has been taking its balances off the market for the last few days. The discount houses have decided not to follow the Bank, as their allowances for deposits were already down to 1 to 1¼ per cent. but the joint banks have reduced their interest upon deposits by ½ per cent. to 1, and now feel more comfortable. It is not nice at any time in business to give 150 per cent. more than one can trust to receive.

The reduction in the Bank rate had little effect, discount rates having steadily declined throughout the week until the rate for three months remitted paper is now no better than 1⅛ per cent. as compared with 1¼ to 1⅜ per cent. a week ago. It is evident now that the July dividends will be anticipated to only a very slight extent by borrowings at the Bank, and consequently the market must look to having two to four millions more cash than usual at its disposal during the dead summer months. A further reduction in the Bank rate must result, and renewed weakness in outside rates may ensue, but consideration for the chances of the autumn will prevent the latter movement being carried to an extremity. The gold demand appears to be just strong enough to prevent gold from going to the Bank, both India and Russia competing at about 77s. 10d. per ounce—the figure at which the outside market must bid in order to take the metal from the Bank. An Indian sterling loan is likely to be introduced soon, and the market is wondering whether it will take the form of a 2½ per cent. or 3 per cent. stock. It is argued that a 3 per cent. issue at about 103 would be preferable to inviting tenders for a 2½ per cent. one at—at what? 90? 88? Assuredly not more than 90 could be obtained for the latter, as the existing 2½ per cents. enjoy no market favour and flop in price at a wink, while a minimum of 103 for a 3 per cent. loan might perhaps bring applications above the figure. We know so little of India that we love and trust it immensely.

A decrease of £888,000 is displayed by the Reserve of the Banking Department in this week's return, and the total is therefore now down to £27,071,000. Why, then, did the Bank rate go down? Because this decrease is only an incident by the way, because the market is flush of funds, £809,000 having been added within the week to the "Other" deposits, making them £45,405,000, and because there is no gold demand on foreign account strong enough to pull large amounts out of the Bank's stock. The truth of the matter also is that the Government has been writing cheques so fast that its balances have run down £1,975,000 within the week, and now amount to only £10,080,000. It is swamping the market, in fact, and that market has in consequence been able to pay £281,000 off "Other" securities while still augmenting its till money. In these circumstances the increase of £933,000 in the note circulation counts for nothing any more than the fall in the proportion of reserve to liabilities from 49$\frac{1}{4}$ per cent. to 48$\frac{5}{8}$ per cent. The absence of any end-of-the-half-year borrowings at the Bank was itself enough to convince the directors that it was quite useless to keep their nominal discount rate at 3 per cent. They might as well have gone to 2 per cent. when they were about it, but conservatism is a good thing in usury.

THURSDAY NIGHT.—Since the above story of the week was written we learn that the Bank had to be applied to yesterday afternoon for considerable sums of money in the aggregate to help the market over the end-of-the-half-year balance-sheet show. The loans were granted till Monday for the most part and at 2$\frac{1}{2}$ per cent. In the open market the same rate was bid for money over-night, but the "squeege" will be at an end to-day.

SILVER.

Buying on account of Spain has continued at intervals throughout the week, and the price of bars for immediate delivery has improved to 27$\frac{1}{8}$d. per ounce. There has also been a moderate amount of purchasing by "bears," while India has been buying for a few weeks ahead. A further decline of 1 per cent. to 8 is notified by both the Banks of Bombay and Bengal, as a result of the improvement in their cash balances this week. The relaxation in the pressure for money—the result rather of the wet season than of any improvement in the position—has caused the exchange to fall to 1s. 3$\frac{31}{32}$d., but the ease is not expected to last for any length of time.

Since the commencement of the financial year on April 1 the India Council has sold Rs.8,22,63·110, realising £5,464,961. As the Budget estimated for £16,000,000 to be drawn in the year, this means that, at 1s. 4d. per rupee, about 40$\frac{1}{2}$ lacs must, in future, be sold per week in order to obtain the amount.

BANK OF ENGLAND.

AN ACCOUNT pursuant to the Act 7 and 8 Vict., cap. 32, for the Week ending on Wednesday, June 29, 1898.

ISSUE DEPARTMENT.

	£		£
Notes Issued	52,958,640	Government Debt	11,015,100
		Other Securities	5,784,900
		Gold Coin and Bullion	36,158,640
		Silver Bullion	—
	£52,958,640		£52,958,640

BANKING DEPARTMENT.

	£		£
Proprietors' Capital	14,553,000	Government Securities	13,497,403
Rest	3,200,022	Other Securities	32,782,260
Public Deposits (including Exchequer, Savings Banks, Commissioners of National Debt, and Dividend Accounts)	10,080,291	Notes	24,695,310
Other Deposits	45,404,650	Gold and Silver Coin	2,375,967
Seven Day and other Bills	112,977		
	£73,350,940		£73,350,940

Dated June 30, 1898.

H. G. BOWEN, *Chief Cashier.*

In the following table will be found the movements compared with the previous week, and also the totals for that week and the corresponding return last year:—

Banking Department.

Last Year. June 30.		June 22, 1898.	June 29, 1898.	Increase.	Decrease.
£	Liabilities.	£	£	£	£
3,097,625	Rest	3,185,998	3,200,022	14,024	—
11,573,624	Pub. Deposits	12,054,927	10,080,291	—	1,974,676
45,143,166	Other do.	44,595,911	45,404,650	808,739	—
149,747	7 Day Bills	108,934	112,977	4,043	—
	Assets.			Decrease.	Increase.
13,948,356	Gov. Securities	13,476,051	13,497,403	—	21,352
35,373,533	Other do.	33,063,346	32,782,260	281,086	—
25,195,273	Total Reserve	27,959,413	27,071,277	888,136	—
				1,996,028	1,996,028
				Increase.	Decrease.
£		£	£	£	£
28,485,230	Note Circulation	27,330,720	28,263,330	932,610	—
44$\frac{5}{8}$ p.c.	Proportion	49$\frac{1}{4}$ p.c.	48$\frac{5}{8}$ p.c.	—	—
2 ,,	Bank Rate	3 ,,	2$\frac{1}{2}$,,	—	—

Foreign Bullion movement for week £67,000 in.

LONDON BANKERS' CLEARING.

Month of	1898.	1897.	Increase.	Decrease.
	£	£	£	£
January	673,281,000	576,558,000	96,723,000	—
February	648,601,000	597,652,000	50,949,000	—
March	799,520,000	729,970,000	69,550,000	—
April	597,410,000	532,508,000	64,902,000	—
Week ending				
May 4	174,057,000	138,987,000	35,070,000	—
,, 11	160,526,000	128,252,000	32,274,000	—
,, 18	171,078,000	152,987,000	18,091,000	—
25	131,037,000	116,372,000	14,665,000	—
June 1	155,655,000	166,981,000	—	11,326,000
,, 8	139,048,000	111,213,000	27,835,000	—
,, 15	164,537,000	148,402,000	16,135,000	—
,, 22	124,723,000	102,454,000	22,269,000	—
,, 29	159,861,000	165,902,000	—	6,041,000
Total to date	4,010,266,000	3,601,143,000	409,123,000	—

BANK AND DISCOUNT RATES ABROAD.

	Bank Rate.	Altered.	Open Market.
Paris	2	March 14, 1895	1$\frac{3}{4}$
Berlin	4	April 9, 1898	3$\frac{1}{4}$
Hamburg	4	April 9, 1898	3$\frac{1}{4}$
Frankfort	4	April 9, 1898	3$\frac{3}{8}$
Amsterdam	3	April 13, 1897	2$\frac{1}{2}$
Brussels	3	April 28, 1896	2$\frac{1}{2}$
Vienna	4	January 22, 1896	4
Rome	5	August 27, 1895	3
St. Petersburg	5$\frac{1}{2}$	January 23, 1898	5
Madrid	5	June 17, 1896	5
Lisbon	6	January 25, 1891	6
Stockholm	5	May 18, 1898	4$\frac{1}{2}$
Copenhagen	4$\frac{1}{2}$	June 2, 1898	4$\frac{1}{2}$
Calcutta	8	June 30, 1898	—
Bombay	8	June 30, 1898	—
New York call money	1 to 1$\frac{1}{2}$	—	—

NEW YORK ASSOCIATED BANKS (dollar at 4s.).

	June 25, 1898.	June 18, 1898.	June 11, 1898.	June 26, 1897.
	£	£	£	£
Specie	36,822,000	36,582,000	35,836,000	18,080,000
Legal tenders	12,498,000	11,822,000	11,142,000	21,622,000
Loans and discounts	123,320,000	122,068,000	122,152,000	104,336,000
Circulation	2,933,200	2,937,400	2,943,800	2,774,000
Net deposits	147,510,000	146,196,000	144,842,000	119,418,000

Legal reserve is 25 per cent. of net deposits; therefore the total reserve (specie and legal tenders) exceeds this sum by £12,442,500, against an excess last week of £11,855,000.

BANK OF SPAIN (25 pesetas to the £).

	June 25, 1898.	June 18, 1898.	June 11, 1898.	June 26, 1897.
	£	£	£	£
Gold	9,833,560	9,833,560	9,833,520	8,919,320
Silver	4,291,400	4,313,640	4,228,040	10,889,600
Bills discounted	33,724,120	33,820,800	31,701,640	9,785,600
Advances and loans	3,613,040	3,692,360	3,878,720	9,382,400
Notes in circulation	52,875,440	52,584,880	2,736,360	44,114,600
Treasury advances, coupon account	28,880	26,840	879,960	218,960
Treasury balances	1,939,280	1,717,720	1,373,760	—

NATIONAL BANK OF BELGIUM (25 francs to the £).

	June 23, 1898.	June 16, 1898.	June 9, 1898.	June 24, 1897.
	£	£	£	£
Coin and bullion	4,369,524	4,399,120	4,355,120	4,090,000
Other securities	16,283,120	15,790,480	15,895,760	16,165,000
Note circulation	18,964,480	19,054,400	19,084,440	18,418,000
Deposits	3,034,960	2,455,000	2,546,640	3,147,000

IMPERIAL BANK OF GERMANY (20 marks to the £).

	June 23, 1898.	June 15, 1898.	June 7, 1898.	June 23, 1897.
	£	£	£	£
Cash in hand	44,774,400	44,528,150	43,594,650	47,038,000
Bills discounted	34,508,100	32,565,250	33,530,850	*36,396,000
Advances on stocks	4,461,650	4,528,800	4,458,300	—
Note circulation	53,498,200	52,002,450	52,583,350	52,400,000
Public deposits	26,824,550	26,098,150	25,087,450	27,812,000

* Includes advances.

AUSTRIAN-HUNGARIAN BANK (1s. 8d. to the florin).

	June 23, 1898.	June 15, 1898.	June 7, 1898.	June 23, 1897.
	£	£	£	£
Gold reserve	29,124,000	29,057,585	29,028,084	20,013,000
Silver reserve	10,526,666	10,515,750	10,484,250	10,557,000
Foreign bills	230,333	205,083	204,410	—
Advances	1,862,000	1,850,666	1,859,500	—
Note circulation	51,232,250	51,020,300	51,168,900	40,713,000
Bills discounted	12,722,000	12,759,183	11,211,181	*10,143,000

* Includes advances.

BANK OF FRANCE (25 francs to the £).

	June 30, 1898.	June 23, 1898.	June 16, 1898.	July 1, 1897.
	£	£	£	£
Gold in hand	75,079,600	75,236,600	75,011,960	80,193,000
Silver in hand	49,528,600	49,497,680	49,390,640	49,290,000
Bills discounted	35,083,640	26,252,520	26,487,880	*43,369,000
Advances	15,840,240	15,464,000	15,431,160	—
Note circulation	148,128,800	143,230,640	145,191,760	146,839,000
Public deposits	11,513,320	9,706,920	8,738,720	8,975,000
Private deposits	18,197,720	19,840,000	18,068,800	21,771,000

Proportion between bullion and circulation 84½ per cent. against 87 per cent. a week ago.

* Includes advances.

FOREIGN RATES OF EXCHANGE ON LONDON.

Place.	Usance.	Last week's.	Latest.	Place.	Usance.	Last week's.	Latest.
Paris	chqs.	25·26	25·24	Italy	sight	27·10	27·08
Brussels	chqs.	25·27	25·25½	Do. gold prem.	..	107·15	107·15
Amsterdam	short	12·04¾	12·05	Constantinople	3 mths	109·20	109·30
Berlin	short	20·39½	20·39½	B. Ayres gd. pm.	..	170·80	178·30
Do.	3 mths	20·39	20·38½	Rio de Janeiro	90 dys	7 5/16d.	7 7/16d.
Hamburg	3 mths	20·30½	20·31½	Valparaiso	90 dys	17d.	17d.
Frankfort	short	20·37	20·38	Calcutta	T. T.	1/3 31/32	1/3 31/32
Vienna	short	11·99½	12·00½	Bombay	T. T.	1/3 31/32	1/3 15/16
St. Petersburg	3 mths	93·95	93·95	Hong Kong	T. T.	1/11	1/11
New York	60 dys	4·84	4·84½	Shanghai	T. T.	2/0⅞	2/7
Lisbon	sight	29½d.	29 5/16d.	Singapore	T. T.	1/10 11/16	1/10⅝
Madrid	sight	47·60	45·45				

LONDON COURSE OF EXCHANGE.

Place.	Usance.	June 21.	June 23.	June 28.	June 30.
Amsterdam and Rotterdam	short	12·1½	12·1½	12·1½	12·1½
Do. do.	3 months	12·3½	12·3½	12·3½	12·3½
Antwerp and Brussels	3 months	25·43¾	25·43¾	25·42½	25·42½
Hamburg	3 months	20·62	20·61	20·60	20·60
Berlin and German B. Places	3 months	20·62	20·61	20·61	20·60
Paris	cheques	25·28¾	25·27½	25·27½	25·25½
Do.	3 months	25·42½	25·41¼	25·41¼	25·40
Marseilles	3 months	25·43¾	25·41	25·41¼	25·40
Switzerland	3 months	25·57½	25·57½	25·57½	25·57½
Austria	3 months	12·13¾	12·15	12·15	12·15
St. Petersburg	3 months	25	25	25	25 1/16
Moscow	3 months	24 15/16	24 15/16	24 15/16	25
Italian Bank Places	3 months	27·37½	27·37½	27·37½	27·37½
New York	60 days	48⅝	48⅝	48⅝	48⅝
Madrid and Spanish B. P.	3 months	25	24¾	25	25½
Lisbon	3 months	28¾	29	29	29⅛
Oporto	3 months	28⅞	29	29	29⅛
Copenhagen	3 months	18·35	18·35	18·34	18·34
Christiania	3 months	18·35	18·35	18·35	18·35
Stockholm	3 months	18·35	18·35	18·35	18·35

OPEN MARKET DISCOUNT.

	Per cent.
Thirty and sixty day remitted bills	1 1/16
Three months ,,	1⅛
Four months ,,	1¼
Six months ,,	1½
Three months fine inland bills	1½—1¾
Four months ,,	1¾—2
Six months ,,	2—2¼

BANK AND DEPOSIT RATES.

	Per cent.
Bank of England minimum discount rate	2½
,, ,, short loan rates	2⅛
Banker's rate on deposits	1
Bill brokers' deposit rate (call)	1
,, 7 and 14 days' notice	1¼
Current rates for 7 day loans	¾–1
,, ,, for call loans	⅝

Stock Market Notes and Comments.

We have got the settlement of a long account over. It has been a tiny affair, for nobody who could help it did any business during its progress. That is often the way with nineteen-day accounts, either that or people take a fit of madness in them and pile up liabilities which end in a mess. Now that the account is behind the market, and the half-year as well, we expect to see more activity, in some of the departments at all events. There will be large sums of dividend money seeking investment, and throughout July this alone should give a good deal more work to many brokers and jobbers. Speculation will also wake up slightly, is showing signs of doing so now under the forcing influence of extremely cheap money. No great passion or fancy of the public in any one direction appears likely to be developed, but there will be little gambles here and there.

We have still, for example, the Chatham gamble with us, and it is fortified by an "official" statement that the "principles" of a working agreement between the Chatham and South-Eastern Companies have been agreed upon. In virtue of this preliminary, the former company alone is straight away going to save £100,000 a year in working expenses. Fiddle-de-dee! The betrothal may end in a wedding—though we have seen the two as near it before and cry off—and still such saving cannot be, if the Chatham line is to be brought into efficiency. As we have never ceased to insist, it is the most disgraceful line in the three kingdoms of any size or pretension to respectability. If money is saved on train mileage by the cessation of useless competition, more than all the Chatham Company's share of the saving will be required to put the line in order and to pay the staff properly. At present it is a staff kept in a position of semi-starvation. Never a man of it gets hurt or dies but what the hat is sent round amongst passengers in order to raise a little money for his widow and family. The company cannot afford superannuation funds, is as near bankruptcy as any line could be short of actually going over the abyss. It carries millions of dead capital and will require a million, at least, to put it in proper physical condition. All this is probably well enough known to the gamblers themselves, but they have run up Chatham second preference to 109½, and may carry the ordinary stock pounds higher than it is now, and see money in the spin. Sensible people will let them have the game to themselves. In several other directions the price of Home railway securities are getting what the market would call "topish." "Heavy" stocks, especially, seem to us rather dear. Great Western has not suffered much in price as yet by the disorganisation of labour in South Wales, nor have Great Northern, Midland, or North Western stocks in any degree felt the influence of the approaching competition of the new Sheffield line into London. That will not be in full swing for some months yet, but it is near enough to be taken into account in any speculation dealing with these securities. They are too dear for investment, all of them, and will be subjected to a more or less severe depression when money becomes dear again. Should they go up now through speculation engendered by cheap money, many possessors ought to sell, sure of being able to buy back again on a favourable market long before 1898 has run its course.

As regards American railroad shares the same counsel seems to be apposite; not but that the gamble in them may carry prices higher than they are now, but they are high enough to make purchases by the unsophisticated public full of risk. The great crop "boom" has been worked for all it is worth in Milwaukee, Great Northern, Northern Pacific, Canadian Pacific, and we may say also in Grand Trunk securities. Moreover, should the volume of traffic fall short of the sanguine estimates, we may be sure rate cutting next autumn and winter will spread rather than diminish. That is a disease certain to remain always with us as long as those railroads are controlled by irresponsible despots, very few of whom appear to have been educated in the principles of common honesty. Some among them of the straighter class have already been warning speculators not to expect too much this coming autumn, and we on this side, at least, will be wise not to neglect these warnings, but to maintain a sceptical mind in regard to the prophecies of great dividends to come on discredited securities. Bonds are, perhaps, in a different category, but speaking in a general way we are inclined to say that most of the speculative class of bonds are also already dear enough from the investor's point of view. It is rarely that such bonds are worth buying for investment above par.

The market for foreign Government stocks has dwindled away almost to vanishing point, and a great blow has been given to it by the latest move of the Spanish Government in the direction of complete default. Spanish Governments may be trusted always to do the wrong thing in a business affair, and in the present instance the narrowness of view characteristic of all Spanish officials has been strikingly illustrated in the decree with reference to the payment, if any, of future coupons on the public debt. Money seems to have been borrowed somewhere to meet this July coupon in gold, both in Spain and abroad, but for the future bonds held in Spain are to get their coupons paid in paper, and only those held abroad will be paid in gold. As we pointed out last week this kills the international market for Spanish bonds, and it is perhaps just as well; but that was not the aim of the Ministry at Madrid. What it was striking at was the Spanish seller. Apparently weeks before anything was publicly known the intention of the Government to partial default leaked out and holders of Spanish bonds in Spain made all haste to sell, "tipping the wink" to their friends here to buy to make their market better. "We must stop this," cried the Ministers, "else we shall have to pay all the coupons in gold in future." And so they launched the decree commented on last week, ordering all bonds in the hands of foreign owners to be sent in for registration by June 30. This forced the price up a pound or two on the London and Paris markets, because that date effectually prevented the Bourse of Barcelona, in particular, from being able to deliver within the time the bonds it had sold abroad. Protests were made at Madrid as to the loss this cunning stroke would cause and the bat-eyed Ministry, whose days are numbered—and the numbering is short—extended the time to the 10th inst. So its purpose in uttering the decree came to nought, but the greater mischief it had not eyes to see remains. It has not only destroyed the international market for Spanish bonds, but has also struck a fatal blow at Spanish credit. How Paris will stand up under this blow we cannot even estimate, but the loss there, actual and impending, must be very great. Here also there will be considerable loss, because the "early information" judiciously sent us caused much buying of these bonds by sanguine people—buying we commented on a fortnight ago as a mystery—who will now have to stick to what they have bought with slender chance of selling again except at a loss. Probably enough the mere payment of stamps in Paris will make bonds held here marketable there and *vice versâ*, but Paris is already enormously overloaded and does not want any more of such stuff; so altogether there is a nice little confusion in this particular foreign security. As for the others there is neither excitement nor business in them. The Brazilian default has hardly excited a ripple of interest, and has produced very little selling. The market for "Brazils," besides, is propped, and will continue to be. By inside influences, prices for the bonds have been kept up, and the exertion required to do so has not been stupendous because of the want of selling. In Italian Rente, again, the "bears" here have been caught, the Continental "bull" operators being too strong for them, and Italy having failed thus far to justify "bear" expectations in the matter of going into default. Bankrupts never do "chuck it" when they ought to. The event is coming all right in Italy, but it won't come in time for those who have been paying "backwardations" account after account; and seeing the price always hoisted against them, they have had to buy back, and Italian has been firm. Argentine securities have weltered about in their own special pool, sometimes up, sometimes down, with no special reason why they should be up or down this week or month more than last. Of the others no mention need be made at present.

The mining market may be almost passed by unnoticed. Prices have been improving a little in South African descriptions, but that is said to be because the Barnato and Consolidated Goldfields groups have to get their balance-sheets ready, the bold fellows they are. We hardly thought the Barnatos at least need have troubled themselves about that. However, they can put prices up if they like, for the sulky public apparently seems to have made up its mind not to sell. Buy it cannot. In the Australian market we are still waiting for some bubbles to burst and may have to wait a few weeks yet: money is so cheap. The public had best wait with us, and whistle, if it likes, to keep its spirits up—something in D flat.

The Week's Stock Markets.

The settlement took up a certain amount of time this week, but although it was the last one of the half-year, it was not a difficult one to arrange, rates again being lighter. Plenty of time was left to devote to new business, if there had been any forthcoming, but apart from a moderate amount of activity in Home railway stocks and in the market for United States railroad shares, there was little or nothing doing, the slight wake up in South African shares soon dying away, and the attendance of members is again very thin. Consols were singularly weak until the "carry over" on Wednesday, when the price rose a little, the rate being only about 1 per cent. Local loans, the Indian sterling loans, and the 2½ per cents. are all slightly weaker, and Home Corporation and Colonial Government stocks have met with little support.

Highest and Lowest this Year.		Last Carrying over Price.	BRITISH FUNDS, &c.	Closing Price.	Rise or Fall.
113⅞	109¼	—	Consols 2¾ p.c. (Money)...	111½	+ 1/16
113 15/16	109½	111¾	Do. Account (Aug. 4)	111 9/16	+ ⅜
106¼	101	105	2½ p.c. Stock red. 1905 ...	104¼	− ⅛
363	341	—	Bank of England Stock...	350½	+ ½
117	111⅜	114	India 3½ p.c. Stk. red. 1931	113	+ ¼
109¼	103⅝	107	Do. 3 p.c. Stk. red. 1948	106¼	− ¼
96⅜	90	93	Do. 2½ p.c. Stk. red. 1926	92	—

Prices in the Home railway market suffered somewhat during the closing hours of last week, sales being affected in view of the settlement, but since then with business a little more active there has been a moderate all-round advance. Considerable dealings have again taken place in the Chatham and South-Eastern Companies' issues, the joint committee having agreed upon the principles contained in the draft agreement for a united working of the two systems. A "clear saving of at least £100,000" a year is considered likely under the new arrangement, and upon the strength of this the price of Chatham second preference has been hoisted a few points higher, but the new issue of debenture stock was badly received, only about half the amount being subscribed.

Highest and Lowest this Year.		Last Carrying over Price.	HOME RAILWAYS.	Closing Price.	Rise or Fall.
186	172½	177	Brighton Def.	176¾	—
59¼	54⅛	58	Caledonian Def.	58¾	+1⅛
23¼	18¼	23	Chatham Ordinary	22⅞	+ ⅞
77¼	62	66	Great Central Pref.	66	—
24⅜	21¼	22	Do. Def.	22¼	—
124½	118	121	Great Eastern	120⅛	− ⅛
61½	50¾	55	Great Northern Def.	55⅝	+ ¼
179⅝	163⅝	165½	Great Western	166⅜	+1⅜
54⅝	45¼	53¼	Hull and Barnsley.........	53½	+ ¼
149¼	145	146	Lanc. and Yorkshire	146½	+ ½
130⅛	127¼	130½	Metropolitan	132	+1½
31	26¾	28½	Metropolitan District......	28½	—
88⅜	82⅛	87	Midland Pref.	87⅜	+ ⅜
95⅜	84½	88½	Do. Def.	89¾	+1¼
93¼	86¾	89⅝	North British Pref.	90½	+ ¾
47½	41¾	44⅝	Do. Def.	45⅝	+1⅛
181½	172¾	178½	North Eastern...............	178¾	+1¼
205½	196¼	199¼	North Western	200¼	+ ¾
117⅛	105½	114¾	South Eastern Def.	115	+1½
98¾	87	92½	South Western Def.	92	−1

Waterloo and City ordinary marks a further recovery, and the line is really to be formally opened on July 11. An increased demand for the stocks of the Scottish companies was due to the statement that additional Government contracts were to be placed at the Clyde yards. All the heavy lines mark substantial gains, North-Western again reaching 200, and "underground" stocks moved up a little on more "electric traction rumours." Hull and Barnsley now stands at about the highest point of the year, the good traffic returns encouraging holders to look for an increased dividend. Continuation rates at the settlement ruled light, the only exception being North-Western, on which nearly ½ per cent. was charged, and on Great Eastern a small contango was paid this time.

In the market for United States railroad shares the most prominent feature has been the introduction of the new securities of the Baltimore and Ohio. This company's common stock quickly fell away when the reorganisation scheme was published, many holders seeing no inducement to pay the assessment at the present price. There was, however, a lot of support forthcoming for the new securities, chiefly on Amsterdam account, and the various gold bonds have risen sharply. Generally speaking, this market has been a dull one, for while the successful landing of troops in Cuba was regarded with satisfaction, and caused a slight advance in prices, rumours of German interference at Manila were again circulated, and another adverse factor was the reported outbreak of yellow fever in Cuba. The new war tax is also expected to act rather as a deterrent to speculative business, and the weakness of the wheat market has also tended to depress prices. Milwaukee and Louisville and Nashville shares have been prominently weak, the former on the decreased earnings for May, and Northern Pacific issues are also lower. Rates of continuation were easier than last time, the general rate being about 3 to 3½ per cent., except that "Milwaukees" were carried over at "even" to 2 per cent. Canadian Pacific shares have exhibited a drooping tendency, the traffic being poor, and the May statement was not a very encouraging one, but Grand Trunk stocks have gone down much more rapidly, the second preference taking the lead, provincial operators apparently taking fright and throwing their stock on a market already overloaded.

Highest and Lowest this Year.		Last Carrying over Price.	CANADIAN AND U.S. RAILWAYS.	Closing Prices.	Rise or Fall.
14 1/16	10⅝	13¾	Atchison Shares	13½	—
35¼	23½	34⅜	Do. Pref.	34½	+ ¼
15⅝	11	14	Central Pacific	13⅞	− ⅛
105	85½	102½	Chic. Mil. & St. Paul	101½	−1
14¼	10	13	Denver Shares	12⅞	− ⅛
54¼	41½	52½	Do. Prefd.	51¾	− ½
16⅝	11¾	13¾	Erie Shares	13½	− ¼
44⅝	29¼	37	Do. Prefd.	36¾	− ⅜
110½	99	107½	Illinois Central	108	+1
62½	45¼	54¼	Louisville & Nashville	53½	− ¾
14½	9 11/16	11¾	Missouri & Texas	11½	− ¼
122¾	108½	119½	New York Central	119¾	+ ¼
57¾	42⅜	53¼	Norfolk & West. Prefd.	52⅝	− ⅝
72¾	59	72¼	Northern Pacific Prefd.	71½	+ ¼
19½	13⅞	15½	Ontario Shares	15⅜	− ⅛
62½	56½	59¼	Pennsylvania	59⅜	—
12½	7 13/16	9¼	Reading Shares	9⅜	− ¼
34¼	24¾	30¾	Southern Prefd.	30½	− ⅝
37⅝	18½	24½	Union Pacific	24¾	+ ⅜
20¾	14⅛	19¾	Wabash Prefd.	19½	− ¼
30¼	21	27⅞	Do. Income Debs.	27½	—
92¾	74	86½	Canadian Pacific	85½	− ¾
79⅝	69⅞	77½	Grand Trunk Guar.	76¾	—
76⅝	57⅛	72¾	Do. 1st Pref.	70¾	−1⅝
58¼	37¾	51¾	Do. 2nd Pref.	48¼	−2⅝
26¾	19¾	23	Do. 3rd Pref.	21¾	−1
107	101½	105	Do. 4 p.c. Deb.	104½ x.d.	—

Highest and Lowest this Year.		Last Carrying over Price.	FOREIGN BONDS.	Closing Price.	Rise or Fall.
94½	84	90½	Argentine 5 p.c. 1886	89½	− ½
92⅝	81⅜	87¾	Do. 6 p.c. Funding	87	—
76¾	64	71½	Do. 5 p.c. B. Ay. Water	70¾	− ¾
61¾	41⅛	53	Brazilian 4 p.c. 1889	52¾	− ¼
69⅝	46	60¼	Do. 5 p.c. 1895	59¾	− ¾
65	42¾	55⅜	Do. 5 p.c. West Minas Ry.	54¾	− ¼
108¾	105½	108	Egyptian 4 p.c. Unified	108	—
104¾	100½	103	Do. 3½ p.c. Pref.	103	—
103	99½	102	French 3 p.c. Rente	102	—
44¾	34½	44	Greek 4 p.c. Monopoly	44	—
93 3/16	88¾	92⅞	Italian 5 p.c. Rente	93⅛	+ ⅜
100	87⅛	98½	Mexican 6 p.c. 1888	99	+ ½
20¾	16	18½	Portuguese 1 p.c.	18⅜	—
62½	29⅜	33¾	Spanish 4 p.c.	34	+ ⅜
47	40	45½	Turkish 1 p.c. "B"	45¾	—
26¾	22¾	26¼	Do. 1 p.c. "C"	26 1/16	− 1/16
22⅜	20	22¼	Do. 1 p.c. "D"	22¼	+ 1/16
46⅝	40	44½	Uruguay 3½ p.c. Bonds	44⅜	—

Prices are very little changed in the Foreign market, and business has been confined within narrow limits. Spanish 4 per cents. were rushed up to 35 owing to some hurried buying by operators for the fall, who did not seem to know quite what the market value of the bonds unstamped by June 30 was. The extension of time to July 10 for bondholders to present their bonds for stamping put a stop to the rush of buyers, and the price was soon back again at the old level. Nothing much has happened on the Paris Bourse, the repeated failures to form a Cabinet being given as the reason why things were so dull, but the announcement of the formation of a Ministry by M. Brisson when it was at last made produced little or no effect, and the tendency was weak throughout. Argentine bonds leave off flat, the gold premium being much higher, due, it was thought, to the wheat crop, having been much over-estimated, and a new issue of Treasury bills is also talked of. Brazilian stocks show but little change, but are, if anything, also rather lower, and Chilian bonds close weak. Turkish groups have hardly been mentioned, but the Chinese 1896 loan has met with support, and the Mexican issues are higher. The rise in the latter case was started by the discovery at the settlement that the bonds were scarce, "even" to a small "back" being quoted. Other rates ranged round about 3 per cent, although Spanish and Italian were continued at charges rather less onerous.

Highest and Lowest this Year.		Last Carrying over Price.	FOREIGN RAILWAYS.	Closing Price.	Rise or Fall.
105½	99	105	Argentine Gt. West. 5 p.c. Pref. Stock	105	—
158½	134	139	B. Ay. Gt. Southern Ord.	140	+1
78½	65	71½	B. Ay. and Rosario Ord.	71½	—
12¼	10¼	10⅜	B. Ay. Western Ord.	10⅛	− ¼
87¼	73	79½	Central Argentine Ord.	80	+ ½
92	76	77	Cordoba and Rosario 6 p.c. Deb.	77	−1
95½	85½	90	Cord. Cent. 4 p.c. Deb. (Cent. Nth. Sec.)	88xd	—
61⅞	42	51	Do. Income Deb. Stk.	51	+ ½
25½	16⅞	20¼	Mexican Ord. Stk.	20½	+ ½
83½	69½	75	Do. 8 p.c. 1st Pref.	75⅝	+1⅛

Among Foreign railways all the leading Brazilian companies' securities have been sold freely, but some of the principal Argentine descriptions are higher. Mexican railway issues advanced during the earlier part of the week, until a disappointing traffic return caused a set back.

As far as investment business is concerned, the Miscellaneous market has done little, but a few of the leading speculative counters have attracted some attention. Brewery stocks have been quieter of late, about the only noticeable move being a rise of 4 in Guinness preference. A further slight recovery is to be recorded in electric lighting companies' shares, but operators are waiting the course of events before launching out again over this class of security. Anglo-Argentine Tramways debenture is 5 higher, and British Electric Traction and Apollinaris shares are slightly firmer. On the other hand, E. & J. Burke debentures dropped 20, the ordinary and preference shares about 2 each, Anglo-Ceylon Estates 5, London Tramways "B" debentures 3, and Jorehaut Tea 5½, these being some of the more important losses. The Assam Railway and Trading Company's various issues also declined on the appearance of the report, and a 5 per cent. dividend on Dunlop deferred failed to do much more than keep the price steady. The Hudson's Bay report was about up to expectations, and hardly affected the price, and holders of Goldsbrough mortgage debentures viewed with equanimity the passing of the "B" debenture interest. East and West India Dock preference is again quoted lower.

Markets closed firm on the whole, without any increase in the volume of business, but the fall in the Bank rate and Lord Salisbury's pacific speech tended to harden the tone generally. Among Home railway stocks Chatham second preference finally closed about ten higher on the week at 109½, but the ordinary left off below the best on profit taking. South Eastern deferred and North Western closed firm, but Great

Eastern and Hull and Barnsley were put lower on some reported trouble in the Yorkshire coalfields. Grand Trunk stocks rallied before the close, and United States shares were also rather firmer, notably Illinois Central, New York Central, and Union Pacific. Spanish 4 per cents. advanced a little on Continental buying, Argentine and Chilian bonds closing dull. Most of the leading Western Australian mining shares picked up rather remarkably just before the finish, and the Mount Lyell group also recovered somewhat sharply.

MINING AND FINANCE COMPANIES.

Professional operators, tired of doing nothing, have tried to impart a little life into the South African market, and the result is that, compared with a week ago, there is quite a long list of rises of ⅛ or so. Paris operators supported East Rand and De Beers shares to a limited extent, and German buying was also reported, but also only to a limited extent, while De Beers were bought on home account in anticipation of the dividend just announced, and close firm. Among Western Australian ventures Hainault advanced on a cable reporting a new discovery, but Golden Horse Shoe and Hannan's Brown Hill are weaker, the continuation rates, for one thing, proving rather more onerous than had been anticipated. Very little has happened in the general mining market. Mount Lyell shares, after being dull, suddenly recovered, and there was a small "back" on the shares at the settlement; Rio Tinto has hardly moved, and Indian shares keep very steady.

THE COUNTERVAIL *VERSUS* SUGAR BOUNTIES.

The International Sugar Bounties Conference, whose sittings have been suspended for some time, looking to the diversity of principles and interests, apart from possible complications, can hardly yield tangible results. A manifesto issued by "The Anti-Bounty League" gives the consumption of sugar per head of the populations as follows: "England, 86 lb.; United States, 65 lb.; Denmark, 44 lb.; France 28 lb.; Germany, 27 lb.; Belgium, 22 lb.; Austria, 17 lb.; and Russia, 11 lb." These figures were presented by "The French Commission of Senate on the Sugar Bill of 1896," and they have generally been accepted as accurate. The sugar question is one closely allied with the principles and policy of Free Trade. The exponents of the legislation sought to be established in defence of English and colonial interests contend that the sugar bounties paid by Continental Governments are ruining the West Indian colonies, which should be protected by the Mother Country, and that this Protection should take the form of countervailing duties. Now the total annual production of sugar by the West Indies is about 270,000 tons, England (after deducting re-exports) taking for home consumption 50,000 tons, and the United States the bulk of the crop. To the extent, therefore, of fully 200,000 tons, the West Indies are protected by the United States, as under the Tariff Law of July, 1897, "the States levy special countervailing duties on bounty-fed sugar."

When simmered down to a residuum, the "vexed question" in the discussion now absorbing a large measure of public attention and upon which no little perplexity is felt is this: Who are the recipients of the benefit derived from the bounties? A little volume, published by Messrs. Cassell, under the title of "Popular Fallacies, being the *Sophismes Economiques* of Bastiat adapted to the Present Time," answers that question thus: "The latest demand has been for countervailing (of course not *protective*) duties to hinder the importation of bounty-fed sugar. Foreign Governments, said the Anti-Bounty League (of 1888), give bounties on refining, and these bounties stimulate the export of refined sugar to this country. True; but the bounties given by foreign countries upon refining were really received by English sugar consumers, who profited by the low price of the commodity, which was the direct result of the bounties. What France, Germany, and others paid to promote refining and to encourage exportation we received. They, in fact, paid tribute to us, and we should receive it gladly." In this explanation of the ultimate destination of the bounties there is no ambiguity. It is clear, explicit, and true.

Advocates of the imposition of the countervail disregard, or at least discreetly keep in the background, the cardinal point that since the cultivation of the beet was entered upon by Continental countries it has become a permanent national industry with all of them. The rental of land in Germany, for example, as a typical case, has risen from 18s. to 54s. an acre, while the refuse beet, or pulp, for cattle feeding yields a revenue of close upon £2,000,000 a year. It is claimed also by experts that the beet-root grower attaches more value to the pulp than to the money he receives for the sugar. Germany—and herein lies the danger—if countervailing duties were imposed, might, and probably would, retaliate by a further increase of the bounties, and we, in defence of our new national policy, would have to follow suit, and countervail still more till we are on a parity not only with Germany, but with all other bounty-giving nations. These reprisals and counter reprisals might be unceasing, and would be equivalent to playing the old-fashioned game of "beggar my neighbour" again. There are many openings through which Germany, in order to adjust the balance, might work. She might, for instance, abolish the land tax, or even give a drawback, a term synonymous with bounty, on her imports of nitrate, a manure of which the beet growing countries on the Continent take nearly ten tons to our one. That form of retaliation might strike the impoverished British farmer rather hard. One salient fact is not open to dispute. Home consumers of sugar, it is estimated, would lose at least £2,000,000 a year, if thus deprived of the cheap sugar they now enjoy. If once the reprisal element is let loose between this country and the Continent, the Englishman, instead of commanding and consuming his allowance of 86 lb. of sugar a year, might perforce be reduced to "short commons," measured by the Frenchman's 28 lb., the German's 27 lb., and the Russian's 11 lb.

But after all said and done, it is necessary to inquire in what does the *rationale* of this compulsory sacrifice of national interests consist? Of our total import of 1,500,000 tons of sugar, 25 per cent. only of cane sugar from all parts of the world (of which not 10 per cent. reaches us from the West Indies) would be directly affected by the projected retaliation. A crucial question on this point, and one rarely considered, is this—what would be the capital expenditure required to restore the "pristine vigour" of the West Indies as sugar producers as it was before these colonies had to face competition with the European Continent? Putting the inquiry in another form, what would be the *cost* of regenerating the sugar industry of the West Indies to a standard approaching that which it had attained in 1874, when protection to colonial grown sugar was abandoned, and when, according to eminent testimony, the plant and appliances of the sugar estates were antiquated, and hastening to the last stage of disintegration and decay? Another pertinent question might be, would it be worth the cost? Of one thing we may be sure—that to enter upon a war of retaliation would tend rather to confirm than shake the faith of Continental Governments in the efficacy of bounties. These Governments are paying heavily for their experience, and it is evident, from the perfunctory nature of the discussions at the International Brussels Conference, that they have not even yet learned their lesson, nor appreciated the tremendous cost of it. But they would not be taught the lesson any more rapidly were we to resort to countervailing duties. That would be but transferring a considerable portion of the expense to our side of the account. Continental Governments will, no doubt, in time see the waste and folly of bounties; but the production of beet sugar is a permanent industry which will now go on with or without them. It is not a matter on which Continental Governments can be forced; and to impose countervailing duties would be but to resort to a kind of force. Why waste time in its discussion? The aims of the countervailers are entirely visionary. They cannot succeed, and even if success were possible, it would be nothing short of a national calamity, for it would mean at least the partial destruction of our free trade policy, by which alone our commerce and industry can be properly developed.

Notice is given to the registered holders of Sultanate of Zanzibar first mortgage bonds, Nos. 1 to 350, for £35,000, that these bonds will be redeemed on January 1, 1899, by payment of the principal sum secured thereon, *plus* a premium of £1 per cent.

Mr. Henry Gerard Philip Hoare, of Messrs. Hoare & Co., bankers, Fleet-street, has been appointed a director of the Provident Clerks' Mutual Life Assurance Association.

The Swiss Bankverein, Switzerland, announce the opening, on July 1, of a branch of their bank in London at 40, Threadneedle-street, E.C., under the style of Swiss Bankverein.

The offices of the Golden Horse Shoe Gold Mining Company, Limited, have been removed to No. 3, Great Winchester-street, E.C.

We are informed that warrants were yesterday posted for the interest on the 4 per cent. consolidated first mortgage debentures of John Barley White & Brothers, Limited, for the six months ended yesterday, and that cheques have also been posted for the thirty-two debentures of £100 each which were drawn for repayment at this date, at a premium of £10 per cent.

The firm of Duff, Bridges, & Watts, of 5, Nicholas-lane, Lombard-street, from July 1 prox. will be carried on as Duff, Watts, & Co.

Prices of Mine and Mining Finance Companies' Shares.

Shares £1 each, except where otherwise stated.

Australian.

Making-Up Price, June 27.	Name	Closing Price.	Rise or Fall.	Making-Up Price, June 27.	Name	Closing Price.	Rise or Fall.
1 1/8	Aladdin	1 1/8		1/8	Hannan's Star	1/8	
3 3/4	Associated	3 11/16		6 5/16	Ivanhoe, New	6 1/4	− 1/16
4/9	Do. Southern	1/2		1/16	Kalgurli Mt.&IronKing, 18/	1/16	
3/4	Brownhill Extended	1		5 3/4	Kalgurli	5 3/4	
1 5/16	Burbank's Birthday	1 1/4		2 7/8	Lady Shenton	2 7/16	
7/8	Central Boulder	7/8		9 3/16	Lake View Cons.	8 7/8	− 3/16
6/	Chaffers, 4/	5/6		8/	Do. Extended	1/16	
1/8	Colonial Finance, 15/	1/8 dis.		1	Do. South	1 1/16	+ 1/16
1/16	Crœsus S. United	7/8		1 5/16	London & Globe Finance	24/	+ 1/
3/8	E. Murchison	3/8		11/16	London&W.A.Exploration	11/16	− 1/16
4/	Golden Arrow fully paid	4/3	+/9	1/16	Do. Investment	1/16	
10 1/4	Golden Horseshoe	9 3/4	− 1/2	3/8	Mainland Consols	3/16	
1/2	Golden Link	7/16		3/8	North Boulder, 10/	3/8	
17/3	Great Boulder, 2/	17/	−/6	1 13/16	North Kalgurli	1 11/16	− 1/16
1 1/8	Do. Main Reef, 10/	1 1/8		11/16	Northern Territories	5/8	
2 13/16	Do. Perseverance	3	+ 1/4	2 7/8	Peak Hill	2 7/8	
5/8	Do. South	5/8		2 3/16	South Kalgurli	2 3/16	
3	Hainault	3 1/8	+ 1/8	1 1/8	W. A. Goldfields	1 3/16	
1/4	Hampton Plains	1/4	− 1/16	11/16	W. A. Joint Stock	11/16	
8 3/4	Hannan's Brownhill	8 3/4	− 1/4	1/9	W. A. Market Trust	1/9	− /3
1/8	Hannan's Oroya	3/16		5/16	W. A. Loan&General Fin.	5/16	
10/6	Do. Proprietary	10/6		3/16	White Feather	3/16	

South African.

Making-Up Price, June 27.	Name	Closing Price.	Rise or Fall.	Making-Up Price, June 27.	Name	Closing Price.	Rise or Fall.
5 7/8	Angelo	5 7/16	+ 1/8	1/6	Lisbon-Berlyn	1/9	
1	Aurora West	1		2 1/16	May Consolidated	2 3/16	+ 1/16
15/16	Bantjes	1	+ 1/16	3 11/16	Meyer and Charlton	4	+ 1/8
8/6	Barrett, 10/	8/	−/6	3 13/16	Modderfontein	3 15/16	+ 1/16
4 1/16	Bonanza	4 1/16		3/4	New Bultfontein	13/16	
3/	Buffelsdoorn	1/8	+ 1/16	3 1/16	New Primrose	3 3/16	+ 1/16
5 13/16	City and Suburban, £4	5 13/16	+ 1/16	1 3/8	Nigel, 15/	1 3/8	− 1/16
2 1/16	Comet (New)	2 3/16	+ 1/8	1	Nigel Deep	1	+ 1/16
3	Con. Deep Level	3		5/16	North Randfontein	3/8	+ 1/16
11 1/4	Crown Deep	11 1/4		4 3/8	Nourse Deep	5	+ 5/8
12 3/4	Crown Reef	13 1/4	+ 1/2	13/16	Porges-Randfontein	15/16	
26 3/4	De Beers, £5	27 1/16	+ 5/16	29 3/4	Rand Mines	29 3/4	+ 1
3 1/8	Driefontein	3 3/16	+ 1/8	1 1/8	Randfontein	1 3/16	
6 1/16	Durban Roodepoort	6 1/4		1 3/8	Rietfontein	1 3/8	+ 1/16
3 3/8	Do. Deep	3 7/16		9 1/2	Robinson Deep	9 9/16	+ 1/16
4 11/16	East Rand	4 7/8	+ 1/8	8	Do. Gold, £5	8 1/4	+ 3/8
24 1/2	Ferreira	25 1/4	+ 3/4	5/8	Do. Randfontein	5/8	
7 5/8	Geldenhuis Deep	7 7/8	+ 1/4	1 1/8	Roodepoort Central Deep	1 1/8	
5 3/8	Do. Estate	5 3/8	+ 1/16	6 1/8	Rose Deep	6 3/8	+ 1/4
1/2	George Goch	9/16		3 5/16	Salisbury	3 3/8	+ 1/16
9 1/4	Ginsberg	9 1/2		1 1/8	Sheba	1 3/16	+ 1/16
1 3/4	Glencairn	2	+ 3/16	3 11/16	Simmer and Jack, £5	3 7/8	+ 1/8
8 1/8	Goldfields Deep	8 3/8	+ 1/4	2 5/8	Transvaal Gold	2 5/8	− 1/8
8 3/8	Griqualand West	8 5/8	+ 1/4	3 3/8	Treasury	3 3/8	+ 1/16
9 3/4	Henry Nourse	10	+ 1/4	3 3/8	United Roodepoort	3 3/8	
7 3/4	Heriot	7 7/8	+ 1/8	1 3/8	Van Ryn	1 7/16	+ 1/8
7 3/8	Jagersfontein	7 5/8	+ 1/4	6	Village Main Reef	6 1/16	
9 3/8	Jubilee	9 1/2	+ 1/8	1 1/8	Vogelstruis	1 1/4	
5	Jumpers	5 1/8	+ 1/8	5/16	Do. Deep	3/8	
2 1/8	Kleinfontein	2 1/4	+ 1/8	10 1/4	Wemmer	10 3/8	
3 3/8	Knight's	3 1/2	+ 1/8	11/16	West Rand	3/4	
2 3/4	Lancaster	2 7/8		5 1/16	Wolhuter, £4	5 3/8	+ 1/8
3	Langlaagte Estate	3		2 3/4	Worcester	2 7/8	

Land Exploration and Rhodesian.

Making-Up Price, June 27.	Name	Closing Price.	Rise or Fall.	Making-Up Price, June 27.	Name	Closing Price.	Rise or Fall.
2 1/16	Anglo-French Ex.	2 3/16	+ 1/8	13/16	Mashonaland Central	13/16	
1 3/8	Barnato Consolidated	1 5/8	+ 1/4	5 1/8	Matabele Gold Reefs	5 3/8	+ 1/4
7/8	Bechuanaland Ex.	7/8		2 1/16	Mozambique	2 3/16	+ 1/16
2 7/8	Chartered B.S.A.	2 15/16		1 1/8	Oceana Consolidated	1 3/16	
5/8	Clark's Cons.	5/8		1 1/16	Rhodesia, Ltd.	1 3/16	
1 1/8	Colenbrander	1 3/16		4	Do. Exploration	4 1/8	+ 1/8
4 1/16	Cons. Goldfields	4 1/4	+ 3/16	13/16	Do. Goldfields	13/16	
1 1/16	Do. Pref.	21/6	+ /6	3 3/8	S. A. Gold Trust	3 5/8	+ 1/4
1 3/8	Exploration	1 3/8		1 1/8	Tati Concessions	1 1/8	
2 1/4	Geelong	2 1/2	+ 1/4	5/8	Transvaal Development	5/8	
13/16	Henderson's Est.	7/8	+ 1/8	1/16	United Rhodesia	1/16	
1 3/8	Johannesburg Con. In.	1 7/16	+ 1/16	1 3/16	Willoughby	1 3/16	
15/16	Do. Water	1	+ 1/16	15/16	Zambesia Explor.	7/8	− 1/16
1 3/16	Mashonaland Agency	1 3/16					

Miscellaneous.

Making-Up Price, June 27.	Name	Closing Price.	Rise or Fall.	Making-Up Price, June 27.	Name	Closing Price.	Rise or Fall.
1	Alamillos, £2	1		7/	Mount Lyell, South	1/16	− 1/8
4 7/8	Anaconda, $25	4 3/8	− 1/2	4 5/8	Mount Morgan, 17s. 6d.	4 11/16	+ 1/8
8/9	Balaghât, fully paid	9/		5 3/8	Mysore, 10s.	5 3/8	
10/	Brilliant, £2	10/		7/6	Mysore Goldfields	8/	− 1/
2 1/16	Do. St. George's	2 1/8		6/	Do. Reefs, 17/	6/	
8/9	British Broken Hill	9/	+ /3	5/6	Do. West	4/6	−1/6
43/	Broken Hill Proprietary	2 1/16		4/6	Do. Wynaad	3/	−1/6
—	Do. Block 10	3		2 3/4	Namaqua, £2	2 13/16	+ 1/16
4 3/8	Cape Copper, £2	4 7/16	+ 1/16	4	Nundydroog	4	
4 5/8	Champion Reef, 10s.	4 11/16	+ 1/16	3 3/8	Ooregum	3 7/16	+ 1/8
2 1/8	Copiapo, £2	2 1/8 x.		3 3/8	Do. Pref.	3 7/16	+ 1/16
2 3/8	Coromandel	2 7/16	+ 1/16	26	Rio Tinto £5	26	+ 1/8
15/	Day Dawn Block	14/6	− /6	6	Do. Pref. £5	6 1/16	
2 1/8	Frontino & Bolivia	2 1/8 x.		1	St. John del Rey	20/6	+ /6
1 3/16	Hall Mines	1 1/8	− 1/16	8/9	Taitipu	1/16	
2	Libiola, £5	2		6	Tharsis, £2	6 1/8	
7 3/8	Linares, £3	7 3/8		9	Tolima "A," £5	9 1/8	+ 1/8
3 3/8	Mason & Barry, £3	3 3/8		4 3/16	Waihi	4 1/8	− 1/16
4 7/8	Mountain Copper, £5	4 7/8		1 3/8	Waitekauri	1 3/8	
8 3/4	Mount Lyell, £3	9 1/8	+ 3/8	16/3	Woodstock (N.Z.)	7/8	
1 3/16	Mount Lyell, North	1 3/8					

The London Tramways Company, Limited, will redeem, on December 31 next its mortgage debenture stock for £180,000 issued in pursuance of the resolution passed at a general meeting of the company, held on April 29, 1880. Payment will be made at the registered offices of the company, and all certificates should be lodged at least ten days before December 31.

Sir Charles Turner, K.C.I.E., has been elected chairman of the Rohilkund and Kumaon Railway Company, Limited, in the place of the late General Alexander Fraser, C.B., R.E., Sir George Allen, K.C.I.E., having declined the office. Colonel T. Gracey, C.S.I., R.E., late Director-General of Railways, and Secretary of the Railway Department of the Government of India, has joined the board of the Rohilkund and Kumaon Railway Company, Limited.

TRAMWAY AND OMNIBUS RECEIPTS.

HOME.

Name.	Period.	Ending.	Amount.	Increase or Decrease on 1897.	Weeks or Months.	Aggregate to Date. Amount.	Inc. or Dec. on 1897.
			£	£		£	£
Aberdeen District	Week	June 25	557	−85	—	—	—
Belfast Street	"	" 25	2,495	−512	—	—	—
Birmingham and Aston	"	" 25	494	−37	—	—	—
Birmingham and Midland	"	" 25	671	−33	—	—	—
Birmingham City	"	" 25	4,001	−177	—	—	—
Birmingham General	"	" 25	1,060	−83	—	—	—
Blessington and Poulaphouca	"	" 26	18	−2	25	314	+22
Bristol Tramways and Carriage	"	" 24	2,829	−1,198	—	—	—
Burnley and District	"	" 25	305	−115	—	—	—
Bury, Rochdale, and Oldham	"	" 25	803	−141	—	—	—
Croydon	"	" 25	384	−118	—	—	+1,090
Dublin and Blessington	"	" 26	138	−32	25	2,664	−8
Dublin and Lucan	"	" 25	75	−11	26	1,355	−377
Dublin United	"	" 24	3,474	−348	—	73,064	+3,222
Dudley and Stourbridge	"	" 25	175	−4	26	4,339	+136
Edinburgh and District	"	" 25	2,626	−504	25	59,111	+4,878
Edinburgh Street	"	" 25	788	−166	25	15,960	+1,662
Gateshead and District	Month	May	935	+66	—	—	—
Glasgow	Week	June 25	2,918	−183	—	—	—
Harrow-road and Paddington	"	" 24	311	−86	—	—	—
Lea Bridge and Leyton	"	" 25	922	+44	—	—	—
London, Deptford, and Greenwich	"	" 25	645	−217	—	14,516	+226
London General Omnibus	"	" 25	24,385	−8,054	—	—	—
London Road Car	"	" 25	7,600	−2,663	†	162,268	−523
London Southern	"	" 25	652	−38	—	—	—
North Staffordshire	"	" 25	426	−51	—	9,934	−215
Provincial	"	" 25	2,592	−1,753	—	—	—
Rossendale Valley	"	" 24	160	−66	—	—	—
Southampton	"	" 25	442	−241	—	—	—
South London	"	" 25	1,932	−659	†	42,214	+217
South Staffordshire	"	" 24	680	−147	25	15,101	−351
Tramways Union	Month	May	12,813	+1,655	5	52,333	+6,150
Wigan and District	Week	June 25	277	−91	—	—	
Woolwich and South East London	"	" 25	450	−166	†	8,846	+160

Jubilee week, 1897. † From January 1. ‡ Strike in 1897.

FOREIGN.

Name.	Period.	Ending.	Amount.	Increase or Decrease on 1897.	Weeks or Months.	Aggregate to Date. Amount.	Inc. or Dec. on 1897.
			£	£		£	£
Anglo-Argentine	Week	May 30	4,480	+771	*	96,199	+10,790
Barcelona	"	June 25	1,210	−481	—	28,607	−5,313
Barcelona, Ensanche y Gracia	"	" 25	276	+14	—	5,679	−25
Bordeaux	"	" 24	2,423	−69	—	52,811	−2,461
Brazilian Street	Month	April (m	lr46,055	+3,871	—	—	—
British Columbia Electric	"	"	$30,729	+$10493	‡	$305,134	—
Do. net	"	"	$10,392	+$4,958	‡	$97,402	—
Buenos Ayres and Belgrano	"	May	5,082	+832	*	24,555	+4,800
Buenos Ayres Grand National	Week	May 28	$23,219	+$2,935	†	—	+$27,456
Buenos Ayres New	Month	March	$70,624	−$864	—	$201,851	−$7,119
Calais	Week	June 25	159	+4	—	—	—
Calcutta	"	" 25	1,239	−23	—	—	—
C'rth'g'na&Herrerias	Month	May	3,609	+173	—	22,418	+1,184
Gothenburg	Week	June 22	343	−4	—	—	—
Lynn and Boston	Month	April	$105,596	+$2,087	7	$727,825	+$30000
Do. net	"	"	$40,418	+$1,912	7	$256,801	+$5,064
Twin City Rapid	"	"	$165,803	+$10411	4	$653,223	+$43912
Do. Net	"	"	$82,629	+$9,356	4	$317,429	+$42582

* From January 1. † From April 1, 1898. ‡ From April 15, 1897. § From October 1, 1897.

THE REVENUE RETURNS.

Budget Estimates for 1898-9.	Increase or Decrease on 1897-8.	—	Revenue for Quarter ended June 30, 1898.	Increase or Decrease on 1897.
£	£		£	£
21,080,000	+ 2,000	Customs	5,005,000	*136,000*
28,950,000	+ 650,000	Excise	6,670,000	70,000
10,670,000	− 430,000	Estate, &c., Duties	3,120,000	200,000
7,600,000	− 50,000	Stamps	1,900,000	*70,000*
925,000	− 15,000	Land Tax	10,000	*5,000*
1,570,000	+ 60,000	House Duty	470,000	35,000
17,700,000	+ 450,000	Prop. and Income Tax	3,060,000	220,000
12,600,000	+ 430,000	Post Office	2,440,000	50,000
3,140,000	+ 130,000	Telegraph Service	775,000	40,000
2,875,000	− 11,000	Miscellaneous	617,846	26,894
107,110,000	+1,176,000		24,087,846	438,894*

Decreases in italics. * Net increase.

Baring Brothers & Co., Limited, have received cable advice from the Banco Comercial, Montevideo, stating that the bank has received from the municipality the sum of $15,000 gold on account of the service of the City of Montevideo sterling loan of 1888.

The numbers are published of sixty-nine bonds of the Otago Harbour Board 6 per cent. sinking fund (1874) loan which have been drawn at the Bank of New Zealand for payment on September 30.

WEST AUSTRALIAN MINE CRUSHINGS.

Capital Issued.	Property.	District or Goldfield.	Name of Company.	February.		March.		April.		May.		Total since Crushing Began.	
£	Acres.			Tons.	Oz.	Tons.	Oz.	Tons.	Oz.	Tons.	Oz.	Tons.	Oz.
450,000	156	Kalgoorlie	Associated G. M. of W. A.	1,800	1,500	1,525	1,520	500	3,250	1,700	1,325	22,838	46,330
90,000	36	Mount Malcolm	Australia United	209	439	145	297	265	538	345	715	1,627	3,846
150,000	51	Nannine	Aust. Champion Reef	373	168	180	195	128	167	125	130	10,649	5,468
240,350	100	Coolgardie	Bayley's United	679	842	690	738	895	1,490	887	892	14,256	69,093
145,000	47	E. Murchison	Bellevue Proprietary	486	604	326	725	528	1,135	241	492	2,771	5,412
150,000	51	Coolgardie	Burbank's Birthday Gift	833	1,126	940	1,290	980	1,437	910	1,240	12,529	27,590
115,000	90	Nannine	Champion Extended	785	396	900	630	1,050	821	750	675	4,333	3,292
113,000	112	Murchison	Consolidated Murchison	789	813	756	790	278	286	505	709	29,631	19,156
100,000	33	Murchison	Cuddingwarra	257	249	227	208	334	287	182	187	1,337	1,378
250,000	117	E. Murchison	East Murchison United	1,290	1,395	—	—	1,800	1,600	2,010	1,456	18,731	25,950
282,380	60	Broad Arrow	Golden Arrow	98	101	—	—	89	137	70	35	990	863
150,000	48	Kanowna	Golden Valley	—	—	300	112	230	108	300	79	2,216	767
220,000	24	Kalgoorlie	Great Boulder Main Reef	590	863	830	1,100	750	486	800	1,200	7,263	15,291
175,000	24	Kalgoorlie	Great Boulder Perseverance	1,019	1,576	1,017	1,701	880	1,044	1,179	1,787	18,682	33,874
160,000	85	Kalgoorlie	Great Boulder Proprietary	2,841	6,513	2,837	6,434	2,880	6,466	2,480	5,542	65,702	200,532
220,000	21	Coolgardie	Hands Across the Sea	165	139	144	96	113	52	120	63	1,209	781
85,000	20	Kalgoorlie	Hannan's Brownhill	994	1,840	1,003	1,830	1,018	2,300	1,065	2,600	10,035	41,149
240,000	36	Kalgoorlie	Hannan's Oroya	832	374	902	545	990	498	891	544	6,796	3,510
1,000,000	24	Kalgoorlie	Ivanhoe	1,722	2,851	1,956	3,005	1,902	2,977	1,751	2,823	28,961	57,412
160,000	36	Menzies	Lady Shenton	552	1,518	900	2,550	609	1,761	600	1,690	9,243	31,807
250,000	48	Kalgoorlie	Lake View Consols	7,850	7,395	8,584	8,039	9,168	8,759	11,061	9,169	61,261	137,142
699,999	67	Coolgardie	Londonderry	330	652	320	477	320	582	450	675	3,249	13,816
224,125	156	Menzies	Menzies Consolidated	650	597	449	363	434	473	554	725	9,251	9,218
193,100	44	Menzies	Menzies Crusoe	330	244	933	799	900	534	—	—	8,698	15,050
173,811	91	Menzies	Menzies Gold Reefs	60	102	1,068	815	70	75	1,151	791	5,029	9,306
200,000	180	Mount Margaret	Mount Malcolm	529	474	660	517	590	371	475	351	3,938	3,703
85,000	84	Nannine	Mount Yagahong	1,201	715	1,060	914	800	784	670	470	7,471	6,302
200,000	174	Dundas	Norseman	697	515	803	704	861	826	715	1,015	6,186	6,358
220,000	19	Kalgoorlie	North Boulder	699	668	737	765	789	724	776	746	10,359	15,912
215,000	143	Mount Margaret	North Star	95	166	100	122	165	181	166	121	4,370	4,471
25,798	36	Coolgardie	Premier	715	345	625	317	550	221	770	337	10,423	11,618
65,003	12	Murchison	Princess Royal	290	219	128	126	515	393	450	319	4,003	3,942
78,984	51	Kanowna	Robinson	415	292	570	143	135	72	—	—	7,662	9,364
100,000	43	Coolgardie	Sherlaws	453	259	149	188	220	194	215	195	2,038	1,929
300,000	168	Mount Malcolm	Sons of Gwalia	960	1,139	990	1,241	960	1,328	940	958	9,797	13,135
200,000	36	Coolgardie	Wealth of Nations	270	256	597	487	650	433	640	396	2,960	2,233
110,993	72	Murchison	Weld-Hercules	363	220	407	226	444	333	553	546	3,359	2,391
200,000	98	Coolgardie	Westralia and East Extension	1,675	1,104	2,326	909	1,782	1,192	1,417	1,271	18,029	24,645
140,300	48	Kanowna	White Feather Main Reef	527	282	580	615	820	1,030	850	1,023	7,581	6,123

WEST AUSTRALIAN MINES.

The total output of gold by the mines of Western Australia—that is to say, "gold, the produce of the colony, entered for export"—continues to grow in bulk, the quantity for May being 83,346 oz., for April 84,083 oz., for March 75,380 oz., for February 53,739 oz., and for January 93,395 oz., but the last total included 12,515 oz. from ore smelted outside the colony. The growth will be better seen from the fact that for the first five months of this year the output was 389,944 oz., as compared with 211,981 oz. for the same five months in 1897, 84,396 oz. in 1896, and 92,151 oz. in 1895. This increase may be attributed entirely to the larger number of companies at work, and the greater mass of ore dealt with. It is of course a fine thing for the colony, but of little benefit to shareholders on this side. As to the fifty or sixty English companies, or companies in which English investors are interested, and which make monthly crushing returns, it is clear that, with a few exceptions, they are a very poor lot, and, as will be seen below, their yield of gold from the ore crushed has been steadily on the down grade for the past year :—

	Tons.	Oz.	Yield per ton. oz.	dwt.
1897.				
July	24,277	38,711	1	12
August	26,214	45,390	1	14
September... ...	31,033	51,860	1	13
October	33,719	51,892	1	11
November	33,147	48,794	1	10
December	36,465	51,166	1	8
1898.				
January	41,208	49,867	1	4
February	39,765	42,919	1	2
March	43,233	52,871	1	4
April	40,153	48,001	1	4
May...	42,849	48,354	1	3

Even from the Great Boulder, which has been the most successful of the English companies, the yield is still getting smaller and smaller. The average from 16,729 tons in 1896 was 3·6 oz. per ton, and from 29,463 tons in 1897 it was 2·16 oz., but it has since fallen gradually to 2·3 oz. The Boulder Perseverance yield keeps up very well, but the Boulder Main Reef, the Ivanhoe, the Lake View, North Boulder, the Associated, Burbank's Birthday Gift, and many other smaller undertakings are all giving poorer returns than the average either of 1897 or 1896. Dividends are also getting scarcer, which, with falling yields and high working charges, is not to be wondered at. The shares of those companies which earn anything for their shareholders stand at greatly inflated prices, and offer no inducement to the speculative investor because he cannot be certain how much more gold there may be in the mine, and also because the price of the shares is so high that in the event of the rich gold giving out in two or three years' time he would stand the chance of losing so much of his capital. Allowing for the companies already defunct and those which are continuing their miserable existence, English investors in West Australian mines have lost more than they have gained, as we said they would do when the speculation was first started. It is the market men and promoters who have derived all the benefit.

NEXT WEEK'S MEETINGS.

MONDAY, JULY 4.

Derby Tea ... ... 28, Fenchurch-street, 11 a.m.
Edinburgh Eastern Cemetery ... Edinburgh, 2 p.m.
Jorehaut Tea ... ... 138, Leadenhall-street, 1 p.m.

TUESDAY, JULY 5.

Great Eastern Railway ... ... Liverpool-street Station, noon.
Johns, Son, & Watts ... ... Guildhall Tavern, 3 p.m.
Lancashire and Yorkshire Bank ... Manchester, noon.
National Bank of New Zealand ... Winchester House, 12.30 p.m.
United River Plate Telephone ... Winchester House, noon.

WEDNESDAY, JULY 6.

Alabama Coal and Iron ... ... Winchester House, noon.
Assam Railways and Trading ... Winchester House, 2.30 p.m.
Mysore West ... ... Winchester House, 3 p.m.
Mysore Wynaad Cons. ... ... Winchester House, 3.30 p.m
Nerbudda Iron and Coal ... ... Winchester House, noon.

THURSDAY, JULY 7.

Colonial Bank... ... ... Winchester House, 2 p.m.
River Plate Fresh Meat ... ... Cannon-street Hotel, 11 a.m.

Mr. Luis Camacho announces the numbers of 180 bonds of the Mexican 6 per cent. consolidated external loan of 1888, and the numbers of fifty-eight bonds of the Mexican 6 per cent. consolidated external loan of 1890, which have been purchased and cancelled.

The statement that the Beira Railway Company, Limited, would postpone interest on Series C coupons till January, 1900, should read that the company are prepared to fund the interest and issue bonds in payment as heretofore.

The Deutsche Bank (Berlin) London agency announce that they are in receipt of the necessary remittance for the service of the 4 per cent. external debt of Guatemala, due 30th inst.

Vice-Admiral George Digby Morant has been elected a director of the Fairfield Shipbuilding and Engineering Company, Limited.

Mr. Edward Birks has resigned his position as manager of the Sheffield Banking Company, Limited, after fifty-two years' service. Mr. William Danthwaite, lately joint manager, has been appointed sole manager.

The registered offices of the Achilles Gold Mines, Limited, have been removed to 6 and 7, Queen-street-place, London, E.C., and Mr. W. F. Garland has been appointed secretary to the company.

The liquidators of the Union Debenture Company, Limited, announce a fourth return to the shareholders of 5s. per share, payable at the offices of Mr. Sydney Cronk, 43 and 44, Lombard-street, E.C., on and after the 30th inst.

The English Association of American Bond and Shareholders, Limited, is prepared to cash coupon No. 10, due January 1, 1896, of the first mortgage bonds of the Muskegon Division of the Grand Rapids and Indiana Railway

ENGLISH RAILWAYS.

Div. for half years. 1896	1896	1897	1897	Last Balance forward.	Amt. to pay 1 p.c. on Ord. for ½ yr.	NAME.	Date.	Gross Traffic for week: Amt.	Inc. or dec. on 1897.	Inc. or dec. on 1896.	No. of weeks	Gross Traffic for half-year to date: Amt.	Inc. or dec. on 1897.	Inc. or dec. on 1896.	Mileage.	Inc. on 1897.	Working	Prior Charges last ½ year.	Prop. add Cap. Exp. this ½ year
				£	£												%	£	£
10	10	10	10	2,707	5,094	Barry	J'ne 25	3,331	−4,324	−4,108	26	160,722	−66,382	−34,633	31	—	8·89	60,665	316,853
nil	nil	nil	nil	—	—	Brecon and Merthyr	" 26	928	−894	−841	26	34,294	−4,344	−7,794	61	—	—	—	—
nil	nil	nil	nil	3,979	4,749	Cambrian	" 26	5,977	+451	−641	*	126,980	+3,871	—	250	—	60·96	63,148	40,000
1½	1½	2	1½	1,510	3,150	City and South London	" 26	986	−127	+95	26	96,518	−127	+2,449	3½	—	56·67	5,559	124,000
	2	1½	2	7,895	13,210	Furness	" 19	10,005	+877	+1,538	*	219,715	+7,333	—	139	—	49·88	97,423	20,910
1	1½	½	1	2,207	27,470	Great Cent. (late M., S., & L.)	" 26	48,009	† +7,504	+3,053	25	1,154,518	+42,393	+67,926	352½	—	57·17	627,386	1,200,000
1½	4½	2	5	51,283	62,865	Great Eastern	" 26	88,682	+262	+5,186	25	2,048,465	+52,213	+168394	1,158½	2	55·35	860,138	250,000
3	5½	3	5	15,094	102,496	Great Northern	" 26	94,760	+12,286	+6,914	26	2,469,173	+89,111	+199402	1,073	10	61·76	641,485	750,000
4½	7½	4½	7½	31,350	121,981	Great Western	" 26	180,510	−1,580	−11,260	25	4,416,120	−67,200	+96,780	2,582	21	51·44	1,486,272	800,000
nil	2	nil	1½	8,951	16,487	Hull and Barnsley	" 26	8,088	+2,391	+1,012	25	181,046	+16,581	+27,434	73	—	58·21	70,290	52,980
5	5½	5	5½	21,495	83,704	Lancashire and Yorkshire	" 26	95,013	+4,491	+4,574	25	2,374,880	+79,545	+91,485	555½	25	56·70	674,745	451,976
4½	8	4½	8½	26,243	43,049	Lon., Brighton, & S. Coast	" 25	64,089	† −5,336	+4,850	26	1,307,657	+29,485	+64,751	476½	—	50·20	407,042	240,735
nil	nil	nil	nil	72,294	56,296	London, Chatham, & Dover	" 26	31,088	−1,576	−1,397	25	710,773	+11,934	+29,927	185½	—	50·65	367,873	nil
6½	8	6½	7½	89,535	204,068	London and North Western	" 26	246,707	+40,360	+14,199	25	5,833,625	+157429	+330204	1,911½	—	56·92	1,404,534	600,000
5	8½	8½	8½	23,038	59,367	London and South Western	" 25	82,448	† −21970	−1,358	25	1,821,015	+20,081	+109848	941	—	51·75	513,740	389,000
2½	6	2½	6½	14,592	6,691	Lon., Tilbury, & Southend	" 26	6,649	−756	+533	26	138,007	+4,350	+25,470	81	—	52·57	39,590	15,000
3½	3½	3½	3½	17,133	26,409	Metropolitan	" 25	19,281	† −873	+3,176	*	418,823	+7,456	—	64	—	43·63	148,047	254,000
nil	nil	nil	nil	4,006	11,250	Metropolitan District	" 26	8,034	† −5,584	+133	25	211,028	−2,063	—	13	—	48·70	119,663	38,450
5	7	5½	6½	38,143	174,582	Midland	" 26	200,110	+44,415	+21,043	26	4,669,017	+173322	+438548	1,354½	15½	57·59	1,216,382	650,000
5½	7½	5½	7	22,374	138,189	North Eastern	" 25	173,231	+7,605	+16,237	25	3,707,486	+82,458	+359148	1,597½	—	58·82	795,077	436,004
7½	7½	7½	7½	7,061	10,102	North London	" 26	8,939	−846	+50	25	234,098	−2,806	—	12	—	50·90	49,973	7,600
4	5	4	4½	4,745	16,150	North Staffordshire	" 26	15,548	+3	−281	26	404,136	+4,601	+10,825	312	—	55·27	118,142	19,605
10	10	11	10	1,642	3,004	Rhymney	" 25	1,620	−2,384	−3,196	26	95,240	−32,062	−24,405	71	—	49·68	29,049	16,700
	6½	3½	6½	4,054	50,215	South Eastern	" 25	49,584	† −1,492	+2,858	*	1,127,667	+46,802	—	448	—	51·88	380,763	250,000
3½	3½	1½	3½	2,315	25,961	Taff Vale	" 25	6,942	−7,755	−7,222	26	289,193	−113589	−91,526	121	—	54·90	94,800	92,000

* From January 1. † Jubilee week in 1897.

SCOTCH RAILWAYS.

Div. 1896	1896	1897	1897	Last Balance forward	Amt. to pay 1 p.c. on Ord. for ½ yr.	Name	Date	Amt.	Inc. or dec. on 1897	Inc. or dec. on 1896	No. of weeks	Amt.	Inc. or dec. on 1897	Inc. or dec. on 1896	Mileage	Inc. on 1897	Working	Prior Charges last ½ year	Prop. add Cap. Exp. this ½ year
5	5	5½	5	9,544	78,066	Caledonian	June 26	76,806	+ 5,083	+ 2,284	21	1,559,956	+ 41,361	—	851½	5	50·38	588,248	441,477
5	5½	5	5	7,364	24,639	Glasgow and South-Western	" 25	31,412	− 248	+ 1,425	21	604,929	+ 19,095	—	393½	—	54·69	221,663	196,145
3½	3½	3½	—	1,291	4,600	Great North of Scotland	" 25	9,408	+ 876	+ 600	21	174,859	+ 1,605	+ 7,714	331	15½	52·03	92,178	60,000
	nil		—	10,477	12,820	Highland	" 26	10,162	− 557	− 73	17	157,193	+ 1,833	—	479½	27½	38·63	78,976	,000
	1½	1	1½	819	45,819	North British	" 26	78,189	+ 6,759	+ 4,555	21	1,534,558	+ 52,703	—	1,230	23	48·62	944,809	40,800

IRISH RAILWAYS.

Div. 1896	1896	1897	1897	Last Balance forward	Amt. to pay 1 p.c. on Ord. for ½ yr.	Name	Date	Amt.	Inc. or dec. on 1897	Inc. or dec. on 1896	No. of weeks	Amt.	Inc. or dec. on 1897	Inc. or dec. on 1896	Mileage	Inc. on 1897	Working	Prior Charges last ½ year	Prop. add Cap. Exp. this ½ year
6½	6½	6½	—	5,466	1,700	Belfast and County Down	June 24	2,860	− 942	− 175	*	56,809	− 1,201	—	76½	—	55·58	17,690	10,000
5½	6½	5½	—	—	4,284	Belfast and Northern Counties	" 24	6,978	− 32	− 151	*	131,798	+ 3,459	[illegible]	249	—	—	—	—
	3	2	—	1,418	1,200	Cork, Bandon, and S. Coast†	" 25	1,517	+ 5	+ 105	*	32,733	− 2,715	—	103	—	54·82	14,436	5,450
	6½	6½	6½	38,776	17,816	Great Northern	" 24	15,654	− 136	+ 147	25	373,702	+ 10,555	+ 22,656	528	—	50·15	88,068	22,000
	5½	5½	5½	30,339	24,855	Great Southern and Western	" 24	—	—	—	not	received	—	—	603	13	51·45	72,800	46,580
	4	4	4½	11,372	11,850	Midland Great Western	" 24	10,811	− 1,891	+ 1,284	25	255,381	+ 5,967	− 2,617	538	—	50·31	83,129	1,800
nil	ni	nil	nil	229	2,822	Waterford and Central	" 24	822	+ 17	− 25	*	—	—	—	59½	—	53·24	6,858	1,900
nil	n	nil	nil	1,936	2,987	Waterford, Limerick & W.	" 24	4,401	− 1,116	− 247	*	—	—	—	350½	—	57·83	42,617	7,075

* From January 1. † Seventeen weeks' strike.

MINING RETURNS.

BROKEN HILL PROPRIETARY COMPANY.—21,357 tons of ore treated, including product from ores purchased; output from the refinery, 1,898 oz. gold (estimated), 427,865 oz. silver, 2,545 tons of lead, and 35 tons antimonial lead (estimated); the copper matte containing 17 tons of copper (estimated), and 22,616 oz. silver (estimated).

MAY CONSOLIDATED GOLD MINING COMPANY.—Yield 3,518 oz.; cyanide, 2,272 oz., inclusive of clean up.

OTTOS KOPJE DIAMOND MINES.—4,751 loads washed, 200 carats of diamonds won.

ST. JOHN DEL REY.—Gold produced June 11 to 20, £7,600. Yield per ton ·92 of an oz. troy.

BAYLEY'S UNITED GOLD MINES.—Cyanide plant treated 890 tons tailings, yielding 946 oz. of gold.

BRILLIANT BLOCK GOLD MINING COMPANY.—1,072 tons for 736 oz. of gold.

FRANK SMITH DIAMOND MINES.—3,600 loads washed producing 211 carats.

ALADDIN'S LAMP GOLD MINING COMPANY.—440 tons of ore crushed, yielding 250 oz., and 9 tons of concentrates, containing 313 oz.

ALASKA TREADWELL.—Bullion shipment, $64,455; ore milled, 22,766 tons; sulphurets treated, 412 tons; bullion from sulphurets, $21,959.

MOUNT USHER.—68 tons of ore crushed, yielded 140 oz. gold.

MYALL'S UNITED.—Crushed 2,200 tons, yielding 451 oz. gold; tailings treated by cyanide yielded 417 oz.

HANNAN'S CRŒSUS.—52 tons crushed, yielded 53 oz.

HAURAKI.—Crushed 150 tons, yielding 440 oz.

BELLEVUE PROPRIETARY.—493 tons crushed, yielding 872 oz.

BRILLIANT BLOCK.—1,072 tons crushed for 736 oz.

QUEEN CROSS REEF.—265 tons crushed, yielding 327 oz.

MOUNT DAVID.—Crushed 404 tons, yielded 670 oz.

VICTORIA AND QUEEN.—280 tons crushed for 588 oz.

LACHLAN GOLDFIELDS.—Crushed 387 tons second class ore, yielding 102 oz.

SUGARLOAF ("25 MILE").—53 tons crushed, yielded 155 oz. of retorted gold.

MAMMOTH COLLINS.—3,000 tons crushed, yielded $10,750.

QUEENSLAND MENZIES.—Crushed 230 tons, yielding 577 oz.

BROCK'S GOLDFIELDS OF THE NORTHERN TERRITORIES OF AUSTRALIA.—Clean up after first crushing of 100 tons for 117 oz. of gold.

DAY DAWN BLOCK AND WYNDHAM GOLD MINING COMPANY.—Tons crushed, 2,400; yield of gold, 1,782 oz., including tailings.

EAGLEHAWK CONSOLIDATED GOLD MINING COMPANY.—Crushed, 230 tons, yielding 141 oz. gold.

NEW AUSTRALIAN BROKEN HILL CONSOLS.—2 tons 13 cwt., containing 4,300 oz of silver.

HIGHLAND CHIEF.—150 tons crushed, yielding 46 oz.

LADY SHENTON.—Crushed 626 tons, yielding 1,890 oz., including 250 oz. from plates.

HOWELL'S CONSOLIDATED GOLD MINES.—1,661 tons of ore crushed for 1,085 oz. of gold.

FRANK SMITH DIAMOND MINES.—3,800 loads washed, producing 200 carats.

WEBSTER'S FIND.—58 oz. gold from 45 tons crushed.

RAILWAY TRAFFIC RETURNS.

ALGECIRAS (GIBRALTAR) RAILWAY.—Traffic for week ended June 18, Ps. 28,920; increase, Ps. 990. Aggregate from July 1, Ps. 1,067,727; increase, Ps. 78,747.

WEST FLANDERS RAILWAY.—Gross receipts for week ending June 26, £2,307; increase, £476. Total from January 1, £61,807; increase, £2,580.

VILLA MARIA AND RUFINO RAILWAY.—Traffic for week ending June 25, £311; increase, £30. Aggregate from January 1, £8,753; increase, £1,640.

BENGAL CENTRAL RAILWAY.—Traffic receipts for week ending June 4, Rs. 16,433; decrease, Rs. 1,296. Aggregate from January 1, Rs. 4,60,372; increase, Rs. 74,081.

ALCOY AND GANDIA RAILWAY AND HARBOUR COMPANY.—Traffic for week, June 25, Ps. 9,900; decrease Ps. 200. Aggregate from January 1, Ps. 224,300; decrease, Ps. 10,770.

WESTERN OF SANTA FE RAILWAYS.—Gross receipts for week ending June 18, $12,103; decrease, $1,287.

BURMA RAILWAYS.—Traffic receipts for week ending May 28, Rs. 1,62,619; decrease Rs. 27,536. Aggregate from January 1, Rs. 43,77,583; decrease, Rs. 52,269.

ROHILKUND AND KUMAON RAILWAY.—Traffic receipts for week ending May 28, Rs. 9,939; increase, Rs. 1,699. Aggregate from January 1, Rs. 1,76,889; increase, Rs. 5,896.

WESTERN OF SANTA FE RAILWAY.—Traffic receipts for week ending June 25, $9,081; decrease, $3,070.

CLEATOR AND WORKINGTON.—Gross receipts for the week ending June 25 amounted to £1,007, an increase of £136. Total receipts from January 1, £26,109, a decrease of £222.

COCKERMOUTH AND KESWICK RAILWAY.—Receipts for the week ending June 25, £1,205; increase, £242. Aggregate from January 1, £22,213; increase, £2,261.

GREAT WESTERN OF BRAZIL.—Traffic receipts for the week ending May 21, $14,375; decrease, $2,679. Aggregate from January 1, $646,699; increase, $81,094.

The numbers are announced of three bonds of £100 each, Series A, and twenty bonds of £20 each, Series B, of the issue of £1,890,000 5 per cent. first mortgage debentures of the Royal Trans-African Railway Company, drawn for redemption, which will be paid on July 1 at the Capital and Counties Bank, Limited, 39, Threadneedle-street, E.C., or at the company's agents in Amsterdam and Brussels, or at the offices of the company in Oporto or Lisbon, but the same will not be payable in Paris as heretofore.

Mr. Joseph Pyke has accepted a seat on the board of the New Tivoli, Limited.

The Southern Pacific Company will, after July 1, against delivery of dividend warrants No. 34 appertaining to certificates of stock of the Central Pacific Railroad Company, pay half of 1 per cent. of the par value of the stock. Holders of the London committee's certificates in England can obtain the amount referred to on presentation of their certificate at Messrs. Glyn, Mills, Currie, & Co.'s, 67, Lombard-street, London, E.C.

Natal and Nova Cruz (Brazilian) Railway, Limited. The registered office of the company is now at 10, Finsbury-circus, London, E.C.

FOREIGN RAILWAYS.

Mileage: Total.	Increase on 1897.	Increase on 1896.	Name	Gross Traffic for Week: Week ending	Amount.	In. or Dec. upon 1897.	In. or Dec. upon 1896.	Gross Traffic to Date: No. of Weeks.	Amount.	In. or Dec. upon 1897.	In. or Dec. upon 1896.
					£	£	£		£	£	£
319	—	—	Argentine Great Western ..	June 10	7,361	+ 1,037	+ 1,547	49	298,715	− 1,238	+ 59,937
76½	—	—	Bahia and San Francisco ..	Apr. 30	2,754	− 131	− 1,437	18	—	—	—
234	48	84	Bahia Blanca and North West..	May 29	287	− 180	—	47	24,892	− 1,614	—
75	1	—	Buenos Ayres and Ensenada ..	June 26	2,768	− 148	—	26	82,787	+ 13,545	—
426	—	—	Buenos Ayres and Pacific ..	June 25	8,033	+ 2,800	+ 539	51	355,300	− 38,866	+ 15,907
914	—	3	Buenos Ayres and Rosario ..	June 25	11,475	+ 443	− 1,441	26	409,388	+ 100,946	+ 68,508
1,499	30	68	Buenos Ayres Great Southern ..	June 26	23,847	+ 3,720	+ 3,738	51	1,500,337	+ 128,705	+ 220,604
602	107	177	Buenos Ayres Western ..	June 26	8,175	− 1,454	− 1,094	51	608,210	− 75,977	− 104,236
845	55	77	Central Argentine..	June 25	13,460	+ 2,320	− 1,455	25	520,413	+ 127,050	+ 60,806
197	—	—	Central Bahia	Apr. 30*	$155,590	+ $35,560	+ $57,258	4	$581,140	+ $60,760	+ $87,881
271	—	—	Central Uruguay of Monte Video	June 25	4,400	+ 831	− 1,116	51	300,580	+ 31,585	− 17,111
228	—	—	Do. Eastern Extension	June 25	715	+ 103	− 174	51	65,000	+ 10,040	+ 131
182	—	—	Do. Northern Extension	June 25	528	− 37	− 114	51	32,142	+ 1,019	− 8,090
180	—	—	Cordoba and Rosario	June 12	1,430	− 500	− 1,050	49	104,500	− 14,085	− 2,725
128	—	—	Cordoba Central	June 12	$22,500	− $6,270	− $16,000	24	$504,830	− $92,670	− $117,210
549	—	—	Do. Northern Extension	June 12	$56,000	− $17,320	− $19,830	24	$1,084,300	− $376,110	− $230,060
137	—	—	Costa Rica	June 11	3,613	− 636	− 607	24	133,294	− 528	+ 11,930
99	—	—	East Argentine	May 1	1,062	+ 496	+ 69	16	13,802	+ 2,131	+ 1,007
386	—	6	Entre Rios	June 25	1,090	+ 341	− 160	51	81,800	+ 25,788	+ 18,847
555	—	24	Inter Oceanic of Mexico.. ..	June 25	$53,800	+ $2,680	+ $8,700	51	$2,973,570	+ $461,160	+ $784,300
23	—	—	La Guaira and Caracas	May 20	1,762	− 607	—	21	41,428	− 6,161	—
321	—	—	Mexican	June 25	$67,100	− $1,900	—	25	$1,027,600	+ $202,750	—
1,846	—	—	Mexican Central	June 21	$255,032	+ $1,694	+ $91,791	25	$6,325,062	+ $102,436	+ $1,746,829
1,217	—	—	Mexican National	June 21	$113,208	+ $2,880	+ $27,419	25	$2,677,984	+ $501,746	+ $598,958
228	—	—	Mexican Southern	June 14	$11,730	− $141	+ $4,192	10	$130,507	− $17,814	+ $34,463
106	—	—	Minas and Rio	Apr. 30*	$142,119	− $22,067	—	10 mos.	$1,740,090	+ $171,787	—
94	—		N. W. Argentine	June 23	1,522	− 127	− 1,304	23	27,351	− 9,465	− 9,031
242	3	—	Nitrate	June 15	13,476	− 5,117	− 13,692	22	164,360	− 5,448	− 83,858
320	—	—	Ottoman	June 25	2,333	− 262	− 1,583	25	112,946	− 23,887	+ 3,371
77½	—	—	Recife and San Francisco ..	Apr. 30	5,313	+ 1,426	+ 463	18	98,559	+ 11,081	− 17,219
86½	—	—	San Paulo	May 15†	15,798	− 7,558	—	18	181,508	—	—
186	—	—	Santa Fe and Cordova	June 25	1,142	− 94	− 478	51	89,690	+ 4,379	− 7,281
110	—	—	Western of Havana	June 25	1,210	− 524	− 690	51	88,235	+ 2,242	+ 5,460

* For month ended. † For fortnight ended.

INDIAN RAILWAYS.

Mileage: Total.	Increase on 1897.	Increase on 1896.	Name.	Gross Traffic for Week: Week ending	Amount.	In. or Dec. on 1897.	In. or Dec. on 1896.	Gross Traffic to Date: No. of Weeks.	Amount.	In. or Dec. on 1897.	In. or Dec. on 1896.
862	—	—	Bengal Nagpur	June 18	Rs.1,00,000	− Rs.11,619	+ Rs.9,774	25	Rs.38,37,446	+ Rs.4,61,064	+ Rs.2,66,488
827	8	63	Bengal and North-Western ..	May 14	Rs.1,64,120	+ Rs.9,345		20	Rs.26,96,385	+ Rs.2,70,581	—
461	—	—	Bombay and Baroda	June 25	£23,283	− £1,593	+ £1,323	25	£791,894	+ £66,755	− £81,574
1,885	2	13	East Indian	June 18	Rs.11,56,000	+ Rs.43,000	+ Rs.2,27,000	25	Rs.3,05,32,000	+ Rs.11,69,000	+ Rs.36,14,000
1,491	—	—	Great Indian Penin.	June 18	£53,763	+ £9,102	+ £3,493	25	£1,719,410	+ £353,356	− £141,363
736	—	—	Indian Midland	June 18	Rs.1,80,040	+ Rs.33,928	+ Rs.81,509	25	Rs.36,89,294	+ Rs.4,51,802	+ Rs.10,17,178
840	—	—	Madras	June 11	£19,983	+ £92	+ £366	23	£450,161	− £22,800	− £4,900
1,042	—	—	South Indian	May 28	Rs.1,77,938	− Rs.2,022	− Rs.12,899	22	Rs.34,05,448	− Rs.3,08,021	− Rs.3,31,22

UNITED STATES AND CANADIAN RAILWAYS.

Mileage: Total.	Increase on 1897.	Increase on 1896.	Name.	Gross Traffic for Week: Period Ending.	Amount.	In. or Dec. on 1897.	Gross Traffic to Date: No. of Weeks.	Amount.	In. or Dec. on 1897.
					dols.	dols.		dols.	dols.
917	—	—	Baltimore & Ohio S. Western ..	June 21	112,646	− 10,605	51	6,691,760	+ 828,591
6,568	92	156	Canadian Pacific	" 7	512,000	+ 43,000	21	9,945,000	+ 1,764,000
922	—	—	Chicago Great Western	" 7	86,141	− 5,281	47	4,998,369	+ 616,273
6,169	—	469	Chicago, Mil., & St. Paul ..	" 21	610,000	− 15,000	25	13,382,001	+ 1,762,800
1,685	—	—	Denver & Rio Grande	" 21	159,400	+ 12,900	51	7,860,100	+ 1,252,600
3,512	—	—	Grand Trunk, Main Line ..	" 14	£71,645	− £1,254	22	£1,701,801	+ £130,333
335	—	—	Do. Chic. & Grand Trunk	" 14	£14,299	+ £2,336	22	£345,802	+ £77,729
189	—	—	Do. Det., G. H. & Mil...	" 14	£3,126	− £529	22	£79,664	− £5,263
2,938	—	—	Louisville & Nashville	" 21	400,000	+ 22,000	25	10,103,175	+ 1,336,620
2,197	137	137	Miss., K., & Texas	" 21	141,803	+ 1,938	51	11,843,047	+ 563,636
477	—	—	N. Y., Ontario, & W.	" 21	73,794	− 3,415	51	3,639,435	+ 66,113
1,570	—	—	Norfolk & Western	" 21	168,000	− 13,000	25	5,135,900	+ 466,433
3,499	336	—	Northern Pacific	" 21	369,000	+ 43,000	25	9,214,775	+ 2,626,552
1,223	—	—	St. Louis S. Western	" 21	113,000	+ 3,000	25	2,403,295	+ 343,928
4,654	—	—	Southern	" 21	356,000	+ 27,000	25	8,695,812	+ 1,777,430
1,979	—	—	Wabash	" 21	231,000	+ 38,000	51	12,863,430	+ 1,256,000

MONTHLY STATEMENTS.

Mileage: Total.	Increase on 1896	Increase on 1895.	Name.	Net Earnings for Month: Month.	Amount.	In. or Dec. on 1897.	In. or Dec. on 1896.	Net Earnings to Date: No. of Months.	Amount.	In. or Dec. on 1897.	In. or Dec. on 1896.
					dols	dols.	dols.		dols.	dols.	dols.
6,935	44	444	Atchison	May	789,000	+ 233,000	+ 309,673	5	3,731,434	+ 1,226,836	+ 776,519
6,547	103	106	Canadian Pacific	May	927,000	+ 51,000	+ 239,510	5	3,337,000	+ 556,000	+ 852,067
6,169	—	469	Chicago, Mil., & St. Paul ..	May	966,000	+ 176,000	+ 294,869	5	4,461,334	+ 420,640	+ 371,794
1,685	—	—	Denver & Rio Grande	April	264,200	+ 11,727	+ 38,988	10	2,777,080	+ 418,762	+ 69,015
1,970	—	—	Erie..	April	554,000	+ 17,000	+ 45,487	4	1,932,600	+ 100,400	− 42,700
3,512	—	—	Grand Trunk, Main Line ..	April	£114,098	+ £16,224	+ £26,710	4	£360,051	+ £78,596	+ £123,527
335	—	—	Do. Chic. & Grand Trunk	April	£11,526	+ £6,424	+ £5,660	4	£50,236	+ £30,706	+ £34,578
189	—	—	Do. Det. G. H. & Mil. ..	April	£4,016	+ £390	+ £2,125	4	£10,544	+ £1,127	+ £8,744
3,127	—	239	Illinois Central	April	531,000	+ 170	+ 95,779	4	2,744,704	+ 535,402	+ 645,318
2,396	—	—	New York Central*	April	3,807,000	+ 302,000	+ 394,152	4	14,602,000	+ 964,000	—
477	—	—	New York Ontario, & W. ..	May	49,000	− 15,500	− 36,070	11	1,029,400	+ 8,000	+ 66,263
1,570	—	—	Norfolk & Western	April	237,000	+ 40,000	+ 96,237	4	1,063,000	+ 105,340	+ 208,139
2,407	—	—	Pennsylvania	April	1,524,200	+ 12,900	+ 236,000	4	5,672,228	+ 121,300	+ 375,900
1,055	—	—	Phil. & Reading	April	623,155	− 12,799	—	10	8,190,418	+ 511,265	—

* Statement of gross traffic.

Prices Quoted on the London Stock Exchange.

Throughout the Investors' Review middle prices alone are quoted, the object being to give the public the approximate current quotations of every security of any consequence in existence. On the markets the buying and selling prices are both given, and are often wide apart where stocks are seldom dealt in. Other particulars will be found in the Investment Index published quarterly—January, April, July, and October—in connection with this Review, price 2s., by post 2s. 2d. Where dividends are paid only once a year, an *italic* type is used to distinguish them. The London Stock Exchange Official List is quoted in the Review almost entire, only very insignificant issues, or bonds falling due within the next two or three years, being omitted. But the list is subdivided into the leading, or active, stocks, and those less frequently dealt in. The former will be found under the head of "Stock Markets," and with more details than it is possible to give for the bulk of securities. By retaining the file of the Investors' Review any subscriber can follow for himself the movements of securities from week to week, and the Investment Index will from time to time help to fill up deficiencies in the information.

Tea Companies and Mines and Mining Finance Stocks are placed in special lists.

Among the abbreviations used are the following:—S.F. Snk. Fd. *sinking fund*; Certs., *certificates*; Debs. or Dbs., *debentures*; Db. or D.Stk., *debenture stock*; Pf. Prf., or Pref., *preference*; Prefd. or Pfd., *preferred*; Dfd., *deferred*; L. or Ltd., *limited*; Sh., *share*; Ans., *annuities*; Cu. or Cm., *cumulative*; Gu or Guar., *guaranteed*; Bds., *bonds*; S., Sr., or Ser., *series*; In., Ins., Insc., *inscribed*; Dr., Drgs., Drwgs., *drawings*; Stg., Strlg., *sterling*; Lia., *liable to*; Sp., Surp., *surplus*; Per., Perp., *perpetual*; Ln. *lien*; Lo. *loan*.

The dates following the names of securities are the years of issue or of redemption. Where shares are not fully paid up, their nominal amount is given with the name so that investors may know the liability upon them.

BRITISH FUNDS, &c.

Rate.	Name.		Price.
2½	2½ p.c.'s (Childers') Red..	1905	106
3	Local Loans Stk.	1912	110½
3	Metro. Police Deb. Stk.	1920	105
—	Red Sea Ind. Tel. Ann.	1908	8½
4	Canada Gv. "Intcl. Rly."	1903	105¼
4	Do. do. ..	1908	111
4	Do. Bonds	1910	112
4	Do. Bonds	1913	117½
3	Egyptian Gov. Gar.		106
3	Mauritius Ins. Stk.	1940	113
4	Turkish Guar. 1855		109
11½	Bank of Ireland Stk.		385
3½	India Rupee Paper		62
3½	Do. 1854-5		62
3	Do. 1896-7	1916	54
3½	Isle of Man Deb.		104
3	Do. Deb. Stk...	1919-29	103

CORPORATION AND COUNTY STOCKS.

FREE OF STAMP DUTY.

Rate.	Name.		Price.
3½	Metropolitan Con.	1929	117½
3	Do.	1941	110
2½	Do.	1920-40	99
2½	L.C.C. Con. Stock	1920	98
3½	Comm. of Sewers, Scp , S.F.	1905	104
3½	Corp. of Lond. Bds...	1898-1902	100½
3	Do.	1898-1912	101
3½	Do , Debs. Scp. ...... S.F.	1916	105
2½	Do., Deb. Stk. Scrip ..	1927-57	97
3	Barnsley	1916-46	103
3	Barry	1914-46	100½
3	Bath	1909-34	103
3	Batley	1914-44	100½
3½	Birmingham	1946	116½
3	Do.	1947	110½
2½	Do.	1926	97
3	Blackburn	1930	103½
3	Bournemouth	1913-33	102
3½	Bradford	1945	115½
3	Do. Deb. Stock ..	1954	108
3	Brighouse..............	1916-46	100
3½	Brighton	1946	117
2½	Do.	1957	96½
3	Burton-on-Trent.........	1913-43	100½
3	Cambridge	1913-43	102
3½	Cardiff	1935	115½
3	Do.	1914-54	102
3	Cheltenham..............	1971	105½
3	Chichester	1916-46	[illegible]
3½	Croydon		126½
3	Do.	1940	107½
3	Derby	1920-50	105½
3	Devon C.C..............	1917-37	104½
3½	Dewsbury	1930	109
3	Do.	1930	103
3	Dorset County	1922-32	106
3	Douglas (I. of Man)	1926	100½
3	Dover	1913-43	101½
3½	Dublin	1944	111½
3	Eastbourne	1920-40	103½
3	Edinburgh	1924	105½
2½	Do.	1927	97
2½	Exeter	1917-57	96
3	Glamorgan County	1914-34	103
3½	Glasgow	1914	109
3	Do.	1921	104½
2½	Do.	1925-40	98
3	Gloster	1915-55	101½
3	Grimsby	1913-43	103
3	Hampshire County	1914-34	105½
3	Hanley	1913-43	102½
3	Harrogate	1914-34	102
3	Hastings	1913-54	103
2½	Hertfordshire C.C.	1916-36	96
3	Heston & Isleworth U.D.C.	1915-35	101
3	Huddersfield	1934	106
3½	Hull (1st iss.)		127½
3	Inverness	1914-44	100
3	Ipswich	1958	106½
3	Lancaster..............	1919-55	101
2½	Leeds	1927	97
3½	Leicester	1934	114
3	Lincoln.................	1919	102
3½	Liverpool..............		131

Corporation, &c. (*continued*):—

Rate.	Name.		Price.
3	Manchester............	1941	107½
3½	Middlesbro'...........	1909	105½
3½	Do.	1911-13	105
3	Do.	1915	104
3	Middlesex C.C.........	1915-35	105
3½	Newcastle	1936	115½
3½	Do. Irred.		127½
2½	Do.	1915-36	99½
3	Newcastle-under-Lyme..	1909-44	100
3	Newport (Mon.)	1915-55	100½
3	Norwich	1952	110
3	Nottingham		113
3	Oxford	1951	108½
3	Penzance	1916-46	100½
3	Plymouth	1942	105
3	Pontypridd U.D.C.	1916-46	98
3	Poole.................	1915-45	101
3½	Portsmouth........1916	24 & 27	111
3	Do.	1913-33	105
3	Ramsey	1920-40	99
3	Ramsgate............	1915-55	102
3½	Reading		129
3	Do.	1962	106
3½	Rhyl U.D.C.	1953	110
3	Richmond (Surrey)	1942	103½
3	River Wear Debt Certs.		99
3	St. Helen's	1915-55	102
3	Scarbro'	1915-50	101
2½	Sheffield	1925-57	94½
3	Shipley U.D.C.........	1915-35	99
3	Somerset Co.	1923-33	104
3	South Shields.........	1915-45	100½
2½	Southampton	1915-45	99½
3	Southend-on-Sea	1916-46	100
3	Staffs C.C.	1915-35	103½
3	Stockport.............	1914-54	101
3	Stockton	1939	104
3	Do.	1915-35	103
3	Surrey Co.	1922-32	105½
3½	Swansea		128½
3	Do.	1955	105
3	Taunton	19183-9-43	101
3	Tees Conserv. Deb. Stk.	1947	99
3	Thames Conserv. "A" Deb. Stk............	1954	102½
3	Do. "B" Deb. Stk.	1954	102½
3	Torquay	1913-43	100½
3	Tunbridge Wells	1931	102½
3	Tynemouth............	1913	99
3	Wakefield............	1929	101½
3	Walsall..............	1932	105½
3	West Bromwich........	1930	105
3½	West Ham	1929	110
3	Do.	1945	105
3	West Sussex C.C.	1915-35	106
3	Weston-s.-Mare Lcl Bd.	1914-44	100½
3	Weymouth & Melc. Regis	1918	99
3	Widnes..............	1915-55	100
3	Wigan	1921	105½
3	Windsor	1918-55	102½
3½	Wisbech	1947	113½
3½	Wolverhampton	1932	117
3	Do.	1924-54	107
3	York	1916-41	105½

SUBJECT TO STAMP DUTY.

Rate.	Name.		Price.
3½	Belfast City & Dis. Watr.	1938	114
3	Do. Red Stk.	1953-6	105
3½	Belfast	1924	102
4	Blackburn Con. Deb. Irred.		140
3½	Do. do. Irred..........		128
3½	Bristol		132
3½	Burnley................	1933	114
2½	Chesterfield Gas & Wtr.	1916-46	96
3½	Douglas Town	1921	103
3	Dover Harb. 1st Deb...	1956	104½
3½	Hull (2nd iss.)		127½
4	Leeds Deb..............	1927	121½
3½	Do.		113½
3	Do.	1927	104
3	Leicester	1919-44	103
4	Manchester..............		145
3	Do.	1928	103½
4½	Middlesboro' Mrts.	1908	110
3½	Sheffield	1898-1916	100½
3½	Do.	1925-36	114
3	Do.	1925	104½
3½	Southampton	S.F.	104½
4½	Stockton Morts.	1908	110½
3½	Worcester............	1950	109

COLONIAL AND PROVINCIAL GOVERNMENT SECURITIES.

Rate.	Name.		Price.
6	British Columbia..........	1907	119½
4½	Do. Debs. ..	1917	111½
3	British Guiana Imgtn. Bds.		98
5	Canada, "Intercol. Rail,"	1903	108½
4	Do. (Bonds)	1904-5-6-8	106
4	Do. Reduced	1910	110
3½	Do. Bnds.	1909-34	107
4	Do. Loan	1910-35	110
3	Do. Loan	1938	103
6	Cape of G. Hope	1900	—
5	Do.	1900	—
4½	Do. red. by an. draw.		108
4½	Do 1879		108
4	Do. 1881		107
4	Dc	1917-23	113
4½	Ceylon		108
4	Do.		106½
4½	Fiji Gov. Deb. Sink. Fd.		104
4	Jamaica Sink. Fd.	1923	105
5	Manitoba Debs..........	1910	113
5	Do. Ster. Bds.	1908	119½
4	Do. Ster. Debs.		105
4	Mauritius, Cons. Debs. 1880...		101½
4½	Natal, Sink. Fd........	1919	118
4	Do. do.	1926	114
3½	Newfoundland Stg. Bds.	1941	100
3½	Do. do. ..	1947	100
3	Do. do.		87
5	New South Wales 1897-1902		104½
4	Do.	1903-5-8-9-1?	106
5	New Zealand	1914	118
5	Do. Cnsls. 1 p.c. per an. Sink. Fd.		105
3½	Nova Scotia Debs.		104
5	Quebec Prov.	1904-6	108
4½	Do. (drgs.)		105
5	Do. Strlg. Bds.	1912	115
4	Do. Strlg. Bds.	1928	110
4	Do. Strlg. Bds.	1934	108
4	Queensland	1913-15	108
4½	St. Lucia Debs...............		102
6	South Australia	1898-1900	103½
6	Do.	1901-1918	116
5	Do.	1911-1920	118½
4	Do.	1899-1916	104½
4	Do.	1929	108½
4	Do.	1916	106½
4	Do.	1917-18-24	110
6	Tasmania	1897-1901	104
4	Do. 1908-11,	1913-14-20	107½
5	Trinidad Debs., an. drw.1 p c...		107
4	Victoria	1899-1901	102½
4½	Do.	1904	107
4	Do. Rail. Loan	1907	107
4	Do. Loans	1908-13	107
4½	West. Austr. 1 p.c. ar. Sink. Fd.		107
4	Do. do.		106

REGISTERED AND INSCRIBED STOCKS.

No stamp duty except for Canada 4 p.c. Reduced (½ per cent.).

Rate.	Name.		Price.
4	Antigua Insc. Stk. Red.	1919-44	111
3½	Barbados Insc. Stk.	1925-42	107
3	British Colum. Insc. Stk.	1941	99
4	British Guiana Insc....	1935	114½
4	Canada Stk. Regd. ..	1904-5-6-8	106
4	Do. 4 p.c. (late 5 p.c.) Regd.	1910	108
3½	Do. 3½ p.c. Stock Regd.	1909-34	107
4	Do. Ln. for 4 milln. stg.	1910-35	108
3	Do. Stk. Regd.	1938	102
2½	Do. Insc...............	1947	92
4	Cape G. Hope Regd. ..	1917-23	113
4	Do. (Ln. of '83) Insc. ..	1923	117
4	Do. Cons. Stk. Insc....	1916-36	114
3½	Do. Consol. Insc. Stock	1929-49	109
4	Ceylon Insc. Stock	1934	120
3	Do.	1940	105
4	Grenada Insc. Stock....	1917-42	110
3½	Hong Kong Insc. Stock	1918-43	104
4	Jamaica Insc. Stock....	1934	118
—	Do.	1922-44	98
4	Mauritius Inscribed	1937	119½
4	Natal Consd. Stk. Insc.	1927	117
4	Do.	1937	119
3½	Do. Inscribed Stock..	1914-39	106
4	Newfoundland Inscribed	1913-38	106
4	Do.	1935	113
4	Do. Consd. Stk. Ins.	1936	113
4	N. S. Wales Stock Insc.	1933	117
3½	Do.	1924	108
3½	Do.	1918	106
3	Do	1935	100

Colonial, &c. (*continued*):—

Rate.	Name.		Price.
4	N. Zealnd. Con. Stk. Ins.	1929	114½
3½	Do	1940	106
3	Do. Inscribed....	1945	98
3	Quebec (Prov.) Ins. Stk.	1937	94
4	Queensland Stock Insc.	1915-24	109½
3½	Do.	1921-4-30	104½
3½	Do.	1945	107
3	Do.	1922-47	98
4	St. Lucia Insc. Stock ..	1919-44	114½
4	S. Austrln. (1882-7) Reg.	1916-36	110½
3½	Do. In. Stk. Reg.	1939	109
3	Do.	1916-26	100
3/	Do.	1916	100
3½	Tasmanian Insc. Stock..	1920-40	108
4	Do.	1920-40	115
4	Trinidad Insc. Stock....	1917-42	110
3	Do.	1922-44	98
4	Victoria Rly. Loan '81, Inscribed Stock	1907	105
4	Victoria Insc. Stock	1908-13-19	108
4	Victoria (1885) Ins. Stk.	1920	112½
3½	Do. Inscribed Stock	1921-3-6	105
4	Do. do.	1911-26	108
4	W. Austral. Insc. Stock	1934	114½
4	Do.	1911-31	109
3½	Do.	1915-35	105
3	Do.	1915-35	98
3	Do.	1916-36	98

FOREIGN STOCKS, BONDS, &c.

COUPONS PAYABLE IN LONDON.

Last Div.	Name.		Price.
36/	Argentine Ry. Loan 6 p.c.	1881	85½
15/	Do. 5 p.c.	1884	67
30/	Do. N. Cent. Ry. Ext. 5 p.c.	1887-8-9	66½
30/	Do. 5 p.c. Trsy. Convs.	1887	66
5/4½	Do. 4½ p.c. Interl. Gld.	1888	63
27/	Do. 4½ p.c. Stlg. Extrl.	1888	64
10/6	Do. 3½ p.c. External ..	1889	47
4	Do. 4 p.c. Ry. Guar. Res....		56½
4½	Brazilian	1883	55
4½	Do. Gold.........	1879	55½
4½	Do.	1888	53
36/	Buenos Ayres	1824	80
6	Do.	1882-3-6	
6	Bulgarian	1888	96
6	Do. Mort. Bonds	1892	95
4½	Chilian	1885	71
4½	Do.	1886	72
4½	Do.	1887	71
4½	Do.	1889	79½
5	Do.	1892	82
4½	Do.	1893	71
4½	Do.	1895	70
5	Do.	1896	80
7	Chinese Silver	1894	98
6	Do. Gold	1895	109
6	Do. Apl. '95 bydwgs.	1901-15	112
5	Do. Red. dwgs. in 36 yr.	1896	99½
5	Do. Do. Regis.	1896	99
1½	Colmbn. 1½ to 3 p.c. Ext. Bds.	1896	18
6	Cordova, Prov.	1886	24
—	Do. Eng. Ass. Certs.		23
—	Do. 6 p.c.	1887-8	24
—	Do. Eng. Ass. Certs.		23
3	Costa Rica "A"		36
2½	Do. "B"		23
3	Danish Gold	1914	99
10/	Ecuador N. Ext. Bds. 4½ p.c. ascn. to 5 p.c..............		25
3½	Egypt'n Ins. Stk. lia. Stp. Dty.	1890	100
4	Do. State Domain	1878	103
4	Do. D. Sanieh, Red. ..	1905	103
6	Entre Rios..............	1886-8	33
6	Do. Fndg. Ln. Bds.	1894-1921	29
6	Do. do. Parana City......		22½
15/	Greek	1881	40
15/	Do.	1884	40
12/	Do. Rentes................		33
15/	Do. (Piræus-Larissa Ry.)		35
2/6	Do. Fundg. Loan		43
4	Guatemala Extl. Debt..........		31
6	Hawaiian		103½
4	Hungarian Gold Rentes.........		102
3	Do.	1895	89½
6	Italian Irriga. Guar.		111½
5	Do. Maremmana		93
5	Japan 5 p.c.		102
5	Mexican (Nat. R. Tehuantp c.)..		94½
6	Do. Extrl.	1890	96

Foreign Stocks, &c. (continued):—

Last Div.	Name.	Price
6	Mexican Extrl. 1893	96
5	Do. Intrnl. Cons. Slvr.	36½
5	Do Intern. Rd. Bds. 2d. Ser.	36½
4	Nicaragua 1886	47½
3½	Norwegian, red. 1937, or earlier	97½
3	Do. do. 1965, do.	99
3½	Do. 3½ p.c. Bnds.	103
1	Paraguay 1 p.c. ris. 3 p.c. 1886-96	17
5	Russian, 1822, £ Strlg.	151
3	Do. 1859	94
4	Do. (Nicolas Ry.) 1867-9	102
3	Do. Transcauc. Ry. 1882	93
4	Do. Con. R. R. Bd. Ser. I., 1889	104
4	Do. Do. II., 1889	104
4	Do. Do. III., 1891	104½
3½	Do. Bonds	101
4	Do. Ln. (Dvinsk and Vitbsk)	101½
6	Salvador 1889	57½
—	S Domingo 4s. Unified: .. 1980	55½
6	San Luis Potosi Stg. 1889	94
5	San Paulo (Brzl.), Stg. 1888	86½
6	Santa Fé 1883-4	32
—	Do. Eng. Ass. Certs. Dep.	31
5	Do. 1888	45
—	Do. Eng. Ass. Certs. Dpsit.	44
5	Do. (W. Cnt. Col. Rly.) Mrt.	24
5	Do. & Reconq. Rly. Mort.	24
5	Spanish Quickslvr Mort. 1870	101½
3½	Swedish 1880	103
3	Do. 1888	99
3	Do. Conversion Loan 1894	99
5	Trans. Gov. Loan Red...1903-42	107
59/	Tucuman (Prov.) 1888	66½
4	Turkish, Secd. on Egypt. Trib.	103
3½	Turkish, Egpt. Trib., Ott. Bd., '94	99½
4	Do. Priority 1890	92
1	Do. Convted Series, "A"	66
5	Do. Customs Ln. 1886	96½
5	Uruguay Bonds 1896	56½
3	Venzuela New Con. Debt 1881	32

COUPONS PAYABLE ABROAD.

Last Div.	Name.	Price
7	Argent. Nat. Cedla. Sries, "B"	32½
5	Austrian Ster. Rnts., ex 10fl., 1870	86
5	Do. do. do.	84
5	Do. Paper do. 1870	85
5	Do. do. do.	85
4	Do. Gld Rentes 1876	102
3	Belgian exchange 25 fr.	100
3½	Danish Int., 1887, Rd. 1896	—
2½	Dutch Certs. ex 12 gldrs.	87
3	Do. Bonds	98
3	Do. Insc. Stk.	97
3½	French Rentes	105
3	Do. 1878, '81-4., Red.	100
3	German Imp. Ln. 1891	95
3	Do. do. 1892-3	95
3	Do. do. 1890-4	95½
5	Japan Cons. Ln., '92, 3, & 5, Red.	48
56/9	Prussian Consols	102
3	Cons. Stg. Ln. 1891	96
4	Utd. States, 1877, Red. 1907	113
4	Do. 1895, 30 yrs.	128
3½	Do. Maschsetts Gl. 1935	113½
3½	Do. Gold Bonds 1923	107½
2	Virginia Cpn. Bds., 3 p.c. from July, 1901	71

BRITISH RAILWAYS.

ORD. SHARES AND STOCKS.

Last Div	Name.	Price.
10	Barry, Ord.	277½
4	Do. Prefd.	126
6	Do. Defd.	154½
5	Caledonian, Ord.	158
3	Do. Prefd.	100
—	Do. Defd. Ord., No. 1	5
	Cambrian, Ord	4½
—	Do. Coast Cons.	4½
32/	Cardiff Ry. Pref. Ord.	114
3/	Central Lond. £10 Ord. Sh.	10
1/9½	Do. do. £6 paid	6
3½d.	Do. Pref. Half-Shares	1½
1/6	Do. Def. do	4½
1½	City and S. London	69½
—	East London, Cons.	7½
2	Furness	65½
2½	Glasgow and S. West. Pfd.	82
2½	Do. do. Dfd.	64½
3	Great Central, Ord....1894	40
32/0	Do. London Exten.	71½
—	Great N. of Scotland, Prfd.	88
—	Do. Dfd.	34
4	Great Northern, Prefd.	119½
—	Do. Consolidated "A"	52
—	Do. do. "B"	191½
2	Highland	74½
4	Isle of Wight, Prefd.	120½
3	Do. Defd.	83½
—	Lancs. Derbys. and E. Cst.	3½
8½	L. Brighton and S. C. Ord.	187
6	Do. Prefd. Ord.	197
10/	Do. Contgt. Rights Certs.	18½
5½	Lond. and S. Western Ord.	225½
4	Do. Preferred	134
6½	Lond., Tilb., and Southend	134½
—	Mersey, £20 shares	½
—	Metropolitan, New Ord.	129
2½	Do. Surplus Lands	91
4	North Cornwall, 4 p.c. Pref.	104½
13/6	Do. Deferred	22½
7½	North London	224½
4½	North Staffordshire	127

British Railways (continued):—

Last Div.	Name.	Price.
3/3	Plymouth, Devenport, and S. W. Junc. £10	8½
3/	Port Talbot £10 Shares	9
9d.	Rhondda Swns. B. £10 Sh.	4½
10	Rhymney, Cons.	265½
4	Do. Prefd.	123
6½	Do. Defd.	145½
1½	Scarboro', Bridlington Junc.	47½
6½	South Eastern, Ord	152
6	Do. Pref.	191
3½	Taff Vale	76
25/	Vale of Glamorgan	127½
3	Waterloo & City	124½

LEASED AT FIXED RENTALS.

Last Div.	Name.	Price.
4	Birkenhead	146
5.19.0	East Lincnshire	202½
5½	Hamsmith. & City Ord.	192½
4½	Lond. and Blackwll.	161½
4½	Do. £100 4½ p. c. Pref.	161½
56/6	Lond. & Green. Ord.	102
5	Do. 5 p. c. Pref.	176½
5	Nor. and Eastn. £50 Ord.	90
6	Do.	104½
3½	N. Cornwall 3½ p. c. Stk.	126½
4 1/8	Nott. & Granthm. R. & C.	145½
3½	Portptk. & Wigtn. Guar. Stk.	121½
9	Vict. Stn. & Pimlico Ord.	307½
4½	Do. 4½ p. c. Pref.	158½
4/	West Lond. £20 Ord. Shs.	14
4 1/8	Weymouth & Portld.	157½

DEBENTURE STOCKS.

Last Div.	Name.	Price.
4	Alexandra Dks. & Ry.	128
3	Barry, Cons.	106
4	Brecon & Mrthyr, New A	124½
4	Do. New B	105
4	Caledonian	148
4	Cambrian "A"	135½
4	Do. "B"	130½
4	Do. "C"	120½
4	Do. "D"	107½
3	Cardiff Rly.	102½
4	City and S. Lond.	137
3½	Cleator & Working Junc.	116½
3	Devon & Som. "A"	103½
16/8	Do. "B" 4 p. c.	36
—	Do. "C" 4 p. c.	10
4	E. Lond. 2nd Ch. 4 p. c. A	134
5/	Do. 2nd B	70½
—	Do. 3rd Ch. 4 p. c.	22½
—	Do. 4th do.	11½
3½	Do. 1st (3½ p. c.)	127½
2½	Do. 2½ p.c. (Whitech. Exn).	86
4	Forth Bridge	141
4	Furness	141
4	Glasgow and S. Western	143
5	Gt. Central	—
4½	Do.	154½
4	Gt. Eastern	146
4	Gt. N. of Scotland	144½
3	Gt. Northern	112
4	Gt. Western	150
4½	Do	156
4½	Do.	166
5	Do.	185
2½	Do.	94½
4	Highland	140½
3	Hull and Barnsley	104
3	Do. 2nd (3-4 p. c).	124
4	Isle of Wight	142½
3	Do. Cent. "A"	91½
4½	Do. "B"	113½
4	Do. "C"	80½
3	Lancs. & Yorkshire	112
4	Lancs. Derbys. & E. Cst.	121½
4½	Ldn. and Blackwall	153
4	Ldn. and Greenwich	142
4	Lond., Brighton, &c.	147
4½	Do.	165
4½	Lond., Chath., &c., Arb.	154½
4½	Do. "B"	152½
4	Do.	136½
4	Do. 1883	136½
3	Do.	104
3	Lond. & N. Western	117
3	Lond. & S. Westn. "A"	113
3	Do. Consld.	113
4	Lond., Til., & Southend	143
—	Mersey, 5 p. c. (Act, 1866)	65
4	Metropolitan	144
4½	Do.	160½
3½	Do.	124½
6	Met. District	205½
4	Do.	136½
2½	Midland	95
4½	Mid-Wales "A"	134½
4	Neath & Brecon 1st	122½
4	Do. "A 1"	117½
3	North British	111
3	Do. 1893	109
3½	N. Cornwall, Launcstn., &c.	126½
4	North Eastern	114

Debenture Stocks (continued):—

Last Div.	Name.	Price.
4½	North London	163½
3	N. Staffordshire	111
4	Plym. Devpt. & S.W. Jn.	139½
4	Rhondda and Swan. Bay	128½
4	Rhymney	142½
4	South-Eastern	147
5	Do.	184
3½	Do.	125½
3	Do.	112½
3	Taff Vale	108½
4	Tottenham & For. Gate	141
3	Vale of Glamorgan	105½
3	West Highld. (Gtd. by N.B.)	107½
4	Wrexham, Mold, &c. "A"	113½
4	Do. "B"	101½
4	Do. "C"	97½

GUARANTEED SHARES AND STOCKS.

Last Div.	Name.	Price.
4	Caledonian	144½
4	Do.	144½
4	Forth Bridge	140½
4	Furness 1881	136½
4	Glasgow & S. Western	143
4	Do. St. Enoch. Rent	141½
6	Gt. Central	198½
4½	Do. 1st Pref.	152½
3½	Do. Pref.	108½
5	Do. Irred. S.Y. Rent	164½
4½	Do. do.	140½
4	Gt. Eastern, Rent	143
5	Do. Metropolitan	176½
4	Do.	145
4	Gt. N. of Scotland	138½
4	Gt. Northern	146½
5	Gt. Western, Rent	186½
5	Do. Cons.	186½
4	Lancs. & Yorkshire	146
5	L., Brighton & S. C.	184
3½	L., Chat. & D. (Shrtlds.)	108½
4	L. & North Western	149
4	L. & South Western .. 1881	147
4½	Met. District, Ealing Rent	151½
4½	Do. Fulham Rent	151½
4	Do. Midland Rent	141½
4	Do. Mid. & Dist. Guar.	130½
2½	Midland, Cons. Perp.	94
3	Mid. & G. N. Jt., "A" Rnt.	106
3	N. British, Lien	109
4	Do Cons. Pref. No. 1	139
3	N. Cornwall, Wadebrge. Gu.	107
4	N. Eastern	146
5	N. Staff. Trent & M. £20 Shs.	36
3½	Nott. Suburban Ord.	123½
20/6	S. E. Perp. Ann.	35
4½	Do. 4½ p.c.	161
3½	S. Yorks. Junc. Ord.	117½
4½	W. Cornwall (G. W., Br., Ex., & S. Dev. Joint Rent	162½
3	W. Highl. Ord. Stk. (Gua., N.B.)	105

PREFERENCE SHARES AND STOCKS.

DIVIDENDS CONTINGENT ON PROFIT OF YEAR.

Last Div.	Name	Price.
4½	Alexandra Dks. & Ry. "A"	126½
5	Barry (First)	169½
4	Do. Consolidated	137½
4	Caledonian Cons., No. 1	143
4	Do. do. No. 2	142
5	Do. do. 1878	177
4	Do. Pref. 1884	141
4	Do. do. 1887 (Conv.)	150½
—	Cambrian, No. 1 4 p.c. Pref.	72½
—	Do. No. 2 do.	37½
—	Do. No. 3 do.	17½
—	Do. No. 4 do.	9
5	City & S. Lond. £10 shares	15½
—	Do. New	14½
4	Furness, Cons. 1881	131½
4	Do. ......"A" 1881	129½
4	Do. ......"B" 1883	127½
4	Glasgow & S. Western	143
4	Do. No. 2	141
4	Do. 1888	139½
4	Do. 1891	139½
5	Gt. Central	159½
4	Do.	133½
5	Do. Conv. 1872	154½
5	Do. do. 1874	153½
5	Do. do. 1876	153½
5	Do. do. 1879	151½
5	Do. do. 1881	148
4	Do. 1889	110½
4	Do. 1891	107½
5	Do. 1894	105½
4	Gt. Eastern, Cons.	143
4	Do. 1886	141½
4	Do. 1881	139½
4	Do. 1884	139½

Preference Shares, &c. (continued):—

Last Div.	Name.	Price.
4	Gt. Eastern, Cons. 1887	139½
4	Do. 1888	139½
3½	Do. 1890	120½
3½	Do. 1891	120½
—	Do. (Int. fr. Jan '99) 189-	117½
4	Gt. North Scotland "A"	133½
4	Do. "B"	133½
4	Gt. Northern, Cons.	145
3	Do. 1896	108
5	Gt. Western Cons.	184
30/11	Hull & Barnsley Red. at 115	113
4	Isle of Wight	133½
3	Lancs. & Yorkshire, Cons.	109
2/2½	Lanc. Drby & E. C. 5 p.c. £10	9½
—	Do. 5 p.c. 2nd £10	9
5	Lond., Bright., &c., Cons.	183
5	Do. and Cons.	182
4½	Lond., Chat. & Dov. Arbitr.	138
25/	Do. 2nd Pref. 4½ p.c.	103
4	Lond. & N. Western	143
4	Lond. & S. Western .. 1881	147
4	Do. 1884	146
3½	Do.	128½
4	Lond., Tilbury & Southend	141½
4	Do. Cons., 1887	141½
4	Do 1891	141½
—	Mersey, 5 p.c. Perp.	—
4	Metropolitan, Perp.	143
4	Do. 1882	140½
4	Do. Irred.	141½
4	Do. 1887	141½
4	Do. New	141½
4½	Do.	146½
3½	Do.	123½
3	Do. Guar.	101½
2½	Metrop. Dist. Exten 5 p.c.	111
2½	Midland, Perp. Pref.	93
4	N. British Cons., No. 2	137
4½	Do. Edin. & Glasgow	153
5	Do. 1865	165½
5	Do. Conv. 1874	166½
4½	Do. 1875	153
4½	Do. Conv. 1875	153
5	Do. do. 1870	166½
4	Do. do. 1884	136½
4	Do. do. 1888	136½
4	Do. do. 1890	136½
4	Do. do. 1892	136½
4	N. Eastern	146
4½	N. Lond., Cons. 1866	174½
4½	Do. 2nd Cons. .. 1875	157½
3	N. Staffordshire	108
4½	Plym. Devpt. & S. W. Junc.	149½
1/5	Port Talbot, &c., 4 p.c. £10 Shares, 4 paid	5
5/	Rhondda & Swansea Bay, 5 p.c. £10 Shares	11
4	Rhymney, Cons.	140½
4½	S. Eastern, Cons.	160½
5	Do. do.	180½
4	Do. Vested Cos.	149
4	Do. 1891	149
3½	Do. 1893	123½
2	Do. 3 p.c. after July 1900	103
4	Taff Vale	138½

INDIAN RAILWAYS.

Last Div.	Name.	Paid.	Price.
3½	Assam Bengal, Ld., (3½ p. c. till June 30, then 3 p.c.)	100	100
4/	Barsi Light, Ld., £10 Shs.	10	10½
4	Bengal and N. West., Ld	100	142½
4/	Do. £10 Shares	10	13½
3/6	Do. 3½ p.c. Cum. Pf. Shs.	10	10½
8½d.	Do.	4	6½
2/3½	Bengal Central, Ld., £10 (3½ p.c. + ¼th net earn)	5	6½
7	Bengal Dooars, Ld.	100	111
4	Bengal Nagpr., Lim. (gua. 4 p.c. + 4th sp. pfts.)	100	112
7½	Bombay, Baroda, and C. I. (gua 5 p.c)	100	216
2½	Burma, Ld. (gua. 2½ p.c. and ½ p.c. add. till 1901)	100	108
7'975d	Do. £10 Shares		3½
5½	Delhi Umb. Kalka, Ld., Gua. 3½ p.c. + net earn.	100	123
4	Do. Deb. Stk., 1890 (1915)	100	111
9/10	Estn. Bengal, "A" An. 1957	—	25
9/	Do. "B" 1957	—	30
4	Do. Gua. Deb. Stock	100	136½
9/7½	East Ind. Ann. "A" (1953)	—	27
8/4½	Do. "C"	—	28
8/11½	Do. "B"	—	30
6 1/10	Do. Def. Ann. Cap. (gua. 4 p.c. + ¼th sp. pfts.)	—	148½
115/9	East Ind. Def. Ann. "D"	—	156
4½	East Ind. Irred. Stock	100	157½
5	Gt. Indian Penin., Gua 5 p.c. + ½ surplus profits	100	176½
4	Do. Irred. 4 p.c. Deb. St.	100	136½
4	Indian Mid., Ld. (gua. 4 p.c. + ¼th surplus pfts.)	100	111
5	Madras Guar. + ½ sp. pfts.	100	162
4½	Do. do.	100	153
4½	Do. do.	100	143
4	Nilgiri, Ld., 1st Deb. Stk.	100	96
51/9	Rohil. and Kumaon, Ld.	100	131
9/11	Scinde, Punj., and Delhi, "A" Ann., 1958	—	25
9/1	Do. "B" do.	—	30

Indian Railways (*continued*):—

Last Div.	Name.	Paid.	Price.
4	South Behar, Ld., £10 shs.	100	98
3½	Do. Deb. Stk. Red.	100	99
4½	South Ind., Gu. Deb. Stk.	100	156½
5	South Indian, Ld. (gua. 3 p.c., and ½ spls. profits)	100	119
5	Sthn. Mahratta, Ld. (3½ p.c. & ¼th net earnings)	100	113½
4	Do. Deb. Stk. Red.	100	121
3½	Southern Punjab, Ld.	100	105
3½	Do. Deb. Stk. Red.	—	104
5	Nizam's Gua. State, Ld.	100	112½
4	Do. Mort. Deb., 1936	100	109
4	Do. do. Reg.	100	107
17/3½	Nizam's Gua. State, Ld., 3½ p.c. Mt. Deb. bearer	—	96½
17/3½	Do. Reg. do.	—	95½
5	W. of India Portgese., Ld.	100	75
5	Do. Deb. Stk., Red	100	102

RAILWAYS.—BRITISH POSSESSIONS.

Last Div.	Name.	Paid.	Price.
5	Atlantic & N.W. Gua. 1 Mt. Bds., 1937	100	126½
5/3	Buff. & L. Huron Ord. Sh.	10	13½
5½	Do. 1st Mt. Perp. Bds. 1879	100	143½
5½	Do. 2nd Mt. Perp. Bds.	100	143½
—	Calgary & Edmon. 6 p.c. 1st Mt. Stg. Bds. Red.	100	82½
5	Canada Cent. 1st Mt. Bds. Red.	100	103
4	Can. Pacific Pref. Stk.	100	102
5	Do. Strl. 1st Mt. Deb. Bds. 1915	100	119
3½	Do. Ld. Grnt. Bds. 1938	100	107
3½	Do. Ld. Grnt. Ins. Stk.	100	106
4	Do. Perp. Cons. Deb. Stk.	100	113
5	Do. Algoma Bch. 1st Mt. Bds., 1937	100	122
3	Demerara, Original Stock	100	47½
7	Do. Perp. Pref. Stk.	100	152½
1/10	Do. 4 p.c. Cum. Ext. Pref. £10 Shs.	4	8
—	Dominion Atlntc. Ord. Stk.	100	33½
5	Do. 5 p.c. Pref. Stk.	100	97½
4	Do. 1st. Deb. Stk.	100	108½
4	Do. 2nd do. Red.	100	100
1/3	EmuBay & Mt. Bischoff, Ld.	5	4½
4½	Do. Irred. Deb. Stk.	100	97
nil.	Gd. Trunk of Canada, Stk.	100	7½
6	Do. 2nd. Equip. Mt. Bds.	100	133
5	Do. Perp. Deb. Stk.	100	139
5	Do. Gt. Westn. Deb. Stk.	100	131½
5	Do. Nthn. of Can. 1st Mt. Bds, 1902	100	104½
4	Do. do. Deb. Stk	100	104
5	Do. G. T. Geor. Bay & L. Erie 1 Mt., 1903	100	105
5	Do. Mid. of Can. Stl. 1st Mt. (Mid. Sec.) 1908	100	106
5	Do. do. Cons. 1 Mt. Bds. 1912	100	108
5	Do. Mont. & Champ. 1 Mt. Bds., 1909	100	104
	Do. Welln., Grey & Brce. 7 p.c. Bds. 1 Mt.	100	110
—	Jamaica 1st Mtg. Bds. Red.	—	103
—	Manitoba & N. W., 6 p.c. 1st Mt. Bds., Red	100	—
—	Do. Ldn. Bdhldrs. Certs.	—	—
5	Manitoba S. W. Col. 1 Mt. Bd., 1934 $1,000 price %	—	119
—	Mid. of W. Aust. Ld. 6 p.c. 1 Mt. Dbs., Red.	100	42½
4	Do. Deb. Bds., Red.	100	104
4	Nakusp & Slocan Bds., 1918	100	106
3	Natal Zululand Ld. Debs.,	100	72½
5	N. Brunswick 1st Mt. Stg. Bds., 1934	100	121
4	Do. Perp. Cons. Deb. Stk.	100	112
—	N. Zealand Mid., Ld., 5 p.c. 1st Mt. Debs.	100	35
6	Ontario & Queb. Cap. Stk.	$100	151½
5	Do. Perm. Deb. Stk.	100	144½
—	Qu'Appelle, L. Lake & Sask. 6 p.c. 1 Mt. Bds. Red.	100	40
	Queb. & L. S. John, 1st Mt. Bds., 1909	100	36½
	Quebec Cent., Prior Ln. Bds., 1908	100	107
1½	Do. 5 p.c. Inc. Bds.	290	36
4	St. Lawr. & Ott. Stl. 1st Mt.	100	111
4	Shuswap & Okan., 1st Mt. Deb. Bds., 1915	100	76
5	Temiscouata, 5 p.c. Stl. 1st Deb. Bds., Red.	100	9½
5	Do. (S. Franc. Brch.) 5 p.c. Stl. 1 Mt. Db. Bds., 1910	100	12
4	Toronto, Grey & B. 1st Mt.	100	112
1/	Well. & Mana. £5 Shs.	1	½
5	Do. Debs., 1908	100	105
5	Do. 2nd Debs., 1908	100	104
5	Do. 3rd do., 1908	100	103
6	Atlnn. & St. Law. Shs., 6 p.c.	100	163½
5	Gd. Trunk Mt. Bds., 1934	100	116½
5	Michigan Air Line, 5 p.c. 1st Mt. Bds., 1902	100	104
4	Minneap., S. P. & S t. Ste. Mar, 1st Mt. Bds., 1938	$1000	100

AMERICAN RAILROAD STOCKS AND SHARES.

Last Div.	Name.	Paid.	Price.
6/	Alab. Gt. Sthn. A 6 p.c. Pref.	10/.	9½
—	Do. do "B" Ord.	10/.	1½
—	Alabma. N. Orl.-Tex. &c., "A" Pref.	10/.	½
—	Do. "B" Def.	10/.	½
5½	Atlant. First Lnd. Ls. Rtl. Trust	Stk.	93½
—	Baltimore & Ohio Com.	$100	15
—	Baltimore Ohio S.W. Pref.	$100	7
—	Chesap. & Ohio Com.	$100	23½
—	Chic. Gt. West. 5 p.c. Pref. Stock "A"	$100	34
—	Do. do. Scrip. In.	—	30½
8/3	Do. 4 p.c. Deb. Stk.	$100	67½
4	Do. Interest in Scrip	$100	63½
$4	Chic. Junc. Rl. & Un. Stk. Yds. Com.	$100	117½
$1½	Do. 6 p.c. Cum. Pref.	$100	117½
$3½	Chic. Mil. & St. P. Pref.	$100	152½
7	Cleve. & Pittsburgh	$10	87½
$1½	Clev., Cincin., Chic., & St. Louis Com.	$100	—
—	Erie 4 p.c. Non-Cum. 1st Pf.	—	36
—	Do. 4 p.c. do. 2nd Pf.	—	19
$1½	Gt. Northern Pref.	$100	180
$4	Illinois Cen. Lsd. Lines	$100	92½
—	Kansas City, Pitts & G.	$100	19
$3	L. Shore & Mich. Sth. C.	$100	190
—	Mex. Cen. Ltd. Com.	$100	5
—	Miss. Kan. & Tex. Pref.	$100	36½
2½	N.Y., Pen. & O. 1st Mt. Tst. Ltd., Ord.	—	47½
4	Do. 1st Mort. Deb. Stk.	$100	92½
2	North Pennsylvania	$50	—
—	Northn. Pacific, Com.	$100	29½
1½	Pitts. F. Wayne & Chic.	$100	173½
—	Reading 1st Pref.	$50	93½
—	Do. 2nd Pref.	$50	12
—	S. Louis & S. Fran. Com.	$100	8
$1	Do. 2nd Pref.	$100	32
6	St. Louis Bridge 1st Pref.	$100	104
3	Do. 2nd Pref.	$100	47½
6	Tunnel Rail. of St. Louis	$100	104
$1½	St. Paul, Min. and Man.	$100	147½
—	Southern, Com.	$100	8½
—	Wabash, Common	$100	8

AMERICAN RAILROAD BONDS. CURRENCY.

Last Div.	Name.		Price.
7	Albany & Susq. 1 Con. Mrt.	1906	118
7	Allegheny Val. 1 Mt.	1910	127½
5	Canada Southern 1 Mt.	1908	110½
5	Chic. & N. West. Sk. Fd. Db.	1933	120½
5	Do. Deb. Coupon	1921	117½
6	Chicago & Tomah	1905	109½
5	Chic. Burl. & Q. Skg. Fd.	1901	102½
4	Do. Nebraska Ext.	—	100½
6	Chic., Mil., & S. Pl., 1 Mt. S.W. Div.	1909	114½
7	Do. (S. Paul Div.) 1 Mt.	1902	129½
5	Do. (La Cross & D.	1919	112½
7	Do. 1 Mt. (Hast. & Dak.)	1910	124½
5	Do. Chic. & Mis. Riv. 1 Mt.	1926	—
6	Det., G. Haven & Mil. Equip	1918	105
6	Do. do. Cons. Mt.	1918	102½
6	Ill. Cent., 1 Mt., Chic. & S.	1898	—
7	Indianap. & Vin., 1 Mt.	1908	125
6	Do. do. 2 Mt.	1900	100½
6	Lehigh Val., Cons. Mt.	1923	114½
—	Mexic. Cent., Ln. 2 Cons. Inc.	—	5
7	N.Y. Cent. & H.R. Mt. Bonds	1903	117½
5	Do. Deb.	1904	111½
6	Penns. Cons. S. F M.	1905	114½
4	West Shore, 1 Mt.	2361	109

DITTO—GOLD.

Last Div.	Name.		Price.
6	Alabama Gt. Sthn. 1 Mt.	1908	111
5	Do. Mid. 1	1928	92
4	Allegheny Val. Gen. Mt.	1942	107½
4	Atch., Top., & S. Fé Gn. Mt.	1995	96
3	Do. Adj. Mt.	1995	69
5	Do. Equipt. Tmst.	—	106
5	Atlantic & Dan. 1 Mt.	1950	94
5	Baltimore & Ohio	1925	115
5	Do. Speyer's Tst. Recpts.	1925	113
5	Do. Cons. Mt.	1988	115½
4½	Do. 4½ p.c. 1 Mt. Term.	1934	92
4½	Do. Brown Shipley's Dep. Cts.	—	92
5	Balt. Belt 5 p.c. 1 Mort.	1990	100½
4½	Balt. & Ohio S.W. 1 Mt.	1990	103
4½	Do. 4½ p.c. 1 Cons. Mt. 1893	1993	77½
—	Do. Inc. Mt. 5 p.c. Cl. A	—	29
—	Do. do. Cl. B	—	10
5	Balt. & Ohio S.W. Term 5 p.c.	1942	97½
6	Balt. & Ptmac (Mn. L.) 1 Mt.	1911	124
6	Do. do. (Tunnel) 1 Mt.	1911	122½
4	Beech Creek 1 Mt.	1936	107
4	Carthage & Adiron 1 Mt.	1981	107

American Railroad Bonds—Gold (*continued*):—

Last Div.	Name.		Price.
5	Cent. of Georgia 1 Mort.	1945	117½
5	Do. Cons. Mt.	1945	90½
5	Cent. of N. Jrsy. Gn. Mt.	1987	114½
6	Central Pacific, 1 Mort.	1898	102
6	Do. Speyer's Certs.	—	102½
5	Do. Land Grant	1900	104
5	Chesap. & Ohio 1st Cons. Mt.	1939	118
4½	Do. Gen. Mt.	1992	86
6	Chic. & W. Ind. Gen. Mt. Skg. Fd.	1932	119½
5	Chic. Mil. & St. Pl. (Chic. & L. Sup.) 1 Mt.	1921	112½
5	Do. Chic. & Pac. W.	1921	118
5	Do. Wisc. & Minn. 1 Mt.	1921	109½
5	Do. Terminal Mt.	1914	112½
4	Do. General Mt.	1989	106
5	Chic. St. L. & N. Orleans	1951	122½
4	Do. 1 Mort. (Memphis)	1951	104
4	Clevel, Cin., Chic. & St. L. 1 Mt. (Cairo)	1939	88
4	Do. 1 Mt. (Cinc., Wab., & Mich.)	1991	88
4	Do. 1 Col. Tst. Mt. (S. Louis)	1990	96
4	Do. General Mt.	1993	80½
4½	Clevel. & Mar. Mt.	1935	109
4½	Clevel. & Pittsburgh	1942	119
4½	Do. Series B.	1942	120
—	Colorado Mid. 1 Mt.	1936	65½
—	Do. Bdhrs.' Comm. Certs.	—	65½
4	Dnvr. & R. Gde. 1 Cons. Mt.	1936	96
5	Do. Imp. Mort.	1928	94
4	Detroit & Mack. 1 Lien	1995	90
5	E. Tennes., Virg., & Grgia. Cons. Mt.	1956	111½
5	Elmira, Cort., & Nthn. Mt.	1914	100
4	Erie 1 Cons. Mt. Pr. Ln.	1996	93½
3	Do. Gen. Lien	1996	75
6	Galvest., Harrisb., &c., 1 Mt.		110
5	Georgia, Car. & N. 1 Mt.	1929	94
4½	Gd. Rpds & Inda. Ex. 1 Mt.	1941	110
5	Do. 1 Mt. (Muskegon)	1926	37½
3½	Illinois Cent. 1 Mt.	1951	102½
4	Do.	1952	105
4	Do. Cairo Bdge.	1950	102
4	Do.	1953	104
4	Do. General Mort.	1904	100½
5	Kans. City, Pitts. & G. 1 M.	1923	73½
3½	L. Shore & Mich. Southern	1997	106½
4½	Lehigh Val. N.Y. 1 Mt.	1940	103½
5	Lehigh Val. Term. 1 Mt.	1941	112
5	Long Island	1931	116
5	Do. Deb.	1934	100
5	Do. (N. Shore Bch.) 1 Cons. Mt.	1932	100
6	Louisville & Nash. G. Mt.	1930	121
6	Do. 2 Mt. Sk. Fd. (S. & N. Alabama	1910	107
6	Do. 1 Mt. N. Orl. & Mb.	1930	122½
5	Do. 1 Mt. Coll. Tst.	1931	106
4	Do. Unified	1940	90
4½	Do. Mobile & Montgy. 1 Mt.	1945	111½
4	Manhattan Cons. Mt.	1990	98
4	Mexican Cent. Cons. Mt.	1911	67
—	Do. 1 Cons. Inc,		14
6	Mexican Nat. 1 Mt.	1927	106½
3½	Do. 2 Mt. 6 p.c. Inc. A	1917	47½
—	Do. do. B.	1917	—
3	Michig. Cnt. (Battle Ck. & S.) 1 Mt.	1989	86
5	Minneap. & S. L. 1 Consold.	1934	107½
4	Minne., Slt. S. M. & A. 1 Mt.	1926	101½
5	Minneapolis Westn. 1 Mt.	1911	102½
4	Miss. Kans. & Tex. 1 Mt.	1990	91
4	Do. 2 do.	1990	65
4	Mobile & Birm. Mt. Inc.	1945	38
5	Do. P. Lien	1945	86
4	Mohawk & Mal. 1 Mt.	1991	108
5	Montana Cent. 1 Mt.	1937	109½
5	Nashv., Chattan., & S. L. 1 Cons. Mt.	1928	102½
5	Nash., Flor., & Shff. Mt.	1937	96½
4	N. Y. & Putnam 1 Cons. Mt.	1993	108
5	N. Y., Brooklyn, & Man. B. 1 Cons. Mt.	1935	107½
4	N. Y. Cent. & Hud. R. Deb. Certs. 1890	1905	106
4	Do. Ext. Debt. Certs.	1905	106
7	N. Y., L. Erie, & W. 1 Cons. Mt. (Erie)	1920	144½
7	Do. 1 Con. Mt. Fd. Coup.	1920	142½
5	N. Y., Onto., & W. Cons. 1 Mt.	—	109
4	Do. 4 p.c. Refund. Mt.	1992	101½
6	Norfolk & West. Gn. Mt.	1931	125½
6	Do. Imp. & Ext.	1934	120
4	Do. 1 Cons. Mt.	—	84
6	N. Pacific Gn. 1 Mt. Ld. Gt.	1921	—
4	Do. P. Ln. Rl. & Ld. Gt.	—	100
3	Do. Gn. Ln. Rl. & Ld. Gt.	—	64
5	Oregon & Calif. 1 Mt.	1927	85½
6	Panama Skg. Fd. Subsidy	1910	106½
4½	Pennsylvania Rlrd.	1913	112
4	Do. Equip. Tst. Ser. A.	1914	104
4	Do. Cons. Mt.	1943	114
4½	Penna. Company 1st Mort.	1921	112½
5	Perkiomen 1 Mrt., 2nd ser.	1918	91½
4½	Pitts., C., C., & St. Ls. Con. Mt. G.B., Ser. A	1940-2	114½
4	Do. Cons. Mort., Ser. D	1945	104½
6	Pittsbgh., Cle., & Toledo	1922	105½
4	Reading, Phil., & R. Genl.	1997	87
5	Richmond & Dan. Equip.	1909	97½
5	Rio Grande Junc. 1st Mort.	1939	90
4	Rio Grande West 1st Tst. Mt.	1939	88
7	S. Louis Bridge 1st Mort	1925	134½
5	S. Louis Mchts. Bdge. Term. 1st Mort.	1930	102½
4	S. Louis S. West 1st Mort.	1989	76½
—	Do. 4 p.c. 2nd Mort. Inc.	1989	30
4½	S. Louis Term. Cupples Sta. & Prop. 1st. Mrt. 4½ p.c.	1908-17	102
4½	St. Paul Minn., & Manit.	1933	109

American Railroad Bonds (*continued*):—

Last Div.	Name.		Price.
6	St. Paul, Minn., & Manit.	1933	129½
6	Shamokin, Sunbury, &c. 2 Mt.	1925	106
5	S. & N. Alabama Cons. Mt.	1936	102
5	Southern 1 Cons. Coup.	1994	96
4	Do. E. Tennes Reorg. Lien	1938	100
6	S. Pacific of Cal. 1 Mt.	1905-12	111½
4½	Trml. Assn. of S. Louis 1 Mt.	1939	112
5	Do. 1 Cons. Mt.	1944	109
5	Texas & Pac. 1 Mt.	2000	106½
—	Do. 5 p.c. 2 Mt. Income	2000	39
5	Toledo & Ohio Cent. 1 Mt. West. Div.	1935	102½
4½	Toledo., Walhon., Val., & Ohio 1 Mt.	1931-3	108½
4	Union Pacific 1 Mt. 4 p.c.	1947	99
—	Union Pac., Linc., & Color. 1 Mt.	1918	—
4	United N. Jersey Gen. Mt.	1944	117½
6	Vicksbrg., Shrevept., & Pac. Pr. Ln. Mt.	1915	102½
5	Wabash 1 Mt.	1939	110
4	Wn. Pennsylvania Mt.	1928	106½
5	W. Virga. & Pittsbg. 1 Mt.	1990	77½
5	Wheeling & L. Erie 1 Mt. (Wheelg. Div.) 5 p.c.	1928	95
5	Do. Extn. Imp. Mt.	1930	90
—	Do. do. Brown Shipley's Cts.		—
5	Willmar & Sioux Falls 1 Mt.	1938	110

STERLING.

Last Div.	Name.		Price.
6	Alabama Gt. Sthn. Deb.	1906	104½
5	Do. Gen. Mort.	1927-8	98
5	Alabama, N. Orl., Tex. & Pac. 5 p.c. "A" Dbs.	1910-40	101
55/	Do. do. "B" do.	1910-40	59
—	Do. do. "C" do.		20
—	Allegheny Valley	1910	132
4	Atlantic 1st Leased Line Perp.		100
6	Baltimore and Ohio	1902	113
6	Do. do.	1910	128
5	Do. do. 1877		112½
—	Do. Morgan's Certs.		112½
4½	Do. do.	1933	106
6	Chicago & Alton Cons. Mt.	1903	112
5	Chic. St. Paul & Kan. City Priority		106½
6	Eastn. of Massachusetts	1906	117½
5	Illinois Cent. Skg. Fd.		104
5	Do.	1905	106
3½	Do.	1950	98½
4	Do. 1 Mt.	1951	114
3	Do. 1 Mt.	1951	93½
6	Louisville & Nash., M. C. & L. Div., 1 Mt.	1902	107
7	Do. 1 Mt. (Memphis & O.)	1901	110
55/8	Mexican Nat. "A" Certs. 5 p.c. Non. cum.		40
—	Do. "B" Certs.		9
6	N.Y. & Canada 1 Mt.	1904	118
6	N. York Cent. & H.R. Mort.	1903	112
4½	N. York, Penns., & Ohio Pr. Ln. Extd.	1935	—
5	Do. Equip. Tst.		108½
5	Do. 5 p.c. Equip. Tst. (1890)		101½
6	Nrthn. Cent. Cons. Gen. Mt.		106
6	Pennsylvania Gen. Mt.	1910	127½
6	Do. Cons. Skg. Fd. Mt.	1905	116½
3½	Do. Cons. Mt.	1945	105
6	Phil. & Erie Cons. Mort	1920	134½
6	Phil. & Reading Gen. Cons. Mort.	1911	124
6	Pittsbg. & Connells. Cons.	1926	125
—	Do. Morgan's Certs.		125
4	St. Paul., Min., & Manitoba (Pac. Extn.)	1940	101
6	S. & N. Alabama	1903	106½
6	Un. N. Jersey & C. Gen. Mt.	1901	109½

FOREIGN RAILWAYS

Last Div.	Name.	Paid.	Price.
12/	Alagoas, Ltd., Shs.	20	6½
5	Do. Deb. Stk., Red.	100	45½
6	Antofagasta, Ltd., Stk.	100	71
4	Do. Perp. Deb. Stk.	100	90
—	Arauco, Ld., Ord. Shs.	10	—
—	Do. 10 p.c. Cum. Pref.	10	—
5	Argentine Gt. W., Ld.,	100	83
5	Do. 5 p.c. Cum. Pref. Shs.	100	106
4	Do. 1 Deb. Stk.	100	103
1/0/0	Argentine N.E., Ltd., 6 p.c. Cum. Pref. Stk.	100	9½
—	Do. 5 p.c. Deb. Stk., Red.	100	28
2/	Arica and Tacna Shs.	20	1½
10/	Bahia & San Fcisco., Ld.,	20	9
6/	Do. Timbo. Bch. Shs.	20	5
12/	Bahia, Blanca, & N.W. Ln. Prf. Cum. 6 p.c.	100	81
4	Do. 4 p.c. 1 Deb. Stk., Red.	100	91
6	Barranquilla R. & P., Ld., 6 p.c. 1 Deb. Stk., Red.	100	93½

Foreign Railways (*continued*):—

Last Div.	Name.	Paid.	Price.
3/	Bilbao Riv. & Cantabn., Ltd., Ord.	3	4½
—	Bolivar, Ltd. Shs.	10	1½
6	Do. 6 p.c. Deb. Stk.	100	96½
4/	Brazil Gt. Southn. Ltd., 7 p.c. Cum. Pref.	20	1½
6	Do. Perm. Deb. Stk	100	51
5½	B. Ayres Gt. Southn. Ld., Ord. Stk.	100	140
5	Do. Pref. Stk.	100	134
4	Do. Deb. Stk.	100	116½
30/	B. Ayres & Ensen. Port., Ltd., Ord. Stk.	100	67
5	Do. Cum. 1 Pref. Stk.	100	117
6/0/0	Do. 6p.c. Con. Pref. Stk.	100	96
4	Do. Deb. Stk., Irred.	100	111
10⁶⁄₁₀	B. Ayres Northern, Ltd., Ord. Stk.	100	260
12¾	Do. Pref. Stk.	100	320
5	Do. 5 p.c. Mt. Deb. Stk., Red.	100	111
3/15/0	B. Ayres & Pac., Ld., 7 p.c. 1 Pref. Stk. (Cum.)	100	91½
4	Do. 1 Deb. Stk.	100	102
5/5/0	Do. 4½ p.c. 2 Deb. Stk.	100	92
3	B. Ayres & Rosario, Ltd., Ord. Stk.	100	71½
7/	Do. 7 p.c. Pref. Shs.	10	17
7/	Do. Sunchales Ext.	10	14½
4	Do. Deb. Stk., Red.	100	108
12/	B. Ayres & Val. Trans., Ltd., 7 p.c. Cum. Pref.	20	6¼
4	Do. 4 p.c. "A" Deb. Stk., Red.	100	68
—	Do. 6 p.c. "B" Deb. Stk. Red.	100	45
3/6	B. Ayres Westn. Ld. Ord.	10	10½
3/	Do. Def. Shs.	10	6½
5	Do. 5 p.c. Pref.	10	13½
4	Do. Deb. Stk	100	109½
6	Cent. Arg. Deb. Sk. Rd.	100	155½
4	Do. Deb. Stk. Rd.	100	109
6	Cent. Bahia L. Ord. Stk.	100	43½
	Do. Deb. Stk., 1934	100	67½
5	Do. Deb. Stk., 1937	100	59
3/6	Cent. Uguy. East. Ext. L. Shs	10	5½
5	Do. Perm. Stk.	100	110
3/6	Do. Nthn. Ext. L. Sh.	10	4
5	Do. Perm. Deb. Stk	100	102
3	Do. of Montev. Ltd., Ord. Stk	100	83
6	Do. Perm. Deb. Stk	100	144
10/	Conde d'Eu, Ltd. Ord.	20	7
—	Cordba & Rosar., Ltd., 6 p.c. Pref. Shs.	100	38
4	Do. 1 Deb. Stk	100	89
75	Do. 6 p.c. Deb. Stk	100	77
—	Cordba Cent., Ltd., 5 p.c. Cu. 1 Pref. Stk	100	78
—	Do. 5 p.c. Non-Cum. 2 Pref. Stk	100	42
5	Do. Deb. Stk	100	118
4/	Costa Rica, Ltd., Shs	10	3½
8/	Dna. Thrsa. Chris., Ltd., 7 p.c. Pref. Shs.	20	3½
20/	E. Argentine, Ltd	100	45
6	Do. Deb. Stk	100	103
1/1	Egyptn. Dlta. Lgt. Rys., Ltd., £10 Pref. Shs.	8	10½
—	Entre Rios, L., Ord. Shs.	5	½
—	Do. Cu. 5 p.c. Pref.	5	2½
6/	Gt. Westn. Brazil, Ltd.,	20	8
6	Do. Perm. Deb. Stk	100	90
6	Do. Extn. Deb. Stk	100	75½
—	Int.-Oceanic Mex., Ltd., 7 p.c. Pref.	10	1½
4	Do. Deb. Stk	100	83
42/6	Do. 7 p.c. "A" Deb. Sk.	100	69
—	Do. 7 p.c. "B" Deb. Sk.	100	30
5/	La Guaira & Carac.	10	7½
5	Do. 5 p.c. Deb. Sk. Red.	100	103
13/3	Lembg.-Czern.-Jassy	30	24½
2/	Lima, Ltd.	20	2½
—	Manila Ltd. 7 p.c. Cu. Pf.	10	½
20/6½	Mexican 2nd Pref. 6 p.c.	100	33
6	Do. Perp Deb. Stk.	100	140½
2/0/0	Mexican Sthrn., Ld., Ord.	100	21
—	Do. 4 p.c. 1 Db. Stk. Rd.	100	85
—	Do. 4 p.c. 2 do.	100	59
—	Mid. Urgy., Ltd.	100	17½
5	Do. Deb. Stk.	100	56
22/	Minas & Rio, Ltd.	20	8
5/2	Namur & Liege	20	13
11/6	Do. Pref.	20	29
6/	Natal & Na. Cruz, Ld., 7 p.c. Cum Pref.	20	5½
6/	Nitrate Ltd., Ord.	10	4½
6/	Do. 7 p.c. Pr. Con. Or.	10	3½
3/	Do. Def. Conv. Ord.	10	½
7/	N.-E. Urgy., Ltd., Ord.	10	14½
7/	Do. 7 p.c. Pref.	10	15
—	N.-W. Argentine Ld., 7 p.c. Pref.	10	2
6	Do. 6 p.c. 1 Deb. Stk.	100	107
—	Do. 2 Deb. Stk.	100	94
-	N.W. Uruguay 6 p.c. 1 Pref. Stk.	100	16
—	Do. 5 p.c. 2 Pref. Stk.	100	7½
6	Do. 6 p.c. Deb. Stk.	100	75½
22/	Ottoman (Sm. Aid.)	20	13
—	Paraguay Cntl., Ld., 5 p.c. Perm. Deb. Stk.	100	10
—	Piræus, Ath., & Pelo.	275	2
4/)	Pto. Alegre & N. Hambg Ld., 7 p.c. Pref. Shs.	20	3½
6	Do. Mt. Deb. Stk. Red.	100	74½
—	Puerto Cabello & Val. Ld.	10	1½
5	Recife & S. Francisco	100	69
14/	R. Claro S. Paulo, Ld., Sh.	10	23
5	Do. Deb. Stk.	100	126
5	Royal Sardinian Ord.	10	11½
7/	Do. Pref.	10	11½

Foreign Railways (*continued*):—

Last Div.	Name.	Paid.	Price.
5/	Sambre & Meuse	20	18
5/6	Do. Pref.	10	12½
22/	San Paulo Ld.	20	33½
2/10½	Do. New Ord. £10 sh.	6	9½
4/8	Do. 5 p.c. Non. Cm. Pref.	10	12
5½	Do. Deb. Stk.	100	131
5	Do. 5 p.c. Deb. Stk.	100	126
—	S. Fé & Cordova, Gt. Sthn., Ld., Shares	100	49
6	Do. Perp. Deb. Stk.	100	118
2/4½	S. Austrian	20	7
12/	Sthn. Braz. R. Gde. do Sul, Ld.	20	7
6	Do. 6 p.c. Deb. Stk.	100	63
4	Swedish Centl, Ld., 4 p.c. Deb. Stk.	100	106½
5	Do. Pref.	100	101
1/3	Taltal, Ld.	5	2¼
—	Uruguay Nthn., Ld. 7 p.c. Pfd. Stk.	100	8
3½	Do. 5 p.c. Deb. Stk.	100	28
—	Villa Maria & Rufino, Ld., 6 p.c. Pref. Shs.	100	17
4	Do. 4 p.c. 1 Deb. Stk.	100	71
6/0/0	Do. 6 p.c. 2 Deb. Stk.	100	42½
5/9	West Flanders	8½	21
5/6	Do. 5½ p.c. Pref.	10	18
3/	Wstn. of Havana, Ld.	10	4½

FOREIGN RAILWAY OBLIGATIONS

Per Cent.	Name.	Price.
6	Alagoas Ld., 6 p.c. Deb., Rd.	82
—	Alcoy & Gandia, Ld., 5 p.c. Debs., Red.	20
5	Arauco., Ld., 5 p.c. 1st Mt., Rd.	64½
—	Do. 6 p.c. Mt. Deb., Rd.	39½
6	Brazil G. Sthn., L., Mt. Dbs., Rd.	89½
6	Do. Mt. Dbs. 1893, Rd.	51
5½	Campos & Caran. Dbs., Rd.	70
6	Central Bahia, L., Dbs., Rd.	87
5½	Conde d'Eu, L., Dbs., Rd.	71
6	Costa Rica, L., 1st Mt. Dbs., Rd.	111
6	Do. 2nd Dbs., Rd.	91
5	Do. Prior Mt. Db., Rd.	104
6	Cucuta Mt. Dbs., Rd.	102
5½	Donna Thrsa. Cris., L., Dbs., Rd.	71
3	Eastn. of France, £20 Dbs., Rd.	18½
4	Egyptn. Delta Light, L., Db., Rd	101
—	Espito. Santo & Cara. 5 p.c. Stl. Dbs., Rd.	38
4	Gd. Russian Nic., Rd.	102
5	Inter-Oceanic Mex., L., 5 p.c. Pr. Ln. Dbs., Rd.	103
3	Ital. 3 p.c. Bds. A & B, Rd.	58½
—	Ituana 6 p.c. Debs., 1918	72½
—	Manila Ltd., 6 p.c. Deb., Red.	21
6	Do. Prior Lien Mt., Rd.	100½
6	Do. Series "B," Rd.	80
7	Matanzas & Sab., Rd.	99½
6	Minas & Rio, L., 6 p.c. Dbs., Rd.	97
5	Mogyana 5 p.c. Deb. Bds., Rd.	101
5	Moscow-Jaros., Rd.	105½
5½	Natal & Na. Cruz Ltd., 5½ p.c. Debs., Red.	74
5	Nitrate, Ltd. Mt. Bds., Red.	86
3	Nthn. France, Red.	19½
4	N. of S. Af. Rep. (Trnsvl.) Gu. Bds. Red.	96
3	Nthn. of Spain £20 Pri. Obs. Red.	7½
6	Ottmn. (Smy to A.) (Kujk) Asnt. Debs., Red.	108
6	Ottmn. (Seraik.) Asg. Debs. Red.	108
6	Ottmn. (Seraik.) Non-Asg. D., Rd	108
5	Ottmn. Kuyjk. Ext. Red.	105
5	Ottmn. Serkeuy. Ext. Red.	102
5	Ottmn. Tireh Ext. 1910	98
5	Ottmn. Debs. 1886, Red.	98½
5	Do. 1888, Red. 1935	98½
5	Do. 1893, Red. 1935	97
5	Ottmn. of Anlia. Debs., Rd.	90½
4	Ottomn. Smyr. & Cas Ext. Bds., Red.	83½
3	Paris, Lyon & Medit. (old sys., £20), Red.	19
3	Paris, Lyon & Medit. (new sys., £20), Red.	18½
50/	Piræus, At. & Pelp., 6 p.c. 1st Mt. Bds., Red.	
3	Do. 5 p.c. Mt. Bds., Red.	99½
4	Pretoria-Pietbg., Ltd., Red.	93½
7	Puerto Cab. & Val., Ltd., 1st Mt. Debs., Red.	81
2	Royal Sardinian, A, Rd. £20	12
3	Royal Sardinian, B., Rd. £20	12
5	Ryl. Trns.-Afric. 5 p.c. 1st Mt. £100 Bds., Red.	48½
4	Sa. Fe & Cor. G.S., Ld. Pr Ln. Bds.	103
5	Sa. Fe, 5 p.c. 2nd Reg. Dbs.	75
3	South Austrian, £20 Red.	15½
3	South Austrian, (Ser. X.)	15½
3	South Italian £20 Obs. (Ser. A to G), Red.	12½
3½	S. W. of Venez. (Barq.), Ltd., 7 p.c. 1st Mt. £100 Debs.	43½
5	Taltal, Ltd., 5 p.c. 1st Ch. Debs., Red.	100
5	Utd. Rwys. Havana, Red.	89½
3	Wtrn. of France, £20 Red.	19

Foreign Rly. Obligations (*continued*):—

Per Cent.	Name.	Price.
6	Wrn. B. Ayres St. Mt. Debs., 1902	108
6	Wrn. B. Ayres, Reg. Cert.	107
5	Do. Mt. Bds.	123
6	Wtrn. of Havna., Ld. Mt. Dbs., Rd.	97
7	Wrn. Ry. San Paulo Red.	101
—	Wrn. Santa Fé, 7 p.c. Red.	41
2/8	Zafra & Huelva, 3 p.c. Red.	2½

BANKS.

Div.	Name.	Paid.	Price.
2/4½	Agra, Ltd.	6	3½
2/9½	Anglo-Argentine, Ltd., £9	7	6
8 fls.	Anglo-Austrian	120f	13
6/	Anglo-Californian, Ltd., £20 Shares	10	11
4/	Anglo-Egyptian, Ltd., £15	5	5½
5/	Anglo-Foreign Bkg., Ltd.	7	7½
7/	Anglo-Italian, Ltd.	5	7
7/6	Bk. of Africa, Ltd., £18¾	6¼	10½
20/	Bk. of Australasia	40	50
10/	Bk. of Brit. Columbia	20	19½
25/	Bk. of Brit. N. America	50	64
20/	Bk. of Egypt, Ltd., £25	12½	18
5/	Bk. of Mauritius, Ltd.	10	9
18/	Bk. of N. S. Wales	20	36½
4 p.c.	Bk. of N. Zland. Gua. Stk.	100	102½
6/	Bk. of Roumania, £20 Shs.	6	7½
2/6	Tarapaca & Ldn., Ltd., £10	5	3½
—	Bque. Fse. de l'Afri. du S.	100f	3½
f.22.50	Bque. Internatle. de Paris	20	23
6/	Brit. Bk. of S. America, Ltd., £20 Shares	10	10½
16/	Capital & Cties., L., £50	10	40½
20/	Chart. of India, &c.	20	30½
10/	City, Ltd., £40 Shares	10	20
18/	Colonial, £100 Shares	30	20½
10/	Delhi and London, Ltd.	25	—
5/	German of London, Ltd.	10	10½
25/	Hong-Kong & Shanghai	28½	46
3/	Imperl. of Persia	6½	3½
10/	Imperl. Ottoman, £20 Shs	10	12½
12/	Intrnatl. of Ldn., Ld., £20	15	11½
10/	Ionian, Ltd.	25	15½
16/	Lloyds, Ltd., £50 Shs.	8	31½
10/	Ldn. & Braziln. Ltd., £20	10	17½
44/	Ldn. & County, Ltd., £80	20	101
9/	Ldn. & Hanseatic, L., £20	10	10½
22/6	Ldn. & Midland, L., £60	12½	53
8/9	Ldn. & Provin., Ltd., £10	5	21½
21/	Ldn. & Riv. Plate, L., £25	15	50½
2/9½	Ldn. & San Fcisco, Ltd.	7	4
28/	Ldn. & Sth. West., L., £50	20	69
26/	Ldn. & Westmins., L., £100	20	57½
5/	Ldn. of Mex. & S. Amer., Ltd., £10 Shs.	6	5½
15/	Ldn. Joint Stk., L., £100	15	34
12/9½	Ldn., Paris & Amer., L. £20	16	25
2/4½	Merchant Bkg., L., £9	4	2½
6/3	Metropn, Ltd., £50 Shs.	5	14½
9/	National, Ltd., £50 Shs.	10	20½
5/11	Natl. of Mexico, $100 Shs.	$35	13
1/3	National of N. Z., L., £7½	2½	2½
12/	National S. Afric. Rep.	10	13½
23/1½	National Provcl. of Eng., Ltd., £75 Shs.	10½	49½
26/4½	Do. do. £60 Shs.	12	56
6/6	North Eastn., Ltd., £20 Shs	6	15
19/	Parr's, Ld., £100 Shs.	20	90
12/6	Prov. of Ireland, L., £100	12½	29½
40/	Stand. of S. Afric., L., £100	25	64
12/6	Union of Australia, L., £75	25	27
4 p.c.	Do. do. Ins. Stk. Dep. 1900	100	102
15/6	Union of Ldn., Ltd., £100	15½	35

BREWERIES AND DISTILLERIES.

Div.	Name.	Paid.	Price.
4½	Albion Prp. 1 Mt. Db. Sk.	100	111
4	All Saints', L., Db. Sk. Rd.	100	97
7	Allsopp, Ltd	100	151
6	Do. Cum. Pref	100	153½
4½	Do. Deb. Stk., Red.	100	115
3½	Do. Deb. Stk., Red.	100	101
4½	Alton & Co., L., Db., Rd	100	107
4½	Do. Mt. Bds., 1896	100	105
—	Arnold, Perrett, Ltd.	10	6
6	Do. Cum. Pref.	10	10½
4½	Do. 1 Mt. Db. Stk., Rd	100	105

Breweries &c. (*continued*):—

Div.	Name.	Paid.	Price
5½	Arrol, A., & Sons, L., Cum. Pref. Shs.	10	10½
4½	Do. 1 Mt. Db. Stk., Rd.	100	108
5	Backus, 1 Mt. Db., Red.	100	59
4	Barclay, Perk., L., Cu. Pf.	10	11½
3½	Do. Mt. Db. Stk., Red.	100	107
—	Barnsley, Ltd.	10	11
6	Do. Cum. Pref.	10	13½
1/3	Barrett's, Ltd	2½	1½
1/3	Do. 5 p.c. Pref.	2½	2½
3/	Bartholomay, Ltd.	10	2½
8	Do. Cum. Pref.	10	6½
6	Do. Deb.	100	96
5	Bass, Ratcliff, Ltd., Cum. Pref. Stk.	100	139½
4½	Do. Mt. Db. Stk., Rd.	100	122
4	Bell, J., L., 1 Mt. D. Stk., R	100	100
—	Benskin's, L., Cum. Pref.	5	—
—	Do. 1 Mt. Db. Stk Red.	100	—
—	Do. "B" Deb. Sk, Rd.	100	—
7/	Bentley's Yorks., Ltd.	10	10½
6/	Do. Cum. Pref.	10	12½
4½	Do. Mt. Debs., Red.	100	110
4½	Do. do. 1892, Red.	100	110
—	Bieckert's, Ltd.	20	2
5	Do. Debs., Red.	100	54
—	Birmingham., Ltd., 6 p.c. Cum. Pref.	5	2½
4½	Do. Mt. Debs., Red.	50	39½
5½	Boardman's, Ld., Cm. Pf.	10	8½
4½	Do., Perp. 1 Mt. Db. Sk.	100	102½
30/9	Brain & Co., Ltd.	100	101
4½	Brakspear, L., 1 D. Stk. Red.	100	108
4	Brandon's, L., 1 D. Stk. Red.	100	102½
21/	Bristol (Georges) Ltd.	10	45
6	Do. Cum. Pref.	10	17
5	Do. Mt. Db. Sk. 1888 Rd.	100	113½
17/6	Bristol United, Ltd.	10	35
6	Do. Cum. Pref.	10	16
4½	Do. Db. Sk. Rd.	100	119½
5½	Buckley's, L., C. Pre-prf.	10	10½
4½	Do. 1 Mt. Db. Stk. Rd.	100	103½
4	Bullard & Sons, Ltd., D. Sk. R.	100	105
6	Bushell, Watk., L., C. Pf.	10	13
4½	Do. 1 Mt. Db. Sk. Rd.	100	111½
5	Camden, Ltd., Cum. Pref.	10	11½
4½	Do. 1 Mt. Db. Sk. Rd.	100	107
5½	Cameron, Ltd., Cm. Prf.	10	13
4½	Do. Mort Deb. Stk.	100	107
3½	Do. Perp Mt. Db. Sk.	100	98½
5	Cam'bell, J'stone, L., C. Pf.	5	5
4½	Do. 4½ p.c. 1 Mt. Db. Sk.	100	102
4	Campbell, Praed, L., Per. 1 Mort. Deb. Stk.	100	105
4	Cannon, L., Mt. Db. Stk.	100	110
4	Do. "B" Deb. Stk.	100	102
5	Castlemaine, L., 1 Mt. Db.	100	94
3½	Charrington, Ltd., Mort. Deb. Stk. Red.	100	107
2/	Cheltnhm. Orig., Ltd.	5	6
3/	Do. Cum. Pref.	5	7½
4	Do. Debs. Red.	100	106
10/	Chicago, Ltd.	10	3½
6	Do. Debs.	100	84½
—	Cincinnati, Cum. Pref.	10	1
10/	City of Baltimore	10	3½
16/	Do. 8 p.c. Cum. Pref	10	7½
14/	City of Chicago, Ltd.	10	1½
8	Do. Cum. Pref.	10	6
13	City of London, Ltd.	100	206½
5	Do. Cum. Pref.	100	126
4	Do. Mt. Deb. Stk., Rd.	100	109½
2/	Colchester, Ltd.	5	4½
7	Do. Pref.	5	6½
4½	Do. Deb. Stk., Red.	100	108
5	Combe, Ltd., Cum. Pref.	10	13½
4	Do. Mt. Db. Stk, Rd.	100	110
3½	Do. Perp. Deb. Stk.	100	106
5	Comm'cial, L., D. Sk., Rd.	100	107½
5	Courage, L., Cm. Pref. Shs.	100	128½
4	Do. Irr. Mt. Deb. Stk.	100	126½
3½	Do. Irr. "B" Mt. Db. Sk.	100	105
8/	Daniell & Sons, Ltd.	10	7
7	Do. Cum. Pref.	10	12
4½	Do. 1 Mt. Perp. Db. Sk.	100	109½
4½	Do. "B" Deb. Stk.	100	99
10d.	Dartford, Ltd.	5	5½
2/9	Do. Cum. Pref.	5	5½
4	Do. 1 Mt. Db. Sk. Rd.	100	99
4	Davenport, Ld., 1 D. Stk.	100	99½
10/	Denver United, Ltd.	10	3½
8	Do. Cum. Pref.	10	8½
6	Do. Debs.	100	98½
4½	Deuchar, L., 1 D. Sk., Rd.	100	109
8/	Distillers, Ltd.	10	25
—	Dublin Distillers, Ltd.	5	1½
6	Do. Cum. Pref.	5	4½
4½	Do. Irr. Deb. Stk.	100	100
5	Eadie, Ltd., Cum. Pref.	10	11½
4	Do. Irr. 1 Mt. Db. Sk.	100	107
6/	Edinbgh. Utd., Ltd.	10	12½
6	Do. Cum. Prf.	10	12½
4	Eldridge, Pope, L. D. St. R.	100	107
—	Emerald & Phœnix, Ltd.	10	1½
8	Do. Cum. Pref.	10	6
6	Empress Ltd., C. Pf.	10	11½
4½	Do. Mt. Deb. Stk.	100	103
6/	Farnham, Ltd.	10	16½
6	Do. Cum. Pref.	10	14½
4	Fenwick, L., 1 D. Sk., Rd.	100	103
4	Flower & Sons, Irr. D. Sk.	100	111
4	Friary, L., 1 Db. Stk., Rd.	100	101½
4	Do. 1 "A" Db. Sk., Rd	100	98½
4½	Groves, L., 1 Db. Sk., Rd.	100	111
14	Guinness, Ltd.	100	590
6	Do. Cum. Prf. Stk.	100	189½
5	Do. Deb. Stk., Red.	100	120
5	Hall's Oxford L., Cm. Pf.	5	5½
6/	Hancock, Ld., Cm. Pf. Ord.	10	14
7.	Do. Def. Ord	10	17½

Breweries, &c. (*continued*) :—

Div.	Name.	Paid.	Price.
6	Hancock, Ld., Cum. Pref.	10	17½
4	Do. 1 Deb. Stk., Rd.	100	110
5	Hoare, Ltd. Cum. Pref...	10	12½
5	Do. "A" Cum. Pref..	10	12
4	Do. Mt. Deb. Stk., Rd.	100	111
3½	Do. do. do. Rd.	100	102
3/6	Hodgson's, Ltd.	5	9½
5	Do. 1 Mt. Db., Red..	—	117½
4	Do. 2 Mt. Db., 1906..	—	100
4½	Hopcraft & N., Ltd., 1 Mt. Deb. Stk., Red. ..	100	101
5	Huggins, Ltd., Cm. Prf..	10	—
4½	Do. 1st D. Stk. Rd...	100	—
4½	Do. "B" Db. Stk. Rd.	100	—
12/	Hull, Ltd.	10	17
7	Do. Cum. Pref.	10	14½
4½	Ind, Coope, L., D.Sk., Rd.	100	117
4	Do. "B" Mt. Db. Stk. Rd.	100	110
8/	Indianapolis, Ltd.	10	3
8	Do. Cm. Prf.	10	8½
5/	Jones, Frank, Ltd.......	10	2½
7½	Do. Cum. Pref.	10	6½
5	Do. 1st Mort. Debs. ..	100	90½
3/	J. Kenward & Co., Ltd...	5	5½
4½	Kingsbury, L., 1 D.Sk., Rd	100	—
4	Lacon, L., D. Stk., Red.	100	108
4	Do. Irrd. "B" D. Sk.	100	106
7/	Lascelles, Ltd.	5	11½
6	Do. Cum. Pref.	5	7½
5	Leney, Ltd., Cum. Pref.	10	11½
4	Do. 1 Mt. Db. Stk. Rd.	100	102
30/7½	Lion, Ltd., £25 shares..	17	49½
10/9½	Do. New £10 shares..	6	17
6	Do. Perp. Pref.	20	33
4	Do. B. Mt. Db. Sk. Rd.	100	107
4½	Lloyd & Y., Ltd., 1 Mt. Deb. Stk., Rd.	100	98½
4½	Locke & S., Ltd., Irr. 1st Mt. Deb. Stk.........	100	101
4½	Lovibond, Ltd., 1st Mt. Deb. Stk., Rd.	100	99½
30/4	Lucas&Co., Ld., Deb.Stk.	100	105
12/	Manchester, Ltd, ...	10	16½
7	Do. Cum. Pref.	10	16½
5/	Marston, J., L., Cm. Prf.	10	10½
4	Do. 1 Mt. Db. Sk., Rd.	100	99½
7/	Massey's Burnley, Ltd...	10	16½
6	Do. Cum. Pref.	10	14½
4½	McCracken, Ltd., 1 Mt. Deb., 1908............	100	80½
5	McEwan, Ltd., Cm. Pref.	10	14
5	Meux, Ltd., Cum. Pref..	10	14½
4	Do. Mt. Db Stk. Red.	100	112
4½	Michell & A., Ltd., 1 Mt. Deb. Stk. Red.....	100	103
4½	MileEndDist. Db. Sk. Rd.	100	109
14/	Milwaukee & Chic., Ltd.	10	1½
4/	Do. Cum. Pref.	10	6
4½	Michell, Toms, L., Db...	50	57
6/	Morgan, Ltd., Cum. Pref.	10	14½
25/	Nalder & Coll., Ltd.....	10	34
6	Do. Cum. Pref..	10	15½
4½	Do. Deb. Red...	100	112
8/	Newcastle, Ltd.	10	19½
6	Do. Cum. Pref......	10	14½
5	Do. 1 Mt. Deb., 1911	100	111½
4	Do. "A" Deb. Stk. Red.	100	106
6	New England, Ltd......	10	4½
8	Do. Cum. Pref......	10	9
6	Do. Debs. Red......	100	101½
4	New London, L., 1 D.Sk.	100	102
7/9	New Westminster, Ltd..	4	10½
2/4½	Do. Pref.........	4	6½
—	New York, Ltd.	10	1
—	Do. 8 p.c. Cum. Pref.	10	3½
6	Do. 1 Mt. Deb. Red.	100	77½
5	Noakes, Ld., Cum. Pref.	10	11½
4	Do. 1 Mt. Db. Stk., Rd.	100	106
4½	Norfolk, L., "A" D.Sk.Rd.	100	107
10/	Northampton, Ld.	10	16½
7	Do. Cum. Pref......	10	15½
6	Do. Cum. Pref......	10	12½
5	Do. 1 Mt. Per. Db. Sk.	100	127
4	Nth. East., L., 1 D.Sk. Rd.	100	100
4½	N. Worcesters., L. Per. 1 Mort. Deb. Stock	100	86½
6	Nottingham, L., Cm. Prf.	10	1½
5	Do. 1 Mt. Deb. Stk., Red.	100	114
17/4	Do. "B" do. Red.	50	109½
6/	Ohlsson' Cape. Ld.......	5	18
7	Do. Cum. Pref.	5	9
4½	Do. 2nd Cum. Pref.	5	5½
5	Do. Deb. Stk., Red.	100	117
4½	Oldfield, L., 1 Mt. Db. Stk.	100	104
6	Page& Overt., L., Cm. Prf.	10	13½
4½	Do. 1 Mt. Dbs., Red.	100	109
10/	Parker's Burslem, Ltd. ..	10	24½
6	Do. Cum. Pref.	10	15
4	Do. 1 Mt. Db. Stk., Red.	100	112
4	Persse, Ld., 1 Mt. Db. Rd.	100	95½
	Phipps, L., Irr. 1 Db. Stk.	100	113
8	Plymouth, L., Min. Cu. Pf.	10	14
4½	Do. Mt. Deb. Stk., Red.	100	107½
4½	Pryor, Reid, L., 1 D.S., R.	100	102½
5	Reid's, Ld., Cm. Pref. Stk.	100	137½
4	Do. Mt. Deb. Stk., Red	100	112
3½	Do. "B" Mt. Db. Stk., Rd	100	105
5	Rhondda Val., L., Cu. Pf	10	10½
4½	Do. 1 Mt. Deb. Stk., Rd	100	106½
5	Robinson, Ld., Cum. Pref.	10	11½
4½	Do. 1 Mt. Perp. Db. Stk.	100	109½
4/	Rochdale, Ltd.	10	6
4½	Do. 1 Mt. Deb. Stk. ..	100	96½
7	Royal, Brentford, Ltd. ..	10	22
	Do. Cum. Pref. ..	10	15
4½	Do. 1 Mt. Dbs. Red	100	106
4/	St. Louis, Ltd.	10	3½
8/	Do. Cum. Pref.	10	8½
14/	St. Paul, Ltd.	10	10
7	Do. Cum. Pref.....	10	11½
4½	Salt (T.), L., 1 Db. Sk. Rd.	100	111
4½	Do. "B" Db. Stk. Red	100	105
—	San Francisco, Ltd.......	10	½
—	Do. 8 p.c. Cum. Pref...	10	½

Breweries, &c. (*continued*) :—

Div.	Name.	Paid.	Price.
4½	Savill Brs., L., D. Sk. Rd.	100	116
4½	Scarboro., Ltd., 1 Db. Stk.	100	101
4	Shaw (Hy.), Ltd., 1 Mt. Db. Stk., Red.........	100	102
8/	Showell's, Ltd...........	10	32
7	Do. Cum. Pref.	10	17½
3/	Do. Gua. Shs.	5	7½
4½	Do. Mt. Db. Stk., Red.	100	112
4	Simonds, L., 1 D. Sk., Rd.	100	111
5/6	Simson & McP., L., Cu. Pf.	10	9½
4½	Do. 1 Mt. Deb. Stk. ..	100	95
5/	Smith, Garrett, L., £20 Shs	10	16½
5	Do. Cum. Pref.	20	25
3½	Do. 3½ p.c. Mt. Db. Stk.	100	107
5	Smith's, Tadcster, L., CPf	10	12
4½	Do. Deb. Stk., Red. ..	100	110
4	Do. Deb. Stk. Red. ..	100	106
4½	Star, L., 1 M. Db. Stk., Rd.	100	103
4	Steward & P., L., 1 D. Sk.	100	111
7/	Strettons Derby, Ltd.....	10	13½
6	Do. Cum. Pref.	10	13
4	Do. Irr. 1 Mt. Db. Stk.	100	102½
4½	Strong, Romsey, L., 1 D.S.	100	113
5	Stroud, L., Db. Sk., Rd.	100	106
4½	Tadcaster To'er, L., D.Sk.	100	109½
8/	Tamplin, Ltd............	10	21½
6	Do. Cum. Pref.	100	15
4	Do. "A" Db. Sk., Rd.	10	108
6	Thorne, Ltd., Cum. Pref.	10	14½
4	Do. Deb. Stk., Red...	100	103½
15/	Threlfall, Ltd.	10	45
6	Do. Cum. Pref.	10	16
5	Do. 1 Mt. Dbs., Red.	100	115
4	Tollemache, L., D. Sk. Rd.	100	103
4	Truman, Hanb., D. Sk., R.	100	109½
3	Do. "B" Mt. Db. Sk., Rd.	100	93
10/	United States, Ltd.......	10	9
8	Do. Cum. Pref.	10	11
6	Do. 1 Mt. Deb........	100	106½
6/	Walker&H., Ld., Cm. Prf.	10	10½
4½	Do. 1 Mt. Deb. Stk., Red.	100	107
5	Walker, Peter, Ld. Cm. Prf.	10	13½
4	Do. 1 Mt. Dbs. Red. ..	100	110
4	Wallingford, L., D. Sk. Rd.	100	105
6	Watney, Ld., Cm. Prf. Sk.	100	171
5	Do. Mt. Db. Sk., Rd.	100	121½
4½	Do. "B" Mt. Db. Sk., Rd.	100	116½
3½	Do. Mt. Db. Stk.	100	105
5	Watney, D., Ld., Cm. Prf.	10	12
4½	Do. 1 Mt. Db. Stk. ..	100	103
10/	Webster & Sons, Ltd. ..	10	16½
6	Do. Cum. Pref. ..	10	13½
5	Wenlock Ltd Pref.	10	12
4	Do. 1 Mt. Db. Sk., Rd.	100	106
5	West Cheshire, L., Cu. Pf.	10	10
4	Do. Irred. 1 Mt. Db. Sk.	100	98
4½	Whitbread, L., Cu. Pf. Sh.	100	123½
4	Do. Db. Stk., Red.	100	110
3½	Do. "B" Db. Stk., Rd.	100	101
8/	Wolverhmpton & D. Ld..	10	18
6	Do. Cum. Pref.......	10	13
4½	Do. 1 Mt. Dbs., Red.	100	108
5½	Worthington, Ld., Cm. Prf.	10	15½
5½	Do. Cum. "B" Pref.	10	13½
4½	Do. Mt. Db. Sk., Rd.	100	113
3½	Do. Irr. "B" Db. Stk.	100	102
6/	Yates's Castle, Ltd.......	10	13
5	Do. Cum. Pref.	10	11
5	Younger W., L., Cu. Pf. Sh.	100	134½

CANALS AND DOCKS.

Last Div.	Name.	Paid.	Price.
4	Birmingham Canal	100	141½
3	E. & W. India Dock	100	19
—	Do. 4 p.c. Prf. Stk.....	100	72
22/8	Do. P.L. Deb. Stk.....	100	101
—	Do. Cons. Deb. Stk. ..	100	89
40/	G. Junction Ord. Shs. ..	100	145½
6/	Do. do. Pref.......	10	18½
4½	King's Lynn Per. Db. Stk.	100	117½
2½	Leeds & L'pool Canal....	100	70
2½	Lndn & St. Kath. Dks. ..	100	54½
4½	Do. Pref.............	100	137½
4½	Do. Pref., 1878	100	131
4½	Do. Pref., 1882	100	130
4	Do. Deb. Stk.	100	131
—	Mchester Ship C. 5 p.c. Pf.	10	1½
3½	Do. 1st Perp. Mt. Deb.	100	100
—	Milford Dks. Db. Stk. "A"	100	20
3½	Millwall Dk..............	100	60
5	Do. Perp. Pref.	100	140½
4½	Do. Pref.	100	106½
5	Do. New Per. Prf., 1887	100	126½
5	Do. Per. Deb. Stk.	100	150½
4/	Newhaven Har.	10	14
2½	N. Metropolitan	100	70
5	Sharpness Nw. Pf. "A" Sk.	100	141½
4	Do. Deb. Stk.	100	115½
5	Sheffiel & S. Yorks Nav. 4½ p.c. Pref Stk.......	100	110½
36.43fr	Suez Canal..............	20	145
7	Surrey Comcl. Dck. Ord.	100	145½
7	Do. Min. 4 p.c. Pref. "A"	110	150
5	Do. Prf. "B"........	100	148½
5	Do do. "C"........	100	148½
5	Do. do. "D"........	100	144
4½	Do Deb. Stk.	100	152½

COMMERCIAL, INDUSTRIAL, &c.

Last Div.	Name.	Paid.	Price.
5	Accles, L., 1 Mt. Db., Red.	100	84½
2/6	Aërated Bread, Ltd.	1	12½
—	African Gold Recovery, L.	1	½
2/	Aluminium, L., "A" Shs.	1	2½
4½	Do. 1 Mt. Db. Stk., Red.	100	97
5½	Amelia Nitr., L., 1 Mort Deb., Red.............	100	82½
14/	Anglo-Chil. Nitrate, Ltd., Cum. Pref............	10	7
4½	Do. Cons. Mt. Bds., Red.	100	79
4½	Anglo-Russian Cotton, Ld., 1 Charge Debs., Red.	100	98
3/9	Angus (G., & Co., L.), £10	7½	16½
6/	Apollinaris, Ltd.	10	10½
5/	Do. 5 p.c. Cum. Pref.	10	10
4	Do. Irred. Deb. Stock	100	101
3/	Argentine Meat Pres., L., 7 p.c. Pref............	10	2½
5	Argentine Refinry, Db. Rd.	100	98
6d.	Armstrong, Whitw., Ltd.	1	3½
4	Do. Cum. Pref.	5	6½
5	Artisans', Labr. Dwllgs., L.	100	127½
4½	Do. Non-Cm. Prf., 1879	100	131½
4½	Do. do. 1884	100	130½
—	Asbestos & Asbestic, Ltd.	10	4
2/7½	Ashley-grdns., L., C. Prf.	5	6½
4½	Do. 1 Mt. Deb. Stk.	100	113½
5/	Assam Rly. & Trdng., L., 8 p.c. Cum. Pref. "A"	10	15
—	Do. Deferrd. "B" Shs.	1	3
—	Do. do. (iss. f. pd)	1	2½
8/	Do. Cum. Pre-Prf. "A"	10	15
6/	Do. New Pref.........	10	11½
5	Do. Debs., Red.	100	106
5	Do. Red. Mort. Debs.	100	110
6	Aust'lian Pastrl, L., Cu. Pf.	10	6½
8d.	Aylesbury Dairy, Ltd. ..	1	1½
4	Do. 4 p.c. Mt. Dbs.	100	104½
10/	Babcock & Wilcox, Ltd.	10	28
6	Do. 6 p.c. Cm. Prf.	10	16
8	Baker (Chs.), L., Cm. Pf.	5	9
8	Do. "B" Cm. Pref.	5	7½
2/1	Barker (John), Ltd.	1	2½
5½	Do. Cum. Pref.	5	7½
4½	Do. Irred. 1 Mt. Db. Stk.	100	123½
2/6	Barnagore Jute, Ltd.....	5	2½
5	Do. Cum. Pref.	5	4½
7½d.	Belgravia Dairy, Ltd. ..	1	1½
5/6	Bell (R.) & Co., Ltd.....	5	4
9½d.	Bell's Asbestos, Ltd.	1	½
5	Do. Mt. Db. Bds., Rd.	100	106
10/	Bengal Mills, Ltd.	10	11
6/	Do. 5 p.c. Cum. Prf.	10	10½
5/	Benson (J. W.) L., Cm. Pf.	10	10½
4	Do. Perp. Mt. Db. Stk.	100	101
6	Bergvik, L., 6 p.c. Cm. Pf.	10	12½
12/	Do. Dfd.	10	11
4½	Do. 1 Dbs., Red. ..	100	105½
5/	Birm'ham Vinegar, Ltd.	5	15
5	Do. Cum. Pref.	5	5½
4½	Do. 1 Mt. Db. Stk., Rd.	100	107½
5	Boake (A.) L., 5 p.c. Cu. Pf.	10	10½
2/6	Bodega, Ltd..............	5	9
4½	Do. Mt. Deb. Stk., Rd.	100	110
12/	Bottomley & Brs., Ltd. ..	10	6
6/	Do. 6 p.c. Pf.	10	9
8½d.	Bovril, Ltd.	1	1
1/0½	Do. Def.	1	½
6½d.	Do. Cum. Pref. ..	1	1½
4½	Do. Deb. Stk. ..	100	100
5/	Bradbury, Gretrex., Ltd., £10 share	8	14
5/	Do. 5 p.c. Cum. Pref.	10	13½
5/	Brewers' Sugar, L., 5 p.c. Cum. Pref............	10	11
3/6	Brighton Grd. Hotel, Ld.	5	4
4	Do Mt. Db. Stk., Red.	100	102
5	Bristol Hotel & Palm. Co., Ltd. 1st Mt. Red. Deb.	100	104½
6d.	British & Bengton's Tea Tr. Asc., Ltd.	1	1
5	Do. Cum. Prf.	5	5½
—	British Deli & Lgkat. Tobacco, Ltd.	1	½
—	Do. Cum. Prf.	1	½
1/3	British Tea Table, Ltd...	1	2½
5½	Do. Cum. Pref.......	1	1½
2/6	Brooke, Ben., & Co., Ltd., Cum. Pref............	5	5½
7/6	Brooke, Bond & Co., Ltd.	5	19
3/	Brown Brs., L., Cum. Pref.	5	5½
10/	Browne & Eagle, Ltd. ..	10	13
5	Do. Cum. Pref.	10	12½
4	Do. Mrt. Db. Sk., Red.	100	106
20/	Brunner, Mond, & Co., Lt.	0	38
10/6	Do. £10 shares.......	3½	14½
7	Do. Cum. Pref.......	10	18
7	Do. £10 shares.......	5	8½
10/	Bryant & May, Ltd.	5	18½
3/	Bucknall, H., & Sons, Lt.	5	7
6	Do. Cum Pref.......	5	7½
3/6	Burke, E. & J., Ltd.	5	5½
3/	Do. Cum. Pref.......	5	6
6	Do. Irred. Deb. Stk...	100	135
1/	Burlington Htls. Co., Ltd	1	1½
/6	Do. Cum. Pref.	1	1
4	Do. Perp. Deb. Stk. ..	100	103½
5	Bush, W. J., & Co., Ltd., Cum. Pref.	5	5½
4	Do. 1 Deb. Stk., Red.	100	102
5½	Callard, Stewart, & Watt, Ltd., Cum. Pref.......	1	1½
4/	Callender's Cable L., Shs.	5	10½
4½	Do. 1 Deb. Stk., Red.	100	109½
—	Campbell, R., & Sons, Lt.	3	2½
6	Cantareira Water, Bd., Rd	100	99½
5	Do. (2nd issue)	100	87½
4	Cartavio Sugar, Ltd., 6 p.c. 1st Debs., Red. ..	80	82½
9/	Cassell & Co., Ltd., £10	9	15
5	Causton, Sir J., & Sons, Ltd., Cum. Pref.......	10	13½

Commercial, &c. (*continued*) :—

Last Div.	Name.	Paid.	Price.
4	Cent. Prod. Mkt. of B.A. 1st Mt. Str. Debs.	100	80
4	Chappell & Co., Ltd., Mt. Deb. Stk. Red....	100	104
6/	Chicago & N.W. Gran. 8 p.c. Cum. Pref.......	10	3
4/	Chicago Packing & Prov.	10	6
8	Do. Cum. Pref....	10	10
6/	City Offices, Ltd........	12	
3½	Do. Mt. Deb. Stk...	100	108½
12/	Cy. London Real Prop., Ltd., £25 shs.	12	21½
9/	Do. £12½ shs........	7½	14½
3½	Do. Deb. Stk. Red...	100	107½
3½	Do. Deb. Stk. Red...	100	106½
3	Do.	100	100½
6/	Cy. of Santos Imprvts., Ltd., 7 p.c. Pref.......	10	8
20/	Clay, Bock, & Co., Ltd...	10	5
8	Do. Cum. Pref......	10	9
6	Do. Mort. Deb.......	100	103½
20/	Coats, J. & P., Ltd.....	10	60
6/	Do. Cum. Pref.	10	18
4½	Do. Deb. Stk. Red.	100	112½
1/2½	Coburg Hotel, Ltd......	1	1½
4	Do. Deb. Stk. Red.	100	100
6	Colonial Consign & Dis., Ltd., Cum. Pref.......	5	4½
4½	Do. 1st Mort. Debs..	100	96½
—	Colorado Nitrate, Ltd. ..	5	½
5/	Co. Gén. des Asphtes. de F., Ltd.............	6	6
5	Do, Non-Cm. Prf. ..	—	5
2/6	Cook, J. W., & Co., Ltd., Cum. Pref...........	5	5½
5	Cook, T., & Son, Egypt, Ltd., 1st Mt. Deb. Red.	100	110½
—	Cork Co., Ltd., 6 p.c. Cum. Pref...........	5	2
5	Cory, W., & Sn, L., Cu. Pf.	5	5½
4	Do. 1st Deb. Stk. Red.	100	109
1/6	Crisp & Co., Ltd........	1	1½
6½	Do. Cum. Pref......	1	1½
—	Crompton & Co., Ltd., 7 p.c. Cum. Pref.......	5	6½
5	Do. 1st Mt. Reg. Deb.	—	90½
4/6	Crossley, J., & Sons, Ltd.	5	8
5	Do. Cum. Pref....	5	6½
—	Crystal Pal. Ord. "A" Stk.	100	6½
—	Do. "B" Red. Stk	100	1½
6	Do. 6 p.c. 1st 1887 Deb. Stk. Red. ..	100	114½
—	Do. 6 p.c. 2nd 1887 Deb. Stk. Red. ..	100	51½
—	Do. 6 p.c. 3rd 1887 Deb. Stk. Red. ..	100	22½
3	Do. 3 p.c. 1st 1895 Deb. Stk........	100	91½
—	Daimler Motor, Ltd.....	10	6
4/	Dalgety & Co., £20 Shs.	5	5½
4½	Do. Deb. Stk.........	100	123
4	Do.	100	112
7/	De Keyser's Ryl. Htl., L.	10	13
5	Do. Cum. Pref......	10	11½
4	Do. Deb. Stk., Red..	100	108
6	Denny, H., & Sons, Ltd., Cum. Pref............	10	14
5/3	Devas, Routledge & Co., L.	7	8½
5	Dickinson, J., & Co., L., Cum. Pref. Stk.	100	123
4½	Domin. Cottn. Mls., Ltd. Mt. Stg. Dbs.	100	97
6/	Dorman, Long & Co., L.	5	4½
—	Eastmans, Ltd..........	10	2½
12/	Do. 8 p.c. Cum. Pref.	10	10½
2/	E. C. Powder, Ltd......	3	4½
1/6	Edison & Swn Utd. Elec. Ltd., "A" £5 Shs....	3	2½
2/6	Do. fully-paid	5	4½
4½	Ekman Pulp & Ppr. Co., Ltd., Mt. Deb., Red..	100	96
1/1½	Electric Construc., Ltd..	2	2½
7	Do. Cum. Pref.......	2	3½
10/	Eley Bros., Ltd.	10	38
—	Elmore's Cop. Deptg., L.	1	½
—	Elmore's Wire Mnfg., L.	2	½
—	Elysée Pal. Hotel Co., L.	5/	½
5 p.c.	Do. 5 p.c. £100 Db., Rd.	70	97½
8½d.	Evans, Ben., & Co., Ltd.	1	1
5	Do. 1 Mt. Db. Sk., Rd.	100	108
1/8½d.	Evans, D. H., & Co., L.	1	2½
6	Do. Cum. Pref.......	1	1½
4½	Do. 1 Mt. Db. Sk., Rd.	100	110
2/6	*Evening News*, L., 5 p.c. Cum. Pref............	5	5½
5/3	Evered & Co., L., £10 Sh.	7	12½
7/6	Do.	10	18
4	Fairbairn Pastoral Co., Aust., L., 1 Mt. Db., Rd.	100	102
6	Fairfield Shipbldg., Ltd., Cum. Pref..........	10	11½
4½	Do. Mort. Deb. Stk	100	113½
6/	Farmer & Co., Ld., 6 p.c. Cum. Pref...........	10	13½
12/	Field, J. C. & J., Ltd. ..	10	10
14/	Do. 7 p.c. Cum. Pref.	10	14
1/3	Fordham, W.B., & Sns, Ld.	1	2
4/6	Fore-st. Warehouse, Ltd.	11	9
4	Do. Regd. Debs., Rd.	100	103½
3/6	Foster, M. B. & Sons, Ltd.	4	6
5	Do. Pref....	10	11
9/	Foster, Porter, & Co., L.	10½	16
4	Fowler, J., & Co. (Leeds), Ltd., 1 Mt. Deb., Red.	100	103½
3/	Fraser & Chalmers, Ltd..	3	1½
4½	Free, Rodwell & Co., Ltd., Deb Stk..........	100	104½
6½d.	Furness, T., & Co., Ltd., 5½ p.c. Cum. Pref.		1
4½	Gartside & Co. (of Manchstr), L., 1 Mt. Db. Sk.	100	111
11	Genl Hydraul Power, L.	100	280

Commercial, &c. (*continued*):—

Last Div.	Name.	Paid.	Price.
8/	Gillman & Spencer, Ltd.	5	2½
6	Do. Pref.	5	4¼
5	Do. Mort. Debs.	50	51
4	Goldsbro., Mort & Co., L., "A" Deb. Stk., Red.	100	67½
—	Do. 3 p.c. "B" Inc. Deb. Stk., Red.	100	12
8/	Gordon Hotels, Ltd.	10	20½
5¾	Do. Cum. Pref.	10	14½
4½	Do. Perp. Deb. Stk.	100	140½
4	Do. do.	100	120½
—	Greenwich Inld. Linoleum Co., Ltd.	1	½
14/	Greenwood & Batley, Ltd., Cum. Pref.	10	9
7½d.	Hagemann & Co., Ltd., 6 p.c. Cum. Pref.	1	1
—	Hammond, Ltd.	10	¼
6/8	Do. 8 p.c. Cum. Pref.	10	2½
—	Do. 6 p.c. Cum. Inc. Stk. Red.	100	56½
	Hampton & Sons, Ltd., 4 p.c. 1 Mt. Db. St. Red.	100	103
—	Hans Crescent Htl., L., 6 p.c. Cum. Pref.	5	3
4	Do. 1 Mt. Deb. Stk.	100	90
6d.	Harmsworth, Ltd., Cum. Pref.	1	1⅛
4/	Harrison, Barber, Ltd.	5	4½
3/	Harrod's Stores, Ltd.	1	4½
2/6	Do. Cum. Pref.	5	7
5½	Hawaiian Comcl. & Sug. 1 Mt. Debs.	100	94½
2/6	Hazell, Watson, L., C. P.	10	11½
18/	Henley's Teleg., Ltd.	10	22
7	Do. Pref. Shs.	10	19
4½	Do. Mt. Db. Stk., Rd.	100	112½
6	Henry, Ltd.	10	11½
5	Do. Cum. Pref.	10	13
4½	Do. Mt. Debs., Red.	50	51
1/4½	Herrmann, Ltd.	1	¾
—	Hildesheimer, Ltd.	3	1¼
1/2½	Holbrn. & Frasca, Ltd.	1	1⅛
5	Do. Cum. Pref.	10	12
4	Do. Deb. Stk.	100	108
6	Home & Col. Stres, L., C.P	5	7½
6	Hood & M.'s Stres., Ltd., Cum. Pref.	1	½
6	Hook, C. T Ltd.	10	6
7/2	Hornsby, Ltd., £10 Shs.	8	3
—	Hotchks. Ordn., Ltd.	10	1
—	Do. 7 p.c Cm. Prf.	10	4½
5	Do. 1 Mt. Dbs., Rd.	100	97½
6	Htl. Cecil, Ld., Cm. Prf.	5	3½
4	Do. 1 Mt. D. Sk., R.	100	100½
8/	Heward & Bulgh, Ltd.	10	38
6	Do. Pref.	10	16
4	Do. Deb. Stk., Red.	100	106
5/	Howell, J., Ltd., £5 Shs.	4	9
—	Howell & Js., Ltd., £3½ Shs.	3	¾
6d.	Humber, Ltd.	1	⅜
6	Do. Cum. Pref.	1	¾
5/6	Hunter, Wilts., Ltd.	5	7
2/6	Hyam Clthg., Ltd., 5 p.c. Cum. Pref.	5	5¾
10/	Impl. Russn. Cotton, L.	5	6
5	Impd. Industl. Dwgs., Ld.	100	131½
6d.	Do. Defrd.	1	1½
25/	Impd. Wood Pave., Ltd.	10	15½
15/	Ind. Rubber, Gutta Per. Telegraph Works, Ltd.	10	22
4	Do. 1 Mt. Debs., Red.	100	104
6	Intern. Tea, Cum. Pref.	5	6½
10½d.	Jays, Ltd.	1	1⅜
5½	Do. Cum. Pref.	5	6½
1/2½d.	Jones & Higgins, Ltd.	1	2½
4½	Do. 1 Mt. Db. Sk., Rd.	100	112
5/	Kelly's Directory, Ltd., 5 p.c. Cum. Pref.	10	12¾
4	Do. Mort. Db. Sk., Rd.	100	105
—	Kent Coal Expirtn. Ltd.	1	⅜
9½d.	King, Howmann, Ltd.	1	1½
4/	Kinloch & Co., Ltd.	5	8¼
6	Do. Pref.	5	7
5	Lady's Pictorial Pub., Ltd., Cum. Pref.	5	5
5 p.c.	La Guaira Harb., Ltd., 5 p.c. Deb. Stk.	100	77½
15/	Do. 2 Mt. 7 p.c. Deb. Stk., Red.	100	25½
4/	Lagunas Nitrate, Ltd.	5	1
2/	Lagunas Syn., Ltd.	5	1
5	Do. 1 Mt. Debs., Red.	100	82½
—	L. Copais Ld., 1 Mt. 6 p.c. Debs., Red.	100	35½
3/	Lautaro Nitrate, Ltd.	5	4½
5	Do. 1 Mt. Debs., Red.	—	100
9/	Lawes Chem. L., £10 shs.	9	5½
14/	Do. N. Cm. Min. Pref.	10	12½
—	Leeds Forge, 7 p.c. Cm. Pf.	5	4
5	Do. 1 Mt. Debs., Red.	50	48
5	Lever Bros., L., Cm. Pf.	10	13
6	Liberty, L., 6 p.c. Cm. Pf.	10	15
60/	Liebig's, Ltd.	20	79
5	Lilley & Sk., L., Cm. Pf.	5	5½
2/6	Linoleum Manftg Ltd.	5	15
3/	Linotype, Ltd., Pre	5	5½
5/	Do. Def.	5	7½
4/	Lister & Co., Ltd.	10	4
5	Do. Cum. Pref.	10	8½
5/	Liverpool. Nitrate	5	5½
—	Liverpool. Warehsg., Ltd	10	3
5½	Do. Cum. Pref.	10	7½
4	Do. 1 Mt. Db. Stk., Rd.	100	105
5½	Lockharts, Ltd., Cm. Pf.	1	1½
4/6	Ldn. & Til. Lightrage £10	9	6½
6/	Ldn. Comcl. Sale Rms., L.	10	17½
3	Do. 1 Mt. Deb. Stk., Red.	100	103
8/4½	London Nitrate, Ltd.	5	1
4/	London Nitrate, Ld. 8 p.c. Cm. Min. Pf.	5	3
8/	London Pavilion, Ltd.	5	7

Commercial, &c. (*continued*):—

Last Div.	Name.	Paid.	Price.
2/6	London. Produce Clg. Ho., Ltd., £10 Shares	2½	3¾
4/	London Stereos., Ltd.	5	3
7½d.	Ldn. Un. Laun. L. Cm. Pf.	1	¾
8½d.	Louise, Ltd.	1	⅜
5½	Do. Cum. Pref.	1	⅝
5/	Lovell & Christmas, Ltd.	5	11½
6	Do. Cum. Pref.	5	7½
4	Do. Mt. Deb. Stk., Red.	100	107
1/9	Lyons, Ltd.	1	4
4½	Do. 1 Mt. Deb., Stk., Rd.	100	111½
10/	Machinery Trust, Ltd.	5	14½
4½	Do. 4½ Deb. Stk.	100	104
6	MacLellan, L., Min. C. Pf.	10	9
5	Do. 1 Mt. Debs., 1900	100	101½
—	McEwan, J. & Co, Ltd.	10	1
6	Do. Mt. Debs., Red.	100	90½
8	McNamara, L., Cm. Pref.	10	9
7½d.	Maison Virot, Ltd.	1	¾
3/	Do. 6 p.c. Cum. Pref.	5	3½
5/	Manbré Sacc., L., Cm. Pf.	10	11½
10/	Mangan Brze., L., £10 Shs.	6	16
2/	Mason & Mason, Ltd.	5	2¾
6	Do. Cum. Pref.	5	5¼
—	Maynards, Ltd.	1	⅜
6	Do. Cum. Pref.	1	¾
9½d.	Mazawattee Tea, Ltd.	1	1⅜
5	Do. Cum. Pref.	5	5¾
3/	Mellin's Food Cum. Pref.	5	6¾
4½	Met. Ascn. Imp. Dwllngs., Ltd.	100	108½
5	Metro. Indus. Dwlgs., Ltd.	5	4½
4	Do. do. Cum. Pref.	5	5½
5	Metro. Prop., L., Cm. Pf.	5	5¾
4½	Do. 1st Mt. Debs. Stk.	100	107½
6	Mexican Cotton 1 Mt. Db.	100	93½
4½	Mid. Class Dwlgs., L., Db.	100	120½
2/	Millars' Karri, Ltd.	1	3
6	Do. Cum. Pref.	1	1½
5/	Milner's Safe, Ltd.	10	20½
10/	Moir & Son, Ltd., Pref.	5	8
6	Morgan Cruc., L., Cm. Pf.	10	14½
1/	Morris, B., Ltd.	3½	3
2/6	Murray L. 5½ p.c. C. Pf.	5	5½
63/4½	Do. 4½ 1 Mt. Db. Sk. Rd.	100	107
1/7½	Nat. Safe Dep., Ltd.	4	3¾
6	Do. Cum. Pref.	1	1
—	Native Guano, Ltd.	5	½
—	Nelson Bros., Ltd.	10	2½
5	Do. Deb. Stk., Red.	100	73
7/	Neuchtel Asph., Ltd.	10	10
10d.	New Darvel Tob., Ltd.	18/	1¼
1/6	New Explosives, Ltd.	3	3
5/3½	New Gd. Htl., Bham, L.	5	4
5½	Do. Pref.	5	4½
4	Do. 1 Mt. Db. Stk., Rd.	100	96½
—	New Julia Nitrate, Ltd.	10/	—
2/	New Ldn. Borneo Tob., L.	16/	¾
1/6	New Premier Cycle, Ltd.	1	⅛
7½	Do. 6 p.c. Cum. Pref.	1	¾
4½	Do. 4½ p.c. 1 Mt. Db. Rd	100	—
—	New Tamargl. Nitr., Ltd	1	1/16
—	Do. 8 p.c. Cum. Pref.	1	1/16
6	Do. 6 p.c. 1 Mt. Dbs. Rd.	100	60
6d.	Newnes, G., L., Cm. Prf.	1	1 1/16
1/3	Nitr. Provision, Ltd.	2½	¾
24/	Nobel-Dynam., Ltd.	10	17
—	North Bram. Sugar, Ltd.	1	¼
15/	Oakey, Ltd.	10	30
6	Do. Cum. Pref.	10	17½
—	Paccha Jazp. Nitr., Ltd.	5	½
5	Pac. Borax, L., 1 Db. Rd.	100	110
—	Palace Hotel, Ltd.	10	5½
5½	Do. Cum. Pref.	10	7½
4	Do. 1 Mt. Deb. Stk.	100	103
—	Palmer, Ltd.	5	¾
6	Do. Cum. Pref.	5	2
1/2½d	Paquin, Ltd.	1	¾
3/	Do. Cum. Pref.	5	3¾
5½	Parnall, Ltd., Cum. Pref.	1	¾
4/6	Pawsons, Ltd., £10 Shs.	6	6¼
4	Do. Mt. Debs., Red.	100	106
7½	Pearks, G. & T., Ltd., 6 p.c. Cum. Pref.	1	¾
9½d.	Pears, Ltd	1	1½
6	Do. Cum. Pref.	10	14
5	Do. Deb. Stk.	100	127
5½	Pearson, C. A., L., Cu. Pf.	5	4¾
4/3	Peebles, Ltd.	5	8
5	Do. Cum. Pref.	5	6½
4½	Do. Mt. Deb. Stk. Red.	100	112½
2/9	Peek Bros., Ltd., 1 Cum. Pref., Nos. 1-60,000	5	6½
3½	Do. 3½ p.c 1 Db. Stk.	100	102½
7½d.	Pegamoid, Ltd.	1	⅝
—	Pillsbury-W. Fl. Mills, L.	10	2
16/	Do. 8 p.c. Cum. Pref.	10	5½
6	Do. 1 Mort. Debs.	100	91½
9½d.	Plummer, Ltd.	1	1½
5	Do. Cum. Pref.	5	5½
17/6	Price's Candle, Ltd.	16	36
6	Priest Marians, L., Cm. Pf.	1	1
6	Pryce Jones, Ld., Cm. Pf.	5	6½
5	Do. Deb. Stk.	100	120
8½d.	Pullman, Ltd.	1	1
6d.	Do. Cum. Pref.	1	1
6d.	Raleigh Cycle, Ltd.	1	1/16
6	Do. Cum. Pref.	1	¾
—	Recife Drnge. Ld. 1 Mt. Debs., R	100	18
6	Redfern, Ltd. Cum. Prf.	10	14
5	Ridgways, Ltd., Cu. Pf.	5	5½
—	R. Janeiro Cy. Imps. Ld.	25	8
5	Do. Debs.	100	84
5	Do. 1880-1893	100	83½
5%	R. Jan Fl. Mills, Ltd.	7	6
5	Do. 1 Mt. Debs., Rd.	100	94
10/	Riv. Plate Meat, Ltd.	5	4
—	Do. Pref.	5	5
8½d.	Roberts, J. R., Ltd.	1	1½
5	Roberts 1 Mt. D. Sk., Rd.	100	108
1/4½	Roberts, T. R., Ltd.	1	2½
5	Do. Cum. Pref.	1	1½

Commercial, &c. (*continued*):—

Last Div.	Name.	Paid.	Price.
3/	Rosario Nit., Ltd.	5	3½
5	Do. Debs., Red.	100	103
1/	Rover Cycle, Ltd.	1	⅝
6/	Ryl. Aquarium, Ltd.	5	4½
6	Do. Pref.	5	5½
5	Ryl. Htl., Edin., Cm. Pf.	1	1⅛
1/2½	Ryl. Niger, Ltd., £10 Sh.	2	2½
6/	Do.	10	15
20/	Russian Petroleum	10	
6½	Do. 6½ p.c. Cm. Prf.	10	
10/	Ruston, Proctor, Ltd.	10	11½
4½	Do. 1 Mort. Debs.	100	108
6/	Sadler, Ltd.	12	7
—	Sal. Carmen Nit., Ltd.	5	3½
9d.	Salmon & Gluck., Ltd.	1	1¼
	Salt Union, Ltd.	10	1¼
1½	Do. 7 p.c. Pref.	10	5½
4½	Do. Deb. Stk.	100	100½
4½	Do. "B" Deb. Sk., Rd.	100	96
—	San Donato Nit., Ltd.	5	½
5/	San Jorge Nit., Ltd.	5	3½
—	San Pablo Nit., Ltd.	5	⅜
—	San Sebastn. Nit., Ltd.	5	⅜
1/9	Sanitas, Ltd	1	2½
—	Sa. Elena Nit., Ltd.	5	⅜
—	Sa. Rita Nit., Ltd.	5	2¾
5/	Savoy Hotel, Ltd.	10	15
7	Do. Pref.	10	13
4	Do. 1 Mt. Deb. Stk.	100	107½
5	Do. Debs., Red	100	102½
5	Do. & Ldn. For. Htl., Ltd., 5 p.c. Debs. Red.	100	99
8½d.	Schweppes, Ltd.	1	1½
2½d.	Do Def.	1	⅝
5	Do. Cum. Pref.	1	1⅛
4	Do. Deb. Stk.	100	105
6d.	Singer Cyc., Ltd.	1	⅝
5½	Do Cum. Pref.	1	¾
—	Smokeless Pwdr., Ltd.	1	⅜
7½d.	S. Eng. Dairies, Ltd., 6 p.c. Cum. Pref.	1	1½
—	Sowler Thos. L.	1	1
3/4½	Do. 5½ Cm. Pf.	5	5½
4/6	Spencer, Turner, & Co. Ltd	5	8½
5	Do. Cum. Pref.	5	6½
5	Spicer, Ld., 5 p.c. Dbs. Rd.	100	65
4/	Spiers & Pond, Ltd.	10	21
5	Do. 1 Mt. Debs., Red.	100	118½
5	Do. "A" Db. Stk., Rd.	100	108½
5	Do. "B" 1 Db. Stk., Rd.	100	109½
4	Do. Fd. "C" 1 Db. S., R.	100	102
7/6	Spratt's, Ltd	5	12½
4	Do. Debs., 1914	—	105
5	Steiner Ld., Cm. Pf.	10	11½
4	Do. 1 Mt. Db. Sk. Rd.	100	105
9/	Stewart & Clydesdale, L.	10	13
6	Do. Cum. Pref.	10	15
5	Sulphide Corp.	100	77
1/	Swan & Edgar, L.	1	1½
1/	Sweetmeat Automatic, L.	1	4
2/9	Teetgen, Ltd., Cum. Pref.	5	5½
24/	Teleg. Construction., Ld.	12	36½
5	Do. Db. Bds., Rd., 1899	100	103½
2/9	Tilling, Ld. 5½ p.c. Cm. Prf.	5	6½
4	Do. 4 p.c. 1 Dbs., Rd.	—	106
1/0½	Tower Tea, Ltd.	1	1½
5	Do. Cum. Pref.	5	5½
5	Travers, Ltd., Cum. Pref.	10	12½
4	Do. 1 Mt. Dbs., Rd.	100	105
6	Tucuman Sug., 1 Dbs., Rd.	100	100
4/	United Alkali, Ltd.	10	1½
7	Do. Cum. Pref.	10	9
5	Do. Mt. Db. Stk., Rd.	100	108½
2½d.	United Horse Shoe, Ltd., Non-Cum. 8 p.c. Pref.	1	1/16
5	Un. Kingm. Tea, Cm. Prf.	5	4½
2/	Un. Lankat Plant., Ltd.	1	2
4/	Un. Limmer Asphlte., Ld.	3	5
13/	Val de Travers Asph., L.	10	15½
3/	V. den Bergh's, L., Cm. P.	5	6
6	Walkers, Park., L., C. Pf.	10	2½
4½	Do. 1 Mt. Debs., Red.	100	90½
4/	Wallis, Thos. & Co., Ltd.	5	14
6	Do. Cum. Pref.	5	8½
5½	Waring, Ltd., Cum. Pref.	5	5¾
4½	Do. 1 Mt. Db. Sk., Red.	100	100
4½	Do. Irred. "B" Db. Stk.	100	103
12/	Waterlow, Dfd. Ord.	10	14
4/	Do. Pref.	10	14
3½	Do. Cum. Pref.	10	10½
10/	Waterlow Bros. & L., Ld.	10	9
5	Do. Pref.	10	12
1/2½	Welford, Ltd.	1	2
4½	Do. Debs., Red.	100	109
1/	Welford's Surrey Dairies, Ltd.	1	1⅜
7½d.	West London Dairy, Ltd.	1	1
4½	Wharncliffe Dwllgs, L., Pf.	10	11½
3	Do. 3 p.c. Irr. Mt. Db. Sk.	100	95
1/	White, A. J., Ltd.	1	¾
6	Do. 6 p.c. Cum. Pref.	1	¾
4	White, J. Bazley, Ltd., 1 Mort. Debs., Red	100	99½
5	White, R., Ltd., 1 Mort. Deb. Stock, Red.	100	104½
11/	White, Tomkins, Ltd	10	10½
5	Do. Cum. Pref.	10	11½
6	White, W. N., L., Cm. Pf.	1	⅜
5/	Wickens, Pease & Co., L.	5	2½
6	Wilkie, Ltd., Cum. Pref.	10	14½
4/	Willans & Robinson, Ltd.	5	8
6	Do. Cum. Pref.	5	7
4½	Do. 1 Mt. Db. Stk., Red.	100	107
7½d.	Williamsons, L., Cm. Prf.	1	1⅛
6	Winterbottm. Book Cloth, Ltd., Cum. Prf.	10	15
4/6	Yates, Ltd.	5	6
6	Do. Cum. Pref.	5	6½
	Young's Paraffin. Ltd.	4	1½

CORPORATION STOCKS—COLONIAL AND FOREIGN.

Per Cent.	Name.	Paid.	Price.
6	Auckland City, '72 1904-24	100	115
6	Do. Cons., '79, Red. 1930	100	135½
5	Do. Deb. Ln., '83 1934-8	100	117
6	Auckland Harb. Debs.	100	111½
5	Do. 1917	100	113½
5	Do. 1936	100	114
5½	Balmain Boro' 1914	—	113½
5	Boston City (U.S.)	100	102½
5	Do. 1902	100	106
5	Brunswick Town 5 c. Debs. 1916-20	100	111
4½	B. Ayres City 4½ p.c.	100	72½
5	Cape Town, City of	100	113
4	Do. 1943	100	115
4	Chicago, City of, Gold 1915	—	110
6	Christchurch 1926	100	131½
—	Cordoba City	100	17
5	Duluth (U.S.) Gold 1926	—	110
6	Dunedin (Otago) 1925	100	127½
6	Do. 1906	100	116
5	Do. Consols 1908	100	111
4	Durban Insc. Stk. 1944	100	109
4	Essex Cnty., N. Jersey 1926	100	114½
5	Fitzroy, Melbrne. 1916-19	100	110
5	Gisborne Harbour 1915	100	109
4	Greymouth Harbour 1925	100	110
4	Hamilton 1934	100	108
5	Hobart Town 1918-30	100	115
4	Do. 1940	100	105
4½	Invercargill Boro. Dbs. 1936	100	111
6	Kimberley Boro., S. A. Debs.	—	102
4	Launceston Twn. Dbs. 1916	100	105
6	Lyttleton, N.Z., Harb. 1929	100	125
4	Melbourne Bd. of Wks. 1921	100	107
5	Melb. City Debs. 1897-1907	100	106½
4½	Do. Debs. 1908-27	100	111½
4	Do. Debs. 1915-20-22	100	106
5	Melbne. Harb. Bds., 1908-9	100	112
4½	Do. do. 1915	100	111
4	Do. do. 1918-21	100	106
4½	Melbrne. Tms, Dbs. 1914-16	100	113
4½	Do. Fire Brig. Db. 1921	100	108
5	Mexico City Stg.	100	93
4	Moncton N. Bruns. City	100	102
5	Montevideo	100	61
5	Montreal Stg.	100	103
5	Do. 1874	100	103
5	Do. 1879	100	104
3½	Do. 1933	100	103
3	Do. Perm. Deb. Stk	100	95
4	Do. Cons. Deb. Stk. 1932	100	112
6	Napier Boro. Consolid. 1914	100	119
5	Napier Harb. Debs. 1920	100	115
5	Do. Debs. 1928	100	107
6	New Plymouth Harb. Debs. 1909	100	107
6	New York City 1901	—	109½
3½	Do. 1910-26	—	103½
4½	Nth. Melbourne Debs. 1-600 1921	100	105
5	Oamaru Boro. Cons. 1920	100	101
6	Do. Harb. Bds. (Reg.)	100	74
25/	Do. 6 p.c. (Bearer) 1919	100	35
6	Otago Harb. Deb. Reg.	100	103
6	Do. 1877	100	107
6	Do. 1881 1921	100	115
5	Do. Debs. 1921	100	107
5	Do. Cons. 1934	100	105
6	Ottawa City	100	109
6	Do. 1904	100	111½
4½	Do. Debs. 1913	100	108½
6	Port Elizabeth Waterworks	100	111
5	Port Louis	100	111
5	Prahran Debs. 1917	100	109
4	Do. Debs. 1919	100	102
6	Quebec C. Coupon. 1875 1905	100	113
6	Do. do. 1878 1908	100	117
4½	Do. Debs. 1914-18	100	108
4	Do. Debs. 1923	200	108
3½	Do. Cns. Rg. Stk., Red.	100	100
5	Richmond (Melb.) Dbs. 1917	100	112
4	Rio Janeiro City	100	59
4	Rome City	100	—
4	Do. 2nd to 8th Iss.	100	93
—	Rosario C.	100	25
—	Do.	100	25
4	St. Catherine (Ont.) 1926	100	101
4	St. John, N.B., Debs. 1934	—	103
4½	St. Kilda (Melb) Dbs. 1918-21	100	105
4	St. Louis C. (Miss.) 1911	100	104
4	Do. 1913	100	103½
3·65	Do. 1915	—	108½
—	Santa Fé City Debs.	100	19
6	Santos City	100	101½
6	Sofia City	100	84
5	Sth. Melbourne Debs. 1915	100	111
4½	Do. Debs. 1919	100	107
5	Sydney City 1904	100	110
4	Do. Debs. 1912-13	100	107
4	Do. do. (1894) 1919	100	109
7	Timaru Boro. 7 p.c. 1910	100	126½
5	Timaru Harb. Debs 1914	100	107
5	Do. Debs. 1916	100	107
6	Toronto City Wtwks 1904-6	100	114
5	Do. G. Cns. Dbs. 1919-20	100	118
4	Do. Strlg. 1922-8	100	107
4	Do. Local Improv.	100	104
3½	Do. 1929	100	106
5½	Valparaiso	100	100
4	Vancouver 1931	100	107
4	Do. 1932	100	108
6	Wanganui Harb. Dbs. 1905	100	107
6	Wellington Con. Deb. 1907	100	117
6	Do. Improv., 1879	100	123
6	Do. Wtrwks. Dbs., 1880	100	123
4½	Do. Debs., 1893 1933	100	114
4½	Wellington Harb. 1907	100	104
4	Westport Harb. Dbs. 1925	100	110
6	Winnipeg City Deb. 1907	—	119
5	Do. 1914	100	117

FINANCIAL, LAND, AND INVESTMENT.

Last Div.	Name.	Paid.	Price.
5	Agncy, Ld. & Fin. Aust., Ltd., Mt. Db. Stk., Rd.	100	88½
6/	Amer. Frehld. Mt. of Lon., Ld., Cum. Pref. Stk. ..	100	85
4½	Do. Deb. Stk., Red. ..	100	91½
1/4½	Anglo-Amer. Db. Cor., L.	2	1
4	Do. Deb. Stk., Red ..	100	106½
	Ang.-Ceylon & Gen. Est., Ltd., Cons. Stk.	100	45
6	Do. Reg. Debs., Red.	100	101½
3/	Ang.-Fch. Explorn., Ltd.	1	2⅛
6	Do. Cum. Pref.	1	1⅛
—	Argent. Ld. & Inv., Ltd. £1 Shares	10/	nil
—	Do. Cum. Pref.	4	1½
1/	Assets Fnders.' Sh., Ltd.,	4	1⅜
4/	Assets Realis., Ltd., Ord.,	5	8½
5	Do. Cum. Pref.	5	6½
26/	Austrln. Agricl. £25 Shs.	21½	61½
4½	Aust. N. Z. Mort., Ltd., Deb. Stk., Red.	100	87½
4	Do. Deb. Stk., Red. ..	100	80½
4½	Australian Est. & Mt., L., 1 Mt. Deb. Stk., Red.	100	103
5	Do. "A" Mort. Deb. Stk., Red.	100	93
5/	Australian Mort., Ld., & Fin., Ltd. £25 Shs. ..	5	5½
3/	Do. New, £25 Shs...	3	3½
4	Do. Deb. Stk	100	109
3	Do. Do.	100	83
5	Bengal Presidy. 1 Mort. Deb., Red.	100	107
25/	British Amer. Ld. "A"	1	22
—	Do. "B"	24	7
2/7½	Brit. & Amer. Mt., Ltd. £10 Shs.	2	1
5/	Do. Pref.	10	10
4	Do. Deb. Stk., Red. ..	100	101
2/3	Brit. & Austrian Tst Ln., Ltd. £25 Shs.	2½	¾
4½	Do. Perm. Debs., Red.	100	104
2½d.	Brit. N. Borneo. £1 Shs.	15/	⅝
2½d.	Do.	1	¾
—	Brit. S. Africa	1	2½
5	Do. Mt. Deb., Red.	—	100
6	B. Aires Harb. Tst., Red.	100	93
22/6	Canada Co.	1	29
—	Canada N. W. Ld., Ltd.	$25	84
—	Do. Pref.	$100	55½
4	Canada Perm. Loan & Sav. Perp. Deb. Stk...	100	98
6	Curamalan Ld., 6 p.c. "A" Scrip	—	92
2/4½	Deb Corp., Ld., £10 Shs	4	3
5	Do. Cum. Pref.	10	11½
4	Do. Perp. Deb. Stk...	100	108
9d.	Deb. Corp. Fders' Sh., Ld.	3	½
4/5⅖	Eastn. Mt. & Agncy, Ld., "A"	10	5½
4½	Do. Deb. Stk., Red.	100	98
8	Equitable Revers. In. Ltd.	100	—
2/6	Exploration, Ltd.	1	1 3/16
/6d.	Freehold Trst. of Austria. Ltd. £10 Shs.	1	¾
4	Do. Perp. Deb. Stk...	100	100
70/	Genl. Reversionary, Ltd.	100	—
3½	Holborn Vi. Land	100	106
4½	House Prop. & Inv.	100	84½
13/	Hudson's Bay	13	20½
—	Hyderabad (Deccan)	5	3
4	Impl. Col. Fin. & Agcy. Corp.	100	93½
4½	Impl. Prop. Inv., Ltd., Deb. Stk., Red.	100	91½
2/6	Internatl. Fincial. Soc., Ltd. £7½ Shs.	2½	1½
4	Do. Deb. Stk., Red...	100	98½
2/4½	Ld. & Mtge. Egypt, Ltd. £18 Shs.	3	2½
5	Do. Debs., Red.	100	101
4½	Do. Debs., Red.	100	100
—	Ld. Corp. of Canada, Ltd.	1	½
4½	Ld. Mtge. Bk. of Texas Deb. Stk.	100	—
3½	Ld. Mtge. Bk. Victoria 4½ p.c. Deb. Stk.	100	75
2/9½	Law Debent. Corp., Ltd., £10 Shs.	2	1½
4½	Do. Cum. Pref., ...	10	12
4	Do. Deb. Stk.	100	113½
—	Law Land, L., 4½ Cm. Prf.	5	5½
1/	Ldn. & Australasian Deb. Corp., Ltd., £4 Shs. ..	2	½
4½	Do. 4½ p.c. Mt. Deb. Stk., Red.	100	99
1/9	Ldn. & Middx. Frhld. Est. £2 Shs.	35/	3
2/6	Lndn. & N. Y. Inv. Corp., Ltd.	5	1½
5	Do. 5 p.c. Cum. Pref...	10	8½
1/6	Ldn. & Nth. Assets Corp., Ltd., £2 Shs.	1½	¾
2	Ldn. & N. Deb. Corp., L.	2	1¼
3/6	Ldn. & S. Afric. Explrn. Ltd.	½	12½
2/	Mtge. Co. of R. Plate, Ltd. £10 Shs.	2	3
4½	Do. Deb. Stk., Red...	100	113
4½	Morton, Rose Est., Ltd., 1st Mort. Debs.	—	100
6/6	Natal Land Col. Ltd. ..	10	7
4/	Do. 8 p.c. Pref., 1870..	5	8½
5/6	Natl. Disct. L., £25 Shs.	5	10½
4½	New Impl. Invest., Ltd. Pref. Stk.	100	67½
	New Impl. Invest., Ltd. Def. Stk.	100	9
3½	N. Zld. Assets Real Deb.	100	101
4	N. Zld. Ln. & Mer. Agcy., Ltd Prf. Ln, Deb. Stk	100	92
2/6	N. Zld. Tst. & Ln. Ltd., £25 Shs.	5	1½

Financial, Land, &c. (*continued*):—

Last Div.	Name.	Paid.	Price.
12/6	N. Zld. Tst. & Ln. Ltd., 5 p.c. Cum. Pref.	25	19
—	N. Brit. Australsn. Ltd...	100	4
—	Do. Irred. Guar.....	100	32½
5	Do. Mort. Debs.....	100	82½
4½	N. Queensld. Mort. & Inv., Ltd., Deb. Stk.	100	93
6	Peel Riv., Ld. & Min. Ltd.	100	90
—	Peruvian Corp., Ltd.	100	2½
—	Do. 4 p.c. Pref.	100	9
3	Do. 6 p.c. 1 Mt. Debs., Red.	100	40½
3/7½	Queensld. Invest. & Ld... Mort. Pref. Ord. Stk...	100	20
3/7	Queensld. Invest. & Ld. Mort. Ord. Shs.	4	3½
4	Queensld. Invest. & Ld. Mort. Perp. Debs.	100	92
3½	Raily. Roll Stk. Tst. Deb., 1903-6	100	100½
50/	Reversiony. Int. Soc., Ltd.	100	—
2/8½	Riv. Plate Trst., Loan & Agcy., L., "A" £10 Shs.	2	4
1/6	Riv. Plate Trst., Loan & Agcy., Ltd., Def. "B"	5	3½
4	Riv. Plate Trst., Loan & Agy., L., Db. Stk., Red.	100	108
—	Santa Fé & Cord. Gt. South Land, Ltd.	20	5
—	Santa Fé Land	10	2½
2/	Scot. Amer. Invest., Ltd. £10 Shs.	2	2½
2½	Scot. Australian Invest., Ltd., Cons.	100	70½
6	Scot. Australian Invest., Ltd., Guar. Pref.	100	133½
5	Scot. Australian Invest., Ltd., Guar. Pref.	100	106½
4	Scot. Australian Invest., Ltd., 4 p.c. Perp. Dbs.	100	106½
5	Sivagunga Zemdy., 1st Mort., Red.	100	101
20/	Sth. Australian	20	48½
3½	Stock Exchange Deb., Rd.	—	101½
—	Strait Develt., Ltd.	1	—
2/6	Texas Land & Mt., Ltd. £10 Shs.	2½	2½
4½	Texas Land & Mt., Ltd., Deb. Stk., Red.	100	104
—	Transvaal Est. & Dev., L.	1	½
—	Transvaal Lands, Ltd., £1 Shs.	15/	1/16
—	Do. F. P.	1	⅛
—	Transvaal Mort., Loan, & Fin., Ltd., £10 Shs. ..	2	1/16
2/	Tst & Agcy. of Austrlsa., Ltd., £10 Shs.	1	1½
7/5	Do. Old, fully paid ..	10	15½
5/7	Do. New, fully paid..	10	12½
5	Do. Cum. Pref.	10	12½
3/	Trust & Loan of Canada, £20 Shs.	5	4½
1/9½	Do. New £20 Shs....	3	2½
4½	Tst. & Mort. of Iowa, Ltd., Deb. Stk. Red...	100	92½
—	Tst., Loan, & Agency of Mexico, Ltd., £10 Shs.	2	½
—	Trsts., Exors, & Sec. Ins. Corp., Ltd., £10 Shs..	7	1½
4	Do. Irred. Deb. Stk.	100	108½
5/	Union Dsc., Ld., £10 Shs.	5	10½
6	Union Mort. & Agcy. of Aust., Ltd., Pref. Stk.	100	30
—	Do. 6 p. Pref. £6 Shs.	2	½
4½	Do. Deb. Stk	100	90
4	Do. Deb. Stk	100	83½
5	Do. Deb. Stk. Red...	100	94
1/6	U.S. Deb. Cor. Ltd., £8 Shs.	1	½
5½	Do. Cum. Pref. Stk..	100	100½
4½	Do. Irred. Deb. Stk..	100	106½
5	U.S. Tst. & Guar. Cor., Ltd., Pref. Stk	100	77½
8/	Van Dieman's	25	16
4	Walker's Prop. Cor., Ltd., Guar. 1 Mt. Deb. Stk..	100	107
4½	Wstr. Mort. & Inv., Ltd., Deb. Stk.	100	92½

FINANCIAL—TRUSTS.

Last Div.	Name.	Paid.	Price.
1/6	Afric City Prop., Ltd...	1	1½
6	Do. Cum. Pref.	1	1 1/16
4	Alliance Invt., Ltd., Cm. 4½ p. c. Prefd.	100	72½
—	Do. Defd	100	12½
4	Do. Deb. Stk. Red...	100	104½
5	Amrcn. Invt., Ltd., Prfd.	100	120½
5	Do. Defd.	100	88½
4	Do. Deb. Stk. Red...	100	114½
2	Army & Navy Invt., Ltd., 5 p.c. Prefd.	100	84½
—	Do. Defd. Stk.	100	16½
4	Do. Deb. Stk.	100	107½
4	Atlas Investment, Ltd., Prefd. Stk.	100	70½
4½	Bankers' Invest., Ltd., Cum. Prefd.	100	103
1/0/0	Do. Defd	100	24½
4	Do. Deb. Stk	100	112
	Brewery & Comml. Inv., Ltd., £10 Shs.	5	6

Financial—Trusts (*continued*):—

Last Div.	Name.	Paid.	Price.
4	British Investment, Ltd., Cum. Prefd.	100	108
5	Do. Defd.	100	103½
4	Do. Deb. Stk.	100	106½
6	Brit. Steam. Invst., Ltd., Prefd	100	121
3/0/0	Do. Defd	100	79½
4½	Do. Perp. Deb. Stk ..	100	121
1/9	Car Trust Invst., Ltd., £10 Shs.	2½	2
5	Do. Pref.	100	99
4	Do. Deb. Stk., 1915..	100	102
4	Cinl. Sec., Ltd., Prefd. ..	100	103½
2⅛	Do. Defd.	100	45½
4	Consolidated, Ltd., Cum. 1st Pref.	100	92
4	Do. 5 p.c. Cm. and do.	100	68½
—	Do. Defd.	100	14½
4½	Do. Deb. Stk.	100	112½
5	Deb. Secs. Invst.	100	106½
4	Do. 4 p.c. Cm. Pf. Sk.	100	106½
4½	Edinburgh Invest., Ltd., Cum. Prefd. Stk.	100	106½
4	Do. Deb. Stk. Red.	100	106½
5	Foreign, Amer. & Gen. Invt., Ltd., Prefd.	100	114
2	Do. Defd.	100	47½
4	Do. Deb. Stk.	100	113½
5	Foreign & Colonial Invt., Ltd., Prefd.	100	137½
5½	Do. Defd.	100	96½
4½	Gas, Water & Gen. Invt., Cum. Prefd. Stk.	100	87½
5	Do. Defd. Stk.	100	37½
4	Do. Deb. Stk.	100	102
5	Gen. & Com. Invt., Ltd., Prefd. Stk.	100	103½
2	Do. Defd. Stk.	100	35½
4	Do. Deb. Stk.	100	111½
2/6	Globe Telegph. & Tst., Ltd.	10	11½
6	Do. do. Pref.	10	17½
4	Govt. & Genl. Invt., Ld., Prefd.	100	82½
3½	Do. Defd.	100	40½
4½	Govts. Stk. & other Secs. Invt., Ltd., Prefd.	100	86½
1	Do. Defd.	100	25
4½	Do. Deb. Stk.	100	108
4	Do. do.	100	102
4½	Guardian Invt., Ltd., Pfd.	100	89½
—	Do. Defd.	100	19½
4	Do. Deb. Stk.	100	104
5	Indian & Gen. Inv., Ltd., Cum. Prefd.	100	108½
3	Do. Defd.	100	58
4½	Do. Deb. Stk.	100	120½
5	Indust. & Gen. Tst., Ltd., Unified	100	98½
3½	Do. Deb. Stk. Red.	100	99½
4½	Internat. Invt., Ltd., Cm. Prefd.	100	64½
—	Do. Defd.	100	7½
4	Do. Deb. Stk.	100	97
4	Invest. Tst. Cor. Ltd. Pfd.	100	100½
6	Do. Defd.	100	88
4	Do. Deb. Stk. Red.	100	102
25/	Ldn. Gen. Invest. Ltd., 5 p.c. Cum. Prefd.	100	111½
37/6	Do. Defd.	100	120
4½	Ldn. Scot. Amer. Ltd. Pfd.	100	106½
£3	Do. Defd.	100	60½
4	Do. Deb. Stk.	100	109
4	Ldn. Tst., Ltd., Cum. Prfd. Stk.	100	101
4	Do. Defd. Stk.	100	67½
4	Do. Deb. Stk., Red.	100	107
3½	Do. Mt. Deb. Stk., Red.	100	100½
5	Mercantile Invt. & Gen., Ltd., Prefd.	100	113
3	Do. Defd.	100	44½
4	Do. Deb. Stk.	100	110½
4	Merchants, Ltd., Pref. Stk.	100	104½
4	Do. Ord.	100	80½
4	Do. Deb. Stk.	100	117½
3½	Municipal, Ltd., Prefd...	100	48½
—	Do. Defd.	100	17½
4½	Do. Debs.	100	111
4½	Do. Debs. "B"....	100	99½
4½	Do. "C" Deb. Stk.	100	91½
3	New Investment, Ltd. Ord.	100	93½
5	Omnium Invest., Ltd., Pfd.	100	89½
1	Do. Defd....	100	26½
4	Do. Deb. Stk.	100	106
5/	Railway Deb. Tst. Ld., £20 Shs.	10	6½
5	Do. Debs., Red. ..	100	108½
4½	Do. Deb. Stk., 1911	100	105½
4	Do. do. 1927	100	106½
4	Railway Invst. Ltd., Prefd.	100	116
17/7	Do. Defd.	100	22
8/	Railway Share Trust & Agency "A"	8	6½
7½	Do. "B" Pref. Stk.	100	148
4½	River Plate & Gen. Invt., Ltd., Prefd.	100	104
£8	Do. Defd.	100	50½
5	Scot. Invst., Ltd., Pfd. Stk.	100	92½
1½	Do. Defd...	100	26½
4	Do. Deb. Stk.	100	106
4½	Sec. Scottish Invst., Ltd., Cum. Prefd.	100	89½
£8	Do. Defd. Stk.	100	32
4	Do. Deb. Stk.	100	106½
5/	Sth. Africa Gold Tst., Ltd.	1	3½
6	Do. Cum. Pref	1	1
5½	Do. 1st Debs., Red.	100	104
/9	Stock Conv. & Invest., Ltd., £5 Shs.	1	1½
4½	Do. do. 4½ p.c. Cm. Prf.	100	114½
3½	Do. Ldn. & N. W. 1st. Charge Prefd.	100	113½
	Do. do. and Chge Prfd.	100	111
4	Do. do. Defd. Charge	100	31½
33/6	Do. N. East. 1 Chge Pfd.	100	91½

Financial—Trusts (*continued*):—

Last Div.	Name.	Paid.	Price.
37/6	Stock N. East Defd. Chge	100	41
6	Submarine Cables	100	138½
5	U.S. & S. Amer. Invest., Ltd., Prefd.	100	99½
20/	Do. Defd.	100	24½
4	Do. Deb. Stk.	100	103½

GAS AND ELECTRIC LIGHTING.

Last Div.	Name.	Paid.	Price.
10/6	Alliance & Dublin Con. 10 p.c. Stand.	10	23½
7/6	Do. 7 p.c. Stand...	10	16½
5	Austln. Gas Lght. (Syd.) Debs. 1909	100	108
5	Bay State of N. Jrsy. Sk. Fd. Tst. Bd., Red. ..	—	92½
3/	Bombay, Ltd.	5	6
2/4½	Do. New	4	4½
12	Brentford Cons.	100	282½
9	Do. New	100	215
5	Do. Pref.	100	142½
4	Do. Deb. Stk. ..	100	132½
11½	Brighton & Hove Gen. Cons. Stk.	100	270½
8½	Do. "A" Cons. Stk.	100	197½
5	Bristol 5 p.c. Max.	100	129½
22/6	British Gas Light, Ltd.	20	55
11/6	Bromley Gas Consumrs.' 10 p.c. Stand.	10	26
8/6	Do. 7 p.c. Stand...	10	21
—	Brush Electl. Enging., L.	—	1½
6	Do. 6 p.c. Pref.	—	2½
4½	Do. Deb. Stk.	100	112
4½	Do. 2 Deb. Stk., Red.	100	100½
7/	B. Ayres (New), Ltd. ..	10	9½
4	Do. Deb. Stk., Rd. ..	—	99
18/6	Cagliari Gas & Wtr., Ltd.	20	31
6/	Cape Town & Dist. Gas Light & Coke, Ltd.	10	15½
4½	Do. Pref.	10	12
6	Do. 1 Mt. Debs. 1910	50	59
4/	Charing Cross & Strand Elec. Sup., Ltd.	5	11½
4½	Do. Cum. Pref.	5	6
2/6	Chelsea Elec. Sup., Ltd.	5	8½
4½	Do. Deb. Stk., Red.	100	114½
5	Chic. Edis'n Co. 1 Mt., Rd.	$1000	106
20/	City of Ldn. Elec. Lht., L.	10	26½
—	Do. New £10 Shs...	5	18½
6	Do. Cum. Pref.	10	15½
5	Do. Deb. Stk., Red.	100	127½
13½	Commercial, Cons.	100	322½
10½	Do. New	100	262½
4½	Do. Deb. Stk.	100	150½
10	Continental Union, Ltd.	100	205½
11	Do. Pref. Stk.	100	192½
—	County of Lon. & Brush Prov. Elec. Lg., Ltd.	10	13
6	Do. Cum. Pref	10	14½
14	Croydon Comcl. Gas, Ld., "A" Stk., 10 p.c...	100	312½
11	Do. "B" Stk., 7 p.c.	100	260
5½	Crystal Pal. Dist. Ord. 5 p.c. Stk.	100	127½
5	Do. Pref. Stk.	100	143½
8/	European, Ltd.	10	24
6/	Do.	7½	17½
12½	Gas Light & Ck Cons. Stk., "A" Ord.	100	292½
4	Do. "B" (4 p.c. Max.)	100	120½
10	Do. "C," "D," & "E" (Pref.)	100	304½
5	Do. "F" (Pref.)	100	152½
7½	Do. "G" (Pref.)	100	222½
7	Do. "H" (7 p.c. Max.)	100	197½
10	Do. "I" (Pref.)	100	302½
6	Do. "K"	100	185½
4	Do. Deb. Stk.	100	131½
4½	Do. do.	100	150½
6	Do. do.	100	200½
8/	Hong Kong & China, Ld.	10	14
4/	House to House Elec. Light Sup., Ltd. ..	5	8½
7	Do. Cum. Pref.	5	10
10	Imperial Continental ..	100	208½
3½	Do. Deb. Stk., Red ..	100	104½
4/	Malta & Medit., Ltd. ..	5	5
7/	Metrop. Elec. Sup., Ltd.	10	15
4½	Do. 1 Mt. Deb. Stk.	100	118
5	Metro. of Melbrne. Dbs. 1908-12	100	111
4½	Do. Debs.. 1918-22-4	100	108
10/	Monte Video, Ltd.	20	14½
9½	Newcastle-upon-Tyne ..	100	237½
—	Do. 3½ p.c. Deb. Stk.	100	117½
18/	Notting Hill Elec. Ltg., Ltd.	10	15½
3/6	Oriental, Ltd.	5	7½
3/1½	Do. New	4½	6½
8½d.	Do. do. 1879	1	1¼
3/6	Ottoman, Ltd.	5	5
6	People's Gas Lt. & C. of Chic. 2 Mt. 1904	100	105½
5	River Plate Elec. Lgt. & Trac., Ltd., 1 Deb. Stk.	—	87½
8s	Royal Elec. of Montreal	—	142½
4½	Do. 1 Mt. Deb. ..	100	104
11/	St. James' & Pall Mall Elec. Light, Ltd. ..	5	16
7	Do. Pref.	5	9½
4	Do. Deb. Stk., Red.	100	106½
10/	San Paulo, Ltd.	10	15

Gas and Electric (*continued*):—

Last Div.	Name.	Paid.	Price.
10	Sheffield Unit. Gas Lt. "A"	100	251½
10	Do. "B"	100	251½
10	Do. "C"	100	251½
—	Sth. Ldn. Elec. Sup., Ld.	2	2¼
5¼	South Metropolitan	100	140½
3	Do. 3 p.c. Deb. Stk.	100	102¾
8	Tottenham & Edmonton Gas Lt. & C., "A"	100	290
9	Do. "B"	100	210
7/	Tuscan, Ltd.	10	13½
5	Do. Debs., Red.	100	101½
5/	West Ham 10 p.c. Stan.	5	12
8/	Wstmnstr. Elec. Sup., Ld.	5	15

INSURANCE.

Last Div.	Name.	Paid.	Price.
4/	Alliance, £20 Shs.	44/	10½
10/	Alliance, Mar., & Gen., Ld., £100 Shs.	25	51
20/	Atlas, £50 Shs.	6	29
8/	British & For. Marine, Ld., £20 Shs.	4	23½
7½d.	British Law Fire, Ltd., £10 Shs.	1	1¼
7/6	Clerical, Med., & Gen. Life £25 Shs.	50/	16½
20/	Commercial Union, Ltd., £50 Shs.	5	43½
4	Do. "W. of Eng." Ter. Deb. Stk.	100	109½
£9	County Fire, £100 Shs.	80	195
5/	Eagle, £50 Shs.	5	½
4/	Employrs' Liability, Ltd., £10 Shs.	2	3½
—	Empress, Ltd., £5 Shs.	1	—
21/	Equity & Law, £100 Shs.	6	23
7/6	General Life, £100 Shs.	5	14½
4½d.	Gresham Life, £5 Shs.	15/	2¼
5/6	Guardian, Ld., £10 Shs.	5	10¼
25/	Imperial, Ltd., £20 Shs.	5	29
5/6	Imperial Life, £20 Shs.	4	6½
6/	Indemnity Mutual Mar., Ltd., £15 Shs.	3	11¾
1/6	Lancashire, £20 Shs.	2	4¾
7½d.	Law Acc. & Contin., Ltd., £5 Shs.	10/	¾
22/6	Law Fire, £100 Shs.	2½	17½
9½d.	Law Guar. & Trust, Ltd., £10 Shs.	1	1¼
9/	Law Life, £20 Shs.	2	24½
2/9	Law Un. & Crown £10Shs	12/	7
4	Do. Deb. Stk., 1942	100	109½
14/6	Legal & General, £50Shs.	8	15
9d.	Lion Fire, Ltd., £8½ Shs.	1½	¾
22/	Liverpool & London & Globe, Stk	2	52
10/	Do. Globe £1 Ann	—	35
35/	London, £25 Shs.	12½	58
8/	Lond. & Lanc. Fire, £25Shs	2½	19
3/6	Lond. & Lanc. Life, £25Shs	2	6¾
1/	Lond. & Prov. Mar., Ld., £10 Shs.	1	⅞
6/	Lond. Guar. & Accident, Ltd., £5 Shs	2	12
10/	Marine, Ltd., £25 Shs.	4½	44
2/	Maritime, Ltd., £10 Shs.	2	4½
1/6	Merc. Mar., Ld., £10 Shs.	2½	2½
10/	N. Brit. & Merc., £25 Shs.	6¼	42
20/	Northern, £100 Shs.	10	79
40/	Norwich Union Fire, £100 Shs.	12	125½
10/	Ocean Acc. & Guar., fy. pd.	5	22½
2/	Do. £5 Shs.	1	3¼
2/6	Ocean, Marine, Ltd.	2½	8¼
2/	Palatine, £10 Shs.	2	3½
2/6	Pelican, £10 Shs.	1	3½
23/	Phœnix, £50 Shs.	5	41½
£6	Provident, £100 Shs.	10	32
5/	Railway Pssngrs., £10Shs.	2	8½
2/6	Rock Life, £5 Shs.	10/	4½
20	Royal Exchange	100	340
18/	Royal, £20 Shs.	3	54
4/6	Sun, £10Shs	10/	11½
3/9	Sun Life, £10 Shs.	7½	15
6	Thames & Mrsey. Marine, Ltd., £20 Shs.	2	10½
10/	Union, £10 Shs.	4	24
3/6	Union Marine, £20 Shs.	2½	9
40/	Universal Life, £100 Shs.	12	40
2/	World Marine, £5 Shs.	2	1½

IRON, COAL, AND STEEL.

Last Div.	Name.	Paid.	Price.
—	Barrow Hæm. Steel, Ltd.	7½	1¾
9/	Do. 6 p.c. 2nd Pref.	7½	6½
10/	Bolck., Vaugh. & C., Ld.	20	17
6/	Do. £8 liab	12	9½
12/6	Brown, J. & Co., Ltd., £20 Shs.	15	19½
7/6	Consett Iron, Ld., £10Shs.	7½	29
7/6	Ebbw Vale Steel, Iron & Coal, Ltd., £23 Shs.	20	5
12/6	General Mining Assn., Ld.	5½	7½
1/7½	Harvey Steel Co. of Gt. Britain, Ltd.	10	2⅜
5	Lehigh V. Coal 1 Mt. 5 p.c. Guar. Gd. Cp. Bds.	—	96
42/6	Nantyglo & Blaina Iron, Ltd., Pref.	$62	96
1/	Nerbudda Coal & Iron, Ltd., £3 Shs.	56/	—
6/	Newport Abrcrn. Bk. Vein Steam Coal, Ltd.	10	6½
5/	New Sharlston Coll., Ltd. Pref.	20	10
4½d.	Nw. Vancvr. Coal & Ld., L.	1	½
2/6	North's Navigation Coll. (1889) Ltd.	5	2½
10/	Do. 10 p.c. Cum. Pref.	5	6½
—	Rhymney Iron, Ltd.	5	1½
	Do. New, £5 Shs.	4½	1
5	Do. Mt. Debs., Red.	100	99½
5	Shelton Irn., Stl. & Cl. Co., Ltd., 1 Chg. Debs., Red.	100	100½
50/	Sth. Hetton Coal, Ltd.	100	—
2/	Vickers & Maxim, Ltd.	1	3⅜
5	Do. 5 p.c. Prfd. Stk.	100	125½

SHIPPING.

Last Div.	Name.	Paid.	Price.
12/	African Stm. Ship, £20 Shs.	16	10½
15/	Do. Fully-paid	20	14½
5/	Amazon Steam Nav., Ltd.	12½	8½
12/	Castle Mail Pakts., Ltd., £20 Shs.	14	15½
3½	Do. 1st Deb. Stk., Red.	100	101
6/	China Mutual Steam, Ltd.	5	3
6	Do. Cum. Pref.	10	10
20/	Cunard, Ltd.	20	9½
5/	Do. £20 Shs.	10	3⅜
4½	Furness, Withy, & Co., Ltd., 1 Mt. Dbs., Red.	100	107
6/	General Steam	15	7½
5/	Do. 5 p.c. Pref., 1874	10	8½
5/	Do. 5 p.c. Pref., 1877	10	8½
26/4½	Leyland & Co., Ltd.	10	26
7/	Do. 7 p.c. Cum. Pref.	10	14½
2/11	Do. 4½ p.c. Cum. Pre-Pf.	3	10½
4	Do. 1st Mt. Dbs., Red.	100	104½
7/6	Mercantile Steam, Ltd.	5	8
6/4½	New Zealand Ship., Ltd.,	6	4½
4	Do. Deb. Stk., Red.	100	102
5/	Orient Steam, Ltd.	10	4½
5	P. & O. Steam, Cum. Prefd.	100	145½
7	Do. Defd.	100	235½
3½	Do. Deb. Stk.	100	117
5	Richelieu & Ont., 1st Mt. Debs., Red.	100	100
30/	Royal Mail, £100 Shs.	60	51
2/6	Shaw, Sav., & Alb., Ltd., "A" Pref.	5	5½
5/	Do. "B" Ord.	5	4
14/	Union Steam, Ltd.	20	19½
7/	Do. New £20 Shs.	10	8½
4	Do. Deb. Stk., Red.	100	106
6/	Union of N.Z., Ltd.	10	9½
5½	Wilson's & Fur.-Ley., 5½ p.c. Cum. Pref.	10	10½
4½	Do. 1 Mt. Db. Sk., Rd.	100	106½

**** Tea Shares will be found in the Special Table following.*

TELEGRAPHS AND TELEPHONES.

Last Div.	Name.	Paid.	Price.
	African Direct, Ltd., Mort. Debs., Red.	100	102
—	Amazon Telegraph, Ltd.	10	6½
15/	Anglo-American, Ltd.	100	65½
30/	Do. 6 p.c. Prefd. Ord.	100	117
—	Do. Defd. Ord.	100	16½
3/	Brazilian Submarine, Ltd.	10	15½
5	Do. Debs., 2 Series	100	114

Telegraphs and Telephones (*continued*):—

Last Div.	Name.	Paid.	Price.
4/	Chili Telephone, Ltd.	5	3
$12	Comcial. Cable, $100 Shs.	—	185
4	Do. Stg. 500-yr. Deb. Stk. Red.	100	106
2½d.	Consd. Telpehone Constr., &c., Ltd.	10/	½
6/	Cuba Submarine, Ltd.	10	7
10/	Do. 10 p.c. Pref.	10	15
2/	Direct Spanish, Ltd.	5	4½
5/	Do. 10 p.c. Cum. Pref.	5	10½
4½	Do. Debs.	50	104½
3/	Direct U.S. Cable, Ltd.	20	10½
2/6	Eastern, Ltd.	10	17½
3/	Do. 6 p.c. Cum. Pref.	10	—
4	Do. Mt. Deb. Stk., Red.	100	125
6/6	Eastern Exten., Aus., & China, Ltd.	10	17½
5	Do. (Aus. Gov. Sub.) Deb., Red.	100	102
5	Do. do. Bearer	100	102½
4	Do. Mort. Deb. Stk.	100	125
5	Eastn. & S. Afric., Ltd., Mort. Deb. 1900	100	102
5	Do. Bearer	100	102
4	Do. Mort. Debs. 1909	100	102½
4	Do. Mort. Debs. (Maur. Subsidy)	25	105½
5/	Grt. Nthn. Copenhagen	10	30
5	Do. Debs., Ser. B., Red.	100	101½
12/6	Indo-European, Ltd.	25	51½
6	London Platino-Brazilian, Ltd., Debs. 1904	100	109½
4/	Montevideo Telpb., Ltd., 6 p.c. Pref.	5	2½
3/	National Telephone, Ltd.	5	5½
6/	Do. Cum. 1 Pref.	10	16
6/	Do. Cum. 2 Pref.	10	16
5	Do. Non-Cum. 3 Pref.	5	5½
3½	Do. Deb. Stk., Red.	100	102½
8d.	Oriental Telephone, Ltd.	1	½
4	Pac. & Euro. Tlg. Dbs., Rd.	100	106½
4/	Reuter's, Ltd.	8	8½
5/	Un. Riv. Plate Telph., Ltd.	5	4½
5	Do. Deb. Stk., Red.	100	104½
—	West African Telg., Ltd.	10	4
5	Do. 5 p.c. Mt. Debs., Red.	100	100½
—	W. Coast of America, Ltd.	10	½
6/9	Western & Brazilian, Ltd.	15	11½
6/	Do. 5 p.c. Pref. Ord.	7½	7½
9d.	Do. Defd. Ord.	7½	4½
4	Do. Deb. Stk., Red.	100	104½
6d.	W. India & Panama, Ltd.	10	½
6	Do. Cum. 1 Pref.	10	7½
6	Do. Cum. 2 Pref.	10	6
	Do. Debs., Red.	100	107½
7	West. Union, 1 Mt. 1902 ($	1000	107½
6	Do. 6 p.c. Stg. Bds., Rd.	100	102½

TRAMWAYS AND OMNIBUS.

Last Div.	Name.	Paid.	Price.
1/6	Anglo-Argentine, Ltd	5	3½
6	Do. Deb. Stk	100	130
4/	Barcelona, Ltd	10	10½
5	Do. Deb., Red.	100	105½
7/6	Belfast Street Trams.	10	16½
—	Blackpl. & Fltwd. Tram., £10 Shs.	8	12½
10/	Bordeaux Tram. & O., Ltd.	10	13
5	Do. Cum. Pref.	10	11
—	Brazilian Street Ry., Ltd.	2	½
—	British Elec. Trac., Ltd.	10	17¾
—	B. Ayres & Belg. Tram., Ltd., 6 p.c. Cum. Pref.	5	—
6	Do. 1 Deb. Stk.	100	—
—	B. Ayres. Gd. Nat., Ltd., 6 p.c 1 Deb. Bds., Red.	100	60½
5½	Do. Pref. Debs., Red.	100	94½
1/	Calais, Ltd.	5	1
—	Calcutta, Ltd.	10	3½
—	Carthngena & Herr., Ltd.	10	2½
5	Do. Deb., Red.	100	90
5	City of B'ham. Trams., Ltd., 5 p.c. Cum. Pref.	5	5
4	Do. 1 Mort. Debs., Rd.	100	105½
3/9	City of B. Ayres, Ltd	5	6½
2/3	Do. Ext. £5 Shs.	3	3½
6	Do. Deb. Stk	100	145
1/4	Edinburgh Street Tram	4	4
1/	Glasgow Tram. & Omni. Ltd., £9 Shs.	8	2½
3/7½	Imperial, Ltd.	6	15
3/	Lond., Deptfd., & Greenwich, Prefd.	5	3½
nil	Do. Defd.	5	1
10½	Lond. Gen. Omni., Ltd.	100	200
4	Do. Deb., Red.	100	113½

Tramways and Omnibus (*continued*):—

Last Div.	Name.	Paid.	Price.
4/9½	London Road Car	6	10
28/6	Do. Red. 1 Mt. Deb. Stk.	100	109½
5	London St. Rly. (Prov., Ont.), Mt. Debs.	100	110
12/6	London St. Trams.	—	2
12/9	London Trams., Ltd	10	9
6/	Do. Non-Cum. Pref.	10	10½
5	Do. Mt. Db. Stk., Rd.	100	101
5	Lynn & Boston 1 Mt. 1924 $	1000	106½
5	Milwaukee Elec. Cons. Mt. $	1000	100½
5	Minneapolis St. 1 Cons. Mt $	1000	92½
5	Montreal St. Dbs., 1908	100	109
4½	Do. Debs., 1922	100	107
6/	Nth. Metropolitan	—	11½
1/9½	Nth. Staffords., Ltd.	6	5
2/6	Provincial, Ltd	10	6
6/	Do. Cum. Pref.	10	12½
5	St. Paul City, 1937 $	1000	92½
5/	Southampton	10	6½
5/	South London	10	5½
7/6	Sunderland, Ltd.	10	6½
4½	Toronto 1 Mt., Red.	100	105
2/6	Tramways Union, Ltd.	5	6½
4½	Do. Deb., Red.	100	109
2/6	Vienna General Omnibus.	5	5
5	Do. 5 p.c. Mt. Deb., Red.	100	103½
4/	Wolverhampton, Ltd	10	5½

WATER WORKS.

Last Div.	Name.	Paid.	Price.
10/	Antwerp, Ltd.	20	22
6/	Cape Town District, Ltd.	5	7½
10½	Chelsea	100	315½
5	Do. Pref. Stk.	100	172½
4½	Do. Pref. Stk, 1875	100	150
4½	Do. Deb. Stk.	100	159½
5/6	City St. Petersburg, Ltd.	11	10½
5/	Colne Valley	14	15½
4	Do. Deb. Stock	100	136½
£4	Consol. of Rosar., Ltd., 4 p.c. 1 Deb. Stk., Red.	100	89
8	East London	100	227½
4½	Do. Deb. Stk.	100	158½
3	Do. Deb. Stk., Red.	100	104
37/6	Grand Junction (Max. 10 p.c.) "A"	50	116½
18/9	Do. "B"	25	
18/9	Do. "C" (Max. 7½ p.c.)	25	53½
35/	Do. "D" (Max. 7 p.c.)	50	95
4	Do. Deb. Stock	100	142½
13	Kent	100	360½
7	Do. New (Max. 7 p.c.)	100	215½
7/	Kimberley, Ltd.	7	4½
6	Do. Debs., Red.	100	104½
6	Do. Deb. Stk., Red.	100	104½
10	Lambeth (Max. 10 p.c.)	100	297½
7½	Do. (Max. 7½ p.c.), 50 & 25	—	227½
4	Do. Deb. Stock	100	142½
3	Do. Red. Deb. Stock	100	103
10/	Montevideo, Ltd.	20	16
5	Do. 1 Deb. Stk.	100	108½
5	Do. 2 Deb. Stk.	100	103½
132/9	New River New	100	434½
4	Do. Deb. Stk.	100	143½
4	Do. Deb. Stk. "B"	100	143½
4	Portland Con. Mt. "B," 1927	—	102½
8/	Seville, Ltd.	20	12
5/6	Southend "Addl." Ord.	10	17
6	Southwark and Vauxhall	100	165½
6	Do. "D" Shares (7½ p.c. max.)	100	154
5	Do. Pref. Stock	100	170
4	Do. "A" Deb. Stock	100	142½
3	Staines Resvirs. Jt. Com. Gua. Deb. Stk., Red.	100	104
8/	Tarapaca, Ltd.	10	8½
10	West Middlesex	100	297½
4½	Do. Deb. Stk.	100	163½
3	Do Deb. Stk	100	105

INDIAN AND CEYLON TEA COMPANIES.

Acres Planted.	Crop. 1897.	Paid up Capital.	Share.	Paid up.	Name.	Dividends. 1894.	1895.	1896.	1897.	Price.	Yield.	Reserve.	Balance Forward.	Working Capital.	Mortgages, Debs. or Pref. Capital not otherwise stated.
	lb.	£	£	£	**INDIAN COMPANIES.**							£	£	£	£
11,240	3,128,000	120,000	10	3	Amalgamated Estates	—	*	10	‡5	3	10	10,000	16,500	D52,950	—
		400,000	10	10	Do. Pref.	—	*	5	5	9½xd	5½				
10,223	3,560,000	187,160	20	20	Assam	20	20	20	17½	54½xd	6½	55,000	264	D11,350	—
6,150	3,278,000	142,500	10	10	Assam Frontier	3	6	6	nil	—	—	—	474	20,000	77,500
		142,500	10	10	Do. Pref.	6	6	6	4	10	4				
2,087	839,000	66,745	5	5	Attaree Khat	12	12	8	5	5	5	3,790	4,114	2,770	—
1,633	583,000	78,170	10	10	Borelli	4	4	5	4	7	6	—	2,558	D270	6,500 Pref.
1,720	812,000	60,825	5	5	British Indian	6	5	5	5	3¼	7½	—	901	12,300	16,500 Pref.
3,223	2,247,000	114,500	5	5	Brahmapootra	20	18	20	15	12	6½	—	28,470	41,600	.
3,754	1,617,000	76,500	10	10	Cachar and Dooars	*	8	7	7	9	7¾	—	1,953	21,240	.
		76,500	10	10	Do. Pref.	*	6	6	6	11	5½				
3,946	2,083,000	72,010	1	1	Chargola	8	7	10	5	⅝xd	8	3,000	2,650	—	—
		81,000	1	1	Do. Pref.	7	7	7	7	1⅛	5¾				
1,071	942,000	33,000	5	5	Chubwa	10	8	10	8	5½	7¼	10,000	2,043	D5,400	—
		33,000	5	5	Do. Pref.	7	7	7	7	6¼	5½				
,250	11,500,000	120,000	10	3	Cons. Tea and Lands	—	*	10	‡5	3½	8½	65,000	14,240	D191,674	—
		1,000,000	10	10	Do. 1st Pref.	—	*	5	5	10½	4¾				
		400,000	10	10	Do. 2nd Pref.	—	*	7	7	11½	5½				
2,230	617,000	135,420	20	20	Darjeeling	5½	5½	6	5	21	4¾	5,552	360	1,7	—
2,114	445,000	60,000	10	10	Darjeeling Cons.	—	*	4/2	nil	5	—	—	1,893	—	—
		60,000	10	10	Do. Pref.	—	*	5	5	9½	5¼				
6,660	3,518,000	150,000	10	10	Dooars	12½	12½	12½	12½	17½	7¼	45,000	300	D32,000	—
		75,000	10	10	Do. Pref.	7	7	7	7	16½	4¼				
3,367	1,811,000	165,000	10	10	Doom Dooma	11½	10	12½	12½	19	6½	30,000	1,965	—	10,000
1,377	582,000	61,120	5	5	Eastern Assam	5	nil.	4	nil	2½	—	—	777	—	10,000
4,038	1,675,000	85,000	10	10	East India and Ceylon	5	nil.	7	3	6	5	—	1,567	—	—
		85,000	10	10	Do. Pref.	*	6	6	6	11	5½				
7,500	3,363,000	219,000	10	10	Empire of India	—	*	6/10	9	10xd	9	14,500	—	27,000	—
		219,000	10	10	Do. Pref.	—	*	5	5	11	4½				
1,180	540,000	94,060	10	10	Indian of Cachar	7	3½	3	2	3¾	5¼	6,450	—	7,120	—
3,050	824,000	83,500	5	5	Jhanzie	10	10	10	8	5½	7	15,800	796	2,700	—
7,980	3,680,000	250,000	10	10	Jokai	10	10	10	8	14xd	6	54,600	4,300	D9,000	—
		100,000	10	10	Do. Pref.	*	6	6	6	14½	4¼				
5,224	1,563,000	100,000	20	20	Jorehaut	20	20	20	—	47½	4¼	36,220	286	3,000	—
1,347	504,000	65,660	10	8	Lebong	15	15	15	12½	15½	6½	12,000	535	8,650	—
5,082	1,709,000	100,000	10	10	Lungla	5	10	6	3	6	5	—	107	D21,000	—
		100,000	10	10	Do. Pref.	*	6	6	6	10	5½				
2,684	885,000	95,970	10	10	Majuli	7	5	5	nil	5	—	—	6,085	560	—
1,375	380,000	91,840	1	1	Makum	—	—	2	—	21	2	—	—	1,200	25,000
2,990	770,000	100,000	1	1	Moabund	—	—	*	—	¾	—	—	50	—	—
		50,000	1	1	Do. Pref.	—	—	*	12½	⅞x	5¼				
1,080	482,000	79,590	10	10	Scottish Assam	7	7	7	—	9½	5¼	4,000	224	9,590	—
4,150	1,456,000	100,000	10	10	Singlo	5	8	5	‡1	8½	6½	—	300	D5,200	—
		80,000	10	10	Do. Pref.	*	6½	6½	13½	13	5				
					CEYLON COMPANIES.										
7,970	1,743,824§	250,000	100	100	Anglo-Ceylon, & Gen.	—	*	5½	—	42½	11	10,992	1,405	D72,844	166,520
1,836	685,741§	50,000	10	10	Associated Tea	—	*	5	12½	7½	6½	—	164	2,478	—
		60,000	10	10	Do. Pref.	—	*	6	‡3	10½	5¾				
10,390	4,000,000	167,380	10	10	Ceylon Tea Plantations	15	15	15	15	23½	6½	90,000	3,122	D30,819	—
		81,080	10	10	Do. Pref.	7	7	7	7	16½xd	4¼				
5,722	1,542,700	55,260	5	3	Ceylon & Oriental Est.	5	8	7	—	2¾	7¼	—	230	D2,047	71,000
		46,000	5	5	Do. Pref.	6	6	6	‡3	5	6				
2,157	801,629§	111,330	5	5	Dimbula Valley	—	*	10	‡5	5½	9	—	—	1,733	6,250
		62,607	5	5	Do. Pref.	—	*	6	‡3	5¼	5½				
11,496	3,635,000	298,250	5	5	Eastern Prod. & Est.	3	5	6¼	7	5½	6½	25,000	10,880	D17,797	102,500
2,193	1,050,000	22,080	10	10	New Dimbula "A"	10	16	16	‡4	24	7	11,000	2,024	2,150	8,400
		55,720	10	10	Do. "B"	18	16	16	‡4	22	7¼				
2,572	570,360§	100,000	10	10	Ouvah	6	8	6	4	8	7½	4,000	396	D1,255	—
2,630	964,963	200,000	10	10	Nuwara Eliya	—	*	6	6	10½	6	9,400	—	—	30,000
2,450	750,000	39,000	10	6	Standard	12½	15	15	15	12	7½	10,000	795	D14,012	4,000
		17,000	10	10	Do.	12½	15	15	15	22	7				

Working-Capital Column.—In working-capital column, D stands for *debit*.

* Company formed this year. † Interim dividends are given as actual distribution made. ‡ Interim div. only. § Crop 1896.

DIVIDENDS ANNOUNCED.

HUMPHREYS.—An interim dividend of 10 per cent. per annum on the ordinary shares.

SOCIETA ITALIANA PER LE STRODE FERRATE DELLA SICILIA (the Italian Company of Silician Railways).—A dividend of lire 12.50 per share, being the second payment on account of the year 1897-98.

DEBENTURE CORPORATION.—An interim dividend on the ordinary shares at the rate of 6 per cent. per annum for the half-year ending the 30th inst.

NEW EXPLOSIVES COMPANY.—An interim dividend for the half-year ending the 30th inst. at the rate of 5 per cent. per annum.

HORNCASTLE WATER COMPANY.—A dividend of 4½ per cent., making 6½ per cent. for the past year.

EASTERN EXTENSION, AUSTRALASIA, AND CHINA TELEGRAPH COMPANY.—An interim dividend for the quarter ended March 31 of 2s. 6d. per share.

UNITED DISCOUNT AND SECURITIES COMPANY.—An interim dividend on the ordinary shares at the rate of 6 per cent. per annum for the half-year ended April 30.

STOCK CONVERSION AND INVESTMENT TRUST.—An interim dividend of 9d. per share on the ordinary shares.

HOME AND COLONIAL STORES.—An interim dividend on the ordinary shares for the quarter ended June 25 of 3s. per share.

NEW TRINIDAD LAKE ASPHALT COMPANY.—An interim dividend of 2 per cent.

LAUTARO NITRATE COMPANY.—A final dividend for the year 1897 of 3s. per share.

DAY DAWN BLOCK AND WYNDHAM GOLD MINING COMPANY.—An interim dividend of 6d. per share.

EDMUNDSONS' ELECTRICITY CORPORATION.—A dividend of 5 per cent. upon the ordinary shares for year ended March 31, carrying forward a balance of £1,012.

DUNLOP PNEUMATIC TYRE COMPANY.—Dividend at the rate of 5 per cent. per annum on the deferred shares.

IMPERIAL OTTOMAN BANK.—A dividend at the rate of 5 per cent.

CANADA COMPANY.—A dividend of £1 per share.

UNITED RIVER PLATE TELEPHONE COMPANY.—Dividend of 6 per cent. on the ordinary shares.

RIVER PLATE FRESH MEAT COMPANY.—Dividend of 10 per cent. on the preference shares, and of 6 per cent. on the ordinary shares.

THOMAS WALLIS & COMPANY.—An interim dividend on the ordinary shares at the rate of 8 per cent. per annum.

NATIONAL BANK OF NEW ZEALAND.—A final dividend at the rate of 5 per cent. per annum, and a bonus of 1 per cent. on the paid-up capital.

EAST SURREY WATER COMPANY.—Dividend at the rate of 6½ per cent. on the ordinary shares.

HOWARD & BULLOUGH.—Dividend of 12 per cent.

COLONIAL BANK.—Dividend at the rate of 6 per cent. per annum.

JOHN CROSSLEY & SONS.—Interim dividend of 5 per cent. on the ordinary and preference shares.

O. C. HAWKES.—Interim dividend at the rate of 8 per cent. per annum on the ordinary shares.

HENRY FORD & CO.—Interim dividend at the rate of 12½ per cent. per annum.

LONDON AND PROVINCIAL MARINE AND GENERAL INSURANCE COMPANY.—Usual payment on account of dividend at the rate of 10 per cent. per annum for half-year ending June 30.

STANHOPE GOLD MINING COMPANY.—Dividend of 10 per cent.

FERREIRA GOLD MINING COMPANY.—Dividend of 150 per cent.

NETTLEFOLDS.—Dividend of 10s. per share, and a bonus of 10s. per share on the ordinary shares.

BODEGA COMPANY.—Final dividend at the rate of 9 per cent. per annum.

JOREHAUT TEA COMPANY.—Dividend of 13 per cent.

NEW EXPLOSIVES COMPANY.—Interim dividend at the rate of 5 per cent. per annum.

PARKER, WINDER, & ACHURCH.—Interim dividend at the rate of 6 per cent. on the preference shares, and 7½ per cent. on the ordinary shares.

SERDANG TABAK MAATSCHAPPY.—Dividend of 11 per cent. on the "A" shares, and 2½ per cent. on the "B" shares.

HUDSON'S BAY COMPANY.—Dividend of 13s. per share.

ASSAM RAILWAYS AND TRADING COMPANY.—Final dividend at the rate of 4½ per cent. per annum.

DE KEYSER'S ROYAL HOTEL.—An interim dividend on the ordinary shares for the half-year ending June 30 at the rate of 6 per cent. per annum.

MOUNT MORGAN GOLD MINING COMPANY.—A dividend of 7d. a share for the month of June.

LADY SHENTON GOLD MINE.—Dividend of 1s. per share.

PERFECTA SEAMLESS TUBE COMPANY.—Dividend at the rate of 2½ per cent. per annum on the ordinary shares, making, with the interim dividend, a total of 5 per cent. for the year.

CHARGOLA TEA ASSOCIATION.—A final dividend at the rate of 2½ per cent., making 5 per cent. for the year, on the ordinary shares.

CITY OF LONDON ELECTRIC LIGHTING COMPANY.—An interim dividend for the six months ending June 30 at the rate of 5 per cent. per annum, on the ordinary shares.

WARING & GILLOW.—An interim dividend on the ordinary shares for the six months ending June 30 at the rate of 10 per cent. per annum, being the same rate as paid for 1897.

JUBILEE GOLD COMPANY.—A dividend of 5s. per share.

DE BEERS CONSOLIDATED MINES.—A dividend of 20s. per share (40 per cent. per annum) for the six months ending June 30.

ARIZONA COPPER COMPANY.—Dividend at the rate of 10 per cent. per annum on the preferred shares.

GENERAL LIFE ASSURANCE COMPANY.—Half-yearly dividend at the rate of 10 per cent. per annum, and a bonus equal to an additional 5 per cent. per annum.

LONDON AND TILBURY LIGHTERAGE, CONTRACTING, AND DREDGING COMPANY.—Dividend at the rate of 5 per cent. per annum.

THOMAS PARKER.—Dividend at the rate of 8 per cent. per annum.

ACCIDENT INSURANCE COMPANY.—An interim dividend for the past half-year at the rate of 5 per cent. per annum.

SINGLETON, BENDA & CO.—Interim dividend of 5 per cent. on the ordinary shares.

NORTHAMPTON BREWERY.—Interim dividend on the ordinary shares at the rate of 8 per cent per annum.

Printed for the Proprietor by LOVE & WYMAN, LTD., Great Queen Street, London, W.C.; and Published by CLEMENT WILSON at Norfolk House, Norfolk Street, Strand, London, W.C.